The Form Book Jumps Annual

Welcome to the 2013-2014 edition of *The Form Book Jumps Annual*, comprising the complete year's results from 28th April 2013 to 26th April 2014.

Race details contain Racing Post Ratings assessing the merit of each individual performance, speed figures for every horse that clocks a worthwhile time, weight-for-age allowances, and the starting price percentage.

Race Focus comments are printed below of most races, along with the results of stewards' enquiries.

• The official record

THE FORM BOOK records comprehensive race details of every domestic race, every major European Group race and every foreign event in which a British-trained runner participated.

MEETING BACK REFERENCE NUMBER is the Raceform number of the last meeting run at the track and is shown to the left of the course name. Abandoned meetings are signified by a dagger.

THE GOING, The Official going, shown at the head of each meeting, is recorded as follows: Turf: Hard; Firm; Good to firm; Good; Good to soft; Soft; Heavy. All-Weather: Fast; Standard to fast; Standard; Standard to slow; Slow. There may be variations for non-British meetings

Where appropriate, a note is included indicating track bias and any differences to the official going indicated by race times.

THE WEATHER is shown below the date for selected meetings.

THE WIND is given as a strength and direction at the Winning Post, classified as follows:
Strength: gale; v.str; str; fresh; mod; slt; almost nil; nil.
Direction: (half) against; (half) bhd; (half) across from or towards stands.

VISIBILITY is good unless otherwise stated.

RACE NUMBERS for Foreign races carry the suffix 'a' in the race header and in the index.

RACE TITLE is the name of the race as shown in the Racing Calendar.

COMPETITIVE RACING CLASSIFICATIONS are shown on a scale from Class 1 to Class 7. All graded races are Class 1.

THE RACE DISTANCE is given for all races to the nearest half-furlong. On All-Weather courses (F) for Fibresand or (P) for Polytrack indicates the nature of the artificial surface on which the race is run.

OFFICIAL RACE TIME as published in the Racing Calendar is followed in parentheses by the time when the race actually started. This is followed by the race class, age restrictions, handicap restrictions and the official rating of the top weight.

PRIZE MONEY shows penalty values down to sixth place (where applicable).

IN THE RACE RESULT, the figures to the far left of each horse (under FORM) show the most recent form figures. The figure in bold is the finishing position in this race as detailed below.

1...40 - finishing positions first to fortieth; **b** - brought down; **c** - carried out; **f** - fell; **p** - pulled up; **r** - refused; **ro** - ran out; **s** - slipped up; **u** - unseated rider; **v** - void race.

THE OFFICIAL DISTANCES between horses are shown on the left-hand side immediately after their position at the finish.

NUMBER OF DAYS SINCE PREVIOUS RUN is the superscript figure immediately following the horse name and suffix.

PREVIOUS RACEFORM RACE NUMBER is the boxed figure to the right of the horse's name.

THE HORSE'S AGE is shown immediately before the weight carried.

WEIGHTS shown are actual weights carried.

OFFICIAL RATING is the figure in bold type directly after the horse's name in the race result. This figure indicates the Official BHA rating, at entry, after the following adjustments had been made:
(i) Overweight carried by the rider.
(ii) The number of pounds out of the handicap (if applicable).
(iii) Penalties incurred after the publication of the weights.
However, no adjustments have been made for:
(i) Weight-for-age.
(ii) Riders' claims.

HEADGEAR is shown immediately before the jockey's name and in parentheses and expressed as: **b** (blinkers); **v** (visor); **h** (hood); **e** (eyeshield); **p** (sheepskin cheekpieces); **t** (tongue-tie).

THE JOCKEY is shown for every runner followed, in superscript, by apprentice allowances in parentheses.

CONDITIONAL JOCKEYS' ALLOWANCES The holders of conditional jockeys' licences, under the provisions of Rule 109(ii) (a) are permitted to claim the following allowances in Jumps races:

7lb until they have won 15 races;

thereafter 5lb until they have won 35 such races;

thereafter 3lb until they have won 65 such Jumps races.

These allowances can be claimed in the steeplechases, hurdle races and National Hunt flat races set out below, with the exception of races confined to conditional jockeys:
(a) All handicaps except the Grand National Steeplechase
(b) All selling races.
(c) All weight-for-age races classified 3, 4, 5, and 6.
(d) All National Hunt Flat races.

RACING POST RATINGS, which record the level of performance attained in this race for each horse, appear in the end column after each horse. These are the work of handicapper Steve Mason, who heads a dedicated team dealing with Jumps races for Raceform and sister publication, the *Racing Post*.

THE TRAINER is shown for every runner.

COMMENT-IN-RUNNING is shown for each horse in an abbreviated form. Details of abbreviations appear later in this section.

STARTING PRICES appear below the jockey in the race result. The favourite indicator appears to the right of the Starting Price; 1 for the favourite, 2 for the second-favourite and 3 for third-favourite. Joint favourites share the same number.

RACE TIMES in Great Britain are official times which are recorded to a tenth of a second. Figures in parentheses following the time show the number of seconds faster or slower than the Raceform Median Time for the course and distance.

RACEFORM MEDIAN TIMES are compiled from all races run over the course and distance in the preceding five years. Times equal to the median are shown as (0.00). Times under the median are preceded by minus, for instance, 1.8 seconds under the median would be shown (-1.8). Record times are displayed as follows (1.2 under best).

GOING CORRECTION appears against each race to allow for changing conditions of the ground. It is shown to a hundredth of a second and indicates the adjustment per furlong against the median time. The going based on the going correction is shown in parentheses and is recorded in the following stages:
Turf: HD (Hard); F (Firm); GF (Good to firm); G (Good); GS (Good to soft); S (Soft); HVY (Heavy). All-Weather: FST (Fast); SF (Standard to fast); STD (Standard); SS (Standard to slow); SLW (Slow)

WEIGHT-FOR-AGE allowances are given where applicable for mixed-age races.

STARTING PRICE PERCENTAGE follows the going correction and weight-for-age details, and gives the total SP percentage of all runners that competed. It precedes the number of runners taking part in the race.

SELLING DETAILS (where applicable) and details of any claim are given. Friendly claims are not detailed.

SPEED RATINGS appear below the race time and going correction. They are the work of time expert Dave Bellingham and differ from conventional ratings systems in that they are an expression of a horse's ability in terms of lengths-per-mile, as opposed to pounds in weight. They are not directly comparable with BHA and Racing Post ratings.

The ratings take no account of the effect of weight, either historically or on the day, and this component is left completely to the user's discretion. What is shown is a speed rating represented in its purest form, rather than one that has been altered for weight using a mathematical formula that treats all types of horses as if they were the same.

A comparison of the rating achieved with the 'par' figure for the grade of race - the rating that should be achievable by an everage winner in that class of race- will both provide an at-a-glance indication of whether or not a race was truly run and also highlight the value of the form from a time perspective.

In theory, if a horse has a best speed figure five points superior to another and both run to their best form in a race over a mile, the first horse should beat the second by five lengths. In a race run over two miles, the margin should be ten lengths and so on.

Before the speed figures can be calculated, it is necessary to establish a set of standard or median times for every distance at every track, and this is done by averaging the times of all winners over a particular trip going back several years. No speed ratings are produced when insufficient races have been run over a distance for a reliable median time to be calculated.

Once a meeting has taken place, a raw unadjusted speed rating is calculated for each winner by calculating how many lengths per mile the winning time was faster or slower than the median for the trip. A difference of 0.2 of a second equals one length. The raw speed ratings of all winners on the card are then compared to the 'par' figure for the class of race. The difference between the 'raw' speed rating and the 'par' figure for each race is then noted, and both the fastest and slowest races are discarded before the rest are averaged to produce the going allowance or track variant. This figure gives an idea as to how much the elements, of which the going is one, have affected the final times of each race.

The figure representing the going allowance (track variant) is then used to adjust the raw speed figures and produce the final ratings, which represent how fast the winners would have run on a perfectly good surface with no external influences, including the weather. The ratings for beaten horses are worked out by taking the number of lengths they were behind the winner, adjusting that to take into account the distance of the race, and deducting from the winner's rating. The reader is left with a rating which provides an instant impression of the value of a time performance.

The speed 'pars' below act as benchmark with which to compare the speed figures earned by each horse in each race. A horse that has already exceeded the 'par' for the class he is about to run in, is of special interest, especially if he has done it more than once, as are horses that have consistently earned higher figures than their rivals.

Class 1 Grade One	117
Class 1 Grade Two	115

Class 1 Grade Three	113
Class 1 Listed	111
Class 2	109
Class 3	107
Class 4	105
Class 5	103
Class 6	101
Class 7	97

Allowances need to be made for younger horses and for fillies. These allowances are as follows.

MONTH	3yo
Jul / Aug	-3
Sep / Oct	-2
Nov / Dec	-1
Races contested by fillies and mares only	-3

Allowances are cumulative.

TOTE prices include £1 stake. Exacta dividends are shown in parentheses. The Computer Straight Forecast dividend is preceded by the letters CSF, Computer Tricast is preceded by CT and Tote Trifecta dividend is preceded by the word Trifecta. Jackpot, Placepot and Quadpot details appear at the end of the meeting to which they refer.

OWNER is followed by the breeder's name and the trainer's location.

STEWARDS' ENQUIRIES are included with the result, and any suspensions and/or fines incurred. Objections by jockeys and officials are included, where relevant.

HISTORICAL FOCUS details occasional points of historical significance.

FOCUS The Focus section has been enhanced to help readers distinguish good races from bad races and reliable form from unreliable form, by drawing together the opinions of handicapper, time expert and paddock watcher and interpreting their views in a punter-friendly manner.

Abbreviations and their meanings

Paddock comments

gd sort – well made, above average on looks
attr – attractive
gd bodied – good bodied, well put together
h.d.w – has done well, improved in looks
wl grwn – well grown, has filled to its frame
lengthy – longer than average for its height
tall – tall
rangy – lengthy and tall but in proportion.
cl cpld – close coupled
scope – scope for physical development
str – strong, powerful looking
w'like – workmanlike, ordinary in looks
lt-f – light-framed, not much substance
cmpt – compact
neat – smallish, well put together
leggy – long legs compared with body
angular – unfurnished behind the saddle, not filled to frame
unf – unfurnished in the midriff, not filled to frame
narrow – not as wide as side appearance would suggest
small – lacks any physical scope
nt grwn – not grown
lw – looked fit and well
bkwd – backward in condition
t – tubed
swtg – sweating
b (off fore or nr fore) – bandaged in front
b.hind (off or nr) – bandaged behind

At the start

stdd s – jockey purposely reins back the horse
dwlt – missed the break and left for a short time
s.s – slow to start, left longer than a horse that dwelt
s.v.s – started very slowly
s.i.s – started on terms but took time to get going
ref to r – does not jump off, or travels a few yards then stops
rel to r – tries to pull itself up in mid-race
w.r.s – whipped round start

Position in the race

led – in lead on its own
disp ld – upsides the leader
w ldr – almost upsides the leader
w ldrs – in a line of three or more disputing the lead
prom – on the heels of the leaders, in front third of the field
trckd ldr(s) – just in behind the leaders giving impression that it could lead if asked
chsd ldr – horse in second place
chsd clr ldrs – horse heads main body of field behind two clear leaders
chsd ldrs – horse is in the first four or five but making more of an effort to stay close to the pace than if it were tracking the leaders.
clsd – closed
in tch – close enough to have a chance
hdwy – making ground on the leader
gd hdwy – making ground quickly on the leader, could be a deliberate move
sme hdwy – making some ground but no real impact on the race
w.w – waited with
stdy hdwy – gradually making ground
ev ch – upsides the leaders when the race starts in earnest
rr – at the back of main group but not detached
bhd – detached from the main body of runners
hld up – restrained as a deliberate tactical move
nt rcvr – lost all chance after interference, mistake etc.
wknd – stride shortened as it began to tire
lost tch – had been in the main body but a gap appeared as it tired

lost pl – remains in main body of runners but lost several positions quickly

Riding

effrt – short-lived effort

pushed along – received urgings with hands only, jockey not using legs

rdn – received urgings from saddle, including use of whip

hrd rdn – received maximum assistance from the saddle including use of whip

drvn – received forceful urgings, jockey putting in a lot of effort and using whip

hrd drvn – jockey very animated, plenty of kicking, pushing and reminders

Finishing comments

jst failed – closing rapidly on the winner and probably would have led a stride after the line

r.o – jockey's efforts usually involved to produce an increase in pace without finding an appreciable turn of speed

r.o wl – jockey's efforts usually involved to produce an obvious increase in pace without finding an appreciable turn of speed

unable qckn – not visibly tiring but does not possess a sufficient change of pace

one pce – not tiring but does not find a turn of speed, from a position further out than unable qckn

nt r.o. – did not consent to respond to pressure

styd on – going on well towards the end, utilising stamina

nvr able to chal – unable to produce sufficient to reach a challenging position

nvr nr to chal – in the opinion of the racereader, the horse was never in a suitable position to challenge.

nrst fin – nearer to the winner in distance beaten than at any time since the race had begun in earnest

nvr nrr – nearer to the winner position-wise than at any time since the race had begun in earnest

rallied – responded to pressure to come back with a chance having lost its place

no ex – unable to sustain its run

bttr for r – likely to improve for the run and experience

rn green – inclined to wander and falter through inexperience

too much to do – left with too much leeway to make up

Winning comments

v.easily – a great deal in hand

easily – plenty in hand

comf – something in hand, always holding the others

pushed out – kept up to its work with hands and heels without jockey resorting to whip or kicking along and wins fairly comfortably

rdn out – pushed and kicked out to the line, with the whip employed

drvn out – pushed and kicked out to the line, with considerable effort and the whip employed

all out – nothing to spare, could not have found any more

jst hld on – holding on to a rapidly diminishing lead, could not have found any more if passed

unchal – must either make all or a majority of the running and not be challenged from an early stage

Complete list of abbreviations

a - always
abt - about
a.p - always prominent
appr - approaching
awrdd - awarded
b.b.v - broke blood-vessel
b.d - brought down
bdly - badly
bef - before
bhd - behind
bk - back
blkd - baulked
blnd - blundered
bmpd - bumped
bnd - bend
btn- beaten
bttr - better
c - came
ch - chance
chal - challenged
chse - chase
chsd - chased
chsng - chasing
circ - circuit
cl - close
clr - clear
clsd - closed
comf - comfortably
cpld - coupled
crse - course
ct - caught
def - definite
dismntd - dismounted
disp - disputed
dist - distance
div - division
drvn - driven
dwlt - dwelt
edgd - edged
effrt - effort
ent - entering
ev ch - every chance
ex - extra
f - furlong
fin - finished
fnd - found
fnl - final
fr - from
gd - good
gng - going
gp - group
grad - gradually
grnd - ground
hd - head
hdd - headed
hdwy - headway
hld - held
hmpd - hampered
imp - impression
ins - inside
j.b - jumped badly
j.w - jumped well
jnd - joined
jst - just
kpt - kept
l - length
ld - lead
ldr - leader
lft - left
mod - moderate
m - mile
m.n.s - made no show
mde - made
mid div - mid division
mstke - mistake
n.d - never dangerous
n.g.t - not go through
n.m.r - not much room
nk - neck
no ex - no extra
nr - near
nrr - nearer
nrst fin - nearest finish
nt - not
nvr - never
one pce - one pace
out - from finish
outpcd - outpaced
p.u - pulled up
pce - pace
pckd - pecked
pl - place

plcd - placed
plld - pulled
press - pressure
prog - progress
prom - prominent
qckly - quickly
qckn - quicken
r - race
racd - raced
rch - reach
rcvr - recover
rdn - ridden
rdr - rider
reard - reared
ref - refused
rn - ran
rnd - round
r.o - ran on
rr - rear
rspnse - response
rt - right
s - start
sddle - saddle
shkn - shaken
slt - slight
sme - some
sn - soo
spd- speed
st - straight
stmbld - stumbled
stdd - steadied
stdy - steady
strly - strongly
styd - stayed
styng - staying
s. u - slipped up
swtchd - switched
swvd - swerved
tk - took
t.k.h - took keen hold
t.o - tailed off
tch - touch
thrght - throughout
trbld - troubled
trckd - tracked
u.p - under pressure
u.str.p-understrongpressure
w - with
w.r.s - whipped round start
wd - wide
whn - when
wknd - weakened
wl - well
wnr - winner
wnt - went
1/2-wy - halfway

Racing Post Ratings

Raceform Ratings for each horse are listed after the Starting Price and indicate the actual level of performance attained in that race. The figure in the back index represents the BEST public form that Raceform's Handicappers still believe the horse capable of reproducing.

To use the ratings constructively in determining those horses best-in in future events, the following procedures should be followed:

(i) In races where all runners are set to carry the same weight, no
calculations are necessary. The horse with the highest rating is best in.

(ii) In races where all runners are set to carry different weights, add one point to the Raceform Rating for every pound less than 12 st to be carried; deduct one point for every pound more than 12 st.

For example,

Horse	Age & Weight	Adj. from 12st	RRbase rating	Adj. rating
Kid Cassidy	7-11-12	+2	150	152
Tanks For That	10-11-9	+5	147	152
Oiseau De Nuit	11-11-8	+6	147	153
Toubab	7-11-7	+7	145	152

Therefore Oiseau De Nuit is top-rated (best-in)

The following symbols are used in conjunction with the ratings:

++: almost certain to prove better

+: likely to prove better

d: disappointing (has run well below best recently)

?: form hard to evaluate

t: tentative rating based on race-time rating may prove unreliable

Weight adjusted ratings for every race are published daily in Raceform Private Handicap.

For subscription terms please contact the Subscription Department on 01933 304858.

Key to racereaders' initials

WG ....Walter Glynn
RL................ Richard Lowther
LM...................Lee McKenzie
TM .... Tim Mitchell
JN .... Jonathan Neesom
DO .... Darren Owen
SP...................... Steve Payne
CR ....Colin Roberts
JR .... Joe Rowntree
AS...................Andrew Sheret
ST .... Steve Taylor
RY...................Richard Young

Raceform median times

Some distances have been omitted where insufficient data exists to establish a reliable median time.

AINTREE
Chase (Mildmay)
2m 4m 0.0
2m4f 5m 8.2
3m1f 6m 30.0

Chase (National)
2m5f110y 5m 36.0
4m4f 9m 20.5

Hurdles
2m110y 4m 4.6
2m4f 5m 0.7
3m110y 6m 16.3

ASCOT
Chase
2m1f 4m 15.0
2m3f 4m 47.0
2m5f110y 5m 26.0
3m 6m 9.0

Hurdles
2m 3m 49.0
2m3f110y 4m 48.0
2m6f 5m 27.0
3m 6m 11.0

AYR
Chase
2m 4m 10.7
2m4f 5m 22.9
3m1f 6m 49.9
4m1f 8m 20.8

Hurdles
2m 4m 3.1
2m4f 5m 12.0
3m110y 6m 31.8

BANGOR-ON-DEE
Chase
2m1f110y 4m 22.1
2m4f110y 5m 09.1
3m110y 6m 19.8
3m6f 7m 55.0

Hurdles
2m1f 4m 10.9
2m4f 4m 57.4
3m 5m 51.0

CARLISLE
Chase
2m 4m 16.1
2m4f 5m 27.4
3m110y 6m 42.4
3m2f 7m 7.2

Hurdles
2m1f 4m 29.8
2m4f 5m 22.8
3m1f 6m 38.2

CARTMEL
Chase
2m1f110y 4m 18.9
2m5f110y 5m 25.4
3m2f 6m 34.9
3m6f 7m 36.2

Hurdles
2m1f110y 4m 13.2
2m6f 5m 29.3
3m2f 6m 26.1

CATTERICK
Chase
2m 4m 0.1
2m3f 4m 48.8
3m1f110y 6m 42.0

Hurdles
2m 3m 52.5
2m3f 4m 46.8
3m1f110y 6m 27.6

CHELTENHAM (NEW)
Chase
2m110y 4m 6.7
2m5f 5m 19.4
3m1f110y 6m 38.2
3m2f110y 6m 54.3
4m1f 8m 49.9

Hurdles
2m1f 4m 11.3
2m4f110y 5m 5.0
2m5f110y 5m 16.6
3m 6m 1.0

CHELTENHAM (OLD)
Chase
2m 3m 58.0
2m4f110y 5m 11.0
3m110y 6m 18.3
3m3f110y 7m 12.6

Hurdles
2m110y 4m 2.0
2m5f 5m 13.4
3m1f110y 6m 30.9

Cross Country Chases
3m7f 8m 38.0

CHEPSTOW
Chase
2m110y 4m 17.1
2m3f110y 5m 11.3
3m 6m 22.0
3m2f110y 7m 2.0
3m5f110y 7m 49.0

Hurdles
2m110y 4m 10.4
2m4f 5m 2.7
3m 6m 16.8

DONCASTER
Chase
2m110y 4m 7.9
2m3f 4m 49.0
3m 6m 12.7
3m2f 6m 40.0

Hurdles
2m110y 4m 4.7
2m3f110y 4m 51.3
3m110y 6m 15.0

EXETER
Chase
2m1f110y 4m 19.0
2m3f110y 4m 57.3
2m7f110y 6m 0.1
3m1f110y 6m 41.1
4m 8m 28.7

Hurdles
2m1f 4m 15.5
2m3f 4m 42.7
2m6f110y 5m 48.0
3m110y 6m 14.4

FAKENHAM
Chase
2m110y 4m 16.6
2m5f110y 5m 41.8
3m110y 6m 35.7

Hurdles
2m 4m 5.4
2m4f 5m 12.6
2m7f110y 6m 4.4

FFOS LAS
Chase
2m 4m 5.0
2m5f 5m 34.0
3m 6m 23.0

Hurdles
2m 3m 54.0
2m4f 4m 52.0
3m 6m 39.0

FONTWELL
Chase
2m2f 4m 34.7
2m4f 5m 7.3
2m6f 5m 43.0
3m2f110y 7m 1.1

Hurdles
2m2f110y 4m 34.3
2m4f 4m 59.4
2m6f110y 5m 42.5
3m3f 6m 52.8

HAYDOCK
Chase
2m 4m 11.0
2m4f 5m 10.0
3m 6m 14.0
3m4f 7m 34.0

Hurdles
2m 4m 0.7
2m4f 4m 56.0
3m 5m 52.0
3m1f 6m 8.0

HEXHAM
Chase
2m110y 4m 9.8
2m4f110y 5m 13.5
3m1f 6m 32.2

Hurdles
2m110y 4m 17.4
2m4f110y 5m 12.5
3m 6m 13.2

HUNTINGDON
Chase
2m110y 4m 10.2
2m4f110y 5m 5.3
3m 6m 10.3

Hurdles
2m110y 3m 54.9
2m4f110y 4m 59.0
2m5f110y 5m 10.6
3m2f 6m 22.9

KELSO
Chase
2m1f 4m 18.0
2m6f110y 5m 44.5
3m1f 6m 31.5
3m4f 7m 25.4

Hurdles
2m110y 4m 1.8
2m2f 4m 27.0
2m6f110y 5m 41.0

KEMPTON
Chase
2m 3m 58.0
2m4f110y 5m 19.5
3m 6m 15.0

Hurdles
2m 4m 0.0
2m5f 5m 24.0
3m 110y 6m 27.5

LEICESTER
Chase
2m 4m 8.2
2m4f110y 5m 18.9
2m7f110y 6m 4.0

Hurdles
2m 4m 1.0
2m4f110y 5m 24.7

LINGFIELD
Chase
2m 4m 7.8
2m4f110y 5m 18.2
3m 6m 23.7

Hurdles
2m110y 4m 14.1
2m3f110y 5m 6.7
2m7f 6m 2.8

LUDLOW
Chase
2m 3m 58.5
2m4f 5m 4.4
3m 6m 8.3

Hurdles
2m 3m 49.5
2m5f 5m 14.8
3m 5m 52.3

MARKET RASEN
Chase
2m2f 4m 35.0
2m4f 5m 5.7
2m6f110y 5m 46.0
3m1f 6m 31.3
3m4f110y 7m 47.1

Hurdles
2m1f110y 4m 19.0
2m3f110y 4m 51.7
2m6f 5m 31.8
3m 6m 7.7

MUSSELBURGH
Chase
2m 3m 52.4
2m4f 5m 1.2
3m 6m 3.4

Hurdles
2m ... 3m 48.4
2m4f ... 4m 51.5
3m110y ... 5m 56.7

NEWBURY
Chase
2m1f ... 4m 13.0
2m2f110y ... 4m 44.0
2m4f ... 5m 12.0
2m6f110y ... 5m 50.3
3m ... 6m 11.0
3m2f110y ... 6m 56.0

Hurdles
2m110y ... 4m 9.9
2m3f ... 4m 50.6
2m5f ... 5m 19.0
3m110y ... 6m 8.3

NEWCASTLE
Chase
2m110y ... 4m 21.1
2m4f ... 5m 27.2
3m ... 6m 22.5
3m6f ... 8m 20.4
4m1f ... 9m 7.8

Hurdles
2m ... 4m 10.0
2m4f ... 5m 21.1
3m ... 6m 14.0

NEWTON ABBOT
Chase
2m110y ... 4m 6.5
2m5f110y ... 5m 21.4
3m2f110y ... 6m 44.6

Hurdles
2m1f ... 4m 5.7
2m3f ... 4m 33.9
2m6f ... 5m 20.3
3m3f ... 6m 41.0

PERTH
Chase
2m ... 4m 2.8
2m4f110y ... 5m 14.0
3m ... 6m 20.4
3m7f ... 8m 11.6

Hurdles
2m110y ... 3m 59.7
2m4f110y ... 5m 6.9
3m110y ... 6m 9.9
3m3f ... 6m 47.6

PLUMPTON
Chase
2m1f ... 4m 25.9
2m4f ... 5m 07.3
3m2f ... 6m 50.7
3m5f ... 7m 40.0

Hurdles
2m ... 4m 0.8
2m5f ... 5m 22.3
3m1f110y ... 6m 28.8

SANDOWN
Chase
2m ... 4m 1.8
2m4f110y ... 5m 18.4
3m110y ... 6m 27.8
3m5f110y ... 7m 44.0

Hurdles
2m110y ... 4m 7.2
2m3f110y ... 5m 1.8
2m6f ... 5m 30.0

SEDGEFIELD
Chase
2m110y ... 4m 8.6
2m4f ... 5m 3.0
2m5f ... 5m 18.0
3m3f ... 6m 49.0

Hurdles
2m1f ... 4m 6.9
2m4f ... 4m 58.7
2m5f110y ... 5m 14.6
3m3f110y ... 6m 52.0

SOUTHWELL
Chase
2m1f ... 4m 7.7
2m4f110y ... 5m 15.0
3m110y ... 6m 26.0
3m2f ... 6m 38.8

Hurdles
2m ... 3m 57.1
2m4f110y ... 5m 10.7
3m110y ... 6m 7.5

STRATFORD
Chase
2m1f110y ... 4m 7.1
2m4f ... 4m 54.2
2m5f110y ... 5m 15.0
2m7f ... 5m 41.6
3m4f ... 7m 13.0

Hurdles
2m110y ... 3m 56.0
2m3f ... 4m 35.3
2m6f110y ... 5m 28.1
3m3f ... 6m 28.6

TAUNTON
Chase
2m110y ... 4m 10.0
2m3f ... 4m 56.5
2m7f110y ... 6m 14.6

Hurdles
2m1f ... 4m 8.0
2m3f110y ... 4m 46.0
3m110y ... 6m 7.1

TOWCESTER
Chase
2m110y ... 4m 16.1
2m3f110y ... 5m 18.2
2m6f ... 5m 53.0
3m110y ... 6m 46.6

Hurdles
2m ... 4m 7.9
2m3f110y ... 4m 9.6
2m5f ... 5m 38.9
3m ... 6m 15.0

UTTOXETER
Chase
2m ... 3m 55.6
2m5f ... 5m 23.5
2m6f110y ... 5m 48.5
3m ... 6m 15.1
3m2f ... 7m 4.0
4m1f110y ... 9m 0.0

Hurdles
2m ... 3m 55.2
2m4f110y ... 5m 4.0
2m6f110y ... 5m 30.9
3m ... 6m 5.0

WARWICK
Chase
2m ... 4m 5.6
2m4f110y ... 5m 21.0
3m110y ... 6m 27.0
3m2f ... 6m 52.7
3m5f ... 7m 41.0

Hurdles
2m ... 3m 56.5
2m3f ... 4m 42.7
2m5f ... 5m 15.0
3m1f ... 6m 27.5

WETHERBY
Chase
2m ... 3m 55.8
2m4f110y ... 5m 7.8
2m7f110y ... 5m 58.5
3m1f ... 6m 15.8

Hurdles
2m110y ... 3m 55.8
2m4f110y ... 5m 15.9
2m6f ... 5m 28.6
3m1f ... 6m 16.5

WINCANTON
Chase
2m ... 3m 59.9
2m5f ... 5m 25.2
3m1f110y ... 6m 39.5
3m3f110y ... 7m 8.2

Hurdles
2m ... 3m 48.9
2m4f ... 5m 0.0
2m6f ... 5m 26.5

WORCESTER
Chase
2m ... 3m 51.6
2m4f110y ... 5m 5.6
2m7f110y ... 5m 55.7

Hurdles
2m ... 3m 47.3
2m4f ... 4m 47.4
3m ... 5m 44.6

Course Descriptions

COURSE	COMMENT
AINTREE	Two left-handed courses. Grand National circuit, 2m2f, is flat and has big fences with a slight drop on the landing side of some and a long run-in. Mildmay Course, 1m3f, flat with conventional fences, is sharper than the hurdles course.
ASCOT	Right-handed, galloping, last mile mainly uphill, with stiff fences. Circuit 1m5f.
AYR	Left-handed, mainly flat. Circuit 1m4f.
BANGOR	Left-handed, sharp and flat with a long run-in. Circuit 1m4f.
CARLISLE	Right-handed, undulating, stiff and galloping. Circuit 1m5f
CARTMEL	Left-handed, sharp and undulating, with stiff fences and a 4f run-in for chases. Circuit 1m.
CATTERICK	Left-handed, sharp and undulating, suiting handy types. Circuit 1m3f.
CHELTENHAM *(old course)*	Left-handed, galloping, undulating and testing track with stiff fences. Circuit 1m4f.
CHELTENHAM *(new course)*	Left-handed, galloping, undulating and testing track with stiff fences. Circuit 1m4½f.
CHEPSTOW	Left-handed and undulating. Going can be very testing. Circuit 1m7f.
DONCASTER	Left-handed, galloping, generally flat. Heavy ground rare. Circuit 2m.
EXETER	Right-handed and undulating. Stiff test of stamina. Circuit 2m.
FAKENHAM	Left-handed, sharp, undulating, suiting nippy types. Circuit 1m.
FFOS LAS	Left-handed, galloping, flat track. Circuit 1m6f.
FONTWELL	Left-handed hurdle course. Figure-of-eight chase course does not suit long-striding gallopers. Ground can be testing. Circuit 1m.
HAYDOCK	Left-handed, flat and galloping but with sharper bends since the course was re-aligned. Circuit 1m5f.
HEXHAM	Left-handed, severe and undulating, emphasis on stamina. Circuit 1m4f.
HUNTINGDON	Right-handed and galloping. Circuit 1m4f.

KELSO	Left-handed and undulating. Hurdles course of 1m1f is sharp, more so than 1m 3f chase track, which has 2f run-in.
KEMPTON	Triangular circuit 1m5f, practically flat. Circuit 1m5f.
LEICESTER	Right-handed and undulating, placing emphasis on stamina. Circuit 1m6f.
LINGFIELD	Left-handed, undulating and sharp. Chase circuit 1m5f, hurdles run on flat course.
LUDLOW	Right-handed. Chase course flat with sharp bends, circuit 1m4f. Hurdles track, 150y longer, slightly undulating, with easier bends.
MARKET RASEN	Right-handed oval, sharp and somewhat undulating. Circuit 1m2f.
MUSSELBURGH	Right-handed virtually flat track with sharp turns. Circuit 1m3f.
NEWBURY	Left-handed, flat and galloping, with stiff fences. Circuit 1m7f.
NEWCASTLE	Left-handed, with uphill finish. Going can be very testing. Circuit 1m6f.
NEWTON ABBOT	Left-handed oval, sharp with short run-in. Circuit 1m2f.
PERTH	Right-handed and flat, with tight bends. Chase course has long run-in. Circuit 1m 2f.
PLUMPTON	Left-handed, undulating, sharp. Circuit 1m1f.
SANDOWN	Right-handed with stiff uphill finish. Chase course tricky, especially for novices. Hurdles run on flat course. Circuit 1m5f.
SEDGEFIELD	Left-handed, undulating oval, sharp bends. Chase course has easy fences. Circuit 1m2f.
SOUTHWELL	Left-handed oval, approx 1m round, with six portable fences. Outside half of jumps course used in summer.
STRATFORD	Left-handed, flat and sharp, with short finishing straight. Circuit 1m2f.
TAUNTON	Right-handed oval, on the sharp side with short run-in. Circuit 1m2f.
TOWCESTER	Right-handed, with last mile uphill. Very testing. Circuit 1m6f.
UTTOXETER	Left-handed with some undulations. Hurdle course is inside chase course. Circuit 1m3f.
WARWICK	Left-handed, with tight turns and short run-in. Circuit 1m5f.
WETHERBY	Left-handed oval, with easy bends. Circuit 1m4f.
WINCANTON	Right-handed rectangular track, mainly flat. Circuit 1m3f.
WORCESTER	Left-handed 1m5f oval, flat with long straights and easy turns.

HUNTINGDON (R-H)

Sunday, April 28

OFFICIAL GOING: Good (chs 6.9; hdl 6.2)

Wind: Fresh; across Weather: Overcast

1 32REDPOKER.COM MARES' "NATIONAL HUNT" NOVICES' HURDLE (10 hdls) 2m 4f 110y

2:20 (2:21) (Class 4) 4-Y-0+ **£3,119** (£915; £457; £228)

Form RPR

350/ **1** **Toubeera**[12] 5339 7-10-12 115 AidanColeman 114+
(Venetia Williams) *chsd clr ldr: clsd to ld 3 out: sn clr and wl in command: mstke last: v easily* **6/4[1]**

22U/ **2** *15* **Pollystone (IRE)**[61] 4434 7-10-9 0 IanPopham(3) 94
(Martin Keighley) *racd keenly: led and sn clr: hdd 3 out: sn outpcd and no ch w wnr: hld on for 2nd flat* **9/2[3]**

55/ **3** *¾* **In By Midnight**[17] 5249 5-10-12 0 GerardTumelty 93
(Tom George) *chsd clr ldng pair: clsd 7th: rdn and btn sn after next: hung bdly lft and pressing for 2nd flat: kpt on same pce* **7/1**

602/ **4** *10* **Gulfport**[25] 5123 4-9-13 0 NickSlatter(7) 77
(Donald McCain) *racd off the pce in midfield: rdn and sme hdwy bef 7th: wknd 3 out* **20/1**

40/ **5** *20* **Miss Duffy**[76] 4163 5-10-12 0 CharlieHuxley 63
(William Kinsey) *racd wl off the pce in last trio: lost tch 6th: t.o after next* **25/1**

00/ **6** *84* **Recway Lass**[27] 5070 5-10-7 0 TrevorWhelan(5)
(John Butler) *a wl bhd: lost tch 6th: wl t.o after next* **66/1**

400/ **U** **Taradrewe**[23] 5163 6-10-9 0 (t) RachaelGreen(3)
(Anthony Honeyball) *midfield whn mstke and uns rdr 1st* **2/1[2]**

000/ **P** **Grafty Girl**[320] 705 6-10-12 0 HaddenFrost
(Roger Curtis) *racd off the pce in midfield: mstke 1st and 5th: dropped to rr after 5th and sn struggling: t.o bef 7th tl p.u 3 out* **100/1**

0/ **P** **Silk Sky**[140] 2953 7-10-12 0 AlexMerriam
(Phil McEntee) *wl off the pce in last trio: sme hdwy 3rd: rdn and dropped to rr bef 6th: lost tch and t.o bef 7th tl p.u 3 out* **66/1**

4m 39.6s (-19.40) **Going Correction** -0.775s/f (Firm)
WFA 4 from 5yo+ 6lb **9** Ran SP% **116.6**
Speed ratings (Par 105): **105,99,99,95,87 55, , ,**
toteswingers 1&2 £2.00, 1&3 £2.30, 2&3 £5.30 CSF £8.68 TOTE £2.00: £1.10, £1.40, £1.80; EX 9.70 Trifecta £37.60 Pool: £1,960.43 - 39.09 winning units..
Owner Richard Britten-Long **Bred** Mrs H I S Calzini **Trained** Kings Caple, H'fords

FOCUS

This became much less competitive when Taradrewe came down at the first flight and it ultimately proved very straightforward for 115-rated winner, who was left with little to beat.

2 32REDBINGO.COM H'CAP HURDLE (10 hdls) 2m 5f 110y

2:50 (2:54) (Class 5) (0-100,99) 4-Y-0+ **£2,053** (£598; £299)

Form RPR

005/ **1** **Deux Etoiles (IRE)**[689] 798 6-10-7 80 JamieMoore 90+
(Gary Moore) *in tch in midfield: mstke 6th: cl 5th and mstke 3 out: ev ch next: hung lft u.p but led fnl 100yds: styd on wl* **12/1**

104/ **2** *2¾* **Overdante**[27] 5083 11-11-1 91 (p) KielanWoods(3) 97
(Charlie Longsdon) *chsd ldrs: rdn and ev ch 2 out: led and wnt lft last: hung lft u.p and hdd fnl 100yds: no ex* **10/1[3]**

530/ **3** *2¼* **Finmerello**[164] 2437 7-11-3 90 NickScholfield 95
(Kim Bailey) *hld up in tch in midfield: wnt 2nd after 7th: led 2 out: hdd last: sn hmpd and swtchd rt: no ex and wknd fnl 75yds* **9/2[2]**

R24/ **4** *4½* **See You Jack**[16] 5275 8-11-12 99 (b[1]) AndrewThornton 101
(Caroline Bailey) *led rdrless to post: v reluctant to line up: led in and rdr vaulted aboard to jump off in midfield: chsd ldrs 2nd: rdn and dropped himself out after 3 out: 6th and wl hld 2 out: styd on wl again fr last* **9/2[2]**

043/ **5** *¾* **Mr Robinson (FR)**[43] 4799 6-10-1 74 AidanColeman 73
(Tony Carroll) *hld up in tch in last trio: hdwy to chse ldrs on outer 7th: rdn and btn after 3 out: wl hld 2 out* **13/8[1]**

644/ **6** *3* **Persian Herald**[27] 5069 5-11-7 99 (v[1]) TrevorWhelan(5) 97
(Neil King) *w ldr tl led 4th: hdd and hit 2 out: btn last: wknd flat* **20/1**

24P/ **7** *11* **Bubbly Braveheart (IRE)**[5] 4774 6-10-12 90 (t) JamesBanks(5) 77
(Phil McEntee) *t.k.h: hld up wl in tch in midfield: rdn and struggling after 7th: wknd 3 out* **33/1**

300/ **8** *32* **Bobbisox (IRE)**[767] 4955 8-10-1 79 KillianMoore(5) 37
(Alex Hales) *wl in tch tl rdn and wknd qckly after 7th: t.o after 3 out* **11/1**

404/ **9** *1* **Tiger's Jacey (IRE)**[31] 4977 6-11-8 95 ConorO'Farrell 52
(James Hughes) *t.k.h: led tl 4th: pressed ldr after: rdn and lost pl qckly after 7th: t.o whn blnd 2 out* **14/1**

006/ **10** *53* **Bally Lagan (IRE)**[110] 3559 5-11-5 92 CharliePoste
(Robin Dickin) *mstkes: hld up in tch in last trio: rdn and no rspnse after 6th: mstke 7th and wl t.o bef next* **20/1**

P06/ **11** *36* **Laidback Leo**[31] 4986 5-10-0 76 WayneKavanagh(3)
(Robin Dickin) *hld up in tch in last trio: rdn and lost tch bef 7th: wl t.o 3 out* **50/1**

5m 1.66s (-8.94) **Going Correction** -0.775s/f (Firm) **11** Ran SP% **120.7**
Speed ratings (Par 103): **85,84,83,81,81 80,76,64,64,44 31**
toteswingers 1&2 £11.80, 1&3 £9.10, 2&3 £7.40 CSF £120.65 CT £632.23 TOTE £12.50: £3.20, £2.70, £1.40; EX 155.40 Trifecta £505.70 Pool: £1,521.67 - 2.25 winning units..
Owner Heart Of The South Racing **Bred** Paget Bloodstock **Trained** Lower Beeding, W Sussex

FOCUS

Very ordinary form, the second and third setting the level.

3 32RED.COM NOVICES' HURDLE (10 hdls) 2m 5f 110y

3:25 (3:26) (Class 4) 4-Y-0+ **£3,119** (£915; £457; £228)

Form RPR

353/ **1** **McIlhatton (IRE)**[80] 4074 5-10-13 0 DarylJacob 116+
(Paul Nicholls) *racd off the pce in midfield: clsd on ldrs 6th: led bef 2 out and sn clr: hung rt between last 2: mstke last: stl hanging but r.o flat: rdn out* **3/1[2]**

PP/ **2** *7* **Now Then Charlie (IRE)**[16] 5265 8-10-6 0 JosephAkehurst(7) 110
(John Ferguson) *chsd clr ldr and clr of field: clsd on ldr 6th: rdn and outpcd after 3 out: pressing for placings but no threat to wnr last: wnt 2nd flat: no imp* **25/1**

212/ **3** *2¼* **Shernando**[43] 4789 6-11-5 135 BarryGeraghty 117+
(Nicky Henderson) *racd off the pce in midfield: clsd on ldrs 6th: clsd enough whn swtchd lft and rdn bef 2 out: fnd little u.p and no threat to wnr after: plugged on to go 3rd flat* **8/15[1]**

U50/ **4** *4½* **Rasheed**[27] 5065 5-10-6 0 ThomasGarner(7) 104
(Lucy Wadham) *led and sn clr: mstke 3rd: rdn and hdd bef 2 out: sn outpcd by wnr and btn: mstke last: wknd and lost 2 pls flat* **33/1**

P0P/ **5** *13* **Buffy The Beatle**[15] 5289 5-10-13 0 (p) NickScholfield 89
(Kim Bailey) *prom in main gp: rdn and clsd on ldrs 6th: cl enough but hrd drvn bef 3 out: wknd wl bef 2 out* **66/1**

03/ **6** *55* **Cappielow Park**[27] 5056 4-10-7 0 (bt[1]) AndrewThornton 28
(Fleur Hawes) *t.k.h: hld up wl off the pce in rr: lost tch and hmpd 7th: sn wl t.o* **66/1**

0/ **7** *7* **Red Mystique (IRE)**[17] 5240 4-10-0 0 NickSlatter(7) 21
(Philip Hide) *hld up wl off the pce in last trio: mstke 6th and 7th: lost tch and hmpd 8th: sn wl t.o* **66/1**

50/ **8** *65* **Clonusker (IRE)**[62] 4426 5-10-13 0 TomCannon
(Linda Jewell) *t.k.h: hld up off the pce in midfield: clsd on ldrs 6th: wknd rapidly bef 3 out: wl t.o after next* **100/1**

65/ **F** **Minellaforlunch (IRE)**[21] 5195 6-10-13 0 HenryOliver
(Henry Oliver) *prom in main gp: mstke 2nd and 3rd: clsd on ldrs 6th: cl 4th whn fell next* **11/2[3]**

4P/ **P** **Kicking Time (IRE)**[15] 5288 7-10-13 0 AidanColeman
(Sarah Humphrey) *t.k.h: hld up wl off the pce in last trio: rdn and struggling after 5th: lost tch next: t.o whn p.u 7th* **66/1**

5m 1.3s (-9.30) **Going Correction** -0.775s/f (Firm)
WFA 4 from 5yo+ 6lb **10** Ran SP% **119.4**
Speed ratings (Par 105): **85,82,81,80,75 55,52,29, ,**
toteswingers 1&2 £8.70, 1&3 £1.10, 2&3 £6.50 CSF £58.30 TOTE £3.50: £1.40, £6.00, £1.02; EX 65.30 Trifecta £138.80 Pool: £2,093.27 - 11.30 winning units..
Owner Giles, Donlon & MacDonald **Bred** Maurice O'Brien **Trained** Ditcheat, Somerset

FOCUS

This was won in emphatic fashion, and the winner is rated in line with his previous best.

4 32REDBET.COM STANDARD OPEN NATIONAL HUNT FLAT RACE 2m 110y

3:55 (3:56) (Class 6) 4-6-Y-O **£1,642** (£478; £239)

Form RPR

6/ **1** **Knock House (IRE)**[152] 2682 4-10-12 0 DominicElsworth 106+
(Mick Channon) *hld up wl in tch: hdwy 6f out: chsd ldrs 4f out: rdn to chse ldr and edging rt wl over 1f out: led fnl 100yds: r.o wl* **13/2**

42/ **2** *2¼* **Keltic Rhythm (IRE)**[27] 5070 6-11-3 0 AlexMerriam 107
(Neil King) *chsd ldr tl lft in ld 10f out: drvn 3f out: kpt battling on u.p tl hdd and no ex fnl 100yds* **3/1[1]**

3 *2* **Arthur's Oak** 5-11-3 0 GerardTumelty 106
(Alan King) *hld up in tch in midfield: hdwy to chse ldrs 5f out: wnt 2nd travelling wl over 2f out: shkn up: rn green and short of room wl over 1f out: styd on same pce fnl f* **10/3[2]**

24/ **4** *4* **Kalucci (IRE)**[102] 3683 4-10-9 0 KielanWoods(3) 97
(Barry Brennan) *hld up in tch in last trio: hdwy 7f out: chsd ldrs 5f out: rdn and unable qck 2f out: styd on same pce after* **7/2[3]**

00/ **5** *17* **Calypso Princess**[27] 5062 6-10-10 0 CharlieHuxley 80
(Alan King) *in tch in rr: rdn 9f out: outpcd and wl btn 5f out: n.d but styd on past btn horses fnl 2f* **40/1**

60U/ **6** *2½* **Dan's Wee Man**[17] 5255 4-10-7 0 JamesBanks(5) 79
(Andy Turnell) *in tch in midfield: rdn 9f out: outpcd 5f out: n.d after but plugged on past btn horses fnl 2f* **25/1**

7 *2½* **Royal Macnab (IRE)**[161] 5-11-0 0 (t) BrendanPowell(3) 82
(Jamie Snowden) *chsd ldrs tl lft upside ldr 10f out: rdn and wknd qckly over 2f out: sn fdd* **12/1**

5/ **8** *1¼* **Giant Hercules (IRE)**[56] 4542 6-11-3 0 SeanFox 81
(Jim Boyle) *led tl rn wd and hdd 10f out: chsd ldrs tl wknd 3f out: sn fdd* **14/1**

9 *13* **Hope Royal**[84] 6-10-10 0 DavidBass 62
(Lawney Hill) *in tch in midfield: rdn and struggling 6f out: lost tch and wl bhd fnl 4f: t.o* **25/1**

10 *8* **The Western Hill (IRE)** 4-10-12 0 FelixDeGiles 57
(Tom Symonds) *chsd ldrs: rdn 9f out: lost pl qckly 5f out: wl bhd fnl 4f: t.o* **20/1**

6/ **11** *9* **Days Gone By**[160] 2534 5-11-3 0 AidanColeman 54
(Emma Lavelle) *chsd ldrs tl rdn and lost pl qckly 5f out: wl bhd fnl 4f: t.o* **16/1**

12 *dist* **Lady Cliche** 4-9-12 0 MrFTett(7)
(Roger Curtis) *in tch in rr tl lost tch qckly 1/2-way: wl t.o fnl 6f* **50/1**

3m 38.0s (-11.10) **Going Correction** -0.775s/f (Firm)
WFA 4 from 5yo+ 5lb **12** Ran SP% **120.7**
Speed ratings: **95,93,93,91,83 81,80,80,74,70 66,**
toteswingers 1&2 £5.00, 1&3 £3.90, 2&3 £3.10 CSF £25.27 TOTE £7.60: £2.10, £1.80, £1.90; EX 30.50 Trifecta £114.30 Pool: £1,033.54 - 6.78 winning units..
Owner Mrs T P Radford **Bred** P Cashman **Trained** West Ilsley, Berks

FOCUS

A low-grade bumper but easy form to rate.

5 32RED CASINO NOVICES' CHASE (16 fncs) 2m 4f 110y

4:30 (4:30) (Class 4) 5-Y-0+ **£3,898** (£1,144; £572; £286)

Form RPR

321/ **1** **Haar**[9] 5382 9-10-7 110 (tp) JamesBanks(5) 115+
(Andy Turnell) *hld up in tch: trckd ldng pair 3 out: led bef next: in command last: idling flat but a doing enough: rdn out mainly hands and heels* **3/1[3]**

3P3/ **2** *1¾* **Refusal**[31] 4997 5-10-12 102 AndrewThornton 113
(Caroline Bailey) *hld up wl in tch: cl 4th and hit 2 out: wnt 3rd and mstke 2 out: chsd wnr last: asked for effrt and nt qckn flat: one pce and a hld* **17/2**

315/ **3** *6* **The Mad Robertson (IRE)**[244] 1379 6-10-12 110 RichieMcLernon 107
(Jonjo O'Neill) *chsd ldrs: wnt 2nd 10th: rdn bef 2 out: pckd and lost 2nd last: no ex and sn outpcd* **11/4[2]**

556/ **4** *15* **Rajamand (FR)**[27] 5080 7-10-12 110 (p) JamieMoore 97
(Gary Moore) *led: mstke 11th: hdd bef 2 out: sn btn and wknd 2 out* **5/2[1]**

0PP/ **5** *17* **Hightown (IRE)**[33] 4965 6-10-9 97 MarkQuinlan(3) 78
(Alison Batchelor) *in tch towards rr: 5th and in tch whn drvn after 3 out: wknd bef next: t.o* **25/1**

223/ **6** *3½* **Itoldyou (IRE)**[75] 4182 7-10-12 101 TomCannon 75
(Linda Jewell) *in tch in rr: mstke 2nd: hung lft and reminders bnd after 10th: struggling after: lost tch 3 out: t.o* **5/1**

P40/ **7** *4½* **Tribal Dance (IRE)**[50] 4660 7-10-9 102 BrendanPowell(3) 71
(John O'Shea) *chsd ldr tl 10th: rdn and lost pl qckly 13th: wl bhd bef 2 out: t.o* **25/1**

005/ **P** **Barry The Barber (IRE)**[4] 5508 7-10-12 76.............(t) MrGBarfoot-Saunt
(Tracey Barfoot-Saunt) *in tch in midfield tl dropped to rr 3rd: sn lost tch: p.u 5th and collapsed: fatally injured* **100/1**

4m 55.5s (-9.80) **Going Correction** -0.275s/f (Good) **8** Ran SP% **116.1**
Speed ratings: **107,106,104,98,91 90,88,**
toteswingers 1&2 £4.60, 1&3 £2.90, 2&3 £4.40 CSF £27.26 TOTE £3.30: £1.80, £2.40, £1.20; EX 25.50 Trifecta £97.40 Pool: £2,017.78 - 15.53 winning units..

Owner Mrs R M Hill **Bred** Gainsborough Stud Management Ltd **Trained** Broad Hinton, Wilts

FOCUS
A reasonable little novice chase. The in-form winner is rated in line with his recent best, but was much better than this in past.

6 32RED H'CAP CHASE (19 fncs) 3m
5:05 (5:05) (Class 2) 5-Y-0+
£14,076 (£4,158; £2,079; £1,039; £519; £261)

Form RPR

301/ **1** **Triolo D'Alene (FR)**[23] 5160 6-10-9 139........................... BarryGeraghty 150+
(Nicky Henderson) *hld up in tch towards rr: hdwy to trck ldng pair 16th: led and j.lft 2 out: rdn and readily asserted between last 2: pushed out: eased towards fin* **2/1**[1]

4PP/ **2** *4½* **Junior**[27] 5098 10-11-12 156...(b) ConorO'Farrell 159
(David Pipe) *chsd ldr: rdn along after 14th: ev ch and drvn bef 2 out: outpcd by wnr 2 out: chsd clr wnr and hit last: kpt on same pce flat* **18/1**

0F5/ **3** *nk* **Billie Magern**[57] 4511 9-9-7 130 oh5............................ RyanHatch(7) 134+
(Nigel Twiston-Davies) *in tch: chsd ldrs 8th: mstke and lost pl 14th: sn drvn: tried to rally 16th: outpcd and btn 2 out: rallied u.p and styd on flat: no ch w wnr* **12/1**

411/ **4** *7* **Galway Jack (IRE)**[25] 5122 8-10-4 134........................ AndrewThornton 128
(Caroline Bailey) *led tl hdd and mstke 2 out: no ex and lost 2nd last: wknd fnl 100yds* **8/1**

352/ **5** *2½* **Niceonefrankie**[15] 5282 7-10-0 130.................................. AidanColeman 123
(Venetia Williams) *in tch: chsd ldrs 5th: rdn and struggling 16th: outpcd bef 2 out: wl hld and plugged on same pce fr 2 out* **10/1**

42U/ **6** *13* **Barlow (IRE)**[44] 4775 6-9-11 130 oh2........................... BrendanPowell(3) 113
(Warren Greatrex) *in tch in midfield: mstke 13th: 4th and rdn 16th: wknd bef 2 out* **3/1**[2]

50U/ **7** *7* **Giorgio Quercus (FR)**[23] 5160 8-10-6 136........................... DavidBass 111
(Nicky Henderson) *hld up in tch: hdwy to chse ldrs 13th: rdn and btn sn after 3 out: wknd next* **14/1**

PP1/ **8** *34* **No Loose Change (IRE)**[12] 5341 8-10-5 135....................(t) DarylJacob 79
(Paul Nicholls) *chsd ldrs tl 5th: steadily lost pl: last but stl wl in tch whn rdn 13th: struggling 16th: wknd after 3 out: t.o* **9/2**[3]

033/ **P** **Holmwood Legend**[24] 5146 12-9-13 132.......................(t) IanPopham(3)
(Neil Mulholland) *dropped to rr 3rd: sn pushed along and nvr gng wl after: blnd 8th: sn rdn and lost tch: t.o whn p.u after 12th* **25/1**

5m 55.5s (-14.80) **Going Correction** -0.275s/f (Good) **9** Ran SP% **120.2**
Speed ratings: **113,111,111,109,108 103,101,90,**
toteswingers 1&2 £8.20, 1&3 £3.80, 2&3 £21.60 CSF £37.02 CT £363.03 TOTE £2.80: £1.10, £4.20, £3.60; EX 41.90 Trifecta £390.70 Pool: £1,905.66 - 3.65 winning units..

Owner Mr & Mrs Sandy Orr **Bred** Louis Couteaudier **Trained** Upper Lambourn, Berks

FOCUS
A quality handicap chase run at a strong pace and this turned into a real stamina test. A step up from the winner with the second more to his mark.

7 32RED BONUS AT 32RED.COM H'CAP CHASE (19 fncs) 3m
5:35 (5:35) (Class 4) (0-110,110) 5-Y-0+ **£3,898** (£1,144; £572; £286)

Form RPR

112/ **1** **City Press (IRE)**[55] 4570 7-11-6 107.......................(tp) BrendanPowell(3) 120+
(Warren Greatrex) *hld up in tch: hdwy to trck ldrs 15th: wnt 2nd and stl travelling strly bef 2 out: asked for effrt and led between last 2: racing v lazily in front and drvn to assert after last: easily* **10/3**[2]

34P/ **2** *5* **Kauto The Roc (FR)**[56] 4539 9-10-13 97..........................(t) CharlieHuxley 105
(Alan King) *chsd ldr tl j. into ld 7th: hdd 9th: reminder after 3 out and sn led: j.lft 2 out: hdd between last 2 and sn outpcd by wnr: one pce flat* **9/1**

P0P/ **3** *9* **Roseneath (IRE)**[43] 4792 9-11-3 101.................................(p) DarylJacob 98
(Alex Hales) *hld up in tch in rr: hdwy to chse ldrs 4th and stl travelling wl enough whn short of room on inner and hmpd bef 2 out: sn swtchd lft and rdn to chse ldng pair: wknd last* **13/2**[3]

P44/ **4** *11* **Global Flyer**[16] 5276 9-11-6 104.................................(b) AndrewThornton 94
(Caroline Bailey) *led tl outj. and hdd 7th: led again 9th: reminders after 11th: hdd and drvn after 3 out: wknd bef next* **9/4**[1]

PP0/ **5** *3¾* **Bishophill Jack (IRE)**[16] 5271 7-11-7 105....................(p) NickScholfield 91
(Kim Bailey) *in tch: lost pl and reminders after 5th: lost several positions after but stl in tch: rdn 12th: struggling u.p 15th: wl hld after 3 out* **14/1**

241/ **6** *nk* **Upton Mead (IRE)**[12] 5336 6-10-1 92........................ ConorShoemark(7) 75
(Kevin Tork) *in tch in midfield: mstke 3rd: 5th and u.p after 15th: struggling 3 out: wknd bef next* **9/1**

523/ **7** *7* **Whistling Senator (IRE)**[109] 3568 6-11-3 101.........(p) RichieMcLernon 80
(Jonjo O'Neill) *chsd ldrs: cl 3rd and blnd 3 out: sn rdn and btn: wkng whn j.lft next* **10/1**

33P/ **8** *10* **Rossbrin (IRE)**[217] 1617 8-11-9 110.................................(t) IanPopham(3) 78
(Anna Brooks) *in tch in midfield: rdn and struggling after 12th: lost tch 3 out: t.o* **12/1**

PPF/ **P** **Samenerve (FR)**[45] 4763 6-11-2 107..................................(t) RyanHatch(7)
(Nigel Twiston-Davies) *in tch in rr: reminders after 4th: more reminders and rdn after 8th: losing tch 14th: eased and p.u next* **14/1**

6m 2.1s (-8.20) **Going Correction** -0.275s/f (Good) **9** Ran SP% **117.3**
Speed ratings: **102,100,97,93,92 92,89,86,**
toteswingers 1&2 £5.00, 1&3 £5.60, 2&3 £10.60 CSF £33.56 CT £187.32 TOTE £4.20: £1.40, £3.10, £2.30; EX 38.90 Trifecta £321.60 Pool: £1,572.33 - 3.66 winning units..

Owner Lewis, Reid, Moss & Luck **Bred** Mrs M Doran **Trained** Upper Lambourn, Berks

FOCUS
A sound gallop to this open-looking handicap chase. The easy winner improved to the level promised by his bumper runs.

T/Plt: £24.30 to a £1 stake. Pool of £62,581.06 - 1,872.54 winning units T/Qpdt: £4.90 to a £1 stake. Pool of £4,635.20 - 695.30 winning units SP

LUDLOW (R-H)
Sunday, April 28

OFFICIAL GOING: Good (7.9)
Wind: Light; half-behind Weather: Cloudy with sunny spells

8 LUDLOW GOLF CLUB MAIDEN HURDLE (9 hdls) 2m
2:10 (2:10) (Class 4) 4-Y-0+ **£3,249** (£954; £477; £238)

Form RPR

22/ **1** **Rayvin Black**[27] 5064 4-10-9 119....................................... LeightonAspell 106
(Oliver Sherwood) *a.p: chsd ldr 3 out: pushed along after next: 2 l down whn lft in ld last: rdn out* **7/4**[1]

0/ **2** *1¼* **Vexillum (IRE)**[138] 2981 4-10-6 0....................................... RyanMahon(3) 103
(Harry Fry) *hld up in tch: rdn after 2 out: lft 2nd last: styd on* **12/1**

250/ **3** *4* **Kings Destiny**[162] 2470 7-11-0 110.................................... AndrewTinkler 105
(Nicky Henderson) *a.p: rdn appr 2 out: lft 3rd last: styd on same pce flat* **9/2**[2]

4/ **4** *2¾* **Hyperlink (IRE)**[44] 4779 4-10-6 0...................................... JackQuinlan(3) 97
(John Ferguson) *chsd ldr: hmpd 4th: lost 2nd 3 out: styd on same pce fr next* **14/1**

66/ **5** *14* **Star Presenter (IRE)**[27] 5064 5-11-0 0............................ LiamTreadwell 90
(Paul Webber) *hld up: hdwy 6th: wkng whn j.rt 3 out* **33/1**

U5/ **6** *9* **Golden Jubilee (USA)**[172] 2267 4-10-9 0.............. SamTwiston-Davies 79
(Nigel Twiston-Davies) *in rr whn blnd 1st: effrt appr 3 out: sn wknd: t.o* **22/1**

7 *1¾* **Swift Blade (IRE)**[163] 5-11-0 0.. RichardJohnson 80
(Lady Herries) *hld up: hdwy 6th: wknd after 3 out: t.o* **20/1**

00/ **8** *16* **Brave Decision**[28] 5032 6-11-0 0.. WillKennedy 65
(Suzy Smith) *hld up: bhd fr 4th: t.o* **100/1**

9 *20* **Sir Trevor (IRE)**[185] 4-10-2 0.................................. MrJamieJenkinson(7) 42
(John Bryan Groucott) *hld up: effrt 5th: wknd after next: t.o* **33/1**

026/ **U** **Panache**[59] 4473 8-10-11 0... MichealNolan(3)
(Angela Clarke) *prom tl hmpd and uns rdr 4th* **33/1**

F/ **P** **Shays River (IRE)**[41] 4840 8-11-0 0..................................... PaulMoloney
(Evan Williams) *hld up: a in rr: bhd fr 4th: t.o whn p.u bef 3 out* **16/1**

40/ **F** **Deia Sunrise (IRE)**[80] 4083 4-10-9 0................................ HarrySkelton 108+
(Paul Webber) *sn led: 2 l clr and looked in command whn fell last* **16/1**

63S/ **U** **Tarmac Girl**[455] 3991 5-9-11 0.................................. ScottBrockbank(10)
(Tim Vaughan) *mid-div: mstke and uns rdr 6th* **50/1**

U42/ **F** **Breaking Bits (IRE)**[28] 5032 6-11-0 112.............................. TomO'Brien
(Jamie Snowden) *trckd ldrs tl fell 4th* **5/1**[3]

3m 48.9s (-0.60) **Going Correction** -0.275s/f (Good)
WFA 4 from 5yo+ 5lb **14** Ran SP% **118.2**
Speed ratings (Par 105): **90,89,87,86,79 74,73,65,55, , , ,**
toteswingers 1&2 £7.60, 1&3 £1.60, 2&3 £11.90 CSF £22.35 TOTE £2.50: £1.30, £3.80, £1.80; EX 25.90 Trifecta £120.70 Pool: £649.94 - 4.03 winning units..

Owner V J Walsh **Bred** Mystic Meg Limited **Trained** Upper Lambourn, Berks

FOCUS
Bends moved to provide fresh ground and stable bend combined. One rider in the first described the ground as "good but a little bit quicker in places" while another was of the opinion that it was "good to firm but consistent". An interesting maiden hurdle run at an ordinary pace. The time was around 11sec outside standard, slow compared with the later handicap. The faller is rated a 2l winner.

9 YOUR FAVOURITE POOL BETS AT TOTEPOOL.COM NOVICES' CHASE (19 fncs) 3m
2:40 (2:40) (Class 3) 5-Y-0+ **£6,330** (£1,870; £935; £468; £234)

Form RPR

P03/ **1** **Bold Chief (IRE)**[59] 4484 8-10-9 0............................(tp) RyanMahon(3) 135+
(Harry Fry) *chsd ldrs: led 2 out: shkn up flat: styd on wl* **9/4**[1]

443/ **2** *6* **Silver Commander**[31] 4989 6-10-12 0.................................(t) JackDoyle 130
(Victor Dartnall) *chsd ldr: ev ch 2 out: styd on same pce flat* **7/1**[3]

621/ **3** *2¼* **Oscargo (IRE)**[22] 5181 9-11-4 130..................................(t) HarrySkelton 134
(Paul Nicholls) *led: blnd and hdd 2 out: no ex last* **11/4**[2]

2P1/ **4** *17* **Victor Leudorum (IRE)**[21] 5196 6-10-13 131............(t) GavinSheehan(5) 122
(Charlie Mann) *hld up: hdwy 12th: pushed along appr 4 out: wknd after next* **11/4**[2]

P0P/ **5** *8* **Spirit River (FR)**[26] 5105 8-10-12 130.............................. AndrewTinkler 104
(Nicky Henderson) *prom: nt fluent 4th: mstke 13th: wknd 4 out: t.o* **10/1**

041/ **P** **Manics Man**[373] 5489 8-10-12 0.. SamThomas
(Helen Nelmes) *a bhd: t.o fr 11th: p.u bef 4 out* **66/1**

5m 59.1s (-9.20) **Going Correction** -0.425s/f (Good) **6** Ran SP% **107.2**
Speed ratings: **98,96,95,89,86**
toteswingers 1&2 £3.50, 1&3 £2.40, 2&3 £4.20 CSF £15.94 TOTE £3.00: £1.70, £2.50; EX 14.80 Trifecta £47.60 Pool: £1,132.77 - 17.83 winning units..

Owner The Eyre Family **Bred** Patrick Carroll **Trained** Seaborough, Dorset

FOCUS
A decent little novice chase. The winner should go on to rate higher.

10 WELSH GUARDS ASSOCIATION H'CAP HURDLE (9 hdls) 2m
3:15 (3:15) (Class 4) (0-120,120) 4-Y-0+ **£5,198** (£1,526; £763; £381)

Form RPR

440/ **1** **Scoglio**[67] 4325 5-11-2 **110**.. LeeEdwards 115+
(Dave Roberts) *a.p: n.m.r 2 out: rdn to ld and hung rt last: styd on u.p* **25/1**

052/ **2** *2* **Candelita**[17] 5252 6-11-1 **109**... MarkGrant 111
(Jo Hughes) *hld up: hdwy 6th: ev ch fr 3 out: hung rt and mstke next: bmpd last: styd on same pce flat* **12/1**

513/ **3** *1¼* **Ladies Dancing**[7] 5435 7-11-4 **112**.. JamesDavies 113
(Chris Down) *chsd ldrs: ev ch fr 3 out tl styd on same pce flat* **4/1**[3]

215/ **4** *1½* **Red Skipper (IRE)**[345] 337 8-11-2 **120**........................ CiaranMckee(10) 122
(John O'Shea) *chsd ldr tl led 6th: rdn and hit 2 out: hdd last: styd on same pce* **14/1**

045/ **5** *nk* **Lemon Drop Red (USA)**[121] 2331 5-11-10 **118**.............. LiamTreadwell 118
(Paul Webber) *a.p: ev ch fr 3 out: rdn and hit last: no ex flat* **8/1**

3P1/ **6** *3¾* **Della Sun (FR)**[22] 5185 7-10-8 **109**.................................. JoshWall(7) 105
(Arthur Whitehead) *chsd ldrs: rdn appr 3 out: wknd bef last* **16/1**

6F0/ **7** *2½* **Aviso (GER)**[8] 4988 9-10-11 **105**......................(p) SamTwiston-Davies 99
(David Evans) *hld up: hdwy appr 3 out: blnd next: wknd appr last* **25/1**

560/ **8** *9* **Early Applause**[57] 4515 5-10-13 **107**................................... DannyCook 94
(Nicky Richards) *hld up: effrt appr 3 out: sn wknd* **25/1**

4F0/ **9** *42* **King Zeal (IRE)**[67] 4325 9-11-4 **112**..............................(t) LiamHeard 60
(Barry Leavy) *led to 6th: rdn and wknd bef next: t.o* **40/1**

The Form Book Jumps, Raceform Ltd, Compton, RG20 6NL.

314/ **10** *54* **Islandmagee (IRE)**[60] 4463 6-11-1 **109**.............................. PaulMoloney 8
(Evan Williams) *mid-div: mstkes: wknd appr 6th: t.o* **7/2**[2]

P **El Gran Torino (IRE)**[38] 4896 5-10-4 **98**....................(t) RichardJohnson
(A J Martin, Ire) *hld up: hdwy appr 3 out: wknd bef next: t.o whn p.u bef last* **11/4**[1]

3m 42.8s (-6.70) **Going Correction** -0.275s/f (Good) 11 Ran SP% **114.2**
Speed ratings (Par 105): **105,104,103,102,102 100,99,94,73,46**
toteswingers 1&2 £32.20, 1&3 £24.40, 2&3 £4.50 CSF £273.03 CT £1459.26 TOTE £44.10: £9.30, £2.40, £1.80; EX 883.60 Trifecta £534.80 Part won. Pool: £713.18 - 0.01 winning units..
Owner D B Roberts **Bred** Henry And Mrs Rosemary Moszkowicz **Trained** Kenley, Shropshire

FOCUS
They went a solid pace in this reasonable handicap hurdle and the form looks sound enough.

11 KING SIZE POOLS AT TOTEPOOL.COM H'CAP CHASE (17 fncs) 2m 4f
3:45 (3:48) (Class 3) (0-135,135) 5-Y-**£9,495** (£2,805; £1,402; £702; £351)

Form RPR
002/ **1** **Fiendish Flame (IRE)**[17] 5251 9-11-12 **135**....................... SeanQuinlan 146+
(Jennie Candlish) *mde all: sn clr: hit 4 out: hung rt flat: unchal* **15/8**[1]

P43/ **2** *6* **Buck Mulligan**[17] 5251 8-11-8 **131**.................................. PaulMoloney 136
(Evan Williams) *racd in 3rd pl tl chsd wnr who was clr 4th: tk clsr order 2 out: rdn and no ex flat* **11/2**

514/ **3** *22* **Cootehill (IRE)**[17] 5251 9-11-8 **131**.......................... SamTwiston-Davies 121
(Nigel Twiston-Davies) *hld up: wnt 3rd 12th: wknd 3 out* **4/1**[2]

1F6/ **4** *21* **Spock (FR)**[267] 1180 8-11-0 **128**...................................(p) HarryDerham(5) 94
(Paul Nicholls) *hld up: pushed along after 9th: nvr on terms: t.o* **6/1**

121/ **5** *4 ½* **Rob Conti (FR)**[169] 2330 8-11-7 **130**............................. RichardJohnson 92
(Philip Hobbs) *hld up and a bhd: blnd 12th: t.o* **5/1**[3]

0PP/ **6** *6* **Campbonnais (FR)**[178] 2154 8-10-9 **121**.........................(b) MPFogarty(3) 78
(John Joseph Hanlon, Ire) *chsd wnr to 4th: racd in 3rd pl to 12th: sn wknd: t.o* **7/1**

4m 51.3s (-13.10) **Going Correction** -0.425s/f (Good) 6 Ran SP% **113.6**
Speed ratings: **109,106,97,89,87 85**
toteswingers 1&2 £2.40, 1&3 £2.60, 2&3 £3.60 CSF £12.77 TOTE £3.60: £1.90, £3.60; EX 13.20 Trifecta £24.80 Pool: £846.12 - 25.51 winning units..
Owner Mrs Hall & Exors of the Late Hall **Bred** Richard Hall **Trained** Basford Green, Staffs

FOCUS
A good handicap chase. The winner is well treated at present and is rated 4lb off his best.

12 FLAT SEASON TEN TO FOLLOW AT TOTEPOOL.COM H'CAP HURDLE (THE SUNDAY £5K BONUS RACE) (11 hdls) 2m 5f
4:20 (4:20) (Class 3) (0-125,125) 4-Y-0 **£6,330** (£1,870; £935; £468; £234)

Form RPR
553/ **1** **Dragon's Den (IRE)**[24] 5148 6-10-9 **108**.......................... LeightonAspell 112+
(Chris Down) *hld up: hdwy after 8th: led 2 out: styd on wl* **7/2**[1]

122/ **2** *2 ¾* **Bravo Bravo**[16] 5269 6-10-11 **115**..............................(b) NicodeBoinville(5) 115
(Mark Gillard) *led to 3rd: chsd ldrs: rdn appr 3 out: hmpd next: rdn to chse wnr bef last: no imp flat* **11/2**[3]

143/ **3** *2 ½* **Gambo (IRE)**[31] 4981 7-11-0 **116**................................. AdamWedge(3) 115
(Evan Williams) *hld up: hdwy after 3 out: hit last: styd on: nt trble ldrs* **7/1**

560/ **4** *1* **Russie With Love**[81] 4069 7-10-9 **108**.............................. JamesDavies 105
(Chris Down) *chsd ldrs: led 7th: rdn and hdd 3 out: styd on same pce flat* **14/1**

UP0/ **5** *1 ¼* **Mark Twain (IRE)**[185] 2013 6-10-13 **112**................(t) SamTwiston-Davies 108
(Kim Bailey) *hld up: hdwy and hmpd 2 out: rdn and hung rt flat: no ex* **16/1**

30P/ **6** *¾* **Midnight Tuesday (FR)**[37] 4902 8-11-4 **124**................(t) KieronEdgar(7) 119
(David Pipe) *chsd ldrs: rdn appr 3 out: n.m.r next: wknd last* **10/1**

41P/ **7** *5* **Chestertern**[29] 5016 6-11-7 **120**.................................... SeanQuinlan 110
(Jennie Candlish) *chsd ldr tl led 3rd: hdd 7th: rdn appr 3 out: wknd bef last* **11/2**[3]

F10/ **8** *1 ½* **Parc Des Princes (USA)**[109] 3570 7-10-8 **107**.................... DannyCook 95
(Nicky Richards) *hld up: mstke 7th: rdn appr 3 out: nvr on terms* **9/2**[2]

UP2/ **9** *1 ¾* **Heavenstown (IRE)**[29] 5019 7-10-13 **112**............................. RhysFlint 100
(John Flint) *hld up: hdwy 8th: led 3 out: rdn and hdd next: wknd last* **10/1**

5m 10.4s (-4.40) **Going Correction** -0.275s/f (Good) 9 Ran SP% **114.4**
Speed ratings (Par 107): **97,95,95,94,94 93,91,91,90**
toteswingers 1&2 £2.30, 1&3 £5.20, 2&3 £4.40 CSF £23.18 CT £126.52 TOTE £4.50: £1.90, £1.80, £2.30; EX 17.00 Trifecta £70.20 Pool: £1,610.51 - 17.20 winning units..
Owner G Waterman **Bred** Thomas Hassett **Trained** Mutterton, Devon

FOCUS
A fair handicap hurdle, but the gallop wasn't strong. Straightforward form.

13 EDDIE MAPP MEMORIAL HUNTERS' CHASE (FOR THE LUDLOW GOLD CUP) (19 fncs) 3m
4:55 (4:55) (Class 6) 6-Y-0+ **£1,871** (£580; £290; £145)

Form RPR
352/ **1** **Lady Myfanwy**[7] 12-10-10 102... MissHLewis(7) 100+
(Mrs Myfanwy Miles) *chsd ldr: mstke 6th: led 12th: shkn up flat: styd on wl* **11/10**[1]

2 *5* **Oh Toodles (IRE)**[14] 6-11-3 0........................... ThomasCheesman(7) 101
(Mrs C J Robinson) *a.p: rdn to chse wnr appr 4 out: styd on same pce flat* **20/1**

34P/ **3** *28* **Coin Of The Realm (IRE)**[12] 5342 8-11-10 102................... MrDMansell 75
(S Flook) *hld up: drvn along appr 4 out: wnt remote 3rd whn blnd last: n.d: t.o* **9/2**[3]

55P/ **4** *15* **Tyup Pompey (IRE)**[15] 12-11-3 81........................... MrNathanCook(7) 62
(Ann Price) *led to 12th: wknd 4 out: t.o* **20/1**

126/ **5** *52* **Captain Marlon (IRE)**[17] 5253 12-11-5 0..................... MrRMcCarthy(5) 60
(Mrs Claire Hitch) *hld up: hdwy 5th: hit 12th: blnd 14th: wknd 3 out: hung rt after next: virtually p.u flat: t.o* **10/1**

252/ **P** **Baddam**[7] 11-11-10 0.. NicodeBoinville
(Martin Jones) *chsd ldrs: mstke 5th: reminders after 8th: bhd fr 12th: t.o whn p.u bef 15th* **3/1**[2]

6m 8.5s (0.20) **Going Correction** -0.425s/f (Good) 6 Ran SP% **109.4**
Speed ratings: **82,80,71,66,48**
toteswingers 1&2 £3.50, 1&3 £1.80, 2&3 £5.00 CSF £18.90 TOTE £2.00: £1.40, £6.80; EX 23.70 Trifecta £89.30 Pool: £1,679.20 - 14.09 winning units..
Owner P B Miles **Bred** A Layton And Miss F Layton **Trained** Kilgetty, Dyfed

FOCUS
Not a strong hunter chase. The winner is rated to her 2012 mark.

14 JENKINSONS CATERERS "NEWCOMERS" STANDARD OPEN NATIONAL HUNT FLAT RACE 2m
5:25 (5:25) (Class 5) 4-6-Y-O **£2,599** (£763; £381; £190)

Form RPR
1 **High Stratos** 4-10-10 0..(b[1]) MPFogarty(3) 97+
(John Joseph Hanlon, Ire) *led: rdn and hdd over 2f out: rallied to ld and hung rt ins fnl f: styd on* **8/1**

2 *2 ½* **My Wigwam Or Yours (IRE)** 4-10-13 0......................... AndrewTinkler 94+
(Nicky Henderson) *hld up: hdwy and hung lft over 3f out: r.o to go 2nd post: nt rch wnr* **11/8**[1]

3 *nk* **Radmores Express** 4-10-3 0....................................... CiaranMckee(10) 93
(John O'Shea) *hld up: hdwy 1/2-way: rdn over 1f out: styd on* **33/1**

4 *2* **Jackthejourneyman (IRE)** 4-10-6 0.............................. PatrickCorbett(7) 95+
(Rebecca Curtis) *a.p: chsd ldr over 3f out: led over 2f out: rdn and hdd whn swvd lft ins fnl f: styd on same pce* **4/1**[2]

5 *¾* **Miller's Maverick** 5-11-4 0.. RichardJohnson 97
(Hughie Morrison) *hld up: hdwy over 5f out: hmpd over 4f out: rdn over 2f out: styd on same pce fr over 1f out* **6/1**[3]

6 *1 ½* **Man Of Steel (IRE)** 4-10-13 0... DonalDevereux 90
(Peter Bowen) *trckd ldrs: racd keenly: rdn over 2f out: styd on same pce appr fnl f* **16/1**

7 *15* **Pembroke House** 6-11-4 0.. WillKennedy 81
(Sarah-Jayne Davies) *mid-div: lost pl over 6f out: hdwy over 3f out: rdn and wknd over 2f out* **50/1**

8 *2 ¾* **Ticket** 4-10-6 0.. SeanQuinlan 67
(Jennie Candlish) *hld up: effrt over 4f out: sn wknd* **20/1**

9 *6* **The Sweetener (IRE)** 4-10-10 0.................................... MichealNolan(3) 68
(Richard Woollacott) *prom: rdn over 3f out: wknd over 2f out: t.o* **10/1**

10 *dist* **Mantles Heath (IRE)** 5-11-4 0... SamThomas 42
(Paul Cowley) *chsd ldrs: rdn over 4f out: wknd over 3f out: t.o* **33/1**

11 *19* **Portrait Gale (IRE)** 6-11-4 0... RhysFlint 25
(Marc Barber) *hld up: a in rr: pushed along 1/2-way: sn lost tch: t.o* **66/1**

12 *5* **Nick The Dove (IRE)** 5-10-13 0... BenPoste(5) 20
(Chris Nenadich) *hld up: pushed along over 7f out: wknd over 5f out: t.o* **66/1**

13 *13* **Haliana** 4-10-1 0.. GavinSheehan(5)
(John Upson) *chsd ldrs tl wknd over 5f out: t.o* **100/1**

3m 40.9s (-3.00) **Going Correction** -0.275s/f (Good)
WFA 4 from 5yo+ 5lb 13 Ran SP% **119.1**
Speed ratings: **96,94,94,93,93 92,84,83,80,63 53,51,44**
toteswingers 1&2 £4.20, 1&3 £41.20, 2&3 £13.00 CSF £18.50 TOTE £10.00: £2.40, £1.20, £8.10; EX 24.70 Trifecta £805.30 Pool: £1,516.52 - 1.41 winning units..
Owner Forever Never Syndicate **Bred** Meon Valley Stud **Trained** Bagenalstown, Co Carlow

FOCUS
No previous form to provide any pointers to this bumper, which featured some green newcomers. They finished in a bit of a heap.
T/Plt: £64.80 to a £1 stake. Pool of £62,412.82 - 702.40 winning units T/Qpdt: £11.00 to a £1 stake. Pool of £4,075.00 - 272.80 winning units CR

WETHERBY (L-H)
Sunday, April 28

OFFICIAL GOING: Good (7.3)
Wind: Fresh; half-behind Weather: Fine but windy; shower Race 4

15 NATIONAL FESTIVAL CIRCUS IS HERE TODAY NOVICES' HURDLE (9 hdls) 2m 110y
2:00 (2:00) (Class 4) 4-Y-0+ **£3,285** (£957; £479)

Form RPR
253/ **1** **Life And Soul (IRE)**[29] 4498 6-10-12 115......................... JasonMaguire 122+
(Donald McCain) *best away: mde all: wnt 13 l clr 4th: lft 8 l clr 3 out: pushed out* **5/2**[2]

3/ **2** *12* **Sea Lord (IRE)**[108] 3591 6-10-12 0.................................. DenisO'Regan 115+
(John Ferguson) *chsd clr ldr: hit 4th: outpcd and lft 8 l 2nd 3 out: hmpd by loose horse appr next: no imp* **7/2**[3]

000/ **3** *13* **Ballycool (IRE)**[120] 3334 6-10-5 0............................(t) GrahamWatters(7) 98
(Lucinda Russell) *j.lft: chsd ldrs: outpcd 6th: lft modest 3rd next* **33/1**

010/ **4** *16* **Rattlin**[268] 1172 5-10-5 0.. RyanMania 79
(Sue Smith) *chsd ldng pair: mstke 1st and 2nd: outpcd after 6th: lft poor 4th 3 out* **28/1**

0/ **5** *5* **Miss Macnamara (IRE)**[21] 5202 4-10-0 0............................. HenryBrooke 67
(Martin Todhunter) *mid-div: outpcd 6th: lft poor 5th 3 out* **66/1**

06P/ **6** *13* **Snow Alert**[61] 4436 7-10-12 0.. FearghalDavis 68
(John Norton) *mid-div: lft poor 6th 3 out: wknd next* **100/1**

06/ **7** *23* **Tukitinyasok (IRE)**[16] 5273 6-10-7 0............................ CallumWhillans(5) 47
(Clive Mulhall) *mid-div: bhd fr 6th* **100/1**

/ **8** *9* **Xclaim**[198] 5-10-7 0.. JoeColliver(5) 39
(Micky Hammond) *chsd ldrs to 3rd: wknd 6th* **40/1**

45/ **9** *8* **Squealy Keely**[27] 5062 5-10-5 0.. PeterBuchanan 25
(James Turner) *in rr: bhd fr 3rd* **100/1**

065/ **10** *10* **Alicesam**[53] 4592 4-10-0 0... RichieMcGrath 11
(Philip Kirby) *nt jump wl in rr: bhd fr 3rd* **50/1**

0/ **11** *16* **Presenting Juno (IRE)**[287] 964 6-10-5 0........................ WilsonRenwick
(Martin Todhunter) *nt jump wl in rr: bhd fr 4th: t.o 3 out* **100/1**

141/ **U** **Fair Trade**[7] 5442 6-11-5 120.. WayneHutchinson 129+
(Alan King) *t.k.h: trckd ldrs 3rd: wnt 2nd 6th: 1 1/2 l down and travelling strly whn blnd bdly and uns rdr next* **10/11**[1]

P **Dicey Vows (USA)**[55] 5-10-9 0.. AlexanderVoy(3)
(Alan Jarvis) *in rr: bhd fr 3rd: t.o whn p.u bef 3 out* **66/1**

3m 57.8s (2.00) **Going Correction** +0.25s/f (Yiel)
WFA 4 from 5yo+ 5lb 13 Ran SP% **120.9**
Speed ratings (Par 105): **105,99,93,85,83 77,66,62,58,53 46,,**
toteswingers 1&2 £1.70, 1&3 £10.80, 2&3 £22.60 CSF £11.75 TOTE £3.10: £1.30, £1.40, £10.40; EX 12.90 Trifecta £176.00 Pool: £1,016.82 - 4.33 winning units..
Owner Matthew Taylor **Bred** Kildaragh Stud **Trained** Cholmondeley, Cheshire

FOCUS
The complexion of what had looked a fair novice hurdle changed dramatically when the strong-travelling Fair Trade departed at the third-last. The winner is entitled to rate higher on Flat form.

16 COMEDY & CURRY NIGHT - FRIDAY 7TH JUNE BEGINNERS' CHASE (THE SUNDAY £5K BONUS RACE) (16 fncs) 2m 4f 110y
2:30 (2:30) (Class 4) 5-Y-O+ **£3,768** (£1,106; £553; £276)

Form RPR
032/ **1** **Muldoon's Picnic (IRE)**[174] 2233 7-11-0 122 JasonMaguire 129
(Kim Bailey) *mde all: drvn 4 out: 4 l ahd whn stmbld on landing last: all out* **1/1**[1]
400/ **2** *nk* **Well Hello There (IRE)**[85] 3986 7-11-0 0 DougieCostello 129
(Jonjo O'Neill) *chsd ldrs: lft clr 2nd and stmbld on landing 2 out: edgd lft and styd on run-in: no ex clsng stages* **8/1**[3]
3/ **3** *dist* **Bafana Choice**[23] 5167 7-11-0 0 DenisO'Regan 94
(Chris Grant) *chsd ldrs: drvn 12th: lost pl appr next: lft distant 3rd 2 out* **25/1**
005/ **4** *dist* **Dramatic Victory (IRE)**[121] 3314 6-10-7 0 PaulNO'Brien(7)
(John Upson) *sn detached in last: t.o 7th: almost p.u appr 3 out: continued in v distant 4th: eventually completed over 45 2nds bhd 3rd* **100/1**
100/ **U** **Olofi (FR)**[44] 4768 7-11-0 0 (t) PaddyBrennan 126
(Tom George) *trckd ldrs: 2 l down and disputing 2nd whn blnd and uns rdr 2 out* **5/4**[2]
0P0/ **P** **About Thyne (IRE)**[56] 4544 8-11-0 0 (t) MichaelMcAlister
(Maurice Barnes) *chsd ldrs: mstke 6th: reminders and lost pl next: sn bhd: t.o 12th: p.u bef next* **50/1**

5m 8.9s (1.10) **Going Correction** +0.25s/f (Yiel) **6** Ran SP% **112.4**
Speed ratings: **107,106,89,,**
toteswingers 1&2 £1.80, 1&3 £1.40, 2&3 £6.40 CSF £9.05 TOTE £2.20: £1.30, £1.80; EX 5.50 Trifecta £30.00 Pool: £790.43 - 19.73 winning units..
Owner Clive Washbourn **Bred** Peter McCrea **Trained** Andoversford, Gloucs
FOCUS
A decent beginners' chase. The winner is rated to his previous chase mark.

17 BOOK YOUR LADIES DAY HOSPITALITY MARQUEE PACKAGE (S) H'CAP HURDLE (11 hdls) 2m 4f
3:05 (3:05) (Class 5) (0-95,93) 4-Y-O+ **£2,053** (£598; £299)

Form RPR
F43/ **1** **Saddlers Mot**[31] 4994 9-11-2 90 (b) JohnDawson(7) 100+
(Karen Tutty) *hld up in mid-div: hdwy 6th: handy 3rd appr 3 out: 2nd 2 out: led last: drvn out* **16/1**
F60/ **2** *1 ½* **I'Ll Be Frank**[51] 4630 8-11-7 88 (t) MichaelMcAlister 95
(Maurice Barnes) *j.lft and hmpd 1st: w ldrs: led 4th: hdd last: no ex last 50yds* **6/1**[3]
000/ **3** *10* **Executive's Hall (IRE)**[200] 1789 9-11-7 88 (p) DougieCostello 86
(Ben Haslam) *t.k.h in rr: hit 5th: stdy hdwy appr 3 out: sn chsng ldrs in 4th: kpt on to take 3rd run-in* **8/1**
45P/ **4** *¾* **Corky Dancer**[23] 5165 8-10-7 74 (p) WilsonRenwick 71
(Andrew Parker) *led to 2nd: chsd ldrs: one pce fr 2 out: 3rd whn hit last* **8/1**
003/ **5** *4* **Grethel (IRE)**[25] 5119 9-10-5 72 BrianHarding 65
(Alan Berry) *in rr: drvn 6th: hdwy 8th: one pce fr next* **16/1**
P0P/ **6** *11* **Sendiym (FR)**[21] 5203 6-10-12 79 (b) JamesReveley 63
(Dianne Sayer) *chsd ldrs 4th: wknd after 3 out* **14/1**
0P0/ **7** *15* **Hoar Frost**[23] 5165 8-10-8 80 (p) SamanthaDrake(5) 49
(Karen Tutty) *chsd ldrs: lost pl 8th: bhd fr 2 out* **18/1**
312/ **8** *hd* **Nicky Nutjob (GER)**[27] 5067 7-11-2 83 (p) JasonMaguire 52
(John O'Shea) *hld up in rr: drvn and hdwy 8th: wknd next* **11/2**[2]
536/ **9** *5* **Kirkhammerton (IRE)**[109] 3578 11-10-3 70 SamJones 35
(Barry Leavy) *prom: drvn 5th: lost pl and mstke 8th* **18/1**
465/ **10** *23* **Long Distance (FR)**[29] 5007 8-11-5 93 (p) CraigNichol(7) 37
(Lucinda Russell) *chsd ldrs: drvn 8th: lost pl bef next: sn bhd: t.o* **25/1**
065/ **11** *34* **Authentic Act (IRE)**[19] 5226 9-10-6 73 DenisO'Regan
(Martin Todhunter) *in rr: drvn 5th: bhd fr 3 out: t.o* **22/1**
111/ **P** **Chilbury Hill (IRE)**[46] 4744 10-10-8 85 (tp) JPKiely(10)
(Tim Vaughan) *in rr: nt jump wl: drvn 5th: bhd next: t.o 8th: p.u bef 3 out: b.b.v* **6/1**[3]
306/ **F** **Majestic Bull (USA)**[5] 5473 7-11-6 92 (p) MissLucyGardner(5)
(Sue Gardner) *trckd ldrs on outer: fell 8th* **5/1**[1]
0P4/ **P** **Royal And Ancient (IRE)**[25] 5118 6-10-1 75 (p) AdamNicol(7)
(David Thompson) *w ldrs: led 2nd to 4th: lost pl 7th: bhd whn mstke next: t.o whn p.u bef 3 out* **40/1**
3P0/ **P** **Venture To War (IRE)**[9] 5384 7-10-13 83 (b[1]) BrianToomey(3)
(Tony Coyle) *w ldrs: j.rt and hmpd 1st: drvn 8th: lost pl bef next: eased and p.u bef 2 out* **28/1**

5m 6.4s (6.90) **Going Correction** +0.25s/f (Yiel) **15** Ran SP% **125.9**
Speed ratings (Par 103): **96,95,91,91,89 85,79,79,77,67 54,,,,**
toteswingers 1&2 £22.40, 1&3 £34.30, 2&3 £13.00 CSF £110.46 CT £853.92 TOTE £33.80: £6.70, £2.80, £3.70; EX 184.10 Trifecta £296.80 Part won. Pool: £395.85 - 0.01 winning units..There was no bid for the winner
Owner Grange Park Racing **Bred** R Winchester And Son **Trained** Osmotherley, N Yorks
FOCUS
An open low-grade handicap. A step up from the winner with the second to his mark.

18 YORKSHIRE POST LADIES EVENING - 30TH MAY H'CAP CHASE (18 fncs) 3m 1f
3:35 (3:41) (Class 3) (0-130,126) 5-Y-O+ **£6,498** (£1,908; £954; £477)

Form RPR
12P/ **1** **Savant Bleu (FR)**[43] 4795 7-11-7 121 JasonMaguire 132+
(Kim Bailey) *trckd ldrs: led 6th: lft clr 3 out: 6 l ahd last: drvn rt out* **9/2**[3]
041/ **2** *3 ½* **Twirling Magnet (IRE)**[58] 4504 7-11-11 125 DougieCostello 131+
(Jonjo O'Neill) *hld up: trckd ldrs: mstke and lft 7 l 2nd 3 out: kpt on same pce run-in* **3/1**[2]
65U/ **3** *3 ¼* **Western Gale (IRE)**[16] 5276 10-10-5 105 LucyAlexander 105
(Martin Todhunter) *chsd ldrs: drvn and lost pl 14th: kpt on and lft modest 3rd 3 out: styd on run-in* **22/1**
01P/ **4** *9* **Everaard (USA)**[51] 4631 7-10-12 112 (tp) RichieMcGrath 104
(Philip Kirby) *led to 6th: drvn 10th: lost pl 13th: sn bhd: t.o 4 out: kpt on to take modest 4th sn after last* **8/1**
256/ **5** *2 ½* **Rich Lord**[27] 5075 9-11-6 120 JamesReveley 112
(Ferdy Murphy, France) *chsd ldrs: outpcd appr 4 out: wknd 2 out* **10/1**
045/ **6** *33* **Time For Spring (IRE)**[24] 5146 9-11-12 126 DenisO'Regan 86
(Charlie Longsdon) *trckd ldrs: blnd 14th: sn lost pl and bhd: eased 2 out: t.o* **10/1**
111/ **F** **Blazing Bull (IRE)**[16] 5276 9-10-1 108 JohnDawson(7) 119
(John Wade) *w ldrs: cl 2nd fr 10th: blnd 14th: upsides whn fell 3 out: fatally injured* **9/4**[1]
1PP/ **P** **Frank The Slink**[58] 4497 7-10-11 111 WilsonRenwick
(Micky Hammond) *chsd ldrs: lost pl 12th: sn bhd: t.o whn p.u bef 4 out* **20/1**

6m 14.6s (5.20) **Going Correction** +0.25s/f (Yiel) **8** Ran SP% **112.4**
Speed ratings: **101,99,98,95,95 84,,**
toteswingers 1&2 £3.20, 1&3 £21.80, 2&3 £21.80 CSF £18.39 CT £260.89 TOTE £4.80: £1.70, £1.70, £5.30; EX 20.00 Trifecta £165.20 Pool: £740.16 - 3.35 winning units..
Owner Kim Bailey Racing Partnership III **Bred** Marc Trinquet And Olivier Trinquet **Trained** Andoversford, Gloucs
FOCUS
A useful handicap chase. The idling winner was value for further.

19 DM KEITH SKODA & SEAT MAIDEN HURDLE (12 hdls) 2m 6f
4:10 (4:10) (Class 5) 4-Y-O+ **£2,053** (£598; £299)

Form RPR
32/ **1** **Silver Eagle (IRE)**[58] 4502 5-11-0 124 (t) JasonMaguire 130+
(Kim Bailey) *hld up: trckd ldrs 4th: led appr 3 out: jnd between last 2: edgd lft run-in: fnd ex clsng stages* **5/6**[1]
144/ **2** *¾* **Letsby Avenue**[128] 3162 5-11-0 118 PaddyBrennan 128
(Alan King) *mid-div: mstke 2nd: chsd ldrs 4th: wnt cl 2nd appr 3 out: upsides between last 2: crowded run-in: kpt on same pce last 30yds* **5/2**[2]
062/ **3** *25* **Northern Executive (IRE)**[21] 5208 5-11-0 0 BrianHughes 103
(Karen McLintock) *hld up towards rr: hdwy 6th: handy 3rd appr 3 out: one pce* **14/1**
445/ **4** *8* **Kilcaskin Star (IRE)**[208] 1711 7-10-7 98 JohnDawson(7) 97
(Karen Tutty) *hld up towards rr: hdwy to trck ldrs 9th: handy 4th whn hit next: one pce: b.b.v* **12/1**[3]
003/ **5** *10* **Exit To Freedom**[25] 5118 7-10-7 85 (p) CallumBewley(7) 85
(John Wainwright) *w ldrs: led 9th: hdd appr next: wknd appr 2 out* **80/1**
6 *dist* **Monbeg (IRE)**[70] 6-11-0 0 DenisO'Regan 50
(Martin Todhunter) *towards rr: bhd fr 9th: t.o* **33/1**
0/ **7** *13* **Captain P K (IRE)**[27] 5072 6-10-7 0 (t) DerekFox(7) 37
(Noel C Kelly, Ire) *j.lft in rr: bhd fr 7th: t.o 9th* **66/1**
65/ **8** *17* **Yukon Delta (IRE)**[27] 5071 6-11-0 0 KennyJohnson 20
(Robert Johnson) *led to 3rd: chsd ldrs: lost pl after 8th: sn bhd: t.o 3 out* **66/1**
00U/ **9** *8* **Dorlesh Way (IRE)**[16] 5273 6-10-11 0 AlexanderVoy(3) 12
(Patrick Holmes) *w ldr: led 3rd: hdd 9th: sn drvn and lost pl: bhd fr 2 out: t.o* **100/1**
24P/ **10** *15* **Radio Nowhere (IRE)**[50] 4657 5-11-0 112 AdrianLane
(Donald McCain) *chsd ldrs: wkng whn hit 8th: bhd fr next: t.o 3 out* **14/1**
440/ **P** **Witch One**[131] 3122 10-10-2 0 SamanthaDrake(5)
(Ashley Dodgson) *in rr: bhd and drvn 6th: t.o next: p.u bef 3 out* **100/1**
060/ **P** **My Mate Paddy**[8] 5408 6-11-0 0 RyanMania
(Ms N M Hugo) *in rr: bhd whn mstke 3rd: sn t.o and p.u: b.b.v* **80/1**
4/ **P** **Serious Mixture**[17] 5241 6-10-7 0 MrSDrinkwater(7)
(Hilary Parrott) *chsd ldrs: lost pl 7th: blnd next: sn t.o and eased: p.u bef 3 out* **16/1**
0/ **P** **Aliking**[109] 3572 6-11-0 0 WilsonRenwick
(Peter Niven) *nt jump wl in rr: bhd and drvn 7th: t.o 9th: p.u bef next* **66/1**

5m 29.8s (3.00) **Going Correction** +0.25s/f (Yiel) **14** Ran SP% **121.9**
Speed ratings (Par 103): **104,103,94,91,88 75,70,64,61,56 ,,,**
toteswingers 1&2 £1.10, 1&3 £5.70, 2&3 £12.80 CSF £2.93 TOTE £1.90: £1.10, £1.30, £2.30; EX 3.50 Trifecta £13.70 Pool: £765.43 - 41.87 winning units..
Owner Kim Bailey Racing Partnership IV **Bred** Martin Cullinane **Trained** Andoversford, Gloucs
FOCUS
The front pair in the market drew a long way clear in a maiden hurdle lacking depth. The winner ran to his mark, with a big step up from the second.

20 BOOK TICKETS ON-LINE @ WETHERBYRACING.CO.UK H'CAP CHASE (16 fncs) 2m 4f 110y
4:45 (4:46) (Class 5) (0-100,100) 5-Y-O+ **£2,144** (£629; £314; £157)

Form RPR
454/ **1** **Lukey Luke**[19] 5224 10-10-10 84 PeterBuchanan 97+
(James Turner) *hld up towards rr: hdwy 11th: handy 2nd appr 4 out: led 2 out: drvn out* **9/1**[3]
54U/ **2** *5* **Cocoa Key (IRE)**[21] 9-11-5 93 RyanMania 100
(Richard Ford) *led: clr w one other 7th to 12th: jnd 3 out: hdd next: kpt on same pce* **14/1**
452/ **3** *1 ¼* **Arrow Barrow (IRE)**[27] 5073 8-10-7 81 WilsonRenwick 85+
(John Wade) *in rr: sme hdwy appr 4 out: 12 l down in 5th last: styd on strly to snatch 3rd nr line* **11/4**[1]
P20/ **4** *1* **Ginger's Lad**[252] 1276 9-10-8 85 JakeGreenall(3) 89
(Michael Easterby) *chsd ldng pair: hit 6th: wnt handy 3rd appr 4 out: kpt on one pce fr next* **10/1**
02P/ **5** *1 ¾* **Doberdan (USA)**[32] 4972 8-10-13 87 (p) RichieMcGrath 90
(Patrick Holmes) *chsd ldrs: rdn and outpcd 12th: rallied next: kpt on same pce: 4th whn stmbld on landing last* **18/1**
643/ **6** *13* **Pistol Basc (FR)**[56] 4548 9-10-8 82 (b) DenisO'Regan 75
(Ferdy Murphy, France) *wore blinkers instead of declared eye-shields: hld up in rr: hdwy 11th: chsng ldrs appr 4 out: wknd 3 out* **9/2**[2]
1P5/ **7** *4* **Knight Woodsman**[25] 5122 9-11-3 98 (p) CallumBewley(7) 85
(R Mike Smith) *chsd ldr: clr w one other 7th to 12th: wknd appr next: sn bhd* **22/1**
064/ **8** *2 ½* **Watledge (FR)**[68] 4301 6-11-7 95 PaddyBrennan 79
(Tom George) *in rr: bhd fr 12th: mstke 3 out* **9/2**[2]
0PP/ **P** **Appeal Denied (IRE)**[53] 4587 11-10-0 74 oh12 (b[1]) AdrianLane
(Sandy Forster) *in rr: bhd whn j. slowly 8th: sn t.o: p.u bef 10th* **100/1**
5F5/ **P** **Ballycracken (IRE)**[51] 4636 9-10-6 85 JoeCornwall(5)
(David Pearson) *in tch: drvn 7th: sn lost pl: bhd whn p.u bef 3 out* **28/1**
PU0/ **P** **Monsoon Music (IRE)**[27] 5073 9-9-7 74 oh2 (p) GrantCockburn(7)
(Lucinda Russell) *in rr: bhd fr 8th: t.o whn p.u bef 12th* **20/1**
P3P/ **P** **Along Came Rosie**[56] 4545 9-11-12 100 DougieCostello
(Andrew Crook) *in rr: sme hdwy 12th: sn wknd: bhd whn p.u bef 3 out* **20/1**
013/ **U** **Drumlang (IRE)**[180] 2119 7-11-7 100 RobertMcCarth(5)
(Ian Williams) *in rr: bhd fr 12th: blnd and uns rdr 3 out* **9/1**[3]
PF6/ **P** **Mia Matriarch**[19] 5226 7-10-5 79 BrianHughes
(Donald Whillans) *in rr: mstke 3rd: bhd fr 8th: t.o whn p.u bef 12th: b.b.v* **33/1**

5m 13.8s (6.00) **Going Correction** +0.25s/f (Yiel) **14** Ran SP% **125.3**
Speed ratings: **98,96,95,95,94 89,88,87,,,,,,**
toteswingers 1&2 £27.70, 1&3 £7.40, 2&3 £9.70 CSF £116.81 CT £447.94 TOTE £9.10: £2.60, £5.10, £1.60; EX 197.00 Trifecta £1359.20 Part won. Pool: £1,812.27 - 0.66 winning units..

The Form Book Jumps, Raceform Ltd, Compton, RG20 6NL.

Owner D M Wordsworth **Bred** J R Wills **Trained** Norton-le-Clay, N Yorks

FOCUS
An open-looking handicap chase that was run at a fair gallop and the field were strung out a long way from home. The winner looks like being a better chaser than hurdler.

21 ROYAL PIGEON RACING ASSOCIATION LADY RIDERS' H'CAP HURDLE (9 hdls) 2m 110y

5:15 (5:15) (Class 5) (0-95,95) 4-Y-0+ **£2,053** (£598; £299)

Form RPR

355/ **1** **Catawollow**[5] 5477 6-9-8 **70**...............................(v[1]) MissBeckySmith(7) 80+
(Richard Guest) *hld up in rr: hdwy 5th: sn chsng ldrs: led after next: styd on wl to forge clr fr 2 out* **12/1**

063/ **2** *13* **Samizdat (FR)**[14] 5311 10-9-9 **71**................................ MissGSwan(7) 69
(John Upson) *chsd ldrs 3rd: led 5th: hdd and outpcd after 6th: modest 6th 2 out: 4th last: kpt on to take 2nd last 50yds* **33/1**

FPP/ **3** *1 1/2* **Talk Of Saafend (IRE)**[19] 5227 8-11-0 **88**..................... EmmaSayer(5) 86
(Dianne Sayer) *in rr: drvn after 3rd: hdwy 3 out: styd on fr next: 5th last: kpt on to go 3rd nr fin* **20/1**

645/ **4** *1* **Lean Burn (USA)**[15] 5290 7-10-12 **88**........................ MissAliceMills(7) 84
(Barry Leavy) *chsd ldrs: reminders and outpcd 6th: hdwy 2 out: 2nd last: one pce* **10/1**

026/ **5** *2* **Vodka Red (IRE)**[25] 5124 5-10-11 **87**..........................(t) MissCWalton(7) 82
(Robert Johnson) *chsd ldrs: hit 4th: one pce fr 2 out* **16/1**

S60/ **6** *3* **Presenting Junior (IRE)**[8] 5412 6-9-12 **70**.................. RachaelGreen(3) 61
(Martin Todhunter) *chsd ldrs: outpcd after 6th: chsng ldrs 2 out: one pce* **8/1**

0/ **7** *13* **Noble Jack (IRE)**[97] 1959 7-11-10 **93**........................... LucyAlexander 73
(Richard Ford) *in rr: drvn and hdwy 6th: outpcd appr next: wknd 2 out* **6/1[3]**

221/ **8** *29* **Arkaim**[5] 5477 5-11-7 **95**.. MissGAndrews(5) 63
(Pam Sly) *hld up: hdwy to trck ldrs 4th: led after 6th: hdd appr 3 out: wknd qckly and eased last: virtually p.u: t.o* **9/4[1]**

544/ **9** *25* **Strathaird (IRE)**[208] 1709 9-9-7 **69** oh1....................(p) MissRMcDonald(7)
(Andrew Crook) *in rr: bhd after 6th: t.o whn virtually p.u run-in* **28/1**

502/ **P** **Rare Coincidence**[53] 4586 12-10-13 **89**................... MissJRRichards(7)
(Alan Berry) *led: hdd 4th: sn lost pl: bhd 7th: blnd 3 out: sn t.o: p.u bef next* **28/1**

003/ **U** **Brother Scott**[58] 4494 6-10-9 **83**............................... SamanthaDrake(5)
(Sue Smith) *w ldrs: led 4th to next: upsides whn mstke and uns rdr 3 out* **3/1[2]**

4m 3.2s (7.40) **Going Correction** +0.25s/f (Yiel) **11** Ran SP% **118.4**
Speed ratings (Par 103): **92,85,85,84,83 82,76,62,50,**
toteswingers 1&2 £27.30, 1&3 £13.20, 2&3 £29.80 CSF £340.72 CT £7590.92 TOTE £16.90: £3.00, £7.30, £5.50; EX 231.50 Trifecta £961.10 Part won. Pool: £1,281.58 - 0.09 winning units..

Owner Miss C Fordham **Bred** Worksop Manor Stud **Trained** Wetherby, W Yorks

FOCUS
A moderate handicap for lady riders'. The winner was very well in on the best of his 2011/12 form.
T/Jkpt: £50,128.30 to a £1 stake. Pool of £529,524.65 - 7.50 winning units T/Plt: £101.50 to a £1 stake. Pool of £85,567.74 - 614.84 winning units T/Qpdt: £40.80 to a £1 stake. Pool of £5,460.00 - 98.90 winning units WG

KELSO (L-H)

Monday, April 29

OFFICIAL GOING: Good (good to soft in places; 6.9)
Wind: Fairly strong, half against Weather: Cloudy, bright

22 LYNTOUN PRIVATE HIRE MAIDEN HURDLE (10 hdls) 2m 2f

2:10 (2:10) (Class 4) 4-Y-0+ **£3,249** (£954; £477; £238)

Form RPR

442/ **1** **Ivan Boru (IRE)**[22] 5202 5-11-0 0.................................... JamesReveley 115
(Keith Reveley) *mde all: rdn whn hrd pressed 2 out: hld on wl fr last* **10/1**

034/ **2** *1 1/4* **Ueueteotl (FR)**[33] 4971 5-11-0 120.............................. BrianHughes 114
(James Ewart) *cl up: effrt and chal 2 out to bef last: kpt on u.p run-in* **5/1[3]**

F5B/ **3** *4* **Lifetime (IRE)**[30] 5013 5-11-0 107.................................(t) DannyCook 110
(Brian Ellison) *trckd ldrs: effrt and pushed along bef 2 out: edgd lft and one pce after last* **11/1**

3/ **4** *1 3/4* **Things Change (IRE)**[33] 4971 5-11-0 0........................ DougieCostello 109
(John Quinn) *t.k.h early: hld up towards rr: hdwy after 3 out: effrt and in tch whn mstke last: no imp* **13/8[1]**

056/ **5** *6* **Plus Jamais (FR)**[10] 5366 6-11-0 0................................[1] RichieMcGrath 102
(Jim Goldie) *hld up in midfield on outside: rdn and outpcd after 3 out: kpt on fr next: no imp* **40/1**

02/ **6** *3 3/4* **Potomac (IRE)**[21] 5220 5-11-0 0.................................... WilsonRenwick 99
(Rose Dobbin) *hld up in midfield: effrt and hdwy after 3 out: rdn and wknd next* **8/1**

00/ **7** *3/4* **Mandarin Sunset (IRE)**[8] 5428 6-11-0 0........................... BrianHarding 98
(James Ewart) *hld up: drvn along after 3 out: plugged on fr next: nvr able to chal* **40/1**

122/ **8** *11* **Vinstar (FR)**[109] 3593 4-10-9 0..................................... JasonMaguire 86+
(Donald McCain) *in tch: effrt after 3 out: drvn and wknd after next* **5/2[2]**

6P0/ **9** *1/2* **Regal Ramirez**[21] 5220 5-11-0 0....................................... BarryKeniry 87
(Michael Smith) *bhd: drvn and outpcd 3 out: btn next* **125/1**

F0/ **10** *8* **Oscar Lateen (IRE)**[21] 5216 5-11-0 0............................. PeterBuchanan 78
(Sandy Thomson) *bhd: struggling fr 4 out: sn btn* **100/1**

00/ **11** *23* **Swindy**[17] 5272 5-11-0 0... RyanMania 55
(Sue Smith) *in tch tl rdn and wknd qckly bef 2 out: t.o* **80/1**

00/ **P** **Sports Model (IRE)**[28] 5071 7-10-7 0........................ GrahamWatters(7)
(Valerie Jackson) *bhd: lost tch bef 6th: t.o whn p.u after next* **250/1**

4m 27.4s (0.40) **Going Correction** -0.275s/f (Good)
WFA 4 from 5yo+ 5lb **12** Ran SP% **120.2**
Speed ratings (Par 105): **88,87,85,84,82 80,80,75,75,71 61,**
toteswingers 1&2 £3.50, 1&3 £16.80, 2&3 £16.80 CSF £60.17 TOTE £9.10: £2.40, £2.00, £4.00; EX 38.50 Trifecta £686.90 Pool: £1185.79 - 1.29 winning units..

Owner Thwaites Furness & Zetland **Bred** Miss Ann Twomey **Trained** Lingdale, Redcar & Cleveland

FOCUS
After 1mm rain overnight the ground was being dried out all the time by the strong, almost head-on wind. After the opener James Reveley described it as "genuine good ground". It paid to race up with the pace in this maiden hurdle, the first three home filling the first three places throughout the final circuit. The second to fourth are rated pretty much to their marks but some of these might be flattered. All rails moved. Chase course on innermost line and all hurdle races increased by about 15yds per circuit.

23 RACEHORSE OWNERS ASSOCIATION H'CAP CHASE (12 fncs) 2m 1f

2:40 (2:40) (Class 4) (0-105,101) 5-Y-0+ **£3,898** (£1,144; £572; £286)

Form RPR

542/ **1** **Prince Tam**[20] 5226 9-10-4 **84**................................... JonathanEngland(5) 95+
(Harriet Graham) *in tch: hdwy to press ldr 6th: effrt and led between last 2: drvn out run-in* **9/2[2]**

405/ **2** *3 3/4* **Freddie Brown**[21] 5219 9-11-12 **101**..................................(t) RyanMania 110+
(George Charlton) *led: nt fluent 6th: rdn bef 2 out: hdd between last 2: kpt on same pce run-in* **9/2[2]**

052/ **3** *2* **Soul Magic (IRE)**[170] 2326 11-10-13 **95**...................... CallumBewley(7) 100
(Harriet Graham) *in tch: rdn and hdwy to chse ldrs bef 2 out: kpt on same pce fr last* **10/1**

F32/ **4** *2 1/2* **Suprise Vendor (IRE)**[21] 5219 7-11-1 **95**................... GaryRutherford(5) 98
(Stuart Coltherd) *hld up: nt fluent and pushed along 5th: effrt 4 out: one pce bef 2 out* **7/4[1]**

P4P/ **5** *11* **Craicneasy (IRE)**[20] 5229 10-10-0 **75** oh16...................... LucyAlexander 70
(Bruce Mactaggart) *hld up: rdn along bef 4 out: no imp fr next* **50/1**

F13/ **6** *11* **Against The Wind**[767] 4961 10-11-9 **98**............................ PeterBuchanan 83
(Lucinda Russell) *hld up in tch: drvn and outpcd 4 out: btn after next* **13/2[3]**

066/ **7** *11* **Schinken Otto (IRE)**[24] 5169 12-11-7 **96**........................... HarryHaynes 76
(Malcolm Jefferson) *chsd ldr to 6th: mstke next: struggling fr 4 out* **22/1**

P04/ **P** **Primrose Time**[21] 5219 10-11-2 **94**............................... AlexanderVoy(3)
(Lucy Normile) *chsd ldrs: outpcd after 5th: struggling next: t.o whn p.u bef 4 out* **10/1**

4m 11.9s (-6.10) **Going Correction** -0.275s/f (Good) **8** Ran SP% **110.6**
Speed ratings: **103,101,100,99,93 88,83,**
toteswingers 1&2 £5.70, 1&3 £1.30, 2&3 £4.70 CSF £23.78 CT £179.32 TOTE £4.10: £1.50, £1.70, £3.00; EX 21.80 Trifecta £262.10 Pool: £960.59 - 2.74 winning units..

Owner Miss G Joughin **Bred** Miss Gail Joughin **Trained** Philip Law, Borders

FOCUS
A modest but truly run handicap chase. The winner is rated in line with his good Carlisle run.

24 PETER & GILLIAN ALLAN CATERING H'CAP HURDLE (11 hdls) 2m 6f 110y

3:10 (3:10) (Class 3) (0-130,130) 4-Y-0+ **£5,523** (£1,621; £810; £405)

Form RPR

004/ **1** **Arctic Court (IRE)**[9] 5405 9-10-13 **117**............................ DenisO'Regan 123+
(Jim Goldie) *in tch: smooth hdwy to chse ldr 3 out: clsd next: shkn up and ev ch whn nt fluent last: rdn and styd on wl to ld last stride* **5/2[1]**

01P/ **2** *nse* **Scotswell**[170] 2322 7-11-4 **122**...................................... LucyAlexander 127
(Harriet Graham) *led at decent gallop: rdn bef 2 out: kpt on gamely fr last: hdd last stride* **16/1**

624/ **3** *15* **Merrydown (IRE)**[67] 4337 10-11-1 **119**........................... DougieCostello 111
(Nicky Richards) *hld up: hdwy to chse ldrs bef 2 out: sn rdn: outpcd whn j. bdly lft last* **10/1**

600/ **4** *11* **Stormin Exit (IRE)**[10] 5369 10-10-10 **114**....................... HenryBrooke 96
(Jim Goldie) *cl up: wnt 2nd 1/2-way to 3 out: rdn and wknd next* **33/1**

600/ **5** *6* **Tornado Bob (IRE)**[11] 5362 8-11-12 **130**......................(p) JasonMaguire 109
(Donald McCain) *nt fluent on occasions: prom tl rdn and wknd bef 2 out* **9/2[2]**

634/ **6** *8* **Latin Connection (IRE)**[51] 4652 7-10-4 **115**...........(t) GrahamWatters(7) 84
(S R B Crawford, Ire) *hld up: rdn after 4 out: sn no imp* **8/1**

506/ **7** *24* **Corkage (IRE)**[28] 5076 10-11-12 **130**............................(b) JamesReveley 77
(Keith Reveley) *midfield: drvn and outpcd 4 out: btn after next* **20/1**

2P1/ **8** *21* **Any Given Moment (IRE)**[115] 3495 7-10-0 **104** oh4...... PeterBuchanan 32
(Sandy Thomson) *hld up: struggling bef 4 out: sn btn* **14/1**

FP0/ **P** **Jukebox Melody (IRE)**[9] 5400 7-10-11 **115**.................. WilsonRenwick
(John Wade) *midfield: stdy hdwy after 7th: struggling bef 4 out: t.o whn p.u bef 2 out* **22/1**

600/ **F** **Kent Street (IRE)**[53] 4608 8-10-13 **117**.................................. RyanMania
(Sue Smith) *midfield: pushed along whn fell heavily 8th* **20/1**

416/ **P** **Quel Elite (FR)**[387] 5275 9-10-5 **109**................................... BrianHarding
(James Moffatt) *bhd: struggling bef 4 out: t.o whn p.u bef 2 out* **14/1**

431/ **F** **Purcell's Bridge (FR)**[30] 5009 6-10-3 **117**.................. ShaunDobbin(10)
(Rose Dobbin) *hld up: fell 8th* **6/1[3]**

460/ **P** **Gymdoli**[22] 5204 6-9-12 **107**.. GaryRutherford(5)
(Rayson Nixon) *in tch: struggling 8th: sn btn: t.o whn p.u bef 2 out* **33/1**

5m 30.3s (-10.70) **Going Correction** -0.275s/f (Good) **13** Ran SP% **120.2**
Speed ratings (Par 107): **107,106,101,97,95 93,84,77, , ,**
toteswingers 1&2 £6.00, 1&3 £8.30, 2&3 £14.70 CSF £38.80 CT £349.15 TOTE £4.20: £1.50, £4.90, £3.50; EX 57.30 Trifecta £429.10 Part won. Pool: £572.19 - 0.96 winning units..

Owner Mr & Mrs Raymond Anderson Green **Bred** Paul Doyle **Trained** Uplawmoor, E Renfrews

FOCUS
A truly run handicap hurdle and only five were still in serious contention at the third-last. The winner rates a small step up on his recent Ayr run.

25 HAPPY 80TH BIRTHDAY JOHN RUST H'CAP CHASE (19 fncs) 3m 2f

3:40 (3:40) (Class 3) (0-125,125) 5-Y-0+ **£6,498** (£1,908; £954; £477)

Form RPR

U02/ **1** **You Know Yourself (IRE)**[8] 5427 10-11-4 **117**.................... RyanMania 127+
(Sue Smith) *led to 14th: styd upsides: led and rdn 2 out: hld on gamely fr last* **10/3[3]**

5FP/ **2** *1 1/4* **Super Ally (IRE)**[20] 5228 8-10-3 **102**............................. WilsonRenwick 110
(Andrew Parker) *in tch: pushed along 12th: rallied next: rdn and outpcd 3 out: styd on u.p fr last: tk 2nd cl home* **3/1[2]**

30P/ **3** *nse* **Captain Americo (IRE)**[9] 5404 11-11-2 **115**.................(p) BrianHughes 123
(James Ewart) *pressed ldr: chal 8th: led 14th to 2 out: rallied: kpt on same pce last 100yds: lost 2nd nr fin* **10/1**

614/ **4** *1 1/2* **Storming Gale (IRE)**[28] 5075 7-11-12 **125**.....................(t) JasonMaguire 132
(Donald McCain) *in tch: stdy hdwy whn hit 4 out: effrt after next: one pce fr last* **5/1**

122/ **5** *19* **Or De Grugy (FR)**[74] 4208 11-10-12 **111**......................... LucyAlexander 100
(N W Alexander) *chsd ldrs tl drvn and outpcd appr 4 out: btn fnl 2* **11/4[1]**

1PP/ **P** **Itzacliche (IRE)**[28] 13-9-8 **100**.................................(b) MissJRRichards(7)
(Nicky Richards) *bhd: pushed along fr 7th: lost tch 12th: p.u bef 14th* **28/1**

01P/ **P** **Flying Squad (UAE)**[33] 4972 9-9-12 **107**....................(t) ShaunDobbin(10)
(Rose Dobbin) *chsd ldrs: lost pl whn hit 6th: outpcd fr 12th: p.u bef 14th* **20/1**

6m 39.2s (-8.00) **Going Correction** -0.275s/f (Good) **7** Ran SP% **108.7**
Speed ratings: **101,100,100,100,94** ,
toteswingers 1&2 £2.80, 1&3 £2.30, 2&3 £11.00 CSF £12.78 TOTE £5.70: £2.50, £2.10; EX 13.70 Trifecta £74.20 Pool: £991.08 - 10.00 winning units..
Owner Mrs S Smith **Bred** Patrick O'Connell **Trained** High Eldwick, W Yorks
■ Stewards' Enquiry : Wilson Renwick two-day ban: used whip above permitted level (May 13-14)

FOCUS
The two leaders took each other on and this proved quite a stern test. Fair form with the winner to his mark.

26 JEDFOREST DEER PARK NOVICES' H'CAP CHASE (12 fncs) 2m 1f

4:10 (4:11) (Class 4) (0-120,120) 5-Y-0+ **£6,498** (£1,908; £954; £477)

Form RPR

221/ **1** **Kykate**[17] 5274 7-11-8 **116**....................(t) CharlieHuxley 122
(William Kinsey) *chsd ldr: hdwy to ld bef 2 out: drvn out fr last* **5/1**[3]

640/ **2** *nk* **Bocamix (FR)**[10] 5386 7-10-2 **96**.................... DougieCostello 102
(Andrew Crook) *hld up: nt fluent and pushed along 3 out: rallied next: chsd wnr last: kpt on: hld towards fin* **22/1**

111/ **3** *2 ½* **Sleep In First (FR)**[7] 5448 7-11-6 **114** 7ex.................... BrianHughes 118
(James Ewart) *trckd ldrs: effrt and rdn bef 2 out: kpt on same pce run-in* **4/5**[1]

20/ **4** *11* **Cloverhill Lad (IRE)**[55] 4581 9-9-9 **94** oh1.................... GaryRutherford(5) 89
(Stuart Coltherd) *mstke 1st: in tch: hit 4th: effrt and drvn after 3 out: sn outpcd: no imp fr next* **14/1**

33F/ **5** *7* **Diocles (IRE)**[61] 4446 7-11-12 **120**.................... JasonMaguire 110+
(Donald McCain) *j.rt on occasions: led to bef 2 out: sn rdn: wknd between last 2* **11/4**[2]

4m 10.7s (-7.30) **Going Correction** -0.275s/f (Good) **5** Ran SP% **109.9**
Speed ratings: **106,105,104,99,96**
CSF £59.70 TOTE £4.10: £1.30, £5.60; EX 30.90 Trifecta £105.60 Pool: £1647.15 - 11.69 winning units..
Owner David Bithell Racing **Bred** B Baggott & H Clewlow **Trained** Ashton, Cheshire

FOCUS
All five runners were still in with a shout at the third-last fence in this ordinary handicap. The first two are rated pretty much to their marks.

27 ISLE OF SKYE BLENDED SCOTCH WHISKEY H'CAP HURDLE (10 hdls) 2m 2f

4:40 (4:40) (Class 4) (0-115,115) 4-Y-0+ **£3,249** (£954; £477; £238)

Form RPR

542/ **1** **All That Remains (IRE)**[8] 5426 8-11-7 **110**....................(t) DannyCook 118+
(Brian Ellison) *cl up: led 4th: mde rest at decent gallop: rdn out fr last* **5/2**[1]

542/ **2** *1 ¼* **Lisbon (IRE)**[21] 5217 5-10-11 **107**....................(t) DerekFox(7) 112
(Patrick Griffin, Ire) *in tch: hdwy after 5th: effrt and chsd wnr last: kpt on: hld towards fin* **4/1**[2]

F04/ **3** *2 ¼* **Bogside (IRE)**[21] 5217 9-11-3 **106**.................... LucyAlexander 110+
(George Charlton) *cl up: effrt and rdn bef 2 out: kpt on same pce fr last* **18/1**

31/ **4** *16* **Waltz Darling (IRE)**[14] 2975 5-11-11 **114**.................... JamesReveley 103
(Keith Reveley) *hld up and bhd: stdy hdwy and in tch bef 2 out: sn pushed along: outpcd between last 2* **5/1**[3]

P03/ **5** *1* **Sam Lord**[20] 5227 9-10-12 **101**....................(p) BrianHarding 89
(James Moffatt) *hld up: rdn bef 3 out: no imp bef next* **14/1**

302/ **6** *1 ¾* **Agricultural**[167] 2407 7-10-8 **97**.................... WilsonRenwick 83
(Lucy Normile) *hld up: drvn and outpcd bef 3 out: n.d after* **20/1**

100/ **7** *½* **Stanley Bridge**[26] 5121 6-10-10 **104**.................... JoeColliver(5) 90
(Barry Murtagh) *mstkes: hld up: outpcd after 4 out: n.d after* **33/1**

334/ **8** *2 ¼* **Ben Akram (IRE)**[28] 5072 5-10-6 **102**.................... GrahamWatters(7) 86
(Lucinda Russell) *midfield: drvn and outpcd after 4 out: btn bef 2 out* **12/1**

630/ **9** *1 ¾* **Maggie Blue (IRE)**[8] 5423 5-9-12 **92**.................... JonathanEngland(5) 74
(Harriet Graham) *hld up: rdn after 5th: hdwy and in tch 3 out: sn rdn and wknd* **33/1**

045/ **P** **Embsay Crag**[38] 4913 7-11-2 **105**.................... RichieMcGrath
(Philip Kirby) *midfield: stdy hdwy after 5th: drvn bef 3 out: wknd bef next: p.u between last 2* **5/1**[3]

1P0/ **P** **War On (IRE)**[22] 5204 6-11-5 **115**....................(b[1]) AdamNicol(7)
(Michael Smith) *led to 4th: blnd bdly 6th: lost pl whn hit next: sn btn: t.o whn p.u 2 out* **16/1**

4m 22.3s (-4.70) **Going Correction** -0.275s/f (Good) **11** Ran SP% **118.1**
Speed ratings (Par 105): **99,98,97,90,89 89,88,87,87,**
toteswingers 1&2 £1.50, 1&3 £10.50, 2&3 £8.90 CSF £12.97 CT £144.43 TOTE £3.60: £1.10, £2.30, £3.90; EX 14.20 Trifecta £131.60 Pool: £1253.01 - 7.14 winning units..
Owner Mrs J A Martin **Bred** Eoin, Patrick And Cian O'Connor **Trained** Norton, N Yorks

FOCUS
Again it paid to race up with the pace. The winner was well in on his recent run and is rated to a similar level.

28 EILDON HILL STABLES NOVICES' HUNTERS' CHASE (FOR THE CHARLIE BROWN TROPHY) (19 fncs) 3m 2f

5:10 (5:10) (Class 5) 5-Y-0+ **£2,495** (£774; £386; £193)

Form RPR

06U/ **1** **Digg Whitaker**[24] 5170 8-11-5 87.................... MrRSmith(7) 102+
(John Wade) *led tl hit and hdd 11th: led 13th: rdn and styd on strly to go clr bef last* **11/1**[3]

P01/ **2** *7* **Buckstruther (IRE)**[23] 11-11-11 99.................... MrJHamilton(5) 101
(Alastair Bell) *hld up towards rr: hdwy and prom 7th: hit and outpcd 14th: rallied bef 4 out: chsd (clr) wnr run-in: no imp* **4/5**[1]

F43/ **3** *1 ¼* **Senor Alco (FR)**[37] 7-11-9 102.................... MrTDavidson(3) 94
(Victor Thompson) *t.k.h: cl up: led 11th to 13th: chsd wnr: drvn after 3 out: no imp bef next: lost 2nd run-in* **5/2**[2]

6/ **4** *33* **Castley Lane**[16] 7-11-5 0.................... MrMJohnson(7) 63
(Sara Ender) *bhd: hdwy to chse wnr 3rd to 11th: cl up: rdn 5 out: wknd after 3 out* **22/1**

5 *25* **Pats Preference (IRE)**[9] 7-11-5 0.................... MrBCampbell(7) 40
(Victor Thompson) *hld up in tch: outpcd fr 13th: btn bef 4 out: t.o* **50/1**

000/ **6** *1* **Maften (IRE)**[8] 10-11-5 0.................... MrNOrpwood(7) 39
(Victor Thompson) *in tch: drvn and outpcd bef 13th: sn lost tch: t.o* **40/1**

0/ **P** **Glen Lord**[8] 10-11-9 0....................(t) MrGCrow(3)
(Mrs N C Neill) *t.k.h: hld up: hdwy and prom 9th: wknd bef 4 out: p.u bef 2 out* **12/1**

5/ **P** **Indian Print (IRE)**[28] 9-11-5 0.................... MrTHamilton(7)
(Victor Thompson) *hld up in tch: mstke 4th: struggling 12th: t.o whn p.u bef 4 out* **16/1**

6m 47.8s (0.60) **Going Correction** -0.275s/f (Good) **8** Ran SP% **114.8**
Speed ratings: **88,85,85,75,67 67,** ,
toteswingers 1&2 £5.30, 1&3 £2.20, 2&3 £2.00 CSF £21.50 TOTE £11.70: £1.90, £1.10, £1.50; EX 30.50 Trifecta £115.90 Pool: £1924.85 - 12.45 winning units..
Owner John Wade **Bred** Helshaw Grange Stud Ltd **Trained** Mordon, Co Durham
■ Stewards' Enquiry : Mr T Davidson two-day ban: careless riding (tbn)

FOCUS
A modest but quite valuable novice hunters' chase. The form is rated around the first two.
T/Plt: £490.20 to a £1 stake. Pool of £51,714.30 - 77.00 winning units T/Qpdt: £68.00 to a £1 stake. Pool of £4108.20 - 44.70 winning units RY

TOWCESTER (R-H)

Monday, April 29

OFFICIAL GOING: Good (10.4)
Wind: blustery and variable Weather: overcast; 12 degrees

29 HAYGAIN HAY STEAMERS CLEAN HEALTHY FORAGE H'CAP HURDLE (11 hdls) 2m 5f

2:00 (2:00) (Class 5) (0-95,95) 4-Y-0+ **£2,053** (£598; £299)

Form RPR

000/ **1** **Sure Thing (FR)**[18] 5248 7-11-12 **95**.................... RichardJohnson 99+
(Henry Daly) *taken down early: tore off in 15 l ld tl 8th: pressed next: rdn and hdd 2 out: rallied bravely to ld again last: sn forged clr and styd on strly* **16/1**

460/ **2** *3 ¼* **Bob Lewis**[5] 5505 7-10-11 **85**....................(t) JamesBanks(5) 86
(Anthony Middleton) *sn cl up: wnt 2nd at 7th and clsd on ldr after indifferent jump next: w ldr whn mstke 2 out: drvn in 3rd at last: edgd rt u.p but sn chsng wnr vainly* **20/1**

F30/ **3** *1 ¼* **Lombardy Boy (IRE)**[32] 4994 8-11-9 **92**....................(p) AlexMerriam 91
(Michael Banks) *chsd clr ldr 3rd tl 7th: 4th and rdn and one pce bef 2 out: plugged on into 3rd flat* **14/1**

054/ **4** *½* **Roseini (IRE)**[6] 5477 7-10-9 **83**.................... TrevorWhelan(5) 83
(Tony Carroll) *bhd: rdn and hdwy after 8th: 8th at next: drvn and clsd qckly to ld and looked wnr next: hdd and mstke last: fading fnl 100yds: awkward ride tactically* **13/2**[3]

534/ **5** *11* **Chilworth Screamer**[29] 5037 5-11-12 **95**.................... TomCannon 84
(Chris Gordon) *hld up: prog to chse ldrs 3 out: wl hld next: wkng after* **10/1**

00U/ **6** *21* **Flame Of Dixie (IRE)**[9] 5412 7-11-2 **85**.................... SeanQuinlan 55
(Jennie Candlish) *hld up towards rr: hdwy to press ldrs whn hit 3 out: floundering and wl btn whn mstke next* **14/1**

65P/ **7** *4 ½* **Highland River**[76] 4178 7-11-2 **85**.................... LeeEdwards 51
(Dave Roberts) *midfield: rdn and btn 3 out: t.o* **16/1**

452/ **8** *2 ¼* **Bellosguardo**[18] 5243 10-11-4 **94**....................(t) MissCBoxall(7) 58
(Kate Buckett) *midfield: rdn and struggling 3 out: t.o* **9/1**

011/ **9** *8* **Zelos Diktator**[16] 5285 7-11-2 **92**.................... MikeyHamill(7) 48
(Sean Curran) *j. slowly 5th: in rr and struggling 8th: t.o* **10/1**

560/ **10** *2 ¼* **Trifollet**[27] 5109 8-11-0 **90**.................... MrJMartin(7) 44
(Andrew J Martin) *towards rr and rdn 5th: struggling 8th: t.o* **16/1**

F64/ **11** *shd* **Western Kate (IRE)**[16] 5285 6-11-7 **95**.................... HarryDerham(5) 49
(John Flint) *hit 2nd: chsd ldrs tl rdn and wknd 8th: t.o* **6/1**[2]

400/ **12** *16* **Cunning Plan (IRE)**[28] 5083 6-10-13 **89**........ MissEmily-JaneHarbour(7) 29
(Raymond York) *in last pair: rdn and lost tch 8th: hopelessly t.o* **100/1**

0P4/ **13** *15* **Perfect Timing**[17] 5271 5-11-11....................(p) HaddenFrost 20
(Kevin Bishop) *midfield: drvn and no rspnse 8th: struggling next: t.o* **11/2**[1]

000/ **P** **Murfreesboro**[75] 3137 10-11-7 **95**.................... MrPYork(5)
(Raymond York) *last pair: nt fluent 8th: hopelessly t.o whn p.u last* **50/1**

53P/ **P** **Vinnie's Girl (IRE)**[165] 2437 6-11-2 **85**.................... SamTwiston-Davies
(Martin Bosley) *prom: 4th whn mstke 6th: lost pl bef 3 out: t.o and p.u last* **8/1**

03U/ **P** **Phar Away Island (IRE)**[29] 5034 5-11-0 **90**............(p) MissBAndrews(7)
(Caroline Fryer) *pressed ldrs on outer tl fdd bdly after 3 out: t.o and p.u next* **50/1**

5m 12.4s (-14.80) **Going Correction** -1.00s/f (Hard) **16** Ran SP% **123.0**
Speed ratings (Par 103): **88,86,86,86,81 73,72,71,68,67 67,61,55,** ,
toteswingers 1&2 £185.20, 1&3 £117.90, 2&3 £105.80 CSF £302.01 CT £4545.56 TOTE £9.50: £3.30, £5.70, £3.80, £1.80; EX 762.30 Trifecta £581.90 Part won. Pool: £775.92 - 0.05 winning units..
Owner Henry Daly **Bred** Mme Karine Colson **Trained** Stanton Lacy, Shropshire

FOCUS
The hurdles course was dolled out to the middle line. Chase and Hurdles on shared bends. A moderate handicap hurdle in which they went a decent gallop on ground officially described as good. The winner improved to the level of his best bumper form.

30 HAYGAIN HAY STEAMERS CLEAN HEALTHY FORAGE MAIDEN CHASE (12 fncs) 2m 110y

2:30 (2:30) (Class 5) 5-Y-0+ **£2,144** (£629; £314; £157)

Form RPR

530/ **1** **Majorica King (FR)**[16] 5293 7-10-7 0.................... ThomasGarner(7) 121+
(Oliver Sherwood) *trckd ldrs gng wl: nt fluent 6th: wnt 2nd at 8th: led 3 out: sn 4 l clr and in command: j.rt last: had it all his own way* **6/1**[3]

2F0/ **2** *12* **Able Deputy**[123] 3287 6-11-0 0....................(t) NickScholfield 113+
(Kim Bailey) *chsd ldrs: 3rd and rdn 3 out: chsd wnr bef next: one pce and nvr looked like getting in a blow* **5/4**[1]

356/ **3** *12* **Tothemoonandback (IRE)**[27] 5109 5-11-0 0.................... JamieMoore 102+
(Gary Moore) *last early: blnd 4th and wl bhd: styd on steadily fr 3 out: modest 3rd whn j.rt last* **17/2**

632/ **4** *1 ½* **Rebel High (IRE)**[52] 4637 9-11-0 92.................... DavidBass 98
(Derek Frankland) *prom: led 7th tl rdn and hdd 3 out: lost 2nd bef next and fdd to lose 3rd at last* **9/1**

440/ **5** *nk* **Sharivarry (FR)**[8] 5426 7-10-4 0.................... DaleIrving(10) 97
(James Ewart) *t.k.h in midfield: making no imp whn nt fluent 8th: no ch after* **12/1**

530/ **6** *18* **Strathcal**[10] 5386 7-11-0 0....................(tp) FelixDeGiles 81
(Tom Symonds) *towards rr: effrt 6th: chsd ldrs next: 4th and u.p 3 out: fading after: t.o* **25/1**

630/ **7** *5* **Snuker**[55] 4581 6-11-0 0.................... JackDoyle 77
(James Ewart) *midfield: rdn 6th: struggling in rr next: t.o* **66/1**

503/ **8** *38* **Tresor De L'Isle (FR)**[8] 5422 6-11-0 0.................... SamThomas 42
(James Ewart) *j. poorly in rr: blnd 4th and continued t.o* **22/1**

060/ **P** **Rogue Dancer (FR)**[32] 4995 8-11-0 0 AlexMerriam
(Michael Banks) *bhd: t.o fr 5th tl p.u 3 out* **100/1**

5PP/ **P** **Hard To Tell (IRE)**[122] 3315 7-11-0 0 AndrewThornton
(Bill Turner) *j. indifferently: led tl 7th: 5th and wkng whn p.u qckly 3 out* **100/1**

366/ **U** **Mezarat (ITY)**[16] 5283 8-10-7 0 (p) MissCareyWilliamson(7)
(Michael Gates) *uns rdr 1st* **125/1**

003/ **P** **Thunder Sheik (IRE)**[16] 5291 5-11-0 112 (bt[1]) PaddyBrennan
(Fergal O'Brien) *w ldr or prom tl lost pl after 5th: gng lft and looking awkward whn eased 7th: t.o and p.u 2 out* **11/2**[2]

3m 57.3s (-18.80) **Going Correction** -1.125s/f (Hard) **12** Ran SP% **114.8**
Speed ratings: **99,93,87,87,86 78,76,58, , ,**
toteswingers 1&2 £2.70, 1&3 £10.40, 2&3 £4.40 CSF £13.73 TOTE £8.30: £1.70, £1.20, £3.40; EX 16.40 Trifecta £138.20 Pool: £1153.20 - 6.25 winning units..
Owner Mrs Sue Griffiths **Bred** S C E A Haras De Clairfeuille **Trained** Upper Lambourn, Berks

FOCUS
A modest maiden chase in which they went a decent clip. The winner is rated in line with the best of his hurdle form.

31 FREE TIPS EVERY DAY AT GG.COM H'CAP HURDLE (8 hdls) 2m
3:00 (3:00) (Class 4) (0-110,110) 4-Y-0+ **£3,119** (£915; £457; £228)

Form RPR

220/ **1** **Jameel (USA)**[124] 3248 5-11-4 **109** (t) JosephAkehurst(7) 119+
(John Ferguson) *t.k.h in ld tl faltered 4th and dropped bk 4th: remained pressing ldrs: regained 2nd 2 out: drvn to ld last: sn asserted* **10/3**[1]

330/ **2** *2* **Brassbound (USA)**[16] 5280 5-11-3 **101** AndrewThornton 108
(Caroline Bailey) *settled in midfield: mstke 5th: effrt after next: drvn to ld bef 2 out: hdd last where clr of rest: nt qckn flat* **7/1**

33P/ **3** *9* **Detour Ahead**[11] 5360 5-11-5 **103** (p) SeanQuinlan 102
(Jennie Candlish) *lft in ld 3rd tl drvn and hdd bef 2 out: 6 l 3rd and wkng whn mstke last* **20/1**

43U/ **4** *3* **Meridiem**[6] 5477 9-10-3 **94** (t) MissBAndrews(7) 89
(Caroline Fryer) *cl up: wnt 2nd at 5th: rdn and ev ch bef 2 out: steadily fdd* **11/2**[3]

2PP/ **5** *10* **Dont Take Me Alive**[27] 5108 4-11-0 **103** (bt[1]) RichardJohnson 83
(Charlie Longsdon) *settled in midfield: effrt 3 out: rdn and pressing ldrs bef next: lost grnd tamely between last two* **8/1**

163/ **6** *9* **Farbreaga (IRE)**[18] 5245 7-11-9 **110** JeremiahMcGrath(3) 86
(Jamie Poulton) *midfield: dropped to rr and rdn after 4th: nt keen and wl bhd fr 3 out* **7/1**

066/ **7** *1 1/2* **Fluter Phil**[10] 5378 6-10-1 **85** MattieBatchelor 62
(Roger Ingram) *dropped out last: impeded 4th: lost tch 3 out* **25/1**

P64/ **8** *1* **Quiet Whisper (IRE)**[23] 5185 7-10-8 **97** (t) EdCookson(5) 72
(Kim Bailey) *cl up: 3rd and drvn whn mstke 3 out: nt run on and sn wl btn* **5/1**[2]

565/ **9** *13* **Herschel (IRE)**[60] 2052 7-11-4 **102** JamieMoore 63
(Gary Moore) *in last trio: struggling whn mstke 3 out: t.o* **50/1**

P40/ **10** *16* **Mccauley (IRE)**[190] 1947 10-10-11 **102** (p) MrMatthewHampton(7) 47
(Robert Walford) *racd up on outer to join ldr 3rd tl 5th: fdd next: t.o* **33/1**

4U2/ **F** **Alwaystheoptimist**[10] 5386 10-11-7 **108** KielanWoods(3)
(Phil Middleton) *hld up in rr tl fell 4th* **8/1**

3m 50.5s (-17.40) **Going Correction** -1.00s/f (Hard)
WFA 4 from 5yo+ 5lb **11** Ran SP% **115.9**
Speed ratings (Par 105): **103,102,97,96,91 86,85,85,78,70**
toteswingers 1&2 £5.70, 1&3 £6.40, 2&3 £22.10 CSF £25.45 CT £403.36 TOTE £3.40: £1.30, £2.40, £4.60; EX 32.40 Trifecta £294.90 Pool: £1326.72 - 3.37 winning units..
Owner Bloomfields **Bred** Darley **Trained** Cowlinge, Suffolk

FOCUS
A modest handicap hurdle in which they went an honest gallop. A step up from the winner, who'll rate higher.

32 REMEMBER COLIN AND SMILE H'CAP CHASE (18 fncs) 3m 110y
3:30 (3:30) (Class 5) (0-100,99) 5-Y-0+ **£2,144** (£629; £314; £157)

Form RPR

P05/ **1** **Time Do (FR)**[27] 5104 6-11-6 **96** (bt) IanPopham(3) 109+
(Caroline Keevil) *mde most tl pckd 10th and rdr lost iron: sn prom again: rdn to go 2nd 14th: blnd bdly 3 out: led bef next: hrd drvn to go clr after last: fine ride* **11/1**

556/ **2** *1 3/4* **D'Gigi**[54] 4587 7-11-9 **96** (t) SamTwiston-Davies 102
(Nigel Twiston-Davies) *trckd ldrs gng wl: clsd grad fr 12th: wnt 2nd bef 2 out: rdn and w wnr 2 out tl last: kpt on wl tl no ex fnl 100yds* **8/1**

4PP/ **3** *11* **Ontheslate (IRE)**[146] 2836 7-10-7 **80** AlexMerriam 77
(Neil King) *prom: rdn and w ldng pair 2 out: wknd bef last* **6/1**[2]

P13/ **4** *3 3/4* **One More Dinar**[68] 4326 10-11-2 **96** NickSlatter(7) 89
(John Bryan Groucott) *cl last at 7th: effrt 15th: rdn after next: sn btn and nt looking v co-operative* **6/1**[2]

535/ **5** *2 1/4* **Von Galen (IRE)**[3] 5542 12-10-1 **74** TomScudamore 65
(Michael Scudamore) *towards rr of bunch: rdn and wknd grad on long run to 2 out* **11/1**

20P/ **6** *33* **Hazy Dawn**[15] 5309 8-10-5 **81** (b[1]) MichealNolan(3) 57
(Richard Woollacott) *on and off bridle: trckd ldrs tl nt fluent 10th and 11th: sn led: hit 15th and rdn: hdd bef 2 out: lost pl v tamely and eased: t.o* **7/1**[3]

PP4/ **7** *15* **Overton Lad**[146] 2838 12-10-7 **80** (bt) JackDoyle 28
(Peter Pritchard) *prom but running in snatches and needing lots of coaxing and reminders: led briefly after 11th: wkng whn blnd next: t.o after 3 out* **25/1**

P00/ **8** *1/2* **Roi De Garde (FR)**[17] 5276 7-11-9 **96** TomMessenger 43
(Chris Bealby) *chsd ldrs: rdn and struggling 14th: t.o after 3 out* **14/1**

05P/ **P** **Moscow Mule**[8] 5443 10-10-0 **80** MarkMarris(7)
(Laura Hurley) *last whn blnd bdly 1st: rdr lost irons and p.u* **66/1**

4UP/ **P** **Jolly Boys Outing (IRE)**[80] 4103 10-11-6 **98** BenPoste(5)
(Rosemary Gasson) *chsd ldrs: rdn 12th: no rspnse: struggling 14th: t.o and p.u 2 out* **11/4**[1]

40P/ **P** **Atherstone Hill (IRE)**[130] 3158 11-11-5 **99** (v) ChristopherWard(7)
(Robin Dickin) *w ldr briefly 5th: rdn and lost pl 7th: reluctant: t.o 10th: p.u 15th* **11/1**

6m 7.6s (-29.30) **Going Correction** -1.125s/f (Hard) **11** Ran SP% **115.9**
Speed ratings: **101,100,96,95,95 84,79,79, , ,**
toteswingers 1&2 £12.30, 1&3 £11.10, 2&3 £8.70 CSF £94.89 CT £582.47 TOTE £12.50: £3.80, £2.30, £2.50; EX 97.50 Trifecta £452.00 Pool: £2050.69 - 3.40 winning units..
Owner Mrs L R Lovell **Bred** R Dugardin & Y Cadoret **Trained** Motcombe, Dorset

FOCUS
A moderate staying handicap chase in which they went a decent gallop. The form is rated around the second.

33 PSP ASSOCIATION NOVICES' HURDLE (8 hdls) 2m
4:00 (4:00) (Class 4) 4-Y-0+ **£3,119** (£915; £457; £228)

Form RPR

342/ **1** **Wild Card**[83] 4045 6-10-12 0 RichardJohnson 104+
(Henry Daly) *settled in midfield: effrt after 3 out: rdn to go 2nd bef 2 out: sustained effrt after: chal last: styd on v gamely to ld fnl 100yds* **13/2**[3]

13/ **2** *nk* **Twelve Roses**[193] 1898 5-10-12 0 NickScholfield 104+
(Kim Bailey) *looked rather green in 2nd: led 3 out: ballooned next and rdn: hdd after last: nt qckn* **8/13**[1]

624/ **3** *6* **Staigue Fort**[90] 3923 5-10-12 0 DominicElsworth 97
(Emma Lavelle) *chsd ldr: outpcd 3 out: tried to rally and wnt 3rd between last two: drifting rt and no imp after* **20/1**

001/ **4** *nk* **Jeano De Toulouse (FR)**[32] 4994 6-10-12 0 LeightonAspell 97
(Oliver Sherwood) *chsd ldrs: effrt in 3rd and rdn 3 out: one pce and no imp after* **8/1**

002/ **5** *3 1/2* **Dougalstar (FR)**[16] 5281 4-10-0 0 MikeyHamill(7) 88
(Sean Curran) *trckd ldrs: rdn after 3 out: one pce and n.d fr next* **33/1**

0P0/ **6** *3/4* **Red Rosso**[40] 4872 8-10-9 0 JamesBest(3) 92
(Rob Summers) *led at v modest pce tl hdd and nt fluent 3 out: sn drvn: lost 3rd between last two: fdd grad* **200/1**

535/ **7** *2 1/4* **Call A Truce (IRE)**[16] 5280 5-10-12 0 DarylJacob 90+
(Ben Case) *a abt same pl: struggling bef 3 out: plugged on* **6/1**[2]

5/ **8** *29* **Frontier Vic**[396] 5144 6-10-12 0 SamTwiston-Davies 61
(Nigel Twiston-Davies) *last trio: blnd bdly 4th whn sme way off pce: nt rcvr: t.o* **20/1**

9 *1/2* **I'Lldoit**[41] 6-10-9 0 JohnKington(3) 61
(Michael Scudamore) *on her toes: hld up in last trio: t.o after 3rd* **100/1**

00/ **P** **Exclusive Rights**[30] 5018 5-10-5 0 AndrewTinkler
(Charlie Longsdon) *plld hrd in last trio: lost tch after 3rd: t.o 3 out: p.u last* **80/1**

3m 58.8s (-9.10) **Going Correction** -1.00s/f (Hard)
WFA 4 from 5yo+ 5lb **10** Ran SP% **115.8**
Speed ratings (Par 105): **82,81,78,78,76 76,75,60,60,**
toteswingers 1&2 £2.70, 1&3 £10.10, 2&3 £6.00 CSF £10.96 TOTE £4.90: £1.30, £1.10, £4.00; EX 16.40 Trifecta £86.80 Pool: £2682.54 - 23.16 winning units..
Owner Evan-Robert Hanbury **Bred** E R Hanbury **Trained** Stanton Lacy, Shropshire

FOCUS
A fair novices' hurdle in which the early gallop was a steady one. The form is given a token rating through the fifth, with the runner-up a stone+ off.

34 BEST RACING BLOGS ON GG.COM H'CAP CHASE (12 fncs) 2m 110y
4:30 (4:30) (Class 5) (0-100,105) 5-Y-0+ **£2,144** (£629; £314; £157)

Form RPR

430/ **1** **Peak Seasons (IRE)**[32] 4992 10-9-4 **72** oh4 GerardGalligan(10) 89+
(Michael Chapman) *midfield: rdr lurchd 4th and lost iron and could nt regain it tl 7th: 5th 3 out: str run to ld next: already clr whn brushed through last: hanging rt flat* **25/1**

564/ **2** *7* **Richo**[10] 5384 7-9-12 **75** TrevorWhelan(5) 86
(Shaun Harris) *quirky abt lining up: detached in last quartet at 5th: effrt after blunder 8th: 4th and on heels of ldrs bef 2 out: plugged on into wl hld 2nd after last* **15/2**

10/ **3** *2 1/4* **Crack At Dawn (IRE)**[16] 5285 12-10-11 **86** (v) AdamWedge(3) 93
(Michael Gates) *settled in rr: hdwy 9th: hit next: drvn and chal 2 out: gng idly in wl hld 2nd after tl fnl 100yds* **12/1**

523/ **4** *4 1/2* **Vosges (FR)**[7] 5448 6-11-5 **98** (p) MrJamesSmith(7) 100
(James Ewart) *sn drvn along and nt gng w gusto: led and j.lft 3rd: hdd 5th: remained prom tl fnd nil fr 2 out* **5/1**[3]

534/ **5** *nk* **Owner Occupier**[6] 5478 8-10-13 **85** (b[1]) TomCannon 87
(Chris Gordon) *drvn most of way: led 5th: hit 3 out: hdd next: fnd nthing after* **9/2**[2]

4P1/ **6** *20* **Henok (FR)**[6] 5478 7-12-5 **105** 7ex (p) ConorO'Farrell 93
(David Pipe) *led tl impeded 3rd: drvn and ev ch 3 out: no rspnse and fdd bdly next: eased* **7/4**[1]

121/ **7** *nk* **Oranger (FR)**[18] 5246 11-11-0 **93** (b) MrJMartin(7) 76
(Andrew J Martin) *sn wl off pce in last quartet: nt travelling fr 6th: remote 3 out* **6/1**

PP/ **8** *11* **Dream Honours (IRE)**[168] 2384 10-10-6 **85** MrLKilgarriff(7) 59
(Clarissa Caroe) *detached in last quartet after 5th: blnd 8th: sn t.o* **50/1**

3m 58.5s (-17.60) **Going Correction** -1.125s/f (Hard) **8** Ran SP% **110.8**
Speed ratings: **96,92,91,89,89 79,79,74**
toteswingers 1&2 £15.70, 1&3 £12.40, 2&3 £6.00 CSF £182.49 CT £2280.99 TOTE £49.70: £6.90, £2.70, £3.40; EX 189.70 Trifecta £1768.20 Part won. Pool: £2357.69 - 0.68 winning units..
Owner J E Reed **Bred** Peter Gleeson **Trained** Market Rasen, Lincs

FOCUS
A modest handicap chase in which there was a strongly contested early gallop. A good time for the grade and the winner's best figure since 2009.

35 GG.COM MARES' STANDARD OPEN NATIONAL HUNT FLAT RACE (DIV I) 2m
5:00 (5:00) (Class 6) 4-6-Y-0 **£1,642** (£478; £239)

Form RPR

010/ **1** **Celestial Island**[24] 5163 6-11-0 0 PeterCarberry(5) 106
(John Gallagher) *trckd ldrs: shkn up 4f out: clsd to ld wl over 1f out: beating off rivals whn hung lft ins fnl f* **8/1**

2 *1* **Western Diva (IRE)** 4-10-7 0 ColinBolger 93
(Pat Murphy) *settled midfield: effrt on inner 3f out: chal 2f out: kpt on wl tl nt qckn ins fnl f* **16/1**

3/ **3** *2 1/4* **Je T'Aime (IRE)**[54] 4592 4-10-7 0 AdrianLane 91
(Donald McCain) *pressed ldr: led over 4f out: drvn and hdd wl over 1f out: no ex fnl f* **8/1**

0/ **4** *1* **Unefille De Guye (FR)**[59] 4507 5-10-5 0 ConorShoemark(7) 95
(Victor Dartnall) *trckd ldrs: effrt over 2f out: drvn to chal over 1f out: nt qckn fnl f* **16/1**

5 *1 1/4* **Lacunae (IRE)** 5-10-9 0 RyanMahon(3) 94
(Seamus Mullins) *towards rr: rdn 4f out: sme prog 3f out: one pce and no real imp fnl 2f* **15/2**[3]

6 *5* **Dungarvan Lass (IRE)** 4-10-7 0 DavidBass 84
(Nicky Henderson) *pressed ldng pair: rdn 2f out: wl hld 5th over 1f out* **15/8**[1]

7 *9* **Cayetina** 4-10-7 0 JackDoyle 76
(Ali Brewer) *midfield: rdn 4f out: outpcd over 2f out* **8/1**

420/ **8** 3¾ **Rising Teal**^{16} 5295 4-10-7 0 .... LeightonAspell 73
(Lucy Wadham) *slt ld in slowly run r tl hdd over 4f out: dropped out qckly over 2f out: t.o* **6/1**^{2}

9 5 **Potkettleblack**^{22} 4-10-7 0 .... TomMessenger 68
(Chris Bealby) *bhd: rdn 4f out: plugged on w no ch fnl 3f: t.o* **20/1**

/ **10** 16 **B B Baloo** 4-10-7 0 .... PaulMoloney 54
(John Wainwright) *plld hrd in last: lost tch 4f out: t.o* **16/1**

3m 52.0s (-10.30) **Going Correction** -1.00s/f (Hard)
WFA 4 from 5yo+ 5lb **10** Ran SP% **116.6**
Speed ratings: **85,84,83,82,82 79,75,73,70,62**
toteswingers 1&2 £20.60, 1&3 £6.80, 2&3 £23.50 CSF £126.97 TOTE £6.90: £1.90, £4.90, £2.70; EX 138.10 Trifecta £698.90 Part won. Pool: £931.97 - 0.73 winning units..
Owner Roy Brown **Bred** H G W Brown **Trained** Chastleton, Oxon
■ Stewards' Enquiry : Peter Carberry two-day ban: used whip above permitted level (May 13-14)

FOCUS
The first division of an ordinary mares' bumper in which they went an even gallop. The winner and fourth were pretty much to their marks.

36 GG.COM MARES' STANDARD OPEN NATIONAL HUNT FLAT RACE (DIV II) 2m
5:30 (5:30) (Class 6) 4-6-Y-0 **£1,642** (£478; £239)

Form RPR

1 **The Govaness** 4-10-7 0 .... PaddyBrennan 97+
(Fergal O'Brien) *trckd ldrs gng wl: led over 2f out: urged clr over 1f out* **8/1**

34/ **2** 2¼ **Bonnet's Vino**^{28} 5062 5-10-12 0 .... SeanQuinlan 99
(Pam Sly) *led tl rdn over 2f out: sn outpcd by wnr and wandering: gamely clung on to 2nd pl* **11/1**

3 nk **No Pushover** 4-10-7 0 .... AndrewTinkler 94+
(Nicky Henderson) *pressed ldrs: drvn over 3f out: slow to respond and wl hld 3rd over 2f out: kpt on steadily ins fnl f* **1/1**^{1}

4 13 **Hortense Mancini** 4-10-7 0 .... LeightonAspell 82
(Lucy Wadham) *v green in rr: passed btn horses fr over 2f out: nvr nr ldrs* **13/2**^{3}

5 1¼ **Tiller Belle** 5-10-9 0 .... JeremiahMcGrath$^{(3)}$ 86
(Nicky Henderson) *midfield: rdn over 3f out: wl btn over 2f out* **6/1**^{2}

6 1½ **Ereyna** 4-10-4 0 .... BrendanPowell$^{(3)}$ 80
(Renee Robeson) *pressed ldr tl rdn 3f out: sn lost pl* **16/1**

60/ **7** 16 **Dervla (IRE)**^{51} 4666 5-10-12 0 .... AndrewThornton 70
(Seamus Mullins) *t.k.h early: towards rr: rdn and btn 3f out: t.o* **14/1**

000/ **8** 9 **Pinnacle Ofpassion (IRE)**^{66} 4377 5-10-12 0 ....^{1} GerardTumelty 62
(Nick Lampard) *nrly a last: lost tch and nt looking keen 1/2-way: t.o fnl 3f* **66/1**

9 13 **Dream Mistress** 4-10-7 0 .... TomMessenger 45
(Chris Bealby) *t.k.h: cl up tl rdn and lost pl bdly 3f out: hopelessly t.o* **25/1**

3m 49.2s (-13.10) **Going Correction** -1.00s/f (Hard)
WFA 4 from 5yo 5lb **9** Ran SP% **115.0**
Speed ratings: **92,90,90,84,83 82,74,70,63**
toteswingers 1&2 £11.30, 1&3 £3.40, 2&3 £4.40 CSF £90.93 TOTE £8.70: £2.60, £1.60, £1.20; EX 82.30 Trifecta £345.90 Pool: £1171.97 - 2.54 winning units..
Owner C B Brookes **Bred** C B Brookes **Trained** Coln St. Dennis, Gloucs

FOCUS
The second division of an ordinary mares' bumper. The second is probably the best guide to the level.
T/Jkpt: Not won. T/Plt: £414.90 to a £1 stake. Pool of £68,464.50 - 120.44 winning units T/Qpdt: £218.00 to a £1 stake. Pool of £5275.00 - 17.90 winning units IM

EXETER (R-H)
Tuesday, April 30
OFFICIAL GOING: Good to firm (good in places)
Wind: mild breeze across Weather: sunny with cloudy periods

37 NEIL CLARK TESTIMONIAL H'CAP HURDLE (8 hdls) 2m 1f
5:35 (5:35) (Class 4) (0-110,108) 4-Y-0+ **£3,249** (£954; £477; £238)

Form RPR

063/ **1** **Party Palace**^{6} 5509 9-10-0 85 .... GilesHawkins$^{(3)}$ 91+
(Stuart Howe) *hld up: reminder after 3rd: rdn after 5th: stdy hdwy fr 3 out: lft in ld last: kpt on wl: drvn out* **9/2**^{3}

PPP/ **2** 5 **Exiles Return (IRE)**^{54} 4614 11-9-11 82 oh20 .... MarkQuinlan$^{(3)}$ 81
(Jacqueline Retter) *led tl 3 out: sn rdn: keeping on at same pce whn lft w ev ch last: no ex* **100/1**

33U/ **3** 8 **No To Trident**^{7} 5464 8-11-9 105 ....(p) RhysFlint 100+
(John Flint) *trckd ldrs: mstke 4th: rdn bef 3 out: lft w ev ch last where bdly hmpd: no ch after* **5/2**^{1}

330/ **4** 2 **Cash Injection**^{7} 4375 4-10-8 95 ....(t) AndrewThornton 78
(Karen George) *hld up: nt fluent 1st: rdn after 5th: hdwy 3 out: styd on same pce fr 2 out: lft 4th at the last* **14/1**

4P0/ **5** 12 **Mighty Monty**^{54} 4616 8-11-7 103 ....(p) JackDoyle 79
(Victor Dartnall) *trckd ldrs: effrt after 3 out: wknd jst bef last* **7/2**^{2}

105/ **6** ¾ **Wild Tonto (IRE)**^{506} 10-11-4 107 .... GeraldQuinn$^{(7)}$ 83
(Nigel Twiston-Davies) *racd keenly: in tch: rdn appr 3 out: sn btn* **18/1**

5P4/ **7** 1½ **Tail Of The Bank (IRE)**^{28} 5103 10-11-12 108 .... LiamHeard 82
(Laura Young) *in tch: rdn appr 3 out: wknd bef 2 out* **6/1**

P65/ **8** 2½ **Zulu Principle**^{189} 1972 6-10-13 95 ....(t) SamThomas 66
(Helen Nelmes) *racd keenly: trckd ldrs: rdn bef 3 out: wknd bef 2 out* **12/1**

U1P/ **F** **Jawhary**^{193} 1924 6-11-6 105 .... BrendanPowell$^{(3)}$ 108
(Robert Walford) *trckd ldr: led 3 out: shkn up in 2 l ld whn hung lft and fell heavily last: fatally injured* **13/2**

3m 59.9s (-15.60) **Going Correction** -1.15s/f (Hard)
WFA 4 from 6yo+ 5lb **9** Ran SP% **117.2**
Speed ratings (Par 105): **90,87,83,82,77 76,76,75,**
toteswingers 1&2 £11.20, 2&3 £0.00, 1&3 £1.90 CSF £218.88 CT £1367.43 TOTE £7.30: £2.10, £16.60, £1.10; EX 728.30 Trifecta £652.90 Part won. Pool: £870.66 - 0.01 winning units..
Owner B P Jones **Bred** Llety Farms **Trained** Oakford, Devon

FOCUS
All races used hurdle bend entering the home straight. The winning time of this opener confirmed the ground was riding fast. Weak handicap form, and they went just a steady pace. The winner is rated in line with her recent run.

38 CHARLES STANLEY NEIL CLARK H'CAP HURDLE (12 hdls) 2m 7f 110y
6:05 (6:05) (Class 4) (0-120,120) 4-Y-0+ **£3,249** (£954; £477; £238)

Form RPR

140/ **1** **Cinevator (IRE)**^{17} 5293 6-11-9 120 ....(p) IanPopham$^{(3)}$ 130+
(Caroline Keevil) *mde all: rdn clr after 2 out: styd on strly: eased towards fin* **11/2**

4P5/ **2** 10 **Phone Home (IRE)**^{28} 5103 6-11-10 118 .... NickScholfield 117
(Nick Mitchell) *hld up bhd: squeezed through gap and hdwy appr 9th: trckd wnr after 3 out: rdn whn mstke 2 out: kpt on same pce* **3/1**^{2}

242/ **3** 1¾ **Wilde Ruby (IRE)**^{9} 5432 6-11-4 112 ....(p) AndrewThornton 107
(Seamus Mullins) *hld up in tch: sltly outpcd appr 3 out: hdwy fr 2 out: wnt 3rd at the last: styd on* **9/2**^{3}

130/ **4** 8 **Elegant Olive**^{109} 3594 10-9-12 99 .... MrFTett$^{(7)}$ 89
(Roger Curtis) *mid-div: hdwy to chse ldrs bef 3 out: sn rdn: styd on same pce* **28/1**

045/ **5** 9 **Comeonginger (IRE)**^{70} 4296 6-11-9 117 ....(t) DarylJacob 101+
(Paul Nicholls) *mid-div: nudged along and hdwy after 8th: rdn bef 3 out: sn one pce: wknd last* **11/5**^{1}

030/ **6** 17 **Frontier Dancer (IRE)**^{31} 5015 9-11-7 115 ....(tp) HarrySkelton 83
(Lawney Hill) *trckd ldrs tl rdn after 9th: btn whn mstke 3 out: sn wknd* **20/1**

336/ **7** 1½ **Stony Road (IRE)**^{33} 4978 6-10-13 107 ....(b^{1}) RhysFlint 70
(John Flint) *mid-div: hdwy after 6th to press wnr fr next tl rdn appr 3 out: wknd after 2 out* **20/1**

6B4/ **8** 30 **Teenage Kicks (IRE)**^{325} 662 8-11-8 119 ....(t) MattGriffiths$^{(3)}$ 55
(Polly Gundry) *struggling 7th: a in rr: t.o* **18/1**

055/ **P** **Be My Light (IRE)**^{16} 5321 7-10-9 106 ....(b^{1}) KielanWoods$^{(3)}$
(Charlie Longsdon) *trckd ldrs tl mstke 8th: sn struggling: losing tch whn p.u bef 3 out: fatally injured* **14/1**

5m 34.9s (-24.10) **Going Correction** -1.15s/f (Hard) **9** Ran SP% **114.7**
Speed ratings (Par 105): **94,90,90,87,84 78,78,68,**
toteswingers 1&2 £3.00, 2&3 £6.30, 1&3 £2.10 CSF £22.09 CT £80.21 TOTE £4.10: £1.70, £1.60, £1.60; EX 27.90 Trifecta £226.80 Pool: £818.96 - 2.70 winning units..
Owner The Optimist & Pessimist Partnership **Bred** Patrick Thompson **Trained** Motcombe, Dorset

FOCUS
Moderate handicap form but it does look a step forward from the easy winner.

39 FRANK TUCKER COMMERCIALS H'CAP CHASE (18 fncs) 3m
6:35 (6:35) (Class 3) (0-140,134) 5-Y-0+ **£6,498** (£1,908; £954; £477)

Form RPR

P3F/ **1** **Top Smart**^{48} 4732 7-10-12 123 .... RyanMahon$^{(3)}$ 133+
(Seamus Mullins) *bhd: hdwy into chsng gp after 4th: disp 3rd 11th: sltly outpcd 13th: hdwy 4 out: chalng whn nt fluent last: sn led: styd on wl: drvn out* **5/2**^{2}

F1F/ **2** ¾ **Lamboro Lad (IRE)**^{242} 1441 8-11-1 123 ....(tp) TomO'Brien 131
(Peter Bowen) *trckd clr ldr 3rd: clsd on ldr 4th: led 10th tl next: led 14th: rdn after 4 out: jnd last: kpt on but no ex whn hdd sn after* **7/1**

P2P/ **3** 7 **Qianshan Leader (IRE)**^{13} 5351 9-11-4 126 ....(v^{1}) DominicElsworth 129
(Emma Lavelle) *lft in ld 1st: clr tl 4th: hdd 10th: led next tl 14th: rdn after 4 out: styd on same pce fr 3 out* **10/1**

024/ **4** 14 **Palace Jester**^{26} 5146 8-10-12 120 ....(t) ConorO'Farrell 111
(David Pipe) *hld up: rdn to cl on ldrs after 14th: chsd ldrs next: one pce fr 3 out* **4/1**^{3}

213/ **5** 69 **Mr Hudson (IRE)**^{377} 5462 8-11-9 131 .... DarylJacob 58
(Paul Nicholls) *trckd ldrs: sltly outpcd whn rchd for 13th: chsd ldrs bef 4 out: sn wknd: eased down fr 2 out* **15/8**^{1}

43P/ **U** **Sarando**^{26} 5146 8-11-1 123 ....(tp) LiamTreadwell
(Paul Webber) *ldng whn hesitant: blnd bdly and uns rdr 1st* **14/1**

5m 44.9s (-24.40) **Going Correction** -1.30s/f (Hard) **6** Ran SP% **111.6**
Speed ratings: **88,87,85,80,57**
toteswingers 1&2 £4.20, 2&3 £2.20, 1&3 £5.80 CSF £18.92 CT £143.26 TOTE £4.00: £2.40, £1.40; EX 19.20 Trifecta £62.10 Pool: £752.74 - 9.08 winning units..
Owner The Calvera Partnership No 2 **Bred** A Price **Trained** Wilsford-Cum-Lake, Wilts

FOCUS
Quite a decent staying handicap. The winner is on a good mark and was close to his best.

40 STILL FORK LIFT TRUCKS H'CAP CHASE (15 fncs) 2m 3f 110y
7:05 (7:05) (Class 4) (0-115,110) 5-Y-0+ **£3,898** (£1,144; £572; £286)

Form RPR

003/ **1** **Brody Bleu (FR)**^{14} 5331 6-11-0 98 .... FelixDeGiles 106+
(Robert Walford) *disp ld tl pushed into def advantage 4 out: drifted lft run-in: r.o strly: rdn out* **9/2**^{3}

003/ **2** 2 **Adrenalin Flight (IRE)**^{42} 4854 7-11-2 100 .... AndrewThornton 108+
(Seamus Mullins) *trckd ldrs: pushed along to chse wnr 3 out: rdn after 2 out: pckd last: kpt on same pce* **13/8**^{1}

666/ **3** 10 **Sound Stage**^{137} 3044 10-11-9 110 ....(p) IanPopham$^{(3)}$ 109
(Caroline Keevil) *disp ld: hit 10th: nt fluent next: rdn whn hdd and hit 4 out: lost 2nd at the next: no ex fr 2 out* **9/4**^{2}

054/ **4** 6 **Cottage Acre (IRE)**^{14} 5330 10-11-9 107 ....(t) LiamHeard 99
(Colin Heard) *trckd ldrs: rdn after 4 out: kpt on same pce fr next* **10/1**

15P/ **5** 16 **Knapp Bridge Boy**^{17} 5286 13-10-13 97 .... LiamTreadwell 71
(James Payne) *racd keenly: sn trcking ldrs: hit 2nd: nt fluent 5th: rdn appr 4 out: wknd bef 2 out* **8/1**

06U/ **6** 2¼ **Cranky Corner**^{37} 4948 9-11-12 110 .... SamThomas 82
(Helen Nelmes) *hld up: effrt to cl on ldrs after 11th: wknd bef 2 out* **25/1**

4m 29.8s (-27.50) **Going Correction** -1.30s/f (Hard) **6** Ran SP% **111.1**
Speed ratings: **103,102,98,95,89 88**
toteswingers 1&2 £1.40, 2&3 £2.60, 1&3 £2.60 CSF £12.57 TOTE £3.60: £1.90, £1.30; EX 16.40 Trifecta £32.80 Pool: £463.26 - 10.58 winning units..
Owner R J Brown **Bred** Pierre Julienne **Trained** Child Okeford, Dorset

FOCUS
The two least exposed runners drew clear in an ordinary handicap, and it was run in a course record time. The winner improved towards the level of his best French hurdle form.

41 CAP CEILINGS AND PARTITIONS LTD MARES' NOVICES' HURDLE (10 hdls) 2m 3f
7:35 (7:35) (Class 4) 4-Y-0+ **£3,249** (£954; £477; £238)

Form RPR

003/ **1** **Emily's Flyer (IRE)**^{56} 4573 6-10-6 0 ....(t) ConorShoemark$^{(7)}$ 106+
(Fergal O'Brien) *mde all: in command whn nt fluent 2 out: pushed out: readily* **10/3**^{3}

4P2/ **2** 5 **Dancing Emily (IRE)**[19] 5249 7-10-13 0 TomO'Brien 99
(Graeme McPherson) *trckd ldrs: pushed along to chse wnr after 3 out: rdn after next: styd on same pce* **11/4**[2]

606/ **3** 3 ¾ **Presenting Me (IRE)**[243] 1426 5-10-10 0 AdamWedge(3) 97+
(Evan Williams) *j. sltly rt at times: trckd wnr tl rdn 3 out: styd on same pce fr next* **40/1**

343/ **4** 3 ¼ **Shady Lane**[24] 5185 6-10-13 100 CharlieHuxley 95
(Alan King) *in tch: blnd 7th: rdn bef 3 out: sn one pce* **9/4**[1]

30/ **5** 2 ½ **Magic Money**[62] 4459 5-10-13 0 NickScholfield 91
(Kim Bailey) *hld up: nt fluent 3rd: struggling in last after 6th: styd on steadily after 3 out: nvr trbld ldrs* **14/1**

602/ **6** 5 **Easter Dancer**[164] 2479 6-10-13 0 DominicElsworth 85
(Lawney Hill) *hld up: effrt appr 3 out: sn one pce: fdd last* **9/2**

23P/ **7** 7 **Call Me April**[62] 4460 5-10-13 0 AndrewThornton 80
(Karen George) *hld up: nt fluent 6th: pushed along and hdwy appr 3 out: wknd after 2 out: awkward last* **40/1**

4m 29.0s (-13.70) **Going Correction** -1.15s/f (Hard) 7 Ran SP% **110.2**
Speed ratings (Par 105): **82,79,78,76,75 73,70**
toteswingers 1&2 £1.40, 2&3 £12.10, 1&3 £12.10 CSF £12.27 TOTE £3.50: £2.80, £2.30; EX 6.30 Trifecta £60.70 Pool: £438.74 - 5.41 winning units..
Owner C Cornes **Bred** Cathal Ennis **Trained** Coln St. Dennis, Gloucs

FOCUS
A modest mares' race which was slowly run and has been given a token rating through the second.

42 LADIES DAY 7TH MAY H'CAP HURDLE (10 hdls) 2m 3f
8:05 (8:05) (Class 5) (0-100,105) 4-Y-0+ **£1,949** (£572; £286; £143)

Form RPR

564/ **1** **High Ville (IRE)**[28] 5108 7-11-10 98 ConorO'Farrell 111+
(David Pipe) *mde all: kicked clr 3 out: kpt on: rdn out* **11/2**[3]

021/ **2** 5 **Castlemorris King**[6] 5509 5-11-11 104 7ex GavinSheehan(5) 112+
(Brian Barr) *hld up bhd: hdwy on outer turning into st: wnt 3rd 3 out: sn rdn: r.o to snatch 2nd nring fin: nvr rching wnr* **15/8**[1]

403/ **3** shd **Get Home Now**[180] 2139 5-10-13 87 (v) TomO'Brien 93
(Peter Bowen) *trckd wnr: rdn bef 3 out: sn hld by wnr: styd on same pce: lost 2nd nring fin* **5/1**[2]

P22/ **4** 9 **Little Eaglet (IRE)**[184] 2078 9-10-12 86 LiamHeard 84
(Colin Heard) *trckd ldrs: rdn after 7th: one pce fr 3 out* **10/1**

PP0/ **5** 15 **Fashion Week**[17] 5285 8-10-11 85 (p) AidanColeman 69
(Sue Gardner) *cl up tl outpcd appr 7th: styd on again fr after 3 out but no ch w ldrs* **5/1**[2]

P40/ **6** 1 ¾ **Shaddaii (FR)**[7] 5473 7-9-11 74 oh5 (t) IanPopham(3) 58
(Caroline Keevil) *hld up: pushed along after 5th: nvr threatened ldrs: wknd 3 out* **33/1**

306/ **7** 10 **Theoystercatcher (IRE)**[168] 2396 7-11-2 97 AlanJohns(7) 71
(Tim Vaughan) *mid-div: hdwy 6th: rdn after 7th: wknd bef 3 out* **28/1**

046/ **8** ½ **Kruseman**[6] 5505 6-11-7 95 (p) AndrewGlassonbury 68
(Richard Woollacott) *trckd ldrs: rdn after 7th: wknd bef 3 out* **12/1**

000/ **9** 6 **Pod**[29] 5083 5-9-12 75 BrendanPowell(3) 47
(Caroline Keevil) *struggling after 7th: a towards rr* **20/1**

313/ **10** 14 **Scales (IRE)**[28] 5108 7-11-7 98 MichealNolan(3) 53
(Richard Lee) *mid-div: blnd 4th: rdn after 6th: sn in rr: wknd after 7th: t.o* **8/1**

4m 19.4s (-23.30) **Going Correction** -1.15s/f (Hard) 10 Ran SP% **122.5**
Speed ratings (Par 103): **103,100,100,97,90 90,85,85,83,77**
toteswingers 1&2 £2.10, 2&3 £2.00, 1&3 £9.80 CSF £17.28 CT £57.90 TOTE £9.00: £3.20, £1.10, £2.00; EX 22.90 Trifecta £121.30 Pool: £513.57 - 3.17 winning units..
Owner G Thompson **Bred** Kevin Foley **Trained** Nicholashayne, Devon

FOCUS
An ordinary handicap and another all-the-way winner, who is rated to the level of hus hurdles form. The second was a few pounds off his latest run.
T/Jkpt: Not won. T/Plt: £60.70 to a £1 stake. Pool of £58791.67 - 706.85 winning tickets. T/Qpdt: £18.60 to a £1 stake. Pool of £5552.50 - 220.40 winning tickets TM

WORCESTER (L-H)
Tuesday, April 30
OFFICIAL GOING: Good (good to firm in places;7.4)
Wind: light breeze Weather: sunny spells; 14 degrees

43 VISITWORCESTERSHIRE.ORG H'CAP CHASE (12 fncs) 2m 110y
5:15 (5:15) (Class 5) (0-100,97) 5-Y-0+ **£2,241** (£658; £329; £164)

Form RPR

000/ **1** **Mount Welcome (IRE)**[65] 4414 9-10-11 87 (t) MrTWeston(5) 98+
(Martin Weston) *midfield: prog to 3rd at 7th: mstke next: led on bit 10th: sn clr: rdn out flat* **22/1**

20F/ **2** 5 **Cruise In Style (IRE)**[104] 3682 7-11-9 97 (p) JamesBest(3) 106+
(Kevin Bishop) *hld up: prog 7th: wnt 3rd after 9th: drvn and jumping and hanging lft fr 3 out: kpt racing awkwardly but won protracted duel for wl hld 2nd after last* **9/2**[2]

232/ **3** 1 **Chestnut Ben (IRE)**[4] 5556 8-11-9 94 JamieMoore 99
(Gary Brown) *2nd tl led 5th: drvn and hdd 10th: hit next: kpt on same pce and finding little after* **4/1**[1]

45U/ **4** 5 **Celtic Intrigue (IRE)**[62] 4446 6-11-5 90 (t) PaddyBrennan 91
(Tom George) *midfield: pushed along bef 5th: rdn and struggling after 9th: styd on wout threatening fr 2 out* **9/2**[2]

455/ **5** ½ **Full Ov Beans**[7] 5478 9-11-1 91 NicodeBoinville(5) 94+
(Michael Gates) *chsd ldrs: blnd bdly 9th and lost pl completely: no ch after but styng on wl after hitting last* **8/1**[3]

3P0/ **6** ¾ **Esteem**[6] 5509 10-11-6 91 (t) AndrewGlassonbury 91
(David Evans) *settled in rr: hdwy 9th: 5th and rdn bef next: btn bef 3 out* **17/2**

004/ **7** 24 **Tom O'Tara**[17] 5291 9-10-9 83 WayneKavanagh(3) 61
(Robin Dickin) *bhd: rdn and struggling after 9th* **10/1**

535/ **8** 7 **Maizy Missile (IRE)**[205] 1772 11-11-4 89 PaulMoloney 67
(Mary Evans) *led tl 5th: w ldr tl blnd bdly 9th: lost pl next: sn eased* **14/1**

PP4/ **9** 7 **Grand Fella (IRE)**[244] 1406 8-10-0 74 oh9 ow3 RobertDunne(3) 39
(Ken Wingrove) *midfield: wknd u.p bef 10th: t.o* **100/1**

00P/ **10** 46 **Benefit Game (IRE)**[147] 2835 9-11-11 96 MattieBatchelor 20
(Richard Hawker) *bhd: lost tch 5th: t.o bef 10th* **50/1**

520/ **P** **The Grey One (IRE)**[187] 2010 10-10-9 85 CharlieWallis(5)
(Milton Bradley) *t.k.h: mstke 3rd: midfield tl blnd 6th: in rr whn p.u 10th* **20/1**

5PP/ **P** **Autumn Haze**[18] 5270 8-10-2 78 KillianMoore(5)
(Phillip Dando) *mstke 1st: chsd ldrs tl 6th: t.o and p.u 10th* **14/1**

4m 6.5s (-7.50) **Going Correction** -0.40s/f (Good) 12 Ran SP% **112.5**
Speed ratings: **101,98,98,95,95 95,83,80,77,55 ,**
toteswingers 1&2 £55.90, 2&3 £3.90, 1&3 £19.70 CSF £112.95 CT £485.44 TOTE £36.00: £7.30, £2.60, £1.50; EX 195.30 Trifecta £380.10 Part won. Pool: £506.81 - 0.22 winning units..
Owner M H Weston **Bred** J Walsh **Trained** Hindlip, Worcs

FOCUS
Both bends set towards outside with run in on stands side. A weak handicap. Solid enough form, but the winner was well in on the best of his Irish efforts.

44 A & A RACING ONCOURSE BOOKMAKERS H'CAP CHASE (18 fncs) 2m 7f
5:45 (5:45) (Class 4) (0-115,114) 5-Y-0+ **£3,768** (£1,106; £553; £276)

Form RPR

660/ **1** **Handsome Buddy (IRE)**[17] 5281 6-9-9 90 (v) CiaranMckee(7) 105+
(Michael Gates) *t.k.h early: hdwy in 4th whn hit 14th and rdn: styd on wl to ld sn after 2 out: readily forged clr: pushed out* **14/1**

146/ **2** 8 **Whispering Jack**[14] 5341 8-11-10 112 (p) RichardJohnson 121
(Keiran Burke) *a 2nd or 3rd: mstke 3rd: v slow 10th: rdn 15th: drvn and ev ch 2 out: outpcd bef last* **7/2**[2]

PPP/ **3** 7 **Strongbows Legend**[14] 5341 8-11-11 113 (v[1]) AndrewTinkler 116
(Charlie Longsdon) *led: qcknd pce 10th: nt fluent 12th: hit 15th: drvn and hdd sn after 2 out: folded tamely* **9/2**[3]

216/ **4** 7 **Waltzing Tornado (IRE)**[18] 5270 9-9-11 90 (p) PeterCarberry(5) 87
(Andy Hobbs) *mstkes 3rd and 5th: in rr tl prog 9th: rdn 14th: wl btn 4th 2 out: j. bdly lft last and nt keen* **6/1**

4P0/ **5** 19 **Francis Du Mesnil (FR)**[55] 4596 11-10-2 90 (tp) JamieMoore 67
(Liam Corcoran) *bhd: mstke 6th: brief effrt 12th: lost tch bef 15th and jumping bdly lft and racing awkwardly after* **40/1**

0PF/ **6** 8 **El Lobo (FR)**[19] 5259 6-11-10 112 (t) TomScudamore 82
(David Pipe) *towards rr tl hdwy 11th: 3rd at 14th: rdn and sn fdd: t.o 3 out* **2/1**[1]

235/ **7** 6 **Sadler's Star (GER)**[19] 5258 10-11-11 113 TomCannon 78
(Michael Blake) *2nd or 3rd tl blnd 11th: nt run on: t.o after 14th* **11/1**

350/ **8** 10 **Nudge And Nurdle (IRE)**[55] 4598 12-11-1 103 SamTwiston-Davies 59
(Nigel Twiston-Davies) *chsd ldrs: rdn after 11th: wknd 13th: t.o after next* **20/1**

5m 50.6s (2.60) **Going Correction** -0.40s/f (Good) 8 Ran SP% **110.2**
Speed ratings: **79,76,73,71,64 61,59,56**
toteswingers 1&2 £7.50, 2&3 £3.40, 1&3 £7.70 CSF £59.64 CT £245.14 TOTE £20.90: £4.20, £1.30, £2.10; EX 85.40 Trifecta £437.90 Pool: £678.15 - 1.16 winning units..
Owner Michael Gates **Bred** Edward Burns **Trained** Clifford Chambers, Warwicks

FOCUS
A modest handicap. The winner is back to the level of his good Warwick run.

45 FIND-A-GROUP.COM HELPING PEOPLE MAKE DECISIONS BEGINNERS' CHASE (15 fncs) 2m 4f
6:15 (6:15) (Class 4) 5-Y-0+ **£3,671** (£1,084; £542; £271; £135)

Form RPR

330/ **1** **Lost Legend (IRE)**[31] 5019 6-11-0 0 RichieMcLernon 115+
(Jonjo O'Neill) *trckd ldrs: cl 3rd st: drvn into 2nd at last: led 150yds out and stormed clr* **9/1**[3]

605/ **2** 2 ¼ **A Bridge Too Far (IRE)**[29] 5076 7-11-0 0 JasonMaguire 113
(Donald McCain) *mstkes: chsd ldrs: drvn 10th: wnt 2nd 2 out: sn hanging and racing awkwardly: ev ch u.p after last: easily outpcd cl home* **5/1**[2]

046/ **3** 1 ¾ **Synthe Davis (FR)**[19] 5252 8-10-7 110 TomCannon 104
(Laura Mongan) *prom: led after 10th: sn 5 l clr and drvn along: hdd and no ex after last* **10/1**

15P/ **4** 32 **Lucky Vic (IRE)**[39] 4907 7-11-0 0 SamTwiston-Davies 89
(Barry Brennan) *led at decent pce: hdd after 10th: mstke next: wknd 3 out: eased* **12/1**

340/ **5** 16 **Brampour (IRE)**[46] 4768 6-10-9 0 HarryDerham(5) 63
(Paul Nicholls) *hit 1st: impeded 2nd whn already wl bhd: tended to jump lft: t.o fr 4th: continued to hack on in own time: fin lame* **8/11**[1]

2PP/ **F** **Princeful (FR)**[72] 4271 10-10-7 107 ChrisDavies(7)
(Milton Bradley) *chsd ldrs: rdn and fdd after 10th: 13 l 5th whn fell next* **40/1**

34P/ **F** **Minella For Steak (IRE)**[13] 5354 6-11-0 0 DougieCostello
(Jonjo O'Neill) *towards rr tl fell 3rd: injured* **10/1**

000/ **F** **Cabo Roche**[273] 1139 6-10-2 0 CharlieWallis(5)
(Milton Bradley) *t.k.h in rr tl fell 2nd* **200/1**

4m 56.6s (-3.40) **Going Correction** -0.40s/f (Good) 8 Ran SP% **113.4**
Speed ratings: **90,89,88,75,69 , ,**
toteswingers 1&2 £3.10, 2&3 £1.50, 1&3 £6.00 CSF £52.81 TOTE £12.00: £2.10, £1.30, £2.50; EX 75.30 Trifecta £439.70 Part won. Pool: £586.32 - 0.67 winning units..
Owner Mrs Gay Smith **Bred** Highfort Stud **Trained** Cheltenham, Gloucs

FOCUS
An eventful beginners' chase. The winner is rated to his hurdles mark.

46 BUSINESSONLINEGROUP.CO.UK INVESTMENT FOR ONLINE BUSINESSES MARES' MAIDEN HURDLE (8 hdls) 2m
6:45 (6:47) (Class 5) 4-Y-0+ **£1,949** (£572; £286; £143)

Form RPR

4/ **1** **Fairyinthewind (IRE)**[18] 5267 4-10-9 0 WayneHutchinson 100+
(Alan King) *settled towards rr of main bunch: impr qckly gng wl bef 3 out: chal and wavered rt next: led last and sn rdn clr* **9/4**[2]

2 7 **Flashy Star**[235] 4-10-9 0 MarcGoldstein 88
(Sheena West) *set slow pce early: led: drvn and jnd 2 out: hdd last: immediately outpcd* **13/2**[3]

040/ **3** 4 **Be My Present**[25] 5163 6-11-0 0 RichardJohnson 90
(Charlie Longsdon) *hld up towards rr of bunch: effrt bef 3 out: rdn and tried to chal next: one pce and btn whn nt fluent last* **15/8**[1]

062/ **4** 2 ¾ **Emerald Rose**[31] 5025 6-11-0 0 SamTwiston-Davies 87
(Julian Smith) *mounted outside paddock: chsd ldrs: drvn bef 3 out: outpcd next: plugged on steadily flat* **8/1**

0F4/ **5** 10 **Just A Whisper**[31] 5025 7-11-0 0 (t) AndrewTinkler 76
(Keiran Burke) *towards rr: struggling fr 3 out* **33/1**

00/ **6** 1 **Queen Spud**[7] 5479 4-10-9 0 PaddyBrennan 70
(Henry Daly) *trckd ldrs: effrt 5th: 2nd briefly but rdn bef next: sn fdd* **16/1**

000/ **7** 5 **Ivebeenthinking**[7] 5479 5-10-9 0 BenPoste(5) 70
(Tom Symonds) *plld hrd and wl detached in last trio: nvr anywhere nr ldrs* **66/1**

0/ **8** 17 **Lucette**[29] 5062 5-11-0 0 JasonMaguire 53
(Kim Bailey) *plld hrd and wl detached in last trio: t.o after 5th* **25/1**

9 ½ **On The Way Home (IRE)** 4-10-9 0 RichieMcLernon 48
(Jonjo O'Neill) *midfield: nt fluent 4th: wl in tch tl bef 3 out* **12/1**

10 *13* **American Kiss (SWE)**[13] 4-10-9 0 .... CharliePoste 35
(Robin Dickin) *chsd ldr at slow pce tl lost pl rapidly after 5th: bdly t.o* **100/1**

11 *11* **Midnight Pearl (USA)**[2473] 10-11-0 0 .... MattieBatchelor 29
(Mark Bradstock) *plld demonically and wl detached in last trio: j. bdly rt 5th and sn wl t.o: continued to jump erratically: eased 2 out* **40/1**

3m 54.1s (6.80) **Going Correction** -0.225s/f (Good)
WFA 4 from 5yo+ 5lb **11** Ran SP% **115.3**
Speed ratings (Par 103): **74,70,68,67,62 61,59,50,50,43 38**
toteswingers 1&2 £4.00, 2&3 £4.00, 1&3 £2.00 CSF £16.44 TOTE £2.90: £1.40, £2.20, £1.10; EX 10.80 Trifecta £52.50 Pool: £1086.86 - 15.51 winning units..
Owner Spittinginthewind Partnership **Bred** J Cullinan **Trained** Barbury Castle, Wilts

FOCUS
A weak mares' maiden run at a slow time. The winner should rate lot higher on Flat form.

47 HOME-XPERTS.CO.UK EXCEPTIONAL ESTATE & LETTING AGENTS (S) HURDLE (10 hdls) 2m 4f
7:15 (7:15) (Class 5) 4-6-Y-O **£1,949** (£572; £286; £143)

Form RPR

20P/ **1** **Well Mett (IRE)**[135] 3091 6-11-0 95 .... (bt[1]) PaddyBrennan 120+
(Fergal O'Brien) *mde all: drew 10 l clr 3 out: unchal after* **5/1**[3]

422/ **2** *14* **Lauberhorn**[19] 5248 6-11-4 106 .... (p) PaulMoloney 107
(Evan Williams) *chsd ldng pair: 10 l bhd at 6th: wnt 2nd but no ch w wnr 3 out tl next: fnd nthing after but coaxed to regain remote 2nd flat* **13/2**

5F5/ **3** *3 1/2* **Polarbrook (IRE)**[21] 5227 6-11-0 110 .... (b[1]) JasonMaguire 103
(Donald McCain) *chsd ldr: rdn and easily outpcd by him bef 3 out: j. modly after and looking reluctant: poor 2nd 2 out tl after last* **5/4**[1]

623/ **4** *2 3/4* **Juno The Muffinman (IRE)**[39] 4908 4-11-2 120 .... RichardJohnson 100
(Tim Vaughan) *a abt same pl: drvn 6th: mstke next: poor 4th and finding nthing fr 3 out* **11/4**[2]

0/ **5** *66* **Up In Flames (IRE)**[25] 5164 4-10-8 0 .... TomSiddall 32
(Martin Keighley) *mstkes in rr: lost tch bef 7th: bdly t.o fr next* **50/1**

030/ **P** **Hurricane Herbie (IRE)**[51] 5-10-7 104 .... (t) MissEKelly[(7)]
(Nick Williams) *bhd: lost tch 6th: bdly t.o whn p.u 3 out* **12/1**

0/ **P** **West End Classic (IRE)**[33] 4991 6-10-9 0 .... BenPoste[(5)]
(Tracey Watkins) *plld hrd in last: hopelessly t.o fr 6th tl p.u 2 out: b.b.v* **100/1**

4m 44.3s (-3.10) **Going Correction** -0.225s/f (Good)
WFA 4 from 5yo+ 6lb **7** Ran SP% **111.8**
Speed ratings: **97,91,90,88,62 ,**
toteswingers 1&2 £4.80, 2&3 £2.10, 1&3 £2.10 CSF £34.61 TOTE £5.40: £2.80, £1.90; EX 18.20 Trifecta £143.90 Pool: £1055.07 - 5.49 winning units..
Owner The Yes No Wait Sorries **Bred** Arctic Tack Stud **Trained** Coln St. Dennis, Gloucs

FOCUS
The winner nicked the seller from the front. A big step up from him in first-time blinkers

48 FOOTBALLCV.COM THE ONLINE DATABASE FOR PLAYERS H'CAP HURDLE (10 hdls) 2m 4f
7:45 (7:46) (Class 4) (0-120,120) 4-Y-0+ **£3,249** (£954; £477; £238)

Form RPR

6F4/ **1** *3* **Jacks Grey**[142] 2951 8-10-10 104 .... (t) PaddyBrennan 108+
(Fergal O'Brien) *trckd ldrs: clsd gng wl on inner bef 3 out: suddenly swtchd to outside then suddenly swtchd bk to ins bef next: chal fr last: ev ch whn cannoned into w 150yds to go and no ch after* **20/1**

326/ **2** **Tuscan Gold**[11] 4907 6-11-5 113 .... TomCannon 117+
(Laura Mongan) *settled in 3rd bhd clr ldr: wnt 2nd and clsng after 7th: led 3 out: sn 3 l clr but drvn and hanging bdly lft and jumping lft after: crashed into rival trying to chal on inner 150yds out: r.o wl* **10/1**[3]

213/ **3** *7* **Be All Man (IRE)**[19] 5257 6-11-6 114 .... JamieMoore 108
(Gary Moore) *chsd clr ldr tl rdn bef 3 out: nt qckn between last two* **2/1**[1]

243/ **4** *6* **Barney Cool**[74] 4230 6-11-11 119 .... (p) TomScudamore 107
(David Pipe) *settled towards rr: rdn bef 3 out: one pce and unable to chal after* **2/1**[1]

643/ **5** *shd* **Likearollingstone (IRE)**[43] 4841 8-11-5 120 .... (t) MikeyHamill[(7)] 109
(Sean Curran) *bhd: rdn and struggling 7th: no ch after* **16/1**

4U1/ **6** *6* **Red Admirable (IRE)**[4] 5543 7-11-7 120 7ex .... KillianMoore[(5)] 103
(Graeme McPherson) *nt a fluent in midfield: drvn and btn 3 out* **11/2**[2]

400/ **7** *20* **Original Star (IRE)**[17] 5293 8-10-6 100 .... DavidBass 65
(Derek Frankland) *bhd: rdn and struggling after 7th: t.o* **25/1**

024/ **8** *1 1/2* **Arrayan**[17] 5283 8-11-2 117 .... (p) ChristopherWard[(7)] 80
(Alexandra Dunn) *led and 10 l clr: nt fluent 5th: wknd bef 3 out where mstke and hdd: wl btn whn blnd next* **14/1**

5PF/ **9** *24* **Elton Fox**[47] 4763 8-10-6 107 .... (bt[1]) MrJarrett[(7)] 49
(John Needham) *a in last: rdn and no rspnse 5th: t.o after 7th* **50/1**

4m 46.4s (-1.00) **Going Correction** -0.225s/f (Good) **9** Ran SP% **114.3**
Speed ratings (Par 105): **91,93,89,86,86 84,76,75,65**
toteswingers 1&2 £14.00, 2&3 £5.30, 1&3 £4.80 CSF £166.18 CT £559.48 TOTE £11.40: £2.10, £3.00, £1.10; EX 73.00 Trifecta £706.20 Pool: £1170.28 - 1.24 winning units..The winner was bought in for 6500gns.
Owner The Yes No Wait Sorries **Bred** Mrs R E Hambro **Trained** Coln St. Dennis, Gloucs
■ Stewards' Enquiry : Tom Cannon six-day ban: careless riding (May 14-19)

FOCUS
A moderate handicap and a tight finish, resulting in a lengthy stewards' enquiry. The second is rated as having dead-heated and to his mark.

49 BUTLERANDGARDENER.COM OUTLET HOME AND GARDEN PRODUCTS H'CAP HURDLE (8 hdls) 2m
8:15 (8:15) (Class 5) (0-100,100) 4-Y-0+ **£1,949** (£572; £286; £143)

Form RPR

554/ **1** **Dresden (IRE)**[45] 4794 5-11-12 100 .... WillKennedy 116+
(Sarah-Jayne Davies) *nt fluent 2nd: hdwy bef 3rd: wnt 2nd bef 5th: led bef 2 out and shot clr: heavily eased flat* **25/1**

065/ **2** *3 1/4* **Ullswater (IRE)**[37] 4944 5-11-1 89 .... (t) GerardTumelty 94
(Andy Turnell) *hld up: 6th and prog st: drvn and str run fr last: snatched 2nd but no ch w v easy wnr* **6/1**[1]

P62/ **3** *1/2* **Green Lightning (IRE)**[61] 4486 6-10-0 74 oh1 .... (b) TomMessenger 80
(Martin Weston) *chsd clr ldr: clsd to ld bef 5th: sn 3 l clr and travelling strly: drvn and hdd bef 2 out: fnd little: lost 2nd fnl strides* **12/1**

000/ **4** *4 1/2* **Foxcub (IRE)**[19] 5241 5-10-12 91 .... BenPoste[(5)] 93
(Tom Symonds) *settled in rr: hdwy 5th: 5th and rdn bef 3 out: kpt on flat but n.d* **20/1**

534/ **5** *nse* **Tiradia (FR)**[57] 4571 6-11-0 88 .... SamTwiston-Davies 90
(J R Jenkins) *bhd: hdwy 5th: 4th bef next: jumping rt after: one pce and n.d* **9/1**

000/ **6** *3 1/4* **Naledi**[60] 2414 9-9-8 74 oh6 ow1 .... ThomasGarner[(7)] 73
(Richard Price) *dropped out last early: passed btn horses fr 3 out: nvr looked like chalng* **25/1**

403/ **7** *7* **Transfer**[17] 5290 8-11-2 90 .... RichardJohnson 82
(Richard Price) *nvr bttr than midfield: btn 3 out* **13/2**[2]

66P/ **8** *7* **Ron**[142] 2952 5-11-4 99 .... DannyBenson[(7)] 87
(Jonjo O'Neill) *chsd ldr: shkn up bef 5th: 8 l 3rd bef 3 out: sn dropped out* **10/1**

355/ **9** *nk* **Jeanry (FR)**[40] 4881 10-10-6 87 .... JoshWall[(7)] 72
(Arthur Whitehead) *prom: j. slowly 3rd: struggling fr 5th* **16/1**

405/ **10** *1* **Commerce**[17] 5283 6-10-4 81 .... RobertDunne[(3)] 65
(Dai Burchell) *midfield: effrt 5th: rdn and fdd bef next* **33/1**

000/ **11** *6* **Diamond Tammy (IRE)**[19] 5248 7-11-6 99 .... PeterCarberry[(5)] 80
(Andy Hobbs) *hit 1st and 2nd: t.o bef 3 out* **33/1**

000/ **12** *18* **Military Precision (IRE)**[62] 4464 7-11-1 89 .... (t) TomScudamore 52
(David Pipe) *hld up in rr: rdn and t.o bef 3 out* **8/1**[3]

0UP/ **13** *10* **Sertao (FR)**[18] 5270 7-9-11 74 oh1 ow2 .... (p) CharlieWallis[(5)] 30
(Milton Bradley) *bhd fr 5th: bdly t.o* **40/1**

000/ **P** **Rampant Ronnie (USA)**[202] 1787 8-11-2 90 .... (t) WayneHutchinson
(Nikki Evans) *plld hrd early and prom tl lost pl and nt fluent 3rd: t.o and p.u after next* **12/1**

PPP/ **P** **Rainbow Haze**[18] 5271 7-11-1 94 .... (b[1]) KillianMoore[(5)]
(Phillip Dando) *led at furious pce and sn 10 l clr: hdd bef 5th and stopped to nil: t.o and p.u 2 out* **14/1**

32/ **P** **Madeira Girl (IRE)**[122] 3335 4-11-3 96 .... RichieMcLernon
(Jonjo O'Neill) *midfield: effrt in 4th after 5th: sn rdn: wkng whn p.u 2 out* **6/1**[1]

3m 43.0s (-4.30) **Going Correction** -0.225s/f (Good)
WFA 4 from 5yo+ 5lb **16** Ran SP% **120.8**
Speed ratings (Par 103): **101,99,99,96,96 95,91,88,88,87 84,75,70, ,**
toteswingers 1&2 £67.60, 2&3 £13.90, 1&3 £56.60 CSF £159.92 CT £1929.06 TOTE £28.30: £5.10, £1.40, £2.50, £6.80; EX 148.10 Trifecta £434.50 Part won. Pool: £579.35 - 0.06 winning units..
Owner Miss Sarah-Jayne Davies **Bred** Diana Webley **Trained** Leominster, H'fords

FOCUS
An ordinary handicap and a very easy winner with the third, fifth and sixth setting the level.
T/Plt: £573.00 to £1 stake. Pool of £60605.30 - 77.20 winning tickets. T/Qpdt: £33.90 to a £1 stake. Pool of £5920.90 - 129.10 winning tickets. IM

50 - 56a (Foreign Racing) - See Raceform Interactive

CHELTENHAM (L-H)
Wednesday, May 1

OFFICIAL GOING: Good (good to soft in places; 7.5)
Wind: Light and variable breeze Weather: Hot and sunny; 16 degrees

57 CHELTENHAM RACECOURSE CONFERENCE AND EVENTS HUNTERS' CHASE (14 fncs) 2m 110y
5:05 (5:06) (Class 5) 5-Y-0+ **£2,183** (£677; £338; £169)

Form RPR

456/ **1** **Himalayan Express**[10] 5436 9-11-9 110 .... (p) MrJMartin[(5)] 121
(Mrs David Plunkett) *trckd ldrs: last of five gng clr at 11th: steadily clsd to go 2nd bef 2 out: styd on wl to ld last: rdn clr* **50/1**

202/ **2** *5* **Marky Bob (IRE)**[10] 5436 8-11-13 114 .... MrMatthewBarber[(5)] 122
(Hugo Froud) *led at furious gallop: hit 5th: 4 l clr 2 out: drvn and hdd last: immediately outstyd by wnr but wl clr of rest* **6/1**[2]

323/ **3** *10* **Rash Move (IRE)**[27] 5138 12-11-13 117 .... MrTEllis[(5)] 112
(F A Hutsby) *trckd ldrs: wnt 2nd at 9th: pressed wnr tl rdn bef 2 out: sn wknd* **6/4**[1]

P32/ **4** *1 3/4* **Swallows Delight (IRE)**[31] 5040 8-11-10 100 .... MrDMansell 103
(Mrs Julie Mansell) *towards rr: kpt on wl past btn horses fr 3 out: ploughed through last: nvr nr ldrs and too much to do* **10/1**

212/ **5** *1 3/4* **What Of It (IRE)**[20] 5253 10-11-7 108 .... MrTDWard[(7)] 104
(Mrs Sarah Ward) *pressed ldr tl 9th: drvn after next: remained cl up tl wknd grad fr 3 out* **9/1**

222/ **6** *11* **Speed Steed (IRE)**[7] 5508 6-11-3 117 .... MrBGibbs[(7)] 91
(Tim Vaughan) *nvr bttr than midfield: no ch w ldng quartet fr 10th* **8/1**[3]

3P4/ **7** *18* **Noble Ben (IRE)**[17] 11-11-3 101 .... (bt[1]) MrJMRidley[(7)] 74
(Mrs H S M Ridley) *chsd ldrs: handy 4th at 11th: sn rdn: dropped rt out fr next* **12/1**

640/ **8** *1 3/4* **Parazar (FR)**[32] 8-11-3 0 .... MrMHeard[(7)] 73
(D Summersby) *midfield: struggling after mstke 8th: t.o 3 out* **100/1**

462/ **9** *2 1/2* **Party Pictures (IRE)**[29] 5106 10-11-3 0 .... MissLeandaTickle[(7)] 71
(Mrs S Westwood) *t.k.h and prom: blnd 2nd: wknd 9th: t.o 3 out* **22/1**

PPP/ **10** *4* **Louis Pasteur (IRE)**[10] 8-11-11 113 .... (b) MrRGHenderson[(3)] 71
(D L Drake) *racd freely and prom: wknd 9th: poor 6th whn mstke 3 out: t.o* **11/1**

23P/ **11** *11* **Bromhead (USA)**[8] 5476 7-11-10 0 .... (t) MrJoshuaGuerriero 57
(S Heard) *t.k.h in rr: lost tch after mstke 8th: t.o 11th* **66/1**

503/ **P** **Caulkin (IRE)**[10] 10-11-7 0 .... MrDKemp[(3)]
(David Kemp) *towards rr: mod hdwy 8th: fading and wl bhd whn blnd 11th and p.u* **20/1**

P/ **P** **Getyouracttogether (IRE)**[18] 9-11-3 0 .... MissAEStirling[(7)]
(C R Willes) *bhd: rdr nrly fell off 4th and struggling after: t.o 10th: p.u 3 out* **100/1**

F/ **P** **Aneda Rose (IRE)**[32] 9-11-0 0 .... (t) MrJRJarrett[(3)]
(G D Hanmer) *j. v erratically and wl bhd: t.o whn blnd 7th and p.u* **80/1**

4m 6.4s (-0.30) **Going Correction** +0.15s/f (Yiel) **14** Ran SP% **116.3**
Speed ratings: **106,103,98,98,97 92,83,82,81,79 74, , ,**
toteswingers: 1&2 £57.00, 1&3 £22.30, 2&3 £3.40. CSF £318.14 TOTE £75.10: £13.80, £1.80, £1.30; EX 347.30 Trifecta £1263.70 Part won. Pool: £1,685.00 - 0.51 winnin units..
Owner Mrs David Plunkett **Bred** The Alchemists **Trained** Banbury, Oxon

FOCUS
A glorious day and the ground was expected to ride a shade quicker than the official going description of good to soft. This specialist hunter chase was always likely to be run at a strong gallop and few emerged from off the pace as those racing handily prospered. The runner-up is rated to the best of his 2012 form, backed up by the fourth to his mark.

58 CONNOLLY'S RED MILLS INTERMEDIATE POINT-TO-POINT CHAMPIONSHIP FINAL HUNTERS' CHASE (21 fncs) 3m 1f 110y
5:40 (5:41) (Class 4) 5-Y-0+ **£4,367** (£1,354; £676; £338)

Form RPR

1 **Harbour Court**[53] 7-11-10 0 .... MrJETudor 115+
(Alan Hill) *dropped out last briefly and v confidently handled: stdy prog 12th: delayed serious effrt tl after 3 out: w ldr on bit 2 out: cruised clr fr last: impressive* **7/2**[2]

The Form Book Jumps, Raceform Ltd, Compton, RG20 6NL.

2 13 **Indiana Bay (IRE)**[24] 6-11-10 0 MrJoshuaGuerriero 100
(Mrs Jill Dennis) *towards rr: hdwy 16th: effrt 3 out: slt ld 2 out: hdd and hit last: kpt on wl but no ch w easy wnr* **9/1**

5/ 3 3 **Chosen Milan (IRE)**[45] 6-10-10 0 (t) AlanJohns(7) 91
(R E Luke) *cl up: 4th whn nt fluent 17th: lft in ld after 3 out: drvn and hdd next: one pce and sn btn* **33/1**

04P/ 4 5 **Quatuor Collonges (FR)**[24] 9-11-3 0 MissAEStirling(7) 91
(C R Willes) *chsd ldrs: handy 6th at 17th: wkng whn j.lft 2 out and last* **50/1**

02/ 5 hd **Bay To Go (IRE)**[15] 5342 7-11-3 113 MissCVHart(7) 90
(Mrs H M Kemp) *racd keenly: cl up: j.rt 2nd: wnt 2nd 11th tl j. into ld 16th: rdn and hdd bef 3 out: wknd fr next* **13/2**[3]

1/ 6 shd **Forest Walker (IRE)**[20] 5253 6-11-9 0 MrAlexEdwards(5) 99
(Philip Rowley) *mstkes towards rr: bdly hmpd 4th: sme hdwy 17th: 5th after next: no imp after slipping on landing 3 out* **11/4**[1]

0/ 7 6 **Fourth In Line (IRE)**[25] 9-11-3 0 (bt) MrABraithwaite(7) 85
(Mrs L Braithwaite) *nvr bttr than midfield: rdn 14th: no ch after* **100/1**

4/ 8 6 **Double Bank (IRE)**[17] 10-11-3 0 MrMWoodward(7) 81
(Ms Emma Oliver) *cl up: 3rd at 16th: led bef 3 out where blnd bdly: sn hdd and lost all ch* **14/1**

4P2/ 9 11 **My Fella (IRE)**[11] 10-11-3 90 MissCPrichard(7) 70
(Andrew Quick) *nvr bttr than midfield: struggling fr 14th* **66/1**

0/ 10 1½ **Oriel Bank (IRE)**[24] 8-10-10 0 MissJoannaMason(7) 61
(I M Mason) *nt fluent 1st: wl bhd: no ch fr 13th: plugged rnd* **100/1**

42P/ 11 6 **Croan Rock (IRE)**[17] 8-11-5 0 (p) NickSlatter(5) 63
(R A Owen) *set modest pce: hdd 16th: rdn and wknd bef 3 out: t.o* **16/1**

3FP/ D 1¾ **Artic Pride (IRE)**[24] 9-11-7 78 MissJCoward(3) 95
(Mrs Emma Clark) *towards rr: plenty to do in 8th at 17th: styng on stoutly at fin but no hope of rching ldrs* **12/1**

F2/ P **Ballyjames (IRE)**[11] 5414 8-11-5 0 MissJCWilliams(5)
(Miss H Brookshaw) *prom tl rdn and nt fluent 9th: t.o and p.u 13th* **20/1**

U **Following Dreams (IRE)**[32] 6-11-5 0 MrLRPayter(5)
(Alastair Ralph) *mstkes: dropped to rr whn hit 11th and uns rdr* **12/1**

P **Hello Mr Kelly (IRE)**[32] 8-11-3 0 MrOWadlow(7)
(Mrs K M Diggle) *prom tl bad mstke 5th: nt rcvr: last after 11th: t.o and p.u 13th* **66/1**

F **Little Cornham (IRE)**[32] 6-11-7 0 MrDEdwards(3)
(Miss C A Tizzard) *pressed ldrs: stl gng wl whn fell heavily 12th* **25/1**

U **Ruapehu (IRE)**[18] 7-11-10 0 MrWBiddick
(Charles Whittaker) *handy whn blnd and uns rdr 4th* **16/1**

6m 44.3s (6.10) **Going Correction** +0.15s/f (Yiel) **17** Ran SP% **124.5**
Speed ratings: **96,92,91,89,88 88,87,85,81,81 79,90,,,,**
toteswingers: 1&2 £8.40, 1&3 £33.80, 2&3 £35.00. CSF £34.09 TOTE £4.80: £2.00, £3.00, £10.80; EX 45.80 Trifecta £828.50 Part won. Pool: £1,104.71 - 0.29 winning units..
Owner Andrew West **Bred** Countess Goess-Saurau & A West **Trained** Aston Rowant, Oxfordshire
■ Stewards' Enquiry : Miss J Coward £200 fine: breach of rules (F)143.3 and 143.4; failed to notify racing calendar office of a winner in Germany and as a result incorrectly claimed 3lbs in this race (for riders' with less than 20 winners)

FOCUS
A belting edition of what is always a highlight in the hunter chase calender and it saw some performance from the exciting winner. The winner was impressive but the time was modest and not form to be confident about.

59 HUNT STAFF BENEFIT SOCIETY HUNTERS' CHASE (FOR UNITED HUNTS CHALLENGE CUP) (21 fncs) 3m 1f 110y
6:10 (6:14) (Class 4) 6-Y-0+ **£3,743** (£1,161; £580; £290)

Form RPR

223/ 1 **Rumbury Grey**[20] 5261 10-11-9 114 NickSlatter(5) 127+
(S Flook) *trckd ldrs: wnt 2nd at 16th: led 3 out: immediately began to draw rt away: unchal* **7/1**[3]

1F2/ 2 24 **Divine Intavention (IRE)**[11] 9-11-11 122 MrMWall(3) 104
(Miss Francesca Moller) *cl up: blnd 4th: 2nd fr 13th tl 16th: drvn 16th: nt fluent next: outpcd by wnr 3 out: regained poor 2nd at next* **6/4**[1]

F5/ 3 4½ **Hameldown Tor**[24] 9-11-7 0 MrEBarrett(7) 103
(E Walker) *mstkes: cl up tl 6 l 4th and getting outpcd at 17th: plugged on to regain poor 3rd at last* **8/1**

P21/ 4 19 **Coombe Hill**[20] 5261 12-12-0 117 MrWBiddick 87
(Miss C A Tizzard) *prom: led 13th: hit 18th and rdn: hdd next: wkng qckly fr 2 out: fin tired* **11/4**[2]

0/ 5 16 **Pertemps Heights**[38] 6-11-7 0 (p) MrSamPainting(7) 69
(M Foley) *towards rr: drvn after 11th: struggled on: t.o fr 18th* **33/1**

013/ P **The General Lee (IRE)**[25] 11-11-9 112 MissJCWilliams(5)
(Philip Rowley) *led tl 13th: wkng rapidly whn hit 16th: p.u next* **12/1**

64/ P **Duke Special (IRE)**[11] 9-12-0 0 MrDMansell
(Miss Hannah James) *last pair and detached: stmbld 9th: t.o 15th: p.u 3 out* **50/1**

01F/ P **Trouble Digger**[40] 4906 8-11-11 0 MrSDrinkwater(3)
(T Lacey) *last pair and nvr looking hopeful: t.o 15th: p.u 17th* **16/1**

6m 37.0s (-1.20) **Going Correction** +0.15s/f (Yiel) **8** Ran SP% **108.8**
Speed ratings: **107,99,98,92,87 ,,**
toteswingers: 1&2 £2.80, 1&3 £10.80, 2&3 £2.90. CSF £17.02 TOTE £7.70: £1.80, £1.10, £2.20; EX 19.10 Trifecta £125.00 Pool: £1,933.47 - 11.59 winning units..
Owner Mrs C M Rogers **Bred** Mrs C M Rogers **Trained** Leominster, Herefordshire

FOCUS
A strong hunter chase, run at a solid gallop and it produced a decent winning time. The winner is rated back to the best of his 2012 form.

60 BONHAMS MEN'S OPEN POINT-TO-POINT CHAMPIONSHIP FINAL HUNTERS' CHASE (22 fncs) 3m 2f 110y
6:45 (6:45) (Class 4) 5-Y-0+ **£4,679** (£1,451; £725; £363)

Form RPR

14/ 1 **Doctor Kingsley**[24] 11-11-7 116 MrPMann(7) 127
(Mrs Pauline Harkin) *handy tl dropped bk qckly after 12th: 4th and rallying but plenty to do 19th: styd on to go 4 l 2nd bef 2 out: coaxed along and sustained run to wear down ldr fnl 75yds: game effrt* **7/2**[2]

2 1¼ **Gunmoney (IRE)**[10] 8-11-5 0 (p) MrJonathanBailey(5) 122
(G T H Bailey) *led: sme stuttering jumps on first circ: jnd and lft 6 l clr 3 out: drvn along w advantage dwindling after: hdd and no ex fnl 75yds* **20/1**

114/ 3 22 **Kirkleigh**[10] 8-11-11 122 MrThomasChanin(7) 113
(R B Chanin) *settled trcking ldrs: pushed along and outpcd in 3rd at 19th: lft 2nd next tl home turn: no imp and wl hld whn landed bdly 2 out* **11/1**

142/ 4 6 **Arbour Hill (IRE)**[24] 11-11-7 0 (p) MrMWall(3) 96
(Miss Francesca Moller) *j. slowly 5th: 2nd tl rdn and lost interest 13th: last at 17th: plodded on* **9/1**

431/ U **Surenaga (IRE)**[18] 11-11-9 123 (b) MrAlexEdwards(5)
(Philip Rowley) *mstke 2nd: in rr tl quick move into 3rd at 10th: wnt 2nd at 13th: upsides ldr and gng bttr than him but wnr stl waiting in the wings whn landed bdly and uns rdr 3 out* **10/3**[1]

33F/ P **Ballyeightra Cross (IRE)**[24] 9-11-7 107 (p) MrJarrett(3)
(G D Hanmer) *rn in snatches: drvn and struggling 19th: t.o and p.u 2 out* **10/1**

133/ P **Ravethebrave (IRE)**[17] 9-11-7 118 MrJoeHill(7)
(Alan Hill) *taken wd in rr: nt a fluent: mstke 7th: nvr looked dangerous fr 12th: struggling 19th: t.o and p.u 2 out* **7/2**[2]

P **Batu Ferringhi (FR)**[30] 7-11-10 0 (p) MrJoshuaGuerriero
(Mrs Claire Hitch) *nvr bttr than midfield: lost tch u.p 19th: t.o and p.u after last* **6/1**[3]

6m 58.4s (4.60) **Going Correction** +0.15s/f (Yiel) **8** Ran SP% **114.0**
Speed ratings: **99,98,92,90, , ,**
toteswingers: 1&2 £7.90, 1&3 £7.60, 27.40. CSF £59.60 TOTE £4.80: £1.70, £2.30, £4.10; EX 109.50 Trifecta £639.50 Pool: £1,003.52 - 1.17 winning units..
Owner Mrs Pauline Harkin **Bred** J M Castle **Trained** Chipping Warden, Northants

FOCUS
This competitive hunter chase saw the first pair dominate up the home straight. The form is difficult to asses but is rated around the winner and third.

61 CHELTENHAM CHAMPION MARES' HUNTERS' CHASE (21 fncs) 3m 1f 110y
7:20 (7:20) (Class 4) 5-Y-0+ **£3,743** (£1,161; £580; £290)

Form RPR

F61/ 1 **Mid Div And Creep**[30] 13-11-11 120 MissGAndrews 125
(Alan Hill) *j. really wl: mde all: drew 7 l clr at 15th: drvn bef 2 out: j.rt last and edgd rt flat but kpt on v gamely* **3/1**[2]

1B2/ 2 5 **Chesnut Annie (IRE)**[24] 12-11-0 106 MissBHampson(7) 117
(Beth Roberts) *pressed wnr tl after 11th and fr 14th: pckd 18th and continued 3rd: 12 l 3rd 2 out: sn regained 2nd: drvn and styd on heroically flat but a hld* **14/1**

3 22 **Popaway**[10] 8-11-0 (t) MrJDocker(7) 99
(Mrs Pauline Harkin) *settled midfield: effrt in 3rd at 16th: wnt 2nd at 18th: unable to cl on wnr whn rdn fr 3 out: lost 2nd after next* **8/1**[3]

2P1/ 4 9 **Lucette Annie**[15] 5332 9-11-11 107 MrJoshuaGuerriero 93
(S J Partridge) *midfield: 5th at 15th: rdn and outpcd fr 17th* **11/4**[1]

42P/ 5 22 **Topless (IRE)**[18] 12-11-2 91 (tp) MissCLWills(5) 69
(C W Loggin) *3rd tl wnt 2nd after 11th tl mstke 14th: losing pl whn j. slowly 16th: t.o fr 18th* **25/1**

414/ P **Keel Road (IRE)**[18] 11-11-0 105 (b[1]) MrDominicSutton(7)
(Mrs Kim Smyly) *bhd: rdn 10th: t.o 13th: p.u 17th* **40/1**

3P/ P **My Lil Ledge (IRE)**[24] 8-11-7 (t) MrDMansell
(Mrs Julie Mansell) *nt a fluent: bhd: lost tch 17th: t.o and p.u 2 out* **12/1**

050/ P **Gemini June (IRE)**[30] 9-11-0 MrSamPainting(7)
(M Foley) *a towards rr: struggling 15th: t.o and p.u 2 out: b.b.v* **22/1**

P **Fruit Fayre**[18] 6-11-7 MrTomDavid
(Mrs Sheila Crow) *cl up: t.k.h early: rdn fr 11th: 4th at16th: no imp whn blnd 18th and rdr nrly c off: t.o and p.u 2 out* **11/4**[1]

6m 45.0s (6.80) **Going Correction** +0.15s/f (Yiel) **9** Ran SP% **114.4**
Speed ratings: **95,93,86,83,77 ,,,**
toteswingers: 1&2 £7.30, 1&3 £4.40, 2&3 £9.20. CSF £39.50 TOTE £4.10: £1.60, £3.40, £2.40; EX 54.70 Trifecta £827.70 Part won. Pool: £1,103.62 - 0.54 winning units..
Owner Mrs K Exall **Bred** Knightsbridge Business Centre (glos) Ltd **Trained** Aston Rowant, Oxfordshire

FOCUS
The first running of this decent mares' hunter chase and there was no hiding place. The winner sets the level rated in line with her 2011 form.

62 JOCKEY CLUB 7.75% RACECOURSE BOND HUNTERS' CHASE (27 fncs) 4m 1f
7:50 (7:52) (Class 4) 5-Y-0+ **£3,743** (£1,161; £580; £290)

Form RPR

0U/ 1 **Charles Bruce (IRE)**[30] 10-11-3 0 CharlieDeutsch(7) 116
(A Campbell) *sme mstkes: led tl 5th: 2nd or 3rd tl led again 14th tl 16th: blnd 18th: led fr 22nd: jnd and pckd 3 out: sn led again: r.o gamely despite edging rt flat: v accomplished ride* **100/1**

F21/ 2 ½ **Special Portrait (IRE)**[6] 5524 9-11-11 109 (t) MrPGerety(7) 122
(Mark Hughes) *settled trcking ldrs: wnt 3rd 3 out: chal next and sn lft 2nd: r.o wl u.p flat: jst hld cl home* **3/1**[1]

3P4/ 3 1¼ **Dammam**[14] 5351 8-11-7 112 MrSDrinkwater(3) 114
(Fergal O'Brien) *led 5th tl 6th: 6th and drvn and outpcd 23rd: plenty to do next: rallied fr 2 out: edgd rt but gaining u.p flat: gave himself too much to do* **10/3**[2]

435/ 4 13 **Thelobstercatcher**[57] 4575 9-11-3 114 (vt) MrBGibbs(7) 104
(Tim Vaughan) *j. slowly 3rd: u.p 20th: bdly outpcd 22nd: plugging on past btn horses fr 3 out: no ch* **8/1**

3P0/ 5 1½ **Keenan's Future (IRE)**[11] 12-11-3 103 (b) MrRHodges(7) 106+
(S Rea) *chsd ldrs: 4th and effrt 3 out: jnd ldr and terrible jump next and rdr almost lost the lot: veered lft and all ch gone* **20/1**

6 12 **Barrick's Hill (IRE)**[17] 8-11-10 0 NicodeBoinville 89
(Mrs Sarah J Bosley) *hld up: stdy prog 17th: mstke 23rd: jnd wnr 3 out: sn drvn: wknd qckly next: nt stay* **22/1**

P21/ 7 1¼ **Oedipe (FR)**[11] 11-11-3 125 (p) MrRJenkins(7) 88
(Mrs N Sheppard) *racd wd: hdwy 16th: wknd 24th* **25/1**

0P3/ 8 8 **Be There In Five (IRE)**[18] 9-11-5 122 (p) MrWEasterby(5) 81
(Mrs Sarah Easterby) *taken down early: midfield: rdn and wknd fr 24th* **16/1**

112/ 9 8 **Freddies Return (IRE)**[11] 12-12-0 115 (t) MrPYork 78
(P York) *hld up: sme hdwy 18th: btn 23rd: t.o* **13/2**[3]

304/ 10 2¼ **James Pine (IRE)**[10] 5436 14-11-3 101 MsAnnabelRoberts(7) 71
(Mrs Annabel Brook) *cl up tl 17th: wknd 22nd: mstke 3 out: t.o* **50/1**

352/ 11 ½ **How's My Friend**[20] 5261 8-11-7 108 MissABush(3) 75
(Grant Cann) *chsd ldrs: struggling 23rd: t.o and hanging bdly rt fr last* **10/1**

4U2/ 12 4½ **Bleuvito (IRE)**[8] 5482 9-11-5 103 MrJMahot(5) 67
(S Turner) *mstkes towards rr: nvr gng wl: blnd 20th: nt keen and t.o* **28/1**

51P/ 13 1 **Deb's Dasher**[30] 8-11-11 113 MrRGHenderson(3) 70
(Miss Kayley Jones) *cl up early: no ch fr 23rd: t.o* **22/1**

24F/ 14 6 **King Of The Road**[38] 11-11-3 0 (b) MrMatthewHampton(7) 61
(Mrs Janet Ackner) *led 6th tl 14th and 16th tl 22nd: blnd next: wknd rapidly: t.o* **66/1**

0P2/ 15 3½ **Crank Hill**[18] 11-11-3 99 MrTHampton(7) 58
(Mrs H M Tory) *sn lost interest: t.o fr 16th* **16/1**

6/ 16 14 **The Rubber Man (IRE)**[4] 9-11-7 0 MrRJarrett(3) 45
(Patrick J Hanly) *blnd 1st: nvr nr ldrs: mstke 8th: t.o 23rd* **80/1**

464/ **17** *23* **Cold Mountain (IRE)**[11] 11-11-3 0................................ MrPBlagg(7) 24
(Paul Blagg) *laboured in rr: j. poorly: mstke 7th and reminders: t.o fr 16th: fin eventually* **66/1**

RR4/ **R** **Zacharova (IRE)**[11] 5414 10-11-3 101.................. MrSDavies-Thomas(7)
(Mrs Jo Messenger) *mulish at s: lost 20 l: a sulking in rr: abt 2 fs bhd whn eventually ref 23rd* **20/1**

244/ **P** **Bell On Bike (IRE)**[8] 5482 10-11-7 0..................................(p) MrMWall(3)
(W M Wanless) *chsd ldrs tl 17th: hopelessly t.o whn p.u 2 out* **66/1**

8m 50.8s (0.90) **Going Correction** +0.15s/f (Yiel) **19** Ran SP% **127.6**
Speed ratings: **104,103,103,100,100 97,96,94,92,92 92,91,90,89,88 85,79, ,**
toteswingers: 1&2 40.50, 1&3 £103.70, 2&3 £3.20. CSF £378.06 TOTE £95.80: £18.90, £2.00, £1.90; EX 679.00 Trifecta £1014.70 Part won. Pool: £1,353.02 - 0.16 winning units..
Owner A Campbell **Bred** Patrick Day **Trained** Moreton-In-Marsh, Gloucs
■ Stewards' Enquiry : Mr S Drinkwater four-day ban: used whip above permitted level (May 15-18)

FOCUS
A searching test and the principals fought out a cracking finish. The runner-up sets the level and the form could be rated higher through those just behind.

63 CHELTENHAM COLLECTION LADIES' HUNTERS' CHASE (17 fncs) 2m 5f
8:20 (8:23) (Class 5) 5-Y-0+ **£2,183** (£677; £338; £169)

Form RPR

02F/ **1** **Rebel Du Maquis (FR)**[27] 5138 8-10-11 137............. MissBAndrews(7) 123+
(Paul Nicholls) *led tl 3rd and fr 7th: drvn 3 l clr 2 out and 5 l ahd at last: kpt on wl: jst clung on* **11/2**

231/ **2** *shd* **Palypso De Creek (FR)**[10] 10-11-1 114................ MissCVHart(7) 126
(Mrs J Dawson) *chsd ldrs: impeded 10th: 7th but wl in tch 13th: pushed into 2nd at next: outpcd by wnr bef 2 out tl drvn and str run flat: mde 5 l fr last but jst failed* **4/1**[2]

P11/ **3** *2 ¾* **Benedictus (IRE)**[15] 5342 8-11-5 129..................... MissLeandaTickle(7) 130+
(Miss Jane Western) *settled chsng ldr: effrt in 3rd bef 3 out where stmbld on landing: nt rcvr but styng on after last* **5/1**[3]

055/ **4** *15* **Big Game Hunter (IRE)**[11] 7-10-11 96..................... MissRPLeyshon(7) 106
(Andrew Leyshon) *plld hrd: w ldrs tl rdn and wknd bef 3 out* **66/1**

432/ **5** *2 ¼* **Cool Friend (IRE)**[27] 5138 10-11-2 114......................... MissJCoward(3) 105
(Oliver Greenall) *chsd ldrs: rdn and outpcd 14th* **8/1**

5U/ **6** *7* **Byerley Bear (IRE)**[87] 8-11-5 0.. MissJBuck(7) 105
(Jackie Du Plessis) *cl up: 2nd 13th tl next: rdn and sn wknd* **20/1**

215/ **7** *5* **Fresh Air And Fun (IRE)**[384] 5377 10-11-3 118........ MissJCWilliams(5) 96
(Alastair Ralph) *j. slowly 1st: nvr gng wl and nt fluent: last at 7th: wl bhd fr 12th* **16/1**

343/ **8** *2 ¼* **Allerford Jack**[24] 5201 9-11-12 120.................................. MissGAndrews 100
(Miss Kayley Jones) *bhd: hit 11th: hdwy to trck ldrs 13th: rdn and wknd bef 3 out where mstke* **16/1**

P15/ **9** *20* **Soulard (USA)**[24] 5201 10-11-5 114..................... MissHannahWatson(3) 86
(Sophie Leech) *a bhd: t.o fr 12th: hit 3 out* **50/1**

10F/ **U** **Taranis (FR)**[38] 12-10-13 0..(t) MissAliceMills(5)
(Charles Whittaker) *rdn whn blnd and uns rdr 9th: fatally injured* **5/2**[1]

PPP/ **U** **Rustic John**[11] 13-10-11 72... MissPFuller(7)
(L J Manners) *slow 1st: uns rdr 2nd* **200/1**

P31/ **U** **Presentandcorrect (IRE)**[10] 5436 12-11-5 106.......... MissAEStirling(7)
(T F Sage) *led 3rd tl 7th: blnd and uns rdr 10th* **16/1**

5m 22.1s (2.70) **Going Correction** +0.15s/f (Yiel) **12** Ran SP% **118.1**
Speed ratings: **100,99,98,93,92 89,87,86,79, ,**
toteswingers: 1&2 £7.60, 1&3 £10.30, 2&3 £5.50. CSF £28.03 TOTE £5.90: £2.40, £1.90, £2.40; EX 35.40 Trifecta £141.80 Pool: £1,093.14 - 5.77 winning units..
Owner Mrs Kathy Stuart & P F Nicholls **Bred** Daniel & Mme Jeannine Laupretre **Trained** Ditcheat, Somerset

FOCUS
There was no hanging about in this lady riders' hunter chase and it served up another thrilling finish. The winner is rated in line with this year's form backed up by the third.
T/Plt: £199.90 to a £1 stake. Pool of £67,441.47 - 246.22 winning tickets. T/Qpdt: £44.40 to a £1 stake. Pool of £5,876.10 - 97.90 winning tickets. IM

SOUTHWELL (L-H)
Wednesday, May 1

OFFICIAL GOING: Good (7.8)
Wind: light 1/2 behind Weather: fine and sunny

64 DOWNLOAD THE BETVICTOR APP NOW H'CAP CHASE (19 fncs) 3m 110y
1:40 (1:40) (Class 5) (0-100,100) 5-Y-0+ **£2,599** (£763; £381; £190)

Form RPR

324/ **1** **Dukeofchesterwood**[108] 3648 11-10-3 77......................(p) BrianHughes 86
(Karen McLintock) *w ldrs: blnd 6th: 2nd 13th: drvn 4 out: styd on run-in: led nr fin* **9/2**[3]

054/ **2** *nk* **Silas Mariner (IRE)**[17] 5314 6-11-12 100.......................(bt) AdamPogson 108
(Mandy Rowland) *trckd ldrs: t.k.h and led after 11th: 2 l ahd last: hdd and no ex nr fin* **33/1**

060/ **3** *25* **Folie A Deux (IRE)**[19] 5275 11-11-8 96..........................(p) CharlieHuxley 83
(William Kinsey) *in rr: reminders 4th: lost pl 14th: kpt on and modest 5th 3 out: tk 3rd nr fin* **12/1**

F32/ **4** *1 ¾* **Caulfields Venture (IRE)**[25] 5182 7-11-8 96.................. NickScholfield 81
(Andy Turnell) *in rr: reminders after 2nd: j. slowly 4th: lost pl 13th: modest 3rd after 4 out: one pce* **6/4**[1]

P0/ **5** *22* **Radsoc De Sivola (FR)**[12] 5386 8-11-1 94........................ JoeCornwall(5) 65
(John Cornwall) *in rr: wnt modest 3rd 15th: wknd qckly 3 out* **66/1**

P43/ **6** *8* **Over And Above (IRE)**[12] 5382 7-10-3 77...................... RichieMcGrath 33
(Henry Hogarth) *chsd ldrs: reminders 11th: lost pl 15th: sn bhd* **3/1**[2]

P25/ **7** *11* **Qualitee**[32] 5023 8-10-10 91...(t) GeraldQuinn(7) 37
(Claire Dyson) *w ldr: led 4th: hdd after 11th: 2nd whn blnd 13th: sn lost pl and mstkes after: t.o 3 out* **10/1**

0F5/ **P** **Farewellatmidnight**[17] 5315 7-11-11 99........................(t) PeterBuchanan
(Alex Hales) *led to 4th: lost pl 14th: t.o 4 out: p.u bef next* **12/1**

6m 23.0s **Going Correction** -0.025s/f (Good) **8** Ran SP% **112.1**
Speed ratings: **99,98,90,90,83 80,77,**
toteswingers 1&2 £8.20, 2&3 £14.90, 1&3 £10.20 CSF £99.05 CT £1641.58 TOTE £3.90: £1.50, £3.50, £3.20; EX 69.60 Trifecta £430.70 Pool: £1021.40 - 1.77 winning units..
Owner Mrs C J Todd **Bred** The Slippery Pigg Partnership **Trained** Ingoe, Northumberland

FOCUS
Fences on the outside rail. The bend into the home straight on outer most line. The Golf club bend on inner most line. A modest staying handicap chase, in which they went an honest gallop on drying ground. The second is rated to his mark and sets the level.

65 BETVICTOR.COM H'CAP CHASE (13 fncs) 2m
2:10 (2:11) (Class 5) (0-100,100) 5-Y-0+ **£2,599** (£763; £381; £190)

Form RPR

601/ **1** **Apache Dawn**[7] 5508 9-10-0 74 7ex...............................(t) TommyPhelan 90+
(Aytach Sadik) *chsd ldr: drvn to ld bef 2 out: drew clr between last 2* **5/1**[3]

241/ **2** *9* **Kayfton Pete**[17] 5311 7-11-12 100....................................(t) AdamPogson 108
(Charles Pogson) *t.k.h in rr: mstke 1st: hdwy to chse ldrs 9th: 3rd appr 3 out: kpt on to take 2nd run-in* **4/1**[2]

2P1/ **3** *1* **Callhimwhatyouwant (IRE)**[5] 5556 8-11-11 99 7ex........(b) TomO'Brien 107+
(Dr Richard Newland) *t.k.h: led: j.lft thrght: hdd bef 2 out: hit last: one pce and lost pl run-in* **11/10**[1]

54/- **4** *7* **Roc De Guye (FR)**[52] 4681 8-10-6 80.............................(p) LiamTreadwell 82
(James Evans) *chsd ldrs: 3rd 9th: wknd and hit 3 out* **12/1**

305/ **5** *10* **Mad Professor (IRE)**[12] 5384 10-9-9 74 oh6...............(b) JoeCornwall(5) 65
(John Cornwall) *in rr: reminders 6th: bhd fr 4 out* **33/1**

403/ **6** *nk* **Reasonable Force**[44] 4839 7-11-7 95..........................(b[1]) JamesReveley 88
(Keith Reveley) *chsd ldng pair: outpcd 8th: rdn and wknd 4 out* **9/1**

503/ **P** **The Black Lion (IRE)**[12] 5384 12-9-10 77....................... PaulNO'Brien(7)
(Nick Kent) *in rr: bhd fr 9th: p.u bef 3 out* **16/1**

4m 1.1s (-0.90) **Going Correction** -0.025s/f (Good) **7** Ran SP% **110.8**
Speed ratings: **101,96,96,92,87 87,**
toteswingers 1&2 £3.10, 2&3 £1.30, 1&3 £2.80 CSF £23.96 TOTE £10.20: £1.90, £2.90; EX 22.90 Trifecta £79.80 Pool: £1213.77 - 11.40 winning units..
Owner A Sadik **Bred** G Reed **Trained** Wolverley, Worcs

FOCUS
A modest handicap chase in which they went a decent gallop. The first two set the level of the form.

66 BETVICTOR CHAMPIONS LEAGUE RED CARD REFUND H'CAP CHASE (16 fncs) 2m 4f 110y
2:40 (2:40) (Class 3) (0-135,135) 5-Y-0+ **£6,498** (£1,908; £954; £477)

Form RPR

134/ **1** **Kings Grey (IRE)**[27] 5139 9-11-12 135.............................. JamesReveley 139+
(Keith Reveley) *led tl appr 10th: led last: styd on wl: readily* **3/1**[2]

230/ **2** *1 ¾* **Montoya's Son (IRE)**[26] 5160 8-10-11 120....................(t) WilsonRenwick 123
(Tim Vaughan) *chsd ldrs: led after 4 out: hdd last: kpt on same pce* **5/2**[1]

P60/ **3** *14* **Pure Faith (IRE)**[166] 2455 9-11-9 132.................................. TomO'Brien 124
(Peter Bowen) *j.lft: chsd wnr: hit 6th: led and increased pce appr 10th: hdd after 4 out: lost pl and last 2 out: tk modest 3rd nr fin* **7/2**[3]

110/ **4** *¾* **Cross Of Honour (IRE)**[34] 4993 6-11-7 130..............(t) RichardJohnson 122
(Charlie Longsdon) *trckd ldrs: t.k.h: j.rt 4 out: sn upsides: wknd and 3rd whn hit last* **7/2**[3]

620/ **5** *2* **Christopher Wren (USA)**[32] 5015 6-10-5 114.................... TomCannon 104
(Nick Gifford) *nt jump wl: awkward and rdr briefly lost iron 1st: chsd ldrs 4 out: 4th and outpcd whn pckd 2 out: sn wknd: mstke last* **7/1**

5m 19.9s (2.90) **Going Correction** -0.025s/f (Good) **5** Ran SP% **110.5**
Speed ratings: **93,92,87,86,85**
CSF £11.12 TOTE £3.90: £1.90, £4.20; EX 11.20 Trifecta £24.80 Pool: £877.99 - 26.49 winning units..
Owner John Wade **Bred** Fred Mackey **Trained** Lingdale, Redcar & Cleveland

FOCUS
A decent small-field handicap chase in which the tempo increased on the final circuit. The winner is rated to his mark, backed up by the runner-up.

67 FOLLOW US ON TWITTER @BETVICTORRACING H'CAP HURDLE (DIV I) (11 hdls) 2m 4f 110y
3:10 (3:10) (Class 5) (0-95,95) 4-Y-0+ **£2,274** (£667; £333; £166)

Form RPR

032/ **1** **Adios Alonso (IRE)**[25] 5183 7-10-13 87.............................. BenPoste(5) 95
(Rosemary Gasson) *w ldrs: led 5th: hdd 7th: led next: hotly chal appr last: hld on wl* **4/1**[1]

000/ **2** *½* **Billing (IRE)**[62] 4473 5-10-0 69 oh2................................ RichieMcLernon 75
(Jonjo O'Neill) *trckd ldrs: cl 2nd 2 out: upsides appr last: no ex in clsng stages* **5/1**[3]

646/ **3** *3* **Storm To Pass**[30] 5060 5-11-12 95....................................(t) HarrySkelton 99
(Caroline Fryer) *mid-div: chsd ldrs 3 out: cl 3rd appr last: kpt on same pce* **12/1**

023/ **4** *9* **Haling Park (UAE)**[12] 5378 7-9-12 72............................ TrevorWhelan(5) 67
(Clarissa Caroe) *in rr: sme hdwy 3 out: one pce and tk modest 4th last* **16/1**

03P/ **5** *3 ¼* **Granwood**[26] 5165 7-11-7 90.......................................(p) PeterBuchanan 82
(Tim Walford) *chsd ldrs: one pce fr 3 out* **14/1**

655/ **6** *2 ¾* **King Mak**[52] 4682 11-11-3 91...(t) KyleJames(5) 84
(Marjorie Fife) *led: blnd and hdd 5th: led 7th: hdd next: lost pl sn after 3 out* **7/1**

053/ **7** *9* **Harrys Whim**[49] 4742 8-10-4 73.. RichieMcGrath 55
(John Weymes) *chsd ldrs: lost pl 3 out: sn bhd: blnd last* **9/2**[2]

U20/ **8** *1 ½* **Benozzo Gozzoli**[71] 4300 7-10-8 77.............................. AndrewThornton 61+
(Simon Earle) *prom: cl up 8th: upsides sn after 3 out: wknd qckly between last 2: eased in clsng stages* **13/2**

P0P/ **9** *20* **Go Teescomponents**[72] 4292 6-10-0 69 oh5...............(t[1]) BrianHughes 31
(Keith Reveley) *stdd s: in rr: bhd fr 6th: t.o 8th* **20/1**

005/ **P** **Greatown (IRE)**[40] 4909 6-11-2 85.....................................(t) CharlieHuxley
(William Kinsey) *t.k.h: trckd ldrs: lost pl3 out: sn bhd: t.o whn p.u between last 2* **12/1**

006/ **P** **Arrowmint**[61] 4496 7-10-12 84... JackQuinlan(3)
(Nicholas Pomfret) *in rr: nt fluent 2nd: bhd fr 7th: t.o 8th: p.u bef 2 out* **100/1**

5m 7.8s (-5.20) **Going Correction** -0.20s/f (Good) **11** Ran SP% **114.4**
Speed ratings (Par 103): **101,100,99,96,95 93,90,89,82,**
toteswingers 1&2 £12.10, 2&3 £18.00, 1&3 £7.60 CSF £23.97 CT £218.46 TOTE £3.80: £1.80, £2.60, £6.10; EX 25.50 Trifecta £228.30 Pool: £527.05 - 1.73 winning units..
Owner Mrs Rosemary Gasson **Bred** Robert Finnegan **Trained** Balscote, Oxon

FOCUS
The first division of a moderate handicap hurdle in which they went a good, even gallop. The winner is rated to his best with the third to his mark.

68 DOWNLOAD THE BETVICTOR SPINCAST APP NOW CONDITIONAL JOCKEYS' TRAINING SERIES H'CAP HURDLE (12 hdls 1 omitted) 3m 110y
3:45 (3:45) (Class 4) (0-110,105) 4-Y-0+ £3,249 (£954; £477; £238)

Form RPR
066/ 1 **Thornton Alice**[30] 5063 8-11-4 100 .... DanielHiskett(3) 100
(Richard Phillips) *trckd ldrs: kpt on same pce between last 2: 5 l down whn lft in narrow ld last: drvn out* **9/1**
P41/ 2 ¾ **Around A Pound (IRE)**[17] 5313 8-11-7 105 .... (p) PaulNO'Brien(5) 104
(Nick Kent) *chsd ldrs: lft in ld 5th: hit 9th: hdd between last 2: lft in cl 2nd last: no ex* **9/2[3]**
606/ 3 8 **Tackler (IRE)**[31] 5035 5-11-9 102 .... (p) DannyBenson 96+
(Jonjo O'Neill) *in tch: trckd ldrs 7th: nt fluent 9th: hrd drvn 3 out: sn chsng ldrs: one pce: 4 l down and lft 3rd whn bdly hmpd last* **9/2[3]**
451/ 4 31 **Earcomesthedream (IRE)**[19] 5271 10-11-9 102 .... (b) KillianMoore 64
(Peter Pritchard) *chsd ldrs: drvn and hit 8th: hmpd by loose horse after next: lost pl 3 out: sn bhd: t.o* **6/1**
345/ F **Mac Steamy (IRE)**[54] 4633 7-11-9 102 .... (t) ThomasGarner 108+
(William Kinsey) *t.k.h: trckd ldrs: hmpd 5th: upsides 3 out: led between last 2: 5 l in front whn stmbld on landing and fell last* **7/2[2]**
222/ U **Lord Luso (IRE)**[19] 5275 7-11-12 105 .... AdamNicol
(Philip Kirby) *led: hit 5th: swvd both ways on landing and uns rdr* **5/2[1]**
6m 14.7s (-0.30) **Going Correction** -0.20s/f (Good) **6** Ran SP% **111.4**
Speed ratings (Par 105): **92,91,89,79,**
toteswingers 1&2 £11.80, 2&3 £3.50, 1&3 £7.20 CSF £46.87 TOTE £14.10: £4.40, £2.00; EX 54.40 Trifecta £534.10 Pool: £1226.55 - 1.72 winning units..
Owner The Listeners **Bred** S P Hudson **Trained** Adlestrop, Gloucs

FOCUS
A modest conditional jockeys' staying handicap hurdle in which they went an honest gallop, and there was plenty of drama. The first two are rated to their marks with the unseater heading for a personal-best.

69 £25 FREE BET AT BETVICTOR.COM NOVICES' HURDLE (9 hdls) 2m
4:20 (4:20) (Class 4) 4-Y-0+ £3,408 (£1,033; £556)

Form RPR
1 **Cool Macavity (IRE)**[186] 5-10-12 0 .... DavidBass 111+
(Nicky Henderson) *trckd ldrs: cl 2nd 3 out: led next: j. slowly last: easily* **4/11[1]**
5/ 2 8 **Midlothian (IRE)**[187] 2026 5-10-12 0 .... DenisO'Regan 99+
(John Ferguson) *trckd ldrs: stmbld on landing 3 out: sn drvn: chsd wnr after 2 out: no imp* **7/2[2]**
00/ 3 39 **Abbraccio**[25] 5180 5-10-12 0 .... (t) PaddyBrennan 62
(Fergal O'Brien) *chsd ldr: lost pl after 3 out: bhd next: lft distant 3rd last* **20/1**
/ U **Audacious**[228] 5-10-12 0 .... AdamPogson 91
(Charles Pogson) *t.k.h: led: hdd 2 out: 4 l down in 3rd whn swvd rt and uns rdr last* **12/1[3]**
3m 57.4s (0.40) **Going Correction** -0.20s/f (Good) **4** Ran SP% **108.0**
Speed ratings (Par 105): **91,87,67,**
CSF £2.06 TOTE £1.40; EX 1.80 Trifecta £5.90 Pool: £1017.55 - 129.19 winning units..
Owner Triermore Stud **Bred** C O P Hanbury **Trained** Upper Lambourn, Berks

FOCUS
A disappointing turnout for the novices' hurdle. The winner is value for further and could rate higher.

70 CHAMPIONS LEAGUE RED CARD REFUND AT BETVICTOR.COM MARES' NOVICES' HURDLE (13 hdls) 3m 110y
4:55 (4:55) (Class 4) 4-Y-0+ £3,249 (£954; £477; £238)

Form RPR
302/ 1 **Midnight Macarena**[19] 5274 8-10-13 0 .... (p) LeightonAspell 110+
(Lucy Wadham) *mde all: increased pce 8th: wnt 6 l clr 2 out: c rt away: eased run-in* **6/4[1]**
263/ 2 19 **Floral Spinner**[20] 5249 6-10-6 113 .... ChrisDavies(7) 94
(Bill Turner) *hld up: nt fluent 5th: shkn up next: drvn to chse ldrs 10th: 2nd 2 out: one pce* **7/4[2]**
6/ 3 ¾ **Strangelittlegirl**[18] 5288 5-10-10 0 .... JackQuinlan(3) 91
(Patrick Gilligan) *t.k.h: j.lft 1st: trckd ldrs: hit 10th: drvn next: one pce appr 2 out* **25/1**
140/ 4 9 **Agent Fedora**[53] 4666 5-10-13 0 .... (t) JasonMaguire 85
(Kim Bailey) *nt fluent: chsd ldrs: 2nd 8th: mstke 10th: rdn next: wknd after 2 out* **11/4[3]**
040/ 5 8 **Une Des Bieffes (FR)**[20] 5249 5-10-13 0 .... (v) TomScudamore 75
(Michael Scudamore) *t.k.h: trckd ldrs: outpcd 9th: sn bhd* **50/1**
6m 21.7s (6.70) **Going Correction** -0.20s/f (Good) **5** Ran SP% **108.8**
Speed ratings (Par 105): **81,74,74,71,69**
CSF £4.51 TOTE £1.90: £1.10, £1.70; EX 4.20 Trifecta £23.20 Pool: £1419.20 - 45.83 winning units..
Owner The Bees **Bred** Mrs Elizabeth Gordon Lennox **Trained** Newmarket, Suffolk

FOCUS
A fair staying mares' novices' hurdle. The winner is rated to her chase mark with the second similar to her previous run and the fourth close to her bumper mark.

71 FOLLOW US ON TWITTER @BETVICTORRACING H'CAP HURDLE (DIV II) (11 hdls) 2m 4f 110y
5:30 (5:30) (Class 5) (0-95,95) 4-Y-0+ £2,274 (£667; £333; £166)

Form RPR
001/ 1 **Starlight Air**[12] 5378 10-11-2 85 .... JamieMoore 90
(John Spearing) *chsd ldrs 5th: drvn 3 out: outpcd appr next: rallied and wnt 2nd after 2 out: styd on wl appr last: lft in ld sn after last: drvn clr* **9/1**
024/ 2 3¼ **Oscar Rainbow**[5] 5538 7-10-1 73 .... RobertDunne(3) 78+
(Dai Burchell) *trckd ldrs: t.k.h: led 3 out: over a l ahd but flagging whn blnd bdly last: sn hdd* **3/1[2]**
250/ 3 4 **Velvet Vic (IRE)**[11] 5412 7-10-8 77 .... (b) BarryKeniry 77
(Richard Guest) *in rr: nt fluent 2nd: stdy hdwy 3 out: hit next: sn 4th: j.lft last: kpt on to take 3rd run-in* **12/1**
0/ 4 1¼ **Grange Boy (IRE)**[46] 4802 5-11-9 95 .... KeithDonoghue(3) 93
(J T R Dreaper, Ire) *hld up in rr: hdwy to chse ldrs 6th: wnt 2nd appr 2 out: kpt on one pce* **7/1**
005/ 5 15 **Brass Monkey (IRE)**[124] 3318 6-11-5 88 .... RichardJohnson 77+
(Charlie Longsdon) *chsd ldrs: drvn 7th: wknd between last 2* **9/4[1]**
0P4/ 6 6 **Music In The Air**[48] 4762 9-10-5 74 .... (p) CharliePoste 52
(Robin Dickin) *w ldrs: led after 1st: nt fluent and hdd next: lost pl appr 2 out* **22/1**
000/ 7 10 **Scheherazadesdream**[63] 4447 6-11-1 84 .... SeanQuinlan 56
(Jennie Candlish) *in rr: drvn 6th: lost pl 3 out* **33/1**
PPF/ 8 1¾ **Pennant Dancer**[25] 5183 6-10-0 69 oh5 .... DonalDevereux 37
(Debra Hamer) *t.k.h: w ldrs: led 2nd: hdd 3 out: wkng whn blnd next* **50/1**
P60/ 9 3¾ **I Can Run Can You (IRE)**[124] 3316 7-11-7 90 .... RichieMcLernon 55
(Jonjo O'Neill) *in rr: drvn 6th: lost pl 3 out: sn bhd* **20/1**
004/ 10 12 **Napoletano (ITY)**[126] 3228 7-10-0 69 .... (v[1]) TomScudamore 23
(Michael Scudamore) *led tl after 1st: w ldrs: wknd appr 2 out: bhd whn eased run-in* **6/1[3]**
5m 10.7s (-2.30) **Going Correction** -0.20s/f (Good) **10** Ran SP% **114.3**
Speed ratings (Par 103): **96,94,93,92,87 84,80,80,79,74**
toteswingers 1&2 £4.00, 2&3 £5.90, 1&3 £8.20 CSF £34.83 CT £328.76 TOTE £6.90: £1.30, £1.70, £3.80; EX 23.60 Trifecta £89.10 Pool: £1564.08 - 13.15 winning units..
Owner Mrs Peter Badger **Bred** Mrs P Badger **Trained** Kinnersley, Worcs

FOCUS
The second division of a moderate handicap hurdle. The first two are rated close to recent form.
T/Plt: £418.90 to a £1 stake. Pool of £50353.44 - 87.73 winning tickets. T/Qpdt: £37.20 to a £1 stake. Pool of £5370.30 - 106.70 winning tickets. WG

SEDGEFIELD (L-H)
Thursday, May 2

OFFICIAL GOING: Good (good to firm in places on hurdle course; chs 7.9; hdl 8.3)
Wind: Breezy, across Weather: Sunny

72 32RED.COM CONDITIONAL JOCKEYS' MAIDEN HURDLE (10 hdls) 2m 5f 110y
2:10 (2:11) (Class 5) 4-Y-0+ £1,949 (£572; £286; £143)

Form RPR
344/ 1 **Welsh Bard (IRE)**[64] 4450 4-10-8 106 .... (b[1]) HenryBrooke(3) 115+
(Donald McCain) *t.k.h: mde all at decent gallop: rdn clr bef 2 out: hrd rdn bef last: kpt on wl* **8/1**
34/ 2 21 **Halifax (IRE)**[19] 5288 5-10-8 0 .... (p) JosephAkehurst(8) 101
(John Ferguson) *nt fluent on occasions: hld up in tch: outpcd 6th: rallied bef 2 out: chsd (clr) wnr after last: no imp* **7/4[1]**
1/ 3 3½ **Four Shuck Men (IRE)**[13] 5388 5-11-2 0 .... HarryDerham 99
(Tim Vaughan) *chsd ldrs: drvn after 3 out: tk modest 2nd whn nt fluent next: sn one pce* **7/2[3]**
UU6/ 4 54 **Two Oscars (IRE)**[8] 5499 7-10-8 90 .... JohnWinston(8) 49
(Andrew Crook) *bhd: pushed along 1/2-way: sme hdwy after 4 out: sn no imp* **25/1**
040/ 5 56 **Escape Artist**[238] 1503 6-11-2 72 .... TonyKelly
(David Thompson) *hld up: struggling fnl circ: t.o* **100/1**
60/ F **Birzali (FR)**[16] 5343 6-11-2 120 .... (bt) MichealNolan 94
(John Joseph Hanlon, Ire) *chsd ldrs: effrt and drvn after 3 out: 30 l 4th and wkng whn fell and down for sme time last* **11/4[2]**
300/ P **Witch Way**[8] 5499 8-10-4 0 .... (p) DiarmuidO'Regan(5)
(Ashley Dodgson) *nt fluent on occasions: hld up: struggling fr 6th: t.o whn p.u bef 2 out* **200/1**
5F4/ P **Shanroe Secret (IRE)**[26] 5193 6-10-8 103 .... LiamMcKenna(8)
(J J Lambe, Ire) *nt fluent in rr: struggling 1/2-way: t.o whn p.u bef 2 out* **17/2**
5m 15.1s (0.50) **Going Correction** +0.225s/f (Yiel)
WFA 4 from 5yo+ 19lb **8** Ran SP% **112.2**
Speed ratings (Par 103): **108,100,99,79,59 , ,**
toteswingers 1&2 £3.30, 2&3 £1.90, 1&3 £4.60 CSF £22.33 TOTE £9.40: £2.40, £1.10, £1.30; EX 18.50 Trifecta £79.10 Pool: £1460.02 - 13.83 winning units..
Owner George Tobitt & Richard Gurney **Bred** Whisperview Trading Ltd **Trained** Cholmondeley, Cheshire
■ Stewards' Enquiry : Henry Brooke two-day ban: used whip when clearly winning (May 16-17)

FOCUS
Divided bends with chases on innermost line and hurdles on outside line. This was nothing more than an ordinary contest, and four of these played no part whatsoever. After riding in the opener Henry Brooke said that they were definitely making a cut, as there was plenty of water in the ground. The second and third are the best guides to the level.

73 PHOENIX SECURITY MAIDEN HURDLE (7 hdls 1 omitted) 2m 1f
2:40 (2:40) (Class 5) 4-Y-0+ £1,949 (£572; £286; £143)

Form RPR
243/ 1 **Aazif (IRE)**[25] 5197 4-10-10 115 .... (t) JasonMaguire 117+
(Donald McCain) *mde all: drvn clr 2 out: kpt on strly* **6/5[1]**
2P/ 2 17 **Cape Explorer**[48] 4767 4-10-10 0 .... DannyCook 97
(Brian Ellison) *prom: hdwy to chse wnr after 3 out (usual 4 out): effrt bef next: sn outpcd* **6/4[2]**
0/ 3 20 **Optical High**[65] 4439 4-10-10 0 .... RyanMania 77
(Sue Smith) *hld up: hdwy and prom bef omitted 3 out: rdn and outpcd fr next* **50/1**
6/ 4 7 **Roxy Beat**[135] 3126 5-10-7 0 .... [1] DougieCostello 70
(John Quinn) *trckd wnr: hmpd by loose horse appr 3 out (usual 4 out): sn lost 2nd: wknd bef 2 out* **18/1**
236/ 5 15 **Langley House (IRE)**[285] 1015 6-10-7 0 .... LucyAlexander 52
(Dianne Sayer) *hld up: short-lived effrt bef omitted 3 out: sn n.d* **22/1**
000/ 6 24 **Bertielicious**[24] 5216 5-10-11 0 .... JohnKington(3) 35
(Jonathan Haynes) *nt fluent in rr: rdn 3 out (usual 4 out): sn btn* **200/1**
40P/ 7 13 **Sunset Song**[333] 9-10-0 0 .... (t) CallumBewley(7) 15
(Theresa Gibson) *midfield: struggling 3 out (usual 4 out): sn btn* **100/1**
0/ 8 13 **Anjum (USA)**[25] 5-10-4 0 .... [1] MichealNolan(3) 2
(John Joseph Hanlon, Ire) *towards rr: mstke 2nd: struggling fr 3 out (usual 4 out)* **50/1**
P43/ 9 4 **Alimure**[399] 5147 7-10-4 0 .... BrianToomey(3)
(Clive Mulhall) *prom tl rdn and wknd 3 out (usual 4 out)* **80/1**
04/ U **Honour System (IRE)**[19] 5281 6-11-0 0 .... DenisO'Regan
(John Ferguson) *in tch: stmbld and uns rdr 1st* **6/1[3]**
U/ U **Stella Marris**[60] 4543 6-10-4 0 .... EwanWhillans(3)
(Christopher Wilson) *nt jump wl: plld hrd: racd wd: w ldr tl uns rdr 4th* **150/1**
00/ U **Billericay Allstar**[65] 4439 5-10-0 0 .... JamesCorbett(7)
(Susan Corbett) *bhd: j. awkwardly and uns rdr 1st* **100/1**
4m 8.2s (1.30) **Going Correction** +0.225s/f (Yiel)
WFA 4 from 5yo+ 18lb **12** Ran SP% **117.6**
Speed ratings (Par 103): **105,97,87,84,77 65,59,53,51, ,**
toteswingers 1&2 £1.30, 2&3 £11.50, 1&3 £20.50 CSF £3.21 TOTE £1.70: £1.10, £1.10, £16.30; EX 3.40 Trifecta £64.90 Pool: £2156.13 - 24.89 winning units..

Owner Askew Dick Hernon Reynard **Bred** Shadwell Estate Company Limited **Trained** Cholmondeley, Cheshire

FOCUS

Not a lot of depth to this race, but it was interesting that the first three home were the only 4-y-os in the contest. What should have been the third-last was bypassed. The winner is rated a slight improver with the second below his best.

74 CHATFIELDS DAF EURO 6 H'CAP CHASE (21 fncs) 3m 3f

3:10 (3:18) (Class 4) (0-105,102) 5-Y-0+ **£3,768** (£1,106; £553; £276)

Form RPR

031/ 1 **Pyjama Game (IRE)**[10] 5450 7-11-4 **87** 7ex.................... WilsonRenwick 99+
(Rose Dobbin) *in tch: hdwy to ld bef 2 out: rdn clr bef last* **7/2**[2]

306/ 2 14 **Frontier Boy (IRE)**[10] 5450 9-11-8 **91**............................(p) BrianHughes 93+
(James Ewart) *prom: hdwy and ev ch 3 out to next: outpcd by wnr bef last* **16/1**

003/ 3 3 1/2 **Moon Melody (GER)**[5] 5570 10-11-0 **83**......................(t) LucyAlexander 82
(Mike Sowersby) *hld up: rdn along 5 out: effrt whn hit 3 out: sn outpcd: kpt on fr next: no imp* **14/1**

605/ 4 15 **Everlasting (IRE)**[23] 5224 6-10-11 **80**............................ RichieMcGrath 66
(Rose Dobbin) *led: rdn and hdd bef 2 out: wknd between last 2* **6/1**

/ 5 51 **Baizically (IRE)**[19] 5300 10-11-3 **86**...........................(b) SeanMcDermott 23
(John Joseph Hanlon, Ire) *hld up: drvn along bef 15th: sn lost tch: t.o* **7/1**

4P0/ P **Esme Rides A Gaine**[10] 5450 11-10-13 **85**.................. EwanWhillans(3)
(Christopher Wilson) *towards rr: sn struggling: t.o whn p.u bef 12th* **22/1**

PP1/ P **Ballyvoneen (IRE)**[6] 5554 8-12-5 **102** 7ex........................(p) AlexMerriam
(Neil King) *hld up: hdwy and prom 1/2-way: wknd 16th: t.o whn p.u bef 2 out* **9/2**[3]

P00/ P **Across The Tweed (IRE)**[10] 5450 7-10-10 **79**..........(t) MichaelMcAlister
(Maurice Barnes) *bhd: reminders 4th: struggling fr 14th: t.o whn p.u after 3 out* **33/1**

00P/ P **Bennys Well (IRE)**[50] 4741 7-10-7 **76**.................................. RyanMania
(Sue Smith) *sn w ldr: rdn and lost pl 16th: nt fluent next: sn wknd: t.o whn p.u 3 out* **3/1**[1]

6m 46.3s (-2.70) **Going Correction** -0.425s/f (Good) **9** Ran SP% **112.0**
Speed ratings: **87,82,81,77,62 , , ,**
toteswingers 1&2 £3.40, 2&3 £13.90, 1&3 £3.90 CSF £51.62 CT £687.28 TOTE £5.50: £1.40, £3.90, £2.60; EX 52.40 Trifecta £289.20 Pool: £1495.14 - 3.87 winning units..
Owner Straightline Construction Ltd **Bred** Peter E Clinton **Trained** South Hazelrigg, Northumbria

FOCUS

A really weak contest that took little winning. The gallop set by the leaders was fairly decent, however. The winner built on a recent success with the placed horses the best guides to the level.

75 MINISTERS INDIAN RESTAURANT SEDGEFIELD H'CAP HURDLE (7 hdls 1 omitted) 2m 1f

3:40 (3:47) (Class 5) (0-100,100) 4-Y-0+ **£1,949** (£572; £286; £143)

Form RPR

266/ 1 **Iktiview**[27] 5166 5-10-9 **88**...(bt[1]) KyleJames(5) 91
(Philip Kirby) *t.k.h early: in tch: hdwy to chse ldr 2 out (usual 3 out): hrd drvn and edgd rt bef next: edgd lft bef omitted last: rdn to ld nr fin* **11/2**[2]

542/ 2 1/2 **Pobs Trophy**[9] 5477 6-9-9 **74** oh9..........................(b) JonathanEngland(5) 81
(Richard Guest) *led at decent gallop: rdn and swtchd sharply lft arnd omitted last: sn jnd: kpt on: hdd nr fin* **11/2**[2]

442/ 3 7 **Shaker Style (USA)**[29] 5124 7-10-4 **78**..........................(p) BrianHughes 80
(Barry Murtagh) *chsd ldrs: hit 1st: effrt 2 out (usual 3 out): cl 3rd whn blnd last: sn one pce* **11/2**[2]

6U4/ 4 6 **Doyenthedecenthing**[29] 5119 5-10-2 **76**............................ AdrianLane 70
(John Davies) *t.k.h: midfield: hdwy 3 out (usual 4 out): rdn and outpcd bef last (usual 2 out)* **10/1**

P/ 5 15 **Do The Bookies**[19] 5298 9-11-5 **100**......................... MissRBlackmore(7) 84
(John Joseph Hanlon, Ire) *prom tl rdn and wknd bef last (usual 2 out)* **4/1**[1]

4P0/ 6 25 **Breeze With Ease (IRE)**[19] 5298 9-11-7 **95**.................(t) EddieO'Connell 53
(J J Lambe, Ire) *hld up: rdn after 3 out (usual 4 out): nvr on terms* **8/1**[3]

260/ 7 13 **Waltham Abbey**[19] 5290 12-10-10 **84**...............................(p) HarryHaynes 31
(Lynsey Kendall) *chsd ldrs: struggling fr 4th: t.o* **18/1**

5PP/ 8 1 **Sunarri (IRE)**[23] 5227 9-10-9 **90**.................................(b) AlistairFindlay(7) 36
(Jane Walton) *bhd: struggling fr 4th: nvr on terms* **50/1**

06P/ 9 28 **One Million**[32] 3605 4-10-12 **90**................................(t) WilsonRenwick 7
(Rose Dobbin) *hld up: pushed along after 3 out (usual 4 out): sn struggling* **40/1**

00P/ P **Weetfromthechaff**[23] 5227 8-11-2 **90**.........................(t) MichaelMcAlister
(Maurice Barnes) *hld up: hit 3rd: struggling and p.u bef 2 out (usual 3 out)* **12/1**

U05/ P **Monashee (IRE)**[24] 5220 8-11-7 **95**..................................... RyanMania
(George Charlton) *chsd ldrs to 3 out (usual 4 out): sn struggling: t.o whn p.u bef 2 out* **25/1**

PP0/ F **Launchpad**[20] 5277 6-11-2 **97**...................................... MrHAABannister(7)
(Kevin Hunter) *hld up in mid-div: fell 3rd: fatally injured* **50/1**

PP6/ P **Encore Un Fois**[288] 989 5-10-0 **74** oh3........................(p) RichieMcGrath
(Henry Hogarth) *s.v.s: t.o thrght: p.u after 4th* **22/1**

0P0/ B **Van Mildert (IRE)**[46] 4815 4-9-7 **78** oh5................ StephenMulqueen(7)
(Evelyn Slack) *hld up: b.d 3rd* **66/1**

4m 9.9s (3.00) **Going Correction** +0.225s/f (Yiel)
WFA 4 from 5yo+ 18lb **14** Ran SP% **115.4**
Speed ratings (Par 103): **101,100,97,94,87 75,69,69,56, , , ,**
toteswingers 1&2 £5.20, 2&3 £2.30, 1&3 £7.90 CSF £32.57 CT £174.41 TOTE £5.80: £2.70, £1.20, £1.90; EX 37.40 Trifecta £188.20 Pool: £1576.70 - 6.28 winning units..
Owner Eastview Thoroughbreds **Bred** Eastview Thoroughbreds **Trained** Middleham, N Yorks
■ Stewards' Enquiry : Jonathan England two-day ban: used whip above permitted level (May 16-17)

FOCUS

Not a race that took much winning but it produced a close finish and the first three ran pretty much to their marks. The final flight was bypassed.

76 MOLSON COORS STANDARD OPEN NATIONAL HUNT FLAT RACE 2m 1f

4:10 (4:13) (Class 6) 4-6-Y-0 **£1,559** (£457; £228; £114)

Form RPR

0/ 1 **Amazing Scenes (IRE)**[107] 3677 4-10-12 0.................. RichardJohnson 92
(Brendan Powell) *trckd ldrs: led 5f out: brought to stands' rail 2f out: drvn out fnl f* **5/1**

2 2 1/4 **Mr Cardle (IRE)** 4-10-12 0... RichieMcGrath 90
(Philip Kirby) *in tch on wd outside: effrt and rn green 4f out: rallied over 2f out: rdn and chsd wnr fnl f: kpt on* **11/4**[1]

3 6 **Howlett (IRE)**[122] 3410 5-10-13 0...................................... MPFogarty(3) 90
(John Joseph Hanlon, Ire) *trckd ldrs: effrt and wnt 2nd over 2f out to 1f out: sn outpcd* **9/2**[3]

50/ 4 18 **Dorset Dora**[23] 5230 5-10-2 0...............................(t) StephenMulqueen(7) 65
(Maurice Barnes) *hld up: hdwy and in tch over 4f out: rdn and wknd wl over 1f out* **33/1**

4S/ 5 10 **Farmer's Friend**[145] 2932 4-10-12 0................................ DonalDevereux 59
(John Mackie) *t.k.h: led at ordinary gallop to 5f out: rdn and wknd 3f out* **11/1**

66/ 6 18 **Genetic Code**[27] 5168 5-10-13 0....................................... BrianToomey(3) 47
(Karen Tutty) *hld up in midfield: drvn along over 5f out: struggling fnl 3f* **50/1**

7 6 **Bollin Bob** 4-10-12 0.. HarryHaynes 38
(Tim Easterby) *hld up: short-lived effrt 5f out: sn struggling* **20/1**

8 nse **Bellorophon (IRE)**[88] 4-10-12 0..................................... WilsonRenwick 38
(Tim Vaughan) *t.k.h early: hld up in tch: stdy hdwy over 5f out: sn rdn and wknd* **3/1**[2]

0/ 9 2 3/4 **If You Wish (IRE)**[89] 4001 5-11-2 0................................ DougieCostello 39
(Tim Easterby) *t.k.h: cl up: drvn and wknd 6f out* **25/1**

060/ 10 11 **Philchezski (IRE)**[29] 5125 6-10-9 0................................ JohnWinston(7) 29
(Andrew Crook) *midfield: drvn along 1/2-way: struggling over 5f out* **20/1**

P/ 11 48 **Big Benjie**[127] 3240 5-10-11 0... TonyKelly(5)
(Edwin Tuer) *hld up: struggling 1/2-way: t.o* **40/1**

4m 11.0s (9.70) **Going Correction** +0.225s/f (Yiel)
WFA 4 from 5yo+ 4lb **11** Ran SP% **115.6**
Speed ratings: **86,84,82,73,68 60,57,57,56,51 28**
toteswingers 1&2 £3.70, 2&3 £3.90, 1&3 £5.50 CSF £17.14 TOTE £3.40: £1.10, £1.70, £2.00; EX 23.70 Trifecta £84.70 Pool: £1694.85 -15.00 winning units..
Owner Let's Get Ready To Rumble Partnership **Bred** Mrs Margaret Reid **Trained** Upper Lambourn, Berks

FOCUS

Just a modest event in which three came clear. A step up from the winner but not an easy contest to rate.

77 32RED CASINO H'CAP CHASE (16 fncs) 2m 4f

4:40 (4:40) (Class 4) (0-120,123) 5-Y-0+ **£3,768** (£1,106; £553; £276)

Form RPR

P46/ 1 **Rudigreen (IRE)**[35] 4979 10-10-0 **91** oh2........................(tp) DougieCostello 104
(John Joseph Hanlon, Ire) *prom: hdwy 4 out: effrt and drvn 2 out: led run-in: styd on wl* **7/1**

5P3/ 2 2 1/2 **My Flora**[24] 5223 9-11-11 **116**... JasonMaguire 129+
(Donald McCain) *chsd ldrs: hdwy to ld after 2 out: sn rdn: hdd run-in: kpt on same pce* **11/4**[1]

P0/ 3 3 1/2 **Attycran (IRE)**[20] 5275 8-10-6 **97**................................(t) MichaelMcAlister 106
(Maurice Barnes) *w ldr: rdn after 3 out: one pce bef last* **12/1**

451/ 4 10 **Tahiti Pearl (IRE)**[8] 5502 9-12-4 **123** 7ex.............................. RyanMania 124
(Sue Smith) *led at reasonable gallop: rdn and hdd after 2 out: wknd bef last* **3/1**[2]

F60/ 5 33 **Willie Hall**[33] 5008 9-10-5 **96**... BrianHarding 65
(William Amos) *hld up in tch: drvn and struggling 5 out: sn btn* **11/1**

5U3/ 6 8 **Predateur (FR)**[16] 5344 10-11-9 **114**............................(t) EddieO'Connell 76
(J J Lambe, Ire) *nt fluent on occasions: hld up: struggling 11th: sn btn* **12/1**

0P5/ P **Rigidity**[47] 4783 6-11-12 **117**...(vt) RichardJohnson
(Tim Vaughan) *in tch: reminders 7th: struggling fr next: t.o whn p.u bef 2 out* **10/3**[3]

4m 51.0s (-12.00) **Going Correction** -0.425s/f (Good) **7** Ran SP% **111.0**
Speed ratings: **107,106,104,100,87 84,**
toteswingers 1&2 £4.10, 2&3 £6.90, 1&3 £7.90 CSF £25.76 TOTE £6.40: £2.60, £2.10; EX 35.10 Trifecta £313.70 Pool: £2529.26 - 6.04 winning units..
Owner John Joseph Hanlon **Bred** John Murphy **Trained** Bagenalstown, Co Carlow

FOCUS

This was an interesting and competitive event, but it produced a slightly surprising result. A big step up from the winner with the third setting the level.

78 32RED H'CAP CHASE (11 fncs 2 omitted) 2m 110y

5:10 (5:10) (Class 4) (0-120,127) 5-Y-0+ **£3,768** (£1,106; £553; £276)

Form RPR

43F/ 1 **Ballybriggan (IRE)**[55] 4632 9-11-9 **117**.............................. JasonMaguire 124+
(Donald McCain) *cl up: led 6th to next: led again after 3 out (usual 4 out): hung lft bef omitted last: drvn clr* **10/11**[1]

1P4/ 2 7 **Monarch's Way**[21] 5250 6-11-3 **118**......................(v) JosephAkehurst(7) 120
(John Ferguson) *led: blnd 5th: hdd next: led 8th: hit 3 out (usual 4 out): drvn and lost 2nd bef last: rallied to take 2nd nr fin: no ch w wnr* **7/2**[3]

016/ 3 1 3/4 **Fred Bojangals (IRE)**[23] 5225 11-11-9 **117**......................(p) BrianHughes 115
(Barbara Butterworth) *t.k.h: trckd ldrs: led 7th to next: effrt and chsd wnr bef last (usual 2 out): one pce appr omitted last* **10/1**

PP1/ 4 11 **Manger Hanagment (IRE)**[8] 5510 8-12-0 **127** 7ex...... GavinSheehan(5) 117
(Barry Brennan) *in tch: mstke and outpcd 6th: styd on fr 2 out (usual 3 out): nvr on terms* **11/4**[2]

4m 4.6s (-4.00) **Going Correction** -0.425s/f (Good) **4** Ran SP% **110.4**
Speed ratings: **92,88,87,82**
CSF £4.60 TOTE £1.60; EX 4.60 Trifecta £12.40 Pool: £1210.01 - 73.05 winning units..
Owner Stewart Andrew & Jim Shaw **Bred** C Kenneally **Trained** Cholmondeley, Cheshire

FOCUS

Only four runners but the early gallop seemed at least fair and the first two are rated to their marks.
T/Plt: £24.70 to a £1 stake. Pool of £63396.28 - 1869.94 winning tickets. T/Qpdt: £15.10 to a £1 stake. Pool of £3820.20 - 186.00 winning tickets. RY

TAUNTON (R-H)

Thursday, May 2

OFFICIAL GOING: Good to firm (good in places; 8.3)

Wind: virtually nil Weather: sunny

79 BATHWICK TYRES TAUNTON AMATEUR RIDERS' MAIDEN HURDLE (12 hdls) 3m 110y

5:20 (5:20) (Class 5) 5-Y-0+ **£2,634** (£810; £405)

Form RPR

4/ 1 **I'm The Article (IRE)**[20] 5264 7-10-11 0.............................. MrJBarber(5) 101+
(Harry Fry) *nvr that fluent: hld up: hdwy 6th: pressed ldr fr next: led 8th: awkward next and 3 out: hdd 2 out: sn rdn to regain ld: v awkward and hdd last: hung lft: rallied to ld nring fin* **13/8**[2]

013/ 2 nk **Captain Kelly (IRE)**[61] 4513 6-11-2 118...........................(t) MrWBiddick 98
(Paul Nicholls) *trckd ldrs: drew clr w wnr fr 9th: led 2 out: sn rdn and hdd: led narrowly sn after last: hdd nring fin* **4/6**[1]

The Form Book Jumps, Raceform Ltd, Compton, RG20 6NL.

460/ **3** *20* **Portmeade**[203] 1804 11-10-9 69... JonPark(7) 79
(Elizabeth Scott) *hld up: struggling in last after 7th: stdy prog past wkng rivals 9th: wnt 3rd next but no ch w ldrs* **50/1**

200/ **4** *27* **Gleannacreim (IRE)**[8] 5506 10-10-9 69.....................(v1) MrCGethings(7) 56
(Carroll Gray) *led tl blnd and hdd 6th: rdr lost iron but rcvrd by next: lost tch bef 9th: t.o* **16/1**

00/ **5** *16* **More Glory (IRE)**[9] 5468 5-10-11 0......................... MrMatthewBarber(5) 35
(Keith Goldsworthy) *trckd ldrs: hmpd 6th: sn struggling: wknd after 8th: t.o* **16/1**

6P0/ **6** *21* **Obscurity (IRE)**[111] 3594 5-10-9 69...............................(p) MrJHarding(7) 14
(Jonathan Portman) *trckd ldrs: pushed along appr 6th: sn in rr: t.o fr 9th* **33/1**

0/ **7** *14* **Trakeur (FR)**[16] 5334 6-11-2 0....................................(b1) NicodeBoinville
(Mark Gillard) *t.k.h: prom: lft in ld 6th: hdd 8th: sn wknd: t.o* **25/1**

40/ **P** **Up Your Game (IRE)**[21] 5241 5-10-11 0....................... MrKevinJones(5)
(Seamus Mullins) *trckd ldrs tl 3rd: in last pair: struggling 8th: blnd next: tailing off whn p.u bef 3 out* **12/1**[3]

5m 47.0s (-17.00) **Going Correction** -0.925s/f (Hard) **8** Ran SP% **126.3**
Speed ratings: **90,89,83,74,69 63,58,**
Tote Swingers: 1&2 £1.10, 1&3 £10.90, 2&3 £12.40 CSF £3.54 TOTE £4.20: £1.30, £1.02, £22.90; EX 3.80 Trifecta £48.70 Pool: £2,638.57 - 40.59 winning units..
Owner The Peckmoor Partnership **Bred** Miss Mary O'Sullivan **Trained** Seaborough, Dorset

FOCUS
Rail moved on bends reducing each circuit by 24yds. 17mm of water had been applied to the course over the previous three days to prevent any jar in the ground. With three horses in the field rated 69 taking on the 118-rated favourite, there was no strength in depth and the two market principals had it between them from midway down the back. The race could be rated higher but the third limits the form.

80 BATHWICK TYRES BRIDGWATER NOVICES' HURDLE (10 hdls) 2m 3f 110y
5:50 (5:50) (Class 4) 4-Y-0+ **£3,422** (£997; £499)

Form RPR

43/ **1** **Courtesy Call (IRE)**[25] 5195 4-10-7 123.......................... AndrewTinkler 114+
(Nicky Henderson) *rn in snatches: w ldr tl 4th: trckd ldng pair: nt fluent 6th: sn nudged along: rdn after 3 out: led sn after 2 out: in command whn rdr dropped whip run-in* **8/13**[1]

451/ **2** *3 ¾* **Forresters Folly**[25] 5195 7-11-5 125.......................(p) WayneHutchinson 123+
(Alan King) *led: rdn whn nt fluent 2 out: sn hdd: hld fr last: kpt on same pce* **15/8**[2]

006/ **3** *46* **Rowanna (IRE)**[6] 5543 5-10-2 0............................ BrendanPowell(3) 60
(Colin Tizzard) *trckd ldrs: pushed along after 6th: lost tch fr next where nt fluent: lft t.o 3rd at the last:* **33/1**

000/ **4** *7* **Mixed Meaning (IRE)**[11] 5441 5-10-9 0......................... GilesHawkins(3) 60
(Stuart Howe) *trckd ldrs: reminders after 5th: wknd after 6th: lft t.o 4th at the last* **150/1**

F **Sir Dylan**[66] 4-10-0 0.. ConorShoemark(7) 104
(Fergal O'Brien) *racd keenly: trckd ldrs: jnd ldr 4th: rdn and ev ch 3 out: keeping on at same pce in 3rd whn fell last* **10/1**[3]

4m 33.0s (-13.00) **Going Correction** -0.925s/f (Hard)
WFA 4 from 5yo+ 18lb **5** Ran SP% **109.4**
Speed ratings (Par 105): **89,87,69,66,**
CSF £2.10 TOTE £1.70: £1.10, £1.30; EX 2.00 Trifecta £5.70 Pool: £2,149.02 - 279.02 winning units..
Owner A D Spence **Bred** Mrs James Wigan **Trained** Upper Lambourn, Berks

FOCUS
The main interest concerned the rematch between market leader Courtesy Call and his Ascot conqueror Forresters Folly, with the former 5lb better off at the weights. The first two are rated close to recent Ascot form.

81 BATHWICK TYRES BATH H'CAP CHASE (12 fncs) 2m 110y
6:20 (6:20) (Class 3) (0-140,140) 5-Y-0+ **£6,498** (£1,908; £954; £477)

Form RPR

404/ **1** **Australia Day (IRE)**[15] 1946 10-11-12 140...................... LiamTreadwell 154+
(Paul Webber) *led 2nd: mde rest: qcknd clr after 4 out: in n.d after: v easily* **5/1**[3]

352/ **2** *11* **Coole River (IRE)**[16] 5331 9-10-11 125........................(tp) AidanColeman 126
(Emma Lavelle) *led tl 2nd: chsd wnr tl 7th: regained 2nd 4 out: sn rdn: no ch w wnr fr bef next: blnd last* **10/3**[2]

612/ **3** *1 ¾* **Sublime Talent (IRE)**[21] 5250 7-10-3 120....................(t) AdamWedge(3) 118
(Evan Williams) *hld up: prog into 3rd after 4 out but no ch w wnr: sn rdn: nvr gng pce to get on terms* **3/1**[1]

6F4/ **4** *10* **Regal D'Estruval (FR)**[18] 5322 8-10-10 124..................1 NickScholfield 111
(Dr Richard Newland) *trckd ldrs: wnt 2nd 7th tl rdn appr 4 out: sn btn* **8/1**

06P/ **5** *4 ½* **Passato (GER)**[49] 4752 9-11-9 137...............................(t) PaddyBrennan 124
(Jo Davis) *chsd ldrs: nudged along after 5th: rdn after 8th: no ch fr 4 out* **9/1**

534/ **6** *38* **Falcon Island**[28] 5144 8-11-4 132.......................................(tp) JoeTizzard 77
(Colin Tizzard) *trckd ldrs tl dropped to last pair 3rd: nvr travelling after: sn lost: lost tch fr 7th: j.lft fr 4 out: t.o* **3/1**[1]

3m 55.9s (-18.10) **Going Correction** -0.825s/f (Firm) **6** Ran SP% **110.9**
Speed ratings: **109,103,103,98,96 78**
Tote Swingers: 1&2 £3.70, 1&3 £2.90, 2&3 £3.00 CSF £21.56 TOTE £5.70: £3.30, £1.60; EX 15.50 Trifecta £52.10 Pool: £1,374.57 - 19.76 winning units..
Owner Skippy & The Partners **Bred** Kenilworth House Stud **Trained** Mollington, Oxon

FOCUS
A small field but most of these liked to race from the front so the pace was set to be fierce, but none could match the winner who made all. The winner is rated back to his best and the race could go higher.

82 BATHWICK TYRES H'CAP HURDLE (9 hdls) 2m 1f
6:50 (6:50) (Class 3) (0-140,132) 4-Y-0+ **£5,393** (£1,583; £791; £395)

Form RPR

320/ **1** **Cry Of Freedom (USA)**[26] 5178 7-11-4 127..............(v1) JackQuinlan(3) 132+
(John Ferguson) *mde all: qcknd up after 3 out: in command fr next: rdn out* **10/1**

U15/ **2** *2 ¼* **Rajnagan (IRE)**[194] 1931 9-11-12 132........................(t) DominicElsworth 133
(Paul Webber) *hld up towards rr: hdwy after 3 out: pushed into 3rd bef next: rdn after 2 out: wnt 2nd at the last: a being hld* **22/1**

000/ **3** *3 ¾* **Ted Spread**[180] 2179 6-11-12 132..............................(tp) DarylJacob 130
(Paul Nicholls) *trckd ldrs: trckd wnr fr 5th: rdn after 3 out: nt pce to get on terms: no ex whn lost 2nd at the last* **3/1**[1]

000/ **4** *3 ¼* **Knight In Purple**[15] 5356 9-11-0 125......................(vt) PeterCarberry(5) 119
(John Mackie) *trckd ldrs: rdn after 3 out: kpt on same pce* **5/1**[3]

251/ **5** *12* **Ulys Du Charmil (FR)**[20] 5277 5-11-5 125................ WayneHutchinson 109
(Alan King) *hld up towards rr of midfield: hdwy 3 out: sn rdn to dispute 3rd: wknd next: mstke last* **4/1**[2]

102/ **6** *30* **Pearls Legend**[16] 5335 6-11-1 121.................................... JamieMoore 73
(John Spearing) *mid-div: rdn after 3 out: sn wknd: t.o* **9/1**

003/ **7** *2 ¾* **Ugo (USA)**[31] 5068 5-11-4 124...(t) PaulMoloney 73
(Evan Williams) *a bhd: wknd 3 out: t.o* **33/1**

000/ **8** *½* **Nampour (FR)**[15] 5356 8-10-9 115.................................(t) JoeTizzard 64
(Colin Tizzard) *trckd wnr tl mstke 5th: dropped to rr rapidly: t.o* **13/2**

626/ **P** **Laudatory**[188] 2024 7-11-7 127... AndrewTinkler
(Nicky Henderson) *in tch: hit 2nd: rdn 3 out: sn losing pl: p.u bef next: dismntd* **12/1**

441/ **F** **Urcalin (FR)**[19] 5280 5-10-13 119.. TomCannon 111
(David Arbuthnot) *hld up towards rr: rdn and stdy prog after 3 out: styng on at same pce in 5th whn fell next* **8/1**

3m 48.1s (-19.90) **Going Correction** -0.925s/f (Hard) **10** Ran SP% **120.2**
Speed ratings (Par 107): **109,107,106,104,99 84,83,83, ,**
Tote Swingers: 1&2 £24.10, 1&3 £12.00, 2&3 £24.50 CSF £196.58 CT £828.04 TOTE £7.30: £2.00, £7.90, £1.40; EX 202.60 Trifecta £828.30 Part won. Pool: £1,104.52 - 0.28 winning units..

Owner Bloomfields **Bred** Clovelly Farms **Trained** Cowlinge, Suffolk

FOCUS
A competitive handicap but, unlike the earlier handicap chase, one with no obvious pacesetters, enabling the winner to dictate affairs. A step up from the winner with the second to his best and the race could be rated higher.

83 BATHWICK TYRES YEOVIL H'CAP HURDLE (10 hdls) 2m 3f 110y
7:20 (7:20) (Class 4) (0-110,105) 4-Y-0+ **£3,422** (£997; £499)

Form RPR

025/ **1** **Lord Of The Dunes**[58] 4574 5-11-4 97..................................(t) JoeTizzard 107+
(Colin Tizzard) *nt a fluent: in tch: tk clsr order 6th: led 3 out: wnt lft last 2: rdn run-in: r.o wl fnl 100yds* **6/4**[1]

154/ **2** *4* **Lady Bridget**[42] 4881 5-9-13 85....................................(bt) JakeHodson(7) 86
(Mark Gillard) *trckd ldrs: jnd ldr after 5th tl rdn after 3 out: rallied bk into 2nd 2 out: kpt on gamely* **7/2**[2]

456/ **3** *1 ¼* **Am I Blue**[137] 3089 7-11-2 102......................... MrMatthewStanley(7) 102
(Mrs D Thomas) *prom: led after 5th tl 3 out: sn rdn: kpt on same pce fr next* **6/1**[3]

P66/ **4** *2 ¼* **Blue Signal (IRE)**[74] 8-11-0 93.. LiamHeard 91
(Colin Heard) *hld up: hdwy 6th: rdn and ev ch briefly after 3 out: kpt on same pce fr next* **18/1**

050/ **5** *3 ¼* **Cantabilly (IRE)**[11] 5437 10-11-4 100.............................. MattGriffiths(3) 94
(Ron Hodges) *chsd ldrs: drvn along fr 6th: styd chsng ldrs but nvr gng pce to threaten* **14/1**

P00/ **6** *4 ½* **Tae Kwon Do (USA)**[200] 1856 7-11-7 100......................... AidanColeman 91
(Tim Vaughan) *hld up but in tch: tk clsr order 3 out: sn rdn: nt pce to get involved* **7/1**

50P/ **P** **Denton (NZ)**[140] 3022 10-11-12 105...................................(tp) TomO'Brien
(Polly Gundry) *j.lft: led tl after 5th: wknd rapidly next: t.o whn p.u bef 2 out* **8/1**

4m 35.6s (-10.40) **Going Correction** -0.925s/f (Hard) **7** Ran SP% **112.0**
Speed ratings (Par 105): **83,81,80,80,78 76,**
Tote Swingers: 1&2 £2.00, 1&3 £3.00, 2&3 £5.30 CSF £7.14 CT £22.52 TOTE £2.80: £2.70, £1.80; EX 5.80 Trifecta £19.90 Pool: £1,007.57 - 37.93 winning units..
Owner Barrow Hill **Bred** Barrow Hill **Trained** Milborne Port, Dorset

FOCUS
A fairly weak affair rated around the placed horses and the fifth.

84 BATHWICK TYRES MIDSOMER NORTON H'CAP CHASE (14 fncs) 2m 3f
7:50 (7:50) (Class 5) (0-95,100) 5-Y-0+ **£2,737** (£798; £399)

Form RPR

050/ **1** **Accessallareas (IRE)**[71] 4324 8-11-3 86............................ WillKennedy 105+
(Sarah-Jayne Davies) *cl up: hmpd 2nd: led 10th: drew clr fr 3 out: hit last: readily* **15/2**

5P6/ **2** *4 ½* **Bolachoir (IRE)**[55] 4644 11-11-6 94............................ NicodeBoinville(5) 103
(Patrick Chamings) *hld up: stdy prog fr 8th: rdn after 10th: chsd wnr after 4 out: a being hld fr last: kpt on same pce* **10/1**

230/ **3** *5* **Kap West (FR)**[68] 4383 8-11-6 89..........................(t) AndrewGlassonbury 94
(Laura Young) *hld up: hdwy 8th: rdn to dispute 2nd after 4 out tl next: regained 3rd last: kpt on same pce* **7/1**[3]

0P1/ **4** *1* **Solitary Palm (IRE)**[8] 5506 10-10-0 69 7ex...................(b) ConorO'Farrell 72
(Brian Forsey) *mid-div: hdwy to trck ldrs 7th: rdn to dispute 2nd after 4 out tl bef next: no ex whn lost 3rd bef last* **7/2**[2]

431/ **5** *10* **Stormyisland Ahead**[9] 5465 8-12-0 100 7ex..............(t) AdamWedge(3) 98
(Evan Williams) *hld up: hdwy into midfield whn hit 9th: sn rdn: 5th and btn whn hit 2 out* **11/4**[1]

3P0/ **6** *4 ½* **Wosayu**[26] 5184 7-10-2 74.. BrendanPowell(3) 63
(Colin Tizzard) *mid-div: drvn along after 7th: sn in rr* **12/1**

156/ **7** *5* **Guns Of Love (IRE)**[149] 2833 11-10-4 76................ WayneKavanagh(3) 60
(Robin Dickin) *led tl 10th: rdn and wknd after 4 out* **25/1**

U6P/ **8** *6* **Spirit Of Lake (IRE)**[72] 4298 11-10-10 79.......................... AndrewThornton 61
(Karen George) *trckd ldr tl pushed along after 7th: wknd after 4 out* **16/1**

063/ **P** **Walls Way**[9] 5478 9-10-13 89...(t) JWStevenson(7)
(Liam Grassick) *chsd ldrs: hit 3rd: lost pl after 7th: sn in rr: t.o whn p.u bef 4 out* **25/1**

604/ **P** **Street Dance (IRE)**[47] 4782 7-11-12 95................................. JackDoyle
(Keith Goldsworthy) *nvr fluent: prom early: bhd 6th: t.o whn p.u bef 10th* **15/2**

4m 34.2s (-17.80) **Going Correction** -0.825s/f (Firm) **10** Ran SP% **115.3**
Speed ratings: **104,102,100,99,95 93,91,88, ,**
Tote Swingers: 1&2 £7.40, 1&3 £8.60, 2&3 £9.90 CSF £77.61 CT £543.61 TOTE £9.10: £3.10, £4.90, £1.80; EX 139.90 Trifecta £542.70 Part won. Pool: £723.71 - 0.06 winning units..
Owner Miss Sarah-Jayne Davies **Bred** Mrs Gail Kidd **Trained** Leominster, H'fords

FOCUS
Reasonable form for the grade with a couple of recent winners in the line-up. The winner is rated to his reappearance form with the second and fourth both below their best.

85 BATHWICK TYRES BRISTOL MARES' STANDARD OPEN NATIONAL HUNT FLAT RACE 2m 1f
8:20 (8:20) (Class 5) 4-6-Y-0 **£2,053** (£598; £299)

Form RPR

25/ **1** **The Pirate's Queen (IRE)**[27] 5163 4-10-10 0........... WayneHutchinson 101+
(Alan King) *mid-div: taking clsr order on inner whn hmpd over 3f out: rdn over 2f out: str run ent fnl f: led nring fin* **8/11**[1]

54/ **2** *hd* **Luci Di Mezzanotte**[21] 5255 5-11-0 0................................ LeightonAspell 105+
(Oliver Sherwood) *trckd ldrs: hmpd on bnd over 3f out: rdn over 2f out: swtchd rt ent fnl f: str run fnl 120yds: snatched 2nd nring fin: jst hld* **8/1**

3/ 3 ½ **Welcometothejungle**[21] 5263 5-11-0 0 NickScholfield 102
(Keiran Burke) *led: qcknd up wl whn rdn over 2f out: kpt on but no ex whn hdd nring fin* **9/2**[2]
0/ 4 5 **Summertime Lady**[21] 5262 5-10-7 0 MrSamPainting(7) 97
(Colin Tizzard) *trckd ldrs: rdn over 2f out: kpt on but nt pce of ldrs ent fnl f* **18/1**
5 3 ¼ **Harriet's Ark** 6-11-0 0 MarkGrant 96+
(Julian Smith) *mid-div: outpcd over 3f out: styd on again fr over 1f out* **25/1**
00/ 6 3 ¾ **Tamarton Tansy**[56] 4621 6-11-0 0 JackDoyle 90
(Ron Hodges) *hld up: hdwy over 4f out: effrt over 2f out: sn one pce* **100/1**
6/ 7 nk **Colin's Nightmare**[18] 5324 5-11-0 0 DarylJacob 90
(Nick Mitchell) *racd keenly: trckd ldr: rdn over 2f out: sn one pce* **33/1**
0/ 8 5 **Maid Of Might (IRE)**[19] 5295 5-11-0 0 TomCannon 85
(Laura Young) *hld up towards rr: rdn 3f out: sn btn* **100/1**
5/ U **Princess Bella (IRE)**[18] 5316 4-10-10 0 PaddyBrennan
(Fergal O'Brien) *in tch: stl cl up whn bdly hmpd and uns rdr over 3f out* **5/1**[3]

3m 57.7s (-4.70) **Going Correction** -0.925s/f (Hard)
WFA 4 from 5yo+ 4lb 9 Ran SP% **117.9**
Speed ratings: **74,73,73,71,69 68,67,65,**
Tote Swingers: 1&2 £2.10, 1&3 £1.60, 2&3 £2.00 CSF £7.70 TOTE £1.50: £1.02, £2.80, £1.30; EX 8.70 Trifecta £21.60 Pool: £765.29 - 26.48 winning units..
Owner Mr & Mrs Christopher Harris **Bred** Regina Anne Hennessy **Trained** Barbury Castle, Wilts

FOCUS
This produced an exciting finish as two horses chased down the long-time leader who had made a bold bid for home. The third and fourth set the level for the time being.
T/Plt: £91.80 to a £1 stake. Pool:£58,998.75 - 468.77 winning tickets. T/Qpdt: £83.80 to a £1 stake. Pool:£4,655.80 - 41.10 winning tickets. TM

86 - 88a (Foreign Racing) - See Raceform Interactive

BANGOR-ON-DEE (L-H)
Friday, May 3

OFFICIAL GOING: Good (7.5)
Wind: Fresh, half behind Weather: Overcast, turning sunny

89 RATHBONES H'CAP HURDLE (12 hdls) 3m
5:45 (5:45) (Class 5) (0-100,102) 4-Y-0+ **£1,949** (£572; £286; £143)

Form RPR
P/1- 1 **Well Mett (IRE)**[3] 47 6-12-0 **102** 7ex (bt) PaddyBrennan 115+
(Fergal O'Brien) *w ldr: led 6th: hit 4 out: clr after 3 out: in command whn nt fluent last: eased down cl home* **11/8**[1]
132/ 2 4 ½ **Barton Gift**[21] 5271 6-11-2 **95** NicodeBoinville(5) 97
(John Spearing) *midfield: hdwy to chse ldrs 5th: pushed along 7th: outpcd bef 3 out: rallied fr 2 out: wnt 2nd last: no ch w wnr* **7/2**[2]
P63/ 3 3 ¼ **Regal Approach (IRE)**[21] 5271 10-11-10 **98** (tp) JasonMaguire 98
(Kim Bailey) *led: hdd 6th: rdn and lost 2nd appr 3 out: sn outpcd: regained 2nd bef 2 out: no imp on wnr: lost 2nd last: no ex run-in* **8/1**[3]
004/ 4 8 **Milosam (IRE)**[14] 5381 6-10-9 **83** (p) TomO'Brien 78
(Philip Hobbs) *in tch: chsd ldrs 8th: wnt 2nd appr 3 out: no imp on wnr: lost 2nd bef 2 out: wl btn whn hit last* **8/1**[3]
PP1/ 5 42 **Laughton Park**[33] 5034 8-11-7 **100** GavinSheehan(5) 54
(Suzy Smith) *chsd ldrs: pushed along and outpcd 7th: n.d after* **10/1**
040/ 6 9 **Blue Cove**[28] 5165 8-10-6 **80** TomSiddall 26
(Lynn Siddall) *hld up: pushed along after 4th: drvn after 7th whn bhd: nvr a threat* **66/1**
056/ 7 1 ¼ **Share Option**[13] 5412 11-10-7 **81** LeeEdwards 26
(Tony Carroll) *hld up: blnd 6th: wnt into midfield but outpcd by ldrs 7th: wl bhd 3 out* **20/1**
062/ P **Illegale (IRE)**[27] 5184 7-10-0 **74** oh2 (t) DougieCostello
(Phillip Dando) *hld up: lost tch appr 8th: n.d whn mstke 3 out: t.o whn p.u bef 2 out* **20/1**
40P/ P **Grovemere (IRE)**[27] 5182 8-11-1 **94** (v) CharlieWallis(5)
(Debra Hamer) *chsd ldrs: rdn and lost pl 5th: t.o whn p.u bef 8th* **33/1**
31P/ U **Cara Court (IRE)**[11] 5450 7-11-2 **95** SamanthaDrake(5)
(Joanne Foster) *hld up in midfield whn uns rdr 1st* **20/1**

5m 43.4s (-7.60) **Going Correction** -0.35s/f (Good) 10 Ran SP% **114.4**
Speed ratings (Par 103): **98,96,95,92,78 75,75,,,**
toteswingers 1&2 £3.30, 1&3 £1.80, 2&3 £6.60 CSF £6.00 CT £26.59 TOTE £2.70: £1.10, £1.60, £1.80; EX 8.00 Trifecta £25.60 Pool: £769.63 - 22.47 winning units..
Owner The Yes No Wait Sorries **Bred** Arctic Tack Stud **Trained** Coln St. Dennis, Gloucs

FOCUS
A one-sided handicap to open proceedings, the winner having the rest of the field beaten a long way out. The next three home are rated pretty much to their marks.

90 MATTHEW CLARK NOVICES' H'CAP CHASE (12 fncs) 2m 1f 110y
6:15 (6:17) (Class 4) (0-110,110) 5-Y-0+ **£3,861** (£1,198; £645)

Form RPR
033/ 1 **Nowurhurlin (IRE)**[12] 5424 6-11-12 **110** (p) JasonMaguire 115
(Donald McCain) *mde all: rdn appr last: edgd rt run-in: kpt on wl towards fin* **3/1**[3]
F42/ 2 1 ¾ **Coeur De Fou (FR)**[21] 5268 8-11-9 **107** (tp) PaddyBrennan 111
(Tom George) *chsd ldrs: dropped to rr 3rd: mstke 4th: wnt 2nd 7th: mstke 4 out: rdn appr last: chalng run-in: hld fnl 50yds: sn eased* **11/10**[1]
460/ 3 24 **Puyol (IRE)**[20] 5293 11-11-4 **102** (p) BrianHughes 86
(Lisa Williamson) *racd in 2nd pl to 7th: mstke 3 out: btn after 2 out* **16/1**
016/ U **Peaks Of Fire (IRE)**[19] 5315 6-11-2 **105** SamanthaDrake(5)
(Joanne Foster) *hld up in rr: wnt cl 3rd at 3rd: mstke and uns rdr 5th* **5/2**[2]

4m 21.4s (-0.70) **Going Correction** -0.30s/f (Good) 4 Ran SP% **107.1**
Speed ratings: **89,88,77,**
CSF £6.89 TOTE £3.20; EX 4.30 Trifecta £11.40 Pool: £497.94 - 32.58 winning units..
Owner The Ground Hurlers **Bred** Thomas Meagher **Trained** Cholmondeley, Cheshire

FOCUS
Clearly a very weak handicap, particularly with Peaks Of Fire unseating before halfway. The form looks suspect with the second the best guide.

91 EMPIRICAL PROPERTY NOVICES' HURDLE (11 hdls) 2m 4f
6:45 (6:45) (Class 4) 4-Y-0+ **£3,119** (£915; £457; £228)

Form RPR
451/ 1 **Tick Tocker (IRE)**[20] 5288 5-10-12 116 JasonMaguire 114+
(Donald McCain) *mde all: rdn appr last: r.o wl and in command run-in* **5/6**[1]
410/ 2 2 ¼ **Scoter Fontaine (FR)**[16] 5352 7-10-12 122 PatrickCorbett(7) 119
(Rebecca Curtis) *a.p: nt fluent 6th: ev ch 3 out: rdn and lugged lft whn nt qckn appr last: no real imp on wnr run-in* **6/4**[2]
06/ 3 4 **Dundee**[21] 5265 5-10-12 0 WayneHutchinson 108+
(Alan King) *midfield: lost pl 7th: hdwy 2 out: styd on to take 3rd towards fin: unable to trble front two* **12/1**
00/ 4 ½ **Trumix**[20] 5288 5-10-12 0 NickScholfield 107
(Kim Bailey) *prom: rdn and outpcd after 3 out: no imp on front two after but kpt on u.p* **66/1**
304/ 5 29 **Cruise Control**[54] 7-10-5 0 MrJamieJenkinson(7) 77
(John Bryan Groucott) *hld up: hmpd 4th: hdwy appr 4 out: ev ch 3 out: sn rdn and wknd* **50/1**
000/ 6 5 **D'Argent Cloud**[115] 3559 5-10-5 0 ThomasGarner(7) 72
(Oliver Sherwood) *hld up: hmpd 4th: hdwy 4 out: ev ch 3 out: rdn and wknd sn after* **40/1**
000/ 7 2 **Crushed Ice**[44] 4863 7-10-12 0 BrianHughes 70
(Malcolm Jefferson) *hld up: pushed along after 6th: struggling bef 3 out: wl btn* **100/1**
60P/ 8 1 ½ **Thefriendlygremlin**[20] 5289 5-10-7 0 (p) GavinSheehan(5) 68
(John Upson) *rdn along most of way: handy tl wknd 3 out* **150/1**
100/ F **Venceremos**[117] 3533 6-10-5 0 (p) SamTwiston-Davies
(Charlie Longsdon) *in tch: fell 4th* **8/1**[3]
550/ F **Nomadic Storm**[61] 4541 7-10-12 0 CharliePoste 70
(Graeme McPherson) *midfield: nt fluent 6th: effrt bef 3 out: sn wknd: no ch whn fell last* **66/1**

4m 52.4s (0.40) **Going Correction** -0.35s/f (Good) 10 Ran SP% **122.4**
Speed ratings (Par 105): **85,84,82,82,70 68,67,67,,**
toteswingers 1&2 £1.10, 1&3 £4.00, 2&3 Not won CSF £2.59 TOTE £2.30: £1.02, £1.10, £2.90; EX 1.60 Trifecta £10.70 Pool: £442.42 - 30.96 winning units..
Owner T G Leslie **Bred** Citadel Stud **Trained** Cholmondeley, Cheshire

FOCUS
A novice predictably dominated by the two market leaders. The winner dictated, quickening a steady pace approaching the third-last. The first two are rated pretty much to their marks, backed up by the fifth and sixth.

92 GREEN ELECTRICIAN H'CAP CHASE (15 fncs) 2m 4f 110y
7:15 (7:15) (Class 4) (0-120,120) 5-Y-0+ **£3,768** (£1,106; £553; £276)

Form RPR
625/ 1 **Cardigan Island (IRE)**[19] 5306 8-10-6 **103** (tp) RobertDunne(3) 115+
(Dai Burchell) *prom: nt fluent 4 out: outpcd after 3 out: rallied after 2 out to ld last: won gng away run-in* **3/1**[2]
250/ 2 8 **Achimota (IRE)**[21] 5269 7-11-4 **119** MrJMRidley(7) 125
(Matt Sheppard) *in tch: hit 11th: rdn whn ev ch appr 2 out: stl chalng bef last: wnt 2nd run-in but unable to go w wnr* **6/1**
342/ 3 1 ½ **Ballywatt (IRE)**[36] 4987 7-11-12 **120** (t) JasonMaguire 123
(Kim Bailey) *hld up in tch: mstke 9th: led appr 2 out: rdn whn hdd last: no ex fnl 100yds* **9/4**[1]
332/ 4 1 ½ **Temple Lord (FR)**[12] 5433 7-11-5 **120** (t) DannyBenson(7) 121
(Jonjo O'Neill) *hld up in tch: effrt whn chsng ldrs appr 2 out: one pce u.p run-in* **9/2**[3]
2U0/ 5 19 **Up To The Mark**[22] 5251 8-11-2 **113** (p) JakeGreenall(3) 100
(Henry Daly) *led: rdn and hdd appr 2 out: wknd between last 2* **11/2**
41P/ 6 38 **Mylord Collonges (FR)**[179] 2236 13-11-5 **113** (p) SamTwiston-Davies 62
(Susan Nock) *hld up: rdn and wknd after 3 out: eased whn wl btn bef last: t.o* **14/1**

5m 9.4s (0.30) **Going Correction** -0.30s/f (Good) 6 Ran SP% **110.3**
Speed ratings: **87,83,83,82,75 61**
toteswingers 1&2 £5.00, 1&3 £3.50, 2&3 £3.20 CSF £19.63 CT £43.26 TOTE £7.10: £3.70, £9.50; EX 34.20 Trifecta £91.10 Pool: £219.78 - 1.80 winning units..
Owner Mrs G Davies **Bred** Patrick John Hughes **Trained** Briery Hill, Blaenau Gwent

FOCUS
A fair handicap rated around those in the frame behind the winner. Plenty were still in with every chance two out but the winner came nicely clear in the end.

93 HAMPDEN H'CAP HURDLE (9 hdls) 2m 1f
7:45 (7:45) (Class 4) (0-120,120) 4-Y-0+ **£3,119** (£915; £457; £228)

Form RPR
0P1/ 1 **Super Collider**[20] 5290 6-11-1 **107** (bt) PaddyBrennan 108+
(Fergal O'Brien) *midfield: hdwy appr 3 out: chalng 2 out: nosed ahd bef last: drvn out run-in* **5/1**[2]
524/ 2 ¾ **Carlton Jack**[32] 5064 6-11-8 **114** RichieMcLernon 115+
(Jonjo O'Neill) *trckd ldrs: blnd 4 out: sn rdn: rallied to chal 2 out: nt qckn bef last: r.o towards fin* **6/1**
260/ 3 1 **Baccalaureate (FR)**[417] 4829 7-10-10 **107** JonathanEngland(5) 105
(Sue Smith) *led: rdn and hdd jst bef last: no ex towards fin* **5/1**[2]
132/ 4 nk **Renoyr (FR)**[74] 4283 8-11-10 **116** HarryHaynes 116+
(Malcolm Jefferson) *hld up: effrt to chse ldrs whn blnd 2 out: styd on and clsd towards fin* **3/1**[1]
023/ 5 nk **Fujin Dancer (FR)**[30] 5121 8-11-4 **117** MissHBethell(7) 116
(Philip Kirby) *hld up in rr: rdn after 3 out and no imp tl prog to chse ldrs bef last: styd on and clsd towards fin* **15/2**
565/ 6 6 **Marley Roca (IRE)**[22] 5251 9-11-12 **118** (b) DominicElsworth 112
(Paul Webber) *prom: nt fluent 4th and 5th: rdn and btn bef 2 out* **14/1**
340/ 7 43 **Tidal Way (IRE)**[26] 5197 4-11-10 **120** (p) SamTwiston-Davies 70
(Charlie Longsdon) *chsd ldrs tl rdn and wknd after 3 out: t.o* **11/2**[3]
S02/ 8 64 **Captain Sully (IRE)**[273] 1170 8-10-1 **93** TommyPhelan
(Jim Wilson) *hld up: struggling 3 out: lost tch bef 2 out: t.o* **20/1**

4m 2.7s (-8.20) **Going Correction** -0.35s/f (Good)
WFA 4 from 6yo+ 18lb 8 Ran SP% **111.2**
Speed ratings (Par 105): **105,104,104,104,103 101,80,50**
toteswingers 1&2 £5.10, 1&3 £5.10, 2&3 £5.10 CSF £32.93 CT £151.22 TOTE £3.50: £1.10, £3.70, £3.00; EX 73.50 Trifecta £189.70 Part won. Pool: £252.98 - 0.32 winning units..
Owner Fergal O'Brien **Bred** Newsells Park Stud **Trained** Coln St. Dennis, Gloucs

FOCUS
A reasonable race for the grade and the form should hold up with the winner back to his old form. The second shaped well.

94 JAMES GRIFFITH MEMORIAL NOVICES' HUNTERS' CHASE (18 fncs) 3m 110y
8:15 (8:16) (Class 6) 5-Y-0+ **£935** (£290; £145; £72)

Form RPR
3P2/ 1 **Findlay's Find (IRE)**[7] 5541 7-11-7 104 (p) MissAEStirling(7) 108
(Mrs Myfanwy Miles) *in tch: j. slowly 4th: struggling and detached fr 10th: styd on fr 2 out: wnt 2nd last: led fnl 150yds: won gng away* **7/4**[1]

2 6 **Time Gentlemen**[26] 8-11-11 0 MrRJarrett(3) 103
(G D Hanmer) *in tch: led bef 4 out: hdd appr 2 out: sn swtchd rt: led after 2 out: hdd fnl 150yds: one pce after* **5/2**[2]

65P/ 3 9 **Chief Heckler (IRE)**[26] 7-11-9 0 MrAlexEdwards(5) 97
(Philip Rowley) *hld up: hdwy appr 12th: prom 14th: led appr 2 out: hdd after 2 out: eased whn no ex fnl 100yds* **17/2**

4 5 **Glidewell**[27] 11-11-7 0 MissADalton(7) 91
(A N Dalton) *led: hdd appr 13th: outpcd bef 4 out: kpt on modly fr 2 out: no imp* **11/1**

0F5/ 5 21 **Glamorous Gg**[20] 8-11-0 0 (b) MrJamieJenkinson(7) 68
(Ms L J Willis) *prom: mstke 7th: led appr 13th: hdd bef 4 out: rdn and wknd bef 3 out* **40/1**

P **Lord Louis**[19] 12-11-11 0 MrWKinsey(3)
(P A Jones) *prom: lost pl 10th: mstke 12th: t.o whn p.u bef 14th* **12/1**

40P/ P **Hinton Indiana**[19] 8-12-0 108 NicodeBoinville
(S Rea) *prom: rdn and wknd appr 3 out: eased bef last and p.u* **5/1**[3]

P **Heels Overhead**[361] 7-11-2 0 NickSlatter(5)
(John Bryan Groucott) *hld up: mstke 1st and 2nd: reminder bef 9th: t.o whn p.u after 10th* **40/1**

6m 10.4s (-9.40) **Going Correction** -0.30s/f (Good) **8** Ran SP% **113.0**
Speed ratings: **103,101,98,96,89** , ,
toteswingers 1&2 £1.50, 1&3 £4.20, 2&3 £4.80 CSF £6.52 TOTE £1.40: £1.02, £1.10, £5.20; EX 5.60 Trifecta £34.80 Pool: £411.27 - 8.84 winning units..
Owner P B Miles **Bred** Ambrose Turnbull **Trained** Kilgetty, Dyfed

FOCUS
The complexion of this novice hunter chase changed dramatically from the second-last. The form could rate a little higher.
T/Plt: £153.00 to a £1 stake. Pool: £51,897.63 - 247.60 winning tickets T/Qpdt: £28.80 to a £1 stake. Pool: £4,768.00 -122.10 winning tickets DO

FONTWELL (L-H)
Friday, May 3

OFFICIAL GOING: Good to firm (good in places) changing to good (good to firm in places) after race 1 (5:00)
Wind: light, across Weather: bright and sunny

95 £32 BONUS AT 32RED.COM MAIDEN HURDLE (10 hdls) 2m 4f
5:00 (5:00) (Class 5) 4-Y-0+ **£1,949** (£572; £286; £143)

Form RPR

553/ 1 **Catch The Rhythm (IRE)**[21] 5272 5-11-0 0 RichardJohnson 109+
(Charlie Longsdon) *t.k.h: chsd ldrs: hmpd 3rd: led 6th and mde rest: drvn after 2 out: j.rt last: kpt on u.p flat: all out towards fin* **4/1**[3]

423/ 2 1 ½ **Phantom Prince (IRE)**[20] 5280 4-10-6 115 BrendanPowell(3) 103+
(Brendan Powell) *chsd ldrs: mstke 4th: trckd wnr sn after 3 out: drvn and little rspnse 2 out: mstke last: wandered u.p flat: plugged on towards fin* **5/4**[1]

5P/- 3 2 ¼ **Border Station (IRE)**[12] 5443 7-10-11 91 MarkQuinlan(3) 104
(Alison Batchelor) *hld up in midfield: j.rt 2nd: hdwy to chse ldng trio 7th: wnt 3rd 2 out: keeping on whn j.rt last: one pce u.p flat* **25/1**

432/ 4 21 **Boss In Boots (IRE)**[44] 4872 5-11-0 110 AndrewThornton 87
(Seamus Mullins) *t.k.h: mstkes: chsd ldrs: wnt 2nd after 4th tl after next: 3rd and btn after 3 out: wknd next* **2/1**[2]

130/ 5 1 ¼ **The Informant**[38] 4964 7-10-11 0 RyanMahon(3) 84
(Seamus Mullins) *hld up in midfield: 6th and wl outpcd sn after 3 out: wl hld but plugged on after* **14/1**

5/ 6 2 ½ **Novel Dancer**[95] 2909 5-11-0 0 MarcGoldstein 83
(Lydia Richards) *in tch in midfield: mstke 2nd and 6th: 5th and outpcd sn after 3 out: wknd bef next: j.rt last* **50/1**

0/ 7 3 ½ **Tang Royal (FR)**[151] 2830 6-11-0 0 AndrewGlassonbury 79
(Richard Rowe) *hld up in tch in last trio: hdwy on outer bef 7th: rdn and btn next: wknd wl bef 2 out* **50/1**

0P0/ 8 6 **Gorhams Gift**[38] 4964 5-10-11 0 JeremiahMcGrath(3) 73
(Jamie Poulton) *hld up in midfield: drvn and wknd sn after 3 out: wl bhd next: t.o* **100/1**

000/ 9 9 **Mac's Grey (IRE)**[17] 5335 6-11-0 0 DaveCrosse 65
(Zoe Davison) *t.k.h: hld up in tch in rr: clsd after 6th: struggling after next: wl bhd bef 2 out: t.o* **100/1**

000/ 10 29 **Strictly Cissbury**[22] 5241 4-10-9 0 LeightonAspell 34
(Philip Hide) *in tch in midfield: mstke 5th: lost pl next: losing tch whn j.rt 3 out: sn t.o* **66/1**

040/ 11 1 ¾ **Juicy Legend**[12] 5441 6-11-0 0 TomCannon 37
(Chris Gordon) *t.k.h: hld up in tch in rr: mstke and struggling 7th: sn wl bhd: t.o after next* **100/1**

000/ 12 ½ **Ricketyrock**[12] 5438 7-11-0 0 DarylJacob 37
(Nick Mitchell) *led: mstke 4th: hdd and hit 6th: losing pl next: wl bhd after 3 out: t.o* **100/1**

50/ 13 8 **Buffy Brosnan**[12] 5438 5-11-0 0 JackDoyle 30
(Chris Gordon) *j.big: chsd ldr tl after 4th: dropped qckly to rr and drvn after 6th: lost tch and t.o 3 out* **100/1**

4m 46.75s (-12.65) **Going Correction** -0.80s/f (Firm)
WFA 4 from 5yo+ 19lb **13** Ran SP% **118.7**
Speed ratings (Par 103): **93,92,91,83,82 81,80,77,74,62 61,61,58**
toteswingers 1&2 £1.90, 1&3 £10.10, 2&3 £6.70 CSF £9.52 TOTE £6.70: £1.30, £1.10, £4.80; EX 12.20 Trifecta £75.70 Pool: £2,483.85 - 24.59 winning units..
Owner Roy Swinburne **Bred** Pat Casey **Trained** Over Norton, Oxon

FOCUS
Fences sited on outer and hurdles on inner. Top bend on inner line and bottom bend common adding 25yds per circuit to chase course. The front three drew clear in a modest maiden hurdle. The third is rated in line with his bumper and chase form.

96 32RED H'CAP CHASE (16 fncs) 2m 6f
5:30 (5:30) (Class 4) (0-120,117) 5-Y-0+ **£4,183** (£1,521)

Form RPR

211/ 1 **Haar**[5] 5 9-11-9 117 7ex (tp) JamesBanks(5) 120+
(Andy Turnell) *chsd ldrs: lft 2nd 10th: mstke 12th and 13th: chal 2 out: sn led: drvn flat: a doing enough to hold rival* **3/1**[2]

560/ 2 ½ **Delgany Gunner**[61] 4539 9-10-9 103 (tp) TrevorWhelan(5) 104
(Neil King) *led: rdn 3 out: hdd sn after next: swtchd rt and drvn flat: kpt on towards fin but a hld* **15/2**

223/ U **Venetian Lad**[14] 5380 8-11-8 111 MarcGoldstein
(Lydia Richards) *chsd ldr tl blnd bdly and uns rdr 10th* **5/1**[3]

121/ F **City Press (IRE)**[5] 7 7-11-8 114 7ex (tp) BrendanPowell(3) 117+
(Warren Greatrex) *hld up in tch in rr: lft 3rd and hmpd 10th: stl travelling wl whn fell 3 out* **4/5**[1]

5m 37.2s (-5.80) **Going Correction** -0.475s/f (Good) **4** Ran SP% **109.0**
Speed ratings: **91,90,** ,
CSF £18.91 TOTE £3.10; EX 17.00 Trifecta £19.80 Pool: £861.82 - 32.49 winning units..
Owner Mrs R M Hill **Bred** Gainsborough Stud Management Ltd **Trained** Broad Hinton, Wilts

FOCUS
Only two got home in an eventful affair and not form to be confident about.

97 PAUL "SPINNER" SMITH LOVE LIFE MEMORIAL H'CAP HURDLE (9 hdls) 2m 2f 110y
6:00 (6:00) (Class 4) (0-115,115) 4-Y-0+ **£3,119** (£915; £457; £228)

Form RPR

605/ 1 **Double Handful (GER)**[17] 5340 7-11-12 115 (t) DavidBass 121+
(Lawney Hill) *in tch in midfield: rdn sn after 3 out: kpt on to press ldrs 2 out: led bef last: styd on wl: drvn out* **11/4**[1]

003/ 2 3 ¾ **Latest Trend (IRE)**[22] 5248 7-11-8 111 RichardJohnson 114+
(Tim Vaughan) *chsd ldng trio: hrd drvn and pressed ldrs after 2 out: chsd clr wnr fnl 100yds: kpt on* **9/2**[3]

P1P/ 3 4 **Marcus Antonius**[49] 4823 6-11-12 115 LeightonAspell 115
(Jim Boyle) *in tch in midfield: hdwy to chal after 3 out: led next: rdn and hdd bef last: nt qckn u.p: lost 2nd and wknd fnl 100yds* **12/1**

003/ 4 2 ½ **Dormouse**[14] 5376 8-11-5 115 (p) KieronEdgar(7) 112
(Anabel K Murphy) *in tch in last pair: rdn bef 3 out: styd on past btn horses between last 2: kpt on but no threat to ldrs* **8/1**

221/ 5 6 **Dubai Glory**[208] 1751 5-11-8 111 MarcGoldstein 104
(Sheena West) *led tl rdn and hdd 2 out: no ex u.p between last 2: wknd last* **6/1**

255/ 6 12 **Deceptive**[121] 2434 5-11-5 108 LiamTreadwell 91
(Paul Webber) *t.k.h: chsd ldr tl 2 out: sn wknd* **8/1**

132/ 7 8 **Guards Chapel**[29] 4604 5-11-7 110 (v) JamieMoore 87
(Gary Moore) *in tch in midfield: mstke 2nd: effrt u.p bef 2 out: fnd little and wknd between last 2: eased towards fin* **4/1**[2]

42U/ 8 46 **Winning Spark (USA)**[58] 229 6-11-7 110 AndrewGlassonbury 42
(Gary Moore) *in tch in rr: mstke 1st and 2nd: lost tch 3 out: t.o* **20/1**

P66/ U **Airedale Lad (IRE)**[151] 2828 12-9-9 91 oh30 ow2. MrJoshuaNewman(7)
(Zoe Davison) *chsd ldrs tl uns rdr 3 out* **100/1**

4m 18.9s (-15.40) **Going Correction** -0.80s/f (Firm) **9** Ran SP% **114.8**
Speed ratings (Par 105): **100,98,96,95,93 88,84,65,**
toteswingers 1&2 £3.50, 1&3 £7.80, 2&3 £6.30 CSF £15.85 CT £125.38 TOTE £3.70: £1.80, £1.70, £3.30; EX 14.80 Trifecta £193.10 Pool: £660.91 - 2.56 winning units..
Owner Fortnum Racing & Alan Hill **Bred** Gestut Gorlsdorf **Trained** Aston Rowant, Oxon

FOCUS
A moderate handicap, run at an ordinary gallop. The first two look well in on the best of last year's form with the third running his best race over hurdles so far.

98 32RED.COM H'CAP CHASE (13 fncs) 2m 2f
6:30 (6:30) (Class 4) (0-115,108) 5-Y-0+ **£3,768** (£1,106; £553; £276)

Form RPR

652/ 1 **Fiftyonefiftyone (IRE)**[14] 5384 9-11-9 105 (p) LeightonAspell 118+
(Oliver Sherwood) *t.k.h: chsd ldrs: wnt 2nd 4th: rdn to ld 2 out: clr last: kpt on u.p flat: rdn out* **9/4**[1]

P36/ 2 4 ½ **Try Catch Me (IRE)**[27] 5186 8-11-0 99 (b) MarkQuinlan(3) 107
(Alison Batchelor) *chsd ldr tl led after 1st: rdn and hdd 2 out: no ex u.p: plugged on same pce flat* **4/1**[2]

P5P/ 3 ¾ **Free World (FR)**[43] 4883 9-11-12 108 (t) RichardJohnson 115
(Tim Vaughan) *hld up in tch in rr of main gp: hdwy to chse ldng pair 10th: rdn and no imp after 2 out: plugged on u.p flat* **7/1**

650/ 4 11 **Morestead (IRE)**[14] 5378 8-11-4 103 (t) BrendanPowell(3) 102
(Brendan Powell) *in tch in midfield: 4th and drvn after 9th: no imp fr 3 out* **14/1**

00P/ 5 16 **Ray Diamond**[17] 5336 8-11-9 105 (v) MarcGoldstein 88
(Michael Madgwick) *in tch in midfield: mstke and rdn along 5th: nvr really travelling after: dropped to rr after 7th: t.o bef 3 out* **16/1**

14P/ 6 6 **Oscar Close (IRE)**[406] 5036 8-11-9 105 TomScudamore 83
(David Bridgwater) *led tl after 1st: chsd ldr tl 4th: steadily lost pl: j.rt and reminders after 7th: lost tch 10th and t.o bef next* **11/2**[3]

442/ 7 25 **Petit Ecuyer (FR)**[53] 4701 7-11-6 102 JamieMoore 57
(Gary Moore) *hld up in detached last: rdn and sme hdwy 9th: 5th and wl btn 3 out: wknd next: t.o and eased flat* **4/1**[2]

4m 24.6s (-10.10) **Going Correction** -0.475s/f (Good) **7** Ran SP% **111.2**
Speed ratings: **103,101,100,95,88 86,74**
toteswingers 1&2 £2.90, 1&3 £3.50, 2&3 £5.20 CSF £11.34 TOTE £2.70: £1.60, £2.80; EX 11.20 Trifecta £39.40 Pool: £583.26 - 11.09 winning units..
Owner A Taylor **Bred** P O'Connell **Trained** Upper Lambourn, Berks

FOCUS
An ordinary handicap, run at a solid gallop. The second to his previous C&D mark, looks the best guide.

99 32REDPOKER.COM H'CAP HURDLE (11 hdls) 2m 6f 110y
7:00 (7:00) (Class 5) (0-100,100) 4-Y-0+ **£1,949** (£572; £286; £143)

Form RPR

PP4/ 1 **Sapphire Rouge (IRE)**[38] 4966 7-10-11 92 (p) MrKevinJones(7) 94+
(Seamus Mullins) *j.rt: mde all: mstke 3rd: c towards centre bef 2 out: rdn and hrd pressed last: edgd lft u.p and bmpd rival fnl 100yds: styd on wl* **14/1**

232/ 2 1 ¼ **Master Cardor Visa (IRE)**[20] 5285 8-11-1 94 JamesBanks(5) 93
(Emma Baker) *hld up in tch in midfield: hdwy to chse ldrs 8th: rdn and chsd wnr sn after 2 out: ev ch last: edgd rt u.p and bmpd wnr fnl 100yds: no ex* **7/1**[2]

0P2/ 3 3 ¾ **Alaccordion**[14] 5378 8-10-0 74 oh2 WillKennedy 70
(Violet M Jordan) *hld up in tch in last quartet: hdwy to chse ldrs 3 out: drvn bef next: 3rd and styd on same pce flat* **12/1**

400/ 4 4 ½ **Spanish Fork (IRE)**[87] 4042 4-11-6 100 MarcGoldstein 86
(Sheena West) *in tch in midfield: lost pl 3rd: rdn and hdwy after 7th: drvn and chsd ldrs after 3 out: wknd last* **7/1**[2]

003/ 5 10 **Twin Bud**[32] 5085 8-11-3 94 AdamWedge(3) 77
(Anna Newton-Smith) *chsd ldrs: drvn after 7th: outpcd and struggling after 3 out: no threat to ldrs but styd on again flat* **16/1**

620/ 6 2 ¼ **Lady From Geneva**[31] 5109 6-11-4 95 (t) BrendanPowell(3) 77
(Brendan Powell) *chsd ldrs: rdn and lost pl bef 3 out: wl btn 2 out but plugged on* **9/1**[3]

004/ 7 5 **Psi (USA)**[22] 5245 8-11-12 100 (p) JamieMoore 79
(Gary Moore) *hld up in tch in last trio: rdn and hdwy bef 8th: struggling and mstke 3 out: sn drvn and btn* **7/4**[1]

0FO/ **8** *4 ½* **Ashmolian (IRE)**[20] 5285 10-10-9 **83**....................(p) DaveCrosse 55
(Zoe Davison) *hld up in tch in rr: j.big 2nd: mstke and rdn 8th: no prog and wl btn after next* **28/1**

64P/ **9** *13* **Dom Lukka (FR)**[150] 2831 5-11-12 **100**.................... RichardJohnson 66
(Charlie Longsdon) *t.k.h: chsd ldr: mstke 5th: hit 7th: rdn and lost 2nd sn after 2 out: 5th and btn whn mstke last: fdd flat* **7/1**[2]

00P/ **10** *17* **Madam Noso**[22] 5257 9-11-12 **100**....................(p) TomCannon 45
(Richard King) *in tch in midfield tl dropped to rr and drvn after 5th: t.o 3 out* **20/1**

406/ **11** *37* **Maison Royale**[19] 5320 5-11-4 **92**....................(tp) ConorO'Farrell 4
(Seamus Durack) *t.k.h: chsd ldrs tl wknd rapidly 3 out: wl t.o and eased flat* **33/1**

POF/ **P** **Amirico (IRE)**[7] 5554 8-11-9 **97**....................(t) AndrewGlassonbury
(Richard Rowe) *in tch in midfield: lost pl and drvn after 7th: lost tch next: t.o 3 out tl p.u last* **25/1**

5m 23.4s (-19.10) **Going Correction** -0.80s/f (Firm)
WFA 4 from 5yo+ 19lb **12** Ran SP% **119.1**
Speed ratings (Par 103): **101,100,99,97,94 93,91,90,85,79 66,**
toteswingers 1&2 £13.60, 1&3 £13.20, 2&3 £7.80 CSF £104.70 CT £1228.69 TOTE £25.20: £5.00, £3.00, £4.40; EX 120.50 Trifecta £494.50 Part won. Pool: £659.43 - 0.53 winning units..

Owner Lake Racing **Bred** James O'Connor **Trained** Wilsford-Cum-Lake, Wilts

FOCUS
A weak handicap with the placed horses setting a modest standard.

100 32RED CASINO H'CAP CHASE (19 fncs) 3m 2f 110y
7:30 (7:31) (Class 5) (0-95,100) 5-Y-0+ **£2,144** (£629; £314; £157)

Form RPR

034/ **1** **Top Benefit (IRE)**[33] 5038 11-11-0 **86**.................... JamesBanks(5) 94
(Richard Harper) *j.rt at times: in tch in midfield: pressed ldr and gng wl bef 3 out: led 2 out: sn drvn and racing awkwardly: forged ahd last: racing v reluctantly and hrd drvn flat: slowing fnl 75yds: jst lasted home* **6/1**

3P1/ **2** *shd* **Might As Well**[32] 5084 10-11-7 **88**....................(p) AndrewThornton 98+
(Seamus Mullins) *chsd ldrs: mstke 7th: led after 15th: rdn wl bef 3 out: hdd and mstke 2 out: hrd drvn and no ex whn mstke last: clsd on slowing ldr fnl 75yds: jst failed* **3/1**[1]

6P5/ **3** *½* **Lajidaal (USA)**[33] 5029 6-11-8 **89**.................... JamieMoore 96
(Gary Moore) *racd off the pce in 5th: rdn along after 10th: clsd after 13th: 3rd and drvn bef 3 out: 4 l down and wl hld last: kpt on fnl 100yds* **5/1**[3]

114/ **4** *39* **Quayside Court (IRE)**[33] 5036 9-10-12 **86**....................(vt) GeraldQuinn(7) 58
(Claire Dyson) *chsd ldr: mstke 6th: led 8th tl 13th: chsd ldr after 15th: ev ch and hit next: wknd u.p bef 3 out: t.o 2 out* **3/1**[1]

PP0/ **5** *18* **Rudinero (IRE)**[50] 4761 11-9-11 **67** oh1....................(t) BrendanPowell(3) 23
(Barry Brennan) *led tl 8th: chsd ldr tl regained ld 13th: hdd and hit 15th: drvn and btn next: t.o bef 2 out* **10/1**

240/ **6** *6* **Current Climate (IRE)**[38] 4967 9-11-2 **83**..........(b) AndrewGlassonbury 34
(Richard Rowe) *nvr gng wl in rr: clsd and in tch after 7th: drvn and struggling after 10th: lost tch after 13th: t.o 16th* **9/2**[2]

0PP/ **U** **Ten More (IRE)**[9] 5506 9-10-3 **77**.................... ChrisDavies(7)
(Bill Turner) *bhd and bucking and broncing on approach to 1st: blnd and uns rdr 1st* **14/1**

6m 47.3s (-13.80) **Going Correction** -0.475s/f (Good) **7** Ran SP% **114.9**
Speed ratings: **101,100,100,89,83 82,**
toteswingers 1&2 £7.30, 1&3 £2.80, 2&3 £2.70 CSF £25.22 CT £96.78 TOTE £5.50: £3.20, £2.50; EX 27.60 Trifecta £280.90 Part won. Pool: £374.63 - 0.90 winning units..

Owner R C Harper **Bred** Frank Tobin **Trained** Kings Sutton, Northants

FOCUS
Another weak handicap with the first three rated pretty much to their marks.

101 32REDBINGO.COM STANDARD OPEN NATIONAL HUNT FLAT RACE 1m 6f
8:00 (8:01) (Class 6) 4-6-Y-0 **£1,559** (£457; £228; £114)

Form RPR

0/ **1** **On The Buckle**[22] 5263 5-10-13 0.................... IanPopham(3) 106+
(Victor Dartnall) *rn green: t.k.h: pressed ldr tl led 3f out: clr over 1f out: in command and rn v green ins fnl f: rdn out* **7/2**[1]

50/ **2** *3 ¾* **Java Rose**[32] 5070 4-10-2 0.................... KielanWoods(3) 88
(Charlie Longsdon) *in tch in last pair: rdn 5f out: outpcd 3f out: plugged on and wnt 4th over 1f out: kpt on fnl f to snatch 2nd last stride: no threat to wnr* **4/1**[2]

3 *shd* **Georgea (IRE)** 4-10-5 0.................... JamieMoore 87
(Gary Moore) *t.k.h: hld up in tch in midfield: rdn and effrt over 3f out: disputing 2nd and unable qck 2f out: styd on same pce after* **8/1**

/ **4** *hd* **Brians Well (IRE)**[186] 6-10-13 0.................... BrendanPowell(3) 98
(Brendan Powell) *chsd ldrs: pressed ldrs 6f out: chsd wnr over 2f out: sn rdn and outpcd: styd on same pce after: lost 2 pls last strides* **4/1**[2]

66/ **5** *5* **The Stig (FR)**[36] 4991 5-11-2 0.................... PaulMoloney 92
(Nick Littmoden) *in tch in last pair: rdn and outpcd 5f out: rallied and sme hdwy 1f out: kpt on same pce fnl f* **12/1**

6 *½* **Top Chief** 5-10-11 0.................... KillianMoore(5) 92
(Mark Rimell) *chsd ldrs tl lost pl and rdn 5f out: rallied over 1f out: kpt on same pce ins fnl f* **7/1**

7 *4 ½* **Star Ride** 4-10-12 0.................... TomScudamore 82
(Mark Bradstock) *rn v green: led tl 3f out: wknd over 2f out: bhd 1f out* **5/1**[3]

3m 20.5s (-10.60) **7** Ran SP% **110.2**
toteswingers 1&2 £5.40, 1&3 £2.10, 2&3 £11.80 CSF £16.27 TOTE £4.90: £2.20, £2.60; EX 20.40 Trifecta £171.80 Pool: £361.53 - 1.57 winning units..

Owner R Allwood **Bred** M Adams **Trained** Brayford, Devon

FOCUS
Modest bumper form rated around the winner and fifth to their pre-race marks.

T/Plt: £160.50 to a £1 stake. Pool: £66,108.28 - 300.53 winning tickets T/Qpdt: £19.20 to a £1 stake. Pool: £5,657.10 - 217.3 winning tickets SP

102 - 108a (Foreign Racing) - See Raceform Interactive

HEXHAM (L-H)
Saturday, May 4

OFFICIAL GOING: Good (good to soft in places; 6.7)
Wind: Strong; half against Weather: Cloudy; bright

109 FRIENDS OF CHOLLERTON H'CAP CHASE (12 fncs) 2m 110y
5:20 (5:20) (Class 5) (0-95,95) 5-Y-0+ **£2,258** (£658; £329)

Form RPR

324/ **1** **Suprise Vendor (IRE)**[5] 23 7-11-7 **95**.................... GaryRutherford(5) 107+
(Stuart Coltherd) *led: hmpd by loose horse appr 4 out: hdd next: led 2 out: drew clr bef last: pushed out* **5/2**[1]

540/ **2** *5* **Zazamix (FR)**[10] 5502 8-10-10 **86**....................(v) JohnWinston(7) 91
(Andrew Crook) *in tch: stdy hdwy 1/2-way: rdn and outpcd 3 out: rallied to chse (clr) wnr bef last: kpt on: no imp* **8/1**

530/ **3** *6* **Gavroche Gaugain (FR)**[12] 5448 9-11-3 **91**.................... TonyKelly(5) 91
(Ferdy Murphy, France) *prom: hdwy to ld 3 out: hdd next: outpcd whn lost 2nd last: one pce* **9/2**[3]

005/ **4** *7* **Justjoe (IRE)**[13] 5424 7-11-7 **90**....................(p) WilsonRenwick 83
(Micky Hammond) *in tch: hdwy to chse wnr bef 4 out to bef next: sn outpcd: no imp fr 2 out* **15/2**

0P3/ **5** *14* **Panthers Run**[27] 5207 13-10-2 **74**....................(t) JohnKington(3) 57
(Jonathan Haynes) *in tch: rdn after 4 out: wknd bef next* **18/1**

055/ **6** *14* **Dodge The Bullet**[27] 5207 7-9-7 **69** oh5.................... JamesCorbett(7) 37
(Susan Corbett) *bhd: struggling 1/2-way: lost tch 4 out: t.o* **25/1**

65F/ **U** **Pete**[27] 5207 10-11-3 **93**....................(tp) GrahamWatters(7)
(Barry Murtagh) *hld up in tch: mstke and uns rdr 6th* **7/1**

44F/ **U** **Turf Trivia**[33] 5073 6-11-0 **83**....................(b) BarryKeniry
(George Moore) *cl up whn hit and uns rdr 1st* **4/1**[2]

4m 18.5s (8.70) **Going Correction** +0.425s/f (Soft) **8** Ran SP% **111.2**
Speed ratings: **96,93,90,87,80 74, ,**
toteswingers 1&2 £5.40, 1&3 £12.00, 2&3 £5.60 CSF £21.34 CT £81.13 TOTE £2.90: £1.60, £2.60, £1.80; EX 27.20 Trifecta £250.20 Pool: £511.45 - 1.53 winning units..
Owner Aidan Gunning **Bred** P Travers **Trained** Selkirk, Borders

FOCUS
Rails and fences moved accordingly. A low-grade handicap chase and not many got in a blow. The winner is rated in line with his previous chasing best, and the form could be rated higher.

110 CARAVAN SITE (S) HURDLE (8 hdls) 2m 110y
5:55 (5:55) (Class 5) 4-Y-0+ **£2,053** (£598; £299)

Form RPR

PU2/ **1** **Milano Supremo (IRE)**[26] 5222 8-10-12 116....................(t) HenryBrooke 92+
(Chris Grant) *cl up: led after 3 out: drvn and edgd lft after last: kpt on wl* **8/13**[1]

350/ **2** *1 ¼* **That'll Do Nicely (IRE)**[37] 4997 10-10-5 105............ MissJRRichards(7) 91
(Nicky Richards) *in tch: hdwy 3 out: effrt and ev ch bef last: kpt on run-in: hld nr fin* **6/1**[3]

306/ **3** *6* **Topo Gigio (FR)**[9] 5520 9-10-5 85.................... CallumBewley(7) 84
(Robert Bewley) *in tch: rdn and outpcd bef 2 out: rallied bef last: kpt on: nt pce of first two* **8/1**

000/ **4** *nse* **Saga De Tercey (FR)**[73] 4323 8-11-3 110....................(b) NickSlatter(7) 96
(Donald McCain) *cl up: ev ch after 3 out: rdn next: outpcd between last 2* **9/2**[2]

PP5/ **5** *6* **Lewlaur Supreme (IRE)**[9] 5520 10-10-5 64.......... StephenMulqueen(7) 80
(William Young Jnr) *hld up in tch: effrt appr 2 out: wknd bef last* **40/1**

P0P/ **6** *8* **Venture To War (IRE)**[6] 17 7-10-2 83....................(b) BrianToomey(3) 65
(Tony Coyle) *in tch: hdwy 3 out: wknd after next* **20/1**

P00/ **P** **Mobane Ali**[12] 5452 5-9-12 70....................(b) JamesCorbett(7)
(Susan Corbett) *bhd: struggling 4th: t.o whn p.u bef 2 out* **80/1**

PP/ **P** **Beyond The Creek**[26] 5220 6-10-5 0.................... JonathonBewley(7)
(George Bewley) *led: hit 3rd: hdd after 3 out: sn wknd: t.o whn p.u bef next* **50/1**

4m 16.4s (-1.00) **Going Correction** +0.075s/f (Yiel) **8** Ran SP% **115.9**
Speed ratings (Par 103): **105,104,101,101,98 94, ,**
toteswingers 1&2 £5.40, 1&3 £12.00, 2&3 £5.60 CSF £4.97 TOTE £1.40: £1.10, £1.70, £1.80; EX 5.40 Trifecta £13.50 Pool: £1,345.54 - 74.37 winning units..There was no bid for the winner
Owner David Armstrong **Bred** Mrs G Galvin **Trained** Newton Bewley, Co Durham

FOCUS
A desperately weak race in which the third and fifth offer the best guides to the level.

111 ARUP MARES' H'CAP HURDLE (10 hdls) 2m 4f 110y
6:25 (6:25) (Class 4) (0-120,122) 4-Y-0+ **£3,119** (£915; £457; £228)

Form RPR

011/ **1** **Mrs Eff**[22] 5275 7-10-1 **100**....................(t) KyleJames(5) 105+
(Philip Kirby) *hld up in tch: stdy hdwy appr 2 out: led whn j.lft last: edgd rt and kpt on strly* **11/8**[1]

U12/ **2** *3 ¾* **Overpriced**[10] 5504 7-10-13 **114**....................(t) StephenMulqueen(7) 115
(Maurice Barnes) *prom: hdwy to ld 4 out: hdd bef last: kpt on run-in: nt pce of wnr* **8/1**

3P3/ **3** *3 ¾* **Detour Ahead**[5] 31 5-10-9 **103**....................(p) SeanQuinlan 102
(Jennie Candlish) *cl up: ev ch bef 2 out: rdn and outpcd bef last* **3/1**[2]

4 *12* **Leish Oscar (IRE)**[66] 4467 7-11-4 **112**.................... BrianHughes 99
(Neil McKnight, Ire) *prom: stdy hdwy bef 2 out: rdn bef last: sn wknd* **17/2**

553/ **5** *17* **Gulf Punch**[10] 5500 6-10-10 **104**.................... HenryBrooke 76
(Donald McCain) *led: hdd and rdn 4 out: outpcd after next: btn fr 2 out* **7/2**[3]

5m 11.4s (-1.10) **Going Correction** +0.075s/f (Yiel) **5** Ran SP% **111.0**
Speed ratings (Par 105): **105,103,102,97,91**
CSF £11.81 TOTE £1.70: £1.30, £2.20; EX 7.90 Trifecta £18.50 Pool: £615.05 - 24.85 winning units..
Owner Mrs K Walton **Bred** Mrs K Walton **Trained** Middleham, N Yorks

FOCUS
A modest mares' handicap hurdle in which the placed horses are rated close to their marks.

112 RAMSIDE HOTELS HEART OF ALL ENGLAND MAIDEN HUNTERS' CHASE (19 fncs) 3m 1f
7:00 (7:00) (Class 6) 5-Y-0+ **£1,871** (£580; £290; £145)

Form RPR

0/ **1** **Show Public (FR)**[35] 7-11-9 0.................... MrJHamilton(5) 115+
(Simon Shirley-Beavan) *hld up in midfield: hdwy and cl up 9th: led 14th: mde rest: drew clr fr 3 out: easily* **4/1**[2]

36/ **2** *21* **A New Rising (IRE)**[13] 11-11-7 65....................(p) MrJLyttle(7) 92
(M E Ellwood) *cl up: led 13th to next: pressed wnr to 3 out: sn one pce* **50/1**

2/ **3** *10* **Barachois Silver**[26] 5221 9-11-4 0 MrGCrow(3) 73
(Mrs J M Hollands) *midfield: pushed along 14th: rallied bef 3 out: kpt on fr last: no ch w first two* **4/1**[2]

233/ **4** *¾* **Beau Traveller**[335] 10-11-7 103 CallumBewley(7) 79
(Miss Bianca Dunk) *led to bef 3rd: cl up: drvn 3 out: outpcd fr next* **7/1**

P02/ **5** *¾* **Soleil D'Avril (FR)**[29] 5167 7-11-9 0 MrWEasterby(5) 79
(Mrs Sarah Easterby) *nt fluent on occasions towards rr: hdwy and prom 4 out: rdn whn blnd next: sn outpcd* **7/2**[1]

040/ **6** *¾* **Newyearsresolution (IRE)**[13] 9-11-7 0 MissAWaugh(7) 78
(Simon Waugh) *midfield: hdwy and prom 14th: drvn and outpcd 3 out: sn n.d* **25/1**

P45/ **P** **Marfleet**[13] 13-11-7 47 MissJWalton(7)
(Mrs D Walton) *nt fluent in rr: struggling fr 1/2-way: t.o whn p.u bef 14th* **33/1**

050/ **P** **Tiger Billy (IRE)**[13] 11-11-7 59 (b) MissSMDoolan(7)
(Miss F J Storey) *a bhd: struggling 1/2-way: no ch whn p.u bef 3 out* **25/1**

2P4/ **P** **Silent Cliche (IRE)**[13] 9-11-7 97 (b) MrDHolmes(7)
(D Holmes) *mstkes: sn bhd: struggling fnl circ: t.o whn p.u bef 3 out* **50/1**

433/ **P** **Senor Alco (FR)**[5] 28 7-11-11 102 MrTDavidson(3)
(Victor Thompson) *trckd ldrs: outpcd bef 14th: t.o whn p.u bef 3 out* **9/2**[3]

P **Sugar Sensation (IRE)**[49] 7-11-7 0 MissRMcDonald(7)
(Alan J Brown) *hld up: mstke 10th: struggling fr 13th: t.o whn p.u bef 4 out* **66/1**

4/ **P** **Thehookybooky (IRE)**[26] 5221 7-11-7 0 MrPGerety(7)
(Miss G E J Anderson) *hld up: struggling bef 14th: t.o whn p.u bef 3 out* **66/1**

P65/ **P** **Darnborough (IRE)**[21] 7-11-9 0 (p) NickSlatter(5)
(Mrs J A Brooke) *cl up: lft in ld 8th: hdd 13th: wknd 4 out: t.o whn p.u bef 2 out* **33/1**

544/ **F** **Merry Minster**[256] 1309 6-11-4 0 MissCWalton(3)
(James Walton) *hdwy to ld bef 3rd: fell 8th* **12/1**

4/ **F** **Who'Slaughingnow (IRE)**[9] 5524 6-11-7 0 MrBCampbell(7)
(D D Ockenden) *mstkes: in tch: outpcd whn blnd 12th: struggling whn fell next* **33/1**

6m 47.8s (15.60) **Going Correction** +0.425s/f (Soft) **15** Ran SP% **124.0**
Speed ratings: **92,85,82,81,81 81, , , , ,**
toteswingers 1&2 £46.10, 1&3 £4.30, 2&3 £46.10 CSF £192.98 TOTE £3.80: £1.60, £23.00, £1.80; EX 419.00 Trifecta £358.30 Part won. Pool: £477.79 - 0.01 winning unit..
Owner Mrs P M Shirley-Beavan **Bred** Jean-Louis Berger And J-F Lamborot **Trained** Abbotrule, Borders

FOCUS
A procession for one of the least exposed runners. The winner looks a fair prospect, with the third and fourth capable of better.

113 JOHN WADE H'CAP CHASE (17 fncs) 2m 7f
7:35 (7:35) (Class 4) (0-120,118) 5-Y-0+ **£3,768** (£1,106; £553; £276)

Form RPR

U34/ **1** **Highrate (IRE)**[25] 5229 7-10-6 **98** RyanMania 115+
(Sue Smith) *chsd ldr: led bef 12th: clr 2 out: drvn out fr last* **5/1**

PP1/ **2** *3* **Dont Tell Sailor (IRE)**[7] 5568 7-10-12 **111** ConorRing(7) 124
(Jennie Candlish) *prom: hdwy to chse wnr 4 out: effrt after 2 out: kpt on same pce fr last* **10/3**[1]

630/ **3** *9* **The Thirsty Bricky (IRE)**[10] 5503 11-11-7 **118** TonyKelly(5) 124
(David Thompson) *hld up: hdwy 12th: effrt and drvn bef 3 out: no imp fr next* **20/1**

565/ **4** *14* **Pena Dorada (IRE)**[12] 5451 6-10-11 **110** (p) GrahamWatters(7) 103
(Lucinda Russell) *prom: effrt and rdn bef 3 out: wknd next* **11/1**

310/ **5** *hd* **Oil Burner**[31] 5122 8-10-11 **103** LucyAlexander 97
(William Amos) *nt fluent: hld up: drvn and outpcd 4 out: n.d after* **9/1**

F43/ **6** *19* **Tutchec (FR)**[33] 5077 6-10-6 **98** BrianHarding 73
(Nicky Richards) *nt fluent: in rr: drvn and outpcd 10th: struggling fr next* **7/2**[2]

0P0/ **7** *2½* **Forzy Origny (FR)**[22] 5276 11-10-12 **104** (v[1]) HenryBrooke 77
(Martin Todhunter) *hld up in tch: hdwy and in tch 12th: drvn and wknd fr 4 out* **28/1**

415/ **8** *7* **Golden View (IRE)**[55] 4678 8-10-11 **103** BrianHughes 70
(Karen McLintock) *prom: blnd and lost pl 5th: struggling fr next: n.d after* **14/1**

2P1/ **P** **Pensnett Bay**[21] 5294 8-11-9 **115** MarkGrant
(Jo Hughes) *led: hit 5th: hdd bef 12th: rdn whn blnd 4 out: sn btn: t.o whn p.u bef 2 out* **4/1**[3]

6m 10.13s (9.33) **Going Correction** +0.425s/f (Soft) **9** Ran SP% **115.2**
Speed ratings: **105,103,100,95,95 89,88,85,**
toteswingers 1&2 £6.20, 1&3 £29.00, 2&3 £25.80 CSF £22.76 CT £305.52 TOTE £6.30: £1.50, £1.70, £4.40; EX 29.30 Trifecta £401.80 Part won. Pool: £535.74 - 0.88 winning units..
Owner Trevor Hemmings **Bred** Oliver And Salome Brennan **Trained** High Eldwick, W Yorks

FOCUS
A modest handicap chase with the winner rated to his Catterick form and the third close to his mark.

114 JIMMY ADAMS 80TH BIRTHDAY NOVICES' CHASE (17 fncs) 2m 7f
8:05 (8:05) (Class 4) 5-Y-0+ **£3,768** (£1,106; £553; £276)

Form RPR

F02/ **1** **Balding Banker (IRE)**[20] 5314 7-10-7 120 TonyKelly(5) 133+
(Ferdy Murphy, France) *in tch: smooth hdwy to chse ldr bef 4 out: led gng wl after next: shkn up and drew wl clr fr 2 out* **15/8**[1]

221/ **2** *34* **Brady (IRE)**[13] 5422 7-10-12 125 HenryBrooke 102
(Donald McCain) *led to 6th: led again bef 11th: blnd 13th: hdd after 3 out: sn no ch w wnr* **2/1**[2]

413/ **3** *31* **Gin Cobbler**[10] 5501 7-10-12 104 MrJHamilton(7) 78
(Victor Thompson) *t.k.h: in tch: nt fluent and outpcd after 4 out: no ch w first two after next* **25/1**

P00/ **4** *8* **Charming Knight (IRE)**[12] 5450 12-10-5 59 AlistairFindlay(7) 63
(Jane Walton) *in tch: drvn and outpcd 11th: n.d after* **125/1**

F63/ **5** *45* **Jat Punjabi**[20] 5307 9-10-12 120 (p) MarkGrant 23
(Jo Hughes) *cl up: led 6th to bef 11th: outpcd 4 out: struggling whn mstke next: t.o* **11/2**[3]

P4P/ **P** **Royal And Ancient (IRE)**[6] 17 6-10-12 75 (p) PeterBuchanan
(David Thompson) *towards rr: struggling 7th: t.o whn p.u bef 11th* **125/1**

6P0/ **P** **Lochore (IRE)**[137] 3121 7-10-12 0 (t) LucyAlexander
(William Amos) *mstkes in rr: t.o whn p.u bef 11th* **66/1**

60P/ **P** **Askalott (IRE)**[353] 309 8-10-12 0 FearghalDavis
(Jean McGregor) *chsd ldrs: outpcd whn hit 9th: t.o whn p.u bef 11th* **100/1**

4F6/ **P** **Stagecoach Jasper**[13] 5423 7-10-12 105 RyanMania
(Sue Smith) *bhd: hmpd 5th: sn struggling: t.o whn p.u after 11th* **7/1**

025/ **F** **Hurraboru (IRE)**[13] 5423 6-10-9 0 (p) JohnKington(3)
(Donald McCain) *hld up: fell 5th* **10/1**

6m 13.5s (12.70) **Going Correction** +0.425s/f (Soft) **10** Ran SP% **113.0**
Speed ratings: **105,93,82,79,63 , , , ,**
toteswingers 1&2 £3.00, 1&3 £4.40, 2&3 £12.90 CSF £5.94 TOTE £3.00: £1.70, £1.10, £3.10; EX 7.50 Trifecta £139.10 Pool: £544.13 - 2.93 winning units..
Owner Club Racing Banker Partnership **Bred** Peter And Ann Downes **Trained** France

FOCUS
This was dominated by the market leaders who were in a different league to the rest. The winner was the form pick but the second was well below his best.

115 ACOMB NOVICES' HURDLE (12 hdls) 3m
8:35 (8:35) (Class 4) 4-Y-0+ **£3,285** (£957; £479)

Form RPR

031/ **1** **Wolf Shield (IRE)**[13] 5423 6-11-5 120 BarryKeniry 107+
(George Moore) *chsd ldr: smooth hdwy to ld bef last: shkn up and wnt clr run-in: easily* **6/5**[1]

1FF/ **2** *6* **Nodforms Violet (IRE)**[9] 5521 9-10-13 0 BrianHughes 91
(Karen McLintock) *chsd ldrs: drvn and outpcd 2 out: styd on fr last to go 2nd nr fin: no ch w wnr* **2/1**[2]

342/ **3** *¾* **Almond Court (IRE)**[12] 5450 10-10-6 70 (p) KennyJohnson 84
(Robert Johnson) *led: clr 5th to 8th: rdn and hdd whn hit last: one pce: lost 2nd cl home* **20/1**

FPP/ **4** *5* **Loose Preformer (IRE)**[51] 4751 7-10-13 122 HenryBrooke 86
(David O'Meara) *hld up in tch: stdy hdwy after 3 out: rdn and outpcd fr next* **9/2**[3]

463/ **5** *30* **Brae On (IRE)**[72] 4336 5-10-6 0 JonathonBewley(7) 59
(George Bewley) *t.k.h: hld up in tch: struggling 4 out: btn after next* **16/1**

40/ **6** *43* **Ballyhoulihan (IRE)**[22] 5279 5-10-13 0 BrianHarding 20
(David O'Meara) *prom: drvn and outpcd after 3 out: struggling bef next* **33/1**

5/ **P** **Master Bud**[27] 5205 8-10-6 0 JamesCorbett(7)
(Susan Corbett) *nt fluent in rr: rdn and effrt 8th: wknd next: t.o whn p.u bef last* **80/1**

6m 18.0s (9.00) **Going Correction** +0.075s/f (Yiel) **7** Ran SP% **111.8**
Speed ratings (Par 105): **88,86,85,84,59 74,**
toteswingers 1&2 £1.20, 1&3 £2.20, 2&3 £11.00 CSF £3.74 TOTE £2.40: £1.80, £1.30; EX 3.80 Trifecta £24.10 Pool: £537.51 - 16.68 winning units..
Owner G R Orchard **Bred** Terence Conroy **Trained** Middleham Moor, N Yorks

FOCUS
A fair novices' hurdle that could rate higher, but the third to his recent chase mark looks the best guide to the level.
T/Plt: £16.00 to a £1 stake. Pool of £55,617.66 - 2,533.76 - winning units T/Qpdt: £13.30 to a £1 stake. Pool of £6,144.40 - 340.60 winning units RY

UTTOXETER (L-H)
Saturday, May 4

OFFICIAL GOING: Good (good to firm in places) changing to good after race 1 (1:55)
Wind: moderate 1/2 against Weather: changeable

116 MUSICMAGPIE.CO.UK "NATIONAL HUNT" MAIDEN HURDLE (9 hdls) 2m
1:55 (1:55) (Class 5) 4-Y-0+ **£2,209** (£648; £324; £162)

Form RPR

532/ **1** **Oyster Shell**[13] 5435 6-10-11 117 JakeGreenall(3) 121+
(Henry Daly) *chsd ldrs: hmpd 3rd: led 3 out: styd on appr last* **3/1**[2]

2/ **2** *2¾* **Deep Trouble (IRE)**[43] 4901 6-11-0 0 [1] DarylJacob 118
(Ben Case) *mid-div: hdwy to chse ldrs 6th: clr 2nd appr 2 out: kpt on same pce run-in* **9/2**[3]

23/ **3** *17* **Definitely Glad (IRE)**[107] 3698 6-10-7 0 DenisO'Regan 97
(Paul Webber) *chsd ldrs: one pce fr 3 out* **25/1**

4 *12* **Bawden Rocks** 4-10-10 0 TommyPhelan 87
(David Bridgwater) *chsd ldrs: one pce fr 3 out: lft modest 4th last* **50/1**

430/ **5** *7* **Picture Post (USA)**[33] 5070 6-11-0 0 DavidBass 86
(Nicky Henderson) *chsd ldrs: wknd 3 out* **16/1**

0/ **6** *4* **Tomibola (IRE)**[62] 4542 5-11-0 0 JamesDavies 82
(Harry Whittington) *in rr: hdwy 4th: outpcd appr 3 out: grad wknd* **66/1**

003/ **7** *1* **Northern Oscar (IRE)**[27] 5202 5-11-0 0 PeterBuchanan 81
(Tim Walford) *in rr: sme hdwy 3 out: nvr on terms* **20/1**

432/ **8** *8* **Cloud Creeper (IRE)**[62] 4543 6-11-0 120 JasonMaguire 73
(Donald McCain) *led: j.lft 3rd: hdd 3 out: wknd bef next: b.b.v* **13/8**[1]

000/ **9** *9* **River Exit (IRE)**[73] 4322 6-11-0 0 SamTwiston-Davies 65
(Nigel Twiston-Davies) *hld up towards rr: sme hdwy 6th: wknd appr next* **33/1**

00/ **10** *11* **Oscars Law**[8] 5543 6-11-0 0 CharliePoste 55
(Matt Sheppard) *a in rr: bhd fr 6th* **125/1**

06/ **11** *5* **Sonny Jim**[206] 1791 5-11-0 0 LiamHeard 51
(John Mackie) *rr-div: sme hdwy 6th: lost pl bef next* **50/1**

PP/ **12** *17* **Oscar Zulu (IRE)**[58] 4617 6-11-0 0 RichardJohnson 36
(Philip Hobbs) *t.k.h in rr: nt jump wl: wl bhd fr 6th: lame* **14/1**

50P/ **13** *24* **Alls It Is**[33] 5071 6-11-0 0 AdrianLane 14
(Donald McCain) *mid-div: lost pl and reminders 3rd: bhd fr 5th: t.o next* **80/1**

4FP/ **F** **Sleeping City (FR)**[23] 5260 6-11-0 118 JackDoyle 92
(Victor Dartnall) *stdd s: hld up in rr: hdwy 5th: disputing 3rd 2 out:4th and wkng whn fell last* **8/1**

500/ **P** **Miss Overbury (IRE)**[23] 5248 7-10-2 0 JamesBanks(5)
(Anthony Middleton) *prom: lost pl 5th: bhd fr 6th: t.o whn p.u bef 2 out* **150/1**

3m 52.5s (0.50) **Going Correction** -0.075s/f (Good)
WFA 4 from 5yo+ 18lb **15** Ran SP% **124.6**
Speed ratings (Par 103): **95,93,85,79,75 73,73,69,64,59 56,48,36, ,**
toteswingers 1&2 £2.00, 1&3 £6.10, 2&3 £3.70 CSF £16.81 TOTE £4.90: £1.80, £1.80, £5.50; EX 19.90 Trifecta £509.30 Part won. Pool: £679.12 - 0.95 winning units..
Owner The Glazeley Partnership 2 **Bred** W P Jenks **Trained** Stanton Lacy, Shropshire

FOCUS
Divided bends with hurdle course 9-12yds off inside line and fences narrowed down from inside. Little depth to this maiden hurdle despite the number of runners and the front two pulled clear. That pair are rated to their marks.

117 BRIAN AND DOROTHY MEATH 50TH ANNIVERSARY H'CAP CHASE (16 fncs) 2m 5f
2:25 (2:25) (Class 5) (0-100,104) 5-Y-0+ **£2,599** (£763; £381; £190)

Form RPR
P44/ 1 **Lemon's Gent**[67] 4441 6-11-9 **97**..........(p) SamJones 109+
(Paul Webber) *led to 4th: led 6th: hit 2 out: styd on wl* **13/2**[2]
642/ 2 4 **Smooth Classic (IRE)**[8] 5552 9-12-2 **104**.......... TomScudamore 112
(David Pipe) *chsd ldrs: mstke 9th: 2nd 11th: kpt on same pce fr 2 out: mstke last* **10/1**
623/ 3 3 ¾ **Winston Churchill (IRE)**[28] 5182 7-11-8 **96**..........(t) PaulMoloney 101
(Sophie Leech) *in rr: hdwy 11th: 4th 3 out: 3rd 2 out: kpt on one pce* **13/2**[2]
442/ 4 5 **Wait No More (IRE)**[190] 2027 8-11-10 **98**..........(p) DougieCostello 96
(Neil Mulholland) *trckd ldrs: led 4th to 6th: outpcd appr 4 out: one pce* **10/1**
650/ 5 8 **Jack Albert (IRE)**[33] 5078 6-10-4 **78** ow1.......... JamesReveley 73
(Dianne Sayer) *in rr: j.rt: hmpd 6th: reminders next: hdwy 11th: 4th 4 out: wknd appr 2 out* **15/2**[3]
443/ 6 32 **Mister Wiseman**[28] 5186 11-11-6 **97**..........(bt) MarkQuinlan(3) 59
(Nigel Hawke) *chsd ldrs: wknd after 12th: t.o 2 out* **9/1**
125/ 7 24 **Witch's Hat (IRE)**[11] 5481 10-11-0 **88**..........(t) MarkGrant 29
(Jim Old) *chsd ldrs: lost pl 11th: bhd whn hit next: t.o 4 out* **14/1**
P03/ 8 6 **Dr Dreamy (IRE)**[14] 5409 6-10-8 **82**.......... NickScholfield 17
(Claire Dyson) *mid-div: hdwy 7th: outpcd whn blnd 10th: sn bhd: t.o 4 out* **11/2**[1]
145/ F **Tisfreetdream (IRE)**[28] 5182 12-10-4 **78**..........(p) JackDoyle
(Peter Pritchard) *in rr: fell 4th* **11/1**
PPP/ P **Gainsborough's Art (IRE)**[241] 1497 8-9-7 **74** oh2.....(p) DanielHiskett(7)
(Harry Chisman) *in rr: bhd fr 9th: t.o 12th: p.u bef 3 out* **50/1**
652/ F **On Gossamer Wings (IRE)**[27] 5207 9-10-10 **84**(p) SamTwiston-Davies
(Ferdy Murphy, France) *mid-div: outpcd whn reminders 5th: lost pl and fell next* **10/1**
2PP/ P **Dot Or Feather (IRE)**[190] 2027 8-11-10 **98**..........(b[1]) DaveCrosse
(Graeme McPherson) *mid-div: lost pl and reminders 7th: bhd fr 9th: t.o whn blnd 10th: p.u bef next* **16/1**
532/ P **Flichity (IRE)**[15] 5383 8-9-9 **74** oh1.......... JoeCornwall(5)
(John Cornwall) *in rr: blnd 1st: hmpd 4th: sn bhd: reminders next: t.o 8th: p.u bef next* **12/1**

5m 22.3s (-0.50) **Going Correction** +0.075s/f (Yiel) 13 Ran SP% **121.6**
Speed ratings: **103,101,100,98,95 82,73,71,, ,,**
toteswingers 1&2 £2.20, 1&3 £1.90, 2&3 £1.90 CSF £71.52 CT £448.48 TOTE £10.10: £3.80, £4.10, £2.30; EX 146.30 Trifecta £278.10 Part won. Pool: £370.91 - 0.74 winning units..
Owner R Waters **Bred** G R Waters **Trained** Mollington, Oxon

FOCUS
An open handicap chase in which the front two raced prominently throughout. The are rated to the best of their hurdles form.

118 PEKTRON BEGINNERS' CHASE (12 fncs) 2m
3:00 (3:01) (Class 4) 5-Y-0+ **£4,431** (£1,309; £654; £327; £163)

Form RPR
543/ 1 **King Spirit (IRE)**[20] 5304 5-10-11 0.......... BrendanPowell(3) 127+
(Brendan Powell) *mde all: styd on wl fr 3 out* **8/1**
240/ 2 5 **Harry Hunt**[50] 4772 6-11-0 0.......... WayneHutchinson 123
(Graeme McPherson) *mid-div: drvn 7th: outpcd bef 4 out: kpt on to take 2nd 2 out: no imp whn hit last* **11/4**[2]
131/ 3 1 ½ **Dance Tempo**[200] 1878 6-11-0 0..........(tp) NickScholfield 119
(Kim Bailey) *chsd ldrs: reminders 6th: outpcd 8th: kpt on one pce fr next: tk 3rd last* **9/2**[3]
6P0/ 4 4 ½ **Sporting Boy (IRE)**[23] 5260 5-11-0 0.......... TomCannon 116
(Michael Blake) *chsd ldrs: reminders 7th: outpcd bef 4 out: one pce* **13/2**
340/ 5 shd **Ubaltique (FR)**[49] 4796 5-11-0 0.......... JasonMaguire 117
(Donald McCain) *hld up: jnd ldrs 6th: upsides 4 out: rdn next: 3rd and one pce whn mstke 2 out* **5/2**[1]
125/ 6 9 **Captain Brown**[272] 1189 5-11-0 0.......... PaulMoloney 109
(Evan Williams) *t.k.h in rr: mstke 5th: hdwy 7th: 3rd and outpcd 4 out: wknd 2 out* **14/1**
360/ 7 24 **Pipe Banner**[468] 3871 9-11-0 0..........(v[1]) CharliePoste 85
(Anthony Middleton) *chsd ldrs: drvn 8th: lost pl next: sn bhd: t.o 2 out* **40/1**
336/ P **Wheres The Hare (IRE)**[14] 5410 6-11-0 0.......... RichieMcLernon
(Jonjo O'Neill) *in rr: drvn 4th: lost pl and j. slowly next: sn p.u* **12/1**

3m 58.2s (3.20) **Going Correction** +0.075s/f (Yiel) 8 Ran SP% **114.7**
Speed ratings: **95,92,91,89,89 84,72,**
toteswingers 1&2 £3.80, 1&3 £2.20, 2&3 £2.50 CSF £31.51 TOTE £7.10: £2.60, £1.20, £1.50; EX 25.80 Trifecta £145.80 Pool: £823.13 - 4.23 winning units..
Owner J J King **Bred** M F Finneran **Trained** Upper Lambourn, Berks

FOCUS
Seven of the eight runners were making their chasing debuts and the winner did it nicely from the front. A fair race for the time of year and the second is rated in line with his previous chasing best.

119 BURTON KIA H'CAP HURDLE (10 hdls) 2m 4f 110y
3:40 (3:40) (Class 3) (0-130,129) 4-Y-0+
£6,256 (£1,848; £924; £462; £231; £116)

Form RPR
254/ 1 **One Lucky Lady**[97] 3904 5-11-0 **122**.......... NicodeBoinville(5) 135+
(Nicky Henderson) *trckd ldrs 4th: chsd ldr sn after 3 out: led last: drvn out* **11/2**[2]
130/ 2 1 ¾ **Lord Grantham (IRE)**[23] 5257 6-10-11 **114**.......... RichardJohnson 126
(Henry Daly) *hld up in rr: hdwy to trck ldrs 6th: led 3 out: hdd and hit last: styd on same pce* **11/2**[2]
211/ 3 26 **Billy Twyford (IRE)**[59] 4595 6-11-12 **129**.......... DavidBass 120
(Lawney Hill) *in rr: nt fluent 4th: hdwy appr 3 out: modest 3rd 2 out: one pce* **5/1**[1]
534/ 4 4 ½ **Trip The Light**[15] 5386 8-10-2 **112**.......... ThomasGarner(7) 96
(Phil Middleton) *in rr: hdwy appr 3 out: kpt on to take poor 4th last* **16/1**
31F/ 5 2 ¼ **Bygones Sovereign (IRE)**[23] 5257 7-11-1 **118**..........(p) TomScudamore 100
(David Pipe) *w ldrs: rdn 7th: outpcd appr 3 out: wknd appr last* **6/1**[3]
312/ 6 23 **Teenage Idol (IRE)**[470] 3833 9-11-6 **128**.......... EmmaSayer(5) 89
(Evelyn Slack) *w ldrs: t.k.h: lost pl after 5th: bhd fr 7th* **33/1**
334/ 7 14 **Jetnova (IRE)**[73] 4319 8-11-10 **127**.......... WayneHutchinson 75
(Alan King) *in rr: rdn 7th: sn bhd: blnd 2 out* **11/2**[2]
200/ P **Quinsman**[17] 5356 7-11-4 **121**.......... AndrewThornton
(Caroline Bailey) *chsd ldrs 4th: lost pl 7th: wl bhd whn p.u bef 2 out* **40/1**
P30/ P **Moonlight Drive (IRE)**[73] 4319 7-11-3 **120**.......... DougieCostello
(Jonjo O'Neill) *nt fluent in rr: sme hdwy 7th: lost pl bef next: bhd whn p.u bef 2 out* **16/1**
201/ P **The Weatherman (IRE)**[335] 564 6-11-5 **122**.......... JasonMaguire
(Donald McCain) *mid-div: lost pl and hit 6th: wl bhd whn p.u bef 2 out* **7/1**
140/ P **Creekside**[90] 4007 5-11-7 **124**.......... DenisO'Regan
(John Ferguson) *led: mstke 6th: hdd and stmbld on landing 3 out: sn wknd: t.o whn p.u bef last* **10/1**
0P/ P **Moyaliff (IRE)**[181] 2215 6-11-11 **128**..........[1] JackDoyle
(Sarah Humphrey) *t.k.h: sn trcking ldrs: hit 3rd: wknd after 6th: bhd whn p.u bef next* **25/1**

4m 53.7s (-5.30) **Going Correction** -0.075s/f (Good) 12 Ran SP% **119.7**
Speed ratings (Par 107): **107,106,96,94,93 85,79,, ,**
toteswingers 1&2 £9.60, 1&3 £7.40, 2&3 £21.60 CSF £36.10 CT £164.03 TOTE £8.40: £3.20, £2.00, £2.00; EX 49.10 Trifecta £95.90 Pool: £807.21 - 6.30 winning units..
Owner S W Group Logistics Limited **Bred** Ken Knox **Trained** Upper Lambourn, Berks

FOCUS
An open looking handicap developed into a two-horse race approaching two out. The first two help set the level andf the form could be rated higher through the third.

120 UTTOXETERTWITTERATI NOVICES' H'CAP CHASE (18 fncs) 3m
4:15 (4:15) (Class 4) (0-115,114) 5-Y-0 **£4,177** (£1,234; £617; £308; £154)

Form RPR
323/ 1 **Patsy Finnegan**[18] 5341 11-11-12 **114**.......... WayneHutchinson 127+
(Alan King) *hld up in mid-div: trckd ldrs 8th: 2nd 3 out: upsides last: sn led: drvn out* **5/1**[2]
446/ 2 1 ¼ **Firm Order (IRE)**[18] 5340 8-11-10 **112**..........(p) DenisO'Regan 125
(Paul Webber) *w ldr: led 6th: jnd last: edgd lft: no ex last 50yds* **8/1**
661/ 3 5 **Blackwell Synergy (FR)**[52] 4741 7-11-3 **105**..........(p) DougieCostello 113
(Jonjo O'Neill) *mid-div: lost pl and drvn 5th: sn bhd: hdwy 14th: 3rd appr 2 out: one pce* **11/1**
640/ 4 2 **Always Bold (IRE)**[15] 5372 8-10-12 **100**..........(v) IanPopham 106
(Martin Keighley) *in rr whn blnd and rdr briefly lost iron 1st: chsd ldrs 4th: one pce fr 4 out* **16/1**
043/ 5 12 **Countess Comet (IRE)**[22] 5274 6-11-5 **107**..........(tp) TomMessenger 102
(Chris Bealby) *hld up towards rr: hdwy 6th: chsng ldrs 10th: wknd appr 2 out* **25/1**
F5P/ 6 20 **Ballycracken (IRE)**[6] 20 9-9-9 **88** oh3.......... JoeCornwall(5) 65
(David Pearson) *towards rr: hdwy to chse ldrs 10th: outpcd 13th: lost pl after next: sn bhd* **66/1**
P21/ 7 7 **Oddjob (IRE)**[28] 5182 9-11-1 **103**.......... TomScudamore 84
(David Pipe) *w ldrs: hmpd 1st: 3rd and hld whn hit 3 out: wknd appr next: bhd whn eased run-in* **15/8**[1]
UUU/ 8 37 **Quel Ballistic**[431] 4562 9-11-1 **103**..........(p) JamieMoore 40
(Peter Bowen) *in rr: bhd fr 12th: t.o 14th: virtually p.u run-in* **11/2**[3]
3P3/ 9 26 **Humphrey Bee (IRE)**[22] 5276 10-11-5 **107**..........(p) RichardJohnson 21
(Charlie Longsdon) *mstke 3rd: chsd ldrs 10th: lost pl after 14th: bhd fr next: t.o whn eased run-in* **11/2**[3]
P65/ P **Chadford**[15] 5382 5-10-7 **95**..........(tp) NickScholfield
(Claire Dyson) *led: reminders 5th: hdd next: lost pl 10th: sn bhd: t.o 12th: p.u bef 4 out* **66/1**

6m 15.3s (0.20) **Going Correction** +0.075s/f (Yiel) 10 Ran SP% **114.4**
Speed ratings: **102,101,99,99,95 88,86,73,65,**
toteswingers 1&2 £9.10, 1&3 £25.30, 2&3 Not won CSF £42.91 CT £415.75 TOTE £3.90: £1.30, £2.60, £3.00; EX 25.20 Trifecta £416.60 Pool: £1,476.57 - 2.65 winning units..
Owner The Wasp Partnership **Bred** J R Bosley And Mrs E Bosley **Trained** Barbury Castle, Wilts

FOCUS
A fair staying handicap with the second to his mark and the third close to his recent winning form.

121 JPW DISTRIBUTION H'CAP HURDLE (12 hdls) 3m
4:50 (4:52) (Class 4) (0-120,118) 4-Y-0 **£3,798** (£1,122; £561; £280; £140)

Form RPR
P23/ 1 **Green Wizard (IRE)**[22] 5275 7-11-4 **115**.......... JonathanEngland(5) 120
(Sue Smith) *chsd ldrs: 2nd 6th: led appr last: styd on* **14/1**
034/ 2 1 ¼ **Sail And Return**[33] 5063 9-10-10 **109**.......... ThomasGarner(7) 114
(Phil Middleton) *in rr: mstke 4th: hdwy 8th: chsng ldrs next: 3rd last: styd on same pce* **16/1**
P66/ 3 1 ½ **Andreo Bambaleo**[15] 5372 9-11-1 **107**..........(p) DannyCook 110
(Brian Ellison) *in rr: hdwy 8th: chsng ldrs next: swtchd rt and 5th last: styd on same pce* **12/1**
50P/ 4 nk **Miss Overdrive**[54] 4713 9-11-4 **110**.......... NickScholfield 114+
(Oliver Sherwood) *led: jnd whn blnd 3 out: hdd and 2nd whn mstke last: kpt on same pce* **9/1**
551/ 5 1 ¼ **Rich Buddy**[21] 5292 7-11-11 **117**.......... IanPopham 120
(Richard Phillips) *in rr: drvn 8th: hdwy to chse ldrs 3 out: kpt on same pce appr last* **7/1**[3]
FPP/ 6 10 **Turtlethomas (IRE)**[32] 5104 7-10-12 **109**..........(tp) GavinSheehan(5) 102
(Lawney Hill) *chsd ldrs: lost pl 9th* **33/1**
132/ 7 17 **Ukrainian Star (IRE)**[21] 5292 10-9-9 **97**..........(b) OllieGarner(10) 74
(Martin Keighley) *chsd ldrs: wknd appr 3 out* **6/1**[2]
450/ 8 3 ¼ **Cyrien Star**[21] 5292 6-11-1 **107**.......... TomO'Brien 81
(Henry Daly) *mid-div: chsd ldrs 8th: lost pl bef 3 out* **20/1**
003/ 9 ½ **Joseph Mercer (IRE)**[54] 4713 6-11-8 **114**.......... RichardJohnson 88
(Philip Hobbs) *in rr: nt fluent and drvn 7th: lost pl bef 3 out: sn bhd* **7/2**[1]
334/ 10 85 **Deise Dynamo (IRE)**[43] 4911 5-11-12 **118**.......... JasonMaguire 15
(Donald McCain) *w ldrs: reminders 6th: lost pl next: bhd 8th: t.o next: virtually p.u run-in* **7/1**[3]
512/ 11 2 **Presenting Paddy (IRE)**[247] 1428 5-11-4 **110**.......... JackDoyle 5
(Sarah Humphrey) *chsd ldrs: lost pl 9th: sn bhd: t.o next: virtually p.u run-in* **20/1**
56/- P **Barenger (IRE)**[71] 4364 6-11-6 **112**.......... AndrewTinkler
(Nicky Henderson) *mid-div: chsd ldrs 5th: lost pl bef 3 out: sn bhd: t.o 10th whn p.u bef last* **10/1**
301/ F **Spoil Me (IRE)**[95] 3924 6-10-13 **105**.......... RichieMcLernon
(Jonjo O'Neill) *in rr: bhd fr 9th: t.o 11th whn fell 2 out* **10/1**

5m 54.9s (4.90) **Going Correction** -0.075s/f (Good) 13 Ran SP% **122.4**
Speed ratings (Par 105): **88,87,87,86,86 83,77,76,76,47 47, ,**
toteswingers 1&2 Not won, 1&3 £49.60, 2&3 Not won CSF £214.01 CT £2773.22 TOTE £20.70: £4.80, £6.60, £4.40; EX 384.40 TRIFECTA Not won..
Owner Mrs S Smith **Bred** Eric Barrett **Trained** High Eldwick, W Yorks

FOCUS
An open handicap and five were in with a chance jumping the last. A narrow personal-best from the winner with the second to his mark.

122 ENJOY STAFFORDSHIRE NOVICES' H'CAP HURDLE (12 hdls) 3m
5:25 (5:25) (Class 5) (0-100,105) 4-Y-0+ **£2,209** (£648; £324; £162)

Form RPR

40P/ **1** **Moscow In April (IRE)**[184] 2148 6-10-6 **80**........................(t) ColinBolger 92+
(Pat Murphy) *hld up in rr: hdwy 9th: sn modest 4th: styd on fr 3 out: chsng ldrs next: led between last 2: forged clr run-in* **20/1**

46F/ **2** *19* **Just Benny (IRE)**[15] 5383 8-11-12 **100**......................... RichardJohnson 99
(Richard Phillips) *in rr: hdwy 8th: 4th 9th: cl 3rd whn blnd 2 out: lft 10 l 2nd and hmpd last* **16/1**

P32/ **3** *6* **Bunratty (IRE)**[20] 5313 7-11-2 **90**................................ JamesReveley 82
(Dianne Sayer) *led: hit 7th: clr after 8th: hdd appr 2 out: mstke: hmpd and lft modest 3rd last* **13/2[3]**

50P/ **4** *6* **Westwire Toby (IRE)**[27] 5205 11-10-0 **74** oh8...................... TomSiddall 58
(Lynn Siddall) *mid-div: hdwy 8th: one pce: lft poor 4th last* **40/1**

362/ **5** *25* **Genny Wren**[89] 4029 7-11-11 **99**..(p) SamJones 61
(Renee Robeson) *chsd ldrs: drvn and lost pl whn hmpd 6th: sn bhd* **11/2[2]**

066/ **6** *½* **Supermightyfine**[15] 5379 6-10-8 **82**..............................(t) TomScudamore 43
(Jo Hughes) *mid-div: chsd ldrs 8th: lost pl sn after next* **16/1**

60/- **7** *79* **Wheelavher**[21] 5285 7-10-4 **78**...(t) NickScholfield
(Claire Dyson) *chsd ldr: wknd 9th: sn bhd: t.o next: virtually p.u: eventually completed* **25/1**

602/ **P** **Iconic Rose**[67] 4437 6-11-7 **95**................................. SamTwiston-Davies
(Pam Sly) *rr-div: bhd fr 8th: sn t.o: p.u bef 3 out* **8/1**

050/ **P** **Cowbridge (IRE)**[13] 5430 7-10-10 **84**................................. HarrySkelton
(Peter Pritchard) *mid-div: lost pl 4th: bhd whn p.u bef 8th* **50/1**

260/ **P** **Harris Garden (IRE)**[112] 3615 6-11-11 **99**........................ DenisO'Regan
(Paul Webber) *stdd s: in rr: hmpd 6th: sn bhd: t.o whn p.u bef 9th* **12/1**

066/ **P** **Hollow Heartbeat (IRE)**[116] 3560 6-10-5 **79**..............(b) RichardKilloran
(Brendan Powell) *chsd ldrs: hmpd 6th: lost pl sn after 9th: t.o whn p.u bef next* **8/1**

50P/ **P** **Black Sambuca**[11] 5477 6-11-2 **90**.................................. TomMessenger
(Chris Bealby) *in rr: nt fluent 4th: bhd and drvn 8th: t.o whn p.u bef 3 out* **25/1**

51/- **F** **Midnight Whisper**[10] 5505 7-12-0 **105**........................... MichealNolan(3) 107
(Richard Woollacott) *chsd ldrs: wnt 2nd 9th: led appr 2 out: hdd and 4 l down whn fell last* **10/3[1]**

350/ **F** **Lord Navits (IRE)**[14] 5412 5-11-3 **91**..............................(p) JasonMaguire
(Donald McCain) *t.k.h: trckd ldrs: fell 6th* **10/1**

5m 57.2s (7.20) **Going Correction** -0.075s/f (Good) **14** Ran SP% **119.4**
Speed ratings (Par 103): **85,78,76,74,66 66,39,,, ,,,**
CSF £286.21 CT £2315.72 TOTE £35.80: £9.30, £6.30, £2.20; EX 316.40 Trifecta £264.10 Part won. Pool: £352.17 - 0.01 winning units..
Owner P G Murphy **Bred** Larry Murphy **Trained** East Garston, Berks

FOCUS
A large-field handicap which was turned into a procession by the winner, who is rated a 10lb improver, with the faller heading a mark in line with his recent win.
T/Plt: £501.50 to a £1 stake. Pool: £82,015.84 - 119.37 winning tickets T/Qpdt: £80.70 to a £1 stake. Pool: £5,218.7 - 47.80 winning tickets WG

123 - 129a (Foreign Racing) - See Raceform Interactive

COMPIEGNE (L-H)
Friday, May 3

OFFICIAL GOING: Turf: very soft

130a PRIX DU GRAND MAITRE (HURDLE) (MAIDEN) (3YO FILLIES) (TURF) 2m
12:50 (12:00) 3-Y-0 **£8,585** (£4,292; £2,504; £1,699; £804)

RPR

1 **Analifet (FR)** 3-10-3 0.. HubertTerrien 114
(S Foucher, France) **34/1**

2 *2½* **Loxlade (FR)** 3-10-3 0.. BenoitGicquel 112
(F Nicolle, France) **78/10[3]**

3 *¾* **Polid'Ajonc (FR)** 3-10-3 0... JanFaltejsek 111
(G Macaire, France) **3/1[1]**

4 *2* **Larabelle (FR)** 3-10-3 0.. ErvanChazelle 109
(Mlle T Puitg, France) **11/1**

5 *1½* **Ladeka (FR)** 3-10-3 0.. AlexisPoirier 108
(Mlle T Puitg, France) **16/1**

6 *3* **Sakina (FR)**[10] 3-10-8 0... HerveJumelle 110
(G Brillet, France) **16/1**

7 *4* **Dolores Delightful (FR)** 3-10-4 0 ow1.............................. JamesReveley 102
(Nick Williams) *hld up towards rr: last tl sme prog appr 2 out: kpt on run-in: nvr in contention* **11/1**

8 *1½* **Kalevala (FR)**[114] 3-10-8 0... LudovicPhilipperon 104
(R Chotard, France) **23/1**

9 *6* **Sky Run (FR)** 3-10-3 0.. MorganRegairaz 93
(C Lerner, France) **11/1**

10 *1½* **Fiorella (FR)**[32] 3-10-3 0.. Mehdi-MikeAridj 92
(P Lenogue, France) **47/1**

0 **Ravissante Du Rheu (FR)** 3-10-3 0............................... AlainDeChitray
(T Trapenard, France) **35/1**

0 **Artiwork (FR)** 3-10-3 0... KevinNabet
(S Foucher, France) **66/1**

0 **Bijou Plage (FR)** 3-10-3 0.. SylvainDehez
(A Lamotte D'Argy, France) **4/1[2]**

P **Tinotara** 3-10-7 0 ow4.. JonathanPlouganou
(R Chotard, France) **8/1**

3m 58.02s (238.02) **14** Ran SP% **117.6**
PARI-MUTUEL (all including 1 euro stakes): WIN 23.30 (coupled with Artiwork); PLACE 8.90, 2.80, 2.00; DF 163.10; SF 388.90.
Owner Scea Des Collines **Bred** Jacques-Emmanuel Cherel **Trained** France

131a PRIX GENERAL DE SAINT-DIDIER (CHASE) (CONDITIONS) (5YO+) (TURF) 2m 5f
2:20 (12:00) 5-Y-0+ **£8,975** (£4,487; £2,617; £1,776; £841)

RPR

1 **Divergont Quirec (FR)**[187] 8-10-8 0........................ JonathanPlouganou 127
(Mlle M-L Mortier, France) **32/5**

2 *3* **Six Des Champs (FR)**[12] 5447 9-11-0 0.......................(b) LenieSuzineau 130
(A Lacombe, France) **48/10[3]**

3 *5* **Ruse Des Planches (FR)**[318] 8-11-7 0........................ ChristopheHerpin 132
(P Chemin, France) **3/1[1]**

4 *6* **Diamond Harry**[153] 2776 10-10-10 0................................ JamesReveley 115
(Nick Williams) *led: set stdy gallop: hdd 3rd and remained prom: led again after 7th: hdd 9th and remained prom: shkn up and nt qckn w ldrs bef 2 out: one pce u.p run-in* **58/10**

5 *2* **Soledad De Monnaie (FR)**[31] 7-10-8 0.......................... GaetanOlivier 111
(P Journiac, France) **17/2**

6 *1½* **Slow Game (FR)**[66] 7-11-3 0..................................... BertrandThelier 119
(G Cherel, France) **9/2[2]**

7 *¾* **Lake World (FR)**[195] 10-10-3 0.................................... PaulLucas(5) 109
(Mlle M-L Mortier, France) **10/1**

P **Hallssio**[21] 5-10-6 0...(b) GaetanMasure
(P Lenogue, France) **13/1**

P **Urlanie (FR)**[8] 5535 5-9-8 0...................................... GaelBarbedette(5)
(Mme A-E Gareau, France) **45/1**

P **Swing De Balme (FR)** 7-10-3 0............................ MaximeFrayssinhes(5)
(Mlle N Pfohl, France) **81/1**

5m 40.21s (340.21) **10** Ran SP% **118.8**
PARI-MUTUEL (all including 1 euro stakes): WIN 7.40; PLACE 2.50, 1.80, 1.60; DF 21.20; SF 42.70.
Owner Jean-Claude Norbert Bignon **Bred** Joseph Coutellec **Trained** France

132 - 139a (Foreign Racing) - See Raceform Interactive

FFOS LAS (L-H)
Monday, May 6

OFFICIAL GOING: Good (7.3)
Wind: Virtually nil Weather: Fine

140 3 A'S LEISURE.COM MAIDEN HURDLE (10 hdls) 2m 4f
2:20 (2:20) (Class 5) 4-Y-0+ **£1,949** (£572; £286; £143)

Form RPR

3/ **1** **Azure Aware (IRE)**[62] 4577 6-11-0 0...............................(t) JasonMaguire 125+
(Kim Bailey) *mde most: nt fluent 3 out: rdn next: hit last: sn hdd: rallied u.p to ld nr fin* **5/2[1]**

225/ **2** *½* **Garryleigh (IRE)**[24] 5265 6-11-0 0..............................(t) TomScudamore 122
(David Pipe) *mid-div: hdwy 3 out: chal and lft in ld last: sn rdn: hdd nr fin* **10/1**

142/ **3** *7* **Third Of The Third**[161] 2671 6-11-0 0............................... ConorO'Farrell 116
(David Pipe) *t.k.h bhd ldrs: chsd wnr 3 out: rdn 2 out: no ex appr last* **5/1[3]**

642/ **4** *17* **Twin Barrels**[24] 5265 6-11-0 117...................................... WillKennedy 100
(Sarah-Jayne Davies) *trckd ldrs: rdn appr 3 out: sn one pce* **7/1**

126/ **5** *hd* **Henri Parry Morgan**[158] 2729 5-11-0 0.......................... DonalDevereux 100
(Peter Bowen) *chsd ldrs: nt fluent 5th: rdn after 7th: wknd after next* **20/1**

222/ **6** *1¼* **Houndscourt (IRE)**[15] 5430 6-11-0 124..........(t) SamTwiston-Davies 100
(Jamie Snowden) *w ldr to 4th: styd in 2nd: rdn after 7th: lost 2nd 3 out: wknd after next* **11/4[2]**

32/ **7** *3¼* **Nodividendsagain**[63] 4565 5-11-0 0................................... PaulMoloney 96
(Evan Williams) *hld up in rr: rdn 7th: styd on fr 3 out: nvr trbld ldrs* **16/1**

404/ **8** *¾* **Kalani King (IRE)**[37] 5021 6-10-11 0................................ RyanMahon(3) 95
(Anthony Honeyball) *towards rr: plugged on past btn rivals fr 3 out* **22/1**

0U/- **9** *8* **Taradrewe**[8] 1 6-10-4 0...(t) RachaelGreen(3) 83
(Anthony Honeyball) *towards rr: hdwy 6th: chalng for 2nd whn j. slowly 3 out: sn wknd* **12/1**

0/ **10** *17* **Macarthur**[738] 156 9-10-11 0..(t) AdamWedge(3) 73
(David Rees) *towards rr: sme hdwy 7th: sn rdn: wknd next: t.o* **25/1**

4/ **11** *7* **Annelko**[15] 5441 6-11-0 0... TomCannon 66
(Michael Blake) *in rr: hdwy 6th: wknd 3 out: t.o* **50/1**

5/ **12** *1* **Mighty Clarets (IRE)**[211] 1768 6-11-0 0............................ JamieMoore 65
(Peter Bowen) *mid-div: wknd appr 3 out: t.o* **40/1**

0P6/ **13** *1¼* **Road Show**[22] 5304 6-10-7 0....................................(t) MrMatthewBarber(7) 64
(Keith Goldsworthy) *chsd ldrs: mstke 6th: rdn next: sn wknd: t.o* **200/1**

000/ **14** *2* **On The Case**[20] 5335 5-11-0 0.. PaddyBrennan 62
(Tom George) *in tch: rdn 5th: sn lost pl: bhd fr 7th: t.o* **80/1**

0PP/ **15** *19* **Gwili Spar**[13] 5463 5-11-0 0.. TomO'Brien 45
(Peter Bowen) *in tch tl wknd 7th: t.o* **100/1**

040/ **16** *16* **Vicator**[158] 2718 5-11-0 0... AidanColeman 31
(Anthony Honeyball) *a in rr: lost tch after 7th: t.o* **80/1**

4m 51.1s (0.20) **Going Correction** +0.05s/f (Yiel) **16** Ran SP% **128.4**
Speed ratings (Par 103): **101,100,98,91,91 90,89,89,85,79 76,75,75,74,66 60**
Tote Swingers 1&2 £0.00, 2&3 £14.00, 1&3 £2.30 CSF £28.23 TOTE £4.20: £1.70, £4.60, £2.70; EX 40.50 Trifecta £246.20 Part won. Pool: £328.30 - 0.66 winning units..
Owner J Perriss **Bred** Miss E Hamilton **Trained** Andoversford, Gloucs

FOCUS
A good turnout and decent novice form for the time of year. The winner can rate higher.

141 EINSLEY AND ANGELA/EH FACTORS H'CAP CHASE (18 fncs) 3m
2:50 (2:50) (Class 5) (0-95,93) 5-Y-0+ **£2,144** (£629; £314; £157)

Form RPR

600/ **1** **Mr Gee Jay**[24] 5270 7-10-11 **78**............................(t) SamTwiston-Davies 96+
(Nigel Twiston-Davies) *chsd ldrs: clsd 11th: led 13th: drew clr fr 2 out: eased towards fin* **7/1**

002/ **2** *9* **Flanagan (IRE)**[403] 5140 9-11-9 **90**............................... DonalDevereux 95
(Peter Bowen) *a.p: trckd wnr 14th: rdn 4 out: no ex appr 2 out* **9/2[1]**

U4P/ **3** *5* **Midnight Charmer**[30] 5182 7-10-3 **75**............................ JamesBanks(5) 76
(Emma Baker) *in tch: hdwy to chse ldng pair 14th: rdn 4 out: kpt on same pce* **5/1[2]**

523/ **4** *4½* **Petroupetrov (FR)**[24] 5270 10-11-12 **93**...................(vt) RichardJohnson 89
(Tim Vaughan) *in rr: sme hdwy 14th: sn one pce and no further imp* **6/1**

043/ **5** *10* **Pacha D'Oudairies (FR)**[13] 5474 10-11-7 **88**........................ TomCannon 75
(Michael Blake) *chsd ldr: led 9th to 13th: sn rdn and outpcd by ldrs: plugged on* **6/1**

P33/ **6** *48* **Bonoman (IRE)**[13] 5467 10-11-1 **89**..............................(b) ConorRing(7) 33
(Evan Williams) *hld up in rr: struggling 12th: t.o* **12/1**

433/ **7** *24* **Proud Times (USA)**[263] 1253 7-11-9 **90**.........................(tp) JackDoyle 13
(Ali Brewer) *mid-div: mstke 1st: rdn 13th: sn wknd: t.o* **17/2**

56P/ **P** **Mercury Bay (IRE)**[20] 5331 8-11-7 **88**..............................(v1) PaulMoloney
(Evan Williams) *led: hit 6th and given reminder: hdd 9th: wknd 14th: wl bhd whn p.u bef 4 out* **7/1**

00P/ **P** **Mister Hendre**[13] 5472 5-11-2 **83**.................................... AidanColeman
(Anthony Honeyball) *towards rr: blnd 3rd: last but stl in tch whn mstke and slithered on landing 8th: p.u bef next* **11/2**[3]

6m 6.5s (-10.90) **Going Correction** -0.25s/f (Good) **9** Ran SP% **122.0**
Speed ratings: **108,105,103,101,98 82,74, ,**
Tote Swingers 1&2 £2.10, 2&3 £4.40, 1&3 £0.00 CSF £41.58 CT £177.26 TOTE £7.80: £2.70, £2.50, £1.80; EX 56.90 Trifecta £97.00 Pool: £134.58 - 1.04 winning units..

Owner The Gary Wheildon Syndicate **Bred** G Wheildon **Trained** Naunton, Gloucs

FOCUS
A moderate staying handicap and a big step up from the easy winner.

142 TRJ - "BUILDING ON A FIRM FOUNDATION" H'CAP CHASE (13 fncs) 2m
3:20 (3:20) (Class 4) (0-115,115) 5-Y-0+ **£3,768** (£1,106; £553; £276)

Form RPR

030/ **1** **Dineur (FR)**[149] 2917 7-11-7 **110**.................................... DonalDevereux 117+
(Peter Bowen) *racd keenly: trckd ldr: rdn 4 out: lft 2nd 2 out: led jst after last: drvn out* **3/1**[2]

P2F/ **2** *2 ½* **True Blue (IRE)**[186] 2144 6-11-5 **108**....................(t) SamTwiston-Davies 114
(Nigel Twiston-Davies) *in tch in 4th: hdwy to chse ldr appr 4 out: led 2 out where lft I up: sn rdn: hdd jst after last: no ex* **3/1**[2]

233/ **3** *1* **Piment D'Estruval (FR)**[193] 2013 10-11-12 **115**.......... RichardJohnson 120
(Tim Vaughan) *hld up in last: 6 l detached 6th: hdwy into 4th and rdn 4 out: unable qck fr next: lft 3rd 2 out: styd on flat* **11/1**

443/ **4** *20* **Smiling Lady (IRE)**[13] 5480 7-10-9 **98**..............................(t) TomO'Brien 87
(David Rees) *a towards rr: rdn after 9th: 5th and no ch whn blnd 4 out: t.o* **6/1**[3]

4P4/ **5** *10* **Bay Central (IRE)**[15] 5439 9-11-4 **107**................................ PaulMoloney 84
(Evan Williams) *led tl after 9th: wkng whn mstke 4 out: t.o* **14/1**

321/ **F** **Sparville (IRE)**[17] 5384 7-11-9 **112**.................................... JasonMaguire 119
(Kim Bailey) *trckd ldrs: chal 8th: led after next: mstke 3 out: hdd and fell next* **7/4**[1]

3m 54.3s (-5.10) **Going Correction** -0.25s/f (Good) **6** Ran SP% **115.6**
Speed ratings: **102,100,100,90,85**
Tote Swingers 1&2 £2.20, 2&3 £2.00, 1&3 £2.10 CSF £13.24 CT £85.41 TOTE £3.00: £1.80, £1.60; EX 13.70 Trifecta £43.40 Pool: £129.66 - 2.23 winning units..

Owner Gwilym J Morris **Bred** Dominique Le Baron **Trained** Little Newcastle, Pembrokes

FOCUS
A modest handicap and there was no hanging about. The form is rated around the second and third.

143 GRWP WRW H'CAP CHASE (17 fncs) 2m 5f
3:55 (3:55) (Class 4) (0-120,118) 5-Y-0+ **£3,768** (£1,106; £553; £276)

Form RPR

542/ **1** **Raduis Bleu (FR)**[13] 5467 8-10-6 **105**.............................. MissLBrooke(7) 114+
(Lady Susan Brooke) *chsd ldrs: wnt 2nd at 12th: drvn to ld appr last: wnt 2 l up flat: idled towards fin* **11/4**[2]

53P/ **2** *½* **Crannaghmore Boy (IRE)**[13] 5467 8-10-0 **92** oh2............. JamieMoore 102
(Keith Goldsworthy) *trckd ldr tl led 9th: blnd 13th: hit 4 out: sn rdn: hdd appr last: kpt on flat* **11/2**

052/ **3** *16* **Western King (IRE)**[30] 5181 6-11-6 **117**..................(tp) GavinSheehan(5) 112
(Charlie Mann) *hld up in tch: clsd 9th: niggled fr 12th: rdn in 3rd and nt run on 4 out: wknd 2 out* **7/4**[1]

10P/ **4** *5* **Accordingtopalm (IRE)**[22] 5307 7-11-6 **115**................(t) AdamWedge(3) 104
(David Rees) *hld up in tch: rdn and wknd appr 4 out* **8/1**

124/ **5** *nse* **Strumble Head (IRE)**[192] 2025 8-11-12 **118**................(p) DonalDevereux 109
(Peter Bowen) *led: mstke 7th: hdd 9th: mstke 11th: wknd after 13th* **3/1**[3]

5m 20.6s (-8.00) **Going Correction** -0.25s/f (Good) **5** Ran SP% **114.5**
Speed ratings: **105,104,98,96,96**
Tote Swinger 1&2 £6.40 CSF £17.37 TOTE £5.10: £1.60, £2.30; EX 17.60 Trifecta £35.80 Pool: £188.93 - 3.95 winning units..

Owner Lady Susan Brooke **Bred** L Chevrollier **Trained** Dolau, Powys

FOCUS
A modest handicap where two came well clear. The form is rated through the second.

144 PARKER PLANT EISTEDDFOD H'CAP HURDLE (12 hdls) 3m
4:25 (4:25) (Class 3) (0-125,124) 4-Y-0+ **£5,393** (£1,583; £791; £395)

Form RPR

010/ **1** **Pension Plan**[17] 5372 9-11-3 **115**......................................(p) TomO'Brien 128+
(Peter Bowen) *in tch: clsd 6th: led appr 9th: styd on strly to draw clr fr 2 out: easily* **7/1**[3]

16/ **2** *11* **Eleven Fifty Nine**[18] 5360 7-11-9 **124**.........................(t) RachaelGreen(3) 121
(Anthony Honeyball) *hld up in rr: hdwy 7th: wnt 2nd after 9th: rdn 3 out: sn no ch w wnr: kpt on one pce* **4/1**[2]

140/ **3** *5* **My Legal Lady**[18] 5360 8-11-0 **112**............................(b) RichardJohnson 105
(Stuart Howe) *hld up towards rr: hit 6th: hdwy 8th: rdn after next: one pce fr 3 out* **14/1**

2P0/ **4** *6* **Tell Me Y (IRE)**[94] 3971 6-11-4 **116**............................(t) RichieMcLernon 104
(Jonjo O'Neill) *hld up in rr: clsd 5th: mstke 9th: sn drvn: styd on one pce fr 3 out* **12/1**

300/ **5** *3 ¼* **Kayf Aramis**[18] 5362 11-11-12 **124**......................(b) SamTwiston-Davies 107
(Nigel Twiston-Davies) *chsd ldrs tl rdn and wknd after 9th* **12/1**

035/ **6** *1 ¾* **Beyond (IRE)**[182] 2234 6-11-3 **115**.............................(t) TomScudamore 98
(David Pipe) *in tch: hdwy to chse ldng pair after 9th: hit 3 out: sn drvn: wknd and lost 3rd appr last* **9/4**[1]

6/3- **7** *9* **Am I Blue**[4] 83 7-9-11 **102**.................................. MrMatthewStanley(7) 76
(Mrs D Thomas) *cl up: rdn 8th: wknd qckly after next: t.o* **11/1**

003/ **8** *51* **Zama Zama**[39] 4978 6-11-0 **115**.................................... AdamWedge(3) 43
(Evan Williams) *led tl hdd appr 9th: wknd qckly: t.o* **4/1**[2]

150/ **P** **Enter Milan (IRE)**[51] 4783 8-11-6 **118**..............................(bt[1]) RhysFlint
(John Flint) *kpt away fr rivals at s: chsd ldrs tl lost pl 7th: struggling next: t.o whn p.u bef 3 out* **20/1**

5m 45.5s (-3.50) **Going Correction** +0.05s/f (Yiel) **9** Ran SP% **118.4**
Speed ratings (Par 107): **107,103,101,99,98 98,95,78,**
Tote Swingers 1&2 £8.00, 2&3 £6.70, 1&3 £8.00 CSF £36.69 CT £388.77 TOTE £10.70: £2.60, £2.00, £5.70; EX 43.20 Trifecta £163.40 Part won. Pool: £217.91 - 0.11 winning units..

Owner The Loppington Five **Bred** Roy David Burden **Trained** Little Newcastle, Pembrokes

FOCUS
This appeared to be a competitive handicap but Pension Plan won easily. The form is rated around the first two.

145 SHADOW SCAFFOLDING H'CAP HURDLE (10 hdls) 2m 4f
4:55 (4:55) (Class 5) (0-100,100) 4-Y-0+ **£1,949** (£572; £286; £143)

Form RPR

006/ **1** **Cawdor House Bert**[348] 410 6-11-9 **97**.............................. PaulMoloney 110+
(David Rees) *hld up in rr: stdy hdwy fr 7th: trckd ldr after 3 out: led sn after last: rdn clr* **8/1**

500/ **2** *7* **My Lad Percy**[161] 2671 5-11-3 **98**.............................. PatrickCorbett(7) 103
(Rebecca Curtis) *in tch in main body of field: wnt 2nd after 7th: led 3 out: sn drvn: hdd sn after last: one pce* **11/4**[1]

F04/ **3** *11* **Maggie Aron**[237] 1544 7-10-13 **87**.................................... ConorO'Farrell 81
(James Hughes) *hld up in rr: hmpd after 7th: stdy hdwy bef next: nt fluent 3 out: wnt 3rd 2 out: no further imp* **9/1**

000/ **4** *8* **Old Pals Act (IRE)**[143] 3039 5-11-12 **100**...................... RichieMcLernon 87
(Jonjo O'Neill) *in tch in main body of field: hdwy 7th: rdn 3 out: sn wknd* **9/1**

0F4/ **5** *9* **Paddleyourowncanoe (IRE)**[54] 4739 12-10-13 **92**...(bt) JamesBanks(5) 71
(Emma Baker) *racd keenly: prom in main body of field: chsd clr ldr after 4th: drvn to ld after 7th: hdd 3 out: sn wknd* **11/1**

500/ **6** *58* **Lucky To Be Alive (IRE)**[51] 4780 6-11-7 **95**........................ JamieMoore 22
(Peter Bowen) *chsd clr ldr tl lost pl after 4th: rdn 6th: lost tch after next: t.o* **6/1**[3]

606/ **7** *2 ¾* **What A Good Night (IRE)**[23] 5285 5-11-4 **92**.....(v) SamTwiston-Davies 16
(Nigel Twiston-Davies) *racd keenly: led: sn clr: c bk to field 5th: hdd after 7th: wknd qckly: t.o* **5/1**[2]

440/ **F** **Mac Beattie**[280] 1124 7-11-4 **95**.. AdamWedge(3)
(Evan Williams) *hld up in main body of field: stl in tch whn bmpd, stmbld and fell a few strides after 7th* **7/1**

003/ **P** **Lucky Sun**[22] 5305 7-10-8 **89**.. GaryDerwin(7)
(Brian Eckley) *chsd along gng to 1st: towards rr: rdn after 4th: lost tch 6th: p.u bef next* **8/1**

4m 49.7s (-1.20) **Going Correction** +0.05s/f (Yiel) **9** Ran SP% **120.7**
Speed ratings (Par 103): **104,101,96,93,90 66,65, ,**
Tote Swingers 1&2 £0.00, 2&3 £6.60, 1&3 £3.30 CSF £32.52 CT £210.34 TOTE £15.30: £5.00, £2.10, £2.20; EX 63.60 Trifecta £200.80 Part won. Pool: £267.78 - 0.02 winning units..
Owner A J & Dai Rees **Bred** Michael S Davies **Trained** Clarbeston, Pembrokes

FOCUS
This ordinary handicap was run at a solid gallop. Big steps up from the first two.

146 2014 CARMARTHENSHIRE NATIONAL EISTEDDFOD STANDARD OPEN NATIONAL HUNT FLAT RACE 2m
5:25 (5:25) (Class 6) 4-6-Y-0 **£1,559** (£457; £228; £114)

Form RPR

22/ **1** **Rolling Maul (IRE)**[23] 5287 5-11-2 0.................................... JamieMoore 118+
(Peter Bowen) *in tch: hdwy to trck ldr after 7f: led 4f out: clr over 1f out: styd on wl* **11/4**[1]

/ **2** *9* **Lily Waugh (IRE)**[72] 6-10-6 0.. RachaelGreen(3) 103
(Anthony Honeyball) *hld up in rr: hdwy 6f out: wnt 2nd over 3f out: rdn 2f out: sn outpcd by wnr: kpt on* **3/1**[2]

03/ **3** *14* **Simply A Legend**[22] 5324 4-10-12 0............................ WayneHutchinson 93
(Alan King) *hld up towards rr: hdwy 5f out: pushed along over 3f out: chsd ldng pair over 2f out: sn one pce* **10/3**[3]

4 *4* **Mr Trilby (IRE)**[386] 6-11-2 0.......................................(b[1]) TomScudamore 93
(David Pipe) *led tl rdn and hdd 4f out: sn dropped to 4th: plugged on one pce* **8/1**

2/ **5** *3* **Solo Jugadores**[65] 4514 5-10-9 0.................................... PatrickCorbett(7) 91
(Rebecca Curtis) *mid-div: hdwy to chse ldrs 1/2-way: rdn 5f out: wknd over 3f out* **3/1**[2]

S64/ **6** *10* **Electric Mayhem**[403] 5144 6-11-2 0.. DarylJacob 82
(Nick Mitchell) *hld up: niggled along 1/2-way: rdn 5f out: sn wknd* **20/1**

0/ **7** *38* **Another Article (IRE)**[22] 5310 5-10-9 0.................. MrMatthewBarber(7) 48
(Marc Barber) *chsd ldr 7f: rdn 6f out: sn wknd: t.o* **50/1**

6/ **8** *2 ¾* **Byronsprincess**[111] 3670 5-10-2 0.. GaryDerwin(7) 38
(Brian Eckley) *chsd ldrs tl rdn and lost pl 1/2-way: lost tch 6f out: t.o* **33/1**

3m 40.2s (-2.70) **Going Correction** +0.05s/f (Yiel)
WFA 4 from 5yo+ 4lb **8** Ran SP% **120.5**
Speed ratings: **108,103,96,94,93 88,69,67**
Tote Swingers 1&2 £3.20, 2&3 £13.30, 1&3 £1.10 CSF £11.89 TOTE £4.20: £1.30, £1.40, £1.60; EX 11.60 Trifecta £28.10 Pool: £252.23 - 6.70 winning units..
Owner Roddy Owen & Paul Fullagar **Bred** Rathmore Stud **Trained** Little Newcastle, Pembrokes

T/Plt: £846.50 to a £1 stake. Pool: £60,964.57 - 52.57 winning tickets. T/Qpdt: £82.50 to a £1 stake. Pool: £4,572.40 - 41.00 winning tickets. RL

147 - 154a (Foreign Racing) - See Raceform Interactive

[37]EXETER (R-H)
Tuesday, May 7

OFFICIAL GOING: Good to firm (firm in places; chs 9.2, hdl 9.1)
Wind: Mild breeze; half-across Weather: Cloudy

155 FARMERS FRIEND OF EXETER MAIDEN HURDLE (8 hdls) 2m 1f
5:55 (5:56) (Class 4) 4-Y-0+ **£3,249** (£954; £477; £238)

Form RPR

02/ **1** **Vexillum (IRE)**[9] 8 4-10-7 0.. RyanMahon(3) 98+
(Harry Fry) *mid-div: travelled wl and hdwy after 3rd: led whn mstke 3 out: sn in command: comf* **1/2**[1]

PP4/ **2** *7* **Present Accepted**[13] 5507 6-10-11 67.................................. JamesBest(3) 93
(Nerys Dutfield) *trckd ldr: led after 5th: hdd 3 out: sn rdn and hld: mstke last: kpt on same pce* **100/1**

006/ **3** *18* **Abbi Jicaro**[14] 5470 6-10-7 74................................(t) AndrewGlassonbury 67
(Mark Shears) *led tl after 5th: sn rdn: hld fr next: wkng whn awkward last* **14/1**

F/ **4** *3 ½* **Sassy Wren**[898] 2554 8-10-7 0.. JamesDavies 64
(Chris Down) *mid-div: hdwy 4th: rdn after next: hld whn nt fluent 3 out: wknd last* **40/1**

04/ **5** *4 ½* **Palmyra (IRE)**[57] 4712 4-10-0 0.................................... BrendanPowell(3) 55
(Martin Hill) *trckd ldr tl rdn after 5th: sn btn: wknd bef last* **10/1**

60/ **6** *35* **Carolingian (USA)**[31] 5180 4-10-10 0.................................. JimmyMcCarthy 27
(Michael Blanshard) *hld up towards rr: rdn after 5th: wkng whn mstke 3 out: t.o* **25/1**

00/ **7** *51* **Haveumistim**[206] 1838 7-10-11 0.................................... MarkQuinlan(3)
(Bernard Llewellyn) *j.lft bdly at times: mid-div tl after 3rd: sn wl bhd: t.o* **33/1**

8 *9* **Best Time Ever**[489] 5-11-0 0.. RichardJohnson
(Philip Hobbs) *plld hrd: a towards rr: rdn and wknd after 5th: t.o* **9/2**[2]

P5U/ **P** **Adajarad (IRE)**[44] 4944 6-11-0 0.. PaulMoloney
(Evan Williams) *nt fluent 2nd: a towards rr: lost tch fr after 3rd: p.u bef 3 out* **8/1**[3]

3m 56.9s (-18.60) **Going Correction** -1.125s/f (Hard)
WFA 4 from 5yo+ 18lb **9** Ran SP% **121.9**
Speed ratings (Par 105): **98,94,86,84,82 66,42,37,**
toteswingers 1&2 £3.10, 1&3 £3.80, 2&3 £8.90 CSF £102.84 TOTE £1.40: £1.02, £6.90, £3.70; EX 42.30 Trifecta £230.50 Pool: £1257.91 - 4.09 winning units..

Owner Hazard Chase Racing **Bred** Rathasker Stud **Trained** Seaborough, Dorset

FOCUS
A weak race. The cosy winner ran to his mark, with a massive step up from the second.

156 32RED.COM "NATIONAL HUNT" NOVICES' HURDLE (10 hdls) 2m 3f
6:25 (6:25) (Class 4) 4-Y-0+ **£3,249** (£954; £477; £238)

Form RPR

403/ **1** **Kentford Legend**[16] 5442 6-10-12 104........................ AndrewThornton 93+
(Seamus Mullins) *hld up bhd ldrs: reminder after 5th: wnt 2nd after next: rdn gng to 3 out: nt fluent 2 out: chal sn after last: led fnl 120yds: styd on: drvn rt out* **2/11**[1]

0P0/ **2** *1 1/4* **Upton Oaks**[11] 5537 7-10-12 0..(t) JamesDavies 88
(Chris Down) *trckd ldr: jnd ldr 3rd: led after 5th: rdn gng to 3 out: kpt 2 l advantage tl hdd fnl 120yds: no ex* **10/1**[3]

5/ **3** *28* **Volio Vincente (FR)**[14] 5475 6-10-12 0.......................... RichardKilloran 62
(Carroll Gray) *led tl after 5th: nt fluent next: rdn after 7th: hld fr 3 out: wnt modest 3rd bef last* **7/1**[2]

0/4- **4** *2* **Mixed Meaning (IRE)**[5] 80 5-10-9 0.......................... GilesHawkins(3) 60
(Stuart Howe) *racd keenly: trckd ldrs: rdn after 7th: hung lft fr 3 out: wknd after 2 out* **25/1**

000/ **P** **General Girling**[11] 5543 6-10-12 0.. IanPopham
(Caroline Keevil) *trckd ldrs: wnt lft and awkward 2nd: nt fluent 6th: sn rdn: wknd after next: t.o whn p.u after 3 out* **16/1**

4m 33.6s (-9.10) **Going Correction** -1.125s/f (Hard) **5** Ran SP% **115.9**
Speed ratings (Par 105): **74,73,61,60,**
CSF £3.66 TOTE £1.10: £1.02, £3.80; EX 3.00 Trifecta £10.40 Pool: £1191.74 - 85.20 winning units..

Owner D I Bare **Bred** D I Bare **Trained** Wilsford-Cum-Lake, Wilts

FOCUS
A poor novice hurdle run in a slow time. The winner was below his best.

157 HEAVITREE BREWERY H'CAP CHASE (15 fncs) 2m 3f 110y
6:55 (6:55) (Class 3) (0-140,136) 5-Y-0+ **£6,498** (£1,908; £954; £477)

Form RPR

600/ **1** **West With The Wind**[33] 5139 8-11-11 135........................ PaulMoloney 148+
(Evan Williams) *j. slickly: mde all: jnd briefly 4 out: shkn up and in command fr next: eased run-in* **6/1**

614/ **2** *7* **Sew On Target (IRE)**[19] 5365 8-11-3 127.............................. JoeTizzard 128
(Colin Tizzard) *trckd ldr tl after 6th: cl 3rd: pushed along after 10th: chalng whn nt fluent 4 out: hld fr next: rchd for 2 out: kpt on same pce* **11/8**[1]

1PP/ **3** *5* **Current Event (FR)**[59] 4658 6-11-6 135........................ HarryDerham(5) 130
(Paul Nicholls) *chsd ldrs: rdn to chse ldng pair gng to 4 out: hit 3 out: kpt on same pce* **3/1**[3]

0/3- **4** *19* **Pure Faith (IRE)**[6] 66 9-11-8 132..................................(v[1]) TomO'Brien 107
(Peter Bowen) *chsd ldrs: wnt lft 1st: chsd wnr after 6th tl rdn gng to 4 out: sn wknd* **11/4**[2]

4m 27.9s (-29.40) **Going Correction** -1.225s/f (Hard) course record **4** Ran SP% **108.1**
Speed ratings: **109,106,104,96**
CSF £14.88 TOTE £5.50; EX 11.60 Trifecta £43.50 Pool: £559.26 - 9.62 winning units..

Owner Mrs Janet Davies **Bred** Newsells Park Stud **Trained** Llancarfan, Vale Of Glamorgan

FOCUS
All of these lined up with something to prove. The winner is rated to the level of the best of his 2012 form.

158 32RED CASINO H'CAP HURDLE (12 hdls) 2m 7f 110y
7:25 (7:25) (Class 3) (0-135,131) 4-Y-0+ **£5,393** (£1,583; £791; £395)

Form RPR

211/ **1** **Big Time Billy (IRE)**[19] 5360 7-11-2 121......................(v) DonalDevereux 135+
(Peter Bowen) *trckd ldrs: rdn to chal gng to 3 out: led last: edgd rt: styd on gamely: drvn out* **3/1**[2]

/11- **2** *2 3/4* **Well Mett (IRE)**[4] 89 6-10-4 109 14ex......................(bt) PaddyBrennan 120
(Fergal O'Brien) *led after 1st: rdn whn hrd pressed fr 3 out: kpt v narrow advantage tl awkward and hdd last: no ex* **11/8**[1]

625/ **3** *42* **Water Garden (FR)**[33] 5145 7-11-5 131......................(p) MikeyEnnis(7) 100
(David Pipe) *hld up in tch: nt fluent 7th: sn rdn: wnt 3rd after 9th but no ch w ldng pair: t.o* **6/1**

0P0/ **4** *15* **Simarian (IRE)**[69] 4448 8-11-8 127..............................(v[1]) PaulMoloney 81
(Evan Williams) *hld up last: rdn into 4th after 9th but nvr any ch: t.o* **16/1**

3P2/ **5** *9* **Abruzzi**[26] 5240 5-11-1 120.. FelixDeGiles 65
(Tom Symonds) *led tl nt fluent 1st: reminder: chsd ldr tl rdn after 8th: sn wknd: t.o* **25/1**

050/ **6** *52* **Laustra Bad (FR)**[192] 2054 10-10-10 122..................(tp) FrancisHayes(7) 15
(David Pipe) *in tch: nudged along fr 3rd: rdn after 7th: sn lost tch: wl t.o* **33/1**

P/U- **R** **Sarando**[7] 39 8-11-0 119..(tp) LiamTreadwell
(Paul Webber) *hld up in last pair: ref 2nd* **22/1**

541/ **P** **Life Of A Luso (IRE)**[19] 5361 9-10-7 112..............................(t) TomO'Brien
(Paul Henderson) *trckd ldrs tl lost action whn p.u after 6th: dismntd* **5/1**[3]

5m 27.3s (-31.70) **Going Correction** -1.125s/f (Hard) **8** Ran SP% **115.1**
Speed ratings (Par 107): **107,106,92,87,84 66, ,**
toteswingers 1&2 £1.10, 1&3 £3.90, 2&3 £2.20 CSF £7.69 CT £21.70 TOTE £3.50: £2.30, £1.10, £1.70; EX 11.30 Trifecta £31.30 Pool: £814.30 - 19.50 winning units..

Owner Miss R L Bryan **Bred** A And C Enterprises **Trained** Little Newcastle, Pembrokes

FOCUS
It paid to race handily here and the first two, who arrived at the top of their game, dominated from four out. The form is rated through the second but could be pitched a lot higher through the others.

159 32RED INTERMEDIATE HUNTERS' CHASE (SERIES FINAL) (18 fncs) 3m
7:55 (7:55) (Class 6) 5-Y-0+ **£1,996** (£619; £309; £154)

Form RPR

1 **King Of Alcatraz (IRE)**[17] 7-11-3 0................................ MissVWade(7) 104+
(R C Smith) *trckd ldrs: travelling wl and mounting chal whn hit rail turning in: bk upsides after next travelling the bttr: led sn after last: qcknd clr: readily* **7/4**[1]

P4/ **2** *6* **Blinding Lights (IRE)**[14] 5476 8-11-3 0.......................... MrJBargary(7) 92
(Mary Sanderson) *disp ld tl clr ldr after 13th: rdn whn hrd pressed after 4 out: hdd sn after last: no ex* **20/1**

2/0- **3** *8* **Party Pictures (IRE)**[6] 57 10-11-3 0.......................... MrCGethings(7) 86
(Mrs S Westwood) *hld up in ast pair but wl in tch: mstke 8th (water) and next: hit 11th: hdwy 13th: effrt 4 out: kpt on same pce fr 3 out* **13/2**[3]

U23/ **4** *4* **Delta Borget (FR)**[14] 5476 8-11-3 99...................... MissLeandaTickle(7) 80
(L Jefford) *hld up in last pair but wl in tch: tk clsr order 13th: effrt gng to 4 out: sn one pce* **7/4**[1]

5 *72* **Buzz Me In (IRE)**[30] 8-11-3 0..(p) MrMHeard(7) 8
(R G Chapman) *disp ld most of way tl after 13th: mstke next: sn rdn: wknd bef 4 out: t.o* **4/1**[2]

5m 56.3s (-13.00) **Going Correction** -1.225s/f (Hard) **5** Ran SP% **110.8**
Speed ratings: **72,70,67,66,42**
CSF £24.55 TOTE £2.70: £2.00, £4.00; EX 28.80 Trifecta £60.90 Pool: £633.19 - 7.79 winning units..

Owner R C Smith **Bred** Kilcornan Stables **Trained** Umberleigh, Devon

■ Stewards' Enquiry : Mr C Gethings two-day ban: used whip above permitted level (May 22,26)

FOCUS
A modest hunter chase, run at a fair gallop. The form of this race probably doesn't amount to much but the winner can rate higher.

160 BECCA BOO BIRTHDAY BUMPER STANDARD OPEN NATIONAL HUNT FLAT RACE 2m 1f
8:25 (8:25) (Class 6) 4-6-Y-0 **£1,624** (£477; £238; £119)

Form RPR

40/ **1** **Nurse Ratched (IRE)**[66] 4528 4-9-12 0.................... ConorShoemark(7) 96+
(Fergal O'Brien) *mde all: styd on wl fnl 2f: asserted fnl 120yds: rdn out* **11/1**

30/ **2** *6* **Straits Of Messina (IRE)**[14] 5469 4-10-12 0...................... FelixDeGiles 97
(Tom Symonds) *trckd ldrs: rdn to chse wnr over 2f out: styd on same pce fnl f* **20/1**

003/ **3** *7* **Quite By Chance**[31] 5187 4-10-12 0...................................... JoeTizzard 90
(Colin Tizzard) *in tch: rdn to chse ldrs 3f out: sn outpcd: styd on to snatch 3rd nring fin* **9/2**[2]

4 *3/4* **Sportsreport (IRE)**[66] 4535 5-11-2 0............................ AndrewThornton 93
(Seamus Mullins) *hld up: stdy prog fr 1/2-way: trckd ldrs over 3f out: rdn 2f out: styd on same pce* **7/1**[3]

43/ **5** *nk* **Guest Of Honour (FR)**[98] 3927 5-11-2 0............................ PaulMoloney 93
(Paul Webber) *trckd ldrs tl lost pl over 7f out: sn pushed along in tch: rdn 3 out: styd on same pce fnl 2f: nvr threatened* **10/11**[1]

6 *15* **Y A Bon (IRE)** 5-10-13 0... BrendanPowell(3) 78
(Martin Hill) *in tch tl wknd wl over 2f out* **20/1**

6/ **7** *13* **Billy My Boy**[21] 5333 4-10-9 0.. GilesHawkins(3) 61
(Chris Down) *hld up: struggling 1/2-way: wknd 4f out* **7/1**[3]

05/ **8** *22* **Higgsy**[57] 4718 5-11-2 0... HaddenFrost 43
(Martin Hill) *in tch tl dropped towards rr 7f out: sn pushed along: wknd 3f out: t.o* **25/1**

020/ **9** *11* **Calverleigh Court (IRE)**[641] 1307 6-10-2 0........................ MrMHeard(7) 25
(Mary Sanderson) *trckd ldr tl rdn 6f out: wknd over 3f out: t.o* **25/1**

3m 49.2s (-19.60) **Going Correction** -1.125s/f (Hard)
WFA 4 from 5yo+ 4lb **9** Ran SP% **121.1**
Speed ratings: **101,98,94,94,94 87,81,70,65**
toteswingers 1&2 £8.40, 1&3 £8.40, 2&3 £8.40 CSF £206.87 TOTE £17.70: £4.40, £4.60, £1.80; EX 56.80 Trifecta £377.50 Part won. Pool: £503.42 - 0.21 winning units..

Owner The Nurse Ratched **Bred** Cathal Ennis **Trained** Coln St. Dennis, Gloucs

FOCUS
An ordinary bumper that was run at a sound tempo. A massive step up from the winner, with the second and fourth setting the level.
T/Plt: £94.20 to a £1 stake. Pool: £44,331.36 - 343.22 winning units T/Qpdt: £42.70 to a £1 stake. Pool: £3,315.16 - 57.40 winning units TM

FAKENHAM (L-H)
Tuesday, May 7

OFFICIAL GOING: Good (7.3)
Wind: Light breeze Weather: Very hot and sunny, 19 degrees

161 COUNTRYSIDE ALLIANCE (S) HURDLE (9 hdls) 2m
2:30 (2:30) (Class 5) 4-Y-0+ **£2,053** (£598; £299)

Form RPR

151/ **1** **Not Til Monday (IRE)**[24] 5283 7-11-8 127......................(v) JasonMaguire 103+
(J R Jenkins) *mde all but dossing bdly w ears pricked thrght: rdn bef 3 out and hit flight: wnt 3 l clr appr last: in command after but making it look unneccesarily hrd work* **4/11**[1]

001/ **2** *1 3/4* **County Zen (FR)**[36] 5056 10-10-12 97........................ MissBAndrews(7) 97
(Caroline Fryer) *w wnr: rdn bef 6th: ev ch tl outpcd u.p bef last* **12/1**

20P/ **3** *3/4* **Wom**[23] 5311 5-10-7 94..(b) TrevorWhelan(5) 89
(Neil King) *str reminders bef 3rd: chsd ldrs: drvn fr 3 out: nt qckn bef last where wnt 2nd briefly: reluctant flat* **6/1**[2]

4 *15* **Global Recovery (IRE)**[335] 6-10-7 0.............................. JamesBanks(5) 76
(Des Donovan) *hit 4th: pressed ldrs tl hrd drvn and fdd 3 out* **25/1**

5/ **5** *6* **Tallevu (IRE)**[16] 5441 4-10-5 0..................................(p) JeremiahMcGrath(3) 68
(Noel Chance) *plentiful awful jumps: drvn and struggling after pecking bdly 5th* **11/1**[3]

000/ **6** *17* **Simplified**[132] 3228 10-9-12 59......................................(t) GerardGalligan(7) 57
(Michael Chapman) *a last and nvr really striding out: mstke 5th and rdn: hit 6th: t.o bef 2 out* **150/1**

3m 58.6s (-6.80) **Going Correction** -0.725s/f (Firm)
WFA 4 from 5yo+ 18lb **6** Ran SP% **108.1**
Speed ratings (Par 103): **88,87,86,79,76 67**
toteswingers 1&2 £1.70, 1&3 £1.10, 2&3 £2.20 CSF £5.33 TOTE £1.20: £1.02, £5.70; EX 5.30 Trifecta £12.40 Pool: £1,416.06 - 85.51 winning units..There was no bid for the winner.

Owner The Three Honest Men **Bred** G J King **Trained** Royston, Herts

FOCUS
There was fresh ground on both tracks all way round. This ordinary seller was run at a good pace. The winner is rated a stone+ off his recent course win.

162 PETER SEXTON 70TH BIRTHDAY H'CAP CHASE (16 fncs) 2m 5f 110y
3:00 (3:00) (Class 5) (0-95,93) 5-Y-0+ **£3,249** (£954; £477; £238)

Form RPR

3F4/ **1** **To Live (FR)**[21] 5336 6-11-12 **93**.. TomCannon 109+
(Nick Gifford) *hld up in tch: lft 2nd at 10th: mstke 13th: sn drvn: slt ld fr next tl hdd bef last where nt fluent as at two previous fences: forced ahd on line: fine ride* **4/1**[2]

301/ **2** *hd* **Peak Seasons (IRE)**[8] 34 10-10-1 **75** 7ex................ GerardGalligan(7) 90
(Michael Chapman) *in rr but in tch: lft 3rd at 10th: pressed for ld fr 12th tl rdn to go nrly 1 length ahd last: pushed along and r.o gamely: pipped on post* **11/2**

245/ **3** *7* **Get Ready To Go (IRE)**[181] 2270 9-10-4 **76**.............(b) TrevorWhelan(5) 85
(Neil King) *lft 2nd at 4th: lft in ld 10th: drvn and hdd 3 out: fnd nil: wl hld 3rd fr next* **7/2**[1]

442/ **4** *69* **Burnt Again (IRE)**[226] 1610 9-11-10 **91**...................(bt[1]) TomScudamore 38
(Jim Best) *led tl after 3rd: plentiful bad jumps after: already rdn whn lft disputing last after being bdly hmpd 10th: t.o whn blnd 12th and 3 out* **4/1**[2]

4F6/ **F** **Monroe Park (IRE)**[18] 5381 8-10-3 **73**............................ JackQuinlan(3)
(Alan Blackmore) *t.k.h: led after 3rd: nt fluent 9th: fell next* **11/2**

246/ **F** **Festival Bound (IRE)**[140] 3133 7-10-13 **80**........................ HarrySkelton
(Caroline Fryer) *trckd ldrs tl bdly hmpd 10th: nt rcvr: mstke 12th: 7 l 4th whn fell next* **5/1**[3]

5m 27.3s (-14.50) **Going Correction** -0.625s/f (Firm) **6** Ran SP% **109.7**
Speed ratings: **101,100,98,73,**
toteswingers 1&2 £3.70, 1&3 £3.60, 2&3 £2.20 CSF £23.91 TOTE £5.50: £3.30, £2.80; EX 17.50 Trifecta £74.90 Pool: £1,050.94 - 10.51 winning units..
Owner John P McManus **Bred** G Berger, S Berger & J M Callier **Trained** Findon, W Sussex

FOCUS
A steady early gallop, the pace quickened after the third-last. Modest form, the winner rated 7lb off his best.

163 SIS NOVICES' HURDLE (13 hdls) 2m 7f 110y
3:30 (3:30) (Class 3) 4-Y-0+ **£5,393** (£1,583; £791; £395)

Form RPR

61/ **1** **Cowards Close (IRE)**[21] 5327 6-11-5 0..............................(t) DarylJacob 125+
(Paul Nicholls) *pressed ldr: gng best 3 out: led and hit next and sn rdn: wnt over 3 l clr bef last: pushed along and styd on wl* **4/9**[1]

304/ **2** *4 1/2* **No Buts**[16] 5430 5-10-13 113.. TomScudamore 115
(David Bridgwater) *led at brisk pce: mstke 2nd: j. path in bk st three times: drvn 3 out: jnd and hit next: outpcd by wnr bef last* **9/2**[2]

335/ **3** *10* **Peterbrown (IRE)**[11] 5553 5-10-13 109.................................. TomCannon 105
(Nick Gifford) *cl up: 3rd and drvn after 9th: struggling in 4th 3 out: plugged on and lft clr 3rd at last* **6/1**[3]

056/ **4** *7* **Native Colony**[11] 5553 5-10-8 100...............................(b) TrevorWhelan(5) 105+
(Neil King) *hld up last: rdn after 10th: wnt 7 l 3rd and blnd 3 out: no ch and finding little after: abt to lose 3rd whn blnd bdly last* **16/1**

3UP/ **5** *27* **Phar Away Island (IRE)**[8] 29 5-10-6 90.............(p) MissBAndrews(7) 74
(Caroline Fryer) *nt a fluent: in tch tl mstke 9th and reminders: completely lft bhd after: t.o 2 out* **80/1**

5m 51.2s (-15.20) **Going Correction** -0.725s/f (Firm) **5** Ran SP% **108.8**
Speed ratings (Par 107): **96,94,91,88,79**
CSF £2.88 TOTE £1.50: £1.10, £1.50; EX 2.90 Trifecta £4.60 Pool: £1,557.87 - 250.52 winning units..
Owner Barry Fulton & Paul K Barber **Bred** Mrs Nichola Kyle **Trained** Ditcheat, Somerset

FOCUS
The pace was sound throughout in this fair novices' hurdle. The winner was the form pick and is rated close to his mark.

164 AT THE RACES NOVICES' CHASE (18 fncs) 3m 110y
4:00 (4:00) (Class 3) 5-Y-0+ **£6,657** (£2,067; £1,113)

Form RPR

531/ **1** **Themilanhorse (IRE)**[18] 5383 7-11-4 132...........................(t) DarylJacob 125
(Paul Nicholls) *tended to lack fluency in 2nd: blnd 14th and rdn and outpcd: 5 l down but clsng valiantly 2 out: styd on to ld bef last where already 5 l clr: rdn out* **9/4**[2]

123/ **2** *9* **Private Equity (FR)**[13] 5494 5-11-4 130........................... AndrewTinkler 116
(Nicky Henderson) *led: mstke 7th: blnd 13th: lft clr next: looked wnr 3 out: 5 l ahd whn blnd next and drvn: hdd home turn: fin v weakly* **10/3**[3]

310/ **3** *12* **Turbo Du Ranch (FR)**[36] 5081 6-10-12 120..................(t) JasonMaguire 97
(Warren Greatrex) *settled in 4th pl and nt travelling: j. slowly 4th: rdn after 7th and lost tch: t.o 11th: lft 3rd at 14th: 45 l 3rd 3 out: fin much the best as ldng pair faltered* **9/2**

055/ **P** **Benefit Evening (IRE)**[16] 8-10-9 0.................................. JackQuinlan(3)
(Noel Quinlan) *a last: pckd 2nd: blnd 5th: t.o 11th: p.u after 13th* **80/1**

014/ **F** **Massini Lotto (IRE)**[52] 4791 6-10-12 0.............................. DougieCostello
(John Quinn) *t.k.h in 3rd: pckd 12th: 5 l down and gng wl whn fell 14th* **15/8**[1]

6m 21.7s (-14.00) **Going Correction** -0.625s/f (Firm) **5** Ran SP% **108.0**
Speed ratings: **97,94,90, ,**
CSF £9.73 TOTE £3.20: £1.50, £1.40; EX 7.40 Trifecta £15.10 Pool: £1,223.75 - 60.74 winning units..
Owner J Hales **Bred** Michael Heskin **Trained** Ditcheat, Somerset

FOCUS
An interesting novices' chase run at a fair gallop, with a slow-motion finish. The winner ran to his chase mark.

165 FAKENHAM LADIES RACEDAY 2ND JUNE FOX HUNTERS' CHASE (FOR THE TURNER FAMILY TROPHY) (18 fncs) 3m 110y
4:30 (4:30) (Class 6) 5-Y-0+ **£1,185** (£364; £182)

Form RPR

1/ **1** **Little Legend**[17] 9-11-7 ....(p) MissCHaydon(7) 120+
(Miss C M E Haydon) *j. economically and mde all: hit 8th: pckd 15th whn gng clr: scampered rt away fr next: pckd last* **4/9**[1]

060/ **2** *36* **Coral Point (IRE)**[16] 7-11-5 .... MissCareyWilliamson(5) 79
(B Dowling) *rdr lost iron briefly 5th: chsd wnr fr 7th: pckd 12th: rdn bef 14th: 10 l down whn hit 3 out: completely outpcd by wnr after: drvn to hold on to remote 2nd* **15/2**[3]

2PP/ **3** *3 1/2* **Hurricane Carter (IRE)**[60] 4644 13-11-3 103.............. MrSRWilliams(7) 77
(S R Williams) *last but in tch: j. slowly 7th: 15 l bhd whn landed w a thud 15th: no ch after but urged into 3rd after last: dismntd after fin* **11/1**

4 *2 1/2* **Kriss William (FR)**[16] 7-11-7 119.. MrJOwen(3) 72
(E Turner) *plld v hrd: many erratic jumps: 2nd tl 7th: no ch fr 15th: 16 l 3rd 2 out: lost 3rd u.p after last* **9/2**[2]

6m 26.9s (-8.80) **Going Correction** -0.625s/f (Firm) **4** Ran SP% **107.5**
Speed ratings: **89,77,76,75**
CSF £4.12 TOTE £1.40; EX 3.90 Trifecta £8.80 Pool: £1,564.13 - 132.41 winning units..
Owner Michael Haydon **Bred** D F Evans **Trained** Aylesbury, Bucks

FOCUS
An uncompetitive hunter chase and the winner made all for an effortless victory. He should rate higher.

166 LAW FERTILISERS MARES' H'CAP HURDLE (11 hdls) 2m 4f
5:00 (5:00) (Class 4) (0-110,110) 4-Y-0+ **£3,249** (£954; £477; £238)

Form RPR

101/ **1** **Brunton Blue**[10] 5567 8-10-8 **92**... LeightonAspell 99+
(Lucy Wadham) *t.k.h and trckd ldrs: nt fluent 3rd: wnt 2nd bef 3 out: cajoled vigorously to ld between last two: in command appr last* **9/4**[1]

3P0/ **2** *7* **Grimley Girl**[16] 5432 7-10-9 **100**....................................... MrJMahot(7) 102
(Sarah-Jayne Davies) *led: nt fluent 3rd: rdn and hdd between last two: sn no ch w wnr but kpt on gamely to remain clr of rest* **3/1**[2]

25/- **3** *7* **Cevaro (IRE)**[38] 5025 5-11-5 **110**.................................. JackSherwood(7) 104
(Nicky Henderson) *hld up in rr: clsd bef 3 out and on heels of ldrs briefly: 6 l 3rd and outpcd next: drvn and racing awkwardly after* **9/2**[3]

0FP/ **4** *3 3/4* **On The Off Chance**[97] 3943 5-11-7 **105**.....................(p) RichieMcLernon 95
(Jonjo O'Neill) *trckd ldrs: drvn after 3 out: 7 l 4th and wl btn next* **7/1**

215/ **5** *6* **Ninfea (IRE)**[139] 5483 5-11-10 **108**................................... TomScudamore 93
(David Bridgwater) *last trio: rdn 3 out: sn struggling* **7/1**

BP0/ **6** *11* **Cairanne**[25] 5267 5-9-11 **84** oh4.. JackQuinlan(3) 59
(Tom Keddy) *pressed ldr tl hit 7th: drvn and lost pl bef 3 out: wl bhd whn blnd 2 out: pckd last* **22/1**

330/ **7** *8* **Osmosia (FR)**[16] 5437 8-11-2 **100**.......................................(t) TomCannon 68
(Chris Gordon) *last trio: rdn after 7th: nt travelling fr next: wl btn 3 out: t.o* **10/1**

4m 56.2s (-16.40) **Going Correction** -0.725s/f (Firm) **7** Ran SP% **112.4**
Speed ratings (Par 105): **103,100,97,95,93 89,85**
toteswingers 1&2 £2.00, 1&3 £3.20, 2&3 £4.10 CSF £9.37 TOTE £2.50: £1.20, £3.40; EX 12.80 Trifecta £32.10 Pool: £1,828.74 - 42.59 winning units..
Owner Mark Law **Bred** G S Shropshire **Trained** Newmarket, Suffolk

FOCUS
This mares' handicap hurdle was run at a fair pace and the front two had it between them from three out. Another step up from the progressive winner.
T/Plt: £9.90 to a £1 stake. Pool: £54,816.92 - 4,031.87 winning units T/Qpdt: £3.40 to a £1 stake. Pool: £2,986.58 - 636.00 winning units IM

[22]KELSO (L-H)
Wednesday, May 8

OFFICIAL GOING: Good (good to firm in places; 8.8)
Wind: Fresh, across Weather: Overcast, drizzly

167 AVER CHARTERED ACCOUNTANTS NOVICES' CHASE (12 fncs) 2m 1f
2:05 (2:05) (Class 4) 5-Y-0+ **£3,898** (£1,144; £572; £286)

Form RPR

251/ **1** **Jack The Gent (IRE)**[30] 5219 9-11-5 125............................... BarryKeniry 128+
(George Moore) *j. boldly on occasions: mde all: clr 2nd to 3 out: rdn next: styd on wl fr last* **5/4**[1]

220/ **2** *2* **Rhymers Ha'**[18] 5400 6-10-5 0.................................... GrahamWatters(7) 119
(Lucinda Russell) *cl up: wnt 2nd 7th: clsd on wnr bef 3 out: effrt next: ch whn nt fluent last: one pce run-in* **4/1**[3]

116/ **3** *16* **Robbie**[49] 4861 9-10-12 0... JamesReveley 106
(Keith Reveley) *novicey on occasions: hld up in tch: outpcd 7th: styd on fr 2 out: no ch w first two* **15/8**[2]

346/ **4** *3 3/4* **My Idea**[16] 5451 7-10-12 0..(t) MichaelMcAlister 102
(Maurice Barnes) *chsd wnr: hit and outpcd 7th: struggling fr 4 out* **22/1**

402/ **5** *42* **Bocamix (FR)**[9] 26 7-10-12 96.. DougieCostello 74
(Andrew Crook) *bhd: outpcd 5th: no ch fr next: t.o* **28/1**

4m 4.0s (-14.00) **Going Correction** -0.80s/f (Firm) **5** Ran SP% **107.0**
Speed ratings: **100,99,91,89,70**
CSF £6.32 TOTE £1.90: £1.50, £2.10; EX 5.70 Trifecta £8.70 Pool: £817.65 - 69.77 winning units..
Owner J B Wallwin **Bred** P O'Connor **Trained** Middleham Moor, N Yorks

FOCUS
Hurdle races increased in distance by about 25yds per circuit. The going was good, good to firm in places. A fair novices' chase for the time of year, run at a sound pace with the winner making all. He's rated to his recent C&D mark.

168 HUNTER PROPERTY FUND MANAGEMENT NOVICES' H'CAP HURDLE (11 hdls) 2m 6f 110y
2:35 (2:35) (Class 4) (0-110,108) 4-Y-0+ **£4,548** (£1,335; £667; £333)

Form RPR

650/ **1** **Unex Canaletto**[26] 5275 4-10-11 **99**..................................... BrianHughes 99+
(James Ewart) *trckd ldrs gng wl: led 2 out: wnt lft appr last: rdn and styd on wl run-in* **25/1**

F05/ **2** *4* **Academy (IRE)**[13] 5522 5-10-12 **94**.................................. LucyAlexander 96
(N W Alexander) *nt fluent on occasions: t.k.h: hld up and bhd: smooth hdwy bef 3 out: pressed wnr after next: effrt and ev ch last: sn one pce* **12/1**

222/ **3** *1 3/4* **Glasson Lad (IRE)**[14] 5495 6-11-1 **102**..........................(p) TonyKelly(5) 102
(Ferdy Murphy, France) *hld up: hdwy and prom bef 3 out: rdn and ev ch next: rdn and edgd lft bef last: one pce* **7/1**

P5P/ **4** *1 1/4* **Farm Pixie (IRE)**[26] 5275 7-10-2 **91**............................ GrahamWatters(7) 89
(Ann Hamilton) *midfield: nt fluent and lost pl 7th: rdn 4 out: styd on fr 2 out: nvr able to chal* **20/1**

040/ **5** *13* **Shady Sadie (IRE)**[30] 5216 6-10-6 **88**.............................(t) RichieMcGrath 74
(Rose Dobbin) *hld up: drvn and effrt after 3 out: no imp fr next* **33/1**

401/ **6** *nse* **Pudsey House**[30] 5222 6-11-5 **101**...................................(b) AdrianLane 87
(John Wade) *cl up: led briefly bef 2 out: wknd after 2 out* **12/1**

036/ **7** *2 1/2* **Ballybroe (IRE)**[39] 5005 6-11-12 **108**.............................(p) DenisO'Regan 93
(Harriet Graham) *in tch: hit 4th: effrt bef 2 out: wknd between last 2* **28/1**

2F5/ **8** *6* **Uncut Stone (IRE)**[26] 5275 5-11-3 **99**............................(b) DannyCook 77
(Peter Niven) *prom: lost pl bef 4 out: sn btn* **6/1**[3]

4/1- **9** *9* **Welsh Bard (IRE)**[6] 72 4-11-4 **106**...............................(b) JasonMaguire 70
(Donald McCain) *led: rdn and hdd bef 2 out: sn wknd* **15/8**[1]

065/ **10** *17* **Kauto Alcazar (FR)**[17] 5426 5-11-6 **102**................................ RyanMania 57
(Sue Smith) *midfield: stdy hdwy 1/2-way: rdn and wknd bef 2 out* **11/2**[2]

The Form Book Jumps, Raceform Ltd, Compton, RG20 6NL.

430/ **P** **Trouble In Paris (IRE)**[39] 5009 6-11-1 **97**.......................... BrianHarding
(Barry Murtagh) *midfield: struggling fr 1/2-way: t.o whn p.u bef 3 out* **20/1**

004/ **U** **Border Phoenix**[30] 5220 6-11-4 **100**................................ TomMessenger
(Sandy Forster) *t.k.h: hld up: pckd and uns rdr 7th* **50/1**

5m 33.0s (-8.00) **Going Correction** -0.275s/f (Good)
WFA 4 from 5yo+ 19lb **12** Ran SP% **114.1**
Speed ratings (Par 105): **102,100,100,99,95 95,94,92,88,83 ,**
toteswingers 1&2 £21.80, 1&3 £8.60, 2&3 £6.20 CSF £259.13 CT £2323.93 TOTE £41.10: £6.70, £3.90, £1.90; EX 365.50 TRIFECTA Not won..
Owner The Craig Farm Syndicate **Bred** Middle Park Stud Ltd **Trained** Langholm, Dumfries & G'way

FOCUS
The race distances on the hurdle course were extended by approximately 25 yards per circuit. Plenty of pace on for this handicap, with the field well strung out at the line. Ordinary form, with the winner rated up a stone.

169 BROWN SHIPLEY WEALTH WELL MANAGED H'CAP CHASE (19 fncs) 3m 2f
3:05 (3:05) (Class 4) (0-115,115) 5-Y-0+ **£5,198** (£1,526; £763; £381)

Form RPR

F00/ **1** **Bobble Hat Bob (FR)**[29] 5229 8-11-2 **105**...................(p) PeterBuchanan 118+
(Lucinda Russell) *midfield: hdwy to chse ldrs 5 out: effrt and led after 2 out: kpt on strly fr last* **12/1**

134/ **2** *3* **Carrigdhoun (IRE)**[13] 5521 8-11-11 **114**.................(tp) MichaelMcAlister 124
(Maurice Barnes) *w ldr: drvn and sltly outpcd bef 2 out: rallied to chse wnr bef last: kpt on same pce run-in* **6/1**[3]

033/ **3** *5* **Markadam**[19] 5372 7-11-12 **115**.. JamesReveley 121
(Dianne Sayer) *prom: effrt after 3 out: hdwy to dispute 2nd pl bef last: outpcd run-in* **7/1**

0P3/ **4** *5* **Captain Americo (IRE)**[9] 25 11-11-5 **115**...........(b) GrahamWatters(7) 115
(James Ewart) *led: rdn 4 out: hdd after 2 out: sn outpcd* **4/1**[1]

502/ **5** *6* **Quinder Spring (FR)**[37] 5077 9-10-3 **99**.................(p) GrantCockburn(7) 94
(Lucinda Russell) *in tch: hit and outpcd 14th: rallied after 4 out: no imp bef 2 out* **8/1**

P50/ **6** *2¾* **Knight Woodsman**[10] 20 9-10-2 **98**.......................... CallumBewley(7) 92
(R Mike Smith) *hld up: mstke 10th: effrt after 5 out: no imp bef 2 out* **22/1**

435/ **7** *8* **General Hardi**[14] 5503 12-11-11 **114**..................................... BrianHughes 99
(John Wade) *chsd ldrs: drvn and outpcd 12th: n.d after* **5/1**[2]

355/ **8** *2¼* **Posh Bird (IRE)**[39] 5012 10-11-11 **114**.............................. HenryBrooke 99
(Peter Niven) *bhd and sn pushed along: nvr on terms fnl circ* **13/2**

00P/ **9** *36* **Solway Bay**[59] 4678 11-11-0 **103**..(t) BrianHarding 54
(Lisa Harrison) *towards rr: drvn and outpcd 12th: struggling fr next: t.o* **12/1**

3F6/ **10** *30* **The Magic Bishop**[14] 5502 8-11-9 **112**............................... HarryHaynes 36
(Malcolm Jefferson) *nt fluent on occasions: hld up: short-lived effrt 14th: sn btn: t.o* **14/1**

6m 31.3s (-15.90) **Going Correction** -0.80s/f (Firm) **10** Ran SP% **114.3**
Speed ratings: **92,91,89,88,86 85,82,82,71,61**
toteswingers 1&2 £15.80, 1&3 £7.80, 2&3 £7.90 CSF £81.57 CT £547.24 TOTE £19.60: £4.40, £2.50, £2.60; EX 165.50 Trifecta £207.60 Pool: £570.46 - 2.06 winning units..
Owner Mrs Carolyn Innes **Bred** Mme M Aubree, D Hanin & Mme G Bozon **Trained** Arlary, Perth & Kinross

FOCUS
This open handicap was run at a fair pace. It paid to race prominently. Ordinary form with the first two pretty much to their marks.

170 BEDMAX H'CAP CHASE (FOR THE HADDINGTON JUBILEE CUP) (17 fncs) 2m 7f 110y
3:35 (3:35) (Class 3) (0-140,140) 5-Y-0+ **£9,747** (£2,862; £1,431; £715)

Form RPR

045/ **1** **De Boitron (FR)**[19] 5369 9-11-1 **129**........................ SamTwiston-Davies 140+
(Ferdy Murphy, France) *hld up: smooth hdwy bef 3 out: rdn to ld run-in: styd on strly towards fin* **12/1**

53P/ **2** *3* **Beneficial Reform (IRE)**[17] 5427 8-10-11 **125**.............(p) NickScholfield 133
(James Ewart) *chsd ldrs: led and rdn 2 out: hdd run-in: kpt on same pce towards fin* **6/1**[2]

44P/ **3** *1¾* **Lets Get Serious (IRE)**[20] 5365 7-10-11 **125**...............(b[1]) BrianHughes 130
(James Ewart) *midfield: rdn and outpcd bef 4 out: rallied u.p after 2 out: kpt on fr last: nt rch first two* **20/1**

2BP/ **4** *½* **Garleton (IRE)**[18] 5404 12-11-11 **139**..........................(t) MichaelMcAlister 145
(Maurice Barnes) *led at decent gallop: rdn and hdd 2 out: kpt on same pce bef last* **7/1**[3]

021/ **5** *11* **You Know Yourself (IRE)**[9] 25 10-10-12 **126** 7ex............ RyanMania 121
(Sue Smith) *prom: hdwy 10th: rdn 4 out: wknd appr 2 out* **9/1**

110/ **6** *hd* **Rolecarr (IRE)**[14] 5496 10-10-10 **131**...................... GrahamWatters(7) 126
(Ann Hamilton) *hld up: rdn along bef 11th: nvr able to chal* **9/1**

221/ **7** *3* **William Money (IRE)**[29] 5229 6-10-8 **122**.......................... HenryBrooke 114
(Chris Grant) *hld up: short-lived effrt bef 4 out: wknd after next* **6/1**[2]

P25/ **8** *7* **Ballycolin**[14] 5496 10-10-2 **116**..................................... DougieCostello 104
(Ian Duncan) *nt fluent in rr: struggling fnl circ: nvr on terms* **8/1**

022/ **9** *49* **Premier Sagas (FR)**[39] 5008 9-10-11 **125**......................... BrianHarding 86
(Nicky Richards) *prom tl rdn and wknd bef 2 out: t.o* **10/1**

01P/ **P** **Always Right (IRE)**[18] 5404 11-11-12 **140**......................... DenisO'Regan
(John Wade) *bhd and nvr gng wl: lost tch and p.u bef 10th* **7/2**[1]

5m 42.6s (-25.40) **Going Correction** -0.80s/f (Firm) **10** Ran SP% **115.9**
Speed ratings: **110,109,108,108,104 104,103,101,84,**
toteswingers 1&2 £13.30, 1&3 £23.80, 2&3 £22.80 CSF £82.69 CT £1436.76 TOTE £11.20: £2.60, £1.90, £5.20; EX 62.80 Trifecta £757.80 Part won. Pool: £1,010.41 - 0.12 winning units..
Owner Mrs J Morgan & Mrs Lindsey J Shaw **Bred** Mme Isabelle Reverseau **Trained** France

FOCUS
A decent field lined up for this valuable event. It was run at a sound pace. The winner had slipped to a good mark and the second is rated back to his best.

171 JAMES EWART RACING & MAURICE FRIEL GROUNDWORKS CONDITIONAL JOCKEYS' H'CAP HURDLE (8 hdls) 2m 110y
4:10 (4:10) (Class 4) (0-120,114) 4-Y-0+ **£3,249** (£954; £477; £238)

Form RPR

112/ **1** **Endeavor**[24] 5311 8-10-10 **98**.. TonyKelly 100+
(Dianne Sayer) *in tch: hdwy bef 3 out: led between last 2: drifted lft u.p and styd on strly fr last* **7/2**[3]

511/ **2** *2* **Musnad (USA)**[19] 5386 5-11-4 **114**...............................(b) CraigGallagher(8) 114
(Brian Ellison) *led: rdn and jnd 2 out: hdd between last 2: rallied: kpt on run-in: nt pce of wnr* **9/4**[2]

200/ **3** *shd* **Smart Ruler (IRE)**[17] 5425 7-11-1 **103**........................... LucyAlexander 104
(James Moffatt) *hld up in tch: stdy hdwy on outside to press ldrs 2 out: kpt on same pce fr last* **15/2**

341/ **4** *3* **Trend Is My Friend (USA)**[14] 5499 4-11-4 **113**............. HenryBrooke(3) 108
(Donald McCain) *t.k.h: nt fluent on occasions: cl up: chal 2 out: sn rdn and hung lft: outpcd fr last* **2/1**[1]

103/ **5** *20* **Millers Reef (IRE)**[254] 1392 7-10-7 **100**........................ GrahamWatters(5) 79
(Andrew Parker) *prom tl rdn and wknd appr 2 out* **9/1**

540/ **6** *31* **Kian's Joy**[18] 3041 4-10-5 **97**...(b) JoeColliver 44
(Jedd O'Keeffe) *chsd ldr to 3 out: rdn and wknd bef next* **33/1**

3m 54.9s (-6.90) **Going Correction** -0.275s/f (Good) **6** Ran SP% **111.0**
Speed ratings (Par 105): **105,104,104,102,93 78**
toteswingers 1&2 £1.70, 1&3 £4.00, 2&3 £2.40 CSF £11.84 TOTE £5.70: £2.80, £1.10; EX 10.40 Trifecta £41.20 Pool: £2,510.53 - 45.66 winning units..
Owner Mrs Margaret Coppola **Bred** Bradmill Meat Ltd **Trained** Hackthorpe, Cumbria

FOCUS
This handicap, confined to conditional riders, was run at a fair pace. Straightforward form.

172 NFU MUTUAL ALNWICK (S) H'CAP CHASE (17 fncs) 2m 7f 110y
4:45 (4:45) (Class 5) (0-95,95) 5-Y-0+ **£3,249** (£954; £477; £238)

Form RPR

P3/ **1** **Borolee (IRE)**[16] 5450 10-10-8 **82**.. TonyKelly(5) 99+
(Ferdy Murphy, France) *hld up: stdy hdwy 5 out: led bef 2 out: sn hrd pressed and rdn: kpt on wl fr last* **9/1**

130/ **2** *8* **Silver Steel (FR)**[19] 5384 10-11-1 **89**........................(t) HarryChalloner(5) 100
(Richard Ford) *hld up: hdwy and in tch 11th: effrt and disp ld bef 2 out: sn rdn: kpt on same pce fr last* **28/1**

005/ **3** *6* **Solway Dornal**[59] 4680 8-9-7 **69** oh2...................(tp) StephenMulqueen(7) 73
(Lisa Harrison) *hld up: hdwy and prom 11th: drvn and outpcd after 3 out: plugged on fr next: no imp* **28/1**

566/ **4** *6* **Flaming Thistle (IRE)**[340] 540 9-9-7 **69** oh2..............(p) MrJHamilton(7) 68
(N W Alexander) *bhd: rdn and effrt whn nt fluent 3 out: plugged on fr next: nvr able to chal* **25/1**

644/ **5** *2½* **More Equity**[30] 5223 11-11-12 **95**.. RyanMania 92
(Dianne Sayer) *chsd ldrs tl drvn and outpcd fr 3 out* **11/2**[2]

PP0/ **6** *8* **Nicky Tam (IRE)**[16] 5450 11-10-5 **74**...................................... AdrianLane 68
(Henry Hogarth) *nt fluent in rr: rdn 5 out: blnd 3 out: n.d* **14/1**

P23/ **7** *15* **Cloudy Dawn**[333] 656 8-9-11 **73**.............................. CallumBewley(7) 49
(Sue Smith) *chsd ldrs: hit and 12th: wknd fr 3 out* **5/2**[1]

24P/ **8** *13* **Bob Will (IRE)**[31] 5206 8-11-1 **84**..(v[1]) HenryBrooke 48
(Chris Grant) *led tl rdn and hdd bef 2 out: sn btn* **9/1**

UP2/ **P** **Melua Maid (IRE)**[26] 5278 11-11-3 **86**................................ BrianHughes
(James Ewart) *chsd ldrs tl lost pl qckly and p.u 6th* **16/1**

2P5/ **P** **Doberdan (USA)**[10] 20 8-11-4 **87**..............................(p) RichieMcGrath
(Patrick Holmes) *in tch: outpcd 5 out: p.u after 3 out* **22/1**

23P/ **P** **Sam Patch**[31] 5206 10-10-1 **73**.. EwanWhillans(3)
(Donald Whillans) *nt fluent in rr: struggling fnl circ: t.o whn p.u bef 4 out: b.b.v* **16/1**

366/ **P** **Copper's Gold (IRE)**[31] 5206 9-10-6 **82**........................(b) CraigNichol(7)
(Lucinda Russell) *chsd ldr: hit and rdn 5 out: outpcd whn blnd 3 out: sn btn: p.u bef 2 out* **13/2**[3]

4P5/ **P** **Craicneasy (IRE)**[9] 23 10-10-0 **69** oh10....................... LucyAlexander
(Bruce Mactaggart) *hld up on outside: hit 4th and 7th: struggling fnl circ: t.o whn p.u bef 4 out* **22/1**

P0P/ **P** **Just Maddie**[31] 5207 9-9-12 **72**....................................... GaryRutherford(5)
(Rayson Nixon) *midfield: rdn 10th: outpcd whn blnd 5 out: lost tch and p.u bef next* **50/1**

5m 52.6s (-15.40) **Going Correction** -0.80s/f (Firm) **14** Ran SP% **117.1**
Speed ratings: **93,90,88,86,85 82,77,73, , ,**
toteswingers 1&2 £44.80, 1&3 £45.90, 2&3 £122.70 CSF £235.88 CT £6584.06 TOTE £11.80: £3.90, £5.30, £9.70; EX 284.40 Trifecta £1196.20 Part won. Pool: £1,595.04 - 0.07 winning units..
Owner Ferdy Murphy **Bred** George Doyle **Trained** France

FOCUS
A desperately weak selling handicap, run at a fair pace. The winner is rated back to the level of his Irish form.

173 D G PRYDE LTD STANDARD OPEN NATIONAL HUNT FLAT RACE 2m 110y
5:20 (5:22) (Class 5) 4-6-Y-O **£2,599** (£763; £381; £190)

Form RPR

5/ **1** **Secrete Stream (IRE)**[125] 3470 4-10-12 0.......................... BrianHughes 113+
(Malcolm Jefferson) *in tch: hdwy to chse ldr after 6f: stl gng wl whn lft in ld over 2f out: pushed clr fnl f* **9/1**

2 *10* **I Got Power** 4-10-12 0.. JamesReveley 104
(Keith Reveley) *hld up in midfield: stdy hdwy 1/2-way: effrt and shkn up whn lft cl 2nd over 2f out: kpt on same pce fnl f* **13/2**[3]

3 *2¼* **Ollie G** 5-11-2 0... DenisO'Regan 107
(Chris Grant) *hld up: smooth hdwy over 4f out: rdn whn lft 3rd and hmpd over 2f out: sn one pce* **10/1**

4 *11* **Oorayvic (IRE)** 6-11-2 0.. RyanMania 98
(Sue Smith) *hld up on outside: smooth hdwy 1/2-way: cl up over 4f out: lft 4th and outpcd over 2f out* **16/1**

03/ **5** *¾* **Rev Up Ruby**[29] 5200 5-10-2 0................................... JonathonBewley(7) 88
(George Bewley) *led: rdn and hdd over 3f out: drvn and outpcd fnl 2f* **4/1**[2]

4/ **6** *14* **Shankhouse Wells (IRE)**[39] 5011 5-10-9 0..................... JasonMaguire 76
(George Charlton) *chsd ldr 6f: cl up tl rdn and outpcd over 5f out: n.d after* **18/1**

7 *8* **Zuileka** 4-10-5 0... BrianHarding 65
(James Moffatt) *bhd: pushed along 1/2-way: sme late hdwy: nvr on terms* **40/1**

P/ **8** *11* **Hurry On Lil (IRE)**[143] 3098 4-10-2 0...................... AlexanderVoy(3) 55
(Patrick Holmes) *bhd: rdn along 1/2-way: nvr on terms* **80/1**

60/ **9** *8* **Be Wise (IRE)**[31] 5208 6-10-11 0................................... GaryRutherford(5) 59
(Harriet Graham) *hld up on outside: rdn after 5f: struggling fr 1/2-way* **50/1**

10 *21* **Poppies Milan (IRE)** 4-10-7 0.. TonyKelly(5) 36
(Ferdy Murphy, France) *bhd and detached: no ch fr 1/2-way: t.o* **14/1**

0/ **11** *22* **Runswick Days (IRE)**[26] 5279 6-10-9 0.......................... JohnDawson(7) 20
(Brian Storey) *chsd ldrs to 1/2-way: sn lost pl and struggling: t.o* **100/1**

00/ **12** *96* **George Almighty**[353] 362 5-10-9 0......................(t) StephenMulqueen(7)
(Maurice Barnes) *hld up towards rr: pushed along and struggling over 4f out: sn btn: virtually p.u fnl f* **40/1**

62/ **U** **Powderonthebonnet (IRE)**[16] 5454 5-10-11 0................ JoeColliver(5) 107+
(Alan Swinbank) *trckd ldrs: led over 3f out: pushed along and jst in front whn stmbld and uns rdr over 2f out* **6/4**[1]

3m 47.9s (-8.30) **Going Correction** -0.275s/f (Good)
WFA 4 from 5yo+ 4lb **13** Ran SP% **119.3**
Speed ratings: **108,103,102,97,96 90,86,81,77,67 57,12,**
toteswingers 1&2 £15.30, 1&3 £14.90, 2&3 £8.40 CSF £65.28 TOTE £6.40: £2.70, £1.70, £3.50; EX 98.50 Trifecta £1126.80 Part won. Pool: £1,502.44 - 0.63 winning units..

Owner Mrs M E Dixon **Bred** Michael Bolger **Trained** Norton, N Yorks

FOCUS

The pace was honest for this bumper with the winner staying on strongly. There was drama turning for home as well-backed favourite Powderonthebonnet stumbled on the level and unseated his rider. The winner looks a fair prospect.

T/Plt: £24,893.90 to a £1 stake. Pool: £52,856.93 - 1.55 winning tickets T/Qpdt: £2,225.20 to a £1 stake. Pool: £3,909.21 - 1.30 winning tickets RY

NEWTON ABBOT (L-H)

Thursday, May 9

OFFICIAL GOING: Good to firm (good to places) changing to good (good to firm in places) after race 5 (4.15)

Wind: very strong headwind Weather: rain

174 SIS SERVING INTERNATIONAL BOOKMAKERS "NATIONAL HUNT" MAIDEN HURDLE (9 hdls) 2m 3f

2:05 (2:05) (Class 4) 4-Y-0+ **£3,508** (£1,030; £515; £257)

Form RPR

226/ 1 **Fergall (IRE)**[141] 3146 6-10-11 118 WayneKavanagh(3) 129+
(Seamus Mullins) *j.rt thrght: mde all: a holding runner-up fr 2 out: pushed out* **5/2**[2]

223/ 2 2½ **Vibrato Valtat (FR)**[102] 3903 4-10-9 0 DarylJacob 121
(Paul Nicholls) *mid-div: hdwy after 5th: wnt 2nd after next: clsd on wnr after 3 out: 2 l down 2 out: sn rdn: fnd little but fin wl clr of remainder* **6/4**[1]

12/ 3 27 **Big Casino**[112] 3711 7-11-0 0 NickScholfield 106+
(Keiran Burke) *trckd ldrs: rdn to chse ldng pair after 3 out: sn outpcd: wknd after next* **11/4**[3]

060/ 4 22 **The Happy Warrior**[23] 5327 5-11-0 0 AndrewGlassonbury 82
(Bob Buckler) *chsd ldrs tl wknd after 6th: t.o* **66/1**

60/ 5 ½ **Milor De La Borie (FR)**[16] 5470 4-10-9 0 HaddenFrost 76
(David Pipe) *nvr impr fr mid-div: wknd after 3 out: t.o* **50/1**

0PP/ 6 12 **Hugo Drax (IRE)**[42] 4977 6-11-0 0 (t) ConorO'Farrell 70
(David Pipe) *trckd clr ldr tl pckd 6th: wknd after 3 out: t.o* **33/1**

600/ 7 16 **Scorer (IRE)**[12] 5566 5-11-0 0 (p) RichieMcLernon 56
(Jonjo O'Neill) *rdn after 6th: a towards rr: t.o* **50/1**

000/ 8 1¾ **Nothing Personal**[23] 5334 6-11-0 0[1] AndrewThornton 54
(Karen George) *j.rt: a in rr: tailing off whn hmpd 6th* **100/1**

05/ 9 ½ **Louis Phillipe (IRE)**[25] 5304 6-10-11 0 MichealNolan(3) 54
(Linda Blackford) *chsd ldrs: rdn appr 6th: sn wknd: t.o* **66/1**

430/ 10 1¾ **Princess Annabelle**[16] 5470 4-10-2 0 JamieMoore 40
(Rod Millman) *towards rr: struggling 4th: t.o whn hmpd 6th* **50/1**

10/ 11 4½ **Jazz Man (IRE)**[201] 1932 6-11-0 0 SamTwiston-Davies 48
(Mark Rimell) *mid-div tl 5th: sn struggling in rr: t.o* **14/1**

30/- F **Clear Mix**[27] 5267 5-10-4 0 MattGriffiths(3)
(Sue Gardner) *hld up towards rr: struggling whn fell 6th* **50/1**

4m 20.0s (-10.00) **Going Correction** -0.575s/f (Firm)
WFA 4 from 5yo+ 18lb 12 Ran SP% **116.7**
Speed ratings (Par 105): **98,96,85,76,76 71,64,63,63,62 60,**
toteswingers 1&2 £1.10, 2&3 £1.40, 1&3 £1.40 CSF £6.53 TOTE £4.30: £1.20, £1.10, £1.30; EX 7.30 Trifecta £18.60 Pool: £875.00 - 35.27 winning units..
Owner Andrew Cocks And Tara Johnson **Bred** Mrs Gail C List **Trained** Wilsford-Cum-Lake, Wilts

FOCUS

All bends moved since last meeting. Plenty took their chance but three dominated the betting and the contest. Fair novice form for the time of year, and it should work out.

175 AT THE RACES H'CAP CHASE (16 fncs) 2m 5f 110y

2:35 (2:35) (Class 4) (0-110,105) 5-Y-0+ **£4,288** (£1,259; £629; £314)

Form RPR

P0P/ 1 **Chase Gate**[198] 1975 8-11-0 93 (p) HaddenFrost 105+
(James Frost) *trckd ldrs: rdn after 4 out: chal next: led between last 2: styd on wl: rdn out* **25/1**

0F4/ 2 1¾ **Cruchain (IRE)**[21] 5363 10-11-8 104 (p) RobertDunne(3) 113
(Dai Burchell) *hld up in tch: tk clsr order 10th: rdn for str chal on outer gng to 2 out tl appr last: kpt on to go 2nd towards fin* **13/2**[3]

P00/ 3 hd **Amuse Me**[121] 3564 7-11-12 105 RichieMcLernon 116
(Jonjo O'Neill) *trckd ldrs: travelling best whn nt clr run: swtchd rt and hit 2 out: sn rdn: swtchd lft bef last: kpt on same pce to go 3rd towards fin* **3/1**[2]

232/ 4 ¾ **For The Staff (IRE)**[63] 4620 9-11-0 96 MichealNolan(3) 105
(Jackie Du Plessis) *j. sltly rt at times: led 1st tl next: prom: led after 7th: rdn whn strly pressed fr 3 out: hdd after next: no ex whn lost 2 pls towards fin* **6/4**[1]

0P3/ 5 5 **Roses Legend**[16] 5465 8-10-13 99 MrPJohn(7) 103
(Reginald Brown) *in tch: struggling 11th: kpt chsng ldrs in 5th but nvr threatened: no ex fr last* **16/1**

3P0/ 6 39 **Iheardu**[20] 5381 7-11-9 102 (p) DougieCostello 71
(Neil Mulholland) *hld up: struggling in last pair fr 9th: nvr a danger: t.o* **16/1**

PP5/ 7 8 **Russian Conquest**[33] 5186 7-11-3 96 (v[1]) AndrewThornton 58
(Seamus Mullins) *led 2nd tl after 5th: prom tl rdn after 11th: wknd after 4 out* **16/1**

6/4- F **Blue Signal (IRE)**[7] 83 8-11-9 102 LiamHeard
(Colin Heard) *prom: led 5th tl 7th: rdn after 10th: sn lost pl: fell 12th* **22/1**

423/ P **Roybuoy**[40] 5024 6-10-7 86 (tp) BrendanPowell
(Derrick Scott) *slow 2nd: nvr travelling in rr: lost tch: 6th: p.u bef 10th* **8/1**

5m 10.7s (-10.70) **Going Correction** -0.375s/f (Good) 9 Ran SP% **115.3**
Speed ratings: **104,103,103,103,101 87,84, ,**
toteswingers 1&2 £13.90, 2&3 £13.90, 1&3 £6.50 CSF £177.76 CT £640.12 TOTE £39.90: £5.60, £2.40, £1.70; EX 305.40 TRIFECTA Not won..
Owner Mrs J F Bury **Bred** A Edwards **Trained** Scorriton, Devon

FOCUS

Probably decent form for the level considering the first three in the betting finished close up. The winner is rated back to his best 2011 form.

176 BHE & ST H'CAP HURDLE (8 hdls) 2m 1f

3:05 (3:07) (Class 3) (0-130,129) 4-Y-0 **£6,076** (£1,795; £897; £449; £224)

Form RPR

053/ 1 **Tzora**[37] 5103 8-10-9 112 HaddenFrost 123+
(Martin Hill) *hld up towards rr: stdy prog appr 5th: led gng to 2 out: pushed clr: readily* **8/1**

051/ 2 14 **Dark And Dangerous (IRE)**[16] 5464 5-11-1 118 (v) BrendanPowell 114
(Brendan Powell) *set str gallop: clr tl 4th: drew clr again bef next: rdn and hdd gng to 2 out: carried lft last: rallied to regain 2nd sn after: no ch w wnr* **16/1**

FUF/ 3 ½ **Akula (IRE)**[152] 2042 6-11-8 125 RichardJohnson 120
(Mark H Tompkins) *chsd clr ldr: clsd on ldr 4th: rdn to ld briefly gng to 2 out: hld between last 2: wnt lft last: lost 2nd run-in: drifted rt nr fin* **28/1**

100/ 4 ¾ **Battlecat**[201] 1930 6-11-0 120 AdamWedge(3) 114
(Evan Williams) *hld up towards rr: rdn and hdwy after 3 out: chsd ldrs next: styng on at same pce disputing 4th whn hmpd nring fin* **16/1**

662/ 5 ½ **Sud Pacifique (IRE)**[22] 5356 5-11-1 125 NickSlatter(7) 118
(Donald McCain) *chsd ldrs: rdn after 3 out: ev ch briefly gng to 2 out: styng on at same pce disputing 4th whn hmpd nring fin* **7/2**[2]

335/ 6 4½ **Dreambrook Lady (IRE)**[26] 5284 7-11-7 124 DominicElsworth 113
(Jeremy Scott) *mid-div: hdwy 5th: rdn to chse ldrs after 3 out: hld in 6th whn hit next* **12/1**

531/ 7 4½ **Dragon's Den (IRE)**[11] 12 6-10-12 115 7ex DarylJacob 100
(Chris Down) *hld up towards rr: rdn 3 out: nvr gng pce to get involved* **10/3**[1]

1P5/ 8 4½ **Shammick Boy (IRE)**[27] 5269 8-11-12 129 JackDoyle 110
(Victor Dartnall) *in tch tl 3rd: sn struggling towards rr of chsng gp: nvr a threat after* **6/1**[3]

13/ 9 14 **Who's Cross (IRE)**[38] 5064 5-11-6 123 AndrewTinkler 92
(Nicky Henderson) *chsd ldrs: rdn after 3 out: sn wknd* **13/2**

PF/- 10 8 **Henry Hurst (IRE)**[69] 4506 7-9-11 105 JamesBanks(5) 66
(Jimmy Fox) *mid-div: hit 5th and 3 out: sn rdn: wknd bef next* **25/1**

P00/ 11 11 **Royal Rationale (IRE)**[99] 3945 9-10-2 105 (b) ConorO'Farrell 57
(David Pipe) *hld up towards rr: rdn after 5th: wknd next: t.o* **14/1**

3m 52.6s (-13.10) **Going Correction** -0.575s/f (Firm) 11 Ran SP% **117.4**
Speed ratings (Par 107): **107,100,100,99,99 97,95,93,86,82 77**
toteswingers 1&2 £20.40, 2&3 £0.00, 1&3 £20.40 CSF £124.15 CT £3379.66 TOTE £11.60: £3.20, £3.00, £7.60; EX 82.60 Trifecta £359.60 Part won. Pool: £479.53 - 0.42 winning units..
Owner Tzora Partners **Bred** Milton Park Stud **Trained** Littlehempston, Devon

FOCUS

This had the appearance of a competitive contest. The winner belatedly built on last year's Stratford win, with the next two close to their marks.

177 SIS INTERNATIONAL NOVICES' H'CAP HURDLE (8 hdls) 2m 1f

3:40 (3:40) (Class 5) (0-95,95) 4-Y-0+ **£2,463** (£718; £359)

Form RPR

000/ 1 **Church Field (IRE)**[23] 5335 5-11-2 85 RichieMcLernon 97+
(Jonjo O'Neill) *hld up towards rr: hdwy after 5th: rdn into 5th after 3 out: swtchd lft after 2 out: led last: r.o wl* **3/1**[1]

60F/ 2 5 **Twyford**[67] 4537 6-11-6 94 MrJoshuaGuerriero(5) 98+
(William Reed) *led tl 3rd: prom: led bef 3 out: rdn after 2 out: narrowly hdd whn landed awkwardly last: no ex* **12/1**

502/ 3 1¼ **Asian Prince (IRE)**[15] 5509 4-11-8 95 (bt) ConorO'Farrell 93
(Alastair Lidderdale) *in tch: chal after 3 out: rdn and ev ch next: kpt on same pce appr last* **7/2**[2]

6P0/ 4 2¾ **Sarenice (FR)**[70] 4486 7-11-3 86 HaddenFrost 85
(James Frost) *hld up towards rr: stdy prog fr after 4th: disp cl 3rd after 3 out: rdn and ch next: hld in 4th whn hit last* **14/1**

050/ 5 9 **Uncle Roger (IRE)**[15] 5509 4-11-8 95 (b) BrendanPowell 81
(Eve Johnson Houghton) *trckd ldrs: rdn bef 2 out: wknd between last 2* **7/1**[3]

420/ 6 18 **Residence And Spa (IRE)**[16] 5473 5-10-10 82 (p) MarkQuinlan(3) 56
(Helen Rees) *dwlt sltly: pushed along early to chse ldrs: led 3rd tl rdn after 5th: wknd after 3 out* **7/2**[2]

004/ 7 1¼ **Oh Dear Oh Dear**[13] 5543 5-11-11 94 (b[1]) JackDoyle 67
(Ron Hodges) *mid-div: rdn to chse ldrs after 3 out: wknd bef next* **20/1**

P44/ 8 2¼ **Taqaat (USA)**[25] 5304 5-11-7 90 (tp) SamTwiston-Davies 61
(Stephen Hughes) *trckd ldrs: rdn after 3 out: wknd bef next* **16/1**

26/- 9 1½ **Clouds Of Mist**[37] 5108 8-11-7 95 MissLucyGardner(5) 65
(Sue Gardner) *nt a fluent: a bhd* **14/1**

FU/ 10 8 **Grace And Beauty (IRE)**[29] 4464 5-11-3 86 TomO'Brien 49
(Paul Henderson) *struggling 5th: a in last pair* **33/1**

004/ 11 19 **Lisahane Bog**[53] 1428 6-10-13 87 CharlieWallis(5) 32
(Peter Hedger) *mid-div: shkn up after 4th: wknd 3 out: t.o* **25/1**

3m 57.1s (-8.60) **Going Correction** -0.575s/f (Firm)
WFA 4 from 5yo+ 18lb 11 Ran SP% **120.4**
Speed ratings (Par 103): **97,94,94,92,88 80,79,78,77,73 65**
toteswingers 1&2 £16.50, 2&3 £17.50, 1&3 £3.60 CSF £38.69 CT £135.01 TOTE £2.10: £1.10, £6.20, £1.60; EX 53.00 Trifecta £654.70 Part won. Pool of £872.99 - 0.10 winning units..
Owner John P McManus **Bred** Mrs Eleanor Hadden **Trained** Cheltenham, Gloucs

FOCUS

This wasn't a strong contest. A massive step up from the winner but the form looks solid.

178 NEWTONABBOTRACING.COM (S) H'CAP HURDLE (10 hdls) 2m 6f

4:15 (4:15) (Class 5) (0-95,95) 4-Y-0+ **£2,463** (£718; £359)

Form RPR

44P/ 1 **Noble Chic**[66] 4560 8-11-5 95 MrJMahot(7) 105+
(Sarah-Jayne Davies) *in tch: rdn to chse ldrs after 3 out: led appr 2 out: drew clr between last 2: styd on strly* **8/1**

046/ 2 13 **Mount Vesuvius (IRE)**[13] 5557 5-11-7 90 TomO'Brien 89
(Paul Henderson) *hld up: hdwy after 6th: travelling wl in cl 3rd after 3 out: rdn to chse wnr bef 2 out: nt gng pce to get on terms* **6/1**[3]

06F/ 3 7 **Majestic Bull (USA)**[11] 17 7-11-3 91 MissLucyGardner(5) 83
(Sue Gardner) *hld up: pushed along after 6th: styd on appr 2 out: wnt 3rd bef last: nvr a threat to ldng pair* **9/2**[2]

000/ 4 7 **Sovereign Spirit (IRE)**[18] 5440 11-11-7 90 (tp) NickScholfield 77
(Michael Blake) *prom: lft in ld on long run between 2nd and 3rd: rdn and hdd bef 2 out: wknd between last 2* **10/1**

0PP/ 5 4 **Detroit Red**[37] 5109 7-11-7 90 (p) HaddenFrost 73
(Martin Hill) *lft w ldr on long run between 2nd and 3rd: rdn and ev ch after 3 out: wknd after next* **14/1**

406/ 6 nk **Millie O'Brien**[241] 1534 5-10-10 79 RichardJohnson 61
(Philip Hobbs) *towards rr: u.p after 4th: nvr on terms* **4/1**[1]

405/ R **The Good Guy (IRE)**[15] 5506 10-11-7 95 (v[1]) KillianMoore(5)
(Graeme McPherson) *led: hung bdly lft: cocked jaw and rn out on long run between 2nd and 3rd* **7/1**

230/ P **Aim**[15] 5505 8-11-5 95 (vt) MikeyHamill(7)
(Sean Curran) *chsd ldrs: drvn along fr after 4th: dropped to rr after 6th: nvr a danger after: t.o whn p.u after 3 out* **14/1**

F60/ P **Yabora (FR)**[12] 8-11-5 95 (bt) MrsAlexDunn(7)
(Alexandra Dunn) *trckd ldrs: hit 3 out: sn rdn and wknd: p.u bef next* **7/1**

The Form Book Jumps, Raceform Ltd, Compton, RG20 6NL.

000/ **P** **Starlife (FR)**[117] 3615 4-10-12 **93**....(v[1]) MrMHeard(7)
(David Pipe) *in tch: trckd ldrs after 6th: rdn after next: wknd 3 out: t.o whn p.u bef last* **14/1**

5m 12.8s (-7.40) **Going Correction** -0.575s/f (Firm)
WFA 4 from 5yo+ 19lb **10** Ran SP% **117.7**
Speed ratings (Par 103): **90,85,82,80,78 78,, , ,**
toteswingers 1&2 £9.80, 2&3 £7.60, 1&3 £8.50 CSF £56.36 CT £245.83 TOTE £13.30: £2.60, £2.70, £2.20; EX 77.90 Trifecta £627.40 Pool: £2089.94 - 2.49 winning units..The winner was bought by R Welsh for £3000.

Owner Miss Sarah-Jayne Davies **Bred** Hesmonds Stud Ltd **Trained** Leominster, H'fords

FOCUS
As sellers go, this looked a moderate one. The first two were pretty much to their marks.

179 NEWTON ABBOT NOVICES' CHASE (16 fncs) 2m 5f 110y
4:50 (4:50) (Class 4) 5-Y-0+ **£3,768** (£1,106; £553; £276)

Form RPR

521/ **1** **Lough Derg Way (IRE)**[594] 1720 7-10-12 0.... BrendanPowell 117+
(Jamie Snowden) *in tch: tk clsr order after 10th to trck ldrs: nt clr run after 3 out tl after 2 out: chal last: sn led: styd on wl: rdn out* **5/1**[2]

354/ **2** *1 ½* **Beckhani**[25] 5313 6-10-12 0.... RichieMcLernon 115+
(Jonjo O'Neill) *mid-div: hdwy 11th: trckd ldrs 4 out: chal on inner 2 out: ev ch whn pckd last: kpt on* **6/1**

245/ **3** *2 ¼* **Starsky Des Mottes (FR)**[62] 4637 7-10-12 104.... JackDoyle 112
(Victor Dartnall) *hld up: midfield after 7th: trckd ldrs 4 out: led narrowly between last 2: rdn and hdd sn after last: no ex* **8/1**

3/2- **4** *6* **Latest Trend (IRE)**[6] 97 7-10-12 0.... RichardJohnson 107
(Tim Vaughan) *sn prom: lft in ld 9th tl 12th: pressed ldr: rdn and ev ch after 3 out tl no ex appr last* **10/3**[1]

423/ **5** *6* **Brockwell Park**[16] 5466 6-10-6 0 ow1.... LiamHeard 96
(Jeremy Scott) *in tch: led 12th: rdn after 3 out: hdd between last 2: fdd* **10/1**

404/ **6** *14* **Niki Royal (FR)**[16] 5479 8-10-5 107.... TomO'Brien 84
(Jamie Snowden) *trckd ldrs: rdn after 4 out: wknd after next* **11/2**[3]

400/ **7** *4* **Minella Fifty (IRE)**[54] 4780 5-10-2 0....(t) JamesHuxham(10) 85
(Jonjo O'Neill) *a in rr* **25/1**

000/ **8** *hd* **Atriptomilan (IRE)**[13] 5538 5-10-12 0....(p) DominicElsworth 85
(Jonjo O'Neill) *mid-div tl 3rd: sn in last pair: nvr on terms after* **16/1**

520/ **F** **Shannon Spirit (IRE)**[37] 5103 8-10-12 105....(b) JamieMoore
(Paul Henderson) *wore blinkers instead of cheek pieces: led tl fell 9th* **16/1**

030/ **U** **Pirans Car**[13] 5538 7-10-9 0....(t) MarkQuinlan(3)
(Nigel Hawke) *hld up towards rr: mstke and uns rdr 12th* **50/1**

P62/ **S** **Caunay**[127] 557 6-10-12 0.... DougieCostello
(Neil Mulholland) *trckd ldrs: pushed along in tch whn slipped up and uns rdr on bnd after winning post after 9th* **33/1**

44P/ **P** **Admiral Boom (IRE)**[71] 4461 7-10-5 0.... MikeyEnnis(7)
(Paul Henderson) *hld up: midfield 9th: wknd bef 4 out: p.u after 3 out* **25/1**

000/ **U** **Whatsupjack (IRE)**[23] 5337 6-10-12 0....(b[1]) SamJones
(Oliver Sherwood) *trcking ldrs: nt fluent 3rd: mstke and uns rdr 6th* **20/1**

5m 14.5s (-6.90) **Going Correction** -0.375s/f (Good) **13** Ran SP% **118.7**
Speed ratings: **97,96,95,93,91 86,84,84,, , ,**
toteswingers 1&2 £9.30, 2&3 £9.10, 1&3 £8.50 CSF £33.16 TOTE £7.20: £2.30, £2.50, £3.10; EX 50.50 Trifecta £332.20 Pool: £1543.62 - 3.48 winning units..

Owner The Folly Partnership **Bred** David And Ann Mooney **Trained** Lambourn, Berks

FOCUS
The first three home all look capable of going on from this, so the form should be at least fair on quick ground. The first two are rated in line with their best hurdle form.

180 INDEPENDENT RACECOURSES LTD, IRL HUNTERS' CHASE (20 fncs) 3m 2f 110y
5:25 (5:25) (Class 6) 6-Y-0+ **£1,383** (£425; £212)

Form RPR

52P/ **1** **Round Tom (FR)**[19] 8-12-0 114....(t) MrWBiddick 115+
(R Barber) *prom: led 3rd: hit 14th: jnd briefly after 3 out: in command fr next: easily* **10/11**[1]

4U6/ **2** *11* **Prince Massini (IRE)**[26] 12-11-7 103.... MissCPrichard(7) 102
(Ian Prichard) *hld up in tch: hdwy fr after 15th: rdn to press wnr after 3 out: sn hld: kpt on same pce* **12/1**

161/ **3** *8* **Parkam Jack**[16] 5476 7-12-1 0.... MikeyEnnis(3) 100
(Miss Kayley Jones) *trckd ldrs: ev ch 4 out: sn rdn: hld fr next: styd on same pce* **11/4**[2]

354/ **4** *1* **Gershwinner (IRE)**[19] 10-11-7 84....(b) MrMWoodward(7) 94
(Ms Emma Oliver) *led tl nt fluent 3rd: w wnr: pushed along 14th: rdn whn lost 2nd gng to 4 out: styd on same pce fr 3 out* **11/2**[3]

265/ **5** *2 ½* **Captain Marlon (IRE)**[11] 13 12-11-7 0.... MrJBargary(7) 91
(Mrs Claire Hitch) *hld up in tch: hit 7th: hdwy 14th: rdn whn hit 3 out: styd on same pce fr next* **20/1**

6 *76* **No Reason Why (IRE)**[12] 9-10-11 0....(p) MissRPLeyshon(7) 12
(Andrew Leyshon) *sltly detached tl lost tch fr 10th: continued t.o* **16/1**

0/0- **P** **Parazar (FR)**[8] 57 8-11-7 0.... MrMHeard(7)
(D Summersby) *trckd ldrs: struggling 11th: wknd after 16th: t.o whn p.u bef 2 out* **40/1**

P6P/ **P** **Tallanstown Boy (IRE)**[23] 5332 8-11-11 84....(b) MrJoshuaGuerriero
(Mrs Rose Partridge) *racd wd: trckd ldrs: disp 2nd after 13th tl rdn after next: wkng wnt hung rt 15th: sn p.u* **18/1**

6m 35.6s (-9.00) **Going Correction** -0.375s/f (Good) **8** Ran SP% **120.5**
Speed ratings: **98,94,92,92,91 68,,**
toteswingers 1&2 £4.60, 2&3 £3.60, 1&3 £2.30 CSF £14.54 TOTE £1.60: £1.02, £2.80, £1.40; EX 11.00 Trifecta £26.40 Pool: £1541.75 - 43.64 winning units..

Owner The Hon Mrs Townshend & J R Townshend **Bred** Didier Besnouin **Trained** Beaminster, Dorset

FOCUS
Uncompetitive stuff. The easy winner stood out and is rated close to his mark.

T/Plt: £349.50 to a £1 stake. Pool of £61622.25- 128.68 winning tickets. T/Qpdt: £86.10 to a £1 stake. Pool of £4492.04- 38.60 winning tickets. TM

[64]SOUTHWELL (L-H)
Thursday, May 9

OFFICIAL GOING: Good (8.2)
Wind: fresh across Weather: overcast, showers, breezy

181 BETVICTOR.COM H'CAP CHASE (16 fncs) 2m 4f 110y
5:35 (5:35) (Class 4) (0-120,123) 5-Y-0+ **£3,768** (£1,106; £553; £276)

Form RPR

33P/ **1** **The Black Baron (IRE)**[26] 5294 11-11-6 **112**.... LeightonAspell 124+
(Lucy Wadham) *trckd ldr: led 4 out: clr whn hit 2 out: j.rt and mstke last: eased nr fin* **4/1**[2]

344/ **2** *8* **That's The Deal (IRE)**[18] 5433 9-10-9 **106**.... JoeCornwall(5) 110
(John Cornwall) *chsd ldrs: lft 3rd and hmpd 11th: tk 6 l 2nd 2 out: one pce* **4/1**[2]

233/ **3** *20* **Clouded Thoughts (IRE)**[26] 5294 7-11-4 **110**....(p) AidanColeman 100
(Venetia Williams) *led: hdd and drvn 4 out: wknd qckly 2 out* **9/4**[1]

06/- **4** *14* **Tasheba**[211] 1780 8-11-12 **118**....(t) PaulMoloney 90
(Sophie Leech) *in rr: drvn 6th: bhd fr 10th: t.o 12th* **9/1**

060/ **5** *1 ¾* **Mr Jay Dee (IRE)**[80] 4291 8-10-6 **105**.... DanielHiskett(7) 76
(Claire Dyson) *j.rt: chsd ldrs: lost pl 8th: t.o 10th* **15/2**

211/ **F** **Kykate**[10] 26 7-11-12 **123** 7ex....(t) HarryChalloner(5)
(William Kinsey) *hld up: chsd ldrs 9th: disputing handy 2nd whn fell 11th* **9/2**[3]

5m 20.3s (3.30) **Going Correction** +0.25s/f (Yiel) **6** Ran SP% **110.7**
Speed ratings: **103,99,92,87,86**
toteswingers 1&2 £2.10, 2&3 £1.80, 1&3 £2.50 CSF £19.63 TOTE £4.20: £1.50, £2.70; EX 18.40 Trifecta £81.60 Pool: £1213.22 - 11.14 winning units..

Owner The Bees **Bred** Mrs Tom O'Donnell **Trained** Newmarket, Suffolk

FOCUS
Bend into home straight at outermost line, Golf Club bend on innermost line as at last meeting. This was a tight opening handicap and they went a sound gallop. The winner's Fakenham win could be rated this high.

182 COLIN FERRY'S 77TH BIRTHDAY BEGINNERS' CHASE (16 fncs) 2m 4f 110y
6:05 (6:05) (Class 4) 5-Y-0+ **£3,768** (£1,106; £553; £276)

Form RPR

020/ **1** **Nagpur (FR)**[21] 5362 7-11-0 0.... AidanColeman 129+
(Venetia Williams) *chsd ldrs: lft 3rd 8th: drvn 4 out: styd on to chse ldng pair 2 out: led last: forged clr* **13/8**[1]

100/ **2** *8* **Bound For Glory (IRE)**[36] 5121 7-11-0 0.... JasonMaguire 120
(Donald McCain) *led to 6th: w ldr: led 11th to 4 out: sn hrd drvn: narrow ld 2 out: hdd last: kpt on same pce* **22/1**

000/ **3** *hd* **Timesawastin (IRE)**[27] 5269 7-11-0 0.... PaulMoloney 122+
(Evan Williams) *w ldrs: led 6th to 11th: narrow ld 4 out: hdd and hit 2 out: 3rd and upsides whn mstke last: hung lft and kpt on same pce* **15/2**

000/ **4** *27* **Secret Edge**[117] 3612 5-11-0 0.... WayneHutchinson 97
(Alan King) *in rr: mstke 6th: sme hdwy 9th: outpcd and lost pl 4 out: distant 4th next* **5/1**[3]

000/ **F** **Paintball (IRE)**[14] 5525 6-11-0 0....(b[1]) TomScudamore
(Charlie Longsdon) *trckd ldrs: handy 3rd whn fell 8th: heavy fall running loose 2 out* **12/1**

34P/ **P** **Rebel Flag (IRE)**[18] 6-11-0 0....(t) TomMessenger
(Chris Bealby) *j.rt: towards rr: lost pl after 9th: sn t.o: p.u bef 3 out* **100/1**

1U2/ **P** **Cloudy Bob (IRE)**[26] 5280 6-11-0 0.... ColinBolger
(Pat Murphy) *j. bdly rt: lft modest 4th 8th: j. violently rt and wknd 3 out: t.o 5th whn p.u bef last* **5/2**[2]

00/ **P** **Raynell**[38] 5-10-11 0....(t) JackQuinlan(3)
(Noel Quinlan) *in rr: reminders 6th: t.o whn reminders 9th: p.u bef 3 out* **100/1**

500/ **P** **Moneymix**[23] 5337 6-11-0 0....(p) DenisO'Regan
(Paul Webber) *in rr: drvn whn hmpd 8th: sme hdwy 10th: lost pl 12th: t.o 3 out: p.u bef next* **50/1**

5m 17.9s (0.90) **Going Correction** +0.25s/f (Yiel) **9** Ran SP% **111.1**
Speed ratings: **108,104,104,94, , , ,**
toteswingers 1&2 £4.00, 2&3 £7.20, 1&3 £2.80 CSF £31.98 TOTE £2.00: £1.30, £5.60, £2.20; EX 26.30 Trifecta £126.20 Pool: £1365.50 - 8.11 winning units..

Owner Miss S Douglas-Pennant **Bred** J Thiebaut, D Moreau & Mme S Moreau **Trained** Kings Caple, H'fords

FOCUS
An interesting beginners' chase for the time of year and there was no hanging about. The winner is rated in line with his French chase figure but is sure to rate higher.

183 £25 FREE BET AT BETVICTOR.COM H'CAP CHASE (13 fncs) 2m
6:35 (6:35) (Class 5) (0-95,94) 5-Y-0+ **£2,144** (£629; £314; £157)

Form RPR

0/1- **1** **Accessallareas (IRE)**[7] 84 8-11-12 **93** 7ex.... WillKennedy 118+
(Sarah-Jayne Davies) *j.rt: trckd ldrs 3rd: upsides 8th: led next: wnt clr bef 2 out: 12 l ahd last: heavily eased* **2/1**[1]

5/5- **2** *6* **Mad Professor (IRE)**[8] 65 10-9-10 **68**....(b) JoeCornwall(5) 79
(John Cornwall) *chsd ldrs: drvn 6th: kpt on fr 4 out: tk modest 2nd 2 out* **20/1**

0/1- **3** *11* **Mount Welcome (IRE)**[9] 43 9-11-8 **94** 7ex....(t) MrTWeston(5) 95
(Martin Weston) *t.k.h: trckd ldrs 3rd: 2nd 3 out: wknd next* **7/1**

4U2/ **4** *8* **Cocoa Key (IRE)**[11] 20 9-11-12 **93**.... RyanMania 88
(Richard Ford) *mstkes: led: hdd 9th: wknd 3 out: blnd last* **4/1**[3]

6/0- **5** *19* **Guns Of Love (IRE)**[7] 84 11-10-9 **76**.... JasonMaguire 52
(Robin Dickin) *chsd ldrs: wknd sn after 9th: bhd fr 3 out* **25/1**

0/P- **6** *2 ¾* **The Grey One (IRE)**[9] 43 10-10-11 **85**.... ChrisDavies(7) 58
(Milton Bradley) *in rr: hdwy 8th: outpcd and j. bdly rt 4 out: sn bhd* **28/1**

0P6/ **7** *4 ½* **Vintage Red**[26] 5290 5-11-1 **82**.... TomMessenger 51
(Chris Bealby) *in tch: lost pl 6th: bhd fr 8th: t.o 3 out* **20/1**

440/ **P** **Strathaird (IRE)**[11] 21 9-10-1 **68**....(p) BrianHughes
(Andrew Crook) *in rr: drvn 6th: sn t.o: p.u bef 3 out* **33/1**

352/ **P** **Youm Jamil (USA)**[66] 4571 6-10-0 **67**.... PaddyBrennan
(Tony Carroll) *in rr: poor 5th 4 out: wknd and p.u bef next* **9/4**[2]

4m 10.3s (8.30) **Going Correction** +0.25s/f (Yiel) **9** Ran SP% **116.4**
Speed ratings: **89,86,80,76,67 65,63, ,**
toteswingers 1&2 £11.90, 2&3 £19.80, 1&3 £3.30 CSF £41.16 CT £241.70 TOTE £3.30: £1.40, £3.80, £1.90; EX 51.70 Trifecta £221.30 Pool: £1499.06 - 5.07 winning units..

Owner Miss Sarah-Jayne Davies **Bred** Mrs Gail Kidd **Trained** Leominster, H'fords

FOCUS
A weak handicap but a fast-improving winner who took another step up.

184 TALK TO VICTOR H'CAP HURDLE (9 hdls) 2m
7:05 (7:06) (Class 5) (0-95,95) 4-Y-0+ **£1,949** (£572; £286; £143)

Form RPR
0/4- **1** **Foxcub (IRE)**[9] 49 5-11-9 **91**........ FelixDeGiles 102+
(Tom Symonds) *chsd ldrs: led 2 out: drvn clr* **6/1**
2/2- **2** *7* **Pobs Trophy**[7] 75 6-10-3 **76**........(b) JonathanEngland(5) 81
(Richard Guest) *j.rt: led: hdd 2 out: styd on same pce* **4/1**[1]
551/ **3** *7* **Catawollow**[5] 21 6-10-9 **77** 7ex........(v) HarryHaynes 75
(Richard Guest) *in rr: hdwy 3 out: 3rd after 2 out: kpt on one pce* **6/1**
053/ **4** *nk* **Argaum (IRE)**[16] 5464 6-11-12 **94**........(t) PaulMoloney 91
(Evan Williams) *in rr: drvn 4th: hdwy 3 out: kpt on to take modest 4th last* **11/1**
2/3- **5** *4* **Green Lightning (IRE)**[9] 49 6-10-5 **73**........(b) TomMessenger 69
(Martin Weston) *trckd ldrs: 3rd and rdn 3 out: wknd last* **9/2**[2]
03F/ **6** *10* **Meglio Ancora**[108] 1392 6-11-5 **92**........ HarryChalloner(5) 77
(Richard Ford) *in rr: hdwy 5th: wknd appr 2 out* **20/1**
000/ **7** *1* **Burns Night**[38] 5064 7-10-8 **79**........ JackQuinlan(3) 63
(Noel Quinlan) *in rr: hdwy 5th: lost pl after 3 out* **16/1**
4/5- **8** *4 ½* **Tiradia (FR)**[9] 49 6-11-6 **88**........ JasonMaguire 68
(J R Jenkins) *j.rt: in rr: hdwy to chse ldrs whn hit 5th: j. violently rt 3 out: lost pl bef next* **5/1**[3]
000/ **9** *17* **Teals Star**[15] 5499 9-10-4 **79**........ MrJohnWilley(7) 44
(C I Ratcliffe) *in rr: sn drvn along: bhd fr 6th: t.o 2 out* **50/1**
050/ **10** *6* **There's No Rules**[12] 5566 4-11-9 **95**........(v[1]) BarryKeniry 50
(Richard Guest) *t.k.h: trckd ldrs 2nd: lost pl bef 3 out: sn bhd: t.o* **40/1**
P00/ **11** *11* **Hoar Frost**[11] 17 8-10-7 **80**........(p) SamanthaDrake(5) 29
(Karen Tutty) *chsd ldrs: lost pl bef 3 out: sn bhd: t.o* **25/1**
P0P/ **U** **Rasteau (IRE)**[16] 5477 5-10-5 **80**........(t) MarkMarris(7)
(Tom Keddy) *chsd ldrs: drvn 4th: lost pl next: mstke and uns rdr 6th* **40/1**
00P/ **P** **Lakota Ghost (USA)**[7] 4272 5-11-2 **84**........(t) AidanColeman
(Seamus Durack) *in rr: bhd fr 5th: t.o whn p.u bef 2 out* **20/1**

4m 2.1s (5.10) **Going Correction** +0.375s/f (Yiel)
WFA 4 from 5yo+ 18lb 13 Ran SP% **117.8**
Speed ratings (Par 103): **102,98,95,94,92 87,87,85,76,73 68, ,**
toteswingers 1&2 £4.80, 2&3 £4.50, 1&3 £9.70 CSF £27.84 CT £152.58 TOTE £5.90: £2.00, £1.60, £3.20; EX 30.70 Trifecta £257.90 Pool: £837.12 - 2.43 winning units..
Owner Celia & Michael Baker **Bred** St Clare Hall Stud **Trained** Harewood End, H'fords

FOCUS
A weak handicap, run at a solid gallop but few landed any sort of a blow in the home straight. The easy winner improved to the level of his best bumper form.

185 BETVICTOR CASINO ON YOUR MOBILE MAIDEN HURDLE (11 hdls) 2m 4f 110y
7:35 (7:35) (Class 5) 4-Y-0+ **£1,949** (£572; £286; £143)

Form RPR
33P/ **1** **Up For An Oscar (IRE)**[152] 2908 6-10-9 114........ EdCookson(5) 118+
(Kim Bailey) *chsd ldrs: led 2 out: narrowly hdd sn after last: styd on to regain ld nr fin* **7/1**[3]
420/ **2** *½* **Mister Newby (IRE)**[123] 3531 7-11-0 0........ SeanQuinlan 118+
(Richard Phillips) *hld up in rr: hdwy 3 out: chsng ldrs whn hmpd on ins appr next: upsides last: sn led narrowly: hdd and no ex nr fin* **12/1**
253/ **3** *¾* **Shuh Shuh Gah (IRE)**[73] 4426 6-11-0 119........ TomScudamore 115
(David Bridgwater) *w ldrs: led 2nd tl after 6th: led 3 out: hdd next: kpt on same pce* **3/1**[1]
33P/ **4** *2 ½* **Jojabean (IRE)**[147] 3022 6-11-0 114........ WayneHutchinson 112
(Alan King) *mid-div: chsd ldrs 3 out: one pce appr last* **3/1**[1]
65F/ **5** *12* **Minellaforlunch (IRE)**[11] 3 6-11-0 0........ HenryOliver 101
(Henry Oliver) *hld up towards rr: hdwy to chse ldrs 6th: drvn 3 out: hmpd and lost pl next* **11/2**[2]
221/ **6** *9* **Bhakti (IRE)**[436] 4564 6-11-0 0........ AidanColeman 93
(Mark Rimell) *led to 2nd: led after 6th to 3 out: wknd next* **20/1**
U03/ **7** *9* **Yazdi (IRE)**[12] 5566 4-10-4 0........(t) GavinSheehan(5) 80
(Charlie Mann) *chsd ldrs 4th: wknd bef 2 out* **14/1**
44/- **8** *12* **Nail 'M (IRE)**[27] 5265 5-11-0 0........ FelixDeGiles 74
(Nigel Hawke) *chsd ldrs: lost pl after 3 out* **40/1**
040/ **9** *3 ½* **Lucanor (IRE)**[19] 5408 5-11-0 0........ HarrySkelton 71
(Paul Webber) *hld up in rr: hdwy 6th: drvn 3 out: sn lost pl* **40/1**
326/ **10** *1 ½* **Fling Me (IRE)**[28] 5241 6-11-0 0........ LeightonAspell 70
(Oliver Sherwood) *hld up towards rr: hdwy to chse ldrs 3 out: sn drvn: wknd 2 out* **22/1**
432/ **11** *24* **Whenindoubtdoit (IRE)**[59] 4698 6-11-0 116........(p) JasonMaguire 48
(David Arbuthnot) *chsd ldrs: reminders 4th: lost pl after 6th: bhd fr 8th: t.o 3 out* **15/2**
12 *19* **Otto Nicolai**[278] 4-10-9 0........ RichardKilloran 26
(Sean Curran) *hld up: mstke 6th: chsng ldrs next: lost pl 3 out: sn bhd: t.o* **100/1**
PP/ **P** **Tibberton Tara**[352] 394 5-10-7 0........ TomMessenger
(Martin Weston) *nt jump wl in rr: bhd fr 6th: t.o whn j. bdly rt 8th: p.u bef next* **150/1**

5m 15.9s (2.90) **Going Correction** +0.375s/f (Yiel)
WFA 4 from 5yo+ 19lb 13 Ran SP% **119.6**
Speed ratings (Par 103): **109,108,108,107,103 99,96,91,90,89 80,73,**
toteswingers 1&2 £11.60, 2&3 £10.10, 1&3 £5.90 CSF £80.34 TOTE £7.10: £3.50, £3.20, £1.10; EX 126.90 Trifecta £461.70 Part won. Pool: £615.71 - 0.85 winning units..
Owner The Hon Mrs Cookson **Bred** S Michael Millar **Trained** Andoversford, Gloucs

FOCUS
An ordinary novice hurdle. The winner and fourth are rated to their marks.

186 DOWNLOAD THE BETVICTOR APP NOW NOVICES' HURDLE (9 hdls) 2m
8:05 (8:05) (Class 4) 4-Y-0+ **£3,119** (£915; £457; £228)

Form RPR
32/ **1** **Sea Lord (IRE)**[11] 15 6-10-12 0........ DenisO'Regan 130+
(John Ferguson) *t.k.h: led to 2nd: led briefly 4th: led again appr next: wnt clr appr last: easily* **1/1**[1]
2 *10* **Daliance (IRE)**[190] 4-10-8 0........ LeightonAspell 110
(Lucy Wadham) *trckd ldrs: wnt cl 2nd appr 2 out: one pce between last 2* **5/1**[3]
325/ **3** *32* **Looking Hopeful (IRE)**[112] 3694 7-10-12 0........ DavidBass 85
(Nicky Henderson) *chsd ldrs: upsides 6th: wknd appr 2 out* **5/2**[2]
526/ **4** *13* **Resourceful Miss**[25] 5316 4-10-1 0........ HarrySkelton 63
(Paul Webber) *in rr: sme hdwy 3 out: modest 4th bef 2 out* **33/1**
500/ **5** *3* **Whispering Harry**[13] 5543 4-10-8 0........ HenryOliver 67
(Henry Oliver) *hld up: hdwy 6th: chsng ldrs next: sn drvn: modest 5th bef 2 out* **50/1**
F5/ **6** *32* **Calypso Star (IRE)**[569] 2038 6-10-12 0........ FelixDeGiles 42
(Nigel Hawke) *hld up in mid-div: drvn and lost pl 3 out: sn bhd: t.o* **66/1**
/ **7** *3 ½* **The Bells O Peover**[225] 5-10-12 0........ JasonMaguire 39
(Donald McCain) *w wnr: pckd landing 1st: led 2nd: hdd and reminders after 4th: sn regained ld: j. slowly and hdd next: rdn and wknd qckly appr 3 out: eased and t.o bef next: virtually p.u* **15/2**
000/ **P** **Captain Wilson**[67] 4536 6-10-12 0........(p) TomScudamore
(Mark Rimell) *chsd ldrs: mstke 2nd: rdn and lost pl 3 out: sn bhd: t.o whn p.u bef next* **66/1**
00P/ **P** **Exclusive Rights**[10] 33 5-10-5 0........ AidanColeman
(Charlie Longsdon) *nt fluent in rr: bhd fr 6th: t.o whn p.u bef 2 out* **66/1**

4m 3.6s (6.60) **Going Correction** +0.375s/f (Yiel)
WFA 4 from 5yo+ 18lb 9 Ran SP% **116.4**
Speed ratings (Par 105): **98,93,77,70,69 53,51, ,**
toteswingers 1&2 £1.70, 2&3 £2.50, 1&3 £1.60 CSF £6.72 TOTE £1.50: £1.10, £1.80, £1.20; EX 7.10 Trifecta £15.30 Pool: £828.34 - 40.53 winning units..
Owner Bloomfields **Bred** Darley **Trained** Cowlinge, Suffolk

FOCUS
A step up from the easy winner but he's entitled to be a lot better than this on Flat form.

187 FOLLOW US ON TWITTER @BETVICTORRACING MARES' MAIDEN NATIONAL HUNT FLAT RACE (CONDITIONALS/AMATEURS) 2m
8:35 (8:35) (Class 6) 4-6-Y-0 **£1,559** (£457; £228; £114)

Form RPR
36/ **1** **Falcon's Present**[52] 4844 5-11-2 0........ HarryChalloner(5) 94+
(Venetia Williams) *mid-div: chsng ldrs 7f out: wl outpcd over 3f out: styd on wl 2f out: led jst ins fnl f: kpt on wl* **7/1**
26/ **2** *2* **Darcey Diva**[164] 2675 5-11-0 0........ KieronEdgar(7) 92
(David Pipe) *mid-div: hdwy 4f out: chal over 1f out: sn led narrowly: hdd jst ins fnl f: styd on same pce* **15/2**
5/ **3** *hd* **Tiller Belle**[10] 36 5-11-4 0........ JeremiahMcGrath(3) 93+
(Nicky Henderson) *led 4f: led 7f out: hdd 3f out sn outpcd: rallied 1f out: styd on towards fin* **6/1**[2]
36/ **4** *shd* **Midnight Cataria**[21] 5364 4-10-10 0........ MrJoshuaNewman(7) 88
(Alan King) *sn trcking ldrs: led narrowly 3f out: hdd narrowly over 1f out: kpt on same pce* **6/4**[1]
4/ **5** *1* **Oscar's Pet (IRE)**[96] 4001 5-11-2 0........ BenPoste(5) 91
(Tom Symonds) *in tch: t.k.h: chsd ldrs 7f out: reminders over 5f out: outpcd over 3f out: hdwy to chse ldrs over 1f out: kpt on one pce* **13/2**[3]
5/ **6** *4* **Rolling Dough (IRE)**[158] 2806 5-11-7 0........ DonalDevereux 87
(Sophie Leech) *chsd ldrs: t.k.h: outpcd over 3f out: one pce fnl 2f* **22/1**
7 *1 ¾* **Langarve Lady (IRE)** 5-10-11 0........ ChrisMeehan(10) 86
(Neil Mulholland) *sn chsng ldrs: upsides over 3f out: wknd fnl f* **25/1**
0/ **8** *2 ½* **Mieuxmix (IRE)**[25] 5316 4-10-10 0........ MrJHamilton(7) 80
(Peter Niven) *in rr: hdwy 6f out: sn pushed along: kpt on: nvr a threat* **25/1**
9 *32* **Miss Redbrook (IRE)** 6-11-0 0........ MrJarrett(7) 55
(Sarah-Jayne Davies) *hld up in rr: t.k.h: outpcd 6f out: lost pl over 3f out: sn bhd: t.o* **20/1**
10 *4 ½* **Langarve Lass (IRE)** 4-10-10 0........ MrLKilgarriff(7) 47
(Neil Mulholland) *towards rr: sn drvn along: kpt on fnl 3f: nvr a factor* **33/1**
00/ **11** *18* **Kicks Milan (IRE)**[76] 4377 6-11-2 0........ TrevorWhelan(5) 35
(Tony Carroll) *sn chsng ldrs: reminders and lost pl 8f out: sn bhd: t.o* **40/1**
0/ **12** *3 ¾* **Home Girl (IRE)**[28] 5254 5-11-4 0........ JakeGreenall(3) 31
(Susan Johnson) *trckd ldrs: led after 4f: hdd 7f out: lost pl 5f out: sn bhd: t.o* **20/1**
P0/ **13** *83* **Foreverbest (IRE)**[16] 5483 4-10-10 0........(t) MrLTorbitt(7)
(Roger Teal) *racd in last: lost tch 6f out: sn wl bhd: t.o 3f out: virtually p.u: eventually completed* **100/1**

4m 4.2s (12.80) **Going Correction** +0.375s/f (Yiel)
WFA 4 from 5yo+ 4lb 13 Ran SP% **119.8**
Speed ratings: **83,82,81,81,81 79,78,77,61,58 49,48,6**
toteswingers 1&2 £3.40, 2&3 £6.70, 1&3 £11.00 CSF £52.01 TOTE £6.20: £3.90, £1.10, £2.50; EX 70.20 Trifecta £366.30 Pool: £898.15 - 1.83 winning units..
Owner Falcon's Line Ltd **Bred** East Burrow Farm **Trained** Kings Caple, H'fords

FOCUS
An ordinary mares' bumper, but the form makes sense.
T/Plt: £29.20 to a £1 stake. Pool of £62952.13 - 1573.26 winning tickets. T/Qpdt: £6.00 to a £1 stake. Pool of £7124.72 - 866.14 winning tickets. WG

WINCANTON (R-H)
Thursday, May 9

OFFICIAL GOING: Good to firm (firm in places; chs 10.2, hdl 10.3)
Wind: Strong, half ahead Weather: Showers

188 DENISE AND BOB'S WEDDING CELEBRATION H'CAP HURDLE (10 hdls) 2m 4f
5:45 (5:46) (Class 5) (0-95,95) 4-Y-0+ **£1,949** (£572; £286; £143)

Form RPR
400/ **1** **Bells Of Berlin**[15] 5509 4-10-6 **90**........(vt) JPKiely(10) 98+
(Tim Vaughan) *chsd ldrs: wnt 2nd after 3 out: chal next: sn led: hit last: easily* **20/1**
345/ **2** *2 ¾* **Chilworth Screamer**[10] 29 5-11-12 **95**........ TomCannon 104
(Chris Gordon) *in tch: chsd ldrs 5th: rdn to chse wnr and hung rt appr last and mstke: styd on same pce* **10/1**
120/ **3** *13* **Capellini**[20] 5379 6-10-12 **81**........(p) MarkGrant 78
(Charles Egerton) *chsd ldr: led 5th: rdn after 3 out: jnd 2 out: hdd sn after and wknd into 3rd bef last* **7/1**
050/ **4** *½* **Shinko Moon**[15] 5509 6-11-7 **90**........ SamTwiston-Davies 87
(Jamie Snowden) *in tch: chsd ldrs fr 3 out: wknd after 2 out* **14/1**
602/ **5** *14* **Bob Lewis**[10] 29 7-10-9 **83**........(t) JamesBanks(5) 70
(Anthony Middleton) *chsd ldrs: rdn bef 2 out: sn wknd* **4/1**[1]
060/ **6** *29* **Venir Rouge**[42] 4997 9-11-0 **83**........ JamesDavies 41
(Harry Whittington) *bhd fr 4th: t.o* **16/1**
4P5/ **7** *15* **Ruby Valentine (FR)**[347] 450 10-10-5 **74**........ TommyPhelan 18
(Jim Wilson) *bhd fr 4th: t.o* **25/1**
24P/ **8** *½* **Kayfrou**[161] 2712 8-11-9 **92**........ DarylJacob 36
(Nick Mitchell) *a bhd: t.o* **5/1**[2]

The Form Book Jumps, Raceform Ltd, Compton, RG20 6NL.

6/3- **P** **Abbi Jicaro**[2] 155 6-10-5 **74**..............(t) AndrewGlassonbury
(Mark Shears) *led to 5th: chsd wnr: styd in 2nd to 3 out: wknd sn after and p.u bef next* **7/1**
133/ **P** **On Alert**[207] 1859 5-10-12 **81**..............(tp) ConorO'Farrell
(Seamus Durack) *chsd ldrs to 5th: no ch whn blnd 3 out: p.u sn after* **11/2**[3]
0P5/ **P** **Theroadtogorey (IRE)**[147] 3026 7-11-1 **84**.............. IanPopham
(Sarah Robinson) *bhd bhd fr 5th: t.o whn p.u bef 2 out* **14/1**
050/ **P** **Lady Sinatra**[16] 5479 5-10-12 **88**..............(t) ThomasGarner[(7)]
(Oliver Sherwood) *hit 1st: chsd ldrs to 5th: wknd after next: t.o whn p.u bef 2 out* **10/1**
000/ **P** **Lanarkshire (IRE)**[26] 5280 4-10-10 **84**..............(t) JoeTizzard
(Jennifer Mason) *bhd fr 4th: t.o whn p.u bef 2 out* **25/1**

4m 38.49s (-18.31) **Going Correction** -0.95s/f (Hard)
WFA 4 from 5yo+ 19lb **13** Ran SP% **126.9**
Speed ratings (Par 103): **98,96,91,91,85 74,68,68, , ,**
toteswingers 1&2 £27.90, 2&3 £9.60, 1&3 £0.00 CSF £214.63 CT £1564.58 TOTE £47.00: £11.80, £1.80, £3.40; EX 382.70 TRIFECTA Not won..
Owner S Grys & M O'Boyle **Bred** Cheveley Park Stud Ltd **Trained** Aberthin, Vale of Glamorgan

FOCUS
A modest handicap hurdle, run in near gale force conditions on very quick ground, and something of an upset. Steps up from the first two.

189 RACING WELFARE GOLF TOURNAMENT NOVICES' HURDLE (11 hdls) 2m 6f
6:15 (6:15) (Class 4) 4-Y-0+ **£3,328** (£1,033; £556)

Form RPR
3/2- **1** **Captain Kelly (IRE)**[7] 79 6-10-12 118..............(t) DarylJacob 122+
(Paul Nicholls) *trckd ldr fr 4th: led on bit 2 out: v easily* **1/4**[1]
105/ **2** *19* **Double Chocolate**[172] 2502 10-10-12 0.............. TommyPhelan 108
(David Bridgwater) *led: rdn after 3 out: hdd next: sn no ch w v easy wnr but wl clr of t.o 3rd* **7/2**[2]
3 *99* **Dancing Royal** 5-10-12 0.............. SamTwiston-Davies 16
(Jamie Snowden) *t.o fr 6th* **12/1**[3]
000/ **F** **Tinelyra (IRE)**[69] 4502 7-10-12 0.............. DavidEngland
(Shaun Lycett) *trckd ldrs: 3 l 3rd whn fell 4 out* **16/1**
600/ **P** **Monte Kaolino (IRE)**[23] 5335 5-10-12 0.............. TomCannon
(Nick Gifford) *chsd ldr to 4th: wknd 6th: t.o whn p.u bef 4 out* **50/1**

5m 5.67s (-20.83) **Going Correction** -0.95s/f (Hard) **5** Ran SP% **117.8**
Speed ratings (Par 105): **99,92,56, ,**
CSF £1.97 TOTE £1.10: £1.02, £1.60; EX 2.00 Trifecta £4.10 Pool: £1004.54 - 180.38 winning units..
Owner Donlon, Doyle, MacDonald & Webb **Bred** Joseph Murphy **Trained** Ditcheat, Somerset

FOCUS
An uncompetitive race, won in a canter by the long odds-on favourite. The first two are rated to their marks.

190 WESSEX WASTE H'CAP CHASE (21 fncs) 3m 1f 110y
6:45 (6:45) (Class 3) (0-130,123) 5-Y-0+ **£6,657** (£2,067; £1,113)

Form RPR
004/ **1** **Bold Perk (IRE)**[28] 5258 11-11-1 **112**.............. HaddenFrost 124+
(Martin Hill) *chsd ldrs: lft 2nd 15th: led next: clr fr 4 out: easily* **5/1**
0P2/ **2** *22* **Key Cutter (FR)**[158] 2813 9-11-4 **115**..............(bt) LiamTreadwell 110
(Paul Webber) *led after 3rd: hdd 11th: j. slowly and lost position 13th (water): lft 3rd 15th: wnt 2nd appr 4 out but nvr any ch w easy wnr* **3/1**[3]
PP2/ **3** *37* **Rossmore Lad (IRE)**[179] 2358 8-11-6 **117**..............(p) RichardJohnson 88
(Charlie Longsdon) *j.lft: led tl after 3rd: hit 6th: chal fr 13th tl lft w ld 15th: hdd next: wknd bef 4 out* **7/4**[1]
021/ **F** **Buck's Bond (FR)**[28] 5242 7-11-9 **123**..............(tp) RyanMahon[(3)]
(Paul Nicholls) *ht 1st: trckd ldr 5th: led 11th: jnd fr 13th but stl gng ok and slt advantage whn fell 15th* **2/1**[2]

6m 23.2s (-16.30) **Going Correction** -0.45s/f (Good) **4** Ran SP% **111.4**
Speed ratings: **107,100,88,**
CSF £19.01 TOTE £6.50; EX 22.00 Trifecta £54.20 Pool: £604.28 - 8.36 winning units..
Owner D Luscombe & M Hill **Bred** Michael O'Mahony **Trained** Littlehempston, Devon

FOCUS
This handicap chase was weak for the grade. The winner is rated back to his best.

191 ROYAL BATH & WEST SHOW NOVICES' H'CAP CHASE (13 fncs) 2m
7:15 (7:16) (Class 4) (0-115,110) 5-Y-0+ **£3,898** (£1,144; £572; £286)

Form RPR
415/ **1** **Miss Tenacious**[23] 5336 6-11-8 **106**.............. JackDoyle 119+
(Ron Hodges) *mde all: c clr fr 4 out: in n.d after: easily* **6/4**[1]
603/ **2** *12* **Teshali (IRE)**[15] 5508 7-11-7 **110**..............(t) JamesBanks[(5)] 108
(Anthony Middleton) *j. slowly in rr 6th: wnt 3rd 8th: chsd wnr 4 out but nvr any ch: wl hld whn hit next* **5/2**[2]
FP4/ **3** *49* **Great Kicker (IRE)**[15] 5510 8-10-13 **100**..............(t) MichealNolan[(3)] 54
(Richard Woollacott) *chsd wnr 6th: rdn 9th: wknd into poor 3rd 4 out: t.o* **6/1**
205/ **4** *2 ½* **Erdeli (IRE)**[19] 9-11-7 **105**..............(vt) TomCannon 57
(Kevin Bishop) *chsd wnr to 6th: wknd 8th* **3/1**[3]

3m 54.72s (-5.18) **Going Correction** -0.45s/f (Good) **4** Ran SP% **107.9**
Speed ratings: **94,88,63,62**
CSF £5.60 TOTE £2.10; EX 2.30 Trifecta £7.20 Pool: £381.12 - 39.46 winning units..
Owner John Frampton & Paul Frampton **Bred** Frampton Farms & Widdin Stud **Trained** Charlton Mackrell, Somerset

FOCUS
A dreadfully weak handicap chase and, with three of the four runners off the bridle and struggling at halfway, it proved plain sailing for the heavily supported winner. She is rated to her mark.

192 WATCH RACING UK ON SKY 432 NOVICES' HURDLE (8 hdls) 2m
7:45 (7:45) (Class 4) 4-Y-0+ **£3,249** (£954; £477; £238)

Form RPR
261/ **1** **Sidney Melbourne (USA)**[18] 5441 6-11-5 118..............(b) DarylJacob 121+
(Paul Nicholls) *trckd ldr: hit 2nd: t.k.h: chal travelling wl 2 out: led sn after: nt fluent last and sn hrd pressed: drvn out fnl 50yds* **2/5**[1]
4F4/ **2** *1* **Qoubilai (FR)**[91] 4079 9-10-12 0..............(t) RichardJohnson 110
(Tim Vaughan) *led: jnd 2 out sn rdn and hdd: rallied to press wnr run-in: no ex u.p fnl 50yds* **9/4**[2]
26U/ **3** *38* **Panache**[11] 8 8-10-9 0.............. MichealNolan[(3)] 83
(Angela Clarke) *hit 3 out: racd in poor 3rd thrght* **16/1**[3]
/ **4** *43* **Sid**[77] 5-10-12 0.............. TommyPhelan 37
(Mark Gillard) *j. slowly 2nd: green and t.o thrght* **50/1**
/ **5** *5* **Bedibyes**[37] 5-10-5 0.............. SamTwiston-Davies 26
(Richard Mitchell) *t.o thrght* **25/1**
000/ **6** *7* **Cardinal Richelieu (IRE)**[75] 4384 5-10-12 0.............. DougieCostello 26
(Tom Gretton) *hit 4 out: t.o thrght* **33/1**

3m 33.0s (-15.90) **Going Correction** -0.95s/f (Hard)
WFA 4 from 5yo+ 18lb **6** Ran SP% **116.8**
Speed ratings (Par 105): **101,100,81,60,57 54**
toteswingers 1&2 £1.02, 2&3 £2.20, 1&3 £2.40 CSF £1.81 TOTE £1.30: £1.10, £1.80; EX 1.40 Trifecta £3.90 Pool: £666.90 - 128.24 winning units..
Owner CGA Racing Partnership 5 **Bred** Sun Valley Farm & Jeffrey Johnson **Trained** Ditcheat, Somerset

FOCUS
A two-horse race according to the market and that proved the case in the race itself. The easy winner is rated to his mark with the second 20lb off his latest chase figure.

193 RACING UK YOUR RACING HOME FROM HOME H'CAP HURDLE (8 hdls) 2m
8:15 (8:15) (Class 5) (0-100,100) 4-Y-0+ **£1,949** (£572; £286; £143)

Form RPR
5P0/ **1** **Nothing Is Forever (IRE)**[197] 1994 9-10-1 **75**.............. JamesDavies 91+
(Chris Down) *disp ld tl led 2nd: drvn 2 out: styd on strly and in n.d after* **7/2**[1]
445/ **2** *11* **Dark Spirit (IRE)**[28] 5252 5-11-5 **96**..............(v[1]) AdamWedge[(3)] 99
(Evan Williams) *chsd ldrs: disp 2nd fr 2 out: tk 2nd u.p after last but nvr any ch w wnr* **7/2**[1]
636/ **3** *1 ½* **Freddy's Star (IRE)**[28] 5243 11-10-11 **90**.............. CharlieWallis[(5)] 93
(Nick Ayliffe) *chsd disp 2nd tl chsd wnr after 3 out: rdn and no imp appr 2 out: styd on same pce into 3rd run-in* **20/1**
536/ **4** *15* **Golden Acorn (IRE)**[28] 5248 4-10-9 **90**..............(t) MarkQuinlan[(3)] 74
(Nigel Hawke) *in rr: rdn 4 out: plenty to do whn hit 3 out: styd on u.p fr 2 out: nt rch ldrs* **10/1**
010/ **5** *hd* **Red Whisper**[211] 1789 9-10-10 **87**.............. JamesBest[(3)] 75
(Rob Summers) *hmpd 2nd: in rr: hdwy 4th: chsd ldrs 3 out: wknd next* **7/1**[3]
304/ **6** *16* **Paupers Present (IRE)**[18] 5442 5-11-7 **95**.............. NickScholfield 69
(Jeremy Scott) *a towards rr* **7/1**[3]
540/ **7** *½* **Walter De La Mare (IRE)**[63] 4343 6-11-5 **100**.............. ThomasGarner[(7)] 73
(Anabel K Murphy) *chsd ldr tl rdn and wknd after 3 out* **12/1**
600/ **8** *39* **Underlay Underlay**[35] 5142 5-10-7 **81**..............(b) JackDoyle 19
(Ron Hodges) *led to 2nd: chsd ldrs tl wknd rapidly after 3 out* **33/1**
500/ **P** **Vacario (GER)**[170] 2535 9-9-10 **75** oh3 ow1..............(tp) KillianMoore[(5)]
(Brian Barr) *sn bhd: t.o 3 out: p.u bef next* **12/1**
242/ **U** **Backhomeinderry (IRE)**[18] 5441 8-11-11 **99**..............(t) MarkGrant
(Kate Buckett) *in rr whn mstke and uns rdr 2nd* **4/1**[2]
P00/ **P** **Picklegend**[25] 5317 7-10-0 **74** oh15..............(p[1]) DaveCrosse
(Richard Woollacott) *bhd and hit 4 out: t.o whn p.u bef 2 out* **50/1**

3m 33.27s (-15.63) **Going Correction** -0.95s/f (Hard)
WFA 4 from 5yo+ 18lb **11** Ran SP% **123.6**
Speed ratings (Par 103): **101,95,94,87,87 79,78,59, ,**
toteswingers 1&2 £4.10, 2&3 £14.00, 1&3 £10.00 CSF £17.19 CT £223.17 TOTE £5.20: £1.60, £2.30, £5.20; EX 25.20 Trifecta £324.40 Part won. Pool: £432.53 - 0.70 winning units..
Owner The Globe Partnership **Bred** Reg Griffin And Jim McGrath **Trained** Mutterton, Devon

FOCUS
A competitive handicap hurdle on paper but it was turned into a procession by a resurgent winner. His nbest fugure since 2011, with the next two pretty much to their marks.
T/Plt: £424.80 to a £1 stake. Pool of £50141.16 - 86.15 winning tickets. T/Qpdt: £53.20 to a £1 stake. Pool of £4738.04 -65.80 winning tickets. ST

194 - 197a (Foreign Racing) - See Raceform Interactive

LE LION-D'ANGERS (R-H)
Thursday, May 9

OFFICIAL GOING: Turf: good to soft

198a PRIX MACKENZIE II (CHASE) (CONDITIONS) (TURF) 2m 4f
4:35 (12:00) Class C 5-Y-0 **£10,536** (£5,268; £3,073; £2,085; £987)

RPR
1 **Ainsivalanour (FR)** 5-10-12 0.............. NoamChevalier 109
(A Vetault, France) **7/2**[1]
2 *5* **Unanime**[22] 5-10-12 0.............. JonathanNattiez 104
(A Adeline De Boisbrunet, France) **43/10**[2]
3 *2* **Jakherphi D'Art (FR)**[20] 5399 5-10-10 0.............. AlexisPoirier 100
(C Plisson, France) **13/1**
4 *10* **Ulrick (FR)**[151] 5-10-10 0.............. ChristopheDubourg 90
(C Dubourg, France) **40/1**
5 *6* **Un Ami (FR)**[25] 5326 5-10-8 0.............. JamesReveley 82
(Nick Williams) *prom: led 4th: hdd after 6th and trckd ldrs: nt qckn w ldng gp bef 3 out: 6th and rdn 2 out: kpt on same pce run-in* **78/10**
6 *8* **Unekaina (FR)**[29] 5239 5-10-10 0..............(b) AlbanDesvaux 76
(E Lecoiffier, France) **15/1**
7 *2 ½* **Valeur Ajoutee (FR)** 5-10-6 0.............. AlainDeChitray 70
(E Leenders, France) **18/1**
8 *1* **Azaro De La Mare (FR)**[183] 5-10-10 0..............(b) HugoLucas 73
(E Leray, France) **10/1**
9 *15* **Sky Flyer (FR)**[395] 5-11-3 0.............. MrAlexandreBaudoin-Boin 65
(J-C Baudoin, France) **57/1**
F **Manaus Opera (FR)**[4] 5-10-12 0..............(p) FabienDehez
(E Lecoiffier, France) **13/1**
F **Rakane Rouge (FR)**[421] 5-10-10 0.............. DavidCottin
(P Cottin, France) **63/10**[3]
P **Miel Cafe (FR)** 5-10-8 0.............. DavidBernier
(Mme C Baron-Losfeld, France) **100/1**
P **Un Reve Du Granval (FR)** 5-10-7 0 ow1.............. JonathanPlouganou
(D Sourdeau De Beauregard, France) **17/2**

5m 0.86s (300.86) **13** Ran SP% **116.7**
PARI-MUTUEL (all including 1 euro stakes): WIN 4.50; PLACE 2.10, 1.90, 3.20; DF 8.10; SF 22.20.
Owner Mme Gilbert Guerot **Bred** E Piednoel **Trained** France

199a PRIX ANJOU-LOIRE CHALLENGE (CROSS-COUNTRY CHASE) (LISTED RACE) (6YO+) (TURF) 4m 4f 110y
5:40 (12:00) 6-Y-O+

£40,975 (£20,032; £11,837; £8,195; £4,552; £3,186)

RPR
1 **Toutancarmont (FR)**[36] 5133 6-10-10 0................. JonathanPlouganou 124
(Mme I Pacault, France) 3/1[2]
2 1 **Phakos (FR)**[249] 1481 10-10-10 0... FabienDehez 123
(P Cottin, France) 12/1
3 nk **Maljimar (IRE)**[25] 5325 13-10-10 0.................................... JamesReveley 123
(Nick Williams) *led: handed clr ld fr the off: jnd 5th: led again 6th: bad mstke 32nd and dropped to midfield: hdwy to chse ldng gp fr 3 out: 4th and rdn 2 out: styd on wl u.p run-in* 32/1
4 1 **Shalimar Fromentro (FR)**[36] 5133 7-10-10 0................ AlainDeChitray 122
(Nick Williams) *midfield: outpcd and dropped to last after 5 out: rdn and prog on outside bef 2 out: styd on wl u.p run-in: nvr on terms* 37/1
5 nse **Posilox (FR)**[36] 5133 7-10-10 0.......................................(b) JonathanViard 122
(W Menuet, France) 17/2[3]
6 3 **Another Jewel (IRE)**[14] 5528 11-10-10 0...........................(p) JohnCullen 119
(Denis Paul Murphy, Ire) *midfield: trckd ldng gp fr 11th: lost pl fr 19th: towards rr whn hdwy appr 3 out: 6th and styng on 2 out: kpt on u.p appr last: no ex fnl 100yds* 18/1
7 20 **Kaid De Lonray (FR)** 11-10-10 0..................................(p) FlorentNeveu 99
(A Le Clerc, France) 69/1
8 10 **Sir Rowan (FR)**[36] 5133 7-10-10 0...................... MarcLamazou-Laresse 89
(J Planque, France) 17/1
F **Chriseti (FR)**[249] 1481 13-10-10 0................................(b) WilfridDenuault
(E Leenders, France) 6/4[1]
P **Silver Whisper (FR)**[357] 333 9-10-10 0....................(b) NicolasMoisson
(A Le Clerc, France) 26/1
P **Bostons Angel (IRE)**[14] 5528 9 10 10 0........................... RobbiePower
(Mrs John Harrington, Ire) *trckd ldng gp: dropped to midfield fr 5th: towards rr fr 14th: bhd fr 24th: p.u 36th* 26/1
P **Rubis D'Albain (FR)**[188] 8-10-10 0.................................. JeromeZuliani
(Patrice Quinton, France) 22/1
P **Sulon (FR)**[36] 5133 7-10-10 0....................................(p) JessyBlandamour
(Patrice Quinton, France) 42/1
F **Picsoudu Bredeloup (FR)**[402] 5212 7-10-10 0............(p) HubertTerrien
(Guy Denuault, France) 51/1

10m 12.31s (612.31) 14 Ran SP% 117.1
PARI-MUTUEL (all including 1 euro stakes): WIN 3.20 (combined with Rubis d'Albain and Sulon); PLACE 2.10, 3.20, 5.70; DF 29.90; SF 45.70.
Owner Mme Patrick Papot **Bred** Scea Haras De Mirande **Trained** France

200a PRIX DE GENE (CROSS-COUNTRY CHASE) (CONDITIONS) (6YO+) (AMATEUR RIDERS) (TURF) 2m 6f
6:45 (12:00) 6-Y-O+ £8,975 (£4,487; £2,617; £1,776; £841)

RPR
1 **Theroadtocroker (IRE)**[32] 9-10-1 0.............................. MrPaulGahan(5) 108
(Denis Paul Murphy, Ire) *trckd ldrs: dropped towards rr 7th: midfield fr 15th: travelling wl on heels of ldrs fr 21st: trckd ldr 4 out: rdn to ld bef 2 out: clr last: pushed out* 87/10
2 10 **Tavenger (FR)**[533] 6-10-6 0.............................(p) MrAlexandreLemarie(4) 102
(A Gregoire, France) 45/1
3 1 **Reve De Kerza (FR)**[357] 332 8-10-3 0..................(b) MrRegisDurand(3) 97
(A Le Clerc, France) 10/1
4 1½ **Santiag (FR)**[357] 332 7-10-10 0................................ MrEdouardMonfort 100
(G Lecomte, France) 5/2[1]
5 3 **Zinnia Des Obeaux (FR)** 6-10-6 0...................(p) MrJeromeFoucher(4) 97
(N Devilder, France) 11/1
6 15 **Diamrock (FR)**[400] 5249 8-10-6 0...........................(b) MrMaximeMercier(4) 82
(E Leenders, France) 68/10[3]
7 3 **Origan Joly (FR)**[2076] 11-10-1 0............................. MrAlmireLefeuvre(5) 75
(Mme A-D Lefeuvre, France) 17/1
8 dist **Wagga Dee Dee (FR)** 9-10-1 0....................(p) MrThomasGuineheux(5)
(P-O Robert, France) 101/1
9 1 **Quadou Ville (FR)** 9-10-10 0 ow4......................... MrYoannLeCourtois
(G Lecomte, France) 34/1
10 3 **Ortax De Maesax (FR)**[707] 11-10-1 0.............(b) MrBenjaminHuchede(5)
(C Macault, France) 88/1
P **Moka De L'Isle (FR)**[95] 4014 13-10-1 0....................(p) MrGCottreau(5)
(Mrs S A Bramall, Ire) *hld up towards rr: wl bhd fr 13th: p.u 16th* 9/1
P **Simonet (FR)**[1894] 10-10-6 0..(b) MrRubensSeror
(E Leenders, France) 16/1
F **Fil's Glory (FR)** 9-10-10 0... MrCCoste
(D Cadot, France) 43/10[2]
P **Hargeisa (FR)** 10-10-1 0... MrBenjaminCaron
(D Bernier, France) 95/1

6m 3.11s (363.11) 14 Ran SP% 117.6
PARI-MUTUEL (all including 1 euro stakes): WIN 9.70; PLACE 4.00, 12.40, 3.50; DF 223.50; SF 549.90.
Owner Michael James Kelly & Simon Donohoe **Bred** Mrs P Kiely **Trained** Enniscorthy, Co Wexford

MARKET RASEN (R-H)
Friday, May 10

OFFICIAL GOING: Good (good to firm in places; chs 9.1; hdl 8.2)
Wind: fresh 1/2 against Weather: overcast, cool and very breezy, becoming fine and sunny

201 WEATHERBYS HAMILTON INSURANCE NOVICES' H'CAP HURDLE (10 hdls) 2m 3f
1:55 (1:55) (Class 4) (0-115,115) 4-Y-O+ £3,119 (£915; £457; £228)

Form RPR
4/2- 1 **Halifax (IRE)**[8] 72 5-11-2 105....................................(v[1]) DenisO'Regan 119+
(John Ferguson) *led: nt fluent 1st: hit 2 out: sn drvn clr: heavily eased last 50yds* 8/1[3]
231/ 2 8 **Full Speed (GER)**[19] 5426 8-11-12 115.......................... RichieMcGrath 116
(Philip Kirby) *trckd ldrs 4th: chsd wnr appr 2 out: kpt on: no imp* 15/8[1]
02/- 3 1¾ **Electric Tiger (GER)**[17] 5473 6-11-4 107........................ TomScudamore 105
(David Bridgwater) *prom: outpcd 7th: styd on appr 2 out: tk 3rd in clsng stages* 12/1
OPP/ 4 1½ **River Purple**[67] 4569 6-10-0 89 oh2...................................(t) DonalDevereux 86
(John Mackie) *hdwy to chse ldrs 6th: 3rd 2 out: one pce* 22/1
6F5/ 5 ¾ **Cut The Cards (IRE)**[66] 4578 6-10-13 102.................... RichieMcLernon 98
(Jonjo O'Neill) *mid-div: drvn to chse ldrs 3 out: kpt on one pce fr next* 8/1[3]
041/ 6 5 **Takaatuf (IRE)**[16] 5498 7-10-10 104............................ SamanthaDrake(5) 97
(John Wade) *chsd wnr: 2nd 5th: 6th and wkng whn hit 2 out* 18/1
000/ 7 1½ **Haljaferia (UAE)**[65] 4590 7-10-1 90.................................... HenryBrooke 80
(Mike Sowersby) *in rr: hdwy 3 out: chsng ldrs next: fdd run-in* 40/1
060/ 8 17 **Euro Trash (IRE)**[19] 5437 7-10-11 100..................... SamTwiston-Davies 75
(Nigel Twiston-Davies) *bhd and drvn 6th: sn t.o* 33/1
15P/ 9 13 **O Crotaigh (IRE)**[16] 5496 9-11-1 111........................... GrahamWatters(7) 74
(Alan Brown) *chsd ldrs: lost pl after 7th: sn bhd* 20/1
360/ 10 11 **Theatrelands**[24] 5335 5-11-4 107..(t) NoelFehily 60
(Charlie Longsdon) *chsd ldrs: wknd 3 out: sn bhd* 9/1
4/1- P **High Ville (IRE)**[10] 42 7-11-2 105 7ex............................ ConorO'Farrell
(David Pipe) *w wnr: lost pl and hit 5th: sn bhd and p.u* 7/2[2]

4m 36.0s (-3.40) **Going Correction** -0.05s/f (Good) 11 Ran SP% 116.7
Speed ratings (Par 105): **105,101,100,100,99 97,97,90,84,79**
toteswingers 1&2 £1.50, 2&3 £6.10, 1&3 £3.70 CSF £22.87 CT £184.52 TOTE £9.10: £2.20, £1.30, £3.40; EX 24.80 Trifecta £483.30 Part won. Pool: £644.52 - 0.45 winning units..
Owner Bloomfields **Bred** Rabbah Bloodstock Limited **Trained** Cowlinge, Suffolk

FOCUS
This modest novice handicap was run at a sound gallop. The form makes sense and the easy winner is entitled to rate a lot higher on Flat form.

202 RACING UK H'CAP HURDLE (8 hdls) 2m 1f
2:25 (2:25) (Class 4) (0-115,115) 4-Y-O+ £3,119 (£915; £457; £228)

Form RPR
0F0/ 1 **Coffee (IRE)**[68] 4540 6-11-8 111...................................... RichieMcLernon 119+
(Jonjo O'Neill) *hld up: hdwy 5th: offrt and swtchd lft appr 2 out: led and hit last: styd on wl* 4/1[1]
154/ 2 2 **Crafty Roberto**[23] 5356 5-11-7 115...................................(t) KillianMoore(5) 120
(Alex Hales) *in rr: hdwy to chse ldrs 3 out: outpcd appr next: 4th last: styd on wl: no imp* 5/1[2]
230/ 3 6 **Muwalla**[220] 1710 6-11-1 104.. BrianHughes 104
(Chris Grant) *trckd ldrs: led appr 2 out: hdd and hit last: one pce* 18/1
213/ 4 1¼ **Helium (FR)**[24] 5330 8-11-4 114... MrsAlexDunn(7) 113
(Alexandra Dunn) *led after 1st: hdd appr 2 out: kpt on same pce* 11/2[3]
266/ 5 2¾ **Outback (IRE)**[13] 5566 4-10-10 108.........................(v[1]) TrevorWhelan(5) 100
(Neil King) *led tl after 1st: chsd ldrs: one pce fr 2 out* 22/1
346/ 6 16 **Bab Al Salam (USA)**[19] 5435 7-11-10 113..................(v[1]) DenisO'Regan 95
(John Ferguson) *chsd ldrs: wknd appr 2 out* 4/1[1]
0P0/ 7 ½ **Smart Catch (IRE)**[27] 5284 7-11-2 105.................................. LeeEdwards 87
(Tony Carroll) *chsd ldrs: hit 3rd: drvn 3 out: lost pl appr next* 14/1
340/ 8 11 **Rocky Rebel**[28] 5277 5-11-4 107....................................(p) TomMessenger 79
(Chris Bealby) *chsd ldrs: outpcd 4th: lost pl 3 out: sn bhd* 28/1
064/ 9 17 **Jawaab (IRE)**[16] 5497 9-11-1 104.....................................(v) RichieMcGrath 60
(Philip Kirby) *in rr: bhd and drvn 3rd: detached and reminders next: t.o 3 out* 8/1
1/3- F **Callhimwhatyouwant (IRE)**[9] 65 8-10-6 102...(b) ChristopherWard(7)
(Dr Richard Newland) *prom: fell 2nd* 9/1

4m 7.6s (0.90) **Going Correction** -0.05s/f (Good)
WFA 4 from 5yo+ 18lb 10 Ran SP% 112.9
Speed ratings (Par 105): **95,94,91,90,89 81,81,76,68,**
toteswingers 1&2 £15.10, 2&3 £15.10, 1&3 £15.10 CSF £23.87 CT £316.32 TOTE £5.70: £2.10, £1.50, £5.10; EX 24.90 Trifecta £479.60 Pool: £1066.16 - 1.66 winning units..
Owner John P McManus **Bred** Ms Margaret Finn **Trained** Cheltenham, Gloucs

FOCUS
This looked an open handicap, but the first pair came clear off the ordinary gallop. The winner was well in on his best form from the autumn and is rated back to that level.

203 WEATHERBYS HAMILTON INSURANCE NOVICES' H'CAP CHASE (14 fncs) 2m 4f
2:55 (2:55) (Class 4) (0-110,110) 5-Y-O+ £3,768 (£1,106; £553; £276)

Form RPR
5P1/ 1 **Badgers Retreat**[16] 5501 7-11-0 98.......................... SamTwiston-Davies 106
(Ferdy Murphy, France) *trckd ldrs 4th: handy 3rd 8th: upsides 3 out: led last: drvn out* 3/1[3]
450/ 2 2 **Nomadic Dreamer**[146] 3057 10-11-7 110.......................(t) KillianMoore(5) 116
(Mark Rimell) *hld up: jnd ldrs 5th: led 4 out: hdd last: kpt on same pce* 8/1
32P/ 3 16 **King's Grace**[41] 5015 7-11-12 110..................................(b) JasonMaguire 105
(Donald McCain) *led: hdd 4 out: wknd appr next* 13/8[1]
UU4/ 4 12 **Xenophon**[13] 5569 5-10-6 90..(t) DaveCrosse 71
(Michael Chapman) *in tch: reminders 5th: drvn 7th: sn wl outpcd: modest 4th 4 out: wl bhd whn blnd 2 out* 28/1
P04/ 5 17 **Advisor (FR)**[16] 5508 7-11-1 104.. MrTWeston(5) 70
(Martin Weston) *chsd ldrs 4th: lost pl 10th: bhd fr 3 out* 20/1
2P3/ P **Special Robon (FR)**[64] 4620 5-11-2 100........................(p) AidanColeman
(Venetia Williams) *chsd ldrs: drvn 8th: nt fluent next: sn lost pl: bhd fr 4 out: t.o whn p.u bef next* 5/2[2]

4m 50.8s (-14.90) **Going Correction** -0.925s/f (Hard) 6 Ran SP% 111.0
Speed ratings: **92,91,84,80,73**
toteswingers 1&2 £4.60, 2&3 £3.80, 1&3 £2.20 CSF £24.19 TOTE £3.40: £1.60, £4.20; EX 23.40 Trifecta £153.80 Pool: £ 1178.27- 5.74 winning units..
Owner Ferdy Murphy **Bred** Wood Farm Stud **Trained** France

FOCUS
A moderate novices' handicap, run at an average gallop and another race where the first pair dominated the finish. The winner comfirmed the merit of his recent win.

204 WEATHERBYS BANK H'CAP CHASE (14 fncs) 2m 4f
3:30 (3:30) (Class 2) 5-Y-O+

£14,076 (£4,158; £2,079; £1,039; £519; £261)

Form RPR
251/ 1 **Bocciani (GER)**[21] 5369 8-11-1 136................................ TomScudamore 143
(Brian Ellison) *mid-div: hdwy and prom 8th: wnt 2nd last: upsides run-in: led nr fin* 14/1
021/ 2 hd **Fiendish Flame (IRE)**[12] 11 9-11-7 142 7ex.................... SeanQuinlan 150
(Jennie Candlish) *set str pce: clr 7th: jnd sn after last: hdd fnl strides* 6/1[2]
261/ 3 5 **Gentleman Anshan (IRE)**[19] 5433 9-10-2 128....................... BenPoste(5) 131
(Rosemary Gasson) *mid-div: hdwy 8th: kpt on fr 3 out: 5th last: tk 3rd last 200yds* 20/1

The Form Book Jumps, Raceform Ltd, Compton, RG20 6NL.

054/ **4** *5* **Joker Choker (IRE)**[29] 5260 8-10-2 **123**.......................... RichardKilloran 122+
(Nicky Henderson) *sn bhd: kpt on fr 4 out: nt rch ldrs* **5/1**[1]

41P/ **5** *3/4* **The Disengager (IRE)**[174] 2468 9-11-5 **140**................ RichardJohnson 137
(Philip Hobbs) *chsd ldrs: one pce fr 3 out* **17/2**

F12/ **6** *nk* **Micheal Flips (IRE)**[15] 5523 9-11-7 **147**.............. JamesBanks(5) 144+
(Andy Turnell) *sn bhd: kpt on fr 4 out: nvr nr to chal* **6/1**[2]

F23/ **7** *6* **Pepite Rose (FR)**[20] 5403 6-11-10 **145**.............................. AidanColeman 140
(Venetia Williams) *hdwy 7th: sn chsng ldrs: 2nd 10th: wknd last* **13/2**[3]

211/ **8** *14* **Aneyeforaneye (IRE)**[14] 5547 7-10-11 **132**......................... BrianHughes 112
(Malcolm Jefferson) *in rr-div: hdwy 10th: lost pl bef 3 out* **7/1**

330/ **9** *4 1/2* **Fistral Beach (IRE)**[35] 5160 10-11-8 **143**.............................. DarylJacob 122
(Paul Nicholls) *mid-div: hdwy to chse ldrs 8th: wkng whn blnd 3 out* **7/1**

105/ **10** *13* **L'Eldorado (FR)**[67] 4567 8-10-3 **124**..............................(t) TomMessenger 87
(Chris Bealby) *in rr: bhd fr 8th: t.o 2 out* **40/1**

P30/ **11** *2 3/4* **Finger Onthe Pulse (IRE)**[57] 4750 12-10-12 **133**........ RichieMcLernon 94
(Jonjo O'Neill) *in rr: bhd fr 4 out: t.o 2 out* **40/1**

232/ **12** *9* **Oscar Hill (IRE)**[70] 4503 7-10-10 **131**.................................... TomO'Brien 84
(Rob Summers) *t.k.h: trckd ldrs: lost pl 7th: sn bhd: t.o 3 out* **20/1**

P16/ **13** *11* **Ostland (GER)**[43] 4993 8-11-8 **143**.......................................(p) NoelFehily 86
(Charlie Longsdon) *chsd ldrs: hit 5th: lost pl 10th: sn bhd: t.o 3 out* **25/1**

4m 41.4s (-24.30) **Going Correction** -0.925s/f (Hard) course record **13** Ran SP% **119.0**
Speed ratings: **111,110,108,106,106 106,104,98,96,91 90,86,82**
toteswingers 1&2 £8.60, 2&3 £26.20, 1&3 £22.00 CSF £90.59 CT £1692.14 TOTE £15.70: £6.40, £3.20, £7.30; EX 154.90 Trifecta £38.00 Pool: £1733.44 - 34.13 winning units..
Owner John Macgregor **Bred** Saturn Stable **Trained** Norton, N Yorks
■ Stewards' Enquiry : Sean Quinlan two-day ban: used whip above permitted level (May 24-25)

FOCUS
A cracking handicap for such an early stage of the season and there was no hiding place off the frantic gallop. Sound form with another step up from the winner.

205 TOTEMIC H'CAP HURDLE (12 hdls) 3m
4:05 (4:06) (Class 3) (0-135,133) 4-Y-0+ **£5,393** (£1,583; £791; £395)

Form RPR

6/3- **1** **Andreo Bambaleo**[6] 121 9-10-0 **107**..........................(p) TomScudamore 111+
(Brian Ellison) *nt fluent in rr: hdwy 9th: styd on fr 2 out: upsides last: led run-in: drvn out* **10/3**[1]

600/ **2** *1 1/4* **Hada Men (USA)**[36] 5141 8-11-9 **130**................................ AidanColeman 132
(Venetia Williams) *chsd ldrs: hit 5th: narrow ld appr 2 out: hdd run-in: no ex* **7/2**[2]

506/ **3** *1* **Ogee**[36] 5145 10-11-12 **133**.. JimmyMcCarthy 134
(Renee Robeson) *chsd ldrs: drvn appr 2 out: 4th whn swtchd lft after last: styd on to take 3rd fnl strides* **12/1**

U00/ **4** *hd* **Topolski (IRE)**[13] 5574 7-11-6 **127**..(t) TomCannon 128
(David Arbuthnot) *trckd ldrs 6th: upsides appr 2 out: kpt on same pce run-in* **28/1**

230/ **5** *17* **Dawn Commander (GER)**[14] 5549 6-11-8 **129**..................(b[1]) NoelFehily 118
(Charlie Longsdon) *led: qcknd pce 3rd and 8th: hdd appr 2 out: sn lost pl: sltly hmpd last* **9/1**

1P1/ **6** *62* **Kellys Brow (IRE)**[71] 4477 6-11-7 **128**..................................(p) AdrianLane 58
(Iain Jardine) *prominenent: drvn 9th: lost pl after next: sn bhd: t.o* **14/1**

P10/ **F** **Bobowen (IRE)**[23] 5352 7-11-5 **133**........................ ChristopherWard(7) 125
(Dr Richard Newland) *hld up: hdwy 3 out: sn pushed along and outpcd: 5th and keeping on same pce whn fell last* **7/2**[2]

411/ **U** **Heronry (IRE)**[65] 4593 5-11-10 **131**................................... AndrewTinkler 120
(Nicky Henderson) *chsd ldrs: drvn 9th: 6th and one pce whn bdly hmpd and uns rdr last* **5/1**[3]

5m 54.2s (3.70) **Going Correction** -0.05s/f (Good) **8** Ran SP% **112.0**
Speed ratings (Par 107): **91,90,90,90,84 63, ,**
toteswingers 1&2 £1.10, 2&3 £10.80, 1&3 £8.30 CSF £15.11 CT £119.80 TOTE £6.20: £2.60, £1.50, £4.70; EX 13.40 Trifecta £127.20 Pool: £1699.02 - 10.01 winning units..
Owner Brian Ellison **Bred** Mrs V McKie **Trained** Norton, N Yorks

FOCUS
A tight staying handicap and sound form. The winner is on a good mark and is rated 2lb off his best.

206 A TORN CONSTRUCTION H'CAP CHASE (17 fncs) 3m 1f
4:40 (4:40) (Class 5) (0-100,100) 5-Y-0+ **£2,258** (£658; £329)

Form RPR

325/ **1** **Foot The Bill**[31] 5229 8-11-4 **92**... BrianHarding 105+
(Patrick Holmes) *rn in snatches: reminders 4th: chsd ldrs 11th: upsides sn after 4 out: hit next: led and hit 2 out: kpt on run-in* **9/1**

342/ **2** *3 1/2* **Ifonlyalfie**[13] 5568 8-11-4 **92**..(bt) TomMessenger 100
(Chris Bealby) *chsd ldrs: drvn 12th: chsd wnr between last 2: kpt on same pce* **7/2**[1]

34P/ **3** *19* **Ratify**[26] 5309 9-11-1 **89**..(t) BrendanPowell 82
(Brendan Powell) *led: hit 4th: hdd 2 out: wknd between last 2* **7/1**[3]

PP3/ **4** *1/2* **Ontheslate (IRE)**[11] 32 7-10-6 **80**.................................... AlexMerriam 71
(Neil King) *chsd ldr: mstke 8th: wknd appr 2 out* **4/1**[2]

P/U- **5** *2 1/2* **Cara Court (IRE)**[7] 89 7-10-12 **91**........................ SamanthaDrake(5) 79
(Joanne Foster) *chsd ldrs: lost pl 5th: reminders 10th: outpcd appr 3 out: kpt on between last 2* **9/1**

4/2- **6** *17* **Silas Mariner (IRE)**[9] 64 6-11-12 **100**.........................(bt) AdamPogson 73
(Mandy Rowland) *trckd ldrs 7th: lost pl sn after 4 out: sn bhd* **7/1**[3]

562/ **7** *8* **D'Gigi**[11] 32 7-11-8 **96**...(t) SamTwiston-Davies 62
(Nigel Twiston-Davies) *gave problems leaving padock: reminders after s: blnd 1st: chsd ldrs 3rd: outpcd and nt fluent 11th: bhd and drvn 4 out* **7/2**[1]

6F5/ **8** *5* **Sycho Fred (IRE)**[189] 2167 12-10-3 **77**................................(t) BrianHughes 38
(Mike Sowersby) *chsd ldrs: drvn 11th: lost pl after 13th: sn bhd* **25/1**

6m 12.6s (-18.70) **Going Correction** -0.925s/f (Hard) **8** Ran SP% **113.3**
Speed ratings: **92,90,84,84,83 78,75,74**
toteswingers 1&2 £5.20, 2&3 £7.10, 1&3 £5.20 CSF £40.83 TOTE £9.60: £2.20, £1.10, £3.70; EX 47.60 Trifecta £294.90 Pool: £1533.36 - 3.89 winning units..
Owner Colin Stirling **Bred** Milton Park Stud Partnership **Trained** Middleham, N Yorks

FOCUS
A weak handicap run at a routine gallop. The first two finished clear and the form is rated around the second.

207 MCFLY PERFORMING HERE ON 31ST AUGUST STANDARD OPEN NATIONAL HUNT FLAT RACE 2m 1f
5:15 (5:15) (Class 6) 4-6-Y-0 **£1,559** (£457; £228; £114)

Form RPR

634/ **1** **Cape York**[41] 5018 5-11-2 **0**.. BrianHughes 104
(Malcolm Jefferson) *led 1f: chsd ldr: led 9f out: styd on wl fnl f* **13/2**

2 *2 3/4* **Factor Fifty (IRE)** 4-10-5 **0**... AdamNicol(7) 97+
(Philip Kirby) *hld up: hdwy 6f out: wnt 2nd over 2f out: 2 l down whn rdn and hung bdly lft jst ins fnl f* **4/1**[3]

0/ **3** *9* **Milan Of Hope (IRE)**[28] 5279 6-11-2 **0**............................. AdamPogson 93
(Charles Pogson) *in rr: drvn 6f out: kpt on fnl 3f: 5th 1f out: tk modest 3rd in clsng stages* **40/1**

5/ **4** *1 1/2* **Fred Le Macon (FR)**[29] 5263 4-10-12 **0**..................... WayneHutchinson 90
(Alan King) *hld up in rr: hdwy to chse ldrs whn stmbld bnd over 3f out: n.m.r over 2f out: one pce* **2/1**[1]

5 *3 1/2* **Balinderry (IRE)**[559] 6-11-2 **0**.. TomScudamore 90
(Steve Gollings) *chsd ldrs: reminders 6f out: 3rd over 2f out: wknd fnl f* **22/1**

6/ **6** *9* **Vodka 'n Tonic (IRE)**[29] 5262 4-10-12 **0**.......................... AndrewTinkler 79
(Nicky Henderson) *trckd ldrs: chsd wnr over 3f out: lost pl over 1f out* **5/2**[2]

36/ **7** *28* **Ballygrooby Bertie (IRE)**[14] 5550 5-10-9 **0**...........(t) ConorShoemark(7) 55
(Fergal O'Brien) *chsd ldrs: drvn over 6f out: lost pl over 3f out: sn bhd: t.o* **9/1**

0/ **8** *75* **Lenderking (IRE)**[13] 5572 5-10-9 **0**............................... GerardGalligan(7)
(Michael Chapman) *led after 1f: hdd 9f out: lost pl 7f out: sn wl bhd: hopelessly t.o* **150/1**

U **Captain Reacher** 4-10-12 **0**... TomMessenger
(Chris Bealby) *t.k.h towards rr: rn wd bnd after 4f: swvd lft and lost tch bnd after 6f: t.o whn swvd and uns rdr over 5f out* **25/1**

4m 1.1s **Going Correction** -0.05s/f (Good)
WFA 4 from 5yo+ 4lb **9** Ran SP% **116.5**
Speed ratings: **98,96,92,91,90 85,72,37,**
toteswingers 1&2 £3.60, 2&3 £16.00, 1&3 £1.60 CSF £31.94 TOTE £5.70: £1.90, £1.80, £6.60; EX 41.30 Trifecta £731.80 Part won. Pool: £975.81 - 0.43 winning units..
Owner J David Abell **Bred** J M Jefferson **Trained** Norton, N Yorks

FOCUS
A modest bumper. The winner and third are on the upgrade.
T/Plt: £562.50 to a £1 stake. Pool of £52101.29 - 67.61 winning tickets. T/Qpdt: £59.30 to a £1 stake. Pool of £3492.19 - 43.55 winning tickets. WG

208 - 214a (Foreign Racing) - See Raceform Interactive

HAYDOCK (L-H)
Saturday, May 11

OFFICIAL GOING: Flat course - good to firm (good in places) changing to good to soft after race 2 (2.25); jumps courses - good
Wind: Moderate, half against Weather: Overcast

215 PERTEMPS NETWORK LONG DISTANCE H'CAP HURDLE 3m
1:50 (1:50) (Class 2) 4-Y-0+
£18,768 (£5,544; £2,772; £1,386; £693; £348)

Form RPR

311/ **1** **Battle Group**[35] 5176 8-11-9 **146**.....................................(p) BrendanPowell 151
(Kevin Bishop) *a.p: rdn to take 2nd appr last: str chal run-in: styd on to ld cl home* **13/2**[2]

532/ **2** *3/4* **Jetson (IRE)**[37] 5141 8-11-1 **143**................................. NicodeBoinville(5) 147
(Mrs John Harrington, Ire) *trckd ldrs: wnt 2nd after 4 out: chalng 2 out: sn led and rdn: pressed run-in: hdd and hld cl home* **6/1**[1]

300/ **3** *1 1/2* **Cross Kennon (IRE)**[15] 5540 9-11-3 **140**.........................(v[1]) SeanQuinlan 143
(Jennie Candlish) *in tch: rdn to chse ldrs appr 2 out: styd on u.p run-in: hld towards fin* **33/1**

421/ **4** *nk* **Araldur (FR)**[29] 5269 9-11-4 **141**................................... WayneHutchinson 144
(Alan King) *hld up: hdwy into midfield 8th: chsng ldrs whn mstke last: styd on u.p towards fin* **16/1**

013/ **5** *1/2* **Fox Appeal (IRE)**[161] 2774 6-11-12 **149**........................ DominicElsworth 152
(Emma Lavelle) *midfield: hdwy appr 4 out: sn chsd ldrs: checked briefly between last 2: effrt after last: styd on u.p: one pce cl home* **16/1**

53P/ **6** *1 3/4* **Double Ross (IRE)**[37] 5141 7-11-2 **139**................... SamTwiston-Davies 139
(Nigel Twiston-Davies) *hld up in rr: hdwy appr 3 out: chsd ldrs bef 2 out: one pce and no imp fnl 100yds* **16/1**

302/ **7** *3 1/4* **Monetary Fund (USA)**[15] 5540 7-10-9 **132**......................... AidanColeman 129
(Venetia Williams) *midfield: hdwy appr 4 out: pushed along whn chsng ldrs bef 3 out: one pce run-in* **14/1**

301/ **8** *2 1/4* **Orsippus (USA)**[21] 5405 7-10-10 **133**................................... DannyCook 129
(Michael Smith) *led: rdn and hdd after 2 out: sn swtchd rt: hit last: no ex fnl 110yds* **16/1**

321/ **9** *7* **Darley Sun (IRE)**[20] 5430 7-10-13 **136**.............................. DenisO'Regan 126
(John Ferguson) *midfield: effrt 2 out: nvr able to chal: plugged on at one pce run-in* **10/1**[3]

5F5/ **10** *3* **Black Thunder (FR)**[14] 5574 6-11-7 **144**................................ DarylJacob 130
(Paul Nicholls) *midfield: lost pl after 6th: hdwy 3 out: kpt on u.p after: no imp on ldrs* **12/1**

411/ **11** *2 1/4* **Whisky Yankee (IRE)**[18] 5463 6-10-4 **132**.................. HarryDerham(5) 116
(Paul Nicholls) *hld up: stdy hdwy appr 4 out: hit 3 out: nvr able to trble ldrs* **12/1**

414/ **12** *nk* **Weekend Millionair (IRE)**[15] 5540 6-10-12 **135**........(p) TomScudamore 119
(David Pipe) *midfield: mstke 4th: rdn and no imp on ldrs 2 out: wknd bef last* **25/1**

000/ **13** *7* **Hollow Tree**[37] 5141 5-10-9 **132**... JasonMaguire 110
(Donald McCain) *prom: rdn after 4 out: wknd bef 2 out* **14/1**

303/ **14** *10* **First Fandango**[37] 5141 6-10-12 **142**................................(t) MrBGibbs(7) 111
(Tim Vaughan) *in tch: mstke 6th: wknd 8th* **16/1**

230/ **15** *16* **Barafundle (IRE)**[37] 5141 9-11-3 **140**................................. SamThomas 94
(Jennie Candlish) *prom tl wknd 8th: toiling 4 out* **12/1**

263/ **16** *2* **Cucumber Run (IRE)**[24] 5352 8-11-6 **143**........................ BarryGeraghty 96
(Nicky Henderson) *in tch: pushed along and lost pl after 4 out: wknd bef next* **11/1**

421/ **17** *5* **Midnight Appeal**[15] 5551 8-10-9 **132**.................................(v) CharlieHuxley 80
(Alan King) *hld up: toiling 4 out: nvr on terms* **33/1**

U01/ **18** *4 1/2* **Pateese (FR)**[22] 5307 8-10-13 **136**.............................(b) RichardJohnson 80
(Philip Hobbs) *hld up: hit 3rd: effrt into midfield appr 3 out: nvr able to get nr ldrs: wknd bef 2 out: eased whn wl btn run-in* **16/1**

600/ **19** *10* **Kells Belle (IRE)**[23] 5360 7-11-0 **137**.................................... DavidBass 72
(Nicky Henderson) *midfield: lost pl bef 7th: toiling 4 out: t.o* **25/1**

U00/ 20 13 **Art Professor (IRE)**[14] 5582 9-10-8 131 .... LiamTreadwell 54
(Venetia Williams) *hld up: hit 3rd: sn reminders: sme hdwy 6th: mstke 8th: wknd bef 4 out: toiling after: t.o* **33/1**

5m 39.9s (-20.10) **Going Correction** -0.70s/f (Firm) **20** Ran SP% **133.3**
Speed ratings (Par 109): **105,104,104,104,103 103,102,101,99,98 97,97,95,91,86 85,84,82,79,74**
toteswingers 1&2 £7.50, 1&3 £96.90, 2&3 £96.90 CSF £46.17 CT £1244.10 TOTE £7.30: £2.00, £1.70, £8.20, £5.40; EX 32.90 Trifecta £1043.20 Part won. Pool: £1,391.00 - 0.30 winning units..

Owner Jolly Boys Outing **Bred** Juddmonte Farms Ltd **Trained** Spaxton, Somerset
■ Stewards' Enquiry : Danny Cook one-day ban: careless riding (May 25)
Brendan Powell four-day ban: used whip above permitted level (May 25-28)

FOCUS
West bend moved out 7m, increasing distances by 22yds. There was 3mm of morning rain on already watered ground. After the opener Nico de Boinville said the hurdles track was riding good, but Brendan Powell thought it was on the slow side of good. This was a highly competitive handicap, run at a reasonable pace, and solid form. Battle Group improved to the level of his Aintree chase win. Opportunities for most of these will be thin on the ground in the next few months, however.

216 PERTEMPS NETWORK H'CAP HURDLE (REGISTERED AS THE SWINTON HURDLE) GRADE 3 — 2m
3:30 (3:30) (Class 1) 4-Y-0+

£34,170 (£12,822; £6,420; £3,198; £1,608; £804)

Form — RPR

014/ 1 **Barizan (IRE)**[63] 4665 7-10-6 126 ....(bt) PaulMoloney 132
(Evan Williams) *chsd ldr: led appr 3 out: rdn and abt 3 l clr last: all out towards fin* **8/1**[2]

1P3/ 2 ½ **Mr Mole (IRE)**[24] 5356 5-11-3 142 ....(t) HarryDerham(5) 148
(Paul Nicholls) *hld up: hdwy 4 out: carried hd awkwardly and chsd ldrs 2 out: wnt 2nd bef last where abt 3 l down: cajoled into action run-in: clsd on wnr towards fin* **11/2**[1]

405/ 3 19 **Local Hero (GER)**[21] 5402 6-11-3 144 ....(p) PaulBohan(7) 132
(Steve Gollings) *hld up in rr: struggling after 4 out: u.p after: hdwy appr last: styd on run-in: tk 3rd cl home: no ch w front two* **12/1**

651/ 4 ½ **Rumble Of Thunder (IRE)**[40] 5076 7-10-8 128 .... RichieMcGrath 116
(Philip Kirby) *chsd ldrs: pushed along appr 2 out: nt qckn bef last: styd on u.p run-in but n.d to front two* **16/1**

162/ 5 1½ **Red Inca**[22] 5367 5-10-7 127 .... DannyCook 114
(Brian Ellison) *in tch: hmpd 3rd: chsd ldrs 2 out: hit last: kpt on u.p but no imp after* **11/1**

001/ 6 1¼ **Starluck (IRE)**[24] 5356 8-11-7 146 ....(b) NicodeBoinville(5) 132
(David Arbuthnot) *hld up: hdwy 4 out: pushed along appr 3 out: chsd ldrs next: no imp whn nt fluent last: plugged on run-in wout threatening* **16/1**

003/ 7 ½ **Silk Hall (UAE)**[21] 5402 8-10-12 132 .... EddieO'Connell 117
(J J Lambe, Ire) *in tch: chsng ldrs appr 3 out: wnt 2nd bef hit 2 out: lost 2nd bef last: no imp after: swtchd rt run-in 1f out: plugged on but n.d* **14/1**

055/ 8 15 **Street Entertainer (IRE)**[189] 2179 6-10-9 129 ....(bt) ConorO'Farrell 101
(David Pipe) *hld up: sn in midfield: styng on abt 7 l off the pce whn blnd 2 out: sn btn* **10/1**[3]

1B1/ 9 6 **Deepsand (IRE)**[17] 5497 4-10-9 133 ....(p) DougieCostello 95
(Tim Easterby) *hld up: hdwy after 4 out: midfield and niggled along whn nt fluent 3 out: n.d after* **12/1**

100/ 10 3½ **Toubab (FR)**[14] 5575 7-11-5 139 .... DarylJacob 102
(Paul Nicholls) *midfield: hmpd 3rd: niggled along after 4 out: sn bhd and outpcd: n.d after: eased whn wl btn run-in* **25/1**

344/ 11 3¼ **Ruler Of All (IRE)**[28] 5284 7-10-2 129 .... MrRWinks(7) 89
(Peter Winks) *led: hdd appr 3 out where mstke and rdr lost iron: wknd after 2 out: eased run-in* **50/1**

0/1- 12 7 **Cry Of Freedom (USA)**[9] 82 7-10-13 133 ....(v) DenisO'Regan 87
(John Ferguson) *midfield: hdwy to chse ldrs after 3rd: wknd 4 out* **10/1**[3]

246/ 13 1½ **Bygones Of Brid (IRE)**[21] 5402 10-11-2 136 .... BrianHughes 88
(Karen McLintock) *chsd ldrs tl wknd qckly appr 2 out* **25/1**

301/ 14 hd **Turn Over Sivola (FR)**[30] 5260 6-10-10 130 .... WayneHutchinson 82
(Alan King) *midfield: hdwy whn nt fluent 3 out: sn btn* **11/2**[1]

350/ 15 25 **Baby Mix (FR)**[91] 4125 5-11-3 137 .... NoelFehily 67
(Tom George) *midfield: pckd 1st: wknd after 4 out: t.o* **14/1**

422/ F **Specialagent Alfie**[41] 5031 7-10-8 128 ....(t) TomCannon
(Nick Gifford) *in tch: fell 3rd* **12/1**

3m 48.5s (-15.70) **Going Correction** -0.70s/f (Firm)
WFA 4 from 5yo+ 18lb **16** Ran SP% **126.2**
Speed ratings (Par 113): **111,110,101,101,100 99,99,91,88,87 85,82,81,81,68**
toteswingers 1&2 £46.30, 1&3 £102.10, 2&3 £46.50 CSF £53.13 CT £546.59 TOTE £9.00: £2.50, £2.00, £3.30, £3.90; EX 75.90 Trifecta £1424.10 Pool: £90,480.12 - 47.65 winning units..
Owner P Conway & John Lee Jones **Bred** His Highness The Aga Khan's Studs S C **Trained** Llancarfan, Vale Of Glamorgan
■ Stewards' Enquiry : Eddie O'Connell caution: careless riding

FOCUS
A good handicap if not quite as competitive as it often is, with the Nicky Henderson pair Forgotten Voice, the morning favourite, and Cape Express taken out because of the ground. Not many got into it off a decent gallop, and the first two were clear. There's a case for rating this form another 10lb higher.

217 PERTEMPS NETWORK INTERMEDIATE H'CAP CHASE — 2m 4f
4:40 (4:40) (Class 2) 5-Y-0+ **£38,988** (£11,448; £5,724; £2,862)

Form — RPR

251/ 1 **Fairy Rath (IRE)**[34] 5198 7-10-6 125 ....(t) TomCannon 132
(Nick Gifford) *in tch: wnt prom 6th: led 4 out: pressed fr 3 out: edgd lft run-in: drvn out and kpt on towards fin* **18/1**

131/ 2 ¾ **Conquisto**[21] 5403 8-11-12 145 .... TomScudamore 151
(Steve Gollings) *chsd ldrs: chalng fr 3 out: rdn bef 2 out: styd on u.p run-in: hld towards fin* **10/1**

230/ 3 2¼ **Tony Star (FR)**[42] 5014 6-11-4 137 .... RichardJohnson 142
(Philip Hobbs) *hld up in rr: nt fluent 8th: hdwy to chse ldrs appr 4 out: tried to chal and ch bef 2 out: nt quiken bef last: kpt on u.p run-in but no imp on front two* **10/1**

3F0/ 4 13 **Poole Master**[24] 5352 8-10-13 132 ....(p) ConorO'Farrell 125
(David Pipe) *disp ld: def advantage 6th: hdd appr 4 out but stl ev ch: outpcd bef 2 out* **16/1**

4F/- 5 4½ **Aikideau (FR)**[136] 3223 6-9-9 119 oh4 .... HarryDerham(5) 107
(Paul Nicholls) *chsd ldrs: lost pl 6th: pushed along appr 10th: outpcd after 11th: styd on u.p fr 2 out: nt trble ldrs* **9/2**[1]

30/- 6 ½ **Tour D'Argent (FR)**[59] 4736 6-10-12 131 .... BarryGeraghty 119
(Nicky Henderson) *hld up in midfield: mstke 1st: lost pl 8th: hdwy into midfield whn hmpd on bnd after 11th: sn lost pl: plugged on fr 2 out wout threatening* **10/1**

321/ 7 7 **Dare Me (IRE)**[42] 5017 9-10-9 128 .... AidanColeman 112
(Venetia Williams) *hld up in midfield: hdwy to chse ldrs 10th: effrt and ev ch 4 out: rdn and wknd bef 2 out* **7/1**[3]

362/ 8 hd **King Of The Night (GER)**[39] 5105 9-11-1 134 .... NoelFehily 115
(Harry Fry) *hld up: hdwy into midfield after 11th: effrt to chse ldrs appr 4 out: jump rt fnl 4: wknd bef 2 out* **8/1**

242/ 9 17 **Elenika (FR)**[20] 5439 5-10-11 130 ....(t) DarylJacob 99
(Paul Nicholls) *racd keenly: disp ld tl 6th: remained w ldr: led appr 4 out where mstke and hdd: sn wknd* **14/1**

2P3/ P **Desert Cry (IRE)**[21] 5401 7-11-9 142 .... JasonMaguire
(Donald McCain) *in tch: mstke 2nd and reminder: wknd after 8th: toiling and bhd 11th: t.o whn p.u bef 4 out* **16/1**

3F5/ P **Ciceron (IRE)**[28] 5291 7-10-6 125 .... LiamTreadwell
(Venetia Williams) *hld up: bdly hmpd and stopped on bnd after 11th: nt rcvr and p.u* **28/1**

330/ P **Attaglance**[35] 5175 7-11-0 133 ....(t) HarryHaynes
(Malcolm Jefferson) *chsd ldrs: lost pl 8th: struggling after: bhd after 11th: t.o whn p.u bef 2 out* **11/2**[2]

25F/ P **Heez A Cracker (FR)**[71] 4503 7-10-3 122 .... AlainCawley
(Tom George) *racd keenly: hld up: hdwy whn bmpd on bnd after 11th: sn u.p and wknd: p.u bef 4 out: dismntd: lame* **16/1**

421/ F **Ulysse Collonges (FR)**[22] 5370 5-11-2 135 .... DenisO'Regan
(Chris Grant) *midfield: hdwy to trck ldrs 9th: wnt wrong on bnd after 11th and fell: fatally injured* **16/1**

4m 57.9s (-12.10) **Going Correction** -0.325s/f (Good) **14** Ran SP% **123.4**
Speed ratings: **111,110,109,104,102 102,99,99,92, , , ,**
toteswingers 1&2 £13.80, 1&3 £24.50, 2&3 £24.50 CSF £192.38 TOTE £24.60: £6.20, £2.30, £3.30; EX 150.60 Trifecta £831.90 Part won. Pool: £11909.30 - 0.21 winning units..
Owner Mrs C L Kyle **Bred** Miss Mary G Cotter **Trained** Findon, W Sussex
■ Stewards' Enquiry : Tom Cannon one-day ban: careless riding (May 25)

FOCUS
The first runnng of this valuable event, one of three similar races put on as part of the revamped novice chase programme introduced last season. Runners must have contested at least two non-handicap novice, beginners' or maiden chases in Britain last term. It attracted a suitably strong line-up and the first three showed useful form in coming clear. The third is the best guide.

[109]HEXHAM (L-H)
Saturday, May 11

OFFICIAL GOING: Good (good to soft in places in back straight; 6.9)
Wind: Fairly strong, half against Weather: Overcast, dull

218 MAYA AND REED BARHAM "NATIONAL HUNT" NOVICES' HURDLE (8 hdls) — 2m 110y
1:55 (1:56) (Class 4) 4-Y-0+ **£3,285** (£957; £479)

Form — RPR

P52/ 1 **Damascus Steel (IRE)**[15] 5544 5-10-12 110 .... BrianHarding 104
(Alison Hamilton) *chsd ldrs: effrt and rdn appr 2 out: led last: hld on wl towards fin* **10/3**[2]

134/ 2 nk **Island Confusion (IRE)**[22] 5373 5-10-5 0 .... GrahamWatters(7) 103
(Lucinda Russell) *t.k.h: cl up: led 3rd: qcknd 2 out: rdn and hdd last: rallied: hld nr fin* **13/8**[1]

606/ 3 12 **Tiny Dancer (IRE)**[19] 5449 5-10-12 0 .... PaddyBrennan 92
(Micky Hammond) *prom: rdn and outpcd after 2 out: kpt on fr last: nt pce of first two* **28/1**

53/ 4 nk **Quest Magic (IRE)**[19] 5449 7-10-5 0 .... JohnDawson(7) 92
(John Wade) *chsd ldr tl drvn and outpcd between last 2: n.d after* **10/3**[2]

400/ 5 8 **Mrs Grass**[34] 5202 6-10-2 0 .... JohnKington(3) 80
(Jonathan Haynes) *hld up in tch: rdn after 3 out: hit and outpcd next* **80/1**

0/ 6 13 **Silver Sophfire**[828] 3903 7-10-0 0 .... JonathanEngland(5) 66
(Sue Smith) *chsd ldrs tl lost pl and struggling appr 4 out: n.d after* **7/1**[3]

306/ 7 28 **Bardeli (IRE)**[15] 5544 6-10-12 0 ....(t) HenryBrooke 48
(Donald McCain) *hld up: hit 2nd: hdwy and in tch bef 2 out: rdn and wknd after 2 out: t.o* **16/1**

050/ 8 3½ **Honourable Gent**[19] 5454 5-10-12 0 .... WilsonRenwick 45
(Rose Dobbin) *nt fluent in rr: stdy hdwy and in tch bef 2 out: sn rdn and wknd* **28/1**

P/0- P **Sunset Song**[9] 73 9-10-5 57 ....(t) PeterBuchanan
(Theresa Gibson) *hld up in tch: drvn and outpcd 4 out: struggling after next: t.o whn p.u bef last* **100/1**

4m 11.1s (-6.30) **Going Correction** -0.075s/f (Good) **9** Ran SP% **111.8**
Speed ratings (Par 105): **111,110,105,105,101 95,82,80,**
toteswingers 1&2 £1.10, 1&3 £6.10, 2&3 Not won CSF £8.96 TOTE £3.70: £1.02, £1.10, £6.00; EX 11.80 Trifecta £61.80 Pool: £434.95 - 5.27 winning units..
Owner J P G Hamilton **Bred** Michael Keane **Trained** Denholm, Borders

FOCUS
Bends and hurdles moved accordingly. A modest novices' hurdle in which they went a steady gallop on ground officially described as good, good to soft in places on an overcast and blustery afternoon.

219 TDR@Q1 (S) HURDLE (8 hdls) — 2m 110y
2:30 (2:30) (Class 5) 4-Y-0+ **£2,053** (£598; £299)

Form — RPR

446/ 1 **Radmores Revenge**[15] 5540 10-10-5 124 ....(p) CiaranMckee(7) 108+
(John O'Shea) *t.k.h: hld up in tch: smooth hdwy to ld after 3 out: pushed along bef last: styd on wl* **4/6**[1]

602/ 2 4½ **I'Ll Be Frank**[13] 17 8-10-5 92 ....(t) StephenMulqueen(7) 102
(Maurice Barnes) *led to after 3 out: sn pushed along and rallied: kpt on fr last: nt pce of wnr* **7/2**[2]

0/2- 3 34 **That'll Do Nicely (IRE)**[7] 110 10-10-5 100 .... MissJRRichards(7) 71
(Nicky Richards) *t.k.h: cl up: nt fluent 3rd: ev ch bef 2 out: rdn after 2 out: wkng whn nt fluent last* **4/1**[3]

000/ 4 7 **Border Tale**[74] 4433 13-10-12 82 .... BrianHarding 65
(James Moffatt) *chsd ldrs: drvn and struggling bef 4 out: no ch after* **28/1**

5/5- 5 2¼ **Lewlaur Supreme (IRE)**[7] 110 10-10-12 67 .... RyanMania 66
(William Young Jnr) *prom: nt fluent 2nd: hdwy to join ldr 4th: hit and rdn 3 out: wknd bef next* **40/1**

4m 12.5s (-4.90) **Going Correction** -0.075s/f (Good) **5** Ran SP% **108.1**
Speed ratings (Par 103): **108,105,89,86,85**
CSF £3.31 TOTE £1.50: £1.10, £1.40; EX 3.70 Trifecta £3.60 Pool: £789.15 - 161.25 winning units..The winner was bought by Sophie Leech 9,500gns
Owner J R Salter **Bred** J R Salter **Trained** Elton, Gloucs

The Form Book Jumps, Raceform Ltd, Compton, RG20 6NL.

FOCUS
A modest selling hurdle. The winner is rated 20lb off his best.

220 BRITAIN IN BLOOM CONDITIONAL JOCKEYS' H'CAP CHASE (15 fncs) 2m 4f 110y
3:05 (3:05) (Class 4) (0-115,112) 5-Y-0+ **£3,969** (£1,157; £578)

Form RPR

332/ **1** **Or D'Oudaires (FR)**[14] 5571 11-10-7 **93**....(t) SamanthaDrake 104+
(Ferdy Murphy, France) *cl up: led after 2nd to 7th: ev ch bef 3 out: rdn to ld last: kpt on wl* **6/1**

34/ **2** 1 1/2 **Sergeant Pink (IRE)**[14] 5571 7-10-9 **95**....(p) TonyKelly 104
(Dianne Sayer) *in tch: hdwy to ld bef 3 out: rdn and hdd last: kpt on: hld towards fin* **8/1**

3F3/ **3** nk **Papa Caruso**[45] 4972 9-11-9 **112**.... JonathanEngland[(3)] 121
(Sue Smith) *hld up in tch on outside: hdwy to chse ldrs whn hit 9th: rallied: outpcd 3 out: styd on fr last: hld towards fin* **11/4[1]**

360/ **4** 23 **Classic Cut**[29] 5276 9-10-8 **99**....(b) GrahamWatters[(5)] 90
(James Ewart) *t.k.h: cl up: led 9th to bef 3 out: wknd bef next* **4/1[3]**

122/ **5** 9 **Ancient Times (USA)**[50] 4909 6-9-11 **89**....(p) AdamNicol[(6)] 69
(Philip Kirby) *in tch: hdwy on ins to ld 7th: hdd 9th: rallied: nt fluent 4 out: rdn and wknd bef next* **7/2[2]**

FP2/ **6** 77 **Civil Unrest (IRE)**[20] 5424 7-10-10 **104**....(b) DaleIrving[(8)] 15
(James Ewart) *mstkes: chsd ldrs: struggling bef 4 out: t.o* **8/1**

146/ **P** **Bene Lad (IRE)**[33] 5219 11-11-10 **110**.... HenryBrooke
(Jim Goldie) *hld up: rdn bef 9th: rallied: lost tch fr 4 out: t.o: p.u after 2 out* **16/1**

1PP/ **P** **Flying Squad (UAE)**[12] 25 9-10-11 **105**....(t) ShaunDobbin[(8)]
(Rose Dobbin) *led to bef 2nd: cl up: lost pl qckly 7th: p.u after next* **33/1**

5m 17.5s (4.00) **Going Correction** +0.10s/f (Yiel) **8 Ran SP% 114.2**
Speed ratings: **96,95,95,86,83 53, ,**
toteswingers 1&2 £2.50, 1&3 £5.10, 2&3 £3.90 CSF £51.29 CT £160.66 TOTE £5.80: £1.40, £2.80, £1.70; EX 25.10 TRIFECTA Pool: £482.24 - 5.16 winning units..
Owner Gay And Peter Hartley **Bred** Comte Michel De Gigou **Trained** France

FOCUS
A fair conditional jockeys' handicap chase. Sound form, and the winner could go in again.

221 MARGARET FERRIES MEMORIAL H'CAP HURDLE (DIV I) (12 hdls) 3m
3:40 (3:40) (Class 5) (0-100,100) 4-Y-0+ **£2,274** (£667; £333; £166)

Form RPR

5P4/ **1** **Corky Dancer**[13] 17 8-10-0 **74** oh2....(v[1]) WilsonRenwick 92+
(Andrew Parker) *j.w: mde all at decent gallop: clr after 2 out: rdn out: unchal* **6/1[3]**

361/ **2** 9 **Solis (GER)**[17] 5500 10-11-3 **96**.... EmmaSayer[(5)] 107
(Dianne Sayer) *hld up: hdwy 3 out: rdn and chsd (clr) wnr bef last: kpt on: nvr able to chal* **4/1[2]**

060/ **3** 28 **Grey Command (USA)**[17] 5495 8-10-4 **83**.... KyleJames[(5)] 71
(Philip Kirby) *prom: chsd wnr 7th: effrt and clsd briefly bef 2 out: sn one pce: lost 2nd bef last: wknd* **9/4[1]**

060/ **4** 9 **Charlie Bucket**[40] 5074 10-10-10 **94**.... RyanNichol[(10)] 71
(Donald Whillans) *midfield on outside: drvn along 8th: outpcd after next: styd on fr 2 out: nt pce to chal* **25/1**

P/4- **5** 1 **Westwire Toby (IRE)**[7] 122 11-10-0 **74** oh8.... TomSiddall 50
(Lynn Siddall) *chsd wnr to 7th: cl up: hit 3 out: struggling fr next* **33/1**

500/ **6** 4 **Political Paddy**[17] 5495 11-10-1 **80**.... GaryRutherford[(5)] 52
(Rayson Nixon) *in tch: drvn and outpcd after 8th: rallied between last 2: no imp* **12/1**

562/ **7** 12 **Weybridge Light**[248] 1497 8-11-7 **100**.... TonyKelly[(5)] 61
(David Thompson) *hld up: stdy hdwy bef 4 out: drvn next: sn struggling* **12/1**

066/ **8** 1 **Western Bound (IRE)**[118] 3647 12-9-9 **76**....(t) MissEButterworth[(7)] 37
(Barbara Butterworth) *bhd: rdn along bef 4 out: nvr on terms* **33/1**

9 4 1/2 **The Bard O Tully (IRE)**[11] 53 5-11-3 **98**....(t) GrahamWatters[(7)] 54
(B Arthey, Ire) *prom: lost pl bef 8th: sn struggling* **25/1**

0F0/ **10** 21 **Overafrica (IRE)**[17] 5495 7-11-9 **97**....(bt) AdrianLane 35
(Donald McCain) *prom tl lost pl 8th: lost tch fr next* **17/2**

0U0/ **11** 96 **Almutaham (USA)**[19] 5451 6-11-4 **92**....[1] HenryBrooke
(Martin Todhunter) *bhd: drvn and struggling fr 8th: virtually p.u run-in* **14/1**

66P/ **P** **Uno Valoroso (FR)**[40] 5074 5-10-12 **86**....(p) PeterBuchanan
(Tim Walford) *hld up: hit 6th: struggling 8th: t.o whn p.u after 2 out* **9/1**

6m 4.8s (-4.20) **Going Correction** -0.075s/f (Good) **12 Ran SP% 121.2**
Speed ratings (Par 103): **104,101,91,88,88 87,83,82,81,74 42,**
toteswingers 1&2 £9.00, 1&3 £3.50, 2&3 £2.00 CSF £30.34 CT £71.00 TOTE £6.20: £2.60, £1.50, £1.60; EX 40.50 Trifecta £114.40 Pool: £528.23 - 3.46 winning units..
Owner Mr & Mrs Raymond Anderson Green **Bred** Design And Planning Consultants Ltd **Trained** Ecclefechan, D'fries & G'way

FOCUS
The first division of a modest staying handicap hurdle in which they went a searching gallop. A hurdles best from the winner.

222 MARGARET FERRIES MEMORIAL H'CAP HURDLE (DIV II) (12 hdls) 3m
4:15 (4:15) (Class 5) (0-100,99) 4-Y-0+ **£2,274** (£667; £333; £166)

Form RPR

4P2/ **1** **Candleford**[40] 5078 8-11-2 **94**.... TonyKelly[(5)] 106+
(Ashley Dodgson) *hld up: gd hdwy bef 2 out: pushed along after 2 out: led whn nt fluent last: kpt on strly* **2/1[1]**

P/5- **2** 4 **Granwood**[10] 67 7-11-0 **87**....(p) PeterBuchanan 93
(Tim Walford) *led to bef 4 out: cl up: rdn bef 2 out: rallied to chse wnr last: kpt on: nt pce to chal* **5/1[3]**

046/ **3** 3 **Bob's Ticket (IRE)**[15] 5546 8-10-6 **86**....(t) AdamNicol[(7)] 89
(Philip Kirby) *chsd ldrs: ev ch bef 2 out: rdn and led briefly bef last: outpcd run-in* **8/1**

431/ **4** 3/4 **Saddlers Mot**[13] 17 9-11-2 **96**....(b) JohnDawson[(7)] 98
(Karen Tutty) *hld up: hdwy and prom bef 2 out: rdn and outpcd after 2 out: no imp fr last* **8/1**

3PF/ **5** 3 1/2 **Raggios Boy**[67] 4581 7-10-4 **77**....(p) HenryBrooke 77
(Barry Murtagh) *cl up: led bef 4 out to bef last: sn rdn: wknd run-in* **12/1**

PP0/ **6** 30 **Nisaal (IRE)**[40] 5074 8-10-0 **73** oh2....(t) AdrianLane 45
(Sandy Forster) *hld up: pushed along after 7th: hdwy next: wknd after 3 out: t.o* **100/1**

1/1- **7** 13 **Pyjama Game (IRE)**[9] 74 7-11-10 **97**.... WilsonRenwick 57
(Rose Dobbin) *prom: drvn and outpcd bef 4 out: wknd after 3 out: t.o* **4/1[2]**

64P/ **P** **Seize**[399] 5283 11-11-12 **99**.... BrianHarding
(James Moffatt) *hld up: rdn and outpcd 7th: lost tch next: t.o whn p.u bef 2 out* **33/1**

P55/ **P** **Teerie Express**[118] 3648 12-11-3 **97**....(p) JonathonBewley[(7)]
(George Bewley) *prom: rdn after 3 out: wknd next: p.u bef last* **28/1**

4PP/ **P** **Heart O' The West (IRE)**[64] 4630 9-10-6 **82**....(p) EwanWhillans[(3)]
(Alistair Whillans) *chsd ldrs to 4 out: struggling fr next: no ch whn p.u bef last* **14/1**

P05/ **P** **Flag Flier**[14] 5570 10-9-7 **73** oh9.... StephenMulqueen[(7)]
(Mike Sowersby) *nt fluent in midfield: lost pl bef 7th: lost tch fr next: t.o whn p.u bef 2 out* **50/1**

00P/ **P** **Roslin Moss**[370] 7-9-8 **74**.... CraigNichol[(7)]
(Donald Whillans) *bhd: rdn and struggling 4 out: t.o whn p.u bef 2 out* **40/1**

6m 12.6s (3.60) **Going Correction** -0.075s/f (Good) **12 Ran SP% 118.4**
Speed ratings (Par 103): **91,89,88,88,87 77,72, , ,**
toteswingers 1&2 £1.40, 1&3 £3.80, 2&3 £11.80 CSF £12.21 CT £67.20 TOTE £2.20: £1.40, £2.10, £2.00; EX 14.80 Trifecta £96.70 Pool: £814.83 - 6.31 winning units..
Owner A C Dodgson **Bred** Miss S E Hall **Trained** Catton, N Yorks

FOCUS
The second division of a modest staying handicap hurdle. The form makes sense.

223 GREGGS CHILDRENS CANCER RUN NOVICES' HURDLE (10 hdls) 2m 4f 110y
4:50 (4:50) (Class 4) 4-Y-0+ **£3,285** (£957; £479)

Form RPR

104/ **1** **Rattlin**[13] 15 5-10-5 0.... RyanMania 94+
(Sue Smith) *cl up: hit 4 out: led appr next and clr to 2 out: sn drvn: hdd briefly run-in: styd on wl towards fin* **10/3[2]**

4/ **2** 1/2 **Azerodegree (IRE)**[17] 5491 4-10-7 0.... AdrianLane 94
(Iain Jardine) *prom: hdwy and carried hd high fr 3 out: effrt and led briefly run-in: hung lft: no ex towards fin* **8/1[3]**

05/ **3** 29 **Miss Macnamara (IRE)**[13] 15 4-10-0 0.... WilsonRenwick 67
(Martin Todhunter) *chsd ldrs: hmpd by faller but lft 3rd 3 out: sn chsng wnr: rdn bef next: wknd bef last* **12/1**

2P6/ **4** 18 **Crabbie's Cloudy (IRE)**[34] 5205 6-10-12 0.... HenryBrooke 57
(Donald McCain) *led to bef 3 out: rdn and wknd bef next* **16/1**

P00/ **5** 8 **Black Velvet Belle (IRE)**[17] 5491 6-10-2 0....(tp) AlexanderVoy[(3)] 43
(Lucy Normile) *nt fluent: bhd: struggling fr 8th: n.d after* **66/1**

0P0/ **6** nk **First Of Never (IRE)**[19] 5449 7-10-12 0.... TomSiddall 49
(Lynn Siddall) *nt fluent in rr: outpcd whn hmpd 3 out: nvr on terms* **150/1**

623/ **F** **Northern Executive (IRE)**[13] 19 5-10-12 0.... PaddyBrennan
(Karen McLintock) *trckd ldrs: pushed along whn fell 3 out* **8/13[1]**

5m 13.2s (0.70) **Going Correction** -0.075s/f (Good)
WFA 4 from 5yo+ 19lb **7 Ran SP% 111.8**
Speed ratings (Par 105): **95,94,83,76,73 73,**
toteswingers 1&2 £3.00, 1&3 £3.50, 2&3 £1.60 CSF £27.58 TOTE £4.00: £1.60, £1.80; EX 24.60 Trifecta £121.20 Pool: £1473.69 - 9.11 winning units..
Owner Broadband Partnership **Bred** R F Broad **Trained** High Eldwick, W Yorks

FOCUS
A modest novices' hurdle in which they went an even gallop. The winner improved in line with the best of her bumper form.

224 LOWGATE NOVICES' H'CAP CHASE (19 fncs) 3m 1f
5:20 (5:20) (Class 4) (0-115,114) 5-Y-0+ **£3,969** (£1,157; £578)

Form RPR

541/ **1** **Lukey Luke**[13] 20 10-10-4 **92**.... PeterBuchanan 96+
(James Turner) *prom: wnt 2nd 4 out: effrt and cl 2nd whn lft 6 l clr 2 out: rdn out fr last* **6/1[3]**

326/ **2** 5 **Bollin Fiona**[33] 5223 9-10-2 **95**.... CallumWhillans[(5)] 93
(Donald Whillans) *nt fluent on occasions: hld up: hdwy and prom 13th: sn rdn: rallied 4 out: lft 6 l 2nd 2 out: one pce fr last* **22/1**

5/4- **3** 1 **Justjoe (IRE)**[7] 109 7-10-0 **88** oh3....(p) WilsonRenwick 86
(Micky Hammond) *nt fluent on occasions: hld up: hdwy bef 14th: effrt whn lft 3rd and sddle slipped bk 2 out: rdr rode wout irons appr last: sn one pce* **11/1**

114/ **U** **Call It On (IRE)**[17] 5503 7-11-7 **114**....(tp) KyleJames[(5)]
(Philip Kirby) *led to 7th: w ldr: outpcd after 4 out: 4th and no imp whn stmbld and uns rdr next* **5/2[1]**

004/ **P** **Dollar Mick (IRE)**[336] 656 8-10-0 **88** oh3.... BrianHarding
(James Moffatt) *hld up in tch: struggling fr 13th: t.o whn p.u bef 4 out* **13/2**

6/P- **F** **Stagecoach Jasper**[7] 114 7-11-3 **105**.... RyanMania 108
(Sue Smith) *cl up: led 7th: rdn 3 out: jst in front and keeping on whn fell next* **11/2[2]**

2U2/ **P** **On Broadway (IRE)**[34] 5203 7-11-1 **110**....(b[1]) CraigNichol[(7)]
(Lucinda Russell) *prom: struggling fr 13th: lost tch and p.u 3 out* **5/2[1]**

6m 38.6s (6.40) **Going Correction** +0.10s/f (Yiel) **7 Ran SP% 112.8**
Speed ratings: **93,91,91, , ,**
CSF £93.28 CT £1400.24 TOTE £4.50: £2.80, £6.20; EX 52.30 Trifecta £108.80 Pool: £327.51 - 2.25 winning units..
Owner D M Wordsworth **Bred** J R Wills **Trained** Norton-le-Clay, N Yorks

FOCUS
A fair staying novices' handicap chase. A step up from the winner with the second to her mark.

225 YARRIDGE HEIGHTS STANDARD OPEN NATIONAL HUNT FLAT RACE 2m 110y
5:50 (5:52) (Class 6) 4-6-Y-0 **£1,642** (£478; £239)

Form RPR

1 **Ziggie (IRE)**[69] 6-11-2 0.... AdrianLane 106+
(Donald McCain) *mde all at stdy pce: qcknd 3f out: rdn and hld on wl fnl f* **5/2[2]**

/ **2** 2 **Line D'Aois (IRE)**[132] 5-11-2 0.... PaddyBrennan 104
(Michael Scudamore) *in tch: hdwy to chse wnr 4f out: sn clr of rest: effrt and drvn 2f out: kpt on same pce last 100yds* **3/1[3]**

/ **3** 39 **Proud Jack** 5-11-2 0.... WilsonRenwick 69
(Ann Hamilton) *trckd ldrs: wnt 2nd 1/2-way: drvn and outpcd over 3f out: hung rt and rallied 2f out: no ch w first two* **5/1**

3/ **4** 2 3/4 **Radmores Express**[13] 14 4-10-5 0.... CiaranMckee[(7)] 63
(John O'Shea) *t.k.h: prom: outpcd and lost pl over 4f out: rallied and hung rt over 2f out: no imp* **9/4[1]**

5 11 **Kajun Thunder (IRE)**[28] 4-10-5 0....(t) GrahamWatters[(7)] 53
(B Arthey, Ire) *hld up in tch: drvn and struggling 1/2-way: plugged on to pass btn rivals in st* **12/1**

0/ **6** nk **Mo Rouge (IRE)**[15] 5550 5-11-2 0.... PeterBuchanan 56
(Mrs Jackie Stephen) *trckd wnr to 1/2-way: rdn and outpcd over 4f out: sn btn* **22/1**

0/ 7 13 **Beyondtemptation**[32] 5230 5-10-6 0 .... JohnKington(3) 38
(Jonathan Haynes) *plld hrd: hld up in tch: hdwy and cl up over 6f out: wknd qckly over 3f out* **100/1**

4m 16.6s (3.90) **Going Correction** -0.075s/f (Good)
WFA 4 from 5yo+ 4lb 7 Ran SP% **114.0**
Speed ratings: **90,89,70,69,64 64,57**
toteswingers 1&2 £2.00, 2&3 £3.40, 1&3 £3.50 CSF £10.42 TOTE £2.90: £2.30, £1.20; EX 7.70 Trifecta £39.70 Pool: £908.99 - 17.16 winning units..
Owner Matthew Sanders **Bred** Gavin Cromwell **Trained** Cholmondeley, Cheshire

FOCUS

They went a sedate gallop. The first two were well clear but this was a weak bumper otherwise.
T/Plt: £26.30 to a £1 stake. Pool: £49770.7 - 1376.98 winning tickets T/Qpdt: £16.60 to a £1 stake. Pool: £3400.30 - 150.70 winning tickets RY

226 - 232a (Foreign Racing) - See Raceform Interactive

KEMPTON (R-H)

Sunday, May 12

OFFICIAL GOING: Good (chs 7.9; hdl 7.7)

Wind: Moderate, across away from stands Weather: Sunny intervals early, light rain from race 4

233 CONOR MAYNARD LIVE AT KEMPTON 14.09.13 NOVICES' HURDLE (10 hdls) 2m 5f

2:20 (2:21) (Class 4) 4-Y-0+ **£3,285** (£957; £479)

Form RPR

506/ 1 **Gold Ingot**[26] 5337 6-10-12 .... WayneHutchinson 110+
(Alan King) *plld hrd in rr of midfield: hdwy 3 out: led appr last: rdn out* **6/1**[3]

5/ 2 2 1/4 **Kadalkin (FR)**[843] 3647 7-10-9 ....(t) MarkQuinlan(3) 107
(Nigel Hawke) *hld up in rr: mstke 4th: hdwy appr 2 out: styd on to take 2nd on line* **66/1**

2P1/ 3 shd **Otto The Great (FR)**[81] 4315 5-10-12 125 .... BarryGeraghty 107
(Nicky Henderson) *chsd ldrs: led 3 out tl appr last: one pce* **4/11**[1]

003/ 4 18 **Proper Villan (IRE)**[31] 5241 8-10-12 .... MarkGrant 92
(Geoffrey Deacon) *bhd: nt fluent 2nd: styd on to take modest 4th appr last* **33/1**

0P5/ 5 4 **Buffy The Beatle**[14] 3 5-10-12 101 ....(v[1]) JasonMaguire 87
(Kim Bailey) *chsd ldrs: wnt cl 3rd 3 out: sn outpcd* **33/1**

55/ 6 1/2 **King Boru (IRE)**[89] 4184 5-10-12 .... DominicElsworth 87
(Emma Lavelle) *bhd: rdn appr 2 out: nvr trbld ldrs* **16/1**

32/ 7 27 **Sonoftheking (IRE)**[43] 5021 5-10-12 .... RichardJohnson 77
(Philip Hobbs) *prom: blnd 2nd: jnd ldr and mstke 3 out: wknd next* **9/2**[2]

8 23 **Rosewood Lad**[75] 6-10-12 .... DarylJacob 42
(J S Moore) *mid-div: mstke 5th: wknd 3 out: bhd whn j.lft next* **50/1**

225/ 9 1 1/2 **Kalmbeforethestorm**[19] 5470 5-10-12 .... SamThomas 40
(Helen Nelmes) *towards rr: nt fluent 7th: mod effrt 3 out: sn wknd: bhd whn j.lft next* **14/1**

0/P- P **Monte Kaolino (IRE)**[3] 189 5-10-12 ....(bt[1]) TomCannon
(Nick Gifford) *led: hdd and losing pl in 4th whn mstke 3 out: sn bhd: p.u bef next* **50/1**

5m 7.7s (-9.80) **Going Correction** -0.425s/f (Good) 10 Ran SP% **129.6**
Speed ratings (Par 105): **101,100,100,93,91 91,81,72,71,**
toteswingers 1&2 £41.90, 2&3 £28.80, 1&3 £2.00 CSF £313.29 TOTE £7.90: £1.60, £20.10, £1.02; EX 743.40 Trifecta £1647.50 Part won. Pool: £2196.72 - 00.47 winning units..
Owner Mrs Sue Welch & Ms Caroline Rowland **Bred** Mrs S C Welch **Trained** Barbury Castle, Wilts

FOCUS

Dual bend configuration and all distances as advertised. Dual bend configuration and all distances as advertised. An additional jump fixture. After 1mm of rain overnight the ground was described as "beautiful" by Wayne Hutchinson after he took this novice hurdle. The gallop was just steady until the third-last flight.

234 LADIES DAY WITH TOBY ANSTIS 07.09.13 BEGINNERS' CHASE (12 fncs) 2m

2:50 (2:51) (Class 4) 5-Y-0+ **£3,705** (£1,118; £576; £305)

Form RPR

00/- 1 **Le Bacardy (FR)**[36] 5178 7-11-0 ....(p) LeeEdwards 126+
(Tony Carroll) *chsd clr ldrs: led appr 3 out: lft wl clr next* **5/2**[2]

6/3- 2 30 **Synthe Davis (FR)**[12] 45 8-10-7 107 .... RichardJohnson 93
(Laura Mongan) *led: hit 4th: hdd & wknd appr 3 out: lft 20 l 2nd at next* **8/1**

F02/ 3 30 **Able Deputy**[13] 30 6-11-0 120 ....(t) NickScholfield 84
(Kim Bailey) *plld hrd in 5th: effrt and blnd 4 out: sn wknd: lft poor 3rd 2 out* **7/2**[3]

6PF/ 4 26 **Carbis Bay**[35] 5196 7-11-0 75 ....(p) MarkGrant 49
(Zoe Davison) *nt a fluent: a bhd: no ch fr 6th* **66/1**

455/ U **Lemon Drop Red (USA)**[14] 10 5-11-0 ....(b[1]) WayneHutchinson 120
(Paul Webber) *hld up in rr: gd hdwy 4 out: chal next: cl 2nd whn blnd and uns rdr 2 out* **12/1**

116/ U **Mulligan's Man (IRE)**[197] 2047 6-11-0 .... JasonMaguire
(Donald McCain) *chsd clr ldrs: mstke 6th: in tch whn blnd and uns rdr 4 out* **2/1**[1]

0/4- F **Sporting Boy (IRE)**[8] 118 5-11-0 123 .... TomCannon
(Michael Blake) *pressed ldr tl fell 4 out* **8/1**

3m 54.3s (-6.00) **Going Correction** -0.275s/f (Good) 7 Ran SP% **115.5**
Speed ratings: **104,89,74,61, ,**
toteswingers 1&2 £4.00, 2&3 £3.50, 1&3 £2.00 CSF £22.48 TOTE £3.50: £1.60, £5.00; EX 25.20 Trifecta £84.20 Pool: £1312.72 - 11.68 winning units..
Owner Carl Hodgson **Bred** Jean-Charles Coude **Trained** Cropthorne, Worcs

FOCUS

A decent performance from the winner.

235 DOWNLOAD THE CORAL APP NOVICES' HURDLE (8 hdls) 2m

3:20 (3:24) (Class 4) 4-Y-0+ **£3,285** (£957; £479)

Form RPR

41U/ 1 **Fair Trade**[14] 15 6-11-5 123 .... WayneHutchinson 128
(Alan King) *hld up in tch: pressed ldr appr 2 out: drvn to ld fnl strides* **9/4**[2]

224/ 2 hd **Seventh Sky (GER)**[15] 5574 6-11-5 128 ....(tp) MarkGrant 128
(Charlie Mann) *t.k.h: chsd ldr: led and chal by wnr appr 2 out: hrd rdn and kpt on wl run-in: hdd fnl strides* **3/1**[3]

40F/ 3 18 **Deia Sunrise (IRE)**[14] 8 4-10-8 0 .... NickScholfield 101
(Paul Webber) *led tl wknd appr 2 out* **7/1**

5/ 4 4 1/2 **Black Spirit (USA)**[78] 4388 6-10-12 0 .... BarryGeraghty 103
(Nicky Henderson) *chsd ldrs: mstke 5th: wknd appr 2 out* **6/4**[1]

00/ 5 19 **Just When**[28] 5317 4-10-8 0 .... TomCannon 79
(Patrick Chamings) *chsd ldrs tl 4th: n.d fr next* **66/1**

55/ 6 2 **Next Oasis (IRE)**[28] 5317 7-10-12 0 .... PaddyBrennan 82
(Paul Henderson) *a bhd* **40/1**

24/ 7 nse **Cape Breton**[783] 4923 7-10-7 0 .... NicodeBoinville(5) 82
(Patrick Chamings) *j. slowly 3rd and 4th: a bhd* **33/1**

8 13 **Jumeirah Liberty**[277] 5-10-12 0 ....(p[1]) DarylJacob 70
(Zoe Davison) *t.k.h in 6th: struggling to stay in tch whn mstke 5th* **100/1**

3m 48.1s (-10.00) **Going Correction** -0.425s/f (Good)
WFA 4 from 5yo+ 18lb 8 Ran SP% **116.1**
Speed ratings (Par 105): **108,107,98,96,87 86,86,79**
toteswingers 1&2 £2.20, 2&3 £4.20, 1&3 £3.30 CSF £9.74 TOTE £4.30: £1.20, £1.30, £2.40; EX 11.60 Trifecta £37.70 Pool: £2355.14 - 46.75winning units..
Owner Raymond Tooth **Bred** Highclere Stud **Trained** Barbury Castle, Wilts

FOCUS

A good-class novice hurdle for the time of year and the two previous winners in the line-up had the finish to themselves.

236 BEST ODDS GUARANTEED AT CORAL.CO.UK H'CAP CHASE (12 fncs) 2m

3:50 (3:53) (Class 3) (0-130,129) 5-Y-0 **£6,330** (£1,870; £935; £468; £234)

Form RPR

204/ 1 **Tindaro (FR)**[174] 2524 6-11-6 123 .... RichieMcLernon 133+
(Paul Webber) *patiently rdn towards rr: hdwy on bit 3 out: led last: pushed clr: comf* **9/2**[2]

555/ 2 3 **Unforgettable (IRE)**[15] 5571 10-11-0 117 ....(bt) CharliePoste 122
(Robin Dickin) *sn prom: led 7th tl last: unable qck* **12/1**

U34/ 3 2 3/4 **Keki Buku (FR)**[43] 5022 10-11-5 122 ....(t) RichardJohnson 125
(Philip Hobbs) *bhd: hdwy 7th: chsd ldrs and drvn along 3 out: hung rt appr last: styd on same pce* **3/1**[1]

363/ 4 4 1/2 **Mibleu (FR)**[21] 5439 13-10-9 112 .... BrendanPowell 110
(Colin Tizzard) *cl up: jnd ldrs 6th: wknd 2 out* **14/1**

45P/ 5 3 1/4 **Gracchus (USA)**[29] 5284 7-11-5 122 .... WayneHutchinson 117
(Tony Carroll) *hld up towards rr: effrt appr 3 out: nvr able to chal* **20/1**

0/ 6 shd **The Sneezer (IRE)**[64] 4672 10-11-12 129 .... NickScholfield 123
(Alexandra Dunn) *chsd ldrs: led 3rd tl 7th: rdn and btn appr 3 out* **25/1**

053/ 7 2 3/4 **Lucy's Legend (IRE)**[24] 5359 7-10-4 107 ....(tp) PaddyBrennan 100
(Paul Henderson) *led tl 3rd: wknd 4 out* **11/2**

3P0/ 8 3/4 **Court In Session (IRE)**[24] 5363 8-11-7 124 .... IanPopham 115
(Martin Keighley) *reluctant to jump off and s.s: bhd: rdn after 4 out: n.d* **10/1**

14P/ 9 2 **Nozic (FR)**[17] 5527 12-11-9 126 .... DarylJacob 116
(Zoe Davison) *chsd ldrs tl wknd after 4 out* **14/1**

330/ 10 nk **Takeroc (FR)**[26] 5341 10-11-10 127 ....(t) TomCannon 116
(Chris Gordon) *mid-div: outpcd 1/2-way: hrd rdn 7th: sn bhd* **10/1**

35P/ 11 16 **Amaury De Lusignan (IRE)**[31] 5244 7-11-11 128 .... SamThomas 103
(Gary Moore) *in tch tl wknd 7th* **25/1**

U11/ U **Anay Turge (FR)**[16] 5545 8-11-7 127 ....(t) MarkQuinlan(3)
(Nigel Hawke) *mid-div whn blnd and uns rdr 1st* **5/1**[3]

3m 56.3s (-4.00) **Going Correction** -0.275s/f (Good) 12 Ran SP% **126.9**
Speed ratings: **99,97,96,93,92 92,90,90,89,89 81,**
toteswingers 1&2 £17.40, 2&3 £12.50, 1&3 £4.60 CSF £59.18 CT £192.35 TOTE £3.00: £1.50, £6.60, £2.10; EX 109.50 Trifecta £574.60 Pool: £1684.60 - 2.19 winning units..
Owner The Tindaro Partnership **Bred** J P Dubois **Trained** Mollington, Oxon

FOCUS

The rain arrived ahead of this competitive 2m handicap chase.

237 KEMPTON.CO.UK H'CAP HURDLE (10 hdls) 2m 5f

4:20 (4:21) (Class 4) (0-115,119) 4-Y-0+ **£3,249** (£954; £477; £238)

Form RPR

4P3/ 1 **Grey Missile**[19] 5470 8-11-2 105 ....(p) NickScholfield 113+
(Jeremy Scott) *hld up in rr: smooth hdwy 7th: led on bit appr 2 out: drvn clr last: styd on wl* **8/1**

402/ 2 3 3/4 **Dalavar (IRE)**[28] 5321 5-11-5 108 .... WayneHutchinson 110
(Alan King) *t.k.h: disp ld tl after 3 out: kpt on same pce* **4/1**[2]

024/ 3 shd **Minella For Party (IRE)**[62] 4714 6-11-6 109 .... RichardJohnson 113+
(Tim Vaughan) *hld up in rr: nt fluent 3rd and 4th: promising hdwy 3 out: one pce fr next* **5/1**[3]

6/1- 4 1 1/4 **Tuscan Gold**[12] 48 6-11-6 119 .... NathanAdams(10) 120
(Laura Mongan) *chsd ldrs: rdn and styd on same pce fr 2 out* **5/1**[3]

/30- 5 6 **Am I Blue**[6] 144 7-10-5 101 .... MrMatthewStanley(7) 97
(Mrs D Thomas) *prom tl outpcd 3 out* **25/1**

046/ 6 7 **Invicta Lake (IRE)**[31] 5245 6-11-4 107 .... PaddyBrennan 102+
(Suzy Smith) *in tch: nt fluent 4th: mstke and lost pl 6th: hit next: towards rr and btn whn hmpd 3 out* **6/1**

P6P/ 7 3 3/4 **Troubletimestwo (FR)**[16] 5538 7-10-5 94 .... LeeEdwards 80
(Tony Carroll) *mid-div: outpcd towards rr 3 out: n.d after* **25/1**

250/ 8 3 1/2 **Catch The Fire**[155] 2908 5-10-11 100 .... BarryGeraghty 87
(Peter Bowen) *hld up towards rr: hdwy 3 out: wknd next* **7/2**[1]

0P0/ 9 3 3/4 **Faha (IRE)**[26] 5330 7-10-13 102 ....(t) BrendanPowell 81
(Andy Turnell) *in tch: pressed ldrs 5th: led after 3 out: sn hdd & wknd* **20/1**

005/ F **Tony Dinozzo (FR)**[364] 247 6-11-2 105 .... RichieMcLernon
(Peter Bowen) *disp ld tl fell 3 out* **12/1**

5m 10.4s (-7.10) **Going Correction** -0.425s/f (Good) 10 Ran SP% **121.1**
Speed ratings (Par 105): **96,94,94,94,91 89,87,86,84,**
toteswingers 1&2 £7.60, 2&3 £4.10, 1&3 £7.70 CSF £41.31 CT £179.45 TOTE £9.70: £1.90, £2.00, £2.00; EX 36.10 Trifecta £260.70 Pool: £2429.76 - 6.98 winning units..
Owner Ian Murray **Bred** Shade Oak Stud **Trained** Brompton Regis, Somerset

FOCUS

An open-looking handicap hurdle. The winner was travelling much the best turning for home. In the end it concerned just the first four home after Tony Dinozzo departed.

238 ARTHUR WALDING H'CAP CHASE (18 fncs) 3m

4:50 (4:51) (Class 3) (0-130,130) 5-Y-0 **£6,330** (£1,870; £935; £468; £234)

Form RPR

51P/ 1 **Merrion Square (IRE)**[45] 4987 7-11-7 125 ....(t) DarylJacob 137
(Paul Nicholls) *trckd ldrs: mstke 14th: chal 3 out: led last: drvn out* **9/2**[3]

1U3/ 2 1 1/4 **Representingceltic (IRE)**[21] 5433 8-10-1 105 .... ColinBolger 116
(Pat Phelan) *t.k.h: chsd ldrs: chalng whn lft in ld 2 out: hdd last: kpt on* **2/1**[1]

21P/ 3 7 **Storm Survivor (IRE)**[36] 5176 7-11-8 126 ....(v) RichieMcLernon 133+
(Jonjo O'Neill) *towards rr: mstke 10th: hrd rdn and styng on whn blnd and lft 3rd 2 out: no imp on first 2* **8/1**

U21/ 4 18 **Flaming Gorge (IRE)**[15] 5569 8-11-12 130 .... BarryGeraghty 121
(Fleur Hawes) *led tl 10th: disp ld after tl wknd qckly 3 out* **8/1**

465/ **5** *nse* **Chasers Chance (IRE)**[86] 4229 10-10-0 104 oh1.......... PaddyBrennan 92
(Paul Henderson) *bhd: gd hdwy 4 out: sn wknd* **16/1**
5/0- **6** *3 1/4* **Sadler's Star (GER)**[12] 44 10-10-5 109.........................(p) TomCannon 95
(Michael Blake) *chsd ldr: disp ld fr 10th tl wknd qckly 3 out* **25/1**
5PP/ **7** *6* **Pentiffic (NZ)**[22] 5404 10-11-7 125.................................(p) AidanColeman 104
(Venetia Williams) *chsd ldrs tl wknd 4 out: sn bhd* **12/1**
464/ **F** **Pantxoa (FR)**[35] 5196 6-11-1 119.......................... WayneHutchinson 131
(Alan King) *hld up in midfield: hdwy on inner to ld 3 out: jst ahd whn fell next* **3/1**[2]

6m 3.7s (-11.70) **Going Correction** -0.275s/f (Good) **8** Ran SP% **116.2**
Speed ratings: **108,107,105,99,99 98,96,**
toteswingers 1&2 £3.70, 2&3 £4.50, 1&3 £5.40 CSF £14.86 CT £69.69 TOTE £5.80: £1.60, £1.30, £2.80; EX 17.80 Trifecta £157.70 Pool: £2161.35 - 10.27 winning units..
Owner The Stewart Family **Bred** Miss Denise Neill **Trained** Ditcheat, Somerset

FOCUS
Plenty had something to prove on recent efforts in this strongly run 3m handicap chase.

239 KEMPTON FOR WEDDINGS STANDARD OPEN NATIONAL HUNT FLAT RACE 2m
5:20 (5:32) (Class 6) 4-6-Y-O **£1,559** (£457; £228; £114)

Form RPR
2/ **1** **Gone Too Far**[164] 2716 5-11-3 0.................................. WayneHutchinson 115+
(Alan King) *in tch: wnt 2nd 4f out: led over 2f out: rdn out* **4/6**[1]
13/ **2** *2 3/4* **Hannibal The Great (IRE)**[175] 2498 5-11-7 0.............(t) KielanWoods(3) 119
(Charlie Longsdon) *prom: chsd wnr over 1f out: unable qck* **8/1**
3 *2 1/4* **Swallowshide** 4-10-13 0.. DominicElsworth 106+
(Emma Lavelle) *mid-div: outpcd and lost pl 5f out: rdn and styd on wl fnl 2f* **16/1**
4 *1 1/4* **In Fairness (IRE)** 4-10-13 0... BarryGeraghty 105
(Nicky Henderson) *in tch: effrt 4f out: disp 2nd 2f out: hld in 3rd whn edgd rt ins fnl f* **3/1**[2]
5/ **5** *11* **Vendredi Trois (FR)**[116] 3683 4-10-13 0.......................... AidanColeman 94
(Emma Lavelle) *led: 6 l clr early: set modest pce: hdd over 2f out: wknd wl over 1f out* **25/1**
1/ **6** *2* **Johnny Og**[122] 3593 4-11-6 0.. IanPopham 99
(Martin Keighley) *hld up towards rr: sme hdwy and in tch 4f out: rdn and btn 2f out* **9/2**[3]
7 *22* **Jacqueline Hyde** 4-10-6 0... ColinBolger 63
(Nigel Dunger) *a bhd* **50/1**
/ **8** *3 1/2* **Goodgoshmsmolly** 4-10-6 0.. RichieMcLernon 62
(Helen Nelmes) *prom tl wknd over 2f out* **40/1**

3m 58.3s (5.80) **Going Correction** -0.425s/f (Good)
WFA 4 from 5yo 4lb **8** Ran SP% **128.4**
Speed ratings: **68,66,65,64,59 58,47,45**
toteswingers 1&2 £2.50, 2&3 £10.30, 1&3 £3.20 CSF £8.93 TOTE £1.70: £1.10, £2.30, £4.10; EX 6.70 Trifecta £36.90 Pool: £2767.76 - 56.14 winning units..
Owner John P McManus **Bred** Richard Evans Bloodstock **Trained** Barbury Castle, Wilts
■ Blue Bear was withdrawn. Price at time of withdrawal 40-1. Rule 4 does not apply.

FOCUS
A much-delayed bumper with two previous winners and four newcomers. The pace was pedestrian until the final half-mile.
T/Plt: £40.60 to a £1 stake. Pool of £63042.18 - 1132.61 winning tickets. T/Qpdt: £6.00 to a £1 stake. Pool of £4047.49 - 492.71 winning tickets. LM

PLUMPTON (L-H)
Sunday, May 12

OFFICIAL GOING: Good (good to soft in places on chase course; good to firm in places on hurdle course)
Wind: medium, across Weather: dry, bright spells, rain last two races

240 MIM HIGGS 80TH MAIDEN HURDLE (9 hdls) 2m
2:00 (2:00) (Class 5) 4-Y-O+ **£2,737** (£798; £399)

Form RPR
6/ **1** **Four Nations (USA)**[36] 5180 5-10-9 0........................(b) TrevorWhelan(5) 103+
(George Baker) *hld up in tch: rdn and clsd on ldrs after 3 out: chal next: led last: styd on strly and drew clr flat* **25/1**
042/ **2** *6* **Somchine**[28] 5317 5-11-0 0.................................... AndrewThornton 99
(Seamus Mullins) *hld up wl in rr: hdwy into midfield after 5th: mstke 3 out: rdn and clsd on ldrs bef next: ev ch and pushed rt bef 2 out: mstke 2 out: stl ev ch last: outpcd flat* **2/1**[1]
0BP/ **3** *1 3/4* **Rachael's Ruby**[32] 4968 6-10-7 0...(v) ColinBolger 89
(Roger Teal) *t.k.h: chsd ldr tl led 2nd: wandered and wnt rt bef 2 out: blnd 2 out: hdd last: outpcd flat* **100/1**
4 *2 1/2* **Western Prize**[211] 5-11-0 0.. RichardKilloran 95
(Tim Vaughan) *t.k.h: chsd ldrs: mstke 5th: rdn and effrt bef 2 out: sltly hmpd and mstke 2 out: 4th and no ex last: wknd flat* **2/1**[1]
045/ **5** *hd* **Amen (IRE)**[21] 5462 5-11-0 104... JamieMoore 93
(Gary Moore) *led tl 2nd: chsd ldr tl drvn and unable qck bef 2 out: wknd jst bef last* **8/1**[3]
62/ **6** *10* **Imperial Stargazer**[21] 5442 4-10-10 0............................... MarcGoldstein 82
(Sheena West) *chsd ldrs: drvn and btn bef 2 out: wknd between last 2* **7/2**[2]
00/ **7** *2* **Cariflora**[23] 5374 6-10-7 0..(t) MattieBatchelor 75
(Nick Gifford) *t.k.h: hld up in last trio: mstke 1st: nt fluent 2nd: rdn and struggling after 6th: n.d after* **50/1**
P **Star Hill**[249] 6-10-7 0.. GerardTumelty
(Alan King) *in tch in midfield: hit 5th: sn lost pl and struggling: t.o next tl p.u 3 out: burst blood vessel* **16/1**
P **Bravo Belle (IRE)**[144] 6-10-2 0...................................... JamesBanks(5)
(Paddy Butler) *t.k.h: hld up in last trio: lost tch after 5th: t.o whn p.u 3 out: burst blood vessel* **200/1**

3m 45.1s (-15.70) **Going Correction** -0.975s/f (Hard)
WFA 4 from 5yo+ 18lb **9** Ran SP% **113.2**
Speed ratings (Par 103): **100,97,96,94,94 89,88, ,**
toteswingers 1&2 £6.70, 2&3 £4.60, 1&3 £27.30 CSF £75.74 TOTE £19.00: £3.80, £1.30, £5.90; EX 50.10 Trifecta £562.70 Pool: £991.99 - 1.32 winning units..
Owner The Transatlantic USA Syndicate **Bred** Kirsten Rausing **Trained** Manton, Wilts

FOCUS
Top bend common to both courses, bottom bends split. A moderate maiden.

241 PLUMPTON ATHLETIC JUNIORS H'CAP HURDLE (12 hdls 2 omitted) 3m 1f 110y
2:30 (2:30) (Class 5) (0-95,95) 4-Y-O+ **£2,737** (£798; £399)

Form RPR
00/- **1** **Marico (FR)**[22] 5412 5-10-7 76...(p) FelixDeGiles 83+
(Tom Symonds) *t.k.h: hld up in tch towards rr: hdwy after 9th: pressed ldrs after 3 out: led next: rdn clr and in command whn dived and mstke last: sn rcvrd and styd on: rdn out* **16/1**
600/ **2** *2 3/4* **Mumbles Pier (IRE)**[21] 5440 8-10-12 81........................(vt) JamieMoore 85
(Peter Bowen) *travelled strly: chsd ldr bypassing 11th: led after 3 out: hdd and blnd 2 out: sn drvn and styd on same pce after* **5/2**[1]
042/ **3** *2* **Sharp Suit (IRE)**[18] 5505 6-11-4 90.......................... WayneKavanagh(3) 91
(Seamus Mullins) *in tch in midfield: cl 4th and drvn after 3 out: styd on same pce fr next* **7/2**[2]
PP3/ **4** *2 1/4* **Conn Man (IRE)**[23] 5381 8-10-6 75.......................... JimmyMcCarthy 74
(Geoffrey Deacon) *chsd ldrs: rdn to chse ldr after 3 out tl bef next: unable qck 2 out: kpt on same pce after* **7/1**[3]
004/ **5** *9* **Go Amwell**[20] 4743 10-11-2 85...(v) HarryHaynes 76
(J R Jenkins) *hld up in tch in rr: rdn and outpcd after 3 out: plugged on but wl hld after* **14/1**
604/ **6** *12* **Bright Light**[23] 5378 6-10-0 69 oh2.. SeanQuinlan 49
(Richard Phillips) *hmpd 1st: in tch in rr: hdwy into midfield after 7th: chsd ldrs bypassing 11th: rdn and wknd bef 2 out* **8/1**
6P6/ **7** *3* **Budsson**[16] 5555 7-9-11 69 oh13..................................... AdamWedge(3) 46
(Anna Newton-Smith) *pressed ldr tl led 10th: hdd and drvn sn after 3 out: wknd bef next* **33/1**
224/ **8** *8* **Absolute Shambles**[16] 5554 9-11-9 92........................(p) MarcGoldstein 62
(Chris Gordon) *led tl 10th: sn drvn: lost pl and towards rr whn nt fluent 3 out: sn wknd* **12/1**
PP/ **F** **Rocky Ryan (IRE)**[200] 1994 10-11-10 93............................(b) JoeTizzard
(Jim Best) *midfield whn fell 1st* **12/1**
0/3- **U** **Portmeade**[10] 79 11-10-7 83.. JonPark(7)
(Elizabeth Scott) *towards rr whn bdly hmpd and uns rdr 1st* **20/1**
P/U- **P** **Ten More (IRE)**[9] 100 9-10-6 82... ChrisDavies(7)
(Bill Turner) *t.k.h: nt fluent: chsd ldrs tl 4th: steadily lost pl: last and lost tch u.p after 7th: t.o whn p.u after 9th* **25/1**
0/5- **P** **Une Des Bieffes (FR)**[11] 70 5-11-1 84...................(v) TomScudamore
(Michael Scudamore) *in tch in midfield: j. slowly and rdn after 7th: lost tch and 10th and t.o whn p.u bef 3 out* **14/1**

6m 9.5s (-15.50) **Going Correction** -0.975s/f (Hard) **12** Ran SP% **120.6**
Speed ratings (Par 103): **84,83,82,81,79 75,74,72, , ,**
toteswingers 1&2 £8.50, 2&3 £1.10, 1&3 £0.00 CSF £57.10 CT £181.79 TOTE £18.20: £5.10, £1.50, £1.50; EX 55.60 Trifecta £377.50 Part won. Pool: £503.39 - 0.32 winning units..
Owner Thomas Symonds Racing Syndicate **Bred** E A R L Haras Du Bosquet **Trained** Harewood End, H'fords

FOCUS
A weak staying handicap.

242 EXPRESSGRASS.COM H'CAP CHASE (THE SUNDAY £5K BONUS RACE) (18 fncs) 3m 2f
3:00 (3:05) (Class 4) (0-110,110) 5-Y-O+ **£6,173** (£1,812; £906; £453)

Form RPR
115/ **1** **Franklin Roosevelt (IRE)**[30] 5276 7-11-8 106...........(b) TomScudamore 114+
(David Pipe) *in tch: chsd ldrs 7th: chsd clr ldr 14th: j. awkwardly next: hit 3 out: 4 l down 2 out: styd on u.p flat to ld towards fin* **9/2**[2]
4P2/ **2** *nk* **Leg Iron (IRE)**[23] 5377 8-11-12 110.................................. MarcGoldstein 118+
(Sheena West) *j.rt at times and mstkes: pressed ldr tl led 7th: hdd 11th: 3rd and rdn bef 15th: rallied between last 2: mstke last: styd on u.p flat to go 2nd cl home* **11/4**[1]
633/ **3** *1/2* **Sea Cadet**[16] 5554 11-10-5 89...(b) HarrySkelton 94
(Laura Mongan) *j.w and travelled strly: pressed ldrs tl led 11th: wnt clr after 14th: 4 l clr and pushed along 2 out: drvn and fnd little flat: hdd and lost 2 pls towards fin* **12/1**
5/3- **4** *18* **Lajidaal (USA)**[9] 100 6-10-5 89..(v[1]) JamieMoore 80
(Gary Moore) *in tch: rdn bef 13th: 4th and keeping on same pce whn mstke 2 out: wknd bef last* **5/1**[3]
1/P- **5** *6* **Ballyvoneen (IRE)**[10] 74 8-11-3 101.............................(p) AlexMerriam 85
(Neil King) *led tl mstke and hdd 7th: rdn and struggling bef 14th: wknd bef 3 out: wl hld whn j.lft 2 out* **6/1**
352/ **6** *4* **Old Dreams (IRE)**[19] 5480 7-10-10 99........................(t) GavinSheehan(5) 79
(Nick Gifford) *in tch towards rr: mstke 2nd: sme hdwy and rdn after 12th: mstke 15th: no prog and wl btn 3 out: wknd 2 out* **9/2**[2]
0/0- **7** *14* **Pipe Banner**[8] 118 9-11-2 105.......................................(p) JamesBanks(5) 72
(Anthony Middleton) *in tch towards rr: mstke 10th: effrt 13th but sn struggling: mstke 14th and lost tch bef next: t.o* **50/1**
OPP/ **0** *2 3/4* **Doctor Ric (IRE)**[19] 6401 0-10-9 93.................................. MattieBatchelor 50
(Gerry Enright) *mstkes: hld up in rr: short-lived effrt after 12th: lost tch after next: t.o* **22/1**
F05/ **P** **Flugzeug**[16] 5552 5-10-6 90.. AndrewThornton
(Seamus Mullins) *in tch: losing pl and blnd 9th: rdn and rallied after 12th: struggling next: lost tch 14th and wl bhd whn p.u 3 out* **14/1**

6m 35.9s (-14.80) **Going Correction** -0.80s/f (Firm) **9** Ran SP% **114.7**
Speed ratings: **90,89,89,84,82 81,76,75,**
toteswingers 1&2 £5.60, 2&3 £5.60, 1&3 £4.90 CSF £17.86 CT £137.29 TOTE £3.60: £1.70, £1.60, £3.40; EX 9.40 Trifecta £23.50 Pool: £1318.15 - 41.89 winning units..
Owner Malcolm C Denmark **Bred** Kenneth Parkhill **Trained** Nicholashayne, Devon

FOCUS
A moderate staying handicap where the principals came well clear.

243 AWARD WINNING EXTECH IT H'CAP HURDLE (9 hdls) 2m
3:30 (3:32) (Class 5) (0-95,95) 4-Y-O+ **£2,737** (£798; £399)

Form RPR
603/ **1** **Hawk Gold (IRE)**[16] 5557 9-9-7 69.........................(b) ConorShoemark(7) 73
(Michelle Bryant) *hld up in rr of main gp: hdwy into midfield after 5th: effrt to chse ldng pair bef 2 out: clsd and wnt 2nd 2 out: gd jump to ld narrowly last: drvn and kpt on fnl 100yds* **15/2**[2]
5/2- **2** *nk* **Ullswater (IRE)**[12] 49 5-11-9 92.................................... GerardTumelty 96
(Andy Turnell) *chsd ldrs and travelled wl: jnd ldr and wnt clr after 3 out: led bef 2 out: mstke and hdd last: ev ch flat: drvn and r.o flat: jst hld* **5/2**[1]
5P/ **3** *8* **Al Amaan**[20] 2536 8-11-2 92 ow2.............................. MrDanielBurchell(7) 89
(Gary Moore) *hld up wl off the pce in rr: clsd and in tch in midfield after 5th: outpcd on downhill run bef 3 out: pushed along and hdwy on outer bef 2 out: kpt on to go 3rd flat: no threat to ldrs* **33/1**

UPP/ **4** *2 ¾* **Drawn Free (IRE)**[38] 5142 5-11-3 **86** .... JoeTizzard 81
(Colin Tizzard) *chsd ldrs tl led 4th: rdn and wnt clr w rival after 3 out: hdd bef next: 3rd and btn between last 2: wknd flat* **14/1**

6/U- **5** *1 ¼* **Airedale Lad (IRE)**[9] 97 12-9-9 **69** oh10 .... (p) JamesBanks(5) 62
(Zoe Davison) *in tch in midfield: rdn and effrt to chse ldrs 3 out: sn outpcd u.p: plugged on but wl hld fr 2 out* **50/1**

0F0/ **6** *1* **Just Beware**[15] 5567 11-10-10 **86** .... (p) MrKevinJones(7) 78
(Zoe Davison) *hld up in tch in midfield: clsd on ldrs after 5th: drvn and outpcd after 3 out: plugged on but no threat to ldrs after* **16/1**

0/3- **7** *4 ½* **Capellini**[3] 188 6-10-7 **81** .... (p) GavinSheehan(5) 69
(Charles Egerton) *led tl after 1st: led again 3rd tl mstke and hdd 4th: chsd ldr tl sn after 3 out: wknd and btn whn mstke next* **5/2**[1]

042/ **8** *27* **Ardmaddy (IRE)**[16] 5557 9-11-12 **95** .... MarcGoldstein 59
(Sheena West) *chsd ldrs: mstke 6th: rdn bef next: wknd wl bef 2 out: t.o and eased flat* **8/1**[3]

565/ **9** *25* **My Boy Ginger**[23] 5378 4-10-12 **85** .... (p) LeightonAspell 22
(Chris Gordon) *in tch towards rr of main gp: rdn and struggling after 5th: lost tch bef 3 out: t.o and eased flat* **10/1**

000/ **P** **Brave Decision**[14] 8 6-10-11 **80** .... (b[1]) ConorO'Farrell
(Suzy Smith) *t.k.h: j.lft and many mstkes: led after 1st: blnd next: blnd bdly and hdd 3rd: lost pl: last and lost tch 6th: t.o whn p.u 2 out* **14/1**

060/ **P** **No Compromise**[57] 4787 4-10-12 **85** .... SeanQuinlan
(Richard Phillips) *in tch in rr of main gp: reminders after 5th: sn lost tch and bhd whn p.u next* **25/1**

3m 44.4s (-16.40) **Going Correction** -0.975s/f (Hard)
WFA 4 from 5yo+ 18lb **11** Ran SP% **117.1**
Speed ratings (Par 103): **102,101,97,96,95 95,93,79,67,**
toteswingers 1&2 £3.00, 2&3 £21.40, 1&3 £21.40 CSF £26.73 CT £595.07 TOTE £9.30: £2.20, £2.10, £14.20; EX 40.60 Trifecta £416.60 Part won. Pool: £555.51- 0.10 winning units..
Owner Miss M Bryant **Bred** Ian Shenkin **Trained** South Common, E Sussex
■ Stewards' Enquiry : Mr Daniel Burchell ten-day ban: failed to take all reasonable and permissable measures to obtain best possible placing (May 26-30,Jun 4,7,15,Jul 24,30)

FOCUS
An ordinary handicap.

244 TAHLIA AND FRANKIE'S RACING EXCELLENCE CONDITIONAL JOCKEYS' TRAINING SERIES FINAL H'CAP HURDLE (12 hdls) 2m 5f

4:00 (4:00) (Class 3) (0-130,125) 4-Y-0+ **£9,747** (£2,862; £1,431; £715)

Form RPR

236/ **1** **Drum Valley**[25] 5352 5-11-7 **125** .... JackSherwood(5) 130
(Oliver Sherwood) *chsd ldrs tl wnt 2nd after 8th: ev ch and mstke 3 out: sn led and rdn: hrd pressed fr 2 out: battled on gamely flat* **7/2**[1]

154/ **2** *hd* **Va'Vite (IRE)**[26] 5339 6-10-6 **113** .... MarkMarris(8) 117
(Anthony Middleton) *in tch in midfield: chsd ldrs 9th: rdn and ev ch 2 out: kpt on wl flat: jst hld* **14/1**

041/ **3** *1* **Sir Fredlot (IRE)**[21] 5435 4-10-10 **117** .... EDLinehan(3) 115
(Brendan Powell) *hld up in tch towards rr: hdwy bef 3 out: clsd on ldrs between last 2: rdn to chal flat: no ex and wknd towards fin* **8/1**[3]

3/3- **4** *3 ½* **Be All Man (IRE)**[12] 48 6-10-9 **113** .... JosephAkehurst(5) 115
(Gary Moore) *chsd ldrs: effrt on inner to press ldrs 3 out: cl 4th and styng on same pce whn mstke last: no ex flat* **9/2**[2]

412/ **5** *2 ¾* **Ironically (IRE)**[15] 5567 4-10-2 **109** .... TrevorWhelan(3) 101
(Neil King) *chsd ldrs: rdn and unable qck bef 2 out: no ex between last 2: wknd flat: fatally injured* **10/1**

040/ **6** *5* **Drussell (IRE)**[31] 5260 7-10-10 **114** .... DanielHiskett(5) 107
(Martin Bosley) *in tch in midfield: rdn and outpcd after 3 out: plugged on same pce and wl hld 2 out* **33/1**

F02/ **7** *7* **Gores Island (IRE)**[16] 5553 7-11-5 **118** .... GavinSheehan 105
(Noel Chance) *in tch in rr: rdn bef 3 out: wknd bef 2 out* **14/1**

011/ **8** *21* **E Street Boy**[16] 5553 7-10-13 **120** .... KieronEdgar(8) 88
(David Pipe) *led tl rdn and hdd after 3 out: dropped out qckly bef next: eased flat: t.o* **9/2**[2]

011/ **9** *8* **Signed Request (IRE)**[22] 5412 6-10-3 **102** .... KillianMoore 63
(Henry Oliver) *in tch in rr: rdn and outpcd bef 3 out: wknd wl bef 2 out: t.o* **9/2**[2]

4/0- **P** **Teenage Kicks (IRE)**[12] 38 8-10-11 **115** .... (t) JamesCowley(5)
(Polly Gundry) *chsd ldr tl after 8th: lost pl bef 3 out: bhd whn p.u 2 out* **25/1**

5m 0.5s (-16.50) **Going Correction** -0.975s/f (Hard)
WFA 4 from 5yo+ 19lb **10** Ran SP% **117.1**
Speed ratings (Par 107): **92,91,91,90,89 87,84,76,73,**
toteswingers 1&2 £0.00, 2&3 £20.10, 1&3 £8.40 CSF £50.76 CT £370.24 TOTE £3.80: £1.40, £4.70, £1.70; EX 58.90 Trifecta £369.40 Part won. Pool: £492.60 - 0.43 winning units..
Owner D J Burke & T Meehan **Bred** Limestone And Tara Studs **Trained** Upper Lambourn, Berks
■ Stewards' Enquiry : Trevor Whelan seven-day ban: used whip contrary to race conditions (May 26,29,Jun 2,10,14,19,23)

FOCUS
A fair handicap, confined to amatuer riders.

245 JARED YOUNG MEMORIAL H'CAP CHASE (14 fncs) 2m 4f

4:30 (4:30) (Class 4) (0-110,109) 5-Y-0+ **£6,173** (£1,812; £906; £453)

Form RPR

3/1- **1** **Brody Bleu (FR)**[12] 40 6-11-9 **106** .... FelixDeGiles 122+
(Robert Walford) *pressed ldr tl led after 3rd: hdd bef 11th: led again and gng best 3 out: rdn and asserted 2 out: styd on wl: readily* **7/2**[2]

2/3- **2** *5* **Chestnut Ben (IRE)**[12] 43 8-10-11 **94** .... JamieMoore 104
(Gary Brown) *in tch: blnd and pckd 10th: lft 3rd next: drvn after 3 out: chsd wnr last: no imp* **11/1**

3/2- **3** *3 ¾* **Adrenalin Flight (IRE)**[12] 40 7-11-8 **105** .... AndrewThornton 113
(Seamus Mullins) *mstkes: in tch: reminders and hdwy after 8th: chsd ldr 10th: led bef next: hdd 3 out: no ex u.p 2 out: mstke and lost 2nd last: wknd flat* **11/4**[1]

233/ **4** *1* **Gandalfe (FR)**[26] 5338 8-11-8 **105** .... LeightonAspell 113
(David Arbuthnot) *nt fluent and mstkes: in tch in rr of main gp: swtchd rt and effrt bef 11th: lft 4th bef 3 out: clsd on ldrs after 3 out: no imp and hld whn mstke last* **13/2**

416/ **5** *17* **Upton Mead (IRE)**[14] 7 6-10-2 **92** .... ConorShoemark(7) 81
(Kevin Tork) *nvr gng wl in rr and sn pushed along: styd in tch tl 10th: sn outpcd and wl btn 3 out: plugged on* **8/1**

502/ **6** *66* **Health Is Wealth (IRE)**[18] 5510 8-11-7 **104** .... (p) JoeTizzard 34
(Colin Tizzard) *racd keenly: pressed ldr tl lost pl after 9th: wl btn 3 out: t.o bef next: eased flat* **4/1**[3]

154/ **P** **Citrus Mark**[199] 2010 8-11-7 **104** .... LiamHeard
(Paul Webber) *in tch: chsd ldng pair and gng wl whn lost action and eased jst bef 11th: had to jump 11th: p.u and dismntd immediately after* **20/1**

1P4/ **P** **Great's Autrechene (FR)**[28] 5315 6-11-12 **109** .... (bt) TomScudamore
(Charlie Longsdon) *led tl after 3rd: chsd ldrs tl lost pl after 9th: lost tch 11th: t.o bef 2 out tl p.u last* **11/1**

4m 56.1s (-11.20) **Going Correction** -0.80s/f (Firm) **8** Ran SP% **114.8**
Speed ratings: **90,88,86,86,79 52,,**
toteswingers 1&2 £14.40, 2&3 £1.70, 1&3 £2.70 CSF £39.39 CT £119.77 TOTE £5.70: £2.10, £3.40, £1.10; EX 44.40 Trifecta £138.80 Pool: £865.35 - 4.67 winning units..
Owner R J Brown **Bred** Pierre Julienne **Trained** Child Okeford, Dorset

FOCUS
A modest handicap.

246 NAGGING BLONDES STANDARD OPEN NATIONAL HUNT FLAT RACE 2m 2f

5:00 (5:02) (Class 6) 4-6-Y-0 **£1,711** (£498; £249)

Form RPR

1 **Bugsy's Girl (IRE)** 5-10-9 0 .... TomScudamore 100+
(Jim Best) *in tch: effrt to chse ldr over 2f out: led: rn green and veered rt over 1f out: rcvrd and r.o wl fnl f* **6/1**[3]

6/ **2** *4 ½* **Just Archie (USA)**[21] 5444 5-11-2 0 .... LeightonAspell 100
(Lady Herries) *chsd ldrs tl led 4f out: rdn and hdd over 1f out: styd on same pce after* **4/1**[2]

260/ **3** *nk* **On The Move**[103] 3921 5-10-6 0 .... RachaelGreen(3) 93
(Anthony Honeyball) *hld up in tch in rr: hdwy over 4f out: chsd ldng pair 2f out: kpt on same pce fnl f* **4/1**[2]

4 *8* **Justanother Muddle** 4-10-12 0 .... MarcGoldstein 89
(Sheena West) *green and rdn leaving s: sn upsides ldr: rdn and outpcd over 3f out: plugged on same pce fnl 2f* **3/1**[1]

0/ **5** *nk* **Steel Summit (IRE)**[41] 5070 4-10-12 0 .... JackDoyle 88
(Ali Brewer) *chsd ldrs: wnt 2nd and rdn over 3f out: outpcd and btn over 2f out: wknd over 1f out* **14/1**

6 *34* **Spiritofchartwell** 5-11-2 0 .... AndrewThornton 62
(Nick Gifford) *led into s: hld up in tch in rr: clsd 6f out: wknd qckly 4f out: t.o* **17/2**

50/ **7** *22* **Giant Hercules (IRE)**[14] 4 6-10-9 0 ....[1] ConorShoemark(7) 42
(Jim Boyle) *wl in tch in midfield: rdn and effrt 5f out: sn struggling: wknd 4f out: t.o* **8/1**

8 *158* **Imperial Cru** 5-11-2 0 .... AlexMerriam
(Diana Grissell) *sn rdn: reminders 12f out: dropped to last 10f out and sn wl t.o* **25/1**

446/ **P** **Business Mover (IRE)**[19] 5483 5-11-2 0 .... MattieBatchelor
(Mark Bradstock) *led: rdn 6f out: hdd 4f out and sn wknd: wl bhd whn lost action and p.u 2f out: fatally injured* **12/1**

4m 12.8s (-12.50) **Going Correction** -0.975s/f (Hard)
WFA 4 from 5yo+ 4lb **9** Ran SP% **119.1**
Speed ratings: **88,86,85,82,82 67,57,,**
toteswingers 1&2 £5.00, 2&3 £1.60, 1&3 £4.90 CSF £31.28 TOTE £7.00: £2.00, £1.90, £1.70; EX 36.00 Trifecta £144.80 Pool: £814.86 - 4.21 winning units..
Owner Mrs Sue Head **Bred** Mrs Patricia Doran **Trained** Lewes, E Sussex

FOCUS
A modest bumper.
T/Jkpt: Not won. T/Plt: £24.70 to a £1 stake. Pool of £81057.89 - 2390.96 winning ticket. T/Qpdt: £12.70 to a £1 stake. Pool of £4772.10 - 276.05 winning tickets. SP

[43]WORCESTER (L-H)

Sunday, May 12

OFFICIAL GOING: Good (good to firm in places; 7.2)
Wind: Light behind Weather: Light rain

247 LADBROKES NOVICES' CHASE (12 fncs) 2m 110y

2:10 (2:10) (Class 4) 5-Y-0+ **£4,093** (£1,202; £601; £300)

Form RPR

U2F/ **1** **Alwaystheoptimist**[13] 31 10-10-9 108 .... KielanWoods(3) 112+
(Phil Middleton) *chsd ldr to 2nd: led 4th: clr fr 6th: nt fluent 4 out: styd on wl* **7/2**[3]

30/ **2** *13* **Stormy Oscar (IRE)**[23] 5386 6-10-7 110 .... HarryDerham(5) 101
(Jamie Snowden) *led to 4th: chsd wnr: blnd 3 out: styd on same pce fr next* **9/4**[2]

040/ **3** *11* **Legend Erry (IRE)**[23] 5379 9-10-12 89 .... LiamTreadwell 91
(Venetia Williams) *hld up: j.rt 2nd: hdwy 7th: mstke 3 out: wknd next* **20/1**

344/ **4** *23* **Massena (IRE)**[19] 5470 6-10-12 104 .... AidanColeman 76
(Venetia Williams) *hld up: nt fluent: hdwy appr 4 out: wknd after next: t.o* **2/1**[1]

0/5- **5** *16* **Fashion Week**[12] 42 8-10-12 84 .... DPFahy 54
(Sue Gardner) *hld up: hit 2nd: bhd fr 5th: t.o whn blnd 3 out* **33/1**

334/ **6** *20* **Zipit (IRE)**[21] 5434 8-10-12 109 .... DougieCostello 36
(Tom Gretton) *hld up: bhd fr 7th: t.o whn hit 3 out* **11/2**

05P/ **U** **Generalise**[43] 5023 7-10-9 79 .... RobertDunne(3) 76
(Venetia Williams) *chsd ldrs: rdn appr 4 out: wkng whn blnd and uns rdr 2 out* **40/1**

4m 6.1s (-7.90) **Going Correction** -0.775s/f (Firm) **7** Ran SP% **111.9**
Speed ratings: **87,80,75,64,57 47,**
toteswingers 1&2 £3.50, 2&3 £12.90, 1&3 £4.50 CSF £11.66 TOTE £4.10: £1.80, £1.70; EX 15.80 Trifecta £79.80 Pool: £1070.52 - 10.04 winning units..
Owner P W Middleton **Bred** Crandon Park Stud **Trained** Dorton, Bucks

FOCUS
Both bends and run-in on inside line. Rain before racing hadn't affected the ground at this stage, Liam Treadwell describing conditions as "a mix of good and good to firm", while Harry Derham thought it "good, quick ground." The time for the opener was 16sec outside the standard. Only one of them had previous experience of fences in what was a weak novice chase. Not many became involved and they finished well strung out. This isn't form to treat too seriously, but the winner and third are rated in line with their hurdles marks..

248 LADBROKES H'CAP CHASE (18 fncs) 2m 7f

2:40 (2:40) (Class 5) (0-95,99) 5-Y-0+ **£2,924** (£858; £429; £214)

Form RPR

13P/ **1** **Royale Knight**[147] 3090 7-11-2 **92** .... ChristopherWard(7) 106+
(Dr Richard Newland) *hld up: nt fluent 2nd: hdwy 10th: led 4 out: styd on wl* **11/4**[1]

6/4- **2** *1* **Waltzing Tornado (IRE)**[12] 44 9-11-5 **88** .... (p) DPFahy 100
(Andy Hobbs) *hld up: hdwy 12th: rdn after 3 out: styd on u.p to go 2nd towards fin* **20/1**

5P2/ **3** *1 ¾* **Maid Of Silk (IRE)**[222] 1081 7-11-7 **90** .... (t) NoelFehily 100
(Neil Mulholland) *prom: mstke 5th: chsd wnr 2 out: sn rdn: styd on same pce flat* **16/1**

The Form Book Jumps, Raceform Ltd, Compton, RG20 6NL.

555/ **4** *14* **Victoria Rose (IRE)**[21] 5431 8-11-9 **92**........................(b[1]) LiamTreadwell 93+
(Richard Woollacott) *chsd ldrs: led and mstke 12th: hit next: hdd 4 out: blnd and wknd next* **16/1**

500/ **5** *7* **Rifleman (IRE)**[36] 5182 13-10-12 **84**..........................(tp) JakeGreenall(3) 75
(Richard Lee) *prom: drvn along appr 4 out: wknd last* **33/1**

0/1- **6** *nk* **Handsome Buddy (IRE)**[12] 44 6-11-9 **99**..............(v) CiaranMckee(7) 89
(Michael Gates) *hld up: hdwy 13th: rdn and wknd after next* **9/2[2]**

210/ **7** *3 1/4* **Oranger (FR)**[13] 34 11-11-3 **93**.......................................(b) MrJMartin(7) 80
(Andrew J Martin) *chsd ldrs: led 3rd: hdd after 9th: remained handy: drvn along 13th: wknd 4 out* **25/1**

22P/ **8** *13* **Derwen Pryde**[64] 4661 9-11-0 **83**.......................................(tp) TomO'Brien 59
(Peter Bowen) *s.i.s: mstke 1st: hdwy 10th: wknd after next: t.o* **10/1**

P06/ **9** *3 1/4* **Lapin Garou (FR)**[18] 5506 6-10-2 **74**..........................(t) RyanMahon(3) 49
(Colin Tizzard) *chsd ldrs: ev ch whn blnd 4 out: wknd next: t.o* **8/1**

350/ **10** *26* **Kilvergan Boy (IRE)**[42] 5038 9-10-5 **74**.................. SamTwiston-Davies 23
(Nigel Twiston-Davies) *prom: lost pl 4th: hdwy after 9th: wknd 13th: t.o whn hmpd 3 out* **11/2[3]**

605/ **11** *12* **Heezagrey (IRE)**[36] 5184 10-10-7 **83**..............................(b) OllieGarner(7) 22
(James Evans) *sn drvn along in rr: bhd fr 4th: t.o* **25/1**

0P6/ **P** **Hazy Dawn**[13] 32 8-10-8 **77**..............................(tp) AndrewGlassonbury
(Richard Woollacott) *hdwy 4th: rdn and wknd appr 4 out: t.o whn p.u bef next* **22/1**

40F/ **F** **Photogenique (FR)**[42] 5036 10-9-12 **70**............................ JamesBest(3)
(Rob Summers) *chsd ldrs: led after 9th: hdd 12th: wkng whn fell 3 out* **33/1**

254/ **P** **Normandy Landings**[179] 2421 10-10-8 **77**..................... DougieCostello
(Neil Mulholland) *a in rr: bhd fr 9th: t.o whn p.u bef 4 out* **25/1**

3PP/ **P** **Himayna**[23] 5382 9-10-7 **76**...(p) TomMessenger
(Christopher Kellett) *led to 3rd: chsd ldrs: lost pl 7th: p.u bef next* **100/1**

004/ **P** **Jomade (IRE)**[23] 5383 7-11-8 **94**.................................... PeterCarberry(3)
(Andy Hobbs) *in rr whn mstke 2nd: blnd 6th: bhd fr 9th: t.o whn p.u bef 4 out* **20/1**

5m 50.7s (2.70) **Going Correction** -0.775s/f (Firm) 16 Ran SP% **124.5**
Speed ratings: **64,63,63,58,55 55,54,49,48,39 35, , , ,**
toteswingers 1&2 £9.70, 2&3 £39.20, 1&3 £12.50 CSF £62.51 CT £783.68 TOTE £3.90: £1.20, £3.80, £3.70, £3.50; EX 75.80 Trifecta £891.20 Part won. Pool: £1188.39 - 0.66 winning units..
Owner C E Stedman & R J Corsan **Bred** R D And Mrs J S Chugg **Trained** Claines, Worcs

FOCUS
A modest handicap chase in which the first three finished clear. The first two are rated to their chase bests.

249 LADBROKES DOWNLOAD THE APP H'CAP CHASE (THE SUNDAY £5K BONUS RACE) (10 fncs 2 omitted) 2m 110y
3:10 (3:12) (Class 2) (0-150,150) 5-Y-0+ **£12,660** (£3,740; £1,870; £936; £468)

Form RPR

006/ **1** **Anquetta (IRE)**[24] 5363 9-10-8 **132**.................................. DavidBass 141+
(Nicky Henderson) *j.rt: chsd ldr tl led 5th: rdn and flashed tail flat: styd on* **10/1**

003/ **2** *1* **Woolcombe Folly (IRE)**[38] 5144 10-11-9 **150**................ RyanMahon(3) 156
(Paul Nicholls) *a.p: rdn to chse wnr flat: styd on* **6/1**

5/2- **3** *3* **Rajnagan (IRE)**[10] 82 9-10-13 **137**..............................(t) LiamTreadwell 141
(Paul Webber) *hld up: hdwy 7th: chsd wnr and hit 4 out: styd on same pce flat* **5/1[3]**

40F/ **4** *7* **Astracad (FR)**[38] 5139 7-11-5 **143**.......................(bt) SamTwiston-Davies 141
(Nigel Twiston-Davies) *prom: racd keenly: mstke 2nd: rdn after 2 out: no ex last* **4/1[1]**

3U/- **5** *13* **Gallox Bridge**[57] 4790 8-10-4 **128**..................................(t) DougieCostello 116
(Tim Vaughan) *led to 5th: j.rt next: wknd appr 2 out* **9/2[2]**

4/1- **6** *8* **Kings Grey (IRE)**[11] 66 9-11-2 **140**................................ JamesReveley 118
(Keith Reveley) *hld up: mstke 5th: wkng whn hit 2 out: t.o* **11/2**

250/ **7** *23* **Trooper Clarence**[190] 2181 9-10-1 **125**.......................... PaulMoloney 82
(Evan Williams) *hld up: a in rr: drvn along after 8th: sn t.o* **20/1**

2PP/ **8** *11* **Mostly Bob (IRE)**[176] 2467 10-10-6 **130**..........................(t) HaddenFrost 77
(Sophie Leech) *sn bhd: t.o* **28/1**

645/ **F** **Doeslessthanme (IRE)**[78] 4381 9-11-2 **145**.............(bt) HarryDerham(5)
(Paul Nicholls) *chsd ldrs: cl 3rd whn hmpd and fell 6th* **8/1**

3m 55.6s (-18.40) **Going Correction** -0.775s/f (Firm) 9 Ran SP% **112.9**
Speed ratings: **112,111,110,106,100 96,86,80,**
toteswingers 1&2 £10.20, 2&3 £8.10, 1&3 £11.20 CSF £67.51 CT £336.46 TOTE £15.50: £4.60, £2.60, £2.60; EX 95.80 Trifecta £770.60 Pool: £1031.98 - 1.00 winning units..
Owner The Ten From Seven **Bred** Gerry Martin **Trained** Upper Lambourn, Berks

FOCUS
The third-last (open ditch) was omitted on both circuits. A valuable handicap chase, particularly with the addition of the Sunday bonus, and it was run at a decent gallop. Solid form, Anquetta rated back to his best.

250 LADBROKES INTERMEDIATE OPEN NATIONAL HUNT FLAT RACE 2m
3:40 (3:40) (Class 6) 4-6-Y-0 **£1,624** (£477; £238; £119)

Form RPR

23/ **1** **Roll On Ruby (IRE)**[245] 1532 5-10-10 0......................... DonalDevereux 101+
(Peter Bowen) *a.p: led 4f out: rdn clr fr over 1f out* **3/1[1]**

2 *6* **No No Romeo (IRE)** 4-10-13 0... NoelFehily 99
(Charlie Longsdon) *hld up: hdwy 1/2-way: rdn to chse wnr fnl 2f: styd on same pce fnl f* **9/2[3]**

0/ **3** *10* **Dahteste**[180] 2402 5-10-10 0.................................. SamTwiston-Davies 87
(Mark Bradstock) *led 4f: chsd ldr tl lft in ld over 5f out: hdd 4f out: wknd fnl f* **14/1**

0/ **4** *1 1/2* **Bandol (IRE)**[213] 1803 5-11-3 0...................................... DougieCostello 92
(Laura Young) *hld up: hdwy over 3f out: nt trble ldrs* **50/1**

5 *5* **Lucky Sovereign (IRE)**[49] 4-10-6 0............................ PatrickCorbett(7) 84
(Rebecca Curtis) *chsd ldrs: rdn over 2f out: wknd wl over 1f out* **9/2[3]**

6 *4 1/2* **Church Hall (IRE)**[29] 5-11-3 0.. AndrewTinkler 84
(Emma Baker) *hld up: hdwy over 4f out: rdn and wknd over 1f out* **20/1**

7 *23* **Flying Native (IRE)** 4-10-13 0.. DavidBass 59
(Nicky Henderson) *chsd ldrs: pushed along 10f out: wknd over 2f out: t.o* **7/2[2]**

8 *6* **Anglingforcharlie** 4-10-13 0.. TomO'Brien 54
(Philip Hobbs) *hld up: hdwy 9f out: wknd over 2f out: t.o* **8/1**

9 *9* **Captain Jinx (IRE)** 6-11-3 0.. HaddenFrost 50
(Carroll Gray) *mid-div: hdwy 1/2-way: wknd over 5f out: t.o* **100/1**

5/ **10** *10* **Jaunty Inflight**[45] 4982 4-10-6 0.................................. GaryDerwin(7) 37
(Brian Eckley) *mid-div: wknd 6f out: t.o* **20/1**

0/ **11** *11* **Stella's Fella**[21] 5444 5-11-3 0..[1] DavidEngland 31
(Giles Smyly) *chsd ldr tl led 12f out: hung rt: hdd & wknd over 5f out: t.o* **33/1**

0/ **12** *70* **Bakari**[31] 5254 5-11-3 0..(t) PaulMoloney
(Graeme McPherson) *mid-div: hdwy 1/2-way: wknd 6f out: t.o* **50/1**

3m 40.7s (-1.00) **Going Correction** -0.125s/f (Good)
WFA 4 from 5yo+ 4lb 12 Ran SP% **118.7**
Speed ratings: **97,94,89,88,85 83,72,69,64,59 54,19**
toteswingers 1&2 £5.10, 2&3 £9.70, 1&3 £8.80 CSF £15.52 TOTE £3.60: £1.20, £3.00, £5.00; EX 24.90 Trifecta £176.30 Pool: £724.41 - 3.08 winning units..
Owner Miss S Munrowd **Bred** Mrs Eleanor Kent **Trained** Little Newcastle, Pembrokes

FOCUS
A modest bumper but probably a step up from the winner.

251 LADBROKES H'CAP HURDLE (8 hdls) 2m
4:10 (4:10) (Class 4) (0-120,120) 4-Y-0+ **£4,114** (£1,215; £607; £304; £152)

Form RPR

266/ **1** **Rime Avec Gentil (FR)**[36] 5185 8-10-1 **100**............... RobertWilliams(5) 107+
(Bernard Llewellyn) *hld up: hdwy and hung lft fr 3 out: rdn to ld fnl 100yds: sn clr: comf* **17/2[3]**

45P/ **2** *3* **Explained (IRE)**[45] 4989 6-11-5 **113**................................ DougieCostello 115
(Tim Vaughan) *led tl after 2nd: chsd ldr: rdn appr 3 out: styd on u.p to go 2nd nr fin* **12/1**

416/ **3** *1/2* **Flying Phoenix**[24] 5358 5-10-9 **106**.............................. RobertDunne(3) 108
(Dai Burchell) *chsd ldrs: rdn appr 3 out: styd on same pce flat* **12/1**

4/1- **4** *1/2* **Dresden (IRE)**[12] 49 5-11-4 **112**....................................... WillKennedy 115+
(Sarah-Jayne Davies) *chsd ldrs: mstke 3 out: led next: rdn: hdd and no ex fnl 100yds* **13/8[1]**

FU5/ **5** *6* **Sky Calling**[18] 5504 10-9-8 **98**..................................(tp) OllieGarner(10) 95
(Martin Keighley) *chsd ldrs: led after 2nd: clr next: hdd 2 out: wknd flat* **14/1**

322/ **6** *6* **Bullet Street (IRE)**[28] 5312 5-11-12 **120**............................ PaulMoloney 110
(Evan Williams) *hld up: nt fluent 3rd: hdwy 3 out: wkng whn j.lft next* **6/1[2]**

401/ **7** *13* **Mr Plod**[17] 2032 8-10-8 **102**.. SamTwiston-Davies 81
(J R Jenkins) *hld up: j.rt 1st: rdn appr 3 out: nvr on terms* **10/1**

U00/ **8** *13* **Looks Like Slim**[120] 3614 6-11-4 **112**.................................... NoelFehily 79
(Ben De Haan) *chsd ldrs: pushed along 4th: rdn and wknd after 3 out: t.o* **14/1**

010/ **9** *33* **Dalmo**[127] 3500 4-10-9 **114**.. ChristopherWard(7) 47
(Dr Richard Newland) *hld up: wknd 4th: t.o* **20/1**

015/ **P** **Walden Prince (IRE)**[30] 5277 6-10-1 **100**....................... HarryDerham(5)
(Tony Carroll) *hld up: a in rr: t.o whn p.u bef 2 out* **10/1**

3m 47.0s (-0.30) **Going Correction** -0.125s/f (Good)
WFA 4 from 5yo+ 18lb 10 Ran SP% **114.6**
Speed ratings (Par 105): **95,93,93,93,90 87,80,74,57,**
toteswingers 1&2 £27.10, 2&3 £11.40, 1&3 £7.50 CSF £101.31 CT £1219.51 TOTE £7.70: £2.00, £5.30, £3.90; EX 130.00 Trifecta £1242.90 Part won. Pool: £1657.28- 0.25 winning units..

Owner Ms S Howell **Bred** Scea Marais Des Pictons **Trained** Fochriw, Caerphilly

FOCUS
A fair handicap hurdle, and soulnd form.

252 NEU-SERVO H'CAP HURDLE (DIV I) (10 hdls) 2m 4f
4:40 (4:40) (Class 5) (0-100,100) 4-Y-0+ **£2,599** (£763; £381; £190)

Form RPR

000/ **1** **Princesse Fleur**[195] 2100 5-10-1 **75**................................ LiamTreadwell 83
(Michael Scudamore) *hld up: hdwy appr 3 out: led after next: drvn out* **25/1**

2/4- **2** *3/4* **Emerald Rose**[12] 46 6-11-9 **97**.................................. SamTwiston-Davies 105
(Julian Smith) *hld up: hdwy 6th: led and blnd 2 out: sn hdd: styd on u.p* **14/1**

3/0- **3** *5* **Transfer**[12] 49 8-11-0 **88**.. DavidBass 90
(Richard Price) *prom: outpcd after 7th: rallied after next: styd on same pce last* **12/1**

4/2- **4** *4 1/2* **Oscar Rainbow**[11] 71 7-10-3 **80**................................... RobertDunne(3) 78
(Dai Burchell) *hld up: mstke 1st: hdwy 7th: outpcd bef next: rallied 2 out: wknd last* **7/2[2]**

0/0- **5** *1/2* **There's No Rules**[3] 184 4-11-2 **95**...................................(e) BarryKeniry 88
(Richard Guest) *hld up: hdwy 7th: rdn and wknd flat* **33/1**

201/ **6** *6* **Ironical (IRE)**[205] 1925 9-11-10 **98**...................................(t) DavidEngland 92
(Shaun Lycett) *chsd ldr tl led 7th: hdd and mstke 2 out: wknd bef last* **16/1**

5/5- **7** *10* **Full Ov Beans**[12] 43 9-10-1 **82**...................................... JakeHodson(7) 65
(Michael Gates) *hld up: effrt appr 3 out: rdn and wknd next* **12/1**

P/0- **8** *8* **Ron**[12] 49 5-11-7 **95**... DougieCostello 71
(Jonjo O'Neill) *prom: rdn appr 3 out: wknd bef next: t.o* **15/2**

1/1- **9** *1 1/2* **Starlight Air**[11] 71 10-11-5 **93**...................................... AndrewTinkler 68
(John Spearing) *chsd ldrs: rdn appr 3 out: wknd bef next: t.o* **8/1**

042/ **10** *2 3/4* **Douchkirk (FR)**[42] 5034 6-11-7 **95**.....................................(p) WillKennedy 67
(John Berry) *prom: mstke 1st: chsd ldr 7th: led 3 out: rdn and hdd next: wknd bef last: eased flat: t.o* **3/1[1]**

005/ **11** *42* **Clarion Call**[21] 5437 5-11-12 **100**...........................(tp) PaulMoloney 34
(Evan Williams) *led to 7th: wknd bef 2 out: eased: t.o* **13/2[3]**

350/ **12** *15* **Only Hope**[29] 5290 9-11-1 **89**...(tp) DPFahy 10
(Andy Hobbs) *hld up: rdn and wknd after 7th: t.o* **40/1**

4m 43.6s (-3.80) **Going Correction** -0.125s/f (Good)
WFA 4 from 5yo+ 19lb 12 Ran SP% **120.6**
Speed ratings (Par 103): **102,101,99,97,97 95,91,88,87,86 69,63**
toteswingers 1&2 £32.10, 2&3 £41.30, 1&3 £73.00 CSF £333.28 CT £4379.94 TOTE £38.10: £5.60, £3.40, £4.40; EX 362.20 Trifecta £1379.10 Part won. Pool: £1838.90 - 0.09 winning units..
Owner The Honfleur Syndicate **Bred** Baker And Readings Partnership **Trained** Bromsash, H'fords

FOCUS
A modest handicap hurdle run at an ordinary gallop. It was over five seconds quicker than the second division. The first two are on the upgrade.

253 NEU-SERVO H'CAP HURDLE (DIV II) (10 hdls) 2m 4f
5:10 (5:10) (Class 5) (0-100,99) 4-Y-0+ **£2,599** (£763; £381; £190)

Form RPR

0/2- **1** **My Lad Percy**[6] 145 5-11-4 **98**................................ PatrickCorbett(7) 106
(Rebecca Curtis) *a.p: chsd ldr 2 out: styd on u.p to ld nr fin* **3/1[1]**

3/3- **2** *nk* **Get Home Now**[12] 42 5-11-3 **90**......................................(v) TomO'Brien 98
(Peter Bowen) *led: mstke 3 out: rdn flat: hdd nr fin* **11/2[3]**

2/1- **3** *7* **Adios Alonso (IRE)**[11] 67 7-10-13 **91**.............................. BenPoste(5) 91
(Rosemary Gasson) *chsd ldr tl rdn appr 3 out: styd on same pce last* **4/1[2]**

0P4/ **4** *1/2* **Conigre**[19] 5473 6-11-12 **99**..(tp) SamJones 99
(Brendan Powell) *hld up: mstke 6th: hdwy next: rdn appr last: styd on same pce* **18/1**

5F6/ **5** *2 ¼* **Crazy Bold (GER)**[16] 5538 10-10-7 **80**.................... SamTwiston-Davies 79
(Tony Carroll) *hld up: hdwy 3 out: sn rdn and hung lft: no ex last* **10/1**
0/0- **6** *8* **Diamond Tammy (IRE)**[12] 49 7-11-4 **94**.................. PeterCarberry(3) 85
(Andy Hobbs) *hld up: hdwy appr 5th: ev ch 3 out: wknd bef last* **33/1**
0/6- **7** *4 ½* **Naledi**[12] 49 9-9-7 **73** oh3.................................... OllieGarner(7) 60
(Richard Price) *hld up: hdwy 6th: rdn and wknd appr 2 out* **25/1**
0/3- **8** *4* **Velvet Vic (IRE)**[11] 71 7-10-4 **77**..(b) BarryKeniry 60
(Richard Guest) *hld up: nvr on terms* **12/1**
320/ **9** *10* **Vicpol (ITY)**[567] 2128 7-11-2 **89**..(p) DougieCostello 63
(Tom Gretton) *hld up: rdn appr 5th: hdwy next: wknd 3 out: t.o* **28/1**
400/ **10** *7* **Dane Cottage**[18] 5505 6-9-9 **73**..................................(p) HarryChalloner(5) 41
(Richard Ford) *hld up: bhd fr 5th: t.o whn mstke 3 out* **40/1**
5/5- **11** *6* **Brass Monkey (IRE)**[11] 71 6-10-11 **84**...........................(b[1]) NoelFehily 46
(Charlie Longsdon) *trckd ldrs: racd keenly: wknd 3 out: t.o* **7/1**
420/ **P** **Gtaab**[19] 5473 7-11-10 **97**..(tp) PaulMoloney
(Sophie Leech) *hld up: mstke and lost tch 5th: t.o whn p.u bef 3 out* **33/1**
545/ **P** **Palio Square (USA)**[85] 2431 6-11-8 **95**.................................(b) RhysFlint
(John Flint) *prom tl mstke and wknd 6th: t.o whn p.u bef 2 out* **22/1**

4m 49.0s (1.60) **Going Correction** -0.125s/f (Good) **13** Ran SP% **114.9**
Speed ratings (Par 103): **91,90,88,87,86 83,81,80,76,73 71,,**
toteswingers 1&2 £5.20, 2&3 £5.40, 1&3 £3.20 CSF £17.34 CT £65.95 TOTE £4.30: £2.20, £2.20, £1.50; EX 18.80 Trifecta £75.40 Pool: £1321.08 - 13.13 winning units..
Owner Davies & Price **Bred** D J M & Mrs Eileen Milligan **Trained** Newport, Dyfed

FOCUS
The slower division by more than five seconds. The winner is rated to his mark.

254 LADBROKES DOWNLOAD THE APP H'CAP HURDLE (12 hdls) 2m 7f
5:40 (5:40) (Class 5) (0-100,99) 4-Y-0+ **£2,599** (£763; £381; £190)

Form RPR
604/ **1** **Kilrush (IRE)**[40] 5109 7-11-12 **99**... NoelFehily 108+
(Neil Mulholland) *hld up: mstke 7th: hdwy appr 3 out: led and pckd next: hung lft flat: all out* **7/1**[3]
P/P- **2** *1* **Grovemere (IRE)**[9] 89 8-11-3 **90**.......................................(tp) TomO'Brien 96
(Debra Hamer) *a.p: chsd ldr 8th: led appr 3 out: hdd next: rdn and ev ch last: unable qck nr fin* **12/1**
2/2- **3** *25* **Master Cardor Visa (IRE)**[9] 99 8-11-4 **98**.................... RyanHatch(7) 82
(Emma Baker) *hld up: drvn along after 6th: hdwy 8th: wknd appr last* **9/2**[1]
236/ **4** *1 ½* **Minella Bliss (IRE)**[30] 5271 8-11-8 **98**............................ RobertDunne(3) 80
(Nikki Evans) *hld up: rdn appr 3 out: nvr on terms* **10/1**
461/ **5** *2 ¼* **Gilded Age**[23] 5085 7-11-11 **98**.............................(tp) SamTwiston-Davies 78
(Chris Gordon) *nt fluent 1st: w ldr tl led 7th: rdn and hdd appr 3 out: wknd after next* **7/1**[3]
003/ **6** *nk* **Ahead Ahead (IRE)**[18] 5505 8-11-8 **95**............................... PaulMoloney 76
(David Rees) *hld up: rdn appr 3 out: n.d* **9/2**[1]
32P/ **7** *57* **Typhon De Guye (FR)**[19] 5471 6-11-2 **99**...................... OllieGarner(10) 28
(Martin Keighley) *chsd ldrs tl rdn and wknd appr 3 out: t.o* **5/1**[2]
500/ **8** *55* **Wak A Turtle (IRE)**[73] 4481 5-11-6 **96**.........................(p) MattGriffiths(3)
(Richard Woollacott) *hld up: hdwy and mstke 5th: wknd 9th: t.o* **20/1**
000/ **P** **Jewellery (IRE)**[16] 5538 6-11-2 **94**..................................(t) HarryDerham(5)
(Kevin Bishop) *led to 7th: wknd next: t.o whn p.u bef 3 out* **14/1**
0/0- **P** **Original Star (IRE)**[12] 48 8-11-8 **95**.................................... DavidBass
(Derek Frankland) *a in rr: bhd fr 5th: t.o whn p.u bef 9th* **28/1**
F43/ **P** **One For The Boss (IRE)**[47] 4965 6-11-3 **90**...............(t) AndrewTinkler
(Brendan Powell) *prom: pushed along approachng 7th: wknd next: t.o whn p.u bef 9th* **12/1**

5m 39.0s (11.00) **Going Correction** -0.125s/f (Good) **11** Ran SP% **117.4**
Speed ratings (Par 103): **75,74,65,65,64 64,44,25,,**
toteswingers 1&2 £5.20, 2&3 £5.40, 1&3 £3.20 CSF £86.51 CT £422.46 TOTE £8.40: £2.20, £3.10, £2.00; EX 117.50 Trifecta £805.50 Part won. Pool of £1074.13 - 0.68 winning units..
Owner Six Shades Of Grey **Bred** J P And Miss M Mangan **Trained** Limpley Stoke, Wilts

FOCUS
A very modest staying handicap hurdle, run at a good gallop. The first two were well clear. The winner was well in on his best Irish form.
T/Plt: £3,329.00 to a £1 stake. Pool of £67720.14 - 14.85 winning tickets. T/Qpdt: £394.90 to a £1 stake. Pool of £4696.15 - 8.80 winning tickets. CR

255 - 261a (Foreign Racing) - See Raceform Interactive

[139]AUTEUIL (L-H)
Friday, May 10

OFFICIAL GOING: Turf: very soft

262a PRIX DE POUILLY (HURDLE) (CONDITIONS) (3YO) (C&G) (TURF) 2m 1f 110y
1:20 (12:00) 3-Y-0 **£18,731** (£9,365; £5,463; £3,707; £1,756)

RPR
1 **King Chop (FR)**[31] 3-10-10 0.. BenoitGicquel 127
(F Nicolle, France) **58/10**[2]
2 *10* **Roxyfet (FR)**[35] 3-10-3 0..(p) BertrandThelier 110
(G Cherel, France) **34/1**
3 *1 ¼* **Abbyssial (IRE)** 3-10-6 0 ow3.. SylvainDehez 112
(M Rolland, France) **11/1**
4 *3* **Fox Norton (FR)**[37] 5134 3-10-8 0.. JamesReveley 111
(Nick Williams) *t.k.h: trckd ldr: led 3rd: jnd 2 out: rdn and hdd appr last where untidy: no ex and dropped to 4th run-in* **68/10**[3]
5 *1 ½* **Garde Ville (FR)**[13] 3-10-3 0.. ErvanChazelle 104
(N Milliere, France) **28/1**
6 *18* **Sun Wild Life (FR)**[32] 3-10-6 0.............................(p) ValentinDevillars(4) 93
(G Cherel, France) **13/1**
7 *5* **Surely Try (FR)**[35] 3-10-3 0.. BorisChameraud 81
(Mme I Pacault, France) **26/1**
8 *dist* **Forsocks D'Ycy (FR)**[19] 3-10-3 0.. AlexisPoirier(5)
(G Cherel, France) **18/1**
P **Azolla De Sivola (FR)**[10] 3-10-3 0.................................. LudovicPhilipperon
(T Trapenard, France) **15/1**
P **Mon Nickson (FR)**[54] 3-10-3 0.. BertrandLestrade
(G Macaire, France) **11/1**
P **Norberix (FR)**[35] 3-10-3 0.. CyrilleGombeau
(G Cherel, France) **8/1**
P **Artiste Rochelais (FR)**[35] 3-9-13 0.........................(b[1]) JonathanGiron(4)
(Mme I Pacault, France) **22/1**
P **Alphanov (FR)**[28] 3-10-1 0.......................................(b) BenoitClaudic(5)
(H Billot, France) **26/1**
F **New Spirit (FR)**[21] 3-10-12 0.. GaetanOlivier
(F Nicolle, France) **5/1**[1]

P **Iris Nobile (FR)** 3-10-8 0.. MlleNathalieDesoutter
(D Guillemin, France) **83/10**

4m 29.3s (269.30) **15** Ran SP% **119.4**
PARI-MUTUEL (all including 1 euro stakes): WIN 6.80; PLACE 2.80, 13.80, 4.80; DF 258.00; SF 435.80.
Owner Alain Chopard **Bred** A Chopard **Trained** France

263a PRIX PRETENTAINE (HURDLE) (CLAIMER) (5YO+) (JOCKEYS WHO HAVEN'T WON 35 RACES) (TURF) 2m 2f
3:25 (12:00) 5-Y-0+ **£8,975** (£4,487; £2,617; £1,776; £841)

RPR
1 **Tempoline (FR)**[30] 5-10-8 0.. AnthonyRenard
(D Sourdeau De Beauregard, France) **172/10**
2 *hd* **Le Temujin (IRE)**[16] 5-10-10 0..(p) AlexisPoirier
(J-Y Artu, France) **68/10**[3]
3 *12* **Bleu Et Rose (FR)**[51] 8-11-3 0...(b) HugoLucas
(E Leray, France) **11/1**
4 *5* **Unique D'Ainay (FR)**[14] 5-10-8 0.................................. NicolasChevreux
(F-M Cottin, France) **14/1**
5 *1* **Sandy Cay (FR)**[16] 6-11-0 0..(b) HerveJumelle
(P Lenogue, France) **25/1**
6 *1 ¾* **Vivacissimo (IRE)**[19] 5447 6-11-3 0.. GeoffreyRe
(Yannick Fouin, France) **7/2**[1]
7 *1 ½* **Goldslic (FR)**[13] 7-11-3 0.. JeremyRey
(Robert Collet, France) **10/1**
8 *2 ½* **Brasero (FR)**[16] 5-10-12 0.. WilfriedLajon
(D Bressou, France) **20/1**
9 *2* **Oracle (GER)**[1056] 9-11-0 0..(p) RaphaelMayeur
(F-M Cottin, France) **17/1**
10 *2 ½* **Fresh Princess (FR)**[16] 7-10-10 0..................................(b) BenjaminPinard
(R Chotard, France) **13/2**[2]
11 *dist* **Majaales (USA)**[44] 4974 10-11-0 0.. AodhaganConlon
(Tom George) *nt fluent: a towards rr: rdn 4 out: dropped to last 3 out: eased and t.o bef last but kpt gng to complete* **9/1**
P **Bella Cara (FR)**[318] 5-10-6 0.. BenoitClaudic
(H Billot, France) **50/1**
P **Lypharez**[579] 6-11-0 0.. StevanBourgois
(Y-M Porzier, France) **15/1**
P **Walk Sibo (FR)**[16] 5-10-12 0.. TeddyCousseau
(D Windrif, France) **11/1**

4m 28.6s (268.60) **14** Ran SP% **118.7**
PARI-MUTUEL (all including 1 euro stakes): WIN 18.20; PLACE 3.90, 1.90, 4.00; DF 28.10; SF 91.20.
Owner Michel Pehu **Bred** Michel Pehu **Trained** France

[29]TOWCESTER (R-H)
Monday, May 13

OFFICIAL GOING: Good (good to firm in places) changing to good after race 2 (6.00) changing to good to soft on hurdle course after race 4 (7.00)
Wind: strong,against Weather: bright spells and showers

264 HAYGAIN HAY STEAMERS CLEAN HEALTHY FORAGE AMATEUR RIDERS' H'CAP HURDLE (10 hdls) 2m 3f 110y
5:25 (5:25) (Class 5) (0-100,100) 4-Y-0+ **£1,871** (£580; £290; £145)

Form RPR
241/ **1** **Prince Pippin (IRE)**[40] 5118 7-11-4 **97**........................(t) MsLucyJones(5) 102
(Lucy Jones) *chsd ldrs: wnt 2nd 4th tl led 7th: clr bef 2 out: styd on wl flat* **17/2**
2/5- **2** *4* **Bob Lewis**[4] 188 7-10-5 **86**..(t) CharlieDeutsch(7) 89
(Anthony Middleton) *hld up in midfield: hdwy bef 3 out: chsd wnr 2 out: pressing wnr whn j.rt and mstke last: no ex flat* **7/1**[2]
150/ **3** *4* **The Fox's Decree**[17] 5538 9-11-3 **98**..................................(tp) MrCDee(7) 97
(Martin Keighley) *in tch in midfield: rdn and effrt after 3 out: chsd clr wnr ent st tl bef 2 out: 3rd whn mstke and pckd 2 out: plugged on same pce after* **16/1**
5P0/ **4** *6* **Highland River**[14] 29 7-9-13 **80**.................................... MissKReynolds(7) 72
(Dave Roberts) *bhd: rdn and effrt after 7th: styd on past btn horses on uphill run bef 2 out: wnt 4th last: nvr trbld ldrs* **20/1**
3U4/ **5** *8* **Meridiem**[14] 31 9-10-12 **93**..(t) MissBAndrews(7) 78
(Caroline Fryer) *chsd ldrs: mstke 4th: effrt to chse ldr after 3 out: no imp and lost 2 pls bef 2 out: wknd 2 out* **15/2**[3]
5F5/ **6** *4* **Mangonel**[24] 5381 9-10-12 **93**..(vt) MrJAPonting(7) 76
(Jo Davis) *led tl 7th: chsd wnr after tl wknd u.p bef 2 out* **25/1**
03/ **7** *1 ½* **Crack At Dawn (IRE)**[14] 34 12-10-3 **84**.......................(v) MrCSmith(7) 64
(Michael Gates) *hld up in rr: stdy hdwy after 5th: chsd ldrs and rdn 3 out: wknd u.p bef next* **25/1**
5P5/ **8** *2 ¼* **Homer Run (IRE)**[30] 5285 6-11-5 **93**.................................. MissGAndrews 71
(Simon Earle) *hld up towards rr: drvn and struggling after 7th: plugged on past btn horses fr 3 out: nvr trbld ldrs* **12/1**
RU0/ **9** *13* **Achieved**[17] 5555 10-9-7 **74** oh10...(v[1]) MrJPearce(7) 41
(Daniel O'Brien) *chsd ldrs tl 7th: wknd sn after next: t.o* **33/1**
632/ **10** *½* **Samizdat (FR)**[15] 21 10-9-7 **74** oh3..................................(p) MissGSwan(7) 40
(John Upson) *chsd ldr tl 4th: rdn and struggling after 7th: wknd sn after next: t.o* **22/1**
600/ **11** *3 ¾* **Tom Sang (FR)**[37] 5184 6-10-5 **86**............................ MrMatthewStanley(7) 49
(Jamie Snowden) *wl in tch: rdn and struggling 3 out: wknd bef next: t.o* **8/1**
564/ **12** *2 ¼* **Marmalade Man**[29] 5318 7-11-7 **100**.............................. MrKevinJones(5) 61
(Seamus Mullins) *hld up in rr: short-lived effrt and no hdwy whn mstke 3 out: n.d: t.o* **9/1**
544/ **13** *hd* **Roseini (IRE)**[14] 29 7-10-4 **83**.................................... ConorShoemark(5) 43
(Tony Carroll) *hld up in midfield: effrt and no rspnse 3 out: wknd and wl btn bef next: t.o* **7/2**[1]
600/ **14** *2 ¼* **Behtarini (IRE)**[60] 4766 6-10-6 **87** ow2......(be) MrJakeThomasCoulson(7) 44
(Christopher Kellett) *a towards rr: mstke 5th: n.d: t.o* **50/1**
400/ **15** *22* **Cian Boy (IRE)**[215] 1790 7-10-10 **87**................................ NickSlatter(3) 26
(Nick Kent) *j.big: chsd ldrs on outer: j.rt and mstke 4th: steadily lost pl: wl bhd after 3 out: t.o* **16/1**
41P/ **16** *24* **Until The Man (IRE)**[24] 5378 6-10-9 **90**.......................... MissKatyLyons(7) 7
(Geoffrey Deacon) *in tch in midfield: bmpd 4th: lost tch 3 out: t.o 2 out* **66/1**

400/ **17** 3 ½ **Mccauley (IRE)**[14] 31 10-11-4 **99**..............................(p) MrTHampton(7) 13
(Robert Walford) *in tch in midfield: lost pl and towards rr whn mstke 7th: lost tch next: t.o 2 out* **50/1**
PPU/ **F** **Massachusetts**[80] 4372 6-9-7 **74** oh15............ MissGeorgiaHenderson(7)
(Rob Summers) *bhd tl fell 6th* **80/1**
4m 45.5s (-24.10) **Going Correction** -0.725s/f (Firm) **18** Ran SP% **124.0**
Speed ratings (Par 103): **103,101,99,97,94 92,92,91,85,85 84,83,83,82,73 63,62,**
Tote Swingers: 1&2 £11.20, 2&3 £21.30 CSF £61.25 CT £958.32 TOTE £7.60: £2.70, £2.60, £3.20, £6.90; EX 66.90 Trifecta £328.80 Part won. Pool: £438.51 - 0.06 winning units..
Owner H D R Harrison-Allen **Bred** William Kane **Trained** Kilgetty, Pembrokeshire

FOCUS
Hurdles track dolled out to widest line. Rather unsettled before racing but the ground remained good, good to firm in places. A true test for this low-grade handicap hurdle for amateur riders with very few managing to get involved. The winner is rated to last season's course best.

265 ENJOY YOUR RETIREMENT STUART PLASKOW H'CAP CHASE (18 fncs) 3m 110y
6:00 (6:00) (Class 4) (0-110,110) 5-Y-0+ **£3,768** (£1,106; £553; £276)

Form RPR
5F2/ **1** **Noble Witness (IRE)**[24] 5382 10-11-9 **107**......................(p) AdamPogson 113
(Charles Pogson) *a.p: mstke 2nd: led 3rd tl 7th: chsd ldr tl after 15th: sn hrd drvn: 5th and looked hld 2 out: rallied gamely to chse ldr last: chalng whn sltly hmpd flat: styd on wl to ld cl home* **8/1**
3U1/ **2** *nk* **Queen Of Mantua (IRE)**[20] 5480 7-11-3 **101**.................. PaddyBrennan 107+
(Fergal O'Brien) *chsd ldrs: wnt 2nd bef 3 out: led 2 out: rdn between last 2: j.rt last: hung lft and bmpd wnr flat: hdd and no ex cl home* **5/2**[1]
P05/ **3** 1 ½ **Bishophill Jack (IRE)**[15] 7 7-11-3 **101**....................(p) NickScholfield 107
(Kim Bailey) *chsd ldrs: mstke 12th: drvn in cl 3rd whn j.rt 2 out: styd on same pce u.p flat* **7/1**
050/ **4** 2 ¼ **River D'Or (FR)**[41] 5104 8-11-10 **108**............................... PaulMoloney 110
(Sophie Leech) *hld up in last trio: clsd on ldrs 10th: mstke 15th: 4th and rdn bef 2 out: keeping on same pce whn slt mstke last: no ex flat* **7/2**[2]
506/ **5** *10* **Monty's Revenge (IRE)**[19] 5500 8-10-11 **95**........................ IanPopham 90
(Martin Keighley) *mainly j.w: led tl 3rd: led again 7th: rdn and hdd 2 out: drvn and no ex between last 2: wknd last* **11/1**
03P/ **P** **Meet The Critics (IRE)**[41] 5104 10-11-8 **106**..............(t) RichieMcLernon
(Jonjo O'Neill) *hld up in last trio: mstke 6th: clsd on ldrs 10th: mstke 13th: rdn and wknd 3 out: wl bhd whn p.u last* **14/1**
133/ **P** **Theophrastus (IRE)**[20] 5481 11-11-12 **110**.......................... TomCannon
(Nick Gifford) *in tch in midfield: dropped to rr but stl wl in tch whn mstke 12th: rdn 14th: wknd 3 out: wl bhd and p.u last* **5/1**[3]
60P/ **P** **Rogue Dancer (FR)**[14] 30 8-9-9 **84** oh15.................. TrevorWhelan(5)
(Michael Banks) *a bhd: rdn and no rspnse after 8th: losing tch and p.u 10th* **33/1**
0F/ **P** **Mongress Boy (IRE)**[24] 5383 8-11-7 **105**.......................... SeanQuinlan
(Andy Hobbs) *nt jump fluently: in tch in midfield: mstke 2nd: reminders and lost pl after 7th: losing tch whn p.u 10th* **25/1**
6m 10.0s (-26.90) **Going Correction** -0.725s/f (Firm) **9** Ran SP% **112.9**
Speed ratings: **98,97,97,96,93 , , ,**
Tote Swingers: 1&2 £4.50, 1&3 £16.60, 2&3 £3.90 CSF £28.79 CT £147.24 TOTE £9.60: £2.20, £1.60, £2.00; EX 35.80 Trifecta £206.80 Pool: £921.56 - 3.34 winning units..
Owner Wordingham Plant Hire & Partner **Bred** Patrick Manning **Trained** Farnsfield, Notts

FOCUS
A fair pace for this staying handicap chase with the front five pulling well clear of the remainder and four of them still holding some sort of chance at the last. Straightforward form.

266 JOHN ABBOTT "HAS GONE FLYING" RETIREMENT (S) HURDLE (8 hdls) 2m
6:30 (6:35) (Class 5) 4-8-Y-0 **£1,949** (£572; £286; £143)

Form RPR
421/ **1** **Molon Labe (IRE)**[17] 5538 6-11-5 107...........................(t) AdamWedge(3) 104+
(David Rees) *hld up wl in tch in last pair: rdn and effrt bef 2 out: rdn to chal last: sn led: styd on wl* **9/4**[1]
P11/ **2** *4* **Paddy Partridge**[55] 781 7-11-8 113............................. RichardJohnson 99
(Tim Vaughan) *racd wd tl after 3rd: lft 3rd next: chsd ldr 5th: ev ch 3 out: led between last 2: sn drvn: dived last: sn hdd and no ex: wknd fnl 100yds* **11/2**
U3/- **3** *shd* **Ajman (IRE)**[30] 5283 8-10-12 105....................................(tp) PaulMoloney 89
(Evan Williams) *hld up wl in tch in last pair: hdwy to chse ldrs 3 out: rdn and unable qck whn edgd rt between last 2: lft 3rd last: kpt on same pce flat* **7/2**[3]
000/ **4** *5* **Inside Knowledge (USA)**[27] 4343 7-10-12 90................. AdamPogson 84
(Garry Woodward) *t.k.h: chsd ldrs: rdn and struggling bef 2 out: wknd between last 2: lft 4th and hmpd last* **28/1**
120/ **5** ½ **Nicky Nutjob (GER)**[15] 17 7-10-10 83.....................(p) CiaranMckee(7) 89
(John O'Shea) *hld up wl in tch in last trio: rdn and effrt after 3 out: no ex next: wknd bef last* **15/2**
0/5- **6** *45* **Up In Flames (IRE)**[13] 47 4-10-8 0.................................(b) TomSiddall 40
(Martin Keighley) *t.k.h: chsd ldrs: lft 2nd 4th tl next: lost tch quickly after 3 out: t.o* **33/1**
6P0/ **U** **Royal Defence (IRE)**[27] 4536 7-10-12 100...................... AndrewTinkler
(Mick Quinn) *pressed ldr tl blnd bdly and uns rdr 4th* **20/1**
026/ **U** **Seaquel**[22] 5432 7-10-5 96.. LeeEdwards 82
(Tony Carroll) *led: rdn bef 2 out: mstke 2 out and sn hdd: stl ev ch but looked to be struggling whn slipped on landing and uns rdr last* **10/3**[2]
3m 56.5s (-11.40) **Going Correction** -0.725s/f (Firm)
WFA 4 from 6yo+ 18lb **8** Ran SP% **114.4**
Speed ratings: **99,97,96,94,94 71, ,**
Tote Swingers: 1&2 £3.00, 1&3 £2.80, 2&3 £3.50 CSF £14.86 TOTE £2.60: £1.10, £1.60, £2.50; EX 14.90 Trifecta £45.30 Pool: £1,324.97 - 21.93 winning units..The winner was bought in for 4,600gns.
Owner D Rees & P Evans **Bred** Swettenham Stud, Carradale Ltd & T Stack **Trained** Clarbeston, Pembrokes

FOCUS
After some heavy showers the ground had now eased to good all round. A trappy selling hurdle. The winner ran to his mark with the next four 10lb+ off.

267 VOLKSWAGEN AMAROK H'CAP HURDLE (8 hdls) 2m
7:00 (7:00) (Class 4) (0-110,110) 4-Y-0+ **£3,119** (£915; £457; £228)

Form RPR
1/2- **1** **Castlemorris King**[13] 42 5-11-4 **107**.......................... GavinSheehan(5) 112
(Brian Barr) *mstkes: w ldr: rdn and ev ch whn mstke 2 out: mstke last: led flat: styd on wl u.p* **9/2**[1]
460/ **2** *nk* **Callisto Moon**[7] 5386 9-11-10 **108**...(p) MarkGrant 113
(Jo Hughes) *led: rdn bef 2 out: mstke last: hdd flat: battled on gamely u.p: jst hld* **12/1**
50F/ **3** *8* **Social Realism (IRE)**[16] 5567 5-10-13 **97**..................(p) RichieMcLernon 95
(Jonjo O'Neill) *hld up in tch towards rr: nt clr run bnd bef 2 out: hdwy bef 2 out: racing awkwardly but styng on whn mstke last: wnt 3rd flat: no threat to ldrs* **20/1**
4/4- **4** 1 ¾ **Trip The Light**[9] 119 8-11-9 **110**...................................(v) KielanWoods(3) 105
(Phil Middleton) *in tch in midfield: mstke 3rd: rdn and effrt to chse ldrs bef 2 out: no ex and btn between last 2: wknd and lost 3rd flat* **9/1**
302/ **5** *8* **Brassbound (USA)**[14] 31 5-11-10 **108**...................... AndrewThornton 96
(Caroline Bailey) *chsd ldng trio: rdn bef 2 out: struggling whn mstke 2 out: sn wknd* **6/1**[3]
20/- **6** ½ **Sun Quest**[32] 5245 9-10-8 **99**...(t) MrLKilgarriff(7) 87
(Steven Dixon) *chsd ldrs: rdn bef 3 out: wknd bef 2 out* **40/1**
050/ **7** *shd* **Hot Spice**[54] 4863 5-11-3 **104**.. JakeGreenall(3) 91
(Michael Easterby) *in tch towards rr: rdn and effrt bef 2 out: no imp and btn 2 out: plugged on* **12/1**
4U0/ **8** *nk* **Pampelonne (IRE)**[22] 5432 7-11-7 **105**.......................(p) NoelFehily 92
(Charlie Longsdon) *in tch: rdn and no ex bef 2 out: wknd 2 out* **20/1**
043/ **9** *1* **Goat Castle (IRE)**[17] 5546 9-10-0 **84** oh1.............(t) SamTwiston-Davies 70
(Nigel Twiston-Davies) *hld up in tch in rr: hdwy on inner bef 3 out: rdn and bef 2 out: wknd 2 out* **10/1**
035/ **10** 4 ½ **Fitandproperjob**[19] 5509 7-9-9 **84** oh1............................(t) JamesBanks(5) 66
(Anthony Middleton) *in tch in rr: hmpd and mstke 3rd: blnd next: rdn and no imp 3 out: n.d* **14/1**
011/ **11** *10* **Weather Babe**[20] 5479 5-11-8 **106**................................... TomScudamore 87+
(David Pipe) *chsd ldrs: drvn and struggling after 5th: losing pl and mstke next: wknd wl bef 2 out* **11/2**[2]
600/ **12** *6* **Shadarpour (IRE)**[36] 5197 4-11-0 **102**.............................(p) JamieMoore 66
(Gary Moore) *in tch in midfield: mstke and blnd 4th: lost pl and drvn whn mstke next: wl bhd bef 2 out* **12/1**
P02/ **13** *48* **Hail Tiberius**[174] 2538 6-10-11 **95**......................................(e[1]) IanPopham 20
(Martin Keighley) *t.k.h: stdd s and hld up in rr: j.lft 4th: lost tch 3 out: t.o 2 out: hit last* **22/1**
14 3 ¾ **Nishay (IRE)**[36] 6-11-7 **105**... PaulMoloney 26
(David Rees) *hld up wl in tch in midfield: lost pl qckly after 5th: bhd next: t.o 2 out* **25/1**
3m 56.5s (-11.40) **Going Correction** -0.725s/f (Firm)
WFA 4 from 5yo+ 18lb **14** Ran SP% **116.8**
Speed ratings (Par 105): **99,98,94,93,89 89,89,89,89,86 81,78,54,52**
Tote Swingers: 1&2 £6.20, 2&3 £17.10 CSF £50.85 CT £982.92 TOTE £4.80: £1.50, £3.00, £8.50; EX 33.50 Trifecta £277.40 Part won. Pool: £369.88 - 0.42 winning units..
Owner Miss Daisy Hitchins **Bred** Peter Storey **Trained** Longburton, Dorset

FOCUS
A competitive handicap hurdle where the winner and runner-up were always to the fore of a generous pace and fought out a cracking finish. A small personal best from the winner.

268 TOWCESTER TEA ROOMS 10TH ANNIVERSARY MARES' MAIDEN HURDLE (11 hdls) 2m 5f
7:30 (7:30) (Class 5) 4-Y-0+ **£2,053** (£598; £299)

Form RPR
562/ **1** **Mrs Peachey (IRE)**[71] 4538 6-10-12 109.......................... JasonMaguire 113+
(Kim Bailey) *j.rt: chsd ldr: mstke 8th: upsides ldr and mstke 3 out: rdn to ld bef 2 out: sn clr: drvn between last 2: kpt on* **6/4**[1]
45/ **2** 2 ¼ **Polly Hopper**[20] 5479 7-10-12 0...........................(t) SamTwiston-Davies 110
(Nigel Twiston-Davies) *mounted on crse: hld up in tch towards rr: mstke 5th: rdn and hdwy after 3 out: hung rt and wnt 2nd 2 out: j.rt last: kpt on wl flat* **12/1**
52/- **3** *8* **Fair Bramble**[31] 5267 7-10-12 102...................................... LeightonAspell 103
(Oliver Sherwood) *led and set stdy gallop: mstke 1st: mstke 8th: rdn and hdd bef 2 out: sn outpcd and btn whn j.rt 2 out: wknd bef last: j.rt last* **7/2**[2]
230/ **4** 1 ¼ **Bebinn (IRE)**[26] 5354 6-10-12 103.......................................(p) DarylJacob 101
(Ben Case) *t.k.h: chsd ldrs: rdn and nt qckn after 3 out: 4th and btn next: plugged on* **5/1**
U43/ **5** 1 ½ **Tea Caddy**[32] 5256 7-10-12 0... TomO'Brien 100
(Jamie Snowden) *t.k.h: hld up in tch in midfield: rdn and effrt 3 out: 5th and btn next* **9/2**[3]
000/ **6** *7* **Lillybrook (IRE)**[75] 4447 7-10-5 0... RyanHatch(7) 93
(Nigel Twiston-Davies) *mstkes: mstke 8th: rdn and struggling bef next: wkng whn mstke next* **33/1**
034/ **7** *43* **Rose Red**[30] 5295 6-10-9 0.. JamesBest(3) 55
(Rob Summers) *t.k.h: hld up in tch in midfield: mstke 2nd: hdwy to chse ldrs 8th: wknd qckly sn after next: t.o* **50/1**
00/ **8** *8* **Myetta**[181] 2402 5-10-12 0... MarcGoldstein 47
(Lydia Richards) *t.k.h: hld up in tch in rr: mstke 3rd: rdn and lost tch bef 3 out: t.o bef 2 out* **100/1**
6/P- **P** **Arrowmint**[12] 67 7-10-7 76... TrevorWhelan(5)
(Nicholas Pomfret) *a bhd: rdn and lost tch after 8th: t.o whn p.u 2 out* **150/1**
11/ **P** **Boracha (IRE)**[19] 5511 5-10-12 0.................................... AndrewThornton
(Seamus Mullins) *t.k.h: chsd ldrs tl 8th: sn lost pl and bhd whn eased bef next: t.o whn p.u 2 out* **25/1**
5m 25.1s (-2.10) **Going Correction** -0.725s/f (Firm) **10** Ran SP% **115.2**
Speed ratings (Par 103): **75,74,71,70,70 67,51,47, ,**
Tote Swingers: 1&2 £7.30, 1&3 £1.80, 2&3 £12.10 CSF £20.30 TOTE £2.70: £1.10, £4.10, £1.80; EX 26.40 Trifecta £50.80 Pool: £458.13 - 6.75 winning units..
Owner The Boom Syndicate **Bred** J Hanly & C Neilan **Trained** Andoversford, Gloucs

FOCUS
Further ease in the ground with the hurdle course now good to soft. An ordinary pace for this mares' novices hurdle. The winner was close to her mark.

269 JIMMY JAMES NOVICES' H'CAP CHASE (12 fncs) 2m 110y
8:00 (8:00) (Class 5) (0-100,99) 5-Y-0+ **£2,144** (£629; £314; £157)

Form RPR
5PP/ **1** **Moscow Mule**[14] 32 10-10-2 **80**... EdCookson(5) 88+
(Laura Hurley) *in tch in midfield: hdwy to chse ldr 8th: led bef 2 out: clr and idling between last 2: edgd lft flat: drvn out* **22/1**
4/0- **2** *5* **Tom O'Tara**[13] 43 9-10-2 **78**.. WayneKavanagh(3) 79
(Robin Dickin) *chsd ldrs tl led 6th: hdd and drvn bef 2 out: kpt on same pce u.p after: j.rt last* **11/2**[3]
306/ **3** ½ **Strathcal**[14] 30 7-11-12 **99**...(tp) FelixDeGiles 100
(Tom Symonds) *sn bhd and pushed along after 2nd: hdwy 7th: chsd ldrs bef 3 out: 3rd and styng on bef 2 out: drvn and styd on same pce between last 2* **10/1**
324/ **4** *15* **Rebel High (IRE)**[14] 30 9-11-5 **92**.. DavidBass 81
(Derek Frankland) *chsd ldrs: drvn and nt qckn bef 2 out: 4th and wknd between last 2* **3/1**[1]

3/4- **5** 8 **Smiling Lady (IRE)**[7] 142 7-11-11 98 (t) PaulMoloney 79
(David Rees) *j.lft: bhd and nt fluent: sme hdwy 3 out but nvr on terms: no imp bef 2 out: wl btn whn hung lft flat* **11/2**[3]

P25/ **6** 9 **Moulin Tour (FR)**[198] 2055 7-10-1 74 HenryOliver 49
(Henry Oliver) *in tch in midfield: mstke 4th and struggling after: no threat to ldrs after: wl bhd 2 out: t.o* **7/2**[2]

400/ **7** 7 **Tribal Dance (IRE)**[15] 5 7-11-2 96 (v) CiaranMckee(7) 62
(John O'Shea) *towards rr: mstke 4th and sn dropped to last: lost tch 6th: sn t.o* **17/2**

P5U/ **P** **Tough Cookie (IRE)**[82] 4326 10-9-12 78 ow2 (v) JakeHodson(7)
(Michael Gates) *w ldr tl 6th: lost pl after mstke next: t.o bef 3 out: p.u 2 out* **25/1**

0PP/ **P** **Daddy'Slittlegirl**[24] 5383 8-9-7 73 oh10 (p) GeraldQuinn(7)
(Claire Dyson) *led tl 6th: chsd ldr tl 8th: wknd rapidly after next: t.o bef 2 out tl p.u last* **16/1**

4m 2.0s (-14.10) **Going Correction** -0.725s/f (Firm) **9** Ran SP% **111.7**
Speed ratings: **101,98,98,91,87 83,80, ,**
Tote Swingers: Not won. CSF £133.54 CT £1283.41 TOTE £48.50: £10.90, £3.30, £1.60; EX 285.60 TRIFECTA Not won..
Owner Mrs R Hurley **Bred** Mrs R Hurley **Trained** Kineton, Warwicks

FOCUS
A good pace but a bit of a shock result for this weak 2m handicap chase. A big step up from the winner.

270 LET'S GIVE THANKS MAIDEN OPEN NATIONAL HUNT FLAT RACE 2m
8:30 (8:30) (Class 6) 4-6-Y-O **£1,559** (£457; £228; £114)

Form RPR

1 **Ulzana's Raid (IRE)** 4-10-12 0 WayneHutchinson 96+
(Alan King) *in tch in midfield: effrt to chse ldng pair over 2f out: str run to ld ins fnl f: edgd rt but r.o strly* **9/2**[3]

2 3 1/4 **Knight Of Noir (IRE)**[44] 4-10-12 0 TomScudamore 93
(David Pipe) *chsd ldr tl led 10f out: hrd pressed and rdn over 2f out: hdd over 1f out: stl ev ch after tl outpcd by wnr ins fnl f: kpt on* **5/1**

2/ **3** nk **Reverb**[24] 5388 4-10-9 0 JeremiahMcGrath(3) 92
(Nicky Henderson) *chsd ldrs: wnt 2nd over 3f out: rdn and ev ch 2f out: led over 1f out: hdd and outpcd by wnr fnl 100yds: kpt on* **11/4**[1]

0/ **4** 4 **Peter**[23] 5413 5-11-2 0 PaulMoloney 93
(Paul Webber) *hld up in tch: hdwy on outer 4f out: outpcd bnd over 2f out and nt clr run 2f out: rallied u.p over 1f out: kpt on* **12/1**

5 1 **Son Of Suzie** 5-11-2 0 PaddyBrennan 92
(Fergal O'Brien) *in tch towards rr: hdwy to chse ldrs 4f out: rdn and outpcd over 2f out: no threat to ldrs but kpt on again fnl f* **12/1**

6 10 **Little Jon** 5-11-2 0 SamTwiston-Davies 85
(Nigel Twiston-Davies) *hld up in tch towards rr: effrt 3f out: outpcd and btn over 2f out: swtchd lft over 1f out: sn wknd* **4/1**[2]

6/ **7** 1 1/4 **Kyles Faith (IRE)**[84] 4293 5-11-2 0 IanPopham 82
(Martin Keighley) *hld up in tch in rr: hdwy into midfield 5f out: rdn and no ex over 2f out: wknd 2f out* **25/1**

8 2 **Mr Shantu (IRE)** 4-10-12 0 NoelFehily 76
(Tony Carroll) *hld up in tch in rr: nt clr run 5f out: effrt 3f out: no real prog whn nt clr run 2f out: wknd over 1f out* **25/1**

0/ **9** 10 **Hope Royal**[15] 4 6-10-9 0 AndrewThornton 64
(Lawney Hill) *racd wd: chsd ldrs: wnt 2nd 10f out tl over 3f out: wknd qckly over 2f out* **40/1**

4/ **10** 13 **Heres Action Man**[16] 5572 5-11-2 0 CharliePoste 59
(John Holt) *chsd ldrs: rdn and lost pl over 4f out: wl bhd fnl 2f: t.o* **33/1**

11 3 3/4 **Flintham** 4-10-12 0 MattieBatchelor 52
(Mark Bradstock) *led tl 10f out: chsd ldrs tl 4f out: sn dropped out and bhd fnl 2f: t.o* **8/1**

0/ **12** 1 1/4 **Mantles Heath (IRE)**[15] 14 5-11-2 0 SamThomas 55
(Paul Cowley) *in tch towards rr: rdn and sme hdwy 4f out: sn wknd: bhd fnl 2f: t.o* **66/1**

13 26 **Deb's Town** 6-10-9 0 LeeEdwards 24
(Tony Carroll) *hld up in tch in rr: effrt and rn green over 4f out: sn wknd: t.o over 2f out* **40/1**

3m 50.85s (-11.45) **Going Correction** -0.725s/f (Firm)
WFA 4 from 5yo+ 4lb **13** Ran SP% **125.0**
Speed ratings: **100,98,98,96,95 90,90,89,84,77 75,75,62**
Tote Swingers: 1&2 £17.20, 1&3 £8.00, 2&3 £1.40 CSF £27.01 TOTE £6.50: £1.90, £2.10, £1.10; EX 34.70 Trifecta £85.40 Pool: £471.69 - 4.13 winning units..
Owner Alan King **Bred** M Brennan **Trained** Barbury Castle, Wilts

FOCUS
An interesting looking bumper run at a decent pace with some top stables being represented with some nice staying prospects for the future. The bare form is probably ordinary.
T/Jkpt: Not won. T/Plt: £225.90 to a £1 stake. Pool: £70,554.14 - 227.90 winning tickets. T/Qpdt: £19.70 to a £1 stake. Pool: £6,350.56 - 238.28 winning tickets. SP

271 - 277a (Foreign Racing) - See Raceform Interactive

[72]SEDGEFIELD (L-H)
Tuesday, May 14

OFFICIAL GOING: Good (7.9)
Wind: fairly strong behind Weather: Mixture of sunshine and cloud

278 PAXTONS & CASE IH A WINNING TEAM NOVICES' HURDLE (8 hdls) 2m 1f
2:00 (2:00) (Class 4) 4-Y-O+ **£3,119** (£915; £457; £228)

Form RPR

3/1- **1** **Aazif (IRE)**[12] 73 4-11-1 120 (t) JasonMaguire 124+
(Donald McCain) *mde all: pushed along between last 2: rdn after last: a in command: eased nr fin* **1/5**[1]

614/ **2** 1 1/4 **Croco Bay (IRE)**[23] 5425 6-11-0 117 HarryChalloner(5) 124
(Peter Atkinson) *trckd ldr in 2nd: rdn 2 out: kpt on but a hld* **11/2**[2]

6/5- **3** 50 **Langley House (IRE)**[12] 73 6-10-5 0 JamesReveley 65
(Dianne Sayer) *in tch in 3rd: grad lft bhd by ldng pair fr 4th: nt fluent 3 out* **25/1**

0/6- **4** 11 **Bertielicious**[12] 73 5-10-9 64 JohnKington(3) 62
(Jonathan Haynes) *hld up: nt fluent 4th: collided w rail sn after 3 out: wnt distant 4th bef 2 out* **250/1**

P/ **5** 41 **Showmehow**[200] 2031 5-10-5 0 AdrianLane 18
(Ray Craggs) *hld up: a bhd* **250/1**

6 2 **Bollin Sam** 7-10-12 0 RyanMania 23
(Sue Smith) *nt fluent: hld up in 4th: wknd after 3 out: t.o* **20/1**[3]

0PF/ **P** **Granny Blackwood**[32] 5273 5-10-5 0 HenryBrooke
(Martin Todhunter) *hld up in rr: t.o whn p.u after 3 out* **100/1**

3m 54.6s (-12.30) **Going Correction** -0.55s/f (Firm) **7** Ran SP% **109.1**
Speed ratings (Par 105): **106,105,81,76,57 56,**
toteswingers 1&2 £1.10, 1&3 £2.40, 2&3 £2.40 CSF £1.45 TOTE £1.10: £1.02, £1.70; EX 1.60 Trifecta £3.70 Pool: £1629.08 - 325.13 winning units..
Owner Askew Dick Hernon Reynard **Bred** Shadwell Estate Company Limited **Trained** Cholmondeley, Cheshire

FOCUS
Common bends dolled off the inside to provide fresher ground. Straightforward novice form, the wuinner rated in line with his recent C&D win.

279 PAXTONS & JCB A WINNING TEAM NOVICES' CHASE (12 fncs 4 omitted) 2m 4f
2:30 (2:30) (Class 4) 5-Y-O+ **£3,768** (£1,106; £553; £276)

Form RPR

200/ **1** **Any Given Day (IRE)**[38] 5175 8-10-12 0 JasonMaguire 118+
(Donald McCain) *mde all: pushed clr extended run-in: eased towards fin: comf* **1/1**[1]

3/3- **2** 9 **Gin Cobbler**[10] 114 7-10-12 104 MrJHamilton(7) 108
(Victor Thompson) *racd keenly: trckd ldrs: rdn after 2 out (normal 3 out): kpt on to go 2nd extended run-in: no ch w wnr* **9/2**[2]

264/ **3** 8 **Chicago Outfit (IRE)**[348] 513 8-10-12 103 (p) BrianHughes 94
(John Wade) *w ldr: rdn and outpcd after 3 out (normal 4 out): nt fluent last (normal 2 out): one pce: wnt modest 3rd passing omitted last* **12/1**

606/ **4** 3/4 **Presenting Junior (IRE)**[16] 21 6-10-5 0 GrahamWatters(7) 92
(Martin Todhunter) *hld up: kpt on after 2 out (normal 3 out): wnt 4th towards fin: nvr threatened* **80/1**

466/ **5** 3 1/4 **Indian Voyage (IRE)**[36] 5216 5-10-12 0 (t) MichaelMcAlister 90
(Maurice Barnes) *trckd ldrs: upsides 9th: rdn 2 out (normal 3 out): wknd and lost 3 pls extended run-in* **10/1**

004/ **6** 2 3/4 **Diddley Dee**[20] 5498 9-10-7 0 GaryRutherford(5) 89
(Lucy Normile) *nt a fluent: nvr bttr than midfield* **16/1**

000/ **7** 19 **Discoverie**[96] 4074 5-10-12 0 RyanMania 70
(Dianne Sayer) *midfield: wknd after 3 out (normal 4 out)* **66/1**

550/ **8** 13 **Prince Blackthorn (IRE)**[41] 5119 7-10-12 0 BrianHarding 58
(William Amos) *trckd ldrs: dropped to midfield by 7th: wknd after 3 out (normal 4 out)* **66/1**

216/ **9** 3/4 **Alba King (IRE)**[92] 4159 7-10-7 0 JonathanEngland(5) 57
(Sue Smith) *midfield: reminder after 6th: lost pl bef next: slow 8th: sn bhd* **11/2**[3]

P/0- **10** 37 **Go Teescomponents**[13] 67 6-10-12 0 (t) JamesReveley 24
(Keith Reveley) *hld up in rr: a bhd: t.o* **33/1**

130/ **F** **Dun To Perfection**[23] 5426 6-10-5 0 StephenMulqueen(7)
(Susan Corbett) *hld up: hdwy after 6th: trckd ldrs whn fell 9th* **40/1**

4m 46.9s (-16.10) **Going Correction** -0.775s/f (Firm) **11** Ran SP% **115.8**
Speed ratings: **101,97,94,93,92 91,83,78,78,63**
toteswingers 1&2 £2.20, 1&3 £6.10, 2&3 £7.90 CSF £5.64 TOTE £1.80: £1.10, £1.70, £2.50; EX 6.40 Trifecta £33.70 Pool: £1066.23 - 23.69 winning units..
Owner T G Leslie **Bred** Ralph And Helen O'Brien **Trained** Cholmondeley, Cheshire

FOCUS
The final fence and the one on the roadside were omitted and meant only six jumps on each circuit were negotiated in all chase races on the card. It also left a massively extended run-in. The easy winner was a 155+ hurdler at best and can probably win more chases.

280 PAXTONS SUPPORTING CUSTOMERS WITH PEREGRINE FINANCE MAIDEN HURDLE (10 hdls) 2m 5f 110y
3:00 (3:00) (Class 5) 4-Y-O+ **£1,949** (£572; £286; £143)

Form RPR

422/ **1** **Valleyofmilan (IRE)**[20] 5491 6-11-0 118 JasonMaguire 114+
(Donald McCain) *midfield: tk clsr order after 4 out: rdn to ld appr 2 out: kpt on* **7/4**[1]

220/ **2** 4 1/2 **Bowie (IRE)**[37] 5195 6-11-0 120 HarryHaynes 108
(Nick Kent) *trckd ldr: rdn to chse wnr after 2 out: kpt on but a hld* **4/1**[3]

2/U- **3** 1 1/4 **Lord Luso (IRE)**[13] 68 7-10-9 105 KyleJames(5) 108
(Philip Kirby) *led: mstke 6th: rdn after 4 out: hdd appr 2 out: one pce in 3rd between last 2* **2/1**[2]

343/ **4** 11 **Trust Thomas**[23] 5423 5-11-0 104 BrianHughes 99
(Ann Hamilton) *midfield: tk clsr order after 4 out: rdn and ev ch appr 2 out: wknd bef last* **6/1**

454/ **5** 42 **Kilcaskin Star (IRE)**[16] 19 7-10-11 98 BrianToomey(3) 59
(Karen Tutty) *hld up: wknd appr 2 out* **25/1**

6 53 **Potts Bridge (IRE)**[65] 4693 7-11-0 0 JamesReveley 11
(Paul Stafford, Ire) *hld up: wknd 3 out: t.o* **150/1**

P **Bunty Boy**[65] 7-11-0 0 RichieMcGrath
(Philip Kirby) *racd wd: in tch: looked reluctant and dropped to rr after 6th: hit next: sn p.u* **100/1**

5m 7.3s (-7.30) **Going Correction** -0.55s/f (Firm) **7** Ran SP% **109.5**
Speed ratings (Par 103): **91,89,88,84,69 50,**
toteswingers 1&2 £1.10, 1&3 £1.10, 2&3 £5.00 CSF £8.48 TOTE £2.00: £1.10, £2.60; EX 6.20 Trifecta £15.30 Pool: £1393.51 - 68.09 winning units..
Owner Tim & Miranda Johnson **Bred** Kenneth William Quinn **Trained** Cholmondeley, Cheshire

FOCUS
An ordinary maiden, run at a sound gallop. The first four were all within a few pounds of their marks.

281 PAXTONS USE ROMERO'S FOR HASSLE FREE INSURANCE H'CAP CHASE (10 fncs 3 omitted) 2m 110y
3:30 (3:30) (Class 5) (0-100,100) 5-Y-O+ **£2,144** (£629; £314; £157)

Form RPR

0P6/ **1** **Sendiym (FR)**[16] 17 6-10-0 74 (b) SeanQuinlan 87+
(Dianne Sayer) *led: mstke last: sn hdd: rallied to ld again towards fin* **4/1**[1]

F/U- **2** 1 3/4 **Turf Trivia**[10] 109 6-10-9 83 (b) BarryKeniry 93
(George Moore) *trckd ldr: rdn to ld extended run-in: no ex fnl 100yds: hdd towards fin* **9/2**[2]

204/ **3** 3 1/4 **Ginger's Lad**[16] 20 9-10-8 85 JakeGreenall(3) 91
(Michael Easterby) *trckd ldr: rdn after 2 out (normal 3 out): kpt on one pce* **5/1**[3]

0/2- **4** 9 **Zazamix (FR)**[10] 109 8-10-5 86 (v) JohnWinston(7) 84
(Andrew Crook) *nt a fluent: midfield: rdn in modest 4th whn hit 2 out (normal 3 out)* **6/1**

405/ **5** 1 3/4 **Sharivarry (FR)**[15] 30 7-11-12 100 BrianHughes 96
(James Ewart) *hld up in midfield: nvr threatened* **4/1**[1]

330/ **6** 3/4 **Frith (IRE)**[200] 2029 11-10-0 74 oh3 DougieCostello 71
(Lucy Normile) *hld up: nt fluent 6th and 7th: nvr threatened* **14/1**

660/ 7 8 **Schinken Otto (IRE)**[15] 23 12-11-5 **93**............................ HarryHaynes 85
(Malcolm Jefferson) *in tch on inner: nt fluent 7th: wknd after next* **9/1**
650/ 8 41 **Authentic Act (IRE)**[16] 17 9-10-0 **74** oh5........................ HenryBrooke 41
(Martin Todhunter) *in tch: mstke 2nd: rdn after 6th: wknd after 3 out (normal 4 out)* **33/1**
040/ P **Bob's Dream (IRE)**[45] 5010 11-11-9 **97**............................(t) BrianHarding
(William Amos) *hld up in rr: reminders after 5th: t.o whn p.u bef 2 out (normal 3 out)* **18/1**
3m 59.5s (-9.10) **Going Correction** -0.775s/f (Firm) **9** Ran SP% **114.0**
Speed ratings: **90,89,87,83,82 82,78,59,**
toteswingers 1&2 £18.80, 1&3 £15.50, 2&3 £4.00 CSF £22.65 CT £90.46 TOTE £6.10: £1.90, £2.10, £2.20; EX 30.50 Trifecta £200.20 Pool: £773.88 - 2.89 winning units..
Owner Tony Ambler **Bred** H H The Aga Khan's Studs Sc **Trained** Hackthorpe, Cumbria
FOCUS
This moderate handicap was an open-looking affair and there was a fair gallop on. The third is best guide to the form.

282 PAXTONS USE SIGNAL TELECOM FOR COMMUNICATIONS H'CAP CHASE (12 fncs 4 omitted) 2m 4f
4:00 (4:00) (Class 4) (0-120,120) 5-Y-0+ **£3,768** (£1,106; £553; £276)

Form RPR
361/ 1 **Riskier**[23] 5424 8-11-4 **112**.. BrianHughes 121
(John Wade) *prom: led 6th: mde rest: rdn extended run-in: a holding on* **4/1**[2]
0/3- 2 1 ¾ **Attycran (IRE)**[12] 77 8-10-3 **97**................................(t) MichaelMcAlister 104
(Maurice Barnes) *in tch: moved upsides after 6th: rdn after 2 out (normal 3 out): one pce and a jst hld extended run-in* **13/2**
6PU/ 3 3 ¼ **Sparkling Tara**[20] 5501 8-10-11 **105**...................................... RyanMania 112+
(Sue Smith) *midfield: hdwy to trck ldrs 7th: rdn in dispute of 2nd whn blnd last (normal 2 out): one pce extended run-in* **10/1**
6/3- 4 10 **Fred Bojangals (IRE)**[12] 78 11-11-7 **115**........................ SeanQuinlan 112
(Barbara Butterworth) *hld up: hdwy 8th: one pce in 4th after 2 out (normal 3 out): wknd fnl 100yds* **18/1**
0/2- 5 17 **Montoya's Son (IRE)**[13] 66 8-11-5 **120**.........................(t) MrBGibbs(7) 100
(Tim Vaughan) *hld up: nvr threatened* **11/2**[3]
010/ 6 1 ¼ **Strobe**[20] 5502 9-10-6 **100**...(p) DougieCostello 79
(Lucy Normile) *trckd ldrs: rdn after 7th: sn struggling to hold pl: wknd after 3 out (normal 4 out)* **33/1**
242/ 7 7 **Twentypoundluck (IRE)**[22] 5448 8-11-4 **112**..............(p) JamesReveley 84
(Patrick Griffin, Ire) *nt a fluent: hld up in midfield: nvr threatened* **3/1**[1]
4/4- 8 4 ½ **Regal D'Estruval (FR)**[12] 81 8-11-12 **120**........................ TomO'Brien 91
(Dr Richard Newland) *led tl blnd 6th: sn dropped into midfield: wknd after 3 out (normal 4 out)* **7/1**
054/ 9 9 **The Panama Kid (IRE)**[41] 5122 9-11-4 **112**...................(b) HarryHaynes 72
(Malcolm Jefferson) *in tch: nt fluent 8th: sn wknd* **17/2**
4m 44.2s (-18.80) **Going Correction** -0.775s/f (Firm) course record **9** Ran SP% **114.0**
Speed ratings: **106,105,104,100,93 92,89,88,84**
toteswingers 1&2 £4.10, 1&3 £13.70, 2&3 £8.50 CSF £30.01 CT £240.52 TOTE £4.60: £1.20, £1.80, £4.10; EX 37.80 Trifecta £675.60 Part won. Pool: £900.82 - 0.44 winning units..
Owner John Wade **Bred** H J Manners **Trained** Mordon, Co Durham
FOCUS
A modest handicap and another open event. It paid to race handy. Straightforward form.

283 PAXTONS & LELY UK MACHINERY & BALERS H'CAP HURDLE (8 hdls) 2m 1f
4:30 (4:30) (Class 5) (0-100,100) 4-Y-0+ **£1,949** (£572; £286; £143)

Form RPR
03U/ 1 **Brother Scott**[16] 21 6-10-2 **83**.................................... CallumBewley(7) 90+
(Sue Smith) *midfield: hdwy to trck ldrs after 4 out: rdn to chal and pushed rt appr last: rdr dropped whip after last: kpt on to ld fnl 100yds* **7/4**[1]
026/ 2 ½ **Agricultural**[15] 27 7-11-7 **95**.. RyanMania 100
(Lucy Normile) *trckd ldr: led appr 2 out: rdn and jnd whn bmpd bef last: hdd fnl 100yds: kpt on* **11/2**[3]
045/ 3 4 **Highland Love**[23] 5426 8-11-12 **100**................................(b) BrianHarding 102
(Jedd O'Keeffe) *led: rdn and hdd appr 2 out: rallied and hung rt appr last: upsides whn blnd last: nt rcvr* **10/1**
230/ 4 3 ½ **Tweedo Paradiso (NZ)**[19] 5520 6-11-5 **93**........................ RichieMcGrath 91
(Rose Dobbin) *hld up: hdwy appr 3 out: wnt 4th 2 out: styd on same pce* **5/1**[2]
F/U- 5 10 **Pete**[10] 109 10-10-9 **90**...(tp) GrahamWatters(7) 79
(Barry Murtagh) *hld up: hdwy appr 3 out: pushed along in 4th after 3 out: mstke 2 out: wknd* **8/1**
560/ 6 39 **Copt Hill**[47] 4995 5-10-5 **82**... AlexanderVoy(3) 35
(Tracy Waggott) *prom: lost pl after 4 out: wknd after 3 out* **10/1**
6P6/ 7 29 **Snow Alert**[16] 15 7-11-5 **93**... FearghalDavis 20
(John Norton) *hld up: bhd after 4th: t.o* **33/1**
P3/- P **Prize Fighter (IRE)**[84] 4300 11-10-10 **84**........................... TomSiddall
(Lynn Siddall) *hld up: sme hdwy whn mstke 3 out: p.u sharply and dismntd* **12/1**
365/ P **Needwood Park**[39] 5166 5-11-5 **100**....................(b[1]) DiarmuidO'Regan(7)
(Ray Craggs) *trckd ldrs: wknd: t.o whn p.u bef 2 out* **14/1**
P66/ P **Teeiygee**[17] 5570 5-9-9 **74** oh5...................................... SamanthaDrake(5)
(Mike Sowersby) *hld up in tch: reminders after 2nd: briefly chsd ldrs after 3rd: wknd next: t.o whn p.u bef 2 out* **40/1**
4m 1.8s (-5.10) **Going Correction** -0.55s/f (Firm) **10** Ran SP% **117.4**
Speed ratings (Par 103): **90,89,87,86,81 63,49,,,**
toteswingers 1&2 £2.60, 1&3 £5.40, 2&3 £6.30 CSF £12.42 CT £75.92 TOTE £2.80: £1.30, £2.50, £2.60; EX 10.70 Trifecta £35.80 Pool: £1335.23 - 27.95 winning units..
Owner Mrs S Smith **Bred** C P E Brooks **Trained** High Eldwick, W Yorks
FOCUS
A weak handicap and a tight finish. The winner can rate higher and should go in again.

284 PAXTONS & SPREAD-A-BALE TOP AIDEN NATIONAL HUNT FLAT RACE (CONDITIONALS/AMATEURS) 2m 1f
5:00 (5:00) (Class 6) 4-6-Y-0 **£1,559** (£457; £228; £114)

Form RPR
1 **Billfromthebar (IRE)**[79] 6-11-4 0.. HenryBrooke 117+
(Donald McCain) *mde all: rdn clr fnl 2f* **3/1**[2]
5/ 2 13 **Robbers Roost (IRE)**[33] 5254 5-10-11 0............................ MrBGibbs(7) 104
(Tim Vaughan) *trckd ldrs: rdn over 2f out: kpt on but no ch w wnr* **13/2**
54/ 3 hd **Rene Le Roi (FR)**[22] 5454 4-10-7 0................................ MrJHamilton(7) 100
(Tim Easterby) *trckd ldrs: briefly chal out wd over 3f out: outpcd over 2f out: kpt on one pce fr over 1f out* **9/2**[3]
4 2 **Mister Jones** 5-10-11 0... CallumBewley(7) 102
(Sue Smith) *hld up: pushed along over 5f out: styd on fnl 2f: nrst fin* **16/1**
5 6 **The Village (IRE)** 4-10-11 0.. MrSCrawford(3) 93
(S R B Crawford, Ire) *midfield: hdwy to trck ldr over 3f out: sn rdn: wknd over 1f out* **7/4**[1]
6 5 **Park House** 4-10-7 0.. DiarmuidO'Regan(7) 87
(Ray Craggs) *hld up in midfield: rdn over 3f out: nvr threatened* **25/1**
0/ 7 nk **Aw Ripe China (IRE)**[214] 1821 5-10-13 0................ JonathanEngland(5) 91
(Simon Waugh) *prom: rdn over 3f out: wknd fnl 2f* **50/1**
8 3 ¼ **Lordenshaws (IRE)**[38] 6-10-11 0.................................... MrTSpeke(7) 87
(Robert Johnson) *trckd ldrs: rdn over 3f out: grad wknd* **50/1**
/ 9 7 **Timber King** 4-10-8 0 ow1.. MrWKitchman(7) 77
(Marjorie Fife) *hld up: nvr threatened* **40/1**
10 3 **Rubber Bullet** 5-10-8 0.. BrianToomey(3) 70
(Tim Etherington) *midfield: rdn over 4f out: sn wknd* **25/1**
0/ 11 48 **Timeforarun (IRE)**[22] 5454 5-10-11 0.................................. MrRSmith(7) 29
(David Thompson) *midfield: lost pl over 5f out: sn bhd* **66/1**
P **Just Once Up** 4-10-7 0.. MrHAABannister(7)
(Kevin Hunter) *sn struggling in rr: t.o whn p.u over 3f out* **33/1**
3m 54.8s (-6.50) **Going Correction** -0.55s/f (Firm)
WFA 4 from 5yo+ 4lb **12** Ran SP% **117.2**
Speed ratings: **93,86,86,85,83 80,80,79,75,74 51,**
toteswingers 1&2 £4.60, 1&3 £4.00, 2&3 £4.60 CSF £21.12 TOTE £3.90: £1.60, £1.80, £2.00; EX 28.90 Trifecta £59.80 Pool: £1459.18 - 18.28 winning units..
Owner D McCain Jnr **Bred** Andrew Pierce **Trained** Cholmondeley, Cheshire
FOCUS
A fair bumper for the track and time of year, and the winner looks a decent recruit.
T/Plt: £15.30 to a £1 stake. Pool: £61,171.25 - 2912.62 winning tickets. T/Qpdt: £15.90 to a £1 stake. Pool: £3713.03 - 172.34 winning tickets. AS

181 SOUTHWELL (L-H)
Tuesday, May 14

OFFICIAL GOING: Good (7.0) changing to good to soft after race 4 (6.55)
Wind: light 1/2 against Weather: overcast, light rain, rain race 1 onwards

285 SYCAMORE BOOKBINDING RESTORATION & CONSERVATION LTD H'CAP CHASE (16 fncs) 2m 4f 110y
5:20 (5:20) (Class 5) (0-95,95) 5-Y-0+ **£2,395** (£698; £349)

Form RPR
523/ 1 **Arrow Barrow (IRE)**[16] 20 8-10-6 **82**............................ JohnDawson(7) 95+
(John Wade) *chsd ldrs: 2nd after 9th: hit 11th: drvn appr 3 out: styd on to ld last: forged clr* **1/1**[1]
2/P- 2 5 **Flichity (IRE)**[10] 117 8-9-13 **73**.. JoeCornwall(5) 80
(John Cornwall) *led: qcknd clr 7th: drvn and 4 l ahd 3 out: hdd last: kpt on same pce* **9/2**[2]
1/2- 3 3 ½ **Peak Seasons (IRE)**[7] 162 10-10-3 **79**...................... GerardGalligan(7) 81
(Michael Chapman) *chsd ldrs 9th: 3rd 11th: one pce fr 3 out: hung rt run-in* **9/2**[2]
3P0/ 4 14 **Kaycee (IRE)**[127] 3551 8-10-0 **69** oh5.................................. JamesDavies 62
(Roger Curtis) *chsd ldrs: drvn 10th: outpcd whn hit 4 out: sn lost pl: blnd last* **12/1**
143/ 5 37 **Streedagh Lady (IRE)**[181] 2427 9-11-7 **95**.......................... DerekFox(5) 51
(Mark Michael McNiff, Ire) *sn detached in last: bhd fr 10th: t.o 4 out* **6/1**[3]
P/P- 6 4 ½ **Gainsborough's Art (IRE)**[10] 117 8-9-7 **69** oh6.......(p) DanielHiskett(7) 21
(Harry Chisman) *chsd ldr tl after 9th: reminders bef next: lost pl 12th: t.o 3 out* **33/1**
5m 26.0s (9.00) **Going Correction** +0.325s/f (Yiel) **6** Ran SP% **111.3**
Speed ratings: **95,93,91,86,72 70**
toteswingers 1&2 £1.50, 1&3 £1.50, 2&3 £4.80 CSF £6.12 TOTE £1.90: £1.10, £2.70; EX 5.60 Trifecta £18.70 Pool: £565.59 - 22.60 winning units..
Owner John Wade **Bred** Mrs Cora Cronin **Trained** Mordon, Co Durham
FOCUS
Fences and bend into the home straight on inside line, Golf Club bend on outside the line used at last meeting to give fresh ground. A modest handicap chase, in which the top-weight was rated 95. The winner is a potential 100+ chaser.

286 BELVOIR EQUINE LASER THERAPY NOVICES' H'CAP CHASE (16 fncs) 2m 4f 110y
5:50 (5:50) (Class 4) (0-120,119) 5-Y-0+ **£3,898** (£1,144; £572; £286)

Form RPR
2P/- 1 **Prolinx (IRE)**[32] 5266 8-11-6 **118**................................ GavinSheehan(5) 130+
(Charlie Mann) *trckd ldrs: wnt 2nd 4 out: upsides next: sn led on bit: wnt clr between last 2: heavily eased run-in* **6/1**[3]
32/- 2 9 **Furrows**[32] 5266 8-11-12 **119**... LeightonAspell 118
(Oliver Sherwood) *hld up: chsd ldrs 11th: wnt 2nd sn after 2 out: no ch w wnr* **4/1**[2]
4U3/ 3 8 **Scampi Boy (IRE)**[31] 5292 9-11-3 **110**.............................. LiamTreadwell 100+
(Paul Webber) *j.lft: led: hdd after 9th: led appr 4 out: hdd after 3 out: 2nd whn stmbld on landing next: sn wknd* **7/4**[1]
332/ 4 2 ¾ **Run Along Boy**[28] 5336 8-11-5 **112**.......................(p) SamTwiston-Davies 104
(Neil Mulholland) *chsd ldrs: hit 6th: mstke 10th: one pce fr 4 out* **4/1**[2]
601/ 5 48 **Chiquilline (FR)**[31] 5286 7-11-8 **115**.................................... JamieMoore 61
(Richard Lee) *t.k.h: w ldr: mstke 3rd: stmbld on landing 7th: led after 9th: hdd bef 4 out: sn lost pl: t.o 2 out: eased run-in* **4/1**[2]
0/5- P **Radsoc De Sivola (FR)**[13] 64 8-9-9 **93** oh11............. JoeCornwall(5)
(John Cornwall) *t.k.h: trckd ldrs: pushed along 6th: lost pl 4 out: sn bhd: p.u bef next* **50/1**
5m 25.0s (8.00) **Going Correction** +0.325s/f (Yiel) **6** Ran SP% **112.6**
Speed ratings: **97,93,90,89,71**
toteswingers 1&2 £4.10, 1&3 £2.70, 2&3 £1.70 CSF £29.87 TOTE £5.90: £1.80, £2.80; EX 18.60 Trifecta £93.10 Pool: £850.23 - 6.84 winning units..
Owner Prolinx Limited **Bred** K Burke **Trained** Upper Lambourn, Berks
FOCUS
Despite the small field, this looked a competitive event. There's a case for rating the form up to 6lb higher through the second.

287 SAVILLS OPEN HUNTERS' CHASE (MIDLANDS POINT-TO-POINT AREA) (16 fncs) 2m 4f 110y
6:20 (6:21) (Class 5) 5-Y-0+ **£2,183** (£677; £338; £169)

Form RPR
602/ 1 **Moon Over Miami (GER)**[38] 12-11-7 123.......................... MrDHolmes(7) 114
(D Holmes) *t.k.h: chsd ldr: outpcd appr 3 out: 5 l down in 4th 2 out: styd on appr last: chalng whn briefly eased clsng stages: rallied to ld post* **6/1**[3]

3/3- **2** *shd* **Rash Move (IRE)**[13] 57 12-12-3 117 .... MrTEllis(5) 124+
(F A Hutsby) *chsd ldrs 7th: hit next: outpcd appr 3 out: styd on between last 2: narrow ld sn after last: hdd post* **2/1**[1]

2/2- **3** *½* **Marky Bob (IRE)**[13] 57 8-12-3 119 .... MrMatthewBarber(5) 122
(Hugo Froud) *led: hdd appr 2 out: led last: sn hdd: no ex nr fin* **2/1**[1]

051/ **4** *3 ¼* **Shrewd Investment**[21] 5482 7-11-11 0 ....(t) MrJoshuaNewman(7) 116
(Miss L Thomas) *drvn 6th: sn chsng ldrs: led appr 2 out: hdd and 3rd whn blnd last: sn fdd* **4/1**[2]

3/ **5** *18* **Discussion Forum**[17] 7-11-7 0 .... MrWBiddick 89
(Mrs C A Coward) *chsd ldrs: wknd 4 out: bhd fr next* **12/1**

50P/ **6** *65* **King Diamond (FR)**[16] 12-11-7 62 ....(p) MrJGoss(7) 35
(J R Goss) *chsd ldrs: drvn 9th: hit next: sn lost pl: t.o after 4 out: eventually completed* **66/1**

004/ **P** **Arumun (IRE)**[257] 1416 12-11-11 80 .... MrSDavies-Thomas(7)
(Alan Phillips) *led to post: hld up: lost pl 10th: sn bhd: t.o whn p.u bef 3 out* **50/1**

0PP/ **P** **Roby De Cimbre (FR)**[23] 10-11-9 0 ....(t) MrJonathanBailey(5)
(S Robinson) *hit 7th: outpcd and reminders 9th: bhd fr next: t.o 6th whn p.u bef 3 out* **50/1**

355/ **P** **Green Du Ciel (FR)**[39] 5167 8-11-7 0 .... MissJoannaMason(7)
(I M Mason) *in rr: hit 7th: sn reminders: bhd fr 10th: sn t.o: p.u bef 3 out* **25/1**

5m 24.4s (7.40) **Going Correction** +0.325s/f (Yiel) **9** Ran SP% **117.9**
Speed ratings: **98,97,97,96,89 64, , ,**
toteswingers 1&2 £3.70, 1&3 £3.20, 2&3 £1.50 CSF £19.39 TOTE £5.30: £2.20, £1.10, £1.02; EX 12.70 Trifecta £71.20 Pool: £747.03 - 7.85 winning units..
Owner D Holmes **Bred** R Kuhne U A **Trained** Morpeth, Northumberland
■ Stewards' Enquiry : Mr D Holmes four-day ban: used whip above permitted level (May 28-30,Jun 4)

FOCUS
Not many had obvious claims in this moderate hunters' chase, which was well run. The winner ran to the level of his Musselburgh run.

288 TFROST.CO.UK SUPPLIERS TO HORSE RACING OPEN HUNTERS' CHASE (19 fncs) 3m 110y
6:55 (6:55) (Class 6) 5-Y-0+ **£1,280** (£419; £225)

Form RPR

211/ **1** **Penmore Mill (IRE)**[43] 5057 8-11-13 119 .... MrTEllis(5) 122+
(F A Hutsby) *hld up in rr: hdwy to trck ldrs 8th: led 4 out: wnt clr run-in: easily* **1/2**[1]

201/ **2** *8* **Impact Zone**[31] 9-11-7 85 .... MissJoannaMason(7) 104
(I M Mason) *chsd ldr: lft in ld 3rd: hit 5th: hdd after 5th: lft in ld bnd after 9th: hdd after 12th: outpcd 2 out: kpt on to take 2nd run-in* **8/1**[3]

333/ **3** *3* **Playing The Field (IRE)**[22] 5453 8-11-11 96 .... MrGBrewer(3) 101
(Mrs Freya Brewer) *trckd ldrs: led after 12th: drvn and hdd 4 out: 2nd and wl hld whn mstke last* **14/1**

F42/ **P** **Point Proven (IRE)**[16] 11-11-3 0 .... MrSDavies-Thomas(7)
(J T B Hunt) *chsd ldrs: drvn 9th: reminders and outpcd 12th: sn bhd: t.o 14th: p.u bef 4 out* **11/2**[2]

P33/ **P** **Alfoisin (IRE)**[31] 9-11-10 0 .... MrWBiddick
(Mrs C A Coward) *chsd ldrs: j.rt 1st: lost pl 6th: rallied 11th: outpcd whn hit 14th: sn wknd: t.o whn p.u bef 2 out* **16/1**

50/- **P** **Defying Gravity (IRE)**[17] 10-11-3 92 .... MissBAndrews(7)
(Mrs L Pomfret) *led to 2nd: chsd ldrs: mstke 6th: reminders 7th: lost pl 12th: t.o 14th: p.u bef 4 out* **20/1**

P **Tegenaria Atrica (USA)**[37] 7-11-3 0 ....(b[1]) MrMJohnson(7)
(Sara Ender) *hung rt and racd v wd: t.k.h: led 2nd: sn rn wd bnd: hit 5th: v wd bnd and hdd after 5th: led next: mstke 8th: j.rt next and sn rn v wd bnd: sn eased and t.o whn p.u bef 10th* **66/1**

6m 38.2s (15.20) **Going Correction** +0.325s/f (Yiel) **7** Ran SP% **112.0**
Speed ratings: **88,85,84, , ,**
toteswingers 1&2 £2.00, 1&3 £4.10, 2&3 £11.10 CSF £5.26 TOTE £1.10: £1.20, £1.60; EX 7.20 Trifecta £16.30 Pool: £1318.54 - 60.64 winning units..
Owner K Hutsby **Bred** P Power **Trained** Stratford-Upon-Avon, Warwicks

FOCUS
Another hunters' chase in which several looked outclassed. It was run in steady rain. The easy winner was value for further.

289 EQUIFORM NUTRITION H'CAP HURDLE (11 hdls) 2m 4f 110y
7:30 (7:30) (Class 4) (0-115,115) 4-Y-0+ **£3,249** (£954; £477; £238)

Form RPR

001/ **1** **Taigan (FR)**[25] 5387 6-11-5 **108** .... DavidEngland 115+
(Giles Smyly) *hld up in mid-div: hdwy to trck ldrs 7th: wnt handy 3rd bef 2 out: led appr last: styd on wl* **11/2**[3]

660/ **2** *1 ¾* **Knockraheen (IRE)**[44] 5039 5-11-9 **112** .... RichieMcLernon 117+
(Jonjo O'Neill) *trckd ldrs: wnt cl 2nd after 3 out: led briefly between last 2: kpt on same pce* **12/1**

POP/ **3** *7* **Jukebox Melody (IRE)**[15] 24 7-11-0 **110** ....(b) JohnDawson(7) 109
(John Wade) *chsd ldr: hit 8th: led after 3 out: hdd between last 2: wkng whn mstke last* **12/1**

003/ **4** *8* **Hi Tide (IRE)**[25] 5386 9-11-5 **108** .... DougieCostello 99
(J R Jenkins) *hld up in rr: mstke 1st: hdwy 8th: modest 4th sn after 2 out: no threat* **14/1**

612/ **5** *10* **Samingarry (FR)**[21] 5471 6-11-1 **107** ....(t) MarkQuinlan(3) 91
(Nigel Hawke) *chsd ldrs: mstke 5th: nt fluent next: drvn 3 out: wknd appr next* **4/1**[1]

640/ **6** *nk* **The Mumper (IRE)**[33] 5245 6-11-10 **113** .... GerardTumelty 95
(Alan King) *chsd ldrs: drvn 3 out: wknd appr next* **7/1**

PFP/ **7** *12* **Bugsy's Boy**[33] 5257 9-11-7 **115** ....(p) TrevorWhelan(5) 86
(George Baker) *led: hdd after 3 out: wknd appr next* **40/1**

400/ **8** *5* **Van Diemens Land (USA)**[67] 4642 6-10-10 **104** ....(t) GavinSheehan(5) 70
(Charlie Mann) *in rr: bhd and rdn 8th* **5/1**[2]

5/6- **9** *9* **Wild Tonto (IRE)**[14] 37 10-10-13 **102** .... SamTwiston-Davies 60
(Nigel Twiston-Davies) *t.k.h: sn trcking ldrs: j.rt 2nd: wknd after 3 out* **25/1**

235/ **10** *30* **Fine Resolve**[221] 1720 4-10-9 **103** ....(t) RichardJohnson 29
(Adrian Wintle) *in rr: outpcd whn mstke 8th: t.o after next* **10/1**

P06/ **P** **Caught By Witness (IRE)**[122] 3624 8-10-11 **100** ....(t) CharliePoste
(Anthony Middleton) *in rr: bhd fr 3 out: p.u bef last* **25/1**

34P/ **P** **Goodtoknow**[47] 4989 5-11-4 **110** .... JakeGreenall(3)
(Richard Lee) *prom: drvn 7th: lost pl 3 out: bhd whn p.u bef 2 out* **7/1**

5m 17.2s (4.20) **Going Correction** +0.325s/f (Yiel)
WFA 4 from 5yo+ 19lb **12** Ran SP% **118.3**
Speed ratings (Par 105): **105,104,101,98,94 94,90,88,84,73 ,**
toteswingers 1&2 £15.50, 1&3 £16.30, 2&3 £19.90 CSF £67.42 CT £766.71 TOTE £4.60: £1.80, £4.30, £4.80; EX 113.30 Trifecta £502.50 Part won. Pool: £670.06 - 0.30 winning units..
Owner M Burford **Bred** Alain Couetil & Jean-Luc Couetil **Trained** Wormington, Worcs

FOCUS
An ordinary handicap hurdle, with the top-weight rated 115, but ultra-competitive on paper. The winner is on the upgrade.

290 COOKS AND COMPANY NEWARK MAIDEN HURDLE (9 hdls) 2m
8:00 (8:00) (Class 5) 4-Y-0+ **£2,274** (£667; £333; £166)

Form RPR

F4/ **1** **Uhlan Bute (FR)**[28] 5335 5-11-0 0 .... AidanColeman 110+
(Venetia Williams) *t.k.h: sn trcking ldrs: led appr 2 out: wnt clr between last 2: easily* **11/4**[1]

60/ **2** *13* **Officially Modern (IRE)**[203] 1971 6-10-7 0 .... ConorShoemark(7) 94
(Fergal O'Brien) *t.k.h: led: hung rt and racd wd: hdd and disputing 2nd whn mstke 2 out: kpt on to take 12 l 2nd appr last* **25/1**

3 *12* **Arkansas Dave (IRE)**[9] 135 6-10-7 0 ....(t) MrSFox(7) 83
(Mark Michael McNiff, Ire) *chsd ldrs: drvn 6th: one pce fr 2 out: tk modest 3rd towards fin* **66/1**

4 *1 ¾* **Cottesmore (USA)**[242] 4-10-7 0 ....(t) JackQuinlan(3) 80
(John Ferguson) *trckd ldrs 3rd: effrt and chsd wnr 2 out: 3rd and wkng whn mstke last* **11/4**[1]

655/ **5** *18* **Bertie's Desire**[28] 5335 5-11-0 0 .... LeightonAspell 72
(Oliver Sherwood) *chsd ldrs: j.rt and wknd 3 out: hung rt run-in* **3/1**[2]

03/ **6** *23* **Sedgemoor Express (IRE)**[20] 5507 5-10-11 0 ....(t) MarkQuinlan(3) 44
(Nigel Hawke) *rr-div: j.rt 2nd: sme hdwy 4th: lost pl and j.rt 3 out: sn bhd: t.o* **33/1**

7 *1* **Mingun Bell (USA)**[15] 6-11-0 0 .... FelixDeGiles 43
(Ed de Giles) *mid-div: chsd ldrs 4th: reminders 6th: wknd appr next: t.o* **6/1**[3]

0P0/ **8** *4 ½* **Camera Shy (IRE)**[62] 4740 9-10-11 0 .... AdamWedge(3) 39
(Kevin Morgan) *in rr: nt fluent 3rd: bhd fr 6th: t.o next* **66/1**

0/ **9** *25* **Minstrel Lad**[12] 5281 5-11-0 0 .... RichieMcLernon 17
(Jonjo O'Neill) *in rr: hdwy 4th: lost pl 6th: sn bhd: hopelessly t.o* **10/1**

6/ **10** *3 ½* **Oakmoss (IRE)**[73] 7-10-9 0 ....(t) DerekFox(5) 13
(Mark Michael McNiff, Ire) *in rr: bhd fr 4th: t.o next* **33/1**

P **Primacy (IRE)**[301] 4-10-3 0 .... DougieCostello
(Neil Mulholland) *t.k.h: trckd ldrs: lost pl 6th: hmpd and blnd next: t.o whn p.u bef 2 out* **40/1**

0/ **P** **Keen's Token**[198] 2073 7-10-11 0 .... BrianToomey(3)
(Clive Mulhall) *nt jump wl in rr: bhd fr 5th: t.o 3 out: p.u bef 2 out* **100/1**

4m 3.8s (6.80) **Going Correction** +0.325s/f (Yiel)
WFA 4 from 5yo+ 18lb **12** Ran SP% **117.9**
Speed ratings (Par 103): **96,89,83,82,73 62,61,59,46,45 ,**
toteswingers 1&2 £12.40, 1&3 £50.40, 2&3 £50.40 CSF £68.68 TOTE £4.60: £1.80, £5.40, £9.50; EX 65.80 Trifecta £435.20 Part won. Pool: £580.32 - 0.09 winning units..
Owner R Elliott & N Coe **Bred** Herve D'Armaille **Trained** Kings Caple, H'fords

FOCUS
A fascinating clutch of first-time hurdlers added spice to this maiden event. Not an easy race to put a figure on but it looks a step up from the winner.

291 SOUTHWELL INTERMEDIATE NATIONAL HUNT FLAT RACE (CONDITIONALS/AMATEURS) 2m
8:30 (8:30) (Class 6) 4-6-Y-0 **£1,642** (£478; £239)

Form RPR

1 **Call The Cops (IRE)** 4-10-9 0 .... NicodeBoinville(5) 106+
(Nicky Henderson) *trckd ldrs: chsd ldr over 2f out: led jst ins fnl f: styd on wl* **1/1**[1]

6/ **2** *3 ¼* **Fond Memory (IRE)**[33] 5254 5-10-11 0 .... GeraldQuinn(7) 105
(Nigel Twiston-Davies) *led 2f: upsides 8f out: led 7f out: qcknd pce 5f out: hdd jst ins fnl f: styd on same pce* **7/1**

5- **3** *½* **Balinderry (IRE)**[4] 207 6-10-11 0 .... PaulBohan(7) 104
(Steve Gollings) *trckd ldrs: effrt over 3f out: hung lft over 1f out: kpt on same pce* **6/1**[3]

4/ **4** *12* **Barney Rubble**[18] 5550 4-10-7 0 .... MissHBethell(7) 88
(Philip Kirby) *chsd ldrs: pushed along 8f out: outpcd and lost pl over 4f out: kpt on fnl 2f: tk modest 4th nr fin* **5/2**[2]

S/5- **5** *hd* **Farmer's Friend**[12] 76 4-11-0 0 ....[1] DonalDevereux 88
(John Mackie) *led at stdy pce after 2f: hdd 7f out: wknd over 1f out* **10/1**

0/0- **6** *72* **Lenderking (IRE)**[4] 207 5-10-11 0 .... GerardGalligan(7) 20
(Michael Chapman) *hld up in rr: drvn over 5f out: sn lost tch: t.o 3f out: eventually completed* **100/1**

006/ **7** *5* **Share The Dosh**[76] 4459 5-10-8 0 .... JackQuinlan(3) 8
(J R Jenkins) *in rr: pushed along after 6f: outpcd 7f out: sn bhd: t.o 4f out: eventually completed* **20/1**

4m 10.2s (18.80) **Going Correction** +0.325s/f (Yiel) **7** Ran SP% **115.9**
Speed ratings: **66,64,64,58,58 22,19**
toteswingers 1&2 £3.40, 1&3 £2.70, 2&3 £2.90 CSF £9.05 TOTE £2.30: £1.60, £2.70; EX 7.20 Trifecta £39.50 Pool: £596.16 - 11.31 winning units..
Owner Matt & Lauren Morgan **Bred** Martin Donnellan **Trained** Upper Lambourn, Berks

FOCUS
Not much worthwhile form evaluate in this small-field finale which was run at slow pace early on. It has been given a token rating through the second.
T/Plt: £70.50 to a £1 stake. Pool: £51,364.86 - 531.19 winning tickets. T/Qpdt: £9.60 to a £1 stake. Pool: £5144.48 - 395.90 winning tickets. WG

188 WINCANTON (R-H)
Tuesday, May 14

OFFICIAL GOING: Good (good to firm in places) changing to good to soft after race 3 (3.20).
Wind: quite strong across Weather: rain, heavy at times

292 BATHWICK TYRES MARES' NOVICES' HURDLE (8 hdls) 2m
2:20 (2:20) (Class 4) 4-Y-0+ **£3,249** (£954; £477; £238)

Form RPR

2/ **1** **Amistress**[21] 5479 5-10-11 0 .... PaddyBrennan 105+
(Renee Robeson) *trckd clr ldr: led appr 2 out: sn rdn: kpt on gamely: drvn out* **5/1**[3]

433/ **2** *1 ¼* **Revaader**[45] 5023 5-10-11 87 .... TommyPhelan 103
(Mark Gillard) *led: clr 2nd: rdn and hdd appr 2 out: looked hld in 3rd between last 2 whn hanging lft: rallied gamely run-in: regained 2nd nr fin* **16/1**

214/ **3** *nk* **Springinherstep (IRE)**[26] 5358 6-11-4 126 .... DavidBass 111
(Nicky Henderson) *mid-div: wnt 3rd 3 out: rdn to cl on ldr appr 2 out: chsd wnr between last 2: kpt on but being hld fr last: lost 2nd nr fin* **4/6**[1]

P/0- **4** *30* **Call Me April**[14] 41 5-10-11 0....................................[1] AndrewThornton 76
(Karen George) *hld up: rdn after 3 out: wnt modest 4th sn after 2 out: nvr on terms w ldrs* **50/1**

604/ **5** *7* **Nurse Brace**[24] 4-10-7 0.. DonalDevereux 65
(David Brace) *mid-div: rdn after 3 out: wknd between last 2: t.o* **33/1**

4/1- **6** *6* **Fairyinthewind (IRE)**[14] 46 4-11-0 0.............................. WayneHutchinson 67
(Alan King) *chsd ldrs: rdn in btn 4th after 3 out: wkng whn hit next: t.o* **11/4**[2]

/5- **7** *13* **Bedibyes**[5] 192 5-10-8 0.. JamesBest(3) 52
(Richard Mitchell) *hld up: nt fluent 3rd: no ch fr 3 out: t.o* **50/1**

6/0- **8** *38* **Colin's Nightmare**[12] 85 5-10-11 0.................................... DarylJacob 18
(Nick Mitchell) *chsd ldrs tl 3rd: struggling in rr fr next: t.o* **33/1**

0/0- **R** **Lucette**[14] 46 5-10-6 0.. EdCookson(5)
(Kim Bailey) *plld hrd: hld up: rn out on bnd after 3rd* **50/1**

3m 45.1s (-3.80) **Going Correction** -0.125s/f (Good)
WFA 4 from 5yo+ 18lb **9** Ran SP% **121.0**
Speed ratings (Par 105): **104,103,103,88,84 81,75,56,**
toteswingers 1&2 £6.90, 1&3 £1.70, 2&3 £6.80 CSF £64.50 TOTE £5.90: £1.70, £4.70, £1.02; EX 40.20 Trifecta £205.20 Pool: £847.50 - 3.09 winning units..
Owner Mrs P Robeson **Bred** Southcourt Stud **Trained** Tyringham, Bucks

FOCUS
Both courses moved out 5yds on to better ground. They were strung out from an early stage in this mares-only novices' hurdle and very few got into it given the quickly deteriorating conditions. The winner improved to the level expected of her Flat form.

293 JOCKEY CLUB CATERING H'CAP HURDLE (10 hdls) 2m 4f
2:50 (2:50) (Class 5) (0-100,100) 4-Y-0+ **£1,949** (£572; £286; £143)

Form RPR

5/2- **1** **Chilworth Screamer**[5] 188 5-11-6 **94**.......................... RichardJohnson 106+
(Chris Gordon) *mid-div on outer: hdwy after 7th: chalng whn wnt rt 2 out: sn led: pushed clr run-in: styd on strly* **11/4**[1]

303/ **2** *10* **Finmerello**[16] 2 7-11-3 **91**.. NickScholfield 95
(Kim Bailey) *trckd ldrs: awkward 2nd: led 3 out: rdn whn pressed bef 2 out: hdd bef last: sn hld: kpt on same pce* **5/1**[3]

4/2- **3** *18* **Lady Bridget**[12] 83 5-10-4 **85**....................................(bt) JakeHodson(7) 71
(Mark Gillard) *prom: disp ld after 5th tl rdn 3 out: hld fr next: styd on same pce to regain 3rd towards fin* **8/1**

055/ **4** *½* **Monderon (FR)**[33] 5241 6-11-9 **100**................................ MattGriffiths(3) 85
(Richard Hawker) *hld up towards rr: hdwy after 7th: rdn into 3rd after 3 out: styd on same pce fr next: lost 3rd towards fin* **25/1**

250/ **5** *10* **Star Of Massini (IRE)**[23] 5440 6-11-5 **100**.................. MrKevinJones(7) 76
(Seamus Mullins) *led tl 3rd: trckd ldrs tl rdn after 3 out: sn btn* **8/1**

4/2- **6** *16* **Present Accepted**[7] 155 6-9-11 **74** oh7.......................... JamesBest(3) 36
(Nerys Dutfield) *hld up towards rr: rdn after 3 out: nvr any imp: wknd 2 out: t.o* **7/2**[2]

POP/ **7** *8* **Nothingbutthetruth (IRE)**[18] 5554 9-11-1 **92**..........(tp) MichealNolan(3) 47
(Richard Woollacott) *trckd ldrs: led 3rd: jnd after 5th: hdd 3 out: sn rdn: wknd bef next: t.o* **20/1**

340/ **8** *5* **Jezza**[21] 2405 7-11-11 **99**.. AndrewThornton 49
(Karen George) *mid-div: nt fluent 7th: wknd after 3 out: t.o* **20/1**

565/ **9** *13* **Dancing Teasel**[476] 3899 6-11-4 **92**............................ DominicElsworth 31
(Emma Lavelle) *a in rr: t.o* **16/1**

036/ **P** **Cnoc Moy (IRE)**[76] 4464 9-10-13 **87**.................................... DaveCrosse
(Helen Rees) *mid-div: pushed along after 6th: wknd after 3 out: t.o whn p.u bef last* **33/1**

U06/ **F** **Glenwood Present (IRE)**[20] 5507 6-9-13 **76** oh5 ow2(t) GilesHawkins(3) 60
(Bob Buckler) *trckd ldrs: rdn whn outpcd after 3 out: no ch after: disputing btn 5th whn fell last* **12/1**

0P0/ **P** **Southfork**[71] 4571 4-10-0 **86**..(t) ThomasGarner(7)
(Brendan Powell) *mid-div tl wknd bef 3 out: t.o whn p.u bef 2 out* **20/1**

4m 53.5s (-3.30) **Going Correction** -0.125s/f (Good)
WFA 4 from 5yo+ 19lb **12** Ran SP% **122.4**
Speed ratings (Par 103): **101,97,89,89,85 79,76,74,68, ,**
toteswingers 1&2 £4.00, 1&3 £1.80, 2&3 £6.20 CSF £16.27 CT £102.29 TOTE £4.10: £2.10, £2.60, £1.70; EX 18.50 Trifecta £29.20 Pool: £694.45 - 17.77 winning units..
Owner 7Rus **Bred** Norman Court Stud **Trained** Morestead, Hants

FOCUS
A moderate handicap hurdle, run at a steady pace in worsening conditions. The first two are rated similar to their good recent runs.

294 RACECOURSEBOND.COM H'CAP CHASE (21 fncs) 3m 1f 110y
3:20 (3:20) (Class 4) (0-120,120) 5-Y-0+ **£3,898** (£1,144; £572; £286)

Form RPR

222/ **1** **Financial Climate (IRE)**[23] 5375 6-10-12 **113**............ ThomasGarner(7) 123+
(Oliver Sherwood) *in tch: disp 2nd 16th: chal 4 out: led appr 3 out: asserted gng to the last: styd on: rdn out* **7/2**[1]

4/4- **2** *2½* **Palace Jester**[14] 39 8-11-8 **116**.................................(t) TomScudamore 123
(David Pipe) *led: rdn whn hdd appr 3 out: j. sltly rt last 3: kpt pressing wnr tl no ex appr last* **4/1**[2]

521/ **3** *¾* **Thomas Wild**[21] 5474 8-11-2 **113**................................... MichealNolan(3) 119
(Philip Hobbs) *trckd ldrs: disp 2nd 15th tl rdn after 4 out: styd on same pce fr next* **7/2**[1]

203/ **4** *74* **Plein Pouvoir (FR)**[53] 4902 10-11-12 **120**........................ AidanColeman 59
(Venetia Williams) *chsd ldrs tl rdn 15th: sn wknd: t.o whn lft 4th and hmpd 2 out* **6/1**[3]

21/ **5** *15* **Dunkelly Castle (IRE)**[188] 2270 9-10-11 **105**...................(t) FelixDeGiles 31
(Brendan Powell) *prom tl rdn after 14th: wknd 17th: t.o* **7/1**

4B4/ **U** **Shake The Barley (IRE)**[31] 5294 10-10-10 **104**...........(p) PaddyBrennan
(Tom George) *trckd ldrs: struggling 16th: wknd after next: modest 4th whn blnd bdly and uns rdr 2 out* **16/1**

1U/- **P** **Addiction**[33] 5259 8-11-9 **117**..(tp) NickScholfield
(Jeremy Scott) *nvr fluent: rarely travelling: j.lft: a last: blnd 2nd: lost tch fr 15th: t.o whn p.u bef 4 out* **4/1**[2]

6m 38.9s (-0.60) **Going Correction** -0.025s/f (Good) **7** Ran SP% **117.1**
Speed ratings: **99,98,98,75,70 ,**
toteswingers 1&2 £2.00, 1&3 £1.70, 2&3 £3.90 CSF £18.93 CT £52.45 TOTE £5.30: £3.00, £2.40; EX 27.10 Trifecta £72.70 Pool: £845.29 - 8.71 winning units..
Owner Mrs Sara Fillery **Bred** Mrs E M Motherway **Trained** Upper Lambourn, Berks

FOCUS
A decent turnout for the feature handicap chase but, with only five finishers and many of these appearing not to cope with the softening ground, it remains to be seen how well the form holds up. It seems sound at face value.

295 SOUTH-WEST RACING CLUB H'CAP HURDLE (11 hdls) 2m 6f
3:50 (3:50) (Class 5) (0-100,100) 4-Y-0+ **£1,949** (£572; £286; £143)

Form RPR

0/- **1** **Titch Strider (IRE)**[23] 5440 8-11-0 **88**............................... ConorO'Farrell 96
(John Panvert) *patiently rdn in last: stdy prog fr 8th: trckd ldr after 2 out: chal last: sn rdn to take narrow advantage: edging clr whn veered rt towards fin* **7/1**[3]

2/4- **2** *1½* **Little Eaglet (IRE)**[14] 42 9-10-12 **86**.................................... LiamHeard 93
(Colin Heard) *trckd ldrs: led after 3 out: wandered whn rdn after 2 out: hdd sn after last: kpt on but hld whn hmpd towards fin* **5/1**[2]

4FP/ **3** *12* **Special Boru (IRE)**[216] 1789 7-10-4 **78**..........................(t) BrendanPowell 74
(Sarah Kerswell) *t.k.h in mid-div: hdwy after 8th: trckd ldr gng to 2 out tl rdn bef last: kpt on same pce* **20/1**

0/4- **4** *15* **Gleannacreim (IRE)**[12] 79 10-9-7 **74** oh5........................ MrMHeard(7) 57
(Carroll Gray) *led tl rdn and hdd sn after 3 out: wknd bef next* **20/1**

00/- **5** *10* **Boomtown Kat**[76] 4461 9-11-12 **100**.........................(b[1]) AndrewThornton 74
(Karen George) *in tch on outer: hdwy after 4th to trck ldrs: rdn after 3 out: wknd bef next* **8/1**

000/ **6** *¾* **Custer Of The West (IRE)**[40] 5148 8-11-8 **96**......(b[1]) WayneHutchinson 69
(Alan King) *kpt tight to inner: mid-div: hdwy 3 out: short of room on bnd sn after: rdn to chse ldng pair briefly gng to 2 out: sn wknd* **3/1**[1]

500/ **7** *shd* **Shot In The Dark (IRE)**[25] 5376 4-11-4 **97**............................ MarkGrant 65
(Jonathan Geake) *hld up: making hdwy whn mstke 7th: chal after 3 out: wknd bef next* **20/1**

0/4- **8** *15* **Spanish Fork (IRE)**[11] 99 4-11-5 **98**............................ MarcGoldstein 52
(Sheena West) *chsd ldrs: rdn after 7th: wknd bef 2 out: t.o* **5/1**[2]

0P0/ **9** *8* **Black Phantom (IRE)**[68] 4614 7-10-13 **87**.....................(t) NickScholfield 39
(Mark Gillard) *chsd ldrs: nudged along after 5th: wknd after 7th: t.o* **7/1**[3]

PP4/ **P** **Notcantdoit (IRE)**[38] 5184 6-10-0 **77**.................................. JamesBest(3)
(Polly Gundry) *trckd ldrs: rchd for 3rd: lost pl next: lost tch qckly after 6th: p.u bef next* **10/1**

5m 21.1s (-5.40) **Going Correction** -0.125s/f (Good)
WFA 4 from 5yo+ 19lb **10** Ran SP% **117.8**
Speed ratings (Par 103): **104,103,99,93,90 89,89,84,81,**
toteswingers 1&2 £4.80, 1&3 £31.30, 2&3 £23.50 CSF £41.49 CT £660.59 TOTE £8.70: £2.30, £1.50, £6.10; EX 26.50 Trifecta £641.70 Part won. Pool: £855.62 - 0.06 winning units..
Owner J F Panvert **Bred** Seamus O'Farrell **Trained** Stoodleigh, Devon

FOCUS
A weak handicap hurdle. The winner is rated in line with his best bumper runs.

296 PIPER HEIDSIECK NOVICES' CHASE (21 fncs) 3m 1f 110y
4:20 (4:20) (Class 4) 5-Y-0+ **£3,994** (£1,240; £667)

Form RPR

130/ **1** **Seven Woods (IRE)**[164] 2773 7-10-12 123........................ PaddyBrennan 130+
(Tom George) *trckd ldrs: rdn after 4 out: clsng whn blnd 2 out: wnt 3 l 2nd bef last: str run fnl 120yds: led fnl strides* **3/1**[3]

213/ **2** *½* **Oscargo (IRE)**[16] 9 9-11-5 128..(t) DarylJacob 134
(Paul Nicholls) *w ldr: wnt sltly lft 4th: led 3 out: sn rdn: 3 l clr last: styd on but no ex whn collared fnl strides* **7/2**

2U6/ **3** *11* **Barlow (IRE)**[16] 6 6-10-12 126.. NoelFehily 120
(Warren Greatrex) *led: j. sltly lft at times: hit 16th: hdd 3 out: sn rdn: no ex whn lost 2nd appr last* **2/1**[1]

512/ **P** **Velator**[26] 5365 6-11-5 128... NickScholfield
(Anthony Honeyball) *trckd ldrs: nudged along after 14th: rdn after 17th: qckly btn: t.o whn p.u bef 3 out* **5/2**[2]

6m 37.6s (-1.90) **Going Correction** -0.025s/f (Good) **4** Ran SP% **109.1**
Speed ratings: **101,100,97,**
CSF £12.68 TOTE £6.00; EX 15.10 Trifecta £27.50 Pool: £1148.76 - 31.31 winning units..
Owner M K George **Bred** Liam Neilan **Trained** Slad, Gloucs
■ Stewards' Enquiry : Paddy Brennan three-day ban: used whip without giving gelding time to respond (May 28-30)

FOCUS
There wasn't a great deal to choose between any of these in the betting and it served up a tremendous finish. The winner has the potential to rate higher if his jumping improves.

297 DOROTHY HALLAM MEMORIAL WESSEX AREA LADY RIDERS' SERIES FINAL HUNTERS' CHASE (17 fncs) 2m 5f
4:50 (4:50) (Class 5) 5-Y-0+ **£2,183** (£677; £338; £169)

Form RPR

PP3/ **1** **Master Medic (IRE)**[16] 12-11-3 0......................... MissEEMacMahon(7) 106+
(Mrs S Alner) *trckd ldr: pushed along fr 11th: rdn after 13th: led 3 out: kpt on and a holding runner-up fr last: rdn out* **4/7**[1]

44F/ **2** *1¼* **Extra Bold**[10] 11-11-7 0.. MissAGoschen(5) 103
(Miss A Goschen) *j.lft at times: led: rdn whn hdd 3 out: rallied appr last: kpt on but a being hld run-in* **6/1**[3]

015/ **3** *11* **Quedillac (FR)**[9] 9-11-10 99.. MissGAndrews 97
(S Penny) *trckd ldrs: rdn to chse ldr after 13th tl hit 4 out: hld fr next: styd on same pce* **3/1**[2]

PP3/ **4** *4½* **Near The Water (IRE)**[16] 9-11-3 0................................. MissJBuck(7) 89
(R J Harraway) *hld up in 5th but wl in tch: rdn whn outpcd gng to 4 out: styd on again fr 2 out but nvr threatened to get bk on terms* **16/1**

PPP/ **P** **Nautical Approach (IRE)**[17] 10-11-3 0......(t) MissEmily-JaneHarbour(7)
(S G Allen) *trckd ldng trio: nt fluent 2nd: mstke 8th: nt fluent next: wknd 12th: t.o whn p.u after 4 out* **50/1**

5m 33.1s (7.90) **Going Correction** -0.025s/f (Good) **5** Ran SP% **110.8**
Speed ratings: **83,82,78,76,**
CSF £4.76 TOTE £1.50: £1.10, £2.40; EX 3.70 Trifecta £5.50 Pool: £1602.12 - 216.66 winning units..
Owner Pell-Mell Partners **Bred** Robert McCarthy **Trained** Droop, Dorset

FOCUS
A class horse (once rated 156 under rules) won nicely and can probably still do better than this.

298 WATCH RACING UK ON SKY 432 STANDARD OPEN NATIONAL HUNT FLAT RACE 2m
5:25 (5:25) (Class 6) 4-6-Y-O **£1,624** (£477; £238; £119)

Form RPR

1 **Hologram** 4-10-12 0.. BrendanPowell 110+
(David Elsworth) *hld up in tch: tk clsr order 5f out: chal over 2f out: led over 1f out: styd on wl: rdn out* **9/2**[3]

6/ **2** 3½ **Zulu Oscar**[33] 5263 4-10-12 0 NoelFehily 107
(Harry Fry) *trckd ldrs: rdn to chal between horses 2f out: kpt on same pce ent fnl f* **5/2**[1]

0/ **3** 1½ **Black Cow (IRE)**[80] 4391 5-11-2 0 DarylJacob 110
(Paul Nicholls) *led: rdn whn pressed over 2f out: hdd over 1f out: kpt on same pce* **7/2**[2]

5/ **4** 20 **Miller's Maverick**[16] 14 5-11-2 0 TomScudamore 92
(Hughie Morrison) *hld up in tch: tk clsr order 1/2-way: chal 3f out: sn rdn: grad fdd* **7/2**[2]

0/ **5** 9 **Upham Running (IRE)**[23] 5444 5-11-2 0 MarkGrant 84
(Kate Buckett) *trckd ldrs: rdn over 2f out: sn wknd* **16/1**

0/ **6** 32 **Flying Quest**[68] 4621 4-10-9 0 MichealNolan(3) 51
(Linda Blackford) *trckd ldrs tl over 4f out: sn wknd: t.o* **50/1**

7 9 **Fereni** 4-10-5 0 NickScholfield 36
(Nick Williams) *hld up last: wknd over 3f out: t.o* **7/1**

0/ **8** 106 **Triple Brandy**[28] 5333 4-10-12 0 AndrewThornton
(Karen George) *trckd ldrs tl wknd over 3f out: hung bdly lft and virtually p.u wl over 2f out* **50/1**

3m 43.4s (0.10) **Going Correction** -0.125s/f (Good)
WFA 4 from 5yo 4lb **8** Ran SP% **113.5**
Speed ratings: **94,92,91,81,77 61,56,**
toteswingers 1&2 £2.80, 1&3 £3.70, 2&3 £2.50 CSF £15.92 TOTE £4.60: £2.20, £1.90, £1.10; EX 13.20 Trifecta £57.30 Pool: £550.92 - 7.20 winning units..
Owner Lordship Stud **Bred** Lordship Stud **Trained** Newmarket, Suffolk

FOCUS
An informative bumper and a likeable performance from the winner, who should go on to rate higher.
T/Plt: £244.90 to a £1 stake. Pool: £52,617.26 - 156.80 winning tickets. T/Qpdt: £95.30 to a £1 stake. Pool: £3028.63 - 23.50 winning tickets. TM

299 - 301a (Foreign Racing) - See Raceform Interactive

[95]FONTWELL (L-H)
Wednesday, May 15

OFFICIAL GOING: Good to soft (6.8)
Wind: fairly light, half behind Weather: bright spells and showers

302 32RED CASINO BEGINNERS' CHASE (16 fncs) 2m 6f
2:05 (2:05) (Class 4) 5-Y-0+ **£3,861** (£1,198; £645)

Form RPR
34P/ **1** **Deireadh Re (IRE)**[136] 3380 7-11-0 123 DarylJacob 130+
(Paul Nicholls) *chsd ldng pair: effrt to chal 3 out: edgd lft and bmpd rival bef next: mstke 2 out: drvn to ld fnl 100yds: styd on wl* **9/4**[2]

432/ **2** 2¼ **Silver Commander**[17] 9 6-11-0 120 (t) JackDoyle 128+
(Victor Dartnall) *chsd ldr: mstke 1st: led on inner after 10th: rdn: hrd pressed and bmpd bef 2 out: hdd fnl 100yds: no ex and wknd towards fin* **7/4**[1]

000/ **3** 2¼ **American Spin**[39] 5175 9-11-0 0 JamieMoore 124+
(Luke Dace) *led tl hdd and rdn after 10th: mstke 12th: drvn and outpcd in 3rd bef 3 out: wl hld 2 out: kpt on again flat* **7/4**[1]

P05/ **P** **Madame Jasmine**[26] 5375 8-10-7 115 ColinBolger
(Suzy Smith) *j.rt: a last and nvr on terms: niggled along after 4th: lost tch 9th: t.o after next tl p.u 13th: dismntd* **16/1**[3]

033/ **P** **Fitz Volonte**[68] 4636 6-10-7 100 MrJMartin(7)
(Andrew J Martin) *a 4th but nvr on terms w ldng trio: rdn and lost tch after 10th: t.o 12th tl p.u last* **33/1**

5m 30.0s (-13.00) **Going Correction** -0.40s/f (Good) **5** Ran SP% **112.3**
Speed ratings: **107,106,105, ,**
CSF £7.05 TOTE £3.00: £1.50, £1.30; EX 5.80 Trifecta £13.20 Pool: £739.04 - 41.73 winning units..
Owner Ian J Fogg & Mrs Wendy Fogg **Bred** Matthew McGoona **Trained** Ditcheat, Somerset

FOCUS
Fences on outer line, hurdles on middle line. A fair beginners' chase, run at a respectable pace.

303 THANKS JO LITTMODEN FOR 10 GREAT YEARS NOVICES' H'CAP CHASE (13 fncs) 2m 2f
2:35 (2:35) (Class 5) (0-95,94) 5-Y-0+ **£2,144** (£629; £314; £157)

Form RPR
P03/ **1** **Time Book (IRE)**[24] 5434 7-10-11 79 (t) BrendanPowell 93+
(Colin Tizzard) *lft in ld 1st: mde virtually all after: mstke 9th: clr 3 out: stdd into last and reduced advantage: drvn and idling flat: hrd pressed towards fin: hdd cl home: led again on post* **2/1**[1]

F03/ **2** nse **Shantou Breeze (IRE)**[24] 5443 6-11-1 83 MarcGoldstein 94
(Michael Madgwick) *chsd wnr 6th: mstke 6th: drvn and unable qck bef 3 out: looked hld 2 out: clsd on wnr last: plugged on and grad clsd on wnr to ld cl home: hdd on post* **5/1**[3]

051/ **3** 8 **Jamesson (IRE)**[19] 5552 8-11-3 90 GavinSheehan(5) 96
(Jamie Snowden) *hld up in tch in rr: mstke 9th: effrt and plenty to do in 4th after next: wnt 3rd and j.lft 3 out and next: no imp* **2/1**[1]

006/ **4** 1 **Dr Thistle (IRE)**[26] 5375 6-11-12 94 (v[1]) JamieMoore 98
(Gary Moore) *j.rt and mstkes: chsd ldrs: rdn after 5th: outpcd 10th: 4th and wl hld whn hmpd 3 out: n.d but plugged on flat* **4/1**[2]

P0P/ **P** **Queen Of The West (IRE)**[19] 5555 6-10-7 75 (t) DaveCrosse
(Jamie Snowden) *j. v awkwardly: led tl j. v awkwardly and hdd 1st: chsd wnr tl 5th: reminders bef next: drvn and dropped to rr after 7th: t.o whn p.u 3 out* **16/1**

4m 41.0s (6.30) **Going Correction** -0.40s/f (Good) **5** Ran SP% **109.2**
Speed ratings: **78,77,74,73,**
CSF £11.62 TOTE £3.10: £2.00, £2.70; EX 11.00 Trifecta £26.30 Pool: £490.10 - 13.93 winning units..
Owner D V Stevens **Bred** Denis McDonnell **Trained** Milborne Port, Dorset

FOCUS
This pace was steady for this modest handicap.

304 FULLERS LONDON PRIDE H'CAP HURDLE (9 hdls) 2m 2f 110y
3:05 (3:05) (Class 3) (0-130,130) 4-Y-0+ **£5,393** (£1,583; £791; £395)

Form RPR
006/ **1** **Taste The Wine (IRE)**[12] 5356 7-9-10 105 RobertWilliams(5) 109
(Bernard Llewellyn) *in tch in midfield: effrt to chse ldr 2 out: rdn and styd on to chal last: drvn and sustained duel w rival tl led fnl 75yds: styd on wl* **9/2**[2]

401/ **2** ¾ **Scoglio**[17] 10 5-10-12 116 LeeEdwards 119
(Dave Roberts) *in tch in midfield: effrt to join ldrs after 3 out: led bef next: hrd pressed last: edgd rt u.p flat: hdd and no ex fnl 75yds* **8/1**

341/ **3** 5 **Kambis**[26] 5376 5-11-7 125 JamieMoore 126+
(Gary Moore) *in tch in midfield: lost pl and dropped to last pair bef 3 out: hdwy bef 2 out: drvn and styd on to chse ldrs whn bmpd last: kpt on same pce flat: wnt 3rd cl home* **5/1**[3]

210/ **4** ½ **Canadian Diamond (IRE)**[39] 5178 6-11-5 123 RichardKilloran 122
(Brendan Powell) *t.k.h: hld up in tch in last pair: hdwy bef 3 out: rdn bef 2 out: drvn and chsd ldng pair between last 2: mstke and wnt lft last: styd on same pce flat: lost 3rd cl home* **4/1**[1]

04P/ **5** 12 **Hi Note**[27] 5360 5-11-12 130 MarcGoldstein 118
(Sheena West) *pressed ldr tl outpcd u.p bef 2 out: 5th and btn between last 2: wknd flat* **6/1**

040/ **6** 4 **Reggie Perrin**[44] 5081 5-9-10 110 PaddyBradley(10) 94
(Pat Phelan) *in tch in rr: rdn after 5th: lost tch 3 out: rallied and styd on past btn horses flat: nvr trbld ldrs* **10/1**

133/ **7** 1 **Ladies Dancing**[17] 10 7-10-11 115 JamesDavies 98
(Chris Down) *chsd ldrs: rdn and struggling after 3 out: btn bef next: wknd between last 2* **8/1**

405/ **8** 1¾ **Darkestbeforedawn (IRE)**[19] 5537 6-11-3 121 TomO'Brien 103
(Caroline Keevil) *led tl bef 2 out: sn outpcd and btn: wknd bef last* **5/1**[3]

660/ **9** 20 **Mohanad (IRE)**[29] 5340 7-11-2 120 LeightonAspell 84
(Philip Hide) *chsd ldrs: mstke 6th: lost pl and rdn sn after next: wknd bef 2 out: wl bhd and eased flat: t.o* **33/1**

4m 25.8s (-8.50) **Going Correction** -0.20s/f (Good) **9** Ran SP% **120.1**
Speed ratings (Par 107): **109,108,106,106,101 99,99,98,90**
toteswingers 1&2 £5.30, 1&3 £13.70, 2&3 £4.10 CSF £41.69 CT £190.39 TOTE £5.50: £1.30, £3.60, £1.90; EX 79.30 Trifecta £558.30 Part won. Pool: £744.46 - 0.98 winning units..
Owner Alan J Williams **Bred** Trevor Reilly **Trained** Fochriw, Caerphilly

FOCUS
A competitive contest, run at a steady pace.

305 32RED H'CAP CHASE (15 fncs) 2m 4f
3:40 (3:40) (Class 5) (0-100,100) 5-Y-0+ **£2,144** (£629; £314; £157)

Form RPR
241/ **1** **Princely Hero (IRE)**[19] 5555 9-11-1 89 (p) BrendanPowell 100
(Chris Gordon) *chsd ldrs: rdn and outpcd after 9th: rdn and chsd ldr after 12th: 7 l down next: fnlly responded to press and styd on last: swtchd rt and led fnl 100yds: sn in command and ears pricked* **3/1**[2]

6/5- **2** 2¼ **Upton Mead (IRE)**[3] 245 6-10-11 92 (b[1]) MrMatthewStanley(7) 102
(Kevin Tork) *chsd ldrs and travelled wl: upsides ldr 8th: led 11th: wnt clr next: 7 l ld whn mstke and pckd 2 out: drvn flat: hdd fnl 100yds: sn btn* **7/1**

/34- **3** 15 **Lajidaal (USA)**[3] 242 6-11-1 89 (v) JamieMoore 84
(Gary Moore) *led tl after 9th: 3rd and drvn next: outpcd 11th: wknd after 12th: lft 4th 3 out: wnt modest 4th between last 2* **7/2**[3]

345/ **4** 12 **Owner Occupier**[16] 34 8-10-7 81 MarcGoldstein 66
(Chris Gordon) *in tch in midfield: drvn and outpcd after 11th: lft modest 5th and hmpd 3 out: wknd* **6/1**

0/4- **5** 3¼ **Morestead (IRE)**[12] 98 8-11-12 100 (vt) TomO'Brien 82
(Brendan Powell) *chsd ldrs tl led after 9th: hdd 11th and sn outpcd by wnr: wkng whn lft 3rd 3 out: lost 3rd and fdd between last 2* **10/1**

06P/ **P** **Curragh Dancer (FR)**[19] 5552 10-9-12 75 oh3 ow1 KielanWoods(3)
(Paddy Butler) *nvr gng wl: in midfield whn j. awkwardly 1st: dropped to rr and rdn 5th: lost tch after 10th: t.o whn p.u bef 3 out* **33/1**

0/5- **P** **Francis Du Mesnil (FR)**[15] 44 11-10-11 85 (bt[1]) DPFahy
(Liam Corcoran) *a towards rr: rdn and lost tch after 10th: t.o whn p.u 3 out* **33/1**

332/ **F** **Inner Steel (IRE)**[19] 5554 8-11-9 97 LeightonAspell
(Lydia Richards) *bhd: mstke 4th: rdn after 9th: sme hdwy u.p 12th: 3rd and stl plenty to do whn fell 3 out* **11/4**[1]

4m 59.6s (-7.70) **Going Correction** -0.40s/f (Good) **8** Ran SP% **115.6**
Speed ratings: **99,98,92,87,86 , ,**
toteswingers 1&2 £7.90, 1&3 £3.90, 2&3 £4.40 CSF £24.52 CT £74.76 TOTE £4.10: £1.10, £3.00, £2.80; EX 33.20 Trifecta £63.60 Pool: £870.17 - 10.25 winning units..
Owner L Gilbert **Bred** Morristown Lattin Stud **Trained** Morestead, Hants

FOCUS
A moderate event run at a fair pace, with few able to get competitive.

306 32RED.COM MAIDEN HURDLE (DIV I) (9 hdls) 2m 2f 110y
4:15 (4:15) (Class 4) 4-Y-0+ **£3,119** (£915; £457; £228)

Form RPR
3/ **1** **Montefeltro**[220] 1766 5-10-11 0 JackQuinlan(3) 113+
(John Ferguson) *t.k.h: chsd ldrs tl led 3 out: sn drew clr w runner-up: blnd 2 out: readily asserted between last 2: in command whn rn green and hung rt and lft flat: pushed out: easily* **1/2**[1]

64P/ **2** 6 **Foxes Bridge**[33] 5264 5-11-0 0 BrendanPowell 104
(Colin Tizzard) *w ldr tl drew clr w wnr sn after 3 out: sn drvn: outpcd and btn between last 2: kpt on* **4/1**[2]

00/ **3** 18 **Agincourt Reef (IRE)**[29] 5335 4-10-9 0 JamieMoore 85
(Gary Moore) *t.k.h: mstke 2nd: rdn and wknd sn after 3 out: 5th and wl btn bef next: plugged on flat to snatch 3rd last strides* **14/1**

400/ **4** hd **Dont Call Me Oscar (IRE)**[22] 5468 6-11-0 0 (t) TommyPhelan 90
(Mark Gillard) *led: mstke 3rd: hdd 3 out: sn outpcd and wl btn next: lost 3rd last strides* **12/1**

P/ **5** 6 **River Sava (IRE)**[70] 4597 6-10-11 0 JeremiahMcGrath(3) 84
(Jamie Poulton) *hld up in tch in rr: mstke 2nd: hdwy after 5th: rdn and outpcd sn after 3 out: 4th and wl btn next* **8/1**[3]

0PP/ **6** 18 **La Madonnina (IRE)**[71] 4573 5-10-7 0 TomO'Brien 59
(Caroline Keevil) *hld up in tch in rr: hdwy after 5th: rdn and wknd sn after 3 out: 6th and wl btn next: t.o* **25/1**

0/0- **7** 44 **Buffy Brosnan**[12] 95 5-11-0 0 JackDoyle 26
(Chris Gordon) *in tch in midfield: dropped to rr and rdn 4th: lost tch 6th: wl t.o after next* **50/1**

00/ **8** 6 **Red Mystique (IRE)**[17] 3 4-10-9 0 (t) AndrewGlassonbury 16
(Philip Hide) *chsd ldrs tl lost pl and rdn after 5th: lost tch 6th: wl t.o after next: virtually p.u flat* **25/1**

0/ **P** **Our Play (IRE)**[19] 5551 5-11-0 0 (v[1]) MarcGoldstein
(Lydia Richards) *wl in tch in midfield: rdn after 5th: wknd qckly 3 out: t.o whn p.u bef next* **25/1**

4m 28.0s (-6.30) **Going Correction** -0.20s/f (Good)
WFA 4 from 5yo+ 18lb **9** Ran SP% **125.6**
Speed ratings (Par 105): **105,102,94,94,92 84,66,63,**
toteswingers 1&2 £1.90, 1&3 £3.00, 2&3 £4.40 CSF £3.27 TOTE £1.30: £1.02, £1.90, £4.10; EX 3.60 Trifecta £17.40 Pool: £2860.05 - 122.67 winning units..
Owner Bloomfields **Bred** Darley **Trained** Cowlinge, Suffolk
■ Stewards' Enquiry : Tommy Phelan two-day ban: used whip above permitted level (May 29-30)

FOCUS
A desperately weak contest run at a sedate pace.

307 32RED.COM MAIDEN HURDLE (DIV II) (9 hdls) 2m 2f 110y
4:50 (4:50) (Class 4) 4-Y-0+ £3,119 (£915; £457; £228)

Form RPR

55/- **1** **Jack By The Hedge**[88] 4246 4-10-9 0 TomO'Brien 93+
(Caroline Keevil) *chsd ldrs: led after 1st tl mstke and hdd 2nd: chsd ldrs after: effrt to chal on inner 2 out: mstke last and sltly outpcd: rallied u.p fnl 100yds: styd on wl and led towards fin* **11/4**[1]

600/ **2** ½ **Port Hill**[88] 4254 6-11-0 100 DPFahy 94
(Liam Corcoran) *hld up wl in tch: hdwy to trck ldrs 3 out: short of room briefly wl bef next: effrt to chal 2 out: led last: sn drvn: kpt on wl tl hdd and unable qck towards fin* **8/1**[3]

025/ **3** 3 **Dougalstar (FR)**[16] 33 4-10-2 0 MikeyHamill(7) 88
(Sean Curran) *w ldr: mstke 2nd and 3 out: led bef next: sn rdn: hdd last: no ex and outpcd fnl 100yds* **11/4**[1]

P30/ **4** 3¼ **Comedy House**[15] 551 5-11-0 0 MarcGoldstein 89
(Michael Madgwick) *t.k.h: hld up wl in tch in rr: hdwy on outer to chal 2 out: mstke last: sn drvn: btn fnl 100yds: wknd towards fin* **8/1**[3]

630/ **5** 17 **Going Twice**[45] 5032 8-11-0 0 LeightonAspell 73
(Steve Woodman) *t.k.h: chsd ldrs tl shuffled bk to rr but stl wl in tch 5th: rdn 3 out: wknd next: mstke last* **8/1**[3]

6 7 **Jakeys Girl**[2] 6-10-7 0 ColinBolger 63
(Pat Phelan) *w ldrs tl led 2nd: hdd bef 2 out: sn struggling and mstke 2 out: wknd qckly bef last* **33/1**

P06/ **7** 20 **Samarkand (IRE)**[106] 3924 5-11-0 0 AlexMerriam 48
(Neil King) *chsd ldrs: pushed along bef 6th: rallied briefly on inner after 3 out: wknd bef next: t.o and eased flat* **3/1**[2]

P/ **8** 1 **Burnbrake**[7] 1433 8-11-0 0 AndrewGlassonbury 48
(Richard Rowe) *j.rt: hld up in tch: hdwy to chse ldrs 5th: mstke 3 out: wknd bef next: t.o and eased flat* **50/1**

4m 35.3s (1.00) **Going Correction** -0.20s/f (Good)
WFA 4 from 5yo+ 18lb **8 Ran SP% 116.6**
Speed ratings (Par 105): **89,88,87,86,79 76,67,67**
toteswingers 1&2 £4.40, 1&3 £1.90, 2&3 £4.10 CSF £25.76 TOTE £3.60: £1.90, £3.00, £1.10; EX 32.40 Trifecta £178.90 Pool: £2107.77 - 8.83 winning units..
Owner K S B Bloodstock **Bred** The Hon Mrs R Pease **Trained** Motcombe, Dorset

FOCUS
The pace was modest for the second division of this maiden hurdle. There were four in a line jumping the last.

308 32REDPOKER.COM H'CAP HURDLE (9 hdls) 2m 2f 110y
5:20 (5:25) (Class 5) (0-95,92) 4-Y-0+ £1,949 (£572; £286; £143)

Form RPR

051/ **1** **Deux Etoiles (IRE)**[17] 2 6-11-6 86 JamieMoore 96+
(Gary Moore) *in tch: chsd ldrs 3 out: swtchd lft and effrt jst bef 2 out: drvn to chse ldr between last 2: led last: sn clr and in command: rdn out* **6/4**[1]

022/ **2** 7 **Benny The Swinger (IRE)**[29] 5338 8-11-11 91 LeightonAspell 93
(Chris Gordon) *hld up in tch in rr: hdwy 6th: chal 2 out and sn led: mstke and hdd last: sn btn and hung lft: wknd fnl 100yds and jst hld on to 2nd* **5/2**[2]

000/ **3** nk **What's For Tea**[19] 5557 8-10-4 73 (vt) KielanWoods(3) 74
(Paddy Butler) *chsd ldr tl led bef 3 out: rdn wl bef 2 out: blnd 2 out and sn hdd: 3rd and btn last: plugged on and pressing for 2nd cl home* **16/1**

500/ **4** 4 **Clonusker (IRE)**[17] 3 5-10-3 69 (t) GerardTumelty 66
(Linda Jewell) *chsd ldrs: jnd ldr and mstke 6th: ev ch and rdn after next: no ex between last 2: wknd last* **20/1**

0P0/ **5** 15 **Charlies Lady**[19] 5557 6-9-7 66 oh2 ThomasGarner(7) 49
(Anna Newton-Smith) *chsd ldrs tl shuffled bk to rr but stl in tch 6th: wknd u.p next* **16/1**

5/0- **6** 10 **My Boy Ginger**[3] 243 4-11-0 85 (b) TomO'Brien 54
(Chris Gordon) *led tl bef 3 out: wknd qckly wl bef 2 out* **9/2**[3]

5/0- **7** 12 **Zulu Principle**[15] 37 6-11-5 92 ChrisDavies(7) 56
(Helen Nelmes) *hld up in tch towards rr: hdwy and trcking ldrs 3 out: rdn and wknd rapidly wl bef next: t.o and eased flat* **12/1**

006/ **8** 13 **Imperial Elegance**[26] 5374 4-11-1 86 (b[1]) MarcGoldstein 33
(Sheena West) *in tch in midfield: reminders and hdwy to chse ldrs after 5th: struggling and dropped to rr after next: t.o after 3 out* **20/1**

P00/ **P** **Saffron Park**[31] 5312 4-10-5 79 (b[1]) AdamWedge(3)
(Anna Newton-Smith) *t.k.h: hld up in tch in rr: rdn and lost tch after 5th: tailing off whn p.u next* **33/1**

P00/ **U** **Roparta Avenue**[34] 5241 6-11-8 88 AlexMerriam
(Diana Grissell) *in tch towards rr whn blnd and uns rdr 2nd* **33/1**

4m 33.8s (-0.50) **Going Correction** -0.20s/f (Good)
WFA 4 from 5yo+ 18lb **10 Ran SP% 121.6**
Speed ratings (Par 103): **93,90,89,88,81 77,72,67, ,**
toteswingers 1&2 £1.40, 1&3 £2.80, 2&3 £6.40 CSF £5.88 CT £41.63 TOTE £2.70: £1.10, £1.10, £2.70; EX 6.00 Trifecta £27.60 Pool: £1763.08 - 47.74 winning units..
Owner Heart Of The South Racing **Bred** Pagct Bloodstock **Trained** Lower Beeding, W Sussex
■ Ede's was withdrawn. Price at time of withdrawal 8-1. Rule 4 applies to bets struck prior to withdrawal but not to SP bets - deduction 10p in the pound. New market formed.
■ Stewards' Enquiry : Kielan Woods two-day ban: used whip above permitted level (May 29-30)

FOCUS
A weak handicap, run at a steady pace.

309 32REDBINGO.COM INTERMEDIATE OPEN NATIONAL HUNT FLAT RACE 1m 6f
5:55 (5:57) (Class 6) 4-6-Y-0 £1,559 (£457; £228; £114)

Form RPR

1 **Lemons Ground** 4-10-12 0 BrendanPowell 88
(Jamie Snowden) *hld up in tch in last pair: trckd ldrs 4f out: rdn to ld 2f out: battled on wl ins fnl f: rdn out* **7/1**[3]

3/ **2** hd **Act Alone**[74] 4528 4-10-12 0 AndrewTinkler 88
(Nicky Henderson) *chsd ldr for 3f and again over 5f out: led over 2f out: sn rdn and hdd 2f out: kpt on ins fnl f: wnt 2nd towards fin* **4/6**[1]

0/ **3** ¾ **Very Noble (FR)**[153] 3028 4-10-12 0 (t) DarylJacob 87
(Paul Nicholls) *hld up in tch in last pair: trckd ldrs and gng best 3f out: ev ch whn shkn up and fnd little jst ins fnl f: drvn and one pce fnl 100yds* **2/1**[2]

4/ **4** 28 **Seabougg**[34] 5247 5-10-13 0 JackQuinlan(3) 58
(James Eustace) *t.k.h: chsd ldrs rdn and wknd qckly 3f out: t.o over 1f out* **20/1**

5 29 **Canarbino Girl** 6-10-9 0 TomO'Brien 16
(Caroline Keevil) *chsd ldrs tl led over 5f out: hdd over 2f out: sn btn and no ch whn hung lft over 1f out: t.o* **25/1**

0/ **6** 55 **Cool Chief**[34] 5247 4-10-5 0 MissECrossman(7)
(Alan Blackmore) *t.k.h: chsd ldr after 3f tl led 8f out: hdd over 5f out: sn lost tch: wl t.o fnl 3f* **100/1**

0/ **7** 2¼ **Indispensabelle**[27] 5364 4-9-12 0 ThomasGarner(7)
(Linda Jewell) *led tl 8f out: sn dropped to rr: wl t.o fnl 4f* **50/1**

3m 24.8s (-6.30) **Going Correction** -0.20s/f (Good) **7 Ran SP% 117.4**
Speed ratings: **101,100,100,84,67 36,35**
toteswingers 1&2 £1.90, 1&3 £2.10, 2&3 £1.10 CSF £12.64 TOTE £10.00: £2.60, £1.10; EX 16.70 Trifecta £34.40 Pool: £1278.87 - 27.86 winning units..
Owner L G Partnership **Bred** William Wallace **Trained** Lambourn, Berks

FOCUS
The pace was solid for this uncompetitive bumper.
T/Plt: £17.30 to a £1 stake. Pool: £51,007.83 - 2143.13 winning tickets. T/Qpdt: £5.10 to a £1 stake. Pool: £3827.14 - 548.10 winning tickets. SP

PERTH (R-H)
Wednesday, May 15

OFFICIAL GOING: Good (8.1)
Wind: Almost nil Weather: Overcast

310 SCOTLAND'S CHARITY AIR AMBULANCE H'CAP HURDLE (12 hdls) 3m 110y
6:00 (6:01) (Class 4) (0-115,115) 4-Y-0+ £4,548 (£1,335; £667; £333)

Form RPR

362/ **1** **Settledoutofcourt (IRE)**[19] 5546 7-10-0 89 oh2 WilsonRenwick 91
(Andrew Parker) *t.k.h: hld up: smooth hdwy 4 out: rdn after next: rallied and c wd bef 2 out: led after last: drvn out* **9/2**[2]

P10/ **2** hd **Any Given Moment (IRE)**[16] 24 7-10-11 100 JamesReveley 102
(Sandy Thomson) *hld up towards rr: drvn after 3 out: rallied next: led briefly last: kpt on u.p: hld nr fin* **10/1**

31/ **3** 2 **Hidden Horizons (IRE)**[23] 5452 7-10-13 102 (p) PeterBuchanan 102
(S R B Crawford, Ire) *cl up: led 4th: rdn bef 2 out: hdd last: kpt on same pce run-in* **9/1**

450/ **4** ¾ **Bescot Springs (IRE)**[26] 5372 8-11-5 115 (v) GrahamWatters(7) 114
(Lucinda Russell) *prom: hdwy and cl up after 3 out: sn drvn: kpt on same pce fr last* **7/2**[1]

346/ **5** 1½ **Dickie Henderhoop (IRE)**[21] 5495 8-9-10 90 SamanthaDrake(5) 88
(Lucy Normile) *hld up in tch: rdn after 3 out: pckd next: kpt on fr last: nt pce to chal* **6/1**[3]

0P5/ **6** 1 **Easement**[37] 5222 10-9-10 92 JonathonBewley(7) 89
(George Bewley) *trckd ldrs: drvn after 3 out: outpcd fr last* **10/1**

2P2/ **7** 3¼ **Lucematic**[21] 5492 7-10-13 112 DiarmuidO'Regan(10) 106
(Chris Grant) *nt fluent on occasions in rr: outpcd bef 4 out: plugged on fr 2 out: nvr on terms* **13/2**

300/ **8** 9 **Ryton Runner (IRE)**[19] 5549 5-11-5 115 (p) CraigNichol(7) 101
(Lucinda Russell) *trckd ldrs: drvn and outpcd after 4 out: struggling fr next* **8/1**

06P/ **9** 45 **Yourlookinathim (IRE)**[21] 5495 7-10-0 89 oh4 HenryBrooke 55
(Jim Goldie) *led to 4th: cl up: mstke 3 out: sn rdn and wknd: t.o* **20/1**

6m 2.0s (-3.00) **Going Correction** +0.025s/f (Yiel) **9 Ran SP% 112.1**
Speed ratings (Par 105): **105,104,104,104,103 103,102,99,84**
toteswingers 1&2 £9.70, 1&3 £15.50, 2&3 £27.50 CSF £45.98 CT £382.97 TOTE £5.10: £1.80, £2.70, £3.00; EX 51.70 Trifecta £309.30 Part won. Pool: £412.47 - 0.18 winning units..
Owner Andrew McAllister **Bred** Sean Naughton **Trained** Ecclefechan, D'fries & G'way
■ Stewards' Enquiry : Graham Watters two-day ban: used whip above permitted level (May 29-30)

FOCUS
All bends and hurdles sited on fresh ground. A fair handicap to kick things off. The close finish suggests none of these are well ahead of their marks, although the third and fourth are possibly a little better than the bare result having possibly done a bit too much too soon out in front.

311 SUNBURST H'CAP CHASE (15 fncs) 2m 4f 110y
6:30 (6:30) (Class 5) (0-95,91) 5-Y-0+ £3,898 (£1,144; £572; £286)

Form RPR

56P/ **1** **Shooting Times**[38] 5206 8-11-1 80 (v[1]) PeterBuchanan 96+
(Lucinda Russell) *trckd ldr: led 10th: pushed along bef 2 out: drvn and kpt on wl fr last* **13/2**

300/ **2** 2¼ **Snuker**[16] 30 6-10-9 74 BrianHughes 86
(James Ewart) *prom: hdwy to chse wnr bef 4 out: effrt whn nt fluent 2 out and last: kpt on run-in* **11/2**

5/3- **3** 26 **Solway Dornal**[7] 172 8-9-9 67 (t) StephenMulqueen(7) 56
(Lisa Harrison) *in tch: drvn along after 4 out: outpcd by first two fr next* **7/2**[1]

3P2/ **4** 16 **Alexander Oats**[68] 4635 10-11-7 91 (p) HarryChalloner(5) 64
(Robert Goldie) *hld up: rdn and outpcd 10th: plugged on fr 2 out: nvr on terms* **9/2**[3]

320/ **5** 1¾ **Great Ocean Road (IRE)**[66] 10-10-1 71 TonyKelly(5) 43
(David Thompson) *hld up in tch: outpcd bef 5 out: struggling fnl 3* **4/1**[2]

0/P- **6** 59 **Lochore (IRE)**[11] 114 7-10-7 72 (t) JamesReveley
(William Amos) *nt fluent in rr: hdwy whn hit 10th: lost tch fr 3 out: t.o* **14/1**

PPP/ **P** **Man Of Principles (IRE)**[83] 4355 10-10-8 78 (v) GaryRutherford(5)
(Stuart Coltherd) *led: rdn 8th: hdd 10th: outpcd whn blnd bdly 4 out: t.o whn p.u bef 2 out* **14/1**

U0P/ **P** **Monsoon Music (IRE)**[17] 20 9-10-4 69 (p) BrianHarding
(Lucinda Russell) *nt fluent in rr: struggling after 8th: t.o whn p.u bef 11th* **22/1**

PP4/ **P** **King Kalium (IRE)**[38] 5207 7-10-5 75 CallumWhillans(5)
(Donald Whillans) *prom: rdn 5 out: wknd 3 out: t.o whn p.u bef last* **16/1**

5m 8.3s (3.30) **Going Correction** +0.325s/f (Yiel) **9 Ran SP% 112.7**
Speed ratings: **106,105,95,89,88 66, , ,**
toteswingers 1&2 £5.40, 1&3 £6.20, 2&3 £5.20 CSF £41.43 CT £144.06 TOTE £7.70: £2.50, £2.70, £1.10; EX 48.50 Trifecta £256.00 Pool: £568.36 - 1.66 winning units..
Owner Mrs I C Lancaster **Bred** Mrs J M Lancaster **Trained** Arlary, Perth & Kinross

FOCUS
A very ordinary handicap.

312 SALUTATION HOTEL PERTH H'CAP CHASE (18 fncs) 3m
7:00 (7:00) (Class 4) (0-120,118) 5-Y-0+ £6,498 (£1,908; £954; £477)

Form RPR

132/ **1** **Wild Geese (IRE)**[20] 5521 6-11-8 114 (p) PeterBuchanan 126+
(Lucinda Russell) *mde all: rdn 4 out: styd on wl fr 2 out* **3/1**[2]

414/ **2** 8 **Bertie Milan (IRE)**[49] 4975 8-10-12 104 WilsonRenwick 108
(N W Alexander) *pressed wnr: effrt and drvn bef 3 out: one pce fr next* **6/1**

232/ **3** 1¾ **Rudemeister (IRE)**[37] 5218 7-11-5 118 GrahamWatters(7) 120
(Andrew Parker) *trckd ldrs: rdn bef 4 out: kpt on same pce after next* **9/4**[1]

004/ **4** 7 **Solway Sam**[66] 4679 10-10-11 **103**...................................... BrianHarding 100
(Lisa Harrison) *hld up: outpcd 10th: rallied and in tch 5 out: nt fluent and rdn next: no imp fr 3 out* **13/2**

016/ **5** ½ **Categorical**[19] 4975 10-11-9 **115**....................................... JamesReveley 112
(Keith Reveley) *hld up: rdn along bef 4 out: no imp bef next* **10/1**

0/3- **6** 41 **The Thirsty Bricky (IRE)**[11] 113 11-11-7 **118**............. TonyKelly(5) 77
(David Thompson) *in tch: outpcd whn hit 5 out: sn btn: t.o* **22/1**

132/ **7** 11 **Seigneur Des Bois (FR)**[31] 5306 7-11-4 **110**...............(p) PaddyBrennan 59
(Tom George) *nt fluent: trckd ldrs tl rdn and wknd bef 4 out: t.o* **5/1**[3]

6m 14.6s (10.60) **Going Correction** +0.325s/f (Yiel) 7 Ran SP% **113.5**
Speed ratings: **95,92,91,89,89 75,71**
toteswingers 1&2 £3.30, 1&3 £2.00, 2&3 £5.10 CSF £20.76 TOTE £3.60: £1.90, £3.70; EX 27.50 Trifecta £107.60 Pool: £870.13 - 6.06 winning units..

Owner Tay Valley Chasers Racing Club **Bred** Darley **Trained** Arlary, Perth & Kinross

FOCUS
Not a particularly strong handicap for the level.

313 STRATHBRAAN BREWERY MAIDEN HURDLE (FOR THE ALAN NORMILE MEMORIAL TROPHY) (10 hdls) 2m 4f 110y

7:30 (7:30) (Class 5) 4-Y-0+ **£3,249** (£954; £477; £238)

Form RPR

1 **Jumbo John (IRE)**[39] 5193 7-11-0 110............................ WilsonRenwick 112+
(Mrs Lorna Fowler, Ire) *trckd ldrs: effrt and rdn after 3 out: led between last 2: hrd pressed fr last: drvn and hld on wl* **7/2**[3]

000/ **2** nk **Mandarin Sunset (IRE)**[16] 22 6-11-0 0.......................... BrianHughes 110
(James Ewart) *in tch: stdy hdwy after 3 out: effrt and chsd wnr last: sn rdn and ev ch: kpt on: hld nr fin* **18/1**

053/ **3** 7 **Clondaw Knight (IRE)**[19] 5544 5-11-0 0......................... PeterBuchanan 105
(Lucinda Russell) *t.k.h early: led: rdn and hdd between last 2: nt fluent last: sn outpcd by first two* **5/2**[1]

342/ **4** 1¾ **Another Mattie (IRE)**[20] 5519 6-11-0 0.............................. BrianHarding 104
(N W Alexander) *mstkes: hld up in tch: hdwy bef 3 out: drvn and one pce whn blnd next: sn no imp* **3/1**[2]

544/ **5** 3½ **Cruachan (IRE)**[21] 5499 4-10-6 108................................ AlexanderVoy(3) 94
(Lucy Normile) *hld up in tch: hdwy and cl up bef 2 out: sn rdn: outpcd whn hit last* **10/1**

4/2- **6** 10 **Azerodegree (IRE)**[4] 223 4-10-9 0....................................(p) AdrianLane 87
(Iain Jardine) *cl up: hit 4 out: rdn whn hit next: wknd bef 2 out* **13/2**

00/ **7** nk **Amethyst Rose (IRE)**[19] 5544 6-10-2 0...................... GaryRutherford(5) 83
(Stuart Coltherd) *hld up on ins: hit 2nd: struggling after 4 out: sme late hdwy: nvr on terms* **80/1**

63/ **8** 3½ **Total Assets**[21] 5491 5-10-2 0.................................... JonathanEngland(5) 80
(Simon Waugh) *plld hrd early: in tch tl rdn and wknd bef 3 out* **20/1**

3/5- **9** 6 **Brae On (IRE)**[11] 115 5-10-7 0.................................. JonathonBewley(7) 81
(George Bewley) *nt fluent in rr: struggling fnl circ: nvr on terms* **33/1**

0P0/ **10** 7 **Karingo**[150] 3098 6-10-9 0... SamanthaDrake(5) 75
(Lucy Normile) *nt fluent in rr: struggling bef 4 out: nvr on terms* **80/1**

00P/ **11** 33 **Here's To Harry**[133] 3457 6-11-0 0.. HarryHaynes 45
(N W Alexander) *towards rr: nt fluent 6th: sn rdn: struggling fr next: t.o* **50/1**

034/ **12** 26 **Mumgos Debut (IRE)**[287] 1146 5-10-7 0..................... GrantCockburn(7) 22
(Lucinda Russell) *nt fluent: plld hrd in rr: struggling whn mstke 4 out: sn btn: t.o* **66/1**

0/ **P** **Northern Warrior**[23] 5454 5-10-7 0................................ ShaunDobbin(7)
(Hugh Burns) *nt fluent towards rr: struggling bef 4 out: t.o whn p.u bef 2 out* **100/1**

5m 6.9s (4.90) **Going Correction** +0.025s/f (Yiel)
WFA 4 from 5yo+ 19lb 13 Ran SP% **118.1**
Speed ratings (Par 103): **91,90,88,87,86 82,82,80,78,76 63,53,**
toteswingers 1&2 £7.80, 1&3 £3.00, 2&3 £17.30 CSF £57.49 TOTE £3.40: £1.40, £5.00, £1.60; EX 63.40 Trifecta £190.20 Pool: £747.48 - 2.94 winning units..

Owner Mrs A Frost & Exors Of Late Lady J Fowler **Bred** Mrs Elizabeth Lawlor **Trained** Summerhill, Co Meath

■ The first training success for Lorna Fowler, who rode plenty of winners under her maiden name Lorna Bradburne.

FOCUS
Fair form from the principals in this maiden hurdle.

314 STEADFAST SCOTLAND NOVICES' H'CAP CHASE (10 fncs 2 omitted) 2m

8:00 (8:03) (Class 5) (0-95,94) 5-Y-0+ **£4,548** (£1,335; £667; £333)

Form RPR

204/ **1** **Cloverhill Lad (IRE)**[16] 26 9-10-12 **85**...................... GaryRutherford(5) 101+
(Stuart Coltherd) *trckd ldrs: led 4th: mde rest: rdn and styd on wl to go clr fr last* **7/1**

U/4- **2** 8 **Celtic Intrigue (IRE)**[15] 43 6-11-6 **88**.......................(tp) PaddyBrennan 97
(Tom George) *cl up: hit 3rd: chal 4th to 2 out: sn drvn: edgd rt and outpcd by wnr fr last* **5/2**[1]

P4B/ **3** 6 **Morning Time (IRE)**[44] 5073 7-10-8 **76**.........................(p) PeterBuchanan 79
(Lucinda Russell) *in tch: stdy hdwy to chse ldrs passing omitted 4 out: effrt next: outpcd whn nt fluent 2 out* **10/3**[2]

0F3/ **4** 14 **Crackerjack Lad (IRE)**[267] 1304 10-10-9 **84**............. GrahamWatters(7) 74
(Lucinda Russell) *hld up: nt fluent 4th: stdy hdwy and prom passing omitted 4 out: rdn and wknd after next* **7/1**

234/ **5** 2 **Vosges (FR)**[16] 34 6-11-2 **94**..(b) DaleIrving(10) 82
(James Ewart) *led to 4th: trckd ldrs: drvn after 4 out (usual 5 out): wknd bef next* **9/2**[3]

642/ **6** 18 **Richo**[16] 34 7-10-2 **75**..(p) TrevorWhelan(5) 47
(Shaun Harris) *nt fluent on occasions: hld up in tch: struggling 4 out (usual 5 out): btn next* **7/1**

PPP/ **7** 15 **Snooze N You Lose**[91] 4185 8-9-9 **68** oh9.............. JonathanEngland(5) 27
(Jean McGregor) *in tch to 4th: struggling fr next: t.o* **66/1**

4m 0.7s (3.70) **Going Correction** +0.325s/f (Yiel) 7 Ran SP% **108.8**
Speed ratings: **103,99,96,89,88 79,71**
toteswingers 1&2 £2.00, 1&3 £6.00, 2&3 £1.40 CSF £23.27 TOTE £9.80: £4.80, £1.90; EX 34.10 Trifecta £151.40 Pool: £691.69 - 3.42 winning units..

Owner Coltherd Turnbull **Bred** D Lynam **Trained** Selkirk, Borders

FOCUS
A weak handicap.

315 BRUCE FARMS HUNTERS' CHASE (FOR THE LINLITHGOW & STIRLINGSHIRE HUNT CHALLENGE TROPHY) (16 fncs 2 omitted) 3m

8:30 (8:30) (Class 6) 5-Y-0+ **£1,871** (£580; £290; £145)

Form RPR

U06/ **1** **Back On The Road (IRE)**[10] 11-11-13 109.......... MrJamieAlexander(7) 110
(N W Alexander) *bhd: stdy hdwy 1/2-way: effrt passing omitted 2 out: wnt 2nd bef 2 out: 8 l down last: styd on wl to ld nr fin* **22/1**

512/ **2** ¾ **Harry Flashman**[23] 5453 12-11-9 115.............................. MrNOrpwood(7) 106
(Greg Aitken) *led to 4th: led 9th to 11th: led 4 out (usual 5 out): rdn bef next: 8 l clr over 2 out and last: wknd and hdd towards fin* **7/2**[2]

65U/ **3** 12 **The Halfway Bar (IRE)**[10] 12-11-5 0.................................. MrPCollins(7) 94
(Miss Gill Boanas) *mstkes in detached last: gd hdwy bef omitted 4 out: rdn and no imp whn mstke next* **14/1**[3]

P5P/ **4** 11 **Waterski**[20] 5524 12-11-5 66.....................................(p) MissAMcGregor(7) 81
(Jean McGregor) *cl up: led 4th to 9th and 11th to 4 out (usual 5 out): chsd ldr to bef 2 out: sn wknd* **100/1**

5 60 **Paddy Curry (IRE)**[10] 11-11-5 0.. MrTHamilton(7) 27
(Mrs E Watson) *in tch: mstke 10th: rdn and wknd fr 4 out (usual 5 out): t.o* **14/1**[3]

3/4- **6** ½ **Beau Traveller**[11] 112 10-11-7 95.. MrSFox(5) 26
(Miss Bianca Dunk) *trckd ldrs: rdn whn slipped appr omitted 4 out: sn wknd: t.o* **14/1**[3]

P0U/ **7** 26 **Barr Head (IRE)**[24] 9-11-5 57..(p) MrRWilson(7) 3
(Lucy Normile) *nt fluent: chsd ldng gp: mstke 9th: struggling fnl circ: t.o* **50/1**

U50/ **U** **Sea Wall**[10] 11-11-5 107.. MrEGTWrigley(7)
(C Storey) *hld up in tch: shkn up and prom whn blnd and uns rdr 12th* **16/1**

1/2- **U** **Special Portrait (IRE)**[14] 62 9-11-13 109.....................(t) MrPGerety(7)
(Mark Hughes) *hld up: hmpd and uns rdr 2nd* **8/13**[1]

6m 22.1s (18.10) **Going Correction** +0.325s/f (Yiel) 9 Ran SP% **117.3**
Speed ratings: **82,81,77,74,54 53,45,,**
toteswingers 1&2 £8.40, 1&3 £27.50, 2&3 £7.10 CSF £101.19 TOTE £26.70: £2.80, £1.40, £3.80; EX 121.70 Trifecta £574.30 Part won. Pool: £765.83 - 0.17 winning units..

Owner Jamie Alexander **Bred** J R And Mrs S Cox **Trained** Kinneston, Perth & Kinross

■ Stewards' Enquiry : Mr P Collins three-day ban: weighed-in 2lb heavy (May 29-30,Jun 4)

FOCUS
A dramatic start and conclusion to this hunter chase.

316 FONAB CASTLE HOTEL NOVICES' H'CAP HURDLE (8 hdls) 2m 110y

9:00 (9:00) (Class 5) (0-95,95) 4-Y-0+ **£4,106** (£1,197; £598)

Form RPR

404/ **1** **Momkinzain (USA)**[19] 5546 6-10-12 **88**..........................(p) CraigNichol(7) 101
(Lucinda Russell) *trckd ldrs: effrt bef 2 out: led bef last: clr whn hung lft run-in: drvn out* **7/1**

002/ **2** 7 **Solway Dandy**[85] 4300 6-11-5 **95**............................ StephenMulqueen(7) 101
(Lisa Harrison) *hld up: hdwy to chse ldrs bef 2 out: wnt 2nd run-in: nt rch wnr* **13/2**[3]

P02/ **3** 2 **Some Lad (IRE)**[20] 5520 8-10-12 **88**............................ GrahamWatters(7) 93
(Alison Hamilton) *midfield: mstke 3rd: effrt and led appr 2 out: rdn and hdd bef last: no ex run-in* **4/1**[1]

2/3- **4** ½ **Shaker Style (USA)**[13] 75 7-10-9 **78**..............................(p) BrianHughes 82
(Barry Murtagh) *midfield: hmpd bnd after 1st: drvn after 3 out: rallied next: no imp run-in* **9/1**

223/ **5** 4½ **Laybach (IRE)**[188] 2284 9-10-5 **74**... HenryBrooke 75
(Jim Goldie) *trckd ldrs: rdn bef 2 out: wknd fr last* **8/1**

440/ **6** 6 **Ravi River (IRE)**[20] 5520 9-10-0 **72**.................................. EwanWhillans(3) 69
(Alistair Whillans) *hld up: effrt u.p after 3 out: no imp fr next: hld whn mstke last* **5/1**[2]

50P/ **7** 2½ **Cigalas**[21] 5495 8-9-9 **69** oh2... SamanthaDrake(5) 61
(Jean McGregor) *midfield: nt fluent 2nd: effrt bef 2 out: sn wknd* **33/1**

000/ **8** 13 **Shivalric (IRE)**[24] 5426 5-11-1 **84**... BrianHarding 65
(Nicky Richards) *led to appr 2 out: sn rdn and wknd* **33/1**

3P0/ **9** ½ **Business Time**[44] 5072 7-11-2 **90**.............................. JonathanEngland(5) 70
(Hugh Burns) *cl up tl rdn and wknd bef 2 out* **33/1**

6/3- **10** 6 **Topo Gigio (FR)**[11] 110 9-10-9 **85**................................... CallumBewley(7) 60
(Robert Bewley) *hld up: struggling after 4 out: nvr on terms* **14/1**

66F/ **11** 2¾ **Glaced Over**[186] 2325 8-11-4 **87**.. AdrianLane 59
(Raymond Shiels) *hld up: hdwy and in tch after 4 out: rdn and wknd bef 2 out* **25/1**

004/ **12** 10 **Silverton**[19] 5544 6-11-8 **94**.. AlexanderVoy(3) 57
(Lucy Normile) *in tch tl lost pl after 4 out: sn btn* **20/1**

604/ **13** 1¾ **Fozy Moss**[20] 5520 7-10-2 **76**....................................... GaryRutherford(5) 38
(Stuart Coltherd) *towards rr: nt fluent 4th: struggling fr next* **8/1**

P05/ **14** 7 **Solway Legend**[309] 908 6-11-2 **85**... HarryHaynes 40
(Lisa Harrison) *bhd: detached bef 4th: nvr on terms* **33/1**

3m 56.2s (-1.80) **Going Correction** +0.025s/f (Yiel) 14 Ran SP% **121.8**
Speed ratings (Par 103): **105,101,100,100,98 95,94,88,88,85 83,79,78,75**
toteswingers 1&2 £11.50, 1&3 £5.70, 2&3 £4.80 CSF £48.80 CT £205.63 TOTE £7.50: £2.30, £2.80, £1.50; EX 66.30 Trifecta £109.80 Pool: £470.04 - 3.21 winning units..

Owner John R Adam & Sons **Bred** Berkshire Stud **Trained** Arlary, Perth & Kinross

FOCUS
Just run-of-the-mill fare, although it probably represents pretty solid form for the grade.
T/Plt: £456.20 to a £1 stake. Pool: £56,779.93 - 90.85 winning tickets. T/Qpdt: £61.20 to a £1 stake. Pool: £5190.40 - 62.75 winning tickets. RY

[116]UTTOXETER (L-H)

Wednesday, May 15

OFFICIAL GOING: Good to soft (soft in places) changing to soft after race 1 (1.55) changing to heavy after race 4 (3.25)
Wind: quite strong against in home straight Weather: overcast; 6 degrees

317 CREWE ALEXANDRA JPT CUP WINNERS CUP "NATIONAL HUNT" NOVICES' HURDLE (12 hdls) 3m

1:55 (1:55) (Class 4) 4-Y-0+ **£3,249** (£954; £477; £238)

Form RPR

321/ **1** **Silver Eagle (IRE)**[17] 19 5-11-5 124..............................(t) JasonMaguire 125+
(Kim Bailey) *trckd ldrs gng wl: wnt 2nd after 9th: led 3 out: gng best after: 3 l clr last: kpt up to work flat* **8/15**[1]

2 2¾ **My Lucky Flame (IRE)**[241] 1576 6-10-6 0................................ MarkGrant 109
(Sean Curran) *2nd or 3rd tl led at 9th: hdd and mstke next: drvn and kpt on gamely after but wl hld* **25/1**

U4/- 3 33 **Wishes And Stars (IRE)**[24] 5432 7-10-6 107.................. ConorO'Farrell 86
(Tim Dennis) *trckd ldrs: effrt in 2 l 3rd bef 3 out: drvn and sn struggling to keep up* **4/1**[2]

253/ 4 28 **Letemgo (IRE)**[24] 5438 5-10-13 0...................................... DavidEngland 61
(Giles Smyly) *midfield: lost tch bef 3 out: sn t.o* **10/1**

400/ P **Any Currency (IRE)**[39] 5177 10-10-13 0...........................(tp) IanPopham
(Martin Keighley) *pressed ldr: reminders after 4th: led 5th tl 9th: sn stopped to nil and looked reluctant: t.o and p.u 2 out* **11/2**[3]

000/ P **Cirrus Coin**[25] 5408 8-10-13 0.. PaulMoloney
(Andrew Hollinshead) *a bhd: t.o after 8th: p.u 2 out* **40/1**

0P0/ P **Missing The Craic**[19] 5537 7-10-8 0..............................(t) CharlieWallis[(5)]
(Sean Curran) *led tl 5th: rdn next: stopped to nil after 7th: t.o and p.u next* **100/1**

0P/ P **Diamond Crescent (IRE)**[358] 394 6-10-13 0........ SamTwiston-Davies
(Nigel Twiston-Davies) *mstkes in last: nvr travelling: drvn 7th: t.o and p.u next* **33/1**

PPP/ P **Master Ted (IRE)**[318] 844 7-10-13 0................................ SeanQuinlan
(Jennie Candlish) *bhd and nt gng wl: mstke 7th and drvn: t.o and p.u next* **80/1**

6m 2.9s (12.90) **Going Correction** +1.35s/f (Heav) 9 Ran SP% **121.2**
Speed ratings (Par 105): **103,102,91,81, , , ,**
toteswingers 1&2 £11.40, 1&3 £1.80, 2&3 £20.40 CSF £21.05 TOTE £1.70: £1.10, £10.50, £1.30; EX 19.20 Trifecta £199.70 Pool: £1086.30 - 4.07 winning units..
Owner Kim Bailey Racing Partnership IV **Bred** Martin Cullinane **Trained** Andoversford, Gloucs

FOCUS
Hurdles course at longest with hurdles on outside adjacent to fences. Common bends. A fair staying novice hurdle in which they went an honest gallop on ground changed to soft after this race.

318 JPW DISTRIBUTION "NATIONAL HUNT" MAIDEN HURDLE (9 hdls) 2m
2:25 (2:25) (Class 5) 4-Y-0+ **£2,079** (£610; £305; £152)

Form RPR

633/ 1 **Clan William (IRE)**[33] 5279 5-11-0 0...................................... RyanMania 106+
(Sue Smith) *settled wl off pce: hdwy whn j.v.slowly 5th: wnt 2nd after next: led wl bef 3 out: jnd and mstke and bmpd last: sn hdd flat: styd on v gamely to ld again fnl 50yds* **5/1**

244/ 2 nk **Kalucci (IRE)**[17] 4 4-10-10 0................................ SamTwiston-Davies 99
(Barry Brennan) *settled wl off pce: effrt after 6th: 2nd and ev ch fr next: drvn and upsides whn wnt lft and bmpd wnr last: sn led flat: kpt edging lft and outbattled and repassed cl home* **10/3**[2]

350/ 3 3¼ **Call A Truce (IRE)**[16] 33 5-10-9 0................................ KillianMoore[(5)] 101
(Ben Case) *hld up in rr: effrt to trck ldrs 6th: cl up tl drvn and no ex between last two* **7/2**[3]

063/ 4 31 **It's Oscar (IRE)**[21] 5498 6-11-0 109.................................(t) JasonMaguire 75
(Donald McCain) *j. and hung rt fr 1/2-way: 20 l 3rd at 4th: effrt and chal and j. bdly rt and reminders 6th: 2nd briefly home turn: lost tch on outer whn drvn bef 3 out: fin w ears pricked* **9/4**[1]

PP3/ 5 16 **Regal County (IRE)**[19] 5543 7-11-0 104............................... NickScholfield 53
(Alexandra Dunn) *led and sn clr: hit 3rd: 15 l ahd whn nt fluent next: pressed after 5th: hdd wl bef 3 out and immediately stopped to nil: t.o* **7/1**

0/0- 6 15 **Nothing Personal**[6] 174 6-11-0 0.............................. AndrewThornton 38
(Karen George) *nrly a last: hit 2nd: t.o fr 6th* **100/1**

7 23 **Carobello (IRE)**[626] 1541 6-11-0 0.............................. WayneHutchinson 15
(Martin Bosley) *in rr and nvr looked hopeful: rdn after 6th: t.o bef 3 out where blnd: fin eventually* **20/1**

5/ U **Desert Sting**[46] 5018 4-10-7 0.. JakeGreenall[(3)]
(Michael Easterby) *blnd and uns rdr 1st* **33/1**

4m 10.5s (18.50) **Going Correction** +1.35s/f (Heav)
WFA 4 from 5yo+ 18lb 8 Ran SP% **113.9**
Speed ratings (Par 103): **107,106,105,89,81 74,62,**
toteswingers 1&2 £3.10, 1&3 £4.40, 2&3 £2.20 CSF £21.98 TOTE £6.80: £2.40, £1.40, £1.40; EX 20.20 Trifecta £88.10 Pool: £1105.13 - 9.40 winning units..
Owner Mrs S Smith **Bred** Patrick Cummins **Trained** High Eldwick, W Yorks

FOCUS
A modest maiden hurdle in which they went a decent gallop.

319 32REDPOKER.COM CONDITIONAL JOCKEYS' (S) HURDLE (10 hdls) 2m 4f 110y
2:55 (2:55) (Class 5) 4-7-Y-0 **£2,130** (£661; £356)

Form RPR

013/ 1 **Molaise Lad (IRE)**[48] 4984 7-11-5 105..............................(v) RyanMahon 112+
(Barry Brennan) *mde all at v stdy pce: flattened 5th: rdn to assert bef 3 out: 5 l ahd next: began to idle bdly between last two: flattened last: unimpressive attitude after but a had enough in hand* **6/4**[2]

311/ 2 2 **Descaro (USA)**[12] 5248 7-11-0 112................................ CiaranMckee[(8)] 110
(John O'Shea) *chsd wnr tl after 2nd and again fr 7th: drvn and floundering in grnd fr bef 3 out: lft w ch briefly last but no further imp* **8/11**[1]

66/- 3 46 **Rum Ginney**[19] 5551 5-10-7 74..(p) GilesHawkins 49
(K F Clutterbuck) *t.k.h early: chsd wnr after 2nd tl j. slowly 7th: drvn and immediately lost tch: t.o next* **25/1**

0/P- R **Gtaab**[3] 253 7-11-0 97...(bt) JamesBest
(Sophie Leech) *mulish at s and ref to r* **12/1**[3]

5m 33.5s (34.50) **Going Correction** +1.35s/f (Heav) 4 Ran SP% **109.4**
Speed ratings: **95,94,76,**
CSF £3.12 TOTE £2.90; EX 3.30 Trifecta £9.60 Pool: £879.85 - 68.06 winning units..There were no bids.
Owner D J Lewin **Bred** Michael Meaney **Trained** Upper Lambourn, Berks

FOCUS
A fair small-field conditional jockeys' selling hurdle in which they went a sensible gallop in worsening conditions.

320 32RED CASINO H'CAP HURDLE (12 hdls) 3m
3:25 (3:25) (Class 5) (0-100,100) 4-Y-0+ **£2,079** (£610; £305; £152)

Form RPR

5P4/ 1 **Indian Citizen (IRE)**[21] 5505 6-10-1 75.............................. DougieCostello 91+
(Arthur Whiting) *mde all at v pedestrian pce: rdn clr fr 3 out: wl on top whn flattened last: battled on slowly* **4/1**[3]

6/3- 2 18 **Storm To Pass**[14] 67 5-11-7 95.................................(t) HarrySkelton 99+
(Caroline Fryer) *in rr trio tl 7th: wnt 2nd at 9th: upsides and briefly looked to be gng best next: sn rdn and fnd nil: in vain pursuit after: eased flat* **3/1**[1]

63P/ 3 10 **Hero's Call**[58] 4842 8-10-0 74 oh4.......................... SamTwiston-Davies 60
(Julian Smith) *hld up last but wl in tch: flattened 7th: outpcd home turn: rdn to go 10 l 3rd 3 out: fading after: 20 l bhd whn hopped through gap in last* **4/1**[3]

044/ 4 2¾ **Little Carmela**[21] 5500 9-11-12 100.................................(vt) WillKennedy 83
(Violet M Jordan) *2nd or 3rd tl rdn bef 8th: rn in snatches after: lost tch after 9th* **6/1**

004/ 5 5 **Handford Henry (IRE)**[58] 4840 7-10-13 90...................... RyanMahon[(3)] 68
(Michael Appleby) *in last trio: rdn and lost tch wl bef 3 out: hit next* **10/1**

PP2/ 6 12 **Chosen Dream (IRE)**[19] 5555 5-11-1 89...................(t) RichieMcLernon 55
(Jonjo O'Neill) *cl up tl drvn and fdd wl bef 3 out: t.o and eased flat* **7/2**[2]

6m 34.6s (44.60) **Going Correction** +1.35s/f (Heav) 6 Ran SP% **110.6**
Speed ratings (Par 103): **76,70,66,65,64 60**
toteswingers 1&2 £3.30, 1&3 £2.70, 2&3 £2.60 CSF £16.07 CT £46.78 TOTE £4.90: £4.60, £1.10; EX 26.10 Trifecta £74.80 Pool: £676.62 - 6.78 winning units..
Owner A J Whiting **Bred** E J O'Sullivan **Trained** North Nibley, Gloucs

FOCUS
A moderate staying handicap hurdle. The ground was changed to heavy after this race.

321 32RED H'CAP CHASE (18 fncs 2 omitted) 3m 2f
4:00 (4:00) (Class 4) (0-115,113) 5-Y-0+ **£3,833** (£1,157; £596; £315)

Form RPR

P05/ 1 **Jaunty Journey**[29] 5329 10-11-7 108....................... SamTwiston-Davies 122+
(Nigel Twiston-Davies) *mde all: began to forge clr bef 3 out: rdn appr last: styd on v stoutly* **10/3**[2]

24/ 2 12 **Merlin's Wish**[31] 5307 8-10-13 100.. IanPopham 102+
(Martin Keighley) *mstkes: prom tl dropped bk last and j. slowly 7th: drvn much of way after: rallied 14th: outpcd in poor 4th next: kpt plugging on wl after and wnt poor 2nd after hitting last* **12/1**

P03/ 3 1¾ **Kilcommon Pride (IRE)**[31] 5306 8-11-2 103....................(t) HaddenFrost 99
(Roger Curtis) *chsd wnr fr 5th: rdn 11th: lost 2nd at 13th: regained it at 15th where wnr sing to go clr: plodded on: relegated to 3rd sn after last* **11/2**

PP1/ 4 7 **Mohi Rahrere (IRE)**[25] 5411 10-11-11 112.............................. SamJones 102
(Barry Leavy) *bhd: rdn 11th: sn giving himself too much to do: modest prog fr 3 out but nvr remotely on terms* **9/1**

324/ P **Tafika**[44] 5066 9-11-12 113..(p) LiamTreadwell
(Paul Webber) *plld much too hrd in rr: clsd to 3rd gng strly at 11th and 2nd at 13th tl lost pl rapidly 15th: fading bdly whn p.u last* **11/4**[1]

51P/ P **Mission Complete (IRE)**[129] 3535 7-11-9 110..........(p) RichieMcLernon
(Jonjo O'Neill) *trckd ldrs tl rdn 12th: lost tch wl bef 15th: t.o and p.u 2 out* **4/1**[3]

PP/ P **Tarraco (FR)**[26] 5380 6-11-6 107... AidanColeman
(Venetia Williams) *cl up early: dropped bk last at 11th: tailing off whn p.u 13th* **8/1**

7m 10.1s (23.70) **Going Correction** +1.00s/f (Soft) 7 Ran SP% **113.9**
Speed ratings: **103,99,98,96, , ,**
toteswingers 1&2 £6.70, 1&3 £4.50, 2&3 £8.60 CSF £37.81 CT £212.99 TOTE £4.00: £1.80, £3.00; EX 30.40 Trifecta £72.50 Pool: £853.45 - 8.81 winning units..
Owner Colin Roberts **Bred** B J Eckley **Trained** Naunton, Gloucs

FOCUS
Fence eight (the last in back straight) was omitted in all chases. A moderate staying handicap chase.

322 WR DAVIES TOYOTA STAFFORD BEGINNERS' CHASE (13 fncs 2 omitted) 2m 4f
4:35 (4:35) (Class 4) 5-Y-0+ **£3,768** (£1,106; £553; £276)

Form RPR

3/1- 1 **Green Wizard (IRE)**[11] 121 7-11-0 0...................................... RyanMania 129+
(Sue Smith) *j. soundly: 2nd tl led 8th: drew rt away fr 3 out: 20 l ahd last: eased flat: impressive* **11/8**[1]

233/ 2 26 **South Stack**[71] 4574 8-11-0 0.. JasonMaguire 106+
(Kim Bailey) *trckd ldrs: j.v.slowly 7th: rallied to go 2nd bef 10th: drvn and sn lost tch w wnr: racing idly after: eased flat* **9/4**[2]

20P/ 3 10 **Jonny Rye (IRE)**[44] 5060 9-10-11 0................................ RyanMahon[(3)] 88
(Michael Appleby) *bhd: pushed along 6th: wknd and mstke 8th: virtually t.o bef 10th tl 2 out: fnlly consented to fin w a real rattle and snatched remote 3rd* **11/1**

325/ 4 hd **Gizzit (IRE)**[29] 5330 7-11-0 0..(p) AndrewThornton 88
(Karen George) *hld up in tch: effrt 9th: pressed ldrs bef next: sn drvn and one pce as wnr and 2nd completely outpcd him: jst lost remote 3rd* **25/1**

505/ 5 ¾ **Lucky Lukey**[157] 2952 7-11-0 0.. SeanQuinlan 87
(Jennie Candlish) *cl up tl 9th: rdn and wknd bef next* **9/1**

0/0- 6 5 **Wheelavher**[11] 122 7-10-9 0 ow2................................(t) NickScholfield 75
(Claire Dyson) *led tl 8th: drvn and lost 2nd bef 10th: steadily dropped rt out* **80/1**

562/ 7 6 **Basford Ben**[98] 4060 5-11-0 0..(p) SamThomas 76
(Jennie Candlish) *in last pair: j.v.slowly 7th: lost tch and mstke next: t.o fr 10th* **5/1**[3]

5m 23.9s (18.40) **Going Correction** +1.00s/f (Soft) 7 Ran SP% **113.0**
Speed ratings: **103,92,88,88,88 86,83**
toteswingers 1&2 £1.50, 1&3 £3.40, 2&3 £3.70 CSF £4.90 TOTE £2.70: £1.60, £1.70; EX 5.90 Trifecta £28.90 Pool: £2001.71 - 51.93 winning units..
Owner Mrs S Smith **Bred** Eric Barrett **Trained** High Eldwick, W Yorks
■ Stewards' Enquiry : Nick Scholfield four-day ban: weighed-in 2lb heavy (May 29-Jun 1)

FOCUS
A fair beginners' chase in which they went a decent gallop on the heavy ground.

323 MOUNT ARGUS OPEN HUNTERS' CHASE (16 fncs 2 omitted) 3m
5:10 (5:10) (Class 6) 5-Y-0+ **£1,114** (£425)

Form RPR

632/ 1 **Vic Venturi (IRE)**[54] 4906 13-11-12 112.......................(vt) NicodeBoinville 123
(S Rea) *mde all at decent pce: rdn but stl 4 l clr and looked to have more to offer whn lft virtually solo 2 out* **5/4**[1]

P/3- 2 65 **Hurricane Carter (IRE)**[8] 165 13-11-5 103................ MrSRWilliams[(7)] 58
(S R Williams) *3rd tl lft 2nd and hit 11th: last and fading rapidly after next: sn nrly a fence bhd: lft 2nd 2 out* **40/1**

1PP/ P **Radetsky March (IRE)**[29] 5342 10-12-1 118.........(p) ConorShoemark[(5)]
(Miss Sally Duckett) *pressed wnr: nt fluent 8th: hanging lft whn lost action bef 11th and p.u* **9/2**[3]

113/ U **Robin Will (FR)**[43] 5106 8-12-6 127......................... MrJoshuaGuerriero 125
(Richard Woollacott) *taken to post v early: t.k.h: cantered along in last tl wnt 2nd after 12th: clsng whn nt fluent 3 out: stl 4 l down and jst coming off bridle whn mstke and uns rdr 2 out* **11/8**[2]

6m 39.3s (24.20) **Going Correction** +1.00s/f (Soft) 4 Ran SP% **107.2**
Speed ratings: **99,77, ,**
CSF £17.86 TOTE £2.00; EX 17.60 Trifecta £19.80 Pool: £1102.81 - 41.59 winning units..

Owner S W Dunn **Bred** Mrs P And C Brabazon **Trained** Belbroughton, Worcs
■ Stewards' Enquiry : Nico de Boinville two-day ban: used whip when clearly winning (May 29-30)
FOCUS
A fair small-field hunter chase.

324 32RED.COM MARES' STANDARD OPEN NATIONAL HUNT FLAT RACE 2m
5:45 (5:45) (Class 6) 4-6-Y-O **£1,559** (£457; £228; £114)

Form RPR
20/ 1 **Keshi Pearl**[40] 5163 5-10-12 0 RichardJohnson 105+
(Henry Daly) *trckd ldrs and t.k.h: effrt to ld over 3f out: sn clr: styd on wl fnl 2f: a in command* **15/8**[1]
13/ 2 6 **Run Ructions Run (IRE)**[31] 5316 4-10-8 0 MrJHamilton(7) 101
(Tim Easterby) *cl up: wnt 2nd 6f out: chsd wnr fr over 3f out: rdn and kpt on steadily but a hld* **8/1**
3 1 1/4 **Shuil Gealach (IRE)** 5-10-12 0 PaulMoloney 97
(Paul Webber) *hld up in midfield: rdn and effrt 3f out: wnt 3rd over 2f out: nvr able to chal and wkng fnl 100yds* **17/2**
4 2 1/4 **Fire Tower** 5-10-12 0 WayneHutchinson 95
(Richard Phillips) *bhd: hdwy 6f out: chsng ldrs over 2f out: rn green: rdn and no imp after* **16/1**
5 17 **Ballyhollow** 6-10-5 0 PatrickCorbett(7) 78
(Rebecca Curtis) *t.k.h: cl up for 12f: sn wknd: eased 2f out: t.o* **5/1**[2]
6 2 **Bad Girls (FR)** 4-10-8 0 TomScudamore 72
(David Pipe) *plld hrd: cl up tl rdn and lost pl 6f out: wl btn 3f out: t.o* **7/1**[3]
6/ 7 20 **Pennies And Pounds**[21] 5511 6-10-12 0 SamTwiston-Davies 56
(Julian Smith) *a bhd: t.o over 2f out* **20/1**
8 10 **Passing Fiesta** 4-10-8 0 WillKennedy 42
(Sarah-Jayne Davies) *t.k.h: cl 2nd tl led 6f out: rdn and hdd over 3f out: fdd rapidly: bdly t.o* **12/1**
9 20 **Valley Road** 5-10-12 0 ConorO'Farrell 26
(Tim Dennis) *last and rdn after 4f: hopelessly t.o fr 1/2-way: v green* **40/1**
10 8 **Wymeswold** 6-10-7 0 JamesBanks(5) 18
(Michael Mullineaux) *ungainly in rr and rdn after 4f: t.o fnl 6f: fin eventually* **66/1**
11 6 **Tara Dove** 5-10-12 0 DavidEngland 12
(Michael Appleby) *t.k.h in slow r: led tl hdd and stopped to nil 6f out: fin eventually* **9/1**

4m 10.3s (23.90) **Going Correction** +1.35s/f (Heav)
WFA 4 from 5yo+ 4lb **11** Ran SP% **117.9**
Speed ratings: **94,91,90,89,80 79,69,64,54,50 47**
toteswingers 1&2 £3.20, 1&3 £6.20, 2&3 £21.50 CSF £17.15 TOTE £3.70: £1.10, £2.90, £2.70; EX 14.10 Trifecta £202.70 Pool: £792.78 - 2.93 winning units..
Owner The Wadeley Partnership **Bred** W P Jenks **Trained** Stanton Lacy, Shropshire
FOCUS
An interesting bumper in which they went a sedate gallop early on.
T/Plt: £48.60 to a £1 stake. Pool: £54,221.23 - 813.91 winning tickets. T/Qpdt: £24.30 to a £1 stake. Pool: £3063.77 - 93.00 winning tickets. IM

302 FONTWELL (L-H)
Thursday, May 16
OFFICIAL GOING: Good (good to soft in places; 7.0)
Wind: virtually nil Weather: sunny

325 32RED.COM NOVICES' HUNTERS' CHASE (FOR THE GUY PEATE MEMORIAL CHALLENGE TROPHY) (19 fncs) 3m 2f 110y
5:10 (5:11) (Class 6) 5-Y-O+ **£1,317** (£405; £202)

Form RPR
1 **Adept Approach (IRE)**[26] 7-11-9 0 MrPGHall(5) 116+
(P G Hall) *hld up: hdwy 7th: trckd ldrs after 13th: pushed along to press ldr 4 out: led narrowly 3 out: awkward on landing 2 out: disputing whn lft clr last: rdn out* **4/6**[1]
2 6 **Alskamatic**[10] 7-11-7 0 MissEEMacMahon(7) 106
(Richard J Bandey) *disp ld most of way tl rdn appr 4 out: styd on same pce fr 3 out: lft 3rd at the last: wnt 2nd run-in* **5/1**[2]
3 3/4 **Rather Curious (IRE)**[10] 9-11-9 99 (p) MrRMcCarthy(5) 106
(David Phelan) *trckd ldrs: rdn after 4 out: styd on same pce fr next: lft 2nd at the last: no ex whn lost 2nd run-in* **25/1**
4 5 **Owenacurra (IRE)**[45] 8-11-7 0 (p) MrStuartRobinson(7) 103
(Miss Rose Grissell) *untidy 1st: mid-div: chsd ldrs 8th tl 10th: rousted along and kpt in tch: styd on same pce fr 3 out: lft 4th at the last* **8/1**[3]
45/ P **Showman (IRE)**[19] 10-11-7 0 (p) ThomasCheesman(7)
(M S Dilworth) *trckd ldrs: hit 9th and 12th: pushed along 14th: wknd next: bhd whn p.u after 4 out* **50/1**
PPP/ P **Buffalo Stampede (IRE)**[19] 10-11-7 0 (t) MrGGorman(7)
(Miss V Collins) *trckd ldrs 2nd tl 10th: sn rdn and dropped to rr: t.o fr14th: p.u after 4 out* **66/1**
02P/ P **Man From Moscow**[26] 10-11-7 79 (v) MrWHickman(7)
(Mrs Alison Hickman) *trckd ldrs tl 4th: hit next: sn struggling in rr: t.o whn p.u bef 14th* **16/1**
P **Oscarsfriend (IRE)**[10] 9-11-9 0 MrJSole(5)
(C J Lawson) *hld up: reminder 9th: hdwy 10th: jst abt in tch but struggling whn p.u after 13th* **14/1**
5/ U **West Cork Flash (IRE)**[26] 9-11-7 97 (p) MrsCLDennis(7) 114+
(Mrs C Dennis) *disp ld most of way: narrowly hdd 3 out: sn pushed along: disputing again w str ch whn mstke and uns rdr last* **10/1**

6m 53.6s (-7.50) **Going Correction** -0.05s/f (Good) **9** Ran SP% **116.7**
Speed ratings: **109,107,107,105, , , ,**
Tote Swingers: 1&2 £2.50, 1&3 £5.60, 2&3 £7.70 CSF £4.66 TOTE £2.00: £1.60, £1.60, £3.70; EX 5.90 Trifecta £40.30 Pool: £1,880.23 - 34.98 winning units..
Owner Christopher Hall **Bred** N J Connors **Trained** Eridge Green, Kent
FOCUS
Fences sited on outer. This hunter chase card used to be run at Folkestone, but since its closure it has now been transferred to Fontwell. A decent novice hunter chase and the winner should win plenty more.

326 32RED CASINO NOVICES' HUNTERS' CHASE (15 fncs) 2m 4f
5:40 (5:40) (Class 6) 5-Y-O+ **£987** (£303; £151)

Form RPR
2/6- 1 **Bay To Go (IRE)**[15] 58 7-12-0 113 MrPYork 98+
(Mrs H M Kemp) *trckd ldrs: jnd ldr 3 out: led appr 2 out: rdn clr run-in* **4/9**[1]
2 4 1/2 **The Rattler Obrien (IRE)**[19] 7-11-7 0 MrBRivett(7) 92
(A Pennock) *trckd ldr: pressed ldr fr 10th tl rdn gng to 3 out: disp cl 2nd fr next: kpt on same pce run-in* **9/2**[2]
3 hd **West Of The Road (IRE)**[19] 7-12-0 0 (v) MissGAndrews 91
(Mrs L Braithwaite) *led: reminder after 5th: rdn after 4 out: hdd bef 2 out: kpt on same pce* **6/1**[3]
4 21 **Marlpit Oak**[19] 8-11-0 0 MrLKilgarriff(7) 68
(J H Young) *trckd ldrs: rdn after 4 out: hld whn mstke 3 out: wknd next* **16/1**
53P/ P **Fitobust (IRE)**[10] 7-11-7 0 MrJoeHill(7)
(Alan Hill) *hld up last but wl in tch: mstke 10th: rdn after 11th: btn 5th whn p.u bef 3 out* **25/1**

5m 13.1s (5.80) **Going Correction** -0.05s/f (Good) **5** Ran SP% **111.4**
Speed ratings: **86,84,84,75,**
CSF £3.19 TOTE £1.60: £1.10, £1.30; EX 3.20 Trifecta £5.00 Pool: £1,053.43 - 155.22 winning units..
Owner Mrs Heather Kemp **Bred** Brett Merry **Trained** Banbury, Oxon
FOCUS
Not a bad hunter chase and the winner didn't need to be anywhere near his best.

327 32RED MAIDEN HUNTERS' CHASE (FOR THE CUCKOO MAIDEN CHALLENGE CUP) (16 fncs) 2m 6f
6:15 (6:15) (Class 6) 5-Y-O+ **£987** (£303; £151)

Form RPR
030/ 1 **Bit Of A Clown (IRE)**[19] 7-11-9 0 MrJSole(5) 104
(Ian Cobb) *in tch: jnd ldr 7th: shkn up 11th: led after 3 out: nt fluent last: styd on wl fnl 100yds: rdn out* **4/1**[3]
322/ 2 3 1/2 **Dusshera (IRE)**[12] 8-11-7 94 MrPYork 96+
(P York) *nvr fluent: j.lft most of way: trcking ldr whn hmpd 2nd: in tch: pushed along fr 9th: rdn after 12th: wnt 2nd 2 out: styd on same pce: no ex fnl 100yds* **5/4**[1]
232/ 3 3 **Earl Grez (FR)**[26] 8-11-7 94 (p) MrJoeHill(7) 97
(Alan Hill) *t.k.h: trckd ldr: led 3rd tl 4th: outpcd gng to 11th: styd on after 3 out. 3rd whn stmbld next: kpt on same pce fr last* **7/2**[2]
4 5 **The Ketchup Kid (IRE)**[26] 5-11-9 0 (p) MrRMcCarthy(5) 94
(David Phelan) *in tch: rdn to chse ldrs after 12th: styd on same pce fr 3 out* **20/1**
5 4 **Just Bridget (IRE)**[12] 7-11-0 0 MissCHaydon(7) 82
(Miss C M E Haydon) *hld up last: reminder after 8th: rdn after 4 out: plugged on but nvr a threat* **10/1**
2/ 6 25 **King's Chase (IRE)**[10] 11-12-0 0 MissGAndrews 77
(N W Padfield) *hld up: hit 10th: reminder: sme prog whn rdn after 4 out: wknd 2 out* **8/1**
P/ 7 5 **Irish Rebel (IRE)**[19] 9-11-7 0 (t) MrRGSpencer(7) 72
(Miss Clare Hobson) *led: wnt rt 2nd: bmpd and hdd 3rd: led 4th: jnd 7th: 1 l clr whn j. into 3 out: sn hdd and rdn: wknd next* **16/1**

5m 49.9s (6.90) **Going Correction** -0.05s/f (Good) **7** Ran SP% **117.5**
Speed ratings: **85,83,82,80,79 70,68**
Tote Swingers: 1&2 £2.90, 1&3 £1.90, 2&3 £3.00 CSF £10.41 TOTE £4.50: £2.40, £2.80; EX 17.20 Trifecta £35.50 Pool: £883.79 - 18.66 winning units..
Owner D Foulkes **Bred** Vincent O'Connor And Adrian Harnett **Trained** Pulborough, W Sussex
FOCUS
A moderate maiden hunter chase. The winner is rated in line with his old hurdles form.

328 32REDBET.COM UNITED HUNTS OPEN CHAMPION HUNTERS' CHASE (21 fncs) 3m 4f
6:50 (6:50) (Class 6) 6-Y-O+ **£1,871** (£580; £290; £145)

Form RPR
2/4- 1 **Arbour Hill (IRE)**[15] 60 11-11-7 99 (p) MrMWall(3) 103+
(Miss Francesca Moller) *w ldr tl 7th: trckd ldrs: led 15th: rdn whn idling fr 3 out: fnd plenty to assert whn jnd after last: drvn out* **9/4**[2]
PP3/ 2 6 **Orfeo Conti (FR)**[19] 11-11-3 0 MrOWedmore(7) 96
(Miss Rose Grissell) *racd in 4th: travelling wl after 4 out: hdwy into 2nd 2 out: rdn to chal idling wnr briefly after last: sn hld* **7/1**
2/0- 3 4 1/2 **Freddies Return (IRE)**[15] 62 12-12-0 113 (t) MrPYork 96
(P York) *j.lft at times: in last trio: nvr travelling fr 7th: drvn after 13th: styd on same pce fr 3 out: wnt 3rd nr fin: nvr trbld ldng pair* **2/1**[1]
060/ 4 1/2 **Duke Of Kentford**[18] 11-11-3 93 (p) MrJDocker(7) 91
(Stuart Morris) *trckd ldrs: jnd ldr 9th: led 11th tl next: lft in ld 13th tl 15th: rdn to chse wnr bef next tl appr 2 out: sn no ex: lost 3rd nr fin* **7/2**[3]
234/ F **Master T (USA)**[12] 14-11-7 0 MrPBull(3)
(Peter Bull) *hld up: blnd bdly 3rd: hdwy briefly 16th: sn lost pl u.p: hld in 5th whn fell heavily 3 out* **50/1**
153/ P **Badger**[39] 13-11-3 0 MrsCLDennis(7)
(Mrs C Dennis) *hld up in last trio: wknd 4 out: sn p.u* **25/1**
545/ F **Pastek (FR)**[19] 10-11-3 80 MrMPeaty(7)
(Martin Peaty) *led tl 11th: led next: crumpled on landing and fell 13th* **16/1**

7m 28.4s (1.10) **Going Correction** -0.05s/f (Good) **7** Ran SP% **110.5**
Speed ratings: **96,94,93,92, , ,**
Tote Swingers: 1&2 £3.50, 1&3 £1.60, 2&3 £5.40 CSF £16.85 TOTE £3.80: £2.00, £5.10; EX 19.50 Trifecta £43.90 Pool: £645.07 - 11.00 winning units..
Owner H Wilson **Bred** Colm O'Leary **Trained** Warwickshire
FOCUS
The feature race on the card was run over a distance 3f shorter than the corresponding race when run at Folkestone. The second and third from last year's race each went one place better this year, which gives a handle on the form.

329 32REDPOKER.COM OPEN HUNTERS' CHASE (FOR THE STUART ADAMSON MEMORIAL TROPHY) (16 fncs) 2m 6f
7:25 (7:25) (Class 6) 5-Y-O+ **£1,317** (£405; £202)

Form RPR
1/ 1 **Hawkeye Native (IRE)**[20] 5541 7-11-13 0 MrMatthewBarber(5) 122+
(M Barber) *trckd ldr: looked to duck out 2nd: trckd ldng pair fr 4th tl led after 10th: rdn after 3 out: styd on wl: rdn out* **6/4**[1]
2/2- 2 2 3/4 **Divine Intavention (IRE)**[15] 59 9-12-5 109 MrMWall(3) 124
(Miss Francesca Moller) *trckd ldrs: jnd ldr after 4th: hmpd next: led 8th tl after 10th: mstke next: sn rdn: chal again 4 out tl next: kpt on but a being hld fr last* **6/4**[1]
2P4/ 3 20 **Start Royal (FR)**[47] 9-11-11 107 MrJoeHill(7) 100
(Alan Hill) *led: j.lft at times: wnt lft and bmpd 5th: hdd 8th: rdn to chse ldng pair after 4 out: wknd 2 out* **5/1**[2]
322/ 4 33 **Armoury House**[18] 12-11-9 96 MissCBoxall(5) 66
(D Buckett) *hld up: wnt 4th after 10th: wknd after 4 out: t.o* **10/1**[3]
3FP/ P **William Butler (IRE)**[10] 13-11-7 108 MrOWedmore(7)
(Mrs Libby Lawson) *hld up: lost tch fr 11th: t.o whn p.u bef 4 out* **33/1**

The Form Book Jumps, Raceform Ltd, Compton, RG20 6NL.

023/ P **Mount Sandel (IRE)**[19] 12-11-7 0 .... MrWHickman(7)
(Mrs Alison Hickman) *trckd ldrs: struggling 9th: wknd bef 11th: bhd whn blnd 4 out: sn p.u* **25/1**
F2P/ P **Le Commencement (IRE)**[12] 11-12-0 0 .... MrPYork
(I Heaney) *trckd ldrs tl awkward 10th: sn rdn and wknd: p.u bef 12th* **25/1**
5m 40.1s (-2.90) **Going Correction** -0.05s/f (Good) **7** Ran SP% **116.4**
Speed ratings: **103,102,94,82,** ,
Tote Swingers: 1&2 £1.40, 1&3 £5.30, 2&3 £3.70 CSF £4.26 TOTE £2.50: £1.70, £2.00; EX 4.10 Trifecta £20.10 Pool: £425.66 - 20.10 winning units..
Owner N Adams **Bred** Albert Wylie **Trained** Narberth, Pembrokeshire
FOCUS
A fair hunter chase, and they finished as the market suggested they should, with three going clear on the final circuit before the joint favourites battled it out in a duel from the home turn. Another step forward from the progressive winner.

330 32RED.COM MARES' HUNTERS' CHASE (19 fncs) 3m 2f 110y
7:55 (7:56) (Class 6) 5-Y-0+ **£987** (£303; £151)

Form RPR
311/ 1 **Double Mead**[10] 11-11-12 121 .... MrsAlexDunn(3) 101+
(Alexandra Dunn) *taken v early to s: hld up 3rd wl off pce early: wnt 2nd 4 out: travelling best whn chal next: mstke 2 out: led bef last: pushed clr* **1/7**[1]
P/5- 2 9 **Topless (IRE)**[15] 61 12-11-2 85 ....(tp) MissCLWills(5) 81
(C W Loggin) *v reluctant to leave paddock: chsd clr ldr: clsd on ldr 4th tl rdn whn ldr wnt clr again after 13th: lost 2nd 4 out: styd on again fr last to snatch 2nd towards fin* **6/1**[2]
403/ 3 ½ **Annie Confidential (IRE)**[19] 10-11-2 72 .... MrKevinJones(5) 81
(M J Jackson) *stole gd advantage and set str pce: diminished advantage after 4th: kicked clr again after 13th tl sn after 4 out: rdn whn jnd next: hdd bef last: sn hld: no ex whn lost 2nd towards fin* **16/1**[3]
7m 1.8s (0.70) **Going Correction** -0.05s/f (Good) **3** Ran SP% **107.7**
Speed ratings: **96,93,93**
CSF £1.62 TOTE £1.10; EX 2.20 Trifecta £1.60 Part won. Pool: £420.60 - 0.78 winning units..
Owner Mrs K R Smith-Maxwell **Bred** Ashfield, Dawson And McGregor **Trained** Wellington, Somerset
FOCUS
An uncompetitive hunter chase and the easy winner was a stone+ off her best. What looked a mere formality for the hot favourite could have turned into controversy as the starter let them go before Double Mead was fully on the course, allowing an opportunistic move from Annie Confidential.

331 32REDBINGO.COM OPEN HUNTERS' CHASE (FOR THE UNITED HUNTS CUP) (13 fncs) 2m 2f
8:25 (8:26) (Class 6) 5-Y-0+ **£1,317** (£405; £202)

Form RPR
2/5- 1 **What Of It (IRE)**[15] 57 10-11-11 108 .... MrTDWard(7) 113+
(Mrs Sarah Ward) *disp ld tl 7th: led 4 out: kpt on wl fr 2 out: rdn out* **7/2**[2]
11P/ 2 2½ **Cedrus Libani (IRE)**[25] 12-11-7 0 .... MrWHickman(7) 106
(Mrs Libby Lawson) *relustant to line up: bhd: hdwy to trck ldrs 4th: rdn and ev ch after 4 out tl next: kpt chsng wnr and a being hld fr 2 out* **12/1**
P05/ 3 1½ **Kikos (FR)**[46] 5040 11-11-7 94 .... MrSDavies-Thomas(7) 104
(Mrs K Lee) *disp ld tl clr ldr 7th: hdd 4 out: sn rdn: kpt on same pce fr next* **20/1**
P22/ 4 6 **Herecomesthetruth (IRE)**[26] 11-12-0 124 .... MrPYork 102
(Chris Gordon) *j.rt: disp ld tl after 4th: chsd ldrs: rdn along fr 7th: kpt on same pce fr 3 out* **5/4**[1]
300/ 5 18 **Qrackers (FR)**[25] 5436 9-11-11 99 ....(t) MissHannahWatson(3) 87
(Miss V Collins) *mid-div: rdn after 4 out: nvr any imp: wknd 2 out* **14/1**
P **Can't Agree**[18] 8-11-2 0 ....(t) MrJonathanBailey(5)
(Stuart Morris) *a in rr: t.o whn p.u after 4 out* **25/1**
036/ P **Alrafid (IRE)**[473] 14-11-7 0 ....(b) MissTWorsley(7)
(Ms G Howell) *mid-div tl 5th: sn bhd: t.o whn p.u bef 8th* **28/1**
046/ P **The Hardy Boy**[26] 13-11-11 0 .... MrPBull(3)
(Miss N Worley) *mid-div tl 6th: sn bhd: t.o whn p.u after 4 out* **40/1**
0F4/ P **Restezen D'Armor (FR)**[12] 8-11-7 122 ....(p) MissCVHart(7)
(Mrs O C Jackson) *chsd ldrs tl rdn after 4 out: wknd next: p.u bef 2 out* **4/1**[3]
4m 40.6s (5.90) **Going Correction** -0.05s/f (Good) **9** Ran SP% **115.5**
Speed ratings: **84,82,82,79,71** , , ,
Tote Swingers: 1&2 £4.50, 1&3 £5.60, 2&3 £5.40 CSF £38.46 TOTE £5.10: £1.70, £1.80, £3.80; EX 35.60 Trifecta £315.40 Part won. Pool: £420.60 - 0.78 winning tickets..
Owner T D Ward **Bred** Mrs Margaret Norris **Trained** East Woodhay, Hampshire
FOCUS
The shortest race on the card and it was duly run at a good pace. The winner was the only one in the field to have previously won a hunter chase this season. A modest hunter chase. The third is perhaps the best guide.
T/Plt: £11.50 to a £1 stake. Pool: £43,418.90 - 2,735.02 winning tickets. T/Qpdt: £11.60 to a £1 stake. Pool: £2,615.65 - 166.10 winning tickets. TM

[8]LUDLOW (R-H)
Thursday, May 16
OFFICIAL GOING: Good (good to firm in places; 8.1)
Wind: Light against Weather: Cloudy with sunny spells

332 BBC RADIO SHROPSHIRE CONDITIONAL JOCKEYS' (S) HURDLE (9 hdls) 2m
5:30 (5:30) (Class 5) 4-8-Y-0 **£2,599** (£763; £381; £190)

Form RPR
440/ 1 **Dantari (IRE)**[218] 1783 8-11-4 110 ....(tp) ConorRing(8) 111
(Evan Williams) *led: rdn appr 3 out: hdd next: edgd lft flat: rallied to ld nr fin* **5/2**[2]
1/2- 2 hd **Descaro (USA)**[1] 319 7-11-0 112 .... CiaranMckee(8) 108
(John O'Shea) *a.p: chsd wnr 4th: led 2 out: rdn and edgd rt flat: hdd nr fin* **2/1**[1]
4/5- 3 15 **Cruise Control**[13] 91 7-10-12 85 .... HarryChalloner 85
(John Bryan Groucott) *hld up: hdwy and mstke 6th: wknd 3 out* **10/1**[3]
F0P/ 4 91 **El Camino Real (IRE)**[33] 5288 5-10-12 0 ....(t) KielanWoods 1
(Barry Leavy) *w ldr tl after 3rd: j.ft and lost 2nd next: wknd 6th: t.o* **18/1**
2/2- U **Lauberhorn**[16] 47 6-11-1 106 ....(v) AdamWedge(3)
(Evan Williams) *chsd ldrs tl blnd and uns rdr 2nd* **2/1**[1]
3m 41.9s (-7.60) **Going Correction** -0.375s/f (Good) **5** Ran SP% **109.6**
Speed ratings: **104,103,96,50,**
CSF £8.04 TOTE £2.50: £1.60, £1.30; EX 9.90 Trifecta £28.10 Pool: £601.52 - 16.00 winning units..No bid for the winner.
Owner D J Burchell **Bred** His Highness The Aga Khan's Studs S C **Trained** Llancarfan, Vale Of Glamorgan
FOCUS
Bends moved to provide best available ground. Stable bend combined. An ordinary seller in which the first three ran pretty much to their marks.

333 LYCETTS INSURANCE BROKERS NOVICES' H'CAP HURDLE (9 hdls) 2m
6:05 (6:05) (Class 4) (0-110,108) 4-Y-0+ **£4,548** (£1,335; £667; £333)

Form RPR
0/1- 1 **Church Field (IRE)**[7] 177 5-11-0 92 7ex .... APMcCoy 104+
(Jonjo O'Neill) *a.p: led appr 3 out: shkn up flat: styd on wl* **1/2**[1]
356/ 2 5 **Eightfold**[14] 5281 4-11-12 108 ....(t) ConorO'Farrell 109+
(Seamus Durack) *hld up: hdwy to join wnr 3 out: mstke last: no ex flat* **16/1**
660/ 3 2½ **Bob's Legend (IRE)**[22] 5509 7-11-6 98 .... SamTwiston-Davies 98
(Martin Bosley) *hld up: hdwy 3 out: sn rdn: styd on same pce: wnt 3rd nr fin* **16/1**
666/ 4 ½ **Honey Of A Kitten (USA)**[17] 279 5-10-13 91 ....(v) AidanColeman 91
(David Evans) *chsd ldrs: rdn bef 3 out: no ex appr last* **7/1**[2]
305/ 5 1¾ **Kayalar (IRE)**[13] 4322 5-11-12 104 .... PaulMoloney 102
(Evan Williams) *chsd ldr to 6th: rdn after 3 out: no ex appr last* **7/1**[2]
006/ 6 40 **Duneen Dream (USA)**[243] 272 8-9-11 78 .... RobertDunne(3) 55
(Nikki Evans) *led: nt fluent: hdd appr 3 out: sn wknd: t.o* **50/1**
630/ B **Blewit (IRE)**[26] 5412 5-10-8 91 .... HarryChalloner(5)
(William Kinsey) *prom: losing pl whn b.d 4th* **12/1**[3]
443/ F **Fairy Alisha**[23] 5479 5-10-10 95 .... JoshWall(7)
(Trevor Wall) *hld up: fell 4th* **14/1**
3m 43.2s (-6.30) **Going Correction** -0.375s/f (Good) **8** Ran SP% **119.8**
Speed ratings (Par 105): **100,97,96,96,95 75,** ,
Tote Swingers: 1&2 £11.80, 1&3 £2.90, 2&3 £5.80 CSF £11.19 CT £75.73 TOTE £1.70: £1.10, £2.90, £3.70; EX 8.30 Trifecta £53.10 Pool: £715.26 - 10.08 winning units..
Owner John P McManus **Bred** Mrs Eleanor Hadden **Trained** Cheltenham, Gloucs
FOCUS
An ordinary novice handicap. The winner was well in but this looks another step up and he can win again.

334 TANNERS WINES H'CAP CHASE (22 fncs) 3m 1f 110y
6:40 (6:40) (Class 3) (0-130,130) 5-Y-£9,495 (£2,805; £1,402; £702; £351)

Form RPR
F53/ 1 **Billie Magern**[18] 6 9-11-12 130 ....(v1) SamTwiston-Davies 144+
(Nigel Twiston-Davies) *led to 6th: chsd ldr tl led again 15th: clr 5 out: easily* **9/2**[2]
433/ 2 14 **Gambo (IRE)**[18] 12 7-11-2 120 .... PaulMoloney 121
(Evan Williams) *hld up: hdwy and mstke 17th: chsd wnr 2 out: mstke last: wknd flat* **4/1**[1]
0U0/ 3 4½ **Giorgio Quercus (FR)**[18] 6 8-11-6 129 ....(b) NicodeBoinville(5) 123
(Nicky Henderson) *prom: rdn 2 out: wknd bef last* **5/1**[3]
4P0/ 4 8 **Rockiteer (IRE)**[39] 5199 10-11-2 120 ....(p) RichardJohnson 106
(Henry Daly) *chsd ldr 3rd tl led 6th: hdd and mstke 15th: rdn and wknd appr 4 out* **5/1**[3]
P5/- 5 11 **Basoda**[30] 5341 10-10-9 113 ....(tp) NickScholfield 90
(Kim Bailey) *prom: mstke and lost pl 6th: wknd 15th: t.o* **11/2**
42/- 6 14 **Prophete De Guye (FR)**[29] 5354 10-11-7 125 .... FelixDeGiles 92
(James Evans) *hld up: wknd 15th: t.o* **10/1**
102/ 7 48 **Sun Tzu (IRE)**[232] 1642 9-11-7 125 ....(v) TomO'Brien 45
(Peter Bowen) *chsd ldrs to 16th: wkng whn blnd 5 out: t.o* **8/1**
521/ F **Point Blank (IRE)**[350] 504 7-11-5 123 .... RichieMcLernon
(Jonjo O'Neill) *hld up: fell 8th* **16/1**
6m 20.5s (-14.80) **Going Correction** -0.375s/f (Good) **8** Ran SP% **113.0**
Speed ratings: **107,102,101,98,95 91,76,**
Tote Swingers: 1&2 £3.60, 1&3 £6.20, 2&3 £6.50 CSF £22.83 CT £91.64 TOTE £4.90: £1.90, £1.50, £1.60; EX 16.10 Trifecta £266.90 Part won. Pool: £355.92 - 0.98 winning units..
Owner Exors of the Late Roger Nicholls **Bred** Roger Nicholls **Trained** Naunton, Gloucs
FOCUS
A decent handicap chase and, at least on paper, it looked competitive. The winner is rated back to his ebst with the second close to his mark.

335 ANN ESP MEMORIAL HUNTERS' CHASE (17 fncs) 2m 4f
7:15 (7:15) (Class 6) 5-Y-0+ **£1,871** (£580; £290; £145)

Form RPR
5/ 1 **Rebel Alliance (IRE)**[19] 8-11-3 0 ....(t) AlanJohns(7) 108+
(Richard A Thomas) *trckd ldrs: racd keenly: led 4th: rdn and edgd lft flat: all out* **17/2**
5PP/ 2 hd **Pathian Prince**[26] 10-11-10 92 .... MrNickWilliams 109+
(F B Clough) *a p: chsd wnr and nt fluent 5 out: sn rdn: ev ch next: looked hld last: rallied flat: jst failed* **10/3**[1]
5/0- 3 7 **Fresh Air And Fun (IRE)**[15] 63 10-11-9 115 .... MrLRPayter(5) 108
(Alastair Ralph) *chsd ldrs: mstkes 4th and 10th: outpcd 12th: rallied to go 3rd 3 out: no imp fr next* **4/1**[2]
164/ 4 10 **Intac (IRE)**[10] 11-11-7 119 ....(b) MrBGibbs(7) 97
(D C Gibbs) *led to 4th: chsd ldrs: rdn after 13th: lost 3rd 3 out: wknd next* **8/1**
05P/ 5 27 **Fairwood Present (IRE)**[42] 5138 15-11-3 104 .... MrBFurnival(7) 67
(John Buxton) *hld up: wknd 10th: t.o* **20/1**
2PP/ 6 4 **Archie Boy (IRE)**[10] 11-11-3 0 ....(t) MrRDPotter(7) 64
(J L Brotherton) *hld up: bhd fr 10th: t.o* **9/2**[3]
3/ 7 8 **Schindler's Prince (IRE)**[39] 8-11-3 0 .... MrJMRidley(7) 56
(Mrs Christine Hardinge) *prom: lost pl after 9th: wknd next: t.o* **8/1**
24F/ P **Thunder Child**[414] 5136 13-11-7 0 ....(t) ConorShoemark(3)
(N K Allin) *prom tl wknd 10th: t.o whn p.u bef 4 out* **14/1**
P **Arguidos (IRE)**[40] 9-11-3 0 .... MrEDavid(7)
(Byron Moorcroft) *hld up: wknd 10th: sn t.o: p.u bef 2 out* **12/1**
P **Porto Prince (IRE)**[19] 7-11-3 0 ....(p) MrJamieJenkinson(7)
(Mrs Belinda Clarke) *hld up: mstke 2nd: hdwy 8th: wknd 10th: mstke next: t.o whn p.u bef 3 out* **33/1**
5m 0.4s (-4.00) **Going Correction** -0.375s/f (Good) **10** Ran SP% **116.1**
Speed ratings: **93,92,90,86,75 73,70,** , ,
Tote Swingers: 1&2 £10.60, 1&3 £6.80, 2&3 £2.20 CSF £38.08 TOTE £10.80: £3.50, £1.60, £2.30; EX 25.50 Trifecta £191.70 Pool: £358.66 - 1.40 winning units..
Owner P J Pitt **Bred** Patrick Condon **Trained** Bromyard, Herefordshire

FOCUS
An ordinary hunter chase. The winner is rated in line with his old hurdles form.

336 LUDLOW RACECOURSE BOOKMAKERS H'CAP HURDLE (12 hdls) 3m
7:45 (7:45) (Class 3) (0-125,125) 4-Y-0 **£6,330** (£1,870; £935; £468; £234)

Form RPR
251/ **1** **Union Saint (FR)**[30] 5330 5-11-0 **113**.................. HaddenFrost 123+
(James Frost) *hld up: racd keenly: hdwy appr 3 out: led next: r.o wl: comf* **20/1**

634/ **2** 3 ½ **Susquehanna River (IRE)**[21] 5522 6-10-8 **107**...... SamTwiston-Davies 109
(Nigel Twiston-Davies) *led to 6th: led next to 8th: rdn appr 2 out: styd on same pce last* **9/1**

23P/ **3** 7 **Kanturk (IRE)**[527] 2989 7-10-4 **103**.................. TomO'Brien 100
(Peter Bowen) *prom: outpcd after 4 out: hdwy and mstke 2 out: rdn and hung lft flat: styd on to go 3rd nr fin* **14/1**

111/ **4** ½ **Oscar Sunset (IRE)**[421] 4995 6-11-12 **125**.................. PaulMoloney 122
(Evan Williams) *hld up: racd keenly: hdwy appr 3 out: rdn after next: nt fluent last: wknd flat* **6/1**[3]

54/- **5** 3 **Phare Isle (IRE)**[42] 5145 8-11-7 **125**..................(tp) KillianMoore(5) 118
(Ben Case) *hld up: hdwy 8th: rdn after 3 out: wknd bef last* **10/1**

550/ **6** 2 ½ **Andhaar**[27] 5372 7-11-9 **122**.................. SeanQuinlan 112
(Richard Phillips) *hld up: pushed along after 8th: nvr trbld ldrs* **20/1**

PP5/ **7** ¾ **Possol (FR)**[28] 5362 10-11-11 **124**.................. RichardJohnson 115
(Henry Daly) *w.r.s: hld up: plld hrd: rdn and wknd appr 3 out* **7/2**[1]

050/ **8** 3 ½ **Oscar's Secret (IRE)**[35] 5257 6-10-11 **110**..................(v[1]) NickScholfield 97
(Kim Bailey) *chsd ldr tl led 6th: hdd next: led 8th: blnd next: hit 3 out: rdn and hdd 2 out: sn wknd* **17/2**

042/ **9** 4 ½ **The Fonz**[26] 5410 7-11-7 **120**..................(p) BrendanPowell 102
(Renee Robeson) *chsd ldrs: rdn appr 3 out: wknd next* **9/2**[2]

41/- **10** 27 **Pyleigh Lass**[35] 5256 7-11-2 **115**.................. IanPopham 91
(Jeremy Scott) *chsd ldrs tl rdn and wknd appr 3 out: t.o* **9/2**[2]

5m 42.2s (-10.10) **Going Correction** -0.375s/f (Good) **10** Ran SP% **118.7**
Speed ratings (Par 107): **101,99,97,97,96 95,95,94,92,83**
Tote Swingers: 1&2 £16.20, 1&3 £49.70, 2&3 £18.70 CSF £189.55 CT £2595.66 TOTE £31.90: £5.60, £3.10, £4.40; EX 181.40 Trifecta £227.10 Part won. Pool: £302.86 - 0.01 winning units..

Owner P Tosh **Bred** Isabelle Garcon & Jean-Pierre Garcon **Trained** Scorriton, Devon

FOCUS
Plenty of these could be given chances. A big step up from the winner with the second setting the level.

337 ST JOHN AMBULANCE NOVICES' HURDLE (11 hdls) 2m 5f
8:15 (8:16) (Class 4) 4-Y-0+ **£4,548** (£1,335; £667; £333)

Form RPR
244/ **1** **Wake Your Dreams (IRE)**[72] 4579 5-10-12 113.................. SeanQuinlan 115+
(Jennie Candlish) *mde all: hit 2 out: rdn clr last: r.o wl* **2/1**[2]

361/ **2** 8 **Top Totti**[34] 5267 5-10-12 0.................. RichardJohnson 110+
(Henry Daly) *chsd wnr: hit 5th: blnd 8th: rdn appr 3 out: styng on same pce whn mstke last* **9/4**[3]

351/ **3** 11 **The Cockney Mackem (IRE)**[20] 5544 7-11-5 127(t) SamTwiston-Davies 104
(Nigel Twiston-Davies) *hld up: hdwy 4th: rdn and wknd appr last* **6/4**[1]

400/ **4** 3 ¼ **Moon Devil (IRE)**[585] 1927 6-10-12 0..................(p) TomO'Brien 95
(Peter Bowen) *prom tl rdn and wknd appr 2 out* **20/1**

456/ **5** 19 **Bad Made (IRE)**[35] 5255 5-10-12 0.................. AidanColeman 80
(David Evans) *chsd ldrs: nt fluent 2nd: lost pl 4th: bhd whn mstke 7th: t.o* **50/1**

5m 4.3s (-10.50) **Going Correction** -0.375s/f (Good) **5** Ran SP% **110.8**
Speed ratings (Par 105): **105,101,97,96,89**
CSF £7.14 TOTE £2.10: £1.80, £1.60; EX 7.20 Trifecta £10.90 Pool: £308.80 - 21.15 winning units..

Owner Pam Beardmore & Alan Baxter **Bred** J R Weston **Trained** Basford Green, Staffs

FOCUS
A modest novice event. The winner is rated to his mark.

338 LION LEINTWARDINE INTERMEDIATE OPEN NATIONAL HUNT FLAT RACE 2m
8:45 (8:45) (Class 5) 4-6-Y-0 **£2,599** (£763; £381; £190)

Form RPR
1/ **1** **Lemony Bay**[74] 4542 4-11-5 0.................. LeightonAspell 103+
(Oliver Sherwood) *hld up: hdwy to chse ldr over 1f out: r.o to ld nr fin* **9/4**[2]

13/ **2** ¾ **Wintered Well (IRE)**[25] 5428 5-11-9 0.................. SeanQuinlan 106
(Jennie Candlish) *led: pushed clr 3f out: rdn and hung lft ins fnl f: hdd nr fin* **8/1**[3]

2/ **3** 7 **My Wigwam Or Yours (IRE)**[18] 14 4-10-12 0.................. APMcCoy 90+
(Nicky Henderson) *trckd ldrs: racd keenly: hung lft fr over 4f out: rdn over 3f out: styd on same pce fnl 2f* **8/11**[1]

4/ **4** ¾ **Alongthewatchtower (IRE)**[150] 3112 5-11-2 0...... SamTwiston-Davies 91
(Barry Brennan) *w ldr to 1/2-way: rdn over 4f out: outpcd fnl 3f* **16/1**

5/ **5** 1 **G'Dai Sydney**[23] 5469 5-11-2 0..................(t) TomO'Brien 90
(Peter Bowen) *hld up: plld hrd: hdwy over 4f out: rdn over 2f out: wknd over 1f out* **16/1**

6 22 **Maisiefantaisie** 6-10-4 0.................. BenPoste(5) 63
(Tom Symonds) *prom: rdn over 3f out: wknd over 2f out: t.o* **20/1**

3m 39.5s (-4.40) **Going Correction** -0.375s/f (Good)
WFA 4 from 5yo+ 4lb **6** Ran SP% **116.3**
Speed ratings: **96,95,92,91,91 80**
Tote Swingers: 1&2 £2.70, 1&3 £1.10, 2&3 £2.30 CSF £20.82 TOTE £2.20: £2.00, £2.70; EX 18.60 Trifecta £19.90 Pool: £407.42 - 15.31 winning units..

Owner R Waters **Bred** G R Waters **Trained** Upper Lambourn, Berks

FOCUS
Not a bad little bumper.

T/Plt: £131.60 to a £1 stake. Pool: £40,436.18 - 224.21 winning tickets. T/Qpdt: £45.60 to a £1 stake. Pool: £3,692.40 - 59.80 winning tickets. CR

[310]PERTH (R-H)
Thursday, May 16

OFFICIAL GOING: Good (8.2)
Wind: Light, half against Weather: Cloudy

339 ST JOHN'S SHOPPING CENTRE PERTH NOVICES' HURDLE (12 hdls) 3m 110y
2:25 (2:25) (Class 4) 4-Y-0+ **£3,249** (£954; £477; £238)

Form RPR
212/ **1** **Indian Castle (IRE)**[45] 5072 5-11-5 129.................. JasonMaguire 120+
(Donald McCain) *j. sltly lft on occasions: mde all: reminders fr 1/2-way: drvn 3 out: nrly 3 l clr last: hld on towards fin* **1/3**[1]

340/ **2** nk **Ballyben (IRE)**[47] 5016 5-10-13 113.................. TomScudamore 113
(Lucinda Russell) *trckd ldrs: wnt 2nd 8th: effrt and hung lft appr 2 out: nrly 3 l down last: kpt on wl last 100yds: jst hld* **3/1**[2]

6/- **3** 28 **Monbeg (IRE)**[18] 19 6-10-13 0.................. WilsonRenwick 92
(Martin Todhunter) *in tch: effrt and chsd ldrs appr 2 out: sn drvn: wknd between last 2* **50/1**

04/ **4** 27 **New Vic (IRE)**[25] 5422 7-10-13 0.................. BrianHarding 64
(Nicky Richards) *prom: rdn and outpcd after 4 out: lost tch fr next* **50/1**

5 11 **Lord Fox (IRE)**[50] 6-10-8 0.................. TrevorWhelan(5) 54
(Shaun Harris) *nt fluent: t.k.h: chsd wnr tl hit 8th: cl up tl rdn and wknd bef 2 out* **18/1**[3]

6m 8.4s (3.40) **Going Correction** -0.375s/f (Good) **5** Ran SP% **109.2**
Speed ratings (Par 105): **79,78,69,61,57**
CSF £1.71 TOTE £1.20: £1.02, £1.70; EX 1.90 Trifecta £6.60 Pool: £1281.10 - 145.41 winning units..

Owner Askew Dick Hernon Reynard **Bred** Robert McCarthy **Trained** Cholmondeley, Cheshire

FOCUS
All bends and hurdles sited on fresh ground. A fair staying novices' hurdle in which they went an even gallop on ground officially described as good. The winner is rated 5lb off his best.

340 TIMOTHY HARDIE JEWELLERS NOVICES' CHASE (18 fncs) 3m
2:55 (2:55) (Class 4) 5-Y-0+ **£5,475** (£1,596; £798)

Form RPR
313/ **1** **Imperial Vic (IRE)**[22] 5493 8-10-12 0.................. DannyCook 137+
(Michael Smith) *mde all: rdn bef 3 out: hung lft run-in: stened and kpt on strly* **85/40**[2]

350/ **2** 10 **Sivola De Sivola (FR)**[96] 4122 7-10-12 0.................. PaddyBrennan 132
(Tom George) *pressed wnr: effrt and drvn bef 3 out: no imp tl rallied appr last: swtchd rt run-in: outpcd last 100yds: eased cl home* **2/1**[1]

P31/ **3** 19 **Fiddlers Reel**[21] 5521 10-11-5 117.................. RyanMania 121
(Jane Clark) *in tch: stdy hdwy 5 out: rdn and wknd fr 3 out* **8/1**

2P1/ **4** 89 **Kris Cross (IRE)**[20] 5549 6-10-12 0.................. PeterBuchanan 31
(Lucinda Russell) *trckd ldrs: mstke 10th: blnd and outpcd 13th: nt fluent after: lost tch fr 4 out* **11/4**[3]

P/P- **P** **Heart O' The West (IRE)**[5] 222 9-10-9 0.................. EwanWhillans(3)
(Alistair Whillans) *mstkes: sn wl bhd: no ch whn p.u bef 12th* **100/1**

300/ **P** **Streams Of Whiskey (IRE)**[25] 5423 6-10-12 0.................. BrianHarding
(Nicky Richards) *hld up bhd ldng gp: struggling fr 12th: t.o whn p.u bef 3 out* **33/1**

000/ **P** **St Gregory (IRE)**[104] 3972 5-10-5 0.................. WilsonRenwick
(Nicky Richards) *nt fluent: bhd and sn struggling: t.o whn p.u bef 12th* **66/1**

6m 2.3s (-1.70) **Going Correction** +0.05s/f (Yiel) **7** Ran SP% **108.5**
Speed ratings: **104,100,94,64,** ,
toteswingers 1&2 £1.10, 1&3 £3.20, 2&3 £5.50 CSF £6.33 TOTE £3.50: £1.50, £1.50; EX 9.40 Trifecta £31.00 Pool: £988.35 - 23.86 winning units..

Owner J Stephenson **Bred** John Ryan **Trained** Kirkheaton, Northumberland

FOCUS
A decent staying novices' chase in which they went a searching gallop. The winner looks like being a better chaser than hurdler.

341 EXPRO H'CAP CHASE (15 fncs) 2m 4f 110y
3:30 (3:30) (Class 4) (0-120,119) 5-Y-0+ **£3,898** (£1,144; £572; £286)

Form RPR
452/ **1** **Hawaii Klass**[22] 5501 8-10-5 **103**..................(b) CallumWhillans(5) 116+
(Donald Whillans) *hld up towards rr: nt fluent 4th: stdy hdwy and prom 9th: effrt and led 2 out: clr last: drvn and kpt on wl* **5/1**

6P5/ **2** 9 **Father Shine (IRE)**[24] 5387 10-10-12 **110**.................. TrevorWhelan(5) 114
(Shaun Harris) *in tch: pushed along bef 5 out: rallied next: effrt 3 out: chsd (clr) wnr run-in: no imp* **25/1**

P55/ **3** 3 ¾ **Blazin White Face (IRE)**[22] 5492 6-11-3 **110**.................. PeterBuchanan 113
(Lucinda Russell) *cl up: led 10th: rdn and hdd 2 out: sn outpcd: lost 2nd run-in* **3/1**[1]

432/ **4** 10 **Gleann Na Ndochais (IRE)**[47] 5010 7-10-8 **104**.......... EwanWhillans(3) 99
(Alistair Whillans) *hld up: stdy hdwy bef 4 out: rdn next: no imp whn mstke 2 out* **7/2**[2]

0PP/ **5** 9 **Lord Redsgirth (IRE)**[22] 5496 8-11-5 **119**.................. MrSFox(7) 102
(Lucy Normile) *led to 10th: disp ld tl wknd after 3 out* **14/1**

B1P/ **6** 63 **Eyre Apparent (IRE)**[50] 4972 8-11-11 **118**..................(p) TomScudamore 45
(Lucinda Russell) *pressed ldr to 9th: drvn and outpcd whn nt fluent 4 out: lost tch next: eased* **9/2**[3]

043/ **P** **Bow School (IRE)**[24] 5451 12-11-11 **118**.................. JasonMaguire
(Alison Hamilton) *hld up in tch: struggling bef 5 out: t.o whn p.u bef 3 out* **7/1**

104/ **P** **Quetzal (IRE)**[162] 2850 8-10-6 **106**.................. GrahamWatters(7)
(Martin Todhunter) *in tch: mstke 8th (water): struggling fr 10th: t.o whn p.u bef 2 out* **16/1**

5m 4.9s (-0.10) **Going Correction** +0.05s/f (Yiel) **8** Ran SP% **111.0**
Speed ratings: **102,98,97,93,89 65,** ,
toteswingers 1&2 £18.10, 1&3 £2.50, 2&3 £7.50 CSF £90.68 CT £419.81 TOTE £5.00: £1.70, £2.90, £1.50; EX 65.30 Trifecta £688.30 Part won. Pool: £917.75 - 0.46 winning units..

Owner Star Racing **Bred** Allan Gilchrist **Trained** Hawick, Borders

FOCUS
A fair handicap chase in which they went a strong, contested gallop. Straightforward form.

342 CRABBIE'S SCOTTISH RASPBERRY ALCOHOLIC GINGER BEER CONDITIONAL JOCKEYS' H'CAP HURDLE (10 hdls) 2m 4f 110y
4:05 (4:05) (Class 4) (0-120,119) 4-Y-0+ **£4,548** (£1,335; £667; £333)

Form RPR
2/2- **1** **Overpriced**[12] 111 7-11-0 **115**..............................(t) StephenMulqueen[(8)] 116
(Maurice Barnes) *chsd ldrs: drvn and outpcd after 3 out: lft 6 l 2nd next: styd on to ld after last: kpt on strly* **15/2**
614/ **2** *1 ½* **Notarfbad (IRE)**[25] 5435 7-11-9 **119**.............................. MattGriffiths[(3)] 122+
(Jeremy Scott) *led: hit 3rd: rdn and jst hdd whn lft 6 l clr 2 out: wnt rt and nt fluent last: sn hdd: rallied: no ex last 50yds* **7/2**[2]
331/ **3** *1 ¾* **King's Chorister**[20] 5546 7-10-0 **93** oh2..............................(t) TonyKelly 91
(Barry Murtagh) *in tch: effrt and drvn whn lft 4th 2 out: kpt on fr last* **8/1**
346/ **4** *2* **Latin Connection (IRE)**[17] 24 7-11-7 **114**................(t) CallumWhillans 111
(S R B Crawford, Ire) *hld up: hdwy and prom 3 out: sn rdn: lft 3rd next: sn one pce* **12/1**
PB/ **5** *8* **Granaruid (IRE)**[24] 5453 10-10-11 **107**......................(p) GrantCockburn[(3)] 98
(Alison Hamilton) *in tch: lost pl 4th: struggling bef 4 out: plugged on fr 2 out: n.d* **50/1**
540/ **6** *15* **Cadore (IRE)**[25] 5425 5-10-10 **103**..................................(p) AlexanderVoy 79
(Lucy Normile) *chsd ldrs: drvn 3 out: outpcd whn mstke next: sn btn* **18/1**
054/ **P** **Signalman**[27] 5367 9-10-10 **103**.. GaryRutherford
(Sandy Thomson) *in tch: outpcd bef 4 out: sn struggling: t.o whn p.u bef 2 out* **25/1**
123/ **P** **Reaping The Reward (IRE)**[26] 5400 9-11-4 **116**....... GrahamWatters[(5)]
(Andrew Parker) *hld up: hdwy and prom whn mstke 3 out: sn rdn and wknd: p.u bef next* **5/2**[1]
431/ **F** **Urban Kode (IRE)**[21] 5520 5-9-9 **96**..............................(v) CraigNichol[(8)] 102+
(Lucinda Russell) *chsd ldr: effrt and jst led whn fell 2 out* **4/1**[3]

4m 58.3s (-3.70) **Going Correction** -0.375s/f (Good) **9** Ran SP% **112.4**
Speed ratings (Par 105): **92,91,90,90,86 81,,,**
toteswingers 1&2 £4.60, 1&3 £8.00, 2&3 £10.30 CSF £33.53 CT £214.90 TOTE £9.00: £2.60, £1.10, £2.90; EX 30.40 Trifecta £556.80 Pool: £1202.05 - 1.61 winning units..
Owner M Barnes **Bred** M A Barnes **Trained** Farlam, Cumbria

FOCUS
A fair conditional jockeys' handicap hurdle in which they went a decent gallop. The faller looked set to follow up and the winner is rated to her mark.

343 MEDIA SHOP 25TH ANNIVERSARY H'CAP CHASE (12 fncs) 2m
4:40 (4:40) (Class 4) (0-115,115) 5-Y-0+ **£5,198** (£1,526; £763; £381)

Form RPR
16P/ **1** **Scotch Warrior**[50] 4972 9-10-10 **106**.............................. CallumBewley[(7)] 116+
(R Mike Smith) *in tch: nt fluent 5th: rdn and outpcd 5 out: rallied bef 3 out: wnt 2nd next: drvn and led run-in: styd on wl* **5/1**
034/ **2** *1 ½* **Kai Broon (IRE)**[24] 5448 6-11-8 **111**..............................(p) PeterBuchanan 119
(Lucinda Russell) *cl up: led and rdn 3 out: hdd run-in: kpt on same pce towards fin* **7/2**[2]
455/ **3** *11* **Al Qeddaaf (IRE)**[20] 5545 7-11-12 **115**.............................. JasonMaguire 113
(Donald McCain) *led tl rdn and hdd 3 out: wknd after next* **4/1**[3]
026/ **4** *9* **Calculaite**[24] 5448 12-11-2 **112**...................................... GrahamWatters[(7)] 102
(Richard Ford) *t.k.h: in tch: effrt and rdn bef 3 out: wknd bef next* **8/1**
54/- **5** *24* **Sophonie (FR)**[125] 3599 7-10-11 **100**...............................(t) PaddyBrennan 68
(Tom George) *nt fluent: hld up: blnd 7th: rallied to chse ldrs bef 4 out: wknd 3 out* **5/2**[1]
343/ **6** *33* **Saddlers Deal (IRE)**[226] 1708 8-11-1 **104**..................(v) WilsonRenwick 43
(Chris Grant) *trckd ldrs: outpcd 5 out: lost tch fr next: t.o* **9/1**

3m 55.5s (-1.50) **Going Correction** +0.05s/f (Yiel) **6** Ran SP% **108.6**
Speed ratings: **105,104,98,94,82 65**
toteswingers 1&2 £3.90, 1&3 £3.90, 2&3 £2.50 CSF £21.36 TOTE £5.80: £3.20, £1.80; EX 25.40 Trifecta £91.70 Pool: £1841.11 - 15.04 winning units..
Owner R Michael Smith **Bred** Miss Jayne Butler **Trained** Galston, E Ayrshire

FOCUS
A modest handicap chase in which they went a strong gallop. The winner is rated back to his best.

344 JOSEPH RIBKOFF AT LORETTA'S COLLECTIONS H'CAP HURDLE (8 hdls) 2m 110y
5:15 (5:15) (Class 3) (0-130,128) 4-Y-0+ **£6,498** (£1,908; £954; £477)

Form RPR
040/ **1** **Bow Badger**[21] 5525 7-11-3 **115**.. BrianHughes 126+
(John Wade) *cl up: led 3rd: mde rest: styd on strly fr 2 out* **7/1**
613/ **2** *10* **Jonny Delta**[27] 5367 6-11-4 **116**.. GaryBartley 118
(Jim Goldie) *hld up: smooth hdwy to chse wnr 2 out: sn rdn: no ex bef last* **5/1**[3]
211/ **3** *10* **Flaming Arrow (IRE)**[24] 5449 5-11-9 **124**...................... BrianToomey[(3)] 116
(Kevin Ryan) *trckd ldrs: drvn 3 out: sn outpcd: hld whn lft modest 4th next: no imp* **5/2**[2]
005/ **4** *5* **Claude Carter**[22] 5497 9-10-7 **108**.................................. EwanWhillans[(3)] 96
(Alistair Whillans) *hld up: rdn and outpcd after 3 out: no imp fr next* **25/1**
P16/ **5** *6* **Parson's Punch**[157] 2978 8-10-9 **110**.............................. AlexanderVoy[(3)] 92
(Lucy Normile) *trckd ldrs: effrt and drvn after 3 out: outpcd and 8 l down whn lft 3rd next: wknd* **10/1**
015/ **F** **Counsel (IRE)**[19] 5573 4-11-12 **128**..................................(t) JasonMaguire 116
(Donald McCain) *led to 3rd: pressed ldr: drvn 3 out: 5 l 3rd whn fell 2 out: fatally injured* **7/4**[1]
361/ **U** **Lone Foot Laddie (IRE)**[21] 5519 4-10-10 **119**.......... GrahamWatters[(7)] 107
(Lucinda Russell) *in tch: hdwy and cl up whn mstke 3 out: rdn and outpcd whn bdly hmpd and uns rdr next* **12/1**

3m 48.5s (-9.50) **Going Correction** -0.375s/f (Good) **7** Ran SP% **114.7**
Speed ratings (Par 107): **107,102,97,95,92**
toteswingers 1&2 £2.90, 1&3 £3.80, 2&3 £2.50 CSF £41.53 TOTE £10.00: £3.40, £1.90; EX 46.70 Trifecta £277.40 Pool: £818.92 - 2.21 winning units..
Owner John Wade **Bred** Juddmonte Farms Ltd **Trained** Mordon, Co Durham

FOCUS
A decent handicap hurdle in which there was no hanging about. The winner is back to the level of his 2011 form.

345 BREAKTHROUGH BREAST CANCER STANDARD OPEN NATIONAL HUNT FLAT RACE 2m 110y
5:45 (5:45) (Class 6) 4-6-Y-0 **£2,053** (£598; £299)

Form RPR
\- **1** **Viacometti (FR)** 4-10-12 0.. PaddyBrennan 97
(Tom George) *prom: effrt 3f out: led and rn green over 1f out: drvn out fnl f* **9/2**[3]
6/ **2** *1 ½* **Craiganee (IRE)**[208] 1932 6-10-13 0.............................. MrSCrawford[(3)] 100
(S R B Crawford, Ire) *t.k.h: hld up in tch: effrt and pushed along 3f out: ev ch and rdn over 1f out: edgd rt ins fnl f: kpt on same pce* **2/1**[2]
3 *3 ½* **Kilbree Chief (IRE)**[102] 5-10-9 0...................................... CraigNichol[(7)] 97
(Lucinda Russell) *chsd ldr to 1/2-way: drvn and outpcd over 5f out: styd on fr 2f out: nt pce to chal* **5/1**
4 *2* **Uppercut De L'Orne (FR)**[95] 5-11-2 0.............................. JasonMaguire 95
(Donald McCain) *led: rdn along over 2f out: hdd over 1f out: sn outpcd* **15/8**[1]
6/ **5** *4 ½* **Tomahawk Wood**[24] 5454 4-10-7 0.............................. CallumWhillans[(5)] 87
(Donald Whillans) *t.k.h: cl up: wnt 2nd 1/2-way: rdn over 2f out: wknd wl over 1f out* **16/1**

3m 48.8s (-3.60) **Going Correction** -0.375s/f (Good)
WFA 4 from 5yo+ 4lb **5** Ran SP% **108.8**
Speed ratings: **93,92,90,89,87**
CSF £13.57 TOTE £4.80: £2.20, £1.60; EX 12.60 Trifecta £45.90 Pool: £413.11 - 6.73 winning units..
Owner S Nelson S O'Donohoe J C Taylor D Taylor **Bred** Mme Laurence Barreaud & Claude Barreaud **Trained** Slad, Gloucs

FOCUS
An ordinary bumper rated through the second. They went an even gallop.
T/Plt: £87.20 to a £1 stake. Pool: £50,066.07 - 418.89 winning tickets. T/Qpdt: £49.30 to a £1 stake. Pool: £2668.50 - 40.00 winning tickets. RY

346 - 352a (Foreign Racing) - See Raceform Interactive

AINTREE (L-H)
Friday, May 17

OFFICIAL GOING: Good (good to soft in places on mildmay course; 7.9)
Wind: Fresh, half behind Weather: Overcast

353 BETDAQ 1ST UK COMMISSION FREE CONDITIONAL JOCKEYS' MARES' H'CAP HURDLE (11 hdls) 2m 4f
5:20 (5:20) (Class 4) (0-120,118) 4-Y-0+ **£4,548** (£1,335; £667; £333)

Form RPR
4/2- **1** **Va'Vite (IRE)**[5] 244 6-10-13 **113**.. MarkMarris[(8)] 122+
(Anthony Middleton) *hld up: clsd 2 out: led appr last: styd on wl to draw clr fnl 75yds* **11/4**[2]
/21- **2** *5* **Chilworth Screamer**[3] 293 5-10-9 **101** 7ex...................... MichealNolan 106
(Chris Gordon) *hld up: trckd ldng pair after 4 out: upsides 3 out: led 2 out: hdd appr last: no ex and no ch w wnr fnl 75yds* **2/1**[1]
214/ **3** *7* **Loyaute (FR)**[29] 5360 6-11-9 **115**.. GilesHawkins 113
(Chris Down) *racd in cl 2nd pl: led 4th: hdd after 5th: regained ld 6th: rdn and hdd 2 out: one pce run-in* **3/1**[3]
3/4- **4** *10* **Shady Lane**[17] 41 6-10-7 **99**.. BrendanPowell 88
(Alan King) *racd keenly: trckd ldrs: effrt on inner 2 out: btn bef last* **9/2**
153/ **5** *14* **Pass The Time**[11] 5252 4-10-12 **109**..............................(p) RichardEvans 81
(Neil Mulholland) *nt fluent and smetimes j.lft: led: hdd 4th: regained ld after 5th: hdd 6th: remained w ldr: rdn and wknd appr 2 out* **14/1**

5m 1.4s (0.70) **Going Correction** -0.20s/f (Good)
WFA 4 from 5yo+ 19lb **5** Ran SP% **109.8**
Speed ratings (Par 105): **90,88,85,81,75**
CSF £8.83 TOTE £3.20: £1.90, £2.00; EX 5.60 Trifecta £32.40 Pool: £439.27 - 10.14 winning units..
Owner Ms B Woodcock & Mrs D Dewbery **Bred** M Conaghan **Trained** Granborough, Bucks

FOCUS
Hurdle bends on stands' side on outer line, adding 70yds per circuit, chase bends moved out, adding 60yds per circuit. They went very steady throughout the first three-quarters of the race and it turned into a bit of a sprint up the straight, so the form is probably nothing to get excited about. It has been rated around the first two.

354 NO PREMIUM CHARGE AT BETDAQ NOVICES' HURDLE (9 hdls) 2m 1f
5:55 (5:55) (Class 3) 4-Y-0+ **£5,848** (£1,717; £858; £429)

Form RPR
531/ **1** **Life And Soul (IRE)**[19] 15 6-11-4 120.............................. JasonMaguire 132+
(Donald McCain) *led: hit 4th: reminder after 4 out: pushed along appr 3 out: hdd 2 out: stl chalng last: rallied to regained ld fnl 150yds: styd on* **15/8**[2]
240/ **2** *2 ¼* **Sky Khan**[40] 5197 4-10-5 121.. JackQuinlan[(3)] 119
(Noel Quinlan) *t.k.h: prom: dropped to rr after 4th: wnt 2nd bef 3 out: led 2 out: rdn appr last: hdd fnl 150yds: no ex towards fin* **7/4**[1]
1- **3** *23* **Cool Macavity (IRE)**[16] 69 5-11-4 0.............................. DavidBass 108
(Nicky Henderson) *prom: rdn and stl there 3 out: outpcd by front two appr last: wknd run-in* **7/1**
F12/ **4** *9* **Bally Rone (IRE)**[24] 5463 5-10-11 123.......................... PatrickCorbett[(7)] 102
(Rebecca Curtis) *hld up: w ldr 5th: bmpd after 4 out: sn lost pl and outpcd in rr: n.d after* **3/1**[3]
00U/ **U** **Mr Burbidge**[21] 5537 5-10-2 0....................................(b[1]) ChrisMeehan[(10)]
(Neil Mulholland) *hld up: j.lft and uns rdr 1st* **100/1**

4m 10.3s (-3.40) **Going Correction** -0.20s/f (Good)
WFA 4 from 5yo+ 18lb **5** Ran SP% **109.6**
Speed ratings (Par 107): **100,98,88,83,**
CSF £5.70 TOTE £3.00: £1.70, £1.10; EX 6.10 Trifecta £21.90 Pool: £1247.48 - 42.68 winning units..
Owner Matthew Taylor **Bred** Kildaragh Stud **Trained** Cholmondeley, Cheshire

FOCUS
They wound things up a lot sooner than in the opener. The winner is entitled to rate higher on Flat form.

355 BETDAQ NEW CUSTOMERS COMMISSION FREE 1ST MONTH H'CAP CHASE (19 fncs) 3m 1f
6:30 (6:30) (Class 3) (0-135,134) 5-Y-0+ **£7,797** (£2,289; £1,144; £572)

Form RPR
P22/ **1** **Lexicon Lad (IRE)**[31] 5341 8-10-11 **119**..........................(t) PaddyBrennan 130+
(Tom George) *a.p: led 10th: abt 5 l clr between last 2: idled run-in: all out towards fin* **7/1**[2]
F1/- **2** *1* **Night In Milan (IRE)**[39] 5218 7-11-4 **126**......................(b) JamesReveley 136
(Keith Reveley) *led: hdd 10th: continued to chse wnr: rdn appr 2 out: abt 5 l down between last 2: rallied and styd on towards fin* **5/1**[1]
4/2- **3** *7* **That's The Deal (IRE)**[8] 181 9-9-9 **108** oh2.................. JoeCornwall[(5)] 111
(John Cornwall) *hld up: hdwy 6th: trckd ldrs 11th: rdn and no imp on front two bef last: kpt on same pce run-in* **25/1**
1P2/ **4** *2 ¼* **Kruzhlinin (GER)**[27] 5409 6-11-12 **134**.............................. JasonMaguire 136
(Donald McCain) *hld up: moved into midfield 12th: hdwy to chse ldrs 4 out: no imp whn j.lft last: kpt on run-in* **14/1**

5P0/ **5** ½ **Major Malarkey (IRE)**[41] 5177 10-11-10 **132**.......(p) SamTwiston-Davies 133
(Nigel Twiston-Davies) *midfield: pushed along to chse ldrs appr 4 out: outpcd 2 out: styd on again towards fin whn no ch* **25/1**

114/ **6** 2½ **Danimix (IRE)**[27] 5406 8-11-9 **131**.......(t) NoelFehily 131
(Anthony Honeyball) *in tch: mstke 12th and 15th: rdn and outpcd bef 2 out: kpt on whn n.d run-in* **11/1**

053/ **7** 6 **Gullible Gordon (IRE)**[23] 5503 10-11-3 **125**....... JamieMoore 119
(Peter Bowen) *hld up in midfield: rdn and outpcd bef 4 out: n.d after* **15/2**[3]

63P/ **8** hd **Triggerman**[90] 4249 11-11-4 **126**.......(p) RichardJohnson 119
(Philip Hobbs) *hld up: j.rt 7th: pushed along bef 14th: u.p bef 3 out: no imp* **7/1**[2]

FPR/ **9** ¾ **Mumbles Head (IRE)**[41] 5177 12-11-11 **133**....... TomO'Brien 127
(Peter Bowen) *hld up: nt fluent early: hdwy 4 out: effrt to chse ldrs 3 out: no imp after 2 out: wknd run-in* **12/1**

5PB/ **10** 12 **Bradley**[27] 5404 9-11-4 **133**....... ConorShoemark(7) 118
(Fergal O'Brien) *j.rt thrght: prom tl rdn and wknd after 4 out* **5/1**[1]

422/ **11** 1¾ **French Ties (IRE)**[23] 5502 11-10-10 **118**.......(p) SeanQuinlan 102
(Jennie Candlish) *hld up in rr: mstke 15th: rdn appr 2 out: no imp: n.d whn hit last* **16/1**

154/ **12** 13 **Kingsmoss (IRE)**[44] 5129 8-10-3 **111**.......(p) BrianHughes 79
(J J Lambe, Ire) *in tch: losing pl whn blnd 15th: sn bhd* **22/1**

P04/ **P** **Door Boy (IRE)**[133] 3496 10-11-4 **126**....... WilsonRenwick
(John Wade) *prom tl lost pl 5th: towards rr 10th: struggling 12th: lost tch 14th: t.o whn p.u bef 4 out* **22/1**

631/ **P** **Dun Masc (IRE)**[26] 5427 8-10-5 **113**.......(p) BrianHarding
(James Moffatt) *towards rr: niggled along after 3rd: struggling bef 7th: t.o after 11th: p.u bef 13th* **20/1**

6m 27.8s (-2.20) **Going Correction** +0.15s/f (Yiel) **14** Ran SP% **119.8**
Speed ratings: **109,108,106,105,105 104,102,102,102,98 98,93, ,**
toteswingers 1&2 £4.90, 1&3 £47.80, 2&3 £35.80 CSF £39.20 CT £830.59 TOTE £8.00: £3.40, £2.30, £7.10; EX 61.70 Trifecta £485.00 Pool: £1463.67 - 2.26 winning units..
Owner C B Compton **Bred** Mrs Elizabeth Lawlor **Trained** Slad, Gloucs

FOCUS
A very competitive handicap for the time of year but nothing got into it from off the pace. Solid form, with the winner on the upgrade.

356 BETDAQ+ MOBILE APPS H'CAP HURDLE (11 hdls) 2m 4f
7:05 (7:05) (Class 2) 4-Y-0+
£12,512 (£3,696; £1,848; £924; £462; £232)

Form RPR

111/ **1** **Party Rock (IRE)**[30] 5352 6-10-4 **128**....... SeanQuinlan 140+
(Jennie Candlish) *in tch: gng wl trcking ldrs bef 3 out: led 2 out: qcknd run-in: r.o wl to draw clr ins fnl 100yds* **9/2**[1]

100/ **2** 5 **Smalib Monterg (FR)**[20] 5178 7-10-0 **124** oh1.....(t) SamTwiston-Davies 130+
(Dr Richard Newland) *in tch: styd on to take 2nd whn mstke last: no imp on wnr fnl 100yds* **25/1**

605/ **3** 7 **One Term (IRE)**[154] 3040 6-9-7 **124** oh4....... PatrickCorbett(7) 123
(Rebecca Curtis) *trckd ldrs: led bef 7th: hdd 2 out: rdn bef last: kpt on same pce run-in* **16/1**

6/1- **4** 1¾ **Drum Valley**[5] 244 5-9-8 **125**....... JackSherwood(7) 122
(Oliver Sherwood) *in tch: hit 5th: effrt whn chsng ldrs bef 2 out: one pce run-in* **5/1**[2]

006/ **5** 6 **Kian's Delight**[27] 5405 5-10-3 **127**....... TomO'Brien 118
(Peter Bowen) *midfield: pushed along whn sme hdwy bef 2 out: mstke last: styd on run-in: nt rch ldrs* **17/2**

041/ **6** ½ **Arctic Court (IRE)**[18] 24 9-10-1 **125**....... RichieMcGrath 115
(Jim Goldie) *hld up: pushed along appr 3 out: prog fr 2 out: styd on run-in: nt rch ldrs* **20/1**

002/ **7** 1¼ **Now This Is It (IRE)**[22] 5525 9-10-8 **135**....... EwanWhillans(3) 124
(S R B Crawford, Ire) *hld up: hdwy appr 3 out: chsd ldng bunch after: styd on towards fin but no ch* **25/1**

103/ **8** 4½ **Native Gallery (IRE)**[20] 5582 8-11-5 **143**....... DarylJacob 128
(Ben De Haan) *prom: chalng 3 out: stl ev ch 2 out: rdn and wknd last* **7/1**[3]

F25/ **9** 1 **Cockney Trucker (IRE)**[70] 4645 11-10-11 **135**....... APMcCoy 119
(Philip Hobbs) *midfield: pushed along appr 3 out: rdn and hung rt bef last whn no imp on ldrs: edgd lft whn wl btn run-in* **12/1**

001/ **10** ¾ **Bar De Ligne (FR)**[22] 5525 7-10-6 **137**.......(p) PaulBohan(7) 121
(Steve Gollings) *in tch: ch 3 out: rdn bef 2 out: wknd appr last* **14/1**

63U/ **11** ¾ **Vendor (FR)**[20] 5574 5-10-8 **132**....... WayneHutchinson 115
(Alan King) *hld up: hdwy to chse ldrs appr 3 out: nt fluent 2 out: wknd bef last* **15/2**

400/ **12** 14 **Bourne**[30] 5352 7-11-0 **138**.......(b) JasonMaguire 108
(Donald McCain) *sn pushed along: nvr travelling in rr: nvr on terms* **20/1**

000/ **13** 1½ **Saphir River (FR)**[27] 5405 7-10-6 **130**.......(tp) PeterBuchanan 99
(Lucinda Russell) *racd keenly: hld up: struggling 6th: rdn whn bhd after 4 out: nvr on terms* **10/1**

F52/ **14** 28 **Trucking Along (IRE)**[27] 5400 7-10-0 **124**....... WilsonRenwick 68
(S R B Crawford, Ire) *hld up: hit 7th: brief effrt into midfield bef 3 out: sn btn: t.o* **28/1**

P36/ **15** 32 **I Hear A Symphony (IRE)**[61] 4831 11-10-0 **124** oh4....... BrianHughes 39
(J J Lambe, Ire) *prom tl rdn and wknd appr 3 out: t.o* **50/1**

100/ **P** **Snap Tie (IRE)**[24] 5486 11-11-12 **150**....... RichardJohnson
(Philip Hobbs) *trckd ldrs: rdn after 4 out: wknd appr 3 out: bhd whn p.u bef 2 out: fatally injured* **33/1**

410/ **P** **Decoy (FR)**[216] 1476 7-10-3 **127**.......(p) TomScudamore
(David Pipe) *led: hdd appr 7th: sn wknd: t.o whn p.u bef 3 out* **25/1**

4m 50.0s (-10.70) **Going Correction** -0.20s/f (Good) **17** Ran SP% **128.4**
Speed ratings (Par 109): **113,111,108,107,105 104,104,102,102,101 101,96,95,84,71 ,**
toteswingers 1&2 £33.00, 1&3 £10.10, 2&3 £112.00 CSF £122.91 CT £1713.80 TOTE £4.50: £2.10, £6.90, £4.10, £2.00; EX 181.10 Trifecta £788.80 Part won. Pool: £1051.85 - 0.12 winning units..
Owner Mrs Pam Beardmore **Bred** Daniel O'Keeffe **Trained** Basford Green, Staffs

FOCUS
The presence of the ill-fated Snap Tie meant that all bar the top three carried less than 11st but even so, this was extremely competitive and looks a hot piece of handicap hurdle form for the time of year. The cosy winner is improving fast and has developed into a smart handicapper.

357 £200 FREE BETS AT BETDAQ OPEN HUNTERS' CHASE (19 fncs) 3m 1f
7:40 (7:40) (Class 6) 5-Y-0+ **£1,871** (£580; £290; £145)

Form RPR

12P/ **1** **What A Laugh**[27] 8-12-1 120....... MrRJarrett(3) 125+
(G D Hanmer) *hld up: gng wl cl up 4 out: wnt 2nd bef 2 out: led appr last: drvn out* **15/8**[2]

3/1- **2** 2¾ **Rumbury Grey**[16] 59 10-12-3 127....... MrMatthewBarber(5) 127
(S Flook) *mainly disp ld tl def advantage after 15th: rdn appr 2 out: hdd bef last: one pce run-in* **4/5**[1]

0/5- **3** 23 **Keenan's Future (IRE)**[16] 62 12-11-7 103.......(v[1]) MrRHodges(7) 98
(S Rea) *chsd ldrs: pushed along and bhd bef 3 out: outpcd after: tk 3rd whn n.d last* **12/1**[3]

2P/- **4** 13 **Cool Mission (IRE)**[27] 5414 9-11-11 115.......(b) NickSlatter(3) 86
(Donald McCain) *mainly disp ld tl after 15th: u.p after: wknd after 2 out* **12/1**[3]

6m 36.3s (6.30) **Going Correction** +0.15s/f (Yiel) **4** Ran SP% **105.7**
Speed ratings: **95,94,86,82**
CSF £3.78 TOTE £2.50; EX 3.90 Trifecta £8.30 Pool: £900.67 - 80.97 winning units..
Owner R P Davies-Cooke **Bred** Miss J C L Needham **Trained** Nantwich, Cheshire

FOCUS
A small-field hunter. The first two were close to their marks and are tough to beat in this grade.

358 WINNERS ARE WELCOME AT BETDAQ H'CAP HURDLE (13 hdls) 3m 110y
8:15 (8:15) (Class 3) (0-135,135) 4-Y-0+ **£5,848** (£1,717; £858; £429)

Form RPR

002/ **1** **Trackmate**[45] 5103 7-11-1 **124**....... LiamTreadwell 130+
(James Evans) *midfield: hdwy appr 3 out: led last: styd on wl to draw clr fnl 150yds* **14/1**

042/ **2** 6 **Howizee**[28] 5372 7-11-5 **128**.......(t) MichaelMcAlister 129
(Maurice Barnes) *handy: led 9th: hdd narrowly after 2 out: stl chalng last: no match for wnr ins fnl 150yds* **10/1**

120/ **3** 1 **Al Co (FR)**[266] 1349 8-11-0 **130**....... MissBAndrews(7) 130
(F Lloyd) *in tch: trckd ldrs after 7th: chalng 3 out: led after 2 out: hdd last: styd on same pce ins fnl 200yds* **50/1**

452/ **4** 2 **Kaysersberg (FR)**[21] 5551 6-11-2 **125**....... AlexMerriam 123
(Neil King) *midfield: hdwy to trck ldrs 8th: rdn bef 2 out: one pce run-in* **33/1**

2P0/ **5** ¾ **Ballyrock (IRE)**[40] 5200 7-11-12 **135**.......(t) AidanColeman 133
(Tim Vaughan) *in rr: pushed along and hdwy appr 3 out: styd on after last: gng on at fin* **14/1**

041/ **6** 2½ **Midnight Prayer**[36] 5257 8-11-0 **123**....... WayneHutchinson 118
(Alan King) *in rr: nt fluent 2nd: hdwy appr 3 out: chsd ldrs 2 out: styd on same pce run-in* **6/1**[1]

361/ **7** 1¼ **Tullyraine (IRE)**[79] 4448 9-11-7 **130**....... SamTwiston-Davies 124
(Nigel Twiston-Davies) *in tch: rdn and outpcd appr 3 out: styd on u.p fr last: nt rch ldrs run-in* **12/1**

441/ **8** 4 **Connectivity (IRE)**[21] 5540 9-11-5 **135**....... ChristopherWard(7) 129
(Dr Richard Newland) *in rr: reminder after 5th: hdwy 7th: handy whn blnd 9th: chalng 3 out: rdn bef next: one pce appr last* **7/1**[2]

P03/ **9** 4 **Tempest River (IRE)**[29] 5360 7-11-3 **126**.......(p) DarylJacob 113
(Ben Case) *hld up: hdwy appr 3 out: chsd ldrs bef 2 out: one pce bef last* **12/1**

0/2- **10** 1¼ **Scoter Fontaine (FR)**[14] 91 7-10-13 **122**....... APMcCoy 111
(Rebecca Curtis) *midfield: hdwy 4 out: chsd ldrs and trying to chal 3 out: wknd qckly after last: sn eased whn btn* **14/1**

042/ **11** 11 **Destroyer Deployed**[29] 5362 7-11-3 **126**.......(v) DougieCostello 102
(Tim Vaughan) *in rr: nvr gng wl: plugged on wout threatening fr 3 out* **8/1**[3]

2FP/ **12** 2 **Ballytober**[62] 4781 7-11-7 **130**....... RichardJohnson 107
(Philip Hobbs) *hld up: hdwy after 4 out: in tch bef next: wknd bef last* **33/1**

42P/ **13** ¾ **Five Star Wilsham (IRE)**[365] 319 9-11-3 **126**....... NickScholfield 100
(Jeremy Scott) *midfield: effrt in tch bef 3 out: wknd after 2 out* **66/1**

6FP/ **14** shd **Mister Hyde (IRE)**[64] 4750 8-10-9 **125**....... DannyBenson(7) 98
(Jonjo O'Neill) *trckd ldrs: effrt 3 out to chal: wknd appr last* **33/1**

333/ **15** 5 **So Fine (IRE)**[21] 5540 7-11-4 **127**....... TomO'Brien 96
(Philip Hobbs) *trckd ldrs: lost pl bef 8th: no imp after: lft bhd after 2 out* **20/1**

010/ **16** 4½ **Akbabend**[182] 2455 7-11-1 **124**....... MarcGoldstein 89
(Chris Gordon) *in tch: lost pl 8th: struggling fr 4 out* **66/1**

4F/- **17** 26 **Problema Tic (FR)**[27] 5404 7-11-6 **129**.......(p) TomScudamore 71
(David Pipe) *towards rr: struggling after 7th: nvr a threat* **10/1**

1P2/ **18** 5 **Scotswell**[18] 24 7-11-6 **129**....... LucyAlexander 66
(Harriet Graham) *trckd ldrs: led 6th: hdd 9th: wknd qckly 4 out* **25/1**

652/ **19** 8 **Mauricetheathlete (IRE)**[57] 4882 10-10-4 **120**....... NickSlatter(7) 50
(Martin Keighley) *prom tl rdn and wknd after 4 out* **50/1**

PP6/ **20** 29 **Keenes Day (FR)**[26] 5430 8-10-11 **120**.......(t) RichieMcLernon 24
(Sophie Leech) *prom tl wknd 9th: t.o* **66/1**

511/ **21** 11 **Super Villan**[33] 5308 8-10-6 **120**....... NicodeBoinville(5) 14
(Mark Bradstock) *led: hdd 9th: wknd bef 4 out: t.o* **20/1**

F22/ **P** **Aibrean (IRE)**[28] 5371 9-11-7 **130**....... JasonMaguire
(S R B Crawford, Ire) *hld up: hdwy after 4 out: pushed along whn chsng ldng bunch bef 3 out: sn wknd: bhd whn p.u bef last* **14/1**

6m 7.8s (-8.50) **Going Correction** -0.20s/f (Good) **22** Ran SP% **128.7**
Speed ratings (Par 107): **105,103,102,102,101 101,100,99,98,97 94,93,93,93,91 90,81,80,77,68 64,**
toteswingers 1&2 £40.00, 1&3 £0.00, 2&3 £0.00 CSF £136.33 CT £6717.29 TOTE £22.00: £3.90, £2.80, £9.20, £9.70; EX 299.10 TRIFECTA Not won..
Owner B Preece **Bred** Silvano Scanu **Trained** Broadwas, Worcs

FOCUS
Another competitive race, but it was won in comfortable fashion. A step up from the winner with the next two close to their marks.

359 CONNOLLY'S RED MILLS FINAL BUMPER CHALLENGE STANDARD OPEN NATIONAL HUNT FLAT RACE 2m 1f
8:50 (8:52) (Class 4) 4-6-Y-0 **£3,898** (£1,144; £572; £286)

Form RPR

41/ **1** **Regal Diamond (IRE)**[28] 5373 5-11-9 0....... TomO'Brien 123+
(Peter Bowen) *mde all: rdn over 1f out: drew clr fnl 150yds: styd on wl* **5/2**[1]

2/ **2** 3¾ **Oscarteea (IRE)**[36] 5263 4-10-12 0....... NoelFehily 109
(Anthony Honeyball) *hld up in midfield: hdwy over 3f out: styd on to take 2nd fnl 120yds: no ch w wnr* **10/3**[2]

/ **3** 2¼ **Hello George (IRE)** 4-10-12 0....... RichardJohnson 107
(Philip Hobbs) *hld up: hdwy 3f out: rdn over 2f out: styd on ins fnl f: tk 3rd cl home: nt gng pce to chal ldrs* **11/2**

4 1¼ **Sign Of A Victory (IRE)** 4-10-12 0....... AndrewTinkler 107
(Nicky Henderson) *midfield: hdwy over 4f out: chsd wnr over 2f out: no imp 1f out: lost 2nd fnl 120yds: no ex* **15/2**

5 7 **Full Throttle (IRE)** 4-10-12 0....... APMcCoy 100
(Jonjo O'Neill) *midfield: hdwy 5f out: effrt over 3f out: one pce 2f out: wl btn after* **4/1**[3]

004/ **6** *9* **Agesilas (FR)**[51] 4976 5-11-2 0.. DougieCostello 95
(Andrew Crook) *hld up: pushed along over 3f out: plugged on fnl 2f: nvr trbld ldrs* **40/1**

0/ **7** *7* **Pol O'Murchu**[40] 5208 6-10-9 0.. JohnWinston(7) 89
(Ferdy Murphy, France) *hld up: rdn 3f out: plugged on fr over 1f out: nvr trbld ldrs* **50/1**

2/ **8** *12* **Allbarnone**[44] 5125 5-11-2 0... CharlieHuxley 78
(William Kinsey) *chsd ldrs: wnt 2nd over 4f out: rdn whn lost 2nd over 2f out: sn wknd* **16/1**

4/ **9** *6* **Jackthejourneyman (IRE)**[19] 14 4-10-5 0............... PatrickCorbett(7) 69
(Rebecca Curtis) *chsd ldrs: losing pl whn n.m.r and hmpd 4f out: sn wknd* **16/1**

0/ **10** *4* **Neville Woods**[419] 5061 6-11-2 0.. SamThomas 69
(William Amos) *chsd wnr tl over 4f out: wknd 3f out* **50/1**

4m 12.3s (4.90) **Going Correction** -0.20s/f (Good)
WFA 4 from 5yo+ 4lb **10** Ran SP% **116.9**
Speed ratings: **80,78,77,76,73 69,65,60,57,55**
toteswingers 1&2 £2.10, 1&3 £8.30, 2&3 £4.30 CSF £10.76 TOTE £3.60: £1.80, £1.60, £1.60; EX 11.90 Trifecta £39.90 Pool: £1053.29 - 19.77 winning units..
Owner Roddy Owen,Paul Fullagar & Karen Bowen **Bred** Brittas House Stud **Trained** Little Newcastle, Pembrokes

FOCUS
This looks quite useful bumper form. The winner is rated similar to his Ayr win.
T/Plt: £1,270.70 to a £1 stake. Pool: £62,563.03 - 35.94 winning tickets T/Qpdt: £449.60 to a £1 stake. Pool: £7,656.82 - 12.60 winning tickets DO

360 - 366a (Foreign Racing) - See Raceform Interactive

[89]BANGOR-ON-DEE (L-H)

Saturday, May 18

OFFICIAL GOING: Good (good to soft in places) changing to good after race 2 (2.30)
Wind: Fresh, half behind Weather: Overcast

367 RACING UK "NATIONAL HUNT" MAIDEN HURDLE (9 hdls) 2m 1f
1:55 (1:56) (Class 4) 4-Y-0+ **£3,119** (£915; £457; £228)

Form RPR

461/ **1** **Just Cameron**[183] 2463 6-11-0 0.. RichieMcGrath 107+
(Philip Kirby) *chsd ldr after 1st: led 3rd: mstke 2 out: pressed last: drvn out and styd on towards fin* **2/1**[1]

204/ **2** *1 ½* **Separate Shadows (FR)**[59] 4864 5-11-0 0.......................... JasonMaguire 104
(Donald McCain) *led to 3rd: remained w wnr: ev ch 3 out: rdn and nt qckn 2 out: rallied to press wnr last: no ex towards fin* **11/4**[2]

0/ **3** *7* **Accordingtojodie (IRE)**[871] 3200 7-11-0 0...................... AndrewTinkler 97
(Nicky Henderson) *prom: chsd ldrs after 1st: effrt whn hit 4 out: rdn and nt qckn appr 2 out: no imp whn j. slowly last: one pce* **9/2**[3]

4 *6* **Star Of Boru (IRE)**[13] 132 6-11-0 0.. AlainCawley 90
(Paul John Gilligan, Ire) *racd keenly: sn chsd ldrs: rdn appr 2 out: one pce after* **14/1**

0/ **5** *5* **Nefyn Bay**[49] 5018 4-10-10 0.. AdrianLane 81
(Donald McCain) *chsd ldrs tl rdn and wknd after 3 out* **28/1**

0- **6** *26* **On The Way Home (IRE)**[18] 46 4-10-3 0................ RichieMcLernon 48
(Jonjo O'Neill) *in tch: outpcd appr 3 out: wl btn after* **20/1**

5/U- **7** *10* **Desert Sting**[3] 318 4-10-7 0.. JakeGreenall(3) 45
(Michael Easterby) *a bhd: toiling bef 5th: nvr a threat* **20/1**

550/ **8** *8* **Flame Of The Glen**[51] 4994 7-11-0 0.. TommyPhelan 41
(Barry Brennan) *unruly bef s: bhd: struggling bef 4th: stl toiling whn blnd 3 out: nvr a threat* **33/1**

05/- **9** *44* **Soeur Blanche (IRE)**[36] 5267 7-10-7 0.................(t) SamTwiston-Davies
(Roy Brotherton) *a bhd: t.o fr 5th* **10/1**

6/ **U** **Over My Head**[137] 3430 5-10-7 0.. DanielHiskett(7)
(Claire Dyson) *hld up in midfield on outer: j. awkwardly and uns rdr 2nd* **50/1**

P **The Iron Curtain (IRE)**[28] 7-11-0 0.. MarkGrant
(Sean Curran) *bhd: j. slowly 3rd: struggling whn p.u bef next* **25/1**

4m 4.0s (-6.90) **Going Correction** -0.175s/f (Good)
WFA 4 from 5yo+ 18lb **11** Ran SP% **115.7**
Speed ratings (Par 105): **109,108,105,102,99 87,82,79,58,**
toteswingers 1&2 £3.10, 2&3 £5.90, 1&3 £2.80 CSF £6.71 TOTE £1.90: £1.10, £1.70, £1.30; EX 8.20 Trifecta £17.20 Pool: £1041.66 - 45.33 winning units..
Owner Mr and Mrs Paul Chapman **Bred** Mrs A E And Miss S J Dixon **Trained** Middleham, N Yorks

FOCUS
Not many could be seriously considered for this maiden hurdle and it was dominated by those towards the head of the market. Modest form but the winner can rate higher.

368 DEVA RACING NOVICES' H'CAP HURDLE (11 hdls) 2m 4f
2:30 (2:30) (Class 5) (0-100,100) 4-Y-0+ **£1,949** (£572; £286; £143)

Form RPR

040/ **1** **Beforeall (IRE)**[37] 5245 5-11-9 **97**.. LeightonAspell 104
(Oliver Sherwood) *mde all: shkn up whn pressed appr 2 out: rdn bef last: styd on wl run-in* **9/2**[2]

065/ **2** *1 ¼* **Feast Of Fire (IRE)**[22] 5543 6-11-12 **100**.. APMcCoy 106
(Jonjo O'Neill) *prom: chsd ldr fr 2nd: rdn whn chalng appr 2 out: wanted to lugg lft u.p bef last: nt qckn run-in: hld towards fin* **11/4**[1]

0F0/ **3** *16* **June French (FR)**[47] 5083 5-10-0 **74**.. HarrySkelton 66
(Ian Williams) *hld up: hdwy 4 out: effrt to chse ldrs appr 3 out: rdn and one pce bef 2 out: kpt on to take 3rd towards fin: no ch w front two* **11/2**[3]

024/ **4** *¾* **Icanmotor**[184] 2431 6-10-6 **80**..(tp) AndrewTinkler 72
(Claire Dyson) *trckd ldrs: rdn whn hit 2 out: no imp after and unable to go w front two: kpt on u.p run-in* **9/2**[2]

433/ **5** *6* **Desert Nova (IRE)**[45] 5124 11-10-6 **80**.. BrianHughes 66
(Mark Campion) *hld up: hdwy 4 out: pushed along and outpcd after 3 out: no imp after* **14/1**

PP5/ **6** *19* **Seymour Legend**[22] 5538 7-10-11 **85**.. HaddenFrost 53
(Jim Wilson) *hld up: struggling 4 out: nvr a threat* **6/1**

066/ **7** *25* **Top Billing**[40] 5220 4-10-10 **89**.. BrianHarding 30
(Nicky Richards) *hld up: niggled along appr 5th: rdn after 6th: lost tch 4 out* **10/1**

00P/ **8** *2 ½* **Princesse Katie (IRE)**[25] 5477 7-9-7 **74** oh1......(t) MrMatthewStanley(7) 18
(James Bennett) *prom tl wknd appr 4 out* **33/1**

000/ **9** *50* **Ashcott Boy**[149] 3155 5-11-10 **98**.. DougieCostello
(Neil Mulholland) *midfield: hdwy to chse ldrs 6th: wknd appr 3 out: eased whn wl btn bef 2 out: t.o* **20/1**

4m 49.0s (-3.00) **Going Correction** -0.175s/f (Good)
WFA 4 from 5yo+ 19lb **9** Ran SP% **116.2**
Speed ratings (Par 103): **99,98,92,91,89 81,71,70,50**
toteswingers 1&2 £5.30, 2&3 £2.50, 1&3 £0.00 CSF £17.87 CT £69.41 TOTE £7.10: £1.90, £1.10, £2.20; EX 19.40 Trifecta £223.70 Pool: £738.32 - 2.36 winning units..
Owner Beforeall Partnership **Bred** Ms Barbara Johnston **Trained** Upper Lambourn, Berks

FOCUS
A desperately weak contest, the form of which is hard to get excited about. The first two are on the upgrade.

369 GET LOGO'D NOVICES' CHASE (12 fncs) 2m 1f 110y
3:05 (3:05) (Class 4) 5-Y-0+ **£3,768** (£1,106; £553; £276)

Form RPR

560/ **1** **Monte Cavallo (SAF)**[37] 5260 8-10-12 0.. APMcCoy 124+
(Rebecca Curtis) *w ldr: led appr 2nd: hdd narrowly 7th: regained ld 4 out: j.rt 2 out: sn rdn: styd on wl to draw clr fnl 150yds* **11/8**[1]

6/U- **2** *7* **Mulligan's Man (IRE)**[6] 234 6-10-12 0.. JasonMaguire 117
(Donald McCain) *led: hdd appr 2nd: chsd ldrs after: wnt 2nd bef 3 out: rdn and tried to chal bef 2 out: swtchd lft after 2 out: nt qckn appr last: no ex and unable to go w wnr fnl 150yds* **7/4**[2]

3/0- **3** *1 ½* **Zama Zama**[12] 144 6-10-9 0.. AdamWedge(3) 116
(Evan Williams) *hld up: hdwy to chse ldrs appr 7th: outpcd bef 2 out: tried to rally between last 2: one pce after last* **12/1**

3/3- **4** *30* **Detour Ahead**[14] 111 5-10-5 0..(p) SeanQuinlan 87
(Jennie Candlish) *j.rt: chsd ldrs: blnd 5th: lost pl appr 7th: struggling after: lost tch 3 out* **14/1**

P40/ **5** *56* **Echo Dancer**[37] 5248 7-10-7 0.. HarryChalloner(5) 38
(Trevor Wall) *sn wl bhd: t.o fr 5th* **100/1**

301/ **F** **Majorica King (FR)**[19] 30 7-11-0 118........................ ThomasGarner(5)
(Oliver Sherwood) *w ldr: led 7th: hdd 4 out: nrly 2 l down disputing 2nd whn fell 3 out* **5/1**[3]

400/ **U** **Mysula**[100] 4090 6-10-5 0..(t) LiamTreadwell
(Claire Dyson) *hld up: blnd and uns rdr 1st* **125/1**

4m 12.9s (-9.20) **Going Correction** -0.40s/f (Good) **7** Ran SP% **111.3**
Speed ratings: **104,100,100,86,62 ,**
toteswingers 1&2 £1.02, 2&3 £6.20, 1&3 £7.20 CSF £4.07 TOTE £1.90: £1.40, £1.40; EX 7.30 Trifecta £20.80 Pool: £1173.66 - 42.21 winning units..
Owner G Costelloe **Bred** Dr M Thomson **Trained** Newport, Dyfed

FOCUS
There wasn't a great deal to choose between the market principals on their hurdles ratings. The winner is a 130+ hurdler at best and can probably match that over fences.

370 WREXHAM LAGER H'CAP CHASE (15 fncs) 2m 4f 110y
3:40 (3:40) (Class 4) (0-115,115) 5-Y-0+ **£3,768** (£1,106; £553; £276)

Form RPR

022/ **1** **Hodgson (IRE)**[25] 5465 8-10-11 **100**..(tp) JamieMoore 112
(Peter Bowen) *a.p: j. slowly 1st: led 11th: rdn whn pressed fr 2 out: fnd ex and styd on towards fin* **7/2**[2]

/11- **2** *1 ¼* **Brody Bleu (FR)**[6] 245 6-11-10 **113** 7ex.. FelixDeGiles 124
(Robert Walford) *hld up in tch: effrt appr 10th: wnt 2nd bef 3 out: rdn and chalng fr 2 out: no ex towards fin* **9/4**[1]

3U/- **3** *50* **Overnight Fame (IRE)**[36] 5274 9-11-1 **104**....................(p) PaddyBrennan 80
(Tom George) *led 2nd to 5th: led 6th to 7th: led 9th: rdn appr 10th: hdd 11th: wknd after 3 out: n.d whn nt fluent 2 out* **6/1**[3]

514/ **4** *31* **Last Shot (FR)**[32] 5338 6-11-9 **112**.. AidanColeman 70
(Venetia Williams) *led to 2nd: led 5th to 6th: led 7th to 9th: rdn appr 10th: wknd bef 4 out: t.o* **7/1**

5/2- **P** **A Bridge Too Far (IRE)**[18] 45 7-11-12 **115**.................. JasonMaguire
(Donald McCain) *prom: blnd 4th: reminder after 5th: sn lost pl: u.p after 6th: bhd 8th: t.o 9th: p.u bef 10th* **7/2**[2]

6PP/ **P** **Sarraco (IRE)**[108] 3942 7-11-2 **105**..(t) TomScudamore
(Richard Lee) *hld up: detached fr 9th: losing tch whn p.u bef 11th* **16/1**

4m 58.0s (-11.10) **Going Correction** -0.40s/f (Good) **6** Ran SP% **107.9**
Speed ratings: **105,104,85,73,**
toteswingers 1&2 £8.00, 2&3 £4.10, 1&3 £9.00 CSF £11.26 CT £36.96 TOTE £3.40: £1.50, £1.10; EX 16.40 Trifecta £61.70 Pool: £1132.45 - 13.75 winning units..
Owner Roddy Owen & Paul Fullagar **Bred** J Landers **Trained** Little Newcastle, Pembrokes

FOCUS
Some improving sorts lined-up for this handicap chase. The winner had slipped to a good mark and is rated back to his best.

371 ALFA AGGREGATES H'CAP HURDLE (9 hdls) 2m 1f
4:15 (4:15) (Class 4) (0-120,120) 4-Y-0+ **£3,119** (£915; £457; £228)

Form RPR

6/1- **1** **Rime Avec Gentil (FR)**[6] 251 8-10-8 **107** 7ex........... RobertWilliams(5) 111+
(Bernard Llewellyn) *prom: hanging lft whn landed awkwardly 4 out: continued to hang lft: sltly outpcd by ldrs appr 2 out: str run fnl 110yds to ld towards fin* **2/1**[2]

050/ **2** *1 ¾* **Gud Day (IRE)**[85] 4368 5-11-4 **112**..(bt) PaddyBrennan 113
(Fergal O'Brien) *nt fluent several times: chsd ldr: led 3 out: rdn appr last: hdd and no ex towards fin* **15/8**[1]

600/ **3** *1 ½* **Early Applause**[20] 10 5-10-8 **102**.. BrianHarding 102
(Nicky Richards) *hld up: impr to chse ldr after 3 out: rdn whn trying to chal between last 2: nt qckn after last: lost 2nd and styd on same pce run-in* **20/1**

003/ **4** *29* **Smadynium (FR)**[24] 5497 5-11-12 **120**.. JasonMaguire 93
(Donald McCain) *led: nt fluent 1st: reminder appr 5th and bef 4 out: hdd 3 out: sn wknd* **9/4**[3]

26P/ **P** **Humbel Ben (IRE)**[164] 2855 10-10-13 **107**........................(p) WillKennedy
(Alan Jones) *in rr: rdn after 4th: lost tch 5th: t.o whn p.u bef 2 out* **14/1**

4m 5.4s (-5.50) **Going Correction** -0.175s/f (Good) **5** Ran SP% **110.3**
Speed ratings (Par 105): **105,104,103,89,**
CSF £6.37 TOTE £2.50: £1.90, £1.10; EX 7.70 Trifecta £26.80 Pool: £1475.49 - 41.23 winning units..
Owner Ms S Howell **Bred** Scea Marais Des Pictons **Trained** Fochriw, Caerphilly

FOCUS
Punters found it hard to split the first three in the market and it duly served up a thrilling finish. The winner is on the upgrade.

372 PATRICK BURLING DEVELOPMENTS MARES' STANDARD OPEN NATIONAL HUNT FLAT RACE 2m 1f
4:50 (4:52) (Class 6) 4-6-Y-O **£1,642** (£478; £239)

Form RPR
1/ **1** **Down Ace (IRE)**[30] 5364 6-11-5 0 JasonMaguire 118+
(Fergal O'Brien) *mde all: rdn over 2f out: kpt on wl* **9/4**[1]
2 *2 3/4* **Handmaid** 4-10-8 0 JamieMoore 104
(Peter Bowen) *trckd ldr: rdn over 3f out: kpt on but a jst hld* **12/1**
3 *9* **Balmusette** 4-10-8 0 JamesReveley 96
(Keith Reveley) *bit slowly away: hld up: stdy hdwy fr over 4f out: pushed along 3f out: wnt 3rd 2f out: kpt on one pce* **16/1**
2/ **4** *2 1/2* **Blue Buttons (IRE)**[24] 5511 5-10-12 0 NoelFehily 97
(Harry Fry) *in tch towards outer: rdn over 4f out: kpt on one pce* **4/1**[2]
- **5** *2* **Ellin's Tower** 4-10-3 0 (t) EdCookson(5) 91
(Kim Bailey) *midfield: rdn 4f out: kpt on one pce* **12/1**
6 *12* **De Grae Clouding (IRE)**[48] 4-10-1 0 PatrickCorbett(7) 81
(Rebecca Curtis) *midfield: hdwy to trck ldr 10f out: rdn over 3f out: wknd over 2f out* **11/1**
5/ **7** *1 3/4* **Notimetowaste (IRE)**[133] 3511 6-10-2 0 PaulO'Brien(10) 83
(Donald McCain) *in tch: rdn over 3f out: wknd over 2f out* **25/1**
8 *8* **Frangipani Lady** 4-10-8 0 DarylJacob 72
(Nick Williams) *racd keenly: in tch: rdn over 3f out: already wkng whn hmpd over 2f out* **10/1**
9 *3* **Playhara (IRE)** 4-10-8 0 DavidBass 69
(Nicky Henderson) *midfield: pushed along 5f out: sn struggling* **9/2**[3]
4/ **10** *7* **Little Dotty**[191] 2291 4-10-3 0 CharlieWallis(5) 63
(Giuseppe Fierro) *hld up: nvr threatened* **66/1**
0/- **11** *1 1/4* **Ticket**[20] 14 4-10-8 0 SeanQuinlan 62
(Jennie Candlish) *midfield: rdn over 4f out: sn wknd* **66/1**
12 *2* **Radmores Return** 5-10-5 0 CiaranMckee(7) 64
(John O'Shea) *hld up: a towards rr* **50/1**
13 *6* **Miss Dimples (IRE)** 4-10-8 0 WillKennedy 54
(Sarah-Jayne Davies) *trckd ldr: wnt wd on bnd after 2f: lost pl 10f out: bhd fnl 6f* **50/1**
14 *1 1/4* **Jayjay Joules** 5-10-12 0 SamThomas 57
(Lisa Williamson) *midfield: rdn over 5f out: sn wknd* **33/1**
0/ **15** *1/2* **Cayetina**[19] 35 4-10-8 0 SamJones 53
(Ali Brewer) *midfield: wknd over 4f out* **66/1**

4m 0.6s (-4.70) **Going Correction** -0.175s/f (Good)
WFA 4 from 5yo+ 4lb **15** Ran SP% **122.8**
Speed ratings: **104,102,98,97,96 90,89,86,84,81 80,79,77,76,76**
toteswingers 1&2 £16.50, 2&3 £56.20, 1&3 £18.50 CSF £31.06 TOTE £2.80: £1.30, £2.60, £2.80; EX 32.80 Trifecta £170.30 Pool: £901.47 - 3.96 winning units..
Owner Paul Sullivan **Bred** Mrs C J Berry **Trained** Coln St. Dennis, Gloucs

FOCUS
An informative bumper, run at a fair pace. The form is rated around the winner and fourth.

373 GAP PERSONNEL HUNTERS' CHASE (18 fncs) 3m 110y
5:20 (5:20) (Class 6) 5-Y-O+ **£987** (£303; £151)

Form RPR
1F1/ **1** **That's Rhythm (FR)**[7] 13-12-1 124 MissPFuller(7) 137+
(Miss Sally Duckett) *trckd ldng pair: led 3 out: pushed clr bef next: comf* **85/40**[3]
1/U- **2** *10* **Surenaga (IRE)**[17] 60 11-11-13 123 (b) MrAlexEdwards(5) 123
(Philip Rowley) *nt a fluent: hld up in tch: outpcd in 4th after 12th: styd on after 3 out: wnt 2nd 2 out: no ch w wnr* **2/1**[2]
2P3/ **3** *26* **Benefit Night (IRE)**[58] 4886 13-11-7 112 (bt) MrPGerety(7) 94
(Mrs Polly Stockton) *led narrowly: hdd 5 out: rdn after 4 out: wknd appr 2 out* **12/1**
P/1- **4** *2* **Round Tom (FR)**[9] 180 8-12-4 120 (t) MrWBiddick 98
(R Barber) *w ldr: briefly dropped to 3rd after 9th: pressed ldr again after 12th: led 5 out: hit 4 out: hdd 3 out: lost 2nd 2 out: wknd* **15/8**[1]
P **Donttellmother (IRE)**[20] 11-11-11 0 ConorShoemark(3)
(Richard Mathias) *in tch: nt fluent 11th: sn pushed along and struggling: wl bhd whn p.u bef 2 out* **25/1**

6m 1.3s (-18.50) **Going Correction** -0.40s/f (Good) **5** Ran SP% **111.7**
Speed ratings: **113,109,101,100,**
CSF £7.17 TOTE £3.20: £1.10, £1.30; EX 6.70 Trifecta £25.60 Pool: £1054.80 - 30.81 winning units..
Owner Mr and Mrs R H F Fuller **Bred** Scea Du Haras Des Sablonets **Trained** Moreton-In-Marsh, Gloucs

FOCUS
A fair hunters' chase, despite the small field. The winner is rated to the level of his February course win.
T/Plt: £7.50 to a £1 stake. Pool of £52265.14 - 5030.78 winning tickets. T/Qpdt: £4.70 to a £1 stake. Pool of £2680.98 - 416.21 winning tickets. DO

[317] UTTOXETER (L-H)
Saturday, May 18

OFFICIAL GOING: Chase course - soft (good to soft in places); hurdle course - good to soft
Wind: moderate 1/2 against Weather: overcast

374 DIRECT TELECOMS NOVICES' HURDLE (10 hdls) 2m 4f 110y
5:35 (5:36) (Class 4) 4-Y-O+ **£3,249** (£954; £477; £238)

Form RPR
01/- **1** **Toubeera**[20] 1 7-10-12 118 AidanColeman 125+
(Venetia Williams) *led after 1st: drew clr fr 3 out: heavily eased run-in (fin 1st)* **9/4**[2]
442/ **2** *23* **Letsby Avenue**[20] 19 5-10-12 122 WayneHutchinson 103
(Alan King) *chsd ldrs: 3rd whn nt fluent 7th: drvn to chse wnr bef next: 5 l down whn mstke 3 out: sn no ch w wnr* **8/13**[1]
045/ **3** *10* **Barton Jubilee**[35] 5288 5-10-12 0 DougieCostello 89
(Neil Mulholland) *led tl after 1st: chsd ldr: reminders 6th: lost pl and modest 3rd whn hit 3 out* **22/1**
0/4- **4** *3/4* **Trumix**[15] 91 5-10-12 0 NickScholfield 89
(Kim Bailey) *led tl after 1st: drvn 6th: sn outpcd and bhd: tk distant 4th 2 out (fin 4th btn 3/4)* **10/1**[3]

140/ **5** *40* **Divine Folly (IRE)**[535] 2872 8-10-12 0 BrendanPowell 53
(Lawney Hill) *chsd ldrs: outpcd whn reminders 6th: bhd fr next: t.o* **28/1**
0/F- **6** *53* **Nomadic Storm**[15] 91 7-10-12 0 CharliePoste 5
(Graeme McPherson) *chsd ldrs: drvn and outpcd 6th: sn bhd: t.o bef 3 out: virtually p.u run-in: eventually completed* **66/1**
P0P/ **P** **Agitation**[405] 5305 9-10-12 68 JamesDavies
(Alan Hollingsworth) *racd in last: reminders after 2nd: detached and nt fluent next: t.o whn p.u bef 5th* **200/1**

4m 54.7s (-4.30) **Going Correction** +0.075s/f (Yiel) **7** Ran SP% **111.6**
Speed ratings (Par 105): **111,102,98,98,82 62,**
toteswingers 1&2 £1.02, 2&3 £3.50, 1&3 £4.20 CSF £3.94 TOTE £2.40: £2.00, £1.10; EX 5.30 Trifecta £17.00 Pool: £907.55 - 39.96 winning units..
Owner Richard Britten-Long **Bred** Mrs H I S Calzini **Trained** Kings Caple, H'fords

FOCUS
The hurdles were placed on the outside, using the full with of the track, adding 68 yards per circuit. The ground rode as advertised on a dry, breezy and overcast evening. They went a decent pace in this weak novice hurdle, which promised to shape like a match between two well-supported rivals. However, the expected duel failed to materialise, resulting in a wide-margin winner. They finished strung out. There's a case for rating the race a lot higher through the second to fourth.

375 MOORLANDS RACING (S) HURDLE (10 hdls) 2m 4f 110y
6:10 (6:10) (Class 5) 4-7-Y-O **£1,949** (£572; £286; £143)

Form RPR
1/1- **1** **Molon Labe (IRE)**[5] 266 6-11-9 107 (t) AdamWedge(3) 109+
(David Rees) *hld up: trckd ldrs 6th: led appr 2 out: wnt clr run-in: eased towards fin* **1/1**[1]
/2U- **2** *13* **Lauberhorn**[2] 332 6-11-7 106 (v) PaulMoloney 96
(Evan Williams) *hld up in last: wnt 3rd after 3 out: 2nd between last 2: 1 1/2 l down whn mstke last: eased whn wl hld in clsng stages* **5/2**[2]
024/ **3** *19* **Gulfport**[20] 1 4-9-9 89 NickSlatter(7) 59
(Donald McCain) *w ldr: drvn to ld bef 3 out: hdd appr 2 out: wknd between last 2* **9/1**
/00- **4** *41* **Ron**[6] 252 5-11-0 95 (b[1]) APMcCoy 45
(Jonjo O'Neill) *led: increased pce 6th: hdd bef 3 out: wknd and eased after 3 out: eventually completed: t.o* **4/1**[3]

5m 2.9s (3.90) **Going Correction** +0.075s/f (Yiel)
WFA 4 from 5yo+ 19lb **4** Ran SP% **108.6**
Speed ratings: **95,90,82,67**
CSF £3.87 TOTE £1.70; EX 2.60 Trifecta £6.60 Pool: £346.53 - 39.01 winning units..There was no bid for the winner.
Owner D Rees & P Evans **Bred** Swettenham Stud, Carradale Ltd & T Stack **Trained** Clarbeston, Pembrokes

FOCUS
A paucity of runners for a run-of-the-mill selling hurdle, for which there was very little pace early on. It produced another wide-margin winner. The form is rated around the first two.

376 BULMERS ORIGINAL H'CAP HURDLE (9 hdls) 2m
6:40 (6:42) (Class 5) (0-100,100) 4-Y-O+ **£2,209** (£648; £324; £162)

Form RPR
000/ **1** **Acapulco Bay**[4] 5290 9-10-3 82 (p) RobertWilliams(5) 97+
(Dai Burchell) *hld up in rr: hdwy 6th: jnd ldr 3 out: sn led: drvn clr appr last: heavily eased in clsng stages* **85/40**[2]
446/ **2** *10* **Persian Herald**[20] 2 5-11-2 95 (v) TrevorWhelan(5) 98
(Neil King) *w ldrs: led 2nd: hdd sn after 3 out: kpt on: no ch w wnr* **12/1**
P65/ **3** *1 1/2* **Eastwell Smiles**[697] 916 9-11-4 95 (t) JamesBest(3) 95
(Sophie Leech) *chsd ldrs: wnt modest 3rd appr last: kpt on one pce* **25/1**
P00/ **4** *9* **Feeling (IRE)**[4] 5290 9-10-6 83 (p) RobertDunne(3) 79
(Dai Burchell) *chsd ldrs drvn 3 out: wknd appr last* **20/1**
/05- **5** *5* **There's No Rules**[6] 252 4-11-0 92 (e) BarryKeniry 76
(Richard Guest) *t.k.h: trckd ldrs: lost pl 6th: kpt on fr 2 out* **16/1**
042/ **6** *8* **Flash Harriet**[28] 5412 9-10-8 82 [1] DonalDevereux 62
(John Mackie) *chsd ldrs: drvn appr 3 out: wknd bef 2 out* **7/1**[3]
P60/ **7** *6* **Onedin Line**[34] 5317 5-11-10 98 AidanColeman 73
(Venetia Williams) *hld up towards rr: hdwy appr 3 out: wknd appr 2 out* **10/1**
136/ **8** *1* **Amazingreyce**[170] 2726 8-9-10 75 GavinSheehan(5) 49
(Christopher Kellett) *mid-div: drvn 4th: lost pl after 6th* **20/1**
404/ **9** *5* **It's A New Day**[59] 4873 5-11-12 100 APMcCoy 70
(Jonjo O'Neill) *hld up in rr: hdwy to chse ldrs 6th: drvn and lost pl appr next: bhd whn eased sn after 2 out* **2/1**[1]
P50/ **10** *36* **Lulu's Gift (IRE)**[164] 2854 7-9-9 74 oh5 JamesBanks(5) 11
(Michael Mullineaux) *led to 2nd: drvn 5th: sn lost pl: bhd after next: t.o 3 out* **25/1**

3m 52.7s (0.70) **Going Correction** +0.075s/f (Yiel)
WFA 4 from 5yo+ 18lb **10** Ran SP% **117.7**
Speed ratings (Par 103): **101,96,95,90,88 84,81,80,78,60**
toteswingers 1&2 £6.40, 2&3 £20.80, 1&3 £25.10 CSF £25.55 CT £493.84 TOTE £3.30: £1.30, £2.70, £7.60; EX 33.40 Trifecta £593.40 Part won. £791.30 - 0.90 winning units..
Owner J Parfitt **Bred** Mrs S Camacho **Trained** Briery Hill, Blaenau Gwent

FOCUS
Two horses were backed almost exclusively to their rivals and after a false start the pace was only fair for this low-grade handicap hurdle, which produced another comfortable winner. He was well treated on his old form.

377 SIR STANLEY CLARKE MEMORIAL H'CAP CHASE (11 fncs 1 omitted) 2m
7:15 (7:15) (Class 4) (0-115,112) 5-Y-O **£3,798** (£1,122; £561; £280; £140)

Form RPR
43P/ **1** **Captain Paulie (IRE)**[36] 5266 10-11-5 112 ConorRing(7) 123+
(Evan Williams) *chsd ldrs: upsides 4 out: led last: drvn out: hld on wl towards fin* **7/2**[3]
/11- **2** *3/4* **Accessallareas (IRE)**[9] 183 8-11-7 107 WillKennedy 116
(Sarah-Jayne Davies) *chsd ldrs: led 2 out: hdd last: styd on: no ex clsng stages* **9/4**[2]
5/0- **3** *3* **Maizy Missile (IRE)**[18] 43 11-10-1 87 PaulMoloney 94
(Mary Evans) *led: j. v big 2nd: hdd 3 out: styd on same pce fr next* **8/1**
2/2- **4** *2 1/4* **Coeur De Fou (FR)**[15] 90 8-11-7 107 (t) PaddyBrennan 111
(Tom George) *w ldr: narrow ld 3 out: hdd next: kpt on one pce* **2/1**[1]
50F/ **5** *33* **Finch Flyer (IRE)**[37] 5250 6-10-13 99 (p) TommyPhelan 70
(Aytach Sadik) *rn in snatches: chsd ldrs 7th: sn outpcd: chsng ldrs next: sn lost pl: bhd fr 2 out: t.o* **14/1**

POP/ 6 nk **Novikov**[207] 1975 9-10-13 **99**..........(t) RichieMcLernon 70
(Sophie Leech) *racd in last: hit 1st: outpcd 7th: lost pl bef next: sn bhd: t.o* **12/1**
4m 5.0s (10.00) **Going Correction** +0.425s/f (Soft) **6** Ran SP% **111.8**
Speed ratings: **92,91,90,89,72 72**
toteswingers 1&2 £1.70, 2&3 £3.10, 1&3 £4.00 CSF £12.14 TOTE £4.50: £2.40, £2.10; EX 11.30 Trifecta £45.90 Pool: £967.13 - 15.78 winning units..
Owner R E R Williams **Bred** John Long **Trained** Llancarfan, Vale Of Glamorgan
FOCUS
They missed out the first fence down the back straight, leaving nine to jump in this modest handicap chase in which they went only a fair pace. The form is rated around the second to fourth.

378 UTTOXETER TOWN FC H'CAP CHASE (13 fncs 2 omitted) 2m 4f
7:45 (7:45) (Class 5) (0-100,100) 5-Y-O+ **£2,599** (£763; £381; £190)

Form RPR
164/ 1 **Le Grand Chene (FR)**[42] 5186 7-11-5 **93**..........(vt) PaulMoloney 102+
(Sophie Leech) *hld up: trckd ldrs 5th: upsides 4 out: led next: sn clr: nudged out* **7/1**
/52- 2 3 **Mad Professor (IRE)**[9] 183 10-9-9 **74** oh6..........(b) JoeCornwall[(5)] 76
(John Cornwall) *drvn 4th: chsd ldrs 7th: lft 2nd sn after 3 out: kpt on run-in: no imp* **14/1**
0/3- 3 27 **Kap West (FR)**[16] 84 8-11-0 **88**..........(t) AndrewGlassonbury 90+
(Laura Young) *chsd ldrs 7th: upsides 4 out: blnd bdly: rdr temporarily lost iron and lost pl: rallied to take distant 3rd nr fin* **4/1**[2]
3/6- 4 1 **Mister Wiseman**[14] 117 11-11-3 **94**..........(bt) MarkQuinlan[(3)] 67
(Nigel Hawke) *led tl after 1st: led next: drvn and jnd 4 out: hdd and hmpd next: sn wknd: lost distant 3rd nr fin* **13/2**[3]
5P6/ P **Evella (IRE)**[22] 5552 9-11-7 **95**..........(p) AlexMerriam
(Neil King) *w ldrs: led after 1st: hdd next: lost pl 9th: sn bhd: t.o next: p.u bef 4 out* **12/1**
PP2/ P **Master Milan (IRE)**[27] 5440 7-11-12 **100**..........(b) APMcCoy
(Jonjo O'Neill) *chsd ldng pair: p.u after 2nd: fatally injured* **1/1**[1]
5m 13.3s (7.80) **Going Correction** +0.425s/f (Soft) **6** Ran SP% **110.2**
Speed ratings: **101,99,89,88,**
toteswingers 1&2 £12.40, 2&3 £8.50, 1&3 £4.20 CSF £74.19 TOTE £8.80: £3.10, £4.30; EX 46.20 Trifecta £129.80 Pool: £861.71 - 4.97 winning units..
Owner T Westmacott & C J Leech **Bred** Joel Degroote **Trained** Elton, Gloucs
FOCUS
They went a strong gallop from the outset in this modest handicap chase. The easy winner is rated similar to his Chepstow win.

379 JPW DISTRIBUTION MARES' H'CAP HURDLE (12 hdls) 3m
8:20 (8:20) (Class 4) (0-120,120) 4-Y-O+ **£3,249** (£954; £477; £238)

Form RPR
1B0/ 1 **Ballinahow Star (IRE)**[32] 5339 7-11-12 **120**..........(t) NickScholfield 126+
(Jeremy Scott) *hld up in last wl in tch: hdwy to trck ldrs 8th: wnt cl 2nd after 3 out: led appr next: 4 l ahd last: drvn out* **11/4**[1]
3/5- 2 1¼ **Twin Bud**[15] 99 8-9-11 **94** oh1.......... AdamWedge[(3)] 97
(Anna Newton-Smith) *w ldrs: led 3 out: hdd appr next: kpt on wl run-in: no real imp* **11/1**
P32/ 3 10 **Kindly Note**[25] 5466 6-11-7 **115**.......... DominicElsworth 109
(Emma Lavelle) *nt fluent: chsd ldrs: drvn 9th: outpcd appr next: kpt on fr 2 out: tk modest 3rd nr fin* **5/1**
604/ 4 ½ **Russie With Love**[20] 12 7-11-0 **108**.......... JamesDavies 101
(Chris Down) *chsd ldrs: cl 2nd 8th: drvn 3 out: one pce and j.rt last 2: lost 3rd nr line* **7/2**[2]
2/1- 5 14 **Midnight Macarena**[17] 70 8-11-2 **110**..........(p) LeightonAspell 96
(Lucy Wadham) *led: j.rt 1st: hdd 3 out: wknd next* **4/1**[3]
320/ 6 33 **Tigresse Bleue**[153] 3089 5-10-13 **107**..........(p) APMcCoy 58
(Jonjo O'Neill) *trckd ldrs: hung lft and lost pl sn after 3 out: bhd next: sn eased: t.o* **9/2**
5m 56.9s (6.90) **Going Correction** +0.075s/f (Yiel) **6** Ran SP% **112.1**
Speed ratings (Par 105): **91,90,87,87,82 71**
toteswingers 1&2 £8.60, 2&3 £14.70, 1&3 £7.90 CSF £28.73 TOTE £3.40: £1.90, £4.80; EX 25.00 Trifecta £123.20 Pool: £757.91 - 4.61 winning units..
Owner Pillhead House Partners **Bred** Roger McLoughlin **Trained** Brompton Regis, Somerset
FOCUS
A modest mares' handicap hurdle run at a fair pace and plenty in with a chance three out. A personal best from the cosy winner.

380 BANNER MARQUEES STANDARD OPEN NATIONAL HUNT FLAT RACE 2m
8:50 (8:50) (Class 6) 4-6-Y-O **£1,559** (£457; £228; £114)

Form RPR
1 **Beau De Tabel (FR)** 5-11-0 0.......... DarylJacob 103+
(Nick Williams) *trckd ldrs: pushed along 6f out: wnt 3rd over 4f out: 2nd over 1f out: led jst ins fnl f: drvn out* **3/1**[2]
2 3½ **When I'm Sixtyfour (IRE)** 4-10-10 0.......... APMcCoy 96
(Jonjo O'Neill) *t.k.h: trckd ldrs: wnt 2nd 4f out: led over 1f out: hdd jst ins fnl f: styd on same pce* **6/4**[1]
5/ 3 5 **Perfect Poison (IRE)**[27] 5429 5-11-0 0.......... JasonMaguire 95
(Donald McCain) *w ldr: led after 4f: hdd over 2f out: kpt on one pce* **9/2**[3]
4 9 **Kilfinichen Bay (IRE)** 5-11-0 0.......... RichardJohnson 87
(Peter Hiatt) *chsd ldrs: modest 4th 3f out: one pce* **6/1**
0/ 5 2½ **Camptown Lady**[30] 5364 4-10-3 0.......... DougieCostello 74
(Laura Young) *hld up: hdwy 7f out: chsng ldrs 4f out: sn wknd* **28/1**
60/ 6 3¾ **Cadgers Hole**[45] 5125 6-11-0 0.......... TomSiddall 81
(Lynn Siddall) *t.k.h in rr: lost pl and carried wd bnd over 4f out: no ch after* **80/1**
7 31 **Alfie Moone** 5-11-0 0.......... LiamHeard 53
(Barry Leavy) *led 4f: w ldrs: outpcd whn hung bdly rt and lost pl bnd over 4f out: sn bhd: t.o* **20/1**
8 1¼ **Revouge** 4-10-10 0.......... MarkGrant 48
(Jim Old) *hld up in rr: drvn 7f out: lost pl 4f out: sn bhd: t.o* **14/1**
P **Cleetons Turn** 6-11-0 0.......... JamesDavies
(Alan Hollingsworth) *sn chsng ldrs: drvn 9f out: lost pl 7f out: sn wl bhd: hopelessly t.o whn p.u 3f out* **66/1**
3m 54.2s (7.80) **Going Correction** +0.075s/f (Yiel)
WFA 4 from 5yo+ 4lb **9** Ran SP% **115.1**
Speed ratings: **83,81,78,74,73 71,55,55,**
toteswingers 1&2 £3.20, 2&3 £1.80, 1&3 £4.30 CSF £7.63 TOTE £4.90: £1.30, £1.10, £1.80; EX 9.70 Trifecta £35.90 Pool: £927.44 - 19.34 winning units..
Owner Larkhills Racing Partnership II **Bred** Peter Jones, Sally Jones & Tobias Jones **Trained** George Nympton, Devon
FOCUS
A good bumper for the track with representatives from a couple of big yards. Run at a fair clip, it should throw up a few winners. The first three look decent types and can rate higher.

T/Plt: £325.00 to a £1 stake. Pool of £59477.13 - 133.58 winning tickets. T/Qpdt: £125.10 to a £1 stake. Pool of £4685.79 - 27.70 winning tickets. WG

381 - 382a (Foreign Racing) - See Raceform Interactive

201 MARKET RASEN (R-H)
Sunday, May 19

OFFICIAL GOING: Good (good to soft in places; chs 8.5, hdl 8.1)
Wind: light 1/2 against Weather: fine and mild

383 INTRO TO RACING MAIDEN HURDLE (8 hdls) 2m 1f
2:00 (2:01) (Class 4) 4-Y-O+ **£3,119** (£915; £457; £228)

Form RPR
1 **Godwit**[278] 5-10-4 0.......... JackQuinlan[(3)] 103+
(Eugene Stanford) *trckd ldng pair: drvn and upsides 2 out: led appr last: edgd lft and forged clr* **25/1**
325/ 2 6 **Yes Daddy (IRE)**[24] 5519 5-10-11 0..........[1] BrianToomey[(3)] 107
(Kevin Ryan) *nt fluent: chsd ldr: led bef 2 out: hdd appr last: kpt on same pce* **11/8**[2]
3 31 **Life And Times (USA)**[1038] 5-11-0 0.......... DenisO'Regan 77
(John Ferguson) *nt fluent: t.k.h: led: hdd bef 2 out: sn wknd* **11/10**[1]
0/ 4 22 **Hubood**[30] 5374 5-10-7 0.......... DaveCrosse 50
(Zoe Davison) *in rr: hdwy 5th: poor 4th 3 out* **66/1**
0/ 5 13 **Xclaim**[21] 15 5-11-0 0.......... JasonMaguire 46
(Micky Hammond) *chsd ldrs: hit 2nd: reminders 5th: wknd next: poor 5th whn blnd 2 out* **9/1**[3]
60P/ 6 52 **Monzino (USA)**[13] 2669 5-10-7 0.......... GerardGalligan[(7)]
(Michael Chapman) *in rr: bhd fr 4th: t.o 3 out* **40/1**
0P0/ P **Rose Of Marron (IRE)**[26] 5483 6-10-9 0.......... GavinSheehan[(5)]
(John Upson) *j.lft: in rr: bhd fr 4th: t.o 3 out: p.u bef next* **150/1**
4m 18.0s (11.30) **Going Correction** +0.65s/f (Soft) **7** Ran SP% **108.2**
Speed ratings (Par 105): **99,96,81,71,65 40,**
toteswingers 1&2 £5.30, 1&3 £5.00, 2&3 £1.02 CSF £56.00 TOTE £24.60: £11.00, £1.10; EX 55.40 Trifecta £269.30 Pool: £1264.89 - 3.52 winning units..
Owner Lemberg Stables **Bred** Sir Thomas Pilkington **Trained** Newmarket, Suffolk
FOCUS
A weak maiden, rated around the second.

384 CALVERTS CARPETS H'CAP HURDLE (8 hdls) 2m 1f
2:30 (2:30) (Class 4) (0-110,109) 4-Y-O+ **£3,119** (£915; £457; £228)

Form RPR
5/0- 1 **Fitandproperjob**[6] 267 7-9-9 **83**..........(t) JamesBanks[(5)] 88+
(Anthony Middleton) *hld up in rr: hdwy 3 out: chsd ldr appr next: led run-in: drvn out* **6/1**
042/ 2 1¾ **Glencree (IRE)**[27] 5451 9-11-12 **109**..........(p) BrianHughes 112
(John Wade) *chsd ldrs: led 3 out: hdd run-in: no ex* **5/1**[2]
45U/ 3 9 **Tracking Time**[49] 5035 6-11-4 **108**.......... MrJMartin[(7)] 103
(Andrew J Martin) *hdwy to chse ldrs 5th: swtchd rt last: kpt on to take modest 3rd run-in* **10/1**
013/ 4 4 **Lindsay's Dream**[28] 5432 7-11-5 **102**..........(p) DaveCrosse 94
(Zoe Davison) *in rr: drvn to chse ldrs 3 out: 3rd whn hit last: fdd* **10/1**
210/ 5 4½ **Arkaim**[21] 21 5-11-0 **102**.......... GavinSheehan[(5)] 91
(Pam Sly) *jnd ldrs 3rd: led appr next: hdd 3 out: cl 3rd whn mstke next: sn wknd* **11/2**[3]
565/ 6 21 **Galley Slave (IRE)**[27] 4433 8-9-7 **83** oh7..........(v[1]) GerardGalligan[(7)] 51
(Michael Chapman) *led: hdd 3rd: sn drvn: lost pl 5th: sn bhd: t.o next* **10/1**
100/ 7 11 **Wheelavit (IRE)**[299] 1065 10-11-3 **100**..........(t) NickScholfield 59
(Claire Dyson) *chsd ldrs: lost pl 4th: bhd whn blnd next: t.o 2 out* **25/1**
133/ 8 31 **Houseparty**[25] 5499 5-11-11 **108**..........(p) DenisO'Regan 39
(John Ferguson) *chsd ldrs: led 3rd: hdd appr next: wknd rapidly bef 2 out: sn wl bhd: hopelessly t.o* **11/4**[1]
033/ P **Chain Of Events**[26] 5312 6-11-8 **105**..........(t) DougieCostello
(Sarah Humphrey) *t.k.h: chsd ldrs: lost pl and p.u bef 2 out* **10/1**
4m 15.4s (8.70) **Going Correction** +0.65s/f (Soft)
WFA 4 from 5yo+ 18lb **9** Ran SP% **113.2**
Speed ratings (Par 105): **105,104,99,98,95 86,80,66,**
toteswingers 1&2 £6.10, 1&3 £0.00, 2&3 £9.50 CSF £35.71 CT £293.02 TOTE £7.10: £2.00, £2.00, £3.40; EX 40.60 Trifecta £573.60 Part won. Pool: £764.90 - 0.85 winning units..
Owner S E D Racing Partnership **Bred** John Allen **Trained** Granborough, Bucks
FOCUS
They finished pretty well strung out in this moderate handicap and the form looks sound.

385 BOOK ONTO RACECOURSE CARAVAN PARK NOVICES' H'CAP CHASE (17 fncs) 3m 1f
3:00 (3:01) (Class 4) (0-110,110) 5-Y-O+ **£3,768** (£1,106; £553; £276)

Form RPR
21P/ 1 **Churchfield Champ (IRE)**[27] 5455 7-11-12 **110**.......... NoelFehily 120
(Paul John Gilligan, Ire) *hld up: hdwy to go 2nd appr 3 out: upsides 2 out: led last: drvn out* **9/2**[2]
U33/ 2 1 **Whiskey Ridge (IRE)**[91] 4279 7-9-12 **85** oh3 ow1.......... BrianToomey[(3)] 94
(Sue Smith) *led: hit 2nd: jnd 2 out: hdd last: rallied last 100yds: a hld* **13/8**[1]
3/0- 3 17 **Dr Dreamy (IRE)**[15] 117 6-10-0 **84** oh5..........(t) LeeEdwards 79
(Claire Dyson) *t.k.h: chsd ldng pair 5th: one pce fr 3 out* **8/1**
024/ 4 6 **Midnight Dove**[23] 5542 8-10-0 **87** ow1.......... RobertDunne[(3)] 75
(Andrew Price) *chsd ldr: drvn 4 out: wknd next* **9/2**[2]
4/4- 5 16 **Xenophon**[9] 203 5-9-8 **85**..........(p) GerardGalligan[(7)] 63
(Michael Chapman) *rn in snatches: nt jump wl: lost pl 11th: bhd fr 4 out* **9/1**
0/0- F **Minella Fifty (IRE)**[10] 179 5-11-3 **101**..........(t) DougieCostello
(Jonjo O'Neill) *hld up: fell 1st* **7/1**[3]
6m 22.5s (-8.80) **Going Correction** -0.475s/f (Good) **6** Ran SP% **108.1**
Speed ratings: **95,94,89,87,82**
toteswingers 1&2 £2.00, 1&3 £6.40, 2&3 £6.40 CSF £11.87 TOTE £4.40: £1.80, £1.60; EX 12.60 Trifecta £62.20 Pool: £1068.35 - 12.88 winning units..
Owner Sean Conroy **Bred** Mrs M Skehan-O'Brien **Trained** Athenry, Co Galway
FOCUS
The first pair came right away in this ordinary novice handicap.

386 CALVERTS CARPETS AND FLOORING H'CAP HURDLE (10 hdls) 2m 5f
3:30 (3:30) (Class 3) (0-125,125) 4-Y-O+ **£5,393** (£1,583; £791; £395)

Form RPR
350/ 1 **Dizzy River (IRE)**[148] 3181 8-10-7 **106**..........(p) DannyCook 111
(Brian Ellison) *chsd ldrs 6th: upsides 2 out: swtchd rt between last 2: led last: drvn out* **6/1**[3]

/21- **2** *1* **Va'Vite (IRE)**[2] 353 6-10-9 **113**.. JamesBanks(5) 117
(Anthony Middleton) *hld up: hdwy 7th: sn w ldrs: upsides 2 out: no ex last 50yds* **7/4**[1]

213/ **3** *7* **Brassick**[151] 3146 6-11-12 **125**..(t) NoelFehily 123
(Charlie Longsdon) *trckd ldr: led 7th: hdd last: kpt on one pce* **9/4**[2]

P30/ **4** *½* **Points Of View**[566] 2238 8-11-6 **119**..................................(t) JasonMaguire 116
(Kim Bailey) *hld up in rr: smooth hdwy 3 out: drvn to chse ldrs next: upsides last: kpt on one pce* **20/1**

404/ **5** *46* **E Major**[262] 1417 8-11-3 **116**.. JimmyMcCarthy 72
(Renee Robeson) *chsd ldrs: drvn and 2nd 7th: wknd 2 out: sn bhd: t.o* **14/1**

P40/ **P** **Iolith (GER)**[36] 5284 8-11-10 **123**...................................... WayneHutchinson
(Alan King) *trckd ldrs: 3rd 7th: wknd and eased after 2 out: p.u bef last: lame* **13/2**

51F/ **P** **Danceintothelight**[12] 5498 6-10-9 **108**..........................(p) WilsonRenwick
(Micky Hammond) *led: hdd 7th: lost pl and j.lft next: sn bhd: t.o whn p.u bef 2 out* **18/1**

5m 23.3s (14.50) **Going Correction** +0.65s/f (Soft) 7 Ran SP% **111.4**
Speed ratings (Par 107): **98,97,94,94,77** ,
toteswingers 1&2 £3.40, 1&3 £2.30, 2&3 £1.70 CSF £16.60 TOTE £5.80: £2.10, £1.50; EX 18.20 Trifecta £56.90 Pool: £1534.62 - 20.19 winning units..
Owner Dan Gilbert **Bred** Oliver Loughlin **Trained** Norton, N Yorks

FOCUS
Not a bad handicap and it proved a lively betting heat. There was a decent gallop on.

387 RUM "N" RASEN H'CAP CHASE (14 fncs) 2m 6f 110y
4:00 (4:00) (Class 4) (0-120,120) 5-Y-0+ **£3,768** (£1,106; £553; £276)

Form RPR

200/ **1** **Brunswick Gold (IRE)**[25] 5496 8-11-12 **120**..............(p) RichardJohnson 130+
(Steve Gollings) *chsd ldrs: led 5th: mde rest: jnd 3 out: drew 7 l clr last: drvn out* **3/1**[2]

62P/ **2** *11* **Peachey Moment (USA)**[160] 2979 8-11-12 **120**.............. JasonMaguire 121
(Nicky Richards) *trckd ldrs: upsides 3 out: kpt on same pce fr next* **17/2**

P10/ **3** *7* **Balinroab (IRE)**[50] 5015 6-11-11 **119**.. APMcCoy 115
(Jonjo O'Neill) *led: nt fluent and hdd 1st: chsd ldrs: reminders 7th: rdn and outpcd 4 out: rallied and 3rd next: kpt on one pce* **9/4**[1]

0/2- **4** *1¾* **Delgany Gunner**[16] 96 9-10-4 **103**........................(tp) TrevorWhelan(5) 94
(Neil King) *chsd ldrs: lost pl 5th: drvn 9th: rallied 4 out: outpcd appr next: kpt on run-in: tk modest 4th clsng stages* **8/1**

252/ **5** *1¾* **Volcan Surprise (FR)**[46] 5122 5-11-5 **113**..............(b) WayneHutchinson 105
(Alan King) *led 1st: hdd 5th: 2nd 8th: drvn 5 out: 3rd and outpcd whn hit 4 out: wknd run-in* **4/1**[3]

035/ **6** *13* **Alpha One (IRE)**[25] 5502 7-11-2 **110**...............................(p) DenisO'Regan 88
(Chris Grant) *mstkes: chsd ldrs: lost pl after 4th: rallied 4 out: lost pl bef next* **14/1**

PP2/ **P** **Masked Man (IRE)**[38] 5259 10-10-8 **112**...................(tp) PaulNO'Brien(10)
(Charlie Mann) *trckd ldrs: lost pl 7th: bhd whn p.u bef next* **10/1**

5m 32.1s (-13.90) **Going Correction** -0.475s/f (Good) 7 Ran SP% **113.2**
Speed ratings: **105,101,98,98,97 93**,
toteswingers 1&2 £5.10, 1&3 £2.70, 2&3 £3.00 CSF £26.57 TOTE £4.10: £2.10, £4.50; EX 36.90 Trifecta £62.70 Pool: £1162.99 - 13.90 winning units..
Owner P J Martin **Bred** J P Murphy **Trained** Scamblesby, Lincs

■ Stewards' Enquiry : Richard Johnson two-day ban; used whip when clearly winning (2nd&4th June).

FOCUS
A modest handicap which was taken apart by the winner.

388 BEAUMONTCOTE HUNTERS' CHASE (14 fncs) 2m 6f 110y
4:30 (4:31) (Class 6) 5-Y-0+ **£935** (£290; £145)

Form RPR

P/4- **1** **Artic Pride (IRE)**[18] 58 9-11-5 78.. MrRSmith(7) 100+
(Mrs Emma Clark) *trckd ldr: led 8th: narrowly hdd 3 out: led last: drvn out* **1/1**[1]

003/ **2** *5* **Farmer Frank**[28] 10-11-5 97.................................. MrSDavies-Thomas(7) 95
(Mrs Jane Kent) *trckd ldrs: wnt cl 2nd after 10th: narrow ld 3 out: hdd last: kpt on same pce* **3/1**[3]

536/ **3** *66* **Bedrock Fred**[21] 7-11-5 0.. MrSamPainting(7) 36
(Miss E J Tanner) *j.rt thrght: led: hdd 8th: lost pl 10th: hung lft and sn wl bhd: t.o next: eventually completed* **9/4**[2]

5m 35.2s (-10.80) **Going Correction** -0.475s/f (Good) 3 Ran SP% **105.8**
Speed ratings: **99,97,74**
toteswingers 1&2 £4.60, 1&3 £12.70, 2&3 £9.00 CSF £3.89 TOTE £2.00; EX 3.70 Trifecta £4.50 Pool: £643.30 - 107.14 winning units..
Owner Charles R Clark **Bred** Brendan Fahey **Trained** Wistow, N Yorks

FOCUS
A tight little hunter chase.

389 WATCH RACING UK ON CHANNEL 432 STANDARD OPEN NATIONAL HUNT FLAT RACE 2m 1f
5:00 (5:00) (Class 6) 4-6-Y-0 **£1,559** (£457; £228; £114)

Form RPR

1 **Make Me A Fortune (IRE)**[84] 5-11-2 0.................................. APMcCoy 113
(Steve Gollings) *trckd ldrs: drvn over 4f out: chal 3f out: sn led: hdd narrowly 2f out: hrd drvn and styd on to ld again nr fin* **2/1**[1]

2 *nk* **Mutanawwer** 4-10-12 0.. BrianHughes 108
(Andrew Crook) *trckd ldrs: upsides 3f out: narrow ld 2f out: hdd and no ex clsng stages* **16/1**

422/ **3** *10* **Keltic Rhythm (IRE)**[21] 4 6-11-2 0.. AlexMerriam 103
(Neil King) *led: qcknd pce 6f out: hdd over 2f out: wknd over 1f out* **11/4**[2]

4 *8* **King's Opus (IRE)** 4-10-12 0.. JasonMaguire 92
(Kim Bailey) *trckd ldrs: outpcd over 2f out: sn wknd* **10/3**[3]

03/ **5** *4½* **Il Testone (FR)**[28] 5429 4-10-2 0................................ DiarmuidO'Regan(10) 88
(Chris Grant) *sn trcking ldrs: reminders 6f out: outpcd 4f out* **20/1**

6/ **6** *2¾* **Ifonlywecud (IRE)**[30] 5388 4-10-12 0.................................... HenryBrooke 86
(Clive Mulhall) *hld up towards rr: hdwy after 6f: drvn 5f out: sn outpcd: lost pl over 3f out* **16/1**

7 *9* **Say When** 5-11-2 0.. WayneHutchinson 81
(Alan King) *gave problems on way to s: hld up in rr: hdwy 9f out: chsng ldrs 6f out: lost pl over 3f out: bhd fnl 2f* **7/1**

00/ **8** *2½* **Sab Le Beau (FR)**[135] 3497 4-10-12 0..................................(t) DannyCook 75
(Alan Brown) *hld up: hdwy after 6f out: outpcd 4f out: sn lost pl* **25/1**

P **Secret Island** 4-10-5 0.. TomMessenger
(Anthony Day) *wnt lft s: t.k.h in rr: hung lft and lost pl 9f out: t.o 6f out: p.u 3f out* **100/1**

4m 15.5s (14.40) **Going Correction** +0.65s/f (Soft)
WFA 4 from 5yo+ 4lb 9 Ran SP% **116.9**
Speed ratings: **92,91,87,83,81 79,75,74**,
toteswingers 1&2 £7.10, 1&3 £1.30, 2&3 £8.20 CSF £36.21 TOTE £2.40: £1.10, £4.90, £1.60; EX 39.90 Trifecta £201.70 Pool: £1637.03 - 6.08 winning units..
Owner P J Martin **Bred** Paddy Fortune & Anna McCarthy **Trained** Scamblesby, Lincs

FOCUS
This was another race where two dominated in the home straight and it saw a cracking finish.
T/Plt: £191.80 to a £1 stake. Pool of £56,082.13 - 213.36 winning tickets T/Qpdt: £38.60 to a £1 stake. Pool of £3344.84 - 64.10 winning tickets WG

STRATFORD (L-H)
Sunday, May 19

OFFICIAL GOING: Good to soft (good in places) changing to good (good to soft in places) after race 3 (3.20)
Wind: light, across Weather: dry, bright spells

390 JONATHAN DAVID ELLIOTT NEWMAN 30TH BIRTHDAY NOVICES' HURDLE (THE SUNDAY £5K BONUS RACE) (8 hdls) 2m 110y
2:20 (2:20) (Class 4) 4-Y-0+ **£3,898** (£1,144; £572; £286)

Form RPR

0/ **1** **The Bay Bandit**[13] 5180 6-10-12 0.............................. SamTwiston-Davies 98+
(Neil Mulholland) *hld up in tch in rr: hdwy to chse ldrs 2 out: gng for gap between ldrs tl swtchd rt jst bef last: qcknd to ld after last: sn in command: comf* **25/1**

2- **2** *1½* **Daliance (IRE)**[10] 186 4-10-8 0.. LeightonAspell 92
(Lucy Wadham) *t.k.h: chsd ldrs tl lft 2nd 3rd: upsides ldr bef 2 out: drvn and fnd little bef last: led last: hdd and immediately outpcd flat* **30/100**[1]

266/ **3** *2½* **Keep The Cash (IRE)**[28] 5438 5-10-12 0.....................(p) ConorO'Farrell 94
(David Pipe) *led and set stdy gallop: nt fluent 3 out: jnd bef next: drvn between last 2: hdd last: no ex flat* **4/1**[2]

0/5- **4** *6* **Milor De La Borie (FR)**[10] 174 4-10-8 0........................ TomScudamore 85
(David Pipe) *t.k.h: hld up in tch in last trio: smooth hdwy to chse ldrs 2 out: rdn and fnd little bef last: sn btn: wknd flat* **14/1**[3]

5FP/ **5** *¾* **Umoristic (FR)**[23] 5538 5-10-5 84.......................................(p) MrPJohn(7) 88
(Reginald Brown) *taken down early and led to s: t.k.h: chsd ldrs: cl 4th and rdn whn mstke 2 out: wknd u.p bef last* **18/1**

P/- **6** *26* **Actodos (IRE)**[35] 5318 9-10-9 0.. MichealNolan(3) 65
(Richard Woollacott) *t.k.h: hld up in tch in midfield: mstke 3 out: rdn and btn bef next: wknd between last 2* **25/1**

7 *nk* **Between The Lines (IRE)**[20] 4-10-8 0.................................... CharliePoste 60
(Anthony Middleton) *t.k.h: chsd ldr: mstke 2nd: j. slowly and lost pl 3rd: styd chsng ldrs: mstke and rdn 3 out: wknd next* **28/1**

8 *14* **Hawk Moth (IRE)**[47] 5-10-12 0.. JamieMoore 52
(John Spearing) *plld hrd: hld up in tch in last trio: mstke 5th: effrt bef 2 out: sn btn and wknd: eased flat: t.o* **16/1**

3m 57.7s (1.70) **Going Correction** +0.025s/f (Yiel)
WFA 4 from 5yo+ 18lb 8 Ran SP% **125.9**
Speed ratings (Par 105): **97,96,95,92,91 79,79,72**
toteswingers 1&2 £7.50, 1&3 £0.00, 2&3 £1.02 CSF £37.74 TOTE £38.60: £7.90, £1.02, £1.10; EX 101.50 Trifecta £452.10 Part won. Pool: £602.90 - 0.37 winning units..
Owner Neil Mulholland Racing Club **Bred** Darley **Trained** Limpley Stoke, Wilts

FOCUS
Rail moved outwards for fresh ground. Sam Twiston-Davies said after the first that the ground was "just on the slow side of good". Smart sorts in Battle Group and Clerk's Choice have won this novice hurdle recently, but this looked a weak race, especially given the bonus money on offer. The pace was modest and the time was 11.7sec slower than standard. The third to fifth set the level with the favourite a stone+ off.

391 STRATFORDCARAVANS.CO.UK MARES' NOVICES' (S) HURDLE (8 hdls) 2m 110y
2:50 (2:50) (Class 5) 4-Y-0+ **£1,949** (£572; £286; £143)

Form RPR

6/4- **1** **Golden Acorn (IRE)**[10] 193 4-10-6 88..................................(t) CharliePoste 85+
(Anthony Middleton) *chsd ldrs: wnt 2nd after 5th: rdn to ld bef last: kpt on wl flat: rdn out* **5/1**[3]

0/6- **2** *2¼* **Lillybrook (IRE)**[6] 268 7-10-10 0.............................. SamTwiston-Davies 86
(Nigel Twiston-Davies) *led: rdn between last 2: hdd and no ex bef last: plugged on same pce flat* **3/1**[2]

0P0/ **3** *3¾* **Turn The Tide**[28] 5435 5-10-10 80...................................... GerardTumelty 82
(Natalie Lloyd-Beavis) *t.k.h: hld up in tch in midfield: hdwy to chse ldng pair bef 2 out: no imp u.p between last 2* **66/1**

6PP/ **4** *nk* **Dazzling Rita**[251] 1534 7-10-10 77..(t) DavidEngland 82
(Shaun Lycett) *chsd ldrs: rdn and kpt on same pce fr 2 out: 4th and hld whn mstke last* **8/1**

600/ **5** *12* **Dervla (IRE)**[20] 36 5-10-3 0.. MrKevinJones(7) 71
(Seamus Mullins) *hld up wl in tch in rr: mstke 4th: effrt and no imp bef 3 out: wknd between last 2* **14/1**

3SU/ **6** *½* **Tarmac Girl**[21] 8 5-10-3 0.. JPKiely(7) 71
(Tim Vaughan) *wl in tch in midfield: 5th and wknd u.p between last 2* **6/1**

2/P- **7** *25* **Madeira Girl (IRE)**[19] 49 4-10-6 96.................................. RichieMcLernon 54
(Jonjo O'Neill) *hld up in tch in midfield: hdwy after 4th: chsd ldrs and rdn bef 2 out: fnd nil and sn struggling: wknd wl bef last: bhd and eased flat: t.o* **5/2**[1]

U **Dansili Dutch (IRE)**[32] 4-10-0 0 ow1.................................. JohnWinston(7)
(Andrew Crook) *hld up in rr: veered bdly rt and uns rdr 2nd* **16/1**

000/ **F** **All Hope**[23] 5543 6-10-5 77..(t) BenPoste(5)
(Pam Ford) *hld up towards rr tl fell 1st* **25/1**

0/F- **U** **Cabo Roche**[19] 45 6-10-5 64.. CharlieWallis(5)
(Milton Bradley) *chsd ldr tl after 5th: rdn and struggling next: dropped to rr and wkng whn blnd and uns rdr 2 out* **100/1**

040/ **P** **Reign Silver (IRE)**[83] 4432 5-10-10 0...................................(p) JamieMoore
(Lee Carter) *t.k.h: chsd ldrs: j. slowly and lost pl 2nd: dropped to rr and lost pl qckly 5th: t.o 3 out tl p.u last* **25/1**

3m 55.0s (-1.00) **Going Correction** +0.025s/f (Yiel)
WFA 4 from 5yo+ 18lb 11 Ran SP% **118.4**
Speed ratings (Par 103): **103,101,100,100,94 94,82**, , ,
toteswingers 1&2 £4.10, 1&3 £26.30, 2&3 £26.30 CSF £20.55 TOTE £3.90: £1.10, £2.20, £19.80; EX 15.30 Trifecta £418.20 Pool: £562.77 - 1.00 winning units..Golden Acorn was bought by John Finch for 4,600gns.
Owner Mr Nic Allen **Bred** Redpender Stud Ltd **Trained** Granborough, Bucks

FOCUS
A weak race of limited relevance for future contests. The time was 2.7sec quicker than the previous novice and the first four were all within a few pounds of their pre-race marks.

392 STRATFORDCARAVANS.CO.UK H'CAP CHASE (14 fncs) 2m 4f
3:20 (3:20) (Class 2) (0-150,150) 5-Y-0+
£11,573 (£3,418; £1,709; £854; £427; £214)

Form RPR
1/3- **1** **Gentleman Anshan (IRE)**[9] 204 9-10-0 **129** .... BenPoste(5) 137
(Rosemary Gasson) *hld up in last trio: hdwy gng wl 10th: led 2 out: rdn clr after 2 out: pressed again last: hld on wl u.p fnl 100yds* **7/1**
3/2- **2** 3/4 **Woolcombe Folly (IRE)**[7] 249 10-11-7 **150** .... HarryDerham(5) 158
(Paul Nicholls) *in tch in midfield: mstke and rdn along 8th: drvn and styng on after 3 out: lft cl 3rd last: pressed wnr fnl 100yds: no ex towards fin* **11/2**
432/ **3** 2 **Buck Mulligan**[21] 11 8-10-7 **131** .... PaulMoloney 136
(Evan Williams) *chsd ldng trio: clsd on ldrs 6th: led bef 12th: hdd 2 out and sn drvn: lft 2nd and pressing wnr last: no ex and outpcd fnl 100yds* **9/2**[2]
3/0- **4** 14 **Pepite Rose (FR)**[9] 204 6-11-5 **143** .... AidanColeman 136
(Venetia Williams) *hld up in last trio: mstke 2nd: clsd on ldrs 6th: chsd ldrs 11th: rdn and wknd sn after 2 out: lft 4th last* **5/1**[3]
5/6- **5** 6 **Marley Roca (IRE)**[16] 93 9-10-0 **124** oh1 ....(p) LiamTreadwell 129+
(Paul Webber) *t.k.h: hld up towards rr: hdwy into midfield 6th: chsd ldrs 3 out: rdn and chsd wnr bef last: clsng whn blnd v bdly last: nt rcvr* **14/1**
P10/ **6** 6 **Pacha Du Polder (FR)**[44] 5160 6-11-12 **150** ....(p) RyanMahon 132
(Paul Nicholls) *w ldr tl after 11th: 6th and struggling u.p after 3 out: wknd next* **13/2**
25U/ **7** 7 **Mahogany Blaze (FR)**[78] 4525 11-11-2 **140** ....(tp) SamTwiston-Davies 117
(Nigel Twiston-Davies) *a in rr and niggled along after 4th: sme hdwy whn blnd 10th: wknd after next* **14/1**
114/ **8** 31 **Galway Jack (IRE)**[21] 6 8-10-8 **132** .... AndrewThornton 80
(Caroline Bailey) *led tl after 11th: sn lost pl: t.o whn mstke 2 out* **4/1**[1]
P/5- **9** 27 **Passato (GER)**[17] 81 9-10-11 **135** ....(t) RichieMcLernon 58
(Jo Davis) *w ldrs tl mstke 5th: lost pl and rdn after 6th: dropped to last and lost tch 9th: t.o 3 out* **18/1**

4m 35.4s (-14.60) **Going Correction** -0.40s/f (Good) 9 Ran SP% **114.7**
Speed ratings: **113,112,111,106,103 101,98,86,75**
toteswingers 1&2 £7.80, 1&3 £7.90, 2&3 £4.80 CSF £45.41 CT £192.72 TOTE £11.00: £3.40, £2.20, £1.10; EX 53.80 Trifecta £514.50 Pool: £1370.89 - 1.99 winning units..
Owner Mrs Rosemary Gasson **Bred** Richard J Hennessy **Trained** Balscote, Oxon

FOCUS
Quite a valuable handicap chase. It was run at a searching gallop in a course record time, and the form looks solid. A small personal best from the winner.

393 STRATFORDCARAVANS.CO.UK H'CAP HURDLE (FOR THE CHARLES LEA MEMORIAL TROPHY) (13 hdls) 3m 3f
3:50 (3:50) (Class 4) (0-115,115) 4-Y-0+ **£3,898** (£1,144; £572; £286)

Form RPR
4/2- **1** **Sail And Return**[15] 121 9-11-7 **110** .... SamTwiston-Davies 121+
(Phil Middleton) *hld up in last: hdwy into midfield after 8th: clsng on ldrs and hit 3 out: chsd ldr and rdn after next: drvn and upsides bef last: led flat: styd on wl* **4/1**[2]
143/ **2** 1 1/2 **Qualviro (FR)**[35] 5321 9-11-11 **114** ....(v) AidanColeman 122
(Tim Vaughan) *led: mstke 7th: wnt 4 l clr 2 out: drvn and hrd pressed jst bef last: hdd and no ex flat* **10/1**
1/P- **3** 18 **Life Of A Luso (IRE)**[12] 158 9-11-9 **112** ....(t) TomO'Brien 104
(Paul Henderson) *hld up in last trio: rdn and outpcd bef 3 out: modest 6th 2 out: kpt on to go 3rd flat: no threat to ldng pair* **6/1**
3/5- **4** 1 1/2 **Roses Legend**[10] 175 8-9-7 **89** oh3 .... MrPJohn(7) 81
(Reginald Brown) *chsd ldrs: mstke 5th: blnd 10th: chsd ldr bef next tl rdn and btn bef 2 out: wl btn and blnd last: lost 3rd flat* **20/1**
5P5/ **5** 1 3/4 **Graduation Night**[29] 5410 7-11-6 **109** ....(v) BrendanPowell 98
(Jamie Snowden) *in tch in midfield: cl 5th 3 out: struggling whn sltly hmpd next: wknd bef last* **7/1**
530/ **6** nse **Munlochy Bay**[70] 4683 9-10-11 **100** ....(p) CharliePoste 89
(Matt Sheppard) *in rr: rdn along briefly 6th: rdn and struggling 10th: sn outpcd and wl btn after 3 out: plugged on between last 2* **28/1**
642/ **7** 10 **Green Bank (IRE)**[201] 2116 7-11-0 **106** ....(t) KielanWoods(3) 90
(Charlie Longsdon) *in tch: chsd ldrs bef 3 out: 4th and u.p whn blnd 2 out: sn btn: fdd bef last* **10/1**
64F/ **8** 35 **Knighton Combe**[42] 5199 13-11-12 **115** ....(p) PaulMoloney 63
(Jamie Snowden) *in tch in midfield: lost pl and dropped to rr after 9th: lost tch 3 out: t.o next* **20/1**
255/ **9** nk **He's The Daddy**[60] 4875 6-10-11 **107** ....(t) RyanHatch(7) 55
(Nigel Twiston-Davies) *chsd ldrs: mstke 8th: drvn and struggling after 10th: wknd rapidly 3 out: t.o after next* **7/2**[1]
2/3- **10** 1 1/2 **Wilde Ruby (IRE)**[19] 38 6-11-? **112** ....(p) MrKevinJones(7) 59
(Seamus Mullins) *in tch in last trio: rdn and no rspnse after 9th: lost tch 3 out: t.o after next: virtually p.u flat* **9/2**[3]
1/4- **11** 34 **Earcomesthedream (IRE)**[18] 68 10-10-13 **102** ....(b) JackDoyle 18
(Peter Pritchard) *chsd ldr tl after 10th: sn dropped out: t.o 2 out: eased flat* **16/1**

6m 25.7s (-2.90) **Going Correction** +0.025s/f (Yiel) 11 Ran SP% **124.2**
Speed ratings (Par 105): **105,104,99,98,98 98,95,84,84,84 74**
toteswingers 1&2 £9.50, 1&3 £3.80, 2&3 £10.60 CSF £44.78 CT £247.13 TOTE £5.60: £2.40, £1.90, £1.90; EX 50.80 Trifecta £239.20 Pool: £829.23 - 2.59 winning units..
Owner P W Middleton **Bred** Andrew And Mrs S R B Davis **Trained** Dorton, Bucks

FOCUS
A marathon handicap hurdle and a true test at the trip. The first two were clear and the winner is on the upgrade.

394 STRATFORDCARAVANS.CO.UK NOVICES' CHASE (14 fncs) 2m 4f
4:20 (4:20) (Class 3) 5-Y-0+ **£6,498** (£1,908; £954; £477)

Form RPR
0/2- **1** **Harry Hunt**[15] 118 6-10-12 126 .... TomScudamore 128+
(Graeme McPherson) *chsd ldrs: cl 4th and drvn after 2 out: led bef last: battled on gamely u.p flat* **13/2**[3]
003/ **2** nk **Buachaill Alainn (IRE)**[44] 5161 6-10-12 0 ....(p) JamieMoore 128+
(Peter Bowen) *chsd ldr tl 6th: rdn and lost pl 9th: rallied u.p to chse ldrs 11th: chsd wnr fnl 100yds: styd on wl* **7/4**[1]
0/1- **3** nk **Nagpur (FR)**[10] 182 7-11-5 134 .... AidanColeman 133
(Venetia Williams) *chsd ldrs: wnt 2nd 6th tl led after 10th: hdd 3 out: drvn after 2 out: stl cl 3rd whn mstke last: no ex towards fin* **15/8**[2]
20F/ **4** 2 1/2 **Roger Beantown (IRE)**[134] 3502 8-10-12 0 .... RyanMahon 123
(Paul Nicholls) *in tch in midfield: chsd ldr bef 11th: led and hit 3 out: rdn between last 2: hdd bef last: no ex: wknd fnl 100yds* **7/1**
3PP/ **5** 17 **Baldadash (IRE)**[35] 5318 8-10-12 0 ....(p) AndrewTinkler 110
(Alison Batchelor) *in tch in last trio: mstke 10th: outpcd after 3 out: wknd next* **50/1**
P/F- **6** 36 **Princeful (FR)**[19] 45 10-10-5 107 .... ChrisDavies(7) 76
(Milton Bradley) *in tch in rr: struggling and mstke 11th: wknd 3 out: t.o* **100/1**
541/ **P** **Di Kaprio (FR)**[76] 4563 7-11-5 128 .... PaulMoloney
(Evan Williams) *j.lft: led: dived and mstke 3rd: hdd after 10th: lost pl qckly 3 out: t.o whn p.u last* **17/2**
006/ **P** **Favoured Nation (IRE)**[186] 2415 6-10-12 0 .... RichieMcLernon
(Jonjo O'Neill) *in tch in rr: pushed along and mstke 7th: j.rt next: losing tch whn p.u bef 9th* **20/1**

4m 48.1s (-1.90) **Going Correction** -0.40s/f (Good) 8 Ran SP% **115.2**
Speed ratings: **87,86,86,85,78 64, ,**
toteswingers 1&2 £3.50, 1&3 £3.20, 2&3 £1.50 CSF £19.20 TOTE £3.50: £1.10, £1.10, £2.40; EX 22.30 Trifecta £64.90 Pool: £1650.38 - 19.05 winning units..
Owner Arion Racing **Bred** Darley **Trained** Upper Oddington, Gloucs

FOCUS
A decent novice chase which will produce winners although it was slow compared with the earlier handicap.

395 STRATFORDCARAVANS.CO.UK STANDARD OPEN NATIONAL HUNT FLAT RACE 2m 110y
4:50 (4:50) (Class 5) 4-6-Y-0 **£1,949** (£572; £286; £143)

Form RPR
1 **Prideofthecastle (IRE)**[142] 3333 6-11-9 0 .... TomScudamore 111
(David Pipe) *led for 2f: styd chsng ldr tl led again over 2f out: drvn and kpt on wl fnl f: holding runner-up whn bmpd fnl 50yds* **5/2**[3]
24/ **2** 3/4 **The Road Ahead**[213] 1904 6-10-9 0 .... TomO'Brien 97+
(Peter Bowen) *chsd ldrs: effrt to chse wnr 2f out: ev ch and edging lft ins fnl f: running into rail whn forced to swerve rt and bmpd wnr fnl 50yds: rdr unbalanced and nt rcvr* **15/8**[1]
3/ **3** 3 **Algernon Pazham (IRE)**[77] 4542 4-10-12 0 .... SamTwiston-Davies 96
(Nigel Twiston-Davies) *hld up in tch: trckd ldrs 5f out: effrt to chse ldng pair 2f out: drvn and unable qck over 1f out: one pce fnl f* **2/1**[2]
3/ **4** 18 **Midnight Chorister**[76] 4572 5-11-2 0 ....(t) RichieMcLernon 84
(Alex Hales) *t.k.h: chsd ldr tl led after 2f: hdd and drvn over 2f out: sn wknd* **11/1**
0/ **5** 8 **Pembroke House**[21] 14 6-11-2 0 .... WillKennedy 77
(Sarah-Jayne Davies) *t.k.h: hld up wl in tch: rdn and struggling over 4f out: lost tch 3f out* **25/1**
6 8 **Ll Cool Horse** 4-10-12 0 .... FelixDeGiles 66
(Tom Gretton) *in tch in rr: rdn over 4f out: lost tch over 3f out* **20/1**

3m 50.0s (-0.40) **Going Correction** +0.025s/f (Yiel)
WFA 4 from 5yo+ 4lb 6 Ran SP% **113.6**
Speed ratings: **101,100,99,90,87 83**
toteswingers 1&2 £1.60, 1&3 £1.50, 2&3 £1.50 CSF £7.79 TOTE £3.20: £2.00, £1.40; EX 8.60 Trifecta £16.30 Pool: £773.82 - 35.44 winning units..
Owner Bryan Drew **Bred** Patrick Cronin **Trained** Nicholashayne, Devon
■ Stewards' Enquiry : Tom Scudamore caution; careless riding.
Tom O'Brien caution; careless riding.

FOCUS
A fair little bumper with a dramatic finish. The riders of the first two were both cautioned for careless riding. Straightforward form.
T/Plt: £11.20 to a £1 stake. Pool of £73,534.81 - 4790.46 winning tickets T/Qpdt: £5.20 to a £1 stake. Pool of £4393.74 - 614.75 winning tickets SP

396 - 405a (Foreign Racing) - See Raceform Interactive

262 AUTEUIL (L-H)
Sunday, May 19

OFFICIAL GOING: Turf: very soft

406a GRAS SAVOYE CORPORATE LIFE PRIX LA BARKA (HURDLE) (GRADE 2) (5YO+) (TURF) 2m 5f 110y
4:45 (12:00) 5-Y-0+
£64,024 (£31,300; £18,495; £12,804; £7,113; £4,979)

RPR
1 **Celestial Halo (IRE)**[43] 5175 9-10-6 0 ....(bt) DarylJacob 156
(Paul Nicholls) *midfield early: prom fr 6th: wnt 3rd 3 out: 2nd and stl gng wl 2 out: rdn to chse ldr after last: styd on to chal ins fnl 100yds: led cl home: hung lft: drvn out* **10/1**
2 1 1/4 **Lord Prestige (FR)**[28] 5446 6-10-6 0 .... JonathanPlouganou 155
(M Rolland, France) *trckd clr ldr: clsd rapidly after 3 out: led on home bnd bef 2 out: rdn flat: styd on wl u.p but hdd cl home* **9/1**
3 5 **Tidara Angel (IRE)**[28] 5446 6-9-13 0 ....(p) AnthonyLecordier 143
(D Windrif, France) *prom: rdn 2 out: wnt 3rd appr last: styd on flat but no imp on front pair* **25/1**
4 2 **Thousand Stars (FR)**[23] 5561 9-10-12 0 .... RWalsh 154
(W P Mullins, Ire) *midfield: dropped towards rr and rdn 3 out: styd on to take n.d 4th ins fnl 75yds* **6/4**[1]
5 1 1/2 **Chuchoteuse (FR)**[30] 5398 8-9-13 0 .... FabienDehez 139
(L Postic, France) *hld up towards rr: hdwy into midfield 7th: rdn bef 2 out: styd on but n.d* **25/1**
6 7 **Nikita Du Berlais (FR)**[182] 2520 6-10-6 0 .... CyrilleGombeau 139
(Robert Collet, France) *midfield: rdn bef 2 out: styd on but n.d* **8/1**[3]
7 2 1/2 **Zaidpour (FR)**[24] 5529 7-10-6 0 .... PaulTownend 137
(W P Mullins, Ire) *hld up and sn towards rr: rdn to try and improve after 3 out: styd on and fin quite strly but nvr remotely dangerous* **7/1**[2]
8 1/2 **Mazuelo (FR)**[22] 5586 5-10-3 0 ow2 .... BertrandThelier 133
(G Cherel, France) *sn prom: mstke 7th: smooth hdwy into 3rd on home bnd after 3 out: rdn 2 out: no ex jumping last and fdd flat* **20/1**
9 3 **So Young (FR)**[23] 5561 7-10-3 0 .... DJCasey 130
(W P Mullins, Ire) *hld up in midfield: mstke 3rd: rdn and outpcd 2 out: plugged on* **16/1**
10 9 **Libaute (FR)**[28] 5446 6-9-13 0 ....(p) AlexisAcker 117
(M Rolland, France) *hld up in midfield: hdwy fr 3 out: disputing 4th and stl ev ch whn bad mstke 2 out: no ex and btn jumping last: eased flat* **33/1**
11 12 **Chegei Has (FR)**[19] 5-9-11 0 .... JonathanNattiez 103
(J-P Gallorini, France) *hld up towards rr: rdn after 3 out: sn t.o but plugged on to complete: nvr a factor* **25/1**

12 *hd* **Lamego (FR)**[22] 5586 6-10-6 0 .... Jean-LucBeaunez 112
(Mme P Butel, France) *hld up towards rr: hdwy fr 5 out: rdn appr 2 out: sn no ex and btn: fdd and t.o but completed* **20/1**

P **Gratia Plena (FR)**[22] 5586 7-10-3 0 .... LudovicPhilipperon
(B De Watrigant, France) *hld up towards rr: rdn and toiling 3 out: eased and p.u bef 2 out* **20/1**

P **Saindor (FR)**[28] 5446 9-10-3 0 .... PaddyBrennan
(Tom George) *led and sn clr: reduced advantage 3 out: rapidly clsd down and hdd on home bnd bef 2 out: qckly btn and wknd: eased and p.u bef last* **12/1**

P **Le Tranquille (FR)**[25] 6-10-6 0 .... RegisSchmidlin
(M Rolland, France) *prom: lost pl 3 out: btn 2 out and sn p.u* **25/1**

P **Monpilou (FR)**[22] 5586 6-10-6 0 .... BertrandLestrade
(G Macaire, France) *prom: lost pl bef 2 out: sn btn and p.u bef last* **14/1**

P **Pierrot Bay (FR)**[28] 5445 6-10-3 0 ....(p) AlainDeChitray
(T Trapenard, France) *midfield: rdn and lost pl 5 out: struggling in rr 3 out: btn and eased 2 out: p.u bef last* **20/1**

P **Defi D'Anjou (FR)**[22] 5586 5-10-1 0 .... JacquesRicou
(L Viel, France) *hld up towards rr: last and btn 3 out: eased and p.u bef 2 out* **25/1**

5m 29.3s (329.30) **18** Ran SP% **144.2**
PARI-MUTUEL (all including 1 euro stakes): WIN 33.20; PLACE 7.60, 3.20, 11.60; DF 171.30; SF 386.70.
Owner The Stewart Family **Bred** Roncon Churchtown Bloodstock & Lane Ltd **Trained** Ditcheat, Somerset

[174]NEWTON ABBOT (L-H)

Monday, May 20

OFFICIAL GOING: Good to firm (8.5)
Wind: Mild breeze; across Weather: Cloudy with sunny periods

407 INDEPENDENT RACECOURSES LTD, IRL H'CAP HURDLE (9 hdls) 2m 3f

2:20 (2:20) (Class 5) (0-95,95) 4-Y-0+ **£2,463** (£718; £359)

Form RPR

614/ 1 **Bach On Tow (IRE)**[26] 5509 6-10-5 **79** .... MissLucyGardner(5) 86+
(Sue Gardner) *hld up towards rr on outside: t.k.h and hdwy after 5th: led after 3 out: r.o wl fr last* **9/2**[1]

2/3- 2 2 ¼ **Asian Prince (IRE)**[11] 177 4-11-7 **95** ....(bt) ConorO'Farrell 94
(Alastair Lidderdale) *in tch: rdn to chse wnr appr 2 out: kpt on but nt pce to get on terms* **5/1**[2]

6/2- 3 ¾ **Mount Vesuvius (IRE)**[11] 178 5-11-7 **90** ....(t) TomO'Brien 94+
(Paul Henderson) *mid-div: tl lost pl 3 out: rdn and hdwy 2 out: r.o wl fr last: wnt 3rd fnl stride* **11/2**[3]

2/P- 4 *nse* **Illegale (IRE)**[17] 89 7-10-3 **72** ....(t) LeightonAspell 75
(Phillip Dando) *prom: led 6th: rdn and hdd bef 2 out: styd on same pce: lost 3rd fnl stride* **16/1**

0/4- 5 ¾ **Cash Injection**[20] 37 4-11-6 **94** ....(t) AndrewThornton 91
(Karen George) *trckd ldrs: rdn after 3 out: kpt on same pce fr next* **14/1**

50P/ 6 ½ **Master Wells (IRE)**[141] 3382 12-10-8 **77** .... HaddenFrost 79
(James Frost) *mid-div: rdn after 3 out: chsd ldrs next: kpt on same pce fr last* **8/1**

0/6- 7 3 ¾ **Tae Kwon Do (USA)**[18] 83 7-11-12 **95** .... RichardJohnson 94
(Tim Vaughan) *mid-div: rdn after 3 out: sn one pce* **11/1**

P45/ 8 11 **Bernisdale**[17] 2723 5-11-12 **95** .... DPFahy 82
(John Flint) *hld up towards rr: sme prog u.p after 3 out: nvr trbld ldrs* **14/1**

000/ 9 ½ **Royal Peak (IRE)**[48] 5107 6-10-10 **79** ....(tp) TomScudamore 67
(David Pipe) *hld up towards rr: sme prog into midfield 2 out: nvr a threat* **16/1**

4/5- 10 3 ¾ **Paddleyourowncanoe (IRE)**[14] 145 12-11-4 **92** .....(bt) JamesBanks(5) 75
(Emma Baker) *mid-div: rdn after 3 out: sn btn* **33/1**

040/ 11 8 **Tiger's Jacey (IRE)**[22] 2 6-11-7 **90** ....(t) PaulMoloney 65
(James Hughes) *trckd ldrs: rdn after 3 out: wknd bef next* **33/1**

P53/ 12 1 ¼ **Jambobo**[152] 3141 4-11-2 **90** .... JamesDavies 59
(Chris Down) *j.lft at times: trckd ldrs: rdn after 3 out: sn wknd* **33/1**

4/5- 13 36 **Palmyra (IRE)**[13] 155 4-10-6 **80** .... BrendanPowell 13
(Martin Hill) *mid-div tl wknd after 3 out: t.o* **14/1**

/44- 14 2 ¼ **Mixed Meaning (IRE)**[13] 156 5-9-13 **71** ow2 .... GilesHawkins(3) 6
(Stuart Howe) *a towards rr: t.o* **33/1**

040/ P **Pour Changer (FR)**[27] 5471 8-10-11 **87** ....(p) JPKiely(7)
(Stephen Hughes) *led tl 6th: wknd after 3 out: bhd whn p.u bef next* **25/1**

F/0- F **Pennant Dancer**[19] 71 6-10-0 **69** oh5 ....(t) DonalDevereux 58
(Debra Hamer) *mid-div: rdn after 3 out: no imp whn fell next* **40/1**

P60/ P **Fanjos Luck (IRE)**[90] 4294 6-11-2 **85** .... WillKennedy
(Alan Jones) *a towards rr: t.o whn p.u bef 6th* **25/1**

560/ P **Comical Red**[46] 5142 5-10-9 **85** ....(p) JakeHodson(7)
(Mark Gillard) *a in rr: t.o fr 5th: p.u bef next* **25/1**

4m 24.4s (-5.60) **Going Correction** -0.425s/f (Good)
WFA 4 from 5yo+ 18lb **18** Ran SP% **127.2**
Speed ratings (Par 103): **94,93,92,92,92 92,90,85,85,84 80,80,65,64, , ,**
toteswingers 1&2 £10.60, 1&3 £12.40, 2&3 £1.70 CSF £25.22 CT £133.40 TOTE £6.20: £2.10, £1.10, £2.00, £6.00; EX 32.50 Trifecta £47.60 Pool: £455.29 - 7.16 winning units..
Owner D V Gardner **Bred** Denis Murphy **Trained** Longdown, Devon

FOCUS
A weak handicap. A step up from the winner, with the second and fourth helping with the level.

408 NEWTONABBOTRACE ON TWITTER NOVICES' H'CAP CHASE (16 fncs) 2m 5f 110y

2:50 (2:50) (Class 5) (0-100,98) 5-Y-0+ **£2,729** (£801; £400; £200)

Form RPR

1/4- 1 **Solitary Palm (IRE)**[18] 84 10-10-5 **77** ....(b) ConorO'Farrell 90+
(Brian Forsey) *led tl 2nd: trckd ldrs: rdn to chal after 3 out: tk ld whn blnd last: styd on wl* **11/4**[2]

P/0- 2 2 ¾ **Spirit Of Lake (IRE)**[18] 84 11-9-10 **75** ow2 ....(t) MrKevinJones(7) 84
(Karen George) *led 2nd: rdn whn strly pressed after 3 out: hdd last: no ex* **11/1**

POP/ 3 18 **Petrarchick (USA)**[39] 5246 6-9-9 **72** oh2 ....(t) JamesBanks(5) 63
(Emma Baker) *hld up bhd ldrs: wnt 3rd 11th: sn rdn: outpcd after 3 out: wknd bef last* **17/2**

0/6- 4 42 **Wosayu**[18] 84 7-10-0 **72** oh2 ....(p) BrendanPowell 21
(Colin Tizzard) *j.lft 1st: pressed ldr tl 6th: reminders: dropped to last pair 9th: nvr travelling after: hmpd 12th: no ch fr next: wnt modest 4th 2 out: t.o* **5/1**[3]

046/ 5 11 **Isthereadifference (IRE)**[113] 3900 6-11-12 **98** .... DougieCostello 36
(Neil Mulholland) *hld up bhd ldrs: nt fluent 7th: rdn after 10th: wknd 3 out: t.o* **2/1**[1]

0/U- F **Pirans Car**[11] 179 7-11-2 **91** ....(t) MarkQuinlan(3)
(Nigel Hawke) *hld up: nt fluent 10th: sn rdn: no imp whn fell 12th* **11/2**

5m 9.9s (-11.50) **Going Correction** -0.60s/f (Firm) **6** Ran SP% **110.9**
Speed ratings: **96,95,88,73,69**
toteswingers 1&2 £7.30, 1&3 £5.80, 2&3 £13.00 CSF £27.57 CT £215.67 TOTE £2.10: £2.00, £4.10; EX 20.20 Trifecta £203.70 Pool: £592.05 - 2.17 winning units..
Owner A Stevens, W McKibbin, B Forsey **Bred** John Byrne **Trained** Ash Priors, Somerset

FOCUS
A weak novice handicap, run at a sound gallop. The first two were very well in on their old form.

409 SIS GREYHOUND CHANNEL H'CAP HURDLE (9 hdls) 2m 3f

3:20 (3:20) (Class 3) (0-135,131) 4-Y-0 **£6,076** (£1,795; £897; £449; £224)

Form RPR

0/2- 1 **Smalib Monterg (FR)**[3] 356 7-11-4 **123** ....(t) SamTwiston-Davies 127+
(Dr Richard Newland) *hld up in tch: tk clsr order 3 out: led narrowly sn after 2 out: rdn and r.o fr last: jst hld on* **11/8**[1]

1/1- 2 *nse* **Union Saint (FR)**[4] 336 5-11-1 **120** 7ex .... HaddenFrost 124+
(James Frost) *led tl 2nd: trckd ldr: led briefly gng wl appr 2 out: rdn bef last: str chal run-in: jst failed* **3/1**[2]

136/ 3 ¾ **Lava Lamp (GER)**[65] 4783 6-10-1 **113** .... ConorRing(7) 116
(Evan Williams) *trckd ldrs: rdn after 3 out: styd on to hold ev ch last: kpt on but no ex* **16/1**

210/ 4 7 **Fear Glic (IRE)**[260] 1476 7-11-1 **123** .... JamesBest(3) 120
(Jackie Du Plessis) *led 2nd: nt fluent 3 out: sn rdn: hdd bef next: kpt on same pce* **11/1**

140/ 5 2 ½ **Special Account (IRE)**[205] 2047 8-11-12 **131** .... NickScholfield 125
(Jeremy Scott) *hld up last: pushed along after 6th: rdn to chse ldrs 2 out: no ex fr last* **6/1**[3]

46U/ 6 1 **Captain Sharpe**[17] 4382 5-9-11 **107** ....(p) RobertWilliams(5) 101
(Bernard Llewellyn) *t.k.h early: trckd ldrs: rdn gng to 2 out: kpt on same pce* **10/1**

P00/ 7 2 ¼ **Kylenoe Fairy (IRE)**[114] 3862 9-11-3 **122** ....(t) TomO'Brien 113
(Paul Henderson) *hld up in tch: rdn after 3 out: outpcd bef next* **12/1**

4m 24.9s (-5.10) **Going Correction** -0.425s/f (Good) **7** Ran SP% **112.4**
Speed ratings (Par 107): **93,92,92,89,88 88,87**
toteswingers 1&2 £1.70, 1&3 £11.50, 2&3 £3.70 CSF £5.96 CT £40.69 TOTE £2.00: £1.50, £2.00; EX 5.20 Trifecta £39.10 Pool: £673.41 - 12.90 winning units..
Owner A P Barwell,Mrs M L Trow & Mrs M J Sanders **Bred** Mr & Mrs Rene Ricous & Mme K Botond **Trained** Claines, Worcs

FOCUS
This modest handicap developed into something of a sprint for home. The form still makes sense.

410 BET TOTEPOOL TEXT TOTE TO 89660 NOVICES' HURDLE (10 hdls) 2m 6f

3:50 (3:50) (Class 4) 4-Y-0+ **£3,508** (£1,030; £515; £257)

Form RPR

P00/ 1 **Theatre Evening (IRE)**[101] 4108 5-10-12 0 ....(t) NoelFehily 111+
(Fergal O'Brien) *hld up bhd ldrs: led 3 out: rdn whn strly pressed bef next: kpt on wl to assert bef last: rdn out* **10/1**[3]

531/ 2 5 **McIlhatton (IRE)**[22] 3 5-11-5 125 .... DarylJacob 113
(Paul Nicholls) *hld up bhd ldrs: awkward 1st: jnd wnr sn after 3 out: shkn up whn mstke 2 out: sn hld: got struck into* **2/7**[1]

0/0- 3 4 ½ **Princess Annabelle**[11] 174 4-9-11 0 ....(b[1]) MarkQuinlan(3) 88
(Rod Millman) *j. sltly rt thrght: prom: hit 6th: sn led: hdd 3 out: rdn and kpt on same pce fr next* **33/1**

406/ 4 37 **Be Marvellous (IRE)**[30] 5407 5-10-12 0 ....(t) BrendanPowell 62
(Colin Tizzard) *trckd ldrs: pushed along after 4th: lost pl 6th: rdn to chse ldrs 3 out: wknd bef next: t.o* **6/1**[2]

0/F- 5 10 **Clear Mix**[11] 174 5-10-5 0 .... DPFahy 45
(Sue Gardner) *hld up: rdn bef 3 out: sn wknd: t.o* **66/1**

0/2- 6 16 **Upton Oaks**[13] 156 7-10-12 95 ....(t) JamesDavies 36
(Chris Down) *trckd ldrs: rdn appr 7th: wknd after 3 out: t.o* **12/1**

U/ 7 97 **No No Cardinal (IRE)**[49] 5079 4-10-7 0 .... TommyPhelan
(Mark Gillard) *racd keenly: led tl after 6th: wknd qckly bef next: sn wl t.o* **50/1**

5m 5.5s (-14.70) **Going Correction** -0.425s/f (Good)
WFA 4 from 5yo+ 19lb **7** Ran SP% **115.2**
Speed ratings (Par 105): **109,107,105,92,88 82,47**
toteswingers 1&2 £2.10, 1&3 £8.90, 2&3 £5.40 CSF £14.41 TOTE £8.90: £4.70, £1.10; EX 21.60 Trifecta £195.30 Pool: £2,723.94 - 10.45 winning units..
Owner Masterson Holdings Limited **Bred** Mrs Juliet Brown **Trained** Coln St. Dennis, Gloucs

FOCUS
There was a turn up in this moderate novice contest. A step up from the winner, with the second in line with his previous best.

411 AT THE RACES SKY 415 H'CAP CHASE (12 fncs 1 omitted) 2m 110y

4:20 (4:21) (Class 4) (0-120,119) 5-Y-0+ **£4,288** (£1,259; £629; £314)

Form RPR

2/1- 1 **Fiftyonefiftyone (IRE)**[17] 98 9-11-5 **112** ....(p) LeightonAspell 125+
(Oliver Sherwood) *mde all: qckly clr after 2 out (usual 3 out): comf* **9/4**[1]

236/ 2 9 **Star Galaxy (IRE)**[31] 5384 13-10-4 **102** ....(b) GavinSheehan(5) 104
(John Flint) *chsd ldrs: rdn after 9th: kpt on fr last (usual 2 out): snatched 2nd towards fin: no ch w wnr* **25/1**

5/1- 3 ¾ **Miss Tenacious**[11] 191 6-11-8 **115** .... JackDoyle 117
(Ron Hodges) *trckd wnr: nt fluent 2 out (usual 3 out): sn rdn: nt pce of wnr: no ex whn lost 2nd towards fin* **9/2**[3]

4/2- 4 4 **Monarch's Way**[18] 78 6-11-11 **118** ....(b) DenisO'Regan 117
(John Ferguson) *trckd ldrs: shkn up after 8th: rdn to chse ldng pair after 3 out (usual 4 out): one pce fr last* **15/2**

413/ 5 6 **Topthorn**[26] 5510 7-10-12 **105** .... WayneHutchinson 96
(Martin Bosley) *in tch: rdn after 3 out(usual 4 out): one pce fr next* **6/1**

2/0- 6 11 **Captain Sully (IRE)**[17] 93 8-11-5 **112** .... HaddenFrost 92
(Jim Wilson) *hld up: effrt 3 out (usual 4 out): hld fr next: wknd by-passing omitted last fence* **33/1**

2/3- P **Sublime Talent (IRE)**[18] 81 7-11-9 **119** ....(t) AdamWedge(3)
(Evan Williams) *hld up: pushed along after 7th: lost tch fr next: p.u bef 4 out* **10/3**[2]

66P/ P **Henry Hook (IRE)**[25] 5521 9-11-8 **115** .... TommyPhelan
(Mark Gillard) *hld up: p.u after 5th: fatally injured* **10/1**

3m 53.4s (-13.10) **Going Correction** -0.60s/f (Firm) **8** Ran SP% **114.0**
Speed ratings: **106,101,101,99,96 91, ,**
toteswingers 1&2 £8.80, 1&3 £2.70, 2&3 £13.20 CSF £46.80 CT £236.04 TOTE £2.70: £1.30, £5.50, £1.80; EX 57.20 Trifecta £298.90 Pool: £2,054.93 - 5.15 winning units..
Owner A Taylor **Bred** P O'Connell **Trained** Upper Lambourn, Berks

FOCUS
There was no hanging around in this modest handicap. The winner is closing in on the best of his 2011 form.

412 NEWTONABBOTRACING.COM STANDARD OPEN NATIONAL HUNT FLAT RACE 2m 1f
4:50 (4:50) (Class 6) 4-6-Y-0 **£2,094** (£610; £305)

Form RPR
\- **1** **Are They Your Own (IRE)**^{29} 5-10-9 0 MissAEStirling$^{(7)}$ 103+
(Fergal O'Brien) *mde all: kpt on strly fnl f: pushed out* **9/1**
0/ **2** 1½ **Talented Kid**^{39} [5262] 4-10-12 0 DenisO'Regan 97
(John Ferguson) *hld up: trckd ldrs 3f out: trckd wnr over 1f out: swtchd lft and shkn up ent fnl f: nt qckn* **7/2^{2}**
6- **3** 7 **Y A Bon (IRE)**^{13} [160] 5-11-2 0 HaddenFrost 94
(Martin Hill) *in tch: cl up 3f out: rdn over 2f out: styd on same pce fr over 1f out* **7/2^{2}**
0/ **4** ½ **Sir Tyto (IRE)**^{128} [3621] 5-11-2 0 SamTwiston-Davies 94
(Ali Brewer) *trckd ldrs: rdn to chse wnr 2f out tl over 1f out: styd on same pce: lost 3rd towards fin* **25/1**
5- **5** 10 **Harriet's Ark**^{18} [85] 6-10-9 0 MarkGrant 77
(Julian Smith) *chsd ldrs: rdn 3f out: wknd fnl f* **8/1^{3}**
6 3¼ **Morpet** 4-10-12 0 TomScudamore 76
(Ron Hodges) *chsd ldrs: rdn over 2f out: wknd jst over 1f out* **14/1**
0/ **7** 16 **Kris Magic (IRE)**^{26} [5511] 6-10-9 0 LiamHeard 57
(Colin Heard) *in tch: pushed along 1/2-way: sn in rr* **33/1**
0/0- **8** ¾ **Triple Brandy**^{6} [298] 4-10-12 0 (p) AndrewThornton 60
(Karen George) *hld up: making prog whn stmbld after being hmpd 2f out: sn wknd* **28/1**
00/ **9** ¾ **Saint Guru**^{27} [5483] 6-10-11 0 GavinSheehan$^{(5)}$ 63
(Barry Brennan) *in tch tl wknd 3f out* **25/1**
10 3½ **My Son Harry (IRE)** 5-11-2 0 JackDoyle 59
(Victor Dartnall) *trckd wnr: rdn over 2f out: wkng whn short of room 2f out* **2/1^{1}**

3m 52.1s (-8.00) **Going Correction** -0.425s/f (Good)
WFA 4 from 5yo+ 4lb **10** Ran SP% **119.6**
Speed ratings: **101,100,97,96,92 90,83,82,82,80**
toteswingers 1&2 £6.00, 1&3 £7.80, 2&3 £2.50 CSF £40.10 TOTE £12.30: £3.30, £3.20, £1.10; EX 53.10 Trifecta £247.20 Pool: £2,169.85 - 6.58 winning units..
Owner Ian Slatter **Bred** William Neville **Trained** Coln St. Dennis, Gloucs

FOCUS
The first pair had it to themselves inside the final furlong in this modest bumper. The form is given a token rating through the second.

413 RONNIE COOK MEMORIAL H'CAP HUNTERS' CHASE (16 fncs) 2m 5f 110y
5:20 (5:22) (Class 4) 5-Y-0+ **£4,117** (£1,277; £638; £319) **Stalls** Far side

Form RPR
31P/ **1** **Chapoturgeon (FR)**^{66} [4771] 9-12-2 **138** MrJBarber$^{(5)}$ 147+
(R Barber) *hld up: hdwy on inner after 9th: cl up whn nt clrest of runs after 3 out: rdn to ld gng to the last: hdd run-in: kpt on strly to ld again towards fin* **11/8^{1}**
1/U- **2** ¾ **Presentandcorrect (IRE)**^{8} 12-10-7 **110** oh3 MrMWall 116
(T F Sage) *in tch: trckd ldrs 5th: rdn appr 11th: led 4 out: hdd bef last: led again run-in: kpt on: hdd towards fin* **4/1^{2}**
342/ **3** 5 **Tiermore (IRE)**^{27} [5476] 9-10-0 **110** oh10 AlanJohns$^{(7)}$ 112
(R E Luke) *in tch: trckd ldrs on inner 8th: chal 4 out: nt clr run after 3 out: swtchd rt: rdn and ev ch 2 out: kpt on same pce* **14/1**
5/4- **4** 3 **Big Game Hunter (IRE)**^{19} [63] 7-10-0 **110** oh14 MissRPLeyshon$^{(7)}$ 108
(Andrew Leyshon) *chsd ldrs: rdn after 4 out: ev ch 2 out: kpt on same pce* **25/1**
521/ **5** 10 **Lady Myfanwy**^{9} 12-10-0 **110** oh8 MissHLewis$^{(7)}$ 98
(Mrs Myfanwy Miles) *chsd clr ldr: led after 9th: hdd 4 out: sn rdn: outpcd after 3 out* **16/1**
2/1- **6** 2 **Findlay's Find (IRE)**^{8} 7-10-0 **110** oh7 MissAEStirling$^{(7)}$ 96
(Mrs Myfanwy Miles) *towards rr on outer: hdwy after 4th: pushed along fr 7th: outpcd after 4 out: sme late prog: nvr trbld ldrs* **8/1**
135/ **7** 8 **Regal Rumpus**^{29} [5436] 11-10-12 **115** (t) MrWBiddick 95
(L Jefford) *hld up bhd: making hdwy whn mstke 12th: rdn after 4 out: wknd 2 out* **16/1**
P/0- **8** 5 **Louis Pasteur (IRE)**^{19} [57] 8-10-7 **113** (b) MrRGHenderson$^{(3)}$ 86
(D L Drake) *racd keenly: j.rt: led tl after 9th: prom tl rdn after 4 out: wknd bef 2 out* **16/1**
5/0- **9** 5 **Soulard (USA)**^{19} [63] 10-10-4 **110** MissHannahWatson$^{(3)}$ 78
(Sophie Leech) *in tch: reminders 6th: trckd ldrs 8th: wknd after 4 out* **33/1**
6/1- **10** ¾ **Himalayan Express**^{19} [57] 9-10-12 **120** (p) MrJMartin$^{(5)}$ 88
(Mrs David Plunkett) *in tch: struggling whn hit 11th: wknd 4 out* **7/1^{3}**
/03- **U** **Party Pictures (IRE)**^{13} [159] 10-10-0 **110** oh9 MissLeandaTickle$^{(7)}$
(Mrs S Westwood) *mid-div: rdn in tch after 4 out: wknd between last 2: blnd and uns rdr last* **40/1**

5m 8.0s (-13.40) **Going Correction** -0.60s/f (Firm) **11** Ran SP% **119.3**
Speed ratings: **100,99,97,96,93 92,89,87,85,85**
toteswingers 1&2 £2.40, 1&3 £3.90, 2&3 £10.00 CSF £7.81 CT £55.22 TOTE £2.30: £1.10, £1.80, £3.20; EX 8.50 Trifecta £72.40 Pool: £1,595.64 - 16.51 winning units..
Owner D A Johnson & P F Nicholls **Bred** Robert Gasche Luc & Michel Boulay **Trained** Beaminster, Dorset

FOCUS
A rare handicap in this sphere and it saw class prevail. Chapoturgeon is the best of the British hunters and is rated to his mark.
T/Plt: £13.30 to a £1 stake. Pool: £66,885.14 - 3,645.08 winning units T/Qpdt: £4.00 to a £1 stake. Pool: £4,168.22 - 764.00 winning units TM

414 - 416a (Foreign Racing) - See Raceform Interactive

264 TOWCESTER (R-H)
Tuesday, May 21

OFFICIAL GOING: Good (9.9)
Wind: Light across Weather: Overcast

417 DON'T MISS OUT WITH GG.COM ALERTS MAIDEN HURDLE (10 hdls) 2m 3f 110y
5:35 (5:35) (Class 5) 4-Y-0+ **£1,949** (£572; £286; £143)

Form RPR
132/ **1** **Twelve Roses**^{22} [33] 5-11-0 119 JasonMaguire 95+
(Kim Bailey) *a.p: mstke 4th: led appr 2 out: clr last: comf* **6/4^{1}**
5/2- **2** 2¼ **Garryleigh (IRE)**^{15} [140] 6-11-0 119 (t) TomScudamore 91+
(David Pipe) *hld up: hdwy to go 2nd and mstke 2 out: styd on: no ch w wnr* **5/2^{2}**
00/ **3** 8 **Tigridia (IRE)**^{85} [4432] 6-10-7 0 MarcGoldstein 76
(Sheena West) *prom: racd keenly: rdn after 3 out: wkng whn mstke last* **50/1**
P/0- **4** 1¼ **Thefriendlygremlin**^{18} [91] 5-10-9 81 (p) GavinSheehan$^{(5)}$ 81
(John Upson) *prom: chsd ldr 6th: ev ch 3 out: wknd appr last* **66/1**
03/ **5** hd **Union Du Chenet (FR)**^{60} [4907] 5-11-0 117 AndrewTinkler 81
(Nicky Henderson) *chsd ldr to 6th: rdn after 3 out: wknd after next* **11/4^{3}**
4B6/ **6** 1¾ **Katnapping**^{40} [5256] 5-10-2 0 MrSWaley-Cohen$^{(5)}$ 72
(Robert Waley-Cohen) *prom: rdn after 3 out: wknd next: j.lft last* **16/1**
0P/- **7** 5 **Shadesofnavy**^{39} [5265] 7-11-0 0 (p) JackDoyle 74
(Peter Pritchard) *led: hung lft on bnd after 4th: hdd appr 2 out: sn wknd* **150/1**
000/ **8** 2 **Played Away**^{79} [4541] 5-11-0 0 HarrySkelton 72
(Caroline Fryer) *hld up: hdwy after 3 out: sn rdn and wknd* **150/1**
50/ **9** 3¾ **Frontier Vic**^{22} [33] 6-11-0 0 SamTwiston-Davies 68
(Nigel Twiston-Davies) *hld up: hdwy after 7th: wknd bef 2 out* **25/1**
000/ **10** hd **Alfie Alexander (IRE)**^{35} [5335] 5-11-0 0 LeightonAspell 68
(Mark Hoad) *hld up: rdn after 6th: wknd 3 out* **100/1**
005/ **11** 17 **Amalric (FR)**^{25} [5551] 6-11-0 0 TomMessenger 51
(Anabel K Murphy) *hld up: racd keenly: hdwy 5th: j.lft and mstke 7th: wknd after 3 out: bhd whn j.lft last: t.o* **66/1**
0/6- **12** 13 **Tomibola (IRE)**^{17} [116] 5-11-0 0 NoelFehily 38
(Harry Whittington) *hld up: a in rr: bhd fr 7th: t.o* **40/1**

4m 44.1s (-25.50) **Going Correction** -1.60s/f (Hard) **12** Ran SP% **114.7**
Speed ratings (Par 103): **87,86,82,82,82 81,79,78,77,77 70,65**
toteswingers 1&2 £1.80, 1&3 £25.50, 2&3 £54.20 CSF £5.20 TOTE £1.90: £1.10, £1.40, £11.50; EX 5.20 Trifecta £373.70 Pool: £967.51 - 1.94 winning units..
Owner Jones Broughtons Wilson Weaver **Bred** Coln Valley Stud **Trained** Andoversford, Gloucs

FOCUS
After a dry night, the ground was officially good. The hurdle course was on its inside line. A maiden hurdle in which very few had obvious claims. It was slowly run and the first two are rated well below their best.

418 HAYGAIN HAY STEAMERS CLEAN HEALTHY FORAGE H'CAP CHASE (12 fncs) 2m 110y
6:05 (6:05) (Class 5) (0-100,100) 5-Y-0+ **£2,144** (£629; £314; £157)

Form RPR
3/0- **1** **Crack At Dawn (IRE)**^{8} [264] 12-10-3 **84** (v) MrCSmith$^{(7)}$ 93
(Michael Gates) *hld up: hdwy 9th: rdn appr last: styd on u.p to ld post* **10/1**
P/1- **2** shd **Moscow Mule**^{8} [269] 10-10-8 **87** 7ex EdCookson$^{(5)}$ 98+
(Laura Hurley) *chsd ldrs: mstke 3rd: wnt 2nd bef 3 out: led appr next: nt fluent last: rdn flat: hdd post* **11/4^{2}**
301/ **3** 2¼ **Orang Outan (FR)**^{50} [5069] 11-11-0 **95** KieronEdgar$^{(7)}$ 102
(Laura Hurley) *led to 2nd: led 3rd to next: chsd ldr tl rdn appr 3 out: no ex towards fin* **9/1**
6/0- **4** 5 **Share Option**^{18} [89] 11-11-3 **91** LeeEdwards 94
(Tony Carroll) *hld up: hdwy 3 out: outpcd bef next: styd on flat* **14/1**
/02- **5** 2 **Tom O'Tara**^{8} [269] 9-10-1 **78** WayneKavanagh$^{(3)}$ 81
(Robin Dickin) *chsd ldr tl led 2nd: hdd next: led again 4th: rdn and hdd appr 2 out: wknd last* **7/2^{3}**
1/2- **6** 8 **Kayfton Pete**^{20} [65] 7-11-12 **100** (t) AdamPogson 96
(Charles Pogson) *s.s: hld up and a in rr: wknd after 3 out* **5/2^{1}**
0/ **7** nk **In The Haven (IRE)**^{32} [5394] 10-11-6 **99** (b) SamanthaDrake$^{(5)}$ 93
(Joanne Foster) *chsd ldrs: drvn along 9th: wknd appr 2 out* **10/1**

3m 52.4s (-23.70) **Going Correction** -1.45s/f (Hard) course record **7** Ran SP% **112.3**
Speed ratings: **97,96,95,93,92 88,88**
toteswingers 1&2 £9.50, 1&3 £9.60, 2&3 £6.90 CSF £37.38 TOTE £21.50: £5.10, £2.60; EX 49.20 Trifecta £457.50 Pool: £610.06 - 3.90 winning units..
Owner Michael Gates **Bred** Austin Rice **Trained** Clifford Chambers, Warwicks
■ Stewards' Enquiry : Mr C Smith four-day ban: use of whip (4-7 June)
Kieron Edgar four-day ban: use of whip (4,7, 15 June, 24 July)

FOCUS
A modest handicap chase, with a top weight rated 100. The winner is rated similar to his C&D run.

419 HAYGAIN HAY STEAMERS CLEAN HEALTHY FORAGE CLAIMING HURDLE (8 hdls) 2m
6:35 (6:35) (Class 5) 4-Y-0+ **£1,949** (£572; £286; £143)

Form RPR
030/ **1** **Dark Energy**^{77} [4574] 9-11-4 102 (t) PaddyBrennan 121+
(Fergal O'Brien) *chsd ldrs: wnt 2nd 5th: tk clsr order bef next: led appr 2 out: sn clr: comf* **11/2**
C21/ **2** 8 **King Fingal (IRE)**^{76} [4586] 8-11-2 110 DougieCostello 111
(John Quinn) *chsd clr ldr to 5th: tk clsr order 3 out: sn rdn: styd on same pce fr next* **5/2^{1}**
3/2- **3** nk **Teshali (IRE)**^{12} [191] 7-10-11 115 (t) JamesBanks$^{(5)}$ 110
(Anthony Middleton) *sn bhd: hdwy appr 2 out: sn rdn: nvr nrr* **4/1^{3}**
064/ **4** 2½ **Right Stuff (FR)**^{25} [5553] 10-11-2 111 JamieMoore 110
(Gary Moore) *hld up: hdwy and blnd 3 out: rdn and mstke next: styd on same pce* **13/2**
66P/ **5** hd **Marodima (FR)**^{40} [5260] 10-12-0 125 (p) TomO'Brien 122
(Jamie Snowden) *led and sn clr: blnd 3rd: c bk to the field 3 out: hdd bef next: wknd last* **11/4^{2}**
/45- **6** 1 **Smiling Lady (IRE)**^{8} [269] 7-10-7 99 (t) PaulMoloney 98
(David Rees) *sn bhd: n.d* **16/1**

3m 41.1s (-26.80) **Going Correction** -1.60s/f (Hard)
WFA 4 from 6yo+ 18lb **6** Ran SP% **109.8**
Speed ratings (Par 103): **103,99,98,97,97 97**
toteswingers 1&2 £3.10, 1&3 £3.90, 2&3 £3.30 CSF £19.11 TOTE £6.00: £2.10, £1.70; EX 18.20 Trifecta £84.10 Pool: £878.01 - 7.82 winning units..
Owner The Yes No Wait Sorries **Bred** Bearstone Stud **Trained** Coln St. Dennis, Gloucs

FOCUS
A claiming hurdle in which a variety of abilities were represented. It was strongly run and the form is rated around the second to fourth.

420 CARLSBERG H'CAP CHASE (18 fncs) 3m 110y
7:05 (7:05) (Class 4) (0-110,110) 5-Y-0+ **£3,768** (£1,106; £553; £276)

Form RPR
5/3- **1** hd **Bishophill Jack (IRE)**^{8} [265] 7-11-3 **101** (p) NickScholfield 110+
(Kim Bailey) *a.p: chsd ldr 4th to 14th: wnt 2nd again 2 out: rdn to ld and hit last: sn hdd: carried lft flat: styd on: fin 2nd: plcd 1st* **7/2^{1}**
53/- **2** **Rebel Swing**^{42} [5228] 7-10-10 **99** SamanthaDrake$^{(5)}$ 109+
(Joanne Foster) *hld up: hdwy 6th: mstke 11th: pushed along next: hit 14th: led flat: sn rdn and hung lft: jst hld on: disqualified and plcd 2nd* **4/1^{2}**

P0/- **3** *11* **Rossbrin (IRE)**[23] 7 8-11-3 **101**..................(t) AndrewTinkler 98
(Anna Brooks) *prom: outpcd 13th: rallied 3 out: styd on same pce fr next* **11/1**

P/3- **4** *4* **Strongbows Legend**[21] 44 8-11-12 **110**..................(v) NoelFehily 104
(Charlie Longsdon) *led: rdn and hdd appr last: wknd flat* **5/1**

226/ **5** *14* **Red Rouble (IRE)**[28] 5481 8-11-7 **105**.................. SamTwiston-Davies 86
(Nigel Twiston-Davies) *chsd ldr to 4th: remained handy: drvn along 13th: wknd after 2 out* **13/2**

2/2- **6** *80* **Smooth Classic (IRE)**[17] 117 9-11-9 **107**.................. TomScudamore 16
(David Pipe) *hld up: hdwy 12th: chsd ldr 14th tl rdn and wknd appr 2 out: clambered over last: t.o* **9/2**[3]

460/ **P** **Watch House (IRE)**[28] 5477 8-10-2 **93**.................. CiaranMckee(7)
(Michael Gates) *hld up: mstkes: wknd 14th: t.o whn p.u bef 2 out* **25/1**

015/ **P** **Brunette'Sonly (IRE)**[25] 5554 8-10-8 **92**.................. AndrewThornton
(Seamus Mullins) *sn bhd: t.o whn p.u after 9th* **8/1**

5m 58.0s (-38.90) **Going Correction** -1.45s/f (Hard) 8 Ran SP% **113.7**
Speed ratings: **103,104,100,99,94 69, ,**
toteswingers 1&2 £3.20, 1&3 £8.40, 2&3 £25.20 CSF £18.20 CT £136.50 TOTE £4.80: £1.30, £1.70, £3.40; EX 18.20 Trifecta £144.20 Pool: £568.30 - 2.95 winning units..
Owner The On The Bridle Partnership **Bred** Greg Lawler **Trained** Andoversford, Gloucs
■ Stewards' Enquiry : Samantha Drake two-day ban: careless riding (4-5 June)

FOCUS
Just an ordinary handicap chase, with the top-weight rated 110, but competitive on paper. Rebel Swing (disqualified), was well treated on his best form, and Bishophill Jack built on his good recent C&D win.

421 VISIT THE FORUM ON GG.COM H'CAP HURDLE (10 hdls) 2m 3f 110y
7:35 (7:37) (Class 4) (0-115,114) 4-Y-O+ **£3,119** (£915; £457; £228)

Form RPR

413/ **1** **Thoresby (IRE)**[38] 5286 7-11-3 **105**..................(p) DarylJacob 106
(Ben Case) *a.p: rdn to ld appr last: styd on u.p* **11/1**

/52- **2** *¾* **Bob Lewis**[8] 264 7-9-9 **88** oh2..................(t) JamesBanks(5) 88
(Anthony Middleton) *hld up: hdwy 5th: ev ch fr 2 out: sn rdn: styd on* **9/2**[2]

1/1- **3** *7* **Prince Pippin (IRE)**[8] 264 7-11-2 **104** 7ex..................(t) APMcCoy 100
(Lucy Jones) *w ldr tl led 7th: rdn and hdd whn n.m.r last: wknd flat* **5/4**[1]

143/ **4** *5* **Midnight Lira**[30] 5440 6-10-8 **96**.................. IanPopham 86
(Caroline Keevil) *chsd ldrs: rdn and ev ch after 3 out: wknd bef last* **16/1**

035/ **5** *1 ½* **Aegean Destiny**[30] 5432 6-10-12 **100**.................. DonalDevereux 88
(John Mackie) *chsd ldrs: lost pl 5th: hdwy 7th: rdn and wknd appr last* **33/1**

2/0- **6** *4* **Guards Chapel**[18] 97 5-11-8 **110**..................(v) JamieMoore 95
(Gary Moore) *hld up: drvn along 7th: hdwy after 3 out: wknd bef last* **28/1**

7 *6* **Moyne Nineoseven (IRE)**[47] 5152 7-10-13 **104**.................. JackQuinlan(3) 83
(Noel Quinlan) *hld up: effrt after 3 out: mstke and wknd next* **25/1**

000/ **8** *2 ½* **Award Winner**[28] 5471 10-10-12 **100**..................(p) BrendanPowell 77
(Brendan Powell) *led to 7th: rdn and wknd appr 2 out* **50/1**

12P/ **9** *hd* **Diamond's Return (IRE)**[94] 4259 9-11-12 **114**..................(tp) ConorO'Farrell 94
(David Pipe) *hld up: hdwy u.p after 3 out: wknd next* **13/2**[3]

1/2- **10** *½* **Around A Pound (IRE)**[20] 68 8-11-3 **105**..................(p) HenryBrooke 81
(Nick Kent) *chsd ldrs: rdn appr 3 out: sn wknd* **22/1**

402/ **P** **Dashing Doc (IRE)**[28] 5464 6-11-3 **105**.................. PaulMoloney
(Evan Williams) *hld up: bhd fr 6th: t.o whn p.u bef 2 out* **10/1**

4m 34.7s (-34.90) **Going Correction** -1.60s/f (Hard) 11 Ran SP% **115.8**
Speed ratings (Par 105): **105,104,101,99,99 97,95,94,94,94**
toteswingers 1&2 £8.90, 1&3 £4.40, 2&3 £2.90 CSF £56.31 CT £106.24 TOTE £9.30: £2.40, £1.70, £1.20; EX 70.80 Trifecta £161.80 Pool: £882.96 - 4.09 winning units..
Owner D Allen **Bred** Patrick Doyle **Trained** Edgcote, Northants

FOCUS
This looked a competitive handicap hurdle despite the presence of a well-backed, short-priced favourite. Ordinary form, but sound enough.

422 BEST RACING BLOGS ON GG.COM NOVICES' CHASE (16 fncs) 2m 6f
8:05 (8:05) (Class 4) 5-Y-O+ **£3,768** (£1,106; £553; £276)

Form RPR

2UP/ **1** **Thanks For Coming**[33] 5365 7-10-12 **125**.................. DavidBass 124+
(Nicky Henderson) *hld up: hit 9th: hdwy 12th: led appr last: styd on wl* **9/4**[2]

423/ **2** *3 ¼* **The Musical Guy (IRE)**[26] 5521 7-10-12 **121**......(b) SamTwiston-Davies 122+
(Nigel Twiston-Davies) *led 2nd: rdn and hdd appr last: styd on same pce flat* **11/8**[1]

10/- **3** *9* **Regal Presence (IRE)**[34] 5354 6-10-12 0..................(p) JackDoyle 112
(Victor Dartnall) *chsd ldrs: mstke 11th: rdn and wknd after 2 out* **11/2**

PP/- **4** *hd* **Accordion Exhibit (IRE)**[101] 4141 7-10-12 0..................(t) NoelFehily 111
(Fergal O'Brien) *chsd ldrs: rdn appr 2 out: wknd bef last* **5/1**[3]

FP0/ **5** *4* **Brough Academy (IRE)**[25] 5553 7-10-12 0.................. AidanColeman 107
(Lawney Hill) *hld up: hdwy appr 3 out: rdn and wknd next* **28/1**

6/6- **6** *41* **Supermightyfine**[17] 122 6-10-12 0.................. MarkGrant 66
(Jo Hughes) *led to 2nd: chsd ldrs: drvn along 13th: wknd after 3 out: t.o* **50/1**

054/ **P** **Dramatic Victory (IRE)**[23] 16 6-10-7 0.................. GavinSheehan(5)
(John Upson) *bhd fr 5th: t.o whn p.u bef 13th* **150/1**

5m 16.9s (-36.10) **Going Correction** -1.45s/f (Hard) 7 Ran SP% **111.0**
Speed ratings: **107,105,102,102,101 86,**
toteswingers 1&2 £1.50, 1&3 £3.70, 2&3 £3.00 CSF £5.67 TOTE £2.60: £1.50, £1.20; EX 6.00 Trifecta £16.50 Pool: £685.43 - 31.13 winning units..
Owner Unchartered Waters **Bred** The National Stud **Trained** Upper Lambourn, Berks

FOCUS
Not many had obvious claims in this fair novice chase. It was steadily run and the first two are rated below their best.

423 FREE TIPS EVERY DAY AT GG.COM CONDITIONAL JOCKEYS' MARES' H'CAP HURDLE (8 hdls) 2m
8:35 (8:35) (Class 5) (0-100,100) 4-Y-O+ **£1,949** (£572; £286; £143)

Form RPR

000/ **1** **Ruby Crown**[28] 5477 11-10-7 **84**..................(p) EdCookson(3) 83
(Kim Bailey) *prom: hit 2nd: outpcd appr 3 out: rallied next: n.m.r last: qcknd to ld nr fin* **4/1**[2]

1/1- **2** *shd* **Brunton Blue**[14] 166 8-11-12 **100**.................. MichealNolan 99
(Lucy Wadham) *hld up: hdwy 3 out: led next: rdn flat: hdd nr fin* **1/1**[1]

P/4- **3** *¾* **On The Off Chance**[14] 166 5-11-6 **100**..................(b[1]) DannyBenson(6) 98
(Jonjo O'Neill) *chsd ldrs: mstke 2 out: rdn appr last: r.o* **6/1**[3]

525/ **4** *¾* **Starlet Mandy (IRE)**[91] 4295 10-10-0 **74** oh5.................. AdamWedge 71
(Nigel Twiston-Davies) *led: rdn and hdd 2 out: styd on same pce flat* **16/1**

2/6- **5** *13* **Flash Harriet**[3] 376 9-10-8 **82**.................. DonalDevereux 67
(John Mackie) *chsd ldrs: ev ch 3 out: rdn and wknd appr last* **9/1**

0/0- **6** *11* **Ivebeenthinking**[21] 46 5-10-9 **86**.................. BenPoste(3) 59
(Tom Symonds) *hld up: hit 5th: effrt after 3 out: sn wknd: hit last* **22/1**

341/ **7** *8* **Definite Lady (IRE)**[376] 183 7-11-8 **96**.................. KillianMoore 61
(Mark Rimell) *chsd ldrs: drvn along 3 out: wknd bef next: t.o* **14/1**

P/P- **8** *1 ½* **Daddy'Slittlegirl**[8] 269 8-9-6 **74** oh11..................(v[1]) DanielHiskett(8) 37
(Claire Dyson) *chsd ldr to appr 3 out: wknd bef next: t.o* **66/1**

3m 47.9s (-20.00) **Going Correction** -1.60s/f (Hard) 8 Ran SP% **112.7**
Speed ratings (Par 103): **86,85,85,85,78 73,69,68**
toteswingers 1&2 £2.10, 1&3 £2.40, 2&3 £2.20 CSF £8.41 CT £21.81 TOTE £4.90: £1.80, £1.10, £2.30; EX 10.00 Trifecta £27.60 Pool: £908.83 - 24.68 winning units..
Owner I F W Buchan **Bred** I F W Buchan **Trained** Andoversford, Gloucs

FOCUS
A modest finale, confined to mares, in which the top weight was rated 100. It was steadily run and the first four ran pretty much to their marks.
T/Plt: £38.80 to a £1 stake. Pool: £77,069.41 - 1446.75 winning units T/Qpdt: £7.80 to a £1 stake. Pool: £6880.42 - 648.45 winning units CR

[1]HUNTINGDON (R-H)
Wednesday, May 22

OFFICIAL GOING: Good (good to firm in places) changing to good to firm after race 2 (2.40)
Wind: light across Weather: overcast; 14 degrees

424 PAUL RACKHAM CHAMPION NOVICES' HUNTERS' CHASE (19 fncs) 3m
2:10 (2:10) (Class 6) 5-Y-O+ **£935** (£290; £145; £72)

Form RPR

1 **Realt Ag Leimt (IRE)**[31] 7-11-5 0.................. MrDPeters(7) 100+
(M R Peters) *racd keenly in 2nd tl led on long run to 2 out: sn 5 l clr: idled flat and drvn out fnl 100yds* **9/4**[2]

2/ **2** *2 ¾* **Galbally King (IRE)**[31] 8-11-5 0.................. MrBRivett(7) 97
(A Pennock) *t.k.h: led at brisk pce tl rdn and hdd on long run to 2 out: tried to rally flat: a wl hld* **8/1**

224/ **3** *49* **French Canadian (FR)**[16] 7-11-9 111.................. MrRJarrett(3) 68
(Mrs C J Robinson) *j.lft 1st: often j. indifferently and nvr really travelling: mostly 3rd fr 8th: hrd rdn and lost tch 3 out: remote 3rd whn j.lft 2 out and last* **1/1**[1]

0/0- **4** *54* **Fourth In Line (IRE)**[21] 58 9-11-5 67..................(bt) MrABraithwaite(7) 4
(Mrs L Braithwaite) *nt fluent 3rd: j. slowly 7th: lost tch 13th: t.o next: eased bef 2 out* **6/1**[3]

00P/ **P** **Departed (IRE)**[3] 9-11-5 69..................(b) MissEKelly(7)
(S G Allen) *last and rdn 8th: sn lost tch: t.o 12th: p.u 14th* **50/1**

5m 50.5s (-19.80) **Going Correction** -0.625s/f (Firm) 5 Ran SP% **108.1**
Speed ratings: **108,107,90,72,**
CSF £17.03 TOTE £3.00: £1.90, £1.90; EX 13.40 Trifecta £27.80 Pool: £929.25 - 25.01 winning units..
Owner M R Peters **Bred** Mrs P Doran **Trained** Sawtry, Cambs

FOCUS
The going was changed to good, good to firm in places from good, good to soft in places before the opener. With both Departed and Fourth In Line playing little to no part, this looks weak form, mainly due to the favourite running well below his previous best. The form is rated through the second.

425 BOOK ONLINE AT NEW LOOK WHITTLEBURYHALL.CO.UK NOVICES' CHASE (12 fncs) 2m 110y
2:40 (2:40) (Class 4) 5-Y-O+ **£3,768** (£1,106; £553; £276)

Form RPR

6/3- **1** **Robbie**[14] 167 9-10-12 132.................. JamesReveley 106+
(Keith Reveley) *mde all and j. soundly: a looked in command fr 2 out* **15/8**[1]

004/ **2** *1 ½* **Uncle Pelder (IRE)**[465] 4274 6-10-12 0.................. DaveCrosse 104
(K F Clutterbuck) *hld up in tch: effrt 3 out: 1 l 4th whn hit next: drvn and ungainly last: chsd wnr after and kpt on but a hld* **100/1**

5/1- **3** *¾* **Double Handful (GER)**[19] 97 7-10-12 0..................(t) DavidBass 102
(Lawney Hill) *pckd bdly 4th: t.k.h: trckd ldrs: wnt 2nd at 6th tl rdn and ev ch bef 2 out: no imp fr last* **15/8**[1]

5/P- **4** *1* **Walden Prince (IRE)**[10] 251 6-10-12 0.................. WayneHutchinson 103+
(Tony Carroll) *t.k.h towards rr of bunch: effrt 3 out: wnt 2nd and hit 2 out: drvn and nt qckn in 3rd fr last* **25/1**[3]

065/ **5** *22* **Cossack Prince**[26] 5557 8-10-12 0.................. TomCannon 81
(Laura Mongan) *2nd tl j. slowly 6th: stl on terms 3 out: rdn and dropped out on long run to next* **80/1**

435/ **6** *16* **Mr Robinson (FR)**[24] 2 6-10-12 0.................. AndrewTinkler 63
(Tony Carroll) *a last: j. slowly 6th: tending to jump lft after: lost tch 8th: t.o 3 out: kpt on after last* **33/1**

1/3- **7** *20* **Kambis**[7] 304 5-10-12 0.................. JamieMoore 73
(Gary Moore) *hit 4th and 5th: cl up tl n.m.r and lost footing after 3 out: nt rcvr: t.o whn mstke last and heavily eased* **9/4**[2]

3m 58.0s (-12.20) **Going Correction** -0.625s/f (Firm) 7 Ran SP% **109.3**
Speed ratings: **103,102,101,101,91 83,74**
Tote Swingers: 1&2 £7.80, 1&3 £1.50, 2&3 £9.00 CSF £117.30 TOTE £2.50: £1.80, £11.80; EX 60.50 Trifecta £587.80 Pool: £824.60 - 1.05 winning units..
Owner Mrs Susan McDonald **Bred** Mrs Susan McDonald **Trained** Lingdale, Redcar & Cleveland

FOCUS
Quite a competitive event for novices, and the early pace looked okay without being strong. The time was ordinary and the form is fairly modest.

426 HOTEL & SPA OFFERS AT WHITTLEBURYHALL.CO.UK H'CAP CHASE (16 fncs) 2m 4f 110y
3:10 (3:10) (Class 4) (0-110,106) 5-Y-O+ **£3,768** (£1,106; £553; £276)

Form RPR

P/6- **1** **Oscar Close (IRE)**[19] 98 8-11-8 **102**..................(tp) TomScudamore 114
(David Bridgwater) *hld up last: hit 9th: clsd grad fr next: wnt 3rd after 3 out: chal next: led last: drvn and hld on gamely flat* **14/1**

3/2- **2** *nk* **Representingceltic (IRE)**[10] 238 8-11-11 **105**.................. ColinBolger 117
(Pat Phelan) *settled wl in tch: wnt 3rd at 12th: led sn after 2 out: drvn and jst hdd last: battled on wl flat but a narrowly hld* **15/8**[1]

/32- **3** *8* **Chestnut Ben (IRE)**[10] 245 8-11-0 **94**.................. JamieMoore 99
(Gary Brown) *hld up trcking ldrs: 4th whn hit 3 out: rdn after next: no rspnse and wl hld bef last* **15/2**

P32/ **4** *2 ½* **Refusal**[24] 5 5-11-11 **105**.................. AndrewThornton 109+
(Caroline Bailey) *led at stdy pce: hit 2 out and sn hdd and drvn: 4th and wkng whn hit last* **6/1**

The Form Book Jumps, Raceform Ltd, Compton, RG20 6NL.

650/ **5** *71* **Another Trump (NZ)**[91] 4324 9-11-12 **106** .... APMcCoy 36
(Jonjo O'Neill) *rn in snatches: coaxed fr 7th: mstke 13th and lost tch: t.o and eased bef 2 out: b.b.v* **9/2**[3]

/5P- **6** *3/4* **Radsoc De Sivola (FR)**[8] 286 8-9-11 **82** .... JoeCornwall(5) 11
(John Cornwall) *rn in snatches: rdn 6th: in rr 11th: t.o 3 out: eased after next* **50/1**

332/ **P** **Porters War (IRE)**[33] 5380 11-11-10 **104** .... NickScholfield
(Jeremy Scott) *pressed ldr: rdn and fdd qckly on long run after 3 out: mod 5th whn p.u 2 out: b.b.v* **7/2**[2]

4m 49.9s (-15.40) **Going Correction** -0.625s/f (Firm) **7** Ran SP% **109.9**
Speed ratings: **104,103,100,99,72 72,**
Tote Swingers: 1&2 £21.60, 1&3 £21.60, 2&3 £1.40 CSF £39.19 CT £202.27 TOTE £12.40: £6.40, £1.90; EX 66.30 Trifecta £533.60 Part won. Pool: £711.59 - 0.75 winning units..
Owner Wayne Hennessey **Bred** Mrs E Moore **Trained** Icomb, Gloucs

FOCUS
The going had dried out to good to firm all round before this race. The winner is rated back to the level of his 2012 form and the second to his mark.

427 SMITHS METAL CENTRES NOVICES' HURDLE (8 hdls) 2m 110y
3:40 (3:47) (Class 4) 4-Y-0+ **£3,119** (£915; £457; £228)

Form RPR

2/1- **1** **Sea Lord (IRE)**[13] 186 6-11-5 119 .... DenisO'Regan 123+
(John Ferguson) *mde all at modest pce: nt a fluent: 5 l clr and wl in command bef 2 out: hrd hld* **4/9**[1]

0/ **2** *3 3/4* **Broughtons Bandit**[20] 5064 6-10-12 0 .... NoelFehily 106
(Willie Musson) *settled in midfield: effrt in 7 l 4th 3 out: wnt 2nd at last and kpt on but no ch w wnr* **33/1**

403/ **3** *4 1/2* **Broughtons Star**[51] 5065 6-10-12 0 .... LeightonAspell 102
(Willie Musson) *trckd ldrs: flattered briefly in 3 l 3rd 3 out: sn chsng wnr vainly: wl hld 3rd fr last* **4/1**[2]

5/ **4** *6* **Spirit Of Xaar (IRE)**[5] 2528 7-10-12 0 .... (p) TomCannon 95
(Linda Jewell) *cl up: wnt 2nd at 5th tl rdn and fdd bef 2 out* **33/1**

4/ **5** *7* **Nelson's Bay**[40] 5273 4-10-5 0 .... (t) JackQuinlan(3) 84
(Noel Quinlan) *midfield: wknd 3 out: wl btn whn j.lft last* **14/1**

2- **6** *4 1/2* **Flashy Star**[22] 46 4-10-1 0 .... MarcGoldstein 72
(Sheena West) *t.k.h: pressed wnr tl 5th: rdn and dropped out tamely after next: b.b.v* **7/1**[3]

0/ **F** **The Wonga Coup (IRE)**[154] 4478 6-10-2 0 .... PaddyBradley(10)
(Pat Phelan) *mounted outside paddock: uns rdr at s: s.s and j. poorly: in last pair: lost tch bef 3 out: remote 9th whn fell next* **33/1**

P **Son Vida (IRE)**[9] 5-10-12 0 .... JamesDavies
(Alan Bailey) *midfield tl 4th: dropped bk last next: t.o and p.u 3 out: b.b.v* **80/1**

100/ **F** **Life Of Laughter (USA)**[47] 3573 5-10-12 0 .... DaveCrosse 83
(Willie Musson) *hld up towards rr: lost tch 3 out: remote 7th whn fell next* **66/1**

P **Checkpoint**[22] 4-10-8 0 .... JamieMoore
(Gary Moore) *lost abt 40 l at s: clsd grad and in tch by 5th: sn fdd again: t.o and p.u 2 out* **16/1**

3m 38.4s (-16.50) **Going Correction** -1.00s/f (Hard)
WFA 4 from 5yo+ 18lb **10** Ran SP% **125.9**
Speed ratings (Par 105): **98,96,94,91,88 85, , , ,**
Tote Swingers: 1&2 £8.40, 1&3 £12.20, 2&3 £6.20 CSF £29.56 TOTE £1.60: £1.02, £8.20, £1.10; EX 25.40 Trifecta £82.40 Pool: £1,266.00 - 11.51 winning units..
Owner Bloomfields **Bred** Darley **Trained** Cowlinge, Suffolk

FOCUS
A modest novice hurdle. A difficult race to rate highly due to the winning distance, and both the winner and third are rated below their best.

428 SHORECLEAN H'CAP HURDLE (12 hdls) 3m 2f
4:10 (4:10) (Class 4) (0-105,106) 4-Y-0+ **£3,119** (£915; £457; £228)

Form RPR

000/ **1** **Salpierre (IRE)**[160] 3023 8-11-12 **105** .... APMcCoy 115
(Jonjo O'Neill) *cl up: j. slowly 3rd: wnt 2nd at 9th: 3 l down 3 out: hrd drvn after: led last: r.o u.str driving flat: all out* **5/4**[1]

400/ **2** *1/2* **Bollin Tahini**[26] 5555 7-10-0 **79** oh3 .... AlexMerriam 88
(Neil King) *set stdy pce: 3 l clr 3 out: rdn next: hdd last: ev ch after but jst hld fnl 100yds* **10/1**

4/5- **3** *1 1/4* **Go Amwell**[10] 241 10-10-6 **85** .... (v) HarryHaynes 92
(J R Jenkins) *settled in 5th pl: effrt in cl 3rd 3 out: ev ch fr last: cajoled along and n.g.t* **13/2**[3]

056/ **4** *23* **Big Sound**[61] 4908 6-11-7 **100** .... (p) PeterBuchanan 86
(Tim Walford) *pressed ldrs: nt fluent 8th: cl 4th whn hmpd and snatched up after 9th: no ch after: mod 5th at next* **5/1**[2]

0/4- **5** *10* **Elegant Olive**[22] 38 10-11-5 **98** .... HaddenFrost 75
(Roger Curtis) *last pair: lost tch after 9th: continued wl bhd: b.b.v* **8/1**

04/- **6** *4 1/2* **Orsm**[26] 5555 6-11-2 **95** .... (t) TomCannon 68
(Laura Mongan) *pressed wnr: rdn 7th: 3rd and drvn at 9th: fdd after 3 out* **16/1**

520/ **P** **Great Hero**[26] 5538 8-11-4 **104** .... ConorShoemark(7)
(Richard Phillips) *last pair: nt fluent 8th and wknd: t.o whn p.u after 3 out: dismntd* **8/1**

5m 59.8s (-23.10) **Going Correction** -1.00s/f (Hard) **7** Ran SP% **111.6**
Speed ratings (Par 105): **95,94,94,87,84 82,**
Tote Swingers: 1&2 £0.00, 2&3 £1.10 CSF £13.41 CT £57.58 TOTE £2.00: £1.30, £4.50; EX 20.90 Trifecta £120.20 Pool: £731.31 - 4.56 winning units..
Owner F Gillespie **Bred** Mrs Mary Furlong **Trained** Cheltenham, Gloucs

FOCUS
The two potential market-leaders were withdrawn during the afternoon due to the quickening ground, meaning this had a moderate look about it. The winner's best figure since 2011.

429 EPDS RACING SUPPORTING RACING WELFARE CONDITIONAL JOCKEYS' (S) H'CAP HURDLE (8 hdls) 2m 110y
4:40 (4:40) (Class 5) (0-95,94) 4-Y-0+ **£1,949** (£572; £286; £143)

Form RPR

P/3- **1** **Wom**[15] 161 5-11-9 **94** .... (v) TrevorWhelan(3) 103+
(Neil King) *midfield: effrt bef 3 out: led appr next: 3 l clr whn wnt rt and hit last: drvn along after: all out but a jst holding 2nd* **9/1**

0/5- **2** *1/2* **Nicky Nutjob (GER)**[9] 266 7-10-7 **83** .... (p) CiaranMckee(8) 90
(John O'Shea) *cl up: wnt 2nd at 5th: rdn and outpcd by wnr whn hit 2 out: 3 l down last: tried to cl again flat: kpt on but nvr quite able to chal* **6/1**[3]

/50- **3** *2* **Tiradia (FR)**[13] 184 6-11-4 **86** .... TomCannon 90
(J R Jenkins) *midfield: rdn and tried to cl after 3 out: 5th bef next: swtchd lft bef last: kpt on after last: a hld* **8/1**

0/4- **4** *2* **Inside Knowledge (USA)**[9] 266 7-11-8 **90** .... RyanMahon 93
(Garry Woodward) *trckd ldrs: drvn and outpcd in 6th whn mstke 2 out: rallied flat: fin wl to snatch 4th* **18/1**

6/3- **5** *1/2* **Freddy's Star (IRE)**[13] 193 11-11-8 **90** .... TonyKelly 92
(Nick Ayliffe) *trckd ldrs: rdn to chal 3 out: one pce fr bef next* **8/1**

/22- **6** *1 1/2* **Pobs Trophy**[13] 184 6-10-12 **80** .... (b) JonathanEngland 80
(Richard Guest) *led: hit 3 out: drvn and hdd bef next: sn btn* **5/1**[2]

060/ **7** *17* **Mightavago**[30] 5449 4-11-4 **93** .... (p) JohnDawson(3) 72
(Tim Walford) *cl up: hit 5th: rdn and wknd next* **20/1**

4P0/ **8** *8* **Bubbly Braveheart (IRE)**[2] 2 6-11-0 **82** .... (p) JackQuinlan 57
(Phil McEntee) *chsd ldrs: rdn after 5th: no rspnse and sn struggling* **40/1**

300/ **9** *13* **Lombok**[274] 1316 7-10-11 **84** .... (v) JosephAkehurst(5) 46
(Gary Moore) *midfield: rdn 5th: no rspnse: btn next: t.o* **16/1**

660/ **10** *nk* **Boogie Dancer**[239] 1635 9-10-9 **77** .... (v) BrendanPowell 38
(Jim Best) *j. slowly 4th: pressed ldr tl hrd drvn 5th: lost pl rapidly bef next: t.o* **9/4**[1]

00P/ **11** *21* **Phoenix Des Mottes (FR)**[70] 4744 10-10-5 **76** .... JoeCornwall(3) 16
(John Cornwall) *bhd: nt fluent 3rd and rdn: wl bhd 5th: t.o next* **80/1**

030/ **P** **Cursum Perficio**[788] 4999 11-11-4 **86** .... GavinSheehan
(John Upson) *sn last: t.o bef 4th tl p.u 2 out* **80/1**

3m 37.1s (-17.80) **Going Correction** -1.00s/f (Hard)
WFA 4 from 5yo+ 18lb **12** Ran SP% **114.8**
Speed ratings (Par 103): **101,100,99,98,98 97,89,86,80,79 70,**
Tote Swingers: 1&2 £8.40, 1&3 £12.20, 2&3 £6.20 CSF £59.31 CT £450.81 TOTE £8.70: £2.80, £2.00, £3.10; EX 41.00 Trifecta £272.10 Pool: £695.11 - 1.91 winning units..No bid for the winner.
Owner Mark & Tracy Harrod **Bred** Genesis Green Stud **Trained** Newmarket, Suffolk

FOCUS
A moderate contest and plenty of these didn't jump fluently, including the winner. The form has a solid look.

T/Plt: £126.10 to a £1 stake. Pool: £50,198.92 - 290.57 winning tickets. T/Qpdt: £11.30 to a £1 stake. Pool: £4,081.12 - 266.49 winning tickets. IM

[247]WORCESTER (L-H)
Wednesday, May 22

OFFICIAL GOING: Good (good to firm in places; 7.0)
2nd fence in the home straight was omitted in all chases due to being damaged.
Wind: Light behind Weather: Cloudy with sunny spells

430 HARGREAVE HALE STOCKBROKERS HUNTERS' CHASE (17 fncs 1 omitted) 2m 7f
5:50 (5:50) (Class 6) 5-Y-0+ **£935** (£290; £145; £72)

Form RPR

1 **Stone (IRE)**[16] 7-11-3 0 .... (t) MrJMRidley(7) 115+
(Miss E Alvis) *a.p: led 10th: clr fr 13th: j.rt 4 out: styd on* **11/2**

453/ **2** *10* **Ice Cool Benny (IRE)**[16] 9-12-0 100 .... (p) MrTWeston 110
(Rachel Hobbs) *hld up: hdwy 8th: rdn 14th: chsd wnr next: no imp fr 2 out* **9/4**[1]

P/5- **3** *24* **Quatuor Collonges (FR)**[21] 58 9-11-3 73 .... MissAEStirling(7) 82
(C R Willes) *hit 1st: nvr gng wl and a bhd: hit 9th: wnt remote 3rd towards fin: t.o* **11/4**[2]

4 *1 1/2* **Bob Almighty (IRE)**[16] 8-11-5 0 .... MrJMartin(5) 81
(A Campbell) *chsd ldr tl lft in ld 7th: hdd 10th: chsd wnr to 4 out: wknd bef next: hung rt flat and lost 3rd nr fin: t.o* **9/2**[3]

P0P/ **P** **The Walnut Tree (IRE)**[3] 12-11-3 0 .... (b) MrCSmith(7)
(David Lewis) *chsd ldrs: lft 2nd 7th: hit 9th: wknd 11th: t.o whn p.u bef 13th* **100/1**

3/4- **F** **Near The Water (IRE)**[8] 297 9-11-3 0 .... MissJBuck(7)
(R J Harraway) *hld up: fell 6th* **20/1**

U **Temair Feis**[31] 10-11-3 0 .... MrRGSpencer(7)
(Miss H Watson) *led tl mstke and uns rdr 7th* **9/1**

PPP/ **P** **Minella (IRE)**[3] 9-11-3 0 .... (p) MrJBargary(7)
(W M Wanless) *chsd ldrs: hmpd 7th: lost pl 9th: sn pushed along: wknd bef next: t.o whn p.u bef 11th* **200/1**

0/ **P** **The Magherally Man (IRE)**[25] 9-11-3 0 .... MrWTelfer(7)
(T P Eades) *bhd: hdwy after 9th: hit 11th: sn wknd: t.o whn p.u bef 4 out* **20/1**

P **Rainbow Trout (IRE)**[53] 7-10-10 0 .... MrRHogg(7)
(Mrs Z Smith) *sn t.o: p.u bef 10th* **50/1**

5m 55.6s (7.60) **Going Correction** -0.575s/f (Firm) **10** Ran SP% **114.0**
Speed ratings: **63,59,51,50, , , , ,**
Tote Swingers: 1&2 £3.20, 1&3 £3.20, 2&3 £2.50 CSF £17.94 TOTE £4.40: £1.70, £1.40, £2.10; EX 15.70 Trifecta £61.10 Pool: £750.42 - 9.19 winning units..
Owner C J Bennett **Bred** Harron Eakin Farms **Trained** Dymock, Gloucs

FOCUS
All bends and run in moved out 3yds adding approximately 17yds to a 2m race. An ordinary hunters' chase in which they went an honest gallop on ground officially described as good. The form is rated through the second and the winner should win more of these.

431 PRINT STRATEGY EUROPE BEGINNERS' CHASE (16 fncs 2 omitted) 2m 7f
6:20 (6:20) (Class 4) 5-Y-0+ **£3,768** (£1,106; £553; £276)

Form RPR

44/- **1** **Double Silver**[39] 5293 6-10-7 105 .... PaddyBrennan 126+
(Fergal O'Brien) *hld up: hdwy 8th: hit 13th: led appr last: sn clr: easily* **7/1**

6/2- **2** *18* **Firm Order (IRE)**[18] 120 8-11-0 115 .... (p) WayneHutchinson 115
(Paul Webber) *chsd ldr: hmpd 3rd: led next: rdn and hdd appr last: wknd flat* **4/1**[3]

234/ **3** *20* **Italian Master (IRE)**[35] 5354 7-11-0 0 .... (t) DarylJacob 100
(Paul Nicholls) *j.rt: led to 4th: chsd ldr: rdn appr 3 out: lost 2nd next: sn wknd: t.o* **5/4**[1]

00/ **4** *8* **Caught Inthe Light**[507] 3502 8-10-11 0 .... MarkQuinlan(3) 89
(Nigel Hawke) *hld up: sme hdwy 10th: wknd next: t.o* **100/1**

P00/ **P** **Carheney River (IRE)**[31] 5440 8-11-0 0 .... LiamHeard
(Colin Heard) *prom to 9th: t.o whn p.u bef 2 out* **80/1**

0P4/ **P** **Jim Job Jones**[33] 5379 9-11-0 0 .... (t) DougieCostello
(Neil Mulholland) *sn bhd: t.o whn p.u bef 11th* **66/1**

3/5- **F** **Likearollingstone (IRE)**[22] 48 8-11-0 0 .... MarkGrant 85
(Sean Curran) *chsd ldrs tl rdn and wknd appr 3 out: t.o whn fell 2 out* **20/1**

1/3- **P** **Dance Tempo**[18] 118 6-11-0 128 ....(tp) JasonMaguire
(Kim Bailey) *chsd ldrs: lost pl 7th: sn rdn: wknd after next: t.o whn p.u bef 11th* **11/4**[2]

5m 41.8s (-6.20) **Going Correction** -0.575s/f (Firm) **8 Ran SP% 112.1**
Speed ratings: **87,80,73,71, , ,**
Tote Swingers: 1&2 £3.10, 1&3 £1.90, 2&3 £2.50 CSF £33.20 TOTE £5.30: £1.90, £2.80, £1.10; EX 31.50 Trifecta £74.10 Pool: £724.87 - 7.33 winning units..
Owner R C Mayall **Bred** Ms Linda Redmond And Mrs Mary Mayall **Trained** Coln St. Dennis, Gloucs

FOCUS
A fair staying beginners' chase in which they went an even gallop. The second fence in the home straight was omitted. The easy winner was a big improver.

432 32RED CASINO H'CAP CHASE (13 fncs 2 omitted) 2m 4f
6:50 (6:50) (Class 3) (0-130,130) 5-Y-O **£6,330** (£1,870; £935; £468; £234)

Form RPR

P5U/ **1** **Hell's Bay (FR)**[34] 5363 11-11-4 **122**..............................(p) NickScholfield 132+
(Keiran Burke) *hld up: hdwy 9th: led last: r.o wl: comf* **8/1**

420/ **2** *9* **Larks Lad (IRE)**[36] 5341 9-11-1 **119**....................................(p) APMcCoy 120
(Jonjo O'Neill) *chsd ldrs: j.lft 1st: led after 10th: hdd next: rdn and ev ch last: no ex flat* **11/2**[3]

100/ **3** *3 1/4* **Donnas Palm (IRE)**[48] 5139 9-11-12 **130**................(v[1]) RichardJohnson 127
(Tim Vaughan) *hld up: hmpd 1st: hdwy 6th: led 3 out: rdn and hdd last: no ex* **14/1**

0P6/ **4** *1* **Midnight Tuesday (FR)**[24] 12 8-10-6 **117**................(t) KieronEdgar[(7)] 113
(David Pipe) *hld up: hdwy 6th: lost pl 8th: hdwy appr 3 out: sn rdn: styd on same pce fr next* **7/2**[2]

45F/ **5** *16* **Fintan**[152] 3163 10-10-11 **118**.. JamesBest[(3)] 99
(Rob Summers) *chsd ldrs: led 6th tl after 10th: ev ch 3 out: wknd next* **20/1**

0/1- **6** *2* **Dineur (FR)**[16] 142 7-10-11 **115**..................................... DonalDevereux 94
(Peter Bowen) *chsd ldr tl led after 4th: hdd 6th: remained handy tl rdn appr 3 out: sn wknd* **5/2**[1]

PD3/ **7** *2 1/4* **Wessex King (IRE)**[34] 5363 9-11-1 **122**......................... JakeGreenall[(3)] 99
(Henry Daly) *led tl after 4th: remained handy: rdn appr 3 out: sn wknd* **10/1**

0/4- **P** **Cross Of Honour (IRE)**[21] 66 6-11-10 **128**.....................(t) NoelFehily
(Charlie Longsdon) *hld up: reminders after 4th: effrt 7th: wknd next: t.o whn p.u bef 3 out* **13/2**

4m 44.1s (-15.90) **Going Correction** -0.575s/f (Firm) **8 Ran SP% 111.1**
Speed ratings: **108,104,103,102,96 95,94,**
Tote Swingers: 1&2 £6.60, 1&3 £13.70, 2&3 £5.00 CSF £48.59 CT £586.43 TOTE £3.90: £1.10, £2.60, £4.80; EX 38.00 Trifecta £162.30 Pool: £480.03 - 2.21 winning units..
Owner A J Norman **Bred** James Patrick Kelly **Trained** Seaborough, Dorset

FOCUS
A decent handicap chase, and solid form. The easy winner was a 150+ novice chaser and this rates his best run since.

433 32RED.COM STANDARD OPEN NATIONAL HUNT FLAT RACE 2m
7:20 (7:20) (Class 6) 4-6-Y-O **£1,559** (£457; £228; £114)

Form RPR

5/ **1** **Irish Cavalier (IRE)**[39] 5287 4-10-12 0.................................. APMcCoy 115+
(Rebecca Curtis) *trckd ldrs: led on bit over 3f out: shkn up and clr fr over 1f out: easily* **2/5**[1]

0/ **2** *3 3/4* **Mountain Of Mourne (IRE)**[76] 4621 4-10-12 0................. IanPopham 101
(Linda Blackford) *prom: pushed along thrght: rdn over 3f out: wnt 2nd 1f out: no ch w wnr* **50/1**

3 *3 3/4* **Miss H Lewiss**[17] 5-10-9 0...................................... SamTwiston-Davies 96+
(Nigel Twiston-Davies) *led: hdd over 3f out: sn rdn: no ex fr over 1f out* **7/1**[3]

64/ **4** *21* **Benefitofhindsight**[29] 5475 4-10-9 0................................ MattGriffiths[(3)] 81
(Jeremy Scott) *hld up: hdwy 1/2-way: wknd over 2f out* **10/1**

5 *2 1/2* **Lennie The Laugh (IRE)**[74] 6-11-2 0...................... WayneHutchinson 81
(Martin Bosley) *hld up: wknd 6f out* **33/1**

0/- **6** *32* **Tenor De Guerre (FR)**[33] 5388 6-11-2 0.....................(t) PaddyBrennan 52
(Fergal O'Brien) *chsd ldrs over 4f out: sn wknd: t.o* **11/2**[2]

0/ **7** *52* **Hopping Hare**[41] 5263 5-11-2 0..................................... DougieCostello 5
(Neil Mulholland) *hld up: bhd fr 1/2-way: t.o* **33/1**

3m 39.8s (-1.90) **Going Correction** -0.125s/f (Good)
WFA 4 from 5yo+ 4lb **7 Ran SP% 116.2**
Speed ratings: **99,97,95,84,83 67,41**
Tote Swingers: 1&2 £0.00, 2&3 £1.10 CSF £36.78 TOTE £1.10: £1.02, £27.20; EX 43.40 Trifecta £572.90 Part won. Pool: £763.87 - 0.71 winning units..
Owner A McIver **Bred** Limetree Stud **Trained** Newport, Dyfed
■ Wotsthecatch (8-1) was withdrawn. Rule 4 applies to board prices prior to withdrawal. Deduction - 10p in the £. New market formed.

FOCUS
An ordinary bumper in which they went an even gallop. The easy winner should win more races.

434 32RED "NATIONAL HUNT" NOVICES' HURDLE (8 hdls) 2m
7:50 (7:50) (Class 4) 4-Y-O+ **£3,119** (£915; £457; £228)

Form RPR

2/2- **1** **Deep Trouble (IRE)**[18] 116 6-10-12 118............................ DarylJacob 115+
(Ben Case) *mde all: j.w: clr fr 2 out* **2/7**[1]

U/3- **2** *19* **Panache**[13] 192 8-10-9 93......................................(p) MichealNolan[(3)] 98
(Angela Clarke) *chsd wnr: rdn appr 3 out: styng on same pce whn blnd next* **9/1**[3]

00P/ **3** *35* **Ata Boy (IRE)**[395] 5527 7-10-12 0.................................... RichardJohnson 76
(Richard Phillips) *hld up: hdwy 5th: wkng whn lft 3rd next: eased fr 2 out: t.o* **18/1**

6/0- **4** *13* **Sonny Jim**[18] 116 5-10-12 0... LiamHeard 55
(John Mackie) *hld up: hdwy 4th: rdn and wknd appr 3 out: t.o* **40/1**

0/0- **5** *4* **Haveumistim**[15] 155 7-10-9 0...................................... MarkQuinlan[(3)] 51
(Bernard Llewellyn) *hld up: wknd after 4th: t.o* **100/1**

0/ **6** *15* **Whats Goin On (IRE)**[119] 3792 4-10-1 0......................... DannyBenson[(7)] 34
(Jonjo O'Neill) *chsd ldrs tl rdn and wknd appr 3 out: t.o* **14/1**

00/- **7** *33* **Vision Of Lights (IRE)**[26] 5543 8-10-12 0.................................. DPFahy 8
(Bernard Llewellyn) *hld up: rdn: wknd 4th: t.o* **33/1**

4- **F** **Bawden Rocks**[18] 116 4-10-8 0...................................... TommyPhelan
(David Bridgwater) *chsd ldrs: rdn after 5th: 5 l 3rd and wkng whn fell 3 out* **9/2**[2]

3m 41.9s (-5.40) **Going Correction** -0.125s/f (Good)
WFA 4 from 5yo+ 18lb **8 Ran SP% 124.2**
Speed ratings (Par 105): **108,98,81,74,72 65,48,**
Tote Swingers: 1&2 £14.50, 1&3 £1.60, 2&3 £4.90 CSF £5.08 TOTE £1.10: £1.02, £2.10, £3.90; EX 6.00 Trifecta £25.30 Pool: £816.98 - 13.94 winning units..
Owner Lady Jane Grosvenor **Bred** Paraig O'Rourke **Trained** Edgcote, Northants

FOCUS
A weak novice hurdle in which they went a decent gallop. The winner stood out and is rated close to his mark.

435 32REDPOKER.COM NOVICES' HURDLE (12 hdls) 2m 7f
8:20 (8:20) (Class 4) 4-Y-O+ **£3,119** (£915; £457; £228)

Form RPR

1 **Academy General (IRE)**[81] 7-10-13 0......................... TomScudamore 115+
(David Bridgwater) *mde virtually all: mstke 7th: clr fr 3 out: easily* **20/1**

F/P- **2** *18* **Mongress Boy (IRE)**[9] 265 8-10-13 105.......................... SeanQuinlan 91
(Andy Hobbs) *prom tl rdn and wknd 8th: wnt mod 2nd towards fin* **33/1**

4/1- **3** *1 1/2* **I'm The Article (IRE)**[20] 79 7-10-12 123......................... MrJBarber[(7)] 97
(Harry Fry) *chsd ldrs: ev ch whn blnd 9th: sn rdn: wknd next* **11/10**[1]

202/ **4** *2* **Sandanski (IRE)**[29] 5468 5-10-13 115...................................(t) APMcCoy 88
(Rebecca Curtis) *chsd ldrs: rdn appr 9th: wknd bef 3 out* **11/8**[2]

460/ **5** *93* **In The Binyanis (IRE)**[91] 4328 6-10-13 0..................... RichieMcLernon 4
(Jonjo O'Neill) *hld up: bhd fr 7th: t.o* **8/1**[3]

0- **6** *1 1/2* **Otto Nicolai**[13] 185 4-10-7 0.. MarkGrant
(Sean Curran) *chsd ldrs tl rdn and wknd after 7th: t.o* **100/1**

5m 44.3s (16.30) **Going Correction** -0.125s/f (Good)
WFA 4 from 5yo+ 19lb **6 Ran SP% 109.5**
Speed ratings (Par 105): **66,59,59,58,26 25**
Tote Swingers: 1&2 £4.10, 2&3 £8.80 CSF £250.86 TOTE £56.40: £15.40, £26.40; EX 123.40 Trifecta £310.40 Part won. Pool: £413.92 - 0.02 winning units..
Owner Mark Bettis **Bred** Ivor And Kieran McGrath **Trained** Icomb, Gloucs

FOCUS
A fair staying novice hurdle. There's a case for rating the form a stone+ higher but this isn't one to be confident about.

436 32REDBET.COM H'CAP HURDLE (10 hdls) 2m 4f
8:50 (8:50) (Class 5) (0-95,95) 4-Y-O+ **£1,949** (£572; £286; £143)

Form RPR

604/ **1** **Don't Be Late (IRE)**[52] 5035 5-11-12 **95**.................................. APMcCoy 111+
(Jonjo O'Neill) *hld up: hdwy appr 3 out: led and mstke last: sn clr: comf* **9/2**[3]

0/1- **2** *4* **Princesse Fleur**[10] 252 5-10-13 **82** 7ex....................... TomScudamore 87
(Michael Scudamore) *hld up: hdwy 7th: rdn after 3 out: styd on same pce flat: wnt 2nd nr fin* **12/1**

0/2- **3** *1* **Mumbles Pier (IRE)**[10] 241 8-10-12 **81**........................(vt) JamieMoore 86
(Peter Bowen) *chsd ldrs: led 2 out: sn rdn and hdd: no ex flat* **4/1**[2]

/P2- **4** *2 1/4* **Grovemere (IRE)**[10] 254 8-11-7 **90**................................(tp) TomO'Brien 92
(Debra Hamer) *a.p: pushed along 5th: rdn 3 out: styd on same pce fr next* **6/1**

10/- **5** *12* **Zelos Diktator**[23] 29 7-11-9 **92**... MarkGrant 85
(Sean Curran) *chsd ldr tl led 3rd: hdd 5th: rdn and ev ch 3 out: wknd bef last* **33/1**

4/0- **6** *9* **Taqaat (USA)**[13] 177 5-11-4 **87**.. DarylJacob 70
(Stephen Hughes) *led to 3rd: led again 5th: rdn and hdd 2 out: sn wknd* **50/1**

4/P- **7** *6* **Notcantdoit (IRE)**[8] 295 6-10-5 **77**.................................. JamesBest[(3)] 55
(Polly Gundry) *hld up: hdwy 6th: rdn and wknd bef 3 out: t.o* **50/1**

05F/ **8** *4 1/2* **Sommersturm (GER)**[9] 3797 9-10-6 **75**.......................(t) AidanColeman 54
(David Evans) *hld up: nt a fluent: reminders after 4th: nvr on terms: t.o* **10/3**[1]

000/ **9** *22* **Anton Dolin (IRE)**[134] 3559 5-11-5 **88**............................. NickScholfield 42
(Dr Richard Newland) *hld up: hdwy 7th: wknd bef next: t.o* **17/2**

0/0- **10** *2 1/4* **Oscars Law**[18] 116 6-10-11 **80**..(p) CharliePoste 32
(Matt Sheppard) *prom: blnd 7th: rdn and wknd bef next: t.o* **66/1**

0/4- **11** *30* **Shinko Moon**[13] 188 6-11-5 **88**.............................. SamTwiston-Davies 13
(Jamie Snowden) *chsd ldrs tl rdn and wknd bef 3 out: t.o* **20/1**

000/ **12** *21* **Whenever**[127] 3673 9-11-3 **86**...(v) RichardJohnson
(Richard Phillips) *in rr and sn pushed along: nt fluent 3rd and 4th: bhd fr 6th: t.o* **9/1**

4m 44.2s (-3.20) **Going Correction** -0.125s/f (Good) **12 Ran SP% 116.9**
Speed ratings (Par 103): **101,99,99,98,93 89,87,85,76,75 63,55**
Tote Swingers: 1&2 £2.80, 1&3 £2.10, 2&3 £5.10 CSF £52.41 CT £234.86 TOTE £7.50: £2.10, £3.30, £1.70; EX 61.10 Trifecta £335.00 Pool: £462.75 - 1.03 winning units..
Owner John P McManus **Bred** Seamus Boyle **Trained** Cheltenham, Gloucs

FOCUS
A moderate handicap hurdle in which they went a decent gallop. The easy winner improved to the level of his bumper form.
T/Plt: £309.60 to a £1 stake. Pool: £67,802.20 - 159.86 winning tickets. T/Qpdt: £22.60 to a £1 stake. Pool: £5,211.50 - 170.60 winning tickets. CR

437 - 443a (Foreign Racing) - See Raceform Interactive

[15]WETHERBY (L-H)
Thursday, May 23

OFFICIAL GOING: Good (7.7)
Wind: fresh 1/2 behind Weather: fine but windy and soccasional showers

444 READ HAYLEY AT RACINGUK.COM EVERY FRIDAY LADY RIDERS' H'CAP HURDLE (13 hdls) 3m 1f
2:10 (2:10) (Class 5) (0-95,95) 4-Y-O+ **£2,053** (£598; £299)

Form RPR

/52- **1** **Granwood**[12] 222 7-11-0 **90**.......................................(p) MissETodd[(7)] 102
(Tim Walford) *chsd ldrs: led after 10th: drvn out* **13/2**[1]

654/ **2** *8* **Minstalad**[33] 9-9-7 **69**... MissLSutcliffe[(7)] 74
(Karen Tutty) *chsd ldrs: kpt on to take 2nd appr 2 out: no imp* **12/1**

530/ **3** *8* **Spaceman**[70] 4762 10-10-2 **78**.................................(v) MissRachelKing[(7)] 80
(Martin Bosley) *hld up towards rr: hdwy 8th: chsd ldrs 10th: 2nd appr 3 out: one pce fr next* **18/1**

0P/- **4** *1* **Eliades Run (IRE)**[31] 5450 7-9-12 **74**.........................(b[1]) MissCWalton[(7)] 71
(Ferdy Murphy, France) *in rr: hdwy 8th: 7th 3 out: kpt on to take modest 4th next: styd on run-in* **16/1**

3/3- **5** *8* **Moon Melody (GER)**[21] 74 10-9-12 **74**..........(t) MissJoannaMason[(7)] 64
(Mike Sowersby) *prom: lost pl 3rd: hdwy 10th: kpt on one pce fr next* **14/1**

/33- **6** *1 1/2* **Solway Dornal**[8] 311 8-10-1 **77**.........................(tp) MissJRRichards[(7)] 67
(Lisa Harrison) *prom: mstke 2nd: outpcd whn hit 7th: hdwy 10th: wknd 3 out* **16/1**

P/0- **7** *18* **Bob Will (IRE)**[15] 172 8-9-12 **72**............................(p) SamanthaDrake[(5)] 44
(Chris Grant) *led tl after 1st: chsd ldrs: reminders 10th: wknd appr next* **7/1**[2]

14P/ **8** *7* **Finbin (IRE)**[46] 5206 11-10-8 **84**.................................. MissSMDoolan[(7)] 50
(Henry Hogarth) *mid-div: drvn 10th: wknd bef next* **10/1**

2/2- **9** *36* **I'Ll Be Frank**[12] 219 8-11-3 **93**..............................(t) MissKellyHarrison(7) 26
(Maurice Barnes) *rr-div: bhd whn hit 8th: t.o 3 out* **7/1**[2]
P/5- **10** *2 ½* **Phar Away Island (IRE)**[16] 163 5-10-9 **85**.............(p) MissBAndrews(7) 16
(Caroline Fryer) *hld up towards rr: hdwy 8th: wknd 10th: sn bhd: t.o* **40/1**
5/P- **11** *10* **Flag Flier**[12] 222 10-9-7 **69** oh5...............................(p) MrsFreyaBrewer(7)
(Mike Sowersby) *sn bhd: mstkes: bhd whn blnd 7th: sn t.o* **66/1**
600/ **F** **Knight Valliant**[33] 5400 10-11-5 **95**.......................... MissEButterworth(7)
(Barbara Butterworth) *sn bhd: hdwy 9th: 7th and no imp whn fell 3 out* **14/1**
053/ **P** **Carmela Maria**[71] 4743 8-11-7 **90**..................................(b) LucyAlexander
(Mike Sowersby) *in rr: bhd and reminders 7th: nvr on terms: p.u bef 2 out* **10/1**
345/ **U** **Andy Vic (IRE)**[29] 5500 10-11-1 **91**.......................... MrsJoanneBrown(7)
(Ian Brown) *chsd ldrs: led 7th: hdd after 10th: wknd next: 8th whn blnd and uns rdr last* **17/2**[3]
0/P- **P** **Yabora (FR)**[14] 178 8-11-0 **90**......................................(bt) MrsAlexDunn(7)
(Alexandra Dunn) *led after 1st: hdd 7th: wknd 9th: sn bhd: t.o whn p.u bef 3 out* **14/1**
P36/ **P** **Sun Lady (FR)**[31] 5452 7-10-5 **81**..................................... MissEYoung(7)
(Jane Walton) *mstkes: chsd ldrs: lost pl whn blnd 8th: sn bhd: t.o 3 out: p.u bef last* **50/1**
00/- **F** **Deportation**[34] 5387 6-11-0 **90**.................................(v) MissRMcDonald(7)
(John Norton) *in tch: fell 3rd* **20/1**
6m 4.4s (-12.10) **Going Correction** -0.50s/f (Good) **17** Ran SP% **122.4**
Speed ratings (Par 103): **99,96,93,93,91 90,84,82,71,70 67, , , ,**
Tote Swingers 1&2 £20.20, 2&3 £42.60, 1&3 £42.60 CSF £80.01 CT £1358.28 TOTE £5.80: £2.00, £4.40, £4.40, £4.10; EX 117.10 Trifecta £226.40 Part won. Pool: £301.87 - 0.02 winning tickets..
Owner Mrs Carol Watson **Bred** Mrs Carol Watson **Trained** Sheriff Hutton, N Yorks
■ Emma Todd's first winner under rules.

FOCUS
Shared bends for Hurdles and Chase course. A moderate staying handicap hurdle for lady riders in which they went an honest gallop. A step up from the winner under a claimer.

445 YORKSHIRE RACING SUMMER FESTIVAL 20TH - 28TH JULY (S) HURDLE (11 hdls) 2m 4f
2:45 (2:45) (Class 5) 4-Y-0+ **£2,053** (£598; £299)

Form RPR
U0F/ **1** **Stand Clear**[195] 2313 8-10-0 99.. TonyKelly(5) 89
(David Thompson) *stdd s: hld up: hmpd 6th: trcking ldrs next: led 2 out: jnd last: hld on nr fin* **11/4**[2]
1/2- **2** *hd* **Paddy Partridge**[10] 266 7-11-8 113.......................... RichardJohnson 106
(Tim Vaughan) *trckd ldrs: upsides last: jst hld* **10/3**[3]
1/2- **3** *7* **County Zen (FR)**[16] 161 10-10-11 102......................... MissBAndrews(7) 97
(Caroline Fryer) *t.k.h: led at stdy pce: increased gallop 8th: hdd next: one pce appr last* **5/1**
/34- **4** *13* **Fred Bojangals (IRE)**[9] 282 11-11-4 105.......................... BrianHughes 87
(Barbara Butterworth) *trckd ldr: narrow ld 3 out: hdd next: 4th and wkng whn blnd last* **7/1**
0PP/ **5** *67* **Bugbug N Booboo**[81] 4543 4-10-2 0.......................... CallumWhillans(5) 13
(Mike Sowersby) *t.k.h: jnd ldrs 2nd: outpcd 6th: rallied next: drvn 8th: sn lost pl: bhd whn blnd 3 out: sn hopelessly t.o* **150/1**
2/1- **F** **Milano Supremo (IRE)**[19] 110 8-11-4 115.....................(t) HenryBrooke
(Chris Grant) *trckd ldrs: fell 6th: fatally injured* **9/4**[1]
4m 59.4s (-0.10) **Going Correction** -0.50s/f (Good)
WFA 4 from 7yo+ 19lb **6** Ran SP% **110.3**
Speed ratings (Par 103): **80,79,77,71,45**
Tote Swingers 1&2 £3.10, 2&3 £2.00, 1&3 £2.90 CSF £12.04 TOTE £3.20: £1.40, £1.90; EX 11.80 Trifecta £54.60 Pool: £805.50 - 11.04 winning tickets..There was no bid for the winner.
Owner T J A Thompson **Bred** Mrs R Crank **Trained** Bolam, Co Durham

FOCUS
An ordinary selling hurdle. The winner is rated back to the best of last season's form.

446 YORKSHIRE POST LADIES EVENING - 30TH MAY NOVICES' CHASE (13 fncs) 2m
3:20 (3:21) (Class 4) 5-Y-0+ **£3,861** (£1,198; £645)

Form RPR
1/1- **1** **Jack The Gent (IRE)**[15] 167 9-11-12 132............................ BarryKeniry 128+
(George Moore) *mde all: sn 10 l clr: hit 9th: rdn between last 2: kpt on: unchal* **5/6**[1]
/10- **2** *3 ½* **Cry Of Freedom (USA)**[12] 216 7-10-12 0....................... DenisO'Regan 110
(John Ferguson) *j.rt: chsd wnr: kpt on and 6 l down 4 out: 3 l down last: no real imp* **11/8**[2]
6/U- **3** *19* **Peaks Of Fire (IRE)**[20] 90 6-11-0 105..................... SamanthaDrake(5) 100
(Joanne Foster) *a detached in last: drvn 8th: lft poor 3rd 3 out* **25/1**
0/3- **F** **Muwalla**[13] 202 6-10-12 0.. BrianHughes 100+
(Chris Grant) *racd in 3rd: 6 l down on runner-up whn fell 3 out* **14/1**[3]
3m 47.0s (-8.80) **Going Correction** -0.375s/f (Good) **4** Ran SP% **107.2**
Speed ratings: **107,105,95,**
CSF £2.39 TOTE £1.60; EX 3.00 Trifecta £10.30 Pool: £765.65 - 55.51 winning tickets..
Owner J B Wallwin **Bred** P O'Connor **Trained** Middleham Moor, N Yorks

FOCUS
A fair small-field novices' chase in which they went a decent gallop. The winner is a decent novice for the time of year and is rated to his mark.

447 WATCH RACING UK ON SKY 432 H'CAP HURDLE (8 hdls 1 omitted) 2m 110y
3:55 (3:55) (Class 3) (0-140,135) 4-Y-0+ **£5,393** (£1,583; £791; £395)

Form RPR
0/4- **1** **Knight In Purple**[21] 82 9-10-10 **122**.........................(vt) PeterCarberry(3) 130+
(John Mackie) *trckd ldrs: led appr 3 out: forged 4 l clr and hit last: drvn out* **7/2**[1]
4/0- **2** *3 ¼* **Ruler Of All (IRE)**[12] 216 7-10-9 **125**.................................. MrRWinks(7) 128
(Peter Winks) *trckd ldrs: upsides appr 3 out: 4 l down last: edgd lft and kpt on same pce* **28/1**
2/5- **3** *6* **Sud Pacifique (IRE)**[14] 176 5-11-2 **125**......................(b) JasonMaguire 123
(Donald McCain) *trckd ldrs: upsides normal 3 out: one pce bef last* **6/1**
4/1- **4** *6* **Tindaro (FR)**[11] 236 6-10-9 **118**... DenisO'Regan 112
(Paul Webber) *trckd ldrs: effrt and 4th normal 3 out: sn drvn: one pce* **5/1**
F/3- **5** *10* **Akula (IRE)**[14] 176 6-11-2 **125**.. ColinBolger 108
(Mark H Tompkins) *led tl after 3rd: outpcd and lost pl appr normal 3 out* **20/1**
421/ **6** *45* **All That Remains (IRE)**[24] 27 8-10-9 **118**.....................(t) DannyCook 61
(Brian Ellison) *w ldr: led sn after 3rd: nt fluent next: rdn after 6th: hdd bef next: sn lost pl and bhd: t.o: b.b.v* **4/1**[2]

00/ **F** **Distant Memories (IRE)**[47] 5178 7-11-2 **125**................ RichardJohnson
(Tim Vaughan) *trckd ldrs: fell 2nd: fatally injured* **9/2**[3]
245/ **B** **Changing The Guard**[36] 5356 7-11-5 **135**............(tp) ChristopherWard(7)
(Dr Richard Newland) *hld up in last: b.d 2nd* **13/2**
3m 43.4s (-12.40) **Going Correction** -0.50s/f (Good) course record **8** Ran SP% **112.9**
Speed ratings (Par 107): **109,107,104,101,97 75, ,**
Tote Swingers 1&2 £16.40, 2&3 £16.40, 1&3 £9.00 CSF £76.58 CT £565.70 TOTE £6.60: £2.20, £11.20, £1.90; EX 165.30 Trifecta £509.20 Pool: £817.87 - 1.20 winning tickets..
Owner A J Wall, G Hicks & N Hooper **Bred** Wood Farm Stud **Trained** Church Broughton , Derbys

FOCUS
A decent handicap hurdle in which the gallop was a solid one. The winner was very well in and is rated back to form.

448 WETHERBYRACING.CO.UK H'CAP CHASE (18 fncs) 3m 1f
4:30 (4:30) (Class 2) 5-Y-0+
£14,076 (£4,158; £2,079; £1,039; £519; £261)

Form RPR
11P/ **1** **Lost Glory (NZ)**[47] 5177 8-10-9 **139**.......................................(t) APMcCoy 145
(Jonjo O'Neill) *trckd ldrs: cl up 6th: led 3 out: jnd last: sn hdd: styd on to ld nr fin* **7/1**
5/1- **2** *nk* **De Boitron (FR)**[15] 170 9-10-6 **136**.. NoelFehily 141
(Ferdy Murphy, France) *hld up: trckd ldrs 14th: upsides last: sn narrow ld: hdd and no ex nr fin* **9/2**[3]
614/ **3** *3 ¾* **Pigeon Island**[29] 5496 10-10-5 **135**......................(bt) SamTwiston-Davies 139
(Nigel Twiston-Davies) *towards rr: outpcd 14th: rallied next: styd on run-in: tk 3rd nr line* **15/2**
P/4- **4** *nk* **Garleton (IRE)**[15] 170 12-10-9 **139**.............................(t) MichaelMcAlister 143
(Maurice Barnes) *led: hdd 3 out: stl cl 3rd whn hit last: kpt on same pce* **7/2**[2]
PP2/ **5** *16* **Junior**[25] 6 10-11-12 **156**...(b) ConorO'Farrell 149
(David Pipe) *chsd ldrs: reminders 6th: hrd drvn 14th: outpcd appr next: modest 5th and wl hld whn blnd bdly 2 out* **15/2**
U63/ **6** *12* **Alfie Spinner (IRE)**[110] 3984 8-10-2 **132**........................ TomScudamore 112
(Nick Williams) *nt fluent: chsd ldrs: outpcd 11th: lost pl 14th* **5/2**[1]
0/6- **7** *3 ¾* **Rolecarr (IRE)**[15] 170 10-10-0 **130**.. WilsonRenwick 104
(Ann Hamilton) *prom: pushed along 5th: lost pl 7th: bhd fr 14th* **28/1**
P/0- **8** *53* **O Crotaigh (IRE)**[13] 201 9-10-0 **130** oh9......................(b) RichieMcGrath 55
(Alan Brown) *stdd s: t.k.h: trckd ldrs 3rd: lost pl and hit 12th: mstke next: sn bhd: t.o 4 out* **80/1**
5m 51.8s (-17.60) **Going Correction** -0.375s/f (Good) **8** Ran SP% **109.7**
Speed ratings: **113,112,111,111,106 102,101,84**
Tote Swingers 1&2 £9.40, 2&3 £3.90, 1&3 £2.40 CSF £35.88 CT £224.03 TOTE £4.80: £1.30, £1.80, £2.90; EX 28.20 Trifecta £71.60 Pool: £1,457.62 - 15.25 winning tickets..
Owner John P McManus **Bred** Keltern Stud Ltd **Trained** Cheltenham, Gloucs

FOCUS
A good staying handicap chase in which they went an even gallop. Solid form, the winner running to his best.

449 WETHERBY RACECOURSE & CONFERENCE CENTRE NOVICES' HURDLE (11 hdls) 2m 4f
5:05 (5:05) (Class 4) 4-Y-0+ **£3,285** (£957; £479)

Form RPR
P/4- **1** **Loose Preformer (IRE)**[19] 115 7-10-12 117.......................... APMcCoy 120+
(David O'Meara) *chsd ldrs: pushed along 8th: hung lft and led appr 3 out: clr 2 out: nudged out* **10/3**[2]
34/ **2** *6* **Indigo Rock (IRE)**[31] 5449 7-10-12 0.................................... DannyCook 113+
(Michael Smith) *chsd ldrs: mstke 5th: kpt on to take 2nd appr last: no imp* **5/1**[3]
3 *6* **Marmas**[27] 4-10-7 0.. BrianHughes 103+
(John Mackie) *j. slowly first 2: chsd ldrs 3rd: chsd wnr 2f out: one pce* **12/1**
/21- **4** *4 ½* **Halifax (IRE)**[13] 201 5-11-5 120.......................................(v) DenisO'Regan 113
(John Ferguson) *led: drvn after 8th: hdd appr next: hung lft and wknd appr last* **5/4**[1]
45/- **5** *18* **The Wicked Kipper**[155] 3139 5-10-5 0...............................(t) IanPopham 79
(Martin Keighley) *chsd ldr: lost pl bef 3 out: modest 5th whn blnd 2 out* **15/2**
500/ **6** *4* **Have You Had Yours (IRE)**[86] 4436 7-10-5 0............. AlistairFindlay(7) 82
(Jane Walton) *chsd ldrs: lost pl 8th: sn bhd* **80/1**
34/ **7** *3 ¾* **Crooked Arrow (IRE)**[132] 3607 5-10-7 0........................(p) KyleJames(5) 78
(Marjorie Fife) *mid-div: drvn 6th: chsd ldrs next: lost pl appr 3 out: bhd whn hit 2 out* **33/1**
0/3- **8** *9* **Optical High**[21] 73 4-10-2 0.................................... JonathanEngland(5) 65
(Sue Smith) *in rr: drvn 5th: bhd fr 8th* **20/1**
00P/ **P** **Direct Approach (IRE)**[40] 5289 9-10-12 64.......................... TomSiddall
(Lynn Siddall) *in rr: bhd and reminders 5th: t.o and j.rt 7th and next: p.u bef 3 out* **100/1**
00P/ **P** **Minkie Moon (IRE)**[143] 3384 5-10-12 74.......................... RichieMcGrath
(Mark Campion) *in rr: bhd fr 6th: blnd next: sn t.o: p.u bef 3 out* **100/1**
0P/- **P** **Aliking**[25] 19 6-10-12 0.. WilsonRenwick
(Peter Niven) *j.rt: reminders after 2nd: chsd ldrs 4th: outpcd 6th: bhd fr 8th: t.o whn p.u bef next* **100/1**
4m 48.3s (-11.20) **Going Correction** -0.50s/f (Good)
WFA 4 from 5yo+ 19lb **11** Ran SP% **115.6**
Speed ratings (Par 105): **102,99,97,95,88 86,85,81, ,**
Tote Swingers 1&2 £2.50, 2&3 £7.20, 1&3 £3.40 CSF £19.41 TOTE £4.70: £2.20, £1.50, £1.50; EX 23.50 Trifecta £142.50 Pool: £1,615.29 - 8.49 winning tickets..
Owner Middleham Park Racing LXIV **Bred** Clare A Kehoe **Trained** Nawton, N Yorks

FOCUS
A fair novices' hurdle in which they went a solid gallop. The winner is rated 140 at best over fences and there may be more to come. The fifth to seventh help with the level.

450 BOOK YORKSHIRE POST LADIES EVENING HOSPITALITY MARES' MAIDEN HURDLE (9 hdls) 2m 110y
5:40 (5:40) (Class 5) 4-Y-0+ **£2,053** (£598; £299)

Form RPR
4/2- **1** **Luci Di Mezzanotte**[21] 85 5-11-0 0.............................. LeightonAspell 106+
(Oliver Sherwood) *trckd ldrs: 2nd 3 out: upsides appr last: drvn clr* **4/1**[2]
3/3- **2** *5* **Definitely Glad (IRE)**[19] 116 6-11-0 0.............................. DenisO'Regan 102
(Paul Webber) *chsd ldr: led appr 3 out: hdd appr last: kpt on same pce* **6/1**
220/ **3** *11* **Dubaianswer**[26] 5567 5-10-11 103.................................. BrianToomey(3) 91
(Tony Coyle) *hld up towards rr: stdy hdwy and modest 4th whn hit 3 out: kpt on to take modest 3rd last* **7/1**

00/ **4** *4 ½* **Flew The Nest (IRE)**[54] 5025 5-11-0 0 APMcCoy 88
(Jonjo O'Neill) *trckd ldrs: wnt 2nd appr 3 out: outpcd 2 out: lost 3rd and j.lft last: wknd* **15/2**

0/6- **5** *1 ¾* **Silver Sophfire**[12] 218 7-10-9 0 JonathanEngland[(5)] 86
(Sue Smith) *chsd ldrs: lost pl 5th: kpt on fr 3 out: 5th 2 out: styd on run-in* **33/1**

00/ **6** *25* **Arisda**[173] 2783 5-11-0 0 DannyCook 63
(Brian Ellison) *mid-div: drvn 6th: sn lost pl and bhd: t.o* **66/1**

2U2/ **7** *½* **Pollystone (IRE)**[25] 1 7-11-0 0 IanPopham 63
(Martin Keighley) *led: clr 3rd to 6th: hdd appr 3 out: hung lft and sn wknd: t.o* **9/2**[3]

2PP/ **8** *29* **Buxom (IRE)**[37] 5339 6-11-0 112 BrendanPowell 36
(Jamie Snowden) *chsd ldrs: pushed along 5th: reminders and outpcd next: lost pl appr 3 out: bhd whn eased between last 2: virtually p.u: t.o* **5/2**[1]

U/ **P** **Royal Gig**[108] 3587 4-10-5 0 KyleJames[(5)]
(Tim Etherington) *in rr: hdwy 4th: lost pl bef 6th: sn bhd: t.o whn p.u bef next* **100/1**

F **David's Folly (IRE)**[48] 4-10-10 0 RichardJohnson
(Tim Vaughan) *hld up in rr: hdwy whn fell 4th: fatally injured* **25/1**

30/ **U** **Captive Moment**[188] 2463 7-10-7 0 MrRSmith[(7)]
(John Norton) *last whn blnd and rdr lost iron 1st: t.o whn j. slowly: wnt rt and uns rdr 2nd* **66/1**

00P/ **P** **Watchmego**[27] 5544 5-11-0 0 (t) MichaelMcAlister
(Maurice Barnes) *in rr: j. violently lft 1st: bhd fr 3rd: t.o 6th: p.u bef next* **100/1**

3m 50.0s (-5.80) **Going Correction** -0.50s/f (Good)
WFA 4 from 5yo+ 18lb 12 Ran SP% **117.1**
Speed ratings (Par 103): **112,109,104,102,101 89,89,75,, ,**
Tote Swingers 1&2 £5.90, 2&3 £7.60, 1&3 £6.40 CSF £27.05 TOTE £3.90: £1.40, £2.00, £2.80; EX 21.30 Trifecta £109.50 Pool: £1,370.44 - 9.38 winning tickets..
Owner P K Gardner **Bred** Springcombe Park Stud **Trained** Upper Lambourn, Berks

FOCUS
A fair mares' maiden hurdle in which there was no hanging about. Ordinary form, the first two rated in line with their bumper marks.
T/Plt: £871.30 to a £1 stake. Pool: £63,416.89 - 53.13 winning tickets. T/Qpdt: £44.20 to a £1 stake. Pool: £4,280.90 - 71.6 winning tickets. WG

451 - 453a (Foreign Racing) - See Raceform Interactive

403 AUTEUIL (L-H)
Thursday, May 23

OFFICIAL GOING: Turf: heavy

454a PRIX JASMIN II (CHASE) (CONDITIONS) (5YO NON-THOROUGHBREDS) (TURF) 2m 5f 110y
1:20 (12:00) 5-Y-0 **£21,463** (£10,731; £6,260; £4,247; £2,012)

RPR

1 **Sizing France (FR)**[18] 5-10-12 0 JacquesRicou 119
(J Bertran De Balanda, France) **13/5**[1]

2 *¾* **Unique D'Ainay (FR)**[13] 263 5-10-6 0 RegisSchmidlin 112
(F-M Cottin, France) **23/1**

3 *1 ¼* **Upsala Collonges (FR)**[32] 5-11-0 0 CyrilleGombeau 119
(G Cherel, France) **9/2**[2]

4 *6* **Ucocotte (FR)**[54] 5-10-6 0 KevinNabet 105
(Guy Denuault, France) **18/1**

5 *3* **Unzing (FR)**[107] 4055 5-10-3 0 BenoitGicquel 99
(F Nicolle, France) **32/5**

6 *1* **Under (FR)**[32] 5-10-7 0 ow1 JonathanPlouganou 102
(F-M Cottin, France) **11/1**

7 *dist* **Un Ami (FR)**[14] 198 5-10-6 0 ow3 JamesReveley
(Nick Williams) *towards rr and t.k.h: in midfield fr 3rd: cl 4th and ev ch 3 out: lost pl on run to 2 out: sn rdn and nt qckn: wknd appr last* **31/1**

8 *dist* **Ulrick (FR)**[14] 198 5-10-3 0 ChristopheDubourg
(C Dubourg, France) **46/1**

P **Up To (FR)**[32] 5-10-3 0 LudovicSolignac
(T Poche, France) **108/1**

F **Ultranet (FR)**[57] 5-10-6 0 (b) RaphaelDelozier
(G Chaignon, France) **20/1**

P **Un Anjou (FR)**[32] 5-10-10 0 PACarberry
(F-M Cottin, France) **14/1**

P **Unrykikipeu (FR)** 5-10-10 0 NoamChevalier
(J Thibault, France) **19/1**

F **Ulex (FR)**[74] 5-10-8 0 HubertTerrien
(Alain Couetil, France) **23/5**[3]

5m 48.52s (1.52) 13 Ran SP% **117.7**
PARI-MUTUEL (all including 1 euro stakes): WIN 3.60; PLACE 1.90, 4.80, 2.30; DF 40.20; SF 52.90.
Owner Alan Potts **Bred** M C Pipe **Trained** France

455a PRIX MELINOIR (HURDLE) (CONDITIONS) (5YO+) (TURF) 2m 2f
3:25 (12:00) 5-Y-0+ **£18,731** (£9,365; £5,463; £3,707; £1,756)

RPR

1 **La Segnora (FR)**[390] 7-10-6 0 JacquesRicou 134
(R Le Gal, France) **17/5**[1]

2 *10* **St Nicolas D'Acy (FR)**[625] 7-10-8 0 CyrilleGombeau 126
(Robert Collet, France) **8/1**

3 *3* **Catch One (FR)**[215] 1940 5-10-10 0 ErvanChazelle 125
(Mlle T Puitg, France) **56/10**[2]

4 *5* **President Jose (FR)**[565] 2349 7-10-8 0 LudovicPhilipperon 118
(Robert Collet, France) **12/1**

5 *3 ½* **Carlain (FR)**[215] 1940 5-10-10 0 (p) SylvainDehez 117
(C Aubert, France) **56/10**[2]

6 *1* **Veinard De Ballon (FR)**[179] 5-10-3 0 KevinNabet 109
(D Retif, France) **50/1**

7 *2* **Lamool (GER)**[34] 5399 6-10-12 0 AnthonyLecordier 116
(F-X De Chevigny, France) **10/1**

8 *1 ¼* **Katnap (FR)**[34] 5397 6-10-8 0 MarcLamazou-Laresse 110
(D Sourdeau De Beauregard, France) **51/1**

9 *2 ½* **Dongarry (FR)**[186] 6-11-3 0 FabienDehez 117
(B Jollivet, France) **43/1**

10 *4* **Magic Guest (FR)**[34] 5399 5-9-13 0 JulienCarayon[(4)] 99
(B Jollivet, France) **101/1**

0 **Tip Dancer (FR)**[737] 7-10-3 0 YohannBourgois[(5)]
(Robert Collet, France) **45/1**

0 **Singapore Sky (FR)**[564] 2371 6-10-8 0 JeremyDaSilva
(Yannick Fouin, France) **31/1**

P **Tenacious Spring (FR)**[23] 6-11-3 0 GaetanOlivier
(F Nicolle, France) **36/5**[3]

P **Danser Encore (FR)**[51] 5-10-9 0 ow3 (p) FabriceBarrao
(Mlle I Gallorini, France) **31/1**

P **Up And Go Banbou (FR)**[371] 331 5-10-3 0 StephanePaillard
(Mme V Seignoux, France) **59/1**

P **Un Bon P'Tit Gars (FR)**[105] 4084 5-10-6 0 ow3 JamesReveley
(Nick Williams) *settled in midfield: toward rr fr 4th: bhd and reminders after 4 out: t.o whn p.u bef 2 out* **16/1**

P **Torrento City (FR)** 6-10-8 0 BertrandBourez
(Y-M Porzier, France) **63/1**

4m 32.14s (272.14) 17 Ran SP% **117.8**
PARI-MUTUEL (all including 1 euro stakes): WIN 4.40; PLACE 2.20, 3.10, 2.20; DF 19.40; SF 30.80.
Owner Paul Sebag **Bred** G Vitse & Mlle C Laignel Porin **Trained** France

417 TOWCESTER (R-H)
Friday, May 24

OFFICIAL GOING: Good to soft (9.8)
Wind: Strong; behind Weather: Showers

456 GLAZERITE WINDOWS LTD NORTH WEST DIVISION H'CAP HURDLE (8 hdls) 2m
5:55 (5:56) (Class 5) (0-100,100) 4-Y-0+ **£1,949** (£572; £286; £143)

Form RPR

/22- **1** **Ullswater (IRE)**[12] 243 5-11-4 **92** (t) NickScholfield 102+
(Andy Turnell) *hld up: hdwy 3 out: chsd ldr and hit next: rdn to ld last: styd on wl* **11/4**[2]

51P/ **2** *2 ¼* **Prime Contender**[1735] 1250 11-11-12 **100** (v[1]) SamThomas 108+
(Jennie Candlish) *chsd ldr tl led 5th: rdn: hdd and hit last: styd on same pce flat* **33/1**

0/5- **3** *5* **Red Whisper**[15] 193 9-10-8 **85** (t) JamesBest[(3)] 87
(Rob Summers) *chsd ldrs: rdn appr 2 out: no ex last* **8/1**

050/ **4** *7* **Spinning Waters**[21] 5538 7-11-3 **94** (p) RobertDunne[(3)] 89
(Dai Burchell) *prom: rdn after 3 out: wknd bef next* **16/1**

522- **5** *1 ¼* **Bob Lewis**[3] 421 7-10-7 **86** (t) JamesBanks[(5)] 81
(Anthony Middleton) *sn pushed along in rr: nvr on terms* **7/4**[1]

P/2- **6** *25* **Exiles Return (IRE)**[24] 37 11-10-5 **82** MarkQuinlan[(3)] 51
(Jacqueline Retter) *led to 5th: hit 3 out: sn rdn and wknd: t.o* **25/1**

4/5- **7** *3 ½* **Meridiem**[11] 264 9-11-5 **93** (t) TomScudamore 58
(Caroline Fryer) *hld up: a in rr: bhd fr 4th: t.o* **11/2**[3]

003/ **8** *½* **Numen (IRE)**[11] 4739 9-11-12 **100** APMcCoy 65
(Barry Brennan) *chsd ldrs tl wknd 3 out: t.o* **12/1**

00/- **P** **Compassion**[115] 3925 5-10-7 **81** (v) DominicElsworth
(Emma Lavelle) *hld up: wknd 4th: t.o whn p.u bef 2 out* **25/1**

3m 48.0s (-19.90) **Going Correction** -1.175s/f (Hard) 9 Ran SP% **113.7**
Speed ratings (Par 103): **102,100,98,94,94 81,80,79,**
toteswingers 1&2 £5.50, 1&3 £3.60, 2&3 £20.20 CSF £83.93 CT £648.23 TOTE £3.70: £1.20, £7.70, £2.30; EX 70.10 Trifecta £906.60 Pool: £1,278.37 - 1.05 winning units..
Owner The Jumping Stars **Bred** J P Dwan **Trained** Broad Hinton, Wilts

FOCUS
Hurdles course on inside line. A wet and windy night. The going was changed to good to soft before this modest handicap. Winning jockey Nick Scholfield reported that the ground was riding close to soft. The winner is on the upgrade and can probably win again.

457 GLAZERITE WINDOWS LTD H'CAP CHASE (14 fncs) 2m 3f 110y
6:25 (6:25) (Class 4) (0-115,115) 5-Y-0+ **£3,768** (£1,106; £553; £276)

Form RPR

3P0/ **1** **Papradon**[87] 4442 9-10-13 **102** (b) SamTwiston-Davies 108
(Nigel Twiston-Davies) *mde all: rdn appr last: styd on u.p* **4/1**[2]

055/ **2** *3 ¾* **Autumm Spirit**[27] 5568 9-11-2 **105** (t) CharliePoste 107
(Robin Dickin) *chsd wnr: ev ch 3 out: sn rdn: styd on same pce flat* **16/1**

23/- **3** *9* **Henry San (IRE)**[43] 5258 6-11-12 **115** WayneHutchinson 110
(Alan King) *prom: nt fluent 1st: mstke 5th: pushed along 9th: rdn appr 2 out: wknd flat* **8/11**[1]

P05/ **4** *11* **Best Lover (FR)**[33] 5439 11-10-13 **107** EdCookson[(5)] 89
(Laura Hurley) *prom: pushed along 9th: rdn and wknd 2 out* **6/1**[3]

P/4- **5** *3 ½* **Accordingtopalm (IRE)**[18] 143 7-11-7 **110** (t) PaulMoloney 89
(David Rees) *hld up: a in rr: rdn and wknd after 3 out* **8/1**

5m 0.3s (-17.90) **Going Correction** -1.00s/f (Hard) 5 Ran SP% **109.2**
Speed ratings: **95,93,89,85,84**
CSF £42.18 TOTE £4.00: £2.00, £3.70; EX 34.70 Trifecta £94.80 Pool: £1,049.54 - 8.30 winning units..
Owner A J Cresser **Bred** B Whitehouse **Trained** Naunton, Gloucs

FOCUS
There was gutsy front-running winner of this small-field handicap. He is rated back to his best 2012 form.

458 KJM GROUP ANDOVER "NATIONAL HUNT" NOVICES' HURDLE (8 hdls) 2m
6:55 (6:55) (Class 4) 4-Y-0+ **£3,119** (£915; £457; £228)

Form RPR

10/ **1** **Tistory (FR)**[48] 5179 6-10-12 0 APMcCoy 120+
(Nicky Henderson) *chsd clr ldr tl tk clsr order 3rd: led 5th: hit 3 out: easily* **2/11**[1]

43/- **2** *3 ½* **Never Says Never**[113] 3961 5-10-12 0 AndrewGlassonbury 106
(Bob Buckler) *hld up: hdwy 5th: sn chsng wnr: rdn after 3 out: styng on same pce whn hit last* **11/2**[2]

04/- **3** *28* **Midnight Thomas**[129] 3677 4-10-8 0 (t) IanPopham 77
(Martin Keighley) *j.lft 1st: sn bhd: hdwy 5th: rdn and wknd appr 2 out: t.o* **25/1**[3]

/00- **4** *32* **Lucette**[10] 292 5-10-5 0 NickScholfield 39
(Kim Bailey) *led: plld hrd and sn clr: j.lft: c bk to the field 3rd: hung lft bef next: hdd 5th: sn wknd: t.o* **40/1**

3m 53.7s (-14.20) **Going Correction** -1.175s/f (Hard)
WFA 4 from 5yo+ 18lb 4 Ran SP% **106.3**
Speed ratings (Par 105): **88,86,72,56**
CSF £1.62 TOTE £1.10; EX 1.70 Trifecta £2.20 Pool: £748.17 - 254.07 winning units..
Owner Mrs Judy Wilson **Bred** Gerard Ferte **Trained** Upper Lambourn, Berks

The Form Book Jumps, Raceform Ltd, Compton, RG20 6NL.

FOCUS
The hot favourite had no trouble taking advantage of a golden opportunity in this novice hurdle. He's the type to rate higher.

459 TEMPLE GLAZING PRODUCTS LTD ALERTS MAIDEN CHASE (14 fncs) 2m 3f 110y
7:25 (7:25) (Class 5) 5-Y-0+ **£2,196** (£682; £367)

Form RPR
530/ **1** **Catch Tammy (IRE)**[302] 1088 7-11-0 0 .... PaddyBrennan 109
(Tom George) *led to 3rd: led 4th to 8th: rdn to ld appr last: hung lft flat: styd on* **13/8[1]**
2 *2 ¼* **High Ron**[363] 8-11-0 0 .... AndrewThornton 108
(Caroline Bailey) *chsd wnr tl led 3rd to next: led again 8th: rdn and hdd whn mstke last: styd on same pce flat* **12/1**
4/4- **3** *76* **Conigre**[12] 253 6-11-0 0 .... (tp) BrendanPowell 31
(Brendan Powell) *hld up: nt fluent: hdwy 6th: outpcd 8th: sme hdwy 3 out: sn rdn and wknd: t.o whn blnd next* **7/4[2]**
P **Coin River (IRE)**[33] 7-11-0 0 .... (t) AndrewGlassonbury
(Bob Buckler) *prom: blnd 6th: sn bhd: hit next: sn p.u* **10/3[3]**
4m 59.5s (-18.70) **Going Correction** -1.00s/f (Hard) 4 Ran SP% **105.2**
Speed ratings: **97,96,65,**
CSF £13.61 TOTE £2.10; EX 10.30 Trifecta £42.30 Pool: £306.49 - 5.42 winning units..
Owner R S Brookhouse **Bred** J A Wilson **Trained** Slad, Gloucs

FOCUS
The first two had a decent battle in this small-field maiden chase. The form could be rated higher.

460 GLAZERITE WINDOWS LTD H'CAP HURDLE (12 hdls) 3m
7:55 (7:55) (Class 5) (0-100,100) 4-Y-0+ **£1,949** (£572; £286; £143)

Form RPR
604/ **1** **Halucha (IRE)**[27] 5570 8-10-13 **90** .... (p) JakeGreenall(3) 99+
(Paul Webber) *chsd ldrs: led appr 3 out: clr next: mstke last: comf* **7/1**
4/6- **2** *6* **Music In The Air**[23] 71 9-10-0 **74** .... (p) CharliePoste 77
(Robin Dickin) *a.p: rdn to chse wnr appr 2 out: no imp whn hit last* **20/1**
5/P- **3** *7* **Brunette'Sonly (IRE)**[3] 420 8-11-2 **90** .... AndrewThornton 88
(Seamus Mullins) *chsd ldr 2nd tl led after 6th: nt fluent 8th: hdd appr 3 out: rdn and wknd bef last* **10/1**
4/4- **4** *1* **Little Carmela**[9] 320 9-11-12 **100** .... (tp) WillKennedy 95
(Violet M Jordan) *hld up: hdwy 7th: rdn after 9th: wknd 2 out* **20/1**
0/6- **5** *4* **Current Climate (IRE)**[21] 100 9-11-5 **93** .... (b) PaddyBrennan 84
(Richard Rowe) *hld up: rdn after 3 out: hung rt after next: n.d* **25/1**
0/1- **6** *8* **Marico (FR)**[12] 241 5-10-9 **83** 7ex .... (p) FelixDeGiles 66
(Tom Symonds) *hld up: hdwy 3 out: rdn and wkng whn mstke next* **3/1[1]**
303/ **7** *3 ¼* **Lombardy Boy (IRE)**[25] 29 8-11-4 **92** .... (p) AlexMerriam 72
(Michael Banks) *hld up: hdwy 7th: rdn and wknd after 3 out* **11/2[3]**
/45- **8** *½* **Westwire Toby (IRE)**[13] 221 11-10-0 **74** oh8 .... TomSiddall 53
(Lynn Siddall) *led tl after 1st: hit next: remained handy: rdn after 7th: wknd appr 3 out* **50/1**
5/0- **9** *8* **Dancing Teasel**[10] 293 6-11-4 **92** .... (p) DominicElsworth 63
(Emma Lavelle) *led after 1st: hit 6th: sn hdd: wknd after 3 out: hmpd after next: t.o* **20/1**
15P/ **10** *5* **The Wee Midget**[229] 1756 8-11-7 **95** .... NickScholfield 61
(Arthur Whiting) *mid-div: hdwy 4th: rdn and wknd after 3 out: hmpd afgter next: t.o* **20/1**
/04- **11** *20* **Thefriendlygremlin**[3] 417 5-10-2 **81** .... (p) GavinSheehan(5) 27
(John Upson) *hld up: hdwy u.p appr 3 out: sn wknd: t.o* **17/2**
000/ **12** *54* **Dreamsoftheatre (IRE)**[111] 3982 5-11-11 **99** .... APMcCoy
(Jonjo O'Neill) *hld up: hdwy 9th: rdn and wknd 3 out: t.o* **4/1[2]**
5m 59.8s (-15.20) **Going Correction** -1.175s/f (Hard) 12 Ran SP% **120.3**
Speed ratings (Par 103): **78,76,73,73,72 69,68,68,65,63 57,39**
toteswingers 1&2 £16.20, 1&3 £11.00, 2&3 £7.40 CSF £139.15 CT £1408.93 TOTE £8.20: £3.00, £6.40, £4.10; EX 182.20 Trifecta £338.60 Part won. Pool: £451.48 - 0.08 winning units..
Owner R W Barnett **Bred** Mrs Mai O'Sullivan **Trained** Mollington, Oxon

FOCUS
There was an emphatic winner of this modest handicap and not many got involved from off the pace. The winner had slipped to a good mark.

461 NETWORK VEKA LTD H'CAP CHASE (18 fncs) 3m 110y
8:25 (8:25) (Class 5) (0-100,99) 5-Y-0+ **£2,599** (£763; £381; £190)

Form RPR
016/ **1** **My Mate Vinnie (IRE)**[237] 1675 6-11-10 **97** .... (t) APMcCoy 109+
(Jonjo O'Neill) *hld up: hdwy 11th: rdn to ld last: styd on wl* **4/1[1]**
F32/ **2** *3 ¾* **Timpo (FR)**[28] 5542 10-11-8 **95** .... (p) RichardJohnson 101
(Henry Daly) *led to 9th: chsd ldr tl led again 15th: rdn and hdd last: styd on same pce* **5/1[2]**
56P/ **3** *3 ½* **The Vicar (IRE)**[53] 10-11-11 **98** .... PaulMoloney 101
(David Rees) *chsd ldrs: j.rt 3rd: led 9th to next: outpcd 15th: rallied appr 2 out: no ex last* **6/1[3]**
33P/ **4** *5* **Pliny (IRE)**[42] 5270 0 10 3 **76** .... (vt) TomO'Brien 70
(Peter Bowen) *chsd ldrs: hmpd 3rd: rdn after 3 out: nt fluent last: wknd flat* **5/1[2]**
1/2- **5** *14* **Might As Well**[21] 100 10-11-1 **88** .... (p) AndrewThornton 77
(Seamus Mullins) *chsd ldr: led 10th to 15th: rdn and wknd after 2 out* **12/1**
626/ **6** *5* **Lupita (IRE)**[33] 5431 9-10-0 **73** oh5 .... (t) BrendanPowell 51
(Derrick Scott) *hld up: hdwy 11th: wknd 3 out: t.o* **33/1**
0P3/ **7** *1* **Roseneath (IRE)**[26] 7 9-11-12 **99** .... (p) DarylJacob 76
(Alex Hales) *prom tl rdn and wknd appr 2 out: t.o* **12/1**
0PP/ **8** *8* **Atherstone Hill (IRE)**[25] 32 11-11-5 **92** .... (v) CharliePoste 66
(Robin Dickin) *in rr whn hmpd 1st: hdwy 3rd: rdn and wknd appr 2 out: t.o* **33/1**
605/ **9** *14* **Notabotheronme (IRE)**[81] 4564 11-10-12 **88** .... (p) RobertDunne(3) 43
(Dai Burchell) *hld up: bhd frokm 10th: t.o* **16/1**
4/1- **P** **Top Benefit (IRE)**[21] 100 11-10-11 **89** .... JamesBanks(5)
(Richard Harper) *mid-div: rdn and wknd 11th: t.o whn p.u bef 2 out* **14/1**
001/ **P** **Ide No Idea (IRE)**[26] 9-10-4 **84** .... (b) MissBAndrews(7)
(Caroline Fryer) *prom whn blnd 1st: sn lost pl: lost tch 11th: t.o whn p.u bef 15th* **6/1[3]**
UP0/ **U** **Best Bette**[35] 5375 8-10-2 **82** .... MrLKilgarriff(7)
(Clarissa Caroe) *bhd fr 4th: t.o whn blnd and uns rdr 12th* **80/1**
6m 10.3s (-26.60) **Going Correction** -1.00s/f (Hard) 12 Ran SP% **117.0**
Speed ratings: **102,100,99,98,93 92,91,89,84, ,**
toteswingers 1&2 £8.80, 1&3 £17.50, 2&3 £13.90 CSF £24.40 CT £119.46 TOTE £4.80: £1.50, £2.40, £3.30; EX 22.10 Trifecta £388.60 Part won. Pool: £518.15 - 0.75 winning units..
Owner G & P Barker Ltd/globe Engineering **Bred** Christoph Amerian **Trained** Cheltenham, Gloucs

FOCUS
The four market leaders filled the first four positions in this minor handicap and the form looks solid. The winner improved towards the level of his best hurdle form.

462 GLAZERITE WINDOWS LTD SOUTH WEST & WALES MARES' INTERMEDIATE OPEN NH FLAT RACE 2m
8:55 (8:55) (Class 6) 4-6-Y-0 **£1,642** (£478; £239)

Form RPR
1 **Reves D'Amour (IRE)**[20] 4-10-7 0 .... MrJoshuaNewman(7) 92
(Polly Gundry) *trckd ldrs: racd keenly: led over 7f out: rdn clr fr over 2f out* **5/1[3]**
0/ **2** *2* **Barrs Lane**[30] 5511 5-11-4 0 .... NickScholfield 94
(Arthur Whiting) *led 2f: chsd ldrs: pushed along 9f out: outpcd over 3f out: rallied over 1f out: r.o to go 2nd wl ins fnl f: nt trble wnr:* **40/1**
04/ **3** *3* **Indiefront**[48] 5187 4-11-0 0 .... RichieMcLernon 87
(Jo Davis) *hld up: racd keenly: hdwy over 4f out: rdn over 2f out: styd on same pce fnl f* **16/1**
4/5- **4** *nk* **Oscar's Pet (IRE)**[15] 187 5-11-4 0 .... FelixDeGiles 91
(Tom Symonds) *chsd ldr: led after 2f: hdd over 7f out: rdn over 2f out: styd on same pce fnl f* **10/3[2]**
5/ **5** *nk* **Lacunae (IRE)**[25] 35 5-11-4 0 .... RyanMahon 91
(Seamus Mullins) *a.p: rdn over 3f out: styd on same pce fnl f* **5/1[3]**
6 *2* **High Holloa** 4-11-0 0 .... AndrewThornton 85
(Caroline Bailey) *hld up: sme hdwy over 2f out: rdn and hung lft fnl f: n.d* **16/1**
04/ **7** *1* **Unefille De Guye (FR)**[25] 35 5-10-11 0 .... ConorShoemark(7) 88
(Victor Dartnall) *hld up: hdwy 1/2-way: rdn over 2f out: wknd ins fnl f* **5/1[3]**
8 *4* **Viking Mistress** 5-11-4 0 .... IanPopham 84
(Martin Keighley) *hld up: hdwy over 4f out: wknd 2f out* **3/1[1]**
9 *3 ½* **Too Trigger Happy** 4-10-11 0 .... WayneKavanagh(3) 76
(Dr Jeremy Naylor) *hld up: plld hrd: a in rr: wknd 3f out* **66/1**
0- **10** *14* **Jacqueline Hyde**[12] 239 4-11-0 0 .... ColinBolger 62
(Nigel Dunger) *prom: rdn over 5f out: wknd over 3f out: t.o* **100/1**
3m 55.1s (-7.20) **Going Correction** -1.175s/f (Hard)
WFA 4 from 5yo 4lb 10 Ran SP% **114.8**
Speed ratings: **71,70,68,68,68 67,66,64,62,55**
toteswingers 1&2 £12.70, 1&3 £12.70, 2&3 £12.70 CSF £174.26 TOTE £7.20: £2.70, £9.50, £3.90; EX 276.30 Trifecta £152.20 Part won. Pool: £203.04 - 0.02 winning units..
Owner Miss Polly Gundry **Bred** Paul Keane **Trained** Ottery St Mary, Devon

FOCUS
A modest mares' bumper which was run at just a fair pace. The form is rated around the third to fifth.
T/Plt: £473.70 to a £1 stake. Pool: £75,210.08 - 115.89 winning units T/Qpdt: £27.80 to a £1 stake. Pool: £6,161.16 - 163.50 winning units CR

463 - 469a (Foreign Racing) - See Raceform Interactive

CARTMEL (L-H)
Saturday, May 25

OFFICIAL GOING: Good to firm (good in places; 7.9)
Wind: light 1/2 against Weather: fine and sunny

470 STICKY TOFFEE PUDDING NOVICES' HURDLE (11 hdls) 2m 6f
5:55 (5:55) (Class 4) 4-Y-0+ **£3,249** (£954; £477; £238)

Form RPR
5/0- **1** **General Hardi**[17] 169 12-10-12 0 .... BrianHughes 108
(John Wade) *chsd wnr: drvn 8th: rallied sn after last: styd on to ld post* **18/1**
1/1- **2** *nse* **Tick Tocker (IRE)**[22] 91 5-11-5 118 .... JasonMaguire 115
(Donald McCain) *led: rdn appr 2 out: kpt on: hdd last stride* **4/9[1]**
0/ **3** *2 ¼* **Antirrhinum**[31] 5499 6-10-7 0 .... TonyKelly(5) 106
(Ferdy Murphy, France) *in rr: drvn to chse ldrs 6th: outpcd between last 2: styd on last 150yds: tk 3rd nr fin* **50/1**
4 *1 ¾* **Twill Stand To Us (IRE)**[19] 6-10-12 0 .... DannyCook 106
(Brian Ellison) *j.rt 1st: chsd ldrs 6th: wnt 2nd between last 2: one pce* **3/1[2]**
5/6- **5** *7* **Alpha One (IRE)**[6] 387 7-10-12 0 .... DenisO'Regan 98
(Chris Grant) *chsd ldrs: drvn 8th: outpcd and lost pl between last 2* **12/1[3]**
6/3- **6** *71* **Monbeg (IRE)**[9] 339 6-10-12 0 .... WilsonRenwick 26
(Martin Todhunter) *prom: lost pl 7th: t.o 3 out: eventually completed* **28/1**
5m 14.9s (-14.40) **Going Correction** -0.70s/f (Firm) 6 Ran SP% **112.6**
Speed ratings (Par 105): **98,97,97,96,93 68**
toteswingers 1&2 £2.40, 1&3 £19.00, 2&3 £7.10 CSF £28.49 TOTE £14.80: £3.80, £1.10; EX 30.70 Trifecta £254.90 Pool: £1395.62 - 4.10 winning units..
Owner John Wade **Bred** Mrs A Yearley **Trained** Mordon, Co Durham

FOCUS
A dry night and warm day saw the ground change to good to firm, good in places. Brian Hughes stated: "It's beautiful ground and just on the quick side." An uncompetitive event in which an ordinary gallop increased from the third-last hurdle. There's a case for rating the form up to 8lb higher.

471 FURNESS BUILDING SOCIETY (S) H'CAP HURDLE (FOR THE ANDREA ROBINSON TROPHY) (11 hdls) 2m 6f
6:25 (6:25) (Class 5) (0-95,95) 4-Y-0+ **£2,599** (£763; £381; £190)

Form RPR
5/0- **1** **The Good Guy (IRE)**[16] 178 10-11-12 **95** .... WayneHutchinson 104
(Graeme McPherson) *trckd ldrs: led 2 out: drvn rt out* **16/1**
646/ **2** *1 ¼* **Worth A King'S**[110] 4031 7-10-12 **81** .... (p) RichieMcGrath 89
(Philip Kirby) *trckd ldrs: chsd wnr 2 out: kpt on run-in: a jst hld* **2/1[1]**
003/ **3** *8* **Executive's Hall (IRE)**[27] 17 9-11-3 **86** .... (p) DougieCostello 88
(Ben Haslam) *hld up in rr: hdwy 6th: modest 4th whn hmpd last: kpt on same pce* **3/1[2]**
0/4- **4** *8* **Border Tale**[14] 219 13-10-13 **82** .... (v) BrianHughes 74
(James Moffatt) *chsd ldrs: outpcd 7th: kpt on fr 3 out: tk modest 4th nr fin* **25/1**
5/P- **5** *nk* **Teerie Express**[14] 222 12-11-2 **92** .... JonathonBewley(7) 84
(George Bewley) *chsd ldrs: drvn 6th: one pce fr 3 out* **33/1**
30/ **6** *3* **Fast Exit (IRE)**[215] 1961 6-11-7 **95** .... (t) DerekFox(5) 84
(Noel C Kelly, Ire) *in rr: hdwy 8th: kpt on one pce fr 2 out* **7/1[3]**
/U5- **7** *4 ½* **Cara Court (IRE)**[15] 206 7-11-6 **94** .... (p) SamanthaDrake(5) 82
(Joanne Foster) *chsd ldr: led after 6th: hdd 2 out: 4th and wkng whn j.rt and mstke last* **9/1**
02P/ **8** *hd* **Rare Coincidence**[12] 21 12-11-6 **89** .... (t) BrianHarding 73
(Alan Berry) *led tl after 6th: wknd appr 2 out* **16/1**
0/4- **9** *5* **Charlie Bucket**[14] 221 10-10-12 **86** .... CallumWhillans(5) 65
(Donald Whillans) *in rr: drvn 3rd: nvr on terms* **14/1**

P/0- **10** 6 **Yourlookinathim (IRE)**[10] 310 7-11-2 **85**.................(v[1]) LucyAlexander 58
(Jim Goldie) *chsd ldrs: lost pl after 7th* **20/1**

540/ **11** 5 **Reckless Romeo (IRE)**[204] 2168 4-10-11 **90**............. HarryChalloner(5) 53
(Richard Ford) *in rr-div: nvr a factor* **20/1**

6PP/ **12** 16 **Pegasus Prince (USA)**[33] 5450 9-10-10 **84**....................(p) TonyKelly(5) 36
(Brian Storey) *prom: lost pl 4th: sn bhd: t.o 3 out* **50/1**

060/ **13** 10 **Ferndale**[33] 5449 4-10-11 **85**... BarryKeniry 22
(Ann Duffield) *mid-div: drvn 7th: lost pl after 8th: sn bhd: t.o: b.b.v* **50/1**

05/- **14** 23 **K Island (IRE)**[36] 5374 5-11-5 **88**.. DavidBass 7
(Richard Price) *in rr: reminders 6th: bhd fr7th: t.o* **16/1**

000/ **15** 4 **Ewe Are Joking**[28] 5570 5-11-1 **84**......................................(t) RyanMania
(Ferdy Murphy, France) *in rr: wl bhd fr 8th: t.o* **16/1**

3/ **U** **Bennative (IRE)**[15] 210 8-11-12 **95**..................................(p) FearghalDavis
(Stephen Francis Magee, Ire) *mid-div: reminders 6th: 9th and styng on whn blnd and uns rdr 3 out* **20/1**

5m 13.7s (-15.60) **Going Correction** -0.70s/f (Firm) course record
WFA 4 from 5yo+ 19lb **16** Ran SP% **136.0**
Speed ratings (Par 103): **100,99,96,93,93 92,90,90,89,86 85,79,75,67,65**
toteswingers 1&2 £9.70, 1&3 £12.40, 2&3 £2.80 CSF £51.18 CT £137.93 TOTE £19.50: £3.10, £1.40, £1.70, £5.20; EX 85.90 Trifecta £447.40 Pool: £821.03 - 1.37 winning units..There was no bid for the winner
Owner The Martins Hill Racing Partnership **Bred** Brian Slattery **Trained** Upper Oddington, Gloucs

FOCUS
Mainly exposed sorts in a moderate selling handicap. The gallop was a reasonable one and the first two pulled clear. The winner's best run since last summer.

472 PRIORY HOTEL CARTMEL H'CAP CHASE (14 fncs) 2m 5f 110y
6:55 (6:55) (Class 4) (0-105,105) 5-Y-O+ **£3,898** (£1,144; £572; £286)

Form RPR

023/ **1** **Glen Countess (IRE)**[81] 4580 6-11-1 **94**......................(t) WilsonRenwick 104+
(Brendan Powell) *chsd ldr: upsides 7th: led last: hrd drvn: hld on towards fin* **3/1**[3]

/23- **2** ¾ **Peak Seasons (IRE)**[11] 285 10-9-7 **79** oh1............... GerardGalligan(7) 87
(Michael Chapman) *in rr: hdwy to chse ldrs 9th: 4th last: styd on and sn chsng wnr: almost upsides fnl f: jst hld* **6/1**

1/1- **3** 3¼ **Badgers Retreat**[15] 203 7-11-5 **105**.............................. MissCWalton(7) 110
(Ferdy Murphy, France) *t.k.h: trckd ldrs: 2nd 2 out: kpt on same pce* **2/1**[1]

33P/ **4** 32 **Salut Honore (FR)**[65] 4884 7-10-12 **91**..............................(t) WillKennedy 64
(Alex Hales) *led: hdd and hit last: sn wknd* **8/1**

600/ **5** 3¼ **Jive Master (IRE)**[150] 3229 8-11-12 **105**.......................... AidanColeman 75
(Tim Vaughan) *chsd ldrs: shkn up 8th: drvn 10th: lost pl 3 out* **11/4**[2]

P/6- **6** ¾ **Novikov**[7] 377 9-11-2 **95**..(t) RichieMcLernon 64
(Sophie Leech) *racd in last: effrt 10th: sn wknd* **25/1**

5m 12.6s (-12.80) **Going Correction** -0.50s/f (Good) **6** Ran SP% **114.2**
Speed ratings: **103,102,101,89,88 88**
toteswingers 1&2 £2.30, 1&3 £2.00, 2&3 £2.50 CSF £20.86 CT £43.05 TOTE £4.10: £1.60, £2.10; EX 20.80 Trifecta £28.90 Pool: £863.32 - 22.39 winning units..
Owner The Naughty Partnership **Bred** David Pim **Trained** Upper Lambourn, Berks

FOCUS
A modest handicap run at just an ordinary gallop. The first three finished a long way clear and are rated close to their marks.

473 WAVE JEWELLERY INTERMEDIATE H'CAP CHASE (18 fncs) 3m 2f
7:30 (7:30) (Class 5) (0-95,94) 5-Y-O+ **£2,599** (£763; £381; £190)

Form RPR

336- **1** **Solway Dornal**[2] 444 8-9-7 **68** oh2.....................(tp) StephenMulqueen(7) 76
(Lisa Harrison) *chsd ldrs: 2nd whn hit 3 out: led over 1f out: hld on wl* **11/1**

3/6- **2** 1¼ **Over And Above (IRE)**[24] 64 7-10-2 **70**...................(t) RichieMcGrath 78
(Henry Hogarth) *chsd ldrs: styd on to chal over 1f out: styd on same pce last 50yds* **7/1**

641/ **3** ¾ **My Friend George**[54] 5077 7-11-9 **91**.............................. JamesReveley 96
(Dianne Sayer) *in rr: outpcd 8th: hdwy 14th: only 5th last: 3rd and chsng ldrs over 1f out: styd on same pce* **3/1**[1]

4/P- **4** ¾ **Dollar Mick (IRE)**[14] 224 8-11-3 **85**.............................(b[1]) BrianHarding 90
(James Moffatt) *led: drvn 3 l clr after 14th: hdd over 1f out: kpt on one pce: lame* **14/1**

4/1- **5** 1¼ **Dukeofchesterwood**[24] 64 11-11-1 **83**.......................(p) BrianHughes 86
(Karen McLintock) *chsd ldrs: one pce fr 2 out* **5/1**[3]

33/- **6** 2½ **Wave Breaker (IRE)**[48] 5203 6-10-11 **79**.....................(p) KennyJohnson 81
(Robert Johnson) *stdd s: detached in last: blnd 6th: hdwy 13th: modest 6th last: one pce* **20/1**

45/- **7** 127 **Runswick Relax**[46] 5228 7-11-10 **92**.............................. WilsonRenwick
(John Wade) *chsd ldrs: outpcd 13th: wknd 4 out: t.o last: eased and eventually completed: b.b.v* **5/1**[3]

P35/ **8** 8 **Samson Collonges (FR)**[33] 5450 7-9-9 **68**............... SamanthaDrake(5)
(Ferdy Murphy, France) *in rr: lost pl 14th: bhd whn mstke 3 out: t.o last: eased: eventually completed* **4/1**[2]

6/2- **P** **Bollin Fiona**[14] 224 9-11-7 **94**.................................... CallumWhillans(5)
(Donald Whillans) *chsd ldrs: lost pl 9th: bhd whn blnd 12th: t.o and sn p.u* **16/1**

5/5- **U** **Glamorous Gg**[13] 8-9-9 **68** oh2.................................(b) HarryChalloner(5)
(John Bryan Groucott) *chsd ldrs: drvn 12th: 6th whn blnd and uns rdr next* **22/1**

6m 19.7s (-15.20) **Going Correction** -0.50s/f (Good) **10** Ran SP% **120.8**
Speed ratings: **103,102,102,102,101 101,,,,**
toteswingers 1&2 £35.30, 1&3 £12.80, 2&3 £6.70 CSF £88.92 CT £295.54 TOTE £13.50: £3.60, £3.00, £1.50; EX 127.90 Trifecta £386.60 Part won. Pool: £515.52 - 0.52 winning units..
Owner David Alan Harrison **Bred** D A Harrison **Trained** Aldoth, Cumbria

FOCUS
A moderate handicap in which an ordinary gallop increased after the third-last fence. The winner is rated 80 over hurdles at best and may match that over fences.

474 SARAH & JON BARRY BIG BIRTHDAY CELEBRATION NOVICES' CHASE (12 fncs) 2m 1f 110y
8:00 (8:00) (Class 4) 5-Y-O+ **£3,898** (£1,144; £572; £286)

Form RPR

020/ **1** **Grey Soldier (IRE)**[155] 3166 8-10-12 0.......................(t) RichieMcLernon 111+
(Sophie Leech) *trckd ldrs 4th: wnt 2nd sn after last: led over 2f out: forged clr* **10/1**

1/0- **2** 8 **Dare Me (IRE)**[14] 217 9-11-5 127.................................... AidanColeman 111+
(Venetia Williams) *wnt 2nd 5th: led 7th: rdn sn after last: hdd over 2f out: kpt on same pce* **5/4**[1]

1/2- **3** 2½ **Musnad (USA)**[17] 171 5-10-12 0.......................................(b) DannyCook 97
(Brian Ellison) *chsd ldrs: cl 2nd 7th: one pce appr last* **5/1**[3]

55/- **4** 13 **Mystified (IRE)**[80] 4587 10-10-12 74...................................... BrianHarding 84
(Alan Berry) *detached in last: wnt modest 4th after 8th: nvr on terms* **50/1**

/ **5** 48 **Bucklemyshoe (IRE)**[798] 12-10-12 0.............................. KennyJohnson 36
(Robert Johnson) *t.k.h: upsides whn lft in ld 1st: hdd 7th: 4th and wkng whn blnd next: sn bhd: t.o 3 out: virtually p.u run-in* **100/1**

301/ **F** **Call Back**[34] 5425 5-10-12 0... JasonMaguire
(Donald McCain) *led: jnd whn fell 1st* **6/4**[2]

4m 9.3s (-9.60) **Going Correction** -0.50s/f (Good) **6** Ran SP% **113.2**
Speed ratings: **101,97,96,90,69**
toteswingers 1&2 £2.10, 1&3 £3.70, 2&3 £2.70 CSF £24.65 TOTE £8.30: £2.00, £1.70; EX 16.80 Trifecta £45.80 Pool: £713.67 - 11.68 winning units..
Owner J O'Brien & C J Leech **Bred** Bering Sl **Trained** Elton, Gloucs

FOCUS
Not a competitive event by any means. The winner is rated 4lb off his best chase fugure with the second a stone+ off. The gallop was fair.

475 FURNESS FISH & GAME MAIDEN HURDLE (8 hdls) 2m 1f 110y
8:35 (8:35) (Class 5) 4-Y-O+ **£2,599** (£763; £381; £190)

Form RPR

422/ **1** **Lisbon (IRE)**[26] 27 5-10-9 112...(t) DerekFox(5) 116+
(Patrick Griffin, Ire) *hld up in mid-div: trckd ldrs 5th: rdn to ld after 2 out: drvn rt out* **5/2**[1]

0/3- **2** 3½ **Smart Ruler (IRE)**[17] 171 7-11-0 103.............................. BrianHarding 112
(James Moffatt) *hld up in rr: hdwy 4th: trcking ldrs 3 out: wnt 2nd sn after last: kpt on: no imp* **14/1**

252/ **3** 12 **Travis County (IRE)**[31] 5499 4-10-10 111...........................(p) DannyCook 100
(Brian Ellison) *led to 2nd: led 4th: j.rt 2 out: sn hdd: 2nd whn j.rt last: sn wknd* **5/2**[1]

635/ **4** 6 **Palus San Marco (IRE)**[8] 4501 4-10-10 114..........(t) WayneHutchinson 90
(Graeme McPherson) *reluctant and led to s: chsd ldrs: wknd between last 2* **11/2**[3]

5 1½ **Exning Halt**[19] 4-10-10 0.. DougieCostello 88
(John Quinn) *mid-div: shkn up 4th: outpcd appr 2 out* **13/2**

265/ **6** 18 **Somerset Island (IRE)**[40] 5225 5-10-/ 100.......................... AdamNicol(7) 74
(Michael Smith) *chsd ldrs: wknd after 2 out* **16/1**

260/ **7** 29 **Mount Hope (IRE)**[34] 5435 6-11-0 107...........................(p) JasonMaguire 45
(Donald McCain) *racd wd: led 2nd: hdd 4th: reminders and lost pl 5th: sn bhd: t.o 2 out* **4/1**[2]

/06- **8** 120 **Lenderking (IRE)**[11] 291 5-10-7 0................................ GerardGalligan(7)
(Michael Chapman) *in rr: bhd fr 3rd: t.o 5th: eventually completed* **150/1**

3m 56.2s (-17.00) **Going Correction** -0.70s/f (Firm) course record
WFA 4 from 5yo+ 18lb **8** Ran SP% **119.1**
Speed ratings (Par 103): **109,107,102,99,98 90,77,**
toteswingers 1&2 £15.30, 1&3 £2.20, 2&3 £22.30 CSF £39.95 TOTE £5.40: £1.30, £2.50, £1.50; EX 45.20 Trifecta £70.90 Pool: £543.89 - 5.75 winning units..
Owner M Deren **Bred** George And Myrtle Grothier **Trained** Oldtown, Co Dublin

FOCUS
An ordinary maiden hurdle in which the gallop was sound throughout. The first two pulled clear and are rated pretty much to their marks.

476 CRABBIE'S ALCOHOLIC GINGER BEER CONDITIONAL JOCKEYS' H'CAP HURDLE (12 hdls) 3m 2f
9:05 (9:05) (Class 4) (0-110,113) 4-Y-O+ **£3,249** (£954; £477; £238)

Form RPR

356/ **1** **Unex Picasso**[31] 5498 5-11-4 **100**.................................... LucyAlexander 103+
(Barry Murtagh) *mde all: jnd whn hit last: kpt on: all out* **33/1**

0/2- **2** hd **Any Given Moment (IRE)**[10] 310 7-11-2 **103**.......... GrahamWatters(5) 105
(Sandy Thomson) *chsd ldrs: 2nd after 3rd: drvn 2 out: upsides fnl f: jst hld* **10/1**

1/1- **3** 2 **Mrs Eff**[21] 111 7-11-6 **108**..(t) AdamNicol(6) 110+
(Philip Kirby) *in rr: hdwy whn hit 7th: modest 4th and drvn 9th: 3rd appr 3 out: styd on same pce last 150yds* **2/1**[1]

0/1- **4** 3 **Dizzy River (IRE)**[6] 386 8-11-9 **113** 7ex...................(p) CraigGallagher(8) 111
(Brian Ellison) *in rr: hdwy and modest 7th last: fin strly* **7/2**[2]

5/6- **5** 2¼ **Easement**[10] 310 10-10-3 **91**..................................(v) JonathonBewley(6) 86
(George Bewley) *w ldrs: outpcd 9th: one pce fr next* **8/1**

3/5- **6** 2 **Gulf Punch**[21] 111 6-11-4 **103**.. HenryBrooke(3) 96
(Donald McCain) *mid-div: drvn 9th: kpt on: one pce* **14/1**

2/3- **7** 10 **Glasson Lad (IRE)**[17] 168 6-11-3 **102**...........................(p) TonyKelly(3) 85
(Ferdy Murphy, France) *chsd ldrs: outpcd 3 out: wknd last* **9/1**

41/- **8** 39 **Gilzean (IRE)**[36] 5381 7-10-12 **94**...................................... KillianMoore 38
(Alex Hales) *mid-div: outpcd 9th: sn bhd: t.o between last 2* **9/2**[3]

14P/ **9** 73 **Painted Sky**[385] 93 10-11-4 **100**... BrianToomey
(Iain Jardine) *in rr: bhd fr 6th: t.o 3 out: eventually completed* **33/1**

6m 4.1s (-22.00) **Going Correction** -0.70s/f (Firm) **9** Ran SP% **116.5**
Speed ratings (Par 105): **105,104,104,103,102 102,99,87,64**
toteswingers 1&2 £14.00, 1&3 £11.20, 2&3 £19.30 CSF £322.34 CT £973.88 TOTE £43.80: £7.40, £3.90, £1.80; EX 190.30 Trifecta £381.50 Part won. Pool: £508.74 - 0.17 winning units..
Owner Mrs Sue Murtagh **Bred** Norelands, Hugo Lascelles & D Clarke **Trained** Low Braithwaite, Cumbria

FOCUS
A fair handicap but, although the gallop was sound throughout, not many got involved. The form is rated around the second and third.
T/Plt: £33.30 to a £1 stake. Pool: £68,258.22 - 1496.34 winning units T/Qpdt: £12.90 to a £1 stake. Pool: £3331.46 - 190.00 winning units WG

140 FFOS LAS (L-H)
Saturday, May 25

OFFICIAL GOING: Good (7.2)
Wind: medium, against Weather: dry

477 FOSTERS NOVICES' HURDLE (8 hdls) 2m
5:40 (5:41) (Class 4) 4-Y-O+ **£3,119** (£915; £457; £228)

Form RPR

1 **Rosie Probert**[344] 4-10-1 0.. AndrewTinkler 84+
(Nicky Henderson) *hld up wl in tch: mstke 1st and 4th: led gng strly between last 2: qckly clr flat: comf* **6/4**[1]

/ **2** 3½ **Shelford (IRE)**[38] 4-10-8 0.. LeeEdwards 86+
(Tony Carroll) *mstkes: wl in tch in midfield: blnd 1st: mstke 4th and 5th: effrt and ev ch whn blnd 2 out: stl ev ch and mstke last: one pce flat* **4/1**[3]

U/6- **3** ½ **Tarmac Girl**[6] 391 5-9-12 0.. JPKiely(7) 79
(Tim Vaughan) *led and set stdy gallop: rdn bef 2 out: hdd between last 2: styd on same pce flat* **8/1**

- 4 6 **Odin (IRE)**[120] 5-10-12 0 LeightonAspell 83+
(Don Cantillon) *mstkes and nvr fluent: hld up bhd: j.rt and mstke 1st: effrt to chse ldrs and blnd 2 out: outpcd and btn between last 2* **7/4**[2]

/05- 5 3 ½ **Haveumistim**[3] 434 7-10-9 0 MarkQuinlan(3) 77
(Bernard Llewellyn) *in tch in last pair: mstke 5th: pushed along and effrt bef 3 out: wknd after 2 out* **50/1**

0P0/ 6 ¾ **Milaneen**[56] 5025 7-10-5 0 RichardKilloran 69
(Tim Vaughan) *pressed ldrs: rdn after 3 out: wknd next* **16/1**

7 6 **Pru** 5-9-12 0 ConorRing(7) 63
(Mary Evans) *chsd ldrs: mstke 4th: mstke and lost pl 3 out: wknd next* **33/1**

0/ 8 4 **Mac Le Couteau**[255] 1561 5-10-9 0 AdamWedge(3) 66
(Evan Williams) *w ldr: j.big 2nd: rdn and no ex after 3 out: wknd next* **20/1**

3m 55.0s (6.50) **Going Correction** +0.225s/f (Yiel)
WFA 4 from 5yo+ 18lb 8 Ran SP% **123.0**
Speed ratings (Par 105): **92,90,90,87,85 84,81,79**
toteswingers 1&2 £1.70, 1&3 £3.40, 2&3 £4.90 CSF £8.95 TOTE £2.50: £1.30, £1.30, £2.10; EX 6.70 Trifecta £37.20 Pool: £1521.99 - 30.65 winning units..
Owner Seasons Holidays **Bred** Seasons Holidays **Trained** Upper Lambourn, Berks

FOCUS
After a dry day on a bright, cool evening, the winning jockey reported the ground rode a little quicker than advertised. They went a very modest gallop for this novices' hurdle, with a decent pace eventually injected turning in. Those with form under jumps rules looked a modest bunch and, as the market suggested, the winner came from one of the four hurdling newcomers. Not form to take too seriously, and it's been given a token rating.

478 FOSTERS H'CAP CHASE (17 fncs) 2m 5f
6:10 (6:10) (Class 5) (0-95,94) 5-Y-O+ **£2,144** (£629; £314; £157)

Form RPR
F5P/ 1 **Forever My Friend (IRE)**[130] 3669 6-11-4 **86** JamieMoore 98+
(Peter Bowen) *chsd ldrs: mstke 12th: chsd ldr and wl clr of field after next: gd jump to ld 14th: clr next: drvn out* **5/2**[2]

3/4- 2 8 **Petroupetrov (FR)**[19] 141 10-11-9 **91** (bt[1]) RichardJohnson 96
(Tim Vaughan) *j.rt: led tl outj. and hdd 14th: sn drvn and styng on same pce whn mstke 2 out: no imp after* **5/1**

0P0/ 3 30 **Fromthetop (IRE)**[110] 4026 7-10-9 **77** (tp) TomScudamore 55
(Michael Scudamore) *chsd ldrs: mstke 8th: chsd ldr whn mstke next: 3rd and struggling whn mstke 13th: wl btn next: t.o* **2/1**[1]

0P3/ 4 28 **Romney Marsh**[29] 5552 12-10-12 **80** HaddenFrost 33
(Roger Curtis) *in tch in midfield: rdn after 8th: rallied u.p and wnt modest 3rd bef 14th: no imp and wl btn whn blnd bdly 3 out: t.o* **8/1**

P34/ 5 4 **Turbulance (IRE)**[41] 5309 11-9-11 **68** oh6 (b) MarkQuinlan(3) 17
(Bernard Llewellyn) *chsd ldr tl 9th: sn rdn: lost tch 14th: t.o next* **14/1**

P/0- P **Benefit Game (IRE)**[25] 43 9-11-9 **94** MattGriffiths(3)
(Richard Hawker) *hld up in tch in rr: rdn and struggling 10th: lost tch 12th: t.o whn p.u bef 14th* **33/1**

P/P- P **Autumn Haze**[25] 43 8-10-4 **72** LeightonAspell
(Phillip Dando) *r wd in last pair: rdn and lost tch 12th: t.o whn p.u bef 14th* **20/1**

0/0- P **I Can Run Can You (IRE)**[24] 71 7-11-3 **85** (t) APMcCoy
(Jonjo O'Neill) *j.rt: chsd ldrs tl lost pl and reminders after 6th: rallied to chse ldrs after 8th: lost pl again and rdn 10th: lost tch 12th: t.o whn p.u bef 14th* **4/1**[3]

5m 15.7s (-12.90) **Going Correction** -0.575s/f (Firm) 8 Ran SP% **124.1**
Speed ratings: **101,97,86,75,74 , ,**
toteswingers 1&2 £4.10, 1&3 £7.10, 2&3 £2.00 CSF £17.44 CT £30.81 TOTE £4.60: £2.60, £1.10, £1.60; EX 14.70 Trifecta £62.30 Pool: £835.03 - 10.03 winning units..
Owner Mickey Bowen **Bred** Eamon Fitzgerald **Trained** Little Newcastle, Pembrokes

FOCUS
A run-of-the-mill handicap chase, run at a decent pace. They finished tired and well strung out. The winner is rated in line with his best hurdles/bumper form.

479 FOSTERS GOLD NOVICES' HURDLE (10 hdls) 2m 4f
6:40 (6:40) (Class 4) 4-Y-0+ **£3,119** (£915; £457; £228)

Form RPR
0/2- 1 **Lord Grantham (IRE)**[21] 119 6-11-2 120 JakeGreenall(3) 123+
(Henry Daly) *in tch: hdwy to ld 5th: mde rest and a gng best after: lft clr 3 out: pushed along and kpt on wl between last 2: comf* **11/8**[1]

414/ 2 4 **Groomed (IRE)**[31] 5502 5-10-12 0 (t) RichardJohnson 111
(Tim Vaughan) *hld up in tch in rr: rdn and effrt to chse ldrs bef 3 out: lft 3rd 3 out and sn chsng wnr: hit next: kpt on same pce after* **6/1**[3]

0/ 3 10 **Waterford Star (IRE)**[199] 2269 5-10-12 0 (p) PaddyBrennan 106+
(Tom George) *in tch in midfield: j. slowly 6th: rdn and struggling whn lft 4th and hmpd 3 out: wl hld next: wnt 3rd last* **12/1**

4 7 **Commitment**[35] 4-10-7 0 NoelFehily 89
(Neil Mulholland) *j. bdly lft 1st: chsd ldr 5th: lft 2nd 3 out: sn 3rd and outpcd by ldrs: lost 3rd and wknd last* **8/1**

5/0- 5 8 **Louis Phillipe (IRE)**[16] 174 6-10-12 0 NickScholfield 85
(Linda Blackford) *t.k.h: hld up in tch in midfield: rdn and struggling after 7th: wkng whn lft 5th next* **66/1**

5/0- 6 120 **Mighty Clarets (IRE)**[19] 140 6-10-12 0 JamieMoore
(Peter Bowen) *a in rr: j. slowly and rdn 5th: lost tch next: wl t.o bef 3 out* **25/1**

0/5- B **More Glory (IRE)**[23] 79 5-10-12 0 TomO'Brien
(Keith Goldsworthy) *led tl 5th: chsd ldr tl after 7th: wkng whn b.d 3 out* **50/1**

2/3- F **Third Of The Third**[19] 140 6-10-12 113 ConorO'Farrell
(David Pipe) *chsd ldrs: rdn and chsd wnr after 7th: 2 l down whn fell next* **6/4**[2]

4m 52.1s (1.20) **Going Correction** +0.225s/f (Yiel)
WFA 4 from 5yo+ 19lb 8 Ran SP% **122.5**
Speed ratings (Par 105): **106,104,100,97,94 , ,**
toteswingers 1&2 £1.40, 1&3 £3.70, 2&3 £6.20 CSF £11.42 TOTE £2.00: £1.20, £1.50, £3.20; EX 13.80 Trifecta £70.70 Pool: £1081.98 - 11.46 winning units..
Owner T F F Nixon **Bred** T F F Nixon **Trained** Stanton Lacy, Shropshire

FOCUS
A muddling pace early on for this ordinary novice hurdle. The first two are rated a bit below their best.

480 PROFESSIONAL SECURITY MANAGEMENT H'CAP HURDLE (3 hdls 5 omitted) 2m
7:15 (7:20) (Class 3) (0-125,125) 4-Y-0+ **£5,393** (£1,583; £791; £395)

Form RPR
042/ 1 **Waterunder (IRE)**[44] 5260 6-11-12 **125** (t) TomScudamore 128
(David Pipe) *in tch in midfield: rdn and effrt over 3f out: hdwy and edging lft over 1f out: led ins fnl f: r.o wl* **5/1**[3]

/02- 2 3 ¼ **Ruler Of All (IRE)**[2] 447 7-11-5 **125** MrRWinks(7) 126+
(Peter Winks) *chsd ldrs: upsides ldr gng wl bypassing 3 out: led over 2f out: rdn over 1f out: hdd, ducked lft and rdr unbalanced ins fnl f: no ex u.p and hung lft after* **4/1**[2]

U/3- 3 nk **No To Trident**[25] 37 8-10-6 **105** (p) DPFahy 105
(John Flint) *in tch in midfield: mstke 4th (actual 2nd): rdn and chsd ldrs 1f out: carried lft and one pce ins fnl f* **12/1**

6/1- 4 nk **Taste The Wine (IRE)**[10] 304 7-10-7 **111** RobertWilliams(5) 110
(Bernard Llewellyn) *chsd ldrs: wnt 2nd 3rd (actual 1st) tl 4f out: sn drvn: kpt on same pce fnl f* **11/2**

1/1- 5 nk **Super Collider**[22] 93 6-10-11 **110** (bt) PaddyBrennan 108
(Fergal O'Brien) *chsd ldr tl mstke and lost pl 3rd (actual 1st): 7th 4f out: swtchd rt and effrt over 2f out: kpt on fnl f* **5/2**[1]

403/ 6 ¾ **Taaresh (IRE)**[262] 4989 8-10-3 **105** AdamWedge(3) 103
(Kevin Morgan) *hld up in last pair: hdwy to trck ldrs 4f out: rdn and nt qckn over 1f out: wknd ins fnl f* **25/1**

1/2- 7 23 **Dark And Dangerous (IRE)**[16] 176 5-11-6 **119** (v) APMcCoy 94
(Brendan Powell) *led: rdn and hdd over 2f out: sn wknd: bhd fnl f* **4/1**[2]

140/ 8 12 **Islandmagee (IRE)**[27] 10 6-10-10 **109** PaulMoloney 72
(Evan Williams) *a in rr: blnd 3rd (actual 1st): lost tch bypassing 3 out: t.o* **14/1**

3m 44.0s (-4.50) **Going Correction** -0.10s/f (Good) 8 Ran SP% **118.8**
Speed ratings (Par 107): **107,105,105,105,104 104,93,87**
toteswingers 1&2 £3.80, 1&3 £6.10, 2&3 £8.10 CSF £26.78 CT £231.64 TOTE £7.00: £1.70, £1.60, £3.10; EX 32.80 Trifecta £474.80 Pool: £920.15 - 1.45 winning units..
Owner Mrs S Clifford **Bred** Charles Clarke **Trained** Nicholashayne, Devon
■ Stewards' Enquiry : Mr R Winks two-day ban; careless riding (tbd).

FOCUS
What should have been a competitive handicap hurdle was turned into a farce because of the setting sun, which resulted in the runners missing out the three hurdles on both occasions up the home straight. They jumped just three hurdles in total and they finished in a heap. Not form to take seriously.

481 BURNS PET NUTRITION H'CAP CHASE (10 fncs 8 omitted) 3m
7:45 (7:47) (Class 4) (0-120,120) 5-Y-0+ **£3,768** (£1,106; £553; £276)

Form RPR
6/2- 1 **Whispering Jack**[25] 44 8-11-4 **112** (p) RichardJohnson 126+
(Keiran Burke) *in tch in midfield: chsd ldrs 5f out: rdn to ld over 3f out: drew clr bypassing 2 out: r.o wl: comf* **9/2**[1]

5/1- 2 10 **Cardigan Island (IRE)**[22] 92 8-11-1 **112** (tp) RobertDunne(3) 116
(Dai Burchell) *chsd ldrs: effrt and chal over 3f out: sn drew clr w wnr: no ex and btn 2f out: wl hld by wnr but kpt on for clr 2nd* **6/1**[3]

P11/ 3 6 **Sir Mattie (IRE)**[32] 5467 8-11-7 **115** PaulMoloney 113
(David Rees) *hld up in rr: hdwy 14th (actual last): 4th and outpcd whn racd awkwardly u.p bypassing 3 out: no ch w ldrs but kpt on to snatch 3rd last strides* **11/2**[2]

363/ 4 shd **Risk (IRE)**[54] 5080 10-10-11 **105** NickScholfield 103
(Jeremy Scott) *hld up in tch in last pair: hdwy 14th (actual last): chsd ldng pair and drvn bypassing 3 out: no imp: lost 3rd last stride* **7/1**

1/5- 5 1 ¾ **Stormyisland Ahead**[23] 84 8-10-8 **105** (t) AdamWedge(3) 102
(Evan Williams) *hld up in tch in midfield: blnd 12th (actual 3 out): rdn and outpcd 4f out: n.d after: plugged on fnl f* **20/1**

2/2- 6 ¾ **Flanagan (IRE)**[19] 141 9-10-0 **94** oh4 DonalDevereux 91
(Peter Bowen) *chsd ldrs: mstke 10th (actual 6th): blnd 12th (actual 3 out) and lost pl: outpcd and btn 4f out: rallied and kpt on fnl f: no threat to ldrs* **10/1**

01/- 7 5 **Mabel Tasman**[191] 2439 7-10-12 **106** SamTwiston-Davies 96
(Neil Mulholland) *in tch towards rr: hdwy 13th (actual 2 out): 5th 5f out: rdn and outpcd 4f out: wknd bypassing 3 out* **7/1**

P04/ 8 11 **Tin Pot Man (IRE)**[32] 5465 7-9-13 **100** (t) ConorRing(7) 79
(Evan Williams) *in tch in midfield: mstke 11th (actual 7th): rdn and struggling 6f out: wknd over 4f out* **33/1**

5/4- 9 10 **Thelobstercatcher**[24] 62 9-10-8 **109** (bt[1]) MrBGibbs(7) 78
(Tim Vaughan) *j.rt: in tch in midfield: dropped to rr and mstke 12th (actual 3 out): sn lost tch and t.o 5f out* **7/1**

620/ 10 13 **Oscar Prairie (IRE)**[39] 5340 8-11-10 **118** (b[1]) NoelFehily 74
(Warren Greatrex) *j.lft at times: mde most tl jst after 14th (actual last): wknd 4f out: t.o fnl 2f* **10/1**

01P/ 11 5 **Very Stylish (IRE)**[169] 2903 9-11-10 **118** (p) APMcCoy 69
(Jonjo O'Neill) *taken down early: w ldr: drvn to ld jst after 14th: hdd over 3f out and sn btn: bhd and eased bypassing 2 out: t.o* **6/1**[3]

5m 54.6s (-22.80) **Going Correction** -0.80s/f (Firm) 11 Ran SP% **125.5**
Speed ratings: **106,102,100,100,100 99,98,94,91,86 85**
toteswingers 1&2 £8.40, 1&3 £8.60, 2&3 £9.90 CSF £34.74 CT £158.55 TOTE £6.20: £1.90, £2.00, £2.30; EX 44.70 Trifecta £132.00 Pool: £505.69 - 2.87 winning units..
Owner Prestige Cars and Couriers **Bred** Miss Kerry Lane **Trained** Seaborough, Dorset

FOCUS
Due to the omission of the fences down the home straight due to the setting sun, only ten of the fences were jumped and it became a tactical battle with very little pace early on. There's a case for rating the form a few pounds higher.

482 FOSTERS H'CAP HURDLE (4 hdls 6 omitted) 2m 4f
8:20 (8:20) (Class 5) (0-100,103) 4-Y-0+ **£1,949** (£572; £286; £143)

Form RPR
061/ 1 **Fuzzy Logic (IRE)**[22] 5102 4-11-0 **98** RobertWilliams(5) 100
(Bernard Llewellyn) *t.k.h: chsd ldr: drew clr w ldr over 2f out: rdn to ld over 1f out: kpt on: rdn out* **14/1**

001/ 2 2 **Sure Thing (FR)**[26] 29 7-11-12 **100** RichardJohnson 105
(Henry Daly) *led: mstke 6th (actual 2 out): rdn and clr w wnr over 2f out: hdd over 1f out: kpt on same pce after* **3/1**[2]

P/0- 3 9 **Gwili Spar**[19] 140 5-10-6 **80** (t) TomO'Brien 78
(Peter Bowen) *hld up in last trio: j.lft 7th (actual last): hdwy over 3f out: chsd clr ldng pair 2f out: hanging lft and pushed along after: no imp* **14/1**

P/P- 4 3 ¾ **Rainbow Haze**[25] 49 7-11-2 **90** LeightonAspell 84
(Phillip Dando) *wl in tch in midfield: chsd ldrs and rdn over 3f out: drvn and outpcd 2f out: plugged on same pce after* **33/1**

062/ 5 3 ¾ **Edgar Jones**[58] 4977 7-11-12 **100** DonalDevereux 90
(Peter Bowen) *t.k.h: chsd ldrs: rdn and outpcd over 2f out: wknd over 1f out* **10/1**

60P/ 6 8 **Sir Benfro**[56] 5023 7-11-5 **93** JamieMoore 76
(Keith Goldsworthy) *chsd ldrs: rdn 7th (actual last): drvn and no ex 4f out: wknd over 2f out* **16/1**

0/1- 7 1 ¼ **Bells Of Berlin**[16] 188 4-11-3 **103** (vt) JPKiely(7) 82
(Tim Vaughan) *in tch in midfield: hdwy to chse ldrs and mstke 6th (actual 2 out) and 7th (actual last): rdn and nt qckn whn flashed tail over 2f out: sn btn* **9/2**[3]

40/ **8** *16* **Arctic Pond (IRE)**[32] 5470 5-11-10 **98** .... APMcCoy 65
(Jonjo O'Neill) *hld up in tch in last trio: hdwy into midfield 5th (actual 2nd): chsd ldrs and drvn over 4f out: no rspnse and wknd over 2f out: bhd and eased ins fnl f: t.o* **2/1**[1]

P00/ **9** *13* **Just The Job (IRE)**[213] 1994 9-11-4 **92** .... NoelFehily 48
(Neil Mulholland) *in tch in midfield: rdn and struggling sn after 7th (actual last): wknd 4f out: bhd and eased ins fnl f: t.o* **33/1**

P/3- **10** *3/4* **Hero's Call**[10] 320 8-10-0 **74** oh4 .... SamTwiston-Davies 29
(Julian Smith) *chsd ldrs: drvn and lost pl qckly sn after 7th (actual last): lost tch 3f out: eased fnl f: t.o* **14/1**

3/4- **11** *14* **Argaum (IRE)**[16] 184 6-11-6 **94** .... (vt) PaulMoloney 36
(Evan Williams) *in tch in rr: struggling bef 7th (actual last): t.o fnl 3f* **12/1**

4m 50.2s (-0.70) **Going Correction** -0.10s/f (Good)
WFA 4 from 5yo+ 19lb 11 Ran SP% **125.1**
Speed ratings (Par 103): **97,96,92,91,89 86,85,79,74,74 68**
toteswingers 1&2 £3.30, 1&3 £14.90, 2&3 £23.60 CSF £60.76 CT £628.58 TOTE £18.90: £4.60, £1.50, £5.90; EX 41.70 Trifecta £474.40 Part won. Pool: £632.55 - 0.05 winning units..
Owner Gethyn Mills **Bred** John Connaughton **Trained** Fochriw, Caerphilly

FOCUS
The low sun resulted in only four of the ten flights being jumped in this modest handicap hurdle and it is largely unsatisfactory, if not futile, for form study purposes. There was little pace until all the flights were jumped and the front pair had it to themselves for much of the race, which produced a protracted duel up the home straight. The winner rates a small personal best.

483 FOSTERS RADLER STANDARD OPEN NATIONAL HUNT FLAT RACE 2m

8:50 (8:50) (Class 6) 4-6-Y-0 **£1,559** (£457; £228; £114)

Form RPR

6/ **1** **Man Of Steel (IRE)**[27] 14 4-10-12 0 .... DonalDevereux 105+
(Peter Bowen) *t.k.h: hld up in tch in rr: hdwy on inner and rn green 3f out: chsd ldng pair over 1f out: styd on wl to ld fnl 50yds* **5/1**[3]

42/ **2** *1* **Oscars Way (IRE)**[58] 4991 5-11-2 0 .... LeightonAspell 107
(Don Cantillon) *t.k.h: chsd ldrs: wnt 2nd 6f out: led and rdn over 3f out: hdd over 1f out: led again ins fnl f: hdd and no ex fnl 50yds* **4/1**[2]

3 *1 1/2* **Laurens Ruby (IRE)** 4-10-5 0 .... DPFahy 95
(John Flint) *t.k.h: in tch: hdwy to chal over 3f out: clr w rival 2f out: rdn and led narrowly over 1f out: hdd ins fnl f: no ex* **20/1**

4 *2 3/4* **Sharon**[32] 5490 4-10-5 0 .... PaddyBrennan 92
(Edward U Hales, Ire) *t.k.h: in tch in midfield: effrt to chse ldrs and rdn over 3f out: 4th and one pce fnl 2f* **6/1**

2/ **5** *5* **Spring Steel (IRE)**[44] 5262 4-10-9 0 .... MattGriffiths(3) 94
(Jeremy Scott) *t.k.h: hld up in tch in rr: hdwy on outer bnd 5f out: chsd ldrs and rdn 4f out: sn outpcd: wknd over 2f out* **2/1**[1]

6 *3 1/4* **Lola Galli** 5-10-9 0 .... (p) TomScudamore 88
(David Pipe) *in tch in midfield: j. path and wnt rt bnd 13f out: rdn and struggling 4f out: wknd 3f out* **6/1**

0/ **7** *9* **Kid Wizzard (USA)**[81] 4585 4-10-12 0 .... (p) APMcCoy 82
(David Pipe) *led: hung rt briefly bnd 13f out: rdn 6f out: drvn and hdd over 3f out: sn wknd* **8/1**

0/ **8** *21* **Hilden**[41] 5316 4-10-5 0 .... (b[1]) NoelFehily 54
(William Muir) *chsd ldr tl 6f out: rdn 4f out: sn wknd: bhd fnl 2f* **25/1**

0/6- **9** *82* **Flying Quest**[11] 298 4-10-12 0 .... NickScholfield
(Linda Blackford) *t.k.h: in tch tl lost pl quicky 1/2-way: sn t.o: sddle slipped* **66/1**

3m 42.6s (-0.30) **Going Correction** +0.225s/f (Yiel)
WFA 4 from 5yo 4lb 9 Ran SP% **119.8**
Speed ratings: **109,108,107,106,103 102,97,87,46**
toteswingers 1&2 £5.90, 1&3 £51.30, 2&3 £51.30 CSF £25.86 TOTE £4.30: £2.10, £1.20, £5.20; EX 23.30 Trifecta £247.60 Pool: £690.42 - 2.09 winning units..
Owner Saith O Ni **Bred** Katie McCarthy **Trained** Little Newcastle, Pembrokes

FOCUS
A largely unprepossessing bunch for a bumper in which they went a fair pace. The front trio did provide some promise, however. The winner is rated up 10lb on his debut run.
T/Plt: £38.30 to a £1 stake. Pool: £69,148.91 - 1314.67 winning units T/Qpdt: £15.70 to a £1 stake. Pool: £5674.80 - 267.30 winning units SP

325 FONTWELL (L-H)

Sunday, May 26

OFFICIAL GOING: Good (good to firm in places) changing to good to firm (good in places) after race 2 (2.55)
The second downhill fence was omitted in all chases.
Wind: light across Weather: sunny and warm

484 FOSTERING SOLUTIONS "NATIONAL HUNT" MAIDEN HURDLE (8 hdls 1 omitted) 2m 2f 110y

2:20 (2:21) (Class 4) 4-Y-0+ **£3,119** (£915; £457; £228)

Form RPR

42F/ **1** **Breaking Bits (IRE)**[28] 8 6-11-0 112 .... TomO'Brien 109+
(Jamie Snowden) *chsd ldr tl led after 5th: mde rest: rdn and mstke 2 out: clr and nt fluent last: pressed whn lft in command fnl 100yds: styd on* **7/1**[3]

151/ **2** *1 1/2* **Azure Fly (IRE)**[260] 1523 5-11-0 0 .... NoelFehily 110+
(Charlie Longsdon) *hld up in tch: 4th and effrt bef 3 out: wnt 3rd and veered sharply lft on landing 2 out: rallied to chse wnr flat: styng on and clsng on wnr whn wnt sharply lft again fnl 100yds: nt rcvr* **5/2**[1]

U/0- **3** *6* **Taradrewe**[20] 140 6-10-4 0 .... RachaelGreen(3) 96
(Anthony Honeyball) *in tch in midfield: j. slowly and lost pl 2nd: rdn and hdwy after 3 out: kpt on steadily between last 2: wnt 3rd flat* **8/1**

2/U- **4** *4* **Backhomeinderry (IRE)**[17] 193 8-11-0 99 .... (t) DarylJacob 98
(Kate Buckett) *chsd ldrs: wnt 2nd and travelling wl after 3 out: rdn and no ex between last 2: lost 2nd sn after last and wknd flat* **14/1**

220/ **5** *25* **Cannon Fodder**[38] 5364 6-10-7 0 .... MarcGoldstein 69
(Sheena West) *mstkes: t.k.h: hld up in midfield: blnd 1st: rdn and struggling after 3 out: wl btn whn hmpd by loose horse next* **8/1**

0/5- **6** *hd* **Going Twice**[11] 307 8-11-0 0 .... LeightonAspell 75
(Steve Woodman) *in tch in midfield: pushed along and lost pl after 3rd: rdn after 5th: outpcd and btn after 3 out: wknd* **66/1**

0/0- **7** *3 3/4* **Mac's Grey (IRE)**[23] 95 6-11-0 0 .... DaveCrosse 72
(Zoe Davison) *hld up in last pair: hdwy after 5th: rdn and mstke 3 out: sn wknd* **200/1**

0/2- **8** *nk* **Officially Modern (IRE)**[12] 290 6-11-0 0 .... PaddyBrennan 72
(Fergal O'Brien) *racd keenly and j.rt at times: led tl after 5th: rdn and wknd after 3 out* **10/1**

9 *4 1/2* **Auld Sthock (IRE)**[80] 4623 5-11-0 0 .... JamieMoore 68
(Gary Moore) *t.k.h: chsd ldrs: j. awkwardly 1st: 3rd and rdn after 3 out: btn next: fdd between last 2: blnd last: eased flat* **7/1**[3]

/4- **10** *7* **Brians Well (IRE)**[23] 101 6-11-0 0 .... APMcCoy 61
(Brendan Powell) *in tch in midfield: rdn after 5th: wknd sn after 3 out: t.o* **14/1**

000/ **11** *3/4* **Pinnacle Ofpassion (IRE)**[27] 36 5-10-0 0 .... MrJoshuaNewman(7) 54
(Nick Lampard) *t.k.h: hld up in rr: j.rt 1st: rdn and struggling after 5th: t.o after 3 out* **200/1**

2/2- **U** **Somchine**[14] 240 5-11-0 110 .... AndrewThornton
(Seamus Mullins) *t.k.h: hld up in rr: bdly hmpd and uns rdr 2nd* **6/1**[2]

0/0- **F** **Cariflora**[14] 240 6-10-7 0 .... (t) TomCannon
(Nick Gifford) *in tch towards rr: hmpd and fell 2nd* **66/1**

4m 21.0s (-13.30) **Going Correction** -0.625s/f (Firm) 13 Ran SP% **116.5**
Speed ratings (Par 105): **103,102,99,98,87 87,85,85,83,81 80, ,**
toteswingers 1&2 £5.40, 1&3 £0.00, 2&3 £11.20 CSF £24.84 TOTE £6.70: £2.30, £1.60, £2.70; EX 31.10 Trifecta £426.20 Part won. Pool: £426.20 - 0.53 winning units..
Owner Colin Peake & John H W Finch Partnership **Bred** Mrs M Farrell **Trained** Lambourn, Berks

FOCUS
Fences on inner, hurdles middle to outer. A key piece of form for this maiden centred around two horses renewing their rivalry after first meeting at Plumpton at the end of March, with the better of the two that day improving to win this time and the other, Somchine, brought down at the second. There was drama at the finish when the favourite wandered about and threw away a potential winning chance.

485 32REDBINGO.COM H'CAP CHASE (14 fncs 2 omitted) 2m 6f

2:55 (2:55) (Class 5) (0-95,96) 5-Y-0+ **£2,144** (£629; £314; £157)

Form RPR

0PP/ **1** **Calypso Bay (IRE)**[138] 3560 7-11-12 **95** .... APMcCoy 106
(Jonjo O'Neill) *towards rr: pushed along and hdwy whn mstke 6th: 5th and drvn after 9th and off the bridle after: wnt 7 l 3rd 11th: chsd wnr 2 out: grad clsd and drvn ahd fnl 100yds: kpt on* **4/1**[2]

P/0- **2** *1* **Nothingbutthetruth (IRE)**[12] 293 9-11-6 **92** .... (tp) MichealNolan(3) 102
(Richard Woollacott) *chsd ldr: led after 3 out: mstke last: drvn and hdd fnl 100yds: no ex* **16/1**

1/1- **3** *11* **Princely Hero (IRE)**[11] 305 9-11-13 **96** .... (p) LeightonAspell 96
(Chris Gordon) *bhd: outpcd after 9th: styd on fr 11th: wnt 18 l 4th 3 out: kpt on to snatch 3rd last stride: nvr trbld ldrs* **7/2**[1]

P/3- **4** *shd* **Ratify**[16] 206 9-11-4 **87** .... (vt[1]) AndrewTinkler 88+
(Brendan Powell) *j.rt at times: led: mstke 7th: hdd sn after 3 out: 3rd and btn next: wknd bef last* **6/1**[3]

P/0- **5** *13* **Doctor Ric (IRE)**[14] 242 8-11-8 **91** .... (p) ColinBolger 78
(Gerry Enright) *taken down early: in tch in midfield: lost pl and j. slowly 6th: outpcd after 9th: nvr on terms after* **20/1**

P/3- **6** *3* **Petrarchick (USA)**[6] 408 6-9-10 **70** .... (t) JamesBanks(5) 55
(Emma Baker) *in tch in midfield: drvn and struggling after 9th: n.d after* **17/2**

343- **7** *25* **Lajidaal (USA)**[11] 305 6-11-4 **87** .... (p) JamieMoore 49
(Gary Moore) *bhd 2nd: rdn and nvr travelling in detached last fr 4th: wl bhd 10th: t.o* **13/2**

6PP/ **8** *25* **Orion Star (IRE)**[259] 1531 11-11-7 **90** .... (p) RyanMahon 30
(Seamus Mullins) *chsd ldrs: lost pl and mstke 6th: rdn and lost tch after 9th: t.o* **25/1**

P **Roisini Bay (IRE)**[14] 9-11-4 **94** .... (p) MrMGCooney(7)
(Richenda Ford) *chsd ldrs: mstke 9th: chsd ldng pair bef next tl 11th: 4th and wl btn bef next: mstke 3 out: wkng and losing pl whn p.u 2 out* **16/1**

2/S- **P** **Caunay**[17] 179 6-11-10 **93** .... (t) DougieCostello
(Neil Mulholland) *a towards rr: mstke 3rd: lost tch after 9th: t.o 11th tl p.u 3 out* **12/1**

3/2- **P** **Shantou Breeze (IRE)**[11] 303 6-11-4 **87** .... MarcGoldstein
(Michael Madgwick) *chsd ldrs: mstke 4th: struggling 10th: wkng whn p.u after 11th* **10/1**

5m 33.6s (-9.40) **Going Correction** -0.475s/f (Good) 11 Ran SP% **117.5**
Speed ratings: **98,97,93,93,88 87,78,69, ,**
toteswingers 1&2 £7.60, 1&3 £8.10, 2&3 £8.10 CSF £63.73 CT £247.29 TOTE £4.50: £1.80, £4.30, £1.70; EX 88.10 Trifecta £309.30 Part won. Pool: £412.51 - 0.93 winning units..
Owner John P McManus **Bred** T Hirschfeld **Trained** Cheltenham, Gloucs
■ Stewards' Enquiry : Micheal Nolan four-day ban; used whip above permitted level (9th-11th, 13th June).

FOCUS
The long-time leaders Nothingbutthetruth and Ratify stretched clear on the final circuit but in the end they had gone a bit too hard and it enabled the winner, assisted by the persistence of AP McCoy, to get up on the line.

486 32RED CASINO H'CAP HURDLE (11 hdls) 2m 6f 110y

3:30 (3:30) (Class 4) (0-120,118) 4-Y-0+ **£3,119** (£915; £457; £228)

Form RPR

6B5/ **1** **Saint Roque (FR)**[151] 3227 7-11-10 **116** .... (t) DarylJacob 131+
(Paul Nicholls) *in tch and a travelling wl: jnd ldr on bit sn after 3 out: led and wnt clr between last 2: in command and edgd rt flat: easily* **2/1**[1]

12/- **2** *14* **Occasionally Yours (IRE)**[37] 5376 9-11-6 **115** .... JackQuinlan(3) 116
(Alan Blackmore) *in tch in midfield: rdn and blnd 8th: 4th and outpcd u.p after 3 out: no ch w wnr but kpt on u.p to go 2nd flat* **15/2**

2/3- **3** *1 1/4* **Electric Tiger (GER)**[16] 201 6-10-8 **107** .... JakeHodson(7) 107
(David Bridgwater) *chsd ldr tl 3rd and outpcd u.p after 3 out: no ch w wnr but kpt on flat to go 3rd cl home* **6/1**[3]

541/ **4** *hd* **Rum And Butter (IRE)**[33] 5473 5-11-3 **109** .... APMcCoy 111
(Jonjo O'Neill) *led: hit 8th: rdn and drew clr after 3 out: hdd between last 2 and sn btn: wknd and lost 2 pls flat* **4/1**[2]

3/1- **5** *11* **Grey Missile**[14] 237 8-11-8 **114** .... (p) NickScholfield 104
(Jeremy Scott) *t.k.h: hld up wl in tch in rr: rdn and effrt sn after 3 out: sn wknd and wl btn next* **4/1**[2]

0/6- **6** *9* **Laustra Bad (FR)**[19] 158 10-11-5 **118** .... (bt) KieronEdgar(7) 100
(David Pipe) *in tch in midfield: dropped to rr and drvn 3 out: sn wknd and wl btn next* **25/1**

003/ **7** *12* **Brilliant Barca**[30] 5553 5-11-9 **115** .... MarcGoldstein 86
(Sheena West) *chsd ldrs: rdn and lost pl after 7th: wknd sn after 3 out: t.o* **12/1**

0/6- **8** *5* **Drussell (IRE)**[14] 244 7-11-1 **112** .... ThomasGarner(5) 79
(Martin Bosley) *hld up in tch in rr: hdwy into midfield after 7th: 5th and rdn after 3 out: sn wknd: t.o and eased flat* **20/1**

230/ **9** *6* **George Woolf**[269] 1417 5-11-11 **117** .... (t) AidanColeman 78
(Tim Vaughan) *t.k.h: chsd ldrs: blnd bdly 8th: wknd next: t.o and eased flat* **33/1**

The Form Book Jumps, Raceform Ltd, Compton, RG20 6NL.

33/ P **Cinematique (IRE)**[30] 5551 5-10-13 **105** JamieMoore
(Laura Mongan) *in tch in rr: rdn and lost tch qckly after 7th: wl t.o whn virtually ref 3 out and immediately p.u* **20/1**

5m 24.5s (-18.00) **Going Correction** -0.625s/f (Firm) 10 Ran SP% **123.4**
Speed ratings (Par 105): **106,101,100,100,96 93,89,87,85,**
toteswingers 1&2 £3.90, 1&3 £3.40, 2&3 £5.90 CSF £17.83 CT £82.64 TOTE £3.70: £2.10, £1.60, £1.80; EX 37.40 Trifecta £102.10 Pool: £581.75 - 4.27 winning units..
Owner Potensis Limited & Chris Giles **Bred** Mme Genevieve Mongin **Trained** Ditcheat, Somerset

FOCUS
A solid-looking handicap with the horses in good recent form running well again, but they were no match for the easy winner.

487 32RED.COM H'CAP CHASE (16 fncs 3 omitted) 3m 2f 110y
4:05 (4:05) (Class 3) (0-140,132) 5-Y-0 **£6,330** (£1,870; £935; £468; £234)

Form RPR

4/1- **1** **Bold Perk (IRE)**[17] 190 11-10-10 **116** HaddenFrost 124+
(Martin Hill) *j.rt: hld up in rr: hdwy to chse ldrs after 11th: wnt 2nd 13th: led and j.rt 2 out: 4 l clr and j.rt last: a doing enough and kpt on flat* **4/1**[2]

00/- **2** 1 3/4 **Eleazar (GER)**[40] 5341 12-10-6 **112** (p) LeightonAspell 116
(Lucy Wadham) *in tch in last pair: reminders after 10th: drvn after 13th: chsd wnr between last 2: 4 l down last: kpt on u.p flat* **7/1**

5/2- **3** 9 **Double Chocolate**[17] 189 10-10-1 **114** (p) JakeHodson[(7)] 110
(David Bridgwater) *j.rt: led and clr tl after 11th: rdn bef 3 out: hdd 2 out: 3rd and btn last: wknd* **9/4**[1]

2/3- **4** 14 **Western King (IRE)**[20] 143 6-10-6 **117** (bt[1]) GavinSheehan[(5)] 103
(Charlie Mann) *chsd ldng pair: mstke and pushed along 12th: racd awkwardly u.p and wknd 3 out* **9/2**[3]

1/1- **5** 7 **Themilanhorse (IRE)**[19] 164 7-11-12 **132** (t) DarylJacob 113
(Paul Nicholls) *chsd ldr: mstke 4th: j.lft 8th: 3rd and drvn 13th: wknd next* **9/4**[1]

6m 42.0s (-19.10) **Going Correction** -0.475s/f (Good) 5 Ran SP% **112.2**
Speed ratings: **109,108,105,101,99**
CSF £27.72 TOTE £4.50: £2.90, £4.70; EX 49.50 Trifecta £68.70 Pool: £647.92 - 7.07 winning units..
Owner D Luscombe & M Hill **Bred** Michael O'Mahony **Trained** Littlehempston, Devon

FOCUS
This was run at a good pace throughout.

488 32RED H'CAP HURDLE (9 hdls) 2m 2f 110y
4:40 (4:40) (Class 4) (0-115,115) 4-Y-0+ **£3,119** (£915; £457; £228)

Form RPR

P/3- **1** **Marcus Antonius**[23] 97 6-11-12 **115** LeightonAspell 119+
(Jim Boyle) *hld up in last pair: hdwy after 5th: chsd ldr bef 2 out: led between last 2: in command but racing awkwardly flat: a doing enough* **10/1**

3/4- **2** 3/4 **Dormouse**[23] 97 8-11-3 **113** (p) KieronEdgar[(7)] 114
(Anabel K Murphy) *in tch in last pair: mstke 2nd: rdn 6th: hdwy after 3 out: chsd ldng pair between last 2: kpt on flat to chse wnr fnl 75yds: nvr quite getting to wnr* **14/1**

0/0- **3** 1 1/2 **Van Diemens Land (USA)**[12] 289 6-10-6 **100** (bt[1]) GavinSheehan[(5)] 103+
(Charlie Mann) *chsd ldr tl led after 1st: blnd 2 out: hdd between last 2: styd on same pce and lost 2nd fnl 100yds* **8/1**[3]

P5/ **4** 1 1/4 **Hired Hand (IRE)**[147] 3377 7-11-7 **110** APMcCoy 110
(Jonjo O'Neill) *in tch in midfield: rdn and chsd ldrs bef 2 out: chsd wnr briefly flat: styd on same pce fnl 100yds* **3/1**[1]

050/ **5** 12 **Billesley Road**[40] 5335 5-10-12 **101** TomO'Brien 89
(Philip Hobbs) *in tch in midfield: rdn and dropped to rr after 5th: lost tch bef 3 out: stl last and mstke 2 out: styd on past btn horses flat: nvr trbld ldrs* **20/1**

0/1- **6** 1 3/4 **Dark Energy**[5] 419 9-11-6 **109** 7ex (t) PaddyBrennan 95
(Fergal O'Brien) *t.k.h: chsd ldrs: mstke 6th: rdn and struggling after 3 out: wknd next* **3/1**[1]

042/ **7** 3/4 **Jaja De Jau**[76] 4712 4-9-12 **95** (t) RachaelGreen[(3)] 76
(Anthony Honeyball) *hld up in tch in last pair: effrt and rdn 3 out: no imp bef next: wknd after 2 out: hung rt flat* **5/1**[2]

650/ **8** 4 1/2 **The Game Is A Foot (IRE)**[65] 4907 6-10-9 **98** AndrewGlassonbury 80
(Gary Moore) *chsd ldrs: lost pl and dropped to rr after 5th: outpcd 3 out: pushed along and sme hdwy between last 2: swtchd rt last: no threat to ldrs and eased fnl 50yds* **8/1**[3]

1/5- **9** 8 **Dubai Glory**[23] 97 5-11-6 **109** MarcGoldstein 84
(Sheena West) *chsd ldrs: rdn 6th: drvn and wknd after next* **14/1**

5/5- **10** 1 1/4 **Amen (IRE)**[14] 240 5-11-1 **104** JamieMoore 77
(Gary Moore) *led tl after 1st: chsd ldr after: ev ch and dived 3 out: wknd qckly bef next* **33/1**

4m 23.5s (-10.80) **Going Correction** -0.625s/f (Firm)
WFA 4 from 5yo+ 18lb 10 Ran SP% **119.0**
Speed ratings (Par 105): **97,96,96,95,90 89,89,87,84,83**
toteswingers 1&2 £28.90, 1&3 £7.20, 2&3 £16.90 CSF £138.34 CT £1183.49 TOTE £14.00: £3.00, £3.50, £3.10; EX 89.10 Trifecta £382.00 Pool: £794.69 - 1.56 winning units..
Owner The Grosvenor Club **Bred** Mrs J J Dye **Trained** Epsom, Surrey

FOCUS
The winner and second met in a similar contest over C&D three weeks ago and give a handle on the form.

489 32REDPOKER.COM H'CAP CHASE (11 fncs 2 omitted) 2m 2f
5:10 (5:10) (Class 5) (0-100,96) 5-Y-0+ **£2,144** (£629; £314; £157)

Form RPR

/45- **1** **Morestead (IRE)**[11] 305 8-11-11 **95** (t) LeightonAspell 102
(Brendan Powell) *in tch towards rr: hdwy into midfield 4th: jnd ldrs 6th: led 8th: edgd lft u.p last: kpt on* **7/1**

/52- **2** 1 1/4 **Upton Mead (IRE)**[11] 305 6-11-4 **95** (b) MrMatthewStanley[(7)] 102+
(Kevin Tork) *t.k.h: hld up wl in tch in midfield: jnd ldrs bef 3 out: chsd wnr 3 out: n.m.r lft: drvn and styd on same pce flat* **4/1**[2]

4/4- **3** 2 **Roc De Guye (FR)**[25] 65 8-10-8 **78** (b) LiamTreadwell 82
(James Evans) *t.k.h: hld up in tch in rr: hdwy into midfield after 6th: rdn and chsd ldng pair 2 out: styd on same pce u.p flat* **6/1**

404/ **4** 14 **Louis Ludwig (IRE)**[211] 2055 8-10-9 **86** AlanJohns[(7)] 79
(Tim Vaughan) *hld up in tch in rr: rdn and hdwy after 8th: wnt 4th and nt fluent 2 out: no imp and wknd flat* **11/2**[3]

3/1- **5** 11 **Time Book (IRE)**[11] 303 7-11-0 **84** (t) TomO'Brien 66
(Colin Tizzard) *mde most tl 8th: drvn and btn bef next: wkng whn j.lft 3 out* **11/4**[1]

4/P- **6** 8 **Normandy Landings**[14] 248 10-10-3 **73** DougieCostello 49
(Neil Mulholland) *w ldr: ev ch bef 3 out: btn after 3 out: wknd next: fdd flat and eased towards fin* **10/1**

344/ **7** 11 **Rosoff (IRE)**[30] 5556 11-11-4 **88** (p) JamieMoore 52
(Laura Mongan) *in tch in rr: drvn and struggling after 6th: bhd and no ch 8th: t.o* **14/1**

600/ **8** 6 **Forest Rhythm (IRE)**[399] 5529 9-11-5 **96** (v) MrKevinJones[(7)] 55
(Seamus Mullins) *t.k.h: chsd ldrs tl lost pl and rdn after 7th: bhd bef 3 out: t.o* **8/1**

4m 33.4s (-1.30) **Going Correction** -0.475s/f (Good) 8 Ran SP% **115.7**
Speed ratings: **83,82,81,75,70 66,62,59**
toteswingers 1&2 £11.20, 1&3 £11.20, 2&3 £6.20 CSF £36.26 CT £179.49 TOTE £8.00: £3.00, £1.10, £2.20; EX 41.60 Trifecta £266.60 Part won. Pool: £355.50 - 0.62 winning units..
Owner L Gilbert **Bred** Declan Hyland And Lillian Montgomery **Trained** Upper Lambourn, Berks

FOCUS
A lively betting heat and a wide-open race.

490 £32 BONUS AT 32RED.COM H'CAP HURDLE (8 hdls 2 omitted) 2m 4f
5:40 (5:40) (Class 5) (0-95,95) 4-Y-0+ **£1,949** (£572; £286; £143)

Form RPR

0/6- **1** **Shaddaii (FR)**[26] 42 7-10-0 **69** oh5 (t) IanPopham 72
(Caroline Keevil) *in tch in midfield: hdwy to chse ldrs 7th: ev ch 2 out (actual last): led and edgd rt ins fnl f: hld on cl home* **16/1**

2/3- **2** shd **Alaccordion**[23] 99 8-10-5 **74** WillKennedy 77
(Violet M Jordan) *chsd ldrs: wnt 2nd 5th: led bef 7th: rdn 2 out (actual last): hdd ins fnl f: battled on wl u.p: jst hld* **6/1**[3]

/U5- **3** 4 1/2 **Airedale Lad (IRE)**[14] 243 12-9-9 **69** oh10 (p) JamesBanks[(5)] 68
(Zoe Davison) *chsd ldrs: j. slowly 7th: drvn after next: chsd ldng pair bypassing last: styd on same pce* **33/1**

P/0- **4** 8 **Dom Lukka (FR)**[23] 99 5-11-12 **95** (t) NoelFehily 88
(Charlie Longsdon) *led tl bef 7th: drvn and no ex 2 out (actual last): wknd bypassing last* **7/1**

0P1/ **5** 2 3/4 **Marie Deja La (FR)**[37] 5379 7-11-10 **93** (b) LeightonAspell 82
(Chris Gordon) *racd on outer: in tch in midfield: rdn and outpcd after 3 out: rallied and kpt on after 2 out (actual last): no threat to ldrs* **5/1**[2]

P/3- **6** 4 **Al Amaan**[14] 243 8-11-7 **90** JamieMoore 77
(Gary Moore) *hld up in tch towards rr: hdwy 5th: chsd ldrs 7th: rdn and no ex 2 out (actual last): wknd on long run-in* **8/1**

5/4- **7** nse **Owner Occupier**[11] 305 8-10-5 **79** (p) HarryDerham[(5)] 65
(Chris Gordon) *in tch in midfield: drvn bef 7th: outpcd u.p 3 out: no threat to ldrs after: plugged on* **12/1**

PP0/ **8** 14 **Hill Forts Gloria (IRE)**[299] 1136 8-9-10 **72** ow2 MrKevinJones[(7)] 45
(Seamus Mullins) *in tch in midfield: rdn and lost pl bypassing 6th: bhd 3 out* **25/1**

000/ **9** 14 **Warsaw Pact (IRE)**[32] 5509 10-11-4 **94** (p) MrLKilgarriff[(7)] 54
(Steven Dixon) *chsd ldr: mstke and pushed along 4th: lost 2nd next: dropped to rr after 7th: wl bhd 2 out (actual last): t.o* **11/1**

654/ **10** shd **Superstición**[24] 5374 4-11-2 **90** MarcGoldstein 45
(Michael Madgwick) *in tch in midfield: mstke 3rd: rdn and struggling 7th: wknd next: t.o* **25/1**

000/ **11** 95 **Classical Twist (IRE)**[80] 4618 5-11-7 **90** APMcCoy
(Jonjo O'Neill) *in tch in rr: mstke and pushed along 3rd: hdwy into midfield bypassing 6th: sn struggling and dropped to rr next: t.o and eased fr next* **11/4**[1]

6/F- **F** **Monroe Park (IRE)**[19] 162 8-10-2 **78** MissECrossman[(7)]
(Alan Blackmore) *t.k.h: hld up towards rr: fell 2nd* **25/1**

0/5- **P** **Charlies Lady**[11] 308 6-9-9 **69** oh5 ThomasGarner[(5)]
(Anna Newton-Smith) *in tch in last trio: rdn bypassing 6th: wknd 3 out: bhd and p.u bef next: dismntd* **50/1**

4m 47.5s (-11.90) **Going Correction** -0.625s/f (Firm)
WFA 4 from 5yo+ 19lb 13 Ran SP% **119.6**
Speed ratings (Par 103): **98,97,96,92,91 90,90,84,79,79 41, ,**
toteswingers 1&2 £15.70, 1&3 £0.00, 2&3 £0.00 CSF £104.33 CT £3149.55 TOTE £19.80: £3.30, £1.80, £9.30; EX 169.90 Trifecta £346.50 Part won. Pool: £462.01 - 0.10 winning units..
Owner Mrs Christine E Davies **Bred** Mme & Nicolas Devilder **Trained** Motcombe, Dorset
■ Stewards' Enquiry : Will Kennedy two-day ban; used whip above permitted level (9th-10th June).

FOCUS
The second-last was omitted after the first circuit due to Monroe Park taking a heavy fall. It led to a right old tussle between the leading pair on the long run to the line.
T/Jkpt: £93,994.50 to a £1 stake. Pool: £198,580.10 - 1.5 winning units T/Plt: £834.70 to a £1 stake. Pool: £94,246.73 - 82.42 winning units T/Qpdt: £81.60 to a £1 stake. Pool: £5483.40 - 49.70 winning units SP

[167]KELSO (L-H)
Sunday, May 26

OFFICIAL GOING: Good to firm (good in places; 8.5)
Wind: Light, half against Weather: Cloudy, warm

491 BORDER FACILITIES NOVICES' H'CAP HURDLE (THE SUNDAY £5K BONUS RACE) (10 hdls) 2m 2f
2:10 (2:10) (Class 3) (0-125,117) 4-Y-0+ **£3,898** (£1,144; £572; £286)

Form RPR

4/2- **1** **Croco Bay (IRE)**[12] 278 6-11-7 **117** TonyKelly[(5)] 124+
(Peter Atkinson) *mde virtually all: rdn clr 2 out: mstke last: kpt on wl* **2/1**[2]

004/ **2** 5 **Groovy Dancer**[32] 5492 6-10-1 **92** WilsonRenwick 92
(Rose Dobbin) *trckd ldrs: rdn and outpcd bef 2 out: rallied and wnt 2nd towards fin: no ch w wnr* **7/1**

540/ **3** 3/4 **Born To Shine (USA)**[21] 2865 5-9-12 **94** GaryRutherford[(5)] 94
(Alan Swinbank) *prom: wnt 2nd 4 out: rdn bef 2 out: one pce whn nt fluent last: no ex and lost 2nd nr fin* **25/1**

B3/- **4** 42 **Lifetime (IRE)**[27] 22 5-11-8 **113** (t) DannyCook 70
(Brian Ellison) *w ldr to 4th: sn drvn along: outpcd after 4 out: btn bef 2 out: t.o* **9/2**[3]

5 10 **Duhallowcountry (IRE)**[21] 7-10-1 **99** MrJHamilton[(7)] 46
(Victor Thompson) *hld up in tch: rdn and outpcd after 4 out: sn struggling: t.o* **20/1**

F00/ **P** **Heart O Annandale (IRE)**[449] 4634 6-10-0 **91** oh6 BrianHughes
(Alistair Whillans) *hld up in tch: outpcd 5th: sn struggling: t.o whn p.u appr 3 out* **33/1**

505/ **P** **Abbey Garth (IRE)**[108] 4078 6-11-0 **105** (t) BrianHarding
(Nicky Richards) *t.k.h: hld up: nt fluent 4th: stmbld bnd after next: rdn bef 6th: lost tch and p.u after next* **7/4**[1]

4m 8.7s (-18.30) **Going Correction** -1.125s/f (Hard) course record 7 Ran SP% **111.9**
Speed ratings (Par 107): **95,92,92,73,69 ,**
toteswingers 1&2 £7.70, 1&3 £7.50, 2&3 £16.90 CSF £14.98 CT £258.04 TOTE £3.00: £2.60, £2.10; EX 15.30 Trifecta £128.10 Pool: £557.43 - 2.30 winning units..
Owner P G Atkinson **Bred** D Caverley **Trained** Yafforth, N Yorks

FOCUS
Rail at innermost position and all distances as advertised. The going had dried out slightly from the overnight description and was good to firm, good in places. The jockeys reported it was riding good to firm. A modest handicap hurdle the feature of which was the support for Abbey Garth.

492 REECE, BEN, JESSICA AND CHARLOTTE COPPOLA H'CAP CHASE (19 fncs) 3m 2f
2:40 (2:40) (Class 5) (0-100,99) 5-Y-0+ **£3,119** (£915; £457; £228)

Form RPR

4/2- **1** **Minstalad**[3] [444] 9-9-11 **73** oh4 BrianToomey(3) 86+
(Karen Tutty) *led: rdn and hdd 3 out: rallied and regained ld next: edgd rt run-in: drvn out* **10/3**[1]

0/2- **2** *1* **Snuker**[11] [311] 6-10-5 **78** BrianHughes 90
(James Ewart) *chsd ldrs: drvn 5 out: outpcd after 3 out: styd on wl fr last to take 2nd nr fin: nt rch wnr* **9/2**[3]

3/1- **3** *½* **Borolee (IRE)**[18] [172] 10-10-12 **90** TonyKelly(5) 100
(Ferdy Murphy, France) *hld up: hit 1st: pushed along 13th: hdwy and ev ch 3 out: sn rdn: kpt on fr last: lost 2nd nr fin* **7/1**

4/5- **4** *shd* **More Equity**[18] [172] 11-11-5 **92** RyanMania 102
(Dianne Sayer) *prom: wnt 2nd 13th: led 3 out to next: kpt on same pce u.p fr last* **10/1**

2P2/ **5** *36* **Sierra Victor (IRE)**[364] [456] 10-10-12 **92** MrJHamilton(7) 70
(Rose Dobbin) *chsd ldrs: mstke 3rd: rdn fr 7th: rallied: wknd fr 5 out: t.o* **14/1**

P/1- **6** *½* **Shooting Times**[11] [311] 8-11-2 **89** (v) PeterBuchanan 66
(Lucinda Russell) *chsd wnr to 13th: rdn and struggling fr 5 out: t.o* **5/1**

3/1- **7** *30* **Rebel Swing**[5] [420] 7-11-7 **99** SamanthaDrake(5) 49
(Joanne Foster) *nt fluent on occasions in rr: struggling fr 13th: t.o* **7/2**[2]

2/5- **8** *3½* **Quinder Spring (FR)**[18] [169] 9-11-4 **98** (p) GrantCockburn(7) 45
(Lucinda Russell) *hld up: rdn and outpcd 14th: sn struggling: t.o* **20/1**

6m 26.4s (-20.80) **Going Correction** -0.675s/f (Firm) **8** Ran SP% **113.2**
Speed ratings: **105,104,104,104,93 93,84,82**
toteswingers 1&2 £3.60, 1&3 £4.20, 2&3 £7.30 CSF £18.76 CT £96.42 TOTE £7.50: £2.20, £1.80, £2.40; EX 36.60 Trifecta £199.20 Pool: £361.30 - 1.36 winning units..
Owner A R Sutcliffe **Bred** A Longbottom **Trained** Osmotherley, N Yorks

FOCUS
A moderate staying handicap chase but a good finish.

493 KOSB NOVICES' H'CAP CHASE (12 fncs) 2m 1f
3:15 (3:15) (Class 4) (0-115,112) 5-Y-0+ **£4,548** (£1,335; £667; £333)

Form RPR

2/1- **1** **Endeavor**[18] [171] 8-11-0 **100** RyanMania 110+
(Dianne Sayer) *trckd ldrs: led after 4 out: drvn and styd on strly fr 2 out* **5/1**[3]

2/3- **2** *9* **Some Lad (IRE)**[11] [316] 8-10-9 **95** DenisO'Regan 97
(Alison Hamilton) *t.k.h early: trckd ldrs: effrt and wnt 2nd 3 out: rdn next: kpt on same pce* **12/1**

36F/ **3** *6* **Beidh Tine Anseo (IRE)**[242] [1640] 7-11-12 **112** (p) PeterBuchanan 108
(Lucinda Russell) *hld up in tch: stdy hdwy bef 4 out: rdn next: outpcd by first two bef 2 out* **12/1**

/32- **4** *9* **Gin Cobbler**[12] [279] 7-10-11 **104** MrJHamilton(7) 92
(Victor Thompson) *hld up in tch: stdy hdwy and cl up 5 out: rdn and outpcd after next: no imp whn lft mod 4th bef 2 out* **9/2**[2]

5/P- **5** *1½* **Craicneasy (IRE)**[18] [172] 10-10-0 **86** oh27 (t) WilsonRenwick 73
(Bruce Mactaggart) *hld up: rdn along 1/2-way: outpcd fr 5 out: n.d after* **100/1**

4/1- **6** *4* **Suprise Vendor (IRE)**[22] [109] 7-10-11 **102** GaryRutherford(5) 87
(Stuart Coltherd) *chsd ldrs: drvn and outpcd 5 out: btn fnl 3* **6/1**

6/0- **7** *½* **Alba King (IRE)**[12] [279] 7-10-0 **91** JonathanEngland(5) 74
(Sue Smith) *prom: rdn and outpcd 7th: n.d after* **9/1**

052/ **P** **Freddie Brown**[27] [23] 9-11-3 **103** (t) LucyAlexander
(George Charlton) *led: hit 4 out: sn rdn and hdd: 4th and outpcd whn p.u bef last* **9/2**[2]

6/4- **U** **My Idea**[18] [167] 7-11-2 **102** (t) MichaelMcAlister
(Maurice Barnes) *hld up: stmbld and uns rdr 3rd* **4/1**[1]

4m 6.5s (-11.50) **Going Correction** -0.675s/f (Firm) **9** Ran SP% **113.7**
Speed ratings: **100,95,92,88,88 86,85, ,**
toteswingers 1&2 £6.60, 1&3 £10.30, 2&3 £17.40 CSF £59.29 CT £678.06 TOTE £4.90: £1.80, £4.00, £2.30; EX 36.30 TRIFECTA Pool: £367.91 - 1.00 winning units..
Owner Mrs Margaret Coppola **Bred** Bradmill Meat Ltd **Trained** Hackthorpe, Cumbria

FOCUS
An ordinary novice handicap chase but an easy success.

494 JACK CLARK SWAN SONG NOVICES' HURDLE (8 hdls) 2m 110y
3:50 (3:50) (Class 4) 4-Y-0+ **£3,898** (£1,144; £572; £286)

Form RPR

1/1- **1** **Life And Soul (IRE)**[9] [354] 6-11-12 127 (p) JasonMaguire 128+
(Donald McCain) *mde all: clr to 3 out: rdn bef next: styd on wl fr last* **8/13**[1]

026/ **2** *3* **Potomac (IRE)**[27] [22] 5-10-12 113 WilsonRenwick 111
(Rose Dobbin) *in tch: hdwy to chse wnr 2 out: sn rdn: one pce fr last* **7/2**[2]

1/U- **3** *16* **Lone Foot Laddie (IRE)**[10] [344] 4-10-8 115 GrahamWatters(7) 99
(Lucinda Russell) *nt fluent on occasions: cl up: effrt and clsd on wnr 3 out: nt fluent and outpcd fr next* **6/1**[3]

0/ **4** *½* **Turtle Watch**[37] [5373] 5-10-12 0 JamesReveley 95
(Pauline Robson) *hld up: stdy hdwy after 3 out: shkn up and outpcd fr next* **22/1**

6/0- **5** *15* **Fling Me (IRE)**[17] [185] 6-10-12 0 BrianHarding 80
(Rose Dobbin) *hld up: rdn and hdwy after 3 out: wknd fr next* **16/1**

0/0- **6** *35* **Honourable Gent**[15] [218] 5-10-12 0 RichieMcGrath 45
(Rose Dobbin) *hld up: rdn after 4 out: nvr on terms* **33/1**

0/P- **7** *55* **Northern Warrior**[11] [313] 5-10-5 0 ShaunDobbin(7)
(Hugh Burns) *nt fluent: sn wl bhd: tailied off fnl circ* **50/1**

100/ **P** **Amisfield Lad**[78] [4654] 4-10-8 0 DannyCook
(Michael Smith) *cl up tl outpcd 4 out: struggling next: p.u bef 2 out* **14/1**

3m 38.9s (-22.90) **Going Correction** -1.125s/f (Hard) course record
WFA 4 from 5yo+ 18lb **8** Ran SP% **120.2**
Speed ratings (Par 105): **108,106,99,98,91 75,49,**
toteswingers 1&2 £1.02, 1&3 £1.02, 2&3 £10.70 CSF £3.39 CT £7.50 TOTE £1.70: £1.10, £1.50, £1.40; EX 4.00 Trifecta £7.50 Pool: £361.05 - 36.08 winning units..
Owner Matthew Taylor **Bred** Kildaragh Stud **Trained** Cholmondeley, Cheshire

FOCUS
A fair novice hurdle for the time of year.

495 JOHN SMITH'S H'CAP CHASE (FOR THE WILFRED & PATRICIA CRAWFORD MEMORIAL TROPHY) (19 fncs) 3m 2f
4:25 (4:25) (Class 3) (0-125,125) 5-Y-0+ **£9,747** (£2,862; £1,431; £715)

Form RPR

P/1- **1** **Royale Knight**[14] [248] 7-10-0 **99** oh1 SamTwiston-Davies 121+
(Dr Richard Newland) *trckd ldrs: led gng wl appr 3 out: clr whn shkn up after next: kpt on strly* **5/2**[1]

4/2- **2** *11* **Carrigdhoun (IRE)**[18] [169] 8-11-4 **117** (tp) MichaelMcAlister 124
(Maurice Barnes) *disp ld: led 4 out to next: outpcd by wnr fnl 2f* **7/1**

P/0- **3** *21* **Solway Bay**[18] [169] 11-10-0 **99** (bt) HarryHaynes 93
(Lisa Harrison) *hld up in tch: stdy hdwy bef 4 out: effrt after next: wknd appr last* **25/1**

644/ **4** *6* **Call Me Mulligan (IRE)**[35] [5427] 9-9-12 **104** (b) JohnDawson(7) 87
(John Wade) *slt ld to 4 out: rdn and wknd after next* **5/1**[3]

3/3- **5** *8* **Papa Caruso**[15] [220] 9-10-13 **112** RyanMania 88
(Sue Smith) *hld up: outpcd whn hit 12th: struggling fr next* **9/2**[2]

P/3- **6** *37* **Lets Get Serious (IRE)**[18] [170] 7-11-12 **125** (b) BrianHughes 67
(James Ewart) *chsd ldrs: drvn and outpcd 14th: lost tch fr next: t.o* **9/2**[2]

F36/ **7** *1* **Nodform Richard**[32] [5503] 7-11-5 **118** (p) JasonMaguire 59
(Donald McCain) *hld up: struggling bef 13th: t.o* **7/1**

6m 25.0s (-22.20) **Going Correction** -0.675s/f (Firm) **7** Ran SP% **110.4**
Speed ratings: **107,103,97,95,92 81,81**
toteswingers 1&2 £1.10, 1&3 £0.00, 2&3 £0.00 CSF £18.54 CT £324.74 TOTE £3.40: £2.10, £3.40; EX 15.50 Trifecta £51.40 Pool: £431.85 - 6.30 winning units..
Owner C E Stedman & R J Corsan **Bred** R D And Mrs J S Chugg **Trained** Claines, Worcs
■ Stewards' Enquiry : John Dawson two-day ban; careless riding (9th-10th June).

FOCUS
Decent prize-money for this feature event but there were several withdrawals on account of the ground. The time was 1.4sec faster than the earlier contest over the trip.

496 ROYAL SCOTS DRAGOON GUARDS CHALLENGE CUP (AN OPEN HUNTERS' CHASE) (19 fncs) 3m 2f
5:00 (5:00) (Class 4) 5-Y-0+ **£3,743** (£1,161; £580; £290)

Form RPR

322/ **1** **Drom**[20] 10-11-11 104 MrWKitchman(7) 113+
(Mrs C Drury) *cl up: led 3rd: mde rest: rdn bef 2 out: styd on gamely* **9/2**[3]

012/ **2** *4½* **Buckstruther (IRE)**[27] [28] 11-11-13 99 (p) MrJHamilton(5) 107
(Alastair Bell) *hld up in midfield: stdy hdwy 5 out: effrt and chsd wnr last: kpt on: no imp* **7/2**[2]

6/1- **3** *1¾* **Back On The Road (IRE)**[11] [315] 11-12-1 109 MrJamieAlexander(7) 110
(N W Alexander) *hld up: hdwy on outside and in tch 8th: hit and outpcd 13th: rdn bef 3 out: styd on fr last: nrst fin* **15/2**

2/2- **4** *6* **Harry Flashman**[11] [315] 12-11-11 107 MrNOrpwood(7) 100
(Greg Aitken) *led to 3rd: chsd wnr: rdn bef 2 out: wknd after last* **3/1**[1]

3/P- **5** *3½* **Senor Alco (FR)**[7] 7-11-11 94 MrCDawson(3) 94
(Victor Thompson) *in tch: mstke 11th: effrt and rdn 3 out: wknd after last* **8/1**

PPP/ **6** *9* **Itzacliche (IRE)**[27] [25] 13-11-13 94 (v[1]) MissJRRichards(5) 88
(Nicky Richards) *cl up: rdn and outpcd bef 4 out: n.d after* **16/1**

P03/ **7** *¾* **Go West (IRE)**[31] [5524] 12-11-7 95 (v) MrTHamilton(7) 84
(A Hamilton) *nt fluent in rr: struggling fnl circ: nvr on terms* **16/1**

6/2- **8** *9* **A New Rising (IRE)**[22] [112] 11-11-7 73 (p) MrJLyttle(7) 76
(M E Ellwood) *hld up: stdy hdwy 1/2-way: outpcd 14th: struggling fr 4 out* **25/1**

P/4- **P** **Waterski**[11] [315] 12-11-7 68 (p) MissAMcGregor(7)
(Jean McGregor) *in tch: lost pl whn hit 8th: lost tch 12th: t.o whn p.u after next* **66/1**

124/ **P** **Pistolet Time (IRE)**[51] [5170] 11-11-11 0 MrGCrow(3)
(Mrs Caroline Crow) *nt fluent in rr: struggling fr 1/2-way: t.o whn p.u bef 2 out* **9/1**

U/0- **P** **Barr Head (IRE)**[11] [315] 9-11-7 57 (p) MrRWilson(7)
(Lucy Normile) *mstkes in midfield: wknd fr 13th: t.o whn p.u bef 2 out* **100/1**

6m 34.8s (-12.40) **Going Correction** -0.675s/f (Firm) **11** Ran SP% **116.4**
Speed ratings: **92,90,90,88,87 84,84,81, ,**
toteswingers 1&2 £2.40, 1&3 £8.80, 2&3 £6.00 CSF £20.96 TOTE £6.10: £2.30, £1.70, £1.50; EX 39.60 Trifecta £103.30 Pool: £390.05 - 2.83 winning units..
Owner Paul Drury **Bred** Miss Ellen Delaney **Trained** Sheriff Hutton, N Yorks

FOCUS
Not a bad hunters' chase, featuring a number of veterans.

497 MERCEDES BENZ OF COLDSTREAM STANDARD OPEN NATIONAL HUNT FLAT RACE (DIV I) 2m 110y
5:30 (5:30) (Class 5) 4-6-Y-0 **£2,599** (£763; £381; £190)

Form RPR

60/ **1** **Magic Present**[33] [5483] 6-11-2 0 BrianHughes 92+
(Malcolm Jefferson) *mde all at stdy pce: rdn along over 2f out: edgd rt ins fnl f: r.o wl* **11/4**[1]

00/- **2** *nk* **Biggar (IRE)**[30] [5550] 5-11-2 0 WilsonRenwick 92
(Andrew Parker) *trckd ldrs: effrt and chsd wnr 2f out: ev ch ins fnl f: kpt on: hld nr fin* **7/2**[2]

/3- **3** *6* **Proud Jack**[15] [225] 5-10-9 0 GrahamWatters(7) 86
(Ann Hamilton) *hld up: rdn over 2f out: kpt on fnl f: nt rch first two* **8/1**

0/4- **4** *½* **Dorset Dora**[24] [76] 5-10-2 0 (t) StephenMulqueen(7) 79
(Maurice Barnes) *hld up in tch: hdwy on outside to chse ldrs over 5f out: rdn over 2f out: outpcd over 1f out* **16/1**

5 *¾* **Chester Legend** 6-10-9 0 JohnDawson(7) 85
(Sue Taylor) *hld up in tch: drvn along over 2f out: sn no ex* **16/1**

6 *7* **Royal Rojo** 4-10-12 0 DenisO'Regan 76+
(Chris Grant) *prom: outpcd whn hung bdly rt 2f out: sn wknd* **5/1**[3]

7 *2½* **Macgregor's Ace** 4-10-12 0 LucyAlexander 71
(N W Alexander) *cl up tl rdn and wknd over 2f out* **7/2**[2]

3m 51.0s (-5.20) **Going Correction** -1.125s/f (Hard)
WFA 4 from 5yo+ 4lb **7** Ran SP% **110.7**
Speed ratings: **67,66,64,63,63 60,58**
toteswingers 1&2 £1.60, 1&3 £2.60, 2&3 £4.60 CSF £11.67 TOTE £3.80: £2.50, £2.00; EX 13.40 Trifecta £50.50 Pool: £625.24 - 9.28 winning units..
Owner P Nelson **Bred** Peter Nelson **Trained** Norton, N Yorks

FOCUS
The first division of this bumper and a race weakened by the absence of the forecast market leaders.

498 MERCEDES BENZ OF COLDSTREAM STANDARD OPEN NATIONAL HUNT FLAT RACE (DIV II) 2m 110y

6:00 (6:00) (Class 5) 4-6-Y-0 **£2,599** (£763; £381; £190)

Form	Pos	Dist	Horse	RPR
	1		**Mr Satco (IRE)**98 5-11-2 0 .... JasonMaguire (Donald McCain) *mde all: rdn 2f out: styd on wl fnl f* **6/1**	103+
2/U-	2	1	**Powderonthebonnet (IRE)**18 [173] 5-11-2 0 .... SamTwiston-Davies (Alan Swinbank) *trckd ldrs: effrt and chsd wnr 2f out: kpt on fnl f: hld towards fin* **13/8**1	102
	3	4 ½	**Lagan Canal (IRE)**56 [5055] 6-11-2 0 .... BrianHughes (A J Martin, Ire) *hld up: smooth hdwy to chse ldrs 3f out: rdn and effrt over 1f out: outpcd ins fnl f* **11/4**2	98
4/	4	2	**Definite Maybe (IRE)**373 [340] 5-11-2 0 .... DenisO'Regan (Martin Todhunter) *chsd wnr to 2f out: edgd lft and outpcd over 1f out: sn no ex* **4/1**3	96
0-	5	20	**Poppies Milan (IRE)**18 [173] 4-10-12 0 .... LucyAlexander (Ferdy Murphy, France) *hld up in tch: rdn over 4f out: no imp fr 2f out* **28/1**	72
/	6	4	**Chanceofa Lifetime (IRE)**7 6-10-9 0 .... MrJHamilton(7) (Victor Thompson) *in tch: rdn and outpcd over 3f out: sn wknd* **18/1**	72
	7	8	**Samandy** 4-9-12 0 .... JamesCorbett(7) (Susan Corbett) *hld up in tch: struggling over 4f out: sn btn* **50/1**	53
6/	P		**Mixed Blend**35 [5428] 4-10-9 0 .... EwanWhillans(3) (Alistair Whillans) *t.k.h: hld up: hdwy and in tch whn broke down 2f out: sn p.u and dismntd* **20/1**	

3m 38.8s (-17.40) **Going Correction** -1.125s/f (Hard)
WFA 4 from 5yo+ 4lb **8** Ran SP% **114.5**
Speed ratings: **95,94,92,91,82 80,76,**
toteswingers 1&2 £4.60, 1&3 £3.10, 2&3 £1.20 CSF £15.96 TOTE £6.30: £1.90, £1.10, £1.60; EX 16.80 Trifecta £81.00 Pool: £1145.13 - 10.59 winning units..
Owner D McCain Jnr **Bred** Lillian Mahon **Trained** Cholmondeley, Cheshire
FOCUS
The second leg of the bumper and the time was 12.2secs faster than the slowly run first leg.
T/Plt: £56.00 to a £1 stake. Pool: £69,951.27 - 911.14 winning units T/Qpdt: £10.30 to a £1 stake. Pool: £4161.64 - 296.78 winning units RY

374 UTTOXETER (L-H)

Sunday, May 26

OFFICIAL GOING: Chase course - good (good to firm in places); hurdle course - good to firm (good in places); (chs 6.2; hdl 6.8)
Wind: light 1/2 against Weather: fine and sunny, warm

499 LISA OLDHAM MAIDEN HURDLE (12 hdls) 3m

2:00 (2:00) (Class 5) 5-Y-0+ **£2,209** (£648; £324; £162)

Form	Pos	Dist	Horse	RPR
6/5-	1		**Henri Parry Morgan**20 [140] 5-11-0 0 .... DonalDevereux (Peter Bowen) *chsd ldrs: hrd drvn to ld 3 out: sn forged wl clr: kpt up to work* **5/2**2	125+
5/3-	2	42	**Polarbrook (IRE)**26 [47] 6-11-0 107 .... HenryBrooke (Donald McCain) *chsd ldrs: 2nd 8th: chsd wnr fr 3 out: one pce* **11/4**3	90
4-	3	8	**Mr Trilby (IRE)**20 [146] 6-11-0 0 ....(b) TomScudamore (David Pipe) *led: reminders and qckned pce after 6th: hdd 3 out: one pce* **13/2**	80
044/	4	14	**Burlington Bertie (IRE)**30 [5551] 5-10-7 0 .... PatrickCorbett(7) (Sarah Humphrey) *trckd ldr: drvn 9th: lost pl next* **12/1**	69
1/3-	5	81	**Four Shuck Men (IRE)**24 [72] 5-11-0 0 .... RichardJohnson (Tim Vaughan) *chsd ldrs: drvn and outpcd 8th: sn lost pl and bhd: t.o 3 out: eventually completed* **2/1**1	
0/P-	P		**Captain Wilson**17 [186] 6-10-9 0 ....(t) KillianMoore(5) (Mark Rimell) *in rr: nt fluent and reminders 4th: bhd next: t.o whn p.u after 7th* **50/1**	
0/6-	P		**Cardinal Richelieu (IRE)**17 [192] 5-10-7 0 ....(b1) FrancisHayes(7) (Tom Gretton) *mstkes: chsd ldrs: reminders 4th: lost pl and blnd next: t.o 6th: blnd bdly next: immediately p.u* **100/1**	

5m 34.8s (-15.20) **Going Correction** -0.40s/f (Good) **7** Ran SP% **112.5**
Speed ratings: **109,95,92,87,60 ,**
toteswingers 1&2 £2.30, 1&3 £7.00, 2&3 £1.60 CSF £9.77 TOTE £3.80: £1.80, £1.50; EX 20.00 Trifecta £50.60 Pool: £868.54 - 12.86 winning units..
Owner Ednyfed & Elizabeth Morgan **Bred** J R Bryan **Trained** Little Newcastle, Pembrokes
FOCUS
Hurdles moved out 3-4 metres from last Saturday's fixture. Divided bends on fresh ground. A one-sided maiden hurdle in the end.

500 ALWAYS WAINING BEGINNERS' CHASE (14 fncs 1 omitted) 2m 4f

2:30 (2:30) (Class 4) 5-Y-0+ **£4,216** (£1,272; £655; £347)

Form	Pos	Dist	Horse	RPR
11P/	1		**Atlanta Falcon (IRE)**219 [1915] 8-11-0 0 ....(t) HenryBrooke (Donald McCain) *t.k.h: led to 3rd: w ldrs: led 3 out: drvn out* **3/1**3	110
335/	2	4	**Duneen Point (IRE)**44 [5271] 9-10-7 0 .... JPKiely(7) (Tim Vaughan) *nt fluent in rr: bhd fr 6th: hdwy 10th: lft modest 3rd and hmpd 2 out: mde up 10 l on run-in to snatch 2nd post* **12/1**	108
232/	3	nse	**Paddy The Hare (IRE)**272 [1391] 8-11-0 118 .... RichardJohnson (Dr Richard Newland) *w ldrs: led 4th to 7th: led 9th to 3 out: kpt on same pce run-in* **9/4**2	107
3/P-	4	49	**Fitz Volonte**11 [302] 6-10-7 100 .... MrJMartin(7) (Andrew J Martin) *t.k.h: led 3rd to next: led 7th to 9th: reminders next: lost pl 10th: bhd next: sn t.o* **33/1**	62
5/F-	F		**Tony Dinozzo (FR)**14 [237] 6-11-0 0 .... DonalDevereux (Peter Bowen) *trckd ldrs 6th: fdd 4 out: 5 l down in 3rd whn fell 2 out* **10/1**	101
PP6/	P		**The Jugopolist (IRE)**83 [4562] 6-10-7 0 .... PatrickCorbett(7) (Rebecca Curtis) *chsd ldrs: pushed along 5th: lost pl next: bhd and reminders 9th: t.o 4 out: p.u bef next* **7/4**1	

4m 57.1s (-8.40) **Going Correction** -0.225s/f (Good) **6** Ran SP% **111.9**
Speed ratings: **107,105,105,85,**
toteswingers 1&2 £5.50, 1&3 £2.80, 2&3 £3.10 CSF £32.01 TOTE £4.40: £2.30, £5.70; EX 39.70 Trifecta £162.00 Pool: £198.82 - 2.30 winning units..
Owner D McCain Jnr **Bred** T D Howley Jnr **Trained** Cholmondeley, Cheshire
FOCUS
Fair form from the principals in this maiden chase.

501 MIDLANDS AIR AMBULANCE CONDITIONAL JOCKEYS' (S) HURDLE (9 hdls) 2m

3:05 (3:05) (Class 5) 4-7-Y-0 **£1,949** (£572; £286; £143)

Form	Pos	Dist	Horse	RPR
/06-	1		**Diamond Tammy (IRE)**14 [253] 7-10-12 91 .... PeterCarberry (Andy Hobbs) *in rr-div: hdwy 3 out: led 2 out: j.lft and lft clr last* **14/1**	90
546/	2	16	**Ghaabesh (IRE)**188 [2523] 6-10-12 110 ....(t) HarryChalloner (Barry Leavy) *hmpd 1st: in rr: hdwy 3 out: upsides whn blnd 2 out: wknd and lft modest 2nd last* **8/1**	80
1/1-	3	1 ¼	**Not Til Monday (IRE)**19 [161] 7-11-8 125 ....(v) AdamWedge (J R Jenkins) *set str pce: mstke 3rd: drvn 6th: hdd appr next: wknd appr 2 out: lft poor 3rd last* **9/4**2	84
542/	4	4	**Quarton (IRE)**392 [1] 6-10-4 108 ....(t) ConorRing(8) (Evan Williams) *lost pl 5th: sn bhd: lft poor 4th last* **10/3**3	71
/3P-	P		**Abbi Jicaro**17 [188] 6-10-0 74 ....(t) OllieGarner(5) (Mark Shears) *hld up: wnt 3rd 4th: chsd ldng pair next: drvn 6th: lost pl and 6th whn mstke 3 out: sn bhd: poor 5th whn bdly hmpd and sddle slipped last: sn p.u* **33/1**	
3/4-	F		**Juno The Muffinman (IRE)**26 [47] 4-10-0 120 ....(v) JPKiely(8) (Tim Vaughan) *j.lft 1st: chsd ldr: led appr 3 out: hdd 2 out: 1 1/2 l down and hld whn fell last* **7/4**1	84

3m 48.2s (-3.80) **Going Correction** -0.40s/f (Good)
WFA 4 from 6yo+ 18lb **6** Ran SP% **110.9**
Speed ratings: **93,85,84,82,**
toteswingers 1&2 £0.00, 1&3 £1.60, 2&3 £0.00 CSF £104.94 TOTE £12.50: £3.30, £3.20; EX 125.30 Trifecta £291.30 Part won. Pool: £388.50 - 0.80 winning units..There was no bid for the winner
Owner Three Counties Racing 2 & A G Hobbs **Bred** Mrs Roisin Reavey **Trained** Hanley Swan, Worcs
FOCUS
Not the easiest race to assess.

502 THREE PEAKS CHALLENGE FOR LISA 14-15 JUNE MARES' MAIDEN HURDLE (10 hdls) 2m 4f 110y

3:40 (3:41) (Class 5) 4-Y-0+ **£2,209** (£648; £324; £162)

Form	Pos	Dist	Horse	RPR
636/	1		**Massannie (IRE)**177 [2751] 5-11-0 0 .... TomScudamore (David Pipe) *gave problems s: hld up: handy 3rd 6th: upsides 3 out: led appr next: drvn clr between last 2: v comf* **3/1**2	121+
2-	2	10	**My Lucky Flame (IRE)**11 [317] 6-11-0 0 .... MarkGrant (Sean Curran) *led: jnd 3 out: hdd appr next: kpt on: no ch w wnr* **5/2**1	109
/42-	3	1 ½	**Emerald Rose**14 [252] 6-11-0 102 .... WayneHutchinson (Julian Smith) *chsd ldrs: drvn 5th: one pce fr 3 out: modest 3rd next* **3/1**2	109
6/3-	4	11	**Presenting Me (IRE)**26 [41] 5-10-7 0 .... ConorRing(7) (Evan Williams) *chsd ldrs: drvn 7th: outpcd next: sn fdd* **20/1**	97
0/F-	5	1	**Venceremos**23 [91] 6-10-11 0 ....(p) KielanWoods(3) (Charlie Longsdon) *chsd ldrs: drvn 7th: outpcd next: sn fdd* **12/1**	96
	6	8	**China Reel (IRE)** 4-10-9 0 .... RichieMcLernon (Jonjo O'Neill) *hld up in rr: hdwy 6th: modest 4th appr 3 out: 5th and wkng whn nt fluent 2 out* **20/1**	86
6/3-	P		**Strangelittlegirl**25 [70] 5-10-7 0 .... MarkMarris(7) (Patrick Gilligan) *t.k.h: trcking ldrs 4th: eased after 6th: bhd whn p.u bef next* **33/1**	
201/	P		**Bypass**81 [4592] 4-10-9 0 .... RichardJohnson (Tim Vaughan) *nt jump wl in rr: bhd and reluactnt 5th: t.o next: p.u bef 2 out* **11/2**3	
0-	P		**Deb's Town**13 [270] 6-11-0 0 .... LeeEdwards (Tony Carroll) *chsd ldrs: blnd 3rd: drvn next: lost pl after 5th: sn bhd: t.o whn p.u bef 7th* **80/1**	

4m 51.2s (-7.80) **Going Correction** -0.40s/f (Good)
WFA 4 from 5yo+ 19lb **9** Ran SP% **115.3**
Speed ratings (Par 103): **98,94,93,89,89 86, , ,**
toteswingers 1&2 £2.30, 1&3 £5.00, 2&3 £1.30 CSF £10.76 TOTE £3.20: £1.10, £1.80, £1.50; EX 21.30 Trifecta £42.10 Pool: £494.22 - 8.79 winning units..
Owner Wayne Clifford **Bred** Mrs S Clifford **Trained** Nicholashayne, Devon
FOCUS
A modest event.

503 DOVE VALLEY FIRST RESPONDER H'CAP HURDLE (10 hdls) 2m 4f 110y

4:15 (4:16) (Class 4) (0-110,110) 4-Y-0+ **£3,249** (£954; £477; £238)

Form	Pos	Dist	Horse	RPR
/21-	1		**My Lad Percy**14 [253] 5-11-0 **105** ....(p) PatrickCorbett(7) (Rebecca Curtis) *chsd ldrs: led appr 2 out: hld on towards fin* **9/2**1	108+
5/5-	2	½	**Lucky Lukey**11 [322] 7-10-11 **95** .... SeanQuinlan (Jennie Candlish) *mid-div: hdwy 7th: sn chsng ldrs: 2nd appr last: styd on: no ex clsng stages* **13/2**	100
P/4-	3	6	**River Purple**16 [201] 6-10-0 **87** ....(t) PeterCarberry(3) (John Mackie) *chsd ldrs: one pce fr 2 out: tk 3rd nr fin* **11/2**3	85
322/	4	nk	**Forever Waining (IRE)**602 [1828] 7-11-0 **98** ....(t) DonalDevereux (Peter Bowen) *trckd ldrs: cl 2nd 2 out: one pce between last 2* **5/1**2	95
0/4-	5	11	**Saga De Tercey (FR)**22 [110] 8-11-7 **105** ....(b) HenryBrooke (Donald McCain) *w ldrs: led bef 3 out: hdd appr 2 out: wknd appr last* **20/1**	92
/11-	6	1 ½	**Molon Labe (IRE)**8 [375] 6-11-9 **110** ....(t) AdamWedge(3) (David Rees) *chsd ldrs: wknd appr 2 out* **7/1**	99+
454/	7	1 ½	**Lean Burn (USA)**28 [21] 7-9-12 **87** .... HarryChalloner(5) (Barry Leavy) *in rr: hdwy 6th: in tch after next: lost pl appr next* **16/1**	72
/44-	8	7	**Trip The Light**13 [267] 8-11-3 **108** ....(p) ConorShoemark(7) (Phil Middleton) *rr-div: drvn and hdwy 6th: wknd appr 3 out* **7/1**	88
3/1-	9	39	**Molaise Lad (IRE)**11 [319] 7-11-11 **109** ....(v) WayneHutchinson (Barry Brennan) *led 2nd: hdd bef 3 out: wkng whn hmpd and lost pl bnd appr 3 out: sn bhd: t.o* **14/1**	52
2/0-	10	9	**Hail Tiberius**13 [267] 6-10-6 **90** ....(e) TomSiddall (Martin Keighley) *t.k.h in rr: bhd fr 6th: t.o 3 out* **40/1**	25
FP0/	11	2	**Honour The World (IRE)**227 [1807] 8-11-7 **105** ....(b) DavidEngland (Shaun Lycett) *in rr: bhd fr 6th: t.o 3 out* **50/1**	38
110/	12	11	**Geminus (IRE)**215 [1974] 5-11-8 **106** ....(t) RichardJohnson (Tim Vaughan) *in rr: bhd fr 6th: t.o 3 out* **12/1**	30
5P/	13	4 ½	**Fred Kennet**77 [4682] 8-11-2 **100** .... GerardTumelty (Paul Fitzsimons) *mid-div: lost pl after 7th: bhd next: t.o* **33/1**	19

404/ **14** *83* **Gap Of Dunloe (IRE)**[33] 5464 5-11-12 **110**......................(t) PaulMoloney
(Evan Williams) *led to 2nd: chsd ldrs: lost pl 4th: sn bhd: t.o 6th: virtually p.u: eventually completed* **50/1**

4m 48.1s (-10.90) **Going Correction** -0.40s/f (Good) **14** Ran SP% **122.9**
Speed ratings (Par 105): **104,103,101,101,97 96,96,93,78,75 74,70,68,36**
toteswingers 1&2 £16.30, 1&3 £3.70, 2&3 £0.00 CSF £33.37 CT £168.32 TOTE £6.00: £2.50, £1.60, £2.90; EX 33.70 Trifecta £215.50 Pool: £304.68 - 1.06 winning units..
Owner Davies & Price **Bred** D J M & Mrs Eileen Milligan **Trained** Newport, Dyfed

FOCUS
This is likely to prove solid form for the level.

504 QUEEN ELIZABETH HOSPITAL BIRMINGHAM H'CAP CHASE (16 fncs 2 omitted) 3m
4:50 (4:51) (Class 4) (0-115,115) 5-Y-0 **£3,924** (£1,159; £579; £290; £145)

Form RPR

0/3- **1** **Turbo Du Ranch (FR)**[19] 164 6-11-10 **113**...........(b) WayneHutchinson 129+
(Warren Greatrex) *hld up in rr: hdwy 11th: handy 3rd 3 out: lft in ld next: j.lft last: drvn clr* **9/1**

1/2- **2** *14* **Dont Tell Sailor (IRE)**[22] 113 7-11-5 **115**......................... ConorRing(7) 119
(Jennie Candlish) *chsd ldrs: hit 1st: lft 2nd 2 out: kpt on same pce* **3/1**[1]

/42- **3** *¾* **Waltzing Tornado (IRE)**[14] 248 9-10-2 **91**...........................(p) DPFahy 100+
(Andy Hobbs) *hld up in rr: hdwy 10th: chsng ldrs whn hit 12th: lft 4th whn hmpd 2 out: kpt on to take modest 3rd nr fin* **15/2**

2/1- **4** *2½* **Hodgson (IRE)**[8] 370 8-11-4 **107**................................(tp) DonalDevereux 111+
(Peter Bowen) *w ldrs: one pce fr 3 out: lft 3rd next* **7/2**[2]

6/P- **5** *17* **Wheres The Hare (IRE)**[22] 118 6-11-11 **114**.........(b[1]) RichieMcLernon 99
(Jonjo O'Neill) *hld up: hdwy 10th: wknd 3 out* **14/1**

0/0- **6** *33* **Oranger (FR)**[14] 248 11-9-10 **90**.......................................(b) BenPoste(5) 45
(Andrew J Martin) *mid-div: hit 7th: lost pl 12th: bhd fr 4 out: t.o 2 out* **22/1**

5P/- **P** **Morning Moment**[39] 5351 11-11-3 **113**.................(p) MrJonathanBailey(7)
(Caroline Bailey) *led to 3rd: drvn 6th: outpcd and reminders 11th: lost pl next: bhd 4 out: p.u bef next* **13/2**[3]

2/2- **P** **Key Cutter (FR)**[17] 190 9-11-7 **113**............................(bt) JakeGreenall(3)
(Paul Webber) *chsd ldrs: drvn 9th: sn lost pl: bhd 11th: t.o whn p.u bef next* **8/1**

3/0- **F** **Humphrey Bee (IRE)**[22] 120 10-11-1 **107**................... KielanWoods(3) 111
(Charlie Longsdon) *led 3rd: jnd whn fell 2 out* **16/1**

FU3/ **P** **Bally Gunner**[29] 5569 8-11-5 **113**...................................... KillianMoore(5)
(Roger Curtis) *stdd s: in rr: sme hdwy 11th: lost pl after next: bhd whn p.u bef 2 out* **20/1**

6m 6.5s (-8.60) **Going Correction** -0.225s/f (Good) **10** Ran SP% **115.1**
Speed ratings: **105,100,100,99,93 82, , , ,**
toteswingers 1&2 £6.80, 1&3 £0.00, 2&3 £4.90 CSF £37.04 CT £215.89 TOTE £11.50: £3.70, £1.30, £1.60; EX 46.00 Trifecta £192.90 Pool: £439.84 - 1.71 winning units..
Owner Ningbo Partnership **Bred** Yannick Berlin & Jean-Michel Peccot **Trained** Upper Lambourn, Berks

FOCUS
A fair handicap. It was soundly run and there's no reason to doubt the form.

505 STAFFORDSHIRE FIRE AND RESCUE H'CAP HURDLE (THE SUNDAY £5K BONUS RACE) (9 hdls) 2m
5:20 (5:21) (Class 4) (0-115,115) 4-Y-0+ **£3,249** (£954; £477; £238)

Form RPR

006/ **1** **Maoi Chinn Tire (IRE)**[228] 1543 6-11-12 **115**...................... SeanQuinlan 119
(Jennie Candlish) *hld up in rr: hdwy 6th: 3rd 2 out: 1 l 2nd last: styd on to ld last 50yds* **12/1**

0/1- **2** *1* **Acapulco Bay**[8] 376 9-10-5 **99**.................................(p) RobertWilliams(5) 102
(Dai Burchell) *hld up: hdwy 5th: 3rd next: led appr 2 out: hdd and no ex run-in* **5/2**[1]

P64/ **3** *1¾* **Royal Opera**[19] 4499 5-11-7 **110**..................................(b) TomScudamore 111
(Brian Ellison) *w ldr: led after 3rd: hdd appr 2 out: styd on same pce run-in* **11/4**[2]

F00/ **4** *3* **King Zeal (IRE)**[28] 10 9-11-4 **107**.......................................(t) LiamHeard 105
(Barry Leavy) *mid-div: hdwy to chse ldrs 3 out: kpt on one pce fr next* **25/1**

036/ **5** *1¾* **Faith Jicaro (IRE)**[202] 2237 6-11-6 **109**.. DPFahy 106
(Andy Hobbs) *in rr: drvn 4th: hit 6th: styd on to chse ldrs next: 5th and outpcd whn hit 2 out: kpt on run-in* **10/1**

06/ **6** *17* **Crescent Beach (IRE)**[94] 4349 6-11-2 **105**.........................(t) HenryOliver 88
(Henry Oliver) *t.k.h: led tl after 3rd: 2nd whn mstke 3 out: sn wknd* **15/2**[3]

310/ **7** *32* **Khazium (IRE)**[71] 4794 4-11-3 **110**..............................(t) RichardJohnson 58
(Claire Dyson) *chsd ldrs: lost pl after 6th: bhd next: t.o* **14/1**

0/P- **8** *2* **Quinsman**[22] 119 7-11-12 **115**.. TomMessenger 65
(Caroline Bailey) *chsd ldrs: outpcd 5th: drvn and lost pl next: sn bhd: t.o 3 out* **20/1**

0/0- **9** *23* **Dalmo**[14] 251 4-10-9 **109**.. ChristopherWard(7) 34
(Dr Richard Newland) *bhd whn mstke 2nd: detached and drvn next: reminders 5th: sn t.o* **9/1**

635/ **F** **Rigid**[20] 1389 6-10-5 **94**... LeeEdwards
(Tony Carroll) *towards rr whn fell 3rd* **12/1**

3m 44.6s (-7.40) **Going Correction** -0.40s/f (Good)
WFA 4 from 5yo+ 18lb **10** Ran SP% **116.8**
Speed ratings (Par 105): **102,101,100,99,98 89,73,72,61,**
toteswingers 1&2 £15.50, 1&3 £1.50, 2&3 £2.50 CSF £43.34 CT £109.85 TOTE £14.00: £4.20, £1.30, £1.60; EX 55.60 Trifecta £260.00 Pool: £790.44 - 2.28 winning units..
Owner Alan Baxter **Bred** Mrs E Thompson **Trained** Basford Green, Staffs

FOCUS
Every reason to believe this will prove a reasonable race for the grade, with the winner potentially well treated and the second and third both arriving in form.
T/Plt: £1213.00 to a £1 stake. Pool: £70,593.28 - 42.48 winning units T/Qpdt: £105.50 to a £1 stake. Pool: £5475.37 - 38.40 winning units WG

470 CARTMEL (L-H)
Monday, May 27

OFFICIAL GOING: Good changing to soft after race 1 (2.00)
Bend after last fenced moved out 2m and bend turning into Woodside moved out 3m to provide fresh ground.
Wind: Moderate; half behind Weather: Rain

506 WATCH RACING UK ON SKY 432 MARES' NOVICES' (S) HURDLE (7 hdls 1 omitted) 2m 1f 110y
2:00 (2:00) (Class 5) 4-Y-0+ **£2,599** (£763; £381; £190)

Form RPR

1 **Binowagh Bay (IRE)**[22] 133 5-10-7 0.................................. DerekFox(5) 85
(Mark Michael McNiff, Ire) *hld up in rr: hdwy 5th: lft 3rd last: styd on to ld fnl 50yds* **9/2**[2]

213/ **2** *1* **Phase Shift**[9] 5504 5-11-8 116..(t) DannyCook 95
(Brian Ellison) *hld up in rr: wnt 2nd omitted 2 out: lft in ld last: hdd and no ex last 50yds* **8/15**[1]

460/ **3** *7* **Tantalized**[46] 5249 4-10-8 78.. RichieMcLernon 75
(Dave Roberts) *chsd ldrs: drvn 4th: one pce whn lft 3rd last* **20/1**

0/0- **4** *1¾* **Dane Cottage**[15] 253 6-10-7 69................................(p) HarryChalloner(5) 78
(Richard Ford) *mid-div: hdwy 5th: sn chsng ldrs: one pce whn lft 2nd last: no ex* **50/1**

035/ **5** *1¼* **Grethel (IRE)**[29] 17 9-10-12 69... BrianHarding 77
(Alan Berry) *mid-div: hdwy 5th: kpt on: lft 5th last: nvr rchd ldrs* **16/1**

4/F- **6** *37* **Merry Minster**[22] 6-10-5 95... MissCWalton(7) 47
(James Walton) *unruly s: chsd ldrs: lost pl normal 3 out: sn bhd: t.o* **14/1**

4/3- **7** *8* **Gulfport**[9] 375 4-10-8 89... JasonMaguire 37
(Donald McCain) *chsd ldrs: wknd qckly after normal 3 out: sn bhd: t.o* **7/1**[3]

8 *52* **True Pleasure (IRE)**[81] 6-10-12 0.................................... FearghalDavis
(James Bethell) *nt fluent in rr: bhd whn mstke 5th: sn t.o: eventually completed* **28/1**

0/ **F** **Bygones For Coins (IRE)**[123] 2031 5-10-12 0............... KennyJohnson 81
(Robert Johnson) *led: hit 3rd: 1 l ahd whn fell last* **50/1**

P **Diamond Sunrise (IRE)**[272] 5-10-7 0 ow2................ NathanMoscrop(7)
(Noel Wilson) *chsd ldrs: drvn 4th: lost pl next: sn bhd: t.o whn p.u bef normal 3 out* **50/1**

4m 19.1s (5.90) **Going Correction** +0.35s/f (Yiel)
WFA 4 from 5yo+ 18lb **10** Ran SP% **122.6**
Speed ratings (Par 103): **100,99,96,95,95 78,75,52, ,**
toteswingers 1&2 £1.20, 1&3 £10.70, 2&3 £3.40 CSF £7.71 TOTE £5.20: £1.60, £1.10, £4.60; EX 14.70 Trifecta £116.80 Pool: £1,064.78 - 6.83 winning units..There was no bid for the winner.
Owner Eugene McMahon **Bred** Patrick Keane **Trained** Sligo, Co. Sligo
■ Stewards' Enquiry : Danny Cook two-day ban: use of whip (10-11 June)

FOCUS
The ground was originally described as good to firm, good in places but after constant rain it had eased to soft all round. An uncompetitive mares' selling hurdle, with the third, fourth and fifth are all rated close to their marks.

507 HALECAT FOUR YEARS OLD NOVICES' HURDLE (8 hdls) 2m 1f 110y
2:30 (2:30) (Class 4) 4-Y-0 **£3,249** (£954; £477; £238)

Form RPR

35/ **1** **Celtic Monarch (IRE)**[38] 5388 4-10-7 0................................ DerekFox(5) 111+
(Mark Michael McNiff, Ire) *in rr: j.rt 3rd: hdwy 5th: styd on wl to ld narrowly last: drvn out* **12/1**

P/2- **2** *7* **Cape Explorer**[25] 73 4-10-12 119....................................... DannyCook 104
(Brian Ellison) *led: j. slowly 1st: hdd 3 out: wnt 2nd sn after last: kpt on same pce* **11/8**[1]

0/ **3** *15* **Rosslyn Castle**[22] 4501 4-10-12 0.. APMcCoy 96
(Gary Brown) *trckd ldr: narrow ld 3 out: hdd last: sn wknd: eased clsng stages* **9/4**[2]

3/ **4** *39* **Allowed**[151] 3281 4-10-12 0... DenisO'Regan 50
(John Ferguson) *t.k.h: trckd ldrs: wknd 2 out: bhd whn virtually p.u run-in: t.o* **5/2**[3]

P **Turned To Gold (IRE)**[19] 4-10-12 0................................ KennyJohnson
(Robert Johnson) *t.k.h: trckd ldrs: nt fluent 1st: lost pl 4th: t.o next: p.u bef last* **100/1**

4m 19.8s (6.60) **Going Correction** +0.55s/f (Soft) **5** Ran SP% **110.1**
Speed ratings: **107,103,97,79,**
CSF £29.98 TOTE £13.70: £4.10, £1.10; EX 26.60 Trifecta £55.80 Pool: £699.65 - 9.39 winning units..
Owner Venue Syndicate **Bred** Airlie Stud **Trained** Sligo, Co. Sligo

FOCUS
An interesting novice hurdle run at just an ordinary early pace which saw a couple of the principals failing to see out the trip. The winner is rated in line with the best of his bumper form.

508 TOTEPOOL H'CAP CHASE (14 fncs) 2m 5f 110y
3:05 (3:05) (Class 3) (0-125,125) 5-Y-0+ **£7,797** (£2,289; £1,144; £572)

Form RPR

243/ **1** **Fine Parchment (IRE)**[46] 5244 10-11-0 **120**.........(tp) MrHAABannister(7) 126
(Charlie Mann) *chsd ldrs: outpcd 2 out: styd on wl fnl 300yds: led last 30yds* **14/1**

04/- **2** *¾* **Iona Days (IRE)**[85] 4539 8-11-1 **114**.......................(v[1]) WayneHutchinson 118
(Julian Smith) *sn chsng ldrs: 2nd 10th: led sn after last: hdd and no ex clsng stages* **4/1**[1]

0P5/ **3** *1¾* **Siberian Tiger (IRE)**[43] 5308 8-11-9 **122**........................... PaulMoloney 125
(Evan Williams) *in rr: hdwy 10th: 6th last: hung rt bnd over 2f out: styd on to take 3rd last 50yds* **10/1**

300/ **4** *6* **Epee Celeste (FR)**[76] 4723 7-10-1 **107**............................ GerardGalligan(7) 105
(Michael Chapman) *led: hdd after last: wknd fnl 100yds* **6/1**[2]

2/4- **5** *9* **Temple Lord (FR)**[24] 92 7-11-6 **119**..................................(t) APMcCoy 107
(Jonjo O'Neill) *chsd ldrs: upsides 2 out: wknd last 200yds* **4/1**[1]

144/ **6** *2½* **Storming Gale (IRE)**[28] 25 7-11-11 **124**...................(t) JasonMaguire 109
(Donald McCain) *in rr: hdwy to chse ldrs 8th: lost pl 10th* **6/1**[2]

R0U/ **7** *7* **Indian Groom (IRE)**[152] 3238 8-11-10 **123**......................... BrianHughes 101
(John Wade) *chsd ldrs: hit 3rd: mstke 8th: lost pl next* **10/1**

013/ **8** *2* **Kilcrea Asla (IRE)**[50] 5199 12-11-7 **125**......................... KillianMoore(5) 109
(Graeme McPherson) *mid-div: chsd ldrs 9th: wknd run-in* **10/1**

/00- **9** *14* **O Crotaigh (IRE)**[4] 448 9-11-8 **121**..............................(b) RichieMcGrath 83
(Alan Brown) *in rr: sme hdwy 9th: wknd 10th* **33/1**

131/ **10** *21* **Diamond Frontier (IRE)**[30] 5571 10-11-2 **122**.............. JohnDawson(7) 63
(John Wade) *chsd ldrs: lost pl 8th: wl bhd fr 10th: t.o* **9/1**[3]

The Form Book Jumps, Raceform Ltd, Compton, RG20 6NL.

6/4- **11** *11* **Tasheba**[18] 181 8-11-4 117....................(tp) RichieMcLernon 47
(Sophie Leech) *mid-div: lost pl 8th: wl bhd fr 10th: t.o* **20/1**

5m 35.1s (9.70) **Going Correction** +0.35s/f (Yiel) **11** Ran SP% **120.2**
Speed ratings: **107,106,106,103,100 99,97,96,91,83 79**
toteswingers 1&2 £23.20, 1&3 £43.10, 2&3 £9.50 CSF £72.90 CT £604.84 TOTE £16.70: £4.40, £1.70, £3.70; EX 84.10 Trifecta £494.00 Part won. Pool: £658.70 - 0.43 winning units..
Owner N W A Bannister **Bred** Timothy Considine **Trained** Upper Lambourn, Berks

FOCUS
A fairly competitive 0-125 handicap chase, run at a decent pace, but once again the ground had a fair say in the outcome. The form could be rated a little higher with the placed horses a few pounds off their best.

509 BURLINGTON STONE GRAND VETERANS' H'CAP CHASE (20 fncs) 3m 6f
3:40 (3:41) (Class 3) (0-130,130) 10-Y-0+ **£9,097** (£2,671; £1,335; £667)

Form RPR

5/0- **1** **Posh Bird (IRE)**[19] 169 10-10-0 111....................(p) MrJHamilton(7) 123+
(Peter Niven) *trckd ldrs: narrow ld 4 out: hdd 2 out: led 3f out: kpt up to work to forge clr fnl f* **12/1**

3/0- **2** *8* **Gullible Gordon (IRE)**[10] 355 10-11-3 121....................(vt1) JamieMoore 126
(Peter Bowen) *chsd ldrs: led 16th: hdd 4 out: led 2 out: hdd run-in: kpt on same pce* **15/2**

01P/ **3** *30* **Neptune Equester**[37] 5404 10-11-8 126.................... DannyCook 100
(Brian Ellison) *mde most to 10th: lost pl 16th: kpt on to take distant 3rd last* **7/1**3

3/4- **4** *13* **Captain Americo (IRE)**[19] 169 11-10-10 114....................(p) JasonMaguire 75
(James Ewart) *chsd ldrs: led 10th: hdd 16th: sn wknd* **10/1**

5U2/ **5** *15* **Incentivise (IRE)**[40] 5351 10-11-0 121.................... MichealNolan(3) 67
(Richard Lee) *mid-div: chsd ldrs 9th: lost pl 14th: t.o 4 out* **10/1**

2P3/ **6** *29* **Earth Planet (IRE)**[164] 3038 11-10-7 111....................(tp) WilsonRenwick 28
(Micky Hammond) *mid-div: hdwy to chse ldrs 9th: wknd 16th* **40/1**

P23/ **7** *dist* **Sea Saffron**[41] 5329 12-11-1 122.................... MattGriffiths(3)
(Sue Gardner) *in rr: blnd 2nd: sn detached: sme hdwy 16th: wknd next: t.o whn virtually p.u run-in: walked fnl 2f* **6/1**2

120/ **P** **Lydon House**[8] 401 14-10-1 105.................... PaddyBrennan
(Barry T Murphy, Ire) *in rr whn bdly hmpd 1st: continued detached: p.u bef 14th* **5/1**1

5/1- **B** **Jaunty Journey**[12] 321 10-10-13 117.................... WayneHutchinson
(Nigel Twiston-Davies) *chsd ldrs: reminders 4th: blnd 9th: lost pl 10th: in rr whn b.d 14th* **9/1**

P/0- **F** **Triggerman**[10] 355 11-11-5 123....................(p) RichardJohnson
(Philip Hobbs) *fell 1st* **8/1**

0/5- **F** **Major Malarkey (IRE)**[10] 355 10-11-11 129....................(p) SamTwiston-Davies
(Nigel Twiston-Davies) *chsd ldrs to 11th: lost pl and fell 10th* **8/1**

P/0- **P** **Mostly Bob (IRE)**[15] 249 10-11-12 130....................(vt) PaulMoloney
(Sophie Leech) *in rr: reminders 5th: sn bhd: t.o whn p.u bef 10th* **20/1**

01P/ **P** **Acrai Rua (IRE)**[31] 5548 10-10-6 110....................(b) BrianHughes
(Tim Fitzgerald) *chsd ldrs: lost pl 13th: t.o 16th* **18/1**

7m 55.3s (19.10) **Going Correction** +0.825s/f (Soft) **13** Ran SP% **125.8**
Speed ratings: **107,104,96,93,89 81,,,, ,,**
toteswingers 1&2 £44.40, 1&3 £20.10, 2&3 £26.40 CSF £105.49 CT £699.25 TOTE £10.60: £2.70, £3.00, £2.40; EX 195.80 Trifecta £372.60 Part won. Pool: £496.89 - 0.20 winning units..
Owner David Bamber **Bred** David Bamber **Trained** Barton-le-Street, N Yorks

FOCUS
A couple of C&D winners mixed in with plenty with solid claims made this a very competitive veterans' marathon handicap chase. The strong pace soon had many struggling and the first two came clear, with the runner-up rated to his mark.

510 SWAN HOTEL & SPA MAIDEN HUNTERS' CHASE (FOR THE FRASER CUP) (14 fncs) 2m 5f 110y
4:10 (4:14) (Class 6) 5-Y-0+ **£1,559** (£483; £241; £121)

Form RPR

1 **Molten Brown**[8] 8-11-5 0.................... MissJWalton(7) 91+
(Miss C Marshall) *trckd ldrs: styd on run-in: led on inner 2f out: edgd rt: drvn out* **28/1**

33/ **2** *1* **Bafana Choice**[29] 16 7-11-5 0....................(p) MrNOrpwood(7) 90
(Chris Grant) *w ldr: led 4 out: hdd 2 out: led 3f out: hdd 2f out: kpt on same pce last 50yds* **5/1**2

3 *3 1/4* **Lucky Lane (IRE)**[16] 8-11-5 0....................(tp) CallumBewley(7) 86
(Jane Clark) *chsd ldrs: outpcd last: kpt on to take 3rd last 50yds* **7/1**

065/ **4** *1 1/2* **Miss Chatterbox**[29] 8-10-12 0.................... MrRSmith(7) 77
(C Dawson) *in rr: hit 1st and rdr briefly lost iron: nt fluent: sme hdwy 9th: styd on to go 3rd 2f out: one pce* **6/1**

5 *12* **One Call (IRE)**[896] 2933 9-11-5 0....................(t) MrSDavies-Thomas(7) 72
(C N Nimmo) *hld up in rr: hdwy 10th: chsng ldrs next: lost pl 3f out* **11/4**1

064/ **6** *3 3/4* **Roman Cruise**[21] 10-11-9 0.................... MrCDawson(3) 69
(Peter Dowson) *set v stdy pce: hdd 5th: led 9th: hdd 4 out: led 2 out: hdd 3f out: sn wknd* **14/1**

U/ **7** *2 1/2* **Mr Shahady (IRE)**[8] 8-11-7 0.................... MrJHamilton(5) 66
(Victor Thompson) *chsd ldrs: led 5th: mstke next: hdd 9th: lost pl 3f out* **16/1**

P **Hand Act Or Part (IRE)**[21] 7-11-5 0....................(b) MrMJohnson(7)
(Lady Susan Watson) *chsd ldrs: sddle slipped after 4th: lost pl 6th: p.u bef next* **11/2**3

0/ **F** **Red Myst (IRE)**[8] 8-11-5 0.................... MrTHamilton(7)
(Victor Thompson) *blnd 1st: fell 2nd* **13/2**

6m 2.8s (37.40) **Going Correction** +0.35s/f (Yiel) **9** Ran SP% **114.8**
Speed ratings: **73,72,71,70,66 65,64,,**
toteswingers 1&2 £24.70, 1&3 £36.80, 2&3 £6.40 CSF £163.36 TOTE £35.20: £6.90, £1.70, £2.40; EX 258.70 Trifecta £876.60 Pool: £1,168.80 - 0.10 winning units..
Owner Tony Hogarth **Bred** M C Byrne **Trained** Galashiels, Scottish Borders

FOCUS
Plenty of winning point-to-point form on offer, but on the whole this was just an ordinary hunter chase. There was a very steady pace which never really increased, resulting with six holding some sort of chance at the last. The race is given a token rating through the runner-up.

511 HADWINS NOVICES' H'CAP HURDLE (11 hdls) 2m 6f
4:45 (4:46) (Class 4) (0-105,105) 4-Y-0+ **£3,249** (£954; £477; £238)

Form RPR

6/0- **1** **Clouds Of Mist**[18] 177 8-10-6 90.................... MissLucyGardner(5) 104+
(Sue Gardner) *sn trcking ldrs: 2nd bef 2 out: led on inner between last 2: forged clr last 200yds: eased nr fin* **8/1**

B/5- **2** *12* **Granaruid (IRE)**[11] 342 10-11-5 105....................(p) GrantCockburn(7) 105
(Alison Hamilton) *set v stdy pce: qcknd gallop 7th: hdd between last 2: styd on same pce run-in* **11/1**

003/ **3** *15* **Vinnie My Boy (IRE)**[34] 5473 5-11-4 97....................(t) JamieMoore 82
(Peter Bowen) *chsd ldrs: pushed along 8th: rdn 2 out: sn btn* **11/8**1

2/2- **4** *3 1/2* **Dancing Emily (IRE)**[27] 41 7-11-12 105.................... WayneHutchinson 87
(Graeme McPherson) *racd wd: hld up: wnt prom 7th: effrt 2 out: sn wknd* **9/2**2

3/4- **5** *3 3/4* **Quest Magic (IRE)**[16] 218 7-11-5 105.................... JohnDawson(7) 83
(John Wade) *chsd ldr: lost pl appr 3 out: sn bhd* **7/1**

202/ **6** *37* **Kingdom Of Munster (IRE)**[54] 5118 6-10-12 96....(p) HarryChalloner(5) 37
(Richard Ford) *in rr: pushed along 8th: lost pl next: sn bhd: t.o* **13/2**3

320/ **P** **Tom Wade (IRE)**[576] 2192 6-11-1 97.................... AdamWedge(3)
(Shaun Harris) *hld up: hit 3rd: lost pl after 8th: t.o whn p.u bef last* **20/1**

5m 52.0s (22.70) **Going Correction** +0.75s/f (Soft) **7** Ran SP% **110.3**
Speed ratings (Par 105): **88,83,78,76,75 62,**
toteswingers 1&2 £12.40, 1&3 £3.70, 2&3 £4.50 CSF £77.57 CT £181.54 TOTE £6.50: £2.60, £7.00; EX 50.50 Trifecta £706.70 Part won. Pool: £942.39 - 0.49 winning units..
Owner P A Tylor **Bred** J B Sumner **Trained** Longdown, Devon

FOCUS
Just a modest pace for this novice handicap hurdle, which cut up slightly with four non-runners. The runner-up is rated close to recent Perth form

512 TOTEPOOL QUICKPICK H'CAP HURDLE (11 hdls) 2m 6f
5:15 (5:16) (Class 3) (0-135,135) 4-Y-0+ **£7,797** (£2,289; £1,144; £572)

Form RPR

6/3- **1** **Lava Lamp (GER)**[7] 409 6-9-11 113.................... ConorRing(7) 119+
(Evan Williams) *trckd ldrs: upsides last: sn led: forged clr* **5/1**2

1/1- **2** *10* **Wolf Shield (IRE)**[23] 115 6-10-11 120.................... BarryKeniry 116
(George Moore) *trckd ldrs: 2nd 3rd: led after 2 out: nt fluent last: sn hdd: kpt on same pce* **4/1**1

024/ **3** *1* **Switched Off**[37] 5410 8-10-10 119....................(b) JasonMaguire 113
(Donald McCain) *hld up towards rr: hdwy 8th: 5th last: kpt on to take 3rd nr fin* **8/1**

2/0- **4** *shd* **Scotswell**[10] 358 7-11-4 127.................... LucyAlexander 121
(Harriet Graham) *led: hdd sn after 2 out: kpt on same pce run-in* **7/1**3

121/ **5** *13* **Humbie (IRE)**[58] 5008 9-10-8 124.................... GrahamWatters(7) 108
(Pauline Robson) *mid-div: chsd ldrs 8th: wknd over 1f out* **7/1**3

P02/ **6** *1/2* **What A Steel (IRE)**[198] 2322 9-10-6 118.................... EwanWhillans(3) 98
(Alistair Whillans) *mid-div: chsd ldrs 8th: wknd after 2 out: sn eased* **12/1**

0/0- **7** *3 1/4* **Bourne**[10] 356 7-11-12 135.................... HenryBrooke 112
(Donald McCain) *in rr: drvn 8th: nvr on terms* **8/1**

16P/ **8** *8* **Quel Elite (FR)**[28] 24 9-10-0 109....................(p) BrianHarding 78
(James Moffatt) *in rr: drvn 5th: bhd fr 7th* **14/1**

/U3- **9** *1* **Lord Luso (IRE)**[13] 280 7-10-1 110.................... RichieMcGrath 78
(Philip Kirby) *chsd ldrs: drvn 6th: lost pl appr 3 out* **10/1**

100/ **P** **No Principles**[170] 2916 10-10-10 119....................(p) SamTwiston-Davies
(Julian Smith) *in rr: bhd and reminders 8th: t.o next: p.u sn after 2 out* **10/1**

5m 44.9s (15.60) **Going Correction** +0.95s/f (Soft) **10** Ran SP% **116.4**
Speed ratings (Par 107): **109,105,105,104,100 100,98,95,95,**
toteswingers 1&2 £6.40, 1&3 £12.80, 2&3 £12.80 CSF £25.81 CT £158.41 TOTE £7.50: £2.80, £1.20, £2.90; EX 33.50 Trifecta £283.80 Pool: £533.81 - 1.41 winning units..
Owner Mrs Janet Davies **Bred** Graf And Grafin Von Stauffenberg **Trained** Llancarfan, Vale Of Glamorgan

FOCUS
A fair 0-135 handicap hurdle in which the runner-up sets the standard.
T/Plt: £7,008.90 to a £1 stake. Pool: £71,529.79 - 7.45 winning units T/Qpdt: Part won. £2,777.60 to a £1 stake. Pool: £3,753.53 - 0.90 winning units. WG

513 - 516a (Foreign Racing) - See Raceform Interactive

407 NEWTON ABBOT (L-H)
Tuesday, May 28

OFFICIAL GOING: Good (good to firm in places; 8.2)
All rails moved out since last meeting, but impact on distances not quantified.
Wind: mild breeze across Weather: overcast

517 LOOK FOR THE SPECIAL OFFER FOR AUGUST 3 MAIDEN HURDLE (8 hdls) 2m 1f
2:20 (2:21) (Class 4) 4-Y-0+ **£3,508** (£1,030; £515; £257)

Form RPR

4/U- **1** **Honour System (IRE)**[26] 73 6-11-0 0.................... DenisO'Regan 118+
(John Ferguson) *hld up towards rr: smooth prog fr after 4th: trckd ldrs 3 out: led on bit gng to 2 out: sn clr: easily* **5/1**2

30P/ **2** *10* **Who's Jeff (IRE)**[35] 5470 5-11-0 102.................... TomO'Brien 104+
(Philip Hobbs) *j.lft thrght: led: hit 3 out: sn rdn: hdd gng to next: sn hld: blnd last: kpt on same pce: no ch w wnr* **7/1**

243/ **3** *hd* **Staigue Fort**[29] 33 5-11-0 0.................... DominicElsworth 101
(Emma Lavelle) *chsd ldrs: rdn after 3 out: ev ch gng to 2 out: styd on same pce* **5/1**2

0/0- **4** *11* **Macarthur**[22] 140 9-11-0 110....................(t) PaulMoloney 90
(David Rees) *mid-div: rdn and stdy prog after 3 out: styd on fr next but nvr trbld ldrs* **16/1**

5/3- **5** *11* **Looking Hopeful (IRE)**[19] 186 7-11-0 0.................... DavidBass 79
(Nicky Henderson) *chsd ldr: chal 5th tl sltly hmpd next: sn rdn: wknd after 2 out* **11/4**1

F/4- **6** *nk* **Sassy Wren**[21] 155 8-10-7 0.................... JamesDavies 71
(Chris Down) *chsd ldrs: rdn after 3 out: wkng whn rchd for 2 out* **28/1**

06P/ **7** *2 1/4* **Holden Caulfield (IRE)**[180] 2717 8-10-9 82.................... CharlieWallis(5) 76
(Nick Ayliffe) *mid-div: nt fluent 2nd: reminders after 3rd: nvr gng pce to get involved: wknd after 3 out* **66/1**

3/6- **7** *dht* **Sedgemoor Express (IRE)**[14] 290 5-10-11 0....................(t) MarkQuinlan(3) 76
(Nigel Hawke) *sme modest late hdwy: mainly towards rr* **66/1**

9 *11* **Greenaway's Eye (FR)**[246] 4-10-10 0.................... HaddenFrost 66
(James Frost) *mid-div: hdwy after 5th: rdn after 3 out: wkng whn stmbld 2 out* **22/1**

10 *10* **Cool Fantasy (IRE)**[399] 4-10-10 0.................... IanPopham 51
(Caroline Keevil) *hld up towards rr of midfield: rdn after 5th: wknd after next: t.o* **50/1**

6/3- **11** *10* **Keep The Cash (IRE)**[9] 390 5-11-0 0.................... TomScudamore 45
(David Pipe) *towards rr of mid-div: nudged along fr 4th: rdn after next: wknd after 3 out: t.o* **11/2**3

0- **12** *31* **Anglingforcharlie**[16] 250 4-10-10 0.................... RichardJohnson 10
(Philip Hobbs) *mid-div tl wknd 5th: t.o* **33/1**

/4- **13** *51* **Sid**[19] 192 5-11-0 0.................... TommyPhelan
(Mark Gillard) *struggling in rr fr 4th: sn t.o* **250/1**

0/ **P** **Petomic (IRE)**[327] 4696 8-11-0 0 APMcCoy
(Paul John Gilligan, Ire) *chsd ldrs tl rdn after 5th: sn wknd: bhd whn p.u bef 2 out* **18/1**

40/- **P** **Snowball (IRE)**[194] 2436 6-11-0 0 AndrewTinkler
(David Arbuthnot) *mid-div: rdn after 3 out: no imp whn p.u bef next (dismntd)* **25/1**

P **Palanour (FR)**[274] 5-11-0 0 DPFahy
(Sue Gardner) *sn struggling in rr: t.o fr 4th: p.u after 3 out* **80/1**

3m 59.4s (-6.30) **Going Correction** -0.325s/f (Good)
WFA 4 from 5yo+ 18lb **16** Ran SP% **120.2**
Speed ratings (Par 105): **101,96,96,91,85 85,84,84,79,74 70,55,31,,**
Tote Swingers: 1&2 £12.60, 1&3 £4.00, 2&3 £10.90 CSF £36.74 TOTE £8.70: £1.80, £3.30, £1.90; EX 44.40 Trifecta £174.50 Pool: £631.93 - 2.71 winning units..
Owner Bloomfields **Bred** Darley **Trained** Cowlinge, Suffolk

FOCUS
Holes could be picked in the form of the majority of these.

518 AT THE RACES VIRGIN 534 BEGINNERS' CHASE (20 fncs) 3m 2f 110y
2:50 (2:51) (Class 4) 5-Y-0+ **£4,288** (£1,259; £629; £314)

Form RPR

0/3- **1** **American Spin**[13] 302 9-11-0 135 (v[1]) JamieMoore 133+
(Luke Dace) *mde all: hit 6th: pushed along fr 14th: tended to jump sltly rt fr 15th: drvn whn pressed after 4 out: hit next: styd on strly whn hit last: drvn out* **7/4**[1]

112- **2** *7* **Well Mett (IRE)**[21] 158 6-11-0 0 (bt) AlainCawley 126
(Fergal O'Brien) *trckd wnr: rdn to chse wnr fr 4 out: ev ch 3 out: styd on tl no ex fr last* **3/1**[3]

20/- **3** *4 ½* **Wayward Glance**[198] 2352 5-11-0 0 (v) APMcCoy 122
(Jim Best) *trckd ldrs: nt best of runs gng to 3 out: sn rdn: nvr quite able to chal: styd on tl no ex fr last* **6/1**

/42- **4** *40* **Palace Jester**[14] 294 8-11-0 116 (t) TomScudamore 84
(David Pipe) *trckd ldrs: j.rt at times: rdn after 14th: outpcd gng to 4 out: no ch after: t.o* **11/4**[2]

5 *1 ½* **Thehorsemaytalk (IRE)**[30] 8-11-0 0 JamesDavies 83
(Mark Shears) *in tch: pushed along to chse ldrs 14th: lost tch fr 16th: t.o* **22/1**

PP4/ **6** *shd* **Russian Song (IRE)**[35] 5471 9-10-7 94 (bt) MrMLegg[(7)] 83
(Colin Tizzard) *in tch: pushed along fr 4th: reminders after 6th: drvn fr 11th: wkng whn hit 16th: t.o* **20/1**

P **Arctic Trail (IRE)**[39] 5391 7-11-0 0 (b[1]) NoelFehily
(Paul John Gilligan, Ire) *nvr travelling but in tch: reminders after 5th: lost tch 13th: p.u bef next* **33/1**

0/P- **F** **Fanjos Luck (IRE)**[8] 407 6-11-0 0 WillKennedy
(Alan Jones) *fell 1st* **100/1**

6m 29.3s (-15.30) **Going Correction** -0.325s/f (Good) **8** Ran SP% **115.4**
Speed ratings: **109,106,105,93,93 93,,**
Tote Swingers: 1&2 £4.20, 1&3 £4.50, 2&3 £3.50 CSF £7.40 TOTE £2.70: £1.20, £1.10, £1.60; EX 9.00 Trifecta £31.50 Pool: £1,364.49 - 32.47 winning units..
Owner G Collacott & R Gadd **Bred** Cheveley Park Stud Ltd **Trained** Five Oaks, W Sussex

FOCUS
An ordinary beginners' chase.

519 BET TOTEPOOL TEXT TOTE TO 89660 "NATIONAL HUNT" NOVICES' HURDLE (9 hdls) 2m 3f
3:20 (3:20) (Class 4) 4-Y-0+ **£3,508** (£1,030; £515; £257)

Form RPR

41/- **1** **Neston Grace**[34] 5511 5-10-5 0 JamesDavies 98+
(Simon Hodgson) *trckd ldr: led gng to 2 out: sn rdn: r.o wl: rdn out* **7/2**[2]

220/ **2** *2 ½* **Lady Lectra**[80] 4666 4-10-0 0 DPFahy 92+
(John Flint) *j.lft at times: in tch: trckd ldng pair after 3 out: wnt bdly lft last 2 whn u.p: kpt on same pce* **9/1**

4/2- **3** *8* **Qoubilai (FR)**[19] 192 9-10-12 110 (t) RichardJohnson 99
(Tim Vaughan) *led: hit 3 out: rdn and hdd bef 2 out where sltly hmpd: kpt on same pce* **4/6**[1]

P/6- **4** *5* **La Madonnina (IRE)**[13] 306 5-10-5 0 IanPopham 84
(Caroline Keevil) *struggling in rr fr 5th: hdwy after 3 out: styd on fr next but nvr threatened to rch ldrs* **50/1**

/00- **5** *15* **Colin's Nightmare**[14] 292 5-10-0 0 GavinSheehan[(5)] 73
(Nick Mitchell) *nt a fluent: chsd ldr tl lost pl appr 6th: sn rdn: one pce fr 3 out: wknd last* **50/1**

0/4- **6** *6* **The Happy Warrior**[19] 174 5-10-12 0 AndrewGlassonbury 72
(Bob Buckler) *mid-div: hdwy after 3rd to trck ldrs: rdn appr 6th: wknd bef 2 out* **14/1**

4- **7** *3 ½* **Sportsreport (IRE)**[21] 160 5-10-12 0 AndrewThornton 70
(Seamus Mullins) *mid-div: awkward 2nd: wnt 4th after 3 out: sn rdn: wknd next* **6/1**[3]

0/P- **8** *9* **General Girling**[21] 156 6-10-9 0 JamesBest[(3)] 61
(Caroline Keevil) *mid-div: rdn after 6th: wknd after 3 out* **80/1**

/06- **9** *3 ¼* **Nothing Personal**[13] 318 6-10-5 0 (t[1]) MrKevinJones[(7)] 58
(Karen George) *hld up towards rr: effrt to cl on ldrs after 6th: wknd after 3 out* **66/1**

5/3- **10** *28* **Volio Vincente (FR)**[21] 156 6-10-12 0 RichardKilloran 33
(Carroll Gray) *hit 3rd: struggling 5th: a in rr: t.o* **33/1**

4m 28.0s (-2.00) **Going Correction** -0.325s/f (Good)
WFA 4 from 5yo+ 18lb **10** Ran SP% **122.8**
Speed ratings (Par 105): **91,89,86,84,78 75,74,70,69,57**
Tote Swingers: 1&2 £4.20, 1&3 £1.10, 2&3 £3.70 CSF £34.38 TOTE £3.70: £1.30, £1.50, £1.20; EX 27.00 Trifecta £64.10 Pool: £1,189.54 - 13.89 winning units..
Owner Dr Nigel Knott **Bred** Dr N J Knott **Trained** Yeovil, Somerset

FOCUS
A weak novices' hurdle.

520 NEWTONABBOTRACES.COM H'CAP CHASE (13 fncs) 2m 110y
3:50 (3:50) (Class 3) (0-140,137) 5-Y-0+ **£4,596** (£2,244; £1,122; £561; £280)

Form RPR

6/1- **1** **Anquetta (IRE)**[16] 249 9-11-7 137 MrSWaley-Cohen[(5)] 147+
(Nicky Henderson) *trckd ldrs: led bef 4 out: in command fr next: wnt rt 2 out: mstke last: rdn out fnl 75yds* **7/2**[2]

5/2- **2** *7* **Unforgettable (IRE)**[16] 236 10-10-3 119 (vt[1]) BenPoste[(5)] 120
(Robin Dickin) *trckd ldr: led after 7th: hdd bef 4 out: sn rdn: kpt on but hld by wnr fr 2 out* **8/1**

15/- **3** *12* **Mister Matt (IRE)**[40] 5363 10-11-5 130 AndrewGlassonbury 122
(Bob Buckler) *led tl after 7th: rdn after 9th: styng on at same pce whn lft 3rd 2 out* **12/1**

3/4- **4** *5* **Mibleu (FR)**[16] 236 13-9-7 111 oh1 MrMLegg[(7)] 99
(Colin Tizzard) *hld up: hdwy after 7th: rdn in disp 2nd whn hit 3 out: wkng whn lft 4th 2 out* **12/1**

11P/ **5** *24* **Green Belt Elite (FR)**[33] 5523 9-11-5 130 AidanColeman 94
(Venetia Williams) *hld up: wkng whn wnt rt 8th: t.o* **10/1**

0/6- **6** *23* **The Sneezer (IRE)**[16] 236 10-11-0 125 NickScholfield 68
(Alexandra Dunn) *chsd ldrs: rdn appr 7th where wnt rt: wknd fr next: t.o* **20/1**

0/0- **P** **Takeroc (FR)**[16] 236 10-10-13 124 (t) APMcCoy
(Chris Gordon) *prom early: lost tch qckly after 6th: p.u after next* **15/2**[3]

/11- **U** **Fiftyonefiftyone (IRE)**[8] 411 9-10-8 119 7ex (p) LeightonAspell 111
(Oliver Sherwood) *trckd ldrs: nudged along fr after 7th: rdn after 9th: disp 2nd next: 3rd and hld whn mstke and uns rdr 2 out* **13/8**[1]

3m 59.9s (-6.60) **Going Correction** -0.325s/f (Good) **8** Ran SP% **112.4**
Speed ratings: **102,98,93,90,79 68,,**
Tote Swingers: 1&2 £11.10, 1&3 £8.30, 2&3 £5.80 CSF £29.86 CT £296.88 TOTE £3.20: £1.40, £2.30, £3.20; EX 29.00 Trifecta £163.90 Pool: £1,587.68 - 7.26 winning units..
Owner Robert Waley-Cohen **Bred** Gerry Martin **Trained** Upper Lambourn, Berks

FOCUS
A competitive race on paper but it was turned into something of procession by Anquetta.

521 NEWTON ABBOT RACECOURSE ON FACEBOOK H'CAP HURDLE (8 hdls) 2m 1f
4:20 (4:20) (Class 4) (0-105,105) 4-Y-0+ **£3,508** (£1,030; £515; £257)

Form RPR

3/1- **1** **Party Palace**[28] 37 9-10-9 91 GilesHawkins[(3)] 98+
(Stuart Howe) *chsd ldrs: blnd 4th: sn pushed along: drvn to ld bef 2 out: kpt on v gamely: drvn out* **12/1**

235/ **2** *1* **Engai (GER)**[56] 5108 7-11-3 103 JakeHodson[(7)] 108
(David Bridgwater) *hld up: hdwy after 5th: rdn to chse ldrs bef 2 out: kpt on into 2nd sn after last: a being hld by wnr* **9/1**[3]

/04- **3** *2 ¾* **Call Me April**[14] 292 5-10-11 90 AndrewThornton 94
(Karen George) *hld up last: smooth hdwy on outer after 3 out: rdn to chse wnr bef 2 out: lost 2nd sn after last: kpt on same pce* **28/1**

5/1- **4** *10* **Lord Of The Dunes**[26] 83 5-11-9 102 (t) APMcCoy 99
(Colin Tizzard) *mid-div: hdwy after 4th: rdn after 3 out to dispute cl 2nd bef next: hld in 4th whn awkward last* **6/4**[1]

P/0- **5** *½* **Kayfrou**[19] 188 8-10-11 90 DarylJacob 83
(Nick Mitchell) *mid-div: pushed along fr after 4th: lost pl 3 out: styd on again fr next* **9/1**[3]

5/P- **6** *1* **Palio Square (USA)**[16] 253 6-10-8 92 (b) GavinSheehan[(5)] 84
(John Flint) *mid-div: rdn after 3 out: styng on in 6th whn mstke 2 out: no further imp* **18/1**

6P0/ **7** *9* **Tamarillo Grove (IRE)**[221] 1919 6-11-12 105 (t) PaulMoloney 90
(Sophie Leech) *mid-div: hdwy 3 out: sn rdn: fdd after next* **11/1**

PP6/ **8** *5* **Umustbejoking (FR)**[37] 5437 5-11-3 99 MichealNolan[(3)] 80
(Michael Blake) *disp ld tl clr ldr 5th: mstke 3 out: rdn and hdd bef next: wknd* **12/1**

0/0- **9** *7* **Jezza**[14] 293 7-10-9 95 (t) MrKevinJones[(7)] 68
(Karen George) *struggling in rr fr 4th: nvr a factor* **33/1**

0/1- **10** *2* **Nothing Is Forever (IRE)**[19] 193 9-10-13 92 JamesDavies 64
(Chris Down) *disp ld tl 5th: rdn after 3 out: sn wknd* **7/2**[2]

404/ **11** *28* **Witchesintune**[101] 4255 6-11-4 97 SamThomas 43
(Helen Nelmes) *mid-div: struggling 4th: wknd after next: t.o* **40/1**

3/5- **12** *28* **Regal County (IRE)**[13] 318 7-11-6 99 NickScholfield 20
(Alexandra Dunn) *disp ld tl 5th: sn rdn: wknd next: t.o* **33/1**

3m 58.8s (-6.90) **Going Correction** -0.325s/f (Good) **12** Ran SP% **123.0**
Speed ratings (Par 105): **103,102,101,96,96 95,91,89,85,85 71,58**
Tote Swingers: 1&2 £6.20, 1&3 £38.90, 2&3 £47.00 CSF £115.12 CT £2979.80 TOTE £11.40: £3.50, £3.30, £8.50; EX 122.70 Trifecta £905.60 Part won. Pool: £1,207.47 - 0.05 winning units..

Owner B P Jones **Bred** Llety Farms **Trained** Oakford, Devon

FOCUS
A competitive race for the grade, but two of the market principals apparently ran a long way below expectations.

522 SIS INTERNATIONAL LADY AMATEUR RIDERS' (S) H'CAP HURDLE (10 hdls) 2m 6f
4:50 (4:50) (Class 5) (0-95,95) 4-Y-0+ **£2,370** (£729; £364)

Form RPR

6/6- **1** **Millie O'Brien**[19] 178 5-9-12 74 MissNatalieParker[(7)] 79+
(Philip Hobbs) *trckd ldrs: led appr 2 out: sn rdn: narrowly hdd last: kpt on to ld again fnl stride* **11/1**

P/6- **2** *hd* **Master Wells (IRE)**[8] 407 12-10-1 77 MissBFrost[(7)] 80+
(James Frost) *mid-div: hdwy 7th: trckd ldrs after 3 out: rdn to chal 2 out: slt ld last: kpt on: hdd fnl stride* **4/1**[2]

000/ **3** *3 ½* **Whatsabillion (IRE)**[39] 5381 11-11-3 91 (tp) MissJoannaMason[(5)] 90
(Anabel K Murphy) *in tch tl outpcd after 3 out: styd on again after next: fin strly to snatch 3rd fnl strides* **25/1**

1P0/ **4** *nk* **Lord Lescribaa (FR)**[245] 1636 10-10-3 77 (tp) MissKHobbs[(5)] 76
(Philip Hobbs) *trckd ldr: led after 7th: rdn and hdd appr 2 out: kpt on same pce: lost 3rd fnl strides* **12/1**

0/5- **5** *3 ¼* **Rifleman (IRE)**[16] 248 13-10-9 81 (tp) MissLBrooke[(3)] 77
(Richard Lee) *in tch: rdn and ev ch after 3 out: styd on same pce fr next* **14/1**

3PP- **6** *2 ¼* **Abbi Jicaro**[2] 501 6-10-2 74 (t) MissCBoxall[(3)] 69
(Mark Shears) *hld up towards rr: hdwy after 3 out: sn rdn to chse ldrs: no ex in 6th whn awkward last* **18/1**

06/- **7** *4* **Jigsaw Financial (IRE)**[54] 5142 7-10-7 76 MissLucyGardner 68
(Laura Young) *hld up towards rr: gd hdwy after 3 out: effrt next: fdd bef last* **16/1**

/44- **8** *2 ¼* **Gleannacreim (IRE)**[14] 295 10-9-9 69 MissLeandaTickle[(5)] 57
(Carroll Gray) *led tl after 7th: rdn after next: sn btn* **12/1**

0/P- **9** *1 ½* **Jewellery (IRE)**[16] 254 6-11-2 90 (v) MissBAndrews[(5)] 77
(Kevin Bishop) *prom tl rdn after 7th: wknd after 3 out: blnd 2 out* **7/1**[3]

/0P- **10** *8* **Benefit Game (IRE)**[3] 478 9-10-9 85 MissCharlotteHawker[(7)] 65
(Richard Hawker) *hld up towards rr: hdwy fr 7th: rdn and ev ch after 3 out: wknd bef next* **40/1**

6/3- **11** *25* **Rowanna (IRE)**[26] 80 5-10-3 79 MissSJBerry[(7)] 36
(Colin Tizzard) *chsd ldrs tl wknd 3 out: t.o* **12/1**

300/ **U** **Dune Shine**59 5019 8-11-12 **95**....(p) MissGAndrews
(Michael Blake) *mid-div: travelling ok whn landed awkwardly, stmbld and uns rdr 7th* **15/8**1

5m 17.6s (-2.60) **Going Correction** -0.325s/f (Good) **12** Ran SP% **122.8**
Speed ratings (Par 103): **91,90,89,89,88 87,86,85,84,81 72,**
Tote Swingers: 1&2 £7.30, 1&3 £57.10, 2&3 £37.10 CSF £57.68 CT £1112.95 TOTE £11.70: £3.70, £1.60, £9.30; EX 81.00 Trifecta £941.80 Part won. Pool: £1,255.77 - 0.01 winning units..No bid for the winner.
Owner Mrs S L Hobbs **Bred** R Johnson **Trained** Withycombe, Somerset

FOCUS
A desperately weak seller and it's unlikely that this took much winning once the favourite departed.

523 TOTNES AND BRIDGETOWN RACES COMPANY NOVICES' HUNTERS' CHASE (16 fncs) 2m 5f 110y
5:20 (5:20) (Class 6) 5-Y-O+ **£1,383** (£425; £212)

Form RPR
2/3- **1** **Tiermore (IRE)**8 413 9-11-5 100.... AlanJohns(7) 112+
(R E Luke) *in tch: tk clsr order 9th: led after 12th: rdn after 3 out: hit next: drvn out run-in* **3/1**2
3/4- **2** *2* **Delta Borget (FR)**21 159 8-11-5 98.... MissLeandaTickle(7) 108
(L Jefford) *hld up: hdwy after 9th: rdn to chse wnr after 4 out: kpt on but a being hld fr last* **9/1**
5/3- **3** *15* **Hameldown Tor**27 59 9-11-5 99.... MrEBarrett(7) 95
(E Walker) *nt a fluent: in tch: pushed along after 9th: nvr able to get on terms w front pair after 4 out: styd on same pce* **7/4**1
0FF/ **4** *16* **Ashclyst (IRE)**13 11-11-5 98....(t) MrThomasChanin(7) 82
(L Jefford) *racd keenly: led tl 3rd: trckd ldr: mstke 5th and 9th: losing pl whn hit 12th: nt a danger after: t.o* **20/1**
1/4- **5** *6* **Shrewd Investment**14 287 7-11-9 0....(t) MrJoshuaNewman(7) 82
(Miss L Thomas) *hld up: in tch but struggling 4 out: sn btn: t.o whn blnd last* **9/2**3
6 *26* **Cousinade (FR)**9 6-11-7 0....(t) MrMatthewBarber(5) 52
(Mrs Kim Thomas) *mid-div tl wknd 4 out: t.o* **20/1**
435/ **P** **Numide (FR)**16 10-11-5 106.... MrCSmith(7)
(G Chambers) *mid-div tl wknd after 12th: t.o whn p.u after 3 out* **20/1**
3/ **P** **Tourist Board (IRE)**44 10-11-5 0....(t) MrMWoodward(7)
(Mrs Ali Sherwin) *j.rt: sn struggling in last: losing tch whn p.u after 7th* **66/1**
466/ **P** **Searree**16 8-10-12 0.... MrMHeard(7)
(Mrs Pauline Geering) *trckd ldrs: pushed along after 9th: rdn after next: wknd 3 out: p.u bef next* **22/1**
0PP/ **P** **Some Slam (IRE)**16 8-11-5 0.... MrMLegg(7)
(Mrs J Bright) *racd keenly: led 3rd tl blnd 12th: sn rdn: wknd 3 out: p.u bef next* **16/1**

5m 17.3s (-4.10) **Going Correction** -0.325s/f (Good) **10** Ran SP% **115.6**
Speed ratings: **94,93,87,82,79 70, , , ,**
Tote Swingers: 1&2 £2.40, 1&3 £2.20, 2&3 £4.60 CSF £25.94 TOTE £4.20: £1.50, £2.70, £1.10; EX 32.90 Trifecta £75.30 Pool: £606.96 - 6.04 winning units..
Owner REL Racing **Bred** Michael Power **Trained** Haverfordwest, Pembrokeshire

FOCUS
Plenty could be fancied in this novices' hunters' chase and the form looks strong.
T/Plt: £250.40 to a £1 stake. Pool: £67,414.47 - 196.51 winning tickets. T/Qpdt: £43.30 to a £1 stake. Pool: £5,178.00 - 88.34 winning tickets. TM

524 - 530a (Foreign Racing) - See Raceform Interactive

506 CARTMEL (L-H)
Wednesday, May 29

OFFICIAL GOING: Soft (heavy in places)
Bend after last fenced moved out 3m and bend turning into Woodside moved out 3m to provide fresh ground.
Wind: fresh 1/2 against Weather: overcast, breezy, shower race 5

531 WATCH RACING UK ON SKY 432 NOVICES' HURDLE (6 hdls 2 omitted) 2m 1f 110y
2:20 (2:20) (Class 4) 4-Y-O+ **£3,249** (£954; £477; £238)

Form RPR
34/ **1** **Things Change (IRE)**30 22 5-10-12 118.... DougieCostello 108+
(John Quinn) *trckd ldr: led appr 2 out: blnd and hdd last: styd on u.p to ld in clsng stages* **3/1**2
112/ **2** *3/4* **Discovery Bay**14 5366 5-11-5 130.... DannyCook 113+
(Brian Ellison) *trckd ldrs: 2nd 2 out: led last: rdn over 1f out: edgd rt: hdd last 30yds* **2/5**1
/04- **3** *20* **Dane Cottage**2 506 6-10-0 69....(v) SamanthaDrake(5) 78
(Richard Ford) *led tl appr 2 out: wknd fnl 3f* **50/1**
55/ **4** *6* **Makellys Blackpool**52 5208 4-9-10 0.... HarryChalloner(5) 68
(Richard Ford) *in rr: n.m.r and stmbld bnd after 3rd: outpcd 4th: kpt on to take poor 4th in clsng stages* **28/1**
4/ **5** *2 1/4* **Tantamount**31 5319 4-10-8 0.... PeterBuchanan 73
(Lucinda Russell) *t.k.h in last: wnt 4th 4th: wknd and lost 4th last 50yds* **12/1**3

4m 27.4s (14.20) **Going Correction** +1.00s/f (Soft)
WFA 4 from 5yo+ 18lb **5** Ran SP% **109.5**
Speed ratings (Par 105): **108,107,98,96,95**
CSF £4.76 TOTE £2.20: £1.30, £1.10; EX 4.90 Trifecta £21.70 Pool: £1107.46 - 38.25 winning units..
Owner Mrs E Wright **Bred** J R Weston **Trained** Settrington, N Yorks

FOCUS
Testing ground with a wind blowing head-on up the straight. The last hurdle and second-last fence were omitted. Only two really mattered in this novices' hurdle and the pair finished a long way clear. The first two are rated below their best with the third setting the standard.

532 DOWNLOAD & WATCH WITH RACING UK'S APP MARES' MAIDEN HURDLE (8 hdls 3 omitted) 2m 6f
2:50 (2:50) (Class 5) 4-Y-O+ **£2,599** (£763; £381; £190)

Form RPR
500/ **1** **The Flaming Matron (IRE)**63 4971 7-11-0 0.... LucyAlexander 95
(N W Alexander) *trckd ldr: led appr 2 out: hld on wl fnl f* **7/2**2
5/2- **2** *1 1/4* **Polly Hopper**16 268 7-11-0 110....(t) SamTwiston-Davies 95
(Nigel Twiston-Davies) *chsd ldrs: cl 2nd and drvn last: upsides whn hung rt bnd over 2f out: kpt on same pce* **4/9**1
5/5- **3** *14* **Grethel (IRE)**2 506 9-11-0 69.... BrianHarding 81
(Alan Berry) *in rr but in tch: one pce and modest 3rd 3f out* **22/1**
PP5/ **4** *11* **Miss Sunflower**37 5452 11-10-9 57....(p) SamanthaDrake(5) 69
(Tina Jackson) *led: hdd appr 2 out: wknd fnl 3f* **66/1**
3/0- **5** *7* **Alimure**27 73 7-10-11 80.... BrianToomey(3) 62
(Clive Mulhall) *chsd ldrs: outpcd 2 out: wknd next* **50/1**
5/0- **P** **Notimetowaste (IRE)**11 372 6-11-0 0.... JasonMaguire
(Donald McCain) *t.k.h in rr but in tch: hit 2nd: lost pl after 6th: t.o whn p.u over 2f out* **15/2**3

5m 52.8s (23.50) **Going Correction** +1.175s/f (Heav) **6** Ran SP% **111.0**
Speed ratings (Par 103): **104,103,98,94,91**
toteswingers 1&2 £1.02, 2&3 £1.90, 1&3 £3.70 CSF £5.61 TOTE £3.10: £1.40, £1.10; EX 7.00 Trifecta £18.60 Pool: £1063.72 - 42.79 winning units..
Owner The Ladies Who **Bred** Joseph and Mark Molloy **Trained** Kinneston, Perth & Kinross

FOCUS
Very weak fare and, like the opener, it turned into a match between the top two in the market. The form is rated around the winner and third.

533 ENGLISH LAKES ICE CREAM H'CAP CHASE (10 fncs 2 omitted) 2m 1f 110y
3:20 (3:20) (Class 4) (0-105,102) 5-Y-O+ **£3,898** (£1,144; £572; £286)

Form RPR
4/2- **1** **Sergeant Pink (IRE)**5 220 7-11-0 95.... EmmaSayer(5) 107+
(Dianne Sayer) *in rr: detached 3rd: hdwy 7th: cl 2nd 3 out: led 3f out: drvn rt out* **3/1**2
4/1- **2** *2* **Cloverhill Lad (IRE)**14 314 9-10-12 93.... GaryRutherford(5) 101
(Stuart Coltherd) *chsd ldr: led after 5th: hdd 3f out: kpt on last 100yds* **4/1**3
3/5- **3** *13* **Laybach (IRE)**14 316 9-10-0 76 oh2.... LucyAlexander 71
(Jim Goldie) *led tl after 5th: outpcd 2 out: kpt on to take modest 3rd 2f out* **5/1**
523/ **4** *8* **Soul Magic (IRE)**30 23 11-10-12 95.... CallumBewley(7) 82
(Harriet Graham) *chsd ldrs: rdn and wknd 3 f out* **5/2**1
6/2- **5** *23* **Star Galaxy (IRE)**9 411 13-11-7 102....(b) GavinSheehan(5) 66
(John Flint) *chsd ldrs: outpcd after 7th: wknd 2f out: eased last 100yds and fin tired* **8/1**
36/- **6** *33* **Against The Wind**30 23 10-11-8 98.... PeterBuchanan 29
(Lucinda Russell) *w ldrs: stmbld on landing and lost pl 3rd: bhd fr 6th: t.o 2 out: virtually p.u last 3f* **10/1**

4m 38.2s (19.30) **Going Correction** +1.175s/f (Heav) **6** Ran SP% **110.4**
Speed ratings: **104,103,97,93,83 68**
toteswingers 1&2 £2.30, 2&3 £3.40, 1&3 £2.30 CSF £14.90 TOTE £3.00: £2.30, £2.40; EX 13.70 Trifecta £60.60 Pool: £801.57 - 9.91 winning units..
Owner Andrew Sayer **Bred** Ring Pink Partnership **Trained** Hackthorpe, Cumbria

FOCUS
Quite a competitive little handicap chase for the grade and the gallop looked reasonable enough given the ground. The placed horses set the level.

534 CARTMEL OLD GRAMMAR BEGINNERS' CHASE (11 fncs 3 omitted) 2m 5f 110y
3:50 (3:50) (Class 4) 5-Y-O+ **£3,898** (£1,144; £572; £286)

Form RPR
0/0- **1** **In The Haven (IRE)**8 418 10-10-9 99....(p) SamanthaDrake(5) 93
(Joanne Foster) *led tl after 1st: led after 5th: edgd rt fnl f: all out* **16/1**
0/5- **2** *nk* **Ubaltique (FR)**25 118 5-11-0 123.... JasonMaguire 95+
(Donald McCain) *trcking ldrs whn blnd 1st: t.k.h and sn hld up: blnd 6th: hdwy to trck ldrs 2 out: chsd wnr 3f out: kpt on fnl f: jst hld* **11/10**1
1/6- **3** *5* **Kellys Brow (IRE)**19 205 6-11-0 0....(p) AdrianLane 90
(Iain Jardine) *hmpd 1st: sn chsng ldrs: wnt 2nd 7th: drvn 2 out: one pce* **9/4**2
065/ **4** *3* **Raifteiri (IRE)**10 6-10-7 69.... MrNOrpwood(7) 85
(William Young Jnr) *led after 1st: hdd after 5th: drvn 3 out: sn outpcd: 5th 3f out: kpt on to take 3rd nr fin* **16/1**
5/4- **5** *3/4* **Mystified (IRE)**4 474 10-11-0 74.... BrianHarding 84
(Alan Berry) *chsd ldrs: one pce fr 2 out* **25/1**
041/ **6** *1 1/2* **Quelle Chance (IRE)**760 166 7-11-0 0.... BrianHughes 83
(John Wade) *prom: drvn 2 out: one pce* **5/1**3
442/ **7** *79* **Lindengrove**74 4799 8-11-0 0.... RichieMcLernon 4
(Dave Roberts) *t.k.h: trckd ldrs: lost pl 8th: t.o whn blnd last: eventually completed* **16/1**

5m 56.2s (30.80) **Going Correction** +1.175s/f (Heav) **7** Ran SP% **116.5**
Speed ratings: **91,90,89,87,87 87,58**
toteswingers 1&2 £4.90, 2&3 £1.10, 1&3 £10.40 CSF £37.40 TOTE £15.20: £6.10, £1.20; EX 48.30 Trifecta £162.00 Pool: £762.75 - 3.53 winning units..
Owner Miss J E Foster **Bred** Thomas Meagher **Trained** Menston, W Yorks

FOCUS
Hard to be positive about this form with the fourth and fifth limiting things.

535 DOWNLOAD FREE RACING UK APP HUNTERS' CHASE (FOR THE HORACE D. PAIN MEMORIAL TROPHY) (12 fncs 6 omitted) 3m 2f
4:25 (4:25) (Class 6) 5-Y-O+ **£1,559** (£483; £241; £121)

Form RPR
/2U- **1** **Special Portrait (IRE)**14 315 9-11-13 109....(t) MrPGerety(7) 102+
(Mark Hughes) *in rr: wnt 3rd 10th: upsides next: led 3f out: edgd rt fnl f: all out* **6/5**1
3/0- **2** *1 1/4* **Go West (IRE)**3 496 12-11-5 95....(v) MrTHamilton(7) 91
(A Hamilton) *led to 1st: lft in ld 4th: hdd 3 out: rallied over 1f out: no ex towards fin* **28/1**
2/3- **3** *3/4* **Barachois Silver**25 112 9-11-0 65.... MrSFox(5) 84
(Mrs J M Hollands) *lost pl 6th: hdwy 10th: wnt 8 l 3rd 4f out: styd on fnl 2f: clsng at fin* **6/1**2
6P0/ **4** *33* **Fiftyfive Degrees (IRE)**18 12-11-5 0.... CallumBewley(7) 56
(Ms Jackie Williamson) *in rr: outpcd whn hit 9th: distant 4th over 2f out: t.o* **14/1**
5 *15* **Howareyougoingon (IRE)**10 9-11-12 0....(p) MrTomDavid 41
(G D Hanmer) *chsd ldrs: hit 2nd: 3rd whn hit 10th: wknd 4f out: sn bhd: t.o* **20/1**
P/4- **6** *2 1/4* **Cool Mission (IRE)**12 357 9-11-9 115....(b) NickSlatter(3) 39
(Donald McCain) *trckd ldrs: rdn 10th: wknd next: t.o* **11/1**
06P/ **P** **Tastes Like More (IRE)**23 11-11-2 0....(p) MrGCrow(3)
(Mrs A R Hewitt) *in rr: bhd whn mstke 8th: sn t.o: p.u over 4f out* **12/1**
3/3- **P** **Benefit Night (IRE)**11 373 13-11-5 109....(bt) CharlieDeutsch(7)
(Mrs Polly Stockton) *led 1st: omitted 4th and immediately p.u* **17/2**3
U1/- **F** **Digg Whitaker**30 28 8-11-9 104.... MrRSmith(7)
(John Wade) *chsd ldr 4th: drvn 8th: wkng whn fell next: fatally injured* **6/1**2

7m 5.1s (30.20) **Going Correction** +1.175s/f (Heav) **9** Ran SP% **115.5**
Speed ratings: **100,99,99,89,84 83, , ,**
toteswingers 1&2 £14.90, 2&3 £5.00, 1&3 £3.80 CSF £34.99 TOTE £2.20: £1.10, £4.50, £2.00; EX 44.80 Trifecta £619.60 Part won. Pool: £826.22 - 0.42 winning units..
Owner Mark Hughes **Bred Trained** Wigton, Cumbria

■ Stewards' Enquiry : Charlie Deutsch twelve-day ban; took wrong course (15th,24th,30th June, 29th Aug & 8 days tbd)

FOCUS

Both the last and second last fences were omitted this time. They were almost walking in the closing stages and the placed horses set the level.

536 CARLSBERG H'CAP HURDLE (6 hdls 2 omitted) 2m 1f 110y

5:00 (5:09) (Class 5) (0-95,93) 4-Y-0+ **£2,599** (£763; £381; £190)

Form RPR

006/ **1** **Logical Approach (IRE)**[56] 5119 6-11-6 **92**.....................(p) TonyKelly(5) 100
(David Thompson) *trckd ldrs: outpcd appr last: 2nd over 3f out: led over 2f out: drvn out* **12/1**

/U5- **2** *8* **Pete**[15] 283 10-11-7 **88**.....................(tp) LucyAlexander 89
(Barry Murtagh) *chsd ldrs: outpcd appr last: kpt on and 4th over 2f out: chsd wnr over 1f out: no imp* **10/1**

6/1- **3** *2 1/4* **Sendiym (FR)**[15] 281 6-10-9 **81**.....................(b) EmmaSayer(5) 79
(Dianne Sayer) *t.k.h: led 1st: hdd 3rd: rdn and lost pl 2 out: rallied fnl 2f: styd on to take modest 3rd nr line* **9/2**[2]

/13- **4** *1/2* **Mount Welcome (IRE)**[20] 183 9-10-11 **83** ow1.............(t) MrTWeston(5) 80
(Martin Weston) *racd wd: t.k.h: trckd ldrs: led appr 2 out: hdd over 2f out: hung lft and fdd* **15/2**

00P/ **5** *1* **Decent Lord (IRE)**[81] 4660 9-10-13 **80**.....................(p) SeanQuinlan 77
(Jennie Candlish) *chsd ldrs: upsides last: one pce fnl 4f* **5/2**[1]

000/ **6** *7* **First Morning (IRE)**[94] 4414 8-11-12 **93**.....................(tp) DougieCostello 82
(Michael Blake) *in rr: sme hdwy after 4th: one pce extended run-in: nvr a threat* **13/2**[3]

/55- **7** *29* **Lewlaur Supreme (IRE)**[18] 219 10-9-7 **67**........... StephenMulqueen(7) 27
(William Young Jnr) *in rr: bhd fr 4th: t.o 4f out: virtually p.u* **8/1**

P00/ **8** *22* **Tropenfeuer (FR)**[8] 4912 6-10-7 **74**..................... BrianHarding 12
(James Moffatt) *in rr: hdwy 4th: lost pl appr next: sn bhd: t.o fnl 4f: virtually p.u* **18/1**

03/- **9** *74* **Hobsons Bay (IRE)**[756] 228 8-11-4 **92**..................... MissCWalton(7)
(Sheena Walton) *led to 1st: led 3rd tl appr 2 out: wknd rapidly: t.o over 3f out: virtually p.u: eventually fin* **22/1**

00/- **P** **History Lesson**[373] 384 7-10-9 **76**..................... WillKennedy
(Alan Jones) *in rr: drvn 3rd: bhd and nt fluent next: t.o 2 out: p.u 4f out* **14/1**

4m 32.3s (19.10) **Going Correction** +1.175s/f (Heav) **10** Ran SP% **116.0**
Speed ratings (Par 103): **104,100,99,99,98 95,82,73,40,**
toteswingers 1&2 £11.10, 2&3 £3.20, 1&3 £10.60 CSF £123.45 CT £626.53 TOTE £17.80: £4.20, £2.30, £1.70; EX 126.20 Trifecta £480.80 Pool: £2323.35 - 3.62 winning units..
Owner A J Duffield **Bred** Albert Wylie **Trained** Bolam, Co Durham

FOCUS

The picture changed dramatically on the home bend as leader Mount Welcome found absolutely zero when coming off the bridle. The winner is rated back to his best with the third below his recent chasing mark.

537 JOHN FLYNN MEMORIAL CONDITIONAL JOCKEYS' H'CAP HURDLE (6 hdls 2 omitted) 2m 1f 110y

5:35 (5:35) (Class 4) (0-120,106) 4-Y-0+ **£3,249** (£954; £477; £238)

Form RPR

52/- **1** **Pret A Thou (FR)**[46] 5293 10-11-12 **106**..................... HarryChalloner 105
(John Bryan Groucott) *w ldrs: led appr 4th: drvn out: hld on nr fin* **15/8**[1]

000/ **2** *3/4* **Stanley Bridge**[30] 27 6-11-8 **102**..................... LucyAlexander 100
(Barry Murtagh) *chsd ldrs: drvn 2 out: 4 l 2nd over 2f out: kpt on: nt quite rch wnr* **3/1**[2]

6/0- **3** *11* **Ballybroe (IRE)**[21] 168 6-11-11 **105**.....................(p) JonathanEngland 94
(Harriet Graham) *chsd ldrs: 2nd 4th: wknd fnl 2f* **3/1**[2]

5/4- **4** *14* **Claude Carter**[13] 344 9-11-10 **104**..................... CallumWhillans 77
(Alistair Whillans) *in rr: drvn and outpcd 4th: poor 4th last* **8/1**

P/0- **5** *9* **Rare Coincidence**[4] 471 12-10-4 **89**.................(tp) StephenMulqueen(5) 53
(Alan Berry) *led tl hdd and lost pl 4th: rallied next: sn wknd* **6/1**[3]

4m 32.8s (19.60) **Going Correction** +1.175s/f (Heav) **5** Ran SP% **110.2**
Speed ratings (Par 105): **103,102,97,91,87**
CSF £8.00 TOTE £2.80: £1.60, £2.30; EX 7.80 Trifecta £19.90 Pool: £901.71 - 33.86 winning units..
Owner C J Tipton **Bred** Mme Robert Jeannin **Trained** Bourton, Shropshire

FOCUS

Moderate stuff rated through the runner-up.

T/Plt: £22.30 to a £1 stake. Pool of £48565.13 - 1589.76 winning tickets. T/Qpdt: £23.10 to a £1 stake. Pool of £3104.86 - 99.14 winning tickets. WG

[484]FONTWELL (L-H)

Wednesday, May 29

OFFICIAL GOING: Good (good to soft in places)

Fences sited on inner and bends moved out 3m to give fresh running line.

Wind: mild breeze behind Weather: cloudy with light rain

538 32REDBINGO.COM NOVICES' HURDLE (11 hdls) 2m 6f 110y

2:10 (2:10) (Class 4) 4-Y-0+ **£3,119** (£915; £457; £228)

Form RPR

P/4- **1** **Jojabean (IRE)**[20] 185 6-10-13 112..................... WayneHutchinson 112+
(Alan King) *trckd ldrs: bad mstke 2nd (did wl to rcvr): nt fluent next: rdn gng to 2 out: led narrowly last: edgd rt: styd on: drvn out* **7/4**[2]

260/ **2** *1 1/4* **Ya Hafed**[33] 5553 5-10-13 105..................... LeightonAspell 108
(Sheena West) *led: rdn whn strly pressed fr 2 out: narrowly hdd last: styd on but a being hld by wnr fnl run-in* **9/1**

56/- **3** *1/2* **Westaway (IRE)**[64] 4964 6-10-13 120..................... TomCannon 108
(David Arbuthnot) *trckd ldr: str chal 2 out: sn rdn: ev ch last: styd on in disp 2nd but a being hld run-in* **8/1**[3]

5/6- **4** *7* **King Boru (IRE)**[17] 233 5-10-13 0..................... DominicElsworth 102
(Emma Lavelle) *trckd ldrs: hit 6th: rdn after 8th: outpcd after 3 out: styng on but no threat whn blnd last: wnt 4th towards fin* **14/1**

3/3- **5** *3/4* **Shuh Shuh Gah (IRE)**[20] 185 6-10-13 117..................... TomScudamore 102
(David Bridgwater) *hld up towards rr: tk clsr order after 7th: rdn in cl 3rd after 3 out: styd on same pce fr next tl fdd and lost 4th fnl 75yds* **5/4**[1]

4P0/ **6** *7* **King Caractacus**[64] 4964 8-10-13 0.....................(t) DavidBass 94
(Lawney Hill) *hld up in tch: rdn after 3 out: sn outpcd: wknd last* **40/1**

7 *dist* **Helloutofdodge (IRE)**[33] 7-10-6 0.....................(t) MrJPO'Sullivan(7)
(R P Rath, Ire) *hld up in last: struggling 8th: t.o fr next: continued: btn 150 l* **50/1**

0/0- **P** **Tang Royal (FR)**[26] 95 6-10-13 0..................... AndrewGlassonbury
(Richard Rowe) *mid-div tl dropped to last trio after 8th: sn rdn: outpcd after 3 out: wknd between last 2: wnt lft last: sn p.u* **50/1**

600/ **U** **Banks Road (IRE)**[520] 3330 8-10-13 0..................... JimmyMcCarthy
(Geoffrey Deacon) *whipped rnd and uns rdr whn tapes wnt bk* **66/1**

5m 46.9s (4.40) **Going Correction** +0.15s/f (Yiel) **9** Ran SP% **116.4**
Speed ratings (Par 105): **98,97,97,94,94 92,,,**
toteswingers 1&2 £3.40, 2&3 £7.80, 1&3 £3.60 CSF £17.50 TOTE £2.80: £1.10, £2.10, £2.10; EX 14.50 Trifecta £78.10 Pool: £1182.32 - 11.34 winning units..
Owner The Dunkley & Reilly Partnership **Bred** Patrick Fennessy **Trained** Barbury Castle, Wilts

FOCUS

"Beautiful ground" according to Wayne Hutchinson. They went a steady pace in this modest novice hurdle. The time was nearly 35sec slower than standard but the first two are rated pretty much to their marks.

539 32RED CASINO NOVICES' CHASE (11 fncs 2 omitted) 2m 2f

2:40 (2:40) (Class 4) 5-Y-0+ **£3,768** (£1,106; £553; £276)

Form RPR

312/ **1** **Suerte Al Salto (IRE)**[35] 5507 6-10-12 0..................... TomCannon 123+
(Chris Gordon) *hld up bhd ldng trio: wnt 2nd after 6th: sltly hmpd whn hit 4 out: shkn up after 3 out: led sn after 2 out: r.o wl fr last: rdn out* **4/1**[2]

10/- **2** *1 3/4* **Prospect Wells (FR)**[55] 5137 8-10-12 0.....................(t) DarylJacob 122+
(Paul Nicholls) *trckd ldrs: led 5th: qcknd pce sltly: nt fluent 4 out: shkn up after 3 out: hdd sn after 2 out whn rdn: nt gng pce to get bk on terms fr last* **1/4**[1]

060/ **3** *13* **Gay Sloane (IRE)**[88] 4526 9-10-9 0..................... MattGriffiths(3) 108
(Richard Woollacott) *led at crawl tl 2nd: dropped to 3rd after 6th: rdn appr 3 out: styd on same pce* **14/1**[3]

0/5- **4** *6* **Star Of Massini (IRE)**[15] 293 6-10-12 0..................... AndrewThornton 102
(Seamus Mullins) *led 2nd: pce remained stdy: hdd 5th: dropped to 4th after next but stl wl in tch: styd on same pce fr 4 out* **25/1**

5m 4.0s (29.30) **Going Correction** +0.075s/f (Yiel) **4** Ran SP% **110.5**
Speed ratings: **37,36,30,27**
CSF £5.99 TOTE £4.90; EX 6.40 Trifecta £11.70 Pool: £963.64 - 61.76 winning units..
Owner David Henery **Bred** M McCabe **Trained** Morestead, Hants

FOCUS

A shock result in this novice chase as Prospect Wells failed to land the odds on his chasing debut. The early pace was very steady as no one really wanted to go on, and the form should not be treated literally.

540 32RED.COM H'CAP HURDLE (9 hdls) 2m 2f 110y

3:10 (3:10) (Class 5) (0-95,95) 4-Y-0+ **£1,949** (£572; £286; £143)

Form RPR

562/ **1** **Windpfeil (IRE)**[16] 1688 7-10-9 **85**.....................(p) MissCBoxall(7) 92
(Dominic Ffrench Davis) *hld up towards rr: hdwy appr 6th: chsd ldrs after 3 out: nt best of runs whn swtchd lft gng to last: rdn and styd on strly run-in: led fnl strides* **28/1**

42F/ **2** *hd* **Wise Hawk**[36] 5472 8-10-6 **78**..................... JamesBest(3) 85
(Jackie Du Plessis) *travelled wl: trckd ldrs: jnd ldr 3 out: led gng to 2 out: wnt sltly lft last: sn rdn: kpt on: collared fnl strides* **9/4**[1]

03/- **3** *3 1/2* **Fair Breeze**[40] 5379 6-10-10 **79**..................... RichardJohnson 82
(Richard Phillips) *mid-div: hdwy appr 6th: rdn to chse ldr 2 out: styd on fr last tl no ex fnl 50yds* **8/1**

3/1- **4** *1/2* **Hawk Gold (IRE)**[17] 243 9-9-12 **74**.....................(b) ConorShoemark(7) 78
(Michelle Bryant) *hld up towards rr: nt fluent 2nd: hdwy 3 out: chsd ldrs next: sn rdn: styd on same pce fr last* **6/1**[2]

62/- **5** *1* **On The Feather**[55] 5142 7-11-8 **91**.....................(v) TomScudamore 93
(Jim Best) *hld up towards rr: hdwy after 3 out: sn rdn: styd on same pce fr last* **8/1**

53/- **6** *14* **Brandy And Pep (IRE)**[33] 9-9-7 **69** oh4.....................(p) MrJPO'Sullivan(7) 58
(R P Rath, Ire) *hld up towards rr: hdwy appr 6th: trckd ldrs 3 out: rdn next: wknd last* **33/1**

050/ **7** *14* **Kijivu**[33] 5557 8-11-4 **87**.....................(bt) ConorO'Farrell 64
(Alastair Lidderdale) *trckd ldr: led after 6th: rdn and hdd bef 2 out: wknd last* **8/1**

0/P- **8** *8* **Lady Sinatra**[20] 188 5-11-0 **83**.....................(p) SamJones 53
(Oliver Sherwood) *led tl appr 6th: wknd bef 3 out: t.o* **16/1**

9 *5* **Patricktom Boru (IRE)**[25] 6-11-9 **92**..................... APMcCoy 57
(Laura Young) *trckd ldr: led appr 6th where mstke: sn rdn and hdd: wknd bef 2 out: t.o* **7/1**[3]

6P4/ **10** *14* **Petie McSweetie (IRE)**[60] 5024 6-10-13 **85**.............(tp) MichealNolan(3) 38
(Richard Woollacott) *mid-div tl after 6th: sn bhd: t.o* **8/1**

0/0- **11** *33* **Osmosia (FR)**[22] 166 8-11-12 **95**.....................(tp) TomCannon 18
(Chris Gordon) *struggling 5th: a in last: lost tch next: t.o* **16/1**

4m 36.4s (2.10) **Going Correction** +0.15s/f (Yiel) **11** Ran SP% **120.2**
Speed ratings (Par 103): **101,100,99,99,98 92,87,83,81,75 61**
toteswingers 1&2 £23.20, 2&3 £5.90, 1&3 £2.70 CSF £95.17 CT £587.98 TOTE £40.30: £11.70, £1.60, £2.70; EX 210.60 Trifecta £442.10 Pool: £589.54 - 0.01 winning units..
Owner Miss Jo Ewell **Bred** Gainsborough Stud Management Ltd **Trained** Lambourn, Berks

FOCUS

A low-grade handicap hurdle run at a fair gallop. The form is rated around the winner and third, backed up by the fifth.

541 32RED NOVICES' H'CAP CHASE (16 fncs 3 omitted) 3m 2f 110y

3:40 (3:40) (Class 4) (0-105,99) 5-Y-0+ **£3,768** (£1,106; £553; £276)

Form RPR

U/0- **1** **Quel Ballistic**[25] 120 9-11-12 **99**.....................(v[1]) RichardJohnson 120+
(Peter Bowen) *led 3rd: mde rest: jnd briefly gng to 3 out: sn bk on top: styd on strly and in command fr 2 out: eased nr fin* **10/1**

213/ **2** *13* **Dimpsy Time**[33] 5542 7-11-6 **93**.....................(tp) BrendanPowell 99
(Colin Tizzard) *prom tl 3rd: chsd ldrs: bmpd 4th: regained 2nd 12th: rdn to chal briefly gng to 3 out: sn hld: styd on same pce: mstke last* **7/2**[1]

2/F- **3** *4* **Inner Steel (IRE)**[14] 305 8-11-10 **97**..................... LeightonAspell 101
(Lydia Richards) *hld up: smooth hdwy 11th: cl 4th whn hit next: sn rdn: chsd ldng pair bef 3 out: styd on same pce fr next: blnd last* **6/1**[3]

0/4- **4** *32* **Kaycee (IRE)**[15] 285 8-10-0 **73** oh9..................... MarkGrant 47
(Roger Curtis) *hld up: hdwy 7th: lost tch after 12th: plugged on to go modest 4th towards fin: t.o* **50/1**

2/6- **5** *2 1/2* **Old Dreams (IRE)**[17] 242 7-11-12 **99**.....................(t) APMcCoy 70
(Nick Gifford) *trckd ldrs: rchd for 4th: rdn after 4 out: wknd next: lost modest 4th towards fin: t.o* **4/1**[2]

6/4- **6** *29* **Dr Thistle (IRE)**[14] 303 6-11-2 **89**..................... JamieMoore 34
(Gary Moore) *in tch: rdn along fr after 8th: wknd after 12th: t.o* **16/1**

433/ **P** **Days Of Pleasure (IRE)**[752] 302 8-11-5 **92**..................... TomCannon
(Chris Gordon) *hld up: struggling fr 6th: sn detached: losing tch whn p.u after 11th* **14/1**

The Form Book Jumps, Raceform Ltd, Compton, RG20 6NL.

022/ **P** **Cool Cascade**[35] 5506 7-10-9 **82** DavidBass
(Lawney Hill) *mid-div: pushed along fr 8th: sn in last pair: wknd after 12th: t.o whn p.u bef 3 out* **7/1**

3/4- **P** **Ontheslate (IRE)**[19] 206 7-10-0 **73** AlexMerriam
(Neil King) *led tl 3rd: chsd ldr tl rdn after 11th: wknd next: t.o whn p.u bef 3 out* **4/1**[2]

7m 1.7s (0.60) **Going Correction** +0.075s/f (Yiel) **9** Ran SP% **112.6**
Speed ratings: **102,98,96,87,86 78, , ,**
toteswingers 1&2 £15.40, 2&3 £4.90, 1&3 £9.00 CSF £45.06 CT £229.78 TOTE £9.60: £3.90, £1.10, £3.20; EX 68.40 Trifecta £287.50 Pool: £956.83 - 2.49 winning units..
Owner H Jones **Bred** Mrs B J Lockhart **Trained** Little Newcastle, Pembrokes

FOCUS
A moderate novices' handicap chase with the winner back to the level of his old form backed up by the runner-up.

542 32REDBET.COM H'CAP CHASE (13 fncs 3 omitted) 2m 6f
4:15 (4:15) (Class 4) (0-115,111) 5-Y-0+ **£3,768** (£1,106; £553; £276)

Form RPR

452/ **1** **Full Of Joy (IRE)**[74] 4782 8-11-11 **110** (t) APMcCoy 121+
(Jonjo O'Neill) *trckd ldrs: lost pl and shkn up briefly 5th: reminder after next: led 10th: rdn after 4 out: wnt bdly lft 3 out: wnt lft last 2: a doing enough* **11/8**[1]

522- **2** *1 1/4* **Upton Mead (IRE)**[3] 489 6-10-3 **95** (b) ConorShoemark[(7)] 102
(Kevin Tork) *hld up: nvr really travelling fr 7th and pushed along: hdwy 10th: sn rdn: styd in 4th tl str run fr last: wnt 2nd towards fin: nvr rching wnr* **3/1**[2]

6/3- **3** *2 1/2* **Sound Stage**[29] 40 10-11-11 **110** (p) IanPopham 114
(Caroline Keevil) *t.k.h: hld up: hdwy to trck ldrs 6th: rdn after 10th: disp 2nd after 4 out tl next: wnt 2nd at the last: a being hld by wnr: lost 2nd towards fin* **7/1**[3]

230/ **4** *4 1/2* **Mic Aubin (FR)**[880] 3260 10-10-9 **94** FelixDeGiles 95
(Jennifer Mason) *racd keenly: trckd ldr: rdn and ev ch after 4 out: sltly hmpd whn chsng wnr next: lost 2nd at the last: no ex fnl 75yds* **16/1**

504/ **5** *18* **Watergate (IRE)**[28] 4594 7-10-7 **92** AndrewGlassonbury 80
(Richard Rowe) *led tl awkward and hdd 10th: sn rdn and lost pl: wknd 3 out* **25/1**

P/2- **6** *28* **Crannaghmore Boy (IRE)**[23] 143 8-10-11 **96** JamieMoore 54
(Keith Goldsworthy) *racd keenly trcking ldrs tl mstke 2nd and lost pl: cl up after 9th: rdn after next: wknd after 3 out: t.o* **11/1**

P/5- **7** *47* **Ray Diamond**[26] 98 8-11-1 **100** RichardJohnson 16
(Michael Madgwick) *trckd ldr tl rdn after 9th: sn last: wknd 4 out: t.o* **20/1**

3/U- **P** **Venetian Lad**[26] 96 8-11-12 **111** MarcGoldstein
(Lydia Richards) *in tch: lost pl whn short of room on bnd after 4th: tk clsr order after 9th: rdn after 4 out: wknd 3 out: p.u bef last* **8/1**

5m 50.1s (7.10) **Going Correction** +0.075s/f (Yiel) **8** Ran SP% **113.5**
Speed ratings: **90,89,88,87,80 70,53,**
toteswingers 1&2 £1.60, 2&3 £4.70, 1&3 £2.80 CSF £6.20 CT £19.55 TOTE £2.40: £1.10, £1.80, £1.70; EX 6.20 Trifecta £31.00 Pool: £1924.74 - 46.50 winning units..
Owner John P McManus **Bred** J D Flood **Trained** Cheltenham, Gloucs

FOCUS
Modest handicap form rated around the placed horses pretty much to their marks.

543 32REDPOKER.COM CONDITIONAL JOCKEYS' H'CAP HURDLE (11 hdls) 2m 6f 110y
4:50 (4:50) (Class 5) (0-95,95) 4-Y-0+ **£1,949** (£572; £286; £143)

Form RPR

/52- **1** **Nicky Nutjob (GER)**[7] 429 7-10-6 **83** (p) CiaranMckee[(8)] 92+
(John O'Shea) *hld up bhd: hdwy 7th: rdn to chse ldng pair gng to 2 out: led bef last: styd on wl* **9/2**[3]

0/4- **2** *9* **Old Pals Act (IRE)**[23] 145 5-11-2 **95** JamesHuxham[(10)] 95
(Jonjo O'Neill) *hld up: hdwy 5th to trck ldrs: chal after 8th: rdn to chse ldr after 3 out: ev ch between last 2: styd on same pce run-in* **7/1**

1/5- **3** *6* **Marie Deja La (FR)**[3] 490 7-11-10 **93** (b) HarryDerham 91
(Chris Gordon) *trckd ldrs: led after 8th: nt fluent 2 out: sn rdn: hdd gng to the last: sn hld: hung rt run-in* **4/1**[2]

6/0- **4** *21* **Budsson**[17] 241 7-10-0 **69** oh13 (p) AdamWedge 45
(Anna Newton-Smith) *trckd ldrs fr 3rd: rdn after mstke 8th: wknd bef last* **33/1**

6/0- **5** *7* **Theoystercatcher (IRE)**[29] 42 7-11-4 **92** NathanAdams[(5)] 61
(Tim Vaughan) *in tch: rdn along after 5th: wknd after 2 out* **20/1**

1/5- **6** *hd* **Gilded Age**[17] 254 7-11-9 **95** (tp) TomCannon[(3)] 64
(Chris Gordon) *disp ld: rn in snatches: drvn along fr 4th: hdd after 8th: wknd after 2 out* **7/2**[1]

F/P- **7** *11* **Amirico (IRE)**[26] 99 8-11-4 **87** JeremiahMcGrath 46
(Richard Rowe) *trckd ldrs: jnd ldr after 7th tl rdn after next: sn btn: wknd after next* **20/1**

/00- **8** *2 3/4* **Buffy Brosnan**[14] 306 5-9-10 **70** JackSherwood[(5)] 27
(Chris Gordon) *rn in snatches on outer: towards rr: midfield after 3rd tl 8th: wknd next* **33/1**

11P/ **9** *63* **Overlay**[160] 3159 9-10-13 **82** BrendanPowell
(Lawney Hill) *disp ld tl after 7th: dropped away rapidly: t.o* **9/2**[3]

460/ **P** **Big Knickers**[535] 3083 8-10-10 **87** (t) ChrisMeehan[(8)]
(Neil Mulholland) *in tch tl lost action and p.u after 7th: fatally injured* **8/1**

5m 47.5s (5.00) **Going Correction** +0.15s/f (Yiel) **10** Ran SP% **117.6**
Speed ratings (Par 103): **97,93,91,84,82 81,78,77,55,**
toteswingers 1&2 £6.80, 2&3 £6.60, 1&3 £4.60 CSF £34.19 CT £135.52 TOTE £3.10: £1.10, £2.40, £1.30; EX 20.40 Trifecta £59.60 Pool: £1735.24 - 21.81 winning units..
Owner Quality Pipe Supports (Q P S) Ltd **Bred** Newsells Park Stud Ltd **Trained** Elton, Gloucs
■ Stewards' Enquiry : Jack Sherwood nine-day ban; used whip above permitted level and when out of contention (13th-15th, 18th-21st, 23rd, 25th June).

FOCUS
A moderate handicap hurdle run at a solid gallop, although the winner is only rated in line with his latest mark.

544 £32 BONUS AT 32RED.COM STANDARD OPEN NATIONAL HUNT FLAT RACE 2m 2f 110y
5:25 (5:27) (Class 6) 4-6-Y-0 **£1,559** (£457; £228; £114)

Form RPR

1 **Father Edward (IRE)** 4-10-13 0 DenisO'Regan 105+
(John Ferguson) *trckd ldrs: led 3f out: nudged clr 2f out: sn in command: comf* **2/1**[1]

2 *2 1/4* **Springhill Lad** 6-11-4 0 JimmyMcCarthy 105
(Geoffrey Deacon) *hld up: hdwy 7f out: rdn and ev ch fr over 2f out tl wl over 1f out: styd on but a being hld fnl f* **50/1**

- **3** *1* **Blue Bear (IRE)** 4-10-13 0 SamThomas 99
(Diana Grissell) *mid-div tl rdn and rn wd on fnl bnd: styd on again nicely in home st: running green but wnt 3rd ins fnl f* **25/1**

4 *1 1/4* **Another Brandy (IRE)**[66] 5-11-4 0 NoelFehily 103
(Neil Mulholland) *hld up: hdwy over 3f out: rdn to chse ldrs over 2f out: styd on same pce fr over 1f out* **14/1**

- **5** *3/4* **When In Roam (IRE)** 4-10-6 0 SamJones 90
(Sean Curran) *mid-div: rdn to chse ldrs 3f out: styd on same pce fnl 2f* **25/1**

5/3- **6** *9* **Tiller Belle**[20] 187 5-10-8 0 JeremiahMcGrath[(3)] 87
(Nicky Henderson) *trckd ldrs: rdn 3f out: one pce fnl 2f* **6/1**

7 *1* **Bow Quest** 6-10-11 0 JamieMoore 86
(Gary Moore) *hld up: hdwy to go in tch: 7f out: rdn over 3f out: one pce fnl 2f* **20/1**

8 *24* **Henwood (IRE)** 5-11-4 0 BrendanPowell 72
(Colin Tizzard) *disp ld: pushed along after 7f: rdn whn hdd 3f out: sn wknd: t.o* **11/4**[2]

6/2- **9** *21* **Just Archie (USA)**[17] 246 5-11-4 0 LeightonAspell 53
(Lady Herries) *disp ld tl over 3f out: wknd over 2f out: t.o* **5/1**[3]

10 *2 3/4* **Wild Legend (IRE)** 4-10-6 0 AndrewGlassonbury 38
(Richard Rowe) *hld up: hdwy to sit promly over 6f out: wknd 3f out: t.o* **66/1**

6- **11** *9* **Top Chief**[26] 101 5-10-13 0 KillianMoore[(5)] 42
(Mark Rimell) *chsd ldrs tl rdn w a circ to go: sn in rr: t.o* **25/1**

12 *shd* **Leyla's Gift** 4-10-6 0 MarcGoldstein 30
(Lydia Richards) *unruly gng to s: a in rr: lost tch u.p fr over 7f out: t.o* **33/1**

13 *13* **Midnight Monkey** 5-11-4 0 AlexMerriam 30
(Lady Anne Connell) *mid-div tl wknd 5f out: t.o* **33/1**

4m 33.7s (5.00) **Going Correction** +0.15s/f (Yiel)
WFA 4 from 5yo+ 4lb **13** Ran SP% **123.3**
Speed ratings: **95,94,93,93,92 89,88,78,69,68 64,64,59**
toteswingers 1&2 £25.70, 2&3 £86.20, 1&3 £17.40 CSF £134.17 TOTE £2.90: £1.50, £19.50, £9.60; EX 136.00 Trifecta £1563.30 Part won, Pool: £2084.48 - 0.18 winning units..
Owner Bloomfields **Bred** Hugh Fitzpatrick **Trained** Cowlinge, Suffolk

FOCUS
This bumper was run over an extended 2m2f and they didn't hang about, so stamina proved important. The form could be rated higher through the sixth.
T/Plt: £154.30 to a £1 stake. Pool of £60764.01 - 287.36 winning tickets. T/Qpdt: £12.60 to a £1 stake. Pool of £6821.51 - 399.60 winning tickets. TM

545 - 551a (Foreign Racing) - See Raceform Interactive

[444]WETHERBY (L-H)
Thursday, May 30

OFFICIAL GOING: Good to soft (soft in places; 6.0)
Third fence in back st omitted in all chases.
Wind: fresh 1/2 against Weather: overcast and breezy

552 READ HAYLEY TURNER EVERY FRIDAY RACINGUK.COM MARES' NOVICES' HURDLE (11 hdls) 2m 4f
6:00 (6:01) (Class 4) 4-Y-0+ **£3,119** (£915; £457; £228)

Form RPR

2/1- **1** **Mrs Peachey (IRE)**[17] 268 6-11-3 113 JasonMaguire 117+
(Kim Bailey) *trckd ldr: led bef 3 out: j.rt and blnd 3 out: clr whn j.rt next: 14 l ahd last: heavily eased* **30/100**[1]

63/- **2** *9* **So Cheeky**[209] 2166 4-10-5 0 (t) BarryKeniry 86
(Richard Guest) *hld up: hdwy 5th: chsd wnr 3 out: no imp* **6/1**[2]

05/- **3** *1/2* **Miss Duffy**[32] 1 5-10-5 0 HarryChalloner[(5)] 90
(William Kinsey) *led: hdd 3 out: kpt on one pce* **11/1**[3]

45/ **4** *8* **Latest Fashion (IRE)**[515] 3494 7-10-10 0 FearghalDavis 84
(Christopher Wilson) *chsd ldrs: drvn 8th: lost pl bef 2 out* **16/1**

0/U- **5** *6* **Captive Moment**[7] 450 7-10-3 0 StephenMulqueen[(7)] 77
(John Norton) *nt fluent: drvn and dropped to rr 4th: bhd whn blnd 7th: tk modest 5th 2 out* **66/1**

6 *dist* **Weeumba**[25] 8-10-10 0 AdrianLane 45
(Sandy Forster) *chsd ldrs: drvn 8th: sn lost pl: wl bhd 2 out: t.o whn heavily eased run-in* **25/1**

05P/ **P** **Bow Fiddle (IRE)**[410] 5432 7-10-7 0 AlexanderVoy[(3)]
(Patrick Holmes) *t.k.h in rr: lost pl 6th: bhd fr 8th: t.o whn p.u bef next* **100/1**

5m 15.1s (15.60) **Going Correction** +0.775s/f (Soft)
WFA 4 from 5yo+ 19lb **7** Ran SP% **111.8**
Speed ratings (Par 105): **99,95,95,92,89 75,**
toteswingers 1&2 £1.30, 1&3 £1.10, 2&3 £3.10 CSF £2.54 TOTE £1.20: £1.10, £2.90; EX 2.30 Trifecta £8.70 Pool: £1457.47 - 125.02 winning units..
Owner The Boom Syndicate **Bred** J Hanly & C Neilan **Trained** Andoversford, Gloucs

FOCUS
A total of 12mm of rain had fallen in the 24 hours leading up to this meeting and the ground was officially good to soft (soft in places), with a GoingStick reading of 6.0. The third fence on the far side was omitted from chases. Racing began, in cool, overcast conditions, with a mares' novices' hurdle that lacked depth. The easy winner still looks to be on the upgrade.

553 LIFE & STYLE NOVICES' CHASE (16 fncs 2 omitted) 3m 1f
6:30 (6:30) (Class 4) 5-Y-0+ **£3,768** (£1,106; £553; £276)

Form RPR

/11- **1** **Green Wizard (IRE)**[15] 322 7-11-5 0 RyanMania 128+
(Sue Smith) *led 2nd: 1 1/2 l ahd whn hit last: jnd last 50yds: hld on gamely* **10/3**[3]

0/1- **2** *hd* **Seven Woods (IRE)**[16] 296 7-11-5 123 (t) AlainCawley 126
(Tom George) *led 1st: mstke and hdd next: chsd ldrs: 2nd and drvn appr 4 out: styd on: swtchd lft and upsides run-in: jst hld* **11/4**[2]

3/2- **3** *1 1/2* **Buachaill Alainn (IRE)**[11] 394 6-10-12 0 (p) JamieMoore 117
(Peter Bowen) *led to 1st: chsd ldrs: drvn 9th: outpcd appr 4 out: styd on fr 2 out: kpt on run-in: nvr quite able to chal* **6/5**[1]

POP/ **4** *27* **War On (IRE)**[31] 27 6-10-12 0 HenryBrooke 93
(Michael Smith) *chsd ldrs: drvn 12th: sn lost pl and bhd* **33/1**

P/6- **5** *18* **Ballycracken (IRE)**[26] 120 9-10-7 77 JoeCornwall[(5)] 82
(David Pearson) *chsd ldrs: drvn 5th: lost pl 11th: mstke next: sn wl bhd* **200/1**

262/ **U** **Sun Cloud (IRE)**[34] 5549 6-10-12 0 BrianHughes
(Malcolm Jefferson) *hld up in last: wl in tch whn blnd and uns rdr 4th* **8/1**

6m 30.5s (21.10) **Going Correction** +0.775s/f (Soft) **6** Ran SP% **109.7**
Speed ratings: **97,96,96,87,82**
toteswingers 1&2 £2.20, 1&3 £1.30, 2&3 £1.40 CSF £12.66 TOTE £3.20: £1.60, £2.40; EX 11.10 Trifecta £19.20 Pool: £1137.18 - 44.29 winning units..
Owner Mrs S Smith **Bred** Eric Barrett **Trained** High Eldwick, W Yorks

FOCUS
A fair novices' chase. The winner is a better chaser than hurdler and can win again.

554 "MILLINERY COLLECTIVE" NOVICES' HURDLE (13 hdls) 3m 1f
7:00 (7:00) (Class 4) 4-Y-0+ **£3,119** (£915; £457; £228)

Form RPR
64/- **1** **Willoughby Hedge**[40] 5408 6-10-13 118 WayneHutchinson 122+
(Alan King) *t.k.h: trckd ldrs: handy 2nd appr 3 out: led 2 out: shkn up wnt clr clr last: easily* **6/4**[2]
/41- **2** *27* **Loose Preformer (IRE)**[7] 449 7-11-5 117 APMcCoy 111
(David O'Meara) *hld up: trckd ldrs 5th: led and hung lft appr 3 out: hit 3 out: hdd and nt fluent 2 out: 7 l down and wl btn whn stmbld on landing last: tired and sn eased* **5/4**[1]
5- **3** *34* **Lord Fox (IRE)**[14] 339 6-10-8 0 TrevorWhelan(5) 67
(Shaun Harris) *led: nt fluent and hdd 2nd: nt fluent next: rdn 10th: hdd & wknd bef next: sn distant 3rd* **40/1**
650/ **4** *10* **Yukon Delta (IRE)**[32] 19 6-10-13 0 KennyJohnson 58
(Robert Johnson) *hld up: trckd ldrs 5th: drvn sn after 10th: sn lost pl and bhd: t.o next* **66/1**
563/ **P** **Harris (IRE)**[141] 3573 6-10-13 110 CharlieHuxley
(William Kinsey) *chsd ldrs: shkn up 5th: hrd drvn 9th: lost pl next: sn bhd: t.o whn p.u bef 3 out* **4/1**[3]
P/P- **P** **Aliking**[7] 449 6-10-13 0 (p) DannyCook
(Peter Niven) *led 2nd to 4th: drvn 7th: reminders and sn lost pl: t.o whn j. slowly next: p.u bef 9th* **100/1**

6m 37.5s (21.00) **Going Correction** +0.775s/f (Soft) **6** Ran SP% **109.4**
Speed ratings (Par 105): **97,88,77,74,**
toteswingers 1&2 £1.10, 1&3 £2.50, 2&3 £4.60 CSF £3.67 TOTE £2.30: £1.40, £1.30; EX 4.00 Trifecta £25.40 Pool: £1357.83 - 39.94 winning units..
Owner J W Haydon **Bred** East Burrow Farm **Trained** Barbury Castle, Wilts

FOCUS
Few had obvious claims in this run-of-the-mill novice hurdle. The easy winner belatedly fulfilled the promise of his Exeter hurdling debut.

555 YORKSHIRE POST MAGAZINE H'CAP CHASE (16 fncs 2 omitted) 2m 6f 110y
7:35 (7:35) (Class 4) (0-105,105) 5-Y-0+ **£3,898** (£1,144; £572; £286)

Form RPR
3/2- **1** **Whiskey Ridge (IRE)**[11] 385 7-9-13 81 BrianToomey(3) 105+
(Sue Smith) *w ldr: led 5th: forged clr fr 12th: pushed out run-in* **3/1**[1]
/32- **2** *23* **Attycran (IRE)**[16] 282 8-11-7 100 (t) MichaelMcAlister 101
(Maurice Barnes) *chsd ldrs: hit 4th: chsd wnr after 12th: kpt on: no imp* **8/1**
5/4- **3** *20* **Everylasting (IRE)**[28] 74 6-10-0 79 oh2 (p) RichieMcGrath 59
(Rose Dobbin) *led to 5th: chsd wnr: nt fluent 10th: outpcd after 12th: 5th 3 out: kpt on to take distant 3rd last* **7/2**[2]
U21/ **4** *3 ¾* **Spot The Ball (IRE)**[177] 2836 8-11-11 104 APMcCoy 81
(Jonjo O'Neill) *hld up in rr: hdwy on outside 9th: drvn and 3rd whn hit next: wknd 3 out: lost distant 3rd last* **7/2**[2]
51P/ **5** *3 ¾* **Mannered**[101] 4285 8-11-2 102 JohnDawson(7) 76
(John Wade) *hld up in rr: sme hdwy 12th: lost pl next* **11/1**
030/ **6** *½* **Tresor De L'Isle (FR)**[31] 30 6-11-5 98 BrianHughes 71
(James Ewart) *trckd ldrs: drvn 12th: sn wknd* **16/1**
/U3- **7** *9* **Peaks Of Fire (IRE)**[7] 446 6-11-7 105 SamanthaDrake(5) 70
(Joanne Foster) *in rr: bhd fr 10th: t.o 4 out* **22/1**
6PP/ **P** **Hever Road (IRE)**[83] 4640 14-9-10 80 JoeCornwall(5)
(David Pearson) *chsd ldrs: drvn 8th: bhd fr next: p.u bef 10th* **80/1**
P/P- **P** **Flying Squad (UAE)**[19] 220 9-11-9 102 (t) RyanMania
(Rose Dobbin) *rn in snatches: chsd ldrs: reminders 5th: lost pl 9th: t.o 12th: p.u bef next* **28/1**
1/1- **P** **Lukey Luke**[19] 224 10-11-7 100 PeterBuchanan
(James Turner) *in rr: sme hdwy 9th: 6th whn blnd 11th: wknd after next: distant 7th whn p.u bef 2 out* **7/1**[3]

5m 52.5s (15.50) **Going Correction** +0.775s/f (Soft) **10** Ran SP% **116.3**
Speed ratings: **104,96,89,87,86 86,83, , ,**
toteswingers 1&2 £5.60, 1&3 £2.60, 2&3 £5.60 CSF £26.76 CT £87.67 TOTE £4.10: £1.30, £2.90, £1.60; EX 21.90 Trifecta £98.60 Pool: £690.18 - 5.24 winning units..
Owner Widdop Wanderers **Bred** Tankardstown Stud **Trained** High Eldwick, W Yorks

FOCUS
A moderate handicap chase, with the top-weight rated 105, but seemingly competitive for the grade despite the seven non-runners. The winner is on the upgrade.

556 JAMES BRINDLEY BEST DRESSED LADY COMPETITION H'CAP HURDLE (11 hdls) 2m 4f
8:10 (8:10) (Class 4) (0-115,114) 4-Y-0+ **£3,249** (£954; £477; £238)

Form RPR
2/1- **1** **Candleford**[19] 222 8-10-9 102 TonyKelly(5) 112+
(Ashley Dodgson) *in rr: mstke 2nd: drvn 6th: hdwy to chse ldrs 8th: outpcd appr next: styd on and 2nd between last 2: lft clr last: all out* **9/2**[2]
/32- **2** *1 ¾* **Get Home Now**[18] 253 5-10-8 96 (v) TomO'Brien 101
(Peter Bowen) *w ldr: led 5th: j.lft 3 out: j.lft and hdd 2 out: lft 3rd last: kpt on to take 2nd clsng stages* **8/1**
4/1- **3** *1 ¼* **Don't Be Late (IRE)**[8] 436 5-11-0 102 7ex APMcCoy 105
(Jonjo O'Neill) *hld up: trckd ldrs 6th: cl 3rd 3 out: kpt on same pce and lft 3 l 2nd last* **5/4**[1]
/20- **4** *10* **I'Ll Be Frank**[7] 444 8-10-5 93 (t) MichaelMcAlister 87
(Maurice Barnes) *chsd ldrs: pushed along 5th: one pce fr 3 out: wl hld and lft modest 4th whn blnd last* **25/1**
2/1- **5** *2 ¾* **Settledoutofcourt (IRE)**[15] 310 7-10-5 93 WilsonRenwick 85
(Andrew Parker) *hld up in rr: hmpd 5th: hdwy next: sn chsng ldrs: wknd appr 3 out* **12/1**
00/- **6** *12* **Secret Dancer (IRE)**[16] 3862 8-11-11 113 WillKennedy 94
(Alan Jones) *led: hit 4th: hdd next: drvn 8th: lost pl bef next* **20/1**
064/ **7** *78* **Nahneh (IRE)**[412] 5395 7-10-6 94 BrianHughes
(John Wade) *hdwy 3rd: chsng ldrs 6th: lost pl and blnd next: t.o 8th: eventually completed* **40/1**
43/- **P** **Victor Lynch (IRE)**[170] 2989 7-11-8 110 RichieMcGrath
(Philip Kirby) *in rr: hdwy 3rd: chsng ldrs 6th: drvn after 7th: lost pl and p.u after next: lame* **15/2**[3]
455/ **F** **Shouldavboughtgold (IRE)**[209] 2163 6-11-4 106 CharlieHuxley
(William Kinsey) *prom: 4th whn fell 5th* **20/1**
4/U- **U** **Border Phoenix**[22] 168 6-10-7 95 AdrianLane 102+
(Sandy Forster) *t.k.h in rr: hdwy to trck ldrs 8th: led 2 out: 1 1/2 l ahd whn blnd bdly, swvd lft and uns rdr last* **80/1**

61/ **P** **Picks Milan (IRE)**[101] 4281 7-11-10 112 BrianHarding
(Philip Kirby) *chsd ldrs: drvn and lost pl after 5th: bhd next: t.o whn p.u bef 7th: b.b.v* **33/1**

5m 15.1s (15.60) **Going Correction** +0.775s/f (Soft)
WFA 4 from 5yo+ 19lb **11** Ran SP% **113.2**
Speed ratings (Par 105): **99,98,97,93,92 87,56, , ,**
toteswingers 1&2 £6.40, 1&3 £3.30, 2&3 £2.10 CSF £34.03 CT £69.28 TOTE £5.40: £1.70, £1.70, £1.20; EX 34.10 Trifecta £51.60 Pool: £665.34 - 9.65 winning units..
Owner A C Dodgson **Bred** Miss S E Hall **Trained** Catton, N Yorks

FOCUS
An ordinary handicap hurdle in which not many had clearcut claims. The winner is rated similar to his recent Hexham win, with the unseater heading for a personal best.

557 WETHERBY RACECOURSE OPEN HUNTERS' CHASE (14 fncs 2 omitted) 2m 4f 110y
8:40 (8:41) (Class 6) 5-Y-0+ **£1,053** (£324; £162)

Form RPR
22P/ **1** **Habbie Simpson**[54] 8-11-7 0 MrTHamilton(7) 110+
(Miss J M Furness) *hld up: stdy hdwy 7th: 4th appr 4 out: led sn after 2 out: drvn clr run-in* **11/4**[2]
210/ **2** *11* **Killary Bay (IRE)**[40] 9-12-1 97 MissHBethell(3) 103
(Mrs T Corrigan) *chsd ldrs: led after 10th: hdd between last 2: 3 l down whn mstke last: no ch w wnr* **25/1**
/32- **3** *2 ½* **Rash Move (IRE)**[16] 287 12-12-3 117 MrTEllis(5) 104
(F A Hutsby) *chsd ldrs: handy 2nd appr 4 out: styd on same pce fr 2 out* **11/10**[1]
3/5- **4** *nk* **Discussion Forum**[16] 287 7-11-2 0 MrJHamilton(5) 88
(Mrs C A Coward) *in rr: chsd ldrs 6th: lost pl after 9th: styd on fr 4 out: 5th last: kpt on* **12/1**
040/ **5** *2 ¼* **Nippy Des Mottes (FR)**[18] 12-11-7 0 MissJGillam(7) 93
(Mrs Jackie Brooke) *in rr: hdwy 10th: styd on 6th last: kpt on* **25/1**
6 *nk* **Siro Demur (FR)**[18] 7-11-9 0 MrAlexEdwards(5) 94
(Philip Rowley) *trckd ldrs 6th: drvn and hit 10th: one pce fr next: 4th last* **6/1**[3]
035/ **7** *dist* **Topinambour (FR)**[19] 13-11-7 0 MrTGreenwood(7) 62
(David Greenwood) *in rr: bhd fr 9th: t.o 2 out* **66/1**
4/ **8** *12* **Blackthirteen (IRE)**[18] 9-11-7 0 CallumBewley(7) 51
(Michael Jones) *chsd ldrs: wknd 10th: poor 7th whn blnd next: t.o 2 out* **33/1**
45F/ **P** **National Petition (IRE)**[18] 11-11-7 0 MissETodd(7)
(Miss Victoria Easterby) *towards rr: outpcd 7th: bhd fr 10th: t.o whn p.u bef next* **40/1**
040/ **P** **Bear Witness (IRE)**[39] 11-11-11 77 (b[1]) MrCDawson(3)
(Lady Susan Watson) *led to 5th: led 7th: hdd after 10th: sn lost pl and bhd: t.o whn p.u bef next* **66/1**
6/ **P** **So It Will Be (IRE)**[39] 9-11-2 0 (b) MrSFox(5)
(Miss G E J Anderson) *w ldrs: led 5th to 7th: wkng whn hit 9th: sn bhd: t.o whn p.u bef 4 out* **100/1**
P- **P** **Tegenaria Atrica (USA)**[16] 288 7-11-7 0 (p) MrMJohnson(7)
(Sara Ender) *sn chsng ldrs: lost pl 8th: bhd fr 10th: t.o whn p.u bef 4 out* **100/1**

5m 31.5s (23.70) **Going Correction** +0.775s/f (Soft) **12** Ran SP% **114.3**
Speed ratings: **85,80,79,79,78 78,65,60, , ,**
toteswingers 1&2 £13.20, 1&3 £1.20, 2&3 £6.90 CSF £61.78 TOTE £4.20: £1.50, £3.30, £1.10; EX 32.90 Trifecta £112.30 Pool: £1044.60 - 6.97 winning units..
Owner Sandy Love **Bred** Moniabrock Farming **Trained** Lauder, Borders

FOCUS
Not much depth to this modest hunter chase. Habbie Simpson should win more of these and they finish ed in a bit of a heap behind him.

558 RACING UK LIVE ON SKY CHANNEL 432 H'CAP HURDLE (9 hdls) 2m 110y
9:10 (9:13) (Class 5) (0-95,94) 4-Y-0+ **£2,053** (£598; £299)

Form RPR
2/3- **1** **Bunratty (IRE)**[26] 122 7-11-1 90 (t[1]) ColmMcCormack(7) 94
(Dianne Sayer) *led 2nd to 6th: kpt on to chal between last 2: led last 40yds: styd on* **11/4**[1]
/34- **2** *2 ¼* **Shaker Style (USA)**[15] 316 7-10-9 77 (p) BrianHughes 81+
(Barry Murtagh) *mid-div: trckd ldrs 6th: led between last 2: jnd and hit last: hdd and no ex run-in* **10/3**[2]
265/ **3** *¾* **Vodka Red (IRE)**[32] 21 5-11-3 85 (t) KennyJohnson 86
(Robert Johnson) *hld up in rr: bhd whn nt fluent 4th: hdwy to trck ldrs 6th: kpt on and 3rd last: styd on towards fin* **20/1**
P/P- **4** *5* **Master Ted (IRE)**[15] 317 7-10-13 81 (vt[1]) SeanQuinlan 79
(Jennie Candlish) *led to 2nd: chsd ldrs: led 6th: hdd between last 2: 4th and wkng whn hit last* **8/1**
0U0/ **5** *11* **Dorlesh Way (IRE)**[32] 19 6-9-12 69 AlexanderVoy(3) 57
(Patrick Holmes) *trckd ldrs: upsides 6th: wknd between last 2* **33/1**
6/4- **6** *1 ¼* **Two Oscars (IRE)**[28] 72 7-11-1 90 JohnWinston(7) 76
(Andrew Crook) *in rr: sme hdwy 3 out: nvr a factor* **25/1**
055- **7** *2 ¼* **There's No Rules**[12] 376 4-11-4 90 (e) BarryKeniry 70
(Richard Guest) *t.k.h in rr: reminders 6th: nvr a factor* **20/1**
2/5- **8** *1 ¼* **Ancient Times (USA)**[19] 220 6-11-5 92 (p) KyleJames(5) 75
(Philip Kirby) *rr-div: bhd and drvn 6th: nvr a factor* **7/1**
0/4- **9** *nse* **Tweedo Paradiso (NZ)**[16] 283 6-11-10 92 RichieMcGrath 75
(Rose Dobbin) *chsd ldrs: drvn 6th: wknd after 3 out* **6/1**[3]
P00/ **10** *4 ½* **Regal Ramirez**[31] 22 5-11-12 94 PeterBuchanan 73
(Michael Smith) *in rr: sme hdwy 6th: lost pl appr next: hit 2 out* **14/1**
F66/ **11** *28* **Think**[46] 5312 6-11-8 90 (t) DenisO'Regan 43
(Clive Mulhall) *mid-dvision: sme hdwy 6th: wknd bef next: t.o last* **28/1**
310/ **P** **Imperial Royale (IRE)**[343] 240 12-10-10 78 DaveCrosse
(Patrick Clinton) *chsd ldrs 3rd: drvn and lost pl 6th: bhd whn j.rt next: t.o whn p.u bef last* **20/1**

4m 8.3s (12.50) **Going Correction** +0.775s/f (Soft)
WFA 4 from 5yo+ 18lb **12** Ran SP% **118.8**
Speed ratings (Par 103): **101,99,99,97,92 91,90,89,89,87 74,**
toteswingers 1&2 £2.60, 1&3 £20.40, 2&3 £22.90 CSF £11.07 CT £153.80 TOTE £3.80: £1.50, £1.50, £5.40; EX 14.50 Trifecta £140.00 Pool: £655.22 - 3.50 winning units..
Owner E G Tunstall **Bred** D Ryan **Trained** Hackthorpe, Cumbria
■ Encore Un Fois was withdrawn. Price at time of withdrawal 40-1. Rule 4 does not apply.

FOCUS
A weak finale in which the top weight was rated 94 and, with Encore Un Fois playing up, the first two attempts to start had to be aborted. The winner is rated back to his best with the second to his mark.

T/Plt: £5.10 to a £1 stake. Pool of £60,534.18 - 8603.27 winning tickets. T/Qpdt: £2.20 to a £1 stake. Pool of £4467.9 - 1464.10 winning tickets. WG

[130]COMPIEGNE (L-H)

Thursday, May 30

OFFICIAL GOING: Turf: heavy

559a PRIX CHAMPAGNE (CHASE) (CONDITIONS) (5YO+) (TURF) 2m 5f

6:55 (12:00) 5-Y-O+ **£9,365** (£4,682; £2,731; £1,853; £878)

RPR

1 **Dasaint (FR)**[1345] 7-10-12 0 .... JanFaltejsek
(G Macaire, France) **6/4**[1]

2 *7* **Vivacissimo (IRE)**[20] 263 6-10-8 0 .... MorganRegairaz
(Yannick Fouin, France) **17/2**

3 *3* **Solkap (FR)**[545] 7-11-0 0 .... RaphaelDelozier
(G Chaignon, France) **17/1**

4 *2* **Une Bonne Fois (FR)**[36] 5-10-0 0 ow1 .... AlexisAcker
(M Rolland, France) **17/1**

5 *2* **Rag Tiger (GER)**[30] 7-10-8 0 .... (p) SylvainDehez
(J Bertran De Balanda, France) **5/2**[2]

6 *4* **Ulis De Vassy (FR)**[35] 5535 5-10-6 0 .... JamesReveley
(Nick Williams) *settled in midfield wl in tch: shkn up to join ldrs on outer 5 out: j. slowly and lost pl 4 out: rejnd ldrs 3 out: rdn and wknd fr 2 out* **11/1**

7 *nse* **Jean D'Angely (FR)**[74] 10-10-8 0 .... JonathanPlouganou
(F Danloux, France) **14/1**

8 *15* **Rock Climber (IRE)**[11] 5-9-13 0 .... YohannBourgois[(4)]
(Y-M Porzier, France) **73/10**[3]

9 *dist* **Last Lulu (FR)**[279] 5-10-0 0 ow1 .... GaelBarbedette[(4)]
(D Grandin, France) **73/1**

5m 44.43s (344.43) **9 Ran SP% 118.6**

PARI-MUTUEL (all including 1 euro stakes): WIN 2.50; PLACE 1.40, 2.30, 2.40; DF 11.90; SF 19.50.

Owner Jacques Crouzillac **Bred** Haras D'Etreham **Trained** Les Mathes, France

[383]MARKET RASEN (R-H)

Friday, May 31

OFFICIAL GOING: Good (8.4)

Both tracks moved in 6m for fresh ground.

Wind: light 1/2 against Weather: fine and sunny, very warm

560 LADIES DAY ON 20TH JULY NOVICES' HURDLE (8 hdls) 2m 1f

1:25 (1:25) (Class 4) 4-Y-O+ **£3,119** (£915; £457; £228)

Form RPR

0/2- 1 **Bowie (IRE)**[17] 280 6-10-12 115 .... HarryHaynes 115
(Nick Kent) *led tl after 2nd: lft in ld 5th: jnd 2 out: kpt on wl last 100yds* **5/1**[3]

221/ 2 *1 1/2* **Rayvin Black**[33] 8 4-11-1 119 .... LeightonAspell 116
(Oliver Sherwood) *hld up in mid-div: t.k.h: hmpd 5th: trckd ldrs next: upsides next: chal and hung rt run-in: styd on same pce last 100yds* **10/3**[2]

2/1- 3 *4* **Oyster Shell**[27] 116 6-11-2 118 .... JakeGreenall[(3)] 117
(Henry Daly) *trckd ldng pair: upsides appr 2 out: cl 3rd whn hit last: kpt on one pce* **1/1**[1]

53- 4 *19* **Balinderry (IRE)**[17] 291 6-10-12 0 .... APMcCoy 92
(Steve Gollings) *mid-div: nt fluent 3rd: drvn 5th: sn wl outpcd* **12/1**

4/3- 5 *1/2* **Rene Le Roi (FR)**[17] 284 4-10-8 0 .... DougieCostello 89
(Tim Easterby) *in rr: outpcd 5th: no ch after* **28/1**

50/ 6 *17* **My Mate Jake (IRE)**[113] 4078 5-10-12 0 .... AndrewTinkler 76
(James Given) *mid-div: nt fluent 2nd: outpcd 4th: wknd appr 3 out* **20/1**

7 *68* **Our Princess Ellie (USA)**[153] 5-9-12 0 .... OllieGarner[(7)] 8
(Derek Shaw) *in rr: bhd fr 3rd: t.o 5th* **200/1**

/U- 8 *18* **Audacious**[30] 69 5-10-12 0 .... AdamPogson
(Charles Pogson) *nt jump wl in rr: bhd fr 4th: t.o whn j. violently rt 2 out* **50/1**

F **Just Fabulous**[26] 4-10-1 0 .... BarryKeniry
(George Moore) *t.k.h: led after 2nd: nt fluent 4th: fell next* **18/1**

4m 4.9s (-1.80) **Going Correction** -0.225s/f (Good)

WFA 4 from 5yo+ 18lb **9 Ran SP% 113.4**

Speed ratings (Par 105): **95,94,92,83,83 75,43,34,**

toteswingers 1&2 £3.10, 1&3 £6.10, 2&3 £10.10 CSF £21.39 TOTE £4.60: £1.20, £1.80, £1.10; EX 19.00 Trifecta £39.50 Pool: £931.92 - 17.68 winning units..

Owner Cynthia Commons,Marina Kent,Nick Kent **Bred** Greentree Stud **Trained** Brigg, Lincs

FOCUS

Fairly useful efforts from the leading trio, who pulled a long way clear of the rest in a race run at a sound pace. Improvement from the first two.

561 LOWMANS NOVICES' H'CAP HURDLE (10 hdls) 2m 3f

1:55 (1:56) (Class 5) (0-100,100) 4-Y-O+ **£1,949** (£572; £286; £143)

Form RPR

000/ 1 **Strongly Suggested**[42] 5387 6-11-10 98 .... (t) APMcCoy 103
(Jonjo O'Neill) *trckd ldrs: cl 2nd 7th: led last 150yds: styd on towards fin* **15/2**

F40/ 2 *3/4* **Rain Mac**[40] 5426 5-11-12 100 .... JasonMaguire 104
(Donald McCain) *hld up in rr: hdwy 7th: trcking ldrs next: cl 3rd appr 2 out: upsides sn after last: no ex clsng stages* **8/1**

00/- 3 *nse* **Apolskapart (IRE)**[56] 5166 5-11-10 98 .... DannyCook 103+
(Michael Smith) *led: j.rt thrght: hdd and no ex last 150yds* **16/1**

265/ 4 *1 1/2* **Blackstone Vegas**[9] 2360 7-11-1 89 .... (v) JamesDavies 92
(Derek Shaw) *chsd ldrs: drvn 6th: upsides sn after last: fdd towards fin* **12/1**

/44- 5 *2 3/4* **Inside Knowledge (USA)**[9] 429 7-11-2 90 .... AdamPogson 91
(Garry Woodward) *nt fluent in rr: hdwy 3 out: styd on between last 2: nt rch ldrs* **10/1**

U/1- 6 *1/2* **Brother Scott**[17] 283 6-10-7 88 .... CallumBewley[(7)] 87
(Sue Smith) *chsd ldrs: drvn appr 2 out: kpt on same pce between last 2* **3/1**[1]

0/3- 7 *9* **Grey Command (USA)**[20] 221 8-10-6 80 .... RichieMcGrath 70
(Philip Kirby) *chsd ldrs: nt fluent 6th: reminders next: outpcd and lost pl 3 out* **5/1**[3]

400/ 8 *26* **Alleged Vanity (IRE)**[381] 285 7-10-0 84 .... DiarmuidO'Regan[(10)] 48
(Chris Grant) *prom: lost pl 3 out: sn bhd: t.o next* **16/1**

/53- 9 *5* **Cruise Control**[15] 332 7-10-4 85 .... MrJamieJenkinson[(7)] 44
(John Bryan Groucott) *hld up in rr: hdwy to chse ldrs whn hit 7th: hit next and sn lost pl: t.o 2 out* **33/1**

000/ 10 *26* **Lady Valtas**[374] 398 5-10-0 74 .... TomMessenger 7
(Martin Bosley) *chsd ldrs: lost pl after 7th: t.o 2 out: eventually completed* **80/1**

0/2- P **Grimley Girl**[24] 166 7-11-5 100 .... MrJMahot[(7)]
(Sarah-Jayne Davies) *chsd ldr: wknd qckly after 3 out: sn eased: t.o whn p.u bef next* **9/2**[2]

4m 35.6s (-3.80) **Going Correction** -0.225s/f (Good) **11 Ran SP% 115.4**

Speed ratings (Par 103): **99,98,98,98,96 96,92,81,79,68**

toteswingers 1&2 £17.60, 1&3 £24.30, 2&3 £0.00 CSF £65.20 CT £933.00 TOTE £8.10: £2.90, £3.80, £5.50; EX 69.10 Trifecta £978.70 Part won. Pool: £1305.00 - 0.89 winning units..

Owner John P McManus **Bred** David Brace **Trained** Cheltenham, Gloucs

FOCUS

Just a modest handicap, but it was competitive enough for the grade. The winner was well in on old form and the fourth is perhaps the best guide.

562 DON NOBLE FAMILY DAY 7TH JULY BEGINNERS' CHASE (14 fncs) 2m 4f

2:30 (2:32) (Class 4) 5-Y-O+ **£3,768** (£1,106; £553; £276)

Form RPR

00/- 1 **Grandads Horse**[34] 5574 7-11-0 0 .... NoelFehily 141+
(Charlie Longsdon) *trckd ldrs: hit 5th: 2nd 11th: sn led: wnt clr fr 3 out: 12 l ahd last: eased: v easily* **9/2**

4/F- 2 *13* **Pantxoa (FR)**[19] 238 6-11-0 119 .... WayneHutchinson 123
(Alan King) *chsd ldrs: chsd wnr 3 out: one pce* **4/1**[3]

003/ 3 *hd* **General Miller**[34] 5574 8-11-0 0 .... (p) AndrewTinkler 124
(Nicky Henderson) *chsd ldrs: nt fluent 4th: drvn 8th: outpcd 11th: one pce fr next* **10/3**[2]

0/2- 4 *9* **Bound For Glory (IRE)**[22] 182 7-11-0 120 .... JasonMaguire 116
(Donald McCain) *led: hdd after 11th: hit next: wknd bef last* **10/1**

1/0- 5 *10* **Bar De Ligne (FR)**[14] 356 7-11-0 0 .... (p) TomScudamore 105
(Steve Gollings) *chsd ldr: rdn 4 out: wknd sn after next* **2/1**[1]

3/0- P **Harrys Whim**[30] 67 8-10-7 0 .... RichieMcGrath
(John Weymes) *in rr: bhd fr 7th: t.o 9th: p.u bef 3 out* **100/1**

4F3/ P **Priest Island (IRE)**[72] 4875 7-11-0 0 .... PaddyBrennan
(Tom George) *nt jump wl: bhd and drvn 6th: t.o 9th: p.u bef 3 out* **16/1**

4m 43.0s (-22.70) **Going Correction** -0.825s/f (Firm) **7 Ran SP% 110.6**

Speed ratings: **112,106,106,103,99 ,**

toteswingers 1&2 £2.80, 1&3 £5.00, 2&3 £4.90 CSF £21.56 TOTE £4.90: £2.40, £2.10; EX 25.50 Trifecta £119.10 Pool: £1422.94 - 8.95 winning units..

Owner Whites Of Coventry Limited **Bred** Wood Farm Stud **Trained** Over Norton, Oxon

FOCUS

This was a good maiden chase for the time of year and it threw up a very impressive winner, who looks a smart novice for time time of year.

563 PATTESON'S GLASS LTD H'CAP HURDLE (10 hdls) 2m 3f

3:05 (3:05) (Class 3) (0-125,124) 4-Y-O+ **£5,393** (£1,583; £791; £395)

Form RPR

006/ 1 **Kayaan**[13] 4777 6-11-5 120 .... KielanWoods[(3)] 127+
(Pam Sly) *trckd ldrs gng wl: led between last 2: hit last: hung lft and c clr* **8/1**

4/1- 2 *6* **Wake Your Dreams (IRE)**[15] 337 5-11-3 115 .... SeanQuinlan 115
(Jennie Candlish) *nt fluent: led: hdd between last 2: kpt on same pce* **11/4**[1]

13/- 3 *2 1/4* **Cool Baranca (GER)**[34] 5567 7-10-2 105 .... EmmaSayer[(5)] 103
(Dianne Sayer) *chsd ldrs: outpcd 3 out: 4th appr 2 out: kpt on to take 3rd clsng stages* **7/1**

304/ 4 *1/2* **Hi George**[62] 5016 5-11-5 117 .... HarryHaynes 114
(Malcolm Jefferson) *chsd ldrs: drvn appr 2 out: one pce: 3rd whn hit last* **4/1**[2]

P20/ 5 *5* **Darenjan (IRE)**[20] 229 10-11-12 124 .... (b) AndrewJMcNamara 116
(John Joseph Hanlon, Ire) *chsd ldrs: fdd appr 2 out* **9/2**[3]

633/ 6 *5* **Rior (IRE)**[47] 5320 6-10-4 102 .... TomO'Brien 89
(Paul Henderson) *in rr: hdwy 7th: chsd ldrs next: wknd 2 out* **7/1**

P/3- 7 *15* **Jukebox Melody (IRE)**[17] 289 7-10-12 110 .... (b) WilsonRenwick 82
(John Wade) *chsd ldrs: 2nd 4th: drvn 3 out: sn lost pl* **10/1**

2F5/ 8 *8* **Halogen**[34] 5566 4-11-1 118 .... JasonMaguire 77
(Donald McCain) *in rr: racd wd: sme hdwy 7th: reminders next: sn wknd* **14/1**

213/ 9 *3/4* **Souter Point (USA)**[154] 1555 7-10-11 109 .... CharlieHuxley 73
(William Kinsey) *nt fluent in rr: bhd fr 7th: sddle slipped* **40/1**

4m 31.7s (-7.70) **Going Correction** -0.225s/f (Good)

WFA 4 from 5yo+ 18lb **9 Ran SP% 119.2**

Speed ratings (Par 107): **107,104,103,103,101 99,92,89,89**

toteswingers 1&2 £14.40, 1&3 £18.50, 2&3 £9.40 CSF £32.09 CT £167.11 TOTE £16.40: £3.80, £1.30, £2.20; EX 56.60 Trifecta £595.30 Pool: £1210.10 - 1.52 winning units..

Owner David L Bayliss **Bred** Shadwell Estate Company Limited **Trained** Thorney, Cambs

FOCUS

A fairly useful handicap which was soundly run. The winner is rated back to the level of last year's course form.

564 LOWMANS H'CAP HURDLE (DIV I) (10 hdls) 2m 5f

3:40 (3:41) (Class 4) (0-105,105) 4-Y-O+ **£3,119** (£915; £457; £228)

Form RPR

/11- 1 **Church Field (IRE)**[15] 333 5-11-10 103 .... APMcCoy 112+
(Jonjo O'Neill) *hld up in rr: effrt 6th: chsng ldrs 3 out: led appr next: jnd last: drvn out* **11/10**[1]

5/6- 2 *1* **Galley Slave (IRE)**[12] 384 8-9-7 79 oh3 .... GerardGalligan[(7)] 80
(Michael Chapman) *in rr: hdwy to chse ldrs 3 out: upsides last: no ex last 50yds* **20/1**

35/- 3 *1* **Exit To Freedom**[33] 19 7-9-13 85 .... (p) CallumBewley[(7)] 85
(John Wainwright) *prom: rdn after 3 out: ev ch 2 out: upsides last: edgd rt: kpt on same pce last 75yds* **25/1**

20/- 4 *3* **Ben Cee Pee M (IRE)**[49] 5275 8-11-7 100 .... (b) LeightonAspell 97
(Oliver Sherwood) *trckd ldrs: effrt appr 2 out: swtchd lft sn after last: one pce* **4/1**[2]

2/0- 5 *1 1/4* **Basford Ben**[16] 322 5-11-12 105 .... (p) SeanQuinlan 104+
(Jennie Candlish) *led: tried to refuse: j.lft and hdd 1st: in rr: mstkes: kpt on fr 2 out: nvr a threat* **20/1**

02/- 6 *7* **Combustible Kate (IRE)**[34] 5570 7-11-1 101 .... PaulNO'Brien[(7)] 90
(Nick Kent) *trckd ldrs: t.k.h: wknd 3 out* **14/1**

000/ 7 *1/2* **Inch Manor (IRE)**[109] 4158 5-10-5 84 .... (t) RichieMcGrath 72
(Philip Kirby) *w ldr: lft in ld 1st: hdd after 4th: lost pl 3 out* **10/1**

411/ 8 37 **Tregaro (FR)**[241] 1708 7-10-13 **92** .... DenisO'Regan 43
(Mike Sowersby) *trckd ldrs: led after 4th: hit 3 out: hdd appr next: sn lost pl and eased: virtually p.u: t.o* **20/1**

/01- U **Fitandproperjob**[12] 384 7-10-4 **88** 7ex .... (t) KyleJames(5)
(Anthony Middleton) *in rr: mstke and uns rdr 7th* **6/1**[3]

5m 15.4s (6.60) **Going Correction** -0.225s/f (Good) 9 Ran SP% **115.8**
Speed ratings (Par 105): **78,77,77,76,75 72,72,58,**
toteswingers 1&2 £14.40, 1&3 £18.50, 2&3 £9.40 CSF £27.21 CT £369.29 TOTE £1.60: £1.40, £5.90, £8.20; EX 17.60 Trifecta £183.20 Pool: £1201.18 - 4.91 winning units..
Owner John P McManus **Bred** Mrs Eleanor Hadden **Trained** Cheltenham, Gloucs

FOCUS
A handicap which went the way of the one progressive sort in the line-up. The winner looked to have a bit in hand and the next two ran to their marks.

565 LOWMANS H'CAP HURDLE (DIV II) (10 hdls) 2m 5f
4:20 (4:20) (Class 4) (0-105,105) 4-Y-0+ **£3,119** (£915; £457; £228)

Form RPR
560/ 1 **Goldan Jess (IRE)**[18] 2978 9-11-2 **102** .... AdamNicol(7) 113+
(Philip Kirby) *mde all: hit 6th: wnt clr after 2 out: eased last 75yds* **4/1**[2]

/13- 2 9 **Adios Alonso (IRE)**[19] 253 7-10-7 **91** .... BenPoste(5) 93
(Rosemary Gasson) *chsd wnr thrght: kpt on same pce fr 2 out* **10/3**[1]

6P4/ 3 3 ¼ **Torran Sound**[22] 5412 6-11-2 **98** .... JackQuinlan(3) 97
(James Eustace) *chsd ldrs: hit 3 out and reminders: kpt on run-in: tk modest 3rd nr line* **9/1**

5/6- 4 hd **King Mak**[30] 67 11-10-3 **87** .... (tp) KyleJames(5) 87
(Marjorie Fife) *mstkes: chsd ldrs: drvn after 5th: one pce appr 2 out* **6/1**[3]

1/ 5 7 **Knockanarrigan (IRE)**[28] 105 5-11-4 **100** .... (p) MichealNolan(3) 93
(John Joseph Hanlon, Ire) *chsd ldrs: wknd between last 2* **4/1**[2]

0PP/ 6 30 **Highland Rain**[93] 4446 5-10-3 **82** .... (p) SeanQuinlan 47
(Jennie Candlish) *in rr: reminders 4th: bhd fr 3 out: t.o whn eased run-in* **4/1**[2]

/45- 7 nse **Xenophon**[12] 385 5-10-4 **90** .... (b) GerardGalligan(7) 54
(Michael Chapman) *chsd ldrs: nt fluent 1st: reminders 4th: lost pl 3 out: sn bhd: t.o* **25/1**

36P/ 8 34 **Tri Nations (UAE)**[175] 1947 8-11-2 **105** .... (tp) MarkMarris(10) 39
(Anthony Middleton) *in rr: pushed along 5th: sn bhd: t.o 2 out* **20/1**

000/ P **Billy Teal**[34] 5570 8-9-7 **79** oh2 .... FrancisHayes(7)
(C I Ratcliffe) *mid-div: lost pl 6th: bhd fr 3 out: t.o whn p.u bef next* **80/1**

5m 9.5s (0.70) **Going Correction** -0.225s/f (Good) 9 Ran SP% **117.2**
Speed ratings (Par 105): **89,85,84,84,81 70,70,57,**
toteswingers 1&2 £4.00, 1&3 £10.10, 2&3 £6.30 CSF £18.12 CT £113.61 TOTE £6.00: £1.50, £1.30, £4.40; EX 22.70 Trifecta £144.50 Pool: £2782.43 - 14.43 winning units..
Owner The Jessies,Colin Fletcher,Philip Kirby **Bred** Bendis Partnership **Trained** Middleham, N Yorks

FOCUS
Just a modest handicap. The winner is rated in line with his recent Flat form.

566 HAPPY 70TH BIRTHDAY RAYMOND THELWELL H'CAP CHASE (14 fncs) 2m 6f 110y
4:55 (4:56) (Class 4) (0-110,110) 5-Y-0+ **£3,768** (£1,106; £553; £276)

Form RPR
2/1- 1 **Or D'Oudairies (FR)**[20] 220 11-10-7 **96** .... (t) SamanthaDrake(5) 109+
(Ferdy Murphy, France) *in rr: hdwy to chse ldrs 4th: cl 2nd after 7th: led 9th: kpt on wl run-in* **8/1**[3]

4/2- 2 1 **Cruchain (IRE)**[22] 175 10-11-7 **105** .... (p) DougieCostello 114
(Dai Burchell) *in rr: hit 6th: hdwy 4 out: chsd wnr between last 2: kpt on* **8/1**[3]

5/0- 3 6 **Golden View (IRE)**[27] 113 8-11-5 **103** .... (p) BrianHughes 107
(Karen McLintock) *chsd ldrs: wnt 2nd appr 3 out: kpt on one pce between last 2* **40/1**

661/ 4 9 **Le Seychellois (FR)**[262] 1541 13-11-2 **100** .... DenisO'Regan 97
(William Kinsey) *in rr: hdwy to chse ldrs 7th: 3rd appr 3 out: wknd between last 2* **33/1**

4/0- 5 1 ¼ **The Panama Kid (IRE)**[17] 282 9-11-11 **109** .... (b) HarryHaynes 103
(Malcolm Jefferson) *chsd ldrs: drvn 4 out: wknd after 3 out* **20/1**

320/ 6 3 ½ **Lukeys Luck**[163] 3135 7-11-12 **110** .... SeanQuinlan 101
(Jennie Candlish) *mid-div: chsng ldrs 4 out: wknd 2 out* **10/1**

P2/- 7 8 **Kauto The Roc (FR)**[33] 7 9-10-13 **97** .... (t) CharlieHuxley 81
(Alan King) *chsd ldrs: wknd bef 3 out* **8/1**[3]

2/3- 8 1 ¼ **Rossmore Lad (IRE)**[22] 190 8-11-11 **109** .... (p) NoelFehily 92
(Charlie Longsdon) *chsd ldrs: j.lft: wknd appr 3 out* **8/1**[3]

9 ¾ **Coolking**[19] 260 6-11-4 **102** .... (p) AndrewJMcNamara 86
(John Joseph Hanlon, Ire) *led: hdd 9th: wkng whn blnd 3 out* **10/3**[1]

4/3- 10 1 ¼ **Chicago Outfit (IRE)**[17] 279 8-11-5 **103** .... (p) WilsonRenwick 84
(John Wade) *sn drvn along in midfield: lost pl 6th: bhd fr 8th: t.o 3 out* **22/1**

P/P- 11 9 **Seize**[20] 222 11-11-6 **104** .... (b) BrianHarding 77
(James Moffatt) *in rr: reminders 9th: sn bhd: t.o 3 out* **66/1**

/54- U **More Equity**[5] 492 11-10-3 **92** .... EmmaSayer(5)
(Dianne Sayer) *detached in rr: hdwy 4 out: in tch and keeping on whn blnd and uns rdr next* **11/1**

U/3- P **Sparkling Tara**[17] 282 8-11-7 **105** .... RyanMania
(Sue Smith) *mid-div: nt fluent 8th: drvn 4 out: btn whn bdly hmpd next: sn p.u* **15/2**[2]

402/ F **Comeragh King**[48] 5294 9-11-4 **102** .... JasonMaguire
(Tim Fitzgerald) *mid-div: hdwy 4 out: keeping on whn fell next* **8/1**[3]

5m 27.3s (-18.70) **Going Correction** -0.825s/f (Firm) 14 Ran SP% **123.8**
Speed ratings: **99,98,96,93,93 91,89,88,88,87 84, , ,**
toteswingers 1&2 £12.90, 1&3 £72.00, 2&3 £52.70 CSF £69.22 CT £2450.22 TOTE £7.10: £2.70, £3.00, £9.70; EX 114.40 Trifecta £1986.00 Part won. Pool: £2648.06 - 0.75 winning units..
Owner Gay And Peter Hartley **Bred** Comte Michel De Gigou **Trained** France

FOCUS
A competitive race for the grade and there's no reason why the form won't hold up. The cosy winner is rated in line with his recent win.

567 RACING UK MARES' STANDARD OPEN NATIONAL HUNT FLAT RACE 2m 1f
5:30 (5:33) (Class 6) 4-6-Y-0 **£1,559** (£457; £228; £114)

Form RPR
4/2- 1 **The Road Ahead**[12] 395 6-11-2 0 .... TomO'Brien 103+
(Peter Bowen) *trckd ldrs: led over 3f out: wnt clr over 1f out: styd on wl* **11/2**[3]

2 6 **Retrieve The Stick** 4-10-12 0 .... BrianHughes 92
(Malcolm Jefferson) *chsd ldrs: drvn 5f out: kpt on to chse wnr over 1f out: no imp* **8/1**

3 nk **Pectora (IRE)** 4-10-12 0 .... LeightonAspell 92
(Oliver Sherwood) *mid-div: pushed along 8f out: drvn 5f out: hdwy over 3f out: 4th over 1f out: styd on wl clsng stages* **11/4**[1]

6/2- 4 3 ½ **Darcey Diva**[22] 187 5-10-9 0 .... KieronEdgar(7) 92
(David Pipe) *in rr-div: hdwy over 3f out: 3rd over 1f out: kpt on one pce* **9/1**

5 10 **Lady Of Provence** 4-10-9 0 .... JeremiahMcGrath(3) 78
(Nicky Henderson) *mid-div: hdwy to trck ldrs 8f out: effrt and 4th 3f out: sn drvn: hung rt and wknd over 1f out* **7/2**[2]

6 ½ **Pamela Lewis** 6-11-2 0 .... HarryHaynes 82
(Pam Sly) *trckd ldrs: effrt over 4f out: wknd 2f out* **25/1**

7 1 **Alco Baba (IRE)** 5-10-11 0 .... TonyKelly(5) 81
(Ferdy Murphy, France) *uns rdr and rn loose bef s: stdd s: in rr: hdwy over 3f out: kpt on: nvr nr ldrs* **33/1**

0- 8 2 ¼ **Wymeswold**[16] 324 6-10-13 0 .... KielanWoods(3) 78
(Michael Mullineaux) *w ldr: wknd over 2f out* **100/1**

9 5 **Agent Louise** 5-11-2 0 .... DenisO'Regan 73
(Mike Sowersby) *stdd s: in rr: drvn 6f out: sn bhd* **40/1**

10 4 ½ **Fennis Moll (IRE)**[15] 351 4-10-9 0 .... MPFogarty(3) 65
(John Joseph Hanlon, Ire) *led: hdd over 3f out: lost pl over 2f out* **13/2**

- 11 2 **Pass Friend** 5-11-2 0 .... JamesDavies 67
(Martin Bosley) *mid-div: hdwy 7f out: lost pl 3f out* **50/1**

12 9 **Roxy Madam** 4-10-12 0 .... AdamPogson 54
(Mandy Rowland) *mid-div: hdwy 8f out: wknd over 2f out* **100/1**

0/ 13 13 **B B Baloo**[32] 35 4-10-12 0 .... (e[1]) BrianHarding 41
(John Wainwright) *stdd s: hld up in rr: sme hdwy 6f out: lost pl over 3f out* **66/1**

- 14 7 **Bartered Bride** 5-10-9 0 .... MissJRRichards(7) 38
(John Norton) *in rr: bhd fnl 6f* **150/1**

P **Ricardo's Girl (IRE)** 4-10-5 0 .... PaulBohan(7)
(Steve Gollings) *in rr: hung lft and wd bnd after 6f: t.o whn p.u 8f out* **10/1**

4m 1.5s (0.40) **Going Correction** -0.225s/f (Good)
WFA 4 from 5yo+ 4lb 15 Ran SP% **123.1**
Speed ratings: **90,87,87,85,80 80,79,78,76,74 73,69,63,59,**
toteswingers 1&2 £11.30, 1&3 £3.90, 2&3 £7.20 CSF £48.18 TOTE £5.70: £1.90, £3.10, £1.60; EX 65.20 Trifecta £381.10 Pool: £2595.81 - 5.10 winning units..
Owner F Lloyd **Bred** F Lloyd **Trained** Little Newcastle, Pembrokes

FOCUS
They finished well strung out in this bumper, which reflects well on the principals. Ordinary form, with a step up from the winner.
T/Plt: £148.60 to a £1 stake. Pool of £48,634.35 - 238.86 winning tickets. T/Qpdt: £14.00 to a £1 stake. Pool of £4689.62 - 246.40 winning tickets. WG

568 - 577a (Foreign Racing) - See Raceform Interactive

[218]HEXHAM (L-H)
Saturday, June 1

OFFICIAL GOING: Good to firm (good in places; 8.1)
As much rail as possible moved to provide best ground and 4 hurdles sited on fresh ground.
Wind: Fresh, half against Weather: Cloudy

578 GREAT RUN ORG (S) HURDLE (8 hdls) 2m 110y
1:40 (1:41) (Class 5) 4-Y-0+ **£2,053** (£598; £299)

Form RPR
U1U/ 1 **Kaolak (USA)**[22] 4342 7-11-0 0 .... (v) HenryBrooke 116
(Jim Goldie) *t.k.h: mde all: sn clr: nt fluent 4th: rdn between last 2: styd on wl run-in* **2/1**[2]

3/3- 2 3 ¼ **Piment D'Estruval (FR)**[26] 142 10-11-0 110 .... RichardKilloran 114
(Tim Vaughan) *in tch: stdy hdwy to chse (clr) wnr 3 out: effrt and clsng whn mstke next: rallied bef last: one pce run-in* **7/4**[1]

6/U- 3 11 **Seaquel**[19] 266 7-10-2 95 .... TrevorWhelan(5) 95
(Tony Carroll) *chsd (clr) wnr to 3 out: rdn and outpcd next: no imp bef last* **9/4**[3]

P/P- 4 44 **Just Maddie**[24] 172 9-10-2 0 .... GaryRutherford(5) 55
(Rayson Nixon) *in tch: rdn and outpcd bef 4 out: n.d after* **80/1**

U- 5 15 **Dansili Dutch (IRE)**[13] 391 4-10-4 0 .... BrianHughes 39
(Andrew Crook) *hld up: struggling 4 out: nvr on terms* **16/1**

4m 4.6s (-12.80) **Going Correction** -0.775s/f (Firm)
WFA 4 from 7yo+ 17lb 5 Ran SP% **107.6**
Speed ratings (Par 103): **99,97,92,71,64**
CSF £5.79 TOTE £4.10: £1.50, £1.50; EX 5.40 Trifecta £11.10 Pool: £397.39 - 26.83 winning units..There was no bid for the winner.
Owner Thomson Fyffe Racing **Bred** Mr And Mrs Robert Courtney Sr Et Al **Trained** Uplawmoor, E Renfrews

FOCUS
The track had been watered, and after the first race winning jockey Henry Brooke described the ground as "on the quick side". The winner dictated the pace and they were strung out from the first. The winner is rated in line with recent Flat runs.

579 JUNIOR NORTH RUN NOVICES' CHASE (15 fncs) 2m 4f 110y
2:15 (2:15) (Class 4) 5-Y-0+ **£4,183** (£1,521)

Form RPR
6/0- 1 **Bygones Of Brid (IRE)**[21] 216 10-10-12 0 .... BrianHughes 113+
(Karen McLintock) *led to 4 out: rdn and ev ch whn lft 13 l clr 2 out: kpt on strly* **9/4**[2]

6/5- 2 28 **Indian Voyage (IRE)**[18] 279 5-10-12 94 .... (t) MichaelMcAlister 94
(Maurice Barnes) *prom: outpcd 4 out: hld whn lft 13 l 2nd 2 out: no imp* **7/1**[3]

322/ R **Monogram**[7] 9-10-5 0 .... MrJHamilton(7)
(Victor Thompson) *hld up in tch: struggling 9th: hung rt bef 4 out: t.o whn rn out bef last* **12/1**

0/0- P **Business Time**[17] 316 7-10-7 0 .... JonathanEngland(5)
(Hugh Burns) *bhd: lost tch and p.u bef 8th* **66/1**

2/3- F **Rudemeister (IRE)**[17] 312 7-10-12 117 .... WilsonRenwick 113+
(Andrew Parker) *pressed ldr: led 4 out: pushed along and jst in front whn fell 2 out* **11/10**[1]

3/2- U **Bafana Choice**[5] 510 7-10-12 0 .... (p) HenryBrooke 97
(Chris Grant) *chsd ldrs: outpcd whn blnd 4 out: lft 6 l 2nd whn hmpd by faller and uns rdr 2 out* **10/1**

5- P **Duhallowcountry (IRE)**[6] 491 7-10-5 0 .... MrTSpeke(7)
(Victor Thompson) *hld up in tch: struggling 1/2-way: t.o whn p.u after 3 out* **66/1**

0/F- **R** **Dun To Perfection**[18] 279 6-10-5 84 .... JamesCorbett(7)
(Susan Corbett) *nt jump wl in rr: t.o whn ref 10th* **33/1**

5m 7.3s (-6.20) **Going Correction** -0.625s/f (Firm) **8** Ran SP% **113.6**
Speed ratings: **86,75, , , , ,**
toteswingers 1&2 £6.20 CSF £17.85 TOTE £2.50: £1.90, £3.30; EX 15.00 Trifecta £12.10 Pool: £1689.75 - 104.65 winning units..
Owner James Callow **Bred** Oliver Brennan **Trained** Ingoe, Northumberland

FOCUS
The market centred around two horses, and they set a scorching pace that burnt off the rest and eventually also found out the favourite. Just two finished. The winner is a 140+ hurdler and probably capable of better than this.

580 GREAT NORTH SWIM H'CAP CHASE (19 fncs) 3m 1f
2:45 (2:48) (Class 5) (0-100,99) 5-Y-0+ **£2,258** (£658; £329)

Form RPR
2/3- **1** **Almond Court (IRE)**[28] 115 10-9-12 74 .... (p) BrianToomey(3) 97+
(Robert Johnson) *j.w: mde all: clr 2 out: styd on strly* **5/1**[1]

044/ **2** *18* **Chernik (IRE)**[40] 5450 12-10-0 73 .... (p) HenryBrooke 80
(Micky Hammond) *prom: wnt 2nd 13th: effrt and rdn after 2 out: sn no ch w wnr* **13/2**[3]

361- **3** *5* **Solway Dornal**[7] 473 8-9-9 73 oh1 ow2 .... (tp) StephenMulqueen(7) 76
(Lisa Harrison) *midfield: stdy hdwy to chse ldrs 14th: effrt and rdn 3 out: outpcd by first two fr next: rdr weighed in 2lb heavy* **10/1**

6/4- **4** *¾* **Presenting Junior (IRE)**[18] 279 6-9-9 75 .... MrJHamilton(7) 77
(Martin Todhunter) *hld up on outside: drvn and outpcd after 4 out: rallied bef last: kpt on run-in* **11/2**[2]

01/ **5** *6* **Oscar Leney (IRE)**[28] 128 7-10-12 85 .... (t) AELynch 82
(J T R Dreaper, Ire) *hld up in midfield: stdy hdwy 1/2-way: rdn 3 out: wknd after next* **8/1**

224/ **6** *14* **Domoly (FR)**[39] 5481 10-10-10 88 .... TonyKelly(5) 72
(Ferdy Murphy, France) *prom: drvn bef 3 out: wknd fr next* **8/1**

3/0- **7** *1 ¾* **Cloudy Dawn**[24] 172 8-9-7 73 oh3 .... CallumBewley(7) 55
(Sue Smith) *prom: hmpd by faller 7th: outpcd bef 4 out: btn fnl 2* **5/1**[1]

0/6- **8** *nk* **Nicky Tam (IRE)**[24] 172 11-10-0 73 oh4 .... RichieMcGrath 55
(Henry Hogarth) *hld up: hmpd by faller 7th: rdn and outpcd after 4 out: nvr on terms* **16/1**

4/6- **9** *36* **Diddley Dee**[18] 279 9-11-7 99 .... GaryRutherford(5) 49
(Lucy Normile) *bhd: outpcd whn blnd 12th: nt fluent next: sn struggling: t.o* **25/1**

255/ **F** **Heez A Steel (IRE)**[71] 4912 12-11-8 95 .... RyanMania
(George Charlton) *chsd ldrs: fell heavily 7th* **12/1**

6/4- **P** **Flaming Thistle (IRE)**[13] 9-10-0 73 oh6 .... (p) LucyAlexander
(N W Alexander) *bhd: hmpd by faller 7th: sn struggling: t.o whn p.u bef 13th* **14/1**

/00- **P** **Go Teescomponents**[18] 279 6-10-0 73 oh9 .... (t) BrianHughes
(Keith Reveley) *chsd wnr to 13th: wknd 15th: t.o whn p.u bef 2 out* **40/1**

6m 16.8s (-15.40) **Going Correction** -0.625s/f (Firm) **12** Ran SP% **119.9**
Speed ratings: **99,93,91,91,89 85,84,84,72, ,**
toteswingers 1&2 £6.80, 2&3 £29.30, 1&3 £10.30 CSF £38.75 CT £319.13 TOTE £5.70: £2.10, £3.00, £2.90; EX 44.70 Trifecta £398.40 Pool: £591.68 - 1.11 winning units..
Owner Alan Kidd **Bred** Martin J Keane **Trained** Newburn, Tyne & Wear

■ Stewards' Enquiry : Stephen Mulqueen three-day ban; weighted in overweight (15th,18th,19th June).

FOCUS
Just a moderate race but the form looks reliable. The winner and second this time round met over C&D in April and that turned out to be a key piece of form, from which the first three there have since gone on to win their next start. The winner is in the form of her life and built on her good recent course form.

581 NOVA INTERNATIONAL H'CAP HURDLE (8 hdls) 2m 110y
3:20 (3:23) (Class 4) (0-120,120) 4-Y-0+
£3,002 (£887; £443; £221; £110; £55)

Form RPR
0/3- **1** **Baccalaureate (FR)**[29] 93 7-10-8 107 .... JonathanEngland(5) 116+
(Sue Smith) *mde all: sn clr: rdn 2 out: kpt on wl fr last* **11/4**[2]

/41- **2** *6* **Foxcub (IRE)**[23] 184 5-10-8 102 .... FelixDeGiles 106
(Tom Symonds) *hld up in tch: stdy hdwy whn mstke 3 out: rallied bef next: chsd (clr) wnr bef last: no imp run-in* **5/1**[3]

3/1- **3** *1* **Montefeltro**[17] 306 5-11-4 115 .... JackQuinlan(3) 119
(John Ferguson) *nt fluent: chsd (clr) wnr: hit 3rd: effrt and drvn 2 out: one pce fr last* **15/8**[1]

6/2- **4** *9* **Agricultural**[18] 283 7-10-4 98 .... RyanMania 94
(Lucy Normile) *hld up in tch: stdy hdwy to chse ldrs 4th: rdn and outpcd fr 2 out* **10/1**

/21- **5** *9* **Overpriced**[16] 342 7-11-5 120 .... (t) StephenMulqueen(7) 106
(Maurice Barnes) *hld up: outpcd bef 3 out: n.d after* **17/2**

030/ **6** *2 ½* **Word Of Warning**[173] 2977 9-10-5 99 .... (p) LucyAlexander 83
(Martin Todhunter) *bhd: outpcd and detached 3rd: sme late hdwy: nvr on terms* **28/1**

1/P- **7** *30* **The Weatherman (IRE)**[28] 119 6-11-10 118 .... HenryBrooke 90
(Donald McCain) *prom: outpcd 1/2-way: struggling fr 3 out: t.o* **6/1**

4m 1.9s (-15.50) **Going Correction** -0.775s/f (Firm) **7** Ran SP% **115.5**
Speed ratings (Par 105): **105,102,101,97,93 92,77**
toteswingers 1&2 £4.00, 2&3 £2.00, 1&3 £2.60 CSF £17.36 CT £31.08 TOTE £4.20: £1.30, £3.10; EX 20.80 Trifecta £73.90 Pool: £1605.88 - 16.29 winning units..
Owner The Cartmel Syndicate **Bred** Elevage Fouchet Loick & Coolmore Stud **Trained** High Eldwick, W Yorks

FOCUS
A fair handicap producing yet another pacesetting winner on the card. The winner is a 120 horse at best and may still be capable of matching that, while the next two are on the upgrade.

582 FILM NOVA JUVENILE HURDLE (8 hdls) 2m 110y
4:20 (4:20) (Class 4) 3-Y-0 **£3,285** (£957; £479)

Form RPR
1 **Akdam (IRE)**[19] 3-10-7 0 .... TrevorWhelan(5) 100+
(Tony Carroll) *mde virtually all: rdn and clr whn mstke last: kpt on wl towards fin* **11/10**[1]

2 *3 ¾* **Lindenhurst (IRE)**[232] 3-10-9 0 .... (t) MarkBolger(3) 94
(John C McConnell, Ire) *t.k.h: chsd ldrs: hdwy to chse (clr) wnr bef last: sn clsd: one pce last 100yds* **16/1**

3 *14* **Hi Candy (IRE)**[39] 3-10-5 0 .... AndrewTinkler 74
(Ben Haslam) *w ldr to 2 out: rdn and wknd bef last* **20/1**

4 *32* **Precision Strike**[21] 3-10-12 0 .... BarryKeniry 52
(Richard Guest) *hld up in tch: rdn along after 3 out: no imp fr next* **9/2**[3]

5 *1* **Luv U Whatever**[24] 3-10-12 0 .... MarkGrant 51
(Jo Hughes) *j.v.slowly 1st: cl up: outpcd whn blnd 4 out: wknd after next* **11/4**[2]

6 *81* **Wild Diamond (IRE)**[278] 3-10-5 0 .... RichardKilloran
(Tim Vaughan) *nt fluent: hld up in tch: outpcd bef 4 out: n.d after* **10/1**

P **Online**[61] 3-10-12 0 .... BrianHughes
(Tracy Waggott) *t.k.h: hld up in tch: struggling 4 out: t.o whn p.u bef last* **66/1**

4m 9.0s (-8.40) **Going Correction** -0.775s/f (Firm) **7** Ran SP% **113.7**
Speed ratings: **88,86,79,64,64 26,**
toteswingers 1&2 £4.90, 2&3 £5.90, 1&3 £3.10 CSF £20.00 TOTE £2.40: £1.10, £3.80; EX 15.20 Trifecta £129.40 Pool: £1594.13 - 9.23 winning units..
Owner Stephen Louch **Bred** His Highness The Aga Khan's Studs S C **Trained** Cropthorne, Worcs

FOCUS
The first juvenile hurdle of the season was the fifth race on the card to be won from the front. The first two were clear. Probably modest form, but nothing to go on bar the slow time.

583 GREAT NORTH CITY H'CAP CHASE (12 fncs) 2m 110y
4:55 (4:55) (Class 4) (0-120,120) 5-Y-0+ **£3,768** (£1,106; £553; £276)

Form RPR
113/ **1** **Sleep In First (FR)**[33] 26 7-11-12 120 .... BrianHughes 128+
(James Ewart) *trckd ldrs: effrt 2 out: led run-in: rdn out* **9/2**[3]

3F5/ **2** *2 ¾* **Exotic Man (FR)**[37] 5521 8-10-11 112 .... JohnDawson(7) 118
(John Wade) *trckd ldrs: led after 2 out: hdd and rdr dropped whip run-in: one pce* **4/1**[2]

/4U- **3** *9* **My Idea**[6] 493 7-10-8 102 .... (t) MichaelMcAlister 102
(Maurice Barnes) *prom: reminders 1/2-way: hdwy and ev ch bef 3 out: sn rdn: outpcd fr last* **11/4**[1]

6/3- **4** *13* **Strathcal**[19] 269 7-10-5 99 .... (bt[1]) FelixDeGiles 85
(Tom Symonds) *led to after 2 out: rdn and wknd bef last* **11/2**

4/2- **5** *5* **Kai Broon (IRE)**[16] 343 6-10-13 114 .... (v[1]) GrantCockburn(7) 95
(Lucinda Russell) *bhd and sn pushed along: sme hdwy 1/2-way: wknd fr 4 out* **5/1**

465/ **6** *19* **Saddle Pack (IRE)**[40] 5448 10-10-1 102 .... MissCWalton(7) 66
(James Walton) *hld up in tch: hit 4th: struggling fr 7th: n.d after* **10/1**

0/6- **7** *12* **Strobe**[18] 282 9-10-4 98 .... (p) RyanMania 51
(Lucy Normile) *chsd ldrs to 4 out: rdn and wknd bef next* **18/1**

3m 56.3s (-13.50) **Going Correction** -0.625s/f (Firm) **7** Ran SP% **111.3**
Speed ratings: **106,104,100,94,92 83,77**
toteswingers 1&2 £7.30, 2&3 £1.20, 1&3 £1.10 CSF £21.84 TOTE £3.20: £2.00, £2.50; EX 29.90 Trifecta £60.30 Pool: £635.46 - 7.90 winning units..
Owner Carruthers, McKenzie, Panther, Wood **Bred** Gilles Chaignon & Jean-Victor Chaignon **Trained** Langholm, Dumfries & G'way

FOCUS
This was run at a fair pace and with three poised to challenge midway down the back, it was the first race on the card not to be won by the pacesetter. A decent time for the grade with the first two to their marks.

584 GREAT NORTH RUN STANDARD OPEN NATIONAL HUNT FLAT RACE 2m 110y
5:30 (5:31) (Class 6) 4-6-Y-0 **£1,642** (£478; £239)

Form RPR
4- **1** **Mister Jones**[18] 284 5-11-1 0 .... RyanMania 105+
(Sue Smith) *a.p: chalng 2f out: styd on to ld fnl 110yds: rdn out* **4/1**[1]

2 *2* **Jimmy The Jetplane (IRE)**[27] 5-11-1 0 .... PeterBuchanan 102
(Alistair Whillans) *led: hdd narrowly 7f out: regained ld 4f out: strly pressed fr 2f out: hdd fnl 110yds: styd on same pce cl home* **9/2**[2]

3 *¾* **Cobajayisland (IRE)**[69] 5-10-8 0 .... CraigNichol(7) 102
(Lucinda Russell) *in tch: trckd ldrs 4f out: chalng over 2f out: rdn over 1f out: nt qckn ins fnl f: kpt on u.p cl home but hld* **4/1**[1]

4 *7* **The Chief Villain** 5-11-1 0 .... (t) AlainCawley 95
(R T J Wilson, Ire) *hld up: hdwy 6f out: trcking ldrs gng ok over 2f out: rdn and one pce over 1f out: no imp after* **9/1**

50/- **5** *½* **Caddells Row**[66] 4976 5-11-1 0 .... BrianHughes 95
(Karen McLintock) *in tch: effrt 4f out: rdn to chse ldrs over 2f out: one pce over 1f out* **11/1**

0/3- **6** *15* **Milan Of Hope (IRE)**[22] 207 6-11-1 0 .... AdamPogson 81
(Charles Pogson) *midfield: rdn and outpcd 4f out: no imp after* **8/1**[3]

40/- **7** *nk* **Central Flame**[36] 5550 5-10-8 0 .... MissCWalton(7) 81
(James Walton) *racd keenly: hld up in midfield: plugged on u.p fnl 2f: nvr a threat* **16/1**

0- **8** *¾* **Lordenshaws (IRE)**[18] 284 6-11-1 0 .... KennyJohnson 80
(Robert Johnson) *hld up in midfield: hdwy to chse ldrs 4f out: wknd over 1f out: sn eased* **66/1**

00/ **9** *39* **Jonefolla**[197] 2463 6 10 8 0 .... (t) JamesCorbett(7) 45
(Susan Corbett) *plld hrd: handy: led narrowly 7f out: hdd 4f out: rdn and wknd qckly over 2f out* **100/1**

10 *10* **Run Brave Run (IRE)** 5-11-1 0 .... HenryBrooke 36
(Martin Todhunter) *in tch: pushed along and wknd over 4f out* **25/1**

11 *nk* **Texit To Nowhere (IRE)** 6-10-1 0 .... GrahamWatters(7) 29
(Ian Duncan) *hld up: struggling 5f out: nvr on terms* **33/1**

12 *15* **Well Related**[34] 6-11-1 0 .... RichieMcGrath 22
(Henry Hogarth) *handy tl wknd 4f out* **10/1**

13 *42* **Mcnulty Wray (IRE)** 5-10-10 0 .... TonyKelly(5)
(Ferdy Murphy, France) *hld up: pushed along after 4f: t.o over 6f out* **12/1**

P- **P** **Just Once Up**[18] 284 4-10-5 0 .... MrTSpeke(7)
(Kevin Hunter) *in rr: rdn after 4f: lost tch over 6f out: t.o whn p.u 2f out* **200/1**

4m 2.1s (-10.60) **Going Correction** -0.775s/f (Firm)
WFA 4 from 5yo+ 3lb **14** Ran SP% **120.1**
Speed ratings: **93,92,91,88,88 81,80,80,62,57 57,50,30,**
toteswingers 1&2 £9.80, 2&3 £2.50, 1&3 £3.00 CSF £21.04 TOTE £3.70: £1.80, £2.10, £2.50; EX 25.40 Trifecta £85.50 Pool: £396.14 - 3.47 winning units..
Owner Mrs S Smith **Bred** J E Abbey **Trained** High Eldwick, W Yorks

FOCUS
An open-looking contest with the three market leaders pulling a little way clear from the home turn. Ordinary form, the winner building on his debut run.

T/Plt: £82.40 to a £1 stake. Pool of £51844.56 - 458.78 winning tickets. T/Qpdt: £28.70 to a £1 stake. Pool of £3580.13 - 92.25 winning tickets. RY

[430]WORCESTER (L-H)

Saturday, June 1

OFFICIAL GOING: Good (good to firm in places; 6.7)

Both bends moved out 6yds from inside line. Second fence in the home straight omitted in all chases.

Wind: Fresh behind Weather: Cloudy with sunny spells

585 JOHN BURKE MEMORIAL NOVICES' H'CAP CHASE (10 fncs 2 omitted) 2m 110y

1:55 (1:55) (Class 4) (0-115,114) 5-Y-0+ **£3,768** (£1,106; £553; £276)

Form RPR

F/2- **1** **True Blue (IRE)**[26] 142 6-11-7 **109**........................(t) SamTwiston-Davies 125
(Nigel Twiston-Davies) *hld up: hdwy 6th: chsd ldr after 3 out: led appr last: drvn out* **4/1**[2]

F/1- **2** ½ **Alwaystheoptimist**[20] 247 10-11-9 **114**........................ KielanWoods(3) 130
(Phil Middleton) *led and j.rt 1st: mstke 4 out: j.rt next: rdn and hdd appr last: r.o u.p* **13/2**

F/2- **3** *18* **Cruise In Style (IRE)**[32] 43 7-10-7 **98**........................(b[1]) JamesBest(3) 97
(Kevin Bishop) *hld up: hdwy 7th: rdn after 2 out: wkng whn j.lft last* **11/1**

0/2- **4** *2¼* **Nomadic Dreamer**[22] 203 10-11-6 **113**........................(t) KillianMoore(5) 109
(Mark Rimell) *hld up: hdwy 6th: ev ch after 4 out: wknd 2 out* **16/1**

043/ **5** *8* **Walcot Lathyrus**[65] 4985 8-11-0 **105**................................ JakeGreenall(3) 95
(Richard Lee) *chsd ldrs: hmpd 1st: rdn appr 3 out: sn wknd: bhd whn hit last* **9/1**

112- **6** *3* **Accessallareas (IRE)**[14] 377 8-11-8 **110**........................ WillKennedy 96
(Sarah-Jayne Davies) *chsd ldrs: rdn appr 3 out: wknd next* **15/2**

/F6- **7** *¾* **Princeful (FR)**[13] 394 10-10-10 **105**................................ ChrisDavies(7) 91
(Milton Bradley) *hld up: hmpd 1st: rdn and wknd 8th* **66/1**

53/ **8** *nse* **Surf And Turf (IRE)**[278] 1378 7-11-5 **107**........................ APMcCoy 93
(Jonjo O'Neill) *hld up: hdwy 8th: rdn and wknd after 3 out* **7/2**[1]

P/4- **9** *79* **Lucky Vic (IRE)**[32] 45 7-11-10 **112**................................ BrendanPowell 27
(Barry Brennan) *hld up: hmpd 1st: wknd 7th: t.o* **20/1**

1/F- **F** **Sparville (IRE)**[26] 142 7-11-11 **113**................................ JasonMaguire 109
(Kim Bailey) *chsd ldrs: rdn and ev ch 3 out: cl up whn fell next* **6/1**[3]

0/2- **U** **Stormy Oscar (IRE)**[20] 247 6-11-3 **110**........................ HarryDerham(5)
(Jamie Snowden) *hmpd and uns rdr 1st* **16/1**

3m 55.7s (-18.30) **Going Correction** -0.95s/f (Hard) 11 Ran SP% **118.0**

Speed ratings: **105,104,96,95,91 90,89,89,52,**

Tote Swingers 1&2 £5.90, 2&3 £4.80, 1&3 £4.90 CSF £30.96 CT £267.83 TOTE £4.60: £1.60, £2.40, £2.30; EX 36.60 Trifecta £369.40 Pool: £611.59 - 1.24 winning tickets..

Owner Middleham Park Racing LVII **Bred** Anthony Walsh **Trained** Naunton, Gloucs

FOCUS

Tony McCoy said the ground was riding good to firm, while Sam Twiston-Davies added that it was "a bit quicker up the home straight but otherwise good ground". A competitive event of its type, run at a good gallop. The first two came clear and are on the upgrade.

586 CROWNGATE FOLLOW US ON FACEBOOK BEGINNERS' CHASE (16 fncs 2 omitted) 2m 7f

2:25 (2:25) (Class 4) 5-Y-0+ **£3,768** (£1,106; £553; £276)

Form RPR

152/ **1** **Ambion Wood (IRE)**[121] 3963 7-11-0 142................................ JackDoyle 127+
(Victor Dartnall) *chsd ldr: mstke 10th: led 2 out: drvn out* **7/4**[1]

2 *2* **Cock And Hen (IRE)**[61] 5089 7-11-0 0........................ RichieMcLernon 125
(Jonjo O'Neill) *chsd ldrs: lost pl 10th: rallied appr 3 out: chsd wnr last: styd on* **10/1**

1/0- **3** *3* **Connectivity (IRE)**[15] 358 9-11-0 0........................ SamTwiston-Davies 123+
(Dr Richard Newland) *hld up in tch: jnd ldrs 10th: led 12th: hdd and mstke 2 out: styd on same pce flat* **2/1**[2]

131/ **4** *42* **Ace Fighter Pilot**[166] 3115 7-11-0 0................................ APMcCoy 99
(Jim Best) *led: mstke 4th: hdd 12th: rdn appr 3 out: sn wknd: t.o* **9/4**[3]

5m 48.9s (0.90) **Going Correction** -0.95s/f (Hard) 4 Ran SP% **109.6**

Speed ratings: **60,59,58,43**

CSF £13.94 TOTE £2.80; EX 23.40 Trifecta £31.40 Pool: £286.23 - 6.82 winning tickets..

Owner O C R Wynne & Mrs S J Wynne **Bred** Michael O'Dwyer **Trained** Brayford, Devon

FOCUS

An interesting beginners' chase. The winner is a 150+ hurdler at best and can do better over fences.

587 CHEMICAL CORPORATION 30TH ANNIVERSARY VALERIE LEWIS MEMORIAL H'CAP CHASE (13 fncs 2 omitted) 2m 4f

3:00 (3:00) (Class 3) (0-135,134) 5-Y-0 **£6,330** (£1,870; £935; £468; £234)

Form RPR

/34- **1** **Pure Faith (IRE)**[25] 157 9-11-3 **125**................................ TomO'Brien 135+
(Peter Bowen) *a.p: chsd ldr 3 out: styd on u.p to ld fnl 100yds* **20/1**

5/P- **2** *2* **Ciceron (IRE)**[21] 217 7-11-3 **125**................................ AidanColeman 133
(Venetia Williams) *hld up: hdwy 9th: led appr 2 out: rdn and hdd fnl 100yds* **16/1**

23/- **3** *3¼* **Have You Seen Me (IRE)**[49] 5282 10-11-4 **126**...(t) SamTwiston-Davies 132
(Nigel Twiston-Davies) *led: nt fluent 4th: rdn and hdd appr 2 out: hung lft flat: styd on same pce* **7/2**[1]

0/P- **4** *6* **Creekside**[28] 119 5-11-2 **124**................................ DenisO'Regan 125
(John Ferguson) *hld up: hdwy appr 3 out: wkng whn j.lft next and last* **18/1**

F/0- **5** *¾* **Problema Tic (FR)**[15] 358 7-11-12 **134**........................(t) TomScudamore 133
(David Pipe) *prom: hit 3rd: rdn appr 3 out: wknd bef next* **10/1**

45/- **6** *16* **Triangular (USA)**[98] 4385 8-11-3 **125**................................(tp) NoelFehily 112
(Tom George) *prom: rdn after 9th: wknd next* **11/2**[3]

215/ **7** *8* **Rob Conti (FR)**[34] 11 8-11-6 **128**................................ RichardJohnson 105
(Philip Hobbs) *hld up: bhd fr 5th: t.o* **9/1**

0/0- **8** *1½* **Finger Onthe Pulse (IRE)**[22] 204 12-11-6 **128**.......... RichieMcLernon 104
(Jonjo O'Neill) *hld up: pushed along 8th: wknd next: t.o* **33/1**

254/ **9** *nk* **Ixora (IRE)**[44] 5359 7-11-5 **127**................................(v) BrendanPowell 103
(Jamie Snowden) *prom: rdn 8th: wknd after next: t.o* **15/2**

2/2- **10** *¾* **Coole River (IRE)**[30] 81 9-11-3 **125**................................(tp) APMcCoy 100
(Emma Lavelle) *prom: stmbld 8th: sn lost pl: t.o* **9/2**[2]

F63/ **11** *9* **The Chazer (IRE)**[65] 4987 8-11-6 **128**................................ JamieMoore 95
(Richard Lee) *hld up: hdwy 5th: rdn after 9th: wkng whn hmpd bnd bef next* **16/1**

3/5- **12** *1½* **Mr Hudson (IRE)**[32] 39 8-11-4 **126**................................(p) DarylJacob 92
(Paul Nicholls) *chsd ldr tl rdn appr 3 out: sn wknd: t.o* **9/1**

4m 40.7s (-19.30) **Going Correction** -0.95s/f (Hard) 12 Ran SP% **121.4**

Speed ratings: **100,99,97,95,95 88,85,85,84,84 80,80**

Tote Swingers 1&2 £16.10, 2&3 £16.10, 1&3 £16.10 CSF £300.58 CT £1399.39 TOTE £15.60: £3.80, £6.10, £1.80; EX 281.80 Trifecta £431.70 Part won. Pool: £575.64 - 0.50 winning tickets..

Owner P Bowling, S Scott & Mrs K Bowen **Bred** P J Carmody **Trained** Little Newcastle, Pembrokes

FOCUS

A decent handicap chase run at a solid pace, and sound form. Pure Faith could still be competitive when reassessed.

588 WEDDINGPEARLS.NET LADIES' DESIGNER OCCASIONWEAR HATS ACCESSORIES INT' OPEN NH FLAT RACE (DIV I) 2m

3:35 (3:35) (Class 6) 4-6-Y-0 **£1,559** (£457; £228; £114)

Form RPR

1 **Most Eligible** 6-11-2 0................................ TomScudamore 114+
(David Pipe) *chsd ldrs: wnt 2nd over 4f out: led over 2f out: rdn clr fr over 1f out* **3/1**[2]

1- **2** *4½* **Billfromthebar (IRE)**[18] 284 6-11-9 0................................ JasonMaguire 114
(Donald McCain) *chsd ldr: rdn over 3f out: nt clr run over 2f out: styd on u.p* **11/10**[1]

66/ **3** *3* **Bay Fortuna**[48] 5310 4-10-13 0................................ WayneHutchinson 101
(Mark Usher) *prom: pushed along 6f out: ev ch over 2f out: sn rdn: styd on same pce fr over 1f out* **5/1**[3]

40/ **4** *3½* **Beaujolais (IRE)**[53] 5230 5-10-9 0........................(v[1]) JosephAkehurst(7) 101
(John Ferguson) *chsd ldrs: rdn over 3f out: hung lft and wknd over 1f out* **8/1**

5 *1¾* **That's Exactly (IRE)** 4-10-6 0................................ DougieCostello 89
(Neil Mulholland) *plld hrd: led: rdn and hdd over 2f out: wknd over 1f out* **18/1**

6 *1¾* **Larks Rising** 5-11-2 0................................ IanPopham 97
(Caroline Keevil) *hld up: hdwy 3f out: hung lft and wknd over 1f out* **14/1**

/60- **7** *13* **Flying Quest**[7] 483 4-10-10 0................................ MichealNolan(3) 81
(Linda Blackford) *hld up: hdwy 1/2-way: wknd over 5f out* **50/1**

0/0- **8** *¾* **Maid Of Might (IRE)**[30] 85 5-10-9 0................................ TomCannon 76
(Laura Young) *hld up: rdn over 4f out: a in rr* **50/1**

9 *38* **Western Dream** 5-10-13 0................................ RobertDunne(3) 45
(Dai Burchell) *hld up: hdwy over 6f out: rdn and wknd over 3f out: t.o* **33/1**

3m 33.5s (-8.20) **Going Correction** -0.425s/f (Good)

WFA 4 from 5yo+ 3lb 9 Ran SP% **119.2**

Speed ratings: **103,100,99,97,96 95,89,88,69**

Tote Swingers 1&2 £2.20, 2&3 £2.30, 1&3 £3.40 CSF £6.84 TOTE £3.50: £1.40, £1.10, £1.40; EX 7.70 Trifecta £25.70 Pool: £962.68 - 28.06 winning tickets..

Owner Skeltools Ltd **Bred** A B Phipps **Trained** Nicholashayne, Devon

FOCUS

A very ordinary bumper overall, run at a steady pace. It was the slower division by 1.4sec but the winner looks a fair recruit.

589 WEDDINGPEARLS.NET LADIES' DESIGNER OCCASIONWEAR HATS ACCESSORIES INT' OPEN NH FLAT RACE (DIV II) 2m

4:35 (4:35) (Class 6) 4-6-Y-0 **£1,559** (£457; £228; £114)

Form RPR

1 **Another Hero (IRE)** 4-10-13 0................................ APMcCoy 110+
(Jonjo O'Neill) *hld up: hdwy 1/2-way: led over 2f out: rdn and hung lft fr over 1f out: styd on wl* **10/11**[1]

0/- **2** *2* **Dr Dalwhinny**[41] 5428 4-10-13 0................................ JasonMaguire 106
(Donald McCain) *hld up: hdwy over 3f out: chsd wnr 2f out: rdn and ev ch 1f out: no ex towards fin* **12/1**

03/- **3** *6* **I'm Not Telling (IRE)**[26] 5-11-2 0................................ TomO'Brien 103
(Grant Cann) *hld up: hdwy 1/2-way: rdn over 1f out: hung lft and styd on same pce fnl f* **25/1**

1/ **4** *5* **High Stratos**[34] 14 4-11-3 0................................(b) MPFogarty(3) 102
(John Joseph Hanlon, Ire) *chsd ldr tl led over 3f out: rdn and hdd over 2f out: wknd over 1f out* **7/2**[2]

4/4- **5** *3¼* **Alongthewatchtower (IRE)**[16] 338 5-11-2 0........ SamTwiston-Davies 94
(Barry Brennan) *led: rdn and hdd over 3f out: wknd over 1f out* **10/1**[3]

6 *1¼* **Katie's Massini (IRE)** 5-10-9 0................................ RichardJohnson 86
(Henry Oliver) *chsd ldrs: rdn over 2f out: wknd over 1f out* **14/1**

- **7** *34* **Sir Harry Hotspur** 5-11-2 0................................ LiamHeard 59
(John Mackie) *prom tl rdn over 4f out: hung rt and wknd over 3f out: t.o* **14/1**

8 *7* **Baksheesh** 4-10-8 0................................ MissLucyGardner(5) 49
(Sue Gardner) *hld up: rdn over 6f out: sn lost tch: t.o* **18/1**

0/ **9** *dist* **Haliana**[34] 14 4-10-1 0................................ GavinSheehan(5)
(John Upson) *chsd ldrs: pushed along and lost pl 12f out: bhd fr 1/2-way: t.o* **150/1**

3m 32.1s (-9.60) **Going Correction** -0.425s/f (Good) 9 Ran SP% **114.5**

Speed ratings: **107,106,103,100,98 98,81,77,**

Tote Swingers 1&2 £4.40, 2&3 £25.60, 1&3 £18.80 CSF £13.71 TOTE £1.70: £1.10, £2.10, £4.30; EX 14.70 Trifecta £93.60 Pool: £1,514.42 - 12.13 winning tickets..

Owner John P McManus **Bred** Miss Noreen Hayes **Trained** Cheltenham, Gloucs

FOCUS

Another modest bumper, but the quicker division by 1.4sec and it should throw up winners.

590 A & A RACING ONCOURSE BOOKMAKERS NOVICES' H'CAP HURDLE (12 hdls) 2m 7f

5:10 (5:10) (Class 5) (0-95,95) 4-Y-0+ **£1,949** (£572; £286; £143)

Form RPR

3/6- **1** **Ahead Ahead (IRE)**[20] 254 8-11-12 **95**................................ PaulMoloney 102+
(David Rees) *hld up: mstke 7th: hdwy appr 3 out: rdn to ld fnl 100yds: styd on* **7/1**[3]

P/1- **2** *1* **Moscow In April (IRE)**[28] 122 6-11-4 **87**........................(t) ColinBolger 92
(Pat Murphy) *mid-div: hdwy 8th: led appr and nt fluent last: rdn and hdd fnl 100yds: styd on same pce* **4/1**[1]

560/ **3** *5* **Sharlene's Quest (IRE)**[35] 5570 7-11-2 **85**........................ ConorO'Farrell 85
(James Hughes) *mid-div: lost pl after 7th: hdwy appr 3 out: rdn after next: styd on same pce flat* **33/1**

4 *¾* **Abolitionist (IRE)**[28] 123 5-11-12 **95**........................ AndrewJMcNamara 94
(John Joseph Hanlon, Ire) *mid-div: hdwy 9th: rdn after 3 out: no ex flat* **8/1**

0/F- **5** *2½* **Lord Navits (IRE)**[28] 122 5-11-8 **91**................................ JasonMaguire 91
(Donald McCain) *hld up: nt fluent 5th: mstke 9th: hdwy bef next: led appr 2 out: hdd bef last: wknd flat* **10/1**

4/1- **6** *2* **Indian Citizen (IRE)**[17] 320 6-10-12 **81**........................ DougieCostello 76
(Arthur Whiting) *chsd ldrs: rdn appr 3 out: wknd bef last* **6/1**[2]

P40/ **7** *7* **Life Long (IRE)**[36] 5555 9-11-3 **86**........................(v[1]) TomMessenger 74
(Anabel K Murphy) *hld up: hdwy u.p appr 3 out: wknd bef next* **25/1**

2/6- **8** *1 ½* **Chosen Dream (IRE)**[17] [320] 5-11-6 **89**..............................(t) APMcCoy 76
(Jonjo O'Neill) *led to 8th: led again 3 out: rdn: hung lft and hdd bef next: wknd appr last* **4/1**[1]
205/ **9** *1 ½* **Southway Queen**[38] [5505] 9-10-10 **84**..................(tp) MissLucyGardner(5) 72
(Sue Gardner) *prom: led 9th: hdd next: wknd 2 out* **8/1**
003/ **10** *9* **Sweet Prince (IRE)**[200] [2390] 6-11-4 **87**........................(t) RichieMcLernon 65
(Jonjo O'Neill) *hld up: hdwy 9th: wknd appr 2 out: t.o* **16/1**
5/0- **11** *24* **Qualitee**[31] [64] 8-11-6 **89**..(t) LiamHeard 45
(Claire Dyson) *chsd ldrs: led 8th to next: rdn and wknd 3 out: t.o* **33/1**
/P0- **12** *28* **Notcantdoit (IRE)**[10] [436] 6-10-5 **74**..................................... TomO'Brien 5
(Polly Gundry) *hld up: rdn and wknd 9th: t.o* **28/1**
P/6- **13** *33* **Sir Benfro**[7] [482] 7-11-2 **85**...(p) JamieMoore
(Keith Goldsworthy) *chsd ldrs tl wknd after 8th: t.o: bled fr nose* **20/1**
0/P- **14** *9* **Cowbridge (IRE)**[28] [122] 7-10-8 **77**.....................(p) SamTwiston-Davies
(Peter Pritchard) *chsd ldrs: reminders after 6th: wknd appr 9th: t.o* **33/1**
/UF- **P** **Pirans Car**[12] [408] 7-11-5 **91**..(t) MarkQuinlan(3)
(Nigel Hawke) *hld up: in rr and rdn 4th: lost tch after 9th: t.o whn p.u bef next* **25/1**
0/F- **P** **All Hope**[13] [391] 6-10-3 **77**...(t) BenPoste(5)
(Pam Ford) *hld up: rdn and wknd 7th: bhd whn p.u and dismntd bef next: bled fr nose* **50/1**

5m 32.8s (4.80) **Going Correction** -0.425s/f (Good) **16** Ran SP% **130.7**
Speed ratings (Par 103): **74,73,71,71,70 70,67,67,66,63 55,45,33,30,**
Tote Swingers 1&2 £18.60, 2&3 £18.60, 1&3 £0.00 CSF £35.00 CT £919.95 TOTE £9.20: £2.30, £1.70, £10.20, £2.60; EX 52.70 Trifecta £548.00 Part won. Pool: £730.75 - 0.05 winning tickets..
Owner Mrs Pauline Lewis **Bred** Aaron Collins **Trained** Clarbeston, Pembrokes
■ Stewards' Enquiry : Andrew J McNamara two-day ban; used whip above permitted level (15th,18th June).

FOCUS
Only modest form, but competitive enough and a truly run race. The form is sound.

591 JOHN WILLIAM DEELEY CLASSIC H'CAP HURDLE (10 hdls) 2m 4f
5:40 (5:40) (Class 3) (0-140,133) 4-Y-0+ **£5,393** (£1,583; £791; £395)

Form RPR
5/1- **1** **Saint Roque (FR)**[6] [486] 7-11-2 **123** 7ex..............................(t) DarylJacob 143+
(Paul Nicholls) *a.p: chsd ldr 3 out: led bef next: sn clr: easily* **11/8**[1]
11/- **2** *14* **Dolatulo (FR)**[36] [5539] 6-11-5 **126**.................................. WayneHutchinson 131
(Warren Greatrex) *chsd ldrs: rdn appr 3 out: outpcd fr next* **11/2**[2]
000/ **3** *¾* **Qulinton (FR)**[217] [2048] 9-10-13 **120**..........................(p) ConorO'Farrell 123
(David Pipe) *chsd ldr after 1st: led appr 3 out: rdn and hdd bef next: sn outpcd* **16/1**
4/1- **4** *2 ¼* **One Lucky Lady**[28] [119] 5-11-7 **133**........................ NicodeBoinville(5) 135
(Nicky Henderson) *hld up: hdwy 5th: rdn appr 2 out: styd on same pce* **13/2**
460/ **5** *6* **Skint**[173] [2978] 7-11-0 **121**.. AidanColeman 117
(Ali Brewer) *hld up: hdwy u.p appr 3 out: wknd next* **20/1**
1/3- **6** *3 ½* **Sir Fredlot (IRE)**[20] [244] 4-10-9 **120**.................................. BrendanPowell 108
(Brendan Powell) *hld up: mstke 6th: hdwy u.p appr 3 out: sn wknd* **20/1**
P/0- **7** *3* **Mister Hyde (IRE)**[15] [358] 8-11-1 **122**..................................(v) APMcCoy 112
(Jonjo O'Neill) *hld up: hdwy and mstke 6th: rdn and wknd appr 3 out* **14/1**
5/3- **8** *12* **One Term (IRE)**[15] [356] 6-10-10 **124**............................ PatrickCorbett(7) 103
(Rebecca Curtis) *led: rdn and hdd appr 3 out: wknd bef next: t.o* **6/1**[3]
403/ **9** *22* **Bathwick Man**[216] [2075] 8-10-13 **120**..............................(p) TomScudamore 79
(David Pipe) *hld up: mstke 5th: rdn and wknd after 7th: t.o* **25/1**
/41- **10** *12* **Knight In Purple**[9] [447] 9-11-6 **130**.............................(vt) PeterCarberry(3) 78
(John Mackie) *chsd ldrs tl wknd appr 3 out: t.o* **20/1**
/4P- **P** **Cross Of Honour (IRE)**[10] [432] 6-11-2 **123**............................ NoelFehily
(Charlie Longsdon) *hld up: stmbld after 2nd: bhd fr 5th: t.o whn p.u bef 3 out* **40/1**

4m 34.1s (-13.30) **Going Correction** -0.425s/f (Good)
WFA 4 from 5yo+ 18lb **11** Ran SP% **118.2**
Speed ratings (Par 107): **109,103,103,102,99 98,97,92,83,78**
Tote Swingers 1&2 £3.60, 2&3 £0.00, 1&3 £0.00 CSF £8.71 CT £86.79 TOTE £2.10: £1.20, £2.40, £5.70; EX 12.30 Trifecta £152.00 Pool: £719.57 - 3.55 winning tickets..
Owner Potensis Limited & Chris Giles **Bred** Mme Genevieve Mongin **Trained** Ditcheat, Somerset

FOCUS
A decent handicap hurdle. The easy winner built on his recent win and should go in again, and there's a case for rating the form higher.

592 TRAMPS & VELVET NIGHTCLUB MAIDEN HURDLE (10 hdls) 2m 4f
6:15 (6:15) (Class 4) 4-Y-0+ **£3,119** (£915; £457; £228)

Form RPR
/22- **1** **Garryleigh (IRE)**[11] [417] 6-11-0 119..........................(t) TomScudamore 116+
(David Pipe) *hld up: nt fluent 2nd: hdwy 6th: nt fluent next: chsd ldr 3 out: mstke next: led last: styd on u.p* **1/1**[1]
422/ **2** *2 ¾* **Cool Hand Luke (IRE)**[8] [2135] 4-10-5 108................(t) RobertMcCarth(5) 107
(Ian Williams) *chsd ldrs: led appr 3 out: rdn and hdd last: no ex towards fin* **6/1**[3]
3 *16* **Dance Floor King (IRE)**[9] [451] 6-11-0 0............... AndrewJMcNamara 101+
(C A Murphy, Ire) *hld up: hdwy 7th: mstke 2 out: sn rdn: hung rt flat: nt run on* **9/4**[2]
24P/ **4** *3 ½* **Record Breaker (IRE)**[251] [1615] 9-11-0 102........................ JasonMaguire 92
(Donald McCain) *chsd ldrs tl rdn and wknd appr 2 out* **12/1**
4/0- **5** *shd* **Nail 'M (IRE)**[23] [185] 5-10-11 0.. MarkQuinlan(3) 92
(Nigel Hawke) *led tl after 1st: chsd ldrs: rdn appr 3 out: wknd bef next* **16/1**
\- **6** *6* **Valkov**[29] 6-10-7 0.. WayneHutchinson 81
(Tony Carroll) *hld up: wknd appr 3 out* **66/1**
0/F- **7** *18* **Tinelyra (IRE)**[23] [189] 7-11-0 0.. DavidEngland 70
(Shaun Lycett) *led after 1st: rdn and hdd appr 3 out: sn wknd: t.o* **33/1**
545/ **8** *9* **Its A Mistake (IRE)**[46] [5334] 6-10-9 0.................................. CharlieWallis(5) 62
(Milton Bradley) *hld up: rdn after 5th: wknd next: t.o* **33/1**
/5B- **9** *6* **More Glory (IRE)**[7] [479] 5-11-0 0.. JamieMoore 57
(Keith Goldsworthy) *prom: drvn along after 5th: wknd next: t.o* **40/1**
004- **10** *2 ¾* **Lucette**[8] [458] 5-10-7 0...(t) TomMessenger 47
(Mark Shears) *plld hrd: hld up and a bhd: lost tch after 7th: t.o* **100/1**

4m 37.8s (-9.60) **Going Correction** -0.425s/f (Good)
WFA 4 from 5yo+ 18lb **10** Ran SP% **119.4**
Speed ratings (Par 105): **102,100,94,93,93 90,83,79,77,76**
Tote Swingers 1&2 £1.30, 2&3 £3.80, 1&3 £1.20 CSF £8.03 TOTE £1.90: £1.10, £1.60, £1.20; EX 8.10 Trifecta £25.70 Pool: £853.50 - 24.87 winning tickets..
Owner Brocade Racing **Bred** Miss Sarah Jane Jones **Trained** Nicholashayne, Devon

FOCUS
No depth to this maiden hurdle, which was run in a time 3.7sec slower than the preceding handicap. The form is rated around the first two, who came clear.
T/Plt: £137.70 to a £1 stake. Pool: £57,114.51 - 302.71 winning tickets. T/Qpdt: £15.00 to a £1 stake. Pool: £3,479.37 - 171.3 winning tickets. CR

161 FAKENHAM (L-H)
Sunday, June 2

OFFICIAL GOING: Good (good to firm in places; 8.8)
Fresh ground on both courses all the way round.
Wind: medium, half behind Weather: dry and bright

593 NORTH NORFOLK RADIO MAIDEN HURDLE (8 hdls 1 omitted) 2m
2:00 (2:04) (Class 4) 4-Y-0+ **£3,249** (£954; £477; £238)

Form RPR
6/- **1** **Lyssio (GER)**[91] [4536] 6-11-0 0... APMcCoy 114+
(Jim Best) *t.k.h: chsd ldrs: j. slowly 1st: chsd ldr after 5th: led 3 out: drew readily clr between last 2: eased ins fnl f: easily* **11/4**[1]
40/ **2** *8* **Ethics Girl (IRE)**[17] [2389] 7-10-0 0.......................(t) ConorShoemark(7) 97
(John Berry) *j.rt 1st: chsd ldrs: chsd wnr 3 out: outpcd and btn sn after next: 3rd whn hung rt bypassing last: plugged on to go 2nd again nr fin* **3/1**[2]
4/0- **3** *¾* **Annelko**[27] [140] 6-11-0 0.. TomCannon 103
(Michael Blake) *hld up in rr: mstke 4th: hdwy after 6th: chsd ldng pair bef 2 out: chsd wnr u.p but no imp between last 2: tired fnl 100yds and lost 2nd nr fin* **16/1**
6/2- **4** *2 ½* **Persian Herald**[15] [376] 5-11-0 97.....................................(v) AlexMerriam 101
(Neil King) *led: mstke 6th: rdn and hdd next: drvn and outpcd bef 2 out: 4th and plugged on same pce u.p between last 2* **20/1**
3/P- **5** *7* **Chain Of Events**[14] [384] 6-11-0 102................................ DougieCostello 94
(Sarah Humphrey) *taken down early: t.k.h: hld up in midfield: sme hdwy 6th: rdn and effrt after next: sn struggling: wknd bef 2 out* **33/1**
0/F- **6** *2 ½* **Birzali (FR)**[31] [72] 6-10-11 110..............................(bt) MichealNolan(3) 91
(John Joseph Hanlon, Ire) *hld up in tch in midfield: hdwy after 5th: chsd ldng trio bef 3 out: rdn and fnd nil wl bef 2 out: sn wknd* **5/1**
7 *10* **Mawaakef (IRE)**[13] 5-11-0 0... HarryHaynes 85
(J R Jenkins) *j.rt and nt fluent: in tch in midfield: j.rt and dropped towards rr 2nd: struggling after 6th: wknd next* **11/2**
6/3- **8** *18* **Rum Ginney**[18] [319] 5-10-7 74..(b[1]) DaveCrosse 59
(K F Clutterbuck) *chsd ldr tl blnd and lost pl 5th: sn drvn and struggling: bhd and lost tch bef 3 out: t.o* **100/1**
4- **9** *21* **Cottesmore (USA)**[19] [290] 4-10-11 0..............................(t) DenisO'Regan 44
(John Ferguson) *hld up in tch in midfield: j.rt 2nd: hdwy bef 3 out: rdn and no rspnse wl bef 2 out: sn wknd: wl bhd and eased fnl f: t.o* **9/2**[3]
0/0- **10** *6* **Played Away**[12] [417] 5-11-0 0... HarrySkelton 42
(Caroline Fryer) *t.k.h: hld up in last pair: lost tch bef 6th: t.o whn blnd next* **150/1**
40/ **P** **Cape Schanck**[420] [5301] 9-11-0 0...................................... JamesDavies
(Alan Coogan) *hld up towards rr: rn wd bnd after 2nd: rdn after 4th: wknd qckly after 5th: wl t.o whn p.u 3 out* **100/1**
U **Plus Fours (USA)**[25] 4-10-11 0... RyanMahon
(Michael Appleby) *in tch in midfield whn hmpd and uns rdr 1st* **80/1**

3m 56.9s (-8.50) **Going Correction** -0.30s/f (Good)
WFA 4 from 5yo+ 17lb **12** Ran SP% **119.4**
Speed ratings (Par 105): **109,105,104,103,99 98,93,84,74,71 ,**
toteswingers 1&2 £5.30, 1&3 £13.50, 2&3 £10.60 CSF £11.27 TOTE £3.20: £1.40, £1.70, £4.30; EX 13.10 Trifecta £118.10 Pool: £1085.07 - 6.84 winning units..
Owner Jack Callaghan **Bred** Gestut Hof Ittlingen **Trained** Lewes, E Sussex
■ There was a sad incident pre-race as Shuh Shuh Gah suffered a fatal heart attack in the paddock.

FOCUS
This looked quite an open race on paper, but not many got into it.

594 SPRING BEGINNERS' CHASE (THE SUNDAY £5K BONUS RACE) (12 fncs) 2m 110y
2:30 (2:32) (Class 4) 5-Y-0+ **£5,198** (£1,526; £763; £381)

Form RPR
6/5- **1** **Kian's Delight**[16] [356] 5-11-0 0.. TomO'Brien 132+
(Peter Bowen) *chsd ldr tl led 8th: gng best whn lft 5 l clr 9th: drew further clr and in n.d after next: easily* **6/5**[1]
/4F- **2** *17* **Sporting Boy (IRE)**[21] [234] 5-11-0 123.............................. TomCannon 116
(Michael Blake) *chsd ldrs: rdn and outpcd after 8th: lft 3rd next: drvn and chsd clr wnr bef 2 out: no imp and wl btn between last 2: plugged on* **8/1**
4/2- **3** *18* **Uncle Pelder (IRE)**[11] [425] 6-11-0 0.................................. DaveCrosse 104
(K F Clutterbuck) *chsd ldrs: mstke 5th: rdn and outpcd after 8th: lft 5 l 2nd and hmpd next: 3rd and wknd after 3 out: j.rt and mstke last* **20/1**
2UP/ **4** *8* **Caravel (IRE)**[79] [4768] 9-11-0 0....................................(t) AidanColeman 95
(Tim Vaughan) *led into s and reluctant to line up: tongue-tie removed and j. off okay: in tch in midfield: lft 4th and hmpd 9th: wknd next: t.o* **4/1**[3]
102- **F** **Cry Of Freedom (USA)**[10] [446] 7-11-0 133..................(v) DenisO'Regan
(John Ferguson) *led into s: j rt and nt a fluent: racd in last trio: rdn and hdwy to chse ldrs 6th: wnt 2nd and reminder sn after 8th: ev ch whn fell next* **5/2**[2]
F **Tulla Emerald (IRE)**[27] 8-10-7 0.................................. MrKevinJones(7)
(Natalie Lloyd-Beavis) *led tl 8th: sn dropped out and last next: t.o 3 out tl fell last* **200/1**
3/0- **F** **Ugo (USA)**[31] [82] 5-11-0 122... PaulMoloney 101
(Evan Williams) *t.k.h: hld up in rr: mstke 1st and 2nd: sme hdwy 8th: struggling whn lft 5th next: 4th and wl btn whn mstke 2 out: fell last* **25/1**

4m 6.4s (-10.20) **Going Correction** -0.70s/f (Firm) **7** Ran SP% **114.2**
Speed ratings: **96,88,79,75, ,**
toteswingers 1&2 £3.30, 1&3 £6.80, 2&3 £13.20 CSF £11.28 TOTE £2.30: £1.20, £3.80; EX 11.10 Trifecta £74.20 Pool: £2131.85 - 21.53 winning units..
Owner Roddy Owen,Paul Fullagar & Karen Bowen **Bred** Mrs J M Quy **Trained** Little Newcastle, Pembrokes

FOCUS
Probably not much of a race and they came home in single file.

595 JUNE NOVICES' H'CAP HURDLE (13 hdls) 2m 7f 110y
3:00 (3:00) (Class 5) (0-100,99) 4-Y-0+ **£3,249** (£954; £477; £238)

Form RPR
0/2- **1** **Bollin Tahini**[11] [428] 7-10-10 **83**.. AlexMerriam 90
(Neil King) *led tl 2nd: chsd ldr tl led again 7th: mde rest: rdn between last 2: kpt on wl* **9/4**[2]
/01- **2** *3 ½* **Clouds Of Mist**[6] [511] 8-11-5 **97** 7ex.......................... MissLucyGardner(5) 101
(Sue Gardner) *hld up wl in tch: chsd wnr 3 out: rdn and effrt between last 2: unable qck and one pce after* **2/1**[1]

6/F- **3** *33* **Festival Bound (IRE)**[26] 162 7-10-0 **80**................(v[1]) MissBAndrews(7) 54
(Caroline Fryer) *chsd ldrs: blnd 9th: drvn and no rspnse bef next: sn outpcd: lft poor 5th 3 out: no ch but plugged on to go poor 3rd bef last* **8/1**

05/- **4** *5* **Renagisha (IRE)**[187] 2678 7-10-13 **86**................................(v[1]) APMcCoy 56
(Jim Best) *in tch towards rr: hdwy to chse ldrs 3rd: mstke 5th: clsd 3rd and rdn 3 out: sn wknd: t.o* **7/1**

00/- **5** *4* **Onwards'N'Upwards**[11] 5557 5-9-9 **73** oh9.................... JoeCornwall(5) 39
(Christine Dunnett) *in tch in last pair: rdn bef 8th: wknd 10th: t.o next* **40/1**

060/ **6** *2 1/4* **The Presidents Man (IRE)**[70] 4944 6-10-1 **79**........... GavinSheehan(5) 43
(Barry Brennan) *hld up in rr: hdwy on inner after 9th: rdn and wknd after next: lft modest 4th 3 out: wknd bef next: t.o* **13/2**[3]

5P/- **U** **Almadan (IRE)**[110] 2377 5-11-7 **99**........................(bt[1]) SamanthaDrake(5)
(Ferdy Murphy, France) *chsd ldr tl led 2nd: hdd 7th: chsd wnr tl after 10th: cl 4th whn mstke and uns rdr 3 out* **10/1**

6m 1.9s (-4.50) **Going Correction** -0.30s/f (Good) 7 Ran SP% **112.6**
Speed ratings (Par 103): **95,93,82,81,79 79,**
toteswingers 1&2 £1.40, 1&3 £5.50, 2&3 £2.70 CSF £7.18 CT £27.46 TOTE £2.40: £2.20, £2.00; EX 6.00 Trifecta £22.00 Pool: £1237.16 - 41.99 winning units..

Owner A W K Merriam **Bred** A W K Merriam **Trained** Newmarket, Suffolk
■ Alex Merriam hung up his boots after this win.

FOCUS
A weak handicap and the two with the best recent form finished miles clear.

596 JULIENNE MCGINLEY & FRIENDS H'CAP CHASE (16 fncs) 2m 5f 110y
3:30 (3:30) (Class 3) (0-130,125) 5-Y-0+ **£7,147** (£2,098; £1,049; £524)

Form RPR

/23- **1** **That's The Deal (IRE)**[16] 355 9-10-2 **106**...................... JoeCornwall(5) 111
(John Cornwall) *in tch in midfield: rdn bef 13th: rallied u.p to chse clr ldr between last 2: styd on wl to ld fnl 100yds: rdn out* **5/1**

P/1- **2** *3/4* **The Black Baron (IRE)**[24] 181 11-11-7 **120**................. LeightonAspell 124
(Lucy Wadham) *j.rt: chsd ldr: upsides ldr and gng best 3 out: led bef next: 4 l clr and rdn between last 2: j.rt last and sn hrd pressed: hdd and no ex fnl 100yds* **10/3**[2]

1/F- **3** *9* **City Press (IRE)**[30] 96 7-11-3 **116**..................................(tp) NoelFehily 114
(Warren Greatrex) *nt a fluent: in tch in rr but niggled along at times: pushed along and effrt whn hit 13th: 5th and stl plenty to do after next: responded to press and hdwy to go 3rd between last 2: no imp last* **3/1**[1]

3/2- **4** *9* **My Flora**[31] 77 9-11-6 **119**.. HenryBrooke 108
(Donald McCain) *chsd ldrs: mstke 12th: drvn and no ex after 3 out: wknd between last 2* **6/1**

1/4- **5** *1 3/4* **Manger Hanagment (IRE)**[31] 78 8-11-7 **125**.......... GavinSheehan(5) 112
(Barry Brennan) *led: rdn after 11th: drvn and hdd bef 2 out: lost 2nd and wknd between last 2* **16/1**

/03- **6** *12* **Zama Zama**[15] 369 6-10-13 **115**...................................... AdamWedge(3) 96
(Evan Williams) *in tch in rr: hmpd 10th: struggling and rdn 13th: 5th and wkng whn hit next: wl btn and mstke next* **4/1**[3]

P/3- **7** *1/2* **Jonny Rye (IRE)**[18] 322 9-10-6 **105**................................. RyanMahon 80
(Michael Appleby) *in tch in midfield: j. slowly 11th: drvn and wknd after next: bhd 2 out* **20/1**

/24- **F** **Monarch's Way**[13] 411 6-11-1 **117**..............................(b) JackQuinlan(3)
(John Ferguson) *in tch in last trio tl fell 10th* **16/1**

5m 22.4s (-19.40) **Going Correction** -0.70s/f (Firm) 8 Ran SP% **115.6**
Speed ratings: **107,106,103,100,99 95,95,**
toteswingers 1&2 £5.80, 1&3 £5.10, 2&3 £2.10 CSF £23.00 CT £58.38 TOTE £7.80: £1.80, £1.90, £1.30; EX 28.60 Trifecta £86.30 Pool: £1461.72 - 12.70 winning units..

Owner J R Cornwall **Bred** P Magill **Trained** Long Clawson, Leics

FOCUS
A competitive event run at a strong gallop, so the form looks solid enough for the level. There were two previous course winners in the field and they finished first and second.

597 LIGHT DRAGOONS H'CAP CHASE (FOR THE PRINCE OF WALES CUP) (18 fncs) 3m 110y
4:00 (4:00) (Class 5) (0-100,97) 5-Y-0+ **£4,548** (£1,335; £667; £333)

Form RPR

025/ **1** **Pairc Na Gcapall (IRE)**[64] 11-10-8 **86**....................... MissBAndrews(7) 84
(Neil King) *racd keenly: led tl 6th: chsd ldr tl after 15th: 3rd and outpcd u.p after next: plugged on to chse clr ldr bef last: 12 l down and wl hld whn lft 3 l clr last: styd on u.p flat* **9/1**

P/4- **2** *3 3/4* **Eliades Run (IRE)**[10] 444 7-9-10 **72**......................... SamanthaDrake(5) 68
(Ferdy Murphy, France) *in tch in midfield: dropped to rr 7th: mstke 13th: rdn and outpcd after next: 6th and wl btn 2 out: lft disputing 5 l 3rd last: kpt on to go 2nd fnl 75yds* **10/3**[1]

/32- **3** *1 1/4* **Hurricane Carter (IRE)**[18] 323 13-11-5 **97**...........(v[1]) MrKevinJones(7) 91
(Natalie Lloyd-Beavis) *chsd ldr: upsides ldr 4th tl led 6th: drvn and hdd after 3 out: sn outpcd and btn: 3rd and wl hld bef last: lft 3 l 2nd last: no ex: lost 2nd fnl 50yds* **28/1**

3/2- **4** *8* **Orfeo Conti (FR)**[17] 328 11-11-0 **92**............................ MrOWedmore(7) 81
(Diana Grissell) *hld up in tch: 5th and outpcd after 15th: wl btn 2 out: lft disputing 5 l 3rd and mstke last: wknd flat* **10/1**

2/2- **5** *4* **Ifonlyalfie**[23] 206 8-11-11 **96**....................................(bt) TomMessenger 79
(Chris Bealby) *chsd ldrs: drvn after 14th: struggling u.p next: wknd sn after 3 out* **7/2**[2]

4/0- **6** *22* **Tin Pot Man (IRE)**[8] 481 7-11-5 **97**.............................(vt[1]) ConorRing(7) 60
(Evan Williams) *in tch in midfield: dropped to rr and blnd 8th: mstke 10th: lost tch 14th: t.o* **9/1**

232- **U** **Peak Seasons (IRE)**[8] 472 10-10-3 **81**..................... GerardGalligan(7) 90
(Michael Chapman) *hld up in tch in rr: gd hdwy 15th: led after next and sn drew clr: 12 l clr and in n.d whn j. sltly rt last and uns rdr* **8/1**

/55- **U** **Fashion Week**[21] 247 8-10-10 **84**.................................. MichealNolan(3)
(Sue Gardner) *in tch: blnd 8th: 4th whn blnd and uns rdr 13th* **10/1**

/P2- **P** **Flichity (IRE)**[19] 285 8-9-11 **73**.. JoeCornwall(5)
(John Cornwall) *hld up in tch: hdwy 11th: rdn and wknd after 14th: t.o whn p.u last* **9/2**[3]

6m 28.9s (-6.80) **Going Correction** -0.70s/f (Firm) 9 Ran SP% **116.2**
Speed ratings: **82,80,80,77,76 69, , ,**
toteswingers 1&2 £6.40, 1&3 £39.00, 2&3 £22.90 CSF £40.65 CT £818.98 TOTE £10.40: £2.60, £1.70, £7.50; EX 48.50 Trifecta £1150.00 Part won. Pool: £1533.42 - 0.44 winning units..

Owner The St Gatien Racing For Fun Partnership **Bred** Hugh Douglas **Trained** Newmarket, Suffolk

FOCUS
Desperate luck for amateur rider Gerard Galligan.

598 AYLSHAM SHOW - AUGUST BANK HOLIDAY - LADY AMATEUR RIDERS' H'CAP HURDLE (10 hdls 1 omitted) 2m 4f
4:30 (4:30) (Class 5) (0-95,95) 4-Y-0+ **£2,634** (£810; £405)

Form RPR

/32- **1** **Storm To Pass**[18] 320 5-11-5 **95**..............................(t) MissBAndrews(7) 100
(Caroline Fryer) *t.k.h: chsd clr ldr tl clsd to ld bypassing 8th: mde rest: rdn between last 2: slt mstke last: drvn flat: all out cl home* **7/4**[1]

4P0/ **2** *hd* **Antihero**[39] 5499 6-10-2 **74**......................................(p) MissCWalton(3) 79
(David Thompson) *hld up wl off the pce in rr: clsd on ldrs after 7th: chsd wnr sn after 3 out: drew clr w wnr and rdn after 2 out: 2 l down last: styd on u.p fnl 100yds: nt quite get up* **25/1**

236/ **3** *13* **Manshoor (IRE)**[40] 5477 8-11-7 **95**.................. MissJoannaMason(5) 88
(Lucy Wadham) *hld up wl off the pce in last trio: clsd on ldrs after 7th: 4th and rdn after 3 out: wknd sn after next* **4/1**[3]

3PP/ **4** *8* **Vinnie's Girl (IRE)**[34] 29 6-10-11 **85**......................... MissAEStirling(5) 71
(Martin Bosley) *chsd clr ldr: clsd and chsd wnr bypassing 8th: 3rd and outpcd after 3 out: wknd sn after next* **8/1**

4/1- **5** *1* **Bach On Tow (IRE)**[13] 407 6-11-4 **87**........................ MissLucyGardner 72
(Sue Gardner) *hld up wl off the pce in last trio: clsd on ldrs after 7th: clhased ldrs and mstke 3 out: 5th and rdn 2 out: sn wknd* **9/4**[2]

6 *99* **An Spailpin Fanach (USA)**[30] 5155 6-11-5 **95**....(b) MissRBlackmore(7)
(John Joseph Hanlon, Ire) *t.k.h: led drew wl clr after 1st: hdd bypassing 8th and sn bhd: wl t.o 3 out* **18/1**

2/0- **U** **Samizdat (FR)**[20] 264 10-9-9 **71**......................................(p) MissGSwan(7)
(John Upson) *racd wl off the pce in 4th tl mstke and uns rdr 4th* **20/1**

5m 8.7s (-3.90) **Going Correction** -0.30s/f (Good) 7 Ran SP% **112.1**
Speed ratings (Par 103): **95,94,89,86,86 46,**
toteswingers 1&2 £7.30, 1&3 £2.20, 2&3 £9.40 CSF £35.29 TOTE £2.80: £2.10, £8.10; EX 38.90 Trifecta £203.80 Pool: £2635.37 - 9.69 winning units..
Owner Mrs S Fryer **Bred** Mickley Stud & E Kearney **Trained** Wymondham, Norfolk
FOCUS
Not form to dwell on.

599 GEOFFREY RICHES MEMORIAL MAIDEN OPEN NATIONAL HUNT FLAT RACE 2m
5:00 (5:00) (Class 6) 4-6-Y-0 **£3,249** (£954; £477; £238)

Form RPR

35/ **1** **Kettlewell**[191] 2610 4-11-0 0.. NoelFehily 98
(Warren Greatrex) *t.k.h: chsd ldr tl led 6f out: hdd over 4f out but styd pressing ldr: drvn to ld again over 1f out: styd on wl and drew clr fnl f* **11/1**

0/2- **2** *4 1/2* **Talented Kid**[13] 412 4-11-0 0.. APMcCoy 94
(John Ferguson) *t.k.h: hld up in tch in midfield: hdwy to ld 4f out: hdd and rdn over 1f out: no ex and btn 1f out: wknd ins fnl f* **11/8**[1]

05/ **3** *1 1/2* **Slaney Star (IRE)**[97] 4432 5-11-3 0............................... MattieBatchelor 95
(Jim Best) *led: hdd and rdn 6f out: styd pressing ldrs tl outpcd 3f out: styd on same pce fnl 2f* **25/1**

3- **4** *6* **Howlett (IRE)**[31] 76 5-11-0 0...................................... MichealNolan(3) 90
(John Joseph Hanlon, Ire) *in tch in midfield: hung lft and rdn 4f out: sn outpcd and btn: plugged on* **4/1**[3]

2/ **5** *10* **Call Him Something (IRE)**[96] 4439 5-11-0 0................. JackQuinlan(3) 81
(Sarah Humphrey) *chsd ldrs: pushed along 1/2-way: rdn and lost pl 5f out: bhd fnl 4f* **2/1**[2]

6 *94* **Tropical Sky (IRE)** 5-10-10 0..................................... GerardGalligan(7)
(Michael Chapman) *in tch in last pair: lost tch qckly 6f out: t.o fnl 4f* **33/1**

P **Mr Lover Lover (IRE)** 4-11-0 0.. PaulMoloney
(John Butler) *hld up in tch in rr: rdn and lost tch over 4f out: wl bhd whn p.u over 1f out: dismntd* **16/1**

3m 58.2s (-1.60) **Going Correction** -0.30s/f (Good)
WFA 4 from 5yo 3lb 7 Ran SP% **116.4**
Speed ratings: **92,89,89,86,81 34,**
toteswingers 1&2 £3.20, 1&3 £9.70, 2&3 £4.90 CSF £27.61 TOTE £12.40: £2.50, £1.50; EX 28.70 Trifecta £290.80 Pool: £2683.48 - 6.91 winning units..
Owner Mark Duthie Partnership **Bred** Giles W Pritchard-Gordon (farming) Ltd **Trained** Upper Lambourn, Berks
FOCUS
More soundly run than many bumpers.
T/Plt: £39.40 to a £1 stake. Pool of £90,662.01 - 1675.67 winning tickets. T/Qpdt: £14.80 to a £1 stake. Pool of £5674.36 - 282.30 winning tickets. SP

[285] SOUTHWELL (L-H)
Sunday, June 2

OFFICIAL GOING: Good (7.8)
Fences on inside rail, bend into home straight was inside and Golf Club bend outside the line raced on May 14th.
Wind: light 1/2 behind Weather: fine and sunny

600 BETVICTOR.COM H'CAP CHASE (16 fncs) 2m 4f 110y
2:15 (2:15) (Class 5) (0-100,100) 5-Y-0+ **£2,144** (£629; £314; £157)

Form RPR

1/3- **1** **Orang Outan (FR)**[12] 418 11-11-0 **95**............................ KieronEdgar(7) 103
(Laura Hurley) *led to 4th: chsd ldr: hit 3 out: led appr last: all out* **16/1**

4/3- **2** *nk* **Ginger's Lad**[19] 281 9-10-8 **85**.......................................(t) JakeGreenall(3) 92
(Michael Easterby) *chsd ldrs: outpcd 10th: drvn 4 out: styd on fr next: 3rd last: no ex towards fin* **15/2**

3/1- **3** *3/4* **Arrow Barrow (IRE)**[19] 285 8-10-9 **90**......................... JohnDawson(7) 97
(John Wade) *in rr: trckd ldrs 6th: outpcd 10th: reminders 4 out: styd on next: hit 2 out: 4th and chsng ldrs last: kpt on* **2/1**[1]

/26- **4** *1 3/4* **Kayfton Pete**[12] 418 7-11-12 **100**..................................(tp) AdamPogson 108+
(Charles Pogson) *j.rt: led 4th: 5 l clr 3 out: hdd appr last: one pce* **9/1**

/43- **5** *nk* **Roc De Guye (FR)**[7] 489 8-10-4 **78**............................(b) LiamTreadwell 82
(James Evans) *t.k.h: chsd ldrs 9th: cl 3rd 4 out: one pce between last 2* **5/1**[2]

22P/ **6** *32* **Reg's Ruby**[202] 2383 7-11-2 **97**..................................... JakeHodson(7) 73
(David Bridgwater) *chsd ldrs: outpcd 11th: bhd fr 13th: t.o* **28/1**

4/U- **7** *6* **Shake The Barley (IRE)**[19] 294 10-11-11 **99**............(p) PaddyBrennan 69
(Tom George) *chsd ldrs: drvn 9th: lost pl and hit next: t.o 4 out* **9/1**

/12- **P** **Moscow Mule**[12] 418 10-10-10 **89**.................................(p) EdCookson(5)
(Laura Hurley) *prom: nt fluent 5th: drvn 7th: bhd and reminders 9th: t.o whn p.u after 10th* **17/2**

3/6- P Reasonable Force[32] 65 7-10-12 89 BrianToomey(3)
(Keith Reveley) *chsd ldrs: outpcd after 9th: lost pl 11th: bhd whn p.u bef 4 out* 7/1[3]

5m 19.4s (2.40) **Going Correction** +0.10s/f (Yiel) **9** Ran SP% **114.1**
Speed ratings: **99,98,98,97,97 85,83, ,**
toteswingers 1&2 £11.80, 1&3 £5.40, 2&3 £3.80 CSF £127.19 CT £347.20 TOTE £16.90: £3.30, £1.90, £1.30; EX 92.10 Trifecta £348.00 Pool: £3061.49 - 6.59 winning units..
Owner Mrs R Hurley **Bred** Pierre De Maleissye Melun **Trained** Kineton, Warwicks

FOCUS
A modest handicap chase which was run at a sound pace.

601 £25 FREE BET AT BETVICTOR.COM H'CAP CHASE (19 fncs) 3m 110y
2:45 (2:47) (Class 5) (0-95,90) 5-Y-0+ **£2,144** (£629; £314; £157)

Form RPR

/13- 1 **Borolee (IRE)**[7] 492 10-11-7 **90** TonyKelly(5) 101
(Ferdy Murphy, France) *hld up in rr: hdwy 12th: 3rd 15th: 5 l 2nd appr 3 out: led between last 2: rdn out* 4/1[2]

/21- 2 2 ¼ **Minstalad**[7] 492 9-10-9 **76** 7ex BrianToomey(3) 86
(Karen Tutty) *led: j.rt: hdd between last 2: kpt on same pce* 5/2[1]

5/0- 3 20 **Sycho Fred (IRE)**[23] 206 12-10-6 **70** (t) BrianHughes 61
(Mike Sowersby) *chsd ldrs: hit 5th: 2nd 12th: one pce fr 4 out* 40/1

63/- 4 3 ¼ **Manadam (FR)**[158] 3243 10-11-3 **86** (v) RobertMcCarth(5) 74
(Ian Williams) *chsd ldrs 6th: one pce fr 4 out* 16/1

/62- 5 4 ½ **Over And Above (IRE)**[8] 473 7-10-7 **71** (t) RichieMcGrath 55
(Henry Hogarth) *chsd ldrs: hit 13th: wknd 15th* 5/1[3]

5/0- 6 10 **Heezagrey (IRE)**[21] 248 10-10-10 **77** (b) MarkQuinlan(3) 52
(James Evans) *in rr: bhd fr 12th: t.o 3 out* 40/1

/35- 7 4 ½ **Moon Melody (GER)**[10] 444 10-11-3 **81** (t) LucyAlexander 52
(Mike Sowersby) *in rr and sn drvn along: sme hdwy 13th: lost pl 15th: distant 6th whn blnd last: eased* 14/1

4/4- 8 36 **Quayside Court (IRE)**[30] 100 9-10-12 **83** (vt) PatrickCorbett(7) 22
(Claire Dyson) *in rr: bhd fr 12th: t.o 4 out* 12/1

5/F- F **Tisfreetdream (IRE)**[29] 117 12-11-0 **78** (p) JackDoyle
(Peter Pritchard) *chsd ldrs: 4th whn fell 6th* 18/1

/30- P **Velvet Vic (IRE)**[21] 253 7-10-13 **77** (b) BarryKeniry
(Richard Guest) *mstkes: lost pl 10th: sn bhd: t.o 12th: p.u after next* 28/1

P/0- R **Derwen Pryde**[21] 248 9-11-1 **79** (vt[1]) JamieMoore
(Peter Bowen) *reluctant to go to s: reluctant to line-up: ref to r: tk no part* 6/1

/06- F **Wheelavher**[18] 322 7-10-9 **73** (t) NickScholfield
(Claire Dyson) *in rr whn fell 3rd* 20/1

6m 25.3s (2.30) **Going Correction** +0.10s/f (Yiel) **12** Ran SP% **118.1**
Speed ratings: **100,99,92,91,90 87,85,74, , ,**
toteswingers 1&2 £3.00, 1&3 £44.20, 2&3 £17.60 CSF £14.36 CT £343.88 TOTE £4.90: £1.90, £1.50, £9.20; EX 15.50 Trifecta £628.00 Pool: £2920.40 - 3.48 winning units..
Owner Ferdy Murphy **Bred** George Doyle **Trained** France

FOCUS
A well-run race, courtesy of the runner-up, which very few ever looked like getting into.

602 TALK TO VICTOR H'CAP CHASE (13 fncs) 2m
3:15 (3:15) (Class 5) (0-95,87) 5-Y-0+ **£2,144** (£629; £314; £157)

Form RPR

5/P- 1 **Darnborough (IRE)**[29] 112 7-10-12 **73** FelixDeGiles 84+
(Tom Symonds) *chsd ldr: led after 6th: hit 9th: drvn clr between last 2* 5/2[2]

UU/- 2 10 **Brannoc (IRE)**[88] 4594 8-11-3 **78** (t) AndrewThornton 83
(Tony Newcombe) *chsd ldrs: reminder 4th: lft 2nd 7th: 3 l down whn hit 2 out: 7 l down and wl hld whn mstke last* 4/1[3]

0/P- 3 11 **Strathaird (IRE)**[24] 183 9-10-5 **66** (v) BrianHughes 59
(Andrew Crook) *in rr: reminders 3rd: drvn 6th: modest 3rd 10th: one pce: 7 l down in 3rd whn mstke last* 14/1

014/ 4 3 ¾ **Escardo (GER)**[194] 2536 10-11-5 **87** JakeHodson(7) 76
(David Bridgwater) *chsd ldrs 7th: hit next: outpcd 10th: in rr whn hit next* 10/1

/P6- 5 48 **Gainsborough's Art (IRE)**[19] 285 8-10-2 **63** (p) IanPopham 9
(Harry Chisman) *chsd ldrs: outpcd whn mstke 9th: sn bhd: t.o 3 out: virtually p.u run-in* 22/1

/P6- B **The Grey One (IRE)**[24] 183 10-11-0 **82** ChrisDavies(7)
(Milton Bradley) *trckd ldrs: disputing 3rd whn b.d 7th* 10/1

/U2- F **Turf Trivia**[19] 281 6-11-11 **86** (b) BarryKeniry
(George Moore) *led tl after 6th: 2nd whn fell next* 15/8[1]

4m 4.5s (2.50) **Going Correction** +0.10s/f (Yiel) **7** Ran SP% **112.6**
Speed ratings: **97,92,86,84,60 ,**
toteswingers 1&2 £2.30, 1&3 £5.20, 2&3 £5.30 CSF £12.84 CT £111.30 TOTE £4.00: £2.00, £2.10; EX 13.60 Trifecta £99.20 Pool: £1358.95 - 10.27 winning units..
Owner Thomas R Symonds **Bred** Bluegate Stud **Trained** Harewood End, H'fords

FOCUS
A weak handicap, even more so once favourite Turf Trivia had departed at halfway.

603 SKYCIG NOVICES' CHASE (16 fncs) 2m 4f 110y
3:45 (3:45) (Class 4) 5-Y-0+ **£3,768** (£1,106; £553)

Form RPR

21/- 1 **Muldoon's Picnic (IRE)**[35] 16 7-11-5 122 NickScholfield 132+
(Kim Bailey) *trckd ldr: led 12th: wnt 4 l clr 3 out: eased towards fin: v comf* 1/1[1]

1/2- 2 11 **Brady (IRE)**[29] 114 7-10-12 120 JasonMaguire 116
(Donald McCain) *led: hdd 12th: reminders next: outpcd appr 3 out: 10 l down and wl hld whn mstke last: eased clsng stages* 11/4[3]

/21- 3 6 **Harry Hunt**[4] 394 6-11-5 129 TomScudamore 117
(Graeme McPherson) *trckd ldng pair: shkn up 10th: outpcd whn hit next: lost pl appr 3 out* 9/4[2]

5m 17.9s (0.90) **Going Correction** +0.10s/f (Yiel) **3** Ran SP% **107.4**
Speed ratings: **102,97,95**
CSF £3.80 TOTE £1.80; EX 3.10 Trifecta £8.50 Pool: £762.44 - 67.23 winning units..
Owner Clive Washbourn **Bred** Peter McCrea **Trained** Andoversford, Gloucs

604 NOTTINGHAM CITY TRANSPORT H'CAP HURDLE (11 hdls) 2m 4f 110y
4:15 (4:15) (Class 4) (0-120,120) 4-Y-0+ **£3,119** (£915; £457; £228)

Form RPR

1/1- 1 **Taigan (FR)**[19] 289 6-11-7 **115** DavidEngland 121+
(Giles Smyly) *hld up in rr: hdwy 7th: led appr 2 out: 3 l clr last: drvn out* 9/4[1]

1P/- 2 6 **Murcar**[10] 2474 8-11-2 **110** DPFahy 110
(Liam Corcoran) *hld up: hdwy 7th: chsd wnr between last 2: no imp* 8/1

4/2- 3 2 ¼ **Jacks Grey**[33] 48 8-11-2 **110** (t) PaddyBrennan 108
(Fergal O'Brien) *chsd ldr: upsides 3 out: styd on same pce fr next* 7/2[2]

10/- 4 4 ½ **Compton Blue**[211] 2176 7-11-6 **114** (b) WayneHutchinson 109
(Alan King) *chsd ldrs: one pce appr 2 out* 13/2[3]

/2P- 5 13 **A Bridge Too Far (IRE)**[15] 370 7-11-5 **113** JasonMaguire 95
(Donald McCain) *led: rdn 3 out: hdd appr next: bhd whn j.rt last* 10/1

331/ 6 36 **Definite Ruby (IRE)**[44] 5374 5-11-7 **115** DavidBass 65
(Nicky Henderson) *chsd ldrs: drvn 7th: lost pl sn after 3 out: sn bhd: t.o* 7/2[2]

0/0- 7 4 ½ **Khazium (IRE)**[7] 505 4-10-12 **110** (tp) NickScholfield 52
(Claire Dyson) *led into s: chsd ldrs: drvn 5th: lost pl bef 7th: bhd fr next: t.o* 40/1

P2/- 8 5 **Lord Gale (IRE)**[27] 7-11-7 **120** (v[1]) HarryChalloner(5) 61
(John Bryan Groucott) *chsd ldrs: drvn 3 out: sn lost pl: t.o* 66/1

5m 9.7s (-3.30) **Going Correction** 0.0s/f (Good)
WFA 4 from 5yo+ 18lb **8** Ran SP% **112.7**
Speed ratings (Par 105): **106,103,102,101,96 82,80,78**
toteswingers 1&2 £4.10, 1&3 £2.60, 2&3 £4.80 CSF £19.95 CT £60.11 TOTE £2.70: £1.10, £2.50, £1.60; EX 24.60 Trifecta £85.30 Pool: £2601.23 - 22.84 winning units..
Owner M Burford **Bred** Alain Couetil & Jean-Luc Couetil **Trained** Wormington, Worcs

FOCUS
A fairly useful handicap.

605 DOWNLOAD THE BETVICTOR APP NOW CONDITIONAL JOCKEYS' H'CAP HURDLE (9 hdls) 2m
4:45 (4:45) (Class 4) (0-110,110) 4-Y-0+ **£3,119** (£915; £457; £228)

Form RPR

000/ 1 **Tinseltown**[9] 3570 7-11-10 **105** (p) LucyAlexander 113
(Brian Rothwell) *mde all: jnd 2 out: edgd lft and forged 2 l clr last: drvn out* 15/2

5/2- 2 2 ¾ **Engai (GER)**[5] 521 7-11-0 **103** JakeHodson(8) 109
(David Bridgwater) *chsd ldrs: cl 2nd 6th: upsides 2 out: styd on same pce appr last* 7/4[1]

3/4- 3 16 **Hi Tide (IRE)**[19] 289 9-11-7 **105** PatrickCorbett(3) 98
(J R Jenkins) *hld up in rr: hdwy 5th: handy 3rd 3 out: one pce appr next* 7/1

523/ 4 1 ¼ **El Toreros (USA)**[240] 1731 5-11-9 **104** JamesBest 94
(Tim Vaughan) *chsd ldrs: rdn 3 out: sn outpcd and lost pl: kpt on run-in: tk poor 4th clsng stages* 25/1

060/ 5 ½ **Aughcarra (IRE)**[213] 2136 8-10-0 **81** oh6 IanPopham 71
(Harry Chisman) *chsd ldrs: outpcd and lost pl 3 out: kpt on run-in to take poor 5th clsng stages* 50/1

6/2- 6 1 **Eightfold**[17] 333 4-11-12 **110** (t) BrendanPowell 97
(Seamus Durack) *hld up in rr: hdwy 5th: sn chsng ldrs: 4th and drvn appr 3 out: wknd run-in and lost 2 pls clsng stages* 6/1[3]

064/ 7 11 **Stadium Of Light (IRE)**[219] 2022 6-10-9 **90** (bt) BenPoste 69
(Shaun Harris) *t.k.h: trckd ldrs: rdn whn stmbld on landing and lost pl 3 out: sn bhd* 25/1

001/ 8 28 **Broctune Papa Gio**[93] 4494 6-11-2 **97** BrianToomey 51
(Keith Reveley) *chsd ldr: nt fluent 6th: mstke next: sn rdn and lost pl: t.o whn eased run-in* 11/4[2]

4m 0.3s (3.30) **Going Correction** 0.0s/f (Good) **8** Ran SP% **111.2**
Speed ratings (Par 105): **91,89,81,81,80 80,74,60**
toteswingers 1&2 £2.60, 1&3 £6.10, 2&3 £2.30 CSF £20.54 CT £92.91 TOTE £12.80: £2.20, £1.10, £2.40; EX 24.40 Trifecta £135.20 Pool: £1629.20 - 9.03 winning units..
Owner Tony Arnott **Bred** Biddestone Stud **Trained** Norton, N Yorks

FOCUS
The leading pair deserve credit for pulling clear.

606 BETVICTOR CASINO ON YOUR MOBILE H'CAP HURDLE (THE SUNDAY £5K BONUS RACE) (13 hdls) 3m 110y
5:15 (5:15) (Class 4) (0-120,120) 4-Y-0+ **£3,119** (£915; £457; £228)

Form RPR

1/3- 1 **Blackwell Synergy (FR)**[29] 120 7-11-7 **115** (p) RichieMcLernon 130+
(Jonjo O'Neill) *mde all: styd on wl fr 2 out: lft wl clr last* 16/1

5/2- 2 30 **Father Shine (IRE)**[17] 341 10-10-3 **102** BenPoste(5) 90
(Shaun Harris) *chsd ldrs: cl 2nd 10th: outpcd bef 2 out: lft 25 l 2nd last* 14/1

0/6- 3 1 ¾ **Frontier Dancer (IRE)**[33] 38 9-11-2 **110** (tp) DavidBass 96
(Lawney Hill) *hld up: chsd ldrs 6th: outpcd and lost pl bef 3 out: poor 4th 2 out: lft 3rd last* 25/1

00/- 4 7 **The Potting Shed (IRE)**[137] 3680 6-11-1 **109** (bt[1]) TomCannon 89
(Emma Lavelle) *chsd ldrs: drvn 10th: wl outpcd next: lft poor 4th last* 7/1

1/5- 5 65 **Rich Buddy**[29] 121 7-11-12 **120** IanPopham 42
(Richard Phillips) *chsd ldrs: drvn 10th: lost pl next: sn bhd: t.o whn eased between last 2: virtually p.u run-in* 6/1

160/ P **The Shy Man (IRE)**[536] 3124 10-11-0 **108** (p) BarryKeniry
(George Moore) *hld up in rr: nt fluent 7th and next: lost pl after 10th: sn bhd: t.o whn p.u bef last* 20/1

0/6- P **Andhaar**[17] 336 7-11-12 **120** JasonMaguire
(Richard Phillips) *chsd wnr 2nd: drvn 8th: lost pl 3 out: sn bhd and eased: t.o whn p.u bef next* 5/1[3]

332/ P **Fortuna Rose**[171] 3023 7-10-11 **105** SamTwiston-Davies
(Julian Smith) *chsd ldrs: drvn 8th: n.m.r bnd bef next: lost pl 10th: sn bhd: t.o whn p.u bef 2 out* 7/2[2]

200/ P **Royal Deal**[43] 5410 6-10-4 **101** JakeGreenall(3)
(Michael Easterby) *in rr: nvr gng wl and nt fluent: j. slowly and reminders 3rd: lost tch after 8th: t.o whn p.u bef next* 10/1

P/1- F **Up For An Oscar (IRE)**[24] 185 6-11-1 **114** EdCookson(5) 123
(Kim Bailey) *chsd ldrs: cl 2nd appr 2 out: 2 1/2 l down and hld whn fell last* 3/1[1]

6m 12.1s (-2.90) **Going Correction** 0.0s/f (Good) **10** Ran SP% **120.9**
Speed ratings (Par 105): **104,94,93,91,70 , , , ,**
toteswingers 1&2 £15.10, 1&3 £14.00, 2&3 £35.20 CSF £218.82 CT £5490.69 TOTE £14.00: £2.90, £4.70, £7.50; EX 152.60 Trifecta £1022.30 Part won. Pool: £1363.16 - 0.23 winning units..
Owner J J Byrne **Bred** Erick Bec De La Motte **Trained** Cheltenham, Gloucs

FOCUS
A handicap in which not too many gave their running.
T/Jkpt: £74,743.50 to a £1 stake. Pool of £105,272.57 - 1.00 winning ticket. T/Plt: £128.10 to a £1 stake. Pool of £91,396.32 - 520.61 winning tickets. T/Qpdt: £30.80 to a £1 stake. Pool of £5337.50 - 128.20 winning tickets. WG

607 - 613a (Foreign Racing) - See Raceform Interactive

DIEPPE (R-H)

Sunday, June 2

OFFICIAL GOING: Turf: good to soft

614a PRIX DE LA VILLE DE BERNEVAL (HURDLE) (CONDITIONS) (3YO COLTS & GELDINGS) (TURF) 2m 1f

2:55 (12:00) 3-Y-0 £8,585 (£4,292; £2,504; £1,699; £804)

RPR

1 **Le Rocher (FR)**38 5534 3-10-4 0 ow1 JamesReveley 115
(Nick Williams) *trckd ldrs thrght: slt mstke 5th: led on run to 3 out: rdn and qcknd clr appr last: pushed out run-in: comf* **127/10**
2 15 **Illico Macias (FR)**39 3-10-3 0 (p) AnthonyLecordier 99
(P Leblanc, France) **103/1**
3 15 **Diable D'Enfer (FR)** 3-10-10 0 OlivierJouin 91
(P Peltier, France) **5/1**2
4 4 **Attawo (FR)**61 3-10-10 0 (p) FabienDehez 87
(A Lamotte D'Argy, France) **12/1**
5 1 **Cesar De La Haulle (FR)**37 3-10-8 0 SylvainDehez 84
(T Trapenard, France) **9/1**3
6 3 ½ **Surely Try (FR)**23 262 3-9-13 0 AnthonyCardine(4) 76
(Mme I Pacault, France) **33/1**
7 6 **Alaparo (FR)**36 3-10-10 0 BertrandLestrade 77
(G Macaire, France) **13/10**1
8 3 **Mister Happy (FR)**58 3-10-3 0 (p) MarcLamazou-Laresse 67
(Mme C De La Soudiere-Niault, France) **16/1**
9 10 **As Du Bosc (FR)**38 5534 3-10-3 0 GregoryAdam 57
(F-M Cottin, France) **34/1**
F **Dreamabad (FR)**38 5534 3-10-1 0 MaximeHevin(5)
(J Bertran De Balanda, France) **39/1**
F **Heaven Ball (FR)** 3-10-8 0 GaetanMasure
(F Nicolle, France) **5/1**2

4m 6.54s (246.54) 11 Ran SP% **116.9**

PARI-MUTUEL (all including 1 euro stakes): WIN 13.70; PLACE 3.80, 14.90, 2.30; DF 339.20; SF 1,097.60.

Owner John White & Anne Underhill **Bred** Mme Sylvie Ringler And Roger Frieh **Trained** George Nympton, Devon

615a PRIX REMY MOUQUET (HURDLE) (CONDITIONS) (3YO FILLIES) (TURF) 2m 1f

3:40 (12:00) 3-Y-0 £8,585 (£4,292; £2,504; £1,699; £804)

RPR

1 **Loin D'Etre Sage (FR)**21 3-10-10 0 GaetanMasure 107
(F Nicolle, France) **14/5**2
2 nk **Rubis De Reve (FR)**10 3-10-6 0 JeremyRey(4) 107
(Robert Collet, France) **13/2**3
3 4 **Ravissante Du Rheu (FR)**30 130 3-10-3 0 SylvainDehez 96
(T Trapenard, France) **66/1**
4 1 ½ **Dolores Delightful (FR)**30 130 3-10-4 0 ow1 JamesReveley 95
(Nick Williams) *trckd ldr on outer: lost pl 7th: 5th and outpcd 3 out: rdn appr last: kpt on wl run-in* **83/10**
5 1 ¼ **Melancholy Hill (FR)**23 3-9-13 0 GeoffreyRe(4) 93
(Yannick Fouin, France) **9/1**
6 1 ½ **Singaminnie (FR)**55 3-10-6 0 BenoitClaudic(4) 98
(H Billot, France) **12/1**
7 1 ¾ **Nulera (FR)**44 3-9-13 0 YohannBourgois(4) 90
(T Castanheira, France) **52/1**
8 2 ½ **Ybarra (FR)**28 3-10-3 0 AnthonyLecordier 87
(D Bressou, France) **23/1**
P **Star D'Authie (FR)**67 3-10-0 0 ow1 PaulLucas(4)
(Y Gourraud, France) **47/1**
P **Lashonara (FR)**55 3-10-4 0 ow1 BertrandBourez
(H Billot, France) **78/1**
P **Nicknack (FR)** 3-10-12 0 (p) OlivierJouin
(P Peltier, France) **9/5**1
P **Cherie Gold (FR)** 3-9-13 0 JessyBlandamour(4)
(Patrice Quinton, France) **29/1**

4m 8.95s (248.95) 12 Ran SP% **118.0**

PARI-MUTUEL (all including 1 euro stakes): WIN 3.80; PLACE 2.10, 2.40, 10.20; DF 13.70; SF 26.10.

Owner Ecurie D Primes **Bred** Ecurie D **Trained** France

616a PRIX DE LA QUINCAILLERIE GUILLEMARRE (CROSS-COUNTRY CHASE) (CONDITIONS) (5YO+) (TURF) 2m 6f 110y

6:45 (12:00) Class C 5-Y-0+ £8,975 (£4,487; £2,617; £1,776; £841)

RPR

1 **Quoquoalco (FR)**274 1472 9-10-10 0 FabienDehez 108
(E Lecoiffier, France) **167/10**
2 6 **Ange Du Lemo (FR)** 6-10-10 0 LudovicSolignac 102
(T Boivin, France) **21/1**
3 dist **Buffalo Pile (FR)** 5-10-3 0 JessyBlandamour(5)
(Patrice Quinton, France) **39/1**
4 10 **Quercy Du Manoir (FR)**17 9-11-0 0 (b) AngeloGasnier
(Jean-Paul Gasnier, France) **20/1**
5 4 **Sparkle (FR)** 7-10-10 0 MarcLamazou-Laresse
(D Sourdeau De Beauregard, France) **6/1**3
6 nk **Zenax Des Brosses (FR)**38 5536 10-11-0 0 (b) RomainBonnet
(J Bigot, France) **16/1**
P **Pouchki De Somoza (FR)**38 5536 10-10-12 0 (p) AlainDeChitray
(Y Gourraud, France) **15/1**
F **Durian (IRE)**1087 8-11-3 0 (p) JulienMorel
(S Foucher, France) **8/1**
U **Sarika (FR)**38 5536 7-11-0 0 (b) JamesReveley
(Nick Williams) *trckd ldrs on inner: 4th whn mstke and uns rdr 5th* **43/10**2
P **Balistix (FR)**38 5536 10-10-10 0 EricMichel
(J-P Carnel, France) **101/1**
P **Print Night (FR)**728 10-10-12 0 ChristopheHerpin
(P Chemin, France) **25/1**
P **Carmona (FR)**33 6-10-12 0 (b) CedricGabard
(D Sourdeau De Beauregard, France) **47/1**
P **Saphir Des Monts (FR)** 7-11-3 0 MrEdouardMonfort
(P Chemin, France) **9/5**1

6m 5.4s (365.40) 13 Ran SP% **116.5**

PARI-MUTUEL (all including 1 euro stakes): WIN 17.70; PLACE 6.20, 7.20, 11.50; DF 140.30; SF 333.30.

Owner Ecurie Bred To Win SC **Bred** P Danard & A Faucheux **Trained** France

617 - 624a (Foreign Racing) - See Raceform Interactive

578 HEXHAM (L-H)

Tuesday, June 4

OFFICIAL GOING: Good (good to firm in places; 7.7)

Bends at bottom of hill moved out 2m for better ground.

Wind: Light; half behind Weather: Hot; sunny

625 BOOK THE PAVILION RESTAURANT NOVICES' CHASE (17 fncs) 2m 7f

6:10 (6:10) (Class 4) 5-Y-0+ £3,768 (£1,106; £553; £276)

Form RPR

0/1- 1 **Bobble Hat Bob (FR)**27 169 8-11-5 113 (p) PeterBuchanan 130
(Lucinda Russell) *hld up: stdy hdwy bef 12th: effrt and chsd clr ldng pair after 2 out: hdwy to ld run-in: styd on wl* **11/1**
1/4- 2 nk **Kris Cross (IRE)**19 340 6-10-12 123 TomScudamore 123
(Lucinda Russell) *cl up: led bef 9th: jnd 3 out: edgd rt and hdd run-in: rallied: hld nr fin* **13/2**3
2/2- 3 19 **Howizee**18 358 7-10-12 0 (t) MichaelMcAlister 112+
(Maurice Barnes) *mstkes in rr: hdwy to chse ldr 12th: lost 2nd whn blnd and outpcd 3 out: hld whn blnd last* **2/1**2
2/1- 4 ¾ **Balding Banker (IRE)**31 114 7-11-0 125 TonyKelly(5) 112
(Ferdy Murphy, France) *in tch: hdwy and ev ch 3 out to last: wknd u.p run-in* **10/11**1
2/6- 5 15 **Kingdom Of Munster (IRE)**8 511 6-10-7 0 HarryChalloner(5) 92
(Richard Ford) *hld up: outpcd bef 4 out: n.d after* **33/1**
0/6- 6 1 ½ **Have You Had Yours (IRE)**12 449 7-10-5 0 AlistairFindlay(7) 90
(Jane Walton) *hld up: shortlived effrt after 12th: wknd fr 4 out* **66/1**
7 22 **Tom's Pride (IRE)**10 10-10-5 0 MrJHamilton(7) 71
(Victor Thompson) *mstkes: in tch: struggling fr 10th: t.o* **28/1**
0/F- 8 25 **Red Myst (IRE)**8 510 8-10-5 0 MrTSpeke(7) 48
(Victor Thompson) *chsd ldrs: wnt 2nd after 9th to 13th: rdn and wknd 4 out: t.o* **66/1**
P/ 9 27 **Paddy The Plumber (IRE)**10 7-10-12 0 (p) RyanMania 24
(Simon Waugh) *chsd ldrs: drvn 13th: wknd after next: t.o* **66/1**
/5- P **Bucklemyshoe (IRE)**10 474 12-10-12 0 KennyJohnson
(Robert Johnson) *plld hrd: sn led: hdd whn mstke 9th: struggling fr next: t.o whn p.u bef 2 out* **200/1**
/P4- P **Just Maddie**3 578 9-10-0 68 (p) GaryRutherford(5)
(Rayson Nixon) *bhd: struggling fr 9th: t.o whn p.u bef 13th* **200/1**

5m 48.3s (-12.50) **Going Correction** -0.55s/f (Firm) 11 Ran SP% **119.2**

Speed ratings: **99,98,92,92,86 86,78,69,60,**

toteswingers 1&2 £7.00, 1&3 £4.50, 2&3 £2.30 CSF £77.33 TOTE £11.60: £2.80, £1.60, £1.40; EX 37.80 Trifecta £207.00 Pool: £1,604.59 - 5.81 winning units..

Owner Mrs Carolyn Innes **Bred** Mme M Aubree, D Hanin & Mme G Bozon **Trained** Arlary, Perth & Kinross

FOCUS

Not a bad novice chase. It saw a one-two for Lucinda Russell and the winner looks on the upgrade.

626 HOWARD COOPER MEMORIAL MARES' H'CAP HURDLE (10 hdls) 2m 4f 110y

6:40 (6:40) (Class 4) (0-115,103) 4-Y-0+ £3,285 (£957; £479)

Form RPR

4/1- 1 **Rattlin**24 223 5-11-7 103 JonathanEngland(5) 110+
(Sue Smith) *t.k.h: cl up: led 3 out: rdn and qcknd after next: kpt on strly fr last* **7/2**2
404/ 2 2 ¾ **Bollin Dolly**41 5504 10-11-9 100 BrianHarding 104
(James Moffatt) *t.k.h: hld up in tch: hdwy bef 2 out: chsd wnr last: kpt on: no imp* **16/1**
5/3- 3 2 ¼ **Blazin White Face (IRE)**19 341 6-11-1 99 GrahamWatters(7) 101
(Lucinda Russell) *cl up: effrt and chsd wnr bef 2 out to last: kpt on same pce run-in* **4/1**3
3PP/ 4 16 **Along Came Rosie**37 20 9-10-5 82 DougieCostello 70
(Andrew Crook) *rn in snatches: hld up: drvn and outpcd bef 2 out: rallied bef last: no ch w first three* **33/1**
F/1- 5 1 ¼ **Stand Clear**12 445 8-11-3 99 TonyKelly(5) 85
(David Thompson) *hld up in tch: effrt bef 2 out: wknd between last 2* **13/2**
4/2- 6 1 ¼ **Groovy Dancer**9 491 6-11-1 92 JasonMaguire 77
(Rose Dobbin) *cl up: hit 2nd: rdn after 3 out: outpcd bef next: sn btn* **9/4**1
14P/ 7 15 **Sparkling Hand**87 4650 7-11-7 103 HarryChalloner(5) 75
(Peter Atkinson) *led to 3 out: sn drvn: wknd bef next* **9/2**

5m 0.9s (-11.60) **Going Correction** -0.625s/f (Firm) 7 Ran SP% **113.3**

Speed ratings (Par 105): **97,95,95,89,88 88,82**

toteswingers 1&2 £5.90, 1&3 £2.90, 2&3 £4.60 CSF £48.98 TOTE £3.50: £1.70, £5.10; EX 27.90 Trifecta £146.00 Pool: £1,061.80 - 5.45 winning units..

Owner Broadband Partnership **Bred** R F Broad **Trained** High Eldwick, W Yorks

FOCUS

A moderate mares' handicap, run at a solid gallop, and the winner looks on the upgrade.

627 JOHN WADE SUPPORTING GRACE IN WINNERS BAR H'CAP CHASE (12 fncs) 2m 110y

7:10 (7:10) (Class 5) (0-100,100) 5-Y-0+ £2,144 (£629; £314; £157)

Form RPR

330/ 1 **Castlelawn (IRE)**66 5010 6-11-3 91 PeterBuchanan 109+
(Lucinda Russell) *mde all at decent gallop: jnd 1/2-way to appr 3 out: rdn and styd on strly fr next* **3/1**2
235/ 2 10 **Pumboo (FR)**216 2127 10-11-0 88 BrianHarding 97
(James Moffatt) *in tch: hdwy to chse wnr 2 out: sn rdn: kpt on same pce fr last* **16/1**
/12- 3 6 **Cloverhill Lad (IRE)**6 533 9-11-0 93 GaryRutherford(5) 99
(Stuart Coltherd) *in tch: effrt and drvn bef 3 out: outpcd after next: no imp fr last* **2/1**1
PP/- 4 7 **Honest And True (IRE)**59 6-9-7 74 oh6 GrantCockburn(7) 71
(Alistair Whillans) *hld up: rdn 4 out: hdwy appr next: no imp fr 2 out* **14/1**
/13- 5 1 **Sendiym (FR)**6 536 6-10-7 81 (bt) SeanQuinlan 78
(Dianne Sayer) *chsd wnr: chal 1/2-way to appr 3 out: wknd after next* **3/1**2
3/5- 6 10 **Panthers Run**31 109 13-9-11 74 oh4 (t) JohnKington(3) 63
(Jonathan Haynes) *in tch: outpcd 1/2-way: n.d after* **33/1**

0/0- **7** *22* **Authentic Act (IRE)**[21] 281 9-10-0 **74** oh5........................ HenryBrooke 42
(Martin Todhunter) *nt fluent on occasions: bhd: struggling 1/2-way: sn no ch* **50/1**

P/0- **8** *13* **Snooze N You Lose**[20] 314 8-9-9 **74** oh15............ JonathanEngland(5) 30
(Jean McGregor) *bhd: struggling 1/2-way: nvr on terms* **100/1**

3/5- **U** **Millers Reef (IRE)**[27] 171 7-11-5 **100**....................(t) GrahamWatters(7)
(Andrew Parker) *hld up towards rr: blnd and uns rdr 6th* **8/1**[3]

3m 59.6s (-10.20) **Going Correction** -0.55s/f (Firm) **9** Ran SP% **112.9**
Speed ratings: **102,97,94,91,90 86,75,69,**
toteswingers 1&2 £9.70, 1&3 £2.20, 2&3 £5.70 CSF £43.53 CT £115.34 TOTE £3.30: £1.30, £2.80, £1.10; EX 25.20 Trifecta £184.70 Pool: £802.76 - 3.25 winning units..
Owner John R Adam **Bred** Mrs Michelle Archdeacon **Trained** Arlary, Perth & Kinross

FOCUS
A weak handicap in which there was a solid gallop on and the form should work out.

628 HEXHAM CARAVAN SITE H'CAP HURDLE (8 hdls 4 omitted) 3m
7:40 (7:42) (Class 5) (0-95,90) 4-Y-0+ **£1,949** (£572; £286; £143)

Form RPR

06P/ **1** **Auberge (IRE)**[111] 4189 9-10-12 **76**....................................... RyanMania 93+
(Dianne Sayer) *prom: stdy hdwy after 3 out: rdn to ld bef last: sn clr* **16/1**

4/1- **2** *9* **Corky Dancer**[24] 221 8-11-4 **82**.................................(v) JasonMaguire 92
(Andrew Parker) *led: mstke 2nd: qcknd bef 4 out: hdd bef last: kpt on same pce* **11/8**[1]

613- **3** *16* **Solway Dornal**[3] 580 8-10-1 **72**........................(tp) StephenMulqueen(7) 67
(Lisa Harrison) *chsd ldrs: effrt and rdn after 3 out: outpcd by first two after next* **15/2**[3]

6/3- **4** *3¾* **Bob's Ticket (IRE)**[24] 222 8-11-1 **86**..............................(t) AdamNicol(7) 77
(Philip Kirby) *hld up: stdy hdwy bef 3 out: rdn and outpcd next: n.d after* **7/2**[2]

450- **5** *2¼* **Westwire Toby (IRE)**[11] 460 11-10-2 **66**........................... TomSiddall 55
(Lynn Siddall) *hld up: drvn to improve 1/2-way: outpcd 4 out: plugged on fr 2 out: no imp* **50/1**

0/6- **6** *43* **Nisaal (IRE)**[24] 222 8-10-5 **69**..(tp) AdrianLane 19
(Sandy Forster) *in tch: rdn along 1/2-way: wknd fr 4 out: t.o: suffered fatal heart attack* **33/1**

5/4- **7** *nk* **Miss Sunflower**[6] 532 11-9-9 **64** oh7......................(p) JonathanEngland(5) 14
(Tina Jackson) *chsd ldr to bef 4 out: wknd after next: t.o* **66/1**

3/6- **8** *2¾* **Wave Breaker (IRE)**[10] 473 6-11-1 **79**.......................(p) KennyJohnson 27
(Robert Johnson) *bhd: drvn along 1/2-way: nvr on terms: t.o* **18/1**

634/ **9** *6* **Shannina**[144] 3603 8-10-7 **76**...(p) TonyKelly(5) 18
(David Thompson) *bhd: drvn along 1/2-way: sn struggling: t.o* **11/1**

P00/ **P** **Vallani (IRE)**[41] 5495 8-11-5 **90**.................................... GrantCockburn(7)
(Lucinda Russell) *sn towards rr: struggling 1/2-way: t.o whn p.u bef last* **33/1**

0FF/ **P** **Ballymacduff (IRE)**[181] 2850 9-11-0 **85**.......................(t) AlistairFindlay(7)
(George Charlton) *chsd ldrs: outpcd whn mstke 3 out: sn struggling: p.u after next: suffered fatal heart attack* **28/1**

0/P- **P** **Across The Tweed (IRE)**[33] 74 7-10-5 **69**............(t) MichaelMcAlister
(Maurice Barnes) *midfield: struggling bef 4 out: t.o whn p.u bef last* **12/1**

0/5- **P** **Black Velvet Belle (IRE)**[24] 223 6-11-0 **81**............(tp) AlexanderVoy(3)
(Lucy Normile) *prom: drvn 1/2-way: wknd 4 out: t.o whn p.u bef last* **66/1**

5m 45.0s (-24.00) **Going Correction** -1.00s/f (Hard) course record **13** Ran SP% **117.5**
Speed ratings (Par 103): **100,97,91,90,89 75,75,74,72, , ,**
toteswingers 1&2 £7.20, 1&3 £8.20, 2&3 £3.00 CSF £37.68 CT £190.97 TOTE £12.90: £4.50, £1.10, £3.00; EX 56.40 Trifecta £591.70 Pool: £856.27 - 1.08 winning units..
Owner Ron Affleck **Bred** David Fenton **Trained** Hackthorpe, Cumbria

FOCUS
A weak staying handicap.but well run and the winner was back to form.

629 BOOK NOW FOR LADIES DAY MAIDEN HURDLE (8 hdls 2 omitted) 2m 4f 110y
8:10 (8:11) (Class 5) 4-Y-0+ **£2,053** (£598; £299)

Form RPR

33/- **1** **Oscar Tanner (IRE)**[38] 5572 5-11-0 0............................. LucyAlexander 117+
(Martin Todhunter) *hld up: stdy hdwy whn nt fluent and pushed along 3 out: clsd bef next: led bef last: sn clr: eased nr fin* **10/1**

0/6- **2** *11* **Arisda**[12] 450 5-9-11 0.. GLavery(10) 95
(Brian Ellison) *hld up: stdy hdwy after 2 out: chsd (clr) wnr run-in: kpt on: no imp* **66/1**

4- **3** *2¼* **Twill Stand To Us (IRE)**[10] 470 6-11-0 0.................... TomScudamore 100
(Brian Ellison) *t.k.h: j.rt on occasions: led: rdn bef 2 out: hdd bef last: outpcd whn lost 2nd run-in* **10/3**[2]

3/F- **4** *3¾* **Northern Executive (IRE)**[24] 223 5-11-0 0..................... BrianHughes 96
(Karen McLintock) *chsd clr ldrs: rdn 3 out: no imp after next* **2/1**[1]

3/0 **5** *1½* **Total Aoooto**[20] 313 6 10 2 0 ow2... MrTSpoko(7) 00
(Simon Waugh) *hld up in midfield: stdy hdwy after 3 out: outpcd between last 2* **25/1**

0/0- **6** *3¾* **Aw Ripe China (IRE)**[21] 284 5-10-11 0......................... JohnKington(3) 93
(Simon Waugh) *hld up in midfield: hdwy after 3 out: rdn and outpcd whn nt fluent last* **80/1**

5/3- **7** *6* **Perfect Poison (IRE)**[17] 380 5-11-0 0............................ JasonMaguire 88
(Donald McCain) *chsd clr ldr fr 3rd: clsd next: effrt and rdn bef 2 out: wkng whn mstke last* **5/1**[3]

6/P- **8** *26* **Sun Lady (FR)**[12] 444 7-10-7 75...................................... DougieCostello 56
(Jane Walton) *bhd: rdn whn hit 4 out: nvr on terms* **40/1**

/65- **9** *6* **Silver Sophfire**[12] 450 7-10-2 0........................... JonathanEngland(5) 50
(Sue Smith) *midfield: drvn and struggling bef 4 out: sn btn* **6/1**

/30- **10** *63* **Optical High**[12] 449 4-10-10 0... RyanMania
(Sue Smith) *mstkes: in tch: struggling 1/2-way: t.o* **18/1**

5/ **P** **Over To You Ruby (IRE)**[110] 4213 6-10-7 0...................... BrianHarding
(Alistair Whillans) *nt fluent in rr: lost tch whn p.u bef 4 out* **25/1**

U **Just Awake** 6-10-7 0.. GrahamWatters(7)
(Sandy Thomson) *bhd: j. awkwardly and uns rdr 2nd* **66/1**

(-12.50) **Going Correction** -0.625s/f (Firm)
WFA 4 from 5yo+ 18lb **12** Ran SP% **116.1**
Speed ratings (Par 103): **98,93,92,91,90 89,87,77,75,51 ,**
toteswingers 1&2 £56.50, 1&3 £11.30, 2&3 £56.50 CSF £512.64 TOTE £10.50: £2.00, £16.70, £1.70; EX 683.50 Trifecta £469.10 Part won. Pool: £625.46 - 0.06 winning units..
Owner Murphy's Law & Vyner-Brooks **Bred** John Mulcahy **Trained** Orton, Cumbria

FOCUS
A strongly run maiden and big steps up from the first two.

630 ST. JOHN LEE AMATEUR RIDERS' NOVICES' H'CAP HURDLE (8 hdls) 2m 110y
8:40 (8:40) (Class 5) (0-95,92) 4-Y-0+ **£1,975** (£607; £303)

Form RPR

B/3- **1** **Morning Time (IRE)**[20] 314 7-10-1 **74**..................(p) MissRMcDonald(7) 79+
(Lucinda Russell) *hld up: smooth hdwy after 2 out: led run-in: drvn and r.o wl* **9/1**

/16- **2** *2* **Brother Scott**[4] 561 6-11-1 **88**.. CallumBewley(7) 91
(Sue Smith) *cl up: led 2 out: sn rdn and qcknd: hdd run-in: kpt on same pce* **2/1**[1]

6/- **3** *8* **The Ferick (IRE)**[68] 4994 7-11-1 **81**.............................(t) NicodeBoinville 77
(Alan Swinbank) *in tch: stdy hdwy to chse ldrs 3 out: effrt after next: one pce bef last* **3/1**[2]

F/5- **4** *2* **Raggios Boy**[24] 222 7-10-6 **75**..(p) NickSlatter(3) 68
(Barry Murtagh) *prom: rdn after 2 out: no ex bef last* **7/2**[3]

P/0- **5** *7* **Cigalas**[20] 316 8-9-8 **67**.. MissAMcGregor(7) 54
(Jean McGregor) *hld up: hit and rdn 3 out: rallied after next: no imp* **50/1**

/64- **6** *¾* **Bertielicious**[21] 278 5-10-0 **66** oh2.............................. MrTomGreenway 53
(Jonathan Haynes) *hld up in tch: stdy hdwy after 3 out: rdn and outpcd after next: no imp whn mstke last* **22/1**

0/6- **7** *7* **Ravi River (IRE)**[20] 316 9-10-0 **71**.................................. MrJHamilton(5) 52
(Alistair Whillans) *chsd ldrs: nt fluent 3 out: rdn and wknd after next* **6/1**

P/P- **8** *14* **Man Of Principles (IRE)**[20] 311 10-10-1 **74**......... MrGaryBeaumont(7) 41
(Stuart Coltherd) *hld up: outpcd bef 4 out: n.d after* **33/1**

500/ **9** *14* **Daniel's Dream**[60] 5164 13-9-7 **66** oh2..............................(p) MrJDixon(7) 21
(John Dixon) *chsd ldrs: outpcd whn hit 4th: rdn 3 out: lost tch fr next* **100/1**

3/0- **10** *3½* **Hobsons Bay (IRE)**[6] 536 8-11-9 **92**............................. MissCWalton(3) 43
(Sheena Walton) *led to 2 out: sn rdn and wknd* **40/1**

4m 6.3s (-11.10) **Going Correction** -0.625s/f (Firm) **10** Ran SP% **117.5**
Speed ratings (Par 103): **101,100,96,95,92 91,88,81,75,73**
toteswingers 1&2 £4.10, 1&3 £6.70, 2&3 £2.80 CSF £27.65 CT £69.29 TOTE £9.30: £3.30, £1.40, £1.20; EX 26.40 Trifecta £80.90 Pool: £750.75 - 6.95 winning units..
Owner Bill Forrester **Bred** Joe O'Flaherty **Trained** Arlary, Perth & Kinross

FOCUS
A typically moderate handicap for amateur riders in which the first pair drew clear after the last.
T/Plt: £96.90 to a £1 stake. Pool: £78,437.86 - 590.56 winning units T/Qpdt: £8.00 to a £1 stake. Pool: £9,161.06 - 837.57 winning units RY

[517] NEWTON ABBOT (L-H)
Wednesday, June 5

OFFICIAL GOING: Good to firm (good in places)
Wind: mild breeze against Weather: sunny

631 FOLLOW TOTEPOOL ON FACEBOOK AND TWITTER NOVICES' HURDLE (8 hdls) 2m 1f
2:20 (2:20) (Class 4) 4-Y-0+ **£3,508** (£1,030; £515; £257)

Form RPR

1/U- **1** **Anay Turge (FR)**[24] 236 8-10-9 0..................................(t) MarkQuinlan(3) 112+
(Nigel Hawke) *in tch: trckd ldrs: 5th: led after 3 out: kpt on wl fr 2 out: rdn out* **7/1**

0/3- **2** *2¾* **Rosslyn Castle**[9] 507 4-10-9 0... APMcCoy 107+
(Gary Brown) *mid-div: hdwy 5th: rdn to chse wnr bef 2 out where awkward: 2 l 2nd but looking hld whn mstke last: kpt on same pce* **9/2**[3]

03P/ **3** *5* **Thunder Sheik (IRE)**[37] 30 5-10-12 112......................... PaddyBrennan 106
(Fergal O'Brien) *trckd ldr: led 5th: rdn and hdd after 3 out: kpt on same pce fr next: nt fluent last* **4/1**[2]

03/ **4** *9* **Sterling Gent (IRE)**[60] 5180 6-10-12 0.................................... DPFahy 95
(Liam Corcoran) *in tch: rdn after 3 out: kpt on same pce* **22/1**

3/2- **5** *13* **Revaader**[22] 292 5-10-5 95.. TommyPhelan 77
(Mark Gillard) *led tl 5th: chsd ldrs: rdn after 3 out: wknd next* **8/1**

000/ **6** *2* **Si Bien (FR)**[42] 5509 8-10-7 84... CharlieWallis(5) 82
(Nick Ayliffe) *trckd ldrs: rdn after 3 out: wknd bef next* **250/1**

0/1- **7** *nk* **The Bay Bandit**[17] 390 6-11-5 0................................. SamTwiston-Davies 89
(Neil Mulholland) *mid-div: nt fluent 1st: hdwy 5th: rdn after 3 out: nvr threatened ldrs: wknd next* **20/1**

2/1- **8** *¾* **Vexillum (IRE)**[29] 155 4-11-2 114.. RyanMahon 86
(Harry Fry) *mid-div: nt fluent 5th: sn nudged along: rdn after 3 out: nvr threatened: wknd tamely: mstke next* **2/1**[1]

/50- **9** *20* **Bedibyes**[22] 292 5-10-2 0... JamesBest(3) 56
(Richard Mitchell) *mid-div on outer tl lost pl after 4th: n.d after: t.o after 3 out* **100/1**

563/ **10** *4½* **River Dancing (IRE)**[45] 5441 6-10-12 0.......................... AidanColeman 59
(Andy Turnell) *mstke 2 out: a towards rr: t.o* **10/1**

11 *3* **Rusty Nail (IRE)**[66] 8-10-12 0.. HaddenFrost 56
(James Frost) *a towards rr: t.o* **40/1**

005- **12** *½* **Colin's Nightmare**[8] 519 5-10-0 0.............................. GavinSheehan(5) 49
(Nick Mitchell) *in tch tl 3rd: sn struggling in rr: t.o* **66/1**

P/ **P** **Countrywide City (IRE)**[118] 4088 7-10-5 0............................. MrCSmith(7)
(Sarah Robinson) *mid-div tl stmbld 4th: sn struggling in rr: t.o whn p.u after 3 out* **250/1**

P **Robber Stone**[32] 5-10-12 0... DonalDevereux
(Debra Hamer) *trckd ldrs tl after 4th: sn struggling in rr: t.o whn p.u after 3 out* **100/1**

0- **P** **Cool Fantasy (IRE)**[8] 517 4-10-9 0.. IanPopham
(Caroline Keevil) *mid-div tl awkward 3rd: sn dropped in rr: p.u after next* **100/1**

3m 54.3s (-11.40) **Going Correction** -0.50s/f (Good)
WFA 4 from 5yo+ 17lb **15** Ran SP% **121.0**
Speed ratings (Par 105): **106,104,102,98,92 91,90,90,81,79 77,77, , ,**
toteswingers 1&2 £7.80, 2&3 £5.30, 1&3 £6.30 CSF £37.64 TOTE £10.60: £3.00, £2.20, £1.30; EX 43.50 Trifecta £413.10 Pool: £817.44 - 1.48 winning units..
Owner Mrs K Wetherall **Bred** Mme Annick Penouilh **Trained** Stoodleigh, Devon

FOCUS
Just a modest event of its type. The pace looked reasonable thanks to Revaader, but plenty still took strong holds while chasing. Tony McCoy reported the going to be "a mix of firm and good to firm". A hurdles best from the winner, but a stone+ off his best chase form.

632 LADIES DAY 25 JUNE H'CAP CHASE (13 fncs) 2m 110y
2:50 (2:50) (Class 4) (0-105,105) 5-Y-0+ **£4,288** (£1,259; £629; £314)

Form RPR
P3/- **1** **Wester Ross (IRE)**52 5315 9-11-9 **105**........................(v) AdamWedge(3) 124+
(Evan Williams) *hld up: hdwy after 7th: trckd ldrs 9th: rdn in cl 3rd after 3 out: chal next: led jst bef last: kpt on wl to assert run-in: rdn out* **8/1**
26/- **2** 4 ½ **Bennys Quest (IRE)**39 5571 10-11-5 **101**.................(tp) PeterCarberry(3) 116
(Andy Hobbs) *in tch: trckd ldrs 8th: led after 3 out: rdn and hdd bef last: kpt on same pce* **7/1**3
323- **3** 4 ½ **Chestnut Ben (IRE)**14 426 8-11-0 **93**..............................(v1) APMcCoy 103
(Gary Brown) *trckd ldrs: pushed along after 8th: led 4 out: rdn and hdd after 3 out: kpt on same pce fr next* **4/1**1
5/0- **4** 4 ½ **Russian Conquest**27 175 7-11-0 **93**.......................(v) AndrewThornton 98
(Seamus Mullins) *nt a fluent: towards rr: hit 2nd: plenty to do 8th: hdwy after 4 out: styd on fr next: wnt 4th bef last: nvr rching ldrs* **16/1**
3/0- **5** 15 **Lucy's Legend (IRE)**24 236 7-11-10 **103**..................(tp) PaddyBrennan 98
(Paul Henderson) *hld up: hdwy 7th: trckd ldrs 9th: rdn after 4 out: sn outpcd: wknd between last 2* **4/1**1
2/6- **6** 7 **Health Is Wealth (IRE)**24 245 8-11-9 **102**................(p) BrendanPowell 85
(Colin Tizzard) *chsd ldrs tl rdn after 8th: sn btn* **10/1**
/64- **7** 9 **Mister Wiseman**18 378 11-10-5 **87**...........................(tp) MarkQuinlan(3) 61
(Nigel Hawke) *led tl 3rd: pressed ldr tl rdn after 9th: wknd after 4 out* **20/1**
4/0- **8** 1 ¾ **Petie McSweetie (IRE)**7 540 6-10-6 **85**.........(bt1) AndrewGlassonbury 57
(Richard Woollacott) *nvr fluent: a in rr* **16/1**
03U- **9** 1 **Party Pictures (IRE)**16 413 10-11-8 **101**.......................... WillKennedy 76
(Miss Jessica Westwood) *prom: led 3rd tl blnd bdly 4 out: sn wknd* **25/1**
/03- **10** 108 **Maizy Missile (IRE)**18 377 11-10-8 **87**........................... PaulMoloney
(Mary Evans) *hld up: pushed along after 6th: t.o fr bef 4 out* **16/1**
2/2- **F** **Benny The Swinger (IRE)**21 308 8-11-3 **96**.................. TomCannon
(Chris Gordon) *hld up: fell 5th* **5/1**2
3m 57.9s (-8.60) **Going Correction** -0.50s/f (Good) **11 Ran SP% 115.6**
Speed ratings: **100,97,95,93,86 83,79,78,77,**
toteswingers 1&2 £11.00, 2&3 £5.70, 1&3 £6.70 CSF £62.59 CT £258.71 TOTE £10.80: £3.00, £2.20, £1.50; EX 107.20 Trifecta £666.20 Pool: £1109.71 - 1.24 winning units..
Owner T Hywel Jones **Bred** Farmers Hill Stud **Trained** Llancarfan, Vale Of Glamorgan

FOCUS
A moderate contest which the majority of the runners came into after a below-par effort. There was a good gallop from the start. The winner should still be competitive off his revised mark.

633 SIS FIRST FOR LATIN AMERICAN RACING NOVICES' HURDLE (10 hdls) 2m 6f
3:20 (3:22) (Class 4) 4-Y-0+ **£3,508** (£1,030; £515; £257)

Form RPR
1/3- **1** **Otto The Great (FR)**24 233 5-10-12 119.............................. APMcCoy 128+
(Nicky Henderson) *led tl 3rd: trckd ldr: shkn up to ld 2 out: styd on wl to assert bef last* **11/8**2
P10/ **2** 5 **No Loose Change (IRE)**38 6 8-10-12 0......................(t) DarylJacob 124
(Paul Nicholls) *w ldr: led 3rd: drew wl clr w wnr fr rest of field after 6th: rdn and hdd 2 out: sn hld: kpt on same pce* **1/1**1
0/1- **3** 49 **Titch Strider (IRE)**22 295 8-10-12 95............................ ConorO'Farrell 79
(John Panvert) *hld up in chsng gp: no ch fr after 6th: wnt modest 3rd after 3 out: t.o* **7/1**3
P/6- **4** 16 **Actodos (IRE)**17 390 9-10-9 0.................................... MichealNolan(3) 65
(Richard Woollacott) *chsd clr ldrs: no ch fr after 6th: lost modest 3rd after 3 out: t.o* **66/1**
0- **5** 25 **Captain Jinx (IRE)**24 250 6-10-12 0.............................. HaddenFrost 43
(Carroll Gray) *racd in 4th: no ch fr after 6th: t.o* **150/1**
0/6- **P** **Carolingian (USA)**29 155 4-10-8 69.............................. JimmyMcCarthy
(Michael Blanshard) *in chsng gp: no ch fr after 6th: t.o whn p.u after 3 out: b.b.v* **100/1**
P **Dartbridge (IRE)** 7-10-5 0... TommyPhelan
(Mark Gillard) *reluctant to go to s: a last in chsng gp: no ch fr after 6th: t.o whn p.u after 3 out* **50/1**
5m 4.5s (-15.70) **Going Correction** -0.50s/f (Good)
WFA 4 from 5yo+ 18lb **7 Ran SP% 109.7**
Speed ratings (Par 105): **108,106,88,82,73 ,**
toteswingers 1&2 £1.02, 2&3 £1.50, 1&3 £1.60 CSF £2.93 TOTE £2.30: £1.10, £1.20; EX 3.30 Trifecta £4.70 Pool: £2431.51 - 380.35 winning units..
Owner Mr And Mrs J D Cotton **Bred** John Dawson Cotton **Trained** Upper Lambourn, Berks

FOCUS
Most of these made no obvious appeal on what they'd done in the past, and the two market leaders dominated throughout. The winner is rated to his best but the second was 20lb+ off his April chase win.

634 VISIT NEWTON ABBOT RACECOURSE ON TWITTER NOVICES' CHASE (13 fncs) 2m 110y
3:50 (3:50) (Class 3) 5-Y-0+ **£7,596** (£2,244; £1,122; £561; £280)

Form RPR
0/0- **1** **Baby Mix (FR)**25 216 5-10-12 0.. NoelFehily 132+
(Tom George) *disp ld tl after 3rd: trckd ldr: led 4 out: r.o wl: rdn out* **13/8**1
233/ **2** 4 ½ **Highway Code (USA)**145 3602 7-10-12 124............... RichardJohnson 128+
(Richard Lee) *trckd ldng pair: hit 4 out: sn rdn: chsd wnr bef 2 out: styd on but a being hld* **3/1**2
5/U- **3** 11 **Lemon Drop Red (USA)**24 234 5-10-12 0................(p) LiamTreadwell 116
(Paul Webber) *in tch: rdn to chse ldng trio after 4 out: chal fr 3rd after next: awkward last: styd on same pce* **9/2**3
046/ **4** ¾ **De Faoithesdream (IRE)**53 5284 7-10-12 0..................... PaulMoloney 114
(Evan Williams) *led: j.rt at times: hdd 4 out: sn rdn: lost 2nd after 3 out: styd on same pce fr next: lost 4th run-in* **9/2**3
5/6- **5** 13 **Next Oasis (IRE)**24 235 7-10-12 0.................................... TomO'Brien 101
(Paul Henderson) *chsd ldrs tl 8th: wknd 4 out* **40/1**
0/ **6** 8 **Redlynch Rock (IRE)**17 5-10-12 0.......................(t) AndrewGlassonbury 93
(Bob Buckler) *nt fluent 1st: j.rt: a in last trio: lost tch fr 8th* **66/1**
3/4- **7** 8 **Midnight Lira**15 421 6-10-5 0.. IanPopham 78
(Caroline Keevil) *a in last trio: lost tch fr 8th* **16/1**
/50- **8** 24 **Amen (IRE)**10 488 5-10-12 0... JamieMoore 61
(Gary Moore) *a in last trio: lost tch fr 8th: t.o* **33/1**
3m 53.3s (-13.20) **Going Correction** -0.50s/f (Good) **8 Ran SP% 112.2**
Speed ratings: **111,108,103,103,97 93,89,78**
toteswingers 1&2 £1.90, 2&3 £3.40, 1&3 £2.80 CSF £6.76 TOTE £2.40: £1.20, £1.60, £1.30; EX 7.00 Trifecta £22.50 Pool: £2415.06 - 80.20 winning units..
Owner Gdm Partnership **Bred** Henrietta Charlet & Danny Charlesworth **Trained** Slad, Gloucs

FOCUS
This looked a decent contest and it produced a classy chasing newcomer. Baby Mix was 7lb off his hurdles best and can probably match that rating over fences.

635 NEWTONABBOTRACING.COM H'CAP HURDLE (8 hdls) 2m 1f
4:20 (4:20) (Class 5) (0-95,93) 4-Y-0+ **£2,463** (£718; £359)

Form RPR
00/- **1** **Planetoid (IRE)**169 3127 5-11-4 **85**.. APMcCoy 102+
(Jim Best) *in tch: tk clsr order 5th: led after 3 out: wnt lft and pckd 2 out: sn clr: easily* **5/6**1
50/- **2** 5 **Dalrymple (IRE)**62 5142 7-10-7 **79**...............................(t) CharlieWallis(5) 86
(Nick Ayliffe) *in tch: rdn and ev ch briefly after 3 out: kpt chsng wnr fr next but a being comf hld* **40/1**
0/6- **3** 1 ¼ **First Morning (IRE)**7 536 8-11-12 **93**......................(tp) DougieCostello 98
(Michael Blake) *hld up towards rr: pushed along bef 3 out: rdn and hdwy bef 2 out: styd on to go 3rd at the last* **14/1**
P/4- **4** 9 **Drawn Free (IRE)**24 243 5-11-1 **82**................................ BrendanPowell 79
(Colin Tizzard) *mid-div: hdwy 3 out: sn rdn to chse ldng pair: fading whn lost 3rd at the last* **4/1**2
560/ **5** 1 **Rolanta (FR)**247 1701 8-11-1 **82**.. HaddenFrost 78
(James Frost) *hld up towards rr: tk clsr order 3 out: sn one pce* **25/1**
/40- **6** ½ **Shinko Moon**14 436 6-11-5 **86**..................................(t) SamTwiston-Davies 82
(Jamie Snowden) *trckd ldrs: rdn after 3 out: sn outpcd* **14/1**
6/0- **7** 9 **Kruseman**36 42 6-11-9 **90**...............................(b1) AndrewGlassonbury 77
(Richard Woollacott) *led: rdn and hdd after 5th: wknd bef 2 out* **14/1**
6/P- **8** 5 **Cnoc Moy (IRE)**22 293 9-10-10 **80**.............................(t) MarkQuinlan(3) 65
(Helen Rees) *trckd ldr: led after 5th: rdn and hdd after 3 out: wknd next* **20/1**
00P/ **P** **Harting Hill**53 5290 8-11-8 **89**...(t) WillKennedy
(Violet M Jordan) *a towards rr: losing tch whn p.u bef 2 out* **66/1**
40/- **P** **Antonius Lad (IRE)**249 1677 6-11-5 **86**............................ PaulMoloney
(Paul Webber) *mid-div tl 5th where jinked rt: sn t.o: p.u after 3 out* **10/1**3
3/0- **P** **Jambobo**16 407 4-11-1 **85**...(tp) JamesDavies
(Chris Down) *mid-div: rdn after 3 out: sn wknd: p.u bef next* **40/1**
3m 55.6s (-10.10) **Going Correction** -0.50s/f (Good)
WFA 4 from 5yo+ 17lb **11 Ran SP% 118.6**
Speed ratings (Par 103): **103,100,100,95,95 95,90,88, ,**
toteswingers 1&2 £12.30, 2&3 £28.60, 1&3 £4.90 CSF £47.95 CT £316.16 TOTE £2.10: £1.90, £8.50, £1.50; EX 47.30 Trifecta £640.30 Pool: £2315.97 - 2.71 winning units..
Owner Planetoid Partnership **Bred** Bjorn Nielsen **Trained** Lewes, E Sussex

FOCUS
A moderate contest, but a couple of runners looked potential improvers off their current marks. The winner was well backed and won easily on his handicap debut. He has the potential to rate a lot higher on his Flat form.

636 SIS LIVE H'CAP CHASE (16 fncs) 2m 5f 110y
4:50 (4:50) (Class 4) (0-115,115) 5-Y-0+ **£4,288** (£1,259; £629; £314)

Form RPR
1/1- **1** **Lough Derg Way (IRE)**27 179 7-11-9 **112**.................... BrendanPowell 122+
(Jamie Snowden) *trckd ldrs: led appr 2 out: pushed clr between last 2: comf* **4/1**2
332/ **2** 8 **Inishrush (IRE)**318 1034 12-10-10 **106**..........................(tp) MrWPotter(7) 107
(Bill Turner) *led: rdn after 4 out: hdd bef 2 out: sn hld: styd on same pce* **20/1**
/33- **3** 2 ½ **Sound Stage**7 542 10-11-7 **110**...(p) IanPopham 107
(Caroline Keevil) *trckd ldr: rdn after 4 out: styd on same pce fr next* **10/1**3
F/5- **4** 5 **Aikideau (FR)**25 217 6-11-12 **115**...................................(p) DarylJacob 109
(Paul Nicholls) *trckd ldrs: chalng whn nt fluent 4 out: rdn in 4th whn short of room sn after: 3rd whn rchd for 2 out: wknd last* **5/2**1
/06- **5** 30 **Sadler's Star (GER)**24 238 10-11-4 **107**........................(p) TomCannon 74
(Michael Blake) *trckd ldr tl pushed along after 10th: wknd 3 out: t.o* **25/1**
P/1- **U** **Noble Chic**27 178 8-10-11 **100**... HaddenFrost
(James Frost) *hld up: bdly hmpd and uns rdr 3rd* **10/1**3
0/3- **F** **Amuse Me**27 175 7-11-4 **107**.. APMcCoy
(Jonjo O'Neill) *trcking ldrs whn fell 3rd* **5/2**1
441/ **P** **Minella Ranger (IRE)**67 5024 7-10-8 **97**............................. TomO'Brien
(Paul Henderson) *nt fluent 2nd: hmpd 3rd: sn detached: t.o fr 9th: p.u after next* **12/1**
5m 7.4s (-14.00) **Going Correction** -0.50s/f (Good) **8 Ran SP% 111.6**
Speed ratings: **105,102,101,99,88 , ,**
toteswingers 1&2 £8.70, 2&3 £10.00, 1&3 £7.20 CSF £64.71 CT £728.29 TOTE £4.00: £1.60, £4.40, £2.60; EX 52.40 Trifecta £282.30 Pool: £893.87 - 2.37 winning units..
Owner The Folly Partnership **Bred** David And Ann Mooney **Trained** Lambourn, Berks
■ Stewards' Enquiry : Mr W Potter three-day ban: careless riding (24, 30, July, 29 Aug)

FOCUS
A decent contest for the level. The winner built on his recent chase win and looks to have more to come.

637 AT THE RACES SKY 415 H'CAP HURDLE (10 hdls) 2m 6f
5:20 (5:20) (Class 5) (0-95,95) 4-Y-0+ **£2,463** (£718; £359)

Form RPR
640/ **1** **Western Kate (IRE)**37 29 6-11-3 **93**............................ MrTomFlint(7) 95
(John Flint) *in tch: jnd ldrs after 6th: led next: rdn and hdd after 3 out: hld in 2nd whn lft in ld and hmpd 2 out: styd on: drvn out: lucky* **8/1**
/4F- **2** 2 ¾ **Blue Signal (IRE)**27 175 8-11-7 **90**..................................... LiamHeard 88
(Colin Heard) *hld up towards rr: hdwy after 7th: rdn to chse ldrs after 3 out: lft 2nd next: styd on same pce* **25/1**
P/0- **3** 6 **The Wee Midget**12 460 8-11-9 **92**...........................(p) RichardJohnson 84
(Arthur Whiting) *led tl after 6th: rdn to chse ldrs after next: styng on at same pce whn lft 3rd 2 out* **9/2**1
644/ **4** ¾ **Ladyvie (FR)**237 1800 6-11-3 **93**...............................(tp) FrancisHayes(7) 86
(David Pipe) *mid-div: pushed along and hdwy 7th: sn drvn: styng on at same pce whn lft 4th 2 out* **7/1**3
6/0- **5** 1 ¾ **Jigsaw Financial (IRE)**8 522 7-10-7 **76**...................... DougieCostello 66
(Laura Young) *hld up towards rr: hdwy after 3 out: sn rdn: styd on same pce fr next* **16/1**
6 7 **Vote For Doodle (IRE)**737 8-11-10 **93**...............................(p) DPFahy 77
(Liam Corcoran) *mid-div: rdn after 3 out: nvr threatened ldrs* **25/1**
/0P- **7** 1 ¾ **I Can Run Can You (IRE)**11 478 7-11-7 **90**...................... APMcCoy 74
(Jonjo O'Neill) *mid-div: hdwy after 6th to trck ldrs: rdn in 3rd after 3 out: wknd bef next* **9/1**
4/6- **8** 3 **Paupers Present (IRE)**27 193 5-11-7 **90**........................ IanPopham 69
(Jeremy Scott) *hld up towards rr on outer: rdn after 7th: nvr any imp on ldrs* **12/1**
000/ **9** 19 **Iron Duke**30 4614 7-11-2 **85**...(bt) DarylJacob 47
(Liam Corcoran) *mid-div: rdn after 3 out: sn wknd: t.o* **25/1**

The Form Book Jumps, Raceform Ltd, Compton, RG20 6NL.

540/ **10** *46* **Miss Tinks**[64] 5106 7-10-13 **85**........................ MichealNolan(3) 6
(Richard Woollacott) *mid-div: mstke 7th: sn wknd: t.o* **25/1**

0/0- **11** *2 ½* **Black Phantom (IRE)**[22] 295 7-10-6 **82**........................(b) JakeHodson(7)
(Mark Gillard) *mid-div tl after 6th: sn t.o* **8/1**

053/ **F** **Orion Express**[43] 5471 12-11-7 **95**........................ MissLucyGardner(5) 103+
(Sue Gardner) *hld up in mid-div: hdwy 7th: led after 3 out: drawing clr and wl in command whn fell 2 out: fatally injured* **5/1**[2]

6PP/ **F** **Wadham Hill**[607] 1893 11-10-6 **82**........................ ChrisDavies(7)
(William Reed) *hld up towards rr: fell 5th* **66/1**

0- **U** **Patricktom Boru (IRE)**[7] 540 6-11-9 **92**.............. AndrewGlassonbury
(Laura Young) *blnd and uns rdr 1st* **20/1**

6/0- **P** **Maison Royale**[33] 99 5-11-4 **87**........................(b1) ConorO'Farrell
(Seamus Durack) *trckd ldr: led 6th tl next: sn rdn: wknd next: p.u bef 2 out* **25/1**

060/ **P** **Mon Reve**[47] 5374 5-10-10 **79**........................ WillKennedy
(Violet M Jordan) *a towards rr: rdn after 7th: t.o whn p.u bef 2 out* **25/1**

5m 14.4s (-5.80) **Going Correction** -0.50s/f (Good) **16** Ran SP% **122.5**
Speed ratings (Par 103): **90,89,86,86,85 83,82,81,74,58 57,,,,**
toteswingers 1&2 £30.40, 2&3 £26.60, 1&3 £9.10 CSF £195.42 CT £1022.64 TOTE £9.00: £1.70, £5.50, £1.60, £2.30; EX 156.70 Trifecta £649.50 Part won. Pool: £866.12 - 0.14 winning units..
Owner Rory Stafford **Bred** Gregg Stafford **Trained** Kenfig Hill, Bridgend

FOCUS
The whole complexion of this race changed at the second-last when clear leader Orion Express took a heavy-looking fall. The fortunate winner is rated to his C&D winning mark.
T/Plt: £25.60 to a £1 stake. Pool of £65514.50 - 1863.97 winning tickets. T/Qpdt: £7.50 to a £1 stake. Pool of £4995.88 - 489.87 winning tickets. TM

[477] FFOS LAS (L-H)
Thursday, June 6

OFFICIAL GOING: Good (good to firm in places; 7.8)
Wind: moderate across Weather: sunny spells

638 32RED.COM NOVICES' HURDLE (11 hdls) 2m 6f
2:20 (2:20) (Class 4) 4-Y-0+ **£3,119** (£915; £457; £228)

Form RPR

/21- **1** **Captain Kelly (IRE)**[28] 189 6-11-5 120........................(t) DarylJacob 126+
(Paul Nicholls) *cl up: dived at 7th: led 3 out where nt fluent: drvn between last 2: styd on to draw away flat* **11/10**[1]

0/4- **2** *7* **Moon Devil (IRE)**[21] 337 6-10-12 0........................(p) TomO'Brien 111
(Peter Bowen) *led: pushed along after 8th: hdd next: drvn 2 out: hld in 2nd whn hit last: one pce* **7/1**[3]

/20- **3** *2* **Scoter Fontaine (FR)**[20] 358 7-11-5 122........................(tp) APMcCoy 117
(Rebecca Curtis) *chsd ldng pair: nt fluent 6th: rdn whn pckd 3 out: disp 2nd appr last: no ex flat* **7/4**[2]

3/2- **4** *4* **Never Says Never**[13] 458 5-10-12 0.................. AndrewGlassonbury 106
(Bob Buckler) *hld up in rr: clsd and wl in tch after 5th: mstke 7th: rdn whn j.lft 2 out: sn wknd* **8/1**

P **Horny Devil** 6-10-12 0........................ DonalDevereux
(Marc Barber) *hld up towards rr: mstke and dropped to last 5th: struggling after next: t.o whn p.u bef 3 out* **66/1**

5m 29.3s (9.30) **Going Correction** +0.175s/f (Yiel) **5** Ran SP% **109.1**
Speed ratings (Par 105): **90,87,86,85,**
Tote Swinger 1&2 £25.70 CSF £8.94 TOTE £2.10: £1.10, £5.30; EX 9.60 Trifecta £21.50 Pool: £1,028.91 - 35.72 winning tickets..
Owner Donlon, Doyle, MacDonald & Webb **Bred** Joseph Murphy **Trained** Ditcheat, Somerset

FOCUS
A modest novice event. The winner was just about the form pick and is rated to his mark.

639 32RED CASINO H'CAP CHASE (17 fncs) 2m 5f
2:50 (2:50) (Class 5) (0-95,94) 5-Y-0+ **£2,144** (£629; £314; £157)

Form RPR

P/1- **1** **Forever My Friend (IRE)**[12] 478 6-11-12 **94**.................. JamieMoore 109+
(Peter Bowen) *trckd ldrs: wnt 2nd at 10th: lft in ld after 13th: jnd briefly 3 out: drawing clr whn mstke last: r.o wl* **15/8**[2]

1/3- **2** *7* **Jamesson (IRE)**[22] 303 8-11-3 **90**........................ GavinSheehan(5) 96
(Jamie Snowden) *hld up in rr: nt fluent 2nd: hdwy to trck wnr after 13th: chal briefly 3 out: swtchd lft next: kpt on same pce* **14/1**

/33- **3** *22* **Kap West (FR)**[19] 378 8-11-6 **88**........................(t) AndrewGlassonbury 75
(Laura Young) *hld up: mstke 3rd: hdwy 10th: carried wd after 13th: sn drvn: wknd 4 out: wnt mod 3rd nr fin* **9/1**

/02- **4** *¾* **Nothingbutthetruth (IRE)**[11] 485 9-11-7 **92**..........(tp) MichealNolan(3) 78
(Richard Woollacott) *trckd ldr: j.lft 7th: lost 2nd at 10th: sn rdn: mstke 13th: wknd appr 2 out: lost mod 3rd nr fin* **7/2**[3]

0/1- **P** **Mr Gee Jay**[31] 141 7-11-10 **92**........................(t) SamTwiston-Davies
(Nigel Twiston-Davies) *led: hit 9th: nt fluent after: p.u sharply and hdd after 13th: fatally injured* **7/4**[1]

5m 25.8s (-2.80) **Going Correction** -0.25s/f (Good) **5** Ran SP% **110.0**
Speed ratings: **95,92,83,83,**
Tote Swinger 1&2 £11.90 CSF £20.89 TOTE £2.40: £1.20, £2.20; EX 18.30 Trifecta £76.70 Pool: £2,321.58 - 2.48 winning tickets..
Owner Mickey Bowen **Bred** Eamon Fitzgerald **Trained** Little Newcastle, Pembrokes

FOCUS
A weak handicap, marred by the injury to Mr Gee Jay. The winner is on the upgrade.

640 32REDPOKER.COM H'CAP HURDLE (10 hdls) 2m 4f
3:25 (3:25) (Class 5) (0-95,95) 4-Y-0+ **£1,949** (£572; £286; £143)

Form RPR

203/ **1** **Man Of Leisure**[54] 5285 9-11-9 **95**........................(t) RachaelGreen(3) 112+
(Anthony Honeyball) *trckd ldrs: wnt 2nd at 7th: led gng wl 3 out: c clr appr last: easily* **5/1**

/03- **2** *12* **Gwili Spar**[12] 482 5-10-11 **80**........................(t) TomO'Brien 82
(Peter Bowen) *chsd ldrs: blnd 4th: styd wl in tch: 3rd whn hit 3 out: wnt 2nd next: one pce and no ch w easy wnr* **6/1**

441/ **3** *1* **Copper Carroll (IRE)**[235] 1859 9-10-7 **83**........................(p) AlanJohns(7) 84
(Beth Roberts) *tended to jump rt: prom: led 6th to 3 out: sn rdn: kpt on same pce* **33/1**

0/0- **4** *1 ½* **Scorer (IRE)**[28] 174 5-10-0 **69**........................(p) RichieMcLernon 69
(Jonjo O'Neill) *mid-div: clsd gng wl 7th: 5 l 4th whn nt fluent and stmbld 3 out: sn rdn: one pce after* **6/1**

521- **5** *1* **Nicky Nutjob (GER)**[8] 543 7-10-11 **87**........................(p) CiaranMckee(7) 85
(John O'Shea) *hld up towards rr: hdwy 6th: rdn and outpcd by ldrs after next: styd on u.p fr 2 out* **9/2**[3]

6/F- **6** *22* **Glenwood Present (IRE)**[23] 293 6-9-7 **69**........(t) MrJoshuaNewman(7) 47
(Bob Buckler) *hld up towards rr: gd hdwy to chse ldrs 6th: rdn appr 3 out: wknd 2 out: t.o* **25/1**

3/0- **7** *8* **Goat Castle (IRE)**[24] 267 9-11-0 **83**....................(t) SamTwiston-Davies 58
(Nigel Twiston-Davies) *hld up towards rr: rdn after 7th: passed wkng rivals but no imp on ldrs: t.o* **20/1**

000/ **8** *4* **Kilrye (IRE)**[162] 3254 6-11-4 **87**........................(p) TomScudamore 54
(David Pipe) *mid-div: mstke 1st: nt fluent next: drvn at times and nvr gng after: wknd 3 out: t.o* **7/2**[1]

052/ **9** *5* **Petrocelli**[212] 5350 6-11-2 **85**........................ AidanColeman 48
(Tim Vaughan) *mid-div: mstke 5th: hit 7th: sn shkn up and lost tch: t.o* **33/1**

0/0- **10** *3* **Tom Sang (FR)**[24] 264 6-11-1 **84**........................ IanPopham 44
(Jamie Snowden) *a towards rr: wknd after 7th: t.o* **33/1**

3/2- **11** *33* **Finmerello**[23] 293 7-11-8 **91**........................ JasonMaguire 21
(Kim Bailey) *led: hdd 6th: mstke next: wknd qckly: t.o* **4/1**[2]

F/3- **12** *½* **Majestic Bull (USA)**[28] 178 7-11-1 **89**.................. MissLucyGardner(5) 19
(Sue Gardner) *mid-div tl lost pl 4th: bhd fr next: t.o* **20/1**

/63- **13** *9* **Tarmac Girl**[12] 477 5-11-1 **84**........................ DougieCostello 6
(Tim Vaughan) *prom tl wknd after 7th: t.o* **33/1**

4m 53.9s (3.00) **Going Correction** +0.175s/f (Yiel) **13** Ran SP% **130.8**
Speed ratings (Par 103): **101,96,95,95,94 86,82,81,79,78 64,64,61**
Tote Swingers 1&2 £10.90, 2&3 £61.90, 1&3 £61.90 CSF £35.80 CT £916.23 TOTE £9.60: £2.40, £2.90, £8.70; EX 43.70 Trifecta £698.80 Part won. Pool: £931.75 - 0.16 winning tickets..
Owner Anthony Honeyball Racing Club Ltd **Bred** Mrs Nerys Dutfield **Trained** Mosterton, Dorset

FOCUS
An ordinary handicap. The easy winner is rated up a stone or or more.

641 32RED NOVICES' H'CAP CHASE (16 fncs 2 omitted) 3m
4:00 (4:00) (Class 4) (0-105,103) 5-Y-0+ **£3,768** (£1,106; £553; £276)

Form RPR

0P/ **1** **Fairwood Massini (IRE)**[68] 5020 8-11-5 **99**..............(tp) MichaelByrne(3) 110+
(Tim Vaughan) *mid-div: hdwy to trck ldr after 12th: rdn to chal 4 out: led narrowly 3 out tl nt fluent next: led last: styd on* **12/1**

/0F- **2** *2 ½* **Minella Fifty (IRE)**[18] 385 5-11-10 **101**....................(t) RichieMcLernon 110+
(Jonjo O'Neill) *led: rdn and jnd 4 out: narrowly hdd next: rallied and tk slt ld 2 out: mstke and hdd last: one pce flat* **16/1**

3/3- **3** *1 ½* **Winston Churchill (IRE)**[33] 117 7-11-5 **96**....................(t) PaulMoloney 102
(Sophie Leech) *hld up in rr: hdwy and nt fluent 9th: wnt 3rd after 12th: drvn 4 out: sn outpcd by ldng pair: styd on flat* **5/1**

1/0- **4** *nk* **Oddjob (IRE)**[33] 120 9-11-12 **103**........................ TomScudamore 109
(David Pipe) *prom: chsd ldr 6th tl after 12th: outpcd by ldng pair fr 4 out: disp 3rd last: styd on flat* **9/2**[3]

/26- **5** *6* **Flanagan (IRE)**[12] 481 9-10-13 **90**........................ DonalDevereux 91
(Peter Bowen) *chsd ldrs: mstke 6th: rdn along 9th: one pce and no imp on ldrs fr 4 out* **11/4**[1]

1/2- **6** *31* **Queen Of Mantua (IRE)**[24] 265 7-11-12 **103**.............. PaddyBrennan 75
(Fergal O'Brien) *hld up in rr: blnd 9th: wknd 4 out: t.o* **4/1**[2]

/66- **7** *18* **Supermightyfine**[16] 422 6-10-1 **78**........................(p) MarkGrant 34
(Jo Hughes) *mainly trckd ldr tl hit 6th: styd prom tl rdn and wknd after 12th: t.o* **16/1**

/55- **8** *8* **Stormyisland Ahead**[12] 481 8-11-5 **103**........................ ConorRing(7) 51
(Evan Williams) *hld up in rr: mstke 2nd: wknd after 12th: t.o* **15/2**

6/5- **P** **Isthereadifference (IRE)**[17] 408 6-11-3 **94**.............. DougieCostello
(Neil Mulholland) *prom tl mstke 2nd: styd in tch: pushed along 8th: wknd 12th: t.o whn p.u bef 2 out* **25/1**

6m 9.5s (-7.90) **Going Correction** -0.25s/f (Good) **9** Ran SP% **116.6**
Speed ratings: **103,102,101,101,99 89,83,80,**
Tote Swingers 1&2 £19.80, 2&3 £15.40, 1&3 £13.10 CSF £170.73 CT £1089.15 TOTE £15.00: £3.80, £3.40, £1.60; EX 415.40 Trifecta £1345.50 Part won. Pool: £1,794.09 - 0.30 winning tickets..
Owner Wayne Jones **Bred** T Kent **Trained** Aberthin, Vale of Glamorgan

FOCUS
Last fence in back straight omitted on both circuits. A moderate novice handicap. The winner is rated in line with the best of his Irish chase form.

642 AT THE RACES H'CAP CHASE (16 fncs 2 omitted) 3m
4:35 (4:35) (Class 3) (0-130,127) 5-Y-0+ **£6,498** (£1,908; £954; £477)

Form RPR

002/ **1** **Well Hello There (IRE)**[39] 16 7-11-5 **120**........................(t) APMcCoy 129+
(Jonjo O'Neill) *hld up in tch: clsd after 12th: chal 3 out: sn led: jnd and stmbld last: rdn to assert towards fin* **7/2**[2]

1/3- **2** *1 ¼* **Sir Mattie (IRE)**[12] 481 8-11-0 **115**........................ PaulMoloney 120
(David Rees) *hld up in rr: hdwy after 12th: trckd ldng pair 3 out: wnt 2nd after next: ev ch last: no ex towards fin* **15/2**

/11- **3** *3 ¾* **Royale Knight**[11] 495 7-10-4 **105** 7ex.................. SamTwiston-Davies 108
(Dr Richard Newland) *in tch: clsd 8th: trckd ldr 12th: led appr 4 out: jnd next: sn hdd: one pce appr last* **6/4**[1]

4/5- **4** *16* **Strumble Head (IRE)**[31] 143 8-11-2 **117**....................(p) DonalDevereux 104
(Peter Bowen) *led to 1st: trckd ldr to 12th: sn drvn along and lost tch w ldrs: plugged on: tk mod 4th nr fin* **14/1**

F64/ **5** *1* **Spock (FR)**[39] 11 8-11-7 **127**........................(p) HarryDerham(5) 113
(Paul Nicholls) *t.k.h: trckd ldrs: rdn after 4 out: wknd 2 out* **20/1**

510/ **6** *10* **Hunters Lodge (IRE)**[50] 5351 7-11-4 **126**........................(b) RyanHatch(7) 103
(Nigel Twiston-Davies) *chsd ldrs tl lost pl after 4th: rdn along fr next: sn in rr: lost tch 11th: t.o* **11/2**[3]

/26- **7** *11* **Crannaghmore Boy (IRE)**[8] 542 8-10-0 **101** oh5.........(p) JamieMoore 68
(Keith Goldsworthy) *led 1st: hit 10th: hdd appr 4 out: wknd qckly: t.o* **33/1**

3/1- **U** **Patsy Finnegan**[33] 120 11-11-5 **120**........................ WayneHutchinson
(Alan King) *hld up towards rr: 6th and in tch whn blnd and uns rdr 11th* **8/1**

6m 7.2s (-10.20) **Going Correction** -0.25s/f (Good) **8** Ran SP% **114.9**
Speed ratings: **107,106,105,100,99 96,92,**
Tote Swingers 1&2 £4.80, 2&3 £3.00, 1&3 £2.40 CSF £29.60 CT £54.29 TOTE £5.00: £2.10, £3.20, £1.10; EX 28.40 Trifecta £66.40 Pool: £2,223.84 - 25.09 winning tickets..
Owner John P McManus **Bred** Denis Noonan **Trained** Cheltenham, Gloucs

FOCUS
Last fence in back straight omitted on both circuits. A modest staying handicap. The winner was value for a bit further and is rated to his mark.

643 YOKOHAMA TYRES H'CAP HURDLE (12 hdls) 3m
5:10 (5:10) (Class 4) (0-115,115) 4-Y-0+ **£3,119** (£915; £457; £228)

Form RPR

P/3- **1** **Kanturk (IRE)**[21] 336 7-11-0 **103**........................(p) TomO'Brien 115+
(Peter Bowen) *hld up in tch: hdwy after 9th: chal 2 out: sn led: clr appr last: easily* **9/4**[1]

2/2- **2** *4 ½* **Dalavar (IRE)**[25] 237 5-11-6 **109** .... WayneHutchinson 112
(Alan King) *trckd ldr: led appr 3 out: sn jnd: hdd after 2 out: kpt on but no ch w easy wnr* **3/1**[2]

350/ **3** *26* **William Hogarth**[3] 5538 8-10-4 **98** .... RobertWilliams(5) 79
(Keith Goldsworthy) *led: hit 6th: drvn after 9th: hdd appr 3 out: sn wknd: hld on to mod 3rd* **12/1**

000/ **4** *9* **Bedouin Bay**[278] 1460 6-11-12 **115** ....(b[1]) IanPopham 88
(Kevin Bishop) *t.k.h: in tch: chsd ldrs after 9th: rdn 3 out: sn wknd: t.o* **16/1**

210/ **5** *16* **Ballybough Gorta (IRE)**[194] 2624 6-11-12 **115** .... JamieMoore 72
(Peter Bowen) *chsd ldrs: rdn 8th: mstke next: wknd appr 3 out: t.o* **5/1**[3]

01/- **P** **Call Me Sir (IRE)**[44] 5471 11-10-9 **103** .... MissLucyGardner(5)
(Sue Gardner) *hld up in rr: blnd 7th: hdwy after 9th: wknd 3 out: mod 5th whn p.u bef last: dismntd* **8/1**

35F/ **P** **Penyfan Dawn (IRE)**[39] 9-11-2 **105** .... DougieCostello
(Polly Gundry) *hld up in rr: mstke 9th: sn wknd: t.o whn p.u bef 3 out* **33/1**

P24- **P** **Grovemere (IRE)**[15] 436 8-10-9 **98** ....(tp) AlainCawley
(Debra Hamer) *in rr: rdn along fr 4th: lost tch 7th: t.o whn p.u bef 9th* **6/1**

216/ **P** **Keep Kicking (IRE)**[9] 3923 6-11-4 **107** .... RichieMcLernon
(Jonjo O'Neill) *chsd ldrs: j. slowly 4th: drvn after 8th: wknd qckly: t.o whn p.u bef 3 out* **20/1**

5m 57.2s (8.20) **Going Correction** +0.175s/f (Yiel) 9 Ran SP% **119.1**
Speed ratings (Par 105): **93,91,82,79,74** , , ,
Tote Swingers 1&2 £2.00, 2&3 £8.20, 1&3 £6.10 CSF £10.17 CT £66.64 TOTE £3.70: £1.40, £1.30, £3.30; EX 10.80 Trifecta £87.70 Pool: £2,371.78 - 20.27 winning tickets..
Owner Ashley Hart **Bred** Mrs Mary O'Connor **Trained** Little Newcastle, Pembrokes

FOCUS
A moderate handicap dominated by the first pair. A step up from the easy winner, with a personal best from the second too.

644 32RED BEST CUSTOMER SERVICE STANDARD OPEN NATIONAL HUNT FLAT RACE 2m

5:40 (5:40) (Class 6) 4-5-Y-O **£1,559** (£457; £228; £114)

Form RPR

2/1- **1** **Rolling Maul (IRE)**[31] 146 5-11-9 0 .... JamieMoore 128+
(Peter Bowen) *mainly in 2nd tl led 6f out: drew clr fnl 3f: v easily* **4/7**[1]

2/2- **2** *25* **Oscars Way (IRE)**[12] 483 5-11-2 0 .... LeightonAspell 96
(Don Cantillon) *mainly racd in 3rd tl wnt 2nd 6f out: shkn up 4f out: sn no ch w easy wnr: wknd fnl f but hld 2nd* **5/2**[2]

3 *1 ½* **Barton Heather** 4-10-6 0 ....(t) DougieCostello 84
(Neil Mulholland) *racd in last: struggling 6f out: sn rdn along: wnt mod 3rd over 2f out: styd on* **16/1**

0/3- **4** *30* **Dahteste**[25] 250 5-10-9 0 .... SamTwiston-Davies 70
(Mark Bradstock) *led at decent gallop: hdd 6f out: sn drvn: grad wknd: t.o* **7/1**[3]

3m 42.5s (-0.40) **Going Correction** +0.175s/f (Yiel)
WFA 4 from 5yo 3lb 4 Ran SP% **110.6**
Speed ratings: **108,95,94,79**
CSF £2.36 TOTE £1.50; EX 1.90 Trifecta £6.40 Pool: £916.91 - 106.25 winning tickets..
Owner Roddy Owen & Paul Fullagar **Bred** Rathmore Stud **Trained** Little Newcastle, Pembrokes

FOCUS
A weakly contested bumper, but the easy winner is improving fast and looks a smart prospect.
T/Plt: £126.40 to a £1 stake. Pool: £52,197.63 - 301.22 winning tickets. T/Qpdt: £49.00 to a £1 stake. Pool: £4,490.52 - 67.7 winning tickets. RL

585 WORCESTER (L-H)

Thursday, June 6

OFFICIAL GOING: Good (good to firm in places; 6.6)
Both bends moved out 9yds from inside line.
Wind: Almost nil Weather: Fine and sunny

645 FREE BETS GALORE AT BOOKMAKERS.CO.UK NOVICES' CHASE (15 fncs) 2m 4f

5:55 (5:55) (Class 4) 5-Y-O+ **£3,898** (£1,144; £572; £286)

Form RPR

150/ **1** **Wiffy Chatsby (IRE)**[56] 5257 6-10-12 0 ....(t) DarylJacob 128+
(Paul Nicholls) *a.p: ev ch whn lft in ld 2 out: styd on wl: comf* **5/2**[3]

0/5- **2** *9* **Special Account (IRE)**[17] 409 8-10-12 0 .... NickScholfield 116
(Jeremy Scott) *hld up: hdwy appr 4 out: lft 2nd 2 out: sn rdn: styd on same pce last* **9/4**[2]

3/3- **3** *4 ½* **Brassick**[18] 386 6-10-12 0 ....(t) NoelFehily 114
(Charlie Longsdon) *chsd ldr tl led appr 2nd: hdd 4th: chsd ldr again tl rdn and ev ch 4 out: lft 3rd 2 out: no ex last* **7/4**[1]

3/5- **4** *11* **Tea Caddy**[24] 268 7-10-5 0 .... BrendanPowell 95
(Jamie Snowden) *chsd ldrs tl rdn and wknd 2 out* **25/1**

00P/ **5** *21* **Standing Ovation (IRE)**[55] 5271 6-10-12 0 ....(t) ConorO'Farrell 83
(David Pipe) *hld up: bhd fr 6th: t.o* **20/1**

5/5- **U** **Ninfea (IRE)**[30] 166 5-10-5 0 ....(p) TommyPhelan 109
(David Bridgwater) *led tl appr 2nd: chsd ldr tl led again 4th: rdn and jnd whn blnd bdly and uns rdr 2 out* **20/1**

6/5- **U** **Bad Made (IRE)**[21] 337 5-10-12 0 .... TomMessenger 83
(David Evans) *chsd ldrs: nt fluent 3rd: mstke next: hit 10th: wknd 4 out: bhd whn blnd and uns rdr 2 out* **100/1**

4m 49.8s (-10.20) **Going Correction** -0.275s/f (Good) 7 Ran SP% **110.1**
Speed ratings: **109,105,103,99,90** ,
Tote Swingers 1&2 £1.10, 2&3 £1.20, 1&3 £1.10 CSF £7.99 TOTE £4.00: £1.60, £1.70; EX 12.50 Trifecta £16.70 Pool: £960.86 - 43.00 winning tickets..
Owner Inch Bloodstock **Bred** Miss Annette McMahon **Trained** Ditcheat, Somerset

FOCUS
Daryl Jacob and Noel Fehily both felt the ground was riding good, good to firm in places. Both bends were out 9yds from the inner line. An ordinary novice chase. The easy winner is rated to the level of his best hurdle form.

646 WIN MORE ON BETTING AT BOOKMAKERS.CO.UK H'CAP CHASE (18 fncs) 2m 7f

6:25 (6:25) (Class 4) (0-120,120) 5-Y-O+ **£4,223** (£1,240; £620; £310)

Form RPR

/01- **1** **Quel Ballistic**[8] 541 9-10-12 **106** 7ex ....(v) RichardJohnson 118+
(Peter Bowen) *chsd ldr: mstke 1st: led 4th to 8th: led 9th: drvn along after 14th: hdd and bmpd 2 out: rallied to ld last: styd on u.p* **13/8**[1]

/16- **2** *2 ½* **Handsome Buddy (IRE)**[25] 248 6-10-4 **98** ....(v) BrendanPowell 105
(Michael Gates) *hld up: hdwy appr 4 out: rdn after 2 out: styd on to go 2nd nr fin* **17/2**

/54- **3** *½* **Roses Legend**[18] 393 8-10-2 **96** .... DPFahy 102
(Reginald Brown) *chsd ldrs: rdn appr 4 out: styd on same pce flat* **8/1**

134/ **4** *5* **Priceless Art (IRE)**[361] 670 8-11-10 **118** .... NickScholfield 121+
(Anthony Honeyball) *prom: chsd wnr 12th: led and wnt lft 2 out: rdn and hdd bef last: wknd flat* **8/1**

/21- **5** *4 ½* **Whispering Jack**[12] 481 8-11-7 **120** ....(p) GavinSheehan(5) 119
(Keiran Burke) *prom: nt fluent 2nd: pushed along 6th: j. slowly 11th: rdn after 14th: sn outpcd* **7/1**[3]

2/1- **6** *3* **Noble Witness (IRE)**[24] 265 10-11-3 **111** ....(p) AdamPogson 105
(Charles Pogson) *led to 4th: chsd wnr tl led 8th: hdd next: styd on 2nd to 12th: rdn after 14th: sn outpcd* **25/1**

/31- **7** *15* **Turbo Du Ranch (FR)**[11] 504 6-11-12 **120** 7ex ....(b) NoelFehily 107
(Warren Greatrex) *hld up: drvn along 13th: sn lost tch: t.o* **11/2**[2]

3/0- **P** **Allerford Jack**[36] 63 9-11-9 **120** .... MichealNolan(3)
(Richard Woollacott) *hld up: hdwy 13th: rdn and wknd after next: t.o whn p.u bef last* **14/1**

5m 50.6s (2.60) **Going Correction** -0.275s/f (Good) 8 Ran SP% **109.2**
Speed ratings: **84,83,82,81,79 78,73,**
Tote Swingers 1&2 £7.20, 2&3 £9.30, 1&3 £2.10 CSF £14.47 CT £75.25 TOTE £2.30: £1.70, £1.70, £2.50; EX 16.20 Trifecta £81.50 Pool: £1,217.56 - 11.20 winning tickets..
Owner H Jones **Bred** Mrs B J Lockhart **Trained** Little Newcastle, Pembrokes

FOCUS
Just a modest handicap, but about as game an effort as you will see from Quel Ballistic. The winner is rated a bit better than the bare result, with the next two to their marks.

647 CLAIRE & DAVE'S 20TH ANNIVERSARY CELEBRATION STANDARD NH FLAT RACE (CONDITIONALS & AMATEURS) 2m

7:00 (7:00) (Class 6) 4-6-Y-O **£1,559** (£457; £228; £114)

Form RPR

4/0- **1** **Little Dotty**[19] 372 4-10-1 0 .... MrKevinJones(7) 85
(Giuseppe Fierro) *hld up: hdwy over 3f out: rdn to ld over 1f out: styd on gamely* **25/1**

2 *hd* **Thatchers Gold (IRE)**[54] 5-10-11 0 .... MrAlexEdwards(7) 95
(Dave Roberts) *chsd ldrs: rdn: edgd lft and ev ch fr over 2f out: styd on* **9/1**[3]

0/ **3** *6* **Imperial Legacy**[56] 5262 5-10-8 0 ....(t) JackSavage(10) 89
(Jo Davis) *prom: rdn over 5f out: sn outpcd: rallied over 3f out: styd on same pce fnl f* **50/1**

1- **4** *¾* **Are They Your Own (IRE)**[17] 412 5-11-4 0 .... NickSlatter(7) 100+
(Fergal O'Brien) *led: hung rt over 3f out: rdn over 2f out: hdd over 1f out: no ex ins fnl f* **4/1**[2]

5 *17* **Grouse Mountain (IRE)** 4-10-12 0 ....(t) KielanWoods(3) 70
(Charlie Longsdon) *hld up: hdwy over 5f out: wknd over 2f out* **7/4**[1]

P **Rubrics (IRE)** 4-11-1 0 .... HenryBrooke
(Donald McCain) *chsd ldr tl pushed along over 5f out: wknd 4f out: sn eased: p.u over 1f out* **7/4**[1]

3m 42.6s (0.90) **Going Correction** -0.275s/f (Good)
WFA 4 from 5yo 3lb 6 Ran SP% **108.5**
Speed ratings: **86,85,82,82,74**
Tote Swingers 1&2 £14.20, 2&3 £14.80, 1&3 £17.40 CSF £199.92 TOTE £22.10: £7.30, £3.60; EX 41.60 Trifecta £466.80 Pool: £830.27 - 1.33 winning tickets..
Owner G Fierro **Bred** Giuseppe Fierro **Trained** Hazelslade, Staffs
■ Giuseppe Fierro's first winner for more than six years.
■ Stewards' Enquiry : Mr Alex Edwards 12 day-ban: use of whip (21, 26 June, 2, 3, 4, 10, 14, 17, 21, 23, 26, 29 July)

FOCUS
A weak bumper, and not form to be confident about.

648 STARTIN YOUNG UNDER 17 DRIVING NOVICES' CLAIMING HURDLE (8 hdls) 2m

7:35 (7:35) (Class 5) 4-Y-O+ **£1,949** (£572; £286; £143)

Form RPR

/15- **1** **Super Collider**[12] 480 6-11-6 110 ....(bt) PaddyBrennan 108+
(Fergal O'Brien) *hld up: hdwy 4th: led after 3 out: shkn up and qcknd clr fnl 100yds* **7/4**[1]

/22- **2** *3* **Descaro (USA)**[21] 332 7-11-2 110 ....(p) RichardJohnson 98
(John O'Shea) *chsd ldrs: rdn after 5th: jnd wnr 2 out: stl ev ch u.p flat: outpcd fnl 100yds* **3/1**[2]

061- **3** *3 ¾* **Diamond Tammy (IRE)**[11] 501 7-10-9 91 .... PeterCarberry(3) 90
(Andy Hobbs) *hld up: hdwy appr 3 out: styd on to go 3rd towards fin: nt trble ldrs* **10/1**

2/0- **4** *1 ¼* **Jaja De Jau**[11] 488 4-10-6 95 ....(t) NickScholfield 83
(Anthony Honeyball) *hld up: hdwy after 3 out: rdn flat: styd on same pce* **12/1**

052/ **5** *hd* **Maraased**[274] 1494 8-10-11 0 .... MichealNolan(3) 91
(Stephen Hughes) *hld up: hdwy appr 3 out: rdn after next: no ex flat* **25/1**

/60- **6** *nk* **Naledi**[10] 253 9-10-5 70 .... ThomasGarner(5) 87
(Richard Price) *hld up: hdwy u.p appr 3 out: no ex flat* **50/1**

2/5- **7** *10* **Solo Jugadores**[31] 146 5-11-6 0 ....(t) APMcCoy 87
(Rebecca Curtis) *prom: chsd ldr 4th tl led and wnt lft 3 out: sn hdd: wknd appr last* **13/2**[3]

6/6- **8** *2 ¾* **Crescent Beach (IRE)**[11] 505 6-10-10 105 ....(t) HenryOliver 74
(Henry Oliver) *chsd ldr tl led 3rd: rdn and hdd 3 out: wknd next* **10/1**

PP6- **9** *7* **Abbi Jicaro**[9] 522 6-9-10 74 ....(t) OllieGarner(7) 60
(Mark Shears) *hld up: rdn appr 3 out: sn wknd* **100/1**

0/3- **10** *2 ¼* **Turn The Tide**[18] 391 5-10-3 80 .... GerardTumelty 58
(Natalie Lloyd-Beavis) *hld up: effrt appr 3 out: sn wknd* **33/1**

11 *8* **Bull Five**[19] 6-10-7 0 ....(p) TrevorWhelan(5) 59
(Nick Littmoden) *chsd ldrs: rdn after 5th: wknd next: t.o* **66/1**

P5P/ **P** **Yellow Duke (FR)**[159] 3334 6-11-6 0 ....(p) AdamPogson
(Charles Pogson) *led to 3rd: rdn and wknd 5th: t.o whn p.u bef 3 out* **20/1**

3m 43.2s (-4.10) **Going Correction** -0.275s/f (Good)
WFA 4 from 5yo+ 17lb 12 Ran SP% **116.6**
Speed ratings (Par 103): **99,97,95,95,94 94,89,88,84,83 79,**
Tote Swingers 1&2 £2.00, 2&3 £4.80, 1&3 £5.80 CSF £6.35 TOTE £2.20: £1.10, £1.70, £3.80; EX 6.70 Trifecta £28.00 Pool: £943.41 - 25.18 winning tickets..There were no claims.
Owner Fergal O'Brien **Bred** Newsells Park Stud **Trained** Coln St. Dennis, Gloucs

The Form Book Jumps, Raceform Ltd, Compton, RG20 6NL.

FOCUS
The market leaders came to the fore in this steadily run claiming hurdle. The winner is rated to his mark but the form is suspect.

649 BEST HORSE RACING ODDS WITH BOOKMAKERS.CO.UK MAIDEN HURDLE (12 hdls) 2m 7f
8:05 (8:05) (Class 5) 4-Y-0+ **£1,949** (£572; £286; £143)

Form RPR
22- **1** **My Lucky Flame (IRE)**11 502 6-10-7 103 MarkGrant 108+
(Sean Curran) *a.p: pushed along appr 3 out: led next: edgd rt flat: drvn out* **5/2**2
534/ **2** *3 ¾* **Letbeso (IRE)**67 5041 5-11-0 0 (p) JamieMoore 111
(Peter Bowen) *chsd ldrs: led 3 out: hdd next: rdn and ev ch last: styd on same pce flat* **11/4**3
/33- **3** *5* **Electric Tiger (GER)**11 486 6-11-0 107 TomScudamore 107
(David Bridgwater) *chsd ldr 3rd: led 8th: j.rt next: hdd 3 out: sn rdn: styd on same pce appr last* **9/4**1
0/P- **4** *20* **West End Classic (IRE)**37 47 6-10-9 0 BenPoste(5) 88
(Tracey Watkins) *hld up: hdwy 8th: rdn appr 3 out: wknd next* **200/1**
0/P- **5** *51* **Cirrus Coin**22 317 8-11-0 0 PaulMoloney 42
(Andrew Hollinshead) *hld up: effrt 8th: wknd next: t.o* **40/1**
/P2- **6** *4 ½* **Mongress Boy (IRE)**15 435 8-11-0 106 SeanQuinlan 38
(Andy Hobbs) *led: j.rt 5th: hdd 8th: sn rdn: wknd next: t.o* **16/1**
7 *6* **Ahcomeretome (IRE)**10 8-10-7 0 MissLBrooke(7) 33
(Lady Susan Brooke) *hld up: hdwy 8th: wknd next: t.o* **100/1**
5/2- **8** *27* **Kadalkin (FR)**25 233 7-10-11 0 (t) MarkQuinlan(3) 8
(Nigel Hawke) *hld up: hdwy 7th: rdn and wknd appr 3 out: t.o* **13/2**
/30- **9** *19* **Volio Vincente (FR)**9 519 6-10-11 0 MichealNolan(3)
(Carroll Gray) *chsd ldrs: mstke 7th: wknd bef next: t.o* **125/1**
0/ **P** **I'Lldoit**38 33 6-11-0 0 AndrewTinkler
(Michael Scudamore) *a in rr: t.o whn p.u bef 3 out* **100/1**
P/0- **P** **Shadesofnavy**16 417 7-11-0 100 (p) JackDoyle
(Peter Pritchard) *w ldr tl after 2nd: rdn 4th: wknd appr 7th: t.o whn p.u bef 3 out* **50/1**
5/- **P** **Amber Beat**47 5413 6-10-4 0 JamesBest(3)
(John Spearing) *mid-div: nt fluent 3rd: sn pushed along: mstke 5th: bhd fr next: sn t.o: p.u bef 3 out* **40/1**

5m 37.1s (9.10) **Going Correction** -0.275s/f (Good) **12** Ran SP% **115.3**
Speed ratings (Par 103): **73,71,69,63,45 43,41,32,25,** ,
Tote Swingers 1&2 £2.50, 2&3 £3.10, 1&3 £1.60 CSF £9.69 TOTE £2.30: £1.20, £1.80, £1.20; EX 12.30 Trifecta £31.30 Pool: £720.26 - 17.23 winning tickets..
Owner Keith Adams **Bred** Rosemary Rooney **Trained** Hatford, Oxon

FOCUS
Moderate maiden hurdle form. The winner and third set the level.

650 NO DEPOSIT FREE BETS WITH BOOKMAKERS.CO.UK H'CAP HURDLE (10 hdls) 2m 4f
8:40 (8:40) (Class 4) (0-110,110) 4-Y-0+ **£3,119** (£915; £457; £228)

Form RPR
120/ **1** **Leath Acra Mor (IRE)**48 5386 7-11-7 110 RobertMcCarth(5) 117+
(Ian Williams) *a.p: led after 7th: hdd bef 2 out: styd on u.p to ld towards fin* **10/1**
/61- **2** *hd* **Oscar Close (IRE)**15 426 8-11-6 104 (tp) TomScudamore 110
(David Bridgwater) *hld up in tch: led appr 2 out: rdn flat: hdd towards fin* **10/1**
4/5- **3** *14* **Advisor (FR)**27 203 7-10-11 100 (b) MrTWeston(5) 93
(Martin Weston) *hld up: hdwy 7th: mstke 2 out: rdn and wknd flat* **66/1**
2/5- **4** *7* **Edgar Jones**12 482 7-11-0 98 DonalDevereux 85
(Peter Bowen) *chsd ldrs: rdn and ev ch appr 3 out: wknd bef last* **7/1**3
625/ **5** *2 ½* **Carhue Princess (IRE)**40 5567 7-10-11 95 FelixDeGiles 80
(Tom Symonds) *led tl after 1st: chsd ldrs: led again 5th: hdd after 7th: wknd appr 2 out* **14/1**
002/ **6** *4 ½* **Sahrati**239 1789 9-11-2 100 TomCannon 81
(Michael Blake) *mid-div: effrt after 7th: wknd bef 2 out* **20/1**
5/6- **7** *2 ¾* **Mangonel**24 264 9-10-8 92 (v) DarylJacob 70
(Jo Davis) *hld up: hdwy 7th: rdn and wknd bef next* **25/1**
550/ **8** *2 ¾* **The Winged Assasin (USA)**24 4223 7-11-5 103 (t) DavidEngland 79
(Shaun Lycett) *hld up: hdwy 6th: rdn and wknd 3 out* **20/1**
F/0- **9** *9* **Henry Hurst (IRE)**28 176 7-11-1 99 AndrewThornton 67
(Jimmy Fox) *chsd ldrs: rdn appr 3 out: wknd after next: t.o* **20/1**
10 *10* **Howya Buddy (IRE)**19 8-11-9 107 RichardJohnson 66
(Adrian Wintle) *led after 1st: hdd and mstke 5th: wknd 8th: t.o* **6/1**2
3/0- **11** *3 ½* **Scales (IRE)**37 42 7-10-11 98 MichealNolan(3) 54
(Richard Lee) *mstke 1st: hld up: nt fluent 3rd: hdwy appr 5th: rdn after 7th: wknd next: t.o* **20/1**
223/ **12** *1* **Wild West (IRE)**279 1437 5-11-10 108 APMcCoy 63
(Jonjo O'Neill) *hld up: mstke and hmpd 1st: nvr on terms: t.o* **6/4**1
4/4- **13** *1 ¼* **Louis Ludwig (IRE)**11 489 8-10-13 97 DPFahy 51
(Tim Vaughan) *hld up: bhd fr 4th: t.o* **33/1**
350/ **14** *37* **Hadron Collider (FR)**217 2136 8-10-0 96 DenPoste(5) 15
(Chris Nenadich) *mid-div: wknd 6th: t.o* **50/1**

4m 44.7s (-2.70) **Going Correction** -0.275s/f (Good) **14** Ran SP% **120.9**
Speed ratings (Par 105): **94,93,88,85,84 82,81,80,76,72 71,71,70,55**
Tote Swingers 1&2 £14.90, 2&3 £22.20, 1&3 £84.30 CSF £92.77 CT £6171.19 TOTE £20.90: £4.40, £2.50, £10.00; EX 138.80 Trifecta £299.80 Part won. Pool: £399.84 - 0.09 winning tickets..
Owner John O'Shea Stephen Hunt Craig Gardner **Bred** Seamus Murphy **Trained** Portway, Worcs
■ Stewards' Enquiry : Robert McCarth seven-day ban: use of whip (23, 24, 25, 26 June)

FOCUS
The front pair drew clear in what was a modest handicap. A step up from the winner under a claimer.

651 BOOKIE FREE BETS WITH BOOKMAKERS.CO.UK H'CAP HURDLE (8 hdls) 2m
9:10 (9:10) (Class 5) (0-100,100) 4-Y-0+ **£1,949** (£572; £286; £143)

Form RPR
F/3- **1** **Social Realism (IRE)**24 267 5-11-9 97 (p) APMcCoy 111+
(Jonjo O'Neill) *hld up: reminders after 2nd: hdwy 5th: led appr 3 out: shkn up flat: styd on* **4/1**2
/35- **2** *1 ½* **Green Lightning (IRE)**28 184 6-10-2 76 (b) TomMessenger 85
(Martin Weston) *a.p: chsd wnr after 3 out: styd on* **14/1**
000/ **3** *12* **Tadabeer**56 2392 5-11-0 88 (t) RichardJohnson 86
(Ian Williams) *hld up: hdwy appr 3 out: sn rdn: styd on same pce fr next* **6/4**1
226- **4** *2 ¼* **Pobs Trophy**15 429 6-10-0 79 (b) JonathanEngland(5) 77
(Richard Guest) *led: hdd appr 3 out: wkng whn j.rt last* **12/1**
PP5/ **5** *7* **Dont Take Me Alive**38 31 4-11-9 100 (bt) NoelFehily 87
(Charlie Longsdon) *mid-div: hdwy appr 3 out: rdn whn mstke next: wknd bef last* **20/1**
0/0- **6** *2 ¼* **Camera Shy (IRE)**23 290 9-9-12 75 AdamWedge(3) 63
(Kevin Morgan) *hld up: hdwy appr 3 out: wknd next* **25/1**
6/0- **7** *2* **Umustbejoking (FR)**9 521 5-11-8 99 MichealNolan(3) 85
(Michael Blake) *hld up: rdn appr 3 out: n.d* **20/1**
F/2- **8** *7* **Twyford**28 177 6-11-10 98 IanPopham 78
(William Reed) *chsd ldrs: rdn after 5th: wknd next: t.o* **8/1**3
4P0/ **9** *1 ¾* **Black Coffee**93 4578 8-11-12 100 (b) PaddyBrennan 78
(Richard Woollacott) *hld up: rdn appr 3 out: n.d: t.o* **28/1**
/43- **10** *3* **Conigre**13 459 6-11-11 99 (vt1) BrendanPowell 75
(Brendan Powell) *hld up: rdn after 5th: n.d: t.o* **25/1**
0/4- **11** *3 ¾* **Feeling (IRE)**19 376 9-10-4 81 (p) RobertDunne(3) 53
(Dai Burchell) *hld up: pushed along 4th: hdwy next: wknd bef 2 out: t.o* **20/1**
/06- **12** *10* **Ivebeenthinking**16 423 5-10-6 80 FelixDeGiles 63
(Tom Symonds) *hld up: hdwy 3 out: rdn and wknd bef next: t.o* **40/1**
P/5- **13** *30* **Umoristic (FR)**18 390 5-10-10 84 DPFahy 20
(Reginald Brown) *chsd ldrs: pushed along 4th: wknd next: t.o* **20/1**
P06/ **14** *2 ½* **Red Rosso**38 33 8-11-9 100 JamesBest(3) 34
(Rob Summers) *chsd ldrs tl wknd after 5th: t.o* **66/1**

3m 42.1s (-5.20) **Going Correction** -0.275s/f (Good)
WFA 4 from 5yo+ 17lb **14** Ran SP% **119.6**
Speed ratings (Par 103): **102,101,95,94,90 89,88,85,84,82 80,75,60,59**
Tote Swingers 1&2 £14.90, 2&3 £22.20, 1&3 £84.30 CSF £46.25 CT £121.29 TOTE £4.30: £2.00, £3.40, £1.50; EX 71.10 Trifecta £310.70 Pool: £565.65 - 1.36 winning tickets..
Owner Mrs Diane Carr **Bred** Darley **Trained** Cheltenham, Gloucs

FOCUS
With the favourite disappointing this low-grade handicap didn't take much winning, but a big step up from Social Realism and she can probably win again.
T/Plt: £675.60 to a £1 stake. Pool: £59,883.10 - 64.7 winning tickets. T/Qpdt: £253.30 to a £1 stake. Pool: £6,471.59 - 18.9 winning tickets. CR

652 - 654a (Foreign Racing) - See Raceform Interactive

390STRATFORD (L-H)
Friday, June 7

OFFICIAL GOING: Good (good to firm in places on hurdle course; 8.5)

655 TECHNICAIR AIR CONDITIONING AND VENTILATION ENGINEERS HUNTERS' CHASE (12 fncs) 2m 1f 110y
5:55 (5:57) (Class 6) 6-Y-0+ **£1,871** (£580; £290; £145)

Form RPR
61P/ **1** **Overlut (FR)**23 11-11-7 105 MissHLewis(7) 113
(S L Bevan) *prom: wnt 2nd after 2 out: rdn to ld bef last: kpt on gamely flat* **15/2**3
/23- **2** *1 ¾* **Marky Bob (IRE)**24 287 8-11-13 119 MrMatthewBarber(5) 116
(Hugo Froud) *racd keenly in ld: drvn and hdd bef last: kpt on gamely but a hld flat* **11/4**2
/42- **3** *3 ¾* **Delta Borget (FR)**10 523 8-11-3 98 MissLeandaTickle(7) 104
(L Jefford) *hld up: hdwy 7th: pressed ldng pair fr 3 out tl rdn and nt qckn fr last* **16/1**
P/2- **4** *4 ½* **Extra Bold**12 11-11-7 97 MissAGoschen(3) 100
(Miss A Goschen) *towards rr: 10 l 5th and styng on 2 out: plugged on but nvr looked like rchng ldrs* **25/1**
4/P- **5** *3 ½* **Arumun (IRE)**24 287 12-11-9 80 MissAEStirling(5) 101
(Alan Phillips) *taken down early and led rnd at s: t.k.h: prom tl 7th: rdn and wl btn 3 out* **150/1**
5/3- **6** *nse* **Kikos (FR)**22 331 11-11-3 94 MrSDavies-Thomas(7) 97
(Mrs K Lee) *t.k.h and prom: rdn bef 2 out: no rspnse: fdd between last two* **25/1**
2/1- **7** *5* **Moon Over Miami (GER)**24 287 12-11-7 123 MrDHolmes(7) 96
(D Holmes) *midfield: pushed along after 6th: no ch whn mstke 3 out* **9/1**
4/4- **8** *2 ½* **Intac (IRE)**11 11-11-7 113 (b) MrBGibbs(7) 94
(D C Gibbs) *hit 1st: sn towards rr: lost tch 9th* **40/1**
/10- **9** *1 ¼* **Himalayan Express**18 413 9-11-13 119 (p) MrJMartin(5) 97
(Mrs David Plunkett) *bhd and nt travelling: blnd 4th: drvn next: no ch after: blnd 2 out* **16/1**
P/5- **P** **Fairwood Present (IRE)**22 335 15-11-3 98 MrBFurnival(7)
(John Buxton) *j.rt in rr: struggling 7th: t.o and p.u last* **100/1**
P/2- **R** **Cedrus Libani (IRE)**22 331 12-11-3 0 MrWHickman(7)
(Mrs Libby Lawson) *v mulish at s and kpt wl away fr the rest: ref to r* **25/1**
001/ **P** **Saphir Des Bois (FR)**61 9-11-9 0 MissBAndrews(5)
(G D Hanmer) *t.k.h: mstkes in midfield: blnd 4th: rdn bef 7th: mstke next: lost tch 3 out: p.u last* **2/1**1
5/1- **P** **Rebel Alliance (IRE)**22 335 8-11-7 0 (t) AlanJohns(7)
(Richard A Thomas) *struggling fr 7th: wl bhd whn p.u 9th* **9/1**

4m 6.0s (-1.10) **Going Correction** -0.325s/f (Good) **13** Ran SP% **119.2**
Speed ratings: **89,88,86,84,83 82,80,79,79,** ,,
toteswingers 1&2 £4.80, 1&3 £14.10, 2&3 £18.30 CSF £28.02 TOTE £7.50: £3.00, £1.20, £4.10; EX 34.60 Trifecta £211.40 Pool: £436.35 - 1.54 winning tickets..
Owner S R Whistance **Bred** Dr I Claude-Meggs & F Cottin **Trained** Bridgend, Bridgend

FOCUS
One of a few hunter chases over the minimum trip through the season. They went an average gallop and it paid to race handily. The winner's best rules figure since 2009.

656 SIMS GARDEN MACHINERY NOVICES' H'CAP CHASE (14 fncs) 2m 4f
6:25 (6:26) (Class 4) (0-120,120) 5-Y-0+ **£3,898** (£1,144; £572; £286)

Form RPR
0/1- **1** **Lost Legend (IRE)**38 45 6-11-12 120 APMcCoy 137+
(Jonjo O'Neill) *cl up: nt fluent 5th: wnt 2nd at 7th: led next: looked to be gng comf: rdn after 2 out: a doing enough flat* **7/4**1
04/ **2** *1 ¾* **Acapulco Gold (IRE)**24 300 6-10-6 100 (tp) DarylJacob 113
(Paul Nolan, Ire) *trckd ldrs: nt fluent 8th: wnt 2nd 3 out: drvn and ev ch last: a jst hld flat* **7/2**3
/23- **3** *19* **Adrenalin Flight (IRE)**26 245 7-10-10 104 RyanMahon 103
(Seamus Mullins) *j. bdly lft first two: rdn and outpcd in detached last tl 2 out: styd on strly to pass four rivals after but no hope of rching ldrs* **10/3**2
/06- **4** *nk* **Captain Sully (IRE)**18 411 8-11-1 109 HaddenFrost 105
(Jim Wilson) *hld up in rr: blnd 9th: wnt 4th at 11th: flattered briefly bef 2 out: wknd appr last: lost 3rd flat* **40/1**
/61- **5** *3 ½* **Bay To Go (IRE)**22 326 7-11-5 113 AndrewTinkler 105
(Mrs H M Kemp) *hld up pressing ldrs tl rdn 10th: lft bhd fr next* **9/1**

3/4- 6 hd **Risk (IRE)**[13] 481 10-10-11 **105**.......................................(t) NickScholfield 97
(Jeremy Scott) *racd keenly: mde most tl 8th: wknd steadily fr 11th* **11/2**

0/P- 7 9 **Watch House (IRE)**[17] 420 8-9-7 **94** oh9....................... CiaranMckee(7) 80
(Michael Gates) *t.k.h early: w ldr tl mstke 7th (water): steadily lost pl: poor last 2 out* **80/1**

4m 40.5s (-9.50) **Going Correction** -0.325s/f (Good) 7 Ran SP% **110.7**
Speed ratings: **106,105,97,97,96 96,92**
toteswingers 1&2 £2.00, 1&3 £1.50, 2&3 £4.90 CSF £8.09 TOTE £2.00: £1.10, £4.80; EX 11.40 Trifecta £23.00 Pool: £680.25 - 22.10 winning tickets..
Owner Mrs Gay Smith **Bred** Highfort Stud **Trained** Cheltenham, Gloucs

FOCUS
A moderate novice handicap in which the first pair had it to themselves from two out. The winner is a much better chaser than hurdler.

657 AGA LADIES OPEN POINT-TO-POINT CHAMPIONSHIP FINAL (HUNTERS' CHASE FOR LADY RIDERS) (20 fncs) 3m 4f

6:55 (6:55) (Class 4) 5-Y-0+ **£6,239** (£1,935; £967; £484)

Form RPR

1/1- 1 **That's Rhythm (FR)**[20] 373 13-11-8 126.......................... MissPFuller(7) 119
(Miss Sally Duckett) *trckd ldrs: wnt prom 11th: tk 3 l 2nd after 2 out: chal last: rdn and led cl home: v game* **11/8**[1]

P4P/ 2 ½ **Swift Counsel (IRE)**[26] 12-11-2 0.......................... MissJCWilliams(5) 111
(Mrs D Williams) *cl up: j.lft 6th: wnt 2nd at 8th and often j. really wl: led fr 12th: rdn 3 l clr sn after 2 out: hrd pressed last: drvn and r.o gallantly but jst ct* **8/1**

1/2- 3 9 **Impact Zone**[24] 288 9-11-6 89.............................. MissJoannaMason(5) 107
(I M Mason) *towards rr: 7th and trying to improve 14th: rdn 17th: outpcd by ldng gp next: styd on again after 2 out: tk 3rd flat but unable to chal* **14/1**

1/5- 4 ¾ **Lady Myfanwy**[18] 413 12-10-11 102.............................. MissHLewis(7) 99
(Mrs Myfanwy Miles) *chsd ldrs: wnt 3rd at 15th: drvn and ev ch 3 out: 6 l 3rd and drvn sn after next: nt qckn after: lost 3rd nr fin* **14/1**

FFF/ 5 10 **Description (IRE)**[12] 11-11-7 0.. MissGAndrews 93
(Alan Hill) *led at fast pce: blnd bdly 2nd: led tl 12th: cl 2nd tl 17th: fdd steadily fr next* **4/1**[2]

216/ 6 10 **Miss Saffron**[47] 10-11-8 0.. MissLucyGardner 85
(Sue Gardner) *nt fluent 1st and 2nd: bhd: gd prog 15th: 5th and pressing ldrs briefly 17th: rdn and wknd next* **11/2**[3]

7 25 **Little Miss Monty**[11] 12-10-7 0.................................. MissRPLeyshon(7) 55
(Mrs S M Farr) *bhd: rdn and struggling 12th: bdly t.o fr 16th but fin w a flourish* **100/1**

42P/ 8 nse **Knight Blaze**[11] 6-10-7 0..(t) MissCPrichard(7) 54
(David Brace) *prom tl bmpd 6th: losing pl whn hit 9th: mstke 15th: bdly t.o fr 16th but fin w a flourish* **25/1**

024/ 9 1½ **Peplum (FR)**[12] 10-11-0 0.. MissHGrissell(7) 65
(Mrs Tina Cook) *prom tl 13th: rdn next: steadily wknd: mstke 16th: t.o* **40/1**

504/ P **Special Occasion**[26] 9-11-0 0.......................................(p) MissLGould(7)
(Miss S L Gould) *clambering over fences and sn tailed himself off: p.u after 6th* **33/1**

24P/ P **Rathcor**[48] 11-11-2 108..(p) MissAEStirling(5)
(S Rea) *bhd: mstke 2nd: struggling whn wnt wrong and p.u sharply 13th (water)* **16/1**

6m 49.6s (-13.40) **Going Correction** -0.325s/f (Good) 11 Ran SP% **118.0**
Speed ratings: **106,105,103,103,100 97,90,90,89,**
toteswingers 1&2 £5.70, 1&3 £10.30, 2&3 £0.00 CSF £13.11 TOTE £2.60: £1.40, £1.90, £3.30; EX 14.20 Trifecta £138.10 Pool: £431.01 - 2.34 winning tickets..
Owner Mr and Mrs R H F Fuller **Bred** Scea Du Haras Des Sablonets **Trained** Moreton-In-Marsh, Gloucs

FOCUS
This lady riders' final wasn't as competitive as the field size might have suggested. The winner is rated a stone+ off this season's best.

658 POINTTOPOINT.CO.UK CHAMPION NOVICES' HUNTERS' CHASE (FOR THE JOHN CORBET CUP) (20 fncs) 3m 4f

7:25 (7:26) (Class 2) 5-Y-0+

£11,992 (£3,746; £1,872; £936; £468; £236)

Form RPR

1- 1 **Harbour Court**[37] 58 7-11-10 0... MrJETudor 114+
(Alan Hill) *hld up in rr and nt a fluent: rdn after 15th: clsd on ldrs fr next: chsd ldr and travelling wl 2 out: led between last 2 and sn in command: rdn out hands and heels flat: readily* **11/8**[1]

/33- 2 4 **Hameldown Tor**[10] 523 9-11-10 99............................. MrRGHenderson 107
(E Walker) *in tch in midfield: dropped to rr and reminder after 6th: bhd and rdn bef 12th: hdwy u.p 3 out: chsd ldrs between last 2: swtchd rt and chsd wnr last: a hld but styd on wl for clr 2nd* **28/1**

1/1- 3 7 **Hawkeye Native (IRE)**[22] 329 7-11-10 0................. MrMatthewBarber 102
(M Barber) *chsd ldrs: wnt 2nd 10th tl led 14th: rdn and hdd between last 2: 3rd and no ex last: wknd but hld on for 3rd flat* **5/1**[2]

4/ 4 1¾ **Ned The Post (IRE)**[12] 9-11-10 0.. MrEBarrett 99
(E Walker) *in tch in midfield: j.rt 11th: 6th after 2 out: rdn bef last and styd on flat: no threat to wnr* **40/1**

/16- 5 nk **Findlay's Find (IRE)**[11] 7-11-10 103............................(p) MissAEStirling 100
(Mrs Myfanwy Miles) *in tch in midfield on outer: mstke and lost pl briefly 5th (water): rdn 3 out and outpcd bef next: 9th looked wl hld sn after 2 out: rallied and j.lft last: styd on flat: no threat to wnr* **11/1**[3]

5/3- 6 ½ **Chosen Milan (IRE)**[19] 6-11-3 0..(t) AlanJohns 91
(R E Luke) *in tch in midfield: hdwy to chse ldrs and travelling wl 14th: rdn and unable qck between last 2: wknd last* **20/1**

1- 7 ¾ **King Of Alcatraz (IRE)**[11] 7-11-10 0.................................. MissVWade 98
(N Harris) *t.k.h: in tch in midfield: mstke 10th and 12th: 5th and no ex whn rdn between last 2: wknd bef last* **20/1**

2/P- 8 8 **Ballyjames (IRE)**[32] 8-11-10 100... NickSlatter 90
(Miss H Brookshaw) *chsd ldrs tl 15th: rdn and lost pl bef 17th: wknd 2 out* **40/1**

2- 9 2 **Time Gentlemen**[19] 8-11-10 0... MrRJarrett 89
(G D Hanmer) *hld up in rr: rdn and effrt bef 17th: no imp 3 out: 8th and wl btn between last 2: wknd* **22/1**

PUP/ 10 1 **Books Review**[20] 9-11-10 105... MrBGibbs 88
(D C Gibbs) *in tch in midfield: mstke 9th and towards rr whn mstke 11th: rdn and struggling after 15th: wknd after 3 out* **66/1**

1- 11 6 **Adept Approach (IRE)**[22] 325 7-11-10 0............................ MrPGHall 82
(P G Hall) *hld up in rr: pushed along and hdwy on inner bef 12th: struggling and mstke 16th: wkng whn j.lft 3 out* **16/1**

243/ 12 12 **Rumbavu (IRE)**[20] 7-11-10 95....................................(b[1]) MrSWaley-Cohen 72
(Robert Waley-Cohen) *j.rt: chsd ldr tl 10th: chsd ldrs tl dropped out qckly bef 2 out: t.o* **12/1**

U/1- P **Charles Bruce (IRE)**[37] 62 10-11-10 103.................... CharlieDeutsch
(A Campbell) *led: mstke 9th: hdd and mstke 14th: lost pl after 16th: bhd 3 out: t.o whn p.u last* **12/1**

2/0- P **Bleuvito (IRE)**[19] 9-11-10 103..(v) MrWBiddick
(S Turner) *in tch in midfield tl lost pl qckly after 14th: lost tch 17th: t.o whn p.u last* **40/1**

3/0- P **Schindler's Prince (IRE)**[22] 335 8-11-10 0......................... MrJMRidley
(Mrs Christine Hardinge) *in tch in midfield: reminder after 6th: mstke 7th and 11th: rdn and struggling 15th: lost tch after next: t.o whn p.u 3 out* **80/1**

/41- P **Artic Pride (IRE)**[19] 388 9-11-10 103.. MrRSmith
(Mrs Emma Clark) *hld up in rr tl eased and p.u 5th: dismntd: p.u lame* **14/1**

6m 53.5s (-9.50) **Going Correction** -0.325s/f (Good) 16 Ran SP% **122.4**
Speed ratings: **100,98,96,96,96 96,95,93,93,92 91,87,,,**
toteswingers 1&2 £16.40, 1&3 £3.40, 2&3 £17.40 CSF £53.96 TOTE £2.30: £1.60, £7.70, £1.80; EX 69.20 Trifecta £308.90 Part won. Pool: £411.86 - 0.31 winning tickets..
Owner Andrew West **Bred** Countess Goess-Saurau & A West **Trained** Aston Rowant, Oxfordshire

FOCUS
This year's John Corbet was all about the favourite, who was so impressive on his rules debut at Cheltenham last month, and he didn't disappoint. He is rated below his recent win. It was much the slowest of the races over the trip.

659 IRISH THOROUGHBRED MARKETING H'CAP HURDLE (13 hdls) 3m 3f

7:55 (7:55) (Class 3) (0-140,134) 4-Y-0+ **£5,523** (£1,621; £810; £405)

Form RPR

/21- 1 **Sail And Return**[19] 393 9-10-10 **118**........................ SamTwiston-Davies 123+
(Phil Middleton) *hld up wl in rr: hdwy after 10th: squeezed through to go 2nd on home turn: hrd drvn after: chal last: sn led flat and qckly asserted* **10/3**[1]

5/0- 2 2¾ **Possol (FR)**[22] 336 10-11-0 **122**.. PaddyBrennan 124
(Henry Daly) *trckd ldrs gng wl: effrt bef 3 out: cajoled to ld whn mstke next: edgd lft home turn: idling in front: hdd jst after last and outbattled* **11/2**[2]

6/3- 3 5 **Ogee**[28] 205 10-11-12 **134**.. JimmyMcCarthy 132
(Renee Robeson) *prom: 3rd and rdn 3 out: 5th st: kpt on to go 3rd and mstke last: nt trble ldrs* **8/1**

P/0- 4 1¼ **Five Star Wilsham (IRE)**[21] 358 9-10-12 **120**............... NickScholfield 114
(Jeremy Scott) *chsd ldrs: drvn and outpcd 3 out: 7th st: styng on wl after last but n.d* **7/1**

65/- 5 3¼ **Lightning Strike (GER)**[131] 3900 10-11-3 **125**............(tp) LiamTreadwell 118
(Paul Webber) *cl up: wnt 2nd at 8th: led 10th: drvn and hdd 2 out: no ex bef last* **20/1**

3/2- 6 2¾ **Qualviro (FR)**[19] 393 9-10-12 **120**..................................(v) RichardJohnson 110
(Tim Vaughan) *pressed ldr: led 6th: hdd 10th: drvn next: wknd bef last* **6/1**[3]

0/4- 7 11 **Points Of View**[19] 386 8-10-11 **119**.................................(t) JasonMaguire 101
(Kim Bailey) *hld up wl in rr: rdn bef 3 out: plodded on and nvr trbld ldrs* **14/1**

1PF/ 8 18 **Helpston**[174] 3063 9-11-3 **130**.. MissGAndrews(5) 93
(Pam Sly) *midfield: 5th and rdn bef 10th: struggling fr next* **16/1**

626/ 9 28 **Our Bomber Harris**[162] 3286 9-11-4 **126**............................(p) NoelFehily 64
(Harry Fry) *in rr and u.p 3rd: nvr looked happy: struggling bef 10th* **6/1**[3]

0/0- 10 4½ **Akbabend**[21] 358 7-10-12 **120**..(t) TomCannon 54
(Chris Gordon) *led at stdy pce: hdd 6th: rdn 8th: sn dropped himself rt out: last at 10th: bdly t.o* **20/1**

6m 19.0s (-9.60) **Going Correction** -0.325s/f (Good) 10 Ran SP% **112.7**
Speed ratings (Par 107): **101,100,98,98,97 96,93,87,79,78**
toteswingers 1&2 £5.70, 1&3 £3.70, 2&3 £6.90 CSF £21.56 CT £132.10 TOTE £4.50: £2.40, £2.50, £2.50; EX 21.80 Trifecta £301.60 Part won. Pool: £402.15 - 0.94 winning tickets..
Owner P W Middleton **Bred** Andrew And Mrs S R B Davis **Trained** Dorton, Bucks
■ Stewards' Enquiry : Paddy Brennan two-day ban; careless riding (21st-23th June).

FOCUS
A fair staying handicap. The winner built on his good recent win, with the next two close to their marks.

660 W+S RECYCLING STRATFORD FOXHUNTERS CHAMPION HUNTERS' CHASE (55TH RUNNING) (20 fncs) 3m 4f

8:30 (8:30) (Class 2) 5-Y-0+

£14,990 (£4,682; £2,340; £1,170; £585; £295)

Form RPR

2FU/ 1 **Mossey Joe (IRE)**[25] 276 10-12-0 0..................................(t) MrDSkehan 159+
(D McNamara, Ire) *mde all at tremendous pce: j. soundly: clr fr 9th: 15 l ld 15th: eased but stl hacking on bridle fr 2 out: lunged through last: cruised home: most impressive* **4/1**[2]

P/1- 2 20 **Chapoturgeon (FR)**[18] 413 9-12-0 140.................................. MrJBarber 143
(R Barber) *settled towards rr: effrt into midfield 13th: wnt 3rd and hit 3 out: rdn bef 2 out where 8 l down briefly: kpt on but no ch w effrtless wnr after* **6/1**

111/ 3 4½ **Salsify (IRE)**[42] 5565 8-12-0 139.. MrCJSweeney 141
(Rodger Sweeney, Ire) *dropped out last early: hdwy 10th: 3rd at 13th: 15 l 2nd whn nt fluent 15th: rdn 3 out: got win 8 l of wnr next but sn 3rd and nt qckn after* **6/5**[1]

P1P/ 4 32 **Rosies Peacock**[11] 10-12-0 98.. MrJETudor 108
(D H Llewellyn) *chsd ldrs: wknd and j. slowly 11th: wl bhd 13th: plugged on after 2 out to go v remote 4th* **66/1**

/12- 5 3¼ **Rumbury Grey**[21] 357 10-12-0 123.. NickSlatter 107
(S Flook) *chsd ldrs: blnd 7th: dropped to rr of main bunch 13th: rdn 15th: plodded on: t.o* **16/1**

402/ 6 12 **Tammys Hill (IRE)**[66] 5116 8-12-0 126.................................. MrJJSmyth 94
(Liam Lennon, Ire) *bhd: hdwy to midfield whn mstke 13th (water): no ch after: t.o 17th* **5/1**[3]

/U2- 7 7 **Presentandcorrect (IRE)**[18] 413 12-12-0 110........................ MrMWall 88
(T F Sage) *prom: chsd long ldr 13th tl 15th: wknd 17th: t.o* **50/1**

/53- 8 1¾ **Keenan's Future (IRE)**[11] 12-12-0 100...........................(p) MissAEStirling 87
(S Rea) *swishing tail bef s: midfield early: t.o fr 15th* **150/1**

P/1- 9 26 **What A Laugh**[21] 357 8-12-0 122.. MrRJarrett 63
(G D Hanmer) *hld up and wl bhd: last at 5th: hdwy to midfield 13th: nvr nr ldrs: 25 l 4th whn blnd 2 out: eased and fin eventually* **16/1**

2/1- P **Vic Venturi (IRE)**[23] 323 13-12-0 112...............................(vt) NicodeBoinville
(S Rea) *cl up: lost pl 11th: t.o 16th: p.u next* **40/1**

The Form Book Jumps, Raceform Ltd, Compton, RG20 6NL.

1/4- P **Coombe Hill**[37] 59 12-12-0 117 .... MrDEdwards
(Miss C A Tizzard) *towards rr and sn pushed along: nvr looked hopeful: lost tch 13th: t.o 16th: p.u last* **80/1**

/U2- P **Surenaga (IRE)**[20] 373 11-12-0 121 .... (b) MrAlexEdwards
(Philip Rowley) *mstke 7th and lost tch rapidly u.p: reluctant and sn t.o: p.u 15th* **40/1**

2/1- P **Drom**[12] 496 10-12-0 104 .... MrWKitchman
(Mrs C Drury) *chsd ldr tl 13th: wknd steadily: t.o and p.u 2 out* **80/1**

6m 38.3s (-24.70) **Going Correction** -0.325s/f (Good) **13** Ran SP% **119.6**
Speed ratings: **122,116,115,105,104 101,99,99,91, , ,**
toteswingers 1&2 £19.20, 1&3 £1.90, 2&3 £2.20 CSF £28.20 TOTE £4.30: £1.90, £2.40, £1.20; EX 24.60 Trifecta £33.80 Pool: £973.72 - 21.60 winning tickets..
Owner William Clifford **Bred** W Clifford **Trained** Cratloe, Co Clare

FOCUS
This was a tremendous running of the Champion Hunters' Chase, and the impressive winner beat the course record. He's rated back to the levl of his novice form and is a potential 160+ horse. Salsify is rated 7kb off his best British figure.

661 LUXURIOUS BOUTIQUE WHITE SWAN HOTEL, STRATFORD H'CAP HURDLE (9 hdls) 2m 3f
9:00 (9:00) (Class 5) (0-95,95) 4-Y-O+ **£1,949** (£572; £286; £143)

Form RPR

/50- **1** **Brass Monkey (IRE)**[26] 253 6-10-10 79 .... NoelFehily 88+
(Charlie Longsdon) *chsd ldrs: wnt 2nd after 3 out: led 2 out: rdn and forged clr between last 2: mstke last: a jst gng to hold on* **7/1**

0/0- **2** ½ **Burns Night**[29] 184 7-10-5 77 .... JackQuinlan(3) 85+
(Noel Quinlan) *hld up in tch in rr: hdwy bef 2 out: wnt 4th and styng on bef last: chsd wnr flat: clsng qckly towards fin but nvr quite getting to wnr* **33/1**

/06- **3** 1 ¼ **Mighty Clarets (IRE)**[13] 479 6-11-6 89 .... JamieMoore 95
(Peter Bowen) *hld up wl in tch in midfield: rdn and effrt to chse wnr after 2 out: nt fluent last: kpt on same pce and lost 2nd flat* **7/1**

06/- **4** 1 ¾ **Maxdelas (FR)**[90] 4660 7-11-3 91 .... (t) JonathanEngland(5) 95
(Roy Brotherton) *travelled wl and hld up in tch in midfield: swtchd rt and hdwy between last 2 out: rdn and chsd ldrs bef last: kpt on same pce flat* **33/1**

0P/- **5** 5 **Sonofagun (FR)**[216] 2176 7-11-7 95 .... RobertMcCarth(5) 94
(Ian Williams) *hld up in tch towards rr: blnd 3rd: effrt 2 out: styng on but stl plenty to do whn j. path and stmbld bef last: kpt on flat: nvr trbld ldrs* **8/1**

6/5- **6** ½ **Crazy Bold (GER)**[26] 253 10-10-10 79 .... WayneHutchinson 78
(Tony Carroll) *hld up in tch in midfield: hdwy to chse ldrs 3 out: rdn and btn between last 2: wknd bef last* **9/2**[1]

0/P- **7** 2 ½ **Harris Garden (IRE)**[34] 122 6-11-9 95 .... (p) JakeGreenall(3) 92
(Paul Webber) *chsd ldr tl led 3 out: hdd next: wknd bef last* **14/1**

25P/ **8** 4 **Tennessee Bird**[67] 5074 5-9-11 71 .... GavinSheehan(5) 64
(Mike Sowersby) *in tch in midfield on outer: j.rt and mstke 4th: wknd u.p after 2 out* **12/1**

01U- **9** 11 **Fitandproperjob**[7] 564 7-11-8 91 .... (t) APMcCoy 74
(Anthony Middleton) *hld up in tch towards rr: hdwy after 5th: chsd ldrs after 3 out: rdn and btn sn after next: no ch and eased flat* **5/1**[2]

0P0- **10** 34 **Benefit Game (IRE)**[10] 522 9-10-9 85 .... (v[1]) MrRobertHawker(7) 38
(Richard Hawker) *hld up in tch in last quartet: rdn and struggling bef 3 out: sn wknd: t.o* **50/1**

0/0- **11** 9 **Wheelavit (IRE)**[19] 384 10-11-12 95 .... (t) NickScholfield 39
(Claire Dyson) *led: j.rt and mstke 5th: hdd 3 out: wknd bef next: t.o and eased flat* **33/1**

0/P- **12** ¾ **Rampant Ronnie (USA)**[38] 49 8-11-1 87 .... (t) RobertDunne(3) 31
(Nikki Evans) *in tch towards rr: dropped to last and struggling 6th: lost tch after next: t.o whn hmpd last* **20/1**

566/ **13** 17 **Dunraven Prince (IRE)**[20] 6-11-6 89 .... (b) TomScudamore 17
(David Brace) *chsd ldrs: losing pl and mstke 4th: sn pushed along: rdn and bhd after 6th: t.o whn hmpd last* **11/1**

P/3- **F** **Special Boru (IRE)**[24] 295 7-10-7 76 .... (t) BrendanPowell
(Sarah Kerswell) *in tch in midfield: mstke 5th: wknd qckly u.p after 2 out: wl btn whn fell last* **13/2**[3]

4m 28.3s (-3.20) **Going Correction** -0.325s/f (Good) **14** Ran SP% **122.5**
Speed ratings (Par 103): **93,92,92,91,89 89,88,86,81,67 63,63,56,**
toteswingers 1&2 £15.40, 1&3 £4.60, 2&3 £15.40 CSF £225.56 CT £1694.09 TOTE £10.30: £3.90, £7.80, £3.10; EX 418.30 Trifecta £119.20 Part won. Pool: £158.96 - 0.01 winning tickets..
Owner The Cheeky Monkeys **Bred** Oliver McDonnell **Trained** Over Norton, Oxon

FOCUS
A wide-open looking handicap. The first four were nicely clear and the winner is entitled to rate higher on bumper form.
T/Plt: £11.00 to a £1 stake. Pool £62,739.69 - 4157.49 winning tickets. T/Qpdt: £3.00 to a £1 stake. Pool £5139.40 - 1227.10 winning tickets. IM

662 - 668a (Foreign Racing) - See Raceform Interactive

[655]STRATFORD (L H)
Saturday, June 8

OFFICIAL GOING: Good to firm (good in places; 9.2)
Rails moved out from meeting the previous day.
Wind: Light behind Weather: Cloudy with sunny spells

669 WILLIAM DEAKIN TESTIMONIAL NOVICES' H'CAP HURDLE (11 hdls) 2m 6f 110y
6:15 (6:16) (Class 5) (0-100,102) 4-Y-O+ **£3,249** (£954; £477; £238)

Form RPR

3/1- **1** **Man Of Leisure**[2] 640 9-11-11 102 7ex .... (t) RachaelGreen(3) 115+
(Anthony Honeyball) *hld up in tch: racd keenly: led after 2 out: clr last: comf* **10/11**[1]

3/3- **2** 5 **Vinnie My Boy (IRE)**[12] 511 5-11-9 97 .... (tp) JamieMoore 102
(Peter Bowen) *a.p: ev ch 2 out: sn rdn: styng on same pce whn wnt 2nd last* **4/1**[2]

5/4- **3** 4 **Blackstone Vegas**[8] 561 7-11-2 90 .... (v) JamesDavies 92
(Derek Shaw) *hld up: mstke 6th: hdwy 8th: led 2 out: sn hdd: no ex whn mstke last* **25/1**

/60- **4** 11 **Chosen Dream (IRE)**[7] 590 5-10-13 87 .... (t) APMcCoy 83+
(Jonjo O'Neill) *hld up: mstke 5th: hdwy 3 out: rdn and wknd appr last* **12/1**

4/5- **5** 13 **Handford Henry (IRE)**[24] 320 7-10-11 85 .... RyanMahon 64
(Michael Appleby) *prom: tl rdn and wknd appr 2 out: t.o* **33/1**

U54/ **6** 1 **Racey Lacey**[42] 5567 6-11-11 99 .... (t) SamTwiston-Davies 81
(Nigel Twiston-Davies) *chsd ldrs: hit 5th: hmpd 7th: rdn and wknd after 2 out: t.o* **10/1**

0- **7** 1 ½ **Moyne Nineoseven (IRE)**[18] 421 7-11-9 100 .... JackQuinlan(3) 77
(Noel Quinlan) *hld up: a in rr: rdn and wknd 3 out: t.o* **33/1**

0/6- **8** 12 **Iheardu**[30] 175 7-11-0 88 .... (p) AndrewThornton 54
(Neil Mulholland) *chsd ldr: lft in ld 7th: rdn and hdd 2 out: wknd bef last: t.o* **50/1**

214/ **9** 4 **Pharaon De Touzaine (FR)**[164] 3209 10-10-9 90 .... CiaranMckee(7) 53
(John O'Shea) *hld up: a in rr: rdn and wknd after 3 out: t.o* **50/1**

5/0- **10** 48 **Fine Resolve**[25] 289 4-11-7 100 .... (p) RichardJohnson 15
(Adrian Wintle) *chsd ldrs: lft 2nd 7th: jnd ldr next: rdn after 3 out: wknd next: t.o* **50/1**

6/6- **11** 20 **Katnapping**[18] 417 5-11-12 100 .... CharliePoste 2
(Robert Waley-Cohen) *hld up: pushed along 6th: rdn and wknd 3 out: bhd whn blnd next: t.o whn mstke last* **40/1**

132- **U** **Adios Alonso (IRE)**[8] 565 7-10-12 91 .... BenPoste(5)
(Rosemary Gasson) *led tl blnd and uns rdr 7th* **8/1**[3]

5m 17.8s (-10.30) **Going Correction** -0.325s/f (Good)
WFA 4 from 5yo+ 18lb **12** Ran SP% **118.3**
Speed ratings (Par 103): **104,102,100,97,92 92,91,87,86,69 62,**
Tote Swingers: 1&2 £1.70, 2&3 £19.10, 1&3 £12.30 CSF £4.73 CT £49.42 TOTE £1.90: £1.10, £1.80, £4.90; EX 6.40 Trifecta £50.60 Pool: £619.88 - 9.17 winning units..
Owner Anthony Honeyball Racing Club Ltd **Bred** Mrs Nerys Dutfield **Trained** Mosterton, Dorset
■ Bob Lewis (25-1) was withdrawn. Rule 4 does not apply.

FOCUS
A pretty uncompetitive affair run at a sedate early pace. The easy winner was well in on his recent win and is rated to a similar level.

670 LLEWELLYN HUMPHREYS H'CAP CHASE (20 fncs) 3m 4f
6:45 (6:45) (Class 3) (0-125,120) 5-Y-**£7,596** (£2,244; £1,122; £561; £280)

Form RPR

0/2- **1** **Eleazar (GER)**[13] 487 12-11-4 112 .... (p) LeightonAspell 119
(Lucy Wadham) *hld up: hdwy 11th: outpcd 16th: rallied u.p after 2 out: styd on to ld fnl 100yds* **7/1**[3]

PP5/ **2** 2 ¾ **I Need A Hero (IRE)**[209] 2358 8-11-2 113 .... (t) JackQuinlan(3) 117
(Sarah Humphrey) *hld up: hdwy 15th: led 3 out: rdn appr last: hdd and unable qck fnl 100yds* **12/1**

2/1- **3** 20 **Full Of Joy (IRE)**[10] 542 8-11-9 117 .... (t) APMcCoy 103
(Jonjo O'Neill) *chsd ldr tl led 10th: hdd next: rdn and wknd 2 out* **9/4**[1]

122- **4** ½ **Well Mett (IRE)**[11] 518 6-11-12 120 .... (bt) PaddyBrennan 126+
(Fergal O'Brien) *led tl mstke and hdd 10th: led again next: hdd 3 out: rdn and ev ch whn slipped on landing last: nt rcvr* **9/4**[1]

131- **5** 7 **Borolee (IRE)**[6] 601 10-9-12 97 7ex .... SamanthaDrake(5) 80
(Ferdy Murphy, France) *chsd ldrs: reminder 13th: mstke 16th: hit next: sn wknd* **3/1**[2]

/30- **P** **Jonny Rye (IRE)**[6] 596 9-10-11 105 .... (p) RyanMahon
(Michael Appleby) *chsd ldrs: lost pl 11th: bhd and rdn next: hit 15th: t.o whn p.u bef 3 out* **18/1**

6m 54.7s (-8.30) **Going Correction** -0.325s/f (Good) **6** Ran SP% **112.0**
Speed ratings: **98,97,91,91,89**
Tote Swingers: 1&2 £6.10, 2&3 £4.40, 1&3 £2.80 CSF £69.67 TOTE £7.90: £2.50, £4.50; EX 92.30 Trifecta £314.80 Pool: £999.84 - 2.38 winning units..
Owner J J W Wadham **Bred** Gestut Rottgen **Trained** Newmarket, Suffolk

FOCUS
A competitive handicap with four of the six in good form coming into this, but overall the level was not that strong. It nevertheless produced a dramatic finish with Well Mett slipping at the last, allowing the winner to swoop by.

671 HOOK NORTON VETERINARY GROUP NOVICES' HURDLE (8 hdls) 2m 110y
7:15 (7:15) (Class 4) 4-Y-O+ **£3,249** (£954; £477; £238)

Form RPR

4- **1** **Odin (IRE)**[14] 477 5-10-12 0 .... LeightonAspell 108+
(Don Cantillon) *mde all: set stdy pce tl qcknd 3 out: rdn clr appr last: comf* **15/2**

2/6- **2** 6 **Imperial Stargazer**[27] 240 4-10-9 104 .... MarcGoldstein 99
(Sheena West) *chsd ldrs: rdn after 2 out: styd on same pce: wnt 2nd last* **16/1**

5/ **3** 6 **Incendo**[16] 1688 7-10-12 0 .... (t) APMcCoy 101+
(Ian Williams) *prom: racd keenly: chsd wnr 5th: ev ch whn mstke 2 out: wkng whn blnd last* **9/4**[1]

6/1- **4** ½ **Four Nations (USA)**[27] 240 5-11-5 0 .... (b) AndrewTinkler 103
(George Baker) *prom: rdn 2 out: wknd appr last* **5/1**

5/4- **5** 11 **Palus San Marco (IRE)**[14] 475 4-10-9 107 .... WayneHutchinson 83
(Graeme McPherson) *chsd ldrs: hit 3rd: rdn and wknd 2 out* **9/2**[3]

6 22 **Gravitate**[51] 4-10-9 0 .... DenisO'Regan 63
(Paul Webber) *chsd wnr to 5th: rdn and wknd appr 2 out: t.o* **7/2**[2]

0/5- **7** 3 ½ **Divine Folly (IRE)**[21] 374 8-10-12 0 .... DavidBass 63
(Lawney Hill) *hld up: bhd fr 5th: t.o* **20/1**

50/- **8** 2 **My Manikato**[56] 5281 6-10-12 0 .... RichardJohnson 62
(Richard Phillips) *hld up: bhd fr 5th: t.o* **33/1**

9 2 ½ **Anrheg**[24] 5-10-2 0 .... RobertDunne(3) 52
(Dai Burchell) *hld up: mstke 2nd: hdwy 5th: rdn and wknd appr 2 out: t.o* **100/1**

00/- **10** 2 ¼ **Elixir Du Lac**[53] 5333 6-10-5 0 .... SamTwiston-Davies 50
(Jo Davis) *hld up: blnd 3rd: j.rt next: sn wknd: t.o* **66/1**

0/4- **11** nk **Hubood**[20] 383 5-10-5 0 .... DaveCrosse 50
(Zoe Davison) *hld up: mstke 4th: bhd fr next: t.o* **100/1**

12 38 **Kims Firebud** 6-10-12 0 .... DPFahy 23
(Dai Burchell) *hld up: hmpd 1st: bhd fr 5th: t.o* **100/1**

U- **13** 3 ¼ **Plus Fours (USA)**[6] 593 4-10-9 0 .... [1] RyanMahon 17
(Michael Appleby) *hld up: j.rt 1st: bhd fr 5th: t.o* **66/1**

F **Wigsy (IRE)** 4-10-9 0 .... JamesDavies
(Gary Brown) *hld up: a in rr: bhd fr 5th: t.o whn fell last* **50/1**

3m 52.4s (-3.60) **Going Correction** -0.325s/f (Good)
WFA 4 from 5yo+ 17lb **14** Ran SP% **121.1**
Speed ratings (Par 105): **95,92,89,89,83 73,71,71,69,68 68,50,49,**
Tote Swingers: 1&2 £15.50, 2&3 £8.40, 1&3 £4.80 CSF £109.50 TOTE £10.70: £2.60, £5.20, £1.70; EX 89.50 Trifecta £545.90 Part won. Pool: £727.91 - 0.30 winning units..
Owner Mrs Catherine Reed **Bred** Littleton Stud **Trained** Newmarket, Suffolk

FOCUS
A reasonable contest featuring some fair ex-Flat racers. It was steadily run and the winner produced a big step up.

672 LIMERICK WARWICKSHIRE HOUND H'CAP CHASE (FOR THE GAMBLING PRINCE TROPHY) (15 fncs) 2m 5f 110y
7:45 (7:45) (Class 2) (0-145,145) 5-Y-0+

£11,573 (£3,418; £1,709; £854; £427; £214)

Form RPR
P/5- **1** **The Disengager (IRE)**[29] 204 9-11-6 **139** .... RichardJohnson 153+
(Philip Hobbs) *led to 3 out: led again next: rdn appr last: styd on u.p* **9/2**[1]
341- **2** *4* **Pure Faith (IRE)**[7] 587 9-10-13 **132** .... TomO'Brien 140+
(Peter Bowen) *chsd ldrs: outpcd 12th: rallied appr last: r.o: nt rch wnr* **9/2**[1]
P/1- **3** *5* **Prolinx (IRE)**[25] 286 8-10-6 **130** .... GavinSheehan(5) 132
(Charlie Mann) *hld up: hdwy 10th: rdn whn lft 2nd last: no ex flat* **10/1**
/23- **4** *nk* **Rajnagan (IRE)**[27] 249 9-11-4 **137** ....(t) DenisO'Regan 140
(Paul Webber) *hld up: hdwy 12th: 2 l down whn mstke last: no ex flat* **7/1**[3]
143/ **5** *7* **Cootehill (IRE)**[41] 11 9-10-11 **130** .... SamTwiston-Davies 126
(Nigel Twiston-Davies) *hld up: drvn along 12th: nvr on terms* **16/1**
U/1- **6** *2 ½* **Hell's Bay (FR)**[17] 432 11-11-0 **133** ....(p) NickScholfield 129
(Keiran Burke) *hld up: nt a fluent: bhd fr 7th* **5/1**[2]
F/1- **7** *11* **Rebel Du Maquis (FR)**[38] 63 8-10-12 **136** .... HarryDerham(5) 121
(Paul Nicholls) *chsd wnr to 3rd: remained handy tl rdn and wknd appr 2 out* **8/1**
/50- **P** **Passato (GER)**[20] 392 9-10-11 **130** ....(vt[1]) WayneHutchinson
(Jo Davis) *chsd ldrs tl rdn and wknd after 9th: t.o whn p.u bef 3 out* **22/1**
/31- **U** **Gentleman Anshan (IRE)**[20] 392 9-10-10 **134** .... BenPoste(5)
(Rosemary Gasson) *prom: disputing 4 l 5th whn blnd and uns rdr 11th* **7/1**[3]
/11- **U** **Anquetta (IRE)**[11] 520 9-11-12 **145** .... DavidBass 147
(Nicky Henderson) *prom: chsd ldr 3rd tl led 3 out: hdd next: rdn and stl ev ch whn blnd and uns rdr last* **14/1**

5m 2.9s (-12.10) **Going Correction** -0.325s/f (Good) **10** Ran SP% **115.1**
Speed ratings: **109,107,105,105,103 102,98,,,**
Tote Swingers: 1&2 £4.00, 2&3 £11.70, 1&3 £11.70 CSF £25.46 CT £191.57 TOTE £3.90: £1.60, £2.10, £3.50; EX 29.20 Trifecta £323.90 Pool: £621.46. - 1.43 winning units..
Owner Govier & Brown **Bred** T Groarke **Trained** Withycombe, Somerset

FOCUS
Some in-form performers in the line-up and the pace was solid. A small personal best from the winner.

673 RED HORSE RUG WASH H'CAP HURDLE (8 hdls) 2m 110y
8:15 (8:15) (Class 2) 4-Y-0+ **£11,710** (£3,459; £1,729; £865; £432)

Form RPR
0/1- **1** **Coffee (IRE)**[29] 202 6-10-3 **119** .... RichieMcLernon 128+
(Jonjo O'Neill) *chsd ldrs: rdn to ld last: r.o wl* **14/1**
1/1- **2** *2 ¼* **Sidney Melbourne (USA)**[30] 192 6-10-2 **118** ....(b) RyanMahon 124+
(Paul Nicholls) *chsd ldr tl led after 3 out: rdn: mstke and hdd last: styd on same pce* **8/1**
/23- **3** *3 ¾* **Teshali (IRE)**[18] 419 7-9-7 **116** oh6..................(t) CharlieDeutsch(7) 116
(Anthony Middleton) *hld up: hdwy 3 out: rdn appr last: styd on same pce flat* **50/1**
/53- **4** *2* **Sud Pacifique (IRE)**[16] 447 5-10-9 **125** .... JasonMaguire 123
(Donald McCain) *hld up: hdwy after 2 out: sn rdn: styd on same pce last* **12/1**
0/2- **5** *½* **Sky Khan**[22] 354 4-9-11 **119** .... JackQuinlan(3) 117+
(Noel Quinlan) *slipped s and lost many l: hdwy 3 out: nt fluent next: rdn appr last: styd on same pce* **5/2**[2]
6/P- **6** *7* **Laudatory**[37] 82 7-10-9 **125** .... AndrewTinkler 120
(Nicky Henderson) *hld up: mstke 4th: nt fluent 2 out: sn rdn: hmpd last: n.d* **14/1**
5/B- **7** *4 ½* **Changing The Guard**[16] 447 7-10-12 **135**.........(tp) ChristopherWard(7) 123
(Dr Richard Newland) *hld up: rdn after 3 out: nvr on terms* **20/1**
0/1- **8** *½* **Monte Cavallo (SAF)**[21] 369 8-10-5 **128**..................(t) PatrickCorbett(7) 115
(Rebecca Curtis) *hld up in tch: effrt appr 2 out: wknd bef last* **13/2**[3]
4/1- **9** *17* **Australia Day (IRE)**[28] 81 10-11-12 **142** .... DenisO'Regan 119
(Paul Webber) *led: j.rt: hdd after 3 out: wknd bef last* **12/1**
10/- **10** *1 ¾* **Cape Express (IRE)**[217] 2179 8-11-3 **133** .... APMcCoy 110
(Nicky Henderson) *prom: ev ch 2 out: sn rdn: wknd bef last* **9/4**[1]
561/ **F** **Screaming Brave**[344] 555 7-10-0 **116**..................(t) MarcGoldstein 111
(Sheena West) *chsd ldrs: ev ch whn mstke 2 out: sn rdn: wkng whn fell last* **66/1**

3m 46.1s (-9.90) **Going Correction** -0.325s/f (Good)
WFA 4 from 5yo+ 17lb **11** Ran SP% **120.7**
Speed ratings (Par 109): **110,108,107,106,106 102,100,100,92,91**
Tote Swingers: 1&2 £24.60, 2&3 £30.40, 1&3 £62.60 CSF £122.30 CT £5395.73 TOTE £8.50: £2.50, £2.40, £10.50; EX 82.70 Trifecta £504.80 Part won. Pool: £673.19 - 0.02 winning units..
Owner John P McManus **Bred** Ms Margaret Finn **Trained** Cheltenham, Gloucs

FOCUS
A highly competitive handicap with guaranteed pace. The third to fifth set the level.

674 LANYARD WARWICKSHIRE HOUND H'CAP CHASE (12 fncs) 2m 1f 110y
8:45 (8:45) (Class 4) (0-120,120) 5-Y-0 **£3,798** (£1,122; £561; £280; £140)

Form RPR
/12- **1** **Alwaystheoptimist**[7] 585 10-11-9 **120** .... KielanWoods(3) 126+
(Phil Middleton) *chsd ldrs: led 9th: blnd next: sn hdd: rallied to ld 2 out: rdn clr appr last: styd on wl* **10/3**[2]
/50- **2** *6* **Full Ov Beans**[27] 252 9-9-7 **94** oh7.................. CiaranMckee(7) 92
(Michael Gates) *hld up and bhd: hdwy after 2 out: wnt 2nd appr last: rdn and r.o flat: nt rch wnr* **25/1**
P55/ **3** *8* **Daneva (IRE)**[151] 3556 9-10-5 **99** ....(tp) CharliePoste 91
(Matt Sheppard) *chsd ldrs: lft in ld after 3 out: hdd next: wknd appr last* **20/1**
3/5- **4** *4 ½* **Topthorn**[19] 411 7-10-9 **103** .... SamTwiston-Davies 90
(Martin Bosley) *hld up: hdwy 3 out: rdn after next: wknd bef last* **8/1**
F/5- **5** *9* **Finch Flyer (IRE)**[21] 377 6-10-1 **95** ....(b) TommyPhelan 74
(Aytach Sadik) *hld up: hdwy 3 out: wkng whn mstke last* **40/1**
F/5- **6** *4 ½* **Fintan**[17] 432 10-11-4 **115** .... JamesBest(3) 94
(Rob Summers) *nt fluent 1st: chsd ldr next tl 8th: rdn and wknd 2 out: t.o* **12/1**
/2F- **7** *11* **Benny The Swinger (IRE)**[3] 632 8-10-2 **96** .... TomCannon 60
(Chris Gordon) *hld up: hdwy 3 out: wknd after next: t.o* **3/1**[1]
P/5- **8** *11* **Gracchus (USA)**[27] 236 7-11-11 **119** .... WayneHutchinson 73
(Tony Carroll) *chsd ldrs: rdn after 3 out: wknd after next: t.o* **6/1**[3]
0/5- **9** *5* **Up To The Mark**[36] 92 8-11-2 **110** ....(b[1]) RichardJohnson 59
(Henry Daly) *led: nt fluent 7th: drvn and hdd 9th: wknd 2 out: t.o* **3/1**[1]

4m 3.1s (-4.00) **Going Correction** -0.325s/f (Good) **9** Ran SP% **117.2**
Speed ratings: **95,92,88,86,82 80,75,71,68**
Tote Swingers: 1&2 £17.30, 2&3 £15.70, 1&3 £3.90 CSF £75.51 CT £1454.62 TOTE £3.50: £1.70, £4.20, £4.00; EX 63.90 Trifecta £274.30 Pool: £680.51 - 1.86 winning units..
Owner P W Middleton **Bred** Crandon Park Stud **Trained** Dorton, Bucks

FOCUS
Not that competitive for the grade, although the pace was sound. Arguably another step up from the winner.

675 SUPPORT HUNT STAFF BENEFIT SOCIETY MAIDEN OPEN NATIONAL HUNT FLAT RACE 2m 110y
9:15 (9:16) (Class 6) 4-6-Y-0 **£1,949** (£572; £286; £143)

Form RPR
4/ **1** **Plain Sailing (IRE)**[182] 2932 4-11-0 0.................. DenisO'Regan 106+
(John Ferguson) *hld up: hdwy over 5f out: chsd ldr over 1f out: shkn up to ld ins fnl f: r.o* **8/1**[3]
2/- **2** *3 ¼* **Clondaw Draft (IRE)**[222] 2101 5-11-3 0.................. JasonMaguire 107+
(Donald McCain) *trckd ldrs: led 2f out: sn rdn: hdd and unable qck ins fnl f* **4/6**[1]
0/4- **3** *16* **Bandol (IRE)**[27] 250 5-11-3 0.................. DougieCostello 92
(Laura Young) *hld up: hdwy over 5f out: rdn over 2f out: wknd over 1f out* **33/1**
4 *2* **Church Bray**[35] 5-11-3 0..................(t) PaddyBrennan 90
(Fergal O'Brien) *prom: chsd ldr9f out: led over 3f out: rdn and hdd 2f out: wknd over 1f out* **20/1**
5 *3 ½* **Port And Ward (IRE)** 4-10-0 0.................. CiaranMckee(7) 77
(John O'Shea) *hld up: hdwy over 1f out: nvr nrr* **50/1**
5- **6** *8* **That's Exactly (IRE)**[7] 588 4-9-11 0.................. ChrisMeehan(10) 70
(Neil Mulholland) *led after 1f: racd keenly: hung rt and hdd over 3f out: wknd wl over 1f out: t.o* **20/1**
0- **7** *8* **Flying Native (IRE)**[27] 250 4-11-0 0.................. DavidBass 70
(Nicky Henderson) *chsd ldrs: pushed along 1/2-way: wknd over 3f out: t.o* **16/1**
8 *¾* **Greek Fire** 4-11-0 0.................. APMcCoy 69
(Dave Morris) *hld up: hdwy over 5f out: wknd over 2f out: t.o* **7/2**[2]
9 *13* **Here's Henry**[49] 4-11-0 0.................. DonalDevereux 57
(David Brace) *hld up: rdn over 5f out: sn wknd: t.o* **66/1**
0- **10** *9* **Fereni**[25] 298 4-10-7 0.................. NickScholfield 42
(Kevin Bishop) *hld up: rdn over 5f out: sn wknd: t.o* **66/1**
0- **11** *3 ½* **Tara Dove**[24] 324 5-10-10 0.................. DavidEngland 42
(Michael Appleby) *plld hrd and prom: lost pl after 3f: bhd fnl 6f: t.o* **50/1**
00/ **12** *12* **Zorro's Blade**[222] 2101 5-11-0 0.................. KielanWoods(3) 38
(Michael Mullineaux) *led 1f: chsd ldrs tl wknd over 5f out: t.o* **150/1**
13 *32* **Game Dorabella** 5-10-5 0.................. EdCookson(5) 2
(Laura Hurley) *mid-div: sn pushed along: lost pl after 6f: bhd fr 1/2-way: t.o* **50/1**

3m 44.2s (-6.20) **Going Correction** -0.325s/f (Good)
WFA 4 from 5yo 3lb **13** Ran SP% **121.2**
Speed ratings: **101,99,91,91,89 85,81,81,75,71 69,63,48**
Tote Swingers: 1&2 £2.60, 2&3 £15.80, 1&3 £32.70 CSF £13.18 TOTE £7.30: £2.00, £1.10, £6.70; EX 17.10 Trifecta £134.40 Pool: £1,091.26 - 5.99 winning units..
Owner Bloomfields **Bred** Darley **Trained** Cowlinge, Suffolk

FOCUS
This was run at a fair pace thanks to the keen-going That's Exactly. Ordinary form, the second and third setting the level.
T/Plt: £1,016.90 to a £1 stake. Pool: £87,692.48 - 62.95 winning tickets. T/Qpdt: £189.60 to a £1 stake. Pool: £7,712.31 - 30.10 winning tickets. CR

339 PERTH (R-H)
Sunday, June 9

OFFICIAL GOING: Good to firm (good in places; 8.6)
Bends and hurdles moved on to fresh ground.
Wind: virtually nil Weather: overcast

676 MURRAYSHALL HOTEL GOLF/RACING BREAK MAIDEN HURDLE (FOR THE PROVOST'S PLATE CHALLENGE TROPHY) (10 hdls) 2m 4f 110y
2:30 (2:30) (Class 5) 4-Y-0+ **£3,249** (£954; £477; £238)

Form RPR
/UU- **1** **Border Phoenix**[10] 556 6-11-0 103.................. AdrianLane 104+
(Sandy Forster) *midfield: wnt 3rd after 7th: rdn after 3 out: lft cl 2nd 2 out: led narrowly last: drvn out* **11/2**[3]
0/2- **2** *½* **Mandarin Sunset (IRE)**[25] 313 6-11-0 0.................. BrianHughes 102
(James Ewart) *trckd ldr: lft in front 2 out: sn rdn: hdd last: drvn and a jst hld run-in* **7/4**[2]
0/0- **3** *9* **Karingo**[25] 313 6-10-9 0.................. SamanthaDrake(5) 93
(Lucy Normile) *in tch: rdn 3 out: sn no imp: lft modest 3rd 2 out* **50/1**
0/6- **4** *6* **Mo Rouge (IRE)**[29] 225 5-11-0 0.................. DenisO'Regan 87
(Mrs Jackie Stephen) *hld up: in rr whn nt fluent 3 out: kpt on after 2 out: nvr threatened ldrs* **33/1**
0/4- **5** *24* **Turtle Watch**[14] 494 5-11-0 0.................. RichieMcGrath 63
(Pauline Robson) *hld up in rr: rdn after 3 out: sn btn* **8/1**
6 *10* **Tim's Approach (IRE)**[15] 8-10-7 0.................. StephenMulqueen(7) 53
(William Young Jnr) *hld up: lft bhd after 3 out* **100/1**
1- **F** **Ziggie (IRE)**[29] 225 6-11-0 0.................. JasonMaguire 102
(Donald McCain) *led: nt a fluent: rdn appr 2 out: 2 l up whn fell 2 out* **7/5**[1]

4m 57.7s (-4.30) **Going Correction** -0.45s/f (Good) **7** Ran SP% **110.4**
Speed ratings (Par 103): **90,89,86,84,74 71,**
Tote Swingers: 1&2 £2.10, 1&3 £13.80, 2&3 £17.30 CSF £14.95 TOTE £8.00: £3.00, £1.50; EX 16.90 Trifecta £199.60 Pool: £1,360.13 - 5.10 winning units..
Owner Anne & Tony Howarth,Dave & Ann Skeldon **Bred** Mrs J K M Oliver **Trained** Kirk Yetholm, Borders

The Form Book Jumps, Raceform Ltd, Compton, RG20 6NL.

FOCUS
Bends and hurdles moved on to fresh ground. After the first race Denis O'Regan said it was good, good to firm in places, though a bit patchy in parts. This very modest maiden hurdle was run at just an average pace.

677 J.D. PIPES GOLD CUP SPECIAL H'CAP CHASE (THE SUNDAY £5K BONUS RACE) (15 fncs) 2m 4f 110y
3:00 (3:00) (Class 3) (0-140,135) 5-Y-O+ **£7,147** (£2,098; £1,049; £524)

Form RPR
P/3- **1** **Current Event (FR)**33 157 6-11-4 **132**......(p) HarryDerham(5) 141
(Paul Nicholls) *hld up in tch: hdwy 3 out: upsides 2 out: led last: rdn and kpt on* **6/1**
560/ **2** 3 **Ultimate**18 5356 7-11-9 **132**......(v1) JasonMaguire 138
(Brian Ellison) *led: rdn after 3 out: jnd 2 out: hdd last: kpt on but a hld by wnr* **9/1**
652/ **3** 2 3/4 **Quito Du Tresor (FR)**44 5545 9-11-0 **123**......(p) TomScudamore 127
(Lucinda Russell) *trckd ldr: rdn 2 out: kpt on one pce* **10/3**2
2/1- **4** 4 **Hawaii Klass**24 341 8-9-12 **112**......(b) CallumWhillans(5) 112
(Donald Whillans) *hld up: reminder after 10th: rdn after 4 out: kpt on one pce: nvr threatened ldrs* **11/2**3
2/0- **5** 7 **Premier Sagas (FR)**32 170 9-10-13 **122**...... BrianHarding 118
(Nicky Richards) *trckd ldr: rdn after 3 out: wknd after 2 out* **9/1**
PUP/ **6** 86 **Degas Art (IRE)**46 5496 10-11-6 **129**......(p) PeterBuchanan 46
(Lucinda Russell) *hld up: pushed along and dropped to rr after 5th: slow 9th: sn bhd: t.o* **14/1**
2/0- **U** **Now This Is It (IRE)**23 356 9-11-12 **135**...... APMcCoy
(S R B Crawford, Ire) *trckd ldr: blnd and uns rdr 5 out* **9/4**1
4m 50.7s (-14.30) **Going Correction** -0.45s/f (Good) **7** Ran SP% **110.2**
Speed ratings: **109,107,106,105,102 69,**
Tote Swingers: 1&2 £33.10, 1&3 £7.00, 2&3 £4.60 CSF £50.22 TOTE £7.20: £3.00, £4.20; EX 57.70 Trifecta £175.40 Pool: £1,335.48 - 5.70 winning units..
Owner Mrs Bunty Millard **Bred** M L Bloodstock Limited **Trained** Ditcheat, Somerset

FOCUS
Not the strongest race for the class or the money or offer, but the pace was sound and the form has a solid look to it.

678 FONAB CASTLE HOTEL NOVICES' H'CAP HURDLE (8 hdls) 2m 110y
3:30 (3:30) (Class 4) (0-105,112) 4-Y-O+ **£3,898** (£1,144; £572; £286)

Form RPR
4/1- **1** **Momkinzain (USA)**25 316 6-10-10 **96**......(p) CraigNichol(7) 98+
(Lucinda Russell) *in tch: led appr 2 out: sn rdn: drvn and kpt on run-in* **3/1**1
0/3- **2** 3 **Early Applause**22 371 5-11-7 **100**...... BrianHarding 99
(Nicky Richards) *hld up: nt fluent 6th: rdn appr 2 out: hdwy to chse wnr between last 2: kpt on* **16/1**
3 1/2 **Lancing**18 439 4-10-9 **91**...... DenisO'Regan 86
(A J Martin, Ire) *midfield: rdn 2 out: chsd wnr between last 2: hit last: one pce run-in* **10/1**
3/1- **4** shd **Sleep In First (FR)**8 583 7-11-9 **112**...... DaleIrving(10) 110
(James Ewart) *midfield: mstke 4th: rdn appr 2 out: kpt on wl fr last* **7/2**2
5/5- **5** 4 **Kayalar (IRE)**24 333 5-11-9 **102**...... PaulMoloney 95
(Evan Williams) *prom: rdn 2 out: wknd after last* **13/2**3
600/ **6** 4 **Garth Mountain**45 5520 6-10-2 **86**......(p) JonathanEngland(5) 75
(Hugh Burns) *trckd ldrs: rdn appr 2 out: grad wknd* **7/1**
0/0- **7** 2 1/2 **Shivalric (IRE)**25 316 5-9-8 **80**......(t) MrJHamilton(7) 66
(Nicky Richards) *led: hdd appr 2 out: wknd* **28/1**
0/2- **8** 22 **Rain Mac**9 561 5-11-10 **103**...... JasonMaguire 71
(Donald McCain) *hld up in rr: sme hdwy 3 out: rdn appr 2 out: sn wknd* **7/2**2
4/0- **9** 13 **Nahneh (IRE)**10 556 7-11-1 **94**...... BrianHughes 45
(John Wade) *hld up: nt fluent 1st: wknd 3 out* **50/1**
3m 46.7s (-11.30) **Going Correction** -0.45s/f (Good)
WFA 4 from 5yo+ 17lb **9** Ran SP% **115.7**
Speed ratings (Par 105): **108,106,106,106,104 102,101,91,84**
Tote Swingers: 1&2 £16.80, 1&3 £8.30, 2&3 £23.40 CSF £47.63 CT £429.07 TOTE £3.40: £1.40, £4.50, £2.00; EX 49.90 Trifecta £592.80 Pool: £1,205.31 - 1.52 winning units..
Owner John R Adam & Sons **Bred** Berkshire Stud **Trained** Arlary, Perth & Kinross

FOCUS
They went a reasonable pace in this ordinary novice handicap.

679 FUGRO SUBSEA SERVICES NOVICES' CHASE (FOR THE SILVER CUP) (12 fncs) 2m
4:00 (4:01) (Class 4) 5-Y-O+ **£5,198** (£1,526; £763; £381)

Form RPR
203/ **1** **Toledo Gold (IRE)**61 5224 7-10-12 100......(t) MichaelMcAlister 115
(Maurice Barnes) *led: jnd after 6th: rdn whn hdd after 3 out: led again jst after last: kpt on* **16/1**
/U2- **2** 6 **Mulligan's Man (IRE)**22 369 6-10-12 127...... JasonMaguire 113+
(Donald McCain) *in tch: hdwy to ld after 3 out: rdn next: 2 l up whn landed awkwardly last and lost momentum: sn hdd and nt rcvr* **11/10**1
F/ **3** 5 **Mourne Paddy (IRE)**9 9-10-12 0...... APMcCoy 104
(S R B Crawford, Ire) *trckd ldr: moved upsides after 6th: rdn appr 3 out: wknd after 2 out* **10/3**2
1/6- **4** 16 **Takaatuf (IRE)**30 201 7-10-12 0...... BrianHughes 90
(John Wade) *hld up: lft remote 4th 4 out: nvr threatened* **9/1**
5/6- **F** **Captain Brown**36 118 5-10-12 118......(t) PaulMoloney
(Evan Williams) *racd keenly hld up: pushed along and 7 l down in 4th whn fell 4 out* **7/2**3
P/P- **P** **Askalott (IRE)**36 114 8-10-12 0...... FearghalDavis
(Jean McGregor) *hld up in rr: a bhd: t.o whn p.u bef 7th* **80/1**
3m 49.5s (-7.50) **Going Correction** -0.45s/f (Good) **6** Ran SP% **110.0**
Speed ratings: **100,97,94,86,**
Tote Swingers: 1&2 £3.30, 1&3 £5.90, 2&3 £1.30 CSF £34.86 TOTE £13.40: £4.30, £1.30; EX 45.10 Trifecta £142.30 Pool: £2,426.55 - 12.78 winning units..
Owner M Barnes, Scott Lowther **Bred** Rathbarry Stud **Trained** Farlam, Cumbria

FOCUS
They went a good gallop in this novice chase.

680 AVIVA CITY OF PERTH GOLD CUP (HANDICAP CHASE) (18 fncs) 3m
4:30 (4:31) (Class 2) 5-Y-O+ **£16,245** (£4,770; £2,385; £1,192)

Form RPR
/05- **1** **Problema Tic (FR)**8 587 7-10-12 **132**......(bt) TomScudamore 140+
(David Pipe) *trckd ldrs: led bef 3 out: jnd last: sn drvn: kpt on wl to assert fnl 100yds* **15/2**
2/3- **2** 3 1/4 **Buck Mulligan**21 392 8-10-9 **132**...... AdamWedge(3) 137
(Evan Williams) *trckd ldrs: wnt 2nd 3 out: rdn and upsides last: sn drvn: one pce and hld fnl 100yds* **10/1**
P/1- **3** 8 **Merrion Square (IRE)**28 238 7-10-13 **133**......(t) RyanMahon 131
(Paul Nicholls) *in tch: wnt 3rd 3 out: sn rdn: one pce and no ch w ldng pair fr between last 2* **15/2**
1/0- **4** 5 **Aneyeforaneye (IRE)**30 204 7-10-12 **132**...... BrianHughes 126
(Malcolm Jefferson) *hld up in midfield: hdwy appr 3 out: wnt 4th 2 out: sn rdn and one pce* **11/1**
P/2- **5** 1 1/4 **Peachey Moment (USA)**21 387 8-10-0 **120**...... DougieCostello 112
(Nicky Richards) *hld up in rr: rdn after 3 out: sme late hdwy: nvr threatened* **18/1**
/12- **6** nk **De Boitron (FR)**17 448 9-11-6 **140**...... NoelFehily 132
(Ferdy Murphy, France) *hld up: sme hdwy 5 out: rdn appr 3 out: sn no imp on ldrs* **12/1**
4/3- **7** 1/2 **Pigeon Island**17 448 10-11-1 **135**......(bt) SamTwiston-Davies 126
(Nigel Twiston-Davies) *hld up: rdn after 5 out: nvr threatened ldrs* **7/1**3
R/0- **8** nk **Mumbles Head (IRE)**23 355 12-10-9 **129**...... TomO'Brien 123
(Peter Bowen) *midfield: rdn 3 out: one pce and no imp on ldrs* **4/1**1
2/1- **9** 10 **Wild Geese (IRE)**25 312 6-10-3 **123**......(p) PeterBuchanan 105
(Lucinda Russell) *midfield: rdn bef 3 out: sn btn* **13/2**2
0/1- **10** 39 **West With The Wind**33 157 8-11-12 **146**...... PaulMoloney 105
(Evan Williams) *led: jst hdd whn blnd 3 out: wknd* **25/1**
/44- **P** **Garleton (IRE)**17 448 12-11-5 **139**......(t) MichaelMcAlister
(Maurice Barnes) *prom: hit 10th: lost pl after next: bhd after 5 out: p.u bef 2 out* **20/1**
0/4- **F** **Simarian (IRE)**33 158 8-9-9 **122**...... ConorRing(7) 95
(Evan Williams) *midfield: rdn appr 3 out: sn no imp: hit 2 out: wl hld whn fell last* **33/1**
2B0/ **P** **Nedzer's Return (IRE)**14 11-11-3 **137**......(t) JasonMaguire
(Gordon Elliott, Ire) *hld up: a in rr: p.u after 11th* **9/1**
5m 46.2s (-17.80) **Going Correction** -0.45s/f (Good) course record **13** Ran SP% **121.3**
Speed ratings: **111,109,107,105,105 105,104,104,101,88 , ,**
Tote Swingers: 1&2 £25.10, 1&3 £6.60, 2&3 £20.10 CSF £79.54 CT £592.70 TOTE £8.70: £3.80, £3.90, £3.10; EX 123.40 Trifecta £1665.20 Part won. Pool: £2,220.30 - 0.34 winning units..
Owner Mrs Jo Tracey **Bred** Julien Merienne & Mrs Maryvonne Merienne **Trained** Nicholashayne, Devon

FOCUS
A suitably competitive field for this valuable handicap chase, and solid form, the first pair coming clear.

681 CRABBIE'S ALCOHOLIC GINGER BEER H'CAP HURDLE (10 hdls) 2m 4f 110y
5:00 (5:03) (Class 4) (0-120,120) 4-Y-O+ **£5,198** (£1,526; £763; £381)

Form RPR
1 **Busted Tycoon (IRE)**57 5296 4-10-8 **106**......(t) DenisO'Regan 119+
(A J Martin, Ire) *hld up in midfield: tk clsr order 6th: smooth hdwy to trck ldr 2 out: upsides on bit last: led fnl 100yds: hrd hld* **5/1**2
00F/ **2** 3/4 **Strongpoint (IRE)**9 569 9-11-2 **110**...... PeterBuchanan 120
(S R B Crawford, Ire) *led: rdn 2 out: jnd last: hdd fnl 100yds: flattered by proximity to wnr* **33/1**
PP3/ **3** 11 **Malin Bay (IRE)**45 5525 8-11-12 **120**...... FearghalDavis 121
(Nicky Richards) *midfield: nt fluent 5th: rdn after 3 out: kpt on: wnt 3rd towards fin: no threat to ldng pair* **10/1**
/31- **4** nk **Andreo Bambaleo**30 205 9-11-5 **113**......(p) TomScudamore 113
(Brian Ellison) *midfield: rdn and outpcd after 3 out: kpt on after 2 out: no threat to ldng pair* **8/1**
1/F- **5** nk **Urban Kode (IRE)**24 342 5-9-11 **98**......(v) CraigNichol(7) 99
(Lucinda Russell) *in tch: rdn to go 3rd 2 out: sn no match ldng pair: nt fluent last: no ex: lost 2 pls cl home* **8/1**
4/5- **6** 4 1/2 **Cruachan (IRE)**25 313 4-10-6 **104**...... DougieCostello 97
(Lucy Normile) *hld up in midfield: rdn after 3 out: sn one pce: hit last 2* **25/1**
503/ **7** 5 **Dj Milan (IRE)**256 1643 7-11-10 **118**......(t) HenryBrooke 109
(Donald McCain) *trckd ldr: rdn after 3 out: wknd after 2 out* **16/1**
2/2- **8** 5 **Glencree (IRE)**21 384 9-11-6 **114**......(p) BrianHughes 101
(John Wade) *midfield: hdwy 7th: rdn 3 out: wknd between last 2* **16/1**
3/3- **9** 2 **Cool Baranca (GER)**9 563 7-10-10 **104**...... LucyAlexander 89
(Dianne Sayer) *hld up: rdn appr 2 out: nvr threatened* **7/1**3
25/ **10** 4 1/2 **Knocklayde Vic (IRE)**29 228 9-11-2 **110**......(p) JasonMaguire 91
(Gordon Elliott, Ire) *hld up in rr: reminders after 3rd: rdn and sme hdwy appr 3 out: wknd 2 out* **5/2**1
6/4- **11** 32 **Latin Connection (IRE)**24 342 7-11-6 **114**......(t) APMcCoy 66
(S R B Crawford, Ire) *hld up: rdn 3 out: nvr threatened* **16/1**
4/P- **12** 27 **Door Boy (IRE)**23 355 10-11-12 **120**......(p) AdrianLane 48
(John Wade) *in tch: lost pl 6th: bhd after next* **40/1**
215- **13** 3/4 **Overpriced**8 581 7-11-4 **119**......(t) StephenMulqueen(7) 46
(Maurice Barnes) *trckd ldr: wknd 3 out* **28/1**
6/5- **14** 70 **Parson's Punch**24 344 8-11-2 **110**...... PaulMoloney
(Lucy Normile) *hld: bhd 1/2-way: t.o* **28/1**
4m 47.4s (-14.60) **Going Correction** -0.45s/f (Good)
WFA 4 from 5yo+ 18lb **14** Ran SP% **122.8**
Speed ratings (Par 105): **109,108,104,104,104 102,100,98,98,96 84,73,73,46**
Tote Swingers: 1&2 £42.60, 1&3 £14.40, 2&3 £76.50 CSF £169.10 CT £1617.45 TOTE £6.40: £2.40, £8.60, £3.30; EX 162.60 Trifecta £735.90 Part won. Pool: £981.30 - 0.12 winning units..
Owner John Breslin **Bred** Swordlestown Little **Trained** Summerhill, Co. Meath
■ Stewards' Enquiry : Jason Maguire five-day ban: use of whip (23, 25, 26, 30 June & 2 July)

FOCUS
They went a sound pace in this fair handicap.

682 WATCH ALL SCOTTISH RACING LIVE ON RACING UK STANDARD OPEN NATIONAL HUNT FLAT RACE 2m 110y
5:30 (5:40) (Class 6) 4-6-Y-O **£2,053** (£598; £299)

Form RPR
3- **1** **Lagan Canal (IRE)**14 498 6-11-1 0...... DenisO'Regan 98
(A J Martin, Ire) *hld up in tch: smooth hdwy to trck ldr 2f out: pushed along to ld post* **9/4**2
2 shd **Vasco Pierji (FR)** 4-10-12 0...... JasonMaguire 95
(Donald McCain) *w ldr: led over 3f out: rdn over 2f out: strly pressed ent fnl f: kpt on: hdd post* **11/4**3
3 4 **Lucky G (IRE)** 4-9-12 0...... CraigNichol(7) 84
(Keith Dalgleish) *trckd ldng pair: rdn 3f out: hung lft: kpt on one pce* **2/1**1
65/- **4** 2 1/2 **Knockturnal (IRE)**71 5011 5-10-8 0......(t) BrianHughes 84
(Malcolm Jefferson) *led narrowly: hdd over 3f out: sn rdn: dropped to 4th 2f out: one pce* **6/1**
0/0- **5** 13 **Jonsfella**8 584 5-10-8 0......(t) JamesCorbett(7) 78
(Susan Corbett) *hld up: tk clsr order 6f out: rdn over 3f out: sn btn* **66/1**

5- **6** *18* **Chester Legend**[14] 497 6-10-10 0........................ TonyKelly(5) 60
(Sue Taylor) *in tch: lost pl 6f out: bhd fnl 4f* **33/1**

7 *75* **Marlee Massie (IRE)** 4-10-12 0........................ LucyAlexander
(N W Alexander) *rn loose befhand: hld up in tch: pushed along and dropped to rr 6f out: sn t.o* **22/1**

3m 50.3s (-2.10) **Going Correction** -0.45s/f (Good)
WFA 4 from 5yo+ 3lb **7** Ran SP% **113.8**
Speed ratings: **86,85,84,82,76 68,33**
Tote Swingers: 1&2 £1.50, 1&3 £1.60, 2&3 £1.90 CSF £8.76 TOTE £2.90: £1.60, £2.00; EX 8.90 Trifecta £14.20 Pool: £2,849.03 - 150.27 winning units..
Owner R Jordan **Bred** Maurice Fenton **Trained** Summerhill, Co. Meath

FOCUS
A modest bumper.
T/Plt: £809.70 to a £1 stake. Pool: £93,643.00 - 84.42 winning tickets. T/Qpdt: £89.10 to a £1 stake. Pool: £7,646.00 - 63.50 winning tickets. AS

454 AUTEUIL (L-H)
Sunday, June 9

OFFICIAL GOING: Turf: very soft

683a PRIX ALAIN DU BREIL - COURSE DE HAIES D'ETE DES QUATRE ANS (HURDLE) (GRADE 1) (4YO) (TURF) 2m 3f 110y
1:30 (12:00) 4-Y-0

£98,780 (£48,292; £28,536; £19,756; £10,975; £7,682)

RPR

1 **Diakali (FR)**[21] 405 4-10-8 0........................ RWalsh 151
(W P Mullins, Ire) *led on run to 1st: hdd bef 3rd: styd prom: led again 4th: mde rest: shkn up after 2 out and asserted: r.o wl u.p run-in: won gng away* **2/1**[2]

2 *7* **Ptit Zig (FR)**[43] 5573 4-10-8 0........................ DarylJacob 144
(Paul Nicholls) *towards rr: prog on inner bef 5 out: trckd ldr in 3rd gng wl 3 out: 2nd and ev ch 2 out: sn rdn and nt qckn w wnr: one pce u.p run-in* **13/2**[3]

3 *½* **Le Grand Luce (FR)**[21] 405 4-10-8 0........................ MlleNathalieDesoutter 143
(J-P Gallorini, France) *hld up towards rr: hdwy to trck ldng gp fr 4 out: cl 3rd whn c stands' side st and lost grnd on front two: 3rd and rdn appr last: kpt on u.p run-in: nt pce to chal* **7/4**[1]

4 *3* **Blue Fashion (IRE)**[49] 4-10-8 0........................ DavidCottin 140
(Nicky Henderson) *trckd ldrs: dropped to 6th bef 3 out: shkn up and wnt 4th whn c stands' side st: sn rdn: one pce run-in* **8/1**

5 *4* **My Maj (FR)**[21] 404 4-10-8 0........................ JeremyDaSilva 136
(Yannick Fouin, France) *pressed ldr: led bef 3rd and qcknd pce: hdd 4th but styd prom bhd ldr: 5th whn c stands' side st: rdn and nt qckn fr 2 out: one pce u.p run-in* **20/1**

6 *8* **Wanaba (FR)**[43] 5585 4-10-8 0........................ Jean-LucBeaunez 128
(Mme P Butel, France) *midfield: cl up fr 4 out: hrd rdn to hold pl on run to 2 out: hrd rdn and no imp between last 2: wknd run-in* **16/1**

7 *20* **Carilo (IRE)**[21] 405 4-10-8 0........................(p) MorganRegairaz 108
(C Lerner, France) *midfield: in rr fr 4th: detached and pushed along fr 5 out: wl bhd whn mstke last* **50/1**

8 *dist* **Dalasiri (IRE)**[46] 5513 4-10-8 0........................ BarryGeraghty
(Sabrina J Harty, Ire) *hld up towards rr: sltly hmpd 2nd: detached and struggling after 4 out: t.o* **16/1**

P **Maghero (FR)**[21] 405 4-10-8 0........................(p) CyrilleGombeau
(P Peltier, France) *trckd ldrs: lost pl appr 3 out: sn wl bhd: p.u bef 2 out* **12/1**

4m 38.4s (-16.60) **9** Ran SP% **120.3**
PARI-MUTUEL (all including 1 euro stakes): WIN 3.10; PLACE 1.40, 2.50, 1.20; DF 24.60; SF 30.60.
Owner Wicklow Bloodstock Limited **Bred** Haras De Son Altesse L'Aga Khan S C E A **Trained** Muine Beag, Co Carlow

685a GRANDE COURSE DE HAIES D'AUTEUIL (HURDLE) (GRADE 1) (5YO+) (TURF) 3m 1f 110y
3:10 (12:00) 5-Y-0+

£135,365 (£66,178; £39,105; £27,073; £15,040; £10,528)

RPR

1 **Gemix (FR)**[43] 5586 5-10-6 0........................ DavidCottin 165
(N Bertran De Balanda, France) *mde most: j.rt 7th: 8th & 9th: hdd 3 out: led again 2 out and racd against nrside rail in st: rdn and styd on strly flat: forged clr* **8/1**[3]

2 *8* **Solwhit (FR)**[64] 5175 9-10-10 0........................ DavyRussell 161
(C Byrnes, Ire) *hld up: smooth hdwy on to heels of ldrs 3 out: rdn and wnt 2nd appr last: styd on flat but sn no imp on wnr* **5/4**[1]

3 *9* **Zaidpour (FR)**[21] 406 7-10-10 0........................(p) PaulTownend 152
(W P Mullins, Ire) *nt fluent: midfield: mstke 3 out and sn rdn: outpcd by ldrs bef 2 out: rallied u.p and styd on to go 3rd fnl strides: no ch w front pair* **22/1**

4 *nk* **Saint Du Chenet (FR)**[43] 5586 7-10-10 0........................(b) RegisSchmidlin 151
(M Rolland, France) *midfield: rdn and ev ch 2 out: outpcd by front pair bef last: styd on but dropped to 4th fnl strides* **33/1**

5 *snk* **Lord Prestige (FR)**[21] 406 6-10-10 0........................ JonathanPlouganou 151
(M Rolland, France) *midfield: clsd and led 3 out: hdd 2 out: sn rdn and outpcd by front pair: styd on* **16/1**

6 *nk* **Celestial Halo (IRE)**[21] 406 9-10-10 0........................(bt) DarylJacob 151
(Paul Nicholls) *midfield: clsd 3 out: rdn and ev ch 2 out: outpcd by front pair bef last: styd on* **8/1**[3]

7 *4* **On His Own (IRE)**[18] 441 9-10-10 0........................ DJCasey 147
(W P Mullins, Ire) *midfield: lost pl 9th and dropped to rr: rdn after 3 out and sn outpcd: plugged on* **33/1**

8 *nk* **Tidara Angel (IRE)**[21] 406 6-10-6 0........................(p) AnthonyLecordier 143
(D Windrif, France) *midfield: rdn and lost pl 5 out: sn bhd and outpcd: plugged on* **33/1**

9 *2½* **Thousand Stars (FR)**[21] 406 9-10-10 0........................ RWalsh 144
(W P Mullins, Ire) *hld up towards rr: hdwy into midfield 8th: rdn after 3 out: outpcd by ldrs after 2 out: no ex flat and fdd* **9/2**[2]

10 *3½* **Mazuelo (FR)**[21] 406 5-10-6 0........................(p) BertrandThelier 137
(G Cherel, France) *trckd ldr: rdn and lost pl after 3 out: outpcd and btn bef last* **50/1**

11 *12* **Reve De Sivola (FR)**[45] 5529 8-10-10 0........................ JamesReveley 129
(Nick Williams) *trckd ldr: rdn and brief effrt to chal after 3 out: lost pl and btn 2 out: eased flat and t.o* **9/1**

12 *15* **Lamego (FR)**[21] 406 6-10-10 0........................ Jean-LucBeaunez 114
(Mme P Butel, France) *hld up in rr: rdn and outpcd bef 2 out: sn btn: eased flat and t.o: nvr a factor* **66/1**

P **Nikita Du Berlais (FR)**[21] 406 6-10-6 0........................ CyrilleGombeau
(Robert Collet, France) *midfield: dropped out rapidly bef 9th and p.u bef next* **16/1**

P **Serienschock (GER)**[35] 139 5-10-6 0........................ KevinNabet
(F-M Cottin, France) *hld up towards rr: last 3 out: sn lost tch and btn: p.u bef 2 out* **20/1**

6m 14.92s (374.92) **14** Ran SP% **128.0**
PARI-MUTUEL (all including 1 euro stakes): WIN 3.90; PLACE 2.20, 2.20, 6.10; DF 8.90; SF 17.30.
Owner Mme Francis Teboul **Bred** Dr V Fremlot & P Dufreche **Trained** France

684 - 685a (Foreign Racing) - See Raceform Interactive

631 NEWTON ABBOT (L-H)
Monday, June 10

OFFICIAL GOING: Good to firm (good in places)
Wind: Strong breeze against Weather: Sunny with cloudy periods

686 PAIGNTON ZOO NOVICES' H'CAP HURDLE (9 hdls) 2m 3f
2:30 (2:30) (Class 5) (0-95,92) 4-Y-0+ **£2,463** (£718; £359)

Form RPR

FFP/ **1** **Just Cloudy**[114] 4260 9-11-8 **88**........................(t) DarylJacob 97+
(Robert Walford) *led tl 2nd: trckd ldr: led after 5th: gng best turning in: rdn after 2 out: awkward last: r.o wl* **11/2**[3]

/23- **2** *2½* **Mount Vesuvius (IRE)**[21] 407 5-11-12 **92**........................(t) TomO'Brien 96
(Paul Henderson) *mid-div: rdn and hdwy after 3 out: nt clr run but sn chsng wnr bef 2 out: styd on same pce* **7/2**[2]

352- **3** *1¼* **Green Lightning (IRE)**[4] 651 6-10-10 **76**........................(b) TomMessenger 80
(Martin Weston) *hld up towards rr: hdwy after 6th: rdn to chse ldrs after 3 out: styd on same pce fr next: wnt 3rd fnl stride* **9/4**[1]

/60- **4** *nse* **Sedgemoor Express (IRE)**[13] 517 5-10-12 **85**(tp) ThomasCheesman(7) 88
(Nigel Hawke) *slowly away: towards rr: hdwy after 5th: rdn to press ldr after 3 out: styd on same pce fr next: lost 3rd fnl stride* **18/1**

P/6- **5** *14* **Hugo Drax (IRE)**[32] 174 6-10-7 **80**........................(t) MrMHeard(7) 70
(David Pipe) *mid-div: hdwy after 6th: rdn and ev ch after 3 out: wknd next* **12/1**

P60- **6** *1½* **Abbi Jicaro**[4] 648 6-10-1 **74**........................(t) OllieGarner(7) 63
(Mark Shears) *hld up towards rr: rdn after 6th: styd on fr after 3 out: nvr threatened to rch ldrs* **50/1**

/26- **7** *7* **Present Accepted**[27] 293 6-11-3 **90**........................ GaryDerwin(7) 75
(Nerys Dutfield) *trckd ldrs: rdn after 3 out: wknd bef next* **33/1**

PPF/ **8** *10* **First Spirit**[58] 5283 7-10-1 **74**........................ MrKevinJones(7) 48
(Sarah Robinson) *mid-div: rdn after 3 out: wknd bef next* **100/1**

055- **9** *nk* **Haveumistim**[16] 477 7-11-6 **89**........................ MarkQuinlan(3) 62
(Bernard Llewellyn) *trckd ldrs: rdn after 6th: sn wknd* **20/1**

/P6- **10** *3¾* **Palio Square (USA)**[13] 521 6-11-4 **91**........................(b) MrTomFlint(7) 61
(John Flint) *j.rt: trckd ldrs: rdn after 6th: sn wknd* **11/2**[3]

0/6- **11** *51* **The Presidents Man (IRE)**[8] 595 6-10-8 **79**........................ GavinSheehan(5) 3
(Barry Brennan) *racd keenly: led 2nd tl after 5th: wknd next: t.o* **50/1**

4PP/ **S** **Plug In Baby**[224] 2100 5-10-6 **72**........................ NickScholfield
(Nick Mitchell) *mid-div tl lost pl 5th: nudged along whn hmpd and slipped up on bnd bef 6th* **20/1**

/00- **P** **Kruseman**[5] 635 6-11-10 **90**........................(bt) AndrewGlassonbury
(Richard Woollacott) *in tch: trckd ldrs 5th: rdn after 3 out: wkng whn p.u bef next: dismntd* **20/1**

4m 29.1s (-0.90) **Going Correction** -0.35s/f (Good) **13** Ran SP% **118.9**
Speed ratings (Par 103): **87,85,85,85,79 78,75,71,71,70 48, ,**
toteswingers 1&2 £6.70, 2&3 £2.60, 1&3 £4.30 CSF £23.58 CT £56.56 TOTE £6.00: £2.20, £1.20, £1.10; EX 31.40 Trifecta £80.80 Pool: £1286.78 - 11.93 winning units..
Owner R Alner **Bred** D Timmis **Trained** Child Okeford, Dorset

FOCUS
The inside rails were out to near their furthest point, in order to provide fresh ground. A modest novices' handicap hurdle run at a steady pace. A big step up from the winner on his previous hurdles form.

687 SIS EARLY MORNING PRODUCT NOVICES' H'CAP CHASE (13 fncs) 2m 110y
3:00 (3:00) (Class 5) (0-100,100) 5-Y-0+ **£2,874** (£837; £419)

Form RPR

134- **1** **Mount Welcome (IRE)**[12] 536 9-11-3 **96**........................(t) MrTWeston(5) 108+
(Martin Weston) *in tch: hdwy after 7th: lft upsides 9th: led on bit after 4 out: in command rdn between last 2: kpt on wl* **5/1**[3]

025- **2** *5* **Tom O'Tara**[20] 418 9-10-2 **79**........................ WayneKavanagh(3) 86
(Robin Dickin) *in tch: hdwy after 7th: hmpd 9th: rdn in cl 3rd after 4 out: chsd wnr gng to 2 out: kpt on but a being hld* **11/2**

325/ **3** *25* **Flowerbud**[174] 3130 8-10-0 **74** oh1........................(b) JamieMoore 56
(Jim Best) *trckd ldr: lft in ld 9th: rdn and hdd after 4 out: sn hld: lost 2nd bef 2 out: wknd* **7/2**[2]

0/0- **4** *15* **Forest Rhythm (IRE)**[15] 489 9-10-11 **92**........................(b) MrKevinJones(7) 61
(Seamus Mullins) *hld up in last trio: struggling after 6th: wnt modest 4th 3 out but nvr any ch w ldrs* **25/1**

6/0- **5** *10* **Lapin Garou (FR)**[29] 248 6-10-0 **74** oh4........................(bt[1]) BrendanPowell 34
(Colin Tizzard) *j.rt at times: led tl drvn after 7th: qckly btn: wknd after 4 out: t.o* **9/4**[1]

F- **P** **Tulla Emerald (IRE)**[8] 594 8-11-3 **91**........................ DaveCrosse
(Natalie Lloyd-Beavis) *trckd ldr tl after 7th: wknd after next: t.o whn p.u bef 2 out* **66/1**

2P/- **P** **Tuskar (USA)**[341] 863 7-10-2 **76**........................ TomO'Brien
(Alan Jones) *nt fluent early: hld up: reminders and lost tch qckly after 6th: p.u bef next: b.b.v* **14/1**

/P4- **F** **Walden Prince (IRE)**[19] 425 6-11-12 **100**........................ WayneHutchinson
(Tony Carroll) *hld up in last trio: hdwy after 7th: narrow advantage and travelling wl whn fell 9th* **5/1**[3]

4m 3.0s (-3.50) **Going Correction** -0.40s/f (Good) **8** Ran SP% **113.7**
Speed ratings: **92,89,77,70,66 , ,**
toteswingers 1&2 £3.60, 2&3 £3.80, 1&3 £3.10 CSF £32.34 CT £107.53 TOTE £5.30: £2.00, £2.00, £1.10; EX 23.10 Trifecta £71.90 Pool: £1705.65 - 17.78 winning units..
Owner M H Weston **Bred** J Walsh **Trained** Hindlip, Worcs

FOCUS
Not a strong contest, this was run at a solid pace with the field well strung out at the line. The winner improved to the level of his best Irish chase form.

688 AT THE RACES SKY 415 NOVICES' HURDLE (9 hdls) 2m 3f
3:30 (3:30) (Class 3) 4-Y-0+ **£6,390** (£1,984; £1,068)

Form RPR

/11- **1** **Saint Roque (FR)**[9] 591 7-11-8 140 (t) DarylJacob 140+
(Paul Nicholls) *trckd ldr: nt fluent 3 out: narrwo ld whn mstke 2 out: nudged clr: comf* **2/5**[1]

/11- **2** *5* **Life And Soul (IRE)**[15] 494 6-11-8 130 (p) JasonMaguire 132
(Donald McCain) *set decent pce: rdn and hdd 2 out: sn hld: kpt on to fin wl clr of 3rd* **11/4**[2]

0/2- **3** *30* **Port Hill**[26] 307 6-10-12 100 DPFahy 98
(Liam Corcoran) *chsd ldng pair tl outpcd after 3 out* **80/1**

311/ **P** **Kim Tian Road (IRE)**[69] 5108 7-11-1 120 HaddenFrost
(Martin Hill) *chsd ldng pair tl wknd 3 out: t.o whn p.u bef 2 out* **9/1**[3]

4m 22.9s (-7.10) **Going Correction** -0.35s/f (Good) 4 Ran SP% **109.3**
Speed ratings (Par 107): **100,97,85,**
CSF £1.97 TOTE £1.40; EX 1.80 Trifecta £11.60 Pool: £1643.44 - 105.93 winning units..
Owner Potensis Limited & Chris Giles **Bred** Mme Genevieve Mongin **Trained** Ditcheat, Somerset

FOCUS
A fair contest despite the small field size, run at an honest pace. The winner is rated similar to his recent best, with the next two pretty much to their marks.

689 FOLLOW NEWTONABBOTRACE ON TWITTER H'CAP CHASE (16 fncs) 2m 5f 110y
4:00 (4:00) (Class 4) (0-105,105) 5-Y-0+ **£4,288** (£1,259; £629; £314)

Form RPR

2/4- **1** **Wait No More (IRE)**[37] 117 8-11-4 97 (p) DougieCostello 105
(Neil Mulholland) *mde all: jnd 9th tl rdn after 3 out: styd on wl to assert fr last: rdn out* **8/1**

/11- **2** *7* **Forever My Friend (IRE)**[4] 639 6-11-8 101 7ex JamieMoore 107+
(Peter Bowen) *in tch: trckd ldrs 8th: drvn in 3rd after 4 out: chsd wnr bef 2 out: 1 l down whn wnt sltly rt last: no ex* **5/4**[1]

/26- **3** *8* **Smooth Classic (IRE)**[20] 420 9-11-12 105 (b[1]) TomScudamore 101
(David Pipe) *trckd wnr: jnd wnr 9th tl nt quite fluent 3 out: sn rdn: lost 2nd bef next: styd on same pce* **9/1**

P/1- **4** *27* **Chase Gate**[32] 175 8-11-5 98 (p) HaddenFrost 76
(James Frost) *trckd ldrs: rdn after 4 out: wknd next: t.o* **9/2**[2]

4/4- **P** **Cottage Acre (IRE)**[41] 40 10-11-8 101 LiamHeard
(Colin Heard) *hld up but wl in tch: trckd ldrs 6th: pushed along after 8th: losing pl whn p.u bef next* **22/1**

3/2- **P** **Ice Cool Benny (IRE)**[19] 430 9-11-7 100 (p) AidanColeman
(Andy Hobbs) *sn niggled along in tch: drvn after 6th: losing tch whn p.u bef 9th* **5/1**[3]

5/2- **P** **Autumn Spirit**[17] 457 9-11-12 105 (t) CharliePoste
(Robin Dickin) *trckd ldrs: reminders after 7th: rdn after 11th: sn wknd: p.u after 3 out* **14/1**

5m 16.4s (-5.00) **Going Correction** -0.40s/f (Good) 7 Ran SP% **111.4**
Speed ratings: **93,90,87,77, , ,**
toteswingers 1&2 £2.90, 2&3 £2.40, 1&3 £6.60 CSF £18.51 TOTE £7.30: £3.70, £1.90; EX 23.30 Trifecta £131.10 Pool: £2968.00 - 16.96 winning units..
Owner John Hobbs **Bred** Sean Naughton **Trained** Limpley Stoke, Wilts

FOCUS
An honest pace for this handicap with the winner making all. The winner is rated to his best.

690 SIS INTERNATIONAL H'CAP HURDLE (11 hdls 1 omitted) 3m 3f
4:30 (4:30) (Class 4) (0-105,105) 4-Y-0+ **£3,508** (£1,030; £515; £257)

Form RPR

/42- **1** **Little Eaglet (IRE)**[27] 295 9-10-11 90 LiamHeard 95+
(Colin Heard) *hld up towards rr on outer: midfield 4th: trckd ldrs 9th: led last (usual 2 out): sn drvn: hld on wl whn strly chal bypassing omitted last: all out* **7/2**[1]

/61- **2** *nk* **Ahead Ahead (IRE)**[9] 590 8-11-10 103 PaulMoloney 108
(David Rees) *hld up towards rr: stdy hdwy fr 9th: rdn to chse ldrs after next: str chal bypassing omitted last: styd on: jst hld* **6/1**[3]

2/0- **3** *4* **Green Bank (IRE)**[22] 393 7-11-12 105 (t) AidanColeman 105
(Charlie Longsdon) *disp tl clr ldr after 4th: rdn after 2 out (usual 3 out): hdd last (usual 2 out): kpt on same pce: jst hld on for 3rd* **4/1**[2]

6/4- **4** *½* **Minella Bliss (IRE)**[29] 254 8-11-0 96 RobertDunne[(3)] 96
(Nikki Evans) *hld up towards rr: stdy prog fr 8th: rdn to chse ldrs after 3 out (usual 2 out): styd on same pce: nrly got up for 3rd* **12/1**

000/ **5** *hd* **Tarvini (IRE)**[126] 4029 8-10-9 95 (p) DannyBenson[(7)] 93
(Jonjo O'Neill) *mid-div: rdn and lost pl after 8th: hdwy after 3 out (usual 2 out): styd on fr last (usual 2 out): nrly snatched 4th fnl strides* **7/1**

0/3- **6** *10* **Fromthetop (IRE)**[16] 478 7-10-0 79 oh5 (t) TomScudamore 70
(Michael Scudamore) *chsd ldrs: rdn after 9th: ev ch tl stmbld after next: sn hld: kpt on same pce* **14/1**

PP0/ **7** *2* **Kasban**[162] 3377 9-11-9 102 (vt[1]) JamieMoore 90
(Jim Best) *trckd ldrs: rdn after 9th: wknd last (usual 2 out)* **7/1**

3/4- **8** *½* **Manadam (FR)**[8] 601 10-10-12 96 (v) RobertMcCarth[(5)] 83
(Ian Williams) *mid-div: rdn after 9th: nvr threatened ldrs* **16/1**

/3U- **9** *4 ½* **Portmeade**[29] 241 11-9-11 83 JonPark[(7)] 66
(Elizabeth Scott) *a towards rr* **66/1**

4/0- **10** *11* **Absolute Shambles**[29] 241 9-10-9 88 (p) TomCannon 61
(Chris Gordon) *disp tl pushed along after 4th: chsd ldrs tl wknd after 8th* **18/1**

/55- **11** *nk* **Rifleman (IRE)**[13] 522 13-9-8 80 (tp) MissLBrooke[(7)] 53
(Richard Lee) *chsd ldrs: rdn after 9th: wknd bef last (usual 2 out)* **25/1**

4/6- **12** *1 ½* **Russian Song (IRE)**[13] 518 9-11-3 103 (bt) MrMLegg[(7)] 75
(Colin Tizzard) *sn pushed along to chse ldrs: lost pl after 4th: in rr fr 8th* **25/1**

0/0- **13** *39* **Whenever**[19] 436 9-10-1 80 (v) DougieCostello 16
(Richard Phillips) *mid-div: rdn after 6th: wknd after 8th: t.o* **16/1**

/5P- **F** **Une Des Bieffes (FR)**[29] 241 5-10-0 79 (p) ConorO'Farrell
(Michael Scudamore) *hld up towards rr: fell 8th* **40/1**

6m 29.3s (-11.70) **Going Correction** -0.35s/f (Good) 14 Ran SP% **124.5**
Speed ratings (Par 105): **103,102,101,101,101 98,97,97,96,93 93,92,81,**
toteswingers 1&2 £5.10, 2&3 £6.50, 1&3 £4.20 CSF £25.29 CT £91.43 TOTE £5.00: £1.80, £1.90, £1.60; EX 16.60 Trifecta £53.90 Pool: £3162.26 - 43.94 winning units..
Owner Mrs Sally White **Bred** Tim & Helen Keoghan **Trained** Boscastle, Cornwall

FOCUS
This moderate but open staying handicap was run at a sound pace. The winner was very well in on his old form, with the third and fourth setting the level.

691 NEWTONABBOTRACING.COM H'CAP HURDLE (8 hdls) 2m 1f
5:00 (5:00) (Class 4) (0-110,110) 4-Y-0+ **£3,508** (£1,030; £515; £257)

Form RPR

/11- **1** **Party Palace**[10] 521 9-10-8 95 GilesHawkins[(3)] 99+
(Stuart Howe) *mid-div: chsd ldr after 4th tl rdn after 3 out: nt clr run 2 out: styd on gamely to ld run-in: drvn out* **11/4**[1]

/04- **2** *1 ¼* **Macarthur**[13] 517 9-11-12 110 (tp) TomO'Brien 113+
(David Rees) *hld up towards rr: hdwy after 5th: led 2 out: sn rdn: wnt lft last: sn hdd: no ex* **17/2**[3]

0/6- **3** *1 ½* **Sun Quest**[28] 267 9-10-7 98 (t) MrLKilgarriff[(7)] 97
(Steven Dixon) *led tl rdn after 3 out: ev ch next: kpt on gamely but nt quite gng pce of ldrs* **20/1**

5/5- **4** *2* **Cut The Cards (IRE)**[31] 201 6-11-3 101 RichieMcLernon 99
(Jonjo O'Neill) *cl up: hit 3rd: hrd drvn after 5th: styd on same pce to go 4th run-in* **11/4**[1]

4P/- **5** *1 ½* **My Lord**[11] 4789 5-10-11 95 ColinBolger 92
(Luke Dace) *racd keenly in midfield: hdwy after 5th: chal 2 out: sn rdn and hld: fdd into 5th run-in* **9/1**

400/ **6** *4 ½* **Kilderry Dean (IRE)**[97] 4574 6-10-10 94 HaddenFrost 87
(James Frost) *hld up towards rr: styd on fr 2 out: nvr a danger* **66/1**

U/6- **7** *½* **Captain Sharpe**[21] 409 5-11-2 103 (p) MarkQuinlan[(3)] 96
(Bernard Llewellyn) *trckd ldrs: rdn after 5th: nt gng pce to chal: wknd last* **11/2**[2]

2/P- **8** *1* **Dashing Doc (IRE)**[20] 421 6-11-7 105 (tp) PaulMoloney 101
(Evan Williams) *trckd ldr: led narrowly after 3 out: sn rdn: hdd next: hld in disp 5th whn blnd last* **12/1**

P/0- **9** *19* **Tri Nations (UAE)**[10] 565 8-11-2 100 (vt) CharliePoste 78
(Anthony Middleton) *a towards rr: t.o after 3 out* **50/1**

5/4- **10** *29* **Erdeli (IRE)**[32] 191 9-11-4 102 (bt[1]) IanPopham 49
(Kevin Bishop) *prom tl 3rd: sn drvn along: bhd fr 5th: t.o* **25/1**

613/ **11** *1 ¼* **Ophelia's Kiss**[484] 4270 6-10-10 94 BrendanPowell 40
(Brendan Powell) *mid-div: rdn after 3 out: sn wknd: t.o* **33/1**

460/ **S** **Oscar Jane (IRE)**[156] 3498 6-11-4 102 TomCannon
(Kevin Bishop) *hld up towards rr: slipped up on bnd bef 5th* **12/1**

4m 1.0s (-4.70) **Going Correction** -0.35s/f (Good) 12 Ran SP% **119.6**
Speed ratings (Par 105): **97,96,95,94,94 91,91,91,82,68 68,**
toteswingers 1&2 £5.50, 2&3 £27.50, 1&3 £13.70 CSF £25.44 CT £400.00 TOTE £4.10: £2.50, £2.10, £6.40; EX 25.90 Trifecta £366.00 Pool: £2200.63 - 4.50 winning units..
Owner B P Jones **Bred** Llety Farms **Trained** Oakford, Devon

FOCUS
Few came into this in much form. The pace was honest and the third anf fifth help set the level.

692 SUNFLOWER DAY NURSERY CONDITIONAL JOCKEYS' H'CAP CHASE (20 fncs) 3m 2f 110y
5:30 (5:30) (Class 5) (0-95,95) 5-Y-0+ **£2,729** (£801; £400; £200)

Form RPR

0/4- **1** **Lord Lescribaa (FR)**[13] 522 10-10-11 88 (tp) ThomasCheesman[(8)] 104+
(Philip Hobbs) *led 2nd tl 5th: chsd clr ldr: led 13th: drew clr after 3 out: rdn out run-in* **12/1**

265- **2** *21* **Flanagan (IRE)**[4] 641 9-11-4 90 (v) DonalDevereux[(3)] 93+
(Peter Bowen) *trckd ldrs: hit 16th: rdn after 4 out: blnd 3 out: sn wl hld: fdd between last 2 but a holding on for 2nd* **3/1**[1]

3/5- **3** *13* **Pacha D'Oudairies (FR)**[35] 141 10-11-4 87 TomCannon 75
(Michael Blake) *hld up towards rr: hdwy after 13th: rdn after 16th: wnt modest 3rd next: no ch w front pair* **9/1**[2]

/25- **4** *9* **Might As Well**[17] 461 10-11-4 87 (b) RyanMahon 64
(Seamus Mullins) *prom early: chsd ldrs fr 5th: rdn after 13th: plugged on and n.d after* **12/1**

55P/ **5** *4 ½* **Upper Deck (IRE)**[205] 2472 8-10-3 72 KielanWoods 45
(Richard Phillips) *mid-div: rdn after 11th: wnt 3rd 16th tl wknd bef 3 out* **16/1**

55/ **6** *11* **Interpleader**[14] 8-11-10 93 (tp) GavinSheehan 56
(Bernard Llewellyn) *led tl 2nd: led 5th: clr tl 12th: hdd next: sn rdn: wkng whn nt fluent 3 out* **10/1**[3]

024/ **P** **Joaaci (IRE)**[35] 13-11-4 87 (b) IanPopham
(Patricia Shaw) *sn outpcd and detached in last: t.o whn p.u after 13th* **20/1**

/42- **P** **Petroupetrov (FR)**[16] 478 10-11-8 91 (bt) KillianMoore
(Tim Vaughan) *prom tl 3rd: chsd ldrs tl dropped in rr 8th: t.o whn p.u after 13th* **9/1**[2]

233/ **P** **Chandlers Cross (IRE)**[14] 11-11-3 86 (tp) AdamWedge
(David Rees) *mid-div: wnt 4th 11th: rdn after 16th: wknd after 4 out: p.u bef 2 out* **16/1**

355/ **P** **Von Galen (IRE)**[42] 32 12-9-9 69 oh1 JackSherwood[(5)]
(Michael Scudamore) *a towards rr: t.o whn p.u after 13th* **40/1**

P53/ **P** **Royal Mile (IRE)**[47] 5506 9-10-2 79 (b[1]) KieronEdgar[(8)]
(David Pipe) *mid-div: hit 4th: lost tch after 14th: t.o whn p.u after 4 out* **9/1**[2]

3/2- **F** **Dimpsy Time**[12] 541 7-11-7 93 (tp) BrendanPowell[(3)]
(Colin Tizzard) *in tch whn fell 3rd* **3/1**[1]

6m 31.8s (-12.80) **Going Correction** -0.40s/f (Good) 12 Ran SP% **123.4**
Speed ratings: **102,95,91,89,87 84, , , , ,**
toteswingers 1&2 £9.70, 2&3 £8.50, 1&3 £38.80 CSF £51.72 CT £357.94 TOTE £13.20: £3.80, £1.50, £3.30; EX 94.60 Trifecta £907.00 Pool: £2034.59 - 1.68 winning units..
Owner Mrs S L Hobbs **Bred** Mme Louis Lafitte **Trained** Withycombe, Somerset

■ Stewards' Enquiry : Thomas Cheesman two-day ban: use of whip (25-26 June)

FOCUS
There was plenty of pace on for this handicap confined to conditional jockeys, with few able to get competitive and the winner benefiting from a fine ride. He produced a step up, and the time was good for the grade.

T/Jkpt: Not won. T/Plt: £7.30 to a £1 stake. Pool of £78611.88 - 7844.99 winning tickets. T/Qpdt: £6.20 to a £1 stake. Pool of £3942.13 - 468.30 winning tickets. TM

600 SOUTHWELL (L-H)

Monday, June 10

OFFICIAL GOING: Good (7.5)

Wind: light 1/2 against Weather: fine

693 PLAY GOLF AT SOUTHWELL GOLF CLUB H'CAP CHASE (16 fncs) 2m 4f 110y

6:10 (6:10) (Class 4) (0-110,110) 5-Y-O+ **£3,768** (£1,106; £553; £276)

Form RPR

/34- 1 **Strongbows Legend**[20] 420 8-11-9 **107**............(v) NoelFehily 124+
(Charlie Longsdon) *led 2nd: mde rest: drew clr fr 3 out* **7/2**[1]

32U- 2 14 **Peak Seasons (IRE)**[8] 597 10-9-7 **84** oh3........ GerardGalligan(7) 87
(Michael Chapman) *chsd ldrs: outpcd and lost pl 9th: hdwy u.p 4 out: modest 5th 3 out: 2nd last: hung rt run-in* **7/1**

/15- 3 5 **Midnight Macarena**[23] 379 8-11-5 **103**..........(p) LeightonAspell 103
(Lucy Wadham) *j.rt: chsd ldrs 5th: 2nd 7th: wknd last* **4/1**[2]

2/6- 4 nse **Civil Unrest (IRE)**[30] 220 7-11-3 **101**..........(p) BrianHughes 100
(James Ewart) *chsd ldrs: hit 10th: one pce fr 3 out* **25/1**

126- 5 16 **Accessallareas (IRE)**[9] 585 8-11-12 **110**............ APMcCoy 94
(Sarah-Jayne Davies) *led to 2nd: chsd ldrs: drvn after 4 out: wknd bef 2 out* **7/2**[1]

1/0- 6 1 1/4 **Tregaro (FR)**[10] 564 7-11-2 **100**..........(t) DenisO'Regan 83
(Mike Sowersby) *hld up in rr: hdwy 10th: trcking ldrs 4 out: rdn and wknd next* **20/1**

/24- 7 31 **Latest Trend (IRE)**[32] 179 7-11-12 **110**........ RichardJohnson 65
(Tim Vaughan) *chsd ldrs 2nd: lost pl 9th: hit next 2: sn bhd: t.o 3 out* **11/2**[3]

444/ 8 6 **Global Flyer**[43] 7 9-11-4 **102**..........(p) AndrewThornton 52
(Caroline Bailey) *in rr: pushed along 6th: lost pl 9th: sn bhd: t.o 4 out* **7/1**

5m 25.0s (8.00) **Going Correction** +0.50s/f (Soft) 8 Ran SP% **113.4**
Speed ratings: **104,98,96,96,90 90,78,76**
toteswingers 1&2 £7.60, 2&3 £2.20, 1&3 £3.30 CSF £27.49 CT £100.41 TOTE £3.30: £1.40, £1.60, £2.30; EX 29.20 Trifecta £147.60 Pool: £1628.04 - 8.26 winning units..
Owner Box A45 **Bred** Mrs F Marriott **Trained** Over Norton, Oxon

FOCUS
Fences sited 5yds off outside rail. Golf Club bend and bend into home straight were outside line raced on June 2nd, adding 36yds to advertised distances. This wasn't overly competitive. The winner's best figure since January 2012.

694 BOOK HOSPITALITY AT SOUTHWELL RACECOURSE H'CAP CHASE (13 fncs) 2m

6:40 (6:40) (Class 5) (0-95,93) 5-Y-O+ **£2,144** (£629; £314; £157)

Form RPR

U2F- 1 **Turf Trivia**[8] 602 6-11-5 **86**..........(b) BarryKeniry 101+
(George Moore) *trckd ldrs: 2nd 9th: led between last 2: 4 l ahd last: sn drew clr* **7/1**

1/1- 2 10 **Apache Dawn**[40] 65 9-11-4 **85**..........(t) TommyPhelan 91
(Aytach Sadik) *chsd ldr: led 7th: 3 l clr and drvn appr 3 out: hdd between last 2: sn btn* **5/2**[2]

522- 3 3 **Mad Professor (IRE)**[23] 378 10-9-10 **68**..........(b) JoeCornwall(5) 70
(John Cornwall) *chsd ldrs: drvn and lost pl 7th: modest 3rd 4 out: kpt on one pce* **11/2**[3]

/P3- 4 17 **Strathaird (IRE)**[8] 602 9-10-0 **67** oh1..........(p) BrianHughes 54
(Andrew Crook) *j.lft: in rr: bhd 3rd: distant 4th sn after 4 out* **22/1**

/01- 5 19 **Crack At Dawn (IRE)**[20] 418 12-10-13 **87**..........(v) MrCSmith(7) 57
(Michael Gates) *in rr: bhd fr 6th: t.o 3 out* **8/1**

P6B- P **The Grey One (IRE)**[8] 602 10-10-8 **82**.......... ChrisDavies(7)
(Milton Bradley) *j.rt: chsd ldrs: lost pl and drvn 6th: t.o next: p.u bef 8th: b.b.v* **25/1**

/66- P **Novikov**[16] 472 9-11-8 **89**.......... AndrewThornton
(Sophie Leech) *in rr: reminders 3rd: bhd fr 6th: t.o 4 out: p.u bef next* **12/1**

BP3/ P **Truckers Benefit (IRE)**[131] 3935 8-11-12 **93**..........(t) RichardJohnson
(Tim Vaughan) *led: hdd after 6th: wknd after 9th: sn bhd: t.o whn p.u bef 3 out* **9/4**[1]

4m 12.4s (10.40) **Going Correction** +0.50s/f (Soft) 8 Ran SP% **114.2**
Speed ratings: **94,89,87,79,69 , ,**
toteswingers 1&2 £12.40, 2&3 £3.40, 1&3 £8.70 CSF £25.82 CT £103.77 TOTE £8.70: £2.60, £1.20, £2.20; EX 30.30 Trifecta £194.50 Pool: £997.58 - 3.84 winning units..
Owner Mrs Mary Hatfield & Mrs Susan Kramer **Bred** London Thoroughbred Services Ltd **Trained** Middleham Moor, N Yorks

FOCUS
They appeared to go a reasonable gallop. The easy winner threatened this sort of figure in the past.

695 GREEN FEE OFFERS AT SOUTHWELLGOLFCLUB.COM "NATIONAL HUNT" MAIDEN HURDLE (11 hdls) 2m 4f 110y

7:10 (7:10) (Class 5) 4-Y-O+ **£1,949** (£572; £286; £143)

Form RPR

PP2/ 1 **Now Then Charlie (IRE)**[43] 3 8-11-0 119.......... DenisO'Regan 110
(John Ferguson) *led: qcknd pce and jnd 7th: hdd after 3 out: lft virtually alone last: eased in clsng stages* **15/8**[2]

4/4- 2 40 **Barney Rubble**[27] 291 4-10-10 0.......... RichieMcGrath 70
(Philip Kirby) *trckd ldng pair: outpcd 8th: tk distant 3rd appr 2 out: lft 2nd last* **14/1**[3]

6- 3 21 **Bollin Sam**[27] 278 7-10-9 0.......... JonathanEngland(5) 55
(Sue Smith) *outpcd whn nt fluent 7th: bhd 3 out: lft distant 3rd last* **25/1**

0/0- 4 35 **Philchezski (IRE)**[39] 76 6-11-0 0.......... BrianHughes 24
(Andrew Crook) *hld up: modest 3rd 8th: wknd qckly appr 2 out: sn t.o* **100/1**

1/2- U **Azure Fly (IRE)**[15] 484 5-11-0 0.......... NoelFehily 126+
(Charlie Longsdon) *trckd ldr: upsides 7th: led after 3 out: hung lft between last 2: 10 l ahd whn swvd violently lft sn after last and uns rdr* **8/13**[1]

P/0- P **Big Benjie**[39] 76 5-11-0 0..........(t) HenryBrooke
(Edwin Tuer) *trckd ldrs: drvn 8th: sn wknd: bhd whn p.u bef 2 out* **100/1**

5m 21.7s (8.70) **Going Correction** +0.225s/f (Yiel)
WFA 4 from 5yo+ 18lb 6 Ran SP% **109.2**
Speed ratings (Par 103): **92,76,68,55,**
toteswingers 1&2 £1.10, 2&3 £11.20, 1&3 £3.10 CSF £20.40 TOTE £2.00: £1.10, £5.30; EX 17.30 Trifecta £69.20 Pool: £1065.02 - 11.52 winning units..
Owner The Bloomfields Partnership **Bred** Miss E Harrington **Trained** Cowlinge, Suffolk

FOCUS
This looked a match and the big two drew clear from a long way out, but there was a dramatic late twist, with Azure Fly, who had readily mastered his market rival, jinking sharply left on touching down after the last and giving Noel Fehily little chance of staying aboard. The winner has been given a token rating to his mark.

696 SOUTHWELL COURT CARE HOME MACMILLAN NOVICES' HURDLE (9 hdls) 2m

7:40 (7:40) (Class 4) 4-Y-O+ **£3,119** (£915; £457; £228)

Form RPR

0/P- 1 **Tom Wade (IRE)**[14] 511 6-10-7 97..........(t) BenPoste(5) 101+
(Shaun Harris) *trckd ldrs: t.k.h: led on bit 2 out: lft over 2 l clr last: idled: jst hld on* **25/1**

1- 2 nk **Rosie Probert**[16] 477 4-10-9 0.......... AndrewTinkler 97+
(Nicky Henderson) *t.k.h: trckd ldrs: shkn up 3 out: upsides next: nt fluent last: rallied towards fin: jst hld* **9/4**[2]

3 1 1/4 **Redoute Star (AUS)**[20] 7-10-12 0.......... PaddyBrennan 97
(Paul D'Arcy) *hld up: hdwy on wd outside to trck ldrs 5th: upsides between last 2: styd on same pce* **14/1**

2/5- 4 2 3/4 **Brassbound (USA)**[28] 267 5-10-12 107.......... AndrewThornton 96
(Caroline Bailey) *trckd ldrs: drvn to ld briefly appr 2 out: one pce between last 2* **1/1**[1]

/04- 5 15 **Sonny Jim**[19] 434 5-10-12 0..........(p) BrianHughes 80
(John Mackie) *led at stdy pce: increased gallop sn after 3 out: hdd appr next: sn lost pl and bhd* **100/1**

1- 6 hd **Godwit**[22] 383 5-10-9 0.......... JackQuinlan(3) 80
(Eugene Stanford) *t.k.h: trckd ldrs: wknd appr 2 out: sn bhd* **5/1**[3]

7 8 **Tatting**[21] 4-10-9 0.......... LeightonAspell 69
(Chris Dwyer) *hld up: outpcd 6th: lost pl bef 2 out: sn bhd* **28/1**

4m 16.0s (19.00) **Going Correction** +0.225s/f (Yiel)
WFA 4 from 5yo+ 17lb 7 Ran SP% **112.4**
Speed ratings (Par 105): **61,60,60,58,51 51,47**
toteswingers 1&2 £9.30, 2&3 £3.50, 1&3 £13.90 CSF £80.25 TOTE £35.00: £9.40, £1.20; EX 142.60 Trifecta £723.60 Part won. Pool: £964.85 - 0.68 winning units..
Owner Paul Tonks **Bred** Denis McDonnell **Trained** Carburton, Notts

FOCUS
Hard to think this was anything other than a modest novice hurdle, with the time slow and the form suspect. The winner is rated to the level of his 2011 form.

697 M & S DECORATORS PAINT GREEN FOR MACMILLAN H'CAP HURDLE (9 hdls) 2m

8:10 (8:10) (Class 4) (0-120,117) 4-Y-O+ **£3,119** (£915; £457; £228)

Form RPR

/31- 1 **Baccalaureate (FR)**[9] 581 7-11-5 **115**.......... JonathanEngland(5) 127+
(Sue Smith) *chsd ldrs: led 4th: drvn clr between last 2: 10 l ahd last: heavily eased in clsng stages* **4/1**[2]

0/1- 2 7 **Tinseltown**[8] 605 7-11-0 **105**..........(p) APMcCoy 110
(Brian Rothwell) *w ldrs: led 3rd: hdd next: reminders 5th: outpcd next: kpt on and 2nd between last 2: no ch w wnr* **5/4**[1]

0/2- 3 2 1/4 **Gud Day (IRE)**[23] 371 5-11-7 **112**..........(bt) PaddyBrennan 114
(Fergal O'Brien) *hld up: wd and trckd ldrs 5th: handy 2nd next: drvn appr 2 out: one pce* **7/1**

440- 4 6 **Trip The Light**[15] 503 8-11-0 **105**.......... SamTwiston-Davies 101
(Phil Middleton) *j.rt and reminders 2nd: chsd ldrs 5th: modest 4th next: one pce* **11/2**[3]

0/0- 5 24 **Tamarillo Grove (IRE)**[13] 521 6-10-9 **103**..........(t) JamesBest(3) 78
(Sophie Leech) *prom: outpcd 5th: lost pl 3 out: sn bhd: t.o* **10/1**

PP/- 6 21 **Red Jade**[102] 4480 8-11-9 **114**..........(p) NickScholfield 70
(Keiran Burke) *mid-div: outpcd and reminders after 4th: lost pl 6th: bhd fr next: t.o* **33/1**

020/ 7 66 **Tornade D'Estruval (FR)**[58] 5291 6-11-6 **114**.......... JackQuinlan(3) 10
(Sarah Humphrey) *led to 3rd: j. slowly and lost pl 5th: t.o whn hmpd 3 out: eventually completed* **33/1**

525/ F **The Tiddly Tadpole**[9] 2164 8-11-7 **117**.......... HarryDerham(5)
(Simon West) *stdd s: hld up detached in last: blnd 4th: modest 6th whn fell 3 out: fatally injured* **18/1**

3m 58.5s (1.50) **Going Correction** +0.225s/f (Yiel) 8 Ran SP% **112.6**
Speed ratings (Par 105): **105,101,100,97,85 74,41,**
toteswingers 1&2 £1.70, 2&3 £2.80, 1&3 £4.30 CSF £9.41 CT £31.39 TOTE £4.50: £1.20, £1.30, £1.90; EX 14.20 Trifecta £34.30 Pool: £759.45 - 16.56 winning units..
Owner The Cartmel Syndicate **Bred** Elevage Fouchet Loick & Coolmore Stud **Trained** High Eldwick, W Yorks

FOCUS
Modest handicap form. A personal best from the winner under a claimer.

698 JAMIE HEMPSALL INTERIORS SUPPORT MACMILLAN H'CAP HURDLE (11 hdls) 2m 4f 110y

8:40 (8:41) (Class 4) (0-120,118) 4-Y-O+ **£3,119** (£915; £457; £228)

Form RPR

2/- 1 **Jewel In The Sun (IRE)**[50] 5423 8-10-8 **100**.......... APMcCoy 108+
(Ben Haslam) *racd wd thrght: trckd ldrs: led sn after 3 out: drvn clr between last 2: j.lft last: styd on wl* **13/8**[2]

00F/ 2 9 **Violets Boy (IRE)**[190] 2816 6-11-6 **112**..........(t) AndrewTinkler 113
(Brendan Powell) *t.k.h: led: hdd after 3 out: rallied and upsides appr next: 6 l down and wl hld whn blnd last* **14/1**

22- 3 1 1/4 **Daliance (IRE)**[22] 390 4-10-8 **104**.......... LeightonAspell 100+
(Lucy Wadham) *trckd ldrs 7th: handy 3rd whn blnd 3 out: one pce appr next* **6/4**[1]

266/ 4 1/2 **Hollins**[62] 5229 9-10-12 **107**.......... JohnKington(3) 103
(Tony Forbes) *hld up: t.k.h: trckd ldrs 7th: rdn and hung lft sn after 3 out: one pce appr next* **16/1**

05/- 5 7 **Mark Twain (IRE)**[43] 12 6-11-6 **112**..........(tp) NickScholfield 102
(Kim Bailey) *sn trcking ldrs: outpcd 6th: outpcd bef 2 out: wknd appr next* **9/1**[3]

31P/ P **Chargen (IRE)**[54] 5354 10-11-0 **116**.......... MikeyHamill(10)
(Sean Curran) *chsd ldrs: drvn 6th: lost pl and reminders 8th: sn bhd: t.o whn p.u bef last* **9/1**[3]

5m 18.9s (5.90) **Going Correction** +0.225s/f (Yiel)
WFA 4 from 6yo+ 18lb 6 Ran SP% **110.6**
Speed ratings (Par 105): **97,93,93,92,90**
toteswingers 1&2 £13.10, 2&3 £4.50, 1&3 £1.10 CSF £20.79 CT £37.05 TOTE £2.70: £1.30, £4.00; EX 22.60 Trifecta £43.70 Pool: £541.55 - 9.29 winning units..
Owner John P McManus **Bred** N McManus **Trained** Middleham Moor, N Yorks

The Form Book Jumps, Raceform Ltd, Compton, RG20 6NL.

FOCUS
Ordinary form for the level. The winner was well in on his best Irish form.

699 SOUTHWELL STANDARD NATIONAL HUNT FLAT RACE (CONDITIONAL JOCKEYS' AND AMATEUR RIDERS' RACE) 2m
9:10 (9:10) (Class 6) 4-6-Y-0 £1,559 (£457; £228; £114)

Form RPR
2- 1 **Factor Fifty (IRE)**31 207 4-10-8 0 AdamNicol(7) 106+
(Philip Kirby) *hld up in mid-div: wnt 3rd over 5f out: 2nd over 2f out: styd on to ld last 75yds* 3/1[2]
0/1- 2 1 3/4 **Nurse Ratched (IRE)**34 160 4-10-8 0 ConorShoemark(7) 105
(Fergal O'Brien) *racd wd: led: rdn over 1f out: hdd and no ex ins fnl f* 3/1[2]
3 8 **Definite Future (IRE)** 4-10-8 0 MrAlexEdwards(7) 97
(Dave Roberts) *hld up in rr: hdwy over 4f out: kpt on to take modest 3rd jst ins fnl f* 10/1
2/3- 4 6 **Reverb**28 270 4-10-12 0 JeremiahMcGrath(3) 92
(Nicky Henderson) *trckd ldrs: 2nd over 5f out: drvn and wknd over 1f out* 15/8[1]
4- 5 14 **Oorayvic (IRE)**33 173 6-10-13 0 JonathanEngland(5) 82
(Sue Smith) *chsd ldrs: drvn and wl outpcd over 4f out* 8/1[3]
0/ 6 3 3/4 **Potkettleblack**42 35 4-10-1 0 MrMatthewStanley(7) 69
(Chris Bealby) *mid-div: outpcd and lost pl over 5f out* 66/1
6- 7 4 **Park House**27 284 4-11-1 0 HenryBrooke 72
(Ray Craggs) *chsd ldrs: drvn and wl outpcd over 5f out* 50/1
8 3/4 **Ginger Mac** 5-11-1 0 PeterCarberry(3) 75
(John Mackie) *mid-div: outpcd and lost pl over 5f out* 20/1
9 7 **Herecomestrouble** 6-11-1 0 BrianToomey(3) 68
(Tim Etherington) *hld up in rr: hdwy 7f out: lost pl over 3f out* 50/1
10 1 3/4 **Coccinnelle (FR)** 5-10-4 0 MrRMorganMurphy(7) 60
(Ferdy Murphy, France) *hld up in rr: sme hdwy 6f out: sn outpcd and lost pl* 20/1
11 24 **Steel Away J (IRE)**71 6-10-11 0 MrJakeThomasCoulson(7) 45
(Christopher Kellett) *chsd ldrs: drvn over 8f out: lost pl 7f out: t.o 4f out* 66/1
6- 12 dist **Tropical Sky (IRE)**8 599 5-10-11 0 (t) GerardGalligan(7)
(Michael Chapman) *chsd ldrs: rdn and lost pl after 6f: t.o 7f out: eventually completed* 100/1

3m 54.2s (2.80) **Going Correction** +0.225s/f (Yiel) 12 Ran SP% 122.4
Speed ratings: **102,101,97,94,87 85,83,82,79,78 66,**
toteswingers 1&2 £1.40, 2&3 £10.20, 1&3 £8.60 CSF £12.31 TOTE £4.10: £1.70, £1.20, £3.50; EX 17.00 Trifecta £82.70 Pool: £968.80 - 8.78 winning units..
Owner The Topspec Partnership **Bred** T J Rooney **Trained** Middleham, N Yorks
FOCUS
The front pair drew clear late on in what was a modest bumper. The fourth and sixth help set the level.
T/Plt: £49.50 to a £1 stake. Pool of £70660.95 - 1040.69 winning tickets. T/Qpdt: £17.60 to a £1 stake. Pool of £5600.48 - 234.90 winning tickets. WG

LYON PARILLY (R-H)
Monday, June 10
OFFICIAL GOING: Turf: good to soft

703a PRIX PAUL VALERIEN PERRIN (HURDLE) 2m 3f
5:10 (12:00) 4-Y-0 £11,707 (£5,853; £3,414; £2,317; £1,097)

RPR
1 **Vivaccio (FR)**19 4-10-10 0 DavidCottin 107
(A Adeline De Boisbrunet, France) 68/10
2 snk **Paris Clermont (FR)**215 4-10-1 0 MlleCelinePicard(5) 103
(H Despont, France) 20/1
3 snk **Grace A Toi Enki (FR)**19 4-11-0 0 MathieuCarroux 111
(A Chaille-Chaille, France) 7/2[1]
4 3 **Volare (FR)**43 4-10-10 0 RegisSchmidlin 104
(M Rolland, France) 13/2[3]
5 1 1/2 **Veauce De Sivola (FR)**114 4247 4-10-6 0 JamesReveley 98
(Nick Williams) *midfield in tch: rdn and lost pl 3 out: towards rr 2 out: rallied u.p and styd on strly flat: wnt 5th post and gng on at fin* 17/1
6 nk **Pyrardini (USA)**239 4-10-12 0 GaetanOlivier 104
(J-L Guillochon, France) 9/2[2]
7 2 **Opaleo (FR)**7 4-10-6 0 KevinNabet 96
(F-M Cottin, France) 52/1
8 1 **Super Pipo (FR)**83 4-10-6 0 GregoryAdam 95
(H Billot, France) 53/1
9 3 **Lovely As (FR)**43 4-10-10 0 JonathanPlouganou 96
(Emmanuel Clayeux, France) 13/2[3]
10 3 1/2 **Karmine (GER)**59 4-10-12 0 BenoitGicquel 95
(F Nicolle, France) 8/1
11 **Garden's Rose (FR)**36 4-10-1 0 DavidBrassil(5) 89
(F-M Cottin, France) 50/1
12 **Grandinas (FR)**44 4-10-12 0 AdrienBetron 95
(X Betron, France) 23/1
P **L'Aumance Girl (FR)**208 4-10-3 0 AlainDeChitray
(A Adeline De Boisbrunet, France) 20/1
P **Limnara (FR)** 4-9-11 0 FrankieLeroy(4)
(Mlle D Schnepp, France) 114/1

4m 41.3s (281.30) 14 Ran SP% 116.8
PARI-MUTUEL (all including 1 euro stakes): WIN 7.80; PLACE 2.50, 5.20, 2.00; DF 68.40; SF 117.70.
Owner Daniel Lassaussaye **Bred** Daniel Lassaussaye **Trained** France

704a PRIX ANDRE BABOIN - GRAND CROSS DE LYON (CROSS-COUNTRY CHASE) (CONDITIONS) (6YO+) (TURF) 3m 2f
6:40 (7:35) 6-Y-0+ £17,170 (£8,585; £5,008; £3,398)

RPR
1 **Yanky Sundown (FR)**1131 190 8-10-10 0 MrChristopheCorduan 123
(M Nicolau, France) 11/10[2]
2 shd **Resistencia (FR)** 8-10-3 0 (p) MarcLamazou-Laresse 116
(E Vagne, France) 23/10[3]
3 6 **Diamond Harry**38 131 10-10-4 0 ow1 JamesReveley 111
(Nick Williams) 1/1[1]
4 3 **Wylder (FR)**1535 9-10-3 0 (p) MlleCelinePicard 107
(Mlle V Crozetiere-Roulet, France) 6/1

7m 6.82s (426.82) 4 Ran SP% 142.2
PARI-MUTUEL (all including 1 euro stakes): WIN 2.10; PLACE 1.10, 1.10, 1.10; DF 2.10; SF 2.80.
Owner Marc Nicolau **Bred** Mme S & C Gesbert & Narvick International **Trained** France

538 FONTWELL (L-H)
Tuesday, June 11
OFFICIAL GOING: Good changing to good to soft (good in places) after race 1 (2.15)
Wind: medium, behind Weather: light rain

705 BET-N-TIP.COM H'CAP CHASE (11 fncs 2 omitted) 2m 2f
2:15 (2:15) (Class 4) (0-120,120) 5-Y-0+ £3,768 (£1,106; £553; £276)

Form RPR
/32- 1 **Synthe Davis (FR)**30 234 8-10-13 107 APMcCoy 121+
(Laura Mongan) *chsd ldrs after 1st: chsd ldr and gng best 8th: led and j.lft 2 out: in command and j.lft again last: styd on: rdn out* 5/1[3]
6/2- 2 8 **Try Catch Me (IRE)**39 98 8-10-3 100 (b) MarkQuinlan(3) 107
(Alison Batchelor) *led: rdn and jnd 3 out: hdd and bmpd next: no ex between last 2: plugged on* 11/4[1]
451- 3 6 **Morestead (IRE)**16 489 8-10-6 100 (t) LeightonAspell 103
(Brendan Powell) *chsd ldrs after 1st: rdn on long run after 7th: chsd ldng pair bef 3 out: plugged on but no imp* 5/1[3]
3/1- 4 29 **Wester Ross (IRE)**6 632 9-11-1 112 7ex (v) AdamWedge(3) 91
(Evan Williams) *hld up in last pair: 4th and outpcd after 7th: no ch fr next: t.o* 4/1[2]
/2U- 5 23 **Stormy Oscar (IRE)**10 585 6-11-2 110 BrendanPowell 71
(Jamie Snowden) *chsd ldr tl 8th: wknd jst bef next: fading and blnd 2 out: t.o* 8/1
P/0- 6 45 **Amaury De Lusignan (IRE)**30 236 7-11-12 120 JamieMoore 45
(Gary Moore) *chsd ldrs tl after 1st: steadily lost pl: last and rdn 6th: lost tch bef next: t.o 8th* 8/1
605/ P **Giant O Murchu (IRE)**208 2433 9-11-4 112 (t) DougieCostello
(Lawney Hill) *a in rr: lost tch after 6th: t.o whn p.u 8th* 10/1

4m 34.95s (0.25) **Going Correction** -0.025s/f (Good) 7 Ran SP% 111.3
Speed ratings: **98,94,91,78,68 48,**
toteswingers 1&2 £2.60, 1&3 £4.60, 2&3 £4.30 CSF £18.71 CT £68.81 TOTE £4.90: £2.60, £1.80; EX 17.40 Trifecta £68.60 Pool: £1470.70 - 16.07 winning units..
Owner Mrs P J Sheen **Bred** Claude Quellier **Trained** Epsom, Surrey
FOCUS
Bends moved to fresh ground. The right horses dominated this modest handicap and the form is believable.

706 3663 FIRST FOR FOOD SERVICE NOVICES' HURDLE (10 hdls) 2m 4f
2:45 (2:45) (Class 4) 4-Y-0+ £3,119 (£915; £457; £228)

Form RPR
2P/ 1 **Experimentalist**88 4779 5-10-12 118 (t) RichardJohnson 109+
(Tim Vaughan) *hld up in tch: trckd ldrs after 7th: upsides ldr 2 out: drvn to ld flat: kpt on: rdn out* 7/4[2]
/21- 2 2 1/4 **Luci Di Mezzanotte**19 450 5-10-12 0 LeightonAspell 111
(Oliver Sherwood) *t.k.h: chsd ldrs: mstke 6th: wnt 2nd 7th: led bef 2 out: rdn between last 2: hdd and one pce flat* 4/5[1]
0/3- 3 1 1/4 **Agincourt Reef (IRE)**27 306 4-10-8 0 JamieMoore 102
(Gary Moore) *t.k.h: chsd ldrs: 3rd and rdn between last 2: styd on same pce flat* 10/1[3]
/0P- 4 25 **Tang Royal (FR)**13 538 6-10-12 0 AndrewGlassonbury 83
(Richard Rowe) *led and set stdy gallop: rdn and hdd bef 2 out: sn btn: wknd between last 2* 66/1
0/3- 5 nk **Tigridia (IRE)**21 417 6-10-5 0 MarcGoldstein 76
(Sheena West) *wl in tch in midfield: mstke 2nd: nt fluent 4th: cl 5th and rdn after 3 out: sn wknd* 14/1
0/0- 6 29 **Pinnacle Ofpassion (IRE)**16 484 5-10-5 0 GerardTumelty 50
(Nick Lampard) *hld up in tch in rr: j. bdly rt 1st: mstke 6th and sn rdn: lost tch after next: t.o bef 2 out* 100/1
7 10 **Michael Michael** 7-10-12 0 ConorO'Farrell 48
(Mick Channon) *nt fluent: chsd ldrs: mstke and lost pl 4th: rdn and struggling 7th: lost tch next: t.o 2 out* 16/1
5/6- 8 10 **Novel Dancer**39 95 5-10-12 0 PaddyBrennan 39
(Lydia Richards) *nt jump wl: pressed ldr tl 7th: wkng qckly whn mstke next: t.o 2 out* 25/1
6- R **Spiritofchartwell**30 246 5-10-12 0 DarylJacob
(Nick Gifford) *whipped arnd and shot off bk into collecting area as tapes wnt up: tk no part* 50/1

5m 2.4s (3.00) **Going Correction** -0.025s/f (Good)
WFA 4 from 5yo+ 18lb 9 Ran SP% 121.8
Speed ratings (Par 105): **93,92,91,81,81 69,65,61,**
toteswingers 1&2 £2.00, 1&3 £2.30, 2&3 £3.20 CSF £3.83 TOTE £2.60: £1.20, £1.10, £1.40; EX 4.10 Trifecta £18.80 Pool: £2246.20 - 89.13 winning units..
Owner Two Gents & An Orange Bloke Racing **Bred** Pigeon House Stud **Trained** Aberthin, Vale of Glamorgan
FOCUS
Modest novice hurdle form and a slow time. The winner was a stone off his Sandown mark.

707 EAZYLAY FLOORING & BEDS - WEST SUSSEX H'CAP CHASE (13 fncs 2 omitted) 2m 4f
3:15 (3:15) (Class 5) (0-95,89) 5-Y-0+ £2,144 (£629; £314; £157)

Form RPR
430- 1 **Lajidaal (USA)**16 485 6-11-8 85 (be) JamieMoore 97
(Gary Moore) *mde virtually all: sn urged along: hdd briefly 5th and sn rdn to ld again: hdd again and rdn after 8th: sn led again and mde rest but a off the bridle: clr and in command 3 out: kpt up to work after* 7/1
/42- 2 7 **Celtic Intrigue (IRE)**27 314 6-11-11 88 (tp) PaddyBrennan 95
(Tom George) *racd in last trio: niggled along after 2nd: 5th and wl outpcd u.p after 9th: styd on to chse wnr after 3 out: no imp* 2/1[1]
5/P- 3 16 **Benefit Evening (IRE)**35 164 8-10-13 79 (b) JackQuinlan(3) 70
(Noel Quinlan) *wl in tch in midfield: drew clr in ldng trio and rdn bef 10th: chsd clr wnr briefly next: 3rd and wl btn next: wknd* 25/1
/P1- 4 17 **Darnborough (IRE)**9 602 7-11-3 80 7ex FelixDeGiles 56
(Tom Symonds) *chsd ldr tl 2nd: styd chsng ldrs: pushed along briefly after 5th: rdn 9th: lost 2nd and btn 3 out: 4th and wkng whn j.rt next: tired flat: t.o* 3/1[3]
50P/ 5 4 **She's Humble (IRE)**97 4594 11-11-8 85 AndrewThornton 57
(Linda Jewell) *a bhd: lost tch 9th: t.o after next* 66/1
0/2- P **Silver Steel (FR)**34 172 10-11-12 89 (bt) APMcCoy
(Richard Ford) *chsd wnr 2nd: led briefly 5th and after 8th: mstke 9th: wknd bef next: t.o whn p.u 3 out* 11/4[2]

3/P- **P** **One For The Boss (IRE)**[30] 254 6-11-8 **85**....................(tp) SamJones
(Brendan Powell) *a in rr: struggling u.p after 8th: t.o whn p.u 3 out* **8/1**

5m 6.85s (-0.45) **Going Correction** -0.025s/f (Good) **7** Ran SP% **113.9**
Speed ratings: **99,96,89,83,81** ,
toteswingers 1&2 £3.20, 1&3 £34.30, 2&3 £10.50 CSF £22.20 CT £331.74 TOTE £6.60: £2.50, £1.60; EX 21.20 Trifecta £301.90 Pool: £1890.66 - 4.69 winning units..

Owner Dedman Properties **Bred** Shadwell Farm LLC **Trained** Lower Beeding, W Sussex

FOCUS
The front pair drew clear in what was a moderate handicap. The winner is rated back to his best.

708 DAVE BRADLEY TRUE BLUE 60TH MEMORIAL NOVICES' H'CAP HURDLE (9 hdls) 2m 2f 110y
3:50 (3:51) (Class 4) (0-105,102) 4-Y-0+ **£3,119** (£915; £457; £228)

Form RPR

P/3- **1** **Border Station (IRE)**[39] 95 7-11-3 **96**.......................... MarkQuinlan(3) 103+
(Alison Batchelor) *prom in chsng gp: chsd ldr after 3rd: clsd 5th: led bef 2 out and gng clr whn hit 2 out: j.rt last: drvn and tiring fnl 100yds: a gng to hold on* **6/1**[2]

0/0- **2** *1 ½* **Pampelonne (IRE)**[29] 267 7-11-9 **102**......................(p) KielanWoods(3) 105
(Charlie Longsdon) *racd in midfield: rdn after 3rd: clsd and in tch 5th: rdn and outpcd next: wnt modest 5th wl bef 2 out: 10 l 3rd last: chsd clr wnr flat: styd on wl but nvr quite getting to wnr* **7/1**[3]

500/ **3** *5* **Seven Summits (IRE)**[22] 5099 6-11-5 **95**.......................... PaulMoloney 93
(Sophie Leech) *hld up towards rr: chsd ldng pair bef 2 out: chsd clr wnr between last 2: kpt on but lost 2nd flat* **25/1**

/36- **4** *27* **Al Amaan**[16] 490 8-10-10 **93** ow3.............................. MrDanielBurchell(7) 67
(Jamie Poulton) *hld up in rr: clsd and in tch after 5th: pushed along and lost tch after 6th: no ch but passed btn horses flat: wnt 4th cl home* **16/1**

0P0/ **5** *1 ½* **Nebula Storm (IRE)**[186] 2904 6-11-8 **98**............................ JamieMoore 71
(Gary Moore) *prom in main gp: clsd and chsd ldrs after 5th: rdn and wknd bef 2 out* **7/1**[3]

P/3- **6** *3* **Rachael's Ruby**[30] 240 6-11-9 **99**......................................(v) ColinBolger 69
(Roger Teal) *led: wnt clr after 1st: c bk to field 5th: mstke 6th: rdn and hdd bef 2 out: hit 2 out: sn wknd* **50/1**

5/6- **7** *14* **Deceptive**[39] 97 5-11-12 **102**.. LiamTreadwell 59
(Paul Webber) *racd in midfield: clsd and in tch 5th: 7th and btn after 3 out: sn wknd: t.o* **12/1**

/64- **8** *13* **La Madonnina (IRE)**[14] 519 5-11-5 **95**................................ IanPopham 41
(Caroline Keevil) *bhd: clsd but rdn after 6th: lost tch after next: t.o bef 2 out* **16/1**

620/ **9** *2 ¼* **Super Duplex**[7] 2470 6-10-13 **99**................................... PaddyBradley(10) 42
(Pat Phelan) *t.k.h: hld up and prom in main gp: clsd and chsd ldrs 5th: wknd 3 out: t.o bef next* **12/1**

430- **P** **Conigre**[5] 651 6-11-9 **99**.. SamJones
(Brendan Powell) *chsd ldr tl after 3rd: rdn and lost pl after 5th: bhd after next: t.o whn p.u 2 out* **14/1**

0/4- **P** **Clonusker (IRE)**[27] 308 5-10-0 **76** oh8........................... PaddyBrennan
(Linda Jewell) *racd off the pce in rr: clsd on ldr 5th: rdn and struggling after next: t.o whn p.u last* **33/1**

000/ **P** **Listen And Learn (IRE)**[148] 3657 5-11-6 **96**......................... APMcCoy
(Jonjo O'Neill) *racd off the pce in midfield: clsd on ldr 5th: rdn and sme hdwy bef 6th: btn sn after 3 out: sn eased and wl bhd whn p.u next* **6/4**[1]

4m 35.5s (1.20) **Going Correction** -0.025s/f (Good) **12** Ran SP% **121.8**
Speed ratings (Par 105): **96,95,93,81,81 80,74,68,67,** ,
toteswingers 1&2 £7.70, 1&3 £22.70, 2&3 £50.00 CSF £48.71 CT £998.19 TOTE £7.20: £2.40, £2.20, £8.30; EX 46.70 Trifecta £1441.10 Pool: £2394.09 - 1.24 winning units..

Owner Mrs Alison Batchelor **Bred** Lac International And Waterside Stud **Trained** Petworth, W Sussex

■ Stewards' Enquiry : Kielan Woods four-day ban: use of whip (25, 26, 30 June, 2 July)

FOCUS
A few of these failed to give their running and the form is just ordinary for the level. The winner was well in on his recent course third and was value for a bit further.

709 32RED H'CAP CHASE (14 fncs 2 omitted) 2m 6f
4:20 (4:20) (Class 5) (0-100,100) 5-Y-0+ **£2,144** (£629; £314; £157)

Form RPR

/04- **1** **Dom Lukka (FR)**[16] 490 5-11-9 **97**......................................(t) NoelFehily 106+
(Charlie Longsdon) *j.rt: led tl 4th: chsd ldrs: blnd 11th: chsd ldr bef next: led 2 out: clr last: kpt on u.p flat: rdn out* **5/1**[2]

/65- **2** *2 ½* **Old Dreams (IRE)**[13] 541 7-11-9 **97**.............................(t) LiamTreadwell 102
(Nick Gifford) *in tch in last quartet: hdwy into midfield after 6th: mstke 9th: lft 3rd 3 out: chsd clr wnr last: kpt on but no imp fnl 100yds* **10/1**

0/5- **3** *8* **Jive Master (IRE)**[17] 472 8-11-12 **100**.......................(v[1]) RichardJohnson 101
(Tim Vaughan) *chsd ldrs tl led 4th: rdn and hdd 2 out: wknd last* **20/1**

6/1- **4** *4 ½* **Rudigreen (IRE)**[32] 212 10-11-7 **98**..........................(tp) JackQuinlan(3) 92
(Noel Quinlan) *hld up in tch in rr: hmpd 11th: sn drvn: struggling u.p after next: lft 5th and hmpd 3 out: 4th and wl hld next* **6/1**

4/0- **5** *43* **Psi (USA)**[39] 99 8-11-12 **100**..(b) JamieMoore 70
(Gary Moore) *in tch in last quartet: j.lft 3rd: in tch and drvn after 10th: wkng whn lft 5th and hmpd 3 out: eased flat: t.o* **7/1**

/13- **P** **Princely Hero (IRE)**[16] 485 9-11-8 **96**..............................(p) PaddyBrennan
(Chris Gordon) *in tch in midfield: pushed along but travelling bttr than usual whn blnd v bdly 10th: nt rcvr: eased and p.u next* **11/2**[3]

61U/ **F** **Bring It On Home**[498] 4017 9-10-7 **81**...........................(b) AidanColeman
(Sarah Kerswell) *in tch in midfield: hdwy to chse ldr 9th: rdn bef 3 out: 3rd and wkng whn fell 3 out* **14/1**

/05- **P** **Doctor Ric (IRE)**[16] 485 8-10-11 **85**...............................(p) ColinBolger
(Gerry Enright) *w ldr tl 3rd: lost pl and rdn after 4th: losing tch whn p.u 10th* **20/1**

/54- **P** **Star Of Massini (IRE)**[13] 539 6-11-9 **97**.......................... RyanMahon
(Seamus Mullins) *in tch in last quartet: rdn and lost tch after 9th: t.o whn p.u 11th* **10/1**

230/ **P** **Whistling Senator (IRE)**[44] 7 6-11-9 **97**.......................(p) APMcCoy
(Jonjo O'Neill) *chsd ldrs: 3rd and drvn after 9th: wkng whn lft 4th and hmpd 3 out: wknd and t.o whn p.u last* **7/2**[1]

5m 47.05s (4.05) **Going Correction** -0.025s/f (Good) **10** Ran SP% **115.4**
Speed ratings: **91,90,87,85,69** , , , ,
toteswingers 1&2 £11.60, 1&3 £13.60, 2&3 £24.20 CSF £52.79 CT £905.08 TOTE £5.60: £2.20, £2.90, £4.30; EX 51.40 Trifecta £1487.00 Part won. Pool: £1982.70 - 0.85 winning units..

Owner Roy Swinburne **Bred** Jean-Claude Janin-Thivos **Trained** Over Norton, Oxon

■ Stewards' Enquiry : Colin Bolger two-day ban: failed to ride out for fourth (25-26 Jun)

FOCUS
Modest handicap form. The winner improved to his best hurdles mark.

710 PLATINUM LACE GENTLEMEN'S CLUB - BRIGHTON H'CAP HURDLE (DIV I) (11 hdls) 2m 6f 110y
4:50 (4:50) (Class 5) (0-95,95) 4-Y-0+ **£1,949** (£572; £286; £143)

Form RPR

000/ **1** **Realta Mo Croi (IRE)**[154] 3556 5-10-0 **69** oh5................ DougieCostello 87+
(Neil Mulholland) *hld up in tch in last quartet: hdwy and gng wl 7th: clr in ldng quartet 3 out: pressed ldr next: led bef last: styd on wl: rdn out* **4/1**[1]

646/ **2** *3 ¼* **Band Of Thunder**[205] 2504 5-9-12 **72**.......................(v) GavinSheehan(5) 85
(Nick Mitchell) *led: rdn and hdd bef last: hung rt and styd on same pce flat* **12/1**

600/ **3** *25* **Franklino (FR)**[10] 4461 6-11-12 **95**.............................. RichardJohnson 86
(Chris Gordon) *hld up in tch in rr: hdwy to chse ldrs 7th: cl 4th and rdn after 3 out: wknd next: wnt modest 3rd last* **6/1**[3]

04U/ **4** *11* **Formedable (IRE)**[53] 5381 11-10-0 **69** oh9.........................(p) SamJones 50
(Violet M Jordan) *in tch: chsd ldr 7th: cl 3rd and rdn 2 out: wknd between last 2: lost 3rd and fdd flat: t.o* **25/1**

U53- **5** *27* **Airedale Lad (IRE)**[16] 490 12-9-7 **69** oh1.........(p) MrJoshuaNewman(7) 25
(Zoe Davison) *j.rt: chsd ldrs: rdn after 8th: lost tch next: t.o 2 out* **8/1**

2/4- **6** *3 ¼* **Burnt Again (IRE)**[35] 162 9-11-3 **86**............................(t) MattieBatchelor 39
(Jim Best) *racd awkwardly: prom but pushed along at times: chsd ldr after 4th tl 7th: wknd bef 3 out: t.o bef 2 out* **8/1**

4/6- **7** *20* **Orsm**[20] 428 6-11-0 **93**..(tp) NathanAdams(10) 28
(Laura Mongan) *in tch in midfield: rdn after 7th: wknd bef 3 out: t.o bef 2 out* **16/1**

/F3- **P** **Festival Bound (IRE)**[9] 595 7-10-4 **80**...................(v) MissBAndrews(7)
(Caroline Fryer) *in tch in last quartet: reminders after 5th: rdn and no rspnse after 7th: lost tch bef 3 out: t.o bef 2 out tl p.u last* **14/1**

P50/ **P** **Midnight Choice**[53] 5378 8-10-3 **75**................................. MarkQuinlan(3)
(James Evans) *in tch towards rr: rdn along briefly after 5th: lost tch u.p bef 3 out: t.o whn p.u 2 out* **4/1**[1]

/40- **P** **Spanish Fork (IRE)**[28] 295 4-11-7 **95**............................ MarcGoldstein
(Sheena West) *chsd ldr tl after 4th: sn rdn: dropped to rr u.p after 7th: t.o 3 out tl p.u next* **9/2**[2]

5m 40.4s (-2.10) **Going Correction** -0.025s/f (Good)
WFA 4 from 5yo+ 18lb **10** Ran SP% **118.8**
Speed ratings (Par 103): **102,100,92,88,78 77,70,** , ,
toteswingers 1&2 £10.20, 1&3 £4.80, 2&3 £15.30 CSF £51.42 CT £289.84 TOTE £4.40: £2.00, £4.80, £2.00; EX 71.30 Trifecta £682.20 Pool: £1991.18 - 2.18 winning units..

Owner Neil Mulholland Racing Ltd **Bred** Mrs Catherine Kenneally **Trained** Limpley Stoke, Wilts

FOCUS
The front pair pulled away up the straight in what was a low-grade handicap hurdle. The winner could go in again and the second is rated back to his 2011 mark.

711 PLATINUM LACE GENTLEMEN'S CLUB - BRIGHTON H'CAP HURDLE (DIV II) (11 hdls) 2m 6f 110y
5:20 (5:20) (Class 5) (0-95,94) 4-Y-0+ **£1,949** (£572; £286; £143)

Form RPR

/53- **1** **Marie Deja La (FR)**[13] 543 7-11-10 **92**.......................(b) MarcGoldstein 101+
(Chris Gordon) *chsd ldr: gng best after 3 out and led bef next: wnt clr between last 2: in command and mstke last: styd on: rdn out* **9/2**[2]

5P5/ **2** *6* **Aaly**[16] 6-9-7 **68** oh9... NathanAdams(7) 71
(Lydia Richards) *j.rt: hld up in rr: rdn and hdwy after 7th: styd on u.p after 3 out: chsd clr wnr bef last: mstke last: styd on wl but no threat to wnr* **8/1**[3]

/P0- **3** *15* **General Girling**[14] 519 6-10-6 **74**.................................... IanPopham 62
(Caroline Keevil) *chsd ldng pair: outpcd 3 out: rallied bef next: mstke 2 out: sn wknd: plugged on to go modest 3rd flat* **50/1**

0/0- **4** *2 ¼* **Shot In The Dark (IRE)**[28] 295 4-11-5 **92**.........................(t) MarkGrant 73
(Jonathan Geake) *in tch in midfield: rdn and dropped to rr after 7th: outpcd bef 3 out: no threat to wnr but plugged on between last 2* **25/1**

0/2- **5** *1 ½* **Billing (IRE)**[41] 67 5-10-4 **72**...................................(b[1]) RichieMcLernon 59
(Jonjo O'Neill) *j.rt: led: hung rt bnd after 3 out: hdd bef next: fnd nil and j.rt 2 out: 3rd and wl hld between last 2: hung rt and wknd flat* **1/1**[1]

P/4- **6** *5* **Dazzling Rita**[23] 391 7-10-11 **79**....................................(t) DavidEngland 61
(Shaun Lycett) *hld up off the pce in last pair: hdwy after 7th: chsd ldrs after 3 out: rdn bef next: wknd sn after 2 out: fdd flat* **12/1**

3/4- **7** *8* **Haling Park (UAE)**[41] 67 7-10-1 **69**............................ TomMessenger 42
(Clarissa Caroe) *in tch in midfield: dropped to rr and mstke 8th: lost tch next: t.o* **16/1**

4/6- **8** *12* **Bright Light**[30] 241 6-10-0 **68** oh4................................... AidanColeman 30
(Richard Phillips) *chsd ldrs: mstke 8th: wknd bef 2 out: fdd between last 2: t.o and eased towards fnish* **10/1**

000/ **P** **Sterling Bill (IRE)**[154] 3556 5-10-0 **68** oh8...................(t) DougieCostello
(Neil Mulholland) *chsd ldrs: mstke 8th: wknd next: t.o whn p.u 2 out* **10/1**

5m 45.1s (2.60) **Going Correction** -0.025s/f (Good)
WFA 4 from 5yo+ 18lb **9** Ran SP% **116.9**
Speed ratings (Par 103): **94,91,86,85,85 83,80,76,**
toteswingers 1&2 £5.20, 1&3 £19.90, 2&3 £73.50 CSF £40.52 CT £1586.50 TOTE £5.70: £1.40, £2.50, £9.90; EX 41.00 Trifecta £536.90 Pool: £844.87 - 1.18 winning units..

Owner Chris Gordon Racing Club **Bred** Ms Louise Collet **Trained** Morestead, Hants

FOCUS
They appeared to go a reasonable gallop in the second division of this handicap. The easy winner is closing in on the best of last year's form.

712 32RED.COM H'CAP CHASE (16 fncs 3 omitted) 3m 2f 110y
5:55 (5:55) (Class 4) (0-110,110) 5-Y-0+ **£3,768** (£1,106; £553; £276)

Form RPR

/F3- **1** **Inner Steel (IRE)**[13] 541 8-10-11 **95**............................ PaddyBrennan 111+
(Lydia Richards) *hld up in last pair: hdwy after 11th: jnd ldr 3 out: led next: sn clr: eased towards fin: easily* **5/1**[3]

5/5- **2** *14* **Basoda**[26] 334 10-11-11 **109**..(tp) NickScholfield 110
(Kim Bailey) *in tch in midfield: hdwy to chse ldrs and mstke 8th: lost pl 13th: rallied u.p after 3 out: styd on to chse wnr flat: no threat to wnr* **8/1**

216/ **3** *2 ½* **Alteranthela (IRE)**[46] 5554 9-10-0 **84** oh2.................(b[1]) DougieCostello 81
(Richard Rowe) *led tl 2nd: chsd ldr after tl led again after 13th: drvn and hdd 2 out sn brushed aside by wnr: lost 2nd flat* **16/1**

3/P- **4** *5* **Days Of Pleasure (IRE)**[13] 541 8-10-4 **88**.......................(v) ColinBolger 81
(Chris Gordon) *chsd ldr tl led 2nd: hdd after 13th: drvn and outpcd 3 out: no threat to wnr but plugged on u.p flat* **25/1**

2/2- **5** *2 ¼* **Leg Iron (IRE)**[30] 242 8-11-12 **110**................................ MarcGoldstein 101
(Sheena West) *chsd ldrs: lost pl and niggled along after 6th: nvr gng wl and a niggled along after: midfield and drvn 12th: outpcd and btn bef 3 out: wknd 2 out* **7/2**[1]

3/3- **6** *nk* **Sea Cadet**[30] 242 11-10-4 **88**......(b) RichardJohnson 78
(Laura Mongan) *in tch in midfield: hdwy to chse ldrs after 6th: 3rd and stl gng wl bef 3 out: rdn and fnd nil after 3 out: wknd between last 2* **8/1**
152/ **7** *22* **Baily Storm (IRE)**[233] 1945 11-11-5 **103**......(tp) DavidBass 74
(Lawney Hill) *in tch in last trio: mstke 7th: rdn and struggling after 12th: lost tch bef 3 out: t.o* **16/1**
5/3- **8** *hd* **Starsky Des Mottes (FR)**[33] 179 7-11-6 **104**...... JackDoyle 74
(Victor Dartnall) *hld up in last pair: clsd on ldrs and gng wl after 12th: 4th bef 3 out: rdn and fnd nil after 3 out: sn wknd: tired flat: t.o* **5/1**[3]
0/4- **P** **River D'Or (FR)**[29] 265 8-11-9 **107**...... PaulMoloney
(Sophie Leech) *in tch in last trio: rdn and struggling after 11th: lost tch 13th: t.o whn p.u next* **9/2**[2]
P60/ **P** **Call At Midnight**[205] 2503 8-11-9 **110**...... JackQuinlan[(3)]
(Sarah Humphrey) *chsd ldrs: lost pl but stl wl in tch after 11th: rdn and wknd wl bef 3 out: p.u bef last* **20/1**

7m 5.2s (4.10) **Going Correction** -0.025s/f (Good) **10** Ran SP% **116.3**
Speed ratings: **92,87,87,85,84 84,78,78, ,**
toteswingers 1&2 £6.60, 1&3 £12.00, 2&3 £22.50 CSF £44.61 CT £597.21 TOTE £5.30: £2.10, £2.50, £4.70; EX 43.20 Trifecta £541.10 Part won. Pool: £721.51 - 0.56 winning units..
Owner The Inner Steel Partnership **Bred** Brendan Caulfield **Trained** Funtington, W Sussex

FOCUS
A good test at the distance on the softened ground.
T/Plt: £655.80 to a £1 stake. Pool of £75,606.54 - 84.15 winning tickets. T/Qpdt: £266.20 to a £1 stake. Pool of £4965.06 - 13.80 winning tickets. SP

645 WORCESTER (L-H)
Tuesday, June 11

OFFICIAL GOING: Good (good to firm in places; 6.5)
Wind: Light against Weather: Overcast

713 FOOTBALL SCORES ON YOUR MOBILE AT FOOTBALLSCORES.COM H'CAP CHASE (18 fncs) 2m 7f
6:10 (6:10) (Class 4) (0-110,108) 5-Y-0+ **£3,898** (£1,144; £572; £286)

Form RPR
55F/ **1** **Basil Fawlty (IRE)**[70] 5104 8-11-6 **102**......(t) TomScudamore 113+
(David Pipe) *hld up: hdwy 11th: led 4 out: hdd 2 out: led again last: rdn and edgd rt flat: styd on* **4/1**[2]
6/1- **2** *hd* **My Mate Vinnie (IRE)**[18] 461 6-11-10 **106**......(t) DominicElsworth 118+
(Jonjo O'Neill) *hld up: blnd 13th: hdwy appr 4 out: rdn and hung lft after next: led 2 out: hdd last: styd on u.p: hmpd towards fin* **7/4**[1]
/05- **3** *18* **Basford Ben**[11] 564 5-11-7 **103**......(p) SeanQuinlan 100
(Jennie Candlish) *hld up: blnd 13th: drvn along appr 4 out: wknd 2 out* **20/1**
P10/ **4** *7* **Junior Jack**[128] 8-11-4 **100**......(t) SamTwiston-Davies 88
(Jennifer Mason) *prom: mstke 8th: rdn appr 3 out: wknd after next* **33/1**
0/3- **5** *16* **Rossbrin (IRE)**[21] 420 8-11-4 **100**......(tp) AndrewTinkler 74
(Anna Brooks) *led: rdn and hdd 4 out: wknd 2 out: t.o* **8/1**
423- **6** *17* **Waltzing Tornado (IRE)**[16] 504 9-10-9 **91**......(p) DPFahy 50
(Andy Hobbs) *hld up: hdwy 10th: rdn and wknd 4 out: t.o whn hit 2 out* **8/1**
P61/ **7** *43* **The Wife's Sister**[384] 406 12-10-1 **88**...... BenPoste[(5)] 8
(James Evans) *chsd ldr tl rdn appr 4 out: sn wknd: t.o* **25/1**
45P/ **P** **Midnight Gold**[229] 2009 13-11-3 **99**......(p) WayneHutchinson
(Julian Smith) *chsd ldrs: rdn appr 13th: wknd next: t.o whn p.u bef 3 out* **15/2**
1/F- **P** **Midnight Whisper**[38] 122 7-11-12 **108**...... AlainCawley
(Richard Woollacott) *hld up: bhd 13th: p.u bef next* **7/1**[3]

5m 54.3s (6.30) **Going Correction** +0.075s/f (Yiel) **9** Ran SP% **114.4**
Speed ratings: **92,91,85,83,77 71,56, ,**
toteswingers 1&2 £2.90, 1&3 £9.40, 2&3 £7.80 CSF £11.58 CT £120.84 TOTE £4.80: £1.70, £1.20, £5.20; EX 12.70 Trifecta £251.10 Pool: £1071.19 - 3.19 winning units..
Owner M C Pipe **Bred** Mrs Margaret Norris **Trained** Nicholashayne, Devon
■ Stewards' Enquiry : Tom Scudamore two-day ban: careless riding (25, 26 June)
Dominic Elsworth two-day ban: use of whip (25, 26 June)

FOCUS
Both bends moved out 12yds from inside line with run-in on stands' side. This moderate handicap was run at an ordinary gallop, but the two market leaders dominated from three out and both came from off the pace. The winner improved and there's probably more to come.

714 COMPARE BOOKMAKERS ON YOUR MOBILE AT BOOKMAKERS.CO.UK H'CAP CHASE (15 fncs) 2m 4f
6:40 (6:40) (Class 4) (0-115,113) 5-Y-0+ **£3,898** (£1,144; £572; £286)

Form RPR
3/0- **1** **Surf And Turf (IRE)**[10] 585 7-11-4 105...... DominicElsworth 125+
(Jonjo O'Neill) *sn prom: led 4th: jnd 4 out: clr 2 out: blnd last: easily* **6/5**[1]
2/4- **2** *20* **Run Along Boy**[28] 286 8-11-9 110......(p) JasonMaguire 97
(Neil Mulholland) *hld up: hit 5th: bhd and pushed along next: rdn 11th: styd on to go remote 2nd nr fin* **5/2**[2]
4/P- **3** *1* **Citrus Mark**[30] 245 8-11-3 104...... LiamHeard 93
(Paul Webber) *prom: ev ch whn mstke 4 out: wkng whn nt fluent 2 out: lost 2nd nr fin* **9/1**
/55- **4** *31* **Finch Flyer (IRE)**[3] 674 6-10-8 95......(b) TommyPhelan 53
(Aytach Sadik) *chsd ldr to 3rd: remained handy tl rdn and wknd appr 4 out: t.o* **16/1**
0/1- **P** **Papradon**[18] 457 9-11-6 107......(b) SamTwiston-Davies
(Nigel Twiston-Davies) *led: blnd and hdd 4th: drvn along 7th: wknd 9th: t.o whn p.u bef 4 out* **4/1**[3]

4m 59.3s (-0.70) **Going Correction** +0.075s/f (Yiel) **5** Ran SP% **109.9**
Speed ratings: **104,96,95,83,**
CSF £4.79 TOTE £1.90: £1.10, £1.40; EX 5.20 Trifecta £15.70 Pool: £760.99 - 36.26 winning units..
Owner John P McManus **Bred** J P Murphy & M Barry Murphy **Trained** Cheltenham, Gloucs

FOCUS
Jumping errors aplenty in this ordinary novice handicap. There's a case for rating the form up to 12lb higher.

715 GET LIVE SPORTS SCORES AT SCORES.CO.UK MARES' STANDARD OPEN NATIONAL HUNT FLAT RACE 2m
7:10 (7:10) (Class 6) 4-6-Y-0 **£1,559** (£457; £228; £114)

Form RPR
3- **1** **Shuil Gealach (IRE)**[27] 324 5-10-12 0...... DenisO'Regan 96+
(Paul Webber) *hld up: drvn along 5f out: styd on u.p fr over 2f out to ld post* **11/8**[1]
2 *hd* **Dardanella** 6-10-12 0...... CharliePoste 95+
(Richard Lee) *hld up: hdwy 10f out: chsd ldr over 2f out: led over 1f out: rdn and edgd rt fnl f: hdd post* **16/1**
6- **3** *1 1/4* **Lola Galli**[17] 483 5-10-12 0......(p) TomScudamore 94
(David Pipe) *chsd ldrs: led over 8f out: hdd over 5f out: led again over 2f out: rdn and hdd over 1f out: kpt on* **13/2**[3]
00/- **4** *3* **Cloudy Lady**[51] 5444 5-10-12 0...... LeightonAspell 91
(Jeremy Gask) *hld up: hdwy over 6f out: rdn over 1f out: styd on same pce fnl f* **9/1**
6/ **5** *11* **Dungarvan Lass (IRE)**[43] 35 4-10-9 0...... AndrewTinkler 78
(Nicky Henderson) *prom: reminders 7f out: wknd 2f out* **9/1**
00- **6** *3 1/4* **Wymeswold**[11] 567 6-10-9 0...... KielanWoods[(3)] 78
(Michael Mullineaux) *chsd ldrs: rdn over 3f out: wknd 2f out* **100/1**
6- **7** *3/4* **Bad Girls (FR)**[27] 324 4-10-2 0......(p) KieronEdgar[(7)] 75
(David Pipe) *chsd ldrs: led over 5f out: hdd & wknd over 2f out* **12/1**
8 *2 1/4* **Just Got Lucky** 5-10-12 0...... DominicElsworth 75
(Emma Lavelle) *hld up: bhd 12f out: nvr nrr* **9/2**[2]
0- **9** *12* **Too Trigger Happy**[18] 462 4-10-6 0...... WayneKavanagh[(3)] 62
(Dr Jeremy Naylor) *hld up: hdwy 1/2-way: rdn and wknd over 4f out: t.o* **100/1**
10 *1 1/2* **Seondeok (IRE)**[100] 5-10-5 0...... MissJodieHughes[(7)] 63
(David Rees) *prom: rdn over 5f out: sn wknd: t.o* **33/1**
0/- **11** *24* **Lady Cliche**[44] 4 4-10-9 0...... HaddenFrost 39
(Roger Curtis) *prom: lost pl 10f out: wknd over 5f out: t.o* **100/1**
0- **12** *3 1/4* **Miss Redbrook (IRE)**[33] 187 6-10-12 0...... WillKennedy 39
(Sarah-Jayne Davies) *chsd ldrs: rdn over 5f out: sn wknd: t.o* **66/1**
6- **13** *6* **High Holloa**[18] 462 4-10-9 0...... AndrewThornton 30
(Caroline Bailey) *hld up: hdwy 1/2-way: wknd over 4f out* **20/1**
0/- **14** *12* **Goldie Horn**[109] 4377 5-10-12 0...... SamTwiston-Davies 23
(Nigel Twiston-Davies) *hld up: rdn over 6f out: sn t.o* **33/1**
0- **P** **Passing Fiesta**[27] 324 4-10-9 0...... BrendanPowell
(Sarah-Jayne Davies) *plld hrd: sn led: sddle slipped and hdd over 8f out: sn p.u* **50/1**

3m 42.1s (0.40) **Going Correction** +0.075s/f (Yiel)
WFA 4 from 5yo+ 3lb **15** Ran SP% **124.3**
Speed ratings: **102,101,101,99,94 92,92,91,85,84 72,70,67,61,**
toteswingers 1&2 £9.20, 1&3 £3.70, 2&3 £10.20 CSF £27.51 TOTE £2.70: £1.10, £6.40, £2.20; EX 49.80 Trifecta £341.60 Pool: £743.31 - 1.63 winning units..
Owner R C Moody **Bred** George Ward **Trained** Mollington, Oxon

FOCUS
There was a fair enough gallop on in this mares' bumper and the first four were nicely clear at the finish. The watered ground looked tacky in places as the runners kicked it up. The form makes sense.

716 COMPARE FREE BETS AT FREEBETS.ORG "NATIONAL HUNT" NOVICES' HURDLE (8 hdls) 2m
7:40 (7:40) (Class 4) 4-Y-0+ **£3,119** (£915; £457; £228)

Form RPR
4/2- **1** **Separate Shadows (FR)**[24] 367 5-10-12 0...... JasonMaguire 109
(Donald McCain) *chsd ldr tl led 6th: shkn up and hung rt after 3 out: hrd rdn flat: all out* **13/8**[1]
/2U- **2** *3/4* **Somchine**[16] 484 5-10-12 110...... AndrewThornton 110+
(Seamus Mullins) *hld up: hdwy 4th: chsd wnr after next: ev ch 3 out: nt clr run and swtchd lft after next: mstke last: edgd lft flat: styd on u.p* **5/2**[2]
0/0- **3** *35* **Frontier Vic**[21] 417 6-10-12 0...... SamTwiston-Davies 77
(Nigel Twiston-Davies) *hld up: pushed along after 5th: styd on to go remote 3rd nr fin: t.o* **20/1**
P/3- **4** *3/4* **Ata Boy (IRE)**[20] 434 7-10-12 0...... AndrewTinkler 76
(Richard Phillips) *hld up: hdwy 5th: rdn and wknd 3 out: t.o* **33/1**
/32- **5** *8* **Panache**[20] 434 8-10-12 93......(p) TomO'Brien 69
(Angela Clarke) *prom: rdn after 5th: wknd bef next: t.o* **5/1**[3]
450/ **6** *7* **Cleeve Cloud (IRE)**[215] 2288 7-10-12 0...... LiamTreadwell 64
(Liam Grassick) *hld up: n.d: t.o* **17/2**
7 *19* **Rockingtimes (IRE)**[65] 5-10-12 0...... HenryOliver 45
(Henry Oliver) *chsd ldrs: rdn after 4th: wknd next: t.o* **13/2**
/50- **8** *29* **Umoristic (FR)**[5] 651 5-10-12 84......(b[1]) DPFahy 19
(Reginald Brown) *led: rdn and hdd 5th: wknd bef next: t.o* **25/1**
00/ **9** *6* **Revupclover (IRE)**[45] 6-10-5 0...... MrEBarrett[(7)] 14
(Polly Gundry) *prom tl rdn and wknd after 4th: t.o* **66/1**
000/ **P** **Chandler Jack**[208] 2436 6-10-9 0...... KielanWoods[(3)]
(Derek Wellicome) *prom: lost pl 3rd: sn bhd: t.o whn p.u bef 2 out* **100/1**
P/ **P** **Harry Dore**[394] 248 7-10-9 0...... AdamWedge[(3)]
(Richard Price) *plld hrd: hld up: bhd fr 3rd: t.o whn p.u bef 5th* **100/1**

3m 45.4s (-1.90) **Going Correction** +0.075s/f (Yiel) **11** Ran SP% **122.2**
Speed ratings (Par 105): **107,106,89,88,84 81,71,57,54,**
totewingers 1&2 £1.90, 1&3 £4.50, 2&3 £12.30 CSF £5.95 TOTE £2.20: £1.40, £1.50, £4.60; EX 7.60 Trifecta £96.50 Pool: £1226.98 - 9.52 winning units..
Owner Howard Spooner **Bred** Mathieu Daguzan-Garros Et Al **Trained** Cholmondeley, Cheshire
■ Stewards' Enquiry : Jason Maguire two-day ban: use of whip (3-4 July)
Henry Oliver seven-day ban: use of whip (25, 26, 30 Jun, 2, 3, 4, 7 July)

FOCUS
A modest novice hurdle, dominated by the two clear market leaders. The winner built on his recent hurdles debut and mistakes cost the second the race.

717 COMPARE BOOKIES FREE BETS AT BOOKMAKERS.CO.UK MARES' MAIDEN HURDLE (10 hdls) 2m 4f
8:10 (8:10) (Class 5) 4-Y-0+ **£1,949** (£572; £286; £143)

Form RPR
P20/ **1** **As I Am (IRE)**[135] 3904 5-11-0 107...... LeightonAspell 120+
(Don Cantillon) *hld up: hdwy 6th: mstke next: led after 3 out: sn clr: easily* **11/10**[1]
33/ **2** *22* **Je T'Aime (IRE)**[43] 35 4-10-10 0...... JasonMaguire 95
(Donald McCain) *chsd ldrs: rdn appr 3 out: wknd bef next* **12/1**
/32- **3** *9* **Definitely Glad (IRE)**[19] 450 6-11-0 110...... DenisO'Regan 90
(Paul Webber) *chsd ldrs: rdn appr 3 out: sn wknd: t.o* **3/1**[2]
0/4- **4** *1 1/4* **Flew The Nest (IRE)**[19] 450 5-11-0 0...... APMcCoy 92+
(Jonjo O'Neill) *hld up: hdwy 5th: led 3 out: sn hdd: j.lft and wknd next: wnt bdly lft last* **10/1**[3]
5 *3 1/4* **Drombeg West**[52] 6-11-0 0...... CharliePoste 86
(Anna Brooks) *hld up: hdwy 7th: rdn and wknd bef next: t.o* **50/1**
026/ **6** *7* **Was My Valentine**[56] 5330 6-10-4 102...... JackSavage[(10)] 80
(Jo Davis) *prom: pushed along 6th: rdn and wknd appr 3 out: t.o whn hmpd next* **12/1**
/2P- **7** *6* **Grimley Girl**[11] 561 7-11-0 100...... WillKennedy 74
(Sarah-Jayne Davies) *chsd ldr tl rdn and wknd appr 3 out: t.o* **14/1**

0/ **8** *6* **Y O Me**^{45} 6-11-0 0 .... DonalDevereux 69
(Sirrell Griffiths) *prom to 6th: t.o* **100/1**

0/3- **9** *2 ¼* **On The Move**^{30} [246] 5-10-11 0 .... RachaelGreen$^{(3)}$ 67
(Anthony Honeyball) *hld up: wknd after 7th: t.o* **16/1**

/03- **10** *3 ½* **Princess Annabelle**^{22} [410] 4-10-7 96 .... (b) MarkQuinlan$^{(3)}$ 60
(Rod Millman) *led: j.rt: hmpd by loose horse after 7th: rdn and hdd 3 out: sn wknd: wnt bdly rt next* **25/1**

5/6- **11** *6* **Rolling Dough (IRE)**^{33} [187] 5-10-7 0 .... KieronEdgar$^{(7)}$ 58
(Sophie Leech) *hld up: bhd fr 4th: t.o* **66/1**

12 *21* **Vic's Moll (IRE)**^{15} 7-10-7 0 .... (p) MrWPotter$^{(7)}$ 39
(Polly Gundry) *prom: mstke and lost pl 3rd: bhd fr 5th: t.o* **33/1**

P- **U** **Heels Overhead**^{39} [94] 7-10-7 0 .... MrJamieJenkinson$^{(7)}$
(John Bryan Groucott) *chsd ldr tl blnd and uns rdr 1st* **100/1**

4m 52.7s (5.30) **Going Correction** +0.075s/f (Yiel)
WFA 4 from 5yo+ 18lb 13 Ran SP% **121.9**
Speed ratings (Par 103): **92,83,79,79,77 75,72,70,69,67 65,57,**
toteswingers 1&2 £6.90, 1&3 £2.50, 2&3 £2.80 CSF £16.57 TOTE £2.00: £1.10, £3.00, £1.80; EX 24.70 Trifecta £147.60 Pool: £648.42 - 3.29 winning units..

Owner Don Cantillon **Bred** Don Cantillon **Trained** Newmarket, Suffolk

FOCUS
There was no strength in depth to this mares' maiden. The winner is rated to the level expect from the best of her bumper form.

718 GET FREE BETS WITH FREEBETS.NET H'CAP HURDLE (12 hdls) 2m 7f
8:40 (8:40) (Class 3) (0-130,130) 4-Y-0+ **£5,523** (£1,621; £810; £405)

Form RPR

005/ **1** **Tornado Bob (IRE)**^{43} [24] 8-11-12 **130** .... (b^{1}) JasonMaguire 140+
(Donald McCain) *mde all at str pce and sn clr: rdn appr last: styd on gamely: unchal* **8/1**

624/ **2** *4* **Mister Dillon**^{65} [5200] 6-11-11 **129** .... AndrewTinkler 134
(Nicky Henderson) *a.p: chsd wnr 4 out: tk clsr order after 3 out: rdn whn mstke last: no imp flat* **7/2^{1}**

P/3- **3** *52* **Storm Survivor (IRE)**^{30} [238] 7-11-8 **126** .... (v) APMcCoy 85
(Jonjo O'Neill) *prom: chsd clr ldr 7th to 4 out: sn rdn and wknd: t.o* **4/1^{2}**

061/ **4** *5* **Sohappyharry**^{432} [5255] 7-10-13 **117** .... DPFahy 71
(Jane Mathias) *hld up: nvr on terms: t.o* **25/1**

1/F- **5** *54* **Point Blank (IRE)**^{26} [334] 7-11-5 **123** .... (t) RichieMcLernon 29
(Jonjo O'Neill) *prom: chsd wnr who was clr 4th to 7th: rdn and wknd next: t.o* **22/1**

4/5- **6** *10* **Phare Isle (IRE)**^{26} [336] 8-11-5 **123** .... (tp) DarylJacob 20
(Ben Case) *hld up: drvn along after 6th: t.o fr next* **9/2^{3}**

U00/ **7** *26* **Home Run (GER)**^{45} [5574] 5-11-4 **122** .... (p) TomScudamore
(David Pipe) *hld up: shkn up after 4th: sme hdwy 7th: wknd next: t.o* **7/1**

333/ **8** *37* **Sainglend**^{203} [2537] 8-11-2 **130** .... MikeyHamill$^{(10)}$
(Sean Curran) *hld up: bhd fr 5th: t.o* **12/1**

2/0- **9** *4 ½* **The Fonz**^{26} [336] 7-11-2 **120** .... (b^{1}) BrendanPowell
(Renee Robeson) *hld up: hdwy 6th: mstke and wknd next: t.o* **7/1**

P/6- **P** **Archie Boy (IRE)**^{26} [335] 11-10-10 **119** .... (tp) JonathanEngland$^{(5)}$
(Roy Brotherton) *chsd wnr who was clr to 4th: lost a pl after next: bhd fr 7th: t.o whn p.u bef 3 out* **66/1**

5m 35.5s (7.50) **Going Correction** +0.075s/f (Yiel) 10 Ran SP% **113.9**
Speed ratings (Par 107): **89,87,69,67,49 45,36,23,22,**
toteswingers 1&2 £8.10, 1&3 £7.70, 2&3 £2.00 CSF £35.38 CT £129.21 TOTE £18.30: £4.10, £1.02, £2.20; EX 50.10 Trifecta £92.20 Pool: £651.44 - 5.29 winning units..

Owner Mrs Diana L Whateley **Bred** Christopher Maye **Trained** Cholmondeley, Cheshire

FOCUS
A fair handicap. They got strung out early on and only two mattered from three out. The winner is rated back to form, with a personal best from the winner.

719 DONATE SOME OF YOUR WINNINGS TO INJUREDJOCKEYS.CO.UK H'CAP HURDLE (10 hdls) 2m 4f
9:10 (9:10) (Class 4) (0-115,115) 4-Y-0+ **£3,119** (£915; £457; £228)

Form RPR

/11- **1** **Man Of Leisure**^{3} [669] 9-11-3 **109** 14ex .... (t) RachaelGreen$^{(3)}$ 122+
(Anthony Honeyball) *trckd ldrs: plld hrd: mstke 3 out: led next: shkn up flat: r.o wl* **1/1^{1}**

1/4- **2** *7* **Rum And Butter (IRE)**^{16} [486] 5-11-6 **109** .... (p) APMcCoy 115+
(Jonjo O'Neill) *a.p: chsd ldr 6th to next: sn wnt 2nd again: ev ch and mstke 2 out: swtchd lft bef last: hung lft flat: styd on same pce* **13/8^{2}**

PP6/ **3** *4 ½* **Nez Rouge (FR)**^{58} [5308] 12-10-11 **100** .... SamTwiston-Davies 99
(Nigel Twiston-Davies) *set stdy pce tl qcknd after 5th: rdn and hdd 2 out: no ex last* **14/1**

/42- **4** *7* **Dormouse**^{16} [488] 8-11-5 **115** .... (p) KieronEdgar$^{(7)}$ 106
(Anabel K Murphy) *hld up: hdwy 7th: wknd next* **12/1^{3}**

060/ **5** *½* **Osric (IRE)**^{38} 10-11-11 **114** .... GerardTumelty 104
(Laura Young) *hld up: wknd 3 out* **40/1**

0/6- **6** *2* **Munlochy Bay**^{23} [393] 9-10-7 **96** .... (p) CharliePoste 86
(Matt Sheppard) *hld up: hdwy 5th: chsd ldr and mstke 7th: sn rdn and lost pl: wknd 3 out* **20/1**

1/6- **7** *19* **Ironical (IRE)**^{30} [252] 9-10-8 **97** .... (t) TomScudamore 66
(Shaun Lycett) *hld up: hdwy and mstke 6th: rdn and wknd appr 3 out: t.o* **14/1**

6/0- **P** **Keenes Day (FR)**^{25} [358] 8-11-12 **115** .... (t) JasonMaguire
(Sophie Leech) *chsd ldr tl pushed along after 5th: wknd next: t.o whn p.u bef 3 out* **20/1**

4m 59.5s (12.10) **Going Correction** +0.075s/f (Yiel) 8 Ran SP% **121.1**
Speed ratings (Par 105): **78,75,73,70,70 69,62,**
toteswingers 1&2 £1.20, 1&3 £5.10, 2&3 £5.90 CSF £3.32 CT £12.60 TOTE £1.60: £1.02, £1.10, £2.60; EX 3.50 Trifecta £29.10 Pool: £1006.04 - 25.91 winning units..

Owner Anthony Honeyball Racing Club Ltd **Bred** Mrs Nerys Dutfield **Trained** Mosterton, Dorset

FOCUS
A moderate handicap. They went a steady early gallop and the principals, who finished clear, were always handy. The easy winner was well in and is rated similar to recent runs.

T/Jkpt: £2741.00 to a £1 stake. Pool of £26,445.25 - 6.85 winning tickets. T/Plt: £7.10 to a £1 stake. Pool of £75,090.10 - 7716.84 winning tickets. T/Qpdt: £2.50 to a £1 stake. Pool of £5596.59 - 1648.67 winning tickets. CR

720 - 724a (Foreign Racing) - See Raceform Interactive

^{499}UTTOXETER (L-H)
Thursday, June 13

OFFICIAL GOING: Good (good to soft in places; 6.9)
Wind: moderate 1/2 against Weather: fine

725 ST14 CONSTRUCTION JUVENILE HURDLE (9 hdls) 2m
6:10 (6:10) (Class 4) 3-Y-0 **£3,378** (£992; £496; £248)

Form RPR

1 **It's Only Business**^{113} 3-10-12 0 .... APMcCoy 107+
(Jim Best) *trckd ldrs: led bef 2 out: pushed clr run-in: v readily* **4/1^{3}**

1- **2** *4 ½* **Akdam (IRE)**^{12} [582] 3-11-0 0 .... TrevorWhelan$^{(5)}$ 105
(Tony Carroll) *led: hdd and drvn 5th: chsd wnr appr 2 out: kpt on same pce appr last* **7/4^{1}**

3 *12* **Sleepy Haven (IRE)**^{34} 3-10-12 0 .... SeanQuinlan 88
(Jennie Candlish) *trckd ldrs: hit 6th: drvn next: one pce appr 2 out* **11/1**

4 *4 ½* **Sirop De Menthe (FR)**^{75} 3-10-12 0 .... RichardJohnson 88+
(Tim Vaughan) *w ldrs: led 5th: hung bdly lft and hdd bef 2 out: wknd and modest 4th whn hit last* **2/1^{2}**

5 *21* **Jawinski (IRE)**^{10} 3-10-12 0 .... AidanColeman 64
(David Evans) *chsd ldrs: lost pl 4th: chsng ldrs next: lost pl 3 out: sn bhd* **16/1**

6 *60* **Mr Blue Nose**^{22} 3-10-12 0 .... AndrewThornton
(Karen George) *j. poorly and bdly rt: in rr: bmpd 3rd: bhd and reminders 5th: sn t.o* **50/1**

7 *1 ¼* **Moorway (IRE)**^{115} 3-10-12 0 .... SamTwiston-Davies
(Andrew Hollinshead) *in rr: reminders 5th: sn bhd: t.o bef 3 out* **20/1**

P **Refuse To Mambo**^{16} 3-10-12 0 .... (p) PaulMoloney
(Andrew Hollinshead) *in rr: bmpd 1st 2: j.rt 3rd: bhd 5th: t.o bef 3 out: p.u bef last* **25/1**

3m 54.2s (2.20) **Going Correction** +0.15s/f (Yiel) 8 Ran SP% **114.5**
Speed ratings: **100,97,91,89,79 49,48,**
Tote Swingers: 1&2 £1.10, 1&3 £8.00, 2&3 £5.10 CSF £11.61 TOTE £3.50: £1.60, £1.10, £2.30; EX 14.50 Trifecta £43.70 Pool: £1,287.03 - 22.04 winning units..

Owner Jack Callaghan **Bred** South Wind Bloodstock **Trained** Lewes, E Sussex

FOCUS
Divided bends on fresh ground and Hurdles moved in 4m. A moderate juvenile hurdle, but a fair winner for the time of year and he should win another.

726 DON AMOTT LEISURE NOVICES' H'CAP CHASE (15 fncs) 2m 4f
6:40 (6:40) (Class 4) (0-115,113) 5-Y-0 **£3,798** (£1,122; £561; £280; £140)

Form RPR

2/3- **1** **Paddy The Hare (IRE)**^{18} [500] 8-11-12 **113** .... (p) SamTwiston-Davies 124+
(Dr Richard Newland) *j.rt: trckd ldr: led 4th: wnt clr 3 out: styd on strly last 100yds* **7/2^{2}**

0/6- **2** *2 ½* **Lukeys Luck**^{13} [566] 7-11-7 **108** .... SeanQuinlan 114
(Jennie Candlish) *chsd ldrs: drvn 11th: chsd wnr next: rallied and 2 l down last: kpt on same pce* **4/1^{3}**

4/2- **3** *20* **Beckhani**^{35} [179] 6-11-6 **107** .... APMcCoy 94
(Jonjo O'Neill) *chsd ldrs: outpcd and drvn 11th: wknd appr 3 out: tk remote 3rd clsng stages* **5/4^{1}**

04/- **4** *nk* **Pure Anticipation (IRE)**^{77} [4985] 8-10-9 **96** .... AidanColeman 85
(Tim Vaughan) *led to 4th: chsd wnr: wknd bef 3 out* **7/1**

P/5- **5** *32* **Baldadash (IRE)**^{25} [394] 8-11-6 **107** .... AndrewTinkler 65
(Barry Brennan) *in rr: blnd 4th: drvn and detached 7th: bhd fr next: t.o whn blnd 11th* **12/1**

4/6- **P** **Zipit (IRE)**^{32} [247] 8-11-2 **103** .... FelixDeGiles
(Tom Gretton) *chsd ldrs: lost pl and nt fluent 6th: drvn next: bhd 8th: t.o whn p.u bef 10th: b.b.v* **50/1**

U30- **P** **Peaks Of Fire (IRE)**^{14} [555] 6-10-11 **103** .... SamanthaDrake$^{(5)}$
(Joanne Foster) *in rr: outpcd 8th: bhd next: t.o 10th: p.u bef 2 out* **20/1**

5m 0.8s (-4.70) **Going Correction** -0.10s/f (Good) 7 Ran SP% **113.6**
Speed ratings: **105,104,96,95,83 ,**
Tote Swingers: 1&2 £2.50, 1&3 £1.50, 2&3 £1.40 CSF £17.95 TOTE £4.40: £1.90, £2.10; EX 12.00 Trifecta £27.30 Pool: £993.02 - 27.22 winning units..

Owner Foxtrot NH Racing Partnership VI **Bred** Cathy Sammon **Trained** Claines, Worcs

FOCUS
An ordinary novice handicap. A step up from the winner, who looked to have a bit in hand.

727 LADIES AT THE RACES (S) HURDLE (9 hdls) 2m
7:10 (7:11) (Class 5) 4-7-Y-0 **£1,949** (£572; £286; £143)

Form RPR

222- **1** **Descaro (USA)**^{7} [648] 7-11-2 110 .... (p) CiaranMckee$^{(7)}$ 120+
(John O'Shea) *trckd ldng pair: 2nd 5th: led sn after next: sn clr: pushed out* **10/3^{3}**

2 *19* **Glenconkeyne (IRE)**^{222} [2197] 6-10-9 0 .... (t) DerekFox$^{(5)}$ 93
(Noel C Kelly, Ire) *in tch: hit 5th: modest 3rd next: chsd clr ldr after 3 out: nvr on terms* **7/4^{1}**

0/0- **3** *18* **Mount Hope (IRE)**^{19} [475] 6-11-0 102 .... (b^{1}) JasonMaguire 79
(Donald McCain) *j. bdly: led: hdd sn after 6th: 3rd and wl btn whn blnd 2 out* **5/1**

6/2- **4** *13* **Ghaabesh (IRE)**^{18} [501] 6-11-0 105 .... (p) HarryChalloner$^{(5)}$ 69
(Barry Leavy) *in rr: bhd fr 5th: distant 4th appr 3 out* **14/1**

5/- **5** *33* **Garryowen Oscar (IRE)**^{71} [5118] 7-10-9 100 .... (t) SamanthaDrake$^{(5)}$ 34
(Joanne Foster) *in rr: drvn 4th: sn bhd: t.o 3 out* **33/1**

/13- **P** **Not Til Monday (IRE)**^{18} [501] 7-11-12 120 .... (v) APMcCoy
(J R Jenkins) *chsd ldr: shkn up after 4th: drvn next: reluctant and sn lost pl: bhd and eased 6th: sn hopelessly t.o: p.u bef 3 out* **3/1^{2}**

3m 52.3s (0.30) **Going Correction** +0.15s/f (Yiel) 6 Ran SP% **110.7**
Speed ratings: **105,95,86,80,63**
Tote Swingers: 1&2 £1.40, 1&3 £3.20, 2&3 £3.80 CSF £9.64 TOTE £4.90: £2.10, £1.70; EX 12.50 Trifecta £37.20 Pool: £750.65 - 15.12 winning units..The winner was bought in for 5,000gns.

Owner The Cross Racing Club **Bred** Langley House Stud **Trained** Elton, Gloucs

FOCUS
No more than two of those who did line up consented to give their all. Arguably a personal best from the winner.

728 MEDIA RESOURCES H'CAP CHASE (18 fncs) 3m
7:40 (7:40) (Class 4) (0-120,117) 5-Y-0 **£3,924** (£1,159; £579; £290; £145)

Form RPR

/12- **1** **Cardigan Island (IRE)**^{19} [481] 8-11-4 **112** .... (tp) RobertDunne$^{(3)}$ 124+
(Dai Burchell) *hld up in rr: hdwy to trck ldrs 9th: led appr 3 out: drvn out* **9/2^{2}**

P/1- **2** *8* **Atlanta Falcon (IRE)**[18] 500 8-11-12 **117**......................(t) JasonMaguire 124+
(Donald McCain) *chsd ldrs: hit 14th: chsd wnr bef 2 out: 2 l down whn hit last: styd on same pce* **9/2**[2]
4/P- **3** *4 1/2* **Quetzal (IRE)**[28] 341 8-10-13 **104**..................................(p) DenisO'Regan 104
(Martin Todhunter) *j.rt: led: hdd appr 3 out: one pce fr 2 out* **16/1**
0/3- **4** *25* **Balinroab (IRE)**[25] 387 6-11-12 **117**.. APMcCoy 94
(Jonjo O'Neill) *chsd ldrs: hit 7th: reminders 10th: wknd bef 2 out: sn eased* **7/2**[1]
/22- **5** *2 1/4* **Dont Tell Sailor (IRE)**[18] 504 7-11-3 **115**........................ ConorRing(7) 90
(Jennie Candlish) *chsd ldrs: lost pl 14th: sn bhd* **9/2**[2]
323- **6** *2* **Hurricane Carter (IRE)**[11] 597 13-9-13 **97**................ MrKevinJones(7) 70
(Natalie Lloyd-Beavis) *in rr: drvn 6th: bhd fr 11th: t.o 14th* **33/1**
/40- **P** **Tasheba**[17] 508 8-11-10 **115**..(t) PaulMoloney
(Sophie Leech) *in rr: blnd 3rd: reminders 6th: bhd 10th: t.o next: p.u bef 3 out* **33/1**
2FP/ **P** **Three Chords (IRE)**[61] 5294 9-11-6 **111**...................... AndrewThornton
(Caroline Bailey) *in rr: prom 11th: drvn next: sn lost pl and bhd: t.o whn p.u bef 3 out* **8/1**
112- **P** **Brody Bleu (FR)**[26] 370 6-11-12 **117**................................... FelixDeGiles
(Robert Walford) *chsd ldr: wknd after 14th: distant 5th whn p.u bef 2 out* **11/2**[3]

6m 10.1s (-5.00) **Going Correction** -0.10s/f (Good) **9** Ran SP% **115.0**
Speed ratings: **104,101,99,91,90 90, , ,**
Tote Swingers: 1&2 £7.20, 1&3 £7.40, 2&3 £18.30 CSF £25.60 CT £290.76 TOTE £6.00: £2.10, £1.90, £3.60; EX 32.90 Trifecta £315.40 Part won. Pool: £201.74 - 0.52 winning units..
Owner Mrs G Davies **Bred** Patrick John Hughes **Trained** Briery Hill, Blaenau Gwent

FOCUS
A moderate handicap. The progressive winner built on the promise of his Bangor win.

729 MEDIA RESOURCES ORACLE NOVICES' H'CAP HURDLE (9 hdls) 2m
8:10 (8:10) (Class 5) (0-100,104) 4-Y-0+ **£2,339** (£686; £343; £171)

Form RPR
0/1- **1** **Planetoid (IRE)**[8] 635 5-11-4 **92** 7ex....................................... APMcCoy 108+
(Jim Best) *chsd ldrs: led 5th: drvn 3 out: forged clr run-in* **1/2**[1]
/P1- **2** *6* **Tom Wade (IRE)**[3] 696 6-11-11 **104** 7ex...........................(t) BenPoste(5) 113
(Shaun Harris) *hld up: trckd ldrs 5th: 1 l down last: rdn and fnd little* **13/2**[2]
3/F- **3** *1/2* **Fairy Alisha**[28] 333 5-11-7 **95**.. RichardJohnson 105+
(Trevor Wall) *trckd ldrs: 2nd after 6th: 3 l 3rd whn blnd last: kpt on clsng stages* **16/1**
043- **4** *23* **Call Me April**[16] 521 5-11-2 **90**................................ AndrewThornton 77
(Karen George) *in rr: hdwy 5th: chsng ldrs next: outpcd appr 3 out: wknd appr 2 out* **8/1**[3]
544/ **5** *11* **Acht (GER)**[218] 2267 4-10-11 **93**.. DerekFox(5) 68
(Noel C Kelly, Ire) *in rr: sme hdwy 6th: sn outpcd: poor 5th 2 out* **20/1**
530- **6** *14* **Cruise Control**[13] 561 7-10-3 **82**.................................. HarryChalloner(5) 47
(John Bryan Groucott) *t.k.h in rr: hdwy 5th: wknd after next* **40/1**
/P4- **7** *25* **Master Ted (IRE)**[14] 558 7-10-7 **81**................................(vt) SeanQuinlan 23
(Jennie Candlish) *led: reminders after 3rd: hdd 5th: lost pl next: sn bhd: t.o next* **14/1**
000/ **8** *12* **Everkingly**[95] 4686 7-10-5 **79**..(tp) CharliePoste 11
(Anna Brooks) *chsd ldrs: drvn 6th: lost pl bef next: sn bhd: t.o* **80/1**
/30- **9** *5* **Turn The Tide**[7] 648 5-10-6 **80**..................................... GerardTumelty
(Natalie Lloyd-Beavis) *trckd ldrs: t.k.h: lost pl after 6th: sn bhd: t.o next* **66/1**
065/ **P** **Fred Willetts (IRE)**[10] 4908 5-11-9 **97**..........................(v) JasonMaguire
(David Evans) *in rr: bhd fr 5th: t.o whn p.u bef 3 out* **14/1**
0- **P** **Nishay (IRE)**[31] 267 6-11-12 **100**.. PaulMoloney
(David Rees) *chsd ldrs: lost pl 5th: sn bhd: t.o whn p.u bef 3 out* **28/1**

3m 52.9s (0.90) **Going Correction** +0.15s/f (Yiel)
WFA 4 from 5yo+ 17lb **11** Ran SP% **123.7**
Speed ratings (Par 103): **103,100,99,88,82 75,63,57,54,**
Tote Swingers: 1&2 £4.10, 1&3 £6.70, 2&3 £11.20 CSF £4.90 CT £31.15 TOTE £1.70: £1.10, £2.10, £2.30; EX 4.50 Trifecta £50.80 Pool: £544.10 - 8.03 winning units..
Owner Planetoid Partnership **Bred** Bjorn Nielsen **Trained** Lewes, E Sussex

FOCUS
A weak handicap and three came clear. The winner is rated similar to his recent win but there should be more to come.

730 JUNGHEINRICH UK LTD 50TH ANNIVERSARY H'CAP HURDLE (10 hdls) 2m 4f 110y
8:40 (8:40) (Class 5) (0-100,107) 4-Y-0+ **£2,339** (£686; £343; £171)

Form RPR
445- **1** **Inside Knowledge (USA)**[13] 561 7-11-2 **90**.................... AdamPogson 98+
(Garry Woodward) *in rr: hdwy after 7th: 4th 2 out: styd on to ld last: kpt on wl towards fin* **16/1**
/42- **2** *3/4* **Old Pals Act (IRE)**[15] 543 5-11-7 **95**...................................... APMcCoy 101
(Jonjo O'Neill) *chsd ldrs: drvnto ld 3 out: narrowly hdd last: no ex clsng stages* **5/2**[1]
/10- **3** *12* **Starlight Air**[32] 252 10-11-5 **93**... JamieMoore 80
(John Spearing) *in rr: gd hdwy 7th: lchal appr 2 out: wknd between last 2* **25/1**
/05- **4** *5* **Kayfrou**[16] 521 8-11-2 **90**.. DarylJacob 82
(Nick Mitchell) *trckd ldrs: chal 3 out: one pce appr next* **7/1**[3]
0/5- **5** *7* **Billesley Road**[18] 488 5-11-11 **99**................................ RichardJohnson 83
(Philip Hobbs) *nt fluent in rr: hdwy 7th: poor 5th appr 2 out: one pce* **14/1**
305- **6** *nk* **Am I Blue**[32] 237 7-11-5 **100**.................................. MrMatthewStanley(7) 84
(Mrs D Thomas) *s.s: reluctant and sn detached in last: sme hdwy appr 3 out: nvr a factor* **28/1**
/43- **7** *nk* **River Purple**[18] 503 6-10-13 **87**.................................(t) DonalDevereux 71
(John Mackie) *chsd ldrs: drvn 7th: lost pl appr next* **5/1**[2]
/F5- **8** *2 1/2* **Lord Navits (IRE)**[12] 590 5-11-2 **90**..............................(b1) JasonMaguire 71
(Donald McCain) *led: hdd appr 2 out: sn wknd* **8/1**
5F3/ **9** *3 1/4* **Lost Arca (FR)**[517] 3706 7-10-4 **83**... EdCookson(5) 61
(Robin Mathew) *in rr: sme hdwy 7th: wknd bef next* **33/1**
506/ **10** *32* **Kristallo (GER)**[310] 991 8-11-1 **92**................................. RobertDunne(3) 42
(Dai Burchell) *in rr: mstke 1st: sme hdwy 7th: sn wknd: t.o next* **33/1**
6/4- **11** *shd* **Honey Of A Kitten (USA)**[3] 333 5-11-3 **91**......................... AidanColeman 41
(David Evans) *in rr: hdwy 7th: wknd next: t.o* **14/1**
4/0- **12** *23* **Stadium Of Light (IRE)**[11] 605 6-10-11 **90**............(bt) TrevorWhelan(5) 19
(Shaun Harris) *chsd ldrs: drvn 7th: lost pl next: sn bhd: t.o* **33/1**
0/0- **13** *20* **Award Winner**[23] 421 10-11-9 **97**...................................(p) BrendanPowell 8
(Brendan Powell) *chsd ldrs: reminders 6th: lost pl next: sn bhd: t.o 2 out* **33/1**
1/3- **14** *12* **King's Chorister**[28] 342 7-11-5 **93**......................................(t) LucyAlexander
(Barry Murtagh) *in rr: bhd fr 6th: t.o 2 out* **10/1**

5/3- **15** *2 3/4* **Eastwell Smiles**[26] 376 9-11-7 **95**...................................(t) PaulMoloney
(Sophie Leech) *chsd ldrs: lost pl after 7th: sn bhd: t.o 2 out* **11/1**

5m 1.4s (2.40) **Going Correction** +0.15s/f (Yiel) **15** Ran SP% **124.5**
Speed ratings (Par 103): **101,100,96,94,91 91,91,90,89,76 76,68,60,55,54**
Tote Swingers: 1&2 £38.60, 1&3 £46.20, 2&3 £10.40 CSF £55.19 CT £1027.10 TOTE £24.70: £5.70, £1.60, £10.00; EX 94.30 Trifecta £347.80 Part won. Pool: £463.75 - 0.04 winning units..
Owner Mrs Elisabeth Cash **Bred** Juddmonte Farms Inc **Trained** Bolham, Notts

FOCUS
A weak handicap. The winner was well in on the best of his hurdles form.

731 SIGNS 2000 STANDARD OPEN NATIONAL HUNT FLAT RACE 2m
9:10 (9:10) (Class 6) 4-6-Y-0 **£1,559** (£457; £228; £114)

Form RPR
1 **Neville**[144] 5-11-1 0.. RichardJohnson 107+
(Philip Hobbs) *trckd ldrs: led over 3f out: hung lft over 1f out: kpt on* **10/1**
2- **2** *2 1/4* **When I'm Sixtyfour (IRE)**[26] 380 4-10-12 0......................... APMcCoy 102+
(Jonjo O'Neill) *hld up in mid-div: trckd ldrs over 7f out: 2nd over 2f out: edgd rt over 1f out: rdn and hung bdly lft fnl f: no real imp* **6/5**[1]
1- **3** *10* **Mr Satco (IRE)**[18] 498 5-11-8 0.................................. JasonMaguire 103
(Donald McCain) *led: drvn over 4f out: hdd over 3f out: edgd rt over 2f out and one pce* **7/4**[2]
4 *4* **Uppingham** 4-10-12 0..[1] BrianHughes 89
(Malcolm Jefferson) *hld up in rr: hdwy 9f out: chsng ldrs 6f out: outpcd over 4f out: one pce* **7/1**[3]
5 *18* **Mount Odell**[40] 5-11-1 0.. NickScholfield 76
(Paul Henderson) *chsd ldrs: outpcd and lost pl over 3f out* **50/1**
6 *2 1/2* **Burmese Jewel** 5-11-1 0.. DenisO'Regan 74
(Martin Todhunter) *chsd ldrs: drvn 9f out: lost pl over 4f out* **25/1**
7 *6* **Seventeen Black (IRE)** 5-11-1 0....................................... DonalDevereux 69
(David Rees) *hld up in rr: lost pl 7f out: sme hdwy 5f out: lost pl over 3f out* **16/1**
/00- **8** *31* **Triple Brandy**[24] 412 4-10-12 0..................................(p) AndrewThornton 38
(Karen George) *hld up in rr: lost pl 7f out: bhd fnl 5f: t.o* **66/1**
9 *22* **Wolmar** 4-10-2 0... PeterCarberry(3) 11
(John Mackie) *mid-div: drvn and lost pl 9f out: t.o 7f out* **50/1**

3m 51.6s (5.20) **Going Correction** +0.15s/f (Yiel)
WFA 4 from 5yo 3lb **9** Ran SP% **118.6**
Speed ratings: **93,91,86,84,75 74,71,56,45**
Tote Swingers: 1&2 £4.70, 1&3 £2.80, 2&3 £1.80 CSF £22.93 TOTE £8.90: £2.10, £1.10, £1.20; EX 30.10 Trifecta £97.20 Pool: £681.13 - 5.25 winning units..
Owner M W Pendarves **Bred** Mrs E A Pendarves **Trained** Withycombe, Somerset

FOCUS
A fair bumper for the time of year. The first two should rate higher.
T/Plt: £52.40 to a £1 stake. Pool: £7,9072.74 - 1,100.64 winning tickets T/Qpdt: £10.50 to a £1 stake. Pool: £6,414.25 - 449.70 winning tickets WG

353 AINTREE (L-H)
Friday, June 14

OFFICIAL GOING: Good to soft
Wind: Blustery Weather: Steady rain after race 2

732 NEW BETDAQ CUSTOMERS COMMISSION FREE 1ST MONTH MAIDEN HURDLE (9 hdls) 2m 1f
5:55 (5:56) (Class 4) 4-Y-0+ **£4,548** (£1,335; £667; £333)

Form RPR
1 **Roc De Prince**[38] 4-10-11 0..(t) BrianHughes 102+
(James Ewart) *trckd ldrs in v slow r: rdn and effrt 2 out: chal last: led 100yds out and sn clr* **20/1**
2 *2 1/4* **Goal (IRE)**[35] 208 5-11-0 0..(t) JasonMaguire 100
(Gordon Elliott, Ire) *midfield and hld up: led 2 out: drvn bef last: hdd and edging lft 100yds out: sn outpcd* **3/1**[2]
3 *3 3/4* **Rock A Doodle Doo (IRE)**[22] 6-11-0 0......................... RichieMcGrath 98
(Sally Hall) *midfield: rdn and effrt after 3 out: ev ch whn mstke next: styd on same pce and btn last* **15/2**[3]
6/2- **4** *3* **Potomac (IRE)**[19] 494 5-11-0 113....................................... APMcCoy 93
(Rose Dobbin) *t.k.h in 2nd: led bef 3 out: rdn and hdd next: fnd nil bef last* **10/11**[1]
5 *nk* **Collingwood (FR)**[353] 7-11-0 0....................................... RichardJohnson 93
(Philip Hobbs) *sweating profusely: t.k.h in last: stl last but only 5 l fr ldr home turn: rdn and one pce whn passing btn horses after: racing awkwardly flat* **8/1**
0/5- **6** *1 1/2* **Nefyn Bay**[27] 367 4-10-11 0.. AdrianLane 88
(Donald McCain) *nt fluent: towards rr but in tch: rdn and fdd after 3 out: mstke last* **33/1**
7 *4 1/2* **Ancient Greece**[30] 6-11-0 0..(t) AndrewTinkler 89
(George Baker) *pressed ldrs: rdn and wknd bef 2 out* **12/1**
P34/ **8** *4* **Best Excuse**[96] 4676 6-11-0 0.. SeanQuinlan 85
(Jennie Candlish) *led and abt 6 l clr but setting v slow pce and wandering into hurdles: blnd 4th: sn pressed: rdn and hdd bef 3 out: dropped out qckly* **25/1**

4m 21.8s (8.10) **Going Correction** +0.30s/f (Yiel)
WFA 4 from 5yo+ 17lb **8** Ran SP% **119.5**
Speed ratings (Par 105): **92,90,89,87,87 86,84,82**
toteswingers: 1&2 £0.00, 1&3 £7.70, 2&3 £2.30 CSF £82.89 TOTE £22.20: £4.40, £1.40, £2.20; EX 93.10 Trifecta £509.90 Part won. Pool: £679.97 - 0.45 winning units..
Owner N M L Ewart **Bred** Mrs James Wigan & London TB Services Ltd **Trained** Langholm, Dumfries & G'way

FOCUS
All bends moved on Mildmay and hurdles tracks. Not a bad maiden, but it was very slowly run and they finished in a heap. Probably not form to get carried away with.

733 VISIT AINTREE'S GOLF DRIVING RANGE CONDITIONAL JOCKEYS' H'CAP CHASE (19 fncs) 3m 1f
6:30 (6:30) (Class 3) (0-135,131) 5-Y-0+ **£6,498** (£1,908; £954; £477)

Form RPR
/02- **1** **Gullible Gordon (IRE)**[18] 509 10-10-13 **121**.........(vt) DonalDevereux(3) 136+
(Peter Bowen) *j. v wl: mde all: easily drew 6 l clr at 16th: cruising along and unchal in long ld after next* **5/2**[1]
21P/ **2** *25* **Russian War (IRE)**[69] 5176 10-11-12 **131**......................(t) GavinSheehan 128+
(Gordon Elliott, Ire) *settled in rr: hdwy 12th to 2nd at 14th: already outpcd by wnr whn hit next two: plugged on to remain clr of rest* **10/1**
231- **3** *16* **That's The Deal (IRE)**[12] 596 9-10-5 **113** 7ex................ JoeCornwall(3) 89
(John Cornwall) *a abt same pl: rdn and outpcd after 15th: no ch w ldng pair fr next* **15/2**

3/2- **4** *18* **The Musical Guy (IRE)**[24] 422 7-10-8 **121**...................(b) RyanHatch(8) 79
(Nigel Twiston-Davies) *pressed wnr tl 14th: sn drvn: struggling whn mstke 16th and again next: all out to hang on to remote 4th* **5/1**

0/4- **5** *¾* **Bescot Springs (IRE)**[30] 310 8-10-7 **120**..............(v) GrahamWatters(8) 77
(Lucinda Russell) *chsd ldrs: pushed along 7th: struggling after: drvn and plugging on after last: t.o* **3/1**[2]

P/1- **P** **Thanks For Coming**[24] 422 7-11-3 **125**................ JeremiahMcGrath(3)
(Nicky Henderson) *nt a fluent on outside: wnt cl up 11th: rdn bef next: wknd tamely 13th: t.o and p.u 3 out* **4/1**[3]

415/ **P** **An Capall Mor (IRE)**[253] 1715 7-10-12 **120**................(tp) HenryBrooke(3)
(Donald McCain) *pressed ldrs tl 11th: rdn and lost tch and hit next: t.o and p.u 16th* **20/1**

6m 37.3s (7.30) **Going Correction** +0.50s/f (Soft) **7** Ran SP% **115.9**
Speed ratings: **108,100,94,89,88** ,
toteswingers: 1&2 £5.70, 1&3 £3.70, 2&3 £13.00 CSF £26.54 TOTE £3.70: £2.00, £4.80; EX 23.80 Trifecta £299.70 Pool: £581.41 - 1.45 winning units..
Owner Yeh Man Partnership **Bred** Mrs Mary Buttimer **Trained** Little Newcastle, Pembrokes

FOCUS
This looked tight, but the winner slammed the field. The winner was a 145+ horse at best and this form could be rated higher.

734 MARK WATSON 50TH BIRTHDAY H'CAP HURDLE (9 hdls) 2m 1f
7:00 (7:03) (Class 3) (0-135,129) 4-Y-0+ **£6,498** (£1,908; £954; £477)

Form RPR

P00/ **1** **First In The Queue (IRE)**[48] 5574 6-11-9 **126**........................ APMcCoy 132+
(Nicky Henderson) *settled cl up: jnd ldr bef 3 out: drvn and stl level last: edgd rt briefly whn jst sing to get upper hand flat: all out* **85/40**[1]

/11- **2** *¾* **Aazif (IRE)**[31] 278 4-11-5 **125**..(t) JasonMaguire 126
(Donald McCain) *2nd or 3rd thrght: rdn and ev ch fr home turn tl hit last: jst hld under driving fnl 100yds* **7/2**[2]

022- **3** *nk* **Ruler Of All (IRE)**[20] 480 7-11-4 **128**.................................. MrRWinks(7) 133+
(Peter Winks) *t.k.h in rr: outpcd in 8 l 6th bef 3 out where impeded sn after flight: swtchd ins bef last where 6 l down: urged along and clsng heroically after: jst too much to do* **8/1**

/35- **4** *13* **Akula (IRE)**[22] 447 6-11-6 **123**....................................... RichardJohnson 115
(Mark H Tompkins) *led tl 5th: rdn and stl ev ch bef 3 out: steadily wknd after* **10/1**

14/- **5** *3 ¾* **Jolly Roger (IRE)**[28] 827 6-11-12 **129**.............................. WillKennedy 119
(Tony Carroll) *hld up towards rr: effrt 6th: rdn and ev ch bef 3 out: fading whn blnd next* **10/1**

3/0- **6** *12* **Majaales (USA)**[35] 263 10-11-4 **121**................................ PaddyBrennan 99
(Tom George) *a midfield: rdn and lost tch wl bef 3 out* **7/1**[3]

60/ **7** *6* **Taruma (FR)**[181] 3060 5-11-6 **123**...(p) BarryKeniry 95
(Simon West) *bhd: mstke 2nd: nt fluent: rdn and racing awkwardly after: t.o bef 3 out* **33/1**

U/0- **8** *6* **Indian Groom (IRE)**[18] 508 8-11-3 **127**........................ JohnDawson(7) 94
(John Wade) *chsd ldrs: rdn and lost tch 5th: t.o next* **25/1**

0/1- **F** **Bow Badger**[29] 344 7-11-10 **127**... BrianHughes
(John Wade) *pressed ldr: led 5th: rdn and jnd home turn: stl w wnr whn stmbld and fell after 3 out* **7/1**[3]

4m 15.2s (1.50) **Going Correction** +0.30s/f (Yiel)
WFA 4 from 5yo+ 17lb **9** Ran SP% **115.3**
Speed ratings (Par 107): **108,107,107,101,99 93,91,88,**
toteswingers: 1&2 £2.70, 1&3 £10.10, 2&3 £5.30 CSF £10.35 CT £48.43 TOTE £3.00: £1.10, £1.50, £2.60; EX 10.00 Trifecta £110.80 Pool: £459.25 - 3.10 winning units..
Owner Liam Breslin **Bred** Holborn Trust Co **Trained** Upper Lambourn, Berks

FOCUS
Not a bad handicap and it was run at a fair gallop. Sound form with the principals coming clear.

735 TROPHIES AT INKERMAN H'CAP CHASE (12 fncs) 2m
7:35 (7:36) (Class 3) (0-140,135) 5-Y-0+ **£7,797** (£2,289; £1,144; £572)

Form RPR

/16- **1** **Dineur (FR)**[23] 432 7-10-6 **115**.. DonalDevereux 128+
(Peter Bowen) *cl up: dropped to 5th briefly but stl gng wl home turn: produced to ld after 3 out: sn rdn clr: comf* **5/2**[1]

/U1- **2** *8* **Anay Turge (FR)**[9] 631 8-11-1 **127**................................(t) MarkQuinlan(3) 132
(Nigel Hawke) *settled in last pair and cl up: wnt 2nd gng wl 3 out: chsd wnr fr bef next: drvn and outpcd bef last* **4/1**[3]

26/- **3** *13* **Nobunaga**[54] 5439 8-11-0 **123**.. AidanColeman 116
(Venetia Williams) *led tl 3rd: 2nd tl led again 8th: drvn and hdd after 3 out: dropped out qckly* **6/1**

11U- **4** *32* **Fiftyonefiftyone (IRE)**[17] 520 9-10-13 **122**.................(p) LeightonAspell 86
(Oliver Sherwood) *racd keenly: cl up: rdn and wknd tamely bef 3 out: t.o next* **7/1**

/11- **5** *18* **Jack The Gent (IRE)**[22] 446 9-11-12 **135**........................... BarryKeniry 83
(George Moore) *led 3rd tl 8th: sn rdn: lost tch bef 3 out: t.o next* **3/1**[2]

/22- **6** *11* **Unforgettable (IRE)**[17] 520 10-10-5 **119**........................(vt) BenPoste(5) 57
(Robin Dickin) *last pair: rdn and lost tch bef 3 out: sn t.o* **6/1**

4m 6.5s (6.50) **Going Correction** +0.50s/f (Soft) **6** Ran SP% **114.6**
Speed ratings: **103,99,92,76,67 62**
toteswingers: 1&2 £16.90, 1&3 £7.50 2&3 £7.50 CSF £13.43 TOTE £4.10: £1.80, £2.70; EX 16.80 Trifecta £59.90 Pool: £284.54 - 3.56 winning units..
Owner Gwilym J Morris **Bred** Dominique Le Baron **Trained** Little Newcastle, Pembrokes

FOCUS
This proved another handicap on the Mildmay course where few landed a serious blow. The winner improved to the level of his best hurdle form.

736 AINTREE INTERACTIVE NOVICES' CHASE (19 fncs) 3m 1f
8:10 (8:10) (Class 4) 5-Y-0+ **£4,758** (£1,636)

Form RPR

0/2- **1** **Sivola De Sivola (FR)**[29] 340 7-10-12 129..................... PaddyBrennan 135+
(Tom George) *j. economically: led fr 4th: gng best fr 12th: 12 l ahd 16th: canter after* **10/11**[1]

0/1- **2** *dist* **Any Given Day (IRE)**[31] 279 8-11-5 0............................... JasonMaguire 92
(Donald McCain) *j. sltly rt in 3rd: mstke 12th: lft 2nd at next: struggling whn mstke 16th: t.o and j. more markedly rt after: trotted across line* **11/8**[2]

P/4- **F** **Accordion Exhibit (IRE)**[24] 422 7-10-12 0........................(t) NoelFehily
(Fergal O'Brien) *led tl 4th: being jnd for 2nd and wnr gng clr whn fell 13th* **7/1**[3]

6m 50.1s (20.10) **Going Correction** +0.50s/f (Soft) **3** Ran SP% **107.0**
Speed ratings: **87**, ,
CSF £2.54 TOTE £1.90; EX 2.70 Trifecta £1.80 Pool: £280.96 - 112.91 winning units..
Owner D O'Donohoe, S & P Nelson & D Silvester **Bred** Gilles Trapenard & Thomas Trapenard **Trained** Slad, Gloucs

FOCUS
A bloodless win for Sivola De Sivola. The easy winner built on the promise of his recent chase debut and is rated in line with his hurdle form.

737 POOLS PANEL CELEBRATING ITS 50TH ANNIVERSARY NOVICES' HURDLE (11 hdls) 2m 4f
8:45 (8:45) (Class 4) 4-Y-0+ **£4,548** (£1,335; £667; £333)

Form RPR

15/ **1** **Killala Quay**[372] 632 6-10-12 0.. NoelFehily 127+
(Charlie Longsdon) *settled trcking ldrs: effrt to go 2nd bef 3 out where hanging lft: led next: rdn clr fr last despite hanging lft* **10/3**[2]

12- **2** *10* **Billfromthebar (IRE)**[13] 588 6-10-12 0........................... JasonMaguire 117
(Donald McCain) *2nd tl led sn after 8th: 3 l clr next: drvn and hdd 2 out: easily outpcd by wnr flat* **3/1**[1]

2/1- **3** *17* **Valleyofmilan (IRE)**[31] 280 6-10-12 118...................... JamesCowley(7) 110
(Donald McCain) *trckd ldrs: ev ch 8th: rdn and wkng whn hit next: sn wl bhd ldng pair* **3/1**[1]

1/6- **4** *26* **Red Admirable (IRE)**[45] 48 7-11-0 114........................ KillianMoore(5) 85
(Graeme McPherson) *trckd ldr: effrt and ev ch after 8th: rdn and fdd tamely next: mstke 2 out: t.o and eased flat* **12/1**

1/1- **5** *9* **Just Cameron**[27] 367 6-11-5 0.. RichieMcGrath 77
(Philip Kirby) *racd keenly and pressed ldrs tl rdn wl bef 3 out: no rspnse and sn dropped rt out: t.o* **9/2**[3]

143/ **6** *2 ½* **Plenty Of Chat (IRE)**[453] 9-10-5 0....................................... MrRWinks(7) 68
(Peter Winks) *sn detached in last: mstke 3rd: rdn and t.o bef 6th: styng on fr hopeless position after last* **20/1**

000/ **7** *2 ¾* **Kukurudu (IRE)**[54] 5428 6-10-12 0.. BarryKeniry 65
(Simon West) *nt fluent in rr: wknd and mstke 6th: t.o and mstke next: eased and blnd 3 out* **66/1**

/21- **P** **Croco Bay (IRE)**[19] 491 6-11-7 124.............................. HarryChalloner(5)
(Peter Atkinson) *led: hit 8th: sn hdd and rdn and wknd: remote 6th whn mstke 2 out: p.u last* **13/2**

5m 7.3s (6.60) **Going Correction** +0.30s/f (Yiel) **8** Ran SP% **118.5**
Speed ratings (Par 105): **98,94,87,76,73 72,71,**
toteswingers: 1&2 £6.10, 1&3 £11.00, 2&3 £1.40 CSF £14.77 TOTE £6.70: £1.60, £1.60, £1.70; EX 20.70 Trifecta £67.20 Pool: £503.54 - 5.61 winning units..
Owner R A H Perkins **Bred** N Franklin **Trained** Over Norton, Oxon

FOCUS
This modest novice hurdle looked an open affair. They went an average gallop and two came well clear from the penultimate flight. The winner looks a decent recruit and should go on to rate higher.

738 MCFLY PLAYING AT AINTREE MARES' H'CAP HURDLE (11 hdls) 2m 4f
9:15 (9:15) (Class 4) (0-120,113) 4-Y-0+ **£4,548** (£1,335; £667; £333)

Form RPR

/31- **1** **Social Realism (IRE)**[8] 651 5-11-3 **104** 7ex........................(p) APMcCoy 111+
(Jonjo O'Neill) *2nd tl led narrowly after 8th: drvn and idling bef last where nt fluent: in command whn hanging lft flat and kpt rt up to work: all out* **9/4**[2]

1/0- **2** *1 ¼* **Definite Lady (IRE)**[24] 423 7-10-5 **92**.......................(b) TomScudamore 97
(Mark Rimell) *cl up: chal for ld after 8th: drvn and pressed wnr fr next: making no imp whn swtchd rt after last* **14/1**

PP4/ **3** *12* **Entertain Me**[52] 5480 9-11-5 **106**.. CharliePoste 100
(Robin Dickin) *hld up towards rr: effrt after 8th: flattered briefly: disp 3rd and rdn and wl hld 2 out* **20/1**

/11- **4** *2 ¾* **Mrs Peachey (IRE)**[15] 552 6-11-12 **113**.......................... JasonMaguire 106
(Kim Bailey) *settled midfield: effrt after 8th: rdn and hit next: one pce and wl hld fr 2 out* **11/4**[3]

1/2- **5** *6* **Top Totti**[29] 337 5-11-7 **108**.. RichardJohnson 96
(Henry Daly) *settled rr of bunch: wl in tch tl rdn bef 3 out: sn wl btn: hit next* **2/1**[1]

/62- **6** *12* **Lillybrook (IRE)**[26] 391 7-10-8 **95**.......................... SamTwiston-Davies 70
(Nigel Twiston-Davies) *led at modest pce tl drvn and hdd after 8th: sn dropped rt out* **12/1**

023/ **7** *1 ¾* **Petit Fleur**[285] 1478 11-11-4 **105**.................................. WayneHutchinson 79
(Julian Smith) *hld up in last pair: drvn and lost tch tamely after 8th: sn wl bhd* **25/1**

5m 17.2s (16.50) **Going Correction** +0.30s/f (Yiel) **7** Ran SP% **113.7**
Speed ratings (Par 105): **79,78,73,72,70 65,64**
CSF £30.18 CT £500.09 TOTE £3.60: £2.30, £3.70; EX 36.90 Trifecta £282.80 Pool: £748.20 - 1.98 winning units..
Owner Mrs Diane Carr **Bred** Darley **Trained** Cheltenham, Gloucs

FOCUS
A modest and steadily run mares' handicap, but it was competitive for the class. The first three are rated pretty much to their marks.
T/Plt: £95.30 to a £1 stake. Pool: £63,466.38 - 486.10 winning tickets T/Qpdt: £8.80 to a £1 stake. Pool: £5,060.13 - 421.45 winning tickets IM

739 - 746a (Foreign Racing) - See Raceform Interactive

625 HEXHAM (L-H)
Saturday, June 15

OFFICIAL GOING: Good (good to firm in places; 7.2)
Wind: Fairly strong, half against Weather: Cloudy

747 CHESTERS FORT NOVICES' HURDLE (12 hdls) 3m
2:10 (2:10) (Class 4) 4-Y-0+ **£3,119** (£915; £457; £228)

Form RPR

4/2- **1** **Indigo Rock (IRE)**[23] 449 7-10-12 105................................. RyanMania 122+
(Michael Smith) *prom: wnt 2nd 8th: led after 3 out: rdn and kpt on strly fr last* **9/2**[2]

2 *3 ¼* **Soweheard (IRE)**[36] 211 6-11-5 115.............................. JasonMaguire 125+
(Gordon Elliott, Ire) *nt fluent on occasions: prom: hdwy to chse wnr between last 2: effrt whn nt fluent last: one pce run-in* **11/10**[1]

3/1- **3** *13* **Oscar Tanner (IRE)**[11] 629 5-11-5 0.............................. LucyAlexander 112
(Martin Todhunter) *hld up in midfield: stdy hdwy and in tch after 3 out: rdn next: one pce bef last* **6/1**[3]

412- **4** *6* **Loose Preformer (IRE)**[16] 554 7-11-5 115........................... APMcCoy 107
(David O'Meara) *in tch: rdn and outpcd after 3 out: rallied between last 2: sn no imp* **9/2**[2]

/01- **5** *2 ½* **General Hardi**[21] 470 12-11-5 112...................................... BrianHughes 105
(John Wade) *chsd ldrs: drvn after 3 out: outpcd fr next* **25/1**

/F6- **6** *3 ¾* **Merry Minster**[19] 506 6-9-12 95.................................... JohnDawson(7) 87
(James Walton) *chsd ldr to 8th: rdn bef 2 out: wknd bef last* **50/1**

5/ **7** *49* **Native Court (IRE)**[24] 442 7-10-7 108............................(t) DerekFox(5) 50
(Mark Michael McNiff, Ire) *hld up: outpcd bef 4 out: nvr on terms: t.o* **25/1**

1- 8 36 **Academy General (IRE)**[24] 435 7-11-5 0 TomScudamore 25
(David Bridgwater) *led to after 3 out: rdn and wknd fr next: t.o* **9/1**
/U0- 9 63 **Desert Sting**[28] 367 4-10-4 0 JakeGreenall(3)
(Michael Easterby) *a bhd: lost tch 1/2-way: continued: t.o* **100/1**
00/ P **Mr Mistopheles (IRE)**[159] 3547 5-10-12 0 HenryBrooke
(Philip Kirby) *a bhd: lost tch 8th: t.o whn p.u bef last* **125/1**
POP/ P **Blue Lodge (IRE)**[116] 4304 7-10-12 0 (v1) BrianHarding
(James Moffatt) *bhd: struggling 1/2-way: t.o whn p.u bef 4 out* **150/1**
P **Sarasola**[21] 6-10-5 0 MrJHamilton(7)
(Alistair Whillans) *nt fluent on occasions: in tch: outpcd 4 out: struggling fr next: t.o whn p.u bef last* **250/1**
P **Trentside William**[14] 6-10-12 0 AndrewThornton
(Mike Sowersby) *bhd: struggling 7th: t.o whn p.u bef 4 out* **250/1**
U- P **Just Awake**[11] 629 6-10-12 0 PeterBuchanan
(Sandy Thomson) *midfield: nt fluent and outpcd 6th: sn struggling: t.o whn p.u bef last* **300/1**

5m 54.2s (-14.80) **Going Correction** -0.425s/f (Good)
WFA 4 from 5yo+ 19lb 14 Ran SP% **121.5**
Speed ratings (Par 105): **107,105,101,99,98 97,81,69,48, , , ,**
toteswingers 1&2 £5.20, 1&3 £2.60, 2&3 £2.00 CSF £10.18 TOTE £5.60: £1.80, £1.10, £2.10; EX 13.30 Trifecta £66.70 Pool: £501.31 - 5.62 winning units..
Owner Sprayclad UK & Cockton Hill Punters Club **Bred** Niall Ryan And Fiona O'Sullivan **Trained** Kirkheaton, Northumberland

FOCUS
Fresh ground on all bends. This well-contested staying novice hurdle was run at a sound gallop and most were feeling the strain before the home turn. The first pair had it to themselves in the home straight and are on the upgrade. The form could be rated up to 5lb higher.

748 ROMAN WALL MARES' NOVICES' HURDLE (8 hdls) 2m 110y
2:45 (2:52) (Class 4) 4-Y-0+ **£3,285** (£957; £479)

Form RPR
416/ 1 **Great Oak (IRE)**[58] 5359 7-10-10 0 RichardJohnson 90+
(Tim Vaughan) *in tch: hdwy to ld 4th: qcknd 2 out: rdn out fr last* **8/13**[1]
1- 2 8 **Binowagh Bay (IRE)**[19] 506 5-10-12 95 DerekFox(5) 89
(Mark Michael McNiff, Ire) *chsd ldrs: outpcd bef 4 out: rallied to chse (clr) wnr last: no imp* **7/2**[2]
F- 3 10 **Just Fabulous**[15] 560 4-10-7 0 BarryKeniry 72
(George Moore) *t.k.h: hld up in last but in tch: hdwy to chse wnr 4 out: effrt and rdn bef last: sn wknd* **4/1**[3]
000/ 4 17 **Beverley Beck**[21] 10-10-10 69 LucyAlexander 55
(Bruce Mactaggart) *chsd ldr to 4th: rdn and outpcd next: n.d after* **16/1**
0P/ 5 36 **Alistorm**[166] 3383 7-10-5 0 SamanthaDrake(5) 19
(Mark Campion) *nt fluent: led to 4th: struggling fr next: t.o* **100/1**

4m 10.5s (-6.90) **Going Correction** -0.425s/f (Good)
WFA 4 from 5yo+ 17lb 5 Ran SP% **111.0**
Speed ratings (Par 105): **99,95,90,82,65**
CSF £3.33 TOTE £1.50: £1.10, £1.80; EX 3.30 Trifecta £4.40 Pool: £1088.48 - 183.25 winning units..
Owner Mrs Monica O'Sullivan **Bred** Miss V McEvoy **Trained** Aberthin, Vale of Glamorgan

FOCUS
Following the defection of Emily's Flyer this took less winning. It was slowly run and the easy winner was a stone+ off his best hurdle figure.

749 VISITHEXHAM.NET H'CAP CHASE (12 fncs) 2m 110y
3:20 (3:20) (Class 5) (0-100,101) 5-Y-0+ **£2,144** (£629; £314; £157)

Form RPR
0/1- 1 **Castlelawn (IRE)**[11] 627 6-11-13 101 PeterBuchanan 116+
(Lucinda Russell) *mde all: hit 6th: drew clr fr 2 out: easily* **15/8**[1]
4/4- 2 10 **Escardo (GER)**[13] 602 10-10-12 86 (p) TomScudamore 91
(David Bridgwater) *nt fluent in rr early on: hdwy bef 4 out: effrt and chsd (clr) wnr bef last: kpt on: no imp* **16/1**
/32- 3 6 **Ginger's Lad**[13] 600 9-10-10 87 (bt) JakeGreenall(3) 87
(Michael Easterby) *chsd wnr: rdn 3 out: lost 2nd bef last: sn btn* **7/1**[3]
/31- 4 12 **Bunratty (IRE)**[16] 558 7-11-5 93 (t) RyanMania 81
(Dianne Sayer) *chsd ldrs: rdn bef 3 out: wknd after next* **11/4**[2]
0/6- 5 ½ **Fast Exit (IRE)**[8] 665 6-10-13 92 (t) DerekFox(5) 79
(Noel C Kelly, Ire) *in tch: lost pl 1/2-way: styd on fr 2 out: nvr rchd ldrs* **20/1**
0/6- 6 1 ¼ **Frith (IRE)**[32] 281 11-10-0 74 oh3 DougieCostello 60
(Lucy Normile) *bhd: pushed along 1/2-way: sme late hdwy: n.d* **25/1**
/50- 7 1 ¾ **Ancient Times (USA)**[16] 558 6-10-8 87 (p) KyleJames(5) 72
(Philip Kirby) *midfield: outpcd after 4 out: btn next* **14/1**
5/2- 8 1 ½ **Pumboo (FR)**[11] 627 10-11-0 88 BrianHarding 71
(James Moffatt) *chsd ldrs: drvn after 4 out: wknd fr next* **7/1**[3]
4/1- 9 ¾ **Le Grand Chene (FR)**[28] 378 7-11-8 96 (vt) PaulMoloney 79
(Sophie Leech) *hld up: shortlived effrt bef 3 out: sn btn* **10/1**
P/4- 10 9 **Honest And True (IRE)**[11] 627 6-9-7 74 oh6 GrantCockburn(7) 49
(Alistair Whillans) *in tch: lost pl 1/2-way: struggling fnl 4* **33/1**

4m 0.3s (-9.50) **Going Correction** -0.50s/f (Good) 10 Ran SP% **119.6**
Speed ratings: **102,97,94,88,88 88,87,86,86,81**
Swingers 1&2 not won, 1&3 £3.40, 2&3 not won CSF £30.75 CT £182.95 TOTE £2.90: £1.10, £3.30, £1.60; EX 27.20 Trifecta £194.60 Pool: £552.65 - 2.12 winning units..
Owner John R Adam **Bred** Mrs Michelle Archdeacon **Trained** Arlary, Perth & Kinross

FOCUS
A moderate, but competitive handicap. Another step forward from the progresssive winner.

750 HEXHAM EDGE OF THE ROMAN EMPIRE H'CAP HURDLE (DIV I) (12 hdls) 3m
3:55 (3:55) (Class 5) (0-100,100) 4-Y-0+ **£1,949** (£572; £286; £143)

Form RPR
1/2- 1 **Solis (GER)**[35] 221 10-11-8 96 RyanMania 107+
(Dianne Sayer) *in tch: smooth hdwy to ld bef 2 out: rdn bef last: styd on strly* **15/8**[1]
1/4- 2 7 **Saddlers Mot**[35] 222 9-11-0 95 (b) JohnDawson(7) 98
(Karen Tutty) *in tch: rdn and effrt 2 out: chsd (clr) wnr bef last: kpt on: no imp* **13/2**[3]
4P5/ 3 ¾ **Via Archimede (USA)**[21] 8-10-3 84 (p) GrantCockburn(7) 86
(Lucinda Russell) *chsd ldrs: drvn and outpcd 4 out: rallied 2 out: kpt on fr last: no imp* **12/1**
603/ 4 2 **It's Me And You**[13] 5-10-4 81 (p) JakeGreenall(3) 81
(Michael Easterby) *chsd ldrs: effrt and drvn bef 2 out: one pce between last 2* **25/1**
0/3- 5 24 **Whatsabillion (IRE)**[18] 522 11-11-3 91 (tp) APMcCoy 78
(Anabel K Murphy) *chsd ldrs: led 3 out to bef next: wknd between last 2* **13/2**[3]
01/- 6 25 **Ahhdehken**[52] 5495 8-10-6 83 EwanWhillans(3) 39
(Alistair Whillans) *hld up: rdn along bef 4 out: wknd bef 2 out* **5/1**[2]
P/0- P **Pegasus Prince (USA)**[21] 471 9-10-2 76 (p) LucyAlexander
(Brian Storey) *sn wl bhd: t.o whn p.u bef 7th* **80/1**
PP0/ P **Aitch Factor**[131] 4031 7-10-0 74 oh3 BrianHughes
(Henry Hogarth) *a bhd: struggling fr 7th: t.o whn p.u bef last* **25/1**
30P- P **Velvet Vic (IRE)**[13] 601 7-10-0 77 (bt) JackQuinlan(3)
(Richard Guest) *bhd: lost tch and p.u 8th: b.b.v* **10/1**
2/6- U **Combustible Kate (IRE)**[15] 564 7-11-10 98 HarryHaynes
(Nick Kent) *chsd ldrs: mstke and uns rdr 3rd* **20/1**
P/U- P **Almadan (IRE)**[13] 595 5-11-6 99 (bt) SamanthaDrake(5)
(Ferdy Murphy, France) *led and sn clr: hdd 3 out: wknd bef next: t.o whn p.u bef last* **20/1**
0/0- P **Alleged Vanity (IRE)**[15] 561 7-9-11 81 DiarmuidO'Regan(10)
(Chris Grant) *mstkes: cl up: wkng whn blnd 4 out: sn btn: t.o whn p.u bef 2 out* **22/1**
U60/ P **George My Friend**[55] 7-10-10 89 JonathanEngland(5)
(Simon Waugh) *midfield: drvn and outpcd bef 4 out: sn struggling: t.o whn p.u bef last* **50/1**

5m 59.4s (-9.60) **Going Correction** -0.425s/f (Good) 13 Ran SP% **119.7**
Speed ratings (Par 103): **99,96,96,95,87 79, , , , ,**
toteswingers 1&2 £2.40, 1&3 £3.30, 2&3 £4.40 CSF £13.16 CT £118.83 TOTE £2.30: £1.60, £3.10, £3.50; EX 14.80 Trifecta £91.70 Pool: £515.63 - 4.21 winning units..
Owner Dennis J Coppola **Bred** Stiftung Gestut Fahrhof **Trained** Hackthorpe, Cumbria

FOCUS
Only five mattered turning for home in this moderate staying handicap. The form is rated through the second and third.

751 HEXHAM EDGE OF THE ROMAN EMPIRE H'CAP HURDLE (DIV II) (12 hdls) 3m
4:25 (4:25) (Class 5) (0-100,100) 4-Y-0+ **£1,949** (£572; £286; £143)

Form RPR
P/1- 1 **Auberge (IRE)**[11] 628 9-11-1 89 RyanMania 100+
(Dianne Sayer) *hld up in tch: hdwy to ld 3 out: rdn after next: kpt on strly fr last* **7/2**[1]
521- 2 5 **Granwood**[23] 444 7-11-12 100 (p) PeterBuchanan 108
(Tim Walford) *led to bef 5th: led 7th to 3 out: chsd wnr: effrt and drvn 2 out: edgd lft and one pce run-in* **4/1**[2]
P/4- 3 12 **Along Came Rosie**[11] 626 9-10-6 80 DougieCostello 78
(Andrew Crook) *nt fluent on occasions: hld up: rdn after 3 out: styd on fr last: nt pce to chal* **20/1**
/65- 4 ¾ **Easement**[21] 476 10-10-9 90 JonathonBewley(7) 85
(George Bewley) *chsd ldrs: drvn 3 out: wknd between last 2* **9/1**
0/0- 5 38 **Reckless Romeo (IRE)**[21] 471 4-10-3 87 (p) HarryChalloner(5) 43
(Richard Ford) *t.k.h: in tch: rdn and outpcd bef 3 out: no imp fr next* **33/1**
350- 6 13 **Moon Melody (GER)**[13] 601 10-9-9 74 oh3 (tp) SamanthaDrake(5) 23
(Mike Sowersby) *chsd ldrs tl rdn and wknd fr 2 out* **25/1**
/31- 7 18 **Almond Court (IRE)**[14] 580 10-10-7 81 (p) KennyJohnson 14
(Robert Johnson) *w ldr: led bef 5th to 7th: cl up tl wknd fr 3 out* **7/2**[1]
P/0- P **Painted Sky**[21] 476 10-11-7 95 AdrianLane
(Iain Jardine) *a bhd: lost tch and p.u bef 4 out* **50/1**
0/6- P **Word Of Warning**[14] 581 9-11-0 95 GrahamWatters(7)
(Martin Todhunter) *prom: outpcd 4 out: struggling after next: t.o whn p.u bef last* **14/1**
55/- P **Delightfully (FR)**[52] 5495 9-11-5 100 (b) GrantCockburn(7)
(Lucinda Russell) *a bhd: lost tch and p.u bef 4 out* **10/1**
0/0- P **Life Long (IRE)**[14] 590 9-10-10 84 (b1) APMcCoy
(Anabel K Murphy) *midfield: struggling 6th: wknd and p.u bef next* **6/1**[3]

5m 57.2s (-11.80) **Going Correction** -0.425s/f (Good)
WFA 4 from 7yo+ 19lb 11 Ran SP% **118.0**
Speed ratings (Par 103): **102,100,96,96,83 79,73, , ,**
toteswingers 1&2 £4.10, 1&3 £14.80, 2&3 not won CSF £17.56 CT £246.07 TOTE £4.90: £1.90, £1.80, £4.10; EX 21.50 Trifecta £273.90 Part won. Pool: £365.31 - 0.10 winning units..
Owner Ron Affleck **Bred** David Fenton **Trained** Hackthorpe, Cumbria

FOCUS
This second division of the staying handicap was the just the weaker of the pair and the front two, both in-form mares, dominated from the third-last. The winner rates a personal best.

752 HEXHAM RACECOURSE PERFECT FOR WEDDINGS AMATEUR RIDERS' H'CAP HURDLE (10 hdls) 2m 4f 110y
4:55 (4:55) (Class 4) (0-120,115) 4-Y-0+ **£2,994** (£928; £464; £232)

Form RPR
/52- 1 **Granaruid (IRE)**[19] 511 10-10-13 105 (p) ConorShoemark(3) 110+
(Alison Hamilton) *chsd ldrs: drvn bef 4 out: rallied and led after 2 out: drvn and idled bef last: edgd lft and drvn out run-in* **3/1**[2]
2/0- 2 1 ¾ **Weybridge Light**[35] 221 8-10-2 98 (b) MrMatthewStanley(7) 101
(David Thompson) *prom: hdwy to ld 5th: hdd 4 out: cl up: outpcd 2 out: rallied to chse wnr bef last: kpt on run-in* **10/1**
533/ 3 3 ¾ **Houston Dynimo (IRE)**[22] 4516 8-11-7 115 MissJRRichards(5) 114
(Nicky Richards) *nt fluent on occasions in rr: pushed along 4 out: hdwy after 2 out: lft modest 3rd last: no imp* **9/1**
/5U- 4 25 **Millers Reef (IRE)**[11] 627 7-10-3 97 (t) MrJHamilton(5) 72
(Andrew Parker) *hld up in tch: hdwy and cl up whn stmbld bef 2 out: sn outpcd: n.d after* **12/1**
FF0/ 5 9 **Dica (FR)**[187] 2974 7-11-3 113 (t) CallumBewley(7) 80
(Patrick Griffin, Ire) *hld up: stmbld and nrly uns rdr after 4th: rdn after 3 out: wknd bef next* **18/1**
/30- 6 9 **Glasson Lad (IRE)**[21] 476 6-10-6 102 (p) MrRMorganMurphy(7) 61
(Ferdy Murphy, France) *nt fluent in rr: struggling bef 4 out: nvr on terms* **7/2**[3]
0/0- 7 21 **Daniel's Dream**[11] 630 13-9-7 89 oh28 (p) MrJDixon(7) 29
(John Dixon) *cl up: led 2nd to 5th: wknd bef 4 out: t.o* **150/1**
0/3- F **Born To Shine (USA)**[20] 491 5-10-5 94 NicodeBoinville 90
(Alan Swinbank) *t.k.h: led to 2nd: led 4 out to after 2 out: 5 l 3rd and one pce whn fell last* **7/4**[1]

5m 7.2s (-5.30) **Going Correction** -0.425s/f (Good) 8 Ran SP% **116.3**
Speed ratings (Par 105): **93,92,90,81,77 74,66,**
toteswingers 1&2 £6.10, 1&3 £6.10, 2&3 £6.10 CSF £32.61 CT £243.94 TOTE £3.60: £1.10, £4.00, £2.20; EX 44.20 Trifecta £204.10 Pool: £430.16 - 1.58 winning units..
Owner J P G Hamilton **Bred** S Donohoe And R Donohoe **Trained** Denholm, Borders

FOCUS
A weak handicap, confined to amateur riders. The winner is a 120 hurdler at best and the next two ran to their marks.

753 BOOK A PRIVATE BOX AT HEXHAM H'CAP CHASE (15 fncs) 2m 4f 110y
5:30 (5:30) (Class 5) (0-100,100) 5-Y-0+ **£2,144** (£629; £314; £157)

Form RPR
/44- **1** **Presenting Junior (IRE)**[14] [580] 6-10-0 **74** oh1............ LucyAlexander 81+
(Martin Todhunter) *in tch: rdn and outpcd after 4 out: rallied after next: styd on wl fr last to ld last stride* **7/2**[2]
322- **2** *shd* **Attycran (IRE)**[16] [555] 8-11-12 **100**..........................(t) MichaelMcAlister 106
(Maurice Barnes) *chsd ldrs: led 4 out: rdn after 2 out: kpt on fr last: hdd last stride* **7/2**[2]
/40- **3** *8* **Miss Sunflower**[11] [628] 11-9-9 **74** oh17...............(p) JonathanEngland[(5)] 73
(Tina Jackson) *bhd: pushed along 10th: hdwy 3 out: rdn and kpt on fr last: nt rch ldrs* **66/1**
/60- **4** *12* **Strobe**[14] [583] 9-11-5 **93**..(p) DougieCostello 81
(Lucy Normile) *bhd: pushed along 1/2-way: kpt on fr 2 out: n.d* **33/1**
/00- **5** *2* **Bob Will (IRE)**[23] [444] 8-9-7 **77**..........................(tp) DiarmuidO'Regan[(10)] 64
(Chris Grant) *t.k.h: cl up tl hit and outpcd 3 out: n.d after* **8/1**
4/2- **6** *5* **Chernik (IRE)**[14] [580] 12-10-0 **74** oh1.............................(p) HenryBrooke 58
(Micky Hammond) *in tch: rdn and outpcd bef 10th: n.d after* **11/4**[1]
/03- **7** *9* **Sycho Fred (IRE)**[13] [601] 12-10-0 **74** oh4.......................(t) BrianHughes 48
(Mike Sowersby) *cl up tl rdn bef 3 out: wknd fr next* **20/1**
625- **8** *8* **Over And Above (IRE)**[13] [601] 7-10-0 **74** oh3.............(t) RichieMcGrath 40
(Henry Hogarth) *chsd ldrs to 1/2-way: sn lost pl: no ch fr 4 out* **14/1**
/2U- **9** *2 3/4* **Bafana Choice**[14] [579] 7-11-10 **98**................................(p) JasonMaguire 66
(Chris Grant) *led to 4 out: rdn and wknd fr 2 out* **11/2**[3]
0/P- **P** **Tiger Billy (IRE)**[14] 11-9-7 **74** oh15.........................(b) MissSMDoolan[(7)]
(Wilf Storey) *nt fluent 1st: sn t.o: p.u 7th* **66/1**
/P5- **P** **Craicneasy (IRE)**[20] [493] 10-9-9 **74** oh12................(t) HarryChalloner[(5)]
(Bruce Mactaggart) *nt fluent in rr: lost tch and p.u bef 10th* **33/1**

5m 7.0s (-6.50) **Going Correction** -0.50s/f (Good) **11** Ran SP% **117.9**
Speed ratings: **92,91,88,84,83 81,78,75,74,**
toteswingers 1&2 £114.60, 1&3 £17.90, 2&3 £68.20 CSF £16.06 CT £677.02 TOTE £5.70: £1.90, £1.70, £12.50; EX 24.30 Trifecta £568.80 Part won. Pool: £758.42 - 0.01 winning units..
Owner W & Mrs J Garnett **Bred** T Horgan **Trained** Orton, Cumbria

FOCUS
A weak handicap, run at a routine gallop. The winner should still be competitive when reassessed.

754 SYCAMORE GAP MARES' STANDARD OPEN NATIONAL HUNT FLAT RACE 2m 110y
6:00 (6:06) (Class 6) 4-6-Y-0 **£1,642** (£478; £239)

Form RPR
1 **Definite Row (IRE)**[24] [443] 4-11-0 0................................ JasonMaguire 103+
(Gordon Elliott, Ire) *mde all at stdy pce: rdn and qcknd clr wl over 1f out: eased ins fnl f* **5/4**[1]
2- **2** *8* **Retrieve The Stick**[15] [567] 4-11-0 0.................................. BrianHughes 92+
(Malcolm Jefferson) *chsd wnr thrght: rdn over 3f out: plugged on same pce fr 2f out* **13/8**[2]
3/5- **3** *4 1/2* **Rev Up Ruby**[38] [173] 5-10-10 0...............................(t) JonathonBewley[(7)] 89+
(George Bewley) *hld up: rdn and hdwy over 2f out: no imp fr over 1f out* **5/1**[3]
0- **4** *nk* **Agent Louise**[15] [567] 5-11-3 0.. HenryBrooke 88
(Mike Sowersby) *t.k.h: trckd ldrs: rdn over 2f out: sn outpcd: n.d after* **40/1**
0/0- **5** *8* **Beyondtemptation**[35] [225] 5-11-0 0................................ JohnKington[(3)] 80
(Jonathan Haynes) *hld up: stdy hdwy over 3f out: rdn and outpcd over 2f out* **80/1**
0- **6** *6* **Coccinnelle (FR)**[5] [699] 5-11-3 0.................................... LucyAlexander 74
(Ferdy Murphy, France) *trckd ldrs: drvn and outpcd over 3f out: n.d after* **28/1**
7 *1 3/4* **Miss Pheebs** 4-10-7 0... CallumBewley[(7)] 69
(Colin Teague) *in tch: struggling wl over 2f out: sn btn* **40/1**
8 *47* **Brave Mouse** 5-11-0 0... JakeGreenall[(3)] 25
(Michael Easterby) *hld up in tch: struggling 3f out: sn wknd and eased* **10/1**

4m 10.9s (-1.80) **Going Correction** -0.425s/f (Good)
WFA 4 from 5yo 3lb **8** Ran SP% **117.9**
Speed ratings: **87,83,81,80,77 74,73,51**
toteswingers 1&2 £1.20, 1&3 £2.50, 2&3 £1.60 CSF £3.59 TOTE £2.30: £1.10, £1.10, £2.00; EX 5.00 Trifecta £9.60 Pool: £751.03 - 58.47 winning units..
Owner Ms Annie Flora Joan Bowles **Bred** Brendan And Mary Fitzpatrick **Trained** Trim, Co Meath

FOCUS
A big step up from the winner in steadily run bumper. The form has been given a token rating through the second.
T/Plt: £19.50 to a £1 stake. Pool: £64,523.16 - 2,407.89 winning units T/Qpdt: £13.20 to a £1 stake. Pool: £4,014.79 - 223.47 winning units RY

669 STRATFORD (L-H)
Tuesday, June 18

OFFICIAL GOING: Good to firm (good in places)
All bends moved out to the maximum.
Wind: almost nil Weather: very warm & sunny; 18 dergrees

755 AT THE RACES MARES' NOVICES' HURDLE (9 hdls) 2m 3f
2:10 (2:10) (Class 4) 4-Y-0+ **£3,119** (£915; £457; £228)

Form RPR
6/1- **1** **Massannie (IRE)**[23] [502] 5-11-5 0.............................. TomScudamore 127+
(David Pipe) *2nd tl led 3 out: easily drew clr after next: 15 l ahd at last: unchal* **2/5**[1]
0/5- **2** *11* **Cannon Fodder**[23] [484] 6-10-12 0.................................. MarcGoldstein 100
(Sheena West) *chsd ldrs: nt a fluent: 6 l 3rd and drvn bef 2 out: no ch w wnr after but chsd her vainly bef last* **7/1**[3]
/22- **3** *1 1/2* **Polly Hopper**[20] [532] 7-10-12 110.......................(tp) SamTwiston-Davies 99
(Nigel Twiston-Davies) *dug toes in and dwlt: sn chsng ldrs: nt fluent 4th: 5th and drvn and outpcd 3 out: plugged into 3rd home turn: ev ch of poor 2nd at last: plodded on* **7/2**[2]
00/ **4** *15* **Terntheothercheek**[125] [3677] 4-10-8 0........................... SeanQuinlan 79
(Jennie Candlish) *wl in tch tl 6th and outpcd 3 out: lft remote 4th at last* **50/1**
4/0- **5** *1 3/4* **Oh Dear Oh Dear**[40] [177] 5-10-12 90...............................(t) JackDoyle 81
(Ron Hodges) *trckd ldrs tl rdn bef 2 out: wknd tamely* **20/1**
6 *3 1/2* **Lucys Girl (IRE)**[388] 6-10-12 0.. BrendanPowell 83
(Jamie Snowden) *led: nt a fluent: rdn and hdd 3 out: 3rd and fading home turn: 25 l 4th whn blnd bdly last* **14/1**
000/ **P** **Podium Dancer**[217] [2402] 6-10-5 0.......................... MrJoshuaNewman[(7)]
(Nick Lampard) *plld hrd for 100yds: hit 2nd and a drvn in rr after: reluctant: t.o after 5th tl p.u 2 out* **100/1**
/06- **P** **Pinnacle Ofpassion (IRE)**[7] [706] 5-10-12 0................. GerardTumelty
(Nick Lampard) *hmpd s: a detached: j.rt 1st: mstke 2nd: sn t.o: p.u 2 out* **100/1**

4m 32.2s (0.70) **Going Correction** -0.10s/f (Good)
WFA 4 from 5yo+ 17lb **8** Ran SP% **121.5**
Speed ratings (Par 105): **94,89,88,82,81 80, ,**
Tote Swingers: 1&2 £1.50, 1&3 £1.02, 2&3 £1.70 CSF £4.71 TOTE £1.30: £1.02, £2.10, £1.10; EX 5.90 Trifecta £9.10 Pool: £1,254.27 - 102.76 winning units..
Owner Wayne Clifford **Bred** Mrs S Clifford **Trained** Nicholashayne, Devon

FOCUS
A moderate mares' novice. The easy winner confirmed the merit of her recent easy win, and was value for further

756 JENKINSONS CATERERS H'CAP HURDLE (8 hdls) 2m 110y
2:45 (2:45) (Class 4) (0-115,115) 4-Y-0+ **£3,249** (£954; £477; £238)

Form RPR
/14- **1** **Dresden (IRE)**[37] [251] 5-11-9 **112**.. WillKennedy 126+
(Sarah-Jayne Davies) *settled handy: effrt 3 out: led next: 5 l clr and wl in command last: pushed out* **12/1**
/21- **2** *5* **Castlemorris King**[36] [267] 5-11-6 **114**......................... GavinSheehan[(5)] 122+
(Brian Barr) *j.rt: led 1st tl after 2nd: led again 3 out tl hdd and hit next: drvn and one pce appr last* **13/2**[3]
412- **3** *7* **Foxcub (IRE)**[17] [581] 5-10-13 **102**.. FelixDeGiles 103
(Tom Symonds) *taken down early: a 2nd or 3rd: drvn 2 out: wl hld bef last: jst hung on to 3rd pl* **4/1**[1]
/11- **4** *nk* **Rime Avec Gentil (FR)**[31] [371] 8-11-3 **111**............... RobertWilliams[(5)] 111
(Bernard Llewellyn) *hld up towards rr: rdn bef 3 out: modest 7th and racing awkwardly next: styd on appr last: nvr threatened ldng pair but nrly snatched 3rd* **8/1**
0/0- **5** *nk* **Hot Spice**[36] [267] 5-10-10 **102**.. JakeGreenall[(3)] 103
(Michael Easterby) *midfield: rdn 3 out: no imp on ldng pair fr next* **16/1**
/FF- **6** *6* **Tony Dinozzo (FR)**[23] [500] 6-11-2 **105**...........................(p) JamieMoore 100
(Peter Bowen) *t.k.h: led after 2nd: j. path bef next: hdd 3 out: drvn and fdd bef last* **11/2**[2]
/13- **7** *24* **Montefeltro**[17] [581] 5-11-12 **115**....................................(p) DenisO'Regan 94
(John Ferguson) *hld up: mstkes 2nd and 3rd: rdn 5th: struggling and nt travelling next: v poor jump 2 out: eased bef last* **4/1**[1]
P/P- **8** *nk* **Humbel Ben (IRE)**[31] [371] 10-10-13 **102**......................(p) NickScholfield 75
(Alan Jones) *unruly: uns rdr in paddock: bhd: mstke 5th: wl in arrrs next* **66/1**
/3F- **9** *35* **Amuse Me**[13] [636] 7-11-8 **111**... APMcCoy 52
(Jonjo O'Neill) *led tl 1st: prom tl hrd drvn and fdd bef 3 out: t.o next: eased after* **16/1**
0/0- **10** *18* **The Winged Assasin (USA)**[12] [650] 7-10-11 **100**....(t) RichardJohnson 25
(Shaun Lycett) *a towards rr: rdn and btn 3 out: t.o* **20/1**
404- **P** **Trip The Light**[8] [697] 8-11-2 **105**..........................(b) SamTwiston-Davies
(Phil Middleton) *chsd ldrs tl rdn and wknd qckly bef 2 out: p.u sharply home turn: fatally injured* **7/1**

3m 51.9s (-4.10) **Going Correction** -0.10s/f (Good) **11** Ran SP% **118.0**
Speed ratings (Par 105): **105,102,99,99,99 96,84,84,68,59**
Tote Swingers: 1&2 £4.50, 1&3 £3.02, 2&3 £4.70 CSF £88.93 CT £374.02 TOTE £24.90: £5.90, £2.30, £2.60; EX 99.60 Trifecta £160.40 Pool: £743.80 - 3.47 winning units..
Owner Dan Lloyd **Bred** Diana Webley **Trained** Leominster, H'fords

FOCUS
An ordinary handicap. The winner is back on the upgrade in the fastest of the hurdle races.

757 GRUNDON WASTE MANAGEMENT H'CAP CHASE (17 fncs) 2m 7f
3:20 (3:20) (Class 4) (0-120,119) 5-Y-0+ **£3,898** (£1,144; £572; £286)

Form RPR
/F3- **1** **City Press (IRE)**[16] [596] 7-11-8 **115**.................................(tp) NoelFehily 124+
(Warren Greatrex) *taken steadily towards rr: stdy prog 11th: 4th at 14: chal gng wl but edgd lft bef last: led last: rdn and kpt on gamely cl home* **6/1**[2]
0/4- **2** *1* **Rockiteer (IRE)**[33] [334] 10-11-10 **117**........................(p) RichardJohnson 125
(Henry Daly) *racd keenly in ld: 8 l clr 9th: pressed fr 14th: hit 3 out and hdd briefly: hdd again last: hrd drvn and kpt on wl: jst hld* **14/1**
/66- **3** *2 1/4* **Health Is Wealth (IRE)**[13] [632] 8-10-7 **100**...............(tp) BrendanPowell 105
(Colin Tizzard) *3rd mostly tl 2nd after 2nd bef 13th tl bef next: rdn and lost pl briefly 3 out: rallied bef last where ev ch briefly: no ex fnl 100yds* **40/1**
/22- **4** *10* **Cruchain (IRE)**[18] [566] 10-10-11 **107**..........................(p) RobertDunne[(3)] 106
(Dai Burchell) *hld up: stdy prog 13th: pressing ldrs whn pckd 2 out: rdn and sn no ex: wl hld whn nt fluent last* **14/1**
323/ **5** *11* **Suburban Bay**[301] [1310] 8-11-5 **112**............................ WayneHutchinson 101
(Alan King) *nt a fluent early: hld up: prog gng wl 9th: wnt 2nd after 13th: led briefly next: lost 2nd whn drvn home turn: fin v weakly* **15/2**[3]
/23- **6** *7* **Double Chocolate**[23] [487] 10-11-6 **113**.......................(p) TomScudamore 95
(David Bridgwater) *hit 7th: chsd ldrs: lost pl 11th: struggling after* **11/1**
341- **7** *4 1/2* **Strongbows Legend**[8] [693] 8-11-0 **114** 7ex...........(v) CharlieDeutsch[(7)] 90
(Charlie Longsdon) *t.k.h in 2nd tl after 12th: rdn and lost pl bef 14th: fnd little and sn no ch* **9/4**[1]
/11- **8** *14* **Or D'Oudairies (FR)**[18] [566] 11-10-6 **104**..............(t) SamanthaDrake[(5)] 67
(Ferdy Murphy, France) *mstke 4th: a towards rr: drvn 11th struggling after: t.o* **11/1**
0/2- **9** *4* **Larks Lad (IRE)**[27] [432] 9-11-12 **119**......................................(p) APMcCoy 79
(Jonjo O'Neill) *chsd ldrs: nt fluent 2nd and 10th (both waters): drvn and nvr hopeful after: lost tch 3 out: sn eased: t.o* **6/1**[2]
3/2- **10** *72* **Farmer Frank**[30] [388] 10-10-4 **97**... HarryHaynes
(Nick Kent) *rdn and dropped to rr 8th: t.o 14th* **20/1**
00P/ **U** **Magical Legend**[201] [2714] 12-11-11 **118**...............................(t) TomO'Brien
(Sarah Kerswell) *midfield tl mstke and uns rdr 5th* **22/1**
24F- **P** **Monarch's Way**[16] [596] 6-11-10 **117**.............................(b) DenisO'Regan
(John Ferguson) *hld up last: struggling 12th: t.o and p.u 3 out* **33/1**

5m 35.1s (-4.10) **Going Correction** -0.10s/f (Good) **12** Ran SP% **115.6**
Speed ratings: **103,102,101,98,94 92,90,85,84,59 ,**
Tote Swingers: 1&2 £24.00 CSF £77.16 CT £3045.72 TOTE £6.40: £2.20, £4.60, £12.20; EX 73.80 Trifecta £661.60 Part won. Pool: £882.17 - 0.01 winning units..
Owner Lewis, Reid, Moss & Luck **Bred** Mrs M Doran **Trained** Upper Lambourn, Berks

FOCUS
An ordinary handicap. The winner is on the upgrade and there is probably still more to come.

758 AT THE RACES NOVICES' HURDLE (8 hdls) 2m 110y
3:55 (3:55) (Class 4) 4-Y-0+ **£3,119** (£915; £457; £228)

Form RPR
061/ 1 **Bright Abbey**58 5437 5-10-12 117 RichardJohnson 108+
(Philip Hobbs) *t.k.h and cl up: wnt 2nd at 4th: led between last two: sn rdn 5 l clr: clipped last: a in command* **4/5**1
41- 2 8 **Odin (IRE)**10 671 5-11-5 0 LeightonAspell 107+
(Don Cantillon) *j. bdly rt: led tl rdn and hdd between last two: immediately outpcd: 5 l 2nd at last* **5/2**2
3 8 **Mayan Flight (IRE)**7 5-10-12 0 NoelFehily 90
(Tony Carroll) *towards rr: effrt on outside after 3 out: disp 3rd at next: sn rdn and no ch w ldng pair: 12 l 3rd at last* **66/1**
0- 4 6 **Carobello (IRE)**34 318 6-10-12 0 SamTwiston-Davies 83
(Martin Bosley) *towards rr: outpcd 3 out: plugged on aftedr next to go poor 4th at last* **66/1**
F/ 5 4 ½ **Danehill Dante (IRE)**283 1519 5-10-12 0 WayneHutchinson 80
(Alan King) *chsd ldrs: rdn 3 out: fdd after next: lost 4th at last* **11/2**3
00/ 6 1 **Ibiza Sunset (IRE)**56 5470 5-10-12 0 (t) BrendanPowell 78
(Sarah Kerswell) *nvr bttr than midfield: hit 3rd: rdn and struggling 3 out* **16/1**
000/ 7 ½ **Cloudy Start**66 5281 7-10-12 89 WillKennedy 77
(Violet M Jordan) *hld up last most of way: struggling 3 out* **250/1**
8 17 **Whispering Boy (IRE)**205 6-10-12 0 TommyPhelan 60
(David Bridgwater) *led tl j. slowly 1st: j. slowly 2nd: prom tl lost pl after 5th: no ch next: t.o* **50/1**
9 13 **Geordie Boy**273 4-10-9 0 MarcGoldstein 44
(Sheena West) *3rd mostly tl rdn and hit 3 out: fdd bdly: t.o* **25/1**

3m 54.5s (-1.50) **Going Correction** -0.10s/f (Good)
WFA 4 from 5yo+ 17lb **9** Ran SP% **114.6**
Speed ratings (Par 105): **99,95,91,88,86 86,85,77,71**
Tote Swingers: 1&2 £1.02, 1&3 £24.50, 2&3 £29.40 CSF £2.99 TOTE £1.70: £1.10, £1.10, £4.90; EX 3.30 Trifecta £27.90 Pool: £1,221.73 - 32.75 winning units..
Owner Mrs Caren Walsh **Bred** Pendley Farm **Trained** Withycombe, Somerset

FOCUS
They went a fair pace for this uncompetitive novices' hurdle and the front pair had it to themselves from the last two flights. The easy winner is rated below his best.

759 AT THE RACES NOVICES' H'CAP CHASE (15 fncs) 2m 5f 110y
4:35 (4:35) (Class 5) (0-95,95) 5-Y-0+ **£2,599** (£763; £381; £190)

Form RPR
/01- 1 **The Good Guy (IRE)**24 471 10-11-4 87 WayneHutchinson 101+
(Graeme McPherson) *settled towards rr: stdy prog fr 11th: wnt 2nd 2 out: rdn to ld bef last where nt fluent: r.o gamely to outbattle rival flat* **11/4**1
5/6- 2 2 ¾ **Mr Robinson (FR)**27 425 6-9-10 70 (v1) TrevorWhelan(5) 81
(Tony Carroll) *chsd ldrs: smooth prog whn mstke 12th: 2nd 3 out: led next: sn 4 l clr: drvn and racd awkwardly and hdd bef last: stl hld a ch last but fnd nthing and wl hld fnl 100yds* **11/2**2
/P0- 3 8 **Watch House (IRE)**11 656 8-10-9 85 CiaranMckee(7) 89
(Michael Gates) *racd keenly and cl up: 3rd at 11th: drvn and outpcd in 6th whn mstke 2 out: rallied and fin wl to go 3rd flat: no ch w ldrs* **25/1**
/0P- 4 1 ¼ **Harrys Whim**18 562 8-10-0 69 RichieMcGrath 70
(John Weymes) *racd keenly: mde most: mstke 5th: drvn and hdd 2 out: sn wknd: 15 l 3rd at last* **14/1**
P/6- 5 7 **Highland Rain**18 565 5-10-8 77 (vt1) SeanQuinlan 77+
(Jennie Candlish) *t.k.h: prom: led and blnd 12th: sn hdd: 3rd whn mstke next: wknd u.p after next* **14/1**
3/6- 6 1 **Brandy And Pep (IRE)**20 540 9-9-7 69 oh4 (p) MrJPO'Sullivan(7) 63
(R P Rath, Ire) *towards rr: hdwy bef 12th: sn rdn: 4th 2 out: fdd wl bef last* **16/1**
644/ 7 3 ½ **Kilshanna (IRE)**22 8-9-9 69 oh7 RobertWilliams(5) 60
(Bernard Llewellyn) *bhd: blnd 5th and reminders: blnd again 9th: mod prog to midfield 12th: nvr on terms* **16/1**
/03- 8 32 **Dr Dreamy (IRE)**30 385 6-10-12 81 ow2 (t) LiamHeard 41
(Claire Dyson) *midfield: mstke 11th: lost tch bef next: t.o* **8/1**
/65- 9 1 ¼ **Kingdom Of Munster (IRE)**14 625 6-11-7 95 HarryChalloner(5) 56
(Richard Ford) *a towards rr: struggling 11th: t.o* **20/1**
3/P- 10 37 **Chandlers Cross (IRE)**8 692 11-11-0 86 (tp) AdamWedge(3) 14
(David Rees) *2nd or 3rd tl 7th: drvn and wknd after 9th: t.o 3 out: fin eventually* **10/1**
5P6- P **Radsoc De Sivola (FR)**27 426 8-10-2 76 JoeCornwall(5)
(John Cornwall) *nt fluent 6th: chsd ldrs tl rdn and lost tch qckly bef 12th: t.o and p.u last* **66/1**
/32- P **Jamesson (IRE)**12 639 8-11-2 90 (t) GavinSheehan(5)
(Jamie Snowden) *nvr jumping or travelling in detached last: 20 l adrift by 5th: t.o and p.u 3 out* **6/1**3
/36- P **Petrarchick (USA)**23 485 6-10-0 69 oh6 (tp) TomScudamore
(Emma Baker) *sweating profusely: bhd: rdn and struggling 9th: t.o and p.u 11th* **20/1**

5m 10.1s (-4.90) **Going Correction** -0.10s/f (Good) **13** Ran SP% **116.5**
Speed ratings: **104,103,100,99,97 96,95,83,83,69 ,,**
Tote Swingers: 1&2 £4.70, 1&3 £28.20, 2&3 £30.10 CSF £17.36 CT £311.95 TOTE £2.80: £1.50, £2.60, £8.50; EX 20.20 Trifecta £783.50 Pool: £1,849.92 - 1.77 winning units..
Owner The Martins Hill Racing Partnership **Bred** Brian Slattery **Trained** Upper Oddington, Gloucs
■ Stewards' Enquiry : Liam Heard two-day ban: weighed in 2lb heavy (Jul 2-3)

FOCUS
A run-of-the-mill novice handicap. The winner was well in on his recent hurdle win and ran to a similar level.

760 GREENWAY INTERMEDIATE OPEN NATIONAL HUNT FLAT RACE 2m 110y
5:10 (5:10) (Class 6) 4-6-Y-0 **£1,559** (£457; £228; £114)

Form RPR
1- 1 **Another Hero (IRE)**17 589 4-11-5 0 APMcCoy 108+
(Jonjo O'Neill) *prom: led 1/2-way: hrd drvn and pressed over 1f out: sn gained upper hand and styd on wl* **4/7**1
5/1- 2 1 ½ **Kettlewell**16 599 4-11-0 0 GavinSheehan(5) 106
(Warren Greatrex) *midfield: 5th and outpcd 5f out: rallied 2f out: kpt on dourly to go 2nd fnl 50yds: nt rch wnr* **13/2**2
3 1 ¼ **Bear Island Flint** 5-11-1 0 SamJones 101
(Brendan Powell) *prom: wnt 2nd over 2f out: rdn and ev ch over 1f out: nt qckn after: lost 2nd 50yds out* **20/1**
4 1 ¾ **Buckhorn Timothy** 4-10-12 0 JoeTizzard 96
(Colin Tizzard) *pressed ldrs: rdn and rn green 3f out: kpt on steadily ins fnl f: do bttr in time* **9/1**3
5 10 **All Riled Up** 5-10-8 0 IanPopham 83
(Harry Chisman) *pushed along in rr: brief effrt 3f out: nvr nr ldrs and plugged on* **100/1**
6 2 **Sarsari (IRE)** 5-10-12 0 AlexanderVoy(3) 89
(Alan Jarvis) *bhd: outpcd 5f out: rallied briefly 3f out: sn btn* **9/1**3
14- 7 7 **Are They Your Own (IRE)**12 647 5-11-1 0 MissAEStirling(7) 89
(Fergal O'Brien) *led tl 1/2-way: rdn and dropped out qckly over 2f out: t.o* **20/1**
8 10 **Much A Doo** 5-11-1 0 RichardJohnson 73
(Paul Henderson) *a bhd: t.o 3f out* **25/1**
9 2 ¼ **Take The Crown**24 4-10-12 0 HenryOliver 68
(Henry Oliver) *t.k.h: prom tl rdn over 3f out: sn lost pl: t.o* **33/1**
00/ 10 27 **Another Journey**184 3098 4-10-12 0 WayneHutchinson 44
(Lisa Williamson) *sweating profusely: t.k.h: a last: t.o 3f out* **100/1**

3m 50.9s (0.50) **Going Correction** -0.10s/f (Good) **10** Ran SP% **115.3**
Speed ratings: **94,93,92,91,87 86,82,78,77,64**
Tote Swingers: 1&2 £3.40, 1&3 £5.50, 2&3 £18.50 CSF £3.92 TOTE £1.50: £1.10, £1.10, £3.40; EX 4.30 Trifecta £40.40 Pool: £2,302.89 - 42.73 winning units..
Owner John P McManus **Bred** Miss Noreen Hayes **Trained** Cheltenham, Gloucs

FOCUS
A moderate bumper rated around the first two.
T/Plt: £35.10 to a £1 stake. Pool: £62,476.00 - 1,297.69 winning units T/Qpdt: £12.70 to a £1 stake. Pool: £3,067.00 - 178.20 winning units IM

725UTTOXETER (L-H)
Wednesday, June 19

OFFICIAL GOING: Good to firm (good in places; 7.8)
Divided bends with hurdle bends moved out 5yds. Hurdles re-sited and moved inwards 4-6 yards on to fresher ground.
Wind: Light against Weather: Overcast

761 TRY OUR NEW CRABBIE'S SCOTTISH RASPBERRY "NATIONAL HUNT" MAIDEN HURDLE (9 hdls) 2m
2:10 (2:10) (Class 5) 4-Y-0+ **£2,339** (£686; £343; £171)

Form RPR
416/ 1 **Bittersweetheart**283 1532 6-10-7 0 TomScudamore 95+
(David Bridgwater) *mid-div: mstke 1st: hdwy 4th: shkn up to ld flat: rdn out* **7/1**
0/2- 2 3 ½ **Dr Dalwhinny**18 589 4-10-11 0 JasonMaguire 95
(Donald McCain) *chsd ldrs: hmpd 3rd: rdn and ev ch last: styd on same pce flat* **5/2**1
4/4- 3 ½ **Definite Maybe (IRE)**24 498 5-11-0 0 DenisO'Regan 98
(Martin Todhunter) *led: rdn and hdd flat: styd on same pce* **7/2**3
2/0- 4 1 ½ **Nodividendsagain**44 140 5-11-0 0 (t) PaulMoloney 96
(Evan Williams) *hld up: hdwy 6th: rdn appr 2 out: styd on* **11/4**2
6R- 5 1 ¾ **Spiritofchartwell**8 706 5-11-0 0 LeightonAspell 93
(Nick Gifford) *hld up: hdwy 6th: outpcd after next: rallied appr last: no ex flat* **66/1**
4/0- 6 12 **Rose Red**37 268 6-10-4 0 JamesBest(3) 74
(Rob Summers) *chsd ldr: hit 3rd: rdn and wknd after 2 out* **28/1**
00/- 7 nk **Mon Homme**173 3310 6-11-0 0 SamTwiston-Davies 81
(Mark Rimell) *hld up: mstke 1st: rdn appr 3 out: blnd and wknd next* **50/1**
03/- 8 nk **Twoways (IRE)**226 2231 7-11-0 106 ConorO'Farrell 81
(Mark Rimell) *hld up: pushed along after 5th: rdn and wknd 3 out* **5/1**
0/P- P **Keen's Token**36 290 7-10-11 0 BrianToomey(3)
(Clive Mulhall) *mid-div: hdwy 3rd: wknd after 5th: t.o whn p.u bef 3 out* **200/1**

3m 51.8s (-0.20) **Going Correction** -0.20s/f (Good)
WFA 4 from 5yo+ 17lb **9** Ran SP% **114.0**
Speed ratings (Par 103): **92,90,90,89,88 82,82,82,**
totewwingers 1&2 £4.70, 1&3 £3.10, 1&3 £4.80 CSF £24.97 TOTE £10.50: £2.10, £1.10, £1.70; EX 24.80 Trifecta £179.50 Pool: £1125.69 - 4.70 winning units..
Owner The Ferandlin Peaches **Bred** Silvano Scanu **Trained** Icomb, Gloucs

FOCUS
The hurdles were sited about 12yds off the inner on fresher ground, and the first fence in the back straight was back last week as a renewed fence. A modest maiden hurdle on ground officially described as good to firm, good in places. It was steadily run and the winner and third are rated in line with their bumper form.

762 THE DOG AND PARTRIDGE MARCHINGTON CONDITIONAL JOCKEYS' (S) HURDLE (10 hdls) 2m 4f 110y
2:45 (2:45) (Class 5) 4-7-Y-0 **£1,949** (£572; £286; £143)

Form RPR
1/P- 1 **Di Kaprio (FR)**31 394 7-10-9 0 (t1) AdamWedge(3) 108
(Evan Williams) *chsd ldrs: wnt 2nd 7th: rdn after 3 out: led last: styd on u.p* **11/2**
221- 2 2 ¼ **Descaro (USA)**6 727 7-11-4 107 (p) CiaranMckee(8) 120
(John O'Shea) *led 2nd: clr 6th: hit next: rdn and hdd last: styd on same pce flat* **7/2**2
333- 3 33 **Electric Tiger (GER)**13 649 6-10-12 107 (tp) BrendanPowell 76
(David Bridgwater) *w ldr to 2nd: remained handy: rdn 6th: wknd next: t.o* **2/1**1
5/P- 4 2 ½ **Rigidity**48 77 6-10-9 121 (vt) MichaelByrne(3) 74
(Tim Vaughan) *led to 2nd: chsd ldr tl rdn 7th: wknd next: t.o* **9/2**
233- 5 6 **Teshali (IRE)**11 673 7-10-4 116 (t) MarkMarris(8) 69
(Anthony Middleton) *hld up: hdwy 6th: wknd 3 out: t.o* **4/1**3
40/- 6 42 **Quiet Whisper (IRE)**51 31 7-10-9 95 EdCookson(3) 31
(Kim Bailey) *hld up: pushed along 6th: sn lost tch: t.o* **20/1**

4m 52.4s (-6.60) **Going Correction** -0.20s/f (Good) **6** Ran SP% **113.9**
Speed ratings: **104,103,90,89,87 71**
toteswingers 1&2 £1.02, 2&3 £3.10, 1&3 £3.20 CSF £25.47 TOTE £5.00: £2.50, £2.20; EX 18.70 Trifecta £120.00 Pool: £987.94 - 6.17 winning units..The winner was bought by B Leavy for 7,200gns.
Owner Mr & Mrs William Rucker **Bred** Mme Dominique Le Drans **Trained** Llancarfan, Vale Of Glamorgan

FOCUS
An interesting contest for a seller with some fair individuals going to post. The form is rated through the second and could be rated a lot higher.

763 #UTTOXETERTWITTERATI NOVICES' H'CAP CHASE (18 fncs) 3m

3:20 (3:20) (Class 4) (0-110,110) 5-Y-0 **£3,798** (£1,122; £561; £280; £140)

Form RPR

/30- **1** **Rossmore Lad (IRE)**[19] 566 8-11-9 **107**............................(p) NoelFehily 130+
(Charlie Longsdon) *mde all: clr 2 out: shkn up flat: styd on wl* **4/1**[1]

4/1- **2** *15* **To Live (FR)**[43] 162 6-11-2 **100**.. APMcCoy 118+
(Nick Gifford) *hld up in tch: mstke 8th: chsd wnr 12th: rdn appr last: eased whn btn flat* **13/2**[3]

4/4- **3** *23* **Solway Sam**[35] 312 10-11-1 **99**.. BrianHarding 88
(Lisa Harrison) *hld up: hdwy 13th: wknd 3 out: t.o* **6/1**[2]

1/3- **4** *17* **Parkam Jack**[23] 7-11-9 **110**.........................(tp) MichealNolan(3) 84
(Richard Woollacott) *prom: rdn appr 4 out: wknd bef next: t.o* **14/1**

162- **5** *2 1/4* **Handsome Buddy (IRE)**[13] 646 6-10-8 **99**..............(v) CiaranMckee(7) 70
(Michael Gates) *hld up: hdwy 5 out: wknd next: t.o* **6/1**[2]

2/0- **6** *7* **D'Gigi**[40] 206 7-11-2 **100**..........................(t) SamTwiston-Davies 65
(Nigel Twiston-Davies) *mstke 1st: mid-div: rdn and wknd 12th: t.o* **16/1**

/43- **7** *13* **Justjoe (IRE)**[39] 224 7-10-1 **85**.......................................(p) HenryBrooke 38
(Micky Hammond) *hld up: effrt 9th: wknd 12th: t.o* **10/1**

053- **8** *3/4* **Basford Ben**[8] 713 5-11-5 **103**.......................................(p) SeanQuinlan 56
(Jennie Candlish) *chsd ldrs: rdn 12th: wknd after next: t.o* **11/1**

1/6- **9** *31* **Quelle Chance (IRE)**[21] 534 7-10-11 **95**.......................... BrianHughes 20
(John Wade) *chsd ldrs: lost pl 6th: wknd 9th: t.o* **14/1**

0/5- **P** **Mr Jay Dee (IRE)**[41] 181 8-11-2 **100**.................................... LiamHeard
(Claire Dyson) *prom: lost pl 5th: wknd 9th: t.o whn p.u bef 12th* **66/1**

/4P- **P** **Ontheslate (IRE)**[21] 541 7-9-7 **84** oh12...................(b) MissBAndrews(7)
(Neil King) *chsd wnr tl rdn 12th: sn wknd: t.o whn p.u bef 14th* **8/1**

3/5- **P** **Walcot Lathyrus**[18] 585 8-11-2 **103**.............................. JakeGreenall(3)
(Richard Lee) *hld up: hdwy 10th: mstke next: blnd 4 out: sn wknd: p.u bef next* **10/1**

6m 5.1s (-10.00) **Going Correction** -0.30s/f (Good) 12 Ran SP% **120.2**
Speed ratings: **104,99,91,85,84 82,78,78,67,** ,
toteswingers 1&2 £5.50, 2&3 £6.10, 1&3 £5.40 CSF £31.44 CT £158.08 TOTE £5.70: £2.30, £2.40, £2.00; EX 35.70 Trifecta £641.80 Part won. Pool: £855.80 - 0.78 winning units..
Owner Biddestone Racing Club **Bred** Miss Lillian Barry **Trained** Over Norton, Oxon

FOCUS
A modest staying novices' handicap chase in which they went a contested gallop. The winner improved to the level of his best hurdles form.

764 BETVICTOR ROYAL ASCOT NO LOSE HUGHES H'CAP HURDLE (DIV I) (10 hdls) 2m 4f 110y

4:00 (4:00) (Class 4) (0-115,115) 4-Y-0+ **£3,378** (£992; £496; £248)

Form RPR

1- **1** **Busted Tycoon (IRE)**[10] 681 4-11-6 **113** 7ex.................. DenisO'Regan 129+
(A J Martin, Ire) *hld up: hdwy 6th: led on bit and mstke 2 out: hrd hld* **5/4**[1]

232- **2** *3* **Mount Vesuvius (IRE)**[9] 686 5-10-3 **92**.......................(t) PaddyBrennan 94
(Paul Henderson) *hld up: hdwy 7th: ev ch 2 out: styd on same pce last* **8/1**

/66- **3** *2 1/4* **Laustra Bad (FR)**[24] 486 10-11-12 **115**....................(bt) TomScudamore 115
(David Pipe) *chsd ldrs: led appr 3 out: hdd next: styd on same pce* **13/2**[3]

/13- **4** *6* **Don't Be Late (IRE)**[20] 556 5-11-7 **110**.................................(p) APMcCoy 105
(Jonjo O'Neill) *hld up: hdwy appr 7th: wknd 3 out* **7/2**[2]

1U0- **5** *3* **Fitandproperjob**[12] 661 7-10-1 **90**...................................(t) PaulMoloney 82
(Anthony Middleton) *hld up: hdwy appr 3 out: sn wknd* **50/1**

2/6- **6** *4* **Speed Steed (IRE)**[49] 57 6-11-12 **115**................... RichardJohnson 103
(Tim Vaughan) *prom: pushed along appr 6th: wknd 3 out* **50/1**

F/1- **7** *9* **Breaking Bits (IRE)**[24] 484 6-11-9 **112**................................ TomO'Brien 92
(Jamie Snowden) *chsd ldr 2nd: led 4th to 6th: led next: rdn and hdd bef 3 out: sn wknd* **12/1**

/FF- **8** *8* **Tisfreetdream (IRE)**[17] 601 12-10-4 **98**.................(p) NicodeBoinville(5) 71
(Peter Pritchard) *chsd ldrs: rdn after 7th: wknd bef next: t.o* **50/1**

450/ **9** *22* **Delphi Mountain (IRE)**[201] 2761 8-11-9 **115**...............(t) MichealNolan(3) 68
(Richard Woollacott) *hld up: hit 5th: hdwy 7th: wknd bef next: t.o* **33/1**

3/0- **10** *3 1/4* **Brilliant Barca**[24] 486 5-11-11 **114**................................ MarcGoldstein 64
(Sheena West) *prom to 7th: t.o* **50/1**

P/6- **P** **Turtlethomas (IRE)**[46] 121 7-10-11 **105**...............(tp) GavinSheehan(5)
(Lawney Hill) *prom to 6th: t.o whn p.u bef 3 out* **12/1**

3- **P** **Dance Floor King (IRE)**[18] 592 6-11-5 **108**....................... DarylJacob
(Nick Mitchell) *led to 4th: led 6th to next: sn wknd: t.o whn p.u bef 2 out* **25/1**

4m 52.8s (-6.20) **Going Correction** -0.20s/f (Good)
WFA 4 from 5yo+ 18lb 12 Ran SP% **121.1**
Speed ratings (Par 105): **103,101,101,98,97 96,92,89,81,79** ,
toteswingers 1&2 £3.30, 2&3 £5.00, 1&3 £3.50 CSF £11.81 CT £48.32 TOTE £2.20: £1.20, £2.60, £1.80; EX 13.60 Trifecta £85.60 Pool: £2843.14 - 24.89 winning units..
Owner John Breslin **Bred** Swordlestown Little **Trained** Summerhill, Co. Meath

FOCUS
The first division of a fair handicap hurdle. The easy winner built on her recent win and should go in again.

765 BETVICTOR ROYAL ASCOT MONEY BACK SPECIAL MARES' H'CAP HURDLE (9 hdls) 2m

4:35 (4:35) (Class 5) (0-100,98) 4-Y-0+ **£2,339** (£686; £343; £171)

Form RPR

2/1- **1** **Amistress**[36] 292 5-11-5 **98**....................................... ConorShoemark(7) 105+
(Renee Robeson) *hld up: hdwy appr 3 out: swtchd rt and rdn bef next: styd on u.p to ld towards fin* **7/4**[1]

/04- **2** *1 1/4* **Jaja De Jau**[13] 648 4-10-12 **90**................................(t) RachaelGreen(3) 93+
(Anthony Honeyball) *hld up: hdwy appr 3 out: led after next: rdn flat: hdd towards fin* **7/1**

/00- **3** *1/2* **Umustbejoking (FR)**[13] 651 5-11-7 **96**...................... MichealNolan(3) 100+
(Michael Blake) *s.s: hld up and bhd: hdwy 3 out: r.o u.p: nt rch ldrs* **20/1**

4 *3/4* **Me And Ben (IRE)**[16] 618 6-11-7 **93**.............................. PaddyBrennan 97+
(Fergal O'Brien) *hld up: hdwy after 6th: rdn 2 out: r.o: nt rch ldrs* **20/1**

0/3- **5** *1 3/4* **June French (FR)**[32] 368 5-10-0 **72**.............................. DougieCostello 74
(Ian Williams) *chsd ldrs: led 6th: rdn and hdd after 2 out: styd on same pce flat* **11/2**[2]

4/4- **6** *8* **Icanmotor**[32] 368 6-10-6 **78**.......................................(tp) NickScholfield 73
(Claire Dyson) *chsd ldrs: ev ch 3 out: sn rdn: wknd last* **13/2**[3]

/0F- **7** *hd* **Cariflora**[24] 484 6-11-4 **90**.......................................(t) LeightonAspell 85
(Nick Gifford) *hld up: hdwy appr 3 out: wknd next* **33/1**

/P0- **8** *1* **Jewellery (IRE)**[22] 522 6-11-0 **86**..................................(v) TomScudamore 80
(Kevin Bishop) *s.i.s: hld up: hdwy 5th: rdn and wknd after 3 out* **25/1**

/41- **9** *6* **Golden Acorn (IRE)**[31] 391 4-10-13 **88**..........................(t) CharliePoste 78+
(Jamie Snowden) *chsd ldrs: rdn 3 out: mstke and wknd next: hit last* **16/1**

/46- **10** *1 3/4* **Sassy Wren**[22] 517 8-11-1 **90**.. GilesHawkins(3) 77
(Chris Down) *hld up: hdwy 5th: wknd 3 out* **50/1**

5/4- **11** *1/2* **Starlet Mandy (IRE)**[29] 423 10-10-1 **73**................ SamTwiston-Davies 59
(Nigel Twiston-Davies) *led to 6th: wknd after 3 out* **17/2**

060- **12** *2 1/4* **Ivebeenthinking**[13] 651 5-10-6 **78**...................................... FelixDeGiles 62
(Tom Symonds) *hld up: bhd fr 5th* **50/1**

F/F- **13** *7* **Photogenique (FR)**[38] 248 10-9-13 **74** oh8 ow2............. JamesBest(3) 52
(Rob Summers) *hld up: pushed along 4th: j. slowly next: sn wknd: t.o* **66/1**

/30- **14** *6* **Gulfport**[23] 506 4-10-7 **89**.. JamesCowley(7) 59
(Donald McCain) *mid-div: pushed along 6th: wknd bef next: t.o* **50/1**

P/ **15** *79* **Eudemis (FR)**[100] 4700 5-11-12 **98**...(p) PaulMoloney
(David Rees) *chsd ldr tl rdn and carried hd to one side appr 6th: nt run on and sn bhd: t.o* **33/1**

3m 47.8s (-4.20) **Going Correction** -0.20s/f (Good)
WFA 4 from 5yo+ 17lb 15 Ran SP% **120.6**
Speed ratings (Par 103): **102,101,101,100,99 95,95,95,92,91 91,90,86,83,44**
toteswingers 1&2 £3.80, 2&3 £30.70, 1&3 £12.70 CSF £12.63 CT £191.86 TOTE £2.50: £1.10, £2.40, £6.80; EX 12.90 Trifecta £201.60 Pool: £1832.91 - 6.81 winning units..
Owner Mrs P Robeson **Bred** Southcourt Stud **Trained** Tyringham, Bucks

FOCUS
A moderate mares' handicap hurdle in which they went a particularly solid gallop. The winner is rated below her Wincanton level.

766 BETVICTOR NO LOSE HUGHES MONEY BACK H'CAP CHASE (20 fncs) 3m 2f

5:10 (5:12) (Class 4) (0-120,120) 5-Y-0 **£3,924** (£1,159; £579; £290; £145)

Form RPR

P05/ **1** **Satou (FR)**[57] 5467 7-10-13 **107**..................................(p) RichardJohnson 121+
(Philip Hobbs) *a.p: led and nt fluent 16th: clr fr 3 out: easily* **5/1**[2]

4/4- **2** *14* **Call Me Mulligan (IRE)**[24] 495 9-10-0 **101**................... JohnDawson(7) 99+
(John Wade) *led to 2nd: chsd ldrs: rdn appr 3 out: styd on same pce* **8/1**

5/1- **3** *3 1/4* **Pairc Na Gcapall (IRE)**[17] 597 11-9-7 **94** oh8.......... MissBAndrews(7) 84
(Neil King) *led 2nd to 14th: rdn 4 out: styd on same pce fr next* **12/1**

2/0- **4** *3/4* **How's My Friend**[17] 8-11-0 **108**....................................... NickScholfield 98
(Grant Cann) *hld up: bhd 5th: styd on fr 2 out: nvr nrr* **14/1**

P/0- **5** *15* **Very Stylish (IRE)**[25] 481 9-11-9 **117**.................................(b[1]) APMcCoy 93
(Jonjo O'Neill) *hld up: hdwy 9th: drvn along 14th: wknd 3 out: t.o* **16/1**

/32- **6** *23* **Sir Mattie (IRE)**[13] 642 8-11-11 **119**.................................. PaulMoloney 75
(David Rees) *hld up: hdwy and hit 15th: rdn after 4 out: blnd and wknd next: t.o* **9/1**

3/6- **7** *17* **Earth Planet (IRE)**[23] 509 11-11-0 **108**.........................(tp) HenryBrooke 48
(Micky Hammond) *hld up: hdwy 8th: rdn and wknd appr 3 out: t.o* **33/1**

5/2- **8** *41* **I Need A Hero (IRE)**[11] 670 8-11-3 **114**.......................(t) JackQuinlan(3) 17
(Sarah Humphrey) *hld up: hdwy 13th: rdn and wknd bef 4 out: t.o* **15/2**

U3/- **P** **Western Gale (IRE)**[52] 18 10-10-9 **103**..............................(p) DenisO'Regan
(Martin Todhunter) *hld up: hdwy 9th: sn pushed along: wknd after 13th: t.o whn p.u bef last* **4/1**[1]

3/P- **P** **Theophrastus (IRE)**[37] 265 11-11-1 **109**.......................(p) LiamTreadwell
(Nick Gifford) *hld up: hdwy 4th: rdn and wknd after 16th: t.o whn p.u bef 3 out* **28/1**

P/P- **P** **Acrai Rua (IRE)**[23] 509 10-11-1 **109**...................................(b) BrianHughes
(Tim Fitzgerald) *prom: hit 6th: wknd 10th: t.o whn p.u bef 3 out* **16/1**

/46- **P** **Cool Mission (IRE)**[21] 535 9-10-13 **107**............................(b) JasonMaguire
(Donald McCain) *mid-div: sn pushed along: bhd fr 6th: t.o whn p.u bef 16th* **25/1**

424- **P** **Palace Jester**[22] 518 8-11-8 **116**....................................(bt[1]) TomScudamore
(David Pipe) *chsd ldrs: led 14th to 16th: wknd bef next: t.o whn p.u bef 3 out* **13/2**[3]

6m 41.3s (-5.10) **Going Correction** -0.30s/f (Good) 13 Ran SP% **119.2**
Speed ratings: **95,90,89,89,84 77,72,59,** , ,
toteswingers 1&2 £12.00, 2&3 £15.50, 1&3 £21.90 CSF £44.30 CT £462.30 TOTE £5.10: £1.90, £3.90, £5.30; EX 63.00 Trifecta £821.10 Pool: £1449.30 - 1.32 winning units..
Owner P J Hobbs **Bred** H D'Armaille **Trained** Withycombe, Somerset

FOCUS
Not a strong handicap chase. The winner is rated back to his best.

767 BETVICTOR ROYAL ASCOT NO LOSE HUGHES H'CAP HURDLE (DIV II) (10 hdls) 2m 4f 110y

5:45 (5:48) (Class 4) (0-115,115) 4-Y-0+ **£3,378** (£992; £496; £248)

Form RPR

322- **1** **Get Home Now**[20] 556 5-10-7 **96**....................................(tp) TomO'Brien 114+
(Peter Bowen) *chsd ldr tl led 7th: clr fr next: easily* **10/3**[1]

366/ **2** *22* **Thegaygardener**[83] 4988 5-11-5 **115**................................... ConorRing(7) 113
(Evan Williams) *hld up: hdwy to chse wnr appr 3 out: blnd and wknd next: mstke last* **5/1**

/1P- **3** *1 3/4* **High Ville (IRE)**[40] 201 7-11-5 **108**................................. ConorO'Farrell 102
(David Pipe) *led to 7th: wknd 3 out* **9/1**

0/0- **4** *8* **George Woolf**[24] 486 5-11-12 **115**...........................(t) RichardJohnson 100
(Tim Vaughan) *hld up: hdwy 5th: rdn after 7th: wknd 3 out: t.o* **14/1**

2/1- **5** *8* **Jewel In The Sun (IRE)**[9] 698 8-11-4 **107** 7ex......................... APMcCoy 85
(Ben Haslam) *chsd ldrs: lost pl after 5th: drvn along appr 7th: wknd bef 3 out: t.o* **9/2**[3]

P/2- **6** *2 1/4* **Murcar**[17] 604 8-11-9 **112**...(bt) DPFahy 88
(Liam Corcoran) *hld up: hit 5th: hdwy next: wknd appr 3 out: t.o* **25/1**

0/6- **7** *6* **King Caractacus**[21] 538 8-10-13 **102**..................................(t) DavidBass 74
(Lawney Hill) *hld up: bhd fr 3rd: t.o* **50/1**

510/ **8** *8* **Vintage Tea**[54] 5553 6-11-9 **115**................................(t) MichealNolan(3) 78
(Richard Woollacott) *chsd ldrs tl rdn and wknd after 7th: t.o* **50/1**

225- **9** *30* **Bob Lewis**[26] 456 7-10-2 **91**..(t) CharliePoste 27
(Anthony Middleton) *hld up: bhd fr 7th: t.o* **16/1**

0/4- **P** **Bedouin Bay**[13] 643 6-11-2 **112**....................................(b) KieronEdgar(7)
(Kevin Bishop) *chsd ldrs tl wknd after 6th: t.o whn p.u bef 2 out* **20/1**

211- **U** **My Lad Percy**[24] 503 5-11-1 **111**..............................(p) PatrickCorbett(7)
(Rebecca Curtis) *mid-div: blnd and uns rdr 2nd* **4/1**[2]

4m 52.1s (-6.90) **Going Correction** -0.20s/f (Good) 11 Ran SP% **114.9**
Speed ratings (Par 105): **105,96,95,92,89 89,86,83,72,**
toteswingers 1&2 £4.90, 2&3 £13.60, 1&3 £6.50 CSF £19.93 CT £134.03 TOTE £3.10: £1.10, £3.00, £2.60; EX 23.40 Trifecta £126.20 Pool: £1245.26 - 7.39 winning units..
Owner Miss Jayne Brace & Gwyn Brace **Bred** Elsdon Farms **Trained** Little Newcastle, Pembrokes

FOCUS
The theme for most of the afternoon continued with another very easy winner off a decent gallop in the second division of a fair handicap hurdle. This was a big step forward from Get Home Now.

768 ROYAL ASCOT MONEY BACK AT BETVICTOR.COM STANDARD OPEN NATIONAL HUNT FLAT RACE 2m
6:15 (6:15) (Class 6) 4-6-Y-O **£1,559** (£457; £228; £114)

Form RPR
6/1- **1** **Man Of Steel (IRE)**[25] 483 4-11-6 0 DonalDevereux 115+
(Peter Bowen) *a.p: led over 3f out: rdn over 1f out: hung lft ins fnl f: styd on* **4/1**[3]
5- **2** *3 ¾* **Full Throttle (IRE)**[33] 359 4-10-13 0 APMcCoy 103
(Jonjo O'Neill) *chsd ldr: chal over 3f out: rdn over 1f out: hung lft ins fnl f: styd on same pce* **6/4**[1]
3 *10* **The Finger Post (IRE)**[26] 469 6-11-2 0 DenisO'Regan 97
(A J Martin, Ire) *hld up: hdwy over 4f out: rdn over 2f out: wknd over 1f out* **7/2**[2]
4 *7* **Keel Haul (IRE)**[46] 5-11-2 0 HenryOliver 91
(Henry Oliver) *hld up: hdwy over 4f out: rdn and wknd wl over 1f out* **20/1**
3/3- **5** *18* **I'm Not Telling (IRE)**[18] 589 5-11-2 0 TomO'Brien 75
(Grant Cann) *hld up: hdwy 11f out: rdn over 4f out: sn wknd: t.o* **14/1**
0/4- **6** *½* **Sir Tyto (IRE)**[30] 412 5-11-2 0 NoelFehily 74
(Ali Brewer) *chsd ldrs tl wknd over 3f out: t.o* **33/1**
3- **7** *24* **Miss H Lewiss**[28] 433 5-10-9 0 SamTwiston-Davies 45
(Nigel Twiston-Davies) *plld hrd and prom: rdn and wknd over 3f out: eased: t.o* **7/1**
8 *3 ¾* **Over The Thyme**[102] 4675 5-11-2 0 JasonMaguire 49
(Karen McLintock) *led: rdn: hdd & wknd over 3f out: eased: t.o* **20/1**
0- **9** *1 ½* **Ginger Mac**[9] 699 5-11-2 0 BrianHughes 48
(John Mackie) *mid-div: wknd over 5f out: t.o* **66/1**
000/ **10** *2 ¼* **Star Belucky**[553] 3133 5-10-4 0 JonathanEngland(5) 39
(Roy Brotherton) *hld up: pushed along over 6f out: sn wknd: t.o* **200/1**
0- **11** *40* **Jayjay Joules**[32] 372 5-10-4 0 MissGAndrews(5) 3
(Lisa Williamson) *hld up: wknd over 6f out: t.o* **200/1**

3m 39.5s (-6.90) **Going Correction** -0.20s/f (Good) 11 Ran SP% **116.3**
Speed ratings: **109,107,102,98,89 89,77,75,74,73 53**
toteswingers 1&2 £2.50, 2&3 £2.20, 1&3 £1.50 CSF £9.78 TOTE £3.10: £1.20, £1.20, £1.60; EX 11.10 Trifecta £51.90 Pool: £1122.13 - 16.19 winning units..
Owner Saith O Ni **Bred** Katie McCarthy **Trained** Little Newcastle, Pembrokes

FOCUS
Another step up from winner who should win more races.
T/Plt: £120.40 to a £1 stake. Pool of £68304.96 - 413.88 winning tickets. T/Qpdt: £23.50 to a £1 stake. Pool of £4077.71 - 128.40 winning tickets. CR

769 - 776a (Foreign Racing) - See Raceform Interactive

[638]FFOS LAS (L-H)
Thursday, June 20

OFFICIAL GOING: Good (8.2)
Wind: rather blustery Weather: raining; 16 degrees

777 SINCLAIR FINANCE AND LEASING NOVICES' HURDLE (11 hdls) 2m 6f
6:00 (6:00) (Class 4) 4-Y-0+ **£3,119** (£915; £457; £228)

Form RPR
/21- **1** **Lord Grantham (IRE)**[26] 479 6-11-9 123 JakeGreenall(3) 126+
(Henry Daly) *settled in 3rd: led bef 6th tl after 8th: chsd ldr after: drvn 2 out: upsides whn lft clr last: rdn out* **11/8**[1]
2 *6* **Our Maimie (IRE)**[29] 437 7-10-5 0 SamTwiston-Davies 98
(R McGlinchey, Ire) *chsd ldrs: effrt to chse ldng pair bef 3 out: rdn and no imp fr next: lft 8 l 2nd and hmpd and swvd last* **12/1**
4- **3** *3 ½* **Commitment**[26] 479 4-10-8 0 NoelFehily 96
(Neil Mulholland) *hld up towards rr: effrt on outer 8th: 4th bef next: kpt on steadily wout threatening after: lft 3rd at last* **6/1**[3]
/P4- **4** *7* **West End Classic (IRE)**[14] 649 6-10-7 0 BenPoste(5) 93
(Tracey Watkins) *hld up: chsd ldrs fr 5th tl fdd bef 3 out: lft poor 4th at last* **50/1**
- **5** *19* **Wynn Darwi (IRE)**[32] 8-10-12 0 DonalDevereux 74
(Debra Hamer) *pressed ldrs tl 7th: wknd after next* **25/1**
00P/ **6** *2 ¼* **Kimora (IRE)**[24] 7-9-12 0 (t) AlanJohns(7) 65
(Marc Barber) *midfield: mstke 7th: no ch fr next* **40/1**
P0P/ **7** *16* **Thistle Stikk**[577] 2666 6-10-12 0 (t) DPFahy 56
(Lucy Jones) *towards rr: mstke 6th: t.o 3 out* **100/1**
PP/ **8** *10* **Celtic Fella (IRE)**[32] 6-10-7 0 CharlieWallis(5) 46
(Debra Hamer) *pressed ldr tl bef 6th: t.o 3 out* **25/1**
9 *27* **Ailanthus**[60] 4-10-1 0 PaddyBrennan 8
(Richard Woollacott) *plld hrd early: a in rr: last and struggling 6th: t.o bef 3 out: fin eventually* **16/1**
/3F- **F** **Third Of The Third**[26] 479 6-10-12 113 ConorO'Farrell 113+
(David Pipe) *led at modest pce tl bef 6th: led again after 8th: rdn home turn: hrd drvn and narrow advantage 2 out: jnd and fell last* **6/4**[2]
0- **P** **Kims Firebud**[12] 671 6-10-12 0 DaveCrosse
(Dai Burchell) *t.k.h early: chsd ldrs and j. erratically: mstke 7th whn wkng: t.o and p.u 3 out* **100/1**

5m 31.1s (11.10) **Going Correction** 0.0s/f (Good)
WFA 4 from 6yo+ 18lb 11 Ran SP% **124.0**
Speed ratings (Par 105): **79,76,75,73,66 65,59,55,46,**
toteswingers 1&2 £7.70, 1&3 £6.40, 2&3 £7.70 CSF £18.86 TOTE £2.30: £1.10, £2.40, £2.30; EX 18.90 Trifecta £154.40 Pool: £460.04 - 2.23 winning units..
Owner T F F Nixon **Bred** T F F Nixon **Trained** Stanton Lacy, Shropshire

FOCUS
After some heavy showers the going was changed to good, good to firm in places. This novice hurdle was weakened by several withdrawals and was run at a steady pace but the two market leaders were involved in a good battle when Third Of The Third fell at the last. Ordinary form.

778 SINCLAIR VOLKSWAGEN COMMERCIAL H'CAP CHASE (18 fncs) 3m
6:30 (6:30) (Class 4) (0-115,113) 5-Y-0+ **£3,768** (£1,106; £553; £276)

Form RPR
52P/ **1** **Power Pack Jack (IRE)**[92] 4874 10-11-4 105 (b) SamTwiston-Davies 118+
(Nigel Twiston-Davies) *rn in snatches: nt fluent 5th and str reminders: 3rd whn mstke 13th: racing awkwardly bef home turn: galvanised to ld 15th: mstke next: urged clr bef last* **14/1**
/04- **2** *6* **Oddjob (IRE)**[14] 641 9-11-2 103 (b[1]) TomScudamore 109
(David Pipe) *cl up: j. slowly 10th: rdn 14th: nt qckn fr next: chsd wnr bef 2 out: no imp* **10/1**
P/1- **3** *2 ½* **Fairwood Massini (IRE)**[14] 641 8-11-2 106 (tp) MichaelByrne(3) 108
(Tim Vaughan) *pressed ldrs: last of five gng clr but rdn 14th: 3rd and btn bef 2 out* **8/1**
/54- **4** *6* **Aikideau (FR)**[15] 636 6-11-12 113 (b[1]) DarylJacob 111
(Paul Nicholls) *pressed ldr: led 14th: hdd and rdn whn nt fluent next: sn btn: lost 3rd bef 2 out* **9/2**[2]
065- **5** *15* **Sadler's Star (GER)**[15] 636 10-11-3 104 TomCannon 86
(Michael Blake) *midfield: rdn and lost tch after 14th* **33/1**
/3P- **6** *5* **Benefit Night (IRE)**[22] 535 13-11-8 109 (bt) APMcCoy 87
(Warren Greatrex) *led: j. slowly 6th and reminders: drvn and hdd 14th: nt run on and rapidly dropped out* **20/1**
531/ **7** *6* **Hobb's Dream (IRE)**[55] 5542 9-9-12 88 (p) MarkQuinlan(3) 61
(Neil Mulholland) *detached last at 1/2-way: nvr nr ldrs after* **20/1**
/41- **8** *11* **Lord Lescribaa (FR)**[10] 692 10-9-5 88 (tp) ThomasCheesman(10) 51
(Philip Hobbs) *prom tl 10th: drvn and lost pl next: t.o 15th* **6/1**[3]
223/ **9** *12* **Sandynow (IRE)**[61] 5411 8-11-0 101 (p) TomO'Brien 53
(Peter Bowen) *blnd 1st: towards rr: mstke 10th: struggling 14th: t.o 3 out* **11/8**[1]
33U/ **F** **Numbercruncher (IRE)**[24] 7-10-5 99 ow1 MrMatthewBarber(7)
(Marc Barber) *nvr bttr than midfield: nt fluent 4th: mstke 10th: struggling in rr whn fell 12th* **14/1**

6m 3.6s (-13.80) **Going Correction** -0.45s/f (Good) 10 Ran SP% **120.6**
Speed ratings: **105,103,102,100,95 93,91,87,83,**
toteswingers 1&2 £8.70, 1&3 £0.00, 2&3 £16.20 CSF £141.19 CT £1212.62 TOTE £13.10: £4.50, £1.90, £3.50; EX 144.90 Trifecta £397.10 Part won. Pool: £529.56 - 0.05 winning units..
Owner N A Twiston-Davies **Bred** Peter Casey **Trained** Naunton, Gloucs

FOCUS
They went a decent pace and finished quite well strung out in this handicap. The winner is rated back to form, with the second to his mark.

779 SINCLAIR VOLKSWAGEN NOVICES' CHASE (15 fncs 2 omitted) 2m 5f
7:05 (7:05) (Class 4) 5-Y-0+ **£3,768** (£1,106; £553; £276)

Form RPR
0/2- **1** **Prospect Wells (FR)**[22] 539 8-10-12 0 (t) DarylJacob 134+
(Paul Nicholls) *trckd ldrs gng wl: wnt 2nd after 13th: led 2 out: rdn and in command flat* **10/11**[1]
034/ **2** *3* **Awaywiththegreys (IRE)**[173] 3352 6-10-12 0 (p) JamieMoore 129+
(Peter Bowen) *tended to jump rt: 2nd tl led 9th: 3 l clr home turn: rdn and hdd 2 out: no imp on wnr whn edgd rt flat* **7/4**[2]
4/2- **3** *8* **Notarfbad (IRE)**[35] 342 7-10-12 0 NickScholfield 122
(Jeremy Scott) *t.k.h: hld up in last pair: effrt 13th: rdn to chse ldng pair fr next: no imp after* **8/1**[3]
213/ **4** *5* **Next Exit (IRE)**[268] 1633 8-10-12 0 (t) RichardJohnson 116
(Tim Vaughan) *cl up tl rdn and lost pl after 13th: plugged on same pce fr next* **14/1**
2U2- **5** *4 ½* **Lauberhorn**[33] 375 6-10-12 0 PaulMoloney 111
(Evan Williams) *hld up in last pair: mstke 4th: struggling whn mstke 13th* **33/1**
/16- **6** *42* **Indian Citizen (IRE)**[19] 590 6-10-5 0 FelixDeGiles 61
(Arthur Whiting) *led tl 9th: drvn and lost pl after 13th: t.o 3 out* **66/1**

5m 18.1s (-10.50) **Going Correction** -0.45s/f (Good) 6 Ran SP% **111.0**
Speed ratings: **102,100,97,95,94 78**
toteswingers 1&2 £1.80, 1&3 £1.10, 2&3 £2.70 CSF £2.90 TOTE £1.80: £1.40, £1.20; EX 2.80 Trifecta £7.00 Pool: £588.77 - 62.84 winning units..
Owner Andrea & Graham Wylie **Bred** Wertheimer & Frere **Trained** Ditcheat, Somerset

FOCUS
The third fence in the back straight was omitted on both circuits. The hot favourite delivered in decent style in this novice chase. The winner is rated 20lb+ off his best hurdles figure.

780 SINCLAIR AUDI H'CAP HURDLE (12 hdls) 3m
7:40 (7:40) (Class 2) (0-150,135) 4-Y-0+ **£9,747** (£2,862; £1,431; £715)

Form RPR
1/1- **1** **Big Time Billy (IRE)**[15] 158 7-11-11 134 (v) DonalDevereux 145+
(Peter Bowen) *led: set sedate pce tl qcknd clr on bit after 3 out: 15 l ahd whn flattened last: heavily eased fnl 150yds* **7/4**[1]
5/3- **2** *4 ½* **Siberian Tiger (IRE)**[24] 508 8-11-1 124 (p) PaulMoloney 121
(Evan Williams) *settled in last trio: hdwy but cajoled along and racing awkwardly fr after 3 out: chal for poor 2nd at last: one pce and no ch w v easy eased wnr* **14/1**
/16- **3** *¾* **Hell's Bay (FR)**[12] 672 11-11-5 128 (p) NickScholfield 124
(Keiran Burke) *midfield tl dropped bk to 7 l last bef home turn: rallied to chse wnr who was already clr after 2 out: lost modest 2nd after sustained duel fr last* **25/1**
0/3- **4** *1 ½* **Donnas Palm (IRE)**[29] 432 9-11-12 135 (v) RichardJohnson 130
(Tim Vaughan) *trckd ldng pair: rdn and outpcd 3 out: styd on again after 2 out: n.d to ldrs* **25/1**
5/0- **5** *7* **Cockney Trucker (IRE)**[34] 356 11-11-11 134 APMcCoy 123
(Philip Hobbs) *pressed wnr tl 3 l down and rdn 3 out: dropped out after next* **5/1**[3]
211- **6** *7* **Sail And Return**[10] 659 9-11-2 125 SamTwiston-Davies 106
(Phil Middleton) *settled in last trio: rdn 3 out: sn lost tch* **4/1**[2]
10/- **7** *3 ¾* **Watergate Bay (IRE)**[79] 5103 7-10-10 119 DarylJacob 96
(Paul Nicholls) *trckd ldrs tl rdn and wknd tamely on long run to 3 out* **8/1**
250/ **8** *hd* **The Tracey Shuffle**[96] 4796 7-11-2 125 TomScudamore 102
(David Pipe) *hld up in last trio: rdn bef 3 out: sn lost tch* **4/1**[2]

6m 5.5s (16.50) **Going Correction** 0.0s/f (Good) 8 Ran SP% **118.5**
Speed ratings (Par 109): **72,70,70,69,67 65,63,63**
toteswingers 1&2 £6.60, 1&3 £0.00, 2&3 £0.00 CSF £26.69 CT £456.79 TOTE £3.60: £1.40, £1.80, £4.30; EX 27.80 Trifecta £264.00 Part won. Pool: £352.09 - 0.69 winning units..
Owner Miss R L Bryan **Bred** A And C Enterprises **Trained** Little Newcastle, Pembrokes

FOCUS
The favourite was an easy winner under a front-running ride in this strong but steadily run handicap. The winner was value for further.

781 SINCLAIR MERCEDES BENZ H'CAP CHASE (13 fncs 2 omitted) 2m 3f 110y
8:15 (8:15) (Class 4) (0-120,120) 5-Y-0+ **£3,768** (£1,106; £553; £276)

Form RPR
/14- **1** **Hodgson (IRE)**[25] 504 8-10-13 107 (tp) JamieMoore 118+
(Peter Bowen) *chsd ldr in fast r: led 6th: dived at 8th: drvn and hrd pressed last: battled on gamely* **9/4**[2]
/01- **2** *2 ½* **Surf And Turf (IRE)**[9] 714 7-11-4 112 7ex APMcCoy 120
(Jonjo O'Neill) *sn trcking ldng pair: wnt 2nd at 9th: drvn and tried to chal last: ev ch briefly: nt qckn and hld fnl 100yds* **6/4**[1]
036- **3** *24* **Zama Zama**[18] 596 6-10-11 112 ConorRing(7) 100
(Evan Williams) *hld up in rr: mstke 8th: no ch after next: lft remote 3rd after casualties in st* **12/1**

4/5- **4** *25* **Bay Central (IRE)**[45] 142 9-10-11 **105**.............................. PaulMoloney 69
(Evan Williams) *taken down early: led at v str gallop tl 6th: wknd qckly 9th: t.o next* **33/1**

4F2- **5** *2 ¾* **Sporting Boy (IRE)**[18] 594 5-11-10 **118**............................ TomCannon 79
(Michael Blake) *cl up: rdn 5th: nvr really travelling after: lost tch 9th: t.o next* **14/1**

/25- **R** **Star Galaxy (IRE)**[22] 533 13-10-2 **101**......................(b) GavinSheehan(5)
(John Flint) *mstke 3rd: last whn blnd 6th: no ch after: remote 4th whn ref 2 out* **33/1**

0/3- **F** **Gay Sloane (IRE)**[22] 539 9-11-7 **115**........................... RichardJohnson
(Richard Woollacott) *settled towards rr: 4th and effrt 9th: 12 l 4th and wkng bef next where fell* **8/1**

/0F- **F** **Ugo (USA)**[18] 594 5-11-6 **117**.......................................(p) AdamWedge(3)
(Evan Williams) *t.k.h in rr: hdwy to midfield whn fell heavily 8th: fatally injured* **40/1**

/21- **F** **True Blue (IRE)**[19] 585 6-11-12 **120**....................(t) SamTwiston-Davies 125
(Nigel Twiston-Davies) *settled midfield: hit 7th: wnt 3rd at 9th: 7 l down bef next: drvn and no imp in 4 l 3rd whn fell 3 out: fatally injured* **5/1**[3]

4m 51.0s (-10.10) **Going Correction** -0.45s/f (Good) **9** Ran SP% **121.2**
Speed ratings: **102,101,91,81,80** , , ,
toteswingers 1&2 £1.10, 1&3 £0.00, 2&3 £2.60 CSF £6.66 CT £32.80 TOTE £4.00: £1.60, £1.30, £3.40; EX 8.40 Trifecta £56.40 Pool: £320.30 - 4.25 winning units..
Owner Roddy Owen & Paul Fullagar **Bred** J Landers **Trained** Little Newcastle, Pembrokes

FOCUS
The two market leaders pulled a long way clear in this handicap.

782 CASTELL HOWELL FOODS H'CAP HURDLE (10 hdls) 2m 4f
8:45 (8:45) (Class 3) (0-135,131) 4-Y-0+ **£5,393** (£1,583; £791; £395)

Form RPR

331/ **1** **Conellie**[735] 870 7-10-7 **112**.......................................(t) APMcCoy 125+
(Rebecca Curtis) *t.k.h in last: shkn up in clsng 3rd bef 2 out: qcknd to ld appr last and sprinted clr: hrd hld* **6/1**[3]

/31- **2** *4 ½* **Kanturk (IRE)**[14] 643 7-10-6 **111**.......................................(p) TomO'Brien 115
(Peter Bowen) *pressed ldr tl led 5th: drvn 2 out: hdd bef last: edgd lft and immediately outpcd* **10/11**[1]

0/5- **3** *2 ½* **Skint**[19] 591 7-11-0 **119**... AidanColeman 121
(Ali Brewer) *trckd ldrs: wnt 2nd gng wl bef 3 out: rdn next: wknd bef last* **10/1**

2/1- **4** *17* **Waterunder (IRE)**[26] 480 6-11-12 **131**.......................(t) TomScudamore 119
(David Pipe) *hld up in 5th pl: effrt bef 3 out: sn rdn and outpcd: wl btn 4th 2 out* **7/2**[2]

/31- **5** *11* **Lava Lamp (GER)**[24] 512 6-10-13 **125**............................. ConorRing(7) 104
(Evan Williams) *hld up: mstkes 4th and 6th: rdn next: last and btn home turn* **12/1**

3/0- **6** *13* **Bathwick Man**[19] 591 8-11-0 **119**.....................................(p) ConorO'Farrell 89
(David Pipe) *set stdy pce: hdd 5th: rdn 7th: cl 2nd home turn: sn lost pl: t.o whn mstke last* **20/1**

5m 0.6s (9.70) **Going Correction** 0.0s/f (Good)
WFA 4 from 6yo+ 18lb **6** Ran SP% **110.4**
Speed ratings (Par 107): **80,78,77,70,66 60**
toteswingers 1&2 £2.40, 1&3 £0.00, 2&3 £1.30 CSF £12.05 CT £48.62 TOTE £5.40: £1.70, £1.10; EX 14.70 Trifecta £95.60 Pool: £298.80 - 2.34 winning units..
Owner Marc Cohen **Bred** Miss K Rausing **Trained** Newport, Dyfed

FOCUS
An interesting handicap, involving four last-time-out winners. They went a decent pace and the winner scored in good style under a hold-up ride on his return from two years off.

783 WALTERS UK H'CAP HURDLE (7 hdls 1 omitted) 2m
9:20 (9:20) (Class 4) (0-110,110) 4-Y-0+ **£3,119** (£915; £457; £228)

Form RPR

/54- **1** **Cut The Cards (IRE)**[10] 691 6-11-3 **101**.............................(p) APMcCoy 111+
(Jonjo O'Neill) *hld up tl 5th: 7th home turn: effrt on outside 3 out: sn rdn: qcknd to ld bef omitted last: easily drew clr* **5/1**[3]

3/3- **2** *5* **Ajman (IRE)**[38] 266 8-10-9 **100**.......................................(bt) ConorRing(7) 105
(Evan Williams) *hld up towards rr: effrt bef 3 out: rdn and ev ch 2 out: nt qckn w wnr bef omitted last: wnt 2nd cl home* **14/1**

/33- **3** *nk* **No To Trident**[26] 480 8-11-2 **105**...............................(p) GavinSheehan(5) 108
(John Flint) *prom: led 2 out tl rdn and hdd bef omitted last: qckly outpcd by wnr: lost 2nd nr fin* **7/1**

/13- **4** *11* **Prince Pippin (IRE)**[30] 421 7-10-12 **103**...................(t) MsLucyJones(7) 96
(Lucy Jones) *nt fluent 1st: j. slowly 3rd: w ldr tl led 4th: rdn and hdd bef 3 out: ev ch next: sn wknd* **5/1**[3]

0/4- **5** *1 ¼* **Spinning Waters**[6] 456 7-10-6 **93**..............................(p) RobertDunne(3) 86
(Dai Burchell) *chsd ldrs: rdn 3 out: wknd next* **20/1**

5PU/ **6** *1 ¾* **Pelennor (FR)**[61] 9-10-6 **90**... LeightonAspell 81
(Stephen Hughes) *bhd: last on home turn: kpt on past btn horses but no ch w ldrs* **33/1**

032- **7** *1 ¾* **Gwili Spar**[14] 640 5-10-0 **84** oh4....................................(t) DonalDevereux 73
(Peter Bowen) *plld hrd and cl up: led bef 3 out: drvn and hdd next: sn fdd* **9/4**[1]

042- **8** *5* **Macarthur**[10] 691 9-11-12 **110**...(tp) TomO'Brien 95
(David Rees) *plld hrd in rr: rdn wl bef 3 out: sn btn* **3/1**[2]

9 *48* **Farley's Risk (IRE)**[20] 570 6-11-0 **98**.................(b) SamTwiston-Davies 39
(Michael McElhone, Ire) *plld hrd in ld: faltered 3rd: hdd 5th: fdd rapidly bef next: t.o* **20/1**

3m 46.7s (-1.80) **Going Correction** 0.0s/f (Good) **9** Ran SP% **120.7**
Speed ratings (Par 105): **104,101,101,95,95 94,93,90,66**
toteswingers 1&2 £10.40, 1&3 £7.10, 2&3 £10.40 CSF £67.91 CT £499.61 TOTE £6.50: £2.60, £2.60, £2.60; EX 52.60 Trifecta £393.60 Part won. Pool: £524.85 - 0.14 winning units..
Owner John P McManus **Bred** Coppice Farm **Trained** Cheltenham, Gloucs

FOCUS
They were tightly bunched around the final turn in this handicap but they finished quite well strung out. The last hurdle was bypassed. A step up from the winner in first-time headgear.

T/Plt: £24.50 to a £1 stake. Pool of £56,788.62 - 1689.67 winning tickets. T/Qpdt: £3.40 to a £1 stake. Pool of £4942.60 - 1045.60 winning tickets. IM

560 MARKET RASEN (R-H)
Friday, June 21

OFFICIAL GOING: Good (good to soft in places; chs 8.4, hdl 8.2)
Wind: almost nil Weather: fine, becoming sunny and very warm

784 DFDS SEAWAYS (S) HURDLE (8 hdls) 2m 1f
2:20 (2:20) (Class 4) 4-6-Y-0 **£3,119** (£915; £457; £228)

Form RPR

F20/ **1** **Meetings Man (IRE)**[13] 4524 6-10-12 120..........................(p) JackDoyle 112+
(Ali Brewer) *trckd ldng pair: cl up 3rd: wnt 2nd after 5th: led appr 2 out: j. slowly and wnt lft last: styd on* **15/8**[1]

4/3- **2** *3 ¾* **Royal Opera**[22] 505 5-11-5 110.................................(b) TomScudamore 115+
(Brian Ellison) *trckd ldr: led 5th: hdd appr 2 out: 1 1/2 l down whn hmpd and swvd lft last: kpt on same pce* **2/1**[2]

/31- **3** *8* **Wom**[30] 429 5-10-7 100..(v) TrevorWhelan(5) 99
(Neil King) *in rr: chsd ldrs 3rd: outpcd and reminders after next: tk modest 3rd bef 2 out* **11/2**[3]

0/U- **4** *14* **Whatsupjack (IRE)**[43] 179 6-10-7 105............................... BenPoste(5) 86
(Shaun Harris) *in rr: mstke 3rd: chsd ldrs next: outpcd after 4th: tk poor 4th between last 2* **20/1**

5/0- **5** *8* **Halogen**[21] 563 4-11-5 113...(b[1]) JasonMaguire 86
(Donald McCain) *led: t.k.h: clr to 3rd: hdd 5th: nt run on: lost pl next: sn bhd* **7/1**

13P/ **6** *dist* **Bathcounty (IRE)**[117] 4411 6-11-5 114............................(p) FelixDeGiles
(Barry Brennan) *chsd ldrs 3rd: drvn next: sn lost pl and bhd: t.o 3 out: eventually completed* **12/1**

4m 10.8s (4.10) **Going Correction** +0.45s/f (Soft) **6** Ran SP% **108.5**
Speed ratings: **108,106,102,95,92**
Tote Swingers 1&2 £1.10, 2&3 £2.70, 1&3 £3.20 CSF £5.69 TOTE £3.00: £1.40, £1.80; EX 4.20 Trifecta £26.40 Pool: £1,180.83 - 33.53 winning tickets..The winner was bought in for 6,000gns. Bathcounty was claimed by Dr Ian Cragg for £6,400.
Owner Miss Ali Brewer **Bred** Hakan Keles **Trained** Eastbury, Berks
■ Ali Brewer's first training success.

FOCUS
Not a bad contest for the grade. It was run at a sound pace, with the market leaders in control from a long way out. The winner was well in and is rated 13lb off his old best.

785 ABP JUVENILE HURDLE (8 hdls) 2m 1f
2:55 (2:55) (Class 4) 3-Y-0 **£3,119** (£915; £457; £228)

Form RPR

1- **1** **It's Only Business**[8] 725 3-11-5 0.. APMcCoy 110+
(Jim Best) *trckd ldrs: t.k.h: j.lft 1st: led appr 2 out: wnt clr between last 2: heavily eased clsng stages* **4/5**[1]

2 *24* **Hanga Roa (IRE)**[53] 3-10-12 0.. JamieMoore 73
(Gary Moore) *w ldr: drvn appr 2 out: kpt on: no ch w wnr* **20/1**

3 *4 ½* **Red Eight (USA)**[17] 3-10-12 0.. DougieCostello 69
(John Butler) *mde most: hdd appr 2 out: one pce* **12/1**

4 *2* **Style Setter** 3-10-5 0... HenryBrooke 59
(Donald McCain) *mid-div: hdwy and modest 4th 2 out: one pce* **8/1**[3]

5 *7* **Walter White (IRE)**[144] 3-10-12 0................................. RichardJohnson 61
(Philip Hobbs) *trckd ldrs: drvn 3 out: wknd and 5th whn mstke 2 out* **5/2**[2]

4- **6** *1* **Precision Strike**[20] 582 3-10-7 0.........................(p) JonathanEngland(5) 58
(Richard Guest) *chsd ldrs to 2nd: rdn and wknd 3 out* **11/1**

7 *42* **Vision Of Judgment**[22] 3-10-12 0.................................... BrianHughes 16
(Ollie Pears) *in rr: bhd fr 4th: t.o whn mstke 2 out* **16/1**

P **Midnight Poet**[325] 3-10-12 0... HarryHaynes
(James Given) *nt jump wl in rr: reminders after 1st: bhd whn j. slowly 2nd: t.o next: p.u after 4th* **40/1**

4m 14.8s (8.10) **Going Correction** +0.45s/f (Soft) **8** Ran SP% **124.3**
Speed ratings: **98,86,84,83,80 79,60,**
Tote Swingers 1&2 £4.00, 2&3 £6.60, 1&3 £3.60 CSF £22.85 TOTE £1.50: £1.10, £5.30, £3.20; EX 20.70 Trifecta £53.50 Pool: £1,959.29 - 27.45 winning tickets..
Owner Jack Callaghan **Bred** South Wind Bloodstock **Trained** Lewes, E Sussex

FOCUS
Only two of the field had run over hurdles before. This uncompetitive contest was run at an honest pace. The easy winner is a decent early juvenile, but the opposition was weak.

786 PD PORTS NOVICES' CHASE (14 fncs) 2m 4f
3:30 (3:31) (Class 4) 5-Y-0+ **£3,768** (£1,106; £553; £276)

Form RPR

/05- **1** **Bar De Ligne (FR)**[21] 562 7-10-12 0.........................(p) TomScudamore 114+
(Steve Gollings) *mde all: styd on fr 3 out: drvn out* **7/2**[2]

0/1- **2** *2 ½* **Grandads Horse**[21] 562 7-11-5 137... NoelFehily 120+
(Charlie Longsdon) *chsd ldng pair: mstke 4th: blnd 3 out: chsd wnr appr next: kpt on same pce run-in* **30/100**[1]

000/ **3** *9* **Bobbisox (IRE)**[54] 2 8-10-0 0.. KillianMoore(5) 94
(Alex Hales) *in rr: styd on fr 4 out: wnt modest 3rd last: one pce* **66/1**

0/0- **4** *2 ¼* **Rocky Rebel**[42] 202 5-10-12 0...................................(p) TomMessenger 98
(Chris Bealby) *mid-div: kpt on and modest 3rd 2 out: one pce* **33/1**

3/4- **5** *9* **It's Me And You**[6] 750 5-10-9 0...................................... JakeGreenall(3) 90
(Michael Easterby) *mid-div: outpcd 4 out: sn bhd* **20/1**[3]

1/0- **F** **Mr Plod**[40] 251 8-10-12 0.. BrendanPowell
(J R Jenkins) *w wnr: blnd 10th: wknd and 4th whn fell heavily 3 out* **22/1**

00P/ **P** **Larkhall**[20] 6-10-12 0... BrianHarding
(Mike Sowersby) *sn bhd: blnd 5th and 7th: t.o next: p.u bef 3 out* **50/1**

4m 53.1s (-12.60) **Going Correction** -0.525s/f (Firm) **7** Ran SP% **114.6**
Speed ratings: **104,103,99,98,94** ,
Tote Swingers 1&2 £1.02, 2&3 £11.70, 1&3 £23.40 CSF £5.20 TOTE £5.30: £1.60, £1.02; EX 6.40 Trifecta £52.60 Pool: £2,978.67 - 42.45 winning tickets..
Owner P J Martin **Bred** Neustrian Associates **Trained** Scamblesby, Lincs

FOCUS
Two dominated the market for this novices' chase, with the second-favourite causing a bit of an upset. A step up from the winner on his chase form, but still a stone below his hurdles best. The runner-up was the best part of 2st off his recent chase course win.

787 GBA GROUP H'CAP CHASE (14 fncs) 2m 6f 110y
4:10 (4:10) (Class 3) (0-140,139) 5-Y-0+ **£9,747** (£2,862; £1,431; £715)

Form RPR

021- **1** **Gullible Gordon (IRE)**[7] 733 10-10-8 **121**.................(vt) DonalDevereux 126
(Peter Bowen) *chsd ldr: drvn 4 out: 2 1/2 l down last: styd on to ld nr fin* **5/6**[1]

3/1- **2** *nk* **Billie Magern**[36] 334 9-11-12 **139**........................(v) SamTwiston-Davies 144
(Nigel Twiston-Davies) *led: hrd drvn 3 out: hdd and no ex nr fin* **9/2**[3]

140/ **3** *10* **Lucky Landing (IRE)**[68] 5313 7-10-9 **125**........................ BrianToomey(3) 123
(Tony Coyle) *hld up: hdwy and 4th after 9th: one pce fr 3 out: 3rd last* **25/1**

/P2- **4** *3* **Ciceron (IRE)**[20] 587 7-11-2 **129**.. AidanColeman 122
(Venetia Williams) *chsd ldrs: lft 3rd 9th: one pce fr 3 out* **8/1**

3/3- **5** *8* **General Miller**[21] 562 8-11-3 **130**..(p) DavidBass 121+
(Nicky Henderson) *chsd ldng pair: blnd and lost pl 9th: rallied 4 out: wknd between last 2* **4/1**[2]

/11- **6** *11* **Bold Perk (IRE)**[26] 487 11-10-11 **124**.................................. HaddenFrost 103
(Martin Hill) *in rr: hdwy 5th: nt fluent 8th: lost pl 10th: bhd fr 4 out* **20/1**

5m 27.8s (-18.20) **Going Correction** -0.525s/f (Firm) **6** Ran SP% **112.5**
Speed ratings: **110,109,106,105,102 98**
Tote Swingers 1&2 £1.80, 2&3 £4.30, 1&3 £4.50 CSF £5.39 TOTE £1.80: £1.10, £2.20; EX 7.30 Trifecta £35.10 Pool: £3,142.88 - 66.96 winning tickets..
Owner Yeh Man Partnership **Bred** Mrs Mary Buttimer **Trained** Little Newcastle, Pembrokes
■ Stewards' Enquiry : Donal Devereux four- day ban: use of whip (7, 8, 9, 10 July)

FOCUS
The pace was honest for this decent handicap, with the front two fighting out a thrilling finish. The winner is rated in line with the best of his form over this trip.

788 SEA CARGO NOVICES' H'CAP HURDLE (8 hdls) 2m 1f
4:45 (4:45) (Class 5) (0-100,98) 4-Y-0+ **£1,949** (£572; £286; £143)

Form RPR

5/5- **1** **Dont Take Me Alive**[15] 651 4-11-9 **98**..................................(tp) NoelFehily 106
(Charlie Longsdon) *hld up in rr: stdy hdwy 3 out: trcking ldrs next: led narrowly last: kpt on u.p* **5/1**[3]

063- **2** *nk* **Mighty Clarets (IRE)**[14] 661 6-11-8 **94**.............................. JamieMoore 105
(Peter Bowen) *chsd ldrs: drvn 4th: led sn after 2 out: hdd last: no ex clsng stages* **3/1**[1]

503- **3** *8* **Tiradia (FR)**[30] 429 6-11-2 **88**.. BrendanPowell 94
(J R Jenkins) *chsd ldrs: led narrowly appr 2 out: blnd and sn hdd: kpt on one pce appr last* **8/1**

0/3- **4** *1 1/4* **Bob's Legend (IRE)**[36] 333 7-11-12 **98**................. SamTwiston-Davies 100
(Martin Bosley) *stdd s: hld up in rr: hrd drvn appr next: kpt on one pce: nvr trbld ldrs* **17/2**

0/0- **5** *3 1/4* **Regal Ramirez**[22] 558 5-11-4 **90**.. APMcCoy 90
(Michael Smith) *trckd ldrs: upsides 3 out: wknd appr last* **7/2**[2]

/00- **6** *2 3/4* **Stadium Of Light (IRE)**[8] 730 6-10-8 **85**......................(bt) BenPoste(5) 82
(Shaun Harris) *chsd ldrs: rdn 3 out: one pce* **22/1**

/24- **7** *1* **Persian Herald**[19] 593 5-11-6 **97**..................................(v) TrevorWhelan(5) 95
(Neil King) *led: hdd appr 2 out: wknd appr last* **7/1**

0/6- **8** *2* **Garth Mountain**[12] 678 6-10-9 **86**........................... JonathanEngland(5) 80
(Hugh Burns) *t.k.h in rr: outpcd 3 out: nvr a threat* **11/1**

6/P- **9** *dist* **Teeiygee**[38] 283 5-9-9 **72** oh3...................................(tp) SamanthaDrake(5) 26
(Mike Sowersby) *chsd ldrs: lost pl 3 out: sn bhd: hopelessly t.o* **80/1**

0/P- **P** **History Lesson**[23] 536 7-10-0 **72** oh3.............................. AidanColeman
(Alan Jones) *nt jump wl in rr: reminders 3rd: sme hdwy next: lost pl 3 out: bhd whn p.u bef next* **7/1**

4m 13.1s (6.40) **Going Correction** +0.45s/f (Soft)
WFA 4 from 5yo+ 17lb **10** Ran SP% **124.4**
Speed ratings (Par 103): **102,101,98,97,95 94,94,93,72,**
Tote Swingers 1&2 £4.90, 2&3 £3.50, 1&3 £5.80 CSF £22.45 CT £124.38 TOTE £7.00: £3.00, £1.10, £3.40; EX 27.30 Trifecta £97.10 Pool: £1,900.14 - 14.66 winning tickets..
Owner Biddestone Racing Club **Bred** Larry Stratton And Plantation Stud **Trained** Over Norton, Oxon

FOCUS
This was not a strong contest, and it was run at a steady pace. The winner and third set the level.

789 GRIMSBY AND IMMINGHAM STEVEDORES NOVICES' H'CAP CHASE (11 fncs 3 omitted) 2m 6f 110y
5:20 (5:21) (Class 4) (0-105,109) 5-Y-0+ **£3,768** (£1,106; £553; £276)

Form RPR

3/1- **1** **Glen Countess (IRE)**[27] 472 6-11-7 **99**........................(t) BrendanPowell 108
(Brendan Powell) *trckd ldrs: led 2 out: 3 l ahd last: drvn rt out* **8/1**

5/1- **2** *1 1/4* **Foot The Bill**[42] 206 8-11-9 **101**....................................... BrianHarding 108
(Patrick Holmes) *chsd ldrs: reminders 5th: outpcd 7th: upsides ldr omitted 4 out: led 3 out: hdd next: styd on fnl 75yds* **6/1**[3]

/15- **3** *2 3/4* **Dukeofchesterwood**[27] 473 11-10-4 **82**.......................(b[1]) BrianHughes 86
(Karen McLintock) *chsd ldrs: upsides 7th: led omitted 4 out: hdd 3 out: kpt on same pce appr last* **14/1**

4/1- **4** *33* **Halucha (IRE)**[28] 460 8-11-0 **95**................................(p) JakeGreenall(3) 79
(Paul Webber) *in last: drvn 3rd: bhd fr 7th: distant 4th whn blnd bdly 3 out: t.o* **8/1**

04P/ **P** **Terfel's Toscar (IRE)**[76] 5182 8-11-3 **95**.......................(t) RichardJohnson
(Tim Vaughan) *led 1st: hdd omitted 4 out: sn wknd: t.o 3 out: p.u bef last* **3/1**[2]

0F2- **P** **Minella Fifty (IRE)**[15] 641 5-11-12 **104**.................................(t) APMcCoy
(Jonjo O'Neill) *led to 1st: chsd ldrs: blnd bdly 3rd: drvn 7th: wknd and eased next: t.o whn p.u bef 3 out* **5/4**[1]

5m 30.6s (-15.40) **Going Correction** -0.525s/f (Firm) **6** Ran SP% **112.6**
Speed ratings: **105,104,103,92,**
Tote Swingers 1&2 £2.40, 2&3 £6.70, 1&3 £6.20 CSF £51.47 CT £657.93 TOTE £9.60: £6.90, £2.00; EX 28.70 Trifecta £180.10 Pool: £2,038.67 - 8.48 winning tickets..
Owner The Naughty Partnership **Bred** David Pim **Trained** Upper Lambourn, Berks

FOCUS
Three last-time-out winners in the field. It was run at a sound pace, with the first of the ditches down the far side omitted. Steps up from the first two with the third to his mark.

790 SVITZER STANDARD OPEN NATIONAL HUNT FLAT RACE 2m 1f
5:55 (5:55) (Class 6) 4-6-Y-0 **£1,559** (£457; £228; £114)

Form RPR

1/ **1** **Clever Cookie**[224] 2319 5-11-9 0.. JasonMaguire 109+
(Peter Niven) *hld up towards rr: hdwy 6f out: chsng ldrs on outer over 2f out: hung rt 1f out: styd on to ld towards fin* **5/2**[2]

6/ **2** *nk* **Western Xpress (IRE)**[85] 4982 5-11-2 0............................ TomO'Brien 102
(Peter Bowen) *led: jnd 3f out: stuck on wl: hdd and no ex nr fin* **5/1**[3]

4/1- **3** *hd* **Plain Sailing (IRE)**[13] 675 4-11-6 0.................................. DenisO'Regan 106+
(John Ferguson) *in tch: effrt over 4f out: chal over 1f out: crowded and no ex clsng stages* **7/4**[1]

0/1- **4** *6* **Magic Present**[26] 497 6-11-9 0.. BrianHughes 104
(Malcolm Jefferson) *trckd ldrs: upsides over 5f out: edgd rt and fdd over 1f out* **18/1**

5 *3/4* **Vasco Du Mee (FR)**[69] 4-10-10 0.................................... JackQuinlan(3) 93
(Richard Pugh, Ire) *trckd ldrs: chal over 2f out: fdd over 1f out* **13/2**

6 *2 1/2* **Countersign** 4-10-13 0.. AdamPogson 91
(Charles Pogson) *stdd s: t.k.h in rr: hdwy over 7f out: in tch over 3f out: one pce* **28/1**

6- **7** *7* **Pamela Lewis**[21] 567 6-10-9 0... HarryHaynes 80
(Pam Sly) *chsd ldrs: drvn 3f out: wknd over 1f out* **20/1**

0/ **8** *1/2* **Nataraja**[163] 3572 4-10-10 0.. BrianToomey(3) 84
(Tony Coyle) *in rr: drvn 5f out: kpt on fnl 3f: nvr a factor* **50/1**

9 *2 1/2* **Not Another Monday (IRE)**[61] 5-11-2 0............................ BarryKeniry 85
(George Moore) *trckd ldrs: effrt over 3f out: wknd over 1f out* **20/1**

0- **10** *8* **Wolmar**[8] 731 4-10-6 0...(p) DonalDevereux 67
(John Mackie) *mid-div: hdwy 7f out: lost pl over 4f out* **66/1**

0/ **11** *3* **Stantastic**[55] 5572 5-10-11 0..................................... SamanthaDrake(5) 75
(Mark Campion) *hld up in rr: hdwy 6f out: drvn over 3f out: lost pl 2f out* **100/1**

0/ **12** *2 1/2* **Wishfull Dancer (IRE)**[115] 4439 5-10-13 0.................... MichaelByrne(3) 73
(John Mackie) *chsd ldrs: drvn and lost pl over 3f out* **33/1**

6- **13** *17* **Royal Rojo**[26] 497 4-10-13 0.. RichieMcGrath 54
(Chris Grant) *mid-div: outpcd 7f out: lost pl 5f out: sn bhd* **50/1**

4m 12.1s (11.00) **Going Correction** +0.45s/f (Soft)
WFA 4 from 5yo+ 3lb **13** Ran SP% **122.5**
Speed ratings: **92,91,91,88,88 87,84,83,82,78 77,76,68**
Tote Swingers 1&2 £3.10, 2&3 £4.00, 1&3 £5.10 CSF £14.65 TOTE £4.40: £1.40, £1.20, £1.70; EX 15.60 Trifecta £45.40 Pool: £871.53 - 14.38 winning tickets..
Owner Francis Green Racing Ltd **Bred** Mrs J A Niven **Trained** Barton-le-Street, N Yorks
■ Stewards' Enquiry : Jason Maguire one-day ban: careless riding (7 July)

FOCUS
A decent bumper run at a fair pace, and the front three pulled clear. The winner third and seventh set the level.
T/Plt: £9.00 to a £1 stake. Pool: £48,413.47 - 3914.61 winning tickets. T/Qpdt: £8.30 to a £1 stake. Pool: £2,504.01 - 222.52 winning tickets. WG

791 - 797a (Foreign Racing) - See Raceform Interactive

[747] HEXHAM (L-H)
Sunday, June 23

OFFICIAL GOING: Good (good to soft in places; 7.5) changing to soft after race 4 (3.30)
Fresh ground on all bends.
Wind: Fresh; half against Weather: Overcast; showers

798 YOUR FAVOURITE POOLS BETS@TOTEPOOL.COM NOVICES' CHASE (12 fncs) 2m 110y
2:00 (2:00) (Class 4) 5-Y-0+ **£3,768** (£1,106; £553; £276)

Form RPR

/01- **1** **Bygones Of Brid (IRE)**[22] 579 10-11-5 0........................... BrianHughes 137+
(Karen McLintock) *chsd clr ldr: smooth hdwy to ld bef last: sn clr* **3/1**[2]

43- **2** *12* **Twill Stand To Us (IRE)**[19] 629 6-10-12 0.................(t) DougieCostello 111
(Brian Ellison) *chsd ldrs: rdn and outpcd after 3 out: rallied bef last: chsd (clr) wnr run-in: no imp* **13/2**

3/1- **3** *4* **Toledo Gold (IRE)**[14] 679 7-11-5 112.......................(t) MichaelMcAlister 115
(Maurice Barnes) *led and clr to 3 out: rdn and hdd bef last: outpcd and lost 2nd run-in* **12/1**

0/1- **4** *3/4* **Grey Soldier (IRE)**[29] 474 8-11-5 125...............................(t) NickScholfield 113
(Sophie Leech) *hld up: rdn along 7th: styd on fr 2 out: nvr rchd ldrs* **5/1**[3]

/24- **5** *11* **Agricultural**[22] 581 7-10-12 0.. RyanMania 95
(Lucy Normile) *bhd: pushed along 4 out: effrt next: wknd after 2 out* **28/1**

/5P- **6** *33* **Bucklemyshoe (IRE)**[19] 625 12-10-5 0............................ JohnDawson(7) 62
(Robert Johnson) *nt fluent: hld up: outpcd whn hit 4 out: t.o* **200/1**

/00- **7** *35* **Alba King (IRE)**[28] 493 7-10-7 87.................................. JonathanEngland(5) 27
(Sue Smith) *a bhd: lost tch 1/2-way: t.o* **66/1**

14P/ **B** **Rathnaroughy (IRE)**[329] 1116 9-10-12 0............................ HarryHaynes
(Malcolm Jefferson) *hld up: b.d 1st* **33/1**

2F1- **U** **Turf Trivia**[13] 694 6-11-5 96...(b) BarryKeniry
(George Moore) *midfield: bdly hmpd and uns rdr 1st* **22/1**

304/ **P** **Bachelor Lad (IRE)**[23] 575 9-10-12 111........................ PeterBuchanan
(C A McBratney, Ire) *in tch to 1/2-way: sn struggling: t.o whn p.u bef 4 out: fin lame* **20/1**

F/P- **F** **Danceintothelight**[35] 386 6-10-12 0................................... BrianHarding
(Micky Hammond) *in tch whn j. slowly and fell 1st* **50/1**

0/2- **U** **Rhymers Ha'**[46] 167 6-10-5 121...................................... GrahamWatters(7)
(Lucinda Russell) *in tch whn stmbld and uns rdr 4th* **7/4**[1]

500/ **F** **Emperor Of Rome (IRE)**[65] 5386 5-10-12 0...............(t[1]) RichieMcGrath
(Tim Fitzgerald) *midfield: fell 1st* **80/1**

0/P- **P** **Heart O Annandale (IRE)**[28] 491 6-10-9 0.................. EwanWhillans(3)
(Alistair Whillans) *hmpd and wl bhd fr 1st: t.o whn p.u bef 7th* **200/1**

4m 3.9s (-5.90) **Going Correction** -0.20s/f (Good) **14** Ran SP% **120.2**
Speed ratings: **105,99,97,97,91 76,59,, , , , ,**
toteswingers 1&2 £7.60, 1&3 £8.20, 2&3 £10.30 CSF £21.29 TOTE £4.20: £1.40, £2.70, £3.70; EX 28.90 Trifecta £327.10 Pool: £703.77 - 1.61 winning units..
Owner James Callow **Bred** Oliver Brennan **Trained** Ingoe, Northumberland

FOCUS
7mm of rain had fallen in the past couple of days and with heavy showers during the day the going had eased to good with good to soft places. An ordinary yet tricky card, with interest boosted by a huge Tote jackpot courtesy of a multiple rollover from Royal Ascot. With four horses falling at the first and the favourite, Rhymers Ha', also departing early, this novice chase did not take much winning in the end.

799 BET TOTEQUADPOT TEXT TOTE TO 89660 CONDITIONAL JOCKEYS' (S) HURDLE (12 hdls) 3m
2:30 (2:30) (Class 5) 4-Y-0+ **£2,053** (£598; £299)

Form RPR

/3P- **1** **Sparkling Tara**[23] 566 8-11-2 0................................ JonathanEngland(3) 101+
(Sue Smith) *prom: hdwy to ld bef last: kpt on strly* **7/2**[2]

212- **2** *4* **Descaro (USA)**[4] 762 7-11-4 120..............................(p) CiaranMckee(8) 103
(John O'Shea) *hld up: hdwy to chal 3 out: led next to bef last: drvn and one pce run-in* **5/4**[1]

5/3- **3** *shd* **Via Archimede (USA)**[8] 750 8-10-11 84.....................(p) CraigNichol(8) 96
(Lucinda Russell) *cl up: led 7th: hdd 2 out: rallied and ev ch bef last: one pce run-in* **7/1**

02U/ **4** *nk* **Mia's Vic (IRE)**[32] 439 8-11-5 109..(t) DerekFox 97+
(Noel C Kelly, Ire) *hld up and bhd: hit 3 out: stdy hdwy after next: sn hrd rdn: kpt on fr last: nvr any ch of rching wnr* **4/1**[3]

40P- **5** *59* **Tasheba**[10] 728 8-10-9 0...(t) KieronEdgar(5) 38
(Sophie Leech) *trckd ldrs: outpcd bef 3 out: lost tch bef next: t.o* **14/1**

/05- **6** *22* **Rare Coincidence**[25] 537 12-11-5 81.........................(tp) AlexanderVoy 23
(Alan Berry) *led to 7th: wknd after next: lost tch fr 4 out: continued* **66/1**

P **Dry Rein (IRE)**[23] 568 8-10-2 0..............................(p) GrahamWatters[(5)]
(B Arthey, Ire) *chsd ldrs: pin c out of stirrup leather and rode wout irons fr 4th: wnt 2nd 7th to 4 out: wknd next: p.u 2 out* **50/1**

0/5- P **Escape Artist**[15] 72 6-11-0 72..............................(p) TonyKelly
(David Thompson) *hld up in tch: rdn and outpcd 3 out: wknd bef next: t.o whn p.u bef last* **100/1**

P26- P **Mongress Boy (IRE)**[17] 649 8-11-0 105.......................(p) PeterCarberry
(Andy Hobbs) *in tch: hdwy to chse ldr 4 out to next: wknd bef 2 out: t.o whn p.u bef last* **16/1**

6m 5.4s (-3.60) **Going Correction** -0.20s/f (Good) **9** Ran SP% **116.2**
Speed ratings (Par 103): **98,96,96,96,76 69, , ,**
toteswingers 1&2 £2.20, 1&3 £6.20, 2&3 £3.00 CSF £8.61 TOTE £4.10: £1.40, £1.40, £1.70; EX 10.10 Trifecta £41.60 Pool: £1,251.05 - 22.51 winning units..There was no bid for the winner
Owner Mrs S Smith **Bred** Victor G And Mrs Izabel Palmer **Trained** High Eldwick, W Yorks
FOCUS
A solid contest for the grade with two well-backed horses and the in-form favourite fighting out the finish.

800 BET TOTEJACKPOT EVERYDAY@TOTEPOOL.COM NOVICES' HURDLE (8 hdls) 2m 110y

3:00 (3:03) (Class 4) 4-Y-0+ **£3,285** (£957; £479)

Form RPR

/ 1 **Howwouldunо (IRE)**[23] 568 5-10-12 0.................... GrahamWatters[(7)] 116+
(Liam Lennon, Ire) *in tch: effrt and rdn after 2 out: led last: edgd lft: kpt on strly* **11/4**[2]

UF5/ 2 1 1/4 **Symphonick (FR)**[15] 7-10-12 0.............................. BrianHughes 107
(Tim Fitzgerald) *led: rdn and hdd last: rallied: kpt on: hld nr fin* **22/1**

4/1- 3 3 1/4 **Things Change (IRE)**[25] 531 5-11-5 120...................... DougieCostello 111
(John Quinn) *prom: hdwy to chse wnr after 3 out to bef last: wnt lft last: one pce run-in* **1/1**[1]

4 13 **Swing Hard (IRE)**[77] 5-10-12 0.. RyanMania 92+
(Sue Smith) *chsd ldr to after 3 out: drvn and outpcd next: styd on fr last: no imp* **14/1**

P/P- 5 1 1/2 **Bow Fiddle (IRE)**[24] 552 7-10-5 0..................................(t) BrianHarding 84
(Patrick Holmes) *hld up: stdy hdwy bef 2 out: rdn and no imp fr last* **100/1**

F04/ 6 14 **Oakwell (IRE)**[46] 5202 5-10-12 105................................. RichieMcGrath 78
(Sally Hall) *chsd ldr to after 3 out: drvn and wknd after next* **12/1**

350/ 7 4 **The Bold Lord (IRE)**[98] 4815 5-10-7 0...................... GaryRutherford[(5)] 75
(Alan Swinbank) *hld up: struggling after 3 out: nvr on terms* **12/1**

/05- 8 12 **Beyondtemptation**[8] 754 5-10-2 0................................ JohnKington[(3)] 57
(Jonathan Haynes) *slowly away: t.k.h in rr: struggling 1/2-way: sn btn* **100/1**

63- 9 27 **Bollin Sam**[13] 695 7-10-7 0...................................... JonathanEngland[(5)] 40
(Sue Smith) *mstkes in rr: struggling fr 4 out: t.o* **40/1**

PPP/ 10 17 **God's County (FR)**[298] 1411 8-10-12 0..........................(t) NickScholfield 24
(Sophie Leech) *midfield: blnd 3rd: struggling fr 3 out: t.o* **8/1**[3]

\- P **More Like Mum** 7-10-0 0...................................... SamanthaDrake[(5)]
(Tina Jackson) *loose bef s: bhd: blnd 2nd: struggling fr 4th: t.o whn p.u after 3 out* **66/1**

4m 11.2s (-6.20) **Going Correction** -0.20s/f (Good) **11** Ran SP% **120.1**
Speed ratings (Par 105): **106,105,103,97,97 90,88,82,70,62**
toteswingers 1&2 £14.40, 1&3 £1.20, 2&3 £8.90 CSF £60.74 TOTE £3.00: £1.30, £5.10, £1.10; EX 70.90 Trifecta £258.60 Pool: £1,817.84 - 5.27 winning units..
Owner James McMullan **Bred** James McMullan **Trained** Newry, Co. Down
FOCUS
Both previous winners were involved in the finish as three pulled clear.

801 TOTEPOOL MOBILE TEXT TOTE TO 89660 H'CAP HURDLE (THE SUNDAY £5K BONUS RACE) (10 hdls) 2m 4f 110y

3:30 (3:30) (Class 4) (0-120,118) 4-Y-0+ **£3,119** (£915; £457; £228)

Form RPR

/56- 1 **Cruachan (IRE)**[14] 681 4-10-6 102................................ DougieCostello 104+
(Lucy Normile) *hld up: hdwy bef 2 out: rdn bef last: led run-in: pushed out* **16/1**

204- 2 1 3/4 **I'Ll Be Frank**[24] 556 8-10-0 92 oh2..........................(t) MichaelMcAlister 95
(Maurice Barnes) *led: pckd after 2nd: rdn and jnd last: sn hdd: kpt on u.p* **11/2**

4/4- 3 hd **Hi George**[23] 563 5-11-10 116.. HarryHaynes 120
(Malcolm Jefferson) *hld up: hdwy to chse ldrs 1/2-way: effrt and ev ch last: sn drvn: one pce run-in* **7/2**[1]

215- 4 10 **Nicky Nutjob (GER)**[17] 640 7-9-7 92..........................(p) CiaranMckee[(7)] 86
(John O'Shea) *hld up: rdn and hdwy after 3 out: kpt on fr last: no ch w first three* **7/1**

/12- 5 1/2 **Wake Your Dreams (IRE)**[23] 563 5-11-10 116................ SeanQuinlan 110
(Jennie Candlish) *chsd ldr to bef last: sn drvn and wknd* **4/1**[2]

/21- 6 3/4 **Sergeant Pink (IRE)**[25] 533 7-10-1 93............................. BrianHughes 86
(Dianne Sayer) *in tch: pushed along after 3 out: shortlived effrt next: sn btn* **8/1**

314- 7 nk **Andreo Bambaleo**[14] 681 9-11-7 113............................(p) RyanMania 106
(Brian Ellison) *in tch: mstke and lost grnd 3 out: rallied bef next: sn no imp* **5/1**[3]

2/6- 8 25 **What A Steel (IRE)**[27] 512 9-11-9 118........................ EwanWhillans[(3)] 88
(Alistair Whillans) *in tch: drvn and outpcd after 3 out: wknd bef next: t.o* **25/1**

0/2- 9 8 **Stanley Bridge**[25] 537 6-10-10 102.................................. LucyAlexander 65
(Barry Murtagh) *t.k.h: in tch: outpcd after 3 out: lost tch fr next: t.o* **16/1**

/15- 10 29 **Stand Clear**[19] 626 8-9-11 96....................................... AdamNicol[(7)] 33
(David Thompson) *hld up: struggling 3 out: sn lost tch: t.o* **25/1**

5m 10.8s (-1.70) **Going Correction** -0.025s/f (Good)
WFA 4 from 5yo+ 18lb **10** Ran SP% **117.3**
Speed ratings (Par 105): **102,101,101,97,97 96,96,87,84,73**
toteswingers 1&2 £8.90, 1&3 £13.40, 2&3 £4.60 CSF £103.10 CT £382.62 TOTE £18.40: £4.00, £2.00, £1.90; EX 133.10 Trifecta £785.40 Part won. Pool: £1,047.32 - 0.01 winning units..
Owner P Carnaby & B Thomson **Bred** Grangecon Stud **Trained** Duncrievie, Perth & Kinross
FOCUS
A open-looking handicap with two well-supported horses having to give best to a 16-1 shot in a three-way battle to the line. This was run in a heavy downpour.

802 KING SIZE POOLS@TOTEPOOL.COM H'CAP CHASE (19 fncs) 3m 1f

4:00 (4:00) (Class 5) (0-100,98) 5-Y-0+ **£2,079** (£610; £305; £152)

Form RPR

2/5- 1 **Sierra Victor (IRE)**[28] 492 10-10-11 90.....................(b[1]) MrJHamilton[(7)] 102+
(Rose Dobbin) *chsd ldr: mstke 13th: effrt 2 out: led last 100yds: styd on wl* **20/1**

/00- 2 3 **Cloudy Dawn**[22] 580 8-9-9 72 oh2........................ JonathanEngland[(5)] 80
(Sue Smith) *led: rdn 2 out: hdd last 100yds: kpt on same pce* **11/2**[1]

5/4- 3 39 **Raifteiri (IRE)**[25] 534 6-9-12 75.................................. GaryRutherford[(5)] 48
(William Young Jnr) *hld up: hdwy bef 14th: rdn and chsd ldng pair after 3 out: wknd bef last* **11/1**

/30- 4 10 **Chicago Outfit (IRE)**[23] 566 8-11-2 95......................(p) JohnDawson[(7)] 54
(John Wade) *chsd ldrs: hit 8th: drvn and outpcd bef 3 out: n.d after* **12/1**

5 1 1/4 **Paddysparks (IRE)**[23] 577 9-10-1 76..........................(p) DJHoward[(3)] 34
(Daniel John Howard, Ire) *hld up: shortlived effrt after 4 out: wknd fr 2 out* **10/1**

/P0- 6 46 **Seize**[23] 566 11-11-12 98..(b) BrianHughes 10
(James Moffatt) *midfield: outpcd 8th: lost tch fr next: continued: t.o* **28/1**

/56- P **Panthers Run**[19] 627 13-9-11 72 oh2..........................(t) JohnKington[(3)]
(Jonathan Haynes) *midfield: struggling fr 6th: t.o whn p.u after 12th* **25/1**

54U- P **More Equity**[23] 566 11-11-6 92..(t) RyanMania
(Dianne Sayer) *hld up: struggling bef 12th: t.o whn p.u bef 14th* **8/1**[3]

55P/ U **Maple Valley Gale (IRE)**[16] 667 9-10-8 87............. GrahamWatters[(7)]
(Liam Lennon, Ire) *hld up: hit 6th: outpcd whn mstke and uns rdr 13th* **6/1**[2]

/33- P **Winston Churchill (IRE)**[17] 641 7-11-10 96................(t) NickScholfield
(Sophie Leech) *hld up: stdy hdwy to chse ldrs 1/2-way: rdn and outpcd whn blnd and sddle slipped two out: sn p.u* **11/2**[1]

/42- P **Eliades Run (IRE)**[21] 597 7-9-9 72 oh1...............(bt) SamanthaDrake[(5)]
(Ferdy Murphy, France) *in tch to 1/2-way: sn struggling: t.o whn p.u bef last* **9/1**

/43- P **Everlylasting (IRE)**[24] 555 6-10-5 77................................(p) RichieMcGrath
(Rose Dobbin) *chsd ldrs: outpcd 13th: struggling fr next: t.o whn p.u bef 3 out* **11/2**[1]

6m 30.0s (-2.20) **Going Correction** -0.025s/f (Good) **12** Ran SP% **118.7**
Speed ratings: **102,101,88,85,84 70, , , ,**
toteswingers 1&2 £20.20, 1&3 £24.20, 2&3 £12.30 CSF £126.69 CT £1297.85 TOTE £20.70: £6.60, £2.00, £2.70; EX 195.00 Trifecta £1247.90 Part won. Pool: £1,663.93 - 0.34 winning units..
Owner M S Borders Racing Club **Bred** Mrs Brenda Cunningham **Trained** South Hazelrigg, Northumbria
■ Stewards' Enquiry : Jonathan England two-day ban: use of whip (7-8 Jul)
FOCUS
The going had changed to soft by this stage and there was a rash of non-runners, including the forecast favourite Presenting Junior. It was run at a good pace and few were able to cope.

803 EXCLUSIVE OFFERS ON TOTEPOOL MOBILE H'CAP HURDLE (8 hdls) 2m 110y

4:30 (4:31) (Class 5) (0-100,100) 4-Y-0+ **£2,053** (£598; £299)

Form RPR

/31- 1 **Morning Time (IRE)**[19] 630 7-10-7 81........................(p) PeterBuchanan 92+
(Lucinda Russell) *hld up in midfield: smooth hdwy to chse (clr) wnr bef 2 out: relentless prog to ld bef last: drvn and styd on wl last 100yds* **6/1**[2]

P/0- 2 3 **Tennessee Bird**[16] 661 5-9-9 74 oh5................................ EDLinehan[(5)] 80
(Mike Sowersby) *chsd ldrs: led 4 out: clr after next: rdn and hdd bef last: rallied: one pce last 100yds* **8/1**

0/0- 3 26 **Waltham Abbey**[52] 75 12-10-4 78.................................... HarryHaynes 61
(Lynsey Kendall) *hld up: outpcd 4 out: rallied bef 2 out: sn no ch w first two* **10/1**

0/6- 4 7 **Cadore (IRE)**[38] 342 5-11-2 97..(p) MrSFox[(7)] 73
(Lucy Normile) *prom: drvn and outpcd bef 3 out: n.d after* **6/1**[2]

314- 5 4 1/2 **Bunratty (IRE)**[8] 749 7-11-3 96.. TonyKelly[(5)] 68
(Dianne Sayer) *led: hit 2nd: hdd 4th: drvn and wknd 2 out* **7/1**[3]

U52- P **Pete**[25] 536 10-11-2 90..(tp) LucyAlexander
(Barry Murtagh) *hld up: struggling bef 3 out: t.o whn p.u bef last* **8/1**

000/ P **Thatwasthepension (IRE)**[75] 5227 7-9-12 79.............(p) CraigNichol[(7)]
(Brian Storey) *in tch to 4th: outpcd whn nt fluent next: sn lost tch: p.u bef 2 out* **33/1**

550- P **Lewlaur Supreme (IRE)**[25] 536 10-9-7 74 oh9............ MrJHamilton[(7)]
(William Young Jnr) *bhd: struggling fr 3rd: sn lost tch: t.o whn p.u bef 2 out* **11/1**

162- P **Brother Scott**[19] 630 6-11-4 92.. RyanMania
(Sue Smith) *cl up: led 4th to next: rdn and wknd bef 2 out: t.o whn p.u bef last* **11/2**[1]

/46- P **Two Oscars (IRE)**[24] 558 7-10-13 87................................ BrianHughes
(Andrew Crook) *hld up: struggling 1/2-way: t.o whn p.u bef 2 out* **15/2**

00P/ P **Ute Antique (FR)**[62] 5452 5-10-1 80.........................(t) SamanthaDrake[(5)]
(Ferdy Murphy, France) *bhd: struggling 3rd: sn lost tch: t.o whn p.u bef 4 out* **16/1**

4m 19.7s (2.30) **Going Correction** +0.175s/f (Yiel) **11** Ran SP% **116.7**
Speed ratings (Par 103): **101,99,87,84,81 , , , ,**
toteswingers 1&2 £16.20, 1&3 £16.60, 2&3 £11.30 CSF £53.15 CT £474.87 TOTE £6.00: £1.90, £2.20, £2.90; EX 84.80 Trifecta £1325.80 Part won. Pool: £1,767.70 - 0.61 winning units..
Owner Bill Forrester **Bred** Joe O'Flaherty **Trained** Arlary, Perth & Kinross
FOCUS
The early pace was reasonable and the few that managed to complete finished strung out. The cosy winner built on his recent win.

804 HEXHAM INTERACTIVE H'CAP HURDLE (12 hdls) 3m

5:00 (5:00) (Class 4) (0-110,112) 4-Y-0+ **£3,038** (£897; £448; £224; £112)

Form RPR

6/4- 1 **Big Sound**[32] 428 6-10-13 97..(p) PeterBuchanan 101
(Tim Walford) *hld up in tch: stdy hdwy after 3 out: led whn mstke last: drvn and styd on strly last 100yds* **7/2**[2]

/11- 2 3 **Auberge (IRE)**[8] 751 9-11-0 98... RyanMania 100
(Dianne Sayer) *led: clr after 3 out: hit next: hdd bef last: rallied: kpt on same pce last 100yds* **6/4**[1]

3/3- 3 3/4 **Executive's Hall (IRE)**[29] 471 9-9-9 86...............(p) CraigGallagher[(7)] 86
(Ben Haslam) *in tch: hdwy 4th: wnt 2nd 3 out: clsd next: rdn and hung lft bef last: rallied run-in: no imp* **4/1**[3]

0/0- 4 40 **Tribal Dance (IRE)**[41] 269 7-10-4 95.........................(b[1]) CiaranMckee[(7)] 59
(John O'Shea) *chsd ldr to 3 out: rdn and lost tch bef next: t.o* **22/1**

521- 5 1 1/4 **Granaruid (IRE)**[8] 752 10-11-7 112......................(p) GrantCockburn[(7)] 75
(Alison Hamilton) *in tch: niggled 6th: drvn and outpcd 8th: sn struggling: t.o* **8/1**

/45- 6 89 **Saga De Tercey (FR)**[28] 503 8-11-4 102..........................(b) AdrianLane
(Donald McCain) *chsd ldrs to 7th: drvn and lost tch fr next: continued: t.o* **12/1**

F66- P **Merry Minster**[8] 747 6-10-4 95..................................... JohnDawson[(7)]
(James Walton) *t.k.h: hld up: rdn and struggling bef 3 out: t.o whn p.u bef last* **20/1**

6m 18.5s (9.50) **Going Correction** +0.175s/f (Yiel) **7** Ran SP% **110.1**
Speed ratings (Par 105): **91,90,89,76,76 46,**
toteswingers 1&2 £2.90, 1&3 £2.50, 2&3 £2.80 CSF £8.77 CT £18.57 TOTE £4.50: £2.80, £1.20; EX 8.60 Trifecta £35.60 Pool: £1,848.84 - 38.85 winning units..

The Form Book Jumps, Raceform Ltd, Compton, RG20 6NL.

Owner A Quirke **Bred** Mr & Mrs W Hodge **Trained** Sheriff Hutton, N Yorks
■ Stewards' Enquiry : Craig Gallagher two-day ban: use of whip (7-8 Jul)

FOCUS
Hexham's final race of the summer produced a tight finish with three in with a chance jumping the last and the hat-trick seeking Augberge just denied. A big step up from the winner.
T/Jkpt: £260,394.10 to a £1 stake. Pool: £1,100,256.82 - 3.00 winning units T/Plt: £236.60 to a £1 stake. Pool: £152,844.39 - 471.56 winning units T/Qpdt: £64.20 to a £1 stake. Pool: £7,203.41 - 82.92 winning units RY

713 WORCESTER (L-H)
Sunday, June 23

OFFICIAL GOING: Good (good to firm in places; 6.5)
All bends and straights on inside line.
Wind: Light behind Weather: Overcast

805 PLAY ROULETTE & BLACKJACK AT TOTEPOOL.COM H'CAP CHASE (15 fncs) 2m 4f
1:50 (1:50) (Class 5) (0-95,95) 5-Y-0+ **£2,274** (£667; £333; £166)

Form RPR
/2P- **1** **Shantou Breeze (IRE)**28 [485] 6-11-1 **84**.......... MarcGoldstein 94
(Michael Madgwick) *a.p: chsd ldr 3 out: rdn to ld last: all out* **9/1**
00P/ **2** *shd* **Quel Bruere (FR)**378 [682] 9-11-7 **95**.......... GavinSheehan(5) 106
(John Upson) *chsd ldr tl led 3rd: hdd after 5th: led again 9th: rdn and hdd last: styd on gamely* **12/1**
435- **3** *12* **Roc De Guyé (FR)**21 [600] 8-10-9 **78**..........1 LiamTreadwell 78
(James Evans) *led to 3rd: led again after 5th: hdd 9th: rdn and wknd appr last* **3/1**2
FP- **4** *18* **Tulla Emerald (IRE)**13 [687] 8-10-7 **83**.......... MrKevinJones(7) 66
(Natalie Lloyd-Beavis) *hld up: hdwy 4 out: blnd next: wknd 2 out: t.o* **66/1**
015- **5** *6* **Crack At Dawn (IRE)**13 [694] 12-11-1 **87**..........(v) AdamWedge(3) 65
(Michael Gates) *hld up: pushed along and hdwy appr 4 out: wknd next: t.o* **7/1**
/06- **6** *4* **Oranger (FR)**28 [504] 11-10-12 **88**..........(b) MrJMartin(7) 62
(Andrew J Martin) *prom: pushed along appr 6th: rdn and wknd after 10th: t.o* **6/1**3
P/6- **7** *2 1/4* **Reg's Ruby**21 [600] 7-11-3 **93**..........(p) JakeHodson(7) 65
(David Bridgwater) *chsd ldrs tl rdn and wknd after 10th: t.o* **12/1**
PP0/ **P** **Dream Honours (IRE)**55 [34] 10-10-1 **77**.......... MrLKilgarriff(7)
(Clarissa Caroe) *chsd ldrs: blnd and rdr lost irons 2nd: pushed along whn hit 6th: sn wknd: t.o whn p.u bef 9th* **66/1**
24P- **P** **Grovemere (IRE)**17 [643] 8-11-11 **94**..........(tp) TomO'Brien
(Debra Hamer) *sn pushed along towards rr: reminders after 2nd: wl bhd fr 5th: t.o whn p.u bef 7th* **9/4**1

4m 47.5s (-12.50) **Going Correction** -0.70s/f (Firm) **9 Ran SP% 110.9**
Speed ratings: **97,96,92,84,82 80,80, ,**
toteswingers 1&2 £8.50, 1&3 £5.70, 2&3 £7.70 CSF £99.51 CT £385.80 TOTE £10.90: £2.90, £2.60, £1.40; EX 122.40 Trifecta £714.80 Part won. Pool: £953.14 - 0.40 winning units..
Owner Ian M McGready **Bred** Miss E Harrington **Trained** Denmead, Hants
■ Stewards' Enquiry : Marc Goldstein seven-day ban: use of whip (8-10, 14, 15, 17 July)

FOCUS
A moderate contest, weakened by a couple of non-runners.

806 LUCKY 15 BONUS AT TOTEPOOL.COM NOVICES' CHASE (15 fncs) 2m 4f
2:20 (2:20) (Class 4) 5-Y-0+ **£3,898** (£1,144; £572; £286)

Form RPR
F/4- **1** **Roger Beantown (IRE)**35 [394] 8-10-12 124.......... DarylJacob 131+
(Paul Nicholls) *a.p: chsd ldr 8th: led 4 out: rdn out* **11/4**2
/13- **2** *5* **Double Handful (GER)**32 [425] 7-10-12 123..........(t) DavidBass 123
(Lawney Hill) *hld up: hdwy 6th: rdn to chse wnr 2 out: blnd last: styd on same pce flat* **9/1**
/32- **3** *14* **Polarbrook (IRE)**28 [499] 6-10-12 0.......... HenryBrooke 112+
(Donald McCain) *hld up: pushed along 6th: hdwy and blnd 4 out: wknd 2 out* **25/1**
541/ **4** *2 1/2* **Fearless Leader**361 [838] 6-10-12 0.......... SamTwiston-Davies 109
(David Bridgwater) *chsd ldrs: rdn after 4 out: wknd 2 out* **12/1**
26/- **5** *15* **My Brother Sylvest**183 [3180] 7-10-12 126..........(b) TomScudamore 94
(David Pipe) *led: j.rt 2nd: nt fluent next: hdd 4 out: wknd appr 2 out: t.o* **15/8**1
460/ **6** *2 1/2* **High Storm (IRE)**219 [2455] 6-10-12 0.......... DPFahy 91
(Bernard Llewellyn) *hld up: bhd fr 10th: t.o* **14/1**
/60- **7** *2 1/4* **Crescent Beach (IRE)**17 [648] 6-10-12 0.......... HenryOliver 89
(Henry Oliver) *hld up: wknd 10th: t.o* **50/1**
FP6/ **8** *1/2* **Theodore Lamb**166 [3564] 8-10-12 105.......... DenisO'Regan 89
(Paul Webber) *hld up: hdwy 5th: wknd after 3 out* **25/1**
/20- **9** *11* **Officially Modern (IRE)**28 [484] 6-10-12 0.......... AlainCawley 79
(Fergal O'Brien) *racd keenly: trckd ldr: j.rt 2nd: blnd 8th: wknd 10th: t.o* **50/1**
543- **10** *89* **Roses Legend**17 [646] 8-10-12 96.......... SamThomas
(Reginald Brown) *hld up: bhd and pushed along 5th: t.o* **33/1**
/03- **P** **Green Bank (IRE)**13 [690] 7-10-12 0..........(t) NoelFehily
(Charlie Longsdon) *hld up: bhd fr 8th: t.o whn p.u bef 3 out* **11/2**3

4m 41.3s (-18.70) **Going Correction** -0.70s/f (Firm) **11 Ran SP% 115.7**
Speed ratings: **109,107,101,100,94 93,92,92,87,52**
toteswingers 1&2 £7.10, 1&3 £17.20, 2&3 £5.40 CSF £25.26 TOTE £3.30: £1.90, £3.00, £4.90; EX 23.80 Trifecta £400.50 Part won. Pool: £534.03 - 0.74 winning units..
Owner Andrea & Graham Wylie **Bred** T Hogan And J Ryan **Trained** Ditcheat, Somerset

FOCUS
A modest novice chase. The third-last fence was bypassed.

807 PLAY DEAL OR NO DEAL AT TOTEPOOL.COM H'CAP CHASE (11 fncs 1 omitted) 2m 110y
2:50 (2:50) (Class 5) (0-100,98) 5-Y-0+ **£2,274** (£667; £333; £166)

Form RPR
0/5- **1** **Echo Dancer**36 [369] 7-9-13 **74** oh4 ow2..........(b1) RobertDunne(3) 93+
(Trevor Wall) *mde all: hit 4th: 8th and 9th: clr last: eased flat* **25/1**
/23- **2** *8* **Cruise In Style (IRE)**22 [585] 7-11-9 **98**..........(b) JamesBest(3) 105
(Kevin Bishop) *mid-div: hdwy 7th: rdn to chse wnr last: no imp* **11/2**3
233- **3** *1* **Chestnut Ben (IRE)**18 [632] 8-11-7 **93**.......... APMcCoy 99
(Gary Brown) *prom: chsd wnr 7th tl rdn appr last: no ex* **7/4**1
/04- **4** *1 3/4* **Russian Conquest**18 [632] 7-11-6 **92**..........(b1) AndrewThornton 96
(Seamus Mullins) *chsd wnr to 7th: mstke next: outpcd appr 4 out: styd on flat* **17/2**
66U/ **5** *3 3/4* **Mezarat (ITY)**55 [30] 8-10-3 **78**..........(p) AdamWedge(3) 79
(Michael Gates) *hld up: nvr on terms* **20/1**
/42- **6** *14* **Escardo (GER)**8 [749] 10-11-1 **87**..........(p) TomScudamore 79
(David Bridgwater) *mid-div: hdwy 7th: hit 4 out: wknd appr 2 out* **9/2**2
223- **7** *1 1/4* **Mad Professor (IRE)**13 [694] 10-9-9 **72** oh5..........(b) JoeCornwall(5) 59
(John Cornwall) *hld up: bhd fr 6th* **12/1**
5/3- **8** *12* **Daneva (IRE)**15 [674] 9-11-12 **98**..........(tp) CharliePoste 75
(Matt Sheppard) *chsd ldrs tl wknd after 9th: t.o* **12/1**
6PP/ **P** **Chapel House**107 [4639] 10-11-3 **94**.......... BenPoste(5)
(Richard Harper) *hld up: blnd 9th: sn t.o: p.u bef next* **14/1**
6UP/ **F** **Lord Wheathill**48 6-10-2 **74**.......... SamJones
(Lisa Williamson) *fell 2nd* **50/1**

4m 0.9s (-13.10) **Going Correction** -0.70s/f (Firm) **10 Ran SP% 113.1**
Speed ratings: **102,98,97,96,95 88,88,82, ,**
toteswingers 1&2 £20.20, 1&3 £11.70, 2&3 £3.20 CSF £152.23 CT £372.19 TOTE £33.30: £6.70, £1.30, £1.30; EX 154.60 Trifecta £530.30 Part won. Pool: £707.10 - 0.36 winning units..
Owner The Wenlock Edge Optimists **Bred** Plantation Stud **Trained** Harton, Shropshire

FOCUS
A weak handicap and suspect form. The third-last was omitted

808 YOUR FAVOURITE RACING BETS AT TOTEPOOL.COM CONDITIONAL JOCKEYS' MAIDEN HURDLE (8 hdls) 2m
3:20 (3:20) (Class 4) 4-Y-0+ **£3,119** (£915; £457; £228)

Form RPR
P/3- **1** **Thunder Sheik (IRE)**18 [631] 5-10-6 112..........(t) ConorShoemark(6) 112+
(Fergal O'Brien) *chsd ldrs: pushed along after 5th: rdn to chse ldr last: styd on u.p to ld fnl 100yds: sn clr* **3/1**1
/22- **2** *4* **Engai (GER)**21 [605] 7-10-4 105.......... JakeHodson(8) 110+
(David Bridgwater) *hld up: hdwy after 3rd: chsd ldr 3 out: led 2 out: hung rt bef last: sn rdn: hdd and no ex fnl 100yds* **10/3**2
360/ **3** *4 1/2* **Orthodox Lad**240 [5193] 5-10-6 0.......... ChristopherWard(6) 104
(Dr Richard Newland) *unruly leaving the paddock: hld up: hdwy appr 3 out: styd on to go 3rd towards fin: nt trble ldrs* **17/2**
44/ **4** *2 1/4* **Hyperlink (IRE)**56 [8] 4-10-6 0.......... JackQuinlan(3) 100
(John Ferguson) *chsd ldr tl led 3rd: hdd and mstke 2 out: wknd flat* **6/1**
066/ **5** *24* **Quadriller (FR)**220 [2441] 6-10-9 0.......... JamesBest(3) 80
(Philip Hobbs) *prom: rdn appr 3 out: wknd bef next: t.o* **5/1**3
30/ **6** *27* **Zafaraban (IRE)**54 [2470] 6-10-12 0.......... GavinSheehan 56
(Tony Carroll) *hld up: nt fluent: a in rr: bhd whn mstke 3rd: t.o* **20/1**
/40- **7** *1 1/2* **Sid**26 [517] 5-10-7 0.......... GaryDerwin(5) 55
(Mark Gillard) *mid-div: pushed along after 3rd: rdn and wknd after 5th: t.o* **100/1**
503/ **8** *shd* **Rifle Shot (IRE)**110 [4579] 6-10-9 113.......... HenryBrooke(3) 55
(Donald McCain) *chsd ldrs tl wknd after 3rd: t.o* **10/1**
3/3- **9** *1* **Staigue Fort**26 [517] 5-10-12 113.......... TomCannon 54
(Emma Lavelle) *hld up: pushed along 4th: wknd after next: t.o* **9/1**
00/ **10** *11* **Di'Philly's Dream**60 [5511] 5-10-5 0.......... RobertWilliams 37
(Lisa Day) *hld up: blnd 4th: sn t.o* **100/1**
2/0- **11** *4 1/2* **Lord Gale (IRE)**21 [604] 7-10-12 115..........(v) HarryChalloner 40
(John Bryan Groucott) *led to 3rd: rdn and wknd after 5th: t.o* **33/1**
F **Force To Spend**541 6-10-5 0.......... GilesHawkins
(Lisa Day) *fell 1st* **100/1**

3m 39.2s (-8.10) **Going Correction** -0.375s/f (Good)
WFA 4 from 5yo+ 17lb **12 Ran SP% 119.3**
Speed ratings (Par 105): **105,103,100,99,87 74,73,73,72,67 65,**
toteswingers 1&2 £2.20, 1&3 £11.70, 2&3 £11.60 CSF £13.10 TOTE £6.20: £2.00, £2.20, £3.20; EX 16.70 Trifecta £71.50 Pool: £627.35 - 6.58 winning units..
Owner R J Rexton **Bred** Janus Bloodstock Inc **Trained** Coln St. Dennis, Gloucs

FOCUS
A modest maiden, confined to conditional riders.

809 PROGRESSIVE CASINO JACKPOTS AT TOTEPOOL.COM NOVICES' H'CAP HURDLE (DIV I) (8 hdls) 2m
3:50 (3:50) (Class 5) (0-95,95) 4-Y-0+ **£1,949** (£572; £286; £143)

Form RPR
000/ **1** **Emerald Glade (IRE)**80 [5142] 6-10-11 **80**.......... APMcCoy 92+
(Jim Best) *trckd ldrs: racd keenly: ev ch fr 3 out: hung lft and led appr last: sn hung rt: drvn out* **9/4**1
0/0- **2** *2 1/4* **Anton Dolin (IRE)**32 [436] 5-11-4 **87**..........(p) SamTwiston-Davies 96
(Dr Richard Newland) *chsd ldr tl led appr 3 out: hdd and nt clr run appr last: swtchd rt: styd on same pce flat* **5/1**3
/00- **3** *11* **Henry Hurst (IRE)**17 [650] 7-11-12 **95**.......... AndrewThornton 94
(Jimmy Fox) *chsd ldrs: rdn appr 3 out: hung lft and wknd bef last* **22/1**
00P/ **4** *3 3/4* **Emeebee**99 [4794] 7-11-2 **85**..........(t) DenisO'Regan 81
(Willie Musson) *hld up: hdwy and mstke 3 out: nt clr run and swtchd rt appr last: sn wknd* **12/1**
/04- **5** *13* **Scorer (IRE)**17 [640] 5-10-0 **69**..........(tp) RichieMcLernon 52
(Jonjo O'Neill) *hld up: hdwy 4th: rdn and wknd appr 3 out: t.o* **11/4**2
606- **6** *2 1/4* **Naledi**17 [648] 9-10-0 **74**.......... ThomasGarner(5) 55
(Richard Price) *hld up: hdwy 3rd: rdn after 5th: wknd bef next: t.o* **8/1**
0/4- **7** *7* **Comedy House**39 [307] 5-11-11 **94**.......... MarcGoldstein 69
(Michael Madgwick) *hld up: rdn and wknd appr 3 out: t.o* **20/1**
/06- **8** *2 1/4* **Camera Shy (IRE)**17 [651] 9-10-0 **72**..........(p) AdamWedge(3) 45
(Kevin Morgan) *chsd ldrs tl rdn and wknd appr 3 out* **20/1**
FP0/ **9** *nk* **Newmans Boy**68 [5337] 6-10-0 **72** oh1 ow3.......... MichaelByrne(3) 45
(Neil Mulholland) *led: rdn and hdd appr 3 out: sn wknd: t.o* **20/1**
300/ **10** *nse* **The Absent Mare**57 [5567] 5-11-7 **90**.......... CharliePoste 63
(Robin Dickin) *hld up: a in rr: t.o whn hmpd last* **25/1**
300- **11** *24* **Turn The Tide**10 [729] 5-10-0 **76**.......... MrKevinJones(7) 27
(Natalie Lloyd-Beavis) *hld up: a in rr: t.o* **33/1**

3m 40.8s (-6.50) **Going Correction** -0.375s/f (Good) **11 Ran SP% 118.3**
Speed ratings (Par 103): **101,99,94,92,86 84,81,80,80,80 68**
toteswingers 1&2 £3.70, 1&3 £8.50, 2&3 £27.20 CSF £12.35 CT £198.70 TOTE £2.80: £1.30, £2.40, £6.80; EX 17.20 Trifecta £185.50 Pool: £1,358.09 - 5.48 winning units..
Owner Emerald Glade Partnership **Bred** J T And Mrs Thomas **Trained** Lewes, E Sussex

FOCUS
A moderate handicap.

810 PROGRESSIVE CASINO JACKPOTS AT TOTEPOOL.COM NOVICES' H'CAP HURDLE (DIV II) (8 hdls) 2m
4:20 (4:20) (Class 5) (0-95,94) 4-Y-0+ **£1,949** (£572; £286; £143)

Form RPR
0/P- **1** **Pour Changer (FR)**34 [407] 8-11-3 **85**.......... LeightonAspell 88+
(Stephen Hughes) *hld up: mstke 4th: hdwy 3 out: led flat: rdn out* **7/1**

0/0- **2** *2* **Ashcott Boy**[36] 368 5-11-12 **94** NoelFehily 94
(Neil Mulholland) *hld up: hdwy appr 3 out: rdn after next: styd on u.p flat* **10/1**
2/1- **3** *3 ¾* **Windpfeil (IRE)**[25] 540 7-11-9 **91** (p) MarkGrant 88
(Dominic Ffrench Davis) *hld up: pushed along and hdwy 3 out: swtchd rt bef next: styd on u.p to go 3rd post: nt rch ldrs* **7/2**[1]
000/ **4** *hd* **Missionaire (USA)**[12] 4372 6-11-7 **89** LeeEdwards 87
(Tony Carroll) *chsd ldrs: led 3 out: rdn and mstke last: hdd and no ex flat* **6/1**[3]
0/0- **5** *10* **Lulu's Gift (IRE)**[9] 376 7-9-11 **68** oh1 BrianToomey(3) 59
(Michael Mullineaux) *chsd ldrs: rdn appr 3 out: wknd last* **16/1**
0/6- **6** *nk* **Si Bien (FR)**[18] 631 8-10-11 **84** CharlieWallis(5) 72
(Nick Ayliffe) *chsd ldr: ev ch 3 out: wknd after next* **16/1**
6/6- **7** *17* **Duneen Dream (USA)**[38] 333 8-10-2 **73** (t) RobertDunne(3) 45
(Nikki Evans) *led: rdn and hdd 3 out: wknd next: t.o* **16/1**
00P/ **8** *6* **Bombel (IRE)**[288] 1519 5-10-2 **70** PaulMoloney 37
(Evan Williams) *hld up: rdn appr 3 out: sn wknd: t.o* **15/2**
5/6- **9** *24* **Calypso Star (IRE)**[45] 186 6-9-12 **69** (bt) MarkQuinlan(3) 14
(Nigel Hawke) *chsd ldrs: rdn and wkng whn blnd 2 out: t.o* **6/1**[3]
0/P- **10** *30* **No Compromise**[42] 243 4-10-8 **79** RichardJohnson
(Richard Phillips) *hld up: rdn and wknd after 5th: t.o* **5/1**[2]

3m 44.1s (-3.20) **Going Correction** -0.375s/f (Good)
WFA 4 from 5yo+ 17lb **10** Ran SP% **118.5**
Speed ratings (Par 103): **93,92,90,90,85 84,76,73,61,46**
toteswingers 1&2 £9.70, 1&3 £6.20, 2&3 £10.00 CSF £75.07 CT £289.34 TOTE £7.60: £1.70, £2.70, £2.00; EX 90.10 Trifecta £702.70 Part won. Pool: £937.00 - 0.84 winning units..
Owner S A Hughes **Bred** Haras D'Ecouves **Trained** Gilfach Goch, Rhondda C Taff
FOCUS
An ordinary handicap.

811 KING SIZE POOLS AT TOTEPOOL.COM MARES' H'CAP HURDLE (12 hdls) 2m 7f
4:50 (4:50) (Class 4) (0-120,117) 4-Y-0+ **£3,119** (£915; £457; £228)

Form RPR
423- **1** **Emerald Rose**[28] 502 6-11-0 **105** SamTwiston-Davies 110
(Julian Smith) *a.p: rdn appr last: swtchd lft flat: styd on u.p to ld nr fin* **9/1**
0/1- **2** *nk* **Western Kate (IRE)**[18] 637 6-10-5 **101** GavinSheehan(5) 105
(John Flint) *hld up: hdwy after 6th: led 2 out: rdn appr last: hdd nr fin* **18/1**
6/1- **3** *7* **Thornton Alice**[53] 68 8-10-9 **100** WayneHutchinson 100
(Richard Phillips) *chsd ldr: led after 3 out: hdd next: rdn and blnd last: no ex* **12/1**
/43- **4** *12* **On The Off Chance**[33] 423 5-10-9 **100** (b) APMcCoy 90+
(Jonjo O'Neill) *prom: led 5th: blnd 3 out: sn hdd: wknd appr last* **3/1**[1]
5/5- **5** *nk* **Aegean Destiny**[33] 421 6-10-6 **97** DonalDevereux 84
(John Mackie) *hld up: hdwy and mstke 8th: wknd 3 out* **20/1**
4/4- **6** *1 ¼* **Russie With Love**[36] 379 7-10-13 **107** GilesHawkins(3) 93
(Chris Down) *hld up: hdwy 8th: rdn appr 3 out: wknd bef next* **12/1**
/66- **7** *1* **Munlochy Bay**[12] 719 9-10-3 **94** (p) CharliePoste 79
(Matt Sheppard) *hld up: mstke 4th: rdn after 9th: wknd 3 out* **25/1**
/44- **8** *13* **Little Carmela**[30] 460 9-10-3 **97** JamesBest(3) 70
(Violet M Jordan) *hld up: pushed along after 3rd: in rr fr 7th: t.o* **11/1**
P6/- **9** *34* **Coronea Lilly (IRE)**[67] 5354 9-11-4 **112** (t) MichaelByrne(3) 55
(Neil Mulholland) *prom: mstke 3rd: lost pl next: hdwy 9th: sn rdn: wknd 3 out: t.o* **5/1**[2]
3/1- **10** *7* **Emily's Flyer (IRE)**[54] 41 6-10-11 **109** (t) ConorShoemark(7) 45
(Fergal O'Brien) *led to 5th: nt fluent next: sn pushed along: rdn and wknd appr 3 out: t.o* **10/1**
2/3- **11** *68* **Kindly Note**[36] 379 6-11-10 **115** RichardJohnson
(Emma Lavelle) *chsd ldrs tl rdn and wknd after 8th: t.o* **15/2**[3]
500/ **P** **Santera (IRE)**[361] 841 9-11-12 **117** JamieMoore
(John Spearing) *prom: mstke and wknd 9th: t.o whn p.u bef next* **40/1**
2P0- **P** **Grimley Girl**[12] 717 7-10-9 **100** WillKennedy
(Sarah-Jayne Davies) *hld up: mstke 5th: in rr fr 8th: t.o whn p.u bef 2 out* **20/1**

5m 32.7s (4.70) **Going Correction** -0.375s/f (Good) **13** Ran SP% **117.3**
Speed ratings (Par 105): **76,75,73,69,69 68,68,63,52,49 25, ,**
toteswingers 1&2 £20.30, 1&3 £19.60, 2&3 £22.60 CSF £143.50 CT £1947.42 TOTE £7.30: £2.00, £5.00, £4.30; EX 108.90 Trifecta £873.30 Part won. Pool: £1,164.51 - 0.46 winning units..

Owner Grand Jury Partnership **Bred** Grand Jury Partnership **Trained** Tirley, Gloucs
■ Stewards' Enquiry : Sam Twiston-Davies two-day ban: use of whip (7-8 July)
FOCUS
A moderate mares' contest that produced a tight finish. The second and third had both won races on their previous outing after the clear leader had come down at the last.

812 VIRTUAL RACING EVERY DAY AT TOTEPOOL.COM H'CAP HURDLE (8 hdls) 2m
5:20 (5:20) (Class 4) (0-120,121) 4-Y-0+ **£3,119** (£915; £457; £228)

Form RPR
/11- **1** **Sea Lord (IRE)**[32] 427 6-11-11 **119** DenisO'Regan 131+
(John Ferguson) *chsd ldr tl led appr 3rd: hdd 3 out: swtchd lft bef next: led again last: rdn clr flat: eased nr fin* **2/1**[1]
111- **2** *7* **Man Of Leisure**[12] 719 9-11-10 **121** (t) RachaelGreen(3) 125+
(Anthony Honeyball) *a.p: racd keenly: chsd wnr and j.rt 4th: mstke next: led 3 out: rdn and hdd whn mstke last: styd on same pce flat* **4/1**[2]
151- **3** *2 ¼* **Super Collider**[17] 648 6-11-6 **114** (bt) AlainCawley 115
(Fergal O'Brien) *a.p: rdn appr 3 out: styd on same pce fr next* **10/1**
/12- **4** *1 ¾* **Acapulco Bay**[28] 505 9-10-2 **101** (p) RobertWilliams(5) 100
(Dai Burchell) *hld up: hdwy 5th: rdn appr 3 out: nt trble ldrs* **12/1**
6/5- **5** *1 ½* **Faith Jicaro (IRE)**[12] 505 6-10-12 **106** DPFahy 104
(Andy Hobbs) *chsd ldrs: hmpd 4th: outpcd after next: styd on flat* **25/1**
006/ **6** *2 ¼* **Taroum (IRE)**[101] 4764 6-10-1 **95** LeeEdwards 91
(Tony Carroll) *hld up: hdwy appr 3 out: wknd next* **25/1**
6/1- **7** *nse* **Maoi Chinn Tire (IRE)**[28] 505 6-11-4 **119** ConorRing(7) 115
(Jennie Candlish) *hld up: rdn appr 3 out: nvr on terms* **16/1**
5/4- **8** *½* **Hired Hand (IRE)**[28] 488 7-11-2 **110** (t) APMcCoy 105
(Jonjo O'Neill) *hld up: hdwy appr 3 out: sn lost pl: no ch whn mstke last* **11/2**[3]
1PP/ **9** *2 ¾* **West Brit (IRE)**[44] 1661 5-11-12 **120** (t) NoelFehily 113
(Charlie Longsdon) *led to appr 3rd: chsd ldrs: rdn bef 3 out: hung lft and wknd bef next* **7/1**
120/ **10** *11* **Dropzone (USA)**[58] 5537 4-11-3 **114** RichardJohnson 94
(Richard Lee) *prom: drvn along 5th: wknd bef next* **33/1**
0F0/ **11** *nse* **Easydoesit (IRE)**[26] 4494 5-10-9 **103** SamTwiston-Davies 86
(Tony Carroll) *mid-div: effrt and nt clr run after 5th: rdn and wknd befoe next* **33/1**
015/ **12** *17* **Nicks Power (IRE)**[397] 396 7-11-1 **109** CharliePoste 77
(Robin Dickin) *hld up: a in rr: bhd fr 5th: t.o* **33/1**
13 *81* **Seaside Shuffle (IRE)**[390] 480 8-10-8 **102** PaulMoloney
(Sophie Leech) *prom: racd keenly: nt fluent 1st and 3rd: wknd next: t.o* **66/1**

3m 41.2s (-6.10) **Going Correction** -0.375s/f (Good)
WFA 4 from 5yo+ 17lb **13** Ran SP% **121.9**
Speed ratings (Par 105): **100,96,95,94,93 92,92,92,90,85 85,76,36**
toteswingers 1&2 £4.20, 1&3 £6.60, 2&3 £9.90 CSF £9.97 CT £67.41 TOTE £2.90: £1.10, £2.10, £2.90; EX 11.60 Trifecta £66.40 Pool: £931.67 - 10.51 winning units..
Owner Bloomfields **Bred** Darley **Trained** Cowlinge, Suffolk
FOCUS
This looked a fair handicap, but few landed a blow.
T/Plt: £38.90 to a £1 stake. Pool: £99,069.75 - 1,858.07 winning units T/Qpdt: £8.70 to a £1 stake. Pool: £5,543.88 - 468.15 winning units CR

813 - 827a (Foreign Racing) - See Raceform Interactive

[686]NEWTON ABBOT (L-H)
Tuesday, June 25

OFFICIAL GOING: Good (good to firm in places)
Wind: mild breeze against Weather: cloudy

828 TRITON GALLERIES MAIDEN HURDLE (10 hdls) 2m 6f
6:00 (6:00) (Class 5) 4-Y-0+ **£2,463** (£718; £359)

Form RPR
4/ **1** **Benefits Well (IRE)**[70] 5333 6-10-9 0 EDLinehan(5) 112
(Brendan Powell) *in tch: rdn to chal after 3 out: led bef next: kpt on: hld on: drvn out* **16/1**
2 *nk* **Kilbree Kid (IRE)**[65] 6-11-0 0 PaddyBrennan 112
(Tom George) *in tch: rdn in clly disp 3rd after 3 out: chsd wnr next: kpt on wl fr last* **4/1**[2]
3 *15* **General Barton (IRE)**[39] 360 7-11-0 0 (p) APMcCoy 98
(Paul W Flynn, Ire) *trckd ldr: nt a fluent: rdn to chal briefly after 3 out: where sn squeezed up: sn btn* **7/2**[1]
0/2- **4** *hd* **Lady Lectra**[28] 519 4-10-3 0 DPFahy 89
(John Flint) *j.lft at times: led: rdn after 3 out: hdd bef next: fading whn mstke 2 out* **7/2**[1]
640- **5** *8* **La Madonnina (IRE)**[14] 708 5-10-7 90 TomO'Brien 84
(Caroline Keevil) *mid-div: pushed along after 5th: hdwy whn rdn after next: styd on wout ever threatening to rch ldrs* **16/1**
/20- **6** *11* **Twyford**[19] 651 6-11-0 98 IanPopham 83
(William Reed) *hld up towards rr: hdwy 4th: rdn after 3 out: wknd bef next* **17/2**
606- **7** *4 ½* **Abbi Jicaro**[15] 686 6-10-7 73 (vt[1]) AndrewGlassonbury 70
(Mark Shears) *hld up towards rr: sme prog after 3 out: wknd bef next* **50/1**
/3F- **8** *13* **Special Boru (IRE)**[18] 661 7-11-0 72 (t) BrendanPowell 65
(Sarah Kerswell) *hld up towards rr: hdwy appr 7th: rdn after 3 out: wknd next: t.o* **28/1**
43- **9** *1 ¾* **Mr Trilby (IRE)**[30] 499 6-10-4 0 (bt) MrSWelton(10) 64
(David Pipe) *mid-div: struggling bef 7th: sn wknd: t.o* **8/1**[3]
10 *15* **Sedgemoor Top Bid (IRE)**[87] 5-10-11 0 (p) MarkQuinlan(3) 50
(Nigel Hawke) *chsd ldrs: rdn 7th: wknd next: t.o* **40/1**
6/ **11** *8* **Rumpleteazer (IRE)**[233] 2218 5-11-0 0 RichardJohnson 43
(Nick Williams) *mid-div tl rdn and wknd after 7th: t.o* **9/1**
0P/ **12** *nk* **Parkham Gent (IRE)**[325] 1179 6-11-0 0 (b[1]) DougieCostello 43
(Laura Young) *mid-div: nt fluent 2nd: bhd fr 6th: t.o* **66/1**
0/0- **13** *2* **Revupclover (IRE)**[14] 716 6-11-0 0 AndrewThornton 41
(Polly Gundry) *mid-div early: towards rr 4th: t.o 7th* **100/1**
P **An Fear Glic (IRE)**[41] 10-11-0 0 (t) WayneHutchinson
(Jo Davis) *a towards rr: t.o whn p.u bef 2 out* **40/1**
0- **U** **Vic's Moll (IRE)**[14] 717 7-10-2 0 ow2 (p) MrWPotter(7)
(Polly Gundry) *racd wd: chsd ldr tl 6th: sn wl t.o: mstke and uns rdr 3 out* **80/1**
P- **P** **Dartbridge (IRE)**[20] 633 7-10-7 0 TommyPhelan
(Mark Gillard) *mid-div tl rdn after 6th: sn wknd: t.o whn p.u after 3 out* **100/1**

5m 15.6s (-4.60) **Going Correction** -0.45s/f (Good)
WFA 4 from 5yo+ 18lb **16** Ran SP% **122.8**
Speed ratings (Par 103): **90,89,84,84,81 77,75,71,70,65 62,61,61, ,**
toteswingers 1&2 £15.30, 2&3 £5.80, 1&3 £19.20 CSF £79.04 TOTE £17.70: £3.70, £1.80, £2.00; EX 101.50 Trifecta £467.00 Pool: £1363.38 - 2.18 winning units..
Owner B G Powell **Bred** John Hayes **Trained** Upper Lambourn, Berks
FOCUS
Probably just an ordinary maiden hurdle. The fourth looks the best guide.

829 DAVE CHILLERY DIVORCE CELEBRATION (S) H'CAP HURDLE (10 hdls) 2m 6f
6:30 (6:31) (Class 5) (0-95,95) 4-Y-0+ **£2,463** (£718; £359)

Form RPR
523- **1** **Green Lightning (IRE)**[15] 686 6-10-9 **83** (b) MrTWeston(5) 102+
(Martin Weston) *mid-div: hdwy after 6th: chal gng strly 3 out: led on bit bef next: sn eased clr* **7/2**[1]
/05- **2** *15* **Theoystercatcher (IRE)**[27] 543 7-11-4 **87** RichardJohnson 91
(Tim Vaughan) *hld up towards rr: hdwy after 6th: chal 3 out: sn rdn: chsd wnr bef next: styd on same pce* **16/1**
0/4- **3** *8* **Sovereign Spirit (IRE)**[47] 178 11-11-4 **87** (tp) TomCannon 83
(Michael Blake) *prom: led 7th: sn drvn: hdd bef 2 out: sn hld: kpt on same pce* **9/2**[2]
P00- **4** *¾* **Jewellery (IRE)**[6] 765 6-11-3 **86** (v) JamieMoore 80
(Kevin Bishop) *in tch: pushed along after 4th: rdn and lost pl after 6th: no ch fr 3 out: styd on fr next but nvr any danger* **9/1**
/35- **5** *1 ¼* **Freddy's Star (IRE)**[34] 429 11-11-2 **90** CharlieWallis(5) 83
(Martin Hill) *hld up towards rr: rdn and stdy hdwy after 7th: styd on fr 2 out: nvr threatened ldrs* **10/1**
0/5- **6** *10* **Boomtown Kat**[42] 295 9-11-12 **95** (v[1]) AndrewThornton 79
(Karen George) *in tch: rdn after 7th: wknd after next* **16/1**
/35- **7** *3 ¼* **Whatsabillion (IRE)**[10] 750 11-11-7 **90** (tp) APMcCoy 71
(Anabel K Murphy) *hld up towards rr: hdwy after 4th to trck ldrs: effrt 7th: wknd sn after next* **10/1**
3U0- **8** *1 ¼* **Portmeade**[15] 690 11-10-3 **79** JonPark(7) 59
(Elizabeth Scott) *towards rr of mid-div: reminders after 4th: rdn after 6th: nvr any danger* **50/1**

/60- **9** ½ **Iheardu**[17] 669 7-11-1 **84**......(tp) NoelFehily 64
(Neil Mulholland) *mid-div: rdn bef 7th: wnt 4th but wl hld after 3 out tl wknd after 3 out* **10/1**

/60- **10** ¾ **Mangonel**[19] 650 9-11-7 **90**......(v) DarylJacob 69
(Jo Davis) *chsd ldrs: rdn to chal briefly 7th: wknd sn after next* **33/1**

0U- **11** nk **Patricktom Boru (IRE)**[20] 637 6-11-7 **90**...... DougieCostello 69
(Laura Young) *hld up towards rr: hdwy after 4th: trckd ldrs 6th: rdn after 7th: wknd after 3 out* **25/1**

/30- **12** 1½ **Majestic Bull (USA)**[19] 640 7-10-13 **87**...... MissLucyGardner(5) 64
(Sue Gardner) *nudged along after 6th: a towards rr: dismntd after fin* **20/1**

/65- **13** 16 **Hugo Drax (IRE)**[15] 686 6-10-11 **80**......(bt[1]) ConorO'Farrell 43
(David Pipe) *mid-div: struggling 7th: sn wknd: t.o* **14/1**

650/ **14** 16 **Downward Spiral (IRE)**[125] 4326 8-11-9 **92**......(b) RhysFlint 40
(John Flint) *led tl 7th: sn rdn: wknd after 3 out: t.o* **8/1**[3]

/60- **15** 1½ **Wild Tonto (IRE)**[42] 289 10-11-12 **95**...... SamTwiston-Davies 42
(Nigel Twiston-Davies) *mid-div: rdn after 7th: blnd bdly next: sn wknd: t.o* **22/1**

0/0- **16** ½ **Hadron Collider (FR)**[19] 650 8-11-2 **90**......(p) BenPoste(5) 37
(Chris Nenadich) *mid-div: rdn after 6th: sn btn: t.o* **50/1**

0/P- **17** 2¾ **Comical Red**[36] 407 5-10-13 **82**...... TommyPhelan 26
(Mark Gillard) *mid-div: mstke 3rd: rdn after 6th: bhd fr after next: t.o* **50/1**

5m 14.6s (-5.60) **Going Correction** -0.45s/f (Good) **17** Ran SP% **129.0**
Speed ratings (Par 103): **92,86,83,83,82 79,78,77,77,77 77,76,70,64,64 64,63**
toteswingers 1&2 £20.70, 2&3 £42.40, 1&3 £4.30 CSF £58.37 CT £267.97 TOTE £4.30: £1.40, £3.70, £2.50, £3.60; EX 76.30 Trifecta £360.80 Part won. Pool: £481.08 - 0.12 winning units..The winner was bought by P Bowen 7,400gns.
Owner M H Weston **Bred** Western Bloodstock **Trained** Hindlip, Worcs

FOCUS
A poor race, but a sizeable gamble landed. The easy winner was up a stone+ for the longer trip and the second was close to his mark.

830 LIMERICK RACECOURSE NOVICES' CHASE (13 fncs) 2m 110y
7:05 (7:05) (Class 3) 5-Y-0+ **£7,596** (£2,244; £1,122; £561; £280)

Form RPR

/B0- **1** **Changing The Guard**[17] 673 7-10-12 0......(t) SamTwiston-Davies 131+
(Dr Richard Newland) *j. sltly rt at times: racd keenly: led 4th: rdn after 3 out: in command after 2 out: kpt on wl* **7/1**[3]

/01- **2** 7 **Baby Mix (FR)**[20] 634 5-11-4 0...... NoelFehily 131+
(Tom George) *led tl 4th: pressed wnr: nudged along 4 out: stl upsides and ev ch whn mstke 2 out: hld after* **5/4**[2]

/51- **3** 7 **Kian's Delight**[23] 594 5-11-4 135...... TomO'Brien 123
(Peter Bowen) *pressed ldr tl 4th: chsd ldng pair: outpcd after 7th: nvr able to get bk on terms: kpt on same pce fr 3 out* **11/10**[1]

0/6- **4** 13 **Redlynch Rock (IRE)**[20] 634 5-10-12 0......(t) AndrewGlassonbury 103
(Bob Buckler) *hld up in last: j.rt at times: wnt 4th after 7th but nvr gng pce to get involved* **66/1**

/16- **5** 5 **Dark Energy**[30] 488 9-10-12 0......(t) AlainCawley 98
(Fergal O'Brien) *racd keenly early: trckd ldrs tl outpcd after 7th: no ch fr next* **18/1**

0/0- **6** 16 **Onedin Line**[38] 376 5-10-12 0...... AidanColeman 87
(Venetia Williams) *hld up in last pair: mstke 6th: outpcd after next: no ch fr 8th: t.o* **50/1**

3m 58.1s (-8.40) **Going Correction** -0.075s/f (Good) **6** Ran SP% **113.3**
Speed ratings: **116,112,109,103,100 93**
toteswingers 1&2 £3.40, 2&3 £1.02, 1&3 £2.60 CSF £17.41 TOTE £10.70: £4.40, £1.30; EX 17.80 Trifecta £25.90 Pool: £1226.77 - 35.39 winning units..
Owner BetterTipster.co.uk **Bred** R A Bonnycastle And Marston Stud **Trained** Claines, Worcs

FOCUS
A decent novice event for the time of year. The winner is the type to keep finding and rate higher.

831 BEAU BOUTIQUE H'CAP HURDLE (8 hdls) 2m 1f
7:35 (7:35) (Class 3) (0-140,133) 4-Y-0+ **£6,238** (£1,831; £915; £457)

Form RPR

3/1- **1** **Tzora**[47] 176 8-11-6 **127**...... HaddenFrost 136+
(Martin Hill) *hld up in last: tk clsr order gng to 3 out: chal 2 out: pushed into ld jst bef last: readily* **5/1**[2]

/12- **2** 2 **Sidney Melbourne (USA)**[17] 673 6-11-1 **122**......(b) DarylJacob 129
(Paul Nicholls) *led: awkward 1st: hdd 4th tl next: hdd 3 out: led bef next: rdn and hdd jst bef last: nt gng pce of wnr* **7/4**[1]

/14- **3** 9 **Taste The Wine (IRE)**[16] 480 7-9-13 **111**...... RobertWilliams(5) 110
(Bernard Llewellyn) *in tch: tk clsr order 3 out: sn rdn: kpt on into 3rd next but nt gng pce of front pair* **8/1**

114- **4** 1½ **Rime Avec Gentil (FR)**[7] 756 8-9-11 **111**...... ConorShoemark(7) 109
(Bernard Llewellyn) *in tch: tk clsr order 3 out: sn rdn: kpt on same pce fr next* **11/2**[3]

4/5- **5** 1 **Jolly Roger (IRE)**[11] 734 6-11-6 **127**...... LeeEdwards 124
(Tony Carroll) *hld up in tch: tk clsr order 3 out: sn rdn: disputing 3rd whn nt fluent 2 out: keeping on at same pce whn awkward last* **16/1**

/P6- **6** hd **Laudatory**[17] 673 7-10-12 **122**...... JeremiahMcGrath(3) 120
(Nicky Henderson) *trckd ldr: sltly hmpd 1st: led 4th tl next: sn rdn: kpt on same pce fr after 3 out* **6/1**

0/0- **7** 10 **Kylenoe Fairy (IRE)**[36] 409 9-10-10 **117**......(t) TomO'Brien 104
(Paul Henderson) *hld up in chsng gp: outpcd 3 out: nvr able to get bk on terms* **10/1**

02F- **8** 3¾ **Cry Of Freedom (USA)**[23] 594 7-11-9 **133**......(v) JackQuinlan(3) 116
(John Ferguson) *led in by handler to s: trckd ldr: hmpd 1st: shkn up to ld 3 out: sn rdn and hdd: fdd fr next* **12/1**

3m 54.0s (-11.70) **Going Correction** -0.45s/f (Good) **8** Ran SP% **116.5**
Speed ratings (Par 107): **109,108,103,103,102 102,97,96**
toteswingers 1&2 £1.30, 2&3 £5.70, 1&3 £11.10 CSF £14.96 CT £69.30 TOTE £5.60: £1.80, £1.40, £2.50; EX 12.70 Trifecta £69.10 Pool: £678.78 - 7.35 winning units..
Owner Tzora Partners **Bred** Milton Park Stud **Trained** Littlehempston, Devon

FOCUS
Not that deeply stocked for a 0-140, with only the top three in the weights rated within 17lb of the maximum permitted. Another big step forward from the winner.

832 NATASHA AND ROGER NISBIT WEDDING ANNIVERSARY H'CAP CHASE (16 fncs) 2m 5f 110y
8:10 (8:10) (Class 4) (0-115,110) 5-Y-0+ **£4,288** (£1,259; £629; £314)

Form RPR

/65- **1** **Next Oasis (IRE)**[20] 634 7-11-6 **104**...... TomO'Brien 118+
(Paul Henderson) *mid-div: trckd ldrs 9th: led 2 out: sn in command: readily* **5/1**[2]

F5/- **2** 5 **Font**[232] 2236 10-11-4 **102**......(t) AidanColeman 109
(Lawney Hill) *hld up but in tch: rdn after 4 out: styd on to go 2nd at the last: no ch w wnr* **10/1**

/05- **3** 2 **Lucy's Legend (IRE)**[20] 632 7-11-3 **101**......(tp) PaddyBrennan 106
(Paul Henderson) *in tch: trckd ldrs 10th: rdn after 4 out: ev ch 2 out: kpt on same pce* **8/1**

P/5- **4** 2 **Standing Ovation (IRE)**[19] 645 6-10-9 **93**......(t) ConorO'Farrell 96
(David Pipe) *t.k.h early: trckd ldr tl after 3rd: in tch: rdn after 4 out: styd on same pce fr next* **10/1**

333- **5** 1½ **Sound Stage**[20] 636 10-11-11 **109**......(p) IanPopham 112
(Caroline Keevil) *trckd ldrs: wnt 2nd after 3rd: rdn into narrow advantage after 4 out: hdd 2 out: kpt on same pce* **7/1**[3]

/41- **6** 1¼ **Wait No More (IRE)**[15] 689 8-11-7 **105**......(p) DougieCostello 105
(Neil Mulholland) *trckd ldrs: rdn after 4 out: kpt on same pce fr next* **5/1**[2]

P/ **7** ¾ **Whiskey And Red (IRE)**[47] 196 8-11-7 **110**......(t) GavinSheehan(5) 110
(Colin Bowe, Ire) *hld up in last but in tch: rdn after 3 out: nt gng pce to get involved* **4/1**[1]

13P/ **8** ¾ **Michigan Assassin (IRE)**[243] 2009 11-11-6 **104**......(p[1]) DonalDevereux 103
(Debra Hamer) *led tl narrowly hdd after 4 out: rdn and ev ch after 3 out tl sn after next: fdd* **14/1**

/10- **9** 14 **Le Grand Chene (FR)**[10] 749 7-10-12 **96**......(tp) PaulMoloney 89
(Sophie Leech) *nt a fluent: mid-div tl 8th: hdwy fr 11th: effrt after 4 out: hld whn mstke 2 out: wknd* **20/1**

5/6- **P** **Interpleader**[15] 692 8-9-11 **88**......(p) ConorShoemark(7)
(Bernard Llewellyn) *mid-div: pushed along fr 4th: awkward next: sddle slipped and sn p.u* **7/1**[3]

5m 19.1s (-2.30) **Going Correction** -0.075s/f (Good) **10** Ran SP% **119.1**
Speed ratings: **101,99,98,97,97 96,96,96,91,**
toteswingers 1&2 £18.20, 2&3 £9.80, 1&3 £9.30 CSF £54.45 CT £399.67 TOTE £4.60: £2.00, £2.90, £2.80; EX 64.00 Trifecta £376.70 Pool: £609.37 - 1.21 winning units..
Owner The Ray Of Hope Partnership **Bred** Barry O'Connor **Trained** Whitsbury, Hants

FOCUS
A moderate event, but one in which everything still held some sort of chance five out with barely six lengths covering them. A step up from the winner, with the second to the best of his recent form.

833 ST AUSTELL BREWERY LADY AMATEUR RIDERS' H'CAP HURDLE (9 hdls) 2m 3f
8:45 (8:45) (Class 4) (0-105,105) 4-Y-0+ **£3,369** (£1,044; £522; £261)

Form RPR

P/5- **1** **Detroit Red**[47] 178 7-10-1 **85**...... MissAliceMills(5) 100+
(Martin Hill) *trckd ldrs: shkn up to ld 2 out: r.o strly to draw clr: readily* **9/1**

1/2- **2** 7 **Sure Thing (FR)**[31] 482 7-11-9 **105**...... MissJCWilliams(3) 110
(Henry Daly) *trckd ldr: nt fluent 5th: led next: rdn and hdd 2 out: kpt on but nt gng pce of wnr* **9/2**[2]

/60- **3** 7 **Captain Sharpe**[11] 691 5-11-1 **101**......(b) MissBHampson(7) 100
(Bernard Llewellyn) *in tch: trckd ldrs 5th: rdn to chse ldng pair after 3 out: kpt on same pce* **16/1**

450/ **4** 10 **Himrayn**[451] 5170 10-10-3 **85**...... MissHannahWatson(3) 75
(Anabel K Murphy) *hld up towards rr: rdn and stdy prog after 3 out: styd on wl fr next: wnt 4th run-in* **33/1**

/10- **5** 1¼ **Bells Of Berlin**[31] 482 4-10-10 **100**......(vt) MissRPLeyshon(7) 85
(Tim Vaughan) *mid-div: hdwy after 5th: rdn after 3 out: styd on same pce* **10/1**

/00- **6** ½ **Tri Nations (UAE)**[15] 691 8-10-13 **95**......(bt) MissCBoxall(3) 83
(Anthony Middleton) *hld up towards rr: rdn and stdy hdwy after 3 out: styd on fr next: nt rch ldrs* **33/1**

604- **7** hd **Sedgemoor Express (IRE)**[15] 686 5-10-5 **89**(tp) MissJoannaMason(5) 78
(Nigel Hawke) *trckd ldrs: rdn after 3 out: 4th and hld next: blnd bdly last* **5/1**[3]

/63- **8** nk **First Morning (IRE)**[20] 635 8-11-0 **93**......(tp) MissLucyGardner 81
(Michael Blake) *hld up bhd wl off pce: styd on steadily whn rdn after 3 out: nvr able to get involved* **3/1**[1]

0/0- **9** 5 **Smart Catch (IRE)**[46] 202 7-11-6 **102**...... MissSallyRandell(3) 85
(Tony Carroll) *hld up towards rr: rdn into midfield sn after 3 out: styd on same pce fr next* **16/1**

/P0- **10** 9 **Dashing Doc (IRE)**[15] 691 6-11-8 **104**......(v[1]) MissLBrooke(3) 79
(Evan Williams) *mid-div: rdn after 3 out: wkng whn mstke 2 out* **12/1**

/66- **11** hd **The Sneezer (IRE)**[28] 520 10-11-6 **99**...... MrsAlexDunn 74
(Alexandra Dunn) *led tl 6th: wknd after 3 out* **20/1**

50P/ **12** dist **Milly Malone (IRE)**[51] 7-10-13 **97**......(t) MissHLewis(5) 36
(Adrian Wintle) *mid-div tl wknd appr 3 out: t.o* **16/1**

P/0- **P** **Holden Caulfield (IRE)**[28] 517 8-10-1 **85**...... MissLeandaTickle(5)
(Nick Ayliffe) *towards rr of midfield: rdn after 6th: wknd after 3 out: p.u bef next* **40/1**

6/P- **P** **Caught By Witness (IRE)**[42] 289 8-10-11 **95**......(tp) MissAEStirling(5)
(Anthony Middleton) *mid-div tl 6th: sn bhd: t.o whn p.u bef 2 out* **20/1**

0/5- **P** **Mighty Monty**[56] 37 8-11-2 **102**......(p) MissSJBerry(7)
(Victor Dartnall) *mid-div tl 6th: sn bhd: t.o whn p.u bef 2 out* **8/1**

4m 23.0s (-7.00) **Going Correction** -0.45s/f (Good)
WFA 4 from 5yo+ 17lb **15** Ran SP% **133.2**
Speed ratings (Par 105): **96,93,90,85,85 85,85,84,82,79 78,62, , ,**
toteswingers 1&2 £19.00, 2&3 £23.40, 1&3 £30.70 CSF £52.13 CT £679.60 TOTE £14.60: £3.60, £1.90, £5.50; EX 91.60 Trifecta £465.50 Part won. Pool: £620.77 - 0.10 winning units..
Owner Martin Hill **Bred** Martin Hill **Trained** Littlehempston, Devon

FOCUS
Another big field to round things off, but very few coped with the decent-looking pace. The winner was rated 110+ in 2010 and can probably win again.
T/Plt: £135.40 to a £1 stake. Pool of £99529.40 - 536.25 winning tickets. T/Qpdt: £45.10 to a £1 stake. Pool of £8389.54 - 137.50 winning tickets. TM

834 - 837a (Foreign Racing) - See Raceform Interactive

683
AUTEUIL (L-H)
Tuesday, June 25

OFFICIAL GOING: Turf: heavy

838a PRIX RIGOLETTO (CHASE) (LISTED RACE) (5YO+) (TURF) 2m 6f
1:35 (1:36) 5-Y-0+ **£44,878** (£22,439; £13,089; £8,882; £4,207)

RPR

1 **Le Bel Anjou (FR)**[16] 5-10-10 0...... KevinNabet 131
(F-M Cottin, France) **98/10**

2 nk **United Park (FR)**[22] 5-10-12 0...... JamesReveley 133
(G Macaire, France) **5/2**[1]

3 2 **Kipour'son (FR)**[22] 5-10-6 0......(p) AnthonyLecordier 125
(M Seror, France) **35/1**

4 ½ **Tiptop Ville (FR)**[12] 6-10-10 0...... AngeloGasnier 128
(L Viel, France) **25/1**

5 3 1/2 **Remember Rose (IRE)**[16] 684 10-10-10 0..............(p) BertrandBourez 125
(Y-M Porzier, France) 31/1
6 3/4 **Wetak (FR)**[16] 684 6-11-0 0.. DavidCottin 128
(F-M Cottin, France) 4/1[3]
7 8 **Princesse Kap (FR)**[16] 684 5-10-10 0......................(p) JonathanNattiez 116
(J-P Gallorini, France) 14/5[2]
8 2 1/2 **Grand Charly (FR)**[37] 403 6-11-7 0..........................(p) RegisSchmidlin 124
(T Civel, France) 15/1
9 1/2 **Rivaliste (FR)**[46] 8-10-10 0.. AlexisAcker 113
(M Rolland, France) 50/1
P **Cornas (NZ)**[65] 5447 11-10-8 0.. AlainDeChitray
(Nick Williams) *t.k.h early: racd in midfield: pckd 10th (water): shkn up and lost pl after 5 out: rdn fr 3 out: bhd whn p.u bef last* 64/1
P **Saga Mome (FR)**[93] 7-10-6 0.. MathieuCarroux
(L Viel, France) 57/1
P **Carlain (FR)**[33] 455 5-10-8 0..(p) SylvainDehez
(C Aubert, France) 31/1
F **Totem Flow (FR)**[37] 6-11-0 0.......................................(b) CyrilleGombeau
(G Cherel, France) 23/1
P **Teejay Flying (FR)**[16] 684 5-10-10 0...................... LudovicPhilipperon
(T Trapenard, France) 22/1

5m 38.43s (-5.57) **14** Ran SP% **117.0**
PARI-MUTUEL (all including 1 euro stakes): WIN 10.80; PLACE 3.10, 1.90, 5.90; DF 20.40; SF 76.10.
Owner Ecurie Centrale **Bred** G Vaillant **Trained** France

805 WORCESTER (L-H)
Wednesday, June 26

OFFICIAL GOING: Good to firm (good in places; 6.6)
Wind: Light behind Weather: Overcast

839 FOLLOW US ON TWITTER @WORCESTERRACES NOVICES' CHASE (18 fncs) 2m 7f
2:10 (2:10) (Class 4) 5-Y-0+ **£3,768** (£1,106; £553; £276)

Form RPR
/23- 1 **Buachaill Alainn (IRE)**[27] 553 6-10-12 134..................(v[1]) JamieMoore 134+
(Peter Bowen) *sn chsng ldrs: ev ch whn lft in ld last: rdn out* 5/2[1]
/33- 2 3 3/4 **Brassick**[20] 645 6-10-12 125...........................(tp) NoelFehily 132
(Charlie Longsdon) *chsd ldrs tl led 3rd: hdd 3 out: rdn and ev ch last: styd on same pce flat* 10/1
/F2- 3 12 **Pantxoa (FR)**[26] 562 6-10-12 119...................... WayneHutchinson 123
(Alan King) *hld up: hit 9th: hdwy 12th: rdn and wkng whn lft 3rd and hmpd last* 5/1[3]
/52- 4 17 **Special Account (IRE)**[20] 645 8-10-12 128.................... NickScholfield 105
(Jeremy Scott) *hld up and bhd: hdwy appr 4 out: sn wknd: t.o* 5/1[3]
2/0- 5 28 **Presenting Paddy (IRE)**[53] 121 5-10-9 0..................... JackQuinlan(3) 80
(Sarah Humphrey) *mid-div: rdn 13th: wknd appr 4 out: t.o* 50/1
/00- 6 2 **Akbabend**[19] 659 7-10-12 0.......................................(tp) TomCannon 78
(Chris Gordon) *chsd ldrs: mstke 8th: rdn and wknd 14th: t.o* 66/1
2- 7 17 **High Ron**[33] 459 8-10-12 0... AndrewThornton 63
(Caroline Bailey) *chsd ldrs tl rdn and wknd 14th: t.o* 40/1
4/0- F **Weekend Millionair (IRE)**[46] 215 6-10-12 0.............(tp) ConorO'Farrell 110+
(David Pipe) *hld up: hdwy 13th: disputing cl 3rd whn fell 3 out* 11/2
412/ F **Twirling Magnet (IRE)**[59] 18 7-11-5 125........................(b[1]) APMcCoy 139
(Jonjo O'Neill) *hld up in tch: chsd ldr 13th: led 3 out: jnd and fell last* 9/2[2]
P46/ P **Supralunary**[337] 1066 7-10-12 0.......................................(tp) LeeEdwards
(Robin Mathew) *led to 3rd: chsd ldrs tl hit 11th: sn wknd: t.o whn p.u bef 3 out* 250/1
P **The Irish Tig (IRE)**[396] 8-10-12 0........................... SamTwiston-Davies
(Graeme McPherson) *in rr: reminders 5th: pushed along thereafter: bhd fr 10th: t.o whn p.u bef 4 out* 125/1

5m 41.4s (-6.60) **Going Correction** -0.925s/f (Hard) **11** Ran SP% **111.6**
Speed ratings: **74,72,68,62,52 52,46, , ,**
Tote Swingers 1&2 £2.20, 2&3 £5.30, 1&3 £5.00 CSF £26.40 TOTE £3.80: £1.60, £2.20, £1.90; EX 31.90 Trifecta £188.90 Pool: £778.87 - 3.09 winning tickets..
Owner Roddy Owen & Paul Fullagar **Bred** T F Duggan **Trained** Little Newcastle, Pembrokes

FOCUS
All bends moved out 3yds from inner line. Fences sited 5yds from inside line. The ground was good to firm in the opinion of riders in the first, a decent novice chase which should produce winners. The winner is entitled to rate higher while the second is rated to his hurdles mark.

840 SUCKLING TRANSPORT H'CAP CHASE (12 fncs) 2m 110y
2:40 (2:40) (Class 3) (0-140,135) 5-Y-0+ **£6,330** (£1,870; £935; £468; £234)

Form RPR
4/3- 1 **Keki Buku (FR)**[45] 236 10-10-13 **122**.........................(t) RichardJohnson 136+
(Philip Hobbs) *hld up: hdwy 8th: chsd ldr 4 out: led next: j.lft last: drvn out* 10/3[2]
/14- 2 7 **Tindaro (FR)**[34] 447 6-11-8 **131**.. DenisO'Regan 140
(Paul Webber) *hld up and bhd: hdwy appr 4 out: chsd wnr 2 out: rdn flat: styd on same pce* 6/1
0U0/ 3 12 **Oceana Gold**[287] 1560 9-11-12 **135**.................................. AidanColeman 134
(Emma Lavelle) *led: hdd and mstke 3rd: nt fluent next: sn led again: hdd 6th: led after 9th: hdd whn blnd 3 out: wknd after next* 9/1
0/0- 4 12 **Trooper Clarence**[45] 249 9-11-0 **123**................................ PaulMoloney 112
(Evan Williams) *chsd ldrs tl rdn and wknd 4 out: t.o whn j.lft 2 out* 12/1
121- 5 19 **Alwaystheoptimist**[18] 674 10-11-5 **128**................. SamTwiston-Davies 96
(Phil Middleton) *w ldr tl led 3rd: hdd after next: led again 6th to 7th: rdn and wknd after 9th: t.o* 4/1[3]
/45- P **Temple Lord (FR)**[30] 508 7-10-9 **118**.................................(bt[1]) APMcCoy
(Jonjo O'Neill) *chsd ldrs: led 7th: hdd after 9th: disputing cl 3rd and pushed along whn blnd 4 out: sn p.u* 15/8[1]

3m 54.1s (-19.90) **Going Correction** -0.925s/f (Hard) **6** Ran SP% **109.8**
Speed ratings: **109,105,100,94,85**
Tote Swingers 1&2 £1.30, 2&3 £12.90, 1&3 £8.70 CSF £21.46 TOTE £4.00: £1.30, £2.00; EX 15.00 Trifecta £134.40 Pool: £1,253.31 - 6.99 winning tickets..
Owner Mrs Diana L Whateley **Bred** Ecurie Passing **Trained** Withycombe, Somerset

FOCUS
They went a decent clip in this good handicap, and the first two came from the rear. The time was quite quick and the form should prove solid, with the second rated to form.

841 NORMAN MACMILLAN CANCER RESEARCH ON FACEBOOK MARES' STANDARD OPEN NATIONAL HUNT FLAT RACE (DIV I) 2m
3:10 (3:10) (Class 6) 4-6-Y-0 **£1,559** (£457; £228; £114)

Form RPR
2- 1 **Handmaid**[39] 372 4-10-10 0.. JamieMoore 98+
(Peter Bowen) *chsd ldrs tl led over 3f out: pushed out* 5/4[1]
2- 2 4 **Dardanella**[15] 715 6-10-13 0.. DenisO'Regan 95
(Richard Lee) *a.p: pushed along over 5f out: rdn over 2f out: chsd wnr over 1f out: styd on same pce* 11/4[2]
1- 3 1 1/2 **Bugsy's Girl (IRE)**[45] 246 5-11-6 0...................................... APMcCoy 101+
(Jim Best) *hld up: hdwy over 4f out: rdn over 2f out: styd on same pce fnl f: wnt 3rd nr fin* 9/2[3]
4 1/2 **Miss Probus** 4-10-10 0.. DarylJacob 90
(Nick Williams) *a.p: led 4f out: sn hdd: rdn and hung lft over 1f out: no ex ins fnl f: lost 3rd nr fin* 10/1
60- 5 3/4 **Bad Girls (FR)**[15] 715 4-10-10 0...................................(t) ConorO'Farrell 89
(David Pipe) *hld up: hdwy over 3f out: rdn over 1f out: styd on* 16/1
0- 6 2 1/4 **Just Got Lucky**[15] 715 5-10-13 0...................................... AidanColeman 90
(Emma Lavelle) *chsd ldrs: rdn over 2f out: styd on same pce fr over 1f out* 14/1
- 7 2 3/4 **Annies Idea** 4-10-10 0... AdamPogson 84
(Mandy Rowland) *hld up: rdn over 2f out: nvr trbld ldrs* 100/1
00/ 8 14 **Spartaculous**[69] 5364 5-10-13 0.................................... AndrewThornton 73
(W De Best-Turner) *hld up: pushed along over 5f out: n.d* 100/1
P- 9 5 **Secret Island**[38] 389 4-10-5 0...................................... KillianMoore(5) 65
(Anthony Day) *set stdy pce tl qcknd over 5f out: hdd 4f out: wknd over 2f out: t.o* 200/1
0- 10 1 1/4 **Miss Dimples (IRE)**[39] 372 4-10-10 0.............................. WillKennedy 64
(Sarah-Jayne Davies) *chsd ldr: rdn over 4f out: wknd over 2f out: t.o* 50/1
5/ 11 29 **Kallina (IRE)**[215] 1990 5-10-13 0.................................... LiamTreadwell 38
(Liam Grassick) *hld up: a in rr: bhd fnl 5f: t.o* 66/1
P/ 12 51 **Ruby Haze**[76] 5262 6-10-13 0.. LeightonAspell
(Phillip Dando) *hld up: bhd fnl 5f: t.o* 66/1

3m 40.6s (-1.10) **Going Correction** -0.45s/f (Good)
WFA 4 from 5yo+ 3lb **12** Ran SP% **118.4**
Speed ratings: **84,82,81,81,80 79,78,71,68,68 53,28**
Tote Swingers 1&2 £1.50, 2&3 £3.10, 1&3 £1.10 CSF £4.62 TOTE £2.70: £1.10, £1.60, £1.10; EX 7.60 Trifecta £7.30 Pool: £1,203.67 - 123.01 winning tickets..
Owner Patrick Burling Developments Ltd **Bred** Patrick And Roslyn Burling **Trained** Little Newcastle, Pembrokes

FOCUS
Probably an above-average race of its type, but the time was slow compared with the second division and the form is rated around the first three.

842 NORMAN MACMILLAN CANCER RESEARCH ON FACEBOOK MARES' STANDARD OPEN NATIONAL HUNT FLAT RACE (DIV II) 2m
3:40 (3:40) (Class 6) 4-6-Y-0 **£1,559** (£457; £228; £114)

Form RPR
3- 1 **Pectora (IRE)**[26] 567 4-10-10 0....................................... LeightonAspell 101+
(Oliver Sherwood) *hld up: hdwy 1/2-way: chsd ldr over 5f out: led over 4f out: rdn and hung rt over 1f out: styd on wl: eased nr fin* 15/8[1]
2 2 1/4 **Dorkas** 4-10-10 0.. SamTwiston-Davies 98+
(J R Jenkins) *prom: lost pl over 6f out: hdwy over 3f out: rdn to chse wnr over 1f out: styd on* 14/1
3- 3 13 **Laurens Ruby (IRE)**[32] 483 4-10-10 0.................................... DPFahy 86
(John Flint) *plld hrd and prom: rdn and hung lft fr over 3f out: wknd over 1f out* 3/1[2]
4 9 **Truckers First** 5-10-13 0... RyanMahon 81
(Richard Phillips) *hld up: hdwy over 5f out: rdn and wknd over 2f out* 18/1
5 2 1/2 **Ilewindelilah** 5-10-6 0... JackSherwood(7) 79
(Gary Brown) *hld up: hdwy 5f out: rdn and wknd over 2f out* 66/1
6 2 1/2 **Ruby's From Milan (IRE)** 5-10-13 0.................... AndrewGlassonbury 77
(Mark Shears) *chsd ldrs tl lost pl and hmpd 7f out: rdn over 4f out: sn wknd* 40/1
7 3 3/4 **The Selector** 4-10-10 0.. TomCannon 70
(Chris Gordon) *prom: chsd ldr over 6f out tl over 5f out: rdn over 3f out: sn wknd: t.o* 33/1
8 6 **Florabury** 4-10-10 0... WillKennedy 65
(Sarah-Jayne Davies) *hld up: drvn along over 6f out: wknd 4f out: t.o* 20/1
9 2 3/4 **Steel A Look** 4-10-10 0...(t) PaddyBrennan 62
(Fergal O'Brien) *hld up: hdwy over 5f out: chsd wnr over 3f out tl wknd and eased over 1f out: t.o* 8/1
10 25 **Miss Treacle** 6-10-8 0.. RobertWilliams(5) 43
(Bernard Llewellyn) *chsd ldr 9f: wknd 6f out: t.o* 33/1
00/ 11 7 **Gilded Article (IRE)**[32] 5-10-13 0.. APMcCoy 37
(A J Martin, Ire) *led over 12f: wknd and eased over 3f out: t.o* 4/1[3]

3m 37.6s (-4.10) **Going Correction** -0.45s/f (Good)
WFA 4 from 5yo+ 3lb **11** Ran SP% **117.4**
Speed ratings: **92,90,84,79,78 77,75,72,71,58 55**
Tote Swingers 1&2 £6.10, 2&3 £3.90, 1&3 £2.90 CSF £29.12 TOTE £3.00: £1.60, £2.60, £1.50; EX 23.70 Trifecta £44.90 Pool: £666.56 - 11.13 winning tickets..
Owner David Redvers **Bred** Miss Elizabeth Kennedy **Trained** Upper Lambourn, Berks

FOCUS
Considerably less previous form to go on than in the first division, and it looked the weaker race on paper, but the time was three seconds quicker. The winner and third offer the best guides to the form.

843 ENJOY THREE EVENING MEETINGS IN JULY NOVICES' HURDLE (8 hdls) 2m
4:15 (4:15) (Class 4) 4-Y-0+ **£3,119** (£915; £457; £228)

Form RPR
13- 1 **Cool Macavity (IRE)**[40] 354 5-11-5 0................................. DavidBass 125+
(Nicky Henderson) *hld up: hdwy 3rd: led after 2 out: qcknd clr flat: easily* 2/1[2]
1/1- 2 9 **Bright Abbey**[8] 758 5-11-5 117..................................... RichardJohnson 116+
(Philip Hobbs) *chsd ldr tl nt fluent 2nd: remained handy: led after 5th: swvd rt appr next: rdn and hdd after 2 out: styd on same pce last* 10/11[1]
3 15 **Renegotiate**[166] 4-10-9 0..................................(p) SamTwiston-Davies 95+
(Dr Richard Newland) *prom: chsd ldr after 2nd: hung lft and hmpd jst bef 3 out: sn ev ch: wkng whn nt fluent last* 5/1[3]
/56- 4 1 1/2 **Nefyn Bay**[12] 732 4-10-9 0.. HenryBrooke 90
(Donald McCain) *prom: lost pl 3rd: hdwy appr 3 out: wknd next* 25/1

The Form Book Jumps, Raceform Ltd, Compton, RG20 6NL.

5 *25* **Gavi**[238] 7-10-12 0 .... AndrewThornton 70
(Karen George) *hld up: mstke 4th: bhd fr next: t.o* **80/1**

6 *16* **Persian Fox (IRE)**[67] 9-10-7 0 .... MrBMoorcroft(5) 55
(Stephen Hughes) *led tl after 5th: sn wknd: t.o* **100/1**

3m 40.6s (-6.70) **Going Correction** -0.45s/f (Good)
WFA 4 from 5yo+ 17lb **6** Ran SP% **108.5**
Speed ratings (Par 105): **98,93,86,85,72 64**
Tote Swingers 1&2 £1.80, 2&3 £1.60, 1&3 £1.20 CSF £4.04 TOTE £2.40: £1.40, £1.10; EX 5.50 Trifecta £12.40 Pool: £2,882.07 - 173.95 winning tickets..
Owner Triermore Stud **Bred** C O P Hanbury **Trained** Upper Lambourn, Berks

FOCUS
They went just a steady early pace in this ordinary novice hurdle. The second is rated to his mark, backed up by the fourth.

844 CHRISTMAS PARTY NIGHTS AT WORCESTER RACECOURSE NOVICES' H'CAP HURDLE (10 hdls) 2m 4f
4:45 (4:45) (Class 5) (0-100,98) 4-Y-0+ **£3,119** (£915; £457; £228)

Form RPR

/02- **1** **Anton Dolin (IRE)**[3] 809 5-11-2 **87** .... (p) SamTwiston-Davies 102+
(Dr Richard Newland) *chsd ldrs: led 7th: rdn and edgd lft flat: styd on wl* **10/11**[1]

/12- **2** *3* **Princesse Fleur**[35] 436 5-11-0 **85** .... LiamTreadwell 94
(Michael Scudamore) *hld up: hdwy 7th: chsd wnr 2 out: rdn last: styd on same pce flat* **13/2**[2]

P/5- **3** *1 3/4* **Sonofagun (FR)**[19] 661 7-11-10 **95** .... RichardJohnson 101
(Ian Williams) *hld up: hdwy 7th: rdn appr last: no ex flat* **8/1**

/P0- **4** *8* **Harris Garden (IRE)**[19] 661 6-11-8 **93** .... (p) DenisO'Regan 92
(Paul Webber) *prom: chsd wnr appr 3 out: sn ev ch: wknd last* **25/1**

/P4- **5** *13* **Rainbow Haze**[32] 482 7-11-3 **88** .... (t) LeightonAspell 76
(Phillip Dando) *hld up: hdwy appr 3 put: wknd next* **20/1**

0/6- **6** *9* **Kilderry Dean (IRE)**[16] 691 6-11-8 **93** .... HaddenFrost 75
(James Frost) *hld up: hdwy 6th: rdn and wknd after 3 out: t.o* **20/1**

604- **7** *5* **Chosen Dream (IRE)**[18] 669 5-11-1 **86** .... (tp) APMcCoy 61
(Jonjo O'Neill) *hld up: mstke 7th: effrt appr 3 out: sn wknd: no ch whn hmpd next* **7/1**[3]

5/0- **8** *3 1/4* **Amalric (FR)**[36] 417 6-11-9 **94** .... TomMessenger 66
(Anabel K Murphy) *hld up: rdn appr 7th: a in rr: t.o* **66/1**

00- **9** *9* **Moyne Nineoseven (IRE)**[18] 669 7-11-9 **97** .... JackQuinlan(3) 61
(Noel Quinlan) *chsd ldrs: rdn after 6th: wknd appr 3 out: t.o* **33/1**

/4P- **10** *5* **Cottage Acre (IRE)**[16] 689 10-11-8 **93** .... (t) LiamHeard 52
(Colin Heard) *led to 7th: wknd after 3 out: t.o* **25/1**

/5P- **11** *2 3/4* **Isthereadifference (IRE)**[20] 641 6-11-10 **95** .... (p) DougieCostello 52
(Neil Mulholland) *mid-div: hdwy 7th: rdn and wknd bef next: t.o* **25/1**

/32- **12** *46* **Asian Prince (IRE)**[37] 407 4-11-9 **98** .... (bt) ConorO'Farrell 10
(Alastair Lidderdale) *prom tl rdn and wknd appr 3 out: t.o* **12/1**

4/3- **13** *18* **Maggie Aron**[51] 145 7-10-13 **87** .... MichaelByrne(3)
(James Hughes) *hld up: a in rr: rdn and wknd after 7th: t.o* **12/1**

306- **F** **Cruise Control**[13] 729 7-10-3 **79** .... HarryChalloner(5) 70
(John Bryan Groucott) *hld up: hdwy appr 3 out: wkng whn fell next* **50/1**

/2P- **P** **Autumm Spirit**[16] 689 9-11-10 **95** .... (bt[1]) CharliePoste
(Robin Dickin) *chsd ldr to 7th: sn rdn and wknd: t.o whn p.u bef 2 out* **33/1**

0/6- **P** **Cleeve Cloud (IRE)**[15] 716 7-11-2 **87** .... AlainCawley
(Liam Grassick) *mid-div: pushed along after 4th: lost pl next: bhd fr 7th: t.o whn p.u bef 3 out* **40/1**

4m 40.2s (-7.20) **Going Correction** -0.45s/f (Good)
WFA 4 from 5yo+ 18lb **16** Ran SP% **137.5**
Speed ratings (Par 103): **96,94,94,90,85 82,80,78,75,73 72,53,46, ,**
Tote Swingers 1&2 £2.90, 2&3 £10.10, 1&3 £4.40 CSF £7.84 CT £41.66 TOTE £2.00: £1.60, £1.80, £1.90, £3.90; EX 11.20 Trifecta £64.40 Pool: £1,871.81 - 21.77 winning tickets..
Owner Mrs M L Trow, Barwell & Newland **Bred** Windflower Overseas Holdings Inc **Trained** Claines, Worcs

FOCUS
A modest novice handicap which centred upon Anton Dolin. The placed horses are rated to their marks in an ordinary handicap.

845 LIKE US ON FACEBOOK WORCESTER RACECOURSE H'CAP HURDLE (12 hdls) 2m 7f
5:15 (5:15) (Class 3) (0-135,130) 4-Y-0+ **£5,393** (£1,583; £791; £395)

Form RPR

211/ **1** **On The Bridge (IRE)**[237] 2139 8-11-2 **120** .... NickScholfield 130+
(Jeremy Scott) *hld up: hdwy after 9th: led appr and wnt lft last: rdn out* **6/1**

03F/ **2** *5* **Sheriff Hutton (IRE)**[51] 10-11-5 **123** .... HaddenFrost 127
(Martin Hill) *hld up: hdwy after 6th: led and mstke 8th: rdn and hdd bef last: styd on same pce flat* **20/1**

0/P- **3** *2 1/4* **No Principles**[30] 512 10-10-11 **115** .... (p) WayneHutchinson 116
(Julian Smith) *hld up: hdwy 8th: rdn after 2 out: no ex flat* **50/1**

/6P- **4** *1 1/2* **Andhaar**[24] 606 7-10-4 **115** .... JackSherwood(7) 115
(Richard Phillips) *hld up: pushed along 4th: swtchd rt and hdwy appr 9th: rdn appr last: no ex flat* **33/1**

/00- **5** *6* **Mister Hyde (IRE)**[25] 591 8-11-2 **120** .... (vt) APMcCoy 116
(Jonjo O'Neill) *hld up: hdwy u.p 3 out: wknd last* **16/1**

0/3- **6** *22* **Qulinton (FR)**[25] 591 9-11-2 **120** .... (b) ConorO'Farrell 95
(David Pipe) *chsd ldrs: rdn after 9th: wknd 3 out: t.o* **7/1**

211- **7** *11* **Captain Kelly (IRE)**[20] 638 6-11-2 **120** .... (t) DarylJacob 85
(Paul Nicholls) *prom: rdn appr 3 out: sn wknd: t.o* **9/2**[2]

4/2- **8** *12* **Mister Dillon**[15] 718 6-11-9 **130** .... JeremiahMcGrath(3) 84
(Nicky Henderson) *chsd ldrs: mstke 3rd: reminder 5th: hit 9th: sn rdn and wknd: t.o* **4/1**[1]

0F6/ **9** *9* **Nataani (IRE)**[61] 5537 10-11-8 **126** .... (vt) RichieMcLernon 72
(Jo Davis) *chsd ldrs tl rdn and wknd appr 3 out: t.o* **25/1**

/42- **10** *27* **Moon Devil (IRE)**[20] 638 6-10-2 **106** .... (tp) TomO'Brien 28
(Peter Bowen) *chsd ldrs: pushed along 9th: rdn and wknd bef next: t.o* **5/1**[3]

0/1- **11** *5* **Leath Acra Mor (IRE)**[20] 650 7-11-1 **119** .... RichardJohnson 36
(Ian Williams) *hld up: drvn and wknd after 9th: t.o* **16/1**

3/0- **12** *shd* **Sainglend**[15] 718 8-11-0 **128** .... MikeyHamill(10) 45
(Sean Curran) *prom: lost pl appr 7th: bhd fr next: t.o* **100/1**

03/- **P** **Hassadin**[67] 5410 7-10-10 **114** .... TomCannon
(Michael Blake) *hld up: bhd fr 5th: t.o whn p.u bef last* **40/1**

0P0/ **P** **What An Oscar (IRE)**[139] 4076 8-11-4 **122** .... (v[1]) SamTwiston-Davies
(Nigel Twiston-Davies) *led to 8th: rdn and wknd next: t.o whn p.u bef last* **10/1**

F14/ **P** **Beggar's Velvet (IRE)**[250] 1916 7-10-6 **117** .... ConorShoemark(7)
(Fergal O'Brien) *prom: pushed along 8th: rdn and wknd next: t.o whn p.u bef 2 out* **25/1**

5m 24.9s (-3.10) **Going Correction** -0.45s/f (Good) **15** Ran SP% **123.3**
Speed ratings (Par 107): **87,85,84,83,81 74,70,66,63,53 51,51, , ,**
Tote Swingers 1&2 £20.80, 2&3 £261.80, 1&3 £60.70 CSF £122.15 CT £5447.95 TOTE £10.20: £2.80, £7.10, £23.70; EX 182.20 Trifecta £1294.10 Part won. Pool: £1,725.53 - 0.12 winning tickets..
Owner Kit James **Bred** J & D Melody **Trained** Brompton Regis, Somerset

FOCUS
A fair, competitive handicap run at an honest pace. The winner is rated to the level of his chasing form with the second to his mark.

846 BOOK TICKETS ONLINE AT WORCESTER-RACECOURSE.CO.UK H'CAP HURDLE (8 hdls) 2m
5:45 (5:45) (Class 4) (0-105,104) 4-Y-0+ **£3,119** (£915; £457; £228)

Form RPR

632- **1** **Mighty Clarets (IRE)**[5] 788 6-11-2 **94** .... (v[1]) JamieMoore 112+
(Peter Bowen) *a.p: chsd ldr 4th: led after next: clr appr 3 out: styd on strly* **2/1**[2]

P/5- **2** *14* **My Lord**[16] 691 5-11-2 **94** .... LiamTreadwell 99+
(Luke Dace) *hld up: mstke 3rd: hdwy appr 3 out: rdn whn mstke 2 out: styd on same pce: wnt 2nd nr fin* **7/1**[3]

0/1- **3** *1/2* **Strongly Suggested**[26] 561 6-11-11 **103** .... (t) APMcCoy 106
(Jonjo O'Neill) *prom: chsd wnr 3 out: sn rdn: no ex flat: lost 2nd nr fin* **7/4**[1]

/03- **4** *shd* **Annelko**[24] 593 6-11-8 **100** .... TomCannon 104
(Michael Blake) *hld up: mstke 5th: hdwy after 3 out: rdn appr last: no ex flat* **14/1**

513- **5** *2* **Morestead (IRE)**[15] 705 8-10-7 **85** .... (t) LeightonAspell 86
(Brendan Powell) *chsd ldrs: rdn appr 3 out: styd on same pce fr next* **10/1**

/43- **6** *5* **Hi Tide (IRE)**[24] 605 9-11-10 **102** .... DougieCostello 99
(J R Jenkins) *hld up: wknd after 3 out* **14/1**

/ **7** *9* **Respectueux (FR)**[17] 7-10-13 **91** .... DonalDevereux 79
(David Brace) *led: mstke 5th: sn hdd: rdn and wknd bef 2 out: t.o* **20/1**

/26- **8** *43* **Exiles Return (IRE)**[33] 456 11-10-1 **82** .... MarkQuinlan(3) 32
(Jacqueline Retter) *chsd ldr to 4th: rdn and wknd after next: t.o* **33/1**

3m 36.5s (-10.80) **Going Correction** -0.45s/f (Good) **8** Ran SP% **112.3**
Speed ratings (Par 105): **109,102,101,101,100 98,93,72**
Tote Swingers 1&2 £3.20, 2&3 £3.70, 1&3 £1.70 CSF £15.99 CT £27.47 TOTE £3.30: £1.10, £2.30, £1.20; EX 20.40 Trifecta £49.50 Pool: £1,287.57 - 19.50 winning tickets..
Owner The Hedonists & Karen Bowen **Bred** Ellesmere Bloodstock Ltd **Trained** Little Newcastle, Pembrokes

FOCUS
An ordinary handicap which was taken apart by Mighty Clarets. The third and fourth look the best guides to the level with the winner an improver in the first-time visor.
T/Plt: £6.90 to a £1 stake. Pool: £74,337.46 - 7846.13 winning tickets. T/Qpdt: £1.30 to a £1 stake. Pool: £6,048.32 - 3221.51 winning tickets. CR

761 UTTOXETER (L-H)
Sunday, June 30

OFFICIAL GOING: Good (good to firm in places; 6.7)
Wind: Fresh against Weather: Cloudy with sunny spells

847 TOTEL SOLUTIONS MAIDEN HURDLE (DIV I) (10 hdls) 2m 4f 110y
1:40 (1:42) (Class 5) 4-Y-0+ **£2,339** (£686; £343; £171)

Form RPR

2/2- **1** **Letsby Avenue**[43] 374 5-11-0 122 .... WayneHutchinson 126+
(Alan King) *a.p: chsd ldr 3 out: led after next: sn clr: easily* **6/4**[1]

/21- **2** *23* **The Road Ahead**[30] 567 6-10-7 0 .... TomO'Brien 98+
(Peter Bowen) *chsd ldrs: mstke 4th: led next: rdn and nt fluent 2 out: sn hdd: wknd last* **5/1**

122- **3** *nk* **Billfromthebar (IRE)**[16] 737 6-11-0 0 .... HenryBrooke 103
(Donald McCain) *led to 2nd: chsd ldr tl rdn appr 3 out: wknd next* **4/1**[3]

0/0- **4** *11* **Kukurudu (IRE)**[16] 737 6-11-0 0 .... (p) BarryKeniry 93
(Simon West) *hld up: hdwy after 7th: rdn and wknd next: t.o* **200/1**

0/ **5** *23* **Themanfromcork**[483] 6-11-0 0 .... (t) BrendanPowell 69
(Brendan Powell) *chsd ldr tl led 2nd: hdd 5th: rdn and wknd appr 3 out: t.o* **22/1**

0/0- **6** *6* **Mon Homme**[11] 761 6-11-0 0 .... SamTwiston-Davies 63
(Mark Rimell) *hld up: rdn and wknd after 7th: t.o* **50/1**

2/ **7** *9* **Rally The Troops (IRE)**[603] 2339 6-11-0 0 .... APMcCoy 54
(Jonjo O'Neill) *prom tl rdn and wknd appr 3 out: t.o* **7/2**[2]

664/ **8** *5* **Multitude Of Sins**[209] 2830 6-11-0 0 .... JoeTizzard 49
(Colin Tizzard) *hld up: bhd fr 6th: sn t.o* **40/1**

45- **9** *26* **Oorayvic (IRE)**[20] 699 6-10-9 0 .... JonathanEngland(5) 23
(Sue Smith) *prom tl rdn and wknd after 7th: t.o* **100/1**

P/P- **P** **Yellow Duke (FR)**[24] 648 6-11-0 81 .... (b[1]) AdamPogson
(Charles Pogson) *hld up: drvn drvn along 6th: sn wknd: t.o whn p.u bef 3 out* **100/1**

P- **F** **Trentside William**[15] 747 6-11-0 0 .... (t) AndrewThornton
(Mike Sowersby) *fell 1st* **200/1**

4m 42.8s (-16.20) **Going Correction** -0.575s/f (Firm) **11** Ran SP% **112.6**
Speed ratings (Par 103): **107,98,98,93,85 82,79,77,67, ,**
toteswingers 1&2 £2.60, 1&3 £1.80, 2&3 £2.40 CSF £8.82 TOTE £2.30: £1.10, £1.80, £1.30; EX 10.00 Trifecta £18.70 Pool: £729.80 - 29.16 winning tickets..
Owner Mrs Peter Prowting **Bred** Mrs E A Prowting **Trained** Barbury Castle, Wilts

FOCUS
Hurdles on inside and course at shortest configuration. Fences at full width and divided bends. The ground was described as good but plenty quick enough by Barry Keniry after the opener.

848 BET365 NOVICES' HURDLE (9 hdls) 2m
2:10 (2:10) (Class 4) 4-Y-0+ **£3,798** (£1,122; £561; £280; £140)

Form RPR

/31- **1** **Thunder Sheik (IRE)**[7] 808 5-10-12 112 .... (t) PaddyBrennan 112+
(Fergal O'Brien) *chsd ldr tl led after 3 out: rdn out* **3/1**[2]

6/1- **2** *4 1/2* **Lyssio (GER)**[28] 593 6-11-5 0 .... APMcCoy 116
(Jim Best) *a.p: chsd wnr after 3 out: sn ev ch: rdn appr last: no ex flat* **11/8**[1]

16- **3** *1 3/4* **Godwit**[20] 696 5-10-9 0 .... JackQuinlan(3) 106
(Eugene Stanford) *led: rdn and hdd after 3 out: styd on same pce appr last* **20/1**

0/ **4** *2 3/4* **Good Of Luck**[145] 4039 4-10-9 0 .... ConorO'Farrell 100
(Mick Channon) *prom: rdn appr 3 out: no ex last* **33/1**

- 5 12 **Cockney Class (USA)**[25] 6-10-12 0 LeeEdwards 93
(Dave Roberts) *hld up: hdwy after 6th: mstke 3 out: sn rdn: wknd after next* **10/1**

6 9 **Portofino Wasp (IRE)** 4-10-9 0 RichieMcLernon 79
(Jonjo O'Neill) *hld up: nvr on terms: t.o* **40/1**

7 5 **Hit The Top (IRE)**[70] 6-10-7 0 JonathanEngland(5) 77
(Sue Smith) *hld up: bhd fr 6th: t.o* **20/1**

/30- 8 6 **Perfect Poison (IRE)**[26] 629 5-10-12 0 HenryBrooke 71
(Donald McCain) *hld up: hmpd 2nd: rdn and wknd after 6th: t.o* **40/1**

45/ 9 4 **Day In The Sun (IRE)**[388] 626 6-10-5 0 DannyBenson(7) 67
(Jonjo O'Neill) *hld up: a in rr: pushed along and wknd after 6th: t.o* **33/1**

0/ 10 21 **Moscow Red (IRE)**[1168] 5283 7-10-12 0 CharliePoste 46
(Matt Sheppard) *chsd ldrs tl rdn and wknd appr 3 out: t.o* **40/1**

0- P **Anrheg**[22] 671 5-10-2 0 (p) RobertDunne(3)
(Dai Burchell) *chsd ldrs: nt fluent 1st: rdn and wknd appr 3 out: t.o whn p.u and dismntd after next: lame* **100/1**

3/2- U **Wintered Well (IRE)**[45] 338 5-10-12 0 SeanQuinlan
(Jennie Candlish) *mid-div: blnd and uns rdr 2nd* **4/1**[3]

3m 43.1s (-8.90) **Going Correction** -0.575s/f (Firm)
WFA 4 from 5yo+ 17lb 12 Ran SP% **119.9**
Speed ratings (Par 105): **99,96,95,94,88 84,81,78,76,66** ,
toteswingers 1&2 £1.10, 1&3 £8.60, 2&3 £11.50 CSF £7.21 TOTE £3.70: £1.30, £1.10, £5.20; EX 7.40 Trifecta £47.10 Pool: £541.98 - 8.62 winning tickets..
Owner R J Rexton **Bred** Janus Bloodstock Inc **Trained** Coln St. Dennis, Gloucs

849 TOTEL SOLUTIONS MAIDEN HURDLE (DIV II) (10 hdls) 2m 4f 110y

2:40 (2:41) (Class 5) 4-Y-O+ **£2,339** (£686; £343; £171)

Form RPR

0/3- 1 **Waterford Star (IRE)**[36] 479 5-11-0 0 (p) PaddyBrennan 116+
(Tom George) *hld up: pushed along and hdwy 7th: rdn appr 3 out: led after next: sn clr: eased nr fin* **2/1**[1]

40/ 2 15 **Mighty Snazy**[635] 1845 9-11-0 110 RichardJohnson 101
(Tim Vaughan) *chsd ldrs: lost pl 5th: rallied 3 out: rdn and ev ch after next: wknd bef last* **4/1**[3]

3/4- 3 1 ¼ **Sterling Gent (IRE)**[25] 631 6-11-0 103 DPFahy 101
(Liam Corcoran) *chsd ldrs: led appr 7th: nt fluent 2 out: sn rdn and hdd: wknd bef last* **15/2**

4 6 **Flatfoot Boogie (FR)** 8-11-0 0 TomO'Brien 95
(N F Glynn, Ire) *hld up: hdwy 4th: rdn appr 3 out: wknd next* **16/1**

P/4- 5 nk **Record Breaker (IRE)**[29] 592 9-11-0 102 (p) HenryBrooke 94
(Donald McCain) *led tl after 1st: chsd ldr: chal 7th: rdn and ev ch after 2 out: wknd bef last* **12/1**

116/ 6 51 **Royal Swain (IRE)**[291] 5129 7-11-0 0 (t) AidanColeman 48
(Anthony Honeyball) *hld up: wknd 3 out: mstke next: t.o* **3/1**[2]

0/U- P **Banks Road (IRE)**[32] 538 8-11-0 0 JimmyMcCarthy
(Geoffrey Deacon) *plld hrd: led after 1st: hdd appr 7th: sn wknd: t.o whn p.u after 3 out* **66/1**

U **Night Of Passion (IRE)** 5-10-7 0 NickScholfield
(Jeremy Scott) *hld up: j. slowly and uns rdr 2nd* **9/1**

4m 49.3s (-9.70) **Going Correction** -0.575s/f (Firm) 8 Ran SP% **115.2**
Speed ratings (Par 103): **95,89,88,86,86 66**, ,
toteswingers 1&2 £2.80, 1&3 £4.00, 2&3 £5.50 CSF £10.61 TOTE £3.10: £1.30, £1.80, £1.70; EX 11.40 Trifecta £42.50 Pool: £603.31 - 10.62 winning tickets..
Owner R S Brookhouse **Bred** Denis McDonnell **Trained** Slad, Gloucs

850 BET365 H'CAP HURDLE (THE SUNDAY £5K BONUS RACE) (9 hdls) 2m

3:10 (3:10) (Class 3) (0-135,132) 4-Y-O+

£6,256 (£1,848; £924; £462; £231; £116)

Form RPR

P12- 1 **Tom Wade (IRE)**[17] 729 6-10-3 114 (t) BenPoste(5) 115+
(Shaun Harris) *a.p: chsd ldr 3 out: led appr last: drvn out* **20/1**

410- 2 ½ **Knight In Purple**[29] 591 9-11-5 128 (vt) PeterCarberry(3) 128
(John Mackie) *chsd ldrs: rdn and nt fluent 2 out: r.o* **16/1**

10P/ 3 hd **Solaras Exhibition (IRE)**[22] 5356 5-11-2 122 RichardJohnson 122
(Tim Vaughan) *hld up: hdwy 2 out: rdn and r.o wl towards fin* **9/1**

311- 4 ½ **Baccalaureate (FR)**[20] 697 7-11-3 128 JonathanEngland(5) 127
(Sue Smith) *led: rdn and hdd appr last: no ex nr fin* **5/1**[1]

223- 5 ½ **Ruler Of All (IRE)**[16] 734 7-11-5 132 MrRWinks(7) 130
(Peter Winks) *hld up: hdwy appr 3 out: rdn bef last: r.o* **11/1**

1/2- 6 4 ½ **Scoglio**[25] 304 5-11-0 120 LeeEdwards 114
(Dave Roberts) *hld up: hdwy after 3 out: sn rdn: styd on same pce appr last* **8/1**[3]

1/3- 7 2 ¼ **Flaming Arrow (IRE)**[14] 344 5-10-11 120 BrianToomey(5) 112
(Kevin Ryan) *prom: rdn appr 3 out: styd on same pce fr next* **12/1**

5P2/ 8 hd **Dontpaytheferryman (USA)**[41] 5007 8-11-1 124 RobertDunne(3) 116
(John Price) *chsd ldr tl rdn appr 3 out: wknd appr last* **22/1**

0/ 9 nse **Teak (IRE)**[22] 2455 6-10-4 110 DougieCostello 102
(Ian Williams) *chsd ldrs: rdn appr 3 out: wknd next* **13/2**[2]

6/2- 10 8 **Thegaygardener**[11] 767 5-10-9 115 (t) PaulMoloney 100
(Evan Williams) *hld up: rdn and wknd 3 out* **13/2**[2]

534- 11 10 **Sud Pacifique (IRE)**[22] 673 5-11-3 123 (p) HenryBrooke 99
(Donald McCain) *hld up: racd keenly: rdn and wknd 3 out* **17/2**

/23- U **Gud Day (IRE)**[20] 697 5-9-13 112 (t) MissAEStirling(7)
(Fergal O'Brien) *mid-div: nt fluent and uns rdr 3rd* **8/1**[3]

3m 39.3s (-12.70) **Going Correction** -0.575s/f (Firm) 12 Ran SP% **117.1**
Speed ratings (Par 107): **108,107,107,107,107 104,103,103,103,99 94**,
toteswingers 1&2 £0.00, 1&3 £20.20, 2&3 £20.20 CSF £296.21 CT £3067.45 TOTE £30.20: £6.70, £5.70, £2.90; EX 402.60 Trifecta £278.90 Part won. Pool: £371.98 - 0.07 winning tickets..
Owner Paul Tonks **Bred** Denis McDonnell **Trained** Carburton, Notts

FOCUS

Plenty in with a chance turning for home.

851 JOHN SMITH'S SUMMER CUP (HANDICAP CHASE) (LISTED RACE) (20 fncs) 3m 2f

3:45 (3:45) (Class 1) 5-Y-O+

£22,780 (£8,548; £4,280; £2,132; £1,072; £536)

Form RPR

/33- 1 **Storm Survivor (IRE)**[19] 718 7-10-1 126 (v) RichieMcLernon 136+
(Jonjo O'Neill) *hld up: hdwy 15th: pushed along after next: rdn to ld flat: styd on wl* **28/1**

412- 2 2 ½ **Pure Faith (IRE)**[22] 672 9-10-9 134 (t) TomO'Brien 142
(Peter Bowen) *hld up in tch: racd keenly: led appr 2 out: rdn and hdd flat: unable qck* **16/1**

P/1- 3 8 **Lost Glory (NZ)**[38] 448 8-11-5 144 (t) APMcCoy 145
(Jonjo O'Neill) *chsd ldrs: rdn appr 4 out: swtchd lft bef next: styd on same pce appr last* **7/1**[2]

PF0/ 4 ¾ **Galaxy Rock (IRE)**[64] 5576 9-10-8 133 (b) DougieCostello 133+
(Jonjo O'Neill) *hld up: hdwy 16th: styd on appr last: nvr nrr* **14/1**

1PB/ 5 1 ¼ **Prince Tom**[87] 5146 9-10-11 136 DarylJacob 135
(Paul Nicholls) *mid-div: hdwy 8th: rdn after 3 out: wknd appr last* **16/1**

260/ 6 1 ½ **Pineau De Re (FR)**[88] 5129 10-11-0 139 SamTwiston-Davies 137
(Dr Richard Newland) *prom: chsd ldr 11th: led 4 out: rdn and hdd appr 2 out: wknd bef last* **11/2**[1]

132/ 7 9 **Victrix Gale (IRE)**[65] 5548 7-10-0 125 BrianHughes 117
(A J Martin, Ire) *hld up: nt fluent 1st: nvr on terms* **8/1**

/32- 8 ½ **Siberian Tiger (IRE)**[10] 780 8-10-0 125 oh1 (v[1]) PaulMoloney 114
(Evan Williams) *hld up: hdwy 16th: rdn and wknd 4 out* **25/1**

/0P- 9 3 ¾ **Mostly Bob (IRE)**[34] 509 10-9-11 125 (t) JamesBest(3) 115
(Sophie Leech) *led to 5th: led again 7th: rdn and hdd 4 out: wkng whn nt fluent and rdr lost irons last: sddle slipped* **66/1**

5P0/ 10 10 **Becauseicouldntsee (IRE)**[64] 5576 10-10-2 127 PaddyBrennan 106
(N F Glynn, Ire) *chsd ldrs: lost pl 6th: hdwy 15th: rdn and wknd 4 out: t.o* **9/1**

104/ 11 8 **Monkerty Tunkerty**[84] 5199 10-10-7 132 WillKennedy 102
(Miss Jessica Westwood) *hld up: rdn 14th: sn wknd: t.o* **16/1**

051- 12 1 **Problema Tic (FR)**[21] 680 7-11-1 140 (bt) TomScudamore 109
(David Pipe) *chsd ldrs: rdn 14th: mstke and wknd next: t.o* **10/1**

PPP/ 13 14 **Weird Al (IRE)**[85] 5177 10-11-12 151 NoelFehily 107
(Donald McCain) *hld up: bhd fr 14th: t.o* **14/1**

/P3- 14 23 **Life Of A Luso (IRE)**[42] 393 9-10-7 132 (t) NickScholfield 67
(Paul Henderson) *hld up: mstke 13th: bhd fr next: sn t.o* **50/1**

F/0- P **Helpston**[23] 659 9-10-3 133 (p) MissGAndrews(5)
(Pam Sly) *chsd ldr tl led 5th: hdd 7th: chsd ldr to 11th: rdn 13th: wkng whn hit 15th: t.o whn p.u bef 3 out* **33/1**

4/6- F **Danimix (IRE)**[44] 355 8-10-4 129 (t) AidanColeman
(Anthony Honeyball) *hld up: hdwy appr 16th: wknd berfore next: no ch whn fell 3 out* **14/1**

P3F/ P **Red Not Blue (IRE)**[77] 5314 10-10-10 135 AndrewThornton
(Simon Earle) *prom tl rdn and wknd 14th: t.o whn p.u bef 16th* **25/1**

P/1- P **Deireadh Re (IRE)**[46] 302 7-9-12 128 HarryDerham(5)
(Paul Nicholls) *hld up: hdwy 13th: wknd after 16th: bhd whn hmpd 3 out: sn p.u* **15/2**[3]

6m 26.3s (-20.10) **Going Correction** -0.425s/f (Good) 18 Ran SP% **125.0**
Speed ratings: **113,112,109,109,109 108,105,105,104,101 99,98,94,87**, , ,
toteswingers 1&2 £15.20, 1&3 £12.60, 2&3 £10.50 CSF £405.50 CT £3485.20 TOTE £44.20: £7.80, £3.20, £2.20, £3.00; EX 444.30 Trifecta £942.10 Part won. Pool: £1256.21 - 0.10 winning tickets..
Owner John P McManus **Bred** James Reeves **Trained** Cheltenham, Gloucs

FOCUS

A strong renewal of this Listed handicap chase and the gallop was unrelenting. It proved another memorable outcome for the Jonjo O'Neill stable, successful with Tominator in the Northumberland Plate the previous day.

852 BET365.COM H'CAP HURDLE (9 hdls) 2m

4:20 (4:20) (Class 5) (0-100,100) 4-Y-O+ **£2,469** (£725; £362; £181)

Form RPR

0/1- 1 **Emerald Glade (IRE)**[7] 809 6-10-13 87 7ex APMcCoy 106+
(Jim Best) *w ldewr: led 6th: wnt clr 3 out: easily* **11/8**[1]

0/0- 2 5 **Kilrye (IRE)**[24] 640 6-10-11 85 (t) TomScudamore 84
(David Pipe) *in rr: styd on fr 3 out: tk 2nd towards fin* **20/1**

2/5- 3 ½ **Maraased**[24] 648 8-11-3 94 MichealNolan(3) 93
(Stephen Hughes) *chsd ldrs: reminders 4th: kpt on same pce fr 3 out* **10/1**

0/3- 4 hd **Tadabeer**[24] 651 5-11-0 88 (t) RichardJohnson 86
(Ian Williams) *chsd ldrs: 2nd 3 out: one pce* **4/1**[2]

6/0- 5 3 ¼ **Snow Alert**[47] 283 7-11-0 88 FearghalDavis 84
(John Norton) *in rr: mstke 3 out: kpt on fr next: nvr a factor* **66/1**

5/0- 6 13 **Homer Run (IRE)**[48] 264 6-11-5 93 AndrewThornton 80
(Simon Earle) *in rr: kpt on fr 2 out: nvr on terms* **16/1**

3/0- 7 6 **Numen (IRE)**[18] 456 9-11-3 98 MissCLWills(7) 76
(Barry Brennan) *led: j.lft: hdd 6th: wknd 2 out* **28/1**

340/ 8 12 **Ivans Back (IRE)**[329] 1187 8-11-7 95 HenryBrooke 63
(Nick Kent) *t.k.h: hdwy 4th: wknd 6th* **50/1**

/03- 9 nse **Van Diemens Land (USA)**[35] 488 6-11-12 100 (bt) NoelFehily 68
(Charlie Mann) *chsd ldrs: wknd appr 2 out* **8/1**

P/0- 10 23 **Until The Man (IRE)**[48] 264 6-10-11 85 DPFahy 32
(Geoffrey Deacon) *a in rr: bhd fr 6th: t.o* **66/1**

/24- 11 4 **Ghaabesh (IRE)**[17] 727 6-11-4 97 HarryChalloner(5) 40
(Barry Leavy) *chsd ldrs: lost pl after 6th* **40/1**

2P4/ P **Vertueux (FR)**[16] 4750 8-11-12 100 WayneHutchinson
(Tony Carroll) *in tch: lost pl 4th: p.u bef 2 out* **33/1**

341- P **Mount Welcome (IRE)**[20] 687 9-10-10 89 (t) MrTWeston(5)
(Martin Weston) *chsd ldrs 4th: lost pl appr 2 out: p.u bef last* **6/1**[3]

3m 48.8s (-3.20) **Going Correction** -0.575s/f (Firm) 13 Ran SP% **121.0**
Speed ratings (Par 103): **85,82,82,82,80 74,71,65,65,53 51**, ,
toteswingers 1&2 £7.80, 1&3 £24.10, 2&3 £0.00 CSF £34.48 CT £215.86 TOTE £2.30: £1.20, £3.60, £2.40; EX 35.40 Trifecta £494.40 Pool: £1281.70 - 1.94 winning tickets..
Owner Emerald Glade Partnership **Bred** J T And Mrs Thomas **Trained** Lewes, E Sussex

853 BET365 H'CAP CHASE (12 fncs) 2m

4:50 (4:50) (Class 4) (0-115,115) 5-Y-O **£5,064** (£1,496; £748; £374; £187)

Form RPR

/44- 1 **Mibleu (FR)**[33] 520 13-11-4 107 BrendanPowell 113
(Colin Tizzard) *chsd ldrs: led appr last: rdn out* **8/1**

/54- 2 ¾ **Bay Central (IRE)**[10] 781 9-11-0 103 (e) PaulMoloney 108
(Evan Williams) *led to 8th: rdn and ev ch appr last: styd on u.p* **11/1**

3 ½ **Another Flutter (IRE)**[85] 5193 9-11-3 106 (p) CharliePoste 111
(Matt Sheppard) *chsd ldr tl led 8th: rdn and hdd appr last: styd on same pce flat* **15/2**

P/3- 4 3 ¾ **Free World (FR)**[58] 98 9-11-5 108 (t) RichardJohnson 111
(Tim Vaughan) *hld up: hdwy 3 out: rdn and wnt lft last: styd on same pce* **4/1**[2]

10/- 5 19 **Milgen Bay**[75] 5338 7-11-11 113 (p) LeightonAspell 102
(Oliver Sherwood) *prom: rdn after 4 out: blnd and wknd 2 out* **6/1**

The Form Book Jumps, Raceform Ltd, Compton, RG20 6NL.

5/P- **6** *2* **An Capall Mor (IRE)**[16] 733 7-11-12 **115**....................(tp) HenryBrooke 98
(Donald McCain) *prom: pushed along after 3rd: drvn along 5th: wknd appr 3 out* **10/1**
6/2- **7** *28* **Bennys Quest (IRE)**[25] 632 10-10-12 **104**...............(tp) PeterCarberry(3) 61
(Andy Hobbs) *hld up: hdwy 5th: rdn and wknd 4 out: t.o* **5/1**[3]
0/1- **P** **Catch Tammy (IRE)**[37] 459 7-11-9 **112**......................... PaddyBrennan
(Tom George) *prom: lost pl 3rd: last whn pckd 5th: rdn and wknd appr 4 out: t.o whn p.u bef 2 out* **7/2**[1]

3m 52.5s (-2.50) **Going Correction** -0.425s/f (Good) **8** Ran SP% **113.5**
Speed ratings: **89,88,88,86,77 76,62,**
toteswingers 1&2 £4.90, 1&3 £25.30, 2&3 £25.30 CSF £84.02 CT £684.28 TOTE £10.60: £2.00, £3.60, £2.60; EX 78.30 Trifecta £299.00 Part won. Pool: £398.75 - 0.02 winning tickets..
Owner Chasing Gold Racing Club **Bred** Haras De La Rousseliere S C E A **Trained** Milborne Port, Dorset

854 CASINO AT BET365 H'CAP HURDLE (10 hdls) 2m 4f 110y
5:20 (5:21) (Class 5) (0-100,100) 4-Y-0+ **£2,339** (£686; £343; £171)

Form RPR
022/ **1** **Kusadasi (IRE)**[186] 3203 8-11-8 **96**............................(b) TomScudamore 103+
(David Pipe) *led after 1st: clr 2 out: mstke last: drvn out* **7/1**[2]
14/- **2** *5* **Bracken House (IRE)**[245] 2078 6-11-6 **94**....................(tp) PaulMoloney 96
(Graeme McPherson) *hld up: hdwy 4th: chsd wnr appr 3 out: sn rdn: styd on same pce last* **9/1**[3]
56P/ **3** *7* **Long Wave (IRE)**[109] 4742 6-11-12 **100**...............................(p) NoelFehily 95
(Charlie Longsdon) *chsd ldrs: rdn appr 3 out: styd on same pce fr next* **7/1**[2]
451- **4** *2 ¼* **Inside Knowledge (USA)**[17] 730 7-11-8 **96**.................. AdamPogson 89
(Garry Woodward) *hld up: rdn after 7th: styd on appr last: nvr nrr* **12/1**
6/4- **5** *12* **Maxdelas (FR)**[23] 661 7-11-1 **94**..........................(t) JonathanEngland(5) 76
(Roy Brotherton) *prom: rdn appr 3 out: wknd next* **16/1**
/53- **6** *10* **Advisor (FR)**[24] 650 7-11-7 **100**..............................(b) MrTWeston(5) 73
(Martin Weston) *led tl after 1st: chsd ldrs tl rdn and wknd 3 out: t.o* **28/1**
0/F- **7** *10* **Mac Beattie**[55] 145 7-11-4 **95**.. AdamWedge(3) 59
(Evan Williams) *hld up: rdn after 7th: wknd bef next: t.o* **20/1**
2/4- **8** *3 ¾* **Forever Waining (IRE)**[35] 503 7-11-10 **98**................(t) DonalDevereux 59
(Peter Bowen) *hld up: sme hdwy appr 3 out: sn wknd* **6/5**[1]
3/4- **9** *½* **El Toreros (USA)**[28] 605 5-11-12 **100**.......................... RichardJohnson 60
(Tim Vaughan) *hld up: rdn after 7th: sn wknd: t.o* **25/1**
050/ **10** *12* **No Woman No Cry**[180] 3425 8-11-6 **94**.............................(tp) JoeTizzard 43
(Colin Tizzard) *mid-div: lost pl 3rd: bhd and rdn 5th: t.o* **14/1**
20P/ **P** **Flexi Time (IRE)**[49] 9-11-4 **95**...................................... MichealNolan(3)
(Stephen Hughes) *mid-div: lost pl and bhd fr 3rd: t.o whn p.u bef 3 out* **50/1**
0/0- **P** **Arctic Pond (IRE)**[36] 482 5-11-10 **98**.................................. APMcCoy
(Jonjo O'Neill) *chsd ldrs to 6th: sn wl bhd: t.o whn p.u bef 3 out* **14/1**

4m 43.8s (-15.20) **Going Correction** -0.575s/f (Firm) **12** Ran SP% **121.4**
Speed ratings (Par 103): **105,103,100,99,95 91,87,85,85,81 ,**
CSF £66.87 CT £466.73 TOTE £5.70: £2.80, £3.30, £2.80; EX 55.80 Trifecta £542.60 Part won. Pool: £723.58 - 0.52 winning tickets..
Owner The Odd Ones Partnership **Bred** Mrs Noeleen And Tom O'Toole **Trained** Nicholashayne, Devon

T/Jkpt: Not won. T/Plt: £98.30 to a £1 stake. Pool: £121567.97 - 902.72 winning tickets T/Qpdt: £71.80 to a £1 stake. Pool: £6575.02 - 67.70 winning tickets CR

CORLAY (R-H)
Sunday, June 30

OFFICIAL GOING: Turf: good

855a GRAND ST-CH-CROSS-COUNTRY DE CORLAY - PRIX CARCARADEC (CROSS-COUNTRY CHASE) (COND'S) (6YO+) (TURF) 3m 4f
3:30 (12:00) 6-Y-0+ **£17,170** (£8,585; £5,008; £3,398; £1,609)

RPR
1 **Adelaide Square (FR)**[664] 1619 7-10-12 0.......................... DavidCottin 116
(G Macaire, France) **29/10**[1]
2 *2* **Racoleur (FR)**[650] 8-10-8 0....................................... DominiqueDelorme 110
(D Delorme, France)
3 *6* **Sulon (FR)**[52] 199 7-11-0 0......................................(p) JeromeZuliani 110
(Patrice Quinton, France)
4 *2* **Shalimar Fromentro (FR)**[52] 199 7-10-10 0................ JamesReveley 104
(Nick Williams)
5 *hd* **Rio Tinto (FR)** 8-10-10 0 ow2.............................. SebastienZuliani 104
(J Follain, France)
6 *4* **Ryvalo Des Brosses (FR)**[66] 5536 8-10-10 0.............. AngeloGasnier 100
(Jean-Paul Gasnier, France)
7 *7* **Sarika (FR)**[28] 616 7-10-8 0..(b) AlainDeChitray 91
(Nick Williams)
8 *dist* **Desirer (FR)**[987] 7-10-6 0.....................................(p) StephanePaillard
(E Lecoiffier, France)
F **Cyclothymique (FR)**[226] 2464 9-10-10 0........................ MehdiDahdouh
(J Bigot, France)
F **Rotterdan (FR)**[1197] 8-10-8 0...................................... LudovicSolignac
(T Boivin, France)
F **Robert's Well (FR)**[308] 8-10-10 0..................................(p) JohnnyCharron
(J Planque, France)
F **Kaid De Lonray (FR)**[52] 199 11-10-10 0.......................(p) NicolasMoisson
(A Le Clerc, France)
F **Trois Huit (FR)** 6-10-8 0...(b) WilfridDenuault
(E Leenders, France)

13 Ran SP% **25.6**
PARI-MUTUEL (all including 1 euro stakes): WIN 3.90; PLACE 1.70, 2.30, 2.30; DF 15.70.
Owner Jean-Yves Touzaint **Bred** Mme H Devin **Trained** Les Mathes, France

755 STRATFORD (L-H)
Tuesday, July 2

OFFICIAL GOING: Good (good to firm in places; 8.7)
Wind: Fresh across Weather: Overcast

856 BASIL NIGHTINGALE MAIDEN HURDLE (DIV I) (7 hdls 1 omitted) 2m 110y
5:40 (5:40) (Class 5) 4-Y-0+ **£2,599** (£763; £381; £190)

Form RPR
550/ **1** **Professeur Emery (FR)**[121] 4540 6-11-0 105........................ NoelFehily 119+
(Warren Greatrex) *mde all: clr fr 3 out: rdn out: unchal* **9/4**[2]
420- **2** *12* **Macarthur**[12] 783 9-11-0 114...(tp) PaulMoloney 108
(David Rees) *hld up: hdwy appr 2 out: rdn to chse wnr fnl f: no imp* **10/1**
/62- **3** *3* **Imperial Stargazer**[24] 671 4-10-12 108........................ MarcGoldstein 104
(Sheena West) *chsd ldrs: hmpd 4th: chsd wnr after 2 out: sn rdn: styd on same pce fnl f* **22/1**
0/2- **4** *¾* **Broughtons Bandit**[41] 427 6-11-0 0.............................. LeightonAspell 105
(Willie Musson) *hld up: hdwy 3 out: rdn after next: styd on same pce appr fnl f* **9/1**
5 *6* **Epic Storm (IRE)**[144] 5-10-4 0.. MikeyHamill(10) 101
(Sean Curran) *chsd wnr: rdn and mstke 2 out: wknd over 1f out* **40/1**
6 *11* **Celebrian**[41] 6-10-2 0..(t) KillianMoore(5) 83
(Alex Hales) *prom: hit 4th: wknd 3 out: t.o* **100/1**
331/ **7** *26* **Claiming Benefits (IRE)**[262] 1845 5-11-0 0....................... TomO'Brien 66
(Ronald O'Leary, Ire) *hld up: sme hdwy whn hmpd 3 out: sn wknd: t.o* **16/1**
5- **8** *5* **Collingwood (FR)**[18] 732 7-11-0 0............................. RichardJohnson 62
(Philip Hobbs) *hld up: hit 3rd: bhd fr 3 out: t.o* **18/1**
3/4- **9** *15* **Allowed**[36] 507 4-10-12 0.. DenisO'Regan 46
(John Ferguson) *hld up: hdwy 3 out: reminder bef next: sn wknd: t.o* **15/2**[3]
10 *46* **Joe The Rogue (IRE)**[18] 741 6-11-0 0.......................... NickScholfield 7
(Paul Henderson) *hld up: bhd fr 5th: t.o* **80/1**
P/P- **F** **Harting Hill**[27] 635 8-11-0 82.....................................(bt[1]) WillKennedy
(Violet M Jordan) *chsd ldrs: rdn and wkng whn fell 2 out* **150/1**
U **Gadreel (IRE)**[342] 4-10-12 0... CharliePoste
(Anthony Middleton) *hld up: a in rr: t.o whn swvd rt and uns rdr jst bef 3 out* **150/1**
/32- **P** **Rosslyn Castle**[27] 631 4-10-12 117... APMcCoy
(Gary Brown) *prom: mstkes: bmpd 4th and next: wknd 3 out: t.o whn p.u and dismntd bef next* **7/4**[1]
P **Flow Jo (IRE)**[244] 5-10-7 0... AndrewThornton
(Karen George) *hld up: bhd fr 3rd: sn drvn along: t.o whn p.u bef 3 out* **250/1**

3m 50.6s (-5.40) **Going Correction** -0.225s/f (Good)
WFA 4 from 5yo+ 15lb **14** Ran SP% **119.9**
Speed ratings (Par 103): **103,97,95,95,92 87,75,73,65,44 , , ,**
Tote Swingers 1&2 £21.60, 2&3 £24.30, 1&3 £12.30 CSF £24.83 TOTE £4.30: £1.60, £2.90, £2.50; EX 37.30 Trifecta £930.20 Pool: £1,282.68 - 1.03 winning tickets..
Owner Gdm Partnership **Bred** E A R L Du Haras De Pierrepont **Trained** Upper Lambourn, Berks

FOCUS
After a dry night, 3mm of water was selectively applied to the track during the morning. Paul Moloney described it as "beautiful ground - it's like a carpet out there." A modest maiden hurdle. The winner is rated to the lvel promised by his best juvenile form. The final flight was bypassed.

857 BASIL NIGHTINGALE MAIDEN HURDLE (DIV II) (8 hdls) 2m 110y
6:10 (6:11) (Class 5) 4-Y-0+ **£2,599** (£763; £381; £190)

Form RPR
/2U- **1** **Azure Fly (IRE)**[22] 695 5-11-0 0....................................(p) NoelFehily 126+
(Charlie Longsdon) *led to 2nd: led 3rd: clr fr 2 out: easily* **5/4**[1]
2 *31* **Ittirad (USA)**[325] 5-11-0 0.. DenisO'Regan 98
(John Ferguson) *chsd wnr tl led 2nd: hdd next: chsd wnr again to 3 out: wknd appr next: wnt 2nd again last: t.o* **7/4**[2]
3 *2 ¼* **Osorios Trial**[609] 6-11-0 0...[1] PaulMoloney 96
(Anthony Middleton) *hld up: plld hrd: styd on appr last: nvr nrr: t.o* **100/1**
5/3- **4** *3* **Incendo**[24] 671 7-11-0 0..(t) APMcCoy 93
(Ian Williams) *prom: chsd wnr 3 out: rdn and wknd after next: lost 2nd last: t.o* **8/1**[3]
3- **5** *3 ¾* **Mayan Flight (IRE)**[14] 758 5-11-0 0.............................. LeeEdwards 90
(Tony Carroll) *hld up: sme hdwy appr 2 out: nvr nr to chal: t.o* **50/1**
563/ **6** *1 ¼* **Special Mix**[10] 5164 5-10-11 0.................................. JakeGreenall(3) 89
(Michael Easterby) *hld up: sme hdwy appr 2 out: nvr nr to chal: t.o* **18/1**
/12- **7** *3 ½* **Nurse Ratched (IRE)**[22] 699 4-9-12 0..................... ConorShoemark(7) 77
(Fergal O'Brien) *hld up: nvr on terms: t.o* **10/1**
0/0- **8** *shd* **Cloudy Start**[14] 758 7-11-0 89.. WillKennedy 86
(Violet M Jordan) *hld up: nvr on terms: t.o* **100/1**
9 *11* **Chapelle du Roi (USA)**[294] 4-10-12 0............................ TomO'Brien 74
(Robert Stephens) *hld up: plld hrd: mstke 1st: bhd fr 5th: t.o* **66/1**
0- **10** *19* **Pass Friend**[32] 567 5-10-7 0..................................... SamTwiston-Davies 52
(Martin Bosley) *plld hrd and prom: lost pl 3rd: bhd fr 5th: t.o* **125/1**
0/ **11** *22* **Sir Trevor (IRE)**[65] 8 4-10-7 0...................................... HarryChalloner(5) 37
(John Bryan Groucott) *mid-div: hmpd 2nd: bhd fr 4th: t.o* **100/1**
6- **P** **Gravitate**[24] 671 4-10-12 0..(t) LiamTreadwell
(Paul Webber) *prom tl wknd after 3 out: t.o whn p.u bef last* **33/1**
0- **P** **Pru**[38] 477 5-10-0 0.. ConorRing(7)
(Mary Evans) *chsd ldrs: j.rt 3rd: sn lost pl: in rr whn hit next: t.o whn p.u bef last* **100/1**

3m 53.9s (-2.10) **Going Correction** -0.225s/f (Good)
WFA 4 from 5yo+ 15lb **13** Ran SP% **117.4**
Speed ratings (Par 103): **95,80,79,77,76 75,73,73,68,59 49, ,**
Tote Swingers 1&2 £1.30, 2&3 £31.50, 1&3 £31.50 CSF £3.52 TOTE £2.60: £1.10, £1.50, £15.20; EX 5.10 Trifecta £195.00 Pool: £1,217.70 - 4.68 winning tickets..
Owner Girls Allowed & David Smith **Bred** Noel Fenton **Trained** Over Norton, Oxon

FOCUS
No one was keen to jump off and the early pace was very steady. The time was 3.3sec slower than the first division. The winner has the potential to do a bit better yet and the form is rated around the fifth.

858 STARS 20TH ANNIVERSARY H'CAP HURDLE (8 hdls) 2m 110y
6:40 (6:40) (Class 4) (0-120,119) 4-Y-0+ **£3,249** (£954; £477; £238)

Form RPR
212- **1** **Castlemorris King**[14] 756 5-11-10 117.............................. APMcCoy 122+
(Brian Barr) *chsd ldr in 2nd tl led after 2 out: sn rdn clr: hit last: hrd drvn flat: all out* **2/1**[1]

/54- **2** ½ **Brassbound (USA)**[22] 696 5-11-0 107 .... AndrewThornton 108
(Caroline Bailey) *hld up: hdwy 3 out: rdn appr last: r.o* **8/1**

356/ **3** 2½ **Ivan Vasilevich (IRE)**[40] 5260 5-11-12 119 .... DougieCostello 119
(John Quinn) *chsd ldrs: mstke 3rd: outpcd whn hit 2 out: rallied appr last: styd on* **7/2**[2]

1/F- **4** nk **Screaming Brave**[24] 673 7-11-7 114 .... (t) MarcGoldstein 113
(Sheena West) *led: mstke 2 out: sn hdd: styd on same pce flat* **7/1**[3]

3F0- **5** 3½ **Amuse Me**[14] 756 7-10-5 108 .... JamesHuxham(10) 103
(Jonjo O'Neill) *chsd ldrs: lost pl 3rd: drvn along 5th: rallied after 2 out: styd on* **16/1**

6/ **6** 15 **Canna (IRE)**[10] 3405 5-11-3 110 .... (p) AidanColeman 92
(Ali Brewer) *prom tl rdn and wknd after 2 out* **16/1**

3P0/ **7** 17 **Gigondas**[207] 2904 4-11-1 110 .... JamieMoore 75
(Gary Moore) *hld up: bhd fr 3rd: t.o* **16/1**

5/5- **8** 7 **Sky Calling**[51] 251 10-10-5 98 .... (tp) IanPopham 58
(Martin Keighley) *hld up: rdn and wknd 3 out: t.o* **14/1**

/10- **9** 5 **Vexillum (IRE)**[27] 631 4-11-2 111 .... RyanMahon 65
(Harry Fry) *prom tl rdn and wknd 3 out: t.o* **8/1**

3m 53.2s (-2.80) **Going Correction** -0.225s/f (Good)
WFA 4 from 5yo+ 15lb **9** Ran SP% **114.6**
Speed ratings (Par 105): **97,96,95,95,93 86,78,75,73**
Tote Swingers 1&2 £2.70, 2&3 £4.00, 1&3 £2.20 CSF £18.59 CT £52.73 TOTE £2.50: £1.10, £3.10, £1.90; EX 15.20 Trifecta £50.30 Pool: £973.78 - 14.50 winning tickets..
Owner Miss Daisy Hitchins **Bred** Peter Storey **Trained** Longburton, Dorset

FOCUS

They went a brisk gallop in this ordinary handicap hurdle. Straightforward form, with the winner value for further.

859 SHEPPARD FAMILY H'CAP CHASE (FOR THE GAY, EVE AND TIM SHEPPARD MEMORIAL CUP) (14 fncs) 2m 4f

7:10 (7:10) (Class 3) (0-130,124) 4-Y-0+ **£6,330** (£1,870; £935; £468; £234)

Form RPR

/00- **1** **Finger Onthe Pulse (IRE)**[31] 587 12-11-11 123 .... (t) APMcCoy 134+
(Jonjo O'Neill) *hld up: hdwy 11th: led appr last: drvn out* **9/1**

064- **2** 2¼ **Captain Sully (IRE)**[25] 656 8-10-9 107 .... HaddenFrost 115
(Jim Wilson) *hld up: hdwy appr 2 out: ev ch last: styd on same pce flat* **66/1**

3/2- **3** 3½ **Highway Code (USA)**[27] 634 7-11-12 124 .... RichardJohnson 129
(Richard Lee) *hld up: in tch: rdn after 2 out: no ex flat* **4/1**[2]

5/P- **4** 1 **Giant O Murchu (IRE)**[21] 705 9-10-11 109 .... DougieCostello 114
(Lawney Hill) *hld up: outpcd after 3 out: rallied appr last: styd on: nt trble ldrs* **33/1**

6/3- **5** 1 **Nobunaga**[18] 735 8-11-10 122 .... AidanColeman 125
(Venetia Williams) *prom: rdn after 3 out: styd on same pce appr last* **12/1**

/11- **6** 2¾ **Lough Derg Way (IRE)**[27] 636 7-11-10 122 .... BrendanPowell 124
(Jamie Snowden) *prom: chsd ldr 7th: rdn appr 2 out: wknd flat* **10/3**[1]

/62- **7** ½ **Lukeys Luck**[19] 726 7-10-5 110 .... (p) ConorRing(7) 110
(Jennie Candlish) *chsd ldrs: rdn appr 2 out: wknd flat* **11/2**[3]

215- **8** 8 **Whispering Jack**[26] 646 8-11-7 119 .... (p) ConorO'Farrell 112
(Keiran Burke) *led to 2nd: led again next: rdn and hdd appr last: sn wknd* **14/1**

4/4- **P** **Priceless Art (IRE)**[26] 646 8-11-6 118 .... NickScholfield
(Anthony Honeyball) *hld up: mstke 2nd: nt fluent 4th: mstke next: bhd fr 9th: t.o whn p.u bef 3 out* **11/2**[3]

/06- **P** **Amaury De Lusignan (IRE)**[21] 705 7-11-2 114 .... (b[1]) JamieMoore
(Gary Moore) *led 2nd to 3rd: chsd ldr: lost pl 6th: wknd after next: t.o whn p.u bef 9th* **20/1**

/P4- **P** **Creekside**[31] 587 5-11-11 123 .... DenisO'Regan
(John Ferguson) *hld up: mstke 3rd: p.u and dismntd after 5th* **10/1**

4m 41.7s (-8.30) **Going Correction** -0.225s/f (Good) **11** Ran SP% **116.5**
Speed ratings (Par 107): **107,106,104,104,103 102,102,99, ,**
Tote Swingers 1&2 £25.00, 2&3 £8.40, 1&3 £5.30 CSF £450.81 CT £2728.29 TOTE £9.10: £3.40, £13.90, £1.80; EX 984.40 Trifecta £518.20 Part won. Pool: £691.03 - 0.04 winning tickets..
Owner John P McManus **Bred** Mary Fanning McCormack **Trained** Cheltenham, Gloucs
■ Stewards' Enquiry : Hadden Frost three-day ban: weighed in heavy (17.20, 21 Jul)

FOCUS

A competitive handicap chase run at a good gallop. Solid form with the winner rated back to the level of his good Cheltenham run.

860 GEORGE STUBBS H'CAP HURDLE (11 hdls) 2m 6f 110y

7:40 (7:40) (Class 5) (0-100,100) 4-Y-0+ **£2,274** (£667; £333; £166)

Form RPR

/32- **1** **Vinnie My Boy (IRE)**[24] 669 5-11-10 98 .... (vt[1]) JamieMoore 118+
(Peter Bowen) *chsd ldrs: nt fluent 5th: led 3 out: clr next: easily* **2/1**[1]

0/0- **2** 20 **Dreamsoftheatre (IRE)**[39] 460 5-11-7 95 .... (t) APMcCoy 92+
(Jonjo O'Neill) *prom: hit 4th: chsd ldr 6th: rdn appr 2 out: sn outpcd* **12/1**[3]

6/3- **3** hd **Nez Rouge (FR)**[21] 719 12-11-12 100 .... SamTwiston-Davies 95
(Nigel Twiston-Davies) *mid-div: hdwy appr 3 out: sn hrd rdn: styd on same pce appr last* **12/1**[3]

04U/ **4** nk **Moorlands Jack**[320] 1245 8-11-11 99 .... NickScholfield 94
(Jeremy Scott) *hld up: hdwy 7th: rdn after 2 out: styd on same pce* **9/2**[2]

0/3- **5** ¾ **The Fox's Decree**[50] 264 9-11-10 98 .... (tp) IanPopham 93
(Martin Keighley) *mid-div: hdwy 4th: rdn to chse wnr 2 out: wkng whn hit last* **20/1**

0/3- **6** 8 **Sharlene's Quest (IRE)**[31] 590 7-10-9 86 .... MichaelByrne(3) 73
(James Hughes) *prom: pushed along 5th: wknd appr 8th* **16/1**

32U- **7** 11 **Adios Alonso (IRE)**[24] 669 7-10-12 91 .... BenPoste(5) 68
(Rosemary Gasson) *chsd ldrs tl rdn and wknd appr 2 out* **14/1**

4/3- **8** 7 **Torran Sound**[32] 565 6-11-9 97 .... (b) PaulMoloney 68
(James Eustace) *led: hit 7th: hdd 3 out: wknd next: t.o* **20/1**

501- **9** 3¼ **Brass Monkey (IRE)**[25] 661 6-10-13 87 .... NoelFehily 55
(Charlie Longsdon) *hld up: hdwy 8th: wknd bef next: t.o* **9/2**[2]

FF0- **10** 1½ **Tisfreetdream (IRE)**[13] 764 12-11-7 95 .... (p) JackDoyle 62
(Peter Pritchard) *hld up: hdwy 6th: rdn and wknd after 8th: t.o* **40/1**

0/P- **11** 8 **Mon Reve**[27] 637 5-10-5 79 .... WillKennedy 38
(Violet M Jordan) *a in rr: bhd fr 5th: t.o* **80/1**

P/4- **12** 2¾ **Vinnie's Girl (IRE)**[30] 598 6-10-9 83 .... WayneHutchinson 40
(Martin Bosley) *hld up: bhd and rdn 5th: t.o* **33/1**

1/3- **13** 2½ **Copper Carroll (IRE)**[26] 640 9-10-2 83 .... (p) AlanJohns(7) 38
(Beth Roberts) *chsd ldrs tl rdn and wknd appr 8th: t.o* **12/1**[3]

U11/ **14** 1¾ **Bollywood (IRE)**[10] 454 10-10-13 87 .... (t) LeightonAspell 40
(Alison Batchelor) *hld up: bhd and rdn 6th: t.o* **40/1**

4/0- **15** 18 **Best Excuse**[18] 732 6-10-13 87 .... SeanQuinlan 24
(Jennie Candlish) *chsd ldrs tl rdn and wknd after 8th: t.o* **25/1**

/00- **P** **Played Away**[30] 593 5-11-2 90 .... (t) HarrySkelton
(Caroline Fryer) *mid-div: pushed along 6th: wknd 8th: t.o whn p.u bef last* **66/1**

5m 20.3s (-7.80) **Going Correction** -0.225s/f (Good) **16** Ran SP% **129.2**
Speed ratings (Par 103): **104,97,96,96,96 93,90,87,86,85 83,82,81,80,74**
Tote Swingers 1&2 £5.10, 2&3 £12.20, 1&3 £5.40 CSF £26.70 CT £256.54 TOTE £3.10: £1.10, £3.30, £3.30, £2.10; EX 38.50 Trifecta £66.40 Pool: £582.96 - 6.57 winning tickets..
Owner Roy Swinburne **Bred** Mrs Kathleen And James Wickham **Trained** Little Newcastle, Pembrokes

FOCUS

A modest handicap hurdle which saw a big step up from the easy winner. Generally sound form.

861 SNAFFLES NOVICES' CHASE (17 fncs) 2m 7f

8:10 (8:10) (Class 4) 5-Y-0+ **£3,898** (£1,144; £572; £286)

Form RPR

031/ **1** **Bold Chief (IRE)**[65] 9 8-11-7 133 .... (tp) NoelFehily 142
(Harry Fry) *mde all: shkn up appr last: drvn out* **6/4**[1]

/21- **2** nk **Prospect Wells (FR)**[12] 779 8-11-7 0 .... (t) DarylJacob 142
(Paul Nicholls) *a.p: racd keenly: chsd wnr 3 out: rdn and ev ch last: styd on u.p* **2/1**[2]

10- **3** 31 **Academy General (IRE)**[17] 747 7-11-0 0 .... TomScudamore 114
(David Bridgwater) *prom: chsd wnr 5th to 8th: wknd after 4 out: t.o* **25/1**

4/2- **4** 20 **Awaywiththegreys (IRE)**[12] 779 6-11-0 133 .... (vt[1]) JamieMoore 101
(Peter Bowen) *nt fluent: chsd wnr to 5th: wnt 2nd again 8th tl rdn 3 out: wknd next: t.o* **7/2**[3]

U/4- **P** **Formedable (IRE)**[21] 710 11-11-0 0 .... (p) WillKennedy
(Violet M Jordan) *a in rr: bhd fr 5th: t.o whn p.u bef 4 out* **200/1**

116- **F** **Sail And Return**[12] 780 9-11-0 0 .... SamTwiston-Davies
(Phil Middleton) *hld up: cl 5th and stl gng okay whn fell 4 out* **7/1**

5m 28.7s (-10.50) **Going Correction** -0.225s/f (Good) **6** Ran SP% **112.4**
Speed ratings: **109,108,98,91,**
Tote Swingers 1&2 £1.02, 2&3 £4.20, 1&3 £13.70 CSF £5.15 TOTE £3.60: £2.00, £1.10; EX 4.60 Trifecta £34.60 Pool: £731.90 - 15.82 winning tickets..
Owner The Fyre Family **Bred** Patrick Carroll **Trained** Seaborough, Dorset

FOCUS

This developed into a fine duel between a pair of useful novice chasers for the time of year, who drew clear. Both are on the upgrade.

862 JOHN FERNELEY STANDARD NATIONAL HUNT FLAT RACE (CONDITIONAL JOCKEYS' AND AMATEUR RIDERS' RACE) 2m 110y

8:40 (8:40) (Class 6) 4-6-Y-0 **£1,559** (£457; £228; £114)

Form RPR

5/5- **1** **G'Dai Sydney**[47] 338 5-11-1 0 .... (t) MichaelByrne(3) 102
(Peter Bowen) *hld up: racd keenly: hdwy 4f out: rdn to ld wl ins fnl f: styd on* **9/2**[3]

2 nk **Radharc Nahabhainn (IRE)**[59] 5-10-11 0 .... (t) ConorShoemark(7) 102
(Fergal O'Brien) *chsd ldrs: led over 2f out: rdn over 1f out: hdd wl ins fnl f: styd on* **14/1**

5/3- **3** 7 **Slaney Star (IRE)**[30] 599 5-11-4 0 .... TomCannon 95
(Jim Best) *chsd ldrs: led 5f out: rdn and hdd over 2f out: wknd ins fnl f* **7/2**[2]

4 3¾ **Crazy Chester (IRE)**[30] 4-10-13 0 .... JakeGreenall(3) 90
(Michael Easterby) *chsd ldrs: pushed along 5f out: styd on same pce fnl 2f* **9/2**[3]

5 14 **Inisheer Boy (IRE)**[247] 6-11-1 0 .... PeterCarberry(3) 77
(Ronald O'Leary, Ire) *trckd ldr: plld hrd: led over 5f out: sn hdd: wknd wl over 2f out* **2/1**[1]

6 nk **Deer Park**[44] 6-11-4 0 .... BrendanPowell 77
(Brendan Powell) *hld up: hdwy over 5f out: wknd over 2f out* **16/1**

0- **7** 3½ **Much A Doo**[14] 760 5-10-11 0 .... MrGBranton(7) 73
(Paul Henderson) *hld up: wknd over 7f out* **66/1**

- **8** 15 **Springhill Boy** 6-10-13 0 .... ThomasGarner(5) 58
(Geoffrey Deacon) *hld up: pushed along 1/2-way: sn bhd: t.o* **33/1**

9 1¾ **Looselipssinkships (IRE)** 6-10-13 0 .... HarryChalloner(5) 57
(William Kinsey) *hld up in tch: pushed along 6f out: wknd 4f out: t.o* **25/1**

10 30 **Highfields Dancer** 5-10-11 0 .... MissHayleyMoore(7) 27
(Gary Moore) *hld up: hdwy 1/2-way: pushed along over 4f out: wknd over 3f out: t.o* **12/1**

11 86 **Organization (IRE)**[114] 5-11-0 0 ow3 .... MrJMahot(7)
(Sarah-Jayne Davies) *led: hdd over 5f out: grad wknd: t.o* **20/1**

3m 51.5s (1.10) **Going Correction** -0.225s/f (Good)
WFA 4 from 5yo+ 2lb **11** Ran SP% **125.2**
Speed ratings: **88,87,84,82,76 76,74,67,66,52 11**
Tote Swingers 1&2 £4.10, 2&3 £7.60, 1&3 £1.90 CSF £66.87 TOTE £7.20: £1.60, £4.30, £1.20; EX 61.70 Trifecta £287.60 Pool: £744.07 - 1.93 winning tickets..
Owner Mrs L J Williams **Bred** Mervyn Williams **Trained** Little Newcastle, Pembrokes

FOCUS

Very modest bumper form, with a big step up from the winner.
T/Jkpt: £7,067.00 to a £1 stake. Pool: £39,814.55 - 4.00 winning tickets. T/Plt: £26.00 to a £1 stake. Pool: £117,492.53 - 3,297.63 winning tickets. T/Qpdt: £5.50 to a £1 stake. Pool: £10,491.65 - 1,388.50 winning tickets. CR

CLAIREFONTAINE (R-H)

Tuesday, July 2

OFFICIAL GOING: Turf: very soft

863a PRIX DE LA VILLE DE BENERVILLE-SUR-MER (PRIX DE PENNEDEPIE) (HURDLE) (CONDITIONS) (5YO+) (TURF) 2m 2f

2:20 (2:24) 5-Y-0+ **£14,048** (£7,024; £4,097; £2,780; £1,317)

RPR

1 **Black Kit (FR)**[587] 5-10-10 0 .... BertrandLestrade 121
(G Macaire, France) **19/10**[1]

2 3 **Stodini (FR)**[74] 5399 7-11-0 0 .... StephanePaillard 122
(Mme V Seignoux, France) **16/1**

3 ¾ **Ninive (FR)**[455] 6-10-8 0 .... GaetanMasure 115
(F Nicolle, France) **20/1**

4 nk **Tulipe De Ballon (FR)**[23] 7-10-6 0 .... KevinNabet 113
(D Retif, France) **17/1**

5 3 **Knockara Beau (IRE)**[73] 5404 10-10-6 0 .... JanFaltejsek 110
(George Charlton) *trckd ldrs: briefly outpcd 5 out: 5th and pushed along 3 out: mstke on outside 2 out and dropped to 10th: rallied appr last: styd on wl u.p run-in* **44/1**

6 2 1/2 **Cigliano (FR)**[44] 7-11-3 0 BenoitGicquel 118
(F Nicolle, France) **48/10**[2]
7 4 **Defile De Mode (FR)**[445] 8-10-10 0 YoannBriant 107
(Mme V Seignoux, France) **41/1**
8 1 1/4 **Flash Jackson**[23] 5-10-8 0 RaymondO'Brien 104
(Mme L Audon, France) **45/1**
9 shd **Jakherphi D'Art (FR)**[12] 5-10-12 0 AlexisPoirier 108
(C Plisson, France) **39/1**
10 1 **Madox (FR)**[223] 2570 9-10-6 0 JacquesRicou 101
(J Bertran De Balanda, France) **9/1**[3]
0 **Bit Of A Madam**[12] 5-10-1 0 ThomasGillet
(F-M Cottin, France) **110/1**
0 **Crios (FR)**[19] 6-10-6 0 (b) AnthonyLecordier
(F-X De Chevigny, France) **30/1**
0 **Discover Du Bourg (FR)**[471] 4963 8-11-3 0 ThierryMajorcryk
(Mme F Gimmi Pellegrino, France) **10/1**
0 **Ma Pretention (FR)**[53] 5-10-3 0 (p) GregoryAdam
(Robert Collet, France) **70/1**
0 **Exotic Flower (FR)**[23] 5-10-8 0 LudovicPhilipperon
(Robert Collet, France) **20/1**
P **Tatispout (FR)**[63] 6-10-8 0 DavidCottin
(R Chotard, France) **9/1**[3]
P **Tedeum De Chamirey (FR)** 6-10-6 0 BertrandBourez
(F-X De Chevigny, France) **149/1**

4m 16.0s (-6.10) **17** Ran SP% **117.3**
PARI-MUTUEL (all including 1 euro stakes): WIN 2.90; PLACE 1.70, 3.30, 4.90; DF 16.90; SF 27.30.
Owner Mme Patrick Papot **Bred** Mme B Gabeur **Trained** Les Mathes, France

676 PERTH (R-H)
Wednesday, July 3

OFFICIAL GOING: Good to firm (good in places; 8.5)
Wind: Breezy, half behind Weather: Overcast

864 PERTH INTERACTIVE H'CAP CHASE (12 fncs) 2m
2:10 (2:10) (Class 4) (0-120,120) 4-Y-0 **£5,064** (£1,496; £748; £374; £187)

Form RPR
216- 1 **Sergeant Pink (IRE)**[10] 801 7-10-7 101 (p) LucyAlexander 113
(Dianne Sayer) *hld up: mstke 4th: stdy hdwy after 5 out: rdn and outpcd bef 3 out: hung rt and rallied to chse clr ldr last: styd on wl to ld cl home* **11/2**[3]
/11- 2 hd **Castlelawn (IRE)**[18] 749 6-11-5 113 PeterBuchanan 125
(Lucinda Russell) *led: rdn 3 out: 4 l clr last: kpt on run-in: hdd cl home* **5/4**[1]
22/- 3 7 **The Paddy Premium (IRE)**[39] 13-9-7 94 oh5 MrJHamilton(7) 99
(N W Alexander) *disp ld to 5 out: rdn and kpt on same pce fr 2 out* **14/1**
140/ 4 1 3/4 **Hidden Future (IRE)**[12] 796 7-11-12 120 (p) DenisO'Regan 123
(C A McBratney, Ire) *hld up: rdn bef 3 out: kpt on fr next: no imp* **10/1**
4/2- 5 3 1/2 **Groomed (IRE)**[39] 479 5-11-5 113 (t) RichardJohnson 113
(Tim Vaughan) *nt fluent on occasions: hld up in tch: lost grnd 4th: styd on fr 2 out: n.d* **4/1**[2]
344- 6 2 1/4 **Fred Bojangals (IRE)**[41] 445 11-11-6 114 (p) SeanQuinlan 112
(Barbara Butterworth) *hld up: hdwy after 5 out: drvn and outpcd 5 out: no imp fr 3 out* **28/1**
0P0/ 7 1 3/4 **Jim Tango (FR)**[9] 1398 9-10-2 96 (p) BrianHughes 94
(Karen McLintock) *chsd ldrs: effrt whn hit 3 out: wknd fr next* **8/1**
3/6- 8 10 **Saddlers Deal (IRE)**[48] 343 8-10-10 104 (v) WilsonRenwick 94
(Chris Grant) *chsd ldrs tl rdn and wknd bef 3 out* **33/1**

3m 44.6s (-12.40) **Going Correction** -0.625s/f (Firm) course record **8** Ran SP% **113.1**
Speed ratings (Par 105): **106,105,102,101,99 98,97,92**
toteswingers: 1&2 £1.90, 1&3 £9.60, 2&3 £6.40 CSF £13.19 CT £89.24 TOTE £9.60: £2.00, £1.30, £3.80; EX 21.00 Trifecta £163.80 Pool: £1,498.59 - 6.85 winning units..
Owner Andrew Sayer **Bred** Ring Pink Partnership **Trained** Hackthorpe, Cumbria

FOCUS
The rails were at their innermost position which, along with the new rules on timing, may help to explain the winner's time. A wide range of abilities were on show here, as the top weight was officially rated some 31lb above the horse at the bottom of the handicap on official figures. The first two ran pretty much to their marks.

865 FONAB CASTLE HOTEL NOVICES' HURDLE (8 hdls) 2m 110y
2:40 (2:40) (Class 4) 4-Y-0+ **£3,249** (£954; £477; £238)

Form RPR
/ 1 **Bayan (IRE)**[11] 514 4-11-3 126 (t) RichardJohnson 112+
(Gordon Elliott, Ire) *chsd ldrs: rdn to ld 2 out: clr last: kpt on strly* **4/5**[1]
2 9 **Wot A Shot (IRE)**[26] 662 4-10-10 107 DenisO'Regan 97+
(C A McBratney, Ire) *hld up in last pl: stdy hdwy to chse (clr) wnr bef last: kpt on run-in: no imp* **14/1**
1/4- 3 3 3/4 **Trend Is My Friend (USA)**[56] 171 4-11-3 111 HenryBrooke 99
(Donald McCain) *plld hrd in tch: effrt and rdn 2 out: kpt on same pce fr last* **11/2**[3]
4/5- 4 6 **Tantamount**[35] 531 4-10-3 0 CraigNichol(7) 86
(Lucinda Russell) *in tch: stdy hdwy whn hit 4 out: rdn and outpcd bef 2 out: no imp fr last* **14/1**
4/0- 5 3 1/4 **Mumgos Debut (IRE)**[49] 313 5-10-12 0 PeterBuchanan 85
(Lucinda Russell) *led at stdy pce: rdn and hdd 2 out: sn btn* **80/1**
OU0/ 6 nse **Dynamic Drive (IRE)**[242] 2183 6-10-5 0 (t) StephenMulqueen(7) 85
(Maurice Barnes) *t.k.h: chsd ldr tl hung rt and wknd fr 2 out* **125/1**
/24- 7 41 **Potomac (IRE)**[19] 732 5-10-12 112 WilsonRenwick 44
(Rose Dobbin) *hld up in tch: nt fluent 3 out: rdn and wknd bef next: t.o* **10/3**[2]

3m 43.5s (-14.50) **Going Correction** -1.00s/f (Hard) **7** Ran SP% **109.4**
Speed ratings (Par 105): **94,89,88,85,83 83,64**
toteswingers: 1&2 £4.00, 1&3 £2.30, 2&3 £3.90 CSF £12.48 TOTE £1.70: £1.40, £2.70; EX 10.80 Trifecta £26.70 Pool: £1,622.24 - 45.53 winning units..
Owner Core Syndicate **Bred** Floors Farming **Trained** Trim, Co Meath

FOCUS
An interesting contest but it was slowly run and the form isn't likely to be that strong in the grand scheme of things. The first four are rated 10lb+ off their best.

866 CRABBIE'S ALCOHOLIC GINGER BEER NOVICES' H'CAP CHASE (15 fncs) 2m 4f 110y
3:10 (3:10) (Class 4) (0-105,105) 4-Y-0 **£4,431** (£1,309; £654; £327; £163)

Form RPR
5/2- 1 **Duneen Point (IRE)**[38] 500 9-11-11 104 RichardJohnson 108+
(Tim Vaughan) *j.lft on occasions: cl up: chal 5 out: led 3 out: hld on wl u.p fr last* **5/1**[2]
/60- 2 1/2 **Diddley Dee**[32] 580 9-10-13 92 DougieCostello 94
(Lucy Normile) *bhd and detached: stdy hdwy 1/2-way: rdn and plenty to do bef 3 out: styd on strly fr last: jst hld* **9/1**
/53- 3 1/2 **Laybach (IRE)**[35] 533 9-10-0 79 oh5 LucyAlexander 82
(Jim Goldie) *led tl hit and hdd 5 out: rallied: chsng wnr whn hit last: kpt on: hld towards fin* **7/1**[3]
/43- 4 2 1/4 **Raifteiri (IRE)**[10] 802 6-9-9 79 oh4 GaryRutherford(5) 79
(William Young Jnr) *prom: drvn and outpcd after 4 out: rallied after 2 out: kpt on run-in* **11/1**
222- 5 1/2 **Attycran (IRE)**[18] 753 8-11-12 105 (t) MichaelMcAlister 105
(Maurice Barnes) *chsd ldrs: led 5 out to 3 out: sn rdn and rallied: outpcd run-in* **5/1**[2]
/10- 6 15 **Pyjama Game (IRE)**[53] 222 7-11-9 102 WilsonRenwick 91
(Rose Dobbin) *chsd ldrs: pushed along 1/2-way: wknd fr 4 out* **8/1**
7 25 **Lusiad (IRE)**[26] 666 11-10-5 84 (b) BrianHughes 47
(Karl Thornton, Ire) *towards rr: rdn 1/2-way: lost tch fr 5 out: t.o* **14/1**
/16- P **Shooting Times**[38] 492 8-10-10 89 (v) PeterBuchanan
(Lucinda Russell) *nvr gng wl: towards rr: nt fluent and outpcd 4th: lost tch fnl circ: t.o whn p.u bef 3 out* **9/4**[1]

4m 55.8s (-9.20) **Going Correction** -0.625s/f (Firm) **8** Ran SP% **112.7**
Speed ratings (Par 105): **92,91,91,90,90 84,75,**
toteswingers: 1&2 £5.50, 1&3 £7.90, 2&3 £7.90 CSF £45.87 CT £311.90 TOTE £5.50: £2.60, £2.90, £2.40; EX 54.40 Trifecta £428.30 Pool: £1,159.07 - 2.02 winning units..
Owner T Vaughan **Bred** Con Troy And David Fenton **Trained** Aberthin, Vale of Glamorgan

FOCUS
A very modest handicap. The winner is rated to his mark.

867 ROBERT MCCONNELL SCOTS GUARDS H'CAP HURDLE (12 hdls) 3m 110y
3:40 (3:40) (Class 4) (0-120,120) 4-Y-0 **£4,431** (£1,309; £654; £327; £163)

Form RPR
3/3- 1 **Malin Bay (IRE)**[24] 681 8-11-12 120 FearghalDavis 127+
(Nicky Richards) *t.k.h early: prom: hdwy to ld bef last: qcknd clr run-in: eased towards fin* **10/3**[1]
6/ 2 4 **Call Box (IRE)**[33] 569 8-11-3 111 PeterBuchanan 111
(S R B Crawford, Ire) *chsd ldr: rdn and ev ch bef 2 out to bef last: kpt on run-in: nt pce of wnr* **7/1**
3/0- 3 hd **Dj Milan (IRE)**[24] 681 7-11-3 118 (t) JamesCowley(7) 118
(Donald McCain) *led: hit 3 out: rdn bef next: hdd whn j.rt last: kpt on same pce* **13/2**
/03- 4 1 **Solway Bay**[38] 495 11-10-0 97 (tp) EwanWhillans(3) 96
(Lisa Harrison) *in tch: nt clr run bef 2 out: sn rdn and outpcd: styd on fr last* **33/1**
0/0- 5 1 3/4 **Taruma (FR)**[19] 734 5-11-7 115 (p) BarryKeniry 112
(Simon West) *hld up towards rr: effrt and pushed along after 3 out: no imp fr next* **25/1**
0/0- 6 3 3/4 **Ryton Runner (IRE)**[49] 310 5-11-2 110 (p) BrianHughes 104
(Lucinda Russell) *chsd ldrs: rdn 4 out: rallied: wknd after 2 out* **10/1**
7 1/2 **Rathmoyle House (IRE)**[26] 666 7-10-2 96 RichardJohnson 89
(Gordon Elliott, Ire) *hld up in tch: stdy hdwy after 4 out: rdn after next: wknd fr 2 out* **9/2**[2]
561- 8 2 1/4 **Cruachan (IRE)**[10] 801 4-10-11 109 7ex DougieCostello 96
(Lucy Normile) *t.k.h: hld up: mstke 5th: nt fluent 8th: rdn after 3 out: n.d* **6/1**
/21- 9 5 **Solis (GER)**[18] 750 10-10-11 105 HenryBrooke 91
(Dianne Sayer) *t.k.h in rr: rdn after 3 out: struggling next: btn whn hit last* **5/1**[3]

5m 49.4s (-15.60) **Going Correction** -1.00s/f (Hard)
WFA 4 from 5yo+ 17lb **9** Ran SP% **113.9**
Speed ratings (Par 105): **84,82,82,82,81 80,80,79,78**
toteswingers: 1&2 £4.30, 1&3 £3.10, 2&3 £9.90 CSF £26.67 CT £142.52 TOTE £4.00: £1.70, £2.10, £1.60; EX 30.50 Trifecta £191.50 Pool: £1,010.87 - 3.95 winning units..
Owner David & Nicky Robinson **Bred** Frank McKevitt **Trained** Greystoke, Cumbria

FOCUS
An open contest run a sedate early gallop. The tempo only lifted with a circuit to go. The easy winner is rated back to his best, with the next four all within a few pounds of their marks.

868 FARMERS MARKET SEPTEMBER 9TH (S) H'CAP HURDLE (10 hdls) 2m 4f 110y
4:10 (4:10) (Class 5) (0-100,95) 4-Y-0+ **£3,249** (£954; £477; £238)

Form RPR
344/ 1 **Feisty Lass (IRE)**[9] 824 7-10-11 80 (bt) WilsonRenwick 91+
(Gordon Elliott, Ire) *prom: hdwy to ld 2 out: rdn and flashed tail run-in: kpt on wl* **4/1**[2]
2 2 3/4 **Sultana Belle (IRE)**[119] 4603 5-11-12 95 PeterBuchanan 102
(S R B Crawford, Ire) *hld up: stdy hdwy to chse wnr after 2 out: sn rdn: kpt on fr last* **25/1**
133- 3 1/2 **Solway Dornal**[29] 628 8-9-10 72 (tp) StephenMulqueen(7) 79
(Lisa Harrison) *chsd ldrs: rdn and outpcd after 3 out: rallied next: kpt on run-in: no imp* **9/1**
123/ 4 1 **Ruttan Lake (IRE)**[274] 1711 10-10-6 75 RichardJohnson 81
(Tim Vaughan) *sn cl up: led 4 out to 2 out: kpt on same pce fr last* **9/4**[1]
/33- 5 8 **Via Archimede (USA)**[10] 799 8-10-8 84 (p) GrantCockburn(7) 85
(Lucinda Russell) *chsd ldrs: rdn 4 out: rallied: outpcd fr 2 out* **9/2**[3]
F/0- 6 22 **Glaced Over**[49] 316 8-11-2 85 (p) AdrianLane 64
(Raymond Shiels) *t.k.h in midfield: effrt after 3 out: wknd fr next* **33/1**
/40- 7 5 **Honest And True (IRE)**[18] 749 6-9-9 69 oh8 CallumWhillans(5) 44
(Alistair Whillans) *midfield: nt fluent 5th: outpcd after next: n.d after* **40/1**
8 nse **Powertakeoff (IRE)**[41] 452 5-11-0 90 [1] MrJCBarry(7) 65
(Karl Thornton, Ire) *hld up: drvn and effrt on outside after 3 out: wknd bef next* **16/1**
6/0- 9 9 **Western Bound (IRE)**[53] 221 12-10-0 69 (tp) SeanQuinlan 35
(Barbara Butterworth) *led: hdd whn hit 4 out: wknd after next* **20/1**
PP3/ 10 7 **Talk Of Saafend (IRE)**[6] 21 8-11-5 88 (p) HenryBrooke 48
(Dianne Sayer) *in tch: drvn bef 3 out: wknd bef next* **8/1**

50P- 11 *12* **Lewlaur Supreme (IRE)**[10] 803 10-9-9 **69** oh4.....(p) GaryRutherford(5) 18
(William Young Jnr) *towards rr: rdn and hdwy whn n.m.r and swtchd lft bnd bef 2 out: sn wknd* **25/1**

42P- P **Eliades Run (IRE)**[10] 802 7-10-2 **71**..........................(bt) LucyAlexander
(Ferdy Murphy, France) *hld up: outpcd bef 4 out: sn btn: t.o whn p.u bef 2 out* **16/1**

4m 48.5s (-13.50) **Going Correction** -1.00s/f (Hard) **12** Ran SP% **119.7**
Speed ratings (Par 103): **85,83,83,83,80 71,70,70,66,63 59,**
toteswingers: 1&2 £17.70, 1&3 £10.50, 2&3 £32.90 CSF £103.90 CT £863.74 TOTE £6.70: £2.40, £6.40, £1.90; EX 88.40 Trifecta £721.60 Part won. Pool: £962.15 - 0.01 winning units..There was no bid for the winner. Glaced Over was claimed by Mr Matthew Taylor for £6,000.
Owner Richard Gilbert **Bred** Paul Barden **Trained** Trim, Co Meath

FOCUS
A weak event. The winner was a bit beloe the level of her recent run with the second back to her best 2012 form.

869 WEATHERBYS HAMILTON INSURANCE H'CAP CHASE (18 fncs) 3m
4:40 (4:40) (Class 3) (0-140,131) 4-Y-0+ **£7,027** (£2,121; £1,092; £579)

Form RPR

0/ 1 **Dantes King (IRE)**[58] 152 8-11-12 **131**.............................. BrianHughes 138+
(Gordon Elliott, Ire) *chsd ldr: led 9th: qcknd clr 4 out: rdn and idled run-in: kpt on wl* **20/1**

011- 2 *2 ¾* **Quel Ballistic**[27] 646 9-10-7 **112**..............................(v) RichardJohnson 114
(Peter Bowen) *in tch: hdwy to chse wnr 11th (water): drvn and outpcd 4 out: rallied bef last: clsd on wnr run-in: one pce towards fin* **11/8**[1]

/25- 3 *16* **Peachey Moment (USA)**[24] 680 8-10-13 **118**............... PaddyBrennan 112
(Nicky Richards) *nt fluent on occasions: prom: hit 5 out: rdn and wknd fr next* **9/2**[3]

P/2- 4 *30* **Russian War (IRE)**[19] 733 10-11-11 **130**.......................(t) DenisO'Regan 100
(Gordon Elliott, Ire) *hld up: stdy hdwy bef 13th: rdn and wknd bef 4 out* **7/2**[2]

/P3- P **Quetzal (IRE)**[20] 728 8-10-0 **105** oh2...........................(p) WilsonRenwick
(Martin Todhunter) *led to 9th: cl up tl wknd fr 12th: t.o whn p.u bef 4 out* **11/1**

/10- P **Wild Geese (IRE)**[24] 680 6-11-3 **122**...........................(p) PeterBuchanan
(Lucinda Russell) *in tch: struggling fnl circ: t.o whn p.u bef 4 out* **5/1**

5m 48.6s (-15.40) **Going Correction** -0.625s/f (Firm) **6** Ran SP% **112.3**
Speed ratings (Par 107): **100,99,93,83,**
toteswingers 1&2 £5.60, 1&3 £11.00, 2&3 £2.70 CSF £50.51 TOTE £18.40: £4.70, £1.60; EX 56.00 Trifecta £286.80 Pool: £2,291.96 - 5.99 winning units..
Owner C Jones **Bred** Donal Kenneally **Trained** Trim, Co Meath

FOCUS
A strong-looking contest run at a solid pace. There's a case for rating the form up to 4lb higher.

870 ABF SOLDIERS CHARITY H'CAP HURDLE (8 hdls) 2m 110y
5:10 (5:10) (Class 4) (0-120,118) 4-Y-0 **£4,431** (£1,309; £654; £327; £163)

Form RPR

2/1- 1 **Lisbon (IRE)**[39] 475 5-11-6 **112**....................................(t) JamesReveley 124+
(Patrick Griffin, Ire) *chsd ldrs: smooth hdwy to ld bef 2 out: sn rdn and styd on strly* **11/4**[1]

10/ 2 *10* **The Ice Factor**[455] 5098 5-11-9 **115**................................. PeterBuchanan 114
(S R B Crawford, Ire) *in tch: hdwy to chse wnr bef 2 out: kpt on same pce fr last* **22/1**

/30- 3 *2 ¼* **Cool Baranca (GER)**[24] 681 7-10-12 **104**........................ HenryBrooke 100
(Dianne Sayer) *in tch: faltered bnd bef 3 out: effrt and drvn bef next: no imp fr last* **11/2**[3]

240- 4 *11* **Latest Trend (IRE)**[23] 693 7-10-12 **114**.......................... AlanJohns(10) 100
(Tim Vaughan) *chsd ldr: clsd after 3rd: rdn and outpcd after 3 out: n.d after* **7/1**

/P0- 5 *nk* **The Weatherman (IRE)**[32] 581 6-11-1 **114**............... JamesCowley(7) 100
(Donald McCain) *in tch: pushed along bef 4 out: rdn and outpcd next: no ch fnl 2* **15/2**

152/ 6 *27* **Outrageous Request**[413] 304 7-11-5 **118**............... GrahamWatters(7) 90
(Lucinda Russell) *led and clr to after 3rd: rdn and hdd bef 2 out: sn wknd* **4/1**[2]

040/ P **Lap Of Honour (IRE)**[399] 493 9-10-8 **100**..................... LucyAlexander
(Ferdy Murphy, France) *bhd: lost tch after 4 out: t.o whn p.u bef 2 out* **20/1**

/32- F **Early Applause**[24] 678 5-10-9 **101**.................................... BrianHarding 87
(Nicky Richards) *hld up: rdn and outpcd after 3 out: 5th and btn whn fell last* **11/2**[3]

3m 38.2s (-19.80) **Going Correction** -1.00s/f (Hard) course record **8** Ran SP% **110.8**
Speed ratings (Par 105): **106,101,100,95,94 82,,**
toteswingers: 1&2 £7.30, 1&3 £4.30, 2&3 £19.9 CSF £50.34 CT £296.61 TOTE £2.70: £2.30, £3.40, £1.50; EX 31.20 Trifecta £234.90 Pool: £2,377.47 - 7.58 winning units..
Owner M Deren **Bred** George And Myrtle Grothier **Trained** Oldtown, Co Dublin

FOCUS
An ordinary handicap hurdle with three of the runners returning from long absences and an easy success for the favourite. Another step up from the winner.
T/Plt: £111.30 to a £1 stake. Pool: £70,269.61. 460.57 winning tickets. T/Qpdt: £69.70 to a £1 stake. Pool: £4,582.30. 48.60 winning tickets. RY

839 WORCESTER (L-H)
Wednesday, July 3

OFFICIAL GOING: Good (good to firm in places; 6.8) changing to good after race 1 (2.20)
Wind: Light, behind Weather: Cloudy with sunny spells

871 WINTERFOLD HOUSE SCHOOL H'CAP CHASE (DIV I) (16 fncs 2 omitted) 2m 7f
2:20 (2:20) (Class 4) (0-110,109) 4-Y-0+ **£3,768** (£1,106; £553; £276)

Form RPR

233- 1 **Adrenalin Flight (IRE)**[26] 656 7-11-6 **103**.................. AndrewThornton 114+
(Seamus Mullins) *chsd ldrs: led 7th: rdn appr last: styd on* **15/2**

P/1- 2 *2* **Calypso Bay (IRE)**[38] 485 7-11-5 **102**................................... APMcCoy 112
(Jonjo O'Neill) *hld up: hdwy 9th: rdn appr 4 out: chsd wnr last: styd on same pce flat* **7/2**[1]

/11- 3 *2* **Glen Countess (IRE)**[12] 789 6-11-8 **105**...................(t) BrendanPowell 112
(Brendan Powell) *chsd ldrs: rdn appr 3 out: styd on same pce flat* **6/1**[3]

112- 4 *1 ½* **Forever My Friend (IRE)**[23] 689 6-11-5 **102**..................... JamieMoore 110
(Peter Bowen) *hld up: hdwy 6th: hit 8th: rdn 3 out: rdr dropped whip flat: no ex* **7/2**[1]

612- 5 *3* **Oscar Close (IRE)**[27] 650 8-11-12 **109**...................(tp) TomScudamore 112
(David Bridgwater) *hld up: hdwy 8th: rdn appr 3 out: styd on same pce fr next* **11/2**[2]

13P- 6 *1 ½* **Princely Hero (IRE)**[22] 709 9-10-13 **96**...........................(p) TomCannon 100
(Chris Gordon) *hld up: hdwy and hit 12th: styd on same pce fr 3 out* **20/1**

/4P- 7 *26* **River D'Or (FR)**[22] 712 8-11-8 **105**..................................... PaulMoloney 89
(Sophie Leech) *prom: lost pl 7th: rdn and wknd after 12th: t.o* **12/1**

5/F- 8 *58* **Pastek (FR)**[24] 10-9-11 **83** oh3............................. WayneKavanagh(3) 9
(Dr Jeremy Naylor) *led to 7th: rdn and wknd 12th: t.o* **25/1**

1/4- P **Le Seychellois (FR)**[33] 566 13-10-11 **99**................. SamanthaDrake(5)
(William Kinsey) *chsd ldrs tl rdn and wknd after 12th: t.o whn p.u bef 2 out* **22/1**

/42- P **Run Along Boy**[22] 714 8-11-9 **109**..............................(p) MichaelByrne(3)
(Neil Mulholland) *hld up: drvn along 10th: wknd 12th: t.o whn p.u bef 2 out* **14/1**

5m 45.8s (-2.20) **Going Correction** -0.375s/f (Good) **10** Ran SP% **113.2**
Speed ratings (Par 105): **88,87,86,86,85 84,75,55,,**
toteswingers: 1&2 £5.30, 1&3 £9.50, 2&3 £4.40 CSF £33.02 CT £167.79 TOTE £8.80: £3.00, £1.50, £2.10; EX 46.10 Trifecta £358.40 Pool: £2,587.11 - 5.41 winning units..
Owner Mark Adams **Bred** Alex Heskin **Trained** Wilsford-Cum-Lake, Wilts

FOCUS
Jockeys after the first reported the watered ground to be good, but with some dead places. Division one of a modest handicap chase, and the quicker by 2sec. A small personal best from the winner.

872 WINTERFOLD HOUSE SCHOOL H'CAP CHASE (DIV II) (16 fncs 2 omitted) 2m 7f
2:50 (2:50) (Class 4) (0-110,109) 4-Y-0+ **£3,768** (£1,106; £553; £276)

Form RPR

2/0- 1 **Baily Storm (IRE)**[22] 712 11-11-5 **102**...............................(vp) DavidBass 112
(Lawney Hill) *hld up: hdwy 9th: hit 12th: sn drvn along and outpcd: rallied appr 3 out: led flat: styd on u.p* **12/1**

P/P- 2 *3 ¾* **Three Chords (IRE)**[20] 728 9-11-12 **109**.................... AndrewThornton 116
(Caroline Bailey) *chsd ldr tl led 6th: jnd 3 out: rdn whn mstke last: hdd and edgd lft flat: styd on same pce* **9/2**[2]

42P- 3 *4* **Petroupetrov (FR)**[23] 692 10-10-4 **90**......................(bt) MichaelByrne(3) 96
(Tim Vaughan) *led to 6th: chsd ldr: hit 10th: sn pushed along: rdn and ev ch fr 3 out tl no ex flat* **9/1**

/16- 4 *15* **Noble Witness (IRE)**[27] 646 10-11-12 **109**...................(p) AdamPogson 100
(Charles Pogson) *chsd ldrs: rdn after 8th: outpcd bef next: rallied u.p appr 4 out: wknd bef next* **12/1**

/54- 5 *10* **Lady Myfanwy**[26] 657 12-10-12 **102**................................ MissHLewis(7) 82
(Adrian Wintle) *hmpd 1st: sn wl bhd: tk clsr order 6th: hdwy 8th: nt fluent 9th: sn pushed along and lost pl: bhd fr 11th: t.o whn hit 4 out* **8/1**

3P6- B **Benefit Night (IRE)**[13] 778 13-11-8 **105**..............................(tp) APMcCoy
(Warren Greatrex) *b.d 1st* **7/1**[3]

530- B **Basford Ben**[14] 763 5-11-2 **99**..(p) SamThomas
(Jennie Candlish) *b.d 1st* **22/1**

041- F **Dom Lukka (FR)**[22] 709 5-11-8 **105**....................................(t) NoelFehily
(Charlie Longsdon) *fell 1st* **6/4**[1]

5m 47.8s (-0.20) **Going Correction** -0.375s/f (Good) **8** Ran SP% **111.5**
Speed ratings (Par 105): **85,83,82,77,73 ,,**
toteswingers: 1&2 £9.60, 1&3 £9.20, 2&3 £6.40 CSF £62.71 CT £503.81 TOTE £11.60: £2.20, £1.50, £2.30; EX 52.00 Trifecta £494.40 Pool: £1,622.24 - 45.53 winning units..
Owner Chasing Gold Racing Club **Bred** J Harold-Barry **Trained** Aston Rowant, Oxon

FOCUS
This was considerably weakened at the first fence where favourite Dom Lukka fell, bringing down Benefit Night and Basford Ben. The time was 2sec slower than the first division, and the form is of very limited value. Arguably a step up on last year's form from the winner.

873 MARTIN NIX MEMORIAL H'CAP CHASE (14 fncs 1 omitted) 2m 4f
3:20 (3:20) (Class 5) (0-100,100) 4-Y-0+ **£2,144** (£629; £314; £157)

Form RPR

11P/ 1 **Chilbury Hill (IRE)**[66] 17 10-10-3 **80**.........................(t) MichaelByrne(3) 95+
(Tim Vaughan) *hld up: mstke 3rd: hdwy and hit 8th: drvn along after next: chsd ldr after 2 out: styd on u.p to ld fnl 100yds* **7/1**

P/2- 2 *1 ½* **Quel Bruere (FR)**[10] 805 9-11-7 **95**....................(p) SamTwiston-Davies 106
(John Upson) *chsd ldrs: led appr 4 out: rdn flat: hdd fnl 100yds* **6/1**[2]

/14- 3 *shd* **Rudigreen (IRE)**[22] 709 10-11-7 **98**.............................(tp) JackQuinlan(3) 109
(Noel Quinlan) *prom: lost pl 5th: hdwy 8th: drvn along appr 4 out: swtchd lft flat: styd on wl* **10/1**

260- 4 *6* **Crannaghmore Boy (IRE)**[27] 642 8-11-7 **95**.................(p) JamieMoore 101
(Keith Goldsworthy) *led tl after 5th: led again 8th: rdn and hdd bef 4 out: hung rt appr 2 out: wknd flat* **15/2**

33P- 5 *8* **Winston Churchill (IRE)**[10] 802 7-11-8 **96**....................(t) PaulMoloney 95
(Sophie Leech) *hld up: rdn after 9th: nvr on terms* **13/2**[3]

U/F- 6 *¾* **Numbercruncher (IRE)**[13] 778 7-11-10 **98**.................... AidanColeman 98
(Marc Barber) *hld up: hdwy 5th: rdn whn mstke 3 out: wkng whn nt fluent next* **14/1**

/45- 7 *¾* **It's Me And You**[12] 786 5-10-4 **81**..................................(t) KielanWoods(3) 78
(Michael Easterby) *hld up: drvn along after 8th: n.d* **6/1**[2]

/65- 8 *6* **Fast Exit (IRE)**[18] 749 6-10-11 **90**...................................(t) DerekFox(5) 82
(Noel C Kelly, Ire) *chsd ldrs tl wknd after 8th* **12/1**

66P- 9 *42* **Novikov**[23] 694 9-10-7 **81**..(tp) RichieMcLernon 35
(Sophie Leech) *chsd ldr tl led after 5th: hdd 8th: rdn and wknd after next: t.o* **40/1**

/5P- 10 *50* **Walcot Lathyrus**[14] 763 8-11-9 **100**................................ JakeGreenall(3) 88
(Richard Lee) *prom: mstke 4 out: sn wknd: virtually p.u flat: t.o* **9/2**[1]

4m 51.3s (-8.70) **Going Correction** -0.375s/f (Good) **10** Ran SP% **110.2**
Speed ratings (Par 103): **102,101,101,98,95 95,95,92,75,55**
toteswingers: 1&2 £3.70, 1&3 £7.20, 2&3 £7.60 CSF £46.01 CT £393.68 TOTE £4.40: £1.20, £2.00, £3.10; EX 22.30 Trifecta £121.40 Pool: £2,288.22 - 14.12 winning units..
Owner B Jones & N Wright **Bred** Barry Murphy **Trained** Aberthin, Vale of Glamorgan

FOCUS
A low-grade handicap chase but a fair time for the grade. The winner is rated to the level of his 2011 course win.

874 £32 BONUS AT 32RED.COM STANDARD OPEN NATIONAL HUNT FLAT RACE 2m
3:50 (3:50) (Class 6) 4-6-Y-0 **£1,559** (£457; £228; £114)

Form RPR

1 **Squeeze Me**[31] 6-10-8 0.. BrendanPowell 101
(F Lloyd) *plld hrd and a.p: led over 3f out: drvn out* **40/1**

1- 2 *¾* **Most Eligible**[32] 588 6-11-8 0.. TomScudamore 114
(David Pipe) *chsd ldrs: rdn over 1f out: styd on* **1/1**[1]

The Form Book Jumps, Raceform Ltd, Compton, RG20 6NL.

3 1 ¼ **Grape Tree Flame**[53] 5-10-8 0 TomO'Brien 99
(F Lloyd) *hld up: plld hrd: hdwy over 3f out: rdn over 1f out: styd on same pce ins fnl f* **50/1**

4 2 **Ressurection Bay** 5-11-1 0 LiamTreadwell 104
(Paul Webber) *hld up: pushed along over 4f out: edgd lft over 2f out: shkn up over 1f out: r.o wl ins fnl f: nvr nr to chal* **8/1**

5 1 ½ **Forget And Forgive (IRE)**[45] 5-11-1 0 PaulMoloney 103
(Anthony Middleton) *hld up: hdwy over 5f out: rdn over 2f out: styd on same pce fr over 1f out* **7/1**[3]

6 15 **The Kings Assassin (IRE)** 5-11-1 0 TomCannon 89
(Chris Gordon) *chsd ldrs: led 4f out: sn hdd: rdn and wknd over 2f out* **16/1**

0/3- 7 10 **Imperial Legacy**[27] 647 5-11-1 0 (t) SamTwiston-Davies 80
(Jo Davis) *chsd ldrs: pushed along 1/2-way: wknd over 4f out: t.o* **16/1**

8 6 **Primitive Dancing** 4-10-13 0 AndrewThornton 73
(Caroline Bailey) *hld up: pushed along 5f out: wknd 4f out: t.o* **33/1**

9 5 **Alpetetim** 4-10-13 0 APMcCoy 68
(Stuart Kittow) *hld up: hdwy over 5f out: wknd 3f out: t.o* **4/1**[2]

0/ 10 17 **Nick The Dove (IRE)**[66] 14 5-10-10 0 BenPoste(5) 55
(Chris Nenadich) *led: rdn and hdd 4f out: sn wknd: t.o* **150/1**

11 50 **Polden Prince** 6-11-1 0 HaddenFrost 10
(James Frost) *hld up: rdn over 6f out: sn bhd: eased: t.o* **125/1**

3m 39.9s (-1.80) **Going Correction** -0.175s/f (Good)
WFA 4 from 5yo+ 2lb **11** Ran SP% **114.2**
Speed ratings: **97,96,96,95,94 86,81,78,76,67 42**
toteswingers: 1&2 £15.80, 1&3 £51.30, 2&3 £21.00 CSF £78.82 TOTE £62.10: £9.00, £1.10, £13.20; EX 109.10 Trifecta £1592.60 Part won. Pool: £2,123.57 - 0.96 winning units..
Owner F Lloyd **Bred** F Lloyd **Trained** Bangor-is-y-coed, Wrexham

FOCUS
A surprise outcome to this very modest bumper but a triumph for Frank Lloyd, who owns, trains and bred both the winner and third. The form is rated around the second and seventh.

875 32RED CASINO (S) HURDLE (8 hdls) 2m
4:20 (4:21) (Class 5) 4-Y-0+ **£1,949** (£572; £286; £143)

Form RPR

016/ 1 **Belle De Fontenay (FR)**[167] 3697 8-10-7 117 (p) TrevorWhelan(5) 114+
(George Baker) *a.p: chsd ldr after 2nd: led 5th: clr next: nt fluent last: sn rdn: jst hld on* **9/2**[3]

0/5- 2 nk **Osric (IRE)**[22] 719 10-10-12 112 (b[1]) APMcCoy 111
(Laura Young) *mid-div: hdwy 4th: rdn appr 3 out: chsd wnr next: styd on wl u.p: jst failed* **3/1**[2]

32/ 3 14 **Mighty Whitey (IRE)**[15] 3461 7-10-7 120 (t) DerekFox(5) 98
(Noel C Kelly, Ire) *chsd ldrs: led after 2nd: hdd 5th: rdn and wknd appr last* **5/1**

4F- 4 3 ¼ **Accordion Exhibit (IRE)**[19] 736 7-10-12 0 (t) NoelFehily 95
(Fergal O'Brien) *mid-div: rdn appr 3 out: hung lft and wknd bef next* **9/4**[1]

/3F- 5 1 ½ **Callhimwhatyouwant (IRE)**[54] 202 8-10-12 102 SamTwiston-Davies 94
(Dr Richard Newland) *led tl after 2nd: chsd ldrs: rdn after 5th: wknd after 3 out* **9/2**[3]

0P0/ 6 19 **Tignello (IRE)**[155] 3924 8-10-12 78 [1] NickScholfield 77
(Emma Baker) *hld up and a in rr: bhd fr 3rd: t.o* **100/1**

0- 7 21 **Rusty Nail (IRE)**[28] 631 8-10-12 0 HaddenFrost 58
(James Frost) *hld up and a in rr: bhd fr 3rd: t.o* **33/1**

8 20 **Dubai Emerald (USA)**[9] 4-10-3 0 FelixDeGiles 31
(Chris Dwyer) *hld up: mstke 1st: a bhd: t.o* **100/1**

000/ 9 26 **Bajan Sunshine (IRE)**[213] 2810 12-10-7 0 CharlieWallis(5) 16
(Chris Dwyer) *chsd ldr to 2nd: drvn along and wknd after 4th: t.o whn j.rt last* **100/1**

3m 45.2s (-2.10) **Going Correction** -0.175s/f (Good)
WFA 4 from 7yo+ 15lb **9** Ran SP% **114.7**
Speed ratings (Par 103): **98,97,90,89,88 78,68,58,45**
toteswingers: 1&2 £3.60, 1&3 £4.90, 2&3 £4.10 CSF £18.63 TOTE £5.70: £1.70, £1.20, £1.60; EX 23.10 Trifecta £75.30 Pool: £1,839.86 - 18.30 winning units..There was no bid for the winner.
Owner George Baker & Partners **Bred** E A R L Elevage Des Loges **Trained** Manton, Wilts

FOCUS
This fair seller was run at a brisk gallop. The winner and fifth help set the level.

876 32RED.COM CONDITIONAL JOCKEYS' NOVICES' H'CAP HURDLE (10 hdls) 2m 4f
4:50 (4:50) (Class 4) (0-105,107) 4-Y-0+ **£3,119** (£915; £457; £228)

Form RPR

/50- 1 **Divine Folly (IRE)**[25] 671 8-10-10 89 BrendanPowell 91+
(Lawney Hill) *chsd ldr to 7th: sn rdn: outpcd bef next: rallied 2 out: swvd rt bef last: mstke last: styd on u.p to ld last 75yds* **11/1**

500/ 2 ¾ **Cruising Bye**[31] 7-10-0 79 oh4 PeterCarberry 81+
(F Lloyd) *mid-div: racd keenly: hdwy 6th: rdn and outpcd bef 3 out: mstke next: rallied: hung rt and lft whn nt fluent last: r.o wl towards fin* **25/1**

/61- 3 hd **Shaddaii (FR)**[38] 490 7-10-0 79 oh6 (t) JamesBest 80
(Caroline Keevil) *led: rdn appr 2 out: hdd and unable qck last 75yds* **8/1**[3]

P/S- 4 2 ¾ **Plug In Baby**[23] 686 5-9-11 79 oh7 (p) ConorShoemark(3) 77
(Nick Mitchell) *mid-div: hdwy 6th: rdn and outpcd appr 3 out: rallied appr last: styd on* **33/1**

321- 5 nk **Mighty Clarets (IRE)**[7] 846 6-12-0 107 7ex (v) MichaelByrne 104
(Peter Bowen) *chsd ldrs: mstke and lost pl 3rd: hdwy 5th: jnd ldr and mstke 7th: rdn appr 2 out: hmpd bef last: no ex flat* **5/4**[1]

P44- 6 ½ **West End Classic (IRE)**[13] 777 6-11-4 97 BenPoste 94
(Tracey Watkins) *hld up: hdwy 3 out: styd on u.p: nt rch ldrs* **20/1**

P03- 7 1 ¼ **General Girling**[22] 711 6-10-0 79 oh5 AdamWedge 75
(Caroline Keevil) *mid-div: hdwy after 4th: pushed along bef next: rdn and outpcd appr 3 out: rallied bef last: styd on same pce flat* **50/1**

UFP- 8 1 **Pirans Car**[32] 590 7-10-4 88 (tp) ThomasCheesman(5) 83
(Nigel Hawke) *hld up: bhd 5th: hdwy appr 3 out: sn rdn: nt trble ldrs* **25/1**

/U4- 9 16 **Whatsupjack (IRE)**[12] 784 6-11-4 97 TrevorWhelan 78
(Shaun Harris) *hld up: rdn appr 5th: a in rr* **33/1**

0/P- 10 ¾ **Royal Deal**[31] 606 6-11-6 99 JakeGreenall 79
(Michael Easterby) *hld up: bhd fr 5th* **12/1**

2/0- 11 65 **Pollystone (IRE)**[41] 450 7-11-3 99 IanPopham(3) 20
(Martin Keighley) *chsd ldrs tl rdn and wknd after 7th: t.o* **12/1**

3/0- P **Wild West (IRE)**[27] 650 5-11-6 105 (tp) DannyBenson(6)
(Jonjo O'Neill) *chsd ldrs: mstke 5th: sn lost pl: wknd 7th: t.o whn p.u bef last* **9/2**[2]

4m 48.1s (0.70) **Going Correction** -0.175s/f (Good) **12** Ran SP% **117.8**
Speed ratings (Par 105): **91,90,90,89,89 89,88,88,81,81 55,**
toteswingers: 1&2 £31.10, 1&3 £5.40, 2&3 £25.20 CSF £248.13 CT £2313.83 TOTE £9.30: £3.30, £8.00, £1.90; EX 250.00 Trifecta £1477.20 Part won. Pool: £1,969.68 - 0.35 winning units..
Owner Mrs Helen Mullineux **Bred** Daryl Deacon **Trained** Aston Rowant, Oxon

FOCUS
A modest event with a frantic finish as the leaders came back. They finished in a heap and three of the first four home were out of the handicap, so this form is of dubious value. The winner may have more to offer.

877 BLAZING SAVILLS H'CAP HURDLE (10 hdls) 2m 4f
5:20 (5:20) (Class 3) (0-135,133) 4-Y-0+ **£5,523** (£1,621; £810; £405)

Form RPR

1/1- 1 **On The Bridge (IRE)**[7] 845 8-11-6 127 7ex NickScholfield 144+
(Jeremy Scott) *hld up: hdwy after 7th: led appr 2 out: pushed clr flat: eased nr fin* **5/2**[1]

/14- 2 8 **One Lucky Lady**[32] 591 5-11-7 133 NicodeBoinville(5) 137
(Nicky Henderson) *chsd ldrs: rdn after 7th: ev ch 2 out: no ex last* **16/1**

121- 3 ½ **Cardigan Island (IRE)**[20] 728 8-10-2 112 (tp) RobertDunne(3) 116
(Dai Burchell) *chsd ldrs: rdn after 7th: styd on same pce appr last* **20/1**

0/P- 4 6 **Decoy (FR)**[47] 356 7-10-11 125 KieronEdgar(7) 124
(David Pipe) *hld up: drvn along after 7th: styd on: nt trble ldrs* **11/1**

1/1- 5 2 ¾ **Conellie**[13] 782 7-11-2 123 (t) APMcCoy 119
(Rebecca Curtis) *hld up: hdwy 7th: rdn and wknd appr last* **9/2**[3]

/53- 6 4 **Skint**[13] 782 7-10-7 119 ThomasGarner(5) 113
(Ali Brewer) *mid-div: hdwy 5th: led appr 3 out: hdd bef next: rdn and wknd last* **11/1**

0/F- 7 nk **Bobowen (IRE)**[54] 205 7-11-11 132 SamTwiston-Davies 127+
(Dr Richard Newland) *hld up in tch: racd keenly: rdn appr 3 out: mstke and wknd next* **20/1**

221- 8 1 ¾ **Get Home Now**[14] 767 5-10-4 111 (tp) TomO'Brien 102
(Peter Bowen) *prom: chsd ldr 5th: ev ch 3 out: sn rdn: wknd appr last* **7/2**[2]

354- 9 ½ **Akula (IRE)**[19] 734 6-11-1 122 ColinBolger 113
(Mark H Tompkins) *hld up: hdwy 6th: rdn and wknd after 3 out* **33/1**

030/ 10 6 **Benbane Head (USA)**[76] 5362 9-11-2 123 (t) IanPopham 108
(Martin Keighley) *hld up: pushed along 6th: wknd after next* **40/1**

/P0- 11 30 **Quinsman**[38] 505 7-10-8 115 AndrewThornton 93
(Caroline Bailey) *prom: racd wd fr 4th: rdn and wknd appr 3 out: t.o* **80/1**

11U- 12 38 **My Lad Percy**[14] 767 5-10-4 111 (p) BrendanPowell 35
(Rebecca Curtis) *led: nt fluent 2nd: hdd & wknd appr 3 out: t.o* **16/1**

/06- 13 20 **Bathwick Man**[13] 782 8-10-10 117 (p) TomScudamore 23
(David Pipe) *chsd ldr 2nd tl pushed along 5th: lost pl next: wknd 7th: sn t.o* **25/1**

4m 39.1s (-8.30) **Going Correction** -0.175s/f (Good) **13** Ran SP% **117.4**
Speed ratings (Par 107): **109,105,105,103,102 100,100,99,99,97 85,69,61**
toteswingers: 1&2 £9.50, 1&3 £8.20, 2&3 £25.90 CSF £36.65 CT £666.18 TOTE £3.20: £1.20, £5.50, £3.40; EX 54.00 Trifecta £461.80 Pool: £1,963.44 - 3.18 winning units..
Owner Kit James **Bred** J & D Melody **Trained** Brompton Regis, Somerset

FOCUS
A decent handicap contested by some in-form horses. Another big step forward from the easy winner who can probably win again.

878 32RED NOVICES' HURDLE (12 hdls) 2m 7f
5:50 (5:50) (Class 4) 4-Y-0+ **£3,249** (£954; £477; £238)

Form RPR

221- 1 **My Lucky Flame (IRE)**[27] 649 6-10-2 109 MikeyHamill(10) 118+
(Sean Curran) *a.p: chsd ldr 9th: mstke 3 out: sn rdn: led flat: drvn out* **5/1**

4/2- 2 1 **Letbeso (IRE)**[27] 649 5-10-12 0 (p) JamieMoore 116+
(Peter Bowen) *a.p: chsd ldr 6th: led next: rdn and hung lft after 2 out: swvd rt bef last: hung rt and hdd flat: styd on u.p* **4/1**[3]

221- 3 17 **Garryleigh (IRE)**[32] 592 6-11-5 118 (t) TomScudamore 107
(David Pipe) *hld up: hdwy 8th: rdn and wknd appr last* **7/2**[2]

0/1- 4 6 **As I Am (IRE)**[22] 717 5-10-12 120 LeightonAspell 94
(Don Cantillon) *hld up: hdwy 7th: rdn and wknd appr 2 out* **15/8**[1]

310- 5 6 **Turbo Du Ranch (FR)**[27] 646 6-11-5 0 (b) WayneHutchinson 97
(Warren Greatrex) *hld up: hdwy 8th: rdn and wknd appr 2 out* **10/1**

6 19 **Golden Squirell (IRE)**[38] 6-10-12 0 BrendanPowell 75
(Brendan Powell) *chsd ldrs tl rdn and wknd 3 out: t.o* **33/1**

0- 7 27 **Whispering Boy (IRE)**[15] 758 6-10-5 0 JakeHodson(7) 48
(David Bridgwater) *prom: chsd ldr 7th to 9th: rdn and wknd bef next: t.o* **100/1**

8 13 **Hopstrings**[58] 5-10-5 0 SamTwiston-Davies 29
(Charlie Brooks) *hld up: hdwy 7th: rdn and wknd appr 3 out* **14/1**

0/P- 9 13 **Moneymix**[55] 182 6-10-12 0 JackDoyle 24
(Ali Brewer) *hld up: bhd and drvn along 7th: t.o* **100/1**

PU- P **Heels Overhead**[22] 717 7-10-0 0 [1] HarryChalloner(5)
(John Bryan Groucott) *plld hrd: led: mstke 3rd: sn hdd: hit 5th: wknd after next: t.o whn p.u bef 9th* **250/1**

P **Coney Choice (IRE)**[33] 5-10-12 0 AlainCawley
(John F O'Neill, Ire) *hld up: rdn and wknd after 8th: t.o whn p.u bef 3 out* **66/1**

0/ P **Katika Kapanga**[172] 3622 6-10-12 0 AdamPogson
(Mandy Rowland) *plld hrd: trckd ldr tl led after 3rd: hdd 7th: sn wknd: t.o whn p.u bef 3 out* **200/1**

5m 34.1s (0.10) **Going Correction** -0.175s/f (Good) **12** Ran SP% **116.7**
Speed ratings (Par 105): **82,81,75,73,71 64,55,51,46, ,**
toteswingers 1&2 £2.80, 1&3 £4.10, 2&3 £4.10 CSF £25.34 TOTE £6.30: £1.80, £1.60, £1.10; EX 34.50 Trifecta £102.50 Pool: £2,495.80 - 18.25 winning units..
Owner Keith Adams **Bred** Rosemary Rooney **Trained** Hatford, Oxon

FOCUS
An ordinary novice hurdle which saw a repeat of the C&D race last month in which My Lucky Flame beat Letbeso. Both stepped up on that form, and there's a case for rating this race a fair but higher.
T/Jkpt: Not won. T/Plt: £458.50 to a £1 stake. Pool: £86,243.69. 137.30 winning tickets. T/Qpdt: £53.40 to a £1 stake. Pool: £6,073.09. 84.10 winning tickets. CR

864 PERTH (R-H)
Thursday, July 4

OFFICIAL GOING: Good (8.7)
Wind: Fairly strong, half behind Weather: Cloudy, bright

879 WATCH ALL SCOTTISH RACING LIVE ON RACING UK NOVICES' H'CAP HURDLE (8 hdls) 2m 110y
2:30 (2:30) (Class 4) (0-105,105) 4-Y-0+ **£3,898** (£1,144; £572; £286)

Form RPR

311- 1 **Morning Time (IRE)**[11] 803 7-10-9 88 7ex (p) PeterBuchanan 94
(Lucinda Russell) *hld up: hdwy after 3 out: rdn and sltly outpcd whn hung lft after 2 out: rallied to ld last 75yds: kpt on wl* **4/1**[2]

2 ¾ **City Line (IRE)**[11] 818 6-11-5 **105**..............(bt) MrJCBarry(7) 109
(Karl Thornton, Ire) *hld up: stdy hdwy 4 out: hrd rdn and chsd wnr fr 2 out: led and hung rt last: hdd last 75yds: kpt on* **7/1**

3 6 **Moonlone Lane (IRE)**[34] 572 6-11-1 **94**..............(bt[1]) APMcCoy 94
(Paul Stafford, Ire) *chsd ldrs: led 3 out: rdn next: nt fluent and hdd last: sn outpcd by first two* **4/1**[2]

5/2- 4 1 **Yes Daddy (IRE)**[22] 383 5-11-9 **105**.............. BrianToomey(3) 104
(Kevin Ryan) *nt fluent: hld up: stdy hdwy and in tch 2 out: rdn and drifted rt bef last: one pce run-in* **5/1**[3]

0- 5 1½ **Powertakeoff (IRE)**[1] 868 5-10-4 **90**..............[1] MrNMcParlan(7) 86
(Karl Thornton, Ire) *hld up in midfield: stdy hdwy and prom bef 3 out: drvn next: sn one pce* **28/1**

605/ 6 1 **Captain Baldwin**[20] 2279 4-10-1 **82** ow1.............. GaryBartley 75
(Jim Goldie) *t.k.h early: hld up: rdn after 3 out: styd on fr last: no imp* **50/1**

/23- 7 3¾ **That'll Do Nicely (IRE)**[54] 219 10-10-6 **92**.............. MissJRRichards(7) 84
(Nicky Richards) *hld up: rdn along after 3 out: no imp fr next* **10/1**

401/ 8 6 **Goodlukin Lucy**[15] 5119 6-10-8 **87**..............(t) HenryBrooke 76
(Dianne Sayer) *led: hit 3rd: hdd 3 out: rdn and wknd fr next* **7/2**[1]

/00- 9 19 **Shivalric (IRE)**[25] 678 5-10-0 **79** oh2..............(t) BrianHarding 49
(Nicky Richards) *nt fluent: cl up tl rdn and wknd fr 3 out* **16/1**

446- 10 19 **Fred Bojangals (IRE)**[1] 864 11-11-7 **100**..............(p) SeanQuinlan 52
(Barbara Butterworth) *prom: hdwy 4 out: rdn and wknd after next* **28/1**

PPP/ 11 44 **Darkan Road**[462] 5146 8-10-0 **79** oh15.............. AdrianLane
(Sandy Forster) *bhd: rdn 4th: lost tch fr next: t.o* **100/1**

3m 48.8s (-9.20) **Going Correction** -0.475s/f (Good)
WFA 4 from 5yo+ 15lb **11** Ran SP% **116.2**
Speed ratings (Par 105): **102,101,98,98,97 97,95,92,83,74 54**
toteswingers 1&2 £3.40, 1&3 £4.20, 2&3 £4.50 CSF £31.02 CT £119.23 TOTE £5.90: £2.20, £1.60, £1.70; EX 23.90 Trifecta £81.50 Pool: £852.70 - 7.84 winning units..
Owner Bill Forrester **Bred** Joe O'Flaherty **Trained** Arlary, Perth & Kinross
■ Stewards' Enquiry : Mr J C Barry 11-day ban; used whip above permitted level (24th&30th July, 29th Aug, 8 other dates tba).

FOCUS
Certainly not form to go overboard about. The winner is rated similar to his recent win, with the second to his mark.

880 ABBA GOLD EVENING ON JULY 30TH MAIDEN HURDLE (9 hdls 1 omitted) 2m 4f 110y
3:00 (3:02) (Class 5) 4-Y-0+ **£3,249** (£954; £477; £238)

Form RPR

1 **Crookstown (IRE)**[68] 6-11-0 0.............. APMcCoy 98+
(Gordon Elliott, Ire) *chsd ldrs: led 3 out (usual 4 out): mstke next: rdn and jst hdd whn lft 5 l clr last (usual 2 out): idled last 150yds: drvn out* **2/1**[1]

604/ 2 ½ **Lady Gargoyle**[7] 3344 5-10-7 0.............. GaryBartley 87
(Jim Goldie) *midfield: stdy hdwy to chse wnr after 3 out (usual 4 out): rdn and outpcd whn lft 5 l 2nd last (usual 2 out): kpt on wl fnl 200yds* **100/1**

3 nk **Ad Man (FR)**[229] 8-11-0 0..............(p) DenisO'Regan 95+
(C A McBratney, Ire) *midfield: hit 3rd: drvn and outpcd 3 out (usual 4 out): lft 11 l 3rd last (usual 2 out): styd on wl fr omitted last* **16/1**

660/ 4 10 **The Mongolian (IRE)**[128] 4436 5-10-7 0.............. WilsonRenwick 78
(Martin Todhunter) *hld up: drvn along 3 out (usual 4 out): drvn and no imp after next* **33/1**

/45- 5 25 **Turtle Watch**[25] 676 5-11-0 0.............. RichieMcGrath 62
(Pauline Robson) *hld up: stdy hdwy after 6th: drvn and outpcd after next: n.d after* **16/1**

1F- 6 28 **Ziggie (IRE)**[25] 676 6-11-0 0.............. HenryBrooke 37
(Donald McCain) *mstkes: led to 4 out: sn rdn and wknd qckly bef next* **3/1**[3]

6- P **Weeumba**[35] 552 8-10-7 0.............. AdrianLane
(Sandy Forster) *bhd: lost tch fnl circ: t.o whn p.u bef 2 out (usual 3 out)* **100/1**

P **Now I Win Again (IRE)**[110] 4807 5-10-7 0.............. PeterBuchanan
(S R B Crawford, Ire) *chsng ldrs whn broke down and p.u after 5th: fatally injured* **9/4**[2]

/05- P **Jonsfella**[25] 682 5-10-7 0..............(t) JamesCorbett(7)
(Susan Corbett) *nt jump wl in rr: lost tch fnl circ: p.u bef 2 out (usual 3 out)* **100/1**

/03- U **Karingo**[25] 676 6-10-9 0.............. SamanthaDrake(5) 98+
(Lucy Normile) *prom: hit and outpcd 2 out (usual 3 out): rallied and led briefly whn stmbld and uns rdr last (usual 2 out)* **10/1**

P **Cabra Boy (IRE)**[59] 148 6-10-7 0.............. MrNMcParlan(7)
(S McParlan, Ire) *hld up in midfield: outpcd whn hit 3 out (usual 4 out): sn struggling: t.o whn p.u after next* **66/1**

4m 55.9s (-6.10) **Going Correction** -0.475s/f (Good) **11** Ran SP% **117.4**
Speed ratings (Par 103): **92,91,91,87,78 67,,,,,**
toteswingers 1&2 £18.20, 1&3 £11.30, 2&3 £31.70 CSF £197.31 TOTE £2.30: £1.10, £12.50, £5.40; EX 55.30 Trifecta £665.80 Pool: £1808.84 - 2.03 winning units..
Owner Ms Annie Flora Joan Bowles **Bred** Vincent Walsh **Trained** Trim, Co Meath

FOCUS
Three of these dominated the betting but this was a messy contest for a number of reasons. The last hurdle was bypassed. The winner was value for further and is rated as haviong dead-heated with Karingo.

881 VIEW MARKETING NOVICES' H'CAP HURDLE (12 hdls) 3m 110y
3:30 (3:32) (Class 4) (0-105,100) 4-Y-0 **£3,798** (£1,122; £561; £280; £140)

Form RPR

231- 1 **Green Lightning (IRE)**[9] 829 6-11-2 **90** 7ex.............. RichardJohnson 108+
(Peter Bowen) *hld up in tch: smooth hdwy to ld bef 2 out: sn qcknd clr: v easily* **6/5**[1]

3P0/ 2 21 **Quacity (FR)**[94] 5077 9-11-4 **92**..............(p) PeterBuchanan 88
(Lucinda Russell) *chsd ldrs: led 4 out to bef 2 out: plugged on: no ch w wnr* **25/1**

00P/ 3 10 **Mill Bay**[34] 570 6-11-8 **99**..............(t) KeithDonoghue(3) 86
(S R B Crawford, Ire) *hld up: hdwy and in tch bef 3 out: one pce next: hld whn lft 3rd last* **50/1**

/26- 4 14 **Groovy Dancer**[30] 626 6-11-4 **92**.............. WilsonRenwick 66
(Rose Dobbin) *hld up on ins: pushed along after 4 out: rdn and wknd bef 2 out* **14/1**

5 7 **Massinimoss (IRE)**[47] 8-11-12 **100**.............. APMcCoy 68
(Ross O'Sullivan, Ire) *in tch on outside: rdn 3 out: wknd bef next* **9/1**

/05- 6 3¼ **Reckless Romeo (IRE)**[19] 751 4-9-13 **82**.............. HarryChalloner(5) 43
(Richard Ford) *cl up tl rdn and wknd after 3 out* **50/1**

005- 7 13 **Bob Will (IRE)**[19] 753 8-9-4 **74** oh5..............(tp) DiarmuidO'Regan(10) 27
(Chris Grant) *in tch: drvn along 8th: rallied: wknd bef 3 out* **22/1**

0P6/ 8 47 **Strandfield Bay (IRE)**[339] 1125 7-11-0 **88**.............. RobbieColgan
(Michael O'Hare, Ire) *hld up: hit 1st: rdn appr 3 out: sn struggling: t.o* **16/1**

02/- P **Birnies Boy**[789] 289 9-10-8 **82**..............(t) RichieMcGrath
(Brian Storey) *led to 4 out: rdn and wknd bef next: t.o whn p.u bef 2 out* **80/1**

5/2- P **Academy (IRE)**[57] 168 5-11-8 **96**.............. LucyAlexander
(N W Alexander) *nt fluent: bhd and detached: hdwy after 4 out: wknd next: hit 2 out: sn p.u* **8/1**[3]

F **Obispo (IRE)**[11] 814 7-11-9 **97**.............. DenisO'Regan 84
(C A McBratney, Ire) *hld up: hdwy to chse ldrs after 3 out: rdn bef next: 21 l 3rd whn fell last* **6/1**[2]

1/3- P **My Friend George**[40] 473 7-11-3 **91**.............. JamesReveley
(Dianne Sayer) *hld up towards rr: rdn bef 4 out: sn lost tch: t.o whn p.u bef 2 out* **10/1**

5m 53.3s (-11.70) **Going Correction** -0.475s/f (Good)
WFA 4 from 5yo+ 17lb **12** Ran SP% **115.8**
Speed ratings (Par 105): **99,92,89,84,82 81,77,62,,**
toteswingers 1&2 £5.90, 1&3 £35.00, 2&3 £40.20 CSF £38.82 CT £1014.83 TOTE £2.30: £1.20, £7.20, £14.30; EX 36.80 Trifecta £1137.10 Part won. Pool: £1516.14 - 0.09 winning units..
Owner H Jones **Bred** Western Bloodstock **Trained** Little Newcastle, Pembrokes

FOCUS
A moderate contest. Arguably another step up from the winner, a potential 120+ hurdler on old Flat form.

882 BOOK YOUR CHRISTMAS PARTY AT PERTH RACECOURSE NOVICES' H'CAP CHASE (11 fncs 1 omitted) 2m
4:00 (4:01) (Class 4) (0-115,115) 4-Y-0+ **£5,198** (£1,526; £763; £381)

Form RPR

314/ 1 **Lord Of Drums (IRE)**[74] 5424 7-10-8 **97**.............. PeterBuchanan 103
(Lucinda Russell) *chsd clr ldr: rdn and led passing omitted 2 out: kpt on wl fr last* **7/2**[2]

2/0- 2 3 **Twentypoundluck (IRE)**[37] 527 8-11-9 **112**..............(p) JamesReveley 114
(Patrick Griffin, Ire) *chsd ldrs: niggled 7th: rdn bef 2 out (usual 3 out): rallied bef last: chsd wnr run-in: no imp* **10/3**[1]

/13- 3 1 **Toledo Gold (IRE)**[11] 798 7-11-9 **112**..............(t) MichaelMcAlister 115
(Maurice Barnes) *led and sn clr: rdn whn hit 2 out (usual 3 out): hdd passing omitted 2 out: one pce and lost 2nd run-in* **10/3**[1]

/11- 4 1 **Endeavor**[20] 493 8-11-7 **110**.............. SeanQuinlan 112
(Dianne Sayer) *hld up in tch: mstke 2nd: outpcd bef 2 out (usual 3 out): drvn and rallied bef last: hung lft run-in: no imp* **7/2**[2]

/3F- 5 24 **Muwalla**[42] 446 6-11-1 **104**.............. BrianHughes 90
(Chris Grant) *hld up: rdn bef 2 out (usual 3 out): sn wknd* **9/1**[3]

U/1- F **Kaolak (USA)**[33] 578 7-11-12 **115**..............(v) HenryBrooke
(Jim Goldie) *hld up: fell 3rd: suffered fatal heart attack* **9/1**[3]

3m 47.9s (-9.10) **Going Correction** -0.425s/f (Good) **6** Ran SP% **110.6**
Speed ratings (Par 105): **105,103,103,102,90**
toteswingers 1&2 £3.70, 1&3 £3.90, 2&3 £3.90 CSF £15.28 TOTE £4.10: £2.60, £2.00; EX 16.70 Trifecta £97.70 Pool: £1691.18 - 12.97 winning units..
Owner The Ormello Way **Bred** Gordon Doyle **Trained** Arlary, Perth & Kinross

FOCUS
A strong gallop was set by the leader, but four of the five remaining in the contest held some sort of chance in the home straight. The second-last was bypassed due to the fatal fall of Kaolak on the previous circuit. The form is sound.

883 NORTHERN MARINE UNDERWRITERS H'CAP CHASE (15 fncs) 2m 4f 110y
4:30 (4:30) (Class 4) (0-120,120) 4-Y-0 **£6,330** (£1,870; £935; £468; £234)

Form RPR

604- 1 **Strobe**[19] 753 9-10-0 **94** oh2..............(p) DougieCostello 101
(Lucy Normile) *cl up: led 4th to 8th: led 4 out: rdn and styd on gamely fr 2 out* **16/1**

/14- 2 ½ **Hawaii Klass**[25] 677 8-10-12 **111**..............(b) CallumWhillans(5) 117
(Donald Whillans) *chsd ldrs: effrt and rdn bef 2 out: chsd wnr run-in: kpt on* **13/2**[2]

112/ 3 5 **Be My Deputy (IRE)**[68] 5569 8-11-11 **119**..............(b) PeterBuchanan 122+
(Lucinda Russell) *led to 4th: cl up: led 8th to 4 out: styd upsides: rdn next: edgd rt and outpcd by first two run-in* **7/2**[1]

256/ 4 1 **Kosta Brava (FR)**[301] 1504 9-11-2 **110**.............. APMcCoy 111
(Michael Smith) *hld up: stdy hdwy and cl up 4 out: rdn next: rallied: outpcd run-in* **16/1**

5 15 **Pistol Jack (IRE)**[40] 11-10-7 **108**..............(p) MrNMcParlan(7) 99
(S McParlan, Ire) *hld up: hdwy and prom 5 out: rdn bef 3 out: wknd bef next* **33/1**

0/5- 6 9 **Dica (FR)**[19] 752 7-11-7 **115**..............(t) JamesReveley 95
(Patrick Griffin, Ire) *hld up in midfield: rdn and outpcd after 4 out: no imp fr next* **25/1**

U13/ 7 1 **Sum Laff (IRE)**[34] 569 9-11-2 **110**..............[1] RichardJohnson 88
(Karl Thornton, Ire) *hld up: outpcd 1/2-way: no imp fr 4 out* **7/2**[1]

/64- 8 2¾ **Civil Unrest (IRE)**[24] 693 7-10-7 **101**..............(p) BrianHughes 77
(James Ewart) *in tch to 1/2-way: sn lost pl: no ch fnl 4* **7/1**[3]

P/5- 9 ½ **Lord Redsgirth (IRE)**[49] 341 8-11-0 **115**..............(p) MrSFox(7) 90
(Lucy Normile) *chsd ldrs: rdn 5 out: wknd fr next* **9/1**

10 21 **Passing Through**[20] 742 9-11-4 **112**..............(p) WilsonRenwick 68
(Gordon Elliott, Ire) *hld up: outpcd whn nt fluent 4 out: btn whn mstke 2 out* **11/1**

0/4- U **Hidden Future (IRE)**[1] 864 7-11-9 **120**..............(p) KeithDonoghue(3)
(C A McBratney, Ire) *hld up: mstke and uns rdr 5th* **10/1**

4m 55.5s (-9.50) **Going Correction** -0.425s/f (Good) **11** Ran SP% **116.3**
Speed ratings (Par 105): **101,100,98,98,92 89,89,87,87,79**
toteswingers 1&2 £10.10, 1&3 £13.40, 2&3 £4.30 CSF £116.45 CT £453.91 TOTE £18.20: £5.10, £1.50, £1.40; EX 145.40 Trifecta £476.90 Pool: £2642.74 - 4.15 winning units..
Owner Miss P A & P J Carnaby **Bred** Old Mill Stud **Trained** Duncrievie, Perth & Kinross
■ Stewards' Enquiry : Callum Whillans four-day ban; used whip above permitted level (20th-23rd July).

FOCUS
A weak contest and only the fourth-placed horse was running without either headgear and/or a tongue-tie. The form is straightforward enough.

884 BOOK NOW FOR 2014 PERTH FESTIVAL CONDITIONAL JOCKEYS' H'CAP HURDLE (10 hdls) 2m 4f 110y
5:00 (5:02) (Class 4) (0-120,120) 4-Y-0 **£4,431** (£1,309; £654; £327; £163)

Form RPR

3/P- 1 **Reaping The Reward (IRE)**[49] 342 9-11-3 **116**.............. CraigNichol(5) 122+
(Andrew Parker) *hld up: stdy hdwy bef 3 out: led gng wl next: drvn clr fr last* **8/1**

F/2- 2 13 **Strongpoint (IRE)**[25] 681 9-11-12 **120**.............. KeithDonoghue 114
(S R B Crawford, Ire) *led: rdn and hdd 2 out: wnt rt last: sn outpcd by wnr* **4/1**[3]

2P5- **3** 1 1/4 **A Bridge Too Far (IRE)**[32] 604 7-10-9 **111**............(b[1]) JamesCowley[(8)] 103
(Donald McCain) *t.k.h early: chsd ldrs: rdn bef 2 out: sn no ex* **12/1**

/02- **4** 11 **Weybridge Light**[19] 752 8-10-5 **102**...............(b) AdamNicol[(3)] 84
(David Thompson) *hld up towards rr: effrt and hdwy 3 out: wknd fr next* **20/1**

U1P/ **5** 9 **Windwood Lad**[280] 1654 8-11-0 **108**.............................. BrendanPowell 82
(Michael O'Hare, Ire) *chsd wnr to after 3 out: rdn and wknd bef next* **8/1**

/0P- **P** **Painted Sky**[19] 751 10-10-0 **94** oh4............................(p) CallumWhillans
(Iain Jardine) *bhd: lost tch fnl circ: t.o whn p.u bef 2 out* **80/1**

/50- **P** **Parson's Punch**[25] 681 8-10-11 **105**........................ SamanthaDrake
(Lucy Normile) *wnt bdly lft s and virtually ref to r: t.o: p.u bef 3rd* **12/1**

/30- **P** **King's Chorister**[21] 730 7-10-0 **94** oh1........................(t) LucyAlexander
(Barry Murtagh) *hld up: rdn along bef 3 out: sn wknd: t.o whn p.u bef 2 out* **16/1**

042- **P** **I'Ll Be Frank**[11] 801 8-9-7 **94** oh4 ow1.................(t) StephenMulqueen[(8)]
(Maurice Barnes) *prom: drvn and outpcd after 4 out: sn btn: t.o whn p.u bef 2 out* **7/2**[2]

2/2- **F** **Solway Dandy**[50] 316 6-10-1 **95**.............................. BrianToomey
(Lisa Harrison) *mstkes in rr: shkn up whn fell heavily 3 out* **11/4**[1]

4m 48.4s (-13.60) **Going Correction** -0.475s/f (Good) **10** Ran SP% **118.4**
Speed ratings (Par 105): **106,101,100,96,92** , , , ,
toteswingers 1&2 £4.50, 1&3 £7.60, 2&3 £9.60 CSF £41.43 CT £390.17 TOTE £9.30: £2.50, £2.20, £3.10; EX 33.90 Trifecta £255.30 Pool: £2508.24 - 7.36 winning units..
Owner Mr & Mrs Raymond Anderson Green **Bred** Paul Lagan **Trained** Ecclefechan, D'fries & G'way

FOCUS
Only two counted turning into the home straight. The easy winner was on a fair mark and is rated back to form.

885 JULY STANDARD OPEN NATIONAL HUNT FLAT RACE 2m 110y
5:30 (5:58) (Class 5) 4-6-Y-0 **£2,053** (£598; £299)

Form RPR

1 **Mike McCann (IRE)** 5-11-2 0.. RobbieColgan 111
(Michael O'Hare, Ire) *trckd ldrs gng wl: led over 2f out: sn hrd pressed and rdn: styd on wl fnl f* **9/2**[3]

1- **2** 2 1/2 **Definite Row (IRE)**[19] 754 4-11-0 0..................................... APMcCoy 106
(Gordon Elliott, Ire) *t.k.h: hld up: smooth hdwy on outside over 4f out: effrt and ev ch over 2f out to over 1f out: one pce ins fnl f* **11/8**[1]

2- **3** 2 1/2 **Mutanawwer**[46] 389 4-11-0 0... BrianHughes 104
(Andrew Crook) *prom: effrt and rdn over 2f out: kpt on same pce fr over 1f out* **7/2**[2]

13- **4** 2 1/2 **Mr Satco (IRE)**[21] 731 5-11-2 0..................................... NickSlatter[(7)] 110
(Donald McCain) *led: rdn and hdd over 2f out: kpt on same pce fr over 1f out* **7/1**

0- **5** 34 **Over The Thyme**[15] 768 5-11-2 0................................. RichardJohnson 69
(Karen McLintock) *hld up on ins: drvn and outpcd over 4f out: n.d after* **50/1**

6 1 **Nearly May** 5-10-4 0.. CallumWhillans[(5)] 61
(Donald Whillans) *bhd: rdn after 6f: sme late hdwy: nvr on terms* **25/1**

4- **7** 2 1/4 **The Chief Villain**[33] 584 5-11-2 0..................................(t) AlainCawley 66
(R T J Wilson, Ire) *plld hrd in rr: hdwy and cl up after 5f: rdn and wknd wl over 2f out* **12/1**

8 74 **Ninetynine (IRE)** 6-10-9 0.....................................(t) MichaelMcAlister
(Maurice Barnes) *bhd: drvn and struggling fr 1/2-way: t.o* **50/1**

9 18 **Mary May** 5-10-2 0.. JamesCorbett[(7)]
(Susan Corbett) *hmpd s: t.k.h on outside: hung lft thrght: rdn and wknd fr 1/2-way: t.o* **100/1**

P0/ **10** 39 **Crispo (IRE)**[342] 1103 5-10-9 0.. AdamNicol[(7)]
(David Thompson) *s.i.s: plld hrd and hdwy to dispute ld after 2f: rdn and wknd over 4f out: t.o* **100/1**

3m 47.3s (-5.10) **Going Correction** -0.475s/f (Good)
WFA 4 from 5yo+ 2lb **10** Ran SP% **112.4**
Speed ratings: **93,91,90,89,73 73,71,37,28,10**
toteswingers 1&2 £2.60, 1&3 £3.40, 2&3 £1.90 CSF £10.46 TOTE £6.40: £2.00, £1.30, £1.20; EX 15.20 Trifecta £48.50 Pool: £3981.70 - 61.52 winning units..
Owner Mrs Tracey O'Hare **Bred** James Larkin **Trained** Castlebellingham, Co. Louth

FOCUS
They went slow early before picking up the tempo in the final third of the contest. Probably a fair bumper for the track and time of year.
T/Plt: £60.80 to a £1 stake. Pool: £79,766.92 - 957.18 winning tickets. T/Qpdt: £15.20 to a £1 stake. Pool: £5603.99 - 272.64 winning tickets. RY

886 - 890a (Foreign Racing) - See Raceform Interactive

769 WEXFORD (R-H)
Friday, July 5

OFFICIAL GOING: Good to firm

891a NICK O'DONNELL MEMORIAL H'CAP HURDLE (11 hdls) 2m
6:10 (6:11) (80-95,93) 4-Y-0+ **£3,926** (£910; £398; £227)

RPR

1 **Luimneach Abu (IRE)**[42] 465 5-11-9 **92**................................. MarkWalsh 108+
(J P Broderick, Ire) *hld up in tch: cl 4th 1/2-way: hdwy to go 2nd 3 out: on terms after next: rdn to ld appr last: kpt on wl run-in* **5/1**[3]

2 2 1/2 **Ice Ice Baby**[28] 662 4-11-3 **92**.. AELynch 100
(John C McConnell, Ire) *hld up in rr of mid-div: prog to go 4th 3 out: styd on wl on outer into 2nd appr last: no ex and styd on same pce run-in* **14/1**

3 1 1/4 **Pennys Tune (IRE)**[16] 772 6-10-13 **89**....................[1] JodyMcGarvey[(7)] 101+
(Matthew J Smith, Ire) *hld up in rr: prog into 5th 2 out: kpt on strly u.p fr bef last: r.o but drifted sltly lft run-in* **3/1**[1]

4 nk **Chinook Run (IRE)**[16] 772 9-11-1 **87**............................... MarkBolger[(3)] 99
(P Cluskey, Ire) *led: wnt clr after 4 out: reduced advantage next: rdn whn pressed for ld after 2 out: hdd appr last: no ex and styd on same pce* **4/1**[2]

5 1/2 **Blue Ridge Lane (IRE)**[8] 605 7-11-0 **90**.............................(t) GerFox[(7)] 101+
(John C McConnell, Ire) *mid-div: 8th 1/2-way: rdn into 6th 2 out: kpt on one pce fr bef last: no ex whn sltly hmpd run-in* **12/1**

6 4 3/4 **Glendaars Best (IRE)**[66] 55 4-10-10 **85**...........................(t) APHeskin 86
(G T Lynch, Ire) *chsd ldrs: 6th 1/2-way: prog to go 3rd 3 out: rdn and sn no ex: styd on same pce after 2 out* **20/1**

7 24 **Flight Control (IRE)**[16] 772 8-10-11 **80**.........................(t) SeanFlanagan 63
(Peter Croke, Ire) *chsd ldrs: 5th 1/2-way: rdn and no imp fr 4 out* **20/1**

8 3/4 **Brabazon (IRE)**[11] 824 10-10-8 **82**.........................(bt) PaddyKennedy[(5)] 64
(Emmet Michael Butterly, Ire) *trckd ldr 2nd 1/2-way: slt mstke 5 out: rdn and no imp fr 3 out* **10/1**

9 3 1/2 **Kitts Delight (IRE)**[11] 824 6-10-12 **81**................................. JohnCullen 59
(M O Quigley, Ire) *chsd ldrs: 7th 1/2-way: rdn and no ex fr bef 3 out* **10/1**

10 1 1/2 **Perfect Focus (IRE)**[21] 743 6-10-12 **88**....................(t) GarethMalone[(7)] 65
(P M Quinlan, Ire) *in rr: last 1/2-way: nvr a factor* **20/1**

11 3 3/4 **Mellow Manner (IRE)**[14] 1809 5-10-11 **85**....................(b) BenDalton[(5)] 58
(A J McNamara, Ire) *lost grnd at s: sn in rr of mid-div: 9th 1/2-way: rdn and no imp fr 4 out* **25/1**

12 3 3/4 **Aves (IRE)**[10] 837 6-10-13 **82**.......................................(p) MichaelDarcy 51
(Timothy Doyle, Ire) *chsd ldrs: 3rd 1/2-way: rdn and lost pl fr 4 out* **20/1**

13 50 **Jabus (IRE)**[28] 662 7-11-5 **88**.. RobbiePower 7
(A Oliver, Ire) *in rr: rdn and wknd fr 5 out: t.o* **13/2**

P **Amana (USA)**[37] 549 9-11-4 **87**... MartinFerris
(P A Fahy, Ire) *in rr: qckly p.u bef 6th* **20/1**

3m 50.1s (-15.10)
WFA 4 from 5yo+ 15lb **14** Ran SP% **135.2**
CSF £70.93 CT £260.85 TOTE £6.40: £1.40, £2.50, £1.70; DF 100.00.
Owner John P McManus **Bred** Hong Kong Breeders Club & Canice Farrell **Trained** Roscrea, Co Tipperary
■ Stewards' Enquiry : Jody McGarvey caution: careless riding

FOCUS
A moderate race.

892 - 896a (Foreign Racing) - See Raceform Interactive

784 MARKET RASEN (R-H)
Sunday, July 7

OFFICIAL GOING: Good (good to firm in places; chs 8.4, hdl 8.6) changing to good to firm (good in places) after race 1 (2.15)
Wind: Light; half behind Weather: Fine and sunny; very warm

897 DONNOBLE.CO.UK NOVICES' HURDLE (10 hdls) 2m 3f
2:15 (2:17) (Class 4) 4-Y-0+ **£3,249** (£954; £477; £238)

Form RPR

3- **1** **Marmas**[45] 449 4-10-9 0.. BrianHughes 105+
(John Mackie) *mde all: 4 l ahd whn blnd last: drvn rt out* **6/4**[2]

2 1 3/4 **Oneofapear (IRE)**[25] 7-10-12 0...................................... DenisO'Regan 103
(Mike Sowersby) *in rr: hdwy to chse ldrs 3 out: 2nd next: kpt on same pce run-in* **25/1**

F3- **3** 12 **Just Fabulous**[22] 748 4-10-2 0.. BarryKeniry 84
(George Moore) *t.k.h: hdwy to trck ldrs 4th: 2nd next: wknd 2 out* **11/1**[3]

/2U- **4** 29 **Wintered Well (IRE)**[7] 848 5-10-12 0................................ SeanQuinlan 69
(Jennie Candlish) *prom: blnd bdly and lost pl 2nd: nt fluent after: bhd fr 7th: t.o whn hung bdly lft run-in* **5/4**[1]

0/0- **5** 1 1/2 **Giant Hercules (IRE)**[56] 246 6-10-9 0........................... JackQuinlan[(3)] 64
(Phil McEntee) *prom: j. slowly 6th: lost pl after 3 out: bhd whn hmpd next: t.o* **50/1**

P/ **6** 86 **Nudge The Nugget**[189] 3376 5-10-9 0......................(b[1]) MarkQuinlan[(3)]
(Nigel Hawke) *chsd ldrs: reminders and lost pl after 5th: sn bhd: t.o 3 out: eventually completed* **33/1**

/04- **B** **Kukurudu (IRE)**[7] 847 6-10-12 0..............................(p) FearghalDavis 77
(Simon West) *hld up in rr: reminders 6th: hdwy to chse ldrs 3 out: wl hld in 5th whn b.d next* **16/1**

0/ **P** **Rearrange**[123] 4588 4-10-2 0... TomMessenger
(Chris Bealby) *chsd ldrs 6th: wknd 3 out: poor 6th whn hmpd next: t.o whn p.u bef last* **12/1**

F **Red Tortue (IRE)** 4-10-9 0.. DougieCostello 74
(Tony Coyle) *chsd ldrs: drvn 3 out: 4th and wl hld whn fell next* **18/1**

4m 36.6s (-2.80) **Going Correction** -0.275s/f (Good)
WFA 4 from 5yo+ 15lb **9** Ran SP% **120.4**
Speed ratings (Par 105): **94,93,88,76,75 39**, , ,
toteswingers 1&2 £6.30, 1&3 £2.70, 2&3 £10.50 CSF £39.70 TOTE £2.50: £1.10, £6.60, £2.50; EX 56.10 Trifecta £243.50 Pool: £1,082.79 - 3.33 winning units.
Owner Gary Shelton **Bred** Shadwell Estate Company Limited **Trained** Church Broughton , Derbys

FOCUS
Plenty of water was put on the track since Wednesday (20mm) with the aim of attaining good ground. Clerk of the course Jane Hedley said prior to racing: "It is mainly good ground. There is just a little bit of good to firm on the point of the bend into the back straight." However, after riding in the opener Sean Quinlan, Barry Keniry and Denis O'Regan all called the ground 'quick'. Only three made any appeal to punters during the morning, but the likely odds-on favourite Killala Quay got taken out twenty minutes before the off leaving two to head the market.

898 MANNY BERNSTEIN FREEPHONE 0800 821821 H'CAP CHASE (12 fncs) 2m 2f
2:45 (3:02) (Class 4) (0-105,104) 4-Y-0+ **£3,898** (£1,144; £572; £286)

Form RPR

640- **1** **Mister Wiseman**[32] 632 11-10-2 **80**..........................(bt) TomScudamore 86
(Nigel Hawke) *led: hdd appr 2 out: styd on to ld again clsng stages* **9/1**

/P3- **2** 2 1/4 **Citrus Mark**[26] 714 8-11-10 **102**.. LiamHeard 106
(Paul Webber) *chsd ldrs: 2nd 8th: led appr 2 out: 1 l ahd last: hdd & wknd last 40yds* **6/1**[3]

/23- **3** 2 **Uncle Pelder (IRE)**[35] 594 6-11-10 **102**............................... DaveCrosse 105
(K F Clutterbuck) *chsd ldrs 5th: 3rd whn hit 3 out: hung lft and kpt on same pce run-in* **15/2**

252- **4** 18 **Tom O'Tara**[27] 687 9-9-12 **79**..................................... WayneKavanagh[(3)] 68
(Robin Dickin) *prom: outpcd and lost pl 5th: modest 4th appr 3 out: nvr a threat* **7/1**

/06- **5** 15 **Tregaro (FR)**[27] 693 7-11-6 **98**..(t) DenisO'Regan 71
(Mike Sowersby) *in rr: poor 5th bef 3 out: nvr on terms* **16/1**

502- **6** 6 **Full Ov Beans**[29] 674 9-10-8 **93**..................................... CiaranMckee[(7)] 60
(Michael Gates) *stdd s: hld up in rr: mstke 4th: nvr on terms* **7/1**

264- **7** 4 1/2 **Kayfton Pete**[35] 600 7-11-8 **100**...........................(tp) AdamPogson 71
(Charles Pogson) *reminders s: chsd ldrs: drvn and mstke 9th: lost pl appr next: poor 5th whn blnd 2 out* **9/2**[1]

6BP- **8** 5 **The Grey One (IRE)**[27] 694 10-10-0 **83** ow1................. CharlieWallis[(5)] 42
(Milton Bradley) *in rr: mstke 2nd: bhd whn mstke 6th* **33/1**

/04- **9** 13 **Rocky Rebel**[16] 786 5-11-10 **102**...............................(p) TomMessenger 49
(Chris Bealby) *in rr: drvn 5th: sn bhd* **12/1**

443/ **P** **Wishes Or Watches (IRE)**[202] 3118 13-9-7 **78** oh18.... PaulNO'Brien[(7)]
(John Upson) *bhd fr 5th: t.o 8th: p.u bef 3 out* **150/1**

/22- **P** **Try Catch Me (IRE)**[26] 705 8-11-5 **100**........................(b) MarkQuinlan[(3)]
(Alison Batchelor) *chsd ldrs: wknd 8th: sn bhd: last whn p.u bef last* **11/2**[2]

4m 13.6s (-21.40) **Going Correction** -0.975s/f (Hard) course record **11** Ran SP% **111.8**
Speed ratings (Par 105): **108,107,106,98,91 88,86,84,78**, ,
toteswingers 1&2 £24.40, 1&3 £25.50, 2&3 £26.20 CSF £60.09 CT £421.09 TOTE £10.20: £3.40, £2.40, £2.70; EX 73.40 Trifecta £319.10 Pool: £1,036.26 - 2.43 winning units.
Owner Mrs K Wetherall **Bred** Mrs D Thomson **Trained** Stoodleigh, Devon

FOCUS
The going was altered to good to firm, good in places prior to this contest. Nothing more than a modest contest, but the track record was lower by the winner.

899 MANNYBERNSTEIN.CO.UK BEGINNERS' CHASE (14 fncs) 2m 4f
3:15 (3:28) (Class 4) 4-Y-0+ **£3,898** (£1,144; £572; £286)

Form RPR

1 **Foreverpresenting (IRE)**35 9-11-10 0..........................(t) BrianHughes 111
(Malcolm Jefferson) *chsd ldrs: hit 2nd: lft in ld 3 out: 2 l ahd last: drvn out: dismntd after line* **16/1**

/24- 2 3 ½ **Nomadic Dreamer**36 585 10-11-10 112..........................(t) PaulMoloney 109
(Sophie Leech) *hld up: shkn up 11th: sn chsng ldrs: lft cl 3rd next: chsd wnr last: styd on same pce* **13/2**

U22- 3 2 ¼ **Mulligan's Man (IRE)**28 679 6-11-10 124.......................... BrianHarding 106
(Donald McCain) *chsd ldrs: drvn 11th: lft cl 2nd next: one pce run-in* **2/1**1

05/ 4 44 **War Of The World (FR)**29 7-11-10 0..........................(p) TomMessenger 66
(Chris Bealby) *led to 3rd: chsd ldrs: drvn 8th: lost pl next: t.o whn lft 4th 2 out* **33/1**

/U3- U **Lemon Drop Red (USA)**32 634 5-11-10 118..............(p) LiamTreadwell 115+
(Paul Webber) *w ldr: led 3rd: 3 l ahd whn collided w loose horse on landing 3 out, stmbld and uns rdr* **9/4**2

0/0- F **The Absent Mare**14 809 5-11-3 0.. CharliePoste 89
(Robin Dickin) *hld up in rr: hdwy 10th: chsng ldrs next: 4th and wkng whn fell 2 out* **40/1**

230/ U **Sunglasses (IRE)**506 4371 6-11-10 0.. DavidBass
(Nicky Henderson) *disputing 3rd whn mstke 1st and uns rdr* **10/3**3

4m 53.0s (-12.70) **Going Correction** -0.975s/f (Hard) **7** Ran SP% **111.8**
Speed ratings (Par 105): **86,84,83,66,** ,
toteswingers 1&2 £21.10, 1&3 £4.90, 2&3 £3.20 CSF £105.45 TOTE £18.90: £6.00, £2.80; EX 98.00 Trifecta £309.80 Pool: £1,560.90 - 3.77 winning units.
Owner Richard Waind **Bred** J P Berry **Trained** Norton, N Yorks

FOCUS
Five held some sort of chance off the final bend.

900 ELISABETH NOBLE MEMORIAL H'CAP CHASE (THE SUNDAY £5K BONUS RACE) (14 fncs) 2m 6f 110y
3:45 (3:56) (Class 3) (0-140,134) 4-Y-0+ **£8,447** (£2,480; £1,240; £620)

Form RPR

/31- 1 **Paddy The Hare (IRE)**24 726 8-10-12 120......................(p) TomO'Brien 135+
(Dr Richard Newland) *led to 1st: chsd ldrs: led 7th: styd on wl to draw clr fr 3 out: eased towards fin* **11/2**3

P6/- 2 12 **Owen Glendower (IRE)**413 365 8-11-6 133............. NicodeBoinville(5) 138
(Nicky Henderson) *prom: drvn 11th: chsd wnr bef 3 out: styd on same pce* **9/2**2

31U- 3 nk **Gentleman Anshan (IRE)**29 672 9-11-7 134.................... BenPoste(5) 137
(Rosemary Gasson) *3rd and trckd ldrs: kpt on same pce fr 3 out* **11/1**

/11- 4 37 **Lost Legend (IRE)**30 656 6-11-8 130.................................... APMcCoy 110
(Jonjo O'Neill) *chsd ldrs: drvn 11th: 4th whn wknd and eased appr next: bhd 2 out: t.o* **5/2**1

0/3- 5 8 **Lucky Landing (IRE)**16 787 7-10-13 124..................... JackQuinlan(3) 87
(Tony Coyle) *in rr: bhd fr 8th: t.o 3 out* **16/1**

0/0- 6 4 **Court In Session (IRE)**56 236 8-11-1 123......................(v1) IanPopham 82
(Martin Keighley) *led into s and reluctant: sme hdwy 6th: lost pl 10th: t.o 3 out: 5th whn blnd last* **16/1**

660- P **The Sneezer (IRE)**12 833 10-10-5 120.....................(b) MrsAlexDunn(7)
(Alexandra Dunn) *j.rt: t.k.h: led 1st: hdd 7th: lost pl next: sn bhd: t.o whn p.u bef 10th* **33/1**

0/1- P **Brunswick Gold (IRE)**49 387 8-11-5 127................(p) RichardJohnson
(Steve Gollings) *chsd ldrs: lost pl 7th: bhd whn p.u bef 9th* **9/2**2

/04- P **Aneyeforaneye (IRE)**28 680 7-11-9 131.......................... BrianHughes
(Malcolm Jefferson) *prom: lost pl 11th: 5th and bhd whn p.u bef next* **8/1**

5m 18.3s (-27.70) **Going Correction** -0.975s/f (Hard) **9** Ran SP% **114.5**
Speed ratings (Par 107): **109,104,104,91,89 87,** , ,
toteswingers 1&2 £5.90, 1&3 £6.60, 2&3 £10.20 CSF £30.88 CT £262.20 TOTE £7.50: £2.00, £2.00, £2.70; EX 31.80 Trifecta £253.50 Pool: £2,101.54 - 5.45 winning units.
Owner Foxtrot NH Racing Partnership VI **Bred** Cathy Sammon **Trained** Claines, Worcs

FOCUS
A really good handicap run at a strong gallop.

901 DON NOBLE H'CAP HURDLE (10 hdls) 2m 3f
4:15 (4:24) (Class 2) (0-150,144) 4-Y-0+ **£9,747** (£2,862; £1,431; £715)

Form RPR

212- 1 **Va'Vite (IRE)**49 386 6-10-5 123.. PaulMoloney 126
(Anthony Middleton) *hld up in rr: hdwy 3 out: lft 2nd 2 out: styd on to ld towards fin* **14/1**

0/1- 2 nk **First In The Queue (IRE)**23 734 6-11-0 132......................... APMcCoy 134
(Nicky Henderson) *t.k.h: led to 3rd: trckd ldrs: led after 3 out: lft clr 2 out: hdd and no ex clsng stages* **7/2**1

144/ 3 4 **Swampfire (IRE)**211 2923 5-10-6 124.......................... RichardJohnson 122
(Tim Vaughan) *chsd ldrs: led 3rd: hdd next: keeping on same pce whn lft 3rd sn after 2 out: kpt on same pce* **11/2**3

211/ 4 6 **Mojolika**30 5225 5-10-2 120.. BrianHarding 113
(Tim Easterby) *in rr: drvn 7th: outpcd next: lft modest 4th sn after 2 out* **8/1**

6/1- 5 6 **Kayaan**37 563 6-10-6 127.. KielanWoods(3) 121+
(Pam Sly) *t.k.h: trckd ldrs whn hit 5th: lft 3rd and bdly hmpd 2 out: wknd and 5th whn hit last* **6/1**

P/4- 6 81 **Caravel (IRE)**35 594 9-9-13 127.................................... AlanJohns(10) 42
(Tim Vaughan) *w ldrs: t.k.h: led 4th to 6th: lost pl 3 out: sn wl bhd: hopelessly t.o* **33/1**

0/0- F **Cape Express (IRE)**29 673 8-10-13 131.............................. DavidBass 134+
(Nicky Henderson) *prom: 2nd appr 2 out: upsides whn fell 2 out* **6/1**

1/4- U **Rumble Of Thunder (IRE)**36 216 7-10-10 128.........(p) RichieMcGrath 117
(Philip Kirby) *w ldrs: led 6th: hdd after 3 out: 6th and hld whn bdly hmpd and uns rdr 2 out* **7/1**

/21- F **Smalib Monterg (FR)**24 409 7-10-13 131......................(tp) TomO'Brien 124
(Dr Richard Newland) *in rr: chsng ldrs 4th: 5th and one pce whn fell 2 out* **5/1**2

4m 30.2s (-9.20) **Going Correction** -0.275s/f (Good) **9** Ran SP% **116.1**
Speed ratings (Par 109): **108,107,106,103,101 67,** , ,
toteswingers 1&2 £9.30, 1&3 £9.00, 2&3 £3.40 CSF £64.15 CT £310.27 TOTE £15.30: £2.90, £1.70, £2.40; EX 60.90 Trifecta £778.40 Pool: £3,255.99 - 3.13 winning units.
Owner Ms B Woodcock & Mrs D Dewbery **Bred** M Conaghan **Trained** Granborough, Bucks

FOCUS
Quite a few had a chance turning in but the whole picture changed at the second-last.

902 TOM HALLIDAY MEMORIAL CONDITIONAL JOCKEYS' H'CAP HURDLE (9 hdls 1 omitted) 2m 5f
4:45 (4:49) (Class 4) (0-120,118) 4-Y-0+ **£3,249** (£954; £477; £238)

Form RPR

0/4- 1 **Compton Blue**35 604 7-11-8 114..................................(b) KillianMoore 119
(Alan King) *chsd ldrs: 3rd and drvn 3 out: swtchd rt and wnt 2nd appr last: styd on to ld run-in: edgd lft: drvn out* **8/1**

250/ 2 1 ½ **Sagredo (USA)**23 2327 9-10-12 110..........................(v1) DannyBenson(6) 114
(Jonjo O'Neill) *trckd ldrs: hmpd and lost pl 2nd: trckd ldrs 4th: led gng wl 2 out: hdd run-in: no ex* **8/1**

F/2- 3 12 **Violets Boy (IRE)**27 698 6-11-6 112..........................(t) BrendanPowell 106
(Brendan Powell) *led: hdd 2 out: wknd last* **7/2**2

/35- 4 3 ¾ **The Fox's Decree**5 860 9-10-3 98...........................(tp) IanPopham(3) 87
(Martin Keighley) *hmpd 2nd: drvn and lost pl 5th: tk modest 4th 2 out* **4/1**3

5/3- 5 3 **Exit To Freedom**37 564 7-9-9 92 oh4.......................(p) CraigNichol(5) 79
(Neville Bycroft) *t.k.h: trckd ldrs: rdn 3 out: sn wknd* **14/1**

/13- 6 6 **Valleyofmilan (IRE)**23 737 6-11-4 118........................ JamesCowley(8) 99
(Donald McCain) *in rr: bhd fr omitted 7th* **3/1**1

6/3- 7 11 **Manshoor (IRE)**35 598 8-10-0 95.................................... MattCrawley(3) 74
(Lucy Wadham) *chsd ldrs: hmpd 2nd: drvn 4th: lost pl omitted 7th: bhd fr 3 out: eased clsng stages* **10/1**

/22- F **Father Shine (IRE)**35 606 10-10-10 102........................ TrevorWhelan
(Shaun Harris) *chsd ldrs: fell 2nd* **10/1**

U05- P **Fitandproperjob**18 764 7-9-9 92 oh3.......................(t) CharlieDeutsch(5)
(Anthony Middleton) *in rr: hdwy 4th: lost pl omitted 7th: sn bhd: t.o whn p.u bef 2 out* **12/1**

5m 6.9s (-1.90) **Going Correction** -0.275s/f (Good) **9** Ran SP% **122.0**
Speed ratings (Par 105): **92,91,86,85,84 82,77,** ,
toteswingers 1&2 £8.80, 1&3 £4.30, 2&3 £8.30 CSF £73.20 CT £270.66 TOTE £8.10: £2.60, £2.10, £1.80; EX 35.90 Trifecta £124.50 Pool: £1,890.64 - 11.38 winning units.
Owner Godfrey Wilson **Bred** Caroline Wilson **Trained** Barbury Castle, Wilts

FOCUS
One of the hurdles in the back straight was bypassed on the second circuit. With a few of these in fair form, it was surprising two came away quite early but they both found little in the final stages.

903 DON NOBLE LADY AMATEUR RIDERS' H'CAP HURDLE (8 hdls) 2m 1f
5:15 (5:18) (Class 5) (0-95,95) 4-Y-0+ **£2,433** (£754; £377; £188)

Form RPR

264- 1 **Pobs Trophy**31 651 6-10-3 79..............................(b) MissBeckySmith(7) 87
(Richard Guest) *chsd clr ldr: led bef 2 out: kpt on wl clsng stages* **7/2**1

2/5- 2 1 ½ **On The Feather**39 540 7-11-8 91.............................(b) MissGAndrews 98
(Jim Best) *hld up in rr-div: hdwy 4th: 3rd 3 out: upsides next: no ex last 50yds* **4/1**2

0/5- 3 4 **Aughcarra (IRE)**35 605 8-10-1 75.............................. MissAEStirling(5) 78
(Harry Chisman) *chsd ldrs: kpt on same pce appr 2 out* **6/1**

U/F- 4 2 ¾ **Massachusetts**55 264 6-9-7 69 oh10............ MissGeorgiaHenderson(7) 70
(Rob Summers) *rr-div: hdwy 3 out: 4th last: one pce* **66/1**

/02- 5 3 ¾ **Tennessee Bird**14 803 5-10-7 81.............................. MissAliceMills(5) 79
(Mike Sowersby) *led: clr after 1st tl after 4th: mstke next: hdd bef 2 out: one pce* **9/2**3

006- 6 13 **Tri Nations (UAE)**12 833 8-11-5 93...........................(vt) MissCBoxall(5) 81
(Anthony Middleton) *mid-div: hdwy 5th: modest 5th 2 out: sn wknd* **11/1**

60/- 7 2 ¼ **Phoenix Eye**248 2136 12-10-7 79.................................... MissHBethell(3) 63
(Michael Mullineaux) *hld up in rr: kpt on fr 2 out: nvr on terms* **16/1**

2/6- 8 6 **Richo**6 314 7-9-12 74.. MissJGillam(7) 52
(Shaun Harris) *prom: lost pl 5th* **9/1**

000/ 9 4 **Cunning Plan (IRE)**69 29 6-10-3 79.......... MissEmily-JaneHarbour(7) 54
(Raymond York) *in rr: bhd fr 4th* **33/1**

0/0- 10 3 ¼ **Walter De La Mare (IRE)**26 193 6-11-9 95...(p) MissHannahWatson(3) 67
(Anabel K Murphy) *mid-div: hdwy to chse ldrs 3 out: sn wknd* **20/1**

/0U- 11 12 **Samizdat (FR)**35 598 10-9-9 71.................................... MissGSwan(7) 32
(John Upson) *chsd ldrs: lost pl 3 out* **20/1**

00P/ 12 29 **Murfreesboro**69 29 10-11-5 91.................................... MrsAlexDunn(3) 26
(Raymond York) *in rr: nt fluent 3rd: bhd fr next: t.o 2 out* **18/1**

4m 3.4s (-3.30) **Going Correction** -0.275s/f (Good) **12** Ran SP% **118.1**
Speed ratings (Par 103): **96,95,93,92,90 84,83,80,78,76 71,57**
toteswingers 1&2 £4.20, 1&3 £6.60, 2&3 £7.40 CSF £17.30 CT £82.14 TOTE £5.00: £1.60, £1.90, £2.40; EX 20.00 Trifecta £90.30 Pool: £1,665.39 - 13.81 winning units.
Owner Miss C Fordham **Bred** Mrs S Joint **Trained** Wetherby, W Yorks

FOCUS
Weak form whatever way you look at it.
T/Jkpt: Not won. T/Plt: £1,299.70 to a £1 stake. Pool: £114,482.56 - 64.30 winning units T/Qpdt: £90.70 to a £1 stake. Pool: £9,511.99 - 77.60 winning units WG

904 - 919a (Foreign Racing) - See Raceform Interactive

828 NEWTON ABBOT (L-H)
Monday, July 8

OFFICIAL GOING: Good to firm (good in places; watered; 8.3)
All rails moved to innermost position.
Wind: Virtually nil Weather: Sunny

920 VISIT NEWTON ABBOT RACECOURSE ON FACEBOOK MAIDEN HURDLE (9 hdls) 2m 3f
2:15 (2:15) (Class 5) 4-Y-0+ **£2,463** (£718; £359)

Form RPR

11- 1 **Another Hero (IRE)**20 760 4-10-11 0.................................... APMcCoy 115+
(Jonjo O'Neill) *mid-div: hdwy after 4th: led bef 2 out where wnt lft: in command whn wnt lft last: comf* **5/4**1

5/0- 2 8 **Kalmbeforethestorm**57 233 5-11-0 0.............................. PaulMoloney 107
(Helen Nelmes) *mid-div: hdwy appr 3 out: rdn to chse wnr sn after 2 out: hld bef last: kpt on same pce* **20/1**

4/0- 3 2 ¾ **Multitude Of Sins**8 847 6-11-0 0.................................. BrendanPowell 104
(Colin Tizzard) *in tch: trckd ldrs after 3 out: rdn in cl 3rd whn wnt lft 2 out: kpt on same pce* **66/1**

/24- 4 11 **Lady Lectra**13 828 4-10-4 103.. TomO'Brien 85
(John Flint) *led: rdn and hdd bef 2 out where mstke: fdd* **11/4**2

5 7 **Alderbrook Lad (IRE)**36 7-11-0 0..............................(t1) NoelFehily 85
(Neil Mulholland) *trckd ldrs: wnt prom 4th: rdn and ev ch after 3 out: hld bef next: fdd* **6/1**3

The Form Book Jumps, Raceform Ltd, Compton, RG20 6NL.

/52- **6** 1 3/4 **Cannon Fodder**[20] 755 6-10-7 0 MattieBatchelor 77
(Sheena West) *hld up towards rr: pushed along after 4th: midfield u.p after 3 out: nvr trbld ldrs* **10/1**

/23- **7** 1 1/4 **Port Hill**[28] 688 6-11-0 100 DPFahy 82
(Liam Corcoran) *a mid-div* **14/1**

605- **8** 2 1/4 **Bad Girls (FR)**[12] 841 4-10-4 0 (t) TomScudamore 70
(David Pipe) *mid-div: rdn after 3 out: nvr any imp on ldrs* **25/1**

9 20 **Broadway Cord (IRE)**[23] 6-11-0 0 HaddenFrost 60
(Martin Hill) *hld up towards rr: prog into midfield after 4th: rdn after 3 out: sn wknd* **50/1**

40- **10** 1 1/4 **Sportsreport (IRE)**[41] 519 5-11-0 0 AndrewThornton 59
(Seamus Mullins) *racd keenly: trckd ldrs: rdn after 3 out: sn wknd* **33/1**

11 7 **Bolberry Springs**[71] 6-11-0 0 JoeTizzard 52
(Colin Tizzard) *trckd ldr tl 4th: cl up: rdn and wknd bef 3 out* **33/1**

/00- **12** dist **Revupclover (IRE)**[13] 828 6-10-11 0 MarkQuinlan(3)
(Polly Gundry) *mid-div: hdwy 3rd: drvn after next: bhd whn hmpd 5th: t.o* **200/1**

/30- **13** 1 **On The Move**[27] 717 5-10-4 0 RachaelGreen(3)
(Anthony Honeyball) *a towards rr: lost tch fr 5th: t.o* **66/1**

4m 17.6s (-12.40) **Going Correction** -0.85s/f (Firm)
WFA 4 from 5yo+ 15lb **13 Ran SP% 121.1**
Speed ratings (Par 103): **92,88,87,82,79 79,78,77,69,68 65,46,46**
toteswingers 1&2 £6.80, 1&3 £48.90, 2&3 £20.10 CSF £32.44 TOTE £2.40: £1.20, £5.00, £12.10; EX 33.60 Trifecta £477.00 Pool: £1,158.08 - 1.82 winning units.
Owner John P McManus **Bred** Miss Noreen Hayes **Trained** Cheltenham, Gloucs

FOCUS
This was not a strong maiden hurdle, but it was run at an honest pace. The easy winner is rated in line with his bumper figures.

921 TRY TOTEQUICKPICK IF YOU'RE FEELING LUCKY BEGINNERS' CHASE (16 fncs) 2m 5f 110y
2:45 (2:45) (Class 4) 5-Y-0+ **£4,288** (£1,259; £629; £314)

Form RPR

1/4- **1** **Ace Fighter Pilot**[37] 586 7-11-0 127 APMcCoy 125+
(Jim Best) *trckd ldr: led narrowly 10th: styd on wl fr 3 out: hit last: pushed out* **7/2**3

121/ **2** 5 **Escudero (IRE)**[65] 8-11-0 0 NickScholfield 119
(Paul Nicholls) *trckd ldrs: rdn to chse wnr after 4 out: a being hld fr 2 out: styd on same pce* **7/2**3

2F3/ **3** 8 **Ballylifen (IRE)**[114] 4789 6-11-0 118 ConorO'Farrell 112
(Mick Channon) *trckd ldrs: rdn after 4 out: wnt 3rd 2 out: styd on same pce* **11/4**2

224- **4** 14 **Well Mett (IRE)**[30] 670 6-11-0 120 (bt) PaddyBrennan 102
(Fergal O'Brien) *j.rt 1st: led: jnd 9th: narrowly hdd next: rchd for 11th: rdn whn lost 2nd after 4 out: fading in 4th whn nt fluent 2 out* **5/2**1

50P/ **5** 3 1/4 **Highbury High (IRE)**[45] 6-11-0 0 TomO'Brien 93
(Paul Henderson) *mid-div: outpcd 11th: styd on fr 3 out but nvr any ch w ldrs* **100/1**

00- **6** 28 **Rusty Nail (IRE)**[5] 875 8-11-0 0 HaddenFrost 65
(James Frost) *a towards rr: lost tch 11th: t.o* **66/1**

5/P- **7** 2 1/4 **Theroadtogorey (IRE)**[60] 188 7-11-0 0 IanPopham 63
(Sarah Robinson) *a towards rr: no ch fr 11th: t.o* **100/1**

/F0- **8** 19 **Mac Beattie**[8] 854 7-10-11 0 AdamWedge(3) 44
(Evan Williams) *mid-div: outpcd 11th: no ch after: t.o* **50/1**

415/ **9** 21 **Miracle House (IRE)**[299] 1558 9-11-0 0 (t) RichardJohnson 23
(Tim Vaughan) *mid-div: outpcd 11th: no ch after: t.o* **12/1**

5- **P** **Thehorsemaytalk (IRE)**[41] 518 8-10-7 0 KevinJones(7)
(Mark Shears) *a towards rr: tailing off whn p.u bef 10th* **50/1**

5m 2.3s (-19.10) **Going Correction** -1.075s/f (Hard) **10 Ran SP% 114.8**
Speed ratings: **91,89,86,81,80 69,69,62,54,**
toteswingers 1&2 £3.80, 1&3 £2.70, 2&3 £2.90 CSF £16.24 TOTE £4.50: £1.50, £1.80, £1.10; EX 20.00 Trifecta £53.30 Pool: £1,317.63 - 18.53 winning units.
Owner Odds On Racing **Bred** P E W Nicholson **Trained** Lewes, E Sussex

FOCUS
Plenty of pace on for this beginners' chase, with the front four home in control a long way out. The cosy winner improved towards the level of his hurdle form.

922 NORTH DEVON HOSPICE MARES' NOVICES' HURDLE (10 hdls) 2m 6f
3:15 (3:15) (Class 4) 4-Y-0+ **£3,508** (£1,030; £515; £257)

Form RPR

/11- **1** **Massannie (IRE)**[20] 755 5-11-10 124 TomScudamore 125+
(David Pipe) *led tl after 2nd: led next: hit 5th: nt fluent and briefly hdd next: drew clr and in total control after 3 out: easily* **4/11**1

231- **2** 18 **Emerald Rose**[15] 811 6-10-12 110 GavinSheehan(5) 92
(Julian Smith) *pressed wnr: led after 2nd tl next: led briefly after 6th: rdn to chse wnr after 3 out: sn outpcd but kpt on for 2nd* **3/1**2

0- **3** 8 **Ailanthus**[18] 777 4-10-7 0 AidanColeman 73
(Richard Woollacott) *hld up: smooth prog into 3rd 3 out: rdn bef next: sn one pce* **66/1**

U- **4** 3 1/4 **Night Of Passion (IRE)**[8] 849 5-10-10 0 NickScholfield 72
(Jeremy Scott) *trckd ldrs: rdn after 3 out: sn one pce* **20/1**

6/5- **5** 6 **Dungarvan Lass (IRE)**[27] 715 4-10-4 0 JeremiahMcGrath(3) 63
(Nicky Henderson) *racd keenly early: trckd ldrs: rdn after 7th: nvr gng pce to threaten: wknd after 2 out* **14/1**3

P **It'syourdeal (IRE)**[785] 8-10-3 0 ThomasCheesman(7)
(Nick Ayliffe) *trckd ldrs: rdn after 7th: wknd after 3 out: p.u bef next* **100/1**

5m 23.3s (3.10) **Going Correction** -0.85s/f (Firm)
WFA 4 from 5yo+ 16lb **6 Ran SP% 112.2**
Speed ratings (Par 105): **60,53,50,49,47**
toteswingers 1&2 £1.10, 1&3 £2.20, 2&3 £6.70 CSF £1.87 TOTE £1.20: £1.10, £1.50; EX 1.90 Trifecta £11.00 Pool: £1,648.10 - 111.36 winning units.
Owner Wayne Clifford **Bred** Mrs S Clifford **Trained** Nicholashayne, Devon

FOCUS
An uncompetitive mares' novices' hurdle, run at a sedate pace. The facile winner stood out in this company.

923 NEWTONABBOTRACE ON TWITTER H'CAP CHASE (20 fncs) 3m 2f 110y
3:45 (3:45) (Class 3) (0-135,133) 4-Y-0+ **£7,596** (£2,244; £1,122; £561; £280)

Form RPR

0/2- **1** **No Loose Change (IRE)**[33] 633 8-11-7 133 (t) HarryDerham(5) 153+
(Paul Nicholls) *j.w: trckd ldrs: led 10th: drew clr after 4 out: comf* **12/1**

113- **2** 13 **Royale Knight**[32] 642 7-10-5 112 TomO'Brien 117
(Dr Richard Newland) *trckd ldrs: rdn after 4 out: styd on same pce fr next: wnt 2nd at the last: no ch w wnr* **9/2**2

F/2- **3** 7 **Sheriff Hutton (IRE)**[12] 845 10-11-4 125 HaddenFrost 126
(Martin Hill) *in tch: trckd ldrs 14th: wnt 2nd after 11th: rdn to chse wnr after 4 out: hld: styd on same pce: no ex whn lost 2nd at the last* **13/2**

0/5- **4** 6 **Ballybough Gorta (IRE)**[32] 643 6-11-1 122 (p) JamieMoore 113
(Peter Bowen) *led tl 10th: sn drvn in midfield: nvr bk on terms: wnt wl hld 4th 2 out* **11/2**3

4/2- **5** 8 **Iona Days (IRE)**[42] 508 8-10-11 118 (p) WayneHutchinson 101
(Julian Smith) *mid-div: rdn and hdwy after 13th: disp 3rd after 15th: wknd after 3 out* **14/1**

5/1- **6** 72 **Satou (FR)**[19] 766 7-11-0 121 (p) RichardJohnson 32
(Philip Hobbs) *mid-div: nt fluent 7th: trckd ldrs 13th tl 15th: sn wknd: t.o* **7/1**

163- **P** **Hell's Bay (FR)**[18] 780 11-11-11 132 (p) FelixDeGiles
(Keiran Burke) *hld up towards rr: p.u bef 13th: dismntd* **20/1**

236- **P** **Double Chocolate**[20] 757 10-9-11 111 (p) JakeHodson(7)
(David Bridgwater) *tended to jump sltly rt at times: mid-div tl struggling after 13th: t.o whn p.u bef 4 out* **25/1**

150- **P** **Whispering Jack**[6] 859 8-10-12 119 (p) ConorO'Farrell
(Keiran Burke) *mid-div: hmpd 2nd: towards rr 7th: rdn after 13th: sn wknd: tailing off whn p.u bef 4 out* **22/1**

P/0- **P** **Deb's Dasher**[23] 8-10-0 107 (p) AidanColeman
(Richard Woollacott) *trckd ldrs tl rdn after 13th: bhd fr next: t.o whn p.u bef 4 out* **20/1**

/04- **P** **Five Star Wilsham (IRE)**[31] 659 9-11-2 123 NickScholfield
(Jeremy Scott) *hld up towards rr of midfield: struggling 13th: losing tch whn p.u bef 15th* **10/1**

F31- **P** **City Press (IRE)**[20] 757 7-11-0 121 (tp) NoelFehily
(Warren Greatrex) *hld up towards rr: hdwy into midfield after 14th: rdn bef 4 out: nvr threatened: wknd next: p.u bef 2 out* **4/1**1

6m 9.5s (-35.10) **Going Correction** -1.075s/f (Hard) course record **12 Ran SP% 120.6**
Speed ratings (Par 107): **109,105,103,101,98 77, , , ,**
toteswingers 1&2 £18.80, 1&3 £19.00, 2&3 £7.30 CSF £64.39 CT £393.67 TOTE £11.90: £5.40, £1.90, £2.50; EX 62.50 Trifecta £463.70 Pool: £1,044.47 - 1.68 winning units.
Owner Donlon, Doyle, MacDonald & Webb **Bred** Stone Electrical Ltd **Trained** Ditcheat, Somerset

FOCUS
A sound pace for this decent handicap. It paid to race prominently. The winner was well treated on his Kempton win but rates a personal best, and the form is solid.

924 VISIT NEWQUAY ZOO H'CAP HURDLE (8 hdls) 2m 1f
4:15 (4:15) (Class 4) (0-115,112) 4-Y-0+ **£3,508** (£1,030; £515; £257)

Form RPR

/05- **1** **Tamarillo Grove (IRE)**[28] 697 6-11-0 100 (t) JasonMaguire 105+
(Sophie Leech) *mde all: rdn after 3 out: styd on gamely: rdn out* **12/1**

/44- **2** 1 1/4 **Drawn Free (IRE)**[33] 635 5-10-0 86 oh5 BrendanPowell 89
(Colin Tizzard) *mid-div: hdwy 5th: trckd wnr after 3 out: rdn bef next: kpt on but a being hld fr last* **14/1**

111- **3** 2 1/4 **Party Palace**[5] 691 9-10-13 102 GilesHawkins(3) 104
(Stuart Howe) *trckd ldrs: rdn after 3 out: nt pce to chal: styd on to go 3rd run-in* **7/1**

/51- **4** 3/4 **Dont Take Me Alive**[17] 788 4-11-4 106 (tp) NoelFehily 104
(Charlie Longsdon) *hld up towards rr: hdwy after 5th: rdn gng to 2 out: styd on to go 4th run-in* **5/1**2

322- **5** 1 **Mount Vesuvius (IRE)**[19] 764 5-10-11 97 (t) TomO'Brien 96
(Paul Henderson) *trckd wnr tl rdn after 3 out: styd on same pce tl no ex and lost 2nd pls run-in* **9/2**1

/55- **6** 15 **Kayalar (IRE)**[29] 678 5-11-1 101 PaulMoloney 85
(Evan Williams) *mid-div: effrt after 3 out: wknd next* **8/1**

23U- **7** 2 3/4 **Gud Day (IRE)**[8] 850 5-11-12 112 (t) PaddyBrennan 93
(Fergal O'Brien) *mid-div: effrt after 3 out: wknd bef 2 out* **5/1**2

042- **8** 2 3/4 **Jaja De Jau**[19] 765 4-10-3 94 (t) RachaelGreen(3) 71
(Anthony Honeyball) *hld up towards rr: hdwy 5th: rdn after 3 out: wknd next* **6/1**3

0/0- **9** 5 **Royal Peak (IRE)**[49] 407 6-10-0 86 oh9 (t) TomScudamore 60
(David Pipe) *a towards rr* **33/1**

0/0- **10** 16 **Warsaw Pact (IRE)**[43] 490 10-9-11 90 (p) MrLKilgarriff(7) 48
(Steven Dixon) *trckd ldrs tl lost pl 5th: sn drvn: wknd after next: t.o* **14/1**

/60- **11** 26 **Calypso Star (IRE)**[15] 810 6-9-11 86 oh20 (bt) MarkQuinlan(3) 18
(Nigel Hawke) *hld up towards rr: rdn bef 3 out: sn wknd: t.o* **100/1**

/00- **P** **Zulu Principle**[54] 308 6-10-1 87 (t) JamieMoore
(Helen Nelmes) *trckd ldrs: rdn after 3 out: wknd bef next: p.u bef last* **28/1**

3m 50.0s (-15.70) **Going Correction** -0.85s/f (Firm)
WFA 4 from 5yo+ 15lb **12 Ran SP% 117.8**
Speed ratings (Par 105): **102,101,100,100,99 92,91,89,87,80 67,**
toteswingers 1&2 £21.20, 1&3 £12.70, 2&3 £23.70 CSF £161.79 CT £1273.02 TOTE £18.00: £4.10, £4.70, £1.30; EX 227.10 Trifecta £1710.10 Part won. Pool: £2,280.17 - 0.89 winning units..
Owner G Doel & C J Leech **Bred** Darley **Trained** Elton, Gloucs

FOCUS
A wide-open handicap hurdle run at a steady pace with the winner making all. The winner was well in on the best of his 2012 form and should still be competitive when reassessed.

925 NEWTON ABBOT RACECOURSE H'CAP HURDLE (9 hdls 1 omitted) 2m 6f
4:45 (4:45) (Class 4) (0-105,105) 4-Y-0+ **£3,508** (£1,030; £515; £257)

Form RPR

4/0- **1** **Gap Of Dunloe (IRE)**[43] 503 5-11-7 100 (tp) RichardJohnson 109
(Peter Bowen) *hld up towards rr: hdwy fr 7th: wnt 3rd after 2 out (usual 3 out): rdn for str chal last (usual 2 out): styd on to ld fnl strides: all out* **9/1**

/51- **2** nk **Detroit Red**[13] 833 7-11-4 97 HaddenFrost 106
(Martin Hill) *mid-div: hdwy after 6th: chal 2 out (usual 3 out): led bef last (usual 2 out): rdn whn strly chal run-in: kpt on: hdd fnl strides* **5/2**1

054- **3** 16 **Kayfrou**[25] 730 8-10-11 90 NickScholfield 83
(Nick Mitchell) *mid-div: hdwy after 7th: rdn after 2 out (usual 3 out): styd on same pce to go 3rd on long run-in: no ch w ldrs* **11/1**

0/P- **4** 3 **Listen And Learn (IRE)**[27] 708 5-11-3 96 (p) APMcCoy 86
(Jonjo O'Neill) *trckd ldrs: led after 7th: rdn and hdd appr last (usual 2 out): no ex* **3/1**2

0/0- **5** 8 **No Woman No Cry**[8] 854 8-11-1 94 (bt) JoeTizzard 76
(Colin Tizzard) *trckd ldrs: rdn after 3 out: sn one pce* **14/1**

PPP/ **6** 1/2 **Choisirez (IRE)**[35] 5509 4-10-0 82 oh5 ConorO'Farrell 60
(John Panvert) *hld up towards rr: pushed along 7th: sme prog after 2 out (usual 3 out): nvr trbld ldrs* **80/1**

531- **7** 6 **Marie Deja La (FR)**[27] 711 7-11-9 102 (b) TomCannon 77
(Chris Gordon) *trckd ldrs: rdn after 6th: sn lost pl* **14/1**

260- **8** 4 **Exiles Return (IRE)**[12] 846 11-9-11 79 oh2 MarkQuinlan(3) 50
(Jacqueline Retter) *led tl rdn after 7th: wknd after 2 out (usual 3 out)* **66/1**

5/0- **9** *2 ¼* **Clarion Call**[57] 252 5-11-5 **98**....................(v) PaulMoloney 67
(Evan Williams) *mid-div: rdn after 2 out: (usual 3 out): nt pce to get involved* **10/1**

5/0- **10** *hd* **Bernisdale**[49] 407 5-11-0 **93**.................... DPFahy 62
(John Flint) *a towards rr* **18/1**

5/0- **11** *nse* **Ruby Valentine (FR)**[60] 188 10-9-7 **79** oh9.............. CharlieDeutsch(7) 48
(Jim Wilson) *a towards rr* **66/1**

/50- **12** *32* **Dubai Glory**[28] 488 5-11-12 **105**.................... IanPopham 42
(Sheena West) *racd keenly: trckd ldrs: rdn after 3 out: sn wknd: t.o* **28/1**

421- **13** *4* **Little Eaglet (IRE)**[28] 690 9-11-2 **95**.................... LiamHeard 28
(Colin Heard) *mid-div: hdwy 5th: wknd 7th: t.o* **6/1**[3]

0- **14** *22* **Howya Buddy (IRE)**[32] 650 8-11-6 **102**.................... MichealNolan(3) 13
(Adrian Wintle) *mid-div: rdn after 5th: wknd after next: t.o* **33/1**

0/0- **P** **Tiger's Jacey (IRE)**[49] 407 6-10-5 **87**....................(t) MichaelByrne(3)
(James Hughes) *hld up towards rr: hit 3rd: p.u bef 6th: dismntd* **50/1**

4m 59.4s (-20.80) **Going Correction** -0.85s/f (Firm)
WFA 4 from 5yo+ 16lb 15 Ran SP% **126.4**
Speed ratings (Par 105): **103,102,97,95,93 92,90,89,88,88 88,76,75,67,**
toteswingers 1&2 £7.20, 1&3 £15.80, 2&3 £7.60 CSF £33.00 CT £268.51 TOTE £12.90: £4.50, £1.80, £4.40; EX 48.00 Trifecta £365.70 Pool: £2,703.87 - 5.54 winning units.
Owner Einsley & Angela Harries **Bred** Dr M V O'Brien **Trained** Little Newcastle, Pembrokes

FOCUS
The final flight was bypassed. A modest handicap run at a steady pace with the front two fighting out a thrilling finish. They were well in on the best of their old form and there's a case for rating the race a bit higher.

926 SIS LIVE CONDITIONAL JOCKEYS' H'CAP CHASE (16 fncs) 2m 5f 110y
5:15 (5:15) (Class 5) (0-95,92) 4-Y-0+ **£2,729** (£801; £400; £200)

Form RPR

4P/- **1** **Five Out Of Five (IRE)**[85] 5309 9-10-10 **79**....................(t) AdamWedge(3) 91+
(Evan Williams) *trckd ldr: jnd ldr after 9th: led appr 4 out: styd on wl fr 2 out: rdn out* **6/1**[3]

2/1- **2** *5* **Kusadasi (IRE)**[8] 854 8-11-4 **92**....................(b) KieronEdgar(8) 100
(David Pipe) *led tl appr 4 out: sn rdn: rallied briefly after 3 out: hld fr next: keeping on at same pce whn mstke last* **11/8**[1]

20P/ **3** *8* **The Goldmeister (IRE)**[78] 6-11-5 **88**.................... KielanWoods(3) 87
(Charlie Longsdon) *trckd ldrs: rdn after 4 out: styd on same pce fr next: nt fluent last* **7/1**

P43/ **4** *3 ½* **Diamond Eclipse (IRE)**[263] 1900 7-11-9 **89**.................... BrendanPowell 84
(Nick Williams) *in tch: disputing 3rd whn nt fluent 12th: rdn after 4 out: no ex whn lost 3rd 2 out* **9/2**[2]

P4/- **5** *18* **Mut'Ab (USA)**[75] 5506 8-10-8 **79**....................(bt) JakeHodson(5) 56
(Mark Gillard) *trckd ldrs tl rdn after 11th: sn btn* **10/1**

/62- **6** *2 ¾* **Mr Robinson (FR)**[20] 759 6-10-9 **75**....................(v) TrevorWhelan 49
(Tony Carroll) *in tch: rdn after 12th: wknd 3 out* **13/2**

63P/ **P** **For Sahkey Moony (IRE)**[23] 8-10-10 **76**....................(bt) TomCannon
(Cathy Hamilton) *sn struggling in last: losing tch whn j.rt 8th: sn t.o: p.u bef 10th* **25/1**

5m 5.8s (-15.60) **Going Correction** -1.075s/f (Hard) 7 Ran SP% **113.3**
Speed ratings (Par 103): **85,83,80,79,72 71,**
toteswingers 1&2 £2.40, 1&3 £4.70, 2&3 £2.60 CSF £15.22 CT £58.40 TOTE £8.80: £3.00, £1.60; EX 18.80 Trifecta £120.90 Pool: £2,448.11 - 15.18 winning units.
Owner D J Burchell **Bred** The Three Rivers Racing Syndicate **Trained** Llancarfan, Vale Of Glamorgan

FOCUS
This weak handicap, confined to conditional riders, was run at a steady pace. The winner belatedly took advantage of a slipping mark.
T/Jkpt: £30,892.60 to a £1 stake. Pool: £304,574.94 - 7.00 winning units T/Plt: £63.90 to a £1 stake. Pool: £113,460.25 - 1,295.36 winning units T/Qpdt: £23.90 to a £1 stake. Pool: £7,597.90 - 235.00 winning units TM

847 UTTOXETER (L-H)
Tuesday, July 9

OFFICIAL GOING: Good to firm (good in places; 7.4)
Hurdles sited 4-5m from inside line and divided bends on fresh ground.
Wind: light 1/2 behind Weather: fine and sunny, very warm

927 MWH DERBY H'CAP HURDLE (9 hdls) 2m
6:15 (6:15) (Class 5) (0-100,100) 4-Y-0+ **£2,209** (£648; £324; £162)

Form RPR

/52- **1** **My Lord**[13] 846 5-11-6 **94**.................... LiamTreadwell 106+
(Luke Dace) *in rr: hdwy 6th: 3rd appr 2 out: 3rd last: sn chsng ldr: styd on wl to ld nr fin* **11/1**

0F1/ **2** *nk* **Next Edition (IRE)**[24] 1714 5-10-13 **94**.................... AdamNicol(7) 107+
(Philip Kirby) *hld up in mid-div: smooth hdwy to trck ldrs 6th: led 2 out: 1 l ahd whn blnd last: hdd nr fin* **7/4**[1]

/11- **3** *3 ½* **Emerald Glade (IRE)**[9] 852 6-11-12 **100** 7ex.................... APMcCoy 107
(Jim Best) *w ldr: led 6th: hdd 2 out: kpt on same pce un-in* **15/8**[2]

313- **4** *13* **Wom**[18] 784 5-11-7 **100**....................(v) TrevorWhelan(5) 94
(Neil King) *in rr: kpt on fr 3 out: nvr a factor* **16/1**

/53- **5** *1 ½* **Red Whisper**[46] 456 9-10-8 **85**....................(t) JamesBest(3) 78
(Rob Summers) *rr-div: hdwy appr 3 out: nvr nr ldrs* **10/1**[3]

003- **6** *5* **Umustbejoking (FR)**[20] 765 5-11-8 **99**.................... MichealNolan(3) 87
(Michael Blake) *in rr: sme hdwy 5th: lost pl next* **14/1**

/45- **7** *10* **Spinning Waters**[19] 783 7-10-13 **90**....................(p) RobertDunne(3) 68
(Dai Burchell) *chsd ldrs: wknd after 3 out* **22/1**

406- **8** *15* **Shinko Moon**[34] 635 6-10-9 **83**....................(p) SamTwiston-Davies 46
(Jamie Snowden) *led to 6th: sn rdn: lost pl after 3 out* **20/1**

/05- **9** *4 ½* **Lulu's Gift (IRE)**[16] 810 7-9-7 **74** oh7.................... StephenMulqueen(7) 32
(Michael Mullineaux) *chsd ldrs: rdn 6th: sn lost pl* **50/1**

/00- **10** *1 ¼* **Cloudy Start**[7] 857 7-11-1 **89**.................... WillKennedy 46
(Violet M Jordan) *in rr: bhd whn mstke 5th* **66/1**

045- **11** *34* **Sonny Jim**[29] 696 5-11-2 **90**....................(p) BrianHughes 13
(John Mackie) *chsd ldrs: lost pl whn j. slowly 6th: sn bhd: t.o 2 out* **50/1**

/00- **12** *3* **Until The Man (IRE)**[9] 852 6-10-11 **85**.................... DPFahy 5
(Geoffrey Deacon) *in rr: bhd fr 5th: t.o next* **100/1**

P00/ **P** **Chippy**[152] 4078 5-10-11 **85**....................(t) CharliePoste
(John Holt) *in rr: bhd fr 5th: t.o after next: p.u bef 2 out* **66/1**

3m 42.1s (-9.90) **Going Correction** -0.55s/f (Firm) 13 Ran SP% **118.1**
Speed ratings (Par 103): **102,101,100,93,92 90,85,77,75,74 57,56,**
Tote Swingers: 1&2 £6.50, 1&3 £3.50, 2&3 £1.70 CSF £29.94 CT £54.81 TOTE £13.10: £3.40, £1.30, £1.20; EX 46.70 Trifecta £61.90 Pool: £1,387.93 - 16.79 winning units..
Owner Mark Benton **Bred** Mrs Monica Teversham **Trained** Five Oaks, W Sussex

FOCUS
This moderate handicap was run at a sound gallop and it only concerned the principals from two out. The first two are on the upgrade and should still be competitive when reassessed.

928 WATER FOR LIFE CONDITIONAL JOCKEYS' NOVICES' HURDLE (9 hdls) 2m
6:45 (6:45) (Class 4) 4-Y-0+ **£3,249** (£954; £477; £238)

Form RPR

/25- **1** **Sky Khan**[31] 673 4-10-4 119....................(p) AdamNicol(6) 118+
(Philip Kirby) *hld up: trckd ldrs 5th: led gng wl between last 2: pushed clr run-in: readily* **4/5**[1]

P/1- **2** *4 ½* **Experimentalist**[28] 706 5-11-2 118....................(t) MichaelByrne(3) 119
(Tim Vaughan) *chsd ldrs: drvn appr 3 out: 2nd between last: kpt on same pce* **9/2**[2]

/22- **3** *1* **Dr Dalwhinny**[20] 761 4-10-2 0.................... JamesCowley(8) 108
(Donald McCain) *trckd ldrs: led bef 3 out: hdd between last 2: kpt on same pce* **9/1**[3]

3- **4** *38* **Renegotiate**[13] 843 4-10-4 0....................(p) ChristopherWard(6) 70
(Dr Richard Newland) *led: nt fluent 4th: hdd bef 3 out: sn lost pl and bhd: t.o* **9/2**[2]

F/5- **5** *33* **Danehill Dante (IRE)**[21] 758 5-10-12 0.................... KillianMoore 39
(Alan King) *chsd ldrs: drvn and nt fluent 6th: lost pl bef next: sn bhd: eased whn t.o run-in* **16/1**

3m 43.4s (-8.60) **Going Correction** -0.55s/f (Firm)
WFA 4 from 5yo+ 15lb 5 Ran SP% **107.8**
Speed ratings (Par 105): **99,96,96,77,60**
CSF £4.59 TOTE £1.50: £1.10, £3.20; EX 4.80 Trifecta £11.50 Pool: £1,088.68 - 70.66 winning units..
Owner The Unique Partnership **Bred** Heather Raw **Trained** Middleham, N Yorks

FOCUS
Straightforward enough novice form. The first two are rated to their marks.

929 MORRISON UTILITY SERVICES (S) HURDLE (9 hdls) 2m
7:15 (7:15) (Class 5) 4-7-Y-0 **£1,949** (£572; £286; £143)

Form RPR

2/3- **1** **Mighty Whitey (IRE)**[6] 875 7-10-7 120....................(t) DerekFox(5) 112+
(Noel C Kelly, Ire) *mde all: j.rt: hit 4th: fnd ex to pull clr run-in* **5/2**[2]

122- **2** *3 ½* **Descaro (USA)**[16] 799 7-11-3 120....................(p) CiaranMckee(7) 120
(John O'Shea) *trckd ldng pair: 2nd 5th: upsides 2 out: 1/2 l down last: fnd little* **7/4**[1]

/50- **3** *17* **Gracchus (USA)**[31] 674 7-10-12 106....................(t) WayneHutchinson 92
(Tony Carroll) *chsd ldrs: t.k.h: drvn 5th: outpcd next: tk modest 3rd between last 2* **4/1**

/6F- **4** *8* **Captain Brown**[30] 679 5-11-5 0....................(vt[1]) PaulMoloney 92
(Evan Williams) *t.k.h in rr: handy 3rd appr 2 out: fnd nthing and mstke 2 out: hung lft and sn wknd* **7/2**[3]

/04- **5** *6* **Tribal Dance (IRE)**[16] 804 7-10-9 90....................(p) JamesBest(3) 79
(John O'Shea) *chsd wnr: reminders 4th: lost pl after 6th: sn bhd* **33/1**

3m 45.0s (-7.00) **Going Correction** -0.55s/f (Firm) 5 Ran SP% **110.1**
Speed ratings: **95,93,84,80,77**
CSF £7.52 TOTE £3.50: £1.50, £1.80; EX 7.10 Trifecta £16.50 Pool: £518.71 - 23.56 winning units..No bid for the winner.
Owner Mrs C Kelly **Bred** Miss Carmel Whelan **Trained** Draperstown, Co. Derry

FOCUS
Not the worst seller and the form makes sense. A step up from the winner on his recent run.

930 MR TAPPY RUN NOVICES' H'CAP CHASE (16 fncs) 2m 5f
7:45 (7:45) (Class 5) (0-100,100) 4-Y-0+ **£2,599** (£763; £381; £190)

Form RPR

6/P- **1** **Favoured Nation (IRE)**[51] 394 6-11-12 **100**.................... APMcCoy 113+
(Jonjo O'Neill) *nt fluent in rr: hit 8th: hdwy 10th: chsng ldrs 3 out: 2nd next: upsides last: sn led: drvn rt out* **4/1**[2]

4/4- **2** *1 ½* **Pure Anticipation (IRE)**[26] 726 8-11-4 **92**....................(v[1]) AidanColeman 101
(Tim Vaughan) *led 2nd: jnd 3 out and last: hdd and kpt on same pce run-in* **10/1**

/65- **3** *12* **Highland Rain**[21] 759 5-10-0 **74**....................(vt) SeanQuinlan 72
(Jennie Candlish) *led to 2nd: chsd ldrs: one pce fr 3 out* **16/1**

225/ **4** *1* **Croco Mister (IRE)**[87] 5286 6-10-3 **82**.................... BenPoste(5) 81
(Rosemary Gasson) *mid-div: chsd ldrs 8th: one pce fr 3 out* **10/1**

143- **5** *8* **Rudigreen (IRE)**[6] 873 10-11-7 **98**....................(tp) JackQuinlan(3) 88
(Noel Quinlan) *chsd ldrs: hmpd on bnd and outpcd 4 out: sn lost pl* **9/2**[3]

PUU/ **6** *15* **Avanos (FR)**[99] 5073 8-10-6 **80**.................... RichieMcGrath 71
(Philip Kirby) *t.k.h in rr: smooth hdwy 10th: cl 2nd whn blnd 3 out: lost pl and sn bhd: fin lame* **5/2**[1]

550- **7** *6* **Stormyisland Ahead**[33] 641 8-11-9 **100**....................(vt[1]) AdamWedge(3) 76
(Evan Williams) *mid-div: chses ldrs 6th: 6th and outpcd whn blnd bdly and rdr briefly lost irons 3 out: sn lost pl* **28/1**

011- **P** **The Good Guy (IRE)**[21] 759 10-11-7 **95**.................... WayneHutchinson
(Graeme McPherson) *in rr: hit 8th: lost pl 10th: sn bhd: t.o whn p.u after 4 out* **8/1**

U46/ **P** **Avenging Ace (IRE)**[81] 5382 7-11-5 **93**....................(t) JasonMaguire
(Donald McCain) *mid-div: chsd ldrs 6th: reminders 11th: lost pl next: t.o whn p.u bef 3 out* **8/1**

6/P- **P** **Supralunary**[13] 839 7-10-0 **74** oh15....................(tp) LeeEdwards
(Robin Mathew) *chsd ldrs: drvn 6th: lost pl 8th: sn bhd: t.o 11th: p.u bef 3 out* **33/1**

5m 4.4s (-18.40) **Going Correction** -0.825s/f (Firm) 10 Ran SP% **119.4**
Speed ratings (Par 103): **102,101,96,96,93 87,85, , ,**
Tote Swingers: 1&2 £15.00, 2&3 £59.20 CSF £44.30 CT £587.35 TOTE £4.20: £1.80, £3.40, £5.30; EX 44.10 Trifecta £473.90 Part won. Pool: £631.89 - 0.14 winning units..
Owner John P McManus **Bred** Miss Penny Downes **Trained** Cheltenham, Gloucs

FOCUS
A moderate novice handicap where two came well clear. The winner improved in line with the best of his bumper form.

931 PUMP UP THE VOLUME H'CAP CHASE (12 fncs) 2m
8:15 (8:15) (Class 4) (0-110,110) 4-Y-0 **£3,798** (£1,122; £561; £280; £140)

Form RPR

542- **1** **Bay Central (IRE)**[9] 853 9-11-5 **103**....................(e) PaulMoloney 113+
(Evan Williams) *t.k.h: mde all: 3 l ahd last: styd on strly: eased towards fin* **5/2**[1]

/5U- **2** *6* **Ninfea (IRE)**[33] 645 5-11-8 **106**....................(p) TomScudamore 109+
(David Bridgwater) *j.lft: chsd ldrs: one pce fr 3 out: kpt on to take 3rd nr fin* **6/1**[3]

The Form Book Jumps, Raceform Ltd, Compton, RG20 6NL.

/20- **3** ½ **Bennys Quest (IRE)**[9] [853] 10-11-3 **104**..................(tp) PeterCarberry(3) 104
(Neil Mulholland) *chsd ldrs: 2nd 4 out: styd on same pce appr last: wknd towards fin* **10/1**

U25- **4** ¾ **Lauberhorn**[19] [779] 6-11-5 **106**......................................(v) AdamWedge(3) 105
(Evan Williams) *hld up in tch: effrt 4 out: 3rd 2 out: one pce: kpt on run-in* **9/1**

2/4- **5** 6 **Quarton (IRE)**[44] [501] 6-10-12 **103**...................................... ConorRing(7) 98
(Evan Williams) *chsd ldrs: 4th and keeping on one pce whn blnd 3 out: sn fdd* **22/1**

/23- **6** 7 **Jacks Grey**[37] [604] 8-11-5 **110**..................................(t) ConorShoemark(7) 98
(Fergal O'Brien) *hit 3rd: chsd ldrs 5th: drvn 7th: outpcd and lost pl 3 out* **3/1**[2]

2U5- **7** 6 **Stormy Oscar (IRE)**[28] [705] 6-11-7 **105**......................... BrendanPowell 87
(Jamie Snowden) *chsd ldrs: hmpd 1st: wknd 3 out* **10/1**

232- **8** 27 **Cruise In Style (IRE)**[16] [807] 7-10-11 **98**.....................(bt) JamesBest(3) 56
(Kevin Bishop) *chsd ldrs: pckd landing 5th: sn outpcd: lost pl 4 out: j.lft 2 out: sn bhd: t.o* **15/2**

3m 49.2s (-5.80) **Going Correction** -0.825s/f (Firm) **8** Ran SP% **112.2**
Speed ratings (Par 105): **81,78,77,77,74 70,67,54**
Tote Swingers: 1&2 £3.80, 1&3 £7.00, 2&3 £13.80 CSF £17.43 CT £124.05 TOTE £3.10: £1.10, £2.50, £3.70; EX 21.70 Trifecta £191.60 Pool: £564.58 - 2.20 winning units..
Owner R E R Williams **Bred** Thomas Kinsella **Trained** Llancarfan, Vale Of Glamorgan

FOCUS
A moderate handicap, run at an average gallop. The winner is rated back to the level of last year's C&D win.

932 MORGAN SINDALL MARES' H'CAP HURDLE (10 hdls) 2m 4f 110y
8:45 (8:45) (Class 4) (0-105,105) 4-Y-O+ **£3,249** (£954; £477; £238)

Form RPR

500/ **1** **Lovey Dovey (IRE)**[565] [3269] 9-11-2 **100**.............................. HarryDerham(5) 109+
(Simon West) *w ldr: led 7th: drvn clr appr 2 out: kpt rt up to work* **9/1**

434- **2** 2 ¼ **On The Off Chance**[16] [811] 5-11-7 **100**................................(b) APMcCoy 107
(Jonjo O'Neill) *led to 7th: drvn upsides appr next: styd on same pce appr last: kpt on run-in* **5/1**[2]

4- **3** 8 **Me And Ben (IRE)**[20] [765] 6-11-2 **95**.............................(t) PaddyBrennan 95
(Fergal O'Brien) *hld up towards rr: hdwy 7th: kpt on to take modest 3rd last* **5/1**[2]

/30- **4** 1 ¼ **Maggie Aron**[13] [844] 7-10-2 **84**....................................(t) MichaelByrne(3) 82
(James Hughes) *hld up in rr: hdwy 7th: one pce fr next* **40/1**

122- **5** 3 ¼ **Princesse Fleur**[13] [844] 5-10-13 **92**.............................. TomScudamore 88
(Michael Scudamore) *chsd ldrs: modest 3rd 2 out: wknd appr last* **13/2**[3]

5/5- **6** 8 **Carhue Princess (IRE)**[33] [650] 7-10-11 **95**......................(p) BenPoste(5) 83
(Tom Symonds) *mid-div: lost pl 7th: kpt on fr 2 out* **22/1**

150- **7** hd **Stand Clear**[16] [801] 8-10-9 **95**..(p) AdamNicol(7) 86
(David Thompson) *hld up in rr: hdwy to trck ldrs 6th: modest 3rd appr 2 out: 6th and wkng whn mstke last* **28/1**

/03- **8** 8 **Taradrewe**[44] [484] 6-11-0 **96**.. RachaelGreen(3) 76
(Anthony Honeyball) *hmpd and lost pl 2nd: hdwy 7th: sn chsng ldrs: wknd next* **9/2**[1]

/24- **9** ¾ **Dancing Emily (IRE)**[43] [511] 7-11-12 **105**................. WayneHutchinson 86
(Graeme McPherson) *chsd ldrs: 3rd and rdn whn hit 3 out: wknd qckly appr next: eased run-in* **13/2**[3]

034/ **10** 11 **Queen Of Epirus**[4] [4588] 5-11-0 **93**...................................... TomO'Brien 63
(Brian Rothwell) *in rr: hdwy 7th: lost pl appr next* **22/1**

12- **11** 2 ¼ **Binowagh Bay (IRE)**[24] [748] 5-11-5 **103**............................ DerekFox(5) 71
(Mark Michael McNiff, Ire) *chsd ldrs: lost pl sn after 3 out* **14/1**

/F0- **P** **Photogenique (FR)**[20] [765] 10-9-13 **81** oh15 ow2........(b) JamesBest(3)
(Rob Summers) *rn in snatches: in rr: hdwy 3rd: lost pl 6th: sn bhd: t.o whn p.u bef 3 out* **100/1**

/P0- **P** **Daddy'Slittlegirl**[49] [423] 8-9-7 **79** oh16.....................(v) DanielHiskett(7)
(Claire Dyson) *chsd ldrs: reminders and lost pl 4th: bhd next: t.o 7th: p.u bef next* **80/1**

/35- **F** **June French (FR)**[20] [765] 5-10-0 **79** oh7............................ AidanColeman
(Ian Williams) *chsng ldrs whn blnd and fell 2nd* **18/1**

/34- **U** **Presenting Me (IRE)**[44] [502] 5-11-3 **99**.......................... AdamWedge(3)
(Evan Williams) *mid-div whn bdly hmpd and uns rdr 2nd* **33/1**

4m 51.7s (-7.30) **Going Correction** -0.55s/f (Firm) **15** Ran SP% **119.9**
Speed ratings (Par 105): **91,90,87,86,85 82,82,79,78,74 73,,,,**
Tote Swingers: 1&2 £16.20, 1&3 £20.20, 2&3 £5.20 CSF £50.60 CT £257.00 TOTE £9.90: £5.10, £2.20, £2.70; EX 74.70 Trifecta £549.40 Part won. Pool: £732.62 - 0.22 winning units..
Owner James-Douglas Gordon **Bred** Hugh Suffern Bloodstock Ltd **Trained** Middleham Moor, N Yorks

FOCUS
A moderate mares' handicap where it paid to be handy. The winner was a 117 hurdler in 2011 and may still match or better that.

933 SEVERN TRENT WATERAID H'CAP HURDLE (12 hdls) 3m
9:15 (9:15) (Class 4) (0-110,110) 4-Y-O+ **£3,249** (£954; £477; £238)

Form RPR

1P3- **1** **High Ville (IRE)**[20] [767] 7-11-9 **107**.............................. ConorO'Farrell 124+
(David Pipe) *t.k.h: mde all: mstke 2nd: sn clr: hit 7th: styd on fr 3 out: unchal* **16/1**

333- **2** 17 **Electric Tiger (GER)**[20] [762] 6-11-9 **107**...................(p) TomScudamore 107
(David Bridgwater) *hld up in rr: hdwy 9th: modest 6th 3 out: styd on to take modest 2nd between last 2* **25/1**

/44- **3** 2 ¼ **Minella Bliss (IRE)**[29] [690] 8-10-9 **96**........................ RobertDunne(3) 94
(Nikki Evans) *hld up in rr: hdwy 9th: kpt on fr 3 out: tk 3rd nr fin* **16/1**

5/2- **4** nk **Feast Of Fire (IRE)**[52] [368] 6-11-8 **106**.................................... APMcCoy 104
(Jonjo O'Neill) *chsd ldrs: modest 2nd whn hit 2 out: one pce* **5/1**[3]

5/0- **5** 2 ½ **Uncut Stone (IRE)**[17] [168] 5-11-0 **98**.......................(b) WilsonRenwick 93
(Peter Niven) *in rr: hdwy 7th: 7th 3 out: kpt on one pce* **33/1**

4/0- **6** 8 **Jawaab (IRE)**[45] [202] 9-11-0 **98**...............................(v) RichieMcGrath 86
(Philip Kirby) *mstkes: chsd ldrs: outpcd and lost pl 8th: no ch after* **4/1**[2]

/55- **7** 20 **Aegean Destiny**[16] [811] 6-10-13 **97**........................ WayneHutchinson 67
(John Mackie) *in rr: sme hdwy 8th: wknd after next* **33/1**

321- **8** 7 **Vinnie My Boy (IRE)**[7] [860] 5-11-7 **105** 7ex...................(vt) JamieMoore 76
(Peter Bowen) *mid-div: hdwy 8th: chsd wnr after next: wknd qckly appr 2 out* **10/11**[1]

430- **9** 4 ½ **River Purple**[26] [730] 6-10-3 **87**......................................(t) BrianHughes 47
(John Mackie) *mid-div: sme hdwy 8th: lost pl after next* **20/1**

3/P- **10** 1 ¼ **Hassadin**[13] [845] 7-11-12 **110**.. TomCannon 69
(Michael Blake) *mid-div: drvn and lost pl 7th: sn bhd* **50/1**

225- **11** 20 **Dont Tell Sailor (IRE)**[26] [728] 7-10-12 **103**..................(p) ConorRing(7) 44
(Jennie Candlish) *chsd ldrs: lost pl appr 2 out: bhd whn eased run-in: t.o* **20/1**

P66/ **12** 9 **He's A Hawker (IRE)**[51] 8-11-1 **102**..............................(p) KielanWoods(3) 35
(Michael Mullineaux) *chsd ldrs: drvn 8th: sn lost pl: bhd fr 3 out: t.o whn eased run-in* **66/1**

5m 37.9s (-12.10) **Going Correction** -0.55s/f (Firm) **12** Ran SP% **123.5**
Speed ratings (Par 105): **98,92,91,91,90 87,81,78,77,77 70,67**
Tote Swingers: 1&2 £21.80, 1&3 £46.80, 2&3 £19.00 CSF £337.14 CT £6366.09 TOTE £16.60: £4.20, £3.90, £3.70; EX 159.00 Trifecta £505.60 Part won. Pool: £674.18 - 0.10 winning units..
Owner G Thompson **Bred** Kevin Foley **Trained** Nicholashayne, Devon

FOCUS
A weak handicap taken apart by the winner, who produced a step up. The form looks sound.
T/Plt: £25.90 to a £1 stake. Pool: £98,081.95 - 2,753.97 winning units. T/Qpdt: £18.60 to a £1 stake. Pool: £7,029.20 - 278.40 winning units. WG

934 - 941a (Foreign Racing) - See Raceform Interactive

[871]WORCESTER (L-H)
Wednesday, July 10

OFFICIAL GOING: Good (good to firm in places; 6.9)
All bends moved out 9yds from inside line.
Wind: Light against Weather: Overcast

942 LOCAL PARKING SECURITIES H'CAP CHASE (18 fncs) 2m 7f
6:10 (6:11) (Class 5) (0-95,95) 4-Y-O+ **£2,144** (£629; £314; £157)

Form RPR

0/P- **1** **Whistling Senator (IRE)**[29] [709] 6-11-12 **95**....................(v[1]) APMcCoy 112+
(Jonjo O'Neill) *a.p: pushed along after 14th: led next: clr last: easily* **5/1**[2]

604- **2** 7 **Crannaghmore Boy (IRE)**[7] [873] 8-11-12 **95**................(p) TomO'Brien 102
(Keith Goldsworthy) *chsd ldrs: led 11th tl after 14th: sn rdn: wnt 2nd again appr last: styd on same pce flat* **14/1**

/5- **3** 4 **Baizically (IRE)**[43] [529] 10-11-2 **85**..............................(b) ConorO'Farrell 88
(John Joseph Hanlon, Ire) *chsd ldrs: led after 14th: rdn and hdd next: chsd wnr to appr last: wknd flat* **12/1**

2/3- **4** 3 ¾ **Maid Of Silk (IRE)**[59] [248] 7-11-8 **91**...................................(t) NoelFehily 92
(Neil Mulholland) *hld up: mstke 2nd: hdwy 14th: mstke 4 out: sn rdn: wknd 2 out* **9/2**[1]

3/0- **5** 9 **Roseneath (IRE)**[47] [461] 9-11-7 **95**...........................(tp) KillianMoore(5) 89
(Alex Hales) *unruly bef s: mid-div: hdwy u.p 14th: wknd appr 2 out* **14/1**

600- **6** 9 **Crescent Beach (IRE)**[17] [806] 6-11-9 **92**.......................... HenryOliver 77
(Henry Oliver) *hld up: hmpd 9th: drvn along after 13th: nvr on terms: t.o* **33/1**

333- **7** 3 ¾ **Chestnut Ben (IRE)**[17] [807] 8-11-2 **92**............................ KevinJones(7) 75
(Gary Brown) *mid-div: hdwy 11th: blnd 14th: rdn and wknd bef next: t.o* **16/1**

650- **8** 19 **Kingdom Of Munster (IRE)**[22] [759] 6-11-0 **88**......(p) HarryChalloner(5) 51
(Richard Ford) *hld up: hdwy 10th: rdn and wknd appr 4 out: t.o* **40/1**

U54/ **9** 33 **Cap Elorn (FR)**[255] [2079] 7-11-6 **89**...................................... DavidBass 23
(Lawney Hill) *prom: mstke 4th: wknd appr 13th: t.o* **9/1**

1/0- **10** 39 **The Wife's Sister**[29] [713] 12-10-10 **84**............................ BenPoste(5)
(James Evans) *mid-div: wknd 10th: t.o* **40/1**

P/P- **P** **Midnight Gold**[29] [713] 13-11-12 **95**..........................(v) WayneHutchinson
(Julian Smith) *chsd ldrs: led 6th to next: led 9th to 11th: wknd 13th: t.o whn p.u bef 4 out* **25/1**

P/0- **P** **Orion Star (IRE)**[45] [485] 11-11-4 **87**.................................(p) RyanMahon
(Seamus Mullins) *led: hit 2nd: hdd next: lost pl 7th: bhd fr 9th: t.o whn p.u bef 12th* **50/1**

652- **P** **Flanagan (IRE)**[30] [692] 9-11-6 **89**...................................(v) JamieMoore
(Peter Bowen) *led 3rd to 6th: led next to 9th: rdn and wknd after 10th: bhd whn p.u bef 12th* **5/1**[2]

/03- **P** **The Wee Midget**[35] [637] 8-11-6 **89**................................. NickScholfield
(Arthur Whiting) *prom: lost pl 4th: bhd fr 6th: t.o whn p.u after 9th* **20/1**

P03- **P** **Watch House (IRE)**[22] [759] 8-10-9 **85**.......................... CiaranMckee(7)
(Michael Gates) *hld up: blnd and rdr lost irons 2nd: sn bhd: t.o whn p.u after 5th* **20/1**

005/ **P** **Captain Scarlett (IRE)**[136] [4417] 7-11-8 **91**............................(p) RhysFlint
(John Flint) *hld up: hdwy 10th: rdn and wkng whn blnd 4 out: t.o whn p.u bef 2 out* **7/1**[3]

5m 45.8s (-2.20) **Going Correction** -0.25s/f (Good) **16** Ran SP% **124.1**
Speed ratings (Par 103): **93,90,89,87,84 81,80,73,62,48 ,,,,,**
toteswingers 1&2 £14.60, 1&3 £18.20, 2&3 £23.00 CSF £67.42 TOTE £6.40: £2.20, £3.20, £3.70, £1.10; EX 92.80 Trifecta £601.80 Pool: £1021.67 - 1.27 winning units..
Owner John P McManus **Bred** Noel O'Brien **Trained** Cheltenham, Gloucs

FOCUS
Following a dry night the official going was good, good to firm in places (watered) with a GoingStick reading of 6.9, and it rode as advertised. This was a well-contested, if poor handicap chase and few came into it in good form. The winner was back to the level promised by last season's Market Rasen fall.

943 MAZAK & POWER PANELS GOING FORWARD TOGETHER H'CAP CHASE (15 fncs) 2m 4f
6:40 (6:40) (Class 3) (0-140,134) 4-Y-O **£6,330** (£1,870; £935; £468; £234)

Form RPR

/12- **1** **Atlanta Falcon (IRE)**[27] [728] 8-10-9 **117**........................(t) JasonMaguire 126+
(Donald McCain) *chsd ldr tl led 4 out: hrd rdn and hung rt flat: hung lft towards fin: all out* **4/1**[2]

/11- **2** hd **On The Bridge (IRE)**[7] [877] 8-11-12 **134**........................ NickScholfield 143+
(Jeremy Scott) *hld up: hdwy 4 out: pckd 2 out: swtchd lft and rdn flat: r.o* **10/11**[1]

/14- **3** 3 **Wester Ross (IRE)**[29] [705] 9-10-3 **114**........................(p) AdamWedge(3) 120
(Evan Williams) *hld up: hdwy 4 out: ev ch 2 out: sn rdn: no ex towards fin* **28/1**

321- **4** 5 **Synthe Davis (FR)**[29] [705] 8-10-7 **115**... APMcCoy 117
(Laura Mongan) *chsd ldrs: rdn appr 4 out: ev ch 2 out: no ex last* **7/1**[3]

4/5- **5** 49 **Spock (FR)**[34] [642] 8-10-11 **119**..............................(tp) HarryDerham(5) 101
(Paul Nicholls) *hld up: hdwy 17th: rdn and wknd appr 4 out: bhd whn hit next: t.o* **7/1**[3]

014/ **P** **Back Bob Back (IRE)**[131] [4506] 8-10-11 **119**..................... PaddyBrennan
(Tom George) *led: rdn and hdd 4 out: p.u bef next: dismntd* **12/1**

4m 50.1s (-9.90) **Going Correction** -0.25s/f (Good) **6** Ran SP% **108.5**
Speed ratings (Par 107): **109,108,107,105,86**
toteswingers 1&2 £1.70, 1&3 £21.30, 2&3 £3.90 CSF £7.96 TOTE £4.50: £2.80, £1.10; EX 9.40 Trifecta £51.00 Pool: £1054.95 - 15.51 winning units..
Owner D McCain Jnr **Bred** T D Howley Jnr **Trained** Cholmondeley, Cheshire

FOCUS
A decent, if poorly contested handicap chase in which they went a reasonable pace. The winner is on the upgrade over fences, with the second in line with his recent hurdles win.

944 PP ELECTRICAL SYSTEMS STANDARD OPEN NATIONAL HUNT FLAT RACE — 2m

7:10 (7:10) (Class 6) 4-6-Y-O **£1,559** (£457; £228; £114)

Form RPR

/13- **1** **Plain Sailing (IRE)**[19] 790 4-11-6 0 .... DenisO'Regan 118+
(John Ferguson) *mde all: edgd rt 2f out: drvn out* **11/8**[1]

2 *3* **Private Malone (IRE)**[88] 4-10-13 0 .... RichardJohnson 106
(A J Kennedy, Ire) *a.p: chsd wnr over 2f out: rdn over 1f out: styd on same pce ins fnl f* **14/1**

5/ **3** *16* **Our Crusade**[98] 5125 6-10-12 0 .... JakeGreenall(3) 93
(Michael Easterby) *hld up: hdwy over 3f out: outpcd fr over 2f out* **11/2**[3]

34- **4** *7* **Howlett (IRE)**[38] 599 5-11-1 0 .... ConorO'Farrell 87
(John Joseph Hanlon, Ire) *prom: racd keenly: trckd wnr over 5f out tl rdn over 2f out: sn wknd* **16/1**

0- **5** *2* **Greek Fire**[32] 675 4-10-13 0 .... (t) JasonMaguire 83
(Dave Morris) *chsd ldrs: rdn over 3f out: wknd over 2f out* **25/1**

0/5- **6** *2 ½* **Caddells Row**[39] 584 5-11-1 0 .... BrianHughes 83
(Karen McLintock) *chsd ldrs: rdn over 4f out: wknd 3f out* **25/1**

0/ **7** *7* **Crow Down (IRE)**[116] 4793 4-10-13 0 .... APMcCoy 75
(Charles Hills) *hld up: pushed along over 4f out: sn wknd: t.o* **3/1**[2]

8 *11* **Give Me The Remote (IRE)**[46] 5-11-1 0 .... WayneHutchinson 67
(Graeme McPherson) *mid-div: effrt over 4f out: wknd over 3f out: t.o* **22/1**

9 *1* **The Debtor (IRE)** 6-11-1 0 .... PaulMoloney 66
(Anthony Middleton) *hld up: a in rr: t.o* **28/1**

4P/ **10** *2 ¼* **Rye Tangle (IRE)**[237] 2436 5-11-1 0 .... LiamTreadwell 64
(Ed de Giles) *hld up: a in rr: t.o* **25/1**

0/ **11** *28* **Portrait Gale (IRE)**[73] 14 6-10-8 0 .... (t) MissJodieHughes(7) 39
(Marc Barber) *w wnr tl pushed along over 6f out: wknd over 4f out: t.o* **250/1**

3m 36.5s (-5.20) **Going Correction** -0.175s/f (Good) **11** Ran SP% **114.8**
Speed ratings: **106,104,96,93,92 90,87,81,81,80 66**
toteswingers 1&2 £7.30, 1&3 £2.50, 2&3 £8.30 CSF £20.11 TOTE £2.20: £1.20, £4.10, £1.90; EX 21.90 Trifecta £88.90 Pool: £897.95 - 7.57 winning units..
Owner Bloomfields **Bred** Darley **Trained** Cowlinge, Suffolk

FOCUS
A very moderate bumper with plenty of dead wood, but run at a decent pace. This rates a step up from the winner.

945 PROMARK T-800 PRINTER FROM PARTEX NOVICES' HURDLE (10 hdls) — 2m 4f

7:40 (7:40) (Class 4) 4-Y-O+ **£3,249** (£954; £477; £238)

Form RPR

203- **1** **Scoter Fontaine (FR)**[34] 638 7-11-5 118 .... APMcCoy 124+
(Rebecca Curtis) *mde all: clr fr 2 out: nt fluent last: eased flat: canter* **8/13**[1]

4- **2** *16* **Keel Haul (IRE)**[21] 768 5-10-12 0 .... HenryOliver 104+
(Henry Oliver) *chsd ldrs: wnt 2nd 6th: rdn appr 3 out: outpcd fr next: eased flat* **7/1**[3]

0/4- **3** *15* **Terntheothercheek**[22] 755 4-10-2 0 .... SeanQuinlan 68
(Jennie Candlish) *prom tl wknd appr 6th: t.o* **16/1**

13P/ **4** *1 ¼* **Mist The Boat**[250] 2163 5-10-12 0 .... RichardJohnson 79
(Tim Vaughan) *hld up in tch: rdn and wknd appr 3 out: blnd next* **10/3**[2]

U00- **5** *79* **Desert Sting**[25] 747 4-10-6 0 .... JakeGreenall(3) 3
(Michael Easterby) *hld up: bhd fr 5th: t.o* **33/1**

0/0- **6** *¾* **Hope Royal**[58] 270 6-10-5 0 .... DavidBass
(Lawney Hill) *chsd wnr to 6th: wknd next: t.o* **12/1**

F50/ **P** **River Rat**[32] 6-10-5 0 .... (t) CharliePoste
(John Holt) *chsd ldrs: 4th and rdn whn wnt wrong after 7th: sn p.u* **33/1**

P **Lightning Bill** 5-10-12 0 .... AndrewThornton
(Caroline Bailey) *nt fluent 1st: sn given reminders and bhd: t.o fr 5th: p.u bef 3 out* **20/1**

4m 43.7s (-3.70) **Going Correction** -0.175s/f (Good)
WFA 4 from 5yo+ 16lb **8** Ran SP% **121.7**
Speed ratings (Par 105): **100,93,87,87,55 55, ,**
toteswingers 1&2 £2.50, 1&3 £1.10, 2&3 £16.50 CSF £6.45 TOTE £1.80: £1.02, £2.20, £3.60; EX 6.70 Trifecta £20.80 Pool: £870.05 - 31.29 winning units..
Owner John P McManus **Bred** Gilbert Mesnil & Mme Louise Mesnil **Trained** Newport, Dyfed

FOCUS
This novice hurdle completely lacked depth.

946 GIVE A HOUND A HOME RGT NOVICES' H'CAP HURDLE (12 hdls) — 2m 7f

8:10 (8:10) (Class 5) (0-95,95) 4-Y-O+ **£1,949** (£572; £286; £143)

Form RPR

6/2- **1** **Band Of Thunder**[29] 710 5-10-5 79 .... (v) GavinSheehan(5) 87+
(Nick Mitchell) *led to 7th: led again appr 3 out: nt fluent 2 out and last: rdn clr flat* **13/2**[3]

040- **2** *8* **Chosen Dream (IRE)**[14] 844 5-11-1 84 .... (t) APMcCoy 84
(Jonjo O'Neill) *a.p: ev ch 3 out: sn rdn: hung lft and no ex flat* **7/2**[1]

000- **3** *11* **Moyne Nineoseven (IRE)**[14] 844 7-11-9 95 .... (t) JackQuinlan(3) 86
(Noel Quinlan) *chsd ldrs: rdn 3 out: wknd appr last* **9/2**[2]

/60- **4** *7* **Orsm**[29] 710 6-11-8 91 .... (tp) TomCannon 74
(Laura Mongan) *hld up: hdwy 8th: rdn and wknd 2 out* **40/1**

/36- **5** *1* **Sharlene's Quest (IRE)**[8] 860 7-11-0 86 .... MichaelByrne(3) 68
(James Hughes) *chsd ldr tl led 7th: rdn and hdd appr 3 out: wknd next* **8/1**

5P0/ **6** *21* **My Friend Riquet (FR)**[141] 4298 6-11-6 89 .... LeeEdwards 52
(Dave Roberts) *prom tl rdn and wknd 3 out: t.o* **33/1**

4/0- **7** *12* **Pharaon De Touzaine (FR)**[32] 669 10-10-10 86 .... CiaranMckee(7) 38
(John O'Shea) *hld up: hdwy 7th: rdn and wknd appr 3 out: t.o* **25/1**

/04- **8** *2* **Shot In The Dark (IRE)**[29] 711 4-11-3 90 .... (t) MarkGrant 36
(Jonathan Geake) *hld up: pushed along whn blnd 8th: no ch whn nt fluent 3 out and next: t.o* **25/1**

4F2- **9** *5* **Blue Signal (IRE)**[35] 637 8-11-12 95 .... LiamHeard 41
(Colin Heard) *hld up: rdn and wknd appr 3 out: t.o* **16/1**

/46- **10** *13* **Dr Thistle (IRE)**[42] 541 6-11-8 91 .... WillKennedy 25
(Sarah-Jayne Davies) *chsd ldrs tl rdn and wknd appr 3 out: t.o* **25/1**

U/6- **P** **Pelennor (FR)**[20] 783 9-11-3 86 .... LeightonAspell
(Stephen Hughes) *hld up: rdn and wknd after 9th: t.o whn p.u and dismntd bef 3 out* **14/1**

0- **P** **Ahcomeretome (IRE)**[34] 649 8-11-5 95 .... MissLBrooke(7)
(Lady Susan Brooke) *hld up: pushed along 6th: bhd fr 8th: t.o whn p.u bef 3 out* **100/1**

/12- **P** **Moscow In April (IRE)**[39] 590 6-11-10 93 .... (t) ColinBolger
(Pat Murphy) *hld up: pushed along and wknd after 8th: t.o whn p.u bef 2 out* **7/2**[1]

5m 35.7s (7.70) **Going Correction** -0.175s/f (Good)
WFA 4 from 5yo+ 16lb **13** Ran SP% **117.5**
Speed ratings (Par 103): **79,76,72,69,69 62,58,57,55,51 , ,**
toteswingers 1&2 £5.30, 1&3 £7.30, 2&3 £13.60 CSF £27.63 TOTE £6.50: £1.50, £9.10, £7.50; EX 29.10 Trifecta £143.90 Pool: £303.99 - 1.58 winning units..
Owner J R Boughey **Bred** John M Troy **Trained** Piddletrenthide, Dorset

FOCUS
A moderate event. The 13 who went to post had 89 hurdles runs between them and only Moscow In April had scored before in this sphere. It paid to be up with the pace, which was decent.

947 COTSWOLD SCAFFOLDING H'CAP HURDLE (8 hdls) — 2m

8:40 (8:40) (Class 4) (0-110,110) 4-Y-O+ **£3,249** (£954; £477; £238)

Form RPR

/16- **1** **Fairyinthewind (IRE)**[57] 292 4-11-5 105 .... WayneHutchinson 110+
(Alan King) *hld up: hdwy 4th: led after 3 out: clr last: styd on wl* **7/1**

3/0- **2** *8* **Houseparty**[52] 384 5-11-6 104 .... DenisO'Regan 104
(John Ferguson) *led: j.rt 1st: hdd next: chsd ldrs: led 5th: rdn and hdd after 3 out: styd on same pce appr last* **6/1**[3]

050/ **3** *hd* **Knockgraffon Lad (USA)**[80] 5437 6-10-10 94 .... AlainCawley 94
(Brendan Powell) *hld up: hdwy appr 3 out: sn chsng wnr: rdn appr last: no ex flat* **8/1**

6/6- **4** *¾* **Taroum (IRE)**[17] 812 6-10-8 92 .... LeeEdwards 91
(Tony Carroll) *hld up: hdwy appr 4th: sn lost pl: rallied bef last: styd on same pce flat* **3/1**[1]

/32- **5** *2 ¼* **Ajman (IRE)**[20] 783 8-10-9 100 .... (bt) ConorRing(7) 98
(Evan Williams) *hld up: hdwy 4th: rdn 3 out: wknd appr last* **13/2**

542- **6** *6* **Brassbound (USA)**[8] 858 5-11-9 107 .... AndrewThornton 101
(Caroline Bailey) *w ldr tl led 2nd: hdd next: jnd ldr 5th: rdn and wknd 2 out* **9/2**[2]

/P1- **7** *9* **Pour Changer (FR)**[17] 810 8-10-7 91 .... LeightonAspell 77
(Stephen Hughes) *prom tl rdn and wknd appr 5th* **16/1**

/44- **8** *17* **Flew The Nest (IRE)**[29] 717 5-11-4 102 .... APMcCoy 84
(Jonjo O'Neill) *hld up: hdwy 5th: wknd 3 out: t.o* **6/1**[3]

265- **9** *26* **Accessallareas (IRE)**[30] 693 8-11-10 108 .... WillKennedy 53
(Sarah-Jayne Davies) *chsd ldrs: led 3rd to 5th: rdn and wknd bef next: t.o* **33/1**

3m 44.9s (-2.40) **Going Correction** -0.175s/f (Good)
WFA 4 from 5yo+ 15lb **9** Ran SP% **117.5**
Speed ratings (Par 105): **99,95,94,94,93 90,85,77,64**
toteswingers 1&2 £4.90, 1&3 £6.30, 2&3 £18.00 CSF £49.60 CT £347.26 TOTE £6.30: £12.10, £13.40, £21.00; EX 50.90 Trifecta £497.20 Pool: £717.47 - 1.08 winning units..
Owner Spittinginthewind Partnership **Bred** J Cullinan **Trained** Barbury Castle, Wilts

FOCUS
A reasonably competitive handicap hurdle.

948 PARTEX LASER ENGRAVED LABELS MAIDEN HURDLE (8 hdls) — 2m

9:10 (9:10) (Class 5) 4-Y-O+ **£1,949** (£572; £286; £143)

Form RPR

222- **1** **Engai (GER)**[17] 808 7-11-0 107 .... TomScudamore 110+
(David Bridgwater) *hld up: hdwy 5th: chsd ldr after 3 out: pckd next: led last: pushed out* **6/4**[1]

0/3- **2** *2 ¾* **Orthodox Lad**[17] 808 5-11-0 106 .... SamTwiston-Davies 107
(Dr Richard Newland) *a.p: led 3 out: j.rt next: rdn and hdd last: styd on same pce flat* **9/4**[2]

P/6- **3** *5* **Kimora (IRE)**[20] 777 7-10-7 0 .... (t) AidanColeman 96
(Marc Barber) *hld up: hdwy appr 3 out: no ex flat* **66/1**

3/4- **4** *7* **It's Oscar (IRE)**[56] 318 6-11-0 107 .... (t) JasonMaguire 96
(Donald McCain) *chsd ldrs: rdn after 3 out: wknd appr last* **7/2**[3]

P- **5** *15* **Robber Stone**[35] 631 5-10-9 0 .... AodhaganConlon(5) 83
(Debra Hamer) *hld up: nvr nrr* **100/1**

0/ **6** *10* **Sedano (FR)**[38] 7-11-0 0 .... BrianHughes 74
(Tim Fitzgerald) *led: hmpd by loose horse 3rd: rdn and hdd whn mstke 3 out: wknd next* **16/1**

7 *1 ½* **On The Cusp (IRE)**[51] 6-11-0 0 .... NoelFehily 72
(Violet M Jordan) *chsd ldrs tl wknd after 3 out* **25/1**

6- **8** *9* **Persian Fox (IRE)**[14] 843 9-11-0 0 .... HaddenFrost 64
(Stephen Hughes) *hld up: hdwy 4th: rdn appr 3 out: wknd bef next: t.o* **66/1**

U **Beyond Dreams (IRE)**[123] 9-10-7 0 .... DPFahy
(Stephen Hughes) *chsd ldr whn mstke and uns rdr 2nd* **40/1**

0PF/ **P** **Catch Me Up (IRE)**[80] 5442 5-11-0 0 .... AlainCawley
(Brendan Powell) *sn bhd and nt fluent: blnd 4th: t.o whn p.u bef 3 out* **25/1**

0- **U** **Take The Crown**[22] 760 4-10-12 0 .... HenryOliver
(Henry Oliver) *hld up: cl 7th whn blnd and almost fell and uns rdr 5th* **50/1**

3m 43.2s (-4.10) **Going Correction** -0.175s/f (Good)
WFA 4 from 5yo+ 15lb **11** Ran SP% **114.9**
Speed ratings (Par 103): **103,101,99,95,88 83,82,77, ,**
toteswingers 1&2 £1.30, 1&3 £24.80, 2&3 £52.10 CSF £4.76 TOTE £2.60: £1.20, £1.10, £20.90; EX 4.70 Trifecta £205.00 Pool: £1026.68 - 3.75 winning units..
Owner Building Bridgies **Bred** Gestut Park Wiedingen **Trained** Icomb, Gloucs

FOCUS
Very little strength in depth for this maiden hurdle and the market proved correct, with the first two home running almost to the pound. The form looks solid.
T/Plt: £44.90 to a £1 stake. Pool: £93,511.03 - 1517.53 winning tickets. T/Qpdt: £17.00 to a £1 stake. Pool: £6431.40 - 278.60 winning tickets. CR

949 - 955a (Foreign Racing) - See Raceform Interactive

879 PERTH (R-H)

Sunday, July 14

OFFICIAL GOING: Good to firm (good in places; watered) changing to good to firm (firm in places) after race 3 (3.00)
Bends moved out on to fresh ground.
Wind: Fresh, half behind Weather: Cloudy, warm

956 WIN BIG WITH TOTEJACKPOT NOVICES' HURDLE (10 hdls) — 2m 4f 110y

2:00 (2:00) (Class 4) 4-Y-O+ **£3,328** (£1,033; £556)

Form RPR

0/1- **1** **Dantes King (IRE)**[11] 869 8-10-12 122 .... JasonMaguire 116+
(Gordon Elliott, Ire) *mde all: rdn bef last: drvn and kpt on wl fr last* **4/9**[1]

The Form Book Jumps, Raceform Ltd, Compton, RG20 6NL.

05P/ **2** 2 ¼ **Ocean Club**[91] 6-10-12 0.. TomO'Brien 113
(Brian Ellison) *chsd ldr to 6th: outpcd whn nt fluent 3 out: rallied next: kpt on to chse wnr towards fin: no imp* **14/1**[3]

/12- **3** 1 ¼ **Experimentalist**[5] 928 5-10-9 118..............................(t) AlanJohns[(10)] 119
(Tim Vaughan) *nt fluent on occasions: chsd ldrs: wnt 2nd 6th: effrt and hung lft bef last: one pce run-in: lost 2nd nr fin* **11/4**[2]

U **Bella Montagna**[674] 5-10-5 0.. BrianHarding
(Sharon Watt) *prom: nt fluent and uns rdr 1st* **40/1**

4m 46.3s (-15.70) **Going Correction** -0.65s/f (Firm) **4** Ran SP% **105.0**
Speed ratings (Par 105): **103,102,101,**
CSF £6.13 TOTE £1.10; EX 4.30 Trifecta £10.60 Pool: £664.50 - 46.66 winning units..
Owner C Jones **Bred** Donal Kenneally **Trained** Trim, Co Meath

FOCUS
Bends moved out on to fresh ground. Straightforward novice form, rated around the third.

957 ROYAL CALEDONIAN HUNT NOVICES' CHASE (15 fncs) 2m 4f 110y
2:30 (2:30) (Class 4) 5-Y-0+ **£5,198** (£1,526; £763; £381)

Form RPR

513- **1** **Kian's Delight**[19] 830 5-11-5 132.. TomO'Brien 127+
(Peter Bowen) *trckd ldrs: led 10th: mde rest: drew clr fr 3 out: easily* **6/5**[1]

245- **2** 11 **Agricultural**[21] 798 7-10-12 97.. WilsonRenwick 102
(Lucy Normile) *in tch: outpcd whn nt fluent 10th: rallied 3 out: chsd (clr) wnr last: no imp* **20/1**

/03- **3** 3 **Dj Milan (IRE)**[11] 867 7-10-12 0..............................(t) JasonMaguire 100
(Donald McCain) *cl up: led 4th to 10th: styd upsides to 4 out: outpcd fr next: lost 2nd last* **9/2**[3]

235/ **4** 65 **Best Served Cold**[64] 230 7-10-12 129..............................(bt) RichardJohnson 33
(Gordon Elliott, Ire) *nt jump wl: led to 4th: cl up tl wknd fr 9th: t.o* **6/4**[2]

UPP/ **P** **Ellandshe (IRE)**[56] 13-10-7 49..............................(b) GaryRutherford[(5)]
(William Young Jnr) *in tch: struggling fr 5th: t.o whn p.u bef 9th* **100/1**

4m 49.3s (-15.70) **Going Correction** -0.65s/f (Firm) **5** Ran SP% **109.4**
Speed ratings: **103,98,97,72,**
CSF £17.77 TOTE £2.40: £1.60, £2.50; EX 15.40 Trifecta £114.00 Pool: £729.31 - 4.79 winning units..
Owner Roddy Owen,Paul Fullagar & Karen Bowen **Bred** Mrs J M Quy **Trained** Little Newcastle, Pembrokes

FOCUS
An ordinary novice chase and the easy winner didn't need to be at his best.

958 TOTEQUADPOT FOUR PLACES IN FOUR RACES H'CAP HURDLE (12 hdls) 3m 110y
3:00 (3:00) (Class 4) (0-115,115) 4-Y-0+ **£5,198** (£1,526; £763; £381)

Form RPR

034- **1** **Solway Bay**[11] 867 11-10-4 96..............................(tp) EwanWhillans[(3)] 100
(Lisa Harrison) *hld up: stdy hdwy and prom 3 out: rdn bef next: rallied to ld run-in: drvn out* **12/1**

4/1- **2** 1 ¼ **Feisty Lass (IRE)**[11] 868 7-10-0 89 oh1..............................(bt) WilsonRenwick 92
(Gordon Elliott, Ire) *hld up in tch: hdwy and cl up whn hit 4 out: led gng wl 2 out: rdn bef last: hdd run-in: kpt on: hld nr fin* **10/3**[2]

/06- **3** 11 **Ryton Runner (IRE)**[11] 867 5-10-12 108..............................(p) CraigNichol[(7)] 100
(Lucinda Russell) *prom: drvn and ev ch bef 2 out: outpcd between last 2* **9/2**[3]

/13- **4** 15 **Fairwood Massini (IRE)**[24] 778 8-10-10 106..............................(vt[1]) JPKiely[(7)] 83
(Tim Vaughan) *cl up: led bef 8th: rdn and hdd 2 out: sn wknd* **9/1**

215- **5** 8 **Granaruid (IRE)**[21] 804 10-11-2 112..............................(p) GrantCockburn[(7)] 81
(Alison Hamilton) *trckd ldrs: hit 8th: drvn and wknd bef 3 out* **33/1**

P4/- **P** **Everaard (USA)**[77] 18 7-11-6 109..............................(tp) RichieMcGrath
(Philip Kirby) *led to bef 8th: rdn and wknd fr next: t.o whn p.u bef 2 out* **9/1**

311- **P** **Green Lightning (IRE)**[10] 881 6-11-12 115.............. RichardJohnson
(Peter Bowen) *trckd ldrs: nt fluent 5th and next: sprawled bdly and dropped to rr 8th: sn p.u* **13/8**[1]

0/0- **P** **The Bold Lord (IRE)**[21] 800 5-10-11 100........................ FearghalDavis
(Alan Swinbank) *hld up: stmbld after 8th: struggling fr next: t.o whn p.u bef 3 out* **25/1**

5m 45.5s (-19.50) **Going Correction** -0.65s/f (Firm) **8** Ran SP% **113.8**
Speed ratings (Par 105): **105,104,101,96,93 , ,**
Tote Swingers: 1&2 £2.80, 1&3 £1.30, 2&3 £14.60 CSF £52.32 CT £210.66 TOTE £14.00: £2.30, £2.20, £1.80; EX 50.60 Trifecta £592.50 Part won. Pool: £292.31 - 0.63 winning units..
Owner David Alan Harrison **Bred** D A Harrison **Trained** Aldoth, Cumbria

FOCUS
A moderate handicap. The winner built on a fair recent C&D run.

959 DREW RUSSELL 65TH BIRTHDAY CELEBRATION MAIDEN HURDLE (8 hdls) 2m 110y
3:30 (3:34) (Class 4) 4-Y-0+ **£3,249** (£954; £477; £238)

Form RPR

2 **1** **Goal (IRE)**[7] 904 6-11-0 112..............................(t) JasonMaguire 113+
(Gordon Elliott, Ire) *trckd ldr: hit 4 out: led gng wl 2 out: qcknd clr fr last: easily* **2/9**[1]

0/6- **2** 18 **Dynamic Drive (IRE)**[11] 865 6-10-7 87..............(t) StephenMulqueen[(7)] 85
(Maurice Barnes) *t.k.h: led: hung lft bnd bef 4th: rdn and hdd 2 out: nt fluent last: no ch w wnr* **9/2**[2]

6- **3** 57 **Tim's Approach (IRE)**[35] 676 8-10-9 0..................(p) GaryRutherford[(5)] 28
(William Young Jnr) *in tch: outpcd whn j.lft 4 out: sn struggling: t.o* **20/1**[3]

/PP- **4** 34 **Askalott (IRE)**[35] 679 8-11-0 0..[1] FearghalDavis
(Jean McGregor) *in tch: struggling bef 4th: sn lost tch: t.o* **40/1**

3m 46.0s (-12.00) **Going Correction** -0.65s/f (Firm) **4** Ran SP% **107.2**
Speed ratings (Par 105): **102,93,66,50**
CSF £1.68 TOTE £1.10; EX 1.40 Trifecta £2.70 Pool: £979.39 - 263.50 winning units..
Owner Willie McKay **Bred** A M F Persse **Trained** Trim, Co Meath

FOCUS
A desperately weak maiden and the winner had little to beat.

960 TOTEPOOL HOME OF KING SIZE POOLS H'CAP CHASE (THE SUNDAY £5K BONUS RACE) (15 fncs) 2m 4f 110y
4:00 (4:00) (Class 4) (0-120,119) 4-Y-0+ **£6,498** (£1,908; £954; £477)

Form RPR

041- **1** **Strobe**[10] 883 9-10-7 100..............................(p) WilsonRenwick 107
(Lucy Normile) *prom: hit 7th: hit and outpcd 4 out: rallied to chse ldr after next: styd on to ld run-in: drvn and kpt on wl* **7/1**

/23- **2** 1 ¼ **Qoubilai (FR)**[47] 519 9-11-12 119..............................(t) RichardJohnson 125
(Tim Vaughan) *t.k.h led: rdn whn mstke last: hdd run-in: kpt on same pce towards fin* **7/2**[3]

432- **3** 20 **Twill Stand To Us (IRE)**[21] 798 6-11-2 109..................(t) TomO'Brien 93
(Brian Ellison) *t.k.h: chsd ldr fr 2nd: blnd next: effrt whn blnd 3 out: sn lost 2nd: wknd next* **9/4**[2]

P01/ **4** 3 **Karinga Queen (IRE)**[72] 107 9-11-6 113........................ JasonMaguire 96
(Gordon Elliott, Ire) *bhd: rdn and sme hdwy after 10th: hung rt and wknd fr 2 out* **11/1**

141- **5** 58 **Hodgson (IRE)**[24] 781 8-11-7 114..............................(tp) JamieMoore 37
(Peter Bowen) *chsd ldr to 2nd: prom: struggling 10th: lost tch after next: t.o* **15/8**[1]

4m 48.2s (-16.80) **Going Correction** -0.65s/f (Firm) course record **5** Ran SP% **108.6**
Speed ratings (Par 105): **106,105,97,96,74**
CSF £29.52 TOTE £7.20: £2.30, £2.80; EX 26.50 Trifecta £76.60 Pool: £559.44 - 5.47 winning units..
Owner Miss P A & P J Carnaby **Bred** Old Mill Stud **Trained** Duncrievie, Perth & Kinross

FOCUS
A modest little handicap in which the first pair drew clear. They are rated pretty much to their marks.

961 ECOSTEEL AND LOTHIAN STEEL CONDITIONAL JOCKEYS' H'CAP HURDLE (8 hdls) 2m 110y
4:30 (4:30) (Class 4) (0-105,105) 4-Y-0+ **£3,898** (£1,144; £572; £286)

Form RPR

50P- **1** **Parson's Punch**[10] 884 8-11-9 105..............................(p) GrantCockburn[(3)] 108
(Lucy Normile) *hung bdly lft and rel to r: hdwy and cl up 2nd: lft in ld bnd bef 3 out: qcknd after next: hld on wl u.p run-in* **8/1**

0/6- **2** 1 **Milaneen**[50] 477 7-9-6 79 oh2.. AlanJohns[(8)] 80
(Tim Vaughan) *chsd ldrs: effrt and drvn bef 2 out: pressed wnr last: kpt on: hld nr fin* **7/2**[2]

/11- **3** nk **Momkinzain (USA)**[35] 678 6-11-0 101..............................(p) CraigNichol[(8)] 103
(Lucinda Russell) *blkd s: cl up: effrt and lft 2nd bef 3 out: drvn bef next: nt fluent last: kpt on wl u.p towards fin* **5/4**[1]

5/6- **4** 4 ½ **Captain Baldwin**[10] 879 4-9-11 81 oh2........................ NickSlatter[(3)] 77
(Jim Goldie) *nt fluent: hmpd s: hld up: checked bnd bef 3 out: effrt and hdwy bef next: no imp run-in* **11/1**

/44- **5** 36 **Claude Carter**[46] 537 9-11-7 100.. CallumWhillans 68
(Alistair Whillans) *hld up in tch: drvn and outpcd whn nt fluent 3 out: struggling bef next: t.o* **10/1**

/3F- **U** **Born To Shine (USA)**[29] 752 5-11-1 94........................ GaryRutherford
(Alan Swinbank) *led: sdle slipped and uns rdr bnd bef 3 out* **5/1**[3]

3m 44.5s (-13.50) **Going Correction** -0.65s/f (Firm)
WFA 4 from 5yo+ 15lb **6** Ran SP% **111.9**
Speed ratings (Par 105): **105,104,104,102,85**
Tote Swingers: 1&2 £32.70, 1&3 £12.50, 2&3 £2.20 CSF £35.55 TOTE £14.60: £3.00, £2.50; EX 53.00 Trifecta £98.20 Pool: £901.59 - 6.88 winning units..
Owner K N R MacNicol **Bred** Peter Ebdon Racing **Trained** Duncrievie, Perth & Kinross

FOCUS
An ordinary handicap, confined to conditional riders. The first four are rated pretty much to their marks.

962 COLLECT TOTEPOOL WINNINGS AT BETFRED SHOPS STANDARD OPEN NATIONAL HUNT FLAT RACE 2m 110y
5:00 (5:00) (Class 6) 4-6-Y-0 **£2,053** (£598; £299)

Form RPR

1 **Henllan Harri (IRE)** 5-11-2 0.. RichardJohnson 109+
(Peter Bowen) *in tch: hdwy over 5f out: rdn and swtchd rt wl over 1f out: led ins fnl f: styd on strly* **7/4**[1]

12- **2** 1 ¼ **Definite Row (IRE)**[10] 885 4-11-0 0.. WilsonRenwick 106
(Gordon Elliott, Ire) *t.k.h: cl up: chal over 2f out: rdn and led over 1f out to ins fnl f: edgd lft: kpt on same pce nr fin* **7/4**[1]

3 1 ½ **Cloudy Joker (IRE)**[98] 5-11-2 0.. JasonMaguire 107
(Donald McCain) *led: rdn and hdd over 1f out: n.m.r ins fnl f: kpt on same pce* **3/1**[2]

4 6 **Dalstontosiloth (IRE)** 5-11-2 0.. LucyAlexander 101
(Barry Murtagh) *hld up in tch: stdy hdwy over 4f out: rdn and outpcd over 2f out: no imp after* **17/2**[3]

0/ **5** dist **Thehoodlum**[247] 2319 6-11-2 0.. FearghalDavis
(Jean McGregor) *cl up: rdn over 6f out: wknd over 4f out: eased whn no ch* **50/1**

3m 46.2s (-6.20) **Going Correction** -0.65s/f (Firm)
WFA 4 from 5yo+ 2lb **5** Ran SP% **110.2**
Speed ratings: **88,87,86,83,**
CSF £5.07 TOTE £2.60: £1.70, £1.10; EX 4.40 Trifecta £2.40 Pool: £838.77 - 251.88 winning units..
Owner Einsley & Angela Harries **Bred** Paul Ryan **Trained** Little Newcastle, Pembrokes
■ Stewards' Enquiry : Wilson Renwick one-day ban: careless riding (Jul 29)

FOCUS
A weak bumper which played out as the market suggested it would. It was steadily run but the second set a fair standard.
T/Plt: £213.00 to a £1 stake. Pool: £50,159.03 - 171.83 winning tickets. T/Qpdt: £78.00 to a £1 stake. Pool: £37,11 63 - 35.20 winning tickets. RY

693 SOUTHWELL (L-H)
Sunday, July 14

OFFICIAL GOING: Good (watered; 7.6)
Fences sited 5yds off outside rail. Both bends moved on to fresh ground since meeting on June 10th.
Wind: Light behind Weather: Fine

963 WOW-24-7 NOVICES' CHASE (19 fncs) 3m 110y
1:40 (2:10) (Class 4) 5-Y-0+ **£3,994** (£1,240; £667)

Form RPR

/12- **1** **Grandads Horse**[23] 786 7-11-5 137..............................(p) NoelFehily 133+
(Charlie Longsdon) *a.p: chsd ldr 7th: mstke 12th: led 15th: shkn up appr last: drvn out* **10/11**[1]

16F- **2** 7 **Sail And Return**[12] 861 9-10-12 125........................ SamTwiston-Davies 117
(Phil Middleton) *hld up: mstke 1st: hdwy appr 10th: chsd wnr after 15th: rdn appr 3 out: styd on same pce fr next* **13/2**[3]

2/1- **3** 83 **Now Then Charlie (IRE)**[34] 695 8-10-12 0.................... DenisO'Regan 42
(John Ferguson) *led: nt fluent 5th: hdd 15th: sn wknd* **13/2**[3]

00/ **P** **Tango In The Night**[147] 6-10-12 0..............................(p) TomMessenger
(Chris Bealby) *chsd ldr tl after 5th: sn rdn: nt fluent 8th: wknd after next: p.u bef 13th* **100/1**

2- **P** **Cock And Hen (IRE)**43 [586] 7-10-12 0 .... APMcCoy
(Jonjo O'Neill) *hld up: hdwy to chse ldr after 5th: lost 2nd 7th: pushed along 13th: sn wknd: p.u bef 15th* **5/2**2

6m 28.2s (5.20) **Going Correction** +0.375s/f (Yiel) **5** Ran SP% **108.6**
Speed ratings: **106,103,77,** ,
CSF £7.00 TOTE £1.90: £1.10, £2.40; EX 6.30 Trifecta £12.00 Pool: £88.75 - 1,422.97 winning units..
Owner Whites Of Coventry Limited **Bred** Wood Farm Stud **Trained** Over Norton, Oxon

FOCUS
Fences sited 5yds off outside rail. Both bends moved on to fresh ground since meeting on June 10th. Plenty of water had been put on the track, 21mm on Wednesday, 20mm on Thursday, 14mm on Friday and 10mm on Saturday, and the going was given as good (GoingStick 7.3). After riding in the first race Denis O'Regan said "It's pretty quick" and Tony McCoy said "It's good to firm", but Noel Fehily said "It's good, beautiful ground." A fair novice chase for the time of year. The winner is rated below the best of his form over shorter.

964 CHAD RETRO H'CAP CHASE (13 fncs) 2m
2:10 (2:40) (Class 5) (0-100,100) 4-Y-0+ **£2,274** (£667; £333; £166)

Form RPR

000- **1** **Alba King (IRE)**21 [798] 7-10-8 **87** .... JonathanEngland(5) 97+
(Sue Smith) *led to 2nd: led again 4th: clr 3 out: rdn flat: eased nr fin* **11/2**

230- **2** *3* **Mad Professor (IRE)**21 [807] 10-9-9 **74** oh7 ....(b) JoeCornwall(5) 76
(John Cornwall) *in rr: mstke 2nd: hdwy 8th: rdn to go 2nd appr 2 out: styd on: nt rch wnr* **12/1**

P14- **3** *11* **Darnborough (IRE)**33 [707] 7-10-8 **82** .... FelixDeGiles 77
(Tom Symonds) *mid-div: j.rt: blnd 2nd: hdwy 6th: sn chsng wnr: rdn appr 3 out: wknd after 3 out* **11/4**1

/53- **4** *23* **Jive Master (IRE)**33 [709] 8-11-9 **100** ....(v) MichaelByrne(3) 72
(Tim Vaughan) *sn pushed along and prom: led 2nd to 4th: sn drvn along: wknd after 8th* **7/2**2

323- **5** *1 ¾* **Ginger's Lad**29 [749] 9-10-12 **86** ....(tp) BrianHughes 56
(Michael Easterby) *in rr: drvn along after 6th: hmpd 10th: nvr on terms* **5/1**

/12- **P** **Apache Dawn**34 [694] 9-10-11 **85** ....(t) TommyPhelan
(Aytach Sadik) *chsd ldrs: mstke 6th: sn pushed along: wknd appr 8th: bhd whn mstke next: p.u bef 10th* **4/1**3

P65- **P** **Gainsborough's Art (IRE)**42 [602] 8-9-7 **74** oh19.....(b) DanielHiskett(7)
(Harry Chisman) *chsd ldrs: rdn appr 7th: wknd bef next: bhd whn p.u bef 10th* **50/1**

5/5- **F** **Garryowen Oscar (IRE)**31 [727] 7-11-2 **95** ....(t) SamanthaDrake(5)
(Joanne Foster) *hld up: hdwy 6th: sn rdn along: wknd after next: bhd whn fell 10th* **20/1**

4m 7.1s (5.10) **Going Correction** +0.375s/f (Yiel) **8** Ran SP% **115.4**
Speed ratings (Par 103): **102,100,95,83,82** , ,
Tote Swingers: 1&2 £25.70, 1&3 £2.90, 2&3 £9.50 CSF £64.21 CT £219.52 TOTE £7.80: £1.50, £4.10, £1.30; EX 84.30 Trifecta £624.30 Part won. Pool: £832.51 - 0.25 winning units..
Owner Mrs S Smith **Bred** John McKillop **Trained** High Eldwick, W Yorks

FOCUS
They went a solid gallop. The easy winner improved in line with his best hurdles form.

965 DISPATCH H'CAP HURDLE (DIV I) (13 hdls) 3m 110y
2:40 (3:10) (Class 5) (0-95,95) 4-Y-0+ **£1,949** (£572; £286; £143)

Form RPR

506- **1** **Moon Melody (GER)**29 [751] 10-9-9 **69** oh1 ....(bt) EDLinehan(5) 82
(Mike Sowersby) *chsd ldrs: led appr last: sn clr: styd on wl* **16/1**

F3P- **2** *16* **Festival Bound (IRE)**33 [710] 7-10-3 **72** .... WillKennedy 72
(Caroline Fryer) *led tl after 1st: w ldr tl led again 6th: rdn and hdd appr last: wkng whn mstke last* **28/1**

/06- **3** *1* **Heezagrey (IRE)**42 [601] 10-9-9 **69** ....(b) BenPoste(5) 67
(James Evans) *prom: drvn along 3 out: wknd next: wnt 3rd flat* **25/1**

/U0- **4** *3 ¼* **Shake The Barley (IRE)**42 [600] 10-11-7 **95**.......(p) AodhaganConlon(5) 91
(Tom George) *hld up: hdwy 6th: pushed along 10th: rdn and wknd after 2 out* **22/1**

430- **5** *25* **Roses Legend**21 [806] 8-11-3 **86** .... DPFahy 58
(Reginald Brown) *prom: ev ch 3 out: sn rdn: wknd next* **16/1**

0/5- **6** *1 ½* **Tarvini (IRE)**34 [690] 8-11-12 **95** ....(p) APMcCoy 66
(Jonjo O'Neill) *reminder after 1st: mid-div: hdwy 4th: drvn along 10th: wknd appr 2 out* **15/8**1

/P0- **7** *½* **Rampant Ronnie (USA)**37 [661] 8-10-10 **82** ....(t) RobertDunne(3) 52
(Nikki Evans) *hld up: hdwy 11th: rdn and wknd bef next* **50/1**

0P/- **P** **Grenoli (FR)**86 [5382] 12-9-9 **69** oh9 ....(bt) JoeCornwall(5)
(John Cornwall) *mid-div: pushed along and lost pl 3rd: bhd fr next: p.u after 8th* **100/1**

003/ **P** **Winged Farasi**13 [4844] 9-11-0 **88** .... SamanthaDrake(5)
(Joanne Foster) *a in rr: bhd and pushed along 5th: p.u bef 7th* **25/1**

P/F- **P** **Rocky Ryan (IRE)**63 [241] 10-11-10 **93** ....(v1) SamTwiston-Davies
(Jim Best) *hld up: rdn appr 9th: wknd next: p.u bef 2 out* **9/1**

212- **P** **Minstalad**42 [601] 9-10-6 **75** .... BrianHughes
(Karen Tutty) *led after 1st tl 6th: remained handy: tl rdn and wknd bef 2 out: p.u bef last* **3/1**2

P/5- **P** **Upper Deck (IRE)**34 [692] 8-10-0 **72** .... KielanWoods(3)
(Richard Phillips) *hld up: drvn along 10th: sn wknd: p.u bef 2 out* **10/1**

/55- **P** **Handford Henry (IRE)**36 [669] 7-10-13 **82** .... RyanMahon
(Michael Appleby) *hld up: drvn along 7th: sn wknd: p.u bef 2 out* **20/1**

3/P- **P** **On Alert**66 [188] 5-10-11 **80** ....(tp) ConorO'Farrell
(Seamus Durack) *prom: drvn along 9th: mstke and wknd next: p.u bef 2 out* **7/1**3

6m 18.7s (3.70) **Going Correction** +0.05s/f (Yiel) **14** Ran SP% **126.3**
Speed ratings (Par 103): **96,90,90,89,81 81,80,** , , , ,
Tote Swingers: 1&2 £0.00, 1&3 £23.00, 2&3 £33.20 CSF £397.34 CT £10637.37 TOTE £21.10: £4.90, £11.50, £5.00; EX 871.70 Trifecta £566.20 Part won. Pool: £754.99 - 0.01 winning units..
Owner Mrs Janet Cooper **Bred** R Hartmann **Trained** Goodmanham, E Yorks

FOCUS
The first division of this stayers' handicap. The winner is rated in line with the best of his recent chase form.

966 HUCKNALLDISPATCH.CO.UK H'CAP HURDLE (11 hdls) 2m 4f 110y
3:10 (3:42) (Class 4) (0-110,110) 4-Y-0+ **£3,898** (£1,144; £572; £286)

Form RPR

/53- **1** **Sonofagun (FR)**18 [844] 7-11-2 **100** .... WillKennedy 106+
(Ian Williams) *hld up: hdwy 8th: led 2 out: clr last: comf* **6/1**3

01U/ **2** *6* **Graceful Descent (FR)**35 [849] 8-10-5 **96** ....(t) JohnDawson(7) 96
(Karen Tutty) *hld up: hdwy 7th: rdn to chse wnr after 2 out: styd on same pce last* **33/1**

/53- **3** *5* **Aughcarra (IRE)**7 [903] 8-9-7 **84** oh9 .... MissAEStirling(7) 80
(Harry Chisman) *chsd ldrs: rdn appr 2 out: styd on same pce* **11/1**

F05- **4** *4* **Amuse Me**12 [858] 7-11-9 **107** .... APMcCoy 100
(Jonjo O'Neill) *chsd ldrs: rdn appr 2 out: wknd bef last* **4/1**2

U/3- **5** *8* **Tracking Time**56 [384] 6-11-3 **108** .... MrJMartin(7) 93
(Andrew J Martin) *prom: pushed along 7th: wknd 3 out* **12/1**

0/0- **6** *28* **Geminus (IRE)**49 [503] 5-11-4 **105** ....(vt1) MichaelByrne(3) 65
(Tim Vaughan) *led: rdn and hdd after 3 out: wknd bef next* **6/1**3

0/4- **7** *6* **Ben Cee Pee M (IRE)**44 [564] 8-11-2 **100** ....(b) TomScudamore 54
(Brian Ellison) *hld up: nt fluent 2nd: hdwy 7th: led after 3 out: rdn and hdd next: sn wknd* **9/4**1

350/ **P** **Mosstown (IRE)**499 [3526] 7-11-12 **110** ....(tp) DPFahy
(Liam Corcoran) *chsd ldr to 8th: wknd after next: bhd whn blnd 2 out: sn p.u* **22/1**

S54/ **P** **Western High**355 [1064] 8-11-6 **104** .... SamTwiston-Davies
(Jim Best) *hld up: drvn along 7th: sn wknd: p.u bef 2 out* **6/1**3

5m 11.7s (-1.30) **Going Correction** +0.05s/f (Yiel) **9** Ran SP% **116.9**
Speed ratings (Par 105): **104,101,99,98,95 84,82,** ,
Tote Swingers: 1&2 £28.80, 1&3 £9.60, 2&3 £31.20 CSF £153.56 CT £2117.10 TOTE £9.30: £1.90, £5.30, £3.30; EX 139.00 Trifecta £664.10 Part won. Pool: £885.54 - 0.02 winning units..
Owner The Piranha Partnership **Bred** Dora Bloodstock Ltd **Trained** Portway, Worcs

FOCUS
Just a modest handicap. The first two are rated back to their best.

967 MANSFIELD CHAD NOVICES' (S) HURDLE (11 hdls) 2m 4f 110y
3:40 (4:10) (Class 5) 4-Y-0+ **£1,949** (£572; £286; £143)

Form RPR

443/ **1** **Raktiman (IRE)**104 [5058] 6-10-12 102 ....(p) TomMessenger 107
(Chris Bealby) *a.p: chsd ldr 2 out: rdn to ld appr last: styd on u.p* **8/1**

124- **2** *1* **Loose Preformer (IRE)**29 [747] 7-11-3 115 ....(p) APMcCoy 111
(David O'Meara) *led to 8th: sn drvn along: led again appr 2 out: hdd bef last: styd on u.p* **6/4**1

3/4- **3** *22* **Lifetime (IRE)**15 [491] 5-10-12 109 ....(tp) TomScudamore 86
(Brian Ellison) *chsd ldrs: rdn after 3 out: wknd next* **4/1**3

/25- **4** *18* **Groomed (IRE)**11 [864] 5-10-9 112 ....(vt1) MichaelByrne(3) 70
(Tim Vaughan) *chsd ldr tl led 8th: rdn and hdd appr 2 out: sn wknd* **15/8**2

PF- **P** **Trentside William**14 [847] 6-10-12 0 ....(t) AndrewThornton
(Mike Sowersby) *sn wl bhd: blnd 8th: p.u bef 2 out* **100/1**

P **Printing Press (IRE)**65 [208] 7-10-7 0 .... JonathanEngland(5)
(Joanne Foster) *sn wl bhd: p.u bef 7th* **22/1**

5m 11.3s (-1.70) **Going Correction** +0.05s/f (Yiel)
WFA 4 from 5yo+ 16lb **6** Ran SP% **111.2**
Speed ratings (Par 103): **105,104,96,89,**
Tote Swingers: 1&2 £2.30, 1&3 £9.30, 2&3 £1.60 CSF £20.82 TOTE £12.40: £4.20, £1.10; EX 27.60 Trifecta £76.60 Pool: £559.44 - 5.47 winning units..Winner bought by John England for 7,000gns. Groom was bought by Sue Smith for 6,000gns.
Owner Michael Hill **Bred** Kilbride Stud Ltd **Trained** Barrowby, Lincs
■ Stewards' Enquiry : Tom Messenger nine-day ban: used whip above permitted level (Jul 29-31,Aug 1-4,13,15)

FOCUS
A bit of a turn-up. The winner is rated to his best.

968 ASHFIELD CHAD H'CAP HURDLE (9 hdls) 2m
4:10 (4:40) (Class 4) (0-115,114) 4-Y-0+ **£3,249** (£954; £477; £238)

Form RPR

541- **1** **Cut The Cards (IRE)**24 [783] 6-11-9 **111** ....(p) APMcCoy 123+
(Jonjo O'Neill) *hld up: hdwy after 4th: chsd ldr 3 out: led appr next: sn clr: comf* **5/4**1

/12- **2** *3 ½* **Tinseltown**15 [697] 7-11-9 **111** ....(p) TomScudamore 113
(Brian Rothwell) *led: rdn and hdd appr 2 out: styd on same pce* **9/2**3

/02- **3** *15* **Houseparty**4 [947] 5-11-2 **104** .... DenisO'Regan 93
(John Ferguson) *hld up: reminders after 3rd: swtchd lft appr 3 out: shkn up and hdwy appr 2 out: sn rdn and wknd* **5/2**2

554- **4** *8* **Finch Flyer (IRE)**9 [714] 6-10-1 **89** ....(p) TommyPhelan 70
(Aytach Sadik) *chsd ldrs: pushed along 6th: rdn and wknd approaching 2 out* **16/1**

4/6- **5** *1 ¾* **Oakwell (IRE)**21 [800] 5-11-3 **105** .... AndrewThornton 85
(Sally Hall) *prom: pushed along and lost pl after 4th: blnd 3 out: sn wknd* **25/1**

62/- **6** *12* **Hilltime (IRE)**2170 [1085] 13-10-5 **100** .... MrJHamilton(7) 69
(Clive Mulhall) *chsd ldr: mstke 3rd: lost 2nd 3 out: wknd bef next* **7/1**

3m 59.7s (2.70) **Going Correction** +0.05s/f (Yiel) **6** Ran SP% **113.4**
Speed ratings (Par 105): **95,93,85,81,80 74**
Tote Swingers: 1&2 £1.30, 1&3 £1.30, 2&3 £1.10 CSF £7.71 CT £11.80 TOTE £2.00: £1.70, £2.30; EX 6.60 Trifecta £10.90 Pool: £1,307.94 - 89.32 winning units..
Owner John P McManus **Bred** Coppice Farm **Trained** Cheltenham, Gloucs

FOCUS
This proved straightforward for the favourite. The easy winner is on the upgrade in headgear and should win again.

969 DISPATCH H'CAP HURDLE (DIV II) (13 hdls) 3m 110y
4:40 (5:10) (Class 5) (0-95,95) 4-Y-0+ **£1,949** (£572; £286; £143)

Form RPR

3/P- **1** **Carmela Maria**52 [444] 8-11-0 **88** ....(p) EDLinehan(5) 91
(Mike Sowersby) *in rr 3rd: hdwy 10th: chsd ldr appr 2 out: led last: rdn and edgd lft flat: styd on* **12/1**

/36- **2** *½* **Fromthetop (IRE)**34 [690] 7-10-5 **74** ....(tp) TomScudamore 77
(Michael Scudamore) *chsd ldrs: led appr 2 out: rdn and hdd last: styd on* **4/1**1

030/ **3** *37* **Radical Bay**222 [2843] 9-10-0 **69** .... ConorO'Farrell 38
(Nicholas Pomfret) *hld up: hdwy 9th: rdn after 3 out: wknd next* **20/1**

P/0- **4** *4 ½* **Overlay**46 [543] 9-10-12 **81** .... DavidBass 46
(Lawney Hill) *chsd ldrs: rdn after 3 out: wknd bef next* **11/2**2

405- **5** *16* **La Madonnina (IRE)**19 [828] 5-11-4 **90** .... JamesBest(3) 41
(Caroline Keevil) *mde most tl rdn: hdd & wknd appr 2 out* **12/1**

0/0- **6** *41* **Phoenix Eye**7 [903] 12-10-7 **79** .... KielanWoods(3)
(Michael Mullineaux) *hld up: hdwy 6th: rdn and wknd after 3 out* **25/1**

/44- **7** *14* **Kaycee (IRE)**46 [541] 8-10-0 **69** oh5 ....(b1) MarkGrant
(Roger Curtis) *sn prom: led briefly 3rd: rdn appr 9th: sn wknd* **25/1**

0/P- **P** **Dream Honours (IRE)**21 [805] 10-10-0 **69** oh1 .... TomMessenger
(Clarissa Caroe) *chsd ldrs: nt fluent 2nd: lost pl 6th: mstke and rdr lost irons next: sn p.u* **100/1**

P/0- **P** **Phoenix Des Mottes (FR)**53 [429] 10-9-11 **71** .... JoeCornwall(5)
(John Cornwall) *mid-div: pushed along and dropped to rr 3rd: bhd whn p.u bef 8th* **50/1**

0/P- **P** **Call At Midnight**33 [712] 8-11-9 **95** .... JackQuinlan(3)
(Sarah Humphrey) *prom: wknd after 6th: p.u bef 9th* **15/2**

46P/ P **Shinrock Beat**[294] [1613] 6-9-7 **69** (t) MrJHamilton(7)
(Barry Brennan) *mid-div: hdwy 4th: rdn and wknd after 3 out: p.u and dismntd bef next* **7/1**[3]

/16- P **Marico (FR)**[51] [460] 5-10-13 **82** (p) FelixDeGiles
(Tom Symonds) *hld up: effrt appr 9th: sn wknd: bhd whn p.u after 3 out* **4/1**[1]

46P- P **Two Oscars (IRE)**[21] [803] 7-10-6 **82** JohnWinston(7)
(Andrew Crook) *hld up: hdwy 4th: wknd and p.u bef 9th* **14/1**

6m 23.4s (8.40) **Going Correction** +0.05s/f (Yiel) **13** Ran SP% **117.1**
Speed ratings (Par 103): **88,87,76,74,69 56,51,, ,, ,,**
Tote Swingers: 1&2 £9.20, 1&3 £41.70, 2&3 £10.90 CSF £56.55 CT £969.76 TOTE £15.80: £3.90, £1.80, £6.50; EX 83.50 Trifecta £607.80 Part won. Pool: £810.52 - 0.19 winning units..
Owner Mrs Janet Cooper & M E Sowersby **Bred** O Pointing **Trained** Goodmanham, E Yorks
■ Stewards' Enquiry : E D Linehan two-day ban: used whip above permitted level (Jul 29-30)

FOCUS
The second division of this stayers' handicap was run in a time 4.7sec slower than the first division. The first two were well clear. The winner's best run since her Catterick win.

970 PROPERTY TODAY.CO.UK MARES' STANDARD OPEN NATIONAL HUNT FLAT RACE 2m
5:10 (5:40) (Class 6) 4-6-Y-O **£1,642** (£478; £239)

Form RPR

1 **Monita Bonita** 4-10-10 0 TomScudamore 94+
(Tim Easterby) *hld up: hdwy over 4f out: led over 1f out: rdn out* **6/1**[3]

2 2 ¼ **Hazel Brook** 4-10-10 0 SamTwiston-Davies 92
(Charlie Brooks) *hld up: hdwy over 4f out: hmpd over 2f out: sn rdn: styd on same pce ins fnl f* **8/1**

3 nse **Inarticulate (IRE)** 5-10-5 0 KevinJones(7) 93
(Seamus Mullins) *hld up: pushed along over 5f out: hdwy over 3f out: rdn whn hmpd over 1f out: styd on* **25/1**

4 hd **Amber Flush** 4-10-10 0 FelixDeGiles 91
(Tom Symonds) *chsd ldrs: led over 9f out: hdd 8f out: led again 6f out: rdn and edgd rt wl over 2f out: sn hung lft: hdd over 1f out: styd on same pce ins fnl f* **25/1**

22- 5 2 ¼ **Retrieve The Stick**[29] [754] 4-10-10 0 BrianHughes 92+
(Malcolm Jefferson) *led 2f: chsd ldrs: rdn and hmpd over 2f out: styd on same pce fnl f* **3/1**[1]

6 ¾ **Noir Girl** 4-10-3 0 AdamNicol(7) 88
(Philip Kirby) *a.p: rdn over 2f out: no ex fnl f* **12/1**

7 8 **Lavella Wells** 5-10-7 0 JonathanEngland(5) 83
(Sue Smith) *prom: rdn whn hmpd over 2f out: wknd over 1f out* **25/1**

04- 8 10 **Agent Louise**[29] [754] 5-10-12 0 DenisO'Regan 74
(Mike Sowersby) *hld up: hdwy over 7f out: wknd over 4f out* **20/1**

06- 9 hd **Just Got Lucky**[18] [841] 5-10-7 0 GavinSheehan(5) 74
(Emma Lavelle) *mid-div: hdwy over 8f out: wknd over 3f out* **17/2**

5- 10 24 **All Riled Up**[26] [760] 5-10-5 0 MissAEStirling(7) 52
(Harry Chisman) *hld up: racd keenly: hdwy to ld after 2f: racd wd: hdd over 9f out: led again 8f out: hdd 6f out: wknd over 4f out* **20/1**

11 3 ¼ **Wave The Grapes** 6-10-12 0 APMcCoy 49
(Peter Bowen) *prom: jnd ldr 6f out: pushed along over 3f out: wknd over 2f out* **4/1**[2]

/ 12 hd **Sooley** 6-10-12 0 RyanMahon 49
(Michael Appleby) *hld up: rdn over 4f out: sn wknd* **40/1**

13 11 **Swincomb Silvalady**[69] 5-10-12 0 AndrewThornton 39
(Robert Walford) *hld up: rdn over 6f out: sn lost tch* **12/1**

3m 55.8s (4.40) **Going Correction** +0.05s/f (Yiel)
WFA 4 from 5yo+ 2lb **13** Ran SP% **119.8**
Speed ratings: **91,89,89,89,88 88,84,79,79,67 65,65,59**
Tote Swingers: 1&2 £29.50, 1&3 £17.80, 2&3 £12.10 CSF £47.77 TOTE £7.90: £2.70, £3.30, £7.40; EX 43.80 Trifecta £623.30 Part won. Pool: £831.12 - 0.19 winning units..
Owner Habton Farms **Bred** E R Hanbury **Trained** Great Habton, N Yorks

FOCUS
There wasn't much of a gallop on early but things picked up down the back straight. Ordinary form rated around the fifth.
T/Jkpt: £50,748.80 to £1 stake. Pool: £142.954.00 - 2.00 winning tickets. T/Plt: £932.30 to £1 stake. Pool: £101,407.68 - 79.40 winning tickets. T/Qpdt: £413.00 to £1 stake. Pool: £5,191.43 - 9.30 winning tickets. CR

856 STRATFORD (L-H)
Sunday, July 14

OFFICIAL GOING: Good to firm (good in places, 9.7)
Rails on inside and all bends split.
Wind: nil Weather: very hot; 28 degrees

971 SGH MARTINEAU "NATIONAL HUNT" NOVICES' HURDLE (8 hdls) 2m 110y
2:20 (2:20) (Class 4) 4-Y-0+ **£3,249** (£954; £477; £238)

Form RPR

6- 1 **Portofino Wasp (IRE)**[14] [848] 4-10-10 0 RichieMcLernon 85+
(Jonjo O'Neill) *racd keenly: hld up gng wl: wnt 2nd 2 out: led nring last: pushed out to assert flat* **6/4**[1]

2 8 **Moscow Me (IRE)**[69] 6-10-12 0 HenryOliver 83
(Henry Oliver) *trckd ldr: led 3 out: rdn next: hdd bef last where nt fluent: easily outpcd flat* **2/1**[2]

6/0- 3 41 **Share The Dosh**[61] [291] 5-10-5 0 BrendanPowell 36
(J R Jenkins) *j. deliberately 2nd and 3rd: settled last: lost tch 3 out: blnd next: wnt v remote 3rd bef last* **14/1**

0/P- 4 10 **Chandler Jack**[33] [716] 6-10-12 0 LeeEdwards 38
(Derek Wellicome) *t.k.h: led at mod pce: j.rt 5th: hdd next: lost 2nd and blnd 2 out: remote last whn blnd body last* **33/1**

0/P- F **Snowball (IRE)**[47] [517] 6-10-12 0 TomCannon
(David Arbuthnot) *disputing 4th and wl in tch whn fell 5th* **3/1**[3]

3m 55.4s (-0.60) **Going Correction** -0.45s/f (Good)
WFA 4 from 5yo+ 15lb **5** Ran SP% **107.9**
Speed ratings (Par 105): **83,79,59,55,**
CSF £4.75 TOTE £2.30: £1.90, £1.30; EX 5.50 Trifecta £13.90 Pool: £510.45 - 27.44 winning units..
Owner Mrs Peter Bond **Bred** J R Weston **Trained** Cheltenham, Gloucs

FOCUS
Rails on inside and all bends split. The watered ground was riding largely as advertised. The time for the opener was 9.4sec slower than standard. This was a very weak novice hurdle, and limited form to say the least.

972 BOURNVILLE COLLEGE H'CAP CHASE (17 fncs) 2m 7f
2:50 (2:50) (Class 4) (0-120,115) 4-Y-0+ **£3,898** (£1,144; £572; £286)

Form RPR

/12- 1 **To Live (FR)**[25] [763] 6-11-2 **105** TomCannon 126+
(Nick Gifford) *hld up towards rr: j. soundly: hdwy 12th: sn chsng ldr: led gng best 3 out: 12 l clr last: v heavily eased flat* **4/1**[1]

334/ 2 14 **Pyracantha**[126] [4678] 8-11-2 **105** (p) SeanQuinlan 111
(Jennie Candlish) *prom: led 11th: hdd and hit 3 out: outj. next: drvn between last two: completely outpcd by wnr after but clr of rest* **9/1**

545- 3 6 **Lady Myfanwy**[11] [872] 12-10-3 **99** MissHLewis(7) 97
(Adrian Wintle) *bhd: rdn 9th: sn outpcd: virtually t.o 13th: stl 18 l 6th 2 out: r.o gamely after: lft 3rd after last: fin wl* **14/1**

625- 4 1 ½ **Handsome Buddy (IRE)**[25] [763] 6-10-6 **98** (v) AdamWedge(3) 94
(Michael Gates) *last pair: rdn and outpcd 3 out: 15 l 5th after next: plugged on* **12/1**

/13- 5 ½ **Pairc Na Gcapall (IRE)**[25] [766] 11-9-7 **89** MissBAndrews(7) 84
(Neil King) *sn led: rdn and hdd 11th: sn dropped himself rt out: remote 7th 2 out: rallied and fin strly fr hopeless position* **5/1**[2]

663- 6 4 ½ **Health Is Wealth (IRE)**[26] [757] 8-10-12 **101** (bt[1]) BrendanPowell 92
(Colin Tizzard) *prom tl lost pl u.p bef 14th: fading fr 2 out* **4/1**[1]

/05- P **Very Stylish (IRE)**[25] [766] 9-11-12 **115** (b) RichieMcLernon
(Jonjo O'Neill) *towards rr: rdn 11th: lost tch next: last whn p.u 13th* **12/1**

/34- P **Western King (IRE)**[49] [487] 6-11-1 **114** (tp) PaulNO'Brien(10)
(Charlie Mann) *j. slowly 2nd (water) and rdn: pressed ldrs tl 12th: 7th and losing tch rapidly whn blnd 14th: t.o and p.u 2 out* **8/1**

/26- U **Queen Of Mantua (IRE)**[38] [641] 7-10-12 **101** PaddyBrennan 102
(Fergal O'Brien) *chsd ldrs: effrt to dispute 2nd after 13th: rdn and wkng in 8 l 3rd after 2 out: 20 l 3rd whn landed awkwardly last and uns rdr* **13/2**[3]

5m 32.2s (-7.00) **Going Correction** -0.175s/f (Good) **9** Ran SP% **113.2**
Speed ratings (Par 105): **105,100,98,97,97 95,, ,**
Tote Swingers: 1&2 £5.90, 1&3 £9.80, 2&3 £7.40 CSF £38.33 CT £452.97 TOTE £4.30: £1.80, £2.90, £3.70; EX 42.50 Trifecta £493.10 Part won. Pool: £657.54 - 0.47 winning units..
Owner John P McManus **Bred** G Berger, S Berger & J M Callier **Trained** Findon, W Sussex
■ Stewards' Enquiry : Sean Quinlan one-day ban: careless riding (Jul 29)

FOCUS
A fair handicap chase run at a decent pace. Another step up from the winner, with the next two close to their marks.

973 PALLASADES H'CAP HURDLE (FOR THE STRATFORD SUMMER SALVER) (8 hdls) 2m 110y
3:20 (3:21) (Class 3) (0-130,125) 4-Y-£4,596 (£2,244; £1,122; £561; £280)

Form RPR

P/3- 1 **Solaras Exhibition (IRE)**[14] [850] 5-11-11 **124** AidanColeman 135+
(Tim Vaughan) *hld up gng wl: effrt 3 out: led and hit next: sn clr: 7 l ahd last: eased* **5/2**[2]

144- 2 5 **Rime Avec Gentil (FR)**[19] [831] 8-10-6 **110** RobertWilliams(5) 111
(Bernard Llewellyn) *t.k.h: cl up tl rdn and let himself get outpcd sn after 2 out: 5th st: 10 l 4th last: consented to run on after and fin strly to pass two rivals cl home* **9/2**[3]

121- 3 ½ **Castlemorris King**[12] [858] 5-11-5 **123** HarryDerham(5) 123
(Brian Barr) *led: rdn and hdd 2 out: lost wl hld 2nd at last and kpt on same pce: snatched 3rd nr fin* **7/4**[1]

/10- 4 shd **Maoi Chinn Tire (IRE)**[21] [812] 6-11-5 **118** SeanQuinlan 119
(Jennie Candlish) *last pair tl rdn and prog after 3 out: tried vainly to cl fr next: wnt 7 l 2nd whn hit last: nt qckn after and lost two pl fnl strides* **10/1**

/55- 5 7 **Jolly Roger (IRE)**[19] [831] 6-11-12 **125** LeeEdwards 120
(Tony Carroll) *pressed ldr tl 3 out: rdn and wknd after next* **13/2**

335- 6 nk **Teshali (IRE)**[25] [762] 7-11-3 **116** (t) PaulMoloney 109
(Anthony Middleton) *last pair: rdn and struggling fr 2 out* **18/1**

3m 50.4s (-5.60) **Going Correction** -0.45s/f (Good) **6** Ran SP% **110.8**
Speed ratings (Par 107): **95,92,92,92,89 88**
Tote Swingers: 1&2 £1.80, 1&3 £2.00, 2&3 £3.80 CSF £13.70 TOTE £2.90: £1.80, £1.30; EX 15.30 Trifecta £37.80 Pool: £1,231.52 - 24.41 winning units..
Owner C Davies **Bred** John Skehan **Trained** Aberthin, Vale of Glamorgan

FOCUS
A reasonable handicap hurdle, albeit one in which the top-weight carried 5lb less than the race maximum. The time was five seconds quicker than the earlier novice hurdle. The easy winner improved in line with the best of his Flat form.

974 BIRMINGHAM POST H'CAP CHASE (FOR THE STRATFORD SUMMER CUP THE SUNDAY £5K BONUS RACE) (12 fncs) 2m 1f 110y
3:50 (3:50) (Class 2) (0-145,145) 4-Y-0+
£11,573 (£3,418; £1,709; £854; £427; £214)

Form RPR

161- 1 **Dineur (FR)**[30] [735] 7-10-6 **125** DonalDevereux 135+
(Peter Bowen) *trckd ldrs: wnt 2nd bef 9th: led 2 out: rdn after: 2 l clr last: hung on bravely* **5/2**[1]

142- 2 ½ **Tindaro (FR)**[18] [840] 6-10-12 **131** RichieMcLernon 140
(Paul Webber) *t.k.h in last pair tl effrt bef 9th: on outside st: wnt 2nd bef last: drvn and clsd grad fr last but nvr looked like overtaking wnr fnl 100yds* **6/1**

234- 3 7 **Rajnagan (IRE)**[36] [672] 9-11-4 **137** (t) LiamTreadwell 141
(Paul Webber) *settled trcking ldrs: nt fluent 3rd: effrt 3 out: rdn and wnt 2nd sn after next tl bef last: sn btn* **11/4**[2]

/10- 4 16 **West With The Wind**[35] [680] 8-11-12 **145** PaulMoloney 133
(Evan Williams) *led tl 7th: lost pl bef 9th: no ch after: snatched poor 4th* **10/1**

11U- 5 ½ **Anquetta (IRE)**[36] [672] 9-11-7 **145** MrSWaley-Cohen(5) 133
(Nicky Henderson) *2nd tl led and mstke 7th: nt fluent 3 out: hdd 2 out: rdn and sn btn: 12 l 4th whn awkward jump last* **3/1**[3]

0/3- 6 18 **Oceana Gold**[18] [840] 9-11-0 **133** AidanColeman 112
(Emma Lavelle) *lacked fluency: j. slowly 3rd: last fr 5th: wl bhd fr 9th* **11/1**

4m 1.5s (-5.60) **Going Correction** -0.175s/f (Good) **6** Ran SP% **111.9**
Speed ratings (Par 109): **105,104,101,94,94 86**
Tote Swingers: 1&2 £6.40, 1&3 £1.10, 2&3 £8.60 CSF £17.12 TOTE £3.70: £2.30, £2.20; EX 14.50 Trifecta £30.70 Pool: £1,090,.07 - 26.58 winning units..
Owner Gwilym J Morris **Bred** Dominique Le Baron **Trained** Little Newcastle, Pembrokes

FOCUS
Quite a valuable handicap chase, run at a fair gallop. The winner is on the upgrade and the second is rated to his best.

975 JOHN LORRIMAN 70TH BIRTHDAY JUVENILE HURDLE (8 hdls) 2m 110y
4:20 (4:22) (Class 4) 3-Y-O £3,249 (£954; £477; £238)

Form RPR
4- 1 **Sirop De Menthe (FR)**31 725 3-10-12 0 BrendanPowell 95+
(Tim Vaughan) *racd keenly and trckd ldrs: 4th and rdn and outpcd 2 out: rallied between last two: led last: sn rdn clr* **14/1**
11- 2 10 **It's Only Business**23 785 3-11-12 0 PaddyBrennan 102+
(Jim Best) *plld hrd and tended to jump rt: mostly 2nd tl led between last two: 3 l clr briefly: rdn and hdd last: immediately outpcd by wnr* **11/10**1
3 1 **Bountiful Bess**67 3-10-5 0 SeanQuinlan 77
(Pam Sly) *toward rr: 6th and outpcd 2 out: wnt 7 l 3rd at last: no ch w wnr but catching 2nd cl home* **20/1**
6- 4 nk **Wild Diamond (IRE)**43 582 3-10-5 0 AidanColeman 77
(Tim Vaughan) *prom: 3rd and rdn 2 out: sn outpcd: 6th between last two: plugged on flat* **50/1**
5- 5 2¾ **Walter White (IRE)**23 785 3-10-9 0 MichealNolan(3) 81
(Philip Hobbs) *midfield: effrt 3 out: cl 5th next: 3rd home turn: drvn and no imp after* **28/1**
3- 6 17 **Red Eight (USA)**23 785 3-10-12 0 LeightonAspell 76
(John Butler) *led tl drvn and hdd between last two: wknd rapidly: blnd bdly last* **16/1**
7 nk **Diamonds A Dancing**21 3-10-12 0 NickScholfield 66
(Rebecca Curtis) *nvr bttr than midfield: struggling after 3 out* **11/1**
P **Double Jeopardy**310 3-10-9 0 AdamWedge(3)
(Dr Jon Scargill) *last whn j. slowly 2nd: t.o after 3 out: p.u last* **50/1**
F **Dark Justice (IRE)**12 3-10-5 0 RichieMcLernon
(Tim Pitt) *kpt clr of rest at s: nt fluent 3rd: pressed ldr on outer tl fell 5th* **50/1**
B **Scepticism (USA)**76 3-10-12 0 NoelFehily
(Charlie Mann) *hld up towards rr: b.d 5th* **13/2**3
P **Town Mouse**29 3-10-7 0 TrevorWhelan(5)
(Neil King) *unruly: uns rdr leaving paddock: led rnd s: s.s and plld frnticaly early: bhd: j. slowly 3rd: impeded 5th and lost tch: t.o and p.u 2 out* **7/2**2
- P **Jd Rockefeller**47 3-10-12 0 HaddenFrost
(Paul D'Arcy) *last whn j. slowly 3rd: v slow next and lost tch: t.o and p.u 3 out* **33/1**

3m 51.9s (-4.10) **Going Correction** -0.45s/f (Good) 12 Ran SP% **121.1**
Speed ratings (Par 102): **91,86,85,85,84 76,76,, ,**
Tote Swingers: 1&2 £5.70, 1&3 £40.00, 2&3 £14.10 CSF £30.19 TOTE £18.10: £2.30, £1.10, £7.80; EX 31.40 Trifecta £602.30 Pool: £2,517.03 - 3.13 winning units..
Owner Straightline Construction Ltd **Bred** Francois-Marie Cottin **Trained** Aberthin, Vale of Glamorgan

FOCUS
A modest juvenile event, rated around the first two.

976 BIRMINGHAM MAIL H'CAP CHASE (14 fncs) 2m 4f
4:50 (4:51) (Class 5) (0-100,100) 4-Y-O+ £2,599 (£763; £381; £190)

Form RPR
/30- 1 **Daneva (IRE)**21 807 9-11-5 93 (tp) CharliePoste 103
(Matt Sheppard) *pressed ldng pair: bumped along bef 11th: led 2 out: drvn after: all out but hung on bravely flat* **13/2**
155- 2 ¾ **Crack At Dawn (IRE)**21 805 12-10-12 86 (b) BrendanPowell 96
(Michael Gates) *last pair: rdn 6th: outpcd 9th: 13 l 4th at next: styd on to go 2nd bef last but hanging rt and v awkward: flattered briefly: outbattled flat* **11/2**3
600- 3 3 **Iheardu**19 829 7-11-12 100 (tp) AidanColeman 107
(Neil Mulholland) *shkn up bef 6th: rdn 9th and outpcd and nt travelling after: 17 l 4th next: clsd 3 out: rdn to go 2nd between last two: flattered briefly: lost 2nd at last and fnd little after* **7/2**2
214/ 4 4½ **Brimham Boy**48 11-11-1 99 (tp) OllieGarner(10) 101
(Martin Keighley) *pressed ldr: rdn to ld 3 out: hdd next: wknd between last two* **3/1**1
655- 5 nse **Sadler's Star (GER)**24 778 10-11-12 100 (p) NickScholfield 102
(Michael Blake) *narrow ld tl rdn and hdd 3 out: fnd little whn fading between last two* **3/1**1
P/U- P **Rustic John**74 63 13-9-8 75 oh2 ow1 MrPJohn(7)
(H Edward Haynes) *t.k.h early: in last pair: rdn and lost tch 8th: t.o and p.u 11th* **11/1**

4m 48.5s (-1.50) **Going Correction** -0.175s/f (Good) 6 Ran SP% **109.3**
Speed ratings (Par 103): **96,95,94,92,92**
Tote Swingers: 1&2 £3.10, 1&3 £4.70, 2&3 £2.90 CSF £37.65 CT £131.82 TOTE £6.80: £3.00, £2.50; EX 20.50 Trifecta £87.50 Pool: £1,690.75 - 14.49 winning units..
Owner Matt Sheppard Racing Club **Bred** Miss Elizabeth Kennedy **Trained** Eastnor, H'fords

FOCUS
A low-grade handicap chase in which solid recent form was thin on the ground, but it produced a decent finish with all bar Rustic John in with a shout heading to the final fence. The winner is rated back to something like her best.

977 COVENTRY TELEGRAPH CONDITIONAL JOCKEYS' H'CAP HURDLE (9 hdls) 2m 3f
5:20 (5:20) (Class 5) (0-100,100) 4-Y-O+ £1,949 (£572; £286; £143)

Form RPR
630- 1 **First Morning (IRE)**19 833 8-11-5 93 MichealNolan 98
(Michael Blake) *chsd ldrs: wnt 2nd 3 out: sn drvn: tk 2nd bef last: styd on steadily and forced ahd fnl strides* **8/1**
6/4- 2 nk **Native Colony**4 163 5-11-9 100 (b) TrevorWhelan(3) 105
(Neil King) *prom: led gng wl between last two: 1 l clr last: urged along and kpt on wl but jst ct* **20/1**
/40- 3 11 **Argaum (IRE)**50 482 6-11-0 91 (bt) AdamWedge(3) 87
(Evan Williams) *led: rdn and hdd between last two: wkng whn nt fluent last* **14/1**
/00- 4 20 **Osmosia (FR)**46 540 8-11-2 93 (vt1) TomCannon(3) 70
(Chris Gordon) *settled towards rr: styd on fr 3 out to go 4th at next: wknd tamely between last two* **22/1**
3/0- 5 1 **Ophelia's Kiss**34 691 6-11-2 90 (t) BrendanPowell 66
(Brendan Powell) *hld up in last pair: effrt 3 out: 5th but struggling after next* **16/1**
3/3- 6 9 **Fair Breeze**25 540 6-10-1 80 DanielHiskett(5) 48
(Richard Phillips) *mstkes: nvr bttr than midfield: t.o 3 out* **6/1**2
/10- 7 15 **Nothing Is Forever (IRE)**47 521 9-11-4 92 GilesHawkins 46
(Chris Down) *plld hrd: prom tl 7th: fdd rapidly bef 2 out: t.o* **15/2**3
50/- U **Saltagioo (ITY)**104 5067 9-10-8 90 (t) MarkMarris(8)
(Anthony Middleton) *bhd: last whn stmbld and uns rdr 6th* **40/1**
021- P **Anton Dolin (IRE)**18 844 5-11-3 97 (p) ChristopherWard(6)
(Dr Richard Newland) *racd wd and keen early: cl up: blnd bdly 3rd: nt fluent 4th: lost pl and hit 5th and rdn: hanging and awkward after: nt run on: t.o whn mstke 3 out: p.u last* **4/5**1

4m 21.6s (-9.90) **Going Correction** -0.45s/f (Good) 9 Ran SP% **116.8**
Speed ratings (Par 103): **102,101,97,88,88 84,78,,**
Tote Swingers 1&2 £12.60, 2&3 £20.80, 1&3 £9.00 CSF £139.65 CT £2193.84 TOTE £9.90: £2.30, £4.70, £3.10; EX 140.20 Trifecta £786.10 Pool: £1,177.72 - 1.12 winning units..
Owner Mark Holder Racing Limited **Bred** Ivan And Mrs Eileen Heanen **Trained** Trowbridge, Wilts

FOCUS
A very modest event. The winner is rated back to the best of his 2012 form.
T/Plt: £62.50 to £1 stake. Pool: £67,372.07 - 786.87 winning tickets. T/Qpdt: £13.00 to £1 stake. Pool: £4,753.03 - 270.15 winning tickets. IM

986 - 992a (Foreign Racing) - See Raceform Interactive

LES LANDES
Sunday, July 14

OFFICIAL GOING: Firm (good to firm in places)

993a 2013 CHAMPION HURDLE 2m 1f
2:30 (2:30) 4-Y-O+ £1,900 (£685; £415)

RPR
1 **If I Had Him (IRE)**13 5462 9-11-2 (v) MattieBatchelor
(George Baker) **11/8**2
2 nk **Landolino (FR)**28 8-11-2 AntonyProcter
(Mrs J L Le Brocq, Jersey) **1/1**1
3 15 **Nordic Affair**16 9-11-2 MrPCollington
(S Arthur, Jersey) **13/2**3
4 dist **Deepika (IRE)**16 5-10-11 (t) ThomasGarner
(Mrs A Malzard, Jersey) **8/1**

3m 58.0s (238.00) 4 Ran SP% **116.5**
.
Owner Sir Alex Ferguson **Bred** Mrs J Morrissey **Trained** Manton, Wilts

920NEWTON ABBOT (L-H)
Monday, July 15

OFFICIAL GOING: Good to firm (good in places; watered; 8.0)
All bends moved out 2-3 metres.
Wind: light breeze across Weather: sunny

994 MR & MRS RICHARDSON WEDDING DAY CELEBRATIONS NOVICES' HURDLE (7 hdls 1 omitted) 2m 1f
2:15 (2:15) (Class 4) 4-Y-O+ £3,594 (£1,116; £601)

Form RPR
/12- 1 **Lyssio (GER)**15 848 6-11-5 114 APMcCoy 116+
(Jim Best) *prom whn lft in ld 1st: drew clr after 3 out: easily* **4/6**1
F- 2 21 **Sir Dylan**45 80 4-10-5 0 EDLinehan(5) 88
(Ronald Harris) *trckd ldrs: jnd wnr after 2nd tl rdn after 3 out: sn hld: lft clr 2nd at the last* **10/1**
P/ 3 26 **Ifan (IRE)**19 4900 5-10-12 0 RichardJohnson 72
(Tim Vaughan) *hld up in tch: hmpd 3rd and on bnd bef omitted 5th: wkng whn wnt bdly lft 3 out: wnt bdly lft 2 out: lft modest 3rd at the last: t.o* **7/1**3
P **Spring Secret**189 7-10-9 0 MichaelByrne(3)
(Tim Vaughan) *trckd ldrs tl after omitted 5th: wknd next: p.u bef last: dismntd* **40/1**
U **Sir Bruno (FR)**189 6-10-5 0 JPKiely(7)
(Tim Vaughan) *in tch whn swvd lft and uns rdr 3rd* **33/1**
0P/- R **Hard House**220 2896 6-10-12 0 TommyPhelan
(Mark Gillard) *led tl rn out 1st* **100/1**
050- P **Bad Girls (FR)**7 920 4-10-3 0 (t) TomScudamore
(David Pipe) *hld up: p.u on bnd bef omitted 5th: fatally injured* **20/1**
/12- F **Kettlewell**27 760 4-10-10 0 NoelFehily
(Warren Greatrex) *trcking ldrs whn overj. and fell 1st* **5/2**2
0- F **Bolberry Springs**7 920 6-10-12 0 JoeTizzard 88
(Colin Tizzard) *trckd ldr: pressed wnr 3 out: sn rdn and hld by wnr: disputing 2nd whn fell last* **50/1**

3m 54.2s (-11.50) **Going Correction** -0.675s/f (Firm)
WFA 4 from 5yo+ 15lb 9 Ran SP% **123.2**
Speed ratings (Par 105): **100,90,77,, , , ,**
toteswingers 1&2 £2.30, 1&3 £1.70, 2&3 £10.50 CSF £9.44 TOTE £1.40: £1.02, £2.90, £2.10; EX 8.10 Trifecta £25.50 Pool: £1960.44 - 57.55 winning units..
Owner Jack Callaghan **Bred** Gestut Hof Ittlingen **Trained** Lewes, E Sussex

FOCUS
With the warm spell continuing the ground was officially good to firm (good in places), after sustained watering, and each bend was moved out by 2-3m. The fifth flight was bypassed. The winner is given a token rating ain a weak novices' hurdle.

995 ATTHERACES SKY415 H'CAP HURDLE (8 hdls) 2m 1f
2:45 (2:45) (Class 4) (0-120,117) 4-Y-O+ £3,508 (£1,030; £515; £257)

Form RPR
113- 1 **Party Palace**7 924 9-10-8 102 GilesHawkins(3) 105
(Stuart Howe) *chsd ldr: pushed along fr sn after 4th: rdn after 3 out: led between last 2: styd on strly: rdn out* **9/2**3
/10- 2 2¼ **Breaking Bits (IRE)**26 764 6-11-7 112 TomO'Brien 114
(Jamie Snowden) *led: rdn whn nt fluent 2 out: hdd bef last: kpt on same pce* **6/1**
P/0- 3 6 **West Brit (IRE)**5 812 5-11-12 117 RichardJohnson 113
(Charlie Longsdon) *hld up in last pair but wl in tch: tk clsr order after 5th: rdn to chse ldr bef 2 out: nt pce to chal: no ex appr last* **11/4**1
/14- 4 16 **Four Nations (USA)**37 671 5-11-4 114 (b) TrevorWhelan(5) 96
(George Baker) *hld up in last but wl in tch: rdn after 5th: nvr gng pce to get involved: wknd after 2 out* **8/1**
363- 5 14 **Zama Zama**25 781 6-11-3 111 AdamWedge(3) 80
(Evan Williams) *trckd ldrs: rdn after 5th: wknd sn after 3 out* **4/1**2

603- **6** *9* **Captain Sharpe**[3] 833 5-10-5 **101**............................(bt) RobertWilliams(5) 62
(Bernard Llewellyn) *trckd ldrs tl dropped to last pair after 4th but stl wl in tch: rdn bef next: wknd sn after 3 out* **4/1**[2]
3m 52.1s (-13.60) **Going Correction** -0.675s/f (Firm) **6** Ran SP% **110.2**
Speed ratings (Par 105): **105,103,101,93,87 82**
toteswingers 1&2 £9.30, 1&3 £2.00, 2&3 £13.00 CSF £28.82 TOTE £3.70: £2.10, £3.70; EX 28.40 Trifecta £197.60 Pool: £1085.43 - 4.11 winning units..
Owner B P Jones **Bred** Llety Farms **Trained** Oakford, Devon

FOCUS

A competitive race for the grade, and a fast gallop throughout meant a quicker time than the opening novice hurdle. The winner is rated to her very best with the third pretty much to his mark.

996 PAIGNTON ZOO H'CAP CHASE (16 fncs) 2m 5f 110y
3:15 (3:15) (Class 3) (0-125,125) 4-Y-O+ **£7,596** (£2,244; £1,122; £561; £280)

Form RPR
/00- **1** **Kylenoe Fairy (IRE)**[20] 831 9-10-8 **107**............................(t) TomO'Brien 115+
(Paul Henderson) *hld up in last but in tch: struggling 4 out: hdwy after 3 out to chse ldrs next: led last: styd on wl: rdn out* **11/1**
/31- **2** *1 1/4* **Tiermore (IRE)**[48] 523 9-10-6 **105**.............................. JamieMoore 112
(Peter Bowen) *trckd ldrs: squeezed up 1st: led after 9th tl next: kpt pressing ldrs: rdn after 3 out: ev ch 2 out whn pckd: stl ev ch fr last: no ex fnl 50yds* **2/1**[1]
3 *2 1/2* **Easily Pleased (IRE)**[49] 7-10-9 **108**.............................. HaddenFrost 112
(Martin Hill) *hld up but wl in tch: hdwy after 10th: led 12th: rdn after 3 out: hdd but ev ch last: no ex* **14/1**
45P- **4** *10* **Temple Lord (FR)**[19] 840 7-11-5 **118**..............................(bt) APMcCoy 114
(Jonjo O'Neill) *hld up but wl in tch: tk clsr order 12th: rdn to chse ldng pair after 3 out: lost 3rd next: fdd* **7/1**
331- **5** *10* **Adrenalin Flight (IRE)**[12] 871 7-10-9 **108**.................. AndrewThornton 94
(Seamus Mullins) *j. sltly rt: led tl 12th: sn rdn: wknd after 3 out* **5/1**[3]
/45- **6** *6* **Manger Hanagment (IRE)**[43] 596 8-11-4 **122**.......... GavinSheehan(5) 102
(Barry Brennan) *trckd ldrs: rdn after 12th: wknd 3 out: mstke last* **25/1**
432/ **7** *4* **Polisky (FR)**[99] 5196 6-11-9 **122**..............................(t) NickScholfield 99
(Paul Nicholls) *trckd ldrs: pushed along briefly whn nt fluent 3rd: rdn after 4 out: sn btn* **3/1**[2]
5/0- **8** *6* **Rob Conti (FR)**[44] 587 8-11-12 **125**.............................. RichardJohnson 96
(Philip Hobbs) *trckd ldrs: rdn after 11th: sn hld: wknd 3 out: eased between last 2* **12/1**
5m 8.2s (-13.20) **Going Correction** -0.60s/f (Firm) **8** Ran SP% **114.0**
Speed ratings (Par 107): **100,99,98,95,91 89,87,85**
toteswingers 1&2 £7.40, 1&3 £23.70, 2&3 £7.40 CSF £34.72 CT £317.32 TOTE £14.20: £2.50, £1.10, £3.20; EX 47.10 Trifecta £296.60 Pool: £895.85 - 2.26 winning units..
Owner The Rockbourne Partnership **Bred** Eamon Hanrahan **Trained** Whitsbury, Hants

FOCUS

A competitive chase, featuring some in-form runners. The gallop was strong. A chasing best from the winner, who can go in again, with the placed horses in line with previous form.

997 SIS LIVE NOVICES' H'CAP HURDLE (10 hdls) 2m 6f
3:45 (3:45) (Class 5) (0-100,100) 4-Y-O+ **£2,463** (£718; £359)

Form RPR
000/ **1** **Bold Raider (IRE)**[123] 4762 6-11-2 **90**.............................. APMcCoy 98+
(Jonjo O'Neill) *mid-div: hdwy after 7th: rdn into 3rd after 3 out: led next: kpt on wl: rdn out* **4/1**[3]
052- **2** *1 1/2* **Theoystercatcher (IRE)**[20] 829 7-10-13 **87**............... RichardJohnson 94+
(Tim Vaughan) *hld up towards rr: sme hdwy whn rdn 7th: styd on after 3 out: wnt 2nd between last 2: kpt on but a being hld* **7/2**[2]
/66- **3** *11* **Kilderry Dean (IRE)**[19] 844 6-11-2 **90**.............................. HaddenFrost 87
(James Frost) *hld up towards rr: pushed along and stdy prog after 3 out: styd on: wnt 3rd run-in but no ch w ldng pair* **20/1**
65/- **4** *1 1/4* **Buddy Love**[181] 3673 6-10-12 **86**..........................(t) SamTwiston-Davies 82
(Nigel Twiston-Davies) *mid-div: hdwy 7th: rdn to ld v briefly bef 5 out: lost 2nd sn after next: no ex whn lost 3rd run-in* **5/2**[1]
P0P/ **5** *1/2* **William Percival (IRE)**[43] 7-10-0 **74**.............................. TommyPhelan 71
(Mark Gillard) *trckd ldr: led bef 7th: rdn and hdd bef 2 out: kpt on same pce* **16/1**
/S4- **6** *26* **Plug In Baby**[12] 876 5-10-5 **79**..(p) NickScholfield 51
(Nick Mitchell) *mid-div tl lost pl u.p after 6th: sn bhd: t.o* **8/1**
030- **7** *1 3/4* **Van Diemens Land (USA)**[15] 852 6-11-12 **100**......(bt) TomScudamore 83+
(Charlie Mann) *mid-div: hdwy after 7th: rdn in cl 4th after 3 out: wkng whn hit 2 out: eased: t.o* **10/1**
4/0- **8** *2* **Kilshanna (IRE)**[27] 759 8-9-9 **74** oh12....................(p) RobertWilliams(5) 43
(Bernard Llewellyn) *trckd ldrs: rdn after 7th: wknd after 3 out: t.o* **50/1**
6/P- **9** *12* **Hollow Heartbeat (IRE)**[72] 122 6-10-0 **74**...................(b) AlainCawley 32
(Brendan Powell) *j.lft: trckd ldrs: rdn after 7th: wknd bef 2 out: t.o* **25/1**
/F6- **P** **Glenwood Present (IRE)**[39] 640 6-10-0 **74** oh7............(t) JamieMoore
(Bob Buckler) *nt fluent: towards rr: drvn after 6th: nvr any imp: wknd after 3 out: p.u bef 2 out* **14/1**
0/0- **P** **Newmans Boy**[22] 809 6-9-12 **74** ow1..................... MichaelByrne(3)
(Neil Mulholland) *led: hit 6th: hdd bef next: sn wknd: p.u bef 3 out* **50/1**
5m 8.4s (-11.80) **Going Correction** -0.675s/f (Firm) **11** Ran SP% **116.1**
Speed ratings (Par 103): **94,93,89,89,88 79,78,78,73,**
toteswingers 1&2 £2.30, 1&3 £15.30, 2&3 £7.90 CSF £17.86 CT £245.30 TOTE £5.90: £1.90, £1.50, £3.70; EX 19.50 Trifecta £293.90 Pool: £1003.29 - 2.56 winning units..
Owner John P McManus **Bred** Aidan Madden **Trained** Cheltenham, Gloucs

FOCUS

There was a steadier gallop in this low-grade novice handicap. A big step up from the winner on the better ground with the runner-up to recent C&D form.

998 NEWTONABBOTRACING.COM H'CAP HURDLE (12 hdls) 3m 3f
4:15 (4:15) (Class 4) (0-120,120) 4-Y-O+ **£3,508** (£1,030; £515; £257)

Form RPR
16P/ **1** **American Legend (IRE)**[158] 4080 5-10-13 **107**.................(v[1]) APMcCoy 115+
(Jonjo O'Neill) *trckd ldrs: wnt 2nd bef 9th: rdn after 3 out: chal 2 out: led jst bef last where awkward: drvn out* **2/1**[1]
/36- **2** *3/4* **Qulinton (FR)**[19] 845 9-11-11 **119**...............................(p) ConorO'Farrell 125
(David Pipe) *j.lft at times: trckd ldr: led 4th: rdn after 3 out: hdd bef last: kpt on run-in* **9/2**[3]
116- **3** *22* **Bold Perk (IRE)**[24] 787 11-11-0 **108**.............................. HaddenFrost 102
(Martin Hill) *racd keenly: hld up: hdwy into 3rd at the 9th: rdn after 3 out: hld bef next: fdd between last 2* **6/1**
612- **4** *21* **Ahead Ahead (IRE)**[35] 690 8-10-13 **107**.............................. PaulMoloney 75
(David Rees) *in tch: rdn after 9th: wknd after 3 out: t.o* **5/2**[2]
/26- **5** *7* **Qualviro (FR)**[38] 659 9-11-12 **120**.............................(b) RichardJohnson 81
(Tim Vaughan) *led tl after 4th: chsd ldr: rdn after 8th: lost 2nd next: wknd after 3 out: t.o* **13/2**

/1U- **6** *7* **Noble Chic**[40] 636 8-10-11 **105**.............................. BrendanPowell 60
(James Frost) *trckd ldrs: losing pl whn nt fluent 3 out: sn wknd: t.o* **16/1**
RP/- **P** **Mobaasher (USA)**[70] 10-10-7 **108**.............................. MikeyEnnis(7)
(Patricia Shaw) *hld up: pushed along fr after 4th: losing tch whn wnt rt 6th: tailing off whn p.u after 8th* **40/1**
6m 24.7s (-16.30) **Going Correction** -0.675s/f (Firm) **7** Ran SP% **116.0**
Speed ratings (Par 105): **97,96,90,84,81 79,**
toteswingers 1&2 £2.70, 1&3 £3.40, 2&3 £3.60 CSF £12.09 CT £45.76 TOTE £3.00: £1.90, £2.10; EX 12.10 Trifecta £67.90 Pool: £2513.48 - 27.76 winning units..
Owner John P McManus **Bred** David Fenton **Trained** Cheltenham, Gloucs

FOCUS

A true run race over this marathon distance, but only two were seriously involved in the home straight. A step up from the winner with the runner-up back to last summer's form.

999 BET TOTEPOOL TEXT TOTE TO 89660 H'CAP CHASE (13 fncs) 2m 110y
4:45 (4:45) (Class 4) (0-120,120) 4-Y-O+ **£4,288** (£1,259; £629; £314)

Form RPR
/32- **1** **Piment D'Estruval (FR)**[44] 578 10-11-7 **115**............... RichardJohnson 125
(Tim Vaughan) *trckd ldrs: wnt 2nd at the 6th: rdn after 3 out: nrly five l down last: str run to ld towards fin: rdn out* **7/1**
6/4- **2** *1* **De Faoithesdream (IRE)**[40] 634 7-11-9 **117**.................. PaulMoloney 129+
(Evan Williams) *led: drew clr after 3 out: rdn after 2 out: nrly 5 l clr whn nt fluent last: jockey briefly stopped riding whn lost iron run-in: hdd towards fin* **5/2**[2]
441- **3** *27* **Mibleu (FR)**[15] 853 13-11-4 **112**.............................. BrendanPowell 102
(Colin Tizzard) *hld up: tk clsr order 5th: cl 3rd after 4 out: awkward next: sn rdn: wknd next* **9/1**
012- **4** *22* **Surf And Turf (IRE)**[25] 781 7-11-7 **115**.............................. APMcCoy 80
(Jonjo O'Neill) *trckd ldr tl 6th: rdn after 9th: wknd after 4 out: stmbld 2 out: t.o* **7/5**[1]
/P4- **5** *8* **Giant O Murchu (IRE)**[13] 859 9-11-0 **108**.............................. DavidBass 66
(Lawney Hill) *hld up but in tch: outpcd after 9th: sn no ch: t.o* **11/2**[3]
0/0- **6** *1/2* **Delphi Mountain (IRE)**[26] 764 8-11-7 **118**................(t) MichealNolan(3) 75
(Richard Woollacott) *trckd ldrs tl after 6th: outpcd 9th: sn no ch: t.o* **25/1**
3m 53.6s (-12.90) **Going Correction** -0.60s/f (Firm) **6** Ran SP% **112.0**
Speed ratings (Par 105): **106,105,92,82,78 78**
toteswingers 1&2 £2.20, 1&3 £3.80, 2&3 £4.70 CSF £25.30 TOTE £5.50: £2.90, £1.50; EX 25.80 Trifecta £147.60 Pool: £2195.57 - 11.15 winning units..
Owner Mrs M J Worgan **Bred** Mme Bernard Le Gentil **Trained** Aberthin, Vale of Glamorgan

FOCUS

A fast-run race with the winner rated to his best.

1000 SIS INTERNATIONAL NOVICES' H'CAP HURDLE (8 hdls) 2m 1f
5:15 (5:15) (Class 5) (0-95,88) 4-Y-O+ **£2,463** (£718; £359)

Form RPR
0/4- **1** **Sarenice (FR)**[67] 177 7-11-9 **85**.............................. HaddenFrost 91+
(James Frost) *in tch: cl up whn nt clr run on bnd after 3 out: led 2 out: r.o wl: rdn out* **11/2**[3]
/14- **2** *2 1/4* **Hawk Gold (IRE)**[47] 540 9-10-8 **77**........................(b) ConorShoemark(7) 80
(Michelle Bryant) *hld up: hdwy after 3 out: rdn to chse wnr next: styd on but a being hld fr last* **11/2**[3]
/P4- **3** *2 1/2* **Illegale (IRE)**[56] 407 7-10-12 **74**..............................(t) LeightonAspell 75
(Phillip Dando) *trckd ldrs: rdn after 3 out: styd on same pce fr next* **6/1**
421- **4** *nk* **Bay Central (IRE)**[6] 931 9-11-12 **88**..............................(e) PaulMoloney 89
(Evan Williams) *taken down early: led: rdn and hdd after 3 out: kpt on same pce fr next* **13/8**[1]
304- **5** *3 3/4* **Maggie Aron**[6] 932 7-11-5 **84**..............................(t) MichaelByrne(3) 82
(James Hughes) *in tch: hdwy after 5th: rdn to ld v briefly bef 2 out: kpt on same pce* **7/2**[2]
/66- **6** *14* **Si Bien (FR)**[22] 810 8-11-3 **84**..............................(t) CharlieWallis(5) 69
(Nick Ayliffe) *hld up: tk clsr order after 4th: rdn after 3 out: wknd bef next* **25/1**
400- **7** *1 1/4* **Sid**[22] 808 5-11-9 **85**..(b[1]) TomCannon 68
(Mark Gillard) *trckd ldrs: reminders after 3rd: drvn to ld after 3 out: hdd bef next: wknd between last 2* **50/1**
460- **8** *30* **Sassy Wren**[26] 765 8-11-5 **81**.............................. JamesDavies 37
(Chris Down) *trckd ldrs tl wknd after 3 out: t.o* **20/1**
3m 57.2s (-8.50) **Going Correction** -0.675s/f (Firm) **8** Ran SP% **115.9**
Speed ratings (Par 103): **93,91,90,90,88 82,81,67**
toteswingers 1&2 £4.30, 1&3 £4.70, 2&3 £2.60 CSF £35.02 CT £188.31 TOTE £5.60: £2.00, £1.50, £2.00; EX 35.70 Trifecta £200.60 Pool: £2564.60 - 9.58 winning units..
Owner Mrs J F Bury **Bred** G Roy & Mme G Roy **Trained** Scorriton, Devon

FOCUS

A modest novice handicap hurdle which was just run at a medium gallop. It is rated around the second and third.

T/Plt: £166.40 to a £1 stake. Pool: £79,179.38 - 347.16 winning tickets T/Qpdt: £87.20 to a £1 stake. Pool: £7519.57 - 63.80 winning tickets TM

299 KILLARNEY (L-H)
Monday, July 15

OFFICIAL GOING: Flat course - good to firm; jumps courses - good to firm (good in places)

1001a RACING POST H'CAP CHASE (12 fncs) 2m 1f
7:40 (7:40) 4-Y-O+ **£12,418** (£3,630; £1,719; £573)

RPR
1 **Prince Of Fire (GER)**[10] 886 8-9-10 **117** oh1.............................. DJCasey 137+
(C F Swan, Ire) *hld up in tch: tk clsr order fr 8th where nt fluent: hdwy bef 3 out: prog between horses to get on terms last and qcknd wl run-in: comf* **6/1**[2]
2 *8 1/2* **Absolutlyfantastic**[65] 229 6-9-13 **120**.............................. AELynch 130
(Henry De Bromhead, Ire) *settled bhd ldrs in 3rd: slt mstke 4th: clsd travelling wl on inner to get on terms 2 out: sn rdn and hdd fr last: sn no ch w wnr: kpt on same pce* **11/10**[1]
3 *1 1/2* **Go All The Way (IRE)**[269] 1914 8-11-2 **140**................ KeithDonoghue(3) 147
(J T R Dreaper, Ire) *disp early: settled bhd ldr fr 2nd: led after 5th: j. fining line w a circ to r and sn lost pl: led again 8th: pressed 3 out where nt fluent: sn rdn and hdd bef last: no ex* **6/1**[2]
4 *1/2* **Mahrajaan (USA)**[10] 886 10-9-9 **119**.............................. MarkEnright(3) 127
(C Byrnes, Ire) *hld up in tch: tk clsr order fr 4 out: hdwy to chal 2 out: sn no ex u.p in 4th: kpt on same pce run-in* **7/1**

5 24 **Tranquil Sea (IRE)**[82] 5517 11-11-12 **147**......................(t) BarryGeraghty 132
(E J O'Grady, Ire) *chsd ldrs: niggled along in 6th after 5th: no imp on ldrs after next: pushed along in mod 6th into st: kpt on one pce in 5th fr 3 out* **11/1**

6 34 **Mister Matt (IRE)**[48] 520 10-10-5 **126**.................... AndrewGlassonbury 81
(Bob Buckler) *disp early: led 2nd tl hdd after 5th: regained advantage after next tl hdd again 8th: sn rdn in 4th and no ex: wknd: t.o* **13/2**[3]

P **Banna Man (IRE)**[10] 888 13-9-10 **117** oh1............................ PhillipEnright
(T J O'Mara, Ire) *hld up towards rr: no imp and trailing whn bad mstke 3 out: p.u bef next* **20/1**

4m 2.1s (242.10) **7** Ran SP% **115.1**
CSF £14.01 CT £41.66 TOTE £6.40: £2.10, £1.60; DF 15.20.
Owner John P McManus **Bred** Gestut Elite **Trained** Cloughjordan, Co Tipperary

FOCUS
The winner had slipped to a great mark and the fourth has been rated to the pick of his form from 2012.

1002 - 1006a (Foreign Racing) - See Raceform Interactive

927 UTTOXETER (L-H)

Wednesday, July 17

OFFICIAL GOING: Good to firm (good in places;7.6)
Hurdles moved out a further 4-5 yds from inside and divided bends to provide fresh ground.
Wind: light 1/2 behind Weather: fine and sunny, very warm

1007 3663 CONDITIONAL JOCKEYS' MAIDEN HURDLE (10 hdls) 2m 4f 110y
2:20 (2:20) (Class 5) 4-Y-0+ **£2,209** (£648; £324; £162)

Form RPR

F33/ **1** **Benefit Of Youth (IRE)**[203] 3205 6-10-11 0.................. MichaelByrne(3) 117+
(Tim Vaughan) *chsd ldr: led bef 3 out: drvn clr 2 out: 11 l ahd whn mstke last: comf* **6/5**[1]

3/2- **2** 11 **Je T'Aime (IRE)**[36] 717 4-9-10 0.................................. JamesCowley(8) 93
(Donald McCain) *chsd ldrs: 2nd appr 2 out: kpt on same pce: no chnce w wnr* **3/1**[2]

00/ **3** 14 **Piper Hill (IRE)**[356] 1089 5-11-0 0....................................... JackQuinlan 93
(Tony Coyle) *hld up towards rr: hmpd 1st: hdwy to chse ldrs 6th: modest 3rd appr 2 out: one pce* **22/1**

/50- **4** 9 **Solo Jugadores**[41] 648 5-11-0 0.................................... BrendanPowell 82
(Richard Guest) *in rr: drvn and hdwy 6th: modest 4th 2 out: one pce* **12/1**

140- **5** 9 **Are They Your Own (IRE)**[29] 760 5-10-11 0..................... NickSlatter(3) 74
(Fergal O'Brien) *led: hdd bef 3 out: wknd 2 out* **20/1**

506/ **6** 3 ½ **Genes Quest**[152] 4232 6-10-7 0.. ThomasGarner 64
(Michael Appleby) *in rr: bhd fr 7th: poor 6th whn j.lft and blnd 2 out* **80/1**

034/ **7** 28 **Fighter Jet**[105] 5125 5-11-0 0.. KillianMoore 46
(Alan King) *hmpd 1st: nt fluent in rr: drvn 4th: reminders next: sme hdwy 7th: sn lost pl and bhd* **4/1**[3]

/30- **8** ½ **Imperial Legacy**[14] 874 5-10-4 0...............................(tp) JackSavage(10) 46
(Jo Davis) *j.lft 1st: chsd ldrs: lost pl 5th: bhd fr 7th: t.o* **66/1**

0/ **P** **Alfinski**[423] 8-11-0 0.. JakeGreenall
(Clive Mulhall) *chsd ldrs: lost ;pl 6th: bhd whn nt fluent next: sn t.o: p.u bef 3 out* **200/1**

6- **P** **The Kings Assassin (IRE)**[14] 874 5-10-11 0.............. TomCannon(3)
(Chris Gordon) *chsd ldrs: rdn and lost pl 7th: bhd whn eased next: t.o whn p.u bef 2 out* **28/1**

4m 54.6s (-4.40) **Going Correction** -0.125s/f (Good)
WFA 4 from 5yo+ 16lb **10** Ran SP% **113.9**
Speed ratings (Par 103): **103,98,93,90,86 85,74,74, ,**
Tote Swingers: 1&2 £1.10, 2&3 £8.40 CSF £4.55 TOTE £2.40: £1.10, £1.60, £5.10; EX 5.40 Trifecta £49.20 Pool: £817.35 - 12.43 winning unit..
Owner Mrs M J Worgan **Bred** Michael Byrnes **Trained** Aberthin, Vale of Glamorgan

FOCUS
The going was good to firm, good in places. The hurdles were moved out 4m from the inside to fresher ground, with the bends also moved out. A modest maiden hurdle, confined to conditional jockeys, run at a fair pace. It paid to race prominently. The easy winner is rated back to his best.

1008 3663 INSPIRED BY YOU NOVICES' HURDLE (9 hdls) 2m
2:50 (2:50) (Class 4) 4-Y-0+ **£3,249** (£954; £477; £238)

Form RPR

1 **Purple 'n Gold (IRE)**[11] 4-10-10 0..............................(p) TomScudamore 108+
(David Pipe) *trckd ldrs: led appr last: drvn 2 l clr run-in: wknd last 60yds: jst hld on* **10/3**[2]

6/1- **2** shd **Bittersweetheart**[28] 761 6-10-12 0.................. SamTwiston-Davies 109
(David Bridgwater) *chsd ldrs: 3rd whn swtchd rt appr last: styd on wl clsng stages: jst hld* **6/1**

311- **3** hd **Thunder Sheik (IRE)**[17] 848 5-11-5 114......................(t) PaddyBrennan 115
(Fergal O'Brien) *w ldr: led bef 3 out: hdd appr last: rallied clsng stages: jst hld* **1/1**[1]

4 12 **The Lodge Road (IRE)**[12] 5-10-12 0............................. WilsonRenwick 96
(Martin Todhunter) *chsd ldrs: drvn 3 out: one pce* **28/1**

5- **5** 22 **Gavi**[21] 843 7-10-12 0... AndrewThornton 74
(Karen George) *hld up in rr: nt fluent and j.rt 5th: outpcd appr 3 out: sn wknd: dsitant 5th whn mstke last* **125/1**

5/2- **6** 1 ¼ **Symphonick (FR)**[24] 800 7-10-12 114................................. BrianHughes 73
(Tim Fitzgerald) *led tl bef 3 out: sn lost pl and bhd* **5/1**[3]

060/ **7** 34 **Hardwick Bay**[171] 3902 7-10-5 0....................................(t) RyanMahon 32
(Michael Appleby) *in rr: reminder after 5th: sn bhd: t.o* **100/1**

3m 52.8s (0.80) **Going Correction** -0.125s/f (Good)
WFA 4 from 5yo+ 15lb **7** Ran SP% **109.3**
Speed ratings (Par 105): **93,92,92,86,75 75,58**
Tote Swingers: 1&2 £1.90, 1&3 £1.20, 2&3 £1.70 CSF £20.54 TOTE £4.50: £2.20, £1.60; EX 13.10 Trifecta £37.00 Pool: £1,274.70 - 25.78 winning unit..
Owner Mrs Lynne Webb **Bred** Stonethorn Stud Farms Ltd **Trained** Nicholashayne, Devon

FOCUS
Not a bad novices' hurdle run at a steady pace. The front three fought out a thrilling finish. The winner is a potential 120+ horse on Flat form.

1009 3663 ONE STOP SHOP (S) HURDLE (9 hdls) 2m
3:20 (3:20) (Class 5) 4-7-Y-0 **£1,949** (£572; £286; £143)

Form RPR

543/ **1** **Bollin Judith**[169] 3925 7-10-10 107.......................................(t) APMcCoy 115+
(Jim Best) *hld up: hdwy to chse ldrs whn nt fluent 6th: led next: 5 l ahd last: drvn out* **6/4**[1]

222- **2** 5 **Descaro (USA)**[8] 929 7-11-1 120...............................(v) CiaranMckee(7) 120
(John O'Shea) *led: clr 4th: hdd narrowly 3 out: kpt on run-in* **3/1**[2]

314/ **3** 7 **Waltz Darling (IRE)**[26] 27 5-11-3 113.............................. BrianHughes 111
(Keith Reveley) *t.k.h: trckd ldrs: 3rd and one pce between last 2* **8/1**

404- **4** 4 **Latest Trend (IRE)**[14] 870 7-11-3 112.....................(v[1]) RichardJohnson 105
(Tim Vaughan) *chsd ldrs: drvn 5th: wknd between last 2* **7/2**[3]

104/ **5** 42 **Fine Kingdom**[22] 4662 4-11-1 119..............................(p) TomScudamore 65
(Brian Ellison) *chsd ldrs: nt fluent 4th: sn lost plac e: reminders next: sn bhd: t.o 2 out* **11/1**

P **Port Of The Oak (IRE)**[40] 662 5-10-12 0........................ PaddyBrennan
(Philip M Byrne, Ire) *chsd ldrs 4th: lost pl and nt fluent 6th: sn bhd: t.o whn p.u bef next* **28/1**

3m 47.9s (-4.10) **Going Correction** -0.125s/f (Good)
WFA 4 from 5yo+ 15lb **6** Ran SP% **110.1**
Speed ratings: **105,102,99,97,76**
Tote Swingers: 1&2 £1.90, 1&3 £1.50, 2&3 £3.10 CSF £6.12 TOTE £2.40: £2.00, £1.50; EX 5.50 Trifecta £24.10 Pool: £1,091.58 - 33.83 winning unit..There was no bid for the winner
Owner Jack Callaghan **Bred** Sir Neil & Exors Of Late Lady Westbrook **Trained** Lewes, E Sussex

FOCUS
This was a fair contest for the grade, run at an honest pace. The winner is rated in line with her previous hurdle best but may be capable of a bit better.

1010 BETVICTOR 8 PLACES ON THE OPEN NOVICES' H'CAP CHASE (18 fncs) 3m
3:50 (3:50) (Class 5) (0-100,100) 4-Y-0+ **£2,599** (£763; £381; £190)

Form RPR

/P0- **1** **Chandlers Cross (IRE)**[29] 759 11-10-5 79...................(tp) PaulMoloney 92
(David Rees) *chsd ldrs 3rd: 2nd 12th: upsides 2 out: sn led: drvn out* **20/1**

0/4- **2** 5 **Always Bold (IRE)**[74] 120 8-11-10 98..................................(v) IanPopham 106
(Martin Keighley) *chsd ldrs: drvn 12th: j.rt 14th: modest 3rd 3 out: tk 2nd run-in* **9/2**[3]

/42- **3** 2 ¼ **Pure Anticipation (IRE)**[8] 930 8-11-4 92.....................(v) AidanColeman 98
(Tim Vaughan) *led: drvn clr 3 out: jnd next: hdd between last 2: one pce* **9/4**[1]

30B- **4** 28 **Basford Ben**[14] 872 5-11-11 99...(p) SeanQuinlan 80
(Jennie Candlish) *in rr: drvn 11th: lost pl 14th: sn bhd: tk distant 4th run-in* **22/1**

P/P- **5** nk **Fitobust (IRE)**[38] 7-10-7 81..(p) DavidBass 62
(Lawney Hill) *chsd ldrs: outpcd and modest 4th appr 3 out: sn wknd* **8/1**

3/ **P** **Euro Farmer (IRE)**[38] 13-10-11 92................................. MikeyHamill(7)
(Barry Brennan) *chsd ldrs: drvn 6th: lost pl 9th: sn bhd: t.o whn p.u after next* **12/1**

/P4- **P** **Days Of Pleasure (IRE)**[36] 712 8-10-11 85...................(v) TomCannon
(Chris Gordon) *chsd ldrs: drvn 4th: lost pl 10th: sn bhd: t.o 13th: p.u bef 2 out* **11/2**

FP4- **P** **Tulla Emerald (IRE)**[24] 805 8-9-12 79.............................. KevinJones(7)
(Natalie Lloyd-Beavis) *chsd ldrs 10th: bmpd 14th: wknd 4 out: sn bhd: t.o whn p.u bef 2 out* **80/1**

0/0- **P** **Atriptomilan (IRE)**[69] 179 5-11-12 100....................(tp) RichieMcLernon
(Jonjo O'Neill) *in rr: j. slowly and rt-handed 8th: bhd and reminders 11th: t.o 14th: p.u bef 2 out* **4/1**[2]

6m 8.2s (-6.90) **Going Correction** -0.125s/f (Good) **9** Ran SP% **113.5**
Speed ratings (Par 103): **106,104,103,94,94 , , ,**
Tote Swingers: 1&2 £27.50, 1&3 £7.10, 2&3 £2.70 CSF £106.08 CT £286.67 TOTE £26.70: £5.20, £1.70, £1.20; EX 146.30 Trifecta £830.30 Part won. Pool: £1,107.17 - 0.86 winning units..

Owner Miss J Price **Bred** Rathbarry Stud **Trained** Clarbeston, Pembrokes

FOCUS
Not a strong contest and run at a steady early pace. Once again the prominent runners dominated. The winner was back to the level of last summer's best, with the second to his mark.

1011 OPEN CHAMPIONSHIP 8 PLACES AT BETVICTOR H'CAP HURDLE (12 hdls) 3m
4:20 (4:20) (Class 4) (0-115,115) 4-Y-0+ **£3,249** (£954; £477; £238)

Form RPR

0/1- **1** **Salpierre (IRE)**[56] 428 8-11-7 110......................................(tp) APMcCoy 120
(Jonjo O'Neill) *chsd ldrs: 2nd 3rd: shkn up 6th: reminders after next: sn drvn: clsd appr 3 out: led appr 2 out: drvn clr run-in: eased nr fin* **11/4**[2]

P31- **2** 8 **High Ville (IRE)**[8] 933 7-11-11 114 7ex.......................... ConorO'Farrell 119
(David Pipe) *t.k.h: led: clr 4th: drkiven appr 3 out: hdd appr 2 out: one pce between last 2: eased nr fin* **4/5**[1]

1/4- **3** 50 **Sohappyharry**[36] 718 7-11-5 115...................................... ConorRing(7) 73
(Jane Mathias) *chsd ldng pair: pushed along 6th: reminders 7th: sn lost pl and bhd: t.o 9th: tk distant 3rd run-in* **5/1**[3]

/40- **4** 12 **Points Of View**[40] 659 8-11-7 115................................(t) EdCookson(5) 62
(Kim Bailey) *hld up in last: wnt modest 3rd 7th: drvn next: wknd appr 3 out: lost distant 3rd run-in and eased* **12/1**

5m 47.2s (-2.80) **Going Correction** -0.125s/f (Good) **4** Ran SP% **106.6**
Speed ratings (Par 105): **99,96,79,75**
CSF £5.47 TOTE £2.80; EX 5.50 Trifecta £8.60 Pool: £1,485.31 - 129.00 winning unit..
Owner F Gillespie **Bred** Mrs Mary Furlong **Trained** Cheltenham, Gloucs

FOCUS
Only four runners but the pace was honest. The winner was a mid 120s horse at his peak, with the second a bit below his recent C&D level.

1012 BETVICTOR OPEN CHAMPIONSHIP 8 PLACES EXCLUSIVE H'CAP CHASE (15 fncs) 2m 4f
4:50 (4:50) (Class 4) (0-115,115) 4-Y-0 **£3,798** (£1,122; £561; £280; £140)

Form RPR

124- **1** **Forever My Friend (IRE)**[14] 871 6-10-13 102.................. JamieMoore 113+
(Peter Bowen) *trckd ldrs 7th: led 4 out: 3 l ahd last: drvn rt out* **11/4**[2]

153/ **2** 1 ¼ **The Mad Robertson (IRE)**[80] 5 6-11-7 110........................ APMcCoy 119
(Jonjo O'Neill) *led to 1st: j.rt and led 3rd: hdd appr next: hit 9th: drvn and outpcd 4 out: 2nd between last 2: kpt on same pce last 50yds* **6/4**[1]

620- **3** 4 ½ **Lukeys Luck**[15] 859 7-10-12 108.......................................(p) ConorRing(7) 114
(Jennie Candlish) *in rr: chsng ldrs whn stmbld on landing 8th: drvn 10th: 3rd and outpcd 3 out: kpt on one pce* **7/2**[3]

3/3- **4** 10 **Henry San (IRE)**[54] 457 6-11-12 115.......................... WayneHutchinson 110
(Alan King) *chsd ldrs 7th: 2nd 3 out: wknd between last 2* **8/1**

F25- **5** 8 **Sporting Boy (IRE)**[27] 781 5-11-12 115............................. TomCannon 104
(Michael Blake) *w ldrs: led appr 4th: hdd 4 out: wknd 2 out* **14/1**

/56- **6** 29 **Fintan**[39] 674 10-11-6 112...(t) JamesBest(3) 74
(Rob Summers) *t.k.h: led 1st: j.lft and hdd 3rd: lost pl appr 4 out: sn bhd: t.o* **22/1**

5m 0.2s (-5.30) **Going Correction** -0.125s/f (Good) **6** Ran SP% **111.0**
Speed ratings (Par 105): **105,104,102,98,95 83**
Tote Swingers: 1&2 £1.20, 1&3 £2.60, 2&3 £1.90 CSF £7.50 TOTE £3.90: £1.60, £2.00; EX 9.20 Trifecta £24.30 Pool: £1,993.52 - 61.45 winning unit..

The Form Book Jumps, Raceform Ltd, Compton, RG20 6NL.

Owner Mickey Bowen **Bred** Eamon Fitzgerald **Trained** Little Newcastle, Pembrokes
FOCUS
Not much pace on for this handicap. The winner is rated to his best.

1013 BETVICTOR 8 PLACES OPEN CHAMPIONSHIP STANDARD OPEN NATIONAL HUNT FLAT RACE 2m
5:20 (5:20) (Class 6) 4-6-Y-O **£1,559** (£457; £228; £114)

Form RPR
/11- **1** **Man Of Steel (IRE)**[28] 768 4-11-10 0..........................(p) DonalDevereux 115+
(Peter Bowen) *trckd ldrs: t.k.h: led over 3f out: rdn over 1f out: styd on wl* **8/11**[1]
2 *3 ½* **Snapchat (IRE)** 6-11-2 0.. ConorO'Farrell 104
(Seamus Durack) *t.k.h: trckd ldrs: cl 2nd 3f out: rdn over 1f out: kpt on same pce* **3/1**[2]
00- **3** *17* **Too Trigger Happy**[36] 715 4-10-4 0.....................(p) WayneKavanagh(3) 80
(Dr Jeremy Naylor) *led: qcknd pce over 5f out: hdd over 3f out: one pce* **80/1**
5- **4** *2 ¼* **Port And Ward (IRE)**[39] 675 4-10-0 0.......................... CiaranMckee(7) 78
(John O'Shea) *in rr: drvn after 6f: outpcd and lost pl 6f out: kpt on to take poor 4th over 1f out* **10/1**
5 *12* **Little Bit Lively (IRE)** 4-10-11 0...................................... JackQuinlan(3) 74
(Sarah Humphrey) *hld up towards rr: drvn 4f out: sn lost pl* **7/1**[3]
6 *9* **Cute Court (IRE)**[45] 6-11-2 0... DPFahy 68
(Liam Corcoran) *trckd ldrs: upsides whn hung bdly lft over 3f out: sn wknd* **12/1**
0/0- **7** *10* **Nataraja**[26] 790 4-11-0 0.. BrianHughes 57
(Tony Coyle) *chsd ldrs: shkn up 8f out: outpcd 4f out: sn lost pl* **20/1**
00- **8** *21* **Wolmar**[26] 790 4-10-7 0..(p) WayneHutchinson 31
(John Mackie) *in rr: drvn after 6f: outpcd over 5f out: sn lost pl and bhd: t.o* **40/1**

3m 46.2s (-0.20) **Going Correction** -0.125s/f (Good) **8** Ran SP% **120.6**
Speed ratings: **95,93,84,83,77 73,68,57**
Tote Swingers: 1&2 £1.40, 1&3 £23.70, 2&3 £24.80 CSF £3.33 TOTE £1.50: £1.02, £1.50, £13.20; EX 4.20 Trifecta £92.50 Pool: £2,194.22 - 17.78 winning unit..
Owner Saith O Ni **Bred** Katie McCarthy **Trained** Little Newcastle, Pembrokes
FOCUS
An uncompetitive bumper, run at a steady pace. The winner is a fair prospect and is rated to his mark.
T/Plt: £37.80 to £1 stake. Pool: £61,411.71 - 1,185.22 winning tickets. T/Qpdt: £9.30 to £1 stake. Pool: £3,498.43 - 276.50 winning tickets. WG

942 WORCESTER (L-H)
Wednesday, July 17
OFFICIAL GOING: Good to firm (good in places; 7.1)
Whole course at innermost configuration.
Wind: Nil Weather: Sunny

1014 COMPARE BOOKMAKERS AT BOOKMAKERS.CO.UK NOVICES' H'CAP CHASE (12 fncs) 2m 110y
5:50 (5:50) (Class 5) (0-95,92) 4-Y-O+ **£2,599** (£763; £381; £190)

Form RPR
4/0- **1** **Cap Elorn (FR)**[7] 942 7-11-4 **89**..............................(b[1]) GavinSheehan(5) 101
(Lawney Hill) *chsd ldr: led 4th to 7th: led 9th: mstke last: drvn out* **6/1**[3]
/40- **2** *1 ¾* **Louis Ludwig (IRE)**[41] 650 8-10-7 **83**..........................(t) AlanJohns(10) 93
(Tim Vaughan) *hld up: hdwy 5th: chsd wnr 4 out: hung rt after 2 out: styd on u.p* **4/1**[2]
/51- **3** *12* **Echo Dancer**[24] 807 7-10-13 **86**..(b) JoshWall(7) 83
(Trevor Wall) *hld up: nt fluent 5th: sn pushed along and outpcd: r.o appr last: nvr nrr* **13/2**
03P- **4** *2* **Watch House (IRE)**[7] 942 8-11-5 **85**............................. BrendanPowell 82
(Michael Gates) *chsd ldrs: pushed along 5th: outpcd fr 9th* **9/1**
544- **5** *25* **Finch Flyer (IRE)**[3] 968 6-10-13 **84**..............................(b) KyleJames(5) 54
(Aytach Sadik) *chsd ldrs: pushed along 6th: rdn after 9th: mstke 4 out: sn wknd* **11/1**
2/P- **F** **Youm Jamil (USA)**[12] 183 6-10-1 **67**.............................. PaddyBrennan 68
(Tony Carroll) *hld up and bhd: hdwy appr 4 out: 4 l 3rd whn fell 2 out* **2/1**[1]
006- **F** **Crescent Beach (IRE)**[7] 942 6-11-12 **92**.......................(b[1]) HenryOliver
(Henry Oliver) *led to 4th: led again 7th: hdd 9th: wkng whn fell 4 out* **8/1**

3m 53.4s (-20.60) **Going Correction** -1.175s/f (Hard) **7** Ran SP% **110.4**
Speed ratings (Par 103): **101,100,94,93,81** ,
Tote Swingers: 1&2 £5.20, 1&3 £6.70, 2&3 £5.60 CSF £28.35 CT £150.82 TOTE £6.70: £2.50, £2.30; EX 40.70 Trifecta £219.90 Pool: £1,249.40 - 4.26 winning units..
Owner Andy Weller **Bred** Jean-Luc Guillerm **Trained** Aston Rowant, Oxon
FOCUS
Whole course at innermost configuration. A low-grade race but a fair time for the level. A small personal best from the winner.

1015 TONBRIE CONSTRUCTION H'CAP CHASE (18 fncs) 2m 7f
6:20 (6:20) (Class 4) (0-110,109) 4-Y-O+ **£4,223** (£1,240; £620; £310)

Form RPR
/P1- **1** **Whistling Senator (IRE)**[7] 942 6-11-5 **102** 7ex.................(v) APMcCoy 115+
(Jonjo O'Neill) *chsd ldrs: rdn appr 4 out: wnt 2nd 3 out: styd on u.p to ld fnl 100yds* **13/8**[1]
0/5- **2** *2 ½* **Brough Academy (IRE)**[57] 422 7-11-8 **105**................(p) AidanColeman 115
(Lawney Hill) *led: mstke 4 out: rdn flat: hdd and styd on same pce fnl 100yds* **14/1**
323- **3** *1 ½* **Polarbrook (IRE)**[24] 806 6-11-8 **105**............................. JasonMaguire 112
(Donald McCain) *hld up: hdwy appr 4 out: rdn after 2 out: styd on* **11/2**[3]
113- **4** *46* **Glen Countess (IRE)**[14] 871 6-11-8 **105**....................(t) BrendanPowell 66
(Brendan Powell) *chsd ldr: rdn and ev ch appr 4 out: wknd next* **8/1**
/52- **P** **Basoda**[36] 712 10-11-12 **109**..(tp) NickScholfield
(Kim Bailey) *hld up: mstke 6th: pushed along 11th: rdn and wknd 13th: p.u bef 3 out* **15/2**
6/5- **P** **Monty's Revenge (IRE)**[65] 265 8-10-11 **94**........................ IanPopham
(Martin Keighley) *prom: pushed along appr 10th: rdn and wknd 13th: p.u bef 3 out* **33/1**
F/1- **F** **Basil Fawlty (IRE)**[36] 713 8-11-12 **109**..........................(t) PaddyBrennan
(David Pipe) *hld up: hdwy 14th: cl 5th whn fell next* **10/3**[2]

5m 32.3s (-15.70) **Going Correction** -1.175s/f (Hard) **7** Ran SP% **109.0**
Speed ratings (Par 105): **80,79,78,62**, ,
Tote Swingers: 1&2 £8.20, 1&3 £2.60, 2&3 £14.70 CSF £20.32 CT £90.56 TOTE £2.20: £1.90, £4.30; EX 25.40 Trifecta £534.80 Pool: £1,029.36 - 1.44 winning units..
Owner John P McManus **Bred** Noel O'Brien **Trained** Cheltenham, Gloucs
FOCUS
A fair handicap and the form looks solid. The winner confirmed the merit of his recent win and ran to a similar level.

1016 GET LIVE FOOTBALL SCORES AT FOOTBALLSCORES.COM STANDARD NH FLAT RACE (CONDITIONALS/AMATEURS) 2m
6:50 (6:50) (Class 6) 4-6-Y-O **£1,559** (£457; £228; £114)

Form RPR
/51- **1** **G'Dai Sydney**[15] 862 5-11-8 0...................................(t) MichaelByrne(3) 102+
(Peter Bowen) *hld up: hdwy over 3f out: led over 1f out: rdn out* **13/8**[1]
2 *4* **Lucky Thirteen** 5-10-11 0.. DanielHiskett(7) 90
(Richard Phillips) *hld up: hdwy 1/2-way: rdn over 2f out: styd on* **10/1**
3 *2 ½* **Itmakessense**[38] 6-11-1 0.. KielanWoods(3) 89
(Charlie Longsdon) *chsd ldrs: led over 4f out: rdn and hdd over 1f out: no ex ins fnl f* **9/2**[3]
4 *1 ¾* **Oldeddietherebel (IRE)** 4-10-9 0........................... ConorShoemark(7) 84
(Barry T Murphy, Ire) *hld up: rdn over 3f out: hdwy and hung lft fr over 2f out: nt trble ldrs* **3/1**[2]
5 *3 ½* **Sava Bridge (IRE)**[54] 469 6-10-11 0.................................. MrGBranton(7) 82
(Paul Henderson) *chsd ldr tl over 4f out: wknd over 1f out* **20/1**
0- **6** *12* **Steel Away J (IRE)**[37] 699 6-10-11 0.......... MrJakeThomasCoulson(7) 70
(Christopher Kellett) *led over 9f: wknd over 2f out* **100/1**
6- **7** *½* **Ruby's From Milan (IRE)**[21] 842 5-10-4 0.................... KevinJones(7) 63
(Mark Shears) *chsd ldrs: lost pl after 5f: wknd 4f out* **25/1**
8 *16* **Mitt'N'Marg** 5-10-11 0... JoshWall(7) 54
(Trevor Wall) *hld up: stmbld over 13f out: pushed along over 5f out: sn wknd: bhd whn hmpd 2f out* **40/1**
R **Uiop** 5-10-11 0.. JakeHodson(7)
(David Bridgwater) *prom: rdn over 3f out: looked hld whn rn out 2f out* **6/1**

3m 39.8s (-1.90) **Going Correction** -0.90s/f (Hard)
WFA 4 from 5yo+ 2lb **9** Ran SP% **116.7**
Speed ratings: **68,66,64,63,62 56,55,47,**
Tote Swingers: 1&2 £3.00, 1&3 £3.50, 2&3 £8.20 CSF £18.97 TOTE £3.50: £2.10, £3.80, £1.10; EX 13.50 Trifecta £77.20 Pool: £1,085.27 - 10.54 winning units..
Owner Mrs L J Williams **Bred** Mervyn Williams **Trained** Little Newcastle, Pembrokes
FOCUS
A moderate looking bumper and they crawled early. It is rated around the third and fifth.

1017 GET LIVE SPORTS SCORES AT SCORES.CO.UK MARES' MAIDEN HURDLE (8 hdls) 2m
7:25 (7:25) (Class 5) 4-Y-O+ **£1,949** (£572; £286; £143)

Form RPR
1 **Crazy (GER)**[60] 4-10-10 0...(p) TomScudamore 94
(David Bridgwater) *hld up: hdwy 5th: chsd ldr 3 out: led appr last: rdn out* **5/1**[3]
/63- **2** *½* **Kimora (IRE)**[7] 948 7-10-12 0.....................................(t) AidanColeman 96
(Marc Barber) *hld up: hdwy appr 3 out: rdn bef last: r.o wl: nt rch wnr* **13/2**
3 *5* **Scarlet Whispers**[44] 4-10-10 0... SeanQuinlan 90
(Pam Sly) *chsd ldrs: led after 4th: hdd next: led again bef 3 out: rdn and hdd appr last: styd on same pce flat* **9/4**[1]
133/ **4** *22* **Bahira (IRE)**[776] 694 6-10-12 0.. JasonMaguire 68
(Donald McCain) *prom: lost pl appr 3rd: hdwy 5th: wknd appr 2 out: j.lft last* **5/2**[2]
P0/ **5** *¾* **Pagham Belle**[111] 4994 5-10-9 0.. MarkQuinlan(3) 67
(Nigel Hawke) *hld up: hdwy 5th: wknd 3 out* **100/1**
5- **6** *5* **Drombeg West**[36] 717 6-10-12 0.. CharliePoste 62
(Anna Brooks) *chsd ldrs: led 5th: hdd bef next: sn wknd* **20/1**
120- **7** *2 ½* **Nurse Ratched (IRE)**[15] 857 4-10-3 0........................ ConorShoemark(7) 58
(Fergal O'Brien) *chsd ldrs tl rdn and wknd appr 3 out* **8/1**
/ **8** *49* **Scommettitrice (IRE)**[23] 5-10-12 0...................................... NickScholfield 11
(Mark Gillard) *hld up: j. slowly 4th: sn wknd* **33/1**
P/ **U** **Desert Fairy**[14] 4309 7-10-5 0... JoshWall(7)
(Trevor Wall) *uns rdr 2nd* **100/1**
U- **P** **Beyond Dreams (IRE)**[7] 948 9-10-5 0..................................... JPKiely(7)
(Stephen Hughes) *led and j.rt 1st: hdd after 4th: wknd next: bhd whn p.u bef 3 out* **33/1**
6- **U** **Lucys Girl (IRE)**[29] 755 6-10-12 0.. BrendanPowell
(Jamie Snowden) *mstke and uns rdr 2nd* **14/1**

3m 36.7s (-10.60) **Going Correction** -0.90s/f (Hard)
WFA 4 from 5yo+ 15lb **11** Ran SP% **119.7**
Speed ratings (Par 103): **90,89,87,76,75 73,72,47**, ,
Tote Swingers: 1&2 £2.20, 1&3 £2.60, 2&3 £3.00 CSF £36.58 TOTE £6.50: £2.30, £2.10, £1.40; EX 41.30 Trifecta £103.80 Pool: £712.67 - 5.14 winning units..
Owner Jobarry Partnership **Bred** J Imm **Trained** Icomb, Gloucs
FOCUS
A very moderate mares' maiden with the first three pulling clear off a steady pace. Early leader Beyond Dreams caused some interference by jumping markedly right-handed which indirectly led to Desert Fairy and Lucys Girl unseating at the second, and slightly impeded the winner later on. The form is rated through the second.

1018 COMPARE FREE BETS AT BOOKMAKERS.CO.UK (S) H'CAP HURDLE (10 hdls) 2m 4f
7:55 (7:55) (Class 5) (0-95,95) 4-Y-O+ **£1,949** (£572; £286; £143)

Form RPR
/05- **1** **Jigsaw Financial (IRE)**[42] 637 7-10-4 **73**........................ GerardTumelty 83
(Laura Young) *hld up: hdwy 6th: led 2 out: rdn out* **20/1**
0/ **2** *1 ½* **Spice Hill (IRE)**[38] 7-10-10 **79**...................................(v[1]) RichardJohnson 88
(Tim Vaughan) *led: rdn and hdd 2 out: styd on* **7/1**[3]
60/- **3** *5* **Neverownup (IRE)**[82] 5557 8-11-6 **89**...........................(t) DaveCrosse 94
(K F Clutterbuck) *chsd ldrs: rdn and mstke 2 out: styd on same pce flat* **33/1**
450- **4** *11* **Spinning Waters**[8] 927 7-11-4 **90**...............................(b) RobertDunne(3) 83
(Dai Burchell) *hld up: hdwy 7th: rdn and wknd 2 out* **20/1**
154- **5** *1* **Nicky Nutjob (GER)**[1] 801 7-11-2 **92**...........................(p) CiaranMckee(7) 84
(John O'Shea) *hld up: drvn along after 7th: nvr on terms* **7/1**[3]
010- **6** *1 ¼* **Brass Monkey (IRE)**[15] 860 6-10-7 **86**..................... CharlieDeutsch(10) 76
(Charlie Longsdon) *prom: chsd ldr 5th: ev ch 3 out: sn rdn: wknd appr last* **8/1**
026- **7** *9* **Full Ov Beans**[10] 898 9-10-8 **82**.. NicodeBoinville(5) 63
(Michael Gates) *hld up: effrt appr 3 out: sn wknd* **20/1**
/0- **8** *1 ¾* **Respectueux (FR)**[21] 846 7-11-3 **86**.................................... DonalDevereux 66
(David Brace) *hld up: hdwy after 4th: rdn and wknd 3 out* **33/1**
410- **9** *26* **Golden Acorn (IRE)**[28] 765 4-10-12 **84**................................(t) CharliePoste 35
(Jamie Snowden) *mid-div: lost pl 5th: bhd whn hmpd 7th* **22/1**

P00- 10 7 **Benefit Game (IRE)**[40] 661 9-10-8 **80** .... JamesBest(3) 27
(Richard Hawker) *hld up: rdn and wknd appr 3 out* **50/1**

00/- 11 30 **Herminella**[268] 1961 5-10-10 **79** .... JackDoyle
(Ali Brewer) *hld up: wknd after 7th* **20/1**

456- P **Saga De Tercey (FR)**[24] 804 8-11-12 **95** .... (v1) JasonMaguire
(Donald McCain) *chsd ldrs: reminder after 3rd: wknd 6th: p.u bef 3 out* **11/2**[2]

0/6- P **Tignello (IRE)**[14] 875 8-10-9 **78** .... (t1) RichieMcLernon
(Emma Baker) *chsd ldr to 5th: sn rdn and wknd: p.u bef 3 out* **40/1**

0/U- P **Dune Shine**[50] 522 8-11-12 **95** .... (p) NickScholfield
(Michael Blake) *hld up: reminders after 4th: sme hdwy bef next: sn wknd: wnt wrong and p.u after 6th* **5/2**[1]

650- P **Hugo Drax (IRE)**[22] 829 6-10-6 **75** .... (tp) TomScudamore
(David Pipe) *prom: rdn and wknd after 7th: p.u bef next* **11/1**

4m 28.7s (-18.70) **Going Correction** -0.90s/f (Hard)
WFA 4 from 5yo+ 16lb **15** Ran SP% **122.1**
Speed ratings (Par 103): **101,100,98,94,93 93,89,88,78,75 63,,,,**
Tote Swingers: 1&2 £19.60, 1&3 £83.00, 2&3 £34.80 CSF £139.97 CT £4602.52 TOTE £17.50: £4.00, £3.20, £11.20; EX 109.20 Trifecta £376.10 Part won. Pool: £501.47 - 0.04 winning units..There was no bid for the winner.
Owner Mrs Laura Young **Bred** Joseph Kent **Trained** Broomfield, Somerset

FOCUS
This was run at a good pace and produced a surprising result. The winner is rated back to the level of his 2011 best.

1019 COMPARE BOOKIES FREE BETS AT BOOKMAKERS.CO.UK MAIDEN HURDLE (12 hdls) 2m 7f
8:30 (8:30) (Class 5) 4-Y-0+ **£1,949** (£572; £286; £143)

Form RPR

223- 1 **Billfromthebar (IRE)**[17] 847 6-11-0 0 .... JasonMaguire 117+
(Donald McCain) *led 2nd: rdn appr 3 out: drvn clr next: eased flat* **9/4**[2]

24/- 2 7 **Prime Location**[117] 4903 7-11-0 114 .... (tp) TomScudamore 103
(David Pipe) *chsd wnr 2nd: rdn appr 3 out: wknd bef last* **6/5**[1]

446- 3 4 **West End Classic (IRE)**[14] 876 6-10-9 97 .... BenPoste(5) 99
(Tracey Watkins) *hld up: hdwy 8th: rdn and wknd 3 out* **16/1**

4 hd **Castle View (IRE)**[115] 6-11-0 0 .... CharliePoste 99
(Anna Brooks) *hdwy 3rd: rdn after 9th: wknd next* **22/1**

2/0- 5 58 **Rally The Troops (IRE)**[17] 847 6-11-0 0 .... APMcCoy 41
(Jonjo O'Neill) *hld up: rdn after 8th: sn wknd* **4/1**[3]

P/0- 6 17 **God's County (FR)**[24] 800 8-11-0 110 .... (tp) PaulMoloney 24
(Sophie Leech) *prom tl rdn and wknd 9th* **20/1**

0- 7 28 **Rockingtimes (IRE)**[36] 716 5-11-0 0 .... HenryOliver
(Henry Oliver) *plld hrd: led to 2nd: remained handy tl wknd appr 8th* **40/1**

00- U **Whispering Boy (IRE)**[14] 878 6-10-7 0 .... JakeHodson(7)
(David Bridgwater) *hld up: hdwy 8th: rdn and cl 3rd whn mstke and uns rdr 3 out* **80/1**

5m 33.2s (5.20) **Going Correction** -0.90s/f (Hard) **8** Ran SP% **114.9**
Speed ratings (Par 103): **54,51,50,50,29 24,14,**
Tote Swingers: 1&2 £1.60, 1&3 £2.20, 2&3 £4.60 CSF £5.37 TOTE £4.00: £1.10, £1.30, £2.70; EX 6.60 Trifecta £23.50 Pool: £905.21 - 28.83 winning units..
Owner Matthew Sanders **Bred** Andrew Pierce **Trained** Cholmondeley, Cheshire

FOCUS
After a sedate early tempo the winner injected some pace in the back straight which soon had most under pressure and they finished strung out. The easy winner was value for further and is rated to his best.

1020 GET FREE BETS WITH BOOKMAKERS.CO.UK H'CAP HURDLE (10 hdls) 2m 4f
9:00 (9:00) (Class 4) (0-120,118) 4-Y-0+ **£3,573** (£1,049; £524; £262)

Form RPR

134- 1 **Don't Be Late (IRE)**[28] 764 5-11-4 **110** .... (p) APMcCoy 115+
(Jonjo O'Neill) *hld up: hdwy after 7th: rdn to ld and mstke last: hdd flat: rallied to ld fnl 50yds* **5/4**[1]

2 ½ **Zalgarry (FR)**[437] 6-10-11 **110** .... JoshWall(7) 114
(Arthur Whitehead) *hld up: hdwy appr 3 out: rdn to ld flat: hdd fnl 50yds* **25/1**

/30- 3 4½ **Staigue Fort**[24] 808 5-10-13 **110** .... GavinSheehan(5) 111
(Emma Lavelle) *chsd ldrs: mstke and rdr lost iron briefly 3 out: ev ch fr next tl rdn and styd* **20/1**

/30- 4 4½ **Flaming Arrow (IRE)**[17] 850 5-11-12 **118** .... BrianHughes 113
(Kevin Ryan) *hld up: hdwy 7th: ev ch 2 out: rdn and wknd last* **9/2**[3]

/04- 5 1 **George Woolf**[28] 767 5-11-7 **113** .... (vt1) RichardJohnson 111+
(Tim Vaughan) *chsd ldr tl led 3rd: mstke and hdd next: remained handy: rdn to ld 2 out: hdd whn blnd last: wknd flat* **8/1**

663- 6 hd **Laustra Bad (FR)**[28] 764 10-11-11 **117** .... (bt) TomScudamore 110
(David Pipe) *led to 3rd: led 4th tl rdn 2 out: wknd last* **4/1**[2]

0/0- 7 26 **Dropzone (USA)**[24] 812 4-11-0 **109** .... CharliePoste 73
(Richard Lee) *prom tl rdn and wknd 3 out* **20/1**

/4P- 8 18 **Priceless Art (IRE)**[15] 859 8-11-12 **118** .... (b1) AidanColeman 67
(Anthony Honeyball) *prom: pushed along 6th: rdn and wknd appr 3 out* **14/1**

4m 32.7s (-14.70) **Going Correction** -0.90s/f (Hard)
WFA 4 from 5yo+ 16lb **8** Ran SP% **113.8**
Speed ratings (Par 105): **93,92,91,89,88 88,78,71**
Tote Swingers 1&2 £11.70, 2&3 £39.70, 1&3 £13.30 CSF £33.69 CT £430.30 TOTE £2.00: £1.30, £6.00, £4.70; EX 52.20 Trifecta £455.40 Part won. Pool: £607.29 - 0.42 winning units..
Owner John P McManus **Bred** Seamus Boyle **Trained** Cheltenham, Gloucs

FOCUS
It looked like any one from five coming to the second last, but in the end the first two pulled a little way clear. The third and fourth help set the level.
T/Plt: £91.50 to a £1 stake. Pool: £67,430.61 - 537.95 winning tickets. T/Qpdt: £9.00 to a £1 stake. Pool: £7,588.55 - 617.20 winning tickets. CR

1021 - 1036a (Foreign Racing) - See Raceform Interactive

531 CARTMEL (L-H)
Saturday, July 20

OFFICIAL GOING: Good to firm (good in places; 8.2)
All rail on innermost line.
Wind: light 1/2 behind Weather: fine and sunny, very warm

1037 HADWINS NOVICES' HURDLE (11 hdls) 2m 6f
2:10 (2:10) (Class 4) 4-Y-0+ **£3,249** (£954; £477; £238)

Form RPR

134- 1 **Mr Satco (IRE)**[16] 885 5-10-12 0 .... JasonMaguire 120+
(Donald McCain) *mde all: rdn wl clr between last 2: heavily eased in clsng stages* **5/1**[3]

2- 2 11 **Soweheard (IRE)**[26] 823 6-10-12 125 .... KieronEdgar(7) 113
(Gordon Elliott, Ire) *nt fluent: chsd ldrs: mstke 7th: drvn next: sn outpcd: kpt on to take modest 2nd 1f out* **4/5**[1]

0- 3 2¼ **Hit The Top (IRE)**[20] 848 6-10-12 0 .... RyanMania 102
(Sue Smith) *chsd ldrs: 2nd between last 2: one pce* **16/1**

F/2- 4 3 **Nodforms Violet (IRE)**[77] 115 9-10-12 118 .... BrianHughes 99
(Karen McLintock) *chsd wnr: hit 3 out: one pce* **9/4**[2]

0/0- 5 dist **Be Wise (IRE)**[73] 173 6-10-5 0 .... CallumBewley(7)
(Harriet Graham) *a in last: mstke 3rd: sn bhd and drvn: t.o 6th: eventually fin* **50/1**

5m 18.2s (-11.10) **Going Correction** -0.425s/f (Good) **5** Ran SP% **110.8**
Speed ratings (Par 105): **103,99,98,97,**
CSF £10.01 TOTE £6.70: £2.50, £1.10; EX 11.30 Trifecta £34.00 Pool: £400.99 - 8.82 winning units..
Owner D McCain Jnr **Bred** Lillian Mahon **Trained** Cholmondeley, Cheshire
■ Stewards' Enquiry : Kieron Edgar two-day ban: used whip above permitted level (Aug 3-4)

FOCUS
All rails on innermost line. With Billfromthebar withdrawn, Jason Maguire switched to the winner. A step up on his bumper form from the easy winner.

1038 CHAMPAGNE LOUIS ROEDERER H'CAP CHASE (17 fncs 1 omitted) 3m 2f
2:45 (2:48) (Class 5) (0-100,94) 4-Y-0+ **£3,249** (£954; £477; £238)

Form RPR

/60- 1 **Nicky Tam (IRE)**[49] 580 11-10-1 **69** .... (p) RichieMcGrath 80
(Henry Hogarth) *in rr: hdwy 14th: 4th omitted last: sn 3rd: wnt 10 l 2nd 2f out: styd on to ld towards fin* **33/1**

/53- 2 ¾ **Baizically (IRE)**[10] 942 10-10-13 **84** .... (b) MichealNolan(3) 94
(John Joseph Hanlon, Ire) *chsd ldrs: 2nd 9th led next: sn clr: tired and hdd towards fin* **10/1**

3 23 **Merrydown Vintage (IRE)**[43] 666 6-11-8 **90** .... PaddyBrennan 80
(D T Hughes, Ire) *in rr-div: hdwy 12th: 12 l 2nd omitted last: wknd fnl 2f* **11/2**[3]

153- 4 8 **Dukeofchesterwood**[29] 789 11-11-0 **82** .... (b) BrianHughes 61
(Karen McLintock) *chsd ldrs: one pce fr 14th* **13/2**

333- 5 nk **Solway Dornal**[17] 868 8-9-11 **72** .... (tp) StephenMulqueen(7) 51
(Lisa Harrison) *in tch: outpcd 12th: no threat after* **7/1**

002- 6 13 **Cloudy Dawn**[27] 802 8-10-0 **75** .... CallumBewley(7) 41
(Sue Smith) *mid-div: outpcd 12th: no threat after* **4/1**[1]

P/4- 7 1 **Pliny (IRE)**[57] 461 9-10-7 **75** .... (bt) JamieMoore 40
(Peter Bowen) *chsd ldrs 6th: 2nd 13th: wknd qckly omitted last* **9/2**[2]

653- 8 5 **Highland Rain**[11] 930 5-10-6 **74** .... (vt) SeanQuinlan 34
(Jennie Candlish) *led to 10th: wknd 14th* **10/1**

P06- 9 4½ **Seize**[27] 802 11-11-12 **94** .... (p) LucyAlexander 49
(James Moffatt) *sn bhd: nvr on terms* **25/1**

/26- P **Chernik (IRE)**[35] 753 12-10-3 **71** .... (p) WilsonRenwick
(Micky Hammond) *in rr: reminders 8th: t.o 12th: p.u bef next* **14/1**

0P0- U **I Can Run Can You (IRE)**[45] 637 7-11-3 **85** .... (bt1) RichieMcLernon
(Jonjo O'Neill) *chsd ldrs: j.rt: blnd and uns rdr 2nd* **14/1**

P **Gibbstown (IRE)**[15] 894 7-11-5 **87** .... (p) FelixDeGiles
(Paul Stafford, Ire) *in rr: hdwy to chse ldrs whn hit 7th: lost pl 9th: sn bhd: t.o whn p.u after 14th* **50/1**

434- F **Raifteiri (IRE)**[17] 866 6-10-5 **78** .... GaryRutherford(5)
(William Young Jnr) *in rr-div: outpcd 9th: bhd whn fell 12th* **20/1**

/66- P **Have You Had Yours (IRE)**[46] 625 7-10-4 **79** .... AlistairFindlay(7)
(Jane Walton) *chsd ldrs: wknd 12th: t.o 14th: p.u bef next* **20/1**

6m 24.2s (-10.70) **Going Correction** -0.55s/f (Firm) **14** Ran SP% **129.2**
Speed ratings (Par 103): **94,93,86,84,84 80,79,78,76,,,,,**
toteswingers 1&2 £35.00, 2&3 £14.10, 1&3 £25.90 CSF £336.94 CT £2131.03 TOTE £47.00: £9.40, £3.50, £2.30; EX 519.00 TRIFECTA Not won..
Owner Hogarth Racing **Bred** Noel O'Brien **Trained** Stillington, N Yorks

FOCUS
A well-contested, if ordinary, staying handicap chase in which the pace was only fair until Baizically quickened the tempo with more than a circuit to go. The first two were very well in on old form.

1039 BROWN HORSE WINSTER VALLEY BREWERY H'CAP CHASE (13 fncs 1 omitted) 2m 5f 110y
3:20 (4:00) (Class 4) (0-110,109) 4-Y-0+ **£3,898** (£1,144; £572; £286)

Form RPR

224- 1 **Cruchain (IRE)**[32] 757 10-11-9 **106** .... (p) RobertDunne(3) 122+
(Dai Burchell) *chsd ldrs 4th: led after 10th: drew clr: run-in: readily* **6/1**[3]

640- 2 17 **Civil Unrest (IRE)**[16] 883 7-11-2 **96** .... (p) BrianHarding 92
(James Ewart) *mid-div: hdwy 8th: chsng ldrs next: wnt 2nd 2 out: no ch w wnr* **18/1**

4UP- 3 4½ **More Equity**[27] 802 11-10-3 **90** .... ColmMcCormack(7) 81
(Dianne Sayer) *in rr: hdwy 8th: tk modest 3rd over 2f out: one pce* **14/1**

P/B- 4 9 **Rathnaroughy (IRE)**[27] 798 9-11-9 **103** .... JasonMaguire 85
(Malcolm Jefferson) *in last whn j. slowly 4th: hdwy 8th: lft modest 5th 10th: tk modest 4th over 1f out* **15/2**

416- 5 9 **Wait No More (IRE)**[25] 832 8-11-11 **105** .... (p) AndrewThornton 78
(Neil Mulholland) *w ldr: led 3rd tl after 10th: wknd fr 2 out* **12/1**

2U2- 6 2½ **Peak Seasons (IRE)**[40] 693 10-10-4 **89** .... JoeCornwall(5) 59
(Michael Chapman) *in rr: hmpd 6th: nvr on terms* **20/1**

/60- P **Earth Planet (IRE)**[31] 766 11-11-8 **102** .... (tp) WilsonRenwick
(Micky Hammond) *in rr: wknd 10th: t.o whn p.u bef last: b.b.v* **25/1**

P01/ F **Baltic Pathfinder (IRE)**[490] 4920 9-11-9 **103** .... RyanMania
(Sue Smith) *chsd ldrs: 4th and outpcd whn fell 11th* **14/1**

2/4- P **Cocoa Key (IRE)**[72] 183 9-10-10 **95** .... HarryChalloner(5)
(Richard Ford) *chsd ldrs: wknd 8th: bhd fr 10th: p.u bef next* **14/1**

The Form Book Jumps, Raceform Ltd, Compton, RG20 6NL.

/03- **P** **Golden View (IRE)**[50] 566 8-11-9 **103**............................(p) BrianHughes
(Karen McLintock) *worst away in ragged s: hdwy 8th: chsng ldrs next: outpcd whn bdly hmpd and lost pl next: p.u bef 11th* **5/1**[2]

241- **F** **Forever My Friend (IRE)**[3] 1012 6-12-1 **109** 7ex................ JamieMoore
(Peter Bowen) *chsd ldrs: fell 6th* **2/1**[1]

5m 10.7s (-14.70) **Going Correction** -0.55s/f (Firm) **11** Ran SP% **117.6**
Speed ratings (Par 105): **104,97,96,92,89 88, , , ,**
toteswingers 1&2 £10.80, 2&3 £0.00, 1&3 £0.00 CSF £102.07 CT £1451.67 TOTE £7.70: £2.40, £5.50, £4.10; EX 135.70 Trifecta £640.60 Part won..
Owner Mr & Mrs A J Mutch **Bred** Dunmanway Breeding Club **Trained** Briery Hill, Blaenau Gwent

FOCUS
A 40-minute delay as the track awaited the air ambulance after Gary Rutherford took a nasty fall in the previous race, and the runners for this competitive 0-110 handicap chase were kept cool by the water-misters supplied by the course. The third-last fence was omitted. An untidy start in an incident-packed race, so the form should be treated with caution. The easy winner was very well in on his best 2012 form and is rated back to that sort of level.

1040 BURLINGTON STONE H'CAP CHASE (18 fncs) 3m 2f
3:55 (4:30) (Class 3) (0-135,130) 4-Y-0+ **£9,747** (£2,862; £1,431; £715)

Form RPR
/54- **1** **Ballybough Gorta (IRE)**[12] 923 6-11-2 **120**.................(v[1]) JamieMoore 132
(Peter Bowen) *mde all: j.lft 12th: drvn 3 l clr over 2f out: all out* **3/1**[2]

132- **2** ½ **Royale Knight**[12] 923 7-10-1 **112**.............................. ChristopherWard(7) 123
(Dr Richard Newland) *trckd ldrs: hit 13th: 2nd 2 out: upsides and drvn last: styd on fnl f: jst hld* **11/10**[1]

320- **3** 13 **Siberian Tiger (IRE)**[20] 851 8-11-4 **122**......................(p) JasonMaguire 119
(Evan Williams) *hld up in last: effrt whn hit 13th: drvn next: outpcd whn nt fluent 4 out: kpt on to take modest 3rd nr fin* **6/1**

/15- **4** shd **Themilanhorse (IRE)**[55] 487 7-11-12 **130**.......................(t) RyanMahon 128
(Paul Nicholls) *chsd wnr: one pce fr 3 out* **8/1**

/13- **5** 47 **Full Of Joy (IRE)**[42] 670 8-10-13 **117**.......................(tp) RichieMcLernon 67
(Jonjo O'Neill) *chsd ldrs: drvn 14th: 4th and wkng whn blnd 2 out: bhd whn eased fnl f: t.o* **5/1**[3]

6m 26.7s (-8.20) **Going Correction** -0.55s/f (Firm) **5** Ran SP% **114.7**
Speed ratings (Par 107): **90,89,85,85,71**
CSF £7.44 TOTE £5.10: £2.30, £1.50; EX 7.50 Trifecta £31.40 Pool: £530.56 - 12.63 winning units..
Owner Yeh Man Partnership **Bred** Jaykayenn Syndicate **Trained** Little Newcastle, Pembrokes
■ Stewards' Enquiry : Christopher Ward seven-day ban: used whip above permitted level (Aug 3-4,13,15,17-19)

FOCUS
An open-looking, decent staying handicap chase. Small personal bests from the first two.

1041 MCGUINNESS FEEDS LADY RIDERS' H'CAP HURDLE (8 hdls) 2m 1f 110y
4:30 (5:05) (Class 3) (0-135,130) 4-Y-0+ **£9,747** (£2,862; £1,431; £715)

Form RPR
112- **1** **Life And Soul (IRE)**[40] 688 6-11-12 **130**....................(p) LucyAlexander 132
(Donald McCain) *led: rdn 2 out: hdd last: styd on to ld in clsng stages* **15/8**[1]

122- **2** ¾ **Sidney Melbourne (USA)**[25] 831 6-11-2 **127**........(b) MissBAndrews(7) 129+
(Paul Nicholls) *trckd wnr: t.k.h: rdn and narrow ld last: no ex and hdd in clsng stages: fin lame* **3/1**[2]

/32- **3** 18 **Orthodox Lad**[10] 948 5-9-8 **105**..................................... MrsAlexDunn(7) 92
(Dr Richard Newland) *nt fluent: chsd ldrs: reminder 4th: 3rd next: one pce* **7/2**[3]

102- **4** 28 **Knight In Purple**[20] 850 9-11-7 **130**.......................(vt) MissGAndrews(5) 84
(John Mackie) *in rr: reminders 5th: sn wl outpcd: tk distant 4th nr fin* **7/1**

6/1- **5** 1½ **Logical Approach (IRE)**[52] 536 6-9-7 **104** oh2...(p) MissJRRichards(7) 57
(David Thompson) *chsd ldrs: outpcd 6th: wknd 2 out: lost distant 4th in clsng stages* **14/1**

215- **6** 11 **Mighty Clarets (IRE)**[9] 876 6-9-13 **110**..............(v) MissRBlackmore(7) 52
(Peter Bowen) *nt fluent in last: drvn 5th: sn wl outpcd and bhd* **6/1**

4m 1.9s (-11.30) **Going Correction** -0.425s/f (Good) **6** Ran SP% **115.5**
Speed ratings (Par 107): **108,107,99,87,86 81**
toteswingers 1&2 £1.10, 2&3 £3.00, 1&3 £2.10 CSF £8.52 TOTE £2.40: £1.80, £1.40; EX 7.90 Trifecta £42.80 Pool: £664.95 - 11.63 winning units..
Owner Matthew Taylor **Bred** Kildaragh Stud **Trained** Cholmondeley, Cheshire

FOCUS
With a couple of confirmed front-runners for this competitive ladies' handicap hurdle the pace was always going to be a strong one with the front pair in the market dominating throughout. They are rated to their marks.

1042 TOTEPOOL.COM CUMBRIA CRYSTAL TROPHY H'CAP HURDLE (11 hdls) 2m 6f
5:05 (5:35) (Class 3) (0-140,135) 4-Y-0+**£17,544** (£5,151; £2,575; £1,287)

Form RPR
111- **1** **Church Field (IRE)**[50] 564 5-10-4 **113**.......................... RichieMcLernon 117+
(Jonjo O'Neill) *trckd ldrs: 2nd 8th: styd on run-in: led nr fin* **7/2**[2]

/11- **2** ½ **Taigan (FR)**[48] 604 6-11-1 **124**.. DavidEngland 126
(Giles Smyly) *hld up in rr: gd hdwy 8th: sn trcking ldrs: led last: hdd and no ex nr fin* **9/1**

/P4- **3** 1¾ **Decoy (FR)**[17] 877 7-10-9 **125**.....................................(p) KieronEdgar(7) 126
(David Pipe) *in rr: hdwy 8th: chsng ldrs appr last: tk 3rd nr fin* **10/3**[1]

5/1- **4** 1½ **Tornado Bob (IRE)**[39] 718 8-11-12 **135**...................(b) JasonMaguire 133
(Donald McCain) *led: hdd last: kpt on same pce fnl f* **5/1**[3]

/31- **5** 3¼ **Malin Bay (IRE)**[17] 867 8-11-5 **128**.................................. FearghalDavis 124
(Nicky Richards) *chsd ldrs: rdn 3 out: wknd fnl f* **10/1**

/04- **6** 7 **Scotswell**[54] 512 7-11-4 **127**.. LucyAlexander 115
(Harriet Graham) *chsd ldrs: drvn and lost pl 3 out: kpt on run-in* **12/1**

110/ **7** 1 **Dartford Warbler (IRE)**[428] 337 6-9-13 **115**............... CallumBewley(7) 103
(Sue Smith) *chsd ldrs: outpcd whn hit 3 out: wknd appr last* **9/1**

315- **8** 1 **Lava Lamp (GER)**[30] 782 6-10-9 **125**............................... ConorRing(7) 111
(Evan Williams) *in rr: drvn 7th: kpt on fr 2 out: nvr a factor* **14/1**

/24- **9** 3¼ **Awaywiththegreys (IRE)**[18] 861 6-11-10 **133**..............(p) JamieMoore 116
(Peter Bowen) *sn detached in rr: drvn 7th: kpt on fr 3 out: nvr on terms* **14/1**

/00- **10** 32 **Sainglend**[15] 845 8-10-6 **125**.......................................(b[1]) MikeyHamill(10) 76
(Sean Curran) *chsd ldrs: outpcd 8th: sn lost pl: bhd whn eased run-in: t.o* **28/1**

104- **11** 5 **Maoi Chinn Tire (IRE)**[6] 973 6-10-9 **118**.......................(p) SeanQuinlan 64
(Jennie Candlish) *in rr: mstke 6th: sme hdwy 8th: sn lost pl: bhd whn eased run-in: t.o* **14/1**

211- **P** **Lord Grantham (IRE)**[30] 777 6-11-2 **128**....................... JakeGreenall(3)
(Henry Daly) *in rr: sme hdwy 8th: sn lost pl: t.o whn p.u bef last* **10/1**

5m 17.6s (-11.70) **Going Correction** -0.425s/f (Good) **12** Ran SP% **131.3**
Speed ratings (Par 107): **104,103,103,102,101 98,98,98,97,85 83,**
toteswingers 1&2 £5.80, 2&3 £16.10, 1&3 £4.40 CSF £39.82 CT £122.18 TOTE £3.80: £2.50, £3.50, £2.10; EX 48.50 Trifecta £259.40 Part won..
Owner John P McManus **Bred** Mrs Eleanor Hadden **Trained** Cheltenham, Gloucs

FOCUS
A decent prize on offer for the track's flagship handicap hurdle with plenty of winners in the field with a decent gallop being set it had quite a few off the bridle a fair way out and only five holding some sort of chance from the last. The first two are on the upgrade.

1043 WILLOW WATER MARES' H'CAP HURDLE (8 hdls) 2m 1f 110y
5:35 (6:05) (Class 4) (0-115,111) 4-Y-0+ **£4,548** (£1,335; £667; £333)

Form RPR
/55- **1** **Faith Jicaro (IRE)**[4] 812 6-11-6 **105**... DPFahy 109+
(James Unett) *hld up: hdwy to trck ldrs 5th: led sn after 2 out: 6 l clr 1f out: idled: pushed out* **11/1**

43- **2** 1¾ **Me And Ben (IRE)**[11] 932 6-10-9 **94**.............................(t) PaddyBrennan 94+
(Fergal O'Brien) *chsd ldrs: 3rd between last 2: kpt on to take 2nd last 150yds: styng on at fin* **7/2**[2]

311- **3** 2¾ **Social Realism (IRE)**[36] 738 5-11-12 **111**..................(p) JasonMaguire 109
(Jonjo O'Neill) *w ldr: kpt on one pce and lost 2nd last 150yds* **3/1**[1]

/53- **4** 2 **Grethel (IRE)**[4] 532 9-10-0 **85** oh13.............................. LucyAlexander 81
(Alan Berry) *in rr: hdwy 3 out: styd on run-in: tk 4th post* **33/1**

566/ **5** hd **Mollyow (IRE)**[274] 1913 5-11-3 **107**.............................. RobertWilliams(5) 102
(Eugene Stanford) *towards rr: hdwy 5th: 4th appr last: one pce* **12/1**

5/3- **6** ½ **Miss Macnamara (IRE)**[17] 223 4-10-1 **88**.................... WilsonRenwick 81
(Martin Todhunter) *chsd ldrs: outpcd whn hmpd bnd after 2 out: kpt on fnl f* **9/2**[3]

4/2- **7** 5 **Bollin Dolly**[46] 626 10-11-3 **102**.. BrianHarding 92
(James Moffatt) *hld up towards rr: hdwy after 5th: drvn and chsng ldrs 2 out: fdd appr last* **11/2**

163- **8** 9 **Godwit**[20] 848 5-11-3 **105**.. JackQuinlan(3) 86
(Eugene Stanford) *led: hdd sn after 2 out: sn wknd* **6/1**

500- **9** 9 **Stand Clear**[11] 932 8-10-1 **93**...(p) AdamNicol(7) 65
(David Thompson) *in rr: reminders 4th: bhd fr 5th* **18/1**

4/5- **10** 1¾ **Acht (GER)**[37] 729 4-10-0 **92**...(t) DerekFox(5) 60
(Noel C Kelly, Ire) *chsd ldrs: drvn 5th: lost pl 2 out* **14/1**

4m 5.7s (-7.50) **Going Correction** -0.425s/f (Good)
WFA 4 from 5yo+ 15lb **10** Ran SP% **126.0**
Speed ratings (Par 105): **99,98,97,96,96 95,93,89,85,84**
toteswingers 1&2 £5.70, 2&3 £3.00, 1&3 £12.60 CSF £54.51 CT £152.70 TOTE £20.50: £5.20, £1.40, £1.20; EX 80.70 Trifecta £318.40 Part won..
Owner Gordon Kendrick **Bred** John Carr **Trained** Tedsmore Hall, Shropshire

FOCUS
A reasonable mares' handicap hurdle where the pace was generous. The third and fourth help set the level.
T/Plt: £207.00 to a £1 stake. Pool of £45649.81 - 160.93 winning tickets. T/Qpdt: £21.70 to a £1 stake. Pool of £2890.10 - 98.20 winning tickets. WG

897 MARKET RASEN (R-H)
Saturday, July 20

OFFICIAL GOING: Chase course - good to firm (good in places); hurdle course - good (good to firm in places)
Fences and hurdles sited at outermost positions and hurdles in home straight moved forward towards Winning Post by 90m and 150m.
Wind: light wind, slightly blustery Weather: overcast; 19 degrees

1044 BETFRED "THE BONUS KING" JUVENILE HURDLE (8 hdls) 2m 1f
1:45 (1:46) (Class 4) 3-Y-0 **£3,898** (£1,144; £572; £286)

Form RPR
1 **Fitzwilly**[58] 3-10-12 0.. WillKennedy 86+
(Mick Channon) *settled in 3rd: shkn up and hit 5th: mstke next and drvn and outpcd: rallied to go 2nd home turn: led bef 2 out: racing v idly in front and stl drvn: 6 l clr last: styd on wl* **10/1**[3]

2- **2** 11 **Hanga Roa (IRE)**[29] 785 3-10-9 0................................ JoshuaMoore(3) 76
(Gary Moore) *racd keenly: mstke 3 out: led and abt 6 l clr tl rdn home turn: hdd bef 2 out where mstke: wl hld by wnr after* **8/1**[2]

4- **3** 5 **Style Setter**[29] 785 3-10-5 0.. AdrianLane 64
(Donald McCain) *racd wl off pce: 20 l 4th after 4th: clsd to heels of ldrs 3 out: sn drvn: no imp in wl hld 3rd fr 2 out* **16/1**

112- **4** 9 **It's Only Business**[6] 975 3-11-8 0.. APMcCoy 77
(Jim Best) *plld hrd: sn 2nd bhd clr ldr: drvn wl bef 2 out: sn fnd nil and lost pl: mstke 2 out in 4th: blnd bdly last* **2/5**[1]

P- **5** 52 **Jd Rockefeller**[6] 975 3-10-9 0......................................(b[1]) JackQuinlan(3) 16
(Paul D'Arcy) *j. slowly in 4th bhd three clr ldrs: lost all tch bef 4th and continued t.o* **50/1**

P **Blue Clumber**[15] 3-10-0 0... BenPoste(5)
(Shaun Harris) *mstkes and wl detached in last pair: rdn 3rd: t.o fr 4th tl p.u 2 out* **66/1**

36- **P** **Red Eight (USA)**[6] 975 3-10-12 0................................. LeightonAspell
(John Butler) *hld up and long way bhd in last pair: mstkes: t.o fr 4th tl p.u 2 out* **20/1**

U **Noble Bacchus (IRE)**[37] 3-10-12 0.................................. AlainCawley
(Fergal O'Brien) *last whn j.v.slowly and uns rdr 1st* **14/1**

P- **U** **Town Mouse**[6] 975 3-10-7 0...[1] TrevorWhelan(5)
(Neil King) *led rnd s: led in, ducked lft and uns rdr* **8/1**[2]

4m 11.4s (4.70) **Going Correction** -0.225s/f (Good) **9** Ran SP% **123.5**
Speed ratings (Par 102): **79,73,71,67,42 , , ,**
toteswingers 1&2 £8.70, 1&3 £13.80, 2&3 £7.30 CSF £89.07 TOTE £13.60: £2.80, £1.90, £3.30; EX 153.90 Trifecta £797.70 Part won..
Owner Peter Taplin **Bred** Imperial & Mike Channon Bloodstock Ltd **Trained** West Ilsley, Berks

FOCUS
Fences and hurdles sited at outermost positions and Hurdles in home straight moved forward towards winning post by 90m and 150m. With It's Only Business seemingly running well below previous levels and the winner very modest on the level, it's likely this form isn't up to much. It was slowly run and the second and third are the best guides.

1045 BETFRED TV H'CAP HURDLE (10 hdls) 2m 5f
2:20 (2:21) (Class 2) (0-150,135) 4-Y-0+ **£10,302** (£3,368; £1,704; £873; £457)

Form RPR
112- **1** **Man Of Leisure**[27] 812 9-10-13 **125**..........................(t) RachaelGreen(3) 131+
(Anthony Honeyball) *confidently rdn in rr: smooth prog on outer home turn: led gng best 2 out: 5 l clr last: pushed out: v comf* **9/2**[3]
/10- **2** *5* **Leath Acra Mor (IRE)**[24] 845 7-10-10 **119**......................... WillKennedy 121
(Ian Williams) *led tl j. slowly 1st: rdn much of way: 2nd or 3rd tl lft jst in front 3 out: hdd by str travelling wnr next: nt qckn and wl hld after* **14/1**
/12- **3** *9* **First In The Queue (IRE)**[13] 901 6-11-12 **135**..................... APMcCoy 130
(Nicky Henderson) *cl up: nt fluent 2nd: lft disputing ld 3 out: rdn wl bef next: limited rspnse: 3rd and btn whn nt fluent 2 out: eased flat* **3/1**[2]
4/3- **4** *4* **Swampfire (IRE)**[13] 901 5-11-1 **124**........................(vt[1]) RichardJohnson 116
(Tim Vaughan) *cl up: rdn 7th: outpcd home turn: 7 l 4th whn blnd 2 out* **11/4**[1]
121- **5** *12* **Va'Vite (IRE)**[13] 901 6-10-9 **128**.. MarkMarris(10) 107
(Anthony Middleton) *detached in last: sn rdn and nvr travelling: lost tch 6th* **6/1**
111- **F** **Massannie (IRE)**[12] 922 5-11-9 **132**............................ TomScudamore
(David Pipe) *lft in ld 1st: hrd pressed whn fell heavily 3 out: returned in horse ambulance* **3/1**[2]

5m 8.5s (-0.30) **Going Correction** -0.225s/f (Good) **6** Ran SP% **115.8**
Speed ratings (Par 109): **91,89,85,84,79**
toteswingers 1&2 £0.00, 1&3 £0.00, 2&3 £5.50 CSF £54.41 TOTE £5.20: £1.80, £7.00; EX 67.50 Trifecta £193.30 Pool: £757.96 - 2.94 winning units..
Owner Anthony Honeyball Racing Club Ltd **Bred** Mrs Nerys Dutfield **Trained** Mosterton, Dorset

FOCUS
A modest handicap. A step up from the winner for the return to a longer trip.

1046 BETFRED MOBILE LOTTO SUMMER HURDLE (H'CAP) (LISTED RACE) (8 hdls) 2m 1f
2:55 (2:55) (Class 1) 4-Y-0+

£19,932 (£7,479; £3,745; £1,865; £938; £469)

Form RPR
111- **1** **Sea Lord (IRE)**[27] 812 6-11-1 **133**................................... DenisO'Regan 143+
(John Ferguson) *trckd ldrs gng wl: j. fluently: led after 3 out and sn clr w runner-up: rdn 2 out: fnd plenty fr last* **9/2**[1]
/11- **2** *1 ½* **Coffee (IRE)**[42] 673 6-10-10 **128**.. APMcCoy 136
(Jonjo O'Neill) *trckd ldrs: effrt in 2nd after 3 out: drew clr w wnr home turn: drvn whn outj. fnl two: nt qckn fr last but remained clr of rest* **9/2**[1]
425/ **3** *5* **Roman Flight (IRE)**[14] 5013 5-10-3 **121**........................(v) AidanColeman 124
(David O'Meara) *settled towards rr: effrt after 3 out: wnt 10 l 3rd next: rdn and styd on wl after but nvr looked like catching ldrs* **10/1**
1/3- **4** *9* **The Cockney Mackem (IRE)**[65] 337 7-10-7 **125** SamTwiston-Davies 120
(Nigel Twiston-Davies) *towards rr: drvn and plenty to do 3 out: styd on to pass tiring rivals fr next: nvr nr principals* **16/1**
136/ **5** *1* **Zarzal (IRE)**[98] 5280 5-10-8 **129**.................................... AdamWedge(3) 123
(Evan Williams) *bhd: mstke 2nd: passed btn horses fr 2 out: nvr a factor* **16/1**
121- **6** *nk* **Tom Wade (IRE)**[20] 850 6-9-9 **118**....................................(t) BenPoste(5) 112
(Shaun Harris) *midfield: 5th and rdn and outpcd home turn: kpt on same pce after* **22/1**
/10- **7** *2 ½* **Australia Day (IRE)**[15] 673 10-11-8 **140**........................ LiamTreadwell 132
(Paul Webber) *taken down early: sn led at fast pce: rdn and hdd after 3 out: dropped out steadily bef next* **14/1**
5/3- **8** *10* **Local Hero (GER)**[70] 216 6-11-5 **144**...............................(p) PaulBohan(7) 129
(Steve Gollings) *towards rr: drvn 5th: struggling after* **7/1**[2]
110/ **9** *4 ½* **Hi Dancer**[22] 2496 10-10-12 **130**.. TomO'Brien 109
(Ben Haslam) *towards rr: rdn 3 out: struggling after* **50/1**
114- **10** *9* **Baccalaureate (FR)**[20] 850 7-10-6 **129**.................. JonathanEngland(5) 99
(Sue Smith) *rdn 3rd: pressed ldr tl bef 3 out: dropped out rapidly* **20/1**
4/1- **11** *29* **Barizan (IRE)**[70] 216 7-11-6 **138**...............................(bt) PaulMoloney 82
(Evan Williams) *hmpd bnd after 1st: prom: rdn bef 4th: lost pl qckly after 3 out: t.o and eased next* **8/1**[3]
014/ **12** *17* **War Singer (USA)**[35] 2179 6-10-6 **124**..........................(t) TomScudamore 53
(David Pipe) *midfield: rdn and wknd 3 out: t.o and eased bef next* **8/1**[3]
/11- **F** **Tzora**[25] 831 8-11-4 **136**... NickScholfield 121
(Martin Hill) *hld up last tl 3 out: stdy prog to midfield between last two: no ch w ldrs whn fell heavily last* **12/1**
5/0- **B** **Street Entertainer (IRE)**[36] 216 6-10-11 **129**.............(bt) ConorO'Farrell 114
(David Pipe) *chsd ldrs: rdn 3 out: flattered briefly in 5 l 3rd home turn: sn wknd: wl bhd whn b.d last* **9/1**

3m 58.0s (-8.70) **Going Correction** -0.225s/f (Good) **14** Ran SP% **127.4**
Speed ratings (Par 111): **111,110,107,103,103 103,101,97,95,90 77,69, ,**
toteswingers 1&2 £6.20, 1&3 £46.80, 2&3 £34.10 CSF £25.85 CT £203.64 TOTE £4.90: £2.20, £1.50, £3.80; EX 30.70 Trifecta £356.80 Pool: £1280.61 - 2.69 winning units..
Owner Bloomfields **Bred** Darley **Trained** Cowlinge, Suffolk

FOCUS
A competitive handicap, but the first pair dominated from some way out. Biggish steps up from the progressive first two, and the form looks solid.

1047 BETFRED SUMMER PLATE (HANDICAP CHASE) (LISTED RACE) (13 fncs 1 omitted) 2m 6f 110y
3:30 (3:31) (Class 1) 4-Y-0+

£28,475 (£10,685; £5,350; £2,665; £1,340; £670)

Form RPR
/F0- **1** **Bobowen (IRE)**[17] 877 7-10-6 **133**............................ SamTwiston-Davies 145+
(Dr Richard Newland) *settled in midfield: 4th and effrt home turn: storming run to ld bef last: easily burst clr* **8/1**
/22- **2** *9* **Woolcombe Folly (IRE)**[62] 392 10-11-7 **153**................ HarryDerham(5) 158
(Paul Nicholls) *hld up: stdy hdwy 10th: 6th st: rdn and kpt on wl fr 3 out: snatched 2nd but no ch w easy wnr* **11/1**
001- **3** *¾* **Finger Onthe Pulse (IRE)**[18] 859 12-9-13 **131**.....(t) MauriceLinehan(5) 134
(Jonjo O'Neill) *travelled v strly on heels of ldrs: led gng wl 3 out: drvn after next: hdd bef last: nt qckn and lost 2nd cl home* **25/1**
611- **4** *2* **Dineur (FR)**[6] 974 7-10-3 **130** 5ex.................................. DonalDevereux 133
(Peter Bowen) *chsd ldrs: 5th and rdn home turn: kpt on gamely but no real imp fr 2 out* **6/1**[2]
1/1- **5** *5* **Bocciani (GER)**[71] 204 8-11-2 **143**..................................(p) AidanColeman 140
(Brian Ellison) *nvr bttr than midfield: drvn bef 3 out: kpt on steadily but nvr looked like threatening* **14/1**
/34- **6** *6* **Donnas Palm (IRE)**[30] 780 9-9-12 **128**......................(b) MichaelByrne(3) 120
(Tim Vaughan) *midfield: drvn 10th: plugged on and no ch w ldrs after* **22/1**
133/ **7** *¾* **King's Legacy (IRE)**[75] 9-10-2 **129**...................................... DavidBass 121
(Lawney Hill) *smetimes j.rt: bhd: drvn and sme prog bef 3 out: nvr rchd ldrs: j.rt last* **12/1**
311- **8** *1* **Paddy The Hare (IRE)**[13] 900 8-10-5 **132**.......................(p) TomO'Brien 124
(Dr Richard Newland) *led at str pce: j. slowly 9th: rdn and hdd 3 out: sn btn* **5/1**[1]
/32- **9** *1 ¼* **Buck Mulligan**[41] 680 8-10-5 **135**.................................. AdamWedge(3) 126
(Evan Williams) *2nd or 3rd tl w ldr briefly 11th: rdn and lost pl bef next* **12/1**
1U3- **10** *4 ½* **Gentleman Anshan (IRE)**[13] 900 9-10-2 **134**.................... BenPoste(5) 119
(Rosemary Gasson) *taken down early: midfield: rdn 10th: sn btn* **25/1**
510- **11** *1* **Problema Tic (FR)**[20] 851 7-10-12 **139**....................(bt) TomScudamore 123
(David Pipe) *prom tl 4th: dropping to rr and struggling 7th: no ch after* **18/1**
0/6- **12** *5* **Pineau De Re (FR)**[20] 851 10-10-10 **137**.................... RichardJohnson 116
(Dr Richard Newland) *prom tl rdn and wknd bef 3 out* **7/1**[3]
1P5/ **13** *7* **Viva Colonia (IRE)**[5] 5139 8-10-13 **140**.................................. NoelFehily 113
(Brian Ellison) *hld up last tl 1/2-way: effrt 10th: chsd ldrs in 7th bef 3 out: rdn and sn btn* **20/1**
1F4/ **14** *¾* **Royale's Charter**[205] 3282 7-10-8 **135**.............................. NickScholfield 108
(Nick Williams) *nt fluent 5th and 6th and rdn: towards rr and nvr looked to be gng wl enough: struggling fr 10th* **16/1**
0/4- **F** **Galaxy Rock (IRE)**[20] 851 9-10-6 **133**................................(b) APMcCoy
(Jonjo O'Neill) *fell 1st: fatally injured* **5/1**[1]
/14- **P** **Grey Soldier (IRE)**[27] 798 8-10-0 **127** oh2......................(t) PaulMoloney
(Sophie Leech) *last and struggling at 8th: t.o whn climbed over 11th: p.u next* **50/1**

5m 16.2s (-29.80) **Going Correction** -0.95s/f (Hard) **16** Ran SP% **131.5**
Speed ratings (Par 111): **113,109,109,108,107 105,104,104,104,102 102,100,97,97,**
toteswingers 1&2 £63.80, 1&3 £182.50, 2&3 £300.30 CSF £93.85 CT £2165.05 TOTE £9.90: £3.10, £4.10, £4.00, £2.10; EX 144.40 Trifecta £4661.30 Pool: £57,490.21 - 9.25 winning units..
Owner Jim Stewart **Bred** Burgage Stud **Trained** Claines, Worcs

FOCUS
The first fence in the back straight was bypassed on the second circuit. This decent handicap was turned into a procession by the winner. He rates a small personal best in a typically solid renewal.

1048 B EYRE & SON LTD FORD NOVICES' HURDLE (8 hdls) 2m 1f
4:05 (4:06) (Class 4) 4-Y-0+ **£3,898** (£1,144; £572; £286)

Form RPR
0/2- **1** **Mighty Snazy**[20] 849 9-10-12 105.................................. RichardJohnson 108+
(Tim Vaughan) *settled in last pair: pushed along after 3 out: effrt on outer to ld wl bef 2 out where 4 l clr: idling in front but nvr looked in any danger* **4/1**[3]
221- **2** *6* **Engai (GER)**[10] 948 7-11-5 110...................................... TomScudamore 110
(David Bridgwater) *2nd tl lft in ld 4th: rejnd 3 out tl rdn and hdd wl bef next: sn btn: chsd wnr vainly fr 2 out* **7/4**[2]
/21- **3** *4 ½* **Separate Shadows (FR)**[39] 716 5-11-5 112.......................... NoelFehily 109
(Donald McCain) *led but kpt jumping v slowly and awkwardly: rousted bef 3rd: wnt rt next and hdd: rejnd ldr 3 out tl wl bef next: lost 2nd 2 out and fin v tamely* **11/8**[1]
513- **4** *18* **Super Collider**[27] 812 6-11-9 116...........................(bt) JamesCorbett(10) 104
(Susan Corbett) *in last pair: rdn and no reponse 3 out: sn wl bhd* **8/1**

4m 11.4s (4.70) **Going Correction** -0.225s/f (Good) **4** Ran SP% **109.6**
Speed ratings (Par 105): **79,76,74,65**
CSF £11.48 TOTE £4.10; EX 10.60 Trifecta £32.10 Pool: £518.83 - 12.10 winning units..
Owner T Vaughan **Bred** Helshaw Grange Farms Ltd **Trained** Aberthin, Vale of Glamorgan

FOCUS
A modest novice hurdle which was steadily run, and the form is suspect.

1049 FUSSEY ENGINEERING AND FUSSEY PILING NOVICES' H'CAP CHASE (14 fncs) 2m 6f 110y
4:40 (4:42) (Class 3) (0-125,125) 4-Y-0+ **£6,498** (£1,908; £954; £477)

Form RPR
/35- **1** **General Miller**[29] 787 8-11-12 **125**......................................(b) DavidBass 137+
(Nicky Henderson) *mde all: fiddled 9th but otherwise j. soundly: 5 l clr and drvn fr 3 out: a in command but lazy and kpt rt up to work* **8/1**
/41- **2** *6* **Roger Beantown (IRE)**[27] 806 8-11-12 **125**................... NickScholfield 132
(Paul Nicholls) *cl up: mstke 6th: wnt 2nd at 11th: rdn bef next: one pce and nvr win 5 l of wnr after* **3/1**[2]
U6P/ **3** *7* **Tough Talkin Man (IRE)**[126] 4782 9-10-0 **99**..............(p) DonalDevereux 100
(Peter Bowen) *nt fluent 3rd: chsd wnr tl 5th and again 7th tl rdn 11th: nt qckn and wl hld after* **3/1**[2]
/12- **4** *18* **My Mate Vinnie (IRE)**[39] 713 6-10-13 **112**........................(t) APMcCoy 99
(Jonjo O'Neill) *t.k.h: in last pair: rdn 10th: struggling fr next* **9/4**[1]
1/4- **P** **Fearless Leader**[27] 806 6-10-7 **106**.............................. TomScudamore
(David Bridgwater) *j. slowly 4th and rdn: last and drvn 8th: t.o 11th: fence bhd whn p.u 2 out* **4/1**[3]

5m 21.9s (-24.10) **Going Correction** -0.95s/f (Hard) **5** Ran SP% **111.9**
Speed ratings (Par 107): **103,100,98,92,**
CSF £31.84 TOTE £8.40: £3.40, £1.50; EX 30.80 Trifecta £103.30 Pool: £555.56 - 4.02 winning units..
Owner W H Ponsonby **Bred** N Shutts **Trained** Upper Lambourn, Berks

FOCUS
Not a bad novice handicap and the time stands up well compared with the other handicap. A big chase best from the winner.

1050 BETFRED SUPER SUNDAY BINGO H'CAP CHASE (12 fncs) 2m 2f
5:15 (5:15) (Class 4) (0-120,120) 4-Y-0+ **£4,548** (£1,335; £667; £333)

Form RPR
165- **1** **Dark Energy**[25] 830 9-11-5 **113**...(t) AlainCawley 125+
(Fergal O'Brien) *chsd clr ldng trio: effrt after 9th: hmpd bef next: swtchd outside 2 out: drvn ahd last: r.o gamely to assert fnl 100yds* **16/1**
536- **2** *½* **Skint**[17] 877 7-11-9 **117**.. AidanColeman 126
(Ali Brewer) *hld up: rdn to go 3rd at 9th: led next: 2 l clr 2 out: drvn and hdd last: outbattled fnl 100yds* **7/4**[1]
3- **3** *8* **Another Flutter (IRE)**[20] 853 9-11-0 **108**............................(p) APMcCoy 111
(Matt Sheppard) *settled in 2nd: blnd 6th: drvn to ld bef 3 out where hdd and mstke: nt qckn fr next* **11/4**[2]

0/5- **4** *5* **Milgen Bay**[20] 853 7-11-4 **112**........(p) LeightonAspell 109
(Oliver Sherwood) *chsd ldrs: pushed along at 5th: drvn whn hit 3 out: one pce and wl hld after* **14/1**

401- **5** *9* **Mister Wiseman**[13] 898 11-10-2 **96** oh7 ow2........(bt) TomScudamore 86
(Nigel Hawke) *led and j.w: rdn and hdd bef 3 out: sn wknd: eased last* **7/1**

113/ **6** *77* **Green To Gold (IRE)**[9] 5250 8-11-12 **120**........(b) PaulMoloney 40
(Don Cantillon) *hit 2nd: in last pair: rdn 7th: wl bhd after: hopelessly t.o and eased fr 3 out* **3/1**[3]

2PP- **P** **Autumn Spirit**[24] 844 9-10-7 **101**........(tp) CharliePoste
(Robin Dickin) *prom: 2nd at 8th: stopped to nil after next: sn bdly t.o: p.u last* **20/1**

4m 16.3s (-18.70) **Going Correction** -0.95s/f (Hard) **7** Ran SP% **117.8**
Speed ratings (Par 105): **103,102,99,97,93 58,**
toteswingers 1&2 £8.70, 1&3 £3.70, 2&3 £3.40 CSF £48.44 TOTE £19.60: £6.40, £1.40; EX 51.00 Trifecta £324.20 Pool: £688.95 - 1.59 winning units..
Owner The Yes No Wait Sorries **Bred** Bearstone Stud **Trained** Coln St. Dennis, Gloucs

FOCUS
The winner was better than the bare result and is rated in line with his best hurdle form.
T/Jkpt: Not won. T/Plt: £4713.90 to a £1 stake. Pool of £80,395.62 - 12.45 winning tickets.
T/Qpdt: £97.50 to a £1 stake. Pool of £7114.40 - 53.95 winning tickets. IM

994 NEWTON ABBOT (L-H)
Sunday, July 21

OFFICIAL GOING: Good to firm (good in places; 8.0)
Wind: fresh across Weather: sunny

1051 SIKYMSA BLOODSTOCK H'CAP HURDLE (12 hdls) 3m 3f
2:20 (2:22) (Class 5) (0-95,95) 4-Y-0+ **£3,119** (£915; £457; £228)

Form RPR

/02- **1** **Dreamsoftheatre (IRE)**[19] 860 5-11-7 95........(t) MauriceLinehan(5) 109+
(Jonjo O'Neill) *in tch: pckd 7th: trckd ldr after 3 out: led 2 out: sn in command: pushed out* **9/2**[2]

5/0- **2** *8* **Southway Queen**[50] 590 9-10-6 82........(tp) NathanAdams(7) 89
(Sue Gardner) *in tch: trckd ldr 7th: led 3 out: sn rdn: hdd bef next: styd on same pce* **12/1**

3/0- **3** *5* **Lost Arca (FR)**[38] 730 7-10-5 79........ EdCookson(5) 81
(Robin Mathew) *hld up: hdwy on inner to trck ldrs after 4th: bk in last trio 6th: hdwy 9th: rdn to chse ldng pair after 3 out: styd on same pce* **8/1**[3]

004- **4** *8* **Jewellery (IRE)**[26] 829 6-11-0 83........(b[1]) JamieMoore 78
(Kevin Bishop) *trckd ldrs: rdn after 8th: sn bhd: styd on again after 3 out but no ch* **8/1**[3]

31P/ **5** *7* **Changing Lanes**[230] 2829 10-11-12 95........(p) TomScudamore 84
(David Rees) *disp ld tl outrt ldr 7th: rdn and hdd 3 out: sn hld: wknd next* **9/1**

340/ **6** *11* **Magical Island**[88] 5505 10-10-4 73........(bt) RyanMahon 52
(Sarah Kerswell) *disp tl 7th: drvn after next: bhd 9th: no ch after* **20/1**

/05- **7** *3 ½* **No Woman No Cry**[13] 925 8-11-6 89........(bt) JoeTizzard 65
(Colin Tizzard) *trcking ldrs whn nt fluent and lost pl 4th: bk trcking ldrs 8th: sn drvn: wknd bef 2 out* **9/2**[2]

/61- **8** *64* **Millie O'Brien**[54] 522 5-10-9 78........ RichardJohnson
(Philip Hobbs) *trckd ldrs: squeezed up 1st: rdn whn awkward 9th: wknd after 3 out: bhd whn blnd last: t.o* **4/1**[1]

1/0- **P** **Bollywood (IRE)**[5] 860 10-10-6 82........(t) MrSHanson(7)
(Alison Batchelor) *struggling 6th: a bhd: t.o whn p.u bef 9th* **40/1**

03P- **P** **The Wee Midget**[11] 942 8-11-6 92........(b) MichealNolan(3)
(Arthur Whiting) *disp ld tl 6th: sn rdn along: wknd after 8th: p.u bef next* **9/1**

6m 29.7s (-11.30) **Going Correction** -0.275s/f (Good) **10** Ran SP% **113.5**
Speed ratings (Par 103): **105,102,101,98,96 93,92,73, ,**
toteswingers 1&2 £0.00, 2&3 £24.10, 1&3 £0.00 CSF £54.71 CT £416.52 TOTE £6.00: £2.30, £4.00, £3.60; EX 71.80 Trifecta £444.40 Part won. Pool: £529.59 - 0.44 winning units..
Owner John P McManus **Bred** Kieran Gleeson **Trained** Cheltenham, Gloucs

FOCUS
Moderate form.

1052 PACKEXE MAIDEN HURDLE (10 hdls) 2m 6f
2:50 (2:50) (Class 4) 4-Y-0+ **£4,061** (£1,192; £596; £298)

Form RPR

2- **1** **Kilbree Kid (IRE)**[26] 828 6-11-0 0........ PaddyBrennan 116+
(Tom George) *trckd ldrs: disp ld fr 4th tl led after 6th: jnd next: rdn bef 2 out: narrow advantage whn edgd rt bef last: styd on wl to assert* **7/4**[1]

0PP/ **2** *3* **Danandy (IRE)**[165] 4067 6-11-0 109........ RichardJohnson 114+
(Philip Hobbs) *in tch: hdwy to dispute ld 7th: rdn after 3 out: sltly hmpd and hdd bef last: hld whn swtchd lft sn after* **7/2**[3]

2U2- **3** *17* **Somchine**[40] 716 5-11-0 110........ AndrewThornton 100
(Seamus Mullins) *racd keenly: hld up: hdwy after 6th: rdn into 3rd after 3 out but no ch w ldng pair: styd on same pce* **11/4**[2]

/03- **4** *6* **Multitude Of Sins**[13] 920 6-11-0 0........ JoeTizzard 92
(Colin Tizzard) *racd keenly: hld up: hdwy whn nt fluent 5th: trckd ldrs next: rdn after 3 out: wknd bef next* **7/1**

000/ **5** *9* **Mister Moonax (IRE)**[49] 13-10-11 0........(tp) GilesHawkins(3) 84
(Chris Down) *led after 2nd: jnd 4th: reminder: rdn and hdd bef 7th: sn btn* **50/1**

34- **6** *2* **Renegotiate**[12] 928 4-10-11 0........(bt[1]) SamTwiston-Davies 79
(Dr Richard Newland) *hld up: rdn bef 7th: no imp: wknd after 3 out* **12/1**

5- **7** *6* **Alderbrook Lad (IRE)**[13] 920 7-10-11 0........(t) MichaelByrne(3) 77
(Neil Mulholland) *trckd ldrs: rdn after 3 out: wknd bef next* **16/1**

P- **P** **It'syourdeal (IRE)**[13] 922 8-10-0 0........ ThomasCheesman(7)
(Nick Ayliffe) *led tl after 2nd: chsd ldrs: rdn after 5th: sn bhd: t.o 7th: p.u bef 3 out* **200/1**

P **Shock N Freaney (IRE)**[50] 6-11-0 0........(p) CharliePoste
(Anthony Middleton) *in tch: rdn after 6th: sn bhd: t.o whn p.u bef 2 out* **50/1**

5m 12.3s (-7.90) **Going Correction** -0.275s/f (Good)
WFA 4 from 5yo+ 16lb **9** Ran SP% **115.7**
Speed ratings (Par 105): **103,101,95,93,90 89,87, ,**
toteswingers 1&2 £5.60, 2&3 £2.10, 1&3 £3.70 CSF £8.39 TOTE £2.80: £1.50, £1.30, £1.20; EX 12.30 Trifecta £37.90 Pool: £1168.04 - 23.09 winning units..
Owner Five Valleys Racing Partnership **Bred** John O'Mahony **Trained** Slad, Gloucs
■ Stewards' Enquiry : Paddy Brennan two-day ban: careless riding (Aug 4,13)

FOCUS
The front pair drew clear in a maiden hurdle lacking depth.

1053 SIS INTERNATIONAL NOVICES' CHASE (13 fncs) 2m 110y
3:20 (3:20) (Class 4) 4-Y-0+ **£4,873** (£1,431; £715; £357)

Form RPR

B01- **1** **Changing The Guard**[26] 830 7-11-8 134........(t) SamTwiston-Davies 138+
(Dr Richard Newland) *chsd ldr: mstke 4th: led bef 4 out: drew wl clr after 3 out: easily* **5/4**[1]

/23- **2** *35* **Highway Code (USA)**[19] 859 7-11-1 124........ RichardJohnson 103+
(Richard Lee) *set quick pce: rchd for 3rd: blnd 7th: hdd bef 4 out: sn rdn and hld: wknd between last 2* **7/4**[2]

40P/ **3** *17* **Featherintheattic (IRE)**[101] 5257 8-11-1 0........(p) JasonMaguire 79
(Warren Greatrex) *chsd clr ldng pair: pushed along fr 7th: nvr any imp on ldrs: wknd after 3 out: t.o* **3/1**[3]

3F0- **4** *4* **Special Boru (IRE)**[26] 828 7-11-1 0........(t) RyanMahon 74
(Sarah Kerswell) *a detached in last pair: did cl on remote 3rd fr 3 out but nvr gng to catch him: t.o* **50/1**

400- **5** *20* **Sportsreport (IRE)**[13] 920 5-11-1 0........ AndrewThornton 64
(Seamus Mullins) *j. v big first circ: a detached: t.o* **28/1**

/P0- **P** **Comical Red**[26] 829 5-10-8 0........ JakeHodson(7)
(Mark Gillard) *nt fluent: immediately t.o: wnt bdly rt and blnd 5th: p.u bef next* **100/1**

3m 56.9s (-9.60) **Going Correction** -0.325s/f (Good) **6** Ran SP% **112.2**
Speed ratings (Par 105): **109,92,84,82,73**
toteswingers 1&2 £1.02, 2&3 £1.20, 1&3 £1.10 CSF £3.99 TOTE £2.00: £1.10, £1.40; EX 3.40 Trifecta £5.10 Pool: £1144.48 - 165.89 winning units..
Owner BetterTipster.co.uk **Bred** R A Bonnycastle And Marston Stud **Trained** Claines, Worcs

FOCUS
The big two in the market went tearing off here and they held a clear advantage throughout.

1054 PACKEXE SHARPSWRAP H'CAP HURDLE (9 hdls) 2m 3f
3:50 (3:50) (Class 3) (0-135,131) 4-Y-0**£7**,**121** (£2,103; £1,051; £526; £263)

Form RPR

/42- **1** **Rum And Butter (IRE)**[40] 719 5-10-8 **113**........(p) MauriceLinehan 126+
(Jonjo O'Neill) *in tch: nt fluent 1st: jnd ldr after 3 out: w.w travelling best: awkward 2 out: led bef last: drifted lft but qcknd sharply clr: readily* **5/2**[1]

200/ **2** *5* **Hunting Tower**[232] 2775 9-11-5 **127**........(t) MichaelByrne(3) 130
(Tim Vaughan) *trckd ldr: led 3 out: sn rdn: hdd bef last: kpt on but nt gng pce of wnr* **7/1**

/12- **3** *1 ¼* **Bright Abbey**[25] 843 5-10-13 **118**........ RichardJohnson 120
(Philip Hobbs) *trckd ldr tl rdn after 3 out: kpt on but nt gng pce to chal* **4/1**[2]

222- **4** *2 ½* **Descaro (USA)**[4] 1009 7-10-8 **120**........(p) CiaranMckee(7) 120
(John O'Shea) *led tl 3 out: sn rdn and hld: kpt on same pce fr next to regain 4th bef last* **9/1**

213- **5** *5* **Castlemorris King**[7] 973 5-10-13 **123**........ HarryDerham(5) 118
(Brian Barr) *in tch: cl up 4th after 3 out: sn rdn: nt gng pce to chal: fading whn lost 4th bef last* **4/1**[2]

/14- **6** *6* **Waterunder (IRE)**[31] 782 6-11-12 **131**........(t) TomScudamore 121
(David Pipe) *hld up but wl in tch: rdn after 3 out: nvr gng pce to get involved: wknd 2 out* **9/2**[3]

356- **7** *1* **Teshali (IRE)**[7] 973 7-10-11 **116**........ SamTwiston-Davies 105
(Anthony Middleton) *hld up but wl in tch: reminders after 5th: hdwy 6th: rdn after 3 out: wknd bef 2 out* **16/1**

4m 20.9s (-9.10) **Going Correction** -0.275s/f (Good) **7** Ran SP% **115.1**
Speed ratings (Par 107): **108,105,105,104,102 99,99**
toteswingers 1&2 £5.80, 2&3 £0.00, 1&3 £8.80 CSF £20.32 CT £67.70 TOTE £2.80: £1.40, £5.80; EX 31.50 Trifecta £107.50 Pool: £585.14 - 4.08 winning units..
Owner John P McManus **Bred** William Hubbert **Trained** Cheltenham, Gloucs

FOCUS
This had looked quite open, but the winner did it readily.

1055 SIS LIVE H'CAP CHASE (20 fncs) 3m 2f 110y
4:20 (4:20) (Class 4) (0-110,110) 4-Y-0+ **£4,873** (£1,431; £715; £357)

Form RPR

410- **1** **Lord Lescribaa (FR)**[31] 778 10-10-12 **96**........(tp) RichardJohnson 106
(Philip Hobbs) *trckd ldrs: led 11th: rdn after 4 out: styd on wl: drvn out* **15/2**

544- **2** *2 ¾* **Aikideau (FR)**[31] 778 6-11-7 **110**........(b) HarryDerham(5) 118
(Paul Nicholls) *hld up in mid-div: stdy prog fr 10th: trcking ldrs whn mstke 13th: wnt 2nd after 14th: rdn after 3 out: flattered briefly jst bef last: a being hld run-in* **11/4**[1]

/42- **3** *25* **Always Bold (IRE)**[4] 1010 8-11-0 **98**........(v) IanPopham 85
(Martin Keighley) *chsd ldrs: drvn along fr 10th: chsd ldng pair in cl enough 3rd after 14th: wknd 3 out: t.o* **7/2**[2]

453- **4** *¾* **Lady Myfanwy**[7] 972 12-10-8 **99**........ MissHLewis(7) 83
(Adrian Wintle) *mid-div: rdn fr 14th: plugged on but nvr any danger to ldrs: t.o* **20/1**

2/2- **P** **Inishrush (IRE)**[46] 636 12-11-1 **106**........(tp) MrWPotter(7)
(Bill Turner) *led tl 11th: sn pushed along: chsd ldrs tl wknd appr 14th: p.u after 15th: lame* **7/1**

/00- **P** **Pharaon De Touzaine (FR)**[11] 946 10-10-4 **95**........ CiaranMckee(7)
(John O'Shea) *nvr travelling in last: tailing off whn p.u after 6th: b.b.vs* **50/1**

3/0- **P** **Sandynow (IRE)**[31] 778 8-11-3 **101**........(v[1]) JamieMoore
(Peter Bowen) *chsd ldrs: chsd wnr 10th tl after 14th: wknd fr next: bhd whn blnd bdly 4 out: sn p.u* **9/2**[3]

1/P- **P** **Minella Ranger (IRE)**[46] 636 7-10-13 **97**........ PaddyBrennan
(Paul Henderson) *nvr travelling in rr: t.o whn p.u bef 4 out* **14/1**

P/P- **P** **Mission Complete (IRE)**[67] 321 7-11-5 **108**........(v[1]) MauriceLinehan(5)
(Jonjo O'Neill) *nvr travelling in rr: lost tch 10th: t.o whn p.u bef 14th* **9/1**

/PP- **P** **Supralunary**[12] 930 7-9-9 **84** oh25........(tp) EdCookson(5)
(Robin Mathew) *prom tl 5th: chsd ldrs tl 13th: sn wknd: t.o whn p.u after 4 out* **66/1**

6m 30.6s (-14.00) **Going Correction** -0.325s/f (Good) **10** Ran SP% **116.2**
Speed ratings (Par 105): **107,106,98,98, , , , ,**
toteswingers 1&2 £5.80, 2&3 £3.30, 1&3 £5.60 CSF £29.09 CT £86.27 TOTE £10.00: £2.60, £1.10, £2.30; EX 37.60 Trifecta £141.10 Pool: £576.12 - 3.06 winning units..
Owner Mrs S L Hobbs **Bred** Mme Louis Lafitte **Trained** Withycombe, Somerset

FOCUS
Less than half of the field finished in what had looked an open handicap chase, with the front pair pulling right away.

1056 AT THE RACES VIRGIN 534 MAIDEN OPEN NATIONAL HUNT FLAT RACE 2m 1f
4:50 (4:50) (Class 5) 4-6-Y-O **£2,309** (£673; £336)

Form RPR
22- **1** **Dardanella**[25] [841] 6-10-9 0 TomScudamore 95+
(Richard Lee) *trckd ldr: rdn to ld jst over 2f out: styd on: rdn out* **5/4**[1]
33- **2** *3 ¼* **Laurens Ruby (IRE)**[25] [842] 4-10-7 0 DPFahy 90
(John Flint) *led after 1f: rdn to qckn pce over 3f out: hdd jst over 2f out: kpt on same pce* **7/2**[2]
4/ **3** *2 ¼* **State Department**[619] [2434] 6-11-2 0 RichardJohnson 97
(Philip Hobbs) *hld up in tch: rdn whn outpcd over 3f out: styd on steadily fnl 2f: wnt 3rd over 1f out: nt quite rchd ldrs* **7/2**[2]
6- **4** *17* **Deer Park**[19] [862] 6-10-11 0 EDLinehan(5) 81
(Brendan Powell) *trckd ldrs: rdn whn outpcd by ldng pair over 3f out: wknd over 1f out* **16/1**
5 *4 ½* **Follow The Tracks (IRE)**[106] 5-10-11 0 KillianMoore(5) 75
(Brian Barr) *led for 1f: trckd ldrs tl rdn 5f out: sn wknd* **25/1**
6 *24* **Petit Hibou** 5-11-2 0 SamTwiston-Davies 51
(Sean Curran) *in tch: rdn 5f out: wknd 3f out: t.o* **16/1**
7 *1 ½* **Tanner Bet** 5-10-2 0 MrWPotter(7) 43
(Polly Gundry) *a in rr: t.o* **40/1**
8 *dist* **Pedrow (IRE)** 5-10-11 0 HarryDerham(5)
(Brian Barr) *hld up in tch: struggling over 6f out: wknd 3f out: t.o* **11/1**[3]

3m 59.7s (-0.40) **Going Correction** -0.275s/f (Good)
WFA 4 from 5yo+ 2lb **8** Ran SP% **115.3**
Speed ratings: **89,87,86,78,76 65,64,**
toteswingers 1&2 £2.00, 2&3 £1.40, 1&3 £1.50 CSF £5.79 TOTE £1.80: £1.10, £2.00, £1.10; EX 5.50 Trifecta £11.90 Pool: £615.95 - 38.81 winning units..
Owner Ray Bailey **Bred** Ray Bailey **Trained** Byton, H'fords

FOCUS
Only three mattered in the betting and the trio drew nicely clear of the remainder.

1057 RICHARD BURSTON'S STAG PARTY WEEKEND H'CAP CHASE (THE SUNDAY £5K BONUS RACE) (13 fncs) 2m 110y
5:20 (5:20) (Class 5) (0-100,96) 4-Y-O+ **£3,249** (£954; £477; £238)

Form RPR
P/1- **1** **Chilbury Hill (IRE)**[18] [873] 10-11-0 **87** (t) MichaelByrne(3) 106+
(Tim Vaughan) *trckd ldrs: pushed along after 7th: led 4 out: drew clr after 3 out: easily* **15/8**[1]
426- **2** *13* **Escardo (GER)**[28] [807] 10-11-2 **86** (p) TomScudamore 91
(David Bridgwater) *in last pair: stdy prog fr after 7th: rdn to chse wnr after 3 out: kpt on but no ch w easy wnr* **6/1**
U/2- **3** *4* **Brannoc (IRE)**[49] [602] 8-10-8 **78** (t) AndrewThornton 77
(Tony Newcombe) *trckd ldrs: pushed along after 8th: wnt 2nd after 4 out: rdn whn nt fluent next: wkng in 3rd whn wnt rt 2 out* **6/1**
2PP/ **4** *5* **Stafford Charlie**[18] [1790] 7-9-7 **70** oh1 CiaranMckee(7) 64
(John O'Shea) *hld up in last: nt fluent 1st: 5th whn stmbld 4 out: plugged on but nvr gng pce to get on terms* **12/1**
354- **5** *7* **The Fox's Decree**[14] [902] 9-11-12 **96** (bt[1]) IanPopham 82
(Martin Keighley) *chsd ldr: sn drvn along: lft in ld 8th: hdd 4 out: wknd next* **5/1**[3]
4B4/ **6** *¾* **Hazeldene**[70] 11-11-8 **95** JeremiahMcGrath(3) 80
(Martin Hill) *led at gd pce tl blnd bdly 8th: nt rcvr and sn btn* **3/1**[2]

4m 0.9s (-5.60) **Going Correction** -0.325s/f (Good) **6** Ran SP% **112.7**
Speed ratings (Par 103): **100,93,92,89,86 86**
toteswingers 1&2 £1.80, 2&3 £9.30, 1&3 £3.10 CSF £13.41 TOTE £1.80: £1.10, £4.50; EX 15.00 Trifecta £34.00 Pool: £971.04 - 21.37 winning units..
Owner B Jones & N Wright **Bred** Barry Murphy **Trained** Aberthin, Vale of Glamorgan

FOCUS
An uncompetitive chase.
T/Plt: £17.50 to a £1 stake. Pool of £63624.43 - 2648.86 winning tickets. T/Qpdt: £3.90 to a £1 stake. Pool of £4677.15 - 872.21 winning tickets. TM

971 STRATFORD (L-H)
Sunday, July 21

OFFICIAL GOING: Good to firm (good in places; watered)
Rails moved on to fresh ground and all bends split.
Wind: almost nil Weather: overcast but brightening; 19 degrees

1058 102 TOUCH FM (S) HURDLE (8 hdls) 2m 110y
2:30 (2:30) (Class 5) 4-6-Y-O **£1,949** (£572; £286; £143)

Form RPR
6/5- **1** **Quadriller (FR)**[28] [808] 6-11-0 104 (t) TomO'Brien 107+
(Philip Hobbs) *settled wl in tch: effrt 3 out: led next: sn in command: 5 l ahd last: rdn out* **11/4**[2]
/10- **2** *2* **The Bay Bandit**[19] [631] 6-11-5 0 NoelFehily 108
(Neil Mulholland) *nt fluent 2nd: in rr of bunch tl effrt 2 out: 5th st: cajoled to go 2nd bef last: kpt on one pce and a looked wl hld* **16/1**
240- **3** *11* **Persian Herald**[30] [788] 5-10-11 96 (v) JackQuinlan(3) 93
(Neil King) *led tl 2 out: sn rdn: lost two pls bef last where lft modest 3rd* **16/1**
5/F- **4** *½* **Rigid**[24] [505] 6-11-0 94 LeeEdwards 94
(Tony Carroll) *t.k.h towards rr: effrt 2 out: disp 2nd and flattered briefly bef last: sn drvn and no rspnse: lft modest 4th at last* **28/1**
/20- **5** *13* **Thegaygardener**[21] [850] 5-11-5 112 (t) PaulMoloney 88
(Evan Williams) *settled in 3rd: mstke 5th: shkn up next: wknd tamely after 3 out: heavily eased bef last* **7/4**[1]
00- **6** *21* **Pass Friend**[19] [857] 5-10-7 0 JamesDavies 55
(Martin Bosley) *plld hrd in rr: rdn and lost tch qckly 3 out: t.o* **100/1**
205/ **7** *11* **Third Half**[175] [3903] 4-11-3 0 (t) AidanColeman 56
(Tim Vaughan) *pressed ldr tl nt fluent 2 out: rdn and dropped out qckly: t.o and virtually p.u flat* **9/2**[3]
134- **U** **Wom**[12] [927] 5-10-9 100 (v) TrevorWhelan(5) 93
(Neil King) *chsd ldrs: effrt 2 out: sn rdn: wnt 8 l 3rd and nt looking keen bef last where mstke and uns rdr* **6/1**

3m 46.9s (-9.10) **Going Correction** -0.375s/f (Good)
WFA 4 from 5yo+ 15lb **8** Ran SP% **111.7**
Speed ratings: **106,105,99,99,93 83,78,**
toteswingers 1&2 £8.40, 1&3 £24.90, 2&3 £38.30 CSF £40.42 TOTE £4.70: £1.50, £2.80, £3.40; EX 49.50 Trifecta £321.80 Part won. Pool: £429.10 - 0.25 winning units..Quadriller was bought by Miss Michelle Ryan for 4,800gns
Owner P J Hobbs **Bred** Brian Moran **Trained** Withycombe, Somerset

FOCUS
A total of 3mm of water was added to the course on the morning of racing, augmenting 0.5mm of rain overnight. All bends were split and all rails were back on the inside to provide fresh ground. A stop-start gallop left most of the field bunched approaching two out in this seller.

1059 JACKIE EBSWORTH MEMORIAL NOVICES' HURDLE (THE SUNDAY £5K BONUS RACE) (8 hdls) 2m 110y
3:00 (3:01) (Class 4) 4-Y-O+ **£3,898** (£1,144; £572; £286)

Form RPR
0/1- **1** **Professeur Emery (FR)**[19] [856] 6-11-5 123 NoelFehily 119+
(Warren Greatrex) *racd freely and j. fluently: mde all and a gng best: 7 l clr last: hrd hld* **1/6**[1]
3- **2** *11* **Osorios Trial**[19] [857] 6-10-12 0 PaulMoloney 97
(Anthony Middleton) *t.k.h: last tl 4th: wnt 2nd 2 out: sn rdn: nvr any ch w effrtless wnr* **11/2**[2]
0- **3** *6* **Geordie Boy**[33] [758] 4-10-10 0 MarcGoldstein 87
(Sheena West) *hld up: in last whn nt fluent 4th: rdn to go 3rd after 2 out: v one pce and no imp on ldng pair after* **16/1**
0- **4** *11* **Chapelle du Roi (USA)**[19] [857] 4-10-10 0 TomO'Brien 76
(Robert Stephens) *j. stickily: chsd wnr tl rdn and mstke 2 out: sn struggling in 4th* **14/1**[3]
P **Highest Red**[632] 4-10-10 0 DavidBass
(Natalie Lloyd-Beavis) *t.k.h early: chsd ldrs tl j.rt 4th: last whn mstke 3 out: sn t.o: p.u last* **50/1**

3m 48.5s (-7.50) **Going Correction** -0.375s/f (Good)
WFA 4 from 5yo+ 15lb **5** Ran SP% **115.6**
Speed ratings (Par 105): **102,96,94,88,**
CSF £2.09 TOTE £1.10: £1.10, £1.30; EX 2.00 Trifecta £3.50 Pool: £1162.44 - 243.24 winning units..
Owner Gdm Partnership **Bred** E A R L Du Haras De Pierrepont **Trained** Upper Lambourn, Berks

FOCUS
The absence of Engai left this looking a paper-thin contest for the enhanced prize-money.

1060 102 TOUCH FM H'CAP CHASE (17 fncs) 2m 7f
3:30 (3:30) (Class 3) (0-125,125) 4-Y-O+ **£9,495** (£2,805; £1,402; £702; £351)

Form RPR
0P0- **1** **Mostly Bob (IRE)**[21] [851] 10-11-7 **123** (t) JamesBest(3) 130
(Sophie Leech) *sn led: hdd 5th: led again 7th: rdn bef 13th: v hrd pressed between last two: battled on gamely flat: all out* **16/1**
4/P- **2** *½* **Beggar's Velvet (IRE)**[25] [845] 7-11-5 **125** ConorShoemark(7) 132
(Fergal O'Brien) *nt fluent 2nd (water): hld up: trckd ldrs fr 8th: 5th 3 out: rdn to chal between last two: disp 2nd w ev ch at last: jst hld fnl 100yds* **16/1**
121- **3** *½* **To Live (FR)**[7] [972] 6-10-13 **112** 7ex APMcCoy 120
(Nick Gifford) *settled towards rr: hdwy to midfield whn blnd 10th (water): wnt 3rd at 13th and 2nd next: drvn fr 2 out: disp cl 2nd at last: nt qckn fnl 100yds* **1/1**[1]
5/2- **4** *3 ¾* **Font**[26] [832] 10-10-5 **104** (t) AidanColeman 107
(Lawney Hill) *sweating profusely: hld up in rr: stdy prog 14th: rdn to chse ldng trio bef last: kpt on steadily but no imp after* **14/1**
/54- **5** *6* **Strumble Head (IRE)**[45] [642] 8-10-13 **112** (v[1]) DonalDevereux 110
(Peter Bowen) *chsd ldrs: rdn 14th: no ex fr 2 out: wl hld 5th between last two* **8/1**[2]
/42- **6** *7* **Rockiteer (IRE)**[33] [757] 10-11-4 **120** (p) JakeGreenall(3) 111
(Henry Daly) *cl up: 4th and looked to be gng wl 14th: rdn next: little rspnse: 6th and wl btn between last two* **9/1**[3]
36P- **7** *13* **Double Chocolate**[13] [923] 10-10-9 **108** SeanQuinlan 88
(David Bridgwater) *mstke 1st: prom: 2nd at 14th tl rdn 3 out: lost pl qckly* **20/1**
642- **8** *29* **Captain Sully (IRE)**[19] [859] 8-11-0 **113** NickScholfield 67
(Jim Wilson) *hld up in rr: short-lived effrt to heels of main bunch 13th: sn wknd: t.o* **25/1**
250- **9** *19* **Dont Tell Sailor (IRE)**[12] [933] 7-10-7 **113** ConorRing(7) 50
(Jennie Candlish) *towards rr: j. slowly 7th: lost tch and blnd 11th: t.o after* **22/1**
P/1- **10** *7* **Power Pack Jack (IRE)**[31] [778] 10-10-8 **114** (v[1]) RyanHatch(7) 44
(Nigel Twiston-Davies) *immediately rdn and nvr wnt a yard: j. slowly: dropped himself bk to last at 8th and continued t.o: fin eventually* **10/1**
1/1- **11** *64* **Haar**[79] [96] 9-11-6 **119** (tp) MarkGrant
(Andy Turnell) *led 5th tl blnd 7th: nt fluent 9th: pressed ldr tl drvn 13th: lost pl rapidly next: t.o and eased after 2 out* **16/1**

5m 29.1s (-10.10) **Going Correction** -0.25s/f (Good) **11** Ran SP% **117.5**
Speed ratings (Par 107): **107,106,106,105,103 100,96,86,79,77 54**
toteswingers 1&2 £47.30, 1&3 £6.00, 2&3 £33.30 CSF £224.68 CT £493.39 TOTE £21.80: £5.30, £5.50, £1.10; EX 362.70 Trifecta £503.60 Pool: £1040.85 - 1.54 winning units..
Owner Bluebirds Racing & Partner **Bred** Mrs Mary Gallagher **Trained** Elton, Gloucs

FOCUS
Competitive for the grade, but the clutch of in-form horses had to give best to a competitor back on a really competitive mark. The pace was generous from flagfall.

1061 GRAMPY'S 65 AND WE'RE GOING RACING! NOVICES' H'CAP HURDLE (9 hdls) 2m 3f
4:00 (4:00) (Class 4) (0-105,105) 4-Y-O+ **£3,898** (£1,144; £572; £286)

Form RPR
/13- **1** **Strongly Suggested**[25] [846] 6-11-10 **103** (t) APMcCoy 114+
(Jonjo O'Neill) *led after 3rd: gng best whn j. slowly 2 out: 3 l clr st: rdn and wl in command whn mstke last* **6/4**[1]
221- **2** *4 ½* **Ullswater (IRE)**[58] [456] 5-11-7 **100** (t) NickScholfield 102
(Andy Turnell) *led tl after 3rd: mostly 2nd after: hit 6th: drvn and no imp fr 2 out* **9/4**[2]
0/6- **3** *1 ½* **Zafaraban (IRE)**[11] [808] 6-11-9 **102** LeeEdwards 102
(Tony Carroll) *rn in snatches: in rr and u.p bef 6th: clsd to 7 l 3rd and drvn after 2 out: no imp after* **25/1**
613- **4** *24* **Diamond Tammy (IRE)**[45] [648] 7-11-7 **103** (t) KielanWoods(3) 81
(Anthony Middleton) *several positions: effrt in 2nd briefly but rdn 3 out: 4th and fading after next* **7/1**[3]

214/ **5** 26 **Riddlestown (IRE)**[93] 5387 6-11-12 **105** HarrySkelton 60
(Caroline Fryer) *chsd ldrs: rdn and wknd 3 out: blnd next: t.o whn mstke last* **7/1**[3]
206- **6** 22 **Twyford**[26] 828 6-11-4 **97** TomCannon 32
(William Reed) *pressed ldr tl 3rd: nt fluent 5th: struggling 3 out: t.o after next* **12/1**
/6P- **P** **Cleeve Cloud (IRE)**[25] 844 7-10-4 **83** (p) LiamTreadwell
(Liam Grassick) *hit 1st: bhd: last and reminders 4th: t.o 6th: p.u 2 out* **22/1**

4m 24.5s (-7.00) **Going Correction** -0.375s/f (Good) 7 Ran SP% **111.7**
Speed ratings (Par 105): **99,97,96,86,75 66,**
toteswingers 1&2 £1.70, 1&3 £4.10, 2&3 £5.40 CSF £5.21 TOTE £2.50: £1.50, £1.60; EX 5.20 Trifecta £41.30 Pool: £2258.02 - 40.94 winning units..
Owner John P McManus **Bred** David Brace **Trained** Cheltenham, Gloucs

FOCUS
Very few ever got meaningfully involved in this ordinary novice handicap.

1062 102 TOUCH FM H'CAP HURDLE (11 hdls) 2m 6f 110y
4:30 (4:30) (Class 4) (0-115,115) 4-Y-0+ **£3,898** (£1,144; £572; £286)

Form RPR
/60- **1** **Ironical (IRE)**[40] 719 9-10-6 **95** (t) AidanColeman 100+
(Shaun Lycett) *settled in midfield: 5th after 3 out: effrt after next: chal on ins and outj. ldr last: sn rdn clr* **20/1**
212- **2** 3 ½ **Chilworth Screamer**[65] 353 5-11-0 **103** TomCannon 106
(Chris Gordon) *midfield: wnt 3rd bef 2 out: rdn to ld between last two: almost jnd whn landed awkwardly last: sn hdd and nt rcvr* **8/1**
31P- **3** 5 **City Press (IRE)**[13] 923 7-11-7 **115** (tp) GavinSheehan(5) 114
(Warren Greatrex) *settled in last pair: nt fluent 4th: shkn up 8th: last whn mstke 3 out and drvn: cajoled to make prog after 2 out: nvr looked like rching ldrs but snatched 3rd* **5/1**[3]
531- **4** nk **Sonofagun (FR)**[7] 966 7-11-2 **105** 7ex WillKennedy 102
(Ian Williams) *settled in 3rd: mostly 2nd fr 8th tl rdn to ld after 2 out: hdd between last two: wknd last: lost 3rd cl home* **6/4**[1]
060- **5** 33 **Bathwick Man**[18] 877 8-11-10 **113** (p) ConorO'Farrell 80
(David Pipe) *led: rdn and hdd after 2 out: fdd tamely and eased bef last* **9/2**[2]
0/2- **6** 9 **Sagredo (USA)**[14] 902 9-11-10 **113** (v) APMcCoy 72
(Jonjo O'Neill) *last pair: blnd bdly 2nd: mstke 7th: slt forward move whn hit 3 out: rdn and fnd nil after: eased and t.o bef last* **9/2**[2]
7 7 **Scenic Route (IRE)**[43] 7-11-6 **114** MrMWall(5) 67
(Giles Smyly) *j.rt and often violently so: mostly 2nd tl rapidly dropped bk to last 2 out: sn t.o* **16/1**

5m 16.3s (-11.80) **Going Correction** -0.375s/f (Good) 7 Ran SP% **114.8**
Speed ratings (Par 105): **105,103,102,101,90 87,84**
toteswingers 1&2 £19.80, 1&3 £12.10, 2&3 £4.50 CSF £160.14 TOTE £24.80: £5.70, £2.90; EX 203.90 Trifecta £539.30 Pool: £2019.05 - 2.80 winning units..
Owner Lady Blyth **Bred** Michael Whitty **Trained** Clapton-on-the-Hill, Gloucs

FOCUS
Five still holding a feasible chance on the turn in, but in the end a fairly clear-cut winner.

1063 102 TOUCH FM NOVICES' H'CAP CHASE (12 fncs) 2m 1f 110y
5:00 (5:00) (Class 4) (0-115,115) 4-Y-0+ **£4,548** (£1,335; £667; £333)

Form RPR
066- **1** **Tri Nations (UAE)**[14] 903 8-10-6 **95** (vt) PaulMoloney 105+
(Anthony Middleton) *hld up: nt fluent 5th (water): effrt gng wl 3 out: disp ld between last two: rdn to forge clr fr last* **10/1**
P4F- **2** 2 ¾ **Walden Prince (IRE)**[41] 687 6-10-11 **100** WayneHutchinson 107
(Tony Carroll) *hld up: effrt 3 out: rdn and w wnr between last two tl last: edgd lft and no ex flat* **4/1**[2]
124- **3** 9 **Surf And Turf (IRE)**[6] 999 7-11-12 **115** (p) APMcCoy 116
(Jonjo O'Neill) *often lacked fluency: sn 2nd: led after 6th: hit 9th: drvn next: hdd and fnd little between last two: eased whn btn flat* **10/11**[1]
5U2- **4** 21 **Ninfea (IRE)**[12] 931 5-11-3 **106** (p) TommyPhelan 86
(David Bridgwater) *led tl rdn and mstke 6th: remained prom but off bridle tl lost tch qckly 3 out* **9/2**[3]
200- **P** **Officially Modern (IRE)**[28] 806 6-10-11 **100** AlainCawley
(Fergal O'Brien) *3rd whn j. slowly 3rd: last next: tailing off whn p.u 7th* **15/2**

4m 5.5s (-1.60) **Going Correction** -0.25s/f (Good) 5 Ran SP% **111.4**
Speed ratings (Par 105): **93,91,87,78,**
CSF £46.71 TOTE £13.00: £4.50, £1.90; EX 48.90 Trifecta £177.80 Pool: £1289.78 - 5.43 winning units..
Owner Miss C Elks & Ms B Woodcock **Bred** Darley **Trained** Granborough, Bucks

FOCUS
A slow-motion finish despite the short trip and fast ground, and victory for the outsider of the quintet.

1064 102 TOUCH FM MARES' STANDARD OPEN NATIONAL HUNT FLAT RACE 2m 110y
5:30 (5:30) (Class 6) 4-6-Y-O **£1,949** (£572; £286; £143)

Form RPR
1 **Miss Sassypants** 4-10-3 0 KevinJones(7) 104+
(Seamus Mullins) *hld up: stdy prog 3f out: pushed into ld wl over 1f out: clr fnl f: styd on determinedly* **9/2**[3]
2- **2** 3 ¼ **Dorkas**[25] 842 4-10-10 0 AidanColeman 101
(J R Jenkins) *cl up: rdn 3f out: led briefly 2f out: one pce and wl hld fnl f* **6/4**[1]
5- **3** 8 **When In Roam (IRE)**[53] 544 4-10-10 0 APMcCoy 96
(John O'Shea) *2nd tl rdn to ld 4f out: drvn and hdd 2f out: wkng fnl f* **13/8**[2]
5- **4** 19 **Ilewindelilah**[25] 842 5-10-5 0 JackSherwood(7) 79
(Gary Brown) *t.k.h: chsd ldrs tl rdn and wknd qckly 3f out: t.o* **20/1**
5 53 **Treelara**[420] 6-10-12 0 TomO'Brien 31
(Miss Imogen Pickard) *led 12f: stopped to nil and sn bdly t.o* **28/1**
5/0- **6** 27 **Kallina (IRE)**[25] 841 5-10-12 0 LiamTreadwell 7
(Liam Grassick) *sweating profusely: in tch tl stopped rapidly 5f out: sn hopelessly t.o* **40/1**
7 71 **Fair Dolly** 5-10-12 0 PaulMoloney
(Sophie Leech) *on her toes: v green and sn hanging and racing awkwardly: last after 4f: lost tch 1/2-way: sn hopelessly t.o* **14/1**

3m 42.1s (-8.30) **Going Correction** -0.375s/f (Good)
WFA 4 from 5yo+ 2lb 7 Ran SP% **113.6**
Speed ratings: **104,102,98,89,64 52,18**
toteswingers 1&2 £2.00, 1&3 £1.80, 2&3 £1.40 CSF £11.55 TOTE £5.60: £2.20, £1.30; EX 12.00 Trifecta £23.10 Pool: £1612.09 - 52.24 winning units..
Owner J T Brown **Bred** J T Brown And Miss Kirsten Rausing **Trained** Wilsford-Cum-Lake, Wilts

FOCUS
Very likely a poor event, but it did at least go to the only trainer represented to have accumulated a double-figure total of bumper winners over the past five seasons.
T/Plt: £168.50 to a £1 stake. Pool of £65,752.71 - 284.81 winning tickets. T/Qpdt: £41.80 to a £1 stake. Pool of £4829.96 - 85.50 winning tickets. IM

1065 - 1066a (Foreign Racing) - See Raceform Interactive

652 TIPPERARY (L-H)
Sunday, July 21

OFFICIAL GOING: Good to firm

1067a KEVIN MCMANUS BOOKMAKER GRIMES HURDLE (GRADE 3) (9 hdls) 2m
3:35 (3:37) 4-Y-0+ **£33,028** (£9,654; £4,573; £1,524)

RPR
1 **Silk Hall (UAE)**[22] 793 8-11-0 128 (b) EddieO'Connell 140
(J J Lambe, Ire) *mde all: rdn whn pressed for ld appr 2 out: kpt on wl u.p fr bef last: hld on wl run-in: gamely* **25/1**
2 ¾ **Steps To Freedom (IRE)**[4] 1021 7-11-9 (t) RobbiePower 149
(Mrs John Harrington, Ire) *hld up in rr: 5th 1/2-way: clsr in 4th after 3 out: rdn to chal 2 out: kpt on wl u.p but no ex fr bef last: styd on same pce run-in* **2/1**[1]
3 ½ **Fosters Cross (IRE)**[10] 5486 11-11-0 139 (t) DavyCondon 139
(Thomas Mullins, Ire) *trckd ldr in 2nd: relegated to 3rd 1/2-way: wnt 2nd again 2 out: sn rdn and 3rd at last: styd on wl u.p but no ex run-in* **2/1**[1]
4 11 **Midnight Game**[29] 5561 6-11-7 147 DavyRussell 135
(W P Mullins, Ire) *chsd ldrs: 2nd 1/2-way: rdn after 3 out and no imp on principals fr next: one pce* **4/1**[2]
5 3 ¼ **Aughnacurraveel (IRE)**[14] 913 9-11-0 119 MrMJO'Connor 125
(Thomas P Cummins, Ire) *chsd ldrs: relegated to rr 1/2-way: sn pushed along: no ex and styd on same pce fr 3 out* **16/1**
6 3 ½ **Ted Dolly (IRE)**[14] 913 9-11-4 117 BarryGeraghty 125
(Edward U Hales, Ire) *in rr: rdn and no ex fr 3 out: one pce* **25/1**
7 12 **Shadow Eile (IRE)**[70] 5580 8-11-2 136 AndrewJMcNamara 111
(Mrs D A Love, Ire) *chsd ldrs: 4th 1/2-way: slt mstke 5th: rdn appr 3 out and no ex: wknd* **6/1**[3]

3m 38.5s (218.50) 7 Ran SP% **114.5**
CSF £77.39 TOTE £37.70: £9.10, £1.80; DF 99.30.
Owner James Callow **Bred** Darley **Trained** Kilmore, Co Armagh

FOCUS
The winner was back to his best, with a personal best from the second in line with his improved Flat form.

1068 - 1071a (Foreign Racing) - See Raceform Interactive

1037 CARTMEL (L-H)
Monday, July 22

OFFICIAL GOING: Good to firm (good in places; watered; 8.1)
Wind: light 1/2 behind Weather: fine and sunny, very warm

1072 BET & WATCH WITH RACING UK'S APP MAIDEN HURDLE (8 hdls) 2m 1f 110y
2:15 (2:15) (Class 5) 4-Y-0+ **£2,599** (£763; £381; £190)

Form RPR
/32- **1** **Smart Ruler (IRE)**[58] 475 7-11-0 107 APMcCoy 113+
(James Moffatt) *trckd ldrs: led 2 out: drvn rt out* **2/1**[1]
4- **2** 4 **Swing Hard (IRE)**[29] 800 5-11-0 0 RyanMania 107
(Sue Smith) *prom: outpcd 5th: styd on fr next: 3rd last: 6 l 2nd over 1f out: kpt on* **20/1**
202- **3** 4 ½ **Macarthur**[20] 856 9-11-0 114 (tp) PaulMoloney 105
(David Rees) *chsd ldrs: wnt 2nd between last 2: kpt on one pce* **3/1**[2]
0/3- **4** 11 **Apolskapart (IRE)**[19] 561 5-11-0 101 BrianHughes 94
(Michael Smith) *chsd ldrs 2nd after 3 out: wknd last* **10/1**
504- **5** 4 ½ **Solo Jugadores**[5] 1007 5-10-11 0 JackQuinlan(3) 89
(Richard Guest) *sn in rr: kpt on fr 3 out: nvr a threat* **25/1**
223- **6** 7 **Dr Dalwhinny**[13] 928 4-10-12 110 JasonMaguire 81
(Donald McCain) *chsd ldrs: reminders 5th: led bef 3 out: hdd 2 out: wknd between last 2* **7/2**[3]
/P5- **7** 22 **Bow Fiddle (IRE)**[29] 800 7-10-0 0 (t) JohnWinston(7) 56
(Patrick Holmes) *mid-div: hdwy 5th: wknd between last 2: eased clsng stages* **66/1**
/43- **8** 26 **Definite Maybe (IRE)**[33] 761 5-11-0 0 DenisO'Regan 40
(Martin Todhunter) *led: hdd bef 3 out: sn bhd: eased bef next: sn t.o* **6/1**
/00- **9** 7 **Daniel's Dream**[37] 752 13-10-7 61 (p) MrJDixon(7) 34
(John Dixon) *s.s: detached in last: t.o 5th* **100/1**

4m 8.7s (-4.50) **Going Correction** -0.05s/f (Good)
WFA 4 from 5yo+ 15lb 9 Ran SP% **115.0**
Speed ratings (Par 103): **108,106,104,99,97 94,84,72,69**
toteswingers 1&2 £7.40, 1&3 £1.70, 2&3 £12.80 CSF £40.88 TOTE £3.30: £1.10, £4.50, £1.40; EX 51.50 Trifecta £344.50 Pool: £1539.70 - 3.35 winning units..
Owner The Vilprano Partnership **Bred** Patrick Cummins **Trained** Cartmel, Cumbria

FOCUS
Rail moved out 3m on both bends. An ordinary maiden hurdle run at a sound gallop. The winner is rated to the level of his latest C&D run, with a big step up from the second.

1073 SEP EVENTS H'CAP HURDLE (11 hdls) 2m 6f
2:45 (2:47) (Class 5) (0-100,100) 4-Y-0+ **£3,249** (£954; £477; £238)

Form RPR
/33- **1** **Executive's Hall (IRE)**[29] 804 9-10-6 **87** (p) CraigGallagher(7) 94
(Ben Haslam) *trckd ldrs: 2nd 5th: led 3 out: styd on strly run-in* **7/2**[1]
/33- **2** 9 **Nez Rouge (FR)**[20] 860 12-11-12 **100** SamTwiston-Davies 99
(Nigel Twiston-Davies) *led to 2nd: chsd ldrs: 2nd after 8th: 2 l down last: kpt on same pce* **7/1**
/62- **3** ¾ **Galley Slave (IRE)**[52] 564 8-10-4 **83** JoeCornwall(5) 81
(Michael Chapman) *chsd ldrs: 3rd 3 out: styd on run-in* **16/1**
335- **4** 15 **Solway Dornal**[2] 1038 8-9-9 **76** (tp) StephenMulqueen(7) 61
(Lisa Harrison) *towards rr: hdwy 7th: one pce fr next* **7/1**
534- **5** 3 ¾ **Grethel (IRE)**[2] 1043 9-10-0 **74** oh2 LucyAlexander 55
(Alan Berry) *in rr: hdwy 7th: 7th whn blnd 3 out: nvr a factor* **8/1**
/64- **6** 15 **King Mak**[52] 565 11-10-6 **85** (bt[1]) KyleJames(5) 55
(Marjorie Fife) *led 2nd: hdd 3 out: sn wknd* **11/2**[3]
/03- **7** 2 ¼ **Waltham Abbey**[29] 803 12-10-3 **77** PeterBuchanan 43
(Lynsey Kendall) *chsd ldrs: outpcd 8th: wknd next* **33/1**
500- **8** 14 **Kingdom Of Munster (IRE)**[12] 942 6-10-11 **90** SamanthaDrake(5) 43
(Richard Ford) *mid-div: outpcd 5th: no threat after* **33/1**

0/5- **9** *41* **Another Trump (NZ)**[61] 426 9-11-10 **98**....(t) APMcCoy 14
(Jonjo O'Neill) *nt fluent in mid-div: reminders 3rd: sn struggling: bhd fr 7th: sn t.o* **9/2**[2]

0PP- **10** *41* **Painted Sky**[18] 884 10-10-13 **87**....(tp) AdrianLane
(Iain Jardine) *in rr: bhd fr 5th: t.o 8th: eventually completed* **66/1**

000/ **P** **Solway Star**[256] 2278 10-10-2 **76**....(p) BrianHarding
(Lisa Harrison) *in rr: bhd fr 5th: t.o whn p.u bef last* **20/1**

0/0- **P** **Inch Manor (IRE)**[52] 564 5-10-7 **81**....(tp) RichieMcGrath
(Philip Kirby) *mid-div: lost pl 8th: sn bhd: t.o whn p.u bef last* **14/1**

5m 26.8s (-2.50) **Going Correction** -0.05s/f (Good) **12** Ran SP% **116.6**
Speed ratings (Par 103): **102,98,98,93,91 86,85,80,65,50**
toteswingers 1&2 £4.50, 1&3 £5.40, 2&3 £4.40 CSF £26.94 CT £347.36 TOTE £3.70: £1.50, £2.20, £4.10; EX 29.70 Trifecta £115.00 Pool: £1015.87 - 6.62 winning units..
Owner Mrs C Barclay **Bred** Mrs Noreen McManus **Trained** Middleham Moor, N Yorks
■ The Mongolian was withdrawn. Price at time of withdrawal 16-1. Rule 4 does not apply.

FOCUS
The majority got taken off their feet in this weak handicap and the principals had it to themselves from three out. The form is sound with the winner rated similarly to his recent C&D run.

1074 CARTMEL CHEESES BEGINNERS' CHASE (14 fncs) 2m 5f 110y
3:20 (3:20) (Class 4) 4-Y-0+ **£3,898** (£1,144; £572; £286)

Form RPR

136- **1** **Valleyofmilan (IRE)**[15] 902 6-11-9 0.... JasonMaguire 109+
(Donald McCain) *mde all: 2 l ahd last: sn drew clr: 15 l ahd whn eased last 75yds* **2/5**[1]

5/ **2** *11* **Black Rock Lake (IRE)**[15] 916 7-11-2 98.... WillKennedy 83+
(T G McCourt, Ire) *chsd ldrs: 2nd 10th: drvn 2 out: one pce run-in* **9/2**[2]

3/P- **3** *1 3/4* **Winged Farasi**[8] 965 9-11-4 0.... SamanthaDrake(5) 86
(Joanne Foster) *chsd ldrs: outpcd 10th: kpt on fnl f: tk modest 3rd last 30yds* **16/1**

/45- **4** *2* **Mystified (IRE)**[25] 534 10-11-9 74.... BrianHarding 84
(Alan Berry) *sn in rr: hdwy 9th: handy 3rd sn after next: one pce: lost 3rd clsng stages* **8/1**[3]

U/ **P** **Bacher Son (IRE)**[17] 895 8-11-6 0....(bt¹) MichealNolan(3)
(Paul Stafford, Ire) *chsd wnr: reminders 8th: 3rd and wkng whn blnd 10th: sn lost pl: bhd whn p.u bef 3 out* **20/1**

P **Tunza The Lion**[488] 6-11-6 0.... JohnKington(3)
(Richard Ford) *nt fluent in last: reminders 4th and 8th: t.o whn p.u bef 9th* **100/1**

5m 24.7s (-0.70) **Going Correction** +0.075s/f (Yiel) **6** Ran SP% **112.4**
Speed ratings (Par 105): **104,100,99,98,**
toteswingers 1&2 £1.10, 1&3 £1.70, 2&3 £5.00 CSF £2.92 TOTE £1.40: £1.30, £1.80; EX 2.60 Trifecta £12.30 Pool: £2473.29 - 149.93 winning units..
Owner Tim & Miranda Johnson **Bred** Kenneth William Quinn **Trained** Cholmondeley, Cheshire

FOCUS
A very weak beginners' chase. The easy winner was value for further and is rated in line with his hurdle form.

1075 UNSWORTH'S YARD H'CAP CHASE (12 fncs) 2m 1f 110y
3:55 (3:55) (Class 5) (0-100,99) 4-Y-0+ **£3,249** (£954; £477; £238)

Form RPR

3/4- **1** **Soul Magic (IRE)**[54] 533 11-11-0 **94**.... CallumBewley(7) 100
(Harriet Graham) *in rr: chsd ldrs 8th: sn outpcd: cl up 3 out: led over 2f out: hld on gamely clsng stages* **7/2**[3]

U26- **2** *3/4* **Peak Seasons (IRE)**[2] 1039 10-10-11 **89**.... JoeCornwall(5) 94
(Michael Chapman) *chsd ldrs: outpcd after 8th: chsng ldrs 3 out: wnt 2 l 2nd 2f out: kpt on clsng stages* **14/1**

/60- **3** *11* **Saddlers Deal (IRE)**[19] 864 8-11-12 **99**....(b¹) WilsonRenwick 94
(Chris Grant) *chsd ldrs: led appr last: hdd over 2f out: one pce* **25/1**

135- **4** *7* **Sendiym (FR)**[14] 627 6-10-8 **81**....(b) DenisO'Regan 71
(Dianne Sayer) *chsd ldrs: cl 2nd whn hit 8th: 2nd last: wknd over 2f out* **11/4**[2]

0/0- **5** *31* **Jim Tango (FR)**[19] 864 9-11-4 **91**....(p) BrianHughes 52
(Karen McLintock) *chsd ldrs: lost pl appr last: sn wl bhd: t.o* **8/1**

/01- **6** *23* **In The Haven (IRE)**[54] 534 10-11-5 **97**....(b) SamanthaDrake(5) 38
(Joanne Foster) *led: hdd appr 4 out: wkng whn hit last: sn bhd: virtually p.u nr fin* **16/1**

001- **7** *3 3/4* **Alba King (IRE)**[8] 964 7-11-2 **94** 7ex.... JonathanEngland(5) 31
(Sue Smith) *in rr: drvn along 3rd: jnd ldrs 7th: led appr 4 out: hdd appr last: wknd sn after last: distant 5th whn heavily eased fnl 100yds: virtually p.u: t.o* **7/4**[1]

4m 22.5s (3.60) **Going Correction** +0.075s/f (Yiel) **7** Ran SP% **112.8**
Speed ratings (Par 103): **95,94,89,86,72 62,61**
toteswingers 1&2 £5.30, 1&3 £6.70, 2&3 £25.50 CSF £43.03 TOTE £4.80: £1.80, £5.70; EX 42.90 Trifecta £909.20 Pool: £1969.39 - 1.62 winning units..
Owner H G Racing **Bred** Robert McCarthy **Trained** Philip Law, Borders

FOCUS
A moderate handicap, run at a fair gallop. The winner is rated 8lb off last season's C&D winning mark, with the second to his mark.

1076 CHAMPAGNE LOUIS ROEDERER H'CAP CHASE (14 fncs) 2m 5f 110y
4:30 (4:30) (Class 3) (0-135,130) 4-Y-0+ **£6,498** (£1,908; £954; £477)

Form RPR

/35- **1** **Papa Caruso**[57] 495 9-10-1 **110**.... JonathanEngland(5) 112
(Sue Smith) *chsd ldrs: pushed along 9th: outpcd 4 out: rallied 2 out: wnt cl 3rd over 1f out: r.o to ld fnl stride* **5/2**[2]

121- **2** *shd* **Atlanta Falcon (IRE)**[12] 943 8-11-4 **122**....(t) JasonMaguire 123
(Donald McCain) *led to 4 out: led 2 out: hrd drvn run-in: hdd post* **7/4**[1]

114- **3** *1/2* **Lost Legend (IRE)**[15] 900 6-11-12 **130**....(p) APMcCoy 131
(Jonjo O'Neill) *chsd ldrs: rdn 3f out: styng on whn nt clr run ins fnl 40yds: styng on at fin* **5/2**[2]

14P- **4** *3/4* **Grey Soldier (IRE)**[2] 1047 8-11-7 **125**....(t) PaddyBrennan 125
(Sophie Leech) *racd wd: chsd ldr 3rd: led narrowly 4 out: hdd 2 out: upsides tl no ex clsng stages* **7/1**[3]

465/ **5** *7* **My Moment (IRE)**[37] 10-11-1 **119**.... DenisO'Regan 113
(Alan Swinbank) *chsd ldrs: outpcd 4 out: rallied 2 out: wknd over 1f out* **25/1**

5m 26.3s (0.90) **Going Correction** +0.075s/f (Yiel) **5** Ran SP% **109.9**
Speed ratings (Par 107): **101,100,100,100,97**
CSF £7.55 TOTE £3.60: £2.10, £1.30; EX 6.30 Trifecta £23.40 Pool: £1852.37 - 59.30 winning units..
Owner Mrs S Smith **Bred** Mrs D L Smith-Hooper **Trained** High Eldwick, W Yorks

FOCUS
This modest little handicap was run at an ordinary early gallop and they finished in a heap. The second and third set the level.

1077 WEATHERBYS HAMILTON INSURANCE H'CAP CHASE (12 fncs) 2m 1f 110y
5:00 (5:00) (Class 3) (0-135,130) 4-Y-0+ **£6,657** (£2,067; £1,113)

Form RPR

161- **1** **Sergeant Pink (IRE)**[19] 864 7-10-3 **107**....(p) LucyAlexander 115
(Dianne Sayer) *drvn along fr 2nd: lost pl and detached in last 6th: reminders after 8th: wnt 12 l 2nd sn after 3 out: 8 l down last: styd on to ld last 100yds* **6/1**

1U4- **2** *3* **Fiftyonefiftyone (IRE)**[38] 735 9-11-2 **120**....(tp) LeightonAspell 125
(Oliver Sherwood) *led: j. soundly: clr 4th: rdn over 2f out: wknd and hdd last 100yds* **9/2**[3]

011- **3** *30* **Bygones Of Brid (IRE)**[29] 798 10-11-12 **130**.... BrianHughes 118
(Karen McLintock) *chsd ldr: hit 6th: wknd 3 out: bhd run-in* **6/4**[1]

6/4- **P** **Kosta Brava (FR)**[18] 883 9-10-6 **110**....(tp) APMcCoy
(Michael Smith) *chsd ldrs hit 2nd: rdn and wknd 8th: bhd whn mstke next: t.o whn p.u bef 2 out: lame* **15/8**[2]

4m 16.3s (-2.60) **Going Correction** +0.075s/f (Yiel) **4** Ran SP% **107.3**
Speed ratings (Par 107): **108,106,93,**
CSF £27.07 TOTE £5.70; EX 14.40 Trifecta £36.90 Pool: £944.02 - 19.16 winning units..
Owner Andrew Sayer **Bred** Ring Pink Partnership **Trained** Hackthorpe, Cumbria

FOCUS
A tight little handicap, run at a strong gallop. The winner is rated similarly to his recent win.

1078 SOMERSBY CIDER H'CAP HURDLE (8 hdls) 2m 1f 110y
5:30 (5:30) (Class 5) (0-100,94) 4-Y-0+ **£3,249** (£954; £477; £238)

Form RPR

40P/ **1** **Lodgician (IRE)**[112] 5067 11-11-5 **87**....(vt¹) SamTwiston-Davies 97+
(Nigel Twiston-Davies) *mde all: stmbld bnd after 5th: styd on wl run-in* **5/1**[3]

056- **2** *9* **Rare Coincidence**[7] 799 12-10-13 **81**....(tp) BrianHarding 81
(Alan Berry) *chsd wnr: outpcd appr 2 out: kpt on to take 2nd last 100yds* **25/1**

62P- **3** *8* **Brother Scott**[29] 803 6-11-3 **92**.... CallumBewley(7) 89
(Sue Smith) *nt fluent: chsd ldrs: 2nd 3 out: sddle slipped: 4 l down last: wandered and wknd last 100yds* **9/4**[2]

52P- **4** *9* **Pete**[29] 803 10-11-8 **90**....(tp) LucyAlexander 76
(Barry Murtagh) *in rr: pushed along 3rd: chsd ldrs whn nt fluent 5th: one pce fr 2 out* **6/1**

3FU- **5** *7* **Born To Shine (USA)**[8] 961 5-11-12 **94**.... APMcCoy 72
(Alan Swinbank) *nt fluent: chsd ldrs 4th: outpcd after 5th: rallied 2 out: sn wknd* **2/1**[1]

0/F- **6** *12* **Emperor Of Rome (IRE)**[29] 798 5-11-11 **93**.... BrianHughes 61
(Tim Fitzgerald) *in rr: hit 3rd: sme hdwy 5th: sn lost pl and bhd* **7/1**

4m 13.2s **Going Correction** -0.05s/f (Good) **6** Ran SP% **111.4**
Speed ratings (Par 103): **98,94,90,86,83 78**
toteswingers 1&2 £4.60, 1&3 £2.50, 2&3 £3.00 CSF £79.85 TOTE £6.60: £3.10, £7.10; EX 63.20 Trifecta £230.90 Pool: £1652.62 - 5.36 winning units..
Owner The Yes No Wait Sorries **Bred** Sir Eric Parker **Trained** Naunton, Gloucs

FOCUS
A weak handicap in which five of the six runners had failed to complete on their latest outings. It was run at a brisk gallop. The winner is rated back to the level of his 2012 form.
T/Plt: £75.50 to a £1 stake. Pool of £78,033.86 - 753.79 winning tickets. T/Qpdt: £19.30 to a £1 stake. Pool of £4019.02 - 154.00 winning tickets. WG

1079 - 1081a (Foreign Racing) - See Raceform Interactive

367
BANGOR-ON-DEE (L-H)
Tuesday, July 23

OFFICIAL GOING: Good to firm (good in places; 7.7)
Wind: Nil Weather: Overcast and Humid

1082 SHADE OAK STUD NOVICES' HURDLE (9 hdls) 2m 1f
6:15 (6:15) (Class 4) 4-Y-0+ **£3,249** (£954; £477; £238)

Form RPR

112- **1** **Aazif (IRE)**[27] 734 4-11-10 129....(t) JasonMaguire 130+
(Donald McCain) *mde all: clr 3rd to 4th: effrtlessly wnt clr again after 3 out: unchal after* **4/6**[1]

12F- **2** *28* **Kettlewell**[8] 994 4-10-10 0.... APMcCoy 89+
(Warren Greatrex) *nt fluent: chsd ldrs: wnt 2nd bef 3rd: clsd on wnr 4th: unable to go w wnr after 3 out: sn eased whn wl btn: hit last* **5/2**[2]

13/- **3** *16* **Bob Tucker (IRE)**[143] 4514 6-10-12 0.... AlainCawley 66
(Brendan Powell) *towards rr: wnt 3rd after 4th: nvr able to get nr ldrs: u.p and no ch fr bef 4 out* **15/2**[3]

2U4- **4** *25* **Wintered Well (IRE)**[16] 897 5-10-12 0.... SeanQuinlan 44
(Jennie Candlish) *nt fluent: chsd wnr: j. awkwardly 1st: wandered appr 2nd: lost 2nd bef next: lost grnd on ldrs fr 4th: struggling after and sn no ch* **16/1**

0P- **5** *45* **Pru**[21] 857 5-9-12 0.... ConorRing(7)
(Mary Evans) *nt fluent: a bhd: t.o fr 4th* **200/1**

3m 56.0s (-14.90) **Going Correction** -0.55s/f (Firm) **5** Ran SP% **106.7**
Speed ratings (Par 105): **113,99,92,80,59**
CSF £2.48 TOTE £1.40: £1.10, £1.50; EX 3.20 Trifecta £9.60 Pool: £1071.85 - 83.30 winning units..
Owner Askew Dick Hernon Reynard **Bred** Shadwell Estate Company Limited **Trained** Cholmondeley, Cheshire

FOCUS
The easy winner stood out on his hurdle form and there's a case for rating the race higher.

1083 PRINTFINE NOVICES' CHASE (15 fncs) 2m 4f 110y
6:45 (6:45) (Class 4) 5-Y-0+ **£3,898** (£1,144; £572; £286)

Form RPR

/30- **1** **One Term (IRE)**[52] 591 6-10-12 0.... APMcCoy 126+
(Rebecca Curtis) *trckd ldrs: led appr 6th: clr after 3 out: styd on wl and a in command after* **6/5**[1]

050/ **2** *4 1/2* **Don't Hang About**[51] 8-10-12 0....(p) TomO'Brien 115+
(F Lloyd) *hld up: bmpd 1st: trckd ldrs appr 7th: outpcd 4 out: mstke 3 out: styd on u.p to take 2nd bef 2 out: no imp on wnr* **33/1**

121/ **3** *22* **Swaledale Lad (IRE)**[107] 5202 6-10-7 0.... HarryChalloner(5) 98
(Richard Ford) *led 1st: hdd 4th: chsd ldrs after: wnt 2nd 11th: lost grnd on wnr after 3 out: wkng whn lost 2nd bef 2 out: wl btn* **5/2**[2]

1U0- **4** *1* **My Lad Percy**[20] 877 5-10-12 0....(p) NickScholfield 95
(Rebecca Curtis) *hld up: bmpd 1st: struggling 11th: mstke 3 out: nvr a threat* **16/1**

/22- **5** *27* **Brady (IRE)**[51] 603 7-10-12 **117**........................ JasonMaguire 70
(Donald McCain) *led tl mstke 1st: chsd ldr tl regained ld 4th: hdd appr 6th: racd in 2nd pl whn j. slowly 9th and 10th: lost 2nd 11th: wknd bef 3 out* **4/1**[3]
130/ **6** *16* **Hit The Switch**[269] 2041 7-10-12 **0**........................(p) SeanQuinlan 56
(Michael Mullineaux) *trckd ldrs: bmpd 1st: lost pl 8th: struggling after 9th: toiling whn j.rt 3 out: wl btn* **33/1**
/24- **P** **Feast Of Fire (IRE)**[14] 933 6-10-7 **0**........................(p) MauriceLinehan(5)
(Jonjo O'Neill) *j. slowly 1st: sn wl bhd: t.o whn p.u after 9th* **20/1**

4m 54.9s (-14.20) **Going Correction** -0.55s/f (Firm) **7** Ran SP% **110.6**
Speed ratings: **105,103,94,94,84 78,**
toteswingers 1&2 £10.70, 2&3 £4.20, 1&3 £1.40 CSF £36.68 TOTE £1.90: £1.30, £15.20; EX 42.30 Trifecta £99.80 Pool: £921.20 - 6.91 winning units..
Owner Miss L Reid & G Costelloe **Bred** Hugh J Holohan **Trained** Newport, Dyfed

FOCUS
An ordinary novice chase. The cosy winner is rated in line with his hurdles form but can rate higher.

1084 YORTON FARM STUD MARES' H'CAP HURDLE (12 hdls) 3m
7:15 (7:16) (Class 4) (0-120,116) 4-Y-0+ **£3,573** (£1,049; £524; £262)

Form RPR
211- **1** **My Lucky Flame (IRE)**[20] 878 6-11-2 **116**........................ MikeyHamill(10) 119
(Sean Curran) *sn chsd ldr: led 4 out: dived at 3 out: pressed appr last: rdn and kpt on gamely run-in* **6/4**[1]
/56- **2** *nk* **Gulf Punch**[59] 476 6-10-3 **100**........................(p) NickSlatter(7) 102
(Donald McCain) *chsd ldrs: big effrt to take 2nd appr 2 out: chalng upsides wnr bef last: nt qckn run-in* **10/3**[2]
3/5- **3** *7* **Pass The Time**[22] 353 4-10-12 **109**........................(p) MichaelByrne(3) 104+
(Neil Mulholland) *blnd 2nd: hld up: outpcd 3 out: rallied to chse front pair 2 out: no real imp whn mstke last: hld after: eased fnl 100yds* **12/1**
440- **4** *18* **Flew The Nest (IRE)**[13] 947 5-10-8 **98**........................ APMcCoy 83
(Jonjo O'Neill) *hld up in rr: clsd 3 out: sn upsides wnr and chalng tl rdn appr 2 out: wknd sn after* **10/3**[2]
236/ **5** *24* **Seedless**[251] 2411 8-11-11 **115**........................ JasonMaguire 73
(Donald McCain) *led: hdd 4 out: rdn and wknd after 3 out* **13/2**[3]

5m 43.1s (-7.90) **Going Correction** -0.55s/f (Firm)
WFA 4 from 5yo+ 17lb **5** Ran SP% **107.2**
Speed ratings (Par 105): **91,90,88,82,74**
CSF £6.57 TOTE £2.30: £1.20, £2.00; EX 6.30 Trifecta £32.00 Pool: £946.40 - 22.17 winning units..
Owner Keith Adams **Bred** Rosemary Rooney **Trained** Hatford, Oxon

FOCUS
Not the strongest of races for the grade, but straightforward form.

1085 PRIMESIGHT H'CAP CHASE (15 fncs) 2m 4f 110y
7:45 (7:47) (Class 3) (0-130,127) 4-Y-0+ **£6,498** (£1,908; £954; £477)

Form RPR
2/F- **1** **Twirling Magnet (IRE)**[27] 839 7-11-12 **127**........................(tp) APMcCoy 143+
(Jonjo O'Neill) *hld up: trckd ldrs gng wl 10th: upsides 2 out: sn led: asserted last: eased down whn clr run-in* **5/2**[2]
14/- **2** *8* **Victor Leudorum (IRE)**[86] 9 6-11-10 **125**........................(t) NickScholfield 129
(Charlie Mann) *a.p: wnt 2nd 9th: led appr 2 out: rdn and hdd sn after fence: no ex last: no ch w wnr run-in* **7/2**[3]
2/0- **3** *6* **French Ties (IRE)**[67] 355 11-11-2 **117**........................(p) SeanQuinlan 120
(Jennie Candlish) *hld up: rdn after 3 out: effrt to chse ldrs after 2 out: one pce fr last* **12/1**
/P6- **4** *8* **An Capall Mor (IRE)**[23] 853 7-10-9 **110**........................(tp) JasonMaguire 104
(Donald McCain) *led to 3rd: remained prom tl regained ld appr 7th: rdn bef 3 out: hdd bef 2 out: wknd sn after* **15/2**
253- **5** *nk* **Peachey Moment (USA)**[20] 869 8-11-0 **115**........................(p) PaddyBrennan 106
(Nicky Richards) *in tch: rdn and wknd after 3 out* **2/1**[1]
1/P- **P** **Saphir Des Bois (FR)**[46] 655 9-11-9 **124**........................ TomO'Brien
(F Lloyd) *prom: led 3rd: hdd appr 7th: mstke 8th: wknd after 9th: in rr whn p.u bef 11th* **16/1**

4m 53.7s (-15.40) **Going Correction** -0.55s/f (Firm) **6** Ran SP% **109.5**
Speed ratings (Par 107): **107,103,101,98,98**
toteswingers 1&2 £1.10, 2&3 £9.10, 1&3 £6.00 CSF £11.26 TOTE £2.20: £1.70, £3.30; EX 9.60 Trifecta £31.30 Pool: £1156.55 - 27.67 winning units..
Owner Mrs Gay Smith **Bred** G Quirk **Trained** Cheltenham, Gloucs

FOCUS
A fair renewal of this feature handicap, despite the small field. The winner was on a fair mark but this rates a step up and he should go in again.

1086 THOROUGHBRED BREEDERS' ASSOCIATION H'CAP CHASE (12 fncs) 2m 1f 110y
8:15 (8:17) (Class 5) (0-100,95) 4-Y-0+ **£2,395** (£698; £349)

Form RPR
030- **1** **Maizy Missile (IRE)**[48] 632 11-11-0 **83**........................ PaulMoloney 96
(Mary Evans) *a.p: led 3 out: rdn and hdd last: styd on u.str driving run-in: regained ld fnl stride* **14/1**
/11- **2** *hd* **Chilbury Hill (IRE)**[2] 1057 10-11-8 **94** 7ex........................(t) MichaelByrne(3) 107
(Tim Vaughan) *hld up in tch: trckd ldrs bef 7th: pushed along bef 3 out: wnt 2nd appr 2 out: rdn to ld last: edgd lft run-in: hdd fnl stride* **10/11**[1]
015- **3** *19* **Mister Wiseman**[3] 1050 11-11-4 **87**........................(bt) TomScudamore 85
(Nigel Hawke) *led: hdd 3 out: rdn and no ex appr last: wl btn run-in* **3/1**[2]
P34- **4** *16* **Strathaird (IRE)**[43] 694 9-10-0 **69** oh10........................(p) BrianHughes 50
(Andrew Crook) *hld up: j. carefully 6th: outpcd 4 out: nvr a threat* **40/1**
/4P- **5** *5* **Cocoa Key (IRE)**[3] 1039 9-11-7 **95**........................ HarryChalloner(5) 72
(Richard Ford) *chsd ldr to 5th: pushed along after 6th: mstke 7th: dropped away 4 out* **11/2**[3]
12P- **6** *1 ½* **Apache Dawn**[9] 964 9-10-11 **85**........................(t) KyleJames(5) 60
(Aytach Sadik) *bhd after 2nd: nvr travelled wl after: t.o* **14/1**

4m 10.4s (-11.70) **Going Correction** -0.55s/f (Firm) **6** Ran SP% **108.5**
Speed ratings (Par 103): **104,103,95,88,86 85**
toteswingers 1&2 £7.00, 2&3 £1.02, 1&3 £9.80 CSF £27.24 TOTE £28.30: £6.30, £1.10; EX 26.20 Trifecta £66.10 Pool: £977.42 - 11.09 winning units..
Owner Mary And Billy Evans **Bred** Mrs M Evans **Trained** Clarbeston Road, Pembrokeshire

FOCUS
Only a modest contest but it served up a pulsating finish. The winner ran to her best, with the second in line with his recent win.

1087 CBS OUTDOOR CONDITIONAL JOCKEYS' H'CAP HURDLE (11 hdls) 2m 4f
8:45 (8:45) (Class 4) (0-115,112) 4-Y-0+ **£3,249** (£954; £477; £238)

Form RPR
6/0- **1** **He's A Hawker (IRE)**[14] 933 8-10-11 **97**........................(b) KielanWoods 108+
(Michael Mullineaux) *mde all: rdn clr appr last: styd on wl* **66/1**
0/2- **2** *12* **Cruising Bye**[20] 876 7-10-0 **86** oh4........................ PeterCarberry 88
(F Lloyd) *t.k.h: hld up in tch: effrt to chse ldrs 3 out: wnt 2nd 2 out: unable to go w wnr and no imp whn hit last: one pce* **9/2**[2]
3/0- **3** *8* **Yazdi (IRE)**[31] 185 4-10-8 **105**........................(tp) PaulNO'Brien(8) 96
(Charlie Mann) *in tch: effrt to take 2nd 4 out: rdn after 3 out: lost 2nd 2 out: one pce bef last* **20/1**
0/ **4** *14* **Vapiano (IRE)**[209] 3265 7-10-11 **105**........................(t) KieronEdgar(8) 95+
(David Pipe) *hld up in rr: mstke 3rd: hdwy 3 out: pushed along and nt picking-up in 4th abt 6 l down whn blnd 2 out: sn wl btn* **5/1**[3]
040- **5** *1 ¾* **Sedgemoor Express (IRE)**[28] 833 5-9-12 **89**(tp) ThomasCheesman(5) 68
(Nigel Hawke) *prom: pushed along bef 4 out: wknd after 3 out* **7/1**
/40- **P** **Hired Hand (IRE)**[30] 812 7-11-6 **109**........................(t) MauriceLinehan(3)
(Jonjo O'Neill) *hld up bhd ldrs: wnt wrong after 6th and sn p.u: fatally injured* **6/4**[1]
6/6- **P** **Canna (IRE)**[21] 858 5-11-7 **107**........................(p) MichaelByrne
(Ali Brewer) *in tch: mstke 3rd: pushed along and outpcd bef 3 out: no imp whn mstke 2 out: sn p.u and dismntd* **20/1**
P05- **U** **The Weatherman (IRE)**[20] 870 6-11-4 **112**........................ JamesCowley(8)
(Donald McCain) *prom tl blnd and uns rdr 4th* **7/1**

4m 43.7s (-8.30) **Going Correction** -0.55s/f (Firm)
WFA 4 from 5yo+ 16lb **8** Ran SP% **110.9**
Speed ratings (Par 105): **94,89,86,80,79 , ,**
toteswingers 1&2 £3.10, 2&3 £10.60, 1&3 £20.60 CSF £324.58 CT £5932.76 TOTE £55.20: £19.30, £1.10, £6.20; EX 197.90 Trifecta £430.10 Part won. Pool: £573.51 - 0.05 winning units..
Owner Bluestone Partnership **Bred** Ms K Murphy **Trained** Alpraham, Cheshire

FOCUS
This race that took very winning, but the form could be rated a little higher.
T/Plt: £113.50 to a £1 stake. Pool of £56531.88 - 363.47 winning tickets. T/Qpdt: £18.00 to a £1 stake. Pool of £3836.15 - 157.70 winning tickets. DO

963 SOUTHWELL (L-H)
Tuesday, July 23

OFFICIAL GOING: Good (good to soft in places) changing to soft (good to soft in places) after race 1 (2.15)
Wind: light 1/2 against Weather: raining until 1pm, now fine and sunny

1088 CONNOLLY'S RED MILLS NOVICES' H'CAP CHASE (19 fncs) 3m 110y
2:15 (2:15) (Class 4) (0-110,110) 4-Y-0+ **£3,898** (£1,144; £572; £286)

Form RPR
03P- **1** **Green Bank (IRE)**[30] 806 7-11-8 **106**........................(t) NoelFehily 124+
(Charlie Longsdon) *w ldr: led 5th: pckd 4 out: drew clr 2 out: eased in clsng stages* **8/1**
/23- **2** *25* **Beckhani**[40] 726 6-11-7 **105**........................(p) APMcCoy 102
(Jonjo O'Neill) *trckd ldrs: 2nd 10th: hit 14th: j.rt 4 out: wknd bef 2 out: fin tired* **15/8**[1]
106- **3** *2* **Pyjama Game (IRE)**[20] 866 7-11-4 **102**........................ WilsonRenwick 94
(Rose Dobbin) *chsd ldrs: outpcd 13th: reminders 15th: kpt on fr 3 out: tk distant 3rd run-in* **25/1**
3P1- **4** *6* **Sparkling Tara**[30] 799 8-11-7 **105**........................ RyanMania 94
(Sue Smith) *in tch: mstke 7th: chsd ldrs 9th: lost pl after 4 out: lost distant 3rd run-in* **7/1**
3/5- **P** **Suburban Bay**[35] 757 8-11-12 **110**........................ WayneHutchinson
(Alan King) *t.k.h: trckd ldrs: outpcd whn hit 4 out: sn lost pl: last whn p.u bef last* **3/1**[2]
00/- **P** **Burnthill (IRE)**[93] 5431 8-10-1 **85**........................(t) IanPopham
(Claire Dyson) *led to 5th: hit 9th: lost pl next: t.o 13th: p.u 4 out* **20/1**
0/U- **P** **Sunglasses (IRE)**[16] 899 6-11-7 **105**........................ DavidBass
(Nicky Henderson) *trckd ldrs: blnd bdly 5th: immediately p.u: fatally injured* **9/2**[3]

6m 46.1s (23.10) **Going Correction** +1.025s/f (Soft) **7** Ran SP% **110.2**
Speed ratings (Par 105): **104,96,95,93, , ,**
toteswingers 1&2 £3.90, 2&3 £5.40, 1&3 £10.30 CSF £22.72 TOTE £10.30: £3.10, £2.30; EX 24.00 Trifecta £289.20 Pool: £1710.06 -4.43 winning units..
Owner Charlie Longsdon **Bred** Andrew Pierce **Trained** Over Norton, Oxon

FOCUS
Golf Club bend on outside and bend into home straight inside the lined utilised on July 14th. After 11mm of rain the going was eased to good, good to soft in places. Not much pace on for this handicap, with the winner making all. A big step up from the winner on his best hurdles form.

1089 COMPARE BOOKMAKERS AT BOOKMAKERS.CO.UK H'CAP CHASE (16 fncs) 2m 4f 110y
2:45 (2:46) (Class 5) (0-100,99) 4-Y-0+ **£2,274** (£667; £333; £166)

Form RPR
030- **1** **Sycho Fred (IRE)**[38] 753 12-10-0 **73** oh3........................(t) BrianHughes 82+
(Mike Sowersby) *chsd ldrs: hit 9th: outpcd 11th: chsng ldrs 12th: led appr 3 out: clr 2 out: drvn out* **11/1**
403- **2** *4 ½* **Miss Sunflower**[38] 753 11-9-9 **73** oh2........................(p) JonathanEngland(5) 73
(Tina Jackson) *led to 4th: led 11th: hdd next: modest 4th and outpcd 4 out: kpt on to take 2nd between last 2: styd on run-in* **13/2**
0/4- **3** *18* **Junior Jack**[42] 713 8-11-12 **99**........................(t) SamTwiston-Davies 84
(Jennifer Mason) *chsd ldrs: hit 10th: led 12th: hdd appr 3 out: wknd between last 2* **15/8**[1]
/20- **4** *3 ½* **Farmer Frank**[35] 757 10-10-9 **89**........................ MissAliceMills(7) 68
(Nick Kent) *in tch: drvn 9th: lost pl appr 3 out* **10/3**[2]
P/5- **5** *¾* **She's Humble (IRE)**[42] 707 11-10-8 **81**........................(p) LeightonAspell 59
(Linda Jewell) *t.k.h: trckd ldrs: ld 4th: hdd 11th: lost pl next: sn bhd* **25/1**
/60- **L** **Richo**[5] 903 7-9-10 **74**........................ TrevorWhelan(5)
(Shaun Harris) *ref to r: lft at s* **8/1**
235- **P** **Ginger's Lad**[9] 964 9-10-10 **86**........................(tp) JakeGreenall(3)
(Michael Easterby) *chsd ldrs: lost pl and reminders 3rd: reminders 5th: bhd whn j. slowly next: sn p.u: b.b.v* **5/1**[3]

5m 50.0s (33.00) **Going Correction** +1.025s/f (Soft) **7** Ran SP% **111.2**
Speed ratings (Par 103): **78,76,69,68,67 ,**
toteswingers 1&2 £6.70, 2&3 £3.00, 1&3 £4.00 CSF £72.65 CT £188.24 TOTE £15.60: £6.90, £3.20; EX 107.30 Trifecta £442.90 Pool: £1985.46 - 3.36 winning units..
Owner Mrs E A Verity **Bred** Finbarr Lordan **Trained** Goodmanham, E Yorks

FOCUS
After the first race the going was changed to soft, good to soft in places. A weak contest, run at a steady pace. The winner is rated in line with his best 2012 form.

1090 CONNIE WHITE MEMORIAL MARES' NOVICES' HURDLE (11 hdls) 2m 4f 110y
3:15 (3:15) (Class 4) 4-Y-0+ **£3,249** (£954; £477; £238)

Form RPR
/14- 1 **As I Am (IRE)**[20] 878 5-11-5 114 LeightonAspell 126+
(Don Cantillon) *mde all: clr fr 2nd: v easily* **4/9**[1]
0- 2 18 **Hopstrings**[20] 878 5-10-12 0 SamTwiston-Davies 96
(Charlie Brooks) *chsd ldng pair: 7 l 2nd 2 out: kpt on: no ch w wnr* **16/1**
3F0/ 3 10 **Hopeand**[158] 4226 8-10-12 81 (t) AdamPogson 86
(Charles Pogson) *t.k.h: trckd wnr: wknd appr 2 out* **25/1**
/24- 4 22 **Darcey Diva**[53] 567 5-10-5 0 (t) KieronEdgar(7) 64
(David Pipe) *t.k.h in rr: hdwy 6th: modest 3rd and rdn 3 out: sn wknd* **7/2**[2]
6- 5 1 1/4 **Celebrian**[21] 856 6-10-7 0 (t) KillianMoore(5) 63
(Alex Hales) *t.k.h in rr: bhd fr 3 out* **20/1**
0/ 6 29 **Tara Dancer**[406] 705 5-10-12 0 (t) PaddyBrennan 34
(Renee Robeson) *t.k.h in rr: sme hdwy 5th: lost pl 7th: sn bhd: t.o 3 out* **9/1**[3]
6U- F **Lucys Girl (IRE)**[6] 1017 6-10-12 0 TomO'Brien
(Jamie Snowden) *trckd ldrs: j.rt: 6th and wkng whn fell 3 out* **16/1**
P **Flamin June** 7-10-9 0 AdamWedge(3)
(Kevin Morgan) *in rr: j. slowly and bhd 7th: t.o whn j.rt 3 out: p.u bef next* **33/1**

5m 31.4s (18.40) **Going Correction** +1.025s/f (Soft) **8** Ran SP% **124.8**
Speed ratings (Par 105): **105,98,94,85,85 74, ,**
toteswingers 1&2 £3.60, 2&3 £22.90, 1&3 £5.10 CSF £11.36 TOTE £1.30: £1.02, £4.40, £4.90; EX 8.10 Trifecta £121.90 Pool: £2048.16 - 12.59 winning units..
Owner Don Cantillon **Bred** Don Cantillon **Trained** Newmarket, Suffolk

FOCUS
The pace was honest for this uncompetitive mares' novices' hurdle. The easy winner stood out and is on a fair mark.

1091 DENIS WRIGHT MEMORIAL H'CAP HURDLE (13 hdls) 3m 110y
3:45 (3:45) (Class 3) (0-140,138) 4-Y-0+ **£5,523** (£1,621; £810)

Form RPR
/33- 1 **Ogee**[46] 659 10-11-8 134 JimmyMcCarthy 130
(Renee Robeson) *trckd other pair: hit 4th: 2nd sn after 3 out: led narrowly next: edgd lft run-in: drvn rt out* **7/4**[2]
F/P- 2 1 1/2 **Red Not Blue (IRE)**[23] 851 10-11-12 138 (p) AndrewThornton 133
(Simon Earle) *led: increased pce 8th: narrowly hdd 2 out: 1 l down whn short of room and swtchd rt run-in: kpt on same pce* **8/1**[3]
15P/ 3 83 **Faultless Feelings (IRE)**[97] 5354 7-10-5 117 IanPopham 29
(Martin Keighley) *t.k.h: w ldr: shkn up 9th: drvn next: lost pl sn after 3 out: t.o whn eased between last 2: virtually p.u: eventually completed* **4/6**[1]

6m 47.4s (32.40) **Going Correction** +1.025s/f (Soft) **3** Ran SP% **107.5**
Speed ratings (Par 107): **89,88,61**
CSF £9.18 TOTE £2.60; EX 6.30 Trifecta £6.00 Pool: £638.37 - 79.60 winning units..
Owner Sir Evelyn De Rothschild **Bred** Hesmonds Stud Ltd **Trained** Tyringham, Bucks
■ Jimmy McCarthy, 43, retired after riding Ogee to victory. He rode his first Flat winner in 1987 and his first over jumps in 1989.

FOCUS
Four non-runners took plenty of interest out of this handicap. It was run at a steady pace and the first two are rated to their marks.

1092 GET LIVE FOOTBALL SCORES AT FOOTBALLSCORES.COM (S) HURDLE (9 hdls) 2m
4:15 (4:15) (Class 5) 4-Y-0+ **£2,395** (£698; £349)

Form RPR
6/1- 1 **Belle De Fontenay (FR)**[20] 875 8-10-10 117 (p) TrevorWhelan(5) 114+
(George Baker) *t.k.h: led to 2nd: led appr 5th: wnt clr after 3 out: 6 l ahd whn j.lft last: jst lasted home* **11/4**[3]
040- 2 3/4 **Rocky Rebel**[16] 898 5-10-12 102 (b) TomMessenger 106
(Chris Bealby) *chsd ldrs: pushed along 4th: outpcd 6th: kpt on fr 2 out: tk 2nd last: styd on* **16/1**
3F5- 3 4 **Callhimwhatyouwant (IRE)**[20] 875 8-10-12 102(b) SamTwiston-Davies 103
(Dr Richard Newland) *chsd ldrs: drvn 6th: 8 l 2nd 2 out: one pce* **11/2**
0/1- 4 9 **Dantari (IRE)**[68] 332 8-10-9 114 (vt[1]) AdamWedge(3) 93
(Evan Williams) *chsd ldrs: reminders and chsd wnr 5th: wknd 2 out* **2/1**[1]
/F4- 5 15 **Screaming Brave**[21] 858 7-11-4 114 (t) MarcGoldstein 94
(Sheena West) *t.k.h: led: hdd appr 5th: lost pl bef 2 out: bhd whn eased in clsng stages* **9/4**[2]

4m 14.9s (17.90) **Going Correction** +1.025s/f (Soft) **5** Ran SP% **112.0**
Speed ratings (Par 103): **96,95,93,89,81**
CSF £32.45 TOTE £3.40: £2.20, £7.20; EX 28.50 Trifecta £73.80 Pool: £1280.94 - 13.01 winning units..There was no bid for the winner. Rocky Rebel was claimed by Michael Blake for £5,000.
Owner George Baker & Partners **Bred** E A R L Elevage Des Loges **Trained** Manton, Wilts

FOCUS
A number of prominent runners in this fair selling hurdle, but the pace was only a steady one. The winner was value for a bit further.

1093 GET LIVE SPORTS SCORES AT SCORES.CO.UK H'CAP HURDLE (9 hdls) 2m
4:45 (4:45) (Class 4) (0-115,118) 4-Y-0+ **£3,249** (£954; £477; £238)

Form RPR
411- 1 **Cut The Cards (IRE)**[9] 968 6-12-1 118 7ex (p) APMcCoy 129+
(Jonjo O'Neill) *racd wd: w ldrs: led 5th: pushed clr between last 2: v readily* **5/6**[1]
514- 2 4 **Dont Take Me Alive**[15] 924 4-11-2 107 (tp) NoelFehily 107
(Charlie Longsdon) *trckd ldrs: wnt 2nd 2 out: no imp* **6/1**[3]
3/6- 3 2 1/4 **Taaresh (IRE)**[59] 480 8-10-12 104 AdamWedge(3) 104
(Kevin Morgan) *hld up in rr: hdwy 5th: trcking ldrs 3 out: 3rd next: kpt on same pce* **20/1**
P00- 4 7 **Quinsman**[20] 877 7-11-7 110 AndrewThornton 103
(Caroline Bailey) *led to 7th: chsd wnr: wknd between last 2* **50/1**
503/ 5 16 **Kings Destiny**[86] 8 7-11-4 107 DavidBass 84
(Nicky Henderson) *chsd ldrs: wknd appr 2 out* **7/2**[2]
21P/ P **Our Choice (IRE)**[130] 4777 11-10-4 100 (t) MissAliceMills(7)
(Nick Kent) *racd wd in rr: bhd and drvn 3 out: t.o whn p.u bef next* **50/1**
436- P **Hi Tide (IRE)**[27] 846 9-10-11 100 (t) TomScudamore
(J R Jenkins) *racd wd in rr: drvn 4th: bhd whn j.v.slowly next: immediately p.u* **8/1**

4m 13.6s (16.60) **Going Correction** +1.025s/f (Soft)
WFA 4 from 5yo+ 15lb **7** Ran SP% **110.9**
Speed ratings (Par 105): **99,97,95,92,84 ,**
toteswingers 1&2 £1.70, 2&3 £12.80, 1&3 £3.60 CSF £6.01 CT £50.30 TOTE £1.70: £1.20, £2.30; EX 7.00 Trifecta £43.50 Pool: £3347.72 - 57.68 winning units..
Owner John P McManus **Bred** Coppice Farm **Trained** Cheltenham, Gloucs

FOCUS
An uncompetitive handicap hurdle run at a fair pace. The winner is on the upgrade and the next two ran to their marks.

1094 COMPARE FREE BETS AT BOOKMAKERS.CO.UK STANDARD OPEN NATIONAL HUNT FLAT RACE 2m
5:15 (5:15) (Class 6) 4-6-Y-0 **£1,642** (£478; £239)

Form RPR
1 **Bennachie (IRE)** 4-11-0 0 RichardJohnson 78+
(Tim Vaughan) *reluctant ldr after field stood stl and 20 2nds bef cantering: hdd after 4f: led 4f out: hung rt and forged clr over 1f out* **6/4**[2]
0- 2 6 **Herecomestrouble**[43] 699 6-11-2 0 AndrewThornton 74
(Tim Etherington) *t.k.h: jnd ldrs after 6f: outpcd 3f out: rallied to chse wnr over 1f out: no imp* **22/1**
3 3 1/4 **Western Way (IRE)** 4-11-0 0 DenisO'Regan 72+
(Don Cantillon) *hld up in rr: shkn up and swtchd ins 5f out: sn rdn and outpcd: hung bdly lft over 1f out: kpt on to take modest 3rd in clsng stages* **10/11**[1]
4 nk **Sgt Bull Berry** 6-10-13 0 JakeGreenall(3) 70
(Peter Maddison) *w ldr: led after 4f: qcknd pce 9f out: hdd 4f out: wknd fnl f* **25/1**
5 10 **Marina Blue** 4-10-7 0 LeeEdwards 51
(Dave Roberts) *trckd ldrs: drvn 5f out: lost pl over 3f out* **11/1**[3]

4m 43.8s (52.40) **Going Correction** +1.025s/f (Soft)
WFA 4 from 6yo 2lb **5** Ran SP% **108.9**
Speed ratings: **10,7,5,5,**
CSF £25.98 TOTE £2.40: £1.20, £2.40; EX 15.70 Trifecta £23.40 Pool: £1846.66 - 59.17 winning units..
Owner Oceans Racing **Bred** Michael Heskin **Trained** Aberthin, Vale of Glamorgan

FOCUS
The pace was sedate for this moderate bumper. The form should be treated with caution.
T/Plt: £158.20 to a £1 stake. Pool of £73,420.14 - 338.65. T/Qpdt: £6.80 to a £1 stake. Pool of £6,937.40 - of 748.50 winning units. WG

1095 - 1102a (Foreign Racing) - See Raceform Interactive

1014 WORCESTER (L-H)
Wednesday, July 24

OFFICIAL GOING: Good (good to soft in places in home straight) changing to good after race 1 (2:20)
Wind: Virtually nil Weather: Sunny spells

1103 WEATHERBYS HAMILTON INSURANCE H'CAP CHASE (18 fncs) 2m 7f
2:20 (2:27) (Class 5) (0-100,97) 4-Y-0+ **£4,223** (£1,240; £620; £310)

Form RPR
/05- 1 **Roseneath (IRE)**[14] 942 9-11-2 92 (tp) KillianMoore(5) 103
(Alex Hales) *in tch: hdwy 12th: chsd ldr appr 4 out: chal u.p last: led sn after: drvn out* **11/1**
/4P- 2 8 **Le Seychellois (FR)**[21] 871 13-11-10 95 DenisO'Regan 98
(William Kinsey) *hld up in rr: stdy hdwy fr 11th: trckd ldrs 4 out: drvn fr next: styd on to take wl-hld 2nd run-in* **20/1**
5- 3 7 **Paddysparks (IRE)**[31] 802 9-10-1 72 (p) PaddyBrennan 71
(Daniel John Howard, Ire) *chsd ldr: chal fr 10th tl mstkes 13th and 14th: no ch after 3 out: kpt on for wl-hld 3rd run-in* **7/2**[2]
2P3- 4 2 **Petroupetrov (FR)**[21] 872 10-11-5 90 (bt) RichardJohnson 96+
(Tim Vaughan) *pressed ldr: led fr 6th: rdn 3 out: hdd sn after last: wknd rapidly: eased to a walk and lost 2 pls fnl 50yds* **6/1**[3]
0P6/ 5 9 **Safe Investment (USA)**[287] 1790 9-11-4 89 (t) DavidBass 74
(Lawney Hill) *chsd ldrs: rdn after 9th: wknd after 10th* **7/1**
550- 6 23 **Rifleman (IRE)**[44] 690 13-10-10 81 (t) TomScudamore 43
(Richard Lee) *in rr: sme hdwy 10th: wknd 14th* **25/1**
024- 7 22 **Nothingbutthetruth (IRE)**[48] 639 9-11-9 97 (tp) MichealNolan(3) 37
(Richard Woollacott) *led to 6th: wknd 12th* **16/1**
P01- P **Chandlers Cross (IRE)**[7] 1010 11-11-1 86 7ex (tp) PaulMoloney
(David Rees) *in rr: sme hdwy 7th: t.o whn p.u bef 4 out* **13/2**
/40- P **Quayside Court (IRE)**[52] 601 9-10-10 81 (vt) LeeEdwards
(Claire Dyson) *rdn and bhd fr 9th: t.o whn p.u bef 4 out* **40/1**
042- F **Crannaghmore Boy (IRE)**[14] 942 8-11-10 95 (p) APMcCoy
(Keith Goldsworthy) *chsd ldrs: hit 1st: 8th: 9th and 10th: rdn 12th: 4th and no imp on ldrs whn fell 3 out* **5/2**[1]

5m 44.34s (-3.66) **Going Correction** -0.675s/f (Firm) **10** Ran SP% **116.2**
Speed ratings (Par 103): **79,76,73,73,69 61,54, , ,**
toteswingers 1&2 £76.70, 1&3 £16.90, 2&3 £22.00 CSF £185.84 CT £930.49 TOTE £16.40: £3.30, £3.40, £1.80; EX 301.50 Trifecta £986.40 Part won. Pool: £1315.29 - 0.15 winning units..
Owner The Strathclyders **Bred** N J Connors **Trained** Edgcote, Northants

FOCUS
The racing line was moved out 4yds from the inside. A modest handicap chase, run at a steady pace. The winner is rated in line with the best of his recent form.

1104 SIS LIVE H'CAP CHASE (15 fncs) 2m 4f
2:50 (2:50) (Class 5) (0-95,94) 4-Y-0+ **£2,144** (£629; £314; £157)

Form RPR
/F6- 1 **Numbercruncher (IRE)**[21] 873 7-11-12 94 AidanColeman 106+
(Marc Barber) *pressed ldr: led 9th: c clr fr 2 out: heavily eased run-in* **5/2**[1]
/4P- 2 15 **Formedable (IRE)**[22] 861 11-10-0 68 oh8 (p) WillKennedy 63
(Violet M Jordan) *chsd ldrs: wnt 2nd appr 4 out: sn rdn: no ch w heavily eased wnr whn blnd 3 out* **12/1**
100- 3 9 **Le Grand Chene (FR)**[29] 832 7-11-12 94 (vt) PaulMoloney 79
(Sophie Leech) *in tch: blnd 8th: no ch w ldrs fr 4 out: wnt 3rd next: blnd 2 out* **9/2**[3]
0P4- 4 5 **Harrys Whim**[36] 759 8-10-0 68 RichieMcGrath 47
(John Weymes) *led to 9th: wknd fr 4 out* **7/2**[2]
0/0- 5 14 **Benozzo Gozzoli**[84] 67 7-10-6 74 AndrewThornton 39
(Simon Earle) *in tch: hit 10th: wknd bef 4 out* **9/2**[3]
/UP- 6 7 **Rustic John**[10] 976 13-9-13 72 NicodeBoinville(5) 30
(H Edward Haynes) *sme hdwy 5th: wknd 10th* **66/1**

32P- **P** **Jamesson (IRE)**[36] 759 8-11-8 **90**.....................................(tp) TomO'Brien
(Jamie Snowden) *a in rr: rdn 10th: t.o fr 4 out: p.u bef last* **11/2**
4m 45.66s (-14.34) **Going Correction** -0.675s/f (Firm) **7** Ran SP% **111.7**
Speed ratings (Par 103): **101,95,91,89,83 81,**
toteswingers 1&2 £7.90, 1&3 £4.80, 2&3 £3.60 CSF £28.06 CT £124.84 TOTE £3.30: £2.20, £7.20; EX 32.40 Trifecta £112.70 Pool: £1051.93 - 6.99 winning units..
Owner G J Barber **Bred** P Magee **Trained** Haverfordwest, Pembrokes
FOCUS
Not much pace for this handicap chase, which suited the prominent runners. A weak race, with the winner rated back to his 2012 level.

1105 COMPARE BOOKMAKERS AT BOOKMAKERS.CO.UK AMATEUR RIDERS' H'CAP HURDLE (12 hdls) 2m 7f
3:20 (3:20) (Class 5) (0-95,94) 4-Y-0+ **£1,871** (£580; £290; £145)

Form RPR
/43- **1** **Sovereign Spirit (IRE)**[29] 829 11-10-12 **85**..........(tp) MissBAndrews[(5)] 91+
(Michael Blake) *trckd ldrs: chal fr 3 out tl slt ld last: pushed out run-in* **2/1**[1]
3P4- **2** 1 ¾ **Watch House (IRE)**[7] 1014 8-10-12 **85**.................... MissAEStirling[(5)] 88
(Michael Gates) *chsd ldrs: wnt 2nd 4 out: slt ld 3 out: jnd fr next: narrowly hdd last: styd on but a hld by wnr* **16/1**
056- **3** 5 **Reckless Romeo (IRE)**[20] 881 4-10-0 **79**................. MrTGreenwood[(7)] 73
(Richard Ford) *chsd ldrs: led 8th: narrowly hdd 3 out: one pce fr 2 out* **12/1**[3]
00P/ **4** 3 **Piece Of Magic**[142] 4569 8-10-5 **76**................................ MrJHamilton[(3)] 71
(Michael Easterby) *in rr: hdwy fr 3 out: styd on run-in: nt rch ldrs* **12/1**[3]
00/- **5** 1 ¼ **Ilewin Kim**[103] 5264 7-10-6 **79**.......................................(p) MissAliceMills[(5)] 73
(Gary Brown) *in tch: pushed along 3 out: styd on appr last: kpt on run-in but nvr any ch* **12/1**[3]
350- **6** 1 ¼ **Whatsabillion (IRE)**[29] 829 11-11-3 **90**...........(tp) MissJoannaMason[(5)] 83
(Anabel K Murphy) *bhd: hdwy fr 3 out: kpt on run-in: nvr rchd ldrs* **14/1**
/00- **7** 2 **Amalric (FR)**[28] 844 6-11-8 **90**.. MrTWeston 83
(Anabel K Murphy) *in rr: hdwy 7th: chsd ldrs and rdn 3 out: wknd fr 2 out* **12/1**[3]
/62- **8** 6 **Master Wells (IRE)**[57] 522 12-10-5 **80**............................. MissBFrost[(7)] 65
(James Frost) *in rr: sme hdwy whn blnd 7th: sn rdn: no ch after* **7/1**[2]
/00- **9** 2 ¼ **Absolute Shambles**[44] 690 9-10-10 **85**..................(p) MissFHickman[(7)] 68
(Chris Gordon) *slt ld after 3rd: hrd pressed tl hdd 8th: sn wknd* **14/1**
U00- **10** 22 **Portmeade**[29] 829 11-10-1 **76**... JonPark[(7)] 37
(Elizabeth Scott) *rdn 6th: a in rr* **25/1**
401/ **11** 4 ½ **The Ginger Man (IRE)**[39] 12-11-3 **92**............................(p) MrEBarrett[(7)] 48
(Michael Scudamore) *chsd ldrs to 8th* **16/1**
/05- **12** dist **Guns Of Love (IRE)**[76] 183 11-9-7 **68** oh3................. MrTWWheeler[(7)]
(Robin Dickin) *led to 3rd: styd pressing ldrs to 6th: t.o* **50/1**
FP/- **F** **Sir John**[934] 3350 7-10-6 **77**.. MrRJarrett[(3)]
(Suzy Smith) *mid-div: fell 2 out* **14/1**
/F4- **F** **Massachusetts**[17] 903 6-9-7 **68** oh2............. MissGeorgiaHenderson[(7)]
(Rob Summers) *mid-div: fell 8th* **16/1**
5m 35.53s (7.53) **Going Correction** -0.50s/f (Good)
WFA 4 from 6yo+ 16lb **14** Ran SP% **120.1**
Speed ratings (Par 103): **66,65,63,62,62 61,61,58,58,50 48, , ,**
toteswingers 1&2 £5.30, 1&3 £9.80, 2&3 £15.20 CSF £35.40 CT £322.10 TOTE £2.60: £1.30, £5.10, £6.10; EX 41.50 Trifecta £537.50 Part won. Pool: £716.78 - 0.38 winning units..
Owner Mark Holder Racing Limited **Bred** Exors Of The Late Mrs I Morris **Trained** Trowbridge, Wilts
FOCUS
A weak handicap hurdle confined to amateur riders. It was run at a steady pace. The winner is rated similar to last season's C&D win.

1106 GET LIVE FOOTBALL SCORES AT FOOTBALLSCORES.COM H'CAP HURDLE (8 hdls) 2m
3:50 (3:50) (Class 5) (0-95,95) 4-Y-0+ **£1,949** (£572; £286; £143)

Form RPR
066- **1** **Naledi**[31] 809 9-9-12 **72**.. ThomasGarner[(5)] 87
(Richard Price) *hld up in rr: stdy hdwy after 4 out: kpt on strly fr 2 out: chsd ldr after 2 out: styd on wl to take slt ld fnl 75yds: hld on all out* **20/1**
00/- **2** hd **Royal Trooper (IRE)**[92] 5470 7-11-0 **83**..................................(t) APMcCoy 99
(Jim Best) *trckd ldr: led 3 out: rdn and nt fluent last: narrowly hdd fnl 75yds: styd chalng but no ex last strides* **8/13**[1]
355- **3** 17 **Freddy's Star (IRE)**[29] 829 11-11-0 **88**............................. CharlieWallis[(5)] 86
(Martin Hill) *chsd ldrs: rdn 4 out: wknd fr 2 out* **10/1**[3]
003- **4** 3 ½ **Henry Hurst (IRE)**[31] 809 7-11-12 **95**.......................... AndrewThornton 89
(Jimmy Fox) *chsd ldrs: rdn appr 3 out: wknd fr 2 out* **10/1**[3]
/30- **5** 10 **Eastwell Smiles**[41] 730 9-11-9 **95**.....................................(t) JamesBest[(3)] 79
(Sophie Leech) *led: hdd 3 out: wknd 2 out* **22/1**
/56- **6** 3 ¾ **Carhue Princess (IRE)**[15] 932 7-11-10 **93**......................... FelixDeGiles 74
(Tom Symonds) *in rr: pushed along 3 out: mod prog fr 2 out* **20/1**
41P- **7** 16 **Mount Welcome (IRE)**[24] 852 9-11-1 **89**.......................(t) MrTWeston[(5)] 54
(Martin Weston) *in tch: chsd ldrs fr 3rd: wknd 3 out* **8/1**[2]
45P/ **8** 20 **Strong Survivor (USA)**[857] 10-11-0 **83**............................. CharliePoste 28
(Evelyn England) *bhd fr 1/2-way: t.o* **50/1**
0/0- **9** 44 **Everkingly**[41] 729 7-10-0 **74**.......................................(tp) GavinSheehan[(5)]
(Anna Brooks) *chsd ldrs: rdn and wknd 4 out: t.o* **100/1**
P10- **10** 25 **Pour Changer (FR)**[14] 947 8-11-7 **90**.............................. LeightonAspell
(Stephen Hughes) *bhd fr 3rd: t.o* **25/1**
0/5- **F** **Rolanta (FR)**[49] 635 8-10-11 **80**.. HaddenFrost
(James Frost) *in rr whn fell 1st* **16/1**
3m 38.95s (-8.35) **Going Correction** -0.50s/f (Good) **11** Ran SP% **117.8**
Speed ratings (Par 103): **100,99,91,89,84 82,74,64,42,30**
toteswingers 1&2 £5.60, 1&3 £35.20, 2&3 £2.50 CSF £32.58 CT £155.29 TOTE £27.40: £4.20, £1.10, £2.10; EX 64.20 Trifecta £630.90 Part won. Pool: £841.32 - 0.54 winning units..
Owner Mrs Janice Thompson **Bred** Genesis Green Stud Ltd **Trained** Ullingswick, H'fords
■ Stewards' Enquiry : Thomas Garner two-day ban: used whip with above the permitted level (Aug 13, 15)
FOCUS
The pace was honest for this modest handicap hurdle. The winner is rated in line with his recent C&D claimer run, and the second is entitled to rate a lot higher on his Flat form.

1107 GET LIVE SPORTS SCORES AT SCORES.CO.UK NOVICES' HURDLE (8 hdls) 2m
4:20 (4:20) (Class 4) 4-Y-0+ **£3,249** (£954; £477; £238)

Form RPR
12- **1** **Rosie Probert**[20] 696 4-10-10 **115**.. APMcCoy 106+
(Nicky Henderson) *led: jnd fr 3rd tl narrowly hdd last: rdn and rallied to ld again sn after: styd on strly clsng stages* **8/15**[1]
121- **2** 2 ½ **Lyssio (GER)**[9] 994 6-11-5 **114**.......................... ConorShoemark[(7)] 116+
(Jim Best) *trckd ldr: chal fr 3rd tl slt ld last: rdn sn after and hdd: no ex u.p* **5/2**[2]
61- **3** 15 **Portofino Wasp (IRE)**[10] 971 4-10-12 0................. MauriceLinehan[(5)] 96+
(Jonjo O'Neill) *chsd ldrs: outpcd by ldng duo fr 2 out* **8/1**[3]
0U- **4** 7 **Take The Crown**[14] 948 4-10-10 0... HenryOliver 78
(Henry Oliver) *in rr: hdwy 4 out: chse ldrs 4 out: wknd 2 out* **33/1**
/20- **5** 2 **Just Archie (USA)**[56] 544 5-10-12 0.................................. LeightonAspell 78
(Lady Herries) *chsd ldrs tl wknd appr 2 out* **14/1**
P5- **6** 2 **Robber Stone**[14] 948 5-10-7 0............................... AodhaganConlon[(5)] 76
(Debra Hamer) *t.k.h: in tch: wknd after 3 out* **50/1**
03- **7** 9 **Ailanthus**[16] 922 4-10-3 0.. AidanColeman 58
(Richard Woollacott) *a in rr* **20/1**
P/P- **8** dist **Harry Dore**[43] 716 7-10-12 0... DonalDevereux
(Richard Price) *in rr: j. slowly 3rd: t.o* **100/1**
P/0- **P** **Hard House**[9] 994 6-10-12 0... TomCannon
(Mark Gillard) *hit 1st: bhd fr 4 out: t.o whn p.u bef 2 out* **100/1**
3m 52.1s (4.80) **Going Correction** -0.50s/f (Good)
WFA 4 from 5yo+ 15lb **9** Ran SP% **123.2**
Speed ratings (Par 105): **68,66,59,55,54 53,49, ,**
toteswingers 1&2 £1.60, 1&3 £2.10, 2&3 £2.20 CSF £2.40 TOTE £1.70: £1.02, £1.10, £1.90; EX 2.60 Trifecta £8.60 Pool: £3123.87 - 269.65 winning units..
Owner Seasons Holidays **Bred** Seasons Holidays **Trained** Upper Lambourn, Berks
■ Stewards' Enquiry : Aidan Coleman ten-day ban: failed to take all reasonable and permissable measures to obtain the best possible placing (Aug 13, 15, 17-24)
FOCUS
Very little pace on for this uncompetitive novices' hurdle, with the market leaders in control from the off. The race has been given a token rating through the second, and the winner can rate higher on Flat form.

1108 COMPARE FREE BETS AT BOOKMAKERS.CO.UK NOVICES' HURDLE (10 hdls) 2m 4f
4:50 (4:50) (Class 4) 4-Y-0+ **£3,249** (£954; £477; £238)

Form RPR
111- **1** **Another Hero (IRE)**[16] 920 4-11-2 0.. APMcCoy 120+
(Jonjo O'Neill) *hld up in rr: hdwy to trck ldrs 4 out: travelling comf fr next: led appr 2 out: in n.d after: eased run-in* **4/9**[1]
/50- **2** 5 **Up To The Mark**[46] 674 8-10-12 0..............................(p) RichardJohnson 104
(Henry Daly) *led: hdd after 4 out: dropped to 3rd 3 out: wnt 2nd again after 2 out: sn rdn and hung lft: styd on as wnr eased run-in* **20/1**
42- **3** 22 **Keel Haul (IRE)**[14] 945 5-10-12 0.. HenryOliver 82
(Henry Oliver) *chsd ldrs: chal 5th tl led after 4 out: rdn bef next: hdd appr 2 out: wknd sn after* **16/1**
322/ **4** 91 **Emrani (USA)**[327] 1437 6-10-12 0....................................(b) JasonMaguire
(Donald McCain) *chsd ldr: rdn along fr 4th: wknd 5th: t.o fr next* **12/1**[3]
125- **P** **Oscar Close (IRE)**[21] 871 8-10-12 **112**....................(tp) TomScudamore
(David Bridgwater) *in tch: chsd ldrs 5th: wknd bef 3 out and p.u sn after* **4/1**[2]
4m 35.11s (-12.29) **Going Correction** -0.50s/f (Good) **5** Ran SP% **107.6**
Speed ratings (Par 105): **104,102,93,56,**
CSF £9.15 TOTE £1.20: £1.20, £4.60; EX 9.70 Trifecta £38.00 Pool: £2002.10 - 39.44 winning units..
Owner John P McManus **Bred** Miss Noreen Hayes **Trained** Cheltenham, Gloucs
FOCUS
A modest event run at a sound pace. The easy winner was value for further.

1109 COMPARE BOOKIES FREE BETS AT BOOKMAKERS.CO.UK H'CAP HURDLE (DIV I) (10 hdls) 2m 4f
5:20 (5:20) (Class 5) (0-100,100) 4-Y-0+ **£2,989** (£877; £438; £219)

Form RPR
051- **1** **Jigsaw Financial (IRE)**[7] 1018 7-10-6 **80** 7ex................. GerardTumelty 87+
(Laura Young) *t.k.h: in tch: hdwy to trck ldrs 4 out: led 2 out: hdd last: rallied run-in to take narrow ld fnl 75yds: hld on all out* **11/4**[2]
422- **2** nk **Old Pals Act (IRE)**[41] 730 5-11-12 **100**................................(p) APMcCoy 106
(Jonjo O'Neill) *led to 3rd: styd chalng: led again 6th: hrd pressed and hung lft 3 out: hdd next: edgd rt sn after: drvn to ld again last: hdd fnl 75yds: no ex u.p clsng stages* **15/8**[1]
4/2- **3** 12 **Bracken House (IRE)**[24] 854 6-11-10 **98**......................(tp) PaulMoloney 94
(Graeme McPherson) *chsd ldrs: rdn 3 out: outpcd by ldng duo fr 2 out* **4/1**[3]
00/ **4** 7 **Mia's Anthem (IRE)**[90] 5520 5-10-6 **85**................................ DerekFox[(5)] 72
(Noel C Kelly, Ire) *w ldr: led 3rd: hrd pressed tl hdd 6th: stl upsides 3 out: wknd after next* **16/1**
2/6- **5** 18 **Sahrati**[48] 650 9-11-10 **98**.. TomCannon 67
(Michael Blake) *chsd ldrs: rdn 5th to 6th: wknd after 4 out* **9/1**
0/3- **6** 30 **William Hogarth**[40] 643 8-11-8 **96**...........(tp) RichardJohnson 35
(Keith Goldsworthy) *chsd ldrs: wknd 4 out* **14/1**
526/ **7** 30 **Attrapeur (FR)**[52] 9-11-7 **98**... JakeGreenall[(3)] 7
(Michael Easterby) *pressed ldrs: reminder 2nd: wknd 4 out* **33/1**
0/4- **F** **Himrayn**[29] 833 10-10-9 **83**.. TomMessenger
(Anabel K Murphy) *in rr: hit 6th: sme hdwy and rdn in bhd ldrs whn fell 4 out* **25/1**
0/0- **P** **Scheherazadesdream**[84] 71 6-10-4 **78**......................(p) SeanQuinlan
(Jennie Candlish) *in rr: rdn 7th: t.o whn p.u bef 2 out* **66/1**
4m 36.36s (-11.04) **Going Correction** -0.50s/f (Good) **9** Ran SP% **112.3**
Speed ratings (Par 103): **102,101,97,94,87 75,63, ,**
toteswingers 1&2 £2.20, 1&3 £2.40, 2&3 £2.20 CSF £8.18 CT £18.61 TOTE £4.00: £1.30, £1.20, £1.50; EX 10.10 Trifecta £26.50 Pool: £1839.29 - 51.92 winning units..
Owner Mrs Laura Young **Bred** Joseph Kent **Trained** Broomfield, Somerset
FOCUS
Not much pace on for this handicap hurdle, with the front two fighting out an exciting finish. The winner built on his recent C&D win.

1110 COMPARE BOOKIES FREE BETS AT BOOKMAKERS.CO.UK H'CAP HURDLE (DIV II) (10 hdls) 2m 4f
5:55 (5:55) (Class 5) (0-100,98) 4-Y-0+ **£2,989** (£877; £438; £219)

Form RPR
536- **1** **Advisor (FR)**[24] 854 7-11-6 **97**...............................(b) MrTWeston[(5)] 106+
(Martin Weston) *in tch: hdwy 4 out: trckd ldr next: led appr 2 out: c clr last: easily* **10/1**
FP0- **2** 12 **Pirans Car**[21] 876 7-10-10 **85**.................................(tp) MarkQuinlan[(3)] 81
(Nigel Hawke) *chsd ldrs: led 4 out: rdn 3 out: hdd appr 2 out: sn no ch w wnr: kpt on wl for 2nd* **16/1**
050/ **3** 3 ¼ **Sangfroid**[205] 3388 9-11-12 **98**...................................(vt) RichardJohnson 91
(Tim Vaughan) *in rr and rdn along fr 4th: styd on again fr 3 out: tk 3rd last: kpt on same pce run-in* **9/2**[3]
056- **4** 2 ½ **Am I Blue**[41] 730 7-11-12 **98**.. APMcCoy 88
(Mrs D Thomas) *led: rdn 5th: hdd next: lost pl u.p after 4 out: styd on again u.p fr 2 out* **10/3**[2]

/45- **5** ¾ **Record Breaker (IRE)**[24] 849 9-11-12 98..................(p) JasonMaguire 88
(Donald McCain) *racd wd: chsd ldrs: chal 5th to 6th: lost pl 4 out: styd on again u.p fr 2 out* **9/1**

0/2- **6** *nk* **Dalrymple (IRE)**[49] 635 7-10-3 80..............................(t) CharlieWallis(5) 69
(Nick Ayliffe) *in rr: hdwy 6th: lost position and rdn after 4 out: styd on again appr last* **12/1**

0U0- **7** *22* **Patricktom Boru (IRE)**[29] 829 6-11-1 87...................... GerardTumelty 54
(Laura Young) *in rr: hdwy 4 out: wknd next* **16/1**

301- **8** *9* **First Morning (IRE)**[10] 977 8-11-4 93.......................... MichealNolan(3) 51
(Michael Blake) *chsd ldrs: led 6th: hdd 4 out: wknd after 3 out* **9/4**[1]

/43- **P** **Terntheothercheek**[14] 945 4-10-10 85............................ SeanQuinlan
(Jennie Candlish) *chsd ldrs: pushed along 5th: in tch whn p.u bef 4 out* **20/1**

4m 40.96s (-6.44) **Going Correction** -0.50s/f (Good)
WFA 4 from 6yo+ 16lb 9 Ran SP% **115.3**
Speed ratings (Par 103): **92,87,85,84,84 84,75,72,**
toteswingers 1&2 £26.20, 1&3 £9.10, 2&3 £19.20 CSF £146.40 CT £821.65 TOTE £16.30: £4.20, £2.90, £1.50; EX 155.80 Trifecta £477.60 Part won. Pool: £596.84 - 0.15 winning units..
Owner M H Weston **Bred** Kilboy Estate **Trained** Hindlip, Worcs

FOCUS
This was not a strong race and the form is suspect, but the winner is rated to the level of his old wins.
T/Jkpt: Not won. T/Plt: £107.20 to a £1 stake. Pool: £79742.74 - 542.67 winning tickets T/Qpdt: £3.40 to a £1 stake. Pool: £5842.67 - 1263.99 winning tickets ST

1111 - 1117a (Foreign Racing) - See Raceform Interactive

1007 UTTOXETER (L-H)

Friday, July 26

OFFICIAL GOING: Good (good to firm in places; selectively watered; chs 6.8, hdl 7.1)
Wind: Light, behind Weather: Cloudy and hot

1118 FRANCESCO GROUP UTTOXETER MAIDEN HURDLE (10 hdls) 2m 4f 110y
2:20 (2:20) (Class 5) 4-Y-0+ **£2,209** (£648; £324; £162)

Form RPR

P/2- **1** **Danandy (IRE)**[5] 1052 6-11-0 109.................................. RichardJohnson 111+
(Philip Hobbs) *a.p: led 3 out: rdn appr next: nt fluent last: pressed fnl 100yds: styd on and in command towards fin* **11/8**[2]

2/2- **2** 1 ½ **Clondaw Draft (IRE)**[48] 675 5-11-0 0............................. JasonMaguire 110+
(Donald McCain) *trckd ldrs: wnt 2nd after 3 out: sn hung lft whn making effrt: nt fluent last: styd on to chal wnr fnl 100yds: no ex whn hit rails towards fin* **5/4**[1]

0/3- **3** 3 ½ **Piper Hill (IRE)**[9] 1007 5-10-11 0.................................... JackQuinlan(3) 106
(Tony Coyle) *hld up: pushed along 4 out: sn impr to chse ldrs: styd on after last: tk 3rd towards fin: no imp on front two* **33/1**

\- **4** ¾ **Oculist**[685] 5-11-0 0... JackDoyle 104
(Ben De Haan) *hld up: hdwy 6th: chsd ldrs and wl there 3 out: rdn bef next: styd on same pce run-in* **50/1**

4- **5** 3 ½ **Western Prize**[75] 240 5-10-11 0.................................... MichaelByrne(3) 102
(Tim Vaughan) *led: mstke 4 out: hdd 3 out: sn rdn: continued to chse ldrs after: wknd after last* **7/1**[3]

34U- **6** ½ **Presenting Me (IRE)**[17] 932 5-10-4 99.......................... AdamWedge(3) 95
(Evan Williams) *in tch: blnd 2nd: mstke 4 out: rdn whn chsng ldrs appr 2 out: wknd after last* **40/1**

/43- **7** *21* **Sterling Gent (IRE)**[26] 849 6-11-0 103..................................... DPFahy 82
(Liam Corcoran) *hld up: hdwy 4 out: effrt whn chsng ldrs 3 out: wknd bef last* **14/1**

00U- **8** *22* **Whispering Boy (IRE)**[9] 1019 6-11-0 0........................ TomScudamore 62
(David Bridgwater) *prom tl rdn and wknd after 4 out* **25/1**

0- **9** *38* **Give Me The Remote (IRE)**[16] 944 5-10-9 0.............. KillianMoore(5) 28
(Graeme McPherson) *midfield: nt fluent 3rd: dropped bhd 5th: mstke 6th: detached and toiling after: t.o* **66/1**

0- **10** *2* **Primitive Dancing**[23] 874 4-10-11 0............................ AndrewThornton 23
(Caroline Bailey) *in tch: mstke 1st: j. slowly 3rd: lost pl and bhd 6th: sn detached and toiling: t.o* **100/1**

P **Indian Ruler (IRE)**[426] 8-10-9 0.. KyleJames(5)
(Philip Kirby) *towards rr: niggled along at times: detached and toiling after 6th: t.o whn p.u bef 3 out* **66/1**

4m 53.1s (-5.90) **Going Correction** -0.20s/f (Good)
WFA 4 from 5yo+ 16lb 11 Ran SP% **120.9**
Speed ratings (Par 103): **103,102,101,100,99 99,91,82,68,67**
toteswingers 1&2 £1.02, 1&3 £21.10, 2&3 £10.90 CSF £3.56 TOTE £2.40: £1.10, £1.10, £6.80; EX 4.40 Trifecta £47.30 Pool: £1325.99 - 20.99 winning units..
Owner Mrs Caren Walsh **Bred** Mrs Mary Motherway **Trained** Withycombe, Somerset

FOCUS
Hurdles sited further towards chase course, common bends on home turn. A modest maiden, run at a routine gallop and the two clear market leaders fought it out. The winner was below the level of his recent run and a stone off his old mark.

1119 LADIES AT THE RACES BEGINNERS' CHASE (16 fncs) 2m 6f 110y
2:55 (2:55) (Class 4) 5-Y-0+ **£3,960** (£1,195; £615; £326)

Form RPR

332- **1** **Brassick**[30] 839 6-11-0 125...(tp) NoelFehily 122+
(Charlie Longsdon) *mainly disp ld tl led appr 3 out: rdn bef 2 out: abt 3 l clr whn drifted lft appr last where nt fluent: sn lft clr: styd on gamely* **4/7**[1]

20- **2** *15* **High Ron**[30] 839 8-11-0 0.. AndrewThornton 109
(Caroline Bailey) *in rr: hit 4th: reminder after 8th: wl bhd after tl styd on fr last: tk 2nd fnl stride: no ch w wnr* **33/1**

0/3- **3** *hd* **Wayward Glance**[59] 518 5-11-0 124....................................(v) APMcCoy 109
(Jim Best) *nt fluent: chsd ldrs: rdn after 8th: hrd at work after: styd on to cl u.str driving after 3 out: abt 6 l down last: no ex run-in: lost 2nd fnl stride* **2/1**[2]

P04- **4** *11* **Harris Garden (IRE)**[30] 844 6-10-11 0.......................(p) JakeGreenall(3) 99
(Paul Webber) *chsd ldrs: nt fluent 12th: sn rdn and wknd* **33/1**

103- **U** **Academy General (IRE)**[24] 861 7-11-0 125............(t) TomScudamore 111
(David Bridgwater) *nt fluent 1st: mainly disp ld tl hdd appr 3 out: rdn bef 2 out: abt 3 l 2nd and u.p whn mstke and uns rdr last* **14/1**[3]

5m 35.6s (-12.90) **Going Correction** -0.20s/f (Good) 5 Ran SP% **109.5**
Speed ratings: **114,108,108,104,**
CSF £14.08 TOTE £1.50: £1.10, £4.30; EX 12.90 Trifecta £52.90 Pool: £1107.16 - 15.68 winning units..
Owner Paul Murphy **Bred** David Jenks **Trained** Over Norton, Oxon

FOCUS
Ordinary novice form. The winner is rated below his recent mark with the second on the upgrade.

1120 TRY NEW CRABBIES RASPBERRY GINGER BEER NOVICES' H'CAP HURDLE (9 hdls) 2m
3:30 (3:30) (Class 5) (0-100,100) 4-Y-0+ **£2,209** (£648; £324; £162)

Form RPR

020/ **1** **Oliver's Gold**[29] 1767 5-11-1 88... PeterBuchanan 96+
(Tim Walford) *a.p: led appr 3 out: hit last: pressed ins fnl 100yds out: kpt on gamely towards fin* **14/1**

034- **2** 1 ¼ **Annelko**[30] 846 6-11-12 99... TomCannon 105
(Michael Blake) *hld up: hdwy appr 3 out: chsd wnr bef 2 out: rdn bef last: styd on to chal ins fnl 100yds: hld towards fin* **5/2**[1]

025- **3** *8* **Tennessee Bird**[19] 903 5-10-3 81.................................. GavinSheehan(5) 80
(Mike Sowersby) *chsd ldrs: nt fluent 4th: rdn and outpcd after 4 out: styd on u.p to take 3rd last: n.d to front two* **7/2**[3]

260/ **4** 2 ¾ **Deny**[484] 5149 5-10-3 76...(p) RichieMcGrath 73
(Henry Hogarth) *t.k.h: hld up: pushed along bef 3 out: kpt on steadily after: n.d to ldrs* **12/1**

0/0- **5** 3 ¾ **Ivans Back (IRE)**[26] 852 8-11-3 90................................(t) JasonMaguire 83
(Nick Kent) *led: hdd appr 3 out where j.big: continued to chse ldrs after: plugged on at one pce run-in* **20/1**

5P0/ **6** 2 ½ **Poetic Power (IRE)**[198] 3577 4-11-4 100...................... DanielHiskett(7) 89
(Claire Dyson) *midfield: hdwy appr 3 out: sn rdn and chsng ldrs: no imp bef 2 out: wknd run-in* **25/1**

/02- **7** *20* **Ashcott Boy**[33] 810 5-11-10 97... NoelFehily 70
(Neil Mulholland) *prom tl pushed along and wknd after 3 out* **11/2**

/00- **8** 3 ½ **Goat Castle (IRE)**[50] 640 9-10-9 82...................(t) SamTwiston-Davies 52
(Nigel Twiston-Davies) *chsd ldrs: mstke 4 out: rdn and wknd bef 3 out* **3/1**[2]

6/0- **9** *24* **Red Rosso**[50] 651 8-11-5 95.. JamesBest(3) 43
(Rob Summers) *hld up: struggling and lft bhd 3 out: t.o* **50/1**

3m 46.3s (-5.70) **Going Correction** -0.20s/f (Good)
WFA 4 from 5yo+ 15lb 9 Ran SP% **116.1**
Speed ratings (Par 103): **106,105,101,100,98 96,86,85,73**
toteswingers 1&2 £36.40, 1&3 £3.00, 2&3 £3.80 CSF £49.81 CT £155.03 TOTE £14.40: £3.20, £1.50, £1.80; EX 57.10 Trifecta £379.90 Pool: £1033.03 - 2.03 winning units..
Owner Quench Racing Partnership **Bred** Bearstone Stud **Trained** Sheriff Hutton, N Yorks

FOCUS
A modest novice handicap, run at an average gallop, and two went clear from the penultimate flight. The winner is rated back to the best of his 2012 form.

1121 BURTON KIA H'CAP HURDLE (12 hdls) 3m
4:05 (4:05) (Class 5) (0-100,100) 4-Y-0+ **£2,209** (£648; £324; £162)

Form RPR

P/3- **1** **Long Wave (IRE)**[26] 854 6-11-12 100.................................(p) NoelFehily 108+
(Charlie Longsdon) *in tch: led appr 5th: pressed fr 3 out: rdn bef 2 out: styd on gamely run-in* **3/1**[2]

061- **2** *2* **Moon Melody (GER)**[12] 965 10-9-10 75 7ex...............(bt) EDLinehan(5) 81
(Mike Sowersby) *racd keenly: prom: hit 8th: pushed along and outpcd whn sltly hmpd 2 out: styd on run-in: tk 2nd towards fin: no imp on wnr* **11/2**[3]

0/1- **3** ½ **Bold Raider (IRE)**[11] 997 6-11-9 97 7ex.............................. APMcCoy 102
(Jonjo O'Neill) *midfield: hdwy to trck ldrs 4th: wnt 2nd appr 4 out: chal fr 3 out: sn rdn: stl ev ch last: no ex run-in: lost 2nd towards fin* **11/4**[1]

443- **4** 2 ¼ **Minella Bliss (IRE)**[17] 933 8-11-4 95........................... RobertDunne(3) 98
(Nikki Evans) *in rr: hdwy and pushed along after 4 out: chsd ldrs next: kpt on u.p: nvr quite able to chal* **17/2**

0/0- **5** *5* **Kasban**[46] 690 9-11-5 100......................................(tp) ConorShoemark(7) 100
(Jim Best) *in tch: rdn after 4 out: chsd ldrs u.p bef next: swvd to avoid faller 2 out: styd on same pce run-in* **16/1**

/53- **6** ¾ **Go Amwell**[16] 428 10-11-0 88.......................................(v) AidanColeman 86
(J R Jenkins) *hld up: rdn and hdwy to chse ldrs appr 3 out: no imp: one pce run-in* **11/1**

0/4- **7** *14* **Highland River**[74] 264 7-10-4 78...................................(p) FelixDeGiles 63
(Dave Roberts) *hld up: hdwy into midfield 7th: trckd ldrs 4 out: rdn bef 3 out: wkng whn swvd to avoid faller 2 out* **20/1**

/40- **8** *5* **Starlet Mandy (IRE)**[37] 765 10-10-0 74 oh3.......... SamTwiston-Davies 55
(Nigel Twiston-Davies) *chsd ldrs tl rdn and wknd after 8th* **20/1**

543- **9** *nk* **Kayfrou**[18] 925 8-11-2 90... NickScholfield 70
(Nick Mitchell) *hld up: rdn and tried to make hdwy appr 3 out: nvr able to trble ldrs* **9/1**

/6U- **10** *6* **Combustible Kate (IRE)**[41] 750 7-11-3 98................... PaulNO'Brien(7) 73
(Nick Kent) *hld up: bhd and u.p after 4 out: nvr a threat* **25/1**

0/6- **11** *8* **My Friend Riquet (FR)**[16] 946 6-10-11 85.....................(p) LeeEdwards 53
(Dave Roberts) *midfield: rdn and wknd after 4 out: t.o* **40/1**

6- **P** **Vote For Doodle (IRE)**[51] 637 8-11-3 91.......................(tp) DPFahy
(Liam Corcoran) *midfield: rdn 7th: struggling and bhd after 8th: t.o whn p.u bef 3 out* **33/1**

0R0/ **P** **Sablazo (FR)**[111] 5183 7-10-0 74 oh6............................ GerardTumelty
(Andy Turnell) *in tch: trckd ldrs 4 out: sn rdn and wknd: wl bhd whn p.u bef 2 out* **50/1**

55P- **F** **Handford Henry (IRE)**[12] 965 7-10-3 82............(p) JonathanEngland(5) 85
(Michael Appleby) *a.p: pushed along appr 3 out: 3rd and jst over 2 l off the pce u.p whn fell 2 out: fatally injured* **40/1**

P0P- **P** **Daddy'Slittlegirl**[17] 932 8-9-7 74 oh11........................(p) DanielHiskett(7)
(Claire Dyson) *led: hdd appr 5th: mstke 6th: wknd bef 4 out: t.o whn p.u bef 3 out* **50/1**

5m 50.1s (0.10) **Going Correction** -0.20s/f (Good) 15 Ran SP% **126.9**
Speed ratings (Par 103): **91,90,90,89,87 87,82,81,81,79 76, , , ,**
toteswingers 1&2 £4.30, 1&3 £1.80, 2&3 £3.40 CSF £19.40 CT £52.77 TOTE £4.40: £1.90, £2.80, £1.80; EX 26.60 Trifecta £48.80 Pool: £1181.81 - 18.13 winning units..
Owner Neysauteur Partnership **Bred** Michael Long **Trained** Over Norton, Oxon

FOCUS
A weak staying handicap. The winner ran to the level promised by his course hurdling debut.

1122 HAYDAYSEVENTS.CO.UK H'CAP CHASE (12 fncs) 2m
4:40 (4:40) (Class 4) (0-120,115) 4-Y-0 **£3,798** (£1,122; £561; £280; £140)

Form RPR

P32- **1** **Citrus Mark**[19] 898 8-11-2 105... LiamHeard 110+
(Paul Webber) *prom: w ldr 5th: chal fr 4 out whn travelling strly: rdn to ld last: styd on run-in: on top towards fin* **3/1**[2]

203- **2** *1* **Bennys Quest (IRE)**[17] 931 10-10-11 103..............(tp) PeterCarberry(3) 107
(Neil Mulholland) *handy: led narrowly 4 out: rdn appr 2 out: hdd last: nt qckn run-in: hld towards fin* **5/1**

255- 3 1 **Sporting Boy (IRE)**9 1012 5-11-12 115 TomCannon 117
(Michael Blake) *prom: w ldr 5th: pushed along after 8th: stl chalng 4 and 3 out: nt qckn sn after: styd on towards fin* 9/2[3]
233- 4 hd **Uncle Pelder (IRE)**19 898 6-11-0 103 (p) DaveCrosse 105
(K F Clutterbuck) *prom: led 5th: hdd narrowly 4 out: sltly outpcd by ldrs appr 2 out: styd on towards fin* 5/2[1]
214- 5 48 **Bay Central (IRE)**11 1000 9-11-9 112 (e) PaulMoloney 71
(Evan Williams) *led: nt fluent and hdd 5th: wknd and bhd bef 7th* 5/1
566- 6 15 **Fintan**9 1012 10-11-6 112 (t) JamesBest(3) 57
(Rob Summers) *racd keenly: hld up: rdn appr 8th: sn lft bhd: t.o* 16/1
3m 49.8s (-5.20) **Going Correction** -0.20s/f (Good) **6** Ran SP% **111.0**
Speed ratings (Par 105): **105,104,104,103,79 72**
toteswingers 1&2 £3.60, 1&3 £2.80, 2&3 £3.60 CSF £17.53 TOTE £3.90: £1.80, £2.20; EX 18.90 Trifecta £81.60 Pool: £2512.03 - 23.07 winning units..
Owner Economic Security **Bred** G R Waters **Trained** Mollington, Oxon

FOCUS
A run-of-the-mill handicap in which the first four jumped three out as one. The second to fourth were all pretty much to their marks.

1123 CARTWRIGHT KING SOLICITORS H'CAP HURDLE (10 hdls) 2m 4f 110y
5:15 (5:15) (Class 4) (0-120,119) 4-Y-0+ **£3,378** (£992; £496; £248)

Form RPR
P16/ 1 **Della Sun (FR)**89 10 7-10-7 107 JoshWall(7) 116
(Arthur Whitehead) *hld up: hdwy appr 3 out: rdn to take 2nd 2 out: jnd ldr last: duelled for ld u.str driving run-in: jst prevailed* 7/1
341- 2 hd **Don't Be Late (IRE)**9 1020 5-11-10 117 7ex (p) APMcCoy 126
(Jonjo O'Neill) *chsd ldrs: led 4 out: rdn appr 2 out: jnd last: duelled for ld u.str driving run-in: jush hld* 13/8[1]
006/ 3 20 **Scottish Boogie (IRE)**16 4853 6-11-0 107 ConorO'Farrell 98
(Seamus Durack) *hld up in rr: hdwy gng wl to take 2nd after 4 out: lost 2nd 2 out: sn rdn and failed to pick-up: wknd run-in* 11/2
/41- 4 24 **Compton Blue**19 902 7-11-12 119 (b) WayneHutchinson 88
(Alan King) *chsd ldrs: lost pl bef 7th: wknd after 3 out* 9/2[2]
636- 5 ½ **Laustra Bad (FR)**9 1020 10-11-10 117 (bt) TomScudamore 86
(David Pipe) *led: reminders after 4th: hdd 4 out: sn rdn and wknd* 5/1[3]
350/ 6 14 **Oscar O'Scar (IRE)**209 3334 5-11-3 110 RichieMcGrath 66
(Philip Kirby) *chsd ldr to 4 out: sn lost pl: bhd bef 3 out* 10/1
4m 51.2s (-7.80) **Going Correction** -0.20s/f (Good) **6** Ran SP% **109.9**
Speed ratings (Par 105): **106,105,98,89,88 83**
CSF £18.65 TOTE £12.70: £4.50, £1.20; EX 26.70 Trifecta £120.20 Pool: £3253.33 - 20.28 winning units..
Owner A J Whitehead **Bred** Mlle Mathilde Lutz **Trained** Aston on Clun, Shropshire

FOCUS
The first pair came right away in this modest handicap.

1124 J & R CONSTRUCTION STANDARD OPEN NATIONAL HUNT FLAT RACE 2m
5:50 (5:50) (Class 6) 4-6-Y-0 **£1,559** (£457; £228; £114)

Form RPR
1 **Minella Hero (IRE)**293 1750 5-10-13 0 JackQuinlan(3) 104
(Sarah Humphrey) *trckd ldrs: pushed along and nt qckn 4f out: styd on to ld 1f out: pushed out towards fin* 15/8[2]
30/ 2 2¾ **H M S Intrepid**41 5-11-2 0 RyanMahon 102
(Anthony Honeyball) *hld up: hdwy u.p 5f out: no imp tl styd on ins fnl f: tk 2nd cl home: nt trble wnr* 15/2[3]
3 ½ **Worth A Go (IRE)**54 6-11-2 0 (t) DPFahy 101
(Liam Corcoran) *led: hdd over 3f out: rdn over 2f out: kpt on ins fnl f but hld* 25/1
3- 4 nk **Bear Island Flint**38 760 5-11-2 0 APMcCoy 101
(Brendan Powell) *hld up in midfield: hdwy 6f out: led over 3f out: rdn over 2f out: hdd 1f out: no ex towards fin: lost 2 pls* 6/5[1]
0- 5 12 **Uiop**9 1016 5-10-9 0 JakeHodson(7) 90
(David Bridgwater) *trckd ldrs tl wknd over 2f out* 16/1
0- 6 7 **Looselipssinkships (IRE)**24 862 6-10-11 0 (t) HarryChalloner(5) 84
(William Kinsey) *midfield: outpcd and lost pl 6f out: plugged on wout threatening fnl 2f* 20/1
0/0- 7 38 **Stantastic**35 790 5-10-11 0 SamanthaDrake(5) 50
(Mark Campion) *in rr: hdwy into midfield 5f out: rdn over 4f out: wknd 3f out* 66/1
04/ 8 5 **Jock Des Mottes (FR)**69 6-10-9 0 MrJMRidley(7) 45
(Elizabeth Juckes) *hld up: pushed along 6f out: bhd after* 12/1
9 28 **Tunnel Vision (IRE)**573 6-10-13 0 RobertDunne(3) 20
(Nikki Evans) *prom tl rdn and wknd 5f out* 25/1
3m 45.7s (-0.70) **Going Correction** -0.20s/f (Good) **9** Ran SP% **119.5**
Speed ratings: **93,91,91,91,85 81,62,60,46**
CSF £16.29 TOTE £2.50: £1.20, £2.80, £4.00; EX 16.10 Trifecta £166.20 Pool: £1344.93 - 6.06 winning units..
Owner P Chapman **Bred** L G Vambeck **Trained** West Wratting, Cambs

FOCUS
An ordinary bumper rated around the winner and the fourth.
T/Plt: £11.90 to a £1 stake. Pool: £69124.59 - 4233.72 winning tickets T/Opdt: £9.10 to a £1 stake. Pool: £4165.00 - 337.85 winning tickets DO

1125 - 1131a (Foreign Racing) - See Raceform Interactive

1118 UTTOXETER (L-H)
Monday, July 29

OFFICIAL GOING: Good to soft (good to soft in places; soft in chute) changing to soft (good to soft in places) after race 2 (6:20)
Wind: nil Weather: heavy rain showers; 19 degrees

1132 SIGNS 2000 MARES' NOVICES' HURDLE (9 hdls) 2m
5:50 (5:50) (Class 4) 4-Y-0+ **£3,249** (£954; £477; £238)

Form RPR
121- 1 **Rosie Probert**5 1107 4-11-8 115 APMcCoy 115+
(Nicky Henderson) *pressed ldr: led bef 3 out: sn hdd: hrd drvn fr 2 out: looked hld last but responded gamely to str driving and forced ahd nr fin* 2/5[1]
/12- 2 nk **Bittersweetheart**12 1008 6-11-3 108 SamTwiston-Davies 109
(David Bridgwater) *trckd ldng pair tl effrt to ld 3 out: mstke next: sn drvn: 3 l clr last: kpt on tl pipped on post* 3/1[2]
/06- 3 12 **Rose Red**40 761 6-10-7 0 JamesBest(3) 90
(Rob Summers) *settled in rr: mstke 5th: rdn and outpcd after 6th: plugged on in poor 3rd fr next* 50/1
U4- 4 22 **Night Of Passion (IRE)**21 922 5-10-10 0 NickScholfield 68
(Jeremy Scott) *settled in rr: lost tch u.p 6th: t.o bef next* 33/1
5 4½ **I Told You So (IRE)**59 4-10-8 0 JasonMaguire 61
(Donald McCain) *t.k.h: led at modest pce tl hdd bef 3 out where nt fluent whn losing grnd rapidly: t.o next* 11/1[3]
6 2¾ **Spanish Trail**10 4-10-8 0 MarkGrant 58
(Christopher Kellett) *t.k.h in last: mstke 5th: mstke next and lost tch: t.o bef 3 out* 125/1
/0- P **Scommettitrice (IRE)**12 1017 5-10-10 0 (t) TomCannon
(Mark Gillard) *t.k.h: cl up tl 5th: sddle slipped and p.u next* 125/1
3m 52.6s (0.60) **Going Correction** +0.10s/f (Yiel) **7** Ran SP% **111.3**
Speed ratings (Par 105): **102,101,95,84,82 81,**
toteswingers 1&2 £1.30, 1&3 £5.20, 2&3 £5.60 CSF £1.85 TOTE £1.40: £1.10, £1.40; EX 2.00 Trifecta £9.00 Pool: £1970.47 - 163.09 winning units..
Owner Seasons Holidays **Bred** Seasons Holidays **Trained** Upper Lambourn, Berks

FOCUS
This ordinary mares' novice hurdle saw the two clear market leaders dominate. The winner can rate higher with the second to her mark.

1133 GORDON BANKS STOKE CITY OLD BOYS BEGINNERS' CHASE (13 fncs 2 omitted) 2m 4f
6:20 (6:20) (Class 4) 4-Y-0+ **£3,798** (£1,122; £561; £280; £140)

Form RPR
0/6- 1 **High Storm (IRE)**36 806 6-11-9 117 SamTwiston-Davies 126+
(Bernard Llewellyn) *racd in 2nd or 3rd: nt fluent 7th: hrd drvn bef 3 out: led next: gained upper hand last where 3 l clr: doing little in front and kpt rt up to work* 12/1
3U0- 2 1½ **Gud Day (IRE)**21 924 5-11-9 0 (t) PaddyBrennan 124
(Fergal O'Brien) *tended to lack fluency: hld up and bhd: mstke 8th: effrt and mstke 10th: chal on inner gng wl 3 out: rdn and ev ch next: outpcd last: clsng again fnl 75yds* 16/1
/23- 3 2½ **Notarfbad (IRE)**39 779 7-11-9 121 NickScholfield 122
(Jeremy Scott) *t.k.h: led: rdn 3 out: hdd next: sn 3rd: nt qckn fr last* 5/2[2]
00/- 4 11 **Trop Fort (FR)**103 5352 6-11-9 0 (t) RichardJohnson 113
(Tim Vaughan) *pressed ldrs tl rdn 3 out: no rspnse and sn modest 4th: eased bef last* 11/8[1]
5 20 **Julie Prince (IRE)**141 4693 7-11-9 0 WillKennedy 90
(Brendan Powell) *trckd ldrs on outer: looked to be gng wl 8th: dropped to rr and hit 10th: kpt on steadily although no ch after* 40/1
242- 6 14 **Nomadic Dreamer**22 899 10-11-9 114 (t) PaulMoloney 76
(Sophie Leech) *bhd: hit 8th: struggling 10th: wnt remote 5th and hit next: t.o* 6/1[3]
7 2½ **Checkmate**79 8-11-9 0 MarkGrant 74
(Christopher Kellett) *last mostly and nt a fluent: lost tch bef 10th: t.o next* 150/1
5/4- 8 1¼ **War Of The World (FR)**22 899 7-11-6 0 (b[1]) AdamWedge(3) 72
(Chris Bealby) *mstke 3rd: 2nd or 3rd tl bef 10th: sn hrd drvn and dropped out: t.o 3 out* 33/1
3/0- 9 shd **Rifle Shot (IRE)**36 808 6-11-9 0 JasonMaguire 72
(Donald McCain) *hld up and nvr bttr than midfield: rdn and lost tch tamely 10th: t.o next* 16/1
5m 7.3s (1.80) **Going Correction** +0.10s/f (Yiel) **9** Ran SP% **110.5**
Speed ratings (Par 105): **100,99,98,94,86 80,79,78,78**
toteswingers 1&2 £9.30, 1&3 £4.30, 2&3 £2.30 CSF £153.23 TOTE £14.30: £3.10, £2.10, £1.20; EX 107.70 Trifecta £598.40 Part won. Pool: £797.98 - 0.52 winning units..
Owner D R James **Bred** Barry Walters Farms **Trained** Fochriw, Caerphilly

FOCUS
A weak beginners' chase. The open ditch (three out) was omitted in all chases due to false ground. The first two are rated in line with the best of their hurdles form while the third is close to his recent chase debut mark.

1134 ANN YATES BIRTHDAY CELEBRATION (S) HURDLE (10 hdls) 2m 4f 110y
6:50 (6:50) (Class 5) 4-7-Y-0 **£1,949** (£572; £286; £143)

Form RPR
223- 1 **Polly Hopper**41 755 7-10-5 109 (tp) SamTwiston-Davies 117+
(Nigel Twiston-Davies) *trckd ldrs: effrt after 7th: led on bit 3 out: cruised clr: hit 2 out and last where 25 l ahd: almost p.u fnl 75yds* 7/2[2]
640- 2 23 **Kayfton Pete**22 898 7-11-8 0 (t) AdamPogson 101
(Charles Pogson) *t.k.h: prom tl rdn and rapidly lost two w ldng pair 3 out: drvn to snatch remote 2nd* 25/1
403- 3 hd **Persian Herald**8 1058 5-10-12 96 (v) JamieMoore 91
(Neil King) *midfield: rdn and racing v awkwardly after 5th: 10 l 4th and u.p home turn: laboured hdwy to go remote 2nd momentarily nr fin* 16/1
242- 4 1¼ **Loose Preformer (IRE)**15 967 7-11-5 113 (b[1]) APMcCoy 97
(David O'Meara) *led: 6 l clr early: drvn bef 3 out where hdd: sn no ch w wnr: lost remote 2nd nr fin* 3/1[1]
/P0- P **Hassadin**20 933 7-11-5 105 TomCannon
(Michael Blake) *drvn and no rspnse after 2nd: nvr wnt a yard: hopelessly t.o fr 5th tl p.u 7th* 0/1[1]
/22- P **Paddy Partridge**67 445 7-11-8 110 RichardJohnson
(Tim Vaughan) *chsd ldrs: rdn after 5th: wkng whn nrly fell 7th: sn t.o and p.u* 11/2[3]
40- P **Lucky Vic (IRE)**58 585 7-11-3 117 (p) GavinSheehan(5)
(Barry Brennan) *j. slowly 2nd: sn bhd and nvr travelling: rdn 4th: mstke 5th: t.o and p.u after 7th* 14/1
5/P- P **Captain Scarlett (IRE)**19 942 7-11-5 0 (p) RhysFlint
(John Flint) *prom tl 5th: lost tch and j. slowly next: t.o and p.u 7th* 10/1
5m 2.5s (3.50) **Going Correction** +0.10s/f (Yiel)
WFA 4 from 5yo+ 16lb **8** Ran SP% **113.1**
Speed ratings: **97,88,88,87, , ,**
toteswingers 1&2 £19.60, 1&3 £8.80, 2&3 £14.40 CSF £71.16 TOTE £5.20: £1.70, £5.00, £4.60; EX 56.00 Trifecta £449.20 Pool: £643.32 - 1.07 winning units..The winner was bought in for 6,200gns.
Owner N A Twiston-Davies **Bred** Mrs Susan Orton **Trained** Naunton, Gloucs

FOCUS
A very weak seller but the winner could rate higher, although not a race to be confident about.

1135 WEATHERBYS HAMILTON INSURANCE H'CAP CHASE (16 fncs 2 omitted) 3m
7:20 (7:21) (Class 4) (0-115,115) 4-Y-0 **£3,798** (£1,122; £561; £280; £140)

Form RPR
/1P- 1 **Papradon**48 714 9-11-4 107 (v) SamTwiston-Davies 119
(Nigel Twiston-Davies) *mstke 3rd: trckd ldrs: wnt 2nd at 12th: chal 3 out: led next: drvn 6 l clr last: kpt up to work and styd on wl* 22/1

34P- 2 9 **Western King (IRE)**15 972 6-11-6 **109**...(tp) NoelFehily 112
(Charlie Mann) *nt fluent 4th: 2nd tl led 8th: drvn 13th: hdd 2 out: sn outpcd by wnr* **16/1**

203- 3 4 ½ **Lukeys Luck**12 1012 7-11-5 **108**... SeanQuinlan 107
(Jennie Candlish) *bhd: sme prog u.p 13th: wnt modest 3rd after 3 out: plugged on and nvr looked like chalng* **17/2**

20P/ 4 15 **Ballyvesey (IRE)**233 2909 8-11-12 **115**...(tp) JamieMoore 99
(Peter Bowen) *midfield: rdn 9th: nt gng wl after: wknd u.p bef 3 out* **14/1**

FF/- 5 12 **Point West (IRE)**57 9-10-8 **97**... NickScholfield 69
(Johnny Farrelly) *bhd: 5th and rdn and 13th: sn lost tch: t.o* **7/2**3

6P0- 6 10 **Double Chocolate**8 1060 10-11-5 **108**...(p) TomCannon 70
(David Bridgwater) *hit 2nd: reminder 3rd: chsd ldrs but nvr travelling: lost tch 10th: t.o next* **20/1**

P/0- P **Michigan Assassin (IRE)**34 832 11-10-8 **102**...(p) AodhaganConlon(5)
(Debra Hamer) *led tl 8th: dropped out qckly u.p 12th: t.o and p.u 3 out* **33/1**

112- P **Quel Ballistic**26 869 9-11-10 **113**...(v) RichardJohnson
(Peter Bowen) *cl up: led briefly 9th: wnt wrong and p.u sharply next* **5/2**1

204/ P **Hoare Abbey (IRE)**108 5266 7-10-11 **100**...(t) PaddyBrennan
(Tom George) *mstkes in rr: struggling whn blnd bdly 10th: t.o and p.u next* **20/1**

/34- P **Balinroab (IRE)**46 728 6-11-12 **115**...(tp) APMcCoy 90
(Jonjo O'Neill) *mstke 1st: rdn 2nd: on and off bridle after and nvr travelling: reminders 8th: chsd ldrs tl 3rd and ch whn blnd 13th: v one pce next: btn 4th whn p.u last* **10/3**2

6m 14.0s (-1.10) **Going Correction** +0.10s/f (Yiel) **10** Ran SP% **113.8**
Speed ratings (Par 105): **105,102,100,95,91 88,,,,**
toteswingers 1&2 £7.80, 1&3 £12.60, 2&3 £27.90 CSF £283.74 CT £3202.84 TOTE £19.60: £3.50, £4.60, £2.10; EX 225.80 Trifecta £497.40 Part won. Pool: £663.32 - 0.12 winning units..
Owner A J Cresser **Bred** B Whitehouse **Trained** Naunton, Gloucs
■ Stewards' Enquiry : Sam Twiston-Davies two-day ban: used whip when clearly winning (Aug 13,15)

FOCUS
A moderate staying handicap, run at a fair gallop and the principals finished well clear. The placed horses are rated close to recent form.

1136 MEDIA RESOURCES H'CAP HURDLE (FOR THE KEN BOULTON MEMORIAL TROPHY) (12 hdls) 3m

7:50 (7:50) (Class 4) (0-105,105) 4-Y-0+ **£3,249** (£954; £477; £238)

Form RPR

/00- 1 **Award Winner**46 730 10-10-13 **92**...(v) APMcCoy 94+
(Brendan Powell) *2nd tl led after 9th: sn given reminders and kpt up to work after: hdd sn after last: led again 100yds out and urged clr* **9/2**2

/63- 2 1 **Zafaraban (IRE)**8 1061 6-11-9 **102**... LeeEdwards 102
(Tony Carroll) *rn in snatches: in rr and drvn 8th: effrt u.p 3 out: wnt 2nd at next: drvn to chal and nt fluent last: sn led: hdd and outbattled fnl 100yds* **16/1**

400/ 3 2 ¼ **Corso Palladio (IRE)**241 2738 11-11-7 **100**...(tp) TomO'Brien 98
(F Lloyd) *bhd: rdn 8th: and nt looked to be gng wl and stl 8th on home turn: laboured prog to go 3rd at last: no further imp on flat* **7/2**1

/13- 4 6 **Thornton Alice**36 811 8-11-7 **100**... RichardJohnson 93
(Richard Phillips) *led: j.rt 6th: hit 7th: drvn and hdd bef 3 out: remained cl up tl between last two: fading after last* **13/2**

F2P- 5 9 **Minella Fifty (IRE)**38 789 5-11-6 **104**...(t) MauriceLinehan(5) 93+
(Jonjo O'Neill) *chsd ldrs: rdn and no imp fr 3 out: 5th and wl hld whn blnd bdly last* **10/1**

U/4- 6 7 **Moorlands Jack**27 860 8-11-6 **99**... NickScholfield 75
(Jeremy Scott) *midfield: effrt 8th: wnt 2nd 3 out tl rdn next: sn wknd* **5/1**3

514- 7 6 **Inside Knowledge (USA)**29 854 7-11-3 **96**... AdamPogson 66
(Garry Woodward) *j. slowly 4th: in rr-div mostly: rdn and modest prog on outer whn mstke 3 out: no ch after* **11/2**

P/5- 8 25 **Windwood Lad**25 884 8-11-5 **105**... MrNMcParlan(7) 50
(Michael O'Hare, Ire) *cl up: nt fluent 5th: mstke 8th: sn rdn: fdd bef 3 out: t.o* **16/1**

0/0- P **Honour The World (IRE)**64 503 8-11-7 **100**...(bt) DavidEngland
(Shaun Lycett) *chsd ldrs: rdn 6th: lost tch 9th: t.o and p.u 3 out* **25/1**

/62- P **Arisda**55 629 5-11-9 **102**... JasonMaguire
(Johnny Farrelly) *bhd: last whn nt fluent 5th and rdn: sn struggling: t.o and p.u 3 out* **10/1**

5m 59.7s (9.70) **Going Correction** +0.40s/f (Soft) **10** Ran SP% **119.6**
Speed ratings (Par 105): **99,98,97,95,92 90,88,80,,**
toteswingers 1&2 £61.20, 1&3 £3.40, 2&3 £61.20 CSF £72.79 CT £284.68 TOTE £5.80: £2.10, £3.90, £2.00; EX 119.70 Trifecta £337.20 Part won. Pool: £449.69 - 0.58 winning units..
Owner John P McManus **Bred** Mrs L M Northover **Trained** Upper Lambourn, Berks
■ Stewards' Enquiry : Lee Edwards four-day ban: used whip above permitted level (Aug 15,17,18)

FOCUS
An open handicap but modest form with the runner-up rated to his mark.

1137 J&R CONSTRUCTION H'CAP HURDLE (9 hdls) 2m

8:20 (8:22) (Class 5) (0-100,94) 4-Y-0+ **£2,339** (£686; £343; £171)

Form RPR

/30- 1 **Capellini**78 243 6-10-6 **78**... GavinSheehan(5) 89
(Charles Egerton) *mstke 5th: 2nd or 3rd tl led bef 2 out: hrd pressed tl last: drvn and grad asserted flat* **8/1**

0/2- 2 1 ½ **Royal Trooper (IRE)**5 1106 7-11-2 **83**...(vt1) APMcCoy 94
(Jim Best) *trckd ldrs: 3rd after 6th: cl 2nd but rdn whn mstke 2 out: ev ch after tl fnd little fr last and wl hld fnl 100yds* **1/2**1

603/ 3 10 **Kingaroo (IRE)**58 3384 7-10-11 **78**... AdamPogson 80
(Garry Woodward) *2nd or 3rd tl led bef 5th: rdn and hdd bef 2 out: btn 4th whn blnd last: wnt 3rd flat* **25/1**

442- 4 3 ½ **Drawn Free (IRE)**21 924 5-11-9 **90**... JoeTizzard 87
(Colin Tizzard) *a abt same pl: rdn 3 out: 3rd whn mstke next: nt qckn after: lost 3rd after last* **7/1**3

P/1- 5 12 **Lodgician (IRE)**7 1078 11-11-13 **94** 7ex...(vt) SamTwiston-Davies 78
(Nigel Twiston-Davies) *led tl racd awkwardly and hdd bef 6th: sn lost pl completely: plugged on w no ch fr 3 out* **4/1**2

200/ 6 46 **Nouailhas**145 4590 7-11-4 **85**... PaulMoloney 23
(Andrew Hollinshead) *a bhd: t.o after 6th* **50/1**

6/0- 7 9 **Strandfield Bay (IRE)**25 881 7-10-10 **84**... MrNMcParlan(7) 13
(Michael O'Hare, Ire) *chsd ldrs tl rdn and fdd 3 out: hopelessly t.o* **25/1**

2/0- 8 5 **Petrocelli**53 640 6-11-4 **85**... RichardJohnson 9
(Tim Vaughan) *nt jump wl in rr: t.o after 6th* **14/1**

0/0- P **Teals Star**81 184 9-10-8 **75**... TommyPhelan
(C I Ratcliffe) *bhd: rdn 3rd: struggling after: hmpd 5th: t.o whn bad mstke 6th: p.u next* **80/1**

550- F **Haveumistim**49 686 7-10-13 **85**... RobertWilliams(5)
(Bernard Llewellyn) *midfield tl fell 5th* **50/1**

3m 57.8s (5.80) **Going Correction** +0.40s/f (Soft) **10** Ran SP% **129.8**
Speed ratings (Par 103): **101,100,95,93,87 64,60,57,,**
toteswingers 1&2 £2.20, 1&3 £31.40, 2&3 £5.70 CSF £14.25 CT £128.58 TOTE £13.00: £2.20, £1.10, £3.10; EX 22.60 Trifecta £226.20 Pool: £1018.17 - 3.37 winning units..
Owner Bruce Pomford & Malcolm Frost **Bred** Wertheimer Et Frere **Trained** Upper Lambourn, Berks

FOCUS
A weak handicap, run at a fair gallop in which two pulled well clear. The winner is rated to his previous winning form, but the race could rate higher through the third and fourth.

1138 #UTTOXETERTWITTERATI SUPPORT THE RAFBF FUND STANDARD OPEN NATIONAL HUNT FLAT RACE 2m

8:50 (8:50) (Class 6) 4-6-Y-0 **£1,559** (£457; £228; £114)

Form RPR

3- 1 **Balmusette**72 372 4-10-5 0... JamesReveley 100+
(Keith Reveley) *trckd ldrs: led gng wl over 3f out: 2 l clr and rdn ins fnl f: eased fnl strides* **11/8**1

23- 2 hd **Mutanawwer**25 885 4-10-12 0... BrianHughes 106
(Andrew Crook) *midfield: effrt and chsd wnr over 2f out: racd awkwardly: hrd drvn and styd on ins fnl f: jst hld* **7/2**2

3 2 ¼ **Grand March** 4-10-7 0... EdCookson(5) 104
(Kim Bailey) *hld up: effrt 4f out: sn pressing ldrs: disp 2nd over 2f out: kpt on steadily wout threatening fr over 1f out* **20/1**

4 1 ¼ **The Winking Prawn (IRE)** 6-11-0 0... JasonMaguire 105
(Kim Bailey) *rn in snatches: effrt on outside home turn: sn outpcd: running green after but plugged on steadily* **12/1**

3- 5 8 **Grape Tree Flame**26 874 5-10-7 0... TomO'Brien 90
(F Lloyd) *rn in snatches: in tch tl rdn and floundering in grnd over 2f out* **12/1**

6 1 ¾ **Ruperra Tom** 5-11-0 0... APMcCoy 95
(Sophie Leech) *settled in rr: hdwy 5f out: 3rd over 3f out: rdn and sn btn* **17/2**

7 2 ¼ **Sebastians Charm (IRE)** 5-10-9 0... GavinSheehan(5) 93
(Warren Greatrex) *drvn 5f out: struggling fnl 3f* **20/1**

8 ¾ **Mighty Leader (IRE)** 5-10-7 0... MrNMcParlan(7) 94
(Michael O'Hare, Ire) *chsd ldr tl home turn: rdn and sn lost pl* **8/1**3

0/ 9 12 **Henrio (IRE)**64 5-11-0 0... AlainCawley 80
(Fergal O'Brien) *set stdy pce tl rdn and hdd over 3f out: sn dropped out: t.o* **50/1**

- 10 21 **Wotsthecatch (IRE)** 5-11-0 0... TomScudamore 59
(Michael Scudamore) *lost tch 6f out: t.o fnl 3f* **25/1**

3m 52.7s (6.30) **Going Correction** +0.40s/f (Soft)
WFA 4 from 5yo+ 2lb **10** Ran SP% **116.7**
Speed ratings: **100,99,98,98,94 93,92,91,85,75**
toteswingers 1&2 £1.20, 1&3 £15.50, 2&3 £13.10 CSF £5.56 TOTE £2.50: £1.10, £1.30, £5.30; EX 5.50 Trifecta £103.90 Pool: £806.06 - 5.81 winning units..
Owner Mr & Mrs W J Williams **Bred** W J & Mrs M Williams **Trained** Lingdale, Redcar & Cleveland
■ Stewards' Enquiry : Brian Hughes seven-day ban: used whip above permitted level (Aug 13,15,17-21)

FOCUS
A modest bumper and a dramatic finish. The winner should have more to come while the second is rated to his mark.
T/Plt: £280.40 to a £1 stake. Pool: £92647.50 - 241.13 winning tickets T/Qpdt: £115.60 to a £1 stake. Pool: £6475.89 - 41.45 winning tickets IM

GALWAY (R-H)
Monday, July 29

OFFICIAL GOING: Flat - yielding (yielding to soft in places); nh - good (good to yielding in places)

1139a GALWAYBAYHOTEL.COM NOVICE HURDLE (9 hdls) 2m

5:10 (5:10) 4-Y-0 **£10,569** (£3,089; £1,463; £487)

RPR

1 **Diplomat (USA)**15 979 4-11-4 125... RWalsh 131+
(D K Weld, Ire) *chsd ldrs: travelled wl to press ldrs in 3rd 2 out: sn led: styd on wl run-in: pushed out clsng stages* **9/10**1

2 1 **Sky Khan**11 928 4-10-11 115...(p) AdamNicol(7) 130+
(Philip Kirby) *trckd ldrs in 4th tl clsd in 3rd last: styd on wl run-in to go clr 2nd: clsng on wnr wout getting on terms* **10/1**3

3 6 **Honourable Emperor (IRE)**24 887 4-11-4 115... DavyCondon 124
(Noel Meade, Ire) *chsd ldrs tl tk clsr order 2 out: clsd to press ldr in 2nd last: no imp and dropped to 3rd run-in* **22/1**

4 3 **Dawerann (IRE)**20 934 4-11-4 118...(t) BarryGeraghty 121
(Michael Hourigan, Ire) *w.w: prog to chse ldrs bef last in 5th: kpt on wl run-in: nvr nrr* **12/1**

5 7 **King Of The Picts (IRE)**24 887 4-11-4 125... AndrewJMcNamara 116
(John Patrick Shanahan, Ire) *sn trckd ldr in 2nd: led appr 2 out: sn hdd: one pce and dropped to 4th appr last* **9/2**2

6 1 ¾ **Celtic Monarch (IRE)**24 887 4-10-13 113... DerekFox(5) 112
(Mark Michael McNiff, Ire) *hld up in rr tl prog 2 out: wnt 7th appr last: kpt on wl run-in: nvr nrr* **50/1**

7 1 ¼ **Green Dragon (FR)**24 887 4-11-4 127... PaulTownend 111
(A J Martin, Ire) *racd in mid-div tl prog to chse ldrs bef 2 out: sn pushed along and no imp appr last* **14/1**

8 31 **Boss's Star (IRE)**84 148 4-11-4 117... AlanCrowe 80
(Peter Casey, Ire) *led and clr tl advantage reduced 3 out: hdd bef next: sn wknd* **16/1**

9 1 ¾ **Ebazan (USA)**34 834 4-10-13 122...(b) BenDalton(5) 78
(Conor O'Dwyer, Ire) *racd in mid-div: pushed along to chse ldrs bef 2 out: sn no ex* **14/1**

10 11 **Zabana (IRE)**36 815 4-11-7 121... RobbieColgan 70
(Andrew Lynch, Ire) *chsd ldrs: clsd to trck ldrs in 3rd w a circ to r: strly drvn bef 2 out: sn no ex* **10/1**3

11 6 **Star For Life (USA)**59 571 4-11-0... RobbieMoran 57
(Eoin Doyle, Ire) *a in rr: no threat after 3 out: t.o* **40/1**

12 37 **Ancelotti (IRE)**6 1095 4-11-0 1... BrianO'Connell 20
(Michael G Cleary, Ire) *a in rr: nvr a factor: t.o* **100/1**

13 9 ½ **Vito De Beauchene (FR)**78 4-11-0... MarkWalsh 11
(F Flood, Ire) *trckd ldrs early: 6th w a circ to r: wknd 3 out: t.o* **28/1**

3m 59.1s (2.40) **13** Ran SP% **129.1**
CSF £12.17 TOTE £1.90: £1.10, £3.00, £4.60; DF 16.90.
Owner Dr R Lambe **Bred** Kenneth L. Ramsey & Sarah K. Ramsey **Trained** The Curragh, Co Kildare

The Form Book Jumps, Raceform Ltd, Compton, RG20 6NL.

FOCUS
The first two came well clear, winner probably value for further.

1140 - 1141a (Foreign Racing) - See Raceform Interactive

956 PERTH (R-H)
Tuesday, July 30

OFFICIAL GOING: Good to soft (good in places; 6.7)
Wind: Breezy, half behind Weather: Overcast, showers

1142 WATCH ALL SCOTTISH RACING LIVE ON RACINGUK NOVICES' HURDLE (12 hdls) 3m 110y
6:00 (6:00) (Class 4) 4-Y-0+ **£3,165** (£935; £467)

Form RPR
231- **1** **Billfromthebar (IRE)**[13] 1019 6-11-5 117 JasonMaguire 129
(Donald McCain) *led: rdn and hdd after 3 out: outpcd and 7 l down next: styd on wl fr last to ld cl home* **15/8**[2]
/31- **2** *1* **Otto The Great (FR)**[55] 633 5-11-0 127 NicodeBoinville(5) 128
(Nicky Henderson) *t.k.h early: w wnr: led after 3 out: 7 l clr next: pushed along and idled run-in: hdd cl home* **8/11**[1]
2/3- **3** *23* **Be My Deputy (IRE)**[26] 883 8-10-12 0 (b) PeterBuchanan 102
(Lucinda Russell) *j.big on occasions: chsd ldrs: outpcd 4 out: n.d after* **13/2**[3]

6m 9.3s (4.30) **Going Correction** -0.25s/f (Good) **3** Ran SP% **106.0**
Speed ratings (Par 105): **83,82,75**
CSF £3.67 TOTE £2.70; EX 3.40 Trifecta £3.50 Pool: £418.78 - 89.27 winning units..
Owner Matthew Sanders **Bred** Andrew Pierce **Trained** Cholmondeley, Cheshire

FOCUS
All bends moved out on to fresh ground. With just a trio of runners this staying novice affair was predictably tactical. The gallop lifted going on to the final lap and it concerned just the first two from four out, but there was a dramatic finish. The form is rated around the principals.

1143 FONAB CASTLE HOTEL AMATEUR RIDERS' H'CAP HURDLE (8 hdls) 2m 110y
6:30 (6:33) (Class 4) (0-105,105) 4-Y-0+ **£3,293** (£1,013; £506)

Form RPR
/64- **1** **Cadore (IRE)**[37] 803 5-10-11 93 (p) MikeyEnnis(3) 98
(Lucy Normile) *hld up: hit 4th: stdy hdwy after 4 out: led bef 2 out: clr bef last: pushed out* **2/1**[2]
111- **2** *6* **Morning Time (IRE)**[26] 879 7-10-9 95 (p) MissRMcDonald(7) 95
(Lucinda Russell) *in tch: effrt bef 2 out: chsng clr wnr whn nt fluent last: no imp run-in* **7/4**[1]
/15- **3** *6* **Logical Approach (IRE)**[10] 1041 6-11-2 102 (p) MrRSmith(7) 97
(David Thompson) *hld up: hdwy bef 3 out: effrt and chsd wnr briefly next: outpcd run-in* **9/1**
/05- **4** *3 ½* **Cigalas**[56] 630 8-9-7 79 oh14 MissAMcGregor(7) 70
(Jean McGregor) *led and clr to 4th: hdd next: led 3 out to bef next: wknd bef last* **80/1**
P40/ **5** *24* **King Brex (DEN)**[96] 5520 10-10-4 90 (v[1]) MrKitAlexander(7) 59
(N W Alexander) *cl up: led 4th to next: rdn and wknd bef 2 out* **15/2**[3]
0/P- **F** **Lap Of Honour (IRE)**[27] 870 9-10-9 95 MrRMorganMurphy(7)
(Ferdy Murphy, France) *hld up: hdwy and prom after 3rd: 4 l 3rd and gng wl whn fell 3 out* **16/1**
000- **P** **Stand Clear**[10] 1043 8-10-4 90 (v[1]) MrPDennis(7)
(David Thompson) *reluctant to go to post: bhd: lost tch after 3 out: p.u next* **25/1**
302/ **P** **Edgware Road**[27] 4980 5-11-5 105 MissBHampson(7)
(Sean Curran) *t.k.h: prom: lost pl after 4th: struggling after 4 out: t.o whn p.u bef 2 out* **8/1**

3m 52.2s (-5.80) **Going Correction** -0.25s/f (Good) **8** Ran SP% **113.5**
Speed ratings (Par 105): **103,100,97,95,84 , ,**
toteswingers 1&2 £1.80, 2&3 £4.50, 1&3 £3.90 CSF £6.01 CT £22.50 TOTE £3.50: £1.40, £1.10, £2.20; EX 6.90 Trifecta £37.80 Pool: £1501.30 - 29.74 winning units..
Owner L B N Racing Club **Bred** Michael O'Callaghan **Trained** Duncrievie, Perth & Kinross

FOCUS
A typically moderate handicap for amateur riders. The horses in the frame behind the winner set the level.

1144 ISLE OF SKYE 8-Y-O BLENDED SCOTCH WHISKY NOVICES' CHASE (12 fncs) 2m
7:00 (7:00) (Class 4) 5-Y-0+ **£4,431** (£1,309; £654; £327)

Form RPR
/02- **1** **Twentypoundluck (IRE)**[26] 882 8-10-12 113 (v[1]) JamesReveley 120
(Patrick Griffin, Ire) *chsd clr ldr: clsd 7th: led 4 out: rdn next: edgd rt run-in: styd on strly* **9/2**[3]
223- **2** *2 ¼* **Mulligan's Man (IRE)**[23] 899 6-10-12 117 JasonMaguire 118
(Donald McCain) *hld up in tch: effrt whn hit 3 out: styd on wl fr last to take 2nd last 50yds: nt rch wnr* **6/4**[2]
/2U- **3** *1 ¾* **Rhymers Ha'**[37] 798 6-10-5 121 GrahamWatters(7) 116
(Lucinda Russell) *chsd ldrs: effrt and wnt 2nd 3 out: rdn and clsd next: one pce run-in: lost 2nd last 50yds* **11/8**[1]
133- **4** *16* **Toledo Gold (IRE)**[26] 882 7-11-5 112 (t) MichaelMcAlister 111
(Maurice Barnes) *t.k.h: led and clr to 7th: hdd 4 out: wknd bef 2 out* **11/1**

3m 50.9s (-6.10) **Going Correction** -0.25s/f (Good) **4** Ran SP% **108.6**
Speed ratings: **105,103,103,95**
CSF £11.83 TOTE £3.90; EX 7.20 Trifecta £15.70 Pool: £391.88 - 18.67winning units..
Owner M Deren **Bred** John Murphy **Trained** Oldtown, Co Dublin

FOCUS
An ordinary novice chase, run at a solid gallop. Steps up from the first two and the form could be rated higher.

1145 WATCH ALL SCOTTISH RACING LIVE ON RACINGUK MAIDEN HURDLE (10 hdls) 2m 4f 110y
7:35 (7:35) (Class 5) 4-Y-0+ **£2,532** (£748; £374; £187; £93)

Form RPR
/54- **1** **Tantamount**[27] 865 4-10-4 98 CraigNichol(7) 109
(Lucinda Russell) *t.k.h: hld up: smooth hdwy and ev ch whn nt fluent 2 out: sn led: hung rt last: kpt on strly* **12/1**
2 *6* **Butney Boy (IRE)**[39] 795 7-11-0 104 (p) DenisO'Regan 107
(C A McBratney, Ire) *prom: hdwy to ld briefly appr 2 out: kpt on fr last: no ch w wnr* **8/1**
2- **3** *1 ¼* **Sultana Belle (IRE)**[16] 984 5-10-4 100 MrSCrawford(3) 98
(S R B Crawford, Ire) *hld up: hdwy and in tch bef 2 out: sn rdn: one pce fr last* **11/4**[2]
3- **4** *9* **Cloudy Joker (IRE)**[16] 962 5-11-0 0 JasonMaguire 99
(Donald McCain) *pressed ldr: led 3 out to bef next: sn rdn and outpcd* **11/8**[1]
5 *26* **Aintnosanityclause (IRE)**[16] 981 5-10-7 0 PeterBuchanan 67
(S R B Crawford, Ire) *midfield: outpcd whn nt fluent 3 out: sn btn* **8/1**
P3P/ **6** *¾* **Vivona Hill**[579] 3423 9-11-0 0 BrianHarding 73
(Nicky Richards) *hld up in tch: stdy hdwy bef 3 out: rdn and wknd bef next* **13/2**[3]
63- **7** *41* **Tim's Approach (IRE)**[16] 959 8-10-11 0 (p) JohnKington(3) 36
(William Young Jnr) *prom to 4 out: sn struggling: lost tch fr next: t.o* **100/1**
/62- **P** **Dynamic Drive (IRE)**[16] 959 6-10-7 87 (t) StephenMulqueen(7)
(Maurice Barnes) *led: qcknd 1/2-way: hdd 3 out: sn wknd: t.o whn p.u after next* **33/1**

4m 58.0s (-4.00) **Going Correction** -0.25s/f (Good)
WFA 4 from 5yo+ 16lb **8** Ran SP% **116.0**
Speed ratings (Par 103): **97,94,94,90,80 80,65,**
toteswingers 1&2 £10.00, 2&3 £4.40, 1&3 £5.70 CSF £102.06 TOTE £13.50: £2.70, £2.20, £1.10; EX 58.70 Trifecta £442.00 Pool: £734.54 - 1.24 winning units..
Owner Mutual Friends **Bred** Juddmonte Farms Ltd **Trained** Arlary, Perth & Kinross

FOCUS
This was a weak maiden. The winner is on the upgrade through and the second is rated to his mark.

1146 ORION GROUP H'CAP CHASE (18 fncs) 3m
8:05 (8:05) (Class 3) (0-140,133) 4-Y-0 **£6,963** (£2,057; £1,028; £514; £257)

Form RPR
/00- **1** **Mumbles Head (IRE)**[51] 680 12-11-7 128 (p) TomO'Brien 139+
(Peter Bowen) *trckd ldrs: lost pl briefly after 4 out: rallied next: ev ch 2 out: led last: drvn out* **11/4**[2]
2/3- **2** *5* **Quito Du Tresor (FR)**[51] 677 9-10-9 123 (p) GrahamWatters(7) 129
(Lucinda Russell) *in tch: smooth hdwy to ld 3 out: rdn and hdd last: kpt on same pce run-in* **11/1**
6/2- **3** *11* **Owen Glendower (IRE)**[23] 900 8-11-7 133 NicodeBoinville(5) 129
(Nicky Henderson) *t.k.h: nt fluent on occasions: chsd ldrs: effrt and ev ch 3 out: sn rdn: outpcd fr next* **11/8**[1]
033- **4** *13* **Dj Milan (IRE)**[16] 957 7-10-11 118 (t) JasonMaguire 104
(Donald McCain) *mde most tl nt fluent and hdd 3 out: sn rdn and wknd* **5/1**[3]
6/2- **5** *9* **Call Box (IRE)**[27] 867 8-11-1 122 PeterBuchanan 101
(S R B Crawford, Ire) *w ldr: effrt and ev ch whn mstke 3 out: sn rdn and wknd* **11/2**

6m 0.8s (-3.20) **Going Correction** -0.25s/f (Good) **5** Ran SP% **109.2**
Speed ratings (Par 107): **95,93,89,85,82**
CSF £24.95 TOTE £5.80: £5.20, £6.70; EX 25.20 Trifecta £20.10 Pool: £548.98 - 20.45 winning units..
Owner Mrs Karen Bowen **Bred** John Sweeney **Trained** Little Newcastle, Pembrokes

FOCUS
They went a routine early gallop in this fair handicap but it lifted near the eighth fence and the first pair dominated from the last. The runner-up is rated in line with recent form.

1147 CONCERTO SPRING BARLEY NOVICES' H'CAP CHASE (15 fncs) 2m 4f 110y
8:35 (8:38) (Class 4) (0-110,110) 4-Y-0 **£3,798** (£1,122; £561; £280; £140)

Form RPR
233- **1** **Polarbrook (IRE)**[13] 1015 6-11-7 105 JasonMaguire 114+
(Donald McCain) *hld up in tch: hit 6th: stdy hdwy bef 3 out: led last: drvn out* **3/1**[2]
4/1- **2** *3* **Lord Of Drums (IRE)**[26] 882 7-11-4 102 PeterBuchanan 105
(Lucinda Russell) *led to 4th: chsd ldr: mstke 8th (water): led bef 3 out: rdn and hdd last: rallied: one pce last 100yds* **7/2**[3]
153/ **3** *14* **Forestside (IRE)**[81] 212 8-11-4 102 BrianHughes 93
(Barry Murtagh) *trckd ldrs: effrt and shkn up 2 out: outpcd fr last* **16/1**
602- **4** *1 ¼* **Diddley Dee**[27] 866 9-10-3 94 MikeyEnnis(7) 87
(Lucy Normile) *nt jump wl in rr: outpcd whn blnd 11th: plugged on fr 2 out: nvr on terms* **7/2**[3]
F/3- **5** *8* **Mourne Paddy (IRE)**[51] 679 9-11-9 110 EwanWhillans(3) 100
(S R B Crawford, Ire) *j.lft thrght: cl up: led 4th: mstke 11th: hdd bef 3 out: drvn whn blnd next: sn btn* **10/1**
/12- **6** *57* **Feisty Lass (IRE)**[16] 958 7-10-11 95 (bt) WilsonRenwick 26
(Gordon Elliott, Ire) *nt jump wl in rr: rdn and flashed tail fr 1/2-way: lost tch fr 11th* **9/4**[1]
/00- **7** *¾* **Snooze N You Lose**[56] 627 8-9-11 84 oh25 (p) JohnKington(3) 14
(Jean McGregor) *chsd ldrs: reminders 1/2-way: wknd 11th: t.o* **100/1**

5m 5.5s (0.50) **Going Correction** -0.25s/f (Good) **7** Ran SP% **116.2**
Speed ratings (Par 105): **89,87,82,82,79 57,57**
toteswingers 1&2 £3.00, 2&3 £5.50, 1&3 £7.40 CSF £14.80 TOTE £3.80: £1.70, £1.80; EX 11.50 Trifecta £163.50 Pool: £992.40 - 4.55 winning units..
Owner Lucky Bln Racing **Bred** Mrs Helen Power Wall **Trained** Cholmondeley, Cheshire

FOCUS
An ordinary novice handicap and another race where two came clear up the run-in. The first two are rated to the level of recent form.

1148 CRABBIE'S ALCOHOLIC GINGER BEER H'CAP HURDLE (8 hdls) 2m 110y
9:05 (9:07) (Class 3) (0-135,126) 4-Y-0 **£5,697** (£1,683; £841; £421; £210)

Form RPR
2/6- **1** **Outrageous Request**[27] 870 7-11-1 115 PeterBuchanan 117
(Lucinda Russell) *hld up: rdn and hdwy bef 2 out: led run-in: drvn out* **5/1**[3]
/1- **2** *½* **Howwoulduno (IRE)**[37] 800 5-10-8 115 GrahamWatters(7) 118
(Liam Lennon, Ire) *cl up on outside: effrt and ev ch whn blkd 2 out: rallied: kpt on wl towards fin* **10/3**[1]
0/ **3** *1 ½* **Toye Native (IRE)**[39] 791 5-11-8 122 DenisO'Regan 123
(C A McBratney, Ire) *trckd ldrs: rdn and outpcd bef 2 out: styd on fr last* **4/1**[2]
/11- **4** *½* **Lisbon (IRE)**[27] 870 5-11-12 126 (t) JamesReveley 127
(Patrick Griffin, Ire) *w ldr: led 4th: rdn whn j.lft 2 out: hdd run-in: kpt on same pce* **4/1**[2]
0/2- **5** *4* **The Ice Factor**[27] 870 5-11-0 117 MrSCrawford(3) 114
(S R B Crawford, Ire) *hld up in tch: drvn and outpcd after 3 out: rallied bef last: no imp* **4/1**[2]
134- **6** *18* **Super Collider**[10] 1048 6-10-5 115 (bt) JamesCorbett(10) 95
(Susan Corbett) *plld hrd: chsd ldrs tl rdn and wknd bef 2 out* **20/1**

045/ 7 61 **Unknown Rebel (IRE)**[234] 2930 5-11-7 121 .... JasonMaguire 47
(Donald McCain) *mde most to 4 out: sn lost pl: lost tch and eased fnl 2* **10/1**

3m 52.6s (-5.40) **Going Correction** -0.25s/f (Good) 7 Ran SP% **113.6**
Speed ratings (Par 107): **102,101,101,100,98 90,61**
toteswingers 1&2 £6.20, 2&3 £2.50, 1&3 £5.20 CSF £22.04 TOTE £7.80: £4.50, £1.60; EX 30.80 Trifecta £399.10 Pool: £764.15 - 1.43 winning units..
Owner Mrs Jo Tracey **Bred** Patrick Eddery Ltd **Trained** Arlary, Perth & Kinross

FOCUS
A modest handicap rated around the first four.
T/Plt: £181.00 to a £1 stake. Pool of £45467.22 - 183.30 winning tickets. T/Qpdt: £42.00 to a £1 stake. Pool of £3632.69, 64.0 winning tickets. RY

1103 WORCESTER (L-H)

Tuesday, July 30

OFFICIAL GOING: Good (6.8)
Wind: Light behind Weather: Overcast

1149 BATHROOM STUDIO & IDEAL CONSTRUCTION H'CAP CHASE (12 fncs) 2m 110y

5:50 (5:50) (Class 5) (0-100,100) 4-Y-0+ **£2,274** (£667; £333; £166)

Form RPR

/01- 1 **Cap Elorn (FR)**[13] 1014 7-11-3 **96** ....(b) GavinSheehan(5) 101+
(Lawney Hill) *chsd ldr tl led after 4th: hdd 6th: led again 8th: clr 2 out: rdn flat: jst hld on* **11/2**[3]

P/4- 2 ½ **Stafford Charlie**[9] 1057 7-9-7 **74** oh5 .... CiaranMckee(7) 78
(John O'Shea) *hld up: hdwy 4 out: rdn to chse wnr last: r.o* **11/1**

06F- 3 2¼ **Crescent Beach (IRE)**[13] 1014 6-10-13 **87** ....(b) HenryOliver 89
(Henry Oliver) *hld up: hdwy 5th: rdn appr last: styd on same pce flat* **8/1**

/45- 4 6 **Quarton (IRE)**[21] 931 6-11-9 **100** ....(p) AdamWedge(3) 98
(Evan Williams) *hld up: blnd 4th: mstke 9th: hdwy next: sn rdn: styd on: nt trble ldrs* **10/1**

U50- 5 13 **Stormy Oscar (IRE)**[21] 931 6-11-12 **100** ....(p) SamTwiston-Davies 89
(Jamie Snowden) *led tl after 4th: led again 6th to 8th: rdn and blnd 3 out: wknd appr last* **13/2**

302- 6 11 **Mad Professor (IRE)**[16] 964 10-9-9 **74** oh3 ....(b) JoeCornwall(5) 49
(John Cornwall) *chsd ldrs: pushed along after 4th: wknd appr 4 out* **10/1**

036- 7 4½ **Umustbejoking (FR)**[21] 927 5-11-5 **96** .... MichealNolan(3) 67
(Michael Blake) *hld up: a in rr: pushed along 9th: wknd bef next* **11/4**[1]

143- 8 42 **Darnborough (IRE)**[16] 964 7-10-4 **78** ....(b[1]) FelixDeGiles 11
(Tom Symonds) *chsd ldrs: j.rt 1st: blnd 6th: wknd appr 4 out* **5/1**[2]

P4P- F **Tulla Emerald (IRE)**[13] 1010 8-9-9 **76** oh3 ow2 .... KevinJones(7)
(Natalie Lloyd-Beavis) *hld up: rdn appr 4 out: 6th and hld whn fell last* **33/1**

3m 55.9s (-18.10) **Going Correction** -1.075s/f (Hard) 9 Ran SP% **112.6**
Speed ratings (Par 103): **99,98,97,94,88 83,81,61,**
toteswingers 1&2 £5.60, 2&3 £20.20, 1&3 £10.50 CSF £59.99 CT £477.57 TOTE £5.10: £1.90, £3.30, £3.30; EX 55.40 Trifecta £280.30 Part won. Pool: £373.79 - 0.11 winning units..
Owner Andy Weller **Bred** Jean-Luc Guillerm **Trained** Aston Rowant, Oxon

FOCUS
The bends had been moved 10yds out from the inside line with the ground, having dried slightly, now given as good. After winning the opener Gavin Sheehan described the ground as "good to soft and patchy". The form is rated around those in the frame behind the winner.

1150 MIDSHIRE COMMUNICATIONS BEGINNERS' CHASE (16 fncs 2 omitted) 2m 7f

6:20 (6:20) (Class 4) 5-Y-0+ **£4,223** (£1,240; £620; £310)

Form RPR

110- 1 **Captain Kelly (IRE)**[34] 845 6-11-0 0 ....(t) RyanMahon 123+
(Paul Nicholls) *mde all: j.w: set stdy pce tl qcknd appr 3 out: shkn up bef next: clr last: styd on wl* **7/4**[2]

240- 2 8 **Awaywiththegreys (IRE)**[10] 1042 6-11-0 129 .... JamieMoore 119
(Peter Bowen) *chsd wnr: nt a fluent: rdn and ev ch 3 out: styd on same pce appr last* **9/4**[3]

524- 3 18 **Special Account (IRE)**[34] 839 8-11-0 123 .... NickScholfield 101
(Jeremy Scott) *hld up: plld hrd: hdwy 6th: wknd 3 out: j.rt last* **6/4**[1]

0- 4 nse **Joe The Rogue (IRE)**[28] 856 6-11-0 0 .... PaddyBrennan 100
(Paul Henderson) *hld up: j.rt 4th: hdwy 11th: mstke 13th: rdn and wknd next: wnt rt last* **50/1**

16P- 5 11 **Marico (FR)**[16] 969 5-11-0 0 ....(p) FelixDeGiles 90
(Tom Symonds) *chsd ldrs: lost pl 6th: bhd 9th: rallied appr 13th: rdn and wknd bef next* **40/1**

5m 51.1s (3.10) **Going Correction** -1.075s/f (Hard) 5 Ran SP% **111.5**
Speed ratings: **51,48,41,41,38**
CSF £6.43 TOTE £3.00: £1.10, £1.40; EX 5.90 Trifecta £8.10 Pool: £902.73 - 82.76 winning units..
Owner Donlon, Doyle, MacDonald & Webb **Bred** Joseph Murphy **Trained** Ditcheat, Somerset

FOCUS
A fair beginners' chase in which only three of the five runners could be given serious consideration. the first two set the level.

1151 PERSHORE PLUM FESTIVAL LAND O'PLUMS H'CAP CHASE (10 fncs 2 omitted) 2m 110y

6:50 (6:50) (Class 3) (0-135,130) 4-Y-0+ **£6,330** (£1,870; £935; £468)

Form RPR

/36- 1 **Oceana Gold**[16] 974 9-11-7 **125** ....(v[1]) AidanColeman 134+
(Emma Lavelle) *mde all: mstke 5th: clr 3 out: comf* **2/1**[1]

/04- 2 10 **Trooper Clarence**[34] 840 9-11-2 **120** .... PaulMoloney 116
(Evan Williams) *chsd ldrs: rdn to go 2nd appr 3 out: styd on same pce* **5/2**[3]

635- 3 3¼ **Zama Zama**[15] 995 6-10-3 **110** ....(p) AdamWedge(3) 103
(Evan Williams) *hld up: drvn along after 8th: wnt 3rd last: nvr trbld ldrs* **9/4**[2]

0P6/ 4 13 **Woody Waller**[95] 5545 8-10-12 **119** .... JamesBest(3) 106
(Sophie Leech) *chsd wnr tl rdn appr 3 out: wknd next* **9/2**

3m 52.5s (-21.50) **Going Correction** -1.075s/f (Hard) course record 4 Ran SP% **110.9**
Speed ratings (Par 107): **107,102,100,94**
CSF £7.45 TOTE £2.00; EX 6.10 Trifecta £10.00 Pool: £414.72 - 30.98 winning units..
Owner The C H F Partnership **Bred** The C H F Partnership **Trained** Hatherden, Hants

FOCUS
With the defection of likely favourite Keki Buku and Captain Paulie this 0-135 handicap chase lost its competitiveness. The winner is rated 6lb off his best.

1152 ROY & CAROLINE HIRONS AND VALE TECHNICAL MAIDEN HURDLE (8 hdls) 2m

7:20 (7:21) (Class 5) 4-Y-0+ **£1,949** (£572; £286; £143)

Form RPR

323- 1 **Orthodox Lad**[10] 1041 5-11-0 105 .... SamTwiston-Davies 114
(Dr Richard Newland) *a.p: led 3 out: clr last: comf* **5/6**[1]

2 10 **Hallings Comet**[348] 4-10-12 0 .... AidanColeman 98
(Adrian Wintle) *plld hrd: trckd ldr tl led 2nd: sn clr and wandered arnd gng into the flights therafter: hdd 3 out: styd on same pce appr last* **20/1**

316/ 3 1¼ **Swift Escape**[263] 2315 6-11-0 0 .... RichardJohnson 98
(Tim Vaughan) *prom: rdn appr 3 out: styd on same pce appr last* **5/1**[2]

4 3¾ **Tempuran**[30] 4-10-12 0 .... TomScudamore 93
(David Bridgwater) *hld up: hdwy 5th: rdn after 3 out: no ex appr last* **10/1**

0/ 5 10 **King Of Forces**[154] 4436 4-10-9 0 .... MichaelByrne(3) 84
(Denis Quinn) *hld up: hdwy u.p 3 out: nt trble ldrs* **33/1**

2- 6 6 **Moscow Me (IRE)**[16] 971 6-11-0 0 .... HenryOliver 80
(Henry Oliver) *hld up: rdn after 5th: n.d* **20/1**

5- 7 11 **Epic Storm (IRE)**[28] 856 5-10-4 0 ....(t[1]) MikeyHamill(10) 70
(Sean Curran) *hld up: rdn 5th: wknd appr 3 out* **7/1**[3]

500/ 8 ½ **Prince Freddie**[204] 2136 5-10-9 0 .... JonathanEngland(5) 70
(Roy Brotherton) *hld up: n.d* **100/1**

55- 9 ½ **Gavi**[13] 1008 7-11-0 0 .... AndrewThornton 69
(Karen George) *hld up: a in rr: bhd whn hmpd 5th* **100/1**

603/ 10 hd **Who Am I**[226] 3087 7-10-11 0 .... RobertDunne(3) 69
(Dai Burchell) *hld up: hdwy 5th: wknd 2 out* **33/1**

56- 11 1¾ **Drombeg West**[13] 1017 6-10-7 0 .... CharliePoste 61
(Anna Brooks) *chsd ldrs to 4th* **50/1**

35- 12 8 **Mayan Flight (IRE)**[28] 867 5-11-0 0 .... LeeEdwards 60
(Tony Carroll) *prom tl wknd appr 3 out* **33/1**

F **Leader Of The Land (IRE)**[760] 6-11-0 0 .... PaddyBrennan
(Robert Stephens) *sn bhd and nt fluent: wl adrift whn fell 2 out* **16/1**

U/0- P **No No Cardinal (IRE)**[71] 410 4-10-12 0 .... TomCannon
(Mark Gillard) *led tl after 2nd: wknd 5th: p.u bef 3 out* **66/1**

3m 35.6s (-11.70) **Going Correction** -0.65s/f (Firm)
WFA 4 from 5yo+ 15lb 14 Ran SP% **122.5**
Speed ratings (Par 103): **103,98,97,95,90 87,82,81,81,81 80,76, ,**
toteswingers 1&2 £8.30, 2&3 £31.00, 1&3 £2.30 CSF £25.21 TOTE £1.70: £1.10, £5.90, £2.10; EX 34.20 Trifecta £222.60 Pool: £815.91 - 2.74 winning units..
Owner Peter Green **Bred** S Nunn **Trained** Claines, Worcs

FOCUS
An ordinary maiden hurdle in which the third and sixth help set the level.

1153 PENSHAM (S) HURDLE (10 hdls) 2m 4f

7:50 (7:50) (Class 5) 4-Y-0+ **£1,949** (£572; £286; £143)

Form RPR

254- 1 **Lauberhorn**[21] 931 6-11-4 105 ....(v) PaulMoloney 111
(Evan Williams) *hld up: hdwy 7th: wnt rt last: edgd lft and styd on u.p to ld fnl 100yds* **6/1**[3]

F53- 2 3 **Callhimwhatyouwant (IRE)**[7] 1092 8-10-12 102... SamTwiston-Davies 103
(Dr Richard Newland) *led: rdn whn mstke 2 out: hdd and unable qck fnl 100yds* **11/4**[2]

42P- 3 1½ **Run Along Boy**[27] 871 8-10-9 0 ....(p) MichaelByrne(3) 102
(Neil Mulholland) *hld up: hdwy 7th: chsd ldr 2 out: ev ch and mstke last: styd on same pce flat* **17/2**

0/3- 4 17 **Neverownup (IRE)**[13] 1018 8-10-12 90 ....(tp) DaveCrosse 86
(K F Clutterbuck) *chsd ldrs: rdn after 5th: wknd 2 out* **17/2**

/56- 5 13 **Boomtown Kat**[35] 829 9-10-12 92 ....(b) AndrewThornton 74
(Karen George) *prom: chsd ldr 5th to 7th: sn rdn and wknd* **25/1**

30/- 6 1 **Illysantachristina**[257] 2438 10-10-5 93 ....(t) APMcCoy 66
(Rebecca Curtis) *hld up: hdwy 6th: chsd ldr next: hung lft and ev ch appr 3 out: rdn and wkng whn wnt lft next* **5/4**[1]

F/0- 7 1¾ **First Spirit**[50] 686 7-9-12 70 .... KevinJones(7) 64
(Sarah Robinson) *chsd ldr to 5th: rdn and wknd after 7th* **100/1**

4m 32.6s (-14.80) **Going Correction** -0.65s/f (Firm) 7 Ran SP% **111.3**
Speed ratings (Par 103): **103,101,101,94,89 88,88**
toteswingers 1&2 £3.10, 2&3 £6.20, 1&3 £9.60 CSF £22.08 TOTE £5.70: £1.80, £2.20; EX 21.50 Trifecta £45.80 Pool: £518.03 - 8.47 winning units..There was no bid for the winner.
Owner Border Pointers **Bred** Grasshopper 2000 Ltd **Trained** Llancarfan, Vale Of Glamorgan

FOCUS
A moderate contest but a step up from the winner with the second rated to his mark.

1154 SGA PROJECT AND COST MANAGEMENT NOVICES' HURDLE (12 hdls) 2m 7f

8:20 (8:20) (Class 4) 4-Y-0+ **£3,249** (£954; £477; £238)

Form RPR

3/1- 1 **Benefit Of Youth (IRE)**[13] 1007 6-10-12 110 .... RichardJohnson 117
(Tim Vaughan) *a.p: chsd ldr 4th tl led after 6th: hdd 8th: rdn appr 2 out: mstke last: styd on to ld flat: drvn out* **5/6**[1]

031- 2 7 **Scoter Fontaine (FR)**[20] 945 7-11-12 122 .... APMcCoy 124
(Rebecca Curtis) *led tl after 6th: led again 8th: rdn and wnt lft 2 out: wnt lft again last: hdd and no ex flat* **11/8**[2]

3 28 **Dbanks (IRE)**[240] 10-10-12 0 .... SamTwiston-Davies 85
(Liam Corcoran) *prom tl rdn and wknd appr 3 out* **16/1**[3]

6- 4 4 **Golden Squirell (IRE)**[27] 878 6-10-12 0 .... TomCannon 81
(Brendan Powell) *prom: rdn after 9th: wknd bef next* **33/1**

6- 5 73 **Cute Court (IRE)**[13] 1013 6-10-12 0 .... DPFahy 16
(Liam Corcoran) *hld up: rdn after 6th: wknd 8th* **66/1**

63P/ 6 77 **Shanks A Lot**[178] 3987 6-10-7 0 .... CharlieWallis(5)
(Lucy Jones) *in rr: reminders after 2nd: bhd fr 7th* **20/1**

P- 7 2¼ **Lightning Bill**[20] 945 5-10-12 0 .... AndrewThornton
(Caroline Bailey) *chsd ldr to appr 4th: remained handy tl wknd 8th* **100/1**

5m 35.3s (7.30) **Going Correction** -0.65s/f (Firm) 7 Ran SP% **112.7**
Speed ratings (Par 105): **61,58,48,47,22 ,**
toteswingers 1&2 £1.10, 2&3 £5.80, 1&3 £5.20 CSF £2.23 TOTE £2.00: £1.10, £1.30; EX 2.10 Trifecta £6.20 Pool: £705.91 - 84.16 winning units..
Owner Mrs M J Worgan **Bred** Michael Byrnes **Trained** Aberthin, Vale of Glamorgan

The Form Book Jumps, Raceform Ltd, Compton, RG20 6NL.

FOCUS
A novice hurdle that was basically a match and so it proved with the two principals having this between them from a fair way out. The pair are rated to their marks.

1155 TIDDESLEY WOOD YELLOW EGG PLUM H'CAP HURDLE (12 hdls) 2m 7f
8:50 (8:50) (Class 3) (0-135,134) 4-Y-O+ **£5,523** (£1,621; £810; £405)

Form | | | | RPR
121- **1** **Man Of Leisure**[10] 1045 9-11-9 **134**..............................(t) RachaelGreen[(3)] 139+
(Anthony Honeyball) *hld up: hdwy 8th: bmpd 3 out: led appr and hmpd next: rdn flat: styd on gamely* **7/4**[1]
/PP- **2** *nk* **Mission Complete (IRE)**[9] 1055 7-9-9 **108**............(p) MauriceLinehan[(5)] 112+
(Jonjo O'Neill) *sn pushed along to ld: rdn and bmpd 3 out: hdd and hmpd next: n.m.r appr last: rallied flat: styd on* **16/1**
/1P- **3** *nk* **Thanks For Coming**[46] 733 7-11-0 **125**................ JeremiahMcGrath[(3)] 127
(Nicky Henderson) *chsd ldr: rdn and ev ch 2 out: edgd lft: styd on u.p* **8/1**
/11- **4** *33* **Salpierre (IRE)**[13] 1011 8-10-13 **121**...................................(tp) APMcCoy 98
(Jonjo O'Neill) *hdwy 3rd: blnd next: pushed along 6th: lost pl after next: drvn and wknd appr 3 out* **9/4**[2]
6P4- **5** *3/4* **Andhaar**[34] 845 7-10-0 **115**.. JackSherwood[(7)] 87
(Richard Phillips) *hld up: pushed along and bhd fr 7th* **4/1**[3]
04P- **6** *16* **Five Star Wilsham (IRE)**[22] 923 9-10-11 **119**............... NickScholfield 76
(Jeremy Scott) *chsd ldrs: rdn after 7th: wknd appr 3 out* **16/1**

5m 27.1s (-0.90) **Going Correction** -0.65s/f (Firm) **6** Ran SP% **110.0**
Speed ratings (Par 107): **75,74,74,63,63 57**
toteswingers 1&2 £6.00, 2&3 £16.90, 1&3 £2.00 CSF £23.93 TOTE £2.00: £1.40, £7.50; EX 36.30 Trifecta £44.00 Pool: £715.68 - 12.18 winning units..
Owner Anthony Honeyball Racing Club Ltd **Bred** Mrs Nerys Dutfield **Trained** Mosterton, Dorset

FOCUS
A good effort by a winner giving lumps of weight away to the runner-up. The third sets the level.
T/Plt: £32.80 to a £1 stake. Pool of £56643.76 - 1257.20 winning tickets. T/Qpdt: £5.40 to a £1 stake. Pool of £5453.79 - 737.09 winning tickets. CR

1156 - (Foreign Racing) - See Raceform Interactive

[1139]GALWAY (R-H)
Tuesday, July 30

OFFICIAL GOING: Flat - yielding; nh - good

1157a LATIN QUARTER CHASE 2m 6f
5:40 (5:43) 5-Y-O+ **£12,418** (£3,630; £1,719; £573)

| | | | RPR
1 **Rathlin**[62] 546 8-11-10 **149**...(t) DavyRussell 158
(M F Morris, Ire) *trckd ldr in 2nd tl on terms 4 out: led bef next and sn clr: styd on wl and extended advantage run-in: easily* **13/8**[2]
2 *6* **Hidden Cyclone (IRE)**[161] 4308 8-11-10 **149**......(p) AndrewJMcNamara 152
(John Joseph Hanlon, Ire) *led at stdy early pce: jnd 4 out and hdd bef next: no imp on wnr after last: kpt on same pce* **7/2**[3]
3 *1 3/4* **Woolcombe Folly (IRE)**[10] 1047 10-11-3 **154**........................... RWalsh 143
(Paul Nicholls) *sn chsd ldrs in 3rd: clsd appr 3 out: pushed along and nt qckn after last: kpt on one pce* **11/8**[1]
4 *38* **Dantes King (IRE)**[16] 956 8-11-3 **128**................................. DavyCondon 105
(Gordon Elliott, Ire) *racd in modest 4th: no imp 4 out* **8/1**
5 *30* **Canaly (IRE)**[97] 5517 8-11-10 **133**...................................... BarryGeraghty 82
(D T Hughes, Ire) *in rr thrght: reminders w a circ to r: adrift 5 out: t.o* **16/1**

5m 33.3s (-6.70) **5** Ran SP% **119.4**
CSF £8.62 TOTE £2.40: £1.60, £2.10; DF 10.70.
Owner Gigginstown House Stud **Bred** Mrs C J Zetter-Wells **Trained** Fethard, Co Tipperary

FOCUS
This was a smart chase for the middle of the summer, though the favourite disappointed. The form is set around the first two.

[1142]PERTH (R-H)
Wednesday, July 31

OFFICIAL GOING: Good to soft (6.6)
Wind: Breezy, half behind Weather: Overcast

1158 WATCH ALL SCOTTISH RACING LIVE ON RACING UK (S) HURDLE (8 hdls) 2m 110y
2:15 (2:15) (Class 5) 4-Y-O+ **£2,599** (£763; £381; £190)

Form | | | | RPR
114/ **1** **Esporao (IRE)**[26] 886 7-11-4 **124**.................................(t) WilsonRenwick 120+
(Gordon Elliott, Ire) *mde all: rdn after 2 out: kpt on wl fr last* **8/11**[1]
4/3- **2** *1 1/2* **Waltz Darling (IRE)**[14] 1009 5-11-4 **113**......................... JamesReveley 118
(Keith Reveley) *chsd wnr thrght: rdn bef 2 out: rallied bef last: kpt on same pce last 75yds* **13/8**[2]
0/5- **3** *36* **King Brex (DEN)**[1] 1143 10-10-5 **90**............................ MrKitAlexander[(7)] 80
(N W Alexander) *bhd: struggling fnl circ: styd on to take modest 3rd run-in: nvr on terms* **25/1**
P02/ **4** *3* **Kirkaig**[452] 89 8-10-9 **102**.. EwanWhillans[(3)] 77
(Alistair Whillans) *chsd clr ldng pair: short-lived effrt bef 3 out: sn outpcd* **12/1**[3]
0P0- **5** *54* **Lewlaur Supreme (IRE)**[28] 868 10-10-12 **62**............(p) PeterBuchanan 28
(William Young Jnr) *sn bhd: lost tch fnl circ: nvr on terms* **100/1**

3m 48.6s (-9.40) **Going Correction** -0.35s/f (Good) **5** Ran SP% **108.5**
Speed ratings (Par 103): **108,107,90,88,63**
CSF £2.18 TOTE £1.20: £1.02, £1.40; EX 2.40 Trifecta £7.70 Pool: £1546.17 - 149.87 winning units..There was no bid for the winner.
Owner Brendan Scully **Bred** J Stan Cosgrove **Trained** Trim, Co Meath

FOCUS
Stands' bend moved out on to fresh ground. A very weak seller.

1159 CONGRATULATIONS TO OUR EARL AND COUNTESS NOVICES' HURDLE (8 hdls) 2m 110y
2:50 (2:50) (Class 4) 4-Y-O+ **£3,422** (£997; £499)

Form | | | | RPR
/12- **1** **Howwoulduno (IRE)**[1] 1148 5-11-5 **115**.................... GrahamWatters[(7)] 123+
(Liam Lennon, Ire) *t.k.h: cl up: led gng wl bef 2 out: nt fluent last: pushed clr: comf* **9/5**[2]
/43- **2** *5* **Trend Is My Friend (USA)**[28] 865 4-10-10 **111**.............. NickSlatter[(7)] 108
(Donald McCain) *in tch: effrt and rdn whn hit 2 out: kpt on fr last to take 2nd nr fin: no ch w wnr* **4/1**[3]
114- **3** *1/2* **Lisbon (IRE)**[1] 1148 5-11-12 **126**......................................(t) JamesReveley 116
(Patrick Griffin, Ire) *pressed ldr: effrt and rdn 2 out: kpt on same pce fr last* **11/10**[1]
/05- **4** *2 1/2* **Mumgos Debut (IRE)**[28] 865 5-10-12 **95**...................... PeterBuchanan 99
(Lucinda Russell) *led at mod gallop: rdn and hdd bef 2 out: outpcd fr last* **22/1**

3m 50.4s (-7.60) **Going Correction** -0.35s/f (Good)
WFA 4 from 5yo 15lb **4** Ran SP% **107.7**
Speed ratings (Par 105): **103,100,100,99**
CSF £8.59 TOTE £2.80; EX 8.20 Trifecta £13.80 Pool: £1216.91 - 66.06 winning units..
Owner James McMullan **Bred** James McMullan **Trained** Newry, Co. Down

FOCUS
A steadily run novice.

1160 PIPE AND PILING SUPPLIES H'CAP CHASE (12 fncs) 2m
3:25 (3:25) (Class 4) (0-110,110) 4-Y-O+ **£4,790** (£1,396; £698)

Form | | | | RPR
2/3- **1** **The Paddy Premium (IRE)**[28] 864 13-10-8 **92**............ LucyAlexander 101+
(N W Alexander) *mde all: clr 2 out: styd on strly: eased run-in* **2/1**[2]
114- **2** *8* **Endeavor**[27] 882 8-11-12 **110**.. RyanMania 112
(Dianne Sayer) *chsd ldr: effrt whn mstke and outpcd 3 out: no imp fr next* **5/6**[1]
66P- **3** *1/2* **Merry Minster**[38] 804 6-10-3 **87**.. BrianHarding 86
(James Walton) *chsd clr ldrs: outpcd 4 out: plugged on fr 2 out: nvr able to chal* **4/1**[3]

3m 54.1s (-2.90) **Going Correction** -0.35s/f (Good) **3** Ran SP% **107.9**
Speed ratings (Par 105): **93,89,88**
CSF £4.15 TOTE £3.10; EX 3.20 Trifecta £4.30 Pool: £748.18 - 130.34 winning units..
Owner Cochrane, Fleming & Alexander **Bred** Patrick Cahalan **Trained** Kinneston, Perth & Kinross

FOCUS
A moderate handicap.

1161 TOAST TO THE NEW PRINCE CONDITIONAL JOCKEYS' H'CAP HURDLE (10 hdls) 2m 4f 110y
4:00 (4:00) (Class 4) (0-110,110) 4-Y-O+ **£4,106** (£1,197; £598)

Form | | | | RPR
134- **1** **Fairwood Massini (IRE)**[17] 958 8-11-1 **102**............(vt) MichaelByrne[(3)] 112+
(Tim Vaughan) *mde virtually all: rdn bef 2 out: styd on strly* **7/2**[2]
264- **2** *2 1/4* **Groovy Dancer**[27] 881 6-10-1 **90**.............................. GrahamWatters[(5)] 97
(Rose Dobbin) *in tch: hit 4 out: effrt and chsd wnr bef 2 out: kpt on same pce run-in* **5/1**
113- **3** *22* **Momkinzain (USA)**[17] 961 6-10-9 **101**...........................(p) CraigNichol[(8)] 93
(Lucinda Russell) *prom: stdy hdwy whn mstke 3 out: rdn bef next: hung lft and wknd between last 2* **2/1**[1]
P53- **4** *9* **A Bridge Too Far (IRE)**[27] 884 7-11-4 **110**.............(b) JamesCowley[(8)] 89
(Donald McCain) *t.k.h: in tch: hdwy to chal after 5th: rdn and wknd after 3 out* **4/1**[3]
00/- **5** *25* **Flying Doctor**[96] 5549 10-11-4 **102**.................................. CallumWhillans 59
(Alistair Whillans) *chsd ldrs: rdn and outpcd 1/2-way: struggling fnl 4* **25/1**
4/2- **P** **Lady Gargoyle**[8] 880 5-10-8 **92**.. LucyAlexander
(Jim Goldie) *chsd ldrs: lost pl and struggling after 5th: t.o whn p.u bef 2 out* **6/1**

4m 56.3s (-5.70) **Going Correction** -0.35s/f (Good) **6** Ran SP% **110.4**
Speed ratings (Par 105): **96,95,86,83,73**
toteswingers 1&2 £5.00, 1&3 £2.00, 2&3 £3.20 CSF £20.04 CT £40.07 TOTE £3.80: £2.00, £2.20; EX 23.50 Trifecta £79.80 Pool: £1936.18 - 18.17 winning units..
Owner Wayne Jones **Bred** T Kent **Trained** Aberthin, Vale of Glamorgan

FOCUS
An ordinary handicap for conditional riders.

1162 SAVILLS' SUMMER H'CAP CHASE (15 fncs) 2m 4f 110y
4:35 (4:35) (Class 4) (0-120,119) 4-Y-O+ **£6,498** (£1,908; £954; £477)

Form | | | | RPR
P/1- **1** **Scotch Warrior**[76] 343 9-10-12 **112**............................. CallumBewley[(7)] 127+
(R Mike Smith) *chsd clr ldng pair: hdwy to chal 5 out: led 3 out: drew clr fr next* **9/2**[3]
/22- **2** *10* **Strongpoint (IRE)**[27] 884 9-11-12 **119**.................................. TomO'Brien 125
(S R B Crawford, Ire) *cl up: hit 3rd: led 6th to 5 out: drvn and outpcd bef 3 out: rallied to chse (clr) wnr after last: no imp* **5/2**[1]
112- **3** *10* **Castlelawn (IRE)**[28] 864 6-11-11 **118**............................ PeterBuchanan 117
(Lucinda Russell) *led at decent gallop to 6th: pressed ldr: led 5 out to 3 out: outpcd next: lost 2nd after last* **11/4**[2]
611- **4** *16* **Sergeant Pink (IRE)**[9] 1077 7-11-7 **114** 7ex.................(p) LucyAlexander 97
(Dianne Sayer) *hld up: outpcd 1/2-way: nvr on terms* **7/1**
/4U- **5** *17* **Hidden Future (IRE)**[27] 883 7-11-10 **117**........................(p) DenisO'Regan 84
(C A McBratney, Ire) *hld up: rdn whn nt fluent 5 out: sn btn* **9/1**
142- **P** **Hawaii Klass**[27] 883 8-11-3 **115**...................................(b) CallumWhillans[(5)]
(Donald Whillans) *in tch: struggling 1/2-way: t.o whn p.u bef 4 out* **5/1**

4m 54.3s (-10.70) **Going Correction** -0.35s/f (Good) **6** Ran SP% **112.6**
Speed ratings (Par 105): **106,102,98,92,85**
toteswingers 1&2 £2.90, 1&3 £3.10, 2&3 £2.00 CSF £16.71 CT £35.39 TOTE £6.10: £2.60, £2.10; EX 18.20 Trifecta £51.70 Pool: £1535.05 - 22.23 winning units..
Owner R Michael Smith **Bred** Miss Jayne Butler **Trained** Galston, E Ayrshire
■ Stewards' Enquiry : Callum Bewley two-day ban: used whip when clearly winning (Aug 29, Oct 18)

FOCUS
A modest handicap.

1163 CRABBIE'S ALCOHOLIC GINGER BEER H'CAP CHASE (17 fncs 1 omitted) 3m
5:10 (5:10) (Class 5) (0-100,99) 4-Y-O+ **£4,106** (£1,197; £598)

Form | | | | RPR
P/P- **1** **Terfel's Toscar (IRE)**[40] 789 8-11-2 **92**......................(t) MichaelByrne[(3)] 103+
(Tim Vaughan) *trckd ldrs: led 4 out: rdn clr fr 2 out* **10/1**
354- **2** *7* **Solway Dornal**[9] 1073 8-9-7 **73** oh2.....................(tp) StephenMulqueen[(7)] 76
(Lisa Harrison) *chsd ldrs: rdn and outpcd after 4 out: chsd (clr) wnr 2 out: kpt on: no imp* **20/1**
436/ **3** *3/4* **Pistol Basc (FR)**[94] 20 9-10-7 **80**...................................... JamesReveley 83
(Ferdy Murphy, France) *hld up: hdwy and prom 4 out: rdn 2 out: kpt on same pce run-in* **16/1**
UP3- **4** *5* **More Equity**[11] 1039 11-11-2 **89**.. RyanMania 88
(Dianne Sayer) *in tch: rdn along after 4 out: styng on whn hit last: no imp* **16/1**

/43- 5 1 3/4 **Solwa Sam**[42] 763 10-11-11 98 ... BrianHarding 94
(Lisa Harrison) *hld up: hit 3rd: hdwy and prom 1/2-way: effrt bef 3 out: outpcd fr next* **3/1**[1]
601- 6 1/2 **Nicky Tam (IRE)**[11] 1038 10-11-0 77 ... (p) RichieMcGrath 74
(Henry Hogarth) *hld up: rdn and outpcd after 5 out: styd on fr 2 out: no imp* **16/1**
P3P- 7 7 **Quetzal (IRE)**[28] 869 8-11-12 99 ... (p) DenisO'Regan 89
(Martin Todhunter) *pressed ldr: led 3rd to 4 out: rdn and wknd after next* **12/1**
335- 8 1 1/2 **Via Archimede (USA)**[28] 868 8-10-2 82 ... (v) CraigNichol(7) 70
(Lucinda Russell) *towards rr: drvn and outpcd after 5 out: n.d after* **13/2**[3]
533- P **Laybach (IRE)**[28] 866 9-10-7 80 ... LucyAlexander
(Jim Goldie) *led to 3rd: cl up tl lost pl after 10th: t.o whn p.u bef 3 out* **9/1**
P **Baby's Hot (IRE)**[18] 991 9-11-9 96 ... PaddyBrennan
(D T Hughes, Ire) *prom tl broke down and p.u after 2nd* **7/2**[2]
34F- P **Raifteiri (IRE)**[11] 1038 6-10-5 78 ... PeterBuchanan
(William Young Jnr) *bhd: outpcd whn blnd 5 out: sn btn: t.o whn p.u bef 3 out* **20/1**

6m 1.0s (-3.00) **Going Correction** -0.35s/f (Good) 11 Ran SP% **114.5**
Speed ratings (Par 103): **91,88,88,86,86 86,83,83, ,**
toteswingers 1&2 £25.50, 1&3 £32.50, 2&3 £42.80 CSF £174.44 CT £3116.50 TOTE £10.80: £3.20, £9.00, £7.40; EX 281.90 Trifecta £901.00 Part won. Pool: £1201.38 - 0.03 winning units..
Owner Alan Peterson **Bred** Miss Jill Farrell **Trained** Aberthin, Vale of Glamorgan

FOCUS
A weak handicap.

1164 WATCH ALL SCOTTISH RACING LIVE ON RACINGUK H'CAP HURDLE (12 hdls) 3m 110y

5:40 (5:40) (Class 4) (0-115,115) 4-Y-0+ **£4,790** (£1,396; £698)

Form RPR
/05- 1 **Taruma (FR)**[28] 867 5-11-10 113 ... (p) BarryKeniry 119+
(Simon West) *trckd ldrs: led and edgd lft bef 2 out: nt fluent last: kpt on wl run-in* **4/1**[3]
5/- 2 3 **Winter Alchemy (IRE)**[168] 4189 8-10-8 97 ... BrianHarding 97
(Nicky Richards) *led: rdn and hdd bef 2 out: rallied: kpt on same pce run-in* **5/2**[2]
341- 3 1/2 **Solway Bay**[17] 958 11-10-7 103 ... (tp) StephenMulqueen(7) 104
(Lisa Harrison) *hld up: rdn and effrt after 3 out: kpt on same pce fr last* **10/1**
/60- 4 8 **What A Steel (IRE)**[38] 801 9-11-9 115 ... EwanWhillans(3) 108
(Alistair Whillans) *hld up: effrt bef 2 out: no imp between last 2* **9/1**
063- 5 2 1/4 **Ryton Runner (IRE)**[17] 958 5-11-2 105 ... (p) TomScudamore 96
(Lucinda Russell) *w ldr tl rdn and outpcd appr 2 out: sn n.d* **9/4**[1]
3/ 6 21 **Street Runner**[6] 1114 7-10-9 98 ... (b) BrianHughes 70
(Karl Thornton, Ire) *prom: hit 4 out: sn rdn: hit next: sn wknd* **9/1**
/ 7 62 **Hit The Road Jack (IRE)**[18] 988 7-10-0 89 oh3 ... (p) PeterBuchanan 5
(S R B Crawford, Ire) *in tch: outpcd 4 out: lost tch fr next: t.o* **14/1**

5m 59.9s (-5.10) **Going Correction** -0.35s/f (Good) 7 Ran SP% **115.1**
Speed ratings (Par 105): **94,93,92,90,89 82,63**
toteswingers 1&2 £1.50, 1&3 £6.40, 2&3 £9.20 CSF £15.03 CT £91.91 TOTE £3.80: £1.20, £2.40; EX 21.60 Trifecta £231.50 Pool: £807.57 - 2.61 winning units..
Owner James-Douglas Gordon **Bred** Francis Montauban **Trained** Middleham Moor, N Yorks

FOCUS
A fair handicap run at a steady pace.
T/Plt: £1256.80. Pool of £46,228.42 - 26.85 winning units. T/Qpdt: £291.60. Pool of £3073.80 - 7.80 winning units. RY

1156 GALWAY (R-H)

Wednesday, July 31

OFFICIAL GOING: Soft changing to soft (soft to heavy in places) on hurdle & flat courses after race 1 (3.00)

1168a WWW.THETOTE.COM GALWAY PLATE (STEEPLECHASE H'CAP) (GRADE A) 2m 6f

5:30 (5:34) 4-Y-0+

£97,865 (£31,199; £14,939; £5,182; £3,556; £1,930)

RPR
1 **Carlingford Lough (IRE)**[79] 275 7-10-7 133 ... APMcCoy 148
(John E Kiely, Ire) *racd in mid-div: slt mstke 3rd: hdwy bef 3 out where slt mstke: clsd u.p in 7th after last: rdn to chal run-in: led narrowly ins fnl f and kpt on wl towards fin* **7/2**[1]
2 1 1/2 **Quantitativeeasing (IRE)**[104] 5362 8-10-11 137 ... NiallPMadden 149
(E Bolger, Ire) *w.w towards rr: gd hdwy fr 4 out to chse ldrs in 3rd on outer bef 2 out: led into st: sn strly pressed and hdd ins fnl f: kpt on same pce* **33/1**
3 7 1/2 **Jacksonslady (IRE)**[55] 5098 8-10-11 137 ... BarryGeraghty 142
(J P Dempsey, Ire) *hld up: clsr in 8th bef 4 out: rdn in 6th after last and sn no imp u.p: kpt on wl u.p into 3rd wl ins fnl f* **12/1**
4 3/4 **Muirhead (IRE)**[19] 949 10-10-9 135 ... DavyCondon 139
(Noel Meade, Ire) *towards rr: hdwy fr 4 out to chse ldrs in 5th after last: rdn and no ex u.p ent fnl f: kpt on same pce* **16/1**
5 3 1/2 **Supreme Doc (IRE)**[24] 917 8-10-9 135 ... (p) PatrickMangan 137
(M T O'Donovan, Ire) *chsd ldrs: clsr in 3rd bef 10th: rdn to chal appr st: sn no ex u.p: one pce towards fin* **20/1**
6 7 **Klepht (IRE)**[15] 5517 8-11-4 144 ... (t) RobbiePower 138
(Thomas Mullins, Ire) *in rr of mid-div: hdwy to chse ldrs in 8th appr 2 out: rdn and no imp on ldrs into st: kpt on same pce* **12/1**
7 1 3/4 **Fosters Cross (IRE)**[10] 1067 11-10-9 135 ... (t) PhillipEnright 127
(Thomas Mullins, Ire) *chsd ldrs in 3rd: cl up bef 10th: led narrowly after 3 out: jnd bef next where j. sltly lft and bmpd rival: wknd u.p fr last* **22/1**
8 nk **Laganbank (IRE)**[10] 1068 7-11-0 140 ... DJCasey 133
(W P Mullins, Ire) *settled in mid-div: sme hdwy fr 3 out to chse ldrs bef next where slt mstke: no ex u.p fr last: kpt on one pce* **25/1**
9 1 1/4 **Lambro (IRE)**[98] 5517 8-11-2 142 ... (p) PaulTownend 132
(W P Mullins, Ire) *hld up: cl 11th bef 4 out: rdn in 7th after next and sn no ex: one pce fr 2 out* **25/1**
10 nk **Terminal (FR)**[96] 5559 6-11-4 144 ... (p) RWalsh 134
(W P Mullins, Ire) *racd in mid-div: t.k.h: clsr in 8th appr 2 out: sn rdn and no ex u.p appr st* **7/1**[2]
11 7 1/2 **Buckers Bridge (IRE)**[97] 5531 7-11-1 141 ... AELynch 123
(Henry De Bromhead, Ire) *in rr of mid-div: rdn fr 3 out and no imp next: kpt on one pce run-in* **9/1**
12 2 **Tranquil Sea (IRE)**[16] 1001 11-11-5 145 ... (t) AndrewJMcNamara 125
(E J O'Grady, Ire) *chsd ldrs: tk clsr order in 3rd after 3 out: got on terms next where bmpd sltly: sn rdn in 2nd and no imp into st: wknd* **25/1**
13 3 **Jamsie Hall (IRE)**[14] 1024 10-10-8 134 ... (tp) RobbieColgan 111
(Gordon Elliott, Ire) *in rr of mid-div for most: rdn and no imp fr 3 out* **33/1**
14 67 **Romanesco (FR)**[121] 5098 8-10-9 135 ... (t) DavyRussell 45
(Gordon Elliott, Ire) *hld up towards rr: plenty to do after 4 out: sn rdn and no imp fr next: wknd: completely t.o* **8/1**[3]
15 8 **Majestic Concorde (IRE)**[32] 1238 10-11-5 145 ... JasonMaguire 47
(D K Weld, Ire) *in rr of mid-div: niggled along in rr fr 8th: n.d next: mstke 5 out: wknd: t.o* **12/1**
16 1/2 **Bob Lingo (IRE)**[14] 5111 11-11-7 147 ... (t) MarkWalsh 49
(Thomas Mullins, Ire) *towards rr: reminders after 9th: n.d 5 out: wknd: t.o* **33/1**
17 1 **Pride Of The Artic (IRE)**[41] 5345 8-10-13 139 ... AndrewLeigh 40
(Peter Fahey, Ire) *chsd ldrs: lost pl after 1/2-way: rdn and no imp fr 3 out: wknd: t.o* **10/1**
18 58 **Mr Cracker (IRE)**[12] 1035 8-10-6 137 ... MrDLQueally(5)
(Michael Hourigan, Ire) *led: sn clr reduced advantage bef 9th: mstke 5 out and hdd: sn wknd: trailing whn bad mstke 2 out: completely t.o* **33/1**
19 1/2 **Imperial Shabra (IRE)**[10] 1068 9-10-2 133 ... JodyMcGarvey(5)
(Patrick O Brady, Ire) *chsd ldrs: cl 4th bef 10th: rdn and sn wknd fr 5 out: wl bhd whn slt mstke 2 out: completely t.o* **40/1**
20 nk **The Disengager (IRE)**[53] 672 9-11-7 147 ... RichardJohnson
(Philip Hobbs) *chsd ldr in 2nd: led narrowly 5 out: mstke 3 out and hdd: sn no ex u.p: eased next: completely t.o* **20/1**
P **Lastoftheleaders (IRE)**[98] 5517 10-11-3 143 ... BMCash
(A L T Moore, Ire) *towards rr: niggled along bef 8th: sn no ex: trailing whn p.u bef 5 out* **20/1**
P **Bobowen (IRE)**[11] 1047 7-11-5 145 ... SamTwiston-Davies
(Dr Richard Newland) *hld up in tch: lost pl after 1/2-way: sn pushed along and no imp whn mstke 4 out: wknd: trailing whn p.u bef next* **16/1**

5m 41.9s (1.90) 22 Ran SP% **144.1**
CSF £132.21 CT £1378.01 TOTE £4.30: £1.80, £9.10, £2.30, £3.40; DF 208.70.
Owner John P McManus **Bred** Kenilworth House Stud **Trained** Dungarvan, Co Waterford

FOCUS
An unforgettable race for owner JP McManus as his colours were carried by the first three home. The winner is rated in line with his hurdles form.

1058 STRATFORD (L-H)

Thursday, August 1

OFFICIAL GOING: Good (good to firm in places) changing to good to firm after race 2 (2.35)
Wind: Light half-against Weather: Fine

1169 TONY AND ANDREA NOVICES' H'CAP HURDLE (DIV I) (11 hdls) 2m 6f 110y

2:05 (2:05) (Class 5) (0-100,102) 4-Y-0+ **£1,949** (£572; £286; £143)

Form RPR
021- 1 **Dreamsoftheatre (IRE)**[11] 1051 5-11-13 102 7ex ... (t) MauriceLinehan(5) 111+
(Jonjo O'Neill) *chsd ldrs: led flat: shkn up and r.o wl* **11/10**[1]
P42- 2 2 1/4 **Watch House (IRE)**[8] 1105 8-10-8 85 ... MissAEStirling(7) 89
(Michael Gates) *hld up: hdwy 3rd: to ld 3rd: clr and nt fluent next: hdd 3 out: led again after next: rdn and hdd flat: styd on same pce* **14/1**
522- 3 4 1/2 **Theoystercatcher (IRE)**[17] 997 7-11-9 93 ... RichardJohnson 94
(Tim Vaughan) *chsd ldrs: lost pl 3rd: hdwy to chse ldr 7th: led 3 out: nt fluent next: sn rdn and hdd: styd on same pce appr last* **4/1**[2]
0/6- 4 10 **Lucky To Be Alive (IRE)**[87] 145 6-11-6 90 ... DonalDevereux 81
(Peter Bowen) *hld up: hdwy 6th: rdn and wknd appr last* **7/1**[3]
600/ 5 1 3/4 **Not A Doctor (IRE)**[53] 10-10-4 74 ... ConorO'Farrell 63
(Polly Gundry) *hld up: hdwy 8th: rdn and wknd after 2 out* **100/1**
434/ 6 7 **Bold Tara**[434] 426 6-11-2 96 ... OllieGarner(10) 79
(Martin Keighley) *prom: rdn appr 8th: wknd 2 out* **20/1**
06P/ 7 5 **Mr Bachster (IRE)**[53] 8-10-3 83 ... JamesJeavons(10) 62
(Richard Lee) *set stdy pce tl hdd 3rd: chsd ldr to 7th: sn lost pl: wknd 2 out* **12/1**
04P/ F **Leyland (IRE)**[122] 5074 4-11-5 92 ... (p) DavidBass
(Lawney Hill) *fell 1st* **8/1**
43P- P **Terntheothercheek**[8] 1110 4-10-12 85 ... SeanQuinlan
(Jennie Candlish) *chsd ldrs to 6th: bhd fr next: p.u bef 3 out* **50/1**

5m 26.4s (-1.70) **Going Correction** -0.575s/f (Firm)
WFA 4 from 5yo+ 14lb 9 Ran SP% **113.3**
Speed ratings (Par 103): **79,78,76,73,72 70,68, ,**
toteswingers 1&2 £3.10, 2&3 £4.00, 1&3 £1.40 CSF £16.35 CT £47.55 TOTE £2.20: £1.10, £2.90, £1.40; EX 13.70 Trifecta £53.80 Pool: £1512.20 - 33.53 winning units..
Owner John P McManus **Bred** Kieran Gleeson **Trained** Cheltenham, Gloucs

FOCUS
Rails on bends moved on to fresh ground. The first division of a modest novices' handicap hurdle in which they initially went very steady on ground officially described as good, good to firm in places on a baking hot afternoon. The cosy winner is on the upgrade and there should be more to come.

1170 TONY AND ANDREA NOVICES' H'CAP HURDLE (DIV II) (11 hdls) 2m 6f 110y

2:35 (2:35) (Class 5) (0-100,97) 4-Y-0+ **£1,949** (£572; £286; £143)

Form RPR
/00- 1 **Royal Peak (IRE)**[24] 924 6-10-6 77 ... (tp) TomScudamore 95+
(David Pipe) *a.p: led 2 out: sn clr: easily* **12/1**
0/2- 2 19 **Spice Hill (IRE)**[15] 1018 7-11-0 85 ... (v) RichardJohnson 88+
(Tim Vaughan) *led: mstke 6th: hdd 2 out: sn rdn and outpcd* **6/4**[1]
40P/ 3 27 **Lost In Newyork (IRE)**[138] 4799 6-11-10 95 ... HarryHaynes 67
(Nick Kent) *hld up: hdwy after 8th: drvn along 3 out: wknd after next* **18/1**
/54- 4 2 1/2 **Edgar Jones**[56] 650 7-11-12 97 ... DonalDevereux 66
(Peter Bowen) *chsd tl rdn after 3 out: j.rt and wknd next* **15/8**[2]
P/0- P **Strong Survivor (USA)**[8] 1106 10-10-12 83 ... CharliePoste
(Evelyn England) *prom: pushed along 6th: wknd appr 8th: p.u bef 3 out* **50/1**
0/0- P **Vicpol (ITY)**[81] 253 7-11-4 89 ... (p) FelixDeGiles
(Tom Gretton) *chsd ldrs: drvn along 4th: sn lost pl: bhd whn p.u bef 6th* **14/1**
12P- P **Moscow In April (IRE)**[22] 946 6-11-8 93 ... ColinBolger
(Pat Murphy) *hld up: drvn along 7th: wknd after next: p.u bef 2 out* **6/1**[3]

5m 15.6s (-12.50) **Going Correction** -0.575s/f (Firm) 7 Ran SP% **110.7**
Speed ratings (Par 103): **98,91,82,81, , ,**
toteswingers 1&2 £3.80, 2&3 £4.20, 1&3 £24.20 CSF £29.56 CT £314.96 TOTE £11.50: £3.20, £1.80; EX 30.10 Trifecta £481.90 Pool: £1781.82 - 2.77 winning units..
Owner G Thompson **Bred** Patrick Moore **Trained** Nicholashayne, Devon

The Form Book Jumps, Raceform Ltd, Compton, RG20 6NL.

FOCUS
The second division of an ordinary novices' handicap hurdle in which they went a good, even gallop. A massive step up from the facile winner.

1171 GEOFF AND JACKIE (S) HURDLE (8 hdls) 2m 110y
3:05 (3:05) (Class 5) 4-7-Y-O £1,949 (£572; £286; £143)

Form RPR
F45- 1 **Screaming Brave**[9] 1092 7-11-4 114..............................(t) MarcGoldstein 113+
(Sheena West) *mde all: rdn clr appr last: styd on wl* **7/2[2]**
/00- 2 8 **Clarion Call**[24] 925 5-11-4 95..(b[1]) PaulMoloney 106
(Evan Williams) *a.p: chsd wnr 2 out: sn rdn: styd on same pce appr last* **11/1**
/51- 3 9 **Quadriller (FR)**[11] 1058 6-11-4 104....................................(t) TomO'Brien 100
(Philip Hobbs) *chsd ldrs: nt fluent 3rd: rdn and wknd appr last* **5/4[1]**
0/ 4 9 **Edgeworth (IRE)**[21] 5050 7-10-12 0.................................. SeanQuinlan 84
(David Bridgwater) *hld up: hdwy appr 2 out: rdn and wknd sn after* **33/1**
361- 5 1 1/4 **Advisor (FR)**[8] 1110 7-10-13 97.......................................(b) MrTWeston(5) 88
(Martin Weston) *chsd wnr tl rdn appr 2 out: wknd sn after* **4/1[3]**
F4F- 6 6 **Massachusetts**[8] 1105 6-10-9 66...................................... JamesBest(3) 77
(Rob Summers) *hld up: rdn and wknd appr 2 out* **100/1**
46/ 7 41 **Mungo Park**[234] 2975 5-10-12 0..................................(p) RichardJohnson 40
(Sophie Leech) *hld up: nt fluent 2nd: mstke next: hdwy 5th: rdn and wknd appr 2 out* **7/1**
50P/ 8 7 **Kealshore Again (IRE)**[166] 4247 4-11-3 112........................ AdrianLane 39
(Danielle McCormick) *hld up: wknd appr 3 out* **16/1**

3m 46.1s (-9.90) **Going Correction** -0.575s/f (Firm)
WFA 4 from 5yo+ 13lb **8 Ran SP% 117.3**
Speed ratings: **100,96,92,87,87 84,65,61**
toteswingers 1&2 £4.00, 2&3 £2.70, 1&3 £2.60 CSF £40.84 TOTE £6.40: £1.60, £3.80, £1.10; EX 53.50 Trifecta £61.80 Pool: £206.18 - 2.5 winning units..There was no bid for the winner.
Owner Tracey Walsom & Alex Woodger **Bred** Norman Court Stud **Trained** Falmer, E Sussex

FOCUS
A fair seller won in a reasonably quick time. The winner was the form pick and is rated 6lb off his best.

1172 JOHN DUNBAR MEMORIAL H'CAP CHASE (17 fncs) 2m 7f
3:35 (3:35) (Class 5) (0-95,101) 4-Y-O+ £2,599 (£763; £381; £190)

Form RPR
P/1- 1 **Five Out Of Five (IRE)**[24] 926 9-11-4 89....................(t) AdamWedge(3) 102+
(Evan Williams) *mde all: clr fr 4th tl appr last: jnd flat: drvn and styd on gamely* **3/1[2]**
F61- 2 1 3/4 **Numbercruncher (IRE)**[8] 1104 7-12-0 101 7ex.............. KillianMoore(5) 111
(Marc Barber) *hld up: hdwy 6th: chsd wnr who was clr 3 out: clsd bef last: rdn and ev ch flat: nt qckn towards fin* **9/4[1]**
0B4- 3 18 **Basford Ben**[15] 1010 5-11-12 94...................................(vt[1]) SeanQuinlan 88
(Jennie Candlish) *hld up: hdwy 12th: wnt remote 3rd appr last: nvr trbld ldrs* **16/1**
11P- 4 9 **The Good Guy (IRE)**[23] 930 10-11-11 93................ WayneHutchinson 79
(Graeme McPherson) *hld up: blnd 1st: hdwy 13th: nvr on terms* **6/1[3]**
2P6- 5 10 **Apache Dawn**[9] 1086 9-10-12 85..................................(t) KyleJames(5) 62
(Aytach Sadik) *prom: chsd wnr who was clr fr 4th: rdn and lost 2nd 3 out: wknd next* **25/1**
P4P- 6 9 **Days Of Pleasure (IRE)**[15] 1010 8-10-13 81.................(b[1]) TomCannon 50
(Chris Gordon) *chsd ldrs: blnd 3rd: lost pl 9th: bhd fr 13th* **12/1**
/P5- 7 17 **Fitobust (IRE)**[15] 1010 7-10-8 76...(p) DavidBass 29
(Lawney Hill) *hld up: drvn along 9th: a in rr* **12/1**
663/ 8 2 3/4 **Feeling Peckish (USA)**[102] 5431 9-9-9 68 oh2............(t) JoeCornwall(5) 19
(Michael Chapman) *chsd ldrs: lost pl 8th: bhd fr 13th* **12/1**
552- 9 6 **Crack At Dawn (IRE)**[18] 976 12-10-13 88.......................(b) MrCSmith(7) 33
(Michael Gates) *hld up: hdwy 6th: wknd 13th* **18/1**
305- 10 17 **Roses Legend**[18] 965 8-11-5 94.. MrJMartin(7) 24
(Reginald Brown) *chsd ldr tl after 3rd: pushed along 6th: wknd after 13th* **14/1**
3/P- P **Wishes Or Watches (IRE)**[25] 898 13-9-9 68 oh8...... GavinSheehan(5)
(John Upson) *hld up: hit 5th: bhd fr next: p.u bef 8th* **80/1**

5m 23.8s (-15.40) **Going Correction** -0.575s/f (Firm) course record **11 Ran SP% 116.0**
Speed ratings (Par 103): **103,102,96,93,89 86,80,79,77,71**
toteswingers 1&2 £3.60, 2&3 £7.00, 1&3 £0.00 CSF £10.45 CT £90.02 TOTE £4.20: £1.50, £1.50, £4.40; EX 10.90 Trifecta £187.20 Pool: £481.75 - 1.93 winning units..
Owner D J Burchell **Bred** The Three Rivers Racing Syndicate **Trained** Llancarfan, Vale Of Glamorgan

FOCUS
A modest staying handicap chase in which the winner made all at a decent tempo throughout. The first two were clear and the winner may still be capable of a bit better.

1173 TONY AND JOSIE H'CAP HURDLE (8 hdls) 2m 110y
4:05 (4:05) (Class 3) (0-125,120) 4-Y-O+ £5,523 (£1,621; £810; £405)

Form RPR
113- 1 **Thunder Sheik (IRE)**[15] 1008 5-11-6 114......................(t) PaddyBrennan 121+
(Fergal O'Brien) *chsd ldr to 2nd: remained handy: wnt 2nd again 4th: rdn to ld appr last: styd on* **4/1[1]**
051- 2 2 1/4 **Tamarillo Grove (IRE)**[24] 924 6-10-13 107..............(t) RichardJohnson 113
(Sophie Leech) *led: hit 2 out: rdn and hdd appr last: styd on same pce flat* **8/1**
442- 3 10 **Rime Avec Gentil (FR)**[18] 973 8-10-11 110........(p) AodhaganConlon(5) 106
(Bernard Llewellyn) *hld up: rdn after 3 out: r.o flat: nvr nrr* **9/1**
340- 4 1 1/4 **Sud Pacifique (IRE)**[32] 850 5-11-5 120......................(p) NickSlatter(7) 115
(Donald McCain) *chsd ldr 2nd to 4th: rdn and wknd after 2 out* **4/1[1]**
521- 5 7 **My Lord**[23] 927 5-10-9 103... LiamTreadwell 94
(Luke Dace) *prom tl rdn and wknd after 2 out* **9/2[2]**
6/3- 6 6 **Flying Phoenix**[81] 251 5-10-7 106................................ CharlieWallis(5) 89
(Dai Burchell) *hld up: rdn and wknd 3 out* **12/1**
216- 7 2 **Tom Wade (IRE)**[12] 1046 6-11-4 117................................(t) BenPoste(5) 98
(Shaun Harris) *prom tl rdn and wknd after 2 out* **5/1[3]**
551- U **Faith Jicaro (IRE)**[12] 1043 6-11-6 114.. DPFahy
(James Unett) *blnd and uns rdr 2nd* **14/1**

3m 43.4s (-12.60) **Going Correction** -0.575s/f (Firm) **8 Ran SP% 110.3**
Speed ratings (Par 107): **106,104,100,99,96 93,92,**
toteswingers 1&2 £2.50, 2&3 £5.00, 1&3 £4.90 CSF £32.70 CT £252.56 TOTE £3.50: £1.30, £2.40, £3.10; EX 20.60 Trifecta £111.50 Pool: £709.68 - 4.77 winning units..
Owner R J Rexton **Bred** Janus Bloodstock Inc **Trained** Coln St. Dennis, Gloucs

FOCUS
The feature race was a fairly good handicap hurdle in which they went an even gallop, and understandably produced comparatively the quickest time on the card so far. A personal best from the winner.

1174 ARKLE FINANCE H'CAP CHASE (14 fncs) 2m 4f
4:40 (4:41) (Class 5) (0-100,100) 4-Y-O+ £2,599 (£763; £381; £190)

Form RPR
435- 1 **Rudigreen (IRE)**[23] 930 10-11-7 98...........................(tp) JackQuinlan(3) 109
(Noel Quinlan) *hld up: hdwy 11th: chsd ldr after 2 out: led last: rdn out* **8/1[3]**
262- 2 2 1/4 **Peak Seasons (IRE)**[10] 1075 10-10-7 86........................ JoeCornwall(5) 94
(Michael Chapman) *sn pushed along in rr: hdwy 2 out: rdn and r.o to go 2nd towards fin: nt rch wnr* **10/1**
26U- 3 2 **Queen Of Mantua (IRE)**[18] 972 7-11-5 100........... ConorShoemark(7) 106
(Fergal O'Brien) *led: rdn and hdd last: no ex flat* **13/2[2]**
4/4- 4 8 **Brimham Boy**[18] 976 11-11-0 98.................................(vt) OllieGarner(10) 98
(Martin Keighley) *mid-div: pushed along after 8th: hdwy 10th: rdn after 2 out: wknd flat* **20/1**
3/4- 5 14 **Diamond Eclipse (IRE)**[24] 926 7-11-0 88.......................... NickScholfield 77
(Nick Williams) *hld up: drvn along after 5th: n.d* **4/1[1]**
F00- 6 3 3/4 **Mac Beattie**[24] 921 7-10-11 88.. AdamWedge(3) 71
(Evan Williams) *prom tl rdn and wknd after 2 out* **8/1[3]**
6P0- 7 nk **Novikov**[29] 873 9-9-11 74..(vt[1]) JamesBest(3) 61
(Sophie Leech) *chsd ldr tl rdn after 2 out: wkng whn hit last* **20/1**
254- 8 7 **Handsome Buddy (IRE)**[18] 972 6-11-8 96.............(v) RichardJohnson 72
(Michael Gates) *hld up: pushed along after 5th: hdwy 10th: wkng whn blnd 3 out* **4/1[1]**
301- 9 44 **Daneva (IRE)**[18] 976 9-11-9 97.......................................(tp) CharliePoste 34
(Matt Sheppard) *chsd ldrs: mstke 11th: wknd bef next* **12/1**
153- P **Mister Wiseman**[9] 1086 11-10-13 87..........................(bt) TomScudamore
(Nigel Hawke) *prom to 9th: bhd whn p.u bef 3 out* **9/1**
/43- P **Junior Jack**[9] 1089 8-11-11 99...(t) FelixDeGiles
(Jennifer Mason) *mid-div: rdn whn hit 10th: sn wknd: bhd whn p.u bef 3 out* **12/1**

4m 38.9s (-11.10) **Going Correction** -0.575s/f (Firm) **11 Ran SP% 119.6**
Speed ratings (Par 103): **99,98,97,94,88 87,86,84,66,,**
toteswingers 1&2 £18.20, 2&3 £15.50, 1&3 £34.20 CSF £85.84 CT £551.37 TOTE £7.70: £3.00, £4.30, £2.90; EX 125.00 TRIFECTA Not won..
Owner Miss M A Quinlan **Bred** John Murphy **Trained** Newmarket, Suffolk

FOCUS
A modest handicap chase in which they went a generous pace. Solid enough form.

1175 SWEEEP KUUSAKOSKI NOVICES' CHASE (12 fncs) 2m 1f 110y
5:10 (5:11) (Class 4) 4-Y-O+ £3,898 (£1,144; £572; £286)

Form RPR
/11- 1 **Professeur Emery (FR)**[11] 1059 6-11-0 0.............................. NoelFehily 127+
(Warren Greatrex) *mde all: j.w: shkn up appr last: rdn out* **1/1[1]**
/10- 2 3 1/4 **Monte Cavallo (SAF)**[54] 673 8-11-6 125............................. JamieMoore 127
(Rebecca Curtis) *chsd wnr: rdn and ev ch 2 out: styd on same pce flat* **9/4[2]**
3/6- 3 18 **Ulis De Vassy (FR)**[63] 559 5-11-0 0................................ NickScholfield 107
(Nick Williams) *hld up: outpcd fr 9th* **10/1**
045- 4 37 **George Woolf**[15] 1020 5-11-0 0....................................(t) RichardJohnson 72
(Tim Vaughan) *prom to 8th* **12/1**
010- P **First Morning (IRE)**[8] 1110 8-11-0 0.................................... TomCannon
(Michael Blake) *in rr whn stirrup leather broke 2nd: sn p.u* **50/1**
535- U **Red Whisper**[23] 927 9-10-11 0..(t) JamesBest(3)
(Rob Summers) *chsd ldrs: cl 3rd whn wnt rt and uns rdr 8th* **50/1**
222- P **Old Pals Act (IRE)**[8] 1109 5-10-9 0.......................... MauriceLinehan(5)
(Jonjo O'Neill) *hld up: a in rr: lost tch 8th: p.u bef 3 out* **15/2[3]**

3m 56.7s (-10.40) **Going Correction** -0.575s/f (Firm) course record **7 Ran SP% 113.2**
Speed ratings (Par 105): **100,98,90,74, , ,**
toteswingers 1&2 £1.10, 2&3 £11.80, 1&3 £8.00 CSF £3.67 TOTE £1.40: £1.10, £2.30; EX 4.60 Trifecta £21.60 Pool: £2018.62 - 69.96 winning units..
Owner Gdm Partnership **Bred** E A R L Du Haras De Pierrepont **Trained** Upper Lambourn, Berks

FOCUS
A fairly good novice chase in which they went an even gallop, and the winning time was quick. The second set a decent standard and the winner looks a fair chase prospect.

1176 IAN AND JUNE MAIDEN HURDLE (9 hdls) 2m 3f
5:45 (5:45) (Class 4) 4-Y-O+ £3,249 (£954; £477; £238)

Form RPR
4/0- 1 **Fighter Jet**[15] 1007 5-11-0 0...................................... WayneHutchinson 112+
(Alan King) *a.p: led appr last: sn clr: styd on wl* **14/1**
632- 2 10 **Kimora (IRE)**[15] 1017 7-10-7 97.....................................(t) AidanColeman 96
(Marc Barber) *hld up: drvn along after 5th: hdwy 3 out: rdn to go 2nd 2nd last: styd on same pce* **3/1[1]**
066/ 3 2 3/4 **Piano Concerto (USA)**[121] 5107 6-11-0 105...................(t) PaulMoloney 101
(Sophie Leech) *hld up: hdwy appr 2 out: swtchd rt bef last: styd on same pce* **5/1[2]**
623- 4 4 1/2 **Imperial Stargazer**[22] 856 4-10-12 108.......................... MarcGoldstein 93
(Sheena West) *prom: chsd ldr 3 out: rdn and ev ch appr last: sn wknd* **5/1[2]**
3- 5 12 **Scarlet Whispers**[15] 1017 4-10-5 0.................................. SeanQuinlan 81
(Pam Sly) *led after 1st: hit 2 out: sn rdn and hdd: wkng whn hit last* **3/1[1]**
65- 6 11 **Celebrian**[9] 1090 6-10-7 0..(t) WillKennedy 68
(Alex Hales) *hld up: hdwy appr 3 out: rdn and wknd bef next* **40/1**
6/6- 7 15 **Genes Quest**[15] 1007 6-10-7 0... RyanMahon 54
(Michael Appleby) *hld up: bhd fr 6th* **66/1**
405- 8 4 1/2 **Are They Your Own (IRE)**[15] 1007 5-10-7 0.................(t) NickSlatter(7) 57
(Fergal O'Brien) *chsd ldrs tl rdn and wknd appr 3 out* **20/1**
00- 9 19 **Give Me The Remote (IRE)**[6] 1118 5-10-9 0................ KillianMoore(5) 40
(Graeme McPherson) *chsd ldrs tl rdn and wknd after 6th* **66/1**
0/0- 10 16 **Mac Le Couteau**[68] 477 5-10-11 0...................................... AdamWedge(3) 26
(Evan Williams) *hld up: wknd 6th* **50/1**
P/P- P **Shinrock Beat**[18] 969 6-10-7 69..(p) MikeyHamill(7)
(Barry Brennan) *led tl after 1st: chsd ldr tl rdn 3 out: wknd befoe next: p.u bef last* **66/1**
P **Endear** 9-10-7 0.. IanPopham
(Martin Keighley) *bhd fr 4th: p.u after 6th* **40/1**

244- F **Darcey Diva**[9] 1090 5-10-0 0 .... (t) KieronEdgar(7)
(David Pipe) *hld up: hdwy appr 3 out: rdn and wknd bef next: bhd whn fell last* **6/1**[3]

4m 23.4s (-8.10) **Going Correction** -0.575s/f (Firm)
WFA 4 from 5yo+ 13lb **13** Ran SP% **120.4**
Speed ratings (Par 105): **94,89,88,86,81 77,70,68,60,54 , ,**
toteswingers 1&2 £6.70, 2&3 £7.20, 1&3 £8.30 CSF £55.74 TOTE £14.60: £5.40, £1.80, £2.70; EX 57.30 Trifecta £453.50 Part won..
Owner Ladas **Bred** Highclere Stud **Trained** Barbury Castle, Wilts

FOCUS
A modest maiden hurdle in which they went just a respectable gallop. The easy winner is on the upgrade and the next two were pretty much to their marks.
T/Plt: £13.60 to a £1 stake. Pool of £64922.34 - 3469.53 winning tickets. T/Qpdt: £8.20 to a £1 stake. Pool of £3619.40, 322.80 winning tickets. CR

1177 - (Foreign Racing) - See Raceform Interactive

1165 GALWAY (R-H)

Thursday, August 1

OFFICIAL GOING: Heavy

1178a GUINNESS MID-STRENGTH NOVICE CHASE (12 fncs) 2m 1f
2:20 (2:20) 5-Y-0+ **£12,154** (£3,552; £1,682; £560)

RPR

1 **Rebel Fitz (FR)**[16] 1004 8-11-9 152 .... BarryGeraghty 148+
(Michael Winters, Ire) *settled bhd ldrs: cl 4th 1/2-way: wnt 3rd after 3 out: pushed along briefly after last: sn clsd gng best between horses into st: hdwy nrside to ld over 1f out: styd on wl: comf* **10/11**[1]

2 3 ¾ **Sizing Italy (IRE)**[15] 1021 6-11-6 138 .... AELynch 138
(Henry De Bromhead, Ire) *settled bhd ldr: cl 3rd 1/2-way: clsr in 2nd after 3 out: disp last and gained narrow advantage into st: sn strly pressed and no ch w wnr: hdd over 1f out: kpt on same pce* **5/2**[2]

3 ¾ **Changing The Guard**[11] 1053 7-11-9 .... (t) SamTwiston-Davies 140
(Dr Richard Newland) *sn led: 2 l clr 1/2-way: reduced advantage after 3 out: brought wd bef next and jnd bef last: hdd narrowly into st: sn no imp on wnr: kpt on same pce in 3rd towards fin* **13/2**[3]

4 10 **He's Our Man (IRE)**[26] 796 8-11-6 130 .... (t) RWalsh 127
(Ross O'Sullivan, Ire) *sn trckd ldr: cl 2nd 1/2-way: slow 4 out and lost pl: pushed along fr last and no imp on ldrs appr st: one pce towards fin* **7/1**

5 17 **Edmundo (IRE)**[16] 1005 7-10-11 99 .... BenDalton(5) 107
(R P Rath, Ire) *hld up in tch: cl 5th 1/2-way: rdn fr last and sn no imp on ldrs in 5th appr st: one pce* **50/1**

6 34 **Miranour**[27] 888 8-11-2 .... EddieO'Connell 72
(Liam Lennon, Ire) *hld up in rr: niggled along fr 8th: detached fr 3 out: wknd: t.o* **33/1**

5m 8.8s (33.30) **6** Ran SP% **111.7**
CSF £3.68 TOTE £1.60: £1.40, £1.70; DF 2.60.
Owner Brian Sweetnam **Bred** Pierre De Maleisseye Melun Et Al **Trained** Kanturk, Co Cork

FOCUS
What we're learning about Rebel Fitz over fences is only coming gradually and again he didn't have to do much more than he needed to in order to complete the hat-trick. They went a steady pace. The form is rated around the second and fifth.

1082 BANGOR-ON-DEE (L-H)

Friday, August 2

OFFICIAL GOING: Good (good to firm in places)
Wind: Breezy, half against Weather: Fine

1182 ESL GROUP JUVENILE HURDLE (9 hdls) 2m 1f
2:05 (2:06) (Class 4) 3-Y-O **£3,422** (£997; £499)

Form RPR

2- 1 **Lindenhurst (IRE)**[62] 582 3-10-9 0 .... (t) MarkBolger(3) 108+
(John C McConnell, Ire) *hld up: chsd ldr 2nd: led 3rd: mde rest: effrtlessly wnt clr after 3 out: easily* **7/2**[2]

41- 2 13 **Sirop De Menthe (FR)**[19] 975 3-11-5 0 .... WilsonRenwick 101
(Tim Vaughan) *hld up: jockey got unbalanced 2nd: wnt 2nd 3 out: sn rdn and unable to go w wnr: no ch after* **2/5**[1]

0- 3 39 **Diamonds A Dancing**[19] 975 3-10-2 0 .... PaulO'Brien(10) 56
(Rebecca Curtis) *led: hdd 3rd: remained prom tl rdn and wknd after 3 out: pressed for 3rd run-in* **10/1**[3]

4 1 **Eyeline**[31] 3-10-12 0 .... (p) PaulMoloney 55
(Andrew Hollinshead) *chsd ldr to 2nd: dropped to rr 3rd: j. slowly most of way: lft bhd fr 4 out: plugged on whn n.d to 3rd horse run-in* **16/1**

4m 0.3s (-10.60) **Going Correction** -0.625s/f (Firm) **4** Ran SP% **108.6**
Speed ratings (Par 102): **99,92,74,74**
CSF £5.66 TOTE £2.40; EX 5.00 Trifecta £9.60 Pool: £678.14 - 52.46 winning units..
Owner Derek Kierans **Bred** K Maginn **Trained** Stamullen, Co Meath

FOCUS
Drying ground described as "good to firm" by two of the riders in the first. This event has been won by two Triumph Hurdle runners-up in recent seasons, Fair Along and Barizan. A step up from the easy winner with the second rated similar to his recent win.

1183 MEADE KING ROBINSON NOVICES' HURDLE (9 hdls) 2m 1f
2:40 (2:40) (Class 4) 4-Y-0+ **£3,249** (£954; £477; £238)

Form RPR

131- 1 **Cool Macavity (IRE)**[37] 843 5-11-12 130 .... DavidBass 134+
(Nicky Henderson) *racd keenly: chsd ldrs: wnt chsng clr ldr fr 3rd: clsd 4 out: led 2 out: clr whn drifted rt jst bef last: eased down run-in* **4/6**[1]

213- 2 13 **Separate Shadows (FR)**[13] 1048 5-11-5 112 .... (b[1]) JasonMaguire 111
(Donald McCain) *led: sn clr: reduced advantage 4 out: mstke 3 out: hdd and hit 2 out: no ch w wnr bef last* **4/1**[2]

3 7 **Bold Revenge (IRE)**[137] 4846 5-10-9 0 .... MarkBolger(3) 97
(John C McConnell, Ire) *chsd clr ldr to 3rd: outpcd bef 5th: u.p and no imp bef 2 out: one pce* **6/1**[3]

0U4- 4 15 **Take The Crown**[9] 1107 4-10-11 0 .... HenryOliver 82
(Henry Oliver) *hld up: plugged on bef 2 out: nvr a threat* **40/1**

04- 5 hd **Carobello (IRE)**[45] 758 6-10-12 0 .... JamesDavies 83
(Martin Bosley) *towards rr: u.p after 3rd: sme hdwy bef 2 out: n.d* **80/1**

U44- 6 ½ **Wintered Well (IRE)**[10] 1082 5-10-12 0 .... SeanQuinlan 83
(Jennie Candlish) *chsd ldrs: outpcd bef 5th: nvr a threat* **33/1**

- P **Isobar (GER)**[674] 7-10-12 0 .... AdrianLane
(Donald McCain) *hld up bhd: rdn appr 4th: t.o whn p.u bef 5th* **25/1**

0/4- P **Good Of Luck**[33] 848 4-10-11 0 .... ConorO'Farrell
(Mick Channon) *hld up bhd: blnd 3rd: t.o whn mstke 4 out: p.u bef 2 out* **7/1**

4m 0.7s (-10.20) **Going Correction** -0.625s/f (Firm)
WFA 4 from 5yo+ 13lb **8** Ran SP% **117.2**
Speed ratings (Par 105): **99,92,89,82,82 82, ,**
toteswingers 1&2 £1.40, 1&3 £2.80, 2&3 £2.80 CSF £3.84 TOTE £1.10: £1.02, £2.00, £2.00; EX 3.60 Trifecta £9.10 Pool: £1791.29 - 147.35 winning units..
Owner Triermore Stud **Bred** C O P Hanbury **Trained** Upper Lambourn, Berks

FOCUS
The field was soon stretched out in this modest novice hurdle, which was run in a slightly slower time than the preceding juvenile event. The easy winner is on the upgrade and closing in on the level expected from the best of his Flat form.

1184 BANGORBET NOVICES' CHASE (15 fncs) 2m 4f 110y
3:15 (3:15) (Class 4) 5-Y-0+ **£3,898** (£1,144; £572; £286)

Form RPR

301- 1 **One Term (IRE)**[10] 1083 6-11-5 0 .... APMcCoy 130+
(Rebecca Curtis) *led to 2nd: chsd ldr after tl regained ld appr 3 out: shkn up to draw clr last: eased down run-in* **1/2**[1]

1- 2 9 **Foreverpresenting (IRE)**[26] 899 9-11-5 0 .... (t) BrianHughes 118
(Malcolm Jefferson) *prom: rdn after 3 out: sn chsd wnr: no real imp appr last: no ch after* **10/1**[3]

P/3- 3 9 **Featherintheattic (IRE)**[12] 1053 8-10-12 0 .... (p) NoelFehily 105
(Warren Greatrex) *prom: led 2nd: hdd appr 3 out: rdn bef 2 out: wknd between last 2* **16/1**

50- 4 53 **Alderbrook Lad (IRE)**[12] 1052 7-10-9 0 .... MichaelByrne(3) 55
(Neil Mulholland) *hld up: blnd 8th: nt fluent 4 out: struggling and lft bhd after: t.o* **50/1**

212- P **Atlanta Falcon (IRE)**[11] 1076 8-11-12 122 .... (t) JasonMaguire
(Donald McCain) *prom to 3rd: dropped to rr 5th: j. slowly 6th: struggling whn mstke 8th: t.o whn p.u after next* **3/1**[2]

/44- F **It's Oscar (IRE)**[23] 948 6-10-12 0 .... (t) BrianHarding
(Donald McCain) *hld up: reminders after 5th: struggling whn fell 4 out* **25/1**

4m 57.2s (-11.90) **Going Correction** -0.50s/f (Good) **6** Ran SP% **112.4**
Speed ratings: **102,98,95,74,**
toteswingers 1&2 £2.40, 1&3 £1.80, 2&3 £3.30 CSF £6.66 TOTE £1.30: £1.02, £4.70; EX 6.60 Trifecta £19.60 Pool: £1843.83 - 70.41 winning units..
Owner Miss L Reid & G Costelloe **Bred** Hugh J Holohan **Trained** Newport, Dyfed

FOCUS
They went a decent pace in this fair novices' chase. The easy winner was the form pick and there should be more to come.

1185 DEBENHAMS OF CHESTER H'CAP HURDLE (9 hdls) 2m 1f
3:50 (3:50) (Class 3) (0-140,130) 4-Y-0+ **£5,393** (£1,583; £791; £395)

Form RPR

100/ 1 **Adelar (GER)**[259] 2455 8-11-2 **120** .... AidanColeman 125+
(Venetia Williams) *a.p: hit 4 out: upsides 2 out: sn rdn to ld: big jump last: r.o and drew away fnl 50yds* **7/2**[2]

/26- 2 2 ¾ **Scoglio**[33] 850 5-11-1 **119** .... LeeEdwards 119
(Dave Roberts) *hld up: effrt to chal appr 2 out: wnt 2nd jst bef last: outpcd by wnr fnl 50yds* **6/1**

000/ 3 1 ¾ **Agent Archie (USA)**[189] 3849 6-11-10 **128** .... JasonMaguire 127
(Donald McCain) *led: rdn whn pressed appr 2 out: hdd jst after 2 out: kpt on same pce run-in* **7/2**[2]

4 1 **Dumbarton (IRE)**[8] 1949 5-11-9 **127** .... (p) RichardJohnson 130+
(Philip Hobbs) *hld up in rr: hdwy 4 out: jst bhd ldrs travelling strly whn blnd 3 out: sn dropped to last: rallied fr 2 out: hanging lft disputing 3rd over 2 l down whn mstke last: one pce run-in* **7/4**[1]

2- 5 13 **Ice Ice Baby**[7] 1126 4-10-0 **105** oh3 .... (t) TomScudamore 92
(John C McConnell, Ire) *in tch: clsd 3 out: dropped to last appr next: btn after: hmpd whn n.d last* **20/1**

024- 6 1 ¾ **Knight In Purple**[13] 1041 9-11-8 **129** .... (vt) PeterCarberry(3) 117
(John Mackie) *prom: rdn to chal appr 2 out: no ex between last 2: btn whn blnd last* **11/2**[3]

3m 56.6s (-14.30) **Going Correction** -0.625s/f (Firm)
WFA 4 from 5yo+ 13lb **6** Ran SP% **115.2**
Speed ratings (Par 107): **108,106,105,105,99 98**
toteswingers 1&2 £6.40, 1&3 £13.10, 2&3 £8.60 CSF £24.40 TOTE £6.70: £2.40, £1.90; EX 32.50 Trifecta £151.50 Pool: £1790.52 - 8.86 winning units..
Owner B Dice & D Jinks **Bred** Gestut Karlshof **Trained** Kings Caple, H'fords

FOCUS
They went a steady pace in this handicap hurdle, which wasn't a strong race for the class. The winner is rated to form with the next two close to their marks.

1186 BANGORBET H'CAP CHASE (12 fncs) 2m 1f 110y
4:25 (4:27) (Class 4) (0-115,114) 4-Y-0+ **£3,898** (£1,144; £572; £286)

Form RPR

143- 1 **Wester Ross (IRE)**[23] 943 9-11-9 **114** .... (p) AdamWedge(3) 126+
(Evan Williams) *hld up: effrt to chse ldr appr 2 out: rdn to ld between last 2: styd on to draw clr ins fnl 75yds* **6/4**[1]

301- 2 5 **Maizy Missile (IRE)**[10] 1086 11-10-2 90 7ex .... PaulMoloney 96
(Mary Evans) *chsd ldr tl appr 2 out: stl ev ch whn rdn between last 2: wnt 2nd jst after last: sn hung lft: no ex fnl 75yds* **3/1**[3]

/54- 3 2 **Milgen Bay**[13] 1050 7-11-8 **110** .... (v[1]) LeightonAspell 115
(Oliver Sherwood) *led: mstke 3 out: pressed 2 out: rdn and hdd between last 2: btn and one pce fnl 100yds: eased towards fin* **2/1**[2]

/40- 4 14 **Highland River**[7] 1121 7-10-0 **88** .... LeeEdwards 82
(Dave Roberts) *hld up in rr: nt fluent 6th: struggling and outpcd appr 3 out: nvr a danger* **13/2**

4m 10.8s (-11.30) **Going Correction** -0.50s/f (Good) **4** Ran SP% **111.7**
Speed ratings (Par 105): **105,102,101,95**
CSF £6.47 TOTE £2.70; EX 7.00 Trifecta £8.90 Pool: £1722.83 - 144.85 winning units..
Owner T Hywel Jones **Bred** Farmers Hill Stud **Trained** Llancarfan, Vale Of Glamorgan

FOCUS
The winner was well in on old form and is rated back to something like his best, with the next two to form.

1187 GOLDFORD STUD MARES' NOVICES' HURDLE (11 hdls) 2m 4f
5:00 (5:00) (Class 4) 4-Y-0+ **£3,249** (£954; £477; £238)

Form RPR

141- 1 **As I Am (IRE)**[10] 1090 5-11-10 114 .... LeightonAspell 117+
(Don Cantillon) *prom: bmpd 1st: led 7th: rdn appr 2 out: drew clr bef last: styd on wl* **40/85**[1]

02- **2** *6* **Hopstrings**[10] 1090 5-10-10 0 .... SamTwiston-Davies 96
(Charlie Brooks) *hld up: sltly outpcd 3 out: effrt appr 2 out: sn wnt 2nd: hung lft bef last: no imp on wnr* **10/1**[3]

00/ **3** *1 3/4* **Duchess Theatre (IRE)**[61] 5-10-7 0 ....(t) JakeGreenall(3) 95
(Michael Easterby) *hld up: hdwy appr 4 out: rdn whn chsng ldrs bef 2 out: nt qckn bef last: kpt on u.p run-in but hld* **33/1**

1- **4** *3 3/4* **Crazy (GER)**[16] 1017 4-11-1 0 ....(p) TomScudamore 97
(David Bridgwater) *racd keenly: trckd ldrs: hit 2nd: wnt 2nd appr 4 out: rdn and lost 2nd bef 2 out: sn wknd* **7/2**[2]

3/ **5** *8* **Nell's Nan (IRE)**[20] 986 5-10-7 93 ....(t) MarkBolger(3) 84
(John C McConnell, Ire) *in tch: lost pl appr 4 out: rdn and outpcd after 3 out: n.d after* **16/1**

3/4- **6** *63* **Bahira (IRE)**[16] 1017 6-10-10 88 .... JasonMaguire 27
(Donald McCain) *led: bmpd 1st: hdd 7th: wknd bef 3 out: t.o* **14/1**

4m 49.1s (-2.90) **Going Correction** -0.625s/f (Firm)
WFA 4 from 5yo+ 14lb 6 Ran SP% **114.8**
Speed ratings (Par 105): **80,77,76,75,72 47**
toteswingers 1&2 £1.40, 1&3 £5.80, 2&3 £6.70 CSF £6.80 TOTE £1.80: £1.10, £5.10; EX 6.20 Trifecta £61.50 Pool: £3205.94 - 39.07 winning units..
Owner Don Cantillon **Bred** Don Cantillon **Trained** Newmarket, Suffolk

FOCUS
Fair mares' form. The winner was the clear form pick and didn't need to be at her best to win again.

1188 R W HOUGH & SONS CONDITIONAL JOCKEYS' H'CAP HURDLE (12 hdls) 3m
5:35 (5:36) (Class 5) (0-95,95) 4-Y-O+ **£2,053** (£598; £299)

Form RPR

/56- **1** **Tarvini (IRE)**[19] 965 8-11-0 **93** ....(p) JamesHuxham(10) 98
(Jonjo O'Neill) *niggled along off the pce: hdwy appr 8th: wnt 2nd 4 out: rdn bef next: chalng 2 out: styd on to ld towards fin* **10/1**

545- **2** *3/4* **Nicky Nutjob (GER)**[16] 1018 7-11-0 **91** ....(p) CiaranMckee(8) 94
(John O'Shea) *hld up in rr: stdy hdwy after 6th: led 8th: pressed 2 out: rdn bef last: hdd towards fin* **9/1**

063- **3** *5* **Heezagrey (IRE)**[19] 965 10-10-0 **69** ....(b) BenPoste 69
(James Evans) *in tch: pushed along chsng ldrs whn nt fluent 4 out: rdn appr 2 out: one pce run-in* **11/1**

331- **4** *21* **Executive's Hall (IRE)**[11] 1073 9-11-6 **94** 7ex ....(p) CraigGallagher(5) 76
(Ben Haslam) *chsd ldrs: lost pl 7th: handy again 8th: one pce whn mstke 2 out: no imp after* **11/2**[3]

P0P/ **5** *2 1/2* **Potters Dream (IRE)**[67] 7-10-1 **76** .... ConorShoemark(6) 53
(Fergal O'Brien) *hld up: hdwy appr 4 out: mstke whn chsng ldrs 3 out: one pce 2 out: no imp after* **12/1**

0/0- **6** *nk* **Almutaham (USA)**[83] 221 6-11-7 **90** .... LucyAlexander 67
(Nicky Richards) *hld up: pushed along whn mstke 7th: kpt on u.p into midfield 3 out: nvr able to trble ldrs* **8/1**

402- **7** *11* **Chosen Dream (IRE)**[23] 946 5-11-3 **89** ....(tp) MauriceLinehan(3) 56
(Jonjo O'Neill) *chsd ldrs: led after 6th: hdd after 7th: rdn and wknd appr 2 out* **7/2**[1]

0/0- **8** *9* **Hill Forts Gloria (IRE)**[68] 490 8-10-0 **69** oh5 ....(t) GavinSheehan 28
(Lawney Hill) *in tch: lost pl 6th: impr to trck ldrs 8th: rdn and wknd 4 out* **4/1**[2]

/05- **9** *hd* **Alimure**[65] 532 7-10-3 **72** .... JakeGreenall 31
(Clive Mulhall) *in tch: rdn and lost pl 7th: racd in midfield but u.p after: wknd 3 out* **40/1**

530- **10** *12* **Highland Rain**[13] 1038 5-9-12 **72** ....(vt) ConorRing(5) 20
(Jennie Candlish) *led to 2nd: led bef 4th: mstke 5th: hdd after 6th: jinked lft appr next: led again sn after: hdd 8th: rdn and wknd bef 3 out* **20/1**

10/- **11** *20* **Dice (IRE)**[514] 4692 7-11-7 **95** ....(p) JackSherwood(5) 25
(Sirrell Griffiths) *midfield: impr to trck ldrs 5th: hit 7th: rdn 4 out: wknd appr 3 out* **25/1**

0/P- **12** *109* **Burnthill (IRE)**[10] 1088 8-10-13 **90** ....(vt1) DanielHiskett(8)
(Claire Dyson) *in rr fr 3rd: nvr travelled: detached 6th: t.o* **20/1**

55P/ **P** **All The Fashion (IRE)**[225] 3159 9-10-0 **69** oh15 .... JamesBest
(Violet M Jordan) *prom: led 2nd: hdd bef 4th: remained handy tl wknd appr 8th: t.o whn p.u bef 4 out* **80/1**

2PP/ **P** **Free Advice (IRE)**[325] 1540 6-11-2 **85** ....(t) MichaelByrne
(Marc Barber) *chsd ldrs: lost pl after 1st: rn in snatches aftertl lost pl after 6th: t.o whn p.u bef 8th* **25/1**

5m 37.7s (-13.30) **Going Correction** -0.625s/f (Firm) 14 Ran SP% **124.7**
Speed ratings (Par 103): **97,96,95,88,87 87,83,80,80,76 69, , ,**
toteswingers 1&2 £12.70, 1&3 £20.40, 2&3 £17.70 CSF £91.95 CT £1031.27 TOTE £10.90: £6.50, £3.90, £3.50; EX 146.80 Trifecta £1106.10 Part won. Pool: £1474.83 - 0.13 winning units..
Owner John P McManus **Bred** His Highness The Aga Khan's Studs S C **Trained** Cheltenham, Gloucs
■ James Huxham's first winner.
■ Stewards' Enquiry : Daniel Hiskett seven-day ban: used whip when out of contention (Aug 17-23)

FOCUS
They went a decent clip in this modest handicap. The winner was on a very good mark and is rated a stone+ off his best here.
T/Plt: £45.60 to a £1 stake. Pool: £46008.11 - 736.15 winning tickets T/Qpdt: £13.10 to a £1 stake. Pool: £2781.81 - 156.30 winning tickets DO

1189 - 1190a (Foreign Racing) - See Raceform Interactive

[1051]NEWTON ABBOT (L-H)
Saturday, August 3

OFFICIAL GOING: Good to firm (good in places; 7.5)
Wind: Fresh breeze; against Weather: Sunny with cloudy periods

1191 BET TOTEJACKPOT AT TOTEPOOL.COM NOVICES' HURDLE (9 hdls) 2m 3f
2:10 (2:11) (Class 3) 4-Y-O+ **£6,330** (£1,870; £935; £468; £234)

Form RPR

131- **1** **Plain Sailing (IRE)**[24] 944 4-10-10 0 .... DenisO'Regan 111+
(John Ferguson) *trckd ldrs: jnd ldr 6th: led after 3 out: hit last: kpt on wl but drifted lft run-in: rdn out* **4/6**[1]

/02- **2** *2 1/4* **Kalmbeforethestorm**[26] 920 5-10-12 115 .... PaulMoloney 107
(Helen Nelmes) *in tch: trckd ldrs 6th: rdn to chse wnr after 3 out: styd on but a being hld fr last* **10/3**[2]

3 *9* **Beachfire**[407] 6-10-9 0 .... JackQuinlan(3) 98
(John Ferguson) *hld up: hdwy appr 3 out: rdn to chse ldng pair bef 2 out: styd on same pce* **4/1**[3]

030- **4** *5* **Ailanthus**[10] 1107 4-10-3 0 .... AidanColeman 84
(Richard Woollacott) *hld up: hdwy appr 3 out: sn rdn: styd on w out troubling ldrs* **16/1**

5 *29* **Amantius**[268] 4-10-10 0 .... NickScholfield 62
(Johnny Farrelly) *in tch: trckd ldrs 5th: nt fluent next: rdn after 3 out: wknd bef next: t.o* **40/1**

0P- **6** *15* **Cool Fantasy (IRE)**[59] 631 4-10-10 0 .... IanPopham 47
(Caroline Keevil) *trckd ldr tl 6th: rdn after 3 out: sn wknd: t.o* **66/1**

64- **7** *2* **Golden Squirell (IRE)**[4] 1154 6-10-12 0 .... TomCannon 47
(Brendan Powell) *led: pushed along at times: drvn 6th: hdd after 3 out: sn btn: t.o* **12/1**

006- **8** *hd* **Rusty Nail (IRE)**[26] 921 8-10-12 0 .... HaddenFrost 47
(James Frost) *pushed along after 6th: a towards rr: t.o after 3 out* **40/1**

4m 27.7s (-2.30) **Going Correction** -0.375s/f (Good)
WFA 4 from 5yo+ 13lb 8 Ran SP% **123.0**
Speed ratings (Par 107): **89,88,84,82,69 63,62,62**
toteswingers 1&2 £1.10, 1&3 £1.30, 2&3 £2.40 CSF £3.79 TOTE £1.70: £1.02, £1.50, £1.20; EX 2.90 Trifecta £7.70 Pool: £533.40 - 51.78 winning units..
Owner Bloomfields **Bred** Darley **Trained** Cowlinge, Suffolk

FOCUS
All bends moved out since last meeting. A fair novice hurdle with four pulling clear off a steady early pace.

1192 TOTESCOOP6 EVERY SATURDAY AT TOTEPOOL.COM NOVICES' H'CAP CHASE (13 fncs) 2m 110y
2:45 (2:45) (Class 4) (0-120,120) 4-Y-£9,495 (£2,805; £1,402; £702; £351)

Form RPR

/42- **1** **De Faoithesdream (IRE)**[19] 999 7-11-12 **120** .... PaulMoloney 128
(Evan Williams) *trckd ldr: nvr as fluent as ldr: hit 8th: led after 4 out: rdn w enough in hand gng to the last: a holding on* **9/4**[1]

541- **2** *3/4* **Lauberhorn**[4] 1153 6-10-8 **105** ....(p) AdamWedge(3) 111
(Evan Williams) *hld up: rdn and stdy prog after 4 out: disp 2nd after 3 out: clsng on wnr fr last: kpt on wl but a being hld run-in* **5/1**

661- **3** *16* **Tri Nations (UAE)**[13] 1063 8-10-7 **101** ....(vt) NickScholfield 95
(Anthony Middleton) *racd in 4th: rdn in 3rd after 4 out: disputing 2nd whn hit 2 out: wknd last* **9/1**

3- **4** *13* **Easily Pleased (IRE)**[19] 996 7-11-2 **110** .... HaddenFrost 92
(Martin Hill) *led: rdn after hdd after 4 out: sn hld: wknd bef 2 out* **7/2**[3]

U24- **5** *12* **Ninfea (IRE)**[13] 1063 5-10-11 **105** ....(p) TomScudamore 74
(David Bridgwater) *nvr fluent: a in rr: t.o* **16/1**

426- **6** *28* **Nomadic Dreamer**[5] 1133 10-11-3 **114** ....(t) JamesBest(3) 58
(Sophie Leech) *chsd ldng pair: hit 5th: rdn after 8th: sn wknd: t.o* **16/1**

651- **P** **Next Oasis (IRE)**[39] 832 7-11-5 **113** .... TomO'Brien
(Paul Henderson) *a in last pair: mstke 1st: strugglng 5th: losing tch whn p.u after 6th: b.b.v* **10/3**[2]

3m 55.8s (-10.70) **Going Correction** -0.375s/f (Good) 7 Ran SP% **114.5**
Speed ratings (Par 105): **110,109,102,96,90 77,**
toteswingers 1&2 not won, 1&3 £6.70, 2&3 not won CSF £14.21 TOTE £3.20: £1.10, £4.30; EX 15.20 Trifecta £64.60 Pool: £677.92 - 7.86 winning units..
Owner R Abbott & M Stavrou **Bred** Pierce Whyte **Trained** Llancarfan, Vale Of Glamorgan

FOCUS
With two horses vying for the early lead a good pace was assured and few got into it.

1193 TOTEPOOL.COM THE HOME OF POOL BETTING JUVENILE HURDLE (8 hdls) 2m 1f
3:20 (3:20) (Class 3) 3-Y-O **£6,388** (£1,928; £993; £526)

Form RPR

55- **1** **Walter White (IRE)**[20] 975 3-10-12 0 ....(t) TomO'Brien 95+
(Philip Hobbs) *trckd ldng pair: cl up and travelling best after 3 out: led 2 out: sn hrd rdn: kpt on wl fr last* **11/1**

12- **2** *4 1/2* **Akdam (IRE)**[23] 725 3-11-4 0 .... APMcCoy 98
(Tony Carroll) *led tl 2nd: pressed ldr: drvn along fr 5th: hmpd 3 out: swtchd rt and sn led: hdd bef 2 out: styd on same pce* **4/7**[1]

64- **3** *15* **Wild Diamond (IRE)**[20] 975 3-10-5 0 .... RichardJohnson 77
(Tim Vaughan) *led 2nd: tended to jump lft: rdn and hdd after 3 out: wknd bef last* **15/2**[3]

B- **4** *66* **Scepticism (USA)**[20] 975 3-10-12 0 .... NoelFehily 18
(Charlie Mann) *trckd ldng trio after being hmpd 1st: rdn after 3 out: sn wknd: t.o* **3/1**[2]

F **Karl Marx (IRE)**[61] 3-10-12 0 .... NickScholfield
(Mark Gillard) *cl up whn swvd lft and fell 1st* **33/1**

4m 5.2s (-0.50) **Going Correction** -0.375s/f (Good) 5 Ran SP% **111.7**
Speed ratings (Par 104): **86,83,76,45,**
CSF £19.27 TOTE £8.40: £4.20, £1.10; EX 19.10 Trifecta £63.90 Pool: £337.48 - 3.95 winning units..
Owner Walter White Partnership **Bred** Catridge Farm Stud & S Von Schilcher **Trained** Withycombe, Somerset

FOCUS
With Akdam and Wild Diamond duelling for over a circuit the race was effectively set up for any closer still in touch. As such the form does not look reliable.

1194 TRY A TOTETRIFECTA AT TOTEPOOL.COM H'CAP CHASE (13 fncs) 2m 110y
3:55 (3:56) (Class 2) (0-145,144) 4-Y-O+
£15,640 (£4,620; £2,310; £1,155; £577; £290)

Form RPR

114- **1** **Dineur (FR)**[14] 1047 7-10-12 **130** .... DonalDevereux 135
(Peter Bowen) *trckd ldrs: slt ld whn nt fluent 3 out: sn hadr pressed and rdn: hld on gamely fr last: all out* **5/2**[1]

362- **2** *1* **Skint**[14] 1050 7-10-5 **123** ....(p) AidanColeman 126
(Ali Brewer) *hld up: hdwy 4 out: rdn for str chal after next: ev ch fr last: kpt on but no ex nring fin* **3/1**[2]

0/0- **3** *22* **Toubab (FR)**[84] 216 7-11-7 **144** .... HarryDerham(5) 128
(Paul Nicholls) *led tl rdn and nt fluent 3 out: fdd fr 2 out but a hanging on for 3rd* **5/2**[1]

456- **4** *3 1/2* **Manger Hanagment (IRE)**[19] 996 8-10-2 **120** ...... SamTwiston-Davies 102
(Barry Brennan) *trckd ldr tl pushed along fr 6th: rdn 8th: sn hld: plugged on* **16/1**

1U5- **5** *4 1/2* **Anquetta (IRE)**[20] 974 9-11-7 **144** .... MrSWaley-Cohen(5) 120
(Nicky Henderson) *trckd ldrs: rdn after 4 out: nt pce to chal: fdd fr 2 out* **8/1**[3]

4P4- **6** *4* **Grey Soldier (IRE)**[12] 1076 8-10-6 **124** ....(t) PaddyBrennan 96
(Sophie Leech) *hld up: rdn after 4 out: nvr any imp: wknd after next: t.o* **10/1**

104- **F** **West With The Wind**[20] 974 8-11-10 **142**........................ PaulMoloney
(Evan Williams) *trckd ldr tl lost action appr 8th: fell: fatally injured* **12/1**

3m 56.8s (-9.70) **Going Correction** -0.375s/f (Good) **7** Ran SP% **115.9**
Speed ratings (Par 109): **107,106,96,94,92 90,**
toteswingers 1&2 £3.90, 2&3 £8.10, 1&3 £1.10 CSF £11.20 TOTE £2.50: £1.10, £2.50; EX 9.70 Trifecta £24.10 Pool: £615.75 - 19.13 winning units..
Owner Gwilym J Morris **Bred** Dominique Le Baron **Trained** Little Newcastle, Pembrokes

FOCUS
No overly competitive and two pulled clear.

1195 MORE FOOTBALL THAN EVER AT TOTEPOOL.COM H'CAP HURDLE (12 hdls) 3m 3f
4:30 (4:32) (Class 3) (0-140,138) 4-Y-O+
£12,512 (£3,696; £1,848; £924; £462; £232)

Form RPR
/23- **1** **Sheriff Hutton (IRE)**[26] 923 10-11-0 **126**.................... RichardJohnson 133
(Martin Hill) *in tch: hdwy after 9th: rdn to ld appr 2 out: styd on wl: rdn out* **16/1**

0/0- **2** *2* **Benbane Head (USA)**[31] 877 9-10-8 **120**........................(t) IanPopham 126
(Martin Keighley) *trckd ldrs: led whn nt fluent 3 out: rdn and hdd whn awkward 2 out: styd on but a being hld* **25/1**

112- **3** *2 3/4* **On The Bridge (IRE)**[24] 943 8-11-11 **137**.................. NickScholfield 141
(Jeremy Scott) *hld up towards rr of midfield: hdwy fr 9th: rdn to chse ldrs after 3 out: styd on same pce fr next* **4/1**[2]

/12- **4** *3/4* **Union Saint (FR)**[75] 409 5-11-2 **128**.................................. HaddenFrost 130
(James Frost) *hld up bhd: hdwy after 8th: rdn to chse ldrs gng to 2 out: styd on fr last* **16/1**

122- **5** *1* **Pure Faith (IRE)**[34] 851 9-11-2 **128**................................ TomO'Brien 129
(Peter Bowen) *trckd ldrs: rdn after 9th: ev ch next: styd on same pce fr 2 out* **8/1**[3]

10P/ **6** *2* **Shoegazer (IRE)**[126] 5014 8-11-12 **138**......................(t) TomScudamore 137
(David Pipe) *mid-div: trckd ldrs 9th: rdn after 3 out: nt quite pce to mount chal: no ex fr last* **20/1**

/02- **7** *20* **Possol (FR)**[57] 659 10-11-0 **126**...................................... PaddyBrennan 107
(Henry Daly) *mid-div: awkward 6th: rdn after 8th: bhd fr next* **14/1**

/05- **8** *1 3/4* **Cockney Trucker (IRE)**[44] 780 11-11-4 **130**........................ APMcCoy 110
(Philip Hobbs) *mid-div: nt a fluent: rdn in tch 3 out: wknd next* **8/1**[3]

362- **9** *1 1/4* **Qulinton (FR)**[19] 998 9-10-10 **122**................................(p) ConorO'Farrell 101
(David Pipe) *led tl rdn and hdd 3 out: sn wknd: t.o* **10/1**

602/ **10** *2* **Cloudy Spirit**[3] 5360 8-11-4 **130**... PaulMoloney 107
(Andrew Hollinshead) *struggling after 8th: a towards rr* **7/2**[1]

1/0- **11** *15* **Darley Sun (IRE)**[84] 215 7-11-10 **136**.............................. DenisO'Regan 99
(John Ferguson) *hld up towards rr: shkn up after 9th: nvr any imp: eased whn btn after 2 out: t.o* **9/1**

442- **P** **Aikideau (FR)**[13] 1055 6-10-4 **121**..............................(b) HarryDerham[(5)]
(Paul Nicholls) *a towards rr: t.o whn p.u bef 2 out* **12/1**

244- **P** **Well Mett (IRE)**[26] 921 6-10-1 **120**.......................(bt) ConorShoemark[(7)]
(Fergal O'Brien) *prom tl nt fluent 8th: sn rdn: bhd fr next: p.u bef 3 out* **16/1**

143- **U** **Lost Legend (IRE)**[12] 1076 6-10-5 **122**..................(p) MauriceLinehan[(5)]
(Jonjo O'Neill) *in tch whn blnd and uns rdr 3rd* **16/1**

6m 23.5s (-17.50) **Going Correction** -0.375s/f (Good) **14** Ran SP% **130.0**
Speed ratings (Par 107): **110,109,108,108,108 107,101,101,100,100 95, , ,**
toteswingers 1&2 not won, 1&3 £11.20, 2&3 not won CSF £375.95 CT £1933.23 TOTE £15.00: £3.80, £8.50, £1.90; EX 555.20 Trifecta £302.10 Part won. Pool: £402.81 - 0.11 winning units..
Owner Russell Dennis **Bred** Joe Slattery **Trained** Littlehempston, Devon

FOCUS
A competitive affair in which they did not get racing until the final circuit.

1196 TOTEEXACTA ON EVERY RACE AT TOTEPOOL.COM STANDARD OPEN NATIONAL HUNT FLAT RACE 2m 1f
5:05 (5:06) (Class 3) 4-6-Y-O **£6,330** (£1,870; £935; £468; £234)

Form RPR
00/- **1** **Rest And Be (IRE)**[261] 2443 6-10-9 0.......................... NickScholfield 94+
(Alan Jones) *hld up in last pair but wl in tch tl tk clsr order over 3f out: led jst over 1f out: rdn clr* **11/2**[2]

34- **2** *6* **Bear Island Flint**[8] 1124 5-11-2 0.. APMcCoy 95
(Brendan Powell) *hld up last but wl in tch: tk clsr order over 6f out: jnd ldr over 2f out: rdn to ld over 1f out: sn hdd: nt pce of wnr* **1/4**[1]

50- **3** *4 1/2* **All Riled Up**[20] 970 5-10-9 0.. LeightonAspell 83
(Harry Chisman) *trckd ldr: led wl over 2f out: rdn and hdd over 1f out: no ex ins fnl f* **12/1**[3]

4 *7* **Mrs Rooney** 6-10-9 0.. DPFahy 76
(Sue Gardner) *trckd ldrs: rdn 4f out: wknd over 1f out* **14/1**

0- **5** *20* **Tanner Bet**[13] 1056 5-10-2 0.. MrWPotter[(7)] 56
(Polly Gundry) *kpt wd: trckd ldr: led over 3f out: sn rdn and hdd: wknd wl over 1f out* **33/1**

0- **6** *45* **Polden Prince**[31] 874 6-11-2 0.. HaddenFrost 18
(James Frost) *led tl rdn 3f out: qckly btn: t.o* **50/1**

4m 17.1s (17.00) **Going Correction** -0.375s/f (Good) **6** Ran SP% **114.6**
Speed ratings: **45,42,40,36,27 6**
toteswingers 1&2 £1.02, 1&3 £9.70, 2&3 £1.02 CSF £7.54 TOTE £1.10: £2.50, £1.02; EX 12.10 Trifecta £25.30 Pool: £771.41 - 22.79 winning units..
Owner T S M S Riley-Smith **Bred** Gerry Burke **Trained** Bickham, Somerset

FOCUS
With one of the market leaders Radharc Nahabhainn a non-runner this looked an uncompetitive event. The pace was an exaggerated crawl for the first mile and the hot favourite was turned over in a sprint to the line.

1197 COLLECT TOTEPOOL WINNINGS AT BETFRED SHOPS H'CAP CHASE (16 fncs) 2m 5f 110y
5:40 (5:40) (Class 4) (0-120,120) 4-Y-O **£6,330** (£1,870; £935; £468; £234)

Form RPR
/34- **1** **Henry San (IRE)**[17] 1012 6-11-5 **113**.........................(p) WayneHutchinson 125
(Alan King) *trckd ldrs tl lost pl 8th: hdwy on outer after 4 out: chal next: led 2 out: hld on: all out* **12/1**

3/2- **2** *hd* **The Mad Robertson (IRE)**[17] 1012 6-11-6 **114**................... APMcCoy 126
(Jonjo O'Neill) *led: dived at 4th: pushed along fr after 10th: rdn after 4 out: hdd 2 out: rallied u.str.p after last: jst hld* **3/1**[1]

/55- **3** *7* **Spock (FR)**[24] 943 8-11-12 **120**..................................(b[1]) RyanMahon 125
(Paul Nicholls) *mid-div: trckd ldrs: rdn after 4 out: wnt 3rd 2 out: styd on same pce* **16/1**

001- **4** *5* **Kylenoe Fairy (IRE)**[19] 996 9-11-6 **114**..........................(t) TomO'Brien 114
(Paul Henderson) *hld up towards rr: rdn and stdy prog fr 4 out: styd on to go 4th 2 out: nvr rchd ldrs* **7/1**[3]

053- **5** *17* **Lucy's Legend (IRE)**[39] 832 7-10-7 **101**...........................(tp) NoelFehily 88
(Paul Henderson) *mid-div: trckd ldrs 6th: rdn in 3rd after 4 out: wknd 2 out* **8/1**

312- **6** *7* **Tiermore (IRE)**[19] 996 9-11-1 **109**.. JamieMoore 88
(Peter Bowen) *trckd ldrs: rdn after 10th: wknd 3 out* **7/2**[2]

/1P- **7** *4* **Catch Tammy (IRE)**[34] 853 7-11-4 **112**........................... PaddyBrennan 87
(Tom George) *prom tl rdn after 4 out: wknd bef 2 out* **20/1**

/21- **8** *4 1/2* **Danandy (IRE)**[8] 1118 6-11-1 **109**................................. RichardJohnson 83
(Philip Hobbs) *mid-div: tk clsr order 8th: rdn and losing pl whn stmbld bdly 12th: sn bhd* **7/2**[2]

4/4- **9** *2* **Ladyvie (FR)**[59] 637 6-10-12 **106**.....................................(t[1]) ConorO'Farrell 75
(David Pipe) *a struggling in rr* **20/1**

P/U- **P** **Magical Legend**[46] 757 12-11-10 **118**..............................(t) AidanColeman
(Sarah Kerswell) *trckd ldr tl 7th: in tch: wknd after 10th: p.u bef 12th* **25/1**

/13- **P** **Now Then Charlie (IRE)**[20] 963 8-11-6 **114**......................... DenisO'Regan
(John Ferguson) *a bhd: reminder after 1st: tailing off whn p.u bef 12th* **14/1**

5m 16.2s (-5.20) **Going Correction** -0.375s/f (Good) **11** Ran SP% **126.7**
Speed ratings (Par 105): **94,93,91,89,83 80,79,77,77,**
toteswingers 1&2 £15.00, 1&3 not won, 2&3 £14.30 CSF £52.27 CT £614.35 TOTE £17.40: £3.10, £1.30, £5.20; EX 57.40 Trifecta £436.50 Part won. Pool: £582.11 - 0.82 winning units..
Owner R M Levitt, G Keirle & A King **Bred** Mrs M C Sweeney **Trained** Barbury Castle, Wilts

FOCUS
A competitive handicap that produced an exciting finish as the first two pulled clear in a battle from the last.
T/Plt: £19.80 to a £1 stake. Pool: £56,829.63 - 2,091.35 winning units T/Qpdt: £9.10 to a £1 stake. Pool: £3,184.30 - 257.80 winning units TM

1198 - (Foreign Racing) - See Raceform Interactive

863 CLAIREFONTAINE (R-H)
Saturday, August 3

OFFICIAL GOING: Turf: very soft

1199a PRIX LE BARON DUTACQ (HURDLE) (CONDITIONS) (4YO) (TURF) 2m 2f
12:30 (12:00) 4-Y-O **£13,268** (£6,634; £3,869; £2,626; £1,243)

RPR
1 **Belenien (FR)**[47] 4-10-10 0... RaymondO'Brien 119
(Y-M Porzier, France) **125/10**

2 *2 1/2* **Sandra Mia (FR)**[255] 4-10-6 0.................................... MichaelDelmares 113
(Mlle J Legatte, France) **71/1**

3 *2* **Aniri (FR)**[312] 4-10-8 0.. GaetanMasure 113
(F Nicolle, France) **15/2**[3]

4 *1 3/4* **Danceur Bresilien (FR)**[272] 2228 4-10-6 0...................(p) GeoffreyRe[(4)] 113
(Yannick Fouin, France) **78/10**

5 *3/4* **Kemaliste (FR)**[104] 4-11-3 0.. BertrandBourez 119
(Y-M Porzier, France) **2/1**[1]

6 *3 1/2* **Jaslinga (FR)**[115] 4-10-10 0..(p) AlexisAcker 109
(M Nigge, France) **29/1**

7 *2 1/2* **Aubusson (FR)** 4-10-6 0.. AlainDeChitray 102
(Nick Williams) *hld up towards rr on inner: in last pair jumping 3 out: rdn after 2 out: styd on wl and tk 7th towards fin but nvr able to chal: do bttr* **56/1**

8 *2 1/2* **Summer Storm (FR)**[47] 4-10-6 0...................................... KevinNabet 100
(Guy Denuault, France) **18/1**

9 *1/2* **Bal Celtique (FR)** 4-10-7 0 ow1.................................. JonathanPlouganou 100
(Mlle M-L Mortier, France) **22/1**

10 *3/4* **Prince Tartare (FR)**[51] 4-10-8 0.................................. LudovicPhilipperon 100
(Robert Collet, France) **24/1**

11 *2 1/2* **Witness (FR)**[44] 4-10-6 0..(p) BenoitClaudic[(4)] 100
(H Billot, France) **33/1**

12 *1* **Volare (FR)**[19] 4-10-10 0.. RegisSchmidlin 99
(M Rolland, France) **44/5**

P **Kick On (FR)**[280] 4-11-0 0.. AnthonyLecordier
(T Clout, France) **9/2**[2]

P **Moskovskaya (FR)**[415] 4-9-13 0.............................. CorentinSmeulders[(2)]
(H Billot, France) **99/1**

4m 17.4s (-4.70) **14** Ran SP% **116.3**
PARI-MUTUEL (all including 1 euro stakes): WIN 13.50; PLACE 4.20, 13.30, 3.40; DF 333.30; SF 438.30.
Owner Denis Grandin **Bred** F Butin **Trained** France

1044 MARKET RASEN (R-H)
Sunday, August 4

OFFICIAL GOING: Good (good to firm in places; watered; chase course 8.3, hurdle course 8.0)
Wind: Fresh across Weather: Mainly fine; quite breezy. Overcast and showers after Race 4

1200 RAF PROLINX CYBER ASSURANCE NOVICES' HURDLE (8 hdls) 2m 1f
2:20 (2:20) (Class 4) 4-Y-O+ **£3,249** (£954; £477; £238)

Form RPR
322/ **1** **Pasture Bay (IRE)**[309] 1672 7-10-5 109...................... ConorShoemark[(7)] 111
(Fergal O'Brien) *chsd ldrs: 2nd 5th: led appr 2 out: forged away clsng stages* **7/4**[1]

232- **2** *1 1/4* **Qoubilai (FR)**[21] 960 9-10-12 111..............................(t) RichardJohnson 110
(Tim Vaughan) *set brisk pce: j. soundly: hdd appr 2 out: rallied and almost upsides last: kpt on same pce* **15/8**[2]

3 *18* **Red Eyes**[17] 5-10-2 0... DiarmuidO'Regan[(10)] 94
(Chris Grant) *in rr: hdwy to chse ldrs 3 out: modest 3rd appr next: one pce* **25/1**

4 *31* **Moon Trip**[330] 4-10-11 0.. DenisO'Regan 75
(John Ferguson) *t.k.h off pce: trckd ldrs 4th: handy 3rd 3 out: lost pl and eased appr next: virtually p.u: t.o* **9/4**[3]

P **Fushicho**[24] 4-10-11 0.. DougieCostello
(Brendan Powell) *in rr: bhd and nt fluent 5th: sn t.o: p.u bef last* **33/1**

The Form Book Jumps, Raceform Ltd, Compton, RG20 6NL.

4/4- **P** **Seabougg**[81] 309 5-10-9 0 .... JackQuinlan(3)
(James Eustace) *chsd ldr to 5th: lost pl after next: t.o whn p.u bef 2 out: b.b.v* **50/1**

4m 7.3s (0.60) **Going Correction** -0.025s/f (Good)
WFA 4 from 5yo+ 13lb **6** Ran SP% **110.7**
Speed ratings (Par 105): **97,96,87,73,**
toteswingers 1&2 £1.10, 1&3 £12.80, 2&3 £9.70 CSF £5.38 TOTE £2.80: £1.50, £1.30; EX 4.70 Trifecta £24.50 Pool: £613.65 - 18.73 winning units.
Owner The Marvellous Partnership **Bred** P Hughes **Trained** Coln St. Dennis, Gloucs

FOCUS
As at the previous fixture the hurdles in the home straight were positioned 90m and 150m closer to wining line than normal. After the first Richard Johnson described the ground as "good to firm". The time for this modest novice hurdle was fairly slow, 12.3sec outside the standard. The first two are rated pretty much to their marks.

1201 RAFBF SPORTING INDEX NOVICES' HURDLE (10 hdls) 2m 5f
2:50 (2:50) (Class 4) 4-Y-0+ **£3,249** (£954; £477; £238)

Form RPR

/21- **1** **Letsby Avenue**[35] 847 5-11-5 129 .... WayneHutchinson 129+
(Alan King) *w ldr: led 2nd: wnt 5 l clr whn mstke 2 out: rdn out* **2/9**[1]

/00- **2** *6* **Rob Conti (FR)**[20] 996 8-10-12 117 .... RichardJohnson 115
(Philip Hobbs) *trckd ldrs: 2nd appr 2 out: kpt on same pce* **6/1**[2]

10- **3** *7* **Emily's Flyer (IRE)**[42] 811 6-10-5 107 .... (t) ConorShoemark(7) 109
(Fergal O'Brien) *j. slowly: led to 2nd: drvn 7th: outpcd after next: kpt on and modest 3rd last* **8/1**[3]

/33- **4** *3 ¼* **Piper Hill (IRE)**[9] 1118 5-10-9 0 .... JackQuinlan(3) 106
(Tony Coyle) *trckd ldrs: 2nd 5th: drvn and wknd appr 2 out: eased clsng stages* **11/1**

/05- **5** *23* **Giant Hercules (IRE)**[28] 897 6-10-5 0 .... JackSherwood(7) 84
(Phil McEntee) *hld up: wnt prom 4th: drvn and nt fluent 7th: lost pl after next: bhd whn eased run-in: t.o* **80/1**

/UP- **6** *16* **Banks Road (IRE)**[35] 849 8-10-12 0 .... [1] MarkGrant 70
(Geoffrey Deacon) *t.k.h in rr: pushed along 4th: lost pl after 3 out: bhd next: t.o whn eased run-in* **100/1**

5m 20.5s (11.70) **Going Correction** -0.025s/f (Good) **6** Ran SP% **117.8**
Speed ratings (Par 105): **76,73,71,69,61 54**
toteswingers 1&2 £1.10, 1&3 £1.30, 2&3 £2.40 CSF £2.76 TOTE £1.10: £1.02, £2.60; EX 2.90 Trifecta £8.30 Pool: £790.45 - 70.78 winning units.
Owner Mrs Peter Prowting **Bred** Mrs E A Prowting **Trained** Barbury Castle, Wilts

FOCUS
They went a steady pace in this ordinary novice hurdle. Straightforward form.

1202 RAFBF MIDSHIRES POWERCHAIRS H'CAP CHASE (17 fncs) 3m 1f
3:25 (3:25) (Class 4) (0-105,105) 4-Y-0+ **£3,898** (£1,144; £572; £286)

Form RPR

/12- **1** **Calypso Bay (IRE)**[32] 871 7-11-11 104 .... APMcCoy 115+
(Jonjo O'Neill) *nt fluent: lost pl 4th: hdwy 8th: outpcd 11th: hdwy next: 3rd and rdn after 4 out: chsd ldr appr next: led 2 out: forged clr run-in* **5/2**[1]

12P- **2** *4 ½* **Minstalad**[21] 965 9-10-1 80 .... (p) DougieCostello 86
(Karen Tutty) *chsd ldr: led sn after 4 out: hdd 2 out: kpt on same pce* **4/1**[2]

40P- **3** *13* **Quayside Court (IRE)**[11] 1103 9-9-7 79 .... (vt) GeraldQuinn(7) 73
(Claire Dyson) *led 2nd: hdd sn after 4 out: one pce appr next* **50/1**

622- **4** *14* **Peak Seasons (IRE)**[3] 1174 10-10-5 89 .... JoeCornwall(5) 70
(Michael Chapman) *sn drvn along in rr: hdwy 10th: outpcd 12th: kpt on fr 3 out: tk modest 5th last: 4th nr fin* **8/1**

204- **5** *3 ¼* **Farmer Frank**[12] 1089 10-9-12 84 .... PaulNO'Brien(7) 63
(Nick Kent) *in rr: hdwy 7th: outpcd 11th: wknd fr 3 out* **12/1**

4/2- **6** *6* **Pyracantha**[21] 972 8-11-12 105 .... (p) SeanQuinlan 77
(Jennie Candlish) *led to 2nd: chsd ldrs: drvn 10th: reminders 12th: sn lost pl* **8/1**

/25- **7** *45* **Ifonlyalfie**[63] 597 8-10-13 95 .... (bt) AdamWedge(3) 27
(Chris Bealby) *in rr: drvn 10th: sn bhd: t.o 4 out* **6/1**[3]

/4P- **8** *3 ¾* **Fearless Leader**[15] 1049 6-11-10 103 .... (bt[1]) TomScudamore 31
(David Bridgwater) *trckd ldrs: wknd qckly 4 out: sn bhd: t.o* **10/1**

4P2- **P** **Le Seychellois (FR)**[11] 1103 13-11-1 94 .... DenisO'Regan
(William Kinsey) *in rr: sme hdwy 10th: sn lost pl: bhd fr 4 out: t.o whn p.u bef next* **16/1**

301- **P** **Sycho Fred (IRE)**[12] 1089 12-10-1 80 .... (t) BrianHughes
(Mike Sowersby) *chsd ldrs: drvn 8th: lost pl 11th: sn bhd: t.o whn p.u bef 2 out* **16/1**

6m 6.3s (-25.00) **Going Correction** -0.925s/f (Hard) **10** Ran SP% **115.6**
Speed ratings (Par 105): **103,101,97,92,91 89,75,74, ,**
toteswingers 1&2 £1.10, 1&3 not won, 2&3 £49.70 CSF £13.39 CT £389.06 TOTE £2.30: £1.10, £2.30, £17.30; EX 17.50 Trifecta £303.90 Pool: £843.71 - 2.08 winning units.
Owner John P McManus **Bred** T Hirschfeld **Trained** Cheltenham, Gloucs

FOCUS
Few got into this modest handicap chase, which was run at a sound gallop. The form is rated through the second.

1203 RAFBF SAFEWAY SCAFFOLD H'CAP HURDLE (10 hdls) 2m 3f
4:00 (4:00) (Class 3) (0-130,125) 4-Y-0+ **£6,498** (£1,908; £954; £477)

Form RPR

210- **1** **Get Home Now**[32] 877 5-10-11 110 .... (tp) TomO'Brien 124+
(Peter Bowen) *trckd ldrs: led appr 2 out: styd on strly to go clr between last 2: eased towards fin* **3/1**[1]

123- **2** *10* **Bright Abbey**[14] 1054 5-11-5 118 .... RichardJohnson 122
(Philip Hobbs) *hld up towards rr: hdwy to trck ldrs 4th: 7 l 2nd whn blnd 2 out: hit last: no imp* **11/2**[3]

/15- **3** *2* **Kayaan**[28] 901 6-11-9 125 .... KielanWoods(3) 127
(Pam Sly) *in rr: hdwy 3 out: 3rd 2 out: kpt on same pce* **15/2**

/23- **4** *8* **Violets Boy (IRE)**[28] 902 6-10-10 109 .... (t) DougieCostello 103
(Brendan Powell) *w ldr: drvn 6th: wknd between last 2* **12/1**

004- **5** *15* **Quinsman**[12] 1093 7-10-9 108 .... AndrewThornton 89
(Caroline Bailey) *chsd ldrs: rdn 3 out: sn lost pl* **16/1**

2/4- **6** *2* **Renoyr (FR)**[93] 93 8-11-3 116 .... BrianHughes 95
(Malcolm Jefferson) *trckd ldrs: drvn 3 out: wknd appr next* **4/1**[2]

512- **7** *1 ¼* **Tamarillo Grove (IRE)**[3] 1173 6-10-8 107 .... (t) JasonMaguire 85
(Sophie Leech) *led: hdd appr 2 out: sn wknd* **4/1**[2]

300- **8** *17* **Van Diemens Land (USA)**[20] 997 6-10-0 99 oh2 ..... (bt) AidanColeman 61
(Charlie Mann) *chsd ldrs: rdn and wknd 3 out: sn bhd* **20/1**

P20/ **P** **Mickelson (IRE)**[24] 4385 7-11-12 125 .... APMcCoy
(Jonjo O'Neill) *in rr: reminders after 5th: bhd whn j.rt 7th: hung rt and sn t.o: p.u bef 2 out* **16/1**

4m 35.2s (-4.20) **Going Correction** -0.025s/f (Good) **9** Ran SP% **116.4**
Speed ratings (Par 107): **107,102,101,98,92 91,90,83,**
toteswingers 1&2 £13.60, 1&3 £21.50, 2&3 £2.80 CSF £20.44 CT £113.26 TOTE £2.70: £1.60, £1.60, £2.50; EX 25.70 Trifecta £86.00 Pool: £932.53 - 8.12 winning units.
Owner Miss Jayne Brace & Gwyn Brace **Bred** Elsdon Farms **Trained** Little Newcastle, Pembrokes
■ Stewards' Enquiry : Tom O'Brien trainer said, regarding apparent improvement in form, that the gelding benefited from being freshened up after a short break.

FOCUS
A fair handicap hurdle, which was truly run. The second and third set the level.

1204 RAFBF PROLINX CLOUD SERVICES H'CAP CHASE (THE SUNDAY £5K BONUS RACE) (14 fncs) 2m 4f
4:35 (4:38) (Class 3) (0-135,132) 4-Y-0+ **£7,797** (£2,289; £1,144; £572)

Form RPR

651- **1** **Dark Energy**[15] 1050 9-11-1 121 .... (t) AlainCawley 129+
(Fergal O'Brien) *hld up in rr: hdwy to trck ldrs 5th: drvn and outpcd after 4 out: styd on 2 out: handy 5th last: styd on gamely to ld towards fin* **9/1**

000- **2** *½* **O Crotaigh (IRE)**[69] 508 9-10-11 117 .... RichardJohnson 125
(Alan Brown) *w ldrs: led 5th to 9th: led 3 out: hdd and no ex clsng stages* **10/1**

/03- **3** *¾* **French Ties (IRE)**[12] 1085 11-10-9 115 .... (p) SeanQuinlan 122
(Jennie Candlish) *hld up in rr: hdwy 5th: sn trcking ldrs: upsides 2 out: no ex last 30yds* **9/1**

/35- **4** *1 ¼* **Lucky Landing (IRE)**[28] 900 7-10-11 120 .... JackQuinlan(3) 127
(Tony Coyle) *chsd ldrs 4th: mstke next: hit 3 out: upsides last: hung rt and kpt on one pce last 50yds* **8/1**[3]

212/ **5** *4 ½* **Wiesentraum (GER)**[208] 3562 7-11-7 127 .... LeightonAspell 129
(Lucy Wadham) *w ldrs: led 9th: hdd 3 out: upsides last: sn fdd* **7/4**[2]

351- **P** **General Miller**[15] 1049 8-11-12 132 .... (b) DavidBass
(Nicky Henderson) *led: hit 2nd: hdd 5th: mstke: lost pl and reminders 7th: dropped to rr 9th: bhd whn hit next: sn t.o: p.u bef 3 out* **13/8**[1]

4m 47.7s (-18.00) **Going Correction** -0.925s/f (Hard) **6** Ran SP% **114.7**
Speed ratings (Par 107): **99,98,98,98,96**
toteswingers 1&2 £5.90, 1&3 £10.50, 2&3 £11.30 CSF £81.14 TOTE £4.60: £2.30, £2.80; EX 63.60 Trifecta £165.40 Pool: £1,743.96 - 7.90 winning units.
Owner The Yes No Wait Sorries **Bred** Bearstone Stud **Trained** Coln St. Dennis, Gloucs

FOCUS
A decent handicap which produced a terrific finish. Solid form.

1205 RAFBF PER ARDUA AD ASTRA H'CAP HURDLE (12 hdls) 3m
5:05 (5:06) (Class 4) (0-115,115) 4-Y-0+ **£3,898** (£1,144; £572; £286)

Form RPR

3P1- **1** **Green Bank (IRE)**[12] 1088 7-11-4 107 .... (t) NoelFehily 113+
(Charlie Longsdon) *trckd ldrs: led after 3 out: styd on u.p run-in: hld on towards fin* **2/1**[1]

6/0- **2** *½* **Coronea Lilly (IRE)**[42] 811 9-11-4 110 .... (t) MichaelByrne(3) 116
(Neil Mulholland) *mid-div: outpcd 8th: hdwy u.p appr 2 out: sn 3rd: cl 2nd last: no ex clsng stages* **20/1**

/42- **3** *3 ¼* **Saddlers Mot**[50] 750 9-10-0 96 .... (b) JohnDawson(7) 99
(Karen Tutty) *hld up in midfield: smooth hdwy to trck ldrs 8th: cl 2nd 2 out: one pce last* **16/1**

6U0- **4** *1 ¾* **Combustible Kate (IRE)**[9] 1121 7-10-5 94 .... HarryHaynes 96
(Nick Kent) *w ldrs: led 5th to 7th: one pce appr 2 out* **33/1**

/35- **5** *6* **Exit To Freedom**[28] 902 7-9-7 89 oh1 .... (p) CallumBewley(7) 85
(Neville Bycroft) *chsd ldrs: one pce appr 2 out* **33/1**

332- **6** *2* **Electric Tiger (GER)**[26] 933 6-11-5 108 .... (p) TomScudamore 102
(David Bridgwater) *chsd ldrs: outpcd 3 out: kpt on one pce fr next* **17/2**

121/ **7** *5* **Milans Well (IRE)**[115] 5259 7-10-12 101 .... DougieCostello 91
(Brendan Powell) *in rr: reminders 5th: kpt on appr 2 out: modest 7th whn mstke last* **10/1**

/20- **8** *3* **Around A Pound (IRE)**[75] 421 8-11-1 104 .... (p) JasonMaguire 91
(Nick Kent) *in rr: drvn 7th: kpt on fr 2 out: nvr on terms* **20/1**

24P- **9** *hd* **Feast Of Fire (IRE)**[12] 1083 6-10-11 105 .... (p) MauriceLinehan(5) 95
(Jonjo O'Neill) *nt jump wl: led: mstke and reminders 3rd: hdd 5th: led 7th: hdd bef 2 out: 7th and wkng whn blnd 2 out* **14/1**

623- **10** *4* **Galley Slave (IRE)**[13] 1073 8-9-9 89 oh6 .... JoeCornwall(5) 72
(Michael Chapman) *rn in snatches: in rr: drvn 5th: hdwy and in tch 3 out: sn lost pl* **22/1**

15- **11** *2 ¾* **Jewel In The Sun (IRE)**[46] 767 8-11-2 105 .... APMcCoy 86
(Ben Haslam) *in rr: hdwy 8th: sn drvn: chsng ldrs 3 out: sn lost pl* **7/1**[3]

210- **12** *39* **Vinnie My Boy (IRE)**[26] 933 5-11-12 115 .... (vt) JamieMoore 61
(Peter Bowen) *prom: drvn 8th: lost pl 3 out: t.o next: eventually completed* **4/1**[2]

2/F- **P** **Comeragh King**[65] 566 9-10-6 95 .... (t) BrianHughes
(Tim Fitzgerald) *mid-div: lost pl 8th: bhd next: t.o whn p.u bef 2 out* **20/1**

5m 57.5s (7.00) **Going Correction** -0.025s/f (Good) **13** Ran SP% **122.6**
Speed ratings (Par 105): **87,86,85,85,83 82,80,79,79,78 77,64,**
toteswingers 1&2 £42.90, 1&3 £7.40, 2&3 £39.50 CSF £50.15 CT £525.30 TOTE £2.60: £1.70, £6.10, £3.90; EX 62.20 Trifecta £748.90 Pool: £1,087.89 - 1.08 winning units.
Owner Charlie Longsdon **Bred** Andrew Pierce **Trained** Over Norton, Oxon
■ Stewards' Enquiry : Maurice Linehan three-day ban: used whip without giving gelding time to respond (Aug 18-20)

FOCUS
This ordinary handicap hurdle was run in a heavy downpour. The pace was sound and the form makes plenty of sense.

1206 RAFBF PROLINX END-USER COMPUTING H'CAP HURDLE (8 hdls) 2m 1f
5:35 (5:37) (Class 4) (0-105,104) 4-Y-0+ **£3,249** (£954; £477; £238)

Form RPR

0/1- **1** **Oliver's Gold**[9] 1120 5-11-5 97 .... PeterBuchanan 104+
(Tim Walford) *hld up in mid-div: hdwy to trck ldrs 4th: led bef 2 out: edgd rt: edgd lft between last 2: drvn out* **11/2**[3]

223- **2** *1 ½* **Daliance (IRE)**[32] 698 4-11-6 104 .... MattCrawley(5) 109+
(Lucy Wadham) *chsd ldrs: wnt 2nd appr 2 out: kpt on same pce run-in* **7/2**[1]

445- **3** *1 ½* **Claude Carter**[21] 961 9-11-2 97 .... EwanWhillans(3) 100
(Alistair Whillans) *in rr: gd hdwy 3 out: 3rd next: styd on same pce* **9/1**

/F6- **4** *13* **Emperor Of Rome (IRE)**[13] 1078 5-10-9 87 .... (t) BrianHughes 79
(Tim Fitzgerald) *in rr: hdwy after 5th: one pce bef 2 out* **22/1**

3F5- **5** *4 ½* **Muwalla**[31] 882 6-11-12 104 .... (tp) DenisO'Regan 92
(Chris Grant) *trckd ldrs 3rd: led briefly bef 2 out: sn swtchd lft and wknd* **16/1**

32F- 6 nk **Early Applause**[32] 870 5-11-8 100 BrianHarding 87
(Nicky Richards) *in rr: hdwy to chse ldrs 3 out: wknd appr next* **8/1**
240- 7 9 **Ghaabesh (IRE)**[35] 852 6-10-6 89 (bt[1]) HarryChalloner(5) 68
(Barry Leavy) *chsd ldrs: drvn 3 out: lost pl bef next* **12/1**
0U0/ 8 10 **The Quantum Kid**[681] 1722 9-10-12 90 LiamTreadwell 60
(Peter Hiatt) *led: hdd bef 2 out: sn lost pl and bhd* **22/1**
0- 9 40 **Seaside Shuffle (IRE)**[42] 812 8-11-5 97 PaulMoloney 31
(Sophie Leech) *gave problems leaving paddock: mid-div: outpcd 4th: bhd after next: t.o 2 out: eventually completed* **22/1**
2/6- P **Hilltime (IRE)**[21] 968 13-10-10 95 MrJHamilton(7)
(Clive Mulhall) *chsd ldrs: wknd 3 out: bhd whn p.u bef next* **33/1**
P/P- P **Our Choice (IRE)**[12] 1093 11-11-3 95 (t) HarryHaynes
(Nick Kent) *mid-div: lost pl after 5th: bhd whn p.u bef 2 out* **50/1**
/00- P **Wheelavit (IRE)**[58] 661 10-10-12 90 (t) LiamHeard
(Claire Dyson) *in rr: reminders 3rd: bhd fr next: t.o 5th: p.u bef 2 out* **33/1**
533- P **Aughcarra (IRE)**[21] 966 8-10-1 79 TomScudamore
(Harry Chisman) *chsd ldrs: wknd 3 out: bhd whn p.u bef next* **9/2**[2]
/55- P **Danehill Dante (IRE)**[26] 928 5-11-5 97 (p) WayneHutchinson
(Alan King) *chsd ldrs: drvn 4th: lost pl after next: sn bhd: t.o whn p.u bef 2 out* **8/1**

4m 10.3s (3.60) **Going Correction** -0.025s/f (Good)
WFA 4 from 5yo+ 13lb **14** Ran SP% **122.5**
Speed ratings (Par 105): **90,89,88,82,80 80,75,71,52, , , ,**
toteswingers 1&2 £5.10, 1&3 £9.00, 2&3 £11.40 CSF £23.89 CT £177.11 TOTE £6.50: £2.00, £2.20, £3.40; EX 28.90 Trifecta £178.00 Pool: £902.31 - 3.79 winning units.
Owner Quench Racing Partnership **Bred** Bearstone Stud **Trained** Sheriff Hutton, N Yorks
FOCUS
A modest handicap. Not many came into it in much form but the winner is on the upgrade.
T/Plt: £55.30 to a £1 stake. Pool: £73,600.77 - 971.05 winning units T/Qpdt: £64.80 to a £1 stake. Pool: £4,757.69 - 54.30 winning units WG

GRANVILLE-ST PAIR SUR MER
Sunday, August 4
OFFICIAL GOING: Turf: good

1214a PRIX DU CONSEIL GENERAL - RENE COUETIL - GRAND CROSS (CROSS-COUNTRY CHASE) (CONDITIONS) (5YO+) (TURF 3m 2f
3:30 (12:00) 5-Y-0+ £11,707 (£5,853; £3,414; £2,317; £1,097)

RPR
1 **Star Des Planches (FR)**[42] 7-10-10 0 WilfridDenuault 101
(P Chemin, France) **77/10**[2]
2 hd **Puncho (FR)**[42] 10-10-10 0 (b) JessyBlandamour 101
(Patrice Quinton, France)
3 shd **Major Dolois (FR)**[112] 5325 7-11-0 0 (b) JeromeZuliani 105
(Patrice Quinton, France)
4 4 **Adelaide Square (FR)**[35] 855 7-11-7 0 DavidCottin 108
(G Macaire, France)
5 6 **Maljimar (IRE)**[87] 199 13-11-5 0 JamesReveley 100
(Nick Williams) **5/1**[1]
6 ½ **Sun Sky Blue (FR)**[1458] 6-10-12 0 (p) Marc-AntoineDragon 93
(G Mousnier, France)
7 20 **Bois D'Auge (FR)**[672] 7-10-8 0 (b) DominiqueDelorme 69
(D Delorme, France)
F **Singapore Gold (FR)**[409] 6-10-8 0 (b) ChristopherCouillaud
(P Cottin, France)
F **Kigreat De La Pree (FR)** 5-10-3 0 (p) BenjaminNey
(G Mousnier, France)

6m 47.18s (407.18) **9** Ran SP% **28.2**
PARI-MUTUEL (all including 1 euro stakes): WIN 8.70; PLACE 1.80, 2.00, 2.00; DF 10.00.
Owner Mme Philippe Chemin **Bred** B Leprovost, Mme A-L Boisson & Mlle D Pestour **Trained** France

1215 - 1249a (Foreign Racing) - See Raceform Interactive

993 LES LANDES
Sunday, August 11
OFFICIAL GOING: Good

1250a LADBROKES ODDS ON! REWARD CARD H'CAP HURDLE 2m 4f
2:30 (2:33) 4-Y-0+ £1,460 (£525; £315)

RPR
1 **If I Had Him (IRE)**[28] 993 9-11-10 (v) MattieBatchelor
(George Baker) **11/10**[2]
2 8 **Landolino (FR)**[14] 993 8-11-4 AntonyProcter
(Mrs J L Le Brocq, Jersey) **4/5**[1]
3 7 **Nordic Affair**[14] 993 9-9-3 MrPCollington
(S Arthur, Jersey) **9/2**[3]

4m 52.0s (292.00) **3** Ran SP% **121.4**

Owner Sir Alex Ferguson **Bred** Mrs J Morrissey **Trained** Manton, Wilts

1251 - 1254a (Foreign Racing) - See Raceform Interactive

1169 STRATFORD (L-H)
Tuesday, August 13
OFFICIAL GOING: Good (good to firm in places)
Wind: Light across Weather: Overcast

1255 102 TOUCH FM MAIDEN HURDLE (9 hdls) 2m 3f
5:20 (5:20) (Class 5) 4-Y-0+ £2,599 (£763; £381; £190)

Form RPR
30/- 1 **Falcarragh (IRE)**[242] 3045 6-11-0 125 RichardJohnson 125+
(Tim Vaughan) *hld up: hdwy 6th: rdn to ld appr last: sn edgd lft: styd on wl* **8/13**[1]
2- 2 8 **Ittirad (USA)**[42] 857 5-11-0 0 DenisO'Regan 116
(John Ferguson) *led: nt fluent 5th: mstke 3 out: rdn and hdd whn swtchd rt bef last: hit last: no ex flat* **4/1**[2]
303- 3 4½ **Staigue Fort**[27] 1020 5-10-9 110 GavinSheehan(5) 110
(Emma Lavelle) *chsd ldrs: ev ch after 2 out: sn rdn: wkng whn j.rt last* **6/1**[3]
/ 4 9 **Dazinski**[17] 7-11-0 0 ColinBolger 101+
(Mark H Tompkins) *chsd ldrs: mstke 2 out: sn rdn and wknd* **9/1**
5 6 **Larteta (FR)**[85] 4-10-9 0 JackQuinlan(3) 93
(Sarah Humphrey) *prom tl rdn and wknd after 2 out* **28/1**
5- 6 16 **Follow The Tracks (IRE)**[23] 1056 5-10-9 0 KillianMoore(5) 79
(Brian Barr) *hld up: hdwy 3 out: wknd bef next* **50/1**
26- 7 ½ **Moscow Me (IRE)**[14] 1152 6-11-0 0 HenryOliver 78
(Henry Oliver) *prom tl rdn and wknd 3 out* **40/1**
0/5- 8 1¾ **King Of Forces**[10] 1152 4-10-12 0 LiamTreadwell 74
(Denis Quinn) *chsd ldrs: pushed along after 5th: blnd and wknd next* **50/1**
0/4- 9 10 **Dont Call Me Oscar (IRE)**[90] 306 6-10-9 0 (t) NicodeBoinville(5) 66
(Mark Gillard) *chsd ldr tl pushed along 5th: rdn and wknd appr 3 out* **40/1**
5- 10 83 **Amantius**[10] 1191 4-10-12 0 HaddenFrost
(Johnny Farrelly) *hit 1st: sn pushed along in rr: bhd fr 6th* **100/1**
00/ 11 13 **Vinnie The Fish (IRE)**[296] 1948 5-11-0 0 (t) DougieCostello
(Brendan Powell) *bhd fr 3rd* **66/1**

4m 26.5s (-5.00) **Going Correction** -0.225s/f (Good)
WFA 4 from 5yo+ 13lb **11** Ran SP% **120.9**
Speed ratings (Par 103): **101,97,95,91,89 82,82,81,77,42 37**
toteswingers 1&2 £1.10, 2&3 £2.10, 1&3 £2.40 CSF £3.47 TOTE £1.90: £1.10, £1.10, £1.60; EX 4.30 Trifecta £11.20 Pool: £854.83 - 56.88 winning units..
Owner Mike Stratford **Bred** Liam McLoughlin **Trained** Aberthin, Vale of Glamorgan
FOCUS
Rail on bends moved out for fresh ground. This opening maiden was all about the winner. The form is taken at face value with the third the key.

1256 MURPHY SALISBURY CHARTERED ACCOUNTANTS "NATIONAL HUNT" NOVICES' HURDLE (8 hdls) 2m 110y
5:50 (5:50) (Class 4) 4-Y-0+ £3,119 (£915; £457; £228)

Form RPR
2F2- 1 **Kettlewell**[21] 1082 4-10-11 0 (t) APMcCoy 111+
(Warren Greatrex) *trckd ldr: racd keenly: led 3 out: mstke next: rdn whn hit last: styd on wl* **3/1**[2]
220/ 2 10 **New Year's Eve**[174] 4318 5-10-12 129 DenisO'Regan 105
(John Ferguson) *hld up: hdwy 3 out: chsd wnr after next: rdn and styng on same pce whn mstke last: eased whn hld flat* **4/9**[1]
423- 3 3 **Keel Haul (IRE)**[20] 1108 5-10-12 0 HenryOliver 99
(Henry Oliver) *chsd ldrs: cl up whn blnd 5th: outpcd after 3 out: styd on flat* **25/1**
3- 4 4½ **Itmakessense**[27] 1016 6-10-12 0 NoelFehily 95
(Charlie Longsdon) *led: hit 2nd: mstke 5th: hdd 3 out: rdn whn hit next: wknd bef last* **20/1**
3/3- 5 38 **Bob Tucker (IRE)**[21] 1082 6-10-12 0 ConorO'Farrell 57
(Brendan Powell) *hld up: nt fluent 3rd: sn given reminders: bhd fr next* **16/1**[3]
0/0- P **Moscow Red (IRE)**[44] 848 7-10-12 0 CharliePoste
(Matt Sheppard) *prom tl wknd after 5th: bhd whn p.u and dismntd bef last* **150/1**

3m 53.1s (-2.90) **Going Correction** -0.225s/f (Good)
WFA 4 from 5yo+ 13lb **6** Ran SP% **109.4**
Speed ratings (Par 105): **97,92,90,88,70**
toteswingers 1&2 £1.10, 2&3 £2.50, 1&3 £3.40 CSF £4.67 TOTE £3.80: £1.50, £1.10; EX 5.60 Trifecta £20.90 Pool: £2000.12 - 71.59 winning units..
Owner Mark Duthie Partnership **Bred** Giles W Pritchard-Gordon (farming) Ltd **Trained** Upper Lambourn, Berks
FOCUS
There was something of a turn up here. The form could be rated higher but looks fluid and so rated cautiously.

1257 STRATFORD FOOD FESTIVAL HERE SEPTEMBER 14/15 H'CAP CHASE (17 fncs) 2m 7f
6:20 (6:21) (Class 4) (0-120,120) 4-Y-0+ £3,898 (£1,144; £572; £286)

Form RPR
F23- 1 **Pantxoa (FR)**[48] 839 6-11-11 119 WayneHutchinson 136+
(Alan King) *chsd ldr tl led 2nd: nt fluent 11th: clr fr 2 out: styd on wl* **15/8**[1]
/1F- 2 24 **Basil Fawlty (IRE)**[27] 1015 8-11-1 109 (t) TomScudamore 104
(David Pipe) *hld up in tch: chsd wnr 2 out: sn rdn: wknd last* **7/2**[2]
105- 3 12 **Turbo Du Ranch (FR)**[41] 878 6-11-7 120 (tp) GavinSheehan(5) 101
(Warren Greatrex) *hld up: pushed along 13th: nvr on terms* **7/1**[3]
124- 4 10 **My Mate Vinnie (IRE)**[24] 1049 6-11-3 111 (t) APMcCoy 82
(Jonjo O'Neill) *prom: chsd ldr fr 3rd tl 2 out: sn wknd* **7/2**[2]
/01- 5 40 **Baily Storm (IRE)**[41] 872 11-11-0 108 (vt) DavidBass 39
(Lawney Hill) *led to 2nd: chsd ldrs: drvn along 12th: blnd and wknd next* **8/1**
U04- F **My Lad Percy**[21] 1083 5-10-6 110 (p) PaulO'Brien(10)
(Rebecca Curtis) *prom: reminders after 5th: wknd appr 14th: bhd whn fell 2 out* **17/2**

5m 24.3s (-14.90) **Going Correction** -0.475s/f (Good) **6** Ran SP% **113.4**
Speed ratings (Par 105): **106,97,93,90,76**
toteswingers 1&2 £2.40, 2&3 £3.70, 1&3 £3.10 CSF £9.32 TOTE £3.40: £1.40, £2.80; EX 9.20 Trifecta £35.80 Pool: £917.99 - 19.22 winning units..
Owner Mrs June Watts **Bred** Pierre De Maleissye Melun **Trained** Barbury Castle, Wilts
FOCUS
A modest staying handicap althopugh thewibnner was quite impressive and is rated an improver.

1258 EDWARD BRAIN PLANT HIRE H'CAP HURDLE (7 hdls 1 omitted) 2m 110y
6:50 (6:50) (Class 4) (0-120,120) 4-Y-0+ £3,119 (£915; £457; £228)

Form RPR
P66- 1 **Laudatory**[49] 831 7-11-7 120 NicodeBoinville(5) 128+
(Nicky Henderson) *mde all: set stdy pce tl qcknd 3 out: rdn and hung lft bef bypassed last: styd on* **11/8**[1]
161- 2 4 **Fairyinthewind (IRE)**[34] 947 4-11-6 115 WayneHutchinson 118+
(Alan King) *a.p: chsd wnr after 2 out: sn rdn: no imp fr bypassed last* **3/1**[2]
412- 3 10 **Odin (IRE)**[46] 758 5-11-7 115 (b[1]) LeightonAspell 108
(Don Cantillon) *chsd wnr tl rdn after 2 out: wknd bef bypassed last* **6/1**[3]
32- 4 shd **Osorios Trial**[23] 1059 6-10-11 105 (t[1]) PaulMoloney 98
(Anthony Middleton) *hld up: hdwy after 3 out: rdn and wknd bef bypassed last* **14/1**
/34- 5 2½ **Bob's Legend (IRE)**[53] 788 7-10-3 97 JamesDavies 87
(Martin Bosley) *hld up: hdwy 5th: rdn and wknd after 2 out* **14/1**
P5/- 6 20 **Cavite Eta (IRE)**[116] 5367 6-11-2 110 [1] DenisO'Regan 80
(Barry Murtagh) *chsd ldrs: pushed along 5th: wknd appr 2 out* **20/1**

431/ **P** **Head Hunted**^{841} [42] 6-10-9 **103**.................................... MattieBatchelor
(Jim Best) *hld up: bhd fr 4th: t.o whn p.u bef bypassed last* **16/1**

/42- **F** **Native Colony**^{30} [977] 5-10-3 **104**..............................(v^{1}) CiaranMckee$^{(7)}$
(John O'Shea) *prom tl fell 3rd* **7/1**

3m 52.2s (-3.80) **Going Correction** -0.225s/f (Good)
WFA 4 from 5yo+ 13lb **8** Ran SP% **117.9**
Speed ratings (Par 105): **99,97,92,92,91 81,** ,
toteswingers 1&2 £3.10, 2&3 £2.90, 1&3 £1.60 CSF £6.50 CT £18.41 TOTE £2.30: £1.10, £1.10, £2.20; EX 7.40 Trifecta £24.10 Pool: £1070.82 - 33.31 winning units..
Owner Eric Newnham and Mrs Julia Newnham **Bred** Whitsbury Manor Stud & Pigeon House Stud **Trained** Upper Lambourn, Berks

FOCUS
This was run at a steady early gallop, but that didn't stop last year's winner. The final flight was bypassed due to the crashing fall of Native Colony first time round. The winner is rated back to his best with the runner-up unexposed over hurdles.

1259 102 TOUCH FM H'CAP HURDLE (11 hdls) 2m 6f 110y
7:20 (7:20) (Class 5) (0-95,94) 4-Y-0+ **£1,949** (£572; £286; £143)

Form RPR

/P4- **1** **Listen And Learn (IRE)**^{36} [925] 5-11-12 **94**.......................(p) APMcCoy 105+
(Jonjo O'Neill) *hld up: hdwy 7th: shkn up to ld whn blnd last: sn hdd: rallied to ld post* **5/2**^{1}

001- **2** *nk* **Royal Peak (IRE)**^{12} [1170] 6-11-10 **92**.......................(tp) TomScudamore 100
(David Pipe) *chsd ldrs: led wl bef last: hdd jst bef last: lft in ld flat: drvn and styd on: hdd post* **5/2**^{1}

106- **3** *8* **Brass Monkey (IRE)**^{27} [1018] 6-10-13 **86**...................... TrevorWhelan$^{(5)}$ 86
(Neil King) *a.p: chsd ldr 8th tl led after 2 out: sn rdn and hdd: styd on same pce* **12/1**^{3}

250- **4** *5* **Bob Lewis**^{55} [767] 7-10-11 **89**......................................(tp) MarkMarris$^{(10)}$ 84
(Anthony Middleton) *hld up: r.o appr last: nvr nrr* **16/1**

253- **5** *14* **Tennessee Bird**^{18} [1120] 5-10-8 **81**.................................. EDLinehan$^{(5)}$ 62
(Mike Sowersby) *j.rt: chsd ldr tl led 5th: mstke 2 out: sn rdn: hdd & wknd* **5/1**^{2}

5/4- **6** *6* **Renagisha (IRE)**^{72} [595] 7-11-4 **86**..................................(b^{1}) JamieMoore 61
(Jim Best) *hld up: hdwy u.p and nt fluent 3 out: wknd after next* **50/1**

000/ **7** *4 ½* **Douglas**^{310} [1757] 8-11-7 **89**.. MarkGrant 60
(Jo Hughes) *chsd ldrs: rdn after 7th: wknd 2 out* **16/1**

P00/ **8** *2 ¾* **Don't Look Bach (IRE)**^{339} [1517] 8-10-13 **86**.............^{1} GavinSheehan$^{(5)}$ 54
(Brian Barr) *led to 5th: chsd ldr to 8th: rdn and wknd 2 out* **25/1**

000- **9** *3* **Cloudy Start**^{35} [927] 7-11-3 **85**... WillKennedy 50
(Violet M Jordan) *hld up: rdn appr 8th: wknd 2 out* **50/1**

420- **10** *15* **Captain Sully (IRE)**^{23} [1060] 8-11-1 **83**.............................. HaddenFrost 33
(Jim Wilson) *hld up: rdn after 3 out: sn wknd* **16/1**

304- **11** *42* **Ailanthus**^{10} [1191] 4-11-6 **94**...................................... MichealNolan$^{(3)}$
(Richard Woollacott) *hld up: a in rr: lost tch after 3 out* **20/1**

2PP/ **P** **Bobbits Way**^{122} [5286] 8-11-4 **89**....................................... JamesBest$^{(3)}$
(Alan Jones) *prom: pushed along after 5th: mstke next: wknd 8th: p.u bef 2 out* **25/1**

P/F- **P** **Leyland (IRE)**^{12} [1169] 4-11-7 **92**... DavidBass
(Lawney Hill) *hld up: drvn along 7th: sn wknd: p.u bef 2 out* **16/1**

5m 22.2s (-5.90) **Going Correction** -0.225s/f (Good)
WFA 4 from 5yo+ 14lb **13** Ran SP% **121.4**
Speed ratings (Par 103): **101,100,98,96,91 89,87,86,85,80 66,** ,
toteswingers 1&2 £2.00, 2&3 £9.80, 1&3 £9.80 CSF £8.67 CT £63.19 TOTE £4.10: £1.80, £1.10, £3.40; EX 8.00 Trifecta £92.80 Pool: £916.60 - 7.40 winning units..
Owner John P McManus **Bred** Micheal Fahy **Trained** Cheltenham, Gloucs

FOCUS
Despite the field size this wasn't that competitive and most were done with before the penultimate flight as the principals dominated. The winner is value for further while the second confirmed his recent effort and can win again.

1260 JENKINSONS CATERERS H'CAP CHASE (14 fncs) 2m 4f
7:50 (7:52) (Class 5) (0-100,98) 4-Y-0+ **£2,144** (£629; £314; £157)

Form RPR

353- **1** **Roc De Guye (FR)**^{51} [805] 8-10-6 **78**..........................(p^{1}) LiamTreadwell 88
(James Evans) *hld up: hdwy 7th: styd on u.p to ld nr fin* **8/1**^{3}

P65- **2** *¾* **Apache Dawn**^{12} [1172] 9-10-5 **82**..............................(t) KyleJames$^{(5)}$ 91
(Aytach Sadik) *a.p: chsd ldr 11th: led 2 out: sn rdn clr: hdd nr fin* **20/1**

402- **3** *3 ¼* **Civil Unrest (IRE)**^{24} [1039] 7-11-9 **95**...........................(p) NickScholfield 101
(James Ewart) *chsd ldrs: lost pl 8th: hdwy and hit 3 out: wnt 3rd last: styd on u.p* **10/3**^{2}

/0P- **4** *3* **Michigan Assassin (IRE)**^{15} [1135] 11-11-7 **98**...(p) AodhaganConlon$^{(5)}$ 101
(Debra Hamer) *led to 4th: chsd ldr tl led again 8th: rdn and hdd 2 out: no ex flat* **16/1**

/02- **5** *7* **Spirit Of Lake (IRE)**^{85} [408] 11-10-0 **79**.......................... KevinJones$^{(7)}$ 75
(Karen George) *hld up: hdwy 9th: rdn and wknd appr last* **20/1**

224- **6** *14* **Peak Seasons (IRE)**^{9} [1202] 10-10-10 **89**.................... MissAliceMills$^{(7)}$ 71
(Michael Chapman) *hld up: bhd fr 8th* **8/1**^{3}

240- **7** *2 ¾* **Nothingbutthetruth (IRE)**^{20} [1103] 9-11-2 **91**...........(tp) MichealNolan$^{(3)}$ 70
(Richard Woollacott) *prom: rdn whn hit 3 out: wknd after next* **9/1**

065- **8** *7* **Tregaro (FR)**^{37} [898] 7-11-10 **96**......................................(t) DenisO'Regan 68
(Mike Sowersby) *hld up: hdwy 3 out: wknd bef last* **11/1**

P/P- **9** *16* **Larkhall**^{53} [786] 6-9-9 **72** oh6.................................. GavinSheehan$^{(5)}$ 28
(Mike Sowersby) *hld up: a in rr: bhd fr 8th* **20/1**

010- **10** *½* **Daneva (IRE)**^{12} [1174] 9-11-11 **97**.....................................(tp) CharliePoste 53
(Matt Sheppard) *chsd ldrs: lost pl 6th: wkng whn hit 11th* **16/1**

423- **11** *8* **Pure Anticipation (IRE)**^{27} [1010] 8-11-11 **97**...............(v) RichardJohnson 45
(Tim Vaughan) *prom: chsd ldr 3rd: led next: mstke 6th: hdd 8th: drvn along 11th: sn wknd* **11/4**^{1}

4m 40.8s (-9.20) **Going Correction** -0.475s/f (Good) **11** Ran SP% **116.4**
Speed ratings (Par 103): **99,98,97,96,93 87,86,83,77,77 74**
toteswingers 1&2 £8.20, 2&3 £13.00, 1&3 £6.80 CSF £148.62 CT £631.73 TOTE £8.30: £2.20, £5.10, £1.10; EX 144.30 Trifecta £451.30 Part won. Pool: £601.78 - 0.21 winning units..
Owner S Crawley, T Crawley **Bred** G A E C Delorme Gerard & Vincent **Trained** Broadwas, Worcs

FOCUS
A weak handicap and the form is straightforward but limited.

1261 102 TOUCH FM INTERMEDIATE OPEN NATIONAL HUNT FLAT RACE 2m 110y
8:20 (8:20) (Class 6) 4-6-Y-0 **£1,559** (£457; £228; £114)

Form RPR

\- **1** **Clondaw Hero (IRE)**^{177} 5-11-1 0.................................... JasonMaguire 107+
(Donald McCain) *mde all: drvn along over 2f out: hung lft over 1f out: hung rt u.p towards fin: styd on gamely* **3/1**^{3}

2 *nk* **Eton Dorney (USA)** 4-11-0 0.. DenisO'Regan 106+
(John Ferguson) *hld up in tch: racd keenly: shkn up to chse wnr over 1f out: rdn and ev ch whn carried rt towards fin: styd on* **2/1**^{2}

2- **3** *5* **Snapchat (IRE)**^{27} [1013] 6-11-1 0.................................... ConorO'Farrell 102
(Seamus Durack) *racd keenly: trckd wnr tl rdn over 1f out: styd on same pce fnl f* **13/8**^{1}

4 *5* **Looks Like Magic** 4-10-9 0.. TrevorWhelan$^{(5)}$ 96
(Neil King) *hld up: hdwy over 3f out: wknd over 1f out* **20/1**

5- **5** *20* **Little Bit Lively (IRE)**^{27} [1013] 4-10-11 0........................ JackQuinlan$^{(3)}$ 76
(Sarah Humphrey) *chsd ldrs: pushed along over 5f out: rdn and wknd over 2f out* **40/1**

6 *6* **Little Fleur (IRE)** 5-10-8 0.. HaddenFrost 64
(Johnny Farrelly) *hld up: effrt over 3f out: wknd over 2f out* **12/1**

3m 49.3s (-1.10) **Going Correction** -0.225s/f (Good)
WFA 4 from 5yo+ 1lb **6** Ran SP% **111.3**
Speed ratings: **93,92,90,88,78 75**
toteswingers 1&2 £1.80, 2&3 £1.10, 1&3 £1.50 CSF £9.27 TOTE £4.10: £2.50, £1.90; EX 11.30 Trifecta £20.40 Pool: £741.67 - 27.19 winning units..
Owner D McCain Jnr **Bred** P J Fortune **Trained** Cholmondeley, Cheshire

FOCUS
There was a very tight finish in this bumper between the first pair and unsurprisingly a stewards' enquiry was called. The third and last year's level provide the best guides.
T/Plt: £7.00 to a £1 stake. Pool of £81883.79 - 8475.21 winning tickets. T/Qpdt: £7.00 to a £1 stake. Pool of £6169.80 - 651.70 winning tickets. CR

1149 WORCESTER (L-H)
Tuesday, August 13

OFFICIAL GOING: Good (good to firm in places; 6.8)
Wind: almost nil Weather: overcast,; 15 degrees

1262 HAYGAIN HAY STEAMERS NOVICES' CHASE (18 fncs) 2m 7f
1:30 (1:30) (Class 4) 5-Y-0+ **£3,768** (£1,106; £553; £276)

Form RPR

4/2- **1** **Victor Leudorum (IRE)**^{21} [1085] 6-11-5 125.........................(t) NoelFehily 130+
(Charlie Mann) *trckd ldng pair: pushed along bef 15th: wnt 2nd 2 out: drvn ahd last: sn edgd clr but nt finding much in front* **6/4**^{2}

101- **2** *3* **Captain Kelly (IRE)**^{14} [1150] 6-11-5 128............................(t) RyanMahon 127
(Paul Nicholls) *slt ld 5th tl 9th: mstke 13th and rdn: pressed ldr tl drvn 15th: wandered rt bef last and hdd: v one pce whn wandering lft flat* **10/11**^{1}

0/5- **3** *22* **Mister Moonax (IRE)**^{23} [1052] 13-10-9 0...................(tp) GilesHawkins$^{(3)}$ 98
(Chris Down) *mstkes in rr bunch: rdn bef 10th and sn lost tch: 30 l 5th at 15th: styng on gamely whn mstke last: fin wl to snatch 3rd: gd effrt* **100/1**

03U- **4** *1* **Academy General (IRE)**^{18} [1119] 7-10-12 120..........(t) TomScudamore 97
(David Bridgwater) *led tl 5th: led again 9th: mstke next: drvn and hdd 15th: lost 2nd 2 out: fin tamely and lost 3rd cl home* **7/1**^{3}

P- **5** *14* **Shock N Freaney (IRE)**^{23} [1052] 6-10-12 0.................(vt^{1}) JamesDavies 83
(Anthony Middleton) *bhd: rdn and struggling 10th: remote 4th at 14th: plodded on* **150/1**

4/0- **P** **Jock Des Mottes (FR)**^{18} [1124] 6-10-5 0........................... MrJMRidley$^{(7)}$
(Elizabeth Juckes) *hld up in rr quartet: brief effrt after hitting 10th: 10 l 4th at next: sn lost tch: t.o and p.u 15th* **50/1**

0/0- **P** **Henrio (IRE)**^{15} [1138] 5-10-12 0... AlainCawley
(Fergal O'Brien) *j. poorly in rr: nvr travelling: rdn and lost tch 10th: t.o 12th: p.u 15th* **66/1**

5m 47.8s (-0.20) **Going Correction** -0.625s/f (Firm) **7** Ran SP% **110.0**
Speed ratings: **75,73,66,65,61** ,
toteswingers 1&2 £1.10, 2&3 £12.70, 1&3 £12.00 CSF £3.12 TOTE £2.60: £1.10, £1.20; EX 3.70 Trifecta £43.50 Pool: £1566.04 - 26.97 winning units..
Owner R Curry, C Leuchars & R Tompkins **Bred** Edmund Vaughan **Trained** Upper Lambourn, Berks

FOCUS
Both bends 3yds outside line used on July 30th. A bumper eight-race card got underway with a quite decent novices' chase in which they went an honest gallop on ground officially described as good, good to firm in places on a murky afternoon with light rain in the air. A fair novices' chase with the runner-up rated to his mark.

1263 PROTEK ENVIROCAIR VETERINARY H'CAP CHASE (12 fncs) 2m 110y
2:00 (2:00) (Class 4) (0-120,117) 4-Y-0+ **£3,768** (£1,106; £553; £276)

Form RPR

5P4- **1** **Temple Lord (FR)**^{29} [996] 7-11-12 **117**...............................(bt) APMcCoy 125
(Jonjo O'Neill) *j. wout any enthusiasm in last tl 8th: plenty to do fr next: u.p fr 2 out: stl 8 l 4th at last: forced ahd nr fin under amazing ride* **7/2**^{2}

33- **2** *½* **Another Flutter (IRE)**^{24} [1050] 9-11-3 **108**.....................(tp) CharliePoste 115
(Matt Sheppard) *tended to jump rt: mde most: j. slowly 6th: drvn 2 out: hdd and mstke last: impeded but lft in front again flat: ct cl home* **8/1**

U02- **3** *1 ¾* **Gud Day (IRE)**^{15} [1133] 5-11-1 **113**..........................(t) ConorShoemark$^{(7)}$ 118
(Fergal O'Brien) *settled in rr: hit 5th: effrt gng wl 9th: 3rd and rdn 3 out: idling on ins bef last: ch flat: fnd little and kpt on same pce* **5/1**^{3}

321- **4** *¾* **Citrus Mark**^{18} [1122] 8-11-3 **108**.. LiamHeard 113
(Paul Webber) *trckd ldrs: mstke 7th: wnt 2nd at 9th: chal next: led last: rdn and hung rt flat: sn hdd and fnd v little* **3/1**^{1}

553- **5** *12* **Sporting Boy (IRE)**^{18} [1122] 5-11-10 **115**..........................(p) TomCannon 108
(Michael Blake) *pressed ldr tl rdn 9th: wknd u.p 3 out* **11/2**

413- **6** *13* **Mibleu (FR)**^{29} [999] 13-11-6 **111**.. JoeTizzard 91
(Colin Tizzard) *chsd ldrs: nt fluent 3rd: rdn and wknd 3 out* **16/1**

06P- **7** *57* **Amaury De Lusignan (IRE)**^{42} [859] 7-11-5 **110**......... RichardJohnson 33
(Paul Henderson) *chsd ldrs: rdn and lost tch qckly 8th: t.o fr 10th* **13/2**

4m 1.0s (-13.00) **Going Correction** -0.625s/f (Firm) **7** Ran SP% **109.6**
Speed ratings (Par 105): **105,104,103,103,97 91,65**
toteswingers 1&2 £6.00, 2&3 £5.80, 1&3 £4.20 CSF £27.50 TOTE £4.10: £2.10, £4.70; EX 29.30 Trifecta £123.90 Pool: £1472.73 - 8.90 winning units..
Owner John P McManus **Bred** M L Bloodstock Limited **Trained** Cheltenham, Gloucs

FOCUS
A fair handicap chase with a twist in the tale. They finished quite bunched and the form is rated negatively.

1264 FLEXINEB NEBULISERS STANDARD OPEN NATIONAL HUNT FLAT RACE 2m
2:30 (2:30) (Class 6) 4-6-Y-0 **£1,559** (£457; £228; £114)

Form RPR

1 **Anger Management (IRE)**^{60} [746] 5-11-1 0.......................... APMcCoy 106+
(Rebecca Curtis) *mde all: set stdy pce: drvn over 1f out: a finding enough fnl f* **4/6**^{1}

3- **2** *1 ¾* **Inarticulate (IRE)**[30] 970 5-10-1 0 .... KevinJones(7) 96
(Seamus Mullins) *cl up tl pushed along 1/2-way: outpcd 5f out: rallied to chse wnr 3f out: kpt on gamely but wl hld fnl f* **9/2**[2]

3- **3** *11* **Western Way (IRE)**[21] 1094 4-11-0 0 .... DenisO'Regan 91+
(Don Cantillon) *racd awkwardly and looking green in rr: rdn 4f out: sn outpcd by ldng trio: sme prog to go modest 3rd wl ins fnl f* **12/1**

4 *2 ¼* **Multiview** 4-10-0 0 .... JakeHodson(7) 82
(David Bridgwater) *last and rdn 10f out: sn outpcd: kpt on steadily fnl 2f: no ch w ldrs* **66/1**

P/0- **5** *1 ½* **Rye Tangle (IRE)**[34] 944 5-11-1 0 .... FelixDeGiles 88
(Ed de Giles) *plld hrd early: 2nd mostly tl rdn 3f out: hanging and losing hind bandage fnl 2f: lost two pls in clsng stages* **50/1**

0/2- **6** *3 ½* **H M S Intrepid**[18] 1124 5-10-12 0 .... RachaelGreen(3) 85
(Anthony Honeyball) *chsd ldrs: rdn 4f out: sn fdd and no ch fnl 3f* **6/1**[3]

7 *62* **Afillycalledlily (IRE)** 4-10-7 0 .... DavidBass 15
(Lawney Hill) *handy tl rdn 5f out: stopped to nil and sn bdly t.o* **16/1**

3m 37.7s (-4.00) **Going Correction** -0.275s/f (Good)
WFA 4 from 5yo+ 1lb 7 Ran SP% **109.5**
Speed ratings: **99,98,92,91,90 89,58**
toteswingers 1&2 £1.10, 2&3 £3.90, 1&3 £2.60 CSF £3.53 TOTE £1.50: £2.40, £1.80; EX 4.80 Trifecta £18.40 Pool: £1629.96 - 66.17 winning units..
Owner G Costelloe **Bred** Kathleen Garry **Trained** Newport, Dyfed

FOCUS
A fair bumper in which they went an even gallop. The winner's previous form and the race averages help set the level.

1265 HAYGAIN HAY STEAMERS MARES' NOVICES' HURDLE (10 hdls) 2m 4f
3:00 (3:00) (Class 4) 4-Y-0+ **£3,119** (£915; £457; £228)

Form RPR

411- **1** **As I Am (IRE)**[11] 1187 5-11-10 114 .... ConorShoemark(7) 126+
(Don Cantillon) *mde all: j. economically and a gng wl: easily scampered clr fr 2 out* **5/6**[1]

2 *19* **Presenting Ruby (IRE)**[835] 178 8-10-10 0 .... DougieCostello 86
(Neil Mulholland) *hld up: hdwy to press ldrs fr 6th: disp 2nd fr 3 out: rdn and disputing 4 l in 2nd next: easily outpcd by wnr after* **8/1**[3]

231- **3** *17* **Polly Hopper**[15] 1134 7-10-10 110 ....(tp) RyanHatch(7) 76
(Nigel Twiston-Davies) *mounted on crse: prom: 2nd fr 5th: drvn fr 3 out: lost tch w wnr next: stl ev ch of modest 2nd at last but wnt lame and slowed markedly flat* **15/8**[2]

4 *8* **Possibly Flora**[584] 8-10-7 0 .... MichealNolan(3) 61
(Richard Woollacott) *j.rt and plld hrd: chsd ldrs: 8 l 4th and rdn and clr of rest bef 3 out: no ch after: eased fnl 100yds* **33/1**

200- **5** *8* **Nurse Ratched (IRE)**[27] 1017 4-10-1 0 .... MissAEStirling(7) 51
(Fergal O'Brien) *t.k.h: wnt 2nd at 3rd tl nt fluent 5th: lost pl rapidly next: t.o bef 3 out* **11/1**

060- **6** *4 ½* **Just Got Lucky**[30] 970 5-10-10 0 .... TomCannon 49
(Emma Lavelle) *chsd ldr tl blnd 2nd and lost pl: struggling u.p 6th: t.o 3 out* **16/1**

050- **7** *19* **Lulu's Gift (IRE)**[35] 927 7-10-3 67 .... StephenMulqueen(7) 30
(Michael Mullineaux) *towards rr: lost tch 7th: sn t.o* **66/1**

8 *8* **Sun Dream**[181] 6-10-10 0 .... MarkGrant 22
(Geoffrey Deacon) *hld up in rr: hdwy 6th: lost tch rapidly after next: hopelessly t.o whn mstke last* **100/1**

5- **P** **Treelara**[23] 1064 6-10-5 0 .... NicodeBoinville(5)
(Miss Imogen Pickard) *stopped to nil bef 4th and sn hopelessly t.o: wnt wrong and dismntd and p.u bef next* **100/1**

/03- **P** **Share The Dosh**[30] 971 5-10-7 0 .... JackQuinlan(3)
(J R Jenkins) *j.lft 1st: nvr travelling in rr: rdn 6th: t.o and mstke next: p.u 2 out* **66/1**

4m 38.4s (-9.00) **Going Correction** -0.275s/f (Good)
WFA 4 from 5yo+ 14lb 10 Ran SP% **122.6**
Speed ratings (Par 105): **107,99,92,89,86 84,76,73, ,**
toteswingers 1&2 £3.40, 2&3 £4.40, 1&3 £1.10 CSF £9.70 TOTE £1.80: £1.10, £3.00, £1.10; EX 13.10 Trifecta £25.90 Pool: £1887.83 - 54.65 winning units..
Owner Don Cantillon **Bred** Don Cantillon **Trained** Newmarket, Suffolk

FOCUS
A fair mares' novices' hurdle best rated through the winner.

1266 PROTEK ENVIROCAIR VETERINARY H'CAP HURDLE (DIV I) (12 hdls) 2m 7f
3:30 (3:30) (Class 5) (0-100,100) 4-Y-0+ **£1,949** (£572; £286; £143)

Form RPR

1 **Harangue (IRE)**[22] 1080 5-10-13 87 .... TomO'Brien 100+
(Paul John Gilligan, Ire) *settled in rr: smooth and stdy prog fr 8th: chal 2 out: sn led: pushed along and stormed clr flat* **33/1**

134- **2** *6* **Thornton Alice**[15] 1136 8-11-4 99 .... DanielHiskett(7) 102
(Richard Phillips) *chsd ldrs: wnt prom 7th: cl 4th and drvn 2 out: wnt 2nd after last and kpt on gamely but no ch w easy wnr* **8/1**

555/ **3** *2 ¼* **Thomas Bell (IRE)**[129] 5183 9-9-7 74 oh2 .... CiaranMckee(7) 75
(John O'Shea) *hld up: stdy prog 8th: chal fr 3 out: ev ch between last: rdn whn mstke last: sn btn* **9/1**

/23- **4** *18* **Bracken House (IRE)**[20] 1109 6-11-10 98 ....(tp) PaulMoloney 81
(Graeme McPherson) *led or disp ld tl def advantage 8th: nrly 3 l clr bef 3 out: rdn next: sn hdd: lost grnd rapidly fr last* **4/1**[2]

564- **5** *7* **Am I Blue**[20] 1110 7-11-3 96 .... CharlieWallis(5) 72
(Mrs D Thomas) *led or disp ld tl 8th: rdn and lost pl rapidly on home turn and sn wl btn: stl plugging away after last* **16/1**

/50- **6** *5* **Another Trump (NZ)**[22] 1073 9-11-7 95 ....(vt[1]) APMcCoy 66
(Jonjo O'Neill) *racd wd: j. slowly 1st and reminders: nvr looked keen: in rr and u.p 6th: sme hdwy 8th: lost tch bef 3 out* **7/1**[3]

0/5- **7** *34* **Ilewin Kim**[20] 1105 7-10-4 78 ....(p) JamieMoore 15
(Gary Brown) *nvr bttr than midfield: pushed along after 6th: last of seven w any ch after mstke 9th: fdd bdly: hopelessly t.o* **9/1**

/5P- **8** *30* **Mr Jay Dee (IRE)**[55] 763 8-11-5 100 .... GeraldQuinn(7) 7
(Claire Dyson) *prom: drvn and reluctant fr 3rd: wkng qckly whn mstke 7th: hopelessly t.o fr 9th* **28/1**

660- **B** **Munlochy Bay**[51] 811 9-11-4 92 ....(p) CharliePoste
(Matt Sheppard) *in rr tl hmpd and b.d 3rd* **10/1**

06/- **P** **Frankie Falco**[874] 4949 7-9-10 77 .... KevinJones(7)
(Giuseppe Fierro) *plld hrd in rr: lost tch 7th: hopelessly t.o whn p.u after 9th* **50/1**

PP0/ **P** **Muzey's Princess**[287] 1174 7-9-10 77 oh15 ow3.(p) StephenMulqueen(7)
(Michael Mullineaux) *mstke 1st: prom tl 7th: hopelessly t.o after 9th: p.u next* **100/1**

S46- **F** **Plug In Baby**[29] 997 5-10-5 79 ....(p) NickScholfield
(Nick Mitchell) *mstke 2nd: j.rt and fell 3rd* **25/1**

0P0/ **P** **Artic Night (FR)**[133] 5109 7-10-11 85 .... NoelFehily
(Nigel Twiston-Davies) *midfield: rdn and lost tch tamely 9th: t.o and p.u next* **3/1**[1]

0P- **P** **Nishay (IRE)**[61] 729 6-11-6 97 .... AdamWedge(3)
(David Rees) *chsd ldrs tl drvn and wknd 8th: t.o and p.u 3 out* **33/1**

5m 32.6s (4.60) **Going Correction** -0.275s/f (Good) 14 Ran SP% **119.7**
Speed ratings (Par 103): **81,78,78,71,69 67,55,45, , , ,**
toteswingers 1&2 £71.60, 2&3 £12.60, 1&3 £53.60 CSF £268.09 CT £2601.67 TOTE £25.80: £11.50, £1.70, £5.30; EX 364.10 Trifecta £744.80 Part won. Pool: £993.15 - 0.01 winning units..
Owner Sean Conroy **Bred** Derrick Fisher **Trained** Athenry, Co Galway

FOCUS
The first division of a modest staying handicap hurdle. The winner looked well handicapped on his old Irish form while the form amongst those behind looks straightforward.

1267 PROTEK ENVIROCAIR VETERINARY H'CAP HURDLE (DIV II) (12 hdls) 2m 7f
4:00 (4:00) (Class 5) (0-100,100) 4-Y-0+ **£1,949** (£572; £286; £143)

Form RPR

362- **1** **Fromthetop (IRE)**[30] 969 7-10-6 80 ....(tp) TomScudamore 85+
(Michael Scudamore) *prom: wnt 2nd at 7th: led 9th: hrd pressed by three rivals 2 out: drvn and hld on gamely flat* **9/2**[3]

511- **2** *4* **Jigsaw Financial (IRE)**[20] 1109 7-10-12 86 .... GerardTumelty 87
(Laura Young) *hld up in rr: gd prog after 9th: rdn to chal 2 out: ev ch last: no ex fnl 150yds* **3/1**[1]

561- **3** *½* **Tarvini (IRE)**[11] 1188 8-11-2 100 ....(p) JamesHuxham(10) 101
(Jonjo O'Neill) *cl up but racing lazily: drvn to go 2nd briefly after 9th: fnd little and plugged on at same pce fr 2 out* **4/1**[2]

034- **4** *4 ½* **Henry Hurst (IRE)**[20] 1106 7-11-6 94 .... AndrewThornton 90
(Jimmy Fox) *settled in rr: hdwy after 9th: rdn to chal 2 out: fnd little bef last: hanging and looking awkward flat* **10/1**

/46- **5** *¾* **Moorlands Jack**[15] 1136 8-11-4 92 .... NickScholfield 87
(Jeremy Scott) *midfield: effrt 7th: trckd ldrs bef 3 out: rdn and no rspnse next: sn btn* **5/1**

P/5- **6** *1* **William Percival (IRE)**[29] 997 7-10-1 75 ow1 .... TomCannon 69
(Mark Gillard) *led tl 9th: stl cl 4th and drvn 3 out: sn wknd* **18/1**

/60- **7** *7* **Bright Light**[63] 711 6-9-12 75 oh13 ow1 .... RobertDunne(3) 62
(Richard Phillips) *bhd most of way: no ch fr 3 out* **50/1**

/06- **8** *1 ¼* **Phoenix Eye**[30] 969 12-9-10 77 .... StephenMulqueen(7) 63
(Michael Mullineaux) *t.k.h in rr: lost tch fr 9th* **33/1**

045- **9** *23* **Tribal Dance (IRE)**[35] 929 7-10-9 90 ....(vt) CiaranMckee(7) 53
(John O'Shea) *unruly leaving paddock: chsd ldrs tl drvn and fdd after 7th: t.o* **40/1**

/36- **10** *3 ¼* **Fair Breeze**[30] 977 6-10-5 79 .... WayneHutchinson 39
(Richard Phillips) *settled in midfield: rdn after 9th: sn btn: t.o* **20/1**

0/3- **11** *11* **Sangfroid**[20] 1110 9-11-6 97 ....(bt) MichaelByrne(3) 46
(Tim Vaughan) *pressed ldr tl drvn bef 7th: fnd nil and sn lost pl: t.o after 9th* **11/1**

P- **P** **Arguidos (IRE)**[89] 335 9-11-5 98 ....(t) AodhaganConlon(5)
(Debra Hamer) *j. slowly 2nd: nvr bttr than midfield: t.o whn p.u 3 out: dismntd* **50/1**

5/P- **P** **Chadford**[101] 120 5-11-10 98 ....(tp) LiamHeard
(Claire Dyson) *chsd ldrs tl drvn and lost pl 7th: t.o and p.u 2 out* **80/1**

5m 37.3s (9.30) **Going Correction** -0.275s/f (Good) 13 Ran SP% **117.8**
Speed ratings (Par 103): **72,70,70,68,68 68,65,65,57,56 52, ,**
toteswingers 1&2 £4.50, 2&3 £5.50, 1&3 £4.90 CSF £17.58 CT £58.93 TOTE £6.70: £2.00, £1.40, £2.10; EX 19.30 Trifecta £83.40 Pool: £ 1313.84- 11.81 winning units..
Owner Mark Blandford **Bred** James O'Connor **Trained** Bromsash, H'fords

FOCUS
The second division of a modest staying handicap hurdle. The winner has more to offer whilst the placed horses set the standard.

1268 HAYGAIN HAY STEAMERS H'CAP HURDLE (10 hdls) 2m 4f
4:30 (4:31) (Class 3) (0-140,138) 4-Y-0+ **£5,393** (£1,583; £791; £395)

Form RPR

412- **1** **Don't Be Late (IRE)**[18] 1123 5-10-8 120 ....(p) APMcCoy 126+
(Jonjo O'Neill) *settled in rr of bunch: mstke 5th: gng wl in cl 6th bef 3 out: wnt 2nd after next: chal and nt fluent last: edging lft u.p but led 100yds out and drvn clr* **6/5**[1]

0/2- **2** *1 ¼* **Hunting Tower**[23] 1054 9-10-13 128 ....(t) MichaelByrne(3) 133
(Tim Vaughan) *settled trcking ldrs: effrt home turn: led sn after 3 out: rdn and drew clr w wnr next: hdd and outpcd fnl 100yds* **11/4**[2]

006/ **3** *30* **The Bull Hayes (IRE)**[10] 4510 7-10-7 119 ....(p) RyanMahon 94
(Michael Appleby) *cl up and t.k.h: disp ld 3 out: sn rdn: 7 l 3rd and fading next* **12/1**

/P2- **4** *3* **Red Not Blue (IRE)**[21] 1091 10-11-12 138 ....(p) AndrewThornton 110
(Simon Earle) *cl up: led briefly 3 out: rdn and qckly lost tch w ldng pair next* **12/1**

/P1- **5** *2 ½* **Di Kaprio (FR)**[55] 762 7-10-11 123 ....(t) LiamHeard 92
(Barry Leavy) *led tl rdn and hdd bef 3 out: wl btn next* **9/1**

345/ **6** *45* **Captain Cardington (IRE)**[32] 4662 4-9-13 120 ....(p) CiaranMckee(7) 42
(John O'Shea) *prom: rdn 7th: fdd bef next: t.o and eased last* **40/1**

0P6/ **7** *14* **Comehomequietly (IRE)**[171] 4382 9-10-4 116 .... PaulMoloney 26
(David Rees) *a in last: drvn bef 5th: sn toiling: t.o 7th: eased next* **8/1**[3]

4m 36.8s (-10.60) **Going Correction** -0.275s/f (Good)
WFA 4 from 5yo+ 14lb 7 Ran SP% **111.1**
Speed ratings (Par 107): **110,109,97,96,95 77,71**
toteswingers 1&2 £1.30, 2&3 £5.30, 1&3 £3.60 CSF £4.81 TOTE £2.60: £1.20, £2.30; EX 5.90 Trifecta £37.20 Pool: £3570.58 - 71.88 winning units..
Owner John P McManus **Bred** Seamus Boyle **Trained** Cheltenham, Gloucs

FOCUS
A good quality handicap hurdle and the feature race on the card, in which they went an even gallop. The winner impressed and the runner-up is the best guide to the form.

1269 FLEXINEB NEBULISERS NOVICES' H'CAP HURDLE (8 hdls) 2m
5:05 (5:05) (Class 5) (0-100,100) 4-Y-0+ **£1,949** (£572; £286; £143)

Form RPR

21P- **1** **Anton Dolin (IRE)**[30] 977 5-11-7 95 ....(p) TomO'Brien 102+
(Dr Richard Newland) *settled in 2nd or 3rd: j. slowly 4th and rdn: cajoled to ld and mstke 2 out: clr but hanging lft flat* **11/8**[1]

0/3- **2** *7* **Knockgraffon Lad (USA)**[34] 947 6-11-7 95 ....(tp) AlainCawley 94
(Brendan Powell) *prom: rdn and chal 2 out: wnt 4 l 2nd last: one pce flat: jst clung on to 2nd* **11/2**[2]

550- **3** *hd* **Gavi**[14] 1152 7-9-11 74 oh1 .... PeterCarberry(3) 73
(Karen George) *chsd ldrs: 7 l 4th home turn: rdn and no real imp after tl lft 3rd at last: kpt on steadily and nrly snatched 2nd* **10/1**

0/U- **4** ½ **Royal Defence (IRE)**[64] 266 7-11-12 **100**.......................... RyanMahon 98
(Mick Quinn) *chsd ldrs: pushed along 4th: bdly outpcd next: rallied bef last: fin stoutly and nrly snatched 3rd* **50/1**
661- **5** 1¼ **Naledi**[20] 1106 9-10-4 **85**.. ConorShoemark(7) 82
(Richard Price) *bhd: shkn up after 5th: no rspnse: kpt on after last but no ch* **7/1**[3]
P56- **6** 1½ **Robber Stone**[20] 1107 5-10-8 **82**..................................[1] PaulMoloney 78
(Debra Hamer) *hld up and t.k.h: in rr tl sme prog 3 out: effrt short lived and nvr cl enough to chal* **18/1**
600- **7** 3¼ **Sassy Wren**[29] 1000 8-10-2 **76**..(t) JamesDavies 68
(Chris Down) *chsd ldr tl rdn and wknd bef 3 out* **33/1**
566- **8** 13 **Carhue Princess (IRE)**[20] 1106 7-11-2 **90**........................ FelixDeGiles 69
(Tom Symonds) *bhd: bmpd along 4th: struggling next* **14/1**
330/ **9** 6 **Slam**[479] 3048 8-10-5 **84**..(t) AodhaganConlon(5) 57
(Tom George) *hld up towards rr: effrt 5th: 5th home turn: rdn and sn wknd: eased flat* **12/1**
/60- **F** **Duneen Dream (USA)**[51] 810 8-9-7 **74** oh4.................... OllieGarner(7) 70
(Nikki Evans) *plld hrd in ld: 3 l clr home turn: rdn and hdd 2 out: cl 3rd but wkng whn fell last* **66/1**
/00- **P** **Petrocelli**[15] 1137 6-10-2 **79**.. MichaelByrne(3)
(Tim Vaughan) *wnt wrong and p.u bef 3rd: dismntd* **12/1**
4/5- **P** **Just A Whisper**[105] 46 7-11-4 **92**.................................(t) NickScholfield
(Keiran Burke) *t.k.h: prom: wnt lft 2nd: wknd rapidly 5th: t.o and p.u next* **16/1**

3m 44.1s (-3.20) **Going Correction** -0.275s/f (Good)
WFA 4 from 5yo+ 13lb 12 Ran SP% **118.7**
Speed ratings (Par 103): **97,93,93,93,92 91,90,83,80, ,**
toteswingers 1&2 £3.20, 2&3 £12.20, 1&3 £5.80 CSF £9.62 CT £56.48 TOTE £1.80: £1.10, £2.40, £4.10; EX 11.40 Trifecta £99.90 Pool: £1334.16 - 10.00 winning units..
Owner Mrs M L Trow, Barwell & Newland **Bred** Windflower Overseas Holdings Inc **Trained** Claines, Worcs

FOCUS
A modest novices' handicap hurdle but the form looks straightforward behind the winner, who looks on the up.
T/Plt: £33.80 to a £1 stake. Pool of £74731.39 - 1611.07 winning tickets. T/Qpdt: £6.40 to a £1 stake. Pool of £6653.97 - 769.14 winning tickets. IM

[705]FONTWELL (L-H)
Thursday, August 15

OFFICIAL GOING: Good to firm (good in places; watered; 7.4)
Wind: Almost nil Weather: Overcast but warm; 21 degrees

1270 SES AUTOPARTS NOVICES' HURDLE (9 hdls) 2m 2f 110y
5:30 (5:30) (Class 4) 4-Y-0+ **£3,119** (£915; £457; £228)

Form RPR
102- **1** **Breaking Bits (IRE)**[31] 995 6-11-5 **112**............................. TomO'Brien 118
(Jamie Snowden) *mde all: drawing clr w one rival whn hit 2 out: rdn bef last: styd on wl flat* **6/4**[2]
450/ **2** 2 **Golanova**[237] 3167 5-10-12 0... JamieMoore 109
(Gary Moore) *prom: drew clr w wnr fr 2 out: looking hld whn plunged over last: kpt on gamely flat: promising* **16/1**
2P1- **3** 22 **Shantou Breeze (IRE)**[53] 805 6-10-5 0....................... RichardJohnson 82
(Michael Madgwick) *a 2nd or 3rd: rdn and lost tch w ldng pair 2 out: 15 l 3rd at last* **16/1**
26- **4** 1 **Flashy Star**[21] 427 4-10-3 0... MarcGoldstein 79
(Sheena West) *chsd ldrs: 5th and rdn and wkng home turn* **20/1**
311- **5** 9 **Plain Sailing (IRE)**[12] 1191 4-11-3 0................................. DenisO'Regan 91
(John Ferguson) *nt a fluent: chsd ldrs: mstke 3 out: 4th and drvn home turn: sn lost tch* **11/10**[1]
205- **6** 3 **Just Archie (USA)**[22] 1107 5-10-12 0.............................. LeightonAspell 78
(Lady Herries) *nt a fluent: chsd ldrs: pushed along after 5th: modest 7th but wl clr of rest home turn: plodded on* **33/1**
/4P- **7** 4½ **Good Of Luck**[13] 1183 4-10-10 0...................................... ConorO'Farrell 76
(Mick Channon) *nvr bttr than midfield: effrt 3 out: 6th and rdn home turn: sn lost tch w ldrs* **12/1**[3]
56- **8** 7 **Follow The Tracks (IRE)**[2] 1255 5-10-7 0...................... KillianMoore(5) 67
(Brian Barr) *mstke 1st: detached in last: passed sme strugglers fr 6th but t.o next* **66/1**
6P- **9** 3½ **The Kings Assassin (IRE)**[29] 1007 5-10-12 0................ PaddyBrennan 64
(Chris Gordon) *j.rt 1st: novicey and wl bhd: j. v awkwardly 3rd: t.o fr 3 out* **66/1**
300- **10** 21 **Imperial Legacy**[29] 1007 5-10-5 0..................................(bt[1]) MikeyHamill(7) 45
(Jo Davis) *chsd ldrs: rdn and struggling bef 6th: t.o next* **100/1**
500- **11** ¾ **Bedibyes**[71] 631 5-10-2 0.. JamesBest(3) 37
(Richard Mitchell) *nvr bttr than midfield: rdn 6th: t.o next* **100/1**
0P6 **12** 7 **Cool Fantasy (IRE)**[12] 1191 4-10-10 0................................. IanPopham 36
(Caroline Keevil) *chsd ldrs tl drvn after 5th: mstke next: t.o 3 out: mstke last and hung bdly lft: fin v slowly* **100/1**
0/ **13** 12 **Lady Barastar (IRE)**[8] 4597 5-10-5 0................................(b) ColinBolger 20
(Amanda Perrett) *chsd ldrs: mstkes 4th and 6th: wknd qckly: t.o next* **40/1**
14 3 **Unsist (FR)**[347] 5-10-12 0... TomCannon 25
(Nick Gifford) *nvr trbld ldrs: drvn 6th: t.o next* **33/1**

4m 16.1s (-18.20) **Going Correction** -0.75s/f (Firm)
WFA 4 from 5yo+ 13lb 14 Ran SP% **126.1**
Speed ratings (Par 105): **108,107,97,97,93 92,90,87,86,77 76,74,68,67**
toteswingers 1&2 £6.80, 1&3 £6.60, 2&3 £17.80 CSF £24.80 TOTE £3.00: £1.10, £4.80, £2.80; EX 32.30 Trifecta £455.40 Pool: £1,253.85 - 2.06 winning units..
Owner Colin Peake & John H W Finch Partnership **Bred** Mrs M Farrell **Trained** Lambourn, Berks

FOCUS
Fences at full width, hurdles middle to inner. Chases increased by 46yds per circuit and hurdles increased by 15yds per circuit. Racing began with a modest novice hurdle, in which two penalised runners dominated the betting. The winner is rated to form and sets the level.

1271 NUFFIELD HEALTH CHICHESTER JUVENILE HURDLE (9 hdls) 2m 2f 110y
6:00 (6:09) (Class 4) 3-Y-0 **£3,119** (£915; £457; £228)

Form RPR
22- **1** **Hanga Roa (IRE)**[26] 1044 3-10-12 0..................................... JamieMoore 86
(Gary Moore) *t.k.h: mde all at slow pce: j. bttr than rivals: 6 l clr and hrd drvn bef 2 out: a in command but only plugging on and unimpressive* **4/5**[1]
2 9 **Sutton Sid**[12] 3-10-12 0.. TomCannon 79
(Chris Gordon) *sn chsng wnr in slowly run r: mstke 3 out: sn rdn: no imp after: 7 l 2nd whn mstke last* **4/1**[2]
F- **3** 9 **Karl Marx (IRE)**[12] 1193 3-10-12 0.................................... TommyPhelan 70
(Mark Gillard) *mstkes and tending to jump rt in rr: rdn 3rd: t.o 6th: wnt 20 l 3rd bef last and plodded on* **25/1**
F- **4** 6 **Dark Justice (IRE)**[32] 975 3-10-5 0................................. DougieCostello 57
(Tim Pitt) *mounted outside paddock and kpt wl away fr rest at s: climbed over 2nd:12 l last at 3rd: nt jump wl: t.o 6th* **8/1**
5 9 **Ruff Luck**[70] 3-9-12 0.. KevinJones(7) 49
(Seamus Mullins) *j.v.slowly 2nd: nt fluent: chsd ldrs: mstke 6th: 9 l 3rd and rdn home turn: fin weakly* **14/1**
U- **6** 32 **Noble Bacchus (IRE)**[26] 1044 3-10-12 0........................... PaddyBrennan 28
(Fergal O'Brien) *chsd ldrs tl rdn and fdd bdly home turn: blnd 2 out and last: hopelessly t.o* **6/1**[3]
P **Running Bull (IRE)**[47] 3-10-5 0....................................... MrFMitchell(7)
(Linda Jewell) *j. v erratically in rr: nvr travelling: t.o 5th: hung violently rt bef next and p.u* **40/1**

4m 27.6s (-6.70) **Going Correction** -0.75s/f (Firm) 7 Ran SP% **113.9**
Speed ratings (Par 102): **84,80,76,73,70 56,**
toteswingers 1&2 £1.60, 1&3 £5.80, 2&3 £11.80 CSF £4.41 TOTE £1.50: £1.10, £2.40; EX 4.40 Trifecta £27.80 Pool: £1,155.10 - 31.14 winning units..
Owner C E Stedman **Bred** M Parrish **Trained** Lower Beeding, W Sussex

FOCUS
A weak juvenile hurdle, the start of which was delayed due to a power failure. The time was slow and the form looks poor.

1272 SOUTHAMPTON MAKES MORE SENSE H'CAP CHASE (16 fncs) 2m 6f
6:30 (6:37) (Class 5) (0-100,100) 4-Y-0+ **£2,144** (£629; £314; £157)

Form RPR
05P- **1** **Doctor Ric (IRE)**[65] 709 8-10-3 **77**................................(b[1]) JamieMoore 98+
(Gerry Enright) *led bef 4th: 6 l clr at 10th: hit 13th: wl in command 3 out: 18 l ahd at last: virtually p.u fnl 100yds* **6/1**
555- **2** 17 **Sadler's Star (GER)**[32] 976 10-11-7 **95**......................(p) NickScholfield 96
(Michael Blake) *a 2nd or 3rd: 6 l 2nd and rdn home turn: no rspnse and sn lost tch w wnr* **5/1**[3]
3P6- **3** 2½ **Princely Hero (IRE)**[43] 871 9-11-6 **94**..........................(p) TomCannon 92
(Chris Gordon) *towards rr: pushed along 10th: drvn and nt keen next: hit 12th: remote 4th whn blnd 2 out: consented to overtake a rival whn keeping on cl home* **9/2**[2]
/55- **4** ¾ **She's Humble (IRE)**[23] 1089 11-9-8 **75**..................... ConorShoemark(7) 73
(Linda Jewell) *chsd ldrs: pushed along after 10th: 10 l 3rd and rdn and btn home turn: lost remote 3rd nr fin* **20/1**
04- **5** 7 **Joe The Rogue (IRE)**[16] 1150 6-10-11 **85**...................... PaddyBrennan 76
(Paul Henderson) *mstkes: in rr and nvr looked to be gng wl: hmpd 6th: mstke next: struggling 13th: t.o next: blnd 2 out* **11/4**[1]
135- **6** 27 **Morestead (IRE)**[50] 846 8-11-10 **98**..........................(t) LeightonAspell 65
(Brendan Powell) *sn led: hdd bef 4th: often j.lft: drvn and lost pl 11th: nt run on: t.o 3 out* **10/1**
P/P- **P** **Curragh Dancer (FR)**[92] 305 10-10-0 **77** oh7 ow3...(v) KielanWoods(3)
(Paddy Butler) *nvr bttr than midfield: struck into and p.u 7th* **25/1**
063/ **U** **Jerry Lee (IRE)**[137] 5033 10-10-0 **74** oh11.................... RichieMcLernon
(Violet M Jordan) *last whn uns rdr 2nd* **33/1**
4P2- **P** **Formedable (IRE)**[22] 1104 11-10-0 **74** oh14..................(p) WillKennedy
(Violet M Jordan) *nt jump wl in rr: drvn 9th: lost tch and mstke 13th: t.o and p.u next* **25/1**
652- **F** **Old Dreams (IRE)**[65] 709 7-11-12 **100**............................(t) APMcCoy
(Nick Gifford) *hld up: chsng ldrs tl fell 6th* **11/4**[1]

5m 34.6s (-8.40) **Going Correction** -0.325s/f (Good) 10 Ran SP% **127.0**
Speed ratings (Par 103): **102,95,94,94,92 82, , , ,**
toteswingers: 1&2 £8.90, 1&3 £6.60, 2&3 £6.10. CSF £38.00 CT £154.93 TOTE £9.90: £2.90, £1.90, £1.30; EX 45.30 Trifecta £407.60 Pool: £805.97 - 1.48 winning units..
Owner M T Forbes-Wood **Bred** P O'Connell **Trained** Lewes, E Sussex

FOCUS
A modest handicap chase, with a 100-rated topweight. The winner is rated back to his best with the placed horses close to more recent marks.

1273 YEOMAN'S HONDA H'CAP HURDLE (9 hdls) 2m 2f 110y
7:00 (7:01) (Class 4) (0-110,110) 4-Y-0+ **£3,119** (£915; £457; £228)

Form RPR
/06- **1** **Guards Chapel**[19] 421 5-11-8 **109**..............................(v) JoshuaMoore(3) 118
(Gary Moore) *hld up: mstke 2nd: pushed along after 5th: effrt 3 out: qcknd to ld wl bef 2 out where already rdn 10 l clr: pushed along flat: unchal* **7/1**
225- **2** 11 **Mount Vesuvius (IRE)**[38] 924 5-10-13 **97**......................(t) TomO'Brien 96
(Paul Henderson) *settled in midfield: effrt 3 out: chsd wnr bef 2 out where wnr 10 l clr: unable to cl: hit last* **7/2**[3]
4U6- **3** 5 **Presenting Me (IRE)**[20] 1118 5-10-10 **97**........................ AdamWedge(3) 92
(Evan Williams) *pressed ldrs: rdn and outpcd whn wnr qcknd bef home turn: wnt 13 l 3rd 2 out: no ch after* **12/1**
605- **4** 9 **Bathwick Man**[25] 1062 8-11-12 **110**..........................(b[1]) TomScudamore 96
(David Pipe) *pressed ldr: led 5th: drvn and hdd bef home turn: immediately lost tch w wnr and fnd nthing after* **3/1**[2]
/00- **5** 9 **Numen (IRE)**[35] 852 9-10-5 **96**......................................(p) MissCLWills(7) 74
(Barry Brennan) *t.k.h: clsd to ld 4th: hdd next: wknd 3 out* **25/1**
060/ **6** 1 **Finding Your Feet (IRE)**[254] 2842 5-11-7 **105**.................... APMcCoy 82
(Jonjo O'Neill) *settled in rr: last at 5th: lost tch qckly bef 6th: sn rdn but no ch after* **7/4**[1]
004- **7** 2 **Osmosia (FR)**[32] 977 8-10-6 **90**..................................(vt) TomCannon 66
(Chris Gordon) *last pair: drvn and lost tch bef 6th: nt run on* **14/1**
/63- **8** 8 **Sun Quest**[66] 691 9-10-9 **100**....................................(t) MrLKilgarriff(7) 68
(Steven Dixon) *set slow pce: hdd 4th: w ldr next: bmpd along and wknd bef 3 out: blnd next: t.o* **12/1**

4m 30.8s (-3.50) **Going Correction** -0.75s/f (Firm) 8 Ran SP% **122.0**
Speed ratings (Par 105): **77,72,70,66,62 62,61,58**
toteswingers 1&2 £3.40, 1&3 £7.10, 2&3 £24.70 CSF £34.51 CT £300.12 TOTE £10.10: £1.70, £1.20, £3.60; EX 40.90 Trifecta £256.00 Pool: £550.42 - 1.61 winning units..
Owner Andrew Bradmore **Bred** Mrs J Chandris **Trained** Lower Beeding, W Sussex

FOCUS
Just a moderate event, but quite competitive on paper. The placed horses are rated pretty much to their marks.

1274 LISA WILSON SCHOLARSHIP FUND NOVICES' H'CAP CHASE (13 fncs) 2m 2f
7:30 (7:30) (Class 4) (0-105,105) 4-Y-0+ **£3,768** (£1,106; £553; £276)

Form RPR
351- **1** **Rudigreen (IRE)**[14] 1174 10-11-9 **105**........................(tp) JackQuinlan(3) 120
(Noel Quinlan) *settled towards rr: stdy prog 7th: wnt 3rd at 9th: 2 l 3rd home turn: led 2 out: 8 l clr last: drvn and styd on wl flat* **4/1**[3]

6/5- **2** *11* **Safe Investment (USA)**[22] 1103 9-10-7 **86**........................(vt) DavidBass 91
(Lawney Hill) *t.k.h: led at str pce tl mstke and hdd 10th: wnt rt bef 2 out: drvn and no ch w wnr after: regained 8 l 2nd and hit last* **8/1**

5- **3** *5* **Julie Prince (IRE)**[17] 1133 7-11-1 **94**....................................... APMcCoy 95
(Brendan Powell) *w ldr 2nd tl nrly fell 3rd and great rcvry: rallied to go 2nd at 6th: shkn up next: hit 8th: led 10th tl drvn and hdd 2 out: lost 2nd at last and fin weakly* **9/4**[1]

613- **4** *19* **Tri Nations (UAE)**[7] 1192 8-11-8 **101**.............................(vt) PaulMoloney 84
(Anthony Middleton) *hld up towards rr: rdn 9th: mstke next: 7 l 4th bef 3 out: sn lost tch* **8/1**

5/5- **5** *25* **Cossack Prince**[85] 425 8-10-0 **79** oh1............................... TomCannon 40
(Laura Mongan) *cl up tl 3rd and rdn after 7th: lost pl 9th: 10 l 5th home turn: drvn and racd awkwardly after: sn t.o* **7/1**

564/ **U** **Dark Oasis**[220] 3548 7-9-10 **82** ow2.................................. KevinJones(7)
(Natalie Lloyd-Beavis) *uns rdr 1st* **10/1**

10P- **U** **First Morning (IRE)**[14] 1175 8-11-5 **98**............................ NickScholfield
(Michael Blake) *hld up last: blnd v bdly and uns rdr 3rd* **12/1**

353- **P** **Zama Zama**[16] 1151 6-11-9 **105**....................................(p) AdamWedge(3)
(Evan Williams) *chsd ldrs tl last and struggling u.p after 7th: t.o fr 9th tl p.u 3 out* **3/1**[2]

4m 30.1s (-4.60) **Going Correction** -0.325s/f (Good) 8 Ran SP% **127.3**
Speed ratings (Par 105): **97,92,89,81,70 , ,**
toteswingers 1&2 £12.10, 1&3 £2.90, 2&3 £6.30 CSF £38.99 CT £93.11 TOTE £7.90: £2.40, £1.90, £1.20; EX 50.90 Trifecta £222.00 Pool: £356.35 - 1.20 winning units..
Owner Miss M A Quinlan **Bred** John Murphy **Trained** Newmarket, Suffolk

FOCUS
A moderate handicap chase, but it got off to a dramatic start. The form looks pretty weak.

1275 CASCADES SHOPPING CENTRE H'CAP HURDLE (10 hdls) 2m 4f
8:00 (8:00) (Class 5) (0-95,95) 4-Y-0+ **£1,949** (£572; £286; £143)

Form RPR

0/3- **1** **Franklino (FR)**[65] 710 6-11-12 **95**....................................(p) TomCannon 103
(Chris Gordon) *a ldng quartet: rdn 4th: led 3 out: sn drvn: 3 l clr whn hit next: ears pricked and a holding rivals after* **14/1**

301- **2** *5* **Capellini**[17] 1137 6-11-3 **91**... GavinSheehan(5) 94
(Charles Egerton) *settled trcking ldrs: effrt and looked gng wl in 4th home turn: sn chsng wnr: rdn and no imp between last two* **5/1**[3]

/30- **3** *5* **Torran Sound**[44] 860 6-11-12 **95**...............................(b) FelixDeGiles 94
(James Eustace) *t.k.h: wnt prom after 2nd: led 8th tl drvn and hdd next: one pce and wl hld fr 2 out* **16/1**

604- **4** *3 ¾* **Orsm**[36] 946 6-11-7 **90**..(tp) DavidBass 85
(Laura Mongan) *sweating bdly: pressed ldr tl led 7th: hdd next: mstke 3 out: lost 2nd bef 2 out and no ch after* **25/1**

002- **5** *1 ¼* **Clarion Call**[14] 1171 5-11-12 **95**..(v) PaulMoloney 89
(Evan Williams) *a abt same pce: drvn and brief effrt to go 3rd briefly on home turn: fnd nthing after* **5/1**[3]

003- **6** *2* **Moyne Nineoseven (IRE)**[36] 946 7-11-9 **95**..............(t) JackQuinlan(3) 87
(Noel Quinlan) *in rr div: sme hdwy 7th: 6th and no ch w ldrs after 3 out: plugged on* **9/2**[2]

P02- **7** *15* **Pirans Car**[22] 1110 7-11-0 **86**..(tp) MarkQuinlan(3) 65
(Nigel Hawke) *nvr bttr than midfield: mstke 4th and reminders: mstke 7th: hmpd 9th: remote 7th next: blnd last* **16/1**

40P- **8** *nk* **Spanish Fork (IRE)**[65] 710 4-11-10 **95**........................ MarcGoldstein 71
(Sheena West) *a towards rr: rdn 6th: remote fr 3 out* **16/1**

0/0- **9** *32* **Don't Look Bach (IRE)**[2] 1259 8-10-12 **86**..................... KillianMoore(5) 36
(Brian Barr) *sweating bdly: t.k.h: led tl hdd and hit 7th: lost pl rapidly: t.o 3 out* **20/1**

/65- **10** *1 ½* **Sahrati**[22] 1109 9-11-12 **95**.. NickScholfield 43
(Michael Blake) *chsd ldrs tl 5th: t.o fr 3 out* **16/1**

/56- **11** *14* **Going Twice**[81] 484 8-11-2 **85**.. LeightonAspell 21
(Steve Woodman) *a bhd: nvr travelling: t.o 3 out* **33/1**

0/5- **12** *12* **Nebula Storm (IRE)**[65] 708 6-11-9 **95**.....................(v[1]) JoshuaMoore(3) 20
(Gary Moore) *rdn 6th: chsd ldrs tl 7th: t.o 3 out* **7/1**

500/ **13** *37* **Filun**[7] 4804 8-11-2 **85**..(vt[1]) RichardJohnson
(Anthony Middleton) *j. v awkwardly 1st and continued t.o: modest prog 8th: sn t.o again* **20/1**

26P/ **14** *5* **Landenstown Star (IRE)**[164] 4560 8-11-2 **85**................. TommyPhelan
(Mark Gillard) *last but one whn mstke 2nd: nvr travelling: rdn 7th: bdly hmpd 8th: t.o and eased after next* **40/1**

404- **F** **Flew The Nest (IRE)**[23] 1084 5-11-11 **94**...........................(p) APMcCoy
(Jonjo O'Neill) *racd wd towards rr: sme hdwy in abt 5 lengths 7th whn fell 8th* **3/1**[1]

4m 43.6s (-15.80) **Going Correction** -0.75s/f (Firm)
WFA 4 from 5yo+ 14lb 15 Ran SP% **138.0**
Speed ratings (Par 103): **101,99,97,95,95 94,88,88,75,74 69,64,49,47,**
toteswingers: 1&2 £24.00, 1&3 £48.10, 2&3 £36.40. CSF £90.11 CT £1201.90 TOTE £12.70: £5.00, £3.40, £4.60; EX 110.10 Trifecta £223.10 Part won. Pool: £297.53 - 0.01 winning units..
Owner L Gilbert **Bred** S C E A Haras Du Ma, Mme & Lengin **Trained** Morestead, Hants

FOCUS
A low-grade finale in which few could boast convincing form. The winner ran to something like his early form with the placed horses close to more recent form.
T/Plt: £85.50 to a £1 stake. Pool: £59,624.17 - 509.00 winning units T/Qpdt: £27.80 to a £1 stake. Pool: £6,455.15 - 171.80 winning units IM

1276 - 1278a (Foreign Racing) - See Raceform Interactive

POMPADOUR (L-H)
Thursday, August 15

OFFICIAL GOING: Turf: good

1279a PRIX BASILE ET BERNARD LACHAUD GRAND CROSS (CROSS-COUNTRY CHASE) (CONDITIONS) (5YO+) (TURF) 3m 1f
5:00 (12:00) 5-Y-0+ **£17,170** (£8,585; £5,008; £3,398; £1,609)

RPR

1 **Beuillac (FR)**[636] 10-10-12 0... JamesReveley 124
(G Macaire, France) **Evs**[1]

2 *9* **Otatou (FR)**[1096] 11-10-10 0.................................. JeremyBesnardiere 113
(F Lagarde, France)

3 *1 ½* **Pegase Du Carcaud (FR)** 10-10-8 0.............................. VincentChenet 110
(F Lagarde, France)

4 *6* **Spead Du Valon (FR)**[641] 2516 7-10-8 0...................... VincentChatellier 104
(F Nicolle, France)

5 *dist* **Bernburg (FR)**[1761] 10-10-8 0....................................(p) FabriceBarrao
(Mlle A Pelletant, France)

F **Janmat (FR)**[3368] 13-10-8 0..(b) MickaelLahlah
(A Mesnil, France)

P **Wedger Pardy (IRE)**[154] 4752 12-10-6 0.......................(p) PeterBuchanan
(Kim Bailey)

P **Petit Bob (FR)** 10-11-5 0.. JanFaltejsek
(G Macaire, France)

6m 50.51s (410.51) 8 Ran SP% **50.0**
PARI-MUTUEL (all including 1 euro stakes): WIN 2.00; PLACE 1.60, 1.90, 4.30.
Owner Jean-Michel Reillier **Bred** J-M Reillier & Mme G Nouard **Trained** Les Mathes, France

[1200]
MARKET RASEN (R-H)
Saturday, August 17

OFFICIAL GOING: Good (good to firm in places; watered; 8.6)
Wind: Breezy Weather: Sunny; 20 degrees

1280 ECHO AND TELEGRAPHS "HANDS AND HEELS" (S) HURDLE (CONDITIONALS/AMATEURS) (RACING EXCELLENCE) (8 hdls) 2m 1f
5:35 (5:35) (Class 5) 4-Y-0+ **£1,949** (£572; £286; £143)

Form RPR

113- **1** **Emerald Glade (IRE)**[14] 927 6-11-1 105........................ JackSherwood 107+
(Jim Best) *2nd or 3rd tl led sn after 3 out: rdn and readily drew clr: 10 l ahd whn unconvincing jumps 2 out and last: sn heavily eased* **10/11**[1]

F55- **2** *5* **Muwalla**[13] 1206 6-11-2 102....................................(tp) DiarmuidO'Regan(3) 104
(Chris Grant) *t.k.h: prom: 4th and outpcd after 3 out: drvn into 2nd bef next: kpt on flat as wnr eaed rt down* **5/1**[2]

0/4- **3** *12* **Edgeworth (IRE)**[16] 1171 7-10-12 0.................................... JakeHodson 84
(David Bridgwater) *chsd ldrs: 3rd after 3 out: rdn and wl hld fr next* **16/1**

F0P- **4** *3* **Photogenique (FR)**[39] 932 10-10-0 64......... MissGeorgiaHenderson(5) 74
(Rob Summers) *immediately lost tch completely: last tl 3 out: 30 l bhd wnr next: passed floundering rivals after to snatch remote 4th* **100/1**

30- **5** *1* **Miss H Lewiss**[59] 768 5-10-2 0..(v) RyanHatch(3) 73
(Nigel Twiston-Davies) *t.k.h: j. slowly 1st: led tl mstke 3 out: sn hdd: drvn and wknd and lost 2nd bef next: lost remote 4th cl home* **14/1**

/PF- **6** *11* **Lap Of Honour (IRE)**[18] 1143 9-10-7 95............. MrRMorganMurphy(5) 71
(Ferdy Murphy, France) *a towards rr: shkn up after 3 out: nvr gng wl enough after* **11/2**[3]

050- **P** **Guns Of Love (IRE)**[24] 1105 11-10-7 65........................ MrTWWheeler(5)
(Robin Dickin) *prom tl stopped to nil after 4th: t.o 3 out: p.u last* **66/1**

5/0- **P** **Third Half**[27] 1058 4-11-1 110..(t) JPKiely(3)
(Tim Vaughan) *a in rr: rdn after 3 out: no rspnse: t.o and p.u last* **6/1**

4m 14.6s (7.90) **Going Correction** +0.325s/f (Yiel)
WFA 4 from 5yo+ 13lb 8 Ran SP% **113.8**
Speed ratings (Par 103): **94,91,86,84,84 78, ,**
toteswingers 1&2 £2.10, 1&3 £4.40, 2&3 £9.20 CSF £5.93 TOTE £1.70: £1.10, £1.20, £4.00; EX 6.00 Trifecta £43.20 Pool: £1,167.17 - 20.21 winning units..There was no bid for the winner.
Owner Emerald Glade Partnership **Bred** J T And Mrs Thomas **Trained** Lewes, E Sussex

FOCUS
An overcast evening and the ground, with a GoingStick reading of 8.7 on the hurdles course, rode as advertised. A weak "hands and heels" selling hurdle to start and they went no gallop early on. Few came into this with any good form. The first three are rated to their marks.

1281 MCFLY PERFORMING HERE LIVE 31ST AUGUST NOVICES' HURDLE (10 hdls) 2m 5f
6:10 (6:11) (Class 4) 4-Y-0+ **£3,898** (£1,144; £572; £286)

Form RPR

125- **1** **Wake Your Dreams (IRE)**[55] 801 5-11-5 115.................. SeanQuinlan 121+
(Jennie Candlish) *mde all: drvn fr 2 out: kpt outbattling chalr after: all out but v game* **6/4**[2]

/34- **2** *2 ¼* **The Cockney Mackem (IRE)**[28] 1046 7-11-5 125. SamTwiston-Davies 119
(Nigel Twiston-Davies) *t.k.h in 2nd or 3rd: chsd wnr gng wl 3 out tl next: sn drvn: nt fluent 2 out: stl ev ch last: declined to overtake flat* **11/10**[1]

2- **3** *3* **Oneofapear (IRE)**[41] 897 7-10-7 0.................................. EDLinehan(5) 108
(Mike Sowersby) *hld up trcking ldrs: wnt 4th on long run to 2 out: sn drvn and no imp after: plugging on after last* **10/1**

P/4- **4** *48* **Mist The Boat**[38] 945 5-10-12 0..................................... RichardJohnson 65
(Tim Vaughan) *mstkes 3rd and 7th: pressed ldr tl 3 out: drvn and fdd wl bef 2 out: t.o whn lft 4th at last* **16/1**

506/ **5** *37* **Miss Mayfair (IRE)**[198] 3956 6-10-5 0....................................... DavidBass 25
(Lawney Hill) *j. slowly thrght: t.k.h early: prom tl lost pl u.p after 5th: lost tch 7th: hopelessly t.o fr next* **33/1**

5/P- **6** *2 ½* **Master Bud**[105] 115 8-10-2 0..................................... JamesCorbett(10) 29
(Susan Corbett) *hld up and detached in last: lost all tch 6th: hopelessly t.o fr 3 out* **100/1**

4PP/ **7** *29* **Kicking Time (IRE)**[111] 3 7-10-9 0..............................[1] JackQuinlan(3) 3
(Sarah Humphrey) *j. slowly 2nd: lost tch 7th: hopelessly t.o fr next* **80/1**

/20- **F** **Kadalkin (FR)**[72] 649 7-10-9 0....................................(t) MarkQuinlan(3) 85
(Nigel Hawke) *wnt cl up at 5th: 2nd briefly after 3 out: sn rdn: wknd bef next whn mstke: remote 4th whn fell heavily last: winded but rcvrd* **9/1**[3]

5m 19.8s (11.00) **Going Correction** +0.325s/f (Yiel) 8 Ran SP% **117.8**
Speed ratings (Par 105): **92,91,90,71,57 56,45,**
toteswingers 1&2 £1.10, 1&3 £3.10, 2&3 £3.40 CSF £3.78 TOTE £2.90: £1.10, £1.10, £2.80; EX 3.90 Trifecta £11.60 Pool: £1,380.95 - 89.18 winning units..
Owner Pam Beardmore & Alan Baxter **Bred** J R Weston **Trained** Basford Green, Staffs

FOCUS
An uncompetitive novices' hurdle run at a fair pace and the market leaders had it to themselves following a protracted duel. The form looks solid enough with the placed horses close to their marks.

1282 FREEBETS.CO.UK DOWNLOAD OUR FREE BETTING APP NOVICES' CHASE (14 fncs) 2m 4f
6:40 (6:40) (Class 4) 4-Y-0+ **£4,548** (£1,335; £667; £333)

Form RPR

234- **1** **Violets Boy (IRE)**[13] 1203 6-11-0 0.................................(t) LeightonAspell 118+
(Brendan Powell) *j.w and racd w zest: w ldr tl led 8th: 4 l clr and rdn 2 out: kpt on stoutly after and a holding chalr* **7/1**

0/4- **2** *1 ¾* **Trop Fort (FR)**[19] 1133 6-11-0 0...............................(t) RichardJohnson 117
(Tim Vaughan) *often j. slowly: w ldrs tl rdn 7th: drvn and outpcd 11th: rallied to chse wnr fr next: no imp fr 2 out* **15/8**[2]

412- **3** *25* **Lauberhorn**[14] 1192 6-11-0 110..(v) PaulMoloney 101
(Evan Williams) *hld up last: mstke 3rd: cajoled along 10th and sn outpcd: blnd 3 out: nt fluent next: poor 3rd after* **6/1**[3]

U3U- 4 41 **Lemon Drop Red (USA)**[41] 899 5-11-0 118...............(p) LiamTreadwell 82
(Paul Webber) *slt ld 4th tl 8th: blnd 10th: chsd wnr after tl rdn bef 3 out: stopped to nil next: t.o and eased flat* 5/4[1]

4m 51.4s (-14.30) **Going Correction** -0.70s/f (Firm) 4 Ran SP% **106.0**
Speed ratings (Par 105): **100,99,89,72**
CSF £19.49 TOTE £7.20; EX 16.80 Trifecta £50.90 Pool: £474.34 - 6.98 winning units..
Owner Harry Redknapp **Bred** Harry Redknapp **Trained** Upper Lambourn, Berks

FOCUS
The GoingStick read 8.5 on the chase course although the jockeys felt the going was more on the good side for this decent little novices' event, where they went a fair pace. The winner is rated to the best of his hurdles form and the form could be rated higher.

1283 JANE CLUGSTON H'CAP CHASE (17 fncs) 3m 1f
7:10 (7:10) (Class 3) (0-140,135) 4-Y-0+ **£7,797** (£2,289; £1,144; £572)

Form RPR
545- 1 **Strumble Head (IRE)**[27] 1060 8-10-2 111....................(b) DonalDevereux 117+
(Peter Bowen) *led 3rd: j.w and travelled strly: 3 l clr fr 3 out: pushed out flat: wl in command* 10/3[2]

/60- 2 3 1/4 **Pineau De Re (FR)**[28] 1047 10-11-12 135.............. SamTwiston-Davies 139
(Dr Richard Newland) *nt a fluent: hld up in last pair: effrt gng wl in 2nd after 14th: drvn bef 2 out: nvr making any imp on ready wnr after* 2/1[1]

/21- 3 15 **Eleazar (GER)**[70] 670 12-10-8 117...............................(p) LeightonAspell 107
(Lucy Wadham) *prom: 2nd briefly bef 11th: rdn and lost tch 13th: plugged on into poor 3rd 2 out* 17/2

346- 4 2 1/4 **Donnas Palm (IRE)**[28] 1047 9-11-4 127....................(b) RichardJohnson 114
(Tim Vaughan) *trckd ldrs: wnt 2nd at 13th tl rdn after next: lost 3rd 2 out where fading tamely and racing awkwardly* 7/1

0/4- 5 14 **Epee Celeste (FR)**[82] 508 7-9-9 109 oh2.............. JoeCornwall(5) 89
(Michael Chapman) *led tl 3rd: rdn 11th: mostly 2nd tl 13th: lost tch after next* 8/1

3/0- P **King's Legacy (IRE)**[28] 1047 9-11-4 127............................... DavidBass
(Lawney Hill) *j.rt: t.k.h in last pair: mstke 11th and qckly lost tch: t.o 14th: p.u 2 out* 7/2[3]

6m 8.0s (-23.30) **Going Correction** -0.70s/f (Firm) 6 Ran SP% **112.8**
Speed ratings (Par 107): **109,107,103,102,97**
toteswingers 1&2 £2.00, 1&3 £3.40, 2&3 £3.40 CSF £10.99 TOTE £4.00: £1.80, £2.00; EX 12.30 Trifecta £78.20 Pool: £515.74 - 4.94 winning units..
Owner Jonathan Martin **Bred** Martin J Dibbs **Trained** Little Newcastle, Pembrokes

FOCUS
The blustery wind had picked up markedly before the start of this decent staying handicap chase. The winner is rated to his best.

1284 RACING UK YOUR RACING HOME FROM HOME H'CAP HURDLE (12 hdls) 3m
7:40 (7:40) (Class 4) (0-120,115) 4-Y-0+ **£3,249** (£954; £477; £238)

Form RPR
PP2- 1 **Mission Complete (IRE)**[18] 1155 7-11-6 109....................(p) APMcCoy 121+
(Jonjo O'Neill) *led or 2nd tl led 8th: rdn home turn: 5 l clr whn wnt lft 2 out and last where in full command: easing off substantially cl home* 2/1[1]

/02- 2 2 3/4 **Coronea Lilly (IRE)**[13] 1205 9-11-12 115...................(p) NoelFehily 119
(Neil Mulholland) *chsd ldrs: 4th whn mstke 7th: kpt on steadily but wl hld by wnr fr 2 out: tk 2nd nr fin: flattered by proximity* 6/1[3]

03- 3 nk **Emily's Flyer (IRE)**[13] 1201 6-10-11 107...............(t) ConorShoemark(7) 109
(Fergal O'Brien) *prom tl drvn and lost pl after 5th: 8th at next: rallied 8th: wnt 2nd 3 out: hrd rdn and no imp whn wnt lft 2 out: lost 2nd nr fin* 18/1

U04- 4 3 1/2 **Combustible Kate (IRE)**[13] 1205 7-9-12 94.................. PaulNO'Brien(7) 93
(Nick Kent) *prom: 4th and rdn after 3 out: kpt on steadily at one pce and wl hld fr next* 12/1

5/2- 5 20 **Dark Spirit (IRE)**[15] 193 5-10-8 97..................................(v) PaulMoloney 78
(Evan Williams) *hld up in last pair tl 7th: hdwy to trck ldrs gng wl enough after 3 out: effrt shortlived: wl btn bef next* 7/1

0/5- 6 4 **Flying Doctor**[17] 1161 10-9-13 93........................... CallumWhillans(5) 70
(Alistair Whillans) *towards rr: bmpd along bef 8th: sn lost tch* 16/1

3/1- 7 4 1/2 **Raktiman (IRE)**[34] 967 6-11-5 108...................................(p) DavidEngland 81
(Michael Appleby) *led rnd s and led in: last pair: j. slowly 4th: drvn and struggling after 7th* 12/1

/43- 8 15 **Sohappyharry**[31] 1011 7-11-10 113... DPFahy 73
(Jane Mathias) *nt fluent 1st: bhd: sme hdwy 6th: lost tch 3 out: t.o and eased last* 33/1

0/P- 9 26 **Santera (IRE)**[55] 811 9-11-9 112......................................(p) WillKennedy 48
(John Spearing) *towards rr: effrt 8th: 3rd briefly but drvn after 3 out: dropped out rapidly bef next: t.o* 22/1

5/6- 10 1/2 **Beyond (IRE)**[17] 144 6-11-9 112...............................(vt[1]) ConorO'Farrell 48
(David Pipe) *led or disp ld tl 8th: lost pl rapidly: eased 3 out and sn t.o* 3/1[2]

5m 57.6s (7.10) **Going Correction** +0.325s/f (Yiel) 10 Ran SP% **118.9**
Speed ratings (Par 105): **101,100,99,98,92 90,89,84,75,75**
toteswingers 1&2 £3.00, 1&3 £45.10, 2&3 £8.70 CSF £15.34 CT £172.10 TOTE £2.80: £1.40, £1.60, £3.30; EX 14.00 Trifecta £52.60 Pool: £555.94 - 7.91 winning units..
Owner John P McManus **Bred** Hubert Carter **Trained** Cheltenham, Gloucs

FOCUS
They went no great pace for this modest contest, but the form looks solid rated around the first three.

1285 CONSTRUCTION DAY HERE ON 21ST NOVEMBER H'CAP HURDLE (10 hdls) 2m 3f
8:10 (8:10) (Class 4) (0-115,115) 4-Y-0+ **£3,249** (£954; £477; £238)

Form RPR
354- 1 **Lucky Landing (IRE)**[13] 1204 7-11-12 115............................ NoelFehily 118
(Tony Coyle) *settled in rr: wnt 4th gng wl after 3 out: tk 2nd next: rdn to ld last: sn clr: gamely* 9/1

131- 2 1 1/2 **Strongly Suggested**[27] 1061 6-11-10 113...........................(t) APMcCoy 118+
(Jonjo O'Neill) *racd keenly and travelled strly: prom: mstke 4th: blnd 3 out: rdn 5 l clr but idling whn mstke next: drvn and hdd last: outbattled flat* 5/4[1]

453- 3 9 **Claude Carter**[13] 1206 9-10-8 100.............................. EwanWhillans(3) 94
(Alistair Whillans) *hld up last tl 7th: rdn and outpcd next: sme prog bef last: wnt modest 3rd flat* 7/2[2]

403- 4 3 1/4 **Argaum (IRE)**[34] 977 6-9-12 90............................(tp) AdamWedge(3) 81
(Evan Williams) *led at str pce: drvn and hdd sn after 3 out: outpcd bef next* 8/1

346- 5 16 **Super Collider**[18] 1148 6-11-1 114.............................. JamesCorbett(10) 92
(Susan Corbett) *nt fluent 6th: pressed ldr tl next: rdn and fdd wl bef 2 out: t.o whn mstke last: eased* 40/1

/21- 6 4 1/2 **Mighty Snazy**[28] 1048 9-11-8 111.................................. RichardJohnson 89
(Tim Vaughan) *towards rr: 5th and drvn after 3 out: one pce and sn btn: t.o and eased last* 9/2[3]

05U- 7 30 **The Weatherman (IRE)**[25] 1087 6-11-9 112........................ AdrianLane 57
(Donald McCain) *in tch tl dropped bk last at 7th: sn struggling: t.o and eased 2 out* 20/1

4m 42.9s (3.50) **Going Correction** +0.325s/f (Yiel) 7 Ran SP% **113.2**
Speed ratings (Par 105): **105,104,100,99,92 90,77**
toteswingers 1&2 £2.40, 1&3 £6.40, 2&3 £4.00 CSF £21.09 CT £47.89 TOTE £7.70: £4.50, £1.10; EX 26.10 Trifecta £43.00 Pool: £723.31 - 12.60 winning units..
Owner Gary Dewhurst & Tony Coyle **Bred** James McGrath **Trained** Norton, N Yorks

FOCUS
The pace was relatively decent for this run-of-the-mill handicap hurdle, which the champion jockey will not look upon as his finest hour. The winner is rated in line with previous course form with the second to recent winning form.
T/Plt: £112.20 to a £1 stake. Pool: £37,971.88 - 247.04 winning units T/Qpdt: £71.00 to a £1 stake. Pool: £2,574.80 - 26.80 winning units IM

1158 PERTH (R-H)
Saturday, August 17

OFFICIAL GOING: Good to firm (good in places; 9.0) changing to good after race 1 (3.00)
Wind: Breezy; half behind Weather: Overcast; showers

1286 TOTEPOOL HOME OF KINGSIZE POOLS NOVICES' H'CAP HURDLE (10 hdls) 2m 4f 110y
3:00 (3:00) (Class 4) (0-110,110) 4-Y-0+ **£4,548** (£1,335; £667; £333)

Form RPR
P30/ 1 **Jimmy The Hat (IRE)**[96] 273 7-11-12 110....................... JasonMaguire 123+
(Gordon Elliott, Ire) *hld up in tch: stdy hdwy after 4 out: effrt and rdn bef 2 out: led appr last: drvn out* 2/1[1]

341- 2 3 3/4 **Fairwood Massini (IRE)**[17] 1161 8-11-6 107............(vt) MichaelByrne(3) 116
(Tim Vaughan) *led: rdn bef 2 out: hdd appr last: kpt on same pce run-in* 3/1[2]

541- 3 22 **Tantamount**[18] 1145 4-10-11 104....................................... CraigNichol(7) 91
(Lucinda Russell) *hld up last: slipped bnd bef 6th: hit 4 out: nt fluent next: rdn and outpcd by first two bef 2 out* 6/1[3]

4 1 1/2 **Dick Dundee**[27] 1065 8-11-11 109.......................................(b[1]) DenisO'Regan 95
(Paul Nolan, Ire) *cl up: rdn and ev ch after 3 out: wknd appr next* 7/1

/22- 5 54 **Je T'Aime (IRE)**[31] 1007 4-10-4 90..................................... HenryBrooke 20
(Donald McCain) *t.k.h: cl up: rdn after 4 out: wknd bef next: t.o* 13/2

630- 6 4 **Tim's Approach (IRE)**[18] 1145 8-9-11 84 oh19............... JohnKington(3) 12
(William Young Jnr) *hld up in tch: drvn along 6th: wknd bef next: t.o* 100/1

P- P **Dry Rein (IRE)**[35] 990 8-9-12 89................................... GrantCockburn(7)
(B Arthey, Ire) *cl up: rdn and outpcd 4 out: sn btn: t.o whn p.u bef 2 out* 66/1

564/ P **Wayne Manor (IRE)**[130] 5227 4-10-12 98....................... PeterBuchanan
(Lucinda Russell) *hld up in tch: struggling 3 out: t.o whn p.u bef next* 7/1

4m 46.6s (-15.40) **Going Correction** -0.875s/f (Firm)
WFA 4 from 7yo+ 14lb 8 Ran SP% **113.4**
Speed ratings (Par 105): **94,92,84,83,63 61, ,**
toteswingers 1&2 £8.90, 1&3 £6.10, 2&3 £3.40 CSF £8.59 CT £28.81 TOTE £3.40: £1.50, £1.20, £2.40; EX 10.40 Trifecta £39.40 Pool: £518.40 - 9.85 winning units..
Owner Ms Annie Flora Joan Bowles **Bred** J F C Maxwell **Trained** Trim, Co Meath

FOCUS
Home bend common and hurdlers used chase bend. A moderate novice handicap with a step up from the winner and the second rated to his recent C&D win.

1287 SPECIAL PIPING MATERIALS (SCOTLAND) LTD NOVICES' H'CAP CHASE (15 fncs) 2m 4f 110y
3:35 (3:35) (Class 4) (0-115,110) 4-Y-0+ **£6,498** (£1,908; £954; £477)

Form RPR
024- 1 **Diddley Dee**[18] 1147 9-10-9 93.. WilsonRenwick 101+
(Lucy Normile) *hld up: rdn and outpcd 7th: mstke 9th: rallied to chse ldr bef 3 out: led next: styd on wl fr last* 7/2[3]

6P3- 2 3 1/2 **Merry Minster**[17] 1160 6-10-0 84....................................... LucyAlexander 87
(James Walton) *hld up: hdwy bef 10th: mstke next: sn rdn: rallied bef 3 out: chsd wnr run-in: kpt on: no imp* 7/1

/12- 3 6 **Lord Of Drums (IRE)**[18] 1147 7-11-6 104...................... PeterBuchanan 105
(Lucinda Russell) *led: mstke and hdd 8th (water): rallied to ld 10th: rdn 3 out: hdd next: outpcd fr last* 9/4[2]

454- 4 dist **George Woolf**[16] 1176 5-11-7 108.................................(vt) MichaelByrne(3)
(Tim Vaughan) *nt fluent on occasions: pressed ldr: lft in ld 8th (water): hdd 10th: rdn and wknd fr 3 out: t.o* 15/2

334- P **Dj Milan (IRE)**[18] 1146 7-11-12 110..................................(t) JasonMaguire
(Donald McCain) *chsd ldrs: rn wd bnd bef 9th: sn pushed along: wknd qckly 5 out: t.o whn p.u bef 3 out* 2/1[1]

4m 59.4s (-5.60) **Going Correction** -0.275s/f (Good) 5 Ran SP% **110.6**
Speed ratings (Par 105): **99,97,95, ,**
CSF £24.24 TOTE £4.70: £2.00, £3.20; EX 26.20 Trifecta £71.50 Pool: £313.10 - 3.28 winning units..
Owner The Fiddlers **Bred** Shaun Moore **Trained** Duncrievie, Perth & Kinross

FOCUS
An ordinary novice handicap rated around the placed horses.

1288 FONAB CASTLE HOTEL NOVICES' HURDLE (8 hdls) 2m 110y
4:10 (4:10) (Class 4) 4-Y-0+ **£3,898** (£1,144; £572; £286)

Form RPR
/1- 1 **Bayan (IRE)**[15] 865 4-11-11 126..................................(tp) JasonMaguire 129
(Gordon Elliott, Ire) *chsd ldr: hdwy to ld between last 2: rdn out run-in* 4/9[1]

2 4 1/2 **Butney Rock**[16] 1179 6-10-12 0.. DenisO'Regan 112
(C A McBratney, Ire) *led: rdn bef 2 out: hdd between last 2: kpt on same pce run-in* 5/2[2]

/ 3 25 **Zambezi Tiger (IRE)**[29] 1031 4-10-11 0......................(t[1]) JamesReveley 85
(Patrick Griffin, Ire) *hld up in tch: stdy hdwy 4 out: rdn and wknd after next* 20/1

020/ 4 21 **High On A Hill (IRE)**[19] 4452 6-10-12 0......................... WilsonRenwick 65
(Iain Jardine) *hld up: struggling after 4 out: wknd fr next* 14/1[3]

P **Jack Kane**[1464] 6-10-5 0 MrRWilson(7)
(Josie Ross) *plld hrd: nt fluent: chsd ldrs to 4th: sn lost tch: t.o whn p.u bef 2 out* **50/1**

3m 42.4s (-15.60) **Going Correction** -0.875s/f (Firm) 5 Ran SP% **111.2**
Speed ratings (Par 105): **101,98,87,77,**
CSF £1.99 TOTE £1.60: £1.10, £1.50; EX 1.90 Trifecta £4.20 Pool: £480.49 - 83.83 winning units..
Owner Core Syndicate **Bred** Floors Farming **Trained** Trim, Co Meath

FOCUS
An uncompetitive novice event and straightforward form, rated through the runner-up.

1289 CPS - PART OF THE GLOBAL ENERGY GROUP H'CAP HURDLE (10 hdls) 2m 4f 110y
4:40 (4:40) (Class 3) (0-125,122) 4-Y-0+ **£6,498** (£1,908; £954; £477)

Form RPR
0/3- 1 **Toye Native (IRE)**[18] 1148 5-11-12 **122** DenisO'Regan 128+
(C A McBratney, Ire) *trckd ldrs: poised to chal 2 out: led and drifted lft bef last: kpt on wl towards fin* **3/1**[2]

232- 2 ½ **Bright Abbey**[13] 1203 5-11-8 **118** LucyAlexander 121
(Dianne Sayer) *t.k.h: prom: rdn and outpcd bef 2 out: rallied to press wnr last: blkd run-in: hld nr fin* **5/1**[3]

0/0- 3 5 **The Tracey Shuffle**[58] 780 7-11-10 **120** TomScudamore 119
(David Pipe) *nt fluent on occasions: mde most to bef last: outpcd run-in* **5/2**[1]

260/ 4 ¾ **Los Nadis (GER)**[114] 5525 9-11-12 **122** HenryBrooke 120
(Jim Goldie) *chsd ldr: ev ch 3 out: outpcd next: no imp fr last* **12/1**

/32- 5 2 **Waltz Darling (IRE)**[17] 1158 5-11-3 **113** JamesReveley 109
(Keith Reveley) *t.k.h: hld up: hit and rdn 3 out: no imp fr next* **10/1**

0P1- S **Parson's Punch**[34] 961 8-10-4 **107** (p) GrantCockburn(7)
(Lucy Normile) *s.v.s: hdwy and prom after 2nd: slipped bdly bnd bef 4 out: fatally injured* **5/1**[3]

/45- S **Bescot Springs (IRE)**[64] 733 8-10 12 **115** GrahamWatters(7)
(Lucinda Russell) *hld up in tch: slipped and fell bnd bef 4 out* **8/1**

4m 51.0s (-11.00) **Going Correction** -0.875s/f (Firm) 7 Ran SP% **114.8**
Speed ratings (Par 107): **85,84,82,82,81 ,**
toteswingers 1&2 £4.10, 1&3 £2.30, 2&3 £1.20 CSF £18.59 TOTE £4.20: £1.80, £2.20; EX 15.10 Trifecta £26.50 Pool: £950.92 - 26.85 winning units..
Owner T I Lindsay **Bred** Terence Donnelly **Trained** Crossgar, Co. Down
■ Stewards' Enquiry : Graham Watters three-day ban: careless riding (Aug 31,Sep 1,4)

FOCUS
The rain arrived before this modest handicap and it proved dramatic with two slipping up. The runner-up sets the level.

1290 STV APPEAL SUMMER CHAMPION HURDLE (A LIMITED H'CAP HURDLE RACE) (FOR THE GOVERNORS CUP) (8 hdls) 2m 110y
5:15 (5:23) (Class 2) 4-Y-0+
£15,640 (£4,620; £2,310; £1,155; £577; £290)

Form RPR
111- 1 **Sea Lord (IRE)**[28] 1046 6-11-10 **146** DenisO'Regan 149+
(John Ferguson) *trckd ldrs: wnt 2nd 4 out: led bef 2 out: sn rdn: kpt on strly fr last* **15/8**[1]

/0U- 2 1½ **Now This Is It (IRE)**[69] 677 9-10-10 **135** MrSCrawford(3) 134
(S R B Crawford, Ire) *cl up: led 3rd: rdn and hdd bef 2 out: rallied: kpt on fr last* **8/1**

004/ 3 1¼ **Shadow Catcher**[16] 1180 5-11-2 **138** (b) WilsonRenwick 136
(Gordon Elliott, Ire) *hld up in tch: stdy hdwy bef 3 out: rdn bef next: edgd rt and kpt on same pce fr last* **9/2**[3]

/61- 4 31 **Outrageous Request**[18] 1148 7-9-11 **126** oh7 CraigNichol(7) 93
(Lucinda Russell) *hld up: hit and outpcd 4 out: effrt u.p after next: wknd bef 2 out* **8/1**

121- 5 30 **Aazif (IRE)**[25] 1082 4-10-6 **129** (t) JasonMaguire 65
(Donald McCain) *chsd ldrs: rdn and wkng whn blnd bdly 2 out: t.o* **11/4**[2]

140/ 6 1¼ **Hawkhill (IRE)**[246] 3045 7-10-8 **133** (t) MichaelByrne(3) 69
(Tim Vaughan) *led to 3rd: chsd ldr to 4 out: wknd next: t.o* **12/1**

3m 38.3s (-19.70) **Going Correction** -0.875s/f (Firm)
WFA 4 from 5yo+ 13lb 6 Ran SP% **109.5**
Speed ratings (Par 109): **111,110,109,95,81 80**
toteswingers 1&2 £6.60, 1&3 £2.40, 2&3 £2.20 CSF £15.54 TOTE £2.10: £1.30, £3.90; EX 12.10 Trifecta £34.10 Pool: £1,490.62 - 32.71 winning units..
Owner Bloomfields **Bred** Darley **Trained** Cowlinge, Suffolk

FOCUS
A decent handicap for the time of year. The placed horses set the level and the form looks solid.

1291 PIPE AND PILING SUPPLIES H'CAP CHASE (15 fncs) 2m 4f 110y
5:50 (5:50) (Class 3) (0-125,123) 4-Y-0+ **£9,097** (£2,671; £1,335; £667)

Form RPR
114- 1 **Sergeant Pink (IRE)**[12] 1162 7-11-1 **112** LucyAlexander 125
(Dianne Sayer) *t.k.h early: in tch: outpcd bef 10th: rallied whn nt fluent next: led 4 out: rdn and styd on wl fr last* **14/1**

/11- 2 2½ **Scotch Warrior**[17] 1162 9-11-4 **122** CallumBewley(7) 132
(R Mike Smith) *hdwy to chse ldrs 3rd: lost pl 9th: rallied and ev ch 4 out: sn chsng wnr: lost 2nd 2 out: rallied to regain 2nd run-in: nt rch wnr* **11/4**[1]

/32- 3 2¼ **Quito Du Tresor (FR)**[18] 1146 9-11-5 **123** (p) GrahamWatters(7) 132
(Lucinda Russell) *trckd ldrs: effrt bef 3 out: wnt 2nd next: hit last: one pce and lost 2nd run-in* **7/2**[2]

4/2- 4 5 **Acapulco Gold (IRE)**[27] 1070 6-11-6 **117** (tp) DenisO'Regan 120
(Paul Nolan, Ire) *hld up in tch: pushed along 9th: stdy hdwy after next: blkd bnd bef 4 out: sn rdn: one pce fr 3 out* **5/1**

/33- 5 41 **Be My Deputy (IRE)**[18] 1142 8-11-8 **119** (b) PeterBuchanan 81
(Lucinda Russell) *cl up: led 10th to 4 out: rdn and wknd bef next: t.o* **8/1**

411- P **Strobe**[34] 960 9-10-7 **104** (p) WilsonRenwick
(Lucy Normile) *led to 10th: hit next: outpcd whn hmpd bnd bef 4 out: sn struggling: lost tch and p.u next* **8/1**

361- P **Valleyofmilan (IRE)**[26] 1074 6-11-5 **116** JasonMaguire
(Donald McCain) *chsd ldrs: lost pl bef 5th: outpcd whn slipped bnd bef 9th: sn lost tch: t.o whn p.u 4 out* **4/1**[3]

4m 55.5s (-9.50) **Going Correction** -0.275s/f (Good) 7 Ran SP% **114.4**
Speed ratings (Par 107): **107,106,105,103,87 ,**
toteswingers 1&2 not won, 1&3 £7.10, 2&3 £3.30 CSF £53.92 TOTE £11.30: £4.40, £2.40; EX 72.80 Trifecta £74.80 Pool: £560.44 - 5.61 winning units..
Owner Andrew Sayer **Bred** Ring Pink Partnership **Trained** Hackthorpe, Cumbria

FOCUS
Not a bad handicap rated around the first three.

1292 THANK YOU FOR SUPPORTING THE STV APPEAL STANDARD OPEN NATIONAL HUNT FLAT RACE 2m 110y
6:20 (6:21) (Class 5) 4-6-Y-0 **£2,053** (£598; £299)

Form RPR
56/ 1 **Bellgrove (IRE)**[118] 5429 5-11-1 0 DenisO'Regan 98
(Ian Semple) *t.k.h: cl up: led 1/2-way: rdn and edgd both ways over 1f out: hld on wl fnl f* **9/1**

2 ¾ **This Thyne Jude** 5-10-8 0 PeterBuchanan 90
(Lucinda Russell) *hld up: stdy hdwy 4f out: effrt and chsd wnr over 1f out: kpt on fnl f: hld nr fin* **13/2**[3]

3 17 **Donna's Pride** 4-10-7 0 JamesReveley 72
(Keith Reveley) *hld up: stdy hdwy to chse wnr over 4f out: rdn: hung rt and wknd wl over 1f out* **6/4**[1]

4 nse **Eurourmrlucky (IRE)**[139] 6-11-1 0 JasonMaguire 80
(Gordon Elliott, Ire) *led to 1/2-way: sn pushed along: bdly outpcd wl over 3f out: sme late hdwy: no imp* **2/1**[2]

4- 5 4 **Dalstontosiloth (IRE)**[34] 962 5-11-1 0 LucyAlexander 76
(Barry Murtagh) *trckd ldrs: rdn and outpcd wl over 3f out: sn btn* **8/1**

6 4½ **Tillernoora (IRE)**[90] 6-10-1 0 (t) GrantCockburn(7) 65
(Patrick Griffin, Ire) *hld up in tch: drvn and struggling over 4f out: btn fnl 2f* **25/1**

3m 41.4s (-11.00) **Going Correction** -0.875s/f (Firm)
WFA 4 from 5yo+ 1lb 6 Ran SP% **111.6**
Speed ratings: **90,89,81,81,79 77**
toteswingers 1&2 £3.60, 1&3 not won, 2&3 £1.90 CSF £62.08 TOTE £10.00: £5.00, £2.00; EX 68.80 Trifecta £123.90 Pool: £464.96 - 2.81 winning units..
Owner M Sawers **Bred** Tim Nolan Jnr **Trained** Carluke, S Lanarks

FOCUS
An ordinary bumper but a step up from the winner.
T/Plt: £173.00 to a £1 stake. Pool: £34,184.27 - 144.17 winning units T/Qpdt: £8.40 to a £1 stake. Pool: £1,754.00 - 153.95 winning units RY

1293 - 1299a (Foreign Racing) - See Raceform Interactive

1088 SOUTHWELL (L-H)
Sunday, August 18

OFFICIAL GOING: Good (7.4)
Wind: moderate 1/2 behind Weather: fine but breezy

1300 FLYING HIRE H'CAP CHASE (19 fncs) 3m 110y
2:00 (2:00) (Class 5) (0-95,92) 4-Y-0+ **£2,144** (£629; £314; £157)

Form RPR
U6P/ 1 **Robobar (FR)**[113] 8-11-11 **91** (v[1]) APMcCoy 108+
(Jim Best) *w ldr: led 8th: mstke 15th: hrd drvn next: styd on fr 3 out: fin tired* **9/4**[1]

045- 2 8 **Farmer Frank**[14] 1202 10-10-6 **79** PaulNO'Brien(7) 89
(Nick Kent) *hld up in rr: stdy hdwy 12th: chsd wnr sn after 4 out: chal next: wknd 2 out* **12/1**

542- 3 20 **Solway Dornal**[18] 1163 8-10-0 **73** (tp) StephenMulqueen(7) 63
(Lisa Harrison) *chsd ldrs: 2nd 15th: wknd 3 out* **12/1**

026- 4 30 **Cloudy Dawn**[29] 1038 8-10-3 **74** JonathanEngland(5) 37
(Sue Smith) *mstkes: chsd ldrs: reinders 5th: blnd 3rd: lost pl 11th: bhd fr 13th: t.o 4 out* **5/1**[2]

01P- P **Sycho Fred (IRE)**[14] 1202 12-11-0 **80** (tp) DenisO'Regan
(Mike Sowersby) *in rr: reminders 6th: bhd 9th: t.o whn p.u after 12th* **20/1**

2P2/ P **Allterrain (IRE)**[713] 1609 10-10-1 **67** (b) JamieMoore
(Gary Moore) *j.lft: led to 8th: lost pl after 14th: t.o 4 out: sn p.u* **6/1**[3]

6/3- P **Pistol Basc (FR)**[18] 1163 9-10-13 **79** SamTwiston-Davies
(Ferdy Murphy, France) *stdd s: t.k.h in rr: sme hdwy 13th: wknd 15th: sn bhd: t.o 3 out: p.u bef last* **17/2**

016- P **In The Haven (IRE)**[27] 1075 10-11-7 **92** (p) SamanthaDrake(5)
(Joanne Foster) *j.rt: mid-div: lost pl 9th: t.o whn p.u after 12th* **50/1**

0/3- F **Bobbisox (IRE)**[58] 786 8-11-0 **85** KillianMoore(5)
(Alex Hales) *j.rt: in rr: fell 6th* **11/1**

1/0- P **Hobb's Dream (IRE)**[59] 778 9-11-3 **86** (p) MichaelByrne(3)
(Neil Mulholland) *in rr: bhd fr 6th: t.o 13th: p.u bef 15th* **25/1**

6P5- P **Marico (FR)**[19] 1150 5-10-10 **76** (p) FelixDeGiles
(Tom Symonds) *j.rt: chsd ldrs 5th: wkng whn mstke 9th: bhd 15th: t.o whn p.u bef 3 out* **10/1**

6m 26.4s (3.40) **Going Correction** -0.075s/f (Good) 11 Ran SP% **115.6**
Speed ratings (Par 103): **91,88,82,72, , , , ,**
Tote Swingers: 1&2 £6.70, 1&3 £6.40, 2&3 £14.70 CSF £28.08 CT £268.75 TOTE £3.30: £1.60, £2.90, £3.60; EX 23.00 Trifecta £505.40 Pool: £991.55 - 1.47 winning units..
Owner Mark Callow & Mark Goldstein **Bred** Y Madiot, L Madiot, E Madiot, S Madiot **Trained** Lewes, E Sussex

FOCUS
Both bends in centre on fresh ground and fences 5yds off outside rail. A drying day and the ground looked on the quick side of good in the opener. This was a weak staying handicap and the majority were in trouble before the fourth-last. The first two look caspable of winning similar races.

1301 TURNBULL HOME IMPROVEMENT NOVICES' CHASE (13 fncs) 2m
2:30 (2:30) (Class 4) 4-Y-0+ **£3,768** (£1,106; £553; £276)

Form RPR
212- 1 **Engai (GER)**[29] 1048 7-11-0 0 TomScudamore 112+
(David Bridgwater) *w ldrs: led 5th: jnd 4 out: wnt clr between last 2: easily* **2/1**[2]

140- 2 6 **Baccalaureate (FR)**[29] 1046 7-10-9 0 JonathanEngland(5) 101
(Sue Smith) *trckd ldrs: 2nd 6th: upsides 4 out: sn rdn: one pce appr 2 out* **8/15**[1]

0/6- 3 34 **Nouailhas**[20] 1137 7-11-0 0 PaulMoloney 70
(Andrew Hollinshead) *led: j. slowly and hdd 5th: outpcd 7th: wnt poor 3rd sn after 4 out* **20/1**

0/P- 4 4½ **Billy Teal**[79] 565 8-11-0 0 (p) CharliePoste 66
(C I Ratcliffe) *outpcd and last 6th: mstke 9th: wnt poor 4th sn after 4 out* **50/1**

POP/ P **Sharadiyn**[121] 5386 10-11-0 0 AndrewThornton
(Clive Mulhall) *w ldrs: led 4th: hdd next: outpcd 7th: mstke 8th: wknd qckly 4 out: t.o whn p.u bef next: b.b.v* **14/1**[3]

4m 6.0s (4.00) **Going Correction** -0.075s/f (Good) 5 Ran SP% **112.0**
Speed ratings (Par 105): **87,84,67,64,**
CSF £3.71 TOTE £2.80: £1.70, £1.10; EX 4.00 Trifecta £9.00 Pool: £1,504.97 - 124.47 winning units..
Owner Building Bridgies **Bred** Gestut Park Wiedingen **Trained** Icomb, Gloucs

The Form Book Jumps, Raceform Ltd, Compton, RG20 6NL.

FOCUS
None of these had previously tackled a fence on the track. It was a novice chase that was a virtual match according to the market after the non-runner and so it played out on the back straight. The winner is rated to the best of his hurdles form and can do better over fences.

1302 AMBITIONS PERSONNEL H'CAP CHASE (16 fncs) 2m 4f 110y
3:00 (3:00) (Class 2) 4-Y-0+ **£14,620** (£4,293; £2,146; £1,073)

Form RPR

2/5- **1** **Wiesentraum (GER)**[14] 1204 7-10-7 **125**........................ LeightonAspell 130+
(Lucy Wadham) *chsd ldrs: wnt cl 2nd 3 out: led narrowly last: styd on wl* **3/1**[2]

013- **2** *1* **Finger Onthe Pulse (IRE)**[29] 1047 12-10-13 **131**................(t) APMcCoy 135
(Jonjo O'Neill) *chsd ldr: drvn to ld sn after 4 out: hdd narrowly last: styd on same pce* **3/1**[2]

341- **3** *nk* **Henry San (IRE)**[15] 1197 6-10-3 **121**......................(v[1]) WayneHutchinson 125
(Alan King) *chsd ldrs: outpcd 10th: styd on to take handy 3rd 3 out: kpt on same pce run-in* **7/1**

/12- **4** *18* **Billie Magern**[58] 787 9-11-12 **144**..........................(v) SamTwiston-Davies 134
(Nigel Twiston-Davies) *led: j.rt: hdd sn after 4 out: wknd next: modest 4th whn hit 2 out* **5/1**[3]

511- **5** *nk* **Dark Energy**[14] 1204 9-10-6 **124**..(t) AlainCawley 112
(Fergal O'Brien) *detached in last: j.rt: drvn and outpcd whn hit 10th: kpt on fr 2 out: tk modest 4th nr fin* **11/1**

622- **6** *3/4* **Skint**[15] 1194 7-10-6 **127**..(p) MichaelByrne(3) 115
(Ali Brewer) *chsd ldrs: drvn 4 out: wknd next: modest 4th whn blnd 2 out* **11/4**[1]

5m 9.6s (-7.40) **Going Correction** -0.075s/f (Good) **6** Ran SP% **114.2**
Speed ratings (Par 109): **111,110,110,103,103 103**
Tote Swingers: 1&2 £2.20, 1&3 £4.60, 2&3 £5.00 CSF £13.05 TOTE £4.40: £2.40, £1.50; EX 18.80 Trifecta £79.20 Pool: £1,434.98 - 13.57 winning units..
Owner G Pascoe & S Brewer **Bred** Gestut Elsetal **Trained** Newmarket, Suffolk

FOCUS
A fair and competitive little handicap. They went a solid gallop thanks to Billie Magern, who paid the price on leaving the back straight. The first three are rated pretty much to their marks.

1303 CMC SUNSHINE BEGINNERS' CHASE (19 fncs) 3m 110y
3:30 (3:30) (Class 4) 5-Y-0+ **£3,768** (£1,106; £553; £276)

Form RPR

4P6/ **1** **According To Trev (IRE)**[122] 5362 7-11-0 0........(t) SamTwiston-Davies 125+
(Nigel Twiston-Davies) *led to 2nd: chsd ldr: led 4 out: sn hrd drvn: forging away whn lft wl clr 2 out: heavily eased run-in* **2/7**[1]

/34- **2** *26* **Neverownup (IRE)**[19] 1153 8-10-9 0............................(t) MattCrawley(5) 99
(K F Clutterbuck) *w ldrs: led 3rd: clr 5th tl after 12th: hdd 4 out: wknd next: lft 16 l 2nd 2 out* **18/1**

202- **3** *5* **High Ron**[23] 1119 8-11-0 110............................... AndrewThornton 95
(Caroline Bailey) *led 2nd: hdd next: outpcd 5th: drvn 9th: hit 11th and reminders: rallied to chse ldrs 14th: wknd 4 out: lft poor 3rd 2 out* **11/2**[2]

0- **4** *58* **Checkmate**[20] 1133 8-11-0 0... MarkGrant 42
(Christopher Kellett) *chsd ldrs: j.lft 4th: outpcd 6th: rallied to chse ldrs 13th: wknd 4 out: sn bhd: t.o whn lft distant 4th 2 out* **100/1**

5P- **5** *5* **Thehorsemaytalk (IRE)**[41] 921 8-11-0 0......................... JamesDavies 37
(Mark Shears) *sn drvn along: lost pl 5th: sn bhd: t.o 13th* **66/1**

4PF/ **F** **Roving Lad (IRE)**[12] 1225 6-11-0 113.................................(t) TomO'Brien 121
(Paul John Gilligan, Ire) *hld up: hit 8th: hdwy to chse ldrs 12th: wnt cl 2nd bef 3 out: rdn and 3 l down and hld whn fell 2 out* **6/1**[3]

6m 24.1s (1.10) **Going Correction** -0.075s/f (Good) **6** Ran SP% **115.2**
Speed ratings: **95,86,85,66,64**
Tote Swingers: 1&2 £3.00, 2&3 £1.80 CSF £7.70 TOTE £1.30: £1.02, £5.40; EX 6.80 Trifecta £22.70 Pool: £1,419.96 - 46.81 winning units..
Owner F J Mills & W Mills **Bred** Sean Harrington **Trained** Naunton, Gloucs

FOCUS
An easy win for the red-hot favourite. The runner-up and faller set the level.

1304 ADVERTISER NEWSPAPERS H'CAP HURDLE (THE SUNDAY £5K BONUS RACE) (13 hdls) 3m 110y
4:05 (4:05) (Class 3) (0-140,126) 4-Y-0+ **£5,393** (£1,583; £791; £395)

Form RPR

225- **1** **Pure Faith (IRE)**[15] 1195 9-11-12 **126**................................(t) TomO'Brien 135+
(Peter Bowen) *chsd ldrs: cl 2nd 9th: led appr 2 out: forged 12 l clr last: eased towards fin* **3/1**[2]

312- **2** *17* **High Ville (IRE)**[32] 1011 7-11-11 **125**.............................. ConorO'Farrell 119
(David Pipe) *t.k.h: led: clr 2nd tl appr 9th: hdd appr 2 out: one pce* **7/1**[3]

P/1- **3** *5* **American Legend (IRE)**[34] 998 5-10-11 **111**.....................(v) APMcCoy 100
(Jonjo O'Neill) *in rr: hdwy 6th: reminders 8th: 3rd and hrd drvn 10th: one pce fr next* **7/4**[1]

4/0- **4** *2 1/2* **Ixora (IRE)**[78] 587 7-11-5 **124**.. GavinSheehan(5) 111
(Jamie Snowden) *in rr: drvn 7th: outpcd 9th: kpt on and distant 4th appr 2 out: nvr on terms* **14/1**

102- **5** *5* **Leath Acra Mor (IRE)**[20] 1045 7-11-7 **121**........................... WillKennedy 103
(Ian Williams) *chsd ldrs: 5th and wkng whn hit 3 out* **10/1**

0/0- **6** *64* **Dartford Warbler (IRE)**[29] 1042 6-10-8 **113**........... JonathanEngland(5) 38
(Sue Smith) *hit 4th and reminders: rallied and chsd ldrs 9th: lost pl 3 out: sn bhd: t.o next: eventually completed* **15/2**

413- **P** **Solway Bay**[18] 1164 11-9-10 **103**.........................(tp) StephenMulqueen(7)
(Lisa Harrison) *in rr: drvn 6th: bhd fr 9th: t.o whn p.u bef 2 out* **16/1**

42/ **P** **Aimigayle**[456] 353 10-11-1 **115**.. ColinBolger
(Suzy Smith) *chsd ldr: wknd 9th: bhd 3 out: t.o whn p.u bef next* **8/1**

6m 5.1s (-9.90) **Going Correction** -0.325s/f (Good) **8** Ran SP% **118.4**
Speed ratings (Par 107): **102,96,94,94,92 72, ,**
Tote Swingers: 1&2 £1.70, 1&3 £4.30, 2&3 £4.90 CSF £25.20 CT £47.42 TOTE £4.10: £1.30, £2.30, £1.50; EX 30.00 Trifecta £88.20 Pool: £1,750.02 - 14.86 winning units..
Owner P Bowling, S Scott & Mrs K Bowen **Bred** P J Carmody **Trained** Little Newcastle, Pembrokes

FOCUS
Not a bad handicap. The second is rated to the level of his most recent run but the race could go higher.

1305 A & V SQUIRES PLANT MARES' NOVICES' HURDLE (9 hdls) 2m
4:35 (4:37) (Class 4) 4-Y-0+ **£3,119** (£915; £457; £228)

Form RPR

122- **1** **Bittersweetheart**[20] 1132 6-11-3 108........................ TomScudamore 107+
(David Bridgwater) *mid-div: hdwy to trck ldrs 4th: 2nd 6th: led appr 2 out: 4 l ahd whn hit last: drvn rt out* **1/2**[1]

0/3- **2** *2 1/2* **Duchess Theatre (IRE)**[16] 1187 5-10-7 0....................(t) JakeGreenall(3) 95
(Michael Easterby) *hld up in rr: hdwy 4th: trckd ldrs 6th: 2nd appr 2 out: kpt on same pce run-in* **6/1**[3]

0/3- **3** *7* **Hopeand**[26] 1090 8-10-10 81.......................................(t) AdamPogson 89
(Charles Pogson) *mid-div: chsd ldrs 4th: drvn 3 out: 4th sn after 2 out: kpt on one pce* **10/1**

4 *3 1/4* **Exclusive Dancer**[99] 4-10-9 0.. BarryKeniry 85
(George Moore) *mid-div: chsd ldrs 4th: one pce fr 3 out: tk 4th between last 2* **16/1**

006/ **5** *10* **Recway Lass**[112] 1 5-10-10 0..................................(tp) DenisO'Regan 77
(Des Donovan) *led: hdd appr 2 out: wknd qckly between last 2* **40/1**

0/5- **6** *3 1/2* **Pagham Belle**[32] 1017 5-10-7 0...(t) MarkQuinlan(3) 74
(Nigel Hawke) *in rr: distant 7th 3 out* **50/1**

35- **7** *25* **Scarlet Whispers**[17] 1176 4-10-9 0.....................................(p) SeanQuinlan 50
(Pam Sly) *chsd ldrs: mstke 5th: rdn next: lost pl 3 out: sn bhd: t.o* **7/2**[2]

6- **8** *7* **Spanish Trail**[20] 1132 4-10-9 0.. MarkGrant 44
(Christopher Kellett) *rr-div: bhd fr 5th: t.o bef 2 out* **100/1**

/0P- **9** *4 1/2* **Scommettitrice (IRE)**[20] 1132 5-10-10 0..........................(t) TomCannon 41
(Mark Gillard) *rr-div: bhd fr 3 out: sn t.o* **50/1**

P- **10** *51* **Flamin June**[26] 1090 7-10-7 0.. AdamWedge(3)
(Kevin Morgan) *s.s: reluctant and reminders after 2nd: t.o 4th: eventually completed* **50/1**

11 *2* **Dapper's Dancer**[760] 4-10-2 0.. JohnDawson(7)
(Chris Grant) *in rr: bhd fr 5th: t.o 3 out: blnd last: eased: virtually p.u* **100/1**

0- **P** **American Kiss (SWE)**[3] 46 4-10-9 0.................................. CharliePoste
(Robin Dickin) *t.k.h: trckd ldrs: lost pl 5th: bhd whn p.u bef 3 out* **66/1**

3m 53.4s (-3.60) **Going Correction** -0.325s/f (Good)
WFA 4 from 5yo+ 13lb **12** Ran SP% **129.9**
Speed ratings (Par 105): **96,94,91,89,84 82,70,66,64,39 38,**
Tote Swingers: 1&2 £2.00, 1&3 £2.50, 2&3 £6.60 CSF £5.18 TOTE £1.70: £1.02, £1.90, £2.90; EX 5.80 Trifecta £17.60 Pool: £3,521.32 - 149.44 winning units..
Owner The Ferandlin Peaches **Bred** Silvano Scanu **Trained** Icomb, Gloucs

FOCUS
An ordinary mares' novice hurdle rated around the first three.

1306 COOPERS MARQUEES H'CAP HURDLE (11 hdls) 2m 4f 110y
5:05 (5:05) (Class 4) (0-105,104) 4-Y-0+ **£3,119** (£915; £457; £228)

Form RPR

1- **1** **Harangue (IRE)**[5] 1266 5-11-2 **94** 7ex.................................... APMcCoy 109+
(Paul John Gilligan, Ire) *hld up in rr: hdwy 6th: trcking ldrs next: led appr 2 out: styd on wl run-in: cosily* **11/8**[1]

/02- **2** *1* **Burns Night**[72] 661 7-9-12 **83**.. AdamNicol(7) 93
(Philip Kirby) *hld up in rr: hdwy 8th: trcking ldrs next: 2nd 2 out: 1 l down and drvn last: styd on same pce* **5/2**[2]

2P3- **3** *15* **Run Along Boy**[19] 1153 8-11-9 **101**..(p) NoelFehily 99
(Neil Mulholland) *in rr: hdwy to chse ldrs 5th: drvn 3 out: one pce fr next: modest 3rd last* **10/1**[3]

4/5- **4** *3 1/2* **Riddlestown (IRE)**[28] 1061 6-11-5 **104**....................... MissBAndrews(7) 97
(Caroline Fryer) *in rr: hdwy to chse ldrs 5th: 3rd 2 out: 4th and wkng whn mstke last* **25/1**

/05- **5** *7* **Snow Alert**[49] 852 7-10-0 **85**....................................... StephenMulqueen(7) 72
(John Norton) *in rr: hdwy 8th: chsng ldrs next: wknd appr 2 out* **33/1**

3/3- **6** *1 1/4* **Kingaroo (IRE)**[20] 1137 7-10-0 **78**.. JamieMoore 64
(Garry Woodward) *mid-div: drvn to chse ldrs 3 out: lost pl appr 2 out* **12/1**

/30- **7** *16* **Keep The Cash (IRE)**[82] 517 5-11-9 **101**..................(p) TomScudamore 73
(David Pipe) *chsd ldr: led 7th: hdd appr 2 out: wknd between last 2: heavily eased run-in: virtually p.u* **12/1**

2P3- **8** *8* **Brother Scott**[27] 1078 6-11-0 **92**... RyanMania 56
(Sue Smith) *chsd ldrs: hit 3rd: wknd appr 2 out* **16/1**

00P- **9** *2* **Officially Modern (IRE)**[28] 1063 6-11-3 **102**............ ConorShoemark(7) 65
(Fergal O'Brien) *led: hdd 7th: lost pl 3 out: sn bhd* **33/1**

500/ **10** *59* **Hammer**[444] 516 8-9-10 **79**...(p) EDLinehan(5)
(Mike Sowersby) *prom: lost pl 7th: sn bhd: t.o 3 out: eventually completed* **40/1**

650/ **P** **Tara Warrior (IRE)**[524] 4820 7-11-7 **102**.......................(v) MichaelByrne(3)
(Tim Vaughan) *chsd ldrs: drvn 6th: lost pl bef next: sn bhd: t.o whn p.u after 3 out* **40/1**

/06- **P** **Geminus (IRE)**[35] 966 5-11-11 **103**..............................(vt) RichardJohnson
(Tim Vaughan) *chsd ldrs: drvn and reluctant 4th: sn lost pl: t.o whn p.u bef 6th* **10/1**[3]

5m 4.2s (-8.80) **Going Correction** -0.325s/f (Good) **12** Ran SP% **124.7**
Speed ratings (Par 105): **103,102,96,95,92 92,86,83,82,60 ,**
Tote Swingers: 1&2 £1.70, 1&3 £3.30, 2&3 £5.60 CSF £5.40 CT £25.30 TOTE £2.50: £1.20, £1.20, £3.10; EX 6.80 Trifecta £33.00 Pool: £2,438.92 - 55.41 winning units..
Owner Sean Conroy **Bred** Derrick Fisher **Trained** Athenry, Co Galway

FOCUS
This was not a bad handicap for the class, run at a routine gallop and the two clear market leaders dominated from two out. The winner is rated in line with the best of his Irish form backed up by the third.
T/Plt: £6.30 to a £1 stake. Pool: £83,533.73 - 9,628.03 winning tickets. T/Qpdt: £3.40 to a £1 stake. Pool: £5,392.73 - 1,173.18 winning tickets. WG

1307 - 1313a (Foreign Racing) - See Raceform Interactive

1262 WORCESTER (L-H)
Monday, August 19

OFFICIAL GOING: Good (good to soft in places; 6.5) changing to good after race 1 (1:45)
Wind: light, half behind Weather: light cloud, bight spells

1314 WORCESTER FESTIVAL H'CAP CHASE (15 fncs) 2m 4f
1:45 (1:45) (Class 5) (0-95,91) 4-Y-0+ **£2,144** (£629; £314; £157)

Form RPR

520- **1** **Crack At Dawn (IRE)**[18] 1172 12-11-2 **88**..................(v) MissAEStirling(7) 98
(Michael Gates) *in tch in rr: hdwy to chse ldrs after 5th: upsides ldr and drew clr 10th: led bef next: clr and idling fr 3 out: 2 l clr last: rdn mainly hands and heels flat: jnd towards fin: fnd enough to prevail on post* **16/1**

PU5/ **2** *nse* **Brousse En Feux (FR)**[251] 2986 10-11-12 **91**......(t) SamTwiston-Davies 99
(Nigel Twiston-Davies) *in tch in midfield: reminders after 5th and rdn along after: outpcd 9th: rallied and clsng on ldng pair bef 11th: chsd clr wnr bef 3 out: 2 l down last: str chal fnl 50yds: jst hld* **5/1**[2]

404- **3** *5* **Highland River**[17] 1186 7-11-5 **84**...(p) LeeEdwards 88
(Dave Roberts) *nt jump wl: dropped to rr and mstke 4th: rdn and lost tch after mstke 7th: poor 5th after 10th: styd on u.p fr 3 out: wnt 3rd last: nt rch ldrs* **10/1**

006- **4** *22* **Mac Beattie**[18] 1174 7-10-13 **81**....................(p) AdamWedge(3) 62
(Evan Williams) *t.k.h: led tl 3rd: styd upsides ldr tl led again 9th: wnt clr w wnr next: hdd bef next: drvn and struggling whn blnd 11th: wknd next* **5/1**[2]

/22- **5** *16* **Spice Hill (IRE)**[18] 1170 7-11-6 **85**....................(v) RichardJohnson 50
(Tim Vaughan) *chsd ldrs: led 3rd tl 9th: struggling next: wknd bef 11th: t.o fr 3 out* **11/8**[1]

0PP/ **P** **Pur De Sivola (FR)**[466] 185 10-11-12 **91**....................(t) GerardTumelty
(Nick Lampard) *racd wd: chsd ldrs tl j. slowly and lost pl 6th: struggling after next: t.o whn p.u 11th* **25/1**

P26/ **P** **Mr Goofy (IRE)**[347] 1502 12-11-7 **86**.................... TomScudamore
(Michael Scudamore) *chsd ldr tl 2nd: in tch in midfield after tl wknd 9th: t.o whn blnd bdly 3 out: p.u next* **6/1**[3]

4/0- **P** **Grand Fella (IRE)**[111] 43 8-10-0 **68** oh3 ow3............(t) RobertDunne(3)
(Ken Wingrove) *hld up in tch in rr: effrt u.p 8th: wknd after next: t.o whn p.u 11th* **100/1**

4m 47.3s (-12.70) **Going Correction** -1.025s/f (Hard) **8** Ran SP% **109.5**
Speed ratings (Par 103): **84,83,81,73,66 , ,**
Tote Swingers 1&2 £2.80, 2&3 £2.70, 1&3 £3.50 CSF £86.59 CT £786.22 TOTE £11.80: £2.20, £1.70, £3.20; EX 60.70 Trifecta £392.00 Pool: £1,139.03 - 2.17 winning tickets..
Owner Michael Gates **Bred** Austin Rice **Trained** Clifford Chambers, Warwicks

■ Stewards' Enquiry : Miss A E Stirling trainer said, regarding the apparent improvement of form, that the gelding was suited by the re-application of of a visor

FOCUS
Both bends moved out 3yds outside the line raced on August 13th with fresh ground in both straights. An eight-race card got underway with a moderate handicap chase in which they went an honest gallop on ground officially changed to plain good after this race. The winner is rated to his best backed up by the third.

1315 QUALITYSOLICITORS PARKINSON WRIGHT NOVICES' H'CAP CHASE (11 fncs 1 omitted) 2m 110y
2:15 (2:15) (Class 4) (0-110,110) 4-Y-0+ **£3,768** (£1,106; £553; £276)

Form RPR

454- **1** **Quarton (IRE)**[20] 1149 6-10-10 **97**....................(p) AdamWedge(3) 111+
(Evan Williams) *chsd ldrs: mstke 1st: lft chsng ldr 4th: clr w wnr after 8th: led bef 2 out: clr and in command last: styd on wl: readily* **11/2**[3]

532- **2** *10* **Callhimwhatyouwant (IRE)**[20] 1153 8-11-4 **102**(b) SamTwiston-Davies 108
(Dr Richard Newland) *t.k.h: w ldr tl led after 3rd: drew clr w wnr after 8th: rdn whn mstke and stmbld next: sn hdd: btn last: wknd flat* **9/4**[2]

6F3- **3** *2* **Crescent Beach (IRE)**[20] 1149 6-10-3 **87**....................(b) HenryOliver 89
(Henry Oliver) *in tch in rr: nt fluent 2nd: wnt 4th 5th: rdn bef 8th: outpcd and wl btn bef 9th (actual 3 out): no ch w wnr but plugged on u.p flat* **11/2**[3]

/33- **4** *26* **Featherintheattic (IRE)**[17] 1184 8-11-8 **106**....................(p) NoelFehily 94
(Warren Greatrex) *led tl after 3rd: blnd bdly and lost 2nd next: drvn and wknd wl bef 9th (actual 3 out): last and wl btn whn blnd 2 out: t.o* **6/4**[1]

/00- **P** **Rifle Shot (IRE)**[21] 1133 6-11-12 **110**.................... JasonMaguire
(Donald McCain) *chsd ldrs: mstke and dropped to last 5th: sn toiling and rdn w no rspnse after next: t.o whn p.u 9th (actual 3 out)* **22/1**

3m 54.75s (-19.25) **Going Correction** -1.025s/f (Hard) **5** Ran SP% **105.9**
Speed ratings (Par 105): **104,99,98,86,**
Tote Swinger 1&2 £2.80 CSF £17.11 TOTE £7.00: £2.80, £1.10; EX 17.10 Trifecta £42.00 Pool: £1,535.88 - 27.39 winning tickets..
Owner Tony Cromwell **Bred** Sean M Collins **Trained** Llancarfan, Vale Of Glamorgan

FOCUS
The second fence in the home straight was omitted. A modest novices' handicap chase in which they went a contested gallop. The placed horses are rated pretty much to their marks.

1316 WORCESTER-RACECOURSE.CO.UK NOVICES' H'CAP CHASE (16 fncs 2 omitted) 2m 7f
2:45 (2:45) (Class 3) (0-125,117) 4-Y-0 **£6,330** (£1,870; £935; £468; £234)

Form RPR

315- **1** **Adrenalin Flight (IRE)**[35] 996 7-11-2 **107**.................... AndrewThornton 112
(Seamus Mullins) *racd in last trio: clsd after 5th: rdn and effrt to chse ldrs bef 14th (actual 3 out): pressing ldr 2 out: drvn to ld fnl 100yds: hld on wl cl home* **15/2**

135- **2** *nk* **Full Of Joy (IRE)**[30] 1040 8-11-10 **115**....................(tp) APMcCoy 121
(Jonjo O'Neill) *mstkes: racd in last trio: clsd after 5th: rdn and hdwy to chse ldrs after 8th: chsd ldr 14th tl after next: drvn and cl 3rd whn mstke next: swtchd lft and ev ch fnl 100yds: nt qckn cl home* **6/1**

/P1- **3** *4* **Terfel's Toscar (IRE)**[19] 1163 8-10-13 **104**....................(t) RichardJohnson 106
(Tim Vaughan) *led and mainly j. boldly: rdn bef 14th (actual 3 out): hdd fnl 100yds: sn btn* **15/2**

/52- **4** *14* **Brough Academy (IRE)**[33] 1015 7-11-2 **107**....................(p) DavidBass 96
(Lawney Hill) *chsd ldr: mstke 7th: lost 2nd next: styd chsng ldrs tl wknd u.p 14th* **3/1**[1]

243- **5** *18* **Special Account (IRE)**[20] 1150 8-11-12 **117**.................... NickScholfield 86
(Jeremy Scott) *hld up in rr: clsd after 5th: chsd ldng trio and cl enought after 14th: rdn: edgd lft and btn bef 2 out: sn wknd* **4/1**[2]

4P2- **6** *43* **Western King (IRE)**[21] 1135 6-11-4 **109**....................(tp) NoelFehily 35
(Charlie Mann) *chsd ldrs: rdn after 12th: dropped to last 14th: sn lost tch: t.o bef 2 out* **9/2**[3]

24P- **P** **Palace Jester**[61] 766 8-11-7 **112**....................(vt[1]) TomScudamore
(David Pipe) *chsd ldrs: wnt 2nd 8th tl bef 14th: sn wknd: t.o whn p.u next (actual 3 out)* **17/2**

5m 37.6s (-10.40) **Going Correction** -1.025s/f (Hard) **7** Ran SP% **111.5**
Speed ratings (Par 107): **77,76,75,70,64 49,**
Tote Swingers 1&2 £6.70, 2&3 £12.20, 1&3 £1.30 CSF £47.76 CT £341.88 TOTE £7.60: £2.90, £1.80; EX 33.80 Trifecta £122.80 Pool: £1,453.11 - 8.87 winning tickets..
Owner Mark Adams **Bred** Alex Heskin **Trained** Wilsford-Cum-Lake, Wilts

FOCUS
The second fence in the home straight was omitted. A fair staying novices' handicap chase was the feature race on the card in which they went a solid gallop. The first three are all rated within a few pounds of their pre-race marks.

1317 SAWYER'S 70TH YEAR WALKABOUT MARES' STANDARD OPEN NATIONAL HUNT FLAT RACE (DIV I) 2m
3:15 (3:15) (Class 6) 4-6-Y-0 **£1,559** (£457; £228; £114)

Form RPR

1- **1** **Miss Sassypants**[29] 1064 4-10-11 0.................... KevinJones(7) 103+
(Seamus Mullins) *t.k.h: hld up wl in tch in rr: hdwy to chse ldrs over 3f out: rdn and ev ch over 1f out: carried rt ins fnl f: hmpd fnl 100yds: sn led and kpt on wl* **2/1**[1]

22- **2** *nk* **Dorkas**[29] 1064 4-10-11 0.................... SamTwiston-Davies 96+
(J R Jenkins) *t.k.h: hld up wl in tch in midfield: shuffled bk 6f out: hdwy on inner to chse ldr 3f out: rdn to ld over 1f out: hung rt fnl f: hdd and styd on same pce wl ins fnl f* **11/4**[2]

3 *6* **Arctic Dixie** 5-10-9 0.................... JamesBest(3) 91
(Rob Summers) *t.k.h: chsd ldrs: rdn over 2f out: unable qck over 1f out: kpt on same pce ins fnl f* **33/1**

4 *½* **Ovilia (IRE)** 4-10-4 0.................... NickSlatter(7) 90
(Donald McCain) *led and crawl tl hdd 12f out: chsd ldr tl led again over 5f out: rdn and hdd over 1f out: 3rd and btn 1f out: one pce after* **9/2**[3]

- **5** *2* **All For Lily** 4-10-11 0.................... AdamPogson 88
(Charles Pogson) *t.k.h: chsd ldrs: wnt 2nd over 5f out tl 3f out: outpcd and btn over 1f out* **33/1**

/ **6** *2½* **Bollin Across** 5-10-12 0.................... PaulMoloney 86
(Andrew Hollinshead) *t.k.h: in tch in rr: outpcd on outer over 4f out: plugged on same pce fnl 2f* **9/1**

7 *5* **Fountains Blossom** 4-10-11 0.................... DavidBass 80
(Lawney Hill) *chsd ldrs: rdn and struggling 5f out: wknd 3f out* **11/1**

0/ **8** *4½* **No Ifs No Buts**[265] 2682 4-10-4 0.................... JakeHodson(7) 76
(David Bridgwater) *t.k.h: wl in tch in midfield: chsng ldrs and travelling wl 4f out: wknd qckly over 2f out* **16/1**

- **9** *34* **A Bit Breezy** 6-10-5 0.................... ConorShoemark(7) 43
(Bill Turner) *t.k.h: chsd ldr tl led and qcknd gallop 12f out: hdd over 5f out and sn dropped out: t.o* **16/1**

10 *½* **Killackey's Pub (IRE)** 5-10-9 0.................... PeterCarberry(3) 42
(Paul Davies) *t.k.h: hld up in rr: rn green whn rdn 6f out: sn lost tch: t.o* **66/1**

3m 56.9s (15.20) **Going Correction** -0.65s/f (Firm)
WFA 4 from 5yo+ 1lb **10** Ran SP% **115.7**
Speed ratings: **36,35,32,32,31 30,27,25,8,8**
Tote Swingers 1&2 £1.10, 2&3 £12.00, 1&3 £11.70 CSF £7.27 TOTE £3.20: £1.50, £1.10, £9.00; EX 7.20 Trifecta £56.50 Pool: £1,649.84 - 21.87 winning tickets..
Owner J T Brown **Bred** J T Brown And Miss Kirsten Rausing **Trained** Wilsford-Cum-Lake, Wilts

■ Stewards' Enquiry : Sam Twiston-Davies two-day ban: careless riding (4-5 Sep)

FOCUS
An ordinary mares' bumper in which they went a farcical gallop until the middle of the back straight, but the two form horses still came to the fore in a rematch from their Stratford rivalry the previous month. The form is rated around the first two.

1318 SAWYER'S 70TH YEAR WALKABOUT MARES' STANDARD OPEN NATIONAL HUNT FLAT RACE (DIV II) 2m
3:45 (3:45) (Class 6) 4-6-Y-0 **£1,559** (£457; £228; £114)

Form RPR

6- **1** **Noir Girl**[36] 970 4-10-4 0.................... AdamNicol(7) 90+
(Philip Kirby) *mde all: rdn clr over 2f out: in command and styd on wl fnl f: comf* **4/1**[2]

2 *4½* **Jazz Thyme (IRE)** 4-10-11 0.................... JamesDavies 85
(Bernard Llewellyn) *in tch in midfield: 5th and rdn 5f out: styd on u.p past btn rivals to chse clr wnr jst over 1f out: no imp* **20/1**

3 *1½* **According To Sarah (IRE)** 5-10-12 0.................... RichardJohnson 86
(Philip Hobbs) *chsd ldr: rdn over 5f out: hanging bdly lft and no imp over 3f out: 3rd and btn whn wnt bdly lft ins fnl f: one pce after* **1/1**[1]

4 *7* **Theatre King'S (IRE)**[13] 1228 4-10-8 0.................... RobertDunne(3) 78
(S J Mahon, Ire) *hld up in rr: hdwy 7f out: chsd ldng pair and rdn 5f out: disputing 2nd whn hmpd and pushed lft 3f out: 4th and btn 1f out: wknd ins fnl f* **15/2**

5 *6* **Comedinewithme** 5-10-12 0.................... TomO'Brien 71
(Jamie Snowden) *in tch towards rr: rn green and wnt lft 6f out: 6th and no imp 5f out: wknd 2f out* **5/1**[3]

6 *53* **Fairy Bay** 6-10-7 0.................... BenPoste(5) 18
(Pam Ford) *in tch towards rr: rdn and struggling 6f out: t.o fnl 4f* **100/1**

7 *8* **Little Windsor** 4-10-11 0.................... LiamTreadwell 9
(Peter Hiatt) *chsd ldrs tl 6f out: sn dropped out: t.o fnl 4f* **16/1**

8 *24* **Fanny Fantastic** 4-10-4 0.................... NickSlatter(7)
(Miss Imogen Pickard) *chsd ldrs tl 6f out: sn dropped out and bhd: t.o fnl 4f* **33/1**

3m 35.3s (-6.40) **Going Correction** -0.65s/f (Firm) **8** Ran SP% **113.0**
Speed ratings: **90,87,87,83,80 54,50,38**
Tote Swingers 1&2 £8.40, 2&3 £4.60, 1&3 £2.10 CSF £73.03 TOTE £4.80: £1.10, £4.70, £1.20; EX 51.80 Trifecta £176.30 Pool: £3,036.05 - 12.90 winning tickets..
Owner The McBar Partnership **Bred** R G Percival And R Kent **Trained** Middleham, N Yorks

FOCUS
The second division of an ordinary mares' bumper in which they went a proper, even gallop. The form is rated around the winner and fourth.

1319 PICK A WINNER WITH ABACUS CARE H'CAP HURDLE (8 hdls) 2m
4:15 (4:15) (Class 4) (0-120,120) 4-Y-0+ **£3,119** (£915; £457; £228)

Form RPR

/63- **1** **Taaresh (IRE)**[27] 1093 8-10-7 **104**.................... AdamWedge(3) 116+
(Kevin Morgan) *a gng wl: hld up in tch in last pair: hdwy to trck ldr on bit 3 out: led and j.rt next: rdn and r.o strly flat* **8/1**[3]

231- **2** *2½* **Orthodox Lad**[20] 1152 5-10-11 **105**.................... SamTwiston-Davies 114+
(Dr Richard Newland) *in tch: dropped towards rr but stl in tch 5th: hdwy to chse ldrs next: chse wnr between last 2: 1 l down last: styd on same pce u.p flat* **4/6**[1]

6/1- **3** *9* **Della Sun (FR)**[24] 1123 7-10-11 **112**.................... JoshWall(7) 110
(Arthur Whitehead) *in tch in last pair: stmbld bnd bef 3rd: rdn and outpcd bef 3 out: rallied between last 2: kpt on to go 3rd flat: no ch w ldrs* **7/1**[2]

425/ **4** *2¾* **Priors Gold**[10] 4774 6-11-5 **113**.................... TomCannon 108
(Laura Mongan) *chsd ldrs: wnt 2nd 3rd: led wl bef 3 out: rdn and hdd whn nt fluent 2 out: 3rd and btn whn j.big last: wknd flat* **18/1**

P/0- **5** *12* **Diamond's Return (IRE)**[90] 421 9-11-3 **111**............(bt[1]) ConorO'Farrell 97
(David Pipe) *t.k.h: chsd ldr tl 2nd: hld up in tch in midfield after: chsd ldr after 5th tl bef next: wknd bef 2 out* **14/1**

502- **6** *3¾* **Up To The Mark**[26] 1108 8-10-13 **107**....................(p) RichardJohnson 87
(Henry Daly) *led tl after 2nd: chsd ldrs: rdn 4th: lost pl and mstke next: wknd bef 3 out* **17/2**

53/- **7** *12* **Watt Broderick (IRE)**[144] 3608 4-10-4 **99**....................(t) WillKennedy 66
(Ian Williams) *t.k.h: hld up in tch in midfield: rdn and effrt to chse ldrs after 5th: wknd bef next: t.o* **12/1**

The Form Book Jumps, Raceform Ltd, Compton, RG20 6NL.

0/ **P** **Ainm Spartacus (IRE)**[7] 906 6-11-9 **120**..................(bt) RobertDunne(3)
(S J Mahon, Ire) *chsd ldrs tl led after 2nd: rdn and hdd after 5th: sn dropped out and bhd next: t.o whn mstke 2 out: p.u last* **50/1**

3m 34.4s (-12.90) **Going Correction** -0.65s/f (Firm)
WFA 4 from 5yo+ 13lb **8** Ran SP% **115.7**
Speed ratings (Par 105): **106,104,100,98,92 91,85,**
Tote Swingers 1&2 £2.70, 2&3 £1.80, 1&3 £4.30 CSF £14.51 CT £41.81 TOTE £9.40: £1.80, £1.10, £1.50; EX 23.50 Trifecta £104.30 Pool: £3,238.34 - 23.27 winning tickets..
Owner Roemex Ltd **Bred** Shadwell Estate Company Limited **Trained** Gazeley, Suffolk

FOCUS
A fair handicap hurdle in which they went a decent gallop. The runner-up is rated to his mark and sets the standard.

1320 LATIMER COURT-BARCHESTER.COM NOVICES' H'CAP HURDLE (12 hdls) 2m 7f
4:45 (4:47) (Class 5) (0-95,94) 4-Y-0+ **£1,949** (£572; £286; £143)

Form RPR

012- **1** **Royal Peak (IRE)**[6] 1259 6-11-10 **92**..........................(tp) TomScudamore 101+
(David Pipe) *chsd ldrs tl led 8th: wnt clr after next: j.lft 3 out: rdn next: hrd pressed last: hdd flat: drvn and led sn led again: and holding runner-up towards fin* **11/4**[1]

000/ **2** *hd* **She Is A Cracker (FR)**[72] 8-10-3 **78**.............................. MrGGorman(7) 86+
(Mrs C M Gorman) *t.k.h: hld up in midfield on inner: effrt in 3rd 3 out: chal last: rdn to ld flat: pricking ears in front and sn hdd: hld towards fin* **4/1**[2]

344- **3** *7* **Henry Hurst (IRE)**[6] 1267 7-11-12 **94**.......................... AndrewThornton 95
(Jimmy Fox) *hld up in rr: stdy hdwy on outer after 9th: cl 3rd between last 2: hung lft and fnd nil flat: wknd* **8/1**[3]

/F0- **4** *4 ½* **Tinelyra (IRE)**[79] 592 7-11-8 **90**...................................... PaddyBrennan 86
(Fergal O'Brien) *in tch towards rr: effrt bef 3 out: wnt 4th between last 2: no imp* **16/1**

365- **5** *8* **Sharlene's Quest (IRE)**[40] 946 7-11-0 **85**.................. MichaelByrne(3) 73
(James Hughes) *chsd ldrs: rdn to chse clr wnr after 9th tl bef 2 out: wknd between last 2* **20/1**

140- **6** *1 ½* **Inside Knowledge (USA)**[21] 1136 7-11-12 **94**.............(p) AdamPogson 81
(Garry Woodward) *t.k.h: hld up in tch towards rr: hdwy after 9th: rdn and no imp next: wknd 2 out* **14/1**

422- **7** *2* **Watch House (IRE)**[18] 1169 8-11-1 **90**...................... MissAEStirling(7) 75
(Michael Gates) *t.k.h: hld up wl in tch in midfield: rdn and outpcd bef 3 out: wknd bef 2 out* **16/1**

0U0- **8** *5* **Whispering Boy (IRE)**[24] 1118 6-11-3 **92**...................... JakeHodson(7) 72
(David Bridgwater) *in tch in midfield: 5th and stl travelling wl after 9th: rdn and fnd nil next: sn wknd* **40/1**

FP0/ **9** *18* **Magical Treasure**[214] 3696 9-11-8 **90**..............................(b) RyanMahon 52
(Sarah Kerswell) *t.k.h: wl in tch in midfield: mstke 6th: lost pl and rdn 6th: wknd bef next: t.o* **40/1**

5PF- **10** *¾* **Une Des Bieffes (FR)**[70] 690 5-10-11 **79**.................(p) LiamTreadwell 40
(Michael Scudamore) *t.k.h: hld up in tch towards rr: effrt but no imp after 9th: wknd next: t.o* **66/1**

501- **11** *24* **Divine Folly (IRE)**[47] 876 8-11-12 **94**.................................. DavidBass 31
(Lawney Hill) *chsd ldr tl 8th: rdn and btn after next: sn wknd: t.o flat* **12/1**

04F- **12** *24* **Flew The Nest (IRE)**[4] 1275 5-11-12 **94**...............................(p) APMcCoy 7
(Jonjo O'Neill) *in tch towards rr: short-lived effrt 9th: wl btn next: t.o whn blnd 2 out* **4/1**[2]

U64/ **13** *6* **Writers Block (IRE)**[24] 10-11-1 **83**..............................(tp) ConorO'Farrell
(John Joseph Hanlon, Ire) *racd wd: in tch: reminders after 4th and 6th: lost pl and bhd 9th: t.o next* **33/1**

4P6/ **P** **Rooftop Rainbow (IRE)**[364] 1295 9-11-4 **86**.................. NickScholfield
(Linda Blackford) *led tl 8th: 3rd and drvn after next: wknd 3 out: wl btn whn lost action and p.u flat: dismntd* **40/1**

6PP- **F** **Two Oscars (IRE)**[36] 969 7-10-7 **78**...........................(p) JohnKington(3)
(Andrew Crook) *hld up in tch towards rr tl fell 2nd* **40/1**

5m 38.4s (10.40) **Going Correction** -0.65s/f (Firm) **15** Ran SP% **122.9**
Speed ratings (Par 103): **55,54,52,50,48 47,46,45,38,38 30,21,19, ,**
Tote Swingers 1&2 £4.30, 2&3 £8.60, 1&3 £6.70 CSF £13.47 CT £81.91 TOTE £4.20: £2.10, £1.90, £2.90; EX 18.30 Trifecta £96.40 Pool: £3,763.79 - 29.26 winning tickets..
Owner M C Pipe **Bred** Patrick Moore **Trained** Nicholashayne, Devon

FOCUS
A moderate staying novices' handicap hurdle. The winner is rated to recent form with the third to his mark and the fourth to his bumper form.

1321 PLEASE SUPPORT THE ALZHEIMER'S SOCIETY MARES' H'CAP HURDLE (10 hdls) 2m 4f
5:15 (5:15) (Class 4) (0-120,121) 4-Y-0+ **£3,119** (£915; £457; £228)

Form RPR

111- **1** **As I Am (IRE)**[6] 1265 5-11-12 **121** 7ex........................ ConorShoemark(7) 135+
(Don Cantillon) *mde all and a gng wl: readily c clr on bit bef 2 out: eased towards fin: v easily* **1/1**[1]

432- **2** *3 ½* **Me And Ben (IRE)**[30] 1043 6-10-9 **97**........................(t) PaddyBrennan 100
(Fergal O'Brien) *hld up in tch in midfield: hdwy to chse ldrs 7th: rdn and disputing 2nd next: no imp on wnr: wnt 2nd flat kpt on but no ch w wnr* **10/1**

512- **3** *1 ¾* **Detroit Red**[42] 925 7-10-9 **104**................................ MissAliceMills(7) 107
(Martin Hill) *t.k.h: in tch in midfield: chsd ldr 5th: rdn and no imp 3 out: mstke last and sn lost 2nd: one pce flat* **13/2**[3]

122- **4** *shd* **Chilworth Screamer**[29] 1062 5-11-3 **105**............................ TomCannon 106
(Chris Gordon) *hld up in tch: rdn and no imp after 7th: 4th and rallied bef 2 out: kpt on u.p flat: no threat to wnr* **12/1**

14- **5** *5* **Crazy (GER)**[17] 1187 4-10-10 **100**................................(p) TomScudamore 94
(David Bridgwater) *hld up in last pair: effrt 3 out: 5th and no hdwy next: wknd flat* **14/1**

342- **6** *25* **On The Off Chance**[41] 932 5-11-3 **105**...............................(b) APMcCoy 81
(Jonjo O'Neill) *chsd wnr after 1st tl 5th: rdn and wknd wl bef 3 out: wl bhd 2 out* **9/2**[2]

/20- **7** *5* **Finmerello**[74] 640 7-10-3 **91**.. NickScholfield 57
(Kim Bailey) *t.k.h: mstke 1st: chsd wnr tl after 1st: grad stdd bk and in tch in last trio after 4th: rdn and effrt to chse ldng trio after 7th: wknd next: t.o and eased flat* **20/1**

020/ **8** *52* **Go Annie**[180] 4323 5-10-2 **90**.................................... SamTwiston-Davies 4
(Jo Davis) *in tch in rr: rdn 6th: lost tch next and sn t.o* **25/1**

4m 31.85s (-15.55) **Going Correction** -0.65s/f (Firm)
WFA 4 from 5yo+ 14lb **8** Ran SP% **113.6**
Speed ratings (Par 105): **105,103,102,102,100 90,88,68**
Tote Swingers 1&2 £3.40, 2&3 £4.10, 1&3 £2.10 CSF £11.81 CT £44.30 TOTE £1.80: £1.10, £2.40, £1.50; EX 11.30 Trifecta £66.40 Pool: £1,813.23 - 20.47 winning tickets..
Owner Don Cantillon **Bred** Don Cantillon **Trained** Newmarket, Suffolk

FOCUS
A fair mares' handicap hurdle concluded proceedings in which they went a good, even gallop throughout. The winner looks on the upgrade with the next four home close to their marks.
T/Plt: £74.10 to a £1 stake. Pool: £78,048.35 - 768.81 winning tickets. T/Qpdt: £6.30 to a £1 stake. Pool: £9,087.69 - 1057.00 winning tickets. SP

1322 - 1324a (Foreign Racing) - See Raceform Interactive

1314 WORCESTER (L-H)
Tuesday, August 20

OFFICIAL GOING: Good to firm (good in places; 6.9)
The second-last fence was omitted in all chases.
Wind: Virtually nil Weather: White cloud

1325 DINE IN THE SEVERN RESTAURANT NOVICES' H'CAP CHASE (16 fncs 2 omitted) 2m 7f
5:10 (5:10) (Class 4) (0-105,112) 5-Y-0+ **£4,223** (£1,240; £620; £310)

Form RPR

334- **1** **Uncle Pelder (IRE)**[25] 1122 6-11-10 **103**.......................(p) DougieCostello 108
(K F Clutterbuck) *t.k.h: hld up in rr: hdwy appr 3 out: drvn to ld appr last: narrowly hdd run-in: styd chalng and led again clsng stages* **7/1**

511- **2** *hd* **Rudigreen (IRE)**[5] 1274 10-12-2 **112** 7ex....................(tp) JackQuinlan(3) 118+
(Noel Quinlan) *in rr but in tch: wnt 3rd 9th: chsd ldr appr 3 out: chsd wnr and hit last: slt ld u.p run-in: hdd and no ex clsng stages* **5/1**[3]

5/0- **3** *12* **Miracle House (IRE)**[43] 921 9-11-12 **105**..................(t) RichardJohnson 101
(Tim Vaughan) *chsd ldr: tendancy to jump rt: led 6th: stmbld bnd appr home st and rdn: hit 2 out: hdd appr last: wknd qckly* **16/1**

232- **4** *3* **Beckhani**[28] 1088 6-11-12 **105**..(tp) APMcCoy 96
(Jonjo O'Neill) *sn chsng ldrs: rdn appr 13th: wknd and hit 3 out* **13/8**[1]

612- **5** *11* **Numbercruncher (IRE)**[19] 1172 7-11-5 **105**.......... MrMatthewBarber(7) 87
(Marc Barber) *chsd ldrs: wnt 2nd and hit 7th: pressing ldr whn hmpd bnd appr home st: sn wknd* **2/1**[2]

0/6- **P** **Hit The Switch**[28] 1083 7-11-6 **99**....................................(tp) SeanQuinlan
(Michael Mullineaux) *j.rt: led: hdd 6th: wknd next: t.o and p.u after 8th* **28/1**

5m 45.49s (-2.51) **Going Correction** -0.925s/f (Hard) **6** Ran SP% **109.9**
Speed ratings: **67,66,62,61,57**
CSF £38.35 TOTE £8.40: £5.80, £1.50; EX 28.70 Trifecta £164.10 Pool: £915.62 - 4.18 winning units..
Owner K F Clutterbuck **Bred** Ms Riona Molony **Trained** Exning, Suffolk
■ Stewards' Enquiry : Mr Matthew Barber one-day ban: careless riding (Sep 9)

FOCUS
Cathedral bend moved in 3yds and Northern bend moved out 3yds from Monday. This was run at an ordinary gallop and the front pair went clear in a battling finish after the last. The second is rated to his mark.

1326 LOCAL PARKING SECURITIES H'CAP CHASE (15 fncs) 2m 4f
5:40 (5:40) (Class 4) (0-120,120) 4-Y-0+ **£4,061** (£1,192; £596; £298)

Form RPR

243- **1** **Surf And Turf (IRE)**[30] 1063 7-11-6 **114**..............................(p) APMcCoy 127+
(Jonjo O'Neill) *led to 3rd: styd trcking ldrs: chal 6th: led appr 2 out: easily* **5/2**[1]

033- **2** *6* **French Ties (IRE)**[16] 1204 11-11-7 **115**...........................(p) SeanQuinlan 121
(Jennie Candlish) *in rr but in tch: hit 5th: hdwy 3 out: chsd wnr last: kpt on u.p but a easily hld* **5/1**[3]

023- **3** *2 ¼* **Gud Day (IRE)**[7] 1263 5-11-5 **113**....................................(t) PaddyBrennan 117
(Fergal O'Brien) *chsd ldrs: j. slowly 5th: chal 6th: led next: rdn 3 out: hdd appr 2 out: no ch w wnr sn after and dropped to 3rd last* **11/2**

553- **4** *6* **Spock (FR)**[17] 1197 8-11-5 **120**....................................(p) MrsAlexDunn(7) 116
(Alexandra Dunn) *t.k.h: led 3rd: hdd 7th: rdn 3 out: wknd after 2 out: mstke last* **5/1**[3]

/5P- **5** *1 ¼* **Suburban Bay**[28] 1088 8-11-0 **108**.............................. WayneHutchinson 105
(Alan King) *t.k.h: early in tch: mstke 3rd: outpcd 6th: hdwy 8th: wknd 3 out: btn whn mstkes 2 out and last* **11/4**[2]

/40- **6** *19* **Intac (IRE)**[66] 11-10-11 **112**.......................................(b) ConorShoemark(7) 91
(Sarah-Jayne Davies) *unruly paddock: in tch tl blnd 7th and sn no ch* **12/1**

4m 49.35s (-10.65) **Going Correction** -0.925s/f (Hard) **6** Ran SP% **111.6**
Speed ratings (Par 105): **84,81,80,78,77 70**
CSF £15.01 TOTE £3.20: £2.10, £3.00; EX 12.60 Trifecta £24.60 Pool: £1,662.83 - 50.65 winning units..
Owner John P McManus **Bred** J P Murphy & M Barry Murphy **Trained** Cheltenham, Gloucs

FOCUS
A trappy little handicap run at a steady gallop through the first half of the race. The placed horses set the level.

1327 LIFEBOATS SAVING LIVES AT SEA H'CAP CHASE (16 fncs 2 omitted) 2m 7f
6:10 (6:10) (Class 4) (0-120,120) 4-Y-0+ **£4,061** (£1,192; £596; £298)

Form RPR

1P1- **1** **Papradon**[22] 1135 9-11-8 **116**..................................(v) SamTwiston-Davies 130+
(Nigel Twiston-Davies) *mde all: drvn: styng on strly and 1 l up whn lft wl clr last: heavily eased fnl 50yds* **12/1**

/21- **2** *10* **Duneen Point (IRE)**[48] 866 9-11-0 **108**...................... RichardJohnson 108
(Tim Vaughan) *pressed wnr tl hit 4th: styd in 2nd: hit 11th: rdn 3f out: wknd into 3rd sn after: lft poor 2nd last: clsd on heavily eased wnr clsng stages* **13/2**[3]

532- **3** *1 ¼* **Baizically (IRE)**[3] 1298 10-9-12 **97** 7ex...........................(b) BrianHayes(5) 96
(John Joseph Hanlon, Ire) *chsd ldrs: dispured 2nd 4 out: sn rdn: wknd bef 3 out: lft mod 3rd last: clsd on heavily eased wnr clsng stages* **5/4**[1]

033- **4** *15* **Lukeys Luck**[22] 1135 7-10-13 **107**.................................(p) SeanQuinlan 95
(Jennie Candlish) *in rr: hit 8th: hdwy 10th: wknd after 4 out: no ch whn hit next: lft poor 4th last* **8/1**

/22- **F** **The Mad Robertson (IRE)**[17] 1197 6-11-12 **120**.................... APMcCoy 130
(Jonjo O'Neill) *in rr but in tch: hdwy appr 3 out and wnt 2nd sn after: drvn 2 out: rdn: flashed tail but styng on and 1 l down whn wnt edgd rt and fell last* **2/1**[2]

5m 39.16s (-8.84) **Going Correction** -0.925s/f (Hard) **5** Ran SP% **109.9**
Speed ratings (Par 105): **78,74,74,68,**
CSF £73.19 TOTE £7.50: £2.80, £2.00; EX 34.90 Trifecta £164.30 Pool: £1,314.16 - 5.99 winning units..
Owner A J Cresser **Bred** B Whitehouse **Trained** Naunton, Gloucs

FOCUS
A modest handicap, run at a routine gallop. The winner looks progressive with the second to his mark.

1328 BIRTHDAY GIRLS H'CAP CHASE (10 fncs 2 omitted) 2m 110y
6:40 (6:40) (Class 5) (0-95,91) 4-Y-0+ **£2,274** (£667; £333; £166)

Form | | | | RPR
504- **1** **Alderbrook Lad (IRE)**[18] 1184 7-11-4 **86**.................... MichaelByrne(3) 102+
(Neil Mulholland) *mde all: hit 4 out: edgd lft after last: drvn out* **5/2**[1]
330- **2** *1* **Chestnut Ben (IRE)**[41] 942 8-11-12 **91**..............................(t) APMcCoy 105
(Gary Brown) *in tch: chsd ldrs 6th: wnt 2nd appr 2 out: sn u.p: crossed and swtchd rt after last: styd on but a hld* **7/2**[2]
402- **3** *15* **Louis Ludwig (IRE)**[34] 1014 8-10-12 **87**......................(t) AlanJohns(10) 86
(Tim Vaughan) *in tch: chsd ldrs fr 5th: disp 2nd fr 4 out tl after 3 out: wknd fr next* **5/1**[3]
/42- **4** *1* **Stafford Charlie**[21] 1149 7-10-4 **76**................................. CiaranMckee(7) 74
(John O'Shea) *in rr but in tch: hdwy 3 out: nvr rchd ldrs and styd on same pce u.p fr 2 out to take 4th run-in* **11/2**
262- **5** *2 1/4* **Escardo (GER)**[30] 1057 10-11-7 **86**......................(tp) TomScudamore 82
(David Bridgwater) *chsd ldrs: disp 2ne fr 4 out to next: wknd sn after* **8/1**
/23- **6** *1/2* **Brannoc (IRE)**[30] 1057 8-10-12 **77**..............................(t) AndrewThornton 72
(Tony Newcombe) *chsd ldr to 7th: wknd 3 out* **8/1**
4PF- **7** *3/4* **Tulla Emerald (IRE)**[21] 1149 8-9-13 **71**............................. KevinJones(7) 66
(Natalie Lloyd-Beavis) *in rr: hdwy 4 out: rdn and wknd next* **25/1**
BP0- **8** *27* **The Grey One (IRE)**[44] 898 10-10-8 **78**........................ CharlieWallis(5) 46
(Milton Bradley) *chsd ldrs: hit 6th and dropped to rr: mstke 4 out and jst in tch: wknd next: mstke 2 out* **33/1**
344- **9** *40* **Strathaird (IRE)**[28] 1086 9-9-11 **65** oh6.........................(p) JohnKington(3)
(Andrew Crook) *hit 6th: a bhd* **25/1**

3m 57.78s (-16.22) **Going Correction** -0.925s/f (Hard) **9** Ran SP% **115.7**
Speed ratings (Par 103): **101,100,93,93,91 91,91,78,59**
Tote Swingers: 1&2 £2.80, 1&3 £4.70, 2&3 £2.20 CSF £11.92 CT £39.92 TOTE £3.90: £1.50, £2.00, £2.00; EX 15.00 Trifecta £55.40 Pool: £1,106.07 - 14.96 winning units..
Owner Wellcroomed T/A eyewearoutlet.co.uk **Bred** A Malone **Trained** Limpley Stoke, Wilts

FOCUS
A weak handicap, run at a fair gallop. The runner-up sets the level.

1329 BOOK HOSPITALITY AT WORCESTER RACECOURSE "NATIONAL HUNT" MAIDEN HURDLE (8 hdls) 2m
7:10 (7:10) (Class 5) 4-Y-0+ **£2,111** (£620; £310; £155)

Form | | | | RPR
/22- **1** **Clondaw Draft (IRE)**[25] 1118 5-11-0 0............................ JasonMaguire 117+
(Donald McCain) *led tl after 1st and again 3rd: drvn clr whn hung lft after 2 out and wnt lft again last but in n.d and eased run-in* **11/10**[1]
3/0- **2** *10* **Who Am I**[21] 1152 7-10-11 92... RobertDunne(3) 100
(Dai Burchell) *in tch: hdwy 4 out: chsd ldr 3 out: rdn after 2 out and no ch but kpt on wl for clr 2nd* **33/1**
322- **3** *10* **Kimora (IRE)**[19] 1176 7-10-7 97..(t) APMcCoy 83
(Marc Barber) *hit 1st: chsd ldrs in 3rd: pushed along 4th: lost pl u.p appr 3 out: styd on to take wl hld 3rd fr 2 out* **11/4**[3]
12- **4** *21* **Most Eligible**[48] 874 6-11-0 0....................................... TomScudamore 69
(David Pipe) *led after 1st: hdd 3rd: wknd fr 3 out* **9/4**[2]
P/6- **5** *30* **Nudge The Nugget**[44] 897 5-10-11 0................................(b) MarkQuinlan(3) 39
(Nigel Hawke) *bhd fr 1/2-way: t.o* **100/1**
00- **6** *17* **Primitive Dancing**[25] 1118 4-10-13 0............................... AndrewThornton 21
(Caroline Bailey) *bhd fr 1/2-way: t.o* **100/1**

3m 36.94s (-10.36) **Going Correction** -0.425s/f (Good)
WFA 4 from 5yo+ 13lb **6** Ran SP% **110.0**
Speed ratings (Par 103): **108,103,98,87,72 64**
Tote Swingers: 1&2 £2.80, 1&3 £1.20, 2&3 £4.60 CSF £20.91 TOTE £2.20: £1.10, £4.80; EX 19.90 Trifecta £91.20 Pool: £1,380.05 - 11.34 winning units..
Owner T G Leslie **Bred** Gerry Ross **Trained** Cholmondeley, Cheshire

FOCUS
The winner was much the best despite being a little wayward. The second is probably the best guide guide to the level.

1330 DOWNLOAD OUR IPHONE APP NOVICES' HURDLE (12 hdls) 2m 7f
7:40 (7:40) (Class 4) 4-Y-0+ **£3,249** (£954; £477; £238)

Form | | | | RPR
43U- **1** **Lost Legend (IRE)**[17] 1195 6-10-12 122..............................(p) APMcCoy 112+
(Jonjo O'Neill) *t.k.h: wnt 2nd fr 5th: stl keen enough 4 out: drvn and one pce 2 out: stl 2 l down last: rallied u.p run-in to ld cl home* **5/4**[1]
/11- **2** *hd* **Benefit Of Youth (IRE)**[21] 1154 6-11-5 116.................. RichardJohnson 117
(Tim Vaughan) *led: rdn 3 out: kpt on wl fr 2 out and 2 l ahd last: hrd rdn run-in: hdd cl home* **7/4**[2]
0/0- **3** *9* **Vinnie The Fish (IRE)**[7] 1255 5-10-12 0...........................(t) TomScudamore 101
(Brendan Powell) *chsd ldrs: lost position 6th: hdwy 4 out: styd on to take 3rd 2 out but no imp on ldng duo* **50/1**
111- **4** *3 3/4* **My Lucky Flame (IRE)**[28] 1084 6-11-2 121.................. MikeyHamill(10) 111
(Sean Curran) *chsd ldr 2nd to 5th: styd pressing for 2nd tl appr 3 out: wknd into 4th 2 out* **10/3**[3]
0/3- **5** *42* **Abbraccio**[15] 69 5-10-12 0...(t) PaddyBrennan 55
(Fergal O'Brien) *in rr: drvn and sme hdwy 4 out: wknd next* **25/1**

5m 27.17s (-0.83) **Going Correction** -0.425s/f (Good)
WFA 4 from 5yo+ 14lb **5** Ran SP% **109.7**
Speed ratings (Par 105): **84,83,80,79,64**
CSF £3.86 TOTE £2.70: £1.20, £1.30; EX 3.40 Trifecta £33.30 Pool: £739.84 - 16.63 winning units..
Owner Mrs Gay Smith **Bred** Highfort Stud **Trained** Cheltenham, Gloucs

FOCUS
This was decimated by non-runners. Just a fair event rated around the first two.

1331 SPONSOR A RACE BY CALLING 01905 25364 CONDITIONAL JOCKEYS' H'CAP HURDLE (8 hdls) 2m
8:10 (8:10) (Class 5) (0-95,95) 4-Y-0+ **£2,111** (£620; £310; £155)

Form | | | | RPR
F40/ **1** **Pindar (GER)**[28] 5509 9-10-5 **77**..........................(b[1]) ConorShoemark(3) 81
(Neil Mulholland) *mde all: hrd pressed fr 2 out: hld on wl u.p run-in* **7/2**[2]
063- **2** *1 1/4* **Rose Red**[22] 1132 6-11-6 **89**.. JamesBest 92
(Rob Summers) *in rr: gd hdwy 3 out: styd on u.p to take 2nd clsng stages but no imp on wnr* **10/1**
504- **3** *hd* **Spinning Waters**[34] 1018 7-11-4 **87**...............................(p) MattGriffiths 90
(Dai Burchell) *in tch: chsd ldrs 3 out: styd on u.p run-in to press for 2nd: no imp one dropped to 3rd clsng stages* **5/1**[3]
0/U- **4** *1* **Saltagioo (ITY)**[37] 977 9-10-8 **85**...................................(t) MarkMarris(8) 87
(Anthony Middleton) *chsd ldrs: drvn to chal 2 out: no ex u.p run-in and one pce into 4th clsng stages* **33/1**
P/0- **5** *20* **Mr Bachster (IRE)**[19] 1169 8-9-13 **78**........................ JamesJeavons(10) 60
(Richard Lee) *in rr: drvn and styd on fr 3 out: kpt on run-in but nvr any threat* **12/1**
00P- **6** *1/2* **Petrocelli**[7] 1269 6-10-2 **79**.. JPKiely(8) 60
(Tim Vaughan) *in rr: mod prog fr 3 out* **16/1**
400- **7** *2* **Ghaabesh (IRE)**[16] 1206 6-11-1 **84**..........................(bt) HarryChalloner 63
(Barry Leavy) *in rr: mod prog fr 3 out* **16/1**
/PF- **8** *3/4* **Youm Jamil (USA)**[34] 1014 6-10-4 **73**.............................. TrevorWhelan 51
(Tony Carroll) *in rr: mod prog fr 3 out* **11/1**
65P- **9** *14* **Gainsborough's Art (IRE)**[37] 964 8-9-9 **69** oh14..(b) JackSherwood(5) 33
(Harry Chisman) *chsd ldrs to 4 out* **66/1**
/62- **10** *3 1/4* **Milaneen**[37] 961 7-10-7 **79**... MichaelByrne(3) 40
(Tim Vaughan) *chsd ldrs: rdn 3 out: wknd next: fin lame* **5/2**[1]
0/0- **11** *nse* **Prince Freddie**[21] 1152 5-10-13 **82**............................... JonathanEngland 43
(Roy Brotherton) *chsd ldrs to 4 out: sn wknd: no ch whn hmpd 3 out* **14/1**
12 *27* **Ned The Vet (IRE)**[29] 1080 6-11-4 **87**............................(bt[1]) MichealNolan 21
(S J Mahon, Ire) *chsd ldrs: wknd after 4 out: no ch whn hmpd 3 out* **33/1**
F **Catcher In The Bog (IRE)**[28] 1097 6-11-12 **95**...........(tp) PeterCarberry
(S J Mahon, Ire) *in rr: hdwy in clsng in bhd ldrs whn fell 3 out: fatally injured* **28/1**

3m 39.95s (-7.35) **Going Correction** -0.425s/f (Good) **13** Ran SP% **121.8**
Speed ratings (Par 103): **101,100,100,99,89 89,88,88,81,79 79,66,**
Tote Swingers 1&2 £11.80, 2&3 £10.90, 1&3 £7.90 CSF £38.31 CT £180.30 TOTE £5.10: £2.30, £1.20, £2.40; EX 47.50 Trifecta £101.60 Pool: £489.95 - 3.61 winning units..
Owner Wellcroomed T/A eyewearoutlet.co.uk **Bred** Gestut Schlenderhan **Trained** Limpley Stoke, Wilts

FOCUS
A moderate handicap, confined to conditional riders. It was run at a solid gallop and the first four had it to themselves from two out. The first three were all within a few pounds of their pre-race marks.
T/Plt: £127.00 to a £1 stake. Pool: £58,859.48 - 338.21 winning tickets. T/Qpdt: £25.70 to a £1 stake. Pool: £6,5087.62 - 187.20 winning tickets. ST

1332 - 1334a (Foreign Racing) - See Raceform Interactive

1191 NEWTON ABBOT (L-H)
Wednesday, August 21

OFFICIAL GOING: Good to firm (good in places; watered; 7.6)
Wind: mild breeze across Weather: sunny

1335 BLUEGLUE GRADUATE JUVENILE MAIDEN HURDLE (8 hdls) 2m 1f
5:40 (5:40) (Class 4) 3-Y-O **£3,508** (£1,030; £515; £257)

Form | | | | RPR
1 **Baltic Blade (IRE)**[12] 3-10-12 0... JamieMoore 87+
(Gary Moore) *trked ldrs tl led 2nd: jnd after 4th: rdn into clr ld appr 2 out: in command whn pckd last: kpt on* **5/2**[2]
2 *11* **Vergality Ridge (IRE)**[37] 3-10-7 0..................................... EDLinehan(5) 75
(Ronald Harris) *hld up in 5th wl in tch: rdn and sltly outpcd after 3 out: styd on steadily fr next: wnt 2nd fnl stride: no ch w wnr* **50/1**
F3- **3** *hd* **Karl Marx (IRE)**[6] 1271 3-10-12 0.................................... TommyPhelan 79
(Mark Gillard) *led tl 1st: j. sltly rt thrght: outpcd after 3 out: rallying whn wandered bdly and awkward 2 out: chsd wnr sn after but no ch: lost 2nd fnl stride* **16/1**
4 *4 1/2* **Relentless (IRE)**[111] 3-10-12 0.. APMcCoy 75+
(Jim Best) *led 1st tl 2nd: trckd ldr: jnd ldr after 4th: rdn after 3 out: hld bef next: wknd bef last* **10/11**[1]
643- **5** *19* **Wild Diamond (IRE)**[18] 1193 3-10-5 98......................... RichardJohnson 47
(Tim Vaughan) *trckd ldrs: hmpd 2nd: dropped to 5th but stl wl in tch after 4th: sn niggled along: wknd after 3 out* **7/2**[3]

4m 3.3s (-2.40) **Going Correction** -0.50s/f (Good) **5** Ran SP% **111.0**
Speed ratings (Par 102): **85,79,79,77,68**
CSF £47.55 TOTE £2.70: £1.30, £12.70; EX 28.70 Trifecta £337.00 Pool: £803.02 - 1.78 winning units..
Owner www.balticbladeracing.com **Bred** J R Craik-White **Trained** Lower Beeding, W Sussex

FOCUS
Rail at innermost position. Dry weather overnight meant good to firm going, and the last flight on the hurdles track was positioned to leave a run-in of just 100 yards. This was a moderate juvenile maiden event and there is little to go on.

1336 BLUEGLUE PRODUCT GURUS H'CAP CHASE (16 fncs) 2m 5f 110y
6:10 (6:10) (Class 5) (0-95,98) 4-Y-0+ **£2,729** (£801; £400; £200)

Form | | | | RPR
/34- **1** **Maid Of Silk (IRE)**[42] 942 7-11-6 **89**..................................(t) NoelFehily 103+
(Neil Mulholland) *racd keenly most of way: trckd ldrs: nudged along to trck ldr after 3 out: chal 2 out: sn led: nt fluent last: styd on wl: pushed out* **7/2**[2]
/44- **2** *7* **Brimham Boy**[20] 1174 11-11-2 **95**.................................(vt) OllieGarner(10) 101
(Martin Keighley) *trckd ldrs: led 7th: rdn after 3 out: hdd after next: kpt on but sn no ex* **14/1**
5/5- **3** *16* **Captain Marlon (IRE)**[104] 180 12-11-4 **87**........................ TomCannon 82
(William Reed) *cl up: hdwy after 11th: effrt 4 out: chsd wnr next tl 2 out: wknd bef last* **16/1**
P/1- **4** *13* **Robobar (FR)**[3] 1300 8-12-1 **98** 7ex.....................................(v) APMcCoy 82
(Jim Best) *led after 2nd tl 7th: pressed ldr: rdn after 11th: wknd bef 3 out* **1/1**[1]
4/6- **5** *1 1/2* **Hazeldene**[31] 1057 11-11-8 **94**.................................... JeremiahMcGrath(3) 73
(Martin Hill) *led tl hit 2nd: trckd ldrs: rdn whn hit 12th: wknd after 4 out* **14/1**
/41- **6** *50* **Solitary Palm (IRE)**[93] 408 10-11-2 **85**.......................(b) ConorO'Farrell 19
(Brian Forsey) *trckd ldrs: rdn after 11th: wknd 4 out: t.o* **14/1**
54/- **P** **West Bay Hoolie**[127] 5331 7-10-0 **69** oh1............................. AlainCawley
(Helen Nelmes) *rdr lost iron whn v awkward 1st: bhd: sn wl detached: p.u bef 7th* **6/1**[3]

5m 10.0s (-11.40) **Going Correction** -0.45s/f (Good) **7** Ran SP% **112.4**
Speed ratings (Par 103): **102,99,93,88,88 70,**
toteswingers 1&2 £7.60, 1&3 £9.70, 2&3 £9.00 CSF £42.76 TOTE £3.90: £2.10, £7.20; EX 39.60 Trifecta £534.50 Pool: £1440.16 - 2.02 winning units..
Owner Donald Bell **Bred** Frank Motherway **Trained** Limpley Stoke, Wilts

The Form Book Jumps, Raceform Ltd, Compton, RG20 6NL.

FOCUS
A moderate handicap run at a good pace. A personal-best from the winner with the second rated in line with recent runs.

1337 BLUEGLUE SOCIAL MEDIA NOVICES' HURDLE (10 hdls) 2m 6f
6:40 (6:40) (Class 4) 4-Y-0+ **£3,508** (£1,030; £515; £257)

Form RPR
21- **1** **Kilbree Kid (IRE)**^{31} [1052] 6-11-5 115............................(t) PaddyBrennan 120
(Tom George) *a.p: led after 6th: rdn after 3 out: sn hrd pressed: gd jump to hold advantage last: kpt on v gamely: all out* **4/5**^{1}
002- **2** ¾ **Rob Conti (FR)**^{17} [1201] 8-10-12 114.............................. RichardJohnson 112
(Philip Hobbs) *travelled wl: trckd ldrs: rdn for str chal appr 2 out: ev ch fr last: kpt on* **9/4**^{2}
123- **3** hd **Experimentalist**^{38} [956] 5-11-2 118............................(t) MichaelByrne(3) 119
(Tim Vaughan) *trckd ldrs: rdn appr 2 out: ev ch last: kpt on* **6/1**^{3}
034- **4** 3 ½ **Multitude Of Sins**^{31} [1052] 6-10-12 110.................................. JoeTizzard 110
(Colin Tizzard) *racd keenly in last but wl in tch: hdwy 3 out: rdn to chal 2 out: no ex fr last* **14/1**
560- **5** 67 **Follow The Tracks (IRE)**^{6} [1270] 5-10-7 0...................... KillianMoore(5) 41
(Brian Barr) *led tl after 6th: rdn after next: sn hld: wknd after 3 out: t.o* **80/1**

5m 22.7s (2.50) **Going Correction** -0.50s/f (Good) **5** Ran SP% **108.5**
Speed ratings (Par 105): **75,74,74,73,49**
CSF £2.87 TOTE £1.60: £1.10, £1.50; EX 2.50 Trifecta £7.50 Pool: £1232.96 - 122.34 winning units..
Owner Five Valleys Racing Partnership **Bred** John O'Mahony **Trained** Slad, Gloucs

FOCUS
A fair novice with the main contenders rated between 110 and 118, and it produced an exciting sprint finish with four in line going to the second last. The first three are rated close to their marks.

1338 BLUEGLUE C-SUITE NOVICES' CHASE (20 fncs) 3m 2f 110y
7:10 (7:10) (Class 3) 4-Y-0+ **£7,783** (£2,431; £1,309)

Form RPR
1/1- **1** **Bold Chief (IRE)**^{50} [861] 8-11-12 139.................................(tp) NoelFehily 138+
(Harry Fry) *j.w: mde all: beginning to be nudged along whn lft wl clr 2 out: heavily eased run-in* **8/15**^{1}
640- **2** dist **Golden Squirell (IRE)**^{18} [1191] 6-11-2 0............................. TomCannon 81
(Brendan Powell) *chsd ldrs: nudged along fr after 5th: rdn whn outpcd 4 out: wknd next: lft remote 2nd 2 out* **28/1**^{3}
300- **3** 9 **Volio Vincente (FR)**^{76} [649] 6-10-13 0......................... MichealNolan(3) 64
(Carroll Gray) *chsd ldrs: struggling 16th: outpcd next: wknd 3 out: lft remote 3rd 2 out* **100/1**
3/2- **F** **Oscargo (IRE)**^{99} [296] 9-11-12 128................................(t) NickScholfield 134
(Paul Nicholls) *trckd wnr: travelling wl enough whn plld out to mount chal and fell heavily 2 out* **13/8**^{2}

6m 33.0s (-11.60) **Going Correction** -0.45s/f (Good) **4** Ran SP% **107.8**
Speed ratings (Par 107): **99,87,84,**
CSF £9.63 TOTE £1.30; EX 12.10 Trifecta £24.60 Pool: £966.98 - 29.38 winning units..
Owner The Eyre Family **Bred** Patrick Carroll **Trained** Seaborough, Dorset

FOCUS
This was effectively a match between two highly-rated novices, and when the pair raised the tempo the others were soon beaten off. The faller was heading for his mark.

1339 BLUEGLUE LINUX SYS ADMIN H'CAP HURDLE (10 hdls) 2m 6f
7:40 (7:40) (Class 5) (0-95,99) 4-Y-0+ **£2,729** (£801; £400; £200)

Form RPR
/56- **1** **William Percival (IRE)**^{8} [1267] 7-10-5 74......................... TommyPhelan 79+
(Mark Gillard) *mid-div: hdwy appr 7th: rdn after 3 out: led sn after 2 out: clr whn nt fluent next: kpt on wl* **16/1**
112- **2** 4 ½ **Jigsaw Financial (IRE)**^{8} [1267] 7-11-3 86....................... GerardTumelty 87
(Laura Young) *cl up: rdn to chse ldr after 3 out: led next: hdd bef last: no ex* **3/1**^{2}
050- **3** 3 ¼ **No Woman No Cry**^{31} [1051] 8-11-2 85.............................(tp) JoeTizzard 83
(Colin Tizzard) *trckd ldrs: rdn whn outpcd sn after 3 out: styd on again fr next: nvr bk on terms w ldng pair* **5/1**^{3}
121- **4** 3 ½ **Royal Peak (IRE)**^{2} [1320] 6-12-2 99 7ex.....................(tp) TomScudamore 94
(David Pipe) *led: rdn after 3 out: hdd bef next: grad fdd* **15/8**^{1}
P00/ **5** 4 ½ **Safferano (IRE)**^{154} [4872] 7-11-5 91............................... MichaelByrne(3) 82
(Tim Vaughan) *hld up towards rr: rdn after 3 out: plugged on but nvr any real imp on ldrs* **40/1**
0/5- **6** nk **Not A Doctor (IRE)**^{20} [1169] 10-10-0 69 oh1..................... ConorO'Farrell 60
(Polly Gundry) *hld up towards rr: hdwy after 6th: rdn after 3 out: wknd 2 out* **50/1**
223- **7** 5 **Theoystercatcher (IRE)**^{20} [1169] 7-11-10 93...........(p) RichardJohnson 79
(Tim Vaughan) *mid-div: rdn after 6th: sn towards rr* **7/1**
46F- **8** 5 **Plug In Baby**^{8} [1266] 5-10-10 79...(p) IanPopham 61
(Nick Mitchell) *trckd ldr tl nudged along fr 5th: rdn after 6th: sn towards rr: nt a factor after* **33/1**
F20- **9** 8 **Blue Signal (IRE)**^{42} [946] 8-11-12 95.................................^{1} LiamHeard 69
(Colin Heard) *hld up and a bhd* **20/1**
045- **P** **Carobello (IRE)**^{19} [1183] 6-11-0 83......................... SamTwiston-Davies
(Martin Bosley) *trckd ldr tl rdn after 6th: blnd bdly next: sn in rr: t.o whn p.u bef 2 out* **12/1**

5m 10.9s (-9.30) **Going Correction** -0.50s/f (Good) **10** Ran SP% **114.6**
Speed ratings (Par 103): **96,94,93,91,90 90,88,86,83,**
toteswingers 1&2 £12.30, 1&3 £21.50, 2&3 £4.20 CSF £62.28 CT £282.51 TOTE £27.00: £3.30, £1.40, £2.00; EX 88.20 Trifecta £156.10 Pool: £1068.58 - 5.13 winning units..
Owner Mrs Jenny Luscombe **Bred** Rockvale Stud **Trained** Holwell, Dorset

FOCUS
A moderate handicap but it was run at a fair pace. The second and fourth are rated to form while the whole race could go higher.

1340 BLUEGLUE LAMP HACKERS CONDITIONAL JOCKEYS' H'CAP HURDLE (12 hdls) 3m 3f
8:10 (8:10) (Class 4) (0-115,115) 4-Y-0+ **£3,508** (£1,030; £515; £257)

Form RPR
211- **1** **Dreamsoftheatre (IRE)**^{20} [1169] 5-11-5 111...........(t) MauriceLinehan(3) 116+
(Jonjo O'Neill) *trckd ldrs tl nt fluent 2nd: in last pair: pushed along fr 6th: rdn and looked btn 3 out: hdwy bef next: disp gng to the last: asserted run-in: drvn out* **6/4**^{1}
/02- **2** ½ **Southway Queen**^{31} [1051] 9-9-9 89 oh7.....................(tp) NathanAdams(5) 93
(Sue Gardner) *trckd ldrs: pressed ldr 9th: led gng wl after 3 out: rdn bef next: jnd bef last: kpt on but no ex whn hdd run-in* **8/1**
P45- **3** 23 **Andhaar**^{22} [1155] 7-11-7 115...(p) JackSherwood(5) 98
(Richard Phillips) *trckd ldrs: rdn in 3rd after 9th: lost 3rd briefly after 3 out: hld fr next: wknd bef last* **10/1**
4/1- **4** 33 **Sapphire Rouge (IRE)**^{110} [99] 7-10-1 98..................(p) KevinJones(8) 51
(Seamus Mullins) *led: clr tl 3rd: j.rt fr 5th: rdn and hdd after 3 out: wknd bef next: t.o* **3/1**^{2}
423- **5** 9 **Always Bold (IRE)**^{31} [1055] 8-11-2 108...........................(v) IanPopham(3) 53
(Martin Keighley) *hld up in last pair: stmbld bdly on bnd appr 6th: nvr travelling after: began to tail off fr bef 9th* **12/1**
4/2- **6** 43 **Prime Location**^{35} [1019] 7-10-13 112.........................(bt^{1}) AnthonyFox(10) 18
(David Pipe) *trckd ldr: hit 1st: rdn after 8th: wknd after next: t.o* **9/2**^{3}

6m 24.0s (-17.00) **Going Correction** -0.50s/f (Good) **6** Ran SP% **111.1**
Speed ratings (Par 105): **105,104,98,88,85 72**
toteswingers 1&2 £1.70, 1&3 £3.70, 2&3 £11.50 CSF £13.15 CT £83.38 TOTE £2.50: £2.50, £2.20; EX 13.00 Trifecta £51.40 Pool: £634.78 - 9.25 winning units..
Owner John P McManus **Bred** Kieran Gleeson **Trained** Cheltenham, Gloucs

FOCUS
A tight finish to a reasonably competitive handicap, though they did not get going until halfway down the back. The first two are rated pretty much to their marks.
T/Plt: £104.00 to a £1 stake. Pool: £56475.31 - 396.04 winning tickets T/Qpdt: £9.10 to a £1 stake. Pool: £5582.3 - 451.00 winning tickets TM

777 FFOS LAS (L-H)
Thursday, August 22

OFFICIAL GOING: Good (7.7)
Wind: light, behind Weather: sunny and warm

1341 BET TOTEJACKPOT AT TOTEPOOL.COM MAIDEN HURDLE (11 hdls) 2m 6f
2:10 (2:10) (Class 5) 4-Y-0+ **£1,949** (£572; £286; £143)

Form RPR
222/ **1** **Koultas King (IRE)**^{153} [4903] 6-11-0 112.....................(t) RichardJohnson 112
(Tim Vaughan) *j.w: mde all: rdn clr bef 3 out: styd on wl: rdn out* **8/11**^{1}
420- **2** 3 ½ **Moon Devil (IRE)**^{57} [845] 6-11-0 106...............................(p) TomO'Brien 108
(Peter Bowen) *chsd ldrs: effrt to chse wnr bef 3 out: drvn and no imp fr 2 out* **9/4**^{2}
3 25 **Slow Train Coming (IRE)**^{315} [1808] 6-11-0 0.................... PaulMoloney 88
(Evan Williams) *t.k.h: hld up in tch in last trio: mstke 6th: 5th and wl in tch after 8th: outpcd and btn next: modest 3rd whn hit 2 out* **10/1**^{3}
4 8 **Toe To Toe (IRE)**^{34} [1031] 5-11-0 0................................. NickScholfield 77
(Lucy Jones) *t.k.h: in tch in midfield: hdwy to join wnr after 5th: rdn and wknd qckly bef 3 out: 5th and wl btn whn mstke 2 out: t.o* **10/1**^{3}
3- **5** 9 **Dbanks (IRE)**^{23} [1154] 10-11-0 99.. DPFahy 72
(Liam Corcoran) *chsd wnr tl after 5th: styd chsng ldrs tl wknd bef 3 out: poor 4th whn mstke 2 out: t.o* **28/1**
00/ **6** 43 **Two Shades Of Blue**^{260} [2858] 6-10-0 0............................ AlanJohns(7) 24
(Beth Roberts) *t.k.h: hld up in tch in last trio: mstke 7th: sn struggling: lost tch and t.o bef 3 out* **100/1**
/00- **7** 57 **Mac Le Couteau**^{21} [1176] 5-10-11 0................................ AdamWedge(3)
(Evan Williams) *nt jump wl: chsd ldrs tl mstke and lost pl 6th: bhd next: wl t.o bef 3 out* **66/1**
8 ½ **Shanksforamillion** 4-10-12 0.. ConorO'Farrell
(David Rees) *t.k.h: hld up in tch in last trio: mstke 6th: sn struggling and lost tch: wl t.o bef 3 out* **50/1**

5m 15.4s (-4.60) **Going Correction** -0.60s/f (Firm)
WFA 4 from 5yo+ 14lb **8** Ran SP% **114.7**
Speed ratings (Par 103): **84,82,73,70,67 51,31,30**
toteswingers 1&2 £1.20, 2&3 £12.50, 1&3 £1.60 CSF £2.63 TOTE £1.70: £1.10, £1.10, £1.40; EX 2.80 Trifecta £9.60 Pool: £1526.34 - 118.86 winning units..
Owner Pearn's Pharmacies Ltd **Bred** Tom McCarthy **Trained** Aberthin, Vale of Glamorgan

FOCUS
The hot favourite beat his main market rival in this modest maiden hurdle and the pair pulled a long way clear. The first two set the level.

1342 YOUR FAVOURITE POOL BETS AT TOTEPOOL.COM CLAIMING HURDLE (8 hdls) 2m
2:45 (2:46) (Class 5) 4-Y-0+ **£1,949** (£572; £286; £143)

Form RPR
665/ **1** **James Pollard (IRE)**^{7} [1608] 8-10-13 0.....................(t) RobertWilliams(5) 101
(Bernard Llewellyn) *t.k.h: hld up wl in tch: rdn and effrt whn hit 2 out: chal last: r.o wl u.p to ld fnl 50yds* **7/1**^{3}
22P- **2** nk **Paddy Partridge**^{24} [1134] 7-10-12 110.........................(b) RichardJohnson 94
(Tim Vaughan) *trckd ldrs: hit 2nd: qcknd to ld after 3 out: hit next: drvn and hrd pressed last: hdd and no ex fnl 50yds* **7/1**^{3}
F04/ **3** 4 **Rayhani (USA)**^{4} [1312] 10-11-0 114.. APMcCoy 93
(J A Nash, Ire) *t.k.h: hld up wl in tch in rr: mstke 1st: hdwy and rdn 3 out: pressed ldrs next: mstke last: no ex and outpcd flat* **2/1**^{1}
555- **4** 1 ¾ **Jolly Roger (IRE)**^{39} [973] 6-11-10 120.................................. LeeEdwards 101+
(Tony Carroll) *t.k.h: hld up wl in tch in midfield: shuffled bk and rdn bef 3 out: no threat to ldng pair but kpt on u.p flat* **5/2**^{2}
325- **5** 1 ½ **Ajman (IRE)**^{43} [947] 8-10-5 100..(bt) ConorRing(7) 87
(Evan Williams) *chsd ldr: mstke 5th: 4th and struggling to qckn whn mstke 2 out: 4th and btn whn mstke last* **7/1**^{3}
PP- **6** 1 ¾ **Arguidos (IRE)**^{9} [1267] 9-10-9 98...........................(t) AodhaganConlon(5) 87
(Debra Hamer) *led and set stdy gallop: rdn bef 3 out: hdd wl bef 2 out and sn outpcd: wknd between last 2* **66/1**
12F/ **7** 5 **Langley**^{30} [5117] 6-10-9 109... MichaelByrne(3) 81
(Tim Vaughan) *wl in tch in midfield: mstke 5th: effrt to join ldr next: struggling to qckn and outpcd whn hit 2 out: wknd between last 2* **16/1**
/02- **F** **Who Am I**^{2} [1329] 7-11-0 92.. SamTwiston-Davies 86
(Dai Burchell) *t.k.h: hld up in tch in rr: rdn and effrt after 3 out: no imp: 7th and wl hld whn fell last* **10/1**

3m 49.6s (1.10) **Going Correction** -0.60s/f (Firm) **8** Ran SP% **115.9**
Speed ratings (Par 103): **73,72,70,69,69 68,65,**
toteswingers 1&2 £10.20, 2&3 £4.20, 1&3 £3.90 CSF £54.90 TOTE £9.40: £2.20, £2.00, £1.10; EX 58.90 Trifecta £199.00 Pool: £1641.87 - 6.18 winning units..
Owner B J Llewellyn **Bred** Gainsborough Stud Management Ltd **Trained** Fochriw, Caerphilly
■ Stewards' Enquiry : A P McCoy caution: careless riding.

FOCUS
They went a steady pace in this competitive claiming hurdle. Most of the runners still had a chance at the second-last and the first two had a good battle in the closing stages. Not form to take too seriously.

1343 BET TOTEQUADPOT AT TOTEPOOL.COM BEGINNERS' CHASE (15 fncs) 2m 3f 110y
3:20 (3:20) (Class 4) 4-Y-0+ **£3,768** (£1,106; £553; £276)

Form RPR
363/ 1 **Red Riverman**[193] [4152] 5-11-7 0 SamTwiston-Davies 128+
(Nigel Twiston-Davies) *chsd ldr and clr of field: upsides and gng best 10th: led bef 12th: in command whn nt fluent 2 out: idling between last 2: drvn and pressed flat: fnd ex fnl 50yds and asserted towards fin* **4/1**[2]
300/ 2 *1* **Ski Sunday**[176] [4448] 8-11-7 0 (t) RichardJohnson 121
(Tim Vaughan) *led and clr of field w wnr: jnd and rdn 10th: hdd bef 12th: looked hld whn hit 2 out: rallied gamely last and chal again fnl 100yds: no ex and hld towards fin* **11/2**[3]
150- 3 *36* **Lava Lamp (GER)**[33] [1042] 6-11-7 0 PaulMoloney 95
(Evan Williams) *chsd ldng pair tl 5th: 4th and outpcd 8th: lft 3rd next: t.o 12th* **11/1**
\- 4 *dist* **Inthelineoffire (IRE)**[131] 8-11-4 0 AdamWedge(3) 57
(David Rees) *a in last: mstke 3rd: losing tch 8th: lft 4th next: wl t.o after 11th* **33/1**
211- F **Man Of Leisure**[23] [1155] 9-11-4 0 (t) RachaelGreen(3)
(Anthony Honeyball) *t.k.h: hld up in 4th: wnt 3rd 5th tl fell 9th* **8/13**[1]

4m 51.25s (-9.85) **Going Correction** -0.825s/f (Firm) **5** Ran SP% **108.6**
Speed ratings (Par 105): **86,85,71,57,**
CSF £22.94 TOTE £3.80: £1.80, £2.10; EX 22.80 Trifecta £30.70 Pool: £1754.14 - 42.78 winning units..
Owner N A Twiston-Davies **Bred** Lady Lonsdale **Trained** Naunton, Gloucs

FOCUS
The hot favourite fell some way out in this beginners' chase but two fair hurdle performers pulled clear and the form looks decent. The idling winner was value for further.

1344 LLEWELLYN HUMPHREYS H'CAP CHASE (18 fncs) 3m
3:55 (3:55) (Class 5) (0-100,100) 4-Y-0+ **£2,144** (£629; £314; £157)

Form RPR
0P4- 1 **Michigan Assassin (IRE)**[9] [1260] 11-11-5 **98** (p) AodhaganConlon(5) 106+
(Debra Hamer) *led tl 5th: dropped to midfield 8th: effrt and pushed along after 14th: lft chsng ldr bef next: chal and pckd last: sn led and forged clr flat: pushed out* **16/1**
506- 2 *2 ½* **Rifleman (IRE)**[29] [1103] 13-10-2 **76** (tp) TomScudamore 82
(Richard Lee) *in tch in midfield: rdn and mstke 14th: sn led: lft 3 l clr bef 15th: drvn bef 2 out: jnd last: sn hdd and no ex flat* **25/1**
500- 3 *4* **Stormyisland Ahead**[44] [930] 8-11-9 **97** (t) PaulMoloney 102
(Evan Williams) *in tch in rr: effrt and hdwy after 14th: lft 3rd and blnd next: styd on same pce u.p fr 2 out* **16/1**
3- 4 *¾* **Merrydown Vintage (IRE)**[33] [1038] 6-11-2 **90** (v[1]) PaddyBrennan 91
(D T Hughes, Ire) *in tch towards rr: rdn along 10th: hdwy to chse ldrs after 14th: lft 4th bef next: plugged on same pce after and hld whn mstke 2 out* **7/2**[2]
0/0- 5 *11* **Kilvergan Boy (IRE)**[102] [248] 9-10-0 **74** oh4 (p) SamTwiston-Davies 67
(Nigel Twiston-Davies) *chsd ldrs: mstke 3rd: rdn after 13th: drvn and lost pl sn after next: lft modest 5th bef 15th: wl btn after* **3/1**[1]
/12- 6 *76* **Kusadasi (IRE)**[45] [926] 8-11-5 **100** (b) MrMatthewBarber(7) 23
(Marc Barber) *chsd ldr tl led 5th: hdd and rdn sn after 14th: immediately dropped out: t.o next* **8/1**
534- P **Lady Myfanwy**[32] [1055] 12-10-13 **94** MissAEStirling(7)
(Adrian Wintle) *dropped to rr 3rd: nvr gng wl after: detached in last fr 5th: lost tch after 9th: t.o whn p.u 11th* **12/1**
P/5- P **Changing Lanes**[32] [1051] 10-11-8 **99** (v) AdamWedge(3)
(David Rees) *in tch towards rr: slt mstke 6th: reminders after next: bhd and struggling 11th: lost tch 13th: t.o whn p.u 15th* **7/1**
F/5- P **Point West (IRE)**[24] [1135] 9-11-7 **95** NickScholfield
(Johnny Farrelly) *in tch in midfield: smooth hdwy to join ldr on bit sn after 14th: lost action: eased and p.u bef next: dismntd* **13/2**[3]
534- P **Jive Master (IRE)**[39] [964] 8-11-7 **95** (b[1]) RichardJohnson
(Tim Vaughan) *bhd early: hdwy to chse ldrs 3rd: wnt 2nd 8th tl sn after 14th: immediately dropped out: t.o whn p.u 3 out* **9/1**

5m 56.25s (-21.15) **Going Correction** -0.825s/f (Firm) **10** Ran SP% **117.5**
Speed ratings (Par 103): **102,101,99,99,95 70,,,,**
toteswingers 1&2 £47.80, 2&3 £17.40, 1&3 £7.40 CSF £313.28 CT £6335.38 TOTE £21.40: £6.10, £5.80, £3.40; EX 462.10 TRIFECTA Not won..
Owner C A Hanbury **Bred** George Ward **Trained** Nantycaws, Carmarthens

FOCUS
Three big-priced runners filled the first three positions in this minor handicap chase. The winner had slipped to a good mark and is rated back to form.

1345 KING SIZE POOLS AT TOTEPOOL.COM H'CAP HURDLE (10 hdls) 2m 4f
4:30 (4:30) (Class 4) (0-120,116) 4-Y-0+ **£5,393** (£1,583; £791; £395)

Form RPR
/13- 1 **Della Sun (FR)**[3] [1319] 7-11-1 **112** JoshWall(7) 121+
(Arthur Whitehead) *hld up in tch in midfield: effrt to chse ldrs bef 2 out: chsd wnr last: led fnl 150yds: r.o strly: rdn out* **4/1**[3]
P41- 2 *1 ¾* **Listen And Learn (IRE)**[9] [1259] 5-10-11 **101** 7ex (p) APMcCoy 108+
(Jonjo O'Neill) *t.k.h: hld up in midfield: effrt to chal bef 2 out: drvn to ld between last 2: dived last: hdd and one pce fnl 150yds* **11/8**[1]
/05- 3 *4 ½* **Diamond's Return (IRE)**[3] [1319] 9-11-7 **111** ConorO'Farrell 114
(David Pipe) *hld up wl off the pce in rr: clsd 5th: effrt after 3 out: no imp tl sme hdwy and bmpd last: styd on flat to go 3rd fnl 50yds: no threat to ldrs* **16/1**
134- 4 *1 ¼* **Prince Pippin (IRE)**[63] [783] 7-10-5 **102** (t) MsLucyJones(7) 103
(Lucy Jones) *t.k.h: chsd ldr tl led 6th: rdn and jnd whn hit 2 out: 3rd and unable qck last: wknd fnl 100yds* **11/1**
423- 5 *1 ¾* **Rime Avec Gentil (FR)**[21] [1173] 8-11-1 **110** AodhaganConlon(5) 110
(Bernard Llewellyn) *t.k.h: chsd ldrs: wnt 2nd 3 out: ev ch and mstke 2 out: no ex and outpcd between last 2: edgd lft and wknd flat* **12/1**
1P1- 6 *4* **Anton Dolin (IRE)**[9] [1269] 5-10-12 **102** 7ex SamTwiston-Davies 99
(Dr Richard Newland) *in tch in midfield: mstke 4th: rdn and j.rt 2 out: 4th and btn whn j.rt again last: wknd flat* **3/1**[2]
604/ 7 *22* **Burnswood (IRE)**[635] [2799] 9-10-7 **97** JoshByrne 71
(Marc Barber) *hld up wl in tch towards rr: rdn 3 out: btn next: wknd qckly between last 2* **50/1**
6/0- 8 *10* **Comehomequietly (IRE)**[9] [1268] 9-11-12 **116** (p) PaulMoloney 80
(David Rees) *led and set stdy gallop: hdd 6th: chsd ldr tl rdn and dropped out bef 3 out: wknd bef 2 out: t.o* **33/1**
614/ P **Knox Overstreet**[50] [5121] 5-10-8 **103** CharlieWallis(5)
(Martin Hill) *lost action and p.u after 1st: dismntd* **22/1**

4m 45.6s (-5.30) **Going Correction** -0.60s/f (Firm) **9** Ran SP% **118.3**
Speed ratings (Par 105): **86,85,83,83,82 80,71,67,**
toteswingers 1&2 £4.80, 2&3 £31.40, 1&3 £34.00 CSF £10.37 CT £79.63 TOTE £11.90: £2.20, £1.30, £3.60; EX 18.50 Trifecta £161.10 Pool: £1961.18 - 9.12 winning units..
Owner A J Whitehead **Bred** Mlle Mathilde Lutz **Trained** Aston on Clun, Shropshire

FOCUS
They went a steady pace in this fair handicap but the well-backed winner stayed on strongly to pick off the favourite and the form looks solid. The winner rates a small personal best.

1346 COLLECT TOTEPOOL WINNINGS AT BETFRED SHOPS H'CAP CHASE (13 fncs) 2m
5:05 (5:07) (Class 2) 4-Y-0+ **£14,242** (£4,207; £2,103; £1,053; £526)

Form RPR
6/5- 1 **My Brother Sylvest**[60] [806] 7-10-8 **124** (b) TomScudamore 132+
(David Pipe) *mde all: j.rt at times: nt fluent 5th: reminders after 8th: hrd pressed between last 2: styd on wl and forged clr again flat: rdn out* **7/1**
431- 2 *2* **Wester Ross (IRE)**[20] [1186] 9-10-1 **120** (v) AdamWedge(3) 126
(Evan Williams) *hld up in tch in rr: mstke 2nd: effrt to chse ldrs 3 out: drvn and pressing wnr between last 2: styd on same pce fr last: wnt 2nd towards fin* **17/2**
141- 3 *¾* **Dineur (FR)**[19] [1194] 7-11-7 **137** DonalDevereux 142
(Peter Bowen) *chsd ldrs: effrt and lft 2nd 10th: rdn and pressing wnr between last 2: no ex and one pce flat: lost 2nd towards fin* **5/2**[1]
/03- 4 *5* **Toubab (FR)**[19] [1194] 7-11-7 **142** HarryDerham(5) 142
(Paul Nicholls) *t.k.h: hld up in tch in midfield: mstke 8th: dropped to rr after mstke 9th: hit next: effrt 3 out: styd on same pce between last 2* **8/1**
/26- 5 *4 ½* **Sagredo (USA)**[32] [1062] 9-10-6 **122** (v) APMcCoy 119
(Jonjo O'Neill) *in tch in last pair: effrt whn mstke and lft 4th 3 out: no imp next: wknd last* **15/2**
314/ 6 *3 ¾* **Rhum (FR)**[145] [5012] 8-10-4 **120** (v[1]) SamTwiston-Davies 115
(Nigel Twiston-Davies) *j.rt and racd wd: chsd ldrs: wnt 2nd 6th tl drvn and blnd 10th: lost pl and wl btn after* **11/2**[3]
421- 7 *35* **De Faoithesdream (IRE)**[19] [1192] 7-10-12 **128** PaulMoloney 89
(Evan Williams) *t.k.h: chsd ldr tl 6th: styd chsng ldrs: lft 2nd 10th: rdn and outpcd whn sprawled on landing and lost all ch next: bhd and j.rt 2 out: virtually p.u flat: t.o* **7/2**[2]

3m 45.6s (-13.80) **Going Correction** -0.825s/f (Firm) **7** Ran SP% **112.1**
Speed ratings (Par 109): **101,100,99,97,94 93,75**
toteswingers 1&2 £8.90, 2&3 £4.40, 1&3 £2.70 CSF £57.68 TOTE £10.10: £2.70, £4.30; EX 51.60 Trifecta £193.90 Pool: £1542.22 - 5.96 winning units..
Owner Teddington Racing Club **Bred** David Brace **Trained** Nicholashayne, Devon

FOCUS
This decent handicap featured several progressive types. A small personal best from the winner with the second in line with his recent win.

1347 IWEC ELECTRICAL MARES' H'CAP HURDLE (8 hdls) 2m
5:35 (5:35) (Class 4) (0-115,111) 4-Y-0+ **£3,119** (£915; £457)

Form RPR
113- 1 **Social Realism (IRE)**[33] [1043] 5-11-12 **111** (p) RichieMcLernon 123+
(Jonjo O'Neill) *w ldr tl led after 2nd: mde rest: hit 5th: clr and in command whn hit 2 out: drew wl clr bef last: easily* **13/8**[2]
6/1- 2 *18* **Great Oak (IRE)**[68] [748] 7-11-9 **108** RichardJohnson 104
(Tim Vaughan) *hld up in 3rd: hdwy to chse clr wnr after 5th: rdn and no imp 2 out: wl btn between last 2* **11/10**[1]
U63- 3 *24* **Presenting Me (IRE)**[7] [1273] 5-10-9 **97** AdamWedge(3) 76
(Evan Williams) *led tl after 2nd: dropped to last and rdn after 5th: lost tch after next: t.o* **7/2**[3]

3m 37.0s (-11.50) **Going Correction** -0.60s/f (Firm)
WFA 4 from 5yo+ 13lb **3** Ran SP% **107.9**
Speed ratings (Par 105): **104,95,83**
CSF £3.83 TOTE £1.70; EX 2.80 Trifecta £3.20 Pool: £405.41 - 94.64 winning units..
Owner Mrs Diane Carr **Bred** Darley **Trained** Cheltenham, Gloucs

FOCUS
The was an easy winner in this small-field mares' handicap. The time was good and it could pay to be positive despite the small field.
T/Plt: £496.30 to a £1 stake. Pool of £55281.04 - 81.30 winning tickets. T/Qpdt: £157.00 to a £1 stake. Pool of £2759.55 - 13.0 winning tickets. SP

1335 NEWTON ABBOT (L-H)
Thursday, August 22

OFFICIAL GOING: Good to firm (7.8)
Wind: mild breeze Weather: sunny

1348 DAVID COOK HAPPY BIRTHDAY MAIDEN HURDLE (8 hdls) 2m 1f
5:25 (5:25) (Class 4) 4-Y-0+ **£3,508** (£1,030; £515; £257)

Form RPR
F- 1 **Leader Of The Land (IRE)**[23] [1152] 6-10-12 0 MichealNolan(3) 105+
(Robert Stephens) *trckd ldr: led bef 2 out: in command whn wnt lft last 2: r.o: comf* **14/1**
324- 2 *6* **Osorios Trial**[9] [1258] 6-11-1 105 NoelFehily 96
(Anthony Middleton) *hld up towards rr: tk clsr order 3 out: sn rdn and lost pl: hdwy appr 2 out: styd on to go 2nd bef last: no ch w wnr* **9/4**[2]
04- 3 *10* **Chapelle du Roi (USA)**[32] [1059] 4-11-0 0 IanPopham 86
(Robert Stephens) *in tch: hmpd 3rd: wnt 3rd under disp 2nd u.p bef 2 out: styd on same pce* **33/1**
0F- 4 *3 ½* **Bolberry Springs**[38] [994] 6-11-1 0 JoeTizzard 88
(Colin Tizzard) *led: bdly hmpd by loose horse 3rd: rdn and hdd bef 2 out: 4th whn nt fluent 2 out: nt fluent last: no ex* **14/1**
360/ 5 *1 ¾* **Portway Flyer (IRE)**[197] [4068] 5-10-10 0 RobertMcCarth(5) 82
(Ian Williams) *hld up towards rr: in tch but struggling 5th: drvn and btn sn after 3 out* **13/8**[1]
6 *3 ¼* **Highlife Dancer**[11] 5-11-1 0 WillKennedy 80
(Mick Channon) *trckd ldrs: nodded on landing 1st: blnd 2nd: rdn bef 3 out: wknd bef next* **7/1**[3]
/35- 7 *10* **Bob Tucker (IRE)**[9] [1256] 6-11-1 0 AlainCawley 70
(Brendan Powell) *mid-div: struggling towards rr 5th: sn no ch* **12/1**
/0P- 8 *4* **No No Cardinal (IRE)**[23] [1152] 4-11-0 0 TommyPhelan 66
(Mark Gillard) *racd keenly in last: hmpd 1st: hdwy 3 out: rdn into 3rd briefly sn after: wknd qckly appr 2 out* **50/1**
U **Keyhole Kate**[15] 4-10-4 0 (p) JamesBest(3)
(Polly Gundry) *wnt rt and v awkward whn uns rdr 1st* **66/1**

The Form Book Jumps, Raceform Ltd, Compton, RG20 6NL.

F **Lily Potts**[15] 4-10-7 0 .... JamesDavies
(Chris Down) *mid-div whn fell 3rd* **12/1**

/65- U **Nudge The Nugget**[2] 1329 5-10-12 0 ....(b) MarkQuinlan(3)
(Nigel Hawke) *trckd ldrs: hmpd whn wnt bdly lft and uns rdr 3rd* **150/1**

4m 0.2s (-5.50) **Going Correction** -0.55s/f (Firm)
WFA 4 from 5yo+ 13lb **11** Ran SP% **117.1**
Speed ratings (Par 105): **90,87,82,80,80 78,73,71, ,**
toteswingers 1&2 £5.50, 2&3 £7.70, 1&3 £20.80 CSF £46.56 TOTE £17.60: £2.90, £1.40, £7.70; EX 51.00 Trifecta £481.20 Pool: £1411.27 - 2.19 winning units..
Owner Mark Duthie & Partners **Bred** Rabbah Bloodstock Limited **Trained** Penhow, Newport
■ The first training success for Robert Stephens.

FOCUS
Rails moved out 2-3yds from Wednesday. This was a modest maiden that proved an eventful heat. It's rated around the second and fourth, and the winner can rate a lot higher on old Flat form.

1349 SIS LIVE H'CAP CHASE (20 fncs) 3m 2f 110y
6:00 (6:00) (Class 5) (0-100,100) 4-Y-0+ **£2,729** (£801; £400; £200)

Form RPR

636- 1 **Health Is Wealth (IRE)**[39] 972 8-11-5 **100** ....(tp) ConorShoemark(7) 109+
(Colin Tizzard) *travelled best: trckd ldr: led 2 out: idling but sn in command: kpt on but rdn out run-in* **11/4**[2]

/5P- 2 *3* **Monty's Revenge (IRE)**[36] 1015 8-11-3 **91** .... IanPopham 96
(Martin Keighley) *led: j.rt thrght bdly at times: pushed along after 15th: rdn after 4 out: hdd 2 out: styd on same pce* **8/1**

434- 3 *13* **Minella Bliss (IRE)**[27] 1121 8-11-2 **90** .... AlainCawley 85
(Nikki Evans) *hld up in last pair: nt fluent 1st or 3rd: slow 4th: pushed along after 14th: struggling and rdn after 16th: wnt 3rd after 3 out: nvr any imp on ldng duo* **2/1**[1]

/PP- 4 *8* **Minella Ranger (IRE)**[32] 1055 7-11-5 **93** .... TomO'Brien 79
(Paul Henderson) *hld up in last pair: struggling after 15th: wnt 4th after 3 out but nvr any imp on ldrs* **9/2**[3]

1P/- P **Paradise Expected**[125] 151 10-11-2 **90** .... TommyPhelan
(Mark Gillard) *trckd ldrs: slow 9th: sn niggled along: dropped to last u.p 14th: sn t.o: p.u bef 4 out* **20/1**

/14- P **Chase Gate**[73] 689 8-11-9 **97** ....(p) HaddenFrost
(James Frost) *trckd ldrs: struggling 16th: wknd after 3 out: p.u bef last* **5/1**

6m 36.1s (-8.50) **Going Correction** -0.55s/f (Firm) **6** Ran SP% **110.7**
Speed ratings (Par 103): **90,89,85,82,**
toteswingers 1&2 £3.40, 2&3 £3.20, 1&3 £1.70 CSF £22.24 TOTE £4.30: £1.90, £4.00; EX 19.60 Trifecta £59.40 Pool: £1044.01 - 13.17 winning units..
Owner Gale Force Five **Bred** Bernard Fenton **Trained** Milborne Port, Dorset

FOCUS
A moderate handicap, dominated by the first pair who are rated to their marks.

1350 NEWTONABBOTRACING.COM H'CAP HURDLE (9 hdls) 2m 3f
6:35 (6:35) (Class 2) (0-150,140) 4-Y-0+ **£10,406** (£3,074; £1,537; £769; £384)

Form RPR

421- 1 **Rum And Butter (IRE)**[32] 1054 5-10-8 **122** ....(p) APMcCoy 132+
(Jonjo O'Neill) *travelled strly thrght: trckd ldr: jnd ldr 3 out: led bef 2 out: qcknd clr: v easily* **11/8**[1]

101- 2 *4 ½* **Get Home Now**[18] 1203 5-10-7 **121** ....(tp) TomO'Brien 124+
(Peter Bowen) *trckd ldrs: nt clr run whn swtchd rt on bnd after 3 out: rdn to chse wnr bef next: readily hld whn nt fluent 2 out: kpt on same pce* **7/2**[2]

121- 3 *16* **Life And Soul (IRE)**[33] 1041 6-11-7 **135** ....(p) JasonMaguire 123
(Donald McCain) *led: drvn whn jnd after 3: hdd bef next: sn fdd in disp 3rd: lft clr 3rd at the last* **7/2**[2]

311- 4 *2 ½* **Cool Macavity (IRE)**[20] 1183 5-11-2 **130** .... DavidBass 114
(Nicky Henderson) *hld up bhd ldrs: nudged along 4th: dsiputed cl 3rd 3 out: rdn bef next: sn fdd: blnd and lost disp 3rd at the last* **6/1**[3]

2/1- 5 *18* **Pasture Bay (IRE)**[18] 1200 7-9-7 **114** .... ConorShoemark(7) 82
(Fergal O'Brien) *kpt wdst: hld up bhd ldrs: rdn after 6th: btn next: t.o* **10/1**

4m 15.2s (-14.80) **Going Correction** -0.55s/f (Firm) **5** Ran SP% **109.9**
Speed ratings (Par 109): **109,107,100,99,91**
CSF £6.67 TOTE £2.30: £1.10, £1.70; EX 6.90 Trifecta £18.40 Pool: £907.46 - 36.91 winning units..
Owner John P McManus **Bred** William Hubbert **Trained** Cheltenham, Gloucs

FOCUS
All five of these had scored last time out so it was obviously a fair event, even if the top weight was rated 15lb lower than the race ceiling. They went a sound gallop and got sorted out from the home turn. The easy winner is improving fast and should win again.

1351 HAPPY 60TH BIRTHDAY SUE ANDREWS H'CAP HURDLE (9 hdls) 2m 3f
7:05 (7:05) (Class 5) (0-95,95) 4-Y-0+ **£2,463** (£718; £359)

Form RPR

0P/- 1 **Sugar Hiccup (IRE)**[239] 3213 5-10-10 **78** .... APMcCoy 92+
(Jim Best) *tended to jump sltly lft: trckd ldrs: led 6th: pushed clr appr 2 out: in n.d after: readily* **5/6**[1]

/4F- 2 *4 ½* **Himrayn**[29] 1109 10-10-10 **83** .... JoshHamer(5) 86
(Anabel K Murphy) *hld up towards rr: hdwy into midfield after 5th: pushed along bef next: rdn and further stdy prog after 3 out: styd on to go 2nd bef last: no ch w wnr* **16/1**

503- 3 *2 ¾* **No Woman No Cry**[1] 1339 8-11-3 **85** ....(tp) JoeTizzard 86
(Colin Tizzard) *mid-div: rdn and hdwy after 3 out: styd on to chse wnr bef 2 out but no ch: lost 2nd bef last: styd on same pce* **4/1**[2]

405- 4 *2* **Sedgemoor Express (IRE)**[30] 1087 5-11-0 **85** ....(tp) MarkQuinlan(3) 84
(Nigel Hawke) *mid-div: hdwy 5th: rdn to chse wnr after 3 out tl next: styd on same pce* **14/1**

P43- 5 *8* **Illegale (IRE)**[38] 1000 7-10-6 **74** ....(t) DougieCostello 68
(Phillip Dando) *led tl 6th: kpt chsng wnr tl appr 2 out: grad fdd* **10/1**

00- 6 *19* **Seaside Shuffle (IRE)**[18] 1206 8-11-9 **94** .... JamesBest(3) 69
(Sophie Leech) *mid-div tl after 6th: sn bhd: t.o* **50/1**

00P- 7 *nk* **Wheelavit (IRE)**[18] 1206 10-11-5 **87** .... LiamHeard 62
(Claire Dyson) *trckd ldrs: rdn and wknd after 3 out: t.o* **50/1**

/45- 8 *nse* **Cash Injection**[94] 407 4-11-8 **95** ....(t) MichealNolan(3) 71
(Richard Woollacott) *mid-div: rdn appr 6th: mstke 3 out: sn wknd: t.o* **8/1**[3]

566- 9 *4 ½* **Robber Stone**[9] 1269 5-11-0 **82** .... PaulMoloney 53
(Debra Hamer) *towards rr: sme prog into midfield whn nt fluent 3 out: sn wknd: t.o* **25/1**

P/F- 10 *3 ½* **Wadham Hill**[78] 637 11-10-7 **82** .... ConorShoemark(7) 49
(William Reed) *struggling 5th: a in rr: t.o* **66/1**

4/6- 11 *5* **Bold Tara**[21] 1169 6-11-6 **88** ....(t) IanPopham 51
(Martin Keighley) *in tch tl rdn after 6th: wknd next: t.o* **16/1**

4m 20.2s (-9.80) **Going Correction** -0.55s/f (Firm)
WFA 4 from 5yo+ 13lb **11** Ran SP% **122.4**
Speed ratings (Par 103): **98,96,94,94,90 82,82,82,80,79 77**
toteswingers 1&2 £8.70, 2&3 £7.80, 1&3 £2.10 CSF £16.32 CT £43.76 TOTE £1.80: £1.20, £3.60, £1.70; EX 24.50 Trifecta £50.00 Pool: £1041.43 - 15.59 winning units..
Owner Jack Callaghan & Christopher Dillon **Bred** Raysiza Partnership **Trained** Lewes, E Sussex

FOCUS
This ordinary handicap was notable for the plunge on Sugar Hiccup and the 5yo fully justified such support with a comfortable success. She can rate a lot higher on Flat form, and the time was good for the grade.

1352 PAIGNTON ZOO H'CAP CHASE (13 fncs) 2m 110y
7:35 (7:35) (Class 4) (0-120,118) 4-Y-0+ **£4,288** (£1,259; £629; £314)

Form RPR

032- 1 **Bennys Quest (IRE)**[27] 1122 10-10-9 **104** ....(p) PeterCarberry(3) 116+
(Neil Mulholland) *trckd ldrs: nt fluent 3rd: trckd ldr after 3 out: rdn to ld bef last: r.o strly* **9/4**[1]

136- 2 *6* **Mibleu (FR)**[9] 1263 13-11-0 **111** .... EDLinehan(5) 116
(Colin Tizzard) *racd keenly: trckd ldrs: wnt prom after 5th: led 7th: rdn between last 2: hdd whn hit last: no ex* **6/1**[3]

564- 3 *13* **Manger Hanagment (IRE)**[19] 1194 8-11-12 **118** ....(p) APMcCoy 109
(Barry Brennan) *trckd ldr: disp fr 3rd tl led after 5th: hdd 7th: rdn after next: kpt chsng ldr tl after 3 out: wknd between last 2* **5/2**[2]

042- 4 *2* **Trooper Clarence**[23] 1151 9-11-12 **118** .... PaulMoloney 108
(Evan Williams) *led: jnd 3rd: blnd and hdd 5th: trckd ldrs but nvr really travelling after: rdn after 9th: wknd between last 2* **5/2**[2]

/06- 5 *10* **Delphi Mountain (IRE)**[38] 999 8-11-3 **112** ....(t) MichealNolan(3) 91
(Richard Woollacott) *trckd ldrs: nt fluent 4th: rdn after 8th: btn 4 out* **12/1**

3m 54.2s (-12.30) **Going Correction** -0.55s/f (Firm) **5** Ran SP% **109.9**
Speed ratings (Par 105): **106,103,97,96,91**
CSF £14.69 TOTE £2.40: £1.60, £2.30; EX 13.70 Trifecta £49.60 Pool: £611.69 - 9.24 winning units..
Owner John Hobbs & Dave Harris **Bred** Patrick J McGrath **Trained** Limpley Stoke, Wilts

FOCUS
A modest little handicap. It was run at a fair gallop and the winner is rated back to his very best for his in-form yard.

1353 IRL INDEPENDENT RACECOURSES LTD INTERMEDIATE OPEN NATIONAL HUNT FLAT RACE 2m 1f
8:05 (8:05) (Class 5) 4-6-Y-0 **£2,094** (£610; £305)

Form RPR

1 **Chalk It Down (IRE)** 4-11-0 0 .... NoelFehily 110+
(Warren Greatrex) *trckd ldr: led gng wl over 1f out: nudged clr: readily* **8/11**[1]

2 *2 ¾* **What A Joke (IRE)**[95] 6-10-8 0 .... ConorShoemark(7) 98
(William Reed) *led: rdn 2f out: hdd over 1f out: kpt on but nt gng pce of ready wnr* **14/1**

2- 3 *1 ¾* **Hazel Brook**[39] 970 4-10-7 0 .... APMcCoy 88
(Mary Hambro) *hld up in 4th: tk clsr order 5f out: rdn to chse ldng pair over 2f out: nt gng pce to get on terms* **7/4**[2]

0/ 4 *16* **Fireweld**[233] 3430 6-10-1 0 .... MikeyEnnis(7) 73
(Patricia Shaw) *trckd ldrs: rdn over 2f out: sn outpcd: wknd fnl f* **33/1**

6- 5 *20* **Ruperra Tom**[24] 1138 5-11-1 0 .... PaulMoloney 60
(Sophie Leech) *hld up in last of 5but wl in tch: effrt wl over 2f out: wknd ent st: t.o* **17/2**[3]

3m 58.0s (-2.10) **Going Correction** -0.55s/f (Firm)
WFA 4 from 5yo+ 1lb **5** Ran SP% **114.4**
Speed ratings: **82,80,79,72,62**
CSF £12.80 TOTE £1.40: £1.10, £3.60; EX 12.60 Trifecta £65.30 Pool: £1089.03 - 12.50 winning units..
Owner Warren Greatrex **Bred** Michael Ryan **Trained** Upper Lambourn, Berks

FOCUS
The market screamed that newcomer Chalk It Down was the one to be with in this moderate bumper and ran out an easy winner. He was value for further.
T/Plt: £82.80 to a £1 state. Pool of £50368.38 - 443.95 winning tickets. T/Qpdt: £9.60 to a £1 stake. Pool of £5143.44 - 395.54 winning tickets. TM

1354 - 1360a (Foreign Racing) - See Raceform Interactive

1341 FFOS LAS (L-H)
Friday, August 23

OFFICIAL GOING: Good (7.7)
Wind: light, across Weather: dry, overcast, showers

1361 EXCLUSIVE OFFERS ON TOTEPOOL MOBILE H'CAP CHASE (17 fncs) 2m 5f
4:05 (4:05) (Class 4) (0-115,110) 4-Y-0+ **£3,861** (£1,198; £645)

Form RPR

412- 1 **Fairwood Massini (IRE)**[6] 1286 8-11-5 **106** ....(vt) MichaelByrne(3) 121+
(Tim Vaughan) *chsd ldrs: led 13th: clr 2 out: r.o wl* **9/4**[2]

41F- 2 *10* **Forever My Friend (IRE)**[34] 1039 6-11-12 **110** .... JamieMoore 118
(Peter Bowen) *chsd ldrs: chsd wnr bef 14th: wknd between last 2* **5/1**[3]

165- 3 *43* **Wait No More (IRE)**[34] 1039 8-11-6 **104** ....(p) DougieCostello 86
(Neil Mulholland) *chsd ldr tl led 10th: hdd 13th: losing tch whn lft poor 3rd next: t.o* **11/1**

F0P/ P **Battlecry**[280] 2456 12-11-10 **108** .... SamTwiston-Davies
(Nigel Twiston-Davies) *led tl 10th: rdn and struggling next: lost tch rapidly 13th: t.o and p.u next* **6/1**

/P1- F **Favoured Nation (IRE)**[45] 930 6-11-10 **108** .... APMcCoy
(Jonjo O'Neill) *nt fluent: hld up in rr: hdwy 11th: cl 3rd whn fell 14th* **11/8**[1]

5m 11.1s (-17.50) **Going Correction** -0.75s/f (Firm) **5** Ran SP% **112.2**
Speed ratings (Par 105): **103,99,82, ,**
CSF £13.39 TOTE £3.10: £1.90, £2.30; EX 12.90 Trifecta £51.30 Pool: £1260.04 - 18.40 winning units..
Owner Wayne Jones **Bred** T Kent **Trained** Aberthin, Vale of Glamorgan

FOCUS
Just a small field, but with Battlecry and Wait No More jostling for the lead they effectively ran themselves out of it. The winner is rated in line with the best of his hurdles form.

1362 COLLECT TOTEPOOL WINNINGS AT BETFRED SHOPS CHASE H'CAP CHASE (19 fncs) 3m 1f 110y
4:40 (4:40) (Class 2) 4-Y-0+ **£14,242** (£4,207; £2,103; £1,053; £526)

Form RPR
231- **1** **Pantxoa (FR)**[10] 1257 6-10-6 **125** 6ex.......................... WayneHutchinson 138+
(Alan King) *mde all: styd on wl: rdn out* **9/4**[1]
/F1- **2** *1 ½* **Twirling Magnet (IRE)**[31] 1085 7-11-4 **137**......................(tp) APMcCoy 147
(Jonjo O'Neill) *midfield: hdwy to chse ldrs 15th: 2nd 3 out: one pce flat* **4/1**[2]
602- **3** *7* **Pineau De Re (FR)**[6] 1283 10-11-2 **135**.................. SamTwiston-Davies 139
(Dr Richard Newland) *hld up in tch towards rr: effrt 3 out: one pce fr next* **5/1**[3]
026/ **4** *nse* **Your Busy (IRE)**[23] 1167 10-10-8 **127**.............................. JasonMaguire 131
(J A Nash, Ire) *t.k.h: hld up towards rr: effrt 3 out: one pce between last 2* **20/1**
203- **5** *4* **Siberian Tiger (IRE)**[34] 1040 8-9-12 **120**........................ AdamWedge(3) 120
(Evan Williams) *hld up in tch in rr: hdwy bef 16th: rdn and little rspnse 3 out: wknd next* **18/1**
/21- **6** *13* **No Loose Change (IRE)**[46] 923 8-11-7 **145**.............(t) HarryDerham(5) 133
(Paul Nicholls) *chsd ldrs: wnt 2nd 14th to 3 out: wknd next* **8/1**
320- **7** *3* **Buck Mulligan**[34] 1047 8-11-0 **133**.................................. PaulMoloney 119
(Evan Williams) *hld up in tch in rr: effrt after 16th: sn btn* **16/1**
31/ **8** *9* **Barel Of Laughs (IRE)**[8] 1276 7-10-6 **125**........................ DenisO'Regan 103
(J H Culloty, Ire) *chsd ldrs: rdn after 16th: wknd next* **8/1**
211- **9** *25* **Gullible Gordon (IRE)**[63] 787 10-11-2 **135**..............(vt) DonalDevereux 90
(Peter Bowen) *chsd ldrs tl 14th: rdn and dropped to rr next: t.o 2 out* **15/2**

6m 14.15s (-26.85) **Going Correction** -0.75s/f (Firm) **9** Ran SP% **117.3**
Speed ratings (Par 109): **111,110,108,108,107 103,102,99,91**
toteswingers 1&2 £3.40, 2&3 £3.70, 1&3 £5.10 CSF £12.49 CT £40.80 TOTE £3.40: £1.20, £1.70, £1.60; EX 19.30 Trifecta £80.60 Pool: £2371.21 - 22.05 winning units..
Owner Mrs June Watts **Bred** Pierre De Maleissye Melun **Trained** Barbury Castle, Wilts

FOCUS
A competitive handicap with three of the recent winners in the field filling the first three places, giving the form a solid look, with the third and fourth setting the level.

1363 TODAROS HAIR BEAUTY AND BARBERS H'CAP HURDLE (12 hdls) 3m
5:15 (5:15) (Class 3) (0-130,123) 4-Y-0+ **£5,393** (£1,583; £791; £395)

Form RPR
/02- **1** **Benbane Head (USA)**[20] 1195 9-11-12 **123**........................(t) IanPopham 130
(Martin Keighley) *chsd ldrs: ev ch 3 out: led next: edgd lft and styd on wl flat* **15/2**[3]
P21- **2** *1* **Mission Complete (IRE)**[6] 1284 7-11-5 **116** 7ex................(p) APMcCoy 122
(Jonjo O'Neill) *led: jnd 3 out: hdd and drvn next: one pce flat* **6/5**[1]
452- **3** *4 ½* **Nicky Nutjob (GER)**[8] 1188 7-9-7 **97** oh1...................(p) CiaranMckee(7) 98
(John O'Shea) *hld up wl in tch: effrt 3 out: outpcd next: kpt on flat* **14/1**
2- **4** *¾* **Zalgarry (FR)**[37] 1020 6-10-11 **115**.. JoshWall(7) 115
(Arthur Whitehead) *hld up wl in tch: hdwy to join ldrs 3 out: btn between last 2: one pce flat* **10/1**
/01- **5** *2 ¾* **Gap Of Dunloe (IRE)**[46] 925 5-10-11 **108**..............(tp) RichardJohnson 107
(Peter Bowen) *wl in tch midfield: ev ch and rdn 3 out: struggling next: wknd bef last* **11/4**[2]
650/ **6** *15* **Royal Riviera**[230] 3502 7-11-1 **112**.......................(t) SamTwiston-Davies 96
(Nigel Twiston-Davies) *t.k.h chsd ldrs: rdn bef 3 out: wknd 2 out* **8/1**

5m 56.3s (7.30) **Going Correction** -0.10s/f (Good) **6** Ran SP% **110.8**
Speed ratings (Par 107): **83,82,81,80,80 75**
toteswingers 1&2 £2.40, 1&3 £5.30, 2&3 £3.10 CSF £17.22 TOTE £6.40: £2.50, £1.70; EX 16.30 Trifecta £84.20 Pool: £1639.72 - 14.59 winning units..
Owner Mrs Louise Jones **Bred** Five Horses Ltd **Trained** Condicote, Gloucs

FOCUS
After a steady first circuit they all had a chance turning in, before the first two pulled clear in a prolonged tussle. The first three are rated pretty much to their marks.

1364 STRADEY PARK H'CAP HURDLE (10 hdls) 2m 4f
5:45 (5:46) (Class 5) (0-95,94) 4-Y-0+ **£1,949** (£572; £286; £143)

Form RPR
5P0- **1** **Isthereadifference (IRE)**[58] 844 6-11-8 **90**........................(p) NoelFehily 95+
(Neil Mulholland) *hld up in midfield: hdwy to ld bef 3 out: clr last: a holding on: rdn out* **12/1**
5/3- **2** *1* **Thomas Bell (IRE)**[10] 1266 9-9-11 **72**.............................. CiaranMckee(7) 75
(John O'Shea) *hld up bhd: hdwy 3 out: wnt 3rdand mstke last: r.o wl flat: too much to do* **12/1**
320- **3** *4 ½* **Gwili Spar**[64] 783 5-10-12 **80**..(t) TomO'Brien 81
(Peter Bowen) *t.k.h: hld up in tch in rr: hdwy 3 out: chal and j.lft next: btn whn mstke last: wknd flat* **4/1**[2]
P40/ **4** *6* **Perfect Timing**[116] 29 5-11-10 **92**.................................... NickScholfield 86
(Johnny Farrelly) *hld up in tch towards rr: reminders after 4th: hdwy 7th: wknd between last 2* **8/1**
043/ **5** *12* **The Nephew (IRE)**[125] 5412 5-11-11 **93**.............................. APMcCoy 76
(Jonjo O'Neill) *led: mstke 3rd: hdd bef 3 out: wknd 2 out* **9/4**[1]
6P/- **6** *3 ¼* **Millenarys Lady (IRE)**[418] 847 6-11-2 **84**.............................. PaulMoloney 64
(David Rees) *hld up in rr: shkn up after 6th: modest late hdwy but n.d* **25/1**
112- **7** *6* **Chilbury Hill (IRE)**[31] 1086 10-11-6 **91**..................(t) MichaelByrne(3) 67
(Tim Vaughan) *in tch in midfield: mstke 5th: drvn to chse ldrs 3 out: wknd next* **6/1**[3]
660/ **8** *½* **Lovely Muck**[148] 4989 8-11-12 **94**............................ SamTwiston-Davies 68
(Nigel Twiston-Davies) *in tch in midfield: rdn after 7th: wknd next* **12/1**
0PP/ **9** *2 ¾* **Mumbles Bay (IRE)**[172] 4559 7-10-1 **69**........................ DonalDevereux 41
(Peter Bowen) *chsd ldr tl wnt 2nd 7th tl bef 3 out: sn wknd* **7/1**
6/0- **10** *6* **Kristallo (GER)**[17] 730 8-11-2 **87**............................(b) RobertDunne(3) 53
(Dai Burchell) *chsd ldr tl 7th: sn wknd and t.o* **28/1**
/30- **11** *10* **Copper Carroll (IRE)**[52] 860 9-10-7 **82**.....................(p) AlanJohns(7) 39
(Beth Roberts) *chsd ldrs: rdn 5th: lost pl next and t.o 3 out* **22/1**
103- **12** *28* **Starlight Air**[71] 730 10-11-11 **93**...................................... JamieMoore 25
(John Spearing) *midfield: lost pl 6th: t.o 3 out* **25/1**

4m 48.0s (-2.90) **Going Correction** -0.10s/f (Good) **12** Ran SP% **127.2**
Speed ratings (Par 103): **101,100,98,96,91 90,87,87,86,84 80,69**
toteswingers 1&2 £13.40, 1&3 £9.30, 2&3 £8.00 CSF £147.04 CT £695.68 TOTE £15.70: £4.40, £4.50, £1.50; EX 178.50 Trifecta £996.60 Part won. Pool: £1328.87 - 0.92 winning units..
Owner The Colony Stable LLC **Bred** Daryl Deacon **Trained** Limpley Stoke, Wilts

FOCUS
A fair race for the grade, run at an honest pace. Straightforward form. The winner was well in on the best of his form and is rated back to that level.

T/Plt: £199.90 to a £1 stake. Pool of £53477.13 -195.20 winning tickets. T/Qpdt: £7.40 to a £1 stake. Pool of £5251.59 - 518.39 winning tickets. SP

1365 - 1372a (Foreign Racing) - See Raceform Interactive

[1072]CARTMEL (L-H)
Saturday, August 24

OFFICIAL GOING: Good (good to soft in places; 7.2)
Wind: light 1/2 against Weather: overcast, becoming warm and sunny after race 2

1373 EBF MARY COOKSON MARES' "NATIONAL HUNT" NOVICES' HURDLE (11 hdls) 2m 6f
2:30 (2:30) (Class 4) 4-Y-0+ **£3,249** (£954; £477; £238)

Form RPR
322- **1** **Me And Ben (IRE)**[5] 1321 6-10-10 97...........................(t) PaddyBrennan 100+
(Fergal O'Brien) *trckd ldrs: pushed along 8th: upsides 2 out: sn led: drvn out* **8/11**[1]
225- **2** *3 ½* **Je T'Aime (IRE)**[7] 1286 4-10-8 90......................................(p) JasonMaguire 92
(Donald McCain) *led: hdd sn after 2 out: kpt on same pce* **11/4**[2]
6- **3** *7* **Tillernoora (IRE)**[7] 1292 6-10-3 0..............................(t) GrantCockburn(7) 88
(Patrick Griffin, Ire) *chsd ldr: one pce appr 2 out* **50/1**
36/ **4** *34* **Mini Muck**[733] 1469 7-10-10 0.................................... SamTwiston-Davies 57
(Nigel Twiston-Davies) *chsng ldrs whn nt fluent and lost pl 4th: outpcd 8th: sn bhd: t.o between last 2* **11/2**[3]
/53- **U** **Langley House (IRE)**[102] 278 6-10-10 90............................ HenryBrooke
(Dianne Sayer) *chsd ldrs 6th: hit 8th: sn drvn and lost pl: distant 5th whn leather broke and uns rdr bef 2 out* **8/1**

5m 30.6s (1.30) **Going Correction** -0.075s/f (Good)
WFA 4 from 6yo+ 14lb **5** Ran SP% **113.0**
Speed ratings (Par 105): **94,92,90,77,**
CSF £3.30 TOTE £1.50: £1.10, £1.60; EX 3.00 Trifecta £26.00 Pool: £478.04 - 13.75 winning units..
Owner M C Fahy **Bred** Micheal Fahy **Trained** Coln St. Dennis, Gloucs
■ Kitnkaboodle was withdrawn. Price at time of withdrawal 25-1. Rule 4 does not apply.

FOCUS
Track at inner configuration. The ground remained good, good to soft in places (a description generally confirmed by jockeys riding in the opener) after only a millimetre of rain fell overnight. An uncompetitive mares' novices' hurdle which was steadily run. It is rated around the first two.

1374 HADWINS H'CAP HURDLE (11 hdls) 2m 6f
3:05 (3:06) (Class 5) (0-95,95) 4-Y-0+ **£2,599** (£763; £381; £190)

Form RPR
2P4- **1** **Pete**[33] 1078 10-10-12 **88**.......................................(tp) GrahamWatters(7) 95
(Barry Murtagh) *trckd ldrs gng wl: 2nd 2 out: led on bit between last 2: drvn fnl f: a doing jst enough* **12/1**
/56- **2** *½* **Flying Doctor**[7] 1284 10-11-4 **90**.................................. EwanWhillans(3) 97
(Alistair Whillans) *w ldrs: led 8th: hdd between last: rallied and kpt on wl fnl f: a jst hld* **5/2**[1]
230- **3** *22* **Galley Slave (IRE)**[20] 1205 8-10-9 **83**................................ JoeCornwall(5) 70
(Michael Chapman) *mid-div: hdwy 3 out: 4th betwen last 2: poor 3rd 1f out* **12/1**
/00- **4** *8* **Western Bound (IRE)**[52] 868 12-10-0 **69** oh5...............(t[1]) SeanQuinlan 49
(Barbara Butterworth) *chsd ldrs: modest 3rd 2 out: one pce* **33/1**
/6P- **5** *7* **Word Of Warning**[14] 751 9-11-8 **91**................................ JasonMaguire 65
(Martin Todhunter) *hld up in rr: sme hdwy 8th: nvr a factor* **10/1**
260- **6** *3* **Moscow Me (IRE)**[11] 1255 6-11-9 **92**................................. HenryOliver 63
(Henry Oliver) *hld up in mid-div: shkn up 6th: upsides 8th: wknd after 2 out* **6/1**[3]
562- **7** *nk* **Rare Coincidence**[14] 1078 12-10-12 **81**........................(tp) BrianHarding 52
(Alan Berry) *led: hdd 8th: sn wknd* **12/1**
314- **8** *8* **Executive's Hall (IRE)**[22] 1188 9-11-5 **95**................(p) CraigGallagher(7) 59
(Ben Haslam) *w ldrs: wknd 2 out* **11/4**[2]
/53- **9** *¾* **King Brex (DEN)**[24] 1158 10-10-5 **81**.........................(p) MrKitAlexander(7) 44
(N W Alexander) *in rr: nt fluent 5th: bhd fr 3 out* **25/1**
/06- **10** *nk* **Almutaham (USA)**[22] 1188 6-11-7 **90**................................ FearghalDavis 53
(Nicky Richards) *in rr: bhd and drvn 5th: nvr a factor* **10/1**
054- **11** *52* **Cigalas**[25] 1143 8-10-1 **70**.. AdrianLane
(Jean McGregor) *chsd ldrs: reminders 5th: lost pl 7th: sn bhd: t.o 2 out: eventually completed* **20/1**
60/- **P** **Taylors Secret**[423] 840 7-10-6 **82**............................. StephenMulqueen(7)
(Patricia Rigby) *in rr: reminders 3rd: t.o whn p.u after 4th* **50/1**

5m 23.7s (-5.60) **Going Correction** -0.075s/f (Good) **12** Ran SP% **124.3**
Speed ratings (Par 103): **107,106,98,95,93 92,92,89,88,88 69,**
toteswingers 1&2 £20.20, 1&3 £20.20, 2&3 £17.10 CSF £43.85 CT £392.38 TOTE £9.20: £2.90, £1.70, £3.00; EX 68.60 Trifecta £316.30 Part won. Pool: £421.80 - 0.01 winning units..
Owner Mrs Sue Murtagh **Bred** Mrs Sue Murtagh And Brian Callaghan **Trained** Low Braithwaite, Cumbria

FOCUS
Plenty of course form on offer for this low-grade handicap hurdle but many of the field were out of sorts. Off a fair pace few got involved with the front pair pulling well clear of the rest. Not form to be confident about.

1375 BURLINGTON STONE EBF BEGINNERS' CHASE (14 fncs) 2m 5f 110y
3:40 (3:40) (Class 4) 4-Y-0+ **£3,768** (£1,106; £553; £276)

Form RPR
234- **1** **Bracken House (IRE)**[11] 1266 6-11-7 0.........................(tp) PaulMoloney 115+
(Graeme McPherson) *t.k.h: blnd 1st: jnd ldrs 9th: blnd and sddle slippedrt bk 2 out: taken wd last: led 2f out: forged clr* **13/2**[2]
216/ **2** *9* **Foundry Square (IRE)**[130] 5327 7-11-7 0............... SamTwiston-Davies 104
(Nigel Twiston-Davies) *led to 4th: w ldr: led 9th: hdd 3 out: rdn to ld sn after last: hdd 2f out: sn btn* **5/4**[1]
232/ **3** *17* **Dannanceys Hill (IRE)**[194] 4160 6-11-7 115.................... JasonMaguire 89
(Donald McCain) *w ldr: led 4th: drvn 8th: hdd next: led 3 out: hdd sn after last: wknd over 2f out* **5/4**[1]
4 *12* **Reef Dancer (IRE)**[125] 10-11-7 0.....................................(p) KennyJohnson 78
(Robert Johnson) *in rr: hdwy 9th: lost pl 11th: sn bhd* **25/1**[3]
/P3- **P** **Winged Farasi**[33] 1074 9-11-2 0..................................... SamanthaDrake(5)
(Joanne Foster) *prom: reminders 2nd: drvn 8th: sn lost pl: bhd whn blnd next: sn p.u* **25/1**[3]
060/ **U** **Cumbrian Farmer**[287] 2320 6-11-0 0.............................. JonathonBewley(7)
(George Bewley) *in rr whn mstke and uns rdr 2nd* **66/1**

5m 27.1s (1.70) **Going Correction** -0.075s/f (Good) **6** Ran SP% **111.4**
Speed ratings (Par 105): **93,89,83,79,**
toteswingers 1&2 £1.80, 1&3 £1.40, 2&3 £1.02 CSF £15.61 TOTE £7.40: £2.40, £1.20; EX 15.70 Trifecta £17.30 Pool: £712.13 - 30.72 winning units..
Owner Ms S Howell **Bred** Patrick Gleeson **Trained** Upper Oddington, Gloucs

FOCUS
The two market leaders appeared to dominate this beginners' chase, which was run at just a modest pace. This was seemingly a step up from the winner but the form is suspect.

1376 GRANT THORNTON H'CAP CHASE (14 fncs) 2m 5f 110y
4:15 (4:15) (Class 5) (0-95,93) 4-Y-0+ **£3,249** (£954; £477; £238)

Form RPR
441- **1** **Presenting Junior (IRE)**[70] 753 6-10-13 **80**................ WilsonRenwick 94
(Martin Todhunter) *chsd ldng pair: wnt 2nd 2 out: styd on to ld last 50yds* **11/2**
32/- **2** *1* **Oh Right (IRE)**[364] 1363 9-10-4 **71**.................................(p) HenryBrooke 84
(Dianne Sayer) *led: 5 l clr 2 out: hdd and no ex clsng stages* **7/2[2]**
264- **3** *16* **Cloudy Dawn**[6] 1300 8-10-2 **74**................................ JonathanEngland[(5)] 73
(Sue Smith) *chsd ldr: one pce fr 3 out* **4/1[3]**
1P4- **4** *2 ½* **The Good Guy (IRE)**[23] 1172 10-11-11 **92**............. SamTwiston-Davies 88
(Graeme McPherson) *in rr-div: poor 5th 10th: wnt modest 4th sn after last* **6/1**
3/P- **5** *43* **Truckers Benefit (IRE)**[75] 694 8-11-12 **93**...............(t) RichardJohnson 51
(Tim Vaughan) *in rr: outpcd 10th: poor 4th 10th: wknd 3 out: sn t.o* **8/1**
P- **6** *12* **Gibbstown (IRE)**[35] 1038 7-11-0 **81**...............................(tp) PaddyBrennan 28
(Paul Stafford, Ire) *stdd s: in rr: nt fluent 5th: sn bhd: t.o 10th* **33/1**
53- **7** *29* **Paddysparks (IRE)**[31] 1103 9-10-3 **70**................................ PaulMoloney
(Henry Oliver) *in rr-div: lost pl 8th: sn bhd: t.o 4 out: eased run-in* **3/1[1]**
16P- **8** *6* **In The Haven (IRE)**[6] 1300 10-11-6 **92**...............(b) SamanthaDrake[(5)] 7
(Joanne Foster) *j. slowly: chsd ldrs: j. slowly and lost pl 3rd: chsd ldrs 8th: sn lost pl: t.o 4 out: eased run-in* **16/1**
5m 21.9s (-3.50) **Going Correction** -0.075s/f (Good) 8 Ran SP% **116.8**
Speed ratings (Par 103): **103,102,96,95,80 75,65,63**
toteswingers 1&2 £3.10, 1&3 £16.00, 2&3 £5.00 CSF £26.39 CT £86.09 TOTE £6.10: £1.60, £1.40, £1.90; EX 20.50 Trifecta £252.10 Pool: £637.01 - 1.89 winning units..
Owner W & Mrs J Garnett **Bred** T Horgan **Trained** Orton, Cumbria

FOCUS
A decent pace for a modest handicap chase in which the first two were rated close to their marks.

1377 TOTEPOOL H'CAP CHASE (FOR THE SADIK MEMORIAL TROPHY) (18 fncs) 3m 2f
4:50 (4:50) (Class 5) (0-100,99) 4-Y-0+ **£3,898** (£1,144; £572; £286)

Form RPR
P34- **1** **More Equity**[24] 1163 11-10-11 **84**.. RyanMania 106+
(Dianne Sayer) *chsd ldrs: lft 2nd 6th: led 8th: forged clr fr 2 out: eased clsng stages* **7/2[1]**
5/ **2** *23* **Mr Duffy (IRE)**[32] 1101 11-11-2 **89**..............................(v) PaddyBrennan 90
(D T Hughes, Ire) *chsd ldrs: clr 2nd 4 out: one pce fr 2 out* **9/2[2]**
423- **3** *11* **Solway Dornal**[6] 1300 8-9-7 **73**...........................(tp) StephenMulqueen[(7)] 64
(Lisa Harrison) *chsd ldrs: 2nd 13th: one pce fr 3 out: mstke last* **7/2[1]**
246- **4** *5* **Peak Seasons (IRE)**[11] 1260 10-10-9 **87**.......................... JoeCornwall[(5)] 74
(Michael Chapman) *in rr: drvn 12th: outpcd and modest 4th 14th: one pce* **10/1**
3/3- **5** *54* **Forestside (IRE)**[25] 1147 8-11-12 **99**................................ BrianHughes 37
(Barry Murtagh) *in rr: outpcd 14th: sn bhd: t.o 3 out* **5/1[3]**
P2P- **6** *36* **Le Seychellois (FR)**[20] 1202 13-11-0 **92**.................... SamanthaDrake[(5)]
(William Kinsey) *led: hdd 8th: nt fluent and lost pl next: mstke 14th: sn bhd: t.o 3 out: virtually p.u run-in: eventually completed* **16/1**
/51- **U** **Sierra Victor (IRE)**[62] 802 10-11-3 **97**.......................(b) MrJHamilton[(7)]
(Rose Dobbin) *chsd ldrs: upsides 5th: blnd and uns rdr next* **7/2[1]**
6m 34.2s (-0.70) **Going Correction** -0.075s/f (Good) 7 Ran SP% **116.5**
Speed ratings (Par 103): **98,90,87,86,69 58,**
toteswingers 1&2 £4.40, 1&3 £2.80, 2&3 £2.80 CSF £20.46 TOTE £5.20: £2.20, £2.00; EX 16.60 Trifecta £67.70 Pool: £772.59 - 8.55 winning units..
Owner Mrs Margaret Coppola **Bred** Mrs A F Tullie **Trained** Hackthorpe, Cumbria

FOCUS
A wide-open 0-100 staying handicap chase with not a great deal of winning form on offer. The winner didn't need to run to her best.

1378 TOTEPOOL.COM CARTMEL CUP H'CAP HURDLE (8 hdls) 2m 1f 110y
5:20 (5:21) (Class 3) (0-130,128) 4-Y-0+ **£7,147** (£2,098; £1,049; £524)

Form RPR
/06- **1** **Dartford Warbler (IRE)**[6] 1304 6-10-11 **113**......................... RyanMania 122+
(Sue Smith) *chsd ldrs: led 2 out: forged clr run-in* **14/1**
322- **2** *8* **Bright Abbey**[7] 1289 5-11-6 **122**.. HenryBrooke 122
(Dianne Sayer) *mid-div: hdwy 3 out: modest 3rd last: styd on to take 2nd nr fin* **9/1**
404- **3** *½* **Sud Pacifique (IRE)**[23] 1173 5-11-1 **117**......................... JasonMaguire 117
(Donald McCain) *mid-div: drvn 5th: modest 4th last: kpt on to take 3rd last strides* **6/1[2]**
122- **4** *nk* **Tinseltown**[8] 968 7-10-10 **112**.. APMcCoy 112+
(Brian Rothwell) *chsd ldrs: upsides 5th: sn led: hdd 2 out: lost 2 pls nr fin* **2/1[1]**
U00/ **5** *4* **Stormy Weather (FR)**[17] 4665 7-11-3 **126**...............(p) CraigGallagher[(7)] 123
(Brian Ellison) *mid-div: drvn and hdwy 5th: kpt on one pce fr next* **8/1[3]**
110/ **6** *9* **Hunters Belt (IRE)**[279] 4490 9-11-4 **127**..............(t) JonathonBewley[(7)] 117
(George Bewley) *mid-div: hdwy 3 out: 6th and one pce whn blnd last: sn wknd* **28/1**
/11- **7** *¾* **Oliver's Gold**[20] 1206 5-10-3 **105**.................................. PeterBuchanan 92
(Tim Walford) *hld up tywards rr: hdwy 3 out: nvr a factor: wknd last* **6/1[2]**
115/ **8** *7* **Indepub**[18] 2166 4-10-12 **115**.. WilsonRenwick 95
(Martin Todhunter) *in rr: sme hdwy 3 out: nvr on terms* **20/1**
0/0- **9** *3* **Hi Dancer**[35] 1046 10-11-4 **125**................................... JoeColliver[(5)] 103
(Ben Haslam) *mid-div: lost pl 5th: sn bhd* **28/1**
505/ **10** *6* **Luggers Hall (IRE)**[19] 3319 5-10-5 **107**................................... LeeEdwards 80
(Tony Carroll) *in rr: drvn 5th: nvr on terms* **8/1[3]**
4- **11** *7* **Dumbarton (IRE)**[22] 1185 5-11-11 **127**...........................(p) BrianHughes 94
(James Moffatt) *chsd ldrs: modest 3rd 2 out: wknd qckly appr last* **14/1**
334- **12** *39* **Toledo Gold (IRE)**[25] 1144 7-9-9 **104**..................(t) StephenMulqueen[(7)] 36
(Maurice Barnes) *led: hdd after 5th: lost pl after next: t.o last: eased: eventually completed* **20/1**
P6P/ **13** *53* **Wild Desert (FR)**[58] 5167 8-10-3 **110**............................. JoshHamer[(5)]
(Tony Carroll) *chsd ldrs: lost pl after 5th: sn bhd: t.o 2 out: sn eased: virtually p.u: eventually completed* **20/1**
P/0- **P** **Kealshore Again (IRE)**[23] 1171 4-10-2 **105**............................ AdrianLane
(Danielle McCormick) *sn bhd: reminders 4th: t.o next: p.u after 3 out* **50/1**
4m 8.6s (-4.60) **Going Correction** -0.075s/f (Good)
WFA 4 from 5yo+ 13lb 14 Ran SP% **130.6**
Speed ratings (Par 107): **107,103,103,103,101 97,96,93,92,89 86,69,45,**
toteswingers 1&2 £28.40, 1&3 £17.10, 2&3 £8.10 CSF £132.11 CT £865.50 TOTE £18.70: £4.20, £3.80, £2.40; EX 147.70 Trifecta £432.70 Part won. Pool: £577.03 - 0.10 winning units..
Owner Mrs S Smith **Bred** John O'Dwyer **Trained** High Eldwick, W Yorks

FOCUS
A decent, competitive handicap hurdle with a strong pace guaranteed with some confirmed front runners in the line-up. Solid form with a big personal best from the impressive winner.

1379 EWGA RACING EXCELLENCE "HANDS AND HEELS" H'CAP HURDLE (FOR CONDITIONAL JOCKEYS & AMATEUR RIDERS) (8 hdls) 2m 1f 110y
5:55 (5:56) (Class 5) (0-95,95) 4-Y-0+ **£2,599** (£763; £381; £190)

Form RPR
/60- **1** **Ravi River (IRE)**[11] 630 9-10-0 **69** oh1................................ KieronEdgar 76
(Alistair Whillans) *led to 2nd: led 3 out: hit next: hdd last: led over 1f out: drvn out* **10/1**
025- **2** *2 ¾* **Clarion Call**[9] 1275 5-11-10 **93**...(b) ConorRing 98
(Evan Williams) *chsd ldrs: 2nd 2 out: led last: hdd over 1f out: kpt on same pce* **9/2[2]**
P30- **3** *7* **Brother Scott**[6] 1306 6-11-9 **92**.. CallumBewley 91
(Sue Smith) *chsd ldrs: nt fluent: one pce fr 2 out: tk 3rd nr fin* **10/1**
345- **4** *½* **Grethel (IRE)**[19] 1073 9-10-2 **74**............................ DiarmuidO'Regan[(3)] 72
(Alan Berry) *s.s: bhd: sme hdwy 3 out: 9th 2 out: 7th last: styd on to take 4th nr fin* **16/1**
306- **5** *½* **Tim's Approach (IRE)**[7] 1286 8-9-11 **69** oh4...............(t) MrTHamilton[(3)] 66
(William Young Jnr) *mid-div: mstke 4th: outpcd next: 8th 2 out: 6th last: styd on to take 5th nr fin* **50/1**
/06- **6** *½* **Glaced Over**[52] 868 8-11-0 **83**.. JamesCowley 80
(Donald McCain) *w ldr: led 2nd: hdd 2 out: wknd and lost 3 pls nr fin* **3/1[1]**
006- **7** *2 ¼* **Stadium Of Light (IRE)**[7] 788 6-10-10 **82**......... WilliamFeatherstone[(3)] 77
(Shaun Harris) *in rr: sme hdwy 5th: one pce fr next* **25/1**
112- **8** *4 ½* **Morning Time (IRE)**[25] 1143 7-11-9 **95**..................(p) MissRMcDonald[(3)] 86
(Lucinda Russell) *in rr: bhd 4th: kpt on fr 2 out: nvr on terms* **7/1**
P/3- **9** *10* **Lost In Newyork (IRE)**[23] 1170 6-11-4 **90**...................... PaulNO'Brien[(3)] 72
(Nick Kent) *chsd ldrs: wknd appr 2 out* **16/1**
3- **10** *3* **Moonlone Lane (IRE)**[51] 879 6-11-11 **94**..................(tp) JackSherwood 73
(Paul Stafford, Ire) *mid-div: hdwy 4th: 7th whn mstke 5th: wknd next* **12/1**
/P0- **11** *3 ¾* **Man Of Principles (IRE)**[81] 630 10-9-9 **69**........... MrGaryBeaumont[(5)] 45
(Stuart Coltherd) *in rr: drvn 4th: bhd fr next* **33/1**
0/6- **12** *hd* **Breeze With Ease (IRE)**[106] 210 9-11-4 **90**.............(t) ShaunDobbin[(3)] 66
(Barry Murtagh) *in rr: bhd fr 5th* **20/1**
13 *2* **Indubitably**[161] 4802 7-11-8 **91**..(bt) MrSFox 65
(Noel C Kelly, Ire) *in rr: nt fluent 1st: bhd fr 5th* **6/1[3]**
62P- **14** *87* **Dynamic Drive (IRE)**[25] 1145 6-11-4 **87**..................(t) StephenMulqueen
(Maurice Barnes) *mid-div: chsd ldrs 3rd: lost pl 5th: sn bhd: t.o 2 out: virtually p.u: eventually completed* **33/1**
/00- **P** **Best Excuse**[53] 860 6-10-7 **79**..(p) RyanHatch[(3)]
(Jennie Candlish) *in rr: bhd and drvn 3rd: t.o whn p.u after 5th: lame* **14/1**
4m 14.6s (1.40) **Going Correction** -0.075s/f (Good) 15 Ran SP% **130.7**
Speed ratings (Par 103): **93,91,88,88,88 88,87,85,80,79 77,77,76,37,**
toteswingers 1&2 £15.40, 1&3 £17.20, 2&3 £17.20 CSF £57.00 CT £488.90 TOTE £12.20: £3.50, £1.80, £4.70; EX 80.10 Trifecta £448.80 Part won. Pool: £598.47 - 0.10 winning units..
Owner Gold Tooth Racing **Bred** Gainsborough Stud Management Ltd **Trained** Newmill-On-Slitrig, Borders

FOCUS
A reasonable pace for this ordinary handicap hurdle for conditionals and amateurs in which the runners finished well strung out. The first two were on decent marks.
T/Plt: £58.00 to a £1 stake. Pool: £61669.84 - 775.71 winning tickets T/Qpdt: £25.90 to a £1 stake. Pool: £2827.90 - 80.75 winning tickets WG

1380 - 1386a (Foreign Racing) - See Raceform Interactive

1182 BANGOR-ON-DEE (L-H)
Monday, August 26

OFFICIAL GOING: Good (good to firm in places; 7.2)
Wind: nil Weather: sunny; 22 degrees

1387 STELLA ARTOIS MAIDEN HURDLE (11 hdls) 2m 4f
2:15 (2:15) (Class 5) 4-Y-0+ **£2,395** (£698; £349)

Form RPR
022- **1** **Hopstrings**[24] 1187 5-10-8 95.................................... WayneHutchinson 101
(Charlie Brooks) *nt a fluent: rdn 4th: mostly 2nd tl rdn bef 7th: outpcd by ldng pair and 4 l down tl rallied to go 2nd bef 2 out: drvn ahd between last two: sn outstyd rivals* **6/4[1]**
6/3- **2** *5* **Swift Escape**[27] 1152 6-11-1 0............................... RichardJohnson 103
(Tim Vaughan) *last pair tl hrd drvn and effrt bef 7th: jnd ldr next: led 3 out: drvn bef next: hdd between last two: fin weakly* **11/4[2]**
33/ **3** *15* **Spitfire Ace (IRE)**[243] 3244 5-11-1 0................................ JasonMaguire 91
(Donald McCain) *led: j.rt 6th: jnd and hit 8th: rdn and hdd 3 out: 3rd and fading tamely bef next* **4/1**
600/ **4** *9* **Midnight Mustang**[375] 1249 6-10-8 0................................ MrJMartin[(7)] 81
(Andrew J Martin) *nt alwys fluent: chsd ldrs tl 7th: lost tch u.p bef next: wl bhd 3 out* **50/1**
221- **5** *1 ½* **Dardanella**[36] 1056 6-10-8 0.. TomScudamore 72
(Richard Lee) *last pair: nt a fluent: last and rdn whn mstke 7th: sn lost tch: wl bhd fr 3 out* **10/3[3]**
4m 48.1s (-3.90) **Going Correction** -0.225s/f (Good) 5 Ran SP% **111.7**
Speed ratings (Par 103): **98,96,90,86,85**
CSF £6.21 TOTE £2.90: £1.10, £1.40; EX 11.80 Trifecta £14.50 Pool: £168.21 - 8.69 winning units..
Owner Mrs S M & G A Newell **Bred** Mrs S M Newell **Trained** Sarsden, Oxon

FOCUS
The form of this maiden may not have been that strong, but it was a tricky contest nonetheless. They went a decent pace from the off. The first four are all rated within a few pounds of their marks.

1388 AEJIS NOVICES' H'CAP HURDLE (12 hdls) 3m
2:50 (2:50) (Class 4) (0-110,106) 4-Y-0+ **£3,422** (£997; £499)

Form RPR
334- **1** **Piper Hill (IRE)**[22] 1201 5-11-12 **106**......................... RichardJohnson 118+
(Tony Coyle) *trckd ldrs: effrt 7th: wnt 2nd next: drvn to ld and mstke 2 out: 6 l clr last: easily* **8/1**
504- **2** *12* **Bob Lewis**[13] 1259 7-10-9 **89**..(tp) PaulMoloney 89
(Anthony Middleton) *j. slowly 2nd and 4th: hld up last tl 8th: clsd to 4th and handy after 3 out: rdn and lft 2nd next: wnr wl in command after* **5/1[3]**
331- **3** *2 ½* **Polarbrook (IRE)**[27] 1147 6-11-11 **105**............................. JasonMaguire 104
(Donald McCain) *nt fluent 3rd and 6th: chsd ldr: rdn and outpcd 8th: rallied to press ldrs wl bef 2 out where hmpd: drvn and plugged on at one pce after* **9/4[2]**

560/ **4** *15* **Lookout Mountain (IRE)**[202] 4040 5-11-10 **104**..................(p) APMcCoy 96
(Jonjo O'Neill) *led at v slow pce: jumping often lacked flair: rdn after slow jump 8th: hdd whn mstke 2 out and landed v bdly and rdr lost iron: nt rcvr and sn eased* **11/8**[1]

/03- **5** *39* **Yazdi (IRE)**[34] 1087 4-11-8 **105**...(t) NoelFehily 46
(Charlie Mann) *nt fluent 3rd: chsd ldr at v slow pce tl 8th: rdn and wkng whn j.lft next: t.o 3 out: eased 2 out* **7/1**

P/P- **P** **Bobbits Way**[13] 1259 8-10-7 **87**.......................................(p) NickScholfield
(Alan Jones) *j. poorly: chsd ldrs tl rdn and outpcd after 7th: t.o bef 3 out: p.u 2 out: fin lame* **18/1**

5m 58.6s (7.60) **Going Correction** -0.225s/f (Good)
WFA 4 from 5yo+ 15lb **6** Ran SP% **118.4**
Speed ratings (Par 105): **78,74,73,68,55**
Tote Swingers 1&2 £0.00, 2&3 £2.80, 1&3 £1.30 CSF £48.16 TOTE £6.20: £6.70, £1.10; EX 20.60 Trifecta £25.50 Pool: £150.25 - 4.40 winning units..
Owner Twenty Four Seven Recruitment **Bred** Kevin Dillon **Trained** Norton, N Yorks

FOCUS
A fairly weak contest run at a crawl early on, gradually picking up through the final circuit. A step up from the winner.

1389 BET AT BANGORSPORT NOVICES' HURDLE (9 hdls) 2m 1f
3:25 (3:27) (Class 4) 4-Y-0+ **£3,422** (£997; £499)

Form RPR

1 **Franciscan**[51] 5-10-12 0.. JasonMaguire 115+
(Donald McCain) *cl 2nd but jumping modly in slow r: chal after 3 out: hrd drvn to join ldr next: led and hung lft w ears pricked last where j.lft: sn in command flat* **4/9**[1]

2 *3 ¾* **Saint Thomas (IRE)**[12] 6-10-12 0..................................... BrianHughes 108
(John Mackie) *led at slow pce: smetimes wandering into hurdles: jnd 2 out: drvn and hdd and wandered last where mstke and crowded: one pce after* **15/2**[3]

1- **3** *4 ½* **Purple 'n Gold (IRE)**[14] 1008 4-11-4 0......................(v) TomScudamore 110
(David Pipe) *trckd ldng pair: rdn after 3 out: chal and landed awkwardly next: sn fnd little and wl hld: landed v awkwardly last* **11/4**[2]

4m 4.3s (-6.60) **Going Correction** -0.225s/f (Good) **3** Ran SP% **107.7**
Speed ratings (Par 105): **106,104,102**
CSF £3.63 TOTE £1.40; EX 6.30 Trifecta £2.70 Pool: £97.88 - 27.11 winning units..
Owner T G Leslie **Bred** Fittocks Stud **Trained** Cholmondeley, Cheshire

FOCUS
A steadily run race. With three ex-Flat performers each scrambling over the last, this did not look too impressive, but they really motored going into the final turn and the form could be a bit better than it looks.

1390 BANGORSPORT IN ASSOCIATION WITH STAN JAMES H'CAP CHASE (12 fncs) 2m 1f 110y
4:00 (4:00) (Class 4) (0-120,120) 4-Y-0+ **£5,475** (£1,596; £798)

Form RPR

541- **1** **Lucky Landing (IRE)**[9] 1285 7-11-12 **120**............................... NoelFehily 131+
(Tony Coyle) *settled trcking ldrs: effrt after 3 out: led gng best next: 5 l clr last: easily: game* **2/1**[2]

145- **2** *7* **Bay Central (IRE)**[31] 1122 9-11-4 **112**.............................(e) PaulMoloney 113
(Evan Williams) *taken down early: led at fair pce: rdn and hdd 2 out: immediately outpcd by wnr but kpt on best in r for 2nd: heavily eased fnl 100yds* **11/1**

232- **3** *5* **Mulligan's Man (IRE)**[27] 1144 6-11-9 **117**......................... JasonMaguire 114
(Donald McCain) *trckd ldng pair: rdn to dispute 2nd w ev ch briefly 2 out: sn fnd little and plugged on* **6/4**[1]

332- **4** *2 ½* **Another Flutter (IRE)**[13] 1263 9-11-2 **110**......................(tp) CharliePoste 106
(Matt Sheppard) *pressed ldr: rdn whn hit 7th: remained cl up tl drvn and no ex bef 2 out* **7/2**[3]

6/5- **P** **Seedless**[34] 1084 8-11-7 **115**.. AdrianLane
(Donald McCain) *hld up last but in tch tl p.u sharply 8th: fin lame* **14/1**

4m 15.1s (-7.00) **Going Correction** -0.225s/f (Good) **5** Ran SP% **110.6**
Speed ratings (Par 105): **106,102,100,99,**
CSF £19.35 TOTE £1.40: £1.10, £6.10; EX 22.30 Trifecta £88.60 Pool: £152.06 - 1.25 winning units..
Owner Gary Dewhurst & Tony Coyle **Bred** James McGrath **Trained** Norton, N Yorks

FOCUS
With several front runners in the field a good pace was assured. The winner is rated to his very best.

1391 AEJIS CORPORATE EVENT MANAGEMENT H'CAP HURDLE (11 hdls) 2m 4f
4:35 (4:35) (Class 4) (0-110,107) 4-Y-0+ **£3,422** (£997; £499)

Form RPR

/01- **1** **He's A Hawker (IRE)**[34] 1087 8-11-11 **106**..........................(b) NoelFehily 111
(Michael Mullineaux) *led: drvn and narrowly hdd 3 out: led again next: hrd pressed fr last: hung on most tenaciously* **9/1**

054- **2** *hd* **Bathwick Man**[11] 1273 8-11-3 **105**.................................. KieronEdgar(7) 111
(David Pipe) *settled in midfield: effrt bef 3 out: sn pressing ldrs: 5th home turn: hit 2 out: wnt 2nd at last: drvn and kpt on but jst hld* **7/1**

045- **3** *2 ¼* **Quinsman**[22] 1203 7-11-8 **103**..................................(p) RichardJohnson 106
(Caroline Bailey) *pressed ldng pair: drvn to ld 3 out: jst hdd whn hit next: stl pressing ldrs last: no imp after* **11/2**[2]

601- **4** *¾* **Ironical (IRE)**[36] 1062 9-11-6 **101**..................................(t) AidanColeman 103
(Shaun Lycett) *hld up in rr gp: stdy prog 8th: cl 3rd home turn: rdn and no ex between last two* **7/1**

60B- **5** *6* **Munlochy Bay**[13] 1266 9-10-11 **92**....................................(p) CharliePoste 89
(Matt Sheppard) *bhd: drvn and lost tch bef 7th: poor 7th home turn: consented to stay on wl after but gave herself an impossible task* **22/1**

0/6- **6** *14* **Finding Your Feet (IRE)**[11] 1273 5-11-10 **105**......................... APMcCoy 92
(Jonjo O'Neill) *j. slowly 1st and 2nd: chsd ldrs: 3rd and ev ch 3 out: rdn w little rspnse bef next: sn btn* **11/4**[1]

31- **7** *3 ¼* **Marmas**[50] 897 4-11-6 **103**.. BrianHughes 82
(John Mackie) *pressed ldr tl bef 7th: rdn and sn dropped out* **6/1**[3]

345- **8** *1* **Bob's Legend (IRE)**[13] 1258 7-11-0 **95**.............................. JamesDavies 75
(Martin Bosley) *pressed ldrs tl rdn bef 3 out: 6th and wl btn home turn* **14/1**

/00- **9** *34* **Dropzone (USA)**[40] 1020 4-11-8 **105**............................. TomScudamore 53
(Richard Lee) *midfield: nt fluent 6th and lost tch: t.o 3 out* **16/1**

P/6- **10** *1 ¾* **Bathcounty (IRE)**[66] 784 6-11-12 **107**......................... WayneHutchinson 55
(Barry Brennan) *prom tl after 6th: sn lost pl: bdly t.o* **28/1**

010/ **11** *86* **Tallulah Mai**[34] 77 6-11-10 **105**.. PaulMoloney
(Paul Fitzsimons) *bhd: short-lived effrt bef 7th: t.o 3 out: fin eventually* **33/1**

455- **P** **Record Breaker (IRE)**[33] 1110 9-11-2 **97**.....................(b) JasonMaguire
(Donald McCain) *last pair: rdn 4th: nvr travelling after: t.o 7th: p.u 3 out* **16/1**

4m 47.6s (-4.40) **Going Correction** -0.225s/f (Good)
WFA 4 from 5yo+ 14lb **12** Ran SP% **120.5**
Speed ratings (Par 105): **99,98,98,97,95 89,88,88,74,73 39,**
Tote Swingers 1&2 £8.60, 2&3 £8.60, 1&3 £8.60 CSF £70.85 CT £387.19 TOTE £15.60: £26.80, £1.30, £2.60; EX 68.60 Trifecta £78.50 Part won. Pool: £104.78 - 0.15 winning units..
Owner Bluestone Partnership **Bred** Ms K Murphy **Trained** Alpraham, Cheshire

FOCUS
An exciting finish with the first four all holding a chance up the home straight. Solid form, the winner rated in line with his best old form.

1392 STELLA ARTOIS INTERMEDIATE NATIONAL HUNT FLAT RACE (CONDITIONAL JOCKEYS' AND AMATEUR RIDERS' RACE) 2m 1f
5:10 (5:10) (Class 6) 4-6-Y-0 **£1,711** (£498; £249)

Form RPR

53- **1** **When In Roam (IRE)**[36] 1064 4-10-3 0.......................... CiaranMckee(7) 103+
(John O'Shea) *settled last pair: effrt to ld 4f out: clr fnl 2f: unchal* **11/4**[2]

1- **2** *11* **Clondaw Hero (IRE)**[13] 1261 5-11-4 0................................ NickSlatter(7) 107
(Donald McCain) *led at brisk pce tl 1/2-way: rdn 6f out: bdly outpcd 3f out: plugged on into poor 2nd but hanging wl over 1f out* **4/6**[1]

4/ **3** *11* **Jayjayrumi (IRE)**[180] 4452 5-10-13 0 ow2..................... MrDerekSmith(7) 97
(Ms N M Hugo) *t.k.h in 2nd: led 1/2-way: 4 l clr 6f out: rdn and hdd 4f out: dropped bk to go 3rd and running green wl over 1f out* **11/2**[3]

4 *75* **Unexpected** 5-10-13 0... HarryChalloner(5) 23
(Donald McCain) *last and rdn after 6f: t.o 4f out: fin a f bhd* **10/1**

3m 53.8s (-11.50) **Going Correction** -0.225s/f (Good)
WFA 4 from 5yo 1lb **4** Ran SP% **111.1**
Speed ratings: **118,112,107,72**
CSF £5.23 TOTE £3.80; EX 8.40 Trifecta £8.20 Pool: £239.35 - 21.66 winning units..
Owner The Cross Racing Club **Bred** Robert McCarthy **Trained** Elton, Gloucs

FOCUS
A moderate bumper run at a fair pace. A step up from the winner.
T/Plt: £532.30 to a £1 stake. Pool: £28,984.95 - 39.75 winning tickets. T/Qpdt: £71.30 to a £1 stake. Pool: £1,456.2 - 15.10 winning tickets. IM

1373 CARTMEL (L-H)
Monday, August 26

OFFICIAL GOING: Good (7.5)
Both bends moved out 4m to provide fresh ground.
Wind: almost nil Weather: fine and sunny, very warm

1393 STICKY TOFFEE PUDDING NOVICES' HURDLE (11 hdls) 2m 6f
2:20 (2:20) (Class 4) 4-Y-0+ **£3,249** (£954; £477; £238)

Form RPR

P/2- **1** **Ocean Club**[18] 956 6-10-12 112... DannyCook 124+
(Brian Ellison) *chsd ldr: led 8th: drvn wl clr fr 2 out: eased nr fin* **7/1**[3]

42- **2** *39* **Swing Hard (IRE)**[35] 1072 5-10-12 112................................. RyanMania 89
(Sue Smith) *chsd ldrs: hrd drvn bef 8th: sn chsng wnr: kpt on one pce fr 2 out* **1/1**[1]

6/0- **3** *13* **Rumpleteazer (IRE)**[62] 828 5-10-7 0.................................. BenPoste(5) 77
(Shaun Harris) *hld up: wnt 3rd 8th: one pce fr 2 out* **33/1**

- **4** *4* **Volcanic Jack (IRE)**[11] 5-10-7 0...................................... JoeCornwall(5) 73
(Michael Chapman) *nt fluent in rr: modest 4th 3 out* **12/1**

341- **5** *23* **Mr Satco (IRE)**[37] 1037 5-11-5 0.....................................(p) HenryBrooke 60
(Donald McCain) *led: hdd 8th: sn lost pl and bhd: t.o 2 out* **7/4**[2]

5m 22.0s (-7.30) **Going Correction** -0.125s/f (Good) **5** Ran SP% **109.5**
Speed ratings (Par 105): **108,93,89,87,79**
CSF £15.01 TOTE £6.60: £2.40, £1.10; EX 13.80 Trifecta £140.70 Part won. Pool: £187.65 - 0.13 winning units..
Owner Brian Ellison **Bred** C C And Mrs D J Buckley **Trained** Norton, N Yorks

FOCUS
Both bends had to moved out 4m onto fresh ground with the going described as good all round. An uncompetitive novices' hurdle. The winner is rated up 10lb on his Perth run with the second a stone+ off.

1394 WICKS WASTE SERVICES JUVENILE HURDLE (8 hdls) 2m 1f 110y
2:55 (2:55) (Class 4) 3-Y-0 **£3,249** (£954; £477; £238)

Form RPR

3- **1** **Hi Candy (IRE)**[86] 582 3-10-0 0... BenPoste(5) 83
(Ben Haslam) *led to 1st: chsd ldr: led appr last: drvn out* **5/1**[3]

2 *4 ½* **Kitchapoly (FR)**[87] 3-11-5 0... JamesCowley(7) 100
(Donald McCain) *led 1st: hdd appr last: kpt on same pce* **15/8**[1]

46- **3** *26* **Precision Strike**[11] 785 3-10-12 0...............................(v) DougieCostello 63
(Richard Guest) *chsd ldrs: hit 5th: sn drvn: 3rd 3 out: sn wknd* **12/1**

4 *31* **Aficionado**[66] 3-10-12 0... WilsonRenwick 35
(Chris Grant) *nt fluent in rr: reminders and lost tch 4th: t.o 3 out* **5/2**[2]

P **Smooth Handle**[14] 3-10-12 0.. FearghalDavis
(Danielle McCormick) *chsd ldrs: reminders 3rd: sn struggling: poor 5th whn p.u bef 3 out: fatally injured* **50/1**

P **Diddy Eric**[14] 3-10-7 0.. JoeColliver(5)
(Micky Hammond) *chsd ldrs: outpcd 4th: bhd whn mstke 3 out: t.o whn blnd next: p.u between last 2* **13/2**

P **Niknad**[29] 3-10-5 0.. DannyCook
(Brian Ellison) *chsd ldrs: 3rd and drvn 5th: wknd next: sn bhd: t.o whn p.u bef last* **8/1**

4m 13.9s (0.70) **Going Correction** -0.125s/f (Good) **7** Ran SP% **114.1**
Speed ratings (Par 102): **93,91,79,65, ,**
toteswingers 1&2 £1.10, 2&3 £4.30, 1&3 £4.00 CSF £15.23 TOTE £4.90: £2.50, £1.80; EX 18.50 Trifecta £91.40 Pool: £165.84 - 1.36 winning units..
Owner Go Alfresco Racing **Bred** Lynn Lodge Stud **Trained** Middleham Moor, N Yorks

FOCUS
Despite Countrywide Flame winning this contest in the past, this was a modest juvenile hurdle where the front pair had the race between themselves from a long way out. Guessy ratings.

1395 WIN A MINI H'CAP CHASE (12 fncs) 2m 1f 110y
3:30 (3:30) (Class 4) (0-105,97) 4-Y-0+ **£3,898** (£1,144; £572; £286)

Form RPR

/41- **1** **Soul Magic (IRE)**[35] 1075 11-11-4 **96**............................. CallumBewley(7) 102
(Harriet Graham) *chsd ldrs: drvn 3 out: styd on to go cl 2nd over 1f out: kpt on gamely to ld towards fin* **5/2**[2]

The Form Book Jumps, Raceform Ltd, Compton, RG20 6NL.

354- **2** *nk* **Sendiym (FR)**21 [1075] 6-10-8 **79**......(b) SeanQuinlan 85
(Dianne Sayer) *chsd ldr: led after 8th: hdd and no ex in clsng stages* **3/1**3

445- **3** *7* **Finch Flyer (IRE)**4 [1014] 6-10-2 **78**......(p) KyleJames(5) 79
(Aytach Sadik) *chsd ldrs: ev ch and hrd rdn run-in tl wknd fnl 150yds* **8/1**

/31- **4** *58* **The Paddy Premium (IRE)**26 [1160] 13-11-12 **97**...... WilsonRenwick 45
(N W Alexander) *led: hdd after 8th: wknd 3 out: sn bhd: eased whn t.o 2f out* **8/1**

P41- **F** **Pete**2 [1374] 10-11-1 **93**......(tp) GrahamWatters(7)
(Barry Murtagh) *chsd ldrs: mstke 2nd: hit 7th: drvn 4 out: outpcd whn fell next* **7/4**1

4m 19.2s (0.30) **Going Correction** -0.125s/f (Good) **5** Ran SP% **112.2**
Speed ratings (Par 105): **94,93,90,64,**
CSF £10.67 TOTE £3.20: £1.70, £1.40; EX 8.10 Trifecta £22.30 Pool: £217.97 - 7.32 winning units..
Owner H G Racing **Bred** Robert McCarthy **Trained** Philip Law, Borders
■ Stewards' Enquiry : Kyle James two-day ban: use of whip (9-10 Sep)

FOCUS
A trappy 0-105 handicap chase where nearly all the runners possessed a rather patchy profile. Straightforward form.

1396 MILLER HOWE CAVENDISH CUP H'CAP CHASE (18 fncs) 3m 2f
4:05 (4:05) (Class 3) (0-130,125) 4-Y-0+ **£8,447** (£2,480; £1,240; £620)

Form RPR

541- **1** **Ballybough Gorta (IRE)**37 [1040] 6-11-9 **122**......(v) JamieMoore 135+
(Peter Bowen) *w ldrs: led 2nd to 4th: led 7th: mde rest: drvn clr 2 out: eased nr fin* **11/4**2

/45- **2** *20* **Epee Celeste (FR)**9 [1283] 7-10-2 **106**...... JoeCornwall(5) 99
(Michael Chapman) *w ldrs: led 6th: hdd next: drvn 13th: 3rd 4 out: wnt 2nd last: kpt on same pce* **8/1**

5/5- **3** *8* **My Moment (IRE)**35 [1076] 10-11-2 **115**...... RyanMania 107
(David Thompson) *chsd ldrs: 2nd 13th: hit next: 3rd and one pce whn blnd last* **16/1**

0/6- **4** *21* **Hunters Lodge (IRE)**81 [642] 7-11-5 **125**......(v) RyanHatch(7) 92
(Nigel Twiston-Davies) *detached in last: nt fluent and reminders 4th: bhd fr 7th: kpt on run-in to take dist 4th last 50yds* **5/1**3

P64- **5** *3 ½* **An Capall Mor (IRE)**34 [1085] 7-10-6 **105**......(tp) HenryBrooke 69
(Donald McCain) *in tch: outpcd and reminders 12th: sme hdwy 13th: wknd 4 out* **14/1**

/16- **6** *3* **Satou (FR)**49 [923] 7-11-4 **120**......(p) JamesBest(3) 86
(Philip Hobbs) *led to 2nd: led 4th to 6th: hit 13th: lost pl and blnd next: bhd fr 4 out* **12/1**

322- **7** *¾* **Royale Knight**37 [1040] 7-10-13 **112**...... SamTwiston-Davies 72
(Dr Richard Newland) *chsd ldrs: drvn and outpcd 9th: bhd fr 13th* **7/4**1

1/P- **P** **Dun Masc (IRE)**101 [355] 8-11-0 **113**......(v1) BrianHarding
(James Moffatt) *mid-div: outpcd 6th: bhd fr 12th: t.o whn p.u after 14th* **16/1**

6m 27.0s (-7.90) **Going Correction** -0.125s/f (Good) **8** Ran SP% **116.9**
Speed ratings (Par 107): **107,100,98,91,90 89,89,**
toteswingers 1&2 £4.30, 2&3 £3.90, 1&3 £8.70 CSF £25.35 CT £299.48 TOTE £4.10: £1.30, £2.20, £3.30; EX 22.10 Trifecta £206.10 Pool: £299.79 - 1.09 winning units..
Owner Yeh Man Partnership **Bred** Jaykayenn Syndicate **Trained** Little Newcastle, Pembrokes

FOCUS
A strong pace for this competitive staying handicap chase. There's a case for rating the form up to 7lb higher.

1397 MARGARET SEXTON AND JULIE GRIMSHAW H'CAP CHASE (THE £5K BONUS RACE) (14 fncs) 2m 5f 110y
4:40 (4:41) (Class 3) (0-130,127) 4-Y-0+ **£7,797** (£2,289; £1,144; £572)

Form RPR

304/ **1** **Sean Airgead (IRE)**84 [622] 8-11-7 **122**......(t) PeterBuchanan 130+
(Mark Michael McNiff, Ire) *detached in last whn mstke 1st: nt fluent 4th: hdwy 9th: 3rd 4 out: upsides sn after last: shkn up to ld 2f out: faltered and hung rt ins fnl f: drvn out* **4/1**3

4F0/ **2** *¾* **Supreme Duke (IRE)**99 11-9-11 **108**...... ThomasCheesman(10) 112
(Philip Hobbs) *led to 3rd: upsides 6th: led 10th: hdd 2f out: keeping on whn carried rt ins fnl f* **5/2**1

3/5- **3** *6* **Cootehill (IRE)**79 [672] 9-11-12 **127**...... SamTwiston-Davies 126
(Nigel Twiston-Davies) *w ldr: led 3rd to 10th: rdn after last: kpt on same pce* **11/4**2

22F- **4** *12* **Father Shine (IRE)**50 [902] 10-10-4 **110**...... BenPoste(5) 98
(Shaun Harris) *chsd ldrs: hit 3 out: one pce* **10/1**

150- **5** *9* **Jewel In The Sun (IRE)**22 [1205] 8-10-8 **109**......(p) DougieCostello 89
(Ben Haslam) *chsd ldrs: outpcd and reminders 9th: lost pl 10th: sn bhd* **15/2**

1/F- **6** *26* **Baltic Pathfinder (IRE)**37 [1039] 9-9-11 **103**...... JonathanEngland(5) 60
(Sue Smith) *chsd ldrs: hit 10th and lost pl: sn bhd: t.o 3 out: virtually p.u in clsng stages* **9/2**

5m 24.6s (-0.80) **Going Correction** -0.125s/f (Good) **6** Ran SP% **114.3**
Speed ratings (Par 107): **96,95,93,89,85 76**
toteswingers 1&2 £1.10, 2&3 £1.50, 1&3 £1.20 CSF £15.24 TOTE £4.10: £2.50, £2.00; EX 15.40 Trifecta £49.20 Pool: £360.97 - 5.49 winning units..
Owner Brendan G Flynn **Bred** J Kehoe **Trained** Sligo, Co. Sligo
■ Stewards' Enquiry : Peter Buchanan cauiton: careless riding

FOCUS
A tight 0-130 handicap run at just a fair pace. A small personal best from the winner.

1398 NEIL & GEMMA FIRST WEDDING ANNIVERSARY H'CAP HURDLE (11 hdls) 2m 6f
5:15 (5:16) (Class 3) (0-130,126) 4-Y-0+ **£6,498** (£1,908; £954; £477)

Form RPR

0/1- **1** **Goldan Jess (IRE)**16 [565] 9-10-10 **115**...... KyleJames(5) 120+
(Philip Kirby) *led to 5th: led after 7th: drvn and styd on wl run-in* **5/1**3

0/0- **2** *3 ¾* **Teak (IRE)**30 [850] 6-10-8 **108**...... SamTwiston-Davies 109
(Ian Williams) *chsd ldrs: 2nd 8th: kpt on same pce between last 2: no imp* **9/2**2

604- **3** *3* **What A Steel (IRE)**26 [1164] 9-10-9 **112**...... EwanWhillans(3) 111
(Alistair Whillans) *chsd ldrs: 3rd 3 out: drvn next: kpt on same pce* **7/2**1

2/0- **4** *9* **Trucking Along (IRE)**101 [356] 7-11-10 **124**...... PeterBuchanan 117
(S R B Crawford, Ire) *hld up in rr: hdwy 6th: chsng ldrs 3 out: sn drvn: wknd fnl f* **10/1**

046- **5** *16* **Scotswell**37 [1042] 7-11-7 **126**...... JonathanEngland(5) 102
(Harriet Graham) *w ldr: led 5th: drvn 8th: lost pl bef 2 out* **6/1**

032/ **6** *8* **Jeu De Roseau (IRE)**46 [2282] 9-10-13 **123**...... DiarmuidO'Regan(10) 92
(Chris Grant) *chsd ldrs: drvn 7th: lost pl next* **20/1**

112- **7** *15* **Auberge (IRE)**64 [804] 9-10-0 **100**...... HenryBrooke 55
(Dianne Sayer) *chsd ldrs: drvn 6th: lost pl 8th: bhd fr 2 out* **5/1**3

/1F- **8** *28* **Up For An Oscar (IRE)**85 [606] 6-11-0 **119**...... EdCookson(5) 49
(Kim Bailey) *hld up in rr: effrt 6th: rdn after next: lost pl 2 out: last whn eased last: t.o* **6/1**

6F4- **F** **Captain Brown**48 [929] 5-11-0 **114**......1 BrianHarding
(James Moffatt) *hld up in rr: sme hdwy 7th: last whn fell next* **28/1**

5m 22.4s (-6.90) **Going Correction** -0.125s/f (Good) **9** Ran SP% **119.6**
Speed ratings (Par 107): **107,105,104,101,95 92,87,76,**
toteswingers 1&2 £7.40, 2&3 £5.20, 1&3 £7.10 CSF £29.30 CT £90.55 TOTE £4.80: £2.30, £1.80, £2.40; EX 40.70 Trifecta £395.00 Pool: £526.78 - 0.62 winning units..
Owner The Jessies,Colin Fletcher,Philip Kirby **Bred** Bendis Partnership **Trained** Middleham, N Yorks

FOCUS
With a couple of confirmed front-runners there was a strong pace for a wide open 0-130 staying handicap hurdle. The winner improved towards the level of his recent Flat win.

1399 SWAN HOTEL & SPA NOVICES' HURDLE (8 hdls) 2m 1f 110y
5:50 (5:50) (Class 4) 4-Y-0+ **£3,249** (£954; £477; £238)

Form RPR

425/ **1** **It's A Mans World**7 [2471] 7-10-2 0...... GLavery(10) 118+
(Brian Ellison) *led to 1st: trckd ldr: led and hit last: drvn clr fnl f* **3/1**3

/16- **2** *12* **Celtic Monarch (IRE)**28 [1139] 4-11-4 125...... PeterBuchanan 112
(Mark Michael McNiff, Ire) *sn chsng ldrs: outpcd 4th: chsd ldrs 2 out: 2nd last: kpt on same pce* **15/8**1

3- **3** *½* **Red Eyes**22 [1200] 5-10-2 0...... DiarmuidO'Regan(10) 106
(Chris Grant) *chsd ldrs: outpcd 4th: hdwy and 4th 3 out: chsd ldrs between last 2: 3rd last: kpt on one pce* **7/1**

4 *6* **Cool Sky**72 4-10-11 0...... HenryBrooke 100
(Donald McCain) *led 1st: drvn between last 2: hdd last: wknd* **2/1**2

454- **F** **Grethel (IRE)**2 [1379] 9-10-5 74...... BrianHarding 72
(Alan Berry) *s.s: in tch: drvn 5th: wknd next: detached in last whn fell last* **20/1**

0PP/ **P** **Rise To Glory (IRE)**115 [2457] 5-10-7 0...... JoeColliver(5)
(Shaun Harris) *lost pl 3rd: t.o next: hmpd by loose horse and p.u bef 2 out* **50/1**

U **Razzle Dazzle 'Em**25 4-10-6 0...... BenPoste(5)
(Shaun Harris) *in last whn blnd bdly and uns rdr 1st* **50/1**

4m 13.6s (0.40) **Going Correction** -0.125s/f (Good) **7** Ran SP% **114.3**
Speed ratings (Par 105): **94,88,88,85, ,**
toteswingers 1&2 £1.60, 2&3 £3.30, 1&3 £5.10 CSF £9.34 TOTE £4.50: £1.90, £1.80; EX 12.70 Trifecta £51.20 Pool: £500.18 - 7.31 winning units..
Owner David Foster & Brian Ellison **Bred** Cheveley Park Stud Ltd **Trained** Norton, N Yorks
■ Stewards' Enquiry : G Lavery two-day ban: careless riding (9-10 Sep)

FOCUS
An interesting novices' hurdle but ordinary form, rated around the front two.
T/Plt: £31.20 to a £1 stake. Pool of £39907.66 - 933.45 winning tickets. T/Qpdt: £10.00 to a £1 stake. Pool of £1959.10 - 144.80 winning tickets. WG

424 HUNTINGDON (R-H)
Monday, August 26

OFFICIAL GOING: Good to soft (good in places) changing to good (good to soft in places) after race 2 (3.10)
Wind: light, half behind Weather: sunny and warm

1400 HOLIDAY INN OPENING ODDS H'CAP HURDLE (8 hdls) 2m 110y
2:35 (2:35) (Class 4) (0-110,110) 4-Y-0+ **£3,119** (£915; £457; £228)

Form RPR

/64- **1** **Taroum (IRE)**47 [947] 6-10-8 **92**...... LeeEdwards 100
(Tony Carroll) *hld up in midfield: effrt and rdn to chse clr ldr sn after 3 out: led between last 2: styd on wl flat: drvn out* **11/4**2

033- **2** *1 ½* **Tiradia (FR)**66 [788] 6-10-4 **88**...... ConorO'Farrell 96
(J R Jenkins) *hld up in tch in midfield: swtchd lft and gd hdwy sn after 3 out: chalng next: mstke last: edgd lft u.p and one pce flat* **11/1**

312- **3** *2 ¼* **Orthodox Lad**7 [1319] 5-11-7 **105**...... TomO'Brien 111
(Dr Richard Newland) *in tch in midfield: hdwy to ld bef 3 out: pressed and mstke next: hdd bef last: one pce flat* **11/8**1

426- **4** *12* **Brassbound (USA)**47 [947] 5-11-11 **109**...... AndrewThornton 103
(Caroline Bailey) *in tch in last quartet: mstke 5th: sn rdn and no imp: styd on past btn horses 2 out: wnt modest 4th last: nvr trbld ldrs* **20/1**

630- **5** *4 ½* **Godwit**37 [1043] 5-11-1 **102**...... JackQuinlan(3) 92
(Eugene Stanford) *chsd ldr tl 3rd: styd chsng ldrs tl wknd u.p bef 2 out* **20/1**

34U- **6** *2 ½* **Wom**36 [1058] 5-10-10 **99**......(v) TrevorWhelan(5) 87
(Neil King) *in tch in rr: reminder after 2nd: hdwy after 5th: 5th and wkng u.p bef 2 out* **20/1**

120- **7** *1 ¼* **Tamarillo Grove (IRE)**22 [1203] 6-11-12 **110**......(t) RichieMcLernon 97
(Sophie Leech) *led tl hdd bef 3 out: drvn and no ex wl bef next: 4th and wl hld whn mstke 2 out: wknd* **20/1**

402- **8** *6* **Kayfton Pete**28 [1134] 7-11-4 **102**......(t) AdamPogson 83
(Charles Pogson) *t.k.h: chsd ldrs: wnt 2nd 3rd tl bef 3 out: mstke 3 out: sn rdn and wknd: mstke 2 out* **20/1**

3/2- **9** *17* **So Cheeky**18 [552] 4-11-1 **100**......(t) DenisO'Regan 65
(Richard Guest) *bhd and nvr gng wl: reminders after 2nd: mstke 4th: rdn and lost tch next: t.o 2 out: hmpd last* **25/1**

U44- **10** *¾* **Take The Crown**24 [1183] 4-10-0 **85** oh2...... HenryOliver 49
(Henry Oliver) *hld up in tch in last quartet: rdn and struggling after 5th: sn wl btn: t.o 2 out* **50/1**

131- **P** **Emerald Glade (IRE)**9 [1280] 6-11-3 **108**...... ConorShoemark(7)
(Jim Best) *chsd ldrs tl lost action bnd after 5th: p.u and dismntd bef 3 out: fatally injured* **8/1**3

0/6- **F** **Poetic Power (IRE)**31 [1120] 4-10-3 **95**...... DanielHiskett(7)
(Claire Dyson) *t.k.h: chsd ldrs: lost pl 4th: lost tch after next: t.o 2 out tl fell last* **50/1**

3m 37.7s (-17.20) **Going Correction** -0.90s/f (Hard)
WFA 4 from 5yo+ 13lb **12** Ran SP% **119.8**
Speed ratings (Par 105): **104,103,102,96,94 93,92,89,81,81 ,**
toteswingers 1&2 £10.00, 2&3 £6.10, 1&3 £2.00 CSF £27.07 CT £58.12 TOTE £4.00: £1.60, £2.70, £1.10; EX 34.70 Trifecta £106.60 Pool: £366.69 - 2.57 winning units..
Owner Jason Tucker **Bred** His Highness The Aga Khan's Studs S C **Trained** Cropthorne, Worcs

FOCUS
A moderate handicap run in a good time for the grade. The winner returned to form.

1401 TONY MONK HAPPY 80TH BIRTHDAY H'CAP CHASE (12 fncs) 2m 110y
3:10 (3:10) (Class 5) (0-100,104) 4-Y-O+ £2,144 (£629; £314; £157)

Form RPR
53- **1** **Julie Prince (IRE)**[11] 1274 7-11-6 **93**........(t) WillKennedy 107+
(Brendan Powell) *mde all and j. bttr than rivals: pushed along and drew clr between last 2: pushed out last* **2/1**[2]

P00- **2** 5 **Novikov**[25] 1174 9-10-0 **73** oh2........(tp) RichieMcLernon 84
(Sophie Leech) *j.lft: chsd ldr 2nd tl 3rd and again 6th: clr w wnr after 3 out: j.lft 2 out: no ex and btn whn j.lft: mstke and pckd last: plugged on same pce flat* **9/1**

F33- **3** 7 **Crescent Beach (IRE)**[7] 1315 6-11-0 **87**........(b) HenryOliver 89
(Henry Oliver) *nt fluent: t.k.h: chsd ldr tl 2nd: styd chsng ldrs: rdn 8th: outpcd by ldng pair sn after 3 out: plugged on but wl hld after* **4/1**[3]

541- **4** 5 **Quarton (IRE)**[7] 1315 6-12-0 **104** 7ex........(p) AdamWedge(3) 104
(Evan Williams) *mstkes: in tch in last pair: shkn up after 4th: rdn 8th: struggling whn blnd 3 out: wl btn whn j.lft and mstke next: mstke last: wnt modest 4th flat* **7/4**[1]

500- **5** 2 **Amen (IRE)**[82] 634 5-11-9 **99**........ JoshuaMoore(3) 95
(Gary Moore) *in tch in last pair: effrt bef 3 out: outpcd by ldng pair wl bef 2 out: 4th and wknd between last 2* **9/1**

0/0- **P** **The Quantum Kid**[22] 1206 9-11-6 **93**........ LiamTreadwell
(Peter Hiatt) *chsd ldrs: wnt 2nd 3rd tl mstke 6th: dropped to last and mstke next: lost tch 3 out: t.o whn p.u next* **20/1**

3m 58.25s (-11.95) **Going Correction** -0.625s/f (Firm) 6 Ran SP% **114.5**
Speed ratings (Par 103): **103,100,97,95,94**
toteswingers 1&2 £5.30, 2&3 £21.60, 1&3 £2.00 CSF £19.16 TOTE £3.70: £2.30, £3.30; EX 20.30 Trifecta £54.00 Pool: £338.62 - 4.70 winning units..
Owner Con Harrington **Bred** Mrs Chris Harrington **Trained** Upper Lambourn, Berks

FOCUS
An ordinary handicap. The winner improved to his hurdle mark.

1402 TONY MCNULTY CONDITIONAL JOCKEYS' (S) HURDLE (10 hdls) 2m 4f 110y
3:45 (3:45) (Class 5) 4-Y-O+ £1,949 (£572; £286; £143)

Form RPR
255- **1** **Ajman (IRE)**[4] 1342 8-10-4 100........(tp) ConorRing(8) 106
(Evan Williams) *hld up wl in tch in rr: hdwy 7th: trckd ldr wl bef next: upsides and mstke 2 out: rdn to ld between last 2: kpt on u.p flat* **2/1**[1]

/14- **2** 1 ¾ **Dantari (IRE)**[34] 1092 8-11-1 114........(p) AdamWedge(3) 110
(Evan Williams) *chsd ldrs tlwnt 2nd 6th: led 7th: clr w wnr bef next: mstke 2 out: hdd between last 2: styd on same pce u.p flat* **11/4**[2]

033- **3** 41 **Persian Herald**[28] 1134 5-10-9 92........(v) TrevorWhelan(3) 68
(Neil King) *chsd ldrs: rdn 6th: outpcd u.p after next and wl btn: wnt modest 3rd bef 2 out: t.o* **5/1**[3]

601/ **4** 1 **Aghill (IRE)**[237] 3431 9-11-4 103........(vt) GavinSheehan 73
(Lawney Hill) *led tl 7th: drvn and btn bef next: 4th and wl btn bef 2 out: t.o* **8/1**

/00- **5** 21 **Khazium (IRE)**[85] 604 4-10-8 104........(tp) DanielHiskett(8) 52
(Claire Dyson) *chsd ldrs tl dropped to last and rdn after 5th: lost tch next: t.o bef 3 out* **14/1**

/ **6** 6 **Cloudgazer (IRE)**[46] 3360 5-11-4 0........(p) KillianMoore 48
(Giles Bravery) *chsd ldr tl lost pl 6th: sn rdn: lost tch qckly sn after next: t.o bef 2 out* **11/2**

4m 37.6s (-21.40) **Going Correction** -0.90s/f (Hard)
WFA 4 from 5yo+ 14lb 6 Ran SP% **109.8**
Speed ratings (Par 103): **104,103,87,87,79 77**
toteswingers 1&2 £1.10, 2&3 £2.50, 1&3 £3.60 CSF £7.54 TOTE £2.70: £1.60, £2.20; EX 9.50 Trifecta £25.50 Pool: £113.70 - 3.33 winning units..There was no bid for the winner.
Owner R P R O'Neil **Bred** Pat McDonnell **Trained** Llancarfan, Vale Of Glamorgan

FOCUS
A very weak seller in which the first two ran pretty much to their marks.

1403 HOLIDAY INN EXPECTATIONS H'CAP CHASE (19 fncs) 3m
4:20 (4:20) (Class 4) (0-120,112) 4-Y-O+ £3,898 (£1,144; £572; £286)

Form RPR
34P- **1** **Balinroab (IRE)**[28] 1135 6-11-11 **111**........ DenisO'Regan 120+
(Richard Guest) *nt a fluent: led and mstke 1st: sn hdd and chsd ldng pair tl wnt 2nd again after 8th tl mstke 14th: cl 3rd tl chal 2 out: pushed into ld flat and sn rdn clr: styd on* **9/4**[2]

015- **2** 2 ¼ **Baily Storm (IRE)**[13] 1257 11-11-7 **107**........(vt) DavidBass 112
(Lawney Hill) *j. boldly: led: rdn and pressed 2 out: drvn last: hdd flat: no ex and styd on same pce fnl 100yds* **12/1**

112- **3** 3 ¾ **Rudigreen (IRE)**[6] 1325 10-11-9 **112**........(tp) JackQuinlan(3) 115
(Noel Quinlan) *in tch in rr: pckd 2nd: hdwy to chse ldrs 10th: trckd ldr 14th: lost 2nd and mstke 2 out: rdn and unable qck between last 2: btn last: one pce flat* **15/8**[1]

/P5- **4** 56 **Ballyvoneen (IRE)**[106] 242 8-10-8 **99**........ TrevorWhelan(5) 50
(Neil King) *a in last pair: 4th and rdn 13th: sn struggling: lost tch 3 out: t.o whn j.lft next* **9/2**

023- **5** 28 **High Ron**[8] 1303 8-11-10 **110**........(p) AndrewThornton 36
(Caroline Bailey) *chsd ldr after 1st tl after 8th: pushed along and lost pl 10th: rallied briefly u.p 11th: struggling next: lost tch 13th: wl t.o fr 15th* **4/1**[3]

5m 57.2s (-13.10) **Going Correction** -0.625s/f (Firm) 5 Ran SP% **111.4**
Speed ratings (Par 105): **96,95,94,75,66**
CSF £22.61 TOTE £3.30: £1.80, £3.80; EX 27.80 Trifecta £48.90 Pool: £321.89 - 4.93 winning units..
Owner Miss C Fordham **Bred** Thomas McGrath **Trained** Wetherby, W Yorks

FOCUS
A fair handicap. The winner is rated back to form for his new yard with the next two close to their marks.

1404 COMING IN FIRST HOLIDAY INN MAIDEN HURDLE (8 hdls) 2m 110y
4:55 (4:55) (Class 4) 4-Y-O+ £3,119 (£915; £457; £228)

Form RPR
3- **1** **Beachfire**[23] 1191 6-10-11 0........ JackQuinlan(3) 124+
(John Ferguson) *hld up in midfield: trckd ldng pair and gng best after 5th: wnt 2nd after next: led and hit 2 out: pushed clr and in command whn wnt rt and hit last: pushed out and r.o wl: comf* **6/1**[3]

0/2- **2** 9 **New Year's Eve**[13] 1256 5-11-0 125........ DenisO'Regan 118
(John Ferguson) *led: blnd 5th: hdd and mstke 2 out: no ex and btn last: eased towards fin* **5/4**[1]

0/2- **3** 8 **Golanova**[11] 1270 5-10-11 0........ JoshuaMoore(3) 108
(Gary Moore) *mstkes: mostly chsd ldr: mstke 2nd and 5th: hit 3 out: rdn and btn bef next: 3rd and wl hld whn mstke 2 out and last* **11/8**[2]

055- **4** 13 **Giant Hercules (IRE)**[22] 1201 6-10-7 0........ JackSherwood(7) 97
(Phil McEntee) *in tch in last pair: outpcd after 5th: wnt modest 4th bef 2 out: plugged on but no threat to ldrs* **66/1**

34- **5** 23 **Itmakessense**[13] 1256 6-10-11 0........(p) KielanWoods(3) 74
(Charlie Longsdon) *chsd ldrs tl rdn and lost pl after 5th: 4th and btn next: wknd: t.o* **14/1**

45/ **6** 1 ¾ **Chankillo**[47] 1920 4-10-13 0........ WillKennedy 71
(Sarah-Jayne Davies) *hld up in rr: clsd and in tch 4th: lost tch rapidly sn after next: t.o after 3 out* **33/1**

3m 36.6s (-18.30) **Going Correction** -0.90s/f (Hard)
WFA 4 from 5yo+ 13lb 6 Ran SP% **111.9**
Speed ratings (Par 105): **107,102,99,92,82 81**
toteswingers 1&2 £1.10, 2&3 £1.10, 1&3 £1.40 CSF £14.45 TOTE £3.70: £1.30, £1.30; EX 10.10 Trifecta £27.20 Pool: £413.96 - 11.39 winning units..
Owner Bloomfields **Bred** Bridgewater Equine Ltd **Trained** Cowlinge, Suffolk

FOCUS
Little strength in depth to this maiden. A big step up from the easy winner but there should be more to come, while his stablemate was again well below his best.

1405 HOLIDAY INN SLEEP EASY H'CAP HURDLE (DIV I) (12 hdls) 3m 2f
5:30 (5:30) (Class 5) (0-95,91) 4-Y-O+ £1,949 (£572; £286; £143)

Form RPR
536- **1** **Go Amwell**[31] 1121 10-11-7 **86**........(v) LeightonAspell 91
(J R Jenkins) *hld up in last trio: hdwy to chse ldrs after 7th: wnt 2nd bef 3 out: ev ch 2 out: led last: drvn and r.o to go clr flat: drvn out* **5/1**[3]

036- **2** 3 ¾ **Moyne Nineoseven (IRE)**[11] 1275 7-11-9 **91**........(t) JackQuinlan(3) 93
(Noel Quinlan) *hld up in midfield: effrt to chse ldrs 3 out: drvn to ld next: hdd and hit last: nt pce of wnr and btn flat: kpt on* **9/2**[2]

/00- **3** 3 **Hill Forts Gloria (IRE)**[24] 1188 8-9-9 **65** oh9........(tp) GavinSheehan(5) 63
(Lawney Hill) *chsd ldrs tl led bef 4th: wnt clr bef 5th: pressed and rdn after 3 out: hdd next: no ex between last 2 and btn last: plugged on same pce flat* **9/1**

563- **4** 8 **Reckless Romeo (IRE)**[33] 1105 4-10-5 **80**........ MrTGreenwood(7) 68
(Richard Ford) *in tch in midfield: hdwy to chse ldr bef 8th tl after 9th: 4th and outpcd u.p after 3 out: wl hld and plugged on same pce fr next* **12/1**

/5P- **5** ¾ **Upper Deck (IRE)**[43] 965 8-9-11 **69**........ DanielHiskett(7) 59
(Richard Phillips) *hld up in last trio: mstke 5th: rdn and struggling after 7th: no threat to ldrs but plugged on u.p fr 2 out* **10/1**

633- **6** 1 **Heezagrey (IRE)**[24] 1188 10-10-1 **69**........(b) MarkQuinlan(3) 59
(James Evans) *in tch in midfield: drvn and outpcd after 9th: 7th and no imp u.p after 3 out: wl hld but plugged on flat* **11/2**

063- **7** 9 **Brass Monkey (IRE)**[13] 1259 6-11-2 **86**........ TrevorWhelan(5) 70
(Neil King) *in tch in midfield: chsd ldr after 7th tl bef next: stl chsng ldrs but drvn whn mstke 3 out: wknd bef next* **7/1**

000- **8** 19 **Absolute Shambles**[33] 1105 9-11-3 **82**........(p) TomCannon 46
(Chris Gordon) *led tl bef 4th: sn rdn along: chsd ldrs tl lost pl after 8th: lost tch bef 3 out: t.o* **14/1**

/03- **9** 11 **Lost Arca (FR)**[36] 1051 7-10-10 **78**........ RobertDunne(3) 32
(Robin Mathew) *hld up in tch in rr: hdwy after 7th: chsd ldrs 9th: rdn and no rspnse next: wknd 3 out: wl btn 2 out: t.o* **4/1**[1]

/P0- **10** 85 **Burnthill (IRE)**[24] 1188 8-10-13 **85**........(tp) GeraldQuinn(7)
(Claire Dyson) *chsd ldr tl lost pl qckly u.p after 7th: bhd next: t.o 9th* **25/1**

6m 2.15s (-20.75) **Going Correction** -0.90s/f (Hard)
WFA 4 from 6yo+ 15lb 10 Ran SP% **120.0**
Speed ratings (Par 103): **95,93,92,90,90 89,87,81,77,51**
toteswingers 1&2 £33.20, 2&3 £16.20, 1&3 £33.20 CSF £29.20 CT £201.52 TOTE £6.60: £2.90, £1.90, £3.90; EX 45.30 Trifecta £298.90 Part won. Pool: £398.65 - 0.44 winning units..
Owner Robin Stevens **Bred** Michael Ng **Trained** Royston, Herts

FOCUS
A weak staying handicap. The winner is rated in line with his May run over C&D.

1406 HOLIDAY INN SLEEP EASY H'CAP HURDLE (DIV II) (12 hdls) 3m 2f
6:00 (6:00) (Class 5) (0-95,90) 4-Y-O+ £1,949 (£572; £286; £143)

Form RPR
P50- **1** **Fitobust (IRE)**[25] 1172 7-10-8 **72**........(v[1]) DavidBass 80
(Lawney Hill) *w ldr tl led after 7th: drvn bef 2 out: hdd and mstke last: lft in ld again flat: sn in command: drvn out* **20/1**

0/2- **2** 5 **She Is A Cracker (FR)**[7] 1320 8-10-7 **78**........ MrGGorman(7) 84+
(Mrs C M Gorman) *t.k.h early: hld up in tch: 4th and gng wl 9th: bmpd along and effrt to chse wnr 2 out: led: j.rt and hit last: pricked ears in front: hung bdly lft and hdd flat: immediately btn and slowed bdly after* **2/1**[1]

/PP- **3** 3 ¾ **Call At Midnight**[43] 969 8-11-5 **90**........ MikeyEnnis(7) 89
(Sarah Humphrey) *t.k.h: in tch: chsd ldr 8th: drvn and unable qck bef 2 out: 3rd and btn between last 2: plugged on* **14/1**

621- **4** nk **Fromthetop (IRE)**[13] 1267 7-11-8 **86**........(tp) LiamTreadwell 85
(Michael Scudamore) *in tch: mstke 5th: rdn and hit 9th: 5th and no imp u.p 3 out: no threat to ldng pair but plugged on u.p flat* **11/4**[2]

0/P- **5** 2 ¾ **Artic Night (FR)**[13] 1266 7-11-7 **85**........(bt) DavidEngland 81
(Nigel Twiston-Davies) *t.k.h: hld up in tch in last pair: hdwy and lft 3rd 8th: drvn and fnd litte bef 2 out: 4th and wknd between last 2* **10/1**

0/3- **6** 23 **Radical Bay**[43] 969 9-10-0 **69**........ TrevorWhelan(5) 45
(Nicholas Pomfret) *in tch in rr: pushed along after 7th and nvr gng wl after: lost tch 9th: wl bhd and hit 2 out: t.o* **16/1**

P/5- **7** 6 **Potters Dream (IRE)**[24] 1188 7-10-3 **67**........ PaddyBrennan 37
(Fergal O'Brien) *led and set stdy gallop tl hdd after 7th: cl 3rd whn blnd 8th: nt rcvr and bhd whn drvn bef next: lost tch 3 out: hit next: t.o* **3/1**[3]

000- **P** **Cloudy Start**[13] 1259 7-11-4 **82**........ WillKennedy
(Violet M Jordan) *chsd ldrs: mstke and lost pl 4th: stl wl in tch in midfield: dropped to rr and rdn 8th: lost tch after next: t.o whn p.u 2 out* **40/1**

6m 7.15s (-15.75) **Going Correction** -0.90s/f (Hard) 8 Ran SP% **113.8**
Speed ratings (Par 103): **88,86,85,85,84 77,75,**
toteswingers 1&2 £11.10, 2&3 £38.80, 1&3 £12.50 CSF £61.57 CT £601.22 TOTE £22.30: £3.20, £1.40, £2.60; EX 81.00 Trifecta £361.60 Part won. Pool: £482.19 - 0.12 winning units..
Owner Alan Hill **Bred** A Byrnes **Trained** Aston Rowant, Oxon

FOCUS
This second division of the weak staying handicap was five seconds slower than the first. The winner was well in on his old form.
T/Plt: £104.20 to a £1 stake. Pool of £31101.55 - 217.76 winning tickets. T/Qpdt: £38.20 to a £1 stake. Pool of £1485.09 - 28.70 winning ticket. SP

1407 - 1413a (Foreign Racing) - See Raceform Interactive

[278]SEDGEFIELD (L-H)

Tuesday, August 27

OFFICIAL GOING: Good to firm (good in places; 7.6)
Divided bends and hurdles sited on outside.
Wind: Virtually nil Weather: Sunny

1414 ALBERTHILL COMMERCIALS CONDITIONAL JOCKEYS' H'CAP HURDLE (10 hdls) 2m 5f 110y
4:55 (4:55) (Class 4) (0-120,112) 4-Y-O+ £3,119 (£915; £457; £228)

Form RPR
/40- 1 **Ben Cee Pee M (IRE)**[44] 966 8-10-6 100..............(v[1]) CraigGallagher(8) 107
(Brian Ellison) *hld up in tch: wnt 3rd 3 out: rdn and hdwy appr 2 out: led last: styd on to go clr* 6/4[1]

/10- 2 8 **Raktiman (IRE)**[10] 1284 6-11-8 108..........................(p) JonathanEngland 107
(Michael Appleby) *in tch: trckd ldr 4th: led 6th: rdn appr 2 out: hit 2 out: strly pressed and wandered between last 2: hdd last: one pce* 6/1

024- 3 nk **Weybridge Light**[14] 884 8-11-0 100...................................(b) TonyKelly 99
(David Thompson) *in tch: nt fluent 2nd: trckd ldrs after 6th: wnt 2nd after 4 out: rdn and ev ch 2 out: one pce run-in* 5/1[3]

144- 4 51 **Four Nations (USA)**[43] 995 5-11-11 111......................(b) TrevorWhelan 59
(George Baker) *nt fluent: sn pushed along along in rr: a bhd: t.o* 8/1

5/6- 5 2 3/4 **Cavite Eta (IRE)**[14] 1258 6-11-4 107.......................... GrahamWatters(3) 52
(Barry Murtagh) *pressed ldr tl 4th: remained in tch tl wknd after 4 out: t.o* 12/1

132- 6 64 **Separate Shadows (FR)**[25] 1183 5-11-6 112.................(b) NickSlatter(6)
(Donald McCain) *led narrowly: hdd 6th: rdn after next: wknd 3 out: t.o* 4/1[2]

5m 1.7s (-12.90) **Going Correction** -0.675s/f (Firm) 6 Ran SP% 109.8
Speed ratings (Par 105): **96,93,92,74,73 50**
toteswingers 1&2 £3.40, 1&3 £2.50, 2&3 £5.80 CSF £10.36 TOTE £2.40: £1.30, £3.80; EX 12.00 Trifecta £55.30 Pool: £2193.62 - 55.30 winning units..
Owner CPM Group Limited **Bred** Daniel Fogarty **Trained** Norton, N Yorks

FOCUS
After a dry night, the ground was officially good to firm, good in places. Bends had been divided and the hurdles were positioned on the outside of the track. Racing began with a moderate handicap hurdle, in which the top weight was rated 112. The early pace looked strong and the winner stayed on best, running not far short of his previous best for Oliver Sherwood.

1415 JARDINES CATERING NOVICES' HURDLE (PAXTONS HURDLE SERIES QUALIFIER) (8 hdls) 2m 1f
5:25 (5:25) (Class 4) 4-Y-O+ £3,119 (£915; £457; £228)

Form RPR
321- 1 **Smart Ruler (IRE)**[36] 1072 7-11-5 117.................................... APMcCoy 115+
(James Moffatt) *mde all: pushed along appr 2 out: drvn between last 2: kpt on wl* 6/4[1]

121- 2 7 **Howwouldyou (IRE)**[27] 1159 5-11-12 117................. GrahamWatters(7) 123
(Liam Lennon, Ire) *trckd ldr: rdn appr 2 out: sn one pce in 2nd* 2/1[2]

3 28 **Knightly Escapade**[73] 5-10-12 0.. DannyCook 82
(Brian Ellison) *in tch: mstke 2nd: nt fluent next: chsd ldng pair whn hit 3 out: sn rdn: wknd 2 out: hit last* 5/2[3]

4- 4 30 **The Lodge Road (IRE)**[4] 1008 5-10-12 0...................... WilsonRenwick 50
(Martin Todhunter) *trckd ldr: rdn and lost pl after 4 out: wknd after 3 out* 25/1

050- 5 11 **Beyondtemptation**[65] 800 5-10-2 0.............................. JohnKington(3) 33
(Jonathan Haynes) *nt fluent in rr: a bhd* 150/1

3m 53.0s (-13.90) **Going Correction** -0.675s/f (Firm)
WFA 4 from 5yo+ 13lb 5 Ran SP% 106.4
Speed ratings (Par 105): **105,101,88,74,69**
CSF £4.62 TOTE £2.10: £1.60, £1.50; EX 4.30 Trifecta £7.10 Pool: £1406.60 - 147.18 winning units..
Owner The Vilprano Partnership **Bred** Patrick Cummins **Trained** Cartmel, Cumbria

FOCUS
The betting suggested only three mattered in this novice hurdle and they filled the significant placings. The form is taken at face value.

1416 WILLS PROPERTY SERVICES NOVICES' H'CAP CHASE (16 fncs) 2m 4f
5:55 (5:55) (Class 5) (0-100,93) 4-Y-O+ £2,144 (£629; £314; £157)

Form RPR
041- 1 **Alderbrook Lad (IRE)**[7] 1328 7-11-9 93 7ex................ MichaelByrne(3) 105+
(Neil Mulholland) *mde all: pushed along after 2 out: a firmly in command: nt fluent last* 11/8[1]

233- 2 7 **Solway Dornal**[3] 1377 8-9-13 73........................(tp) StephenMulqueen(7) 76
(Lisa Harrison) *trckd wnr in 2nd: rdn after 3 out: sn one pce and no ch w wnr* 11/4[2]

044- 3 11 **Harris Garden (IRE)**[32] 1119 6-11-9 93.......................... JackQuinlan(3) 89
(Paul Cowley) *in tch in 3rd: rdn after 3 out: sn no imp: hit last* 7/2[3]

0/0- 4 25 **Cian Boy (IRE)**[10b] 264 7-11-0 81...................................... HarryHaynes 51
(Nick Kent) *j.rt and none too fluently in rr: bhd after 10th* 8/1

/P0- F **Larkhall**[14] 1260 6-9-9 67 oh1.. GavinSheehan(5)
(Mike Sowersby) *trckd ldrs: fell 1st* 16/1

4m 46.9s (-16.10) **Going Correction** -0.675s/f (Firm) 5 Ran SP% 108.0
Speed ratings (Par 103): **105,102,97,87,**
CSF £5.50 TOTE £2.00: £1.10, £1.50; EX 5.30 Trifecta £10.90 Pool: £397.88 - 27.19 winning units..
Owner Wellcroomed T/A eyewearoutlet.co.uk **Bred** A Malone **Trained** Limpley Stoke, Wilts

FOCUS
A low-grade handicap chase, but an improving winner and the runner-up is the key to the form.

1417 SANTANDER H'CAP CHASE (13 fncs) 2m 110y
6:25 (6:26) (Class 4) (0-110,111) 4-Y-O+ £3,768 (£1,106; £553; £276)

Form RPR
321- 1 **Bennys Quest (IRE)**[5] 1352 10-11-11 111 7ex..........(p) PeterCarberry(3) 118+
(Neil Mulholland) *in tch: wnt 2nd 8th: led narrowly on bit jst after 2 out: drvn run-in: hld on all out* 2/1[1]

552- 2 nk **Muwalla**[10] 1280 6-11-5 102..(tp) DenisO'Regan 108
(Chris Grant) *hld up: hdwy to trck ldr 9th: rdn 2 out: sn upsides: drvn appr last: kpt on: jst hld* 8/1[3]

323- 3 19 **Twill Stand To Us (IRE)**[44] 960 6-11-12 109..................(t) DannyCook 102
(Brian Ellison) *led: often j. sltly rt: j. bdly rt and hit 2 out: sn hdd: wknd: hit last* 2/1[1]

35P- 4 19 **Ginger's Lad**[35] 1089 9-9-9 85.................................... MrHAABannister(7) 57
(Michael Easterby) *trckd ldrs: wknd after 4 out* 16/1

010- P **Alba King (IRE)**[36] 1075 7-10-4 92........................... JonathanEngland(5)
(Sue Smith) *trckd ldr: reminder after 4th: lost pl after 8th: sn wknd: wl bhd whn p.u after 3 out* 11/4[2]

3m 57.5s (-11.10) **Going Correction** -0.675s/f (Firm) 5 Ran SP% 110.3
Speed ratings (Par 105): **99,98,89,80,**
CSF £15.96 TOTE £2.50: £1.50, £2.60; EX 12.30 Trifecta £28.60 Pool: £1267.65 - 33.23 winning units..
Owner John Hobbs & Dave Harris **Bred** Patrick J McGrath **Trained** Limpley Stoke, Wilts
■ Merry Minster was withdrawn. Price at time of withdrawal 17-2. Rule 4 applies to bets placed prior to withdrawal but no to SP bets - deduction 10p in the pound. New market formed.

FOCUS
Just a small field, but a competitive event nonetheless, and the early pace looked decent. The winner is in great form and is value for more that the official margin.

1418 ROFLOW VENTILATION FOR NATION NOVICES' HURDLE (PAXTONS HURDLE SERIES QUALIFIER) (10 hdls) 2m 4f
6:55 (6:55) (Class 4) 4-Y-O+ £3,119 (£915; £457; £228)

Form RPR
512- 1 **Sky Khan**[29] 1139 4-10-5 119...(p) AdamNicol(5) 119+
(Philip Kirby) *trckd ldng pajr: nt fluent 6th: led narrowly on bit after 2 out: nt extended to assert run-in* 1/4[1]

03- 2 3 3/4 **Hit The Top (IRE)**[38] 1037 6-10-12 0....................................... RyanMania 107
(Sue Smith) *trckd ldng pair: rdn and upsides after 2 out but wnr a gng much bttr: one pce run-in* 10/1[3]

5- 3 7 **Larteta (FR)**[14] 1255 4-10-7 0.. JackQuinlan(3) 98
(Sarah Humphrey) *w ldr: led 4 out: rdn and hdd after 2 out: wknd* 33/1

34- 4 1 1/2 **Cloudy Joker (IRE)**[28] 1145 5-10-12 0................................ JasonMaguire 99
(Donald McCain) *hld up: rdn after 3 out: sn one pce* 14/1

0/5- 5 68 **Mrs Grass**[108] 218 6-10-2 0.. JohnKington(3) 24
(Jonathan Haynes) *hld up: wknd after 4 out: t.o* 100/1

6- P **Miranour**[17] 1240 8-11-12 112... APMcCoy
(Liam Lennon, Ire) *in tch: wnt wrong and p.u after 3rd* 11/2[2]

P- P **Indian Ruler (IRE)**[32] 1118 8-10-7 0................................ KyleJames(5)
(Philip Kirby) *led narrowly: hdd 4 out: sn wknd: p.u bef 2 out* 100/1

4m 42.1s (-10.60) **Going Correction** -0.675s/f (Firm)
WFA 4 from 5yo+ 14lb 7 Ran SP% 116.1
Speed ratings (Par 105): **94,92,89,89,61 ,**
CSF £4.31 TOTE £1.30: £1.10, £4.10; EX 3.60 TRIFECTA Pool: £1245.07 - 19.03 winning units..
Owner Two Ladies And A Gentleman **Bred** Heather Raw **Trained** Middleham, N Yorks

FOCUS
A lop-sided market for this novice hurdle, won easily by the long odds-on favourite. he is value for ten lengths with the form straightforward rated around those in the frame behind him.

1419 BE PREMIERE HAIR H'CAP HURDLE (8 hdls) 2m 1f
7:25 (7:25) (Class 5) (0-100,100) 4-Y-O+ £1,949 (£572; £286; £143)

Form RPR
0/4- 1 **Deny**[32] 1120 5-10-2 76..(p) RichieMcGrath 76
(Henry Hogarth) *hld up in midfield: hdwy 3 out: sn trckd ldr: rdn and ev ch 2 out: led last: sn drvn: idled: jst hld on* 8/1

0/P- 2 shd **Mr Mistopheles (IRE)**[73] 747 5-10-0 74 oh19.............(b[1]) HenryBrooke 74
(Philip Kirby) *prom: sltly hmpd after 3 out: rdn 2 out: kpt on run-in: jst failed* 9/1

0U3/ 3 2 1/4 **Forster Street (IRE)**[146] 5123 4-11-8 97.................................. APMcCoy 94
(James Moffatt) *midfield: hdwy 3 out: lft in front after 3 out: rdn appr 2 out: sn strly pressed: hdd last: no ex fnl 100yds* 6/1[3]

646- 4 8 **King Mak**[36] 1073 11-10-4 83...(bt) KyleJames(5) 74
(Marjorie Fife) *trckd ldrs: rdn and outpcd after 3 out: plugged on fr between last 2* 8/1

5U4- 5 19 **Millers Reef (IRE)**[73] 752 7-11-7 95..........................(t) WilsonRenwick 66
(Andrew Parker) *in tch: rdn after 3 out: wknd 2 out* 10/1

533- U **Claude Carter**[10] 1285 9-11-8 99................................ EwanWhillans(3)
(Alistair Whillans) *hld up: mstke and uns rdr 3 out* 11/4[1]

550/ P **Valantino Oyster (IRE)**[12] 993 6-10-8 82.................(p) DougieCostello
(Tracy Waggott) *in tch: mstke 1st: rdr lost iron: p.u bef 2nd* 9/1

2P0- U **Dynamic Drive (IRE)**[3] 1379 6-10-6 87..............(tp) StephenMulqueen(7)
(Maurice Barnes) *hld up: hmpd and uns rdr 3 out* 25/1

/34- P **Apolskapart (IRE)**[36] 1072 5-11-12 100................................ RyanMania
(Michael Smith) *led: wnt wrong and p.u after 3 out* 5/1[2]

3m 58.9s (-8.00) **Going Correction** -0.675s/f (Firm)
WFA 4 from 5yo+ 13lb 9 Ran SP% 112.8
Speed ratings (Par 103): **91,90,89,86,77 , , ,**
toteswingers 1&2 £10.20, 1&3 £8.30, 2&3 £9.20 CSF £74.32 CT £460.80 TOTE £6.10: £1.50, £1.40, £2.90; EX 80.30 Trifecta £616.80 Part won. Pool: £822.43 - 0.74 winning units..
Owner Hogarth Racing **Bred** James Wigan **Trained** Stillington, N Yorks

FOCUS
A modest handicap hurdle, with the top weight rated 100, but a thrilling finish. The form looks weak though.

1420 CAPITAL FM STANDARD OPEN NATIONAL HUNT FLAT RACE 2m 1f
7:55 (7:55) (Class 6) 4-6-Y-O £1,559 (£457; £228; £114)

Form RPR
232- 1 **Mutanawwer**[29] 1138 4-11-0 0.. BrianHughes 108+
(Andrew Crook) *mde all: pushed clr over 1f out: comf* 11/10[1]

2 6 **Abel J Tasman (IRE)** 5-11-1 0.. BrianHarding 101+
(James Moffatt) *hld up in tch: hdwy over 6f out: rdn and outpcd over 3f out: kpt on fr over 1f out: wnt 2nd fnl 100yds* 25/1

45- 3 1 3/4 **Dalstontosiloth (IRE)**[10] 1292 5-11-1 0.................................. APMcCoy 99
(Barry Murtagh) *hld up in tch: hdwy to trck ldr over 6f out: rdn over 3f out: sn one pce: lost 2nd fnl 100yds* 10/1

5/3- 4 2 3/4 **Our Crusade**[48] 944 6-10-12 0....................................... JakeGreenall(3) 97
(Michael Easterby) *trckd ldrs: rdn over 3f out: one pce* 11/4[2]

5 3 **Lacocodanza** 4-10-7 0.. BarryKeniry 86
(George Moore) *in tch: lost pl over 6f out: rdn and outpcd over 3f out: kpt on fnl f* 3/1[3]

0/0- 6 29 **Crispo (IRE)**[54] 885 5-10-10 0....................................... TonyKelly(5) 68
(David Thompson) *hld up: rdn 4f out: sn wknd* 100/1

0- 7 99 **Ninetynine (IRE)**[54] 885 6-10-1 0........................(t) StephenMulqueen(7)
(Maurice Barnes) *trckd ldr: lost pl over 6f out: sn bhd: t.o fnl 4f* 50/1

3m 54.9s (-6.40) **Going Correction** -0.675s/f (Firm)
WFA 4 from 5yo+ 1lb 7 Ran SP% 115.2
Speed ratings: **88,85,84,83,81 68,21**
toteswingers 1&2 £7.10, 1&3 £2.60, 2&3 £8.30 CSF £31.40 TOTE £2.60: £1.30, £10.40; EX 33.90 Trifecta £418.10 Pool: £1211.07 - 2.17 winning units..
Owner RA Syndicate **Bred** Shadwell Estate Company Limited **Trained** Middleham Moor, N Yorks

FOCUS
Not much worthwhile form to evaluate in this concluding bumper. The third and fourth help set the level.

T/Plt: £39.50 to a £1 stake. Pool: £48365.82 - 892.95 winning tickets T/Qpdt: £12.70 to a £1 stake. Pool: £4090.05 - 237.99 winning tickets AS

1421 - 1423a (Foreign Racing) - See Raceform Interactive

WAREGEM (R-H)
Tuesday, August 27

OFFICIAL GOING: Turf: good

1424a ING GROTE STEEPLE-CHASE VAN VLAANDEREN (CHASE) (H'CAP) (6YO+) (TURF) 2m 7f
3:40 (12:00) 6-Y-O+ £40,650 (£16,260; £10,162; £6,097; £4,065)

RPR

1 **Martalin (FR)**[147] 7-10-3 0 ow2 (p) JeromeZuliani 11
(Patrice Quinton, France) 6/1[3]
2 8 **Pop Island (FR)**[311] 10-9-11 0 MaximeLeGalliard 2
(A Chaille-Chaille, France) 2/1[1]
3 9 **Royal Fou (FR)**[728] 1569 8-10-6 0 JordanDuchene 9
(Patrice Quinton, France) 19/5[2]
4 dist **Alanco (GER)**[436] 743 12-10-10 0 CevinChan 4
(O W Seiler, Germany) 12/1
5 9 **Quintos (FR)**[512] 5213 9-9-11 0 (b) KevinNabet 6
(Guy Denuault, France) 15/1
6 1 ¾ **Cafe De Paris (FR)**[139] 8-10-1 0 ow4 (b) ArnoldCisel 8
(S Foucher, France) 17/1
7 2 ½ **Puncho (FR)**[23] 1214 10-10-1 0 ow4 (b) Marc-AntoineDragon 5
(Patrice Quinton, France) 11/1
8 4 **Politeo (FR)**[164] 4784 7-10-8 0 JamesReveley 1
(Nick Williams) *t.k.h: prom early: sn hld up towards rr: tk clsr order to chse ldng quartet fr 10th: lost pl 13th: wl bhd fr 5 out: t.o* 10/1
F **General Tete Jaune (FR)**[402] 9-9-11 0 MorganRegairaz 12
(Y Fertillet, France) 9/1
F **Tyquaveron (FR)**[690] 1896 6-9-11 0 (b) StephanePaillard 3
(J Planque, France) 34/1

5m 38.43s (338.43) 10 Ran SP% 118.2
PARI-MUTUEL (all including 1 euro stakes): WIN 2.30 (combined with Royal Fou and Puncho); PLACE 2.40, 1.40, 1.80; DF 9.30; SF 23.40.
Owner Ecurie Des Dunes **Bred** Mme Henri Devin & Peter Spiller **Trained** France

1325 WORCESTER (L-H)
Wednesday, August 28

OFFICIAL GOING: Good (good to firm in places; 7.2)
Both bends and fences/hurdles on inside line.
Wind: Light behind Weather: Overcast

1425 WORCESTER-RACECOURSE.CO.UK H'CAP CHASE (18 fncs) 2m 7f
2:20 (2:20) (Class 3) (0-140,132) 4-Y-0 £6,330 (£1,870; £935; £468; £234)

Form RPR

P11- 1 **Whistling Senator (IRE)**[42] 1015 6-10-2 108 (v) RichieMcLernon 117
(Jonjo O'Neill) *a.p: chsd ldr 5th: led 13th: shkn up after 4 out: rdn appr 2 out: styd on wl* 11/4[2]
1F2- 2 1 **Forever My Friend (IRE)**[5] 1361 6-10-4 110 JamieMoore 118
(Peter Bowen) *hld up: hdwy 14th: rdn bef next: ev ch last: unable qck towards fin* 9/4[1]
232- 3 8 **Highway Code (USA)**[38] 1053 7-11-2 122 RichardJohnson 122
(Richard Lee) *hld up: hdwy to chse wnr appr 4 out: ev ch fr next tl rdn appr last: no ex flat* 5/1
/21- 4 3 ¼ **Victor Leudorum (IRE)**[15] 1262 6-11-12 132 (t) NoelFehily 129
(Charlie Mann) *chsd ldr to 5th: remained handy: rdn appr 4 out: styd on same pce fr 2 out* 7/2[3]
P11- 5 59 **Papradon**[8] 1327 9-11-3 123 7ex (v) SamTwiston-Davies 61
(Nigel Twiston-Davies) *led to 13th: mstke next: sn lost pl: wknd appr 4 out* 15/2

5m 29.7s (-18.30) **Going Correction** -0.90s/f (Hard) course record 5 Ran SP% 108.1
Speed ratings (Par 107): **95,94,91,90,70**
CSF £9.22 TOTE £3.80: £1.70, £1.30; EX 9.70 Trifecta £28.10 Pool: £1150.60 - 30.70 winning units..
Owner John P McManus **Bred** Noel O'Brien **Trained** Cheltenham, Gloucs

FOCUS
The ground was riding much as advertised. A competitive handicap chase, featuring three last-time-out winners over C&D, if not the strongest race for the grade. The finish was fought out by the bottom pair, who were in receipt of a lot of weight from the others. The runner-up is rated to form.

1426 A & A RACING ONCOURSE BOOKMAKERS NOVICES' CHASE (12 fncs) 2m 110y
2:50 (2:50) (Class 4) 4-Y-0+ £3,994 (£1,240; £667)

Form RPR

342- 1 **The Cockney Mackem (IRE)**[11] 1281 7-11-0 0 SamTwiston-Davies 131+
(Nigel Twiston-Davies) *chsd clr ldrs: mstke 2nd: wnt 2nd 5th: led appr 4 out: hit next: rdn appr last: styd on wl* 2/1[2]
522/ 2 9 **Candelita**[26] 10 6-10-7 110 MarkGrant 113
(Jo Hughes) *hld up: hdwy 7th: chsd wnr 4 out: rdn appr 2 out: styd on same pce* 10/1
102- 3 16 **Monte Cavallo (SAF)**[27] 1175 8-11-6 125 APMcCoy 114
(Rebecca Curtis) *chsd clr ldrs: j.rt: lft 2nd 4th tl nt fluent next: pushed along appr 4 out: mstke and wknd 2 out* 6/4[1]
U **Longwood Lad (IRE)**[1241] 11-11-0 0 SeanQuinlan
(Carole Ikin) *led: plld hrd: hdd whn blnd and uns rdr 4th* 100/1
4/1- P **Esporao (IRE)**[28] 1158 7-11-6 0 (t) TomO'Brien
(Rob Summers) *chsd ldr tl led and lft clr 4th: hdd appr 4 out: wkng whn blnd 3 out: sn p.u* 16/1
020- F **Pirans Car**[13] 1275 7-10-11 0 (bt[1]) MarkQuinlan[(3)]
(Nigel Hawke) *j.rt: sn wl bhd: fell 7th* 100/1
0/4- P **Canadian Diamond (IRE)**[105] 304 6-11-0 0 AlainCawley
(Brendan Powell) *sn wl bhd: p.u bef 9th* 4/1[3]

3m 56.1s (-17.90) **Going Correction** -0.90s/f (Hard) 7 Ran SP% 110.3
Speed ratings (Par 105): **106,101,94,, ,**
toteswingers 1&2 £4.70, 1&3 £1.10, 2&3 £3.50 CSF £19.61 TOTE £3.30: £2.80, £2.20; EX 21.00 Trifecta £41.20 Pool: £1887.61 - 34.30 winning units..
Owner Mills & Mason Partnership **Bred** Albert Sherwood **Trained** Naunton, Gloucs

FOCUS
They went a decent gallop and were soon spread out in this ordinary novice chase. The winner is value for a little extra.

1427 PHIL SHARP 50TH BIRTHDAY STANDARD OPEN NATIONAL HUNT FLAT RACE 2m
3:20 (3:20) (Class 6) 4-6-Y-O £1,559 (£457; £228; £114)

Form RPR

1/ 1 **Cole Harden (IRE)**[159] 4914 4-11-2 0 GavinSheehan[(5)] 115
(Warren Greatrex) *trckd ldrs: t.k.h: wnt 2nd over 10f out: rdn to ld over 1f out: styd on* 7/2[3]
33- 2 1 ¼ **Western Way (IRE)**[15] 1264 4-11-0 0 DenisO'Regan 107
(Don Cantillon) *hld up: hdwy 6f out: rdn and hung lft fr over 1f out: r.o to go 2nd wl ins fnl f: nt quite rch wnr* 14/1
1- 3 3 ¼ **Anger Management (IRE)**[15] 1264 5-11-8 0 APMcCoy 112
(Rebecca Curtis) *led: rdn and hdd over 1f out: no ex ins fnl f* 11/8[1]
4/3- 4 8 **State Department**[38] 1056 6-11-1 0 RichardJohnson 97
(Philip Hobbs) *trckd ldrs: t.k.h: rdn and hung lft over 2f out: styd on same pce* 8/1
23- 5 21 **Snapchat (IRE)**[15] 1261 6-11-1 0 ConorO'Farrell 76
(Seamus Durack) *trckd ldr tl over 10f out: remained handy tl wknd 2f out* 10/3[2]
4- 6 4 ½ **Multiview**[15] 1264 4-10-0 0 JakeHodson[(7)] 63
(David Bridgwater) *chsd ldrs: pushed along over 9f out: wknd over 5f out* 50/1
0/0- 7 39 **Nick The Dove (IRE)**[56] 874 5-10-8 0 MrFMitchell[(7)] 32
(Chris Nenadich) *in rr: pushed along 10f out: rdn: wknd over 6f out* 200/1
8 5 **Septenarius (USA)** 4-11-0 0 TommyPhelan 26
(Brian Baugh) *hld up: a in rr: rdn and wknd over 6f out* 28/1
0/ 9 ¾ **Charles Onze (FR)**[494] 5518 6-11-1 0 LeeEdwards 26
(Dave Roberts) *hld up: plld hrd: rdn over 6f out: sn wknd* 25/1

3m 30.1s (-11.60) **Going Correction** -0.90s/f (Hard)
WFA 4 from 5yo+ 1lb 9 Ran SP% 114.9
Speed ratings: **102,101,99,95,85 83,63,61,60**
toteswingers 1&2 £11.50, 1&3 £1.80, 2&3 £7.60 CSF £47.27 TOTE £3.70: £1.30, £2.90, £1.40; EX 63.90 Trifecta £492.90 Pool: £1179.46 - 1.79 winning units..
Owner Mrs Jill Eynon & Robin Eynon **Bred** Mrs J O'Callaghan **Trained** Upper Lambourn, Berks

FOCUS
Not a bad summer bumper, run at a reasonable gallop. The third is rated close to his pre-race mark.

1428 LIFEBOATS SAVING LIVES AT SEA (S) H'CAP HURDLE (8 hdls) 2m
3:50 (3:50) (Class 5) (0-95,95) 4-Y-0+ £1,949 (£572; £286; £143)

Form RPR

120- 1 **Chilbury Hill (IRE)**[5] 1364 10-11-5 91 (t) MichaelByrne[(3)] 97
(Tim Vaughan) *chsd ldrs: rdn appr 3 out: swtchd rt flat: r.o to ld towards fin* 10/1
034- 2 1 ¼ **Argaum (IRE)**[11] 1285 6-11-4 87 (tp) PaulMoloney 92
(Evan Williams) *trckd ldr to appr 3 out: wnt 2nd again bef next: shkn up to ld appr last: rdn flat: hdd towards fin* 13/2[2]
/52- 3 1 ½ **On The Feather**[52] 903 7-11-5 95 (p) KieronEdgar[(7)] 98
(Jim Best) *hld up: nt fluent 4th: hdwy 2 out: rdn flat: styd on* 7/1[3]
0/1- 4 7 **Pindar (GER)**[8] 1331 9-10-1 77 (b) ConorShoemark[(7)] 73
(Neil Mulholland) *led: nt fluent 3 out: rdn: hung lft and hdd appr last: no ex flat* 1/1[1]
615- 5 3 **Naledi**[15] 1269 9-10-10 84 ThomasGarner[(5)] 77
(Richard Price) *hld up: hdwy appr 5th: sn outpcd: rallied 2 out: rdn: n.m.r and wknd flat* 16/1
/50- 6 nk **Nebula Storm (IRE)**[13] 1275 6-11-2 88 JoshuaMoore[(3)] 81
(Gary Moore) *hld up: hdwy 5th: chsd ldr appr 3 out: sn rdn: lost 2nd bef next: wknd flat* 16/1
/33- 7 5 **Hopeand**[10] 1305 8-10-12 81 (t) AdamPogson 69
(Charles Pogson) *mid-div: hdwy 4th: rdn appr 2 out: wknd last* 15/2
/00- 8 2 **Hadron Collider (FR)**[64] 829 8-10-8 84 (p) MrFMitchell[(7)] 70
(Chris Nenadich) *chsd ldrs: pushed along and wknd after 5th* 66/1
46/- 9 1 ¾ **Bazart**[27] 2262 11-11-0 88 (tp) RobertWilliams[(5)] 72
(Bernard Llewellyn) *mid-div: rdn appr 5th: wknd bef next* 25/1

3m 33.4s (-13.90) **Going Correction** -0.90s/f (Hard) course record 9 Ran SP% 113.8
Speed ratings (Par 103): **98,97,96,93,91 91,88,87,87**
toteswingers 1&2 £9.00, 1&3 £6.10, 2&3 £2.40 CSF £72.23 CT £486.67 TOTE £8.40: £1.70, £2.50, £1.10; EX 49.30 Trifecta £276.70 Pool: £1541.58 - 4.17 winning units..There was no bid for the winner.
Owner B Jones & N Wright **Bred** Barry Murphy **Trained** Aberthin, Vale of Glamorgan

FOCUS
Not a bad seller and the form looks reasonable for the grade, with the third helping to srt the level.

1429 BOOK CHRISTMAS PARTIES AT WORCESTER RACECOURSE CLAIMING HURDLE (10 hdls) 2m 4f
4:20 (4:20) (Class 5) 4-Y-0+ £1,949 (£572; £286; £143)

Form RPR

/33- 1 **Wayward Glance**[33] 1119 5-11-10 0 (p) APMcCoy 117
(Jim Best) *sn pushed along to chse ldrs: wnt 2nd 5th: led next: rdn after 3 out: styd on u.p* 2/1[1]
116- 2 3 **Molon Labe (IRE)**[94] 503 6-10-12 107 (t) AdamWedge[(3)] 105
(David Rees) *hld up: hdwy appr 3 out: edgd lft bef next: chsd wnr and nt fluent last: sn rdn: edgd lft and styd on same pce flat* 10/3[2]
/15- 3 1 ¼ **Lodgician (IRE)**[30] 1137 11-10-2 96 (vt) RyanHatch[(7)] 98
(Nigel Twiston-Davies) *led to 6th: rdn after next: hmpd appr 2 out: styd on same pce flat* 20/1
4P0- 4 5 **Priceless Art (IRE)**[42] 1020 8-10-6 113 (t) RachaelGreen[(3)] 93
(Anthony Honeyball) *hld up: pushed along appr 3 out: r.o flat: nvr nrr* 7/1
100- 5 ¾ **Vexillum (IRE)**[57] 858 4-9-11 107 (t) MartinMcIntyre[(10)] 90
(Harry Fry) *hld up: hdwy 7th: n.m.r appr 2 out: sn rdn: wknd flat* 7/2[3]
1P0- 6 4 ½ **Catch Tammy (IRE)**[25] 1197 7-10-9 0 (tp) PaddyBrennan 88
(Tom George) *hld up: hdwy 5th: chsd wnr appr 3 out tl rdn next: wknd last* 9/1
/56- 7 2 ¼ **Gilded Age**[70] 543 7-11-1 94 JamesBest[(3)] 95
(Rob Summers) *hld up: hdwy 5th: mstke 2 out: sn rdn and wknd* 40/1
/26- 8 12 **H M S Intrepid**[15] 1264 5-10-9 0 RyanMahon 74
(Anthony Honeyball) *hld up: a in rr* 25/1
406- 9 88 **Intac (IRE)**[8] 1326 11-11-0 0 (p) MrJMahot[(7)]
(Sarah-Jayne Davies) *chsd ldr tl pushed along 5th: wknd after next* 50/1

4m 29.6s (-17.80) **Going Correction** -0.90s/f (Hard)
WFA 4 from 5yo+ 14lb 9 Ran SP% 114.1
Speed ratings (Par 103): **105,103,103,101,101 99,98,93,58**
toteswingers 1&2 £2.50, 1&3 £9.60, 2&3 £19.20 CSF £8.46 TOTE £2.90: £1.20, £1.20, £4.10; EX 8.90 Trifecta £65.50 Pool: £1864.82 - 21.35 winning units..

The Form Book Jumps, Raceform Ltd, Compton, RG20 6NL.

Owner Jack Callaghan **Bred** The Queen **Trained** Lewes, E Sussex
FOCUS
There were doubts over plenty of these in this claimer, which was run at a solid pace. The third and seventh offer perspective.

1430 FOLLOW US ON TWITTER @WORCESTERRACES H'CAP HURDLE (12 hdls) 2m 7f
4:55 (4:55) (Class 3) (0-140,135) 4-Y-0+ **£5,697** (£1,683; £841; £421)

Form RPR
331- **1** **Ogee**[36] 1091 10-11-12 **135** .... JamieMoore 137+
(Renee Robeson) *chsd ldrs: shkn up appr 3 out: r.o u.p to ld towards fin* **11/4**[2]
3/0- **2** *1 ½* **So Fine (IRE)**[103] 358 7-11-2 **125** .... RichardJohnson 125
(Philip Hobbs) *trckd ldr tl pushed along to ld and wnt lft 3 out: rdn flat: hdd towards fin* **6/4**[1]
P24- **3** *2 ¼* **Red Not Blue (IRE)**[15] 1268 10-11-12 **135** ....(p) APMcCoy 133
(Simon Earle) *set stdy pce tl qcknd after 9th: hdd 3 out: rdn and ev ch flat: no ex towards fin* **4/1**[3]
315- **4** *9* **Malin Bay (IRE)**[39] 1042 8-11-5 **128** .... FearghalDavis 117
(Nicky Richards) *chsd ldrs: pushed along after 9th: rdn and hung lft appr last: wknd flat* **4/1**[3]
5m 31.1s (3.10) **Going Correction** -0.90s/f (Hard) 4 Ran SP% **106.7**
Speed ratings (Par 107): **58,57,56,53**
CSF £7.24 TOTE £3.40; EX 9.60 Trifecta £16.20 Pool: £622.36 - 28.65 winning units..
Owner Sir Evelyn De Rothschild **Bred** Hesmonds Stud Ltd **Trained** Tyringham, Bucks
■ Stewards' Enquiry : Jamie Moore eight-day ban: gelding sustained moderate weals from use of whip (Sep 24-28,30, Oct 1,3)
FOCUS
Not a strong race for the grade, this was run at a fairly steady pace until picking up after the fourth-last. The winner used to be better than this and might do better again, while the form in behind is straightforward.

1431 SPONSOR A RACE BY CALLING 01905 25364 NOVICES' HURDLE (10 hdls) 2m 4f
5:30 (5:33) (Class 4) 4-Y-0+ **£3,249** (£954; £477; £238)

Form RPR
0/1- **1** **Falcarragh (IRE)**[15] 1255 6-11-5 125 .... RichardJohnson 99+
(Tim Vaughan) *mde all: nt fluent 1st: clr 2nd tl nt fluent 5th: j.rt 6th and 7th: rdn appr 2 out: drvn out* **1/4**[1]
330/ **2** *1 ¾* **Castle Beach (IRE)**[137] 5288 4-10-10 0 .... APMcCoy 85+
(Rebecca Curtis) *trckd wnr: j.rt 6th: t.k.h: rdn flat: styd on same pce* **10/3**[2]
UP6- **3** *2* **Banks Road (IRE)**[24] 1201 8-10-12 0 .... MarkGrant 85
(Geoffrey Deacon) *hld up: pushed along appr 3 out: mstke next: styd on to go 3rd flat: nt trble ldrs* **66/1**[3]
0/0- **4** *2 ½* **Trakeur (FR)**[118] 79 6-10-12 0 .... JamesDavies 83
(Simon Hodgson) *trckd ldrs: mstke 4th: rdn appr 3 out: styd on same pce last* **66/1**[3]
4m 42.2s (-5.20) **Going Correction** -0.90s/f (Hard)
WFA 4 from 6yo+ 14lb 4 Ran SP% **106.1**
Speed ratings (Par 105): **74,73,72,71**
CSF £1.42 TOTE £1.10; EX 1.30 Trifecta £3.90 Pool: £1016.50 - 195.05 winning units..
Owner Mike Stratford **Bred** Liam McLoughlin **Trained** Aberthin, Vale of Glamorgan
FOCUS
A weak novice hurdle which was run at a sedate pace, and the form is of very limited value and not a race to place much faith in.
T/Plt: £113.40 to a £1 stake. Pool: £60,989.31 - 392.30 winning tickets T/Qpdt: £17.30 to a £1 stake. Pool: £4983.28 - 212 winning tickets CR

1270 FONTWELL (L-H)
Thursday, August 29

OFFICIAL GOING: Good to firm (good in places; 7.3)
Rail movement increased chases by 45yds per circuit and hurdles by 30yds per circuit. Fences at full width and hurdles middle/inner.
Wind: strong breeze behind Weather: sunny

1432 CHANCELLOR OF THE FORMCHECKER MARES' NOVICES' HURDLE (10 hdls) 2m 4f
2:30 (2:30) (Class 4) 4-Y-0+ **£3,119** (£915; £457; £228)

Form RPR
6UF- **1** **Lucys Girl (IRE)**[37] 1090 6-10-10 0 .... TomO'Brien 89
(Jamie Snowden) *tended to jump rt: trckd ldrs: chal 3 out tl rdn bef next: styd on to ld sn after last: kpt on wl to assert* **20/1**
221- **2** *1 ¾* **Hopstrings**[3] 1387 5-10-10 95 .... ConorShoemark[(7)] 96
(Charlie Brooks) *led: bked off hurdles and rdn into them fr 3rd: reminder whn 10 l clr after 6th: rdn after 3 out: hdd sn after last: no ex* **5/4**[2]
P13- **3** *13* **Shantou Breeze (IRE)**[14] 1270 6-10-10 95 .... MarcGoldstein 77
(Michael Madgwick) *trckd ldr tl 3 out: sn rdn to chse ldng pair: styd on same pce fr pce* **14/1**[3]
4 *21* **Money Money Money**[419] 7-10-10 0 .... APMcCoy 63
(Jim Best) *nvr fluent: racd keenly bhd ldng trio: hit 2nd: struggling whn hit 7th: btn 3 out: t.o* **10/11**[1]
4m 50.0s (-9.40) **Going Correction** -0.475s/f (Good) 4 Ran SP% **108.3**
Speed ratings (Par 105): **99,98,93,84**
CSF £45.93 TOTE £11.40; EX 25.90 Trifecta £55.60 Pool: £1,072.71 - 14.46 winning units..
Owner John H W Finch **Bred** T Desmond **Trained** Lambourn, Berks
FOCUS
Not form to put much faith in, with the favourite running poorly, and it went to the outsider of the field. The form is rated around the first two.

1433 LYNN DAVIES 40TH / ROGER DAVIES MEMORIAL BEGINNERS' CHASE (13 fncs) 2m 2f
3:00 (3:00) (Class 4) 4-Y-0+ **£3,861** (£1,198; £645)

Form RPR
0/1- **1** **Cinevator (IRE)**[121] 38 6-11-6 0 ....(p) IanPopham 95+
(Caroline Keevil) *trckd ldr: lft disputing ld 5th: lft in ld 3 out: shkn up but in command fr next: styd on* **9/5**[2]
0/0- **2** *6* **Wak A Turtle (IRE)**[109] 254 5-11-3 0 .... MichealNolan[(3)] 86
(Richard Woollacott) *j.rt bdly at times: trckd ldrs: bdly hmpd and did wl to stand up 6th: chal 4 out: rdn whn wnt bdly rt: mstke and nrly uns rdr next: kpt on for 2nd but hld after* **33/1**
430- **3** *12* **Kayfrou**[34] 1121 8-11-3 0 .... JamesBest[(3)] 72
(Nick Mitchell) *trckd ldrs: lft disputing ld 5th tl 4 out: outpcd whn mstke next: hit 2 out: wknd last* **16/1**[3]
11F- **U** **Man Of Leisure**[7] 1343 9-11-3 0 ....(t) RachaelGreen[(3)]
(Anthony Honeyball) *tended to jump sltly rt: led tl blnd and uns rdr 5th* **4/7**[1]
4m 45.3s (10.60) **Going Correction** -0.225s/f (Good) 4 Ran SP% **108.2**
Speed ratings (Par 105): **67,64,59,**
CSF £21.89 TOTE £3.20; EX 14.40 Trifecta £56.80 Pool: £1144.88 - 15.09 winning units..
Owner The Optimist & Pessimist Partnership **Bred** Patrick Thompson **Trained** Motcombe, Dorset
FOCUS
What had looked a straight match never had a chance to develop. The time was very slow and not an easy race to put a level on.

1434 MALCOLM "HAIRY" ROBERTS MEMORIAL NOVICES' H'CAP HURDLE (11 hdls) 2m 6f 110y
3:30 (3:30) (Class 4) (0-115,102) 4-Y-0+ **£3,119** (£915; £457; £228)

Form RPR
/13- **1** **Bold Raider (IRE)**[34] 1121 6-11-9 **99** .... APMcCoy 101+
(Jonjo O'Neill) *trckd ldng pair: chal after 3 out: drvn between last 2: nt fluent last: styd on u.str.p to ld fnl 75yds: all out* **5/6**[1]
/31- **2** *nk* **Franklino (FR)**[14] 1275 6-11-12 **102** ....(p) TomCannon 104
(Chris Gordon) *disp ld: nt fluent 3rd: outrt ldr after 3 out but sn hrd pressed: drvn next: gamely hld narrow advantage: hit last: hdd fnl 75yds: kpt on* **7/2**[2]
5P1- **3** *17* **Doctor Ric (IRE)**[14] 1272 8-10-12 **88** ....(b) JamieMoore 75
(Gerry Enright) *disp ld: wnt lft 5th: pushed along after 8th: rdn and hdd sn after 3 out: hld fr next: wkng wnt wnt lft last* **8/1**[3]
/32- **4** *nk* **Thomas Bell (IRE)**[6] 1364 9-9-7 **76** oh3 .... CiaranMckee[(7)] 62
(John O'Shea) *racd keenly trcking ldng pair: nt fluent 7th: sn struggling to hold pl: hld after 3 out: wknd last* **7/2**[2]
5m 30.0s (-12.50) **Going Correction** -0.475s/f (Good) 4 Ran SP% **110.1**
Speed ratings (Par 105): **102,101,95,95**
CSF £4.26 TOTE £1.70; EX 4.60 Trifecta £6.60 Pool: £1557.71 - 175.07 winning units..
Owner John P McManus **Bred** Aidan Madden **Trained** Cheltenham, Gloucs
■ Stewards' Enquiry : Tom Cannon one-day ban: careless riding (Sep 13)
FOCUS
The front pair drew clear from the end of the back straight and they are rated pretty much to their marks.

1435 OVERLAND TRAVEL H'CAP CHASE (13 fncs) 2m 2f
4:00 (4:00) (Class 4) (0-105,100) 4-Y-0+ **£3,768** (£1,106; £553; £276)

Form RPR
/52- **1** **Safe Investment (USA)**[14] 1274 9-10-13 **86** ....(vt) DavidBass 95
(Lawney Hill) *trckd ldr tl rdn after 7th: regained 2nd sn after 4 out: looked hld whn wnt rt 3 out: beginning str run whn 3 1/2 l down last: led towards fin: won gng away* **7/1**
411- **2** *1 ¼* **Alderbrook Lad (IRE)**[2] 1416 7-11-10 **100** 14ex .... MichaelByrne[(3)] 109+
(Neil Mulholland) *sn led: 3 1/2 l clr whn rdn after last: no ex whn hdd towards fin* **11/8**[1]
P00- **3** *43* **The Grey One (IRE)**[9] 1328 10-10-5 **78** .... JamieMoore 47
(Milton Bradley) *j.rt bdly at times: hld up but wl in tch: blnd bdly 7th: sn trcking ldr: wnt bdly rt 9th: rdn whn lost 2nd after 4 out: wknd fr next: t.o* **25/1**
356- **4** *2* **Morestead (IRE)**[14] 1272 8-11-10 **97** ....(vt) LeightonAspell 64
(Brendan Powell) *chsd ldrs: pressing ldr whn nt fluent and lost pl again 4th: hmpd 7th: sn rdn along: no ch fr 4 out: plugged on fr 3 out: wnt poor 4th run-in: t.o* **9/1**
505- **5** *6* **Stormy Oscar (IRE)**[30] 1149 6-11-5 **92** ....(t[1]) TomO'Brien 54
(Jamie Snowden) *hld up but wl in tch: hit 1st: short-lived effrt whn hit 4 out: sn rdn: wknd fr next: t.o* **3/1**[2]
22P- **U** **Try Catch Me (IRE)**[53] 898 8-11-9 **99** ....(b) MarkQuinlan[(3)]
(Alison Batchelor) *trckd ldrs: wnt rt and hit 5th: slt adantage whn wnt rt: blnd and uns rdr 7th* **9/2**[3]
4m 33.7s (-1.00) **Going Correction** -0.225s/f (Good) 6 Ran SP% **111.6**
Speed ratings (Par 105): **93,92,73,72,69**
toteswingers 1&2 £1.80, 2&3 £7.30, 1&3 £10.50 CSF £17.80 TOTE £6.10: £2.40, £1.40; EX 16.70 Trifecta £199.60 Pool: £2466.78 - 9.26 winning units..
Owner Alan Hill **Bred** Juddmonte Farms Inc **Trained** Aston Rowant, Oxon
FOCUS
Jumping errors did for a few of these in what was a modest handicap chase run at a good gallop. The front pair pulled well clear, the winner is on a good mark and is rated back to form.

1436 CHANCELLOR OF THE FORMCHECKER 40@40 CLUB H'CAP HURDLE (11 hdls) 2m 6f 110y
4:30 (4:30) (Class 4) (0-120,107) 4-Y-0+ **£3,119** (£915; £457; £228)

Form RPR
523 **1** **Nicky Nutjob (GER)**[6] 1363 7-10-8 **96** ....(p) CiaranMckee[(7)] 100
(John O'Shea) *hld up: plld hrd: led 3rd: hit 7th: rdn bef 2 out: edgd lft run-in: kpt on wl: rdn out* **9/4**[2]
526- **2** *1 ¼* **Cannon Fodder**[52] 920 6-11-5 **100** .... MarcGoldstein 103
(Sheena West) *trckd ldr: hit 8th: sn rdn: styng on whn swtchd rt fnl 120yds: kpt on but hld towards fin* **8/1**
0/0- **3** *2 ½* **Gigondas**[58] 858 4-11-8 **106** .... JamieMoore 105
(Gary Moore) *led at stdy pce tl 3rd: trckd ldr: nt fluent 5th: pushed along in 3rd after 7th: drvn after 3 out: mounting chal whn nt fluent next: kpt on same pce fr last* **6/1**[3]
310- **4** *24* **Marie Deja La (FR)**[52] 925 7-11-0 **102** ....(b) JackSherwood[(7)] 85
(Chris Gordon) *trckd ldrs: nt fluent 4th: struggling whn hit 8th: drvn in disp 4th after 3 out: wknd between last 2* **13/2**
/60- **5** *11* **Beyond (IRE)**[12] 1284 6-11-5 **107** .... KieronEdgar[(7)] 76
(David Pipe) *trckd ldrs: dropped to last pair but in tch 3rd: pushed along after 6th: in rr and no threat fr next* **9/5**[1]
445/ **P** **Pistolet Noir (FR)**[140] 5253 7-11-9 **107** .... MichealNolan[(3)]
(Richard Woollacott) *hld up: nudged along whn clsng on ldrs after 8th: rdn after 3 out: wknd qckly: p.u bef last* **11/1**
5m 35.3s (-7.20) **Going Correction** -0.475s/f (Good)
WFA 4 from 6yo+ 14lb 6 Ran SP% **113.5**
Speed ratings (Par 105): **93,92,91,83,79**
toteswingers 1&2 £6.50, 2&3 £5.20, 1&3 £2.00 CSF £19.67 TOTE £3.00: £1.60, £2.80; EX 14.20 Trifecta £91.90 Pool: £1977.43 - 16.13 winning units..
Owner Quality Pipe Supports (Q P S) Ltd **Bred** Newsells Park Stud Ltd **Trained** Elton, Gloucs

FOCUS
They dawdled through the early stages of this moderate handicap. The first two are rated to their marks.

1437 TOM CANNON, FONTWELL'S CHAMPION JOCKEY H'CAP CHASE (19 fncs) 3m 2f 110y
5:00 (5:00) (Class 5) (0-95,96) 4-Y-0+ **£2,144** (£629; £314; £157)

Form RPR
0/0- **1** **Douglas**[16] 1259 8-11-6 **87**.. MarkGrant 99
(Jo Hughes) *trckd ldrs: led after 12th: rdn whn pressed after 4 out: styd on strly to assert appr last* **12/1**
P63- **2** *12* **Princely Hero (IRE)**[14] 1272 9-11-12 **93**....................(p) TomCannon 94
(Chris Gordon) *chsd ldrs early: pushed along in tch fr 3rd: wnt 3rd bef 14th tl lost pl after 4 out: plenty to do whn untidy 2 out: r.o again fr last: wnt 2nd towards fin: no ch w wnr* **5/1**[3]
/36- **3** *3* **Sea Cadet**[79] 712 11-11-6 **87**....................................(b) DavidBass 85
(Laura Mongan) *in tch: pushed along in last after 6th: reminders after next: rdn to chse wnr after 4 out: hld 2 out: no ex whn lost 2nd towards fin* **9/2**[2]
400- **4** *10* **Nothingbutthetruth (IRE)**[16] 1260 9-11-5 **89**..........(tp) MichealNolan(3) 79
(Richard Woollacott) *hld up early: trckd ldrs 4th: prom 8th: rdn whn lost 2nd after 4 out: wkng whn wnt rt last* **12/1**
/0P- **P** **Orion Star (IRE)**[50] 942 11-10-12 **79**...........................(p) RyanMahon
(Seamus Mullins) *j.rt: prom tl 2nd: chsd ldrs: reminders after next: slow jump 10th: sn struggling in rr: tailing off whn p.u bef 14th* **9/1**
P/P- **P** **Chapel House**[67] 807 10-11-7 **88**................................ AndrewThornton
(Richard Harper) *j.rt most of way: led tl after 12th: wknd qckly: p.u bef 14th* **22/1**
341- **P** **Maid Of Silk (IRE)**[8] 1336 7-12-1 **96** 7ex............................(t) NoelFehily
(Neil Mulholland) *hld up: hmpd 7th: cl enough in disp 4th 14th: wknd qckly bef 4 out: p.u bef 3 out* **1/1**[1]

6m 53.1s (-8.00) **Going Correction** -0.225s/f (Good) 7 Ran SP% **114.6**
Speed ratings (Par 103): **102,98,97,94, ,**
toteswingers 1&2 £5.90, 2&3 £2.20, 1&3 £6.10 CSF £69.67 TOTE £12.50: £5.00, £2.60; EX 76.50 Trifecta £403.00 Pool: £1888.54 - 3.51 winning units..
Owner John Wardle **Bred** T J Wardle **Trained** Lambourn, Berks
■ Stewards' Enquiry : Mark Grant two-day ban: used whip when clearly winning (Sep 13,17)

FOCUS
Weak staying chase form but a personal-best from the winner, with the runner-up rated in line with recent form.

1438 CHANCELLOR'S SERVICES FOR THE THINKING PUNTER H'CAP HURDLE (9 hdls) 2m 2f 110y
5:30 (5:31) (Class 5) (0-95,94) 4-Y-0+ **£1,949** (£572; £286; £143)

Form RPR
P/1- **1** **Sugar Hiccup (IRE)**[7] 1351 5-11-5 **85** 7ex.............................. APMcCoy 99+
(Jim Best) *mde all: wl in command and clr appr 2 out: comf* **4/11**[1]
142- **2** *8* **Hawk Gold (IRE)**[45] 1000 9-10-7 **80**......................(b) ConorShoemark(7) 82
(Michelle Bryant) *in tch: hdwy appr 6th: rdn after 3 out: sn chsng wnr but a being comf hld: kpt on wl for clr 2nd* **8/1**[2]
040- **3** *16* **Osmosia (FR)**[14] 1273 8-11-2 **82**...............................(tp) TomCannon 70
(Chris Gordon) *trckd ldrs: pressed wnr after 4th tl rdn appr 3 out: outpcd bef 2 out: plugged on to regain 3rd run-in* **12/1**
364- **4** *1 ¼* **Al Amaan**[79] 708 8-11-10 **90**.. MattieBatchelor 76
(Jamie Poulton) *hld up: rdn and stdy prog on main bunch fr after 3 out: wnt 4th run-in: nvr trbld ldrs* **20/1**
0/3- **5** *2 ¼* **What's For Tea**[106] 308 8-10-0 **73**..........................(vt) CiaranMckee(7) 57
(Paddy Butler) *w wnr tl after 4th: sn lost pl: plugged on fr 2 out but nvr any danger* **14/1**
264- **6** *1* **Flashy Star**[14] 1270 4-11-12 **94**...................................... MarcGoldstein 76
(Sheena West) *trckd ldrs: blnd 3rd: rdn after 6th: styd on same pce fr after 3 out* **12/1**
0/0- **7** *6* **Lombok**[23] 429 7-10-11 **80**..(v) JoshuaMoore(3) 61
(Gary Moore) *hld up: hdwy after 5th: rdn to chse wnr after 3 out tl bef next: wknd bef last: lost 4 pls run-in* **10/1**[3]
535- **P** **Airedale Lad (IRE)**[79] 710 12-9-9 **68**...............(p) MrJoshuaNewman(7)
(Zoe Davison) *trckd ldrs: rdn after 5th: wknd after next: t.o whn p.u bef last* **25/1**

4m 26.1s (-8.20) **Going Correction** -0.475s/f (Good) 8 Ran SP% **124.2**
Speed ratings (Par 103): **98,94,87,87,86 86,83,**
toteswingers 1&2 £2.40, 2&3 £5.60, 1&3 £3.10 CSF £5.51 CT £20.91 TOTE £1.40: £1.10, £1.40, £3.30; EX 4.40 Trifecta £23.20 Pool: £1800.61 - 58.02 winning units..
Owner Jack Callaghan & Christopher Dillon **Bred** Raysiza Partnership **Trained** Lewes, E Sussex

FOCUS
A moderate handicap that took little winning. The second is rated to his mark.
T/Plt: £4,906.00 to a £1 stake. Pool of £50068.23 - 7.45 winning tickets. T/Qpdt: £28.50 to a £1 stake. Pool of £4071.05 - 105.60 winning tickets. TM

1255 STRATFORD (L-H)
Thursday, August 29

OFFICIAL GOING: Good (good to firm in places)
All bends on fresh ground
Wind: Light against Weather: Cloudy with sunny spells

1439 ALBERT BRASSEY JUVENILE HURDLE (8 hdls) 2m 110y
2:20 (2:20) (Class 4) 3-Y-0 **£3,249** (£954; £477; £238)

Form RPR
1 **Refer**[108] 3-10-9 0.. KielanWoods(3) 100
(Phil Middleton) *a.p: hmpd after 4th: j.rt next: lft 2nd bnd appr 3 out: led after next: rdn and hdd bef last: rallied to ld flat: r.o* **2/1**[2]
2 *½* **Instinctual**[21] 3-10-12 0.. AlainCawley 100
(Brendan Powell) *hld up: hdwy 3 out: rdn to ld appr last: hdd flat: styd on* **10/1**
122- **3** *¾* **Akdam (IRE)**[26] 1193 3-11-0 113..........................(p) TrevorWhelan(5) 107
(Tony Carroll) *chsd ldrs: hmpd bnd appr 3 out: rdn after next: r.o* **13/8**[1]
4 *14* **Wooly Bully**[36] 3-10-12 0.. WayneHutchinson 89
(Alan King) *hld up: mstke 3rd: pushed along after next: rdn 2 out: nt clr run bnd appr last: nvr trbld ldrs* **6/1**[3]
5 *10* **Many Levels**[33] 3-10-12 0.. DougieCostello 79
(John Quinn) *hld up: racd keenly: mstke 2nd: hmpd bnd appr 3 out: hdwy bef next: rdn and wknd appr last* **14/1**
2- **6** *2* **Vergality Ridge (IRE)**[8] 1335 3-10-7 0.............................. EDLinehan(5) 76
(Ronald Harris) *chsd ldrs tl rdn and wknd after 2 out* **16/1**
- **7** *25* **Arabougg**[176] 3-10-9 0.. RobertDunne(3) 53
(Nikki Evans) *led: racd keenly: mstke 2nd: hit 2 out: sn rdn: hdd & wknd* **66/1**
5- **U** **Ruff Luck**[14] 1271 3-9-12 0.. KevinJones(7)
(Seamus Mullins) *chsd ldr tl slipped and uns rdr bnd appr 3 out* **33/1**

3m 57.1s (1.10) **Going Correction** -0.25s/f (Good) 8 Ran SP% **111.8**
Speed ratings (Par 102): **87,86,86,79,75 74,62,**
toteswingers 1&2 £6.70, 2&3 £3.10, 1&3 £1.10 CSF £21.00 TOTE £4.40: £1.10, £2.10, £1.10; EX 25.60 Trifecta £51.60 Pool: £1653.37 - 23.99 winning units..
Owner P W Middleton **Bred** Juddmonte Farms Ltd **Trained** Dorton, Bucks

FOCUS
Impossible to know exactly what to make of the form, but the winner looks a decent type for the time of year and, along with the sixth, helps set the level.

1440 REGINALD CORBET NOVICES' HURDLE (11 hdls) 2m 6f 110y
2:50 (2:50) (Class 4) 4-Y-0+ **£3,249** (£954; £477; £238)

Form RPR
/01- **1** **Fighter Jet**[28] 1176 5-11-5 0.. WayneHutchinson 118
(Alan King) *chsd ldrs: blnd 3rd: pushed along after 5th: rdn appr 3 out: led flat: edgd lft drvn out* **5/2**[2]
/4- **2** *1 ½* **Dazinski**[16] 1255 7-10-12 0.. ColinBolger 109
(Mark H Tompkins) *a.p: j.rt 7th: rdn and ev ch appr last: nt clr run flat: styd on* **7/1**[3]
112- **3** *nk* **Benefit Of Youth (IRE)**[9] 1330 6-11-5 116.................... RichardJohnson 117
(Tim Vaughan) *led: mstke 5th: rdn and jnd whn blnd last: sn hdd: styd on same pce flat* **5/6**[1]
053- **4** *9* **Turbo Du Ranch (FR)**[16] 1257 6-11-0 117................(p) GavinSheehan(5) 108
(Warren Greatrex) *chsd ldr: ev ch fr 3 out: sn drvn along: wknd appr last* **17/2**
P5- **P** **Shock N Freaney (IRE)**[16] 1262 6-10-12 0..................(tp) PaulMoloney
(Anthony Middleton) *a in rr: lost tch fr 6th: p.u bef last* **150/1**

5m 18.1s (-10.00) **Going Correction** -0.25s/f (Good) 5 Ran SP% **106.8**
Speed ratings (Par 105): **107,106,106,103,**
CSF £16.99 TOTE £3.70: £1.40, £2.30; EX 11.80 Trifecta £17.90 Pool: £1504.47 - 62.85 winning units..
Owner Ladas **Bred** Highclere Stud **Trained** Barbury Castle, Wilts
■ Stewards' Enquiry : Wayne Hutchinson one-day ban: careless riding (Sep 13)

FOCUS
Rated around the balance of the first three, this doesn't appear strong form.

1441 JOHN MYTTON H'CAP CHASE (12 fncs) 2m 1f 110y
3:20 (3:20) (Class 3) (0-130,122) 4-Y-0+ **£6,498** (£1,908; £954; £477)

Form RPR
/63- **1** **Ulis De Vassy (FR)**[28] 1175 5-11-2 **112**........................ NickScholfield 123+
(Nick Williams) *mde all: mstke 9th: shkn up appr last: rdn out* **13/8**[1]
P41- **2** *3* **Temple Lord (FR)**[16] 1263 7-11-11 **121**....................(bt) RichieMcLernon 128
(Jonjo O'Neill) *hld up: hdwy 8th: chsd wnr 3 out: rdn appr last: styd on same pce flat* **4/1**[2]
P45- **3** *12* **Giant O Murchu (IRE)**[45] 999 9-10-11 **107**...............(p) DougieCostello 105
(Lawney Hill) *chsd ldrs: wnt 2nd 8th to 3 out: sn rdn: wknd appr last* **5/1**[3]
P46- **4** *4* **Grey Soldier (IRE)**[26] 1194 8-11-12 **122**.........................(t) PaddyBrennan 115
(Sophie Leech) *chsd wnr to 8th: sn pushed along: rdn and wknd after 2 out* **4/1**[2]
134- **5** *nk* **Tri Nations (UAE)**[14] 1274 8-10-3 **99**............................(bt) PaulMoloney 91
(Anthony Middleton) *hld up: hdwy u.p 2 out: wknd sn after* **13/2**

4m 3.8s (-3.30) **Going Correction** -0.25s/f (Good) 5 Ran SP% **108.1**
Speed ratings (Par 107): **97,95,90,88,88**
CSF £8.16 TOTE £3.10: £1.40, £1.80; EX 10.00 Trifecta £33.50 Pool: £1541.04 - 34.44 winning units..
Owner Len&White,Hewlett,Robinson,Banyard&Booth **Bred** Nicolas Ferrand **Trained** George Nympton, Devon

FOCUS
A fair handicap chase with a big step up on recent form from the winner, while the second is rated to the level of his recent win.

1442 BAY MIDDLETON H'CAP HURDLE (9 hdls) 2m 3f
3:50 (3:50) (Class 5) (0-95,99) 4-Y-0+ **£2,599** (£763; £381; £190)

Form RPR
022- **1** **Burns Night**[11] 1306 7-10-10 **83**..................................(p) AdamNicol(5) 86+
(Philip Kirby) *sn prom: shkn up appr last: r.o u.p to ld nr fin* **4/5**[1]
641- **2** *¾* **Taroum (IRE)**[3] 1400 6-12-3 **99** 7ex.............................. LeeEdwards 100
(Tony Carroll) *trckd ldrs: wnt 2nd after 3 out: rdn appr last: led flat: edgd lft and hdd nr fin* **11/4**[2]
3/P- **3** *5* **Walls Way**[119] 84 9-9-9 **70**.. JWStevenson(7) 69
(Tracey Barfoot-Saunt) *led: rdn and jnd whn blnd last: sn hdd and no ex* **66/1**
/43- **4** *5* **Blackstone Vegas**[11] 669 7-11-8 **90**..............................(v) JamesDavies 82
(Derek Shaw) *hld up: hdwy after 4th: rdn appr 2 out: nvr trbld ldrs* **10/1**
060- **5** *3* **Phoenix Eye**[16] 1267 12-10-3 **74**...................................... KielanWoods(3) 63
(Michael Mullineaux) *hld up: rdn 3 out: wknd after next* **25/1**
/00- **6** *14* **The Winged Assasin (USA)**[72] 756 7-11-12 **94**........(t) AidanColeman 71
(Shaun Lycett) *hld up: hdwy 3 out: rdn and wknd appr last* **25/1**
0/3- **7** *6* **Gavroche Gaugain (FR)**[117] 109 9-10-10 **78**...............(p) HarrySkelton 49
(Dan Skelton) *racd keenly: trckd ldr tl pushed along after 3 out: wknd after next* **5/1**[3]
0/0- **P** **Filun**[14] 1275 8-10-12 **80**..(vt) PaulMoloney
(Anthony Middleton) *prom: mstke 3rd: sn pushed along: rdn and wknd 6th: bhd whn p.u bef last* **50/1**

4m 30.5s (-1.00) **Going Correction** -0.25s/f (Good) 8 Ran SP% **119.1**
Speed ratings (Par 103): **92,91,89,87,86 80,77,**
toteswingers 1&2 £1.10, 2&3 £28.60, 1&3 £11.80 CSF £3.72 CT £74.75 TOTE £2.10: £1.10, £1.50, £5.40; EX 4.30 Trifecta £91.90 Pool: £1932.79 - 15.77 winning units..
Owner Two Ladies And A Gentleman **Bred** Highclere Stud And Floors Farming **Trained** Middleham, N Yorks

FOCUS
A moderate event and the early gallop didn't appear strong. The placed horses are rated pretty much to their marks.

1443 SQUIRE OSBALDESTON AMATEUR RIDERS' H'CAP HURDLE (8 hdls) 2m 110y
4:20 (4:20) (Class 5) (0-100,100) 4-Y-0+ **£1,871** (£580; £290; £145)

Form RPR
252- **1** **Mount Vesuvius (IRE)**[14] 1273 5-11-2 **97**......................(t) MrGBranton(7) 104+
(Paul Henderson) *hld up: hdwy after 4th: led after next: rdn out* **4/1**[3]
551- **2** *2 ¼* **Ajman (IRE)**[3] 1402 8-11-7 **100**..............................(tp) MrFMitchell(5) 104
(Evan Williams) *a.p: rdn to chse wnr appr last: styd on same pce flat* **3/1**[2]

The Form Book Jumps, Raceform Ltd, Compton, RG20 6NL.

0P1/ **3** 21 **Masterful Act (USA)**[62] 4993 6-11-7 **100**............... MrMatthewBarber(5) 85
(Alan McCabe) *chsd ldrs: pushed along 4th: chsd wnr 3 out tl rdn and wknd appr last* **13/8**[1]

524/ **4** 4 **Isola Bella**[10] 5142 4-10-13 **95**.. MrJHarding(7) 76
(Jonathan Portman) *chsd ldrs: led 4th hdd and mstke next: rdn and wknd after 2 out* **20/1**

/00- **5** 2 **Warsaw Pact (IRE)**[52] 924 10-10-4 **85**........................(p) MrLKilgarriff(7) 65
(Steven Dixon) *hld up: hdwy appr 2 out: sn rdn and wknd* **8/1**

005- **6** ½ **Numen (IRE)**[14] 1273 9-10-11 **90**..................................(p) MissCLWills(5) 69
(Barry Brennan) *prom: lost pl 4th: rdn 3 out: wknd after next* **16/1**

4/U- **7** 5 **Dark Oasis**[14] 1274 7-9-13 **80**.. MrSamPainting(7) 55
(Natalie Lloyd-Beavis) *led to 3rd: rdn after 5th: wknd 2 out* **16/1**

2P2/ **8** 99 **Our Guardian Angel (IRE)**[787] 1002 9-10-13 **94**
MrJakeThomasCoulson(7)
(Christopher Kellett) *racd keenly: trckd ldr tl led 3rd: hdd next: led 5th: sn hdd: nt clr run bnd sn after: rdn and wknd appr 2 out* **40/1**

3m 53.5s (-2.50) **Going Correction** -0.25s/f (Good)
WFA 4 from 5yo+ 13lb **8** Ran SP% **113.2**
Speed ratings (Par 103): **95,93,84,82,81 81,78,32**
toteswingers 1&2 £4.00, 2&3 £4.00, 1&3 £3.60 CSF £16.48 CT £26.03 TOTE £4.20: £1.20, £1.40, £1.70; EX 11.00 Trifecta £23.00 Pool: £1227.0 - 39.91 winning units..
Owner The Ray Of Hope Partnership **Bred** Parker's Cove Syndicate **Trained** Whitsbury, Hants

FOCUS
An ordinary handicap in which the early leaders helped to set a reasonable pace, which suited the three with the best form. A personal-best from the winner with the second setting the level.

1444 TOM FIRR H'CAP CHASE (17 fncs) 2m 7f
4:50 (4:50) (Class 4) (0-115,115) 4-Y-0+ **£3,898** (£1,144; £572; £286)

Form RPR

/24- **1** **Font**[39] 1060 10-11-1 **104**...(t) AidanColeman 110
(Lawney Hill) *a.p: pushed along to chse ldr 3 out: rdn appr last: led flat: drvn out* **15/8**[2]

254/ **2** 2¼ **Qaspal (FR)**[422] 854 9-11-12 **115**.................................. RichardJohnson 120
(Philip Hobbs) *hld up: hdwy and mstke 3 out: rdn appr last: r.o: nt rch wnr* **11/2**[3]

126- **3** 3¼ **Tiermore (IRE)**[26] 1197 9-11-6 **109**...............................(p) DonalDevereux 112
(Peter Bowen) *led: rdn whn nt fluent last: hdd and unable qck flat* **5/4**[1]

6P0- **4** 34 **Amaury De Lusignan (IRE)**[16] 1263 7-11-1 **104**..........(t) PaddyBrennan 74
(Paul Henderson) *trckd ldr tl rdn 3 out: wknd bef next* **7/1**

5m 30.1s (-9.10) **Going Correction** -0.25s/f (Good) **4** Ran SP% **107.1**
Speed ratings (Par 105): **105,104,103,91**
CSF £10.56 TOTE £2.10; EX 7.00 Trifecta £10.00 Pool: £796.04 - 59.15 winning units..
Owner A Hill, S Florey, H Webb **Bred** Cheveley Park Stud Ltd **Trained** Aston Rowant, Oxon

FOCUS
The first three are rated to their marks in an ordinary handicap.

1445 SIS LIVE MARES' STANDARD OPEN NATIONAL HUNT FLAT RACE 2m 110y
5:20 (5:20) (Class 6) 4-6-Y-0 **£1,624** (£477; £238; £119)

Form RPR

222- **1** **Dorkas**[10] 1317 4-10-11 0... SamTwiston-Davies 101
(J R Jenkins) *trckd ldrs: wnt 2nd over 4f out: pushed along over 2f out: rdn to ld 1f out: r.o wl* **5/6**[1]

63- **2** 6 **Lola Galli**[79] 715 5-10-12 0..(p) TomScudamore 97
(David Pipe) *led: rdn and hdd 1f out: no ex ins fnl f* **6/4**[2]

0- **3** 3¼ **Wave The Grapes**[46] 970 6-10-12 0...........................(t) DonalDevereux 94
(Peter Bowen) *hld up: plld hrd: hdwy over 4f out: rdn over 2f out: styd on same pce appr fnl f* **12/1**[3]

0/4- **4** 23 **Fireweld**[7] 1353 6-10-5 0.. MikeyEnnis(7) 73
(Patricia Shaw) *trckd ldrs: racd keenly: rdn over 4f out: wknd 3f out* **40/1**

0- **5** 37 **Little Windsor**[10] 1318 4-10-11 0.. LiamTreadwell 39
(Peter Hiatt) *racd keenly: w ldr tl rdn over 5f out: wknd over 3f out* **66/1**

6 63 **Musselwick Bay** 5-10-12 0... AidanColeman
(Marc Barber) *hld up: pushed along over 7f out: rdn and wknd over 5f out* **20/1**

3m 48.7s (-1.70) **Going Correction** -0.25s/f (Good)
WFA 4 from 5yo+ 1lb **6** Ran SP% **110.9**
Speed ratings: **94,91,89,78,61 31**
toteswingers 1&2 £1.10, 2&3 £1.90, 1&3 £1.60 CSF £2.21 TOTE £2.00: £1.10, £1.60; EX 3.40 Trifecta £8.20 Pool: £1773.21 - 161.35 winning units..
Owner P J Kirkpatrick **Bred** Peter Kirkpatrick **Trained** Royston, Herts

FOCUS
Fireweld, Little Windsor and Musselwick Bay were beaten miles from home, and the remaining three came a long way clear. The winner and third set the level in a modest contest.
T/Plt: £16.60 to a £1 stake. Pool of £62080.73 - 2727.47 winning tickets T/Qpdt: £4.60 to a £1 stake. Pool of £3338.18 - 533.19 winning tickets. CR

1446 - 1463a (Foreign Racing) - See Raceform Interactive

614 DIEPPE (R-H)
Friday, August 30

OFFICIAL GOING: Turf: soft

1464a GRAND STEEPLE-CHASE NORMANDIE-DIMANCHE (CHASE) (CONDITIONS) (5YO+) (TURF) 2m 6f
2:20 (12:00) 5-Y-0+ **£10,146** (£5,073; £2,959; £2,008; £951)

RPR

1 **Kauto Sweety (FR)**[122] 6-11-0 0.. JacquesRicou 113
(J Bertran De Balanda, France) **54/10**[3]

2 2½ **Land Of Soprani (FR)**[438] 744 8-10-6 0......................... RegisSchmidlin 103
(F-M Cottin, France) **10/1**

3 ½ **Tel Pere Tel Fils (FR)**[642] 2831 6-11-3 0.................... BertrandLestrade 113
(G Macaire, France) **4/5**[1]

4 9 **Sadyjaune (FR)**[507] 7-10-6 0... ThierryMajorcryk 93
(E Lecoiffier, France) **33/1**

5 5 **George Nympton (IRE)**[196] 4234 7-10-8 0......................... JamesReveley 90
(Nick Williams) *t.k.h early stages: midfield in tch on outer: rdn after 3 out: outpcd by ldrs fr 2 out: plugged on for mod 5th* **26/1**

6 **Salamix (FR)**[703] 7-10-6 0... AlainDeChitray 88
(Mme I Pacault, France) **37/1**

7 **Renne Du Houx (FR)** 8-10-8 0.. YoannLecourt 90
(J Merienne, France) **9/1**

P **Sous Officier (FR)**[71] 7-10-12 0...................................(p) BertrandThelier
(G Cherel, France) **9/2**[2]

P **Windsor Brook (IRE)**[845] 6-10-10 0.. BorisDulong
(L Buyl, Belgium) **73/1**

5m 35.9s (335.90) **9** Ran SP% **119.1**
PARI-MUTUEL (all including 1 euro stakes): WIN 6.40; PLACE 1.60, 1.90, 1.20; DF 15.30; SF 34.20.
Owner Simon Munir **Bred** D & J Aubert **Trained** France

1465a PRIX PARIS-NORMANDIE (CHASE) (CONDITIONS) (4YO) (TURF) 2m 1f 110y
3:25 (12:00) 4-Y-0 **£9,756** (£4,878; £2,845; £1,930; £914)

RPR

1 **Milord Thomas (FR)**[66] 4-10-8 0.. JacquesRicou 115
(D Bressou, France) **21/10**[2]

2 6 **Star Flight (FR)**[103] 405 4-10-1 0 ow2............................ MathieuCarroux 102
(A Chaille-Chaille, France) **9/5**[1]

3 shd **Volare (FR)**[27] 1199 4-10-3 0.. RegisSchmidlin 104
(M Rolland, France) **73/10**

4 2½ **Vintage Mag (FR)** 4-10-8 0... BenoitGicquel 106
(F Nicolle, France) **19/5**[3]

5 4 **Rio De Sivola (FR)**[196] 4233 4-10-6 0 ow3........................ JamesReveley 100
(Nick Williams) *led: nt fluent 8th (water): rdn after 3 out: untidy and hdd 2 out: no ex and fdd flat* **83/10**

6 **A Suivre (FR)**[150] 4-10-3 0... AlbanDesvaux 97
(A Lamotte D'Argy, France) **37/1**

P **Kadella (FR)** 4-10-4 0 ow1.. BertrandLestrade
(E Lecoiffier, France) **48/1**

4m 25.6s (265.60) **7** Ran SP% **116.3**
PARI-MUTUEL (all including 1 euro stakes): WIN 3.10; PLACE 1.40, 1.30, 1.50; DF 3.10; SF 7.20.
Owner Mme Magalen Bryant **Bred** S Boucheron **Trained** France

1280 MARKET RASEN (R-H)
Saturday, August 31

OFFICIAL GOING: Good (good to firm in places; watered; chs 8.1, hdl 7.9)
Rail moved to outermost position.
Wind: Light; across Weather: Sunny intervals; 17 degrees

1466 EXPERT GUIDE AT MARKETRASENRACECOURSETIPS.CO.UK NOVICES' HURDLE (8 hdls) 2m 1f
4:20 (4:21) (Class 4) 4-Y-0+ **£3,898** (£1,144; £572; £286)

Form RPR

22- **1** **Ittirad (USA)**[18] 1255 5-10-9 117.. JackQuinlan(3) 119+
(John Ferguson) *led wl bef 2nd and a travelling strly: toying w rival 2 out: firmly in command last* **8/13**[1]

123- **2** 4½ **Odin (IRE)**[18] 1258 5-10-12 115.................................(p) ConorShoemark(7) 116
(Don Cantillon) *chsd wnr wl bef 2nd: drvn upsides whn hit 2 out: nvr any danger to wnr after* **3/1**[2]

432- **3** 15 **Trend Is My Friend (USA)**[31] 1159 4-11-4 109............. JasonMaguire 100
(Donald McCain) *hld up: wnt 3rd bef 5th: drvn after next: 10 l 3rd and toiling 2 out: wnt lft last* **9/2**[3]

345- **4** 26 **Itmakessense**[5] 1404 6-10-12 0...(p) NoelFehily 73
(Charlie Longsdon) *led at pedestrian pce tl wl bef 2nd: nt jump wl: dropped bk last and blnd 5th: sn remote: t.o bef 2 out* **16/1**

4m 20.3s (13.60) **Going Correction** +0.45s/f (Soft) **4** Ran SP% **111.0**
Speed ratings (Par 105): **86,83,76,64**
CSF £3.01 TOTE £1.40; EX 3.00 Trifecta £3.20 Pool: £1131.71 - 263.17 winning units..
Owner Bloomfields **Bred** Darley **Trained** Cowlinge, Suffolk

FOCUS
The last two flights of hurdles were both sited in an advanced position up the home straight, and the run-in was no more than about 150 yards. The time of this opener won't count for much, as the field stood still for over five seconds and then dawdled until Jack Quinlan grabbed the race by the throat approaching the second. The winner is value for further.

1467 COASTAL LOANS NOVICES' HURDLE (10 hdls) 2m 5f
4:55 (4:55) (Class 4) 4-Y-0+ **£3,898** (£1,144; £572; £286)

Form RPR

251- **1** **Wake Your Dreams (IRE)**[14] 1281 5-11-12 121................ SeanQuinlan 120+
(Jennie Candlish) *mde all: mstke 3 out: slow pce tl qcknd clr wl bef next where rdn and 10 l ahd: mstke last: looked all out but v game* **5/4**[2]

222- **2** 5 **Bright Abbey**[7] 1378 5-11-5 125... HenryBrooke 108+
(Dianne Sayer) *2nd mostly: drvn and outpcd after 3 out: clsd u.p 2 out to be 6 l down whn hit last: no further imp* **4/5**[1]

406- **3** 9 **Inside Knowledge (USA)**[12] 1320 7-11-5 94................(p) AdamPogson 98
(Garry Woodward) *wnt 2nd briefly bef 6th where j. deliberately: drvn and outpcd after 3 out: 17 l 3rd and struggling next* **16/1**[3]

006/ **4** 7 **Silver Dragon**[152] 5071 5-10-12 0.. NoelFehily 84
(Tony Coyle) *awkward at ev flight: a last: blnd 7th and remote after but did keep plugging away steadily fr 2 out* **25/1**

5m 31.4s (22.60) **Going Correction** +0.45s/f (Soft) **4** Ran SP% **109.7**
Speed ratings (Par 105): **74,72,68,66**
CSF £2.76 TOTE £2.50; EX 2.90 Trifecta £3.20 Pool: £941.21 - 217.02 winning units..
Owner Pam Beardmore & Alan Baxter **Bred** J R Weston **Trained** Basford Green, Staffs

FOCUS
Two reasonable performers for the time of year locked horns. The winner is rated close to his mark, with the second more than a stone off his best.

1468 HENDERSON JAMBOREE H'CAP HURDLE (12 hdls) 3m
5:25 (5:25) (Class 4) (0-115,115) 4-Y-0+ **£3,119** (£915; £457; £228)

Form RPR

022- **1** **Coronea Lilly (IRE)**[14] 1284 9-11-12 115...........................(tp) NoelFehily 121+
(Neil Mulholland) *cl up tl led bef 8th: drew clr after 3 out: rdn next: kpt on gamely and a gng bttr than pursuer after: nt fluent last* **2/1**[1]

P/F- **2** 15 **Minella For Steak (IRE)**[123] 45 6-11-5 108....................(p) APMcCoy 108
(Jonjo O'Neill) *settled cl up: nt fluent 5th: wnt 2nd bef 8th: rdn after 3 out: little rspnse and outpcd bef home turn: no imp whn hit 2 out: 5 l down whn wnt lft and on his nose last* **2/1**[1]

6/5- **3** 15 **Outback (IRE)**[11] 202 4-10-11 108...........................(v) TrevorWhelan(5) 84
(Neil King) *cl last but u.p 7th: nvr travelling after: 3rd and losing tch w ldng pair 9th: 15 l 3rd 2 out: no ex* **14/1**

044- **4** 26 **Combustible Kate (IRE)**[14] 1284 7-10-4 93..................(p) HarryHaynes 49
(Nick Kent) *led: nt fluent 7th: rdn and hdd bef next: last fr 9th: sn t.o* **5/1**[3]

5/2- **P** **Winter Alchemy (IRE)**[31] 1164 8-10-9 98........................ BrianHarding
(Nicky Richards) *cl up tl rdn and lost tch rapidly bef 9th: hopelessly t.o whn p.u after next* **9/2**[2]

5m 58.3s (7.80) **Going Correction** +0.45s/f (Soft)
WFA 4 from 6yo+ 15lb **5** Ran SP% **108.2**
Speed ratings (Par 105): **105,100,95,86,**
CSF £6.34 TOTE £3.00: £1.50, £2.00; EX 6.80 Trifecta £23.50 Pool: £229.12 - 7.30 winning units..
Owner Wellcroomed T/A eyewearoutlet.co.uk **Bred** Connor Giles Partnership **Trained** Limpley Stoke, Wilts

FOCUS
A clear-cut winner for in-form connections, and the second successive race in which a kick for home after three out proved decisive. The second is rated to his mark and sets the level.

1469 CALVERTS CARPETS YORK H'CAP CHASE (17 fncs) 3m 1f
6:00 (6:01) (Class 4) (0-115,115) 4-Y-0+ **£4,548** (£1,335; £667; £333)

Form RPR

341- **1** **More Equity**[7] 1377 11-10-8 97........................ HenryBrooke 108+
(Dianne Sayer) *trckd ldrs: led after 14th: gng clr w ears pricked fr next: styng on stoutly whn brushed through 2 out and last* **8/1**

P11- **2** *10* **Green Bank (IRE)**[27] 1205 7-11-12 115........................(t) NoelFehily 117
(Charlie Longsdon) *led tl rdn and hdd after 14th: lost tch w wnr next: 9 l 2nd whn mstke last* **15/8**[1]

121- **3** *3/4* **Calypso Bay (IRE)**[27] 1202 7-11-9 112........................ APMcCoy 115
(Jonjo O'Neill) *trckd ldrs: mstke 4th: hit 5th and 10th: nvr looked to be gng w sufficient zest after: hit 12th: btn 3rd and u.p whn j.rt 3 out: hit last* **15/8**[1]

023- **4** *17* **Civil Unrest (IRE)**[18] 1260 7-10-6 95........................(p) BrianHarding 82
(James Ewart) *pressed ldr 5th tl mstke 13th: sn rdn: dropped bk last 3 out: struggling after* **5/1**[2]

13P- **P** **Solway Bay**[13] 1304 11-10-3 95........................(tp) EwanWhillans(3)
(Lisa Harrison) *a last: lost tch tamely 11th: tailing off whn p.u 13th* **13/2**[3]

6m 9.3s (-22.00) **Going Correction** -0.75s/f (Firm) **5** Ran SP% **110.7**
Speed ratings (Par 105): **105,101,101,96,**
CSF £24.07 TOTE £4.20: £2.80, £1.40; EX 31.10 Trifecta £41.50 Pool: £656.59 - 11.86 winning units..
Owner Mrs Margaret Coppola **Bred** Mrs A F Tullie **Trained** Hackthorpe, Cumbria

FOCUS
The three last-time winners filled the frame, though not in the order expected. The winner built on a recent easy success, with the third rated similar to his recent C&D winning mark.

1470 FRONT ROW FENCING H'CAP CHASE (14 fncs) 2m 4f
6:30 (6:30) (Class 4) (0-120,127) 4-Y-0+ **£4,548** (£1,335; £667; £333)

Form RPR

426- **1** **Rockiteer (IRE)**[41] 1060 10-11-7 118........................(p) JakeGreenall(3) 123
(Henry Daly) *2nd tl led 5th: drvn and hdd 2 out: looked hld tl ldr fluffed last: sn in front again and r.o wl for driving* **6/1**

411- **2** *nk* **Lucky Landing (IRE)**[5] 1390 7-12-5 127 7ex........................ NoelFehily 133
(Tony Coyle) *settled in rr: hit 8th: rdn bef 12th: clsd to ld w ears pricked 2 out: over 1 l clr whn mstke last: sn hdd: battled on wl but jst hld fnl 100yds* **2/1**[1]

341- **3** *5* **Violets Boy (IRE)**[14] 1282 6-11-9 117........................(t) LeightonAspell 118
(Brendan Powell) *settled in midfield: rdn to go 3rd bef 3 out: kpt on same pce and hld fr next* **11/4**[2]

650- **4** *7* **Tregaro (FR)**[18] 1260 7-10-0 94........................(t) BrianHughes 88
(Mike Sowersby) *hld up last tl after 11th: effrt bef 2 out: rdn and sn no further imp* **20/1**

431- **5** *2* **Surf And Turf (IRE)**[11] 1326 7-12-0 122........................(p) APMcCoy 118
(Jonjo O'Neill) *trckd ldrs: nt fluent 11th: drvn to go 2nd briefly wl bef 3 out: outpcd by ldng pair next: eased after last* **5/1**[3]

002- **6** *4 1/2* **O Crotaigh (IRE)**[27] 1204 9-11-10 118........................ RichieMcGrath 106
(Alan Brown) *led tl 5th: 3rd and pushed along after 7th: last and struggling bef 3 out* **7/1**

U42- **7** *30* **Fiftyonefiftyone (IRE)**[40] 1077 9-11-7 120........................(p) JoeCornwall(5) 81
(John Cornwall) *cl up: nt fluent 4th: wnt 2nd fr 7th tl rdn and lost pl qckly wl bef 3 out: bttr for r* **16/1**

4m 50.9s (-14.80) **Going Correction** -0.75s/f (Firm) **7** Ran SP% **114.1**
Speed ratings (Par 105): **99,98,96,94,93 91,79**
toteswingers 1&2 £3.10, 1&3 £3.20, 2&3 £1.90 CSF £19.16 TOTE £4.80: £4.50, £3.00; EX 24.10 Trifecta £66.80 Pool: £1395.02 - 15.64 winning units..
Owner Michael O'Flynn & John Nesbitt **Bred** R C A Latta **Trained** Stanton Lacy, Shropshire

FOCUS
Two of the main protagonists came into the race rated above the 120 ceiling, but it was one of the more exposed alternatives that obliged in a driving finish.

1471 EMERALD GREEN FEEDS H'CAP HURDLE (8 hdls) 2m 1f
7:00 (7:00) (Class 4) (0-120,117) 4-Y-0+ **£3,249** (£954; £477; £238)

Form RPR

312- **1** **Strongly Suggested**[14] 1285 6-11-12 117........................(t) APMcCoy 119+
(Jonjo O'Neill) *cl up: pushed into 2nd at 4th: delayed effrt tl led wl bef 2 out: sn rdn: abt 2 l clr after and kpt finding enough* **8/11**[1]

142- **2** *2* **Dont Take Me Alive**[39] 1093 4-11-3 109........................(tp) NoelFehily 107
(Charlie Longsdon) *travelled wl: last tl after 3 out: wnt 2nd wl bef next where hit flight: sn rdn: abt 2 l down and making no imp after* **5/2**[2]

145- **3** *12* **Bunratty (IRE)**[69] 803 7-10-3 94........................ HenryBrooke 82
(Dianne Sayer) *t.k.h: led after 1st: nt fluent 3 out: rdn and hdd bef next and hit flight whn already wl btn* **8/1**

0/2- **4** *25* **Callisto Moon**[110] 267 9-11-8 113........................(p) MarkGrant 86
(Jo Hughes) *led tl after 1st: rdn and dropped bk last after 3 out: sn wl btn: mstke next: t.o and eased flat* **6/1**[3]

4m 16.4s (9.70) **Going Correction** +0.45s/f (Soft)
WFA 4 from 6yo+ 13lb **4** Ran SP% **111.9**
Speed ratings (Par 105): **95,94,88,76**
CSF £3.19 TOTE £1.50; EX 3.20 Trifecta £8.00 Pool: £782.74 - 72.59 winning units..
Owner John P McManus **Bred** David Brace **Trained** Cheltenham, Gloucs

FOCUS
A modest handicap hurdle with the first two rated in line with their recent best.

1472 CHESTNUT HOMES EXCLUSIVE NEW DEVELOPMENT MARES' INTERMEDIATE OPEN NATIONAL HUNT FLAT RACE 2m 1f
7:30 (7:30) (Class 6) 4-6-Y-0 **£1,642** (£478; £239)

Form RPR

1 **Hannah's Princess (IRE)** 4-10-11 0........................ NoelFehily 100+
(Brian Storey) *settled last pair: effrt 3f out: led wl over 1f out: urged along and kpt gng gamely: clr ins fnl f* **3/1**[3]

225- **2** *9* **Retrieve The Stick**[48] 970 4-10-11 0........................(p) BrianHughes 92
(Malcolm Jefferson) *pressed ldr: led 3f out: drvn and hdd wl over 1f out: sn outpcd: fin weakly* **11/4**[2]

324/ **3** *9* **Pastoral**[156] 4991 4-10-11 0........................ APMcCoy 84
(Tony Coyle) *led at decent pce: drvn and hdd 3f out: fnd nthing and wl btn 3rd 2f out* **2/1**[1]

/ **4** *4* **Arakelton** 5-10-12 0........................ ColinBolger 81
(Mark H Tompkins) *settled last pair: rdn over 4f out: nvr gng wl enough after and plodded on fnl 2f* **14/1**

5- **5** *28* **All For Lily**[12] 1317 4-10-11 0........................ AdamPogson 55
(Charles Pogson) *t.k.h: chsd ldrs: rdn 1/2-way: fdd bdly 4f out: t.o over 2f out* **6/1**

503- **6** *49* **All Riled Up**[28] 1196 5-10-12 0........................ LeightonAspell 12
(Harry Chisman) *t.k.h: pressed ldrs for 11f: stopped to nil and sn hopelessly t.o* **12/1**

4m 8.4s (7.30) **Going Correction** +0.45s/f (Soft)
WFA 4 from 5yo 1lb **6** Ran SP% **113.6**
Speed ratings: **100,95,91,89,76 53**
toteswingers 1&2 £2.30, 1&3 £2.50, 2&3 £1.90 CSF £11.92 TOTE £4.10: £3.00, £2.40; EX 10.30 Trifecta £44.70 Pool: £978.38 - 16.39 winning units..
Owner Andrew Kitching **Bred** Gary Adams **Trained** Boltonfellend, Cumbria

FOCUS
Not too many regular sources of bumper winners represented here, barring the trainer of the runner-up, but a visually impressive winner at least. The placed horses set the level.
T/Plt: £78.10 to a £1 stake. Pool: £24,663.69 - 230.49 winning units T/Qpdt: £9.90 to a £1 stake. Pool: £2,584.70 - 192.40 winning units IM

1348 NEWTON ABBOT (L-H)
Saturday, August 31

OFFICIAL GOING: Good (good to firm in places; 7.5)
All bends moved but impact on distances not notified.
Wind: Mild breeze; across Weather: Sunny

1473 EMMA JUVENILE HURDLE (8 hdls) 2m 1f
2:10 (2:10) (Class 4) 3-Y-0 **£4,061** (£1,192; £596; £298)

Form RPR

551- **1** **Walter White (IRE)**[28] 1193 3-11-5 114........................(t) TomO'Brien 111+
(Philip Hobbs) *led 2nd: mde rest: drew wl clr after 3 out: easily* **4/11**[1]

F33- **2** *32* **Karl Marx (IRE)**[10] 1335 3-10-12 0........................(p) TommyPhelan 75
(Mark Gillard) *nt a fluent: led tl 2nd: rdn along to chse ldrs after next: regained 2nd 5th: no ch w wnr fr after 3 out: wknd between last 2* **8/1**[3]

3 *30* **Castell Avon**[134] 3-9-12 0........................ MrFTett(7) 41
(Milton Bradley) *trckd ldr: wnt 2nd after 4th tl next: wknd after 3 out: t.o* **50/1**

4 *5* **Complexity**[59] 3-10-12 0........................ AndrewThornton 44
(Seamus Mullins) *t.k.h: trckd ldrs: tended to jump lft: nt fluent 3 out: sn wknd: t.o* **5/1**[2]

P **Studfarmer**[95] 3-10-7 0........................ RobertWilliams(5)
(Martin Hill) *t.k.h: trckd ldrs: wknd 5th: t.o whn p.u after 3 out* **11/1**

4m 3.2s (-2.50) **Going Correction** -0.225s/f (Good) **5** Ran SP% **111.4**
Speed ratings (Par 102): **96,80,66,64,**
CSF £4.25 TOTE £1.20: £1.10, £1.50; EX 3.40 Trifecta £20.40 Pool: £938.09 - 34.38 winning units..
Owner Walter White Partnership **Bred** Catridge Farm Stud & S Von Schilcher **Trained** Withycombe, Somerset

FOCUS
A weak juvenile hurdle with the second rated to his mark.

1474 DAVID WHITTON HAPPY 70TH BIRTHDAY NOVICES' H'CAP CHASE (20 fncs) 3m 2f 110y
2:45 (2:45) (Class 5) (0-95,92) 4-Y-0+ **£3,249** (£954; £477; £238)

Form RPR

55P/ **1** **Jayandbee (IRE)**[151] 5104 6-11-12 92........................ RichardJohnson 103
(Philip Hobbs) *trckd ldr but nt a as fluent: led sn after 3 out: styd on dourly: rdn out* **11/4**[1]

/66- **2** *2* **Brandy And Pep (IRE)**[74] 759 9-10-0 66 oh1........................(p) PaddyBrennan 75
(R P Rath, Ire) *trckd ldrs: cl 3rd fr 15th tl after 4 out: clsd on ldrs again u.p after 3 out: flattered between last 2: styd on same pce and a being hld run-in* **11/1**

416- **3** *6* **Solitary Palm (IRE)**[10] 1336 10-11-1 81........................(b) ConorO'Farrell 86
(Brian Forsey) *led: hit 8th: nt fluent 3 out: sn rdn and hdd: lost 2nd bef next: styd on same pce* **12/1**

/45- **4** *31* **Diamond Eclipse (IRE)**[30] 1174 7-11-4 84........................ NickScholfield 59
(Nick Williams) *hld up: hmpd 1st: struggling 14th: wnt modest 4th 4 out: nvr a threat: t.o* **6/1**[3]

003- **5** *4 1/2* **Volio Vincente (FR)**[10] 1338 6-10-0 66........................ IanPopham 37
(Carroll Gray) *trckd ldrs: rdn after 15th: sn btn: t.o* **18/1**

343- **6** *27* **Minella Bliss (IRE)**[9] 1349 8-11-4 87........................(p) RobertDunne(3) 34
(Nikki Evans) *j.rt 1st: towards rr of gp wl in tch: struggling after 15th: sn btn: t.o* **7/2**[2]

033- **P** **No Woman No Cry**[9] 1351 8-11-2 82........................(tp) JoeTizzard
(Colin Tizzard) *nt fluent early: in last pair fr 3rd: lost tch after 13th: p.u after next* **7/2**[2]

PP4- **U** **Minella Ranger (IRE)**[9] 1349 7-11-10 90........................ TomO'Brien
(Paul Henderson) *blnd bdly (virtually falling) whn unseating rdr 2nd* **9/1**

6m 36.8s (-7.80) **Going Correction** -0.225s/f (Good) **8** Ran SP% **116.7**
Speed ratings (Par 103): **102,101,99,90,89 81, ,**
toteswingers 1&2 £8.40, 1&3 £11.00, 2&3 £20.30 CSF £32.13 CT £315.57 TOTE £3.00: £1.10, £5.70, £2.70; EX 39.20 Trifecta £692.60 Pool: £925.85 - 1.00 winning unit..
Owner J & B Gibbs & Sons Ltd **Bred** Miss E Violet Sweeney **Trained** Withycombe, Somerset

FOCUS
An open staying handicap in which the first three pulled well clear. The winner improved to the level of its hurdles form, with the third helping to set the level.

1475 TRY TOTEQUICKPICK IF YOU'RE FEELING LUCKY NOVICES' H'CAP HURDLE (8 hdls) 2m 1f
3:20 (3:21) (Class 4) (0-110,110) 4-Y-0+ **£4,061** (£1,192; £596; £298)

Form RPR

P35/ **1** **Vimiero (USA)**[85] 3854 6-11-12 110........................ RichieMcLernon 113+
(Jonjo O'Neill) *hld up bhd ldrs: trckd ldr travelling wl after 3 out: chal 2 out: sn shkn up to ld: wandered appr last: r.o: rdn out* **9/2**[3]

The Form Book Jumps, Raceform Ltd, Compton, RG20 6NL.

513- **2** 2 1/2 **Quadriller (FR)**30 1171 6-11-7 **105**.....(t) TomO'Brien 104
(Philip Hobbs) *trckd ldr: led 3 out: rdn bef next: hdd between last 2 out: ev ch last: kpt on same pce* **15/8**1

4P0- **3** 23 **Good Of Luck**16 1270 4-11-0 **99**..... ConorO'Farrell 76
(Mick Channon) *racd keenly trcking ldr: rdn in v cl 3rd after 3 out tl rdr eased off momentarily and lost pl: hld after: wknd between last 2* **15/2**

0F/- **4** 3 1/4 **Koralsdarling (IRE)**331 1714 9-9-11 **84** oh1..... JamesBest(3) 59
(Alan Jones) *racd keenly trcking ldrs: rdn after 3 out: sn hld: wkng whn awkward 2 out* **12/1**

P16- **5** 2 3/4 **Anton Dolin (IRE)**9 1345 5-11-7 **105**.....(b1) SamTwiston-Davies 78
(Dr Richard Newland) *led: nt a fluent: rdn after 5th: hdd next: qckly btn* **11/4**2

242- **P** **Osorios Trial**9 1348 6-11-6 **104**..... PaulMoloney
(Anthony Middleton) *hld up bhd ldrs: struggling after 4th: lost tch bef next: t.o whn p.u bef 2 out: lame* **15/2**

3m 58.9s (-6.80) **Going Correction** -0.225s/f (Good)
WFA 4 from 5yo+ 13lb **6** Ran SP% **110.9**
Speed ratings (Par 105): **107,105,95,93,92**
toteswingers 1&2 £2.00, 1&3 £1.40, 2&3 £3.50 CSF £13.43 TOTE £7.10: £4.60, £1.10; EX 13.90 Trifecta £64.60 Pool: £1,012.36 - 11.74 winning units..
Owner Diane Carr & John Cockcroft **Bred** Stonestreet Thoroughbred Holdings LLC **Trained** Cheltenham, Gloucs

FOCUS
A moderate handicap hurdle, but the winner has the potential to rate higher, and the second is rated to his mark.

1476 LORD MILDMAY MEMORIAL H'CAP CHASE (LISTED RACE) (16 fncs) 2m 5f 110y
3:55 (3:55) (Class 1) 4-Y-0+
£19,761 (£7,451; £3,724; £1,858; £934; £465)

Form RPR
510- **1** **The Disengager (IRE)**31 1168 9-11-12 **147**..... RichardJohnson 155+
(Philip Hobbs) *mde all: tended to jump rt: rdn after 2 out: styd on v gamely* **10/1**

022- **2** 1 1/4 **Rob Conti (FR)**10 1337 8-9-12 **122**..... JamesBest(3) 129
(Philip Hobbs) *trckd wnr thrght: rdn after 3 out: nvr quite able to mount chal: styd on* **8/1**

P/6- **3** 2 1/4 **Shoegazer (IRE)**28 1195 8-11-10 **145**.....(t) TomScudamore 149
(David Pipe) *in tch: trckd ldrs after 10th: rdn after 3 out: wnt 3rd between last 2: styd on same pce: bloke blood vessel* **5/1**2

124- **4** nk **Billie Magern**13 1302 9-11-0 **142**.....(v) RyanHatch(7) 145
(Nigel Twiston-Davies) *trckd ldrs: rdn after 3 out: nt pce to mount chal: styd on* **20/1**

F12- **5** 2 3/4 **Twirling Magnet (IRE)**8 1362 7-11-9 **144**.....(tp) RichieMcLernon 146
(Jonjo O'Neill) *hld up in last pair: smooth hdwy 12th: rdn after 3 out: nt pce to mount chal: styng on at same pce whn nt fluent last: no ex* **8/1**

131- **6** 1 **Kian's Delight**48 957 5-10-11 **132**..... TomO'Brien 132
(Peter Bowen) *mid-div: lost pl whn nudged along after 11th: styd on again fr after 3 out but nvr threatening to rch ldrs* **3/1**1

200- **7** 2 1/4 **Buck Mulligan**8 1362 8-10-9 **130**..... PaulMoloney 128
(Evan Williams) *hld up towards rr: effrt to cl 3 out: sn rdn: grad fdd between last 2* **12/1**

01P- **8** 3 **Bobowen (IRE)**31 1168 7-11-7 **142**..... SamTwiston-Davies 139
(Dr Richard Newland) *mid-div: slow 6th: hdwy 4 out: rdn after next: wknd between last 2* **7/1**3

P30- **9** 3 1/2 **Life Of A Luso (IRE)**62 851 9-10-11 **132**.....(t) PaddyBrennan 126
(Paul Henderson) *hld up towards rr: hit 9th: effrt 3 out: wknd after next* **40/1**

4/0- **10** 6 **Royale's Charter**42 1047 7-10-12 **133**..... NickScholfield 120
(Nick Williams) *trckd ldrs: losing pl whn nt fluent 4 out: wknd after next* **8/1**

034- **11** 1/2 **Toubab (FR)**9 1346 7-11-0 **140**..... HarryDerham(5) 126
(Paul Nicholls) *hld up towards rr: rdn bef 4 out: nvr threatened: wknd after 3 out* **10/1**

5m 10.0s (-11.40) **Going Correction** -0.225s/f (Good) **11** Ran SP% **120.6**
Speed ratings (Par 111): **111,110,109,109,108 108,107,106,105,102 102**
toteswingers 1&2 £9.10, 1&3 £8.90, 2&3 £6.60 CSF £89.88 CT £456.32 TOTE £9.90: £3.20, £3.00, £1.40; EX 60.10 Trifecta £585.20 Part won. Pool: £780.36 - 0.99 winning units..
Owner Govier & Brown **Bred** T Groarke **Trained** Withycombe, Somerset

FOCUS
A competitive Listed handicap chase. The pace was ordinary and several were still in contention once in the home straight. The form looks solid enough with the third to sixth helping to set the level.

1477 AT THE RACES SKY 415 H'CAP HURDLE (12 hdls) 3m 3f
4:30 (4:30) (Class 4) (0-105,100) 4-Y-0+ **£4,061** (£1,192; £596; £298)

Form RPR
613- **1** **Tarvini (IRE)**18 1267 8-11-2 **100**.....(p) JamesHuxham(10) 104+
(Jonjo O'Neill) *pressed ldr thrght: nudged along to draw clr w ldr after 8th: rdn bef 2 out: drew ahd appr last: drifted lft run-in: rdn out* **9/4**1

342- **2** 2 3/4 **Thornton Alice**18 1266 8-11-5 **100**..... DanielHiskett(7) 102
(Richard Phillips) *led: drew clr w wnr after 8th: rdn appr 2 out: hdd between last 2: styd on for clr 2nd but no ex* **9/2**3

/53- **3** 12 **Mister Moonax (IRE)**18 1262 13-11-9 **100**.....(bt1) GilesHawkins(3) 92
(Chris Down) *chsd ldrs tl pushed along fr 5th: last and rdn after 8th: styd on appr 2 out to go 3rd towards fin but nvr any ch w ldng pair* **22/1**

022- **4** 1 **Southway Queen**10 1340 9-10-13 **94**.....(tp) NathanAdams(7) 84
(Sue Gardner) *chsd ldrs: rdn to chse clr ldrs appr 9th: nvr any imp: no ex whn lost 3rd run-in* **7/2**2

200- **5** 12 **Blue Signal (IRE)**10 1339 8-11-2 **90**..... IanPopham 70
(Colin Heard) *hld up in chsng gp: rdn bef 9th: nvr any imp: wknd 2 out* **12/1**

561- **6** 1 **William Percival (IRE)**10 1339 7-10-9 **83**..... TommyPhelan 62
(Mark Gillard) *chsd ldrs: mstke 7th: rdn to chse clr ldrs appr 9th: nt fluent 3 out: nvr threatened: wknd 2 out* **6/1**

210- **P** **Little Eaglet (IRE)**54 925 9-11-5 **93**..... LiamHeard
(Colin Heard) *hld up in chsng gp: struggling 6th: t.o whn p.u after 3 out* **5/1**

6m 38.2s (-2.80) **Going Correction** -0.225s/f (Good) **7** Ran SP% **114.2**
Speed ratings (Par 105): **95,94,90,90,86 86,**
toteswingers 1&2 £3.10, 1&3 £8.90, 2&3 £18.00 CSF £13.01 CT £171.46 TOTE £3.10: £2.30, £3.30; EX 12.40 Trifecta £76.60 Pool: £685.96 - 6.70 winning units..
Owner John P McManus **Bred** His Highness The Aga Khan's Studs S C **Trained** Cheltenham, Gloucs

FOCUS
An ordinary staying handicap which developed into a match over the final circuit. The second is rated to her mark, with the third rated close to his recent chasing mark.

1478 SIS LIVE H'CAP CHASE (13 fncs) 2m 110y
5:05 (5:05) (Class 4) (0-120,121) 4-Y-0+ **£4,873** (£1,431; £715; £357)

Form RPR
34- **1** **Easily Pleased (IRE)**28 1192 7-11-2 **110**..... HaddenFrost 124+
(Martin Hill) *wnt to s early: t.k.h: hld up last: smooth hdwy to ld sn after 4 out: clr bef last: easily* **11/4**2

312- **2** 7 **Wester Ross (IRE)**9 1346 9-11-10 **121**.....(v) AdamWedge(3) 126
(Evan Williams) *trckd clr ldr: clsd on ldr 8th but lost 2nd: chsd ldrs: ev ch 4 out tl rdn to chse wnr after next: kpt on same pce* **4/1**3

53P- **3** 14 **Zama Zama**16 1274 6-10-1 **102**..... ConorRing(7) 95
(Evan Williams) *led: clr tl 8th: hdd 4 out: sn rdn: grad fdd fr 2 out* **4/1**3

362- **4** 13 **Mibleu (FR)**9 1352 13-10-11 **110**..... EDLinehan(5) 91
(Colin Tizzard) *racd keenly bhd ldng pair: hit 6th: clsd on ldr 8th: rdn after 4 out: wknd after next* **6/1**

121- **5** nk **Engai (GER)**13 1301 7-11-10 **118**..... TomScudamore 102
(David Bridgwater) *hld up bhd ldng pair: clsd on clr ldr 8th: led whn mstke 4 out: sn hdd: nt fluent next: sn btn* **2/1**1

4m 3.6s (-2.90) **Going Correction** -0.225s/f (Good) **5** Ran SP% **114.3**
Speed ratings (Par 105): **97,93,87,81,80**
CSF £14.20 TOTE £6.10: £3.30, £3.70; EX 19.10 Trifecta £51.50 Pool: £762.54 - 11.09 winning units..
Owner Roger Oliver & Claire Harding **Bred** Mrs Eleanor Hadden **Trained** Littlehempston, Devon

FOCUS
What looked an open handicap chase was turned into a procession by the easy winner. A big step up from that gelding with the second rated to his mark.

1479 NEWTONABBOTRACING.COM H'CAP HURDLE (9 hdls) 2m 3f
5:35 (5:35) (Class 5) (0-95,94) 4-Y-0+ **£2,842** (£834; £417; £208)

Form RPR
054- **1** **Sedgemoor Express (IRE)**9 1351 5-11-4 **85**.....(tp) TomScudamore 96+
(Nigel Hawke) *hld up in last trio: wnt 2nd after 6th: led after 3 out: rdn clr bef last: r.o* **4/1**3

4F2- **2** 8 **Himrayn**9 1351 10-11-0 **86**..... JoshHamer(5) 92
(Anabel K Murphy) *hld up in tch: last trio: pushed along bef 6th: rdn to chal after 3 out: outpcd by wnr bef last* **5/2**2

435- **3** 19 **Illegale (IRE)**9 1351 7-10-7 **74**.....(t) RichardJohnson 61
(Phillip Dando) *hld up: wnt 3rd after 3rd tl rdn after 3 out: wknd after next* **7/1**

00- **4** 123 **Exiles Return (IRE)**54 925 11-10-7 **74**..... NickScholfield
(Jacqueline Retter) *j.rt: chsd ldrs tl awkward 2nd: in last pair 4th: sn lost tch: continued t.o* **18/1**

000- **P** **Sassy Wren**18 1269 8-10-6 **73**.....(t) JamesDavies
(Chris Down) *hld up last: pushed along bef 6th: wknd bef 3 out: t.o whn lft remote 4th bef 2 out: p.u bef last* **16/1**

3/5- **P** **The Nephew (IRE)**8 1364 5-11-12 **93**.....(v1) RichieMcLernon
(Jonjo O'Neill) *led: clr tl awkward 3rd: clr again next: rdn and hdd after 3 out: qckly btn: p.u bef next* **2/1**1

040- **P** **Lucette**91 592 5-10-5 **75**.....(tp1) MichealNolan(3)
(Richard Woollacott) *wnt lft 1st: chsd ldrs: jnd ldr 3rd tl bef next: wknd 6th: t.o whn p.u bef 2 out* **25/1**

4m 26.5s (-3.50) **Going Correction** -0.225s/f (Good)
WFA 4 from 5yo+ 13lb **7** Ran SP% **109.4**
Speed ratings (Par 103): **98,94,86, ,**
toteswingers 1&2 £3.20, 1&3 £11.40, 2&3 £2.50 CSF £13.49 CT £59.27 TOTE £4.00: £3.00, £2.90; EX 15.70 Trifecta £52.10 Pool: £470.89 - 6.77 winning units..
Owner Pearce Bros 2 **Bred** Seamus Cooney **Trained** Stoodleigh, Devon

FOCUS
An uncompetitive handicap but a big step up from the winner.
T/Plt: £60.80 to a £1 stake. Pool: £58,034.51 - 696.52 winning units T/Qpdt: £27.60 to a £1 stake. Pool: £3,769.90 - 101.00 winning units TM

1480 - 1482a (Foreign Racing) - See Raceform Interactive

1473 NEWTON ABBOT (L-H)
Sunday, September 1

OFFICIAL GOING: Good to firm (7.8)
All bends moved from previous day.
Wind: virtually nil Weather: dry and sunny

1483 TOTEPLACEPOT RACING'S FAVOURITE BET NOVICES' HURDLE (9 hdls) 2m 3f
2:20 (2:20) (Class 4) 4-Y-0+ **£4,508** (£1,639)

Form RPR
/11- **1** **Falcarragh (IRE)**4 1431 6-11-2 125..... AlanJohns(10) 124
(Tim Vaughan) *t.k.h: hld up in tch: chsd clr ldr after 3rd: led and gng best bef 2 out: idling and racing v awkwardly whn 2 l clr between last 2: landed awkwardly last: hung rt and flashed tail flat: a jst holding rival* **5/6**1

42F- **2** hd **Native Colony**19 1258 5-10-5 104.....(v) CiaranMckee(7) 109
(John O'Shea) *chsd ldr tl led 2nd: sn clr: mstke 4th: clr w wnr 3 out: rdn and hdd bef next: 2 l down 2 out: pressing idling wnr again flat: edgd rt and hld towards fin* **11/4**2

F- **F** **Lily Potts**10 1348 4-10-4 0..... JamesDavies
(Chris Down) *nt fluent: chsd ldrs whn j. violently rt 1st: modest 4th fr 4th: lost tch 3 out: t.o next: fell last* **16/1**

3- **F** **The Finger Post (IRE)**50 989 6-11-5 0..... PaulMoloney 87
(Helen Nelmes) *hld up in last: chsd clr ldng pair 4th: nvr on terms: rdn and lost tch 3 out: t.o next: fell last* **4/1**3

65U- **P** **Nudge The Nugget**10 1348 5-10-12 0.....(b) TomScudamore
(Nigel Hawke) *rdn along early: led tl 2nd: steadily lost pl: last 4th and sn lost tch: t.o whn p.u 6th* **66/1**

4m 27.5s (-2.50) **Going Correction** -0.60s/f (Firm)
WFA 4 from 5yo+ 11lb **5** Ran SP% **108.6**
Speed ratings (Par 105): **81,80, , ,**
CSF £3.42 TOTE £1.70: £1.10, £1.40; EX 3.10 Trifecta £3.70 Pool: £1042.97 - 206.28 winning units..
Owner Mike Stratford **Bred** Liam McLoughlin **Trained** Aberthin, Vale of Glamorgan

FOCUS
All bends moved from yesterday. The ground had dried out overnight and was riding a little quicker than on Saturday. This weak novice hurdle was run at a modest pace. Straightforward enough novice form, rated around the finishers.

1484 TRY A TOTETRIFECTA NOVICES' CHASE (16 fncs) 2m 5f 110y
2:50 (2:50) (Class 3) 4-Y-O+ **£8,703** (£2,571; £1,285)

Form RPR
413- **1** **Dineur (FR)**[10] 1346 7-11-12 137 DonalDevereux 133
(Peter Bowen) *led: mstke 9th: drvn and hdd after 3 out: j.rt next: swtchd lft between last 2: swtchd bk rt flashed tail u.p but drvn to ld again fnl 100yds: hld on* **5/6**[1]

1/0- **2** *hd* **Pateese (FR)**[113] 215 8-11-8 129 (b) RichardJohnson 128
(Philip Hobbs) *chsd wnr: upsides and rdn 12th: led after 3 out: 1 l ahd next: hdd flat: kpt on same pce after* **5/4**[2]

464- **3** *33* **Grey Soldier (IRE)**[3] 1441 8-11-8 122 (t) RichieMcLernon 98
(Sophie Leech) *in tch in last: rdn after 9th: struggling next: lost tch bef 3 out: t.o* **10/1**[3]

5m 18.1s (-3.30) **Going Correction** -0.60s/f (Firm) **3** Ran SP% **108.1**
Speed ratings (Par 107): **82,81,69**
CSF £2.31 TOTE £1.60; EX 2.00 Trifecta £3.80 Pool: £482.86 - 94.65 winning units..
Owner Gwilym J Morris **Bred** Dominique Le Baron **Trained** Little Newcastle, Pembrokes
■ Stewards' Enquiry : Donal Devereux two-day ban: used whip above permitted level (Sep 17,22)

FOCUS
A disappointing turn out for this decent novices' chase. The first two were locked together through the final circuit. The winner is rated to the level of his previous run over the trip with the second to his mark.

1485 TOTEQUADPOT FOUR PLACES IN FOUR RACES H'CAP HURDLE (10 hdls) 2m 6f
3:20 (3:20) (Class 2) 4-Y-O+
£16,265 (£4,804; £2,402; £1,201; £600; £301)

Form RPR
453/ **1** **Kangaroo Court (IRE)**[63] 4628 9-11-0 128 NoelFehily 138+
(Emma Lavelle) *hld up in rr of tightly gped field: hdwy after 3 out: rdn to ld between last 2: looked wnr whn lft in command last: r.o wl: comf* **16/1**

211- **2** *4 ½* **Rum And Butter (IRE)**[10] 1350 5-11-12 140 (p) APMcCoy 145+
(Jonjo O'Neill) *hld up in tch towards rr: hdwy 6th: chsd ldrs after 3 out: rdn to ld next: hdd between last 2: keeping on same pce whn blnd last: wl hld by wnr after* **3/1**[1]

/02- **3** *6* **Teak (IRE)**[6] 1398 6-9-9 114 oh6 GavinSheehan(5) 111
(Ian Williams) *chsd ldr tl after 3 out: drvn and outpcd ldng pair 2 out: kpt on to hold 3rd flat* **9/1**

012- **4** *nk* **Get Home Now**[10] 1350 5-10-13 127 (tp) TomO'Brien 124
(Peter Bowen) *in tch towards rr: effrt and n.m.r after 3 out: hdwy u.p bef 3 out: no ex and styd on same pce between last 2* **7/1**[3]

/51- **5** *3 ¼* **My Brother Sylvest**[10] 1346 7-10-9 123 (b) TomScudamore 120
(David Pipe) *j.rt: led: drvn and hdd bef 2 out: 3rd and outpcd 2 out: wknd between last 2* **14/1**

640/ **6** *1* **American Trilogy (IRE)**[171] 4747 9-11-7 135 HarrySkelton 128
(Dan Skelton) *hld up in tch towards rr: j.big 3 out: sn rdn and effrt whn nt clr run on inner after 3 out: rdn and no hdwy next: wknd between last 2* **33/1**

111- **7** *nk* **Church Field (IRE)**[43] 1042 5-10-8 122 RichieMcLernon 115
(Jonjo O'Neill) *chsd ldrs: rdn and sltly outpcd after 3 out: rallied briefly and swtchd rt bef next: wknd between last 2* **6/1**[2]

231- **8** *¾* **Sheriff Hutton (IRE)**[29] 1195 10-11-7 135 HaddenFrost 127
(Martin Hill) *t.k.h: chsd ldrs: rdn and outpcd sn after 3 out: rallied u.p bef next: no ex and wknd between last 2* **9/1**

6U/- **9** *2 ½* **Gauvain (GER)**[309] 2040 11-11-12 140 RichardJohnson 130
(Philip Hobbs) *in tch in midfield: effrt u.p on outer after 3 out: btn bef next: bhd 2 out* **16/1**

/0B- **10** *11* **Street Entertainer (IRE)**[43] 1046 6-10-10 124 (bt) ConorO'Farrell 104
(David Pipe) *hld up in tch towards rr: hdwy on outer after 7th: chsd ldrs sn after 3 out: rdn and fnd little bef next: wknd qckly between last 2* **8/1**

P43- **11** *4 ½* **Decoy (FR)**[43] 1042 7-10-8 129 (b) KieronEdgar(7) 105
(David Pipe) *t.k.h: in tch in midfield: lost pl and rdn 7th: bhd after 3 out: wknd* **9/1**

/61- **12** *11* **High Storm (IRE)**[34] 1133 6-10-6 120 SamTwiston-Davies 86
(Bernard Llewellyn) *chsd ldrs tl 3 out: sn rdn and struggling: wknd bef next: bhd 2 out: t.o* **28/1**

014- **P** **Kylenoe Fairy (IRE)**[29] 1197 9-10-0 114 (t) PaddyBrennan
(Paul Henderson) *in tch in rr: rdn bef 7th: no hdwy and wknd bef 2 out: bhd whn eased and p.u after 2 out* **22/1**

5m 1.5s (-18.70) **Going Correction** -0.60s/f (Firm) **13** Ran SP% **122.1**
Speed ratings (Par 109): **110,108,106,106,104 104,104,104,103,99 97,93,**
toteswingers 1&2 £25.20, 1&3 £45.40, 2&3 £11.70 CSF £65.22 CT £482.54 TOTE £21.80: £5.80, £1.90, £2.80; EX 149.20 Trifecta £1171.20 Part won. Pool: £1561.69 - 0.33 winning units..
Owner Nicholas Mustoe **Bred** Brian Wilson **Trained** Hatherden, Hants

FOCUS
A valuable and well contested handicap, with nearly all still in with a chance three from home. The time was quick and it is solid form, rated around the third and fourth.

1486 TOTEPOOL KING SIZE POOLS H'CAP CHASE (THE SUNDAY £5K BONUS RACE) (20 fncs) 3m 2f 110y
3:50 (3:50) (Class 4) (0-115,110) 4-Y-O+ **£4,873** (£1,431; £715; £357)

Form RPR
P26- **1** **Western King (IRE)**[13] 1316 6-11-9 107 (tp) NoelFehily 117
(Charlie Mann) *mde all: rdn whn chal bef 2 out: a doing enough to hold runner-up: styd on wl to assert fr last: rdn out* **14/1**

244- **2** *3 ¼* **My Mate Vinnie (IRE)**[19] 1257 6-11-10 108 (t) APMcCoy 116
(Jonjo O'Neill) *awkward 1st: plld hrd: in tch tl restrained in last after 5th: hdwy 16th: wnt 2nd after 4 out: rdn to chal after 3 out tl next: renewed chal gng to last where ev ch: sn swtchd rt and no ex* **4/1**[2]

P/4- **3** *dist* **Ballyvesey (IRE)**[34] 1135 8-11-9 107 (vt) JamieMoore 78
(Peter Bowen) *trckd wnr: pressed wnr 12th tl pushed along 14th: rdn after next: hld bef 3 out: wknd 2 out: t.o* **3/1**[1]

P13- **4** *13* **Terfel's Toscar (IRE)**[13] 1316 8-11-6 104 (t) RichardJohnson 63
(Tim Vaughan) *sn trcking ldrs: hit 12th and next: rdn after 16th: hld after 4 out: wkng whn mstke 2 out: fin tired: t.o* **9/2**[3]

/U0- **5** *2 ½* **Sarika (FR)**[63] 855 7-11-5 110 (b) MissEKelly(7) 67
(Nick Williams) *trckd ldrs: struggling 4 out: sn btn: t.o* **12/1**

30/- **P** **Sanpor (IRE)**[133] 10-10-0 84 oh2 (b) PaddyBrennan
(R P Rath, Ire) *hld up: pushed along briefly whn tried to push loose horse off crse after 9th: sme prog whe mstke 14th: wknd next: bhd whn p.u bef 2 out* **25/1**

101- **P** **Lord Lescribaa (FR)**[42] 1055 10-10-9 103 (tp) ThomasCheesman(10)
(Philip Hobbs) *trckd ldrs: pushed along after 13th: wknd 15th: t.o whn p.u bef 3 out* **6/1**

1F2- **U** **Basil Fawlty (IRE)**[19] 1257 8-11-10 108 (t[1]) TomScudamore
(David Pipe) *mstke and uns rdr 1st* **11/2**

6m 27.7s (-16.90) **Going Correction** -0.60s/f (Firm) **8** Ran SP% **111.1**
Speed ratings (Par 105): **101,100,88,84,83 , ,**
toteswingers 1&2 £9.10, 1&3 £7.20, 2&3 £2.70 CSF £66.49 CT £208.78 TOTE £11.40: £3.20, £2.00, £1.50; EX 58.60 Trifecta £211.20 Pool: £1526.57 - 5.42 winning units..
Owner The Western King Partnership **Bred** David Kennedy **Trained** Upper Lambourn, Berks

FOCUS
Afair handicap chase in which the first two finished well clear. The winner is rated back to his best and the runner-up to his mark.

1487 TOTEQUICKPICK CONDITIONAL JOCKEYS' MAIDEN HURDLE (8 hdls) 2m 1f
4:25 (4:25) (Class 5) 4-Y-O+ **£2,912** (£904; £486)

Form RPR
0/ **1** **To The Sky (IRE)**[91] 5053 5-10-6 0 CiaranMckee(8) 103
(John O'Shea) *racd freely and sn clr: mde all: rdn after 3 out: jnd between last 2: bttr jump at the last to assert run-in* **2/1**[2]

556- **2** *1 ¾* **Kayalar (IRE)**[31] 924 5-10-11 100 (tp) AdamWedge(3) 102
(Evan Williams) *trckd clr ldr in disp 2nd: wnt clr 2nd after 4th: rdn and steadily clsd on wnr after 3 out: chal between last 2: ev ch whn mstke last: no ex* **10/11**[1]

/43- **3** *57* **Edgeworth (IRE)**[15] 1280 7-10-6 83 (p) JakeHodson(8) 50
(David Bridgwater) *trckd clr ldr in disp 2nd tl pushed along after 4th: wknd bef next where lft modest 3rd: wl t.o* **4/1**[3]

P/ **P** **Ma Ridge**[509] 9-11-0 0 BenPoste
(Sarah-Jayne Davies) *trckd clr ldr in disp 2nd tl after 4th: wknd next: t.o whn p.u bef 2 out* **33/1**

0P0- **U** **No No Cardinal (IRE)**[10] 1348 4-11-0 0 TomCannon
(Mark Gillard) *hld up: wnt 3rd after 4th: stl a bit to do whn blnd bdly and uns rdr next* **25/1**

3m 58.5s (-7.20) **Going Correction** -0.60s/f (Firm) **5** Ran SP% **112.5**
Speed ratings (Par 103): **92,91,64, ,**
CSF £4.51 TOTE £3.20: £1.50, £1.20; EX 4.00 Trifecta £5.60 Pool: £2993.50 - 397.20 winning units..
Owner J R Salter **Bred** John McEnery **Trained** Elton, Gloucs

FOCUS
A moderate maiden hurdle, confined to conditional riders. The winner was again below the best of his Irish form with the second to his mark.

1488 COLLECT TOTEPOOL WINNINGS AT BETFRED SHOPS H'CAP HURDLE (10 hdls) 2m 6f
4:55 (4:55) (Class 4) (0-110,110) 4-Y-O+ **£4,061** (£1,192; £596; £298)

Form RPR
033- **1** **Staigue Fort**[19] 1255 5-11-7 110 GavinSheehan(5) 118+
(Emma Lavelle) *t.k.h: hld up: hdwy 7th: trckd ldng pair after 3 out: chal between last 2: rdn to ld run-in: edgd rt: r.o* **5/1**

542- **2** *½* **Bathwick Man**[6] 1391 8-11-0 105 KieronEdgar(7) 111+
(David Pipe) *hld up: hdwy after 6th: jnd ldr after next: led bef 2 out: sn rdn: jnd between last 2: hdd sn after last: kpt on* **2/1**[1]

123- **3** *6* **Detroit Red**[13] 1321 7-11-6 104 HaddenFrost 106
(Martin Hill) *in tch: trckd ldrs 5th: led 7th: rdn and hdd bef 2 out: no ex between last 2* **3/1**[2]

0/0- **4** *6* **Catch The Fire**[112] 237 5-11-0 98 [1] DonalDevereux 93
(Peter Bowen) *in tch: nudged along fr 2nd: rdn bef 7th: kpt chsng ldrs tl outpcd in disp 3rd bef 2 out* **8/1**

P0P- **5** *14* **Hassadin**[34] 1134 7-11-4 102 TomCannon 85
(Michael Blake) *led tl 7th: sn rdn: wknd appr 2 out* **14/1**

122- **6** *2 ½* **Jigsaw Financial (IRE)**[11] 1339 7-10-5 89 GerardTumelty 69
(Laura Young) *hld up in tch: pushed along 7th: effrt 3 out: wknd bef next* **9/2**[3]

430- **7** *35* **Sohappyharry**[15] 1284 7-11-12 110 DPFahy 59
(Jane Mathias) *trckd ldr tl 5th: sn in last but in tch: pushed along bef 7th: wknd 3 out: t.o* **20/1**

P/0- **8** *3 ¾* **Landenstown Star (IRE)**[17] 1275 8-10-0 84 oh3 TommyPhelan 29
(Mark Gillard) *trckd ldr tl 7th: dropped away v tamely: t.o* **40/1**

5m 9.1s (-11.10) **Going Correction** -0.60s/f (Firm) **8** Ran SP% **118.2**
Speed ratings (Par 105): **96,95,93,91,86 85,72,71**
toteswingers 1&2 £3.80, 1&3 £4.70, 2&3 £1.90 CSF £16.51 CT £35.67 TOTE £7.40: £1.80, £1.40, £1.50; EX 20.60 Trifecta £80.80 Pool: £1393.89 - 12.92 winning units..
Owner Lady Bland **Bred** Lady Bland **Trained** Hatherden, Hants

FOCUS
An ordinary handicap hurdle run in a time 7.6sec slower than the earlier Class 2 event. The second is rated in line with his recent run and the third to her mark.

1489 FOLLOW TOTEPOOL ON FACEBOOK AND TWITTER STANDARD OPEN NATIONAL HUNT FLAT RACE 2m 1f
5:25 (5:25) (Class 5) 4-6-Y-O **£2,309** (£673; £336)

Form RPR
0- **1** **Sebastians Charm (IRE)**[34] 1138 5-11-2 0 NoelFehily 101+
(Warren Greatrex) *trckd ldrs: pushed along 3f out: barged through gap on rails sn after: rdn to ld 2f out: hung rt: kpt on wl fnl f* **3/1**[2]

0/1- **2** *¾* **Rest And Be (IRE)**[29] 1196 6-11-2 0 NickScholfield 101
(Alan Jones) *hld up in 4th: nudged along to cl on ldrs over 3f out: chal wl over 1f out: rdn ent fnl f: kpt on but nt qckn* **11/4**[1]

2- **3** *2 ½* **What A Joke (IRE)**[10] 1353 6-10-9 0 ConorShoemark(7) 98
(William Reed) *trckd ldr: bmpd on bnd whn u.p over 2f out: ev ch briefly sn after: styng on at same pce whn hung lft jst over 1f out* **11/4**[1]

3- **4** *4* **Worth A Go (IRE)**[37] 1124 6-11-2 0 (t) DPFahy 94
(Liam Corcoran) *led: rdn and hdd 2f out: sn one pce* **4/1**[3]

5 *15* **Sovinnie (IRE)** 4-10-9 0 (t) ConorRing(7) 81
(Jane Mathias) *hld up 5th: pushed along 6f out: rdn 3f out: sn wknd* **8/1**

3m 57.6s (-2.50) **Going Correction** -0.60s/f (Firm)
WFA 4 from 5yo+ 11lb **5** Ran SP% **109.4**
Speed ratings: **81,80,79,77,70**
CSF £11.38 TOTE £3.20: £2.50, £1.70; EX 12.60 Trifecta £23.10 Pool: £1384.94 - 44.78 winning units..
Owner Furze Hill Partnership **Bred** Mrs Ann Hogan **Trained** Upper Lambourn, Berks

The Form Book Jumps, Raceform Ltd, Compton, RG20 6NL.

FOCUS
Some decent horses have taken this bumper, most notably Ghizao, but this looked an ordinary event. Steps up from the first two and the third to his mark.
T/Plt: £13.60 to a £1 stake. Pool: £87,226.37 - 4673.43 winning units T/Qpdt: £7.20 to a £1 stake. Pool: £6422.19 - 655.34 winning units TM

1490 - 1492a (Foreign Racing) - See Raceform Interactive

1300 SOUTHWELL (L-H)
Wednesday, September 4

OFFICIAL GOING: Good (7.7)
Wind: light 1/2 against Weather: fine, sunny and very warm

1493 SIS LIVE H'CAP CHASE (16 fncs) 2m 4f 110y
2:10 (2:10) (Class 4) (0-120,120) 4-Y-0+ **£3,768** (£1,106; £553; £276)

Form RPR
322- **1** **Callhimwhatyouwant (IRE)**[16] 1315 8-10-8 **102**.............(b) TomO'Brien 122+
(Dr Richard Newland) *j.lft: led: nt fluent and hdd 2nd: led 5th: drvn clr fr 4 out: eased clsng stages* **11/4**[1]
404- **2** *21* **Points Of View**[49] 1011 8-11-6 **114**.................................(t) JasonMaguire 113
(Kim Bailey) *nt fluent in rr: reminders 3rd: hdwy 11th: wnt modest 2nd sn after 3 out* **5/1**[3]
312/ **3** *10* **Park Lane**[13] 7-11-7 **118**.. JackQuinlan(3) 108
(Noel Quinlan) *hld up in rr: hdwy 10th: chsd wnr next: blnd 3 out: sn wknd* **7/2**[2]
313- **4** *6* **That's The Deal (IRE)**[82] 733 9-10-12 **111**.................... JoeCornwall(5) 96
(John Cornwall) *chsd ldrs: pushed along 9th: outpcd 12th* **7/2**[2]
643- **5** *10* **Manger Hanagment (IRE)**[13] 1352 8-11-2 **115**.......(p) GavinSheehan(5) 91
(Barry Brennan) *led 2nd: hdd 5th: lost pl and blnd 10th: sn bhd* **10/1**
534- **P** **Spock (FR)**[15] 1326 8-11-5 **120**..................................(p) MrsAlexDunn(7)
(Alexandra Dunn) *chsd ldrs: reminders 11th: outpcd next: wknd 4 out: last whn p.u bef 2 out* **6/1**
5m 17.7s (0.70) **Going Correction** -0.05s/f (Good) **6** Ran SP% **111.2**
Speed ratings (Par 105): **96,88,84,81,78**
toteswingers 1&2 £2.80, 1&3 £2.10, 2&3 £6.00 CSF £16.23 TOTE £2.80: £3.00, £2.60; EX 18.60 Trifecta £58.10 Pool: £1198.03 - 15.45 winning units..
Owner Prof D E Newland & R J L Newland **Bred** John McGovern **Trained** Claines, Worcs

FOCUS
Golf Club bend outside and home straight bend inside the lines raced on August 18th. Fences sited 3yds outside the line used that day. A modest yet open handicap run at a fair pace. A big step up from the easy winner and a case for rating the form up to 3lb higher.

1494 32RED NOVICES' CHASE (19 fncs) 3m 110y
2:40 (2:40) (Class 4) 4-Y-0+ **£3,768** (£1,106; £553; £276)

Form RPR
6/1- **1** **According To Trev (IRE)**[17] 1303 7-10-13 0.................(t) RyanHatch(7) 120+
(Nigel Twiston-Davies) *trckd ldr: led 4 out: drvn next: styd on strly run-in* **4/5**[1]
321- **2** *2 1/4* **Brassick**[40] 1119 6-11-6 125...(t) PaulMoloney 118+
(Evan Williams) *trckd ldr: t.k.h: led 14th: hdd 4 out: kpt on same pce between last 2* **6/5**[2]
005/ **3** *12* **Inandover**[296] 2387 8-11-0 0...(t) BrianHughes 100
(John Mackie) *led: hdd 14th: one pce whn hit 3 out* **66/1**
3/4- **4** *56* **Next Exit (IRE)**[76] 779 8-10-9 118.................................. JoeCornwall(5) 44
(John Cornwall) *j.big: chsd ldrs: drvn 10th: outpcd 13th: bhd fr 4 out: sn t.o* **16/1**[3]
/P4- **P** **Billy Teal**[17] 1301 8-11-0 68.. CharliePoste
(C I Ratcliffe) *in rr: mstke 11th: lost pl before 13th: eased and bhd 14th: p.u bef 4 out* **100/1**
6m 35.8s (12.80) **Going Correction** -0.05s/f (Good) **5** Ran SP% **109.4**
Speed ratings (Par 105): **77,76,72,54,**
CSF £2.16 TOTE £1.70: £1.10, £1.10; EX 2.40 Trifecta £11.00 Pool: £2229.99 - 151.71 winning units..
Owner F J Mills & W Mills **Bred** Sean Harrington **Trained** Naunton, Gloucs

FOCUS
This looked a match on the book and the market rivals pulled clear up the straight. The winner was a 140 hurdler and can probably match that over fences.

1495 32RED CASINO H'CAP HURDLE (9 hdls) 2m
3:10 (3:10) (Class 5) (0-100,103) 4-Y-0+ **£1,949** (£572; £286; £143)

Form RPR
11- **1** **Sugar Hiccup (IRE)**[6] 1438 5-12-1 **103** 7ex........................... APMcCoy 111
(Jim Best) *trckd ldrs: led appr 2 out: drvn rt out* **6/4**[1]
36P- **2** *1 1/4* **Hi Tide (IRE)**[43] 1093 9-11-12 **100**..................................... AidanColeman 107
(J R Jenkins) *hld up in rr: hit 5th: trcking ldrs 3 out: cl 2nd appr next: upsides last: no ex clsng stages* **9/1**
/41- **3** *20* **Deny**[8] 1419 5-10-9 **83** 7ex..(p) RichieMcGrath 72
(Henry Hogarth) *hit 3rd: reminders and chsng ldrs 6th: outpcd appr 2 out: tk poor 3rd appr last* **12/1**
/32- **4** *10* **Duchess Theatre (IRE)**[17] 1305 5-11-2 **93**..................(t) JakeGreenall(3) 73
(Michael Easterby) *hdwy to chse ldrs 4th: drvn 3 out: lost pl appr next: lft poor 4th last* **4/1**[2]
552/ **5** *15* **My Oh Mount Brown (IRE)**[413] 988 6-11-7 **95**.......... RichardJohnson 62
(Tim Vaughan) *uns rdr and rn loose in paddock: led to 2nd: chsd ldrs: lost pl appr 2 out: 6th and eased between last 2* **9/2**[3]
665/ **6** *nk* **Sanctuary**[908] 4707 7-10-8 **82**...(t) JasonMaguire 48
(Kim Bailey) *hld up in rr: sme hdwy 6th: sn drvn: lost pl bef 2 out: sn bhd* **9/1**
P00/ **7** *28* **Fairview Sue**[379] 1314 9-10-11 **85**.......................................(t) LiamHeard 26
(Claire Dyson) *chsd ldrs: drvn 6th: lost pl bef next: sn bhd: t.o 2 out* **33/1**
0/0- **8** *3/4* **Hammer**[17] 1306 8-9-9 **74**... EDLinehan(5) 14
(Mike Sowersby) *in rr: bhd and drvn 4th: t.o 3 out* **40/1**
056- **F** **Numen (IRE)**[6] 1443 9-10-11 **90**..............................(b[1]) GavinSheehan(5) 73
(Barry Brennan) *t.k.h: led 2nd: hdd appr 2 out: 4th and wkng whn fell heavily last* **25/1**
3m 54.7s (-2.30) **Going Correction** -0.05s/f (Good) **9** Ran SP% **115.1**
Speed ratings (Par 103): **103,102,92,87,79 79,65,65,**
toteswingers 1&2 £3.60, 1&3 £4.10, 2&3 £5.30 CSF £15.29 CT £119.90 TOTE £2.10: £1.20, £3.00, £2.60; EX 18.20 Trifecta £115.40 Pool: £1282.59 - 8.33 winning units..
Owner Jack Callaghan & Christopher Dillon **Bred** Raysiza Partnership **Trained** Lewes, E Sussex

FOCUS
Plenty of pace on for this handicap with the front two fighting out an exciting finish. Another step forward from the progressive winner but she can rate higher on Flat form. The overall form is solid.

1496 SIMON & EDWINA'S WEDDING DAY NOVICES' HURDLE (9 hdls) 2m
3:40 (3:45) (Class 4) 4-Y-0+ **£3,195** (£992; £534)

Form RPR
233- **1** **Experimentalist**[14] 1337 5-11-5 118..........................(vt[1]) RichardJohnson 110
(Tim Vaughan) *wnt 2nd 4th: hit 3 out: sn drvn: swtchd lft appr 2 out: hung lft: upsides whn lft virtually alone last: heavily eased clsng stages* **2/13**[1]
6/5- **2** *44* **Recway Lass**[17] 1305 5-10-5 0.......................................(p) PaulMoloney 63
(Des Donovan) *led tl after 2nd: drvn 6th: lost pl next: sn bhd: lft 35 l 2nd and j.rt last: eased run-in* **16/1**[3]
U- **3** *34* **Razzle Dazzle 'Em**[9] 1399 4-10-7 0.................................. BenPoste(5) 33
(Shaun Harris) *chsd ldrs: outpcd whn hit 6th: bhd next: t.o 2 out* **100/1**
4- **F** **Exclusive Dancer**[17] 1305 4-10-5 0...................................... BarryKeniry 96
(George Moore) *t.k.h: trckd ldrs: led after 2nd: drvn appr 2 out: reminders between last 2: jnd whn fell last* **7/1**[2]
4m 1.7s (4.70) **Going Correction** -0.05s/f (Good)
WFA 4 from 5yo 11lb **4** Ran SP% **106.0**
Speed ratings (Par 105): **86,64,47,**
CSF £3.40 TOTE £1.10; EX 3.40 Trifecta £10.60 Pool: £1318.68 - 93.11 winning units..
Owner Two Gents & An Orange Bloke Racing **Bred** Pigeon House Stud **Trained** Aberthin, Vale of Glamorgan

FOCUS
What had seemed an uncompetitive contest was run at a steady pace. There was drama at the final flight with Exclusive Dancer falling while upsides the winner, leaving the short-priced favourite clear. The form is rated around the winner and faller.

1497 £32 BONUS AT 32RED.COM MAIDEN HURDLE (13 hdls) 3m 110y
4:10 (4:11) (Class 5) 4-Y-0+ **£1,949** (£572; £286; £143)

Form RPR
/03- **1** **Vinnie The Fish (IRE)**[15] 1330 5-11-0 0................................(t) APMcCoy 121+
(Brendan Powell) *led tl appr 2nd: w ldrs: led 10th: drvn appr 2 out: sn drew clr: 16 l ahd last: eased clsng stages* **9/2**
326- **2** *18* **Electric Tiger (GER)**[31] 1205 6-11-0 106...................... TomScudamore 101
(David Bridgwater) *sn trcking ldrs: chsd wnr briefly appr 2 out: faltered between last 2: kpt on run-in to regain 2nd nr fin: lame* **2/1**[1]
240/ **3** *nk* **Ballymoat**[195] 4349 6-11-0 108.....................................(t) RichardJohnson 101
(Tim Vaughan) *w ldrs: led appr 9th: hdd next: one pce appr 2 out* **5/2**[2]
223- **4** *16* **Kimora (IRE)**[15] 1329 7-10-7 97......................................(t) AidanColeman 80
(Marc Barber) *chsd ldrs: 4th and drvn 3 out: wknd appr next* **10/1**
/56- **P** **Not A Doctor (IRE)**[14] 1339 10-11-0 65.........................(p) ConorO'Farrell
(Polly Gundry) *in rr 3rd: hit 5th: bhd fr 9th: t.o 3 out: p.u bef next* **100/1**
/36- **P** **Radical Bay**[9] 1406 9-10-9 69.. TrevorWhelan(5)
(Nicholas Pomfret) *in rr: hit 6th: drvn 8th: bhd next: t.o 3 out: p.u bef next* **100/1**
P **Not Many Know That (IRE)**[123] 7-11-0 0...................(t) NickScholfield
(Marc Barber) *sn in rr: bhd and reminders 7th: t.o 9th: p.u bef next* **50/1**
P0F- **P** **Larkhall**[8] 1416 6-10-9 0..(t) GavinSheehan(5)
(Mike Sowersby) *trckd ldrs: t.k.h: outpcd 9th: wknd next: bhd after 3 out: t.o 5th whn p.u bef next* **100/1**
12- **P** **Clondaw Hero (IRE)**[9] 1392 5-11-0 0.................................. JasonMaguire
(Donald McCain) *t.k.h: led appr 2nd: reminders 8th: hdd appr next: sn lost pl: bhd 3 out: t.o 6th whn p.u bef 2 out* **7/2**[3]
6m 21.6s (6.60) **Going Correction** -0.05s/f (Good) **9** Ran SP% **116.3**
Speed ratings (Par 103): **87,81,81,76, , , ,**
toteswingers 1&2 £2.20, 1&3 £3.90, 2&3 £2.30 CSF £14.56 TOTE £7.30: £1.50, £1.10, £1.10; EX 16.40 Trifecta £51.20 Pool: £2427.02 - 35.52 winning units..
Owner Mr & Mrs A Mutch & Mr & Mrs J King **Bred** Michael Slattery Jnr **Trained** Upper Lambourn, Berks

FOCUS
A weak maiden hurdle, run at a steady pace. A big step up from the easy winner and a case for rating the form up to 6lb higher through the second and third.

1498 32RED.COM H'CAP HURDLE (13 hdls) 3m 110y
4:40 (4:40) (Class 4) (0-120,118) 4-Y-0+ **£3,119** (£915; £457; £228)

Form RPR
341- **1** **Piper Hill (IRE)**[9] 1388 5-11-7 **113** 7ex........................... RichardJohnson 120+
(Tony Coyle) *chsd ldrs 8th: led after next: drvn appr 2 out: hung lft between last 2: styd on* **6/5**[1]
414- **2** *4* **Compton Blue**[40] 1123 7-11-12 **118**.........................(b) WayneHutchinson 119
(Alan King) *chsd ldrs 8th: chsd wnr 10th: drvn next: kpt on same pce: no imp* **3/1**[2]
415- **3** *69* **Hodgson (IRE)**[52] 960 8-11-6 **112**.................................(tp) JamieMoore 51
(Peter Bowen) *chsd clr ldr: drvn to ld briefly appr 9th: reminders 10th: sn lost pl: t.o 2 out* **10/3**[3]
/P1- **4** *8* **Carmela Maria**[52] 969 8-10-3 **100**...............................(b) EDLinehan(5) 32
(Mike Sowersby) *best away: clr ld to 7th: j.rt: hdd and lost pl appr 9th: sn bhd: t.o 3 out* **11/2**
6m 18.9s (3.90) **Going Correction** -0.05s/f (Good) **4** Ran SP% **108.9**
Speed ratings (Par 105): **91,89,67,65**
CSF £5.18 TOTE £1.70; EX 5.00 Trifecta £8.20 Pool: £1288.00 - 117.67 winning units..
Owner Twenty Four Seven Recruitment **Bred** Kevin Dillon **Trained** Norton, N Yorks

FOCUS
Not a bad contest despite the small field. It was run at a fierce gallop. The winner confirmed the merit of his recent easy win.

1499 32REDPOKER.COM MAIDEN OPEN NATIONAL HUNT FLAT RACE 2m
5:10 (5:10) (Class 6) 4-6-Y-O **£1,559** (£457; £228; £114)

Form RPR
1 **Tara Muck** 6-10-4 0.. RyanHatch(7) 90+
(Nigel Twiston-Davies) *trckd ldrs: 2nd over 5f out: rdn to ld over 1f out: styd on gamely towards fin* **7/2**[3]
2 *1 1/4* **A Tail Of Intrigue (IRE)**[157] 5-11-4 0................................ APMcCoy 94
(Paul W Flynn, Ire) *hld up: hdwy on outside 6f out: 3rd and drvn over 3f out: 2nd 1f out: upsides 100yds out: no ex* **10/3**[2]
6/6- **3** *3 1/4* **Ifonlywecud (IRE)**[108] 389 4-11-4 0................................ BrianHughes 91
(Clive Mulhall) *led: qcknd pce 7f out: hdd over 1f out: kpt on one pce* **14/1**
4 *21* **Vrombel (FR)** 4-11-4 0.. RichieMcLernon 70
(Jonjo O'Neill) *t.k.h: trckd ldrs: outpcd 4f out: modest 4th and hung rt 3f out* **9/1**
0- **5** *7* **Wotsthecatch (IRE)**[37] 1138 5-11-4 0............................ TomScudamore 63
(Michael Scudamore) *chsd ldrs: drvn over 6f out: lost pl over 4f out: sn bhd* **50/1**

2- 6 hd **Eton Dorney (USA)**[22] 1261 4-11-1 0 JackQuinlan(3) 63
(John Ferguson) *hld up in rr: t.k.h: hdwy over 6f out: drvn over 3f out: sn btn* 5/4[1]
7 83 **Lily Marie** 4-10-11 0 TomO'Brien
(Mike Hammond) *chsd ldrs: drvn and lost pl 8f out: sn bhd: t.o 4f out: eventually completed* 14/1
0- P **Rubber Bullet**[113] 284 5-10-11 0 AndrewThornton
(Tim Etherington) *in rr: reminders after 6f: sn lost pl and bhd: t.o whn p.u 9f out: lame* 50/1
3m 58.1s (6.70) **Going Correction** -0.05s/f (Good) **8** Ran SP% **117.0**
Speed ratings: **81,80,78,68,64 64,23,**
toteswingers 1&2 £1.70, 1&3 £11.20, 2&3 £7.00 CSF £16.06 TOTE £4.90: £1.90, £1.40, £4.30; EX 17.10 Trifecta £146.40 Pool: £2293.19 - 11.74 winning units..
Owner N A Twiston-Davies **Bred** N A Twiston-Davies **Trained** Naunton, Gloucs
FOCUS
The pace was steady for this maiden bumper and the time was slow. The form is rated around the third and fifth.
T/Plt: £9.80 to a £1 stake. Pool: £60,913.57 - 4503.42 winning units T/Qpdt: £4.80 to a £1 stake. Pool: £3120.00 - 472.75 winning units WG

1414 SEDGEFIELD (L-H)
Thursday, September 5

OFFICIAL GOING: Good to firm (good in places; 7.3)
Wind: Fresh; behind Weather: Sunny initially, turning cloudy

1500 NETTING SERVICES SUPPORTS MILES FOR MEN NOVICES' HURDLE (PAXTONS HURDLE SERIES QUALIFIER) (10 hdls) 2m 4f
2:20 (2:20) (Class 4) 4-Y-0+ **£3,119** (£915; £457; £228)

Form RPR
33- 1 **Red Eyes**[10] 1399 5-10-2 0 DiarmuidO'Regan(10) 105+
(Chris Grant) *trckd ldr: pckd 3 out: led 2 out: sn rdn: kpt on to go clr* 10/3[3]
344- 2 7 **Cloudy Joker (IRE)**[9] 1418 5-10-12 0 JasonMaguire 99
(Donald McCain) *led: rdn whn hdd 2 out: one pce and sn no ch w wnr* 15/8[2]
216- 3 4 ½ **Mighty Snazy**[19] 1285 9-11-5 110 RichardJohnson 102
(Tim Vaughan) *hld up in tch in 4th: rdn and outpcd after 3 out: wnt modest 3rd after 2 out: plugged on* 5/4[1]
63- 4 1 ½ **Tillernoora (IRE)**[12] 1373 6-10-6 0 ow1 (t) JamesReveley 88
(Patrick Griffin, Ire) *trckd ldr: rdn after 3 out: wknd after 2 out* 28/1
0/ 5 3 ¾ **Eila Wheeler**[20] 943 6-9-12 0 (t) StephenMulqueen(7) 85
(Maurice Barnes) *racd keenly: hld up: awkward 2nd and rdr briefly lost iron: hit 4 out: rdn bef 2 out: sn btn* 100/1
4m 47.9s (-4.80) **Going Correction** -0.40s/f (Good) **5** Ran SP% **106.7**
Speed ratings (Par 105): **93,90,88,87,86**
CSF £9.60 TOTE £5.10: £1.70, £1.20; EX 9.70 Trifecta £18.90 Pool: £994.56 - 39.30 winning units..
Owner Brian Morton & Sara Hattersley **Bred** Roger Charlton And Floors Farming **Trained** Newton Bewley, Co Durham
FOCUS
Hurdles on outside and fresh ground provided on divided bends. A weak event, in which only three of the five could be given an obvious chance. The first two are rated to their marks.

1501 PHOENIX SECURITY JUVENILE MAIDEN HURDLE (PAXTONS HURDLE SERIES QUALIFIER) (8 hdls) 2m 1f
2:50 (2:50) (Class 5) 3-Y-0 **£1,949** (£572; £286; £143)

Form RPR
4- 1 **Aficionado**[10] 1394 3-10-12 0 WilsonRenwick 92+
(Chris Grant) *trckd ldr: led appr 2 out: rdn to assert between last 2 out: drvn out run-in* 13/8[1]
2 5 **Tinctoria**[26] 3-10-5 0 BrianHughes 80
(Kevin Ryan) *trckd ldr: reminders after 2nd: rdn after 3 out: wnt 2nd bef 2 out: plugged on but a hld by wnr* 7/2[3]
3 28 **Joeluke**[9] 3-10-7 0 AdamNicol(5) 62
(Philip Kirby) *led: rdn whn hdd appr 2 out: wknd* 8/1
P- 4 nk **Niknad**[10] 1394 3-9-9 0 GLavery(10) 55
(Brian Ellison) *hld up in tch: rdn after 3 out: sn btn* 6/1
P **Sakhees Romance**[33] 3-10-5 0 RichieMcGrath
(Philip Kirby) *hld up in rr: slow 3rd: a bhd: p.u bef last* 3/1[2]
4m 6.1s (-0.80) **Going Correction** -0.40s/f (Good) **5** Ran SP% **110.7**
Speed ratings (Par 101): **85,82,69,69,**
CSF £7.74 TOTE £2.10: £1.60, £1.80; EX 5.70 Trifecta £29.10 Pool: £1,046.76 - 26.95 winning units..
Owner Straightline Construction Ltd **Bred** Bloomsbury Stud **Trained** Newton Bewley, Co Durham
FOCUS
Weak juvenile form and not one could be confident about.

1502 MB DISTRIBUTION SUPPORTS MILES FOR MEN H'CAP CHASE (17 fncs) 2m 6f
3:25 (3:25) (Class 4) (0-120,115) 4-Y-0+ **£3,768** (£1,106; £553; £276)

Form RPR
054- 1 **Amuse Me**[53] 966 7-11-4 107 APMcCoy 118+
(Jonjo O'Neill) *trckd ldr on inner: led gng wl 2 out: pushed out run-in: comf* 2/1[2]
304- 2 5 **Chicago Outfit (IRE)**[74] 802 8-10-3 92 (p) BrianHughes 94
(John Wade) *trckd ldr: rdn and outpcd in 3rd after 3 out: plugged on to go 2nd appr last: no ch w wnr* 11/2[3]
/11- 3 6 **Five Out Of Five (IRE)**[35] 1172 9-10-5 97 (t) AdamWedge(3) 93
(Evan Williams) *j.w in ld: rdn appr 2 out: hdd 2 out: wknd and lost 2nd appr last* 11/8[1]
/F6- 4 57 **Baltic Pathfinder (IRE)**[10] 1397 9-10-9 103 JonathanEngland(5) 47
(Sue Smith) *hld up: reminders after 8th: lost tch after 11th: t.o* 16/1
354/ 5 ¾ **Apache Blue (IRE)**[369] 1459 9-10-12 108 JohnDawson(7) 52
(John Wade) *hld up: blnd 5 out: sn wknd: t.o* 15/2
5m 14.4s (-18.60) **Going Correction** -0.675s/f (Firm) **5** Ran SP% **108.5**
Speed ratings (Par 105): **106,104,102,81,81**
CSF £12.18 TOTE £2.90: £1.70, £2.00; EX 8.40 Trifecta £26.50 Pool: £1,249.36 - 35.33 winning units..
Owner John P McManus **Bred** Whatton Manor Stud **Trained** Cheltenham, Gloucs
FOCUS
Not a great race for a 0-120, as when Valleyofmilan was declared a non-runner the highest-rated horse left had a mark of just 108. The cosy winner was value for further and is back to the best of his 2012 chase form.

1503 STY ELECTRICAL H'CAP CHASE (13 fncs) 2m 110y
3:55 (3:55) (Class 4) (0-120,119) 4-Y-0+ **£3,768** (£1,106; £553; £276)

Form RPR
522- 1 **Muwalla**[9] 1417 6-10-9 102 (tp) DenisO'Regan 109+
(Chris Grant) *trckd ldr: led 2 out: pushed along to assert between last 2: rdn out run-in* 15/8[1]
265- 2 6 **Sagredo (USA)**[14] 1346 9-11-12 119 (v) APMcCoy 120
(Jonjo O'Neill) *hld up in rr: tk clsr order appr 2 out: rdn to dispute 2nd appr last: lft clr 2nd last: kpt on but no threat wnr* 3/1[3]
2/2- 3 3 ¼ **Candelita**[8] 1426 6-11-3 110 MarkGrant 110
(Jo Hughes) *in tch in 3rd: rdn 2 out: disputing 2nd whn hit last: nt rcvr* 9/4[2]
452- 4 4 ½ **Bay Central (IRE)**[10] 1390 9-11-5 112 (e) PaulMoloney 106
(Evan Williams) *led: hdd 2 out: sn wknd* 13/2
040- F **Maoi Chinn Tire (IRE)**[14] 1042 6-11-6 113 (p) SeanQuinlan
(Jennie Candlish) *hld up: fell 5th* 16/1
4m 1.3s (-7.30) **Going Correction** -0.675s/f (Firm) **5** Ran SP% **109.8**
Speed ratings (Par 105): **90,87,85,83,**
CSF £7.98 TOTE £3.00: £2.10, £1.60; EX 8.30 Trifecta £14.70 Pool: £1,565.10 - 79.38 winning units..
Owner Elliott Brothers And Peacock **Bred** S P Burke **Trained** Newton Bewley, Co Durham
FOCUS
All four that completed had a chance rounding the final bend, suggesting this turned into a sprint. The winner confirmed the merit of his recent C&D run and to a similar level.

1504 JARDINES CATERING H'CAP HURDLE (8 hdls) 2m 1f
4:30 (4:31) (Class 3) (0-130,128) 4-Y-0+ **£5,393** (£1,583; £791; £395)

Form RPR
521- 1 **Mount Vesuvius (IRE)**[7] 1443 5-10-2 104 7ex (t) TomO'Brien 106
(Paul Henderson) *hld up: smooth hdwy 3 out: sn trckd ldng pair: rdn to ld appr last: drvn out run-in* 9/4[1]
143- 2 1 ¼ **Lisbon (IRE)**[36] 1159 5-11-10 126 (t) JamesReveley 127
(Patrick Griffin, Ire) *trckd ldr: led narrowly 3 out: rdn 2 out: hdd appr last: kpt on but a hld run-in* 11/4[2]
0/5- 3 3 ½ **Stormy Weather (FR)**[12] 1378 7-11-0 126 (p) GLavery(10) 124
(Brian Ellison) *in tch: hdwy to dispute ld 3 out: rdn and dropped to 3rd 2 out: plugged on* 7/2[3]
0/3- 4 10 **Agent Archie (USA)**[34] 1185 6-11-12 128 JasonMaguire 117
(Donald McCain) *led: hdd appr 3 out: sn btn* 5/1
5/0- 5 ½ **Indepub**[12] 1378 4-10-10 112 WilsonRenwick 100
(Martin Todhunter) *hld up: pushed along after 4th: a towards rr* 18/1
/00- 6 15 **Hi Dancer**[12] 1378 10-11-6 122 APMcCoy 102
(Ben Haslam) *trckd ldr: wknd 3 out* 10/1
3m 56.3s (-10.60) **Going Correction** -0.40s/f (Good)
WFA 4 from 5yo+ 11lb **6** Ran SP% **110.7**
Speed ratings (Par 107): **108,107,105,101,100 93**
toteswingers 1&2 £1.10, 1&3 £20.10, 2&3 £2.00 CSF £8.82 TOTE £2.70: £1.80, £1.80; EX 8.10 Trifecta £21.20 Pool: £1,367.87 - 48.38 winning units..
Owner The Ray Of Hope Partnership **Bred** Parker's Cove Syndicate **Trained** Whitsbury, Hants
FOCUS
The best race on the card, albeit an ordinary handicap, was run at an even gallop. Another step forward from the winner.

1505 32RED H'CAP CHASE (21 fncs) 3m 3f
5:00 (5:00) (Class 5) (0-100,100) 4-Y-0+ **£2,144** (£629; £314; £157)

Form RPR
063- 1 **Pyjama Game (IRE)**[44] 1088 7-11-12 100 WilsonRenwick 111
(Rose Dobbin) *in tch: reminders 9th: rdn after 13th: chal 4 out: led appr 2 out: styd on* 13/2
332- 2 11 **Solway Dornal**[9] 1416 8-9-7 74 oh2 (tp) StephenMulqueen(7) 76
(Lisa Harrison) *prom: led 7th: rdn whn hdd appr 2 out: no ex* 7/2[3]
51U- 3 8 **Sierra Victor (IRE)**[12] 1377 10-11-9 97 (b) JasonMaguire 93
(Rose Dobbin) *trckd ldr: rdn 4 out: sn btn in 3rd* 9/2
324/ 4 69 **Cilliseal (IRE)**[151] 5206 8-11-4 97 (t) DerekFox(5) 29
(Noel C Kelly, Ire) *hld up in rr: a bhd: t.o* 11/4[2]
/01- P **Douglas**[7] 1437 8-11-6 94 7ex MarkGrant
(Jo Hughes) *led: hdd after mstke 7th: nt fluent next: reminders after 12th: wkng whn anther mstke 14th: sn wl bhd: p.u bef last* 5/2[1]
6m 38.3s (-10.70) **Going Correction** -0.675s/f (Firm) **5** Ran SP% **109.0**
Speed ratings (Par 103): **88,84,82,61,**
CSF £27.67 TOTE £9.30: £3.10, £2.20; EX 18.90 Trifecta £84.70 Pool: £1,049.22 - 9.28 winning units..
Owner Straightline Construction Ltd **Bred** Peter E Clinton **Trained** South Hazelrigg, Northumbria
FOCUS
A moderate staying contest. A big step forward from the winner, with the second to his mark.

1506 INJURED JOCKEYS FUND H'CAP HURDLE (10 hdls) 2m 4f
5:30 (5:30) (Class 5) (0-100,100) 4-Y-0+ **£1,949** (£572; £286; £143)

Form RPR
401- 1 **Ben Cee Pee M (IRE)**[9] 1414 8-11-5 100 (v) CraigGallagher(7) 110+
(Brian Ellison) *in tch: smooth hdwy 3 out: led narrowly on bit 2 out: drvn and kpt on run-in* 5/2[2]
620/ 2 1 ¼ **Quadrato (GER)**[139] 5387 6-11-12 100 (t) RichardJohnson 105
(Tim Vaughan) *trckd ldr: rdn 2 out: ev ch last: kpt on: hld towards fin* 14/1
045- 3 6 **Solo Jugadores**[45] 1072 5-11-4 92 (v[1]) DenisO'Regan 92
(Richard Guest) *in tch: rdn to chse ldng pair after 2 out: one pce* 7/1[3]
140- 4 8 **Executive's Hall (IRE)**[12] 1374 9-11-5 93 (p) APMcCoy 87
(Ben Haslam) *trckd ldr: rdn 3 out: wknd after 2 out* 14/1
00P- 5 2 ¼ **Stand Clear**[37] 1143 8-10-11 90 TonyKelly(5) 81
(David Thompson) *hld up in midfield: rdn after 3 out: nvr threatened ldrs* 28/1
412- 6 nk **Taroum (IRE)**[7] 1442 6-11-6 99 7ex JoshHamer(5) 90
(Tony Carroll) *midfield: rdn after 3 out: wknd 2 out* 9/4[1]
423- 7 7 **Saddlers Mot**[32] 1205 9-11-3 98 (b) JohnDawson(7) 84
(Karen Tutty) *midfield: wknd appr 2 out* 10/1
065- 8 6 **Tim's Approach (IRE)**[12] 1379 8-9-11 74 oh6 (t) JohnKington(3) 53
(William Young Jnr) *hld up: nt fluent 1st: wnt midfield after 3rd: wknd after 3 out* 50/1
U50- 9 1 **Cara Court (IRE)**[103] 471 7-10-12 91 SamanthaDrake(5) 69
(Joanne Foster) *hld up in midfield: wknd after 3 out* 20/1

The Form Book Jumps, Raceform Ltd, Compton, RG20 6NL.

2PP/ **10** *16* **Jewelled Dagger (IRE)**[41] 3927 9-11-6 **94**.....................(b) BrianHarding 58
(Sharon Watt) *led: hdd 2 out: wknd* **40/1**

U/2- **11** *½* **Graceful Descent (FR)**[53] 966 8-11-8 **96**...................(t) DougieCostello 59
(Karen Tutty) *hld up: a towards rr* **16/1**

P/P- **12** *7* **Bennys Well (IRE)**[126] 74 7-9-9 **74** oh4............... JonathanEngland(5) 31
(Sue Smith) *hld up: a towards rr* **16/1**

4m 44.3s (-8.40) **Going Correction** -0.40s/f (Good) **12** Ran SP% **118.6**
Speed ratings (Par 103): **100,99,97,93,93 92,90,87,87,80 80,77**
toteswingers 1&2 £13.90, 1&3 £6.80, 2&3 £8.20 CSF £35.50 CT £223.97 TOTE £2.70: £1.10, £6.70, £3.70; EX 46.80 Trifecta £616.60 Pool: £859.39 - 1.04 winning units..
Owner CPM Group Limited **Bred** Daniel Fogarty **Trained** Norton, N Yorks

FOCUS
Quite a competitive contest for moderate performers run at a sound gallop. The cosy winner built on his recent C&D win.
T/Plt: £100.60 to a £1 stake. Pool: £58,484.91 - 424.01 winning units T/Qpdt: £31.90 to a £1 stake. Pool: £4,123.07 - 95.40 winning units AS

1507 - 1516a (Foreign Racing) - See Raceform Interactive

1439 STRATFORD (L-H)
Saturday, September 7

OFFICIAL GOING: Good to firm (good in places; 9.8)
Wind: Almost nil Weather: Sunny; 17 degrees

1517 LUXURIOUS BOUTIQUE WHITE SWAN HOTEL STRATFORD CONDITIONAL JOCKEYS' (S) H'CAP HURDLE (8 hdls 1 omitted) 2m 3f
2:10 (2:10) (Class 5) (0-95,96) 4-7-Y-O **£1,949** (£572; £286; £143)

Form RPR

523- **1** **On The Feather**[10] 1428 7-11-10 **96**.................................. KieronEdgar(3) 96
(Jim Best) *settled in rr: blnd 2nd: nt fluent 3 out: sn drvn: nt giving rdr much help after: wnt 2nd bef omitted last: fnlly wore down ldr fnl stride* **15/8**[1]

4/4- **2** *shd* **Isola Bella**[9] 1443 4-11-7 **91**... GavinSheehan 89
(Jonathan Portman) *mde most tl 5th and fr 3 out: rdn fr 2 out: had to switch rt to skirt omitted last: kpt on gamely to maintain advantage tl pipped on post* **10/1**

060- **3** *2½* **Nothing Personal**[102] 519 6-9-11 **71**.............................(t) KevinJones(5) 68
(Karen George) *j.rt 1st: settled in rr: mstke 4th: clsd to ld narrowly 5th tl rdn and hit 3 out: drvn and lost 2nd bef last: plodded on* **25/1**

/60- **4** *11* **Bold Tara**[16] 1351 6-10-13 **85**...(p) IanPopham(3) 74
(Martin Keighley) *j.rt: w ldr tl 3rd: in last and drvn next: fnd nil after: struggling 3 out: plugged on into poor 4th bef omitted last* **7/1**

/46- **5** *8* **Bahira (IRE)**[36] 1187 6-10-9 **84**.. NickSlatter(6) 64
(Donald McCain) *prom tl drvn 2 out: lost tch tamely: lost poor 4th bef omitted last* **6/1**[3]

42F/ **U** **Wicklewood**[362] 1536 7-11-0 **83**... JamesBest
(John Flint) *hit 1st: hld up in rr tl uns rdr 4th* **11/2**[2]

P/6- **B** **Millenarys Lady (IRE)**[15] 1364 6-10-13 **82**............................ AdamWedge
(David Rees) *hld up and bhd tl b.d 3rd* **6/1**[3]

450- **F** **Cash Injection**[16] 1351 4-11-10 **94**.................................(t) MichealNolan
(Richard Woollacott) *t.k.h: cl up tl hmpd and fell 3rd* **12/1**

4m 33.9s (2.40) **Going Correction** -0.45s/f (Good) **8** Ran SP% **111.9**
Speed ratings: **76,75,74,70,66 ,,**
toteswingers: 1&2 £4.50, £9.40, £2&3 £7.70. CSF £19.83 CT £342.79 TOTE £2.60: £1.10, £2.10, £7.80; EX 28.60 Trifecta £90.80 Pool: £726.46 - 5.99 winning units..There was no bid for the winner.
Owner Elten Barker & Chris Dillon **Bred** Mrs Jenny Willment **Trained** Lewes, E Sussex

FOCUS
The final flight was bypassed. All bends moved but impact on distances not notified. Not a strong race, even for the level, and it was weakened further with over a circuit to go when Cash Injection fell and brought down Millenarys Lady, while Wicklewood unseated at the fourth.

1518 ZYDA LAW CHARITY CHALLENGE BEGINNERS' CHASE (14 fncs) 2m 4f
2:45 (2:45) (Class 4) 4-Y-0+ **£3,898** (£1,144; £572; £286)

Form RPR

043/ **1** **Jimbill (IRE)**[309] 2159 7-11-6 0.. RichardJohnson 117+
(Tim Vaughan) *nt fluent 5th but often j.w: led fr 3rd and travelled strly: in command bef last: easily* **4/6**[1]

463/ **2** *7* **Another Kate (IRE)**[344] 1662 9-10-13 0...................................... DPFahy 102
(David Richards) *trckd ldng pair: effrt to go 2nd and drawing clr of rest fr 3 out: flattered briefly next: sn rdn: 7 l down and outpcd bef last where nt fluent* **25/1**

6/2- **3** *14* **Foundry Square (IRE)**[14] 1375 7-11-6 0.............(p) SamTwiston-Davies 98
(Nigel Twiston-Davies) *t.k.h: led tl j.v.slowly 3rd: drvn bef 11th: lost 2nd and hit 3 out: sn wknd* **5/2**[2]

F04- **4** *1¾* **Tinelyra (IRE)**[19] 1320 7-11-6 0.. PaddyBrennan 94
(Fergal O'Brien) *t.k.h: hld up off pce in last pair: pushed along bef 11th: nvr nr ldrs: poor 4th 2 out* **20/1**

/54- **5** *21* **Riddlestown (IRE)**[20] 1306 6-11-6 0.................................. HarrySkelton 75
(Caroline Fryer) *last pair: nt a fluent: last and struggling 8th: lost tch and hit 11th: t.o 3 out* **33/1**

3U4- **6** *3¼* **Academy General (IRE)**[25] 1262 7-11-6 120............... TomScudamore 72
(David Bridgwater) *settled in 3rd or 4th: blnd 3rd: hit 7th (water): mstke 8th: rdn and fdd tamely 3 out: t.o and eased bef last* **7/1**[3]

4m 40.9s (-9.10) **Going Correction** -0.275s/f (Good) **6** Ran SP% **112.6**
Speed ratings (Par 105): **107,104,98,97,89 88**
toteswingers: 1&2 £5.20, 1&3 £1.10, 2&3 £7.10. CSF £17.67 TOTE £1.60: £1.30, £3.30; EX 21.60 Trifecta £33.30 Pool: £739.17 - 16.63 winning units..
Owner M E Moore & B Ead **Bred** Mrs Marion Condren **Trained** Aberthin, Vale of Glamorgan

FOCUS
Apart from the winner, who can rate higher, it's best to presume this is modest form until proven otherwise.

1519 D.W. CLARK DRAINAGE NOVICES' HURDLE (7 hdls 1 omitted) 2m 110y
3:20 (3:20) (Class 4) 4-Y-0+ **£3,249** (£954; £477; £238)

Form RPR

6/ **1** **Jonnie Skull (IRE)**[4] 988 7-10-9 0...............................(t) JackQuinlan(3) 115+
(Phil McEntee) *tore off in front w only two others ever able to keep up: occasionally j.rt: forged rt away fr 2 out: 40 l ahd last: v game* **12/1**

0P/ **2** *42* **Lordship (IRE)**[32] 2216 9-10-12 0.. FelixDeGiles 75
(Tom Gretton) *settled wl off pce: no ch fr 5th: began to pick up faders fr bef 2 out: wnt 40 l 2nd bef last* **50/1**

3 *14* **Iguacu**[25] 9-10-12 0...(p) RichardJohnson 62
(Richard Price) *hld up wl off pce: wnt poor 3rd bef 3 out: tk 10 l 2nd and rdn bef next: rapidly lost tch w wnr and lost remote 2nd bef last* **10/1**[3]

244- **4** *7* **Lady Lectra**[61] 920 4-10-5 103.. DPFahy 50
(John Flint) *hit 3rd: 15 l 4th whn hit 4th: t.o after mstke 2 out: veered lft bef line and collapsed after fin: fatally injured* **5/2**[2]

0/2- **5** *2¾* **Castle Beach (IRE)**[10] 1431 4-10-12 115.............................(p) APMcCoy 55
(Rebecca Curtis) *pressed ldr at furious pce tl drvn and stopped to nil bef 2 out where blnd bdly: t.o bef last* **8/11**[1]

0/0- **6** *13* **No Ifs No Buts**[19] 1317 4-10-5 0.................................... TomScudamore 34
(David Bridgwater) *j. bdly: nvr gng pce of ldng trio: t.o after 5th* **16/1**

4/3- **7** *hd* **Midnight Thomas**[106] 458 4-10-2 0...............................[1] OllieGarner(10) 41
(Martin Keighley) *mounted on crse: last and struggling whn mstke 2nd: j. slowly 3rd: t.o fr 5th* **14/1**

0- **P** **Sun Dream**[25] 1265 6-10-5 0.. MarkGrant
(Geoffrey Deacon) *sweating profusely and taken down early: plld hrd early but nvr nr ldng trio: mod 5th whn mstke 2nd: hit 4th and lost tch: t.o last next: p.u bef omitted 3 out* **66/1**

P- **P** **Fushicho**[17] 1200 4-10-12 0... WillKennedy
(Brendan Powell) *taken down early: j. bdly in 2nd or 3rd and clr of rest tl mstke 5th and rdn: sn t.o: p.u 2 out* **33/1**

3m 47.6s (-8.40) **Going Correction** -0.45s/f (Good) **9** Ran SP% **122.2**
Speed ratings (Par 105): **101,81,74,71,70 63,63, ,**
toteswingers: 1&2 not won, 1&3 £3.30, 2&3 £6.20. CSF £402.71 TOTE £8.90: £2.20, £10.00, £2.50; EX 388.10 Trifecta £714.70 Part won. Pool of £953.00 - 0.01 winning units..
Owner Eventmaker Racehorses **Bred** Canice Farrell Jnr **Trained** Newmarket, Suffolk

FOCUS
The third-last was omitted. Only one horse mattered throughout and the winner can score again over hurdle. There's a case for rating the race a lot higher.

1520 CHARLIELONGSDONRACING.COM H'CAP HURDLE (8 hdls) 2m 110y
3:55 (3:55) (Class 2) (0-150,140) 4-Y-0+
£9,384 (£2,772; £1,386; £693; £346; £174)

Form RPR

661- **1** **Laudatory**[25] 1258 7-10-7 **126**....................................... NicodeBoinville(5) 135+
(Nicky Henderson) *mde all: racd enthusiastically: dived at 5th: stdy pce tl qcknd clr after 2 out: 8 l ahd last: pushed out* **11/4**[1]

0/6- **2** *9* **Hawkhill (IRE)**[21] 1290 7-11-0 **128**...............................(t) RichardJohnson 129
(Tim Vaughan) *chsd ldrs: prom fr 4th: wnt 2nd bef 2 out: sn outpcd by wnr: 3rd whn hit last but lft modest 2nd after blunder of rival* **11/1**

6/5- **3** *1¼* **Zarzal (IRE)**[49] 1046 5-10-11 **128**..................................... AdamWedge(3) 129
(Evan Williams) *settled in midfield: blnd 2nd: wnt 3rd and hit 2 out: sn rdn: tk 2nd bef home turn tl pckd last: wl hld 3rd after* **9/2**[2]

121/ **4** *nk* **Ahyaknowyerself (IRE)**[317] 2004 7-11-0 **128**......... SamTwiston-Davies 127
(Dr Richard Newland) *chsd ldrs 5th: drvn and bdly outpcd after 2 out: rallied and styd on stoutly after last: nrly snatched 3rd* **5/1**[3]

221/ **5** *6* **Alfraamsey**[9] 1754 5-10-11 **125**...................................... MarcGoldstein 119
(Sheena West) *hit 1st and 3rd: cl up: j. slowly 5th and rdn: wknd fr 2 out* **7/1**

2/0- **6** *1¾* **Dontpaytheferryman (USA)**[69] 850 8-10-3 **122**....... RobertWilliams(5) 114
(John Price) *pressed ldr tl drvn and lost pl fr 3 out* **12/1**

2F0- **7** *3¼* **Cry Of Freedom (USA)**[74] 831 7-11-5 **133**..................(p) DenisO'Regan 122
(John Ferguson) *taken wd early: towards rr whn blnd 3rd: rdn after 5th: no rspnse and sn wl btn* **12/1**

20U/ **8** *13* **Escort'men (FR)**[136] 5510 7-10-3 **117**...............................(t) PaulMoloney 94
(Anthony Middleton) *tk hold and j. modly in last pair: lost tch tamely fr 3 out* **14/1**

51P/ **P** **First Avenue**[38] 4772 8-11-12 **140**.. APMcCoy
(Laura Mongan) *hld up in last pair: lost tch qckly bef 3 out: p.u next* **8/1**

3m 43.8s (-12.20) **Going Correction** -0.45s/f (Good) **9** Ran SP% **115.5**
Speed ratings (Par 109): **110,105,105,105,102 101,99,93,**
toteswingers: 1&2 £3.90, 1&3 £2.90, 2&3 £6.70. CSF £32.57 CT £132.63 TOTE £3.40: £1.70, £3.30, £1.60; EX 32.10 Trifecta £264.50 Part won. Pool of £352.74 - 0.87 winning units..
Owner E R Newnham **Bred** Whitsbury Manor Stud & Pigeon House Stud **Trained** Upper Lambourn, Berks

FOCUS
A useful event on the figures but a few of these had a bit to prove. The time was good and the form is solid enough, if modest for the class.

1521 H.L. BARNES H'CAP CHASE (17 fncs) 2m 7f
4:30 (4:30) (Class 3) (0-125,122) 4-Y-0+ **£6,330** (£1,870; £935; £468)

Form RPR

121- **1** **Fairwood Massini (IRE)**[15] 1361 8-11-2 **115**............(vt) MichaelByrne(3) 121+
(Tim Vaughan) *settled in last pair: nt fluent 6th: hit 12th: qcknd to ld 14th: 5 l clr 2 out tl drvn and nt fluent last: idling bdly flat and kpt rt up to work* **11/8**[1]

413- **2** *2¼* **Henry San (IRE)**[20] 1302 6-11-12 **122**......................(v) WayneHutchinson 125+
(Alan King) *settled in last pair: reminder 11th: wnt 2nd and blnd 3 out: drvn and no real imp after: 5 l bhd at last: kpt on u.p but flattered by proximity to idling wnr* **5/2**[2]

4/6- **3** *17* **Rhum (FR)**[16] 1346 8-11-9 **119**..............................(v) SamTwiston-Davies 106
(Nigel Twiston-Davies) *tended to jump and drift rt: led tl j.rt 5th: pressed ldr tl led 13th tl drvn and hdd and hit 14th: fnd little after: lost tch qckly fr 2 out* **9/2**

263- **4** *58* **Tiermore (IRE)**[9] 1444 9-10-12 **108**............................(tp) DonalDevereux 40
(Peter Bowen) *nt fluent 1st and 2nd: lft in ld 5th: hit 10th (water): hdd 13th and dropped out v rapidly fr 3 out: bdly t.o* **4/1**[3]

5m 28.3s (-10.90) **Going Correction** -0.275s/f (Good) **4** Ran SP% **108.9**
Speed ratings (Par 107): **107,106,100,80**
CSF £5.25 TOTE £2.40; EX 3.30 Trifecta £7.10 Pool: £320.18 - 33.47 winning units..
Owner Wayne Jones **Bred** T Kent **Trained** Aberthin, Vale of Glamorgan

FOCUS
Only four runners, but it had appeared competitive contest. Straightforward form.

1522 KEOGH AND HOWS H'CAP CHASE (FOR THE KEOGH AND HOWS CHALLENGE TROPHY) (12 fncs) 2m 1f 110y
5:05 (5:05) (Class 4) (0-115,115) 4-Y-0+ **£3,898** (£1,144; £572; £286)

Form RPR

453- **1** **Giant O Murchu (IRE)**[9] 1441 9-11-3 **106**.....................(p) AidanColeman 116+
(Lawney Hill) *trckd ldrs gng wl: 3rd 2 out: produced to ld between last two: sn 6 l clr: pushed out: readily* **7/2**[3]

211- **2** *7* **Bennys Quest (IRE)**[11] 1417 10-11-9 **115**..................(p) PeterCarberry(3) 118
(Neil Mulholland) *trckd ldrs: 4th whn blnd 8th: nvr really rcvrd: rdn whn hit 3 out: drvn into 2nd bef last: no imp on wnr after* **5/2**[2]

214- **3** *1½* **Synthe Davis (FR)**[59] 943 8-11-11 **114**.. APMcCoy 117
(Laura Mongan) *mstke 1st: j. slowly 2nd: led 3rd and t.k.h: urged bef 2 out: drvn and hdd between last two: easily brushed aside by wnr and lost 2nd bef last* **2/1**[1]

345- **4** *2 1/4* **Tri Nations (UAE)**[9] 1441 8-10-8 **97**....................(vt) PaulMoloney 97
(Anthony Middleton) *hld up in last: mstke 2nd: nt fluent 8th: 6 l last 2 out: rdn and no rspnse after: plugged on flat* **9/1**

2PU- **5** *8* **Try Catch Me (IRE)**[9] 1435 8-10-10 **99**.................... LeightonAspell 93
(Alison Batchelor) *led tl 3rd: pressed ldr: rdn 3 out: drvn and lost 2nd after next: sn dropped out* **11/2**

4m 10.1s (3.00) **Going Correction** -0.275s/f (Good) **5** Ran SP% **109.5**
Speed ratings (Par 105): **82,78,78,77,73**
CSF £12.65 TOTE £3.90: £1.50, £2.00; EX 14.60 Trifecta £30.90 Pool: £630.55 - 15.30 winning units..
Owner Diana Clark & Alan Hill **Bred** P D Hickey **Trained** Aston Rowant, Oxon

FOCUS
Not a strong contest by any means. The winner was well in on last year's C&D win, and is rated below that level here.

1523 BORDEAUX UNDISCOVERED SUPPORTING OWNERS AND TRAINERS STANDARD OPEN NATIONAL HUNT FLAT RACE 2m 110y

5:40 (5:40) (Class 6) 4-6-Y-O **£1,949** (£572; £286; £143)

Form				RPR
	1		**Garnock (IRE)** 5-10-0 0.................... JakeHodson(7)	91+
			(David Bridgwater) *hld up: outpcd and pushed along over 2f out: swtchd rt and rallied 1f out: urged past ldng pair nr fin* **14/1**	
	2	*1 1/4*	**In A Heartbeat** 4-10-7 0.................... IanPopham	90
			(Martin Keighley) *hld up: effrt to dispute 2nd 5f out: ev ch but drvn whn ducked lft bhd ldr 1f out: sn stened to have ev ch tl no ex fnl 50yds* **13/2**	
20/	**3**	*3/4*	**Keppel Isle (IRE)**[234] 3683 4-11-0 0.................... TomCannon	96
			(Laura Mongan) *gifted 7 l ld at s: set modest pce: pressed 2f out: hrd drvn over 1f out: ct fnl 50yds* **5/1**	
03-	**4**	*2*	**Wave The Grapes**[9] 1445 6-10-7 0....................(t) DonalDevereux	87
			(Peter Bowen) *hld up in last: effrt 4f out: sn pushed along: on heels of ldrs over 1f out: one pce after* **9/4**[1]	
	5	*3*	**Master Dennis** 4-11-0 0.................... HarrySkelton	91
			(Dan Skelton) *chsd ldrs: drvn and racd awkwardly fr 3f out: no imp fnl 2f: v green* **7/2**[2]	
	6	*27*	**Alfies Gift** 4-10-4 0.................... RobertDunne(3)	57
			(Dai Burchell) *chsd ldrs: dropped to rr 4f out: t.o fnl 2f* **14/1**	
/6-	**7**	*6*	**Bollin Across**[19] 1317 5-10-7 0.................... PaulMoloney	51
			(Andrew Hollinshead) *plld hrd: wnt 2nd bhd clr ldr after 2f: rdn and lost pl tamely 5f out: virtually p.u over 1f out: t.o* **9/2**[3]	
	P		**Gabbys Star** 6-10-7 0.................... DavidEngland	
			(Shaun Lycett) *t.k.h: prom for 6f: dropped bk last and cocked jaw ent bk st: immediately p.u* **20/1**	

3m 50.0s (-0.40) **Going Correction** -0.45s/f (Good) **8** Ran SP% **119.3**
Speed ratings: **82,81,81,80,78 66,63,**
toteswingers: 1&2 £11.70, 1&3 £11.70, 2&3 not won CSF £105.08 TOTE £21.00: £3.20, £2.50, £2.10; EX 143.20 Trifecta £425.00 Part won. Pool of £566.69 - 0.13 winning units..
Owner Mrs Margaret Turner **Bred** Mrs M Turner, C White & G M McCourt **Trained** Icomb, Gloucs

FOCUS
This was steadily run and the form is modest.
T/Plt: £382.50 to a £1 stake. Pool of £54,928.72 - 104.82 winning tickets. T/Qpdt: £189.70 to a £1 stake. Pool of £3,359.30 - 13.10 winning tickets. IM

1432 FONTWELL (L-H)

Sunday, September 8

OFFICIAL GOING: Good (7.0) changing to good to soft after race 4 (3.45)
Wind: Breezy Weather: Overcast & damp; light rain; 15 degrees

1524 BUTLINS BOGNOR REGIS DAYS OUT JUVENILE HURDLE (9 hdls) 2m 2f 110y

2:10 (2:11) (Class 4) 3-Y-O **£3,573** (£1,049; £524; £262)

Form				RPR
4-	**1**		**Wooly Bully**[10] 1439 3-10-12 0.................... WayneHutchinson	97
			(Alan King) *pressed ldrs: 4 l 3rd and rdn and sltly outpcd home turn: drvn to ld and hit last: edgd clr* **9/2**[2]	
	2	*2*	**Alanjou (FR)**[41] 3-10-12 0.................... TomO'Brien	96
			(Jamie Snowden) *j.w: led: rdn whn wnt rt and sprawled bdly 2 out: sn hanging lft: hdd last: nt qckn flat: promising* **2/1**[1]	
1-	**3**	*7*	**Baltic Blade (IRE)**[18] 1335 3-11-2 0.................... JoshuaMoore(3)	97
			(Gary Moore) *t.k.h: pressed ldr: hit 5th: drvn bef 2 out: wknd appr last* **2/1**[1]	
	4	*9*	**Down Time (USA)**[100] 3-10-12 0....................(t) AndrewJMcNamara	80
			(John Joseph Hanlon, Ire) *midfield: rdn 3 out: sn outpcd and 15 l 5th on home turn* **5/1**[3]	
	5	*31*	**Fiachra (IRE)** 3-10-12 0.................... DavidBass	52
			(Natalie Lloyd-Beavis) *unruly at s: bhd: mstke 3rd: hdwy to midfield whn mstke 6th: drvn and lost tch bef next: t.o bef 2 out* **80/1**	
5U-	**6**	*40*	**Ruff Luck**[10] 1439 3-9-12 0.................... KevinJones(7)	9
			(Seamus Mullins) *nt a fluent: cl up tl lost pl and mstke 6th: t.o after next* **33/1**	
	7	*12*	**Dude Alert (IRE)**[82] 3-10-9 0.................... AdamWedge(3)	
			(Anna Newton-Smith) *j.lft 1st: in rr whn j. bdly lft 3rd: drvn and nvr travelling in last pair after: lost tch 6th: hopelessly t.o 3 out* **25/1**	
3-	**P**		**Castell Avon**[8] 1473 3-9-12 0.................... MrFTett(7)	
			(Milton Bradley) *towards rr whn blnd 4th and drvn: nvr travelling after: hopelessly t.o 3 out: p.u last* **100/1**	
	F		**Ron Waverly (IRE)** 3-10-2 0.................... PaddyBradley(10)	78
			(Pat Phelan) *chsd ldrs: rdn 3 out: 4th and outpcd home turn: disputing 17 l 4th whn fell heavily last: winded* **50/1**	

4m 31.7s (-2.60) **Going Correction** -0.10s/f (Good) **9** Ran SP% **112.5**
Speed ratings (Par 103): **101,100,97,93,80 63,58,,**
toteswingers 1&2 £2.10, 1&3 £2.10, 2&3 £1.80 CSF £13.62 TOTE £5.10: £1.40, £1.20, £1.10; EX 14.60 Trifecta £30.70 Pool: £1,441.69 - 35.14 winning units..
Owner W A Harrison-Allan **Bred** W A Harrison-Allan **Trained** Barbury Castle, Wilts

FOCUS
Rail movement added 48yds per circuit to chases and 33yds per circuit to Hurdles. Fences at full width, hurdles middle to inner. Modest juvenile form, and the first few finished really tired. A step up from the winner.

1525 HAPPY FIFTIETH BIRTHDAY KATE LIVERMORE NOVICES' HURDLE (8 hdls 1 omitted) 2m 2f 110y

2:40 (2:41) (Class 4) 4-Y-O+ **£3,573** (£1,049; £524; £262)

Form				RPR
123-	**1**		**Orthodox Lad**[13] 1400 5-10-12 111.................... ChristopherWard(7)	114+
			(Dr Richard Newland) *mounted outside paddock: plld hrd: a gng strly: 15 l 3rd after 2nd: lft 2nd at next: clr w one rival bef 3 out: led bef next: drew rt away appr last* **1/3**[1]	
F2-	**2**	*38*	**Sir Dylan**[55] 994 4-10-6 0.................... CharlieWallis(5)	68
			(Ronald Harris) *t.k.h: wnt 2nd bef 4th where mstke and hmpd by unseater but lft in ld: bdly hmpd by loose horse after 5th: rdn and hdd bef 2 out: immediately outpcd: tired and 25 l 2nd whn unbalanced at last: hung rt flat* **8/1**[2]	
0-	**3**	*49*	**Unsist (FR)**[24] 1270 5-10-12 0.................... DominicElsworth	20
			(Nick Gifford) *j. v erratically: chsd ldrs tl blnd 4th and rdr lost iron: struggling after mstke 6th: 15 l 3rd home turn: hopelessly t.o whn j.rt last* **20/1**	
0-	**4**	*78*	**My Son Harry (IRE)**[111] 412 5-10-12 0.................... JackDoyle	
			(Victor Dartnall) *taken down early: nt fluent 1st: detached last early: mstke 5th: blnd 6th: sn hopelessly t.o: blnd 2 out* **8/1**[2]	
	P		**Courageous (IRE)**[2] 7-10-5 0.................... MrFTett(7)	
			(Milton Bradley) *plld v hrd early: mstke 3rd: chsd ldr tl bef 4th: stopped to nil after 5th: t.o whn p.u 2 out* **66/1**	
	U		**Kilcolman Wizard (IRE)**[98] 7-10-12 0.................... DPFahy	
			(Liam Corcoran) *kpt jumping rt: led tl j.rt 4th and uns rdr* **50/1**	
6P0-	**U**		**The Kings Assassin (IRE)**[24] 1270 5-10-12 0.................... TomCannon	
			(Chris Gordon) *j.rt and uns rdr 1st* **14/1**[3]	

4m 35.9s (1.60) **Going Correction** +0.20s/f (Yiel)
WFA 4 from 5yo+ 11lb **7** Ran SP% **112.1**
Speed ratings (Par 105): **104,88,67,34, ,**
toteswingers 1&2 £1.70, 1&3 £2.90, 2&3 £5.10 CSF £3.58 TOTE £1.20: £1.10, £2.20; EX 3.60 Trifecta £18.30 Pool: £1,862.96 - 76.24 winning units..
Owner Peter Green **Bred** S Nunn **Trained** Claines, Worcs

FOCUS
The third-last hurdle was omitted due to damage. The Kings Assassin unseated at the first, while Kilcolman Wizard and Courageous went clear early before being caught. The facile winner is given a token rating in this weak race.

1526 DEREK & COLLEEN COLLINS GOLDEN WEDDING ANNIVERSARY H'CAP CHASE (16 fncs) 2m 6f

3:10 (3:10) (Class 4) (0-110,108) 4-Y-O+ **£4,223** (£1,240; £620; £310)

Form				RPR
004-	**1**		**Nothingbutthetruth (IRE)**[10] 1437 9-10-3 **85**....................(tp) TomScudamore	90+
			(Richard Woollacott) *trckd ldrs: prom fr 7th: wnt clr 2nd at 9th: hit 12th: led bef 3 out: rdn and doing nthing in front fr 2 out: 5 l clr last: jst lasted* **6/1**	
5/5-	**2**	*nse*	**Chasers Chance (IRE)**[119] 238 10-11-7 **103**.................... TomO'Brien	106
			(Paul Henderson) *off bridle fr 2nd: drvn in 10 l last after 4th: j. slowly 7th: hdwy u.p after 13th to go 8 l 3rd 2 out: mde 6 l fr last and almost pipped idling wnr* **8/1**	
P13-	**3**	*3 1/2*	**Doctor Ric (IRE)**[10] 1434 8-10-11 **93**....................(b) JamieMoore	92
			(Gerry Enright) *sn 2nd: led 8th tl drvn and hdd bef 3 out: plugged on and wl hld after: lost 2nd after last* **4/1**[2]	
524-	**4**	*2 1/2*	**Brough Academy (IRE)**[20] 1316 7-11-11 **107**....................(p) AidanColeman	104
			(Lawney Hill) *led tl after 1st: mstke 6th: dropped towards rr and u.p 8th: hit 12th: remote 5th 3 out: plugging on after last* **3/1**[1]	
212-	**5**	*8*	**Duneen Point (IRE)**[19] 1327 9-11-9 **108**.................... MichaelByrne(3)	98
			(Tim Vaughan) *mstke 2nd and drvn: j. modly and nvr travelling: chsd ldrs tl hit 12th: 10 l 3rd and struggling next: plodded on* **11/2**[3]	
323-	**6**	*20*	**Baizically (IRE)**[19] 1327 10-11-7 **103**....................(b) AndrewJMcNamara	74
			(John Joseph Hanlon, Ire) *led after 1st: set stdy pce: hdd 8th: blnd next: sn lost interest: hit 12th: remote last bef 3 out* **8/1**	
222-	**P**		**Upton Mead (IRE)**[102] 542 6-11-1 **97**.................... TomCannon	
			(Kevin Tork) *towards rr: off bridle and reminders several stages: struggling u.p after 10th: t.o and p.u 13th* **13/2**	

5m 52.1s (9.10) **Going Correction** +0.525s/f (Soft) **7** Ran SP% **110.2**
Speed ratings (Par 105): **104,103,102,101,98 91,**
toteswingers 1&2 £5.10, 1&3 £4.80, 2&3 £6.70 CSF £46.26 TOTE £9.30: £3.10, £4.30; EX 54.10 Trifecta £304.80 Pool: £1,154.67 - 2.84 winning units..
Owner J Pike & G Pike **Bred** P A Byrne **Trained** South Molton, Devon
■ Stewards' Enquiry : Tom O'Brien two-day ban: used whip above permitted level (Sep 22,24)

FOCUS
A modest handicap. The idling winner din't need to be at his best.

1527 32RED CASINO H'CAP HURDLE (10 hdls) 2m 4f

3:45 (3:45) (Class 3) (0-125,120) 4-Y-O+ **£6,498** (£1,908; £954; £477)

Form				RPR
224-	**1**		**Chilworth Screamer**[20] 1321 5-10-11 **105**.................... TomCannon	106
			(Chris Gordon) *pressed ldr fr 3rd: flattened 3 out: led next: maintained narrow advantage: hung on gamely u.p cl home* **7/2**[2]	
131-	**2**	*1/2*	**Della Sun (FR)**[17] 1345 7-11-3 **118**.................... JoshWall(7)	119
			(Arthur Whitehead) *last but cl up whn pushed along after 4th: effrt after 3 out: 4 l 4th and briefly outpcd whn mstke 2 out: hrd drvn and rallied and nt fluent last: tried valiantly flat: jst hld cl home* **4/1**[3]	
061-	**3**	*2*	**Guards Chapel**[9] 1273 5-11-9 **120**....................(v) JoshuaMoore(3)	119
			(Gary Moore) *settled in rr of bunch: wnt 3rd 3 out: rdn fr next: tl ev ch last: outbattled fnl 100yds* **6/1**	
/03-	**4**	*11*	**The Tracey Shuffle**[22] 1289 7-11-11 **119**.................... TomScudamore	110
			(David Pipe) *racd keenly in ld: rdn and hdd 2 out: fdd bef last* **5/2**[1]	
/22-	**5**	*31*	**Representingceltic (IRE)**[109] 426 8-11-2 **110**.................... ColinBolger	81
			(Pat Phelan) *settled handy: mstke 5th: cl 4th but hrd drvn home turn: fdd bdly after 2 out: tired whn j. violently lft last* **9/2**	
213/	**P**		**Don't Stop Me Now (IRE)**[16] 1370 8-11-0 **108**....(b) AndrewJMcNamara	
			(John Joseph Hanlon, Ire) *cl up tl p.u qckly after 6th: dismntd: lame* **20/1**	
2/6-	**P**		**Prophete De Guye (FR)**[115] 334 10-11-4 **112**.................... FelixDeGiles	
			(James Evans) *racd wd and t.k.h towards rr: bmpd along and lost tch bef 7th: sn lost action: bdly t.o and p.u 2 out: removed by horse ambulance* **16/1**	

5m 0.4s (1.00) **Going Correction** +0.20s/f (Yiel) **7** Ran SP% **113.9**
Speed ratings (Par 107): **106,105,105,100,88 ,**
toteswingers 1&2 £3.30, 1&3 £4.00, 2&3 £5.40 CSF £17.95 CT £79.76 TOTE £3.90: £2.50, £3.00; EX 19.40 Trifecta £99.90 Pool: £1,384.37 - 10.39 winning units..

Owner 7Rus **Bred** Norman Court Stud **Trained** Morestead, Hants
FOCUS
They mainly raced in a bunch for much of this contest until the tempo increased on the final circuit. Straightforward form.

1528 32RED.COM H'CAP CHASE (19 fncs) 3m 2f 110y
4:15 (4:15) (Class 4) (0-105,93) 4-Y-0+ **£4,223** (£1,240; £620; £310)

Form RPR
045- 1 **Joe The Rogue (IRE)**24 1272 6-11-4 **85** NickScholfield 106+
(Paul Henderson) *nt a fluent: bhd tl wnt 3rd at 12th: 2nd next: mstke 15th: gng best after: led 2 out: 12 l ahd whn mstke last: heavily eased fnl f* **11/4**3
402- 2 *19* **Golden Squirell (IRE)**18 1338 6-10-9 **76** (v1) TomCannon 76
(Brendan Powell) *led: mstke 9th: 5 l ld and gng clr w wnr whn pckd 16th: sn drvn and looking reluctant: hdd 2 out and immediately btn* **9/4**2
632- 3 *16* **Princely Hero (IRE)**10 1437 9-11-12 **93** (v) APMcCoy 78
(Chris Gordon) *on and off bridle: nvr travelling: mstke 8th: 2nd tl nt fluent 13th: tried to pull himself up u.p bef next and continued a remote 3rd: blnd 16th* **7/4**1
P5P- 4 *68* **Shock N Freaney (IRE)**10 1440 6-10-8 **85** (vt) MarkMarris(10) 8
(Anthony Middleton) *mstkes: in last pair and nvr gng wl: drvn 11th: struggling 13th: blnd 16th: continued hopelessly t.o: fnlly walked past post* **16/1**
4/5- P **Watergate (IRE)**102 542 7-11-6 **87** LeightonAspell
(Richard Rowe) *chsd ldng pair tl 12th: last fr next: hopelessly t.o whn p.u 3 out* **10/1**
7m 15.0s (13.90) **Going Correction** +0.525s/f (Soft) **5 Ran SP% 108.8**
Speed ratings (Par 105): **100,94,89,69,**
CSF £9.34 TOTE £2.90: £2.40, £1.60; EX 9.10 Trifecta £18.50 Pool: £1,950.48 - 79.01 winning units..
Owner Antell, Coles & Finch **Bred** Patrick Gibbons **Trained** Whitsbury, Hants
FOCUS
Really moderate fare. There's a case for rating the form up to 5lb higher through the second.

1529 £32 FREE AT 32RED.COM MARES' H'CAP HURDLE (THE SUNDAY £5K BONUS RACE) (11 hdls) 2m 6f 110y
4:50 (4:50) (Class 4) (0-115,110) 4-Y-0+ **£3,573** (£1,049; £524; £262)

Form RPR
262- 1 **Cannon Fodder**10 1436 6-11-4 **102** MarcGoldstein 104
(Sheena West) *sn pressing ldr: nt fluent 8th: drvn to ld on home turn: kpt finding more after and styd on gamely flat: all out* **6/1**3
221- 2 *1 3/4* **Me And Ben (IRE)**15 1373 6-11-1 **99** (t) PaddyBrennan 100
(Fergal O'Brien) *settled midfield: nt fluent 8th: effrt on outer after 3 out: sn rdn to chse wnr: swtchd lft nring last where ev ch: kpt on but no imp fnl 100yds* **5/2**1
312- 3 *1 1/4* **Emerald Rose**62 922 6-11-12 **110** SamTwiston-Davies 111
(Julian Smith) *settled in 3rd or 4th: ev ch home turn: sn rdn: nt qckn appr last* **8/1**
/14- 4 *nk* **Sapphire Rouge (IRE)**18 1340 7-10-6 **97** (p) KevinJones(7) 96
(Seamus Mullins) *led: nt fluent 6th and reminders: kpt up to work after: hdd u.p bef 2 out: sn outpcd: rallied and styng on wl after last* **9/1**
2/ 5 *3/4* **Coosan Belle (IRE)**8 1482 7-11-1 **99** AndrewJMcNamara 97
(John Joseph Hanlon, Ire) *settled last pair: effrt after 3 out: 6 l 6th home turn: drvn and kpt on same pce after* **10/1**
UF1- 6 *3* **Lucys Girl (IRE)**10 1432 6-10-10 **94** TomO'Brien 89
(Jamie Snowden) *hld up in last pair: effrt 3 out: rdn and on heels of ldrs home turn: nt qckn bef last* **6/1**3
2- 7 *62* **Presenting Ruby (IRE)**26 1265 8-11-2 **100** DougieCostello 40
(Neil Mulholland) *chsd ldrs: j. slowly 4th: rdn 7th: wknd next: wl t.o bef 2 out* **5/1**2
52F- P **Old Dreams (IRE)**24 1272 7-11-2 **100** (t) TomCannon
(Nick Gifford) *j.lft 3rd: pushed along after 6th: chsd ldrs tl stmbld bdly and nrly uns rdr after 7th: rdr lost iron and p.u* **12/1**
5m 44.1s (1.60) **Going Correction** +0.20s/f (Yiel)
WFA 4 from 6yo+ 12lb **8 Ran SP% 111.7**
Speed ratings (Par 105): **105,104,103,103,103 102,80,**
toteswingers 1&2 £2.30, 1&3 £5.50, 2&3 £2.80 CSF £20.94 CT £117.54 TOTE £6.20: £2.30, £1.50, £1.70; EX 24.30 Trifecta £131.30 Pool: £2,167.22 - 12.37 winning units..
Owner The Cheapskates **Bred** Andrew And Mrs S R B Davis **Trained** Falmer, E Sussex
FOCUS
Ordinary form with a step up from the winner.

1530 32RED H'CAP CHASE (13 fncs) 2m 2f
5:20 (5:20) (Class 5) (0-95,95) 4-Y-0+ **£2,469** (£725; £362; £181)

Form RPR
302- 1 **Chestnut Ben (IRE)**19 1328 8-11-12 **95** (t) APMcCoy 105+
(Gary Brown) *hld up trcking ldrs: impeded 10th: sn wnt 2nd: nt fluent 2 out: rdr holding on to him tl chal last: sn led and pushed along to assert* **2/1**1
403- 2 *4* **Osmosia (FR)**10 1438 8-11-9 **92** (tp) TomCannon 95
(Chris Gordon) *led: 3 l clr and pushed along 3 out: drvn next: hdd last: sn outpcd flat* **11/1**
/02- 3 *20* **Wak A Turtle (IRE)**10 1433 5-11-7 **93** MichealNolan(3) 83
(Richard Woollacott) *t.k.h in rr: hdwy after 7th: 3rd and gng wl after 10th: rdn and fdd bef 2 out and hit fence: 10 l 3rd whn j.rt last: fin tired* **7/1**
521- 4 *2* **Safe Investment (USA)**10 1435 9-11-11 **94** (vt) DavidBass 77
(Lawney Hill) *prom early but nvr gng w relish: lost pl u.p 3rd: n.d fr 8th: wnt lft bef last* **11/4**2
554- 5 *9* **She's Humble (IRE)**24 1272 11-10-4 **73** (p) LeightonAspell 48
(Linda Jewell) *prom: 2nd after 7th: j.lft next two whn losing pl: 5th and struggling after 10th* **14/1**
003- 6 *7* **The Grey One (IRE)**10 1435 10-10-2 **71** JamieMoore 44
(Milton Bradley) *blnd 3rd: rn in snatches and several positions: rdn after 7th: effrt in 3rd 3 out: 15 l 4th and fading whn j. bdly rt last* **20/1**
002- 7 *53* **Novikov**13 1401 9-10-6 **75** (tp) PaulMoloney
(Sophie Leech) *bhd: last and rdn after 7th: t.o after 10th: j.lft 2 out and bdly so at last* **5/1**3
236/ U **Celtic Charlie (FR)**157 4763 8-10-10 **79** ColinBolger
(Pat Phelan) *hit 1st and uns rdr* **25/1**
4m 53.2s (18.50) **Going Correction** +0.525s/f (Soft) **8 Ran SP% 112.8**
Speed ratings (Par 103): **79,77,68,67,63 60,36,**
toteswingers 1&2 £5.60, 1&3 £2.40, 2&3 £8.50 CSF £22.89 CT £127.87 TOTE £2.60: £1.30, £3.20, £2.70; EX 25.20 Trifecta £271.80 Pool: £2,282.53 - 6.29 winning units..
Owner Russell H Lee **Bred** Sean Deu Burca **Trained** Lambourn, Berks

FOCUS
The cosy winner is rated to his mark in this weak handicap.

1531 32REDPOKER.COM MARES' STANDARD OPEN NATIONAL HUNT FLAT RACE 1m 6f
5:50 (5:51) (Class 6) 4-6-Y-0 **£1,559** (£457; £228; £114)

Form RPR
23- 1 *1 1/4* **Hazel Brook**17 1353 4-10-12 0 SamTwiston-Davies 97+
(Mary Hambro) *pressed ldr: drvn to dispute ld 2f out: u.p but stl ev ch whn barged into rails by rival ins fnl 100yds: lost all ch: fin 2nd: awrdd the r* **5/1**3
2 **Centoria (IRE)** 5-10-12 0 TomO'Brien 96+
(Jamie Snowden) *cl up: effrt 3f out: duelled w rival fr 2f out: edging rt 1f out: ducked rt and bdly hmpd rival ins fnl 100yds and lft clr: fin first: disqualified and plcd 2nd* **5/2**1
4- 3 *12* **Ovilia (IRE)**20 1317 4-10-12 0 JasonMaguire 81
(Donald McCain) *trckd ldrs: led over 3f out: sn rdn: hdd 2f out and immediately lft bhd by ldng pair* **4/1**2
4 *3/4* **Beatrix Kiddo (IRE)** 4-10-12 0 HarrySkelton 80
(Dan Skelton) *in rr of bunch: drvn and outpcd 4f out: mod 5th home turn* **5/1**3
10/ 5 *2* **Miss Lilly Lewis**341 1712 5-10-12 0 DanielHiskett(7) 85
(Richard Phillips) *chsd ldrs: 4th and drvn bef home turn: sn floundering* **11/2**
0- 6 *54* **Afillycalledlily (IRE)**26 1264 4-10-12 0 DavidBass 13
(Lawney Hill) *led: rdn and hdd over 3f out: stopped to nil: bdly t.o* **20/1**
7 *27* **Garlands Quest** 4-10-12 0 AndrewThornton
(Richenda Ford) *rdn and hopelessly t.o fnl 6f: fin eventually* **33/1**
/- 8 *32* **Ragtime Lady** 5-10-5 0 MrLKilgarriff(7)
(Steven Dixon) *plld hrd early: chsd ldrs tl shkn up 1/2-way: hopelessly t.o fnl 6f: fin eventually* **50/1**
U **Libation** 4-10-12 0 RhysFlint
(John Flint) *unruly and uns rdr sn after s* **14/1**
3m 23.9s (-7.20) **9 Ran SP% 113.6**
toteswingers 1&2 £2.80, 1&3 £3.10, 2&3 £3.50 CSF £17.26 TOTE £5.10: £1.90, £1.40, £1.70; EX 17.80 Trifecta £90.30 Pool: £2,629.86 - 21.82 winning units..
Owner Mrs Richard Hambro **Bred** Cotswold Stud **Trained** Bourton-on-the-Hill, Gloucs
■ Stewards' Enquiry : Tom O'Brien four-day ban: careless riding (Sep 25-28)
FOCUS
What looked an ordinary end to the card produced a dramatic finish. The form is rated around the placed horses.
T/Plt: £76.90 to a £1 stake. Pool: £91,026.15 - 864.02 winning units T/Qpdt: £60.70 to a £1 stake. Pool: £5,862.20 - 71.40 winning units IM

CRAON (R-H)
Sunday, September 8
OFFICIAL GOING: Turf: good to soft

1532a GRAND CROSS COUNTRY DE CRAON - CRYSTAL CUP (CROSS-COUNTRY CHASE) (LISTED RACE) (5YO+) (TURF) 3m 6f
4:30 (12:00) 5-Y-0+ **£29,268** (£14,634; £8,536; £5,792; £2,743)

RPR
1 **Balthazar King (IRE)**134 5576 9-10-10 0 RichardJohnson 137
(Philip Hobbs) *w.w towards rr: nt fluent 16th: tk clsr order 22nd to r in midfield: nt fluent 3 out: 5th and styng on after 2 out: sn rdn: led jumping last: edgd rt but r.o run-in: drvn clr* **15/1**
2 *2 1/2* **Quick Baby (FR)**158 5133 9-10-10 0 AnthonyThierry 135
(J Follain, France) **17/2**
3 *2 1/2* **Beuillac (FR)**24 1279 10-10-10 0 JamesReveley 132
(G Macaire, France) **7/1**3
4 *5* **Chriseti (FR)**122 199 13-10-10 0 (b) WilfridDenuault 127
(E Leenders, France) **5/2**1
5 *4* **Shalimar Fromentro (FR)**70 855 7-10-10 0 AlainDeChitray 123
(Nick Williams) *midfield but in tch: outpcd 17th and dropped to rr: prog after 3 out: 7th and styng on last: kpt on wl run-in: tk 5th fnl strides* **17/1**
6 *1/2* **Posilox (FR)**122 199 7-10-10 0 (b) OlivierJouin 123
(W Menuet, France) **13/1**
7 *20* **Phakos (FR)**55 10-10-10 0 DavidCottin 103
(P Cottin, France) **48/10**2
8 *5* **Hades Des Mottes (FR)**296 2464 8-10-10 0 StephanePaillard 98
(E Lecoiffier, France) **14/1**
P **Naschador (FR)**824 789 9-10-10 0 Marc-AntoineDragon
(E Leray, France) **17/1**
P **Major Dolois (FR)**35 1214 7-10-10 0 (b) JeromeZuliani
(Patrice Quinton, France) **17/1**
F **Quoquoalco (FR)**55 9-10-10 0 HubertTerrien
(E Lecoiffier, France) **17/1**
F **Racoleur (FR)**70 855 8-10-10 0 (p) DominiqueDelorme
(D Delorme, France) **40/1**
P **Resistencia (FR)**90 704 8-10-6 0 (b) ThomasBeaurain
(E Vagne, France) **66/1**
F **Trois Huit (FR)**70 855 6-10-10 0 (b) RomainJulliot
(E Leenders, France) **40/1**
8m 4.36s (484.36) **14 Ran SP% 117.5**
PARI-MUTUEL (all including 1 euro stakes): WIN 16.00; PLACE 4.40, 2.90, 3.10; DF 65.00; SF 153.60.
Owner The Brushmakers **Bred** Sunnyhill Stud **Trained** Withycombe, Somerset

1400 HUNTINGDON (R-H)
Monday, September 9
OFFICIAL GOING: Good (watered; chs 7.5, hdl 7.6)
Wind: Light against Weather: Overcast

1533 TAM ASSET MANAGEMENT NOVICES' HURDLE (10 hdls) 2m 4f 110y
2:10 (2:10) (Class 4) 4-Y-0+ **£3,898** (£1,144; £572)

Form RPR
2/1- 1 **Koultas King (IRE)**18 1341 6-11-5 112 (t) RichardJohnson 112+
(Tim Vaughan) *mde all: shkn up appr 3 out: jnd sn after: styd on to go clr appr last: rdn out* **4/11**1

4- **2** *9* **Moon Trip**[36] 1200 4-10-11 0 DenisO'Regan 98
(John Ferguson) *trckd ldrs: mstke 1st: chal gng wl after 3 out: shkn up appr last: no ex* **5/2**[2]

/U4- **3** *9* **Royal Defence (IRE)**[27] 1269 7-10-12 100 RyanMahon 90
(Mick Quinn) *trckd wnr tl rdn 3 out: wknd appr next* **18/1**[3]

4m 46.7s (-12.30) **Going Correction** -0.375s/f (Good)
WFA 4 from 6yo+ 12lb 3 Ran SP% **107.1**
Speed ratings (Par 105): **108,104,101**
CSF £1.66 TOTE £1.20; EX 1.80 Trifecta £1.70 Pool: £857.62 - 368.09 winning units..
Owner Pearn's Pharmacies Ltd **Bred** Tom McCarthy **Trained** Aberthin, Vale of Glamorgan

FOCUS
Stands' bend moved on to fresh ground. A modest novice event, with the winner rated up to his mark.

1534 INGREBOURNE VALLEY H'CAP CHASE (16 fncs) 2m 4f 110y
2:40 (2:40) (Class 5) (0-100,99) 4-Y-0+ **£2,209** (£648; £324; £162)

Form RPR

442- **1** **Brimham Boy**[19] 1336 11-10-12 95 (vt) OllieGarner(10) 104
(Martin Keighley) *chsd ldrs: lft 2nd 3rd: rdn after 3 out: 4 l 2nd and styng on same pce whn lft in ld last: drvn out* **5/1**[3]

452- **2** *7* **Farmer Frank**[22] 1300 10-10-0 80 PaulNO'Brien(7) 84
(Nick Kent) *hld up: hdwy appr 2 out: rdn whn lft 2nd last: hung rt and no ex flat* **11/4**[1]

342- **3** *5* **Neverownup (IRE)**[22] 1303 8-11-3 90 (t) DaveCrosse 88
(K F Clutterbuck) *prom: mstke 13th: drvn along after next: mstke 2 out: wkng whn lft 3rd last* **4/1**[2]

/U0- **4** *13* **Dark Oasis**[11] 1443 7-10-0 73 oh1 JamieMoore 63
(Natalie Lloyd-Beavis) *hld up: bhd fr 9th* **18/1**

564- **5** *23* **Morestead (IRE)**[11] 1435 8-11-9 96 (tp) LeightonAspell 64
(Brendan Powell) *hld up: a in rr: bhd fr 8th* **16/1**

06R/ **U** **Ajzal (IRE)**[222] 3937 9-11-12 99 (b) LiamTreadwell
(Ed de Giles) *led tl after 2nd: blnd and uns rdr next* **13/2**

325/ **P** **Knock Boy (IRE)**[519] 5295 11-9-11 73 oh2 (v) GavinSheehan(3)
(Linda Jewell) *chsd ldrs: mstke 7th: nt fluent and lost pl next: sn bhd: p.u bef 2 out* **25/1**

333- **U** **Crescent Beach (IRE)**[14] 1401 6-10-12 85 (b) HenryOliver
(Henry Oliver) *w ldrs whn slipped on landing and uns rdr 1st* **17/2**

430- **F** **Darnborough (IRE)**[41] 1149 7-10-1 74 (p) FelixDeGiles 84
(Tom Symonds) *w ldr tl led after 2nd: mstke 9th: rdn appr 2 out: 4 l ld and looked in control whn fell last* **9/1**

4m 53.6s (-11.70) **Going Correction** -0.50s/f (Good) 9 Ran SP% **112.2**
Speed ratings (Par 103): **102,99,97,92,83 , , ,**
toteswingers 1&2 £2.30, 1&3 £4.40, 2&3 £3.70 CSF £19.18 CT £58.78 TOTE £4.50: £1.30, £1.70, £1.90; EX 13.50 Trifecta £41.20 Pool: £1605.35 - 29.18 winning units..
Owner D A Thorpe **Bred** Miss T M Hammond **Trained** Condicote, Gloucs

FOCUS
This low-grade handicap saw a dramatic finish. The faller is rated as a 3l winner, with the winner 5lb off his old mark.

1535 HOUSE OF FLAGS H'CAP HURDLE (8 hdls) 2m 110y
3:10 (3:10) (Class 4) (0-120,117) 4-Y-0+ **£3,249** (£954; £477; £238)

Form RPR

/03- **1** **West Brit (IRE)**[56] 995 5-11-10 115 (t) NoelFehily 119+
(Charlie Longsdon) *hld up: hdwy after 3 out: shkn up to ld flat: hung lft: r.o: readily* **5/2**[2]

232- **2** *1 ½* **Odin (IRE)**[9] 1466 5-11-3 115 (p) ConorShoemark(7) 116+
(Don Cantillon) *chsd ldrs: wnt 2nd after 5th: led 2 out: rdn and hdd flat: styd on* **11/2**

030/ **3** *14* **King Of Wing (IRE)**[7] 4843 4-10-5 99 (p) JackQuinlan(3) 87
(Phil McEntee) *led: mstke 5th: rdn and hdd 2 out: wknd flat* **33/1**

215- **4** *6* **Alwaystheoptimist**[75] 840 10-11-9 117 KielanWoods(3) 102
(Phil Middleton) *hld up: hdwy 3 out: rdn and hit 2 out: wknd appr last* **14/1**

5 *38* **Tangolan (IRE)**[62] 934 5-11-2 112 (p) ThomasGarner(5) 61
(Phil Middleton) *prom: disp cl 2nd after 3 out: sn rdn and wknd* **15/8**[1]

442/ **6** *41* **Tiny Tenor (IRE)**[190] 4540 7-11-12 117 NickScholfield 29
(David Dennis) *trckd ldr: hit 4th: nt fluent next: sn lost 2nd: wkng whn nt fluent 3 out* **7/2**[3]

3m 46.2s (-8.70) **Going Correction** -0.375s/f (Good)
WFA 4 from 5yo+ 11lb 6 Ran SP% **110.6**
Speed ratings (Par 105): **105,104,97,94,77 57**
toteswingers 1&2 £4.40, 1&3 £2.30, 2&3 £3.70 CSF £15.73 TOTE £3.50: £1.40, £2.90; EX 14.10 Trifecta £188.10 Pool: £1633.02 - 6.51 winning units..
Owner Tyrone Hanlon **Bred** R N Auld **Trained** Over Norton, Oxon

FOCUS
Quite a competitive handicap hurdle on paper. A step up from the winner with the second to his mark.

1536 FLAGS.CO.UK JUVENILE HURDLE (8 hdls) 2m 110y
3:40 (3:40) (Class 4) 3-Y-O **£3,119** (£915; £457; £228)

Form RPR

PU- **1** **Town Mouse**[10] 1044 3-10-7 0 TrevorWhelan(5) 100+
(Neil King) *hld up: plld hrd: hdwy 3 out: led and wandered arnd next: r.o wl* **50/1**

511- **2** *7* **Walter White (IRE)**[9] 1473 3-11-12 120 (t) TomO'Brien 108+
(Philip Hobbs) *chsd ldrs: bdly hmpd 2nd: shkn up to go 2nd last: rdn and styd on same pce flat* **13/8**[1]

2- **3** *3 ½* **Kitchapoly (FR)**[14] 1394 3-11-5 0 JamesCowley(7) 102
(Donald McCain) *hld up in tch: lft trcking ldr after 2nd: led after 3 out: rdn and hdd next: no ex last* **2/1**[2]

221- **4** *3 ¼* **Hanga Roa (IRE)**[25] 1271 3-11-5 0 JamieMoore 94
(Gary Moore) *plld hrd: led: hit 3 out: sn hdd: hit next: wknd last* **12/1**

P- **5** *9* **Double Jeopardy**[57] 975 3-10-9 0 JackQuinlan(3) 78
(Dr Jon Scargill) *chsd ldrs: rdn appr 2 out: wkng whn blnd last* **125/1**

6 *6* **Getaway Car**[38] 3-10-12 0 (p) DenisO'Regan 75
(Gerard Butler) *chsd ldr tl j. bdly rt and rdr lost irons 2nd: sn lost pl and nt fluent next: rdr got irons bk sn after: wknd appr 3 out* **3/1**[3]

7 *½* **Day In Day Out**[56] 3-10-12 0 AndrewThornton 70
(Seamus Mullins) *hld up: pushed along 5th: wknd after 3 out* **28/1**

3m 50.6s (-4.30) **Going Correction** -0.375s/f (Good) 7 Ran SP% **110.3**
Speed ratings (Par 103): **95,91,90,88,84 81,81**
toteswingers 1&2 £14.00, 1&3 £26.50, 2&3 £2.30 CSF £126.47 TOTE £46.10: £11.70, £1.40; EX 146.40 Trifecta £542.50 Pool: £1706.20 - 2.35 winning units..
Owner Brian Bell & John Smith **Bred** Bishop Wilton Stud **Trained** Newmarket, Suffolk

FOCUS
An ordinary juvenile contest and a surprise winner. The winner can rate higher with the second 7lb off and the third close to his recent mark.

1537 32RED CASINO H'CAP CHASE (12 fncs) 2m 110y
4:10 (4:10) (Class 4) (0-120,119) 4-Y-0+ **£3,898** (£1,144; £572; £286)

Form RPR

011- **1** **Cap Elorn (FR)**[41] 1149 7-10-5 101 (b) GavinSheehan(3) 118+
(Lawney Hill) *trckd ldr tl led after 7th: clr 9th: eased flat* **15/8**[2]

201- **2** *17* **Chilbury Hill (IRE)**[12] 1428 10-10-3 99 (t) MichaelByrne(3) 99
(Tim Vaughan) *chsd ldrs: j.lft: reminder after 3rd: outpcd fr 8th: wnt remote 2nd appr last* **7/4**[1]

420- **3** *17* **Fiftyonefiftyone (IRE)**[9] 1470 9-11-7 119 (tp) JoeCornwall(5) 100
(John Cornwall) *led tl after 7th: wknd appr 2 out: lost 2nd bef last* **12/1**

123- **4** *6* **Lauberhorn**[23] 1282 6-11-3 110 PaulMoloney 86
(Evan Williams) *hld up: pushed along after 5th: sn wl bhd: hit last* **5/2**[3]

3m 59.1s (-11.10) **Going Correction** -0.50s/f (Good) 4 Ran SP% **107.4**
Speed ratings (Par 105): **106,98,90,87**
CSF £5.60 TOTE £3.00; EX 4.90 Trifecta £23.50 Pool: £1117.84 - 35.61 winning units..
Owner Andy Weller **Bred** Jean-Luc Guillerm **Trained** Aston Rowant, Oxon

FOCUS
An ordinary handicap chase but they were strung out a long way from home. The form is rated around the first two.

1538 32RED.COM H'CAP HURDLE (12 hdls) 3m 2f
4:40 (4:40) (Class 5) (0-100,100) 4-Y-0+ **£2,079** (£610; £305; £152)

Form RPR

361- **1** **Go Amwell**[14] 1405 10-11-7 95 (v) LeightonAspell 100
(J R Jenkins) *hld up: pushed along after 7th: hdwy after 9th: chsd ldr next: led 2 out: sn rdn: styd on u.p* **8/1**[3]

501- **2** *¾* **Fitobust (IRE)**[14] 1406 7-10-6 80 (v) DavidBass 85
(Lawney Hill) *chsd ldrs: mstke 8th: led next: mstke 3 out: rdn and hdd 2 out: ev ch whn wnt rt last: styd on u.p* **6/1**[2]

336- **3** *2 ¼* **Heezagrey (IRE)**[14] 1405 10-9-9 74 oh5 (b) BenPoste(5) 75
(James Evans) *mid-div: hdwy 5th: pushed allong 7th: rdn appr 2 out: styd on* **12/1**

0P0- **4** *8* **Spanish Fork (IRE)**[25] 1275 4-11-0 90 MarcGoldstein 82
(Sheena West) *prom: pushed along 6th: rdn appr 3 out: styd on same pce fr next* **12/1**

362- **5** *nk* **Moyne Nineoseven (IRE)**[14] 1405 7-11-4 95 (tp) JackQuinlan(3) 90
(Noel Quinlan) *hld up: hdwy after 9th: rdn appr 2 out: wkng whn mstke last* **10/3**[1]

231- **6** *16* **Nicky Nutjob (GER)**[11] 1436 7-11-5 100 (p) CiaranMckee(7) 79
(John O'Shea) *hld up: pushed along appr 2 out: nvr on terms* **6/1**[2]

560- **7** *4 ½* **Gilded Age**[12] 1429 7-11-3 94 (t) JamesBest(3) 69
(Rob Summers) *led to 2nd chsd ldr: chal 9th: rdn and wknd appr 2 out* **16/1**

1/4- **8** *19* **Aghill (IRE)**[14] 1402 9-11-9 97 (vt) AidanColeman 55
(Lawney Hill) *hld up: rdn after 9th: a in rr* **14/1**

/35- **9** *80* **Rossbrin (IRE)**[90] 713 8-11-3 91 (tp) CharliePoste
(Anna Brooks) *chsd ldrs: pushed along after 7th: rdn and wknd appr 3 out: nt fluent next: eased* **14/1**

003- **P** **Hill Forts Gloria (IRE)**[14] 1405 8-9-11 74 oh8 (tp) GavinSheehan(3)
(Lawney Hill) *led 2nd to 9th: sn rdn and wknd: bhd whn p.u bef 2 out* **6/1**[2]

/46- **P** **Renagisha (IRE)**[27] 1259 7-10-9 83 (b) JamieMoore
(Jim Best) *mid-div: hdwy 5th: rdn and wknd appr 3 out: bhd whn p.u bef next* **25/1**

6m 13.2s (-9.70) **Going Correction** -0.375s/f (Good)
WFA 4 from 7yo+ 13lb 11 Ran SP% **115.5**
Speed ratings (Par 103): **99,98,98,95,95 90,89,83,58, ,**
toteswingers 1&2 £6.10, 1&3 £18.30, 2&3 £11.90 CSF £55.00 CT £576.06 TOTE £7.60: £2.80, £2.60, £3.00; EX 34.00 Trifecta £340.20 Pool: £2701.64 - 5.95 winning units..
Owner Robin Stevens **Bred** Michael Ng **Trained** Royston, Herts

■ Stewards' Enquiry : David Bass four-day ban: use of whip (24-27 Sept)

FOCUS
A moderate stayers' handicap hurdle in which the finish was dominated by two recent course winners. This was the winner's best effort since March 2012 with the second to his best and the third to last season's C&D mark.

1539 32RED STANDARD OPEN NATIONAL HUNT FLAT RACE 2m 110y
5:10 (5:11) (Class 6) 4-6-Y-O **£1,559** (£457; £228; £114)

Form RPR

332- **1** **Western Way (IRE)**[12] 1427 4-11-0 0 (b1) DenisO'Regan 118+
(Don Cantillon) *led after 2f: qcknd clr over 2f out: easily* **13/8**[2]

21- **2** *27* **Handmaid**[75] 841 4-11-0 0 JamieMoore 101+
(Peter Bowen) *led 2f: chsd wnr: rdn over 3f out: sn outpcd: eased fnl f* **1/1**[1]

3 *37* **Private Jones** 4-11-0 0 RichardJohnson 61
(Miss Imogen Pickard) *plld hrd and prom: rdn over 3f out: sn wknd* **14/1**

5/ **4** *1* **Motorhead**[270] 3028 4-11-0 0 NickScholfield 60
(Bob Buckler) *hld up: pushed along 6f out: wknd 4f out* **7/1**[3]

P- **5** *99* **Gabbys Star**[2] 1523 6-10-7 0 AidanColeman
(Shaun Lycett) *hld up: pushed along 10f out: bhd fr 1/2-way* **66/1**

3m 46.0s (-3.10) **Going Correction** -0.375s/f (Good) 5 Ran SP% **108.8**
Speed ratings: **92,79,61,61,14**
CSF £3.49 TOTE £2.20: £1.50, £1.10; EX 3.80 Trifecta £13.20 Pool: £2434.45 - 137.78 winning units..
Owner Don Cantillon **Bred** Don Cantillon **Trained** Newmarket, Suffolk

FOCUS
This was one-way traffic for Western Way. This is a step forward with the second to his mark.

T/Plt: £38.90 to a £1 stake. Pool: £50231.24 - 940.32 winning tickets T/Qpdt: £30.40 to a £1 stakee. Pool: £2590.59 - 63.00 winning tickets CR

[1286] PERTH (R-H)

Monday, September 9

OFFICIAL GOING: Good (8.1)

Wind: Light, half behind Weather: Cloudy, bright

1540 TUV-SUD CONSULTING ENGINEERS NOVICES' HURDLE (8 hdls) 2m 110y
2:20 (2:20) (Class 4) 4-Y-0+ **£3,249** (£954; £477; £238)

Form RPR

5/1- **1** **It's A Mans World**[14] 1399 7-10-12 118........................ CraigGallagher(7) 120+
(Brian Ellison) *trckd ldrs: wnt 2nd 4 out: led bef 2 out: pushed clr bef last: comf* **15/8**[2]

211- **2** *7* **Smart Ruler (IRE)**[13] 1415 7-11-12 117.................................. APMcCoy 118
(James Moffatt) *chsd ldr to 2nd: cl up: effrt and chsd wnr bef 2 out: sn rdn: edgd rt bef last: kpt on same pce* **6/4**[1]

P/ **3** *8* **Ultra Du Chatelet (FR)**[256] 3288 5-10-12 0..................(t) PeterBuchanan 97
(Lucinda Russell) *hld up: stdy hdwy whn mstke 4 out: drvn and outpcd next: kpt on fr last: no ch w first two* **7/1**

5/ **4** *¾* **King Kurt (IRE)**[15] 1396 5-10-12 0...................................... BrianHughes 95
(Kevin Ryan) *led: rdn and hdd bef 2 out: sn outpcd* **9/2**[3]

5 *1 ¾* **Whinstone Dee (IRE)**[187] 4606 5-10-5 0.................(t) GrahamWatters(7) 94
(Miss Clare Louise Cannon, Ire) *hld up: stdy hdwy 4 out: rdn and outpcd bef 2 out: n.d after* **20/1**

/06- **6** *47* **Honourable Gent**[106] 494 5-10-12 0............................ WilsonRenwick 51
(Rose Dobbin) *t.k.h: chsd ldr 2nd to 4 out: lost tch fr next: t.o* **100/1**

3m 49.0s (-9.00) **Going Correction** -0.30s/f (Good) 6 Ran SP% **111.2**

Speed ratings (Par 105): **109,105,101,101,100 78**

toteswingers 1&2 £1.20, 1&3 £2.90, 2&3 £2.30 CSF £5.17 TOTE £3.00: £1.20, £1.80; EX 5.10 Trifecta £19.90 Pool: £2730.96 - 102.69 winning units..

Owner David Foster & Brian Ellison **Bred** Cheveley Park Stud Ltd **Trained** Norton, N Yorks

FOCUS

Stands' bend moved on to fresh ground. This opening novice hurdle was run at a reasonable gallop. The first two are rated pretty much to their marks.

1541 MONESS ESTATE H'CAP HURDLE (12 hdls) 3m 110y
2:50 (2:50) (Class 3) (0-135,128) 4-Y-0+ **£5,848** (£1,717; £858; £429)

Form RPR

033- **1** **Emily's Flyer (IRE)**[23] 1284 6-10-5 107..........................(t) PaddyBrennan 115+
(Fergal O'Brien) *mde all: rdn bef 2 out: clr whn hit last: styd on strly* **6/1**[3]

/31- **2** *5* **Toye Native (IRE)**[23] 1289 5-11-12 128.................................. APMcCoy 130
(C A McBratney, Ire) *hld up in tch: nt fluent 2nd: hdwy to chse wnr 4 out: effrt bef 2 out: hung lft: one pce last* **5/2**[2]

0/1- **3** *8* **Jimmy The Hat (IRE)**[23] 1286 7-11-4 120..........................(p) JasonMaguire 118
(Gordon Elliott, Ire) *chsd ldrs: wnt 2nd bef 6th: hit 8th: carried tail awkwardly and outpcd 3 out: no imp fr next* **1/1**[1]

0/4- **4** *22* **Los Nadis (GER)**[23] 1289 9-11-4 120................................... HenryBrooke 95
(Jim Goldie) *pressed wnr to bef 6th: drvn and outpcd bef 3 out: sn lost tch* **7/1**

5m 54.2s (-10.80) **Going Correction** -0.30s/f (Good) 4 Ran SP% **105.4**

Speed ratings (Par 107): **105,103,100,93**

CSF £19.28 TOTE £4.90; EX 10.80 Trifecta £19.30 Pool: £1204.33 - 46.76 winning units..

Owner C Cornes **Bred** Cathal Ennis **Trained** Coln St. Dennis, Gloucs

FOCUS

Modest form rated though the runner-up to her recent course mark, but a step up from the winner.

1542 TUV-SUD CONSULTING ENGINEERS H'CAP CHASE (18 fncs) 3m
3:20 (3:20) (Class 4) (0-120,120) 4-Y-0+ **£4,548** (£1,335; £667; £333)

Form RPR

/24- **1** **Acapulco Gold (IRE)**[23] 1291 6-11-7 115...........................(tp) APMcCoy 126+
(Paul Nolan, Ire) *trckd ldrs: effrt and drvn bef 3 out: led whn hit 2 out: hit last: drvn clr* **4/1**[3]

10P- **2** *6* **Wild Geese (IRE)**[68] 869 6-11-12 120.........................(p) PeterBuchanan 126
(Lucinda Russell) *pressed ldr: drvn and ev ch bef 2 out to last: one pce run-in* **8/1**

241- **3** *5* **Diddley Dee**[23] 1287 9-10-5 99.. WilsonRenwick 103+
(Lucy Normile) *hld up: drvn along fr 1/2-way: outpcd 4 out: plugged on fr 2 out: no imp* **7/2**[2]

026- **4** *¾* **O Crotaigh (IRE)**[9] 1470 9-11-9 117.................................. JasonMaguire 117
(Alan Brown) *led to appr 2 out: sn rdn and outpcd bef last* **16/1**

435- **U** **Solway Sam**[40] 1163 10-9-7 94.............................. StephenMulqueen(7)
(Lisa Harrison) *hld up in tch: pushed along 4 out: in tch whn slipped and uns rdr bnd bef next* **7/2**[2]

0- **F** **Rathmoyle House (IRE)**[11] 1448 7-10-1 95..................(p) BrianHughes
(Gordon Elliott, Ire) *chsd ldrs: drvn along and cl 4th whn fell 4 out* **13/5**[1]

5m 56.9s (-7.10) **Going Correction** -0.15s/f (Good) 6 Ran SP% **109.2**

Speed ratings (Par 105): **105,103,101,101,**

toteswingers 1&2 £3.20, 1&3 £2.90, 2&3 £2.90 CSF £30.56 TOTE £4.40: £2.30, £3.90; EX 18.70 Trifecta £58.50 Pool: £2188.49 - 28.04 winning units..

Owner G Murtagh **Bred** Corduff Stud **Trained** Enniscorthy, Co. Wexford

FOCUS

A competitive handicap chase and it was run at a true gallop. The winner improved to the level of his best hurdle mark with the second back to form and the third close to his recent winning rating.

1543 CRABBIE'S ALCOHOLIC GINGER BEER AMATEUR RIDERS' H'CAP HURDLE (10 hdls) 2m 4f 110y
3:50 (3:50) (Class 4) (0-120,115) 4-Y-0+ **£3,898** (£1,144; £572; £286)

Form RPR

/25- **1** **Call Box (IRE)**[41] 1146 8-11-8 111.................................. MrSCrawford 116
(S R B Crawford, Ire) *trckd ldrs: chal 4 out: led after next: rdn and styd on wl fr last* **3/1**[2]

2 *1 ¼* **Hold Em Cowboy (IRE)**[14] 1408 9-10-7 99...................... MikeyEnnis(3) 103
(Gordon Elliott, Ire) *hld up in tch: stdy hdwy to chse wnr bef 2 out: rdn bef last: one pce run-in* **4/5**[1]

45S- **3** *18* **Bescot Springs (IRE)**[23] 1289 8-11-7 115............................ MrSFox(5) 103
(Lucinda Russell) *in tch: hdwy and cl up 4 out: outpcd next: rallied bef 2 out: wknd between last 2* **8/1**

650- **4** *24* **Tim's Approach (IRE)**[4] 1506 8-9-7 89 oh21..............(t) MrTHamilton(7) 55
(William Young Jnr) *t.k.h: cl up: hit 5th: lost pl after 4 out: struggling fr next* **66/1**

054- **5** *1* **Mumgos Debut (IRE)**[40] 1159 5-9-13 95................... MissRMcDonald(7) 60
(Lucinda Russell) *t.k.h: mde most to after 3 out: rdn and wknd qckly appr next* **5/1**[3]

4m 54.1s (-7.90) **Going Correction** -0.30s/f (Good) 5 Ran SP% **109.8**

Speed ratings (Par 105): **103,102,95,86,86**

CSF £6.05 TOTE £3.60: £1.50, £1.10; EX 5.90 Trifecta £15.50 Pool: £1791.68 - 86.50 winning units..

Owner Pircan Partnership **Bred** David Fenton **Trained** Larne, Co Antrim

FOCUS

A modest handicap hurdle, confined to amateur riders. The form is rated around the first two.

1544 TUV-SUD CONSULTING ENGINEERS H'CAP HURDLE (8 hdls) 2m 110y
4:20 (4:20) (Class 4) (0-120,119) 4-Y-0+ **£3,898** (£1,144; £572; £286)

Form RPR

000/ **1** **Dhaular Dhar (IRE)**[19] 3519 11-10-6 99................................ GaryBartley 106+
(Jim Goldie) *hld up: stdy hdwy to trck ldrs bef 2 out: hdwy to ld whn nt fluent last: pushed out* **25/1**

30- **2** *4* **Moonlone Lane (IRE)**[16] 1379 6-10-0 93.......................(vt[1]) BrianHughes 95
(Paul Stafford, Ire) *trckd ldrs: smooth hdwy to ld appr 2 out: rdn and hdd appr last: kpt on same pce run-in* **10/1**

142- **3** *2* **Endeavor**[40] 1160 8-10-11 104.. HenryBrooke 104
(Dianne Sayer) *prom: nt fluent 3rd: effrt and drvn after 3 out: kpt on same pce fr last* **6/1**

614- **4** *hd* **Outrageous Request**[23] 1290 7-11-5 119......................(p) CraigNichol(7) 120
(Lucinda Russell) *led tl hdd appr 2 out: rallied: kpt on same pce fr last* **5/2**[2]

F- **5** *10* **Obispo (IRE)**[29] 1246 7-10-12 105.. APMcCoy 98
(C A McBratney, Ire) *t.k.h: trckd ldrs tl wknd bef 2 out* **9/4**[1]

0P3/ **6** *33* **Lillioftheballet (IRE)**[138] 5492 6-10-2 95......................... WilsonRenwick 56
(Jim Goldie) *cl up: drvn 1/2-way: rallied and ev ch 3 out: wknd bef next: t.o* **9/2**[3]

465- **7** *8* **Super Collider**[14] 1285 6-10-5 108...........................(bt) JamesCorbett(10) 62
(Susan Corbett) *hld up: outpcd whn hit 4 out: sn struggling: t.o* **25/1**

3m 50.3s (-7.70) **Going Correction** -0.30s/f (Good) 7 Ran SP% **108.6**

Speed ratings (Par 105): **106,104,103,103,98 82,79**

toteswingers 1&2 £29.30, 1&3 £19.40, 2&3 £12.50 CSF £209.68 TOTE £18.80: £8.90, £3.50; EX 131.50 Trifecta £723.90 Pool: £1621.63 - 1.68 winning units..

Owner Johnnie Delta Racing **Bred** Gainsborough Stud Management Ltd **Trained** Uplawmoor, E Renfrews

FOCUS

A competitive event for the grade on paper, but scratch the surface and there was plenty of question marks over the protagonists. It was just a reasonable gallop, but those in the frame behind the winner are rated pretty much to their marks.

1545 PRESTIGE H'CAP CHASE (15 fncs) 2m 4f 110y
4:50 (4:50) (Class 3) (0-140,137) 4-Y-0+ **£6,498** (£1,908; £954; £477)

Form RPR

112- **1** **Scotch Warrior**[23] 1291 9-10-5 123.............................. CallumBewley(7) 132
(R Mike Smith) *chsd ldr to 7th: nt fluent 10th: rallied to ld 2 out: edgd rt run-in: hld on gamely* **5/2**[1]

141- **2** *hd* **Sergeant Pink (IRE)**[23] 1291 7-10-7 118........................... HenryBrooke 128
(Dianne Sayer) *nt fluent: prom: wnt 2nd 7th: effrt and chal fr 2 out: kpt on run-in: jst hld* **7/1**[3]

115- **3** *2 ¼* **Dark Energy**[22] 1302 9-10-12 123...................................(t) AlainCawley 129
(Fergal O'Brien) *chsd ldrs: hit 1st and 9th: pushed along and effrt bef 3 out: kpt on same pce run-in* **10/1**

323- **4** *8* **Quito Du Tresor (FR)**[23] 1291 9-10-11 122..............(p) TomScudamore 121
(Lucinda Russell) *mde most to bef 2 out: outpcd between last 2* **4/1**[2]

622/ **5** *5* **Maggio (FR)**[140] 5449 8-11-7 132.................................(t) JamesReveley 128
(Patrick Griffin, Ire) *nt fluent: hld up in tch: stdy hdwy 11th: rdn 3 out: wknd next* **4/1**[2]

0/0- **6** *8* **Jamsie Hall (IRE)**[14] 1410 10-11-12 137.......................(tp) JasonMaguire 126
(Gordon Elliott, Ire) *t.k.h: hld up in tch: outpcd 11th: btn bef 2 out* **4/1**[2]

4m 56.9s (-8.10) **Going Correction** -0.15s/f (Good) 6 Ran SP% **110.2**

Speed ratings (Par 107): **109,108,108,105,103 100**

toteswingers 1&2 £3.70, 1&3 £4.40, 2&3 £4.20 CSF £18.42 TOTE £3.10: £1.60, £2.20; EX 10.30 Trifecta £65.40 Pool: £1557.03 - 17.83 winning units..

Owner R Michael Smith **Bred** Miss Jayne Butler **Trained** Galston, E Ayrshire

FOCUS

A competitive handicap chase, and some old adversaries renewing rivalry. The winner is rated close to his recent course mark, backed up by the third to form.

1546 PIPE AND PILING SUPPLIES STANDARD OPEN NATIONAL HUNT FLAT RACE 2m 110y
5:20 (5:20) (Class 5) 4-6-Y-0 **£2,053** (£598; £299)

Form RPR

4/ **1** **It's All An Act (IRE)**[287] 2675 5-11-0 0.................................. APMcCoy 108+
(John Joseph Hanlon, Ire) *mde all at stdy pce: pushed along over 4f out: styd on strly to go clr fr over 2f out: easily* **4/6**[1]

2 *11* **Indian Winter (IRE)**[403] 1166 6-10-7 0............................ MrSFMagee(7) 95
(Stephen Francis Magee, Ire) *chsd ldrs: effrt over 3f out: chsd (clr) wnr 2f out: sn no imp* **7/1**[3]

3 *13* **Sharp** 4-11-0 0.. JasonMaguire 86
(Donald McCain) *chsd wnr: rdn wl over 2f out: wknd over 1f out* **2/1**[2]

3m 57.1s (4.70) **Going Correction** -0.30s/f (Good)

WFA 4 from 5yo+ 11lb 3 Ran SP% **105.8**

Speed ratings: **76,70,64**

CSF £4.76 TOTE £1.70; EX 6.20 Trifecta £3.50 Pool: £576.33 - 123.44 winning units..

Owner Miss Rachel O'Neill **Bred** Patrick Doyle **Trained** Bagenalstown, Co Carlow

FOCUS

Ordinary bumper form rated through the runner-up for the time being.

T/Plt: £567.30 to a £1 stake. Pool: £54756.46 - 70.46 winning tickets T/Qpdt: £129.30 to a £1 stake. Pool: £3162.77 - 18.10 winning tickets RY

[1425]WORCESTER (L-H)

Tuesday, September 10

OFFICIAL GOING: Good (7.1)

Wind: almost nil Weather: overcast; 16 degrees

1547 DOWNLOAD OUR IPHONE APP H'CAP CHASE (12 fncs) 2m 110y

2:10 (2:10) (Class 5) (0-95,102) 4-Y-O+ **£2,274** (£667; £333; £166)

Form RPR

4PP/ 1 **Shalamiyr (FR)**[463] 8-11-4 **87** WillKennedy 101+
(Sarah-Jayne Davies) *prom and travelled wl: lft in ld bef 5th: abt 5 l clr fr 10th: pushed along and nvr seriously trbld after* **16/1**

201- 2 5 **Crack At Dawn (IRE)**[22] 1314 12-11-3 **93** (v) MissAEStirling(7) 98
(Michael Gates) *chsd ldrs: wnt 2nd at 9th: drvn and nvr able to bridge 5 l gap fr next* **10/1**

453- 3 10 **Finch Flyer (IRE)**[10] 1395 6-10-5 **74** (p) LeeEdwards 72
(Aytach Sadik) *trckd ldrs: 5th and drvn after 9th: wnt modest 3rd next but nvr threatened ldng pair after* **4/1**[2]

625- 4 5 **Escardo (GER)**[21] 1328 10-10-8 **84** (p) JakeHodson(7) 76
(David Bridgwater) *bhd: 8th and lot to do after 9th: plodded on up st: nvr looked like getting in a blow* **10/1**

100- 5 1 ¾ **Daneva (IRE)**[28] 1260 9-11-5 **95** (tp) MrJMRidley(7) 85
(Matt Sheppard) *prom: lft 2nd bef 5th tl 9th: rdn and sn outpcd by ldng pair: wl btn whn hit next* **16/1**

/63- 6 5 **Nouailhas**[23] 1301 7-10-12 **81** (p) PaulMoloney 67
(Andrew Hollinshead) *hld up in rr: 7th and struggling after 9th: wl btn whn hanging and jumping lft fr next* **16/1**

3PU/ 7 18 **Go On Arch (IRE)**[190] 4563 7-11-4 **87** SamTwiston-Davies 68+
(Nigel Twiston-Davies) *on his toes: countless errors: stdd to chse ldrs: 4th and drvn w no rspnse after 9th: already struggling whn blnd bdly 3 out: eased last* **11/10**[1]

/0P- 8 ½ **Grand Fella (IRE)**[22] 1314 8-10-0 **69** oh7 (b) JamesDavies 38
(Ken Wingrove) *chsd ldrs tl rdn and lost tch 9th: t.o whn j.rt 2 out* **80/1**

40P/ 9 94 **Cash In Hand (IRE)**[297] 2472 13-10-0 **69** oh10 MarkGrant
(Christopher Kellett) *rdn and lost tch 6th: t.o fr 9th: fin eventually* **66/1**

U- P **Longwood Lad (IRE)**[13] 1426 11-10-13 **85** PeterCarberry(3)
(Carole Ikin) *sweating bdly: reluctant to line up and led in: plld ferociously in clr ld tl stopped to nil bef 5th: t.o and p.u next* **50/1**

513- F **Echo Dancer**[55] 1014 7-10-9 **85** (b) JoshWall(7)
(Trevor Wall) *2nd whn fell heavily 2nd* **7/1**[3]

3m 58.7s (-15.30) **Going Correction** -0.95s/f (Hard) 11 Ran SP% **120.6**
Speed ratings (Par 103): **98,95,90,88,87 85,76,76,32,**
Tote Swingers: 1&2 £11.90, 1&3 £22.90, 2&3 £8.00 CSF £165.73 CT £776.42 TOTE £20.70: £6.20, £2.20, £1.60; EX 306.50 Trifecta £525.50 Part won. Pool: £700.78 - 0.10 winning units..
Owner Miss Sarah-Jayne Davies **Bred** H H The Aga Khan's Studs Sc **Trained** Leominster, H'fords

FOCUS
Both bends moved out 3yds off inside line. This was a weak opening handicap, run at an average gallop and the runner-up sets the standard. The ground looked to be riding as officially advertised.

1548 SEVERN RESTAURANT "HANDS AND HEELS" H'CAP CHASE (CONDITIONALS/AMATEURS) (RACING EXCELLENCE) (17 fncs 1 omitted) 2m 7f

2:40 (2:41) (Class 5) (0-95,95) 4-Y-O+ **£2,274** (£667; £333; £166)

Form RPR

220- 1 **Watch House (IRE)**[22] 1320 8-10-10 **79** MissAEStirling 100+
(Michael Gates) *2nd or 3rd tl led 12th: drawing clr and gng best bef 15th: 12 l ahd whn hit last: unchal* **7/1**[3]

552- 2 22 **Sadler's Star (GER)**[26] 1272 10-11-12 **95** KieronEdgar 95
(Michael Blake) *rn in snatches: effrt in 6th after 14th: sn rdn: hit 3 out and bdly outpcd: 20 l 5th at last but consented to run on late and overtk three floundering rivals after and snatched 2nd* **10/1**

530- 3 hd **Paddysparks (IRE)**[17] 1376 9-10-0 **69** oh2 (p) ConorRing 72
(Henry Oliver) *midfield: hmpd 8th: nt a fluent after: wnt 2nd at 14th: 4 l down and drvn next: sn lost tch w wnr: hit 3 out: plugged on: lost 2nd fnl strides* **11/2**[2]

214- 4 1 **Fromthetop (IRE)**[15] 1406 7-11-0 **83** (tp) JackSherwood 83
(Michael Scudamore) *rn in snatches: lost pl 7th: hit 11th: rallied to 3rd and mstke 12th: urged along after: 4th home turn: one pce after* **11/4**[1]

5P5- 5 1 **Upper Deck (IRE)**[15] 1405 8-10-0 **69** oh3 DanielHiskett 67
(Richard Phillips) *chsd ldr: 5th and rdn after 14th: plodded on same pce and n.d after* **14/1**

062- 6 2 ¾ **Rifleman (IRE)**[19] 1344 13-10-5 **79** (tp) JamesJeavons(5) 75
(Richard Lee) *towards rr and rdn 1/2-way: sme hdwy after 14th: rdn and no imp on ldrs fr next* **14/1**

363- 7 14 **Sea Cadet**[12] 1437 11-11-0 **86** (v[1]) NathanAdams(3) 69
(Laura Mongan) *last whn mstkes 3rd and 4th: nvr travelling: t.o fr 11th* **9/1**

230- 8 5 **Pure Anticipation (IRE)**[28] 1260 8-11-9 **95** (v) MrBGibbs(3) 74
(Tim Vaughan) *blnd 1st: sn chsng ldrs: wnt 2nd fr 12th tl 14th: rdn and fdd tamely bef next: eased and t.o* **14/1**

4P5- 9 5 **Cocoa Key (IRE)**[49] 1086 9-11-2 **90** MrTGreenwood(5) 64
(Richard Ford) *led tl 12th: dropped out rapidly: t.o fr 15th* **20/1**

2/P- 10 2 ¼ **Allterrain (IRE)**[23] 1300 10-9-9 **69** oh3 (b) MrGGorman(5) 41
(Gary Moore) *dropped to rr after being impeded 8th: t.o after blunder 14th* **9/1**

50P- F **Guns Of Love (IRE)**[24] 1280 11-10-0 **74** MrTWWheeler(5)
(Robin Dickin) *chsd ldrs tl fell heavily 8th* **50/1**

0P3- P **Quayside Court (IRE)**[37] 1202 9-10-10 **79** (vt) RyanHatch
(Claire Dyson) *in rr and drvn and looking reluctant after 9th: t.o 11th tl p.u 15th* **14/1**

5m 40.0s (-8.00) **Going Correction** -0.95s/f (Hard) 12 Ran SP% **117.0**
Speed ratings (Par 103): **75,67,67,66,66 65,60,59,57,56** ,
Tote Swingers: 1&2 £28.70, 1&3 £14.20, 2&3 £24.50 CSF £74.04 CT £415.96 TOTE £9.20: £2.70, £2.90, £2.30; EX 110.30 Trifecta £738.30 Part won. Pool: £984.47 - 0.42 winning units..
Owner Michael Gates **Bred** T Reeves **Trained** Clifford Chambers, Warwicks

■ Stewards' Enquiry : Mr T Greenwood two-day ban: ignored starters' instructions (Oct 18,22)

FOCUS
An ordinary handicap which was confined to conditional/amateur riders and their whips, while carried, were not permitted to be used. The second-last fence was bypassed. The placed horses are rated in line with recent form.

1549 WORCESTER-RACECOURSE.CO.UK NOVICES' H'CAP CHASE (15 fncs) 2m 4f

3:10 (3:11) (Class 4) (0-115,115) 4-Y-O+ **£4,223** (£1,240; £620; £310)

Form RPR

465- 1 **Moorlands Jack**[28] 1267 8-10-5 **94** (p) NickScholfield 108+
(Jeremy Scott) *racd keenly in 2nd: j. slowly 6th: led 8th: gng wl fr next but getting rather low at the fences: battled bttr than two chalrs fr 2 out: in command last: eased cl home* **85/40**[1]

233- 2 4 ½ **Gud Day (IRE)**[21] 1326 5-11-9 **112** (t) PaddyBrennan 120
(Fergal O'Brien) *trckd ldrs: j. slowly 7th: effrt and ev ch gng wl fr 12th: rdn 2 out and v little rspnse: wl hld 2nd fr last* **7/2**[3]

6/4- 3 1 **Midnight Tuesday (FR)**[111] 432 8-11-12 **115** (t[1]) HarrySkelton 121
(Dan Skelton) *plld hrd in 3rd on outer: chal 12th: ev ch tl rdn and racd awkwardly fr 2 out: wandering and wl hld after* **11/4**[2]

61P- 4 22 **Valleyofmilan (IRE)**[24] 1291 6-11-12 **115** JasonMaguire 101
(Donald McCain) *led at stdy pce: hdd 8th: lost tch rapidly bef 12th: drvn flat: snatched remote 4th* **6/1**

0PU- 5 nk **First Morning (IRE)**[26] 1274 8-10-9 **98** TomCannon 87
(Michael Blake) *nt jump wl in last pair: wnt 4th after 10th but rdn and sn struggling: poor 4th whn hit 2 out and last* **20/1**

123- 6 60 **Rudigreen (IRE)**[15] 1403 10-11-9 **115** (tp) JackQuinlan(3) 47
(Noel Quinlan) *last pair: reminder after 5th: j. slowly 6th: nvr travelling after: last at 7th: t.o fr 9th* **13/2**

4m 38.2s (-21.80) **Going Correction** -0.95s/f (Hard) course record 6 Ran SP% **113.3**
Speed ratings (Par 105): **105,103,102,94,93 69**
Tote Swingers: 1&2 £1.10, 1&3 £2.20, 2&3 £1.30 CSF £10.43 TOTE £2.40: £1.70, £2.00; EX 11.20 Trifecta £32.50 Pool: £1,545.09 - 30.96 winning units..
Owner Mrs Lynda M Williams **Bred** Mrs L M Williams **Trained** Brompton Regis, Somerset

FOCUS
A moderate novice handicap, run at a routine pace. A step up from the winner with the placed horses to their marks.

1550 FOLLOW US ON TWITTER @WORCESTERRACES NOVICES' CHASE (12 fncs) 2m 110y

3:40 (3:40) (Class 4) 4-Y-O+ **£3,898** (£1,144; £572; £286)

Form RPR

011- 1 **One Term (IRE)**[39] 1184 6-11-7 133 PaulO'Brien(10) 125+
(Rebecca Curtis) *mde all: rdn 2 out: jnd and nt fluent last: galloped on resolutely flat* **2/1**[2]

421- 2 1 ¼ **The Cockney Mackem (IRE)**[13] 1426 7-11-11 0.. SamTwiston-Davies 119+
(Nigel Twiston-Davies) *rdn to s wout irons: planted and lost 20 l whn tapes rose: rcvrd to chse ldrs fr 4th: tk 2nd gng wl after 9th: drvn 2 out: upsides wnr last: hld fnl 100yds* **7/4**[1]

1/3- 3 4 ½ **Swaledale Lad (IRE)**[49] 1083 6-11-0 125 HarryChalloner(5) 107
(Richard Ford) *t.k.h: hit 1st: pressed wnr tl after 9th: 3rd and nt qckn fr 3 out: hit last* **4/1**[3]

5/0- 4 4 ½ **Nicks Power (IRE)**[79] 812 7-11-5 0 CharliePoste 104
(Robin Dickin) *midfield: mstke 9th and rdn: sn outpcd: trying to rally whn wnt lft last: kpt on wout threatening* **40/1**

0/P- 5 12 **Mosstown (IRE)**[58] 966 7-11-5 0 (tp) DPFahy 92
(Liam Corcoran) *last pair: rdn and outpcd after 9th: plugged on* **50/1**

/00- 6 2 ¼ **Red Rosso**[46] 1120 8-10-12 0 JakeHodson(7) 91
(Rob Summers) *plld hrd: pressed ldrs: pushed along bef 10th: sn btn* **100/1**

/5P- 7 12 **The Nephew (IRE)**[10] 1479 5-11-5 0 (t) RichieMcLernon 79
(Jonjo O'Neill) *hld up and wl in rr: j.rt 2nd: looked promising hdwy to chse ldrs bef 10th: sn losing grnd and nt pushed* **20/1**

04- 8 2 ½ **Checkmate**[23] 1303 8-11-5 0 MarkGrant 77
(Christopher Kellett) *hmpd s: a in last trio: mstke 7th: rdn and struggling fr 9th* **100/1**

P/ F **Train Of Thought (IRE)**[50] 1582 5-11-5 0 PaulMoloney 91
(Evan Williams) *prom: 3rd whn mstke 6th: rdn bef 10th: disputing 12 l 4th whn fell 2 out* **5/1**

4m 1.3s (-12.70) **Going Correction** -0.95s/f (Hard) 9 Ran SP% **117.5**
Speed ratings (Par 105): **91,90,88,86,80 79,73,72,**
Tote Swingers: 1&2 £1.02, 1&3 £2.60, 2&3 £1.40 CSF £6.20 TOTE £2.40: £1.10, £1.30, £1.40; EX 6.00 Trifecta £13.30 Pool: £1,230.12 - 68.86 winning units..
Owner Miss L Reid & G Costelloe **Bred** Hugh J Holohan **Trained** Newport, Dyfed

FOCUS
The two market leaders dominated the finish of this novice chase and it's straightforward form with the first four all entitled to rate this high.

1551 COLIN PRICE 60TH BIRTHDAY CELEBRATIONS H'CAP HURDLE (8 hdls) 2m

4:10 (4:10) (Class 4) (0-110,110) 4-Y-O+ **£3,249** (£954; £477; £238)

Form RPR

215- 1 **My Lord**[10] 1173 5-11-5 **103** LiamTreadwell 110
(Luke Dace) *trckd ldrs: wnt 2nd bef 3 out: rdn to ld and nt fluent last: drvn and kpt on wl flat* **8/1**

000/ 2 1 **Judiciary (IRE)**[157] 5185 6-11-2 **110** PaulO'Brien(10) 116
(Rebecca Curtis) *t.k.h: led 2nd: rdn 2 out: hdd nring last: no imp flat* **4/1**[3]

6P2- 3 2 ½ **Hi Tide (IRE)**[6] 1495 9-11-2 **100** AidanColeman 103
(J R Jenkins) *t.k.h in rr: effrt in 4th 3 out: sn rdn: 5 l 3rd 2 out: racd awkwardly and wl hld after* **11/4**[2]

022- 4 2 ¾ **The Bay Bandit**[15] 1827 6-11-10 **108** (p) NoelFehily 110
(Neil Mulholland) *settled in rr: effrt after 5th: rdn next: 6 l 4th and nt fluent last: styd on one pce* **12/1**

/60- 5 4 ½ **Bathcounty (IRE)**[15] 1391 6-11-4 **102** SamTwiston-Davies 99
(Barry Brennan) *towards rr: effrt 5th: rdn next: no imp after: wl hld between last two* **40/1**

456/ 6 ¾ **Last Shadow**[215] 4083 4-11-12 **110** APMcCoy 106
(Jonjo O'Neill) *hld up in rr: prog after 5th: effrt and looked to be gng wl on heels of ldrs home turn: sn drvn and no rspnse: edging lft and looking awkward after* **5/2**[1]

/00- 7 7 **Comehomequietly (IRE)**[19] 1345 9-11-10 **108** LeightonAspell 98
(David Rees) *prom tl 5th: rdn and dropped out bef next* **33/1**

264- 8 1 **Brassbound (USA)**[15] 1400 5-11-11 **109** AndrewThornton 98
(Caroline Bailey) *rdn and dropped bk last at 4th: no ch after* **20/1**

666- 9 12 **Fintan**[46] 1122 10-11-3 **104** (t) JamesBest(3) 82
(Rob Summers) *mounted on crse: plld hrd in 2nd or 3rd tl drvn and lost pl tamely bef 3 out* **50/1**

4/0- **10** *44* **Burnswood (IRE)**[19] 1345 9-10-8 **92**................................ RichardJohnson 31
(Marc Barber) *chsd ldrs: nt fluent 3rd: lost tch 5th: t.o next* **33/1**

0/4- **P** **Vapiano (IRE)**[49] 1087 7-11-4 **102**.................................... TomScudamore
(David Pipe) *led tl sprawled on landing 2nd: prom tl drvn and blnd 5th: stopped qckly: t.o next: p.u 2 out* **12/1**

3m 37.6s (-9.70) **Going Correction** -0.50s/f (Good) **11** Ran SP% **116.8**
Speed ratings (Par 105): **104,103,102,100,98 98,94,94,88,66**
Tote Swingers: 1&2 £18.50, 1&3 £4.30, 2&3 £6.70 CSF £38.41 CT £111.98 TOTE £6.50: £1.60, £2.20, £1.60; EX 85.40 Trifecta £639.50 Part won. Pool: £852.71 - 0.10 winning units..
Owner Mark Benton **Bred** Mrs Monica Teversham **Trained** Five Oaks, W Sussex

FOCUS
A moderate handicap, run at an ordinary gallop. The first two are on the upgrade with the fourth the best guide.

1552 BOOK HOSPITALITY AT WORCESTER RACECOURSE NOVICES' HURDLE (12 hdls) 2m 7f
4:40 (4:40) (Class 4) 4-Y-0+ **£3,249** (£954; £477; £238)

Form RPR

216- **1** **No Loose Change (IRE)**[18] 1362 8-10-7 131..............(t) HarryDerham(5) 119+
(Paul Nicholls) *mde all: qng strly home turn: 6 l clr last: hrd hld* **2/5**[1]

/64- **2** *5* **King Boru (IRE)**[104] 538 5-10-9 0................................ GavinSheehan(3) 109+
(Emma Lavelle) *dropped out last: 8 l last and clsng whn nt fluent 7th: smooth prog to go 2nd after 9th: rdn and no match w wnr fr next but wl clr of rest fr 2 out* **9/4**[2]

6/5- **3** *26* **Miss Mayfair (IRE)**[24] 1281 6-10-5 0....................................... DavidBass 77
(Lawney Hill) *chsd ldrs: hmpd 8th: rdn and outpcd by ldng pair whn nt fluent 3rd out: plugged on to take remote 3rd sn after last* **16/1**

65- **4** *1 1/4* **Cute Court (IRE)**[42] 1154 6-10-12 0.. DPFahy 84
(Liam Corcoran) *settled last quartet: sme hdwy 3 out: wnt remote 3rd 2 out tl sn after mstke last* **33/1**

20F- **5** *12* **Pirans Car**[13] 1426 7-10-12 85..(t) TomScudamore 77
(Nigel Hawke) *settled rr quartet: hdwy 7th: disp 2nd home turn: drvn whn mstke 3 out: fading after: t.o* **16/1**

4- **6** *37* **Possibly Flora**[28] 1265 8-10-2 0..................................... MichealNolan(3) 32
(Richard Woollacott) *bhd: lost tch tamely 9th: t.o fr next: sn eased* **18/1**

- **P** **Phantom Ranch**[43] 4-10-10 0... WillKennedy
(Alastair Lidderdale) *pressed wnr tl 9th: drvn and rapidly bec t.o: p.u 2 out* **33/1**

056- **F** **Just Archie (USA)**[26] 1270 5-10-12 0................................ LeightonAspell
(Lady Herries) *chsd ldrs and wl in tch tl fell 8th* **14/1**[3]

5m 34.8s (6.80) **Going Correction** -0.50s/f (Good)
WFA 4 from 5yo+ 12lb **8** Ran SP% **131.8**
Speed ratings (Par 105): **68,66,57,56,52 39, ,**
Tote Swingers: 1&2 £1.10, 1&3 £3.80, 2&3 £3.70 CSF £2.21 TOTE £1.10: £1.02, £1.10, £4.30; EX 2.20 Trifecta £11.00 Pool: £1,088.35 - 74.14 winning units..
Owner Donlon, Doyle, MacDonald & Webb **Bred** Stone Electrical Ltd **Trained** Ditcheat, Somerset

FOCUS
The winner stood out in this otherwise modest novice hurdle, although the runner-up is on the upgrade.

1553 SPONSOR A RACE BY CALLING 01905 25364 MAIDEN HURDLE (8 hdls) 2m
5:10 (5:10) (Class 5) 4-Y-0+ **£1,949** (£572; £286; £143)

Form RPR

2- **1** **Hallings Comet**[42] 1152 4-11-0 0.. AidanColeman 125+
(Adrian Wintle) *taken down early: plld hrd and sn clr: nvr less than 5 l ahd: pushed along bef last: wl in command between last two: rdn out* **4/1**[2]

4/2- **2** *9* **Carlton Jack**[130] 93 6-11-0 115.. APMcCoy 120+
(Jonjo O'Neill) *chsd wnr but many awkward jumps: drvn bef 3 out: sn hanging lft: fnd nthing and wl hld between last two* **30/100**[1]

6F6/ **3** *13* **Next Sensation (IRE)**[150] 5291 6-11-0 0.....................(t) TomScudamore 106
(Michael Scudamore) *a 3rd or 4th: 6 l 3rd home turn: rdn and plodded on and wl hld after* **9/1**[3]

/04- **4** *24* **Trakeur (FR)**[13] 1431 6-11-0 0.. JamesDavies 83
(Simon Hodgson) *chsd ldrs: rdn and lost tch after 5th: t.o bef 2 out* **33/1**

5 *23* **Quernstone (USA)**[685] 4-10-11 0................................ JeremiahMcGrath(3) 62
(Harry Whittington) *last pair: t.o fr 4th* **33/1**

P **The Last Bullit**[878] 7-10-7 0.....................................(t) MrMatthewBarber(7)
(Marc Barber) *j. v poorly in last pair: t.o fr 4th tl p.u 3 out* **50/1**

3m 38.2s (-9.10) **Going Correction** -0.50s/f (Good)
WFA 4 from 5yo+ 11lb **6** Ran SP% **114.8**
Speed ratings (Par 103): **102,97,91,79,67**
Tote Swingers 1&2 £1.10, 2&3 £1.40, 1&3 £1.40 CSF £6.06 TOTE £5.20: £1.60, £1.10; EX 5.90 Trifecta £12.80 Pool: £595.22 - 34.77 winning units..
Owner Lord Blyth **Bred** Lord Blyth **Trained** Westbury-On-Severn, Gloucs

FOCUS
An uncompetitive maiden hurdle with a big step up from the winner and the others in the frame rated close to their marks.
T/Plt: £32.80 to a £1 stake. Pool: £70,297.41 - 1,560.40 winning units. T/Qpdt: £3.00 to a £1 stake. Pool: £6,013.96 - 1,463.63 winning units. IM

1554 - 1560a (Foreign Racing) - See Raceform Interactive

1132 UTTOXETER (L-H)
Wednesday, September 11

OFFICIAL GOING: Chase course - good (good to firm in places); hurdle course - good to firm (good in places) changing to good all over after race 3 (3:15)
moderate 1/2 against**overcast, light rain, persistent rain race 3 onwards**

1561 BET365.COM MAIDEN HURDLE (10 hdls) 2m 4f 110y
2:10 (2:10) (Class 5) 4-Y-0+ **£2,339** (£686; £343; £171)

Form RPR

30F/ **1** **Toughness Danon**[44] 4872 7-10-9 105........................ RobertMcCarth(5) 111+
(Ian Williams) *rel to r and hopelessly detached in last: hdwy and in tch 3rd: effrt appr 3 out: chsd ldr appr 2 out: led last: drvn out* **16/1**

4- **2** *3* **Oculist**[47] 1118 5-11-0 0.. JackDoyle 106
(Ben De Haan) *trckd ldrs: led 3 out: hdd last: no ex* **6/1**

5/5- **3** *5* **The Wicked Kipper**[111] 449 5-10-7 0.................................. IanPopham 95
(Martin Keighley) *chsd ldrs: drvn and outpcd 3 out: styd on to take 3rd appr last* **20/1**

45- **4** *4* **Western Prize**[47] 1118 5-10-4 0...................................... AlanJohns(10) 97
(Tim Vaughan) *led: j.rt: hdd 3 out: wknd run-in* **4/1**[2]

/32- **5** *hd* **Swift Escape**[16] 1387 6-11-0 100...........................(p) RichardJohnson 98
(Tim Vaughan) *t.k.h: trckd ldrs: hit 3 out: wknd appr next* **5/1**[3]

2- **6** *5* **Our Maimie (IRE)**[22] 1334 7-10-7 103...................... SamTwiston-Davies 86
(R McGlinchey, Ire) *chsd ldrs: drvn appr 3 out: wknd appr next* **7/4**[1]

623/ **7** *6* **Berea Boru (IRE)**[409] 1118 5-11-0 0................................ DonalDevereux 87
(Peter Bowen) *t.k.h: mstke 2nd: chsd ldrs 5th: wknd 3 out* **16/1**

3/3- **8** *13* **Spitfire Ace (IRE)**[16] 1387 5-11-0 0.................................. JasonMaguire 75
(Donald McCain) *chsd ldr: wknd appr 2 out* **14/1**

P63- **9** *26* **Banks Road (IRE)**[14] 1431 8-11-0 0.. MarkGrant 52
(Geoffrey Deacon) *in rr: hit 4th: reminders after 7th: sn lost pl: t.o 2 out* **80/1**

P **Astrogold**[75] 4-10-6 0... ColinBolger
(Mark H Tompkins) *t.k.h: nt fluent in rr: rn v wd and lost pl bnd bef 3 out: t.o whn p.u bef 3 out* **66/1**

0- **P** **Shanksforamillion**[20] 1341 4-10-13 0................................. PaulMoloney
(David Rees) *t.k.h: lost pl 6th: hopelessly t.o next: p.u after 3 out: b.b.v* **100/1**

5m 2.0s (3.00) **Going Correction** -0.075s/f (Good)
WFA 4 from 5yo+ 12lb **11** Ran SP% **114.2**
Speed ratings (Par 103): **91,89,87,86,86 84,82,77,67,**
toteswingers 1&2 £38.00, 1&3 £38.00, 2&3 £38.00 CSF £104.58 TOTE £42.50: £8.80, £1.40, £3.90; EX 234.70 Trifecta £563.80 Part won..
Owner Paul Frank Barry **Bred** Stiftung Gestut Fahrhof **Trained** Portway, Worcs

FOCUS
Significant drainage work had taken place since the last meeting in July and racing lines utilised were away from those areas where possible. Hurdles well off inside line and some divided bends. Conditions had eased slightly from the overnight description. After the first Ian Popham said the ground was "a bit quicker than good in places - lovely ground". They went a very steady gallop in this modest maiden hurdle and the time was slow. The winner can rate higher on Flat form.

1562 BET365.COM CONDITIONAL JOCKEYS' (S) HURDLE (9 hdls) 2m
2:40 (2:40) (Class 5) 4-8-Y-0 **£1,949** (£572; £286)

Form RPR

/11- **1** **Belle De Fontenay (FR)**[50] 1092 8-11-5 117..................(p) TrevorWhelan 119+
(George Baker) *led: clr to 5th: styd on wl fr 3 out: unchal* **5/2**[3]

3/1- **2** *6* **Bollin Judith**[34] 1009 7-11-1 115...(t) TomCannon 111
(Jim Best) *hdwy to chse ldrs 6th: 2nd appr 2 out: 3 l down whn hit last: no imp* **2/1**[2]

5/1- **3** *8* **Vimiero (USA)**[11] 1475 6-11-2 116.............................. MauriceLinehan(3) 109
(Jonjo O'Neill) *trckd wnr: j.rt: t.k.h: drvn and 3rd whn hit 2 out: sn btn* **5/4**[1]

3m 52.4s (0.40) **Going Correction** -0.075s/f (Good)
WFA 4 from 6yo+ 11lb **3** Ran SP% **106.3**
Speed ratings: **96,93,89**
CSF £7.00 TOTE £2.70; EX 4.20 Trifecta £5.50 Pool: £524.63 - 70.33 winning units..There was no bid for the winner.
Owner George Baker & Partners **Bred** E A R L Elevage Des Loges **Trained** Manton, Wilts

FOCUS
This was hit by non-runners but was still a decent race of its type. The three that remained, all winners last time over hurdles, were closely matched on the figures. The form is rated around the first two.

1563 CASINO AT BET365 BEGINNERS' CHASE (18 fncs) 3m
3:15 (3:15) (Class 4) 4-Y-0+ **£4,177** (£1,234; £617; £308; £154)

Form RPR

P/3- **1** **Faultless Feelings (IRE)**[50] 1091 7-11-7 0.......................... IanPopham 131+
(Martin Keighley) *mde all: j. soundly: drvn clr appr 2 out: 10 l ld last: styd on strly: eased nr fin* **11/4**[3]

0FP/ **2** *18* **Civil Disobedience**[548] 4822 9-11-4 120........................ MichealNolan(3) 118
(Richard Woollacott) *chsd wnr fr 5th: upsides 4 out: kpt on same pce appr 2 out* **9/4**[2]

/42- **3** *19* **Trop Fort (FR)**[25] 1282 6-11-7 125................................(t) RichardJohnson 104
(Tim Vaughan) *nt fluent: chsd wnr to 5th: hmpd 7th: j. slowly next: outpcd and drvn 11th: reminders 13th: modest 3rd 3 out* **6/5**[1]

35- **4** *20* **Dbanks (IRE)**[20] 1341 10-11-7 0.. DPFahy 80
(Liam Corcoran) *hld up wl in tch: chsd ldrs 13th: modest 3rd 4 out: wknd next* **25/1**

4- **5** *7* **Reef Dancer (IRE)**[18] 1375 10-11-7 0..............................(p) KennyJohnson 73
(Robert Johnson) *t.k.h: 3rd whn wnt lft and mstke 7th: wknd after 14th: sn bhd: t.o 2 out* **66/1**

P6P- **P** **Radsoc De Sivola (FR)**[85] 759 8-11-2 71......................... JoeCornwall(5)
(John Cornwall) *in tch: pushed along 11th: lost pl 14th: t.o whn p.u bef 3 out* **100/1**

6m 11.3s (-3.80) **Going Correction** -0.075s/f (Good) **6** Ran SP% **109.2**
Speed ratings (Par 105): **103,97,90,84,81**
toteswingers 1&2 £1.10, 1&3 £1.10, 2&3 £1.50 CSF £9.04 TOTE £3.70: £1.50, £2.10; EX 11.10 Trifecta £24.70 Pool: £2193.71 - 66.58 winning units..
Owner Mrs Peter Prowting **Bred** Finbar Leahy **Trained** Condicote, Gloucs

FOCUS
A fair beginners' chase, but it lacked depth. The winner is rated up 8lb on the best of his hurdle form but there should be more to come.

1564 BET365 H'CAP HURDLE (10 hdls) 2m 4f 110y
3:50 (3:50) (Class 3) (0-140,137) 4-Y-0+
£5,630 (£1,663; £831; £415; £207; £104)

Form RPR

061- **1** **Dartford Warbler (IRE)**[18] 1378 6-11-0 **125**.......................... RyanMania 127+
(Sue Smith) *chsd ldrs: led appr 3 out: edgd lft run-in: hld on gamely* **7/1**

1FU- **2** *1 1/2* **Man Of Leisure**[13] 1433 9-11-9 **137**.........................(t) RachaelGreen(3) 137
(Anthony Honeyball) *hld up in rr but wl in tch: t.k.h: hdwy to trck ldrs 7th: cl 2nd whn hit 2 out: styd on same pce last 50yds* **11/2**[3]

123- **3** *3/4* **First In The Queue (IRE)**[53] 1045 6-11-6 **134**........ JeremiahMcGrath(3) 132
(Nicky Henderson) *chsd ldrs: cl 2nd 3 out: kpt on same pce last 75yds* **8/1**

400/ **4** *3 1/2* **Dooney Rock (IRE)**[34] 1233 9-10-10 **121**..............(p) SamTwiston-Davies 118
(Michael McElhone, Ire) *chsd ldrs: drvn 4th: reminders after next: n.m.r and lost pl bnd bef 6th: sn lost pl: kpt on fr 2 out: 6th last: tk 4th nr fin* **12/1**

023- **5** *1 1/4* **Teak (IRE)**[10] 1485 6-10-0 **111**..(p) WillKennedy 106
(Ian Williams) *led: hdd appr 3 out: outpcd after next: kpt on fr 2 out* **9/2**[2]

P/ **6** *nk* **Bombadero (IRE)**[44] 1140 6-9-13 **117**....................(t) ChristopherWard(7) 111
(Dr Richard Newland) *t.k.h: trckd ldrs: lost pl and reminders after 6th: kpt on fr 2 out* **8/1**

131- **7** *60* **Social Realism (IRE)**[20] 1347 5-10-6 **117**..............................(p) APMcCoy 93
(Jonjo O'Neill) *chsd ldr: hit 5th: j.rt and reminders next: lost pl 7th: bhd and eased bef 2 out: sn t.o: eventually completed* **2/1**[1]

4m 52.3s (-6.70) **Going Correction** -0.075s/f (Good) **7** Ran SP% **109.3**
Speed ratings (Par 107): **109,108,108,106,106 106,83**
toteswingers 1&2 £4.20, 1&3 £6.10, 2&3 £2.50 CSF £40.47 CT £286.78 TOTE £8.10: £2.40, £2.00; EX 33.30 Trifecta £286.40 Pool: £1386.95 - 3.63 winning units..

Owner Mrs S Smith **Bred** John O'Dwyer **Trained** High Eldwick, W Yorks

FOCUS

The rain was starting to get into the ground, and the official going was amended to good all round before this race. This decent handicap was run at a strong pace, putting the emphasis on stamina, and the form looks sound. Another step up from the winner.

1565 BET365.COM H'CAP HURDLE (12 hdls) 3m
4:25 (4:25) (Class 4) (0-115,111) 4-Y-0+ **£3,249** (£954; £477; £238)

Form RPR

053- **1** **Diamond's Return (IRE)**[20] 1345 9-11-12 **111**................. ConorO'Farrell 121+
(David Pipe) *hld up in rr: smooth hdwy after 9th: led appr last: wnt clr: eased towards fin* **16/1**

3/6- **2** *2 ¾* **Street Runner**[12] 1455 7-11-5 **104**................(p) BrianHughes 106
(Karl Thornton, Ire) *hld up in mid-div: hdwy to chse ldrs appr 3 out: wnt 2nd appr last: no ch w wnr* **9/1**

/31- **3** *2* **Long Wave (IRE)**[47] 1121 6-11-7 **106**................(p) NoelFehily 107
(Charlie Longsdon) *in rr: chsd ldrs 4th: led appr 3 out: hdd 2 out: kpt on same pce* **13/8**[1]

120- **4** *nk* **Auberge (IRE)**[16] 1398 9-11-1 **100**................ RyanMania 100
(Evelyn Slack) *chsd ldrs: drvn appr 3 out: hit last: kpt on same pce* **22/1**

/64- **5** *2 ¾* **Lucky To Be Alive (IRE)**[41] 1169 6-10-1 **86**................ DonalDevereux 84
(Peter Bowen) *prom: drvn and outpcd whn hit 3 out: kpt on fr next* **20/1**

562- **6** *1* **Flying Doctor**[18] 1374 10-10-11 **99**................ EwanWhillans(3) 96
(Alistair Whillans) *w ldrs: one pce fr 3 out* **7/1**[3]

53- **7** *nk* **Larteta (FR)**[15] 1418 4-11-2 **106**................ JackQuinlan(3) 102+
(Sarah Humphrey) *led to 3rd: chsd ldrs: led 2 out: hdd and nt fluent last: one pce* **33/1**

/F2- **8** *1 ¾* **Minella For Steak (IRE)**[11] 1468 6-11-9 **108**................(tp) APMcCoy 104
(Jonjo O'Neill) *hld up in mid-div: chsd ldrs 8th: drvn appr 3 out: swtchd lft between last 2: one pce* **11/2**[2]

/52- **9** *5* **Twin Bud**[116] 379 8-10-7 **95**................ AdamWedge(3) 87
(Anna Newton-Smith) *chsd ldrs 4th: wknd 3 out* **20/1**

/5P- **10** *hd* **Changing Lanes**[20] 1344 10-10-5 **90**................(v) PaulMoloney 80
(David Rees) *t.k.h: led 3rd: hdd appr 3 out: sn wknd* **28/1**

612- **11** *24* **Moon Melody (GER)**[47] 1121 10-9-9 **85** oh4................(bt) EDLinehan(5) 53
(Mike Sowersby) *prom 4th: lost pl after 9th: sn bhd* **25/1**

3/1- **12** *7* **Thoresby (IRE)**[113] 421 7-11-6 **110**................(p) KillianMoore(5) 72
(Ben Case) *in rr: drvn 9th: bhd fr next* **14/1**

P04- **13** *12* **Priceless Art (IRE)**[14] 1429 8-11-3 **105**................(t) RachaelGreen(3) 56
(Anthony Honeyball) *hld up in rr: bhd fr 9th* **25/1**

030- **14** *32* **Starlight Air**[19] 1364 10-10-6 **91**................(p) JamieMoore 14
(John Spearing) *hld up in rr: sme hdwy 9th: lost pl bef next: bhd whn virtually p.u run-in: t.o* **40/1**

5m 53.7s (3.70) **Going Correction** -0.075s/f (Good)
WFA 4 from 6yo+ 13lb **14** Ran SP% **118.9**
Speed ratings (Par 105): **90,89,88,88,87 87,86,86,84,84 76,74,70,59**
wingers 1&2 £51.40, 1&3 £14.20, 2&3 £2.70 CSF £131.92 CT £367.09 TOTE £23.50: £5.00, £2.70, £1.20; EX 230.40 Trifecta £1102.80 Part won. Pool: £1470.47 - 0.34 winning units..
Owner Seamus O'Farrell **Bred** Seamus O'Farrell **Trained** Nicholashayne, Devon

FOCUS

Quite a competitive handicap on paper, run at a reasonable gallop. Solid form with the easy winner value for further and back to his best 2012 form.

1566 BET365 H'CAP CHASE (15 fncs) 2m 4f
4:55 (4:55) (Class 4) (0-120,118) 4-Y-0+ **£3,924** (£1,159; £579; £290)

Form RPR

504- **1** **Tregaro (FR)**[11] 1470 7-10-0 **92**................ BrianHughes 103+
(Mike Sowersby) *rn wout declared tongue strap: hld up in last but wl in tch: jnd ldrs 4 out: led 2 out: wnt clr run-in* **6/1**[3]

/20- **2** *12* **Larks Lad (IRE)**[85] 757 9-11-12 **118**................(p) APMcCoy 120
(Jonjo O'Neill) *chsd ldr: j.lft 3rd: drvn 9th: outpcd 11th: n.m.r bef next: chsd ldrs 3 out: 2nd whn hit fnl fence: no ch w wnr* **15/8**[2]

324- **3** *9* **Another Flutter (IRE)**[16] 1390 9-11-3 **109**................(tp) CharliePoste 105
(Matt Sheppard) *chsd ldrs: hmpd 3rd: 2nd 7th: drvn and hit 9th: led bef 4 out: hdd 2 out: wknd between last 2* **6/1**[3]

221- **4** *36* **Callhimwhatyouwant (IRE)**[7] 1493 8-11-3 **109** 7ex(b)
SamTwiston-Davies 69
(Dr Richard Newland) *j.lft: led: hdd bef 4 out: sn lost pl: t.o 3 out* **6/5**[1]

5m 1.7s (-3.80) **Going Correction** -0.075s/f (Good) **4** Ran SP% **108.8**
Speed ratings (Par 105): **104,99,95,81**
CSF £17.38 TOTE £6.60; EX 12.70 Trifecta £54.90 Pool: £1273.01 - 17.37 winning units..
Owner Alan R Lyons **Bred** Jean-Charles Haimet & J-Pascal Liberge **Trained** Goodmanham, E Yorks

FOCUS

Fair handicap chase form. The winner is rated back to his best.

1567 POKER AT BET365 H'CAP HURDLE (9 hdls) 2m
5:25 (5:27) (Class 5) (0-100,100) 4-Y-0+ **£2,209** (£648; £324; £162)

Form RPR

/00- **1** **Pollystone (IRE)**[70] 876 7-11-4 **92**................ IanPopham 99+
(Martin Keighley) *chsd ldrs: hung lft appr 2 out: 2nd last: sn led: drvn out* **12/1**

4U6- **2** *2* **Wom**[16] 1400 5-11-2 **95**................(b) TrevorWhelan(5) 99
(Neil King) *hld up in rr: hdwy to trck ldrs 6th: led 3 out: hdd next: kpt on run-in: tk 2nd last 75yds* **10/1**

/22- **3** *3 ¼* **Royal Trooper (IRE)**[44] 1137 7-11-8 **96**................(vt) APMcCoy 99+
(Jim Best) *racd wd: hld up in rr: hdwy to trck ldrs after 5th: led 2 out: hit last: hdd and no ex last 100yds* **11/8**[1]

33U- **4** *¾* **Claude Carter**[15] 1419 9-11-8 **99**................ EwanWhillans(3) 100
(Alistair Whillans) *chsd ldrs: upsides 3 out: kpt on one pce fr next* **11/2**[2]

33P- **5** *3* **Laybach (IRE)**[42] 1163 9-10-0 **74** oh2................ HenryBrooke 73
(Jim Goldie) *led: hdd 3 out: one pce fr next* **12/1**

P03- **6** *1 ½* **Good Of Luck**[11] 1475 4-11-9 **97**................ AidanColeman 93
(Mick Channon) *chsd ldrs: drvn appr 3 out: one pce* **11/1**

632- **7** *nse* **Rose Red**[22] 1331 6-11-3 **94**................ JamesBest(3) 90
(Rob Summers) *in rr: hdwy to chse ldrs 3 out: sn outpcd: kpt on between last 2* **8/1**[3]

623/ **8** *38* **Prickles**[187] 4642 8-11-9 **100**................(t[1]) MichealNolan(3) 62
(Richard Woollacott) *in rr: drvn 5th: bhd fr 3 out: t.o* **10/1**

/FP- **9** *24* **Leyland (IRE)**[29] 1259 4-11-1 **89**................(b) DavidBass 29
(Lawney Hill) *w ldrs: drvn 5th: lost pl 6th: sn bhd: t.o next* **20/1**

3m 54.2s (2.20) **Going Correction** -0.075s/f (Good)
WFA 4 from 5yo+ 11lb **9** Ran SP% **115.3**
Speed ratings (Par 103): **91,90,88,88,86 85,85,66,54**
toteswingers 1&2 £12.20, 1&3 £9.40, 2&3 £4.70 CSF £121.81 CT £270.60 TOTE £13.70: £4.30, £3.10, £1.10; EX 155.30 Trifecta £1021.70 Part won. Pool: £1362.35 - 0.94 winning units..
Owner R T Crellin **Bred** James Bowe **Trained** Condicote, Gloucs

FOCUS

A modest handicap hurdle run in deteriorating conditions. The winner improved in line with the best of his bumper form.

T/Plt: £2,658.40 to a £1 stake. Pool: £70649.89 - 19.40 winning tickets T/Qpdt: £123.10 to a £1 stake. Pool: £6238.48 - 37.50 winning tickets WG

1568 - 1571a (Foreign Racing) - See Raceform Interactive

[1554] GALWAY (R-H)
Wednesday, September 11

OFFICIAL GOING: Good to firm (good in places)

1572a RYANS CLEANING CHASE 2m 6f
6:30 (6:31) 5-Y-0+ **£11,626** (£3,398; £1,609; £536)

RPR

1 **Your Busy (IRE)**[19] 1362 10-11-5 123................ DJCasey 117+
(J A Nash, Ire) *led and disp: awkward 2nd and j.lft at times: narrow advantage 1/2-way: wnt bdly lft bef 2 out: sn rdn and wnt 2 l clr into st: reduced advantage and strly pressed nr fin: kpt on wl* **2/1**[2]

2 *¾* **Schelm (GER)**[9] 1491 11-11-0................ JodyMcGarvey(5) 116+
(Ronald O'Leary, Ire) *chsd ldrs: 4th 1/2-way: hdwy bef 2 out to trck ldr in 2nd into st: sn rdn and clsd u.p to strly press wnr nr fin: hld* **7/1**

3 *1 ¼* **Bob Lingo (IRE)**[42] 1168 11-11-5 145................(t) MarkWalsh 115+
(Thomas Mullins, Ire) *chsd ldrs: 3rd 1/2-way: tk clsr order on inner fr last where n.m.r: sn rdn in mod 3rd: kpt on wl nr fin wout threatening principals* **3/1**[3]

4 *14* **Shock N Freaney (IRE)**[3] 1528 6-11-5 81................(vt) BMCash 101?
(Anthony Middleton) *reluctant to line up: hld up and niggled along early: 5th 1/2-way: reminders fr 10th: rdn and no imp on ldrs bef st: kpt on same pce into mod 4th nr fin* **100/1**

5 *2 ½* **Sin Palo (IRE)**[27] 1277 9-11-12 132................ RWalsh 106
(W P Mullins, Ire) *led and disp: cl 2nd 1/2-way: forced lft 2 out and got on terms briefly fr last: rdn and dropped to 4th bef st: carried hd high: no ex and hung run-in: dropped to mod 5th nr fin* **13/8**[1]

6 *21* **Chaninbar (FR)**[541] 2490 10-11-5................(vt) NickScholfield 78
(Anthony Middleton) *reluctant to s and lost grnd w rdr wout irons briefly: detached in rr thrght: nvr a factor* **16/1**

5m 39.3s (-0.70) **6** Ran SP% **115.8**
CSF £16.35 TOTE £3.10: £1.90, £4.20; DF 15.60.
Owner J A Nash **Bred** Miss Catriona Cagney **Trained** The Curragh, Co. Kildare

FOCUS

Not the most straightforward of races and pretty uncompetitive, but it was won by a very uncomplicated horse at his best. The form is rated around the second.

1573 - 1574a (Foreign Racing) - See Raceform Interactive

[1387] BANGOR-ON-DEE (L-H)
Friday, September 13

OFFICIAL GOING: Good (6.9)
Wind: moderate 1/2 behind Weather: raining

1575 BANGORBET NOVICES' H'CAP HURDLE (9 hdls) 2m 1f
1:50 (1:50) (Class 4) (0-105,104) 4-Y-0+ **£3,422** (£997; £499)

Form RPR

000- **1** **Goat Castle (IRE)**[49] 1120 9-10-1 **79**................(t) SamTwiston-Davies 83
(Nigel Twiston-Davies) *chsd ldrs 3rd: 2nd 3 out: led next: drvn out* **7/1**

5/6- **2** *5* **Chankillo**[18] 1404 4-10-7 **85**................ WillKennedy 85
(Sarah-Jayne Davies) *led after 1st: hdd 2 out: kpt on same pce* **33/1**

1/F- **3** *4* **Spoil Me (IRE)**[132] 121 6-11-12 **104**................ RichieMcLernon 100
(Jonjo O'Neill) *hld up in rr: hdwy to chse ldrs 3 out: 3rd and kpt on one pce next* **12/1**

324- **4** *5* **Duchess Theatre (IRE)**[9] 1495 5-10-12 **93**................(t) JakeGreenall(3) 84
(Michael Easterby) *led tl after 1st: drvn 3 out: one pce* **15/2**

453- **5** *5* **Solo Jugadores**[8] 1506 5-11-0 **92**................(b[1]) DenisO'Regan 80
(Richard Guest) *hld up in rr: hdwy to chse ldrs 5th: wkng whn mstke 2 out* **9/2**[1]

601- **6** *27* **Ravi River (IRE)**[20] 1379 9-9-9 **80**................ KieronEdgar(7) 43
(Alistair Whillans) *nt jump wl: blnd 2nd: sme hdwy 5th: sn wknd: t.o 2 out* **5/1**[2]

340/ **7** *55* **Quantique (FR)**[1411] 2038 9-10-6 **84**................ AidanColeman
(Venetia Williams) *in rr: bhd fr 6th: t.o 2 out* **11/2**[3]

3P2/ **8** *21* **Pampanito**[614] 3645 7-11-7 **99**................ JasonMaguire
(Donald McCain) *chsd ldrs: reminders 4th: nt fluent and lost pl next: sn bhd: t.o 3 out* **10/1**

506/ **P** **Ma Toolan (IRE)**[139] 5567 6-11-8 **100**................ AlainCawley
(John Mackie) *chsd ldrs: p.u after 5th: fatally injured* **9/2**[1]

4m 3.7s (-7.20) **Going Correction** -0.325s/f (Good)
WFA 4 from 5yo+ 11lb **9** Ran SP% **112.4**
Speed ratings (Par 105): **103,100,98,96,94 81,55,45,**
toteswingers 1&2 Not won, 1&3 Not won, 2&3 Not won CSF £170.66 CT £2678.63 TOTE £8.70: £2.40, £10.80, £4.80; EX 141.20 Trifecta £411.90 Part won. Pool: £549.21 - 0.01 winning units..
Owner N A Twiston-Davies **Bred** Edward Lacy **Trained** Naunton, Gloucs

FOCUS

A modest novice handicap hurdle run at an ordinary pace. The winner is rated to his best form for the last year.

1576 DEVA RACING NOVICES' HURDLE (11 hdls) 2m 4f
2:20 (2:20) (Class 4) 4-Y-0+ **£3,249** (£954; £477; £238)

Form RPR

221- **1** **Clondaw Draft (IRE)**[24] 1329 5-11-5 116................ JasonMaguire 133+
(Donald McCain) *j. soundly: mde all: qcknd pce 6th: drvn appr 2 out: styd on strly: eased towards fin* **11/2**[3]

111- **2** *11* **Another Hero (IRE)**[51] 1108 4-11-11 0................ APMcCoy 128
(Jonjo O'Neill) *hld up in rr: 3rd after 6th: chsd wnr 8th: drvn after 3 out: kpt on same pce appr 2 out* **13/8**[1]

/21- **3** *5* **Ocean Club**[18] 1393 6-10-12 120................ CraigGallagher(7) 117
(Brian Ellison) *chsd ldrs: nt fluent 5th: outpcd and lost pl 7th: wnt modest 3rd after 3 out: kpt on* **5/2**[2]

464/ **4** *24* **Splash Of Ginge**[146] 5407 5-10-12 0................ SamTwiston-Davies 88
(Nigel Twiston-Davies) *nt fluent: chsd wnr: wknd 3 out: sn bhd* **8/1**

U30- **5** *54* **Gentleman Anshan (IRE)**[55] 1047 9-10-7 0........................ BenPoste(5) 39
(Rosemary Gasson) *t.k.h towaerds rr: pushed along 4th: outpcd 7th: sn bhd: t.o 3 out: lame* **7/1**

4m 46.1s (-5.90) **Going Correction** -0.325s/f (Good) **5** Ran SP% **105.7**
Speed ratings (Par 105): **98,93,91,82,60**
CSF £14.06 TOTE £6.00: £1.80, £1.10; EX 10.30 Trifecta £28.50 Pool: £1156.43 - 30.34 winning units..
Owner T G Leslie **Bred** Gerry Ross **Trained** Cholmondeley, Cheshire

FOCUS
An interesting novice hurdle in which the winner made all. The winner is on the upgrade and should win more races.

1577 BROOKE RANKIN ACCOUNTANTS SILVER JUBLIEE H'CAP CHASE (15 fncs) 2m 4f 110y
2:50 (2:51) (Class 4) (0-105,105) 4-Y-0+ **£5,198** (£1,526; £763; £381)

Form RPR
531- **1** **Roc De Guye (FR)**[31] 1260 8-10-4 **83**............................(p) LiamTreadwell 106+
(James Evans) *racd wd: hdwy 5th: chsng ldrs next: clr 2nd appr 3 out: led appr 2 out: sn drew clr: eased towards fin* **8/1**

5P5- **2** *10* **Suburban Bay**[24] 1326 8-11-11 **104**.............................. WayneHutchinson 114
(Alan King) *chsd ldrs: reminder 10th: outpcd 3 out: 3rd appr next: kpt on to take 2nd last 100yds* **5/1**

22P- **3** *4 ½* **Old Pals Act (IRE)**[43] 1175 5-11-12 **105**................................(p) APMcCoy 112
(Jonjo O'Neill) *sn chsng ldr: led after 12th: hdd appr 2 out: lost 2nd run-in* **9/2**[3]

P/3- **4** *8* **Tough Talkin Man (IRE)**[55] 1049 9-11-4 **97**................(p) DonalDevereux 96
(Peter Bowen) *sn chsng ldrs: drvn 12th: sn outpcd: wknd appr 2 out* **7/2**[1]

026- **5** *½* **Up To The Mark**[25] 1319 8-11-12 **105**........................(p) RichardJohnson 103
(Henry Daly) *chsd ldrs: pushed along 9th: lost pl 11th: kpt on run-in* **9/1**

P41- **6** *3 ¾* **Michigan Assassin (IRE)**[22] 1344 11-11-7 **105**...(p) AodhaganConlon(5) 100
(Debra Hamer) *led: hdd after 12th: wknd bef 2 out* **16/1**

/P3- **7** *19* **Walls Way**[15] 1442 9-9-11 **83**.. JWStevenson(7) 61
(Tracey Barfoot-Saunt) *chsd ldrs: outpcd and lost pl 7th: bhd fr 11th: t.o 2 out* **16/1**

334- **8** *15* **Featherintheattic (IRE)**[25] 1315 8-11-10 **103**.....................(p) NoelFehily 67
(Warren Greatrex) *in rr: sme hdwy 9th: lost pl 11th: sn bhd: t.o 2 out* **4/1**[2]

5P4- **P** **Ginger's Lad**[17] 1417 9-9-10 **82**.................................. MrHAABannister(7)
(Michael Easterby) *sn in rr: bhd and reminders 3rd: t.o 5th: p.u bef 7th* **25/1**

5m 5.4s (-3.70) **Going Correction** -0.20s/f (Good) **9** Ran SP% **113.8**
Speed ratings (Par 105): **99,95,93,90,90 88,81,75,**
toteswingers 1&2 £5.70, 1&3 £3.70, 2&3 £7.10 CSF £47.74 CT £202.44 TOTE £8.60: £2.00, £1.70, £2.80; EX 62.50 Trifecta £309.40 Pool: £1065.74 - 2.58 winning units..
Owner S Crawley, T Crawley **Bred** G A E C Delorme Gerard & Vincent **Trained** Broadwas, Worcs

FOCUS
A moderate handicap chase. The winner is rated back to his old best.

1578 PTARMIGAN OF CHESTER AND SALES@PTARMIGANCLOTHING.CO.UK MAIDEN HURDLE (9 hdls) 2m 1f
3:25 (3:25) (Class 5) 4-Y-0+ **£2,395** (£698; £349)

Form RPR
2- **1** **Saint Thomas (IRE)**[18] 1389 6-11-0 0.................................. BrianHughes 121+
(John Mackie) *trckd ldr: led 2 out: clr between last 2: eased towards fin* **5/2**[1]

150/ **2** *15* **Little Pop**[181] 4800 5-11-0 0.. SamTwiston-Davies 106
(Nigel Twiston-Davies) *led: j.rt and hit 5th: hdd 2 out: kpt on same pce* **5/2**[1]

3 *6* **Apollo Eleven (IRE)**[127] 4-11-0 0...................................... JasonMaguire 99
(Donald McCain) *chsd ldrs 5th: 3rd and drvn 3 out: one pce* **10/3**[2]

332- **4** *13* **Laurens Ruby (IRE)**[54] 1056 4-10-7 0.. DPFahy 80
(John Flint) *nt fluent: trckd ldrs: mstke 1st: hit 10th: sn outpcd and drvn: wknd appr 2 out* **12/1**

0/4- **5** *1 ¾* **Midnight Mustang**[18] 1387 6-10-7 82.................................. MrJMartin(7) 85
(Andrew J Martin) *mid-div: chsd ldrs 5th: outpcd and lost pl after next* **50/1**

0/6- **6** *21* **Queen Spud**[136] 46 4-10-7 0.. RichardJohnson 59
(Henry Daly) *in rr: sme hdwy 5th: lost pl next: bhd whn hit 2 out* **14/1**

7 *19* **Qasser (IRE)**[87] 4-11-0 0.. NoelFehily 49
(Harry Whittington) *t.k.h in rr: hdwy 5th: outpcd after next: wknd appr 2 out: sn bhd* **8/1**[3]

/34- **8** *3* **Our Crusade**[17] 1420 6-10-11 0.. JakeGreenall(3) 47
(Michael Easterby) *nt jump wl in rr: sme hdwy 5th: sn lost pl and bhd: t.o 3 out* **20/1**

50/- **F** **Miss Beattie**[155] 5249 6-10-4 0.................................... RobertDunne(3)
(Andrew Price) *mid-div: chsd ldrs 5th: lost pl next: bhd whn hit 2 out: poor 5th whn fell last: fatally injured* **100/1**

4m 5.2s (-5.70) **Going Correction** -0.325s/f (Good)
WFA 4 from 5yo+ 11lb **9** Ran SP% **113.4**
Speed ratings (Par 103): **100,92,90,84,83 73,64,62,**
toteswingers 1&2 £3.10, 1&3 £2.70, 2&3 £4.10 CSF £8.73 TOTE £3.00: £1.80, £1.10, £1.30; EX 14.30 Trifecta £49.90 Pool: £1240.13 - 18.61 winning units..
Owner P Riley **Bred** S Coughlan **Trained** Church Broughton , Derbys

FOCUS
Little depth to this maiden hurdle. The easy winner was the form pick.

1579 GENESIS WEALTH MANAGEMENT H'CAP CHASE (18 fncs) 3m 110y
4:00 (4:01) (Class 3) (0-135,133) 4-Y-0+ **£6,498** (£1,908; £954; £477)

Form RPR
352- **1** **Full Of Joy (IRE)**[25] 1316 8-10-12 **119**................................(tp) APMcCoy 126+
(Jonjo O'Neill) *chsd ldrs: cl 2nd 14th: led appr 2 out: j.lft last: drvn out* **9/2**[3]

411- **2** *5* **Ballybough Gorta (IRE)**[18] 1396 6-11-11 **132**................(v) JamieMoore 135
(Peter Bowen) *chsd ldrs: j.lft and mstke 2nd: drvn and lost pl 8th: reminders next: plld wd bef 10th: sn chsng ldrs: 3rd and wl outpcd 3 out: rallied and upsides next: 4 l down whn j.lft last* **2/1**[1]

6/0- **3** *4 ½* **Nataani (IRE)**[79] 845 10-11-5 **133**..................................(t) MikeyHamill(7) 131
(Jo Davis) *t.k.h: trckd ldrs: hit 9th: outpcd and lost pl 14th: rallied and 3rd appr 2 out: one pce* **9/1**

P01- **4** *17* **Mostly Bob (IRE)**[54] 1060 10-11-5 **129**............................(t) JamesBest(3) 111
(Sophie Leech) *j.rt: led: hdd appr 2 out: sn wknd* **10/1**

UPP/ **5** *4* **Tuskar Rock (FR)**[439] 845 10-10-0 **107**.............................. AidanColeman 85
(Venetia Williams) *hld up: jnd ldrs 10th: pushed along 12th: lost pl and reminders next* **9/1**

116- **P** **Lough Derg Way (IRE)**[73] 859 7-10-13 **120**.......... SamTwiston-Davies
(Jamie Snowden) *in rr: chsd ldrs 10th: drvn next: wknd 14th: sn bhd: t.o whn p.u bef 2 out* **9/4**[2]

6m 8.6s (-11.20) **Going Correction** -0.20s/f (Good) **6** Ran SP% **111.4**
Speed ratings (Par 107): **109,107,105,100,99**
toteswingers 1&2 £1.70, 1&3 £5.00, 2&3 £3.70 CSF £14.26 TOTE £4.80: £1.70, £2.10; EX 11.40 Trifecta £68.00 Pool: £1951.92 - 21.52 winning units..
Owner John P McManus **Bred** J D Flood **Trained** Cheltenham, Gloucs

FOCUS
An open handicap in which several had a chance turning in. The winner was a 129 horse in the past and may be capable of bettering that.

1580 RACING UK H'CAP HURDLE (DIV I) (11 hdls) 2m 4f
4:35 (4:35) (Class 5) (0-100,100) 4-Y-0+ **£2,274** (£667; £333; £166)

Form RPR
450- **1** **Tribal Dance (IRE)**[31] 1267 7-10-4 **85**............................ CiaranMckee(7) 95
(John O'Shea) *t.k.h: led: jnd last: all out* **16/1**

/44- **2** *hd* **Mist The Boat**[27] 1281 5-10-9 **83**.................................... RichardJohnson 94
(Tim Vaughan) *in rr-div: chsd ldrs 5th: drvn 3 out: chalng whn nt fluent 2 out: upsides last: jst hld* **7/1**

6/0- **3** *14* **What A Good Night (IRE)**[130] 145 5-11-2 **90**....(v) SamTwiston-Davies 87
(Nigel Twiston-Davies) *t.k.h towards rr: hdwy to chse ldrs 7th: hit next: kpt on one pce fr 2 out to take modest 3rd last* **9/2**[1]

41F- **4** *1 ¾* **Pete**[18] 1395 10-11-3 **98**....................................(tp) CraigGallagher(7) 94
(Barry Murtagh) *trckd ldrs: upsides 3 out: one pce fr next* **9/1**

303- **5** *5* **Torran Sound**[29] 1275 6-11-7 **95**..(b) FelixDeGiles 86
(James Eustace) *towards rr: hdwy 6th: outpcd appr 3 out: kpt on between last 2* **9/1**

/05- **6** *1 ½* **Mr Bachster (IRE)**[24] 1331 8-10-0 **74**.............................. TomScudamore 64
(Richard Lee) *chsd ldrs: outpcd appr 2 out: wknd appr last* **11/1**

0P/- **7** *3 ¼* **Rigolo Ville (FR)**[152] 5321 8-11-5 **100**......................(p) ConorShoemark(7) 87
(Richard Hobson) *hld up in rr: sme hdwy 3 out: nvr a factor* **13/2**[3]

506- **8** *11* **Another Trump (NZ)**[31] 1266 9-11-5 **93**..............................(vt) APMcCoy 70
(Jonjo O'Neill) *mid-div: hdwy to chse ldrs 6th: reminders next: wknd 2 out* **8/1**

/P0- **9** *20* **Humbel Ben (IRE)**[87] 756 10-11-11 **99**.............................. NickScholfield 58
(Alan Jones) *t.k.h in rr: sme hdwy 3 out: lost pl appr next: sn bhd: t.o* **25/1**

/40- **10** *14* **Dont Call Me Oscar (IRE)**[31] 1255 6-10-9 **88**.........(t) NicodeBoinville(5) 34
(Mark Gillard) *nt fluent in rr: bhd fr 7th: t.o 3 out* **14/1**

0P4/ **11** *5* **Orange Gizmo (IRE)**[504] 5634 9-10-0 **74** oh2.................... AidanColeman 16
(Venetia Williams) *chsd ldrs: lost pl 7th: sn bhd: t.o 2 out* **20/1**

464- **P** **King Mak**[17] 1419 11-10-3 **80**..(bt) KyleJames(3)
(Marjorie Fife) *w ldrs: nt fluent and lost pl 7th: bhd whn hit 3 out: sn t.o: p.u bef next* **6/1**[2]

4m 55.3s (3.30) **Going Correction** -0.325s/f (Good) **12** Ran SP% **118.9**
Speed ratings (Par 103): **80,79,74,73,71 71,69,65,57,51 49,**
toteswingers 1&2 £56.50, 1&3 £31.20, 2&3 £13.00 CSF £125.16 CT £599.59 TOTE £21.00: £6.40, £2.60, £2.30; EX 198.00 Trifecta £726.60 Part won. Pool: £968.87 - 0.43 winning units..
Owner Quality Pipe Supports (Q P S) Ltd **Bred** Liam O'Regan **Trained** Elton, Gloucs

FOCUS
An ordinary handicap in which the first two pulled clear.

1581 BANGOR-ON-DEE H'CAP HURDLE (12 hdls) 3m
5:10 (5:10) (Class 3) (0-130,130) 4-Y-0+ **£5,253** (£1,552; £776; £388; £194)

Form RPR
51P- **1** **General Miller**[40] 1204 8-11-7 **130**............................(b) NicodeBoinville(5) 140+
(Nicky Henderson) *led: hdd briefly appr 2 out: forged clr appr last: drvn out* **15/2**

FF6- **2** *12* **Tony Dinozzo (FR)**[87] 756 6-10-0 **104** oh1......................(p) JamieMoore 105
(Peter Bowen) *chsd ldrs: 2nd appr 9th: led briefly appr 2 out: wknd between last 2* **5/1**[2]

020- **3** *4 ½* **Possol (FR)**[41] 1195 10-11-8 **126**.................................... PaddyBrennan 121
(Henry Daly) *in rr: sme hdwy 5th: drvn and outpcd 7th: reminders next: tk modest 3rd 2 out* **8/1**

6/4- **4** *24* **Hollins**[95] 698 9-9-13 **106**.. JohnKington(3) 79
(Tony Forbes) *chsd wnr: hit 8th: outpcd 3 out: wknd next* **28/1**

/04- **5** *15* **Ixora (IRE)**[26] 1304 7-11-1 **122**......................................(v) GavinSheehan(3) 82
(Jamie Snowden) *chsd ldrs: mstke and lost pl 4th: sme hdwy 8th: lost pl bef 3 out* **16/1**

3U1- **6** *39* **Lost Legend (IRE)**[24] 1330 6-11-4 **122**................................(p) APMcCoy 47
(Jonjo O'Neill) *in rr: hdwy 5th: chsng ldrs 7th: reminders next: sn lost pl: wl bhd whn mstke 3 out: sn eased and hopelessly t.o* **6/1**[3]

531- **P** **Diamond's Return (IRE)**[2] 1565 9-11-0 **118** 7ex.............. ConorO'Farrell
(David Pipe) *detached in last: nt fluent 1st: sme hdwy 7th: reminders next: sn lost pl and bhd: t.o whn p.u bef 3 out* **11/10**[1]

5m 50.2s (-0.80) **Going Correction** -0.325s/f (Good) **7** Ran SP% **110.8**
Speed ratings (Par 107): **88,84,82,74,69 56,**
toteswingers 1&2 £5.90, 1&3 £6.90, 2&3 £4.50 CSF £41.43 TOTE £6.50: £4.50, £1.70; EX 42.60 Trifecta £228.00 Pool: £2368.04 - 7.78 winning units..
Owner W H Ponsonby **Bred** N Shutts **Trained** Upper Lambourn, Berks

FOCUS
A good handicap hurdle, but the favourite was making a quick reappearance and ran very flat. The winner was a 150+ novice hurdler but is rated more in line with the best of his recent chase runs.

1582 RACING UK H'CAP HURDLE (DIV II) (11 hdls) 2m 4f
5:40 (5:40) (Class 5) (0-100,100) 4-Y-0+ **£2,274** (£667; £333; £166)

Form RPR
345/ **1** **Flicka Williams (IRE)**[296] 2550 6-11-12 **100**.......................... NoelFehily 107+
(Tony Coyle) *t.k.h in rr: hdwy 6th: led appr 2 out: styd on wl* **5/2**[2]

5/0- **2** *2* **Jeanry (FR)**[136] 49 10-10-2 **83**.. JoshWall(7) 86
(Arthur Whitehead) *led to 2nd: chsd ldr: 2nd 3 out: kpt on: no real imp* **8/1**

203- **3** *13* **Gwili Spar**[21] 1364 5-10-6 **80**..(t) TomO'Brien 73
(Peter Bowen) *t.k.h: trckd ldrs: 2nd appr 2 out: one pce: hit last* **2/1**[1]

043- **4** *3 ¾* **Chapelle du Roi (USA)**[22] 1348 4-11-5 **94**............................. IanPopham 81
(Robert Stephens) *hld up in mid-div: drvn 7th: outpcd next: tk modest 4th last* **28/1**

324- **5** *1 ¾* **Thomas Bell (IRE)**[15] 1434 9-9-7 **74** oh1......................(p) CiaranMckee(7) 61
(John O'Shea) *hld 2nd: hdd 7th: one pce appr 2 out* **17/2**

4/0- **6** *37* **Roseini (IRE)**[123] 264 7-10-4 **83**................................ JoshHamer(5) 36
(Tony Carroll) *in rr: bhd fr 8th: t.o 2 out* **22/1**

0/P- **7** *4* **Tara Warrior (IRE)**[26] 1306 7-11-7 **98**.........................(v) MichaelByrne(3) 48
(Tim Vaughan) *chsd ldrs: wknd appr 2 out: sn bhd: t.o* **33/1**

F22- **8** *20* **Himrayn**[13] 1479 10-10-12 **86**.. APMcCoy 18
(Anabel K Murphy) *hld up in rr: racd wd: sme hdwy 6th: drvn next: sn lost pl and bhd: t.o 2 out: hit last: virtually p.u* **5/1**[3]

/32- **9** *4* **Knockgraffon Lad (USA)**[31] 1269 6-11-8 **96**................(tp) AlainCawley 24
(Brendan Powell) *t.k.h in rr: jnd ldr after 6th: led next: hdd 3 out: wknd qckly: t.o next: virtually p.u* **14/1**

5m 4.6s (12.60) **Going Correction** -0.325s/f (Good)
WFA 4 from 5yo+ 12lb **9** Ran SP% **117.6**
Speed ratings (Par 103): **61,60,55,53,52 38,36,28,26**
toteswingers 1&2 £8.80, 1&3 £5.70, 2&3 £8.30 CSF £22.68 CT £47.40 TOTE £4.40: £2.80, £3.40, £1.10; EX 28.50 Trifecta £165.00 Pool: £1213.70 - 5.51 winning units..
Owner Twenty Four Seven Recruitment **Bred** Tony Hickey **Trained** Norton, N Yorks

FOCUS
The second division of an ordinary handicap. A personal best from the winner.
T/Plt: £148.00 to a £1 stake. Pool: £54486.37 - 268.64 winning tickets T/Qpdt: £10.90 to a £1 stake. Pool: £5464.90 - 370.80 winning tickets WG

ENGHIEN (L-H)
Friday, September 13

OFFICIAL GOING: Turf: very soft

1583a PRIX DES ROUGES TERRES (CHASE) (CONDITIONS) (5YO+) (TURF) 2m 3f
1:30 (1:31) 5-Y-O+ **£21,463** (£10,731; £6,260; £4,247; £2,012)

RPR
1 **Saindor (FR)**[117] 406 9-10-6 0.. DavidCottin 128
(R Chotard, France) **27/10**[2]
2 *shd* **Chegei Has (FR)**[117] 406 5-10-10 0.......................... BertrandLestrade 132
(J-P Gallorini, France) **7/2**[3]
3 *10* **Lachlan Bridge (GER)**[344] 5-10-12 0.......................... MathieuCarroux 124
(A Chaille-Chaille, France) **23/10**[1]
4 *3* **Rafale Precieux (FR)**[505] 8-11-0 0.............................. AlbanDesvaux 123
(Mme M Desvaux, France) **36/1**
5 *6* **Cornas (NZ)**[80] 838 11-11-0 0.. JamesReveley 117
(Nick Williams) *prom: dropped to 4th 1/2-way: rdn and outpcd in 5th bef 2 out: styd on but no threat to ldrs* **14/1**
6 *1* **Serienschock (GER)**[80] 5-10-6 0.................................. RegisSchmidlin 108
(F-M Cottin, France) **15/2**
P **Ma Pretention (FR)**[73] 863 5-10-3 0...................(p) LudovicPhilipperon
(Robert Collet, France) **37/1**
P **Titanesque (FR)**[352] 6-11-0 0.. JacquesRicou
(J Bertran De Balanda, France) **13/2**

4m 32.6s (-14.40) **8** Ran SP% **116.7**
PARI-MUTUEL (all including 1 euro stakes): WIN 3.70; PLACE 1.60, 1.70, 1.30; DF 7.30; SF 15.80.
Owner P E Atkinson & Mrs L M Kemble **Bred** Andre Vagne **Trained** France

1584 - 1593a (Foreign Racing) - See Raceform Interactive

[1517]
STRATFORD (L-H)
Tuesday, September 17

OFFICIAL GOING: Hurdle course - good to soft (soft in places); chase course - soft (good to soft in places)
Wind: Light across Weather: Raining

1594 AT THE RACES SKY 415 NOVICES' CHASE (17 fncs) 2m 7f
4:35 (4:35) (Class 4) 5-Y-O+ **£5,198** (£1,526; £763; £381)

Form RPR
103/ **1** **Big Talk**[701] 2034 6-11-0 0.. TomScudamore 120+
(David Bridgwater) *a.p: chsd ldr 3 out: led appr last: sn rdn: styd on wl* **25/1**
3/2- **2** *6* **Another Kate (IRE)**[10] 1518 9-10-7 0.................................... DPFahy 106
(David Richards) *led: rdn and hdd appr last: btn whn hit last* **8/1**
/30- **3** *2 ¾* **Kindly Note**[86] 811 6-10-7 0.. AidanColeman 104
(Emma Lavelle) *prom: mstke 2nd (water): rdn after 2 out: styd on same pce appr last* **7/1**
6F2- **4** *9* **Sail And Return**[65] 963 9-11-0 123...................... SamTwiston-Davies 101
(Phil Middleton) *hld up: hdwy 3 out: nt fluent next: sn rdn and wknd* **11/4**[2]
/02- **5** *8* **Pateese (FR)**[16] 1484 8-11-7 129...............................(b) RichardJohnson 103
(Philip Hobbs) *chsd ldrs: mstke 14th: sn drvn along: blnd next: wknd bef 2 out* **9/4**[1]
205/ **6** *22* **Maller Tree**[29] 1324 6-11-0 129...................................... APMcCoy 70
(David Dennis) *trckd ldr to 3 out: wknd bef next* **7/2**[3]
/50- **7** *5* **Potters Dream (IRE)**[22] 1406 7-11-0 0............................ PaddyBrennan 65
(Fergal O'Brien) *hld up: a in rr: mstke 13th: sn lost tch* **100/1**
542/ **P** **Mountaineer (FR)**[1616] 5037 8-11-0 0.............................. JamieMoore
(Gary Moore) *hld up: plld hrd: mstke 13th: sn p.u* **12/1**

5m 51.2s (12.00) **Going Correction** +0.675s/f (Soft) **8** Ran SP% **115.8**
Speed ratings: **106,103,102,99,97 89,87,**
Tote Swingers: 1&2 £10.80, 1&3 £10.60, 2&3 £5.50 CSF £204.37 TOTE £17.60: £7.00, £1.90, £2.70; EX 246.90 Trifecta £248.80 Part won. Pool: £331.83 - 0.65 winning units..
Owner Deauville Daze Partnership **Bred** Miss K Rausing **Trained** Icomb, Gloucs

FOCUS
Bends moved onto fresh ground. The forecast rain had arrived with the ground easing to good to soft, soft in places on the hurdle course and soft, good to soft in places on the chase course. A fair novice chase with only a modest pace and the second is rated in line with his hurdles mark, while the form could rate higher through the fourth and fifth.

1595 AT THE RACES VIRGIN 534 NOVICES' HURDLE (8 hdls) 2m 110y
5:05 (5:07) (Class 4) 4-Y-O+ **£3,898** (£1,144; £572; £286)

Form RPR
F21- **1** **Kettlewell**[35] 1256 4-11-5 113.......................................(t) APMcCoy 111+
(Warren Greatrex) *mde all: hit 2nd: mstke 5th: nt fluent 3 out: hit next: sn drvn along: unchal* **4/1**[2]
R/ **2** *9* **L Frank Baum (IRE)**[17] 1833 6-10-12 0............................ PaulMoloney 95
(Bernard Llewellyn) *chsd ldrs: rdn to go 2nd after 2 out: styng on same pce whn hung lft appr last* **25/1**
4- **3** *10* **Volcanic Jack (IRE)**[22] 1393 5-10-7 0.......................... JoeCornwall(5) 84
(Michael Chapman) *chsd ldrs: rdn appr 2 out: wknd bef last* **50/1**
2/0- **4** *¾* **Sonofthekiing (IRE)**[128] 233 5-10-12 0.............................. TomO'Brien 82
(Philip Hobbs) *chsd wnr tl rdn and wknd after 2 out* **7/1**[3]
0/P- **5** *6* **Rearrange**[72] 897 4-10-5 0.. TomMessenger 69
(Chris Bealby) *hld up: hdwy after 3 out: rdn and wknd after next* **66/1**

/30- **6** *47* **Midnight Thomas**[10] 1519 4-10-12 0...................................... IanPopham 29
(Martin Keighley) *plld hrd and prom: rdn and wknd after 2 out* **33/1**
0P- **7** *69* **Kims Firebud**[89] 777 6-10-9 0.................................. RobertDunne(3)
(Dai Burchell) *hld up: plld hrd: mstke 3rd: rdn and wknd appr 3 out* **50/1**
/05- **P** **Rye Tangle (IRE)**[35] 1264 5-10-12 0..........................(t) RichieMcLernon
(Sophie Leech) *hld up: blnd 5th: rdn and wknd 2 out: bhd whn p.u bef last* **33/1**
51/ **P** **Killyglass (IRE)**[164] 5179 6-10-12 0...................................... NoelFehily
(Emma Lavelle) *hld up: p.u after 3rd: fatally injured* **2/7**[1]

4m 0.5s (4.50) **Going Correction** +0.25s/f (Yiel) **9** Ran SP% **125.4**
Speed ratings (Par 105): **99,94,90,89,86 64,32, ,**
Tote Swingers: 1&2 £12.00, 1&3 £5.80, 2&3 £50.20 CSF £77.32 TOTE £5.90: £1.30, £5.70, £6.30; EX 56.60 Trifecta £516.50 Pool: £1,496.74 - 2.17 winning units..
Owner Mark Duthie Partnership **Bred** Giles W Pritchard-Gordon (farming) Ltd **Trained** Upper Lambourn, Berks

FOCUS
A race that revolved around the smart bumper performer Killyglass, but he sadly suffered a fatal injury at an early stage. The winner was left with little to beat and is rated to his mark.

1596 FOLLOW @ATTHERACES ON TWITTER H'CAP CHASE (12 fncs) 2m 1f 110y
5:35 (5:35) (Class 4) (0-115,115) 4-Y-O+ **£3,898** (£1,144; £572; £286)

Form RPR
P06- **1** **Catch Tammy (IRE)**[20] 1429 7-11-7 110........................ PaddyBrennan 120+
(Tom George) *mde virtually all: shkn up appr last: styd on wl* **8/1**
214/ **2** *10* **Olympian Boy (IRE)**[193] 4643 9-11-12 115.................... JasonMaguire 114
(Sophie Leech) *hld up: hdwy 3 out: rdn appr last: styd on same pce: wnt 2nd flat* **11/4**[2]
320- **3** *6* **Cruise In Style (IRE)**[70] 931 7-10-5 97.........................(bt) JamesBest(3) 91
(Kevin Bishop) *chsd ldrs: wnt 2nd 3 out: rdn appr last: hung lft and wknd flat* **10/1**
235- **4** *11* **Rime Avec Gentil (FR)**[26] 1345 8-11-6 109...................... PaulMoloney 91
(Bernard Llewellyn) *chsd ldrs tl rdn and wknd after 3 out* **3/1**[3]
531- **5** *2* **Julie Prince (IRE)**[22] 1401 7-10-12 101................................(t) APMcCoy 81
(Brendan Powell) *chsd ldr to 3 out: sn drvn along: wknd after next: eased* **7/4**[1]
/PP- **6** *21* **Bobbits Way**[22] 1388 8-10-0 89 oh2...........................(p) TomMessenger 48
(Alan Jones) *hld up: mstkes 9th and 3 out: sn wknd* **25/1**

4m 16.8s (9.70) **Going Correction** +0.675s/f (Soft) **6** Ran SP% **112.1**
Speed ratings (Par 105): **105,100,97,93,92 82**
Tote Swingers: 1&2 £8.00, 1&3 £11.30, 2&3 £4.50 CSF £30.62 TOTE £4.50: £2.80, £1.20; EX 37.70 Trifecta £129.90 Pool: £737.85 - 4.25 winning units..
Owner R S Brookhouse **Bred** J A Wilson **Trained** Slad, Gloucs

FOCUS
Modest handicap form but the winner could be rated better than this, with the second well off his best.

1597 AT THE RACES ON FACEBOOK H'CAP HURDLE (11 hdls) 2m 6f 110y
6:05 (6:05) (Class 3) (0-135,129) 4-Y-O **£6,330** (£1,870; £935; £468; £234)

Form RPR
211- **1** **Letsby Avenue**[44] 1201 5-11-12 129.......................... RobertThornton 138+
(Alan King) *trckd ldrs: led and mstke 2 out: rdn clr whn nt fluent last: styd on wl* **3/1**[1]
021- **2** *5* **Benbane Head (USA)**[25] 1363 9-11-11 128........................(t) IanPopham 130
(Martin Keighley) *trckd ldrs: led 6th: rdn and hdd 2 out: hung lft appr last: styd on same pce* **9/2**[3]
050/ **3** *3 ¾* **Marju King (IRE)**[397] 1246 7-10-2 105.................. SamTwiston-Davies 104
(Phil Middleton) *hld up: hdwy 3 out: rdn after next: styng on same pce whn nt clr run appr last* **16/1**
331- **4** *23* **Staigue Fort**[16] 1488 5-10-10 116................................. GavinSheehan(3) 91
(Emma Lavelle) *hld up: sme hdwy appr 2 out: sn wknd* **5/1**
115/ **5** *3 ¼* **Dirty Bertie (FR)**[426] 991 7-9-9 105................................. JakeHodson(7) 77
(David Bridgwater) *trckd ldrs: racd keenly: pushed along 8th: wknd appr 2 out* **7/1**
014- **6** *1* **Ironical (IRE)**[22] 1391 9-10-0 103....................................(t) AidanColeman 74
(Shaun Lycett) *hld up: hdwy appr 2 out: sn wknd* **12/1**
100- **7** *20* **Vinnie My Boy (IRE)**[44] 1205 5-10-12 115......................(vt) JamieMoore 66
(Peter Bowen) *led and nt fluent 1st: hdd next: led again 3rd to 5th: ev ch 3 out: sn rdn and wknd* **7/2**[2]
0/4- **8** *34* **Topolski (IRE)**[11] 205 7-11-11 128.................................... TomCannon 45
(David Arbuthnot) *w ldr: led 2nd to next: led 5th to next: rdn after 8th: wknd after 3 out: hit next* **14/1**
/06- **P** **Court In Session (IRE)**[72] 900 8-11-5 122...................... RichardJohnson
(Martin Keighley) *hld up: wknd 3 out: bhd whn p.u bef last* **20/1**

5m 28.7s (0.60) **Going Correction** +0.25s/f (Yiel) **9** Ran SP% **119.6**
Speed ratings (Par 107): **108,106,104,96,95 95,88,76,**
Tote Swingers: 1&2 £2.80, 1&3 £13.80, 2&3 £15.70 CSF £18.06 CT £188.86 TOTE £3.90: £1.40, £2.10, £3.30; EX 16.40 Trifecta £104.00 Pool: £1,479.93 - 10.66 winning units..
Owner Mrs Peter Prowting **Bred** Mrs E A Prowting **Trained** Barbury Castle, Wilts
■ A winner for Robert Thornton on his first ride back since being injured in March.

FOCUS
Only a reasonable pace for this competitive, if ordinary, looking staying handicap hurdle with the first three pulling well clear of some rather tired rivals. The winner is on the upgrade while the placed horses set the level.

1598 VISIT ATTHERACES.COM/MOBILE H'CAP CHASE (17 fncs) 2m 7f
6:35 (6:35) (Class 4) (0-115,115) 4-Y-O+ **£3,898** (£1,144; £572; £286)

Form RPR
412/ **1** **Al Alfa**[185] 4792 6-11-9 112.. RichardJohnson 123+
(Philip Hobbs) *mde all: rdn appr last: styd on u.p* **11/10**[1]
U46- **2** *3 ½* **Academy General (IRE)**[10] 1518 7-11-5 115..............(p) JakeHodson(7) 120
(David Bridgwater) *hld up: mstke 9th: hdwy 13th: chsd wnr appr 2 out: rdn bef last: styd on same pce flat* **20/1**
451- **3** *19* **Joe The Rogue (IRE)**[9] 1528 6-10-3 92 7ex...................... NickScholfield 78
(Paul Henderson) *bhd: hdwy 13th: rdn and wknd appr last* **6/4**[2]
U04- **4** *10* **Dark Oasis**[8] 1534 7-10-0 89 oh17.. JamieMoore 65
(Natalie Lloyd-Beavis) *chsd ldrs: wnt 2nd 7th tl rdn after 3 out: pckd next: sn wknd* **33/1**
452- **5** *11* **Epee Celeste (FR)**[22] 1396 7-10-12 106.......................... JoeCornwall(5) 71
(Michael Chapman) *chsd wnr to 7th: drvn along 12th: wknd 14th* **8/1**[3]
P0/- **P** **Tiquer (FR)**[323] 2096 5-11-1 104.. TomMessenger
(Alan Jones) *hld up: pushed along 10th: sn lost tch: p.u bef 13th* **33/1**

5m 51.9s (12.70) **Going Correction** +0.675s/f (Soft) **6** Ran SP% **109.4**
Speed ratings (Par 105): **104,102,96,92,88**
Tote Swingers: 1&2 £2.60, 1&3 £1.10, 2&3 £4.60 CSF £17.79 CT £30.21 TOTE £2.00: £1.20, £6.50; EX 24.20 Trifecta £96.10 Pool: £1,786.35 - 13.93 winning units..
Owner James Drummond **Bred** Countess Goess-Saurau **Trained** Withycombe, Somerset

The Form Book Jumps, Raceform Ltd, Compton, RG20 6NL.

FOCUS
A staying handicap chase which looked competitive before half the field defected. However, it was a decent front-running performance from Al Alfa. The first two are on the upgrade and the form could rate higher.

1599 ATTHERACES.COM EXCLUSIVE WILLIAM BUICK BLOG STANDARD OPEN NATIONAL HUNT FLAT RACE 2m 110y

7:05 (7:05) (Class 6) 4-6-Y-O **£1,949** (£572; £286; £143)

Form RPR
4/ **1** **Mrs Jordan (IRE)**[207] 4377 5-10-7 0 AidanColeman 109+
(Venetia Williams) *chsd ldrs: led 2f out: rdn clr fr over 1f out* **7/4**[1]
2 *11* **Perfect Romance** 4-10-2 0 NicodeBoinville(5) 97
(Patrick Chamings) *hld up: pushed along and hdwy over 5f out: styd on to go 2nd ins fnl f: no ch w wnr* **25/1**
3- **3** *3 ½* **Grand March**[50] 1138 4-11-0 0 JasonMaguire 101
(Kim Bailey) *trckd ldrs: rdn over 2f out: wknd over 1f out* **9/2**[2]
4 *½* **Seamus Rua (IRE)**[67] 954 5-10-11 0 KielanWoods(3) 100
(Charlie Longsdon) *led after 2f: rdn and hdd 2f out: wknd fnl f* **12/1**
2- **5** *3 ¼* **In A Heartbeat**[10] 1523 4-10-7 0 IanPopham 90
(Martin Keighley) *hld up: racd keenly: hdwy over 7f out: rdn whn hmpd over 2f out: sn wknd* **20/1**
6 *2* **Max Ward (IRE)** 4-11-0 0 SamTwiston-Davies 95
(Charlie Brooks) *prom: rdn over 2f out: wknd over 1f out* **7/1**[3]
5- **7** *6* **Sava Bridge (IRE)**[62] 1016 6-10-7 0 MrCSmith(7) 89
(Paul Henderson) *hld up: pushed along 1/2-way: wknd over 4f out* **50/1**
3/ **8** *1 ½* **Our Boy Ben**[196] 4585 4-11-0 0 BrianHughes 88
(Malcolm Jefferson) *led 2f: trckd ldrs: rdn and wknd over 2f out* **9/2**[2]
0/0- **9** *5* **Wishfull Dancer (IRE)**[88] 790 5-10-11 0 (t) MichaelByrne(3) 83
(John Mackie) *hld up: rdn over 5f out: sn wknd* **50/1**
320/ **10** *1 ¾* **Cash For Steel (IRE)**[245] 3670 6-10-0 0 CiaranMckee(7) 74
(Richard Phillips) *prom: pushed along over 6f out: wknd 5f out* **16/1**
11 *16* **Borkum (IRE)** 5-10-7 0 ChrisDavies(7) 65
(Philip Hobbs) *prom: lost pl after 3f: hdwy 1/2-way: rdn and wknd over 4f out* **16/1**
- **12** *82* **Twice Shy (IRE)** 5-10-2 0 BenPoste(5)
(Mike Hammond) *mid-div: pushed along and lost pl over 8f out: sn bhd* **50/1**
13 *19* **Silver B** 5-10-7 0 DavidBass
(Mark Brisbourne) *prom: lost pl 10f out: bhd fr 1/2-way* **33/1**

3m 58.6s (8.20) **Going Correction** +0.25s/f (Yiel) **13** Ran SP% **122.1**
Speed ratings: **90,84,83,82,81 80,77,76,74,73 66,27,18**
Tote Swingers 1&2 £18.00, 2&3 £34.00, 1&3 £2.60 CSF £61.71 TOTE £3.20: £1.30, £8.70, £2.10; EX 51.40 Trifecta £743.50 Pool: £1,757.37 - 1.77 winning units..
Owner James Drummond **Bred** R Lynch **Trained** Kings Caple, H'fords

FOCUS
A truly run race and fairly solid form, with the the third, fifth, seventh and eighth all close to their pre-race marks.
T/Plt: £464.20 to a £1 stake. Pool: £73,281.55 - 115.24 winning tickets. T/Qpdt: £7.70 to a £1 stake. Pool: £9,219.69 - 882.70 winning tickets. CR

1600 - 1603a (Foreign Racing) - See Raceform Interactive

1600 LISTOWEL (L-H)

Wednesday, September 18

OFFICIAL GOING: Flat course - heavy; jumps courses - soft

1604a GUINNESS KERRY NATIONAL H'CAP CHASE (GRADE A) (18 fncs) 3m

5:10 (5:11) 4-Y-0+

£78,333 (£25,000; £11,991; £4,186; £2,886; £1,585)

RPR
1 **White Star Line (IRE)**[19] 1459 9-10-4 130 AELynch 141+
(D T Hughes, Ire) *w.w towards rr: gd hdwy fr 13th to chse ldrs fr next: clsd travelling wl to ld into st: sn clr: styd on wl: comf* **16/1**
2 *5* **Carlingford Lough (IRE)**[49] 1168 7-11-7 147 APMcCoy 151+
(John E Kiely, Ire) *chsd ldrs: pushed along fr 3 out and no imp on wnr in 5th fr next: kpt on wl fr last into nvr threatening 2nd cl home* **10/1**[3]
3 *½* **Muirhead (IRE)**[49] 1168 10-10-9 135 (p) DavyCondon 139
(Noel Meade, Ire) *led: hdd fr 5th tl regained advantage fr 4 out: mstke next and hdd: rdn in 4th into st and sn no imp on wnr in 2nd: kpt on same pce fr 2 out and dropped to 3rd cl home* **12/1**
4 *¾* **Questions Answered (IRE)**[147] 5512 8-10-5 131 RobbiePower 134
(E McNamara, Ire) *w.w in rr of mid-div: hdwy fr 12th to chse ldrs: rdn in 6th into st and sn no imp on wnr: kpt on same pce fr 2 out* **10/1**[3]
5 *4 ½* **Shot From The Hip (GER)**[19] 1462 9-10-11 137 (t) MarkWalsh 135
(E J O'Grady, Ire) *chsd ldrs: rdn in 7th into st and no imp on ldrs bef 2 out: kpt on fr last into mod 5th run-in* **12/1**
6 *4 ½* **Gift Of Dgab (IRE)**[528] 5321 9-10-12 138 (t) DavyRussell 132
(A J Martin, Ire) *trckd ldr in 2nd: t.k.h: led fr 5th: jnd bef 4 out and sn hdd: rdn in 2nd into st and no imp on wnr: dropped to 5th bef last where mstke: kpt on one pce* **14/1**
7 *nse* **Wise Oscar (IRE)**[61] 1035 9-10-4 130 BryanCooper 124
(D T Hughes, Ire) *w.w in rr of mid-div: tk clsr order whn mstke 4 out: rdn in 10th into st and kpt on u.p fr 2 out: jst hld for 6th: nvr nrr* **4/1**[1]
8 *1 ¾* **Jamsie Hall (IRE)**[9] 1545 10-10-7 133 (bt[1]) RobbieColgan 125
(Gordon Elliott, Ire) *chsd ldrs: pushed along in 10th bef st and sn no ex u.p: kpt on one pce fr 2 out* **33/1**
9 *nk* **Forpadydeplasterer (IRE)**[165] 5177 11-11-4 144.. AndrewJMcNamara 136
(Thomas Cooper, Ire) *hld up in tch: tk clsr order fr 12th: rdn in 3rd into st and sn no ex u.p whn mstke 2 out: wknd* **33/1**
10 *nk* **Like Your Style (IRE)**[41] 1233 9-10-3 134 JodyMcGarvey(5) 125
(Edward P Harty, Ire) *nvr bttr than mid-div: rdn and no imp fr 3 out* **20/1**
11 *½* **Jacksonslady (IRE)**[49] 1168 8-10-13 139 BarryGeraghty 130
(J P Dempsey, Ire) *in rr of mid-div: tk clsr order after 1/2-way: pushed along fr 13th and no imp on ldrs fr 3 out: one pce after* **10/1**[3]
12 *1 ½* **He'llberemembered (IRE)**[19] 1459 10-10-6 136 ow1 ShaneButler(5) 126
(P G Fahey, Ire) *in rr of mid-div: mstkes 11th and 13th: n.d fr 3 out: wknd* **9/1**[2]
13 *4 ½* **Sweet My Lord (FR)**[30] 1324 7-10-5 131 (p) DJCasey 116
(W P Mullins, Ire) *racd in mid-div: tk clsr order fr 9th: impr on outer at 12th where nt fluent: rdn in 5th into st and sn no ex u.p: wknd bef 2 out* **14/1**
14 *½* **Romanesco (FR)**[49] 1168 8-10-8 134 (tp) ConorO'Farrell 118
(Gordon Elliott, Ire) *in rr of mid-div: rdn and no imp fr 3 out* **14/1**
15 *21* **Chartreux (FR)**[145] 5547 8-10-9 135 PaddyBrennan 98
(Tom George) *on toes befhand: trckd ldrs in 3rd: pushed along and wknd bef 3 out* **16/1**
16 *20* **Quantitativeeasing (IRE)**[49] 1168 8-11-4 144 NiallPMadden 87
(E Bolger, Ire) *towards rr: tk clsr order fr 10th: rdn and no imp fr 3 out: wknd* **12/1**
P **Lambro (IRE)**[49] 1168 8-11-1 141 (p) PaulTownend
(W P Mullins, Ire) *in rr of mid-div: mstke 8th and lost pl: wknd towards rr after 10th: p.u bef 3 out* **25/1**
P **Terminal (FR)**[49] 1168 6-11-4 144 (p) RWalsh
(W P Mullins, Ire) *trckd ldrs in 4th: nt fluent 7th and lost pl: sn pushed along and wknd: no ex u.p fr 4 out: trailing whn p.u bef 2 out* **12/1**

5m 52.1s (-7.80) **18** Ran SP% **134.3**
CSF £176.14 CT £2034.69 TOTE £20.80: £3.70, £3.10, £2.80, £2.50; DF 163.50.
Owner P A Byrne **Bred** Louis Vambeck **Trained** The Curragh, Co Kildare
■ Stewards' Enquiry : Shane Butler one-day ban: weighed in 1lb heavy (Oct 2)

FOCUS
A highly competititive handicap with a tight finish for a three-miler. The standard is set around the winner, third and seventh.

1605 - 1612a (Foreign Racing) - See Raceform Interactive

1609 LISTOWEL (L-H)

Friday, September 20

OFFICIAL GOING: Flat course - heavy (soft to heavy in places); jumps courses - soft (yielding in places)

1613a SOUTHAMPTON GOODWILL CHASE (15 fncs) 2m 4f

5:15 (5:16) 5-Y-0+ **£11,626** (£3,398; £1,609; £536)

RPR
1 **Hidden Cyclone (IRE)**[52] 1157 8-11-6 148 AndrewJMcNamara 154+
(John Joseph Hanlon, Ire) *trckd ldr in 2nd: nt fluent 1st and 3rd: clsr in 2nd whn nt fluent again 8th: got on terms next and led 4 out: extended advantage fr 3 out and sn clr: mstke last: rdn and kpt on wl run-in* **2/1**[2]
2 *2* **Forpadydeplasterer (IRE)**[2] 1604 11-11-2 143 BryanCooper 144
(Thomas Cooper, Ire) *hld up in tch: tk clsr order and disp 3rd at 9th: nt fluent 3 out and sn pushed along in 3rd: wnt mod 2nd fr 2 out where nt fluent: kpt on wl fr last to cl on wnr: a hld* **7/2**[3]
3 *4* **Spring Heeled (IRE)**[22] 1447 6-10-13 130 (p) DavyRussell 137
(J H Culloty, Ire) *chsd ldrs in 3rd: slt mstke 3rd: mstke in 4th at 6th and lost pl: drvn in 5th fr 4 out and wnt mod 3rd between last 2: j. sltly lft last and kpt on same pce* **15/8**[1]
4 *9 ½* **Tribes And Banner (IRE)**[20] 1481 9-11-2 145 JohnCullen 131
(C F Swan, Ire) *hld up in tch: slt mstke 6th: clsr in 3rd fr 7th: wnt 2nd 3 out and rdn into st: sn no imp on wnr and wknd* **8/1**
5 *7* **Bob Lingo (IRE)**[9] 1572 11-11-2 142 (t) MarkWalsh 124
(Thomas Mullins, Ire) *led: jnd at 9th and hdd 4 out: sn pushed along and no imp fr next: wknd* **8/1**
R **Chaninbar (FR)**[9] 1572 10-11-2 140 (vt) PaulMoloney
(Anthony Middleton) *ref to r* **33/1**
P **Schelm (GER)**[9] 1572 11-10-11 JodyMcGarvey(5)
(Ronald O'Leary, Ire) *racd in rr: nt fluent 1st: slow 5th and mstke 7th: n.d fr 4 out and trailing whn p.u bef 2 out* **16/1**

4m 49.7s (-27.30) **7** Ran SP% **121.4**
CSF £10.76 TOTE £3.10: £1.80, £1.80; DF 14.20 Trifecta £60.90.
Owner Mrs A F Mee & David Mee **Bred** Ronald O'Neill **Trained** Bagenalstown, Co Carlow

FOCUS
A return to form for Hidden Cyclone, but no matter how he performs he always leaves a bit of doubt in the mind. The form choice winner did not need to repeat his best and the form is rated in line with the top end of the race averages.

1614 - 1622a (Foreign Racing) - See Raceform Interactive

1532 CRAON (R-H)

Saturday, September 21

OFFICIAL GOING: Turf: soft

1623a PRIX DE L'OUDON (CHASE) (CLAIMER) (5YO+) (TURF) 2m 4f

4:40 (12:00) 5-Y-0+ **£7,024** (£3,512; £2,048; £1,390; £658)

RPR
1 **Simson (FR)**[100] 7-11-0 0 LudovicSolignac 93
(T Boivin, France) **44/5**
2 *1* **Marcomax (FR)**[1421] 7-10-8 0 (b) DavidCottin 86
(J Planque, France) **2/1**[1]
3 *5* **Kigreat De La Pree (FR)**[48] 1214 5-10-3 0 (p) RaphaelDelozier 76
(G Mousnier, France) **17/1**
4 *snk* **Glazig Du Graglan (FR)**[1112] 8-10-1 0 MaximeNey(9) 83
(Christian Le Galliard, France) **7/2**[2]
5 *2 ½* **White Singer (FR)**[1014] 7-10-1 0 FlorentNeveu(9) 80
(A Le Clerc, France) **63/10**
6 *dist* **Cafe De Paris (FR)**[25] 1424 8-10-10 0 (b) YoannBriant(9)
(S Foucher, France) **68/10**
7 *4* **George Nympton (IRE)**[22] 1464 7-11-0 0 JamesReveley
(Nick Williams) *led: j. slowly 4th and 6th: sn dropped to midfield: rdn and outpcd in rr fr 2 out: sn bhd and btn: t.o* **58/10**[3]
F **Talisasoto (FR)**[357] 6-10-6 0 ow3 (p) MathiasSolier
(T Boivin, France) **66/1**
P **Renko (FR)** 8-11-0 0 ArnoldCisel
(X-L Le Stang, France) **39/1**

5m 8.02s (308.02) **9** Ran SP% **116.5**
PARI-MUTUEL (all including 1 euro stakes): WIN 8.50 (coupled with Talisasoto); PLACE 2.40, 1.80, 3.50; DF 12.20; SF 31.00.
Owner Tanguy Boivin **Bred** P Adenot **Trained** France

[240]PLUMPTON (L-H)

Sunday, September 22

OFFICIAL GOING: Good to firm (good in places; watered; hdl 8.3, chs 8.7)
Wind: Almost nil Weather: Overcast, warm

1624 EVIE AND LOIS @MARATHONBET_UK JUVENILE HURDLE (9 hdls) 2m
2:30 (2:30) (Class 4) 3-Y-O **£4,548** (£1,335; £667; £333)

Form RPR

1 **Orla's Rainbow (IRE)**[13] 3-10-9 0..............................(b) JoshuaMoore(3) 87
(Gary Moore) *trckd ldng pair: rdn after 3 out: wnt 2nd between last 2: styd on u.p to ld nr fin* **9/2**[3]

2 *nk* **Raven's Tower (USA)**[158] 3-10-12 0.. DavidBass 86
(Ben Pauling) *trckd ldr: gd jump to ld 3 out: pressed after 2 out: drvn flat: hdd nr fin* **3/1**[1]

3 *1 3/4* **Unidexter (IRE)**[102] 3-10-12 0.. MarcGoldstein 85
(Sheena West) *trckd ldng pair: rdn to chse ldr sn after 3 out: lost 2nd between last 2 but stl cl enough: one pce flat* **10/3**[2]

4- 4 *17* **Complexity**[22] 1473 3-10-12 0.. AndrewThornton 73
(Seamus Mullins) *plld hrd early and hld up in last: prog to midfield at 6th: nudged along to take 4th 2 out: no imp on ldng trio* **10/1**

B4- 5 *7* **Scepticism (USA)**[50] 1193 3-10-12 0.. MarkGrant 63
(Charlie Mann) *led to 3 out: steadily wknd* **6/1**

5- 6 *3 1/2* **Fiachra (IRE)**[14] 1524 3-10-9 0.. MichaelByrne(3) 60
(Natalie Lloyd-Beavis) *t.k.h early: hld up in tch: 6th 3 out: sn wknd* **33/1**

7 *50* **Moonlit Orchard (FR)** 3-10-5 0.. TomCannon
(Michael Blake) *a in rr: t.o bef 3 out* **10/1**

P **Until Midnight (IRE)**[130] 3-10-5 0.. KevinJones(7)
(Alexandra Dunn) *in rr: mstke 4th: mstke 6th and wknd: t.o whn p.u bef 2 out* **12/1**

P **Get Going**[23] 3-10-9 0.. JackQuinlan(3)
(Paul Cowley) *j. slowly 1st: dropped to last and struggling 3rd: sn t.o: j. violently rt 2 out and p.u* **20/1**

3m 40.4s (-20.40) **Going Correction** -1.40s/f (Hard) **9** Ran SP% **114.1**
Speed ratings (Par 103): **95,94,93,85,81 80,55, ,**
Tote Swingers: 1&2 £3.20, 1&3 £3.40, 2&3 £2.40 CSF £18.63 TOTE £4.10: £1.70, £1.30, £1.60; EX 20.20 Trifecta £148.50 Pool: £458.82 - 2.31 winning units..
Owner The Alhambra Partnership **Bred** Patrick Peare **Trained** Lower Beeding, W Sussex

FOCUS
Common bends for all races. There had been £30,000 of drainage work to the track on the railway turn and the going was good to firm with good patches and watered. Not a strong juvenile contest to kick off Plumpton's new season, but it produced a good finish with three in line at the last.

1625 HEPWORTH BREWERY NOVICES' HURDLE (10 hdls) 2m 2f
3:00 (3:02) (Class 4) 4-Y-0+ **£4,548** (£1,335; £667; £333)

Form RPR

/23- 1 **Golanova**[27] 1404 5-10-12 106.. JamieMoore 108+
(Gary Moore) *mde virtually all: rdn to assert fr 2 out: nt fluent last: drvn out* **1/1**[1]

331- 2 *2* **Experimentalist**[18] 1496 5-11-2 118..............................(t) AlanJohns(10) 119
(Tim Vaughan) *trckd ldng pair: wnt 2nd 3 out: rdn and tried to chal fr 2 out: kpt on but a hld* **3/1**[2]

234- 3 *8* **Imperial Stargazer**[52] 1176 4-10-12 108.. MarcGoldstein 101
(Sheena West) *trckd ldng pair: rdn after 3 out: cl 3rd whn mstke 2 out: steadily fdd* **4/1**[3]

PP5/ 4 *13* **Hightown (IRE)**[147] 5 6-10-12 97.. LeightonAspell 87
(Alison Batchelor) *w wnr tl 3 out: steadily wknd: nt fluent last* **20/1**

5 *2 1/2* **Micquus (IRE)**[142] 4-10-12 0.. MarkGrant 84
(Jonathan Geake) *wl in tch in midfield: outpcd bef 3 out: shuffled along and nvr on terms after* **50/1**

POU- 6 *hd* **The Kings Assassin (IRE)**[14] 1525 5-10-12 0.. TomCannon 84
(Chris Gordon) *wl in tch: outpcd and struggling 7th: no ch 3 out: plugged on fr next* **33/1**

7 *2 1/4* **Evergreen Forest (IRE)**[8] 5-10-12 0.. DavidBass 82
(Natalie Lloyd-Beavis) *w ldrs to 7th: steadily wknd bef 3 out* **50/1**

0- 8 *7* **Jumeirah Liberty**[133] 235 5-10-12 0..............................(p) DaveCrosse 76
(Zoe Davison) *hld up in last trio: stdy prog into midfield at 7th: outpcd by ldrs 3 out: nvr on terms after* **100/1**

/06- 9 *7* **No Ifs No Buts**[15] 1519 4-10-0 0 ow2.. JakeHodson(7) 64
(David Bridgwater) *hld up wl in rr: stdy prog into midfield bef 7th: outpcd and nt fluent 3 out: fdd* **40/1**

03- 10 *1 3/4* **Unsist (FR)**[14] 1525 5-10-12 0.. DominicElsworth 68
(Nick Gifford) *a in rr: rdn and lost tch after 6th: wl bhd after next* **50/1**

5- 11 *18* **Quernstone (USA)**[12] 1553 4-10-9 0.. JeremiahMcGrath(3) 51
(Harry Whittington) *nvr bttr than midfield: first one in trble by 1/2-way: t.o after 7th* **100/1**

5/4- 12 *40* **Spirit Of Xaar (IRE)**[110] 427 7-10-12 0.. AndrewThornton 15
(Linda Jewell) *a towards rr: wknd 7th: t.o* **25/1**

P **Silent Owner**[329] 5-10-2 0.. KielanWoods(3)
(Paddy Butler) *a wl in rr: wknd after 6th: t.o after next: p.u bef 2 out* **100/1**

4m 10.5s (-20.40) **Going Correction** -1.40s/f (Hard)
WFA 4 from 5yo+ 11lb **13** Ran SP% **117.8**
Speed ratings (Par 105): **89,88,84,78,77 77,76,73,70,69 61,43,**
Tote Swingers: 1&2 £1.40, 1&3 £1.50, 2&3 £2.30 CSF £3.73 TOTE £2.20: £1.10, £1.60, £1.50; EX 4.40 Trifecta £6.90 Pool: £852.04 - 91.49 winning units..
Owner Galloping On The South Downs Partnership **Bred** R D And Mrs J S Chugg **Trained** Lower Beeding, W Sussex

FOCUS
Not too many got into this novice, which was weakened somewhat with forecast favourite Billy No Name being a non-runner. Four fought it out half a circuit from home.

1626 ANDREW "SUPER WACK" JACKSON MEMORIAL H'CAP CHASE (18 fncs) 3m 2f
3:30 (3:30) (Class 4) (0-110,107) 4-Y-0+ **£4,548** (£1,335; £667; £333)

Form RPR

2FP- 1 **Old Dreams (IRE)**[14] 1529 7-11-5 100..............................(t) TomCannon 114+
(Nick Gifford) *w.w in rr: sltly hmpd 2nd: prog fr 12th to trck ldng pair after next: shkn up and quick move to ld after 3 out: sn rdn wl clr* **16/1**

/43- 2 *21* **Ballyvesey (IRE)**[21] 1486 8-11-12 107..............................(vt) JamieMoore 101
(Peter Bowen) *pressed ldr: led 10th: drvn 4 out: hdd after 3 out: sn outpcd and btn* **6/1**[3]

361- 3 *3* **Health Is Wealth (IRE)**[31] 1349 8-11-3 105..........(tp) ConorShoemark(7) 97
(Colin Tizzard) *sltly hmpd 2nd: sn trckd ldrs: wnt 2nd at 11th: stl appeared to be gng wl 3 out: wnr shot past sn after: rdn and wknd tamely* **9/2**[2]

01P- 4 *14* **Douglas**[17] 1505 8-11-2 97.. MarkGrant 80
(Jo Hughes) *led: urged into several fences: slow and hdd 10th: rdn 12th: wl btn 4th fr 14th* **16/1**

133- 5 *9* **Doctor Ric (IRE)**[14] 1526 8-10-9 93..............................(p) JoshuaMoore(3) 64
(Gerry Enright) *sltly hmpd 2nd: nvr on terms w ldrs: rdn in 5th after 12th: sn btn* **8/1**

P54- 6 *11* **Ballyvoneen (IRE)**[27] 1403 8-11-3 98..............................(p) AndrewThornton 59
(Neil King) *j. slowly 2nd: nvr gng wl: struggling in 6th fr 12th: no ch after* **12/1**

653- 7 *3/4* **Wait No More (IRE)**[30] 1361 8-11-7 102..............................(p) DougieCostello 62
(Neil Mulholland) *sltly hmpd 2nd: a in rr: nt fluent 8th: blnd 12th: wl btn in last after* **12/1**

P/1- F **Jayandbee (IRE)**[22] 1474 6-11-5 100.. RichardJohnson
(Philip Hobbs) *in tch whn hmpd and fell 2nd* **11/8**[1]

6m 38.6s (-12.10) **Going Correction** -0.925s/f (Hard) **8** Ran SP% **112.8**
Speed ratings (Par 105): **81,74,73,69,66 63,62,**
Tote Swingers: 1&2 £3.20, 1&3 £5.80, 2&3 £3.90 CSF £104.48 CT £508.53 TOTE £11.80: £3.30, £1.80, £1.40; EX 143.70 Trifecta £401.50 Part won. Pool: £535.35 - 0.22 winning units..
Owner Nick Gifford Racing Club **Bred** Rachel Ryan **Trained** Findon, W Sussex

FOCUS
The complexion of this moderate race changed early on when warm favourite Jayandbee departed early.

1627 FREEBETS.CO.UK MOBILE BETTING H'CAP HURDLE (9 hdls) 2m
4:00 (4:00) (Class 3) (0-135,130) 4-Y-O+ **£8,122** (£2,385; £1,192; £596)

Form RPR

1/5- 1 **Alfraamsey**[15] 1520 5-11-4 122.. MarcGoldstein 123
(Sheena West) *led to 2nd: pushed along 6th: rallied to ld after 3 out: hrd pressed after 2 out: battled on gamely* **6/1**[3]

231- 2 *1* **Orthodox Lad**[14] 1525 5-10-0 111.. ChristopherWard(7) 112
(Dr Richard Newland) *t.k.h early: cl up: chal and upsides 3 out: lost pl bef 2 out: renewed effrt to chse wnr sn after last: hanging and outbattled flat* **2/1**[1]

13- 3 *1* **Purple 'n Gold (IRE)**[22] 1389 4-10-6 110..............................(p) TomScudamore 110+
(David Pipe) *hld up in rr: stdy prog fr 6th: trckd wnr 2 out and poised to chal: rdn last: fnd nil* **4/1**[2]

/24- 4 *1* **Callisto Moon**[7] 1471 9-10-5 109..............................(p) MarkGrant 108
(Jo Hughes) *prom: pressed ldr fr 4th: led bef 3 out tl after 3 out: kpt on same pce u.p* **16/1**

422- 5 *1 3/4* **Dont Take Me Alive**[22] 1471 4-10-5 112..............................(tp) KielanWoods(3) 110
(Charlie Longsdon) *hld up towards rr: prog after 6th: cl up bef 2 out: nt qckn bef last: fdd flat* **12/1**

613- 6 *hd* **Guards Chapel**[14] 1527 5-11-2 123..............................(v) JoshuaMoore(3) 120
(Gary Moore) *hld up in last: pushed along and prog fr 6th: tried to latch on to ldng gp bef 2 out: nt qckn but kpt on fr last* **12/1**

5/1- 7 *16* **James Pollard (IRE)**[19] 1342 8-10-7 116..............................(t) RobertWilliams(5) 98
(Bernard Llewellyn) *w.w in tch: shkn up after 6th: lost tch w ldrs fr 3 out: no ch after* **16/1**

/62- 8 *31* **Hawkhill (IRE)**[15] 1520 7-11-10 128..............................(t) RichardJohnson 83
(Tim Vaughan) *wl in tch tl rdn and wknd after 6th: eased bef 2 out: t.o* **10/1**

212- P **Lyssio (GER)**[60] 1107 6-10-11 115.. JamieMoore
(Jim Best) *t.k.h early: cl up: nt fluent 2nd: rdn and wknd after 6th: t.o whn p.u bef 2 out* **6/1**[3]

/36- P **Rachael's Ruby**[103] 708 6-10-0 104 oh5..............................(v) ColinBolger
(Roger Teal) *racd freely: led 2nd tl bef 3 out: dropped out rapidly: t.o whn p.u bef next* **50/1**

3m 37.0s (-23.80) **Going Correction** -1.40s/f (Hard)
WFA 4 from 5yo+ 11lb **10** Ran SP% **120.1**
Speed ratings (Par 107): **103,102,102,101,100 100,92,77, ,**
Tote Swingers: 1&2 £6.70, 1&3 £5.30, 2&3 £6.90 CSF £19.52 CT £55.82 TOTE £7.80: £2.70, £1.40, £1.90; EX 28.30 Trifecta £76.10 Pool: £469.75 - 4.62 winning units..
Owner Tapestry Partnership **Bred** G Hedley & Mike Channon Bloodstock Limited **Trained** Falmer, E Sussex

FOCUS
A competitive handicap with several vying for the lead, ensuring it was run at a sound pace throughout.

1628 FREEBETS.CO.UK DOWNLOAD OUR FREE APP H'CAP HURDLE (14 hdls) 3m 1f 110y
4:30 (4:30) (Class 3) (0-140,133) 4-Y-O+ **£9,747** (£2,862; £1,431; £715)

Form RPR

2/P- 1 **Aimigayle**[35] 1304 10-10-5 112.. ColinBolger 118+
(Suzy Smith) *mde all: set mod pce: mstke 4 out: sn kicked on: rdn after 3 out: styd on gamely* **5/1**[3]

0/5- 2 *2 1/4* **Dawn Commander (GER)**[135] 205 6-11-4 125.. JasonMaguire 128
(Charlie Longsdon) *nt fluent: in tch: shoved along 10th: outpcd bef 3 out: rallied next: styd on to take 2nd flat: unable to chal* **11/4**[1]

621- 3 *3/4* **Cannon Fodder**[14] 1529 6-10-0 107 oh1.. MarcGoldstein 110
(Sheena West) *chsd wnr: nt fluent 8th and 9th: chal 3 out: rdn and nt qckn bef 2 out: lost 2nd nr fin* **5/1**[3]

/02- 4 *4 1/2* **So Fine (IRE)**[25] 1430 7-11-4 125.. RichardJohnson 124
(Philip Hobbs) *trckd wnr: chal and mstke 3 out: sn rdn: nt qckn bef next: fdd* **3/1**[2]

213- 5 *1* **To Live (FR)**[63] 1060 6-10-5 112.. TomCannon 109
(Nick Gifford) *hld up in last: outpcd bef 3 out and pushed along: kpt on steadily fr 2 out: nvr involved* **6/1**

F24- 6 *4 1/2* **Sail And Return**[5] 1594 9-11-1 125..............................(t) KielanWoods(3) 120
(Phil Middleton) *hld up in tch: outpcd and pushed along bef 3 out: no imp after: fdd* **6/1**

6m 0.15s (-24.85) **Going Correction** -1.40s/f (Hard) **6** Ran SP% **113.6**
Speed ratings (Par 107): **82,81,81,79,79 78**
Tote Swingers: 1&2 £3.50, 1&3 £5.50, 2&3 £2.80 CSF £19.76 TOTE £6.80: £2.70, £2.10; EX 25.40 Trifecta £160.70 Pool: £942.14 - 4.39 winning units..
Owner David Cliff, Phillipa Clunes & P Mercer **Bred** P J Mercer **Trained** Lewes, E Sussex

The Form Book Jumps, Raceform Ltd, Compton, RG20 6NL.

FOCUS
A steadily run affair dictated by the winner.

1629 BONUS.CO.UK ONLINE CASINO BONUSES NOVICES' H'CAP CHASE (14 fncs) 2m 4f
5:00 (5:00) (Class 4) (0-105,105) 4-Y-0+ **£4,223** (£1,240; £620; £310)

Form RPR
4P0- **1** **Fearless Leader**[49] 1202 6-11-7 **100**..........(b) TomScudamore 114+
(David Bridgwater) *trckd ldrs: lost pl 9th but stl gng wl: prog to chal whn j.rt 4 out and next: led bef 2 out: pushed clr: comf* **9/2**[3]
112- **2** *10* **Alderbrook Lad (IRE)**[24] 1435 7-11-9 **105**.......... MichaelByrne(3) 109
(Neil Mulholland) *mde most to 9th: rdn 4 out: sn lost 2nd and outpcd: kpt on fr 2 out to snatch 2nd post* **7/2**[2]
265/ **3** *nse* **Red Rock (FR)**[213] 4356 8-10-13 **95**.......... GavinSheehan(3) 100
(Emma Lavelle) *hld up in last: blnd 6th: rapid prog after next to ld 9th: hdd and fnd nil bef 2 out: lost 2nd post* **5/2**[1]
545- **4** *3 ¾* **Riddlestown (IRE)**[15] 1518 6-11-9 **102**.......... HarrySkelton 104
(Caroline Fryer) *hld up in rr: nt fluent 4th: prog and prom 9th: nt fluent next: outpcd and rdn 4 out: one pce after* **14/1**
/40- **5** *30* **Midnight Lira**[109] 634 6-10-13 **95**.......... JamesBest(3) 68
(Caroline Keevil) *chsd ldrs: rdn after 9th: sn wknd: t.o* **5/1**
214- **P** **Safe Investment (USA)**[14] 1530 9-11-0 **93**..........(vt) DavidBass
(Lawney Hill) *w ldr tl mstke 8th: gave up and t.o after 10th: crawled over 3 out and p.u* **8/1**
P44- **U** **Shock N Freaney (IRE)**[11] 1572 6-10-3 **85**..........(vt) KielanWoods(3)
(Anthony Middleton) *chsd ldrs: rdn after 9th: struggling next: wl hld in 5th whn stmbld and uns rdr 3 out* **8/1**

5m 1.6s (-5.70) **Going Correction** -0.925s/f (Hard) **7** Ran SP% **114.5**
Speed ratings (Par 105): **74,70,69,68,56** ,
Tote Swingers 1&2 £2.70, 2&3 £3.20, 1&3 £2.90 CSF £21.12 CT £47.16 TOTE £5.90: £3.00, £2.30; EX 25.80 Trifecta £89.40 Pool: £975.84 - 8.18 winning units..
Owner The Ferandlin Peaches **Bred** Kingwood Bloodstock **Trained** Icomb, Gloucs

FOCUS
A reasonably competitive novice handicap.

1630 AT THE RACES H'CAP HURDLE (9 hdls) 2m
5:30 (5:30) (Class 5) (0-95,99) 4-Y-0+ **£2,395** (£698; £349)

Form RPR
012- **1** **Capellini**[38] 1275 6-11-7 **93**.......... GavinSheehan(3) 98+
(Charles Egerton) *disp ld: rdn after 3 out: narrow advantage next: hdd last: rallied wl to ld fnl strides* **3/1**[1]
/0P- **2** *nk* **The Quantum Kid**[27] 1401 9-11-3 **86**.......... LiamTreadwell 89
(Peter Hiatt) *trckd ldrs: shkn up after 3 out: quick move to chal 2 out: led last: styd on but hdd fnl strides* **25/1**
422- **3** *7* **Hawk Gold (IRE)**[24] 1438 9-10-8 **84**..........(b) ConorShoemark(7) 81
(Michelle Bryant) *hld up in rr: prog after 6th: rdn in 8th and last of those w any ch after 3 out: kpt on to take 3rd last: no ch w ldng pair* **5/1**[3]
646- **4** *¾* **Flashy Star**[24] 1438 4-11-6 **89**..........(p) MarcGoldstein 85
(Sheena West) *trckd ldrs: blnd 5th: rdn and stl cl up 3 out: outpcd but disp 3rd after 2 out: plugged on* **12/1**
506- **5** *1 ½* **Nebula Storm (IRE)**[25] 1428 6-10-13 **85**.......... JoshuaMoore(3) 81
(Gary Moore) *hld up in rr: prog 6th: jnd ldng gp whn nt fluent 3 out: sn drvn: outpcd but disp 3rd after 2 out: one pce* **8/1**
/52- **6** *3 ½* **Recway Lass**[18] 1496 5-10-10 **79**..........(tp) DenisO'Regan 72
(Des Donovan) *trckd ldrs: effrt to chal and mstke 3 out: w wnr bef next: lost pl qckly and eased* **18/1**
032- **7** *shd* **Osmosia (FR)**[14] 1530 8-10-5 **84**..........(tp) LouisMuspratt(10) 76
(Chris Gordon) *settled in midfield: rdn and cl up after 3 out: 6th bef next: no hdwy after* **7/2**[2]
630- **8** *10* **Brass Monkey (IRE)**[27] 1405 6-10-13 **85**.......... JackQuinlan(3) 68
(Neil King) *disp ld: rousted along after 4th: lost pl and wknd sn after 3 out* **6/1**
644- **9** *6* **Al Amaan**[24] 1438 8-10-13 **89**..........(p) MrDanielBurchell(7) 66
(Jamie Poulton) *hld up and detached in last: rn wd bnds: allowed to come home in own time* **16/1**
/35- **10** *17* **What's For Tea**[24] 1438 8-9-9 **71**..........(vt) CiaranMckee(7) 33
(Paddy Butler) *a in rr: rdn and wknd after 5th: t.o* **25/1**
6/U- **11** *1 ½* **Celtic Charlie (FR)**[14] 1530 8-11-0 **83**.......... ColinBolger 44
(Pat Phelan) *hld up towards rr: nudged along and losing tch w ldrs whn mstke 3 out: sn eased and t.o* **33/1**

3m 40.5s (-20.30) **Going Correction** -1.40s/f (Hard)
WFA 4 from 5yo+ 11lb **11** Ran SP% **118.8**
Speed ratings (Par 103): **94,93,90,89,89 87,87,82,79,70 70**
Tote Swingers 1&2 £11.30, 2&3 £28.90, 1&3 £3.50 CSF £76.81 CT £372.47 TOTE £3.90: £1.90, £5.80, £1.70; EX 81.50 Trifecta £193.80 Pool: £634.09 - 2.45 winning units..
Owner Bruce Pomford & Malcolm Frost **Bred** Wertheimer Et Frere **Trained** Upper Lambourn, Berks

FOCUS
The first two pulled clear in a duel up the home straight.
T/Plt: £39.80 to a £1 stake. Pool: £62,045.01 - 1,135.81 winning tickets. T/Qpdt: £23.60 to a £1 stake. Pool: £4,484.59 - 140.20 winning tickets. JN

1561 UTTOXETER (L-H)
Sunday, September 22

OFFICIAL GOING: Good (good to firm in places; 6.6)
Wind: moderate 1/2 against Weather: fine and sunny

1631 DEREK FOWER TRANSPORT NOVICES' H'CAP HURDLE (DIV I) (12 hdls) 3m
1:40 (1:40) (Class 5) (0-100,100) 4-Y-0+ **£2,209** (£648; £324; £162)

Form RPR
0/4- **1** **Mia's Anthem (IRE)**[22] 1482 5-10-4 **83**.......... DerekFox(5) 93+
(Noel C Kelly, Ire) *in rr: gd hdwy 9th: chsng ldrs next: lft cl 2nd 2 out: led appr last: forged clr* **8/1**
0/4- **2** *5* **Perfect Timing**[30] 1364 5-11-4 **92**..........(v[1]) NickScholfield 96
(Johnny Farrelly) *mid-div: chsd ldrs 5th: lft in ld 2 out: hdd appr last: wl hld whn hit last* **3/1**[1]
/53- **3** *28* **The Wicked Kipper**[11] 1561 5-11-3 **98**.......... OllieGarner(7) 78
(Martin Keighley) *chsd ldrs: led briefly appr 3 out: hit 3 out: lft modest 3rd next: hung rt and wknd between last 2* **11/2**[3]
355- **4** *2 ½* **Exit To Freedom**[49] 1205 7-10-13 **87**..........(p) HarryHaynes 63
(John Wainwright) *chsd ldrs: wknd 3 out: lft poor 4th next* **16/1**
6F0- **5** *5* **Plug In Baby**[32] 1339 5-10-3 **77**.......... IanPopham 48
(Nick Mitchell) *towards rr: drvn 4th: bhd fr 8th* **25/1**
/60- **6** *4* **My Friend Riquet (FR)**[58] 1121 6-10-1 **75**..........(b[1]) LeeEdwards 42
(Dave Roberts) *led: hit 1st: hdd appr 3 out: sn lost pl* **25/1**
214- **7** *21* **Royal Peak (IRE)**[32] 1339 6-11-12 **100**..........(p) ConorO'Farrell 57
(David Pipe) *chsd ldrs: mstke 5th: outpcd whn mitskae 9th: lost pl appr next: bhd whn bdly hmpd 2 out: eased run-in: t.o* **4/1**[2]
400/ **8** *68* **Be Kind**[332] 2011 7-9-7 **74** oh5.......... MrPJohn(7)
(Natalie Lloyd-Beavis) *mid-div: chsd ldrs 7th: lost pl and mstke next: sn bhd: t.o 9th: eventually completed* **80/1**
/0F- **P** **Pennant Dancer**[125] 407 6-10-0 **74** oh10..........(p) AlainCawley
(Debra Hamer) *in rr: drvn 3rd: sn bhd: t.o whn p.u after 5th* **66/1**
645- **F** **Lucky To Be Alive (IRE)**[11] 1565 6-10-12 **86**..........(p) NoelFehily 90
(Peter Bowen) *hld up: hdwy to chse ldrs 7th: led 3 out: jnd whn fell next* **3/1**[1]

5m 51.0s (1.00) **Going Correction** +0.025s/f (Yiel) **10** Ran SP% **112.8**
Speed ratings (Par 103): **99,97,88,87,85 84,77,54,** ,
Tote Swingers: 1&2 £5.70, 1&3 £6.30, 2&3 £5.80 CSF £31.12 CT £143.35 TOTE £10.60: £3.60, £2.40, £3.10; EX 40.80 Trifecta £209.80 Pool: £1,123.71 - 4.01 winning units..
Owner Don't Ask Now Syndicate **Bred** Cornelius Walsh **Trained** Draperstown, Co. Derry

FOCUS
The rail was moved where possible for fresher ground and to avoid the majority of drainage scars. The first fence in the back straight was omitted in all chases. The ground had dried out a little from its overnight designation as good. They went a reasonable pace in this modest novice handicap, and it was much the quicker of the two divisions. A big step up from the winner in a fair time for the grade.

1632 UTTOXETER AND CHEADLE VOICE MAIDEN HURDLE (10 hdls) 2m 4f 110y
2:10 (2:10) (Class 5) 4-Y-0+ **£2,209** (£648; £324; £162)

Form RPR
05/ **1** **Drop Out Joe**[161] 5323 5-11-0 0.......... NoelFehily 117+
(Charlie Longsdon) *chsd ldr: led 5th: styd on wl fr 2 out: pushed out* **8/1**
2/3- **2** *2 ¼* **Keltic Rhythm (IRE)**[126] 389 6-10-9 0.......... TrevorWhelan(5) 113
(Neil King) *chsd ldrs: cl 2nd 3 out: sn rdn: styd on same pce between last 2* **5/1**[3]
00/ **3** *11* **Exemplary**[209] 4426 6-11-0 0.......... NickScholfield 103
(Marc Barber) *trckd ldrs: effrt 3 out: sn chsng ldng pair: one pce* **6/4**[1]
/33- **4** *16* **Slaney Star (IRE)**[82] 862 5-11-0 0.......... SamTwiston-Davies 88
(Jim Best) *mid-div: drvn to chse ldrs 6th: 4th and one pce 3 out* **16/1**
13- **5** *11* **Anger Management (IRE)**[25] 1427 5-11-0 0.......... APMcCoy 83
(Rebecca Curtis) *stdd s: plld hrd in rr: nt fluent 4th: hdwy 6th: sn trcking ldrs: wknd qckly 3 out* **9/4**[2]
0/5- **6** *29* **Portway Flyer (IRE)**[31] 1348 5-10-10 0 ow1.......... RobertMcCarth(5) 53
(Ian Williams) *trckd ldrs: drigven 6th: lost pl next: t.o 2 out* **14/1**
0/ **7** *2 ¾* **Mortlestown (IRE)**[149] 5537 5-11-0 0.......... IanPopham 49
(Martin Keighley) *in rr: lost pl 7th: hung rt and sn bhd: t.o 2 out* **7/1**
P- **8** *6* **Not Many Know That (IRE)**[18] 1497 7-10-7 0....(t) MrMatthewBarber(7) 44
(Marc Barber) *in rr: drvn 6th: sn bhd: t.o 2 out* **66/1**
U3- **9** *7* **Razzle Dazzle 'Em**[18] 1496 4-10-8 0..........(t) BenPoste(5) 37
(Shaun Harris) *in rr: bhd fr 7th: sn t.o* **125/1**
45P- **10** *5* **Carobello (IRE)**[32] 1339 6-11-0 83..........[1] JamesDavies 33
(Martin Bosley) *led to 5th: lost pl appr 3 out: sn bhd: t.o 2 out* **50/1**
P/U- **U** **Desert Fairy**[67] 1017 7-10-0 0.......... JoshWall(7)
(Trevor Wall) *t.k.h in rr: blnd and uns rdr 5th* **150/1**

5m 1.0s (2.00) **Going Correction** +0.025s/f (Yiel)
WFA 4 from 5yo+ 12lb **11** Ran SP% **128.5**
Speed ratings (Par 103): **97,96,91,85,81 70,69,67,64,62**
Tote Swingers: 1&2 £12.40, 1&3 £15.30, 2&3 £6.20 CSF £52.86 TOTE £12.10: £3.00, £2.20, £1.30; EX 76.80 Trifecta £476.00 Pool: £1,616.86 - 2.54 winning units..
Owner The Jesters **Bred** Jethro Bloodstock **Trained** Over Norton, Oxon

FOCUS
A modest maiden hurdle. A big step up from the winner on his bumper form.

1633 DEREK FOWER TRANSPORT NOVICES' H'CAP HURDLE (9 hdls) 2m
2:40 (2:40) (Class 5) (0-100,100) 4-Y-0+ **£2,209** (£648; £324; £162)

Form RPR
541- **1** **Sedgemoor Express (IRE)**[22] 1479 5-11-3 **94**..........(tp) MarkQuinlan(3) 106+
(Nigel Hawke) *trckd ldrs: led bef 2 out: forged clr* **6/1**[3]
13F- **2** *12* **Echo Dancer**[12] 1547 7-9-10 **77**..........(b) JoshWall(7) 78
(Trevor Wall) *in rr: hdwy 6th: led appr next: hdd appr 2 out: wl hld whn nt fluent last* **16/1**
450- **3** *2 ½* **Bob's Legend (IRE)**[27] 1391 7-11-5 **93**.......... SamTwiston-Davies 92
(Martin Bosley) *t.k.h in rr: hdwy 6th: 3rd 2 out: kpt on same pce* **8/1**
155- **4** *1 ½* **Naledi**[25] 1428 9-10-2 **83**.......... KieronEdgar(7) 79
(Richard Price) *in rr: sme hdwy 3 out: styd on wl run-in* **16/1**
060- **5** *1* **Stadium Of Light (IRE)**[29] 1379 6-10-1 **80**.......... BenPoste(5) 76
(Shaun Harris) *chsd ldrs 4th: wknd 2 out* **16/1**
001- **6** *3 ¼* **Pollystone (IRE)**[11] 1567 7-11-11 **99**.......... IanPopham 93
(Martin Keighley) *trckd ldrs: t.k.h: rdn 6th: hung lft: lost pl appr next* **9/2**[2]
503- **7** *¾* **Gavi**[40] 1269 7-9-12 **75**.......... PeterCarberry(3) 69
(Karen George) *mid-div: nt fluent 6th: kpt on fr 2 out: nvr a factor* **8/1**
P/2- **8** *9* **Lordship (IRE)**[15] 1519 9-10-11 **85**.......... FelixDeGiles 69
(Tom Gretton) *in rr: sme hdwy appr 3 out: wknd between last 2* **25/1**
0/0- **9** *2 ¼* **Theatrelands**[135] 201 5-11-12 **100**.......... NoelFehily 82
(Charlie Longsdon) *in rr: j.rt 1st: chsd ldrs 4th: hit 3 out: lost pl bef next* **5/2**[1]
333- **10** *9* **Persian Herald**[27] 1402 5-10-13 **92**..........(v) TrevorWhelan(5) 66
(Neil King) *chsd ldrs: led 6th: hdd appr next: sn lost pl* **14/1**
/0P- **P** **Teals Star**[55] 1137 9-10-0 **74** oh9.......... TommyPhelan
(C I Ratcliffe) *in rr: reminders 5th: sn bhd: t.o whn p.u bef 3 out* **100/1**
0/3- **P** **King Of Wing (IRE)**[13] 1535 4-11-7 **95**..........(p) APMcCoy
(Phil McEntee) *led: reminders after 5th: hdd next: sn lost pl: t.o whn p.u bef 3 out* **10/1**

3m 52.5s (0.50) **Going Correction** +0.025s/f (Yiel)
WFA 4 from 5yo+ 11lb **12** Ran SP% **121.5**
Speed ratings (Par 103): **99,93,91,91,90 88,88,84,82,78** ,
Tote Swingers: 1&2 £13.00, 1&3 £7.70, 2&3 £20.20 CSF £98.25 CT £785.41 TOTE £6.00: £2.50, £5.30, £2.70; EX 133.00 Trifecta £676.80 Part won. Pool: £676.80 - 0.94 winning units..
Owner Pearce Bros 2 **Bred** Seamus Cooney **Trained** Stoodleigh, Devon

FOCUS
Ordinary novice handicap form. Another step up from the winner with the second to his mark.

1634 ADVERTISE IN THE UTTOXETER AND CHEADLE VOICE H'CAP HURDLE (10 hdls) 2m 4f 110y
3:10 (3:10) (Class 4) (0-120,120) 4-Y-0+ **£3,249** (£954; £477; £238)

Form RPR
0/1- **1** **Lovey Dovey (IRE)**[75] 932 9-10-9 **108** HarryDerham(5) 115+
(Simon West) *trckd ldrs: chsd ldr after 7th: led after 3 out: sn clr: drvn rt out* **9/2**[1]
1F0- **2** 1 3/4 **Up For An Oscar (IRE)**[27] 1398 6-11-6 **119** (p) EdCookson(5) 123+
(Kim Bailey) *chsd ldrs: chsd wnr appr 2 out: styd on same pce run-in* **16/1**
422- **3** 1 1/4 **Bathwick Man**[21] 1488 8-10-9 **110** KieronEdgar(7) 111
(David Pipe) *in rr: hit 2nd: stdy hdwy 7th: 3rd appr 2 out: kpt on run-in* **7/1**[2]
0/6- **4** 3/4 **Oscar O'Scar (IRE)**[58] 1123 5-10-10 **104** RichieMcGrath 104
(Philip Kirby) *in rr: hdwy after 7th: modest 4th appr 2 out: styd on wl run-in* **16/1**
/44- **5** 3 1/4 **Hollins**[9] 1581 9-10-6 **103** JohnKington(3) 100
(Tony Forbes) *in rr: hdwy to chse ldrs 6th: 5th and rdn 3 out: one pce* **33/1**
235- **6** 4 **Always Bold (IRE)**[32] 1340 8-10-8 **102** IanPopham 96
(Martin Keighley) *in rr: bhd and rdn 7th: kpt on fr 2 out* **14/1**
506/ **7** 9 **Josies Orders (IRE)**[265] 3383 5-11-2 **110** APMcCoy 97
(Jonjo O'Neill) *mid-div: effrt appr 3 out: nvr a factor* **8/1**[3]
3/6- **8** 4 **Green To Gold (IRE)**[23] 1050 8-11-10 **118** (b) PaulMoloney 100
(Don Cantillon) *in rr: hdwy 6th: chsng ldrs next: wknd 3 out* **11/1**
0/2- **9** 1/2 **Judiciary (IRE)**[12] 1551 6-10-11 **115** PaulO'Brien(10) 100+
(Rebecca Curtis) *chsd ldrs: led appr 3rd: clr next: hdd after 3 out: sn wknd* **7/1**[2]
346/ **10** 3 1/2 **Dealing River**[375] 1560 6-11-9 **117** RobertThornton 96
(Caroline Bailey) *mid-div: sme hdwy 7th: lost pl bef next* **20/1**
/52- **11** nk **Osric (IRE)**[81] 875 10-11-8 **116** (b) NickScholfield 94
(Laura Young) *in rr: bhd fr 7th* **20/1**
P15- **12** 26 **Di Kaprio (FR)**[40] 1268 7-11-9 **117** [1] LiamHeard 72
(Barry Leavy) *in rr: sme hdwy 6th lost pl bef next: t.o 3 out* **20/1**
F/1- **L** **Toughness Danon**[11] 1561 7-10-13 **112** RobertMcCarth(5)
(Ian Williams) *ref to r: lft at s* **10/1**
011- **P** **He's A Hawker (IRE)**[27] 1391 8-11-4 **112** (b) NoelFehily
(Michael Mullineaux) *mid-div: lost pl after 6th: sn bhd: t.o whn p.u bef 3 out* **8/1**[3]
/53- **P** **Outback (IRE)**[22] 1468 4-10-3 **103** (v) TrevorWhelan(5)
(Neil King) *led: hdd approachibng 3rd: chsd ldr: reminders after 5th: wknd appr 3 out: t.o whn p.u bef 2 out* **25/1**

5m 0.9s (1.90) **Going Correction** +0.025s/f (Yiel)
WFA 4 from 5yo+ 12lb **15 Ran SP% 122.3**
Speed ratings (Par 105): **97,96,95,95,94 92,89,87,87,86 86,76,,,**
Tote Swingers: 1&2 £33.30, 1&3 £6.60, 2&3 £47.00 CSF £69.18 CT £510.44 TOTE £7.00: £2.10, £7.10, £2.40; EX 132.00 Trifecta £573.00 Part won. Pool: £764.02 - 0.19 winning units..
Owner James-Douglas Gordon **Bred** Hugh Suffern Bloodstock Ltd **Trained** Middleham Moor, N Yorks

FOCUS
A modest handicap, run in an almost identical time to the earlier maiden hurdle. Pretty solid form.

1635 DEREK FOWER TRANSPORT NOVICES' H'CAP HURDLE (DIV II) (12 hdls) 3m
3:40 (3:40) (Class 5) (0-100,100) 4-Y-0+ **£2,209** (£648; £324; £162)

Form RPR
P5P- **1** **Marico (FR)**[35] 1300 5-10-6 **80** (p) FelixDeGiles 86
(Tom Symonds) *racd wd: trckd ldr: hit 6th: led appr 3 out: 2 l clr last: all out* **8/1**
212- **2** nk **Hopstrings**[24] 1432 5-11-10 **98** SamTwiston-Davies 104
(Charlie Brooks) *chsd ldrs: drvn 8th: chsd wnr between last 2: styd on run-in: jst hld* **4/1**[2]
434- **3** 3 1/2 **Blackstone Vegas**[24] 1442 7-11-1 **89** (v) JamesDavies 92
(Derek Shaw) *in rr: hdwy 5th: sn chsng ldrs: 4th 2 out: kpty on run-in: tk 3rd nr fin* **6/1**
055- **4** 3/4 **Snow Alert**[35] 1306 7-10-2 **83** StephenMulqueen(7) 86
(John Norton) *j.lft 1st: chsd ldrs 6th: cl 2nd 3 out: one pce appr last* **12/1**
P/0- **5** 30 **Princesse Katie (IRE)**[127] 368 7-9-7 **74** oh5 (t) MrMatthewStanley(7) 49
(James Bennett) *in rr: hdwy to chse ldrs 8th: rdn whn hit 3 out: sn wknd and eased: t.o* **33/1**
225- **6** 11 **Spice Hill (IRE)**[34] 1314 7-10-1 **85** (v) NathanAdams(10) 50
(Tim Vaughan) *chsd ldr: drvn to ld 8th: hdd appr 3 out: sn wknd* **5/1**[3]
/0P- **7** 33 **Vicpol (ITY)**[52] 1170 7-10-12 **86** (v[1]) LeeEdwards 21
(Tom Gretton) *led: hdd 8th: lost pl appr 2 out: bhd whn eased between last 2: t.o* **10/1**
P/P- **P** **All The Fashion (IRE)**[51] 1188 9-10-0 **77** oh20 ow3 RobertDunne(3)
(Violet M Jordan) *in rr: hdwy 8th: lost pl next: sn bhd: t.o whn p.u bef 2 out* **66/1**
0/2- **P** **Antihero**[112] 598 6-9-11 **76** TonyKelly(5)
(David Thompson) *nt fluent in rr: bhd and reminders 6th: t.o whn p.u bef 8th: lame* **8/1**
03/- **U** **Ballycool (IRE)**[147] 15 6-11-5 **100** (t) MrSFox(7)
(Lucinda Russell) *w ldrs: mstke and uns rdr 3rd* **3/1**[1]

5m 59.2s (9.20) **Going Correction** +0.025s/f (Yiel) **10 Ran SP% 119.4**
Speed ratings (Par 103): **85,84,83,83,73 69,58,,,**
Tote Swingers: 1&2 £30.90, 1&3 £23.40, 2&3 £8.30 CSF £41.80 CT £211.08 TOTE £10.70: £3.60, £1.80, £2.70; EX 52.60 Trifecta £272.30 Pool: £660.13 - 1.81 winning units..
Owner Thomas Symonds Racing Syndicate **Bred** E A R L Haras Du Bosquet **Trained** Harewood End, H'fords

FOCUS
This was run in a time 8.2sec slower than the first division, and the form is very limited. The third and fourth help set the level.

1636 UTTOXETER AND CHEADLE VOICE H'CAP CHASE (THE SUNDAY £5K BONUS RACE) (14 fncs 2 omitted) 2m 5f
4:10 (4:10) (Class 3) (0-130,130) 4-Y-0+
£6,256 (£1,848; £924; £462; £231; £116)

Form RPR
412- **1** **Sergeant Pink (IRE)**[13] 1545 7-11-3 **121** HenryBrooke 130
(Dianne Sayer) *chsd ldrs: wnt 2nd appr 4 out: lft in narrow ld 3 out: sn hdd: upsides last: r.o to ld run-in: drvn rt out* **10/1**
000- **2** 1 1/2 **Buck Mulligan**[22] 1476 8-11-9 **127** PaulMoloney 135
(Evan Williams) *hld up in rr: hdwy 10th: sn trcking ldrs: chalng whn lft upsides 3 out: sn led: jnd last: hdd and no ex run-in* **4/1**[3]
211- **3** 25 **Fairwood Massini (IRE)**[15] 1521 8-10-11 **122** (vt) JPKiely(7) 107
(Tim Vaughan) *chsd ldrs 7th: drvn 10th: outpcd, hmpd and lft 3rd 3 out: sn wknd* **5/1**
413- **4** 15 **Violets Boy (IRE)**[22] 1470 6-10-13 **117** (t) APMcCoy 92
(Brendan Powell) *chsd ldrs: wknd 4 out: lft poor 4th and hmpd next* **7/2**[2]
134- **5** nk **That's The Deal (IRE)**[18] 1493 9-10-1 **110** JoeCornwall(5) 81
(John Cornwall) *chsd ldrs: outpcd 10th: lost pl bef next: sn bhd* **20/1**
200/ **6** 26 **Sir Frank (IRE)**[176] 5015 8-11-0 **118** (b[1]) ConorO'Farrell 66
(David Pipe) *led tl after 1st: chsd ldrs: rdn and lost pl 10th: sn bhd: t.o 2 out* **3/1**[1]
2F4- **B** **Father Shine (IRE)**[27] 1397 10-9-13 **108** BenPoste(5)
(Shaun Harris) *hld up in rr: b.d 8th* **25/1**
041- **F** **Tregaro (FR)**[11] 1566 7-10-0 **104** oh3 (t) BrianHughes
(Mike Sowersby) *t.k.h in rr: fell 8th* **14/1**
51P- **F** **Next Oasis (IRE)**[50] 1192 7-10-9 **113** PaddyBrennan 118
(Paul Henderson) *led after 1st: sticking on whn fell 3 out* **9/1**

5m 14.0s (-8.80) **Going Correction** -0.20s/f (Good) **9 Ran SP% 118.3**
Speed ratings (Par 107): **108,107,97,92,92 82,,,**
Tote Swingers: 1&2 £6.60, 1&3 £2.50, 2&3 £4.90 CSF £52.24 CT £229.50 TOTE £5.40: £1.90, £2.20, £1.60; EX 47.90 Trifecta £127.10 Pool: £1,336.75 - 7.88 winning units..
Owner Andrew Sayer **Bred** Ring Pink Partnership **Trained** Hackthorpe, Cumbria

FOCUS
The first chase of the day was a decent handicap, run at a fair pace. The leader's fall left the first two clear. The faller and the second are rated pretty much to their marks.

1637 DEREK FOWER TRANSPORT NOVICES' H'CAP CHASE (16 fncs 2 omitted) 3m
4:40 (4:40) (Class 4) (0-115,115) 4-Y-0+ **£3,833** (£1,157; £596; £315)

Form RPR
201- **1** **Watch House (IRE)**[12] 1548 8-9-11 93 MissAEStirling(7) 106+
(Michael Gates) *j.lft 1st: chsd ldrs 6th: cl 2nd 10th: led sn after 3 out: drew rt away run-in* **5/1**
111- **2** 14 **Whistling Senator (IRE)**[25] 1425 6-11-12 115 (v) APMcCoy 119
(Jonjo O'Neill) *chsd ldr 2nd: led 8th: jnd whn blnd 3 out: sn hdd: upsides next: 4 l down and wl hld last: sn eased* **4/1**[3]
112- **3** 39 **Green Bank (IRE)**[22] 1469 7-11-12 115 (tp) NoelFehily 80
(Charlie Longsdon) *led: hdd 8th: drvn 10th: outpcd whn hit 11th: sn bhd: t.o 4 out* **10/3**[2]
244- **4** 6 **Brough Academy (IRE)**[14] 1526 7-11-3 106 (tp) AidanColeman 66
(Lawney Hill) *chsd ldrs: reminders 3rd: drvn 5th: bhd fr 10th: hit 12th: t.o next* **8/1**
/54- **F** **Standing Ovation (IRE)**[89] 832 6-10-3 92 (t) ConorO'Farrell
(David Pipe) *4th whn fell 2nd* **7/4**[1]

6m 5.7s (-9.40) **Going Correction** -0.20s/f (Good) **5 Ran SP% 107.2**
Speed ratings (Par 105): **107,102,89,87,**
CSF £22.67 TOTE £4.60: £2.00, £1.40; EX 11.60 Trifecta £20.10 Pool: £1,350.55 - 50.17 winning units..
Owner Michael Gates **Bred** T Reeves **Trained** Clifford Chambers, Warwicks

FOCUS
This novice handicap rather fell apart, beginning with favourite Standing Ovation hitting the deck at the second. There's a case for rating the form a few pounds higher.

1638 NIGEL TITTERTON AND DEREK FOWER H'CAP CHASE (11 fncs 1 omitted) 2m
5:10 (5:10) (Class 5) (0-100,98) 4-Y-0+ **£2,599** (£763; £381; £190)

Form RPR
5P0- **1** **The Nephew (IRE)**[12] 1550 5-11-5 **91** (t) RichieMcLernon 105+
(Jonjo O'Neill) *stdd s: hld up in rr: hdwy 7th: trcking ldrs next: handy 3rd whn blnd 3 out: cl 2nd last: r.o to ld last 30yds* **3/1**[2]
0/0- **2** 1 3/4 **Schinken Otto (IRE)**[131] 281 12-11-4 **90** HarryHaynes 99
(Malcolm Jefferson) *led: jnd 2 out: hdd and no ex clsng stages* **10/1**
13U/ **3** 1 1/4 **Drumlang (IRE)**[147] 20 7-11-7 **98** RobertMcCarth(5) 107
(Ian Williams) *chsd ldrs: upsides 2 out: kpt on same pce appr last* **11/4**[1]
012- **4** 26 **Maizy Missile (IRE)**[51] 1186 11-11-3 **89** PaulMoloney 76
(Mary Evans) *chsd ldr: wknd 4 out: wl bhd fr 2 out: t.o* **8/1**
454- **5** 9 **Tri Nations (UAE)**[15] 1522 8-11-10 **96** (vt) NickScholfield 72
(Anthony Middleton) *in rr: drvn 6th: sn bhd: t.o 3 out* **7/1**
6PP- **6** 3/4 **Radsoc De Sivola (FR)**[11] 1563 8-9-9 **72** oh1 JoeCornwall(5) 48
(John Cornwall) *chsd ldrs: drvn 9th: lost pl appr 4 out: sn bhd: t.o 2 out* **9/1**
012- **P** **Crack At Dawn (IRE)**[12] 1547 12-11-2 **95** (v) MissAEStirling(7)
(Michael Gates) *chsd ldrs: lost pl 7th: sn bhd: t.o whn p.u bef 3 out* **4/1**[3]

3m 56.6s (1.60) **Going Correction** -0.20s/f (Good) **7 Ran SP% 114.4**
Speed ratings (Par 103): **88,87,86,73,69 68,**
Tote Swingers 1&2 £7.90, 2&3 £7.00, 1&3 £3.90 CSF £30.48 CT £90.48 TOTE £5.00: £2.70, £4.80; EX 50.20 Trifecta £437.50 Pool: £1,561.85 - 2.67 winning units..
Owner Mrs Gay Smith **Bred** Nicholas Teehan **Trained** Cheltenham, Gloucs

FOCUS
A moderate event but the form seems sound enough. The winner was up 7lb on the best of his hurdles form but looks sure to rate higher still over fences.
T/Jkpt: Not won. T/Plt: £226.40 to a £1 stake. Pool: £81,110.00 - 261.50 winning tickets. T/Qpdt: £23.90 to a £1 stake. Pool: £5,521.42 - 170.90 winning tickets. WG

1483 NEWTON ABBOT (L-H)
Tuesday, September 24

OFFICIAL GOING: Good to firm (good in places; 7.7)
Wind: mild breeze half across Weather: sunny with some cloud

1639 NEWTONABBOTRACING.COM MARES' NOVICES' HURDLE (9 hdls) 2m 3f
2:20 (2:20) (Class 4) 4-Y-0+ **£3,508** (£1,030; £515; £257)

Form RPR
/25- **1** **Top Totti**[102] 738 5-11-5 108 RichardJohnson 106+
(Henry Daly) *trckd ldrs: chal after 3 out: sn rdn: led sn after 2 out: drifted lft: r.o wl fr last: rdn out* **5/4**[1]
633- **2** 2 1/4 **Presenting Me (IRE)**[33] 1347 5-10-5 92 ConorRing(7) 97
(Evan Williams) *trckd ldrs: nudged along after 5th: rdn after 3 out: ev ch briefly between last 2: nt pce of wnr fr last* **6/1**[3]
1/1- **3** 3 **Neston Grace**[119] 519 5-11-5 0 JamesDavies 102
(Simon Hodgson) *trckd ldr: led bef 4th and qcknd pce: pushed along whn hit 2 out: sn hdd no ex* **2/1**[2]

/56- **4** *16* **Pagham Belle**[37] 1305 5-10-9 83....(t) MarkQuinlan(3) 80
(Nigel Hawke) *led at stdy pce tl hdd 4th: trckd ldr: rdn after 3 out: hld whn lft 4th next: wknd between last 2* **33/1**

5 *3 ½* **Pandorica**[9] 5-10-12 0.... PaulMoloney 77
(Bernard Llewellyn) *hld up bhd ldrs: rchd for 5th: struggling after next: wkng whn lft 5th 2 out* **16/1**

00/ **F** **Diddypurptoon**[313] 2443 7-10-9 0.... JamesBest(3)
(Jackie Du Plessis) *hld up bhd ldrs: rdn to chse ldng pair after 3 out: hld in 4th whn fell next* **50/1**

R **Sea Island Pearl**[71] 4-10-8 0.... MichealNolan(3)
(Philip Hobbs) *ref to r: tk no part* **14/1**

4m 34.2s (4.20) **Going Correction** -0.25s/f (Good)
WFA 4 from 5yo+ 11lb **7** Ran SP% **109.5**
Speed ratings (Par 105): **81,80,78,72,70** ,
Tote Swingers: 1&2 £2.20, 1&3 £1.10, 2&3 £2.00 CSF £8.71 TOTE £2.00: £1.60, £2.40; EX 6.80 Trifecta £14.50 Pool: £2,006.62 - 103.39 winning units..
Owner Hamer, Hawkes & Hellin **Bred** E R Hanbury **Trained** Stanton Lacy, Shropshire

FOCUS
All races on shared bends. After a dry night, the ground was officially good to firm, good in places. A mares' novices' hurdle that lacked depth. The early pace was very steady and the winner is rated 7lb off her best.

1640 PAUL NEWBOLD 50TH BIRTHDAY CELEBRATIONS NOVICES' CHASE (13 fncs) 2m 110y
2:50 (2:50) (Class 4) 4-Y-0+ **£4,288** (£1,259; £629; £314)

Form RPR

210- **1** **De Faoithesdream (IRE)**[33] 1346 7-11-11 128.... PaulMoloney 132+
(Evan Williams) *mde all: qckbd clr after 4 out: in command fr next: eased run-in* **2/1**[2]

2/6- **2** *12* **Tiny Tenor (IRE)**[15] 1535 7-11-4 0.... NickScholfield 110
(David Dennis) *trckd wnr: rdn after 4 out: hld whn nt fluent next: keeping on at same pce whn lost 2nd between last 2: regained 2nd nring fin* **10/1**[3]

26/- **3** *nk* **If I Were A Boy (IRE)**[31] 3593 6-10-11 0.... MarkGrant 103
(Dominic Ffrench Davis) *trckd ldng pair: rdn whn outpcd after 4 out: styd on again appr 2 out: wnt 2nd bef last: lost 2nd nring fin* **20/1**

1PP/ **4** *31* **Mr Watson (IRE)**[150] 5574 6-11-4.... APMcCoy 101
(Jonjo O'Neill) *hld up bhd ldng trio: nt that fluent: reminders after 8th: nvr any imp: outpcd after 4 out: slow next: wknd and eased* **4/7**[1]

3m 56.9s (-9.60) **Going Correction** -0.45s/f (Good) **4** Ran SP% **110.8**
Speed ratings (Par 105): **104,98,98,83**
CSF £15.60 TOTE £3.40; EX 9.30 Trifecta £14.00 Pool: £1,059.97 - 56.51 winning units..
Owner R Abbott & M Stavrou **Bred** Pierce Whyte **Trained** Llancarfan, Vale Of Glamorgan

FOCUS
Only one of these had previous chasing form and he scored convincingly. He was value for further and rated to his mark.

1641 PAIGNTON ZOO NOVICES' HURDLE (10 hdls) 2m 6f
3:20 (3:20) (Class 4) 4-Y-0+ **£3,508** (£1,030; £515; £257)

Form RPR

236/ **1** **Angles Hill (IRE)**[237] 3946 6-10-9 123.... MichealNolan(3) 105
(Richard Woollacott) *trckd ldr: chal after 3 out: hrd rdn between last 2: narrowly led sn after last: drifted lft: jst hld on: all out* **8/13**[1]

0/2- **2** *shd* **Quadrato (GER)**[19] 1506 6-10-12 105....(t) RichardJohnson 105
(Tim Vaughan) *led: rdn whn chal after 3 out: narrowly hdd sn after last: carried sltly lft: rallying nr fin where lightly bmpd: jst hld* **13/8**[2]

4P0- **3** *11* **Cottage Acre (IRE)**[90] 844 10-10-12 90.... LiamHeard 95
(Colin Heard) *trckd ldr: pushed along after 7th: outpcd after 3 out: wl hld 3rd whn wnt sltly rt next* **33/1**

0/6- **4** *7* **Ibiza Sunset (IRE)**[98] 758 5-10-12 96....(t) RyanMahon 90
(Sarah Kerswell) *slowly away: racd in 4th but wl in tch: rdn after 3 out: sn outpcd: wknd between last 2* **20/1**[3]

5m 22.2s (2.00) **Going Correction** -0.25s/f (Good) **4** Ran SP% **107.7**
Speed ratings (Par 105): **86,85,81,79**
CSF £1.97 TOTE £1.60; EX 2.10 Trifecta £6.60 Pool: £819.98 - 92.56 winning units..
Owner R G Westacott **Bred** D Roche **Trained** South Molton, Devon

FOCUS
A novices' hurdle deprived of significant interest when hat-trick-seeking Koultas King defected. There was, however, a thrilling finish. The winner is rated a stone+ off his best, with the second and third setting the level.

1642 SIS OUR DATA BRINGS BETTING TO LIFE H'CAP CHASE (20 fncs) 3m 2f 110y
3:50 (3:50) (Class 3) (0-135,130) 4-Y-£7,596 (£2,244; £1,122; £561; £280)

Form RPR

300- **1** **Life Of A Luso (IRE)**[24] 1476 9-11-10 128....(t) PaddyBrennan 135
(Paul Henderson) *hld up bhd: nudged along after 14th: stdy hdwy fr next: rdn in disp 3rd whn nt fluent 3 out: swtchd rt appr last where lft clr 2nd: styd on strly to ld run-in: drvn out* **9/1**

0P6/ **2** *½* **Inside Dealer (IRE)**[173] 5146 9-11-2 120....(tp) JoeTizzard 125
(Colin Tizzard) *trckd ldrs: wnt 2nd after 15th: rdn after 4 out: led 2 out: styd on but no ex whn hdd run-in* **13/2**

261- **3** *6* **Western King (IRE)**[23] 1486 6-10-11 115....(tp) NoelFehily 117
(Charlie Mann) *hld up: reminders after 13th: plenty to do fr next: sn rdn: stdy prog fr after 4 out: wnt 4th after 2 out: styng on at same pce whn lft 3rd at the last* **7/2**[1]

012- **4** *8* **Captain Kelly (IRE)**[42] 1262 6-11-10 128....(t) RyanMahon 124
(Paul Nicholls) *mid-div: pushed along after 16th: rdn in disp 3rd after 4 out: fading in 5th whn lft 4th at the last* **5/1**[3]

01P- **5** *11* **Lord Lescribaa (FR)**[23] 1486 10-9-4 104 oh2..(tp) ThomasCheesman(10) 87
(Philip Hobbs) *trckd ldr: led bef 5th: rdn and hdd bef 15th: wknd after 3 out* **14/1**

451- **6** *16* **Strumble Head (IRE)**[38] 1283 8-10-13 117....(v) DonalDevereux 86
(Peter Bowen) *in tch: reminders after 9th and 12th: drvn after 14th: wknd after 3 out* **11/2**

620- **F** **Qulinton (FR)**[52] 1195 9-11-12 130....(bt) JasonMaguire 132
(Johnny Farrelly) *j. sltly lft: led tl appr 5th: trckd ldr: led appr 15th: rdn whn hrd pressed after 3 out: hdd next: hld in 2nd whn fell last* **7/1**

P/3- **P** **Qianshan Leader (IRE)**[147] 39 9-11-4 125.... GavinSheehan(3)
(Emma Lavelle) *in tch: pushed along after 12th: rdn in last pair after next: wkng whn slow 3 out: p.u bef next* **9/2**[2]

6m 25.7s (-18.90) **Going Correction** -0.45s/f (Good) **8** Ran SP% **115.0**
Speed ratings (Par 107): **110,109,108,105,102 97**, ,
Tote Swingers: 1&2 £22.80, 1&3 £8.50, 2&3 £25.60 CSF £65.41 CT £245.39 TOTE £10.00: £1.90, £2.80, £1.30; EX 88.90 Trifecta £478.50 Pool: £1,002.78 - 1.57 winning units..
Owner Mareildar Racing Part 1 **Bred** Mrs Mona Costelloe **Trained** Whitsbury, Hants

FOCUS
A competitive event, in which few could be confidently discounted. The winner is rated to his best.

1643 BET TOTEPOOL TEXT TOTE TO 89660 (S) H'CAP HURDLE (8 hdls) 2m 1f
4:20 (4:20) (Class 5) (0-95,94) 4-Y-0+ **£2,463** (£718; £359)

Form RPR

342- **1** **Argaum (IRE)**[27] 1428 6-11-1 90....(vt) ConorRing(7) 97+
(Evan Williams) *trckd ldrs: led briefly 3 out: rdn to ld again bef 2 out: slt advantage whn mstke last: hld on: all out* **7/2**[1]

6/0- **2** *nk* **Bazart**[27] 1428 11-10-11 84....(tp) RobertWilliams(5) 90
(Bernard Llewellyn) *in tch: rdn to chse ldng pair after 3 out: chal next: ev ch whn nt fluent last: kpt on* **14/1**

/14- **3** *3 ½* **Pindar (GER)**[27] 1428 9-10-5 80....(p) ConorShoemark(7) 86+
(Neil Mulholland) *led tl 5th: sn rdn: outpcd after 3 out: styd on again fr 2 out: wnt 3rd between last 2: nvr rching ldng pair* **9/2**[2]

50F- **4** *7* **Cash Injection**[17] 1517 4-11-9 94....(t) MichealNolan(3) 92
(Richard Woollacott) *hld up towards rr: rdn and stdy prog fr 3 out: styng on wl whn gng 4th between last 2: nt fluent last: no further imp* **20/1**

/00- **5** *2 ¼* **Lombok**[26] 1438 7-10-7 78....(v) JoshuaMoore(3) 74
(Gary Moore) *mid-div: hdwy after 5th: rdn and ch whn wnt rt 2 out: hld after: wnt rt last* **6/1**[3]

33P- **6** *6* **No Woman No Cry**[24] 1474 8-11-3 85....(bt) JoeTizzard 74
(Colin Tizzard) *mid-div tl dropped to rr u.p 5th: plugged on after 3 out* **7/1**

/62- **7** *7* **Chankillo**[11] 1575 4-11-5 87.... WillKennedy 70
(Sarah-Jayne Davies) *trckd ldrs tl lost pl bef 5th: sn rdn but nvr a danger after* **7/1**

POU- **8** *nk* **No No Cardinal (IRE)**[23] 1487 4-11-1 83.... TommyPhelan 69+
(Mark Gillard) *racd keenly: mid-div: trckd ldrs 3rd: led travelling wl sn after 3 out: rdn and hdd bef next: fnd little: sn wknd* **33/1**

F/U- **9** *8* **Wicklewood**[17] 1517 7-11-1 83.... RhysFlint 58
(John Flint) *a towards rr: t.o* **16/1**

P60- **10** *15* **Cool Fantasy (IRE)**[40] 1270 4-10-0 68 oh3....(p) IanPopham 30
(Caroline Keevil) *mid-div tl 5th: sn rdn: wknd next: t.o* **25/1**

242/ **11** *1 ½* **Supernoverre (IRE)**[812] 1018 7-11-8 93....(p) GavinSheehan(3) 53
(Alan Jones) *a towards rr: t.o fr 3 out* **14/1**

020- **P** **Novikov**[16] 1530 9-11-6 88....(bt) PaulMoloney
(Sophie Leech) *mid-div: rdn after 4th: sn in rr: p.u bef next* **22/1**

/0P- **P** **Holden Caulfield (IRE)**[91] 833 8-10-9 82.... CharlieWallis(5)
(Nick Ayliffe) *drvn along to hold midfeild position tl wknd 5th: t.o whn p.u bef 2 out* **20/1**

55P- **P** **Danehill Dante (IRE)**[41] 1206 5-11-12 94.... TomCannon
(Chris Gordon) *prom: led 5th tl next: wknd qckly: p.u bef 2 out* **25/1**

3m 56.9s (-8.80) **Going Correction** -0.25s/f (Good)
WFA 4 from 5yo+ 11lb **14** Ran SP% **123.4**
Speed ratings (Par 103): **110,109,108,104,103 101,97,97,93,86 86**, , ,
Tote Swingers: 1&2 £16.70, 2&3 £5.30 CSF £46.89 CT £232.94 TOTE £4.70: £2.00, £5.70, £2.20; EX 81.00 Trifecta £316.30 Pool: £657.95 - 1.56 winning units..No bid for the winner.
Owner George Houghton **Bred** Pendley Farm **Trained** Llancarfan, Vale Of Glamorgan

FOCUS
A modest contest, with the top weight rated just 94, but competitive on paper and solid form for the grade.

1644 HAPPY 25TH ANNIVERSARY IAN AND TRACEY BORTHWICK H'CAP CHASE (16 fncs) 2m 5f 110y
4:50 (4:50) (Class 5) (0-95,95) 4-Y-0+ **£2,729** (£801; £400; £200)

Form RPR

522- **1** **Sadler's Star (GER)**[14] 1548 10-11-10 93....(p) NickScholfield 102+
(Michael Blake) *disp ld tl clr ldr after 10th: in command but pushed along fr 3 out: comf* **3/1**[2]

060- **2** *13* **Rusty Nail (IRE)**[52] 1191 8-10-3 72.... FelixDeGiles 69
(James Frost) *hld up bhd ldng 4: disp 3rd after 9th: mstke next: wnt 2nd 4 out: sn rdn: hld fr next: styd on same pce* **7/2**

0/0- **3** *½* **Magical Treasure**[36] 1320 9-11-12 95....(bt) RyanMahon 91
(Sarah Kerswell) *trckd ldrs: nt fluent 1st: sltly hmpd whn blnd 2nd: hit 5th and 9th: sn struggling but stl in tch: no imp tl styd on fr last to go 3rd towards fin: clsng fast on 2nd* **12/1**

041- **4** *2 ½* **Nothingbutthetruth (IRE)**[16] 1526 9-11-8 91....(tp) TomScudamore 85
(Richard Woollacott) *trckd ldrs: wnt lft 2nd: pushed along after 12th: rdn after 4 out: nt pce to get involved: no ex whn lost 3rd nring fin* **9/4**[1]

/P0- **P** **Allterrain (IRE)**[14] 1548 10-10-0 72 oh3 ow3....(p) JoshuaMoore(3)
(Gary Moore) *disp ld tl after 10th: sn rdn: wknd after 4 out: wnt lft 2 out: p.u bef last* **10/3**[3]

5m 17.8s (-3.60) **Going Correction** -0.45s/f (Good) **5** Ran SP% **108.8**
Speed ratings (Par 103): **88,83,83,82**,
CSF £13.28 TOTE £2.60: £3.30, £2.10; EX 12.20 Trifecta £81.90 Pool: £1,030.48 - 9.43 winning units..
Owner Mrs J M Haines **Bred** R Haag And H Schniepp **Trained** Trowbridge, Wilts

FOCUS
A weak handicap chase, made all the more uncompetitive by the late defection of likely favourite Roc de Guye. The easy winner is rated in line with his 2013 best.

1645 LIVING COASTS TORQUAY H'CAP HURDLE (10 hdls) 2m 6f
5:20 (5:22) (Class 4) (0-115,115) 4-Y-0+ **£3,508** (£1,030; £515; £257)

Form RPR

412- **1** **Listen And Learn (IRE)**[33] 1345 5-11-4 107....(p) APMcCoy 115+
(Jonjo O'Neill) *hld up in gp: swtchd to outer after 6th: hdwy next: led 3 out: drew clr fr next: mstke last: comf* **9/4**[1]

612/ **2** *5* **Buckhorn Tom**[171] 5185 5-11-11 114.... JoeTizzard 113+
(Colin Tizzard) *trckd ldrs: chal 7th: sn rdn: dropped to 3rd after 3 out: styd on to regain 2nd gng to the last: no ch w wnr* **5/2**[2]

F62- **3** *3 ¼* **Tony Dinozzo (FR)**[11] 1581 6-11-0 103....(p) DonalDevereux 99
(Peter Bowen) *trckd ldrs: rdn to chse wnr after 3 out: nt pce to get on terms: no ex whn lost 2nd at the last* **7/2**[3]

104- **4** *1 ¾* **Marie Deja La (FR)**[26] 1436 7-10-11 100....(p) TomCannon 94
(Chris Gordon) *mid-div: hdwy 6th to trck ldrs: outpcd after 3 out: styd on after next to go 4th at the last* **16/1**

/26- **5** *2 ¼* **Prime Location**[34] 1340 7-10-5 104....(tp) AnthonyFox(10) 95
(David Pipe) *trckd ldr: led 5th tl 3 out: sn rdn: one pce fr next* **11/2**

0P5- **6** *4* **Hassadin**[23] 1488 7-10-11 100....(p) NickScholfield 88
(Michael Blake) *hld up: lost tch 6th: stdy prog u.p after 3 out: styd on same pce fr next bt nvr any threat* **12/1**

/00- **7** *13* **Landenstown Star (IRE)**[23] 1488 8-10-0 89 oh12....(t) TommyPhelan 70
(Mark Gillard) *led tl 5th: struggling bef 7th: wknd 3 out* **66/1**

004- **P** **Exiles Return (IRE)**[24] 1479 11-9-11 **89** oh20................. MarkQuinlan(3)
(Jacqueline Retter) *hld up: wnt rt 1st: hdwy after 6th: wknd 3 out: wnt bdly rt 2 out: p.u bef last* **66/1**

5m 10.3s (-9.90) **Going Correction** -0.25s/f (Good) 8 Ran SP% **113.5**
Speed ratings (Par 105): **108,106,105,104,103 102,97,**
Tote Swingers 1&2 £1.02, 2&3 £3.90, 1&3 £1.90 CSF £8.46 CT £17.46 TOTE £2.50: £1.50, £1.10, £1.30; EX 8.40 Trifecta £28.10 Pool: £1,845.64 - 49.09 winning units..
Owner John P McManus **Bred** Micheal Fahy **Trained** Cheltenham, Gloucs

FOCUS
Just a handful appeared to have realistic chances in this low-key finale. Another step forward from the easy winner.
T/Plt: £97.40 to a £1 stake. Pool: £62,080.25 - 464.87 winning tickets. T/Qpdt: £19.20 to a £1 stake. Pool: £4,415.30 - 169.35 winning tickets. TM

1646 - 1653a (Foreign Racing) - See Raceform Interactive

1540 PERTH (R-H)

Wednesday, September 25

OFFICIAL GOING: Good (good to soft in places; 7.9) changing to good to soft after race 2 (2.50)
Wind: Moderate, half behind Weather: Overcast

1654 HUGH AND JEAN BROGAN MEMORIAL NOVICES' HURDLE (9 hdls 1 omitted) 2m 4f 110y
2:20 (2:20) (Class 4) 4-Y-0+ **£3,249** (£954; £477; £238)

Form RPR

3/- **1** **Mysteree (IRE)**[152] 5550 5-10-12 0.................................. PeterBuchanan 116+
(Lucinda Russell) *t.k.h: prom: rdn and outpcd 2 out (usual 3 out): rallied and chsd ldr last: led last 100yds: styd on* **8/1**[3]

2- **2** *5* **Butney Rock**[39] 1288 6-10-12 111.................................. DenisO'Regan 112+
(C A McBratney, Ire) *led to 3rd: w ldr: led 3 out (usual 4 out): qcknd after next: 8 l clr last (usual 2 out): no and hdd last 100yds* **8/13**[1]

3 *14* **Station Closed (IRE)**[68] 1030 5-10-5 0.......................... WilsonRenwick 91
(Mrs Lorna Fowler, Ire) *hld up in tch: stdy hdwy 1/2-way: effrt and chsd (clr) ldr briefly appr last (usual 2 out): wknd bef omitted last* **16/1**

4 *3/4* **Mister D (IRE)**[220] 7-10-5 0.. JonathonBewley(7) 98
(George Bewley) *t.k.h: cl up: led 3rd: hdd whn hit 3 out (usual 4 out): wknd bef last (usual 2 out)* **66/1**

64P/ **5** *3 1/4* **Rossini's Dancer**[152] 5545 8-10-12 0............................(p) LucyAlexander 95
(N W Alexander) *prom: lost pl bef 6th: sn struggling: n.d after* **9/1**

331- **6** *10* **Red Eyes**[20] 1500 5-10-9 112.................................. DiarmuidO'Regan(10) 95
(Chris Grant) *mstkes: chsd ldrs tl wknd 2 out (usual 3 out)* **4/1**[2]

\- **7** *91* **Badged**[145] 4-10-11 0... RyanMania 3
(Lucy Normile) *in tch tl rdn and lost tch fr 2 out (usual 3 out)* **40/1**

\- **P** **Kitnkaboodle (IRE)** 8-9-12 0.. MrDFBourke(7)
(Stuart Coltherd) *nt fluent in rr: struggling fr 3rd: lost tch whn p.u 3 out (usual 4 out)* **66/1**

5m 7.0s (5.00) **Going Correction** +0.225s/f (Yiel)
WFA 4 from 5yo+ 12lb 8 Ran SP% **114.3**
Speed ratings (Par 105): **99,97,91,91,90 86,51,**
toteswingers 1&2 £2.50, 1&3 £12.90, 2&3 £2.40 CSF £13.98 TOTE £6.20: £2.10, £1.02, £3.20; EX 21.50 Trifecta £73.60 Pool: £737.34 - 7.51 winning units..
Owner Mrs Lynne Maclennan **Bred** Lar & Fiona Cloke **Trained** Arlary, Perth & Kinross

FOCUS
Bends moved on to fresh ground. The winning rider in the first said the going was "lovely, good to soft ground". A modest novice hurdle, run at an ordinary pace, and there are doubts over the form. The final flight was bypassed. It's been rated around the second and third.

1655 SCOTTISH CHARITY AIR AMBULANCE H'CAP CHASE (18 fncs) 3m
2:50 (2:50) (Class 5) (0-100,99) 4-Y-0+ **£3,898** (£1,144; £572; £286)

Form RPR

/05- **1** **Kilvergan Boy (IRE)**[34] 1344 9-10-0 73 oh3........(p) SamTwiston-Davies 80
(Nigel Twiston-Davies) *chsd ldrs: wnt 2nd bef 14th: nt fluent next: sn rdn: 4 l down 2 out: led run-in: styd on wl* **11/4**[1]

/50- **2** *1 1/4* **Quinder Spring (FR)**[122] 492 9-11-3 **97**.................(p) GrantCockburn(7) 103
(Lucinda Russell) *in tch: stdy hdwy bef 4 out: rdn bef next: no imp tl styd on wl fr last: tk 2nd post* **10/1**

2/2- **3** *nse* **Oh Right (IRE)**[32] 1376 9-10-4 **77**................................(p) HenryBrooke 83
(Dianne Sayer) *cl up: led 13th: rdn bef 3 out: 4 l clr next: edgd rt after last: hdd run-in: kpt on same pce: lost 2nd last stride* **11/4**[1]

322- **4** *23* **Solway Dornal**[20] 1505 8-9-7 **73** oh1...................(tp) StephenMulqueen(7) 56
(Lisa Harrison) *chsd ldrs: drvn 4 out: wknd bef next* **5/1**[2]

0/6- **5** *7* **Knight Woodsman**[140] 169 9-11-0 **94**........................ CallumBewley(7) 71
(R Mike Smith) *hld up in tch: outpcd bef 13th: struggling fr 4 out* **6/1**[3]

236- **6** *8* **Baizically (IRE)**[4] 1618 10-11-12 **99**................................(v[1]) ConorO'Farrell 69
(John Joseph Hanlon, Ire) *led to 13th: rdn bef next: wknd after 4 out* **15/2**

4/4- **7** *15* **Cilliseal (IRE)**[20] 1505 8-11-1 **95**...(t) MrSFox(7) 51
(Noel C Kelly, Ire) *bhd and sn pushed along: lost tch fr 1/2-way: t.o* **10/1**

P00- **P** **Man Of Principles (IRE)**[32] 1379 10-9-8 **74**........... DiarmuidO'Regan(7)
(Stuart Coltherd) *bhd: struggling fr 7th: t.o whn p.u bef 13th* **28/1**

6m 16.3s (12.30) **Going Correction** +0.275s/f (Yiel) 8 Ran SP% **117.7**
Speed ratings (Par 103): **90,89,89,81,79 76,71,**
toteswingers 1&2 £14.70, 1&3 £3.30, 2&3 £4.30 CSF £30.19 CT £83.26 TOTE £3.80: £1.70, £2.90, £1.20; EX 38.10 Trifecta £127.50 Pool: £927.05 - 5.45 winning units..
Owner The Yes No Wait Sorries **Bred** J J Behan **Trained** Naunton, Gloucs

FOCUS
A moderate handicap chase. The winner was a 100+ horse in 2012 but was nowhere near that level here, and the second and third look the best guide.

1656 CRABBIE'S ALCOHOLIC GINGER BEER CLAIMING HURDLE (8 hdls) 2m 110y
3:25 (3:25) (Class 4) 4-Y-0+ **£3,898** (£1,144; £572; £286)

Form RPR

0/- **1** **Formal Bid (IRE)**[19] 1511 6-11-4 116............................(bt) JasonMaguire 113+
(Gordon Elliott, Ire) *hld up: stdy hdwy after 3 out: effrt between last 2: led last 50yds: drvn out* **6/4**[1]

144- **2** *nk* **Outrageous Request**[16] 1544 7-11-4 119....................... PeterBuchanan 113
(Lucinda Russell) *hld up: hdwy bef 2 out: led bef last to last 50yds: kpt on: hld nr fin* **11/4**[2]

/11- **3** *2* **It's A Mans World**[16] 1540 7-11-4 120.............................. GLavery(10) 122
(Brian Ellison) *chsd ldrs: hdwy and ev ch 2 out to last: kpt on same pce run-in* **5/1**[3]

45R/ **4** *3* **Hide The Evidence (IRE)**[52] 1211 12-10-7 114............ RobertDunne(3) 101
(Michael McElhone, Ire) *chsd ldr: led bef 2 out to between last 2: nt fluent last: sn outpcd* **12/1**

U45- **5** *6* **Millers Reef (IRE)**[29] 1419 7-10-12 90..........................(t) WilsonRenwick 97
(Andrew Parker) *prom: rdn bef 2 out: wknd fr last* **50/1**

PFP/ **6** *25* **Wind Shuffle (GER)**[27] 1145 10-10-4 0 ow1...........(p) GrahamWatters(7) 74
(Lucinda Russell) *led: hdd and outpcd whn mstke last: sn btn: t.o* **40/1**

30P/ **7** *1 1/4* **Makhzoon (USA)**[156] 5451 9-10-10 119.........................(p) LucyAlexander 71
(N W Alexander) *hld up: struggling 3 out: sn btn: t.o* **11/2**

8 *11* **Belle Noverre (IRE)**[60] 981 9-10-3 0.............................. ConorO'Farrell 55
(John Carr) *bhd: rdn bef 3 out: nvr on terms: t.o* **66/1**

3m 58.3s (0.30) **Going Correction** +0.225s/f (Yiel) 8 Ran SP% **112.3**
Speed ratings (Par 105): **108,107,106,105,102 90,90,85**
toteswingers 1&2 £1.50, 1&3 £2.60, 2&3 £2.20 CSF £5.68 TOTE £2.40: £1.10, £1.10, £2.00; EX 6.70 Trifecta £14.00 Pool: £1523.17 - 81.26 winning units..
Owner Ms Annie Flora Joan Bowles **Bred** Neville O'Byrne & John Weld **Trained** Trim, Co Meath

FOCUS
The ground was officially changed to good to soft before this event, a fair claiming hurdle. The first two are probably the best guide to the level. The third has been rated as running a personal best.

1657 PIPE AND PILING SUPPLIES NOVICES' H'CAP CHASE (12 fncs) 2m
4:00 (4:00) (Class 4) (0-115,112) 4-Y-0+ **£3,898** (£1,144; £572; £286)

Form RPR

332- **1** **Gud Day (IRE)**[15] 1549 5-11-12 **112**...............................(tp) PaddyBrennan 123+
(Fergal O'Brien) *chsd ldrs: smooth hdwy 4 out: led gng wl 2 out: rdn last: kpt on strly* **13/8**[1]

452- **2** *4 1/2* **Agricultural**[73] 957 7-10-11 **97**... WilsonRenwick 102
(Lucy Normile) *chsd ldr: rdn to ld 3 out: hdd next: rallied and ev ch last: one pce run-in* **15/8**[2]

/60- **3** *23* **Breeze With Ease (IRE)**[32] 1379 9-10-12 **98**..................(t) BrianHughes 82
(Barry Murtagh) *hld up in tch: stdy hdwy bef 3 out: rdn and wknd fr next* **9/1**

340- **4** *2 1/4* **Toledo Gold (IRE)**[32] 1378 7-11-5 **112**...............(t[1]) StephenMulqueen(7) 94
(Maurice Barnes) *led tl rdn and hdd 3 out: wknd fr next* **3/1**[3]

3m 58.4s (1.40) **Going Correction** +0.275s/f (Yiel) 4 Ran SP% **107.9**
Speed ratings (Par 105): **107,104,93,92**
CSF £5.13 TOTE £2.20; EX 3.70 Trifecta £10.50 Pool: £1201.08 - 85.10 winning units..
Owner The People's Horse **Bred** Patrick M Ryan **Trained** Coln St. Dennis, Gloucs

FOCUS
Ordinary novice handicap form. The second has been rated to his mark.

1658 ABERDEEN & GLASGOW PA JUVENILE HURDLE (8 hdls) 2m 110y
4:35 (4:36) (Class 4) 3-Y-0 **£3,249** (£954; £477; £238)

Form RPR

1 **Estinaad (USA)**[4] 3-10-8 0 ow3.. DannyCook 93+
(Brian Ellison) *in tch: stdy hdwy 3 out: effrt and slt ld next: kpt on gamely u.p towards fin* **4/1**[2]

223- **2** *1/2* **Akdam (IRE)**[27] 1439 3-11-0 113.....................................(p) JoshHamer(5) 104
(Tony Carroll) *cl up: led appr 3 out: hdd next: styd upsides: hit last: kpt on: hld nr fin* **11/4**[1]

4- **3** *15* **Down Time (USA)**[10] 1585 3-10-7 0...............................(t) BrianHayes(5) 83
(John Joseph Hanlon, Ire) *chsd ldrs: drvn and outpcd 2 out: no imp fr last* **14/1**

4 *1 1/2* **Most Honourable** 3-10-12 0.. RyanMania 81
(Michael Smith) *prom: effrt and drvn bef 2 out: sn outpcd* **7/1**

41- **5** *1* **Aficionado**[20] 1501 3-11-5 0... WilsonRenwick 88
(Chris Grant) *prom on outside: nt fluent 4 out: drvn after next: outpcd bef 2 out* **15/2**

6 *6* **Chloe's Image**[29] 3-10-5 0... RichieMcGrath 68
(Philip Kirby) *plld hrd: in tch: struggling 3 out: btn next* **11/2**[3]

F **Snoqualmie Chief**[62] 3-10-12 0......................................(t[1]) JasonMaguire 78
(Gordon Elliott, Ire) *hld up last: stdy hdwy bef 2 out: nt fluent and rdn 2 out: sn fnd little: disputing 5th and btn whn fell heavily last* **11/2**[3]

2- **P** **Tinctoria**[20] 1501 3-10-5 0..(b) BrianHughes
(Kevin Ryan) *led: hit and blkd 3rd: stmbld 4 out: wandered and hdd appr next: sn struggling: t.o whn p.u bef 2 out* **14/1**

4m 2.3s (4.30) **Going Correction** +0.225s/f (Yiel) 8 Ran SP% **115.0**
Speed ratings (Par 103): **98,97,90,90,89 86, ,**
toteswingers 1&2 £4.20, 1&3 £24.70, 2&3 £14.30 CSF £15.97 TOTE £4.70: £1.80, £1.10, £3.00; EX 17.70 Trifecta £234.00 Pool: £1679.98 - 5.38 winning units..
Owner L S Keys **Bred** Shadwell Farm LLC **Trained** Norton, N Yorks

FOCUS
A weak juvenile hurdle run at a fairly steady pace. The first two drew clear. The second and third are the best guide.

1659 GS GROUP GALLOP H'CAP CHASE (FOR THE DUKE OF ATHOLL CHALLENGE CUP) (18 fncs) 3m
5:10 (5:10) (Class 3) (0-130,130) 4-Y-0+ **£7,147** (£2,098; £1,049; £524)

Form RPR

222/ **1** **Raajih**[19] 1515 5-11-1 **119**...(bt) JasonMaguire 125
(Gordon Elliott, Ire) *in tch: smooth hdwy to chse ldr 3 out: effrt next: led run-in: drvn out* **17/2**

/63- **2** *1 1/4* **Rhum (FR)**[18] 1521 8-10-13 **117**...........................(vt) SamTwiston-Davies 123
(Nigel Twiston-Davies) *led: rdn 3 out: edgd rt after last: hdd run-in: kpt on: hld nr fin* **7/1**[3]

04P- **3** *2 1/2* **Aneyeforaneye (IRE)**[80] 900 7-11-12 **130**........................ BrianHughes 134
(Malcolm Jefferson) *hld up towards rr: hdwy and prom fnl circ: effrt and drvn 3 out: one pce fr last* **10/1**

411- **4** *1* **More Equity**[25] 1469 11-10-4 **108**...................................... HenryBrooke 110
(Dianne Sayer) *midfield: lost pl 12th: drvn bef 4 out: styd on fr 2 out: nvr able to chal* **22/1**

153- **5** *2 1/2* **Dark Energy**[16] 1545 9-11-5 **123**...(t) AlainCawley 125
(Fergal O'Brien) *t.k.h: chsd ldrs: lost pl bef 12th: rallied bef 3 out: one pce between last 2* **20/1**

121- **6** *6* **Scotch Warrior**[16] 1545 9-11-2 **127**.............................. CallumBewley(7) 122
(R Mike Smith) *midfield: lost pl 12th: rdn 4 out: hmpd by faller next: nvr on terms* **13/2**[2]

61U/ **7** *26* **Palos Conti (FR)**[156] 5453 10-10-8 **112**................................ DannyCook 90
(Brian Ellison) *nt fluent: t.k.h in rr: mstke 5th: hdwy and cl up 12th: rdn whn hit 3 out: sn wknd* **5/2**[1]

234- **8** *14* **Quito Du Tresor (FR)**[16] 1545 9-11-2 **120**..................... TomScudamore 78
(Lucinda Russell) *hld up: stdy hdwy after 4 out: rdn and wknd fr next* **10/1**

4/2- **U** **Qaspal (FR)**[27] 1444 9-10-11 **115**.. APMcCoy
(Philip Hobbs) *mstke and nrly uns rdr 1st: hld up: blnd and uns rdr 13th* **13/2**[2]

0P2- **F** **Wild Geese (IRE)**[16] 1542 6-11-2 **120**..........................(p) PeterBuchanan
(Lucinda Russell) *pressed ldr: rdn whn blnd 4 out: sixth and wkng whn fell heavily next* **7/1**[3]

6m 14.0s (10.00) **Going Correction** +0.275s/f (Yiel) **10** Ran SP% **118.1**
Speed ratings (Par 107): **94,93,92,92,91 89,80,76, ,**
toteswingers 1&2 £8.60, 1&3 £95.80, 2&3 £17.40 CSF £67.82 CT £611.33 TOTE £9.60: £3.10, £2.70, £3.10; EX 87.70 Trifecta £1049.10 Pool: £1398.92 - 0.83 winning units..
Owner Sideways Syndicate **Bred** Shadwell Estate Co Ltd **Trained** Trim, Co Meath

FOCUS
A decent handicap chase run in a time 2.3sec quicker than the earlier 0-100 handicap. Sound form. The second, third and fourth help set the level.

1660 BET WITH THE DEWHURST RING BOOKMAKERS H'CAP HURDLE (12 hdls) 3m 110y
5:40 (5:40) (Class 3) (0-125,125) 4-Y-0+ **£5,393** (£1,583; £791; £395)

Form RPR
331- **1** **Emily's Flyer (IRE)**[16] 1541 6-11-0 **113**..........................(t) PaddyBrennan 119+
(Fergal O'Brien) *mde all: pushed clr fr 4 out: rdn whn hit 2 out: wnt rt last: hld on gamely* **6/1**[3]

5S3- **2** ¾ **Bescot Springs (IRE)**[16] 1543 8-11-0 **113**................(v) TomScudamore 116
(Lucinda Russell) *in tch: hit 7th: rdn bef 3 out: hdwy bef next: rallied to chse wnr after last: kpt on fin* **20/1**

154- **3** 3 **Malin Bay (IRE)**[28] 1430 8-11-12 **125**................................ FearghalDavis 125
(Nicky Richards) *cl up: wnt 2nd 4 out: rdn after next: one pce fr last* **20/1**

043- **4** 5 **What A Steel (IRE)**[30] 1398 9-10-13 **112**........................ WilsonRenwick 108
(Alistair Whillans) *midfield: reminders and lost pl 6th: struggling 8th: styd on wl fr 2 out: nrst fin* **8/1**

35U- **5** 3 **Solway Sam**[16] 1542 10-10-1 **100**.. BrianHarding 94
(Lisa Harrison) *chsd ldrs: drvn after 4 out: outpcd fr 2 out* **22/1**

0/6- **6** 3 **Royal Riviera**[33] 1363 7-10-9 **108**.....................(t) SamTwiston-Davies 98
(Nigel Twiston-Davies) *hld up: rdn and hdwy bef 3 out: no imp bef next* **17/2**

2/6- **7** 3 **Jeu De Roseau (IRE)**[30] 1398 9-10-11 **120**.......... DiarmuidO'Regan[(10)] 107
(Chris Grant) *bhd: drvn along 1/2-way: sme late hdwy: nvr on terms* **28/1**

1/5- **8** 1½ **Knockanarrigan (IRE)**[31] 1385 5-10-1 **105**...................(p) BrianHayes[(5)] 91
(John Joseph Hanlon, Ire) *hld up in midfield: smooth hdwy 4 out: rdn after next: wknd bef 2 out* **6/1**[3]

050- **9** 4½ **Cockney Trucker (IRE)**[53] 1195 11-11-12 **125**...................... APMcCoy 107
(Philip Hobbs) *hld up: stdy hdwy after 8th: rdn after 4 out: wknd after next* **11/2**[2]

2/U- **10** 10 **Sun Cloud (IRE)**[118] 553 6-11-5 **118**................................ BrianHughes 91
(Malcolm Jefferson) *hld up: rdn after 4 out: struggling fr next* **9/1**

5P2/ **11** 20 **Drop Anchor (IRE)**[33] 1369 10-10-3 **102**......................... ConorO'Farrell 57
(Edward Cawley, Ire) *bhd: struggling fnl circ: t.o* **40/1**

0/2- **P** **Ballyben (IRE)**[132] 339 5-11-0 **113**.................................... JasonMaguire
(Lucinda Russell) *chsd ldrs tl rdn and wknd 3 out: t.o whn p.u bef last* **10/3**[1]

6m 7.1s (2.10) **Going Correction** +0.225s/f (Yiel) **12** Ran SP% **118.4**
Speed ratings (Par 107): **105,104,103,102,101 100,99,98,97,94 87,**
toteswingers 1&2 £24.00, 1&3 £27.30, 2&3 £61.40 CSF £120.34 CT £2253.73 TOTE £7.60: £2.40, £5.30, £6.60; EX 116.20 Trifecta £459.00 Pool: £986.38 - 1.61 winning units..
Owner C Cornes **Bred** Cathal Ennis **Trained** Coln St. Dennis, Gloucs

FOCUS
An open handicap hurdle, and probably ordinary form for the grade. The second has been rated to his mark, with the third a bit below his best.
T/Plt: £15.10 to £1 stake. Pool: £72,579.47 - 3489.80 winning tickets. T/Qpdt: £14.40 to £1 stake. Pool: £4894.70 - 251.25 winning tickets. RY

1654 PERTH (R-H)
Thursday, September 26
OFFICIAL GOING: Good to soft (7.7)
Wind: Almost nil Weather: Cloudy

1661 ISLE OF SKYE 8-Y-O BLENDED WHISKY NOVICES' HURDLE (8 hdls) 2m 110y
2:45 (2:46) (Class 4) 4-Y-0+ **£3,249** (£954; £477; £238)

Form RPR
406/ **1** **Castletown Bridge (IRE)**[112] 653 6-10-12 119...........(t) JasonMaguire 116+
(Gordon Elliott, Ire) *t.k.h: in tch: nt fluent 4 out: smooth hdwy to ld appr 2 out: sn hrd pressed: hit last: drvn out* **3/1**[3]

212- **2** ½ **The Cockney Mackem (IRE)**[16] 1550 7-11-5 120. SamTwiston-Davies 121
(Nigel Twiston-Davies) *chsd ldr: smooth hdwy and disp ld appr 2 out: sn rdn: kpt on u.p fr last: jst hld* **2/1**[1]

0/ **3** 9 **Call Of Duty (IRE)**[15] 2376 8-10-12 0................................ HenryBrooke 105
(Dianne Sayer) *nt fluent in rr: hdwy after 3 out: rdn and no imp fr next* **66/1**

220/ **4** 4 **Hallmark Star**[154] 5522 4-10-12 118............................ TomScudamore 102
(Lucinda Russell) *led: rdn and hdd appr 2 out: sn outpcd* **9/4**[2]

5 9 **Trois Vallees (USA)**[183] 4-10-12 0.................................. PeterBuchanan 93
(Lucinda Russell) *midfield: rdn and outpcd 3 out: n.d after* **16/1**

6 7 **Military Call**[23] 6-10-5 0.. CallumBewley[(7)] 85
(R Mike Smith) *hld up: rdn and outpcd 4 out: n.d after* **100/1**

2- **7** 2 **Wot A Shot (IRE)**[27] 1450 4-10-12 108..................................[1] DenisO'Regan 83
(C A McBratney, Ire) *t.k.h: hld up: hdwy to ld after 3rd: hdd 4 out: wknd bef 2 out* **20/1**

0/1- **8** 1 **On The Buckle**[146] 101 5-10-12 0.................................. WilsonRenwick 84
(Rose Dobbin) *t.k.h in midfield: effrt and rdn bef 2 out: sn btn* **12/1**

9 3¾ **Firethorn (IRE)**[100] 720 4-10-12 0...................................... BrianHughes 78
(C A McBratney, Ire) *t.k.h: hld up: rdn and outpcd 3 out: n.d after* **100/1**

/53- **10** 9 **Rev Up Ruby**[103] 754 5-9-12 0.................................. JonathonBewley[(7)] 62
(George Bewley) *sn wl bhd: no ch fr 1/2-way* **28/1**

4m 1.8s (3.80) **Going Correction** +0.20s/f (Yiel)
WFA 4 from 5yo+ 11lb **10** Ran SP% **114.4**
Speed ratings (Par 105): **99,98,94,92,88 85,84,83,81,77**
toteswingers 1&2 £2.20, 2&3 £15.60, 1&3 £18.60 CSF £9.21 TOTE £4.60: £2.00, £1.10, £12.10; EX 11.60 Trifecta £376.40 Pool: £940.98 - 1.87 winning units..
Owner M J Wasylocha **Bred** M Cummins **Trained** Trim, Co Meath

FOCUS
The majority of these runners are nothing more than modest performers, and the early gallop was sedate. The first two have run pretty much to their marks, with the third in line with his Flat form.

1662 GS GROUP GALLOP NOVICES' HURDLE (12 hdls) 3m 110y
3:20 (3:20) (Class 4) 4-Y-0+ **£3,249** (£954; £477; £238)

Form RPR
211- **1** **Kilbree Kid (IRE)**[36] 1337 6-11-12 119..........................(t) PaddyBrennan 124+
(Tom George) *t.k.h: trckd ldrs: led and rdn 2 out: rdn and hld on gamely fr last* **11/8**[1]

213- **2** 2¾ **Ocean Club**[13] 1576 6-11-5 120.. DannyCook 116
(Brian Ellison) *pressed ldr: led 8th: rdn 3 out: hdd next: rallied: ch last: one pce run-in* **11/8**[1]

3- **3** 23 **Cobajayisland (IRE)**[117] 584 5-10-12 0...................... TomScudamore 92+
(Lucinda Russell) *in tch: effrt after 3 out: wknd fr next* **6/1**[2]

0/U- **4** 5 **Cumbrian Farmer**[33] 1375 6-10-5 0........................... JonathonBewley[(7)] 83
(George Bewley) *led at slow gallop: hdd 8th: outpcd after 4 out: n.d after* **150/1**

064/ **5** ¾ **Saudi Pearl (IRE)**[495] 341 5-10-12 0.................... SamTwiston-Davies 82
(Nigel Twiston-Davies) *prom tl rdn and wknd after 3 out* **10/1**[3]

6m 15.9s (10.90) **Going Correction** +0.20s/f (Yiel) **5** Ran SP% **108.2**
Speed ratings (Par 105): **90,89,81,80,79**
CSF £3.45 TOTE £1.90: £1.30, £1.10; EX 3.80 Trifecta £6.60 Pool: £1047.66 - 117.31 winning units..
Owner Five Valleys Racing Partnership **Bred** John O'Mahony **Trained** Slad, Gloucs

FOCUS
Nothing of significance happened until the last 6f of the contest. The first two are likely to make fair staying chasers in time. The winner is on the upgrade and there's a case for rating him up to 5lb higher through the runner-up.

1663 TIMOTHY HARDIE JEWELLERS NOVICES' CHASE (FOR THE CENTENARY SILVER PLATE) (15 fncs) 2m 4f 110y
3:55 (3:55) (Class 3) 4-Y-0+ **£7,147** (£2,098; £1,049; £524)

Form RPR
P/6- **1** **Double Ross (IRE)**[138] 215 7-11-2 0.................... SamTwiston-Davies 130+
(Nigel Twiston-Davies) *led to 6th: led again 9th: mde rest: rdn 3 out: hrd pressed fr next: hld on gamely run-in* **8/13**[1]

0/P- **2** 1¾ **Attaglance**[138] 217 7-11-2 133.......................................(t) HarryHaynes 129+
(Malcolm Jefferson) *nt fluent on occasions: chsd ldrs: wnt 2nd 5 out: effrt and ev ch 2 out to run-in: kpt on same pce towards fin* **11/4**[2]

2/1- **3** 4½ **Raajih**[1] 1659 5-11-12 119...(bt) JasonMaguire 134
(Gordon Elliott, Ire) *hld up in tch: hdwy to chse ldrs bef 2 out: sn rdn: outpcd between last 2* **7/1**[3]

535- **4** 20 **Dark Energy**[1] 1659 9-11-12 123...(t) AlainCawley 121
(Fergal O'Brien) *t.k.h: prom: hdwy to ld 6th: hdd 9th: rdn and wknd appr 3 out* **20/1**

0P/- **P** **Glen Lord**[150] 28 10-11-2 0...(t) AdrianLane
(Sandy Forster) *t.k.h in rr: struggling: whn mstke 8th (water) t.o whn p.u bef next* **100/1**

5m 4.7s (-0.30) **Going Correction** +0.20s/f (Yiel) **5** Ran SP% **106.8**
Speed ratings (Par 107): **108,107,105,98,**
CSF £2.59 TOTE £1.40: £1.10, £2.00; EX 2.50 Trifecta £4.60 Pool: £2068.98 - 331.83 winning units..
Owner Options O Syndicate **Bred** T McIlhagga **Trained** Naunton, Gloucs

FOCUS
An interesting contest but it would be surprising if any of these took high rank during the winter. The winner is a 140 hurdler but has only been rated in line with his previous chase best here.

1664 CELEBRATING 40 YEARS OF EXPRO NOVICES' H'CAP HURDLE (10 hdls) 2m 4f 110y
4:30 (4:30) (Class 4) (0-110,110) 4-Y-0+ **£4,548** (£1,335; £667; £333)

Form RPR
/03- **1** **Frontier Vic**[107] 716 6-10-0 **84**................................ SamTwiston-Davies 94+
(Nigel Twiston-Davies) *chsd ldrs: led after 3 out: hrd pressed whn nt fluent next: styd on wl fr last* **11/4**[1]

413- **2** 4½ **Tantamount**[40] 1286 4-10-12 **104**.. CraigNichol[(7)] 105
(Lucinda Russell) *hld up: hdwy and prom 4 out: ev ch whn nt fluent 2 out and last: kpt on same pce run-in* **11/2**[3]

610- **3** 2¼ **Cruachan (IRE)**[85] 867 4-11-8 **107**................................ DougieCostello 107
(Lucy Normile) *hld up: rdn and hdwy to chse clr ldng pair bef 2 out: kpt on fr last* **11/1**

456/ **4** 13 **Rockchasebullett (IRE)**[167] 5264 5-11-12 **110**.............. PaddyBrennan 103+
(Fergal O'Brien) *t.k.h: hld up: stdy hdwy whn mstke 3 out: rdn bef next: no imp* **7/2**[2]

304/ **5** 6 **La Bacouetteuse (FR)**[23] 3421 8-11-1 **99**..........................(p) AdrianLane 80
(Iain Jardine) *hld up: stdy hdwy bef 3 out: sn rdn: wknd bef next* **12/1**

03U- **6** nse **Karingo**[84] 880 6-10-13 **102**.. SamanthaDrake[(5)] 85
(Lucy Normile) *nt fluent 1st: midfield: pushed along 3 out: btn next* **25/1**

333/ **7** 1 **Lady Of Verona (IRE)**[157] 5452 6-10-1 **92**................. GrahamWatters[(7)] 74
(Lucinda Russell) *cl up: led after 4 out to after next: wknd 2 out* **7/1**

P **Steviekey (IRE)**[130] 7-10-8 **92**.......................................(t) ConorO'Farrell
(John Joseph Hanlon, Ire) *bhd: struggling 4 out: t.o whn p.u bef 2 out* **20/1**

504- **F** **Tim's Approach (IRE)**[17] 1543 8-9-11 **84** oh16............(t) JohnKington[(3)]
(William Young Jnr) *chsd ldr: fell 4th* **100/1**

4/P- **P** **Wayne Manor (IRE)**[31] 1286 4-10-13 **98**..................(bt[1]) PeterBuchanan
(Lucinda Russell) *t.k.h: led and clr to 4th: hdd after 4 out: wknd fr next: t.o whn p.u bef 2 out* **22/1**

/2P- **P** **Lady Gargoyle**[20] 1161 5-10-8 **92**... GaryBartley
(Jim Goldie) *hld up: hmpd by faller 4th: struggling 6th: t.o whn p.u bef 4 out* **28/1**

000/ **P** **Oscar Stanley (IRE)**[170] 5227 6-10-1 **85**...................(b[1]) WilsonRenwick
(Rose Dobbin) *hld up in midfield: hdwy to chse ldrs 5th: wknd bef 3 out: t.o whn p.u bef next* **12/1**

5m 3.9s (1.90) **Going Correction** +0.20s/f (Yiel)
WFA 4 from 5yo+ 12lb **12** Ran SP% **117.9**
Speed ratings (Par 105): **104,102,101,96,94 94,93, , , ,**
toteswingers 1&2 £3.50, 2&3 £6.90, 1&3 £6.00 CSF £17.11 CT £145.53 TOTE £4.00: £2.50, £2.40, £2.50; EX 21.50 Trifecta £299.90 Pool: £1123.81 - 2.81 winning units..
Owner Jump For Fun Racing **Bred** B Mayoh, Eskdale Thoroughbreds **Trained** Naunton, Gloucs

FOCUS
Moderate fare but the pace was sound from the start thanks to the free-running Wayne Manor, who was in blinkers for the first time. The winner has been rated as improving markedly on his previous hurdles form. The time was decent and he should win again.

1665 ANDERSON ANDERSON AND BROWN H'CAP HURDLE (8 hdls) 2m 110y
5:05 (5:05) (Class 4) (0-120,120) 4-Y-0+ **£4,548** (£1,335; £667; £333)

Form RPR
303- **1** **Cool Baranca (GER)**[85] 870 7-10-10 **104**.......................... RyanMania 117+
(Dianne Sayer) *in tch: smooth hdwy to ld whn j.rt 2 out: sn clr: easily* **5/2**[1]
4U3- **2** *14* **My Idea**[117] 583 7-10-6 **107**.................................(t) StephenMulqueen[(7)] 106+
(Maurice Barnes) *chsd ldr to 4 out: rdn whn hit next: rallied to chse (clr) wnr bef 2 out: hit last: no imp* **14/1**
0/1- **3** *8* **Dhaular Dhar (IRE)**[17] 1544 11-10-13 **107**.......................... GaryBartley 96
(Jim Goldie) *hld up: stdy hdwy bef 3 out: rdn bef next: styd on fr last: no imp* **12/1**
/05- **4** *½* **Indepub**[21] 1504 4-11-1 **109**... WilsonRenwick 97
(Martin Todhunter) *hld up: rdn bef 3 out: styd on fr last: nvr able to chal* **20/1**
605/ **5** *nk* **De Bee Keeper (IRE)**[193] 4815 5-10-3 **97**...................... PeterBuchanan 85
(Lucinda Russell) *hld up: outpcd and drvn along 4 out: styd on fr last: nvr able to chal* **4/1**[2]
/31- **6** *nk* **Marcus Antonius**[63] 488 6-11-12 **120**.......................... TomScudamore 109
(Jim Boyle) *t.k.h: cl up: wnt 2nd 4 out to bef 2 out: sn drvn and wknd* **17/2**[3]
POP/ **7** *nk* **Flogarose (FR)**[155] 5492 4-9-8 **95**................................ GrantCockburn[(7)] 83
(Lucy Normile) *led to bef 2 out: rdn and sn btn* **20/1**
641- **8** *4 ½* **Cadore (IRE)**[58] 1143 5-10-1 **102**...................................(p) MikeyEnnis[(7)] 88
(Lucy Normile) *midfield: pushed along and hdwy bef 3 out: mstke and wknd next* **5/2**[1]
640/ **9** *5* **Leroy Parker (IRE)**[122] 2112 5-11-7 **115**......................... LucyAlexander 94
(Barry Murtagh) *hld up: rdn along after 4 out: struggling fr next* **25/1**

4m 0.6s (2.60) **Going Correction** +0.20s/f (Yiel)
WFA 4 from 5yo+ 11lb **9** Ran SP% **115.4**
Speed ratings (Par 105): **101,94,90,90,90 90,89,87,85**
toteswingers 1&2 £9.20, 2&3 £16.60, 1&3 £6.60 CSF £34.06 CT £356.25 TOTE £3.70: £1.40, £3.80, £2.40; EX 38.90 Trifecta £267.10 Pool: £2381.18 - 6.68 winning units..
Owner Dennis J Coppola **Bred** Stiftung Gestut Fahrhof **Trained** Hackthorpe, Cumbria

FOCUS
This should be reliable form considering Flogarose set a decent gallop. The easy winner was thrown in on the best of her 2012 form, and she's been rated back to a similar level following a break, with the second rated close to his mark.

1666 CRABBIE'S ALCOHOLIC GINGER BEER H'CAP CHASE (15 fncs) 2m 4f 110y
5:35 (5:35) (Class 4) (0-115,115) 4-Y-0+ **£5,198** (£1,526; £763; £381)

Form RPR
11P- **1** **Strobe**[40] 1291 9-10-13 **102**..(p) DougieCostello 107
(Lucy Normile) *led to 3rd: led 7th to 9th: chsng ldr whn mstke 5 out: effrt bef 3 out: led run-in: styd on gamely* **8/1**
6/4- **2** *2* **Woody Waller**[58] 1151 8-11-9 **112**....................................(t) PaulMoloney 114
(Sophie Leech) *hld up towards rr: effrt and rdn bef 3 out: chsd wnr last 50yds: kpt on* **18/1**
423- **3** *1 ¾* **Endeavor**[17] 1544 8-11-6 **109**... RyanMania 111
(Dianne Sayer) *cl up: led 9th: rdn bef 3 out: hdd run-in: kpt on: hld towards fin* **10/1**
3P0/ **4** *2 ¼* **Good Egg (IRE)**[160] 5395 10-11-12 **115**......................... WilsonRenwick 114
(Mrs Lorna Fowler, Ire) *hld up: mstke 5 out: nt fluent next: effrt bef 3 out: one pce fr last* **6/1**[3]
12P/ **5** *4 ½* **Etxalar (FR)**[153] 5548 10-11-5 **108**................................(t) PeterBuchanan 105
(Lucinda Russell) *hld up: nt fluent 5th: rdn along after 4 out: plugged on fr next: no imp* **15/2**
233- **6** *7* **Twill Stand To Us (IRE)**[30] 1417 6-11-4 **107**...................(t) DannyCook 102+
(Brian Ellison) *hld up: mstke 8th (water): stdy hdwy to chse ldrs bef 4 out: effrt whn blnd bdly and sddle slipped briefly next: nt rcvr* **4/1**[2]
314- **7** *21* **The Paddy Premium (IRE)**[31] 1395 13-10-7 **96**............. LucyAlexander 70
(N W Alexander) *cl up: led 3rd to 7th: hit next (water): hit and rdn 5 out: wknd next* **22/1**
P/6- **8** *9* **Eyre Apparent (IRE)**[133] 341 8-11-12 **115**.......................(tp) APMcCoy 79
(Lucinda Russell) *chsd ldrs: drvn along 9th: wknd fr 4 out* **7/2**[1]
212/ **P** **Ring Bo Ree (IRE)**[575] 4586 10-11-12 **115**....................... PaddyBrennan
(Tom George) *hld up: stdy hdwy and in tch 5 out: nt fluent next: sn wknd: p.u bef 2 out* **7/1**
P **Western Island (IRE)**[350] 1813 10-10-8 **97**...................... ConorO'Farrell
(Edward Cawley, Ire) *in tch to 9th: sn struggling: t.o whn p.u bef 3 out* **20/1**

5m 12.2s (7.20) **Going Correction** +0.20s/f (Yiel) **10** Ran SP% **115.3**
Speed ratings (Par 105): **94,93,92,91,90 87,79,75, ,**
toteswingers 1&2 £19.80, 2&3 £33.30, 1&3 £9.20 CSF £129.12 CT £1449.01 TOTE £7.20: £2.80, £5.30, £3.30; EX 144.20 Trifecta £1107.30 Pool: £1970.99 - 1.33 winning units..
Owner Miss P A & P J Carnaby **Bred** Old Mill Stud **Trained** Duncrievie, Perth & Kinross

FOCUS
A good finish to this modest chase saw four hold some sort of chance at the final fence. The winner has been rated to his last C&D win, with the third and fourth close to their marks.

1667 BOOK NOW FOR APRIL FESTIVAL STANDARD OPEN NATIONAL HUNT FLAT RACE 2m 110y
6:05 (6:07) (Class 5) 4-6-Y-0 **£2,053** (£598; £299)

Form RPR
4/1- **1** **It's All An Act (IRE)**[17] 1546 5-11-9 0.............................. APMcCoy 112+
(John Joseph Hanlon, Ire) *led to 1/2-way: cl up: led again over 1f out: drvn and styd on wl fnl f* **9/2**[3]
2 *2* **Owen Na View (IRE)**[138] 5-11-2 0................................ PaddyBrennan 103+
(Fergal O'Brien) *t.k.h: prom: hdwy to chse clr ldr 7f out: led over 3f out: rdn and hdd over 1f out: kpt on same pce ins fnl f* **14/1**
3 *1 ½* **Muckle Roe (IRE)** 4-11-2 0...................................... SamTwiston-Davies 102
(Nigel Twiston-Davies) *in tch: rdn and sltly outpcd 3f out: rallied and edgd rt over 1f out: kpt on fnl f: nrst fin* **5/2**[2]
6/1- **4** *2 ¼* **Bellgrove (IRE)**[40] 1292 5-11-9 0.................................. DenisO'Regan 107
(Ian Semple) *hld up in midfield: stdy hdwy 4f out: rdn and edgd rt 2f out: sn one pce* **16/1**
5/1- **5** *9* **Secrete Stream (IRE)**[141] 173 4-11-9 0............................ BrianHughes 99+
(Malcolm Jefferson) *t.k.h early: chsd ldrs: outpcd over 3f out: no imp fr 2f out* **2/1**[1]
0/ **6** *1 ¼* **Innocent Girl (IRE)**[257] 3628 4-10-2 0............................ CraigNichol[(7)] 84
(Lucinda Russell) *hld up: pushed along and stdy hdwy over 4f out: rdn and no imp fr 3f out* **20/1**
301/ **7** *½* **Orchard Road (USA)**[165] 5324 6-11-2 0.......................(t) GrantCockburn[(7)] 97
(Lucinda Russell) *t.k.h: hld up: hdwy 4f out: sn rdn: no imp fr over 2f out* **14/1**
8 *5* **Dark Caviar (IRE)**[95] 819 5-10-9 0..........................[1] JonathonBewley[(7)] 87
(George Bewley) *plld hrd in rr: hdwy to ld 1/2-way: sn clr: hdd over 3f out: wknd 2f out* **16/1**
9 *2 ½* **Dunkirk's First (IRE)** 5-11-2 0...................................... WilsonRenwick 84
(C A McBratney, Ire) *hld up: rdn and outpcd over 4f out: n.d after* **66/1**
10 *10* **Dr Paddy (IRE)**[144] 6-11-2 0...................................... DougieCostello 75
(Lucy Normile) *cl up tl lost pl over 6f out: sn struggling* **50/1**
11 *nk* **Amilliontimes (IRE)**[130] 5-11-2 0.................................. LucyAlexander 74
(Mrs Jackie Stephen) *hld up towards rr: rdn over 4f out: nvr on terms* **25/1**
U0/ **12** *54* **Quick Brew**[199] 4718 5-10-9 0...............................(t) StephenMulqueen[(7)] 26
(Maurice Barnes) *plld hrd towards rr: struggling over 4f out: t.o* **150/1**

3m 59.9s (7.50) **Going Correction** +0.20s/f (Yiel)
WFA 4 from 5yo+ 11lb **12** Ran SP% **117.9**
Speed ratings: **90,89,88,87,83 82,82,79,78,74 73,48**
toteswingers 1&2 £12.20, 2&3 £7.60, 1&3 £3.30 CSF £61.92 TOTE £5.40: £1.30, £3.90, £1.50; EX 69.70 Trifecta £271.60 Pool: £2182.63 - 6.02 winning units..
Owner Miss Rachel O'Neill **Bred** Patrick Doyle **Trained** Bagenalstown, Co Carlow

FOCUS
Potentially quite a decent bumper with five last-time-out winners in the line-up. The form should work out, the second and third being up to winning something similar and the fourth taking a big step forward.
T/Plt: £13.60 to a £1 stake. Pool of £49184.45 - 2630.54 winning tickets. T/Qpdt: £7.30 to a £1 stake. Pool of £3392.80 - 341.95 winning tickets. RY

1547 WORCESTER (L-H)
Friday, September 27

OFFICIAL GOING: Good (good to firm in places; watered; 7.2)
Wind: almost nil Weather: bright & sunny; 16 degrees

1668 SUPPORT SOLDIERS OFF THE STREET H'CAP CHASE (15 fncs) 2m 4f
1:50 (1:50) (Class 5) (0-95,98) 4-Y-0+ **£2,274** (£667; £333; £166)

Form RPR
P01- **1** **The Nephew (IRE)**[5] 1638 5-12-1 **98** 7ex.....................(t) RichieMcLernon 114+
(Jonjo O'Neill) *settled in detached last: mstkes 2nd: 4th and 6th: smooth prog fr 10th: wnt 3rd home turn: led on bit 2 out: sn clr* **5/2**[1]
636- **2** *9* **Nouailhas**[17] 1547 7-10-0 **76**.......................................(v[1]) MissAEStirling[(7)] 85+
(Andrew Hollinshead) *prom: jnd ldr 10th: ev ch whn sddle slipped and rdr wobbled next: gd rcvry: stl ev ch 2 out: kpt on steadily but no ch w wnr whn lunged at last and blnd bdly* **33/1**
443- **3** *3 ½* **Harris Garden (IRE)**[31] 1416 6-11-5 **91**..........................(p) JackQuinlan[(3)] 96
(Paul Cowley) *hld up: stdy prog whn blnd 8th: disp ld after 10th tl drvn and hdd and blnd 2 out: sn btn* **25/1**
234- **4** *10* **Civil Unrest (IRE)**[27] 1469 7-11-0 **93**............................(b) DaleIrving[(10)] 89
(James Ewart) *chsd ldrs: rdn after 5th: mstke 7th: struggling 10th: plodded on* **7/1**[3]
220- **5** *1* **Himrayn**[14] 1582 10-11-7 **95**... JoshHamer[(5)] 87
(Anabel K Murphy) *hld up and bhd: effrt 8th: 5th and struggling home turn* **25/1**
P30- **6** *14* **Walls Way**[14] 1577 9-10-5 **81**.. JWStevenson[(7)] 61
(Tracey Barfoot-Saunt) *prom: led bef 6th tl sn after 10th: 4th and struggling home turn* **50/1**
5P3/ **7** *nk* **Mistic Academy (IRE)**[146] 8-10-0 **69** oh6.......................... TomScudamore 48
(Jim Best) *led tl after 1st: lost pl 7th: remote fr 3 out* **5/2**[1]
040- **8** *9* **Checkmate**[17] 1550 8-10-8 **77**...(p) MarkGrant 48
(Christopher Kellett) *towards rr: struggling 9th: t.o whn mstke 2 out* **100/1**
5/3- **9** *13* **Inandover**[23] 1494 8-10-9 **78**..(t) BrianHughes 37
(John Mackie) *lost pl 4th: last after next: t.o fr 8th* **9/2**[2]
213/ **P** **Sumner (IRE)**[801] 1157 9-11-11 **94**..(t) CharliePoste
(William Davies) *chsd ldrs tl 7th: struggling 9th: t.o and p.u 11th* **33/1**
423- **P** **Neverownup (IRE)**[18] 1534 8-11-5 **88**.................................(t) DaveCrosse
(K F Clutterbuck) *set off too fast: led after 1st: hdd whn hit 6th: t.o fr 10th: p.u next* **8/1**

4m 44.4s (-15.60) **Going Correction** -0.725s/f (Firm) **11** Ran SP% **115.5**
Speed ratings (Par 103): **102,98,97,93,92 87,86,83,78,**
toteswingers 1&2 £31.50, 1&3 £9.40, 2&3 £31.50 CSF £81.78 CT £1681.50 TOTE £4.10: £2.40, £8.00, £4.50; EX 68.40 Trifecta £476.80 Part won. Pool: £635.78 - 0.13 winning units..
Owner Mrs Gay Smith **Bred** Nicholas Teehan **Trained** Cheltenham, Gloucs

FOCUS
Rails about 9yds off the inside line. A progressive 5yo completed a double in good style in this low-grade handicap chase. The winner is much better over fences and can probably win again, while the second has improved for the fitting of a visor, but was better than this over hurdles and can improve further.

1669 BOB LOVE "KING OF DIRT" MEMORIAL BEGINNERS' CHASE (18 fncs) 2m 7f
2:20 (2:20) (Class 4) 4-Y-0+ **£4,327** (£1,343; £723)

Form RPR
/03- **1** **Connectivity (IRE)**[118] 586 9-11-6 130..............................(b[1]) APMcCoy 123+
(Dr Richard Newland) *w ldr fr 4th tl def advantage fr 7th: rdn 2 out: in command last but kpt up to work* **5/6**[1]
0/P- **2** *2 ½* **What An Oscar (IRE)**[93] 845 8-11-6 0...............(p) SamTwiston-Davies 119
(Nigel Twiston-Davies) *mstke 2nd: j. slowly 11th: trckd ldng pair tl wnt 2nd at 13th: hrd drvn fr 2 out: 4 l down and no imp whn hit last* **3/1**[2]
533- **3** *dist* **Finch Flyer (IRE)**[17] 1547 6-11-6 74...................................(p) LeeEdwards
(Aytach Sadik) *mstke 4th: hit 12th: in last pair: t.o fr 13th: stl between last two fences as wnr fin* **50/1**[3]
120/ **P** **Abbey Storm (IRE)**[155] 5522 7-11-6 0.................................. JasonMaguire
(Donald McCain) *tended to jump rt: led or disp ld to 7th: lost 2nd at 13th: stopped to nil after next: t.o and p.u 15th* **3/1**[2]

5m 42.7s (-5.30) **Going Correction** -0.725s/f (Firm) **4** Ran SP% **106.5**
Speed ratings (Par 105): **80,79, ,**
CSF £3.66 TOTE £2.00; EX 4.20 Trifecta £16.70 Pool: £1187.84 - 53.14 winning units..
Owner Paul L Drinkwater **Bred** Mrs K Healy **Trained** Claines, Worcs

FOCUS
A fairly useful type put in a professional display to justify odds-on favouritism in this beginners' chase. The second has been raed to his hurdles mark.

1670 HAPPY WEDDING ANNIVERSARY FRANK & FIONA H'CAP CHASE
(12 fncs) **2m 110y**
2:50 (2:50) (Class 3) (0-135,130) 4-Y-0 **£6,330** (£1,870; £935; £468; £234)

Form RPR
34P- **1** **Spock (FR)**[23] 1493 8-10-4 **115**.....................(b) MrsAlexDunn(7) 122+
(Alexandra Dunn) *t.k.h: mstke 3rd: pressed ldr tl mde most fr 5th: hrd pressed whn barged through last and rdr temporarily unbalanced: sn hdd: rallied gamely: edgd rt but got up cl home* **8/1**
/00- **2** 1/2 **Royale's Charter**[27] 1476 7-11-12 **130**..................... NickScholfield 137
(Nick Williams) *led tl 5th: mostly cl 2nd after: hrd rdn fr 2 out: lft in ld sn after last: nt qckn and ct cl home* **2/1**[1]
214- **3** 3/4 **Citrus Mark**[45] 1263 8-10-4 **108**..................... LiamHeard 113
(Paul Webber) *cl up in 3rd: effrt 3 out: rdn and styng on same pce whn lft w ev ch at last: hld whn impeded fnl 50yds* **3/1**[2]
3P3/ **4** 3 **Wings Of Smoke (IRE)**[181] 5017 8-11-4 **125**..............(t) MichaelByrne(3) 128
(Tim Vaughan) *nt a fluent and tended to be too deliberate: settled in last trio: mstke 9th: rdn and effrt 3 out: pressing ldrs at last: wknd fnl 100yds* **5/1**[3]
/0P- **5** 1 3/4 **Takeroc (FR)**[122] 520 10-11-1 **119**.....................(t) PaulMoloney 122
(Sophie Leech) *hld up in last trio: stl last after mstke 10th: effrt 3 out: plugged on same pce fr bef last* **8/1**
652- **6** 8 **Sagredo (USA)**[22] 1503 9-11-1 **119**.....................(v) APMcCoy 117
(Jonjo O'Neill) *hld up in last trio: nt fluent 7th: mstke 8th: clsd gng wl win himself bef 10th: fnd nil immediately he was rdn: btn 3 out* **5/1**[3]

4m 2.1s (-11.90) **Going Correction** -0.725s/f (Firm) **6** Ran SP% **113.9**
Speed ratings (Par 107): **99,98,98,97,96 92**
toteswingers 1&2 £16.90, 1&3 £9.50, 2&3 £9.50 CSF £25.82 TOTE £11.60: £6.90, £1.50; EX 72.30 Trifecta £127.90 Pool: £1368.20 - 8.01 winning units..
Owner Mrs K R Smith-Maxwell **Bred** Jaques Cypres Et Al **Trained** Wellington, Somerset

FOCUS
There was an exciting finish in this decent handicap. The first two are on good marks and the fourth has been rated close to best of last season's form.

1671 BRUNO'S BIRTHDAY INTERMEDIATE OPEN NATIONAL HUNT FLAT RACE
2m
3:25 (3:26) (Class 6) 4-6-Y-0 **£1,624** (£477; £238; £119)

Form RPR
533/ **1** **Indian Stream**[231] 4105 4-10-4 0..................... RobertDunne(3) 105+
(Peter Bowen) *2nd tl led 7f out: rdn and edgd lft fr 2f out: a doing enough and styd on gamely* **12/1**
2 2 **Notnowivorheadache** 4-10-7 0..................... SamJones 102
(Paul Webber) *uns rdr gng to s: chsd ldrs: rdn and sltly outpcd 6f out: rallied 4f out: chsd wnr u.p over 2f out: no imp fnl f* **25/1**
3 nk **Germany Calling (IRE)**[180] 4-11-0 0..................... NoelFehily 109+
(Charlie Longsdon) *t.k.h towards rr: hdwy 5f out: sltly outpcd 3f out: rdn and styd nicely fnl 2f: nrly snatched 2nd: promising* **5/2**[2]
1- **4** 2 **Chalk It Down (IRE)**[36] 1353 4-11-7 0..................... APMcCoy 114
(Warren Greatrex) *on his toes at s: hld up and wl bhd: hdwy 6f out: sn rdn and outpcd: wd up st: chsd ldng trio over 2f out: plugged on same pce and no imp after* **15/8**[1]
5 15 **Wistari Rocks (IRE)** 4-11-0 0..................... RichardJohnson 99+
(Tim Vaughan) *hld up in midfield: effrt 6f out: 4th home turn: rdn and on heels of ldrs 2f out: sn btn: eased 1f out* **8/1**
50/ **6** 3 **Monasterevin (IRE)**[270] 3389 5-10-11 0.....................(b[1]) JackQuinlan(3) 91
(Noel Quinlan) *on his toes in paddock: plld hrd: cl up: effrt to dispute 2nd 5f out tl rdn and reluctant 3f out: edgd lft and sn btn: t.o* **50/1**
33/ **7** 1/2 **Hare In A Round (IRE)**[316] 2443 5-11-0..................... TomScudamore 90
(Rebecca Curtis) *prom: 3rd and rdn home turn: fdd over 3f out: t.o* **4/1**[3]
3- **8** 9 **Arctic Dixie**[39] 1317 5-10-4 0..................... JamesBest(3) 75
(Rob Summers) *t.k.h in midfield: rdn and lost pl 5f out: t.o* **33/1**
6- **9** 12 **Katie's Massini (IRE)**[118] 589 5-10-7 0..................... RobertThornton 64
(Henry Oliver) *chsd ldrs: drvn 7f out: wknd 5f out: t.o* **16/1**
6- **10** 5 **Fairy Bay**[39] 1318 6-10-0 0..................... MissAEStirling(7) 60
(Pam Ford) *dropped bk last at 1/2-way and sn t.o* **200/1**
05- **11** 1 1/4 **Little Windsor**[29] 1445 4-10-2 0..................... TrevorWhelan(5) 59
(Peter Hiatt) *midfield: pushed along after 6f: nt travelling after: bdly t.o fnl 4f* **200/1**
000/ **12** 2 **On The Raz**[897] 5306 6-10-4 0..................... MarkQuinlan(3) 57
(Jacqueline Retter) *last trio: t.o fnl 5f* **100/1**
0/0- **13** 13 **Charles Onze (FR)**[30] 1427 6-11-0 0..................... LeeEdwards 52
(Dave Roberts) *t.k.h in rr: lost tch 5f out: hopelessly t.o* **200/1**
0- **14** 53 **Septenarius (USA)**[30] 1427 4-11-0 0..................... TommyPhelan 5
(Brian Baugh) *led tl hdd 7f out: stopped to nil and sn hopelessly t.o and eased* **200/1**

3m 36.7s (-5.00) **Going Correction** -0.55s/f (Firm) **14** Ran SP% **119.8**
Speed ratings: **90,89,88,87,80 78,78,74,68,65 64,63,57,30**
toteswingers 1&2 £35.30, 1&3 £6.70, 2&3 £11.70 CSF £273.05 TOTE £11.90: £4.90, £3.50, £1.40; EX 322.30 Trifecta £981.60 Pool: £1460.46 - 1.11 winning units..
Owner Mrs G Davies **Bred** A W Buller **Trained** Little Newcastle, Pembrokes

FOCUS
They went a modest pace early on in this bumper. There was a 12-1 winner and the market leaders couldn't make a big impact. The fourth has been rated in line with his recent win.

1672 HAPPY 70TH BIRTHDAY PATRICK MCNALLY MAIDEN HURDLE
(10 hdls) **2m 4f**
4:00 (4:00) (Class 5) 4-Y-0+ **£1,949** (£572; £286; £143)

Form RPR
604/ **1** **Village Vic (IRE)**[173] 5195 6-11-0 128..................... RichardJohnson 115+
(Philip Hobbs) *pressed ldr: led bef 3 out: hrd pressed fr next: rdn and kpt on gamely cl home: all out* **4/11**[1]
2 1/2 **Hurakan (IRE)**[13] 7-11-0 0..................... AidanColeman 114+
(Richard Price) *prom: wnt 2nd bef 2 out but wandering arnd after: upsides fr last tl outbattled fnl 75yds* **16/1**[3]
350- **3** 3 **Bob Tucker (IRE)**[36] 1348 6-11-0 0..................... AlainCawley 112+
(Brendan Powell) *reluctant ldr at slow pce: j.rt and markedly so at 6th: rdn and hdd bef 3 out: 3rd and wl hld between last two* **25/1**
/42- **4** 6 **Dazinski**[29] 1440 7-11-0 117..................... ColinBolger 105
(Mark H Tompkins) *chsd ldrs: 5th but rdn and outpcd by ldng trio home turn: n.d after but styd on after last* **9/2**[2]
3/0- **5** 4 1/2 **Berea Boru (IRE)**[16] 1561 5-11-0 0.....................(t) DonalDevereux 101
(Peter Bowen) *chsd ldrs tl 4th and drvn home turn: plugged on as ldng trio wnt clr 3 out* **33/1**
6/0- **6** 1/2 **Kyles Faith (IRE)**[137] 270 5-11-0 0..................... IanPopham 100
(Martin Keighley) *midfield: rdn after 7th: btn bef next* **20/1**
324- **7** 2 1/2 **Laurens Ruby (IRE)**[14] 1578 4-10-6 0..................... WillKennedy 91
(John Flint) *plld hrd in rr: short-lived effrt after 7th: no ch fr next: mstke last* **50/1**
0/- **8** 4 1/2 **Native Brian (IRE)**[635] 3508 7-11-0 0..................... NickScholfield 96+
(Jeremy Scott) *t.k.h: chsd ldrs tl 6th and losing pl home turn: stmbld and landed bdly last* **33/1**
U- **9** 9 **Kilcolman Wizard (IRE)**[19] 1525 7-11-0 0..................... ConorO'Farrell 84
(Liam Corcoran) *nt a fluent: a wl bhd: no ch bef 3 out* **50/1**
6- **10** 3 **Alfies Gift**[20] 1523 4-10-3 0..................... RobertDunne(3) 73
(Dai Burchell) *a bhd: struggling after 7th* **66/1**
5U4/ **11** 4 1/2 **Hamilton Hill**[10] 5537 6-10-9 0..................... RobertWilliams(5) 77
(Bernard Llewellyn) *midfield tl rdn and fdd wl bef 3 out: t.o* **50/1**
150/ **12** 9 **Bens Moor (IRE)**[173] 8-10-11 0..................... MichaelByrne(3) 68
(Tim Vaughan) *bhd: rdn and struggling 7th: t.o and eased 2 out* **33/1**
4- **13** nk **Money Money Money**[29] 1432 7-10-7 0..................... MattieBatchelor 60
(Jim Best) *sweating bdly: several awful jumps in last mostly: nvr in tch w ldrs: rdn briefly 7th: heavily eased after 3 out* **33/1**

4m 47.5s (0.10) **Going Correction** -0.55s/f (Firm)
WFA 4 from 5yo+ 12lb **13** Ran SP% **125.1**
Speed ratings (Par 103): **77,76,75,73,71 71,70,68,64,63 61,58,58**
toteswingers 1&2 £3.20, 1&3 £8.30, 2&3 £15.90 CSF £7.80 TOTE £1.70: £1.10, £3.50, £5.60; EX 12.20 Trifecta £161.10 Pool: £2639.21 - 12.28 winning units..
Owner Alan Peterson **Bred** Tom Curran **Trained** Withycombe, Somerset

FOCUS
The hot odds-on favourite had to work hard to deny a persistent challenger in this maiden hurdle. The winner has been rated 20lb off his best, and a few of those in behind could be flattered, but the second, fifth and seventh have been rated in line with their bumper form, and the fourth to a similar level to his recent runs, so it's given the benefit of the doubt for now.

1673 PAMELA ANN H'CAP HURDLE (DIV I) (12 hdls) **2m 7f**
4:35 (4:37) (Class 5) (0-100,100) 4-Y-0+ **£3,249** (£954; £477; £238)

Form RPR
/P5- **1** **Artic Night (FR)**[32] 1406 7-10-8 **82**.....................(bt) SamTwiston-Davies 91+
(Nigel Twiston-Davies) *bhd: last after 6th: stdy hdwy bef 9th: stl 8th home turn and sn hrd drvn: remorseless prog after: wnt 3rd 2 out: led after last and drew clr* **5/1**[2]
221- **2** 2 1/4 **Burns Night**[11] 1442 7-10-12 **91**.....................(p) AdamNicol(5) 98
(Philip Kirby) *settled midfield and gng wl: tk clsr order 7th: wnt 2nd 3 out: led on bit next: rdn last: no reponse: edgd lft: hdd and outpcd fnl 200yds* **7/2**[1]
41F- **3** 2 1/4 **Dom Lukka (FR)**[86] 872 5-11-9 **97**..................... NoelFehily 102
(Charlie Longsdon) *led: rdn 3 out: jst hdd next: stl w ldr last: wknd fnl 100yds* **5/1**[2]
540- **4** 2 1/4 **Handsome Buddy (IRE)**[57] 1174 6-10-9 **90**..................... MissAEStirling(7) 92
(Michael Gates) *prom and t.k.h: wnt 2nd at 7th tl rdn 3 out: fdd steadily fr next* **10/1**
U/0- **5** 8 **Go On Arch (IRE)**[17] 1547 7-11-5 **100**..................... RyanHatch(7) 95
(Nigel Twiston-Davies) *blnd 1st: cl up: nt a fluent: t.k.h: cl up tl rdn bef 3 out: one pce and wl hld bef next* **20/1**
0/3- **6** 3 1/4 **Corso Palladio (IRE)**[60] 1136 11-11-12 **100**..............(tp) DougieCostello 92
(Peter Bowen) *j.v.slowly 2nd: pressed ldrs tl pushed along after 6th: rdn and lost pl next: virtually t.o after 9th: passed btn horses fr 2 out* **8/1**
442- **7** 3/4 **Mist The Boat**[14] 1580 5-11-2 **90**..................... RichardJohnson 89+
(Tim Vaughan) *hld up and bhd: hdwy 9th: on heels of ldrs whn blnd bdly 3 out and lost all ch* **11/2**[3]
606- **8** 3/4 **My Friend Riquet (FR)**[5] 1631 6-10-1 **75**..................... LeeEdwards 65
(Dave Roberts) *last pair tl 7th: modest prog 9th: rdn and wl hld fr next* **12/1**
354- **9** 11 **Dbanks (IRE)**[16] 1563 10-11-6 **94**..................... ConorO'Farrell 75
(Liam Corcoran) *hld up towards rr: hdwy to chse ldrs 7th: rdn bef 9th: sn lost pl: eased last* **50/1**
PP0- **10** 39 **Painted Sky**[67] 1073 10-10-5 **79**.....................(b[1]) AdrianLane 24
(Iain Jardine) *bhd: rdn after 8th: nt keen: t.o after next* **14/1**
PP6/ **P** **No Regrets (FR)**[1653] 4587 12-10-5 **82**..................... MichaelByrne(3)
(Angela Clarke) *plld hrd in rr and on outside tl p.u qckly 6th* **33/1**
6PP/ **P** **Edgevine**[305] 2674 9-10-2 **76** oh4 ow2..................... PaulMoloney
(Lisa Day) *cl up tl 6th: struggling after next: t.o and p.u after 9th* **50/1**

5m 39.6s (11.60) **Going Correction** -0.55s/f (Firm) **12** Ran SP% **117.1**
Speed ratings (Par 103): **57,56,55,54,51 50,50,50,46,32 ,**
toteswingers 1&2 £4.50, 1&3 £4.70, 2&3 £4.10 CSF £22.30 CT £91.74 TOTE £5.60: £2.40, £2.10, £2.20; EX 31.10 Trifecta £164.30 Pool: £2639.21 - 12.28 winning units..
Owner The I O U Partnership **Bred** Remi Sabatier And Arnaud Poirier **Trained** Naunton, Gloucs

FOCUS
The winner finished well to win this competitive minor handicap hurdle. There may be more to come from the winner for his new yard, while the second remains on the upgrade and may be a bit better back over shorter. The third is on a winning mark and the fourth is another well in on his chase form.

1674 SUPPORT MACMILLAN CANCER BUCKET COLLECTION TODAY NOVICES' H'CAP HURDLE (8 hdls)
2m
5:10 (5:10) (Class 4) (0-110,108) 4-Y-0+ **£3,249** (£954; £477; £238)

Form RPR
606- **1** **Moscow Me (IRE)**[34] 1374 6-10-8 **90**..................... PaulMoloney 96
(Henry Oliver) *sn prom: racd on outer: 2nd or 3rd fr 5th: rdn 3 out: 3rd and racing awkwardly u.p bef last: persuaded to surge ahd cl home* **25/1**
2F0- **2** 3/4 **Benny The Swinger (IRE)**[111] 674 8-10-10 **92**..................... TomCannon 97
(Chris Gordon) *settled midfield: clsd gng wl 3 out: sn 2nd: led sn after last but drvn and edgd lft flat: ct nr fin* **25/1**
320- **3** 1 1/2 **Knockgraffon Lad (USA)**[14] 1582 6-10-13 **95**..............(tp) AlainCawley 99
(Brendan Powell) *hld up in rr: smooth prog bef 3 out: led appr next: rdn and hrd pressed whn hit last and hdd: nt qckn after* **20/1**
0F0/ **4** 2 **Investissement**[77] 3437 7-11-1 **97**..................... NoelFehily 99
(Charlie Longsdon) *mstke 1st: settled in rr: prog wd fr bef 2 out: rdn and one pce appr last* **9/2**[2]
/F3- **5** 7 **Spoil Me (IRE)**[14] 1575 6-11-8 **104**..................... RichieMcLernon 100
(Jonjo O'Neill) *towards rr: rdn and outpcd 3 out: plugged on after* **10/1**
411- **6** 1 1/2 **Sedgemoor Express (IRE)**[5] 1633 5-11-2 **101** 7ex...(tp) MarkQuinlan(3) 95
(Nigel Hawke) *towards rr: drvn after 5th: laboured prog next: no imp and wl hld fr 2 out* **15/8**[1]
602/ **7** 2 3/4 **Kalamill (IRE)**[144] 3985 6-11-9 **105**.....................(t) AidanColeman 97
(Shaun Lycett) *prom: chsd long ldr 3rd tl 5th: drvn and sn wknd* **16/1**
325- **8** 2 **Panache**[108] 716 8-10-8 **93**..................... MichaelByrne(3) 84
(Angela Clarke) *chsd ldrs: rdn bef 3 out: sn btn* **28/1**

001- 9 3 ¼ **Goat Castle (IRE)**[14] 1575 9-10-5 **87**...................... SamTwiston-Davies 76
(Nigel Twiston-Davies) *t.k.h: prom in chsng gp: wnt 20 l 2nd at 5th: rdn and fnd nil after next: sn dropped out* **7/1**[3]
/26- 10 20 **Symphonick (FR)**[72] 1008 7-11-9 **105**...................... BrianHughes 74
(Tim Fitzgerald) *chsd long ldr tl 3rd: drvn and wknd bef 5th: sn t.o* **16/1**
/00- 11 1 ¾ **Hail Tiberius**[124] 503 6-10-1 **83**......................................(t[1]) IanPopham 51
(Martin Keighley) *bolted off in big ld: stl 20 l ahd at 5th: rdn and hdd bef 2 out and immediately dropped rt out: blnd last* **7/1**[3]

3m 37.2s (-10.10) **Going Correction** -0.55s/f (Firm) 11 Ran SP% **114.7**
Speed ratings (Par 105): **103,102,101,100,97 96,95,94,92,82 81**
toteswingers 1&2 £29.90, 1&3 £58.60, 2&3 £30.90 CSF £485.16 CT £12013.79 TOTE £30.40: £5.60, £5.20, £5.20; EX 397.80 Trifecta £1022.80 Part won. Pool: £1363.76 - 0.20 winning units..
Owner Ms S Howell **Bred** Egmont Stud **Trained** Broomhall, Worcs
■ Stewards' Enquiry : Alain Cawley two-day ban: used whip above permitted level (Oct 11-12)

FOCUS
There was a tight finish between two 25-1 runners in this novices' handicap. Okay time for the grade and the form might work out, with the fifth in line with his recent form and fourth potentially well in on his Flat form.

1675 PAMELA ANN H'CAP HURDLE (DIV II) (12 hdls) 2m 7f
5:45 (5:45) (Class 5) (0-100,100) 4-Y-O+ **£3,249** (£954; £477; £238)

Form RPR
000- 1 **Absolute Shambles**[32] 1405 9-10-3 **77**...........................(p) TomCannon 85
(Chris Gordon) *rdn 7th: a 2nd or 3rd tl drvn ahd 3 out: hrd pressed fr next: put his hd down and battled on wl after last to assert nr fin* **16/1**
225- 2 ¾ **Princesse Fleur**[27] 932 5-11-2 **90**...................................... TomScudamore 97
(Michael Scudamore) *hld up towards rr: smooth prog 3 out: chal gng wl next: ev ch flat: jst hld fnl 100yds* **6/1**[3]
/03- 3 4 ½ **What A Good Night (IRE)**[14] 1580 5-11-2 **90**........ SamTwiston-Davies 93
(Nigel Twiston-Davies) *settled pressing ldrs: rdn 3 out: disp 3rd and outpcd and edgd lft last* **8/1**
/03- 4 1 ¼ **Transfer**[17] 252 8-11-0 **88**.. APMcCoy 90
(Richard Price) *last trio: hit 7th and cajoled along on outer: effrt bef 3 out: sn drvn: one pce and no imp fr next* **14/1**
043- 5 4 ½ **Highland River**[39] 1314 7-10-0 **74** oh3................................... LeeEdwards 72
(Dave Roberts) *rn in snatches: nt fluent 6th: j. slowly 7th and drvn: sn bhd: kpt on wout threatening fr 2 out* **14/1**
645- 6 11 **Morestead (IRE)**[18] 1534 8-10-8 **82**................................ LeightonAspell 72
(Brendan Powell) *slt ld mostly tl rdn and hdd 3 out: sn lost pl: eased flat* **25/1**
20- 7 2 ½ **Presenting Ruby (IRE)**[19] 1529 8-11-7 **95**...................(t) DougieCostello 82
(Neil Mulholland) *nt fluent 2nd: nvr trbld ldrs: lost tch u.p 9th: hit last* **16/1**
/60- 8 3 **Tae Kwon Do (USA)**[130] 407 7-11-5 **93**...................(t) RichardJohnson 80
(Tim Vaughan) *mstke 1st: t.k.h: hld up in midfield: rdn and outpcd 3 out: hmpd next* **11/2**[2]
6P5- 9 3 ½ **Word Of Warning**[34] 1374 9-10-10 **89**............................(p) AdamNicol(5) 71
(Philip Kirby) *trckd ldrs: looked to be gng wl tl 9th: fading whn mstke next* **4/1**[1]
610- 10 nse **Millie O'Brien**[68] 1051 5-9-13 **76**... JamesBest(3) 56
(Philip Hobbs) *2nd or 3rd tl hrd drvn and lost pl on long run to 3 out* **20/1**
/40- 11 4 ½ **Forever Waining (IRE)**[89] 854 7-11-10 **98**..............(tp) DonalDevereux 74
(Peter Bowen) *t.k.h: chsd ldrs tl 9th: drvn and struggling next* **6/1**[3]
0/4- P **High On A Hill (IRE)**[11] 1288 6-11-12 **100**.........................(p) AdrianLane
(Iain Jardine) *a wl bhd: struggling 7th: t.o and p.u 3 out: dismntd* **25/1**
604- F **Bold Tara**[20] 1517 6-10-6 **80**.. IanPopham
(Martin Keighley) *sn cl up: rdn and wknd 3 out: 7 l fr ldr whn fell next* **14/1**

5m 37.4s (9.40) **Going Correction** -0.55s/f (Firm) 13 Ran SP% **119.3**
Speed ratings (Par 103): **61,60,59,58,57 53,52,51,50,50 48, ,**
toteswingers 1&2 £11.30, 1&3 £35.40, 2&3 £7.50 CSF £107.53 CT £835.90 TOTE £21.20: £7.00, £2.30, £1.70; EX 171.60 Trifecta £312.90 Part won. Pool: £417.33 - 0.11 winning units..
Owner Chris Gordon Racing Club **Bred** R Bowers **Trained** Morestead, Hants

FOCUS
The pace was not very strong in the second division of this handicap but the first two had a good battle and pulled clear. The second and third are the best guide to the level.
T/Plt: £56.40 to a £1 stake. Pool: £64149.06 - 829.12 winning tickets T/Qpdt: £16.40 to a £1 stake. Pool: £5499.25 - 247.30 winning tickets IM

1676 - 1682a (Foreign Racing) - See Raceform Interactive

MERANO
Friday, September 27

OFFICIAL GOING: Turf: soft

1683a LXIX PREMIO DELLE NAZIONI - MEMORIAL MARCO ROCCA (CROSS-COUNTRY CHASE) (GRADE 2) (5YO+) (TURF) 3m 6f
4:05 (12:00) 5-Y-O+ **£11,086** (£4,878; £2,660; £1,330)

RPR
1 **Wan (FR)**[393] 6-10-12 0.. RRomano
(P Favero, Italy) **19/10**[2]
2 1 ¾ **Nils (IRE)**[1867] 7-10-8 0... JosefBartos
(P Favero, Italy) **84/10**
3 2 ¼ **Maljimar (IRE)**[54] 1214 13-10-8 0... JamesReveley
(Nick Williams) *led: rn v wd turn after 22nd: led again 24th: hdd 4 out: cl 3rd and rdn 2 out: styd on at same pce* **11/10**[1]
4 1 ¼ **Arman (GER)**[1426] 8-10-8 0.. MStromsky
(J Vana Jr, Czech Republic) **111/10**
5 6 **Pareto (CZE)** 6-10-8 0.. JMyska
(Cestmir Olehla, Czech Republic) **57/10**[3]
6 2 ¼ **Ilion (POL)** 9-10-8 0.. DColumbu
(J Vana Jr, Czech Republic) **54/1**
7 dist **Sarika (FR)**[26] 1486 7-10-8 0...(b) ColmMcCormack
(Nick Williams) *chsd ldr: lost pl 16th: continued towards rr: wl bhd fr 28th: t.o* **11/10**[1]
F **Val Sugana (IRE)** 6-10-8 0.. APollioni
(P Favero, Italy) **29/4**

8m 45.8s (525.80) 8 Ran SP% **177.5**
PARI-MUTUEL (all including 1 euro stakes): WIN 2.90; PLACE 1.30, 1.75, 1.24; DF 12.08.
Owner Scuderia Vama Di Renzo Dolzan **Bred** P Nataf **Trained** Italy

1466 MARKET RASEN (R-H)
Saturday, September 28

OFFICIAL GOING: Good (watered; chs 8.1, hdl 7.8)
Wind: Almost nil Weather: Very bright and sunny; 18 degrees

1684 WIN BIG WITH THE TOTEJACKPOT JUVENILE HURDLE (8 hdls) 2m 1f
1:45 (1:46) (Class 2) 3-Y-O **£10,396** (£3,052; £1,526; £763)

Form RPR
1 **Royal Irish Hussar (IRE)**[64] 3-10-12 0.................................. DavidBass 113+
(Nicky Henderson) *trckd ldrs: novicey: 3rd whn blnd 5th and lost grnd: sn rallied: wnt 2nd and mstke 2 out: 2 l down whn nt fluent last: hrd drvn and responded gamely: got up cl home* **15/8**[1]
1/4- 2 nk **Fox Norton (FR)**[141] 262 3-11-6 0.................................... NoelFehily 118+
(Nick Williams) *sn prom and travelled wl: wnt 2nd at 4th: led bef 2 out: drvn whn v untidy last: kpt on wl but jst ct* **5/1**[3]
PU1- 3 10 **Town Mouse**[19] 1536 3-11-3 0... TrevorWhelan 106+
(Neil King) *mounted on crse and taken to post v early: reluctant to s and lost over 20 l: clsd grad to be in tch after 3rd: wnt 6 l 4th on home turn: drvn and no imp after: wnt wl hld 3rd bef last* **14/1**
4 12 **Durable Man**[22] 3-10-12 0.. RobertThornton 91
(Alan King) *mde most at decent pce tl rdn and hdd bef 2 out: dropped away tamely: lost 3rd bef last* **11/4**[2]
23- 5 2 ½ **Kitchapoly (FR)**[19] 1536 3-11-6 0.. JasonMaguire 95
(Donald McCain) *a towards rr: rdn and struggling after 3 out* **14/1**
6 5 **Jubilee Games**[49] 3-10-12 0... BrianHughes 82
(Richard Fahey) *hld up towards rr: hdwy 5th: cl 4th and gng wl after next: fdd tamely sn after home turn: hit 2 out* **28/1**
7 32 **Couloir Extreme (IRE)**[23] 3-10-12 0.................................... JoshuaMoore 53
(Gary Moore) *chsd ldrs: j. slowly 4th: rdn and wknd after 3 out: bdly t.o: eased last* **7/1**
8 81 **Shesnotforturning (IRE)**[64] 3-10-5 0................................... BarryKeniry
(Ben Haslam) *lost pl 3rd: struggling next: hopelessly t.o fr 3 out: fin eventually* **125/1**
31- P **Hi Candy (IRE)**[33] 1394 3-10-10 0.. APMcCoy
(Ben Haslam) *w ldr tl 3rd: lost pl 5th: t.o and p.u 2 out* **12/1**
P5- P **Double Jeopardy**[19] 1536 3-10-12 0..................................... JackQuinlan
(Dr Jon Scargill) *last after 3rd: t.o after 3 out: p.u next* **150/1**

4m 11.0s (4.30) **Going Correction** +0.125s/f (Yiel) 10 Ran SP% **116.5**
Speed ratings (Par 107): **94,93,89,83,82 79,64,26, ,**
toteswingers 1&2 £9.50, 1&3 £9.50, 2&3 £9.00 CSF £11.86 TOTE £2.50: £1.40, £2.00, £3.80; EX 10.90 Trifecta £139.50 Pool: £1,002.24 - 5.38 winning units.
Owner Triermore Stud **Bred** Adjalisa Syndicate **Trained** Upper Lambourn, Berks

FOCUS
All fences and hurdles sited on fresh ground on inner line of Summer track and hurdles in home straight returned to normal positions. This juvenile hurdle has been the springboard for some high-class jumpers, with Katchit, Franchoek and Silencio sent out to win for Alan King, as well as Barizan for Evan Williams in recent years. This renewal produced a driving finish up the straight with two pulling clear. They are probably above average, while the third also has the potential to be.

1685 BET TOTESCOOP6 AT TOTEPOOL.COM HURDLE (H'CAP) (LISTED RACE) (8 hdls) 2m 1f
2:15 (2:15) (Class 1) 4-Y-O+
£19,932 (£7,479; £3,745; £1,865; £938; £469)

Form RPR
1/4- 1 **Ahyaknowyerself (IRE)**[21] 1520 7-11-4 **128**.......(b) SamTwiston-Davies 148+
(Dr Richard Newland) *2nd and clr of rest in v strly run r: hit 3rd: led bef next: hit 3 out but sn drew clr: 9 l ahd whn untidy 2 out and 12 l up whn even more so at last but nvr looked like being ct in fnl 3f: eased bef fin* **7/1**
312- 2 14 **Orthodox Lad**[6] 1627 5-10-1 **111**..................................... TomScudamore 114
(Dr Richard Newland) *racd keenly in rr: sed to pick off rivals fr after 3 out: 4th 2 out: drvn and kpt on wl to go 2nd after last but nvr nr wnr* **11/2**[3]
212/ 3 3 ½ **Prompter**[31] 1807 6-10-12 **122**.. APMcCoy 123
(Jonjo O'Neill) *settled off pce in midfield: clsd gng wl after 3 out: nudged into 2nd home turn: nvr win striking dist of wnr: rdn in 12 l 2nd whn hit last: lost 2nd fnl 100yds* **5/1**[2]
631- 4 1 ¾ **Taaresh (IRE)**[18] 1319 8-10-2 **115**.................................... AdamWedge(3) 113
(Kevin Morgan) *last early: stl plenty to do 3 out: rdn and kpt on wl after next but nvr got in a blow* **28/1**
611- 5 1 ¾ **Laudatory**[21] 1520 7-11-7 **136**...................................... NicodeBoinville(5) 133
(Nicky Henderson) *set v str gallop tl hdd bef 4th: rdn and lost 2nd over 3f out: stuck on steadily at same pce after* **7/1**
/53- 6 2 ¼ **Stormy Weather (FR)**[23] 1504 7-11-2 **126**......................(p) DannyCook 121
(Brian Ellison) *bhd and wl off pce: modest prog to midfield after 3 out: rdn and no further imp bef next* **16/1**
221- 7 2 **Ittirad (USA)**[28] 1466 5-10-9 **119**...................................... DenisO'Regan 112
(John Ferguson) *midfield: drvn after 3 out: styd on one pce and wl hld after* **9/2**[1]
620- 8 8 **Hawkhill (IRE)**[6] 1627 7-10-11 **128**...................................(t) JPKiely(7) 114
(Tim Vaughan) *prom in chsng bunch tl 5th: rdn and struggling after next: mstke 2 out* **25/1**
011/ 9 18 **Watered Silk**[11] 5566 5-11-0 **124**... LeightonAspell 93
(Lucy Wadham) *10 l 3rd at 3rd: hld pl tl rdn after 3 out: sn wknd: t.o* **5/1**[2]
/31- 10 29 **Solaras Exhibition (IRE)**[13] 973 5-11-0 **134**...................... AlanJohns(10) 77
(Tim Vaughan) *towards rr and wl off pce: poor last and drvn 3 out: hopelessly t.o and eased* **20/1**
111- 11 8 **Falcarragh (IRE)**[27] 1483 6-11-1 **125**..........................(p) RichardJohnson 61
(Tim Vaughan) *midfield tl 5th: drvn and losing pl whn n.m.r after next: hopelessly t.o and eased* **10/1**

4m 4.8s (-1.90) **Going Correction** +0.125s/f (Yiel) 11 Ran SP% **118.9**
Speed ratings (Par 111): **109,102,100,99,99 98,97,93,84,71 67**
toteswingers 1&2 £10.00, 1&3 £10.00, 2&3 not won CSF £45.20 CT £213.57 TOTE £7.70: £2.90, £2.50, £2.10; EX 42.70 Trifecta £191.70 Pool: £454.03 - 1.77 winning units.
Owner G Carstairs & R Marker **Bred** Tim Hegarty **Trained** Claines, Worcs

The Form Book Jumps, Raceform Ltd, Compton, RG20 6NL.

FOCUS

Not the strongest competition for Listed grade, but with several front-runners in the field it was likely to be run at a sound pace. In the event the winner set a punishing tempo which no one else could live with. He was on a decent mark but this has to rate a big step up, backed up by the time. The second has run to his recent level and the third can win off this mark.

1686 TOTEPOOL HOME OF KING SIZE POOLS H'CAP CHASE (LISTED RACE) (14 fncs) 2m 6f 110y

2:50 (2:50) (Class 1) 4-Y-0+

£28,475 (£10,685; £5,350; £2,665; £1,340; £670)

Form RPR

030/ **1** **Bouggler**[32] 4747 8-10-11 **137**..(p) AidanColeman 151+
(Emma Lavelle) *cl up and travelled wl: mstke 10th: led after 11th w only one rival able to keep up after: rdn home turn: asserting whn nt fluent 2 out: nrly 5 l clr last: rdn out* **22/1**

222- **2** *4 ½* **Rob Conti (FR)**[28] 1476 8-9-11 **126** oh2.............................. JamesBest(3) 135
(Philip Hobbs) *2nd or 3rd tl led bef 11th where nt fluent: hdd next: rdn and outpcd by wnr 2 out but a clr of rest in st* **25/1**

316- **3** *8* **Kian's Delight**[28] 1476 5-10-4 **130**.................................... DonalDevereux 132
(Peter Bowen) *cl up: rdn and outpcd whn ldng pair drew clr fr 11th: rallied gamely clsng stages to pass two rivals after last* **12/1**

101- **4** *1* **The Disengager (IRE)**[28] 1476 9-11-12 **152**................ RichardJohnson 153
(Philip Hobbs) *led: j. slowly 2nd: hdd bef 11th: drvn and sn outpcd by ldng pair: 12 l 3rd 3 out: kpt on same pce* **10/1**

0/3- **5** *½* **Al Co (FR)**[134] 358 8-10-10 **136**.. DougieCostello 136
(Peter Bowen) *towards rr: seemed to lose interest after 1/2-way: hrd drvn and wl off pce 9th: picked up bit after 3 out: fin v strly w ears pricked: gave himself no ch* **11/1**

2/0- **6** *nk* **King Of The Night (GER)**[140] 217 9-10-6 **132**................ BrianHughes 132
(Malcolm Jefferson) *dropped out last but one: stdy prog fr 9th: rdn and disp 12 l 3rd 3 out: sn no further imp* **16/1**

121- **7** *4* **Grandads Horse**[76] 963 7-10-11 **137**..................................(p) NoelFehily 136
(Charlie Longsdon) *midfield: rdn and outpcd fr 11th: wl btn whn mstke next* **9/2[2]**

132- **8** *8* **Finger Onthe Pulse (IRE)**[41] 1302 12-10-1 **132**.....(t) MauriceLinehan(5) 121
(Jonjo O'Neill) *racd keenly and chsd ldrs: rdn after 11th: one pce and sn btn: 15 l 5th 3 out: racing awkwardly next* **25/1**

/11- **9** *2* **Bold Chief (IRE)**[38] 1338 8-10-13 **139**..............................(tp) RyanMahon 127
(Harry Fry) *hld up off pce: gd hdwy 10th: chsd ldrs after next: rdn and outpcd home turn: wknd clsng stages* **8/1[3]**

/51- **10** *nse* **Wiesentraum (GER)**[41] 1302 7-10-2 **128**........................ LeightonAspell 116
(Lucy Wadham) *hld up and wl in rr: rdn and short-lived effrt 10th: nvr in contention* **14/1**

22U/ **11** *3 ¾* **Well Regarded (IRE)**[174] 5196 8-10-1 **130**.................. GavinSheehan(3) 114
(Emma Lavelle) *hld up and bhd: sme hdwy 10th: drvn after next: sn no ch* **12/1**

/23- **12** *26* **Owen Glendower (IRE)**[60] 1146 8-10-7 **133**.............(t) RichieMcLernon 94
(Sophie Leech) *2nd or 3rd tl 10th: dropped out tamely fr next: t.o* **40/1**

002- **13** *5* **Buck Mulligan**[6] 1636 8-10-1 **127**.. PaulMoloney 83
(Evan Williams) *hld up in last: no ch fr 8th: bdly t.o and hacking along fr bef 3 out* **12/1**

125- **14** *19* **Twirling Magnet (IRE)**[28] 1476 7-11-3 **143**........................(tp) APMcCoy 82
(Jonjo O'Neill) *nt fluent towards rr: drvn and struggling after 10th: eased 3 out: t.o and virtually p.u flat* **14/1**

616/ **P** **Dover's Hill**[518] 5652 11-10-9 **135**..........................(t) SamTwiston-Davies
(Nigel Twiston-Davies) *midfield: rdn 6th: u.p after next: nt travelling after: blnd bdly 9th and dropped bk last: t.o and p.u 11th* **4/1[1]**

1P0- **P** **Bobowen (IRE)**[28] 1476 7-11-1 **141**.................................... JasonMaguire
(Dr Richard Newland) *chsd ldrs tl 8th: struggling u.p 10th: t.o and p.u 3 out* **16/1**

5m 20.9s (-25.10) **Going Correction** -0.70s/f (Firm) **16** Ran SP% **129.4**
Speed ratings (Par 111): **115,113,110,110,110 110,108,105,105,105 103,94,93,86,**,
toteswingers 1&2 £29.90, 1&3 £14.90, 2&3 £29.90 CSF £480.24 CT £6766.71 TOTE £26.60: £6.40, £4.90, £4.90, £3.40; EX 1016.10 TRIFECTA Not won..
Owner Axom (XXI) **Bred** David Brown, Slatch Farm Stud & G B Turnbull Ltd **Trained** Hatherden, Hants

■ Stewards' Enquiry : Donal Devereux two-day ban: used whip above permitted level (Oct 12-13)

FOCUS

Another competitive renewal of this end-of-the-summer highlight. A key piece of form was the Listed handicap chase at Newton Abbot four weeks earlier with six of the first eight home there lining up for battle once again. The runner-up on that occasion filled the same spot again as he came clear with the winner, who bypassed the Newton Abbot contest. The surprise winner has been rated up 8lb on his old chase form, but in line with his best hurdles form, and it looks believable with the second, third and fourth giving it a solid look.

1687 COLLECT TOTEPOOL WINNINGS AT BETFRED SHOPS H'CAP CHASE (14 fncs) 2m 6f 110y

3:20 (3:22) (Class 4) (0-115,115) 4-Y-0+ **£6,190** (£1,520; £760; £381)

Form RPR

165/ **1** **Little Chip (IRE)**[161] 5411 6-11-6 **109**.. NoelFehily 127+
(Charlie Longsdon) *j. soundly: closed to ld after 7th: travelled strly after: drew rt away fr 3 out: 15 l ahd last: heavily eased fnl 100yds* **3/1[1]**

264- **2** *17* **O Crotaigh (IRE)**[19] 1542 9-11-12 **115**.................................. DannyCook 119+
(Alan Brown) *led tl after 7th: chsd wnr after: rdn and completely outpcd fr 3 out: lunged over next: wnt rt last: plugged on gamely* **7/2[2]**

153- **3** *16* **Hodgson (IRE)**[24] 1498 8-11-11 **114**..........................(tp) DonalDevereux 100
(Peter Bowen) *pressed ldr tl reminders after 7th: drvn and lft bhd by ldng pair bef 3 out* **8/1**

541- **4** *36* **Amuse Me**[23] 1502 7-11-12 **115**.. APMcCoy 69
(Jonjo O'Neill) *j. slowly 2nd: nt a fluent and nvr travelling wl enough: rdn and struggling 1/2-way: modest 4th bef 3 out: fin v slowly flat* **5/1[3]**

042- **P** **Points Of View**[24] 1493 8-11-9 **112**................................(tp) JasonMaguire
(Kim Bailey) *a wl bhd: rdn and struggling 1/2-way: tailed 10th: p.u 3 out* **9/1**

421- **P** **Brimham Boy**[19] 1534 11-10-0 **96**....................................(vt) OllieGarner(7)
(Martin Keighley) *sn pushed along: nvr gng wl enough: hit 5th: dropped to rr and struggling whn j. slowly 8th: t.o whn hit 11th and p.u* **6/1**

044- **P** **Dark Oasis**[11] 1598 7-9-11 **89** oh22.. JamesBest(3)
(Natalie Lloyd-Beavis) *sn toiling in rr: drvn 1/2-way: t.o 10th: p.u 2 out* **50/1**

/03- **P** **Miracle House (IRE)**[39] 1325 9-11-2 **105**....................(t) RichardJohnson
(Tim Vaughan) *j. slowly 4th: wl bhd and nvr gng wl: t.o 10th: p.u 3 out* **12/1**

50P/ **P** **Icy Colt (ARG)**[463] 784 7-11-12 **115**..................................(p) DenisO'Regan
(Paul Webber) *chsd ldrs: gng wl 1/2-way: rdn and fdd rapidly after 11th: t.o and p.u 2 out* **11/1**

5m 29.8s (-16.20) **Going Correction** -0.70s/f (Firm) **9** Ran SP% **117.3**
Speed ratings (Par 105): **100,94,88,76,** , , ,
toteswingers 1&2 £2.90, 1&3 £8.00, 2&3 £6.90 CSF £14.78 CT £76.12 TOTE £3.20: £1.80, £1.80, £1.90; EX 15.70 Trifecta £63.00 Pool: £551.55 - 6.56 winning units.
Owner L Dens (Shipbrokers) Limited **Bred** Fintan Kealy **Trained** Over Norton, Oxon

FOCUS

Few got into this and the first two had this between them with a circuit to go. Only four finished. The easy winner clearly goes well here and there's a case for rating him 6lb higher through the second.

1688 EMERALD GREEN FEEDS NOVICES' HURDLE (8 hdls) 2m 1f

3:55 (3:57) (Class 4) 4-Y-0+ **£3,898** (£1,144; £572; £286)

Form RPR

332/ **1** **Spirit Of Shankly**[202] 4676 5-10-12 127.................................... NoelFehily 121+
(Charlie Longsdon) *settled in midfield: effrt in 3rd after hitting 3 out: wnt 2nd bef next: rdn to chal and knocked last flat: sn urged to ld and readily asserted* **5/6[1]**

/13- **2** *3 ¼* **Oyster Shell**[120] 560 6-11-2 118.. JakeGreenall(3) 121
(Henry Daly) *trckd ldr: led 3f out and tried to qckn clr: hit next: sn drvn and hrd pressed: hdd and nt qckn after last* **4/1[2]**

051/ **3** *14* **Benefit Cut (IRE)**[165] 5335 7-11-5 0.................................. PaddyBrennan 110
(Renee Robeson) *led at stdy pce: hit 5th: rdn after next: hdd 3f out and sn outpcd by ldng pair: hit 2 out* **6/1**

322- **4** *4* **Odin (IRE)**[19] 1535 5-10-12 117..................................(p) ConorShoemark(7) 105
(Don Cantillon) *settled in 4th pl: rdn after 3 out: no rspnse: wl hld whn hit next* **5/1[3]**

43- **5** *26* **Volcanic Jack (IRE)**[11] 1595 5-10-7 0.............................. JoeCornwall(5) 74
(Michael Chapman) *chsd ldrs: rdn 5th: drvn and wknd bef home turn: sn t.o* **40/1**

6 *9* **Storey Hill (USA)**[59] 8-10-12 0.. HarryHaynes 66
(Richard Guest) *dropped out last: hit 2nd: nt fluent 3rd: no ch fr 4th: t.o after 3 out* **100/1**

0/0- **7** *76* **Hardwick Bay**[73] 1008 7-10-5 0..(t) RyanMahon
(Michael Appleby) *towards rr: rdn and outpcd 4th: hopelessly t.o 3 out* **100/1**

10/ **8** *¾* **Dubai Kiss**[162] 5373 4-10-12 0.. AidanColeman
(Harry Whittington) *hld up in last trio: stamina evaporated 3 out and sn hopelessly t.o* **16/1**

4m 8.2s (1.50) **Going Correction** +0.125s/f (Yiel)
WFA 4 from 5yo+ 11lb **8** Ran SP% **115.8**
Speed ratings (Par 105): **101,99,92,91,78 74,38,38**
toteswingers 1&2 £1.50, 1&3 £1.10, 2&3 £4.10 CSF £4.76 TOTE £1.80: £1.10, £1.10, £2.20; EX 5.10 Trifecta £14.00 Pool: £562.18 - 30.03 winning units.
Owner Alan Halsall **Bred** Mrs S M Newell **Trained** Over Norton, Oxon

FOCUS

Just a fair novice contest that was run to form with the first two pulling clear. The second and third have been rated close to their marks.

1689 YOUR FAVOURITE POOL BETS AT TOTEPOOL.COM H'CAP HURDLE (10 hdls) 2m 3f

4:30 (4:30) (Class 4) (0-120,120) 4-Y-0+ **£5,198** (£1,526; £763; £381)

Form RPR

310- **1** **Marmas**[33] 1391 4-10-7 **102**.. BrianHughes 108+
(John Mackie) *a ldng pair: led 5th tl 7th and again after 3 out: hrd pressed next where nt fluent: styd on strly and in command fr last* **4/1[2]**

031- **2** *¾* **Cool Baranca (GER)**[2] 1665 7-11-3 **111** 7ex........................ RyanMania 117+
(Dianne Sayer) *settled trcking ldrs and gng wl: hit 3 out: wnt 2nd 4f out: chal and wnt rt 2 out: sn stened but rdn: tried to chal last: kpt on wl but no imp flat* **6/5[1]**

002/ **3** *17* **Elsafeer (IRE)**[485] 506 8-11-10 **118**.............................. RichardJohnson 108
(Tim Vaughan) *bhd: nt fluent 2nd: j. deliberately 6th: gd prog next: disp 3rd after 3 out: rdn and lost tch w ldng pair bef next* **17/2**

234/ **4** *1* **Danvilla**[31] 2011 6-11-4 **112**..(p) DenisO'Regan 101
(Paul Webber) *chsd ldrs: drvn after 3 out: lost tch w ldng pair wl bef next* **15/2**

303- **5** *16* **Galley Slave (IRE)**[35] 1374 8-9-7 **94** oh11........................ MrJHamilton(7) 69
(Michael Chapman) *in rr quartet: rdn 7th: last and completely outpcd wl bef 3 out: plugged past three rivals fnl 200yds* **25/1**

011/ **6** *1* **Monkey Milan (IRE)**[531] 5433 7-11-12 **120**........................ BarryKeniry 94
(Philip Kirby) *last away: a bhd: pushed along 7th: struggling after next* **5/1[3]**

605- **7** *1 ¼* **Phoenix Eye**[30] 1442 12-9-7 **94** oh22..................(p) StephenMulqueen(7) 67
(Michael Mullineaux) *t.k.h in last quartet: short-lived effrt 7th: rdn and wknd after next* **50/1**

P/0- **8** *10* **Wild Desert (FR)**[35] 1378 8-10-6 **105**.............................. JoshHamer(5) 69
(Tony Carroll) *led tl 5th: led 7th tl rdn and hdd after 3 out: sn lost pl: j. slowly 2 out: eased and t.o flat* **18/1**

4m 42.5s (3.10) **Going Correction** +0.125s/f (Yiel)
WFA 4 from 6yo+ 11lb **8** Ran SP% **115.5**
Speed ratings (Par 105): **98,97,90,90,83 82,82,78**
toteswingers 1&2 £2.50, 1&3 £9.50, 2&3 £1.10 CSF £9.64 CT £37.43 TOTE £3.70: £1.10, £1.10, £3.40; EX 9.20 Trifecta £72.90 Pool: £714.26 - 7.34 winning units.
Owner Gary Shelton **Bred** Shadwell Estate Company Limited **Trained** Church Broughton , Derbys

FOCUS

A steadily-run moderate handicap. The winner has been rated as improving a little, and he can go higher based on his Flat form, while the runner-up has been rated close to her recent win.

1690 BETFRED/TOTEPOOL RACING'S BIGGEST SUPPORTER STANDARD NATIONAL HUNT FLAT RACE (CONDITIONALS/AMATEURS) 2m 1f

5:05 (5:07) (Class 6) 4-6-Y-0 **£1,559** (£457; £228; £114)

Form RPR

24/ **1** **Long Lunch**[169] 5279 4-10-4 0.................................... CharlieDeutsch(10) 100+
(Charlie Longsdon) *hld up chsng ldrs: hdwy in 6 l 3rd home turn: pushed into ld wl over 1f out: sn clr but carrying hd high: rdn out* **5/6[1]**

2 *4 ½* **Lawsons Thorns (IRE)** 4-10-11 0.................................. GavinSheehan(3) 95
(Peter Niven) *racd keenly in 2nd: effrt to ld over 2f out: sn rdn: hdd wl over 1f out: kpt on steadily at same pce* **7/2[2]**

50/ **3** *3 ¼* **Frankie Four Feet**[404] 1296 5-10-11 0.............................. KielanWoods(3) 91
(Michael Mullineaux) *led: 3 l clr home turn: rdn and hdd over 2f out: nt qckn after: btn 1f out* **33/1**

4 11 **Looking Tanned** 4-10-9 0 JonathanEngland(5) 80
(Michael Appleby) *chsd ldrs: drvn 6f out: sn struggling: remote 5th home turn* **20/1**
2/ 5 6 **Operatic Heights (IRE)**192 4864 4-10-11 0 MichaelByrne(3) 74
(Tim Vaughan) *2nd or 3rd tl rdn 6f out: drvn in poor 4th and floundering home turn: t.o* **11/2**3
6 4 1/2 **Rossington** 4-10-7 0 GLavery(7) 70
(John Wainwright) *last away: struggling fr 1/2-way: t.o fnl 4f* **40/1**
7 8 **Torrington Deal** 5-10-0 0 MrJTeal(7) 55
(Malcolm Jefferson) *last pair: t.o fr 1/2-way: penny dropped and sprinting ins fnl f* **16/1**
8 8 **Up To Al (IRE)** 5-10-7 0 MrJHamilton(7) 54
(John Wainwright) *t.o fr 1/2-way* **28/1**
60- U **Tropical Sky (IRE)**110 699 5-10-9 0 (t) JoeCornwall(5)
(Michael Chapman) *hopelessly t.o fr 1/2-way: abt 2f bhd whn jinked and uns rdr 2f out* **100/1**
P **Never Another (USA)** 4-10-7 0 MrRBirkett(7)
(Julia Feilden) *lost pl rapidly and collapsed 1/2-way: fatally injured* **12/1**

4m 8.5s (7.40) **Going Correction** +0.125s/f (Yiel) **10** Ran SP% **120.3**
Speed ratings: **87,84,83,78,75 73,69,65, ,**
toteswingers 1&2 £2.10, 1&3 £9.70, 2&3 £16.30 CSF £3.78 TOTE £1.90: £1.10, £1.50, £7.80; EX 5.10 Trifecta £84.30 Pool: £903.30 - 8.03 winning units.
Owner Battersby, Birchall, Halsall & Vestey **Bred** Overbury Stallions Ltd **Trained** Over Norton, Oxon

FOCUS
An emphatic victory for the well-backed favourite to give his trainer a treble on the day. The winner has been rated to his mark in what was an ordinary bumper.
T/Plt: £56.30 to a £1 stake. Pool: £72,962.75 - 945.39 winning units T/Qpdt: £17.10 to a £1 stake. Pool: £3,593.10 - 154.90 winning units IM

1691 - 1694a (Foreign Racing) - See Raceform Interactive

1639
NEWTON ABBOT (L-H)
Monday, September 30

OFFICIAL GOING: Good to soft (soft in places; 6.6)
Wind: mild across Weather: overcast

1695 HAPPY BIRTHDAY MUM "NATIONAL HUNT" NOVICES' HURDLE (9 hdls) 2m 3f
2:20 (2:20) (Class 4) 4-Y-0+ **£3,508** (£1,030; £515; £257)

Form RPR
221/ 1 **Oscar Magic (IRE)**184 5016 6-11-5 129 SamTwiston-Davies 130+
(Nigel Twiston-Davies) *j.lft: mde all: rdn after 3 out: hung off rails bef next: styd on: drvn out* **1/10**1
3/3- 2 3 **Quite By Chance**146 160 4-10-11 0 JoeTizzard 117
(Colin Tizzard) *trckd wnr: swtchd rt and ch appr 2 out: sn rdn: kpt on but nt quite pce to chal* **9/1**3
400/ 3 48 **Here Comes Moss**442 965 6-10-12 0 RhysFlint 75
(John Flint) *hld up bhd ldng trio: nudged along after 5th: lost tch after next: wnt modest 3rd bef last* **50/1**
/34- 4 1 **State Department**33 1427 6-10-12 0 RichardJohnson 74
(Philip Hobbs) *hld up bhd ldng trio: struggling after 6th: wknd after next: wnt modest 4th bef last* **7/1**2
0/4- 5 6 **Cloudy Lady**111 715 5-10-5 0 IanPopham 62
(Caroline Keevil) *trckd wnr: awkward 2nd: rdn after 6th: wknd after next: lost modest 3rd whn mstke last* **16/1**

4m 34.8s (4.80) **Going Correction** +0.175s/f (Yiel)
WFA 4 from 5yo+ 11lb **5** Ran SP% **121.3**
Speed ratings (Par 105): **96,94,74,74,71**
CSF £3.04 TOTE £1.10: £1.02, £3.60; EX 3.20 Trifecta £24.50 Pool: £1,691.15 - 51.70 winning units.
Owner Mrs Lorna Berryman **Bred** NIALL RADFORD **Trained** Naunton, Gloucs

FOCUS
All races on shared bends. A workmanlike success for the long odds-on Oscar Magic. He was seemingly close to his mark with a big step up from the second.

1696 WELCOME BACK SEAN DOONER H'CAP CHASE (13 fncs) 2m 110y
2:50 (2:51) (Class 4) (0-115,122) 4-Y-0+ **£4,288** (£1,259; £629; £314)

Form RPR
203- 1 **Cruise In Style (IRE)**13 1596 7-10-4 96 (bt) JamesBest(3) 103+
(Kevin Bishop) *trckd ldrs: chalng whn nt fluent 2 out: led last: rdn and r.o wl to assert towards fin* **2/1**2
112- 2 1 1/4 **Bennys Quest (IRE)**23 1522 10-11-5 115 (p) ConorShoemark(7) 118
(Neil Mulholland) *trckd ldrs: led 2 out: rdn and hdd last: kpt on but no ex* **5/4**1
P00- 3 3/4 **Humbel Ben (IRE)**17 1580 10-11-4 107 (p) NickScholfield 109
(Alan Jones) *trckd ldrs: led after 4 out: rdn and hdd 2 out: kpt on same pce* **12/1**
424- 4 1 1/2 **Trooper Clarence**39 1352 9-11-12 115 PaulMoloney 116
(Evan Williams) *led at stdy pce: hdd after 4 out: rdn after next: kpt on same pce* **10/3**3

4m 26.7s (20.20) **Going Correction** +0.325s/f (Yiel) **4** Ran SP% **108.5**
Speed ratings (Par 105): **65,64,64,63**
CSF £5.09 TOTE £3.40; EX 4.80 Trifecta £29.10 Pool: £1,511.43 - 38.82 winning units.
Owner Steve Atkinson **Bred** Swordlestown Stud **Trained** Spaxton, Somerset

FOCUS
A steadily run handicap and the winner did not have to be at her best.

1697 SIS OUR DATA BRINGS BETTING TO LIFE NOVICES' H'CAP HURDLE (8 hdls) 2m 1f
3:20 (3:20) (Class 3) (0-125,120) 4-Y-0 **£6,076** (£1,795; £897; £449; £224)

Form RPR
344- 1 **Multitude Of Sins**40 1337 6-11-2 110 (p) JoeTizzard 120+
(Colin Tizzard) *chsd clr ldr tl lost pl whn nt fluent 4th: sltly outpcd next: styd on strly u.p to cl on ldng pair after 3 out: led bef 2 out where nt fluent: in command whn hit last: drew clr: comf* **11/2**
133- 2 9 **Purple 'n Gold (IRE)**8 1627 4-11-2 110 (p) TomScudamore 110
(David Pipe) *trckd ldrs in chsng gp tl disp 2nd after 4th: rdn and ev ch briefly bef 2 out: no ex appr last* **3/1**2
132- 3 8 **Quadriller (FR)**30 1475 6-10-13 107 (t) TomO'Brien 101
(Philip Hobbs) *chsd clr ldr: led whn nt fluent 3 out: rdn and hdd bef 2 out: kpt on same pce* **9/4**1
0/1- 4 3 **To The Sky (IRE)**29 1487 5-10-11 112 (p) CiaranMckee(7) 101
(John O'Shea) *led: sn clr: rdn and hdd after 3 out: one pce fr next* **7/1**
0/0- 5 23 **Super Duplex**67 708 6-10-5 99 ColinBolger 67
(Pat Phelan) *hld up in chsng gp: tk clsr order after 4th: rdn after next: wknd after 3 out: t.o* **25/1**

612- P **Fairyinthewind (IRE)**48 1258 4-11-12 120 WayneHutchinson
(Alan King) *trckd ldrs in chsng gp tl dropped to last and struggling after 4th: wknd next: t.o whn p.u bef 2 out* **4/1**3
3- P **Slow Train Coming (IRE)**39 1341 6-10-6 100 PaulMoloney
(Evan Williams) *hld up in chsng gp: rdn after 5th: wknd after next: p.u bef 2 out* **10/1**

4m 5.6s (-0.10) **Going Correction** +0.175s/f (Yiel) **7** Ran SP% **116.6**
Speed ratings (Par 107): **107,102,99,97,86 ,**
toteswingers 1&2 £3.20, 1&3 £3.10, 2&3 £2.20 CSF £23.55 CT £47.94 TOTE £6.00: £3.50, £2.00; EX 28.30 Trifecta £53.00 Pool: £1,537.62 - 21.73 winning units.
Owner Tizzard Racing One **Bred** Barrow Hill **Trained** Milborne Port, Dorset

FOCUS
The pace was decent in this ordinary handicap. A step up from the easy winner.

1698 OLIVE AND JACK OLIVER MEMORIAL NOVICES' CHASE (13 fncs) 2m 110y
3:50 (3:50) (Class 4) 4-Y-0+ **£4,288** (£1,259; £629; £314)

Form RPR
300/ 1 **Ivor's King (IRE)**192 4905 6-11-4 0 JoeTizzard 135+
(Colin Tizzard) *mde all: shkn up between last 2: r.o wl fr last: readily* **5/2**2
633/ 2 5 **Valco De Touzaine (FR)**206 4647 4-10-7 0 DarylJacob 117+
(Paul Nicholls) *racd keenly: trckd wnr: shkn up after 3 out: rdn between last 2: nt pce to chal: no ex fr last* **8/11**1
/53- 3 6 **Zarzal (IRE)**23 1520 5-11-4 0 PaulMoloney 122
(Evan Williams) *trckd ldrs: rdn after 4 out: kpt on same pce fr next* **6/1**3
/06- 4 12 **Dontpaytheferryman (USA)**23 1520 8-11-1 0 (b1) RobertDunne(3) 111
(John Price) *trckd ldrs: rdn after 4 out: wknd 2 out* **25/1**
0/- U **Hansupfordetroit (IRE)**125 529 8-11-4 125 DPFahy
(Bernard Llewellyn) *trckd ldng 4 fr 4th: cl enough but pushed along whn awkward and uns rdr 9th* **12/1**

4m 8.8s (2.30) **Going Correction** +0.325s/f (Yiel)
WFA 4 from 5yo+ 11lb **5** Ran SP% **112.3**
Speed ratings (Par 105): **107,104,101,96,**
CSF £5.13 TOTE £3.90: £1.90, £1.20; EX 5.60 Trifecta £13.20 Pool: £2,446.82 - 138.45 winning units.
Owner W I M Perry **Bred** W Bourke **Trained** Milborne Port, Dorset

FOCUS
Not a bad little novice chase for the track.

1699 AT THE RACES SKY 415 H'CAP HURDLE (9 hdls) 2m 3f
4:20 (4:21) (Class 4) (0-115,115) 4-Y-0+ **£3,508** (£1,030; £515; £257)

Form RPR
535- 1 **Sporting Boy (IRE)**48 1263 5-11-12 115 (t) NickScholfield 126+
(Johnny Farrelly) *trckd ldrs: rdn into clr ld after 3 out: in command after: comf* **15/2**
24- 2 8 **Zalgarry (FR)**38 1363 6-11-4 114 JoshWall(7) 119+
(Arthur Whitehead) *mid-div: hdwy after 3 out: rdn to chse wnr bef next: styd on but no ch w wnr* **5/2**2
211- 3 9 **Mount Vesuvius (IRE)**25 1504 5-11-8 111 (t) TomO'Brien 107
(Paul Henderson) *hld up towards rr: hdwy 6th: rdn to chse wnr after 3 out tl bef next: styd on same pce* **7/1**
U/0- 4 2 **Escort'men (FR)**23 1520 7-11-9 112 (t) PaulMoloney 106
(Anthony Middleton) *hld up towards rr: hdwy after 6th: rdn after 3 out: wnt 4th and styd on same pce fr next: nvr threatened* **25/1**
065- 5 4 1/2 **Delphi Mountain (IRE)**39 1352 8-10-12 104 MichealNolan(3) 95
(Richard Woollacott) *trckd ldrs: rdn after 3 out: fdd fr next* **20/1**
5P6/ 6 15 **Bold Cuffs**213 4501 4-10-13 103 JoeTizzard 79
(Colin Tizzard) *racd keenly early: trckd ldr: led 6th: rdn and hdd after 3 out: fnd little: wknd bef next* **9/4**1
004/ 7 1/2 **Matako (FR)**481 623 10-10-13 102 IanPopham 78
(Caroline Keevil) *mid-div: rdn after 6th: wknd bef 2 out* **33/1**
233- 8 1 3/4 **Detroit Red**29 1488 7-11-1 104 HaddenFrost 79
(Martin Hill) *towards rr of mid-div: rdn 3 out: wknd bef next* **5/1**3
630- 9 2 1/2 **Sun Quest**46 1273 9-10-2 98 (t) MrLKilgarriff(7) 70
(Steven Dixon) *chsd ldrs: pushed along after 5th: wknd after 3 out* **33/1**
/P0- P **Santera (IRE)**44 1284 9-11-4 107 (b1) WillKennedy
(John Spearing) *led tl 6th: wknd qckly: t.o whn p.u bef 2 out* **33/1**
/P5- P **Mosstown (IRE)**20 1550 7-11-1 104 (vt1) DPFahy
(Liam Corcoran) *towards rr of mid-div: struggling in rr after 5th: tailing off whn wnt bdly lft next: sn p.u* **22/1**

4m 30.9s (0.90) **Going Correction** +0.175s/f (Yiel)
WFA 4 from 5yo+ 11lb **11** Ran SP% **122.1**
Speed ratings (Par 105): **105,101,97,97,95 88,88,87,86,**
toteswingers 1&2 £4.80, 1&3 £3.90, 2&3 £4.20 CSF £26.10 CT £139.57 TOTE £8.60: £2.20, £1.40, £1.80; EX 34.80 Trifecta £122.90 Pool: £1,991.73 - 12.15 winning units.
Owner Wayne Clifford **Bred** Joe & June Staunton **Trained** Bridgwater, Somerset

FOCUS
A modest handicap with an easy winner who had slipped to a very good mark.

1700 TRY TOTEQUICKPICK IF YOU'RE FEELING LUCKY H'CAP HURDLE (8 hdls) 2m 1f
4:50 (4:50) (Class 5) (0-95,91) 4-Y-0+ **£2,463** (£718; £359)

Form RPR
5P/- 1 **North London**184 5023 6-10-12 77 HaddenFrost 85+
(James Frost) *mid-div in chsng gp: hdwy after 6th: led gng to 2 out: r.o: rdn out* **12/1**
620- 2 1 1/4 **Chankillo**6 1643 4-11-8 87 WillKennedy 92
(Sarah-Jayne Davies) *led chsng gp: clsd on clr ldrs 5th: led 6th tl sltly outpcd sn after 3 out: rallied gamely between last 2 to hold ch sn after last: kpt on* **16/1**
360- 3 7 **Fair Breeze**26 1267 6-10-11 76 RichardJohnson 76
(Richard Phillips) *mid-div in chsng gp: hdwy 5th: chal after 3 out tl awkward next: styd on same pce* **20/1**
/- 4 1 1/4 **Lets Get Cracking (FR)**1732 4484 9-10-6 71 NickScholfield 69
(Alan Jones) *hld up bhd: rdn and stdy prog after 3 out: wnt 4th bef last: styd on wout threatening ldrs* **25/1**
/00- 5 6 **Bernisdale**84 925 5-11-9 88 RhysFlint 83
(John Flint) *mid-div: rdn and hdwy after 3 out: mstke next: no further imp* **10/1**
0F4- 6 11 **Bolberry Springs**39 1348 6-11-12 91 (t) JoeTizzard 74
(Colin Tizzard) *trckd ldr in chsng gp: clsd on ldrs 5th: led after 3 out: rdn and hdd bef 2 out: sn wknd* **7/1**3
0/0- 7 3/4 **Lovely Muck**38 1364 8-11-11 90 SamTwiston-Davies 72
(Nigel Twiston-Davies) *mid-div in chasign gp: reminder after 4th: nvr travelling after: no threat fr 3 out* **15/8**1

041/ **8** 3/4 **Rock Peak (IRE)**[46] 2594 8-10-13 **83**........................(b) RobertWilliams(5) 64
(Bernard Llewellyn) *mstke 5th: nvr bttr than mid-div of chsng gp: wknd bef 2 out* **7/1**[3]

005- **9** 5 **Warsaw Pact (IRE)**[32] 1443 10-10-8 **80**........................(p) MrLKilgarriff(7) 57
(Steven Dixon) *sn struggling: a in rr* **14/1**

3FP/ **P** **Jazz City**[2365] 4847 13-11-7 **86**.. MarkGrant
(Michael Blanshard) *mid-div in chsng gp tl wknd after 6th: t.o whn p.u bef 2 out* **50/1**

04P- **P** **Exiles Return (IRE)**[6] 1645 11-10-1 **69**........................... MarkQuinlan(3)
(Jacqueline Retter) *led tl mstke 6th: wknd qckly: tailing off whn p.u bef 2 out* **33/1**

P41/ **P** **Doheny Bar (IRE)**[183] 5029 10-10-12 **77**.............................. TomO'Brien
(Paul Henderson) *trckd ldr: clr of remainder tl wknd 6th: sn bhd: t.o whn p.u bef 2 out* **12/1**

P00/ **P** **Jawahal Du Mathan (FR)**[180] 5119 5-10-0 **72**.................... JoshWall(7)
(Arthur Whitehead) *mid-div in chsng gp tl wknd after 3 out: bhd whn p.u bef next* **11/2**[2]

4m 9.9s (4.20) **Going Correction** +0.175s/f (Yiel)
WFA 4 from 5yo+ 11lb **13** Ran SP% **125.7**
Speed ratings (Par 103): **97,96,93,92,89 84,84,83,81, , ,**
toteswingers 1&2 £26.10, 1&3 £44.30, 2&3 £21.80 CSF £185.22 CT £3807.05 TOTE £18.10: £5.10, £5.20, £5.20; EX 285.20 Trifecta £745.00 Pool: £1,740.39 - 1.75 winning units.
Owner Tim Russell **Bred** J D Frost **Trained** Scorriton, Devon

FOCUS
A weak handicap, but the first two looked to step up.

1701 NEWTON ABBOT RACES CONDITIONAL JOCKEYS' H'CAP CHASE (20 fncs) 3m 2f 110y
5:20 (5:21) (Class 5) (0-95,95) 4-Y-0+ **£2,729** (£801; £400; £200)

Form RPR

035- **1** **Volio Vincente (FR)**[30] 1474 6-9-9 **69** oh8............................. JonPark(5) 75
(Carroll Gray) *hld up: wnt 3rd w plenty to do 15th: hdwy fr 3 out: 12 l down 2 out: 10 l down last: str run to ld nring fin* **16/1**

022- **2** 2 **Golden Squirell (IRE)**[22] 1528 6-10-6 **75**........................(v) TomCannon 82
(Brendan Powell) *prom: pushed along fr 8th: reminders after 10th: led after 13th: drvn after 4 out: 10 l clr last: no ex whn hdd nring fin* **2/1**[1]

P/3- **3** 4 **The Goldmeister (IRE)**[84] 926 6-11-2 **88**.................(p) KielanWoods(3) 90
(Charlie Longsdon) *trckd ldrs: rdn along after 13th: chal fr 15th tl 3 out: plugged on: lost 2nd run-in* **3/1**[2]

P55- **4** 73 **Upper Deck (IRE)**[20] 1548 8-9-9 **69** oh4...................... DanielHiskett(5) 4
(Richard Phillips) *hld up: lost tch after 14th: continued t.o* **11/1**

163- **F** **Solitary Palm (IRE)**[30] 1474 10-10-12 **81**......................(b) MichealNolan
(Brian Forsey) *led tl rdn and hdd after 13th: wknd 15th: fell next* **7/1**[3]

/03- **R** **Magical Treasure**[6] 1644 9-11-12 **95**...............................(bt) JamesBest
(Sarah Kerswell) *prom: pushed along fr 13th: rdn and stl upsides whn ref 15th* **14/1**

/0P- **B** **Hobb's Dream (IRE)**[43] 1300 9-10-13 **85**..............(p) ConorShoemark(3)
(Neil Mulholland) *hld up: struggling after 13th: bhd whn b.d 16th* **7/1**[3]

P- **P** **Roisini Bay (IRE)**[127] 485 9-11-2 **90**.......................(p) JackSherwood(5)
(Richenda Ford) *in tch tl wknd after 13th: t.o whn p.u after next* **20/1**

/P0- **P** **Theroadtogorey (IRE)**[84] 921 7-11-1 **84**........................... IanPopham
(Sarah Robinson) *mid-div tl after 13th: tailing off whn p.u after next* **33/1**

5P5- **P** **Thehorsemaytalk (IRE)**[43] 1303 8-10-4 **78**.................(v[1]) KevinJones(5)
(Mark Shears) *hld up: struggling 11th: wkng whn bdly hmpd 15th: sn p.u* **9/1**

7m 6.9s (22.30) **Going Correction** +0.325s/f (Yiel) **10** Ran SP% **121.9**
Speed ratings (Par 103): **79,78,77,55, , , , ,**
toteswingers 1&2 £11.00, 1&3 £11.40, 2&3 £3.00 CSF £52.71 CT £131.66 TOTE £21.10: £4.80, £1.40, £1.70; EX 67.20 Trifecta £357.20 Pool: £1,496.37 - 3.14 winning units.
Owner optimumracing.co.uk **Bred** Classic Breeding Sarl Et Al **Trained** Moorland, Somerset
■ Stewards' Enquiry : Kielan Woods six-day ban: used whip above permitted level (Oct 15-20)
Tom Cannon seven-day ban: used whip above permitted level (Oct 15-21)

FOCUS
A very weak handicap, confined to conditional riders. Improvement from the winner.
T/Plt: £165.20 to a £1 stake. Pool: £75,946.06 - 335.58 winning units T/Qpdt: £81.30 to a £1 stake. Pool: £5,426.97 - 49.35 winning units TM

1490 ROSCOMMON (R-H)
Monday, September 30

OFFICIAL GOING: Flat course - good (good to firm in places); chase course - good to firm (good in places)

1702a KILBEGNET EUROPEAN BREEDERS FUND NOVICE CHASE (GRADE 3) (10 fncs) 2m
4:35 (4:35) 4-Y-0+ **£18,495** (£5,406; £2,560; £853)

RPR

1 **Darwins Fox (FR)**[57] 1207 7-11-1 .... AELynch 142+
(Henry De Bromhead, Ire) *hld up in tch: keen early: 4th 1/2-way: tk clsr order in 3rd after 4 out: prog gng wl to ld fr 2 out: sn drew clr: easily* **9/4**[1]

2 13 **Cootamundra (IRE)**[157] 5559 10-11-2 135 ow1................. RobbieMoran 127
(J A Berry, Ire) *hld up towards rr: 6th 1/2-way: hdwy bef 3 out into 4th: sn rdn and wnt mod 2nd at last: kpt on same pce run-in wout ever troubling easy wnr* **8/1**[3]

3 1 1/2 **Ballyfinboy (IRE)**[30] 1482 7-11-1 121.............................. EddieO'Connell 126
(J R Finn, Ire) *hld up towards rr: nt fluent 5th: pushed along in 6th bef 3 out where nt fluent: wnt mod 4th at last and kpt on u.p into 3rd run-in wout ever troubling easy wnr* **20/1**

4 2 **Boxer Beat (IRE)**[19] 1573 6-11-2 121 ow1..................(p) KeithDonoghue 124
(Paul W Flynn, Ire) *chsd ldrs in 3rd: 2nd 1/2-way: tk clsr order fr 4 out: pushed along bef st and sn lost pl: no ex u.p in 4th fr 2 out: kpt on same pce* **11/1**

5 1/2 **The Folkes Choice**[24] 1512 7-10-8 112............................ PhillipEnright 116
(Henry De Bromhead, Ire) *led: over 2 l clr 1/2-way: reduced advantage fr 4 out: strly pressed into st and hdd fr 2 out: sn no imp on easy wnr and dropped to 3rd bef last: dropped to 5th run-in* **33/1**

6 2 3/4 **He's Our Man (IRE)**[17] 1178 8-11-1 129.......................(t) DavyCondon 120
(Ross O'Sullivan, Ire) *hld up in tch: lost pl and reminders in rr after 4th: rdn in mod 6th 2 out and kpt on one pce u.p* **8/1**[3]

7 15 **Toostrong (FR)**[15] 1589 6-11-1 126................................(t) RWalsh 105
(W P Mullins, Ire) *chsd ldr in 2nd: 3rd 1/2-way: niggled along fr 6th and lost pl fr next: pushed along in 4th bef st and sn no ex u.p: wknd* **10/3**[2]

8 3 3/4 **Shadow Eile (IRE)**[20] 1558 8-10-8 .... AndrewJMcNamara 95
(Mrs D A Love, Ire) *chsd ldrs: nt fluent in 5th at 5th: pushed along in 5th bef 3 out and sn no ex u.p: wknd qckly bef 2 out: slt mstke last: lame* **9/4**[1]

3m 48.6s (228.60) **8** Ran SP% **122.9**
CSF £22.82 TOTE £3.20: £1.02, £2.40, £3.70; DF 18.00 Trifecta £62.60.
Owner John J Brennan **Bred** Jean-Pierre Dubois **Trained** Knockeen, Co Waterford

FOCUS
Baily Green won this last year before going on to give Simonsig his biggest scare in the Arkle and other noteworthy winners include Conna Castle (2007) and Kalderon (2008). This year's renewal was weakened considerably by the defection of The Real Article but even that 141-rated performer would have struggled to cope with this winner. He's rated close to his Galway figure.

1703 - 1705a (Foreign Racing) - See Raceform Interactive

CHEPSTOW (L-H)
Tuesday, October 1

OFFICIAL GOING: Good (good to soft in places; chs 7.4, hdl 7.5)
Wind: Virtually nil Weather: Overcast

1706 WESTERN DAILY PRESS MAIDEN HURDLE (11 hdls) 2m 4f
2:00 (2:01) (Class 5) 4-Y-0+ **£1,949** (£572; £286; £143)

Form RPR

F22/ **1** **Creepy (IRE)**[167] 5352 5-11-0 131... IanPopham 135+
(Martin Keighley) *t.k.h: led 2nd: hung rt bnd after 4th: shkn up last and nt fluent: sn rcvrd: comf* **10/11**[1]

4/4- **2** 2 1/4 **Splash Of Ginge**[18] 1576 5-11-0 0......................... SamTwiston-Davies 127
(Nigel Twiston-Davies) *chsd ldrs: wnt 2nd 3 out: drvn fr 2 out: rallied after last: no imp on wnr* **10/1**[3]

2P2/ **3** 11 **Gassin Golf**[24] 5513 4-11-0 131...................................... RichardJohnson 118
(Richard Lee) *t.k.h: in tch: hdwy after 4th: trckd ldrs fr next: chsd wnr 4 out to next: fading whn hit last* **15/8**[2]

3/ **4** 14 **Tijori (IRE)**[16] 2415 5-10-9 0.. RobertWilliams(5) 108
(Bernard Llewellyn) *chsd ldrs: rdn bef 4 out: wknd sn after* **16/1**

654- **5** 16 **Cute Court (IRE)**[21] 1552 6-11-0 0.................................... ConorO'Farrell 91
(Liam Corcoran) *in rr whn hmpd bnd after 4th: rdn 6th: mod prog fr 3 out* **100/1**

400- **6** 7 **Dont Call Me Oscar (IRE)**[18] 1580 6-10-9 83........... NicodeBoinville(5) 84
(Mark Gillard) *led to 2nd: chsd wnr tl after 7th: wknd 3 out* **100/1**

40P/ **7** 6 **Peter Muck**[1516] 1161 10-10-7 0.. RyanHatch(7) 78
(Nigel Twiston-Davies) *towards rr: sme hdwy 7th: wknd 4 out* **50/1**

8 5 **Maxi's Lady (IRE)**[100] 814 6-10-7 0.............................. DonalDevereux 67
(David Rees) *mid-dvision to 7th* **100/1**

0/0- **9** 1/2 **Cash For Steel (IRE)**[14] 1599 6-10-0 0....................... CharlieDeutsch(7) 73
(Richard Phillips) *in rr: stl bhd whn bdly hmpd bnd appr 4 out* **100/1**

0/6- **10** 8 **Two Shades Of Blue**[40] 1341 6-10-4 0.............................. AdamWedge(3) 59
(Beth Roberts) *a in rr* **150/1**

P/P- **11** 44 **Flexi Time (IRE)**[93] 854 9-10-7 90... JPKiely(7) 27
(Stephen Hughes) *rdn 5th: a bhd: t.o* **100/1**

4/ **12** 7 **Josie's Dream (IRE)**[82] 577 5-11-0 0.. MarkGrant 20
(Jo Hughes) *chsd ldrs: wnt 2nd after 7th: btn whn hit 4 out: t.o* **66/1**

F/5- **S** **Minellaforlunch (IRE)**[145] 185 6-11-0 0.............................. HenryOliver
(Henry Oliver) *in rr: hdwy 7th: styng on and in tch w ldrs whn slipped up bnd bef 4 out* **14/1**

0/ **P** **Daizy (IRE)**[183] 5070 4-11-0 0... LiamTreadwell
(Hilary Parrott) *in rr whn hung bdly rt bnd after 4th: p.u bef next* **66/1**

4m 45.79s (-16.01) **Going Correction** -0.80s/f (Firm) **14** Ran SP% **119.4**
Speed ratings (Par 103): **100,99,94,89,82 79,77,75,75,72 54,51, ,**
toteswingers 1&2 £3.00, 2&3 £2.90, 1&3 £1.60 CSF £12.13 TOTE £2.40: £1.10, £3.40, £1.10; EX 12.90 Trifecta £36.30 Pool: £4597.44 - 94.76 winning units..
Owner M Boothright, T Hanlon, S Harman **Bred** Gareth Metcalfe **Trained** Condicote, Gloucs

FOCUS
This interesting maiden hurdle was run at a steady pace with the cosy winner rated a bit below his best.

1707 COUNTY MARQUEES H'CAP HURDLE (12 hdls) 3m
2:30 (3:06) (Class 4) (0-115,115) 4-Y-0+ **£3,119** (£915; £457; £228)

Form RPR

24/- **1** **Sinbad The Sailor**[7] 704 8-11-5 **113**............................... TrevorWhelan(5) 121+
(George Baker) *hld up in rr: hdwy appr 4 out: hit 3 out chal 2 out: sn led: drvn out run-in* **10/1**

131- **2** 1 **Tarvini (IRE)**[31] 1477 8-10-7 **106**.............................(p) JamesHuxham(10) 113
(Jonjo O'Neill) *chsd ldrs: led 4 out: jnd 2 out: sn hdd: kpt on wl run-in but a hld* **7/1**

003/ **3** 7 **Fix It Right (IRE)**[183] 5081 5-11-5 **111**........................... GavinSheehan(3) 112
(Emma Lavelle) *chsd ldrs: wnt 3rd 4 out: sn rdden: styd on same pce* **9/2**[2]

046/ **4** hd **Glenwood Prince (IRE)**[196] 4857 7-10-6 **95**..................(t) NickScholfield 95
(Jeremy Scott) *in rr: hdwy fr 4 out: styd on fr 2 out to take 4th appr last: kpt on to cl on 3rd nr fin but no ch w ldng duo* **5/1**[3]

422- **5** 12 **Thornton Alice**[31] 1477 8-10-13 **102**............................ WayneHutchinson 93
(Richard Phillips) *in rr: hdwy appr 4 out: sn rdn: btn 3 out* **10/1**

5P0- **6** nse **Changing Lanes**[20] 1565 10-10-1 **90** oh1 ow1..............(vt) PaulMoloney 81
(David Rees) *led: jnd 4th to 5th: hdd 4 out: wknd after next: btn whn hit 2 out* **25/1**

131- **7** 6 **Bold Raider (IRE)**[33] 1434 6-11-3 **106**................................. APMcCoy 92
(Jonjo O'Neill) *chsd ldrs: chal 4 out: sn rdn: wknd after 3 out* **4/1**[1]

124/ **8** 10 **Blowing A Hoolie (IRE)**[464] 798 5-10-12 **104**.............(p) JamesBest(3) 79
(Sophie Leech) *in rr: hdwy 6th: wknd after 8th* **50/1**

332- **9** 6 **Nez Rouge (FR)**[71] 1073 12-10-11 **100**..................... SamTwiston-Davies 69
(Nigel Twiston-Davies) *chsd ldrs: wknd 4 out* **12/1**

222/ **10** 3/4 **Bravo Bravo**[12] 12 6-11-7 **115**..............................(b) NicodeBoinville(5) 85
(Mark Gillard) *sn drvn: chsd ldrs: chal 4th to 5th: rdn fr 7th: wknd 4 out* **10/1**

015- **11** 27 **Gap Of Dunloe (IRE)**[39] 1363 5-11-4 **107**.................(tp) RichardJohnson 51
(Peter Bowen) *blnd 3rd: a towards rr* **8/1**

5m 51.7s (-10.50) **Going Correction** -0.80s/f (Firm) **11** Ran SP% **119.2**
Speed ratings (Par 105): **85,84,82,82,78 78,76,72,70,70 61**
toteswingers 1&2 £12.20, 2&3 £6.80, 1&3 £12.10 CSF £79.83 CT £365.60 TOTE £14.00: £4.00, £2.00, £2.40; EX 93.50 Trifecta £1076.20 Pool: £3784.68 - 2.63 winning units..
Owner Baker, Coleman, Wand & Williams **Bred** Sir Eric Parker **Trained** Manton, Wilts

FOCUS
The second race was delayed as officials and trainers went to check the home bend after a number of runners slipped in the first race. This competitive handicap was run at a steady pace. The first two were very well in on their old form.

1708 PORTABLE TOILETS LTD (S) HURDLE (11 hdls) 2m 4f
3:05 (3:50) (Class 5) 4-7-Y-O **£1,949** (£572; £286; £143)

Form RPR
/25- **1** **Dark Spirit (IRE)**[45] 1284 5-10-2 97 (p) AdamWedge[(3)] 110+
(Evan Williams) *in rr: hdwy 6th: trckd ldrs in 3rd 4 out: drvn to chal after ldr blnd 2 out: led appr last: drvn out* **3/1**[2]
P/6- **2** *4* **Bombadero (IRE)**[20] 1564 6-10-12 115 (t) APMcCoy 116+
(Dr Richard Newland) *chsd ldrs in 3rd: led appr 4 out: rdn bef next: blnd 2 out: hdd u.p appr last: no ex u.p* **11/8**[1]
331- **3** *2* **Wayward Glance**[34] 1429 5-11-4 119 (v) TomScudamore 117
(Jim Best) *led to 2nd: styd pressing ldr: led briefly after 7th: rdn and one pce disputing 3rd fr 4 out: no imp on ldng duo fr 2 out* **5/1**[3]
/13- **4** *12* **Vimiero (USA)**[20] 1562 6-11-4 115 RichieMcLernon 108
(Jonjo O'Neill) *in rr: hdwy 7th: nvr rchd ldrs and no ch fr 3 out* **11/1**
234- **5** *5* **Lauberhorn**[22] 1537 6-11-8 113 (v) PaulMoloney 109
(Evan Williams) *hit 2nd: in rr: sme hdwy fr 7th: wknd 4 out* **16/1**
UF0/ **6** *5* **Mister Carter (IRE)**[7] 3981 6-10-12 0 (tp) WillKennedy 92
(Ian Williams) *hit 3rd: bhd most of way* **12/1**
/25- **7** *18* **Castle Beach (IRE)**[24] 1519 4-10-12 107 RichardJohnson 75
(Rebecca Curtis) *chsd ldrs: wknd 4 out* **20/1**
0FP- **8** *42* **Pennant Dancer**[9] 1631 6-10-12 64 (vt[1]) DonalDevereux 37
(Debra Hamer) *t.k.h: led 2nd but jnd tl hdd & wknd qckly after 7th* **100/1**

4m 43.8s (-18.00) **Going Correction** -0.80s/f (Firm)
WFA 4 from 5yo+ 10lb **8** Ran SP% **111.4**
Speed ratings: **104,102,101,96,94 92,85,68**
toteswingers 1&2 £1.80, 2&3 £2.30, 1&3 £3.00 CSF £7.35 TOTE £4.00: £1.60, £1.10, £1.60; EX 9.50 Trifecta £30.30 Pool: £41701.52 - 103.03 winning units..The winner was bought in for £4200.
Owner Richard Abbott & Mario Stavrou **Bred** Thomas G N Burrage **Trained** Llancarfan, Vale Of Glamorgan

FOCUS
Not a bad contest for the grade. It was run at a fair pace.

1709 32RED NOVICES' LIMITED H'CAP CHASE (18 fncs) 3m
3:40 (4:15) (Class 3) (0-140,136) 5-Y-0+ **£6,498** (£1,908; £954; £477)

Form RPR
311- **1** **Pantxoa (FR)**[39] 1362 6-11-5 **136** WayneHutchinson 146+
(Alan King) *mde all: pushed along fr 2 out: rdn and r.o strly run-in* **6/1**[3]
212- **2** *1 ¼* **Brassick**[27] 1494 6-10-8 **125** (t) PaulMoloney 134+
(Evan Williams) *chsd ldrs: rdn in cl 4th 3 out: styd on u.p run-in and fin strly to take 2nd in clsng stages but no imp on wnr* **4/1**[2]
430/ **3** *1 ¼* **Gas Line Boy (IRE)**[195] 4863 7-10-8 **125** RichardJohnson 132
(Philip Hobbs) *in rr: blnd 1st: mstkes 3rd and 4th: hit 12th: hdwy after 13th: chsd ldrs 14th: chsd wnr u.p last but no imp: lost 2nd in clsng stages* **6/1**[3]
2/0- **4** *3 ¾* **Polisky (FR)**[78] 996 6-10-5 **122** oh2 (tp) DarylJacob 126
(Paul Nicholls) *chsd wnr fr 5th: rdn 3 out: wknd after 2 out* **8/1**
114/ **5** *13* **Annacotty (IRE)**[167] 5350 5-10-11 **128** IanPopham 119
(Martin Keighley) *chsd ldrs: wknd and hit 4 out* **2/1**[1]
521- **6** *15* **Full Of Joy (IRE)**[18] 1579 8-10-8 **125** (tp) APMcCoy 107+
(Jonjo O'Neill) *in rr but in tch: hit 6th: j. slowly 12th: hit 13th: hdwy and mstke 14th: sn btn* **7/1**
266- **7** *28* **Nomadic Dreamer**[59] 1192 10-10-5 **122** oh13 (t) RichieMcLernon 68
(Sophie Leech) *hit 10th and 12th: a in rr* **100/1**
/11- **8** *24* **Cinevator (IRE)**[33] 1433 6-11-1 **132** (p) TomO'Brien 54
(Caroline Keevil) *pushed along 8th: no ch fr next: t.o* **16/1**

5m 58.56s (-23.44) **Going Correction** -0.925s/f (Hard) **8** Ran SP% **112.4**
Speed ratings: **102,101,101,99,95 90,81,73**
toteswingers 1&2 £4.40, 2&3 £5.00, 1&3 £5.70 CSF £29.79 CT £148.55 TOTE £6.30: £1.50, £1.80, £1.90; EX 30.80 Trifecta £214.30 Pool: £3966.68 - 13.87 winning units..
Owner Mrs June Watts **Bred** Pierre De Maleissye Melun **Trained** Barbury Castle, Wilts

FOCUS
A cracking contest for this time of year. It was run at a sound gallop and the first three all look useful.

1710 LLEWELLYN HUMPHREYS H'CAP CHASE (12 fncs) 2m 110y
4:15 (4:50) (Class 4) (0-105,105) 4-Y-0+ **£3,768** (£1,106; £553; £276)

Form RPR
6P4/ **1** **Take Of Shoc'S (IRE)**[211] 4561 9-11-6 **97** (t) PaulMoloney 105
(Sophie Leech) *led: wl clr 2nd: pushed along fr 3 out: styd on gamely u.p run-in: edgd rt fnl 75yds: all out* **4/1**[3]
021- **2** *nk* **Chestnut Ben (IRE)**[23] 1530 8-11-12 **103** (t) APMcCoy 113+
(Gary Brown) *racd in 3rd bhd clr ldr and subsiquent wnr: hit 7th and wnt 2nd: blnd 8th: rallied fr 2 out: kpt on wl u.p run-in: jst hld* **15/2**
011- **3** *5* **The Nephew (IRE)**[4] 1668 5-12-0 **105** 14ex (t) RichieMcLernon 108
(Jonjo O'Neill) *hld up in rr and wl off pce bhd clr ldr and subsequent wnr: hit 4th: hdwy 8th: styd on to take 3rd u.p fr 3 out: no imp last* **7/4**[1]
5/4- **4** *3 ½* **Gizzit (IRE)**[139] 322 7-11-7 **98** AndrewThornton 98
(Karen George) *in rr: sme hdwy whn mstke 8th: styd on fr 3 out but nvr a danger* **12/1**
5/3- **5** *½* **Red Rock (FR)**[9] 1629 8-11-1 **95** GavinSheehan[(3)] 96
(Emma Lavelle) *chsd clr ldr and subsequent wnr: hit 6th: dropped to 3rd 7th: wknd 4 out* **7/2**[2]
333- **6** *38* **Finch Flyer (IRE)**[4] 1669 6-9-11 **77** oh3 (p) PeterCarberry[(3)] 42
(Aytach Sadik) *chsd ldrs early: bhd fr 3rd* **8/1**
036- **F** **The Grey One (IRE)**[23] 1530 10-10-0 **77** oh11 LiamTreadwell
(Milton Bradley) *hit 5th: sn bhd: t.o whn fell 4 out* **40/1**

(-17.10) **Going Correction** -0.925s/f (Hard) **7** Ran SP% **111.6**
Speed ratings (Par 105): **103,102,100,98,98 80,**
toteswingers 1&2 £3.90, 2&3 £2.20, 1&3 £2.70 CSF £30.84 CT £67.87 TOTE £6.20: £3.10, £1.90; EX 31.90 Trifecta £81.50 Pool: £3803.10 - 34.96 winning units..
Owner C J Leech **Bred** Frank Ryan **Trained** Elton, Gloucs

FOCUS
Plenty of pace for this modest handicap with the well-backed winner making all.

1711 CASTELL HOWELL FOODS LTD H'CAP HURDLE (8 hdls) 2m 110y
4:50 (5:20) (Class 5) (0-100,100) 4-Y-0+ **£1,949** (£572; £286; £143)

Form RPR
000- **1** **Hail Tiberius**[4] 1674 6-10-9 **83** (t) TomSiddall 91+
(Martin Keighley) *t.k.h and hld up in rr: stdy hdwy appr 4 out: hit next: led last: drvn out* **5/1**[3]
252- **2** *2 ½* **Clarion Call**[19] 1379 5-11-7 **100** (p) KillianMoore[(5)] 106+
(Graeme McPherson) *chsd ldrs: drvn fr 2 out: styd on u.p to chse wnr last: no imp run-in* **7/2**[1]
134/ **3** *1* **Supercilliary**[17] 5557 4-11-7 **95** TomCannon 100
(Chris Gordon) *chsd ldrs: drvn to ld 2 out: narrowly hdd last: no ex and styd on same pce for 3rd run-in* **9/2**[2]
243- **4** *2 ¾* **Another Flutter (IRE)**[20] 1566 9-11-10 **98** (tp) CharliePoste 100
(Matt Sheppard) *trckd ldrs: led 4 out: hdd 2 out: wknd last* **10/1**
0F5- **5** *10* **Pirans Car**[21] 1552 7-10-11 **85** (t) SamTwiston-Davies 78
(Nigel Hawke) *towards rr: sme hdwy appr 4 out: sn wknd* **14/1**
006- **6** *2* **Seaside Shuffle (IRE)**[40] 1351 8-11-2 **90** (tp) PaulMoloney 80
(Sophie Leech) *in tch sme hdwy 4 out: sn wknd* **8/1**
/26- **7** *5* **Dalrymple (IRE)**[69] 1110 7-10-1 **80** (t) CharlieWallis[(5)] 69
(Nick Ayliffe) *chsd ldrs: hit 4 out: wknd 3 out: mstke next* **16/1**
0/0- **8** *9* **Go Annie**[43] 1321 5-10-13 **87** (bt[1]) DominicElsworth 63
(Jo Davis) *a in rr* **8/1**
0PP/ **9** *5* **The Young Master**[216] 4464 4-11-9 **97** NoelFehily 68
(Neil Mulholland) *in rr: sme hdwy appr 4 out: sn wknd* **20/1**
043/ **10** *25* **Old Magic (IRE)**[226] 4272 8-11-4 **92** RichieMcLernon 38
(Sophie Leech) *led: hdd & wknd appr 4 out* **8/1**
100- **P** **Pour Changer (FR)**[69] 1106 8-10-9 **90** JPKiely[(7)]
(Stephen Hughes) *chsd ldrs early: wknd after 4th: t.o whn p.u bef 4 out* **16/1**

3m 55.8s (-14.80) **Going Correction** -0.80s/f (Firm)
WFA 4 from 5yo+ 9lb **11** Ran SP% **122.7**
Speed ratings (Par 103): **102,100,100,99,94 93,91,86,84,72**
toteswingers 1&2 £6.30, 2&3 £4.80, 1&3 £7.50 CSF £24.48 CT £87.63 TOTE £8.80: £2.40, £2.00, £2.00; EX 37.60 Trifecta £176.30 Pool: £2052.91 - 8.73 winning units..
Owner Tim Exell **Bred** Mr And Mrs Geoff Bonson **Trained** Condicote, Gloucs

FOCUS
A modest handicap run at a steady pace.

1712 32RED.COM STANDARD NATIONAL HUNT FLAT RACE (CONDITIONAL JOCKEYS' AND AMATEUR RIDERS' RACE) 2m 110y
5:20 (5:55) (Class 6) 4-6-Y-O **£1,559** (£457; £228; £114)

Form RPR
1 **Take A Bow** 4-11-1 0 PeterCarberry[(3)] 109+
(Nicky Henderson) *towards rr: hdwy on outside bnd 5f out: pushed along and hdwy 4f out: led over 2f out: styd on wl fnl f* **9/2**[2]
1/ **2** *2 ¾* **Southfield Vic (IRE)**[168] 5334 4-11-4 0 MissMNicholls[(7)] 112+
(Paul Nicholls) *trckd ldrs: wd into st bnd 5f out: pushed along and hdwy over 2f out: chsd wnr over 1f out: kpt on but a hld* **11/4**[1]
3 *4* **Master Butcher (IRE)**[157] 6-11-1 0 JoshuaMoore[(3)] 100
(Rebecca Curtis) *led after 2f: hdd 9f out: styd pressing ldr tl outpcd u.p 3f out: styd on again over 1f out and kpt on wl to take 3rd fnl 110yds: no imp on ldng duo* **10/1**
6- **4** *1 ¼* **Little Jon**[141] 270 5-10-11 0 RyanHatch[(7)] 99
(Nigel Twiston-Davies) *led 2f: styd chsng ldr tl led again 9f out: rdn over 3f out: hdd over 2f out: outpcd by ldng duo over 1f out: dropped to 4th fnl 110yds* **25/1**
5 *½* **Powerful Action (IRE)**[68] 1117 5-11-1 0 JamesBest[(3)] 98
(Philip Hobbs) *in rr: hdwy 7f out: pressed ldrs 3f out: styd on same pce fnl 2f* **5/1**[3]
6 *1* **Its A Long Road**[135] 5-11-1 0 MichealNolan[(3)] 97
(Tim Dennis) *t.k.h: chsd ldrs: rdn over 3f out: outpcd fnl 2f* **33/1**
7 *7* **Moorlands George** 5-11-1 0 MattGriffiths[(3)] 90
(Jeremy Scott) *in rr: hdwy to chse ldrs 1/2-way: wknd ins fnl 3f* **25/1**
2- **8** *1 ¼* **Radharc Nahabhainn (IRE)**[91] 862 5-10-11 0 NickSlatter[(7)] 89
(Fergal O'Brien) *chsd ldrs: hmpd on rails and lost position 6f out: kpt on frtom 3f out but nvr a threat* **8/1**
0/ **9** *shd* **Merchant Of Milan**[311] 2617 5-10-13 0 EDLinehan[(5)] 89
(Brendan Powell) *chsd ldrs: drvn 5f out: wknd over 3f out* **28/1**
1/6- **10** *6* **Johnny Og**[142] 239 4-11-4 0 OllieGarner[(7)] 90
(Martin Keighley) *in rr: sme hdwy on outer bnd 5f out: nvr rchd ldrs and no ch fnl 3f* **11/2**
05/ **11** *5* **Major Martin (IRE)**[189] 4970 4-11-1 0 GavinSheehan[(3)] 78
(Charlie Brooks) *chsd ldrs: hmpd in rails and lost pl 6f out: no ch after* **40/1**
0- **12** *nk* **Borkum (IRE)**[14] 1599 5-10-11 0 (t) MrCSmith[(7)] 77
(Philip Hobbs) *a in rr* **50/1**
13 *2 ¾* **Hearditbefore (IRE)**[122] 5-10-4 0 (p) MrStanSheppard[(7)] 68
(Matt Sheppard) *bhd most of way* **66/1**
14 *51* **Lord Farquaad** 4-10-11 0 (t) MissPJeffrey[(7)] 24
(Robin Dickin) *sn bhd: t.o fnl 5f* **66/1**

3m 51.72s (-13.28) **Going Correction** -0.80s/f (Firm) **14** Ran SP% **118.6**
Speed ratings: **99,97,95,95,95 94,91,90,90,87 85,85,83,59**
toteswingers 1&2 £3.50, 2&3 £6.70, 1&3 £6.30 CSF £15.66 TOTE £6.20: £2.20, £2.10, £2.90; EX 21.50 Trifecta £172.90 Pool: £1339.59 - 5.81 winning units..
Owner Michael Buckley **Bred** Upton Viva Stud **Trained** Upper Lambourn, Berks

FOCUS
Plenty of big stables were in opposition and this bumper was run at a fair pace with the front two looking useful.
T/Plt: £37.50 to a £1 stake. Pool of £93047.83 - 1809.30 winning tickets. T/Qpdt: £15.40 to a £1 stake. Pool of £5757.38 - 276.50 winning tickets. ST

1500 SEDGEFIELD (L-H)
Tuesday, October 1

OFFICIAL GOING: Good to firm (good in places) changing to good (good to firm in places) after race 1 (2.20)
Wind: fresh 1/2 against Weather: ffine but very breezy

1713 CUMMINS DIESEL DASH NOVICES' HURDLE (PAXTONS HURDLE SERIES QUALIFIER) (8 hdls) 2m 1f
2:20 (2:20) (Class 4) 4-Y-0+ **£3,119** (£915; £457; £228)

Form RPR
21- **1** **Saint Thomas (IRE)**[18] 1578 6-11-5 0 BrianHughes 121+
(John Mackie) *mde all: pushed out* **5/4**[1]
2 *4* **Wakanda (IRE)**[79] 978 4-11-5 0 RyanMania 117+
(Sue Smith) *mstke 1st: chsd ldrs: 2nd appr 2 out: kpt on same pce between last 2: no imp* **9/4**[2]
3 *5* **Downtown Boy (IRE)**[92] 5-10-12 0 PaddyBrennan 103
(Chris Grant) *mid-div: chsd ldrs 5th: one pce fr 2 out* **20/1**

The Form Book Jumps, Raceform Ltd, Compton, RG20 6NL.

4 7 **Satanic Beat (IRE)**[12] 4-10-12 0 BrianHarding 97
(Jedd O'Keeffe) *chsd ldrs: drvn 3 out: wknd after 2 out: j.lft last* 5/1[3]

4F- 5 4 **Exclusive Dancer**[27] 1496 4-10-5 0 BarryKeniry 85
(George Moore) *chsd ldrs: wknd 2 out* 12/1

44- 6 ¾ **The Lodge Road (IRE)**[35] 1415 5-10-12 0 (t) WilsonRenwick 91
(Martin Todhunter) *chsd ldrs: wknd 2 out* 22/1

2/ 7 15 **Omid**[118] 2613 5-10-12 0 HenryBrooke 76
(Evelyn Slack) *in rr: drvn 2nd: bhd fr 4th: t.o 3 out* 40/1

8 11 **District Attorney (IRE)**[34] 4-10-12 0 DougieCostello 65
(Chris Fairhurst) *in rr: bhd fr 3 out: t.o next* 33/1

- P **Touching History (IRE)**[68] 4-10-12 0 AndrewTinkler
(Tim Etherington) *t.k.h in rr: hmpd 1st: mstke and lost pl 4th: sn bhd: t.o 3 out: p.u bef next* 100/1

3m 58.7s (-8.20) **Going Correction** -0.25s/f (Good) 9 Ran SP% 115.1
Speed ratings (Par 105): **109,107,104,101,99 99,92,87,**
toteswingers 1&2 £1.70, 2&3 £2.50, 1&3 £13.20 CSF £4.04 TOTE £2.70: £1.50, £1.40, £1.60; EX 5.40 Trifecta £37.40 Pool: £1628.80 - 32.63 winning units..
Owner P Riley **Bred** S Coughlan **Trained** Church Broughton , Derbys

FOCUS
Shared bends and hurdles on outside. This modest opening novice hurdle saw six in with a chance of sorts turning for home, but they got sorted out from the penultimate flight and the form ought to work out.

1714 SANTANDER SUPPORTS J AMER & M SWEENEY NOVICES' HURDLE (PAXTONS HURDLE SERIES QUALIFIER) (10 hdls) 2m 5f 110y
2:50 (2:50) (Class 4) 4-Y-0+ **£3,119** (£915; £457; £228)

Form RPR
222- 1 **Bright Abbey**[11] 1467 5-11-5 125 LucyAlexander 110+
(Dianne Sayer) *chsd ldrs: shkn up 6th: chsd wnr appr 2 out: rdn and chalng whn nt fluent last: styd on to ld last 50yds* 6/4[1]

442- 2 ¾ **Cloudy Joker (IRE)**[26] 1500 5-10-12 105 JasonMaguire 99
(Donald McCain) *led: qcknd pce 7th: hit 2 out: jnd last: hdd and no ex in clsng stages* 9/2[3]

500/ 3 12 **Sohcahtoa (IRE)**[28] 5520 7-10-9 89 (p) JohnKington(3) 87
(Andrew Crook) *in rr: slipped bnd after 5th: hdwy 3 out: wnt modest 3rd appr 2 out: one pce* 66/1

530- 4 17 **Larteta (FR)**[20] 1565 4-10-9 106 JackQuinlan(3) 74
(Sarah Humphrey) *chsd ldr: rdn 3 out: wknd appr next: sn bhd* 7/4[2]

5 8 **Harrison's Cave**[41] 5-10-12 0 HenryBrooke 65
(Chris Grant) *trckd ldrs: rdn 3 out: lost pl appr next: sn bhd* 13/2

5m 6.7s (-7.90) **Going Correction** -0.25s/f (Good)
WFA 4 from 5yo+ 10lb 5 Ran SP% 109.4
Speed ratings (Par 105): **104,103,99,93,90**
CSF £8.50 TOTE £2.50: £1.70, £1.60; EX 6.20 Trifecta £37.80 Pool: £1943.26 - 38.55 winning units..
Owner Anthony White **Bred** Pendley Farm **Trained** Hackthorpe, Cumbria

FOCUS
This was markedly weakened by the withdrawal of hat-trick-seeking Koultas King. The winner was a stone off his best.

1715 DURHAM ARMY CADET FORCE H'CAP CHASE (16 fncs) 2m 4f
3:25 (3:25) (Class 4) (0-110,104) 4-Y-0+ **£3,768** (£1,106; £553; £276)

Form RPR
344- 1 **Civil Unrest (IRE)**[4] 1668 7-11-1 93 (p) BrianHarding 101+
(James Ewart) *led: j. slowly: reminders and hdd 3rd: led 5th: styd on fr 2 out: rdn and kpt on wl run-in* 9/4[1]

225- 2 4½ **Attycran (IRE)**[90] 866 8-11-5 104 (t) StephenMulqueen(7) 107+
(Maurice Barnes) *j.rt: chsd ldrs: led 3rd: hdd next: outpcd 9th: rdn and outpcd 12th: wnt 5 l 2nd between last 2: no imp* 5/2[2]

/64- 3 10 **Takaatuf (IRE)**[114] 679 7-11-10 102 BrianHughes 95
(John Wade) *w ldrs: led 4th: hdd next: rdn 3 out: wknd between last 2* 4/1[3]

1PP- 4 8 **Sycho Fred (IRE)**[44] 1300 12-9-7 78 oh1 (t) MrJHamilton(7) 65
(Mike Sowersby) *in tch: outpcd 9th: drvn next: sn bhd* 8/1

/66- 5 20 **Frith (IRE)**[108] 749 11-10-0 78 oh10 DougieCostello 55
(Lucy Normile) *racd wd: in tch: drvn and lost pl 9th: sn bhd: blnd 2 out: t.o: b.b.v* 12/1

464- U **Peak Seasons (IRE)**[38] 1377 10-10-3 86 JoeCornwall(5)
(Michael Chapman) *w ldr whn blnd and uns rdr 2nd* 8/1

4m 55.9s (-7.10) **Going Correction** -0.25s/f (Good) 6 Ran SP% 109.3
Speed ratings (Par 105): **104,102,98,95,87**
toteswingers 1&2 £2.20, 2&3 £1.10, 1&3 £2.00 CSF £8.14 TOTE £2.90: £1.50, £2.40; EX 8.40 Trifecta £22.70 Pool of £2004.20 - 65.95 winning units..
Owner J P L Ewart **Bred** D And Mrs Noonan **Trained** Langholm, Dumfries & G'way

FOCUS
A weak handicap in which the routine gallop lifted sharply around six from home. The winner was a stone of his best.

1716 C & A PUMPS NOVICES' H'CAP CHASE (13 fncs) 2m 110y
4:00 (4:00) (Class 5) (0-100,96) 4-Y-0+ **£2,209** (£648; £324; £162)

Form RPR
542- 1 **Sendiym (FR)**[21] 1395 6-10-9 79 (b) BrianHughes 93+
(Dianne Sayer) *chsd ldr: led 8th: drew clr fr 2 out: heavily eased nr fin* 6/4[1]

500- 2 9 **Cara Court (IRE)**[26] 1506 7-11-0 89 (p) SamanthaDrake(5) 93
(Joanne Foster) *j.rt: led: hdd 8th: lost pl 10th: kpt on fr 2 out: tk modest 2nd nr fin* 9/1

F1U- 3 nk **Turf Trivia**[100] 798 6-11-12 96 BarryKeniry 101
(George Moore) *wnt 2nd 10th: rdn next: one pce fr 2 out: lost 2nd nr line* 5/1[3]

060/ 4 7 **Newdane Dancer (IRE)**[207] 4633 6-11-2 86 HenryBrooke 82
(Dianne Sayer) *last whn mstke 1st: drvn and sme hdwy 8th: lost pl and reminders next* 8/1

500- 5 5 **Potters Dream (IRE)**[14] 1594 7-10-0 70 oh3 (t) PaddyBrennan 65
(Fergal O'Brien) *chsng ldrs whn hit 5th: reminders 10th: sn outpcd: 3rd whn mstke 2 out: sn wknd* 9/4[2]

4m 4.1s (-4.50) **Going Correction** -0.25s/f (Good) 5 Ran SP% 108.5
Speed ratings (Par 103): **100,95,95,92,89**
CSF £13.02 TOTE £2.30: £1.10, £3.00; EX 9.70 Trifecta £25.20 Pool: £2046.34 - 60.87 winning units..
Owner United Five Racing & Andrew Sayer **Bred** H H The Aga Khan's Studs Sc **Trained** Hackthorpe, Cumbria

FOCUS
Another weak handicap, run at solid early pace.

1717 JOHN DENHOLM MELDRUM MEMORIAL CLASSIC H'CAP HURDLE (9 hdls 1 omitted) 2m 4f
4:35 (4:35) (Class 4) (0-110,110) 4-Y-0+ **£3,195** (£992; £534)

Form RPR
243- 1 **Weybridge Light**[24] 1414 8-11-2 100 (b) PaddyBrennan 104+
(David Thompson) *chsd ldr: upsides on bit 2 out: sn led: rdn and kpt on run-in: all out* 8/1

454- 2 nk **Western Prize**[20] 1561 5-11-1 102 (v[1]) MichaelByrne(3) 105
(Tim Vaughan) *led: drvn 4 out: hdd sn after 2 out: upsides last: kpt on nr fin* 4/1[3]

3/4- 3 93 **Trust Thomas**[140] 280 5-11-4 102 BrianHughes 21
(Ann Hamilton) *chsd ldng pair: outpcd 4 out: sn lost pl and bhd: t.o next: eventually completed* 11/4[2]

0P5- B **Stand Clear**[26] 1506 8-10-4 88 LucyAlexander
(David Thompson) *b.d 1st* 16/1

011- B **Ben Cee Pee M (IRE)**[26] 1506 8-11-5 110 (v) CraigGallagher(7)
(Brian Ellison) *b.d 1st* 11/8[1]

/05- F **Total Assets**[119] 629 5-11-1 102 JohnKington(3)
(Simon Waugh) *4th whn fell 1st* 50/1

4m 46.6s (-6.10) **Going Correction** -0.25s/f (Good) 6 Ran SP% 107.7
Speed ratings (Par 105): **102,101,64, ,**
toteswingers 1&2 £3.80, 2&3 £1.70, 1&3 £3.30 CSF £36.15 TOTE £7.00: £2.60, £2.10; EX 34.80 Trifecta £86.10 Pool: £3261.52 - 28.38 winning units..
Owner J A Moore **Bred** Hascombe And Valiant Studs **Trained** Bolam, Co Durham

FOCUS
Carnage after the very first flight saw 50% of the runners depart and so this form should be treated with some caution.

1718 COMPARE BOOKMAKERS AT BOOKMAKERS.CO.UK "HANDS AND HEELS" NOVICES' H'CAP HURDLE (C'TIONALS/A'TEURS) (10 hdls) 2m 5f 110y
5:10 (5:10) (Class 5) (0-100,100) 4-Y-0+ **£1,949** (£572; £286; £143)

Form RPR
2/5- 1 **My Oh Mount Brown (IRE)**[27] 1495 6-11-1 92 MrBGibbs(3) 99+
(Tim Vaughan) *gave problems leaving paddock: w ldr: led 4th: qcknd pce next: styd on wl fr 2 out: drvn out* 9/2[3]

/42- 2 3¾ **Perfect Timing**[9] 1631 5-11-1 92 (v) MrRobertHawker(3) 96
(Johnny Farrelly) *t.k.h: sn trcking ldrs: hit 5th: drvn and hit 7th: kpt on fr 2 out: tk 2nd run-in* 11/8[1]

23- 3 2¼ **Sultana Belle (IRE)**[36] 1407 5-11-9 100 MrBGCrawford(3) 101
(S R B Crawford, Ire) *trckd ldrs: handy 2nd appr 2 out: swtchd lft between last 2: wknd run-in* 7/2[2]

005- 4 8 **Nurse Ratched (IRE)**[49] 1265 4-10-3 82 MrRHogg(5) 76
(Fergal O'Brien) *t.k.h: trckd ldrs: drvn 3 out: wknd appr next* 11/2

0P4- 5 2¼ **Photogenique (FR)**[45] 1280 10-9-9 74 oh10.. MissGeorgiaHenderson(5) 66
(Rob Summers) *in rr: detached 3rd: t.o 6th: styd on fr 2 out: 6th last: kpt on wl* 20/1

04F- 6 8 **Tim's Approach (IRE)**[5] 1664 8-10-0 74 oh6 (t) StephenMulqueen 59
(William Young Jnr) *set v stdy pce: t.k.h: hdd 4th: drvn 3 out: wknd appr next* 12/1

0FP- 7 8 **Larkhall**[27] 1497 6-9-11 74 oh8 (t) MrRLindsay(3) 51
(Mike Sowersby) *t.k.h in rr: hdwy 5th: drvn and lost pl after 3 out* 40/1

5m 18.1s (3.50) **Going Correction** -0.25s/f (Good)
WFA 4 from 5yo+ 10lb 7 Ran SP% 112.8
Speed ratings (Par 103): **83,81,80,77,77 74,71**
toteswingers 1&2 £1.80, 2&3 £1.60, 1&3 £1.60 CSF £11.21 TOTE £5.70: £2.80, £1.10; EX 12.70 Trifecta £33.30 Pool: £3321.33 - 74.69 winning units..
Owner Craig Buckingham **Bred** James Dillon **Trained** Aberthin, Vale of Glamorgan

■ Stewards' Enquiry : Miss Georgia Henderson ten-day ban: failed to take all reasonable and permissable measures to obtain best possible placing (Oct 18,22,24,26, Nov 14,15,18,24,30, Dec 1)

FOCUS
An ordinary "hands and heels" novice handicap in which they went an overly steady pace early.

1719 BOOKMAKERS FREE BETS AT BOOKMAKERS.CO.UK MARES' STANDARD OPEN NATIONAL HUNT FLAT RACE 2m 1f
5:40 (5:40) (Class 6) 4-6-Y-0 **£1,559** (£457; £228; £114)

Form RPR
006- 1 **Wymeswold**[112] 715 6-10-9 0 KielanWoods(3) 100+
(Michael Mullineaux) *trckd ldrs: handy 2nd over 3f out: led over 1f out: dived rt jst ins fnl f: rdn out* 14/1

2 3 **Lilywhite Gesture (IRE)**[21] 1560 4-10-12 0 PaddyBrennan 98+
(Fergal O'Brien) *hdwy to trck ldrs 10f out: led 6f out: hdd over 1f out: swtchd lft jst ins fnl f: kpt on same pce* 6/1[3]

5- 3 15 **Lacocodanza**[35] 1420 4-10-12 0 BarryKeniry 84
(George Moore) *chsd ldrs: drvn over 3f out: sn outpcd: kpt on to take modest 3rd last 75yds* 8/1

4 8 **Alys Rock (IRE)** 4-10-12 0 RyanMahon 77
(Michael Appleby) *sn trcking ldrs: wnt modest 3rd over 2f out: wknd ins fnl f* 4/1[2]

0/0- 5 3½ **Mieuxmix (IRE)**[145] 187 4-10-5 0 MrJHamilton(7) 74
(Peter Niven) *hld up wl in tch: drvn 5f out: lost pl 3f out* 8/1

43- 6 3¼ **Ovilia (IRE)**[23] 1531 4-10-12 0 JasonMaguire 71
(Donald McCain) *trckd ldrs: drvn 7f out: lost pl 4f out* 7/4[1]

7 3¾ **Furie Glory (IRE)**[496] 419 5-10-12 0 DougieCostello 67
(Denis Coakley) *led tl 6f out: wknd over 2f out* 8/1

8 5 **Bracing** 4-10-12 0 PeterBuchanan 63
(Susan Corbett) *in rr: bhd and drvn 7f out: nvr on terms* 40/1

3m 56.1s (-5.20) **Going Correction** -0.25s/f (Good) 8 Ran SP% 113.1
Speed ratings: **102,100,93,89,88 86,84,82**
toteswingers 1&2 £5.10, 2&3 £0.00, 1&3 £9.80 CSF £92.60 TOTE £13.80: £3.10, £1.80, £1.60; EX 154.40 Trifecta £1007.50 Pool: £1916.03 - 1.42 winning units..
Owner The Hon Mrs S Pakenham **Bred** Mrs C S Wilson **Trained** Alpraham, Cheshire

FOCUS
The first pair came clear late on in this moderate mares' bumper.
T/Plt: £22.90 to a £1 stake. Pool of £66607.13 - 2120.89 winning tickets. T/Qpdt: £14.30 to a £1 stake. Pool of £3878.0 - 200.10 winning tickets. WG

1720 - 1726a (Foreign Racing) - See Raceform Interactive

1575 BANGOR-ON-DEE (L-H)

Thursday, October 3

OFFICIAL GOING: Good changing to good to soft (soft in places) after race 1 (2.20) changing to soft after race 4 (3.50)

Wind: Nil Weather: Heavy Rain

1727 RIPPLEFFECT JUVENILE HURDLE (9 hdls) 2m 1f
2:20 (2:22) (Class 4) 3-Y-O **£3,249** (£954; £477; £238)

Form RPR

1 **Dispour (IRE)**[120] 3-10-12 0 .... JasonMaguire 112+
(Donald McCain) *mde all: mstke 4 out: rdn appr 2 out whn jnd: plld out more fnl 100yds: kpt on wl towards fin* **8/15**[1]

2 1 ¾ **Herod The Great**[38] 3-10-12 0 .... RobertThornton 112+
(Alan King) *nt fluent 1st: prom: racd in cl 2nd pl fr 2nd: upsides pressing wnr whn hit 2 out: sn rdn: nt qckn run-in: no ex towards fin* **5/2**[2]

3 31 **Nellie Forbush**[49] 3-10-5 0 .... PaulMoloney 86
(Sophie Leech) *hld up: j. slowly 1st: wnt mod 3rd appr 4 out: lost grnd on front pair after: allowed to coast home and nvr a danger* **16/1**[3]

4 50 **Moaning Butcher**[38] 3-10-12 0 ....(v) LeeEdwards 45
(Dave Roberts) *j. poorly: chsd wnr to 2nd: nvr travelled: rdn appr 5th: wknd bef 4 out: t.o* **22/1**

P **Big John Cannon (IRE)**[86] 3-10-12 0 .... WillKennedy
(Sarah-Jayne Davies) *t.k.h: hld up: rdn and bhd after 4th: sn toiling: lost tch bef 4 out: t.o whn p.u bef 2 out* **28/1**

4m 23.0s (12.10) **Going Correction** +0.65s/f (Soft) 5 Ran SP% **107.5**
Speed ratings (Par 103): **97,96,81,58,**
CSF £2.07 TOTE £1.60: £1.10, £1.20; EX 2.40 Trifecta £4.90 Pool: £2123.78 - 322.10 winning units..
Owner Paul & Clare Rooney **Bred** His Highness The Aga Khan's Studs S C **Trained** Cholmondeley, Cheshire

FOCUS
None of these had jumped hurdles in public, and it rained quite hard before the off. The going was altered from good after this contest. Punters only wanted to know about two of these, and they pulled miles clear. They look above-average early season juveniles and should rate higher.

1728 BREWIN DOLPHIN NOVICES' CHASE (15 fncs) 2m 4f 110y
2:50 (2:50) (Class 4) 4-Y-0+ **£3,898** (£1,144; £572; £286)

Form RPR

12P/ 1 **Dursey Sound (IRE)**[264] [3619] 5-10-12 0 .... APMcCoy 141+
(Jonjo O'Neill) *trckd ldrs: j.big 3rd: mstke 11th: wnt cl 2nd after 3 out: mstke and led 2 out: pressed appr last: styd on and in command towards fin* **13/8**[1]

/23- 2 1 ¾ **Foundry Square (IRE)**[26] [1518] 7-10-12 0 .... SamTwiston-Davies 135
(Nigel Twiston-Davies) *cl up: rdn and sltly outpcd appr 2 out: clsd to take 2nd and chal bef last: no ex towards fin* **16/1**

140/ 3 16 **Boyfromnowhere (IRE)**[243] [3983] 6-10-12 0 .... TomScudamore 123+
(Rebecca Curtis) *led to 4th: continued to chse ldr: regained ld 3 out: pushed along and hdd 2 out: wknd fr last* **9/4**[2]

3/1- 4 47 **Jimbill (IRE)**[26] [1518] 7-11-5 0 .... RichardJohnson 110
(Tim Vaughan) *handy: nt fluent 1st: blnd 2nd: led 4th: mstke and hdd 3 out: stopped qckly: eased* **3/1**[3]

5 41 **Terry Tibbs (IRE)**[137] [399] 8-10-12 0 .... RichieMcGrath 41
(J T R Dreaper, Ire) *a bhd: lost tch 9th: t.o* **50/1**

000/ P **Son Of Flicka**[264] [3612] 9-10-12 0 .... NoelFehily
(Tony Coyle) *hld up: nt fluent 5th: lost tch bef 11th: t.o whn p.u bef 3 out* **9/1**

060- P **My Friend Riquet (FR)**[6] [1673] 6-10-12 0 .... LeeEdwards
(Dave Roberts) *hld up: niggled along after 6th: rdn appr 8th: struggling 10th: t.o whn p.u bef 2 out* **150/1**

5m 17.5s (8.40) **Going Correction** +0.65s/f (Soft)
WFA 4 from 5yo+ 10lb 7 Ran SP% **112.4**
Speed ratings (Par 105): **110,109,103,85,69 ,**
toteswingers 1&2 £2.00, 2&3 £10.80, 1&3 £2.20 CSF £24.64 TOTE £3.80: £2.60, £3.90; EX 16.00 Trifecta £81.00 Pool: £995.19 - 9.20 winning units..
Owner John P McManus **Bred** Billy Kenneally **Trained** Cheltenham, Gloucs

FOCUS
A decent contest for the time of year. The cosy winner is rated in line with the best of his hurdle form and should rate higher.

1729 WREXHAM LAGER H'CAP HURDLE (9 hdls) 2m 1f
3:20 (3:22) (Class 4) (0-120,119) 4-Y-0+ **£4,223** (£1,240; £620; £310)

Form RPR

0/0- 1 **Tidal Way (IRE)**[153] [93] 4-11-9 **116** ....(p) NoelFehily 122+
(Charlie Longsdon) *in tch: wnt cl 2nd 5th: led jst bef 2 out: rdn clr bef last: styd on wl* **3/1**[2]

554- 2 3 **Jolly Roger (IRE)**[42] [1342] 6-11-10 **117** .... LeeEdwards 120+
(Tony Carroll) *prom: mstke 3 out: sn rdn: big effrt 2 out: styd on to take 2nd bef last: no imp on wnr* **4/1**[3]

5U0- 3 6 **The Weatherman (IRE)**[47] [1285] 6-10-12 **105** .... HenryBrooke 104
(Donald McCain) *led: mstke 2nd: rdn and hdd jst bef 2 out where mstke: wl hld in 3rd whn mstke last* **5/1**

221/ 4 ¾ **Pippa Greene**[505] [298] 9-11-6 **118** .... NicodeBoinville(5) 113
(Nicky Henderson) *t.k.h: hld up in rr: hdwy 4 out: rdn whn chsng ldrs after 3 out: one pce and no imp bef 2 out: kpt on towards fin whn no ch* **5/2**[1]

51U- 5 4 ½ **Faith Jicaro (IRE)**[63] [1173] 6-11-7 **114** .... DonalDevereux 105
(James Unett) *hld up in midfield: pushed along 3 out: sn wknd* **16/1**

3/4- 6 10 **Smadynium (FR)**[138] [371] 5-11-8 **115** .... JasonMaguire 97
(Donald McCain) *t.k.h: hld up in midfield: wknd 3 out* **8/1**

0/ 7 1 ½ **Hartside (GER)**[86] [937] 4-11-0 **114** .... MrRWinks(7) 95
(Peter Winks) *hld up: struggling bef 3 out: nvr a threat* **33/1**

01F/ 8 14 **Natural High (IRE)**[27] [2054] 8-11-12 **119** ....(t) APMcCoy 87
(Sean Curran) *prom: mstke 4 out: rdn bef 3 out: sn wknd* **16/1**

4m 23.3s (12.40) **Going Correction** +0.85s/f (Soft)
WFA 4 from 5yo+ 9lb 8 Ran SP% **116.1**
Speed ratings (Par 105): **104,102,99,99,97 92,91,85**
toteswingers 1&2 £3.70, 2&3 £5.90, 1&3 £4.30 CSF £16.07 CT £57.63 TOTE £2.40: £1.10, £1.80, £2.50; EX 20.00 Trifecta £160.30 Pool: £1147.99 - 5.36 winning units..
Owner Harold Peachey & Saddleworth Players **Bred** Tallyho Stud, J Delahooke & P Twoomey **Trained** Over Norton, Oxon

FOCUS
Quite a competitive event. The winner improved towards the level of his best Flat form.

1730 BREWIN DOLPHIN H'CAP CHASE (15 fncs) 2m 4f 110y
3:50 (3:51) (Class 3) (0-140,133) 4-Y-0+ **£6,498** (£1,908; £954; £477)

Form RPR

PPF/ 1 **Hazy Tom (IRE)**[160] [5547] 7-11-12 **133** .... NoelFehily 142+
(Charlie Longsdon) *mde all: mstke 10th: rdn appr last: drew clr and styd on wl run-in* **11/8**[1]

F/2- 2 9 **Lamboro Lad (IRE)**[156] [39] 8-11-2 **123** ....(tp) TomO'Brien 124
(Peter Bowen) *chsd wnr: chal fr 3 out: rdn bef 2 out where stl ev ch: one pce fr last* **3/1**[3]

112- 3 16 **Lucky Landing (IRE)**[33] [1470] 7-11-11 **132** .... RichardJohnson 123
(Tony Coyle) *hld up in rr: wnt 3rd 4 out: rdn and no imp on ldrs after 3 out* **5/1**

3P0/ 4 27 **Gus Macrae (IRE)**[181] [5160] 9-11-7 **128** ....(tp) APMcCoy 100
(Rebecca Curtis) *chsd ldrs: j. slowly 1st: reminder bef 10th: dropped to rr 4 out: sn wknd: t.o* **11/4**[2]

5m 21.8s (12.70) **Going Correction** +0.85s/f (Soft) 4 Ran SP% **110.4**
Speed ratings (Par 107): **109,105,99,89**
CSF £5.93 TOTE £2.90; EX 6.70 Trifecta £21.60 Pool: £1088.21 - 37.71 winning units..
Owner Alan Halsall **Bred** Messrs T & J Hayes **Trained** Over Norton, Oxon

FOCUS
Fairly useful form but probably not a race to get carried away with.

1731 STAN JAMES MARES' NOVICES' HURDLE (11 hdls) 2m 4f
4:20 (4:25) (Class 4) 4-Y-0+ **£3,249** (£954; £477; £238)

Form RPR

6/4- 1 **Mini Muck**[40] [1373] 7-10-10 0 .... SamTwiston-Davies 99+
(Nigel Twiston-Davies) *hld up: hdwy 4 out: swtchd rt between last 2: led jst bef last: styd on wl to draw clr run-in: won gng away* **11/1**

212- 2 8 **Me And Ben (IRE)**[25] [1529] 6-11-3 100 ....(t) PaddyBrennan 100
(Fergal O'Brien) *trckd ldrs: led appr 2 out: rdn and hdd jst bef last: unable to go w wnr run-in and no ch* **2/1**[2]

/12- 3 6 **Great Oak (IRE)**[42] [1347] 7-11-3 108 .... RichardJohnson 93
(Tim Vaughan) *hld up: hdwy 4 out: effrt and tried to chal 2 out: nt qckn between last 2: one pce fr last* **13/8**[1]

46- 4 5 **Possibly Flora**[23] [1552] 8-10-7 0 .... MichealNolan(3) 81
(Richard Woollacott) *chsd ldr: led briefly appr 2 out: wknd bef last* **50/1**

5- 5 7 **I Told You So (IRE)**[66] [1132] 4-10-10 0 .... AdrianLane 73
(Donald McCain) *hld up: rdn appr 2 out: no imp* **25/1**

- 6 2 **Anchoretta Eyre (IRE)**[592] 7-10-10 0 .... AlainCawley 71
(Fergal O'Brien) *led: rdn and hdd appr 2 out: sn wknd* **33/1**

3/ 7 43 **Carolina Wren**[173] [5295] 4-10-10 0 .... SamJones 28
(Renee Robeson) *trckd ldrs: rdn and j. awkwardly 4 out: sn wknd: t.o* **3/1**[3]

/60- P **Rolling Dough (IRE)**[114] [717] 5-10-10 0 .... RichieMcLernon
(Sophie Leech) *hld up: mstke 3rd: struggling whn j.rt 4 out: t.o whn p.u bef 2 out* **66/1**

5m 20.8s (28.80) **Going Correction** +1.05s/f (Soft)
WFA 4 from 5yo+ 10lb 8 Ran SP% **115.0**
Speed ratings (Par 105): **84,80,78,76,73 72,55,**
toteswingers 1&2 £5.50, 2&3 £1.70, 1&3 £4.90 CSF £33.88 TOTE £9.60: £2.50, £1.10, £1.10; EX 36.30 Trifecta £143.40 Pool: £2221.36 - 11.61 winning units..
Owner N A Twiston-Davies **Bred** N A Twiston-Davies **Trained** Naunton, Gloucs

FOCUS
A modest mares' event rated through the second.

1732 MATTHEW CLARK STANDARD NATIONAL HUNT FLAT RACE (CONDITIONAL JOCKEYS AND AMATEUR RIDERS) 2m 1f
4:50 (4:54) (Class 6) 4-6-Y-O **£1,711** (£498; £249)

Form RPR

1 **Cloud Brook (IRE)**[138] 5-10-11 0 .... PatrickCorbett(7) 115+
(Rebecca Curtis) *hld up: hdwy 6f out: led 4f out: drew clr fnl f: styd on wl* **1/1**[1]

2- 2 10 **A Tail Of Intrigue (IRE)**[29] [1499] 5-10-13 0 .... HarryDerham(5) 103
(Ian Williams) *prom: pushed along 3f out: wnt 2nd 2f out: rdn and hung lft over 1f out: no ch w wnr fnl f* **8/1**[3]

531- 3 2 ¾ **When In Roam (IRE)**[38] [1392] 4-10-11 0 .... CiaranMckee(7) 100
(John O'Shea) *in tch: clsd 9f out: led 6f out: rdn and hdd 4f out: one pce over 1f out* **4/1**[2]

50- 4 15 **Sava Bridge (IRE)**[16] [1599] 6-10-11 0 .... MrGBranton(7) 85
(Paul Henderson) *led: hdd 6f out: rdn and wknd over 2f out* **25/1**

5 5 **Gonalston Cloud (IRE)** 6-11-1 0 .... AdamWedge(3) 80
(Nick Kent) *hld up in rr: outpcd over 4f out: nvr a threat* **40/1**

6 1 ¾ **Shantou Tiger (IRE)** 4-10-11 0 .... NickSlatter(7) 78
(Donald McCain) *hld up: struggling over 4f out: nvr a threat* **4/1**[2]

7 dist **Our Dawn** 5-10-8 0 .... KielanWoods(3)
(Michael Mullineaux) *prom: rdn and lost pl qckly over 9f out: t.o* **14/1**

4m 21.6s (16.30) **Going Correction** +1.05s/f (Soft)
WFA 4 from 5yo+ 9lb 7 Ran SP% **114.1**
Speed ratings: **103,98,97,89,87 86,**
toteswingers 1&2 £1.70, 2&3 £2.30, 1&3 £1.40 CSF £10.11 TOTE £2.20: £1.20, £2.30; EX 7.60 Trifecta £16.20 Pool: £2111.84 - 97.50 winning units..
Owner R J H Geffen **Bred** Edward & Mrs Bernadette Walsh **Trained** Newport, Dyfed

FOCUS
Not a competitive bumper but the winner looks a decent recruit.
T/Plt: £17.30 to a £1 stake. Pool of £60572.45 - 2548.06 winning tickets. T/Qpdt: £7.90 to a £1 stake. Pool: £3094.35 - 288.60 winning tickets. DO

1733 - 1739a (Foreign Racing) - See Raceform Interactive

1607 AUTEUIL (L-H)

Thursday, October 3

OFFICIAL GOING: Turf: very soft

1740a PRIX DE SALERS (CHASE) (CLAIMER) (5YO+) (TURF) 2m 5f 110y
11:45 (11:45) 5-Y-0+ **£8,975** (£4,487; £2,617; £1,776; £841)

RPR

1 **River Choice (FR)**[20] 10-11-0 0 ....(b) GeoffreyRe(9) 130
(Yannick Fouin, France) **19/10**[1]

2 4 ½ **Sous Officier (FR)**[34] [1464] 7-10-6 0 ....(p) AnthonyCardine(8) 117
(G Cherel, France) **33/10**[2]

3 4 **Anik De Maspie (FR)**[108] 11-10-1 0 ....(p) HugoLucas(9) 109
(E Leray, France) **33/10**[2]

4 *7* **Osso Bello (FR)**[15] 5-10-12 0.. RegisSchmidlin 104
(F-M Cottin, France) **73/10**[3]
5 *3* **Boulevard Auteuil (FR)**[27] 5-10-8 0....................(p) NicolasChevreux(9) 106
(T Civel, France) **13/1**
6 *dist* **Politeo (FR)**[37] 1424 7-11-3 0.. JamesReveley
(Nick Williams) *hld up: dropped to last 5 out: rdn and bhd fr 4 out: t.o after 2 out but completed for remote 6th* **17/1**
7 *6* **Temoin Du Calif (FR)**[15] 6-10-12 0.......................... JonathanPlouganou
(Mme I Pacault, France) **18/1**
8 *15* **Prio Royal (FR)**[8] 5-10-10 0.......................................(p) RaymondO'Brien
(Y-M Porzier, France) **18/1**
P **Roi Du Tango (FR)**[1589] 7-10-6 0............................ VincentRoisnard(8)
(J Bigot, France) **56/1**

5m 37.01s (-9.99) **9** Ran SP% **118.0**
PARI-MUTUEL (all including 1 euro stake): WIN 2.90; PLACE 1.20, 1.50, 1.30; DF 7.40; SF 11.80.
Owner Maurice Lamour **Bred** *unknown **Trained** France

1741a PRIX PIOMARES (HURDLE) (CONDITIONS) (3YO COLTS & GELDINGS) (TURF) 2m 1f 110y
12:15 (12:18) 3-Y-O **£18,731** (£9,365; £5,463; £3,707; £1,756)

RPR
1 **Le Rocher (FR)**[123] 614 3-10-6 0.................................... JamesReveley 125
(Nick Williams) *midfield: clsd 3 out: pushed along to chal and led 2 out: hung lft appr last and jnd: rdn on landing: styd on strly and asserted flat* **18/5**[3]
2 *3* **L'Ami Serge (IRE)**[21] 3-10-6 0.. JacquesRicou 122
(G Macaire, France) **33/10**[2]
3 *8* **Mannish Boy (FR)**[21] 3-10-3 0.. GregoryAdam 111
(F-M Cottin, France) **18/1**
4 *2 ½* **Bullet Tooth (IRE)**[21] 3-10-3 0.................................. CyrilleGombeau 109
(G Cherel, France) **10/1**
5 *½* **Kenasie (FR)**[21] 3-10-3 0.. JonathanNattiez 108
(J-P Gallorini, France) **11/2**
6 *4* **Alleu (FR)** 3-10-6 0 ow3.. JonathanPlouganou 107
(Mme I Pacault, France) **48/1**
7 *2* **Sultan Silk (FR)**[8] 3-10-3 0.. MorganRegairaz 102
(T Doumen, France) **80/1**
8 *2 ½* **Savanas (FR)**[21] 3-10-3 0...(b¹) GeoffreyRe 100
(Yannick Fouin, France) **57/1**
9 *dist* **Mick Staraco (FR)**[21] 3-10-3 0..............................(b¹) AlexandreSeigneul
(Mme E Siavy-Julien, France) **186/1**
10 *dist* **Tyriac (FR)**[21] 3-10-3 0.................................... MlleMaelleDaubry-Barbier
(J-P Gallorini, France) **79/1**
P **Sarjinsky (IRE)**[164] 3-10-6 0 ow3.. SylvainDupuis
(Mlle C Comte, France) **79/1**
P **Lie To Me (FR)**[21] 3-10-3 0.. YohannBourgois
(E Lellouche, France) **66/1**
F **Aladin Du Chenet (FR)**[21] 3-10-6 0.................................... RegisSchmidlin
(M Rolland, France) **5/2**[1]
P **Orcenhac (FR)** 3-10-3 0..(b¹) ErvanChazelle
(C Scandella, France) **66/1**
P **Ascott Rock (FR)** 3-10-3 0......................................(b¹) Jean-LucBeaunez
(Mme P Butel, France) **40/1**

4m 14.09s (254.09) **15** Ran SP% **116.8**
PARI-MUTUEL (all including 1 euro stake): WIN 4.60; PLACE 2.40, 1.90, 3.70; DF 8.10; SF 15.00.
Owner John White & Anne Underhill **Bred** Mme Sylvie Ringler And Roger Frieh **Trained** George Nympton, Devon

1742a PRIX BAYONNET (CHASE) (CONDITIONS) (4YO) (TURF) 2m 5f 110y
1:20 (1:23) 4-Y-O **£25,365** (£12,682; £7,398; £5,020; £2,378)

RPR
1 **Milord Thomas (FR)**[20] 4-10-6 0.................................... MorganRegairaz 125
(D Bressou, France) **4/1**[3]
2 *5* **The Reader (FR)**[116] 4-10-8 0............................(p) JonathanPlouganou 122
(J-P Gallorini, France) **17/1**
3 *3* **Notario Has (FR)**[187] 5026 4-10-10 0.............................. JacquesRicou 121
(P Peltier, France) **14/5**[1]
4 *2* **Pour Toi Georges (FR)**[21] 4-10-6 0.................................. WilfridDenuault 115
(E Leenders, France) **20/1**
5 *20* **Silver Chop (FR)**[9] 4-10-10 0.. BenoitGicquel 99
(F Nicolle, France) **63/10**
6 *1 ½* **Sanouva (FR)**[159] 5584 4-10-8 0.................................... JonathanNattiez 96
(J-P Gallorini, France) **8/1**
7 *10* **Vent Sombre (FR)**[122] 4-10-8 0...................................... CyrilleGombeau 86
(G Cherel, France) **3/1**[2]
8 *3 ½* **Rio De Sivola (FR)**[34] 1465 4-10-6 0 ow3.......................... JamesReveley 80
(Nick Williams) *restrained and hld up in last: several untidy jumps: hdwy into midfield after 3 out: rdn after 2 out: sn outpcd and btn: eased and t.o* **32/1**
9 *4* **Forgeon (FR)**[21] 4-10-8 0.. JulienTabary 78
(T Civel, France) **20/1**
P **Tell Everyone (FR)**[21] 4-10-10 0...................................... BertrandThelier
(G Cherel, France) **47/1**

5m 44.96s (-2.04) **10** Ran SP% **116.3**
PARI-MUTUEL (all including 1 euro stake): WIN 5.00; PLACE 2.00, 3.30, 1.80; DF 41.40; SF 83.90.
Owner Mme Magalen Bryant **Bred** S Boucheron **Trained** France

1524 FONTWELL (L-H)
Friday, October 4

OFFICIAL GOING: Good (good to soft in places; 6.6)
Wind: strong behind Weather: overcast

1743 SHOREHAM PORT AUTHORITY JUVENILE MAIDEN HURDLE (9 hdls) 2m 2f 110y
2:10 (2:11) (Class 4) 3-Y-O **£3,119** (£915; £457; £228)

Form RPR
1 **Halling's Wish**[49] 3-10-9 0.. JoshuaMoore(3) 104+
(Gary Moore) *hld up towards rr: hdwy 4th: led sn after 3 out: stmbld bdly next and rdr lost iron (rcvrd jst bef last): drvn run-in: styd on wl towards fin* **10/1**
2- 2 *1 ½* **Instinctual**[36] 1439 3-10-12 0.. AlainCawley 99
(Brendan Powell) *mstke 1st: in last pair after: hdwy appr 6th: rdn to chse ldng pair after 3 out: ev ch last: kpt on but no ex towards fin* **7/2**[2]
3- 3 *13* **Unidexter (IRE)**[12] 1624 3-10-12 0.............................. MarcGoldstein 88
(Sheena West) *mid-div whn mstke 1st: in last pair: hdwy appr 6th: rdn after 3 out: chsd ldng pair next: ev ch last: kpt on but no ex towards fin* **8/1**
2- 4 *8* **Alanjou (FR)**[26] 1524 3-10-12 0.. TomO'Brien 80
(Jamie Snowden) *hung rt thrght: prom: led after 6th: j.rt next: rdn and hdd sn after 3 out: wknd next* **1/1**[1]
332- 5 *½* **Karl Marx (IRE)**[34] 1473 3-10-12 94.............................. TommyPhelan 82
(Mark Gillard) *mid-div: blnd 3rd: rdn along fr after 5th: nvr a threat* **50/1**
26- 6 *1* **Vergality Ridge (IRE)**[36] 1439 3-10-7 0........................ CharlieWallis(5) 79
(Ronald Harris) *trckd ldrs: mstke 1st: rdn after 3 out: wknd bef next* **80/1**
56- 7 *42* **Fiachra (IRE)**[12] 1624 3-10-12 0.. DavidBass 41
(Natalie Lloyd-Beavis) *led by handler to s: led: wandered abt at hurdles: hdd after 5th: rdn after next: wknd bef 3 out: t.o* **150/1**
0- 8 *7* **Dude Alert (IRE)**[26] 1524 3-10-9 0.................................. AdamWedge(3) 35
(Anna Newton-Smith) *in tch: drvn along fr after 3rd: bhd fr 6th: t.o* **100/1**
0- 9 *3* **Day In Day Out**[25] 1536 3-10-12 0.............................. AndrewThornton 32
(Seamus Mullins) *mid-div tl wknd appr 3 out: t.o* **33/1**
U **Mighty Thor**[59] 3-10-12 0.. LeightonAspell
(Lydia Richards) *hld up bhd: nt fluent whn stmbld bdly and uns rdr 2nd* **66/1**
P **Maypole Joe (IRE)**[230] 3-10-12 0...................................... TomCannon
(Raymond York) *a towards rr: t.o whn p.u after 3 out* **80/1**
P **Mick Duggan**[35] 3-10-12 0.. NickScholfield
(Simon Hodgson) *in tch: nt fluent 1st: pckd bdly 2nd: nvr really travelling after: reminders after 4th: dropped to rr qckly: p.u after next* **11/2**[3]

4m 23.5s (-10.80) **Going Correction** -0.65s/f (Firm) **12** Ran SP% **118.3**
Speed ratings (Par 103): **96,95,89,86,86 85,68,65,64, ,**
toteswingers 1&2 £7.80, 1&3 £7.70, 2&3 £6.70 CSF £45.43 TOTE £12.00: £3.00, £1.30, £2.40; EX 62.60 Trifecta £242.80 Pool: £1,149.66 - 3.55 winning units..
Owner WBC Partnership **Bred** B R Marsden **Trained** Lower Beeding, W Sussex

FOCUS
Fences at full width, hurdles inner, and bottom bend common. Rail movement increased chases by 15yds per circuit. There was 5mm of overnight rain and the ground was described as good to soft, good in places prior to this modest juvenile maiden. The winner is rated a bit better than the bare result.

1744 NICOLA COY APPRECIATION SOCIETY BREAKTHROUGH NOVICES' CHASE (16 fncs) 2m 6f
2:40 (2:40) (Class 4) 4-Y-O+ **£4,659** (£1,446; £779)

Form RPR
P6U/ 1 **Kings Lodge**[217] 4504 7-11-4 115.................................. AndrewTinkler 124+
(Nicky Henderson) *disp ld tl trckd ldrs after 3rd: prom 7th: led 4 out: in command fr next: rdn after last: styd on wl: eased nr fin* **5/2**[2]
0/2- 2 *6* **Ski Sunday**[43] 1343 8-11-4 117....................................(t) RichardJohnson 116
(Tim Vaughan) *disp ld tl trckd ldr 2nd and mstke: led after 7th: rdn and hdd and dropped to 3rd 3 out: sn bk chsng wnr: styd on same pce fr next* **7/2**[3]
5/5- 3 *7* **Dirty Bertie (FR)**[17] 1597 7-11-4 0.............................. TomScudamore 111
(David Bridgwater) *j.lft at times: disp tl led after 3rd: wnt lft 6th: hdd after next: trckd ldrs: rdn bk into 3rd whn hit 3 out: kpt on same pce fr next* **7/1**
100/ U **Virginia Ash (IRE)**[170] 5354 5-11-4 0..............................(b¹) JoeTizzard
(Colin Tizzard) *disputing ld whn mstke and uns rdr 2nd* **2/1**[1]
FP1- P **Old Dreams (IRE)**[12] 1626 7-11-4 100..............................(t) TomCannon
(Nick Gifford) *trckd ldrs: pushed along fr 10th: rdn to chal 4 out: wknd bef next: p.u bef 2 out: b.b.v* **8/1**
P- P **Silent Owner**[12] 1625 5-10-8 0...................................... KielanWoods(3)
(Paddy Butler) *hld up bhd ldrs: blnd 6th: lost tch fr 8th: t.o whn p.u bef 3 out* **150/1**

5m 43.5s (0.50) **Going Correction** -0.325s/f (Good) **6** Ran SP% **108.4**
Speed ratings (Par 105): **86,83,81, ,**
toteswingers 1&2 £2.50, 1&3 £2.40, 2&3 £3.20 CSF £11.02 TOTE £2.70: £1.80, £2.30; EX 11.60 Trifecta £70.10 Pool: £945.27 - 10.10 winning units..
Owner W H Ponsonby **Bred** R D And Mrs J S Chugg **Trained** Upper Lambourn, Berks

FOCUS
A modest novice chase which changed complexion after the early departure of the well-fancied Virginia Ash. The winner is rated similar to his Doncaster fall, with the second to his mark.

1745 "ELIXIR" NEW ALBUM BY OCASAN H'CAP HURDLE (9 hdls) 2m 2f 110y
3:15 (3:15) (Class 3) (0-130,128) 4-Y-O+ **£5,393** (£1,583; £791; £395)

Form RPR
123- 1 **Foxcub (IRE)**[108] 756 5-10-0 **102**.................................... FelixDeGiles 119+
(Tom Symonds) *trckd ldrs: led sn after 3 out: rdn clr bef next: wl in command whn hung rt run-in: rdn out* **16/1**
P/5- 2 *14* **Hi Note**[15] 304 5-11-12 **128**.. MarcGoldstein 132
(Sheena West) *trckd ldr: ev ch 3 out: sn rdn and hld by wnr: kpt on same pce* **14/1**
000/ 3 *6* **Cabimas**[186] 5081 6-10-11 **113**....................................(p) JamieMoore 113
(Gary Moore) *in tch: nudged along 4th: rdn after 3 out: wnt 3rd next: nvr any ch w front pair: kpt on same pce* **7/1**[3]
0B0- 4 *11* **Street Entertainer (IRE)**[33] 1485 6-11-5 **121**................(bt) APMcCoy 111
(David Pipe) *trckd ldrs: chal 3 out: sn rdn: qckly btn* **7/2**[2]
122- 5 *shd* **Orthodox Lad**[6] 1685 5-10-9 **111**.............................. SamTwiston-Davies 100
(Dr Richard Newland) *mid-div: rdn after 3 out: nvr any imp: chal for modest 4th run-in* **5/2**[1]
244- 6 *4* **Callisto Moon**[12] 1627 9-10-7 **109**....................................(v) MarkGrant 94
(Jo Hughes) *sn pushed into ld: nt fluent 3rd: mstke next: rdn 6th: hdd sn after 3 out: wknd bef next* **20/1**
/4P- 7 *3 ¼* **Canadian Diamond (IRE)**[37] 1426 6-11-7 **123**.................. AlainCawley 105
(Brendan Powell) *mid-div tl dropped to last trio 3rd: rdn after 6th: nvr any threat* **25/1**
000/ 8 *11* **Kingcora (FR)**[239] 4084 5-11-4 **120**.............................. AidanColeman 92
(Venetia Williams) *hld up towards rr of mid-div: rdn after 6th: nvr any imp: wknd after 3 out: t.o* **16/1**
FPP/ 9 *3* **Cnoc Seoda (IRE)**[60] 1220 8-10-3 **105**..........................(t) RichardJohnson 74
(Paul Henderson) *a towards rr: t.o* **9/1**
2/P- 10 *65* **Cloudy Bob (IRE)**[148] 182 6-11-6 **122**.............................. ColinBolger 33
(Pat Murphy) *a towards rr: t.o fr 3 out* **16/1**
6/6- F **Invicta Lake (IRE)**[145] 237 6-10-3 **105**........................(p) PaddyBrennan
(Suzy Smith) *mid-div tl fell heavily 6th* **7/1**[3]

4m 17.9s (-16.40) **Going Correction** -0.65s/f (Firm) **11** Ran SP% **118.7**
Speed ratings (Par 107): **108,102,99,94,94 93,91,87,85,58**
toteswingers 1&2 £34.20, 1&3 £18.40, 2&3 £2.80 CSF £217.53 CT £1719.99 TOTE £19.60: £3.40, £3.40, £2.60; EX 149.90 Trifecta £683.30 Pool: £911.09 - 0.02 winning units..

Owner Celia & Michael Baker **Bred** St Clare Hall Stud **Trained** Harewood End, H'fords

FOCUS
Not a bad handicap. They went a solid pace and it proved hard work for most from three out. A big step up from the easy winner, with the second to form.

1746 FULLER'S LONDON PRIDE H'CAP CHASE (13 fncs) 2m 2f
3:50 (3:52) (Class 2) (0-145,145) 4-Y-0+ **£11,710** (£3,459; £1,729; £865; £432)

Form RPR

422- **1** **Tindaro (FR)**[82] [974] 6-11-1 **134**.....(t) APMcCoy 139+
(Paul Webber) *hld up: hdwy after 6th: wnt 3rd 4 out: rdn to chse ldr 2 out: led sn after last: drvn rt out* **4/1**[3]

021/ **2** ¾ **King Edmund**[166] [5439] 10-11-6 **139**.....(t) TomCannon 142
(Chris Gordon) *in tch: wnt 2nd 7th: chal 4 out: led bef 3 out: sn rdn: hit last and hdd: rallied but hld nring fin* **11/2**

412- **3** ½ **Temple Lord (FR)**[36] [1441] 7-10-4 **123**.....(bt) RichieMcLernon 128+
(Jonjo O'Neill) *hld up: hdwy after 7th: hit 9th: slow whn lost pl sltly 4 out: rdn to chse ldng pair 2 out: swtchd rt last: styd on* **9/1**

4/2- **4** 4 ½ **Olympian Boy (IRE)**[17] [1596] 9-10-0 **119** oh4..... PaulMoloney 118
(Sophie Leech) *hld up bhd: hdwy after 4 out: rdn bef next: styd on same pce fr 2 out: hit last* **15/2**

/36- **5** 6 **Mister Matt (IRE)**[81] [1001] 10-10-7 **126**..... RichardJohnson 120
(Bob Buckler) *led: clr tl 8th: rdn and hdd after 4 out: wkng whn wnt lft 2 out* **20/1**

521/ **6** 2 ¼ **Fruity O'Rooney**[176] [5244] 10-11-7 **140**..... JamieMoore 133
(Gary Moore) *in tch: hit 2nd: outpcd and dropped to rr next: hdwy after 7th to latch on to main gp: hld appr 3 out: fdd 2 out* **3/1**[1]

50P- **7** 11 **Passato (GER)**[118] [672] 9-10-6 **125**.....(t) DominicElsworth 107
(Jo Davis) *trckd ldr: rdn after 4 out: wknd bef next* **16/1**

4/6- **8** 15 **Falcon Island**[155] [81] 8-10-13 **132**..... JoeTizzard 105
(Colin Tizzard) *trckd ldr tl 8th: sn pushed along: rdn after next: wknd bef 3 out: t.o* **7/2**[2]

4m 26.4s (-8.30) **Going Correction** -0.325s/f (Good) **8** Ran SP% **115.0**
Speed ratings (Par 109): **105,104,104,102,99 98,93,87**
toteswingers 1&2 £5.80, 1&3 £3.00, 2&3 £6.80 CSF £26.63 CT £185.77 TOTE £3.80: £1.80, £2.50, £3.10; EX 23.70 Trifecta £153.60 Pool: £1,482.12 - 7.23 winning units..
Owner The Tindaro Partnership **Bred** J P Dubois **Trained** Mollington, Oxon

FOCUS
A fair handicap rrun at a decent pace. The first three are allrated to their marks.

1747 BLACKSMITH BOB H'CAP HURDLE (13 hdls) 3m 3f
4:25 (4:25) (Class 3) (0-135,133) 4-Y-0+ **£5,393** (£1,583; £791; £395)

Form RPR

024- **1** **So Fine (IRE)**[12] [1628] 7-11-4 **125**..... RichardJohnson 133+
(Philip Hobbs) *trckd ldrs: jnd ldr 5th: led 10th where mstke: in command 2 out: rdn whn wnt lft and mstke last: styd on* **9/2**[2]

6U2/ **2** 6 **Royal Native (IRE)**[222] [4406] 5-10-5 **112**.....(t) AidanColeman 113
(Anthony Honeyball) *hld up bhd ldrs: drvn along fr after 10th: nvr fnd pce to get on terms but styd on to chse wnr fr last: a being hld* **9/2**[2]

211/ **3** 4 **Theologist (IRE)**[616] [3954] 7-11-2 **126**.....(b) JoshuaMoore[(3)] 123
(Dr Richard Newland) *led tl 10th: rdn in disp 2nd after 3 out: regained clr 2nd 2 out tl last but a being hld by wnr: no ex run-in* **8/1**[3]

243- **4** 5 **Red Not Blue (IRE)**[37] [1430] 10-11-5 **133**..... RyanHatch[(7)] 126
(Simon Earle) *hld up bhd ldrs: nudged along fr 8th: rdn after 3 out: rdr dropped whip: styd on but nvr finding pce to get on terms* **16/1**

146/ **5** 18 **Brackloon High (IRE)**[230] [4242] 8-11-4 **125**..... APMcCoy 108
(Brendan Powell) *kpt to outer: pressed ldr tl 5th: trckd ldrs: rdn after 10th: disp 2nd after 3 out tl wknd next* **5/2**[1]

111- **P** **Dreamsoftheatre (IRE)**[44] [1340] 5-10-5 **117**.....(t) MauriceLinehan[(5)]
(Jonjo O'Neill) *trckd ldrs: struggling in last whn rdn after 6th: lost tch rapidly u.str.p after next: p.u bef 8th* **5/2**[1]

6m 36.6s (-16.20) **Going Correction** -0.65s/f (Firm) **6** Ran SP% **110.5**
Speed ratings (Par 107): **98,96,95,93,88**
CSF £23.68 TOTE £5.20: £2.60, £3.60; EX 25.20 Trifecta £156.30 Pool: £2,311.86 - 11.08 winning units..
Owner Mrs L R Lovell **Bred** Patrick And John O'Connor **Trained** Withycombe, Somerset

FOCUS
This fair staying handicap was run at a steady gallop. The winner is rated in line with his old hurdles best, with a step up from the second.

1748 JAMES TODD CHARTERED ACCOUNTANTS CONDITIONAL JOCKEYS' H'CAP CHASE (19 fncs) 3m 2f 110y
5:00 (5:00) (Class 4) (0-120,120) 4-Y-0+ **£3,768** (£1,106; £553; £276)

Form RPR

213- **1** **Eleazar (GER)**[48] [1283] 12-11-5 **116**.....(p) MattCrawley[(3)] 125+
(Lucy Wadham) *trckd ldrs: led sn after 4 out: styd on wl fr 2 out: rdn out* **16/1**

241- **2** 4 **Font**[36] [1444] 10-11-0 **108**.....(t) JoshuaMoore 111
(Lawney Hill) *hld up but in tch: hdwy after 13th: rdn to dispute 2nd fr 3 out: a being hld by wnr: styd on same pce* **14/1**

5/1- **3** nse **Little Chip (IRE)**[6] [1687] 6-11-5 **116** 7ex..... KielanWoods[(3)] 122+
(Charlie Longsdon) *in tch: trcking ldrs whn hit 4th: led 15th: hdd whn slow and mstke next: sn rdn: styd on same pce fr 3 out* **1/1**[1]

52- **4** 4 ½ **Chasers Chance (IRE)**[26] [1526] 10-10-13 **107**..... JamesBest 106
(Paul Henderson) *trckd ldrs tl 13th: in tch: hdwy 4 out: rdn bef next: styd on same pce* **14/1**

152- **5** 22 **Baily Storm (IRE)**[39] [1403] 11-11-0 **108**.....(vt) GavinSheehan 92
(Lawney Hill) *led tl nt fluent 4th: trckd ldr: lft in ld 13th: hdd whn mstke 15th: sn rdn: wknd fr 3 out: t.o* **20/1**

462- **6** 11 **Academy General (IRE)**[17] [1598] 7-10-13 **115**.....(p) JakeHodson[(8)] 84
(David Bridgwater) *hld up but in tch: hdwy 13th: rdn after 4 out: wknd next: t.o* **8/1**[3]

632- **U** **Rhum (FR)**[9] [1659] 8-11-1 **117**.....(vt) RyanHatch[(8)]
(Nigel Twiston-Davies) *j.rt bdly at times: led after 4th: stmbld 12th: mstke and uns rdr next* **4/1**[2]

P/P- **U** **Tarraco (FR)**[142] [321] 6-10-5 **102**..... HarryChalloner[(3)]
(Venetia Williams) *hld up in tch: hdwy 13th: rdn after next: wknd after 4 out: bhd whn nt fluent and uns rdr next* **10/1**

6m 48.5s (-12.60) **Going Correction** -0.325s/f (Good) **8** Ran SP% **114.2**
Speed ratings (Par 105): **105,103,103,102,95 92, ,**
CSF £193.69 CT £430.08 TOTE £17.00: £3.10, £2.20, £1.40; EX 100.50 Trifecta £663.70 Pool: £2,037.05 - 2.30 winning units..
Owner J J W Wadham **Bred** Gestut Rottgen **Trained** Newmarket, Suffolk

FOCUS
A modest staying handicap confined to conditional riders that was run at a fair gallop. The form is rated through the second.

1749 SOUTHERN WATER SUPPORTING MACMILLAN MAIDEN HURDLE (11 hdls) 2m 6f 110y
5:30 (5:30) (Class 4) 4-Y-0+ **£3,119** (£915; £457; £228)

Form RPR

12F/ **1** **Kings Palace (IRE)**[254] [3787] 5-10-13 0..... TomScudamore 130+
(David Pipe) *mde all: hit 2 out: nt fluent last: rdn whn hung rt towards exit run-in: styd on wl* **15/8**[2]

5/ **2** 1 **Kaki De La Pree (FR)**[308] [2756] 6-10-13 0..... FelixDeGiles 126
(Tom Symonds) *trckd ldrs: rdn after 3 out: swtchd rt bef next: chsd wnr between last 2: kpt on: hld towards fin* **10/1**

22/- **3** 15 **Billy No Name (IRE)**[176] [5257] 5-10-13 121..... JoeTizzard 116+
(Colin Tizzard) *trckd wnr: rdn after 3 out: lost 2nd next: sn outpcd* **5/6**[1]

56F- **4** 23 **Just Archie (USA)**[24] [1552] 5-10-13 0..... LeightonAspell 95
(Lady Herries) *mid-div: wnt 4th after 3 out: sn rdn but nvr any ch: wknd between last 2: t.o* **33/1**

334- **5** 12 **Slaney Star (IRE)**[12] [1632] 5-10-13 0..... MattieBatchelor 81
(Jim Best) *towards rr and struggling after 3rd: nvr a factor: t.o fr 3 out* **50/1**

433/ **6** 18 **King Of Glory**[175] [5265] 5-10-13 112..... AidanColeman 65
(Venetia Williams) *trckd ldrs: rdn whn mstke 3 out: sn wknd: t.o* **8/1**[3]

050/ **7** 6 **Rule Of Thumb**[171] [5335] 5-10-13 0..... NickScholfield 60
(Paul Henderson) *a towards rr: t.o fr 3 out* **25/1**

05/ **8** 1 **Chendiyr (FR)**[297] [2981] 4-10-9 0..... JackQuinlan[(3)] 58
(Sarah Humphrey) *hld up: midfield 7th: lost tch bef 3 out: t.o* **80/1**

3- **9** 47 **Dancing Royal**[148] [189] 5-10-13 0..... SamTwiston-Davies 16
(Jamie Snowden) *in tch tl lost pl after 7th: lost tch qckly after next: sn t.o* **33/1**

U **Lady Oaksey**[647] 7-10-6 0..... GerardTumelty
(Bob Buckler) *hld up: v awkward whn uns rdr 1st* **100/1**

60/- **P** **Lascaux**[176] [5241] 4-10-5 0..... LiamTreadwell
(Luke Dace) *a towards rr: t.o after 8th: p.u bef 2 out* **100/1**

5m 22.5s (-20.00) **Going Correction** -0.65s/f (Firm)
WFA 4 from 5yo+ 10lb **11** Ran SP% **124.4**
Speed ratings (Par 105): **108,107,102,94,90 84,81,81,65,**
toteswingers 1&2 £4.10, 1&3 £1.10, 2&3 £3.50 CSF £20.97 TOTE £2.20: £1.10, £3.00, £1.10; EX 27.30 Trifecta £54.60 Pool: £3,735.05 - 37.54 winning units..
Owner Drew, George & Johnson Family **Bred** Kahill Burke Racing **Trained** Nicholashayne, Devon

FOCUS
The winner is rated to the level of his bumper form, with the favourite a stone+ off.
T/Plt: £313.20 to a £1 stake. Pool: £70693.56 - 164.75 winning tickets T/Qpdt: £90.70 to a £1 stake. Pool: £6525.45 - 53.20 winning tickets TM

798 HEXHAM (L-H)
Friday, October 4

OFFICIAL GOING: Good (good to soft in places) changing to good to soft (good in places) after race 1 (2:55)
Wind: Light, half against Weather: Overcast, showers

1750 KINTAIL LUXURY HOLIDAY COTTAGE NOVICES' LIMITED H'CAP CHASE (15 fncs) 2m 4f 110y
2:20 (2:20) (Class 3) (0-125,123) 4-Y-0+ **£6,844** (£1,995; £998)

Form RPR

/3F- **1** **Rudemeister (IRE)**[125] [579] 7-10-13 **117**.....(t) WilsonRenwick 126+
(Lucinda Russell) *hld up in tch: hdwy 1/2-way: effrt and led whn nt fluent last: drvn and styd on wl towards fin* **13/8**[1]

/14- **2** ¾ **Balding Banker (IRE)**[122] [625] 7-10-13 **122**..... TonyKelly[(5)] 128
(Rebecca Menzies) *taken early to s: t.k.h: in tch: nt fluent 7th: hdwy to chse ldr bef 2 out: led after 2 out: rdn and hdd last: rallied: hld nr fin* **3/1**[2]

021- **3** 11 **Twentypoundluck (IRE)**[66] [1144] 8-11-5 **123**.....(v) JamesReveley 120
(Patrick Griffin, Ire) *sn led: blnd bdly 3 out (usual 4 out): hdd after next: outpcd fr last* **14/1**

643- **4** 1 ¾ **Grey Soldier (IRE)**[33] [1484] 8-11-2 **120**.....(t) DougieCostello 115
(Sophie Leech) *chsd ldrs: rdn and outpcd appr 3 out (usual 4 out): rallied after next: no imp bef last* **22/1**

/22- **5** 2 ¼ **Carrigdhoun (IRE)**[131] [495] 8-10-6 **117**.....(tp) StephenMulqueen[(7)] 110
(Maurice Barnes) *chsd ldr to bef 2 out: rdn and wknd after 2 out* **7/1**

313- **6** 29 **Polarbrook (IRE)**[39] [1388] 6-10-8 **112**..... JasonMaguire 79
(Donald McCain) *nt fluent in rr: pushed along fr 1/2-way: drvn and struggling whn hit 3 out (usual 4 out): n.d after* **7/2**[3]

5m 4.8s (-8.70) **Going Correction** -0.225s/f (Good) **6** Ran SP% **108.8**
Speed ratings (Par 107): **107,106,102,101,101 89**
toteswingers 1&2 £1.20, 1&3 £4.80, 2&3 £7.30 CSF £6.72 TOTE £2.70: £1.40, £1.80; EX 10.80 Trifecta £32.90 Pool: £1,378.82 - 31.36 winning units..
Owner Andrew McAllister **Bred** Bernard And Deirdre Brady **Trained** Arlary, Perth & Kinross

FOCUS
A competitive opener run at a strong pace. A step up from the winner, and the second is on a very good mark.

1751 BHEST RACING TO SCHOOL (S) HURDLE (10 hdls) 2m 4f 110y
2:55 (2:55) (Class 5) 4-Y-0+ **£2,053** (£598; £299)

Form RPR

006/ **1** **Moufatango (FR)**[179] [5217] 7-11-0 93..... BrianHarding 110+
(Nicky Richards) *mde all at stdy gallop: rdn and qcknd clr bef last: drvn out run-in* **9/2**

000/ **2** 13 **Spiekeroog**[13] [5013] 7-11-5 111..... FearghalDavis 104
(David O'Meara) *t.k.h: prom: nt fluent 6th: rdn to chse wnr between last 2: outpcd bef last* **7/2**[2]

P5B- **3** 9 **Stand Clear**[3] [1717] 8-10-7 88..... TonyKelly[(5)] 88
(David Thompson) *hld up in tch: rdn bef 2 out: rallied to chse clr ldng pair bef last: no imp* **4/1**[3]

U/4- **4** ¾ **Mia's Vic (IRE)**[89] [910] 8-10-12 102.....(t) MrSFox[(7)] 95
(Noel C Kelly, Ire) *chsd ldrs: effrt and rdn 2 out: wknd bef last* **7/2**[2]

544- **5** 16 **George Woolf**[48] [1287] 5-11-2 108.....(vt) MichaelByrne[(3)] 80
(Tim Vaughan) *chsd wnr tl rdn and outpcd between last 2: sn btn* **11/4**[1]

00/ **P** **Jordans Day**[1446] [1838] 8-10-7 0..... BrianHughes
(Susan Corbett) *bhd: struggling 3 out: t.o whn p.u after next* **100/1**

5m 8.6s (-3.90) **Going Correction** -0.35s/f (Good) **6** Ran SP% **110.3**
Speed ratings (Par 103): **93,88,84,84,78**
toteswingers 1&2 £3.20, 1&3 £6.80, 2&3 £5.00 CSF £19.84 TOTE £5.50: £2.60, £2.30; EX 22.60 Trifecta £67.60 Pool: £1,996.61 - 22.12 winning units..There was no bid for the winner.
Owner Miss J R Richards **Bred** Olivier Le Quere **Trained** Greystoke, Cumbria

The Form Book Jumps, Raceform Ltd, Compton, RG20 6NL.

FOCUS
The official going description was changed from Good, to Good to soft after the opener. This was a desperately weak affair, even accounting for the grade. The winner dictated a steady pace and is rated back to his best.

1752 YOUNGS RPS H'CAP HURDLE (10 hdls) 2m 4f 110y
3:30 (3:30) (Class 3) (0-130,129) 4-Y-0+ **£5,393** (£1,583; £791; £395)

Form RPR
F02- **1** **Up For An Oscar (IRE)**[12] 1634 6-10-11 **119**..............(tp) EdCookson(5) 123+
(Kim Bailey) *in tch: hit 6th: rdn and outpcd bef 2 out: rallied between last 2: led and edgd lft run-in: drvn out* **6/1**

430- **2** 2 **Decoy (FR)**[33] 1485 7-11-8 **125**..(p) ConorO'Farrell 126
(David Pipe) *t.k.h: led to 2nd: cl up: effrt after 2 out: ev ch last: chsd wnr run-in: kpt on: hld nr fin* **4/1**[2]

251- **3** 1 ¾ **Call Box (IRE)**[25] 1543 8-10-12 **118**................................. MrSCrawford(3) 117
(S R B Crawford, Ire) *t.k.h: cl up: led 4 out: rdn and edgd lft bef last: hdd run-in: kpt on same pce* **9/2**[3]

2/5- **4** 9 **Maggio (FR)**[25] 1545 8-11-12 **129**....................................(t) JamesReveley 122
(Patrick Griffin, Ire) *cl up: led 2nd to 6th: cl up tl rdn and wknd between last 2* **7/1**

422- **5** 10 **Swing Hard (IRE)**[39] 1393 5-10-9 **112**.................................. RyanMania 97
(Sue Smith) *prom: outpcd whn mstke 3 out: no imp fr next* **7/1**

/12- **6** 6 **Wolf Shield (IRE)**[130] 512 6-11-3 **120**................................ BarryKeniry 97
(George Moore) *hld up in tch: rdn and outpcd 4 out: n.d after* **7/2**[1]

/04- **7** 11 **Trucking Along (IRE)**[39] 1398 7-11-6 **123**..................... PeterBuchanan 90
(S R B Crawford, Ire) *mstkes: hld up: stdy hdwy after 3 out: rdn and wknd bef next* **7/1**

5m 0.56s (-11.94) **Going Correction** -0.35s/f (Good) 7 Ran SP% **112.2**
Speed ratings (Par 107): **108,107,106,103,99 97,92**
toteswingers 1&2 £3.20, 1&3 £6.80, 2&3 £5.00 CSF £29.14 TOTE £8.20: £3.30, £3.40; EX 38.30 Trifecta £429.40 Pool: £1,900.80 - 3.31 winning units..
Owner The Hon Mrs Cookson **Bred** S Michael Millar **Trained** Andoversford, Gloucs

FOCUS
Steadily deteriorating conditions for this competitive feature. Decent form for the track, with the second and third to their marks.

1753 CAMPBELL GILLIES MEMORIAL H'CAP CHASE (10 fncs 2 omitted) 2m 110y
4:05 (4:05) (Class 4) (0-120,120) 4-Y-0+ **£3,969** (£1,157; £578)

Form RPR
1/1- **1** **Riskier**[143] 282 8-11-12 **120**.. BrianHughes 132+
(John Wade) *j.w: mde all: qcknd clr bef last: kpt on strly run-in* **2/1**[2]

323- **2** 9 **Mulligan's Man (IRE)**[39] 1390 6-11-6 **114**.......................... JasonMaguire 118
(Donald McCain) *prom: hdwy to chse wnr bef last: sn one pce* **5/2**[3]

2U3- **3** 3 **Rhymers Ha**[66] 1144 6-11-11 **119**.................................... PeterBuchanan 119
(Lucinda Russell) *t.k.h early: chsd wnr tl rdn and edgd lft bef last: outpcd whn nt fluent last* **7/4**[1]

421/ **4** shd **Prince Tam**[158] 23 9-9-9 **94** oh3.............................. JonathanEngland(5) 94
(Harriet Graham) *chsd ldrs: drvn and outpcd passing omitted 3 out: n.d after* **10/1**

4m 5.0s (-4.80) **Going Correction** -0.225s/f (Good) 4 Ran SP% **107.4**
Speed ratings (Par 105): **102,97,96,96**
CSF £7.19 TOTE £2.30; EX 6.10 Trifecta £9.80 Pool: £1,506.81 - 114.23 winning units..
Owner John Wade **Bred** H J Manners **Trained** Mordon, Co Durham

FOCUS
Fair form, and seemingly a big step forward from the easy winner.

1754 RAY HAWKEY MEMORIAL MAIDEN HURDLE (8 hdls) 2m 110y
4:40 (4:41) (Class 5) 4-Y-0+ **£2,053** (£598; £299)

Form RPR
633/ **1** **Revocation**[187] 5041 5-11-0 0... PeterBuchanan 114+
(Lucinda Russell) *t.k.h in midfield: gd hdwy after 2 out: led bef last: sn clr: kpt on strly* **7/1**

4/ **2** 7 **Spin Cast**[60] 2457 5-10-7 0.. MissHBethell(7) 108+
(Philip Kirby) *hld up and bhd: stdy hdwy after 2 out: effrt and chsd (clr) wnr last: edgd lft and kpt on run-in: nvr any ch of rching ldr* **7/2**[2]

3 7 **Kodicil (IRE)**[15] 5-11-0 0.. DougieCostello 103
(Tim Walford) *prom: pushed along 1/2-way: outpcd after 3 out: rallied next: drvn and one pce bef last* **3/1**[1]

42- **4** 2 ¾ **Moon Trip**[25] 1533 4-11-0 0.. DenisO'Regan 100
(John Ferguson) *trckd ldrs: led appr 2 out: rdn and hdd bef last: sn outpcd* **7/2**[2]

/06- **5** 9 **Aw Ripe China (IRE)**[122] 629 5-10-11 0......................... JohnKington(3) 91
(Simon Waugh) *cl up: chal briefly appr 2 out: rdn and wknd bef last* **66/1**

0/3- **6** 3 **Call Of Duty (IRE)**[8] 1661 8-11-0 0.................................. HenryBrooke 88
(Dianne Sayer) *nt fluent on occasions: hld up in tch: effrt and hdwy bef 2 out: wknd bef last* **6/1**[3]

6 **7** 9 **Whinstone Dee (IRE)**[25] 1540 5-11-0 0..........................(t) JamesReveley 80
(Miss Clare Louise Cannon, Ire) *hld up in midfield: rdn and outpcd 4 out: n.d after* **14/1**

00/ **8** 7 **Just Tyn (IRE)**[340] 2099 6-11-0 0.................................... WilsonRenwick 74
(Martin Todhunter) *hld up: struggling after 3 out: nvr on terms* **100/1**

0/ **9** 14 **Moheebb (IRE)**[14] 4060 9-11-0 0.................................(p) KennyJohnson 61
(Robert Johnson) *nt fluent on occasions: hld up and bhd: struggling bef 3 out: nvr on terms* **40/1**

F56/ **10** 4 **Oddsmaker (IRE)**[121] 2421 12-10-7 86................(t) StephenMulqueen(7) 58
(Maurice Barnes) *t.k.h: led and sn clr: hdd appr 2 out: sn btn* **40/1**

F **Shirls Son Sam**[39] 5-11-0 0.. BarryKeniry
(Chris Fairhurst) *hld up: fell 4 out* **25/1**

4m 7.8s (-9.60) **Going Correction** -0.35s/f (Good)
WFA 4 from 5yo+ 9lb 11 Ran SP% **114.1**
Speed ratings (Par 103): **108,104,101,100,95 94,90,86,80,78**
toteswingers 1&2 £6.60, 1&3 £3.90, 2&3 £3.30 CSF £30.47 TOTE £7.30: £2.90, £1.40, £1.50; EX 36.20 Trifecta £149.10 Pool: £3,463.94 - 149.10 winning units..
Owner Michael & Lady Jane Kaplan **Bred** Ms W T Futter **Trained** Arlary, Perth & Kinross

FOCUS
An informative, if probably only ordinary maiden hurdle but it was run a searing pace in the softening conditions. The winner built on his best novice form.

1755 TDR APPRENTICESHIPS NOVICES' HURDLE (12 hdls) 3m
5:15 (5:15) (Class 4) 4-Y-0+ **£3,285** (£957; £479)

Form RPR
311- **1** **Billfromthebar (IRE)**[66] 1142 6-11-5 122........................... NickSlatter(7) 132+
(Donald McCain) *w ldr: led 8th: rdn 2 out: jnd bef last: hld on gamely u.p run-in* **7/2**[3]

21/ **2** nse **Simarthur**[180] 5208 6-10-12 0.. PeterBuchanan 117
(Lucinda Russell) *prom: pushed along fr 8th: hdwy bef 2 out: chal appr last: kpt on run-in: jst hld* **15/8**[2]

/21- **3** 4 ½ **Indigo Rock (IRE)**[111] 747 7-11-5 120.................................. RyanMania 120
(Michael Smith) *chsd ldrs: effrt and drvn bef 2 out: outpcd bef last* **7/4**[1]

123- **4** 8 **Benefit Of Youth (IRE)**[36] 1440 6-11-5 125.................... DougieCostello 114
(Tim Vaughan) *t.k.h early: led to 8th: w ldr to after 2 out: rdn and wknd bef last* **9/2**

6m 2.1s (-6.90) **Going Correction** -0.35s/f (Good) 4 Ran SP% **111.6**
Speed ratings (Par 105): **97,96,95,92**
CSF £10.68 TOTE £3.20; EX 12.20 Trifecta £29.50 Pool: £1,514.14 - 38.44 winning units..
Owner Matthew Sanders **Bred** Andrew Pierce **Trained** Cholmondeley, Cheshire

FOCUS
Three last-time-out winners in this small field and the form looks rock solid. Another step forward from the winner.

1756 WELCOME TO HEXHAM RACECOURSE H'CAP CHASE (15 fncs 4 omitted) 3m 1f
5:45 (5:45) (Class 4) (0-115,109) 4-Y-0 **£3,671** (£1,084; £542; £271; £135)

Form RPR
631- **1** **Pyjama Game (IRE)**[29] 1505 7-11-10 107....................... WilsonRenwick 115+
(Rose Dobbin) *led or disp ld thrght: asserted 2 out: hld on wl u.p fr last* **4/1**[3]

F64- **2** nk **Baltic Pathfinder (IRE)**[29] 1502 9-10-11 99........... JonathanEngland(5) 105
(Sue Smith) *hld up: pushed along and outpcd after 3 out (usual 4 out): rallied whn nt clr run between last 2: styd on strly fr last: jst hld* **9/1**

22F/ **3** 1 **The Friary (IRE)**[213] 4580 6-11-12 109..........................(t) PeterBuchanan 116+
(Lucinda Russell) *nt fluent on occasions: chsd ldrs: drvn along bef 2 out: kpt on u.p fr last* **3/1**[1]

4/5- **4** hd **Apache Blue (IRE)**[29] 1502 9-11-1 105.......................... JohnDawson(7) 110
(John Wade) *led or disp ld to 2 out: sn rdn: kpt on u.p fr last* **14/1**

644/ **5** 1 ¾ **Badger Foot (IRE)**[495] 454 8-10-8 98...................(t) GrantCockburn(7) 103
(Lucinda Russell) *hld up in tch: hdwy and ev ch whn sprawled on landing 2 out: sn rdn and rallied: one pce fnl 100yds* **7/2**[2]

626- **6** 3 ¼ **Flying Doctor**[23] 1565 10-11-10 107.............................. JasonMaguire 107
(Alistair Whillans) *chsd ldrs: lost pl bef 12th: hit and outpcd 3 out (usual 4 out): kpt on fr last: no imp* **6/1**

/35- **7** 2 **Forestside (IRE)**[41] 1377 8-10-12 95................................... BrianHughes 93
(Barry Murtagh) *prom tl rdn and wknd bef last* **7/1**

6m 30.5s (-1.70) **Going Correction** -0.225s/f (Good) 7 Ran SP% **110.7**
Speed ratings (Par 105): **93,92,92,92,91 90,90**
toteswingers 1&2 £7.80, 1&3 £2.40, 2&3 £6.80 CSF £34.57 TOTE £2.70: £1.70, £5.30; EX 31.60 Trifecta £131.00 Pool: £1,836.29 - 10.50 winning units..
Owner Straightline Construction Ltd **Bred** Peter E Clinton **Trained** South Hazelrigg, Northumbria
■ Stewards' Enquiry : Jonathan England four-day ban; used whip above permitted level (18th-21st Oct).

FOCUS
A fair staying handicap chase and it served up a thrilling finish. They finished in a bit of a heap but the winner is on the upgrade.
T/Plt: £318.10 to a £1 stake. Pool: £52124.64 - 119.60 winning tickets T/Qpdt: £65.10 to a £1 stake. Pool: £3599.10 - 40.90 winning tickets RY

1757 - 1763a (Foreign Racing) - See Raceform Interactive

[1743]FONTWELL (L-H)
Saturday, October 5

OFFICIAL GOING: Good (good to soft; 6.7)
Wind: mild breeze behind Weather: cloudy with sunny periods

1764 4D AND ST BARNABAS HOUSE NOVICES' HURDLE (10 hdls) 2m 4f
1:55 (1:55) (Class 4) 4-Y-0+ **£3,573** (£1,049; £524; £262)

Form RPR
3/2- **1** **Hannibal The Great (IRE)**[146] 239 5-10-12 0..................(t) NoelFehily 125+
(Charlie Longsdon) *travelled wl in mid-div: smooth hdwy after 3 out to press ldr next: led last: nudged clr: easily* **10/11**[1]

2 12 **Gate Please (IRE)**[388] 1568 8-10-12 0.................................. APMcCoy 114+
(Rebecca Curtis) *trckd ldrs: led sn after 7th: rdn whn jnd 2 out: hdd last: sn hld by wnr: eased towards fin* **7/2**[2]

3 7 **Gun Shy (IRE)**[148] 214 5-10-9 0...................................... JoshuaMoore(3) 105+
(Gary Moore) *in tch: rdn into 3rd after 3 out: sddle slipped bef next: hld 5th whn hmpd last: rdn and styd on strly to go 3rd sn after but ldrs out of rch* **7/1**

23/- **4** 7 **Sash Of Honour (IRE)**[187] 5079 4-10-12 115............(v) RichardJohnson 97
(Tim Vaughan) *in tch after 3 out: wnt 3rd next: one pce whn blnd last: no ex* **6/1**[3]

4/0- **5** 1 ¼ **Superstición**[132] 490 4-10-5 86.. MarcGoldstein 86
(Michael Madgwick) *mid-div: rdn after 3 out: disp hld 4th after next: fdd run-in* **100/1**

5- **6** 2 ¾ **Mount Odell**[114] 731 5-10-12 0.. JamieMoore 91
(Gary Moore) *hld up towards rr: effrt into midfield after 3 out: nvr trbld ldrs* **33/1**

000/ **7** 15 **Pullmen**[200] 4219 5-10-12 0... NickScholfield 77
(Paul Henderson) *t.k.h: a towards rr* **66/1**

000/ **8** 3 **Sylvan Legend**[271] 3547 5-10-12 0...................................... IanPopham 74
(Caroline Keevil) *diputed ld tl sn after 7th: rdn after 3 out: wknd bef next* **100/1**

0/3- **9** 21 **Keppel Isle (IRE)**[28] 1523 4-10-12 0................................... TomCannon 55
(Laura Mongan) *racd keenly disputing ld: hdd 3 out: sn rdn: wknd bef next: t.o* **33/1**

6/4- **10** 9 **Be Marvellous (IRE)**[138] 410 5-10-12 0...........................(t) JoeTizzard 47
(Colin Tizzard) *hld up towards rr: lost tch tamely bef 7th: t.o* **14/1**

50- **11** 5 **Quernstone (USA)**[13] 1625 4-10-12 0............................... AidanColeman 43
(Harry Whittington) *trckd ldrs 2nd tl 4th: sn drvn along in rr: t.o after 3 out* **100/1**

4m 51.6s (-7.80) **Going Correction** -0.25s/f (Good) 11 Ran SP% **118.4**
Speed ratings (Par 105): **105,100,97,94,94 93,87,85,77,73 71**
Tote Swingers: 1&2 £1.30, 1&3 £11.10, 2&3 £3.00 CSF £4.29 TOTE £2.10: £1.10, £1.60, £2.10; EX 5.50 Trifecta £21.10 Pool: £580.09 - 20.55 winning units..
Owner The Pantechnicons **Bred** Mrs Mary Gallagher **Trained** Over Norton, Oxon

FOCUS
Hurdles moved out two sections from Friday, bends on fresh line. Chases increased by 20yds per circuit and hurdles increased by 5yds per circuit. After a dry night the ground had dried out slightly but was still riding on the easy side of good. The bends had been moved out to provide fresh ground. A steady pace until setting out on to the final circuit. The easy winner looks a decent recruit.

1765 BTU SUPPORTING CHESTNUT TREE HOUSE NOVICES' H'CAP CHASE (15 fncs) 2m 4f
2:30 (2:30) (Class 4) (0-110,107) 4-Y-0+ **£3,768** (£1,106; £553; £276)

Form RPR
2/4- **1** **Caulfields Venture (IRE)**[157] 64 7-11-0 **95**..............(p) NickScholfield 98
(Andy Turnell) *chsd ldrs: outpcd after 4 out: hdwy into cl 4th appr last: str run up ins rail run-in: led fnl strides* **3/1**[1]

312- **2** *hd* **Franklino (FR)**[37] 1434 6-11-12 **107**.................................... TomCannon 110
(Chris Gordon) *led: jnd after 9th: rdn clr after 4 out tl jnd again next: hdd last: kpt on gamely to ld again fnl 75yds: hdd fnl strides* **9/2**[3]

0/3- **3** *1 ¼* **Ballymoat**[31] 1497 6-11-10 **105**..........................(t) RichardJohnson 108
(Tim Vaughan) *trckd ldrs: disp after 9th tl after 4 out: rdn bk upsides 3 out: narrow ld whn mstke last: hdd fnl 75yds: no ex* **6/1**

2/P- **4** *2 ¼* **Mountaineer (FR)**[18] 1594 8-11-10 **105**.............................. JamieMoore 107
(Gary Moore) *hld up: hdwy 9th: rdn whn short of room briefly on bnd after 4 out: ev ch next tl after 2 out: swtchd rt sn after last: styd on same pce* **7/2**[2]

/15- **5** *17* **Time Book (IRE)**[132] 489 7-10-0 **81**............................(t) BrendanPowell 73
(Colin Tizzard) *trckd ldrs: pckd 2nd: rdn in cl 4th after 4 out: wknd after 2 out* **9/2**[3]

53P- **6** *17* **Outback (IRE)**[13] 1634 4-10-1 **98**..............................(tp) TrevorWhelan(5) 56
(Neil King) *hld up towards rr: struggling and detached after 10th: nvr a threat after: t.o* **10/1**

350- **7** *9* **What's For Tea**[13] 1630 8-9-11 **81** oh14 ow2.................(vt) EDLinehan(5) 44
(Paddy Butler) *hld up towards rr: lost tch fr after 10th: t.o* **50/1**

/55- **P** **Cossack Prince**[51] 1274 8-10-0 **81** oh8.......................... HarrySkelton
(Laura Mongan) *trcking ldrs whn blnd v bdly 7th: in rr after: nvr rcvrd: t.o whn p.u bef 3 out: b.b.v* **28/1**

5m 7.6s (0.30) **Going Correction** -0.025s/f (Good)
WFA 4 from 6yo+ 10lb 8 Ran SP% **112.4**
Speed ratings (Par 105): **98,97,97,96,89 82,79,**
Tote Swingers: 1&2 £2.80, 1&3 £2.90, 2&3 £6.00 CSF £16.73 CT £73.71 TOTE £4.20: £1.40, £1.20, £2.20; EX 12.70 Trifecta £34.50 Pool: £738.39 - 16.01 winning units..
Owner C F Colquhoun **Bred** Michael Crean **Trained** Broad Hinton, Wilts

FOCUS
A weak novice handicap chase run at a sound gallop. The winner was on a good mark and is rated below his best, with the next three in line with their hurdles form.

1766 MOTT MACDONALD SUPPORTING ST BARNABAS HOUSE H'CAP HURDLE (10 hdls) 2m 4f
3:05 (3:07) (Class 2) (0-145,144) 4-Y-0 **£5,811** (£2,898; £1,449; £725; £362)

Form RPR
505/ **1** **Princely Player (IRE)**[217] 4524 6-10-12 **130**................ RichardJohnson 132+
(Philip Hobbs) *v reluctant to line up: hld up bhd ldrs: blnd 6th: nudged along after 7th: swtchd out appr 2 out: hdwy to chse ldr appr last: hrd drvn run-in: styd on to ld nring fin* **3/1**[1]

/52- **2** *nk* **Hi Note**[1] 1745 5-10-10 **128**... MarcGoldstein 129
(Sheena West) *prom: led 3rd: rdn after 3 out: stuck to her task extremely gamely whn jnd again 2 out: 2 l up last* **5/1**

63/- **3** *3 ½* **Ashbrittle**[357] 1476 6-9-11 **120**..................................(p) TrevorWhelan(5) 119
(Neil King) *led tl nt flent 3rd: trckd ldr: rdn to dispute ld gng to 2 out tl appr last: kpt on same pce* **9/2**[3]

312- **4** *2 ¼* **Experimentalist**[13] 1625 5-10-2 **120**...........................(t) AidanColeman 116
(Tim Vaughan) *trckd ldrs: rdn after 3 out: nt quite pce to mount chal: kpt on but no ex fr last* **8/1**

500/ **5** *2 ½* **Act Of Kalanisi (IRE)**[188] 5031 7-10-12 **130**.........(t) SamTwiston-Davies 124
(Dr Richard Newland) *trckd ldrs: rdn after 3 out: kpt on same pce fr next* **4/1**[2]

46F/ **6** *10* **Peckhamecho (IRE)**[168] 5409 7-11-5 **144**.................... PatrickCorbett(7) 133
(Rebecca Curtis) *hld up bhd ldrs: awkward 2nd: effrt in cl 3rd after 3 out: outpcd after next* **6/1**

03P/ **P** **Havingotascoobydo (IRE)**[204] 4772 8-11-0 **132**................ IanPopham
(Martin Keighley) *hld up bhd ldrs: pushed along after 5th: outpcd aftetr 7th: no ch whn p.u after 3 out* **6/1**

4m 48.5s (-10.90) **Going Correction** -0.25s/f (Good) 7 Ran SP% **119.5**
Speed ratings (Par 109): **111,110,109,108,107 103,**
Tote Swingers: 1&2 £8.40, 1&3 £4.00, 2&3 £3.90 CSF £19.63 CT £67.99 TOTE £4.60: £2.40, £3.10; EX 28.40 Trifecta £129.80 Pool: £1,352.86 - 7.81 winning units..
Owner Thurloe 52 **Bred** Patrick Burling Developments Ltd **Trained** Withycombe, Somerset

FOCUS
A tight class 2 handicap hurdle and all but one still in with a big shout two out. Straightforward form.

1767 CLANCY DOCWRA SUPPORTING CHESTNUT TREE HOUSE H'CAP CHASE (15 fncs) 2m 4f
3:40 (3:40) (Class 4) (0-120,115) 4-Y-0+ **£3,768** (£1,106; £553; £276)

Form RPR
441/ **1** **Dorset Naga**[415] 1245 7-11-12 **115**..............................(t) AidanColeman 127+
(Anthony Honeyball) *hld up: smooth hdwy after 4 out: chal 2 out: sn rdn into clr advantage: styd on wl: readily* **2/1**[1]

143- **2** *5* **Synthe Davis (FR)**[28] 1522 8-11-10 **113**...........................(p) APMcCoy 117
(Laura Mongan) *mid-div: tk clsr order after 11th: cl 3rd 3 out: sn rdn: styd on to go 2nd run-in but no ch w wnr* **6/1**[3]

543- **3** *1 ¼* **Milgen Bay**[64] 1186 7-11-4 **107**...................................(p) LeightonAspell 111
(Oliver Sherwood) *led: pckd 10th: rdn after 3 out: hdd after next: styd on same pce: no ex whn lost 2nd run-in* **8/1**

535- **4** *16* **Lucy's Legend (IRE)**[63] 1197 7-10-11 **100**..................(tp) PaddyBrennan 90
(Paul Henderson) *chsd ldrs: nt fluent 5th: struggling whn lost pl 10th: wl hld after: pluged on into modest 4th at the last* **7/1**

P01- **5** *9* **Fearless Leader**[13] 1629 6-11-7 **110**..........................(b) TomScudamore 91
(David Bridgwater) *trckd ldrs: wnt 2nd after 9th: pressed ldr after 4 out tl rdn next: wkng whn lft 4th 2 out* **9/2**[2]

531- **6** *7* **Giant O Murchu (IRE)**[28] 1522 9-11-9 **115**...............(p) GavinSheehan(3) 89
(Lawney Hill) *hld up bhd: effrt to cl on ldrs appr 3 out: little imp and nvr threatened: wknd 2 out* **10/1**

P04- **7** *6* **Amaury De Lusignan (IRE)**[37] 1444 7-10-12 **101**...(tp) RichardJohnson 70
(Paul Henderson) *pressed ldr tl after 9th: chsd ldrs: rdn after 4 out: sn wknd* **16/1**

PU5- **U** **Try Catch Me (IRE)**[28] 1522 8-10-5 **97**.......................... MarkQuinlan(3) 100
(Alison Batchelor) *mid-div: nt fluent 8th: hdwy after 11th: nt fluent 4 out: sn rdn: styng on at same pce in 4th whn stmbld v bdly and uns rdr 2 out* **14/1**

5m 4.3s (-3.00) **Going Correction** -0.025s/f (Good) 8 Ran SP% **111.1**
Speed ratings (Par 105): **105,103,102,96,92 89,87,**
Tote Swingers: 1&2 £2.20, 1&3 £7.20, 2&3 £8.80 CSF £13.87 CT £73.64 TOTE £3.80: £1.80, £1.50, £2.50; EX 13.00 Trifecta £85.30 Pool: £805.79 - 7.07 winning units..
Owner Steve & Jackie Fleetham **Bred** R Jenks **Trained** Mosterton, Dorset

FOCUS
Ordinary form. The cosy winner is on the upgrade and there should be more to come.

1768 MORRISON UTILITY SERVICES SUPPORTING ST BARNABAS HOUSE H'CAP HURDLE (12 hdls 1 omitted) 3m 3f
4:15 (4:15) (Class 5) (0-100,100) 4-Y-0+ **£3,119** (£915; £457; £228)

Form RPR
001- **1** **Absolute Shambles**[8] 1675 9-10-9 **83**.............................(p) TomCannon 88
(Chris Gordon) *trckd ldrs: led 10th: rdn after next: jnd last (usual 2 out): styd on wl u.p to draw ahd by-passing omitted last* **7/2**[2]

630- **2** *2 ¼* **Sea Cadet**[25] 1548 11-10-0 **74** oh1...................................... HarrySkelton 77
(Laura Mongan) *trckd ldrs: jnd wnr travelling wl whn nt fluent 2 out (usual 3 out): ev ch last (usual 2 out): sn rdn: no ex and hld by-passing omitted last* **5/1**

/36- **3** *12* **Corso Palladio (IRE)**[8] 1673 11-11-12 **100**.....................(tp) TomO'Brien 92
(Peter Bowen) *trckd ldrs tl rdn after 10th: plugged on fr 2 out (usual 3 out) to go 3rd at the last (usual 2 out): nvr threatening to rch ldrs* **3/1**[1]

144- **4** *17* **Sapphire Rouge (IRE)**[27] 1529 7-11-2 **97**...................(p) KevinJones(7) 74
(Seamus Mullins) *disp ld: hit 3rd: hdd 10th: sn drvn: lost 3rd at the last (usual 2 out) wknd* **9/2**[3]

2/5- **5** *32* **Genny Wren**[154] 122 7-11-11 **99**.. SamJones 47
(Renee Robeson) *disp ld most of way tl after 9th: struggling after next: wknd after 2 out (usual 3 out): t.o* **5/1**

45/ **6** *5* **Sovereigns Legacy**[408] 1332 6-10 2 **76**.......................... ConorO'Farrell 20
(John Panvert) *hld up bhd ldng gp: nt fluent 8th: struggling after next: wknd after 2 out (usual 3 out): t.o* **20/1**

103/ **F** **Royal Kicks (FR)**[162] 5555 12-11-0 **91**....................(bt) GavinSheehan(3)
(Suzy Smith) *in tch: racd wd 9th and fell: fatally injured* **8/1**

6m 44.4s (-8.40) **Going Correction** -0.25s/f (Good) 7 Ran SP% **114.6**
Speed ratings (Par 103): **102,101,97,92,83 81,**
Tote Swingers: 1&2 £6.40, 1&3 £1.40, 2&3 £14.80 CSF £21.40 CT £57.51 TOTE £4.10: £2.30, £3.00; EX 21.00 Trifecta £56.40 Pool: £331.24 - 4.40 winning units..
Owner Chris Gordon Racing Club **Bred** R Bowers **Trained** Morestead, Hants

FOCUS
This weak handicap hurdle was a severe test of stamina despite the steady early pace. The final flight had to be bypassed.

1769 MTS SPONSORING CHESTNUT TREE HOUSE CONDITIONAL JOCKEYS' H'CAP CHASE (16 fncs) 2m 6f
4:50 (4:50) (Class 5) (0-95,95) 4-Y-0+ **£2,144** (£629; £314; £157)

Form RPR
405- **1** **Midnight Lira**[13] 1629 6-11-7 **90**.. JamesBest 97+
(Caroline Keevil) *trckd ldr: pckd 3rd: chal 4 out: rdn after next: kpt on gamely run-in: led fnl 75yds: drvn rt out* **7/2**[3]

3/3- **2** *1 ½* **Annie Confidential (IRE)**[142] 330 10-9-12 **72**............... KevinJones(5) 77
(Miss Imogen Pickard) *led: rdn whn chal after 4 out: kpt on gamely: no ex whn hdd fnl 75yds fin* **5/2**[2]

456- **3** *37* **Morestead (IRE)**[8] 1675 8-11-12 **95**..................................... EDLinehan 67
(Brendan Powell) *trckd ldrs: drvn along after 10th: lost tch bef 4 out: t.o whn lft 4th 2 out: snatched poor 3rd fnl stride* **7/2**[3]

/PP- **4** *shd* **Curragh Dancer (FR)**[51] 1272 10-10-0 **69** oh2..............(v) KielanWoods 41
(Paddy Butler) *trckd ldrs: rdn appr 11th: wknd 4 out: lft modest 3rd 2 out tl fnl stride* **14/1**

3P/- **F** **Finnegan Paddy (IRE)**[210] 4661 7-11-1 **87**.................. MichaelByrne(3) 67
(Tim Vaughan) *trckd ldrs: squeezed up 4th: rdn after 11th: no ch w front pair after 4 out: wkng whn fell 2 out* **9/4**[1]

5m 43.5s (0.50) **Going Correction** -0.025s/f (Good) 5 Ran SP% **110.5**
Speed ratings (Par 103): **98,97,84,83,**
CSF £12.84 TOTE £5.10: £1.70, £1.60; EX 12.70 Trifecta £24.70 Pool: £630.17 - 19.07 winning units..
Owner Brian Derrick **Bred** B Derrick And P R Rodford **Trained** Motcombe, Dorset

FOCUS
A weak conditional jockeys' handicap chase and just two seriously involved early on the final circuit. The winner improved in line with her hurdles form, with the second close to her mark.

1770 BLACK & VEATCH SUPPORTING TODAY'S CHARITIES STANDARD OPEN NATIONAL HUNT FLAT RACE (DIV I) 2m 2f 110y
5:20 (5:20) (Class 6) 4-6-Y-0 **£1,559** (£457; £228; £114)

Form RPR
102/ **1** **Seedling**[217] 4528 4-11-7 0..[1] SamTwiston-Davies 105+
(Charles Egerton) *patiently rdn in rr: smooth hdwy fr 6f out: chsd ldr over 2f out: led over 1f out: r.o wl: rdn out* **7/2**[2]

2 *3* **Doing Fine (IRE)**[188] 5-11-0 0... APMcCoy 94
(Rebecca Curtis) *trckd ldr: led 1/2-way: pushed along whn jinked lft over 2f out: rdn and hdd over 1f out: styd on same pce* **7/4**[1]

0/0- **3** *18* **Stella's Fella**[146] 250 5-11-0 0...................................... DavidEngland 78
(Giles Smyly) *racd freely: led tl 1/2-way: w ldr tl rdn over 2f out: sn outpcd: regained 3rd fnl strides* **100/1**

4 *nk* **Vikekhal (FR)**[195] 4-11-0 0.. JamieMoore 78
(Gary Moore) *trckd ldrs: rdn to chse ldng pair over 2f out: sn outpcd: no ex whn lost 3rd fnl strides* **7/2**[2]

0/ **5** *4 ½* **The Master Remover (IRE)**[167] 5444 4-11-0 0................... TomCannon 74
(Chris Gordon) *in tch: rdn over 2f out: sn one pce* **20/1**

6 *26* **Harry's Choice** 5-10-7 0.............................. MissEmily-JaneHarbour(7) 50
(Raymond York) *trckd ldrs tl over 5f out: rdn over 3f out: sn btn: t.o* **66/1**

55- **7** *22* **Little Bit Lively (IRE)**[53] 1261 4-10-11 0......................... JackQuinlan(3) 30
(Sarah Humphrey) *mid-div tl 7f out: sn bhd: t.o* **40/1**

33/ **8** *3 ½* **Move Along**[553] 5179 6-10-4 0...................................... RachaelGreen(3) 20
(Anthony Honeyball) *hld up towards rr: hdwy fr 6f out: hung rt on bnd over 3f out: sn wknd: t.o* **6/1**[3]

06- **9** *47* **Afillycalledlily (IRE)**[27] 1531 4-10-7 0..............................(t) DavidBass
(Lawney Hill) *mid-div tl 7f out: sn wl bhd: t.o* **33/1**

10 *87* **Queen Avalon** 4-10-2 0...[1] MattCrawley(5)
(Lucy Wadham) *a bhd: t.o fr 5f out: virtually p.u fnl 2f* **12/1**

4m 23.5s (-5.20) **Going Correction** -0.25s/f (Good) 10 Ran SP% **115.4**
Speed ratings: **100,98,91,91,89 78,68,67,47,11**
Tote Swingers: 1&2 £2.20, 2&3 £22.60 CSF £9.55 TOTE £4.80: £1.50, £1.10, £8.70; EX 13.10 Trifecta £440.50 Pool: £738.32 - 1.25 winning units..

The Form Book Jumps, Raceform Ltd, Compton, RG20 6NL.

Owner Equis & Christopher Spence **Bred** Chieveley Manor Stud **Trained** Upper Lambourn, Berks

FOCUS

First division of a bumper which was run at a sound pace. A step up from the winner with the third to his mark.

1771 BLACK & VEATCH SUPPORTING TODAY'S CHARITIES STANDARD OPEN NATIONAL HUNT FLAT RACE (DIV II) 2m 2f 110y

5:50 (5:51) (Class 6) 4-6-Y-O **£1,559** (£457; £228; £114)

Form RPR

/2- **1** **Lily Waugh (IRE)**[152] 146 6-10-4 0 RachaelGreen(3) 105+
(Anthony Honeyball) *trckd ldrs: chal gng wl 2f out: sn led: rdn and kpt on wl fnl f* **7/2**[3]

3/ **2** *1 1/4* **Third Act (IRE)**[165] 5475 4-11-0 0 JoeTizzard 109+
(Colin Tizzard) *travelled wl: trckd ldrs: disp ld fr over 5f out: outrt ldr over 2f out: rdn and hdd wl over 1f out: kpt on but a being hld fnl f* **7/4**[1]

3 *12* **Coco Shambhala** 5-10-7 0 LeightonAspell 91
(Oliver Sherwood) *mid-div: hdwy 5f out: sltly outpcd over 3f out: hdwy to chse ldng pair 2f out: styd on same pce* **7/1**

4 *6* **Badger Wood**[160] 4-11-0 0 DavidEngland 93
(Giles Smyly) *trckd ldrs: rdn over 2f out: one pce fnl 2f* **25/1**

- **5** *18* **Eddy** 4-11-0 0 ConorO'Farrell 77
(John Panvert) *hld up bhd: sme prog over 4f out: nvr threatened ldrs: wknd over 2f out* **66/1**

0/ **6** *16* **Saffron Wells (IRE)**[283] 3273 5-10-9 0 TrevorWhelan(5) 77
(Neil King) *racd keenly: disp ld tl rdn over 2f out: sn wknd: t.o* **3/1**[2]

7 *10* **Pursuitofhappiness (IRE)**[188] 5-11-0 0 NoelFehily 53
(Neil Mulholland) *mid-div: hdwy to trck ldrs over 4f out: effrt over 3f out: sn wknd: t.o* **16/1**

3/5- **8** *37* **Guest Of Honour (FR)**[151] 160 5-11-0 0 JamieMoore 20
(Renee Robeson) *disp ld tl over 5f out: sn wknd: t.o* **14/1**

0/ **9** *2 1/2* **Utaly (FR)**[222] 4432 5-11-0 0 MarcGoldstein 18
(Michael Roberts) *mid-div tl over 5f out: sn bhd: t.o* **33/1**

4m 25.8s (-2.90) **Going Correction** -0.25s/f (Good) 9 Ran SP% **116.9**
Speed ratings: **96,95,90,87,80 73,69,53,52**
Tote Swingers: 1&2 £2.10, 1&3 £4.50, 2&3 £4.00 CSF £10.03 TOTE £4.60: £1.70, £1.10, £2.60; EX 10.70 Trifecta £44.30 Pool: £1,312.90 - 22.18 winning units..
Owner Go To War **Bred** F Boyd **Trained** Mosterton, Dorset

FOCUS

Part two and the gallop in the first half of the race was much steadier, resulting in a slower time. The winner is rated to her Ffos Las level.

T/Plt: £37.70 to a £1 stake. Pool: £75,672.44 - 1,461.81 winning tickets. T/Qpdt: £29.90 to a £1 stake. Pool: £3,796.30 - 93.93 winning tickets. TM

1772 - 1775a (Foreign Racing) - See Raceform Interactive

1757 GOWRAN PARK (R-H)

Saturday, October 5

OFFICIAL GOING: Hurdle course - yielding; chase course - good

1776a PWC CHAMPION CHASE (GRADE 2) (14 fncs) 2m 4f

4:40 (4:40) 5-Y-O+ **£20,609** (£6,024; £2,853; £951)

RPR

1 **Sizing Europe (IRE)**[165] 5487 11-11-10 169 AELynch 159+
(Henry De Bromhead, Ire) *chsd ldr in 2nd tl almost on terms 3 out: led next: pushed out run-in and styd on wl* **4/5**[1]

2 *1 1/4* **Baily Green (IRE)**[163] 5531 7-11-8 154 (t) DJCasey 157
(M F Morris, Ire) *chsd ldrs: prog into 3rd after 4 out: styd on wl run-in to go 2nd clsng strides* **8/1**

3 *nk* **Rubi Light (FR)**[164] 5517 8-11-10 158 BarryGeraghty 158+
(Robert Alan Hennessy, Ire) *sn clr ldr: advantage reduced 1/2-way: sn extended again: pressed 3 out and hdd next: kpt on same pce run-in: dropped to 3rd clsng strides* **4/1**[2]

4 *4* **Laganbank (IRE)**[24] 1573 7-11-3 138 RWalsh 147
(W P Mullins, Ire) *hld up in rr: tk clsr order in 4th 2 out: sn no imp on ldrs: kpt on same pce run-in* **25/1**

5 *10* **Tribes And Banner (IRE)**[15] 1613 9-11-3 144 JohnCullen 139
(C F Swan, Ire) *w.w: no imp after 3 out: lft 5th next* **33/1**

6 *9* **Sumkindasuprstar (IRE)**[164] 5517 9-11-8 132 (tp) BenDalton 133
(John O Clifford, Ire) *chsd ldrs in 4th tl nt qckn and dropped to rr after 3 out: sn no imp* **66/1**

F **Quito De La Roque (FR)**[164] 5515 9-11-10 159 (p) DavyRussell 152+
(C A Murphy, Ire) *sn chsd ldrs in 3rd: clsd 1/2-way: pushed along and nt qckn bef 3 out: no ex in 6th whn fell next* **8/1**

F **Roi Du Mee (FR)**[188] 5046 8-11-8 157 (t) DavyCondon 149+
(Gordon Elliott, Ire) *w.w towards rr tl prog to chse ldrs bef 3 out: no imp in 5th whn fell next* **6/1**[3]

4m 46.5s (-24.80) 8 Ran SP% **120.3**
CSF £0.00 TOTE £1.80: £1.70, £2.80, £1.70; DF 9.40 Trifecta £25.30.
Owner Ann & Alan Potts Partnership **Bred** Mrs Angela Bracken **Trained** Knockeen, Co Waterford

FOCUS

A good renewal, but the tight finish and the fourth to sixth limit the form a little. Sizing Europe has improved 11lb+ for his seasonal debut in the last three years.

1777 - 1778a (Foreign Racing) - See Raceform Interactive

1533 HUNTINGDON (R-H)

Sunday, October 6

OFFICIAL GOING: Good (watered; chs 7.5, hdl 7.3)

Wind: Light; across Weather: Very bright and sunny; 18 degrees

1779 THOMAS MORRIS (SALES & LETTINGS) NOVICES' HURDLE (8 hdls) 2m 110y

2:10 (2:10) (Class 4) 4-Y-O+ **£3,898** (£1,144; £572; £286)

Form RPR

2U1- **1** **Azure Fly (IRE)**[96] 857 5-11-5 135 (tp) AidanColeman 128+
(Charlie Longsdon) *chsd clr ldr: clsd after 3rd: a gng strly after: hit 5th: led on bit after 3 out: 5 l clr last: edgd lft briefly flat: hrd hld* **1/1**[1]

04/ **2** *10* **Uriah Heep (FR)**[11] 4787 4-10-12 0 RobertThornton 107+
(Alan King) *hld up in chsng gp: effrt in 4th whn blnd 3 out: sn drvn: no ch w wnr fr next: untidy jump last but tk 2nd flat* **9/2**[2]

6/5- **3** *1 1/4* **The Stig (FR)**[156] 101 5-10-12 0 RichieMcLernon 104
(Nick Littmoden) *hld up in midfield: wnt 4th and gng wl after 5th: tk 2nd 2 out: rdn and no ch w wnr after: lost 2nd after last* **80/1**

4 *9* **Kaafel (IRE)**[13] 4-10-12 0 TomCannon 97
(Peter Hedger) *t.k.h: hld up in midfield: rdn and tried to cl 3 out: one pce fr next* **33/1**

5 *3 1/2* **Ashdown Lad**[100] 4-10-12 0 AlainCawley 96+
(Tom Symonds) *t.k.h: chsd ldrs: rdn 3 out: suddenly heavily eased bef next* **9/2**[2]

6 *1 3/4* **Uramazin (IRE)**[686] 7-10-12 0 LeightonAspell 92
(Philip Hide) *mstkes: midfield: rdn and no ex after 3 out: mstke last: plugged on* **14/1**

6/1- **7** *3 1/4* **Jonnie Skull (IRE)**[9] 1519 7-11-5 0 (t) SamTwiston-Davies 96
(Phil McEntee) *led at fast pce and clr tl 3rd: rdn and hdd after 3 out: sn lost pl* **7/1**[3]

5/ **8** *1* **Waving**[34] 2430 4-10-7 0 (t) JoshHamer(5) 87
(Tony Carroll) *hld up: prog after 5th: chal next: 2nd and drvn home turn: lost pl qckly* **33/1**

9 *32* **Mishrif (USA)**[25] 7-10-2 0 (v) StevieSanders(10) 59
(J R Jenkins) *mstkes in rr: poor last and drvn after 3rd: hdwy bef next: sn chsng ldrs: drvn and fdd after 5th: t.o bef 2 out* **66/1**

6/4- **10** *50* **Resourceful Miss**[150] 186 4-10-5 0 PaulMoloney
(Paul Webber) *mstke 1st: towards rr: mstke 4th: drvn and floundering after next: jumping last as wnr fin* **50/1**

11 *2* **My Best Man**[20] 7-10-12 0 LeeEdwards
(Tony Carroll) *struggling fr 4th: t.o after bad blunder next: jumping last as wnr fin* **150/1**

P **Thecornishwren (IRE)**[13] 4-10-5 0 (t) JamieMoore
(John Ryan) *mstke 2nd: nvr travelling: last and struggling after 3rd: t.o and p.u 3 out* **150/1**

3m 44.5s (-10.40) **Going Correction** -0.575s/f (Firm)
WFA 4 from 5yo+ 9lb 12 Ran SP% **117.4**
Speed ratings (Par 105): **101,96,95,91,89 89,87,87,71,48 47,**
toteswingers 1&2 £1.10, 1&3 £37.60, 2&3 £37.60 CSF £5.62 TOTE £2.20: £1.10, £1.80, £9.70; EX 6.80 Trifecta £326.70 Pool: £691.65 - 1.58 winning units.
Owner Girls Allowed **Bred** Noel Fenton **Trained** Over Norton, Oxon

■ Stewards' Enquiry : Alain Cawley 10-day ban; failing to take all reasonable measures to obtain best possible placing (20th-29th Oct).

FOCUS

A glorious day and ground expected to be just on the quick side of good, but it was evident after a race that it was a watered surface.

1780 PARTNERS FINANCIAL H'CAP CHASE (THE SUNDAY £5K BONUS RACE) (12 fncs) 2m 110y

2:45 (2:45) (Class 4) (0-120,117) 4-Y-O+ **£3,898** (£1,144; £572; £286)

Form RPR

111- **1** **Cap Elorn (FR)**[27] 1537 7-11-5 110 (b) SamTwiston-Davies 125+
(Lawney Hill) *j. fast and low: mde virtually all at brisk pce: at least 6 l clr fr 8th: styd on strly fr 2 out: brushed through last: unchal* **9/4**[2]

/43- **2** *7* **Midnight Tuesday (FR)**[26] 1549 8-11-9 114 (t) HarrySkelton 122+
(Dan Skelton) *plld hrd and racd awkwardly in rr: mstkes 2nd and 6th: mostly jumping bdly lft fr 1/2-way: 10 l 4th home turn: plugged on after 2 out: hit last but sn wnt poor 2nd flat* **15/8**[1]

P/1- **3** *6* **Captain Paulie (IRE)**[141] 377 10-11-9 117 AdamWedge(3) 117
(Evan Williams) *chsd ldng pair: wnt 2nd after 3 out: sn hrd drvn and nvr rchd wnr: lost mod 2nd after last* **8/1**

06P- **4** *22* **Court In Session (IRE)**[19] 1597 8-11-12 117 IanPopham 101
(Martin Keighley) *t.k.h early: w wnr tl outj. 4th: outpcd by him fr 1/2-way: rdn and lost 2nd after 3 out: fin v weakly: t.o* **7/2**[3]

203- **P** **Fiftyonefiftyone (IRE)**[27] 1537 9-11-5 115 (p) JoeCornwall(5)
(John Cornwall) *midfield: rdn and lost pl 7th: t.o and p.u 3 out* **16/1**

40F- **P** **Maoi Chinn Tire (IRE)**[15] 1503 6-11-8 113 SeanQuinlan
(Jennie Candlish) *mstkes and j.ffr in detached last: nvr travelling: t.o fr 5th tl p.u 2 out* **12/1**

3m 59.6s (-10.60) **Going Correction** -0.475s/f (Good) 6 Ran SP% **112.5**
Speed ratings (Par 105): **105,101,98,88,**
toteswingers 1&2 £1.02, 1&3 £1.70, 2&3 £4.40 CSF £7.27 TOTE £3.00: £1.90, £1.90; EX 7.80 Trifecta £16.30 Pool: £433.27 - 19.81 winning units.
Owner Andy Weller **Bred** Jean-Luc Guillerm **Trained** Aston Rowant, Oxon

FOCUS

A modest handicap.

1781 THOMAS MORRIS CONVEYANCING JUVENILE HURDLE (8 hdls) 2m 110y

3:25 (3:25) (Class 4) 3-Y-O **£3,249** (£954; £477; £238)

Form RPR

214- **1** **Hanga Roa (IRE)**[27] 1536 3-11-5 0 JamieMoore 105+
(Gary Moore) *pressed ldr tl led 3rd: drvn clr after 3 out: 18 l ahd whn bungled last: unchal* **4/1**[2]

1- **2** *15* **Refer**[38] 1439 3-11-5 0 SamTwiston-Davies 91
(Phil Middleton) *i. bdly rt 2nd: prom: hit 3rd: drvn 5th: wnt 7 l 2nd bef 3 out: no ch w wnr whn mstke next* **8/11**[1]

3 *11* **Rancher (IRE)**[41] 3-10-12 0 (b) LeeEdwards 73
(Tony Carroll) *t.k.h: hmpd 2nd: sn towards rr: 4th whn hit 3 out: sn vainly chsng ldng pair: mstke last* **33/1**

4 *13* **Ravens Nest**[184] 3-10-12 0 (p) DavidBass 64
(Ben Pauling) *3rd tl wnt 2nd bef 4th: rdn 5th: lost pl and j.rt next: blnd last: fin weakly* **20/1**

5 *10* **Unmoothaj**[18] 3-10-12 0 SeanQuinlan 50
(Pam Sly) *t.k.h: hmpd and mstke 1st: bmpd 2nd: chsd ldrs: 5th and btn whn mstke 3 out* **9/2**[3]

6 *6* **Royal Caper**[4] 3-10-12 0 (t) MattieBatchelor 45
(John Ryan) *sn last: j.rt 2nd: struggling 4th: t.o after next* **25/1**

7 *54* **Barnaby Brook (CAN)**[37] 3-10-12 0 PaulMoloney
(Nick Littmoden) *hmpd 2nd: bhd: rdn and lost tch 5th: sn t.o* **20/1**

P **Minimee**[3] 3-10-5 0 JackSherwood(7)
(Phil McEntee) *cl up: hmpd 2nd: drvn 3 out: dropped out rapidly: t.o and p.u next* **20/1**

0- **P** **Arabougg**[38] 1439 3-10-9 0 RobertDunne(3)
(Nikki Evans) *led at stdy pce: hdd 3rd: wkng whn mstke next: t.o 3 out: p.u last* **100/1**

3m 50.4s (-4.50) **Going Correction** -0.575s/f (Firm) 9 Ran SP% **118.1**
Speed ratings (Par 103): **87,79,74,68,63 61,35, ,**
toteswingers 1&2 £1.30, 1&3 £42.00, 2&3 £15.30 CSF £7.23 TOTE £6.10: £1.50, £1.10, £5.90; EX 9.50 Trifecta £171.00 Pool: £1,955.66 - 8.57 winning units.
Owner C E Stedman **Bred** M Parrish **Trained** Lower Beeding, W Sussex

FOCUS
This was a weak juvenile hurdle.

1782 RELOCATION AGENT NETWORK NOVICES' LIMITED H'CAP CHASE (12 fncs) 2m 110y
3:55 (3:55) (Class 3) (0-140,132) 4-Y-O+ **£7,797** (£2,289; £1,144; £572)

Form RPR
515- **1** **My Brother Sylvest**[35] 1485 7-11-1 **128**......................(b) TomScudamore 138+
(David Pipe) *led tl 4th: led again bef 8th: pushed clr after 3 out: 10 l ahd whn nudged last: eased fnl 100yds* **7/4**[1]

3/1- **2** *20* **Red Riverman**[45] 1343 5-10-11 **124**........................ SamTwiston-Davies 112
(Nigel Twiston-Davies) *settled in 3rd: nt fluent 8th: wnt 2nd next: lost tch w wnr u.p after 3 out: mod 2nd whn mstke next* **15/8**[2]

412/ **3** *14* **Netherby**[583] 4614 7-11-0 **130**........................ JoshuaMoore[(3)] 108
(Gary Moore) *mstkes: chsd ldrs: drvn and outpcd after 3 out: mstkes 2 out and last* **10/3**[3]

PP6- **4** *97* **Radsoc De Sivola (FR)**[14] 1638 8-10-0 **118** oh50........... JoeCornwall[(5)] 5
(John Cornwall) *mstkes and tended to jump lft: 20 l last at 4th: t.o fr 6th: fence bhd whn blnd over 2 out and last* **100/1**

115- **P** **Jack The Gent (IRE)**[114] 735 9-11-5 **132**........................ BarryKeniry
(George Moore) *mstke 2nd: led at str pce 4th tl bef 8th: stopped to nil bef 3 out: remote 4th and p.u sn after fence* **7/1**

4m 1.6s (-8.60) **Going Correction** -0.475s/f (Good) **5** Ran SP% **107.7**
Speed ratings (Par 107): **101,91,85,39,**
CSF £5.40 TOTE £2.80: £1.50, £1.60; EX 5.10 Trifecta £13.50 Pool: £726.45 - 40.21 winning units.
Owner Teddington Racing Club **Bred** David Brace **Trained** Nicholashayne, Devon

FOCUS
A moderate novice handicap.

1783 FINE & COUNTRY H'CAP HURDLE (10 hdls) 2m 4f 110y
4:25 (4:25) (Class 4) (0-120,117) 4-Y-O+ **£3,249** (£954; £477; £238)

Form RPR
114- **1** **Mrs Peachey (IRE)**[114] 738 6-11-8 **113**........................ AidanColeman 126+
(Kim Bailey) *confidently rdn in rr: smooth prog after 7th: wnt 2nd 3 out: sn led and gng clr: j.rt 2 out: 6 l ahd whn j.rt last: kpt on strly* **4/1**[1]

5/4- **2** *8* **Priors Gold**[24] 1319 6-10-9 **110**........................ NathanAdams[(10)] 115
(Laura Mongan) *prom: disp 2nd fr after 3 out: rdn and no imp fr next: wl hld 2nd whn hit last* **8/1**

0/3- **3** *4 ½* **Marju King (IRE)**[19] 1597 7-11-0 **105**........................ SamTwiston-Davies 106
(Phil Middleton) *settled towards rr: stdy prog 7th: rdn to vie for 2nd fr bef 2 out: sn one pce and nvr rchd wnr* **9/2**[2]

305- **4** *8* **Godwit**[41] 1400 5-10-9 **100**........................ BrendanPowell 94
(Eugene Stanford) *led: rdn and hdd sn after 3 out: wknd to wl btn 4th at next* **12/1**

453- **5** *16* **Quinsman**[41] 1391 7-11-1 **106**........................ RobertThornton 84
(Caroline Bailey) *3rd tl wnt 2nd bef 6th: rdn and lost pl tamely 3 out: poor 5th at next* **11/2**[3]

F65/ **6** *4* **Norse Wren**[216] 4568 5-10-12 **103**........................ SamJones 78
(Renee Robeson) *j. deliberately 2nd and 3rd: midfield: rdn and effrt 6th: pressed ldrs after next: lost tch qckly after 3 out* **22/1**

554- **7** *5* **Giant Hercules (IRE)**[41] 1404 6-9-11 **95**........................ JackSherwood[(7)] 65
(Phil McEntee) *mounted outside paddock: chsd ldrs: nt fluent 5th: hit 7th and drvn: struggling after: t.o* **25/1**

2/0- **8** *7* **Gores Island (IRE)**[147] 244 7-11-12 **117**........................ JamieMoore 81
(Gary Moore) *bhd: rdn 7th: struggling next: t.o after 3 out* **11/2**[3]

665/ **9** *76* **Star Presenter (IRE)**[161] 8 5-10-13 **104**........................ PaulMoloney
(Paul Webber) *a last: rdn 8th: hopelessly t.o fr 3 out* **10/1**

320/ **P** **King Ozzy (IRE)**[352] 1919 9-11-8 **113**........................(tp) DavidBass
(Lawney Hill) *pressed ldr tl bef 6th: stopped to nil next: t.o and p.u 2 out* **20/1**

200- **P** **Captain Sully (IRE)**[54] 1259 8-9-7 **91** oh12........................ CharlieDeutsch[(7)]
(Jim Wilson) *nvr bttr than midfield: rdn 6th: struggling next: t.o and p.u last* **16/1**

4m 44.0s (-15.00) **Going Correction** -0.575s/f (Firm) **11** Ran SP% **115.7**
Speed ratings (Par 105): **105,101,100,97,91 89,87,85,56,**
toteswingers 1&2 £8.30, 1&3 £4.10, 2&3 £11.30 CSF £34.43 CT £149.58 TOTE £4.90: £2.50, £3.00, £1.60; EX 37.90 Trifecta £388.50 Pool: £1,178.09 - 2.27 winning units.
Owner The Boom Syndicate **Bred** J Hanly & C Neilan **Trained** Andoversford, Gloucs

FOCUS
This looked competitive, but Mrs Peachey ran out a most decisive winner on her return from a 114-day absence.

1784 MAGPAS H'CAP HURDLE (12 hdls) 3m 2f
4:55 (4:55) (Class 5) (0-95,95) 4-Y-O+ **£2,274** (£667; £333; £166)

Form RPR
224- **1** **Southway Queen**[36] 1477 9-11-2 **92**........................(tp) PatrickCorbett[(7)] 95
(Sue Gardner) *trckd ldrs: wnt 2nd at 6th: led bef 8th: hit next: drvn 2 out: 3 l clr fr 2 out tl last: hung on to dwindling advantage after: gamely fnd ex fnl 100yds* **5/1**[3]

/45- **2** *½* **Midnight Mustang**[23] 1578 6-10-6 **82**........................ MrJMartin[(7)] 85
(Andrew J Martin) *chsd ldrs but rn in snatches: drvn and outpcd by ldng pair bef 3 out: wnt 2nd at next: 3 l down whn hit last: styd on u.p tl no ex fnl 75yds* **9/1**

/05- **3** *1 ¼* **Princesse Katie (IRE)**[14] 1635 7-9-7 **69**........................(t) MrMatthewStanley[(7)] 70
(James Bennett) *settled in detached last tl 1/2-way: drvn and prog 8th: chsd ldng pair fr 2 out: no imp whn edgd lft flat* **33/1**

P04- **4** *3 ¼* **Spanish Fork (IRE)**[27] 1538 4-11-5 **89**........................ MarcGoldstein 86
(Sheena West) *hit 4th and rdn: nvr bttr than midfield or gng wl enough: drvn again after 7th: plugged on fr 2 out: nvr looked like getting in a blow* **3/1**[1]

044- **5** *9* **Orsm**[52] 1275 6-11-6 **89**........................(tp) TomCannon 79
(Laura Mongan) *trckd ldrs: wnt 3rd after 7th: cl 2nd fr next tl hrd drvn home turn: fdd tamely fr 2 out* **7/1**

436- **6** *3 ¼* **Minella Bliss (IRE)**[36] 1474 8-11-9 **95**........................ RobertDunne[(3)] 82
(Nikki Evans) *settled towards rr: stdy hdwy 8th: pressed ldrs briefly next: fading tamely whn hit 3 out* **8/1**

363- **7** *¾* **Heezagrey (IRE)**[27] 1538 10-10-6 **75**........................(b) WayneHutchinson 61
(James Evans) *sn sulking in rr and urged along: last pair mostly: remote fr 7th: plugged on* **4/1**[2]

2P6- **P** **Le Seychellois (FR)**[43] 1377 13-9-9 **69** oh2........................ HarryChalloner[(5)]
(Richard Ford) *lft in ld 5th: hdd 8th: rdn and wkng rapidly whn blnd next: hopelessly t.o whn p.u after 3 out* **9/1**

/1P- **P** **Top Benefit (IRE)**[135] 461 11-10-7 **83**........................ MrPJohn[(7)]
(Richard Harper) *prom tl rdn and lost pl bef 8th: hopelessly t.o whn hopped over 3 out and p.u* **25/1**

P00- **P** **Burnthill (IRE)**[41] 1405 8-10-13 **82**........................(tp) LiamHeard
(Claire Dyson) *led tl j. slowly 5th: sn drvn and lost pl: nt keen: t.o fr 7th: p.u 3 out* **20/1**

6m 19.8s (-3.10) **Going Correction** -0.575s/f (Firm)
WFA 4 from 6yo+ 11lb **10** Ran SP% **116.8**
Speed ratings (Par 103): **81,80,80,79,76 75,75,,,**
toteswingers 1&2 £7.80, 1&3 £10.70, 2&3 £44.80 CSF £47.58 CT £1341.86 TOTE £5.40: £2.10, £4.40, £3.40; EX 78.40 Trifecta £662.80 Part won. Pool: £883.83 - 0.67 winning units..
Owner Clear Racing **Bred** T R Watts **Trained** Longdown, Devon

FOCUS
An ordinary staying handicap.
T/Plt: £15.70 to a £1 stake. Pool: £58,062.65 - 2,683.09 winning units T/Qpdt: £10.90 to a £1 stake. Pool: £3,127.55 - 210.90 winning units IM

[491] KELSO (L-H)
Sunday, October 6

OFFICIAL GOING: Good (good to firm in places; 8.0)
Wind: Breezy; half against Weather: Cloudy

1785 RADIO BORDERS H'CAP HURDLE (8 hdls) 2m 110y
2:00 (2:00) (Class 4) (0-120,118) 4-Y-O+ **£3,898** (£1,144; £572; £286)

Form RPR
/20- **1** **Glencree (IRE)**[119] 681 9-11-6 **112**........................(p) BrianHughes 115
(John Wade) *cl up: led after 4 out: rdn bef 2 out: hld on wl run-in* **14/1**

500/ **2** *hd* **Bright Applause**[15] 3122 5-10-7 **99**........................ DougieCostello 102
(Tracy Waggott) *midfield: stdy hdwy after 3 out: effrt and rdn next: chsd wnr run-in: kpt on wl: jst hld* **22/1**

233- **3** *1 ¾* **Endeavor**[10] 1666 8-10-7 **104**........................ TonyKelly[(5)] 105
(Dianne Sayer) *t.k.h: prom: wnt 2nd after 3 out: effrt and rdn next: lost 2nd run-in: kpt on same pce* **5/1**[2]

5/P- **4** *2 ½* **Abbey Garth (IRE)**[133] 491 6-10-13 **105**........................ BrianHarding 104
(Nicky Richards) *hld up and bhd: stdy hdwy and prom 2 out: pushed along and outpcd run-in* **10/1**[3]

/65- **5** *6* **Cavite Eta (IRE)**[40] 1414 6-10-12 **104**........................ JasonMaguire 97
(Barry Murtagh) *cl up: chal 2nd to after 4 out: rdn and outpcd whn drifted rt fr last* **22/1**

465/ **6** *½* **Talkin Thomas (IRE)**[168] 5425 7-10-11 **110**........................ MissJRRichards[(7)] 103
(Nicky Richards) *hld up in midfield: stdy hdwy and prom 3 out: mstke next: sn rdn and outpcd* **5/1**[2]

1/2- **7** *2 ½* **Next Edition (IRE)**[19] 927 5-10-5 **102**........................ AdamNicol[(5)] 95
(Philip Kirby) *nt fluent: hld up: rdn along bef 3 out: no imp bef next* **15/8**[1]

150- **8** *1 ¼* **Overpriced**[119] 681 7-11-5 **118**........................(t) StephenMulqueen[(7)] 107
(Maurice Barnes) *towards rr: drvn along and outpcd after 4 out: rallied appr 2 out: no imp* **40/1**

/3- **9** *1* **Zambezi Tiger (IRE)**[50] 1288 4-10-9 **101**........................(t) JamesReveley 89
(Patrick Griffin, Ire) *hld up: stdy hdwy and in tch bef 2 out: sn rdn and wknd* **50/1**

455- **10** *10* **Millers Reef (IRE)**[11] 1656 7-10-0 **92** oh2........................(t) WilsonRenwick 70
(Andrew Parker) *prom tl rdn and wknd bef 2 out* **14/1**

455- **11** *¾* **Turtle Watch**[94] 880 5-10-3 **95**........................ RichieMcGrath 72
(Jim Goldie) *t.k.h: prom tl rdn and wknd bef 2 out* **20/1**

3/6- **12** *½* **Lillioftheballet (IRE)**[27] 1544 6-10-0 **92** oh3........................ LucyAlexander 68
(Jim Goldie) *hld up: struggling after 4 out: btn bef 2 out* **22/1**

/03- **P** **Ballybroe (IRE)**[130] 537 6-10-8 **103**........................ EwanWhillans[(3)]
(Harriet Graham) *mde most to after 4 out: struggling next: t.o whn p.u and dismntd run-in* **28/1**

3m 44.1s (-17.70) **Going Correction** -0.875s/f (Firm)
WFA 4 from 5yo+ 9lb **13** Ran SP% **116.2**
Speed ratings (Par 105): **106,105,105,103,101 100,99,99,98,93 93,93,**
toteswingers 1&2 £40.40, 1&3 £10.80, 2&3 £40.40 CSF £271.52 CT £1752.57 TOTE £19.00: £5.50, £9.70, £2.20; EX 310.50 Trifecta £496.50 Part won. Pool: £662.00 - 0.01 winning units..
Owner John Wade **Bred** P J Doyle **Trained** Mordon, Co Durham

FOCUS
A soundly run, competitive handicap.

1786 URWIN FAMILY JUVENILE HURDLE (8 hdls) 2m 110y
2:35 (2:35) (Class 4) 3-Y-O **£3,898** (£1,144; £572; £286)

Form RPR
235- **1** **Kitchapoly (FR)**[8] 1684 3-11-12 118........................ JasonMaguire 113+
(Donald McCain) *midfield on ins: smooth hdwy to ld bef 2 out: clr last: easily* **7/2**[2]

1- **2** *5* **Estinaad (USA)**[11] 1658 3-10-12 0........................ DannyCook 92
(Brian Ellison) *in tch: stdy hdwy 3 out: effrt and rdn whn hit next: kpt on fr last: nt rch wnr* **7/4**[1]

3 *8* **Aneedh**[16] 3-10-12 0........................ BrianHarding 85
(Jedd O'Keeffe) *t.k.h early: prom: hdwy and ev ch briefly bef 2 out: sn rdn: wknd fr last* **7/2**[2]

4 *14* **Brookland Breeze (IRE)**[47] 3-9-12 0........................ LiamMcKenna[(7)] 64
(J J Lambe, Ire) *in tch: mstke 1st: nt fluent next: rdn and outpcd whn hit 3 out: plugged on fr next: n.d* **33/1**

6- **5** *8* **Chloe's Image**[11] 1658 3-10-5 0........................ RichieMcGrath 54
(Philip Kirby) *cl up: led briefly 1st: rdn and wknd bef 2 out* **20/1**

6 *6* **Hazza The Jazza**[5] 3-10-12 0........................(p) WilsonRenwick 55
(Richard Guest) *hld up: rdn and outpcd after 4 out: n.d after* **12/1**

7 *16* **Duchess Of Dreams**[1] 3-10-0 0........................ AdamNicol[(5)] 32
(Richard Guest) *plld hrd in rr: hdwy and led after 1st: j.lft 4th: hdd bef 2 out: sn wknd* **66/1**

8 *5* **Jebulani**[15] 3-10-12 0........................ BrianHughes 34
(Barry Murtagh) *t.k.h: led to 1st: cl up tl nt fluent and wknd fr 3 out* **20/1**

9 *14* **Ihtikar (USA)**[179] 3-10-12 0........................ DougieCostello 20
(Lucy Normile) *hld up: nt fluent 3rd: mstke and struggling next: n.d after* **9/1**[3]

10 *60* **Classic Orange** 3-10-2 0........................ JohnKington[(3)]
(Simon Waugh) *hld up: struggling 1/2-way: sn lost tch: t.o* **100/1**

3m 47.5s (-14.30) **Going Correction** -0.875s/f (Firm) **10** Ran SP% **113.4**
Speed ratings (Par 103): **98,95,91,85,81 78,71,68,62,34**
toteswingers 1&2 £1.50, 1&3 £1.90, 2&3 £1.70 CSF £9.53 TOTE £3.60: £2.00, £1.10, £1.70; EX 9.80 Trifecta £29.70 Pool: £1,284.82 - 32.36 winning units.
Owner Paul & Clare Rooney **Bred** S C P Haras Des Coudraies **Trained** Cholmondeley, Cheshire

The Form Book Jumps, Raceform Ltd, Compton, RG20 6NL.

FOCUS
A soundly-run juvenile with the first three in the market pulling clear.

1787 TIGER MCELRATH NOVICES' LIMITED H'CAP CHASE (17 fncs) 2m 7f 110y
3:05 (3:05) (Class 3) (0-125,123) 4-Y-0+ **£6,498** (£1,908; £954)

Form RPR
225- **1** **Carrigdhoun (IRE)**[2] 1750 8-10-6 **117**.................(tp) StephenMulqueen(7) 125
(Maurice Barnes) *j. hesitantly on occasions: led: reminder 7th: hdd 4 out: sn rdn: rallied bef 2 out: regained ld last: styd on wl* **3/1**[3]
12P- **2** *8* **Atlanta Falcon (IRE)**[65] 1184 8-11-5 **123**.......................(t) JasonMaguire 126
(Donald McCain) *chsd ldrs: smooth hdwy to ld 4 out: rdn 2 out: hdd last: outpcd run-in* **9/4**[2]
/42- **3** *11* **Kris Cross (IRE)**[124] 625 6-11-2 **120**............................ PeterBuchanan 114+
(Lucinda Russell) *chsd wnr: effrt and ev ch 5 out: outpcd next: rallied bef 2 out: 5 l 3rd and outpcd whn blnd bdly last: wknd* **1/1**[1]
5m 50.0s (-18.00) **Going Correction** -0.725s/f (Firm) **3** Ran SP% **105.8**
Speed ratings (Par 107): **101,98,94**
CSF £8.60 TOTE £2.50; EX 5.50 Trifecta £8.00 Pool: £968.83 - 90.81 winning units.
Owner M Barnes **Bred** The Geraghtys Boys **Trained** Farlam, Cumbria

FOCUS
The race began in earnest from four out and all three had a chance at some stage.

1788 NSPCC SCHOOL SERVICE INTERMEDIATE HURDLE (THE SUNDAY £5K BONUS RACE) (11 hdls) 2m 6f 110y
3:45 (3:45) (Class 4) 4-Y-0+ **£5,198** (£1,526; £763; £381)

Form RPR
/54- **1** **Maggio (FR)**[2] 1752 8-11-7 129...(t) DerekFox(5) 131+
(Patrick Griffin, Ire) *prom: wnt 2nd 3rd: effrt 2 out: led run-in: pushed out towards fin* **9/4**[1]
013/ **2** *1 3/4* **Our Joey (IRE)**[200] 4863 5-10-12 120........................ JonathonBewley(7) 122
(George Bewley) *led at ordinary gallop: rdn 2 out: hdd run-in: kpt on: hld nr fin* **9/4**[1]
3 *4 1/2* **Full Jack (FR)**[119] 684 6-10-12 0..................................(b) JamesReveley 113
(Pauline Robson) *t.k.h: prom: stdy hdwy 3 out: effrt whn nt fluent next: sn rdn and one pce last* **9/4**[1]
221- **4** *9* **Bright Abbey**[5] 1714 5-11-12 125..................................... LucyAlexander 118
(Dianne Sayer) *hld up in tch: drvn along after 4 out: rallied: outpcd fr 2 out* **5/1**[2]
P- **5** *94* **Kitnkaboodle (IRE)**[11] 1654 8-9-13 0 ow1...................... MrDFBourke(7)
(Stuart Coltherd) *nt jump wl: cl up to 3rd: sn lost pl: t.o fnl circ* **200/1**
/05- **6** *2 1/2* **Be Wise (IRE)**[78] 1037 6-10-5 0..................................... CallumBewley(7)
(Harriet Graham) *sn bhd and struggling: t.o fnl circ* **125/1**[3]
5m 23.5s (-17.50) **Going Correction** -0.875s/f (Firm) **6** Ran SP% **110.3**
Speed ratings (Par 105): **95,94,92,89,57 56**
toteswingers 1&2 £1.20, 1&3 £1.60, 2&3 £1.50 CSF £7.52 TOTE £3.50: £2.10, £1.80; EX 9.50 Trifecta £18.30 Pool: £1,620.73 - 66.39 winning units.
Owner M Deren **Bred** Haras Du Reuilly **Trained** Oldtown, Co Dublin

FOCUS
Not that competitive and after a steady early pace it gradually wound up on the final circuit as the three co-favourites pulled clear.

1789 FLEET BAR EYEMOUTH H'CAP CHASE (17 fncs) 2m 7f 110y
4:15 (4:15) (Class 5) (0-95,95) 4-Y-0+ **£3,249** (£954; £477; £238)

Form RPR
042- **1** **Chicago Outfit (IRE)**[31] 1502 8-11-9 **92**.........................(p) BrianHughes 100+
(John Wade) *chsd ldrs: rdn and outpcd bef 4 out: rallied bef 2 out: led run-in: styd on wl* **3/1**[1]
411- **2** *2 1/2* **Presenting Junior (IRE)**[43] 1376 6-11-6 **89**.................. WilsonRenwick 92
(Martin Todhunter) *hld up bhd ldng gp: stdy hdwy 5 out: chal 3 out: led and rdn next: hdd run-in: kpt on same pce* **10/3**[2]
004- **3** *3/4* **Western Bound (IRE)**[43] 1374 12-10-0 **69** oh5............(t) DougieCostello 71
(Barbara Butterworth) *hld up: stdy hdwy 12th: rdn and effrt 3 out: kpt on fr last: nrst fin* **22/1**
/2P- **4** *6* **Winter Alchemy (IRE)**[36] 1468 8-11-12 **95**....................(p) BrianHarding 93
(Nicky Richards) *cl up: led 10th: rdn and hdd whn mstke 2 out: sn outpcd* **8/1**
5/2- **5** *23* **Mr Duffy (IRE)**[9] 1681 11-11-6 **89**...................................(v) JasonMaguire 62
(D T Hughes, Ire) *towards rr and nvr gng wl: struggling fnl circ: nvr on terms: lft modest 5th last* **11/2**[3]
/65- **6** *24* **Knight Woodsman**[11] 1655 9-11-2 **92**.......................(p) CallumBewley(7) 41
(R Mike Smith) *mstkes: prom tl hit and wknd 3 out: lost tch fr next* **16/1**
310- **P** **Almond Court (IRE)**[113] 751 10-11-5 **88**.........................(p) KennyJohnson
(Robert Johnson) *led to 10th: cl up tl wknd 5 out: t.o whn p.u bef 2 out* **20/1**
224- **U** **Solway Dornal**[11] 1655 8-9-8 **70**..........................(tp) StephenMulqueen(7) 65
(Lisa Harrison) *chsd ldrs: wnt 2nd after 10th to 5 out: outpcd bef 2 out: 8 l 5th and hld whn blnd and uns rdr last* **7/1**
16P- **P** **Shooting Times**[95] 866 8-11-6 **89**..................................(v) PeterBuchanan
(Lucinda Russell) *a bhd and nvr gng wl: t.o fnl circ: p.u bef last* **8/1**
000- **P** **Snooze N You Lose**[68] 1147 8-9-11 **69** oh10................. JohnKington(3)
(Jean McGregor) *in tch: drvn and outpcd 10th: struggling fr next: t.o whn p.u after 2 out* **100/1**
5m 49.6s (-18.40) **Going Correction** -0.725s/f (Firm) **10** Ran SP% **114.2**
Speed ratings (Par 103): **101,100,99,97,90 82, , , ,**
toteswingers 1&2 £2.60, 1&3 £17.00, 2&3 £24.10 CSF £13.36 CT £180.15 TOTE £4.40: £1.60, £1.80, £5.20; EX 13.80 Trifecta £238.20 Pool: £1,086.84 - 3.42 winning units.
Owner John Wade **Bred** Roger Ryan **Trained** Mordon, Co Durham

FOCUS
A reasonably competitive handicap for the grade.

1790 KATIE SCOTT POINTING & EMMA DUNKLEY'S 18TH NOVICES' H'CAP HURDLE (DIV I) (10 hdls) 2m 2f
4:45 (4:45) (Class 5) (0-95,95) 3-Y-0+ **£2,599** (£763; £381; £190)

Form RPR
066- **1** **Honourable Gent**[27] 1540 5-10-6 **75**.............................[1] WilsonRenwick 81
(Rose Dobbin) *hld up: stdy hdwy 3 out: effrt between last 2: styd on wl to ld nr fin* **28/1**
421- **2** *1* **Sendiym (FR)**[5] 1716 6-10-10 **79**......................................(b) BrianHughes 84
(Dianne Sayer) *led: rdn bef 2 out: rdr dropped whip and edgd lft run-in: kpt on: hdd nr fin* **2/1**[1]
POU- **3** *3* **Dynamic Drive (IRE)**[40] 1419 6-10-8 **84**............(t[1]) StephenMulqueen(7) 87
(Maurice Barnes) *hld up bhd ldng gp: stdy hdwy bef 3 out: effrt and ev ch next: drifted rt bef last* **40/1**
5/3- **4** *hd* **Vodka Red (IRE)**[129] 558 5-11-3 **86**..............................(t) KennyJohnson 88
(Robert Johnson) *hld up: smooth hdwy to chse ldrs bef 3 out: rdn and one pce after next* **11/1**

000/ **5** *9* **Rhymers Stone**[218] 4515 5-11-5 **95**............................ GrantCockburn(7) 88
(Lucinda Russell) *hld up on ins: rdn bef 3 out: no imp bef next* **8/1**[3]
/P2- **6** *7* **Mr Mistopheles (IRE)**[40] 1419 5-10-10 **79**.................(bt) RichieMcGrath 65
(Philip Kirby) *cl up tl rdn and wknd bef 2 out* **4/1**[2]
450/ **7** *1 1/2* **Blue Kascade (IRE)**[168] 5423 6-11-9 **92**.......................... JamesReveley 77
(Sandy Thomson) *hld up: nt fluent 3rd: outpcd whn nt fluent 3 out: n.d* **4/1**[2]
300/ **8** *3 1/4* **Maggie Blue (IRE)**[160] 27 5-10-13 **89**........................ CallumBewley(7) 70
(Harriet Graham) *in tch: hdwy 5th: rdn and wknd bef 2 out* **22/1**
463- **9** *5* **Precision Strike**[9] 1394 3-9-9 **86** oh1..............................(v) AdamNicol(5) 45
(Richard Guest) *trckd ldrs: mstke 6th: nt fluent next: wknd bef 3 out* **10/1**
/55- **10** *45* **Mrs Grass**[40] 1418 6-11-1 **87**... JohnKington(3) 18
(Jonathan Haynes) *chsd ldrs: hit 5th: lost pl next: sn struggling: t.o* **100/1**
4m 17.2s (-9.80) **Going Correction** -0.875s/f (Firm)
WFA 3 from 5yo+ 17lb **10** Ran SP% **113.1**
Speed ratings (Par 103): **86,85,84,84,80 77,76,74,72,52**
toteswingers 1&2 £18.50, 1&3 £63.40, 2&3 £23.90 CSF £82.54 CT £2313.57 TOTE £36.60: £5.80, £1.60, £8.30; EX 148.50 Trifecta £1000.50 Part won. Pool: £1,334.11 - 0.18 winning units..
Owner Mr & Mrs Duncan Davidson **Bred** Mrs P Wright **Trained** South Hazelrigg, Northumbria

FOCUS
A moderate affair but it was run at a good pace which enabled the winner to swoop late.

1791 KATIE SCOTT POINTING & EMMA DUNKLEY'S 18TH NOVICES' H'CAP HURDLE (DIV II) (10 hdls) 2m 2f
5:15 (5:17) (Class 5) (0-95,94) 3-Y-0+ **£2,599** (£763; £381; £190)

Form RPR
0P/ **1** **Push Me (IRE)**[34] 4704 6-11-2 **84**.. AdrianLane 92+
(Iain Jardine) *hld up: smooth hdwy after 3 out: led last: rdn and qcknd clr: readily* **20/1**
0/0- **2** *4 1/2* **Discoverie**[145] 279 5-10-2 **70**... BrianHughes 74
(Dianne Sayer) *chsd ldrs: led gng wl bef 2 out: rdn and hdd last: kpt on same pce run-in* **4/1**[2]
3/P- **3** *13* **Lucky Sun**[153] 145 7-11-5 **87**.. RichieMcGrath 78
(Philip Kirby) *prom: nt fluent 1st: reminder 4th: effrt and ch bef 2 out: outpcd by first two bef last* **3/1**[1]
6/0- **4** *1/2* **Top Billing**[141] 368 4-11-3 **85**..(p) BrianHarding 75
(Nicky Richards) *hld up bhd ldng gp: rdn along after 3 out: plugged on same pce fr next* **8/1**
3P5- **5** *3/4* **Laybach (IRE)**[25] 1567 9-10-4 **72**................................. LucyAlexander 61
(Jim Goldie) *t.k.h: cl up tl rdn and wknd appr 2 out* **5/1**[3]
605- **6** *1 1/4* **Stadium Of Light (IRE)**[14] 1633 6-10-11 **79**.................. DougieCostello 67
(Shaun Harris) *nt fluent: bhd: struggling after 4 out: nvr on terms* **9/1**
/50- **7** *11* **Brae On (IRE)**[144] 313 5-10-13 **88**........................... JonathonBewley(7) 65
(George Bewley) *cl up: led 5th to 4 out: rdn after next: wknd bef 2 out* **9/1**
545- **8** *9* **Mumgos Debut (IRE)**[27] 1543 5-11-8 **90**...................... PeterBuchanan 58
(Lucinda Russell) *led to 5th: cl up: led 4 out to bef 2 out: sn wknd* **8/1**
/05- **U** **Fling Me (IRE)**[133] 494 6-11-12 **94**............................. WilsonRenwick
(Rose Dobbin) *hld up in tch: stdy hdwy and prom bef 3 out: cl sixth but outpcd whn nt fluent, sprawled and uns rdr next* **11/1**
4m 16.5s (-10.50) **Going Correction** -0.875s/f (Firm)
WFA 4 from 5yo+ 9lb **9** Ran SP% **117.0**
Speed ratings (Par 103): **88,86,80,80,79 79,74,70,**
toteswingers 1&2 £27.20, 1&3 £10.20, 2&3 £3.80 CSF £101.09 CT £317.28 TOTE £10.70: £3.60, £2.20, £1.90; EX 160.90 Trifecta £1192.80 Part won. Pool: £1,590.43 - 0.27 winning units..
Owner Alex and Janet Card **Bred** Mrs Dolores Gleeson **Trained** Bonchester Bridge, Borders

FOCUS
This looked the weaker of the two divisions of the novice handicap hurdle.

1792 CITY ROOFING LTD STANDARD OPEN NATIONAL HUNT FLAT RACE 2m 110y
5:45 (5:48) (Class 5) 4-6-Y-O **£2,599** (£763; £381; £190)

Form RPR
1 **Mont Royale** 5-11-0 0.. DannyCook 101+
(Michael Smith) *chsd ldrs: hdwy to ld over 1f out: pushed clr ins fnl f* **16/1**
2 *6* **Lord De Beaufai (FR)**[139] 414 5-10-7 0...................... LiamMcKenna(7) 95
(J J Lambe, Ire) *hld up in midfield: stdy hdwy over 2f out: rdn and chsd wnr fnl f: kpt on: no imp* **4/1**[2]
3 *shd* **Cousin Guillaume (FR)** 4-11-0 0................................... JasonMaguire 94
(Karen McLintock) *t.k.h early: trckd ldrs: rdn and effrt 2f out: edgd lft and one pce ins fnl f* **8/1**[3]
21- **4** *6* **Factor Fifty (IRE)**[118] 699 4-11-2 0.................................. AdamNicol(5) 95
(Philip Kirby) *in tch: effrt and rdn 2 out: wknd ins fnl f* **3/1**[1]
5 *1 1/2* **Final Assault (IRE)**[189] 4-10-7 0.................................. GrantCockburn(7) 87
(Lucinda Russell) *led at ordinary gallop: rdn and hdd over 1f out: sn wknd* **8/1**[3]
0- **6** *1 1/2* **Dark Caviar (IRE)**[10] 1667 5-11-0 0............................... DougieCostello 85
(George Bewley) *hld up: stdy hdwy 3f out: shkn up and wknd over 1f out* **22/1**
7 *hd* **Mr Selby** 4-11-0 0... BrianHarding 85
(Nicky Richards) *hld up in midfield: stdy hdwy over 3f out: rdn drifted lft over 1f out: sn btn* **16/1**
2- **8** *2* **This Thyne Jude**[50] 1292 5-10-7 0.................................... PeterBuchanan 76
(Lucinda Russell) *hld up in midfield on ins: pushed along and outpcd over 3f out: n.d after* **4/1**[2]
00/ **9** *1 1/4* **Ronald Gee (IRE)**[256] 3792 6-11-0 0................................... GaryBartley 82
(Jim Goldie) *hld up: rdn along 3f out: sn struggling* **50/1**
0/0- **10** *hd* **Runswick Days (IRE)**[151] 173 6-10-7 0........................ JohnDawson(7) 82
(John Wade) *prom tl rdn and wknd over 2f out* **80/1**
11 *hd* **Kalanessa** 4-10-7 0... LucyAlexander 75
(Jim Goldie) *hld up: struggling over 3f out: nvr on terms* **9/1**
12 *36* **Oscar Too (IRE)** 4-11-0 0... JamesReveley 46
(Sandy Thomson) *towards rr: struggling over 4f out: sn btn: t.o* **25/1**
3m 45.5s (-10.70) **Going Correction** -0.875s/f (Firm) **12** Ran SP% **120.4**
Speed ratings: **90,87,87,84,83 82,82,81,81,81 81,64**
toteswingers 1&2 £13.10, 1&3 £21.30, 2&3 £8.80 CSF £78.27 TOTE £18.30: £5.50, £2.10, £2.80; EX 111.50 Trifecta £1159.00 Part won. Pool: £1,545.35 - 0.51 winning units..
Owner Mrs Sandra Smith **Bred** D J And Mrs Deer **Trained** Kirkheaton, Northumberland

FOCUS
The first three home were all ridden near the head of affairs and they fought out the finish, with the winner coming clear.
T/Plt: £55.80 to a £1 stake. Pool: £61,112.93 - 798.13 winning units T/Qpdt: £10.80 to a £1 stake. Pool: £3,330.30 - 226.15 winning units RY

1631 UTTOXETER (L-H)

Sunday, October 6

OFFICIAL GOING: Chase course - good to soft (good in places; 6.2); hurdle course - good (good to soft in places; 6.5)

Wind: Light; half against Weather: Fine and sunny; warm

1793 ENSOR GROUP MAIDEN HURDLE (FOR THE STAFFORDSHIRE REGIMENT CHALLENGE CUP) (DIV I) (9 hdls) 2m

1:50 (1:50) (Class 5) 4-Y-0+ **£2,209** (£648; £324; £162)

Form RPR

112/ 1 **Ballyalton (IRE)**[328] 2389 6-11-0 0........ WillKennedy 123+
(Ian Williams) *chsd ldng pair: 2nd 6th: led next: lft clr 2 out: nt fluent last: easily* **2/1**[2]

2 15 **Curzon Line**[212] 4-11-0 0........ DenisO'Regan 105+
(John Ferguson) *mid-div: hdwy 6th: lft modest 2nd 2 out: no ch w wnr* **10/1**

3 5 **Vujiyama (FR)**[152] 4-11-0 0........ APMcCoy 102
(Jonjo O'Neill) *nt fluent in rr: hdwy 5th: modest 3rd whn mstke 3 out: lft modest 3rd next* **7/1**[3]

235- 4 2 ¾ **Snapchat (IRE)**[39] 1427 6-11-0 0........ ConorO'Farrell 97
(Seamus Durack) *stdd s: hld up in rr: hdwy 3 out: styd on run-in* **40/1**

P- 5 8 **Astrogold**[25] 1561 4-10-7 0........ ColinBolger 85
(Mark H Tompkins) *led to 2nd: w ldrs: wknd appr 3 out: lft modest 4th and hmpd next* **100/1**

U30- 6 3 ¼ **Razzle Dazzle 'Em**[14] 1632 4-10-9 0........(t) BenPoste[(5)] 89
(Shaun Harris) *prom: outpcd appr 3 out: sn wknd* **150/1**

220/ 7 1 ¾ **Vinstar (FR)**[160] 22 4-11-0 0........ HenryBrooke 85
(Donald McCain) *prom: drvn 6th: lost pl bef next* **12/1**

- 8 1 **Filatore (IRE)**[21] 4-11-0 0........ JamesDavies 84
(Bernard Llewellyn) *mid-div: drvn and outpcd whn mstke 6th: no ch whn hmpd 2 out* **40/1**

66/ 9 hd **Fly By Knight**[190] 5018 4-11-0 0........ DarylJacob 84
(Tim Walford) *stdd s: bhd: kpt on fr 3 out: nvr on terms* **66/1**

0/2- 10 12 **Straits Of Messina (IRE)**[152] 160 4-11-0 0........ FelixDeGiles 73
(Tom Symonds) *mid-div: sme hdwy 6th: lost pl bef next* **20/1**

200/ 11 ½ **Swing State**[911] 5211 8-11-0 0........ DavidEngland 72
(Tom Gretton) *in rr: bhd fr 5th* **100/1**

12 15 **Mattie's Passion (IRE)**[134] 6-11-0 0........ SamThomas 59
(Jennie Candlish) *mid-div: drvn 6th: sn wknd* **100/1**

13 12 **Arcas (IRE)**[99] 4-11-0 0........ TomO'Brien 48
(Alan Jones) *in rr: bhd fr 5th: t.o 3 out* **80/1**

634/ F **Milord (GER)**[207] 4737 4-11-0 126........ NickScholfield 108
(Kim Bailey) *trckd ldr: led 2nd: hdd 3 out: clr 2nd but wl hld whn fell next* **7/4**[1]

3m 45.9s (-6.10) **Going Correction** -0.65s/f (Firm) **14** Ran SP% **115.0**
Speed ratings (Par 103): **89,81,79,77,73 72,71,70,70,64 64,56,50,**
toteswingers 1&2 £3.50, 1&3 £2.30, 2&3 £6.80 CSF £19.93 TOTE £2.80: £1.10, £2.00, £2.90; EX 22.90 Trifecta £61.30 Pool: £969.85 - 11.85 winning units.
Owner John Westwood **Bred** P Doyle **Trained** Portway, Worcs

FOCUS
Hurdles on inside with course at shortest with divided bends. Ground on the easy side of good. A few of these look interesting in this sphere but the two with the best hurdles form in the book had it between them from the home turn.

1794 ANDREW HALL BIRTHDAY CELEBRATION CONDITIONAL JOCKEYS' MAIDEN HURDLE (10 hdls) 2m 4f 110y

2:20 (2:20) (Class 5) 4-Y-0+ **£2,209** (£648; £324; £162)

Form RPR

/22- 1 **Carlton Jack**[26] 1553 6-10-11 115........ MauriceLinehan[(3)] 117+
(Jonjo O'Neill) *chsd ldrs: chalng whn nt fluent 2 lout: swtchd rt appr last: r.o wl to ld last 30yds* **9/2**[2]

/32- 2 2 **Keltic Rhythm (IRE)**[14] 1632 6-10-11 0........ TrevorWhelan[(3)] 112
(Neil King) *led: hdd and no ex clsng stages* **7/1**

10/ 3 9 **Il Presidente (GER)**[540] 5408 6-11-0 0........ MichealNolan 107+
(Ian Williams) *hdwy and chsd ldrs 4th: cl 3rd whn blnd 2 out: kpt on one pce* **11/2**[3]

333/ 4 1 ½ **Cleve Cottage**[181] 5220 5-11-0 0........ JonathanEngland 104
(Philip Kirby) *w ldr: drvn appr 3 out: one pce* **12/1**

5 4 **Rally**[89] 941 4-10-11 0........ JeremiahMcGrath[(3)] 99
(Nicky Henderson) *chsd ldrs: hrd drvn and outpcd 6th: one pce fr 3 out* **15/8**[1]

5/ 6 4 ½ **Demographic (USA)**[348] 1977 4-11-0 0........ GavinSheehan 96
(Emma Lavelle) *chsd ldrs: drvn appr 3 out: 5th and wkng whn hit last* **33/1**

2P0/ 7 3 ¾ **Soliwery (FR)**[529] 5592 5-10-8 120........ KieronEdgar[(6)] 92
(David Pipe) *in rr-div: hdwy 5th: drvn appr 3 out: wknd between last 2* **14/1**

1- 8 6 **Minella Hero (IRE)**[72] 1124 5-11-0 0........(t) JackQuinlan 87
(Sarah Humphrey) *mid-div: hdwy 7th: chsng ldrs next: sn wknd* **12/1**

042/ 9 34 **West End (IRE)**[155] 6-10-11 0........ EdCookson[(3)] 56
(Kim Bailey) *mid-div: hdwy to chse ldrs 4th: lost pl bef 3 out: sn bhd: t.o* **16/1**

10 nse **Dancing Lancer**[694] 4-11-0 0........(p) JakeGreenall 56
(Tim Walford) *mid-div: drvn after 5th: lost pl after next: sn bhd: t.o* **80/1**

0- 11 15 **Evergreen Forest (IRE)**[14] 1625 5-11-0 0........ MichaelByrne 42
(Natalie Lloyd-Beavis) *in rr: mstke 7th: sn bhd: t.o* **100/1**

00/- 12 18 **Storm Quest**[58] 5364 6-10-7 0........(t) BenPoste 19
(Robin Dickin) *nt jump wl in rr: bhd fr 6th: sn bhd: t.o 3 out* **100/1**

00/ 13 37 **Tilt Du Chatelier (FR)**[252] 3899 6-10-6 0........ JosephPalmowski[(8)]
(Robin Dickin) *rn wout declared tongue-tie: in rr: bhd fr 6th: t.o 3 out* **66/1**

0/P- 14 15 **Rose Of Marron (IRE)**[140] 383 6-10-9 0........ RyanHatch[(5)]
(John Upson) *nt fluent in rr: bhd fr 6th: t.o 3 out* **100/1**

F **Gloshen (IRE)** 7-10-11 0........ NathanMoscrop[(3)]
(Philip Kirby) *in rr: drvn and sme hdwy 6th: lost pl after next: sn bhd: t.o whn fell 3 out* **100/1**

4m 42.3s (-16.70) **Going Correction** -0.65s/f (Firm)
WFA 4 from 5yo+ 10lb **15** Ran SP% **118.4**
Speed ratings (Par 103): **105,104,100,100,98 97,95,93,80,80 74,67,53,47,**
toteswingers 1&2 £5.20, 1&3 £6.30, 2&3 £14.00 CSF £35.21 TOTE £5.20: £1.90, £1.70, £3.40; EX 23.20 Trifecta £220.60 Pool: £1,070.58 - 3.63 winning units.
Owner John P McManus **Bred** A J Wall **Trained** Cheltenham, Gloucs

FOCUS
Quite a competitive maiden hurdle with several having a sound chance on paper.

1795 ENSOR GROUP MAIDEN HURDLE (FOR THE STAFFORDSHIRE REGIMENT CHALLENGE CUP) (DIV II) (9 hdls) 2m

2:55 (2:55) (Class 5) 4-Y-0+ **£2,209** (£648; £324; £162)

Form RPR

1 **Timesremembered (IRE)**[189] 5055 5-10-11 0........ GavinSheehan[(3)] 111+
(Emma Lavelle) *mde all: mstkes: clr after 5th: jnd whn hit last: styd on wl* **11/2**[3]

251/ 2 1 ¾ **No No Mac (IRE)**[192] 4991 4-11-0 0........ NoelFehily 107+
(Charlie Longsdon) *chsd ldrs: clr 2nd 4th: upsides whn hit last: styd on same pce* **3/1**[2]

115/ 3 11 **Dakar Run**[183] 5179 4-11-0 0........ APMcCoy 97
(Jonjo O'Neill) *chsd ldrs: drvn 3 out: one pce* **11/8**[1]

023/ 4 2 ¾ **Mystifiable**[178] 5255 5-11-0 0........(t) PaddyBrennan 94
(Fergal O'Brien) *t.k.h in rr: gd hdwy 6th: 4th next: one pce* **12/1**

4- 5 1 **Tempuran**[68] 1152 4-11-0 0........ RichardJohnson 93
(David Bridgwater) *in rr-div: kpt on fr 3 out: nvr nr ldrs* **9/1**

6 3 **Tweedle Dee**[52] 4-10-4 0........ JackQuinlan[(3)] 83
(Noel Quinlan) *mid-div: hdwy to chse ldrs 6th: 5th and wkng whn hit last* **50/1**

7 nk **Stag Hill (IRE)**[13] 4-10-9 0........ RobertWilliams[(5)] 90
(Bernard Llewellyn) *in rr: mstke 1st: kpt on fr 3 out: nvr a factor* **66/1**

6- 8 ½ **Church Hall (IRE)**[147] 250 5-10-9 0........ JamesBanks[(5)] 90
(Emma Baker) *mid-div: chsd ldrs 6th: wknd appr next* **100/1**

40/ 9 4 ½ **Ghost Of A Smile (IRE)**[228] 4321 5-10-9 0........ RobertMcCarth[(5)] 86
(Ian Williams) *hld up: hdwy 6th: 5th 3 out: sn fdd* **20/1**

3- 10 2 **Iguacu**[6] 1519 9-11-0 0........ DarylJacob 84
(Richard Price) *plld hrd towards rr: nvr a factor* **50/1**

11 21 **Drummond**[20] 4-11-0 0........ JamesDavies 65
(Bernard Llewellyn) *in rr: bhd and drvn 6th* **80/1**

344- 12 5 **State Department**[6] 1695 6-11-0 0........ TomO'Brien 60
(Philip Hobbs) *in rr-div: reminders 5th: sn bhd* **40/1**

13 2 ½ **Eanans Bay (IRE)**[20] 4-11-0 0........ ColinBolger 58
(Mark H Tompkins) *nt jump wl: chsd ldrs: reminders 5th: j. slowly next: sn lost pl and bhd* **100/1**

/00- 14 36 **Wishfull Dancer (IRE)**[19] 1599 5-10-11 0........(t) MichaelByrne[(3)] 26
(John Mackie) *chsd wnr: j.lft 1st: lost pl 5th: sn bhd: t.o 3 out* **100/1**

3m 47.0s (-5.00) **Going Correction** -0.65s/f (Firm) **14** Ran SP% **117.0**
Speed ratings (Par 103): **86,85,79,78,77 76,76,75,73,72 62,59,58,40**
toteswingers 1&2 £11.50, 1&3 £2.50, 2&3 £1.10 CSF £21.36 TOTE £7.30: £1.60, £1.50, £1.60; EX 23.40 Trifecta £37.00 Pool: £1,082.36 - 21.92 winning units.
Owner Tim Syder & Sarah Prior **Bred** Jarlath Glynn **Trained** Hatherden, Hants

FOCUS
Very few got into this and it developed into a match by the home straight.

1796 KALAHARI KING BEGINNERS' CHASE (15 fncs) 2m 4f

3:35 (3:35) (Class 4) 4-Y-0+

£6,256 (£1,848; £924; £462; £231; £116)

Form RPR

264/ 1 **Le Bec (FR)**[173] 5337 5-11-4 0........ NoelFehily 145+
(Emma Lavelle) *chsd ldrs: j.rt 3rd: led narrowly 11th: hdd next: led 3 out: drvn clr appr last: styd on strly* **7/4**[2]

16P/ 2 7 **Bear's Affair (IRE)**[183] 5175 7-11-4 0........ APMcCoy 139
(Nicky Henderson) *w ldrs: led 2nd: narrowly hdd 11th: led narrowly next: hdd 3 out: kpt on same pce between last 2* **13/8**[1]

0/3- 3 ¾ **Tony Star (FR)**[148] 217 6-11-4 140........ RichardJohnson 139
(Philip Hobbs) *hld up in rr: hdwy to chse ldrs 11th: disp 2nd 2 out: kpt on same pce* **7/2**[3]

252/ 4 19 **Ballinvarrig (IRE)**[176] 5289 6-11-4 0........ PaddyBrennan 121
(Tom George) *chsd ldrs: hit 8th: wknd 4 out: bhd whn j.rt 2 out* **33/1**

611- 5 14 **Dartford Warbler (IRE)**[25] 1564 6-11-4 0........ RyanMania 107
(Sue Smith) *chsd ldrs: outpcd 11th: lost pl bef next: sn wl bhd* **11/1**

41/- 6 47 **Spanish Optimist (IRE)**[511] 237 7-11-1 0........ MichaelByrne[(3)] 65
(Tim Vaughan) *in rr: bhd fr 9th: t.o 4 out: eventually completed* **40/1**

4m 52.1s (-13.40) **Going Correction** -0.45s/f (Good) **6** Ran SP% **110.4**
Speed ratings (Par 105): **108,105,104,97,91 72**
toteswingers 1&2 £1.02, 1&3 £1.30, 2&3 £1.10 CSF £5.07 TOTE £2.90: £2.10, £1.70; EX 6.00 Trifecta £15.10 Pool: £2,113.18 - 104.90 winning units.
Owner Tim Syder **Bred** N Madamet, I Kellitt & D Thomlinson **Trained** Hatherden, Hants

FOCUS
A warm beginners' chase featuring two classy hurdles recruits.

1797 FRISBY SOLICITORS H'CAP HURDLE (FOR THE ROYAL MERCIAN & LANCASTRIAN YEOMANRY CHALLENGE CUP) (11 hdls 1 omitted) 3m

4:05 (4:05) (Class 4) (0-120,119) 4-Y-0**£3,544** (£1,047; £523; £262; £131)

Form RPR

5/1- 1 **Flicka Williams (IRE)**[23] 1582 6-11-3 **110**........ NoelFehily 119+
(Tony Coyle) *hld up towards rr: hdwy 7th: trcking ldrs next: led appr 2 out: drvn out* **10/3**[1]

635/ 2 3 ½ **Bertie Boru (IRE)**[168] 5438 6-11-5 **115**........ MichealNolan[(3)] 121+
(Philip Hobbs) *in rr: hdwy 7th: chsng ldrs whn mstke 3 out: wnt 2nd between last 2: kpt on same pce* **12/1**

642- 3 6 **King Boru (IRE)**[26] 1552 5-11-5 **115**........ GavinSheehan[(3)] 114
(Emma Lavelle) *chsd ldrs: drvn 8th: kpt on same pce appr 2 out: tk 3rd nr fin* **6/1**[3]

204- 4 1 **Auberge (IRE)**[25] 1565 9-10-8 **101**........ RyanMania 100
(Evelyn Slack) *led: hit 3 out: hdd appr nxt: one pce* **9/1**

0/6- 5 2 ¼ **Sir Frank (IRE)**[14] 1636 8-11-8 **115**........ ConorO'Farrell 111
(David Pipe) *rr-div: hdwy 7th: one pce fr 3 out* **20/1**

343- 6 ½ **Blackstone Vegas**[14] 1635 7-10-0 **93** oh3........(v) JamesDavies 89
(Derek Shaw) *nt fluent: in rr: hdwy 8th: kpt on one pce fr next* **14/1**

PP0/ 7 7 **Fidelor (FR)**[168] 5440 7-10-5 **98**........ WillKennedy 87
(Alex Hales) *chsd ldrs: 2nd after 8th: wknd appr 2 out* **20/1**

340/ 8 1 ½ **Mallusk (IRE)**[310] 2752 8-10-5 **98**........ DominicElsworth 86
(Shaun Lycett) *chsd ldrs: lost pl 8th: no ch after* **14/1**

445- 9 nk **Hollins**[14] 1634 9-10-2 **102**........ JoshWall[(7)] 90
(Tony Forbes) *chsd ldrs: drvn 8th: wknd appr 2 out* **12/1**

2/0- 10 21 **Mauricetheathlete (IRE)**[142] 358 10-11-5 **119**........ NickSlatter[(7)] 88
(Martin Keighley) *chsd ldrs: outpcd and lost pl 8th: rallied briefly next: sn wknd and bhd* **20/1**

P/6- P **Vivona Hill**[68] 1145 9-10-2 **95**........ PaddyBrennan
(Nicky Richards) *in rr: drvn 8th: sn bhd: t.o whn p.u bef last* **11/1**

The Form Book Jumps, Raceform Ltd, Compton, RG20 6NL.

213- **P** **Calypso Bay (IRE)**[36] 1469 7-11-5 112 .... APMcCoy
(Jonjo O'Neill) *in rr: chsd ldrs 4th: upsides whn p.u after 6th: fatally injured* **4/1**[2]

5m 39.2s (-10.80) **Going Correction** -0.65s/f (Firm) **12** Ran SP% **118.7**
Speed ratings (Par 105): **92,90,88,88,87 87,85,84,84,77 ,**
toteswingers 1&2 £22.50, 1&3 £4.40, 2&3 £7.00 CSF £41.67 CT £226.90 TOTE £5.00: £1.70, £3.80, £2.40; EX 51.30 Trifecta £67.00 Pool: £1,315.02 - 14.69 winning units.
Owner Twenty Four Seven Recruitment **Bred** Tony Hickey **Trained** Norton, N Yorks

FOCUS
An open-looking handicap on paper and they went steadily early on.

1798 GORDON HORNER 80TH BIRTHDAY H'CAP CHASE (FOR QUEEN'S ROYAL LANCERS CHALLENGE CUP) (SUNDAY £5K BONUS) (18 fncs) 3m
4:35 (4:35) (Class 4) (0-105,103) 4-Y-0 **£4,177** (£1,234; £617; £308; £154)

Form RPR

311- **1** **Roc De Guye (FR)**[23] 1577 8-11-1 **92** ....(p) LiamTreadwell 102+
(James Evans) *hld up in rr: gd hdwy to chse ldrs 13th: led appr 3 out: drvn rt out* **11/2**[2]

/P0- **2** 2 ½ **Bennys Well (IRE)**[31] 1506 7-9-9 **77** oh7.................. JonathanEngland(5) 83
(Sue Smith) *led: hdd narrowly 12th: chsd wnr after: styd on same pce fr 2 out* **12/1**

221- **3** *hd* **Sadler's Star (GER)**[12] 1644 10-11-12 **103**..........................(p) NoelFehily 108
(Michael Blake) *chsd ldrs: lost pl 13th: rallied and lft modest 6th 4 out: styd on and 3rd last: kpt on same pce* **16/1**

U24/ **4** *7* **Kilcascan**[177] 5270 9-10-6 **88**.. BenPoste(5) 86
(Rosemary Gasson) *mid-div: hdwy to chse ldrs 13th: lft modest 4th 4 out: sn wknd* **9/1**[3]

134- **5** *1* **Terfel's Toscar (IRE)**[35] 1486 8-11-12 **103**................(t) RichardJohnson 100
(Tim Vaughan) *chsd ldrs: led 12th: hdd appr 3 out: wknd last* **11/2**[2]

1P5- **6** *21* **Lord Lescribaa (FR)**[12] 1642 10-11-1 **102**.......(tp) ThomasCheesman(10) 80
(Philip Hobbs) *prom: outpcd and lost pl 11th: bhd fr 14th* **16/1**

3PP- **7** *41* **Solway Bay**[36] 1469 11-11-1 **92**..(t) HarryHaynes 34
(Lisa Harrison) *in rr: hdwy 11th: drvn 13th: lost pl bef 4 out: sn bhd: t.o* **16/1**

350- **P** **Rossbrin (IRE)**[27] 1538 8-11-2 **93**...................................(bt[1]) AndrewTinkler
(Anna Brooks) *chsd ldrs: drvn 8th: sn lost pl and bhd: t.o 11th: p.u bef next* **22/1**

011- **F** **Watch House (IRE)**[14] 1637 8-11-4 **102**...................... MissAEStirling(7)
(Michael Gates) *hld up: trckd ldrs 4th: hit 7th: 4th and hld whn fell 4 out* **4/1**[1]

546- **P** **Ballyvoneen (IRE)**[14] 1626 8-11-0 **96**..........................(p) TrevorWhelan(5)
(Neil King) *in rr: reminders 5th: bhd fr 11th: t.o whn p.u bef 14th* **20/1**

/3P- **P** **My Friend George**[94] 881 7-11-0 **91**.................................... HenryBrooke
(Dianne Sayer) *in rr: reminders 5th and 7th: bhd fr 10th: t.o whn p.u bef 12th* **4/1**[1]

6m 9.8s (-5.30) **Going Correction** -0.45s/f (Good) **11** Ran SP% **115.2**
Speed ratings (Par 105): **90,89,89,86,86 79,65, , ,**
toteswingers 1&2 £22.80, 1&3 £3.50, 2&3 £19.40 CSF £67.00 CT £991.14 TOTE £5.60: £2.40, £3.60, £3.70; EX 74.40 Trifecta £344.60 Pool: £1,131.13 - 2.46 winning units.
Owner S Crawley, T Crawley **Bred** G A E C Delorme Gerard & Vincent **Trained** Broadwas, Worcs

FOCUS
Quite a competitive handicap.

1799 MOORLANDS RACING H'CAP HURDLE (9 hdls) 2m
5:05 (5:05) (Class 5) (0-100,100) 4-Y-0+ **£2,339** (£686; £343; £171)

Form RPR

001- **1** **Hail Tiberius**[5] 1711 6-10-11 **85** 7ex..............................(t) TomSiddall 92+
(Martin Keighley) *stdd s: hld up in last: stmbld and hit rail after 4th: smooth hdwy bef 3 out: led on bit and hit last: rdn out* **11/4**[1]

U62- **2** 3 ¼ **Wom**[25] 1567 5-11-6 **99**...(b) TrevorWhelan(5) 101
(Neil King) *chsd ldrs: lost pl 5th: hdwy appr 3 out: sn chsng ldrs: cl 3rd whn blnd last: styd on to take 2nd last 40yds* **8/1**

3F2- **3** 1 ½ **Echo Dancer**[14] 1633 7-9-11 **78**..(b) JoshWall(7) 78
(Trevor Wall) *mid-div: hdwy 6th: sn chsng ldrs: kpt on run-in to take 3rd last 30yds* **16/1**

212- **4** *2* **Ullswater (IRE)**[77] 1061 5-11-7 **100**.................................(t) JamesBanks(5) 100
(Andy Turnell) *chsd ldrs: led bef 2 out: hdd and hit last: wknd last 50yds* **3/1**[2]

/P0- **5** *½* **Tara Warrior (IRE)**[23] 1582 7-11-3 **94**..........................(b) MichaelByrne(3) 92
(Tim Vaughan) *led: hdd appr 2 out: one pce* **40/1**

063- **6** *2* **Inside Knowledge (USA)**[17] 1467 7-11-6 **94**...............(p) AdamPogson 90
(Garry Woodward) *chsd ldrs: drvn 6th: sn wl outpcd: kpt on fr 2 out* **11/1**

660- **7** *hd* **Carhue Princess (IRE)**[54] 1269 7-10-10 **84**..................... FelixDeGiles 79
(Tom Symonds) *chsd ldrs: drvn appr 3 out: one pce* **5/1**[3]

564- **8** *shd* **Pagham Belle**[12] 1639 5-10-6 **83**...................................(t) MarkQuinlan(3) 78
(Nigel Hawke) *chsd ldrs: drvn bef 3 out: one pce* **28/1**

/6F- **9** 4 ½ **Poetic Power (IRE)**[41] 1400 4-10-8 **89**............................. GeraldQuinn(7) 80
(Claire Dyson) *stdd s: hld up in rr-div: kpt on fr 3 out: nvr a factor* **50/1**

0/5- **10** *9* **Whispering Harry**[150] 186 4-10-10 **84**................................ HenryOliver 67
(Henry Oliver) *in rr: mstke 5th: sme hdwy on outside bef 3 out: sn wknd* **25/1**

650/ **11** *nse* **Song Of Pride (GER)**[20] 5174 9-10-3 **77**.................(b[1]) TomMessenger 60
(Mandy Rowland) *prom: wknd appr 3 out* **50/1**

0P0- **12** 2 ¾ **Wheelavit (IRE)**[45] 1351 10-10-8 **82**.................................... LiamTreadwell 63
(Claire Dyson) *mid-div: effrt on outside after 6th: lost pl bef next* **33/1**

554- **13** *6* **Naledi**[14] 1633 9-10-2 **83**.. KevinJones(7) 58
(Richard Price) *in rr: bhd fr 3 out* **25/1**

450- **14** *39* **Sonny Jim**[89] 927 5-10-12 **86**...(p) NoelFehily 26
(John Mackie) *mid-div: j. slowly 6th: sme hdwy on outside bef next: sn wknd: t.o 2 out* **16/1**

3m 44.8s (-7.20) **Going Correction** -0.65s/f (Firm)
WFA 4 from 5yo+ 9lb **14** Ran SP% **120.0**
Speed ratings (Par 103): **92,90,89,88,88 87,87,87,84,80 80,79,76,56**
toteswingers 1&2 £14.00, 1&3 £21.30, 2&3 £10.10 CSF £23.45 CT £301.62 TOTE £4.00: £2.00, £3.10, £2.90; EX 21.10 Trifecta £235.70 Pool: £1,002.74 - 3.18 winning units.
Owner Tim Exell **Bred** Mr And Mrs Geoff Bonson **Trained** Condicote, Gloucs

FOCUS
Just an ordinary handicap.

1800 TAX AND WEALTH H'CAP CHASE (16 fncs) 2m 5f
5:35 (5:35) (Class 5) (0-100,89) 4-Y-0+ **£2,729** (£801; £400; £200)

Form RPR

P/3- **1** **Midnight Charmer**[153] 141 7-10-6 **74**................................. JamesBanks(5) 87+
(Emma Baker) *mid-div: hdwy to chse ldrs 9th: upsides bef 3 out: styd on wl to ld last 100yds* **7/1**

5/4- **2** 4 ½ **Croco Mister (IRE)**[89] 930 6-10-13 **81**................................ BenPoste(5) 89
(Rosemary Gasson) *chsd clr ldr: led after 4 out: hdd and no ex last 100yds* **10/1**

044- **3** *15* **Tinelyra (IRE)**[29] 1518 7-11-12 **89**..................................(t) PaddyBrennan 88
(Fergal O'Brien) *led: clr 2nd to 8th: hdd after 4 out: 3rd and btn whn hit next: eased clsng stages* **7/4**[1]

433- **4** *7* **Harris Garden (IRE)**[9] 1668 6-11-9 **89**........................(p) JackQuinlan(3) 78
(Paul Cowley) *blnd 1st: in rr: reminders 11th: modest 4th whn hit 4 out: sn wknd* **8/1**

P/0- **5** *¾* **Milly Malone (IRE)**[103] 833 7-11-7 **84**.......................(t) RichardJohnson 71
(Adrian Wintle) *in rr: sme hdwy 11th: wknd appr 4 out* **16/1**

522- **6** *21* **Farmer Frank**[27] 1534 10-11-3 **80**...................................... DenisO'Regan 48
(Nick Kent) *chsd ldrs 9th: drvn 12th: lost pl bef next: bhd whn eased 2 out* **9/2**[2]

3F/- **7** 3 ¾ **Molko Jack (FR)**[217] 4549 9-11-5 **85**.............................. KielanWoods(3) 49
(Michael Mullineaux) *mid-div: lost pl 8th: bhd fr 12th* **25/1**

/23- **8** *¾* **Oh Right (IRE)**[11] 1655 9-11-2 **79**....................................(p) HenryBrooke 43
(Dianne Sayer) *chsd clr ldr: wknd appr 4 out: bhd whn eased run-in* **6/1**[3]

P/P- **9** *5* **Paradise Expected**[45] 1349 10-11-6 **86**.....................(t) MichaelByrne(3) 45
(Mark Gillard) *j. slowly 1st: lost pl 7th: sn bhd: t.o 11th* **33/1**

5m 13.0s (-9.80) **Going Correction** -0.45s/f (Good) **9** Ran SP% **114.2**
Speed ratings (Par 103): **100,98,92,89,89 81,80,79,78**
toteswingers 1&2 £9.60, 1&3 £3.50, 2&3 £5.60 CSF £71.34 CT £174.68 TOTE £7.70: £3.20, £2.10, £1.60; EX 66.70 Trifecta £753.60 Pool: £1,670.19 - 1.66 winning units.
Owner Mrs M J Arnold **Bred** Mrs J Hoskins And Brian Wilson **Trained** Naunton, Gloucs

FOCUS
A modest finale.
T/Jkpt: £13,395.90 to a £1 stake. Pool: £37,735.04 - 2.00 winning units T/Plt: £53.70 to a £1 stake. Pool: £100,330.54 - 1,363.89 winning units T/Qpdt: £7.20 to a £1 stake. Pool: £7,434.27 - 763.66 winning units WG

1065 TIPPERARY (L-H)
Sunday, October 6

OFFICIAL GOING: Flat course - yielding; jumps courses - good

1801a FRIENDS OF TIPPERARY HURDLE (GRADE 2) (9 hdls) 2m
3:50 (3:50) 4-Y-0+ **£27,743** (£8,109; £3,841; £1,280)

RPR

1 **Captain Cee Bee (IRE)**[252] 3909 12-11-10 **150**.................... MarkWalsh 157+
(Edward P Harty, Ire) *chsd ldrs: 4th 1/2-way: tk clsr order 3 out: hdwy to chal gng best bef 2 out: sn led and wnt clr bef last: eased cl home: easily* **15/8**[1]

2 5 ½ **Midnight Game**[66] 1180 6-11-7 **144**.. DavyRussell 147
(W P Mullins, Ire) *w.w towards rr: mstke in 6th 4 out: pushed along bef 2 out and clsd u.p into mod 3rd between last 2: kpt on into 2nd run-in wout ever troubling easy wnr* **3/1**[2]

3 *½* **False Economy (IRE)**[13] 1421 8-11-4 **130**..................... BarryGeraghty 144
(Michael Hourigan, Ire) *hld up in rr: nt fluent 4th: sme hdwy fr 4 out: pushed along fr next and on terms bef 2 out: rdn and no imp on wnr in 2nd between last 2: dropped to 3rd run-in: kpt on same pce* **14/1**

4 3 ½ **Moon Dice (IRE)**[37] 1462 8-11-4 **137**................................... RobbiePower 140
(Paul W Flynn, Ire) *led and sn clr: reduced advantage whn slow at 4th: jnd 3 out where slt mstke: pushed along w narrow advantage into st: mstke 2 out and hdd: no ex in 4th bef last: kpt on one pce* **12/1**

5 2 ¾ **Fosters Cross (IRE)**[25] 1573 11-11-4 **138**......................(t) BryanCooper 137
(Thomas Mullins, Ire) *trckd ldr: clsr in 2nd bef 1/2-way: dropped to 3rd bef 4 out: got on terms next: pushed along in 2nd bef st and no ex u.p 2 out: dropped to 5th bef last where slt mstke: one pce run-in* **11/2**

6 *½* **Foildubh (IRE)**[162] 5582 9-11-4 **139**...................................... PaulTownend 137
(John Patrick Ryan, Ire) *hld up: 5th 1/2-way: rdn on outer bef 2 out and no imp on ldrs: kpt on one pce fr last* **7/2**[3]

7 1 ¼ **Miley Shah (IRE)**[17] 1610 8-11-7 **132**....................................(p) AELynch 139
(J P Kenny, Ire) *chsd ldrs: 3rd 1/2-way: wnt 2nd bef 4 out and sn on terms: pushed along in 3rd bef st and sn lost pl: wknd bef 2 out* **16/1**

3m 45.3s (225.30) **7** Ran SP% **117.6**
CSF £8.34 TOTE £2.90: £1.30, £2.10; DF 9.10 Trifecta £34.80.
Owner John P McManus **Bred** Maurice Stack **Trained** Curragh, Co Kildare

FOCUS
A disappointing renewal with recent form thin on the ground. The third helps the standard.

1802a DOLORES PURCELL MEMORIAL NOVICE HURDLE (GRADE 3) (9 hdls) 2m
4:20 (4:20) 4-Y-0+ **£14,532** (£4,247; £2,012; £670)

RPR

1 **King Of The Picts (IRE)**[16] 1614 4-10-12 **128** ow1. AndrewJMcNamara 133
(John Patrick Shanahan, Ire) *chsd ldr in 2nd: tk clsr order fr 3 out and hdwy to ld fr next: styd on wl u.p fr last* **12/1**

2 1 ½ **Que Pasa (IRE)**[26] 1556 5-11-1 **130**................................... BarryGeraghty 135
(David Harry Kelly, Ire) *hld up towards rr: tk clsr order fr 4 out: hdwy in 5th 2 out to chal in cl 3rd at last: kpt on u.p into 2nd run-in: a hld* **11/4**[1]

3 1 ½ **Shamar (FR)**[16] 1614 5-11-5 **134**..(t) RWalsh 138
(W P Mullins, Ire) *chsd ldrs: 3rd 1/2-way: tk clsr order bef st and almost on terms on inner 2 out: sn rdn in cl 2nd: no ex u.p fr last and dropped to 3rd run-in* **10/1**

4 *5* **The Mighty Milan (IRE)**[165] 5516 6-11-1 .... BryanCooper 129
(T J Nagle Jr, Ire) *hld up in tch: tk clsr order in 4th 1/2-way: clsr in 3rd bef st: sn rdn and no imp on ldrs in 5th whn nt fluent last: kpt on same pce* **13/2**[3]

5 1 ¼ **Curley Bill (IRE)**[21] 1586 5-11-5 .... DavyCondon 131
(Noel Meade, Ire) *hld up towards rr: pushed along in 7th after 3 out where nt fluent: no imp on ldrs next: kpt on fr last* **11/4**[1]

6 *¾* **Un Beau Roman (FR)**[21] 1586 5-11-5 **131**........................ PaulTownend 131
(W P Mullins, Ire) *led and sn clr: keen: reduced advantage bef 5th where slt mstke: pressed into st and hdd fr 2 out: sn no ex u.p and dropped to 4th bef last: one pce run-in* **8/1**

7 1 ¾ **Honey Bach (IRE)**[126] 609 6-10-8 **114**................................. MrDGLavery 118
(B R Hamilton, Ire) *chsd ldrs: nt fluent 5th: niggled along in 5th after 3 out: nt fluent next and no imp after in 6th: one pce run-in* **20/1**

8 7 **One Fine Day (IRE)**[19] 1601 4-10-11 127 (t) RobbiePower 114
(Mrs John Harrington, Ire) *hld up: t.k.h: nt fluent 1st and next: mstke 4th: pushed along in rr fr 4 out: slt mstke again next: rdn and no imp bef st* **9/2**[2]

3m 46.1s (226.10)
WFA 4 from 5yo+ 9lb **8** Ran SP% **117.5**
CSF £47.48 TOTE £9.40: £3.30, £1.60, £3.30; DF 48.20 Trifecta £452.60.
Owner Thistle Bloodstock Limited **Bred** Longfort Stud **Trained** Danesfort, Co. Kilkenny

FOCUS
This had more a feel of a late summer hurdle race, as opposed to one with a major bearing on the main jumps season. The pacesetter was soon clear. A bit of a sprint and a tight finish.

1804a LIKE A BUTTERFLY NOVICE CHASE (GRADE 3) (14 fncs) 2m 4f
5:25 (5:25) 4-Y-0+ **£14,532** (£4,247; £2,012; £670)

RPR
1 **Rebel Fitz (FR)**[26] 1558 8-11-8 152 BarryGeraghty 149+
(Michael Winters, Ire) *sweated up befhand: settled bhd ldrs in 3rd: hdwy on outer travelling wl to ld bef st: wnt clr bef 2 out: nt extended* **2/5**[1]
2 3 ½ **Owega Star (IRE)**[17] 1609 6-11-2 (t) AndrewLeigh 133
(Peter Fahey, Ire) *w.w in rr: tk clsr order in 4th fr 5 out: bad mstke 3 out: sn rdn and wnt 3rd on outer bef 2 out: kpt on into 2nd between last 2: no ch w easy wnr: kpt on same pce* **4/1**[2]
3 4 ¼ **Clar Na Mionn (IRE)**[139] 415 6-11-2 APHeskin 129
(V T O'Brien, Ire) *hld up in tch: pushed along in 6th after 3 out and clsd into mod 5th bef next: rdn between last 2 and clsd u.p into nvr threatening 3rd cl home* **20/1**
4 1 **Boxer Beat (IRE)**[6] 1702 6-11-2 121 RobbiePower 128
(Paul W Flynn, Ire) *led and disp: pushed along w narrow advantage bef 3 out: pushed along and hdd bef st: no ch w wnr: dropped to 3rd fr 2 out and wknd towards fin* **33/1**
5 1 ½ **Run With The Wind (IRE)**[15] 1616 7-11-2 RWalsh 126
(Michael Hourigan, Ire) *hld up: pushed along in 5th after 3 out: wnt mod 4th next: sn no ex u.p and lost pl after last: kpt on same pce* **10/1**[3]
6 28 **Caoimhe's Delight (IRE)**[145] 301 7-10-9 DavyCondon 91
(Sean O'Brien, Ire) *hld up towards rr: pushed along and struggling fr 5 out: detached and wl bhd fr 3 out: nvr a factor* **33/1**
P **Toostrong (FR)**[6] 1702 6-11-2 125 (t) DavyRussell
(W P Mullins, Ire) *led and disp: pushed along in 3rd bef st and wknd u.p into 6th whn bad mstke 2 out: no ex and p.u bef last* **16/1**

4m 52.3s (292.30) **7** Ran SP% **117.0**
CSF £2.72 TOTE £1.80: £1.40, £2.40; DF 3.20 Trifecta £15.00.
Owner Brian Sweetnam **Bred** Pierre De Maleisseye Melun Et Al **Trained** Kanturk, Co Cork

FOCUS
The front-running fourth limits the form. He's been rated to the best view of his previous efforts. The winner costed in.

1803 - 1812a (Foreign Racing) - See Raceform Interactive

[332] LUDLOW (R-H)
Wednesday, October 9

OFFICIAL GOING: Good (good to firm in places; chs 7.9, hdl 7.9)
Wind: breezy Weather: overcast; 14 degrees

1813 RACING TO SCHOOL JUVENILE MAIDEN HURDLE (9 hdls) 2m
2:10 (2:10) (Class 4) 3-Y-0 **£3,898** (£1,144; £572; £286)

Form RPR
1 **Ballyglasheen (IRE)**[24] 1585 3-10-12 0 PaulMoloney 104+
(Evan Williams) *trckd ldr: tk slt ld 3 out: drvn and jst hdd next: sustained effrt flat: got up cl home* **4/1**[3]
2- 2 ½ **Raven's Tower (USA)**[17] 1624 3-10-12 0 DavidBass 103
(Ben Pauling) *settled in 3rd tl wnt 2nd wl bef 3 out: rdn and slt ld next: nk ahd after last: kpt on gamely but jst ct* **9/2**
3 9 **Saint Jerome (IRE)**[25] 3-10-12 0 JackDoyle 95+
(Jamie Osborne) *plld hrd: led and sn 10 l clr: j.lft 4th and pressed fr next: hit 6th: rdn and hdd 3 out: btn whn wnt rt after next* **11/4**[2]
4 5 **Maxi Mac (IRE)**[65] 3-10-5 0 JoshWall(7) 91
(Trevor Wall) *last tl home turn where only 6 l fr ldr: blnd 3 out and n.d after: mstke last* **66/1**
5 13 **Ocean Applause**[11] 3-10-12 0 (t) APMcCoy 81
(John Ryan) *jumping a lacked conviction: chsd ldrs: effrt in cl 4th home turn: sn rdn: mstke 3 out and n.d after: blnd last: eased flat* **2/1**[1]
6 ¾ **Major Parkes**[427] 3-10-12 0 JasonMaguire 75
(Donald McCain) *hld up in rr: nt fluent 5th and 6th and pushed along: stl in tch home turn: rdn and sn wknd* **16/1**
7 nse **Exclusion (USA)**[40] 3-10-2 0 (b) JackQuinlan(3) 68
(Noel Quinlan) *midfield: stl wl in tch home turn: rdn and wknd 3 out* **14/1**

3m 41.3s (-8.20) **Going Correction** -0.75s/f (Firm) **7** Ran SP% **112.2**
Speed ratings (Par 103): **90,89,85,82,76 75,75**
toteswingers 1&2 £6.50, 2&3 £3.00, 1&3 £2.50 CSF £21.51 TOTE £5.30: £2.10, £2.40; EX 10.20 Trifecta £79.60 Pool: £250.94 - 2.36 winning units..
Owner R J Gambarini **Bred** Mrs Evie Stockwell **Trained** Llancarfan, Vale Of Glamorgan

FOCUS
Stable bend combined and hurdles on inside line in straight. Paul Moloney said it was "perfect ground" after partnering the opening winner, while the general view was that it was good, but on the fast side in places. They went no great pace in this modest juvenile event, and all seven were still involved turning to face up to the last three flights before the dash for home began. The form is rated around the first two.

1814 UK FOREST PRODUCTS ASSOCIATION MARES' NOVICES' HURDLE (11 hdls) 2m 5f
2:40 (2:40) (Class 4) 4-Y-0+ **£3,898** (£1,144; £572; £286)

Form RPR
0/5- 1 **Magic Money**[162] 41 5-10-10 0 JasonMaguire 109+
(Kim Bailey) *pressed ldr tl led 3 out: rdn and wandering lft fr bef last: hld on gamely but all out* **12/1**
40/- 2 ¾ **Dreams And Songs**[174] 5364 5-10-10 0 RichardJohnson 108+
(Philip Hobbs) *t.k.h in rr: effrt on outer and 4th whn hmpd 3 out: swtchd ins and rallied to chse wnr bef last: rn green but kpt on wl: rather unlucky* **5/1**[3]
332- 3 9 **Presenting Me (IRE)**[15] 1639 5-10-7 97 AdamWedge(3) 97
(Evan Williams) *chsd ldrs: drvn and outpcd in 5th after 8th: rallied to 4 l 2nd 2 out tl bef last: easily outpcd flat* **8/1**
212- 4 1 ¾ **The Road Ahead**[101] 847 6-10-10 0 TomO'Brien 99+
(Peter Bowen) *trckd ldrs: nt fluent 1st and 7th: shkn up after next: ev ch whn ducked bdly lft nring 3 out and racd awkwardly after flight: one pce and no imp after* **6/4**[1]
/ 5 21 **Kathleen Frances**[48] 1354 6-10-10 0 (t) JackDoyle 89
(Ali Brewer) *led at sedate pce: tried to qckn 8th: rdn and hdd 3 out: fdd tamely* **2/1**[2]
240- 6 25 **Laurens Ruby (IRE)**[12] 1672 4-10-10 0 RhysFlint 49
(John Flint) *nt fluent 2nd: plld hrd in rr: brief effrt 6th but edging lft: rdn after 8th: sn lost tch: bdly t.o* **28/1**
06/ 7 2 **Fair Gun Lady**[243] 4105 5-10-10 0 ConorO'Farrell 47
(Michael Scudamore) *towards rr: struggling 6th: lost tch after 8th: bdly t.o whn mstke last* **100/1**

5m 0.9s (-13.90) **Going Correction** -0.75s/f (Firm) **7** Ran SP% **113.2**
Speed ratings (Par 105): **96,95,92,91,83 74,73**
toteswingers 1&2 £6.70, 2&3 £3.90, 1&3 £8.60 CSF £68.24 TOTE £10.40: £2.30, £3.70; EX 57.30 Trifecta £102.50 Pool: £872.27 - 6.38 winning units..
Owner David Jenks **Bred** Hartshill Stud **Trained** Andoversford, Gloucs

FOCUS
Ordinary mares' form, rated therough the third. The time was slow.

1815 BETFAIR CASH OUT H'CAP CHASE (22 fncs) 3m 1f 110y
3:10 (3:11) (Class 3) (0-130,130) 4-Y-0+ **£9,495** (£2,805; £1,402; £702; £351)

Form RPR
465/ 1 **Imperial Circus (IRE)**[175] 5351 7-11-0 118 (p) RichardJohnson 128+
(Philip Hobbs) *gng wl in cl 3rd or 4th: mstke 2nd: hit next: looked in command last tl drvn and idled flat: plld out ex cl home* **15/8**[1]
261- 2 ½ **Rockiteer (IRE)**[39] 1470 10-11-3 124 (p) JakeGreenall(3) 130
(Henry Daly) *led: nt fluent 5th (water): hdd 8th: led 10th tl 15th and again bef 19th: drvn and hdd 3 out: trying to rally whn lunged at last: hung fire flat: jst hld by idling wnr fnl 50yds* **12/1**
6/2- 3 4 ½ **Inside Dealer (IRE)**[15] 1642 9-11-6 124 (tp) JoeTizzard 125
(Colin Tizzard) *ldng pair: led 8th tl 10th and 15th tl bef 19th: drvn and ev ch 2 out: nt qckn bef last* **7/1**[3]
2P1/ 4 1 ¾ **Savant Bleu (FR)**[164] 18 7-11-9 127 JasonMaguire 126
(Kim Bailey) *a in 3rd or 4th: mstke 2nd: gng wl and ev ch tl 19th: rdn 2 out: sn wknd: j. sltly rt last* **4/1**[2]
/53- 5 2 **Cootehill (IRE)**[44] 1397 9-11-9 127 SamTwiston-Davies 125
(Nigel Twiston-Davies) *towards rr: nt fluent 15th: rdn 17th: no imp 19th: kpt on same pce* **7/1**[3]
020- 6 6 **Buck Mulligan**[11] 1686 8-11-12 130 PaulMoloney 122
(Evan Williams) *nrly a in last: detached after 18th* **8/1**
035- P **Siberian Tiger (IRE)**[47] 1362 8-10-12 119 (b) AdamWedge(3)
(Evan Williams) *hld up wl in tch: hit 16th: on heels of ldrs whn wnt wrong and p.u 3 out: fatally injured* **8/1**

6m 27.1s (-8.20) **Going Correction** -0.425s/f (Good) **7** Ran SP% **109.7**
Speed ratings (Par 107): **95,94,93,92,92 90,**
toteswingers 1&2 £5.10, 2&3 £8.50, 1&3 £2.30 CSF £20.90 TOTE £2.90: £2.20, £5.70; EX 24.00 Trifecta £178.80 Pool: £962.78 - 4.03 winning units..
Owner R A S Offer **Bred** K Riordan **Trained** Withycombe, Somerset

FOCUS
Decent prize money for this fair handicap chase, which was run at a modest gallop. The idling winner was value for further, and is rated in line with the best of his form.

1816 LUDLOW RACING PARTNERSHIP H'CAP HURDLE (9 hdls) 2m
3:40 (3:42) (Class 4) (0-110,110) 4-Y-0+ **£4,548** (£1,335; £667; £333)

Form RPR
154- 1 **Alwaystheoptimist**[30] 1535 10-11-10 108 SamTwiston-Davies 119+
(Phil Middleton) *settled towards rr: smooth prog to 2nd and bmpd rival 3 out: led between last two and readily qcknd clr: heavily eased fnl 100yds* **9/1**
/11- 2 7 **Planetoid (IRE)**[118] 729 5-11-10 108 APMcCoy 111+
(Jim Best) *disp 2nd and racd keenly tl lft in ld bef 4th: hit 6th: rdn 4 l clr home turn: hdd between last two and immediately outpcd by wnr: hit last: nudged along to hold poor 2nd flat* **5/4**[1]
153- 3 1 ½ **Lodgician (IRE)**[42] 1429 11-10-6 97 (vt) RyanHatch(7) 98
(Nigel Twiston-Davies) *mstke 2nd: a in 2nd or in 3rd: hit 5th: drvn and outpcd by ldr bef home turn: bmpd 3 out: plugged on and n.d after* **6/1**[2]
4/P- 4 10 **Vertueux (FR)**[35] 852 8-11-2 100 (p) LeeEdwards 91
(Tony Carroll) *midfield: dropped to rr and drvn wl bef 3 out: n.d after* **10/1**
224- 5 3 ¼ **The Bay Bandit**[29] 1551 6-11-10 108 (p) DarylJacob 94
(Neil Mulholland) *midfield: brief effrt on long run to 3 out: sn rdn and lost pl: btn next* **7/1**[3]
/26- 6 64 **Eightfold**[27] 605 4-11-12 110 (t) ConorO'Farrell 72
(Seamus Durack) *racd in last but one: rdn bef 3 out: sn lost tch: t.o and virtually p.u flat* **18/1**
540/ P **Educated Son**[304] 2441 5-11-12 110 JackDoyle
(Ben De Haan) *a in last: lost tch 6th: sn t.o: p.u in last* **33/1**
P/2- F **Who's Jeff (IRE)**[134] 517 5-11-12 110 TomO'Brien
(Philip Hobbs) *taken down early: tk fierce hold and rushed 12 l clr: j.lft: hung bdly lft to stables after 3rd: sn hdd: fiddled next: fdd wl bef 3 out: 25 l 6th whn stmbld and fell after next* **6/1**[2]

3m 35.9s (-13.60) **Going Correction** -0.75s/f (Firm) course record
WFA 4 from 5yo+ 9lb **8** Ran SP% **112.8**
Speed ratings (Par 105): **104,100,99,94,93 61,,**
toteswingers 1&2 £2.40, 2&3 £2.70, 1&3 £7.40 CSF £20.89 CT £74.25 TOTE £10.20: £2.80, £1.10, £2.70; EX 28.40 Trifecta £250.60 Pool: £1174.90 - 3.51 winning units..
Owner P W Middleton **Bred** Crandon Park Stud **Trained** Dorton, Bucks

FOCUS
A modest handicap hurdle, run at a brisk pace. Sound form, the winner rated back to his best.

1817 OCTOBER NOVICES' LIMITED H'CAP CHASE (17 fncs) 2m 4f
4:10 (4:10) (Class 3) (0-140,130) 4-Y-0+ **£7,783** (£2,431; £1,309)

Form RPR
503- 1 **Lava Lamp (GER)**[48] 1343 6-10-2 116 oh1 AdamWedge(3) 116+
(Evan Williams) *detached tl 9th and hld up last tl bef 14th: sn lft 2nd and sustained effrt after: rdn bef last: led and forged clr fnl 120yds* **8/1**
101- 2 2 ¼ **De Faoithesdream (IRE)**[15] 1640 7-11-5 130 PaulMoloney 129
(Evan Williams) *t.k.h: led at brisk pce but wavered into several obstacles: lft 3 l clr 14th: hrd drvn and wandered rt bef last: hdd and nt qckn flat* **15/8**[2]
/34- 3 30 **Agent Archie (USA)**[34] 1504 6-11-1 126 JasonMaguire 99
(Donald McCain) *pressed ldr tl 12th: ev ch tl drvn bef 14th: sn fdd v tamely: eased flat* **4/1**[3]
13/- U **Woodbank**[509] 335 6-10-5 116 AndrewTinkler 116
(Nicky Henderson) *t.k.h in 3rd tl wnt 2nd at 12th: stl gng strly and looking wnr whn blnd 14th and uns rdr* **11/8**[1]

4m 51.5s (-12.90) **Going Correction** -0.425s/f (Good) **4** Ran SP% **108.0**
Speed ratings (Par 107): **108,107,95,**
CSF £22.76 TOTE £8.70; EX 13.80 Trifecta £36.30 Pool: £225.35 - 4.65 winning units..

Owner Mrs Janet Davies **Bred** Graf And Grafin Von Stauffenberg **Trained** Llancarfan, Vale Of Glamorgan

FOCUS

Not a strong race for the grade or the money on offer. It produced a 1-2 for Evan Williams. The winner improved to his hurdle mark.

1818 RACING UK MARES' H'CAP HURDLE (12 hdls) 3m

4:40 (4:40) (Class 3) (0-130,130) 4-Y-O **£6,330** (£1,870; £935; £468; £234)

Form RPR

251- **1** **Dark Spirit (IRE)**[8] 1708 5-9-11 **104** 7ex........................(p) AdamWedge(3) 111+
(Evan Williams) *settled towards rr: effrt gng wl bef 3 out: sn wnt 2nd: produced to ld jst after last: sn asserted: rdn out* **9/2**[2]

123- **2** *3 ¾* **Emerald Rose**[31] 1529 6-10-6 **110**........................... SamTwiston-Davies 111
(Julian Smith) *rn in snatches: lost gd pl 6th: drvn bef 8th: rallied bef 3 out: styd on but no real imp fr 2 out: nt fluent last: wnt wl hld 2nd flat* **7/2**[1]

311- **3** *1 ¼* **Emily's Flyer (IRE)**[14] 1660 6-11-2 **120**.........................(t) PaddyBrennan 119
(Fergal O'Brien) *hit 4th and 5th: led at gd pce and abt 6 l clr tl 6th: pushed along home turn: 2 l ahd but rdn 2 out: sn hdd and outpcd flat: lost 2nd in clsng stages* **9/2**[2]

215- **4** *7* **Va'Vite (IRE)**[81] 1045 6-10-12 **126**..................................... MarkMarris(10) 119
(Anthony Middleton) *pckd 2nd: nt fluent 5th: hld up last tl 8th: rdn and tried to get on terms home turn: sn no imp* **10/1**

221- **5** *nk* **Coronea Lilly (IRE)**[39] 1468 9-11-6 **124**.............................(tp) APMcCoy 115
(Neil Mulholland) *2nd or 3rd bhd clr ldr: nt fluent 7th and rdn: drvn and lost 2nd on long run to 3 out and sn btn* **7/2**[1]

114- **6** *1 ¾* **My Lucky Flame (IRE)**[50] 1330 6-10-7 **121**.................... MikeyHamill(10) 113
(Sean Curran) *midfield: pressed ldrs fr 7th: 4th and drvn home turn: sn struggling: mstkes 3 out and last* **6/1**[3]

562- **7** *38* **Gulf Punch**[78] 1084 6-9-7 **104**..(p) NickSlatter(7) 56
(Donald McCain) *chsd ldr tl 8th: rdn and fdd qckly and t.o last after next* **14/1**

5m 33.3s (-19.00) **Going Correction** -0.75s/f (Firm) course record **7** Ran SP% **110.9**
Speed ratings (Par 107): **101,99,99,97,96 96,83**
toteswingers 1&2 £1.30, 2&3 £2.10, 1&3 £5.20 CSF £19.59 CT £70.10 TOTE £4.80: £3.20, £2.60; EX 17.10 Trifecta £95.40 Pool: £436.58 - 3.42 winning units..
Owner Richard Abbott & Mario Stavrou **Bred** Thomas G N Burrage **Trained** Llancarfan, Vale Of Glamorgan

FOCUS

A competitive handicap for mares on paper. The form looks solid enough.

1819 CHRISTMAS PARTIES INTERMEDIATE OPEN NATIONAL HUNT FLAT RACE 2m

5:10 (5:10) (Class 5) 4-5-Y-O **£2,599** (£763; £381; £190)

Form RPR

1 **On Tour (IRE)**[143] 5-11-2 0.. PaulMoloney 104+
(Evan Williams) *trckd ldrs gng wl: wnt 2nd over 3f out: rdn to ld over 1f out: sn in command and styd on resolutely* **2/1**[1]

2 *5* **Flying Eagle (IRE)** 5-11-2 0................................... RichardJohnson 97
(Peter Bowen) *settled in midfield: effrt over 3f out: drvn to chse wnr over 1f out: kpt on but in vain pursuit after* **9/4**[2]

3/4- **3** *4* **Radmores Express**[151] 225 4-10-9 0............................ CiaranMckee(7) 93
(John O'Shea) *midfield: drvn to try to cl on outer over 3f out: no imp after: wnt mod 3rd 1f out* **16/1**

4 *3 ½* **Stormbay Bomber (IRE)** 4-11-2 0.. APMcCoy 90
(Rebecca Curtis) *chsd ldr: drvn to ld over 3f out: labouring to hold advantage after: hdd over 1f out and fdd qckly* **3/1**[3]

6- **5** *18* **Max Ward (IRE)**[22] 1599 4-11-2 0............................ SamTwiston-Davies 75
(Charlie Brooks) *racd freely in ld: rdn and hdd over 3f out: hung lft and racd awkwardly after: eased over 1f out: t.o* **6/1**

6 *8* **Retroson (IRE)**[304] 5-11-2 0.. AndrewTinkler 64
(Michael Scudamore) *bhd: struggling 4f out: t.o fnl 3f* **33/1**

/60- **7** *17* **Bollin Across**[32] 1523 5-10-2 0................................ MissAEStirling(7) 40
(Andrew Hollinshead) *t.k.h in poor last: t.o fnl 6f* **33/1**

0- **P** **Mitt'N'Marg**[84] 1016 5-10-9 0.. JoshWall(7)
(Trevor Wall) *in last pair: rdn 1/2-way: hopelessly t.o 7f out: p.u and dismntd over 3f out* **100/1**

3m 30.0s (-13.90) **Going Correction** -0.75s/f (Firm) **8** Ran SP% **116.1**
Speed ratings: **104,101,99,97,88 84,76,**
Swingers 1&2 £1.10, 2&3 £9.40, 1&3 £14.40 CSF £6.86 TOTE £3.40: £1.50, £1.20, £3.50; EX 6.80 Trifecta £41.30 Pool: £431.90 - 7.82 winning units..
Owner T Hywel Jones **Bred** Mrs Meliosa Walshe **Trained** Llancarfan, Vale Of Glamorgan

FOCUS

Just a modest bumper, the third setting the level.

T/Plt: £1,731.10 to a £1 stake. Pool of £49562.74 - 20.90 winning tickets. T/Qpdt: £73.30 to a £1 stake. Pool of £4252.55 - 42.90 winning tickets. IM

456 TOWCESTER (R-H)

Wednesday, October 9

OFFICIAL GOING: Good to firm (good in places; 8.7)

Wind: medium to fresh, across Weather: overcast

1820 MICK WHITE 70TH BIRTHDAY "NATIONAL HUNT" NOVICES' H'CAP HURDLE (11 hdls) 2m 5f

2:20 (2:20) (Class 5) (0-100,100) 3-Y-O+ **£1,949** (£572; £286; £143)

Form RPR

/51- **1** **My Oh Mount Brown (IRE)**[8] 1718 6-11-1 **92**............. MichaelByrne(3) 102+
(Tim Vaughan) *mounted on crse and taken down early: in tch in midfield: hdwy 6th: chsd ldr after next: led 3 out: hrd pressed and drvn between last 2: hdd flat: kpt on gamely and ld again fnl 50yds: all out* **11/4**[1]

P00/ **2** *nk* **Val D'Allier (FR)**[171] 5438 4-11-12 **100**................................(t) MarkGrant 110+
(Jim Old) *hld up in tch in last trio: hdwy and hit 5th: chsd wnr and effrt after 3 out: drvn and ev ch between last 2: led flat: hdd and no ex fnl 50yds* **20/1**

060/ **3** *22* **Bally Lagan (IRE)**[164] 2 5-10-13 **87**................................. CharliePoste 76
(Robin Dickin) *chsd ldrs: edgd rt after 6th: 3rd and drvn after 3 out: btn next and wknd between last 2: plugged on to go modest 3rd again flat* **25/1**

033- **4** *hd* **Gwili Spar**[26] 1582 5-10-6 **80**..................................(t) DonalDevereux 71
(Peter Bowen) *hld up in tch in rr: hdwy bef 3 out: drvn and chsd ldrs after 3 out: wnt 3rd but btn next: wknd between last 2: mstke last and lost modest 3rd flat* **11/4**[1]

040- **5** *3 ¼* **Thefriendlygremlin**[138] 460 5-10-11 **88**...................(p) GavinSheehan(3) 74
(John Upson) *chsd ldrs: lft 2nd 6th tl after next: rdn and wknd bef 2 out* **40/1**

5P1- **6** *11* **Marico (FR)**[17] 1635 5-10-11 **85**..(p) FelixDeGiles 61
(Tom Symonds) *t.k.h: hld up in tch towards rr: rdn and outpcd 8th: wknd sn after next* **9/2**[2]

2/0- **7** *7* **Douchkirk (FR)**[150] 252 6-11-5 **93**...................................... WillKennedy 63
(John Berry) *in tch towards rr: rdn and struggling after 7th: wknd sn after 3 out: wl btn whn nt fluent next: t.o* **6/1**[3]

054- **8** *32* **Nurse Ratched (IRE)**[8] 1718 4-10-8 **82**............................... AlainCawley 35
(Fergal O'Brien) *led tl mstke and hdd 2nd: chsd ldr tl j.rt 6th: lost pl and hmpd on inner sn after: last next: wknd 3 out: eased next: t.o* **10/1**

/30- **F** **Lost In Newyork (IRE)**[46] 1379 6-10-13 **87**......................(p) HarryHaynes
(Nick Kent) *t.k.h: hld up in midfield: hdwy to ld 2nd: blnd 6th: hdd and mstke 3 out: sn fdd and bhd whn fell next* **14/1**

5m 6.9s (-20.30) **Going Correction** -1.70s/f (Hard) **9** Ran SP% **112.6**
Speed ratings (Par 103): **70,69,61,61,60 56,53,41,**
toteswingers 1&2 £7.10, 2&3 £28.30, 1&3 £10.50 CSF £52.29 CT £1121.60 TOTE £4.10: £1.70, £7.30, £6.90; EX 69.40 Trifecta £374.50 Pool: £1075.77 - 2.15 winning units..
Owner Craig Buckingham **Bred** James Dillon **Trained** Aberthin, Vale of Glamorgan
■ Stewards' Enquiry : Michael Byrne one-day ban: careless riding (Oct 23)

FOCUS

Chase and Hurdle course on shared bends. Hurdles course on inside line. They came home at long intervals in this steadily run novices' handicap hurdle. The winner ran to the level of his recent win with a big step up from the second.

1821 FLEXINEB NEBULISERS NOVICES' CHASE (12 fncs) 2m 110y

2:50 (2:50) (Class 4) 4-Y-O+ **£4,548** (£1,335; £667; £333)

Form RPR

001/ **1** **Claret Cloak (IRE)**[179] 5284 6-11-3 0.................................. AidanColeman 137+
(Emma Lavelle) *t.k.h: a gng wl and j.w: chsd ldr after 2nd tl next: chsd ldrs after tl clsd and j. into ld 3 out: cruised clr bef next: in command whn slt mstke last: v easily* **1/3**[1]

225- **2** *14* **Dont Take Me Alive**[17] 1627 4-10-9 0 ow2.........................(tp) NoelFehily 107+
(Charlie Longsdon) *t.k.h: hld up in midfield: hdwy 7th: led sn after 9th: mstke and hdd next: brushed aside by wnr and btn next: plugged on* **8/1**[3]

540- **3** *6* **Akula (IRE)**[98] 877 6-11-3 0... ColinBolger 109
(Mark H Tompkins) *j.lft: chsd ldrs: hmpd 2nd: chsd clr ldr 3rd tl 3 out: 3rd and wknd bef next: plugged on* **25/1**

210/ **4** *16* **Chicklemix**[249] 3995 7-10-10 0.. SeanQuinlan 92
(Pam Sly) *t.k.h: hld up off the pce in last pair: sme hdwy bef 3 out: wnt modest 4th bef 2 out: no imp and wl hld whn mstke last* **22/1**

/31- **5** *13* **American Spin**[109] 518 9-11-10 135....................................... JamieMoore 85
(Luke Dace) *j.rt: chsd ldr tl j.rt and bmpd rival 2nd: sn lost 2nd and nvr gng wl after: steadily lost pl: 6th and t.o 3 out* **13/2**[2]

/1P- **6** *26* **Esporao (IRE)**[42] 1426 7-11-7 124.................................(t) JamesBest(3) 59
(Rob Summers) *led and sn clr: mstke 9th and sn hdd: 4th and btn next: sn fdd and t.o 2 out* **33/1**

0/0- **7** *6* **Be Kind**[17] 1631 7-10-3 0.. MrPJohn(7) 39
(Natalie Lloyd-Beavis) *a in rr and nvr on terms: mstke and pckd 4th: losing tch and blnd 8th: t.o bef 3 out* **150/1**

3m 54.75s (-21.35) **Going Correction** -1.20s/f (Hard)
WFA 4 from 6yo+ 9lb **7** Ran SP% **111.3**
Speed ratings (Par 105): **102,95,92,85,78 66,63**
toteswingers 1&2 £1.40, 2&3 £13.30, 1&3 £3.70 CSF £3.35 TOTE £1.30: £1.20, £2.90; EX 4.10 Trifecta £22.30 Pool: £1538.54 - 49.45 winning units..
Owner Hawksmoor Partnership **Bred** W H Neville **Trained** Hatherden, Hants
■ Stewards' Enquiry : Noel Fehily three-day ban: weighed-in 2lb heavy (Oct 23-25)

FOCUS

This was a case of mission accomplished for the winner, who looks a smart recruit to fences.

1822 PARKWAY MK H'CAP HURDLE (8 hdls) 2m

3:20 (3:20) (Class 5) (0-100,99) 4-Y-O+ **£1,949** (£572; £286; £143)

Form RPR

/00- **1** **Theatrelands**[17] 1633 5-11-11 **98**...(p) NoelFehily 104+
(Charlie Longsdon) *t.k.h: chsd ldrs: led and gng best whn lft clr 2 out: hit last: r.o strly flat: readily* **5/2**[2]

203- **2** *5* **Knockgraffon Lad (USA)**[12] 1674 6-11-10 **97**...............(tp) AlainCawley 99
(Brendan Powell) *t.k.h: hld up bhd: hdwy after 3 out: chsng ldrs whn hmpd next: chsd clr wnr between last 2: styd on but no imp* **15/2**

011- **3** *4* **Hail Tiberius**[3] 1799 6-11-5 **92** 14ex.....................................(t) TomSiddall 89
(Martin Keighley) *t.k.h: hld up in last pair: blnd 6th: hdwy next: rdn and no prog bef 2 out: plugged on to go 3rd between last 2: no threat to wnr* **9/4**[1]

0/0- **4** *2* **Shadarpour (IRE)**[149] 267 4-11-10 **97**................................ JamieMoore 91
(Gary Moore) *led: j. slowly and jnd 3rd: j. slowly again and hdd next: styd upsides ldr: rdn and unable qck whn lft 2nd 2 out: wknd and lost 2 pls between last 2* **12/1**

320- **5** *½* **Osmosia (FR)**[17] 1630 8-10-8 **81**..(tp) TomCannon 78+
(Chris Gordon) *hld up in tch in midfield: rdn and effrt bef 2 out: stl handy whn hmpd 2 out: wknd bef last* **5/1**[3]

545- **6** *17* **Tri Nations (UAE)**[17] 1638 8-11-1 **93**..........................(vt) JamesBanks(5) 70
(Anthony Middleton) *in tch in midfield: rdn and after 3 out: struggling and btn whn hmpd next: sn wknd* **33/1**

231- **7** *15* **On The Feather**[32] 1517 7-11-7 **99**............................(b) TrevorWhelan(5) 61
(Jim Best) *in tch in midfield: rdn and no rspnse after 3 out: wknd bef next: t.o* **10/1**

5/4- **F** **Hightown (IRE)**[17] 1625 6-11-10 **97**................................ LeightonAspell 91
(Alison Batchelor) *chsd ldr tl j. into ld 4th: rdn and hdd whn fell 2 out* **16/1**

3m 48.25s (-19.65) **Going Correction** -1.70s/f (Hard)
WFA 4 from 5yo+ 9lb **8** Ran SP% **113.4**
Speed ratings (Par 103): **81,78,76,75,75 66,59,**
toteswingers 1&2 £3.50, 2&3 £3.10, 1&3 £3.90 CSF £21.18 CT £46.59 TOTE £4.40: £1.50, £2.70, £1.30; EX 23.30 Trifecta £67.10 Pool: £956.11 - 10.67 winning units..
Owner N Davies & S Crowley **Bred** Juddmonte Farms Ltd **Trained** Over Norton, Oxon

FOCUS

A fair race for the modest grade. The winner can do better still and the second is rated to form.

1823 THOROUGHBRED BREEDERS' ASSOCIATION MARES' "NATIONAL HUNT" NOVICES' HURDLE (8 hdls) 2m

3:50 (3:50) (Class 4) 4-Y-O+ **£3,898** (£1,144; £572; £286)

Form RPR

046/ **1** **Blase Chevalier (IRE)**[442] 1064 7-10-9 0............... WayneKavanagh(3) 103+
(Seamus Mullins) *t.k.h: nt a fluent: hld up in tch in midfield: rdn and effrt after 3 out: chsd ldr and j.lft 2 out: swtchd rt between last 2: led and j.lft last: styd on wl u.p flat* **4/1**[3]

1- **2** *1* **Reves D'Amour (IRE)**[138] 462 4-10-12 0............................ BrendanPowell 99
(Jamie Snowden) *led and set stdy gallop: rdn and hit 2 out: hdd last: kpt on same pce u.p flat* **5/2**[2]

332/ **3** *15* **Amazing D'Azy (IRE)**330 2402 5-10-12 0.......................... NickScholfield 85
(Kim Bailey) *t.k.h: chsd ldrs: 4th and effrt after 3 out: wnt 3rd but struggling whn mstke next: sn outpcd and btn: plugged on* **7/4**1

1- **4** *5* **Garnock (IRE)**32 1523 5-10-12 0.......................... TomScudamore 79
(David Bridgwater) *mstkes: chsd ldr tl after 2nd: styd chsng ldrs: 5th and outpcd whn nt fluent 3 out: wl hld and plugged on same pce fr next* **15/2**

60- **5** *1 1/2* **Katie's Massini (IRE)**12 1671 5-10-12 0.......................... RobertThornton 80
(Henry Oliver) *chsd ldrs: hit 1st: chsd ldr after 2nd tl jst bef 2 out: 4th and btn whn mstke 2 out: wknd between last 2* **28/1**

5/5- **6** *15* **Lacunae (IRE)**138 462 5-10-12 0.......................... RyanMahon 66
(Seamus Mullins) *bhd: hmpd and mstke 2nd: detached in last 4th: lost tch 3 out* **12/1**

060- **7** *1* **No Ifs No Buts**17 1625 4-10-5 0.......................... JakeHodson(7) 62
(David Bridgwater) *t.k.h: hld up wl in tch in last trio: rdn and struggling bef 3 out: lost tch wl bef 2 out* **33/1**

8 *18* **Scolt Head Island** 7-10-12 0.......................... AndrewThornton 44
(Caroline Bailey) *t.k.h: hld up wl in tch in last trio: struggling after 6th: lost tch sn after next: t.o* **50/1**

3m 54.55s (-13.35) **Going Correction** -1.70s/f (Hard)
WFA 4 from 5yo+ 9lb **8** Ran SP% **112.7**
Speed ratings (Par 105): **65,64,57,54,53 46,45,36**
toteswingers 1&2 £3.10, 2&3 £1.10, 1&3 £2.20 CSF £14.35 TOTE £6.10: £1.10, £1.70, £1.10; EX 17.30 Trifecta £59.20 Pool: £1379.45 - 17.47 winning units..
Owner Andrew Cocks And Tara Johnson **Bred** Newtownbarry House Stud **Trained** Wilsford-Cum-Lake, Wilts

FOCUS
With nobody keen to make the early running and the race only developing shortly after halfway, it remains to be seen what the form is worth. The winner is rated to the level of her 2012 form.

1824 HAYGAIN HAY STEAMERS CLEAN HEALTHY FORAGE H'CAP HURDLE (10 hdls) 2m 3f 110y
4:20 (4:21) (Class 5) (0-95,95) 4-Y-0+ **£1,949** (£572; £286; £143)

Form RPR

0/5- **1** **Safferano (IRE)**49 1339 7-11-2 **80**.......................... MichaelByrne(3) 92
(Tim Vaughan) *hld up off the pce in last trio: rdn and hdwy after 8th: chsd ldng pair and clsng bef 2 out: sltly hmpd and swtchd rt 2 out: chalng last: led fnl50yds: styd on: rdn out* **8/1**

035- **2** *1/2* **Torran Sound**26 1580 6-11-11 **94**.......................... (p) FelixDeGiles 98
(James Eustace) *prom in main gp: chsd clr ldr after 5th: pressing ldr next: mstke 3 out: rdn to ld 2 out: str pressed and hit last: hdd and unable qck fnl 50yds* **5/1**2

535/ **3** *13* **Grand Article (IRE)**136 9-10-0 **69** oh4.......................... AidanColeman 64+
(Paul Cowley) *led and handed clr ld s: c bk to rivals after 5th: rdn after 3 out: hdd and hit 2 out: wknd bef last* **10/1**

/4P- **4** *7* **High On A Hill (IRE)**12 1675 6-11-12 **95**.......................... (p) AdrianLane 81
(Iain Jardine) *hld up wl off the pce in rr: clsd after 5th: rdn and effrt after 8th: no imp: plugged on past btn horses after 3 out: wnt modest 4th between last 2: nvr trbld ldrs* **8/1**

F16- **5** *11* **Lucys Girl (IRE)**31 1529 6-11-9 **92**.......................... BrendanPowell 68
(Jamie Snowden) *hld up off the pce in midfield: clsd after 5th: rdn and effrt after 8th: no hdwy 3 out: 4th and wl btn next* **3/1**1

0P2- **6** *25* **The Quantum Kid**17 1630 9-11-7 **90**.......................... LiamTreadwell 54
(Peter Hiatt) *hld up off the pce in midfield: clsd after 5th: 3rd bef 3 out: rdn and btn wl bef 2 out: fdd: t.o* **13/2**3

600- **7** *17* **Gilded Age**30 1538 7-11-8 **94**.......................... (t) JamesBest(3) 32
(Rob Summers) *prom: clsd after 5th: lost pl and rdn 7th: lost tch 3 out: t.o next* **9/1**

/66- **8** *4* **Queen Spud**26 1578 4-11-4 **87**.......................... RobertThornton 22
(Henry Daly) *prom in main gp: clsd after 5th: rdn and btn whn j.lft 3 out: sn wknd: blnd next: t.o* **12/1**

/PP- **P** **Chapel House**41 1437 10-10-3 **79**.......................... (t) MrPJohn(7)
(Richard Harper) *chsd clr ldr tl after 5th: lost pl after 7th: lost tch 3 out: t.o whn p.u next* **20/1**

U0- **P** **Kilcolman Wizard (IRE)**12 1672 7-11-12 **95**.......................... NoelFehily
(Liam Corcoran) *hld up wl off the pce in rr: clsd after 5th: rdn after 8th: sn btn: t.o whn p.u 2 out* **18/1**

4m 34.65s (-34.95) **Going Correction** -1.70s/f (Hard)
WFA 4 from 6yo+ 9lb **10** Ran SP% **114.0**
Speed ratings (Par 103): **101,100,95,92,88 78,71,70,,**
toteswingers 1&2 £5.40, 2&3 £8.30, 1&3 £10.50 CSF £47.31 CT £404.89 TOTE £10.70: £2.70, £2.10, £2.70; EX 52.60 Trifecta £514.20 Pool: £2040.69 - 2.97 winning units..
Owner Exors of the Late R H D Smith **Bred** John Irish **Trained** Aberthin, Vale of Glamorgan

FOCUS
A weak race with very little in the way of recent form to go on, but it was run at a searching pace. A big step forward from the winner, with the second to form.

1825 BILL MOORE 80TH BIRTHDAY H'CAP CHASE (18 fncs) 3m 110y
4:50 (4:52) (Class 5) (0-95,95) 4-Y-0+ **£2,144** (£629; £314; £157)

Form RPR

5/P- **1** **Von Galen (IRE)**121 692 12-10-0 **69** oh8.......................... (p) LiamTreadwell 85+
(Michael Scudamore) *hld up in last pair: hdwy gng wl 10th: jnd ldr and stl travelling wl 3 out: rdn to ld bef next and sn drew clr: eased flat: v easily* **12/1**

626- **2** *15* **Rifleman (IRE)**29 1548 13-10-7 **76**.......................... (tp) TomScudamore 76
(Richard Lee) *chsd ldrs: wnt 2nd 8th tl cocked jaw and hung lft 11th: styd chsng ldrs: rdn and chsd clr ldng pair after 3 out: no threat to wnr but plugged on to go 2nd last* **7/1**3

P3P- **3** *10* **Quayside Court (IRE)**29 1548 9-10-0 **76**.......................... (vt) GeraldQuinn(7) 68
(Claire Dyson) *chsd ldrs tl led 3rd: mde most after: mstke 12th: drvn and hdd after 3 out: btn and j.lft next: wknd and lost 2nd last* **8/1**

44P- **4** *6* **Dark Oasis**11 1687 7-10-0 **69** oh2.......................... JamieMoore 52
(Natalie Lloyd-Beavis) *chsd ldrs: led 2nd tl 3rd: styd chsng ldrs: mstke 13th: rdn and no ex bef 3 out: wknd bef 2 out* **12/1**

44U- **5** *1 3/4* **Shock N Freaney (IRE)**17 1629 6-10-7 **81**.......................... (vt) JamesBanks(5) 63
(Anthony Middleton) *hld up in rr: hdwy into midfield after 11th: rdn and no hdwy bef 3 out: wknd wl bef 2 out* **17/2**

40/- **6** *15* **Overton Lad**163 32 12-10-5 **74**.......................... (b) HarrySkelton 42
(Peter Pritchard) *led tl 2nd: chsd ldrs after: pressing ldrs and mstke 12th: rdn 14th: outpcd 3 out: 4th and wl btn next: fdd: t.o* **16/1**

1P4- **7** *28* **Douglas**17 1626 8-11-12 **95**.......................... MarkGrant 38
(Jo Hughes) *hmpd 1st: chsd ldr 5th tl 8th: lost pl and bhd 12th: lost tch 14th: t.o after 3 out* **11/1**

540- **8** *10* **Dbanks (IRE)**12 1673 10-11-4 **87**.......................... NoelFehily 21
(Liam Corcoran) *j.lft: hmpd 1st: a towards rr: lost tch 14th: t.o after 3 out* **8/1**

/14- **P** **Halucha (IRE)**110 789 8-11-4 **90**.......................... (p) PeterCarberry(3)
(Paul Webber) *dropped to rr and rdn 3rd: nvr travelling after: losing tch whn blnd 10th: t.o whn p.u next* **9/2**2

445/ **P** **Kevin Fancy (IRE)**169 5480 7-9-11 **69** oh13.......................... GavinSheehan(3)
(John Upson) *racd wd: hmpd 1st: chsd ldrs 5th tl lost pl bnd after 9th: bhd 11th: t.o whn p.u 3 out* **40/1**

/30- **F** **Inandover**12 1668 8-10-2 **71**.......................... (t) BrianHughes
(John Mackie) *midfield whn fell 1st* **4/1**1

6m 5.75s (-31.15) **Going Correction** -1.20s/f (Hard) **11** Ran SP% **115.5**
Speed ratings (Par 103): **101,96,93,91,90 85,76,73,,**
toteswingers 1&2 £25.10, 2&3 £16.20, 1&3 £20.40 CSF £92.66 CT £718.69 TOTE £17.40: £3.60, £2.60, £2.40; EX 87.90 Trifecta £1458.60 Part won. Pool: £1944.92 - 0.70 winning units..
Owner Mrs Bettine Evans **Bred** Donal Turner **Trained** Bromsash, H'fords

FOCUS
A poor staying handicap and a nightmare for punters with Inandover getting no further than the first fence. The winner's best figure since 2010.

1826 BEST RACING BLOGS ON GG.COM MAIDEN OPEN NATIONAL HUNT FLAT RACE 1m 5f 110y
5:20 (5:20) (Class 6) 4-6-Y-0 **£1,559** (£457; £228; £114)

Form RPR

00/ **1** **Wyfield Rose**173 5388 4-10-9 0.......................... NoelFehily 94+
(Jamie Snowden) *chsd ldrs tl led over 2f out: rdn and styd on wl fr over 1f out* **11/2**3

6- **2** *2* **Countersign**110 790 4-11-2 0.......................... 1 AdamPogson 98
(Charles Pogson) *taken down early: hld up wl off the pce in rr: clsd 1/2-way: effrt to chse wnr 2f out: kpt on but a hld* **9/2**2

3 *3 3/4* **Di's Gift** 4-11-2 0.......................... DenisO'Regan 93
(Richard Guest) *hld up wl off the pce in rr: clsd 1/2-way: effrt to chse ldrs and edgd rt wl over 1f out: one pce after* **9/2**2

3/ **4** *12* **Newforge House (IRE)**287 3215 5-11-2 0.......................... BrendanPowell 78
(Brendan Powell) *t.k.h: hld up wl off the pce towards rr: clsd 1/2-way: trcking ldrs 4f out: rdn and outpcd jst over 2f out: wknd over 1f out* **7/2**1

4- **5** *2 3/4* **Seamus Rua (IRE)**22 1599 5-10-13 0.......................... KielanWoods(3) 74
(Charlie Longsdon) *led tl 5f out: styd handy tl rdn and no ex ent fnl 2f: wknd over 1f out* **7/2**1

25- **6** *3/4* **In A Heartbeat**22 1599 4-10-9 0.......................... IanPopham 66
(Martin Keighley) *hld up wl off the pce towards rr: clsd 1/2-way: rdn and effrt 3f out: wknd 2f out* **9/1**

0/6- **7** *3 3/4* **Monasterevin (IRE)**12 1671 5-10-13 0.......................... (p) JackQuinlan(3) 68
(Noel Quinlan) *hung lft thrght: chsd ldr tl led 5f out: hdd: hung lft and v wd bnd over 2f out: sn wknd* **16/1**

8 *15* **Swanage Bay (IRE)** 6-10-11 0.......................... JamesBanks(5) 49
(Anthony Middleton) *hld up wl off the pce towards rr: clsd 1/2-way: lost pl and bhd 4f out: wknd 3f out* **33/1**

9 *7* **Alwayslookback (IRE)**129 4-10-11 0.......................... BenPoste(5) 40
(Rosemary Gasson) *t.k.h: chsd clr ldng pair: clsd 1/2-way: dropped to rr 4f out: lost tch 3f out* **66/1**

3m 6.9s (-33.70) **9** Ran SP% **116.5**
toteswingers 1&2 £6.00, 2&3 £6.20, 1&3 £6.90 CSF £30.76 TOTE £6.10: £1.70, £2.50, £2.30; EX 36.30 Trifecta £232.90 Pool: £1686.13 - 5.42 winning units..
Owner Mrs Nicholas Jones & Friends **Bred** Coln Valley Stud **Trained** Lambourn, Berks

FOCUS
A stronger early pace than is often the case in races of this nature. A big step up from the winner but the form could be a few pounds out either way.
T/Plt: £32.40 to a £1 stake. Pool of £72613.08 - 1632.97 winning tickets. T/Qpdt: £8.90 to a £1 stake. Pool of £5698.70 - 473.30 winning tickets. SP

1250 LES LANDES
Monday, August 26

OFFICIAL GOING: Good (good to firm in places)

1827a FINE ART H'CAP HURDLE 2m
2:30 (2:30) 3-Y-0+ **£1,460** (£525; £315)

RPR

1 **If I Had Him (IRE)**15 1250 9-11-10.......................... (v) MattieBatchelor
(George Baker) *trckd ldrs: jnd ldr and mstke 5th: led after 3 out: hdd after 2 out: nt fluent last: rallied to ld nr fin* **7/4**2

2 *1/2* **The Bay Bandit**36 1058 6-10-13.......................... (p) GerardTumelty
(Neil Mulholland) *hld up: j. deliberately early: smooth hdwy fr 3 out: led after 2 out: fnd little run-in: hdd nr fin* **4/6**1

3 *5* **Azaria (FR)**59 7-9-3.......................... ThomasGarner
(Mrs A Malzard, Jersey) *trckd ldr: outpcd appr 3 out: kpt on one pce fr 2 out* **6/1**

4 *2* **Landolino (FR)**15 1250 8-10-12.......................... AntonyProcter
(Mrs J L Le Brocq, Jersey) *mainly led: jnd 5th: hdd after 3 out: btn fr 2 out* **7/2**3

5 *15* **Nordic Affair**15 1250 9-9-3.......................... MrPCollington
(S Arthur, Jersey) *a in rr: outpcd appr 3 out: t.o* **20/1**

6 *15* **Deepika (IRE)**43 993 5-9-9.......................... (t) MrFTett
(Mrs A Malzard, Jersey) *t.k.h: trckd ldrs tl outpcd fr 5th t.o* **9/1**

3m 52.0s (-9.00) **6** Ran SP% **147.6**
.
Owner Sir Alex Ferguson **Bred** Mrs J Morrissey **Trained** Manton, Wilts

155 EXETER (R-H)
Thursday, October 10

OFFICIAL GOING: Good to firm (chs 6.9, hdl 6.9)
Wind: strong breeze against (in relation to straight) Weather: bright and sunny

1828 BATHWICK TYRES PLYMOUTH H'CAP HURDLE (10 hdls) 2m 3f
2:20 (2:21) (Class 4) (0-120,119) 4-Y-0+ **£3,249** (£954; £477; £238)

Form RPR

314- **1** **Staigue Fort**23 1597 5-11-9 **116**.......................... AidanColeman 127+
(Emma Lavelle) *mde all: rdn appr 3 out: a holding runner-up: styd on strly* **7/2**3

2/1- **2** *3* **Twelve Roses**142 417 5-11-12 **119**.......................... JasonMaguire 126
(Kim Bailey) *trckd wnr thrght: rdn appr 3 out: kpt on but a being hld* **7/4**1

The Form Book Jumps, Raceforム Ltd, Compton, RG20 6NL.

022- **3** *11* **Kalmbeforethestorm**[68] 1191 5-11-1 **115**........................ ChrisDavies(7) 112
(Helen Nelmes) *trckd ldrs: nt fluent 6th: rdn after 7th: styd on same pce fr next* **10/1**

3/0- **4** *8* **Ladies Dancing**[148] 304 7-11-7 **114**.................................. JamesDavies 103
(Chris Down) *hld up bhd ldrs: rdn after 7th: styd on same pce to go 4th at the last: nvr trbld ldrs* **25/1**

223- **5** *1* **Bathwick Man**[18] 1634 8-10-10 **110**.................................. KieronEdgar(7) 101
(David Pipe) *hld up bhd ldrs: taking clsr order whn hit 5th: rdn after 7th: one pce fr next* **3/1**[2]

131- **6** *3/4* **Party Palace**[87] 995 9-10-10 **106**.................................. GilesHawkins(3) 93
(Stuart Howe) *trckd ldrs: rdn after 7th: sn one pce* **11/1**

/04- **7** *23* **Sonoftheking (IRE)**[23] 1595 5-10-11 **104**.......................... TomO'Brien 71
(Philip Hobbs) *trckd ldrs: nt fluent 3rd: pushed along after 6th: rdn after next: sn wknd: t.o* **10/1**

4m 21.5s (-21.20) **Going Correction** -1.175s/f (Hard) 7 Ran SP% **113.9**
Speed ratings (Par 105): **97,95,91,87,87 87,77**
toteswingers 1&2 £2.00, 2&3 £5.00, 1&3 £7.30 CSF £10.33 TOTE £3.30: £1.90, £2.20; EX 10.50 Trifecta £78.40 Pool: £1621.98 - 15.50 winning units..
Owner Lady Bland **Bred** Lady Bland **Trained** Hatherden, Hants

FOCUS
Aidan Coleman said of the ground: "It's on the quick side of good". The two at the head of the weights, who were on the pace throughout, dominated what was probably a reasonable race for the grade. The form is rated around the second and third.

1829 ILFRACOMBE FOOD SERVICE NOVICES' H'CAP HURDLE (11 hdls) 2m 5f 110y
2:50 (2:50) (Class 4) (0-105,103) 3-Y-0+ **£3,249** (£954; £477; £238)

Form RPR

/22- **1** **Cruising Bye**[79] 1087 7-10-6 **83**..[1] TomO'Brien 94+
(Peter Bowen) *trckd ldrs: rdn appr 3 out: led 2 out: styd on wl to assert fr last: rdn out* **10/3**[2]

542- **2** *7* **Western Prize**[9] 1717 5-11-11 **102**.................................(v) AidanColeman 102
(Tim Vaughan) *trckd ldr: rdn bef 3 out: ev ch 2 out: sn hld: styd on same pce* **11/4**[1]

6/6- **3** *1* **Bold Cuffs**[10] 1699 4-11-12 **103**.. JoeTizzard 103
(Colin Tizzard) *hld up bhd ldrs: hdwy after 8th: rdn bef next: styd on same pce: wnt 3rd bef last* **7/1**

P03- **4** *12* **Cottage Acre (IRE)**[16] 1641 10-10-13 **90**............................ LiamHeard 78
(Colin Heard) *trckd ldrs: disp 2nd fr 7th tl rdn appr 3 out: wkng whn swtchd lft bef last* **20/1**

140- **5** *1 1/4* **Royal Peak (IRE)**[18] 1631 6-11-8 **99**..........................(tp) TomScudamore 92+
(David Pipe) *led: j. and hung lft fr 5th: rdn bef 3 out: wnt lft and hit 2 out whn hdd: wknd last* **6/1**

335/ **P** **Ifyouthinkso**[185] 5218 6-11-9 **100**....................................(t) JasonMaguire
(Lucy Jones) *trckd ldrs: reminders after 4th: sn in rr: t.o whn p.u bef 8th* **6/1**

122- **P** **Hopstrings**[18] 1635 5-11-11 **102**.................................. WayneHutchinson
(Charlie Brooks) *trckd ldrs tl swtchd wd and lost pl after 4th: reminders after next: wknd 6th: t.o whn p.u bef 8th* **9/2**[3]

5m 5.7s (-27.30) **Going Correction** -1.175s/f (Hard) course record 7 Ran SP% **113.8**
Speed ratings (Par 105): **102,99,99,94,94 ,**
toteswingers 1&2 £2.10, 2&3 £4.10, 1&3 £4.90 CSF £13.14 CT £58.31 TOTE £3.30: £2.00, £2.00; EX 12.30 Trifecta £67.90 Pool: £745.56 - 8.23 winning units..
Owner F Lloyd **Bred** F Lloyd **Trained** Little Newcastle, Pembrokes

FOCUS
Modest form. There's probably more to come from the winner.

1830 GREAT POINT MEDIA INVESTMENTS H'CAP CHASE (18 fncs) 3m
3:20 (3:20) (Class 4) (0-120,120) 4-Y-0+ **£5,848** (£1,717; £858; £429)

Form RPR

54F- **1** **Standing Ovation (IRE)**[18] 1637 6-10-0 **94** oh2............(t) ConorO'Farrell 104+
(David Pipe) *nt a fluent: hld up: pushed along and hdwy 11th: str reminders bef next whn lost pl: pushed along: disp cl 3rd after 14th: drvn to chal 2 out: led w gd jump last: hld on: drvn rt out* **9/4**[1]

/3P- **2** *nk* **Qianshan Leader (IRE)**[16] 1642 9-11-12 **120**...............(p) AidanColeman 127
(Emma Lavelle) *led: rdn whn hrd pressed fr 4 out: narrowly hdd last: kpt on gamely w ev ch: hld nring fin* **9/2**[2]

112- **3** *4 1/2* **Whistling Senator (IRE)**[18] 1637 6-11-7 **115**............(v) RichieMcLernon 119
(Jonjo O'Neill) *trckd ldr: rdn appr 4 out: ev ch 2 out: swtchd lft and hld in 4th bef last: styd on to snatch 3rd fnl strides* **7/1**

F2U- **4** *shd* **Basil Fawlty (IRE)**[39] 1486 8-11-0 **108**........................(t) TomScudamore 113+
(David Pipe) *hld up: nt fluent 1st: stdy prog fr 12th: cl up after 14th: rdn and ev ch 2 out tl last: no ex: lost 3rd fnl stride* **6/1**[3]

/32- **5** *13* **Bishophill Jack (IRE)**[142] 420 7-11-0 **108**...................... NickScholfield 102
(Kim Bailey) *trcking ldrs whn blnd bdly 1st and rdr lost iron briefly: in tch: cl up whn rdn after 14th: hld fr after next: wknd 2 out* **9/1**

134- **6** *3* **Violets Boy (IRE)**[18] 1636 6-11-7 **115**.........................(t) LeightonAspell 103
(Brendan Powell) *hld up: hit 6th: hdwy after 14th but nvr threatened ldrs: rdn after 4 out: wknd 2 out* **9/1**

613- **7** *34* **Health Is Wealth (IRE)**[18] 1626 8-10-5 **104**.....................(tp) EDLinehan(5) 62
(Colin Tizzard) *in tch: rdn after 11th: sn wknd: t.o* **14/1**

432- **8** *shd* **Ballyvesey (IRE)**[18] 1626 8-10-13 **107**..........................(bt[1]) JamieMoore 65
(Peter Bowen) *chsd ldrs tl rdn after 12th: sn in rr: t.o* **9/1**

533- **U** **Mister Moonax (IRE)**[40] 1477 13-10-2 **99**.....................(tp) GilesHawkins(3)
(Chris Down) *hld up: nt fluent 7th: in last pair whn blnd and uns rdr 9th* **33/1**

5m 47.0s (-22.30) **Going Correction** -0.775s/f (Firm) 9 Ran SP% **115.3**
Speed ratings (Par 105): **106,105,104,104,100 99,87,87,**
toteswingers 1&2 £1.50, 2&3 £7.80, 1&3 £6.60 CSF £13.35 CT £60.34 TOTE £2.70: £1.10, £1.40, £2.10; EX 18.50 Trifecta £99.00 Pool: £900.02 - 6.81 winning units..
Owner The Bravo Partnership **Bred** Patrick McGrath **Trained** Nicholashayne, Devon

FOCUS
A good test at the distance, and faur form. The winner can rate higher if his jumping improves.

1831 BATHWICK TYRES BRIDGWATER BEGINNERS' CHASE (18 fncs) 3m
3:50 (3:50) (Class 4) 4-Y-0+ **£4,659** (£1,446; £778)

Form RPR

/52- **1** **Dawn Commander (GER)**[18] 1628 6-11-5 118............... JasonMaguire 125+
(Charlie Longsdon) *j. sltly rt: nt a fluent: pressed ldr thrght: lost pl briefly w a slow jump 14th: sn bk upsides: led 4 out: sn wl clr: heavily eased run-in* **15/8**[2]

2/2- **2** *34* **Silver Commander**[148] 302 6-11-5 124................................. JackDoyle 88+
(Victor Dartnall) *led tl hdd 4 out: qckly btn: t.o* **6/5**[1]

/64- **3** *34* **Redlynch Rock (IRE)**[107] 830 5-11-2 0...................... GilesHawkins(3) 52
(Bob Buckler) *nt a fluent: chsd ldrs tl mstke 9th and 10th: sn t.o* **20/1**

0/U- **P** **Virginia Ash (IRE)**[6] 1744 5-11-5 0.......................................(p) JoeTizzard
(Colin Tizzard) *j. v poorly: sn detached and drvn: blnd 5th: v slow 8th (water): p.u bef next* **7/2**[3]

5m 48.4s (-20.90) **Going Correction** -0.775s/f (Firm) 4 Ran SP% **107.2**
Speed ratings (Par 105): **103,91,80,**
CSF £4.64 TOTE £2.10; EX 3.90 Trifecta £11.80 Pool: £1100.64 - 69.77 winning units..
Owner Alan Halsall **Bred** W Lohmann Jr **Trained** Over Norton, Oxon

FOCUS
Not form to put any faith in, with Virginia Ash being in trouble after a very slow jump at the first, and favourite Silver Commander stopping quickly once headed. However the winner is probably capable of at least matching his hurdle best of 130+.

1832 BATHWICK TYRES TAUNTON NOVICES' HURDLE (8 hdls) 2m 1f
4:20 (4:20) (Class 4) 4-Y-0+ **£3,249** (£954; £477; £238)

Form RPR

1/2- **1** **Rayvin Black**[132] 560 4-11-5 119............................... LeightonAspell 115+
(Oliver Sherwood) *mde all: drew clr w ease fr 3 out: unextended* **4/7**[1]

R- **2** *10* **Sea Island Pearl**[16] 1639 4-10-5 0...[1] TomO'Brien 85+
(Philip Hobbs) *prom whn bmpd 1st: trckd wnr fr after 2nd: rdn after 3 out but nvr any ch w v easy wnr* **20/1**

445/ **3** *7* **Reyes Magos (IRE)**[208] 4787 7-10-12 0........................(t) ConorO'Farrell 84
(Seamus Durack) *trckd ldrs: rdn after 3 out: lost 3rd next: styd on same pce to regain 3rd at the last* **4/1**[2]

50- **4** *2 1/2* **Amantius**[21] 1255 4-10-12 0.. NickScholfield 81
(Johnny Farrelly) *mid-div: hdwy into 4th u.p after 5th tl next: sn one pce: regained 4th whn hit last* **14/1**

FF- **5** *1 1/2* **Lily Potts**[39] 1483 4-10-2 0..(p) GilesHawkins(3) 73
(Chris Down) *mid-div: rdn in last pair of gp after 5th: plugged on* **33/1**

6 *hd* **Frozen Over**[21] 5-10-12 0.. JamesDavies 80
(Chris Down) *hld up: hdwy into 5th after 5th: sn rdn: wnt 3rd 2 out: wknd run-in* **6/1**[3]

0/F- **7** *3/4* **Diddypurptoon**[16] 1639 7-10-2 0...................................... JamesBest(3) 72
(Jackie Du Plessis) *hld up: rdn gng to 3 out: nvr any imp* **25/1**

0/P- **8** *16* **Daizy (IRE)**[9] 1706 4-10-12 0.. JackDoyle 63
(Hilary Parrott) *prom whn wnt lft and bmpd 1st: chsd ldrs tl wknd after 5th: t.o* **50/1**

430- **9** *dist* **Mr Trilby (IRE)**[107] 828 6-10-5 0.................................(tp) MrSWelton(7)
(David Pipe) *t.o after 2nd: continued* **12/1**

3m 52.7s (-22.80) **Going Correction** -1.175s/f (Hard) 9 Ran SP% **125.8**
Speed ratings (Par 105): **106,101,98,96,96 96,95,88,**
toteswingers 1&2 £3.50, 2&3 £7.60, 1&3 £1.02 CSF £19.81 TOTE £2.00: £1.10, £7.20, £1.10; EX 14.80 Trifecta £92.50 Pool: £999.38 - 8.10 winning units..
Owner V J Walsh **Bred** Mystic Meg Limited **Trained** Upper Lambourn, Berks

FOCUS
There was little depth to this novice hurdle. The winner was value for further and is rated close to his mark.

1833 BATHWICK TYRES CONDITIONAL JOCKEYS' H'CAP HURDLE (8 hdls) 2m 1f
4:50 (4:52) (Class 4) (0-105,104) 4-Y-0+ **£3,249** (£954; £477; £238)

Form RPR

522- **1** **Clarion Call**[9] 1711 5-11-5 **100**......................................(p) KillianMoore(3) 104
(Graeme McPherson) *t.k.h: trckd ldrs: chal 2 out: rdn to ld last: drifted lft: drvn out* **5/2**[1]

01F/ **2** *1/2* **Key To Milan**[191] 5108 7-11-2 **94**..................................(tp) GilesHawkins 98
(Chris Down) *j.lft: disp ld fr 2nd: clr ldr after 5th: rdn next: hdd last: kpt on* **7/1**

/50- **3** *7* **Ray Diamond**[134] 542 8-11-3 **95**... JamesBest 92
(Jackie Du Plessis) *led tl 5th: pressed ldr: rdn appr 3 out: styd on same pce fr 2 out* **7/2**[2]

0F4- **4** *15* **Cash Injection**[16] 1643 4-11-2 **94**.....................................(t) MichealNolan 78
(Richard Woollacott) *hld up wl in tch: rdn appr 3 out: wknd 2 out* **12/1**

/4P- **5** *3/4* **Bedouin Bay**[113] 767 6-11-7 **104**..........................(b) ThomasCheesman(5) 87
(Johnny Farrelly) *t.k.h: trckd ldrs: rdn appr 3 out: wknd 2 out* **5/1**

/02- **6** *33* **Bazart**[16] 1643 11-10-8 **89**....................................(tp) RobertWilliams(3) 42
(Bernard Llewellyn) *prom tl 4th: chsd ldrs: rdn after 5th: sn wknd: t.o* **8/1**

0/6- **S** **Residence And Spa (IRE)**[154] 177 5-10-2 **80**.............(tp) JackQuinlan
(Helen Rees) *trckd ldrs on outer: jst coming u.p whn slipped up on bnd after 5th* **9/2**[3]

3m 54.0s (-21.50) **Going Correction** -1.175s/f (Hard)
WFA 4 from 5yo+ 9lb 7 Ran SP% **116.9**
Speed ratings (Par 105): **103,102,99,92,92 76,**
toteswingers 1&2 £2.80, 2&3 £2.40, 1&3 £14.50 CSF £20.82 CT £61.77 TOTE £2.70: £1.60, £3.80; EX 12.90 Trifecta £96.70 Pool: £1252.88 - 9.71 winning units..
Owner The Maugersbury Racegoers **Bred** Grasshopper 2000 Ltd **Trained** Upper Oddington, Gloucs

FOCUS
Quite modest handicap form. The winner is rated in line with his Chepstow run.
T/Plt: £26.30 to a £1 stake. Pool of £60183.29 - 1667.93 winning tickets. T/Qpdt: £8.90 to a £1 stake. Pool of £3001.0 - 247.45 winning tickets. TM

1668 WORCESTER (L-H)
Thursday, October 10

OFFICIAL GOING: Good (good to firm in places; 7.3)
Wind: strong behind Weather: very bright and sunny; 11 degrees

1834 LADBROKES CONDITIONAL JOCKEYS' NOVICES' H'CAP CHASE (14 fncs 1 omitted) 2m 4f
2:30 (2:30) (Class 4) (0-110,106) 4-Y-0+ **£3,898** (£1,144; £572; £286)

Form RPR

0/4- **1** **The Potting Shed (IRE)**[130] 606 6-11-12 **106**............(p) GavinSheehan 120+
(Emma Lavelle) *nt a fluent: mde all: drvn and wandering rt bef last where hrd pressed briefly: a looked to be idling but sn asserted flat* **3/1**[2]

/34- **2** *6* **Tough Talkin Man (IRE)**[27] 1577 9-11-0 **94**...................(p) JoshuaMoore 100
(Peter Bowen) *pressed wnr fr 5th: drvn 2 out: tried to chal and ev ch u.p last: sn outpcd flat* **7/1**

5/5- **3** *30* **Bertie's Desire**[149] 290 5-10-13 **96**.............................. ThomasGarner(3) 80+
(Oliver Sherwood) *j. bdly rt: 2nd tl 5th: 3rd after: blnd 8th: drvn bef 11th: sn labouring: no ch 2 out* **6/1**

/04- **4** *3 1/2* **Nicks Power (IRE)**[30] 1550 7-11-11 **105**.................................. BenPoste 81
(Robin Dickin) *dropped out wl off pce: detached in last trio 5th: nrly 15 l 4th and rdn 11th: nvr remotely hopeful* **5/1**[3]

05P- **5** *1* **Fitandproperjob**[95] 902 7-10-7 **87**..................................(t) KielanWoods 62
(Anthony Middleton) *detaced in last trio 5th: last next: t.o fr 11th* **33/1**

044- 6 *11* **Trakeur (FR)**[30] 1553 6-10-7 **87** PeterCarberry 52
(Simon Hodgson) *hmpd 4th: detached in last trio next: remote fr 7th: mstke 10th: continued t.o* **50/1**

651- U **Moorlands Jack**[30] 1549 8-11-5 **102** (p) MattGriffiths[(3)]
(Jeremy Scott) *landed awkwardly 1st and uns rdr* **5/2**[1]

/22- F **Quadrato (GER)**[16] 1641 6-11-8 **105** (t) MichaelByrne[(3)]
(Tim Vaughan) *mstke 3rd: fell heavily 4th: fatally injured* **7/1**

4m 43.3s (-16.70) **Going Correction** -0.75s/f (Firm) 8 Ran SP% **114.4**
Speed ratings (Par 105): **103,100,88,87,86 82, ,**
toteswingers 1&2 £2.60, 2&3 £7.90, 1&3 £5.10 CSF £24.24 CT £117.65 TOTE £4.20: £1.80, £1.60, £2.30; EX 27.10 Trifecta £72.40 Pool: £1195.90 - 12.38 winning units..
Owner N Mustoe & Tim Syder **Bred** Mrs Eileen O'Brien **Trained** Hatherden, Hants

FOCUS
Both bends set 9yds off inside line. The second-last fence was bypassed. A moderate event, run in a decent-looking time. The easy winner produced a big step up on his hurdles form for his in-form yard.

1835 LADBROKES H'CAP CHASE (12 fncs) 2m 110y
3:00 (3:00) (Class 5) (0-100,99) 4-Y-0+ **£2,599** (£763; £381; £190)

Form RPR

5P0- 1 **Walcot Lathyrus**[99] 873 8-11-7 **97** JakeGreenall[(3)] 109+
(Richard Lee) *hld up trcking ldrs: effrt 7th: wnt 2nd at 10th: led 3 out: sn rdn clr: 3 l in front last: doing little in front but comf maintained advantage* **7/2**[2]

P/1- 2 *2 ½* **Shalamiyr (FR)**[30] 1547 8-11-9 **96** WillKennedy 103
(Sarah-Jayne Davies) *pressed ldr tl rdn 10th: outpcd by wnr and finding little fr next: hit last: plugged into 2nd fnl strides* **9/4**[1]

315- 3 *shd* **Julie Prince (IRE)**[23] 1596 7-11-12 **99** (t) BrendanPowell 107
(Brendan Powell) *led: 6 l clr early: drvn and hdd 3 out: plugged on and wl hld after: blnd last: lost 2nd on line* **4/1**[3]

260- 4 *18* **Full Ov Beans**[85] 1018 9-10-12 **90** NicodeBoinville[(5)] 82
(Michael Gates) *nt a fluent: last early: rdn 8th: struggling fr 10th: hit last* **5/1**

3/P- 5 *7* **Sumner (IRE)**[13] 1668 9-11-5 **92** (t) CharliePoste 77
(William Davies) *handy early: lost pl 7th: remote last at 10th: plugged on and overtk two stragglers nr fin* **20/1**

36F- 6 *nk* **The Grey One (IRE)**[9] 1710 10-10-0 **73** oh7 DonalDevereux 60
(Milton Bradley) *t.k.h: last whn mstke 6th: brief effrt but rdn 9th: fading bef next and jumping bdly rt after* **50/1**

006- 6 *dht* **Red Rosso**[30] 1550 8-10-12 **92** JakeHodson[(7)] 76
(Rob Summers) *t.k.h: hdwy 7th: 4th at 9th: rdn and fdd bef next: j. indifferently after* **12/1**

12P- P **Crack At Dawn (IRE)**[18] 1638 12-11-1 **95** (v) MissAEStirling[(7)]
(Michael Gates) *chsd ldrs: j. slowly 5th: rdn and fading 9th: wl bhd whn p.u 10th: dismntd* **12/1**

4m 1.1s (-12.90) **Going Correction** -0.75s/f (Firm) 8 Ran SP% **111.8**
Speed ratings (Par 103): **100,98,98,90,87 86,86,**
toteswingers 1&2 £3.10, 2&3 £2.60, 1&3 £4.20 CSF £11.77 CT £30.61 TOTE £3.80: £1.70, £1.10, £2.30; EX 15.70 Trifecta £60.50 Pool: £1370.27 - 16.97 winning units..
Owner D Pugh **Bred** Edward Crow **Trained** Byton, H'fords

FOCUS
Not a strong race by any means. The winner was on a decent mark andis rated to his best, but there may be more to come.

1836 GARLOCK GYLON GALLOP INTERMEDIATE OPEN NATIONAL HUNT FLAT RACE 2m
3:30 (3:30) (Class 6) 4-6-Y-0 **£1,559** (£457; £228; £114)

Form RPR

1 **Our Kaempfer (IRE)**[249] 4-11-4 0 NoelFehily 110+
(Charlie Longsdon) *hacked along bhd ldng pair: wnt 2nd 4f out: led on bit 3f out: immediately clr: green fnl f: jinked rt to paddock gate 100yds out* **4/11**[1]

2 *7* **My Boy George (IRE)** 5-10-11 0 CiaranMckee[(7)] 96
(John O'Shea) *trckd ldrs: rdn 5f out: lost tch wnr 3f out: vied for 2nd fnl f and snatched it on line* **22/1**

0/2- 3 *shd* **Barrs Lane**[139] 462 5-10-11 0 (p) RobertThornton 89
(Arthur Whiting) *pressed ldr who was gng slowly: rdn after 5f and v idle after: outpcd by wnr over 2f out: racd awkwardly: lost 2nd fnl strides* **6/1**[2]

3- 4 *5* **Barton Heather**[126] 644 4-10-8 0 (t) MichaelByrne[(3)] 84
(Neil Mulholland) *trckd ldr: rdn and outpcd 5f out: struggling after* **14/1**

0/ 5 *3 ¾* **Barton Rose**[180] 5295 4-10-11 0 DougieCostello 80
(Neil Mulholland) *led at v modest pce: rdn and hdd 3f out: fdd wl over 1f out* **8/1**[3]

3m 40.7s (-1.00) **Going Correction** -0.45s/f (Good) 5 Ran SP% **109.7**
Speed ratings: **84,80,80,77,76**
CSF £10.21 TOTE £1.30: £1.10, £4.00; EX 10.80 Trifecta £33.10 Pool: £1623.24 - 36.72 winning units..
Owner Swanee River Partnership **Bred** P Hore **Trained** Over Norton, Oxon

FOCUS
One-way traffic down the home straight for the final time. The overall form is modest but the easy winner should rate higher and win more races.

1837 LADBROKES (S) H'CAP HURDLE (12 hdls) 2m 7f
4:00 (4:00) (Class 5) (0-95,92) 4-Y-0+ **£1,949** (£572; £286; £143)

Form RPR

034- 1 **Transfer**[13] 1675 8-11-10 **88** APMcCoy 90
(Richard Price) *settled towards rr: stdy prog 9th: 6 l 3rd home turn: cajoled to chal and nt fluent 2 out: sn drvn: led and clipped last: drvn and all out* **4/1**[2]

/06- 2 *1 ¼* **Tin Pot Man (IRE)**[130] 597 7-11-7 **85** (t) PaulMoloney 85
(Evan Williams) *handy early: dropped to rr 6th: rallied 9th: 4th home turn: chal 2 out: drvn and jinked lft last: sn chsng wnr but no imp* **7/1**

630- 3 *½* **Banks Road (IRE)**[29] 1561 8-11-12 **90** MarkGrant 89
(Geoffrey Deacon) *hld up wl in rr: hdwy 3 out: chal next: drvn and ev ch last: sn hanging rt: nt qckn fnl 100yds* **25/1**

245- 4 *6* **Thomas Bell (IRE)**[27] 1582 9-10-1 **72** CiaranMckee[(7)] 68
(John O'Shea) *plld hrd: set off in rr: wnt prom 3rd: led bef next: 3 l clr but rdn home turn: hrd pressed 2 out: hdd last: sn carried rt and gave up* **7/2**[1]

FP0- 5 *19* **Pennant Dancer**[9] 1708 6-10-0 **64** (tp) DonalDevereux 41
(Debra Hamer) *led tl bef 4th: clr w one rival tl 7th: nt fluent 9th: 2nd and hrd drvn home turn: sn dropped rt out* **33/1**

303- 6 *13* **Paddysparks (IRE)**[30] 1548 9-10-3 **67** (p) PaddyBrennan 32
(Henry Oliver) *chsd ldrs in midfield: brief effrt 7th: rdn and floundering bef 3 out: t.o and racing awkwardly next* **5/1**[3]

005- 7 *3 ¾* **Potters Dream (IRE)**[9] 1716 7-10-3 **67** (t) AlainCawley 28
(Fergal O'Brien) *wl bhd fr 6th: t.o 3 out* **10/1**

6/P- P **No Regrets (FR)**[13] 1673 12-11-4 **82** RobertThornton
(Angela Clarke) *midfield tl p.u sharply after 6th* **33/1**

000- P **Hadron Collider (FR)**[43] 1428 8-10-12 **79** (p) RobertDunne[(3)]
(Chris Nenadich) *a wl bhd: t.o and p.u 8th* **16/1**

03R- P **Magical Treasure**[10] 1701 9-11-9 **87** (t) RyanMahon
(Sarah Kerswell) *dropped bk last and rdn 6th: blnd next: t.o and p.u after 8th* **25/1**

P4P/ P **Presenting Dr T (IRE)**[167] 5542 7-10-11 **82** CharlieDeutsch[(7)]
(Harry Chisman) *chsd ldrs: blnd 5th and rdr lost iron briefly: rdn and fdd 8th: t.o and p.u 3 out* **33/1**

02P/ P **Ledbury Star (IRE)**[174] 5381 7-11-2 **80** CharliePoste
(Matt Sheppard) *2nd or 3rd tl pushed along after 6th: struggling next: t.o 9th: p.u next* **8/1**

5m 33.7s (5.70) **Going Correction** -0.45s/f (Good) 12 Ran SP% **114.0**
Speed ratings (Par 103): **72,71,71,69,62 58,56, , ,**
toteswingers 1&2 £5.00, 2&3 £10.90, 1&3 £9.10 CSF £28.83 CT £605.00 TOTE £3.40: £1.80, £3.00, £5.40; EX 28.20 Trifecta £139.90 Pool: £1875.73 - 10.05 winning units..There was no bid for the winner.
Owner G Ivall & R J Price **Bred** Kingsclere Stud **Trained** Ullingswick, H'fords

FOCUS
A competitive event for the grade, run at a strong gallop. The first three are rated pretty much to their marks.

1838 LADBROKES MAIDEN HURDLE (12 hdls) 2m 7f
4:30 (4:31) (Class 5) 4-Y-0+ **£2,662** (£826; £445)

Form RPR

503- 1 **Bob Tucker (IRE)**[13] 1672 6-10-12 117 APMcCoy 89+
(Brendan Powell) *pressed ldr: blnd 9th and sprawled bdly on landing: ev ch whn lft in ld next: mstke 2 out: drew clr bef last* **11/10**[2]

056- 2 *25* **Mr Bachster (IRE)**[27] 1580 8-10-5 72 MissLBrooke[(7)] 69
(Richard Lee) *chsd clr ldng pair: clsng whn lft 2nd 3 out: 2 l down next: rdn and wkng whn j.rt last: eased* **16/1**[3]

3 *99* **Spike Mac (IRE)**[145] 8-10-12 0 AndrewThornton
(Richard Harper) *sn t.o: hurdle bhd fr 1/2-way: stl persevering although fs adrift whn flag man intervened and stopped horse 3 out: missed out flight but continued to eventually complete* **50/1**

1/ F **Court Appeal (IRE)**[204] 4878 6-10-12 0 NoelFehily
(Charlie Longsdon) *t.k.h and j.rt: narrow ldr tl slipped and fell 3 out: winded but rcvrd* **10/11**[1]

5m 35.3s (7.30) **Going Correction** -0.45s/f (Good) 4 Ran SP% **107.8**
Speed ratings (Par 103): **69,60,25,**
CSF £12.23 TOTE £2.90; EX 8.70 Trifecta £31.70 Pool: £2378.62 - 56.20 winning units..
Owner Nigel M Davies **Bred** Mrs Mary Mangan **Trained** Upper Lambourn, Berks

FOCUS
Not form to dwell on, with the winner rated 20lb+ off his best.

1839 E B F STALLIONS LADBROKES "NATIONAL HUNT" NOVICES' HURDLE (QUALIFIER) (8 hdls) 2m
5:00 (5:00) (Class 4) 4-6-Y-0 **£3,443** (£1,011)

Form RPR

/22- 1 **New Year's Eve**[45] 1404 5-10-12 123 DenisO'Regan 122+
(John Ferguson) *mde all: v stdy pce: in full command 2 out: hrd hld and tk sme pulling up after fin* **1/2**[1]

110/ 2 *3 ¾* **Alphabetical Order**[187] 5179 5-10-12 0 RichardJohnson 111
(Tim Vaughan) *nt often fluent: chsd rival: mstke 3 out: rdn and racd awkwardly fr next: struggling after* **7/4**[2]

3m 54.9s (7.60) **Going Correction** -0.45s/f (Good) 2 Ran SP% **103.0**
Speed ratings: **63,61**
TOTE £1.40; EX 1.30.
Owner Bloomfields **Bred** Newsells Park Stud **Trained** Cowlinge, Suffolk

FOCUS
This developed into a sprint from the third-last and the time was very slow. Difficult form to put a figure on.

1840 LADBROKES H'CAP HURDLE (8 hdls) 2m
5:30 (5:30) (Class 4) (0-120,115) 4-Y-0+ **£3,119** (£915; £457; £228)

Form RPR

P23- 1 **Hi Tide (IRE)**[30] 1551 9-11-2 **105** BrendanPowell 107
(J R Jenkins) *dropped out in last pair: stdy run after 3 out: 4 l 3rd and drvn whn hit last: styd on wl to ld fnl strides* **8/1**

/62- 2 *shd* **Bombadero (IRE)**[9] 1708 6-11-12 **115** (t) SamTwiston-Davies 116
(Dr Richard Newland) *racd keenly in 2nd: drvn and upsides bef 2 out tl tk slt advantage after last: ct cl home* **11/4**[1]

3 *½* **Codoor (GER)**[116] 6-11-4 **107** NoelFehily 109
(Charlie Longsdon) *hld up in rr tl smooth prog on outer after 5th: led after 3 out: sn hrd pressed: drvn and hdd after last: nt qckn fnl 50yds* **5/1**[2]

322- 4 *8* **Qoubilai (FR)**[67] 1200 9-11-8 **111** (t) RichardJohnson 104
(Tim Vaughan) *led: rdn whn hit 3 out: sn hdd: btn 4th bef last* **8/1**

126- 5 *7* **Taroum (IRE)**[35] 1506 6-11-0 **103** LeeEdwards 92
(Tony Carroll) *chsd ldr: rdn bef 3 out: btn next: hanging rt whn mstke last and v unbalanced after* **8/1**

151- 6 *22* **My Lord**[13] 1551 5-11-8 **111** LiamTreadwell 78
(Luke Dace) *off bridle after 3rd: towards rr and nvr really travelling after: rdn and struggling bef 3 out* **7/1**

/20- 7 *1 ¾* **Judiciary (IRE)**[18] 1634 6-11-12 **115** APMcCoy 81
(Rebecca Curtis) *t.k.h: chsd ldrs: nt fluent 3rd: struggling bef 3 out: heavily eased next* **5/1**[2]

5- U **Tangolan (IRE)**[31] 1535 5-11-6 **112** (p) KielanWoods[(3)]
(Phil Middleton) *midfield tl blnd and uns rdr 4th* **6/1**[3]

3m 37.9s (-9.40) **Going Correction** -0.45s/f (Good) 8 Ran SP% **120.1**
Speed ratings (Par 105): **105,104,104,100,97 86,85,**
toteswingers 1&2 £5.80, 2&3 £3.50, 1&3 £9.30 CSF £32.67 CT £125.92 TOTE £11.60: £3.00, £2.00, £2.70; EX 39.90 Trifecta £61.70 Pool: £2033.62 - 24.70 winning units..
Owner Mrs Wendy Jenkins **Bred** D H W Dobson **Trained** Royston, Herts

FOCUS
A modest contest, in which the gallop looked respectable. The first two are rated pretrty much to their marks.

T/Plt: £67.40 to a £1 stake. Pool of £65992.46 - 714.27 winning tickets. T/Qpdt: £11.70 to a £1 stake. Pool of £4515.64 -284.62 winning tickets. IM

The Form Book Jumps, Raceform Ltd, Compton, RG20 6NL.

1841 - 1847a (Foreign Racing) - See Raceform Interactive

CARLISLE (R-H)

Friday, October 11

OFFICIAL GOING: Good (good to firm in places on chase course; chs 7.7, hdl 7.1)

Wind: Breezy, half behind Weather: Overcast

1848 EPDS RACING SUPPORTING RACING WELFARE #BTO2013 CONDITIONAL JOCKEYS' H'CAP HURDLE (9 hdls) 2m 1f

2:10 (2:10) (Class 4) (0-105,107) 4-Y-0+ **£3,249** (£954; £477; £238)

Form RPR

/40- **1** **Tweedo Paradiso (NZ)**[134] 558 6-10-3 **89** ShaunDobbin(8) 91+
(Rose Dobbin) *t.k.h: hld up: hdwy bef 3 out: led last 100yds: styd on wl* **3/1**[1]

133- **2** *nk* **Momkinzain (USA)**[72] 1161 6-11-3 **101** (p) CraigNichol(6) 103
(Lucinda Russell) *in tch: hdwy to ld bef 2 out: sn rdn: hdd last 100yds: rallied: hld nr fin* **5/1**[3]

413- **3** *1* **Deny**[37] 1495 5-10-4 **82** (p) HarryChalloner 82
(Henry Hogarth) *hld up: hdwy and ev ch bef 2 out: kpt on fr last: hld nr fin* **15/2**

000/ **4** *10* **Blue Sea Of Ibrox (IRE)**[191] 5119 5-9-9 **78** oh1 GLavery(5) 69
(Alan Brown) *in tch: rdn and outpcd after 4 out: plugged on fr 2 out: nt pce to chal* **66/1**

3/0- **5** *1 ¼* **Souter Point (USA)**[34] 563 7-11-7 **104** JackSherwood(5) 94
(William Kinsey) *chsd ldrs: rdn bef 3 out: edgd rt and outpcd after next* **20/1**

312/ **6** *20* **Letterpress (IRE)**[492] 618 9-10-11 **95** JohnDawson(6) 67
(John Wade) *mde most to bef 2 out: sn rdn: disputing 4th and outpcd whn blnd bdly last: nt rcvr* **7/2**[2]

603- **7** *3 ¼* **Breeze With Ease (IRE)**[16] 1657 9-10-4 **85** GrahamWatters(3) 54
(Barry Murtagh) *chsd ldr: rdn bef 3 out: wknd fr next* **16/1**

02P/ **8** *13* **Formulation (IRE)**[189] 5166 6-11-9 **104** TonyKelly(3) 61
(Rebecca Menzies) *nt fluent in rr: struggling 4 out: btn next: t.o* **7/2**[2]

50P/ **9** *10* **Bernix**[151] 2861 11-9-9 **78** oh4 CraigGallagher(5) 26
(Julie Camacho) *in tch: reminders bef 5th: struggling fr 4 out: t.o* **33/1**

4m 10.8s (-16.90) **Going Correction** -1.10s/f (Hard) course record **9** Ran SP% **113.0**
Speed ratings (Par 105): **99,98,98,93,93 83,82,76,71**
toteswingers 1&2 £4.10, 1&3 £5.60, 2&3 £7.40 CSF £17.86 CT £100.22 TOTE £5.30: £1.40, £1.90, £2.70; EX 28.50 Trifecta £160.30 Pool: £1323.51 - 6.19 winning units..
Owner J Dickson **Bred** Glazeley Farms Trust **Trained** South Hazelrigg, Northumbria

FOCUS
All hurdles races on Flat course. All bends moved out 4yds and hurdles sited on outside. The first two home were both returning from a break and are rated pretty much to their marks. The pace was steady.

1849 GEN II TRAINING NOVICES' LIMITED H'CAP CHASE (12 fncs) 2m

2:45 (2:45) (Class 3) (0-140,130) 4-Y-0+ **£6,498** (£1,908; £954; £477)

Form RPR

2P1/ **1** **Up To Something (FR)**[183] 5240 5-11-5 **130** (p) NoelFehily 139+
(Charlie Longsdon) *j.w: chsd ldrs: led 6th: clr 8th: rdn and kpt on wl fr 2 out: unchal* **6/4**[1]

/33- **2** *3 ¼* **Swaledale Lad (IRE)**[31] 1550 6-10-4 **120** HarryChalloner(5) 128+
(Richard Ford) *hld up in tch: hdwy to chse (clr) wnr bef 3 out: sn rdn: kpt on fr last: nt gng pce to chal* **6/1**[2]

213- **3** *11* **Twentypoundluck (IRE)**[7] 1750 8-10-12 **123** (v) JamesReveley 120
(Patrick Griffin, Ire) *hld up: outpcd 4th: rallied bef 3 out: sn rdn: no imp fr next* **10/1**

001/ **4** *32* **Star In Flight**[332] 2409 6-11-1 **126** JasonMaguire 93
(Donald McCain) *cl up: chal 5th: chsd wnr fr next to bef 3 out: wknd fr 2 out: t.o* **18/1**

442- **5** *8* **Outrageous Request**[16] 1656 7-10-8 **119** PeterBuchanan 79
(Lucinda Russell) *bhd whn hmpd by faller 1st: sn t.o: nvr on terms* **14/1**

404- **6** *25* **Toledo Gold (IRE)**[16] 1657 7-9-12 **116** oh6 (t) StephenMulqueen(7) 54
(Maurice Barnes) *led: hit and stmbld bdly 4th: hdd 6th: rallied: nt fluent and outpcd 4 out: wkng whn hit next: t.o* **28/1**

113- **R** **Bygones Of Brid (IRE)**[81] 1077 10-11-3 **128** (p) BrianHughes
(Karen McLintock) *nt fluent and mostly j.lft: hld up in tch: struggling 1/2-way: 5th and no ch whn ref 2 out* **8/1**

336/ **U** **Jet Master (IRE)**[169] 5525 7-11-0 **125** (t) LucyAlexander
(N W Alexander) *s.i.s: bhd whn jinked to avoid faller and uns rdr 1st* **12/1**

31P/ **F** **Simply Ned (IRE)**[189] 5162 6-11-5 **130** FearghalDavis
(Nicky Richards) *hld up: fell 1st* **13/2**[3]

3m 54.5s (-21.60) **Going Correction** -1.10s/f (Hard) **9** Ran SP% **110.9**
Speed ratings (Par 107): **110,108,102,86,82 70,,,**
toteswingers 1&2 £2.30, 1&3 £3.20, 2&3 £9.10 CSF £10.71 CT £60.96 TOTE £2.10: £1.20, £2.60, £3.10; EX 9.90 Trifecta £53.20 Pool: £2245.69 - 31.60 winning units..
Owner E M G Roberts **Bred** Marc Trinquet And Olivier Trinquet **Trained** Over Norton, Oxon

FOCUS
There were some handy performers in this novice chase, which was run at a solid pace, with the winner making his first appearance over fences. He looks a good novice and bettered his decent hurdle form.

1850 DERWENT "NATIONAL HUNT" NOVICES' HURDLE (11 hdls) 2m 4f

3:20 (3:20) (Class 4) 4-Y-0+ **£3,249** (£954; £477; £238)

Form RPR

5/1- **1** **Drop Out Joe**[19] 1632 5-11-5 0 NoelFehily 124+
(Charlie Longsdon) *pressed ldr: led 4 out: pushed along whn nt fluent next: styd on strly fnl 2* **11/10**[1]

542/ **2** *6* **Desgrey**[182] 5277 5-10-12 114 DannyCook 111
(Peter Niven) *prom: effrt and chsng wnr whn nt fluent 3 out: kpt on same pce fr next* **9/2**[3]

3 *16* **Lakefield Rebel (IRE)**[523] 7-10-12 0 RichieMcGrath 95
(Henry Hogarth) *t.k.h: hld up in tch: rdn and outpcd bef 3 out: plugged on after next: no imp* **28/1**

03/- **4** *¾* **Swift Arrow (IRE)**[168] 5547 7-10-12 0 JasonMaguire 94
(Donald McCain) *t.k.h: hld up: hdwy and in tch bef 3 out: sn rdn: wknd between last 2* **11/4**[2]

6U1/ **5** *4* **Standintheband (IRE)**[170] 5491 6-11-5 119 LucyAlexander 99
(N W Alexander) *led to 4 out: sn drvn along: outpcd fr next: 4th and hld whn mstke last* **8/1**

/U4- **6** *19* **Cumbrian Farmer**[15] 1662 6-10-5 0 JonathonBewley(7) 73
(George Bewley) *t.k.h: hld up in tch: struggling bef 4 out: sn btn: t.o* **100/1**

7 *28* **Cloudy Deal (IRE)**[160] 6-10-12 0 WilsonRenwick 48
(Martin Todhunter) *hld up: rdn and outpcd after 4 out: wknd fr next: t.o* **66/1**

4m 56.9s (296.90) **Going Correction** -1.10s/f (Hard) **7** Ran SP% **109.5**
Speed ratings (Par 105): **107,104,98,97,96 88,77**
toteswingers 1&2 £1.40, 1&3 £11.80, 2&3 £14.00 CSF £6.00 TOTE £2.40: £1.30, £2.60; EX 6.40 Trifecta £55.70 Pool: £3281.02 - 44.10 winning units..
Owner The Jesters **Bred** Jethro Bloodstock **Trained** Over Norton, Oxon

FOCUS
The pace was modest but there were some fair sorts in the line-up. The winner built on his recent win, with the second to his mark.

1851 PARK GATE "ELECTRIC MOTORS R US" NOVICES' CHASE (16 fncs) 2m 4f

3:55 (3:55) (Class 4) 4-Y-0+ **£4,548** (£1,335; £667; £333)

Form RPR

014/ **1** **Beeves (IRE)**[170] 5493 6-11-4 0 JasonMaguire 131+
(Donald McCain) *mde all: rdn 5 out: styd on gamely fr 2 out* **5/2**[2]

11P/ **2** *3 ¾* **Superior Quality (IRE)**[210] 4769 8-11-4 0 NoelFehily 130+
(Charlie Longsdon) *t.k.h: hld up: stmbld 3rd: hdwy to chse ldrs 9th: wnt 2nd 11th: stl gng wl 2 out: rdn bef last: one pce run-in* **5/6**[1]

/22- **3** *3 ¼* **Hunting Tower**[43] 1268 9-11-4 0 (t) WilsonRenwick 124
(Tim Vaughan) *hld up in tch on outside: stdy hdwy 1/2-way: effrt and rdn 3 out: one pce fr next* **8/1**[3]

341- **4** *29* **Bracken House (IRE)**[48] 1375 6-11-11 0 (tp) PaulMoloney 108+
(Graeme McPherson) *nt fluent: prom: rdn and outpcd 11th: no imp fr 4 out* **14/1**

400/ **5** *8* **Book'Em Danno (IRE)**[601] 4377 7-11-4 0 JamieMoore 87
(Peter Bowen) *t.k.h: chsd wnr to 6 out: rdn and wknd fr 3 out* **11/1**

45- **6** *2 ¼* **Reef Dancer (IRE)**[30] 1563 10-11-4 0 (p) KennyJohnson 85
(Robert Johnson) *t.k.h: cl up: lost pl 1/2-way: struggling fr 5 out* **200/1**

66P- **7** *25* **Have You Had Yours (IRE)**[83] 1038 7-10-11 76 AlistairFindlay(7) 60
(Jane Walton) *hld up in tch: mstke 8th: struggling fr 10th: t.o fr 4 out* **200/1**

5m 7.0s (-20.40) **Going Correction** -1.10s/f (Hard) **7** Ran SP% **110.2**
Speed ratings (Par 105): **96,94,93,81,78 77,67**
toteswingers 1&2 £1.10, 1&3 £2.70, 2&3 £1.70 CSF £4.82 TOTE £3.20: £1.90, £1.10; EX 6.90 Trifecta £16.80 Pool: £3161.50 - 140.77 winning units..
Owner Paul & Clare Rooney **Bred** Donal O'Brien **Trained** Cholmondeley, Cheshire

FOCUS
The first two home were developing into high-class hurdlers last season, so this looks a novice chase to note. The first three should all win races.

1852 EDEN H'CAP CHASE (18 fncs) 3m 110y

4:30 (4:30) (Class 3) (0-135,127) 4-Y-0+ **£6,498** (£1,908; £954; £477)

Form RPR

0PP/ **1** **Harouet (FR)**[251] 3984 8-11-11 **126** (p) JamieMoore 132+
(Peter Bowen) *hld up in tch: nt fluent 10th: rdn and outpcd bef 4 out: rallied after next: styd on wl u.p fr last to ld post* **9/1**

3FP/ **2** *nse* **Lively Baron (IRE)**[168] 5548 8-11-9 **124** (tp) JasonMaguire 128
(Donald McCain) *cl up: led 9th: rdn after 5 out: kpt on wl fr last: hdd post* **9/4**[2]

121- **3** *6* **Sergeant Pink (IRE)**[19] 1636 7-11-12 **127** HenryBrooke 126
(Dianne Sayer) *prom on outside: smooth hdwy to chse ldr 13th: chal gng wl 3 out: rdn after next: wknd run-in* **6/1**[3]

456/ **4** *1 ½* **Time For Spring (IRE)**[166] 18 9-11-8 **123** NoelFehily 122
(Charlie Longsdon) *t.k.h: prom: hdwy and ch 3 out: rdn next: hit last: edgd rt and wknd run-in* **11/8**[1]

225/ **5** *38* **Or De Grugy (FR)**[165] 25 11-10-8 **109** LucyAlexander 72
(N W Alexander) *led: hit 8th: hdd next: rallied: n.m.r and lost pl 13th: lost tch fr 4 out: t.o* **8/1**

6m 15.1s (-27.50) **Going Correction** -1.10s/f (Hard) **5** Ran SP% **108.3**
Speed ratings (Par 107): **100,99,98,97,85**
CSF £28.80 TOTE £9.90: £3.50, £1.70; EX 29.60 Trifecta £136.60 Pool: £2911.92 - 15.98 winning units..
Owner Egan Waste & Karen Bowen **Bred** Jean Pierre Roussel **Trained** Little Newcastle, Pembrokes

FOCUS
The first two both have potential over much further than this, but stamina is always a factor on this course. The winner is rated similar to his previous course win.

1853 DAVID ALLEN ACCOUNTANTS NOVICES' HURDLE (9 hdls) 2m 1f

5:00 (5:01) (Class 4) 4-Y-0+ **£3,249** (£954; £477; £238)

Form RPR

23/ **1** **Sergeant Mattie (IRE)**[199] 4970 5-10-12 0 NoelFehily 117+
(Charlie Longsdon) *mde all: nt fluent 3 out: rdn and styd on strly fr last* **10/11**[1]

F23/ **2** *7* **Blades Lad**[29] 3437 4-10-12 123 DenisO'Regan 112+
(Peter Niven) *trckd ldrs: stdy hdwy and wnt 2nd 3 out: effrt after next: outpcd by wnr fr last* **7/2**[2]

3 *8* **Tourtiere**[21] 5-10-12 0 BarryKeniry 102+
(George Moore) *t.k.h in midfield: hdwy bef 3 out: rdn: edgd rt and one pce fr next* **33/1**

03/ **4** *2 ¼* **Politeness (FR)**[227] 4439 4-10-12 0 WilsonRenwick 98
(Rose Dobbin) *hld up: shkn up and hdwy bef 3 out: pushed along and no imp fr next* **12/1**

0/2- **5** *3* **Biggar (IRE)**[138] 497 5-10-12 0 PeterBuchanan 95
(Lucinda Russell) *in tch: rdn and outpcd 4 out: rallied after next: nvr able to chal* **6/1**[3]

4/0- **6** *5* **Crooked Arrow (IRE)**[141] 449 5-10-9 0 KyleJames(3) 93
(Marjorie Fife) *pressed wnr to 3 out: rdn and outpcd whn mstke next: sn btn* **20/1**

0/5- **7** *15* **Eila Wheeler**[36] 1500 6-9-12 0 (t) StephenMulqueen(7) 68
(Maurice Barnes) *nt fluent in rr: rdn and hdwy bef 3 out: sn no imp* **40/1**

530- **8** *6* **Rev Up Ruby**[15] 1661 5-9-12 0 JonathonBewley(7) 62
(George Bewley) *hld up: outpcd 1/2-way: n.d after* **22/1**

0- **9** *10* **District Attorney (IRE)**[10] 1713 4-10-12 0 BrianHarding 59
(Chris Fairhurst) *in tch: rdn after 4 out: wknd fr next* **33/1**

0/0- **10** *¾* **Just Tyn (IRE)**[7] 1754 6-10-12 0 LucyAlexander 58
(Martin Todhunter) *hld up towards rr: struggling whn nt fluent 5th: sn btn* **100/1**

0- **11** *11* **Run Brave Run (IRE)**[132] 584 5-10-12 0 HenryBrooke 47
(Martin Todhunter) *midfield: rdn and outpcd after 4 out: sn btn* **100/1**

646- **12** *2 ¾* **Bertielicious**[129] 630 5-10-9 64 JohnKington(3) 45
(Jonathan Haynes) *plld hrd: mstkes in rr: struggling fr 1/2-way: nvr on terms* **200/1**

13 *26* **Just Poppy (IRE)**[105] 4-10-5 0 .... AdrianLane 12
(Iain Jardine) *t.k.h: nt fluent in rr: struggling fr 1/2-way: t.o* **33/1**

4m 13.5s (-14.20) **Going Correction** -1.10s/f (Hard)
WFA 4 from 5yo+ 9lb 13 Ran SP% **119.4**
Speed ratings (Par 105): **92,88,84,83,82 80,73,70,65,65 60,58,46**
toteswingers 1&2 £1.80, 1&3 £13.90, 2&3 £25.70 CSF £3.71 TOTE £2.00: £1.40, £1.20, £8.50; EX 7.00 Trifecta £105.20 Pool: £2445.93 - 17.42 winning units..
Owner Swanee River Partnership **Bred** Miss Patricia Kirke **Trained** Over Norton, Oxon

FOCUS
The runner-up sets a decent standard based on his second run over hurdles, which is a compliment to the winner, though there wasn't much previous jumps form among those who finished behind them. The second sets the standard.

1854 WEDDINGS AT CARLISLE RACECOURSE STANDARD OPEN NATIONAL HUNT FLAT RACE 2m 1f
5:30 (5:30) (Class 6) 4-6-Y-O **£1,559** (£457; £228; £114)

Form RPR

1 **Ocean Waves (IRE)** 4-11-0 0 .... JasonMaguire 105+
(Ronald O'Leary, Ire) *in tch: stdy hdwy 1/2-way: drvn and outpcd over 3f out: rallied over 1f out: led last 100yds: kpt on wl* **5/4**[1]

2 *½* **Kilcooley (IRE)**[207] 4-11-0 0 .... NoelFehily 104+
(Charlie Longsdon) *t.k.h: trckd ldrs: led after 6f: rdn and qcknd over 2f out: hdd last 100yds: kpt on* **2/1**[2]

3 *8* **Crown And Glory (IRE)**[158] 6-11-0 0 .... PeterBuchanan 96
(Karen Tutty) *led 6f: chsd ldr: drvn over 2f out: no ex over 1f out* **20/1**

4 *6* **Utopian** 4-11-0 0 .... WilsonRenwick 91
(Rose Dobbin) *t.k.h: in tch: rdn and outpcd over 4f out: rallied over 2f out: sn no imp* **8/1**

5 *10* **Golden Calf (IRE)**[173] 6-11-0 0 .... JamieMoore 82
(Peter Bowen) *hld up: drvn along 1/2-way: no imp fr over 3f out* **7/1**[3]

6 *7* **Cockney Lacey** 4-10-7 0 .... GrantCockburn(7) 76
(Lucinda Russell) *hld up: struggling over 4f out: sn btn* **16/1**

7 *4* **Westend Theatre (IRE)**[166] 4-10-7 0 .... AlistairFindlay(7) 72
(Jane Walton) *hld up: rdn and outpcd over 4f out: nvr on terms* **50/1**

60/ 8 *10* **Vodka Moon**[280] 3497 4-11-0 0 .... BrianHarding 63
(Sharon Watt) *cl up tl lost pl 5f out: sn struggling* **25/1**

4m 12.0s (-12.20) **Going Correction** -1.10s/f (Hard) 8 Ran SP% **117.8**
Speed ratings: **84,83,80,77,72 69,67,62**
toteswingers 1&2 £1.10, 1&3 £6.20, 2&3 £11.00 CSF £3.95 TOTE £2.10: £1.60, £1.40, £3.80; EX 5.00 Trifecta £43.50 Pool: £1720.51 - 29.64 winning units..
Owner Mrs Ronald O'Leary **Bred** David Cox **Trained** Killaloe, Co. Clare

FOCUS
The market vibes were in favour of the winner and against the runner-up. Not much rules form to go on.
T/Plt: £15.90 to a £1 stake. Pool: £54102.92 - 2478.78 winning tickets T/Qpdt: £5.50 to a £1 stake. Pool: £3483.70 - 466.00 winning tickets RY

1695 NEWTON ABBOT (L-H)
Friday, October 11

OFFICIAL GOING: Good (good to soft in places; 6.7)
Wind: fresh behind Weather: sunny with cloudy periods becoming overcast

1855 EMMA BIRTHDAY TURTLE JUVENILE HURDLE (8 hdls) 2m 1f
1:50 (1:51) (Class 4) 3-Y-O **£3,508** (£1,030; £515; £257)

Form RPR

1 **Harristown**[101] 3-10-9 0 .... KielanWoods(3) 116+
(Charlie Longsdon) *trckd ldrs: wnt 2nd after 3 out: qcknd to ld next: r.o strly: readily* **5/1**[3]

2 *9* **Abracadabra Sivola (FR)** 3-10-12 0 .... DarylJacob 106+
(Nick Williams) *racd green and nt a fluent: in rr but in tch: rdn after 5th: chsd ldng pair after 3 out: styd on same pce fr next: wnt 2nd at the last* **9/4**[2]

3 *9* **Keychain (IRE)**[42] 1457 3-10-12 0 .... BrendanPowell 101+
(Brendan Powell) *led tl after 4th: led sn after 3 out: rdn whn outpcd and hdd by wnr 2 out: lost 2nd bef stumbling at the last* **6/5**[1]

325- 4 *23* **Karl Marx (IRE)**[7] 1743 3-10-12 94 .... TommyPhelan 76
(Mark Gillard) *trckd ldrs tl pushed along after 4th: nt danger fr next: wnt modest 4th after 3 out: t.o* **16/1**

5 *1 ½* **Boogie De Bispo**[98] 3-10-5 0 .... TomScudamore 68
(Stuart Kittow) *trckd ldrs: pushed along after 4th: rdn after next: sn btn: t.o* **20/1**

44- 6 *60* **Complexity**[19] 1624 3-10-12 0 .... AndrewThornton 21
(Seamus Mullins) *tk str hold in rr: hdwy after 3rd to ld after next: hdd sn after 3 out: wknd qckly: t.o* **14/1**

P- P **Until Midnight (IRE)**[13] 1624 3-10-12 0 .... (t) NickScholfield
(Alexandra Dunn) *w ldr tl rdn after 4th: wknd next: t.o whn p.u after 3 out* **66/1**

4m 7.3s (1.60) **Going Correction** +0.50s/f (Soft) 7 Ran SP% **111.7**
Speed ratings (Par 103): **116,111,107,96,96 67,**
toteswingers 1&2 £1.80, 1&3 £1.80, 2&3 £1.10 CSF £16.33 TOTE £4.40: £2.00, £2.50; EX 17.90 Trifecta £33.90 Pool: £1882.13 - 41.54 winning units..
Owner Kyuna Memories **Bred** Juddmonte Farms Ltd **Trained** Over Norton, Oxon

FOCUS
All rail moved since last fixture and bottom bend from back straight to home straight split as normal. An informative, if probably only ordinary juvenile hurdle. Harristown looks decent and should win more races.

1856 E B F "NATIONAL HUNT" NOVICES' HURDLE (QUALIFIER) (9 hdls) 2m 3f
2:20 (2:20) (Class 4) 4-6-Y-O **£3,508** (£1,030; £515; £257)

Form RPR

231/ 1 **The Skyfarmer**[173] 5444 5-10-12 0 .... RichardJohnson 113+
(Philip Hobbs) *travelled wl: trckd ldrs: disputing whn nt fluent 6th: led 3 out: (nvr that fluent whn hitting the front): idling between last 2 but a in command: readily* **10/11**[1]

2 *3 ¾* **Back In June**[145] 5-10-12 0 .... TomO'Brien 105
(Paul Henderson) *hld up bhd ldrs: hdwy 3 out: sn rdn: styd on to go 2nd jst bef the last: a being hld by wnr* **50/1**

1- 3 *5* **Beau De Tabel (FR)**[146] 380 5-10-12 0 .... DarylJacob 100+
(Nick Williams) *hld up bhd ldrs: tk clsr after 6th: rdn to chse ldng pair after 3 out: styd on same pce* **6/1**[3]

146/ 4 *¾* **Even If**[218] 4618 5-10-12 0 .... APMcCoy 99
(Jonjo O'Neill) *disp ld untl jst hdd 3 out: rdn to chse wnr bef next: styd on same pce tl no ex fr last* **7/1**

111- 5 *12* **Man Of Steel (IRE)**[86] 1013 4-10-12 0 .... (p) DonalDevereux 89
(Peter Bowen) *trckd ldrs: rdn after 3 out: wknd next* **11/4**[2]

23- 6 *57* **What A Joke (IRE)**[40] 1489 6-10-9 0 .... MarkQuinlan(3) 37
(William Reed) *nvr fluent: disp ld tl after 5th: wknd 3 out: t.o* **50/1**

4m 37.6s (7.60) **Going Correction** +0.50s/f (Soft)
WFA 4 from 5yo+ 9lb 6 Ran SP% **109.8**
Speed ratings: **104,102,100,100,94 70**
toteswingers 1&2 £5.80, 1&3 £1.70, 2&3 £4.00 CSF £31.83 TOTE £2.10: £1.10, £9.00; EX 35.90 Trifecta £120.50 Pool: £1831.01 - 11.38 winning units..
Owner Mrs Joanna Peppiatt **Bred** Barkfold Manor Stud **Trained** Withycombe, Somerset

FOCUS
A fair novice hurdle. The cosy winner should rate higher.

1857 SOUTH WEST RACING CLUB NOVICES' LIMITED H'CAP CHASE (13 fncs) 2m 110y
2:55 (2:55) (Class 3) (0-125,129) 4-Y-**£7,596** (£2,244; £1,122; £561; £280)

Form RPR

233- 1 **Notarfbad (IRE)**[74] 1133 7-11-4 **121** .... RichardJohnson 132+
(Jeremy Scott) *t.k.h: trckd ldr: led 7th: jnd whn hit 2 out: sn pushed clr: r.o wl: pushed out* **9/1**

341- 2 *3 ¼* **Easily Pleased (IRE)**[41] 1478 7-11-2 **119** .... HaddenFrost 125
(Martin Hill) *hld up: smooth hdwy fr 8th: trckd wnr 3 out: chal next: sn rdn: kpt on but nt pce of wnr* **6/1**

2/1- 3 *4 ½* **Suerte Al Salto (IRE)**[135] 539 6-11-5 **122** .... TomCannon 124
(Chris Gordon) *hld up: hdwy after 4 out: wnt cl 3rd after next: effrt 2 out: kpt on same pce* **14/1**

0/1- 4 *6* **Ivor's King (IRE)**[11] 1698 6-11-12 **129** 7ex .... JoeTizzard 128
(Colin Tizzard) *led: rchd for 1st: hdd 7th: chsd ldr tl outpcd after 4 out: styd on again to regained 4th 2 out: wnt rt last* **2/1**[1]

631- 5 *8* **Ulis De Vassy (FR)**[43] 1441 5-11-1 **118** .... NickScholfield 109
(Nick Williams) *in tch: struggling whn awkward 4 out: nvr gng pce to get on terms* **5/1**[3]

6 *14* **Vesperal Dream (FR)**[184] 4-10-12 **125** .... DarylJacob 95
(Paul Nicholls) *trckd ldrs: rdn after 4 out: sn outpcd: jst lost 4th whn hit 2 out: wknd* **5/2**[2]

5/0- 7 *6* **Darkestbeforedawn (IRE)**[149] 304 6-11-0 **117** .... IanPopham 88
(Caroline Keevil) *in tch: rdn after 8th: wknd 4 out* **16/1**

4m 0.7s (-5.80) **Going Correction** -0.15s/f (Good)
WFA 4 from 5yo+ 9lb 7 Ran SP% **115.4**
Speed ratings (Par 107): **107,105,103,100,96 90,87**
toteswingers 1&2 £12.20, 1&3 £19.10, 2&3 £16.40 CSF £60.74 CT £754.79 TOTE £10.30: £3.90, £2.90; EX 68.40 Trifecta £278.00 Pool: £1599.65 - 4.31 winning units..
Owner Govier & Brown **Bred** Brian Groarke **Trained** Brompton Regis, Somerset

FOCUS
A competitive race, despite the relatively small field. A big step up from the easy winner, and the form looks solid.

1858 SOUTH WEST RACING CLUB H'CAP HURDLE (10 hdls) 2m 6f
3:30 (3:30) (Class 2) (0-145,139) 4-Y-**£10,406** (£3,074; £1,537; £769; £384)

Form RPR

3/1- 1 **Kangaroo Court (IRE)**[40] 1485 9-11-9 **139** .... GavinSheehan(3) 143+
(Emma Lavelle) *travelled strly: hld up: tk clsr order on outer after 7th: chal gng best 2 out: shkn up to edge ahd run-in* **11/4**[2]

201/ 2 *nk* **Uncle Jimmy (IRE)**[229] 4406 6-10-11 **124** .... RichardJohnson 128+
(Philip Hobbs) *trckd ldrs: rdn to ld appr 2 out: sn jnd: looked to be fighting losing battle but dug deep: hdd nring fin* **7/2**[3]

1/0- 3 *10* **Dragon's Den (IRE)**[155] 176 6-10-1 **114** .... TomScudamore 110
(Chris Down) *hld up: squeezed way through to chal 3 out: led briefly bef rdn gng to 2 out: kpt on same pce* **11/1**

2/0- 4 *20* **Bravo Bravo**[10] 1707 6-9-11 **115** .... (b) NicodeBoinville(5) 91
(Mark Gillard) *j.lft: led: jinked lft 3rd: hdd after 3 out: sn wknd: lft 4th modest next* **14/1**

P06/ 5 *12* **Wayward Prince**[190] 5136 9-11-12 **139** .... (t) JackDoyle 104
(Hilary Parrott) *trckd ldr tl 5th: cl up: rdn after 3 out: wknd bef next* **10/1**

310/ U **Wilton Milan (IRE)**[190] 5141 5-11-8 **135** .... DarylJacob 126
(Paul Nicholls) *trckd ldrs: sltly hmpd 3rd: jnd ldr 5th: nt fluent next: led after 3 out: sn rdn and hdd: hld in 4th whn blnd and uns rdr 2 out* **13/8**[1]

5m 25.4s (5.20) **Going Correction** +0.50s/f (Soft) 6 Ran SP% **111.1**
Speed ratings (Par 109): **110,109,106,98,94**
toteswingers 1&2 £2.70, 1&3 £9.20, 2&3 £10.00 CSF £12.63 TOTE £4.10: £1.60, £2.20; EX 8.20 Trifecta £51.10 Pool: £1531.50 - 22.46 winning units..
Owner Nicholas Mustoe **Bred** Brian Wilson **Trained** Hatherden, Hants

FOCUS
Not the strongest of races for the grade. A small step up from the winner on his previous C&D win, and the second is probably still on the upgrade.

1859 SOUTH WEST RACING CLUB H'CAP CHASE (20 fncs) 3m 2f 110y
4:05 (4:05) (Class 5) (0-100,100) 4-Y-0+ **£2,729** (£801; £400; £200)

Form RPR

P66/ 1 **Orange Nassau (FR)**[199] 4967 7-11-10 **98** .... AidanColeman 117
(Charlie Longsdon) *mde all: pushed clr after 3 out: styd on wl* **9/4**[1]

/1F- 2 *12* **Jayandbee (IRE)**[19] 1626 6-11-12 **100** .... RichardJohnson 108
(Philip Hobbs) *trckd wnr fr 9th: pushed along after 16th: rdn after 4 out: j. sltly rt: styd on same pce fr next* **3/1**[2]

051- 3 *4* **Kilvergan Boy (IRE)**[16] 1655 9-10-4 **78** .... (p) SamTwiston-Davies 82
(Nigel Twiston-Davies) *trckd wnr: landed steeply 3rd: dropped to 3rd 9th: nt fluent next: rdn 4 out: styd on same pce fr 3 out: hit last 2* **10/3**[3]

513- 4 *13* **Joe The Rogue (IRE)**[24] 1598 6-11-9 **97** .... NickScholfield 90
(Paul Henderson) *j.rt: hld up in last: sme prog into 4th after 15th: sn rdn: disp 3rd after 3 out: wknd bewtween last 2* **6/1**

F4P/ 5 *47* **Ballyegan (IRE)**[201] 4946 8-11-9 **97** .... SamJones 47
(Bob Buckler) *in tch: pushed along fr 11th: wknd after 15th: t.o* **14/1**

4/P- 6 *5* **Joaaci (IRE)**[123] 692 13-10-4 **85** .... (b) MikeyEnnis(7) 31
(Patricia Shaw) *in tch: niggled along fr 13th: grad lost tch fr 15th: t.o* **12/1**

PPP/ P **Tom Bach (IRE)**[137] 9-10-4 **78** .... (b) LiamTreadwell
(Hywel Evans) *nvr travelling: in tch tl 9th: tailing off whn p.u after next* **14/1**

6m 39.4s (-5.20) **Going Correction** -0.15s/f (Good) 7 Ran SP% **114.2**
Speed ratings (Par 103): **101,97,96,92,78 77,**
toteswingers 1&2 £2.60, 1&3 £3.00, 2&3 £1.10 CSF £9.80 TOTE £3.10: £2.00, £1.60; EX 10.30 Trifecta £23.40 Pool: £2040.38 - 65.23 winning units..
Owner The Ferandlin Peaches **Bred** E A R L La Dariole **Trained** Over Norton, Oxon

FOCUS
A moderate contest. The form is rated around the second.

1860 SOUTH WEST RACING CLUB (S) HURDLE (9 hdls) 2m 3f
4:40 (4:40) (Class 5) 4-Y-0+ **£2,463** (£718; £359)

Form RPR
P33- **1** **Run Along Boy**[54] 1306 8-10-11 101..........................(tp) MichaelByrne(3) 113+
(Neil Mulholland) *travelled wl: midfield: smooth hdwy after 6th: trckd ldrs gng to 2 out: swtchd lft and qcknd up wl between last 2: chalng whn lft clr last* **9/2**
134- **2** *12* **Vimiero (USA)**[10] 1708 6-11-6 115.................................. RichieMcLernon 108
(Jonjo O'Neill) *travelled wl most of way: trckd ldr: chal after 3 out: rdn gng to 2 out: fnd little and sn btn: lft 2nd at the last* **4/1**[3]
/00- **3** *20* **Ruby Valentine (FR)**[95] 925 10-10-7 70........................ NickScholfield 74
(Jim Wilson) *hld up: pushed along after 5th: rdn and hdwy after 3 out: wnt 4th bef next: wknd between last 2: lft 3rd at the last* **50/1**
135- **4** *15* **Anger Management (IRE)**[19] 1632 5-11-0 0.......................... APMcCoy 69
(Rebecca Curtis) *wnt rt s: led: rdn and hdd wl after 3 out: wknd qckly: t.o* **3/1**[2]
P/0- **5** *23* **Peter Muck**[10] 1706 10-11-0 0.................................. SamTwiston-Davies 43
(Nigel Twiston-Davies) *mid-div: rdn after 5th: wknd bef 3 out: t.o* **14/1**
P/P- **P** **Jazz City**[11] 1700 13-11-0 86.. MarkGrant
(Michael Blanshard) *nt a fluent: trckd ldrs: mstke 5th: sn rdn: wknd after next: t.o whn p.u bef 2 out* **100/1**
666- **P** **Si Bien (FR)**[88] 1000 8-10-9 80.. CharlieWallis(5)
(Nick Ayliffe) *hld up: rdn after 5th: wknd after next: t.o whn p.u after 3 out* **50/1**
311/ **F** **Hes Our Lad (IRE)**[417] 1291 7-11-6 130.........................(t) AidanColeman 119
(Anthony Honeyball) *travelled wl in midfield: trckd ldrs 5th: led wl after 3 out: nt fluent next: shkn up and jnd whn fell last: fin lame* **5/4**[1]

4m 35.7s (5.70) **Going Correction** +0.50s/f (Soft)
WFA 4 from 5yo+ 9lb **8** Ran SP% **119.2**
Speed ratings (Par 103): **108,102,94,88,78 , ,**
toteswingers 1&2 £3.30, 1&3 £16.40, 2&3 £11.00 CSF £24.03 TOTE £5.50: £1.60, £1.30, £5.70; EX 20.30 Trifecta £455.80 Pool: £2421.44 - 3.98 winning units..There was no bid for the winner.
Owner John Hobbs **Bred** Helshaw Grange Stud Ltd **Trained** Limpley Stoke, Wilts

FOCUS
A decent race for the grade. The winner is rated back to something like his best, with the faller heading for a mark a stone off his best.

1861 SOUTH WEST RACING CLUB STANDARD OPEN NATIONAL HUNT FLAT RACE 2m 1f
5:10 (5:11) (Class 6) 4-6-Y-0 **£2,094** (£610; £305)

Form RPR
1 **Champagne At Tara**[209] 4-11-3 0... APMcCoy 117+
(Jonjo O'Neill) *racd keenly: a.p: led 5f out: qcknd up wl over 2f out: shkn up and r.o strly fnl f: nice prospect* **11/4**[1]
3/ **2** *1 ¾* **Assam Black (IRE)**[183] 5262 5-11-3 0................................ RyanMahon 114
(Harry Fry) *mid-div: smooth hdwy fr 4f out to trck ldrs 3f out: trckd wnr over 2f out: sn rdn and hung lft: drifted rt fnl f: kpt on wl but nt pce to chal: nice prospect* **3/1**[2]
4- **3** *9* **Another Brandy (IRE)**[135] 544 5-11-0 0.......................... MichaelByrne(3) 106
(Neil Mulholland) *mid-div: pushed along and hdwy 4f out: rdn to chse ldng pair 2f out: kpt on but nt pce of ldrs* **12/1**
4 *2 ½* **Glowinginthedark (IRE)**[347] 5-11-0 0............................ KielanWoods(3) 104
(Charlie Longsdon) *trckd ldrs tl dropped to midfield over 6f out: hdwy to chse ldrs but nt clr run on inner fr over 3f out: nvr gng pce to get on terms* **11/2**
252/ **5** *1 ¼* **August Hill (IRE)**[214] 4718 5-10-10 0...........................(t) RichardJohnson 96
(Philip Hobbs) *plld hrd: towards rr: swtchd out and hdwy to ld over 8f out: hdd 5f out: rdn over 3f out: styd on same pce fnl 2f* **5/1**[3]
232- **6** *7* **Hazel Brook**[33] 1531 4-11-3 0.................................... SamTwiston-Davies 96
(Mary Hambro) *trckd ldrs: outpcd whn rdn over 4f out: styd on again over 2f out but no threat* **16/1**
5/ **7** *17* **Fourth Act (IRE)**[218] 4621 4-11-3 0... JoeTizzard 81
(Colin Tizzard) *chsd ldrs tl rdn 4f out: wknd 3f out: t.o* **6/1**
8 *¾* **Sutes** 5-11-3 0.. DarylJacob 80
(Alan Jones) *towards rr of mid-div: pushed along 1/2-way: nvr a factor: t.o* **33/1**
9 *3 ¼* **Businessmoney Jive** 6-10-10 0.. NickScholfield 70
(Keiran Burke) *mid-div: hdwy 4f out: sn rdn: wknd 3f out: t.o* **20/1**
10 *14* **J R Hawk (IRE)** 5-10-12 0... PatrickCorbett(5) 65
(William Reed) *mid-div tl 7f out: sn bhd: t.o* **66/1**
11 *nk* **Dbobe**[174] 4-11-3 0.. DonalDevereux 65
(David Brace) *a towards rr: wknd 3f out: t.o* **33/1**
/44- **12** *19* **Fireweld**[43] 1445 6-10-3 0..(p) MikeyEnnis(7) 40
(Patricia Shaw) *led tl over 8f out: prom tl rdn and wknd over 5f out: t.o* **100/1**

4m 6.4s (6.30) **Going Correction** +0.50s/f (Soft)
WFA 4 from 5yo+ 9lb **12** Ran SP% **124.7**
Speed ratings: **105,104,99,98,98 94,86,86,85,78 78,69**
toteswingers 1&2 £4.40, 1&3 £5.10, 2&3 £6.10 CSF £11.33 TOTE £3.20: £3.20, £1.50, £4.30; EX 18.70 Trifecta £117.80 Pool: £2000.91 - 12.73 winning units..
Owner John P McManus **Bred** A M Armitage **Trained** Cheltenham, Gloucs

FOCUS
A decent-looking bumper for the track. The first two look above average.
T/Plt: £253.90 to a £1 stake. Pool: £63041.68 - 181.25 winning tickets T/Qpdt: £32.30 to a £1 stake. Pool: £5477.75 - 125.45 winning tickets TM

1706 CHEPSTOW (L-H)
Saturday, October 12

OFFICIAL GOING: Good (chs 7.1, hdl 7.4)
Race 1: Charity Flat race over 1m7f, not under rules, won by Jimmy Frost on Court In Session.
Wind: fresh, half behind Weather: dry and breezy

1862 HICKS LOGISTICS JUVENILE HURDLE (8 hdls) 2m 110y
2:25 (2:29) (Class 4) 3-Y-0 **£3,898** (£1,144; £572; £286)

Form RPR
1 **Keltus (FR)**[171] 3-10-12 0.. DarylJacob 106+
(Paul Nicholls) *mde all: travelling best bef 2 out: rdn and readily drew clr between last 2: comf* **10/11**[1]
41- **2** *5* **Wooly Bully**[34] 1524 3-11-5 0...................................... WayneHutchinson 105
(Alan King) *chsd ldng pair: pressed wnr 5th: rdn and unable qck 2 out: styd on same pce after* **9/2**[2]
232- **3** *2 ¼* **Akdam (IRE)**[17] 1658 3-11-0 119.....................................(p) JoshHamer(5) 104
(Tony Carroll) *w wnr tl mstke 5th: 3rd and outpcd hit 2 out: kpt on same pce after* **7/1**
12- **4** *3 ¾* **Refer**[6] 1781 3-11-2 0.. KielanWoods(3) 100
(Phil Middleton) *in tch in 4th: rdn and effrt 3 out: no imp whn mstke 2 out: wknd bef last* **10/1**
5 *45* **After Eight Sivola (FR)** 3-10-12 0................................... NickScholfield 51
(Nick Williams) *t.k.h: nt jump wl: hld up in tch in rr: lost tch 3 out: t.o next* **5/1**[3]

3m 58.4s (-12.20) **Going Correction** -0.925s/f (Hard) **5** Ran SP% **108.8**
Speed ratings (Par 103): **91,88,87,85,64**
CSF £5.26 TOTE £1.60: £1.10, £2.10; EX 5.40 Trifecta £19.60 Pool: £602.25 - 22.96 winning units..
Owner Donlon & MacDonald **Bred** Roland Peyres & Madame Regine Peyres **Trained** Ditcheat, Somerset
■ Daryl Jacob's first winner since shoulder surgery, and his first as stable jockey to Paul Nicholls.

FOCUS
A race that has produced plenty of decent hurdlers in the past, including last year's Triumph Hurdle runner-up Far West. However, there wasn't much early pace, which casts a slight doubt about the reliability of the form. The third, fourth and the time limit enthusiasm.

1863 HICKS LOGISTICS 35TH ANNIVERSARY NOVICES' HURDLE (DIV I) (10 hdls 1 omitted) 2m 4f
3:00 (3:00) (Class 4) 4-Y-0+ **£3,898** (£1,144; £572; £286)

Form RPR
5/1- **1** **Killala Quay**[120] 737 6-11-5 0.. NoelFehily 127+
(Charlie Longsdon) *t.k.h: in tch in midfield: clsd and pressed ldr after 3 out: led jst after bypassing 2 out: asserting and gd jump last: r.o strly: readily* **8/11**[1]
304/ **2** *6* **Perfect Candidate (IRE)**[182] 5289 6-10-12 119............. PaddyBrennan 113
(Fergal O'Brien) *led: jnd and rdn after 3 out: hdd sn after bypassing 2 out: no ex and styd on same pce fr last* **16/1**
3 *2* **Twice Returned (IRE)**[235] 4307 7-10-12 0......................... HarrySkelton 110
(Dan Skelton) *chsd ldrs: 3rd and rdn whn outpcd bypassing 2 out: styd on same pce after* **8/1**[3]
225/ **4** *6* **I Am Colin**[172] 5483 4-10-12 0.................................. SamTwiston-Davies 107+
(Nigel Twiston-Davies) *nt a fluent: in tch in midfield: mstke 5th: clr in ldng quartet after 8th: rdn and outpcd bypassing 2 out: wknd flat* **12/1**
/11- **5** *8* **Rolling Maul (IRE)**[128] 644 5-10-12 0.............................. JamieMoore 101+
(Peter Bowen) *nt fluent: chsd ldrs: mstke 7th: 5th and outpcd sn after next: wl hld bypassing 2 out* **2/1**[2]
/40- **6** *14* **Be Marvellous (IRE)**[7] 1764 5-10-12 0..............................(t) JoeTizzard 87
(Colin Tizzard) *hld up in last trio: nt fluent 1st: outpcd after 7th: wknd and no ch fr next: t.o* **40/1**
7 *hd* **Flemengo (IRE)** 4-10-5 0... RichieMcLernon 78
(Jonjo O'Neill) *mstkes: hld up in last trio: short-lived effrt after 7th: wknd next: t.o* **28/1**
006- **8** *½* **Dont Call Me Oscar (IRE)**[11] 1706 6-10-7 83...........(t) PatrickCorbett(5) 84
(Mark Gillard) *chsd ldrs tl after 7th: lost pl and wknd next: t.o* **66/1**
5- **9** *1 ¼* **Wynn Darwi (IRE)**[114] 777 8-10-7 0........................ AodhaganConlon(5) 83
(Debra Hamer) *a in rr: lost tch bef 8th: t.o* **66/1**

4m 53.9s (-7.90) **Going Correction** -0.925s/f (Hard)
WFA 4 from 5yo+ 10lb **9** Ran SP% **124.8**
Speed ratings (Par 105): **78,75,74,72,69 63,63,63,62**
toteswingers 1&2 £3.30, 1&3 £2.60, 2&3 £13.70 CSF £16.56 TOTE £1.70: £1.10, £2.40, £2.30; EX 11.10 Trifecta £41.80 Pool: £1318.42 - 23.60 winning units..
Owner Richard & Mrs Susan Perkins **Bred** N Franklin **Trained** Over Norton, Oxon

FOCUS
What should have been the second-last was omitted due to damage for the remainder of the meeting. An interesting contest, but it was won in some style by the penalised winner. The first two are rated pretty much to their marks.

1864 HICKS LOGISTICS 35TH ANNIVERSARY NOVICES' HURDLE (DIV II) (11 hdls) 2m 4f
3:35 (3:35) (Class 4) 4-Y-0+ **£3,898** (£1,144; £572; £286)

Form RPR
3/4- **1** **Tijori (IRE)**[11] 1706 5-10-7 110.......................... RobertWilliams(5) 119+
(Bernard Llewellyn) *in tch in midfield: rdn and effrt 3 out: chsd ldr bef next: led bef last: r.o gamely u.p flat* **20/1**
001/ **2** *nk* **Berkeley Barron (IRE)**[225] 4502 5-11-5 0.................... RichardJohnson 129+
(Philip Hobbs) *t.k.h: hld up towards rr: hdwy 8th: chalng whn outj. last: rallied wl fnl 75yds and wnt 2nd last strides* **1/1**[1]
3 *hd* **Potters Cross**[161] 129 6-10-12 0... APMcCoy 122
(Rebecca Curtis) *j.big at times: led: rdn and wnt 6 l clr whn mstke 3 out: blnd next: hdd bef last: kpt on but unable qck flat: lost 2nd last strides* **11/4**[2]
01/ **4** *6* **Amore Alato**[189] 5187 4-10-12 0.. NickScholfield 114
(Nick Williams) *t.k.h: hld up in midfield: hdwy to chse ldrs after 7th: rdn and cl 3rd whn blnd 2 out: wknd last* **6/1**[3]
5 *3 ¾* **Spookydooky (IRE)**[216] 5-10-12 0.................................. RichieMcLernon 110
(Jonjo O'Neill) *nt a fluent: chsd ldrs: wnt 2nd after 4th: mstke 7th: lost 2nd after 3 out: 5th and unable qck whn hit next: wknd bef last* **16/1**
0/3- **6** *12* **Exemplary**[20] 1632 6-10-12 0... AidanColeman 99
(Marc Barber) *t.k.h: hld up in tch in midfield: hdwy to chse ldrs 5th: rdn and struggling after 8th: wknd after next* **14/1**
5/ **7** *6* **Lightentertainment (IRE)**[247] 4092 5-10-12 0..................... RyanMahon 94
(Paul Nicholls) *t.k.h: hld up in rr: hdwy after 7th: rdn and blnd 8th: wknd bef next* **14/1**
0/0- **8** *19* **Native Brian (IRE)**[15] 1672 7-10-9 0............................ MattGriffiths(3) 77
(Jeremy Scott) *t.k.h: hld up in last trio: mstke 3rd: lost tch bef 8th: t.o 3 out* **50/1**
P60/ **9** *20* **Puerto Azul (IRE)**[916] 5234 9-10-9 100.......................... MichealNolan(3) 59
(Bernard Scriven) *taken down early: t.k.h: hld up in rr: hdwy into midfield after 4th: wknd rapidly bef 8th: t.o 3 out* **80/1**
P/0- **10** *17* **Celtic Fella (IRE)**[114] 777 6-10-7 0.................................. CharlieWallis(5) 43
(Debra Hamer) *chsd ldr tl after 4th: steadily lost pl: last and lost tch after 7th: t.o next* **100/1**

0/ **U** **Echoes Of Joy**[252] 4-10-5 0 .... JoshWall(7)
(David Evans) *t.k.h: hld up in midfield: stmbld and uns rdr bnd after 4th* **66/1**

4m 45.3s (-16.50) **Going Correction** -0.925s/f (Hard)
WFA 4 from 5yo+ 10lb **11** Ran SP% **120.6**
Speed ratings (Par 105): **96,95,95,93,91 87,84,77,69,62**
toteswingers 1&2 £8.40, 1&3 £9.50, 2&3 £1.30 CSF £42.65 TOTE £18.30: £3.30, £1.10, £1.70; EX 67.20 Trifecta £669.60 Part won. Pool: £1021.52 - 1.14 winning units..
Owner B J Llewellyn **Bred** Polish Belle Partnership **Trained** Fochriw, Caerphilly

FOCUS

An unsatisfactory result due to the jumping of the market leaders. The winner improved towards the level of his bumper form.

1865 BETVICTOR ROBERT MOTTRAM MEMORIAL TROPHY NOVICES' CHASE (16 fncs) 2m 3f 110y

4:15 (4:15) (Class 2) 4-Y-0+ **£12,996** (£3,816; £1,908; £954)

Form RPR

3U5/ **1** **Balder Succes (FR)**[19] 5031 5-11-4 0 .... RobertThornton 145+
(Alan King) *chsd ldr: jnd ldr 5th: qcknd clr w ldr and led bef 3 out: clr and in command between last: kpt up to work flat: a doing enough* **5/2**[2]

400/ **2** ¾ **The Romford Pele (IRE)**[178] 5352 6-11-4 0 .... APMcCoy 144
(Rebecca Curtis) *hld up in last pair: wnt 4th 9th: 4 l down and rdn 3 out: low but fast jump to go 2nd last: styd on wl fnl 100yds* **7/1**[3]

/61- **3** 9 **Double Ross (IRE)**[16] 1663 7-11-9 137 .... SamTwiston-Davies 142
(Nigel Twiston-Davies) *led: jnd 5th: qcknd clr w wnr but hdd bef 3 out: lost 2nd and btn last: wknd flat* **5/2**[2]

210/ **4** 13 **Easter Day (FR)**[191] 5141 5-11-4 0 .... DarylJacob 127+
(Paul Nicholls) *chsd ldng pair: 3rd and outpcd whn dived and mstke 3 out: 4th and btn next: wknd* **7/4**[1]

/22- **5** 31 **Another Kate (IRE)**[25] 1594 9-10-11 107 .... AidanColeman 89
(David Richards) *hld up in last pair: dropped to last 9th: rdn and lost tch bef 12th: t.o whn hit 2 out* **33/1**

4m 42.5s (-28.80) **Going Correction** -0.925s/f (Hard) course record **5** Ran SP% **108.9**
Speed ratings (Par 109): **120,119,116,110,98**
CSF £17.47 TOTE £4.30: £1.60, £2.40; EX 19.80 Trifecta £63.90 Pool: £845.91 - 9.91 winning units..
Owner Masterson Holdings Limited **Bred** Damien Bellanger Et Al **Trained** Barbury Castle, Wilts

FOCUS

Smart novice form. The previous two winners of this were Fingal Bay and Cue Card, so there is every chance that this winner is going to develop into an above-average sort as a chaser. He's rated 5lb off his hurdles best.

1866 DOWNLOAD THE BETVICTOR APP HURDLE (A LIMITED H'CAP) (6 hdls 2 omitted) 2m 110y

4:45 (4:47) (Class 2) 4-Y-0 **£16,245** (£4,770; £2,385; £1,192)

Form RPR

253/ **1** **Handazan (IRE)**[164] 4501 4-10-10 126 ....(p) RobertThornton 135+
(Alan King) *mde all: rdn and 2 l clr bypassing 2 out: in command last: styd onn strly: readily* **5/1**[3]

112- **2** 11 **Another Hero (IRE)**[29] 1576 4-10-11 127 .... APMcCoy 128
(Jonjo O'Neill) *hld up in tch in last pair: hdwy and clr in ldng quartet after 4th: rdn bef next: lft chsng wnr 2 out: no ex bef last: wknd flat* **6/4**[1]

22/ **3** 6 **For Two (FR)**[280] 3513 4-10-13 129 .... DarylJacob 124
(Paul Nicholls) *chsd ldrs: wnt 2nd but hanging lft 3 out: hit next and lost 2nd: wknd bypassing 2 out* **11/4**[2]

11P/ **4** 2½ **Pistol (IRE)**[213] 4737 4-11-2 132 .... RichardJohnson 123
(Philip Hobbs) *chsd ldr tl 3rd: dropped bit and lost pl after 4th: 5th and wl btn next: no ch but styd on again bef last* **10/1**

105/ **5** 53 **In The Crowd (IRE)**[27] 5435 4-10-4 120 oh6 .... DavidBass 63
(Richard Price) *in tch in last pair: dropped to last 3rd: lost tch next: t.o bef 5th (actual 3 out)* **40/1**

F30/ **F** **Swnymor (IRE)**[211] 4767 4-11-5 140 .... PatrickCorbett(5)
(Rebecca Curtis) *t.k.h: chsd ldng pair tl wnt 2nd 3rd tl 5th (actual 3 out): wknd after next: bhd whn fell last* **11/2**

3m 50.3s (-20.30) **Going Correction** -0.925s/f (Hard) **6** Ran SP% **110.2**
Speed ratings: **110,104,102,100,75**
toteswingers 1&2 £2.00, 1&3 £3.40, 2&3 £1.80 CSF £12.93 CT £22.13 TOTE £5.70: £2.40, £1.50; EX 13.10 Trifecta £34.50 Pool: £1285.24 - 27.90 winning units..
Owner McNeill Family **Bred** His Highness The Aga Khan's Studs S C **Trained** Barbury Castle, Wilts

FOCUS

This looked a strong renewal of a long-established event. A big step forward from the winner who's a potential 150+ horse on Flat form. The next three were pretty much to their marks.

1867 BETVICTOR BACK OF THE NET OFFER H'CAP HURDLE (9 hdls 2 omitted) 2m 4f

5:15 (5:17) (Class 3) (0-140,137) 4-Y-0+ **£9,747** (£2,862; £1,431; £715)

Form RPR

210/ **1** **Hidden Identity (IRE)**[177] 5358 7-10-9 120 .... AidanColeman 128+
(Tim Vaughan) *patiently rdn: hld up wl in tch in rr: hdwy and hmpd 3 out (actual 2 out): chsd ldng pair bypassing next: chal and fast jump last: led fnl 100yds: r.o wl* **14/1**

201/ **2** nk **Open Day (IRE)**[222] 4562 7-11-3 128 .... APMcCoy 135
(Jonjo O'Neill) *t.k.h: mostly chsd ldr: rdn and ev ch 3 out (actual 2 out): drvn and forged ahd bef last: hrd pressed last: hdd and unable qck fnl 100yds* **9/2**[2]

/P0- **3** 8 **Cloudy Bob (IRE)**[8] 1745 6-10-9 120 .... ColinBolger 120
(Pat Murphy) *mde most: rdn after 3 out (actual 2 out): hdd and no ex bef last: 3rd and wknd last* **20/1**

U/0- **4** 1 **Gauvain (GER)**[41] 1485 11-11-12 137 ....(t) RichardJohnson 138+
(Philip Hobbs) *hld up wl in tch in midfield: stl wl in tch whn bdly hmpd 3 out (actual 2 out): 9th and looked wl btn bypassing 2 out: rallied bef last: r.o strly flat* **14/1**

011- **5** ¾ **Fighter Jet**[44] 1440 5-11-0 125 ....(v[1]) WayneHutchinson 122
(Alan King) *wl in tch in midfield: rdn and effrt after 3 out (actual 2 out): outpcd bypassing 2 out: plugged on same pce after* **12/1**

32F/ **6** 3½ **Carrigmorna King (IRE)**[169] 5539 7-11-2 127 ....(t) TomO'Brien 121
(Philip Hobbs) *t.k.h: hld up wl in tch towards rr: effrt and hdd 3 out (actual 2 out): outpcd u.p by passing 2 out: wknd bef last* **7/1**

165/ **7** ¾ **Kitegen (IRE)**[273] 3619 7-10-11 122 .... CharliePoste 116
(Robin Dickin) *chsd ldrs: rdn and unable qck after 3 out (actual 2 out): wknd and wl hld whn mstke last* **12/1**

224- **8** ¾ **Descaro (USA)**[25] 1054 7-10-2 120 ....(p) CiaranMckee(7) 114
(John O'Shea) *hld up wl in tch in last trio: sltly hmpd 3 out (actual 2 out): effrt and sn no imp: wknd bef last* **33/1**

0/6- **9** 23 **American Trilogy (IRE)**[41] 1485 9-11-7 132 ....(b) HarrySkelton 114
(Dan Skelton) *chsd ldrs: outpcd after 3 out (actual 2 out): wkng whn short of room and swtchd rt bypassing 2 out: sn wl btn: bhd and eased flat: t.o* **9/1**

P/F- **10** 66 **Train Of Thought (IRE)**[32] 1550 5-11-0 125 .... PaulMoloney 38
(Evan Williams) *hld up wl in tch in last trio: lost tch bef 3 out (actaul 2 out): t.o bypassing 2 out: virtually p.u flat* **25/1**

012/ **F** **Fox Run (IRE)**[191] 5143 5-10-12 128 .... HarryDerham(5)
(Paul Nicholls) *t.k.h: chsd ldrs: cl 3rd and travelling strly whn crashing fall 3 out: fatally injured* **6/1**[3]

313/ **U** **God's Own (IRE)**[210] 4791 5-11-3 128 .... PaddyBrennan
(Tom George) *wl in tch in midfield: cl 4th and stl gng wl whn bdly hmpd and uns rdr 3 out (actual 2 out)* **7/2**[1]

4m 44.7s (-17.10) **Going Correction** -0.925s/f (Hard) **12** Ran SP% **117.5**
Speed ratings (Par 107): **97,96,93,93,92 91,91,90,81,55 ,**
toteswingers 1&2 £12.50, 1&3 £44.00, 2&3 £40.70 CSF £74.82 CT £1281.20 TOTE £18.30: £4.70, £1.80, £5.70; EX 167.30 Trifecta £426.00 Part won. Pool: £568.10 - 0.13 winning units..
Owner Paul Bowtell **Bred** J P Kiely **Trained** Aberthin, Vale of Glamorgan

FOCUS

A competitive handicap which saw a nasty incident at what was the second-last, as Fox Run over-jumped the hurdle, sadly suffering a fatal injury, and came down, giving God's Own nowhere to go.

1868 FOLLOW US ON TWITTER @BETVICTORRACING H'CAP CHASE (18 fncs) 3m

5:45 (5:47) (Class 2) (0-150,148) 4-Y-0+**£16,245** (£4,770; £1,788; £1,788)

Form RPR

/35- **1** **Al Co (FR)**[14] 1686 8-11-0 136 .... TomO'Brien 139
(Peter Bowen) *in tch in midfield: rdn and effrt bef 3 out: styng on whn lft jst over 3 l 4th last: r.o u.p flat to ld towards fin* **12/1**[3]

216/ **2** ½ **What A Warrior (IRE)**[177] 5361 6-10-12 134 .... SamTwiston-Davies 136
(Nigel Twiston-Davies) *in tch in midfield: rdn and effrt after 14th: edging lft u.p but hdwy 3 out: styng on whn lft 3 l 2nd last: r.o u.p: ev ch towards fin: snatched 2nd last strides* **20/1**

1P0/ **3** nk **Court By Surprise (IRE)**[212] 4751 8-10-8 130 .... AidanColeman 132
(Emma Lavelle) *chsd ldrs tl led bef 14th: rdn bef 2 out: lft 3 l clr last: drvn and worn down flat: hdd and lost 2 pl towards fin* **11/4**[1]

331- **3** dht **Storm Survivor (IRE)**[104] 851 7-10-12 134 ....(v) APMcCoy 136
(Jonjo O'Neill) *in tch in midfield: rdn to chse ldrs bef 14th: drvn 15th: keeping on whn lft 3rd last: styd on u.p flat* **14/1**

6R3/ **5** 2¼ **Alvarado (IRE)**[177] 5361 8-10-8 130 .... PaulMoloney 130
(Fergal O'Brien) *t.k.h: hld up in tch towards rr: hdwy bef 14th: no imp whn lft 5th last: kpt on flat* **16/1**

360/ **6** 10 **Duke Of Lucca (IRE)**[168] 5576 8-11-2 138 ....(t) RichardJohnson 129
(Philip Hobbs) *chsd ldr tl led 6th: hdd bef 14th: 4th and btn 3 out: wknd next* **6/1**[2]

120/ **7** 2¼ **Rebeccas Choice (IRE)**[175] 5404 10-10-1 126 ....(p) RobertDunne(3) 115
(Dai Burchell) *hld up in tch in rr: rdn and hdwy bef 13th: no imp and btn 15th: plugged on same pce after* **33/1**

/03- **8** 12 **Nataani (IRE)**[29] 1579 10-10-10 132 ....(bt) DominicElsworth 110
(Jo Davis) *hld up in rr: hdwy into midfield 7th: rdn and struggling 11th: wknd 14th* **50/1**

2P0/ **9** ½ **Join Together (IRE)**[189] 5177 8-11-7 148 ....(p) HarryDerham(5) 125
(Paul Nicholls) *a in rr: in tch: struggling after 13th: wl btn nextn.d* **33/1**

3/6- **10** 4½ **Alfie Spinner (IRE)**[142] 448 8-10-8 130 .... TomScudamore 103
(Nick Williams) *hld up towards rr: rdn and struggling after 13th: wknd next* **14/1**

/13- **11** 6 **Merrion Square (IRE)**[125] 680 7-10-11 133 ....(t) DarylJacob 103
(Paul Nicholls) *in tch in midfield: effrt whn blnd 14th: wl btn after: wknd 3 out* **14/1**

P11/ **12** 20 **Theatrical Star**[176] 5375 7-11-4 140 .... JoeTizzard 92
(Colin Tizzard) *t.k.h: led tl 6th: chsd ldr: mstke 12th: lost 2nd after next: lost pl qckly 14th: t.o 2 out* **12/1**[3]

3P0/ **F** **Pete The Feat (IRE)**[214] 4721 9-10-13 135 .... NoelFehily 135
(Charlie Longsdon) *j.rt: t.k.h: chsd ldrs: wnt 2nd bef 15th: 1 l down and hit 2 out: keeping on and stl 1 l down whn fell last* **11/4**[1]

014- **P** **Mostly Bob (IRE)**[29] 1579 10-10-3 128 ....(t) JamesBest(3)
(Sophie Leech) *chsd ldrs tl stdd bk into midfield after 2nd: lost pl qckly and p.u bef 8th: dismntd* **50/1**

5m 55.5s (-26.50) **Going Correction** -0.925s/f (Hard) **14** Ran SP% **123.5**
Speed ratings (Par 109): **107,106,106,106,105 102,101,97,97,96 94,87, ,**
PLACE: Court By Surprise £0.70, Storm Surviver £1.30. T/C: AC&WAW&CBS £428.79. AC&WAW&SS £1691.45. toteswingers 1&2 £41.40, 1&SS £6.60, 1&CBS £4.20, 2&CBD £9.10, 2&SS £8.80 CSF £226.52 TOTE £14.20: £4.10, £5.80; EX 343.50.
Owner F Lloyd **Bred** Jacky Rauch & Mme Colette Rauch **Trained** Little Newcastle, Pembrokes

FOCUS

The majority of these were returning from a break, and it was all change from the last. A competiitve handicap, and sound form.

1869 £25 FREE BET #BACKOFTHENET STANDARD OPEN NATIONAL HUNT FLAT RACE 2m 110y

6:10 (6:15) (Class 5) 4-6-Y-0 **£1,949** (£572; £286; £143)

Form RPR

2/2- **1** **Oscarteea (IRE)**[148] 359 4-11-0 0 .... AidanColeman 110+
(Anthony Honeyball) *t.k.h: hld up in tch in midfield: hdwy to chse ldrs 5f out: rdn to ld and edgd lft 2f out: r.o wl* **7/2**[1]

/3- **2** 1 **Hello George (IRE)**[148] 359 4-11-0 0 .... RichardJohnson 107
(Philip Hobbs) *t.k.h: hld up in tch towards rr: hdwy to chse ldrs on inner 4f out: chsd wnr u.p 1f out: r.o* **6/1**

24/ **3** 2¼ **Trevaylor Boy (IRE)**[290] 3259 6-11-0 0 .... WillKennedy 105
(Sue Gardner) *chsd ldrs tl led 3f out: rdn and hdd 2f out: 3rd and styd on same pce fnl f* **25/1**

4 5 **Thomas Brown**[196] 4-11-0 0 .... NoelFehily 100
(Harry Fry) *t.k.h: led for 3f: styd chsng ldrs: rdn and outpcd 3f out: no threat to ldrs but kpt on again ins fnl f* **4/1**[2]

5 ¾ **Minella On Line (IRE)**[202] 4-11-0 0 .... JamieMoore 100
(Rebecca Curtis) *chsd ldrs: stl travelling wl 5f out: 4th and outpcd whn rn green and hung lft over 1f out: plugged on but hld after* **12/1**

6 2½ **Minella Scamp (IRE)**[199] 4-11-0 0 .... TomScudamore 98
(David Pipe) *t.k.h: miostly chsd ldr tl led over 5f out: hdd 3f out: rdn and outpcd whn rn green and hung lft over 1f out: wknd fnl f* **9/2**[3]

1/ **7** 8 **Comte D'Anjou**[309] 2898 4-11-7 0 .... NickScholfield 97
(Nick Williams) *hld up in tch in midfield: rdn and outpcd 3f out: no threat to ldrs after* **14/1**

8 3 **Spending Time** 4-11-0 0 JoeTizzard 88
(Colin Tizzard) *hld up in tch towards rr: hdwy 5f out: rdn and outpcd over 3f out: wknd over 2f out* **14/1**

0/3- 9 1 ¼ **Very Noble (FR)**[150] 309 4-11-0 0 DarylJacob 87
(Paul Nicholls) *t.k.h: hld up in tch towards rr: hdwy into midfield 7f out: rdn and btn over 3f out: wknd over 2f out* **16/1**

10 2 ¾ **Back By Midnight** 4-10-9 0 JamesBanks(5) 84
(Emma Baker) *wl in tch in midfield: rdn and outpcd over 3f out: wknd over 2f out* **66/1**

11 ½ **Matripajo (IRE)** 4-11-0 0 APMcCoy 84
(Jonjo O'Neill) *hld up in midfield: rdn and outpcd over 3f out: sn wknd* **14/1**

3/ 12 7 **Trillerin Minella (IRE)**[174] 5444 5-11-0 0 WayneHutchinson 77
(Graeme McPherson) *chsd ldr tl led after 3f: hdd over 5f out: lost pl over 3f out: sn wknd* **25/1**

- 13 3 ½ **You Too Pet (IRE)**[153] 5-11-0 0 PaddyBrennan 74
(Fergal O'Brien) *in tch towards rr: struggling 6f out: bhd fnl 4f: t.o* **50/1**

14 nk **Lymm Grey** 4-10-7 0 DominicElsworth 67
(Jo Davis) *in tch towards rr: struggling 6f out: bhd fnl 4f: t.o* **66/1**

15 4 ½ **Joe Bugg (IRE)**[181] 4-10-9 0 NicodeBoinville(5) 70
(Roy Brotherton) *hld up in rr: rdn and btn 6f out: bhd fnl 4f: t.o* **33/1**

3m 52.5s (-12.50) **Going Correction** -0.925s/f (Hard) **15** Ran SP% **123.8**
Speed ratings: **92,91,90,88,87 86,82,81,80,79 79,76,74,74,72**
toteswingers 1&2 £2.40, 1&3 £53.80, 2&3 £24.90 CSF £23.65 TOTE £4.30: £1.80, £2.60, £5.30; EX 26.60 Trifecta £157.50 Pool: £760.70 - 3.62 winning units..
Owner Steve & Jackie Fleetham **Bred** Cathal Ennis **Trained** Mosterton, Dorset

FOCUS
This is usually won by an above-average performer, as Regal Encore proved last year, but this was perhaps not the strongest renewal. The first three were pretty much in line with their pre-race marks.

T/Plt: £33.20 to a £1 stake. Pool: £85446.42 - 1873.82 winning tickets T/Qpdt: £18.10 to a £1 stake. Pool: £4242.74 - 172.95 winning tickets SP

1750 HEXHAM (L-H)
Saturday, October 12

OFFICIAL GOING: Good (7.6)
Second fence and penultimate fence in back straight omitted; ground under repair.
Wind: Breezy, half behind Weather: Overcast

1870 INTU METROCENTRE ALWAYS A WINNER NOVICES' H'CAP CHASE (11 fncs 4 omitted) 2m 4f 110y
2:15 (2:15) (Class 4) (0-110,110) 4-Y-0+ **£3,768** (£1,106; £553; £276)

Form RPR

0/P- 1 **Streams Of Whiskey (IRE)**[149] 340 6-11-12 **110** BrianHarding 123+
(Nicky Richards) *led to 2nd: cl up: effrt and led bef last: sn rdn: edgd lft run-in: styd on wl* **9/1**

P/5- 2 3 **Highbury High (IRE)**[96] 921 6-10-4 **88** BrianHughes 99+
(Paul Henderson) *hld up: stdy hdwy and in tch 3 out (usual 4 out): stmbld next: sn rcvrd and smooth hdwy to chse wnr last: effrt whn n.m.r and swtchd rt run-in: one pce* **6/1**[3]

522- 3 6 **Agricultural**[17] 1657 7-10-13 **97** DougieCostello 100
(Lucy Normile) *t.k.h: prom: effrt and rdn after 2 out: kpt on fr last: nt pce of first two* **5/1**[2]

/30- 4 1 ½ **Spitfire Ace (IRE)**[31] 1561 5-10-9 **93** JasonMaguire 95
(Donald McCain) *t.k.h: chsd ldrs: drvn after 2 out: kpt on same pce fr last* **6/1**[3]

3/U- 5 7 **Ballycool (IRE)**[20] 1635 6-10-9 **100** (t) MrSFox(7) 97
(Lucinda Russell) *t.k.h: cl up: led 2nd: hit 4th: rdn after 2 out: hdd bef last: wknd run-in* **4/1**[1]

0/4- 6 7 **Newdane Dancer (IRE)**[11] 1716 6-10-0 **84** HenryBrooke 75
(Dianne Sayer) *hld up: outpcd 8th: rallied after 2 out: no imp whn nt fluent last* **16/1**

B15/ 7 14 **Milan Royale**[194] 5077 8-10-9 **93** HarryHaynes 69
(Kevin Hunter) *bhd: struggling fr 1/2-way: nvr on terms* **14/1**

400/ 8 52 **The Shrimp (IRE)**[218] 4630 6-10-0 **84** oh4 PeterBuchanan 14
(Sandy Thomson) *prom: lost pl 5th: lost tch fr 7th: t.o* **14/1**

30P- F **King's Chorister**[100] 884 7-10-2 **91** (t) TonyKelly(5)
(Barry Murtagh) *hld up in tch: nt fluent and outpcd 3 out (usual 4 out): rallied: cl 5th and gng wl whn fell next* **33/1**

054/ F **Acordingtoscript (IRE)**[280] 3509 7-10-8 **92** WilsonRenwick
(Martin Todhunter) *midfield: unsighted and mstke 1st: towards rr whn fell next* **9/1**

00P/ U **Court Red (IRE)**[174] 5422 7-10-0 **91** JohnDawson(7)
(John Wade) *prom: j.lft 1st: mstke and lost pl 3rd: nt fluent and uns rdr next* **14/1**

5m 1.5s (-12.00) **Going Correction** -0.45s/f (Good) **11** Ran SP% **114.1**
Speed ratings (Par 105): **104,102,100,100,97 94,80,60,,,**
toteswingers 1&2 £8.60, 1&3 £11.10, 2&3 £16.30 CSF £61.30 CT £301.26 TOTE £14.70: £3.70, £1.60, £2.00; EX 57.40 Trifecta £492.90 Part won. Pool: £657.28 - 0.48 winning units..
Owner Mr & Mrs R Kelvin Hughes **Bred** Miss Ann Hennessy **Trained** Greystoke, Cumbria
■ Stewards' Enquiry : Brian Harding caution: careless riding.

FOCUS
All bends moved on to fresh ground. Back straight down hill widened to provide fresh ground. The second and second-last fences in the back straight were omitted. A fair novices' handicap chase in which they went a decent gallop on ground officially described as good.

1871 INTU ELDON SQUARE ALIVE AFTER FIVE MARES' NOVICES' HURDLE (8 hdls) 2m 110y
2:45 (2:45) (Class 4) 4-Y-0+ **£3,195** (£992; £534)

Form RPR

233- 1 **Sultana Belle (IRE)**[11] 1718 5-10-10 100 PeterBuchanan 102
(S R B Crawford, Ire) *mde all at modest gallop: rdn clr bef last: styd on wl* **7/4**[2]

0/ 2 10 **Rathvawn Belle (IRE)**[190] 5163 6-10-10 0 WilsonRenwick 95
(Lucinda Russell) *t.k.h: chsd wnr: nt fluent 3rd: hit 5th: effrt and ev ch bef 2 out: outpcd bef last: sn no imp* **8/15**[1]

0/P- 3 77 **Jordans Day**[8] 1751 8-10-10 0 BrianHughes 24
(Susan Corbett) *prom: outpcd whn nt fluent 3 out: sn lost tch: t.o* **100/1**

306/ U **Cinnomhor**[196] 5011 5-10-10 0 DenisO'Regan
(Chris Grant) *t.k.h: hld up in tch: mstke 1st: swvd both ways and uns rdr next* **20/1**[3]

4m 6.2s (-11.20) **Going Correction** -0.80s/f (Firm) **4** Ran SP% **107.3**
Speed ratings (Par 105): **94,89,53,**
CSF £3.15 TOTE £2.40; EX 3.70 Trifecta £9.80 Pool: £1293.53 - 98.48 winning units..
Owner D J McCormack **Bred** Eugene McCormack **Trained** Larne, Co Antrim

FOCUS
A modest mares' novices' hurdle in which they went a steady gallop until halfway down the back straight. The winner is rated to her mark.

1872 INTU METROCENTRE JUST KEEPS GETTING BETTER H'CAP CHASE (11 fncs 4 omitted) 2m 4f 110y
3:20 (3:20) (Class 4) (0-120,118) 4-Y-0+ **£3,768** (£1,106; £553; £276)

Form RPR

P/5- 1 **Rossini's Dancer**[17] 1654 8-11-5 **118** (v) MrKitAlexander(7) 123+
(N W Alexander) *w ldr: led 4th: mde rest: clr bef last: rdn out* **12/1**

34P/ 2 8 **Allanard (IRE)**[192] 5122 9-11-6 **112** (v) LucyAlexander 110
(Martin Todhunter) *nt fluent on occasions: in tch: drvn fr 1/2-way: rallied: chsd (clr) wnr between last 2: no imp run-in* **15/2**

P/5- 3 ¾ **Etxalar (FR)**[16] 1666 10-10-8 **107** (t) MrSFox(7) 104
(Lucinda Russell) *hld up: stdy hdwy bef 2 out: rdn between last 2: kpt on fr last: nt pce to chal* **5/1**[3]

P/3- 4 6 **Ultra Du Chatelet (FR)**[33] 1540 5-11-9 **115** (t) PeterBuchanan 107
(Lucinda Russell) *chsd ldrs: drvn and outpcd after 2 out: no imp fr last* **3/1**[1]

41F- 5 hd **Tregaro (FR)**[20] 1636 7-10-9 **101** (t) DenisO'Regan 93
(Mike Sowersby) *hld up: hit 3 out (usual 4 out): stdy hdwy bef next: rdn and wknd last* **6/1**

1P1- 6 4 ½ **Strobe**[16] 1666 9-11-2 **108** (p) DougieCostello 95
(Lucy Normile) *led to 4th: w ldr to bef 2 out: wknd between last 2* **7/1**

252- 7 ½ **Attycran (IRE)**[11] 1715 8-10-5 **104** (t) StephenMulqueen(7) 90
(Maurice Barnes) *chsd ldrs: drvn along fr 1/2-way: rallied: wknd after 2 out* **7/2**[2]

5m 0.6s (-12.90) **Going Correction** -0.45s/f (Good) **7** Ran SP% **110.1**
Speed ratings (Par 105): **106,102,102,100,100 98,98**
toteswingers 1&2 £22.10, 1&3 £21.40, 2&3 £3.30 CSF £85.83 TOTE £10.60: £5.70, £3.80; EX 84.00 Trifecta £214.70 Pool: £1206.87 - 4.21 winning units..
Owner Turcan Barber Fletcher Dunning **Bred** Heather Raw **Trained** Kinneston, Perth & Kinross

FOCUS
A fair handicap chase in which they went a decent, contested gallop. The winner had slipped to a good mark and is rated back to form.

1873 INTU ELDON SQUARE HEART OF THE COMMUNITY H'CAP HURDLE (DIV I) (12 hdls) 3m
4:00 (4:00) (Class 5) (0-100,100) 4-Y-0+ **£2,053** (£598; £299)

Form RPR

300/ 1 **Hartforth**[81] 4569 5-10-4 **83** CallumWhillans(5) 92+
(Donald Whillans) *plld hrd: hld up: hdwy 4th: rdn to ld bef last: styd on wl run-in* **10/1**

6/4- 2 1 ¾ **Silver Dragon**[42] 1467 5-10-11 **85** DougieCostello 91
(Tony Coyle) *nt fluent: in tch on outside: rdn and effrt between last 2: rallied to chse wnr run-in: kpt on: nt pce to chal* **5/2**[1]

260- 3 1 ¾ **Symphonick (FR)**[15] 1674 7-11-12 **100** BrianHughes 104
(Tim Fitzgerald) *led at modest gallop: rdn after 2 out: hdd whn nt fluent last: kpt on same pce run-in* **14/1**

F53/ 4 ½ **Amore Mio (GER)**[308] 2928 8-11-10 **98** (tp) PeterBuchanan 103
(Lucinda Russell) *chsd ldr: rdn bef 2 out: rallied and ev ch bef last: edgd lft and one pce run-in* **3/1**[2]

5/P- 5 5 **Delightfully (FR)**[119] 751 9-11-1 **96** (p) GrantCockburn(7) 94
(Lucinda Russell) *hld up: stdy hdwy bef 2 out: kpt on fr last: nvr able to chal* **8/1**[3]

/40- 6 2 ¾ **Cilliseal (IRE)**[17] 1655 8-11-0 **93** (t) DerekFox(5) 89
(Noel C Kelly, Ire) *prom: nt fluent and lost grnd 5th: rdn and outpcd after 4 out: styd on fr 2 out: n.d* **8/1**[3]

/36- 7 5 **Monbeg (IRE)**[140] 470 6-11-2 **90** (p) WilsonRenwick 84
(Martin Todhunter) *t.k.h: chsd ldrs tl rdn and wknd after 2 out* **16/1**

FP0- 8 15 **Larkhall**[11] 1718 6-9-10 **77** oh8 ow3 (t) MrRLindsay(7) 55
(Mike Sowersby) *t.k.h: hld up: stdy hdwy and in tch after 3 out: rdn and wknd next* **100/1**

4/5- 9 ¾ **La Bacouetteuse (FR)**[16] 1664 8-11-7 **95** (p) AdrianLane 72
(Iain Jardine) *hld up: rdn and outpcd bef 3 out: n.d after* **12/1**

0/P- 10 3 ½ **St Gregory (IRE)**[149] 340 5-10-2 **76** BrianHarding 50
(Nicky Richards) *in tch: lost pl 1/2-way: struggling fr 4 out* **10/1**

6m 0.9s (-8.10) **Going Correction** -0.80s/f (Firm) **10** Ran SP% **115.2**
Speed ratings (Par 103): **81,80,79,79,78 77,75,70,70,69**
toteswingers 1&2 £3.30, 1&3 Not won, 2&3 £4.40 CSF £35.72 CT £357.58 TOTE £9.50: £3.30, £1.50, £3.10; EX 55.10 Trifecta £430.20 Part won. Pool: £573.69 - 0.41 winning units..
Owner The Brave Lads Partnership **Bred** Bishop Wilton Stud **Trained** Hawick, Borders

FOCUS
The first division of a very modest staying handicap hurdle in which they went an ordinary gallop. The first two are rated to their marks.

1874 INTU ELDON SQUARE HEART OF THE COMMUNITY H'CAP HURDLE (DIV II) (12 hdls) 3m
4:30 (4:31) (Class 5) (0-100,99) 4-Y-0+ **£2,053** (£598; £299)

Form RPR

42P- 1 **I'Ll Be Frank**[100] 884 8-11-1 **95** (t) StephenMulqueen(7) 102+
(Maurice Barnes) *chsd ldrs: hdwy to ld bef last: sn clr: hld on wl towards fin* **9/2**[1]

230- 2 ¾ **Saddlers Mot**[37] 1506 9-11-1 **95** (b) JohnDawson(7) 99
(Karen Tutty) *hld up in tch: stdy hdwy bef 2 out: chsd wnr run-in: kpt on fin* **6/1**[3]

266- 3 4 ½ **Flying Doctor**[8] 1756 10-11-9 **99** EwanWhillans(3) 100
(Alistair Whillans) *chsd ldr: led briefly bef last: outpcd run-in* **5/1**[2]

060- 4 5 **Almutaham (USA)**[49] 1374 6-11-0 **87** (p) DenisO'Regan 83
(Nicky Richards) *led: rdn and hdd bef last: wknd run-in* **5/1**[2]

120- 5 2 ¼ **Moon Melody (GER)**[31] 1565 10-10-2 **80** (tp) EDLinehan(5) 73
(Mike Sowersby) *t.k.h: cl up: hit 8th: rdn and outpcd after 2 out: n.d after* **11/1**

0/P- 6 shd **Vallani (IRE)**[130] 628 8-10-6 **86** GrantCockburn(7) 80
(Lucinda Russell) *hld up: rdn and outpcd 4 out: no imp fr 2 out* **12/1**

040/ 7 99 **Morello Mist**[504] 8-9-9 **73** oh4 SamanthaDrake(5)
(Richard Drake) *hld up: rdn and hdwy after 3 out: wknd fr next: virtually p.u run-in* **5/1**[2]

000/ P **Stormion (IRE)**[171] 5495 8-11-5 **99** (p) CraigNichol(7)
(Lucinda Russell) *in tch: drvn along fr 1/2-way: lost tch and p.u bef 3 out* **6/1**[3]

5m 58.4s (-10.60) **Going Correction** -0.80s/f (Firm) **8** Ran SP% **112.8**
Speed ratings (Par 103): **85,84,83,81,80 80,47,**
toteswingers 1&2 Not won, 1&3 £8.40, 2&3 £11.50 CSF £30.64 CT £137.92 TOTE £3.60: £1.70, £1.90, £1.80; EX 37.10 Trifecta £49.30 Pool: £424.17 - 6.44 winning units..
Owner M D Townson **Bred** Gallant Denco Wallace Whittle **Trained** Farlam, Cumbria

FOCUS
The second division of a modest staying handicap hurdle in which they went an initially decent, but muddling pace. The winner is rated in line with the best of her recent course form over shorter.

1875 INTU METROCENTRE ALWAYS A HOT FAVOURITE MAIDEN HURDLE (10 hdls) 2m 4f 110y
5:00 (5:00) (Class 5) 4-Y-O+ **£1,949** (£572; £286; £143)

Form RPR
/2P- **1** **Ballyben (IRE)**^{17} 1660 5-10-7 113 CraigNichol$^{(7)}$ 113
(Lucinda Russell) *mde all: rdn bef last: styd on wl run-in* **5/2^{1}**
2PP/ **2** 1¾ **Milano Magic (IRE)**^{196} 5009 7-11-0 109 LucyAlexander 111
(N W Alexander) *pressed wnr: effrt and rdn after 2 out: kpt on u.p run-in* **5/1^{3}**
F4/ **3** 1 **Shimla Dawn (IRE)**^{329} 2483 5-11-0 0 PeterBuchanan 111
(Tim Walford) *t.k.h: chsd ldrs: effrt and rdn after 2 out: kpt on run-in* **9/2^{2}**
4 5 **Redpender (IRE)**^{160} 7-11-0 0 BrianHarding 106
(James Moffatt) *hld up: hdwy and in tch bef 2 out: rdn and no imp bef last* **25/1**
23- **5** 39 **Oneofapear (IRE)**^{56} 1281 7-11-0 112 DenisO'Regan 89
(Mike Sowersby) *hld up in midfield: stdy hdwy and in tch 3 out: wknd bef next* **5/1^{3}**
0P/ **6** 2¾ **Danebrook Lad (IRE)**^{174} 7-11-0 0 RyanMania 68
(Sandy Thomson) *bhd: drvn along 1/2-way: nvr on terms* **50/1**
7 6 **Print Shiraz (IRE)**^{140} 5-11-0 0 WilsonRenwick 63
(Rose Dobbin) *hld up: stdy hdwy bef 4 out: rdn and wknd bef 2 out* **11/1**
45/ **8** 34 **Spanish Fleet**^{173} 5454 5-11-0 0 BrianHughes 72
(John Wade) *nt fluent: in tch tl rdn and wknd after 3 out: t.o* **16/1**
0- **9** dist **Amilliontimes (IRE)**^{16} 1667 5-11-0 0 HenryBrooke
(Mrs Jackie Stephen) *t.k.h early: in tch tl rdn and wknd after 3 out: t.o* **66/1**
0- **P** **Dr Paddy (IRE)**^{16} 1667 6-11-0 0 DougieCostello
(Lucy Normile) *a bhd: struggling bef 4 out: t.o whn p.u run-in* **50/1**
146/ **P** **Sankyouplease (IRE)**^{178} 5350 5-11-0 0 AndrewTinkler
(Michael Scudamore) *in tch tl rdn and wknd after 2 out: p.u run-in* **7/1**

4m 58.7s (-13.80) **Going Correction** -0.80s/f (Firm) **11** Ran SP% **116.1**
Speed ratings (Par 103): **94,93,92,91,76 75,72,59, ,**
toteswingers 1&2 £2.10, 1&3 £1.80, 2&3 £3.70 CSF £14.63 TOTE £3.40: £1.70, £1.60, £2.20; EX 16.60 Trifecta £59.40 Pool: £305.01 - 3.84 winning units..
Owner Drew & Ailsa Russell **Bred** G Williams **Trained** Arlary, Perth & Kinross

FOCUS
A fair maiden hurdle in which they went an even gallop. The first three were close to their marks.

1876 INTU ELDON SQUARE WORLD ERVICE H'CAP CHASE (10 fncs 2 omitted) 2m 110y
5:30 (5:30) (Class 5) (0-95,95) 4-Y-O+ **£2,144** (£629; £314; £157)

Form RPR
504/ **1** **Local Present (IRE)**^{176} 5382 10-10-8 77 BarryKeniry 85+
(James Turner) *chsd ldrs: wnt 2nd 7th: led bef last: sn rdn: styd on wl run-in* **10/1**
1/4- **2** 2¼ **Prince Tam**^{8} 1753 9-11-3 91 JonathanEngland$^{(5)}$ 96
(Harriet Graham) *led: rdn and hdd bef last: rallied: kpt on same pce last 100yds* **6/1^{3}**
120- **3** ¾ **Morning Time (IRE)**^{49} 1379 7-11-5 88 (p) PeterBuchanan 92
(Lucinda Russell) *in tch: rdn and hdwy after 2 out: drifted rt u.p run-in: kpt on: no imp* **11/4^{1}**
P/P- **4** 5 **Glen Lord**^{16} 1663 10-10-3 72 (t) LucyAlexander 74
(Sandy Forster) *rn in snatches: hld up: hdwy after 3 out: sltly outpcd next: rallied bef last: kpt on run-in: nt pce to chal* **4/1^{2}**
302- **5** 2¼ **Moonlone Lane (IRE)**^{15} 1679 6-11-7 95 (vt) DerekFox$^{(5)}$ 94
(Paul Stafford, Ire) *in tch: mstke and lost grnd 1st: hit 4th: stdy hdwy bef 7th: outpcd bef 2 out: plugged on fr last: no imp* **8/1**
/05- **6** 1¼ **Jim Tango (FR)**^{82} 1075 9-11-2 85 (p) BrianHughes 82
(Karen McLintock) *chsd ldrs: drvn and outpcd after 2 out: btn run-in* **7/1**
1UP/ **7** 6 **Vardas Supreme (IRE)**^{210} 4798 10-11-3 91 (tp) SamanthaDrake$^{(5)}$ 82
(Richard Drake) *chsd ldr to 7th: cl up tl rdn and wknd after 2 out* **9/1**
56P- **8** ½ **Panthers Run**^{111} 802 13-10-0 69 (t) HenryBrooke 60
(Jonathan Haynes) *bhd: struggling 1/2-way: nvr on terms* **11/1**
440- **9** 15 **Strathaird (IRE)**^{53} 1328 9-9-11 69 oh15 (p) JohnKington$^{(3)}$ 46
(Andrew Crook) *hld up in tch on ins: struggling bef 2 out: sn btn* **40/1**

4m 0.4s (-9.40) **Going Correction** -0.45s/f (Good) **9** Ran SP% **114.4**
Speed ratings (Par 103): **104,102,102,100,99 98,95,95,88**
CSF £68.38 CT £211.36 TOTE £15.00: £2.20, £2.00, £1.70; EX 73.60 Trifecta £176.70 Part won. Pool: £235.69 - 0.11 winning units..
Owner J R Turner **Bred** John Quane **Trained** Norton-le-Clay, N Yorks

FOCUS
A moderate handicap chase in which they went a decent gallop. The form is rated around the second.

1877 INTU METROCENTRE ALWAYS A SAFE BET INTERMEDIATE NATIONAL HUNT FLAT RACE (CONDITIONAL/AMATEUR RIDERS) 2m 110y
6:00 (6:00) (Class 6) 4-6-Y-O **£1,642** (£478; £239)

Form RPR
/2- **1** **Line D'Aois (IRE)**^{154} 225 5-10-11 0 JackSherwood$^{(7)}$ 108+
(Michael Scudamore) *in tch: n.m.r briefly 1/2-way: effrt whn n.m.r over 3f out: hdwy to ld wl over 1f out: pushed out fnl f* **15/8^{1}**
- **2** 3¾ **Royal Ripple (IRE)**^{133} 5-10-11 0 MrGBranton$^{(7)}$ 102
(Paul Henderson) *in tch: hdwy to ld over 3f out: rdn and hdd wl over 1f out: kpt on same pce fnl f* **8/1^{3}**
3 14 **You'resomedreamer (IRE)**^{199} 5-10-11 0 GrantCockburn$^{(7)}$ 89
(Lucinda Russell) *hld up towards rr: rdn over 5f out: styd on fr over 2f out: no ch w first two* **14/1**
0- **4** 1½ **Dunkirk's First (IRE)**^{16} 1667 5-10-8 0 ShaunDobbin$^{(10)}$ 88
(Rose Dobbin) *chsd ldrs: led 1/2-way: rdn and hdd over 3f out: outpcd by ldrs fr 2f out* **25/1**
5 2¼ **Shine A Diamond (IRE)**^{146} 5-10-11 0 GrahamWatters$^{(7)}$ 86
(Lucinda Russell) *hld up in tch: hdwy and cl up over 5f out: effrt 3f out: outpcd fr 2f out* **9/4^{2}**
2- **6** 15 **Abel J Tasman (IRE)**^{46} 1420 5-10-13 0 TonyKelly$^{(5)}$ 72
(James Moffatt) *hld up: rdn over 5f out: sme late hdwy: nvr on terms* **17/2**
7 4 **Thatildee (IRE)** 5-10-8 0 DiarmuidO'Regan$^{(10)}$ 69
(Chris Grant) *in tch: hdwy over 5f out: rdn and wknd over 3f out* **9/1**
0- **8** 1½ **Up To Al (IRE)**^{14} 1690 5-10-11 0 (p) MissETodd$^{(7)}$ 67
(John Wainwright) *hld up towards rr: outpcd over 6f out: n.d after* **100/1**
9 nk **Mr Kealshore** 4-11-1 0 JakeGreenall$^{(3)}$ 67
(George Moore) *bhd: struggling 7f out: nvr on terms* **20/1**
10 16 **Bob Bo Jangles (IRE)**^{15} 1682 5-10-13 0 DerekFox$^{(5)}$ 53
(Paul Stafford, Ire) *led to 1/2-way: cl up tl rdn and wknd fr 4f out: t.o* **25/1**
11 6 **Just A Gin** 5-10-4 0 MissJWalton$^{(7)}$ 40
(Iain Jardine) *a bhd: struggling fr 1/2-way: t.o* **50/1**
12 38 **Wind Echo** 5-10-13 0 JonathanEngland$^{(5)}$ 13
(Rayson Nixon) *chsd ldr: led briefly 1/2-way: rdn and wknd fr over 6f out: t.o* **50/1**

3m 58.6s (-14.10) **Going Correction** -0.80s/f (Firm) **12** Ran SP% **121.2**
Speed ratings: **101,99,92,91,90 83,81,81,81,73 70,52**
CSF £16.98 TOTE £3.40: £1.80, £4.80, £1.50; EX 29.90 Trifecta £225.10 Part won. Pool: £300.21 - 0.13 winning units..
Owner S M Smith **Bred** S O'Keeffe **Trained** Bromsash, H'fords

FOCUS
An ordinary bumper for conditional/amateur riders. The winner was the form pick but this was arguably a step up.
T/Plt: £440.90 to a £1 stake. Pool: £54328.26 - 89.95 winning tickets T/Qpdt: £87.10 to a £1 stake. Pool: £4181.50 - 35.50 winning tickets RY

1878 - 1884a (Foreign Racing) - See Raceform Interactive

1361 FFOS LAS (L-H)
Sunday, October 13

OFFICIAL GOING: Good changing to good to soft after race 2 (2.45)
Wind: virtually nil Weather: rain

1885 IWEC ELECTRICAL MARES' "NATIONAL HUNT" MAIDEN HURDLE (8 hdls) 2m
2:15 (2:16) (Class 4) 4-Y-O+ **£3,119** (£915; £457; £228)

Form RPR
161/ **1** **Joanne One (IRE)**^{195} 5070 5-10-12 0 (t) BrendanPowell 110+
(Jamie Snowden) *in tch in midfield: effrt to chse ldrs bef 3 out: wnt 2nd 2 out: led bef last and sn asserted: gng clr whn gd jump last: r.o strly: readily* **11/4^{2}**
3/1- **2** 9 **Indian Stream**^{16} 1671 4-10-9 0 RobertDunne$^{(3)}$ 101
(Peter Bowen) *chsd ldr after 4th tl led wl bef 3 out: drvn and hdd between last 2: sn outpcd by wnr and btn whn j.big last: plugged on to hold 2nd flat* **6/1^{3}**
30/ **3** 1 **Tenmoku**^{226} 4507 4-10-12 0 NoelFehily 100
(Jonjo O'Neill) *t.k.h: hld up in tch towards rr: hdwy into midfield bef 3 out: pushed along to go 3rd after 2 out: mstke last: styd on same pce flat* **33/1**
215- **4** 7 **Dardanella**^{48} 1387 6-10-12 0 TomScudamore 95
(Richard Lee) *in tch in midfield: effrt whn stmbld sn after 3 out: no threat to ldrs but plugged on to go 4th flat* **14/1**
110/ **5** 2½ **Midnight Minx**^{218} 4666 6-10-9 0 (t) RachaelGreen$^{(3)}$ 91
(Anthony Honeyball) *hld up in tch: mstke 1st: hdwy to trck ldrs and looked to be gng wl bef 3 out: wnt 2nd 3 out and effrt bef next: mstke 2 out: nudged along and sn btn: wknd bef last: hung rt flat* **6/4^{1}**
1- **6** 2 **Tara Muck**^{39} 1499 6-10-12 0 SamTwiston-Davies 90
(Nigel Twiston-Davies) *t.k.h: hld up towards rr: mstke 2nd and 3rd: rdn and no prog 3 out: wknd next* **8/1**
345/ **7** 1¼ **Benefique Royale**^{190} 5187 5-10-12 0 DarylJacob 88
(Nick Williams) *t.k.h: chsd ldr after 2nd tl led 4th: hdd next: wknd after 3 out* **16/1**
234- **8** ¾ **Kimora (IRE)**^{39} 1497 7-10-12 95 (t) RhysFlint 87
(Marc Barber) *led tl 4th: lost pl u.p after next: wknd 3 out* **22/1**
0- **9** dist **Maxi's Lady (IRE)**^{12} 1706 6-10-9 0 MichaelByrne$^{(3)}$ 42
(David Rees) *chsd ldr tl after 2nd: steadily lost pl: bhd and lost tch 5th: t.o* **100/1**
/60- **10** ½ **Two Shades Of Blue**^{12} 1706 6-10-9 0 AdamWedge$^{(3)}$ 42
(Beth Roberts) *in tch in rr tl rdn and lost tch 5th: t.o* **250/1**
0/0- **11** 68 **Home Girl (IRE)**^{157} 187 5-10-12 0 RichardJohnson
(Susan Johnson) *a bhd: t.o 5th* **80/1**

3m 49.6s (1.10) **Going Correction** +0.15s/f (Yiel)
WFA 4 from 5yo+ 9lb **11** Ran SP% **114.5**
Speed ratings (Par 105): **103,98,98,94,93 92,91,91,66,66 32**
toteswingers 1&2 £4.10, 1&3 £47.20, 2&3 £17.00 CSF £18.74 TOTE £4.40: £1.80, £2.00, £9.80; EX 21.30 Trifecta £551.60 Pool: £1236.34 - 1.68 winning units..
Owner Sir Chips Keswick **Bred** Gerry Burke **Trained** Lambourn, Berks

FOCUS
A decent race of its type and a few of these should go on to land a novice or two. After riding in the first, Noel Fehily said about the ground; "It's good to soft and may be soft quite soon."

1886 TANNERS WINES H'CAP CHASE (17 fncs) 2m 5f
2:45 (2:45) (Class 4) (0-120,118) 4-Y-O+ **£3,768** (£1,106; £553; £276)

Form RPR
1 **Mister Grez (FR)**^{186} 7-11-7 113 HarrySkelton 129+
(Dan Skelton) *a travelling strly: in tch in midfield: clsd on bit and j. into ld 13th: drew clr fr next: in n.d whn blnd last: eased towards fin* **7/1^{3}**
U43/ **2** 18 **Taffy Thomas**^{402} 1504 9-11-1 107 (t) TomO'Brien 107
(Peter Bowen) *in tch in midfield: hdwy and wnt clr w wnr after 13th: rdn and struggling to stay w wnr whn hit next: btn after: j.rt 2 out: plugged on for clr 2nd* **11/4^{2}**
2/P- **3** 17 **Ring Bo Ree (IRE)**^{17} 1666 10-11-6 112 PaddyBrennan 93
(Tom George) *hld up in detached last pair: clsd and in tch 12th: 4th and wknd u.p after 13th: wnt modest 3rd last* **8/1**
P16/ **4** 2 **Material Boy**^{222} 4575 6-11-3 109 (vt) DarylJacob 88
(Nick Williams) *led tl after 2nd: chsd ldr after tl 8th: wnt 2nd again 9th: led 11th tl outj. and hdd 13th: sn drvn and wknd: no ch whn mstke 3 out* **5/2^{1}**
320- **5** 2 **Nez Rouge (FR)**^{12} 1707 12-11-9 115 SamTwiston-Davies 96
(Nigel Twiston-Davies) *chsd ldrs: cl 3rd after 13th: drvn and btn bef next: lost modest 3rd last* **9/1**
526- **P** **Sagredo (USA)**^{16} 1670 9-11-2 118 (v) JamesHuxham$^{(10)}$
(Jonjo O'Neill) *a in rr: rdn and lost tch 9th: tailing off whn p.u 11th* **10/1**
064- **P** **Dontpaytheferryman (USA)**^{13} 1698 8-11-2 111 (b) RobertDunne$^{(3)}$
(John Price) *led: j.lft and hdd 11th: lost pl after next: lost tch wl bef 14th: t.o whn p.u 3 out* **10/1**
F0P/ **P** **Moulin De La Croix**^{177} 5380 9-10-13 112 JackSherwood$^{(7)}$
(Oliver Sherwood) *hld up towards rr early: hdwy to chse ldrs after 2nd: wnt 2nd 8th tl 9th: lost tch 13th: t.o whn p.u 3 out* **14/1**

5m 22.6s (-6.00) **Going Correction** -0.125s/f (Good) **8** Ran SP% **113.7**
Speed ratings (Par 105): **106,99,92,91,91 , ,**
toteswingers 1&2 £6.40, 1&3 £13.40, 2&3 £3.50 CSF £27.26 CT £157.45 TOTE £6.60: £2.00, £1.90, £2.80; EX 44.40 Trifecta £326.30 Pool: £1003.25 - 2.30 winning units..
Owner Gilmans Point Racing Syndicate **Bred** Mme Sylvie Isaac-Nonn & Jerome Reboul **Trained** Alcester, Warwicks
■ The first winner for Dan Skelton, who was previously assistant to Paul Nicholls.

FOCUS
Quite a good gallop was set in this modest handicap.

1887 FESTIVAL RACING THE JUMP RACING BOOKMAKER H'CAP HURDLE (10 hdls) 2m 4f
3:20 (3:21) (Class 4) (0-110,107) 4-Y-0+ **£3,119** (£915; £457; £228)

Form RPR
/00- **1** **Scales (IRE)**^{129} [650] 7-11-0 **98**..................................... MichealNolan$^{(3)}$ 104+
(Richard Lee) *hld up in tch in rr: clsd and travelling wl bef 3 out: led and rdn clr between last 2: 2 l clr and blnd last: idled flat: rdn out* **25/1**
/66- **2** *¾* **Finding Your Feet (IRE)**^{48} [1391] 5-11-3 **103**.........(p) MauriceLinehan$^{(5)}$ 108+
(Jonjo O'Neill) *in tch in midfield: hdwy to chse ldrs 6th: wnt 2nd 3 out: led u.p after next: hdd between last 2: 2 l down and mstke last: rallied u.p fnl 100yds: styd on* **7/1**^{3}
316- **3** *2 ½* **Nicky Nutjob (GER)**^{34} [1538] 7-10-11 **99**....................(p) CiaranMckee$^{(7)}$ 102
(John O'Shea) *hld up in tch in last trio: rdn and hdwy bef 3 out: chsng ldrs whn blnd bdly and lost pl 2 out: rallied and wnt 3rd last: kpt on* **16/1**
344- **4** *7* **Prince Pippin (IRE)**^{52} [1345] 7-11-1 **103**......................(t) MsLucyJones$^{(7)}$ 100
(Lucy Jones) *chsd ldr tl led after 2nd: hdd 6th: styd w ldrs tl no ex after 2 out: wknd flat* **10/1**
031- **5** *½* **Frontier Vic**^{17} [1664] 6-10-12 **93**................................. SamTwiston-Davies 89
(Nigel Twiston-Davies) *t.k.h: in tch in midfield: slt mstke and outpcd 3 out: hrd drvn next: kpt on flat but no threat to ldrs* **5/4**^{1}
0FP/ **6** *¾* **Night Alliance (IRE)**^{604} [4355] 8-11-9 **104**.........................(b) TomO'Brien 100
(Dr Richard Newland) *chsd ldrs tl led 6th: drvn whn j.lft 2 out: sn hdd and no ex: wknd bef last* **10/1**
2/5- **7** *12* **Samingarry (FR)**^{152} [289] 6-11-9 **107**............................ MarkQuinlan$^{(3)}$ 92
(Nigel Hawke) *in tch in midfield: drvn and no imp after 7th: wknd after 3 out* **16/1**
351/ **8** *7* **The Rockies (IRE)**^{321} [2673] 6-11-7 **102**..........................(t) PaulMoloney 80
(Evan Williams) *hld up in tch in rr: clsd and wl in tch after 7th: wknd qckly sn after 3 out* **10/1**
PP6- **9** *30* **Arguidos (IRE)**^{52} [1342] 9-10-9 **95**.........................(tp) AodhaganConlon$^{(5)}$ 46
(Debra Hamer) *in tch in midfield: lost pl u.p after 7th: t.o between last 2* **25/1**
126- **10** *27* **Kusadasi (IRE)**^{52} [1344] 8-11-3 **105**......................(b) MrMatthewBarber$^{(7)}$ 32
(Marc Barber) *led tl after 1st: chsd ldrs tl lost pl and bhd 7th: lost tch wl bef 3 out: t.o next* **33/1**
/44- **P** **Trumix**^{148} [374] 5-11-12 **107**... JasonMaguire
(Kim Bailey) *chsd ldrs: lost pl and midfield whn mstke 3rd: reminder after 4th: dropped to last after next: lost tch 7th: t.o bef next tl p.u last* **13/2**^{2}
4m 59.75s (8.85) **Going Correction** +0.15s/f (Yiel) 11 Ran SP% **119.9**
Speed ratings (Par 105): **88,87,86,83,83 83,78,75,63,53**
toteswingers 1&2 £46.10, 1&3 £46.10, 2&3 £17.30 CSF £192.10 CT £2914.11 TOTE £26.90: £5.70, £2.20, £4.40; EX 259.60 Trifecta £1062.70 Part won. Pool: £1416.94 - 0.24 winning units..
Owner A Beard B Beard S Ripley **Bred** Michael Long **Trained** Byton, H'fords

FOCUS
Quite a few of these knew how to win, albeit not on a regular basis, so this wasn't a bad race for the class.

1888 BURNS PET NUTRITION NOVICES' LIMITED H'CAP CHASE (18 fncs) 3m
3:55 (3:58) (Class 3) (0-140,132) 4-Y-0+ **£6,657** (£2,067; £1,113)

Form RPR
/21- **1** **Sivola De Sivola (FR)**^{121} [736] 7-11-5 **132**.................... PaddyBrennan 139+
(Tom George) *led tl after 9th: 3 l 2nd and drvn bef 15th: keeping on whn lft in ld 3 out: edgd rt u.p flat: styd on: drvn out* **6/5**^{1}
0/U- **2** *¾* **Hansupfordetroit (IRE)**^{13} [1698] 8-10-7 **125**.............. RobertWilliams$^{(5)}$ 133+
(Bernard Llewellyn) *t.k.h: hld up in tch in last tl hdwy to ld after 9th: rdn whn j. v awkwardly: rdr unbalanced and hdd 3 out: rallied last: pressing wnr fnl 100yds: kpt on* **8/1**
/P2- **3** *42* **What An Oscar (IRE)**^{16} [1669] 8-10-7 **120**............(p) SamTwiston-Davies 88
(Nigel Twiston-Davies) *chsd ldr tl after 9th: lft 3rd 12th: rdn and wknd bef 15th: t.o 2 out* **7/2**^{3}
2/1- **F** **Well Hello There (IRE)**^{129} [642] 7-10-11 **129**.........(t) MauriceLinehan$^{(5)}$
(Jonjo O'Neill) *racd in cl 3rd: hit 8th: mstke 11th: fell 12th* **5/2**^{2}
6m 17.0s (-0.40) **Going Correction** -0.125s/f (Good) 4 Ran SP% **107.4**
Speed ratings (Par 107): **95,94,80,**
CSF £9.01 TOTE £2.00; EX 9.00 Trifecta £27.70 Pool: £1691.00 - 45.69 winning units..
Owner D O'Donohoe, S & P Nelson & D Silvester **Bred** Gilles Trapenard & Thomas Trapenard **Trained** Slad, Gloucs

FOCUS
Not form to trust.

1889 TRUSTMARK DESIGN AND PRINT H'CAP HURDLE (THE SUNDAY £5K BONUS RACE) (8 hdls) 2m
4:30 (4:31) (Class 3) (0-140,129) 4-Y-0+ **£5,393** (£1,583; £791; £395)

Form RPR
622- **1** **Bombadero (IRE)**^{3} [1840] 6-10-11 **114**...................(t) SamTwiston-Davies 119+
(Dr Richard Newland) *chsd clr ldr: mstke 2nd: grad clsd fr 3rd: led sn after 2 out: rdn and qcknd clr bef last: r.o wl: comf* **11/10**^{1}
/04- **2** *9* **Escort'men (FR)**^{13} [1699] 7-10-6 **109**...............................(t) PaulMoloney 106+
(Anthony Middleton) *hld up off the pce in midfield: grad clsd fr 3rd: trckd wnr after 2 out: shkn up and little rspnse bef last: rdn and no hdwy flat: eased towards fin* **11/1**
340- **3** *4 ½* **Toubab (FR)**^{43} [1476] 7-11-12 **129**.. HarrySkelton 121
(Dan Skelton) *led and sn wl clr: grad c bk to field and 2 l clr bef 3 out: hdd and mstke 2 out: wknd bef last* **9/1**
/10- **4** *20* **James Pollard (IRE)**^{21} [1627] 8-10-7 **115**.................(t) RobertWilliams$^{(5)}$ 88
(Bernard Llewellyn) *hmpd s: hld up wl off the pce in last pair: stdy hdwy 3rd: wl in tch 5th: rdn and struggling bef next: wknd next* **16/1**
542- **5** *8* **Jolly Roger (IRE)**^{10} [1729] 6-11-3 **120**.................................. LeeEdwards 86
(Tony Carroll) *racd off the pce in 3rd: grad clsd fr 3rd: rdn and btn 3 out: 4th and wkng whn blnd bdly next: t.o* **11/2**^{3}
1F/- **P** **One For Joules (IRE)**^{26} [1990] 6-11-8 **125**............................... RhysFlint
(John Flint) *stdd s: hld up wl off the pce in last pair: steadily clsd fr 3rd: wl in tch 5th: rdn and wknd bef next: t.o whn p.u last* **16/1**
61P/ **R** **Lordofthehouse (IRE)**^{177} [5399] 5-11-12 **129**................. PaddyBrennan
(Tom George) *virtually ref to racd and nt respond to press: barely cantered up to 1st and ref* **9/2**^{2}
3m 47.65s (-0.85) **Going Correction** +0.15s/f (Yiel) 7 Ran SP% **111.3**
Speed ratings (Par 107): **108,103,101,91,87 ,**
toteswingers 1&2 £4.00, 1&3 £2.90, 2&3 £5.10 CSF £12.84 TOTE £1.80: £1.10, £5.30; EX 13.90 Trifecta £94.10 Pool: £3466.48 - 27.60 winning units..
Owner The Berrow Hill Partnership **Bred** Windflower Overseas Holdings Inc **Trained** Claines, Worcs

FOCUS
Quite a few reasons to oppose some of these.

1890 32RED CONDITIONAL JOCKEYS' H'CAP HURDLE (12 hdls) 3m
5:00 (5:00) (Class 5) (0-100,100) 4-Y-0+ **£1,949** (£572; £286; £143)

Form RPR
01P/ **1** **Jump Up**^{641} [3679] 7-11-7 **95**.. MichaelByrne 101+
(Peter Bowen) *in tch in midfield: chsd ldrs 8th: 3rd and drvn after next: chal and hit 3 out: forged ahd after last: rdn out* **5/1**^{2}
500/ **2** *2 ¾* **Captain Moonman (IRE)**^{195} [5078] 8-10-10 **90**.........(p) PatrickCorbett$^{(6)}$ 92
(Rebecca Curtis) *in tch in midfield: hdwy to chse ldrs 6th: wnt 2nd 7th: j. into ld 3 out but immediately idling in front: hit next and hdd bef last: drvn and fnd nil after last: fnd ex whn pressed for 2nd fnl 100yds: styd on* **3/1**^{1}
501- **3** *1* **Tribal Dance (IRE)**^{30} [1580] 7-11-0 **94**............................. CiaranMckee$^{(6)}$ 94
(John O'Shea) *chsd ldr tl led 2nd: outj. and hdd 3 out: 3rd and outpcd next: plugged on and pressing for 2nd fnl 100yds: one pce* **6/1**^{3}
P06- **4** *3 ¾* **Changing Lanes**^{12} [1707] 10-11-0 **88**..............................(vt) AdamWedge 85
(David Rees) *chsd ldrs: 4th and outpcd u.p wl bef 3 out: plugged on u.p between last 2* **5/1**^{2}
146/ **5** *14* **Dancing Daffodil**^{213} [4766] 8-10-8 **90**..................... JosephPalmowski$^{(8)}$ 73
(Robin Dickin) *in tch in rr: rdn along 7th: sme hdwy 9th: no hdwy bef next: wknd after 3 out* **7/1**
P56- **6** *9* **Hassadin**^{19} [1645] 7-11-5 **98**.. JoshWall$^{(5)}$ 73
(Michael Blake) *in tch in midfield: rdn and struggling after 9th: wknd bef next* **12/1**
040/ **7** *134* **The Wee Lass**^{190} [5183] 6-10-8 **82**.. MichealNolan
(Arthur Whiting) *a in rr: mstke 7th: lost tch after next: wl t.o bef 3 out* **12/1**
/00- **P** **Burnswood (IRE)**^{33} [1551] 9-10-13 **87**.........................(p) MauriceLinehan
(Marc Barber) *led tl 2nd: chsd ldr tl 7th: dropped out rapidly next: t.o whn p.u 9th* **33/1**
1/P- **P** **Head Hunted**^{61} [1258] 6-11-12 **100**... JamesBest
(Jim Best) *chsd ldrs: rdn after 8th: fdd rapidly wl bef 3 out: t.o whn p.u 3 out* **10/1**
605- **P** **Follow The Tracks (IRE)**^{53} [1337] 5-11-2 **90**....................... KillianMoore
(Brian Barr) *in tch in rr: struggling whn mstke 9th: sn lost tch: t.o whn p.u 2 out* **14/1**
6m 9.65s (20.65) **Going Correction** +0.15s/f (Yiel) 10 Ran SP% **119.2**
Speed ratings (Par 103): **71,70,69,68,63 60, , , ,**
toteswingers 1&2 £5.00, 1&3 £6.60, 2&3 £5.20 CSF £21.41 CT £93.97 TOTE £6.60: £2.90, £1.40, £2.70; EX 34.80 Trifecta £153.40 Pool: £1644.20 - 8.03 winning units..
Owner Ashley Hart **Bred** D J And Mrs Deer **Trained** Little Newcastle, Pembrokes

FOCUS
Not many got into this, in what looked to be tiring conditions.

1891 32RED.COM MAIDEN OPEN NATIONAL HUNT FLAT RACE 2m
5:30 (5:30) (Class 6) 4-6-Y-0 **£1,642** (£478; £239)

Form RPR
32/ **1** **Solstice Son**^{175} [5444] 4-10-11 0..................................(t) RachaelGreen$^{(3)}$ 105+
(Anthony Honeyball) *hld up in tch: hdwy to ld on bit over 3f out: drew clr 2f out: v easily* **6/4**^{1}
2 *13* **Driving Well (IRE)** 5-11-0 0... NickScholfield 91
(Arthur Whiting) *in tch in midfield: hdwy to ld over 4f out: hdd and rdn over 3f out: brushed aside by wnr 2f out: tired but hld on for 2nd fnl f* **20/1**^{3}
3 *16* **Mission To Mars (IRE)**^{196} 4-11-0 0....................... SamTwiston-Davies 81
(Nigel Twiston-Davies) *plld v hrd: chsd ldr tl led over 5f out: hdd over 4f out: 4th and btn 3f out: plugged on: lft 3rd last strides* **11/4**^{2}
4 *17* **Iouascore (IRE)**^{160} 6-10-7 0.. MissLBrooke$^{(7)}$ 62
(Lady Susan Brooke) *t.k.h early: in tch: dropped to last 9f out: sn toiling: lost tch 6f out: plugged on past btn horses fnl 3f: lft 4th last strides: t.o* **80/1**
0- **5** *7* **Tunnel Vision (IRE)**^{79} [1124] 6-10-7 0.................................. OllieGarner$^{(7)}$ 55
(Nikki Evans) *led tl over 5f out: sn rdn and dropped out: t.o over 2f out: lft 5th last strides* **66/1**
F **Relentless Dreamer (IRE)** 4-11-0 0.................................. RichardJohnson 88
(Rebecca Curtis) *chsd ldrs: 3rd and outpcd u.p over 3f out: no ch w wnr but plugged on same pce fnl 2f: 3rd and wl hld whn stmbld and fell cl home* **6/4**^{1}
P **Just Lewis** 6-10-11 0.. RobertDunne$^{(3)}$
(Nikki Evans) *hld up in tch in rr: lost tch rapidly 5f out: wl t.o whn hung bdly rt fnl 4f: p.u 1f out* **25/1**
3m 49.8s (6.90) **Going Correction** +0.15s/f (Yiel)
WFA 4 from 5yo+ 9lb 7 Ran SP% **118.0**
Speed ratings: **88,81,73,65,61 ,**
toteswingers 1&2 £6.20, 1&3 £1.60, 2&3 £5.20 CSF £31.38 TOTE £3.30: £1.80, £6.60; EX 26.10 Trifecta £89.20 Pool: £3022.03 - 25.39 winning units..
Owner The Summer Solstice **Bred** R W Russell **Trained** Mosterton, Dorset

FOCUS
Almost certainly not a strong race.
T/Plt: £383.10 to a £1 stake. Pool: £98,538.76 - 187.72 winning tickets T/Qpdt: £107.00 to a £1 stake. Pool: £7214.51 - 49.89 winning tickets SP

1111 LIMERICK (R-H)
Sunday, October 13

OFFICIAL GOING: Good

1893a FERGUS O'TOOLE MEMORIAL NOVICE HURDLE (GRADE 3) (12 hdls) 2m 5f
2:35 (2:36) 4-Y-0+ **£14,532** (£4,247; £2,012; £670)

RPR
1 **Indevan**^{33} [1556] 5-11-5 132.. RWalsh 143+
(W P Mullins, Ire) *sn led at stdy pce: almost jnd bef 2 out: styd on wl to extend advantage between fnl 2 flights: pushed out run-in* **5/4**^{1}
2 *2 ¾* **Lots Of Memories (IRE)**^{25} [1603] 6-11-2 .... ShaneButler 136
(P G Fahey, Ire) *slow 1st: racd in 4th tl clsd after 3 out: travelled wl to press ldr in 2nd appr 2 out: sn pushed along and nt qckn: kpt on same pce run-in* **3/1**^{2}
3 *2 ¾* **Little King Robin (IRE)**^{9} [1760] 5-10-9 115.........................(t) MarkWalsh 126
(Colin Bowe, Ire) *t.k.h and trckd ldr on inner in 2nd tl 3rd w under a circ to r: ev ch appr 2 out: no imp on wnr whn nt fluent last: kpt on same pce* **14/1**

4 6 ½ **Silver Tassie (IRE)**[10] 1735 5-11-5 126.............................. DavyCondon 130
(Noel Meade, Ire) *hld up in rr: nt fluent 6 out and 5 out: clsd to chse rivals bef 2 out: sn nt qckn: kpt on one pce* **6/1**

5 8 **Tropical Three (IRE)**[27] 1591 5-10-12 119...................... BarryGeraghty 116
(Michael Hourigan, Ire) *trckd ldrs in 3rd: clsd in 2nd w under a circ to r: almost on terms after 3 out: sn pushed along and wknd appr 2 out* **7/2**[3]

5m 4.9s (304.90)
WFA 4 from 5yo+ 10lb **5** Ran SP% **112.6**
CSF £5.59 TOTE £1.90: £1.60, £2.30; DF 7.00 Trifecta £30.80.
Owner Mrs S Ricci **Bred** D J And Mrs Brown **Trained** Muine Beag, Co Carlow

FOCUS
A smart type of race but little more than a farce in terms of the gallop. It was a glorified sprint in the end and deeply unsatisfactory. The winner did not need to repeat his best.

1896a PRICEWATERHOUSECOOPERS CHASE (GRADE 3) (14 fncs) 2m 3f 120y
4:20 (4:21) 4-Y-0+ **£15,325** (£4,479)

RPR

1 **Far Away So Close (IRE)**[24] 1610 8-11-5 134.................. DavyRussell 130
(Paul Nolan, Ire) *nt fluent 2nd and hdd: led again 4th: mstke 6 out: extended advantage 4 out and sn wl clr: nt extended* **1/5**[1]

2 42 **New Phase (IRE)**[22] 1616 9-10-10 .... SeanMcDermott 88
(A J McNamara, Ire) *led 2nd tl 4th: no match for wnr fr 4 out in remote 2nd: eased* **7/2**[2]

4m 47.1s (287.10) **2** Ran SP% **105.6**
TOTE £1.20.
Owner Gigginstown House Stud **Bred** B Higgins **Trained** Enniscorthy, Co. Wexford

FOCUS
This cut up to an extremely weak race for the grade.

1897a LADBROKES MUNSTER NATIONAL H'CAP CHASE (GRADE A) (16 fncs) 3m
4:50 (4:50) 4-Y-0+
£48,780 (£15,447; £7,317; £2,439; £1,626; £813)

RPR

1 **Double Seven (IRE)**[64] 1241 7-11-4 138...........................(tp) MarkWalsh 153+
(Martin Brassil, Ire) *w.w: travelled wl to trck ldrs 3 out: short of room bef 2 out but sn led: mstke last: styd on strly run-in* **8/1**[3]

2 2 **Spring Heeled (IRE)**[23] 1613 6-11-1 135...........................(p) BarryGeraghty 147
(J H Culloty, Ire) *trckd ldrs: impr into cl 2nd 3 out: disp bef next: sn hdd: kpt on wl run-in* **11/2**[1]

3 1 ½ **Jamsie Hall (IRE)**[25] 1604 10-10-12 132.....................(tp) KeithDonoghue 143
(Gordon Elliott, Ire) *racd in mid-div tl tk clsr order after 3 out to trck ldrs: pushed along in 5th 2 out: styd on strly into 3rd last: kpt on wl run-in* **33/1**

4 5 **Shot From The Hip (GER)**[25] 1604 9-11-3 137...................(t) APMcCoy 143
(E J O'Grady, Ire) *racd in mid-div: pushed along to chse ldrs 4 out: prog to press ldrs in 4th 2 out: no imp appr last: kpt on same pce* **7/1**[2]

5 ¾ **Heaney (IRE)**[10] 1737 6-10-10 130 14ex........................ PaulTownend 135
(T J Taaffe, Ire) *w.w towards rr tl tk clsr order after 3 out: chsd ldrs whn awkward 2 out: styd on wl run-in* **9/1**

6 1 ½ **Wise Oscar (IRE)**[25] 1604 9-10-10 130.............................. BryanCooper 133
(D T Hughes, Ire) *chsd ldrs: prog 4 out: led next: wandered and hdd appr 2 out: sn one pce* **7/1**[2]

7 3 ¾ **Sin Palo (IRE)**[32] 1572 9-10-9 129.. RWalsh 129
(W P Mullins, Ire) *hld up towards rr: sme hdwy on inner after 3 out: sn no imp: kpt on one pce* **16/1**

8 6 ½ **Forpadydeplasterer (IRE)**[23] 1613 11-11-7 141............ DenisO'Regan 134
(Thomas Cooper, Ire) *hld up in rr whn hmpd 5th: niggled along w a circ to r: hdwy to chse ldrs after 3 out: no imp next* **16/1**

9 ¾ **Tom Horn (IRE)**[86] 1035 7-10-10 130.............................. NiallPMadden 122
(Noel Meade, Ire) *w.w: nt fluent at times but gd hdwy to press ldrs in 3rd 3 out: wknd qckly bef next* **7/1**[2]

10 1 ¾ **Go All The Way (IRE)**[11] 1723 8-11-4 138.......................... AELynch 129
(J T R Dreaper, Ire) *a towards rr: sme prog after 3 out: no imp appr next* **16/1**

11 21 **Whodoyouthink (IRE)**[8] 1775 8-11-2 136.....................(v[1]) MichaelDarcy 106
(Oliver McKiernan, Ire) *led and clr bef 3rd tl reduced advantage 5 out: sn hdd & wknd* **33/1**

12 23 **Sumkindasuprstar (IRE)**[8] 1776 9-10-9 132.................(tp) BenDalton[(3)] 79
(John O Clifford, Ire) *chsd ldrs tl mstke 7 out: no ex and wknd bef 3 out* **20/1**

13 hd **Muirhead (IRE)**[25] 1604 10-11-3 137...............................(p) DavyCondon 83
(Noel Meade, Ire) *trckd ldrs tl after 4 out: nt fluent next: sn wknd* **8/1**[3]

14 5 ½ **Bob Lingo (IRE)**[23] 1613 11-11-3 137.......................................(t) DJCasey 78
(Thomas Mullins, Ire) *trckd ldr in 2nd: mstke 5 out: sn wknd* **33/1**

F **Questions Answered (IRE)**[25] 1604 8-10-12 132........... RobbiePower
(E McNamara, Ire) *w.w whn fell 5th* **8/1**[3]

5m 52.7s (-42.30) **15** Ran SP% **127.5**
CSF £53.55 CT £1404.19 TOTE £9.20: £3.10, £2.40, £7.50; DF 67.10.
Owner John P McManus **Bred** M Doran **Trained** Dunmurray, Co Kildare

FOCUS
Unusually quick ground for this race which made all the difference to the winner. The pace was generous and the Kerry National form was put to the test, with the horses who filled positions third to ninth in Listowel all declared (one a non-runner).

1899 - 1900a (Foreign Racing) - See Raceform Interactive

[1740]AUTEUIL (L-H)
Sunday, October 13

OFFICIAL GOING: Turf: very soft

1901a PRIX CARMARTHEN (HURDLE) (GRADE 3) (5YO+) (TURF) 2m 3f 110y
3:20 (12:00) 5-Y-0+
£49,390 (£24,146; £9,878; £5,487; £3,841)

RPR

1 **Ceasar's Palace (FR)**[19] 6-10-3 0.............................. BertrandLestrade 143
(J-P Gallorini, France) **1/1**[1]

2 6 **Prince Oui Oui (FR)**[19] 7-10-3 0.................................. JacquesRicou 137
(P Peltier, France) **83/10**

3 3 ½ **Dulce Leo (FR)**[25] 1608 7-10-3 0.............................. JonathanNattiez 134
(J-P Gallorini, France) **42/1**

4 hd **Lord Prestige (FR)**[25] 1608 6-10-10 0.................... JonathanPlouganou 140
(M Rolland, France) **7/2**[2]

5 1 ¼ **Monpilou (FR)**[25] 1608 6-10-6 0............................ VincentCheminaud 135
(G Macaire, France) **12/1**

6 ¾ **Une Vague (FR)**[25] 1608 5-9-11 0.................................... WilfridDenuault 125
(E Leenders, France) **34/1**

7 2 **Lamego (FR)**[25] 1608 6-10-3 0...................................... Jean-LucBeaunez 129
(Mme P Butel, France) **26/1**

8 10 **Solix (FR)**[212] 4772 7-10-3 0.. JamesReveley 119
(Ian Williams) *midfield: mstke 4 out: rdn after 2 out: sn outpcd and dropped to rr: eased whn btn flat* **62/1**

F **Saint Du Chenet (FR)**[126] 685 7-10-10 0..................(b) RegisSchmidlin
(M Rolland, France) **13/2**[3]

P **Blingless (FR)**[10] 5-10-1 0.. KevinNabet
(J Bertran De Balanda, France) **37/1**

4m 39.32s (-15.68) **10** Ran SP% **117.1**
PARI-MUTUEL (all including 1 euro stake): WIN 2.00; PLACE 1.50, 2.10, 5.60; DF 7.20; SF 8.00.
Owner J-P Gallorini **Bred** J P Gallorini **Trained** France

1902a PRIX HEROS XII (CHASE) (GRADE 3) (5YO+) (TURF) 2m 6f
4:00 (12:00) 5-Y-0+
£58,536 (£28,617; £16,910; £11,707; £6,504; £4,552)

RPR

1 **Saint Palois (FR)**[40] 5-10-3 0... JamesReveley 137
(J Ortet, France) **25/1**

2 snk **Quart Monde (FR)**[21] 9-10-3 0...................................... GaetanOlivier 137
(F Nicolle, France) **12/1**

3 2 **Farlow Des Mottes (FR)**[147] 403 5-10-3 0......................... KevinNabet 135
(F Nicolle, France) **2/1**[1]

4 1 ¾ **Reglis Brunel (FR)**[19] 8-10-3 0................................. ThierryMajorcryk 133
(E Lecoiffier, France) **12/1**

5 shd **Shannon Rock (FR)**[31] 7-11-0 0............................(p) BertrandLestrade 144
(J-P Gallorini, France) **6/1**[3]

6 2 **Ozamo (FR)**[31] 6-10-6 0.. JonathanPlouganou 134
(P Peltier, France) **6/1**[3]

7 1 ¾ **Parigny (FR)**[31] 7-10-6 0..(p) DavidCottin 132
(F-M Cottin, France) **33/1**

8 1 ½ **Sadler'Sflaure (FR)**[322] 2661 7-10-3 0........................(p) CyrilleGombeau 128
(N Bertran De Balanda, France) **21/1**

9 10 **Princesse Kap (FR)**[31] 5-9-13 0...............................(p) JonathanNattiez 114
(J-P Gallorini, France) **48/10**[2]

10 shd **Dragon Mask (FR)**[147] 403 7-10-6 0..................(b) Marc-AntoineBillard 121
(J-P Gallorini, France) **37/1**

P **Remember Rose (IRE)**[10] 10-10-3 0.........................(p) BertrandBourez
(Y-M Porzier, France) **16/1**

P **Rubis Sur Ongle (FR)**[19] 8-10-8 0................................ BertrandThelier
(G Cherel, France) **37/1**

P **Halley (FR)**[186] 5239 6-10-3 0... AlainCawley
(Tom George) *led or disp ld: slt mstke 1st: hdd and lost pl 10th: pushed along bef next: in rr bef 5 out: bhd and btn whn p.u bef 2 out* **110/1**

5m 38.64s (-5.36) **13** Ran SP% **117.9**
PARI-MUTUEL (all including 1 euro stake): WIN 5.50 (coupled with Ozamo); PLACE 4.20, 3.60, 1.90; DF 104.10; SF 299.20.
Owner Mme Patrick Papot **Bred** Earl Haras Du Luy **Trained** France

1903 - (Foreign Racing) - See Raceform Interactive

PARDUBICE (L-H)
Sunday, October 13

OFFICIAL GOING: Turf: good

1904a CENA SPOLECNOSTI VCES - CENA LABE (CROSS-COUNTRY CHASE) (LISTED RACE) (5YO+) (TURF) 3m 2f
1:50 (12:00) 5-Y-0+ **£10,521** (£4,839; £3,156; £1,262; £1,262)

RPR

1 **Sarika (FR)**[16] 1683 7-10-10 0...................................... AlainDeChitray 114
(Nick Williams) *hld up towards rr: tk clsr order 8th to r in midfield but wl in tch: nt fluent 6 out: chsd ldng pair fr 5 out: rdn to chal appr last: led run-in: sn clr: comf* **16/1**

2 7 **Rubin (CZE)**[1099] 1811 11-10-10 0... PKasny 107
(Martina Ruzickova, Czech Republic) **30/1**

3 3 ¼ **Ter Mill (CZE)** 7-10-3 0.. MichalKohl 97
(Antonin Novak, Czech Republic) **14/1**

4 1 ¼ **Universe Of Gracie (GER)**[1086] 8-10-10 0............................ JKousek 103
(Petr Juranek, Czech Republic) **25/1**

4 dht **Borderland (IRE)** 7-10-10 0... DusanAndres 103
(S Popelka Jr, Czech Republic) **17/2**

6 2 ¾ **Silver Regent (USA)**[1775] 8-10-10 0.. JVanalll 100
(J Vana Jr, Czech Republic) **9/5**[1]

7 9 **Dracula (CZE)** 5-10-10 0... JanFaltejsek 91
(J Vana Jr, Czech Republic) **7/2**[2]

8 18 **Cmana (CZE)** 8-10-10 0.. JosefBartos 73
(V Luka Jr, Czech Republic) **12/1**

9 2 **Sortina (CZE)** 6-10-6 0.. MrFMitchell 67
(J Votava, Czech Republic) **25/1**

10 3 ¼ **Loire (CZE)** 5-10-6 0.. TBoyer 64
(Pavel Slozil, Czech Republic) **30/1**

F **Lorain (CZE)** 6-10-10 0.. JMyska
(Stepanka Sedlackova, Czech Republic) **16/1**

U **Mlyn (CZE)** 7-10-10 0.. MNovak
(F Kovacik, Czech Republic) **25/1**

F **Amaragon (CZE)** 8-10-10 0... JKratochvil
(S Popelka Jr, Czech Republic) **78/10**

F **Moula (CZE)** 5-10-10 0.. LMatusky
(J Uhl, Czech Republic) **4/1**[3]

7m 3.71s (423.71) **14** Ran SP% **143.9**
WIN: 17.00; PLACE IN TOP THREE: 5.00, 7.00, 4.50.
Owner Mrs Jane Williams **Bred** Peter Drew Jones Et Al **Trained** George Nympton, Devon

1905a VELKA PARDUBICKA SPONSORED BY CESKOU POJISTOVNOU (CROSS-COUNTRY CHASE) (LISTED RACE) (6YO+) (TURF) 4m 2f 110y

3:30 (12:00) 6-Y-O+

£64,745 (£35,610; £22,661; £16,186; £11,330; £6,474)

RPR

1 **Orphee Des Blins (FR)**[331] 2454 11-10-6 0........................ JanFaltejsek 143
(G Wroblewski, Czech Republic) **3/1**[1]

2 *dist* **Nikas (CZE)**[365] 1853 8-10-10 0.......................... DusanAndres
(S Popelka Jr, Czech Republic) **35/1**

3 *3 1/2* **Klaus (POL)**[365] 1853 8-10-10 0.......................... JMyska
(Cestmir Olehla, Czech Republic) **13/1**

4 *1 1/2* **Kasim (CZE)** 8-10-10 0.......................... MNovak
(Premek Kejzlar, Czech Republic) **50/1**

5 *8* **Peintre Abstrait (IRE)**[1438] 7-10-10 0.......................... LMatusky
(R Holcak, Czech Republic) **150/1**

6 *nk* **Tropic De Brion (FR)**[559] 5212 6-10-10 0............. Marc-AntoineDragon
(Pavel Vitek, Czech Republic) **30/1**

F **Freneys Well**[25] 1603 13-10-10 0.......................... MartinFerris
(E Bolger, Ire) *towards rr: fell 7th* **30/1**

U **Budapest (IRE)**[834] 1045 8-10-10 0.......................... JVanaIII
(J Vana Jr, Czech Republic) **7/1**[2]

U **Zest For Life (IRE)**[25] 1603 9-10-10 0.......................... MrSWaley-Cohen
(E Bolger, Ire) *slipped and fell cantering to post: midfield: wl in tch whn mstke: hmpd and uns rdr 15th* **20/1**

U **Tiumen (POL)**[365] 1853 12-10-10 0.......................... JVanaJr
(J Vana Jr, Czech Republic) **3/1**[1]

U **Tomis (CZE)**[365] 1853 12-10-3 0.......................... OndrejVelek
(Antonin Novak, Czech Republic) **77/1**

U **Shalimar Fromentro (FR)**[35] 1532 7-10-10 0................ AlainDeChitray
(Nick Williams) *midfield: mstke and uns rdr 10th* **12/1**[3]

F **Mount Sion (IRE)**[19] 1653 7-10-10 0.......................... RichieMcLernon
(E Bolger, Ire) *midfield: fell 3rd (water)* **22/1**

F **Trezor (POL)**[365] 1853 9-10-10 0.......................... JosefBartos
(Hana Kabelkova, Czech Republic) **3/1**[1]

P **Seslost (CZE)** 9-10-6 0.......................... LiamTreadwell
(Z Matysik, Czech Republic) **35/1**

U **Speranza (CZE)** 8-10-10 0.......................... TBoyer
(Jaroslav Pechacek, Czech Republic) **50/1**

P **Bodyguard (POL)** 7-10-10 0.......................... JBrecka
(Michal Rocak, Czech Republic) **150/1**

U **Al Jaz (CZE)** 7-10-10 0.......................... MichalKohl
(J Blecha, Czech Republic) **30/1**

U **Cantridara (SLO)** 7-10-6 0.......................... MrFMitchell
(J Papousek, Czech Republic) **150/1**

U **Status Quo (CZE)** 7-10-10 0.......................... PKasny
(Miroslav Sevcik, Czech Republic) **40/1**

9m 33.22s (573.22) **20** Ran SP% **136.3**
WIN: 4.00 PLACE IN TOP THREE: 2.50, 6.00, 3.50.
Owner DS Pegas **Bred** Suc. G Cahu **Trained** Czechoslovakia

[1779]HUNTINGDON (R-H)

Tuesday, October 15

OFFICIAL GOING: Soft (good to soft in places; 5.9)
Water jump omitted in all chases.
Wind: light across in relation to home straight Weather: overcast but brightening; 13 degrees

1913 1ST SECURITY SOLUTIONS H'CAP HURDLE (8 hdls) 2m 110y

2:20 (2:26) (Class 4) (0-115,114) 4-Y-O+ **£3,249** (£954; £477; £238)

Form RPR

26/- 1 **Makari**[179] 5386 6-11-10 **112**.......................... AndrewTinkler 127+
(Nicky Henderson) *mstke 2nd: hld up in rr: hdwy to go cl up after hitting 5th: cruised into ld bef 2 out: 5 l clr last: hrd hld* **11/8**[1]

U43- 2 *5* **Royal Defence (IRE)**[29] 1533 7-10-11 **99**.......................... RyanMahon 98
(Mick Quinn) *chsd ldrs: drvn bef 4th: outpcd 3 out: 10 l 6th 2 out tl last: battled on v gamely to snatch 2nd bhd heavily eased wnr* **25/1**

232- 3 *shd* **Daliance (IRE)**[72] 1206 4-11-1 **108**.......................... MattCrawley(5) 108
(Lucy Wadham) *towards rr: hit 3 out and rdn and outpcd: kpt on to go 3rd at last: no ch w effrtless wnr: ev ch of 2nd tl fnl stride* **9/2**[2]

0/0- 4 *1/2* **Hartside (GER)**[12] 1729 4-11-1 **110**.......................... MrRWinks(7) 109
(Peter Winks) *towards rr: mstke 4th: rdn and outpcd by ldng trio after 3 out: plugged on gamely to go 2nd briefly after last: lost two pl fnl 100yds* **50/1**

13P- 5 *1 1/4* **Not Til Monday (IRE)**[49] 727 7-11-12 **114**..................(v) JasonMaguire 111
(J R Jenkins) *2nd or 3rd tl 3rd and drvn and outpcd by ldng pair home turn: btn bef last* **7/1**[3]

211- 6 *hd* **Kettlewell**[28] 1595 4-11-11 **113**..........................(t) APMcCoy 112
(Warren Greatrex) *led tl after 1st: nt fluent: hit 3rd: led bef next: hit 3 out and drvn: hdd bef next: stl 2nd at last but no ex* **9/2**[2]

3/0- 7 *1/2* **Twoways (IRE)**[118] 761 7-11-3 **105**.......................... NickScholfield 101
(Mark Rimell) *t.k.h early: midfield: chsd ldrs tl mstke 3 out: rdn and plugged on and n.d after: blnd last* **28/1**

6/0- 8 *31* **Dealing River**[23] 1634 6-11-12 **114**.......................... AndrewThornton 79
(Caroline Bailey) *t.k.h early: chsd ldrs tl 5th: fdd rapidly u.p bef next: sn t.o* **14/1**

PP/- 9 *61* **Eighteen Carat (IRE)**[329] 2537 9-10-7 **100**.......................... JoeCornwall(5) 4
(John Cornwall) *j. slowly 1st: last and drvn and struggling after 3rd: t.o whn mstkes next two: fin nrly two hurdles bhd* **100/1**

U65/ P **Mr Lando**[53] 5272 4-11-8 **110**.......................... WayneHutchinson
(Tony Carroll) *bolted leaving paddock and overshot s by 5f: allowed to compete: last away but bolted into ld after 1st: 8 l clr after 3rd: hdd bef next and stopped to nil: t.o and p.u 5th* **12/1**

3m 55.4s (0.50) **Going Correction** +0.025s/f (Yiel)
WFA 4 from 6yo+ 9lb **10** Ran SP% **115.6**
Speed ratings (Par 105): **99,96,96,96,95 95,95,80,52,**
toteswingers 1&2 £17.10, 1&3 £1.60, 2&3 £23.30 CSF £38.59 CT £130.01 TOTE £3.20: £1.60, £5.30, £1.60; EX 41.30 Trifecta £322.50 Pool: £1547.01 - 3.59 winning units..
Owner Matt & Lauren Morgan **Bred** Longdon Stud Ltd **Trained** Upper Lambourn, Berks

FOCUS
One-way traffic for the progressive winner. The second to fourth set the level.

1914 32RED.COM H'CAP CHASE (14 fncs 2 omitted) 2m 4f 110y

2:50 (2:51) (Class 4) (0-105,103) 4-Y-O+ **£3,898** (£1,144; £572; £286)

Form RPR

454- 1 **Riddlestown (IRE)**[23] 1629 6-11-8 **99**.......................... HarrySkelton 106
(Caroline Fryer) *pckd bdly 1st: towards rr and wl off pce of ldng pair tl clsd to 4th and mstke 11th: tk 3rd next and 2nd on home turn: brought wd to chal 2 out: ev ch after: wore down ldr fnl strides* **9/1**

666/ 2 *nk* **Plum Pudding (FR)**[196] 5104 10-11-8 **99**..................(p) TomScudamore 107+
(David Bridgwater) *cl 2nd mostly tl led 6th: hrd pressed fr 2 out: sn drvn: costly mstke last: ct cl home* **5/2**[1]

212/ 3 *24* **Allerton (IRE)**[362] 1900 6-11-12 **103**..........................(t) PaddyBrennan 89
(Fergal O'Brien) *towards rr and wl off pce of ldrs: rdn 7th: sme prog into 12 l 3rd at 10th: sn struggling: 20 l 3rd whn mstke 2 out* **5/2**[1]

30F- 4 *1* **Darnborough (IRE)**[36] 1534 7-10-2 **79**..........................(p) FelixDeGiles 62
(Tom Symonds) *t.k.h: mstkes 1st and 3rd: mde most tl 6th: j. slowly next: pressed ldr tl drvn 3 out: lost 2nd home turn and dropped rt out* **6/1**[2]

64U- 5 *5* **Peak Seasons (IRE)**[14] 1715 10-10-4 **86**.......................... JoeCornwall(5) 63
(Michael Chapman) *wl bhd: rdn 7th: no ch fr 9th: t.o 11th: plugged on after last* **33/1**

362- P **Nouailhas**[18] 1668 7-9-8 **78** oh1 ow1..........................(v) MissAEStirling(7)
(Andrew Hollinshead) *j.lft: a wl bhd: struggling 7th: j. slowly 9th: sn t.o: p.u 2 out* **7/1**[3]

PPP- P **Autumm Spirit**[87] 1050 9-11-6 **97**..........................(t) CharliePoste
(Robin Dickin) *chsd ldng pair tl wknd and j.v.slowly 7th: rdn and t.o 10th: p.u 2 out* **12/1**

P/P- P **Hinton Indiana**[165] 94 8-11-4 **100**..........................(t) NicodeBoinville(5)
(Adrian Wintle) *a wl bhd: disp last and hrd drvn after 8th: sn t.o: p.u 2 out* **8/1**

5m 6.3s (1.00) **Going Correction** -0.15s/f (Good) **8** Ran SP% **115.7**
Speed ratings (Par 105): **92,91,82,82,80 , ,**
toteswingers 1&2 £25.80, 1&3 £10.10, 2&3 £2.60 CSF £33.47 CT £74.58 TOTE £7.80: £2.60, £2.00, £1.30; EX 46.90 Trifecta £109.40 Pool: £606.19 - 4.15 winning units..
Owner J Ward **Bred** Jeremiah O'Brien **Trained** Wymondham, Norfolk

FOCUS
This moderate handicap was run at a frantic early pace and the first pair were well clear at the finish. The ground looked sounder on the chase course, and was backed up by the winning time. The winner is rated to his hurdles mark.

1915 32RED CASINO NOVICES' HURDLE (10 hdls) 2m 4f 110y

3:20 (3:22) (Class 4) 4-Y-O+ **£3,898** (£1,144; £572; £286)

Form RPR

41/ 1 **Oscar Fortune (IRE)**[186] 5279 5-10-12.......................... APMcCoy 125+
(Jonjo O'Neill) *settled in 3rd pl: chal and hit 3 out: sn led and rdn: nt fluent last: battled on wl flat* **4/1**

31- 2 *1/2* **Beachfire**[50] 1404 6-11-5 128.......................... DenisO'Regan 131
(John Ferguson) *hld up towards rr: effrt 3 out: sn pushed along: wnt 2nd after next: chal and sltly impeded last: ev ch tl outbattled fnl 100yds* **7/2**[3]

422/ 3 *9* **Present View**[315] 2842 5-10-12.......................... BrendanPowell 116
(Jamie Snowden) *chsd ldrs: effrt 3 out: wnt 2nd and rdn bef next: wknd between last two* **2/1**[1]

4 *1/2* **Patsys Castle (IRE)**[219] 6-10-12.......................... JasonMaguire 115
(Kim Bailey) *chsd ldrs tl hit 6th and drvn: sn outpcd: plugged on again wout threatening fr 2 out* **33/1**

0/4- 5 *11* **Beaujolais (IRE)**[136] 588 5-10-9.......................... JackQuinlan(3) 104
(John Ferguson) *hld up towards rr: no ch fr 3 out* **33/1**

01P/ 6 *25* **Gallic Warrior (FR)**[185] 5287 6-10-12.......................... PaddyBrennan 89
(Fergal O'Brien) *t.k.h: chsd ldrs tl 6th: rdn and struggling after mstk next: j.b rt 2 out: t.o and eased* **28/1**

123/ 7 *12* **No No Charlie (IRE)**[271] 3697 6-10-12.......................... NoelFehily 82
(Charlie Longsdon) *plld hrd: chsd ldr tl led 6th: drvn and hdd 3 out: stopped to nil: t.o whn mstke last* **5/2**[2]

8 *6* **Great Link**[20] 4-11-0..........................(bt) JoshHamer(5) 68
(Tony Carroll) *t.k.h: led and 4 l clr: hdd 6th: rdn and nt keen next: sn tailed himself off* **50/1**

P/0- 9 *23* **Kicking Time (IRE)**[59] 1281 7-10-12.......................... ConorO'Farrell 38
(Sarah Humphrey) *taken down early: midfield: struggling after mstke 7th: t.o whn j. bdly rt 2 out: eased after* **200/1**

0/P- P **Cape Schanck**[124] 593 9-10-12.......................... DaveCrosse
(Alan Coogan) *a bhd: t.o after 6th: p.u 3 out* **200/1**

40- P **Money Money Money**[18] 1672 7-10-5..........................[1] MattieBatchelor
(Jim Best) *anchored in last and j. v awkwardly: lost all tch after 5th: eventually p.u 2 out* **100/1**

0/0- P **Jazz Man (IRE)**[159] 174 6-10-12.......................... NickScholfield
(Mark Rimell) *wl bhd in fnl pair: mstke 3rd and reminder: t.o after 6th: p.u bef 2 out* **100/1**

4m 54.6s (-4.40) **Going Correction** +0.025s/f (Yiel)
WFA 4 from 5yo+ 10lb **12** Ran SP% **118.4**
Speed ratings (Par 105): **109,108,105,105,101 91,86,84,75, ,**
toteswingers 1&2 £2.60, 1&3 £2.20, 2&3 £1.50 CSF £18.22 TOTE £7.20: £2.20, £1.20, £1.60; EX 25.60 Trifecta £79.20 Pool: £1124.32 - 10.64 winning units..
Owner The Jackdaws Strangers **Bred** John Hennessy **Trained** Cheltenham, Gloucs

FOCUS
An interesting novice hurdle, run at a sound gallop. A step up from the winner on his bumper form but he's the type to rate higher.

1916 NYMAN LIBSON PAUL 80TH ANNIVERSARY NOVICES' LIMITED H'CAP CHASE (14 fncs 2 omitted) 2m 4f 110y

3:50 (3:50) (Class 3) (0-125,122) 4-Y-O+ **£6,498** (£1,908; £954; £477)

Form RPR

34/- 1 **Avoca Promise (IRE)**[252] 4041 8-11-3 **120**.......................... FelixDeGiles 127+
(Tom Symonds) *hld up in rr early: prog to 2nd bef 9th: rdn bef 2 out: sustained chal after: got up cl home* **17/2**

613/ 2 *1* **Loudmouth (IRE)**[182] 5327 6-10-10 **113**.......................... NoelFehily 118+
(Charlie Longsdon) *2nd or 3rd tl lft in ld 6th: 1 l in front and drvn on home turn: hrd pressed fr 2 out: hdd fnl 50yds* **5/4**[1]

246- 3 *10* **Sail And Return**[23] 1628 9-11-3 **120**..........................(t) SamTwiston-Davies 115
(Phil Middleton) *dropped out last early: stdy prog 9th: 4th and drvn home turn: sn btn: lft 3rd after 2 out* **20/1**

00/- 4 *2 3/4* **Bucking The Trend**[214] 4769 5-11-5 **122**.......................... RichardJohnson 119+
(Tim Vaughan) *hld up towards rr: stdy hdwy 9th: nt fluent 3 out: sn rdn: cl 3rd whn blnd bdly next and lost all ch* **11/4**[2]

/44- P **Next Exit (IRE)**[41] 1494 8-10-6 **114**..........................(t) JoeCornwall(5)
(John Cornwall) *dropped bk last after 8th: t.o and p.u 10th* **66/1**

/15- **P** **Pasture Bay (IRE)**54 [1350] 7-10-9 **112** AlainCawley
(Fergal O'Brien) *towards rr: struggling 9th: p.u next: b.b.v* **10/1**

/62- **P** **Tiny Tenor (IRE)**21 [1640] 7-11-0 **117** NickScholfield
(David Dennis) *chsd ldr tl 6th: lost tch 11th: t.o and p.u 2 out: collapsed and died: heart attack* **25/1**

225- **P** **Brady (IRE)**84 [1083] 7-10-9 **112** (p) JasonMaguire
(Donald McCain) *j.lft: led tl j.lft and pckd bdly 6th: sed to hang violently lft and almost unrideable fr 10th: blnd next: t.o and p.u 2 out* **8/1**[3]

4m 58.0s (-7.30) **Going Correction** -0.15s/f (Good) **8** Ran SP% **111.9**
Speed ratings (Par 107): **107,106,102,101, , ,**
toteswingers 1&2 £4.20, 1&3 £19.10, 2&3 £2.60 CSF £19.82 CT £206.52 TOTE £8.20: £1.80, £1.30, £3.20; EX 20.00 Trifecta £66.30 Pool: £730.42 - 8.25 winning units..
Owner Bailey-Carvill Equine **Bred** Kenneth Parkhill **Trained** Harewood End, H'fords
■ Stewards' Enquiry : Noel Fehily four-day ban: used whip above permitted level (Oct 29-Nov 1)

FOCUS
A fair novice handicap for the class. They started racing a long way from home and just four managed to complete. The winner is rated to the best of his form for his previous yard.

1917 32RED FREE AT 32RED.COM H'CAP HURDLE (12 hdls) 3m 2f
4:20 (4:20) (Class 4) (0-110,108) 4-Y-0+ **£3,249** (£954; £477; £238)

Form RPR

1F3- **1** **Dom Lukka (FR)**18 [1673] 5-11-3 **99** NoelFehily 105+
(Charlie Longsdon) *pressed ldr gng wl: led 8th: wnt 3 l clr after 3 out: rdn bef last: clipped flight: styd on gamely flat but all out* **5/2**[1]

F20- **2** *1* **Minella For Steak (IRE)**34 [1565] 6-11-11 **107** (tp) APMcCoy 112+
(Jonjo O'Neill) *prom on outer and nt a fluent: chsd wnr fr 9th: hrd drvn and tried to chal and blnd 3 out: pckd next: racing awkwardly after: 3 l down at last: r.o u.p but a hld* **7/2**[2]

611- **3** *1 3/4* **Go Amwell**36 [1538] 10-11-3 **99** (v) LeightonAspell 101
(J R Jenkins) *t.k.h in rr: effrt bef 3 out: wnt 3rd home turn: drvn and tried to chal last: kpt on but no imp fnl 100yds* **8/1**

45F- **4** *6* **Lucky To Be Alive (IRE)**23 [1631] 6-10-7 **89** (p) DonalDevereux 86
(Peter Bowen) *nt a fluent: midfield: mstke 7th: 5th and rdn bef 3 out: sn no imp: hit last* **6/1**[3]

4/1- **5** *4 1/2* **Kilrush (IRE)**156 [254] 7-11-9 **108** MichaelByrne(3) 100
(Neil Mulholland) *dropped out in last trio: short-lived effrt 9th: sn drvn: wl-btn 6th on home turn* **12/1**

364/ **6** *8* **Flemi Two Toes (IRE)**211 [4841] 7-11-6 **105** (p) JackQuinlan(3) 90
(Sarah Humphrey) *prom: rdn whn hit 3 out: wknd bef next* **16/1**

3/0- **7** *2* **Lombardy Boy (IRE)**144 [460] 8-10-5 **92** TrevorWhelan(5) 74
(Michael Banks) *dropped bk to 8 l last bef 8th: sn rdn: nvr gng wl enough after* **18/1**

035- **8** *2 1/4* **Galley Slave (IRE)**17 [1689] 8-9-10 **83** JoeCornwall(5) 63
(Michael Chapman) *nvr bttr than midfield: rdn and struggling after 9th* **50/1**

32F/ **9** *nk* **Thedeboftheyear**182 [5328] 9-11-4 **100** JamesDavies 79
(Chris Down) *several positions: effrt 9th: rdn and btn whn mstke next* **10/1**

0B5- **10** *16* **Munlochy Bay**50 [1391] 9-10-10 **92** (p) CharliePoste 55
(Matt Sheppard) *last pair mostly: mstke and pushed along 7th: drvn and lost tch bef 3 out* **16/1**

164- **11** *36* **Noble Witness (IRE)**104 [872] 10-11-7 **103** (p) AdamPogson 30
(Charles Pogson) *j. slowly 4th: led tl 8th: stopped to nil after next and sn t.o* **40/1**

/45- **P** **Elegant Olive**146 [428] 10-11-2 **98** HaddenFrost
(Roger Curtis) *towards rr: lost tch bef 3 out: t.o and p.u last* **20/1**

6m 32.7s (9.80) **Going Correction** +0.025s/f (Yiel) **12** Ran SP% **119.2**
Speed ratings (Par 105): **85,84,84,82,80 78,77,77,77,72 61,**
toteswingers 1&2 £1.40, 1&3 £5.60, 2&3 £4.90 CSF £11.71 CT £61.82 TOTE £3.10: £1.50, £1.20, £2.30; EX 13.30 Trifecta £41.10 Pool: £633.24 - 11.52 winning units..
Owner Roy Swinburne **Bred** Jean-Claude Janin-Thivos **Trained** Over Norton, Oxon

FOCUS
An ordinary staying handicap in which it paid to race handily. The winner improved to his chase mark.

1918 32RED H'CAP CHASE (17 fncs 2 omitted) 3m
4:50 (4:50) (Class 3) (0-135,132) 4-Y-0+ **£8,656** (£3,148)

Form RPR

1/1- **1** **Muldoon's Picnic (IRE)**135 [603] 7-11-12 **132** JasonMaguire 140+
(Kim Bailey) *j. slowly 2nd: blnd 14th: hld up last tl effrt after 3 out: chal apparently gng best next and lft virtually solo: heavily eased fr last* **5/1**[3]

534/ **2** *53* **Tigre D'Aron (FR)**325 [2612] 6-10-10 **116** APMcCoy 71
(Chris Gordon) *t.k.h: led 2nd tl 7th: led and hit 10th: nt fluent 13th: hdd next: wknd rapidly: already t.o whn lft 2nd and clambered over 2 out: j.lft last* **11/4**[2]

421/ **U** **Ballypatrick (IRE)**242 [4227] 7-11-7 **127** ConorO'Farrell 113
(Mick Channon) *chsd ldng pair and hld up: nt fluent 11th: wnt 2nd 3 out tl tired qckly bef next: lft 12 l 2nd but hmpd and uns rdr 2 out* **2/1**[1]

410- **F** **Strongbows Legend**119 [757] 8-10-12 **118** (v) NoelFehily 119
(Charlie Longsdon) *led tl 2nd: led 7th tl 10th and 14th tl jnd and fell heavily 2 out: fatally injured* **2/1**[1]

6m 13.1s (2.80) **Going Correction** -0.15s/f (Good) **4** Ran SP% **110.0**
Speed ratings (Par 107): **89,71, ,**
CSF £17.97 TOTE £4.40; EX 8.00 Trifecta £13.60 Pool: £330.15 - 18.10 winning units..
Owner Clive Washbourn **Bred** Peter McCrea **Trained** Andoversford, Gloucs

FOCUS
A dramatic affair. The winner is on the upgrade but not a race to be confident about.

1919 32RED ON THE APP STORE STANDARD OPEN NATIONAL HUNT FLAT RACE 2m 110y
5:20 (5:20) (Class 6) 4-6-Y-0 **£1,559** (£457; £228; £114)

Form RPR

14/ **1** **Wadswick Court (IRE)**239 [4293] 5-10-11 **0** CharlieDeutsch(10) 117+
(Charlie Longsdon) *plld hrd in midfield: effrt in 4th home turn: swtchd lft bhd horses to chal over 1f out: rdn and swtchd rt to ld ins fnl f: r.o stoutly: impressive* **3/1**[2]

154/ **2** *3/4* **Purple Bay (IRE)**192 [5179] 4-11-7 **0** DenisO'Regan 114+
(John Ferguson) *settled towards rr: 5th and clsng gng wl home turn: led w rdr looking rnd over 1f out: sn rdn: hdd ins fnl f: no imp after* **10/11**[1]

50/ **3** *7* **Chase The Spud**234 [4384] 5-11-0 **0** PaddyBrennan 100
(Fergal O'Brien) *taken down early: a abt same pl: drvn over 2f out: ev ch over 1f out: sn lft bhd by ldng pair* **33/1**

1- **4** *2 3/4* **Make Me A Fortune (IRE)**149 [389] 5-11-0 **0** PaulBohan(7) 105
(Steve Gollings) *led or w ldr: rdn and hdd over 1f out: sn wknd* **8/1**[3]

5 *1/2* **Kilkenny Kim (IRE)** 4-10-2 **0** KillianMoore(5) 90
(Jennie Candlish) *towards rr: rdn 6f out: no ch w ldrs fnl 3f* **33/1**

6 *2 1/4* **Cusheen Bridge (IRE)**137 5-11-0 **0** AdamPogson 95
(Charles Pogson) *w ldr: drvn 2f out: sn lost pl* **50/1**

0/ **7** *5* **Grand Gigolo (FR)**279 [3572] 4-11-0 **0** NoelFehily 90
(Ian Williams) *t.k.h towards rr: lost tch and edgd lft over 4f out* **33/1**

8 *15* **Fine Lily** 4-10-7 **0** AidanColeman 68
(Venetia Williams) *t.k.h early: midfield for 10f: struggling over 3f out: t.o* **16/1**

9 *35* **Little Pudding** 5-10-7 **0** DarylJacob 33
(Mary Hambro) *nrly a last: rdn 4f out: sn t.o* **12/1**

U **Dorton Lad (IRE)** 4-11-0 **0** SamTwiston-Davies
(Phil Middleton) *plld hrd and hung lft: dashed up to ld briefly after 4f: lost pl rapidly and virtually unrideable 5f out: veered violently lft and uns rdr 4f out* **20/1**

3m 54.6s (5.50) **Going Correction** +0.025s/f (Yiel) **10** Ran SP% **117.6**
Speed ratings: **88,87,84,83,82 81,79,72,55,**
toteswingers 1&2 £1.10, 1&3 £15.60, 2&3 £8.90 CSF £5.78 TOTE £4.80: £1.30, £1.10, £7.00; EX 7.40 Trifecta £165.00 Pool: £605.57 - 2.75 winning units..
Owner The Chosen Few **Bred** L W Doran **Trained** Over Norton, Oxon

FOCUS
Not a bad bumper and the first two are above average.
T/Plt: £35.10. Pool of £72,158.73 - 1500.34 winning units. T/Qpdt: £11.70. Pool of £4098.00 - 259.00 winning units. IM

552 WETHERBY (L-H)
Wednesday, October 16

OFFICIAL GOING: Good changing to good to soft after race 2 (2:50)
Wind: Blustery, half against Weather: Rain

1920 SPINAL RESEARCH RACHEL WRIGHT MEMORIAL HURDLE (JUVENILE MAIDEN HURDLE) (9 hdls) 2m 110y
2:20 (2:20) (Class 5) 3-Y-0 **£2,053** (£598; £299)

Form RPR

1 **Mixed Message (IRE)**35 3-10-5 **0** DannyCook 88+
(Brian Ellison) *chsd ldrs: j. slowly 4th: mstke 5th: led 3 out: pressed to last: drvn out whn edgd lft and kpt on run-in* **15/8**[1]

3- **2** *1 1/4* **Nellie Forbush**13 [1727] 3-10-5 **0** PaulMoloney 86
(Sophie Leech) *midfield: nt fluent 6th: sn rdn: hdwy 3 out: carried hd high u.p: r.o and tk 2nd towards fin: nt rch wnr* **6/1**[3]

2P- **3** *3/4* **Tinctoria**21 [1658] 3-10-5 **0** (p) BrianHughes 83
(Kevin Ryan) *chsd ldr: chalng 3 out: rdn and lugged lft appr last: nt qckn run-in: no ex and lost 2nd towards fin* **12/1**

6- **4** *7* **Hazza The Jazza**10 [1786] 3-10-9 **0** (p) JakeGreenall(3) 84
(Richard Guest) *hld up in midfield: effrt to chse ldrs 2 out: one pce and no imp run-in* **16/1**

5 *hd* **Eton Rambler (USA)**18 3-10-12 **0** (p) AndrewTinkler 86
(George Baker) *trckd ldrs: stmbld 3 out: sn rdn and outpcd: nt fluent last: kpt on run-in but no ch* **4/1**[2]

4- **6** *hd* **Ravens Nest**10 [1781] 3-10-12 **0** DavidBass 83
(Ben Pauling) *hld up: pushed along whn hit 3 out: styd on u.p fr last: nt trble ldrs* **20/1**

7 *6* **Attansky (IRE)**27 3-10-12 **0** HarryHaynes 79
(Tim Easterby) *hld up: pushed along appr 3 out: nvr on terms* **15/2**

0- **8** *5* **Duchess Of Dreams**10 [1786] 3-10-5 **0** WilsonRenwick 67
(Richard Guest) *racd keenly: hld up: u.p 3 out: n.d whn bmpd last* **100/1**

65- **9** *6* **Chloe's Image**10 [1786] 3-10-5 **0** RichieMcGrath 63
(Philip Kirby) *led: pushed along and hdd 3 out: wkng whn blnd 2 out* **14/1**

10 *2* **Green Special (ITY)**114 3-10-12 **0** LeeEdwards 66
(Frank Sheridan) *chsd ldrs: rdn and wknd after 2 out* **33/1**

R **Multilicious**44 3-10-5 **0** DougieCostello
(Tim Easterby) *nvr gng wl: a in rr: no imp whn rn out 3 out* **20/1**

3m 58.6s (2.80) **Going Correction** -0.10s/f (Good) **11** Ran SP% **114.5**
Speed ratings (Par 101): **89,88,88,84,84 84,81,79,76,75**
toteswingers 1&2 £2.20, 1&3 £21.70, 2&3 £21.70 CSF £12.30 TOTE £3.10: £1.50, £1.50, £3.80; EX 13.50 Trifecta £101.90 Pool: £796.08 - 5.85 winning units..
Owner W I Bloomfield **Bred** J Costello **Trained** Norton, N Yorks

FOCUS
It had been raining since an hour or so before racing, and the ground looked to be riding easier than the official description at this stage. Just an ordinary juvenile hurdle in which the gallop was a reasonably steady one. The first three home are all fillies. The form is rated around the second and third.

1921 CLAIM YOUR FREE BETS AT WELOVEFREEBETS.CO.UK H'CAP CHASE (13 fncs) 2m
2:50 (2:51) (Class 3) (0-135,135) 4-Y-0+ **£6,844** (£1,995; £998)

Form RPR

123- **1** **Lucky Landing (IRE)**13 [1730] 7-11-7 **130** NoelFehily 135
(Tony Coyle) *hld up in rr: mstke 6th: 7th and no imp on ldrs whn j.rt 3 out: clsd appr last: r.o to ld fnl 110yds: drvn out* **13/2**

BU5/ **2** *2 1/4* **Stagecoach Pearl**179 [5403] 9-11-7 **135** JonathanEngland(5) 137
(Sue Smith) *led to 2nd: remained prom: led 4 out: rdn whn hdd next: looked hld appr last: rallied run-in but no imp on wnr* **10/3**[2]

123- **3** *1 3/4* **Temple Lord (FR)**12 [1746] 7-11-0 **123** (bt) APMcCoy 124
(Jonjo O'Neill) *hld up in rr: hdwy 9th: led 3 out: rdn whn 2 l ahd appr last: hdd fnl 110yds: no ex* **5/1**[3]

213/ **4** *2 1/4* **Granville Island (IRE)**173 [5539] 6-11-1 **124** SeanQuinlan 122
(Jennie Candlish) *racd keenly: in tch: stl travelling wl bhd ldrs bef 4 out: effrt appr 2 out: kpt on u.p and edgd rt run-in: no imp towards fin* **8/1**

4P1- **5** *4* **Spock (FR)**19 [1670] 8-10-4 **120** (b) MrsAlexDunn(7) 115
(Alexandra Dunn) *chsd ldrs: lost pl appr 4 out: no imp on ldrs after: mstke whn hld last* **22/1**

2U4/ **6** *12* **Kealigolane (IRE)**180 [5370] 9-11-4 **127** BrianHughes 112
(Barry Murtagh) *prom: led 2nd: nt fluent 8th: hdd 4 out: wknd appr last* **25/1**

1/0- **7** *nk* **Diamond Frontier (IRE)**142 [508] 10-10-6 **122** JohnDawson(7) 105
(John Wade) *hld up in tch: lost pl qckly 9th: sn u.p and n.d* **14/1**

624- **8** *7* **Mibleu (FR)**46 [1478] 13-10-0 **109** BrendanPowell 88
(Colin Tizzard) *hld up: sme hdwy 4 out: hit 3 out: n.d after* **16/1**

123- **9** *45* **Castlelawn (IRE)**77 [1162] 6-10-9 **118** PeterBuchanan 55
(Lucinda Russell) *carried hd high and t.k.h: handy tl rdn and wknd appr 4 out: t.o* **3/1**[1]

The Form Book Jumps, Raceform Ltd, Compton, RG20 6NL.

15P- **10** *11* **Jack The Gent (IRE)**[10] 1782 9-11-9 **132**............................ BarryKeniry 59
(George Moore) *racd keenly: sn trckd ldrs: rdn and wknd bef 4 out: t.o*
22/1

3m 46.8s (-9.00) **Going Correction** -0.325s/f (Good) **10** Ran SP% **114.3**
Speed ratings (Par 107): **109,107,107,105,103 97,97,94,71,66**
toteswingers 1&2 £7.00, 1&3 £2.90, 2&3 £5.60 CSF £28.03 CT £117.33 TOTE £7.70: £1.60, £1.70, £2.50; EX 29.70 Trifecta £90.30 Pool: £848.00 - 7.03 winning units..
Owner Gary Dewhurst & Tony Coyle **Bred** James McGrath **Trained** Norton, N Yorks

FOCUS
A decent handicap chase and solid form, with a personal best from the winner. It was run at a fast pace.

1922 READ RACINGUK.COM/COLUMNISTS H'CAP HURDLE (9 hdls) 2m 110y
3:25 (3:25) (Class 3) (0-135,132) 4-Y-0+ **£5,523** (£1,621; £810; £405)

Form RPR

536- **1** **Stormy Weather (FR)**[18] 1685 7-10-11 **124**...........(p) NathanMoscrop[(7)] 128
(Brian Ellison) *hld up: hdwy after 6f out: rdn after 3 out: r.o after last: led post*
17/2

246- **2** *shd* **Knight In Purple**[75] 1185 9-11-4 **127**.......................(vt) PeterCarberry[(3)] 130
(John Mackie) *in tch: effrt to chal 2 out: led last: hrd pressed clsng stages: hdd post*
22/1

40- **3** *2 ½* **Dumbarton (IRE)**[53] 1378 5-11-5 **125**................................ BrianHughes 127+
(James Moffatt) *midfield: hdwy whn stmbld 3 out: sltly short of room after last: sn rdn: kpt on: no imp on front pair towards fin*
28/1

454/ **4** *2 ½* **Pas Trop Tard (FR)**[174] 5525 6-11-5 **132**.............(t) StephenMulqueen[(7)] 131
(Maurice Barnes) *chsd ldr: led 5th: rdn and hdd after 2 out: stl wl there last: one pce fnl 100yds*
28/1

221/ **5** *1* **Big Water (IRE)**[213] 4815 5-11-5 **125**............................... PaddyBrennan 123
(Alan Swinbank) *midfield: hdwy after 6th: rdn to ld after 2 out: hdd last: wknd fnl 100yds*
6/1[3]

224- **6** *5* **Tinseltown**[25] 1378 7-10-8 **114**... LucyAlexander 108
(Brian Rothwell) *led: hdd 5th: pushed along and lost pl bef 3 out: n.d after*
8/1

314- **7** *nk* **Taaresh (IRE)**[18] 1685 8-10-5 **114**................................. AdamWedge[(3)] 107
(Kevin Morgan) *nt fluent 1st: hld up: rdn appr 2 out: no imp on ldrs* **12/1**

12F/ **8** *4 ½* **Blackwater King (IRE)**[250] 4100 5-10-12 **118**................. JasonMaguire 107
(Donald McCain) *racd keenly: chsd ldrs: ev ch 3 out: rdn and wknd qckly after 2 out*
11/4[1]

505/ **9** *2 ¾* **Coverholder (IRE)**[179] 5400 6-10-5 **116**................. JonathanEngland[(5)] 102
(Sue Smith) *in tch: lost pl after 6th: n.d after*
8/1

121- **10** *18* **Strongly Suggested**[46] 1471 6-11-4 **124**............................(t) APMcCoy 99
(Jonjo O'Neill) *hld up: pushed along appr 3 out: nvr a threat* **5/1**[2]

/43- **11** *6* **Lifetime (IRE)**[94] 967 5-10-1 **107**.................................... AidanColeman 80
(Brian Ellison) *hld up in rr: niggled along whn nt fluent 5th: toiling bef 3 out*
25/1

3m 55.0s (-0.80) **Going Correction** +0.20s/f (Yiel) **11** Ran SP% **113.2**
Speed ratings (Par 107): **109,108,107,106,106 103,103,101,100,91 88**
toteswingers 1&2 £37.80, 1&3 £18.60, 2&3 £21.90 CSF £170.66 CT £4865.09 TOTE £11.60: £3.10, £4.50, £8.40; EX 222.10 Trifecta £470.30 Part won. Pool: £627.11 - 0.04 winning units..
Owner Keith Hanson & Steve Catchpole **Bred** Ecurie Skymarc Farm **Trained** Norton, N Yorks

FOCUS
With rain continuing to fall the official going was changed to Good to soft before this race. This competitive handicap hurdle was run at a fair pace and there were five fighting it out at the last.

1923 BOBBY RENTON H'CAP CHASE (16 fncs) 2m 4f 110y
3:55 (3:56) (Class 3) (0-135,135) 4-Y-0+
£6,256 (£1,848; £924; £462; £231; £116)

Form RPR

210- **1** **Grandads Horse**[18] 1686 7-11-12 **135**................................(p) NoelFehily 138+
(Charlie Longsdon) *in tch: mstke 5th: effrt bef 2 out: led last: styd on wl*
2/1[1]

211/ **2** *1 ¼* **Tara Rose**[181] 5359 8-11-0 **123**..............................(t) SamTwiston-Davies 126+
(Nigel Twiston-Davies) *hld up: hdwy appr 4 out: effrt 2 out: ev ch whn bmpd and pckd last: lost momentum: rallied to take 2nd towards fin* **13/2**

31F/ **3** *nk* **No Planning**[179] 5406 6-11-3 **126**... RyanMania 127
(Sue Smith) *chsd clr ldr: clsd 8th: upsides whn hit 4 out: led between last 2: hdd last: styd on but hld run-in*
6/1[3]

3F1- **4** *2 ¾* **Rudemeister (IRE)**[12] 1750 7-11-0 **123**.......................(t) WilsonRenwick 121
(Lucinda Russell) *chsd ldrs: rdn and nt qckn appr last: kpt on same pce run-in*
6/1[3]

230- **5** *3* **Owen Glendower (IRE)**[18] 1686 8-11-9 **132**...................(t) PaulMoloney 127
(Sophie Leech) *hld up in rr: struggling bef 4 out: styd on after last: nvr trbld ldrs*
50/1

F21/ **6** *4 ½* **Golden Call (IRE)**[515] 343 9-11-10 **133**.......................... PaddyBrennan 128+
(Tom George) *led: clr to 8th: pressed 4 out: hdd between last 2: lost gound gng in to last: wknd run-in*
8/1

P53/ **7** *34* **Riguez Dancer**[172] 5571 9-10-11 **120**............................... JasonMaguire 80
(Donald McCain) *racd keenly: hld up: rdn after 12th: sn toiling: lost tch bef 3 out: t.o*
12/1

1/1- **F** **Dorset Naga**[11] 1767 7-11-1 **124**.......................................(t) AidanColeman
(Anthony Honeyball) *hld up: rdn in 6th and 6 l off pce whn fell 3 out* **5/1**[2]

5m 2.2s (-5.60) **Going Correction** -0.025s/f (Good) **8** Ran SP% **112.7**
Speed ratings (Par 107): **109,108,108,107,106 104,91,**
toteswingers 1&2 £2.90, 1&3 £4.80, 2&3 £7.00 CSF £15.24 CT £64.96 TOTE £3.00: £1.60, £1.60, £2.10; EX 14.30 Trifecta £59.50 Pool: £965.50 - 12.16 winning units..
Owner Whites Of Coventry Limited **Bred** Wood Farm Stud **Trained** Over Norton, Oxon

FOCUS
Sound form to this handicap chase, which should produce winners. The winner is on a good mark and is rated below his best, while the secon was unlucky and the next two ran to their marks.

1924 POPLAR FARM CARAVAN PARK NOVICES' HURDLE (11 hdls) 2m 4f
4:30 (4:30) (Class 4) 4-Y-0+ **£3,249** (£954; £477; £238)

Form RPR

340/ **1** **Three Kingdoms (IRE)**[217] 4737 4-10-12 120................. DenisO'Regan 121+
(John Ferguson) *trckd ldrs: wnt 2nd appr 3 out: led on bit bef last: easily drew clr run-in*
9/4[1]

3- **2** *2 ¾* **Kilbree Chief (IRE)**[153] 345 5-10-12 0......................... PeterBuchanan 113
(Lucinda Russell) *led: nt fluent 1st: hdd 2nd: chsd ldr tl rdn appr 3 out: nt qckn u.p bef 2 out: kpt on to take 2nd run-in: no ch w wnr*
8/1[3]

421/ **3** *8* **Wild Card**[170] 33 6-11-5 0.. JasonMaguire 115+
(Donald McCain) *prom: led 2nd: hit 3 out: rdn whn jnd bef 2 out: hdd appr last: lost 2nd run-in: no ex*
10/3[2]

200/ **4** *6* **Herostatus**[77] 2930 6-10-12 0... BrianHughes 102
(Jason Ward) *midfield: sme hdwy appr 3 out: u.p bef next: nvr able to trble ldrs*
14/1

00/ **5** *6* **Alaplee**[178] 5428 5-10-12 0... HenryBrooke 95
(Chris Grant) *in rr: sme hdwy appr 3 out: plugged on but n.d*
200/1

600/ **6** *6* **Jokers And Rogues (IRE)**[223] 4613 5-10-5 0.............. JohnDawson[(7)] 90
(John Wade) *midfield: outpcd bef 2 out: nvr on terms w ldrs*
50/1

3- **7** *¾* **Rock A Doodle Doo (IRE)**[88] 732 6-10-12 0............... RichieMcGrath 89
(Sally Hall) *midfield: niggled along and outpcd bef 2 out: nvr threatened ldrs*
14/1

465/ **8** *3 ½* **Mister Bricolage (IRE)**[176] 5468 6-10-12 115...............(t) PaddyBrennan 90
(Fergal O'Brien) *in tch: outpcd bef 2 out: hanging lft and wl btn whn mstke last*
10/3[2]

/06- **9** *21* **Crooked Arrow (IRE)**[5] 1853 5-10-9 0............................. KyleJames[(3)] 67
(Marjorie Fife) *hld up: struggling bef 3 out: nvr on terms*
40/1

4/6- **10** *19* **Agesilas (FR)**[152] 359 5-10-9 0...................................... JohnKington[(3)] 50
(Andrew Crook) *in rr: sme hdwy into midfield 7th: wknd next: t.o* **100/1**

11 *8* **Rocky Island (IRE)**[164] 5-10-12 0..................................... SeanQuinlan 43
(Jennie Candlish) *racd keenly: trckd ldrs tl wknd appr 3 out: t.o* **25/1**

050/ **12** *½* **Darlington County (IRE)**[200] 5009 5-10-12 110.................. AdrianLane 42
(Donald McCain) *hld up: struggling bef 3 out: nvr on terms: t.o* **28/1**

6/ **13** *21* **Rayadour (IRE)**[72] 2329 4-10-12 0................................ WilsonRenwick 23
(Micky Hammond) *hld up: struggling bef 3 out: nvr on terms: t.o* **50/1**

5m 0.2s (0.70) **Going Correction** +0.20s/f (Yiel)
WFA 4 from 5yo+ 10lb **13** Ran SP% **116.5**
Speed ratings (Par 105): **106,104,101,99,96 94,94,92,84,76 73,73,65**
toteswingers 1&2 £5.40, 1&3 £3.10, 2&3 £4.80 CSF £20.00 TOTE £2.70: £1.60, £2.50, £1.50; EX 17.20 Trifecta £105.90 Pool: £1143.49 - 8.09 winning units..
Owner Bloomfields **Bred** Darley **Trained** Cowlinge, Suffolk

FOCUS
This ordinary novice hurdle was run at a modest pace which only lifted on the home turn. Nothing got into it from the back. The easy winner is on the upgrade.

1925 WETHERBY RACECOURSE & CONFERENCE CENTRE NOVICES' H'CAP CHASE (18 fncs) 3m 1f
5:00 (5:03) (Class 4) (0-110,109) 4-Y-0+ **£3,898** (£1,144; £572; £286)

Form RPR

4/2- **1** **Susquehanna River (IRE)**[153] 336 6-11-12 **109**.. SamTwiston-Davies 114
(Nigel Twiston-Davies) *mainly disp ld: def advantage appr 4 out: rdn bef last: all out towards fin*
9/4[2]

534- **2** *nk* **Dukeofchesterwood**[88] 1038 11-10-0 **83** oh2.................(p) BrianHughes 88
(Karen McLintock) *mainly disp ld: hdd appr 4 out: rallied bef 2 out: tk 2nd last: r.o and clsd on wnr towards fin*
15/2

/15- **3** *6* **Settledoutofcourt (IRE)**[139] 556 7-10-10 **93**................ PeterBuchanan 93
(Lucinda Russell) *hld up bhd ldrs: wnt 2nd appr 4 out: rdn whn lost 2nd last: no ex fnl 100yds*
3/1[3]

P00/ **4** *1 ¾* **Cornish Ice**[186] 5292 9-11-7 **104**.. CharliePoste 102
(Robin Dickin) *hld up bhd ldrs: effrt 4 out: rdn appr last: one pce run-in*
16/1

4PP/ **5** *13* **Dark Glacier (IRE)**[222] 4631 8-11-9 **106**...........................(p) JamieMoore 97
(Peter Bowen) *prom to 2nd: sn in rr: mstke 12th: struggling bef 4 out: no imp after*
7/4[1]

6m 22.0s (12.60) **Going Correction** +0.075s/f (Yiel) **5** Ran SP% **109.8**
Speed ratings (Par 105): **82,81,79,79,75**
CSF £16.86 TOTE £2.40: £1.20, £1.90; EX 11.00 Trifecta £38.00 Pool: £1563.45 - 30.79 winning units..
Owner The Wasting Assets **Bred** J W Nicholson **Trained** Naunton, Gloucs

FOCUS
This modest novice handicap was run at a steady pace, but still became rather a slog in the deteriorating conditions. The form is rated through the second.

1926 DON'T MISS THE BET365 CHARLIE HALL MEETING H'CAP HURDLE (12 hdls) 2m 6f
5:30 (5:31) (Class 3) (0-140,133) 4-Y-0+ **£5,817** (£1,695; £848)

Form RPR

02P/ **1** **Lie Forrit (IRE)**[291] 3339 9-11-10 **131**............................. PeterBuchanan 135+
(Lucinda Russell) *mde all: shkn up appr 3 out: gd jump last: styd on wl*
13/2

31F/ **2** *3 ½* **Purcell's Bridge (FR)**[170] 24 6-10-0 **117**................. ShaunDobbin[(10)] 118
(Rose Dobbin) *in tch: wnt 2nd 9th: rdn appr last: no imp on wnr run-in*
7/2[2]

165/ **3** *12* **Devotion To Duty (IRE)**[174] 5523 7-11-4 **125**................ RichieMcGrath 117
(Philip Kirby) *chsd wnr to 9th: rdn appr 3 out: one pce fr 2 out* **16/1**

040- **4** *¾* **Trucking Along (IRE)**[12] 1752 7-11-0 **121**............................. APMcCoy 113+
(S R B Crawford, Ire) *t.k.h: hld up in rr: nt fluent 8th: hdwy bef 3 out: rdn and no imp on ldrs appr 2 out: wl btn whn mstke last*
7/4[1]

/PF- **5** *3 ¼* **Danceintothelight**[8] 798 6-9-7 **107** oh1............... MissBeckySmith[(7)] 94
(Micky Hammond) *t.k.h: hld up in rr: hdwy to go prom 6th: nt fluent 7th: wknd after 9th*
18/1

/00- **6** *18* **Bourne**[142] 512 7-11-11 **132**... JasonMaguire 106
(Donald McCain) *hld up: u.p fr bef 7th: n.d after*
11/2[3]

/23- **7** *10* **Howizee**[134] 625 7-11-1 **129**...................................(t) StephenMulqueen[(7)] 98
(Maurice Barnes) *chsd ldrs: rdn appr 3 out: wkng whn blnd 2 out* **13/2**

5m 28.8s (2.00) **Going Correction** +0.30s/f (Yiel)
WFA 4 from 6yo+ 10lb **7** Ran SP% **111.8**
Speed ratings (Par 107): **108,106,102,102,100 94,90**
toteswingers 1&2 £3.70, 1&3 £10.70, 2&3 £14.50 CSF £28.44 CT £342.17 TOTE £7.20: £3.80, £2.60; EX 38.70 Trifecta £355.30 Pool: £1659.18 - 3.50 winning units..
Owner JW McNeill C McNeill Ms L Gillies **Bred** Niall McGrady **Trained** Arlary, Perth & Kinross

FOCUS
This fair handicap hurdle was run in fading light and in the worst of the ground.
T/Plt: £333.60 to a £1 stake. Pool: £66220.19 - 144.88 winning tickets T/Qpdt: £89.60 to a £1 stake. Pool: £4701.50 - 38.80 winning tickets DO

[1793]UTTOXETER (L-H)
Thursday, October 17

OFFICIAL GOING: Chase course - soft (good to soft in places); hurdle course - good to soft (soft in places; chs 5.8, hdl 6.0)
Wind: Light to moderate, against Weather: Overcast

1934 TEENAGE CANCER TRUST JUVENILE HURDLE (9 hdls) 2m
2:00 (2:00) (Class 4) 3-Y-0 **£3,378** (£992; £496; £248)

Form RPR

2- **1** **Herod The Great**[14] 1727 3-10-12 0.............................. RobertThornton 107+
(Alan King) *in tch: pushed along appr 3 out: moved upsides to chal 2 out: led appr last: styd on wl run-in*
4/11[1]

22- 2 2 ¾ **Instinctual**[13] [1743] 3-10-12 116..........(p) APMcCoy 100
(Brendan Powell) *led: pressed 2 out: rdn and hdd appr last: one pce run-in* **4/1**[2]
3 10 **War Lord (IRE)**[53] 3-10-12 0.......... BarryKeniry 91
(Philip Kirby) *trckd ldrs: rdn and outpcd whn mstke 2 out: tk mod 3rd last: no ch after* **10/1**[3]
4 3 **Green And White (ITY)**[64] 3-10-12 0.......... LeeEdwards 87
(Frank Sheridan) *hld up: nt fluent 4th: struggling 2 out: nvr a threat* **100/1**
- 5 ¾ **Innoko (FR)**[94] 3-10-7 0.......... JoshHamer(5) 85
(Tony Carroll) *hld up: nt fluent 3rd: j. slowly 6th and pushed along: nvr a threat* **25/1**
6 ½ **Bugsy**[332] 3-10-12 0..........(t) JasonMaguire 87
(Seamus Durack) *prom: j. slowly 5th: rdn and wknd 2 out* **40/1**
U **Lady Bonanova (IRE)**[156] 3-10-5 0.......... SamTwiston-Davies
(J R Jenkins) *plld hrd: hld up: struggling whn blnd and uns rdr 3 out* **66/1**

3m 57.0s (5.00) **Going Correction** +0.075s/f (Yiel) 7 Ran SP% **111.2**
Speed ratings (Par 103): **90,88,83,82,81 81,**
toteswingers 1&2 £1.10, 2&3 £2.00, 1&3 £1.50 CSF £2.05 TOTE £1.30: £1.10, £1.70; EX 2.40 Trifecta £6.00 Pool: £2260.82 - 280.80 winning units..
Owner S M Smith & D Minton **Bred** Whitsbury Manor Stud **Trained** Barbury Castle, Wilts

FOCUS
A weak juvenile hurdle run in a slow time. The form is rated around around the first two.

1935 EBF STALLIONS "NATIONAL HUNT" NOVICES' HURDLE (QUALIFIER) (9 hdls) 2m
2:30 (2:30) (Class 4) 4-6-Y-O **£3,798** (£1,122; £561; £280; £140)

Form RPR
0/2- 1 **Little Pop**[34] [1578] 5-10-12 0.......... SamTwiston-Davies 109+
(Nigel Twiston-Davies) *racd keenly: mde all: sn clr: pushed out and r.o wl after last* **7/2**[1]
26/ 2 3 **Vinnieslittle Lamb (IRE)**[238] [4347] 5-10-5 0.......... AlainCawley 99
(David Bridgwater) *chsd wnr: rdn appr 2 out: kpt on but no imp* **7/1**
32/- 3 4 **John Reel (FR)**[189] [5254] 4-10-12 0.......... HarrySkelton 105+
(Dan Skelton) *chsd ldrs: blnd 3 out: styd on same pce fr 2 out* **4/1**[2]
14- 4 8 **Chalk It Down (IRE)**[20] [1671] 4-10-12 0.......... APMcCoy 100+
(Warren Greatrex) *racd keenly: trckd ldrs: outpcd whn nt fluent 2 out: one pce and no imp after* **4/1**[2]
2/0- 5 hd **West End (IRE)**[11] [1794] 6-10-7 0.......... EdCookson(5) 95
(Kim Bailey) *midfield: stdy hdwy fr 2 out: kpt on wout threatening* **33/1**
530/ 6 4 ½ **Fairweather Friend**[180] [5413] 4-10-5 0.......... SeanQuinlan 85
(Jennie Candlish) *in rr: blnd 2nd: hdwy whn mstke 3 out: rdn after 2 out: kpt on steadily: no imp on ldrs: one pce run-in* **50/1**
400/ 7 10 **Celtic Abbey**[200] [5035] 6-10-12 115.......... JasonMaguire 82
(Donald McCain) *hld up: hdwy travelling wl after 6th: 5th 3 out: sn rdn: wknd after 2 out* **9/2**[3]
535/ 8 1 ¼ **Fiddleesticks (IRE)**[200] [5039] 5-10-12 0.......... CharlieHuxley 81
(William Kinsey) *towards rr: pushed along after 4th: plugged on fr 3 out: nvr bttr than midfield: n.d* **20/1**
33- 9 6 **Grand March**[30] [1599] 4-10-12 0.......... DougieCostello 76
(Kim Bailey) *midfield: mstke 1st: wknd 3 out* **20/1**
10 1 ¾ **Midnight Request** 4-10-12 0.......... FelixDeGiles 74
(Tom Symonds) *nt fluent: in rr: struggling after 4th: nvr on terms* **33/1**
0- 11 nk **Mattie's Passion (IRE)**[11] [1793] 6-10-12 0.......... SamThomas 74
(Jennie Candlish) *in rr-div: struggling after 4th: nvr on terms* **100/1**
12 18 **Keen Eye (IRE)** 4-10-7 0.......... MauriceLinehan(5) 58
(Jonjo O'Neill) *midfield: pushed along after 4th: wknd after 6th: t.o* **20/1**
13 4 ½ **No Routine (IRE)** 4-10-12 0.......... RichieMcLernon 54
(Jonjo O'Neill) *chsd ldrs: blnd 5th: wkng whn mstke 3 out: t.o* **20/1**

3m 51.8s (-0.20) **Going Correction** +0.075s/f (Yiel) 13 Ran SP% **120.8**
Speed ratings: **103,101,99,95,95 93,88,87,84,83 83,74,72**
toteswingers 1&2 £5.30, 2&3 £4.80, 1&3 £5.00 CSF £25.56 TOTE £5.80: £1.90, £3.50, £1.80; EX 44.50 Trifecta £133.80 Pool: £1166.55 - 6.53 winning units..
Owner Mrs S Such **Bred** Jethro Bloodstock **Trained** Naunton, Gloucs

FOCUS
An ordinary novice hurdle, with small steps up from the first two. The third and fourth can rate higher on bumper form.

1936 HILTON HOTELS IN THE MIDLANDS H'CAP CHASE (18 fncs) 3m
3:00 (3:00) (Class 5) (0-100,99) 4-Y-0+ **£2,599** (£763; £381; £190)

Form RPR
P02- 1 **Bennys Well (IRE)**[11] [1798] 7-9-9 73 oh3.......... JonathanEngland(5) 83+
(Sue Smith) *mde all: rdn appr last: kpt on wl: a in control run-in* **3/1**[1]
356- 2 1 ¼ **Always Bold (IRE)**[25] [1634] 8-11-11 98..........(v) IanPopham 105
(Martin Keighley) *hld up: hdwy 13th: rdn to chse ldrs bef 4 out but no imp tl styd on to take 2nd last: clsd on wnr towards fin: nvr gng to get there* **9/2**[3]
4/4- 3 6 **Kilcascan**[11] [1798] 9-10-10 88.......... BenPoste(5) 90
(Rosemary Gasson) *handy: pushed along after 14th: wnt 2nd 4 out: unable to get to wnr: rdn bef 2 out: lost 2nd last: one pce run-in* **7/2**[2]
5/2- 4 4 ½ **Brousse En Feux (FR)**[59] [1314] 10-11-8 95........(vt) SamTwiston-Davies 93
(Nigel Twiston-Davies) *chsd wnr to 4 out: rdn bef 2 out: no ex after last* **12/1**
/3F- 5 4 **Bobbisox (IRE)**[60] [1300] 8-10-7 85.......... KillianMoore(5) 78
(Alex Hales) *hld up: pushed along appr 14th: nvr able to get on terms w ldrs* **16/1**
502- 6 shd **Quinder Spring (FR)**[22] [1655] 9-11-5 99..........(p) GrantCockburn(7) 93
(Lucinda Russell) *hld up: hdwy appr 4 out: rdn whn chsng ldrs bef 3 out: sn no imp: wknd bef last* **13/2**
166- 7 ½ **Indian Citizen (IRE)**[119] [779] 6-10-8 81.......... DougieCostello 74
(Arthur Whiting) *prom: mstke 7th: lost pl 8th: rdn after 10th: su.p and struggling to get on terms w ldrs bef 4 out: blnd 2 out: mstke whn no ch last* **9/2**[3]
250- 8 28 **Ifonlyalfie**[74] [1202] 8-11-5 92..........(bt) TomMessenger 59
(Chris Bealby) *in tch: pushed along whn lost pl 12th: u.p after and n.d* **14/1**

6m 19.8s (4.70) **Going Correction** +0.25s/f (Yiel) 8 Ran SP% **117.2**
Speed ratings (Par 103): **102,101,99,98,96 96,96,87**
toteswingers 1&2 £4.90, 2&3 £5.30, 1&3 £3.90 CSF £17.87 CT £49.17 TOTE £4.00: £3.00, £1.10, £2.40; EX 18.00 Trifecta £80.20 Pool: £1228.06 - 11.47 winning units..
Owner Mrs A Ellis **Bred** J Costello **Trained** High Eldwick, W Yorks

FOCUS
A modest staying handicap. The winner was well in on his best form.

1937 CLUB WEMBLEY NOVICES' HURDLE (10 hdls) 2m 4f 110y
3:30 (3:30) (Class 4) 4-Y-0+ **£3,378** (£992; £496; £248)

Form RPR
1 **Flemenson (IRE)**[204] 4-10-12 0.......... APMcCoy 120+
(Jonjo O'Neill) *chsd ldrs: wnt 2nd 3 out: str chal 2 out: rdn to ld narrowly last: kpt on and fnd ex cl home* **11/4**[2]
11P/ 2 ¾ **Ashes House (IRE)**[342] [2310] 7-10-12 0.......... RobertThornton 120+
(Rebecca Curtis) *chsd ldr: led 2nd: hit 3 out: pressed fr 2 out: rdn whn rdr dropped whip appr last where hdd narrowly: continued to chal run-in: no ex cl home* **7/1**[3]
2/ 3 7 **Rio Milan (IRE)**[906] [50] 7-10-12 0..........(t) PaddyBrennan 113
(Fergal O'Brien) *hld up: in midfield 6th: effrt to chse ldrs appr 3 out: no imp on front pair: kpt on u.p fr 2 out but no ch* **20/1**
4 ¾ **By The Boardwalk (IRE)**[368] 5-10-12 0.......... SamTwiston-Davies 113
(Kim Bailey) *hld up: hdwy 7th: rdn whn chsng ldrs but no imp bef 2 out: kpt on u.p after but no ch w front pair* **14/1**
5 15 **Man In Black (FR)**[187] 4-10-12 0.......... DarylJacob 102
(Nick Williams) *chsd ldrs: unable to go w front pair appr 2 out: wknd bef last* **8/1**
/5S- 6 8 **Minellaforlunch (IRE)**[16] [1706] 6-10-12 0.......... DenisO'Regan 94
(Henry Oliver) *unruly gng to post: midfield: rdn and wknd 3 out* **10/1**
12/ 7 17 **Halo Moon**[288] [3458] 5-10-12 0.......... JasonMaguire 76
(Donald McCain) *led to 2nd: chsd ldr tl pushed along appr 3 out: wknd qckly* **6/4**[1]
8 8 **Oak Wood (IRE)**[172] 5-10-12 0.......... LeeEdwards 69
(John Upson) *midfield: wknd 7th* **100/1**
0- 9 5 **Dancing Lancer**[11] [1794] 4-10-9 0.......... JakeGreenall(3) 64
(Tim Walford) *midfield: rdn and wknd 7th* **100/1**
4P0/ 10 33 **Radio Nowhere (IRE)**[172] [19] 5-10-12 110.......... AdrianLane 35
(Donald McCain) *hld up: rdn after 7th: nvr a threat: t.o* **40/1**
160/ P **Shipton**[224] [4613] 4-10-12 0.......... AlainCawley
(Brendan Powell) *a bhd: struggling and lost tch after 6th: t.o whn p.u after 2 out* **66/1**
05- P **Wotsthecatch (IRE)**[43] [1499] 5-10-12 0.......... AndrewTinkler
(Michael Scudamore) *hld up: struggling 7th: t.o whn p.u bef 2 out* **100/1**

4m 57.3s (-1.70) **Going Correction** +0.075s/f (Yiel)
WFA 4 from 5yo+ 10lb 12 Ran SP% **117.7**
Speed ratings (Par 105): **106,105,103,102,97 94,87,84,82,70 ,**
toteswingers 1&2 £5.70, 2&3 £20.70, 1&3 £28.10 CSF £21.50 TOTE £3.40: £1.60, £1.90, £4.70; EX 26.50 Trifecta £214.60 Pool: £1048.41 - 3.66 winning units..
Owner Mrs Gay Smith **Bred** Grange Stud **Trained** Cheltenham, Gloucs

FOCUS
A fair novices' hurdle in which they went a decent gallop. The first two are probably a bit better than average.

1938 ST GEORGE'S PARK H'CAP HURDLE (9 hdls) 2m
4:00 (4:03) (Class 5) (0-100,100) 4-Y-0+ **£2,209** (£648; £324; £162)

Form RPR
600- 1 **Ivebeenthinking**[120] [765] 5-10-0 74 oh3.......... FelixDeGiles 83+
(Tom Symonds) *hld up: hit 4th: sltly hmpd 6th: rdn 3 out: stl 10th and no real imp 2 out: hdwy bef last where lft in ld: styd on wl run-in: sn drew clr* **25/1**
020- 2 5 **Kayfton Pete**[52] [1400] 7-11-11 99..........(t[1]) AdamPogson 103
(Charles Pogson) *nt fluent 1st: trckd ldrs: rdn appr 2 out: hmpd last: styd on to take 2nd towards fin: no ch win wnr* **25/1**
622- 3 ½ **Wom**[11] [1799] 5-11-6 99..........(b) TrevorWhelan(5) 101
(Neil King) *midfield: hdwy 5th: led 3 out: hdd 2 out: rdn whn stl wl there last: kpt on u.p run-in but hld* **8/1**
066- 4 ¾ **Seaside Shuffle (IRE)**[16] [1711] 8-10-13 87..........(tp) PaulMoloney 88
(Sophie Leech) *midfield: hdwy u.p 2 out: styd on run-in but nt quite able to chal* **16/1**
032- 5 1 ¼ **Knockgraffon Lad (USA)**[8] [1822] 6-11-9 97..........(tp) AlainCawley 99+
(Brendan Powell) *hld up: hdwy travelling wl appr 3 out: rdn to try and chal bef last where over 2 l down and hmpd by faller: no ex fnl 100yds* **7/1**[2]
430/ 6 6 **Tyrur Ted**[35] [4582] 8-11-10 98..........(t) LeeEdwards 93
(Frank Sheridan) *midfield: outpcd bef 3 out: styd on fr bef last: no imp on ldrs* **66/1**
202- 7 10 **Chankillo**[17] [1700] 4-11-2 90.......... WillKennedy 76
(Sarah-Jayne Davies) *midfield: pushed along bef 2 out: no imp on ldrs* **10/1**
53P/ 8 hd **Blake Dean**[451] [1050] 5-9-11 76.......... JonathanEngland(5) 62
(Sue Smith) *prom tl rdn and wknd appr 2 out* **4/1**[1]
9 nk **Born To Benefit (IRE)**[354] [2090] 7-11-7 95..........(t) PaddyBrennan 80
(Fergal O'Brien) *hld up: hdwy into midfield bef 3 out: no imp on ldrs: wknd 2 out* **20/1**
3/0- 10 2 ¾ **Prickles**[36] [1567] 8-11-6 97.......... MichealNolan(3) 80
(Richard Woollacott) *trckd ldrs tl rdn and wknd appr 3 out* **20/1**
/36- 11 nse **Kingaroo (IRE)**[60] [1306] 7-10-2 76.......... RyanMahon 59
(Garry Woodward) *trckd ldrs tl wknd after 6th* **8/1**
325- 12 2 ¼ **Swift Escape**[36] [1561] 6-11-9 100..........(p) MichaelByrne(3) 81
(Tim Vaughan) *led: hdd 3 out: rdn and wknd bef last* **15/2**[3]
/45- 13 3 **Maxdelas (FR)**[109] [854] 7-11-6 94..........(t) TomSiddall 72
(Roy Brotherton) *hld up: bhd whn mstke 6th: struggling after and n.d* **20/1**
/P5- 14 47 **Rearrange**[30] [1595] 4-10-0 74..........(t) TomMessenger 10
(Chris Bealby) *hld up: struggling after 6th: t.o 3 out* **33/1**
605- F **Bathcounty (IRE)**[37] [1551] 6-11-12 100.......... SamTwiston-Davies 107
(Barry Brennan) *chsd ldrs: led 2 out: rdn and over 2 l clr whn fell last* **9/1**
500/ U **My Nosy Rosy**[227] [4569] 5-11-0 88..........(t) DarylJacob
(Ben Case) *midfield tl blnd and uns rdr 6th* **12/1**

3m 52.8s (0.80) **Going Correction** +0.075s/f (Yiel)
WFA 4 from 5yo+ 9lb 16 Ran SP% **125.6**
Speed ratings (Par 103): **101,98,98,97,97 94,89,89,89,87 87,86,84,61,**
toteswingers 1&2 £0.00, 2&3 £68.50, 1&3 £0.00 CSF £520.68 CT £5377.42 TOTE £44.60: £7.90, £7.30, £1.70, £3.50; EX 1480.50 TRIFECTA Not won..
Owner Mrs V J Norbury **Bred** Mrs V J Norbury **Trained** Harewood End, H'fords

■ Stewards' Enquiry : Trevor Whelan caution: careless riding.

FOCUS
A moderate handicap with a dramatic end. The winner can probably go in again, and the next four were pretty much to their marks. The faller should win off this mark.

1939 BOWMER & KIRKLAND NOVICES' H'CAP CHASE (12 fncs) 2m
4:30 (4:31) (Class 4) (0-110,107) 4-Y-0 **£4,304** (£1,271; £635; £318; £159)

Form RPR
450/ **1** **Pinkneys Prince**[231] 4477 6-11-10 **105**................................. DarylJacob 113+
(Nick Williams) *hld up: hdwy 6th: chalng 3 out: led and mstke 2 out: r.o gamely whn duelled for ld run-in: gamely prevailed* **14/1**
360/ **2** *nse* **Foundation Man (IRE)**[321] 2756 6-11-12 **107**......................... APMcCoy 114
(Jonjo O'Neill) *a.p: led appr 3 out: rdn and hdd 2 out: stl chalng last: r.o u.p whn duelled for the ld run-in: jst hld* **13/8**[1]
066/ **3** *4 ½* **Strawberry Hill (IRE)**[308] 3023 7-11-5 **100**............................ IanPopham 103
(Caroline Keevil) *in tch: effrt whn chsng ldrs appr 4 out: rdn bef 2 out: kpt on same pce run-in* **25/1**
0/4- **4** *nse* **Missionaire (USA)**[35] 810 6-10-3 **89**................................ JoshHamer(5) 92
(Tony Carroll) *hld up: hdwy appr 4 out: styd on run-in but no imp on front pair* **25/1**
031- **5** *10* **Cruise In Style (IRE)**[17] 1696 7-11-1 **99**.........................(bt) JamesBest(3) 97
(Kevin Bishop) *in tch: clsd 6th: chal 3 out: rdn bef last: wknd run-in* **10/1**[3]
505/ **6** *nse* **Rozolenn (FR)**[950] 4719 8-10-10 **96**................................ HarryChalloner(5) 91
(Venetia Williams) *midfield: rdn 7th: plugged fr 4 out: no imp on ldrs* **12/1**
533- **7** *1* **Lodgician (IRE)**[8] 1816 11-11-2 **97**......................(vt) SamTwiston-Davies 90
(Nigel Twiston-Davies) *trckd ldrs: outpcd bef 3 out: n.d after* **14/1**
/00- **8** *9* **Smart Catch (IRE)**[114] 833 7-11-4 **99**................................ LeeEdwards 86
(Tony Carroll) *hld up: mstke 4th and 6th: plugged on wout threatening fr 3 out* **33/1**
450- **9** *hd* **Hollins**[11] 1797 9-11-0 **102**.. JoshWall(7) 90
(Tony Forbes) *midfield: hmpd 5th: nt fluent 7th and pushed along: wknd 8th* **25/1**
P5/ **10** *2 ¼* **Unik De Nougi (FR)**[306] 3066 5-11-11 **106**...................(p) PaddyBrennan 91
(Tom George) *led: hdd appr 3 out: wknd bef 2 out* **10/1**[3]
6/4- **11** *10* **Rockchasebullett (IRE)**[21] 1664 5-11-12 **107**..................(t) AlainCawley 81
(Fergal O'Brien) *midfield: rdn appr 4 out: sn wknd* **14/1**
605/ **12** *25* **Classic Case (IRE)**[313] 2905 6-10-11 **92**.............................. WillKennedy 43
(Ian Williams) *in rr: struggling bef 8th: nvr on terms: t.o* **14/1**
6/3- **P** **Scottish Boogie (IRE)**[83] 1123 6-11-12 **107**.................(t) JasonMaguire
(Seamus Durack) *hld up in rr: hdwy 7th: nvr nr ldrs: wknd 3 out: t.o whn p.u bef last* **13/2**[2]
300/ **F** **Snowed In (IRE)**[203] 4992 4-11-1 **105**...........................(p) SeanQuinlan
(Jennie Candlish) *prom: cl 3rd whn fell 5th* **25/1**

3m 59.8s (4.80) **Going Correction** +0.25s/f (Yiel)
WFA 4 from 5yo+ 9lb **14 Ran SP% 122.3**
Speed ratings (Par 105): **98,97,95,95,90 90,90,85,85,84 79,66, ,**
toteswingers 1&2 £14.50, 2&3 £26.50, 1&3 £54.00 CSF £36.94 CT £612.28 TOTE £19.30: £3.10, £1.30, £10.50; EX 55.60 Trifecta £541.00 Part won. Pool: £721.43 - 0.03 winning units..
Owner Michael Stenning **Bred** Paul Brewer **Trained** George Nympton, Devon

FOCUS
An ordinary handicap with two well-treated chasers coming clear. The first three stepped up on their hurdles form.

1940 TEENAGE CANCER TRUST H'CAP HURDLE (10 hdls) 2m 4f 110y
5:00 (5:00) (Class 5) (0-100,100) 4-Y-0+ **£2,209** (£648; £324; £162)

Form RPR
/42- **1** **Silver Dragon**[5] 1873 5-10-11 **85**...................................... DougieCostello 91+
(Tony Coyle) *hld up: hdwy 5th: mstke 6th: sn rdn: styd on to ld last: in command cl home* **11/4**[1]
2 *1 ½* **Texas Rose (IRE)**[23] 1648 6-11-7 **100**................................ TonyKelly(5) 103
(Rebecca Menzies) *hld up: hdwy 7th: led 3 out: rdn and hdd last: stl ev ch run-in: one pce cl home* **16/1**
110/ **3** *10* **Nicene Creed**[174] 5538 8-11-12 **100**...............................(tp) PaulMoloney 94
(Sophie Leech) *midfield: chsd ldrs after 5th: outpcd bef 3 out: rallied u.p after 2 out: styd on run-in: no ch w front two* **20/1**
636- **4** *¾* **Inside Knowledge (USA)**[11] 1799 7-11-6 **94**.................(p) AdamPogson 89
(Garry Woodward) *prom: outpcd whn nt fluent 2 out: styd on same pce after* **10/1**
/UP- **5** *4* **Almadan (IRE)**[124] 750 5-11-5 **93**...........................(t) SamTwiston-Davies 85
(Kim Bailey) *hld up: hmpd 5th: outpcd bef 7th: rdn and hdwy appr 3 out: styd on bef last: one pce run-in* **5/1**[3]
001- **6** *11* **Award Winner**[80] 1136 10-11-8 **96**.................................(v) APMcCoy 78
(Brendan Powell) *led: hdd after 2nd: remained prom: ev ch 3 out: wknd bef last* **9/2**[2]
000/ **7** *8* **Ebony River (IRE)**[180] 5410 7-11-12 **100**........................... SeanQuinlan 73
(Jennie Candlish) *trckd ldrs: rdn appr 3 out: wkng whn hit 2 out* **20/1**
4/0- **8** *1* **Matako (FR)**[17] 1699 10-11-9 **97**.. IanPopham 69
(Caroline Keevil) *midfield: hmpd 5th: pushed along appr 7th: wknd bef 3 out* **25/1**
/U0- **9** *13* **Wicklewood**[23] 1643 7-10-3 **80**... AdamWedge(3) 40
(John Flint) *midfield: hmpd 5th: sn towards rr: pushed along appr 7th: btn bef 3 out* **40/1**
P50- **10** *3 ¼* **Word Of Warning**[20] 1675 9-10-10 **89**..............................(p) AdamNicol(5) 46
(Philip Kirby) *prom: led after 2nd: hdd 3 out: wknd bef 2 out* **9/1**
0U0- **P** **Samizdat (FR)**[102] 903 10-10-0 **74** oh8................................ LeeEdwards
(John Upson) *midfield: nt a fluent: hmpd 5th: sn in rr: t.o whn p.u bef last* **66/1**
0/0- **F** **Song Of Pride (GER)**[11] 1799 9-10-3 **77**.....................(b) TomMessenger
(Mandy Rowland) *trckd ldrs tl fell 5th* **80/1**
436- **B** **Blackstone Vegas**[11] 1797 7-10-9 **90**..............................(v) OllieGarner(7)
(Derek Shaw) *hld up: b.d 5th* **10/1**
2/0- **P** **Pampanito**[34] 1575 7-11-8 **96**.. JasonMaguire
(Donald McCain) *a bhd: t.o whn p.u bef 3 out* **22/1**

4m 59.4s (0.40) **Going Correction** +0.075s/f (Yiel)
WFA 4 from 5yo+ 10lb **14 Ran SP% 118.5**
Speed ratings (Par 103): **102,101,97,97,95 91,88,88,83,82 , , ,**
toteswingers 1&2 £16.90, 2&3 £31.80, 1&3 £27.30 CSF £41.39 CT £750.07 TOTE £5.00: £1.80, £3.90, £4.70; EX 55.30 Trifecta £554.00 Part won. Pool: £738.77 - 0.68 winning units..
Owner Tony Coyle **Bred** D L Pearcy **Trained** Norton, N Yorks

FOCUS
The concluding contest was a modest handicap hurdle. The winner built on his good Hexham run, with the second to his mark.
T/Jkpt: Not won. T/Plt: £86.90 to a £1 stake. Pool of £87,595.29 - 735.58 winning tickets. T/Qpdt: £50.00 to a £1 stake. Pool of £5,614.26 - 83.05 winning tickets. DO

[292]WINCANTON (R-H)
Thursday, October 17

OFFICIAL GOING: Good (good to firm in places; 9.7)
Wind: virtually nil Weather: mainly sunny with occasional shower

1941 BATHWICK TYRES BATH NOVICES' H'CAP HURDLE (10 hdls) 2m 4f
2:20 (2:20) (Class 4) (0-115,115) 3-Y-0+ **£3,249** (£954; £477; £238)

Form RPR
3/4- **1** **Letemgo (IRE)**[155] 317 5-11-5 **108**................................... DavidEngland 112
(Giles Smyly) *trckd ldr: chal 2 out: rdn to ld last: r.o wl* **40/1**
532/ **2** *2* **Upton Wood**[174] 5538 7-10-11 **103**................................ GilesHawkins(3) 106
(Chris Down) *racd keenly: led: jnd 2 out: sn rdn and hdd: nt fluent last: kpt on gamely but no ex* **16/1**
231- **3** *hd* **Golanova**[25] 1625 5-11-3 **109**... JoshuaMoore(3) 113+
(Gary Moore) *sn mid-div: hdwy after 3 out: chalng whn hit next: sn rdn and hung rt: ev ch last: kpt on but no ex* **9/2**[1]
111- **4** *2 ½* **Sugar Hiccup (IRE)**[43] 1495 5-11-8 **111**.......................... TomScudamore 111
(Jim Best) *trckd ldrs: rdn bef 2 out: styd on same pce* **8/1**
5/3- **5** *1 ¼* **Barton Jubilee**[152] 374 5-11-9 **112**......................................(t) NoelFehily 110
(Neil Mulholland) *mid-div: hdwy after 6th: rdn to chse ldrs appr 2 out: styd on same pce* **20/1**
3/6- **6** *1* **Rior (IRE)**[139] 563 6-10-10 **99**.. TomO'Brien 99
(Paul Henderson) *hld up towards rr: rdn and hdwy after 3 out to chse ldrs next: styd on same pce* **7/1**[3]
014/ **7** *18* **Jeano De Toulouse (FR)**[171] 33 6-11-7 **110**.............. LeightonAspell 91
(Oliver Sherwood) *mid-div: hdwy after 3 out: rdn bef next: wknd between last 2* **16/1**
2/2- **8** *18* **Buckhorn Tom**[23] 1645 5-11-12 **115**..................................... JoeTizzard 80
(Colin Tizzard) *trckd ldrs: pushed along after 6th: sn lost pl: wknd after 3 out: t.o* **5/1**[2]
F46- **9** *2* **Bolberry Springs**[17] 1700 6-10-0 **89**...........................(t) BrendanPowell 52
(Colin Tizzard) *towards rr: pushed along briefly after 2nd: sme prog u.str.p after 3 out: wknd next: t.o* **20/1**
04/- **10** *32* **Best Boy Barney (IRE)**[177] 5468 7-11-9 **112**...............(t) NickScholfield 47
(Jeremy Scott) *bhd fr 4th: t.o* **16/1**
/13- **11** *9* **Neston Grace**[23] 1639 5-11-1 **104**....................................... JamesDavies 30
(Simon Hodgson) *in tch: reminders after 6th: wknd bef 3 out: t.o* **10/1**
241- **F** **Chilworth Screamer**[39] 1527 5-11-8 **111**......................... RichardJohnson
(Chris Gordon) *mid-div: making hdwy whn fell 7th* **5/1**[2]
116- **U** **Sedgemoor Express (IRE)**[20] 1674 5-11-1 **107**........(tp) MarkQuinlan(3)
(Nigel Hawke) *towards rr whn stmbld and uns rdr 1st* **20/1**

4m 35.3s (-21.50) **Going Correction** -1.10s/f (Hard) **13 Ran SP% 118.6**
Speed ratings (Par 105): **99,98,98,97,96 96,89,81,81,68 64, ,**
toteswingers 1&2 £49.50, 2&3 £20.90, 1&3 £36.60 CSF £544.26 CT £3435.96 TOTE £27.90: £8.90, £5.20, £1.60; EX 251.60 Trifecta £410.20 Part won. Pool: £547.03 - 0.03 winning units..
Owner Anthony Ward-Thomas **Bred** Mrs Sharon Slattery **Trained** Wormington, Worcs

FOCUS
David England described the going as "nice, good ground". Sand had to be applied to bends after the stands, with one or two riders feeling the ground was a bit slippery where the grass was so lush. Little got into this modest handicap hurdle. Straightforward form.

1942 BATHWICK TYRES MIDSOMER NORTON NOVICES' H'CAP CHASE (21 fncs) 3m 1f 110y
2:50 (2:51) (Class 4) (0-110,105) 4-Y-0+ **£3,898** (£1,144; £572; £286)

Form RPR
4F1- **1** **Standing Ovation (IRE)**[7] 1830 6-11-6 **99** 7ex............(tp) ConorO'Farrell 114+
(David Pipe) *led 3rd: mde rest: nt fluent 9th and 4 out: shkn up and r.o stry after last: eased nr fin: readily* **3/1**[2]
563/ **2** *1 ½* **Tothemoonandback (IRE)**[171] 30 5-11-9 **102**............... JamieMoore 112+
(Gary Moore) *trckd ldrs: trckd wnr fr 12th: rdn after 4 out: lugging rt whn hit next and 2 out: flattered briefly after last: sn outpcd* **8/1**
6/4- **3** *13* **Glenwood Prince (IRE)**[16] 1707 7-11-2 **95**.................(t) NickScholfield 96+
(Jeremy Scott) *led tl 3rd: trckd wnr tl 12th: chsd ldng pair: nudged along whn stmbld bdly 4 out: sn rdn: styd on same pce fr next* **9/4**[1]
41P- **4** *39* **Maid Of Silk (IRE)**[49] 1437 7-11-4 **97**.................................(t) NoelFehily 58
(Neil Mulholland) *j.rt thrght: hld up in last but in tch: lost tch fr 14th: t.o* **9/1**
330/ **5** *13* **Zava River (IRE)**[181] 5387 6-11-12 **105**............................ BrendanPowell 55
(Jamie Snowden) *hld up bhd ldrs: rdn after 16th: sn no ch: wknd after 3 out: t.o* **16/1**
36P/ **U** **Ballyhilty Bridge**[235] 4417 7-11-5 **98**...................................... TomO'Brien
(Paul Henderson) *in tch: hit 12th: blnd bdly and uns rdr 15th* **8/1**
4/4- **P** **Milosam (IRE)**[167] 89 6-10-1 **80**.. JamesDavies
(Philip Hobbs) *trckd ldrs tl 14th: wknd 17th: t.o whn p.u bef 3 out* **4/1**[3]

6m 26.4s (-13.10) **Going Correction** -0.675s/f (Firm) **7 Ran SP% 113.9**
Speed ratings (Par 105): **93,92,88,76,72 ,**
toteswingers 1&2 £6.00, 2&3 £5.30, 1&3 £3.70 CSF £25.76 TOTE £3.40: £2.70, £3.70; EX 23.60 Trifecta £47.00 Pool: £773.11 - 12.33 winning units..
Owner The Bravo Partnership **Bred** Patrick McGrath **Trained** Nicholashayne, Devon

FOCUS
A good test of both stamina and jumping for these novices. The front pair were in control from a long way out. The winner can rate higher.

1943 BATHWICK TYRES BRIDGWATER H'CAP HURDLE (8 hdls) 2m
3:20 (3:24) (Class 3) (0-130,130) 4-Y-0 **£6,330** (£1,870; £935; £468; £234)

Form RPR
541- **1** **Alwaystheoptimist**[8] 1816 10-10-4 **115** 7ex...................... RyanHatch(7) 122+
(Phil Middleton) *hld up in last pair: hdwy 3 out: rdn to chal between last 2: led last: r.o wl* **11/4**[2]
151- **2** *2 ½* **My Brother Sylvest**[11] 1782 7-11-2 **120**.....................(b) TomScudamore 125
(David Pipe) *led: sn clr: rdn after 2 out: hdd whn nt fluent last: kpt on same pce* **7/4**[1]
113- **3** *7* **Mount Vesuvius (IRE)**[17] 1699 5-10-5 **109**.........................(t) TomO'Brien 107
(Paul Henderson) *chsd ldr: rdn bef 2 out: lost 2nd sn after: kpt on same pce* **4/1**[3]
10/ **4** *4* **Right Step**[34] 5388 6-11-1 **119**.. JamieMoore 113
(Alan Jarvis) *racd in 4th: rdn after 3 out: kpt on same pce fr next* **33/1**
0/0- **5** *4 ½* **Oscar Prairie (IRE)**[145] 481 8-11-7 **128**........................ GavinSheehan(3) 118
(Warren Greatrex) *outpcd in last: styd on same pce fr 2 out wout ever threatening to get involved* **14/1**

441- 6 20 **Multitude Of Sins**[17] 1697 6-11-5 123..........(p) JoeTizzard 95
(Colin Tizzard) *chsd ldr tl nt fluent 5th: drvn after 3 out: sn wknd: t.o* 5/1
3m 28.0s (-20.90) **Going Correction** -1.10s/f (Hard) 6 Ran SP% **109.3**
Speed ratings (Par 107): **108,106,103,101,99 89**
toteswingers 1&2 £4.90, 2&3 £5.30, 1&3 £3.90 CSF £7.80 CT £15.34 TOTE £4.50: £2.60, £1.50; EX 8.50 Trifecta £29.80 Pool: £1663.47 - 41.72 winning units..
Owner P W Middleton **Bred** Crandon Park Stud **Trained** Dorton, Bucks
FOCUS
No hanging around here. The winner may be capable of a bit better yet.

1944 BATHWICK TYRES YEOVIL H'CAP CHASE (17 fncs) 2m 5f
3:50 (3:50) (Class 3) (0-130,130) 4-Y-£4,920 (£4,920; £1,122; £561; £280)

Form RPR
14P/ 1 **Goring One (IRE)**[189] 5259 8-10-9 113.......... AndrewThornton 117
(Anna Newton-Smith) *trckd ldr: mstke 4th: losing pl and struggling 10th: lft 4th 4 out: hdwy after 2 out: led sn after last: kpt on: jnd on line* 20/1
123/ 1 dht **Jump City (FR)**[186] 5322 7-11-7 130.......... MrWBiddick(5) 139+
(Paul Nicholls) *trckd ldrs: wnt 2nd 8th: pushed along fr 11th: lft disputing ld whn nodded on landing 4 out: outrt ldr u.p after 3 out: idling gng to last: hdd run-in: rallied to join wnr on line* 7/2[2]
213- 3 1 1/2 **Cardigan Island (IRE)**[106] 877 8-10-13 120..........(tp) RobertDunne(3) 122
(Dai Burchell) *hld up in tch: rdn along fr after 9th: lft 3rd 4 out: ev ch last: styd on same but no ex* 10/1
354- 4 3 1/2 **Dark Energy**[21] 1663 9-11-5 123..........(t) TomScudamore 123
(Fergal O'Brien) *chsd ldrs: hit 5th: lost pl u.p 11th: plenty to do 4 out: styd on fr after 3 out but nvr rchd ldrs* 14/1
514/ 5 35 **Shuil Royale (IRE)**[184] 5341 8-11-4 122.......... LeightonAspell 98
(David Arbuthnot) *nvr fluent in last: nudged along whn mstke 12th: wknd after 4 out: t.o* 4/1[3]
2/P- 6 2 1/4 **Velator**[156] 296 6-11-9 127.......... AidanColeman 116+
(Anthony Honeyball) *hld up: pckd 8th: hdwy 10th: rdn after 13th: lft disputing ld 4 out tl blnd 3 out: wknd bef last: eased run-in: t.o* 4/1[3]
2/1- U **Al Alfa**[30] 1598 6-11-1 119.......... RichardJohnson
(Philip Hobbs) *j.w: led: 3 l clr and travelling best whn slipped on landing and uns rdr 4 out: unlucky* 5/2[1]
5m 6.5s (-18.70) **Going Correction** -0.675s/f (Firm) 7 Ran SP% **111.3**
Speed ratings (Par 107): **108,108,107,106,92 91,** WIN: GO £8.30, JC £2.30; PL: GO £6.20, JC £2.90; EX: JC/GO £23.00 GO/JC £56.30; CSF: GO/JC £42.54, JC/GO £26.44; TRI: JC/GO/CI£308.66 GO/JC/CI £368.99; TF: JC/GO/CI £167.90 GO/CI/JC £523.90. toteswinger: 1&1 £6.40, GO&3 £19.90, JC&3 £6.60 TR27 Owner.
Owner Mrs Angela Tincknell & W Tincknell **Bred** Erich Schmid **Trained** Ditcheat, Somerset
FOCUS
A decent but eventful handicap chase, with the bold front-running Al Alfa departing four out and then Velator, who was duelling with Jump City, losing his chance with a notable blunder at the next. Jump City is rated better than the bare result, with Goring One to his mark. Unseater Al Alfa looked the likely winner.

1945 BATHWICK TYRES TAUNTON H'CAP HURDLE (11 hdls) 2m 6f
4:20 (4:23) (Class 4) (0-105,103) 4-Y-0+ £3,249 (£954; £477; £238)

Form RPR
2- 1 **The Rattler Obrien (IRE)**[154] 326 7-11-4 95.......... HaddenFrost 103
(Martin Hill) *hld up towards rr: stdy prog fr 7th: chal gng to 2 out: led sn after last: nudged ahd: readily* 9/1[3]
3/4- 2 3/4 **Proper Villan (IRE)**[158] 233 8-11-12 103.......... MarkGrant 111
(Geoffrey Deacon) *mid-div: hdwy after 7th: led after 3 out: rdn after 2 out: pckd and hdd last: kpt on but a being hld by wnr* 25/1
422- 3 8 **Perfect Timing**[16] 1718 5-11-5 96..........(b[1]) BrendanPowell 96
(Johnny Farrelly) *trckd ldrs: rdn bef 2 out: kpt on same pce* 7/2[1]
43- 4 1 **Commitment**[119] 777 4-11-10 101.......... NoelFehily 100
(Neil Mulholland) *hld up on outer towards rr of midfield: nudged along and nt travelling after 6th: hdwy after next: rdn to chse ldrs 2 out: styd on same pce* 9/2[2]
600- 5 3 1/4 **Tae Kwon Do (USA)**[20] 1675 7-11-1 92..........(t) RichardJohnson 90
(Tim Vaughan) *hld up towards rr: rdn and stdy prog after 3 out: wnt 5th between last 2: wnt lft last: no further imp* 14/1
6 8 **Moon Prince (IRE)**[9] 1808 11-11-11 102 7ex..........(p) MartinFerris 94
(Michael Winters, Ire) *mid-div: hdwy after 7th: chal 3 out: rdn and ev ch bef next: sn outpcd: wknd between last 2* 7/2[1]
P44- 7 3 3/4 **The Good Guy (IRE)**[54] 1376 10-11-10 101.......... WayneHutchinson 87
(Graeme McPherson) *trckd ldrs: led 7th tl sn after 3 out: wknd between last 2* 16/1
P/P- 8 4 1/2 **Admiral Boom (IRE)**[161] 179 7-11-7 98.......... TomO'Brien 80
(Paul Henderson) *hld up towards rr: hdwy into midfield after 3 out: sn rdn: wknd next* 16/1
044- 9 hd **Marie Deja La (FR)**[23] 1645 7-10-12 99..........(p) LouisMuspratt(10) 80
(Chris Gordon) *trckd ldrs: rdn after 3 out: wknd next* 14/1
/23- 10 9 **Master Cardor Visa (IRE)**[158] 254 8-11-2 98.......... JamesBanks(5) 71
(Emma Baker) *mid-div: rdn after 3 out: wknd next* 10/1
/46- 11 8 **The Happy Warrior**[142] 519 5-10-3 83.......... GilesHawkins(3) 49
(Bob Buckler) *mid-div: hdwy 4th: led after 5th: nt fluent next: hdd 7th: wknd after 3 out: t.o* 16/1
5/6- 12 24 **Sovereigns Legacy**[12] 1768 6-10-0 77 oh5.......... ConorO'Farrell 21
(John Panvert) *led: j. bdly lft progively worse: hdd after 5th: wknd after 3 out: t.o* 33/1
5m 2.1s (-24.40) **Going Correction** -1.10s/f (Hard)
WFA 4 from 5yo+ 10lb 12 Ran SP% **119.5**
Speed ratings (Par 105): **100,99,96,96,95 92,91,89,89,86 83,74**
toteswingers 1&2 £46.30, 2&3 £16.30, 1&3 £5.50 CSF £202.56 CT £944.11 TOTE £8.30: £2.70, £7.00, £1.90; EX 351.90 Trifecta £1073.40 Part won. Pool: £1431.29 - 0.71 winning units..
Owner Spirit Of Devon **Bred** James Maher **Trained** Littlehempston, Devon
FOCUS
The front pair drew clear, and probably fair form for the level.

1946 BATHWICK TYRES SALISBURY MAIDEN HURDLE (11 hdls) 2m 6f
4:50 (4:55) (Class 5) 4-Y-0+ £2,599 (£763; £381; £190)

Form RPR
2/3- 1 **Billy No Name (IRE)**[13] 1749 5-11-0 121.......... JoeTizzard 116+
(Colin Tizzard) *mde all: in command whn blnd last: comf* 4/9[1]
3/2- 2 8 **Floral Spinner**[169] 70 6-10-7 110.......... BrendanPowell 98
(Bill Turner) *trckd ldrs: nudged along after 7th: rdn to chse wnr appr 2 out: styd on same pce* 7/2[2]
60- 3 14 **Church Hall (IRE)**[11] 1795 5-10-9 0.......... JamesBanks(5) 95
(Emma Baker) *trckd wnr tl rdn appr 2 out: sn one pce* 10/1
5- 4 1 3/4 **Micquus (IRE)**[25] 1625 4-11-0 0.......... MarkGrant 92
(Jonathan Geake) *trckd wnr tl rdn after 3 out: wknd bef next* 16/1
/24- 5 20 **Never Says Never**[133] 638 5-11-0 0.......... SamJones 81+
(Bob Buckler) *t.k.h: j.lft: hld up: hdwy 3 out: sn rdn: wknd bef next: t.o* 6/1[3]
00- 6 14 **Evergreen Forest (IRE)**[11] 1794 5-11-0 0.......... DavidBass 58
(Natalie Lloyd-Beavis) *in tch: effrt 3 out: wknd bef next: t.o* 50/1
7 83 **Spabreaksdotcom (IRE)**[1928] 8-10-7 0.......... ConorO'Farrell
(Liam Corcoran) *hld up: wknd after 7th: sn t.o* 80/1
P **With Hindsight (IRE)**[178] 5-10-9 0.......... CharlieWallis(5)
(Alan Jones) *hld up bhd: blnd 1st: wknd after 8th: t.o whn p.u between last 2: dismntd* 25/1
5m 4.2s (-22.30) **Going Correction** -1.10s/f (Hard)
WFA 4 from 5yo+ 10lb 8 Ran SP% **127.8**
Speed ratings (Par 103): **96,93,88,87,80 75,44,**
toteswingers 1&2 £1.30, 2&3 £3.50, 1&3 £2.30 CSF £3.10 TOTE £1.40: £1.02, £1.70, £2.60; EX 2.20 Trifecta £13.40 Pool: £2774.29 - 154.86 winning units..
Owner Mrs Jean R Bishop **Bred** Seamus O'Farrell **Trained** Milborne Port, Dorset
FOCUS
A weak maiden hurdle, lacking in depth. The easy winner stood out and is rated below his best, with the second 12lb off.
T/Plt: £120.30 to a £1 stake. Pool of £63444.34 - 384.95 winning tickets. T/Qpdt: £14.90 to a £1 stake. Pool of £4564.16 - 225.46 winning tickets. TM

1947 - (Foreign Racing) - See Raceform Interactive

[1927]PUNCHESTOWN (R-H)
Thursday, October 17
OFFICIAL GOING: Good

1948a GRABEL MARES HURDLE (GRADE 3) (11 hdls) 2m 2f
2:45 (2:45) 4-Y-0+ £14,532 (£4,247; £2,012; £670)

RPR
1 **Cailin Annamh (IRE)**[13] 1760 5-11-2 132..........(t) BarryGeraghty 142+
(Mrs John Harrington, Ire) *settled bhd ldrs in 4th: nt fluent 2 out and next: qcknd into st and swtchd to far side to chal: led bef last and drvn clr: eased cl home: comf* 8/11[1]
2 5 **Little King Robin (IRE)**[4] 1893 5-10-9 115..........(t) MarkWalsh 127
(Colin Bowe, Ire) *trckd ldr: 2nd 1/2-way got on terms fr 4th and led narrowly into st: sn strly pressed and hdd bef last where mstke: no imp on wnr: kpt on same pce run-in to hold 2nd* 11/2[3]
3 shd **Takeyourcapoff (IRE)**[34] 1459 8-10-13 118..........(tp) RobbiePower 131
(Mrs John Harrington, Ire) *trckd ldrs: 3rd 1/2-way: pushed along fr 2 out and clsd on outer to chal bef last: sn no imp on wnr: kpt on same pce fr last: jst hld for 2nd* 16/1
4 17 **Top Madam (IRE)**[12] 1775 7-11-6 134..........(t) MrHDDunne 124
(Donal Coffey, Ire) *led: 2 l clr at 1/2-way: reduced advantage whn mstke 4 out: sn jnd and hdd narrowly into st: no imp u.p bef last and dropped to 4th: wknd run-in* 3/1[2]
5 2 1/2 **Diyala (IRE)**[9] 1806 4-10-5..........(t) DavyCondon 103
(Gordon Elliott, Ire) *hld up towards rr: t.k.h: pckd sltly 4th: mstke in 5th at 7th and j.lft next: nt fluent 3 out and no imp in rr: kpt on fr last* 10/1
6 23 **Oscar's Passion (IRE)**[70] 1235 4-10-5.......... BryanCooper 80
(David Harry Kelly, Ire) *w.w in rr: nt fluent 6th: sltly hmpd 4 out: wnt mod 5th bef 3 out: no imp on ldrs bef next: one pce after and dropped to rr bef last* 66/1
4m 23.5s (-12.50)
WFA 4 from 5yo+ 9lb 6 Ran SP% **114.8**
CSF £5.78 TOTE £1.70: £1.02, £2.90; DF 4.00 Trifecta £28.30.
Owner Flyers Syndicate **Bred** A J Nevin **Trained** Moone, Co Kildare
FOCUS
An ordinary race for the grade and the pace was steady early on. The last five renewals have all been strong and the third helps with the standard.

1950a BUCK HOUSE NOVICE CHASE (GRADE 3) (13 fncs) 2m 2f
3:45 (3:47) 4-Y-0+ £14,532 (£4,247; £2,012)

RPR
1 **Art Of Logistics (IRE)**[12] 1778 5-11-0.......... BryanCooper 138+
(D T Hughes, Ire) *trckd ldr: t.k.h early: cl 2nd 1/2-way: led narrowly bef 7th tl hdd 5 out: clsd gng best into st to regain advantage 2 out: sn clr: kpt on wl fr last: comf* 1/1[1]
2 5 1/2 **Six Stone Ned (IRE)**[36] 1570 7-11-1 130..........(t) DavyCondon 132
(Noel Meade, Ire) *led: narrow advantage 1/2-way: hdd bef 7th tl regained advantage 5 out where nt fluent: strly pressed into st and hdd again 2 out: sn no ch w wnr: slt mstke last: kpt on one pce* 12/1
3 4 3/4 **Darwins Fox (FR)**[17] 1702 7-11-8.......... AELynch 135+
(Henry De Bromhead, Ire) *settled bhd ldrs: 3rd 1/2-way: nt fluent 4 out: pushed along fr next and no imp on ldrs fr 2 out: kpt on one pce* 13/8[2]
F **Takestan (IRE)**[5] 1882 10-11-1.......... APHeskin
(Patrick O Brady, Ire) *chsd ldrs in 4th: fell heavily 1st* 66/1
U **Saint Gervais (IRE)**[37] 1558 8-11-1.......... AndrewJMcNamara
(John E Kiely, Ire) *hld up in rr: j.rt at times: jinked sltly and uns rdr 4th* 11/2[3]
4m 28.2s (-13.10) 5 Ran SP% **112.7**
CSF £12.08 TOTE £2.30: £1.40, £2.00; DF 13.50 Trifecta £26.40.
Owner Munnelly Support Services Ltd **Bred** Butlersgrove Stud **Trained** The Curragh, Co Kildare
FOCUS
The winner was the form choice, but is rated only to his best. The form doesn't rate highly on the race averages.

1951a STAR BEST FOR RACING COVERAGE CHASE (GRADE 3) 2m 7f
4:15 (4:16) 5-Y-0+ £15,589 (£4,556; £2,158; £719)

RPR
1 **Toner D'Oudairies (FR)**[15] 1723 6-11-6 140..........(tp) BryanCooper 151+
(Gordon Elliott, Ire) *hld up: slt mstke 2nd and j. sltly lft at 11th: tk clsr order on outer in 3rd bef 4 out: clsd gng best on nr side to chal last: rdn and kpt on wl to ld nr fin* 8/1[3]
2 3/4 **Roi Du Mee (FR)**[12] 1776 8-11-8 156..........(t) DavyCondon 152+
(Gordon Elliott, Ire) *led narrowly tl hdd bef 3rd: regained advantage bef 5th: pushed along into st and strly pressed fr 2 out: hdd u.p run-in and no ex cl home* 2/1[2]
3 2 **First Lieutenant (IRE)**[176] 5515 8-11-10 170..........(p) DavyRussell 152+
(M F Morris, Ire) *trckd ldrs: clsr in 2nd for most after 7th: rdn in cl 3rd fr 2 out on far side: no ex u.p run-in: eased nr fin* 4/5[1]
4 11 **Noble Prince (GER)**[158] 259 9-11-6 146.......... BarryGeraghty 137
(Paul Nolan, Ire) *hld up towards rr: clsd bhd ldrs in 4th 3 out: sn pushed along and no imp fr next: wknd* 8/1[3]

5 7 ½ **Shabra Charity (IRE)**[15] 1723 8-10-10 111...............................(t) APHeskin 120
(Patrick O Brady, Ire) *trckd ldr tl led bef 3rd: hdd bef 5th and remained prom tl dropped towards rr bef 4 out: no imp u.p fr next: wknd* **66/1**

6m 3.8s (6.30) **5** Ran SP% **112.6**
CSF £25.35 TOTE £7.10: £2.20, £1.40; DF 23.20 Trifecta £48.80.
Owner Gigginstown House Stud **Bred** Comte Michel De Gigou **Trained** Trim, Co Meath

FOCUS
Gigginstown House Stud's dominance of this event continued but it was the outsider of their three runners leading home a one-two-three for Irish jumps racing's champion owners who were winning the event for the fourth time since 2008. The form is rated around the fourth and fifth. Toner D'Oudairies is progressing, but First Lieutenant was some way below his best.

1952 - 1953a (Foreign Racing) - See Raceform Interactive

[57] CHELTENHAM (L-H)
Friday, October 18

OFFICIAL GOING: Good (7.0)
All races on Round course, firm ground in chute.
Wind: Virtually nil Weather: Low cloud

1954 NEPTUNE INVESTMENT MANAGEMENT NOVICES' HURDLE (10 hdls) 2m 5f
2:10 (2:10) (Class 2) 4-Y-0+
£10,635 (£3,141; £1,570; £785; £392; £197)

Form RPR
111- 1 **Saint Roque (FR)**[130] 688 7-11-6 140...............................(t) DarylJacob 146+
(Paul Nicholls) *lw: trckd ldr: led appr last: drvn and hld on wl run-in* **11/4**[2]
112- 2 ½ **Rum And Butter (IRE)**[47] 1485 5-11-6 145...............................(p) APMcCoy 145+
(Jonjo O'Neill) *in rr but in tch: hdwy fr 6th: trckd ldrs 2 out: chsd wnr last: hrd drvn and kpt on wl run-in: styd on clsng stages but a hld* **2/1**[1]
211- 3 9 **Clondaw Draft (IRE)**[35] 1576 5-11-6 132............................ JasonMaguire 136
(Donald McCain) *led: rdn after 2 out: hdd appr last: wknd u.p run-in* **7/1**
465/ 4 5 **Pure Science (IRE)**[182] 5373 5-10-12 0................. SamTwiston-Davies 125+
(Nigel Twiston-Davies) *trckd ldrs in cl 3rd: j. slowly 7th: hit 3 out and rdn: j. slowly and wknd 2 out* **4/1**[3]
1- 5 hd **Cloud Brook (IRE)**[15] 1732 5-10-12 0.................................... NoelFehily 124
(Rebecca Curtis) *lw: in tch: rdn and nt fluent 3 out: lost pl next: sme prog again run-in* **7/1**
FU2- 6 4 ½ **Man Of Leisure**[37] 1564 9-11-6 139...............................(t) RachaelGreen 128
(Anthony Honeyball) *in rr: j. slowly 6th: hdwy 4 out: wl in tch next: wknd after 2 out* **16/1**

5m 8.86s (-4.54) **Going Correction** -0.425s/f (Good) **6** Ran SP% **110.9**
Speed ratings (Par 109): **91,90,87,85,85 83**
toteswingers 1&2 £1.10, 1&3 £2.00, 2&3 £2.60 CSF £8.72 TOTE £3.90: £2.20, £1.10; EX 7.40 Trifecta £28.90 Pool: £2,370.14 - 61.35 winning units..
Owner Chris Giles & Ian Fogg **Bred** Mme Genevieve Mongin **Trained** Ditcheat, Somerset

FOCUS
The forecast rain failed to materialise and it was good ground all over for the opening meeting here of the 2013/14 season. An intriguing little novice hurdle in so much that 50% of the field brought useful handicap form to the table, adding to the promise of the trio who were more unexposed. They went a fair enough gallop and the first pair fought it out from the last. Solid form, with the first two both decent novices.

1955 CHELTENHAM ANNUAL MEMBERS NOVICES' CHASE (14 fncs) 2m 4f
2:40 (2:40) (Class 2) 4-Y-0+ **£12,512** (£3,696)

Form RPR
262/ 1 **Third Intention (IRE)**[196] 5158 6-11-3 151...........................(t) JoeTizzard 148+
(Colin Tizzard) *mde all: shkn up run-in and styd on strly under hand riding* **11/8**[2]
/11- 2 1 ¼ **Rebel Fitz (FR)**[12] 1804 8-11-11 152................................. BarryGeraghty 155
(Michael Winters, Ire) *lw: j.big 1st and 2nd: trckd ldr: hit 3 out and lost momentum: drvn and rallied fr 2 out: kpt on u.p run-in but no imp on wnr* **4/7**[1]

4m 57.49s (-5.91) **Going Correction** -0.175s/f (Good) **2** Ran SP% **105.8**
Speed ratings (Par 109): **104,103**
TOTE £1.70.
Owner Robert And Sarah Tizzard **Bred** Richard Klay And Dr M Klay **Trained** Milborne Port, Dorset

FOCUS
Even before the defection of Taquin De Seuil this was a badly contested novice chase. However, it still served up an informative tactical match between two smart performers who were closely matched over both hurdles and fences. The winner was the form pick at the weights and this is probably not one to read too much into.

1956 PERTEMPS NETWORK H'CAP HURDLE (SERIES QUALIFIER) (12 hdls) 3m
3:15 (3:15) (Class 2) 4-Y-0+
£12,512 (£3,606; £1,848; £924; £462; £232)

Form RPR
2/1- 1 **Trackmate**[154] 358 7-11-4 **132**.. LiamTreadwell 138+
(James Evans) *in rr but in tch: hdwy 3 out: drvn appr last: qcknd run-in to ld fnl 110yds: hld on wl* **9/1**[3]
212- 2 hd **Benbane Head (USA)**[31] 1597 9-11-2 **130**.........................(t) IanPopham 136
(Martin Keighley) *chsd ldrs: chsd ldr 8th: led 4 out: rdn and jnd bef last: hdd fnl 110yds: rallied clsng stages but a jst hld* **16/1**
241- 3 2 **So Fine (IRE)**[14] 1747 7-11-2 **130**............................ RichardJohnson 133
(Philip Hobbs) *chsd ldrs: rdn 6th: drvn to chse ldrs 2 out: ev ch after last: one pce clsng stages* **16/1**
123- 4 ¾ **On The Bridge (IRE)**[76] 1195 8-11-11 **139**.......................... NickScholfield 141
(Jeremy Scott) *in rr: hdwy 8th: styd on fr 2 out: kpt on u.p run-in but nt rch ldrs* **12/1**
021- 5 2 ¾ **Up For An Oscar (IRE)**[14] 1752 6-10-4 **123**.................(tp) EdCookson[(5)] 123
(Kim Bailey) *lw: chsd ldrs: drvn to chal after 2 out: wknd fnl 150yds* **16/1**
0/5- 6 ¾ **Act Of Kalanisi (IRE)**[13] 1766 7-10-7 **128**............(bt) ChristopherWard[(7)] 127
(Dr Richard Newland) *in rr: hdwy to cl on ldrs 3 out: one pce run-in* **14/1**
045/ 7 5 **Rare Bob (IRE)**[14] 1761 11-10-12 **126**..........................(p) BryanCooper 121
(D T Hughes, Ire) *in tch: hdwy 2 out: sn rdn: styd on same pce appr last* **14/1**
0/3- 8 ½ **Cross Kennon (IRE)**[160] 215 9-11-12 **140**......................... SeanQuinlan 134
(Jennie Candlish) *in tch fr 6th: chsd ldrs 4 out: wknd bef last* **25/1**
4/1- 9 ¾ **Sinbad The Sailor**[17] 1707 8-10-3 **122**........................... TrevorWhelan[(5)] 116
(George Baker) *in rr: hdwy 4 out: chsd ldrs fr next: wknd bef last* **25/1**
2/0- 10 1 ¾ **Monetary Fund (USA)**[160] 215 7-11-2 **130**........................ AidanColeman 122
(Venetia Williams) *b.bkwd: in rr: drvn and sme hdwy 2 out: wknd bef last* **25/1**
154- 11 ¾ **Va'Vite (IRE)**[9] 1818 6-10-7 **126**.................................... JamesBanks[(5)] 117
(Anthony Middleton) *mid-div: hdwy 8th: wknd 2 out* **40/1**
212- 12 4 **Mission Complete (IRE)**[56] 1363 7-10-8 **122**.....................(p) APMcCoy 110
(Jonjo O'Neill) *chsd ldrs to 3 out: wknd next* **20/1**
F22/ 13 7 **Captain Sunshine**[218] 4747 7-11-9 **140**......................... GavinSheehan[(3)] 126+
(Emma Lavelle) *lw: in rr: hit 5th: mod hdwy and rdn whn hit 3 out: sn btn* **3/1**[1]
25P/ 14 1 **Viking Blond (FR)**[195] 5177 8-11-1 **129**...............(v[1]) SamTwiston-Davies 110
(Nigel Twiston-Davies) *led to 2nd: styd w ldr: led again 4th: hdd 4 out: wknd after 3 out* **8/1**[2]
251- 15 3 ¼ **Pure Faith (IRE)**[61] 1304 9-11-10 **138**...............................(t) TomO'Brien 116
(Peter Bowen) *hdwy 6th: chsd ldrs 4 out: wknd next* **22/1**
203- 16 1 ¾ **Possol (FR)**[35] 1581 10-10-10 **124**.............................. RobertThornton 100
(Henry Daly) *lw: chsd ldrs to 3 out: sn wknd* **33/1**
50/- 17 10 **Kilmacowen (IRE)**[320] 2810 7-11-0 **128**............................ PaddyBrennan 95
(Fergal O'Brien) *in rr: hdwy 8th: wknd after 3 out* **33/1**
150/ 18 5 **Tweedledrum**[183] 5360 6-9-12 **117**.....................................(p) BenPoste[(5)] 80
(Tom Symonds) *rdn 6th: bhd most of way* **16/1**
20F- 19 31 **Qulinton (FR)**[24] 1642 9-10-7 **121**................................(bt) BrendanPowell 56
(Johnny Farrelly) *led 2nd: hdd 4th: wknd 8th* **20/1**
03P/ 20 3 ¾ **Restless Harry**[175] 5540 9-11-4 **132**.................................... CharliePoste 63
(Robin Dickin) *lw: chsd ldrs to 6th* **22/1**

5m 46.96s (-16.44) **Going Correction** -0.425s/f (Good) course record**20** Ran SP% **128.7**
Speed ratings (Par 109): **110,109,109,109,108 107,106,106,105,105 104,103,101,100,99 99,95,94,83,82**
toteswingers 1&2 £88.60, 1&3 £49.50, 2&3 £26.90 CSF £127.92 CT £2307.85 TOTE £12.00: £3.30, £4.50, £4.20, £3.40; EX 235.50 Trifecta £1500.20 Part won. Pool: £2,000.37 - 0.51 winning units..
Owner B Preece **Bred** Silvano Scanu **Trained** Broadwas, Worcs

FOCUS
Another very competitive running of this staying handicap, the opening qualifier for the final back here at the festival in March, for which the first eight home qualify. It proved a proper test and the majority were in trouble from three out. Another step forward from the progressive winner, and the form has a solid look.

1957 RYMAN STATIONERY CHELTENHAM BUSINESS CLUB NOVICES' CHASE (19 fncs) 3m 110y
3:50 (3:50) (Class 2) 5-Y-0+
£12,512 (£3,696; £1,848; £924; £462; £232)

Form RPR
250- 1 **Twirling Magnet (IRE)**[20] 1686 7-11-8 142.........................(tp) APMcCoy 147+
(Jonjo O'Neill) *lw: in rr but in tch: impr fr 13th: styd on wl fr 3 out: chal last: sn led: styd on strly* **7/1**[3]
111- 2 4 ½ **Pantxoa (FR)**[17] 1709 6-11-8 142................................ WayneHutchinson 142+
(Alan King) *led: tendency to jump rt: rdn 3 out: blnd next: jnd last: sn hdd: no ex and styd on same pce run-in* **7/2**[1]
/11- 3 2 ¼ **According To Trev (IRE)**[44] 1494 7-11-8 0.........(t) SamTwiston-Davies 138
(Nigel Twiston-Davies) *in rr: hdwy to 4 out to trck ldrs 3 out and sn rdn: nt fluent 2 out: styd on same pce fr last to take 3rd fnl 50yds* **4/1**[2]
6/ 4 3 **Minella For Value (IRE)**[13] 1777 7-11-8 139............................ NoelFehily 136
(John Butler) *in tch: hdwy 15th: chsd ldr 3 out: sn rdn: dropped to 3rd last: wknd into 4th fnl 50yds* **8/1**
/2F- 5 3 ½ **Oscargo (IRE)**[58] 1338 9-11-5 128...............................(t) DarylJacob 129
(Paul Nicholls) *lw: in tch: hdwy 15th: trckd ldrs 3 out: wknd 2 out* **10/1**
/31- 6 nk **Faultless Feelings (IRE)**[37] 1563 7-11-5 127........................ IanPopham 130
(Martin Keighley) *chsd ldrs: hit 15th: lost pl 3 out: kpt on again run-in but nvr a threat* **10/1**
15/ 7 nk **Sizing Symphony (IRE)**[31] 1600 7-11-5 133............................... AELynch 129
(Henry De Bromhead, Ire) *it tch: hit 7th: drvn and hdwy 4 out: chsd ldrs next: wknd 2 out* **7/2**[1]
/13- 8 14 **Raajih**[22] 1663 5-11-8 130...(bt) JasonMaguire 122
(Gordon Elliott, Ire) *rdn 14th: a bhd: blnd 3 out* **25/1**
9 66 **Ultragold (FR)**[180] 5-11-8 125.. JoeTizzard 60
(Colin Tizzard) *chsd ldr fr 3rd: j. slowly and wknd 16th: t.o whn blnd 3 out* **20/1**

6m 6.43s (-11.87) **Going Correction** -0.175s/f (Good) **9** Ran SP% **114.8**
Speed ratings: **111,109,108,107,106 106,106,102,80**
toteswingers 1&2 £2.90, 1&3 £10.50, 2&3 £2.00 CSF £32.55 TOTE £8.30: £2.50, £1.70, £1.70; EX 27.00 Trifecta £89.80 Pool: £1,762.64 - 14.71 winning units..
Owner Mrs Gay Smith **Bred** G Quirk **Trained** Cheltenham, Gloucs

FOCUS
A fair and competitive staying novice chase. There was a sound gallop on and the form should work out. The cosy winner was the form pick but this was probably a step up.

1958 JACK DEE HERE ON 31ST OCTOBER MAIDEN HURDLE (8 hdls) 2m 110y
4:25 (4:25) (Class 3) 4-Y-0+
£6,256 (£1,848; £924; £462; £231; £116)

Form RPR
230/ 1 **Lac Fontana (FR)**[217] 4767 4-11-0 130................................ DarylJacob 116+
(Paul Nicholls) *lw: led and sn cl: mde all: drvn run in: unchal* **8/13**[1]
3- 2 4 ½ **Germany Calling (IRE)**[21] 1671 4-11-0 0.............................(t) NoelFehily 113+
(Charlie Longsdon) *in tch: hit 2nd: hdwy 3 out: chsd wnr next: kpt on u.p run-in but no imp* **4/1**[2]
3- 3 8 **Apollo Eleven (IRE)**[35] 1578 4-11-0 0.............................. JasonMaguire 105
(Donald McCain) *w'like: chsd wnr fr 2nd: rdn 3 out: dropped to 3rd next: sn no ch w ldng duo* **20/1**
2/ 4 6 **Hawaii Five Nil (IRE)**[226] 4599 5-11-0 0................................ APMcCoy 102+
(Jonjo O'Neill) *lw: j. slowly 2nd: in tch: j. slowly 3rd: outpcd 3 out: drvn and sme prog again run-in* **5/1**[3]
3/4- 5 5 **Mystifiable**[12] 1795 5-11-0 0...(t) PaddyBrennan 97
(Fergal O'Brien) *in rr: hit 3rd: hdwy and wl in tch 3 out: rdn and 4th next: nvr any ch w wnr and wknd sn after* **25/1**
435- 6 11 **Volcanic Jack (IRE)**[20] 1688 5-10-9 88................................ JoeCornwall[(5)] 85
(Michael Chapman) *towards rr most of way* **100/1**
/00- 7 2 ¼ **Cash For Steel (IRE)**[17] 1706 6-10-0 0.............................. DanielHiskett[(7)] 76
(Richard Phillips) *lw: chsd ldrs to 3rd: bhd fr next* **66/1**
5- 8 2 ¾ **Trois Vallees (USA)**[22] 1661 4-11-0 0.............................. PeterBuchanan 84
(Lucinda Russell) *in rr: hdwy 3 out: wknd next* **33/1**
212/ 9 12 **Be Bop Boru (IRE)**[286] 3504 6-11-0 0............................. RichardJohnson 70
(Tim Vaughan) *towards rr most of way* **9/1**
10 8 **Into The Wind**[60] 6-10-2 0....................................... TrevorWhelan[(5)] 56
(Jim Best) *b.bkwd: a in rr* **66/1**

3m 55.06s (-6.94) **Going Correction** -0.425s/f (Good) **10** Ran SP% **124.1**
Speed ratings (Par 107): **99,96,93,90,87 82,81,80,74,71**
CSF £3.70 TOTE £1.70: £1.10, £1.50, £4.40; EX 5.70 Trifecta £19.80 Pool: £2,468.11 - 93.02 winning units..

Owner Potensis Limited **Bred** S C A La Perrigne **Trained** Ditcheat, Somerset

FOCUS

This was all about Lac Fontana and he didn't disappoint, although he is rated a stone off his best in victory. The second is rated in line with his recent bumper win.

1959 FINE & COUNTRY NORTH COTSWOLDS AMATEUR RIDERS' H'CAP CHASE (19 fncs) 3m 110y

5:00 (5:00) (Class 3) (0-125,125) 4-Y-0+

£7,195 (£2,247; £1,123; £561; £280; £141)

Form RPR

/64- **1** **Hunters Lodge (IRE)**[53] 1396 7-11-3 **123**........................ MrJBargary(7) 130
(Nigel Twiston-Davies) *chsd ldrs tl lost pl 4 out: rallied fr 2 out: stl plenty to do last: fin wl to ld cl home* **8/1**

4P6- **2** *¾* **Five Star Wilsham (IRE)**[80] 1155 9-10-11 **117**............... MissVWade(7) 121
(Jeremy Scott) *chsd ldrs: rdn and outpcd after 3 out: plenty to do appr last but styd on wl to take 2nd clsng stages: nt quite pce of wnr* **50/1**

P/2- **3** *1* **Civil Disobedience**[37] 1563 9-11-4 **117**.............................. MrJTCarroll 120
(Richard Woollacott) *chsd ldrs: rdn and outpcd fr 3 out: styd on appr last: fin wl to take 3rd clsng stages: nt pce of ldng duo* **11/1**

130/ **4** *½* **Handy Andy (IRE)**[184] 5351 7-11-3 **123**...........................(t) MrMLegg(7) 129+
(Colin Tizzard) *in tch: hdwy to chse ldr 15th: chalng whn lft in ld 3 out: narrowly hdd whn lft 6 l clr last: wknd and lost three pls clsng stages* **16/1**

503/ **5** *¾* **Fredo (IRE)**[184] 5351 9-11-9 **122**.............................. MrSWaley-Cohen 128+
(Ian Williams) *lw: chsd ldrs: drvn to chal 2 out: upsides whn blnd last: rallied to chse wnr: no imp and wknd clsng stages* **7/1[3]**

4P0- **6** *2 ½* **River D'Or (FR)**[107] 871 8-10-0 **102**........................ MrFMitchell(3) 102
(Sophie Leech) *in rr: plenty to do fr 3 out: kpt on last: fin wl: nt rch ldrs* **20/1**

355/ **7** *1* **Our Island (IRE)**[219] 4732 8-11-7 **125**.............................(v) MrBGibbs(5) 125
(Tim Vaughan) *lw: in tch: lost pl 15th: styd on again u.p fr 3 out: kpt on run-in* **7/1[3]**

24- **8** *19* **Chasers Chance (IRE)**[14] 1748 10-9-13 **105**.................. MrGBranton(7) 87
(Paul Henderson) *bhd fr 14th* **33/1**

4/3- **9** *1 ¼* **Dammam**[170] 62 8-10-8 **112**...................................(p) MissAEStirling(5) 94
(Fergal O'Brien) *pressed ldr: led 7th: styd hrd pressed: hdd 13th: wknd 16th: mstke 4 out* **11/2[2]**

412- **10** *20* **Font**[14] 1748 10-10-9 **108**..(t) MissGAndrews 71
(Lawney Hill) *towards rr most of way* **16/1**

3/U- **11** *13* **Robin Will (FR)**[156] 323 8-11-6 **119**........................... MrDerekO'Connor 70
(Richard Woollacott) *lw: hit 12th and 16th: bhd most of way* **5/1[1]**

11F- **12** *14* **Watch House (IRE)**[12] 1798 8-9-10 **102**.................. MrHAABannister(7) 41
(Michael Gates) *hit 3rd: a towards rr* **25/1**

344/ **13** *2 ¼* **The Big Freeze (IRE)**[180] 5443 7-10-3 **107** ow1............(vt) MrAJDoyle(5) 44
(Tim Vaughan) *in tch to 14th* **20/1**

342/ **F** **Oscar Davy (IRE)**[195] 5186 7-10-9 **115**........................... MrCGethings(7) 125+
(Philip Hobbs) *in tch: hdwy 11th: drvn to chal 2 out: slt ld and styng on whn fell last* **10/1**

\- **U** **Rockshandy (IRE)**[13] 1777 7-11-2 **122**.................. MissMMMcElligott(7)
(Patrick Neville, Ire) *led to 7th: styd pressing ldr: led again 13th: pushed along and stl narrow ldr whn blnd and uns rdr 3 out* **16/1**

6m 15.34s (-2.96) **Going Correction** -0.175s/f (Good) **15** Ran SP% **121.5**
Speed ratings (Par 107): **97,96,96,96,96 95,94,88,88,82 77,73,72, ,**
toteswingers 1&2 £69.70, 1&3 £23.70, 2&3 £69.30 CSF £366.39 CT £4368.30 TOTE £10.00: £2.70, £14.30, £3.80; EX 443.40 Trifecta £2056.30 Part won. Pool: £2,741.82 - 0.12 winning units..

Owner Exors of the Late Roger Nicholls **Bred** Rodney Deacon **Trained** Naunton, Gloucs

■ Jamie Bargary's first winner under rules.

FOCUS

This is always an open-looking handicap for amatuer riders. They went a solid gallop and, as is often the case at this venue, there was changing fortunes in the home straight. The winner might easily have finished fourth but for last-fence incidents but is rated to his C&D mark.

1960 REWARDS4RACING REWARDING YOUR PASSION CONDITIONAL JOCKEYS' H'CAP HURDLE (8 hdls) 2m 110y

5:30 (5:31) (Class 3) (0-140,135) 4-Y-0+

£6,256 (£1,848; £924; £462; £231; £116)

Form RPR

233- **1** **First In The Queue (IRE)**[37] 1564 6-11-9 **135**........ JeremiahMcGrath(3) 143+
(Nicky Henderson) *chsd ldrs: led bef 2 out: drvn clr run-in* **10/1**

4P0- **2** *7* **Canadian Diamond (IRE)**[14] 1745 6-10-11 **120**..........(p) MichealNolan 122
(Brendan Powell) *t.k.h: chsd ldrs: pressed wnr 2 out: outpcd bef last but kpt on wl for 2nd* **10/1**

231- **3** *6* **Foxcub (IRE)**[14] 1745 5-10-7 **119**.................................... BenPoste(3) 117
(Tom Symonds) *lw: chsd ldrs: hit 4th: styd on same pce for 3rd after 2 out* **3/1[1]**

2/3- **4** *5* **For Two (FR)**[6] 1866 4-10-12 **129**..........................(t) AndriasGuerin(8) 123
(Paul Nicholls) *lw: chsd ldrs: hit 3rd and 4 out: wl hld in 4th whn mstke last* **5/1[2]**

U12- **5** *1* **Anay Turge (FR)**[126] 735 8-10-9 **121**..............................(t) KieronEdgar(3) 112
(Nigel Hawke) *in rr: pushed along 4 out: styd on fr 2 out: nvr a threat* **16/1**

115- **6** *½* **Laudatory**[20] 1685 7-11-8 **134**... NicodeBoinville(3) 125
(Nicky Henderson) *chsd ldr tl appr 2 out: wknd sn after* **11/1**

312- **7** *hd* **Della Sun (FR)**[40] 1527 7-10-9 **123**... JoshWall(5) 114
(Arthur Whitehead) *in rr: sme hdwy fr 3 out: nvr rchd ldrs* **11/1**

443/ **8** *3 ¾* **Lancetto (FR)**[258] 3989 8-11-5 **131**.................................... AdamWedge(3) 118
(Evan Williams) *bhd most of way* **25/1**

111- **9** *5* **Belle De Fontenay (FR)**[37] 1562 8-10-13 **122**..............(p) TrevorWhelan 106
(George Baker) *led: hrd pressed 3 out: hdd bef next and wknd* **25/1**

043- **10** *8* **Sud Pacifique (IRE)**[55] 1378 5-10-4 **119**............................ NickSlatter(6) 94
(Donald McCain) *in tch tl wknd 4 out* **7/1[3]**

6/1- **11** *nk* **Castletown Bridge (IRE)**[22] 1661 6-10-12 **124**.......(t) KeithDonoghue(3) 99
(Gordon Elliott, Ire) *a in rr* **9/1**

210/ **P** **Leviathan**[204] 4988 6-10-8 **120**... HarryChalloner(3)
(Venetia Williams) *in tch: wknd 4 out: blnd next: p.u after 2 out* **16/1**

3m 51.05s (-10.95) **Going Correction** -0.425s/f (Good) course record
WFA 4 from 5yo+ 9lb **12** Ran SP% **118.5**
Speed ratings (Par 107): **108,104,101,99,99 98,98,96,94,90 90,**
toteswingers 1&2 £18.20, 1&3 £5.20, 2&3 £10.30 CSF £105.77 CT £374.43 TOTE £12.20: £3.50, £2.60, £2.10; EX 141.20 Trifecta £688.40 Pool: £1,468.30 - 1.59 winning units..

Owner Liam Breslin **Bred** Holborn Trust Co **Trained** Upper Lambourn, Berks

FOCUS

This looked to be another competitive handicap. A surprise step up from the impressive winner, but backed up by a good time and the second to fifth give the form a solid enough look.

T/Jkpt: Not won. T/Plt: £141.30 to a £1 stake. Pool: £157,807.38 - 815.00 winning units. T/Qpdt: £25.80 to a £1 stake. Pool: £8,690.60 - 248.35 winning units. ST

1961 - 1967a (Foreign Racing) - See Raceform Interactive

1954 CHELTENHAM (L-H)

Saturday, October 19

OFFICIAL GOING: Good changing to good to soft (soft in places) after race 4 (3.45)

All races on Round course, firm ground in chute.

Wind: Virtually nil Weather: Low cloud

1968 JOOLS HOLLAND HERE ON 9TH NOVEMBER NOVICES' HURDLE (13 hdls) 3m 1f 110y

2:00 (2:00) (Class 3) 4-Y-0+

£6,256 (£1,848; £924; £462; £231; £116)

Form RPR

F/1- **1** **Kings Palace (IRE)**[15] 1749 5-11-3 0.............................. TomScudamore 149+
(David Pipe) *led 3rd: clr 3 out: pushed out run-in: easily* **5/1**

2/1- **2** *18* **Creepy (IRE)**[18] 1706 5-11-3 131... IanPopham 132
(Martin Keighley) *chsd ldrs: wnt 2nd 3 out: no imp whn hit 2 out: no ch w wnr after* **10/3[1]**

13P/ **3** *2* **Monbeg Dude (IRE)**[218] 4770 8-10-12 0.............................. JamieMoore 126
(Michael Scudamore) *in rr: hit 9th: hdwy sn after: wnt 3rd 3 out: nvr any ch w wnr and j. slowly last: kpt on to go cl 3rd nr fin* **25/1**

111- **4** *13* **Kilbree Kid (IRE)**[23] 1662 6-11-6 130.......................(t) PaddyBrennan 122
(Tom George) *chsd ldrs: lost pl 4 out: styd on again appr last* **12/1**

412/ **5** *13* **Neltara**[178] 5493 9-11-3 132.. NickScholfield 107
(Claire Dyson) *led to 3rd: wknd 4 out* **25/1**

5/ **6** *1 ¾* **Minella Fiveo (IRE)**[21] 1693 5-11-6 115................................(p) NoelFehily 108
(John Butler) *in rr 7th: hdwy 9th: chsd wnr 4 out: wknd after 3 out* **50/1**

626/ **7** *4 ½* **Aerial (FR)**[258] 4003 7-10-12 0... DarylJacob 96
(Paul Nicholls) *in tch: slipped 6th: hdwy 9th: wknd 4 out* **11/2**

550/ **P** **Hold On Julio (IRE)**[175] 5576 10-10-12 132.................. RobertThornton
(Alan King) *in rr: reminders and hdwy after 7th: wknd u.p 4 out: t.o whn p.u bef 2 out* **9/2[3]**

1/1- **P** **Oscar Magic (IRE)**[19] 1695 6-11-6 129.................. SamTwiston-Davies
(Nigel Twiston-Davies) *chsd ldrs: hit 8th: wknd 4 out: no ch whn mstke 3 out: p.u bef next* **4/1[2]**

031- **P** **Vinnie The Fish (IRE)**[45] 1497 5-11-3 122....................(t) BrendanPowell
(Brendan Powell) *chsd ldrs early: rdn and bhd 7th: t.o whn p.u bef 3 out* **40/1**

6m 24.84s (-1.26) **Going Correction** +0.075s/f (Yiel) **10** Ran SP% **113.1**
Speed ratings (Par 107): **104,98,97,93,89 89,87, , ,**
toteswingers: 1&2 £4.70, 1&3 £7.10, 2&3 £15.70. CSF £21.03 TOTE £6.10: £2.10, £1.60, £5.00; EX 23.10 Trifecta £525.90 Pool: £11,63.56 - 1.65 winning units..

Owner Drew, George & Johnson Family **Bred** Kahill Burke Racing **Trained** Nicholashayne, Devon

FOCUS

Good ground and overcast conditions following 4mm of rain overnight. Six of the line-up had won last time out during the preceding six weeks, but the race didn't prove as competitive as might have been expected. A step up from the winner, who rates a smart novice.

1969 EQUUS-FINE DINING AT THE FESTIVAL H'CAP CHASE (14 fncs) 2m 4f

2:35 (2:38) (Class 2) 4-Y-0+

£31,280 (£9,240; £4,620; £2,310; £1,155; £580)

Form RPR

033/ **1** **Johns Spirit (IRE)**[182] 5406 6-10-3 **129**........................ RichieMcLernon 141+
(Jonjo O'Neill) *hld up in rr: hmpd 9th: stdy hdwy 3 out: led after 2 out: pushed out run-in: readily* **5/1[2]**

222- **2** *3 ½* **Rob Conti (FR)**[21] 1686 8-10-1 **130**.................................... JamesBest(3) 136
(Philip Hobbs) *chsd ldrs: wnt 2nd 3 out: ev ch 2 out: chsd wnr bef last: no imp but kpt on run-in* **16/1**

4/2- **3** *1* **Sew On Target (IRE)**[165] 157 8-10-1 **127**...................... BrendanPowell 132
(Colin Tizzard) *led: hdd 4 out: outpcd after 3 out but styd wl there: rallied and kpt on to take 3rd after last to cl on 2nd but no ch w wnr* **25/1**

43F/ **4** *nk* **Tartak (FR)**[197] 5160 10-10-4 **130**..(t) JackDoyle 135
(Victor Dartnall) *chsd ldrs: rdn 3 out: outpcd bef next: kpt on again run-in* **11/1**

F/4- **5** *½* **Astracad (FR)**[160] 249 7-11-2 **142**.............................. SamTwiston-Davies 146
(Nigel Twiston-Davies) *mid-div: hdwy to chse ldrs 10th: rdn and one pce after 3 out: kpt on again run-in* **10/1[3]**

223- **6** *1* **Woolcombe Folly (IRE)**[81] 1157 10-11-7 **152**................ MrWBiddick(5) 157+
(Paul Nicholls) *chsd ldrs: rdn 3 out: chsng wnr but u.p whn blnd last: nt rcvr* **22/1**

006/ **7** *7* **Renard (FR)**[177] 5523 8-10-6 **132**...................................... AidanColeman 129
(Venetia Williams) *chsd ldrs: wnt 2nd 10th: led 4 out: rdn and hit 2 out: hdd sn after: wknd bef last* **33/1**

/33- **8** *7* **Tony Star (FR)**[13] 1796 6-10-11 **137**.............................. RichardJohnson 133
(Philip Hobbs) *in rr: hit 1st: blnd 3rd: sme hdwy and mstke 3 out: mod progres again whn blnd 2 out* **11/1**

320- **9** *1* **Finger Onthe Pulse (IRE)**[21] 1686 12-9-9 **131**.......(t) JamesHuxham(10) 121
(Jonjo O'Neill) *chsd ldr: chal 6th to 9th: wknd bef 2 out* **28/1**

25F/ **10** *4 ½* **Kumbeshwar**[218] 4773 6-11-10 **150**............................ WayneHutchinson 136
(Alan King) *chsd ldrs: wknd 4 out* **25/1**

320/ **11** *½* **Vulcanite (IRE)**[221] 4724 6-10-11 **137**.. APMcCoy 126
(Charlie Longsdon) *in rr: blnd 3rd: hit 4th: sme hdwy whn hit 3 out: no ch whn blnd 2 out* **5/1[2]**

120/ **12** *11* **Malt Master (IRE)**[177] 5526 6-11-1 **141**........................ AndrewTinkler 116
(Nicky Henderson) *hit 2nd: in tch: btn whn blnd 4 out* **20/1**

PPP/ **13** *37* **Kingsmere**[195] 5196 8-10-2 **128**.. TomO'Brien 70
(Henry Daly) *hit 1st: in rr: blnd 11th and sn t.o* **16/1**

P20/ **P** **Tanks For That (IRE)**[175] 5575 10-11-10 **150**................. BarryGeraghty
(Nicky Henderson) *towards rr: hdwy 7th: wknd qckly 3 out: p.u bef next* **16/1**

125/ **U** **Vino Griego (FR)**[197] 5158 8-11-11 **151**.................................. JamieMoore
(Gary Moore) *in rr: hit 7th: stl bhd whn blnd and uns rdr 9th* **16/1**

214/ **P** **Easter Meteor**[185] 5353 7-11-4 **144**.. NoelFehily
(Emma Lavelle) *chsd ldrs: blnd 2nd and next: rdr lost iron: lost pl 6th: hit next and 8th: sn t.o: p.u bef 3 out* **7/2[1]**

4m 51.51s (-11.89) **Going Correction** -0.20s/f (Good) **16** Ran SP% **128.0**
Speed ratings (Par 109): **115,113,113,113,112 112,109,106,106,104 104,100,85, ,**
toteswingers: 1&2 £4.00, 1&3 £15.40, 2&3 £27.30. CSF £76.30 CT £1882.34 TOTE £6.10: £1.80, £2.50, £6.80, £3.90; EX 99.70 TRIFECTA Not won..

Owner Christopher W T Johnston **Bred** Arctic Tack Stud & Crossogue Stud **Trained** Cheltenham, Gloucs

FOCUS
The first of many ultra-competitive 2m4f-2m5f handicap chases to be held at Cheltenham during the season. As on the preceding day's racing, the 2m4f/4m chute was not in use owing to firm going. The cosy winner is rated to his best.

1970 MASTERSON HOLDINGS HURDLE (8 hdls) 2m 110y
3:10 (3:10) (Class 2) 4-Y-O
£18,768 (£5,544; £2,772; £1,386; £693; £348)

Form RPR
332/ 1 **Sametegal (FR)**[182] 5402 4-11-6 144 .... DarylJacob 143+
(Paul Nicholls) *cl up on outer: wnt 2nd 3 out: led on bit sn after next: rdn fnl 100yds: hld on gamely* **7/4**[1]
/11- 2 *nk* **Bayan (IRE)**[32] 1601 4-11-2 138 ....(tp) DavyCondon 139+
(Gordon Elliott, Ire) *trckd ldrs: nt fluent 2nd: gng wl 3 out: mstke next: rdn to go 2 l 2nd bef last: str chal to look dangerous 100yds out: jst hld after* **4/1**[2]
3/1- 3 *11* **Handazan (IRE)**[7] 1866 4-10-12 134 ....(p) RobertThornton 123
(Alan King) *led at stdy pce tl 4th: sn rdn and nvr looked to be gng wl enough after: led u.p after 5th tl sn after 2 out: wknd bef last: tk modest 3rd cl home* **7/4**[1]
2/3- 4 *¾* **Gassin Golf**[18] 1706 4-10-12 128 .... RichardJohnson 124
(Richard Lee) *hld up in last: mstke 3rd: effrt whn hit 3 out: cl 3rd after next: outpcd bef last: lost 3rd nr fin* **8/1**[3]
5/5- 5 *32* **In The Crowd (IRE)**[7] 1866 4-10-12 114 ....(t) RobertDunne 90
(Richard Price) *cl up: nt fluent 5th: rdn and struggling next: t.o bef 2 out* **100/1**
13/- 6 *34* **Leo Luna**[18] 5573 4-10-12 135 .... JamieMoore 56
(Gary Moore) *2nd tl led narrowly 4th tl 5th: rdn 3 out: stopped rapidly after next: t.o between last two: eased* **16/1**

3m 58.3s (-3.70) **Going Correction** +0.075s/f (Yiel) **6** Ran SP% **110.7**
Speed ratings: **111,110,105,105,90 74**
toteswingers: 1&2 £2.20, 1&3 £1.02, 2&3 £2.30. CSF £9.16 TOTE £2.30: £1.60, £2.30; EX 7.80 Trifecta £17.20 Pool: £1,875.04 - 81.67 winning units..
Owner Mr And Mrs J D Cotton **Bred** Pierre De Maleissye Melun Et Al **Trained** Ditcheat, Somerset

FOCUS
A competitive event, though in recent times not one to prove much of a springboard to major honours back here in March, as the last four winners all subsequently finished unplaced in either the Champion or Supreme Novices' Hurdle. The form is rated around the first two.

1971 SHOWCASE TROPHY (HANDICAP CHASE) (19 fncs) 3m 110y
3:45 (3:46) (Class 2) 4-Y-O+
£31,280 (£9,240; £4,620; £2,310; £1,155; £580)

Form RPR
P/1- 1 **Balthazar King (IRE)**[41] 1532 9-11-6 139 .... RichardJohnson 152+
(Philip Hobbs) *sn led: mde rest: forged clr bef 2 out: unchal* **7/2**[1]
004/ 2 *7* **Tour Des Champs (FR)**[182] 5404 6-11-0 133 .... SamTwiston-Davies 137
(Nigel Twiston-Davies) *chsd ldrs: wnt 2nd 8th to 3 out: sn rdn and one pce: rallied fr 2 out and kpt on wl to take 2nd clsng stages: no ch w wnr* **11/2**[2]
4U0/ 3 *¾* **Tullamore Dew (IRE)**[184] 5361 11-10-8 127 .... NoelFehily 130
(Nick Gifford) *in tch: hdwy to cl on ldrs 4 out: chsd wnr 3 out tl appr next: styd on wl to regain 3rd run-in* **20/1**
1- 4 *hd* **Mister Grez (FR)**[6] 1886 7-10-0 119 6ex .... HarrySkelton 125+
(Dan Skelton) *in rr: hdwy 12th: disputing 2nd whn blnd 3 out: chsd wnr again appr next: hung rt u.p run-in and lost two pls clsng stages* **13/2**[3]
B/0- 5 *3 ½* **Bradley**[155] 355 9-10-11 130 .... PaddyBrennan 131
(Fergal O'Brien) *in rr: hdwy fr 4 out: styd on fr 2 out and kpt on run-in: nt rch ldrs* **11/1**
053/ 6 *5* **Queiros Bleu (FR)**[50] 1459 9-10-9 128 .... AELynch 126
(Henry De Bromhead, Ire) *in rr and blnd 3rd: blnd 11th: hdwy and wnt lft and bmpd rival 3 out: keeping on again whn blnd 2 out: nt rcvr* **14/1**
163- 7 *17* **Kian's Delight**[21] 1686 5-10-11 130 .... TomO'Brien 110
(Peter Bowen) *chsd ldrs: wknd 4 out: no ch whn mstke next* **14/1**
661/ 8 *7* **Pickamus (FR)**[567] 5171 10-11-2 135 .... AndrewTinkler 109
(Henry Daly) *chsd ldrs: blnd 15th: wknd 4 out* **66/1**
203/ 9 *5* **Sire Collonges (FR)**[185] 5355 7-11-7 145 .... MrWBiddick[(5)] 114
(Paul Nicholls) *chsd wnr to 7th: wknd after 4 out* **10/1**
001- 10 *1 ¾* **Life Of A Luso (IRE)**[25] 1642 9-11-1 134 ....(t) NickScholfield 102
(Paul Henderson) *hit 4th: a in rr* **40/1**
0/0- 11 *16* **Becauseicouldntsee (IRE)**[16] 1735 10-10-5 124 ....(p) MartinFerris 77
(N F Glynn, Ire) *mstkes 15th and 4 out: a towards rr* **14/1**
12 *17* **Vif Argent (FR)**[121] 4-10-0 130 .... TomScudamore 57
(David Pipe) *in rr: blnd 11th: hdwy 14th: wknd after 4 out: mstke next* **8/1**
3P/- 13 *10* **Ace High**[350] 2180 9-11-3 136 .... JackDoyle 65
(Victor Dartnall) *chsd ldrs: wkng whn bmpd 3 out: no ch after* **14/1**
1P/- 14 *7* **Well Refreshed**[175] 5576 9-11-5 141 .... JoshuaMoore[(3)] 64
(Gary Moore) *mstke 3rd: a in rr* **25/1**
/13- 15 *2 ¼* **Lost Glory (NZ)**[111] 851 8-11-11 144 ....(t) APMcCoy 64
(Jonjo O'Neill) *bhd fr 7th: mstke 12th* **14/1**
031- P **Connectivity (IRE)**[22] 1669 9-10-11 130 ....(b) AidanColeman
(Dr Richard Newland) *chsd ldrs: wknd 10th: blnd 12th: p.u bef 15th* **16/1**

6m 11.59s (-6.71) **Going Correction** +0.025s/f (Yiel) **16** Ran SP% **131.2**
WFA 4 from 5yo+ 1lb
Speed ratings (Par 109): **111,108,108,108,107 105,100,98,96,95 90,85,82,79,79**
toteswingers 1&2 £6.60, 1&3 £20.00, 2&3 £25.50. CSF £24.98 CT £363.43 TOTE £4.60: £2.10, £1.70, £4.50, £2.20; EX 32.50 Trifecta £1042.20 Pool: £1,707.41 - 1.22 winning units..
Owner The Brushmakers **Bred** Sunnyhill Stud **Trained** Withycombe, Somerset

FOCUS
A really searching test. A step up from the impressive winner and the form looks solid.

1972 GO RACING WITH MCPHERSONRACING.CO.UK H'CAP HURDLE (10 hdls) 2m 5f
4:25 (4:28) (Class 3) (0-140,139) 4-Y-O+
£7,507 (£2,217; £1,108; £554; £277; £139)

Form RPR
10P/ 1 **Thomas Crapper**[224] 4663 6-10-9 122 .... CharliePoste 129+
(Robin Dickin) *t.k.h in midfield on outer: chal and nt fluent 3 out: led gng wl and hit next: 3 l clr last: hung on gamely cl home* **12/1**
1/1- 2 *¾* **Silver Eagle (IRE)**[157] 317 5-11-3 130 ....(t) NickScholfield 136+
(Kim Bailey) *cl up: drvn bef 2 out and sltly outpcd: rallied u.p to go 2nd last: styd on wl to make over 2 l fr last but wnr a jst had enough in hand* **3/1**[1]
5/1- 3 *nse* **Princely Player (IRE)**[14] 1766 6-11-7 134 .... RichardJohnson 138
(Philip Hobbs) *midfield: mstke 2nd: drvn hrd and gave himself too much to do fr 3 out: wnt 8 l 3rd at last: kpt on wl flat but nvr quite looked like making it* **12/1**
045- 4 *5* **Ixora (IRE)**[36] 1581 7-10-3 119 ....(v) GavinSheehan[(3)] 119
(Jamie Snowden) *midfield: effrt 8th: led bef 3 out and hit flight: drvn and hdd and hit next: nt qckn bef last* **20/1**
10/- 5 *6* **Phoenix Flight (IRE)**[32] 2386 8-10-2 115 .... LiamTreadwell 111
(James Evans) *plld hrd in last: nt fluent 2nd and whn sing to improve 8th: chsd ldrs in 4th briefly bef 2 out: sn no further imp* **25/1**
F/5- 6 *4* **Bygones Sovereign (IRE)**[168] 119 7-10-4 117 ....(p) TomScudamore 108
(David Pipe) *led: stdy pce early: rdn and hdd bef 3 out: no ex between last two* **7/1**[3]
/03- 7 *4* **Dragon's Den (IRE)**[8] 1858 6-10-0 113 .... AidanColeman 100
(Chris Down) *t.k.h: towards rr mostly: rdn and btn 3 out* **20/1**
110- 8 *31* **Church Field (IRE)**[48] 1485 5-10-6 119 .... RichieMcLernon 78
(Jonjo O'Neill) *settled in rr: hit 2nd: sme hdwy after 8th: chsd ldrs in 7th but bit to do bef 3 out: no further imp* **6/1**[2]
434- 9 *29* **Red Not Blue (IRE)**[15] 1747 10-11-5 132 .... AndrewThornton 65
(Simon Earle) *cl up tl mstke 7th and rdn: struggling after next: t.o and eased* **33/1**
6P4- 10 *5* **Court In Session (IRE)**[13] 1780 8-10-0 113 oh1 .... IanPopham 42
(Martin Keighley) *racd keenly and prom: ev ch whn hit 3 out: fdd tamely bef next: eased and hopelessly t.o* **20/1**
124- 11 *1* **Get Home Now**[48] 1485 5-11-0 127 ....(tp) TomO'Brien 55
(Peter Bowen) *midfield: mstke 8th: struggling whn mstke 3 out: eased and hopelessly t.o* **12/1**
235- 12 *16* **Teak (IRE)**[28] 1564 6-9-11 115 ow1 .... RobertMcCarth[(5)] 28
(Ian Williams) *prom and t.k.h tl 7th: stopped to nil and t.o after next: fin eventually* **12/1**
202- 13 *39* **Larks Lad (IRE)**[38] 1566 9-9-13 117 ....(b[1]) MauriceLinehan[(5)]
(Jonjo O'Neill) *bhd: last and struggling u.p bef 8th: sn hopelessly t.o: fin eventually* **25/1**
0/2- 14 *55* **Mister Newby (IRE)**[163] 185 7-10-5 118 .... SeanQuinlan
(Richard Phillips) *plld hrd in rr: lost tch 8th: sn t.o: walked up the hill fr last* **14/1**
1P/- U **Mickie**[186] 5339 5-11-3 130 .... RobertThornton 122
(Henry Daly) *cl up on inner: ev ch tl rdn 2 out: 7 l 4th whn stmbld on landing and uns rdr last* **8/1**

5m 26.1s (12.70) **Going Correction** +0.30s/f (Yiel) **15** Ran SP% **125.3**
Speed ratings (Par 107): **87,86,86,84,82 80,79,67,56,54 54,48,33,12,**
toteswingers: 1&2 £22.10, 1&3 £11.50, 2&3 £9.20. CSF £45.67 CT £467.94 TOTE £8.70: £2.80, £2.30, £3.50; EX 50.20 Trifecta £275.40 Pool: £1,145.94 - 3.12 winning units..
Owner apis.uk.com **Bred** Mrs J A Carr-Evans **Trained** Alcester, Warwicks

FOCUS
Driving rain had set in by the time of this race, which was delayed by three minutes after Bygones Sovereign originally appeared without any declared cheekpieces. The first two were on decent marks and are rated in line with their previous bests.

1973 ROYAL GLOUCESTERSHIRE HUSSARS NOVICES' CHASE (13 fncs) 2m
5:00 (5:00) (Class 2) 4-Y-O+ £12,685 (£3,869; £2,021; £1,097)

Form RPR
143/ 1 **Dark Lover (GER)**[237] 4409 8-11-2 0 .... DarylJacob 141+
(Paul Nicholls) *disp 2nd to 5th: mstke next: chsd ldr fr 9th: hit 3 out: 3 l down: pushed along and styng on but possibly nt gng as wl as ldr whn lft clr 2 out: n.d after* **7/4**[1]
2- 2 *28* **Sizing Italy (IRE)**[79] 1178 6-11-7 144 .... AELynch 121
(Henry De Bromhead, Ire) *in rr: hit 5th: j.big 8th: no ch w ldrs fr 4 out: lft disputing poor 2nd whn hmpd 2 out: kpt on same pce* **7/2**[2]
P/4- 3 *6* **Mr Watson (IRE)**[25] 1640 6-11-2 0 ....(b[1]) APMcCoy 111
(Jonjo O'Neill) *t.k.h: hit 5th: j. slowly and hdd 6th: j. slowly again next: hit 8th: wknd 4 out: lft poor 4th 2 out: styd on for mod 3rd run-in* **14/1**[3]
321- 4 *4* **Gud Day (IRE)**[24] 1657 5-11-7 118 ....(tp) PaddyBrennan 115
(Fergal O'Brien) *in rr: mstkes 6th and 8th: blnd 4 out: sme hdwy whn blnd next: lft poor 3rd 2 out: wknd into 4th run-in* **50/1**
122- F **The Cockney Mackem (IRE)**[23] 1661 7-11-7 132(v[1]) SamTwiston-Davies 120
(Nigel Twiston-Davies) *chsd ldrs: blnd 9th: u.p and hld in 3rd whn fell 2 out* **14/1**[3]
5/1- F **Balder Succes (FR)**[7] 1865 5-11-10 145 .... RobertThornton 151+
(Alan King) *disp 2nd tl led 6th: 3 l ahd and styng on strly whn fell 2 out* **7/4**[1]

4m 5.59s (7.59) **Going Correction** +0.25s/f (Yiel) **6** Ran SP% **110.2**
Speed ratings (Par 109): **91,77,74,72,**
toteswingers: 1&2 £1.10, 1&3 £4.10, 2&3 £6.30. CSF £8.22 TOTE £2.80: £1.90, £2.30; EX 8.30 Trifecta £66.40 Pool: £1,273.80 - 14.38 winning units..
Owner Des Nichols & Peter Hart **Bred** W Lohmann Jr **Trained** Ditcheat, Somerset
■ Stewards' Enquiry : Daryl Jacob two-day ban: used whip when clearly winning (Nov 2-3)

FOCUS
Not a race usually won by horses who go on to collect the season's major novice chase honours, though Arkle third His Excellency did take it 12 months earlier and Poquelin and Snap Tie in recent years as well. The winner is rated 10lb off his best hurdle figure with the faller looking set to win.

1974 HAVE YOUR CHRISTMAS PARTIES HERE STANDARD OPEN NATIONAL HUNT FLAT RACE 2m 110y
5:30 (5:31) (Class 4) 4-6-Y-O £4,548 (£1,335; £667; £333)

Form RPR
1/ 1 **Carningli (IRE)**[188] 5310 4-11-7 0 .... APMcCoy 121+
(Rebecca Curtis) *trckd ldrs: narrow advantage but jnd fr 5f out: drvn and styd on strly to assert over 1f out* **7/1**[3]
22/ 2 *3 ½* **Chase The Wind (IRE)**[188] 5324 4-11-0 0 .... NoelFehily 111+
(Warren Greatrex) *in rr: hdwy fr 5f out: drvn to dispute 2nd wl over 1f out: kpt on wl to hold that position fnl f but no imp on wnr* **14/1**
3 *¾* **Vazaro Delafayette (FR)**[217] 4-11-0 0 .... TomScudamore 110
(David Pipe) *trckd ldrs: drvn to dispute 2nd over 1f out: no imp on wnr and styd on same pce for 3rd fnl f* **9/2**[2]
2/3- 4 *1* **My Wigwam Or Yours (IRE)**[156] 338 4-11-0 0 .... BarryGeraghty 109
(Nicky Henderson) *in tch: hdwy to chse ldrs over 4f out: rdn and effrt fr 2f out: nvr gng pce to rch wnr and styd on same pce fnl f* **17/2**
1/ 5 *2* **The Govaness**[173] 36 4-11-0 0 .... PaddyBrennan 108
(Fergal O'Brien) *in rr: hdwy 5f out: chsd ldrs 3f out: sn rdn: styd on same pce fnl 2f* **25/1**
1/1- 6 *1 ½* **Regal Diamond (IRE)**[155] 359 5-11-10 0 .... TomO'Brien 116
(Peter Bowen) *chsd ldrs: pressed wnr fr 5f out to 2f out: wknd u.p fnl f* **7/2**[1]

22/ **7** *3 ½* **Brother Brian (IRE)**[179] 5483 5-11-0 0 DougieCostello 103
(Hughie Morrison) *in rr: hdwy fr 3f out: kpt on wl fnl 2f: nt rch ldrs* **20/1**

14/ **8** *5* **Gentleman Jon**[193] 5230 5-11-7 0 BrendanPowell 106
(Colin Tizzard) *in tch and drvn fr 5f out: styd on fnl 2f: nvr a threat* **16/1**

9 *4 ½* **Trickaway (IRE)**[195] 5-11-0 0 RichardJohnson 94
(Philip Hobbs) *t.k.h: led 3f: styd chsng ldrs: lost position 5f out: mod prog again fnl 2f* **11/1**

6/2- **10** *6* **Craiganee (IRE)**[156] 345 6-11-0 0 LeightonAspell 90
(Chris Down) *in rr: brief effrt 5f out: sn dropped away* **50/1**

2/ **11** *2* **The Kvilleken**[197] 5168 5-11-0 0 IanPopham 87
(Martin Keighley) *nvr beyond mid-div* **66/1**

66/ **12** *3 ¾* **Ma'Ire Rua (IRE)**[226] 4621 6-11-0 0 DarylJacob 84
(Alan Jones) *towards rr most of way* **100/1**

31/ **13** *1 ½* **Werenearlyoutofit (IRE)**[314] 2953 5-11-7 0 WayneHutchinson 90
(Graeme McPherson) *t.k.h: chsd ldrs 10f* **33/1**

0/6- **14** *3* **Innocent Girl (IRE)**[23] 1667 4-10-7 0 RobertThornton 73
(Lucinda Russell) *sme hdwy and in tch 6f out: sn wknd* **66/1**

331/ **15** *2* **Chill Factor (IRE)**[179] 5469 4-11-4 0 RachaelGreen(3) 85
(Anthony Honeyball) *in rr: sme hdwy 6f out: sn wknd* **10/1**

20- **16** *1* **Radharc Nahabhainn (IRE)**[18] 1712 5-10-7 0 NickSlatter(7) 77
(Fergal O'Brien) *bhd fr 1/2-way* **100/1**

17 *25* **Midnight Thunder (IRE)**[223] 4-11-0 0 JoeTizzard 55
(Colin Tizzard) *t.k.h: chsd ldrs 11f* **7/1**[3]

3- **18** *8* **Muckle Roe (IRE)**[23] 1667 4-11-0 0 SamTwiston-Davies 47
(Nigel Twiston-Davies) *led after 3f: hdd 5f out: sn btn* **25/1**

3m 57.95s (1.55) **Going Correction** +0.30s/f (Yiel)
WFA 4 from 5yo+ 9lb **18** Ran SP% **128.2**
Speed ratings: **108,106,106,105,104 103,102,99,97,94 94,92,91,90,89 88,76,73**
toteswingers: 1&2 £9.80, 1&3 £14.60, 2&3 £22.70. CSF £97.75 TOTE £7.80: £2.40, £4.10, £2.90; EX 102.00 Trifecta £1166.30 Pool: £2,044.99 - 1.31 winning units..
Owner The Newport Partnership **Bred** Butlersgrove Stud **Trained** Newport, Dyfed

FOCUS
A good-looking bumper run at a better pace than many, and six had gone clear by the turn for home. The winner looks a decent prospect.
T/Plt: £97.40 to a £1 stake. Pool: £175,161.58 - 1,311.84 winning units. T/Qpdt: £9.10 to a £1 stake. Pool: £9,176.15 - 744.50 winning units. ST

1785 KELSO (L-H)
Saturday, October 19

OFFICIAL GOING: Good to soft (soft in places; 6.4)
Fresh ground around bends on hurdles course.
Wind: Almost nil Weather: Overcast

1975 DALKEITH BOWLING CLUB "NATIONAL HUNT" MAIDEN HURDLE (DIV I) (8 hdls) 2m 110y
1:35 (1:36) (Class 5) 4-Y-0+ **£2,599** (£763; £381; £190)

Form RPR

1/ **1** **Plan Again (IRE)**[248] 4192 6-11-0 0 JasonMaguire 107+
(Donald McCain) *t.k.h: trckd ldrs: wnt 2nd bef 4th: led gng wl appr 2 out: sn clr: kpt on strly* **1/1**[1]

606/ **2** *6* **Bernardelli (IRE)**[279] 3643 5-11-0 0 DenisO'Regan 98+
(Nicky Richards) *hld up: hdwy 3 out: effrt and chsd (clr) wnr after next: kpt on: no imp* **9/1**

160/ **3** *8* **Spitz (FR)**[196] 5179 5-11-0 0 WilsonRenwick 89
(Rose Dobbin) *prom: stdy hdwy after 3 out: effrt next: sn outpcd* **11/2**[3]

360/ **4** *1 ¼* **Ellistrin Belle**[195] 5202 5-10-2 0 CallumWhillans(5) 82
(Donald Whillans) *chsd clr ldr: hit 3rd: rdn and lost 2nd bef next: drvn and outpcd after 3 out: no imp fr next* **80/1**

065- **5** *hd* **Aw Ripe China (IRE)**[15] 1754 5-10-11 0 JohnKington(3) 89
(Simon Waugh) *led and clr to 3rd: hdd whn mstke 2 out: sn btn* **22/1**

25/ **6** *13* **Lord Brendy**[190] 5279 5-11-0 0 KennyJohnson 80+
(Robert Johnson) *t.k.h: hld up and bhd: stdy hdwy bef 2 out: n.d* **16/1**

300- **7** *4 ½* **Rev Up Ruby**[8] 1853 5-10-0 0 JonathonBewley(7) 64
(George Bewley) *bhd: nt fluent 2nd: drvn and outpcd after next: nvr on terms* **40/1**

311/ **U** **Frankie's Promise (IRE)**[176] 5550 5-11-0 0 LucyAlexander
(N W Alexander) *prom on outside: mstke 1st: nt fluent and uns rdr next* **11/4**[2]

0/0- **U** **Quick Brew**[23] 1667 5-10-7 0 (t[1]) StephenMulqueen(7)
(Maurice Barnes) *hld up towards rr: outpcd whn blnd and uns rdr 4th* **200/1**

F- **P** **Gloshen (IRE)**[13] 1794 7-10-7 0 NathanMoscrop(7)
(Philip Kirby) *a wl bhd: no ch whn p.u bef 3 out* **100/1**

4m 1.0s (-0.80) **Going Correction** -0.30s/f (Good) **10** Ran SP% **117.4**
Speed ratings (Par 103): **89,86,82,81,81 75,73, , ,**
Tote Swingers: 1&2 £2.80, 1&3 £1.80, 2&3 £8.00 CSF £11.43 TOTE £1.90: £1.10, £2.00, £2.20; EX 10.70 Trifecta £24.70 Pool: £535.28 - 16.21 winning units..
Owner Paul & Clare Rooney **Bred** Mrs B Byrne **Trained** Cholmondeley, Cheshire

FOCUS
After 6mm of overnight rain and a heavy shower before the opener the ground was reckoned to be on the soft side of good. An ordinary maiden hurdle which was steadiily run. The wasy winner was value for further and can rate higher.

1976 CLIFFORD & MARTIN FIRTH MEMORIAL NOVICES' CHASE (16 fncs 1 omitted) 2m 7f 110y
2:10 (2:10) (Class 4) 4-Y-0+ **£4,548** (£1,335; £667; £333)

Form RPR

522/ **1** **Green Flag (IRE)**[182] 5405 6-11-4 0 PeterBuchanan 133+
(Lucinda Russell) *hld up: hdwy and prom 10th: wnt 2nd after 4 out (usual 5 out): rdn to ld bef last: hld on wl run-in* **12/5**[1]

3/1- **2** *nk* **Imperial Vic (IRE)**[156] 340 8-11-11 135 DannyCook 140+
(Michael Smith) *w ldr: led 11th: rdn after 4 out (usual 5 out): hdd bef last: rallied: hld cl home* **3/1**[2]

3- **3** *20* **Full Jack (FR)**[13] 1788 6-11-11 143 (b) DenisO'Regan 123
(Pauline Robson) *hld up in midfield on ins: nt fluent 7th: hdwy and prom after next: outpcd 3 out (usual 4 out): no imp fr next* **6/1**[3]

142- **4** *9* **Balding Banker (IRE)**[15] 1750 7-11-6 125 TonyKelly(5) 120
(Rebecca Menzies) *hld up: nt fluent 4th: stdy hdwy and prom 4 out (usual 5 out): outpcd after 2 out (usual 3 out): lft mod 3rd last* **10/1**

441/ **P** **Netminder (IRE)**[182] 5406 7-11-11 127 RyanMania
(Sandy Thomson) *mstkes in midfield: struggling fr 10th: t.o whn p.u bef 4 out (usual 5 out)* **16/1**

232- **F** **Foundry Square (IRE)**[16] 1728 7-10-11 135 (p) RyanHatch(7) 130
(Nigel Twiston-Davies) *chsd ldrs: nt fluent 4 out (usual 5 out): effrt after 2 out (usual 3 out): 3 l 3rd and one pce whn fell heavily last* **8/1**

343/ **P** **Witness In Court (IRE)**[182] 5408 6-11-4 0 JasonMaguire
(Donald McCain) *led to 11th: rallied: wknd qckly after 4 out (usual 5 out): p.u next* **6/1**[3]

0/1- **U** **Show Public (FR)**[168] 112 7-11-11 0 BarryKeniry
(Simon Shirley-Beavan) *midfield: blnd and uns rdr 8th* **25/1**

0P0/ **P** **Sagliere**[315] 2926 8-11-4 0 BrianHughes
(John Wade) *nt fluent in rr: lost tch 4th: t.o whn p.u after 9th* **250/1**

00/ **P** **Big George**[167] 6-11-1 0 JohnKington(3)
(Simon Waugh) *mstkes: in midfield: struggling fr 10th: t.o whn p.u bef 12th* **50/1**

5m 48.0s (-20.00) **Going Correction** -0.55s/f (Firm) **10** Ran SP% **115.3**
Speed ratings (Par 105): **111,110,104,101, , , , ,**
Tote Swingers: 1&2 £1.60, 1&3 £3.70, 2&3 £2.60 CSF £9.95 TOTE £3.30: £1.40, £1.70, £2.20; EX 10.00 Trifecta £36.60 Pool: £916.40 - 102.54 winning units..
Owner John R Adam **Bred** L M Walshe **Trained** Arlary, Perth & Kinross

FOCUS
A good-class novice chase. The two pacesetters set a very strong gallop and only six were still in contention at the normal five out. The second-last fence had to be omitted having been damaged on the first circuit. The winner looks a good recruit and this is solid novice form for the class.

1977 DALKEITH BOWLING CLUB "NATIONAL HUNT" MAIDEN HURDLE (DIV II) (8 hdls) 2m 110y
2:45 (2:45) (Class 5) 4-Y-0+ **£2,599** (£763; £381; £190)

Form RPR

1 **Vinny Gambini (IRE)**[944] 6-11-0 0 WilsonRenwick 107
(Rose Dobbin) *hld up in tch: stdy hdwy 3 out: effrt next: led run-in: drvn and hld on wl* **28/1**

342/ **2** *nk* **Ueueteotl (FR)**[173] 22 5-11-0 118 BrianHughes 109+
(James Ewart) *pressed ldr: led bef 3 out: rdn whn nt fluent next: jst in front whn mstke last: hdd run-in: rallied: jst hld* **5/4**[1]

1/0- **3** *1 ¾* **Orchard Road (USA)**[23] 1667 6-11-0 0 (t) PeterBuchanan 106
(Lucinda Russell) *prom: hdwy to press ldr bef 2 out: effrt and ev ch last: kpt on: hld nr fin* **12/1**

2/ **4** *1 ¼* **Gold Futures (IRE)**[181] 5428 4-11-0 0 BrianHarding 104
(Nicky Richards) *hld up: stdy hdwy to chse ldrs bef 2 out: rdn and one pce fr last* **9/2**[3]

0/ **5** *11* **Heart Dancer (FR)**[727] 2124 7-11-0 0[1] BarryKeniry 97
(Simon Shirley-Beavan) *hld up: effrt and pushed along after 3 out: outpcd fr next* **16/1**

6 *12* **Milan Flyer (IRE)**[150] 440 7-10-9 0 DerekFox(5) 83
(Noel C Kelly, Ire) *in tch: lost pl 3rd: struggling next: n.d after* **12/1**

7 *5* **Brighton Road (IRE)**[224] 4675 6-10-7 0 CallumBewley(7) 79
(R Mike Smith) *prom: effrt and rdn 3 out: wknd bef next* **66/1**

4P3/ **P** **Arizona River**[190] 5273 7-10-4 99 (t) KyleJames(3)
(Jason Ward) *t.k.h: led to after 4 out: sn wknd: t.o whn p.u bef 2 out* **50/1**

2/4- **P** **Another Mattie (IRE)**[157] 313 6-11-0 110 RyanMania
(N W Alexander) *hld up: rdn after 3 out: sn struggling: t.o whn p.u after next* **10/3**[2]

0/ **P** **Tchatchaco Ya Ya**[224] 4654 6-11-0 0 HarryHaynes
(Nicky Richards) *t.k.h: cl up to 4 out: sn struggling: t.o whn p.u after next* **100/1**

4m 0.2s (-1.60) **Going Correction** -0.30s/f (Good) **10** Ran SP% **114.9**
Speed ratings (Par 103): **91,90,90,89,84 78,76, , ,**
Tote Swingers: 1&2 £9.00, 1&3 £20.90, 2&3 £5.70 CSF £64.63 TOTE £30.20: £3.80, £1.10, £2.60; EX 102.70 Trifecta £275.70 Part won. Pool: £367.73 - 0.10 winning units..
Owner Mr & Mrs Duncan Davidson **Bred** Brian Mulcahy **Trained** South Hazelrigg, Northumbria

FOCUS
Division two of this ordinary maiden, and weaker than the first. The second was well below his best.

1978 EDF-ER FALLAGO RIG H'CAP CHASE (FOR THE MARSHALL TROPHY) (19 fncs) 3m 2f
3:20 (3:20) (Class 3) (0-140,139) 4-Y-0+ **£9,747** (£2,862; £1,431; £715)

Form RPR

P/5- **1** **Knockara Beau (IRE)**[109] 863 10-11-12 **139** JanFaltejsek 150+
(George Charlton) *led to 3rd: chsd ldr to 13th: rallied and led 3 out: clr after next: eased run-in* **7/1**

S32- **2** *2 ¾* **Bescot Springs (IRE)**[24] 1660 8-9-12 **118** (v) CraigNichol(7) 121
(Lucinda Russell) *chsd ldrs: drvn and outpcd 5 out: rallied to chse (clr) wnr bef last: no imp* **10/3**[2]

114- **3** *1 ½* **More Equity**[24] 1659 11-9-9 **113** oh5 HarryChalloner(5) 114
(Dianne Sayer) *hld up on ins: hdwy to chse ldr 13th: rdn and outpcd whn nt fluent 3 out: kpt on fr next* **20/1**

266/ **4** *3 ¼* **Pettifour (IRE)**[176] 5548 11-9-11 **117** (v[1]) RyanHatch(7) 118
(Nigel Twiston-Davies) *bhd and nvr gng wl: hdwy u.p bef 4 out: plugged on fr last: no imp* **5/2**[1]

110/ **5** *21* **Rapidolyte De Ladalka (FR)**[201] 5098 8-11-0 **127** BarryKeniry 110
(Simon Shirley-Beavan) *chsd ldrs: nt fluent 12th: effrt and ev ch 4 out to next: wkng whn hit last* **9/2**[3]

44P- **6** *9* **Garleton (IRE)**[132] 680 12-11-4 **138** (t) StephenMulqueen(7) 115
(Maurice Barnes) *led to 3rd: cl up: rdn 4 out: wknd after 2 out* **10/1**

02/ **P** **Wicklow Lad**[175] 5579 9-10-9 **122** BrianHarding
(N W Alexander) *hld up in tch on outside: rdn and outpcd 4 out: t.o whn p.u after 2 out* **12/1**

215/ **F** **Micro Mission (IRE)**[183] 5371 7-10-2 **115** HenryBrooke
(Chris Grant) *hld up: fell 6th* **17/2**

6m 48.0s (0.80) **Going Correction** -0.55s/f (Firm) **8** Ran SP% **114.4**
Speed ratings (Par 107): **76,75,74,73,67 64, ,**
Tote Swingers: 1&2 £2.10, 1&3 £20.20, 2&3 £6.60 CSF £31.50 CT £446.06 TOTE £9.90: £2.50, £2.30, £3.10; EX 33.80 Trifecta £79.70 Pool: £267.19 -2.51 winning units..
Owner J I A Charlton **Bred** George Durrheim & Mrs Maria Mulcahy Durr **Trained** Stocksfield, Northumberland

FOCUS
A competitive and quite a valuable stayers' handicap, run at a sound gallop, and a very comfortable winner. He was on a good mark and is rated to the level of last season's course win.

1979 PETER DOYLE H'CAP HURDLE (8 hdls) 2m 110y
3:55 (3:55) (Class 4) (0-115,115) 4-Y-0+ **£3,249** (£954; £477; £238)

Form RPR

550- **1** **Turtle Watch**[13] 1785 5-10-3 **92** WilsonRenwick 102+
(Jim Goldie) *hld up and bhd: smooth hdwy to chse clr ldr bef 2 out: led run-in: sn rdn and edgd rt: kpt on wl* **12/1**

F4F- **2** *4* **Captain Brown**[27] 1398 5-11-11 **114**.................................. BrianHughes 120
(James Moffatt) *led and clr tl given breather 4th: qcknd clr bef 3 out: rdn next: hdd run-in: kpt on same pce* **40/1**

043/ **3** *7* **Bogside (IRE)**[173] 27 9-11-6 **109**...................................... JanFaltejsek 110
(George Charlton) *hld up in midfield: stdy hdwy and cl up in chsng gp bef 2 out: hung lft and no imp fr last* **10/1**

0/4- **4** *10* **Hallmark Star**[23] 1661 4-11-5 **115**...................................... CraigNichol(7) 106
(Lucinda Russell) *chsd ldrs: effrt and disp 2nd pl 3 out: drvn and wknd between last 2* **6/1**[3]

2/4- **5** *hd* **Kirkaig**[80] 1158 8-10-3 **95** ow1.. EwanWhillans(3) 86
(Alistair Whillans) *t.k.h: hld up: rdn bef 3 out: kpt on fr last: nvr able to chal* **33/1**

645/ **6** *20* **Clondaw Flicka (IRE)**[183] 5366 5-11-4 **107**.................... PeterBuchanan 80
(Lucinda Russell) *bhd: drvn and outpcd 4 out: nvr on terms* **11/1**

530/ **7** *½* **Bollin Julie**[506] 335 6-9-10 **90**.......................... CallumWhillans(5) 62
(Donald Whillans) *hld up: rdn and outpcd 4 out: sn btn* **40/1**

P/1- **8** *10* **Push Me (IRE)**[13] 1791 6-10-8 **97**.. AdrianLane 60
(Iain Jardine) *hld up and bhd: stdy hdwy after 4 out: wknd after next* **7/1**

/20- **9** *23* **Stanley Bridge**[118] 801 6-10-13 **102**................................. BrianHarding 44
(Barry Murtagh) *midfield: drvn along 3 out: sn btn* **18/1**

333- **P** **Endeavor**[13] 1785 8-11-3 **106**.. RyanMania
(Dianne Sayer) *prom: effrt and wnt 2nd 3 out to bef next: sn btn: p.u and dismntd bef last* **7/2**[1]

P **Seattle Drive (IRE)**[33] 1549 5-11-4 **114**........................... MikeyEnnis(7)
(David Pipe) *t.k.h: prom to 3 out: sn rdn and btn: p.u bef last* **5/1**[2]

P/0- **P** **Flogarose (FR)**[23] 1665 4-9-8 **90**............................ GrantCockburn(7)
(Lucy Normile) *chsd clr ldr to 3 out: sn struggling: t.o whn p.u bef next* **5/1**[2]

3m 54.5s (-7.30) **Going Correction** -0.30s/f (Good)
WFA 4 from 5yo+ 9lb **12** Ran SP% **120.5**
Speed ratings (Par 105): **105,103,99,95,95 85,85,80,69,** ,
Tote Swingers: 1&2 £15.70 CSF £395.41 CT £4889.79 TOTE £17.30: £3.70, £13.30, £2.70; EX 724.60 Trifecta £219.30 Part won. Pool: £292.45 - 0.01 winning units..
Owner Mr & Mrs Raymond Anderson Green **Bred** Design And Planning Consultants Ltd **Trained** Uplawmoor, E Renfrews
■ Stewards' Enquiry : Mikey Ennis one-day ban: careless riding (Nov 2)

FOCUS
They went a strong gallop in this open-looking 2m handicap hurdle and the eventual winner came from last to first. A good time for the grade and the form is rated through the third.

1980 ROYAL SMITHFIELD CLUB NOVICES' HURDLE (11 hdls) 2m 6f 110y
4:35 (4:35) (Class 4) 4-Y-0+ **£3,898** (£1,144; £572; £286)

Form RPR

1 **Kilgefin Star (IRE)**[122] 769 5-10-12 0.................................. DannyCook 121+
(Michael Smith) *pressed ldr and sn clr of rest: led 5 out: rdn bef 2 out: styd on strly: unchal* **6/1**[3]

3/1- **2** *3 ¼* **Mysteree (IRE)**[24] 1654 5-11-5 0...................................... PeterBuchanan 124
(Lucinda Russell) *chsd ldrs: effrt and wnt 2nd bef 2 out: clsd last: kpt on same pce last 100yds* **11/10**[1]

42P/ **3** *25* **Shanen (IRE)**[224] 4648 7-10-12 115.................................(t) DenisO'Regan 94
(Pauline Robson) *hld up in tch: stdy hdwy gng wl 3 out: pushed along bef next: sn wknd* **7/4**[2]

4- **4** *4 ½* **Mister D (IRE)**[24] 1654 7-10-5 0........................... JonathonBewley(7) 89
(George Bewley) *led to 5 out: chsd wnr tl rdn and wknd bef 2 out* **14/1**

/64- **5** *10* **Mo Rouge (IRE)**[132] 676 5-10-12 0....................................... BarryKeniry 80
(Mrs Jackie Stephen) *hld up in tch: outpcd whn j.lft and mstke 4 out: sn n.d* **33/1**

F00/ **6** *43* **Oscar Lateen (IRE)**[173] 22 5-10-12 0.................................... RyanMania 42
(Sandy Thomson) *hld up towards rr: rdn and outpcd after 4 out: btn bef 2 out: t.o* **18/1**

7 *1* **Generous Chief (IRE)**[202] 5-10-12 0.................................. BrianHughes 41
(Chris Grant) *hld up in midfield: drvn and outpcd bef 4 out: btn after next: t.o* **25/1**

8 *22* **Boric**[230] 5-10-9 0.. JohnKington(3) 21
(Simon Waugh) *hld up in midfield: drvn and outpcd bef 4 out: sn struggling: t.o* **22/1**

0PP/ **P** **Fleet Fox**[228] 4579 6-10-12 0.. BrianHarding
(N W Alexander) *prom: struggling 5 out: t.o whn p.u bef 3 out* **50/1**

0/ **P** **Flaybay**[180] 5454 5-10-5 0.. HenryBrooke
(Chris Grant) *t.k.h in rr: struggling 5 out: t.o whn p.u bef 3 out* **66/1**

056- **P** **Be Wise (IRE)**[13] 1788 6-10-5 0.................................... CallumBewley(7)
(Harriet Graham) *bhd: struggling 5 out: t.o whn p.u bef 2 out* **100/1**

5m 40.7s (-0.30) **Going Correction** -0.30s/f (Good) **11** Ran SP% **125.8**
Speed ratings (Par 105): **88,86,78,76,73 58,57,50,** ,
Tote Swingers: 1&2 £2.60, 1&3 £7.50, 2&3 £1.10 CSF £14.00 TOTE £5.40: £2.20, £1.10, £1.10; EX 16.70 Trifecta £29.00 Pool: £562.20 - 14.50 winning units..
Owner J Stephenson **Bred** John F Gibbons **Trained** Kirkheaton, Northumberland

FOCUS
Plenty of deadwood in this moderately run novice hurdle. A big step up from the winner but it looks believable.

1981 SIR MAXWELL HARPER GOW MEMORIAL NOVICES' H'CAP CHASE (12 fncs) 2m 1f
5:10 (5:10) (Class 4) (0-110,105) 4-Y-0+ **£4,873** (£1,431; £715; £357)

Form RPR

212- **1** **Sendiym (FR)**[13] 1790 6-10-10 **89**.................................(b) BrianHughes 99
(Dianne Sayer) *led to 2nd: w ldr: led 6th: mde rest: drvn bef last: hld on gamely towards fin* **7/2**[2]

/66- **2** *¾* **Royal Riviera**[24] 1660 7-11-5 **105**................................(t) RyanHatch(7) 113
(Nigel Twiston-Davies) *prom: hdwy on outside bef 4 out: effrt and ev ch last: kpt on: hld towards fin* **5/1**

U32- **3** *1 ¾* **My Idea**[23] 1665 7-11-2 **102**.................................(t) StephenMulqueen(7) 108
(Maurice Barnes) *prom: effrt and rdn bef 2 out: kpt on same pce fr last* **4/1**[3]

30P- **4** *17* **Peaks Of Fire (IRE)**[11] 726 6-11-1 **99**....................(p) SamanthaDrake(5) 94
(Joanne Foster) *s.i.s and early reminders: hdwy to ld 2nd: hdd 6th: styd upsides tl wknd bef 2 out* **20/1**

340/ **5** *18* **Ben Akram (IRE)**[173] 27 5-11-3 **96**.................................. PeterBuchanan 77
(Lucinda Russell) *nt jump wl and nvr gng wl in rr: lost tch fr 5 out* **11/4**[1]

643- **P** **Takaatuf (IRE)**[18] 1715 7-11-0 **100**................................. JohnDawson(7)
(John Wade) *in tch: blnd bdly 3rd: sn p.u* **17/2**

655- **U** **Cavite Eta (IRE)**[13] 1785 6-11-9 **102**.................................. HenryBrooke
(Barry Murtagh) *in tch whn blnd and uns rdr 7th* **15/2**

4m 18.8s (0.80) **Going Correction** -0.55s/f (Firm) **7** Ran SP% **112.6**
Speed ratings (Par 105): **76,75,74,66,58** ,
Tote Swingers: 1&2 £10.40, 1&3 £1.80, 2&3 £1.10 CSF £20.67 TOTE £3.70: £2.10, £3.10; EX 15.40 Trifecta £21.80 Pool: £736.11 - 25.31 winning units..
Owner United Five Racing & Andrew Sayer **Bred** H H The Aga Khan's Studs Sc **Trained** Hackthorpe, Cumbria

FOCUS
A low-grade novice handicap chase and some of the jumping on show left plenty to be desired. A personal best from the in-form winner.

1982 MAXWELL CELEBRATION CONDITIONAL JOCKEYS' TRAINING SERIES H'CAP HURDLE (RACING EXCELLENCE I'TIVE) (11 hdls) 2m 6f 110y
5:40 (5:49) (Class 5) (0-100,100) 4-Y-0+ **£2,599** (£763; £381; £190)

Form RPR

043/ **1** **Capital Venture (IRE)**[201] 5078 7-11-2 **95**.............. DiarmuidO'Regan(5) 104
(N W Alexander) *trckd ldrs: led 3 out: hrd pressed fr next: styd on gamely run-in* **5/1**[2]

/04- **2** *½* **Top Billing**[13] 1791 4-10-9 **84**.......................................(p) GrahamWatters 92
(Nicky Richards) *hld up: nt fluent 4 out: stdy hdwy next: chal 2 out to run-in: kpt on: hld nr fin* **16/1**

2- **3** *10* **Texas Rose (IRE)**[2] 1940 6-11-5 **100**.................................... SDBohan(7) 100
(Rebecca Menzies) *hld up: stdy hdwy and prom 4 out: effrt and ev ch 2 out: outpcd by first two appr last* **11/4**[1]

/41- **4** *1 ¼* **Mia's Anthem (IRE)**[27] 1631 5-11-4 **92**.............................. JohnDawson 91
(Noel C Kelly, Ire) *hld up: stdy hdwy to chse ldrs after 3 out: rdn next: hung lft and outpcd bef last* **7/1**

PP0- **5** *14* **Solway Bay**[13] 1798 11-11-6 **97**...................................(t) CraigGallagher(3) 83
(Lisa Harrison) *bhd: drvn along 1/2-way: styd on fr 3 out: nvr able to chal* **28/1**

0- **6** *3* **Indubitably**[56] 1379 7-11-2 **90**......................................(bt) GrantCockburn 75
(Noel C Kelly, Ire) *mstkes: sn towards rr: hdwy u.p after 3 out: outpcd fr next* **20/1**

00/ **7** *3 ¼* **Captain P K (IRE)**[174] 19 6-10-10 **84**..............................(t) CiaranMckee 64
(Noel C Kelly, Ire) *chsd ldrs tl rdn and wknd bef 2 out* **40/1**

012/ **8** *23* **Solway Silver**[708] 2457 7-10-6 **80**................................ StephenMulqueen 45
(Lisa Harrison) *led: mstke and hdd 3 out: sn rdn and wknd* **7/1**

P5/- **9** *8* **Dundock**[211] 4903 12-10-11 **85**.. KieronEdgar 37
(Alistair Whillans) *chsd ldrs: drvn along fr 4 out: wknd after next* **20/1**

050/ **10** *6* **Robin's Command (IRE)**[181] 5423 6-10-4 **83**.................. ShaunDobbin(5) 30
(Rose Dobbin) *hld up IN midfield: stdy hdwy and prom bef 3 out: sn rdn: wknd bef 2 out* **13/2**[3]

6P0- **11** *18* **In The Haven (IRE)**[56] 1376 10-11-1 **92**....................(p) CallumBewley(3) 23
(Joanne Foster) *prom: lost pl bef 4 out: struggling fr next* **66/1**

/02- **12** *¾* **Discoverie**[13] 1791 5-10-3 **77**... CraigNichol 7
(Dianne Sayer) *in tch: drvn and outpcd fr 8th: btn fr 3 out* **9/1**

05U- **P** **Fling Me (IRE)**[13] 1791 6-11-1 **92**.................................. JamesCowley(3)
(Rose Dobbin) *bhd: lost tch and p.u bef 8th* **16/1**

5m 39.3s (-1.70) **Going Correction** -0.30s/f (Good)
WFA 4 from 5yo+ 10lb **13** Ran SP% **120.3**
Speed ratings (Par 103): **90,89,86,85,81 80,78,70,68,66 59,59,**
Tote Swingers: 1&2 £14.60, 1&3 £3.60, 2&3 £11.90 CSF £74.51 CT £267.52 TOTE £4.30: £1.60, £6.20, £1.70; EX 95.00 Trifecta £405.40 Part won. Pool: £540.65 - 0.62 winning units..
Owner Mrs Ray Calder & Mrs Jan Scott **Bred** Gerald Mitchell **Trained** Kinneston, Perth & Kinross

FOCUS
An ordinary handicap, confined to conditional riders. Steps up from the first two but both are entitled to rate higher on their bumper/Flat form.
T/Plt: £88.10 to a £1 stake. Pool: £59,196.75 - 490.45 winning tickets. T/Qpdt: £48.00 to a £1 stake. Pool: £3,526.40 - 54.35 winning tickets. RY

1899 AUTEUIL (L-H)
Saturday, October 19
OFFICIAL GOING: Turf: very soft

1983a PRIX PIERRE DE LASSUS (HURDLE) (GRADE 3) (4YO) (TURF) 2m 3f 110y
1:00 (12:00) 4-Y-0

£49,390 (£24,146; £14,268; £9,878; £5,487; £3,841)

RPR

1 **Yankee Hill (FR)**[21] 4-10-1 0.. ErvanChazelle 130
(Mlle T Puitg, France) **8/1**

2 *3* **Le Grand Luce (FR)**[21] 4-10-10 0.................................. BertrandLestrade 136
(J-P Gallorini, France) **6/4**[1]

3 *5* **My Maj (FR)**[21] 4-10-8 0... GeoffreyRe 129
(Yannick Fouin, France) **47/1**

4 *1 ¾* **Storminator (FR)**[18] 4-10-3 0...................................... JonathanNattiez 122
(J-P Gallorini, France) **3/1**[2]

5 *10* **Singapore Sling (FR)**[21] 4-10-6 0.. KevinNabet 115
(A Bonin, France) **27/1**

6 *2* **Jolipoulinderuins (FR)**[25] 4-10-7 0 ow4................................ DavidCottin 114
(F Cheyer, France) **9/1**

7 *1 ½* **Kemaliste (FR)**[21] 4-10-0 0.. BertrandBourez 112
(Y-M Porzier, France) **14/1**

8 *dist* **Extreme Cara (FR)**[19] 2228 4-10-8 0...........................(p) BertrandThelier
(G Cherel, France) **78/10**[3]

P **Orcus (FR)**[18] 4-10-3 0.. VincentCheminaud
(M Seror, France) **26/1**

P **Laskaline (FR)**[21] 4-10-1 0.....................................(p) CyrilleGombeau
(G Cherel, France) **26/1**

P **Voiladenuo (FR)**[21] 4-10-8 0.. JonathanPlouganou
(Guy Denuault, France) **49/1**

4m 39.47s (-15.53) **11** Ran SP% **119.2**
PARI-MUTUEL (all including 1 euro stake): WIN 9.00; PLACE 2.20, 1.20, 6.10; DF 8.60; SF 19.90.
Owner Ecurie Victoria Dreams **Bred** Ecurie Liberty **Trained** France

1984a PRIX MONTGOMERY (CHASE) (GRADE 3 H'CAP) (5YO+) (TURF) 2m 7f 110y
2:08 (12:00) 5-Y-0+

£64,024 (£31,300; £18,495; £12,804; £7,113; £4,979)

RPR

1 **Tito Dela Barriere (FR)**[21] 6-9-11 **0**............................ ThierryMajorcryk 125
(E Lecoiffier, France) **9/1**

2 *1 ¾* **Northwest Du Lys (FR)**[21] 8-10-6 **0**............................ JonathanPlouganou 132
(J-L Guillochon, France) **5/1**[1]

3 *8* **Upwelling (FR)**[21] 5-9-11 **0**...................................(p) VincentCheminaud 115
(J-P Gallorini, France) **16/1**

4 *6* **United Park (FR)**[46] 5-11-0 **0**.. JamesReveley 126
(G Macaire, France) **78/10**[3]

5	¾	**River Choice (FR)**[16] [1740] 10-10-13 0 (b) GeoffreyRe (Yannick Fouin, France)	**33/1**	124
6	1 ½	**Nom De D'La (FR)**[21] 7-10-1 0 (b) JonathanNattiez (J-P Gallorini, France)	**22/1**	111
7	¾	**Pharly De Kerser (FR)**[21] 10-10-8 0 (b) JeromeZuliani (Patrice Quinton, France)	**55/1**	117
8	1 ¼	**Symphonie D'Anjou (FR)**[25] 5-10-10 0 MathieuCarroux (A Chaille-Chaille, France)	**6/1**[2]	118
9	1 ½	**Sundahia (FR)**[21] 6-10-10 0 (b) KevinNabet (J-D Marion, France)	**9/1**	116
10	dist	**Sadyjaune (FR)**[27] 7-9-12 0 ow1 RaymondLeeO'Brien (E Lecoiffier, France)	**48/1**	
P		**Cokydal (FR)**[25] 8-10-4 0 (p) CyrilleGombeau (G Cherel, France)	**83/10**	
P		**Monetaire (FR)**[51] 7-10-4 0 JacquesRicou (J Bertran De Balanda, France)	**9/1**	
P		**Colorado Seven (FR)**[37] 6-9-11 0 (b) GaetanMasure (J-L Gay, France)	**35/1**	
P		**Vivacissimo (IRE)**[21] 6-9-13 0 MorganRegairaz (Yannick Fouin, France)	**27/1**	
P		**Mukonzi Has (FR)**[21] 5-9-13 0 (p) AlexisAcker (M Rolland, France)	**13/1**	
P		**Snooze (FR)**[23] 7-10-8 0 (p) ThomasGueguen (F Nicolle, France)	**35/1**	
P		**Upsala Collonges (FR)**[21] 5-9-11 0 AlainDeChitray (G Cherel, France)	**89/1**	

6m 9.24s (369.24) **17** Ran SP% **117.4**
PARI-MUTUEL (all including 1 euro stake): WIN 8.60 (coupled with Sadyjaune); PLACE 3.30, 2.40, 4.80; DF 24.30; SF 52.40.
Owner Eric Lecoiffier **Bred** S Duchene **Trained** France

233 KEMPTON (R-H)

Sunday, October 20

OFFICIAL GOING: Good (good to soft on bend adjacent to lake) changing to good to soft after race 2 (2.45)
Dual bend alignment utilised for this meeting.
Wind: medium, across Weather: showers

1985 WILLIAM HILL - DOWNLOAD THE APP JUVENILE HURDLE (8 hdls) 2m

2:15 (2:16) (Class 3) 3-Y-0 **£5,848** (£1,717; £858; £429)

Form					RPR
4-	1		**Duroble Man**[22] [1684] 3-10-12 0 RobertThornton (Alan King) *prom in main gp: clsd on ldrs 5th: rdn to chal between last 2: drvn to ld flat: styd on wl: rdn out*	**2/1**[1]	104+
U13-	2	1 ¾	**Town Mouse**[22] [1684] 3-10-13 123 TrevorWhelan(5) (Neil King) *taken down early: t.k.h: chsd ldr tl clsd and led after 5th: rdn and pressed 2 out: drvn between last 2: hdd and one pce flat*	**11/2**	109
	3	1 ½	**Aldopicgros (FR)**[189] 3-10-12 0 DarylJacob (Paul Nicholls) *chsd clr ldng pair: mstke 2nd: clsd 5th: wnt 2nd sn after 3 out: chal next: rdn and unable qck in 3rd whn mstke last: one pce flat*	**11/4**[2]	103+
	4	4 ½	**Handsome Stranger (IRE)**[9] 3-10-12 0 JamesDavies (Alan Bailey) *hld up in midfield: clsd on ldrs 5th: 4th and rdn after 3 out: outpcd bef next: plugged on same pce fr 2 out*	**66/1**	97
	5	25	**Exclusive Waters (IRE)**[30] 3-10-12 0 JamieMoore (Gary Moore) *hld up in midfield: clsd on ldrs 5th: rdn and struggling after 3 out: wkng whn j.rt and mstke next: wl btn whn j.rt again last*	**8/1**	74
	6	6	**Dark Emerald (IRE)**[21] 3-10-12 0 (t) BrendanPowell (Brendan Powell) *t.k.h: hld up in last trio: mstke 1st: clsd on ldrs 5th: rdn and btn after 3 out: wknd bef next: t.o*	**5/1**[3]	69
F-	7	6	**Ron Waverly (IRE)**[42] [1524] 3-10-9 0 JoshuaMoore(3) (Pat Phelan) *hld up in last trio: clsd on ldrs 5th: rdn and wknd after 3 out: t.o 2 out*	**100/1**	63
	8	29	**Assembly**[39] 3-10-12 0 ColinBolger (Pat Phelan) *t.k.h: hld up towards rr: bmpd 1st: clsd on ldrs 5th: rdn and wknd qckly after 3 out: t.o next*	**50/1**	37
	9	67	**Minister Of Mayhem**[86] 3-10-12 0 NickScholfield (Nick Mitchell) *hld up in midfield: wandered and blnd 1st: lost pl 5th and sn drvn in rr: lost tch and t.o after 3 out*	**14/1**	
446-	P		**Complexity**[9] [1855] 3-10-12 0 [1] AndrewThornton (Seamus Mullins) *t.k.h: led: j. bdly lft and then hung lft 5th: j.lft again and hdd next: hung bdly lft and sn p.u*	**66/1**	

3m 58.6s (0.50) **Going Correction** +0.275s/f (Yiel) **10** Ran SP% **115.8**
Speed ratings (Par 105): **109,108,107,105,92 89,86,72,38,**
toteswingers 1&2 £3.00, 1&3 £2.30, 2&3 £3.20 CSF £13.62 TOTE £2.40: £1.10, £1.80, £1.70; EX 14.30 Trifecta £44.10 Pool: £2739.00 - 46.51 winning units..
Owner McNeill Family **Bred** D A Yardy **Trained** Barbury Castle, Wilts

FOCUS
Rain was falling during this ordinary juvenile hurdle. It was run at reasonable pace but a lot of these pulled for their heads in the first part of the race. A big step up from the winner, who can rate higher on his Flat form.

1986 WILLIAM HILL - IN APP STORE BEGINNERS' CHASE (THE SUNDAY £5K BONUS RACE) (12 fncs) 2m

2:45 (2:45) (Class 4) 4-Y-0+ **£4,548** (£1,335; £667; £333)

Form					RPR
300/	1		**Dodging Bullets**[197] [5173] 5-11-2 0 DarylJacob (Paul Nicholls) *chsd ldrs: j.lft 1st: clsd and trckd ldrs 6th: chal and j. into ld 3 out: shkn up and lft in command next: 3 l clr last: pushed out*	**8/11**[1]	136+
1/0-	2	4	**Turn Over Sivola (FR)**[162] [216] 6-11-2 0 RobertThornton (Alan King) *chsd ldrs: clsd to press ldrs 6th: led after 9th: outj. and hdd next: ev ch and travelling as wl as wnr whn mstke and landed awkwardly 2 out: 3 l down and mstke last: one pce*	**5/2**[2]	134+
3F/-	3	13	**Earls Quarter (IRE)**[447] [5318] 7-11-2 0 (t) AidanColeman (Ian Williams) *t.k.h: j.lft: led: mstke 4th: hdd next but styd pressing ldr: stl cl up whn j.lft and mstke 3 out: btn next: plugged on*	**20/1**	118
/34-	4	23	**Be All Man (IRE)**[161] [244] 6-11-2 113 JamieMoore (Gary Moore) *w ldr tl led after 5th: mstke 7th and 8th: rdn and hdd after 9th: btn 3 out: fdd*	**8/1**[3]	101
2U3/	5	4 ½	**Grab The Glory (IRE)**[611] [4363] 7-10-13 0 JoshuaMoore(3) (Gary Moore) *a wl off the pce in last: lost tch 8th: t.o after next*	**12/1**	94

4m 1.8s (1.50) **Going Correction** +0.275s/f (Yiel) **5** Ran SP% **110.0**
Speed ratings (Par 105): **107,105,98,87,84**
CSF £3.06 TOTE £2.10: £1.30, £1.40; EX 2.80 Trifecta £9.20 Pool: £1804.55 - 146.66 winning units..
Owner Martin Broughton & Friends **Bred** L Dettori **Trained** Ditcheat, Somerset

FOCUS
Some decent novices have won this event in recent years. Dodging Bullets was a 150 novice hurdler and there should be more to come, with Turn Over Sivola in line with his hurdles form.

1987 WILLIAM HILL - ON YOUR MOBILE NOVICES' HURDLE (LISTED RACE) (8 hdls) 2m

3:20 (3:20) (Class 1) 4-Y-0+ **£9,681** (£3,632; £1,819; £906; £455)

Form					RPR
111-	1		**Sea Lord (IRE)**[64] [1290] 6-11-8 150 DenisO'Regan (John Ferguson) *j.rt at times: hld up wl off the pce in last trio: mstke 2nd: clsd on ldrs 3 out: chsd ldr bef next: rdn to ld between last 2: styd on wl: eased towards fin*	**1/1**[1]	141+
213-	2	9	**Life And Soul (IRE)**[59] [1350] 6-11-8 134 (p) JasonMaguire (Donald McCain) *chsd clr ldr and clr of field: led bef 3 out: drvn bef 2 out: hdd and no ex between last 2: wknd flat*	**7/1**[3]	132
U11-	3	8	**Azure Fly (IRE)**[14] [1779] 5-11-6 135 (tp) NoelFehily (Charlie Longsdon) *j.lft: hld up wl off the pce in last: clsd 3 out: chsd ldr briefly bef next: stl handy in 3rd whn veered sharply lft and reluctant on landing 2 out: wl hld whn wnt lft again last*	**2/1**[2]	128+
114-	4	29	**Cool Macavity (IRE)**[59] [1350] 5-11-6 129 DavidBass (Nicky Henderson) *chsd clr ldng pair: mstke 5th: rdn and clsd on ldrs whn blnd next: sn btn and wl bhd next: t.o*	**8/1**	96
21-	5	18	**Hallings Comet**[40] [1553] 4-11-4 0 AidanColeman (Adrian Wintle) *taken down early: t.k.h: led and clr tl hdd bef 3 out: sn wknd: t.o 2 out*	**20/1**	84

3m 58.75s (0.65) **Going Correction** +0.275s/f (Yiel)
WFA 4 from 5yo+ 9lb **5** Ran SP% **111.7**
Speed ratings (Par 111): **109,104,100,86,77**
CSF £8.62 TOTE £1.90: £1.10, £3.00; EX 5.80 Trifecta £9.40 Pool: £1506.89 - 119.01 winning units..
Owner Bloomfields **Bred** Darley **Trained** Cowlinge, Suffolk

FOCUS
With 5mm of rain having fallen in half an hour, the official going description was changed to good to soft all round before this race. A good edition of this Listed novice hurdle. The field was soon stretched out, with Hallings Comet going off at a rate of knots. The easy winner is rated below his best, with the next two close to their marks.

1988 WILLIAM HILL - IPHONE, IPAD, IPAD MINI H'CAP CHASE (16 fncs 2 omitted) 3m

3:50 (3:50) (Class 4) (0-115,115) 4-Y-0+ **£4,548** (£1,335; £667; £333)

Form					RPR
/22-	1		**Firm Order (IRE)**[151] [431] 8-11-12 **115** (p) DenisO'Regan (Paul Webber) *patiently rdn: hld up in last trio: stdy hdwy 12th: trckd ldrs after 15th: rdn to ld and readily wnt clr bef last: eased towards fin: comf*	**12/1**	135+
P52-	2	9	**Suburban Bay**[37] [1577] 8-11-0 **103** WayneHutchinson (Alan King) *chsd ldrs: wnt 2nd 4th: mstke 15th: drvn to ld bef bypassed 2 out: hdd and no ex bef last: no ch w wnr and one pce after*	**4/1**[2]	116
044/	3	4 ½	**Moleskin (IRE)**[183] [5411] 10-11-6 **109** (bt) JackDoyle (Victor Dartnall) *chsd ldr tl led 2nd: drvn and hrd pressed bef bypassed 3 out: hdd bef bypassed 2 out and sn outpcd: wknd bef last*	**11/2**	115
43P/	4	2 ¼	**Be Definite (IRE)**[178] [5521] 9-11-11 **114** (p) PaddyBrennan (Tom George) *chsd ldrs: rdn and outpcd bef bypassed 3 out: 4th and wl hld whn mstke last*	**12/1**	119
213-	5	¾	**Sadler's Star (GER)**[14] [1798] 10-11-2 **105** (tp) APMcCoy (Michael Blake) *in tch in midfield: rdn after 15th: outpcd and btn bypassing 3 out: n.d but plugged on fr bypassed 3 out*	**14/1**	108
433-	6	3 ¾	**Milgen Bay**[15] [1767] 7-11-4 **107** LeightonAspell (Oliver Sherwood) *in tch in midfield: struggling whn mstke and pckd 13th: n.d after but plugged on fr bypassed 2 out*	**14/1**	109
415/	7	shd	**Bally Sands (IRE)**[177] [5548] 9-11-1 **109** (p) EdCookson(5) (Robin Mathew) *nt fluent: led tl 2nd: j. slowly and dropped to midfield 5th: rdn and struggling 14th: wl hld but plugged on fr bypassed 3 out*	**16/1**	109
2/P-	8	33	**Porters War (IRE)**[151] [426] 11-11-1 **104** NickScholfield (Jeremy Scott) *in tch in midfield: 6th and rdn after 15th: sn struggling and btn bypassing next: wknd: eased flat*	**16/1**	74
525-	9	18	**Baily Storm (IRE)**[16] [1748] 11-11-5 **108** (vt) DavidBass (Lawney Hill) *in tch towards rr: dropped to last and rdn 1/2-way: struggling whn hit 13th: lost tch 15th: t.o after 15th*	**33/1**	62
123-	10	25	**Green Bank (IRE)**[28] [1637] 7-11-11 **114** (t) NoelFehily (Charlie Longsdon) *mstkes: in tch in midfield: dropped to last and mstke 11th: lost tch 13th: t.o after 15th*	**5/1**[3]	45
4/1-	P		**Highrate (IRE)**[169] [113] 7-11-3 **106** JasonMaguire (Kim Bailey) *hld up in last trio: lost action and p.u after 7th: fatally injured.*	**7/2**[1]	

6m 18.9s (3.50) **Going Correction** +0.275s/f (Yiel) **11** Ran SP% **117.7**
Speed ratings (Par 105): **105,102,100,99,99 98,98,87,81,72**
toteswingers 1&2 £21.80, 1&3 £12.60, 2&3 £4.90 CSF £61.38 CT £301.64 TOTE £10.80: £3.70, £2.10, £2.40; EX 93.70 Trifecta £299.40 Pool: £938.81 - 2.35 winning units..
Owner The Syndicators **Bred** Edmund Arthur **Trained** Mollington, Oxon

FOCUS
Just an ordinary handicap chase. The third-last and second-last fences were bypassed on the final circuit. A step up from the winner, and the second and third could win off their current marks.

1989 WILLIAM HILL - DOWNLOAD THE APP HURDLE (LISTED RACE) (8 hdls) 2m

4:25 (4:25) (Class 1) 4-Y-0+ **£14,237** (£5,342; £2,675; £1,332)

Form					RPR
212/	1		**The New One (IRE)**[199] [5137] 5-11-8 165 SamTwiston-Davies (Nigel Twiston-Davies) *j.rt: hld up in 3rd tl chsd ldr bef 5th: shkn up and j. into ld 2 out: rdn and readily qcknd clr between last 2: eased towards fin: impressive*	**1/2**[1]	166+
123/	2	10	**Rock On Ruby (IRE)**[177] [5561] 8-11-8 170 (t) NoelFehily (Harry Fry) *chsd ldr tl led after 3rd: mstke and hdd next: sn led again: outj. and hdd 2 out: sn rdn and outpcd: wl hld whn j.rt last*	**7/4**[2]	157
400/	3	40	**Quaddick Lake (IRE)**[176] [5574] 10-11-0 130 NickScholfield (Jeremy Scott) *t.k.h: hld up in last: lost tch w ldng pair 3 out: modest 3rd bef next: t.o*	**80/1**[3]	108

215- **4** *19* **Coronea Lilly (IRE)**[11] [1818] 9-10-7 124........................(tp) MichaelByrne 82
(Neil Mulholland) *led tl after 3rd: lft in ld again next: sn hdd: 3rd and struggling bef 3 out: t.o last bef 2 out* **150/1**

3m 53.5s (-4.60) **Going Correction** +0.275s/f (Yiel) **4** Ran SP% **104.9**
Speed ratings (Par 111): **122,117,97,87**
CSF £1.61 TOTE £1.30; EX 1.50 Trifecta £1.80 Pool: £1496.53 - 593.59 winning units..
Owner Mrs S Such **Bred** R Brown & Ballylinch Stud **Trained** Naunton, Gloucs

FOCUS
This event held Listed status for the first time. Rooster Booster took the race in 2002 and went on to win the Champion Hurdle later in the season, while Katchit was beaten as reigning champion on his seasonal reappearance in this in 2008. This was an early festival trial, with 2012 Champion Hurdle winner and last season's runner-up Rock On Ruby up against young pretender The New One. The withdrawal of Australia Day meant the race lacked an obvious pacemaker, but they went a reasonable gallop anyway and the time was a full five seconds faster than that recorded by Sea Lord in the Listed novice hurdle. The New One did it impressively but Rock On Ruby is rated 13lb off his best.

1990 WILLIAM HILL - EXCLUSIVE MOBILE OFFERS H'CAP CHASE (12 fncs) 2m
5:00 (5:00) (Class 3) (0-135,133) 4-Y-0+ **£6,498** (£1,908; £954; £477)

Form RPR

U/5- **1** **Gallox Bridge**[161] [249] 8-11-6 **127**................................(t) RichardJohnson 132+
(Tim Vaughan) *prom in main gp: chsd clr ldr 6th: steadily clsd and led 9th: outj. and hdd next: drvn and looked hld 2 out: rallied and pressing ldr last: sn led and styd on wl* **15/8**[1]

2/3- **2** *2 3/4* **Able Deputy**[161] [234] 6-10-13 **120**....................................(t) JasonMaguire 124+
(Kim Bailey) *hld up off the pce in last pair: clsd and wnt 2nd 9th: j. into ld: pushed clr and looked in command 2 out: pressed last: sn hdd and drvn: fnd nil and immediately btn: eased towards fin* **3/1**[2]

111- **3** *2 1/2* **Cap Elorn (FR)**[14] [1780] 7-10-9 **119**................................. GavinSheehan(3) 119
(Lawney Hill) *racd off the pce in main gp: clsd and trcking ldrs 9th: rdn and wnt 3rd 3 out: outpcd and btn next: kpt on flat* **4/1**[3]

2/0- **4** *21* **Oscar Hill (IRE)**[163] [204] 7-11-9 **130**....................................(t) TomO'Brien 111
(Rob Summers) *led and sn wl clr: hit 1st: hdd 9th: stl cl 3rd and rdn bef next: wknd sn after 3 out* **8/1**

404/ **5** *1* **Oh Crick (FR)**[183] [5403] 10-11-5 **133**..................... MrJoshuaNewman(7) 114
(Alan King) *racd off the pce in main gp: clsd to chse ldrs and rdn after 9th: btn next: wkng whn mstke 2 out* **5/1**

316- **6** *31* **Giant O Murchu (IRE)**[15] [1767] 9-10-8 **115**...................(p) AidanColeman 75
(Lawney Hill) *a last: struggling and mstke 9th: lost tch bef next: t.o* **20/1**

4m 3.9s (3.60) **Going Correction** +0.275s/f (Yiel) **6** Ran SP% **112.3**
Speed ratings (Par 107): **102,100,99,88,88 72**
toteswingers 1&2 £1.60, 1&3 £2.30, 2&3 £2.90 CSF £8.25 TOTE £3.10: £2.00, £1.70; EX 7.90 Trifecta £29.60 Pool: £1811.07 - 45.86 winning units..
Owner D W Fox **Bred** R J Tompkins **Trained** Aberthin, Vale of Glamorgan

FOCUS
A fair handicap chase. Oscar Hill was very keen and quickly opened up a long lead, largely ignored by the others. The winner is rated below his best, with the second in line with his hurdles form.

1991 WILLIAM HILL RADIO - DOWNLOAD THE APP "NATIONAL HUNT" NOVICES' HURDLE (10 hdls) 2m 5f
5:30 (5:31) (Class 4) 4-Y-0+ **£3,898** (£1,144; £572; £286)

Form RPR

422/ **1** **Warden Hill (IRE)**[196] [5195] 5-10-12 124........................ DominicElsworth 113+
(Mick Channon) *in tch in midfield: swtchd lft and effrt after 2 out: rdn and ev ch last: led flat and styd on wl* **11/4**[1]

220/ **2** *1* **Carole's Destrier**[254] [4113] 5-10-12 0.............................. DougieCostello 112+
(Neil Mulholland) *in tch in midfield: hdwy to chse ldrs bef 3 out: ev ch 2 out: drvn and sltly outpcd sn after last: rallied towards fin to go 2nd again last strides* **16/1**

032/ **3** *nk* **Master Benjamin**[204] [5013] 6-10-12 119.........................(p) NickScholfield 112+
(Jeremy Scott) *hld up in tch in midfield: clsd to trck ldrs 2 out: rdn and ld last: drvn and hdd flat: one pce and lost 2nd last strides* **7/2**[2]

4 *2 3/4* **Andy Kelly (IRE)**[203] 4-10-9 0.................................. GavinSheehan(3) 111+
(Emma Lavelle) *t.k.h: chsd ldr after 1st tl led bef 2 out: wandered 2 out: hrd pressed whn mstke and hdd last: outpcd flat* **7/1**

32P/ **5** *5* **Mr Moss (IRE)**[176] [5576] 8-10-12 0....................................... PaulMoloney 104
(Evan Williams) *chsd ldr tl after 1st: styd chsng ldrs: rdn and unable qck 2 out: styd on same pce between last 2* **12/1**

6 *1 1/2* **Ballinalacken (IRE)**[119] [813] 5-11-0 0.......................... JamesBanks(5) 110
(Anthony Middleton) *hld up in tch towards rr: clsd on ldrs 3 out: drvn bef next: outpcd 2 out: plugged on same pce after* **33/1**

7 *2 1/2* **Gallery Exhibition (IRE)**[182] 6-10-12 0......................... JasonMaguire 100
(Kim Bailey) *hld up in tch in midfield: clsd to trck ldrs after 3 out: rdn next: unable qck and wknd bef last* **25/1**

2- **8** *10* **Owen Na View (IRE)**[24] [1667] 5-10-12 0....................... PaddyBrennan 93
(Fergal O'Brien) *hld up in tch towards rr: clsd and in midfield 3 out: rdn and no ex bef 2 out: wknd 2 out* **20/1**

P/ **9** *25* **Ergo Sum**[293] [3389] 6-10-9 0.. RobertDunne(3) 65
(Robin Mathew) *led tl bef 2 out: sn btn and dropped out: bhd and eased flat: t.o* **150/1**

6/1- **10** *hd* **Gold Ingot**[161] [233] 6-11-5 118.................................. WayneHutchinson 72
(Alan King) *in tch in midfield: rdn and lost pl after 3 out: wl btn next: t.o* **9/1**

1/ **11** *23* **Howlongisafoot (IRE)**[180] [5475] 4-10-12 0............................. DarylJacob 42
(Paul Nicholls) *hld up in tch in last quartet: rdn after 3 out: sn wknd: t.o* **4/1**[3]

12 *34* **Donapollo** 5-10-12 0... WillKennedy 8
(Ian Williams) *in tch in rr: rdn bef 3 out: wknd 3 out: t.o next* **50/1**

5m 20.5s (3.00) **Going Correction** +0.275s/f (Yiel)
WFA 4 from 5yo+ 10lb **12** Ran SP% **119.1**
Speed ratings (Par 105): **105,104,104,103,101 100,100,96,86,86 77,64**
toteswingers 1&2 £13.20, 1&3 £2.30, 2&3 £12.80 CSF £45.22 TOTE £3.90: £1.70, £6.20, £1.30; EX 64.10 Trifecta £280.20 Pool: £1809.05 - 4.84 winning units..
Owner Mrs T P Radford **Bred** Aaron Metcalfe **Trained** West Ilsley, Berks

FOCUS
Winners should come out of this novice hurdle, which was run at a modest pace. There were plenty still involved between the last two flights. The winner and third are rated below their best, with the second in line with his hurdles form.

T/Plt: £7.50. Pool: £88,110.73 - 8558.98 winning units. T/Qpdt: £8.90. Pool: £5105.19 - 421.53 winning units. SP

1992 - 2001a (Foreign Racing) - See Raceform Interactive

[1624] PLUMPTON (L-H)

Monday, October 21

OFFICIAL GOING: Soft (hdl 6.1, chs 6.3)
Wind: medium, against Weather: dry

2002 BETFAIR LONG TERM SUPPORTER OF MOORCROFT MAIDEN HURDLE (9 hdls) 2m
2:20 (2:20) (Class 5) 4-Y-0+ **£2,053** (£598; £299)

Form RPR

4/1- **1** **Long Lunch**[23] [1690] 4-11-0 0... NoelFehily 114+
(Charlie Longsdon) *chsd ldrs: effrt to ld and rn green jst bef 2 out: quick jump and asserted last: r.o wl: rdn out* **7/4**[2]

0- **2** *2 3/4* **Auld Sthock (IRE)**[148] [484] 5-11-0 0................................. JamieMoore 108
(Gary Moore) *chsd ldrs: trcking ldrs and travelling wl after 3 out: rdn and ev ch 2 out: stl ev ch whn outj. last: r.o same pce flat* **5/1**[3]

3 *7* **Macbeth (IRE)**[90] [1095] 4-11-0 0.............................(t) RichardJohnson 102
(Tim Vaughan) *pressed ldr: mstke 4th: rdn to ld bnd bef 2 out: hdd and struggling to qckn in 3rd whn hit 2 out: outpcd and btn last* **6/4**[1]

355/ **4** *3 1/4* **Noble Friend (IRE)**[229] [4593] 5-11-0 0............................ GerardTumelty 98
(Chris Gordon) *plld v hrd early: hld up in rr: prog after 5th: chsd ldng quartet and dived 3 out: lft 4th bef 2 out: no ex between last 2: plugged on* **25/1**

354- **5** *2 1/2* **Snapchat (IRE)**[15] [1793] 6-11-0 0................................ ConorO'Farrell 95
(Seamus Durack) *hld up in last quartet: hdwy bef 3 out: rdn and lft 5th bef 2 out: sn no imp: wknd between last 2* **20/1**

30/ **6** *8* **Wah Wah Taysee (IRE)**[246] [4280] 6-11-0 0................... TomScudamore 87
(David Bridgwater) *t.k.h: hld up in midfield: reminders after 6th: sme hdwy next: no imp whn wnt lft 2 out: nvr trbld ldrs* **20/1**

345- **7** *3/4* **Slaney Star (IRE)**[17] [1749] 5-11-0 0................................ MattieBatchelor 87
(Jim Best) *hld up in last quartet: last whn j.rt and rdn 5th: hdwy past btn horses bef 2 out: nvr trbld ldrs* **66/1**

60- **8** *hd* **Top Chief**[145] [544] 5-11-0 0... NickScholfield 86
(Mark Rimell) *hld up in last quartet: lost tch in last pair after 6th: hdwy past btn horses whn short of room on inner 2 out: nvr trbld ldrs* **100/1**

440- **9** *1 3/4* **State Department**[15] [1795] 6-11-0 0.................................... TomO'Brien 85
(Philip Hobbs) *nt a fluent: racd in midfield: rdn and no hdwy 3 out: wknd bef next* **50/1**

3- **10** *14* **Blue Bear (IRE)**[145] [544] 4-11-0 0...................................... SamThomas 86+
(Diana Grissell) *led: mstke 6th: hdd wl bef 2 out and immediately hung rt and reluctant: lost all ch: wkng whn hit 2 out: bhd and eased flat: t.o* **14/1**

11 *1 3/4* **Heading To First**[119] 6-10-11 0.............................(p) MichaelByrne(3) 69
(Paddy Butler) *t.k.h: hld up in midfield: rdn and btn 3 out: wknd bef next: bhd and eased flat: t.o* **100/1**

3m 57.9s (-2.90) **Going Correction** -0.575s/f (Firm)
WFA 4 from 5yo+ 9lb **11** Ran SP% **118.5**
Speed ratings (Par 103): **84,82,79,77,76 72,71,71,70,63 63**
toteswingers 1&2 £7.10, 1&3 £11.30, 2&3 £4.70 CSF £10.57 TOTE £2.60: £1.10, £1.90, £1.20; EX 12.50 Trifecta £23.60 Pool: £1763.16 - 55.92 winning units..
Owner Battersby, Birchall, Halsall & Vestey **Bred** Overbury Stallions Ltd **Trained** Over Norton, Oxon

FOCUS
Split bends for all races. A gloomy morning and 3mm of rain saw the going changed to Soft all over prior to this opening maiden event. The general opinion of the riders afterwards was that it wasn't too holding, though. This was run at an ordinary gallop and no doubt it proved an advantage to race handily. The winner stepped up on his hurdles form, with the next few close to their marks.

2003 FRIENDS OF JOSH GIFFORD H'CAP CHASE (FOR THE JOSH GIFFORD MEMORIAL TROPHY) (14 fncs) 2m 4f
2:50 (2:50) (Class 5) (0-95,95) 4-Y-0+ **£2,599** (£763; £381; £190)

Form RPR

22P- **1** **Upton Mead (IRE)**[43] [1526] 6-11-12 **95**.......................(b) RichardJohnson 105
(Kevin Tork) *chsd ldrs: wnt 2nd 7th tl led bef 3 out: drvn and hdd bef 2 out: led again between last: pricked ears in front but sn drvn clr: idling and drvn out flat* **3/1**[1]

1/P- **2** *4 1/2* **Doheny Bar (IRE)**[21] [1700] 10-10-8 **77**.................................. TomO'Brien 83
(Paul Henderson) *led tl 3rd: chsd ldr tl 7th: styd prom: chsd wnr bef 3 out: led and looked to travelling best bef 2 out: j.rt 2 out: hdd and no ex between last 2: tired but hld on to 2nd cl home* **7/2**[3]

205- **3** *nk* **Osmosia (FR)**[12] [1822] 8-11-12 **95**...........................(tp) MarcGoldstein 100
(Chris Gordon) *chsd ldrs: short of room 2nd: drvn and chsd ldng pair sn after 3 out: mstke 2 out: tired but plugged on flat and pressing for 2nd cl home* **5/1**

/5P- **4** *9* **Watergate (IRE)**[43] [1528] 7-10-10 **79**............................... LeightonAspell 76
(Richard Rowe) *w ldr tl led 3rd: clr after 6th: hdd after 11th and sn struggling: hit 3 out: 4th and wl hld bef next* **10/3**[2]

PP4- **5** *hd* **Curragh Dancer (FR)**[16] [1769] 10-9-11 **69** oh5............(v) AdamWedge(3) 65
(Paddy Butler) *in tch in midfield: rdn and struggling after 8th: 6th and lost tch 10th: plugged on u.p and battling for modest 4th flat* **33/1**

000/ **6** *1/2* **Badb Catha (IRE)**[405] [1540] 7-9-9 **71**...................................(t) MrFTett(7) 67
(Roger Curtis) *mstkes: in tch in midfield: 5th and outpcd after 10th: n.d after but plugged on and battling for modest 4th flat* **10/1**

545- **P** **She's Humble (IRE)**[43] [1530] 11-10-1 **70**.........................(v) JamieMoore
(Linda Jewell) *nvr travelling wl in rr: rdn 5th: lost tch after 8th: p.u bef 10th* **15/2**

500- **P** **What's For Tea**[16] [1765] 8-9-9 **69** oh2...............................(vt) EDLinehan(5)
(Paddy Butler) *chsd ldrs: mstke 2nd: lost pl next: dropped to last and rdn after 4th: lost tch 6th: t.o whn p.u bef 10th* **22/1**

5m 10.3s (3.00) **Going Correction** -0.15s/f (Good) **8** Ran SP% **115.1**
Speed ratings (Par 103): **88,86,86,82,82 82, ,**
toteswingers 1&2 £2.10, 1&3 £1.10, 2&3 £2.40 CSF £14.58 CT £49.85 TOTE £3.60: £1.10, £1.80, £1.80; EX 14.10 Trifecta £21.50 Pool: £1771.70 - 61.73 winning units..
Owner Tork Racing **Bred** Francis Small **Trained** Leigh, Surrey

FOCUS
A weak handicap that was run at an average gallop and produced a tired finish. The first three were all pretty close to their marks.

2004 RETIREMENT VILLAGES NOVICES' H'CAP HURDLE (9 hdls) 2m
3:20 (3:20) (Class 5) (0-100,100) 3-Y-0+ **£2,053** (£598; £299)

Form RPR

0/5- **1** **Just When**[162] [235] 4-11-7 **100**..................................(v) NicodeBoinville(5) 121+
(Patrick Chamings) *chsd ldr tl led after 5th: mde rest: rdn and qcknd clr after 3 out: hit next: eased flat: easily* **10/1**

22/- **2** *15* **Meirig's Dream (IRE)**[185] 5379 7-10-0 **74** oh3.................. JamesDavies 76
(Philip Hobbs) *chsd ldrs: j.rt 5th: wnt 2nd after 6th: drvn and outpcd by wnr after 3 out: no ch w wnr whn j.rt 2 out and last: hld on for 2nd u.p flat* **3/1**[1]

001- **3** *1* **Ivebeenthinking**[4] 1938 5-10-4 **78** 7ex................................ FelixDeGiles 77
(Tom Symonds) *hld up off the pce in last quartet: hdwy after 6th: 7th and styng on after 3 out: wnt 3rd between last 2: kpt on: no ch w wnr* **4/1**[2]

555/ **4** *1 ¾* **Coup De Grace (IRE)**[185] 5376 4-11-9 **100**.................. JoshuaMoore(3) 97
(Pat Phelan) *hld up off the pce in last quartet: rdn and effrt after 6th: styd on between last 2: swtchd lft and past btn horses flat: nvr trbld ldrs* **33/1**

F02- **5** *¾* **Benny The Swinger (IRE)**[24] 1674 8-11-8 **96**............... MarcGoldstein 93
(Chris Gordon) *j.rt: hld up in midfield: 5th and no imp after 3 out: wnt 3rd bef 2 out tl between last 2: plugged on same pce* **5/1**[3]

0P6- **6** *¾* **Petrocelli**[62] 1331 6-9-8 **75**.. JPKiely(7) 74
(Tim Vaughan) *chsd ldrs: rdn in 3rd whn blnd and pckd 3 out: wl hld and plugged on same pce after* **8/1**

223- **7** *shd* **Royal Trooper (IRE)**[8] 1567 7-11-9 **97**......................(vt) MattieBatchelor 93
(Jim Best) *hld up in last quartet: hdwy on downhill run after 6th: no imp bef 2 out: nvr trbld ldrs* **16/1**

306- **8** *1 ¾* **Midnight Thomas**[34] 1595 4-10-3 **77**.................................(t[1]) IanPopham 71
(Martin Keighley) *racd in midfield: effrt u.p bef 3 out: wnt modest 3rd after 3 out tl bef next: wknd between last 2* **14/1**

U44- **9** *1 ½* **Night Of Passion (IRE)**[84] 1132 5-10-3 **77**................... NickScholfield 69
(Jeremy Scott) *racd in midfield: pushed along and lost pl after 4th: drvn and struggling after next: n.d after: plugged on flat* **8/1**

020- **10** *2 ¼* **Ashcott Boy**[87] 1120 5-11-7 **95**..(p) NoelFehily 85
(Neil Mulholland) *racd in midfield: rdn and no hdwy after 6th: plugged on but no threat fr next* **16/1**

30/- **11** *7* **Nemo Spirit (IRE)**[227] 4642 8-11-5 **100**.......................(tp) JamesO'Neill(7) 83
(Jim Best) *hld up in rr: mstke 2nd: lost tch bef 3 out: n.d* **16/1**

/40- **12** *9* **Hubood**[118] 671 5-10-5 **79**..(p) DaveCrosse 53
(Zoe Davison) *racd in midfield: nt fluent 3rd: rdn and struggling after 6th: bhd after next: t.o* **100/1**

36P- **P** **Rachael's Ruby**[29] 1627 6-11-11 **99**................................ (p) ColinBolger
(Roger Teal) *led tl after 5th: wknd bef next: t.o whn p.u 2 out* **50/1**

3m 50.5s (-10.30) **Going Correction** -0.575s/f (Firm)
WFA 4 from 5yo+ 9lb **13** Ran SP% **123.2**
Speed ratings (Par 103): **102,94,94,93,92 92,92,91,90,89 86,81,**
toteswingers 1&2 £10.90, 1&3 £12.30, 2&3 £3.00 CSF £41.99 CT £147.30 TOTE £15.30: £4.00, £1.90, £1.70; EX 66.70 Trifecta £536.00 Pool: £898.99 - 1.25 winning units..
Owner Inhurst Players **Bred** George Strawbridge Stables **Trained** Baughurst, Hants

FOCUS
A moderate novice handicap, run at a fair gallop and in a good time for the grade. A massive step up from the winner on his previous hurdle form but but he's entitled to rate higher on visored Flat form.

2005 GERALD KARN-SMITH MEMORIAL NOVICES' LIMITED H'CAP CHASE (14 fncs) 2m 4f
3:50 (3:50) (Class 3) (0-140,137) 4-Y-0+ **£8,122** (£2,385; £1,192; £596)

Form RPR

315/ **1** **Uxizandre (FR)**[199] 5161 5-11-3 **135**... APMcCoy 142+
(Alan King) *t.k.h: mostly j. fast and accurately: chsd ldr tl led bef 3 out: gng best whn dived, blnd bdly and hdd 2 out: swtchd rt and rallied u.p to chal: led flat: r.o wl* **11/10**[1]

FF/- **2** *nk* **De Blacksmith (IRE)**[188] 5340 5-10-5 **123** oh1.................... JamieMoore 125
(Gary Moore) *chsd ldng pair: mstke 11th: lft chsng wnr 3 out: rdn and effrt to press wnr whn lft in ld 2 out: drvn and pressed last: hdd flat: kpt on but no ex fnl 75yds* **15/2**

1P0/ **3** *26* **Loose Chips**[222] 4736 7-11-5 **137**...(b) NoelFehily 113
(Charlie Longsdon) *j.rt at times: led tl after 11th: blnd and dropped to 3rd 3 out: wknd u.p bef 2 out* **2/1**[2]

6/3- **4** *¾* **Barlow (IRE)**[160] 296 6-10-2 **123** oh1.......................... GavinSheehan(3) 99
(Warren Greatrex) *a in last: mstke and pushed along 8th: lost tch after 3 out: wl btn and mstke last* **9/2**[3]

4m 58.95s (-8.35) **Going Correction** -0.15s/f (Good) **4** Ran SP% **110.9**
Speed ratings (Par 107): **110,109,99,99**
CSF £8.41 TOTE £1.70; EX 7.90 Trifecta £13.60 Pool: £783.03 - 42.98 winning units..
Owner John P McManus **Bred** Frederic Aimez **Trained** Barbury Castle, Wilts

FOCUS
A good-quality novice handicap in which three of the four were having a first taste of chasing. They went a fair gallop. The winner looks a better chaser than hurdler, and the second stepped up on his best hurdles form.

2006 SIS H'CAP HURDLE (14 hdls) 3m 1f 110y
4:20 (4:20) (Class 3) (0-130,122) 4-Y-0+ **£6,498** (£1,908; £954; £477)

Form RPR

213- **1** **Cannon Fodder**[29] 1628 6-10-11 **107**............................... MarcGoldstein 117+
(Sheena West) *in tch in midfield: hdwy to chse ldrs 10th: led after next: mstke 3 out: drvn and kpt on gamely between last 2* **10/3**[1]

2/5- **2** *1 ¾* **Abruzzi**[167] 158 5-11-5 **115**.. FelixDeGiles 122
(Tom Symonds) *in tch in midfield: chsd ldr after 9th: rdn and pressing wnr 2 out: kpt on same pce u.p flat* **8/1**

331/ **3** *9* **Ballyculla (IRE)**[181] 5468 6-11-9 **119**.................................... NoelFehily 119
(Warren Greatrex) *hld up in tch towards rr: hdwy after 10th: chsd ldng pair and drvn after 3 out: no imp: wknd last* **5/1**

0/3- **4** *3 ¾* **Cabimas**[17] 1745 6-11-0 **113**... JoshuaMoore(3) 107
(Gary Moore) *hld up in rr: hdwy after 11th: rdn and no imp after 3 out: wknd 2 out: wnt modest 4th last* **4/1**[2]

/03- **5** *10* **Gigondas**[53] 1436 4-10-9 **106**.. JamieMoore 89
(Gary Moore) *in tch in last trio: rdn 11th: wknd next* **16/1**

/11- **6** *1 ¼* **Koultas King (IRE)**[42] 1533 6-11-2 **112**......................(t) RichardJohnson 98
(Tim Vaughan) *chsd ldrs: cl 4th and mstke 3 out: wkng whn mstke next: fdd flat* **9/2**[3]

520- **7** *17* **Twin Bud**[40] 1565 8-9-11 **96** oh2................................. AdamWedge(3) 62
(Anna Newton-Smith) *w ldr tl led 4th: rdn and hdd after 11th: sn dropped out: bhd bef 2 out: t.o: lame* **6/1**

006- **8** *1 ¾* **Akbabend**[117] 839 7-10-12 **118**..............................(tp) LouisMuspratt(10) 82
(Chris Gordon) *in tch in midfield: lost pl and dropped to rr 7th: rdn next: wknd bef 3 out: t.o* **25/1**

P/ **P** **Wolf Hall (IRE)**[369] 1885 6-11-3 **113**...................................... WillKennedy
(Violet M Jordan) *led tl mstke and hdd 4th: styd chsng ldr tl rdn and lost pl qckly 9th: tailing off whn p.u after next* **66/1**

6m 16.7s (-8.30) **Going Correction** -0.575s/f (Firm)
WFA 4 from 5yo+ 11lb **9** Ran SP% **114.5**
Speed ratings (Par 107): **89,88,85,84,81 81,75,75,**
toteswingers 1&2 £7.90, 1&3 £4.20, 2&3 £11.50 CSF £29.86 CT £131.03 TOTE £4.50: £1.40, £3.10, £1.90; EX 32.40 Trifecta £235.80 Pool: £1692.46 - 5.38 winning units..
Owner The Cheapskates **Bred** Andrew And Mrs S R B Davis **Trained** Falmer, E Sussex

FOCUS
This ordinary staying handicap was run at a routine gallop and two came clear off the home bend. The winner is rated in line with his recent C&D run, with the second to his mark.

2007 BETFRED/TOTEPOOL RACING'S BIGGEST SUPPORTER NOVICES' H'CAP CHASE (12 fncs) 2m 1f
4:50 (4:50) (Class 4) (0-110,110) 4-Y-0+ **£3,898** (£1,144; £572; £286)

Form RPR

6/3- **1** **Next Sensation (IRE)**[41] 1553 6-11-7 **105**..................(t) TomScudamore 125+
(Michael Scudamore) *j.w: mde all: lft clr 2nd: clr w runner-up fr 8th: readily drew clr bef 2 out: eased flat: easily* **4/1**[1]

51U- **2** *10* **Moorlands Jack**[11] 1834 8-11-4 **102**..............................(p) NickScholfield 108
(Jeremy Scott) *chsd ldrs: lft chsng wnr 2nd: clsd and clr w wnr fr 8th: rdn and btn bef 2 out: wl hld after but kpt on for clr 2nd* **4/1**[1]

P- **3** *8* **Un Anjou (FR)**[151] 454 5-11-6 **104**... NoelFehily 102
(David Dennis) *hld up in last trio: 6th and outpcd whn mstke 8th: wnt modest 3rd 3 out: plugged on but no threat to ldrs* **10/1**

323- **4** *4 ½* **Quadriller (FR)**[21] 1697 6-11-7 **105**....................................(t) TomO'Brien 99
(Philip Hobbs) *hld up in last trio: sme hdwy 7th: outpcd and no threat to ldrs fr next: plugged on same pce fr 3 out* **5/1**[3]

155- **5** *27* **Time Book (IRE)**[16] 1765 7-10-0 **84** oh4.......................(t) BrendanPowell 51
(Colin Tizzard) *chsd ldrs: mstke 1st: lft 3rd next: rdn and lost pl 7th: bhd next: t.o 3 out* **8/1**

2/3- **6** *¾* **Fair Bramble**[161] 268 7-11-5 **103**..................................... LeightonAspell 69
(Oliver Sherwood) *racd in midfield: mstke 1st: 4th and outpcd 8th: struggling bef next: lost tch after 3 out: heavily eased flat: t.o* **9/2**[2]

150/ **7** *7* **Rocky Elsom (USA)**[191] 5284 6-11-10 **108**........................... DarylJacob 67
(David Arbuthnot) *hld up in last trio: hdwy to chse ldrs 7th: outpcd next: wknd bef 3 out: t.o* **12/1**

0P6/ **F** **Should I Stay (FR)**[242] 4345 5-11-12 **110**........................ PaddyBrennan
(Tom George) *chsd ldr tl fell 2nd* **7/1**

4m 17.6s (-5.40) **Going Correction** -0.15s/f (Good) **8** Ran SP% **115.2**
Speed ratings (Par 105): **106,101,97,95,82 82,79,**
toteswingers 1&2 £3.40, 1&3 £6.20, 2&3 £11.00 CSF £21.10 CT £148.32 TOTE £6.10: £2.20, £2.60, £4.20; EX 25.50 Trifecta £150.60 Pool: £1709.55 - 8.50 winning units..
Owner Mark Blandford **Bred** Mrs Regina McAuliffe **Trained** Bromsash, H'fords

FOCUS
An ordinary novice handicap. There was a sound gallop on and all bar the first pair were in trouble three from home. A big step up from the impressive winner with the next two pretty much to their marks.

2008 GOOD LUCK CLAIRE H'CAP HURDLE (12 hdls) 2m 5f
5:20 (5:20) (Class 5) (0-100,100) 4-Y-0+ **£2,053** (£598; £299)

Form RPR

44P/ **1** **Hopatina (IRE)**[247] 4260 7-11-4 **95**............................... MichaelByrne(3) 105
(Neil Mulholland) *hld up in rr: stdy prog after 8th: rdn and chsd ldrs after 3 out: j. into ld next: styd on wl flat: rdn out* **20/1**

10/- **2** *3* **Sandy's Double**[202] 5104 7-11-12 **100**..................... SamTwiston-Davies 106
(Jamie Snowden) *led tl 2nd: chsd ldr after: drvn after 3 out: pressing ldrs next: unable qck and kpt on same pce flat* **4/1**[2]

P/1- **3** *1 ¾* **Just Cloudy**[133] 686 9-11-8 **96**..(t) DarylJacob 100
(Robert Walford) *chsd ldrs: 3rd and drvn after 3 out: kpt on u.p flat to go 3rd last strides* **3/1**[1]

04F- **4** *hd* **Bold Tara**[24] 1675 6-9-10 **77**...(p) OllieGarner(7) 82
(Martin Keighley) *j.rt: chsd ldr tl led 2nd: clr at 4th: rdn bef 2 out: outj. and hdd next: no ex and j.rt last: one pce and lost 2 pls flat* **8/1**[3]

P/P- **5** *10* **Presenting Dr T (IRE)**[11] 1837 7-10-1 **75**......................(p) JamieMoore 69
(Harry Chisman) *hld up towards rr: rdn and hdwy bef 3 out: no imp bef 2 out: plugged on* **25/1**

P01- **6** *16* **Isthereadifference (IRE)**[59] 1364 6-11-7 **95**......................(p) NoelFehily 73
(Neil Mulholland) *in tch in midfield: hdwy after 8th: rdn and effrt bef 3 out: wknd bef 2 out* **4/1**[2]

46P- **7** *shd* **Renagisha (IRE)**[42] 1538 7-9-10 **75**..........................(v) TrevorWhelan(5) 53
(Jim Best) *hld up towards rr: rdn and dropped out after 8th: styd on past btn horses after 3 out: no threat to ldrs* **50/1**

030- **8** *16* **Unsist (FR)**[29] 1625 5-10-0 **74** oh1.................................... LiamTreadwell 36
(Nick Gifford) *in tch in midfield: mstke 5th: 6th and btn whn mstke 3 out: wknd bef next: t.o* **8/1**[3]

/PP- **9** *2 ¼* **Head Hunted**[8] 1890 6-11-12 **100**...................................... MattieBatchelor 59
(Jim Best) *hld up in last trio: mstke 2nd: mstke and rdn 7th: struggling after next: t.o after 3 out* **33/1**

406- **10** *6* **Be Marvellous (IRE)**[9] 1863 5-11-7 **95**.........................(tp) BrendanPowell 48
(Colin Tizzard) *in tch in midfield: rdn after 8th: struggling next: wknd 3 out: t.o* **14/1**

3/4- **11** *½* **Romney Marsh**[149] 478 12-11-8 **96**..................................... HaddenFrost 49
(Roger Curtis) *in tch in midfield: outpcd next: wknd bef 3 out: t.o* **25/1**

/00- **12** *10* **Mac's Grey (IRE)**[148] 484 6-10-9 **83**.................................... DaveCrosse 26
(Zoe Davison) *t.k.h: hld up in rr: rdn and struggling after 8th: lost tch after next: t.o after 3 out* **66/1**

440- **13** *12* **Al Amaan**[29] 1630 8-10-11 **85**...(p) LeightonAspell 16
(Jamie Poulton) *t.k.h: chsd ldrs tl 8th: lost pl bef next: t.o bef 2 out* **20/1**

360/ **14** *16* **Oscar Baby (IRE)**[265] 3925 7-11-8 **96**............................. MarcGoldstein 11
(Diana Grissell) *in tch in midfield: rdn and lost pl after 7th: t.o fr 9th* **20/1**

5m 11.1s (-5.90) **Going Correction** -0.575s/f (Firm) **14** Ran SP% **122.3**
Speed ratings (Par 103): **88,86,86,86,82 76,76,70,69,66 66,62,58,52**
toteswingers 1&2 £24.70, 1&3 £16.10, 2&3 £3.20 CSF £94.40 CT £321.52 TOTE £30.40: £8.20, £1.80, £1.80; EX 118.60 Trifecta £871.30 Pool: £2048.35 - 1.76 winning units..
Owner J R Baigent **Bred** Avon Thoroughbreds **Trained** Limpley Stoke, Wilts

FOCUS
A moderate handicap, run at a fair gallop. The winner is rated up 10lb on his 2011 best, with the next three to their marks.

T/Plt: £11.70 to a £1 stake. Pool: £97850.21 - 6102.07 winning tickets T/Qpdt: £9.60 to a £1 stake. Pool: £4253.20 - 325.62 winning tickets SP

1828 EXETER (R-H)

Tuesday, October 22

OFFICIAL GOING: Good to soft (soft in places; 6.2)

Wind: strong behind Weather: overcast with heavy showers

2009 HAVE YOUR CHRISTMAS PARTY HERE AMATEUR RIDERS' NOVICES' HURDLE (12 hdls) 2m 7f 110y

2:10 (2:11) (Class 4) 4-Y-0+ **£3,119** (£967; £483; £242)

Form RPR

31P/ 1 **Masters Hill (IRE)**[339] 2466 7-10-11 0 MrMLegg(7) 123+
(Colin Tizzard) *racd wd: trckd ldrs: trckd ldr after 5th: chal 3 out: led between last 2: rchd for last: styd on wl: pushed out* **5/4**[1]

2 5 **Lumpys Gold**[185] 5-11-4 0 MrWBiddick 116+
(Paul Nicholls) *racd keenly trcking ldrs: settled in front after 5th tl lit up by loose horse and drew clr bef 7th: rdn and hdd between last 2: styd on but no ex* **7/2**[3]

3 10 **Wither Yenot (IRE)**[169] 154 6-10-11 0 MrMJPKendrick(7) 105
(Ben Case) *mid-div: hdwy whn lft 3rd at the 6th: rdn bef 3 out: sn outpcd by ldrs: j.big and wnt lft 2 out* **25/1**

320/ 4 4 **Kastani Beach (IRE)**[191] 5321 7-10-13 103 MissAliceMills(5) 101
(Seamus Mullins) *mid-div: rdn and hdwy to chse ldrs appr 3 out: sn one pce* **12/1**

3/0- 5 7 **Hare In A Round (IRE)**[25] 1671 5-11-1 0 MrFMitchell(3) 94
(Rebecca Curtis) *mid-div: shkn up and hdwy after 7th: rdn to chse ldrs bef 3 out: wknd after 2 out* **14/1**

25/ 6 12 **Degenerate (FR)**[156] 6-10-11 0 MrCGethings(7) 82
(Jeremy Scott) *hld up towards rr of midfield: sme prog after 9th: sn rdn: wkng whn rchd for 2 out* **20/1**

/00- 7 8 **Native Brian (IRE)**[10] 1864 7-10-11 0 (t) MissVWade(7) 77
(Jeremy Scott) *in tch: lft 4th at the 6th: rdn bef 3 out: wknd 2 out* **50/1**

504- 8 12 **Sava Bridge (IRE)**[19] 1732 6-10-11 0 MrGBranton(7) 62
(Paul Henderson) *a towards rr* **100/1**

6- 9 23 **Anchoretta Eyre (IRE)**[19] 1731 7-10-4 0 MrHBeswick(7) 32
(Fergal O'Brien) *virtually ref to r: t.o thrght* **66/1**

U- F **Lady Oaksey**[18] 1749 7-10-4 0 MrEBarrett(7)
(Bob Buckler) *trckd ldrs tl lost pl 6th: struggling in rr fr after next: t.o whn fell heavily 2 out* **200/1**

/50- U **Un Ami (FR)**[152] 454 5-10-11 118 MrCWilliams(7)
(Nick Williams) *hld up towards rr: blnd and uns rdr 3rd* **3/1**[2]

0- P **Hearditbefore (IRE)**[21] 1712 5-10-4 0 (p) MrStanSheppard(7)
(Matt Sheppard) *led tl after 5th: stmbld bdly next: sn p.u: fatally injured* **66/1**

5m 45.1s (-13.90) **Going Correction** -0.425s/f (Good) 12 Ran SP% **121.1**
Speed ratings (Par 105): **106,104,101,99,97 93,90,86,79, ,**
toteswingers 1&2 £2.90, 2&3 £10.30, 1&3 £11.00 CSF £5.86 TOTE £3.10: £1.10, £1.40, £3.70; EX 10.20 Trifecta £145.60 Pool: £1100.85 - 5.66 winning units..
Owner K S B, M Doughty & Mrs Sarah Tizzard **Bred** S McElroy **Trained** Milborne Port, Dorset

FOCUS
A total of 26mm of rain had fallen in the 24 hours leading up to the morning of this fixture and the ground was officially good to soft, soft in places. Racing began in cloudy, damp and windy conditions, with a novice hurdle in which just a handful had obvious claims. A hurdles best from the winner, but below the level of his chase win.

2010 YOUR FAVOURITE POOL BETS AT TOTEPOOL.COM BEGINNERS' CHASE (18 fncs) 3m

2:40 (2:40) (Class 4) 4-Y-0+ **£5,580** (£1,908)

Form RPR

25F/ 1 **Sonofvic (IRE)**[586] 4862 8-11-4 0 DarylJacob 147+
(Paul Nicholls) *lft in ld 2nd: mde rest: pushed along and in command fr 3 out: styd on wl* **13/8**[2]

403/ 2 12 **Kentford Grey Lady**[186] 5371 7-10-11 0 NoelFehily 128+
(Emma Lavelle) *trckd wnr fr 2nd: travelled wl tl rching for 12th: nt so fluent at fences after: shkn up after 4 out: sn hld* **10/11**[1]

3PP/ F **Rendl Beach (IRE)**[310] 3085 6-11-4 0 APMcCoy
(Rebecca Curtis) *led tl fell 2nd* **11/2**[3]

6m 0.1s (-9.20) **Going Correction** -0.425s/f (Good) 3 Ran SP% **105.9**
Speed ratings (Par 105): **98,94,**
CSF £3.48 TOTE £2.50; EX 3.60 Trifecta £3.90 Pool: £694.37 - 133.04 winning units..
Owner Mrs Angela Hart **Bred** Mrs Rosemary Ross **Trained** Ditcheat, Somerset

FOCUS
A fascinating beginners' chase, despite the small field. The winner is rated to the level of his best 2011 chase run.

2011 GREYSTONE NOVICES' HURDLE (8 hdls) 2m 1f

3:10 (3:11) (Class 4) 4-Y-0+ **£3,249** (£954; £477; £238)

Form RPR

1S2/ 1 **Horizontal Speed (IRE)**[220] 4787 5-10-12 0 RichardJohnson 120+
(Philip Hobbs) *in tch: tk clsr order 4th: led 2 out: sn rdn: styd on: drvn out* **1/1**[1]

2 ¾ **Minella Friend (IRE)**[153] 443 4-10-12 0 PaulMoloney 118+
(Evan Williams) *disp ld tl 5th: chsd ldrs: nt best of runs briefly turning in: rdn whn swtchd lft bef 2 out: styd on to regain 2nd run-in: clsng on wnr nring fin* **5/2**[2]

/32- 3 2½ **Quite By Chance**[22] 1695 4-10-12 0 JoeTizzard 114
(Colin Tizzard) *disp tl clr ldr 5th: rdn and hdd whn hit 2 out: styd on tl no ex towards fin* **15/2**[3]

F4/ 4 9 **Brinestine (USA)**[229] 4617 4-10-12 0 DarylJacob 105
(Paul Nicholls) *mid-div: hdwy after 5th to trck ldrs next: styd on same pce fr 2 out* **10/1**

5/1- 5 hd **Jack By The Hedge**[160] 307 4-11-5 0 IanPopham 112
(Caroline Keevil) *mid-div: hdwy after 5th: rdn to chse ldrs next: styd on same pce* **40/1**

4/- 6 2¼ **Dream Deal**[191] 5324 5-10-12 0 NickScholfield 103
(Jeremy Scott) *mid-div: struggling whn lost pl 5th: prog bk into midfield 3 out: no further imp fr next* **16/1**

205/ 7 ½ **Somerset Lias (IRE)**[191] 5324 5-10-12 0 SamJones 103
(Bob Buckler) *mid-div: struggling in rr after 4th: styd on again fr 3 out: nvr threatened ldrs* **66/1**

245/ 8 6 **Absolutely Bygones (IRE)**[322] 2844 5-10-9 0 JamesBest(3) 97
(Jackie Du Plessis) *racd on outer: rdn appr 3 out: nvr bttr than mid-div* **66/1**

0/0- 9 11 **Puerto Azul (IRE)**[10] 1864 9-10-9 97 MichealNolan(3) 86
(Bernard Scriven) *hld up towards rr: hdwy after 4th: rdn in midfield gng to 3 out: sn wknd* **100/1**

4/5- 10 7 **Saudi Pearl (IRE)**[26] 1662 5-10-12 0 SamTwiston-Davies 79
(Nigel Twiston-Davies) *mid-div: rdn after 4th: sn bhd: t.o* **50/1**

11 nk **Ernest Speak (IRE)**[61] 4-10-12 0 HaddenFrost 78
(Martin Hill) *t.k.h: trckd ldrs: chal 5th: rdn bef next: sn wknd: t.o* **100/1**

R/2- 12 24 **L Frank Baum (IRE)**[35] 1595 6-10-12 0 JamesDavies 54
(Bernard Llewellyn) *struggling in rr 3rd: t.o fr after 5th* **33/1**

0- 13 9 **Drummond**[16] 1795 4-10-7 0 RobertWilliams(5) 45
(Bernard Llewellyn) *a towards rr: wknd 3 out: t.o* **100/1**

000/ U **Salut L'As (FR)**[324] 7-10-12 0 WillKennedy 80
(Sue Gardner) *in tch: j.lft at times: chsd ldrs 5th: rdn and wknd bef next: bhd whn wkng and uns rdr last* **100/1**

- U **Luckwell Bridge** 8-10-2 0 JonPark(10)
(Kevin Bishop) *hld up towards rr: nt fluent bef eventually bucking rdr off after 1st* **50/1**

4m 3.6s (-11.90) **Going Correction** -0.425s/f (Good) 15 Ran SP% **121.6**
Speed ratings (Par 105): **111,110,109,105,105 104,103,101,95,92 92,81,76, ,**
toteswingers 1&2 £1.20, 2&3 £2.90, 1&3 £1.10 CSF £3.40 TOTE £2.70: £1.10, £1.70, £1.70; EX 5.20 Trifecta £19.20 Pool: £1570.93 - 61.14 winning units..
Owner Favourites Racing **Bred** Dick White **Trained** Withycombe, Somerset

FOCUS
Not a lot of obvious depth to this nonetheless interesting novice hurdle. Heavy rain accompanied the race and the early pace was steady. There's a case for rating the form a bit higher through the winner.

2012 TOTEPOOL MOBILE BEST MATE NOVICES' LIMITED H'CAP CHASE (12 fncs) 2m 1f 110y

3:40 (3:40) (Class 3) (0-140,132) 4-Y-0+ [illegible] (£2,244; £1,122; £561; £280)

Form RPR

/12- 1 **Red Riverman**[16] 1782 5-10-9 **122** SamTwiston-Davies 128
(Nigel Twiston-Davies) *hld up in last but in tch: wnt 5th at the 5th: trckd ldrs 4 out: shkn up appr last: led run-in: drifted rt: drvn out* **10/1**

126/ 2 ¾ **The Italian Yob (IRE)**[227] 4663 5-10-11 **124** NoelFehily 129
(Nick Williams) *led: jnd 4 out: pushed along whn blnd and hdd 2 out: rallied to press wnr after last: drifted rt: hld nring fin* **11/4**[2]

2P0/ 3 1¼ **Funny Star (FR)**[185] 5405 5-11-5 **132** (t) DarylJacob 137+
(Paul Nicholls) *trckd ldrs: hmpd 3rd: wnt 2nd after next: chal 4 out: led 2 out: rdn whn nt fluent last: qckly hdd and swtchd lft: no ex* **10/1**

11P/ 4 1½ **Barrakilla (IRE)**[227] 4663 6-11-3 **130** PaulMoloney 134
(Evan Williams) *trckd ldrs: shkn up after 4 out: mstke 2 out: styng on at same pce whn lft 4th at the last* **3/1**[3]

4/5- 5 13 **Annacotty (IRE)**[21] 1709 5-11-0 **127** IanPopham 120
(Martin Keighley) *nvr fluent: trckd ldrs tl awkward and dropped to last pair after 3rd: bhd fr 5th: nvr bk on terms* **9/4**[1]

320/ F **Flaming Charmer (IRE)**[206] 5013 5-10-5 **118** oh3 (t) BrendanPowell 120
(Colin Tizzard) *trckd ldrs: rdn after 4 out: styng on at same pce in hld 4th whn fell heavily last* **7/1**

4m 11.7s (-7.30) **Going Correction** -0.425s/f (Good) 6 Ran SP% **113.1**
Speed ratings (Par 107): **99,98,98,97,91**
toteswingers 1&2 £6.00, 2&3 £12.60, 1&3 £3.00 CSF £38.70 TOTE £6.50: £2.10, £2.00; EX 16.40 Trifecta £66.40 Pool: £2076.74 - 23.45 winning units..
Owner N A Twiston-Davies **Bred** Lady Lonsdale **Trained** Naunton, Gloucs

FOCUS
Just two of these had previous chasing form. They finished in a heap but the race should produce winners.

2013 EXETER H'CAP HURDLE (10 hdls) 2m 3f

4:10 (4:10) (Class 4) (0-115,115) 4-Y-0+ **£3,249** (£954; £477; £238)

Form RPR

503- 1 **Ray Diamond**[12] 1833 8-10-3 **95** JamesBest(3) 98+
(Jackie Du Plessis) *mid-div: hdwy to trck ldr 5th: led 3 out: styd on wl: rdn out* **7/2**[1]

/P4- 2 2¼ **Mountaineer (FR)**[17] 1765 8-11-2 **105** JamieMoore 106
(Gary Moore) *t.k.h in midfield: hdwy after 6th: rdn to chse wnr and hung lft fr 3 out: styd on but hld fr 2 out* **8/1**

032/ 3 5 **Amok (IRE)**[253] 4159 5-11-11 **114** (t) RichardJohnson 112
(Tim Vaughan) *racd neely: hld up towards rr: taken wd in bk st: hdwy on outer appr 3 out: sn rdn: nt fluent 2 out: wnt 3rd whn rching for last: styd on same pce* **5/1**[3]

F55- 4 ¾ **Pirans Car**[21] 1711 7-10-0 **89** oh6 (t) SamTwiston-Davies 85
(Nigel Hawke) *hld up towards rr: rdn appr 3 out: styd on fr 2 out: snatched 4th fnl stride* **33/1**

446- 5 nse **Callisto Moon**[18] 1745 9-11-5 **108** MarkGrant 103
(Jo Hughes) *hld up in tch: pushed along after 7th: rdn bef 3 out: styd on same pce: lost 4th fnl stride* **25/1**

124- 6 1 **Ullswater (IRE)**[16] 1799 5-10-11 **100** (t) NickScholfield 95
(Andy Turnell) *hld up towards rr: hdwy appr 3 out: sn rdn: styd on same pce fr 2 out* **6/1**

0/S- 7 5 **Oscar Jane (IRE)**[134] 691 6-10-9 **98** BrendanPowell 87
(Johnny Farrelly) *mid-div: trckd ldrs after 4th: rdn appr 3 out: wknd bef 2 out* **10/1**

1/0- 8 2½ **Pyleigh Lass**[159] 336 7-11-12 **115** IanPopham 102
(Jeremy Scott) *trckd ldrs: struggling whn lost pl 6th: wknd bef 2 out* **9/2**[2]

313/ 9 10 **Eseej (USA)**[138] 1357 8-11-9 **112** NoelFehily 89
(Geoffrey Deacon) *j.lft: led tl rdn 3 out: sn wknd* **40/1**

315- 10 10 **Surf And Turf (IRE)**[52] 1470 7-11-12 **115** (p) APMcCoy 82
(Jonjo O'Neill) *racd wd: in tch: rdn bef 3 out: sn wknd* **11/1**

0LP/ 11 4½ **Light The World (FR)**[248] 4260 5-10-6 **95** DougieCostello 57
(Kevin Frost) *mid-div: rdn and wkng whn j.lft fr 3 out* **10/1**

4m 34.6s (-8.10) **Going Correction** -0.425s/f (Good) 11 Ran SP% **118.2**
Speed ratings (Par 105): **100,99,96,96,96 96,94,93,88,84 82**
toteswingers 1&2 £9.10, 2&3 £5.40, 1&3 £3.10 CSF £31.49 CT £141.61 TOTE £6.50: £3.20, £4.30, £1.10; EX 43.40 Trifecta £150.60 Pool: £915.37 - 4.55 winning units..
Owner Miss J Du Plessis **Bred** H H L Bloodstock **Trained** Trehan, Cornwall

FOCUS
A wide-open handicap hurdle on paper, with a top weight rated 115. The early pace was steady. Quite a weak race, rated around the third and fourth.

2014 HALDON H'CAP CHASE (15 fncs) 2m 3f 110y

4:40 (4:40) (Class 4) (0-120,118) 4-Y-0+ **£3,898** (£1,144; £572; £286)

Form RPR

435- 1 **Special Account (IRE)**[64] 1316 8-11-9 **115** NickScholfield 123+
(Jeremy Scott) *travelled wl: hld up: smooth hdwy fr 4 out: chal 2 out: led last: rdn out* **4/1**[2]

1F/- **2** 3/4 **Bendant**[179] 5539 8-11-6 **112**........(v) PaddyBrennan 120+
(Debra Hamer) *nt a fluent: j.rt at times: led 4th: rdn and j. bdly rt fr 4 out: hdd last: drifted rt: kpt on* **5/1**[3]

315/ **3** 2 3/4 **O'Callaghan Strand (AUS)**[262] 3993 7-11-12 **118**........ APMcCoy 122
(Jonjo O'Neill) *trckd ldrs: rdn after 4 out: styd on same pce* **4/1**[2]

/42- **4** 7 **Woody Waller**[26] 1666 8-11-9 **115**........(t) PaulMoloney 113
(Sophie Leech) *led tl 4th: trckd ldrs: rdn appr 4 out: hdwy after 2 out* **7/1**

003- **5** 3 3/4 **Humbel Ben (IRE)**[22] 1696 10-11-0 **106**........(p) TomO'Brien 102
(Alan Jones) *hld up in last pair: hit 3rd: rdn whn outpcd bef 4 out: mstke 2 out* **25/1**

23F/ **6** 18 **Milarrow (IRE)**[212] 4948 6-11-10 **116**........ JoeTizzard 99
(Colin Tizzard) *nt fluent early: trckd ldrs: pressed ldr fr 10th: rdn appr 4 out: wknd after 3 out* **13/8**[1]

4m 45.6s (-11.70) **Going Correction** -0.425s/f (Good) **6** Ran SP% **111.1**
Speed ratings (Par 105): **106,105,104,101,100 93**
toteswingers 1&2 £3.50, 2&3 £2.50, 1&3 £7.00 CSF £23.00 TOTE £6.90: £2.70, £2.70; EX 27.70 Trifecta £233.30 Pool: £1720.05 - 5.52 winning units..
Owner Mrs Jenny Perry **Bred** M Murphy **Trained** Brompton Regis, Somerset

FOCUS
Few could be confidently discounted in this competitive handicap chase. The winner improved to his hurdles mark.

2015 CONNOLLY'S RED MILLS BUMPER CHALLENGE "JUNIOR" STANDARD OPEN NATIONAL HUNT FLAT RACE 1m 5f
5:10 (5:10) (Class 6) 3-Y-0 **£1,559** (£457; £228; £114)

Form RPR

1 **Modus** 3-10-12 0........ TomO'Brien 103+
(Robert Stephens) *racd keenly towards rr of mid-div: hdwy fr 3f out: short of room but squeezed through to ld ent fnl f: r.o strly: readily* **9/1**

2 5 **Flamenco Lad** 3-10-12 0........ HaddenFrost 94
(Martin Hill) *mid-div: hdwy 4f out: rdn over 2f out: styd on to go 3rd ent fnl f: sn chsng wnr but readily hld* **40/1**

3 3/4 **Looks Like Power (IRE)** 3-10-12 0........ JamieMoore 93
(Debra Hamer) *led: rdn over 2f out: hdd ent fnl f: sn lost 2nd: no ex* **16/1**

4 4 1/2 **Leviche** 3-10-12 0........(t) RobertThornton 87
(Alan King) *mid-div: hdwy 3f out: sn rdn to chse ldrs* **9/4**[1]

5 hd **Anwyl House** 3-10-12 0........ MarkGrant 86
(Jo Hughes) *trckd ldrs: wnt 2nd over 3f out: sn rdn and rn green: no ex ent fnl f* **33/1**

6 6 **Carraig Rock** 3-10-12 0........ DougieCostello 79
(Hughie Morrison) *nvr bttr than mid-div* **7/2**[2]

7 8 **State The Blend** 3-10-5 0........ WillKennedy 61
(Sue Gardner) *towards rr: struggling over 5f out: nvr a threat* **16/1**

8 5 **Henri De Boistron (FR)** 3-10-12 0........ PaddyBrennan 62
(Tom George) *racd keenly: trckd ldrs: rdn over 3f out: wknd 2f out* **5/1**[3]

9 10 **Alfa Red** 3-10-2 0........(b[1]) MikeyHamill(10) 49
(Sean Curran) *trckd ldrs tl rn wd and lost pl ent st: nt a threat after: wknd 2f out* **25/1**

10 5 **Kayf Charmer** 3-10-5 0........ TomScudamore 35
(Stuart Howe) *trckd ldr: rdn over 3f out: sn wknd* **16/1**

11 1 **Ceevee** 3-10-12 0........(t) RichardJohnson 41
(Tim Vaughan) *struggling over 5f out: a towards rr* **8/1**

3m 2.7s (-14.00) **11** Ran SP% **117.6**
toteswingers 1&2 £7.30, 2&3 £39.90, 1&3 £39.90 CSF £324.73 TOTE £12.50: £3.30, £4.60, £3.70; EX 303.50 Trifecta £571.00 Pool: £1337.80 - 1.75 winning units..
Owner D J Deer **Bred** D J And Mrs Deer **Trained** Penhow, Newport

FOCUS
No form to go on in this newcomers' bumper, but several of the runners came from yards with a decent record in the discipline. The early pace, as is so often the case in these events, was very steady.
T/Plt: £132.00 to a £1 stake. Pool of £68814.65 - 380.42 winning tickets. T/Qpdt: £39.00 to a £1 stake. Pool of £4694.34 - 89.05 winning tickets. TM

1764 FONTWELL (L-H)
Wednesday, October 23

OFFICIAL GOING: Soft (heavy in the odd place; 5.5)
Wind: stiff breeze across Weather: sunny periods

2016 £32 BONUS AT 32RED.COM CONDITIONAL JOCKEYS' NOVICES' H'CAP HURDLE (8 hdls 2 omitted) 2m 4f
2:20 (2:20) (Class 5) (0-95,95) 3-Y-0+ **£1,949** (£572; £286; £143)

Form RPR

000/ **1** **Easy Beesy**[193] 5280 5-11-0 **83**........ GavinSheehan 101+
(Charles Egerton) *kpt wd on far side: trckd ldrs: led 4th: drew clr fr last (usual 2 out): comfortaby* **7/1**

434- **2** 27 **Chapelle du Roi (USA)**[40] 1582 4-11-10 **93**........(p) MichealNolan 81
(Robert Stephens) *trckd ldrs: rdn to chse wnr after 2 out (usual 3 out): fdd run-in but a clr of remainder* **11/2**[2]

554/ **3** 14 **Mighty Mambo**[594] 4723 6-11-12 **95**........ AdamWedge 69
(Lawney Hill) *kpt wd on far side: trckd ldrs: rdn after 2 out (usual 3 out): wknd last (usual 2 out): t.o* **12/1**

600- **4** 2 3/4 **No Ifs No Buts**[14] 1823 4-10-8 **85**........ JakeHodson(8) 56
(David Bridgwater) *mid-div: rdn after 2 out (usual 3 out): nvr threatened: plugged on for modest 4th fr last (usual 2 out): t.o* **33/1**

/50- **5** 1 1/2 **Phar Away Island (IRE)**[153] 444 5-10-11 **80**........(p) KillianMoore 50
(Charlie Brooks) *trckd ldrs: rdn appr 3 out (usual 7th) wknd bef last (usual 2 out): t.o* **7/1**

460/ **6** 1 3/4 **Regal Park (IRE)**[567] 5242 6-11-6 **92**........(p) JoshuaMoore(3) 60
(Gary Moore) *hld up towards rr: hmpd 2nd: nt travelling fr 4th: nvr a danger: t.o* **13/2**[3]

020- **7** 29 **Chankillo**[6] 1938 4-11-7 **90**........ JoshHamer 29
(Sarah-Jayne Davies) *led: nt fluent 1st: hdd 4th: trckd ldrs: rdn after 3 out (usual 7th): wknd next: t.o* **8/1**

/05- **8** 9 **Superstición**[18] 1764 4-11-3 **86**........ ThomasGarner 16
(Michael Madgwick) *a towards rr: t.o fr 2 out (usual 3 out)* **20/1**

/51- **9** 16 **Safferano (IRE)**[14] 1824 7-11-7 **93**........ MichaelByrne(3) 7
(Tim Vaughan) *struggling in rr 4th: nvr threatened: t.o fr 2 out (usual 3 out)* **3/1**[1]

5/0- **10** 2 1/4 **Chendiyr (FR)**[19] 1749 4-11-2 **85**........ JackQuinlan
(Sarah Humphrey) *a towards rr: t.o fr 2 out (usual 3 out)* **20/1**

/FP- **P** **All Hope**[144] 590 6-10-5 **74**........ BenPoste
(Paul Davies) *prom whn awkward 1st: mid-div: rdn and dropped to rr qckly w a circ to run: p.u bef next: b.b.v* **25/1**

03F/ **F** **Oh So Charming**[318] 2947 4-11-3 **89**........ TomBellamy(3)
(Mark Gillard) *mid-div whn fell 2nd: fatally injured* **40/1**

5m 16.2s (16.80) **Going Correction** +0.925s/f (Soft)
WFA 4 from 5yo+ 10lb **12** Ran SP% **116.3**
Speed ratings (Par 103): **103,92,86,85,84 84,72,69,62,61** ,
CSF £41.56 CT £457.79 TOTE £11.00: £3.20, £2.60, £2.50; EX 55.50 TRIFECTA Not won..
Owner Mrs Sandra A Roe **Bred** Mrs Sandra A Roe **Trained** Upper Lambourn, Berks

FOCUS
Bottom bend divided. Chases on inner line and Hurdles on outer. Despite having missed the heaviest of the overnight thunderstorms, there had been plenty of rain and the ground changed to Soft (Heavy in Places). There was little pace on in this modest conditional jockeys' novices' handicap and they finished well strung out. Due to an early casualty, the final hurdle on both circuits was omitted, making a long run-in. A big step up from the easy winner and there's a case for rating it a bit higher through the beaten horses.

2017 CHRISTOPHER ANNAND 50TH BIRTHDAY H'CAP CHASE (16 fncs) 2m 6f
2:50 (2:57) (Class 4) (0-115,114) 4-Y-0+ **£3,768** (£1,106; £553; £276)

Form RPR

2PU/ **1** **Kind Of Easy (IRE)**[241] 4408 7-11-12 **114**........(p) AidanColeman 130+
(Emma Lavelle) *nt a fluent: prom tl 3rd: trckd ldrs: pressed ldr fr 11th: led 4 out: awkward and v nrly uns rdr 3 out: rcvrd iron by next: in command whn blnd last: pushed out* **5/2**[2]

P06- **2** 8 **Double Chocolate**[86] 1135 10-10-5 **100**........(p) CiaranMckee(7) 104
(John O'Shea) *j.rt at times: sn led: blnd 2nd: hdd 4 out: sn rdn and hld: styd on same pce fr next* **2/1**[1]

/UP- **3** 23 **Venetian Lad**[147] 542 8-11-6 **108**........ MarcGoldstein 88
(Lydia Richards) *trckd ldrs: rdn after 3 out: sn hld: grad fdd fr 3 out* **9/2**[3]

0/1- **4** 1 1/4 **Bit Of A Clown (IRE)**[160] 327 7-10-8 **103**........ MrJSole(7) 82
(Nick Gifford) *trckd ldrs: pckd 12th: sn rdn: wl hld after 4 out: plugged on* **6/1**

323- **5** 3 1/4 **Princely Hero (IRE)**[45] 1528 9-9-6 **90**........(tp) LouisMuspratt(10) 66
(Chris Gordon) *sn pushed along to stay in tch: no ch fr 11th: plugged on* **8/1**

P56- **6** 62 **Lord Lescribaa (FR)**[17] 1798 10-10-1 **99**........(tp) ThomasCheesman(10) 13
(Philip Hobbs) *prom tl 4th: trckd ldr tl 8th: sn struggling in rr: t.o fr 12th* **20/1**

5m 49.4s (6.40) **Going Correction** +0.425s/f (Soft) **6** Ran SP% **110.2**
Speed ratings (Par 105): **105,102,93,93,92 69**
toteswingers 1&2 £2.20, 1&3 £6.20, 2&3 £3.10 CSF £7.97 TOTE £3.60: £2.00, £2.00; EX 8.20 Trifecta £27.80 Pool: £1732.21 - 46.63 winning units..
Owner T D J Syder & N Mustoe **Bred** John Murphy **Trained** Hatherden, Hants

FOCUS
A weak event but the gallop was sound for the conditions and the form might prove reliable. The easy winner is on the upgrade and should go in again.

2018 32RED.COM NOVICES' HURDLE (9 hdls) 2m 2f 110y
3:25 (3:26) (Class 4) 4-Y-0+ **£3,898** (£1,144; £572; £286)

Form RPR

4/ **1** **Shantou Magic (IRE)**[249] 4246 6-10-12 0........ AidanColeman 123+
(Charlie Longsdon) *trckd ldrs: jnd ldr after 6th: led gng to 2 out: styd on strly and clr last: eased nring fin* **9/4**[1]

3/3- **2** 9 **Simply A Legend**[170] 146 4-10-12 0........ RobertThornton 109
(Alan King) *mid-div: hdwy 6th: rdn to dispute 3rd after 3 out: wnt 2nd between last 2: styd on but no ch w wnr* **9/1**

11/- **3** 1 1/2 **Anteros (IRE)**[240] 4432 5-10-12 0........ PaulMoloney 108+
(Sophie Leech) *mid-div: hdwy after 6th: rdn to dispute 3rd after 3 out: styd on same pce fr next* **5/1**[3]

1/1- **4** 2 1/2 **Cole Harden (IRE)**[56] 1427 4-10-9 0........ GavinSheehan(3) 107+
(Warren Greatrex) *led: wandered and nt fluent 2nd and 3rd: clr tl 5th: rdn and hdd bef 2 out: lost 2nd between last 2: styd on same pce* **4/1**[2]

2/ **5** 3 3/4 **Generous Ransom (IRE)**[292] 3490 5-10-12 0........ DarylJacob 104
(Nick Gifford) *mid-div: hdwy after 6th: rdn to dispute 3rd on bnd whn hmpd after 3 out and hld after* **16/1**

56- **6** 2 3/4 **Mount Odell**[18] 1764 5-10-12 0........ JamieMoore 98
(Gary Moore) *hld up towards rr: hdwy u.p after 3 out: styd on same pce fr next: nvr threatened ldrs* **80/1**

4- **7** 13 **Kaafel (IRE)**[17] 1779 4-10-12 0........ LeightonAspell 90
(Peter Hedger) *hld up towards rr: sme prog 3 out: nvr threatened: wknd next* **33/1**

/60- **8** 8 **Tomibola (IRE)**[155] 417 5-10-12 0........ JamesDavies 77
(Harry Whittington) *mid-div: rdn after 3 out: no imp: wknd next* **250/1**

5/5- **9** 8 **Vendredi Trois (FR)**[164] 239 4-10-12 0........ WayneHutchinson 69
(Emma Lavelle) *trckd ldrs: awkward and stmbld 2nd: nt fluent 6th: wknd next: t.o* **16/1**

/40- **10** 9 **Brians Well (IRE)**[150] 484 6-10-12 0........ AndrewTinkler 60
(Brendan Powell) *trckd ldr tl 4th: rdn after 6th: sn wknd: t.o* **100/1**

4/1- **11** 5 **Benefits Well (IRE)**[120] 828 6-11-5 0........ BrendanPowell 62
(Brendan Powell) *pushed along after 3rd: a towards rr: t.o 3 out* **16/1**

40/- **12** 46 **Jigsaw Puzzle (IRE)**[607] 4496 7-10-12 0........ TomScudamore 9
(David Pipe) *mid-div tl 5th: sn struggling in rr: t.o fr next* **9/1**

13 56 **Standing Strong (IRE)**[78] 5-10-12 0........(p) DaveCrosse
(Zoe Davison) *towards rr: struggling after 5th: sn t.o* **250/1**

1/ **P** **Dark Desire**[246] 4299 4-10-12 0........ JoeTizzard
(Colin Tizzard) *in tch tl 6th: sn struggling in rr: t.o whn p.u bef last* **12/1**

4m 49.6s (15.30) **Going Correction** +0.925s/f (Soft)
WFA 4 from 5yo+ 9lb **14** Ran SP% **118.7**
Speed ratings (Par 105): **104,100,99,98,96 95,90,86,83,79 77,58,34,**
toteswingers 1&2 £9.50, 1&3 £5.40, 2&3 £23.90 CSF £23.39 TOTE £4.00: £1.60, £3.10, £1.80; EX 30.60 Trifecta £205.30 Pool: £1143.79 - 4.17 winning units..
Owner Owners For Owners: Shantou Magic **Bred** Daniel Fogarty **Trained** Over Norton, Oxon

FOCUS
A decent gallop on for what was a well contested, fair novice hurdle. There should be subsequent winners coming out of it, with the third to fifth all rated similar to their bumper marks.

2019 32RED BEGINNERS' CHASE (15 fncs) 2m 4f
4:00 (4:00) (Class 4) 4-Y-0+ **£4,659** (£1,446; £779)

Form RPR

5/0- **1** **Black Thunder (FR)**[165] 215 6-11-3 0........ DarylJacob 146+
(Paul Nicholls) *trckd ldrs: chal sn after 4 out: rdn after 2 out: rchd and hit last: drvn and carried rt run-in: styd on wl to ld fnl 75yds* **11/4**[2]

3/5- **2** nk **Fox Appeal (IRE)**[165] 215 6-11-3 0........ AidanColeman 145+
(Emma Lavelle) *t.k.h: hld up: hdwy to dispute ld 3rd: outrt ldr 10th: pckd 4 out: sn jnd: rdn after 2 out: slt ld last: hung rt run-in: kpt on but no ex whn hdd fnl 75yds* **7/4**[1]

23P/ 3 35 **Ohio Gold (IRE)**[207] 5014 7-11-3 134 .... JoeTizzard 113
(Colin Tizzard) *led: jnd 3rd: j.lft at times fr 7th: hdd 10th: pressed ldr untl rdn after 4 out: sn btn* **9/2**

52/- U **Orzare (IRE)**[551] 5519 7-11-0 0 .... JoshuaMoore(3)
(Philip Hide) *trckd ldrs: propped on landing 1st: hit 11th: abt to mount chal whn bdly hmpd and uns rdr 4 out* **50/1**

255/ F **Baby Shine (IRE)**[188] 5360 7-10-10 132 .... LeightonAspell
(Lucy Wadham) *hld up bhd ldrs: travelling wl enough and mounting chal whn fell 4 out* **14/1**

1/U- P **Heronry (IRE)**[166] 205 5-11-3 128 .... BarryGeraghty
(Nicky Henderson) *trckd ldrs: stmbld 5th: jumping rt and nt travelling in last fr 7th: tailing off whn p.u bef 10th* **4/1**[3]

5m 11.6s (4.30) **Going Correction** +0.425s/f (Soft) **6** Ran SP% **109.8**
Speed ratings (Par 105): **108,107,93, ,**
toteswingers 1&2 £6.60, 1&3 £4.30, 2&3 £1.80 CSF £7.99 TOTE £4.30: £2.60, £1.10; EX 8.70 Trifecta £23.30 Pool: £1725.45 - 55.51 winning units..
Owner Donlon, MacDonald, Fulton & Webb **Bred** Mickael Keane **Trained** Ditcheat, Somerset

FOCUS
A decent beginners' chase and, while only three finished, the form looks solid. It produced a cracking finish between the top two in the market, who were rated in the mid 140s over hurdles. The winner is rated in line with his hurdles form with the second 8lb off his hurdling best.

2020 32RED CASINO H'CAP HURDLE (11 hdls) 2m 6f 110y
4:30 (4:30) (Class 3) (0-135,130) 4-Y-0+ **£5,393** (£1,583; £791; £395)

Form RPR

1U6/ 1 **Bally Legend**[194] 5269 8-11-12 **130** .... IanPopham 139+
(Caroline Keevil) *trckd ldr tl after 7th: rdn whn regained 3rd after 3 out: styd on to ld between last 2: drew clr run-in* **20/1**

163- 2 10 **Nicky Nutjob (GER)**[10] 1887 7-9-7 **104** oh5 .... (p) CiaranMckee(7) 102
(John O'Shea) *hld up in rr: pushed along and stdy prog after 3 out: rdn after next: wnt 3rd whn hanging rt run-in: styd on to go 2nd towards fin: nvr any ch w wnr* **16/1**

430/ 3 1 3/4 **Cocacobana (IRE)**[245] 4319 8-10-12 **121** .... KillianMoore(5) 118
(Graeme McPherson) *mid-div: nt fluent 4th: hdwy 8th where nt fluent: lft in ld on bnd after 3 out: rdn and hdd between last 2: no ex whn lost 2nd towards fin* **10/1**

143/ 4 9 **San Telm (IRE)**[305] 3184 8-11-6 **124** .... BrendanPowell 110
(Renee Robeson) *trckd ldrs: wnt 2nd after 7th: rdn after 3 out: ev ch briefly between last 2: no ex fr last* **5/1**[2]

210/ 5 1 **Alberobello (IRE)**[258] 4076 5-11-1 **119** .... (t) NickScholfield 104
(Jeremy Scott) *hld up towards rr: nt fluent 2nd: sme hdwy 7th: lost pl u.p next: plugged on again fr 2 out* **12/1**

302- 6 3 1/2 **Decoy (FR)**[19] 1752 7-11-9 **127** .... (b) TomScudamore 114
(David Pipe) *led: nt fluent 3 out: hindered by loose horse whn stumbling and hdd on bnd sn after: stmbld again then rdn to chse ldng trio: nvr bk on terms: wknd last* **6/1**

/04- P **Bravo Bravo**[12] 1858 6-10-4 **113** .... (b) NicodeBoinville(5)
(Mark Gillard) *trckd ldr: reminders after 5th: rdn after next: sn bhd: t.o whn p.u after 8th* **20/1**

033/ F **Kartanian (IRE)**[279] 3706 7-10-9 **113** .... TomO'Brien
(Philip Hobbs) *fell 1st* **11/2**[3]

600/ U **Hayjack**[188] 5362 8-11-1 **119** .... AidanColeman
(Charlie Longsdon) *bdly hmpd whn unseating rdr 1st* **2/1**[1]

2/4- P **Bally Rone (IRE)**[159] 354 5-11-2 **123** .... JackQuinlan(3)
(Sarah Humphrey) *mid-div: hit 5th: rdn after 7th: sn bhd: t.o whn p.u after 3 out* **33/1**

5m 58.8s (16.30) **Going Correction** +0.925s/f (Soft) **10** Ran SP% **114.8**
Speed ratings (Par 107): **108,104,103,100,100 99, , , ,**
toteswingers 1&2 £15.30, 1&3 £47.70, 2&3 £22.50 CSF £279.84 CT £3360.55 TOTE £22.40: £5.70, £2.90, £3.40; EX 185.80 Trifecta £894.00 Part won. Pool: £1192.02 - 0.20 winning units..
Owner Brian Derrick **Bred** V Thorne, B Derrick And P R Rodford **Trained** Motcombe, Dorset

FOCUS
A reasonable handicap hurdle, not lacking in drama. The winner was a 139-rated hurdler at his peak, and the second is rated to his mark.

2021 32REDBINGO.COM H'CAP CHASE (13 fncs) 2m 2f
5:05 (5:05) (Class 4) (0-105,102) 4-Y-0+ **£3,768** (£1,106; £553; £276)

Form RPR

/35- 1 **Red Rock (FR)**[22] 1710 8-11-1 **94** .... GavinSheehan(3) 108+
(Emma Lavelle) *led after 1st: mde rest: asserted between last 2: comf* **9/4**[2]

53P- 2 9 **Mister Wiseman**[83] 1174 11-10-8 **84** .... (bt) TomScudamore 86
(Nigel Hawke) *led tl after 1st: trckd wnr: effrt after 4 out: a being hld fr next: styd on same pce* **13/2**

563- 3 23 **Morestead (IRE)**[18] 1769 8-11-2 **92** .... (bt) LeightonAspell 70
(Brendan Powell) *chsd ldrs: rdn after 7th: no ch fr after next: plugged on into modest 3rd between last 2* **5/1**[3]

4/6- 4 26 **Niki Royal (FR)**[167] 179 8-11-12 **102** .... BrendanPowell 54
(Jamie Snowden) *chsd ldrs: nudged along fr 4th: rdn and wknd after 4 out: lost modest 3rd between last 2* **11/8**[1]

616/ P **Edlomond (IRE)**[458] 1030 7-11-5 **100** .... (t) TomO'Connor(5)
(Bill Turner) *hld up bhd ldrs: pckd 2nd: mstke 3rd: lost tch fr 7th: t.o whn p.u bef 3 out* **16/1**

4m 53.6s (18.90) **Going Correction** +0.425s/f (Soft) **5** Ran SP% **108.8**
Speed ratings (Par 105): **75,71,60,49,**
CSF £15.13 TOTE £3.20: £2.50, £3.20; EX 8.60 Trifecta £26.50 Pool: £1782.54 - 50.29 winning units..
Owner Mrs Sarah Stevens **Bred** Mme M Cochonneau & Mme M V D Broele **Trained** Hatherden, Hants

FOCUS
A small field for this weak handicap chase, run at a fair gallop for the conditions and they finished very tired. The winner was on a decent mark but this was arguably a small personal best.

2022 32RED ON THE APP STORE MARES' INTERMEDIATE OPEN NATIONAL HUNT FLAT RACE 1m 6f
5:40 (5:40) (Class 6) 4-6-Y-0 **£1,642** (£478; £239)

Form RPR

/- 1 **Rouquine Sauvage** 5-10-9 0 .... (t) RachaelGreen(3) 108+
(Anthony Honeyball) *hld up bhd: rn wd on bnd after 2f: smooth hdwy fr 5f out: chal over 2f out: led jst over 1f out: kpt on wl: readily* **4/1**[2]

4/0- 2 6 **Unefille De Guye (FR)**[152] 462 5-10-12 0 .... JackDoyle 98
(Victor Dartnall) *mid-div: hdwy 6f out: led over 2f out: sn rdn and strly pressed: hdd jst over 1f out: kpt on but sn hld* **16/1**

1- 3 5 **Centoria (IRE)**[45] 1531 5-10-12 0 .... BrendanPowell 92
(Jamie Snowden) *hld up towards rr: hdwy fr 6f out: rdn 3f out: ev ch briefly 2f out: styd on same pce* **7/1**[3]

2/ 4 13 **A Shade Of Bay**[193] 5295 5-10-7 0 .... EdCookson(5) 76
(Kim Bailey) *trckd ldrs: jnd ldr over 4f out tl over 3f out: rdn to chal again briefly 2f out: sn outpcd* **11/4**[1]

5 7 **Frank N Fair** 5-10-12 0 .... DaveCrosse 68
(Zoe Davison) *hld up towards rr: hdwy fr 1/2-way: rdn 6f out: led over 3f out tl over 2f out: sn wknd* **200/1**

3- 6 hd **Georgea (IRE)**[173] 101 4-10-12 0 .... JamieMoore 68
(Gary Moore) *hld up towards rr: hdwy fr 6f out: rdn to chse ldrs 3f out: grad fdd fnl 2f* **14/1**

3/ 7 9 **Party Girls (FR)**[511] 495 5-10-12 0 .... (t) TomScudamore 57
(David Pipe) *trckd ldr: led over 4f out tl over 3f out: sn wknd* **10/1**

4- 8 9 **Amber Flush**[101] 970 4-10-7 0 .... BenPoste(5) 46
(Tom Symonds) *mid-div: hdwy over 4f out: rdn 3f out: wknd 2f out: t.o* **9/1**

2- 9 1 1/2 **Perfect Romance**[36] 1599 4-10-7 0 .... NicodeBoinville(5) 44
(Patrick Chamings) *mid-div tl rdn along over 7f out: sn in rr: t.o* **8/1**

0- 10 29 **Businessmoney Jive**[12] 1861 6-10-12 0 .... NickScholfield 10
(Keiran Burke) *trckd ldrs tl pushed along over 6f out: sn bhd: t.o* **33/1**

4/ 11 5 **Salford Lady**[330] 2682 4-10-12 0 .... TomO'Brien 4
(Philip Hobbs) *led tl over 4f out: sn wknd: t.o* **8/1**

0- 12 27 **Fanny Fantastic**[65] 1318 4-10-9 0 .... RobertDunne(3)
(Miss Imogen Pickard) *mid-div tl wknd over 4f out: t.o* **125/1**

0- 13 5 **Garlands Quest**[45] 1531 4-10-12 0 .... RichieMcLernon
(Richenda Ford) *chsd ldrs for 7f: sn bhd: t.o* **200/1**

3m 31.1s **13** Ran SP% **117.8**
toteswingers 1&2 £21.60, 1&3 £12.90, 2&3 £34.90 CSF £65.32 TOTE £7.10: £2.40, £4.80, £2.80; EX 96.50 Trifecta £1185.30 Part won. Pool: £1580.41 - 0.52 winning units..
Owner Anthony Honeyball Racing Club Ltd **Bred** Mrs Corinna Turner **Trained** Mosterton, Dorset

FOCUS
A mares' bumper with very little depth and a few were keen early on. Again they finished well strung out. The cosy winner is the type to rate higher.
T/Plt: £636.60. Pool: £75,889.17 - 87.01 winning units. T/Qpdt: £78.40. Pool: £6120.54 - 57.70 winning units. TM

[1834]WORCESTER (L-H)
Wednesday, October 23

OFFICIAL GOING: Soft (heavy in places)
Wind: almost nil Weather: sunny spells; 15 degrees

2023 RICHARD WRIGHT MEMORIAL H'CAP CHASE (18 fncs) 2m 7f
2:10 (2:10) (Class 5) (0-95,95) 4-Y-0+ **£2,144** (£629; £314; £157)

Form RPR

4P6- 1 **Days Of Pleasure (IRE)**[83] 1172 8-10-8 **77** .... (b) TomCannon 89
(Chris Gordon) *2nd tl led 11th: rdn and hdd bef 15th: drvn and racing quite awkwardly after: chal again last: sn led and cajoled clr* **10/3**[2]

333- 2 4 **Kap West (FR)**[139] 639 8-11-1 **84** .... (t) DougieCostello 93
(Laura Young) *mstke 4th: towards rr: stdy prog to 3rd and hit 14th: drvn and no real imp after tl clsd on tiring ldr last: wnt 2nd but sn outpcd by wnr flat* **7/2**[3]

225/ 3 2 1/4 **Royaume Bleu (FR)**[187] 5377 8-11-8 **91** .... PaddyBrennan 98
(Alex Hales) *led tl hdd and hit 11th: led again bef 15th: edgd rt next and rdn: floundering last and sn hdd & wknd* **11/4**[1]

404- 4 23 **Handsome Buddy (IRE)**[26] 1673 6-11-5 **95** .... MissAEStirling(7) 78
(Michael Gates) *chsd ldrs tl struggling and racing v idly fr 14th: remote 4th whn mstke next* **4/1**

/P0- P **Paradise Expected**[17] 1800 10-10-13 **82** .... (t) RichardJohnson
(Mark Gillard) *last whn nt fluent 8th: sn hrd drvn and no reponse: t.o fr 10th tl p.u 15th* **20/1**

4PP/ P **Laughing Game**[206] 5033 9-9-11 **69** oh8 .... PeterCarberry(3)
(Laura Hurley) *t.k.h briefly: bhd fr 5th: nt fluent 9th and struggling after: t.o 11th tl p.u next* **10/1**

/00- P **Be Kind**[14] 1821 7-9-7 **69** oh5 .... (p) MrJohn(7)
(Natalie Lloyd-Beavis) *mstke 1st: nt fluent: in tch tl 10th: rdn 13th: t.o next: p.u 15th* **40/1**

6m 11.8s (23.80) **Going Correction** +0.175s/f (Yiel) **7** Ran SP% **108.3**
Speed ratings (Par 103): **65,63,62,54, , ,**
toteswingers 1&2 £4.80, 1&3 £4.20, 2&3 £1.90 CSF £14.09 TOTE £4.00: £1.70, £2.10; EX 16.20 Trifecta £47.70 Pool: £901.70 - 14.15 winning units..
Owner E J Farrant **Bred** Shay White **Trained** Morestead, Hants

FOCUS
Bends 12yds off inner line adding circa 50yds to a 2m race. Tom Cannon described the ground as "soft and a bit loose on the bends", with Paddy Brennan calling it "heavy". Conditions certainly looked testing. This weak handicap chase produced a three-way scrap over the last couple of fences. There could be a bit more t ocome from the winner based on his old form.

2024 FRED RIMELL MEMORIAL NOVICES' LIMITED H'CAP CHASE (18 fncs) 2m 7f
2:40 (2:40) (Class 3) (0-125,123) 5-Y-0 **£6,330** (£1,870; £935; £468; £234)

Form RPR

421/ 1 **Trafalgar (FR)**[693] 2881 6-10-12 **116** .... SamTwiston-Davies 125+
(Nigel Twiston-Davies) *a ldng pair: led 9th: gng wl 14th: jst hdd and hit next: pressed rival hrd tl led again last: sn in command and styd on stoutly* **9/2**[2]

13P/ 2 1 3/4 **Winds And Waves (IRE)**[190] 5328 7-10-11 **118** .... JakeGreenall(3) 123
(Henry Daly) *midfield: effrt 14th: 3rd bhd clr ldng pair fr next: 6 l down at last: styd on really willingly to go 2nd fnl 100yds: nt rch wnr* **10/1**

350/ 3 1 3/4 **Spanish Arch (IRE)**[207] 5013 6-10-7 **114** .... (p) KielanWoods(3) 117
(Charlie Longsdon) *towards rr: hdwy 11th: 2nd at 14th: slt ld next: drvn and hdd last: edgd lft and wknd flat: lost 2nd cl home* **5/1**[3]

1/0- 4 10 **Tullyraine (IRE)**[159] 358 9-10-9 **120** .... RyanHatch(7) 114
(Nigel Twiston-Davies) *chsd ldrs: rdn 13th: sn outpcd: plugged on again wout threatening fr 3 out* **13/2**

5/5- 5 7 **Comeonginger (IRE)**[176] 38 6-10-11 **115** .... (t) TomCannon 101
(Chris Gordon) *towards rr: rdn and outpcd bef 15th but kpt plugging on steadily after: no threat but encouraging effrt* **20/1**

0/2- 6 6 **Achimota (IRE)**[173] 92 7-10-8 **119** .... MrJMRidley(7) 99
(Matt Sheppard) *chsd ldrs: u.p 12th: wknd bef 15th* **10/1**

626- 7 dist **Academy General (IRE)**[19] 1748 7-10-11 **115** .... (p) SeanQuinlan
(David Bridgwater) *nvr bttr than midfield: mstke 9th: hmpd 13th: rdn and lost tch after next: t.o after mstke 2 out* **20/1**

014/ 8 8 **Stow**[209] 4981 8-11-5 **123** .... ConorO'Farrell
(Michael Blake) *nt fluent in rr: struggling after mstkes 10th and 11th: t.o bef 15th* **25/1**

226/ **F** **Big Society (IRE)**[207] 5016 7-11-5 **123**............................ PaddyBrennan
(Tom George) *several clumsy jumps: led tl 9th: prom tl lost pl rapidly bef 15th: last but one and stopping qckly whn fell 3 out* **4/1**[1]

2/4- **P** **Sandanski (IRE)**[154] 435 5-10-11 **115**................................(t) FelixDeGiles
(Tom Gretton) *in rr div on outer: struggling 10th: t.o whn hit 14th: sn p.u* **50/1**

3/1- **F** **Azure Aware (IRE)**[170] 140 6-11-2 **120**.........................(t) JasonMaguire
(Kim Bailey) *cl 2nd or 3rd tl fell 13th* **6/1**

6m 5.0s (17.00) **Going Correction** +0.175s/f (Yiel) **11** Ran SP% **116.0**
Speed ratings: **77,76,75,72,69 67, , , ,**
toteswingers 1&2 £20.20, 1&3 £6.00, 2&3 £35.30 CSF £44.62 CT £233.92 TOTE £5.00: £2.20, £4.90, £1.70; EX 70.80 Trifecta £317.80 Pool: £1084.20 - 2.55 winning units..
Owner Mr & Mrs Gordon Pink **Bred** Anthony Bromley **Trained** Naunton, Gloucs

FOCUS
One of a number of novice chases converted into limited handicaps this season, the Fred Rimell had a distinguished role of honour in its former guise. All but three of this field were making their chasing debuts, and plenty of winners should emerge from this event. The winner is the type to rate higher, and the next two are rated in line with their hurdles mark.

2025 RICHARD DAVIS MEMORIAL H'CAP CHASE (11 fncs 1 omitted) 2m 110y
3:15 (3:15) (Class 4) (0-120,120) 4-Y-0+ **£3,898** (£1,144; £572; £286)

Form RPR
0/5- **1** **Christopher Wren (USA)**[33] 66 6-11-4 **112**......................... APMcCoy 123+
(Nick Gifford) *settled towards rr: lacked fluency: mstke 7th: u.p and nt looking keen: wnt 3rd after next: tk slt ld 2 out but edging lft: forced clr after last: jinked rt towards paddock gate 100yds out: unimpressive* **5/2**[1]

434- **2** *1 ¾* **Another Flutter (IRE)**[22] 1711 9-10-13 **107**....................(tp) CharliePoste 114
(Matt Sheppard) *nrly a 2nd: pushed along after 8th: w wnr and racing awkwardly fr 2 out tl last: one pce* **10/1**

432- **3** *5* **Midnight Tuesday (FR)**[17] 1780 8-11-6 **114**...................(t) HarrySkelton 119
(Dan Skelton) *t.k.h: led: terrible jump 4th: hdd 2 out and immediately gave up: plugged home* **11/4**[2]

3/2- **4** *3 ¼* **South Stack**[161] 322 8-11-9 **117**.. JasonMaguire 116
(Kim Bailey) *bhd: rdn 6th and no reponse: no ch fr 8th but plugging on after last* **6/1**

/50- **5** *3 ¾* **George Nympton (IRE)**[32] 1623 7-11-12 **120**............... RichardJohnson 115
(Nick Williams) *pressed ldrs: struggling whn blnd bdly 8th: n.d after* **8/1**

604- **6** *14* **Full Ov Beans**[13] 1835 9-9-11 **94** oh7............................. PeterCarberry(3) 79
(Michael Gates) *last pair: lost tch 8th* **25/1**

6/F- **P** **Should I Stay (FR)**[2] 2007 5-11-2 **110**............................. PaddyBrennan
(Tom George) *chsd ldrs tl 4th and drvn after 8th: dropping out rapidly whn p.u next* **5/1**[3]

4m 14.2s (0.20) **Going Correction** +0.175s/f (Yiel) **7** Ran SP% **110.2**
Speed ratings (Par 105): **106,105,102,101,99 92,**
toteswingers 1&2 £4.40, 1&3 £1.70, 2&3 £2.90 CSF £23.97 TOTE £4.00: £2.40, £2.80; EX 27.70 Trifecta £220.40 Pool: £1746.69 - 5.94 winning units..
Owner John P McManus **Bred** Rod D'Elia **Trained** Findon, W Sussex

FOCUS
A very modest race, run at a decent clip in the conditions. The winner is rated in line with his best hurdles form, with the second to his mark.

2026 MYSON RADIATORS "NEWCOMERS" STANDARD OPEN NATIONAL HUNT FLAT RACE 2m
3:50 (3:50) (Class 6) 3-5-Y-0 **£1,559** (£457; £228; £114)

Form RPR
1 **Sidbury Hill** 5-11-3 0.. KevinJones(7) 110
(Seamus Mullins) *dropped out last: pushed along and stdy prog 6f out: chal on inner home turn: chsd ldr over 2 out and gamely wore him down to ld fnl 100yds* **20/1**

2 *¾* **Binge Drinker (IRE)** 4-11-10 0... APMcCoy 109
(Rebecca Curtis) *2nd tl led 1/2-way: rdn and hrd pressed fr 2f out: kpt on wl tl hdd and nt qckn fnl 100yds* **7/4**[1]

/ **3** *2 ½* **Rose Of The World (IRE)** 5-11-3 0.........................(t) DominicElsworth 100
(Jo Davis) *chsd ldrs: effrt 5f out: pressed ldng pair over 2f out: sn rdn: rn green and no imp after but kpt on steadily* **20/1**

4 *18* **Closest Friend** 4-11-10 0....................................... SamTwiston-Davies 89
(J R Jenkins) *t.k.h and chsd ldrs: effrt in cl 3rd home turn: rdn and fdd over 2f out to fin poor 4th* **4/1**[2]

5 *10* **Buckboru (IRE)** 5-11-3 0... DougieCostello 72
(Laura Young) *plld hrd in midfield: effrt 5f out: lost tch w ldng quartet over 2f out: t.o* **50/1**

6 *1 ¾* **Barton Antix** 4-11-10 0... RichardJohnson 77
(Neil Mulholland) *trckd ldrs gng wl: wnt 2nd home turn: rdn and fdd wl over 2f out: t.o* **12/1**

7 *1 ¼* **Grilyne (FR)** 4-11-10 0.. FelixDeGiles 76
(Tom Symonds) *led at modest pce tl 1/2-way: sn rdn: fdd 4f out: t.o* **14/1**

8 *7* **Bonds Conquest** 4-11-10 0.. AndrewThornton 69
(Seamus Mullins) *a bhd: t.o fnl 4f* **12/1**

9 *2 ¾* **Venez Horace (FR)** 4-11-10 0.. DavidEngland 66
(Giles Smyly) *chsd ldrs 11f: sn wknd: t.o fnl 4f* **16/1**

10 *½* **Nicki's Nipper** 5-10-12 0... JonathanEngland(5) 59
(Shaun Lycett) *bhd tl hdwy to go prom after 6f: lost pl rapidly over 4f out: t.o* **40/1**

11 *17* **Mullinavat (IRE)** 4-11-5 0.. AodhaganConlon(5) 49
(Tom George) *nvr trbld ldrs: t.o fnl 4f* **10/1**[3]

12 *22* **Modeligo (IRE)** 4-11-10 0.. CharliePoste 27
(Matt Sheppard) *uns rdr leaving paddock: a bhd: t.o fnl 5f* **33/1**

13 *15* **Glacial Roes (IRE)** 5-11-3 0... WillKennedy
(Sarah-Jayne Davies) *cl up tl 1/2-way: hopelessly t.o fnl 5f* **25/1**

14 *85* **Grapetree** 3-10-7 0.. TomMessenger
(David Evans) *bhd: hopelessly t.o fr 1/2-way: eventually walked past the post* **20/1**

3m 52.7s (11.00) **Going Correction** +0.875s/f (Soft)
WFA 3 from 4yo+ 17lb **14** Ran SP% **118.9**
Speed ratings (Par 101): **107,106,105,96,91 90,89,86,85,84 76,65,57,15**
toteswingers 1&2 £11.10, 1&3 £43.30, 2&3 £8.90 CSF £51.01 TOTE £26.90: £7.00, £1.10, £6.70; EX 94.10 Trifecta £511.00 Part won. Pool: £681.46 - 0.20 winning units..
Owner S J Rawlins **Bred** Mr And Mrs S J Rawlins **Trained** Wilsford-Cum-Lake, Wilts

FOCUS
A steady gallop and no racecourse form to go on, but the time was reasonable.

2027 HAYGAIN HAYSTEAMERS FOR CLEAN, HEALTHY FORAGE MARES' NOVICES' HURDLE (8 hdls) 2m
4:20 (4:20) (Class 4) 4-Y-0+ **£3,119** (£915; £457; £228)

Form RPR
553/ **1** **In By Midnight**[178] 1 5-10-10 0....................................... PaddyBrennan 102+
(Tom George) *prom on wd outside: sme rt handed jumps: led 3 out: rdn and racing awkwardly fr next: hrd pressed tl sn tk command after last and wl on top by fin* **2/1**[1]

5/0- **2** *2 ½* **Benefique Royale**[10] 1885 5-10-10 0........................... RichardJohnson 98
(Nick Williams) *t.k.h: trckd ldrs: effrt after 5th: pressed wnr fr bef 2 out: wavering and racing awkwardly tl edgd lft and ev ch last: outpcd fnl 100yds* **7/2**[2]

/54- **3** *3* **Oscar's Pet (IRE)**[152] 462 5-10-10 0..................................... FelixDeGiles 96
(Tom Symonds) *chsd ldrs: rdn bef 3 out: 4 l 3rd next: one pce and no imp after* **9/1**

04/ **4** *8* **Siksika (IRE)**[192] 5316 5-10-10 0.. HarrySkelton 90
(Dan Skelton) *a abt same pl: rdn bef 3 out: btn next: eased flat* **12/1**

0/4- **5** *2 ¼* **Agent Fedora**[175] 70 5-10-10 0......................................(t) JasonMaguire 85
(Kim Bailey) *prom tl drvn bef 3 out: sn struggling bhd ldng quartet* **5/1**[3]

00/ **6** *4* **Allez Zane**[182] 5511 4-10-10 0...(t) DavidEngland 81+
(Giles Smyly) *unruly s: hld up in last pair: passed fading rivals fr 3 out but nvr on terms* **33/1**

14- **7** *2* **Garnock (IRE)**[14] 1823 5-10-10 0....................................(p) SeanQuinlan 79
(David Bridgwater) *midfield: rdn and lost tch after 5th* **28/1**

063/ **8** *5* **Chambray Dancer (IRE)**[267] 3921 5-10-10 0............. AndrewThornton 74
(Seamus Mullins) *hld up in last pair: lost tch 5th: t.o next* **16/1**

\- **9** *7* **Balady (IRE)**[41] 4-10-10 0... MarkGrant 67
(Dominic Ffrench Davis) *led at slow pce and isolated on inner tl rdn and hdd 3 out: sn dropped rt out: t.o whn mstke last* **10/1**

/F5- **10** *2 ¼* **Clear Mix**[156] 410 5-10-10 0... WillKennedy 65
(Sue Gardner) *towards rr: pushed along and lost tch 5th: t.o next* **66/1**

50P/ **11** *41* **Crowcombe Park**[320] 2895 5-10-0 0..................................... JonPark(10) 24
(Kevin Bishop) *dropped to rr: wandering and all over the pl whn t.o fr 5th: fin eventually* **66/1**

4m 4.5s (17.20) **Going Correction** +0.875s/f (Soft)
WFA 4 from 5yo 9lb **11** Ran SP% **114.3**
Speed ratings (Par 105): **92,90,89,85,84 82,81,78,75,74 53**
toteswingers 1&2 £2.10, 1&3 £10.70, 2&3 £9.60 CSF £8.41 TOTE £3.30: £1.10, £1.60, £2.80; EX 11.70 Trifecta £63.30 Pool: £860.58 - 10.18 winning units..
Owner Silkword Racing Partnership **Bred** Mrs Caroline George **Trained** Slad, Gloucs

FOCUS
A modest event confined to mares. A small step up from the winner with the next two rated to their bumper form.

2028 HAYGAIN HAYSTEAMERS FOR CLEAN, HEALTHY FORAGE MAIDEN HURDLE (10 hdls) 2m 4f
4:55 (4:55) (Class 5) 4-Y-0+ **£1,949** (£572; £286; £143)

Form RPR
1 **Premier Portrait (IRE)**[151] 6-11-0 0................................. JasonMaguire 111+
(Kim Bailey) *trckd ldrs in v slowly run r: wnt cl 2nd 2 out: rdn and sustained effrt after: sn led flat and clr fnl 100yds* **4/1**[3]

/F5- **2** *2 ½* **Venceremos**[150] 502 6-10-4 0....................................(p) KielanWoods(3) 100
(Charlie Longsdon) *trckd ldrs: wnt 2nd after 6th: rdn and led narrowly 2 out tl after last: outpcd fnl 100yds* **3/1**[2]

1- **3** *4* **Neville**[132] 731 5-11-0 0.. RichardJohnson 104
(Philip Hobbs) *mstke 3rd: settled towards rr: hdwy after 6th: chal next: w ldr briefly but hanging lft 2 out: one pce: 3rd and btn whn stl hanging at last: plugged on* **13/8**[1]

4/ **4** *4 ½* **Audacious Plan (IRE)**[183] 5469 4-11-0 0................................ APMcCoy 101
(Rebecca Curtis) *sn chsng clr ldr: clsd 5th and led next: rdn and hdd bef 2 out and sn dropped bk to btn 4th* **5/1**

5 *3 ½* **Troufion (FR)**[36] 4-11-0 0..(t) HarrySkelton 95
(Dan Skelton) *hld up in midfield: effrt after 7th: cl 6th home turn: sn rdn and wl btn* **33/1**

6 *13* **Here's Herbie**[241] 5-10-9 0... MissLucyGardner(5) 82
(Sue Gardner) *bhd: effrt wd to midfield at 5th: lost tch 7th: styng on nicely after last* **50/1**

0/U- **7** *2* **Echoes Of Joy**[11] 1864 4-11-0 0... TomMessenger 81
(David Evans) *plld hrd in rr: effrt 7th: cl 5th on home turn: sn floundering: mstke 2 out and eased* **100/1**

P **Stickers**[703] 6-11-0 0... DougieCostello
(Alan Jessop) *in tch tl 6th: struggling next: hopelessly t.o whn p.u 3 out* **40/1**

0/0- **P** **Tilt Du Chatelier (FR)**[17] 1794 6-10-4 0.............. JosephPalmowski(10)
(Robin Dickin) *reluctant but clr ldr tl 4th: pressed whn nt fluent next: drvn and hdd 6th: hopelessly t.o after next: p.u 3 out* **100/1**

P **Typical Oscar (IRE)**[241] 6-11-0 0.. TomCannon
(Michael Blake) *prom tl lost pl qckly 6th: hopelessly t.o whn p.u 3 out* **16/1**

5m 3.0s (15.60) **Going Correction** +0.875s/f (Soft) **10** Ran SP% **115.0**
Speed ratings (Par 103): **103,102,100,98,97 92,91, , ,**
toteswingers 1&2 £4.40, 1&3 £4.80, 2&3 £3.00 CSF £16.27 TOTE £5.20: £1.60, £1.02, £2.10; EX 18.10 Trifecta £44.50 Pool: £1307.02 - 21.98 winning units..
Owner Mrs Penny Perriss **Bred** Joe Fogarty **Trained** Andoversford, Gloucs

FOCUS
That smart mare Sparky May won this event three years ago. This looked just an ordinary maiden hurdle, and it was run at a very steady gallop. The winner may be capable of a bit better.

2029 HAYGAIN HAYSTEAMERS FOR CLEAN, HEALTHY FORAGE MARES' H'CAP HURDLE (10 hdls) 2m 4f
5:30 (5:30) (Class 4) (0-120,118) 4-Y-0+ **£3,119** (£915; £457; £228)

Form RPR
15/- **1** **Midnight Belle**[205] 5063 6-11-1 **107**..................................... FelixDeGiles 114+
(Tom Symonds) *led after 1st: set mod pce: at least 6 l clr fr 3 out and nvr looked like being ct: kpt on gamely flat* **5/2**[2]

132/ **2** *7* **Jean Fleming (IRE)**[187] 5374 6-11-12 **118**................... RichardJohnson 119
(Jamie Snowden) *often lacked fluency in 2nd or 3rd: rdn after mstke 7th where wnr drew clr: no imp fr 2 out but plugged on flat* **4/1**[3]

6/6- **3** *21* **Miss Saffron**[138] 657 10-10-10 **102**..................................... WillKennedy 84
(Sue Gardner) *settled in rr: effrt 6th: disp 3rd and rdn after next: wknd after 3 out: heavily eased fnl 100yds and nrly lost 3rd* **16/1**

The Form Book Jumps, Raceform Ltd, Compton, RG20 6NL.

14P/ **4** ¾ **Combustible Lady (IRE)**[287] 3576 8-11-0 **106**............ AndrewThornton 84+
(Seamus Mullins) *dropped out last and wl bhd: often switching fr outer to inner and bk again fr 1/2-way: 25 l 5th after 7th: str run after last where stl 5th and almost tk 3rd* **16/1**

5/ **5** 2¼ **Teochew (IRE)**[184] 5457 5-11-9 **115**.. APMcCoy 91
(Warren Greatrex) *reluctant ldr tl after 1st: cl up tl drvn home turn: dropped out rapidly: lost remote 4th after last* **7/4**[1]

250/ **6** 75 **Wychwoods Mist**[365] 1974 6-9-11 **96**.............................. GeraldQuinn(7)
(Claire Dyson) *2nd or 3rd tl rdn and stopped to nil after 7th: sn hopelessly t.o* **16/1**

233/ **P** **Just Spot**[211] 4968 6-9-12 **100**.. JonPark(10)
(Kevin Bishop) *bhd: last and rdn 6th: hopelessly t.o whn p.u 3 out* **12/1**

5m 6.7s (19.30) **Going Correction** +0.875s/f (Soft) 7 Ran SP% **110.3**
Speed ratings (Par 105): **96,93,84,84,83 53,**
toteswingers 1&2 £3.70, 1&3 £5.90, 2&3 £5.00 CSF £12.18 TOTE £4.00: £1.90, £2.60; EX 17.80 Trifecta £161.60 Pool: £1524.61 - 7.07 winning units..
Owner Mrs Patricia Holtorp **Bred** Mrs Patricia Ellen Holtorp **Trained** Harewood End, H'fords

FOCUS
A very modest hurdle for mares, run in a time 3.7sec slower than the preceding maiden hurdle. None of the seven came here with a recent outing under their belt. The form is rated around the first two.
T/Plt: £38.00. Pool: £64,226.44 - 1231.28 winning units. T/Qpdt: £6.20. Pool: £4978.70 - 591.20 winning units. IM

1848 CARLISLE (R-H)
Thursday, October 24

OFFICIAL GOING: Good to soft (soft in places; 6.7)
Wind: Breezy, half against Weather: Sunny, warm

2030 STARSPORTSBET.CO.UK NOVICES' HURDLE (11 hdls) 2m 4f
1:50 (1:50) (Class 4) 4-Y-O+ **£3,898** (£1,144; £572; £286)

Form RPR

1 **Milan Bound (IRE)**[243] 4405 5-10-12 0.................................... APMcCoy 125+
(Jonjo O'Neill) *nt fluent at any stage: hld up in tch: stdy hdwy whn hit 3 out: mstke next: effrt and swtchd rt last: led last 100yds: styd on wl* **6/4**[2]

2 ½ **Fayette County (IRE)**[222] 4807 6-10-12 0.................. WilsonRenwick 119
(Tim Vaughan) *chsd ldrs: wnt 2nd bef 3 out: effrt and ev ch next: led last: hdd last 100yds: kpt on: hld nr fin* **7/1**[3]

3 1½ **Blakemount (IRE)**[186] 5-10-12 0.. RyanMania 118
(Sue Smith) *led: rdn bef 3 out: hdd last: kpt on same pce last 100yds* **16/1**

6/3- **4** 26 **Tiny Dancer (IRE)**[166] 218 5-10-12 100........................... BrianHughes 97
(Alan Swinbank) *chsd ldrs: wnt 2nd 6th to bef 3 out: wknd next: hld whn nt fluent last* **20/1**

1/2- **5** 12 **Simarthur**[20] 1755 6-10-12 0..................................... PeterBuchanan 84
(Lucinda Russell) *chsd ldr: hit 5th and nt fluent after: lost 2nd next: rdn and wknd bef 3 out* **11/10**[1]

2/0- **6** ¾ **Omid**[23] 1713 5-10-12 0.. HenryBrooke 83
(Evelyn Slack) *nt fluent in rr: rdn and sme hdwy after 4 out: wknd fr next* **100/1**

/00- **7** 29 **Runswick Days (IRE)**[18] 1792 6-10-5 0.......................... JohnDawson(7) 57
(John Wade) *hld up in tch: struggling bef 4 out: lost tch bef next: t.o* **100/1**

55/ **8** 7 **Fiddler Onthe Hoof (IRE)**[218] 4864 4-10-12 0..................... DannyCook 51
(Martin Todhunter) *nt fluent in rr: struggling fr 6th: t.o* **50/1**

6/0- **9** 75 **Rayadour (IRE)**[8] 1924 4-10-12 0............................(t) JasonMaguire
(Micky Hammond) *hld up: struggling 6th: t.o* **50/1**

5m 3.0s (-19.80) **Going Correction** -0.725s/f (Firm) 9 Ran SP% **116.7**
Speed ratings (Par 105): **110,109,109,98,94 93,82,79,49**
toteswingers 1&2 £1.50, 2&3 £6.20, 1&3 £4.80 CSF £12.08 TOTE £1.70: £1.10, £3.30, £4.40; EX 14.10 Trifecta £40.90 Pool: £1697.19 - 31.09 winning units..
Owner John P McManus **Bred** T J Nagle **Trained** Cheltenham, Gloucs

FOCUS
All Hurdle races run on Flat course. Ordinary novice hurdle form and a race littered with jumping errors.

2031 CALL STAR SPORTS ON 08000 521 321 BEGINNERS' CHASE (12 fncs) 2m
2:20 (2:23) (Class 4) 4-Y-O+ **£4,548** (£1,335; £667; £333)

Form RPR

120/ **1** **Pendra (IRE)**[225] 4736 5-11-2 139... APMcCoy 135+
(Charlie Longsdon) *t.k.h: trckd ldrs: wnt 2nd 6th: led and hrd pressed 3 out: lft clr next: easily* **4/5**[1]

124/ **2** 3¾ **Eduard (IRE)**[201] 5173 5-11-2 0.. BrianHarding 131+
(Nicky Richards) *hld up in tch: smooth hdwy 1/2-way: effrt and ev ch 3 out: upsides whn sprawled bdly and lost all ch next: shkn up and kpt on run-in: no ch w wnr* **7/4**[2]

1P0/ **3** 3 **Chestertern**[179] 12 6-11-2 0.. SeanQuinlan 117
(Jennie Candlish) *prom: drvn and outpcd 1/2-way: plenty to do 4 out: styd on wl fr 2 out: no ch w first two* **40/1**

0/6- **4** 1¾ **Tour D'Argent (FR)**[166] 217 6-11-2 130.......................... JasonMaguire 115
(Donald McCain) *t.k.h: led: jnd 5 out: rdn and hdd 3 out: outpcd fr next* **9/1**[3]

323- **5** 7 **My Idea**[5] 1981 7-10-9 102...............................(t) StephenMulqueen(7) 109
(Maurice Barnes) *chsd ldr: hit and lost 2nd 6th: rdn 5 out: outpcd fr next* **66/1**

62P/ **P** **Gold Cygnet (IRE)**[185] 5448 8-11-2 112........................ PeterBuchanan
(Theresa Gibson) *bhd: lost tch bef 5th: t.o whn p.u 5 out* **100/1**

6/U- **U** **Jet Master (IRE)**[13] 1849 7-11-2 125................................ BrianHughes
(N W Alexander) *hld up in tch: stdy hdwy 1/2-way: less than 3 l 4th and gng wl whn mstke: stmbld and uns rdr 2 out* **40/1**

4m 1.5s (-14.60) **Going Correction** -0.725s/f (Firm) 7 Ran SP% **109.3**
Speed ratings (Par 105): **107,105,103,102,99 , ,**
toteswingers 1&2 £1.10, 2&3 £8.40, 1&3 £7.10 CSF £2.34 TOTE £1.40: £1.10, £1.50; EX 3.00 Trifecta £22.30 Pool: £2876.34 - 96.56 winning units..
Owner John P McManus **Bred** P Murphy **Trained** Over Norton, Oxon

FOCUS
A good beginners' chase, with a pair of 139-rated hurdlers facing off, and it was shaping up nicely into a duel between the pair, who were alongside and seemingly travelling equally as well, when Eduard sprawled on landing two out and handed the contest to Pendra.

2032 STAR SPORTS FOLLOW US ON TWITTER @STAR_SPORTSBET INTERMEDIATE H'CAP HURDLE (9 hdls) 2m 1f
2:55 (2:55) (Class 3) (0-125,122) 4-Y-O+ **£6,498** (£1,908; £954; £477)

Form RPR

341/ **1** **Upswing (IRE)**[221] 4819 5-11-4 **114**.. APMcCoy 125+
(Jonjo O'Neill) *hld up in tch: smooth hdwy to chse ldr after 3 out: led gng wl last: shkn up briefly run-in: comf* **7/4**[1]

5/0- **2** ¾ **Coverholder (IRE)**[8] 1922 6-11-1 **116**...................... JonathanEngland(5) 119
(Sue Smith) *led: rdn 3 out: hdd last: kpt on last 100yds: nt gng pce of wnr* **5/1**[3]

1PP/ **3** 4 **One For Harry (IRE)**[200] 5204 5-11-8 **118**......................... BrianHarding 118
(Nicky Richards) *nt fluent on occasions: hld up in tch: effrt and rdn bef 2 out: one pce fr last* **7/1**

/46- **4** 13 **Smadynium (FR)**[21] 1729 5-11-3 **113**............................... JasonMaguire 102
(Donald McCain) *nt fluent in rr: effrt u.p bef 3 out: no imp fr next* **16/1**

225/ **5** 1¼ **Yorkist (IRE)**[183] 5499 5-10-12 **108**.. DannyCook 95
(Brian Ellison) *t.k.h: cl up: effrt and rdn bef 3 out: wknd between last 2* **2/1**[2]

521/ **6** 3¾ **Phoenix Returns (IRE)**[199] 5216 5-11-12 **122**.................. NickScholfield 106
(Alan Swinbank) *chsd ldr to after 3 out: sn rdn: wknd fr next* **16/1**

500- **U** **Overpriced**[18] 1785 7-11-0 **117**...............................(t) StephenMulqueen(7)
(Maurice Barnes) *prom whn mstke and uns rdr 2nd* **28/1**

4m 15.5s (-12.20) **Going Correction** -0.725s/f (Firm) 7 Ran SP% **114.1**
Speed ratings (Par 107): **103,102,100,94,94 92,**
toteswingers 1&2 £2.50, 2&3 £8.20, 1&3 £2.70 CSF £11.16 TOTE £2.60: £1.80, £3.10; EX 12.70 Trifecta £68.00 Pool: £2878.22 - 31.71 winning units..
Owner John P McManus **Bred** Darren Quaid **Trained** Cheltenham, Gloucs

FOCUS
Not the most competitive handicap, but the cosy winner should have more to offer.

2033 STAR SPORTS TRADER BETIQUETTE H'CAP CHASE (19 fncs) 3m 2f
3:25 (3:25) (Class 3) (0-125,125) 4-Y-O+ **£7,147** (£2,098; £1,049; £524)

Form RPR

251- **1** **Carrigdhoun (IRE)**[18] 1787 8-11-5 **125**...............(tp) StephenMulqueen(7) 131
(Maurice Barnes) *pressed ldr: led 9th: rdn 3 out: hld on gamely fr last* **10/1**

/1P- **2** ¾ **Vic Venturi (IRE)**[139] 660 13-10-13 **112**..................(vt) JasonMaguire 116
(Adrian Wintle) *chsd ldrs: wnt 2nd 10th: drvn along and ev ch 4 out: edgd lft and kpt on u.p fr last* **5/1**[3]

F/3- **3** ¾ **The Friary (IRE)**[20] 1756 6-10-10 **109**..........................(tp) PeterBuchanan 117+
(Lucinda Russell) *nt fluent on occasions: prom: hdwy to chse wnr briefly whn hit 3 out: sn outpcd: rallied last: edgd lft and kpt on* **7/2**[1]

311- **4** 7 **Pyjama Game (IRE)**[20] 1756 7-10-11 **110**...................... WilsonRenwick 107
(Rose Dobbin) *prom: rdn fr 11th: drvn and outpcd bef 4 out: no imp fr next* **9/1**

/PP- **P** **Dun Masc (IRE)**[59] 1396 8-10-12 **111**.................................(p) BrianHughes
(James Moffatt) *led to 9th: rdn and lost pl qckly after next: sn lost tch and p.u* **9/1**

22/ **P** **Moyode Wood**[427] 1328 8-10-10 **109**.. DannyCook
(Brian Ellison) *hld up in tch: rdn 11th: wknd qckly after 13th: p.u bef next* **7/2**[1]

23P/ **P** **Abnaki (IRE)**[208] 5012 8-11-10 **123**..(p) APMcCoy
(Jonjo O'Neill) *nt fluent: hld up in tch on outside: reminders 8th: pckd 11th: outpcd whn blnd 13th: sn btn: p.u after 5 out* **9/2**[2]

6m 51.7s (-15.50) **Going Correction** -0.725s/f (Firm) 7 Ran SP% **108.4**
Speed ratings (Par 107): **94,93,93,91, ,**
toteswingers 1&2 £5.10, 2&3 £5.00, 1&3 £5.80 CSF £52.52 TOTE £12.60: £4.80, £1.60; EX 78.70 Trifecta £382.20 Pool: £1354.94 - 2.65 winning units..
Owner M Barnes **Bred** The Geraghtys Boys **Trained** Farlam, Cumbria
■ Stewards' Enquiry : Stephen Mulqueen two-day ban: used whip above permitted level (Nov 7-8)

FOCUS
A good test at the distance, but probably not the strongest form.

2034 STAR SPORTS BE KNOWLEDGEABLE H'CAP HURDLE (DIV I) (11 hdls) 2m 4f
3:55 (3:57) (Class 4) (0-110,110) 4-Y-O+ **£3,898** (£1,144; £572; £286)

Form RPR

662- **1** **Finding Your Feet (IRE)**[11] 1887 5-11-5 **103**......................(p) APMcCoy 110+
(Jonjo O'Neill) *cl up: led gng wl 3 out: hdd next: rallied: lft cl 2nd last: sn led: rdn and r.o strly* **6/4**[1]

04F/ **2** 4 **Rocking Blues (FR)**[211] 4974 8-11-12 **110**...................... WilsonRenwick 112
(Rose Dobbin) *in tch: stdy hdwy bef 3 out: ev ch next: cl 2nd whn lft in ld briefly last: kpt on: nt gng pce of wnr* **17/2**

603- **3** 16 **Symphonick (FR)**[12] 1873 7-11-2 **100**................................ BrianHughes 90
(Tim Fitzgerald) *j.lft: led to 6th: cl up: drvn and outpcd bef 3 out: no imp whn lft modest 3rd last* **7/1**

332/ **4** 11 **Romany Ryme**[230] 4633 7-11-0 **105**.......................... JonathonBewley(7) 83
(George Bewley) *mstkes: cl up: led 6th: hdd 3 out: wknd next: lft modest 4th last* **11/2**[2]

125/ **5** 1¼ **Northern Acres**[16] 5546 7-10-13 **97**.. HenryBrooke 74
(N W Alexander) *t.k.h in rr: effrt and pushed along after 4 out: wknd fr next* **16/1**

0/3- **6** ½ **Sohcahtoa (IRE)**[23] 1714 7-10-2 **89**................................(p) JohnKington(3) 66
(Andrew Crook) *hld up: struggling bef 4 out: btn next* **33/1**

6/5- **F** **Dickie Henderhoop (IRE)**[162] 310 8-9-13 **90**.......... GrantCockburn(7) 97
(Lucy Normile) *trckd ldrs: effrt and led 2 out: jst in front but keeping on whn fell heavily last* **6/1**[3]

P **Ballyreesode (IRE)**[161] 347 8-10-11 **105**.................... JamesCorbett(10)
(Susan Corbett) *t.k.h: hld up: stdy hdwy after 5th: wknd next: t.o whn p.u bef 3 out* **14/1**

054- **P** **Indepub**[28] 1665 4-11-2 **107**.. CraigNichol(7)
(Martin Todhunter) *hld up: struggling bef 4 out: t.o whn p.u bef next* **16/1**

5m 7.5s (-15.30) **Going Correction** -0.725s/f (Firm)
WFA 4 from 5yo+ 10lb 9 Ran SP% **114.1**
Speed ratings (Par 105): **101,99,93,88,88 87, , ,**
toteswingers 1&2 £3.10, 2&3 £9.70, 1&3 £3.40 CSF £14.96 CT £68.71 TOTE £2.60: £1.60, £1.80, £2.00; EX 15.00 Trifecta £102.90 Pool: £1718.35 - 12.52 winning units..
Owner John P McManus **Bred** L Wright **Trained** Cheltenham, Gloucs

FOCUS
Drama late on, with Dickie Henderhoop crashing out at the last when holding a narrow lead. The winner looks on the upgrade.

2035 STAR SPORTS BE KNOWLEDGEABLE H'CAP HURDLE (DIV II) (11 hdls) 2m 4f
4:30 (4:30) (Class 4) (0-110,109) 4-Y-0+ **£3,898** (£1,144; £572; £286)

Form RPR

6/1- **1** **Moufatango (FR)**[20] [1751] 7-11-8 **105**.................................. BrianHarding 113+
(Nicky Richards) *mde all: jnd after 3 out: rdn and kpt on strly fr last* **5/1**[2]

1F4- **2** *4* **Pete**[41] [1580] 10-10-8 **98**..(tp) GrahamWatters(7) 99
(Barry Murtagh) *hld up in tch: mstke 3rd: smooth hdwy to chal after 3 out: rdn last: sn no ex* **16/1**

044- **3** *11* **Auberge (IRE)**[18] [1797] 9-10-13 **101**.......................... ColmMcCormack(5) 93
(Evelyn Slack) *chsd ldrs: hit and outpcd 4 out: rallied next: kpt on fr 2 out: nvr able to chal* **14/1**

0/0- **4** *hd* **Blue Kascade (IRE)**[18] [1790] 6-10-9 **92**................................ RyanMania 82
(Sandy Thomson) *trckd ldrs: effort and rdn bef 3 out: outpcd fr next* **9/1**

103- **5** *9* **Cruachan (IRE)**[28] [1664] 4-11-10 **107**.............................. DougieCostello 94
(Lucy Normile) *hld up: stdy hdwy 4 out: effrt whn mstke 2 out: sn btn* **9/2**[1]

066/ **6** *20* **Bold Slasher (IRE)**[218] [4863] 5-10-2 **90**................. JonathanEngland(5) 54
(Sue Smith) *chsd wnr tl rdn and wknd fr 3 out: t.o* **7/1**

3PP/ **7** *63* **Billy Cuckoo (IRE)**[186] [5427] 7-11-5 **109**........................ MrMJohnson(7) 16
(Tony Coyle) *sn pushed along in rr: struggling bef 4 out: t.o* **6/1**[3]

/46- **F** **Newdane Dancer (IRE)**[12] [1870] 6-10-2 **85**....................(p) HenryBrooke
(Dianne Sayer) *hld up: struggling bef 6th: btn whn fell 4 out* **12/1**

3/P- **P** **Harris (IRE)**[147] [554] 6-11-4 **106**................................... HarryChalloner(5)
(William Kinsey) *in tch whn sprawled bdly and lost pl 3rd: nt rcvr: t.o whn p.u 4 out* **7/1**

455/ **P** **Markem (IRE)**[183] [5491] 6-11-5 **102**.............................. WilsonRenwick
(Rose Dobbin) *hld up in tch: struggling 6th: p.u appr next* **6/1**[3]

5m 6.1s (-16.70) **Going Correction** -0.725s/f (Firm) **10** Ran SP% **118.7**
Speed ratings (Par 105): **104,102,98,97,94 86,61, , ,**
toteswingers 1&2 £8.30, 2&3 £9.10, 1&3 £10.40 CSF £79.70 CT £1060.15 TOTE £5.30: £2.00, £5.20, £3.10; EX 77.50 Trifecta £351.90 Pool: £1613.01 - 3.43 winning units..
Owner Miss J R Richards **Bred** Olivier Le Quere **Trained** Greystoke, Cumbria

FOCUS
The front pair drew clear in what was perhaps the stronger of the two divisions. The winner looks to have more to come.

2036 STAR SPORTS BE POLITE H'CAP CHASE (16 fncs) 2m 4f
5:00 (5:02) (Class 4) (0-110,107) 4-Y-0+ **£4,873** (£1,431; £715; £357)

Form RPR

3/6- **1** **Tutchec (FR)**[173] [113] 6-11-2 **97**... APMcCoy 114+
(Nicky Richards) *nt fluent on occasions: mde all: mstke 8th: rdn bef 2 out: kpt on strly fr last* **3/1**[1]

4/2- **2** *5* **Bertie Milan (IRE)**[162] [312] 8-11-9 **104**............................ BrianHarding 112
(N W Alexander) *hld up in tch: swvd to avoid faller 8th: rdn after 10th: hdwy 4 out: styd on fr last to take 2nd nr fin: no ch w wnr* **6/1**[3]

6PP/ **3** *1 ½* **Twice Lucky**[200] [5206] 9-9-11 **83**............................ JonathanEngland(5) 90
(Sue Smith) *pressed wnr: effrt and rdn 3 out: one pce between last 2: lost 2nd towards fin* **3/1**[1]

PPP/ **4** *6* **Frank The Slink**[179] [18] 7-11-12 **107**................................ HenryBrooke 108
(Micky Hammond) *bhd and detached: shkn up and hdwy 3 out: kpt on fr last: nvr nr ldrs* **14/1**

421- **5** *nse* **Chicago Outfit (IRE)**[18] [1789] 8-11-3 **98**.........................(p) BrianHughes 100
(John Wade) *prom: rdn and outpcd 10th: rallied 5 out: nt fluent next: sn n.d* **13/2**

/34- **6** *6* **Detour Ahead**[159] [369] 5-11-6 **101**....................................(p) SeanQuinlan 98
(Jennie Candlish) *chsd ldrs: drvn whn mstke 5 out: rallied next: wknd fr 2 out* **25/1**

350- **P** **Forestside (IRE)**[20] [1756] 8-10-9 **90**.................................. JasonMaguire
(Barry Murtagh) *nt fluent on occasions: hld up in tch: struggling fr 11th: no ch whn hit 3 out: sn p.u* **12/1**

112- **F** **Presenting Junior (IRE)**[18] [1789] 6-10-9 **90**.................. WilsonRenwick
(Martin Todhunter) *in tch whn fell 8th* **9/2**[2]

5m 12.0s (-15.40) **Going Correction** -0.725s/f (Firm) **8** Ran SP% **114.0**
Speed ratings (Par 105): **101,99,98,96,95 93, ,**
toteswingers 1&2 £7.50, 2&3 £6.10, 1&3 £2.50 CSF £21.40 CT £57.30 TOTE £5.00: £2.00, £1.40, £1.60; EX 13.90 Trifecta £107.20 Pool: £2114.48 - 14.78 winning units..
Owner Club 4 Racing **Bred** William Ewart **Trained** Greystoke, Cumbria

FOCUS
A modest handicap chase, but the winner looks capable of better.

2037 STAR SPORTS DON'T BE RUSHED STANDARD OPEN NATIONAL HUNT FLAT RACE 2m 1f
5:30 (5:32) (Class 6) 4-6-Y-0 **£1,624** (£477; £238; £119)

Form RPR

1 **Five In A Row (IRE)**[26] 5-11-0 0.. DannyCook 112+
(Brian Ellison) *trckd ldrs: led 3f out: rdn and drew clr fr over 1f out* **6/1**[3]

2 *9* **The Last Samuri (IRE)**[166] 5-11-0 0................................... JasonMaguire 103
(Donald McCain) *t.k.h: cl up: led over 4f out to 3f out: one pce fr over 1f out* **3/1**[2]

3 *½* **Emral Silk** 5-11-0 0.. RyanMania 102
(Sue Smith) *prom: effrt and ev ch 3f out: one pce fr over 1f out* **25/1**

4 *3 ¼* **Landecker (IRE)**[172] 5-11-0 0... BrianHarding 99
(N W Alexander) *midfield: effrt and pushed along over 3f out: no imp fr 2f out* **33/1**

53- **5** *1 ¼* **Lacocodanza**[23] [1719] 4-10-2 0.. JoeColliver(5) 91
(George Moore) *hld up: pushed along over 6f out: rallied over 3f out: kpt on: nvr able to chal* **50/1**

230/ **6** *18* **Bobs Lady Tamure**[181] [5550] 6-10-0 0..................(t) StephenMulqueen(7) 75
(Maurice Barnes) *t.k.h early: hld up: stdy hdwy 1/2-way: c wd over 4f out: sn struggling* **14/1**

3- **7** *nse* **Crown And Glory (IRE)**[13] [1854] 6-11-0 0......................... PeterBuchanan 82
(Karen Tutty) *in tch: effrt and drvn 4f out: wknd over 2f out* **14/1**

235/ **8** *2 ¼* **Ultiep (FR)**[377] [1821] 5-11-0 0...(p) BrianHughes 80
(Karen McLintock) *led to over 4f out: rdn and wknd 3f out* **25/1**

9 *3 ¾* **Voyage A New York (FR)**[172] 4-11-0 0.............................. WilsonRenwick 76
(Tim Vaughan) *in tch tl rdn and wknd over 4f out* **13/2**

- **10** *2 ¼* **Dubai Sonnet** 4-11-0 0.. APMcCoy 74
(Alan Swinbank) *t.k.h: sn midfield on outside: hdwy and cl up after 6f: wknd over 3f out* **5/2**[1]

11 *27* **Casual Cavalier (IRE)** 5-10-7 0...................................... JohnDawson(7) 50
(John Wade) *hld up: struggling over 5f out: sn btn: t.o* **50/1**

0- **12** *25* **Wind Echo**[12] [1877] 5-10-7 0.. DaraghBourke(7) 28
(Rayson Nixon) *bhd: struggling fr 1/2-way: t.o* **250/1**

0- **13** *13* **Marlee Massie (IRE)**[137] [682] 4-11-0 0.................................. HenryBrooke 16
(N W Alexander) *a bhd: struggling after 6f: t.o* **50/1**

2/ **U** **Marrakech Trader (NZ)**[211] [4976] 6-10-7 0..................... TomBellamy(7)
(Rose Dobbin) *plld hrd in midfield: jinked: hit rail and uns rdr bnd after 5f* **15/2**

4m 16.2s (-8.00) **Going Correction** -0.725s/f (Firm)
WFA 4 from 5yo+ 9lb **14** Ran SP% **123.2**
Speed ratings: **89,84,84,83,82 73,73,72,71,70 57,45,39,**
toteswingers 1&2 £6.50, 2&3 £23.50, 1&3 £19.10 CSF £23.83 TOTE £5.30: £1.90, £1.70, £8.60; EX 27.10 Trifecta £965.70 Pool: £1504.80 - 1.16 winning units..
Owner P J Martin **Bred** Ms M Maher **Trained** Norton, N Yorks

FOCUS
This looked a fair bumper beforehand, but the front two in the market did themselves few favours by refusing to settle.
T/Plt: £117.60 to a £1 stake. Pool of £51394.03 - 318.80 winning tickets. T/Qpdt: £32.90 to a £1 stake. Pool of £3893.40 - 87.40 winning tickets. RY

1813 LUDLOW (R-H)
Thursday, October 24

OFFICIAL GOING: Good (good to soft in places; 7.7)
Wind: almost nil Weather: sunny; 12 degrees

2038 RACING WELFARE WEEK JUVENILE CLAIMING HURDLE (9 hdls) 2m
1:40 (1:40) (Class 4) 3-Y-O **£3,898** (£1,144; £572; £286)

Form RPR

1- **1** **Ballyglasheen (IRE)**[15] [1813] 3-11-8 108.............................. PaulMoloney 110
(Evan Williams) *prom: j. slowly 4th and lost pl briefly: rallied next: gng wl on inner home turn: chal and hrd drvn 2 out: sn led flat: kpt on wl but all out* **2/1**[1]

2 *nk* **Aglaophonos**[8] 3-11-2 0..(p) AidanColeman 106+
(Ian Williams) *pressed ldrs: effrt 3 out: led next: drvn and hit last: sn hdd: rallied flat: kpt on wl cl home but jst hld* **4/1**[3]

141- **3** *11* **Hanga Roa (IRE)**[7] [1781] 3-11-7 123..................................... JamieMoore 100
(Gary Moore) *led at decent pce: drvn bef 3 out: hdd and nt fluent next: btn last* **11/4**[2]

4- **4** *2 ¾* **Eyeline**[24] [1182] 3-10-0 0...(tp) JamesCowley(7) 82
(Andrew Hollinshead) *t.k.h towards rr: rdn after 6th: struggling bef 2 out* **20/1**

2- **5** *6* **Sutton Sid**[7] [1271] 3-10-10 0...(p) TomCannon 81
(Chris Gordon) *hld up and rn in snatches: last whn mstke 5th: drvn bef 3 out: no reponse and sn wl btn* **9/2**

6 *1 ¾* **Herbalist**[21] 3-10-7 0.. DavidBass 79
(Ben Pauling) *j. slowly 4th: towards rr: rdn and sing to struggle whn blnd bdly 3 out* **16/1**

P- **7** *29* **Big John Cannon (IRE)**[21] [1727] 3-10-8 0............................. WillKennedy 50
(Sarah-Jayne Davies) *prom: rdn after 6th: fdd tamely next: t.o and eased* **50/1**

3m 44.8s (-4.70) **Going Correction** 0.0s/f (Good) **7** Ran SP% **110.8**
Speed ratings (Par 103): **111,110,105,103,100 100,85**
toteswingers 1&2 £3.40, 2&3 £2.30, 1&3 £1.30 CSF £9.88 TOTE £3.80: £1.70, £3.50; EX 10.70 Trifecta £16.70 Pool: £894.28 - 40.03 winning units..
Owner R J Gambarini **Bred** Mrs Evie Stockwell **Trained** Llancarfan, Vale Of Glamorgan

FOCUS
All rails as for last meeting and Hurdles on inside line in straight. A fair race for the grade and, with the very easy-to-back Hanga Roa ensuring a solid gallop throughout, there were positives to be gleaned by the performances of the principals, who pulled well clear.

2039 BLUEFIN NOVICES' H'CAP CHASE (13 fncs) 2m
2:10 (2:10) (Class 5) (0-100,100) 4-Y-O+ **£3,249** (£954; £477; £238)

Form RPR

U/3- **1** **Drumlang (IRE)**[32] [1638] 7-11-7 **100**.............................. RobertMcCarth(5) 112+
(Ian Williams) *pressed ldrs and t.k.h: effrt and lft 2nd bef 10th: led and dived at 3 out: kpt rt up to work after and hld on wl: all out* **5/1**[3]

066/ **2** *½* **Think Its All Over (USA)**[183] [5509] 6-10-13 **90**.............. AdamWedge(3) 104+
(Evan Williams) *prom: 2nd whn bdly hmpd on long run to 10th: dropped bk 3rd: rallied and drvn to chal 3 out: ev ch after: jst hld fnl 100yds* **4/1**[2]

/12- **3** *9* **Shalamiyr (FR)**[14] [1835] 8-11-8 **96**.. WillKennedy 99
(Sarah-Jayne Davies) *led tl 6th and 7th tl next: sn led again: lft 5 l clr on long run to 10th: rdn and hdd 3 out: fnd little fr next and plugged on in wl hld 3rd* **8/1**

443- **4** *23* **Tinelyra (IRE)**[18] [1800] 7-10-13 **87**...........................(t) SamTwiston-Davies 68
(Fergal O'Brien) *mstke 1st: hld up in midfield: lost tch after being hmpd after 9th: mstke next: drvn into remote 4th bef last* **3/1**[1]

5P0- **5** *2* **Carobello (IRE)**[32] [1632] 6-10-9 **83**....................................(t) JamesDavies 62
(Martin Bosley) *blnd bdly 1st: nt jump wl in rr: struggling after 9th: j.lft 3 out* **33/1**

/0F- **6** *3 ¼* **The Absent Mare**[109] [899] 5-10-6 **85**.................................. BenPoste(5) 61
(Robin Dickin) *nvr bttr than midfield: nt fluent early: rdn after 9th: sn struggling and no ch fr next* **16/1**

/P4- **7** *20* **Vertueux (FR)**[15] [1816] 8-11-4 **92**.......................................(p) LeeEdwards 50
(Tony Carroll) *sn bhd and nt looking keen: in last whn blnd 7th and unbalanced: remote after: blnd again 10th* **12/1**

0/0- **F** **Quantique (FR)**[41] [1575] 9-10-8 82..................................... AidanColeman
(Venetia Williams) *mstke 1st: in rr whn fell 2nd* **14/1**

/00- **S** **Prickles**[7] [1938] 8-11-6 **97**... MichealNolan(3)
(Richard Woollacott) *midfield: rdn bef 6th and nt keen: struggling whn slipped up on long run bef 10th* **20/1**

153- **S** **Julie Prince (IRE)**[14] [1835] 7-11-11 **99**...........................(t) BrendanPowell
(Brendan Powell) *led tl 3rd: 6th tl 7th and 8th: cl 2nd whn slipped up on long run to 10th* **6/1**

3m 57.1s (-1.40) **Going Correction** 0.0s/f (Good) **10** Ran SP% **115.0**
Speed ratings (Par 103): **103,102,98,86,85 84,74, , ,**
toteswingers 1&2 £9.10, 2&3 £4.90, 1&3 £5.20 CSF £25.75 CT £157.18 TOTE £7.30: £3.60, £1.40, £2.70; EX 46.20 Trifecta £204.00 Pool: £790.53 - 2.90 winning units..
Owner M Roberts J O'Shea S Hunt R Stearman **Bred** Sandra Hodgins **Trained** Portway, Worcs

The Form Book Jumps, Raceform Ltd, Compton, RG20 6NL.

FOCUS
A moderate novices' chase, but the winner was stepping up. Plenty of drama with Quantique crashing out at an early stage and the still-in-contention Julie Prince slipping up on the penultimate bend and causing significant interference to the runner-up.

2040 HAPPY 70TH BIRTHDAY KEITH TAMPIN NOVICES' HURDLE (9 hdls) 2m
2:40 (2:40) (Class 4) 4-Y-0+ **£3,898** (£1,144; £572; £286)

Form RPR

2- **1** **Curzon Line**[18] 1793 4-10-12 0 DenisO'Regan 112+
(John Ferguson) *sn chsng clr ldr: clsd bef 3 out where led on bit: sn clr and in command: rdn out flat* **11/4**[1]

5- **2** *3 ¼* **Ashdown Lad**[18] 1779 4-10-12 0 FelixDeGiles 108+
(Tom Symonds) *racd freely in ld: nt fluent 4th: sn clr: 8 l ahd on long run to 3 out where rdn and hdd and hit flight: mstke next: no ch w wnr but kpt on wl to remain ahd of rest* **5/1**

45- **3** *6* **Tempuran**[18] 1795 4-10-12 0 TomScudamore 103
(David Bridgwater) *chsd ldrs: effrt 6th: wnt 3rd home turn but rdn and clouted fnl three: unable to get in a blow* **12/1**

6/0- **4** *3 ¼* **Ballygrooby Bertie (IRE)**[167] 207 5-10-12 0 (t) SamTwiston-Davies 99
(Fergal O'Brien) *t.k.h early: bhd: picked off btn horses fr 6th: rdn and no further imp fr after next: mstke 2 out* **50/1**

523/ **5** *3 ¼* **Devil's Dyke (USA)**[193] 5310 5-10-12 0 PaulMoloney 95
(Evan Williams) *a abt same pl: 4th and rdn on long run to 3 out: one pce and wl hld after* **3/1**[2]

0/ **6** *9* **Six One Away (IRE)**[235] 4542 4-10-9 0 JakeGreenall(3) 87
(Paul Webber) *chsd ldrs: rdn bef 3 out: kpt on same pce and n.d after* **50/1**

0/ **7** *3 ¼* **Veratan (FR)**[609] 4474 6-10-7 0 CallumWhillans(5) 86
(Venetia Williams) *nt fluent: in rr after slow jump 4th: plugging on after last* **33/1**

55/ **8** *¾* **Cane Cat (IRE)**[26] 364 6-10-5 0 (t) LeeEdwards 77
(Tony Carroll) *nvr bttr than midfield: hit 5th: rdn and btn bef 3 out* **33/1**

/P0- **9** *1* **Daizy (IRE)**[14] 1832 4-10-12 0 JackDoyle 84
(Hilary Parrott) *prom tl rdn and fdd on long run to 3 out* **100/1**

06/ **10** *hd* **Young Lou**[195] 5267 4-9-9 0 JosephPalmowski(10) 75
(Robin Dickin) *nvr trbld ldrs: struggling bef 3 out* **80/1**

0- **11** *2 ¼* **Stag Hill (IRE)**[18] 1795 4-10-7 0 RobertWilliams(5) 80
(Bernard Llewellyn) *midfield: lost tch bef 3 out: mstke next* **50/1**

035/ **12** *nk* **Lone Ranger (FR)**[218] 4872 5-10-12 0 AidanColeman 80
(Venetia Williams) *nt a fluent: effrt 6th: chsd ldrs bef next: btn 3 out: eased flat* **7/2**[3]

/20- **13** *29* **Straits Of Messina (IRE)**[18] 1793 4-10-7 0 BenPoste(5) 54
(Tom Symonds) *hld up in last and wl off pce: t.o 6th: eased next* **25/1**

530/ **14** *32* **Kings Music (IRE)**[357] 2142 7-10-2 0 ThomasCheesman(10) 25
(Philip Hobbs) *j. poorly and wl bhd: t.o fr 6th* **16/1**

3m 44.9s (-4.60) **Going Correction** 0.0s/f (Good) 14 Ran SP% **122.0**
Speed ratings (Par 105): **111,109,106,104,103 98,97,96,96,96 94,94,80,64**
toteswingers 1&2 £3.80, 2&3 £8.00, 1&3 £5.30 CSF £16.55 TOTE £4.00: £1.50, £1.70, £2.50; EX 15.50 Trifecta £108.40 Pool: £923.59 - 6.38 winning units..
Owner Bloomfields **Bred** Darley **Trained** Cowlinge, Suffolk

FOCUS
An informative, if probably only ordinary novices' event.

2041 THOROUGHBRED BREEDERS ASSOCIATION CUP (HANDICAP CHASE) (19 fncs) 3m
3:15 (3:15) (Class 4) (0-120,119) 4-Y-0+ **£6,498** (£1,908; £954; £477)

Form RPR

613- **1** **Western King (IRE)**[30] 1642 6-11-8 **115** (tp) SamTwiston-Davies 125+
(Charlie Mann) *chsd ldr: dropped himself out 11th where mod 5th: rallied in 3rd gng wl bef 16th: drvn ahd bef next: idling bdly and carrying hd awkwardly after: 3 l clr at last: a holding rival flat* **7/2**[2]

2/1- **2** *3* **Raduis Bleu (FR)**[171] 143 8-10-12 **112** MissLBrooke(7) 116
(Lady Susan Brooke) *sn in 2nd: slt ld fr 8th: hdd after 3 out and pushed along: kpt on gamely but a hld fr last* **12/1**

416- **3** *6* **Michigan Assassin (IRE)**[41] 1577 11-10-4 **102** (p) AodhaganConlon(5) 103
(Debra Hamer) *led 2nd tl 8th: w ldr tl 12th and again briefly bef 16th: rdn and fdd after next: hit last* **16/1**

434- **4** *16* **Grey Soldier (IRE)**[20] 1750 8-11-8 **115** (tp) DenisO'Regan 99
(Sophie Leech) *bhd: rdn and tailed himself off after 11th: consented to pass two rivals in clsng stages to go remote 4th at last* **16/1**

05P/ **5** *13* **Ringa Bay**[228] 4687 8-11-12 **119** TomScudamore 97
(David Bridgwater) *led and hit 1st: sn hdd: j. deliberately 3rd: 7 l 3rd at 11th: struggling fr next: t.o and eased* **3/1**[1]

326/ **6** *27* **Rocky Bender (IRE)**[184] 5471 8-11-3 **110** AidanColeman 73
(Venetia Williams) *often j. slowly: nvr bttr than midfield: brief effrt 12th: struggling fr 16th: t.o and eased* **10/1**

1/0- **P** **The Rockies (IRE)**[11] 1887 6-10-11 **104** (t) PaulMoloney
(Evan Williams) *hld up in rr: rdn after 11th: t.o 13th: p.u 16th* **9/2**[3]

210- **P** **Danandy (IRE)**[82] 1197 6-10-13 **106** TomO'Brien
(Philip Hobbs) *hit 3rd: midfield tl p.u 7th: sddle slipped* **9/2**[3]

6m 4.2s (-4.10) **Going Correction** 0.0s/f (Good) 8 Ran SP% **112.1**
Speed ratings (Par 105): **106,105,103,97,93 84, ,**
toteswingers 1&2 £2.30, 2&3 £21.50, 1&3 £15.80 CSF £40.23 CT £583.38 TOTE £5.00: £1.90, £2.30, £5.20; EX 25.30 Trifecta £520.10 Pool: £1466.47 - 2.11 winning units..
Owner The Western King Partnership **Bred** David Kennedy **Trained** Upper Lambourn, Berks

FOCUS
Not the strongest of races for the grade and, with the well-supported Danandy forced out with a slipping saddle, it remains to be seen how well the form will work out.

2042 BLUEFIN INSURANCE SOLUTIONS WELSHPOOL NOVICES' LIMITED H'CAP CHASE (13 fncs) 2m
3:45 (3:45) (Class 3) (0-125,121) 4-Y-0+ **£6,963** (£2,057; £1,028; £514)

Form RPR

344- **1** **Be All Man (IRE)**[4] 1986 6-10-11 **113** JamieMoore 119+
(Gary Moore) *pressed ldr: nt fluent 9th: led next: hrd drvn and hrd pressed fr 2 out: mstke last: battled on gamely: all out* **9/1**

3/U- **2** *½* **Woodbank**[15] 1817 6-11-0 **116** AndrewTinkler 126+
(Nicky Henderson) *t.k.h in last: blnd 1st: blnd bdly 8th: hrd drvn fr 3 out: clsd and chal last: ev ch 100yds out: out battled nr fin* **7/4**[1]

132- **3** *1 ¾* **Oyster Shell**[26] 1688 6-11-2 **121** JakeGreenall(3) 124
(Henry Daly) *often j. indifferently tl 1/2-way: cl up: 2nd and ev ch 3 out tl last: rdn and no ex flat* **15/8**[2]

310/ **4** *1 ½* **Tornado In Milan (IRE)**[208] 5016 7-11-4 **120** PaulMoloney 122
(Evan Williams) *led down to s early: led: set mod pce: nt fluent 5th (water): hdd 10th: being cajoled along w little rspnse whn mstke 2 out: btn last* **11/4**[3]

4m 1.1s (2.60) **Going Correction** 0.0s/f (Good) 4 Ran SP% **107.8**
Speed ratings (Par 107): **93,92,91,91**
CSF £24.61 TOTE £4.30; EX 30.30 Trifecta £53.70 Pool: £1332.82 - 18.58 winning units..
Owner A Head, R Lockwood & M Burne **Bred** Howard Barton Stud **Trained** Lower Beeding, W Sussex

FOCUS
Steadily run with sprint finish and suspect form, but winner in line with best of hurdle form; second would have won bar errors.

2043 TBA MARES' NOVICES' HURDLE (11 hdls) 2m 5f
4:15 (4:15) (Class 4) 4-Y-0+ **£4,992** (£1,550; £834)

Form RPR

6/4- **1** **Midnight Cataria**[168] 187 4-10-10 0 WayneHutchinson 110+
(Alan King) *settled in 2nd or in 3rd in v slowly run r: rdn and effrt after 3 out: hit next: flat out after and being sltly leant on by rival: drew level 100yds out and jst prevailed* **11/10**[1]

2 *hd* **Forgivienne**[180] 6-10-7 0 AdamWedge(3) 107
(Evan Williams) *j. sltly lft: led at slow pce: pushed along bef 3 out: hrd drvn and edging lft and crowding rival after next: jnd flat: pipped nr fin* **9/2**[3]

62/ **3** *8* **Ellnando Queen**[193] 5316 5-10-7 0 GavinSheehan(3) 100
(Warren Greatrex) *wnt 2nd after 5th: rdn bef 3 out: lost 2nd next: sn wknd: eased flat* **6/4**[2]

/UU- **P** **Desert Fairy**[32] 1632 7-10-3 0 (t) JoshWall(7)
(Trevor Wall) *in last pair: floundering 6th: hopelessly t.o whn p.u after 8th* **33/1**

0/0- **P** **Haliana**[145] 589 4-10-10 0 LeeEdwards
(John Upson) *nt jump wl: 2nd tl bef 3rd: dropped bk last and blnd 6th: could nt raise a gallop after and eventually p.u after 8th* **100/1**

5m 13.9s (-0.90) **Going Correction** 0.0s/f (Good)
WFA 4 from 5yo+ 10lb 5 Ran SP% **109.7**
Speed ratings (Par 105): **101,100,97, ,**
CSF £6.59 TOTE £2.10: £1.30, £2.50; EX 6.10 Trifecta £6.50 Pool: £1959.63 - 223.48 winning units..
Owner Mrs K Holmes **Bred** Pitchall Stud **Trained** Barbury Castle, Wilts

FOCUS
A race weakened by the absence of the likely odds-on favourite Toubeera, but the likelihood is it still took some winning.

2044 AMATEUR JOCKEYS' ASSOCIATION AMATEUR RIDERS' H'CAP CHASE (FOR THE COURT OF HILL CHALLENGE) (17 fncs) 2m 4f
4:50 (4:50) (Class 5) (0-95,94) 4-Y-0+ **£3,743** (£1,161; £580; £290)

Form RPR

562- **1** **Mr Bachster (IRE)**[14] 1838 8-9-13 **72** MissLBrooke(5) 84+
(Richard Lee) *settled in rr early: gd hdwy to press ldrs 9th: led gng wl bef 14th: rdn and slt advantage fr next: hit last: styd on gamely cl home* **6/1**[3]

336- **2** *1* **Finch Flyer (IRE)**[23] 1710 6-9-12 **71** (p) MrAlexEdwards(5) 79
(Aytach Sadik) *settled in midfield: hit 7th and rdn: hdwy on inner whn nt fluent 11th: led briefly after 13th: pressed wnr w ev ch fr next tl pushed along and outstyd fnl 100yds* **8/1**

62P- **3** *3 ¼* **Nouailhas**[9] 1914 7-10-3 **76** (v) MissAEStirling(5) 83
(Andrew Hollinshead) *j.lft and rn in snatches: led bef 9th tl 11th: rdn and outpcd 14th: 7 l fr ldng pair whn v awkward 2 out and last: rallied flat and styd on* **6/1**[3]

5P5- **4** *½* **Fitandproperjob**[14] 1834 7-10-7 **78** (t) MrFMitchell(3) 85
(Anthony Middleton) *dropped out last early: hdwy 9th: cl 5th home turn: rdn w no rspnse whn lurchd 2 out: kpt on again after last* **5/1**[2]

1PP- **5** *½* **Top Benefit (IRE)**[18] 1784 11-10-12 **87** MrJBargary(7) 91
(Richard Harper) *rn in snatches: lost gd pl 9th: drvn and rallied 13th: pressed ldrs bef next: kpt on same pce after* **16/1**

/PP- **6** *10* **One For The Boss (IRE)**[135] 707 6-10-9 **82** MrMatthewBarber(5) 78
(Dai Burchell) *drvn after 4th: in rr and nvr travelling w purpose: struggling bef 14th* **7/2**[1]

4P4- **7** *17* **Dark Oasis**[15] 1825 7-9-7 **68** oh8 (v[1]) MrPJohn(7) 53
(Natalie Lloyd-Beavis) *sn prom: hit 8th: led 11th tl sn after 13th: dropped out qckly u.p: t.o and eased 2 out* **10/1**

005- **8** *12* **Daneva (IRE)**[44] 1547 9-11-7 **94** (tp) MrJMRidley(5) 68
(Matt Sheppard) *settled wl in rr: effrt 10th: 6th and rdn after 13th: sn struggling: t.o* **10/1**

0PF- **9** *27* **Guns Of Love (IRE)**[44] 1548 11-9-13 **74** MrTWWheeler(7) 19
(Robin Dickin) *prom briefly: dropped to rr and rdn 9th: t.o fr next: fin eventually* **33/1**

/32- **P** **Annie Confidential (IRE)**[19] 1769 10-10-3 **76** MissAliceMills(5)
(Miss Imogen Pickard) *led: j.lft 2nd: hdd bef 9th: drvn and lost pl rapidly 12th: t.o next: p.u 3 out* **5/1**[2]

5m 8.8s (4.40) **Going Correction** 0.0s/f (Good) 10 Ran SP% **122.2**
Speed ratings (Par 103): **91,90,89,89,88 84,78,73,62,**
toteswingers 1&2 £7.10, 2&3 £9.30, 1&3 £10.20 CSF £55.77 CT £308.16 TOTE £8.10: £2.00, £1.20, £3.00; EX 58.80 Trifecta £505.10 Pool: £2164.91 - 3.21 winning units..
Owner Richard Lee **Bred** Mrs Anne Caplice **Trained** Byton, H'fords

FOCUS
A devilishly competitive, if very ordinary contest.

2045 AIUA/BLUEFIN AGRICULTURAL INSURANCE SPECIALISTS H'CAP HURDLE (9 hdls) 2m
5:20 (5:20) (Class 4) (0-115,119) 4-Y-0+ **£4,873** (£1,431; £715; £357)

Form RPR

6/1- **1** **Makari**[9] 1913 6-11-13 **119** 7ex NicodeBoinville(5) 132+
(Nicky Henderson) *t.k.h: settled in rr: cruised into contention home turn: led on bit 2 out: hrd hld after* **1/3**[1]

16U- **2** *3 ½* **Sedgemoor Express (IRE)**[7] 1941 5-11-3 **107** (tp) MarkQuinlan(3) 106
(Nigel Hawke) *wnt 2nd after 5th: led 3 out: rdn and hdd next: kpt on to jst hold 2nd but flattered by proximity to effrtless wnr* **10/1**

023- **3** *nk* **Macarthur**[94] 1072 9-11-10 **111** (v[1]) PaulMoloney 110
(David Rees) *prom and t.k.h: ev ch on inner 3 out: rdn and racing awkwardly fr next: kpt on after last but wnr only cantering* **7/1**[2]

266- **4** *¾* **Eightfold**[15] 1816 4-11-5 **106** (t) ConorO'Farrell 104
(Seamus Durack) *settled towards rr: effrt 3 out: chsd ldrs but no imp fr next* **20/1**

3/0- **5** *6* **Old Magic (IRE)**[23] 1711 8-10-3 **90** JamesDavies 82
(Sophie Leech) *got flier and abt 6 l clr tl 4th: pressed fr next: rdn and hdd 3 out: dropped out steadily: j.rt 2 out* **20/1**

16/- **6** *4* **Western Approaches**[396] 1608 6-11-4 **110**.............(t) RobertMcCarth(5) 99
(Ian Williams) *t.k.h in 2nd or 3rd: ev ch bef 3 out: rdn and btn next: blnd last* **8/1**[3]

5F/- **7** *3 ½* **Nether Stream (IRE)**[183] 5508 9-11-12 **113**.................... TommyPhelan 97
(David Dennis) *j. v poorly in rr: rdn and struggling bef 3 out* **40/1**

440/ **8** *26* **Bin End**[176] 4275 7-11-4 **105**....................................(p) SamTwiston-Davies 63
(Barry Brennan) *swvd bdly lft s and forfeited many l: nt fluent 2nd: in tch by 3rd: a in last pair: rdn and fdd bef 3 out: sn t.o and eased* **11/1**

3m 46.8s (-2.70) **Going Correction** 0.0s/f (Good)
WFA 4 from 5yo+ 9lb **8** Ran SP% **128.0**
Speed ratings (Par 105): **106,104,104,103,100 98,96,83**
toteswingers 1&2 £2.60, 2&3 £8.00, 1&3 £1.30 CSF £6.27 CT £16.66 TOTE £1.40: £1.02, £2.90, £2.20; EX 5.90 Trifecta £25.30 Pool: £3054.63 - 90.43 winning units..
Owner Matt & Lauren Morgan **Bred** Longdon Stud Ltd **Trained** Upper Lambourn, Berks

FOCUS
This was nothing more than piece of work for the facile winner.
T/Plt: £351.00 to a £1 stake. Pool of £46724.0 - 97.15 winning tickets. T/Qpdt: £82.90 to a £1 stake. Pool of £3868.49 - 34.50 winning tickets. IM

1493 SOUTHWELL (L-H)

Thursday, October 24

OFFICIAL GOING: Good to soft (good in places; 6.8)
Wind: almost nil Weather: fine and sunny

2046 32RED NOVICES' H'CAP CHASE (19 fncs) 3m 110y

1:30 (1:30) (Class 4) (0-110,110) 4-Y-0+ **£3,768** (£1,106; £553; £276)

Form RPR

023/ **1** **Shockingtimes (IRE)**[318] 2972 6-11-11 **109**.......................... MarkGrant 125+
(Charlie Mann) *trckd ldrs: t.k.h: hit 9th: led 14th: drew clr fr 3 out: pushed out* **6/1**[3]

00P/ **2** *13* **Moorland Sunset**[184] 5471 6-11-12 **110**................................ IanPopham 112
(Caroline Keevil) *t.k.h: trckd ldr to 12th: regained 2nd sn after 4 out: no imp* **25/1**

313- **3** *6* **Long Wave (IRE)**[43] 1565 6-11-9 **107**.........................(p) RichardJohnson 103
(Charlie Longsdon) *led to 14th: outpcd 4 out: modest 3rd next: one pce* **15/8**[1]

342- **4** *7* **Tough Talkin Man (IRE)**[14] 1834 9-10-10 **94**.............(p) DonalDevereux 88
(Peter Bowen) *chsd ldrs: pushed along 13th: 5th whn blnd 4 out: sn wl outpcd: modest 4th 3 out: wknd last* **9/2**[2]

056/ **5** *24* **Tickatack (IRE)**[299] 3348 8-11-4 **107**........................... KillianMoore(5) 75
(Graeme McPherson) *trckd ldrs: 2nd 12th: rdn and wknd 4 out: t.o next* **9/2**[2]

412/ **U** **Forgotten Symphony (IRE)**[445] 1190 9-11-5 **110**.... NathanMoscrop(7)
(Brian Ellison) *t.k.h in rr: hit 2nd: blnd and uns rdr 3rd* **7/1**

300- **F** **River Purple**[107] 933 6-9-11 **84** oh1.........................(t) PeterCarberry(3)
(John Mackie) *in rr: outpcd 11th: bhd whn fell 15th* **12/1**

6m 30.6s (7.60) **Going Correction** +0.425s/f (Soft) **7** Ran SP% **109.5**
Speed ratings (Par 105): **104,99,97,95,88** ,
toteswingers 1&2 £28.40, 2&3 £5.60, 1&3 £3.30 CSF £95.36 CT £354.10 TOTE £8.60: £3.30, £10.50; EX 119.10 Trifecta £733.00 Part won. Pool: £977.45 - 0.75 winning units..
Owner S Beccle,J Maynard,Lady Hart,Boscobel EL **Bred** Brendan Healy **Trained** Upper Lambourn, Berks

FOCUS
Golf Club bend on outside line, Home turn bend inside line. Home straight on inside and Fences on outside rail. They went no gallop for most of the first circuit. It wasn't a particularly strong handicap, but it was taken in really good style by the lightly raced winner.

2047 32REDPOKER.COM H'CAP CHASE (21 fncs) 3m 2f

2:00 (2:00) (Class 5) (0-95,94) 5-Y-0+ **£2,144** (£629; £314; £157)

Form RPR

30F- **1** **Inandover**[15] 1825 8-10-3 **71**...(t) DonalDevereux 80+
(John Mackie) *prom: reminders 7th: drvn 14th: outpcd and hit next: lft modest 4th 3 out: styd on strly run-in: led last 50yds: won gloing rt away* **11/2**[2]

4U5- **2** *3 ½* **Shock N Freaney (IRE)**[15] 1825 6-10-3 **76**.............(bt[1]) JamesBanks(5) 82
(Anthony Middleton) *chsd ldrs: 2nd 17th: led sn after next: hdd and no ex last 50yds* **10/1**

643- **3** *½* **Cloudy Dawn**[61] 1376 8-9-11 **72**.............................. CallumBewley(7) 76
(Sue Smith) *towards rr: hdwy to chse ldrs 6th: lft modest 3rd 3 out: kpt on same pce run-in* **7/2**[1]

46P- **4** *4 ½* **Ballyvoneen (IRE)**[18] 1798 8-11-12 **94**......................(b) TomMessenger 97
(Neil King) *trckd ldrs: led bnd bef 15th: blnd 4 out: sn hdd: upsides next: wknd last* **20/1**

254- **5** *31* **Might As Well**[136] 692 10-11-3 **85**..............................(p) AndrewThornton 77
(Seamus Mullins) *led to 4th: blnd 11th: outpcd and lost pl 4 out: blnd bdly 2 out: sn eased: t.o* **15/2**

P40- **6** *46* **Douglas**[15] 1825 8-11-9 **91**...(v[1]) MarkGrant 21
(Jo Hughes) *chsd ldrs: outpcd whn hit 10th: lost pl 13th: sn bhd: t.o whn mstke 17th: eventually completed* **20/1**

3/0- **P** **Feeling Peckish (USA)**[84] 1172 9-9-9 **68** oh2..............(t) JoeCornwall(5)
(Michael Chapman) *in rr: hit 5th: bhd fr 12th: t.o whn p.u bef 15th* **16/1**

630- **P** **Heezagrey (IRE)**[18] 1784 10-10-7 **75**..............................(b) LiamTreadwell
(James Evans) *sn detached in last: bhd and reminders 8th: t.o whn p.u bef 14th* **15/2**

250- **P** **Over And Above (IRE)**[131] 753 7-10-1 **69**.................(t) RichieMcGrath
(Henry Hogarth) *in rr: pckd 7th: bhd fr 12th: t.o whn p.u bef 15th* **11/2**[2]

002- **U** **Cara Court (IRE)**[23] 1716 7-11-2 **89**.....................(p) SamanthaDrake(5) 89
(Joanne Foster) *j.rt: led 4th: hung rt and hdd bnd bef 15th: 3rd and one pce whn blnd and uns rdr 3 out* **7/1**[3]

6m 56.9s (10.90) **Going Correction** +0.425s/f (Soft) **10** Ran SP% **113.5**
Speed ratings: **100,98,98,97,87 73**, , , ,
toteswingers 1&2 £17.50, 2&3 £13.70, 1&3 £5.20 CSF £56.84 CT £216.75 TOTE £5.80: £2.60, £2.40, £2.50; EX 61.30 Trifecta £274.00 Pool: £876.38 - 2.39 winning units..
Owner Mrs K Oliver **Bred** Miss M E Rowland **Trained** Church Broughton , Derbys

FOCUS
A weak race in which the picture changed dramatically after the last, where the leader ran out of petrol.

2048 BRAMLEY APPLE H'CAP CHASE (13 fncs) 2m

2:30 (2:31) (Class 5) (0-100,96) 5-Y-0+ **£2,144** (£629; £314; £157)

Form RPR

F/0- **1** **Molko Jack (FR)**[18] 1800 9-10-6 **79**.............................. KielanWoods(3) 86
(Michael Mullineaux) *chsd ldrs 3rd: outpcd and reminder next: hdwy to chse ldrs 8th: cl 3rd whn mstke 3 out: 2nd appr next: swtchd lft appr last: styd on to ld last 30yds* **3/1**[2]

1U3- **2** *¾* **Turf Trivia**[23] 1716 6-11-11 **95**.......................................(b) BarryKeniry 101
(George Moore) *trckd ldr 3rd: led 3 out: hdd and no ex last 30yds* **4/1**[3]

044- **3** *10* **Nicks Power (IRE)**[14] 1834 7-11-12 **96**................................ CharliePoste 92
(Robin Dickin) *last whn hmpd 2nd: drvn 5th: hdwy to chse ldrs 8th: rdn 4 out: one pce fr next: tk modest 3rd last 50yds* **5/4**[1]

P64- **4** *1 ¼* **Radsoc De Sivola (FR)**[18] 1782 8-9-9 **70** oh20............. JoeCornwall(5) 66
(John Cornwall) *led: drvn 7th: hdd 3 out: wl outpcd next: wknd and lost 3rd in clsng stages* **16/1**

P/0- **P** **Vardas Supreme (IRE)**[12] 1876 10-11-0 **89**.........(tp) SamanthaDrake(5)
(Richard Drake) *j. bdly lft 2nd: last and pushed along next: bhd fr 5th: t.o 7th: p.u bef next* **15/2**

4m 15.6s (13.60) **Going Correction** +0.425s/f (Soft) **5** Ran SP% **107.1**
Speed ratings: **83,82,77,77,**
CSF £14.00 TOTE £5.10: £2.00, £1.30; EX 13.90 Trifecta £35.00 Pool: £1292.53 - 27.68 winning units..
Owner David Ashbrook **Bred** Mme Jacqueline Vuillard **Trained** Alpraham, Cheshire

FOCUS
Another weak event and the leader appeared to set quite a strong pace which set things up for a finisher. The winner had slipped to a good mark and will probably still be competitive once reassessed.

2049 32RED.COM "NATIONAL HUNT" NOVICES' HURDLE (9 hdls) 2m

3:05 (3:05) (Class 4) 4-Y-0+ **£3,119** (£915; £457; £228)

Form RPR

150/ **1** **Parsnip Pete**[223] 4773 7-10-12 0.. PaddyBrennan 117
(Tom George) *led to 4th: led 2 out: hdd between last 2: rallied and upsides whn lft clr last: drvn out* **7/2**[3]

/21- **2** *9* **Deep Trouble (IRE)**[155] 434 6-11-5 118.............................. DarylJacob 118
(Ben Case) *t.k.h: trckd ldr 3rd: led next: hdd 2 out: lft 7 l 2nd and hmpd last* **11/4**[2]

2/ **3** *¾* **Comeback Colin**[544] 5648 5-10-5 0............................... CallumBewley(7) 108
(Sue Smith) *mid-div: chsd ldrs 3 out: one pce fr next: lft 3rd last* **15/2**

115- **4** *22* **Man Of Steel (IRE)**[13] 1856 4-10-12 0..........................(p) DonalDevereux 88
(Peter Bowen) *chsd ldrs: hrd drvn 3 out: lost pl appr next: lft distant 4th last* **9/2**

5 *25* **Fiddler's Flight (IRE)** 7-10-12 0.. AdrianLane 65
(John Norton) *j. bdly in rr: bhd fr 5th: t.o 3 out* **100/1**

6PP/ **6** *18* **Why Always Me (IRE)**[248] 4289 5-10-12 0............................. TomMessenger 49
(Chris Bealby) *chsd ldrs: lost pl 3rd: sn bhd: t.o 3 out* **100/1**

220/ **F** **Key To The West (IRE)**[200] 5195 6-10-12 123............. RichardJohnson 117
(David Dennis) *chsd ldrs: drvn 3 out: led between last 2: jnd whn fell last* **85/40**[1]

0- **P** **Well Related**[145] 584 6-10-12 0.. RichieMcGrath
(Henry Hogarth) *in rr: drvn 2nd: bhd and reminders after next: t.o whn p.u bef 5th* **80/1**

3m 57.8s (0.80) **Going Correction** +0.05s/f (Yiel)
WFA 4 from 5yo+ 9lb **8** Ran SP% **114.1**
Speed ratings (Par 105): **100,95,95,84,71 62**, ,
toteswingers 1&2 £3.00, 2&3 £2.60, 1&3 £5.80 CSF £13.84 TOTE £6.00: £2.20, £1.30, £3.50; EX 13.40 Trifecta £58.70 Pool: £2406.65 - 30.72 winning units..
Owner The Parsnips **Bred** A E Smith And Co **Trained** Slad, Gloucs

FOCUS
An interesting novices' event.

2050 32RED CASINO H'CAP HURDLE (11 hdls) 2m 4f 110y

3:35 (3:35) (Class 4) (0-120,120) 4-Y-0+ **£3,119** (£915; £457; £228)

Form RPR

P10/ **1** **Capellanus (IRE)**[119] 5013 7-11-5 **120**........................ CraigGallagher(7) 125+
(Brian Ellison) *mid-div: chsd clr ldr 8th: swtchd lft between last 2: led last: drvn out* **8/1**

1/3- **2** *2 ½* **Benefit Cut (IRE)**[26] 1688 7-11-5 **113**................................ PaddyBrennan 117
(Renee Robeson) *led: clr 2nd: rdn appr 2 out: edgd rt between last 2: hdd and blnd last: kpt on same pce* **17/2**

121- **3** *17* **Listen And Learn (IRE)**[30] 1645 5-11-7 **115**..............(p) RichieMcLernon 103
(Jonjo O'Neill) *mid-div: chsd ldrs 7th: one pce fr 3 out* **7/1**

16F/ **4** *½* **King Helissio (IRE)**[194] 5289 5-11-5 **116**...................... MichaelByrne(3) 103
(Neil Mulholland) *mid-div: hdwy 8th: drvn next: one pce* **6/1**[3]

126- **5** *34* **Wolf Shield (IRE)**[20] 1752 6-11-12 **120**............................... BarryKeniry 77
(George Moore) *in rr: bhd whn reminders 7th: t.o 2 out* **12/1**

0PO/ **6** *1 ¼* **Tealissio**[188] 5376 7-11-2 **110**... LeightonAspell 66
(Lucy Wadham) *chsd ldrs: lost pl appr 3 out: sn bhd: t.o 2 out* **16/1**

/23- **7** *21* **Candelita**[49] 1503 6-11-4 **112**... MarkGrant 49
(Jo Hughes) *in rr: hdwy 7th: lost pl next: bhd 3 out: t.o next* **40/1**

11P- **P** **He's A Hawker (IRE)**[32] 1634 8-11-1 **112**..................(b) KielanWoods(3)
(Michael Mullineaux) *chsd clr ldr to 4th: drvn 6th: lost pl bef next: sn bhd: t.o whn p.u bef 3 out* **33/1**

103/ **U** **Hollow Penny**[203] 5143 5-11-10 **118**................................ RobertThornton
(Alan King) *trckd ldrs: uns rdr 1st* **5/2**[1]

411- **P** **Piper Hill (IRE)**[50] 1498 5-11-11 **119**.............................. RichardJohnson
(Tony Coyle) *trckd ldrs: p.u after 6th: lame* **9/2**[2]

5m 15.3s (2.30) **Going Correction** +0.05s/f (Yiel) **10** Ran SP% **114.1**
Speed ratings (Par 105): **97,96,89,89,76 75,67**, , ,
toteswingers 1&2 £16.20, 2&3 £6.70, 1&3 £13.50 CSF £72.19 CT £499.36 TOTE £10.70: £3.20, £2.60, £2.60; EX 82.80 Trifecta £1183.00 Pool: £1849.16 - 1.17 winning units..
Owner Mrs Claire Ellison **Bred** C H Wacker Iii **Trained** Norton, N Yorks

FOCUS
This looked a decent event on paper, but very few got involved. The winner is on a very good mark.

2051 £32 BONUS AT 32RED.COM H'CAP HURDLE (9 hdls) 2m

4:05 (4:05) (Class 4) (0-105,105) 4-Y-0+ **£3,119** (£915; £457; £228)

Form RPR

061- **1** **Moscow Me (IRE)**[27] 1674 6-11-3 **96**................................ PaddyBrennan 107+
(Henry Oliver) *racd wd: trckd ldrs: upsides 5th: 2nd 3 out: led between last 2: styd on* **11/2**[2]

202- **2** *3* **Kayfton Pete**[7] 1938 7-11-6 **99**.......(t) AdamPogson 106
(Charles Pogson) *mid-div: trckd ldrs 4th: led appr 3 out: mstke next: hdd between last 2: no ex* **6/1**[3]

431- **3** *10* **Weybridge Light**[23] 1717 8-11-4 **102**.......(b) TonyKelly(5) 98
(David Thompson) *chsd ldrs: 3rd and drvn after 3 out: kpt on same pce* **16/1**

0/4- **4** *1 ¾* **Investissement**[27] 1674 7-11-4 **97**....... RichardJohnson 93
(Charlie Longsdon) *in rr: hit 3rd: hdwy next: sn chsng ldrs: 4th and drvn after 3 out: one pce* **5/2**[1]

225/ **5** *3 ½* **White Diamond**[17] 4843 6-11-3 **96**....... RyanMahon 87
(Michael Appleby) *chsd ldrs: modest 5th appr 2 out: one pce* **20/1**

424- **6** *9* **Moon Trip**[20] 1754 4-11-6 **102**.......(p) JackQuinlan(3) 85
(John Ferguson) *trckd ldrs: drvn 3 out: wknd appr next* **6/1**[3]

5P0- **7** *11* **Gainsborough's Art (IRE)**[65] 1331 8-9-7 **79** oh24....... DanielHiskett(7) 52
(Harry Chisman) *in rr: reminders bef 3rd: sn drvn: sme hdwy after 6th: nvr on terms* **100/1**

660- **8** *33* **Fintan**[44] 1551 10-11-0 **100**.......[1] JakeHodson(7) 44
(Rob Summers) *chsd ldrs: drvn 5th: lost pl after next: sn bhd: t.o 2 out* **33/1**

PU0/ **9** *8* **Swiss Art (IRE)**[257] 4132 7-11-3 **103**....... CallumBewley(7) 39
(Sue Smith) *in rr: bhd fr 3 out: t.o whn heavily eased run-in* **12/1**

306- **10** *2 ½* **Razzle Dazzle 'Em**[18] 1793 4-10-11 **90**.......(t) CharliePoste 24
(Shaun Harris) *in rr: bhd fr 5th: t.o 2 out* **66/1**

/45- **11** *7* **Palus San Marco (IRE)**[138] 671 4-11-7 **105**....... KillianMoore(5) 33
(Graeme McPherson) *in rr: bhd fr 6th: t.o 2 out* **9/1**

360- **P** **Kingaroo (IRE)**[7] 1938 7-9-9 **79** oh3....... TrevorWhelan(5)
(Garry Woodward) *led: reminders after 4th: hdd and mstke 3 out: lost pl and poor 7th whn p.u bef 2 out* **10/1**

P/0- **P** **Eighteen Carat (IRE)**[9] 1913 9-11-2 **100**.......(b[1]) JoeCornwall(5)
(John Cornwall) *chsd ldrs: sn drvn along: hit 3rd: sn reminders and lost pl: detached last whn p.u after next* **100/1**

3m 56.6s (-0.40) **Going Correction** +0.05s/f (Yiel) **13** Ran SP% **116.4**
Speed ratings (Par 105): **103,101,96,95,93 89,83,67,63,62 58,,**
toteswingers 1&2 £7.50, 2&3 £9.70, 1&3 £14.00 CSF £36.66 CT £496.99 TOTE £7.80: £1.10, £5.10, £2.90; EX 43.30 Trifecta £352.10 Pool: £1545.67 - 3.29 winning units..
Owner Ms S Howell **Bred** Egmont Stud **Trained** Broomhall, Worcs

FOCUS
This looked fairly open on paper, but the field thinned right out by the home turn. The winner took another step forward and can win again.

2052 32REDBINGO.COM MAIDEN OPEN NATIONAL HUNT FLAT RACE (DIV I) 2m
4:40 (4:40) (Class 6) 4-6-Y-0 **£1,559** (£457; £228; £114)

Form RPR

1 **Truckers Steel (IRE)**[220] 5-11-4 0....... PaddyBrennan 110+
(Tom George) *mde all: wnt clr over 1f out: heavily eased last 100yds* **11/4**[2]

62- **2** *6* **Countersign**[15] 1826 4-11-4 0....... AdamPogson 100
(Charles Pogson) *trckd ldrs: t.k.h: wnt 2nd over 5f out: kpt on: no ch w easy wnr* **7/2**[3]

3- **3** *5* **Cousin Guillaume (FR)**[18] 1792 4-11-4 0....... RichardJohnson 96
(Karen McLintock) *trckd wnr: drvn and outpcd over 3f out: kpt on to take modest 3rd over 1f out* **7/4**[1]

4 *10* **Garrahalish (IRE)**[207] 5-11-4 0....... CharliePoste 87
(Robin Dickin) *chsd ldrs: outpcd 4f out: wknd over 2f out* **8/1**

5 *2* **Billy The Bandit (IRE)** 5-11-4 0....... SamThomas 85
(Jennie Candlish) *stdd s: t.k.h in rr: hdwy to trck ldrs 7f out: 3rd over 4f out: wknd fnl 2f* **9/1**

6 *6* **Island Whisper (IRE)** 6-10-1 0....... RyanLynam(10) 72
(Ben Case) *trckd ldrs on outer: lost pl 4f out* **33/1**

7 *67* **Shadow Of The Day** 6-11-1 0....... KyleJames(3) 19
(Lee James) *hld up in rr: drvn 8f out: lost pl over 6f out: sn bhd: t.o over 4f out: eventually completed* **100/1**

3m 55.8s (4.40) **Going Correction** +0.05s/f (Yiel)
WFA 4 from 5yo+ 9lb **7** Ran SP% **110.3**
Speed ratings: **91,88,85,80,79 76,43**
toteswingers 1&2 £2.00, 2&3 £1.60, 1&3 £1.50 CSF £11.84 TOTE £3.50: £2.10, £2.40; EX 8.80 Trifecta £23.90 Pool: £2444.11 - 76.59 winning units..
Owner Crossed Fingers Partnership **Bred** Ailish Cunningham **Trained** Slad, Gloucs

FOCUS
No depth to this bumper, but the winner looks a fair recruit.

2053 32REDBINGO.COM MAIDEN OPEN NATIONAL HUNT FLAT RACE (DIV II) 2m
5:10 (5:10) (Class 6) 4-6-Y-0 **£1,559** (£457; £228; £114)

Form RPR

1 **Cogry**[180] 4-10-11 0....... RyanHatch(7) 103+
(Nigel Twiston-Davies) *trckd ldrs: led 3f out: jnd over 1f out: drvn and styd on wl* **11/4**[2]

3/ **2** *1 ½* **Masquerade (IRE)**[210] 4991 4-11-4 0....... DarylJacob 102
(Warren Greatrex) *trckd ldrs: 2nd over 2f out: upsides over 1f out: styd on same pce* **4/1**[3]

3- **3** *4 ½* **Di's Gift**[15] 1826 4-11-4 0....... RobertThornton 98
(Richard Guest) *stdd s: hld up in rr: hdwy over 5f out: handy 3rd over 2f out: fdd fnl f* **8/1**

0/3- **4** *15* **Frankie Four Feet**[26] 1690 5-11-1 0....... KielanWoods(3) 85
(Michael Mullineaux) *led: hdd 3f out: wknd 2f out* **9/1**

5 *5* **Cadeau George**[171] 4-11-4 0....... DavidBass 80
(Ben Pauling) *w ldrs: drvn over 5f out: lost pl over 4f out* **20/1**

0- **6** *½* **Langarve Lady (IRE)**[168] 187 5-10-8 0....... MichaelByrne(3) 73
(Neil Mulholland) *hld up towards rr: pushed along 5f out: sn outpcd: lost pl over 2f out* **50/1**

7 *2* **Valseur Du Granval (FR)**[168] 4-11-4 0....... PaddyBrennan 78
(Tom George) *hld up towards rr: hdwy on outside 6f out: sn trcking ldrs: outpcd over 2f out: sn wknd* **2/1**[1]

50/ **8** *12* **Honour A Promise**[187] 5407 5-10-11 0....... LiamHeard 60
(Paul Webber) *trckd ldrs: drvn 7f out: lost pl over 5f out: t.o 4f out* **20/1**

4- **9** *2* **Looking Tanned**[26] 1690 4-11-4 0....... RyanMahon 65
(Michael Appleby) *trckd ldrs: drvn 9f out: lost pl over 7f out: t.o 4f out* **50/1**

3m 54.8s (3.40) **Going Correction** +0.05s/f (Yiel) **9** Ran SP% **114.6**
Speed ratings: **93,92,90,82,80 79,78,72,71**
toteswingers 1&2 £3.40, 2&3 £5.10, 1&3 £4.90 CSF £13.42 TOTE £4.90: £1.40, £1.60, £2.00; EX 16.10 Trifecta £81.50 Pool: £2134.77 - 19.64 winning units..
Owner N A Twiston-Davies **Bred** R D And Mrs J S Chugg **Trained** Naunton, Gloucs

FOCUS
A more evenly run bumper than is often the case and a few of these looked interesting on paper. This didn't look a particularly strong heat, but the first three came clear and look useful types.

T/Plt: £357.30 to a £1 stake. Pool of £64338.59 - 131.44 winning tickets. T/Qpdt: £14.30 to a £1 stake. Pool of £6070.75 - 312.58 winning tickets. WG

2054 - 2061a (Foreign Racing) - See Raceform Interactive

[593]FAKENHAM (L-H)
Friday, October 25

OFFICIAL GOING: Good (good to soft in places; 7.1)
Wind: light, against Weather: dry

2062 PUDDING NORTON CONDITIONAL JOCKEYS' (S) H'CAP HURDLE (9 hdls) 2m
1:50 (1:50) (Class 5) (0-95,95) 4-Y-0+ **£2,053** (£598; £299)

Form RPR

330- **1** **Persian Herald**[33] 1633 5-11-3 **89**.......(bt) TrevorWhelan(3) 93
(Neil King) *aggressively rdn: led tl drvn and hdd bef 6th: 8 l 3rd and no imp u.p 2 out: clsd on slowing ldng pair and j. into ld last: plugged on* **7/2**[3]

143- **2** *2* **Pindar (GER)**[31] 1643 9-10-12 **81**.......(p) MichaelByrne 83
(Neil Mulholland) *chsd ldr tl led and travelling wl bef 6th: hdd and mstke next: 4 l down and nt finding for press next: clsd on slowing ldr to ld jst bef last: j.lft and hdd last: one pce* **11/4**[2]

065- **3** *6* **Nebula Storm (IRE)**[33] 1630 6-10-11 **83**.......(v) JoshuaMoore(3) 81
(Gary Moore) *niggled along in rr early: hdwy fr 3rd: wnt 2nd after 6th: led next: sn rdn 4 l clr but looked reluctant: slowed bnd bef last and hdd jst bef last: sn btn and wknd flat* **9/4**[1]

/FF- **4** *17* **Monroe Park (IRE)**[152] 490 8-10-9 **78**.......(p) JackQuinlan 59
(Alan Blackmore) *trckd ldrs and travelled wl: rdn after 6th: fnd nil and sn btn: mstke and wknd fr next* **14/1**

450- **5** *11* **Xenophon**[31] 565 5-11-2 **85**....... JoeCornwall 56
(Michael Chapman) *sn rdn along in rr: lost tch u.p after 5th: t.o bef 3 out: plugged on* **25/1**

023- **6** *20* **Louis Ludwig (IRE)**[66] 1328 8-11-4 **95**.......(t) AlanJohns(8) 48
(Tim Vaughan) *in tch towards rr: niggled along and nt travelling wl fr 4th: drvn and btn after next: t.o after 3 out* **7/1**

540- **7** *17* **Giant Hercules (IRE)**[19] 1783 6-11-7 **95**.......(b[1]) JackSherwood(5) 33
(Phil McEntee) *j.rt and mstkes: chsd ldrs tl lost pl qckly 5th: sn lost tch u.p: t.o after 3 out* **12/1**

4m 14.25s (8.85) **Going Correction** +0.30s/f (Yiel) **7** Ran SP% **110.4**
Speed ratings (Par 103): **89,88,85,76,71 61,52**
toteswingers 1&2 £1.10, 1&3 £1.60, 2&3 £1.40 CSF £12.89 TOTE £4.00: £3.00, £1.50; EX 17.10 Trifecta £43.90 Pool: £1117.06 - 19.06 winning units..There was no bid for the winner.
Owner The St Gatien Racing For Fun Partnership **Bred** J W P Clark **Trained** Newmarket, Suffolk

FOCUS
A typically weak selling handicap run at a sound pace. The winner was well in on his best form.

2063 FAKENHAM NOVICES' CHASE (16 fncs) 2m 5f 110y
2:20 (2:20) (Class 3) 4-Y-0+ **£6,989** (£2,170; £1,168)

Form RPR

10/ **1** **Wonderful Charm (FR)**[225] 4749 5-11-3 0.......(t) DarylJacob 155+
(Paul Nicholls) *j. accurately: chsd ldrs tl lft 2nd 3rd: j. into ld 13th: slt mstke and hdd next but stl travelling bttr than rival: led bef last: readily wnt clr flat: easily* **8/11**[1]

P/2- **2** *8* **Bear's Affair (IRE)**[19] 1796 7-11-3 138....... APMcCoy 142
(Nicky Henderson) *nt fluent and mstkes: led: qcknd gallop 12th: mstke and hdd 12th: rdn and led again next: drvn bef 2 out: hdd bef last: hrd drvn 1 l down whn mstke last: sn outpcd* **85/40**[2]

/06- **3** *30* **King Of The Night (GER)**[27] 1686 9-11-3 132....... BrianHughes 117
(Malcolm Jefferson) *hld up in last: bdly hmpd 1st and nt a fluent after: lft 3rd and in tch 3rd: outpcd 12th: wl btn 3 out* **10/1**[3]

44P- **U** **Next Exit (IRE)**[10] 1916 8-10-12 114.......(t) JoeCornwall(5)
(John Cornwall) *hmpd: blnd v bdly and uns rdr 1st* **125/1**

1P1/ **U** **Le Reve (IRE)**[192] 5337 5-11-3 0....... LeightonAspell
(Lucy Wadham) *chsd ldr: j. slowly: j. bdly lft 1st: blnd and uns rdr 3rd* **10/1**[3]

5m 40.4s (-1.40) **Going Correction** +0.20s/f (Yiel) **5** Ran SP% **108.9**
Speed ratings (Par 107): **110,107,96,,**
CSF £2.69 TOTE £1.70: £1.10, £1.60; EX 3.50 Trifecta £5.30 Pool: £1319.28 - 185.33 winning units..
Owner R J H Geffen **Bred** Jean-Philippe Dubois **Trained** Ditcheat, Somerset

FOCUS
A fascinating contest run at a steady pace. The winner looks exciting.

2064 AUTUMN H'CAP HURDLE (9 hdls) 2m
2:50 (2:51) (Class 3) (0-135,135) 4-Y-0+ **£5,718** (£1,679; £839; £419)

Form RPR

331- **1** **First In The Queue (IRE)**[7] 1960 6-11-9 **135** ....JeremiahMcGrath(3) 137
(Nicky Henderson) *in tch in midfield: n.m.r 1st: hdwy to chse ldr 6th: ev ch and hit next: drvn bef 2 out: led jst bef last and forged ahd last: drvn and a jst doing enough flat* **10/11**[1]

1/6- **2** *½* **All That Remains (IRE)**[155] 447 8-10-9 **118**.......(t) DannyCook 120+
(Brian Ellison) *hld up in last pair: hdwy to chse ldng pair after 6th: j.rt and mstke next: clsd to press ldrs and trying for impossible run on inner whn forced to switch rt bnd bef last: hit last: sn chsng wnr: styd on wl* **10/1**[3]

210- **3** *2 ¾* **Ittirad (USA)**[27] 1685 5-10-7 **116**....... DenisO'Regan 116
(John Ferguson) *chsd ldrs tl led bef 6th: jnd and hit 3 out: rdn bef next: hdd jst bef last: mstke last: kpt on same pce flat* **5/2**[2]

6/3- **4** *13* **The Bull Hayes (IRE)**[73] 1268 7-10-7 **116**.......(p) RyanMahon 102
(Michael Appleby) *chsd ldrs: nt fluent 3rd: rdn and struggling after 6th: wl btn next: plugged on* **20/1**

2/2- **5** *23* **Occasionally Yours (IRE)**[152] 486 9-10-6 **115**....... MarcGoldstein 81
(Alan Blackmore) *chsd ldrs tl led 2nd: hdd after next: chsd ldr tl rdn and lost pl after 5th: wl bhd 3 out: t.o after 3 out* **20/1**

21/- **6** *8* **Lightening Rod**[205] 5121 8-11-0 **126**....... JakeGreenall(3) 84
(Michael Easterby) *hld up in rr: hdwy into 4th and shkn up bef 3 out: no hdwy and sn btn: wknd next: t.o* **12/1**

/10- **7** *30* **Jonnie Skull (IRE)**[19] 1779 7-10-5 **117**.......(t) JackQuinlan(3) 48
(Phil McEntee) *j.rt: led tl 2nd: chsd ldr tl led again after 3rd: hdd and rdn bef 6th: sn dropped out and bhd: t.o after 3 out* **33/1**

4m 6.6s (1.20) **Going Correction** +0.30s/f (Yiel) **7** Ran SP% **110.2**
Speed ratings (Par 107): **109,108,107,100,89 85,70**
toteswingers 1&2 £1.90, 1&3 £1.10, 2&3 £2.70 CSF £9.32 TOTE £2.10: £1.30, £3.30; EX 7.80 Trifecta £30.50 Pool: £1509.50 - 37.05 winning units..
Owner Liam Breslin **Bred** Holborn Trust Co **Trained** Upper Lambourn, Berks

FOCUS
A fair handicap, despite the small field, run at a sound pace.

2065 OCTOBER H'CAP CHASE (18 fncs) 3m 110y
3:25 (3:25) (Class 3) (0-140,139) 4-Y-0+ **£6,989** (£2,170; £1,168)

Form RPR
510- **1** **Wiesentraum (GER)**[27] 1686 7-11-0 **127**.......................... LeightonAspell 132+
(Lucy Wadham) *in tch towards rr: hdwy 6th: chsd ldrs and mstke 14th: cl 3rd and drvn after 3 out: chal bef last: pushed rt and lft 3 l clr last: idled and slowly bdly fnl 75yds a jst lasting home* **7/1**[3]
4UP/ **2** *nk* **The Rainbow Hunter**[181] 5576 9-11-9 **136**........................ NickScholfield 140+
(Kim Bailey) *t.k.h: hld up in rr: mstke 11th: effrt and mstke 14th: rdn next: lft 8 l 5th 3 out: styd on between last 2: lft 4 l 3rd last: r.o to go 2nd and clsd qckly on idling wnr towards fin* **9/1**
/31- **3** *½* **Current Event (FR)**[138] 677 6-11-7 **139**.....................(p) HarryDerham[(5)] 140
(Paul Nicholls) *hld up in tch in last trio: hdwy to chse ldrs 14th: lft cl 4th and hmpd 3 out: drvn and chsd ldng pair bef last: lft 3 l 2nd last: styd on and clsng on idling wnr fnl 100yds: lost 2nd towards fin* **16/1**
6/P- **P** **Dover's Hill**[27] 1686 11-11-7 **134**..............................(t) SamTwiston-Davies
(Nigel Twiston-Davies) *chsd ldrs tl led 4th: hdd 7th: rdn and lost pl rapidly after next: t.o whn p.u after 10th* **10/1**
345- **F** **That's The Deal (IRE)**[33] 1636 9-9-9 **113** oh5.................. JoeCornwall[(5)]
(John Cornwall) *in tch in midfield tl fell 3rd* **33/1**
U01/ **U** **Forgotten Gold (IRE)**[194] 5314 7-11-6 **133**......................... PaddyBrennan 138+
(Tom George) *j.rt and mstkes: chsd ldr tl 4th: chsd ldr tl led again 7th: rdn and mstke 15th: 1/2 l ahd whn blnd: slipped on landing and uns rdr last* **9/4**[1]
4P3- **F** **Aneyeforaneye (IRE)**[30] 1659 7-11-3 **130**.......................... BrianHughes
(Malcolm Jefferson) *chsd ldrs: cl 4th whn fell 3 out* **12/1**
115/ **P** **Arbeo (IRE)**[190] 5365 7-10-12 **125** ow1................................ SamThomas
(Diana Grissell) *in tch in midfield: mstke 1st: lost pl and bhd whn mstke 9th: rdn and wknd after 13th: j. slowly 15th: t.o and p.u next* **12/1**
214- **P** **Victor Leudorum (IRE)**[58] 1425 6-11-3 **130**.........................(t) APMcCoy
(Charlie Mann) *in tch in midfield: chsd ldrs after 7th: ev ch and drvn after 3 out: wknd qckly between last 2: fading whn eased and p.u last* **8/1**
521- **P** **Dawn Commander (GER)**[15] 1831 6-11-2 **129**................ JasonMaguire
(Charlie Longsdon) *nt jump wl: led tl mstke and hdd 4th: chsd ldrs lost pl 7th: wknd after 13th: wl bhd and p.u 3 out* **5/1**[2]

6m 34.3s (-1.40) **Going Correction** +0.20s/f (Yiel) **10** Ran SP% **114.3**
Speed ratings (Par 107): **110,109,109, , , , , , ,**
toteswingers 1&2 £30.50, 1&3 £34.20, 2&3 £16.30 CSF £66.38 CT £968.92 TOTE £8.40: £2.70, £3.30, £3.60; EX 78.50 Trifecta £533.70 Pool: £1233.96 - 1.73 winning units..
Owner G Pascoe & S Brewer **Bred** Gestut Elsetal **Trained** Newmarket, Suffolk
FOCUS
There was plenty of pace on for this competitive contest which saw a thrilling finish, but the form is probably ordinary for the level.

2066 NORFOLK FILLIES' JUVENILE HURDLE (9 hdls) 2m
4:00 (4:00) (Class 3) 3-Y-0 **£5,718** (£1,679; £839; £419)

Form RPR
32- **1** **Nellie Forbush**[9] 1920 3-10-12 0.......................................(p) PaulMoloney 86
(Sophie Leech) *chsd ldrs tl lost pl after 4th: rdn and outpcd bef 6th: 7 l 4th 2 out: plugged on as ldrs slowed between last 2: clsng last: led flat: sn in command: styd on* **5/1**[3]
2 *1½* **Chasse En Mer (FR)**[38] 3-11-8 0.................................... RobertThornton 96
(Caroline Bailey) *chsd ldr: blnd 5th: rdn: clr w rival and ev ch 3 out: sustained duel after tl forged ahd but allout between last 2: hdd flat and sn btn* **7/2**[2]
3 *3* **Ariane Nopolis (FR)**[131] 3-11-8 0..............................(t[1]) JasonMaguire 93
(Gordon Elliott, Ire) *led: clr w rival whn mstke 3 out: sn rdn and sustained duel w rival tl hdd between last 2: drvn and slowing after: stl pressing ldr last: wknd flat* **8/11**[1]
4 *6* **Taming The Tweet**[204] 3-10-2 0.................................. StevieSanders[(10)] 79
(J R Jenkins) *t.k.h: hld up in tch: hdwy to chse ldrs 5th: 3rd and rdn bef 3 out: mstke 3 out: plugged on tl btn jst bef last: wknd flat* **66/1**
5 *7* **Jacobella**[11] 3-10-12 0.. SamJones 70
(Jonathan Portman) *mstkes: racd in midfield: 4th and drvn 6th: no prog: 5th and btn 2 out* **10/1**
00- **P** **Duchess Of Dreams**[9] 1920 3-10-12 0.............................. DenisO'Regan
(Richard Guest) *hld up in rr: short-lived effrt after 6th: btn next: sn btn: t.o whn p.u last* **66/1**

4m 21.35s (15.95) **Going Correction** +0.30s/f (Yiel) **6** Ran SP% **108.9**
Speed ratings (Par 102): **72,71,69,66,63**
toteswingers 1&2 £1.50, 1&3 £3.10, 2&3 £1.60 CSF £21.38 TOTE £5.00: £2.70, £2.30; EX 15.70 Trifecta £17.40 Pool: £1676.47 - 71.89 winning units..
Owner C J Leech **Bred** J C & S R Hitchins **Trained** Elton, Gloucs
FOCUS
Another exciting finish, but a slow time and the form looks very modest.

2067 BURNHAM MARKET H'CAP CHASE (16 fncs) 2m 5f 110y
4:30 (4:30) (Class 5) (0-100,106) 4-Y-0+ **£2,599** (£763; £381; £190)

Form RPR
/31- **1** **Midnight Charmer**[19] 1800 7-10-3 **81**.............................. JamesBanks[(5)] 88
(Emma Baker) *in tch in midfield: hdwy to chse ldrs 6th: rdn and chsd ldr bef 2 out: drvn to ld bef last: kpt on wl: drvn out* **9/4**[2]
6/2- **2** *¾* **Plum Pudding (FR)**[10] 1914 10-11-12 **99**...................(p) TomScudamore 108+
(David Bridgwater) *led: mstke 8th: hdd and hit 11th: rdn to ld again bef 3 out: hrd pressed and drvn 2 out: hdd bef last: no ex and one pce flat* **6/4**[1]
3P6- **3** *15* **Outback (IRE)**[20] 1765 4-10-5 **93**..............................(bt) TrevorWhelan[(5)] 76
(Neil King) *chsd ldr: j. slowly and reminder 5th: led 11th: rdn and hdd bef 3 out: 3rd whn drvn and nt qckn bef 2 out: wknd bef last* **33/1**
111- **4** *7* **Roc De Guye (FR)**[19] 1798 8-11-12 **99**........................(p) LiamTreadwell 88
(James Evans) *t.k.h: chsd ldrs: rdn and outpcd after 12th: lft 4th and hmpd 3 out: no imp 2 out: wknd bef last* **11/2**[3]
4U5- **5** *24* **Peak Seasons (IRE)**[10] 1914 10-10-8 **86**......................... JoeCornwall[(5)] 51
(Michael Chapman) *a in last pair: rdn and nvr travelling wl fr 5th: t.o 3 out* **25/1**
14P- **6** *22* **Safe Investment (USA)**[33] 1629 9-11-5 **92**...........................(vt) DavidBass 37
(Lawney Hill) *a in last pair: mstke 10th: lost tch u.p after next: t.o 3 out* **16/1**
541- **F** **Riddlestown (IRE)**[10] 1914 6-11-12 **106** 7ex..................(p) MikeyEnnis[(7)]
(Caroline Fryer) *chsd ldrs: reminder after 12th: cl 4th whn fell 3 out* **7/1**

5m 45.2s (3.40) **Going Correction** +0.20s/f (Yiel)
WFA 4 from 6yo+ 10lb **7** Ran SP% **111.3**
Speed ratings (Par 103): **101,100,95,92,84 76,**
toteswingers 1&2 £1.70, 1&3 £8.30, 2&3 £7.80 CSF £5.99 TOTE £3.00: £1.70, £2.20; EX 6.10 Trifecta £70.90 Pool: £2278.74 - 24.08 winning units..
Owner Mrs M J Arnold **Bred** Mrs J Hoskins And Brian Wilson **Trained** Naunton, Gloucs
■ Stewards' Enquiry : James Banks seven-day ban: use of whip (8-14 Nov)
FOCUS
A moderate handicap, run at a steady pace, with once again a decent finish.

2068 EAST ANGLIA NOVICES' HURDLE (9 hdls) 2m
5:00 (5:00) (Class 4) 4-Y-0+ **£3,249** (£954; £477; £238)

Form RPR
/53- **1** **The Stig (FR)**[19] 1779 5-10-12 0.. PaulMoloney 110
(Nick Littmoden) *mad all: rdn and wnt 2 l clr bef last: kpt on: rdn out* **10/1**[3]
113- **2** *1* **It's A Mans World**[30] 1656 7-11-2 124.................................. GLavery[(10)] 122
(Brian Ellison) *in tch in midfield: rdn 3 out: no imp and looked hld between last 2: rallied last: kpt on u.p flat to go 2nd last strides* **11/4**[2]
/45- **3** *hd* **Beaujolais (IRE)**[10] 1915 5-10-9 0.................................. JackQuinlan[(3)] 108
(John Ferguson) *chsd wnr: rdn and ev ch bef 3 out: outpcd and 2 l down whn j.lft last: kpt on same pce and lost 2nd last strides* **14/1**
54/ **4** *2¾* **My Guardian Angel**[31] 1942 4-10-12 0............................... ColinBolger 106
(Mark H Tompkins) *t.k.h: chsd ldrs: rdn bef 3 out: kpt on same pce between last 2* **28/1**
5 *3½* **Prince Siegfried (FR)**[356] 7-10-12 0.............................. DenisO'Regan 105
(John Ferguson) *nt a fluent: hld up in tch: wnt 3rd and effrt after 2 out: fnd nil and dropped to last whn mstke last: wknd flat* **8/13**[1]
P **Churt**[10] 4-10-12 0.. TomMessenger
(Christopher Kellett) *mstkes: hld up in last: rdn and lost tch after 5th: t.o whn p.u 3 out* **150/1**

4m 14.4s (9.00) **Going Correction** +0.30s/f (Yiel)
WFA 4 from 5yo+ 9lb **6** Ran SP% **108.5**
Speed ratings (Par 105): **89,88,88,87,85**
toteswingers 1&2 £1.50, 1&3 £3.80, 2&3 £4.40 CSF £35.47 TOTE £6.30: £2.70, £1.70; EX 18.40 Trifecta £58.00 Pool: £2609.77 - 33.72 winning units..
Owner A A Goodman **Bred** Peter Jones, Sally Jones & Tobias Jones **Trained** Newmarket, Suffolk
FOCUS
Not much pace on for this uncompetitive novices' hurdle with the winner making all.
T/Plt: £51.00 to a £1 stake. Pool: £69990.25 - 1000.37 winning tickets T/Qpdt: £19.20 to a £1 stake. Pool: £5172.60 - 199.20 winning tickets SP

[732]AINTREE (L-H)
Saturday, October 26

OFFICIAL GOING: Mildmay course - good (good to soft in places; 7.1); hurdle course - good to soft (good in places; 6.7)
Wind: Fresh; across Weather: Cloudy Rails: All bends and hurdles on inside line

2069 BETFRED GOALS GALORE H'CAP HURDLE (9 hdls) 2m 1f
1:55 (1:55) (Class 2) (0-150,143) 4-Y-0+
£12,512 (£3,696; £1,848; £924; £462; £232)

Form RPR
111/ **1** **Karinga Dancer**[205] 5143 7-11-4 **135**..............................(t) NickScholfield 143+
(Harry Fry) *hld up: hdwy appr 3 out: trckd ldrs gng wl 2 out: led and hit last: styd on wl and drew clr fnl 150yds* **4/1**[1]
13R- **2** *8* **Bygones Of Brid (IRE)**[15] 1849 10-10-10 **127**................(p) BrianHughes 125
(Karen McLintock) *a.p: wnt 2nd 6th: ch fr 3 out: rdn bef last whn nt qckn and lost 2nd: regained 2nd run-in 1f out: no ch w wnr* **22/1**
10F/ **3** *1¾* **Ifandbutwhynot (IRE)**[189] 5402 7-11-2 **133**........................ APMcCoy 130
(David O'Meara) *hld up: nt fluent 5th: smooth hdwy 3 out: led 2 out: hdd last: rdn and edgd lft run-in: kpt on same pce but no ch after* **4/1**[1]
455/ **4** *4½* **Special Catch (IRE)**[203] 5178 6-10-10 **127**...................... JamesReveley 121
(Keith Reveley) *in tch: mstke 6th: wl there 3 out: rdn after 2 out and no imp: wl hld whn j.lft last: kpt on u.p run-in wout threatening* **4/1**[1]
1/0- **5** *8* **Deepsand (IRE)**[168] 216 4-11-2 **133**..............................(p) HarryHaynes 119
(Tim Easterby) *midfield: hdwy 6th: chsd ldrs 3 out: rdn bef next: nt qckn: btn whn mstke last* **16/1**
502/ **6** *4½* **Liberty's Gift (IRE)**[20] 1803 5-10-11 **128**.........................(t) JasonMaguire 111
(Paul W Flynn, Ire) *chsd ldr: led after 3rd: pressed fr 3 out: hdd 2 out: wknd appr last* **10/1**
312- **7** *7* **Cool Baranca (GER)**[28] 1689 7-10-5 **122**............................... RyanMania 96
(Dianne Sayer) *chsd ldrs tl rdn and wknd appr 2 out* **20/1**
503/ **8** *10* **Star Of Aragon (IRE)**[6] 2000 7-10-5 **122**.....................(p) RobertThornton 87
(J A Nash, Ire) *in rr: rdn after 6th: toiling after* **7/1**[2]
561/ **9** *42* **Mwaleshi**[238] 4518 8-11-7 **143**...................................... JonathanEngland[(5)] 71
(Sue Smith) *racd freely: led: hdd after 3rd: coninued to chse ldr to 6th: sn wknd* **9/1**[3]
02/- **10** *35* **Bob's World**[182] 5573 4-10-8 **125**.. SeanQuinlan 21
(Jennie Candlish) *hld up: pushed along and hit 5th: lost tch bef 3 out: t.o* **14/1**

4m 9.7s (-4.00) **Going Correction** +0.05s/f (Yiel)
WFA 4 from 5yo+ 9lb **10** Ran SP% **113.2**
Speed ratings (Par 109): **111,107,106,104,100 98,95,90,70,54**
toteswingers 1&2 £15.10, 1&3 £1.80, 2&3 £18.80 CSF £80.02 CT £371.19 TOTE £4.80: £2.40, £5.50, £2.00; EX 89.90 Trifecta £249.40 Pool: £671.65 - 2.01 winning units..
Owner H B Geddes **Bred** Mr & Mrs J K S Cresswell **Trained** Seaborough, Dorset
FOCUS
All bends and Hurdles on inside line. This was run at a sound gallop and the principals dominated from two out. Sound form with the winner well in on his handicap debut.

2070 BETFRED MOBILE SPORTS VETERANS' H'CAP CHASE (19 fncs) 3m 1f
2:30 (2:32) (Class 2) (0-145,142)
10-Y-0+
£13,763 (£4,065; £2,032; £1,016; £508; £255)

Form RPR
603- **1** **Jamsie Hall (IRE)**[13] 1897 10-11-5 **138**...................(tp) KeithDonoghue[(3)] 141
(Gordon Elliott, Ire) *hld up: smooth hdwy 15th: led 2 out: sn rdn: fiddled last: hrd pressed run-in: hld on gamley cl home* **10/1**
/30- **2** *nk* **Pigeon Island**[139] 680 10-11-4 **134**..................(vt[1]) SamTwiston-Davies 136
(Nigel Twiston-Davies) *chsd ldr to 13th: rdn and outpcd bef 4 out: rallied to chal 2 out: r.o u.p whn strly chalng wnr and upsides run-in: jst hld* **9/2**[3]
6/5- **3** *1¼* **Categorical**[8] 312 10-10-0 **116** oh4.. BrianHughes 119
(Keith Reveley) *hld up: mstke and bmpd 1st: nt fluent 13th: sn outpcd: prog appr last: styd on and chalng run-in: one pce and hld cl home* **12/1**
52P/ **4** *5* **Hey Big Spender (IRE)**[228] 4721 10-11-12 **142**.................(t) JoeTizzard 138
(Colin Tizzard) *in tch: bmpd 1st: wnt prom 12th: wnt 2nd 13th: upsides ldr gng wl 14th: led 3 out: hdd 2 out: sn rdn: one pce appr last* **9/2**[3]

The Form Book Jumps, Raceform Ltd, Compton, RG20 6NL.

1/6- **5** *4* **Fruity O'Rooney**[22] 1746 10-11-5 **138**........................(p) JoshuaMoore(3) 133
(Gary Moore) *led: pushed along appr 4 out: hdd 3 out: rdn and stl there 2 out: no ex appr last* **7/2**[2]

/41- **6** *5* **Your Busy (IRE)**[45] 1572 10-10-11 **127**........................(t) APMcCoy 117
(J A Nash, Ire) *chsd ldrs: mstke and lost pl 15th: outpcd sn after: chsd ldrs 2 out: wknd appr last* **13/2**

/0F- **R** **Triggerman**[152] 509 11-10-7 **123**........................(p) RichardJohnson
(Philip Hobbs) *mstke 2nd: j. slowly 3rd: hld up after: tk clsr order 13th: rdn 14th: outpcd sn after: wl bhd whn ref last* **3/1**[1]

6m 23.7s (-6.30) **Going Correction** -0.30s/f (Good) **7** Ran SP% **113.7**
Speed ratings: **98,97,97,95,94 93,**
toteswingers 1&2 £5.00, 1&3 £23.40, 2&3 £23.40 CSF £53.48 TOTE £9.40: £3.20, £3.00; EX 72.00 Trifecta £409.90 Pool: £994.25 - 1.81 winning units..
Owner Mrs Teresa Mangan **Bred** Mrs Rosemary Swan **Trained** Trim, Co Meath

FOCUS
A good-quality veterans' chase, run at an ordinary gallop.

2071 BETFRED MONET'S GARDEN OLD ROAN CHASE (A LIMITED H'CAP) (GRADE 2) (16 fncs) 2m 4f
3:05 (3:05) (Class 1) 4-Y-0+

£42,202 (£15,900; £7,957; £3,975; £1,995; £997)

Form RPR

1/2- **1** **Conquisto**[168] 217 8-11-0 **150**........................ APMcCoy 156+
(Steve Gollings) *chsd ldrs: rdn to ld last: r.o gamely and in command cl home* **17/2**

/45- **2** *1 1/4* **Astracad (FR)**[7] 1969 7-10-5 **141**........................(t) SamTwiston-Davies 146
(Nigel Twiston-Davies) *led: hit 4 out: rdn and hdd last: r.o u.p tl no ex cl home* **4/1**[2]

5/0- **3** *1* **Viva Colonia (IRE)**[98] 1047 8-10-4 **140** oh1........................ DannyCook 143
(Brian Ellison) *hld up: hdwy 11th: effrt whn chsng ldrs and swtchd lft appr last: tk 3rd run-in: styd on but nt quite able to chal front two* **16/1**

4P2/ **4** *5* **Mr Moonshine (IRE)**[190] 5369 9-10-4 **140** oh5........................ RyanMania 140
(Sue Smith) *a.p: ev ch fr 3 out tl rdn and nt qckn appr last: no ex run-in* **8/1**

314/ **5** *11* **Oiseau De Nuit (FR)**[182] 5575 11-11-8 **158**........................(t) JoeTizzard 149
(Colin Tizzard) *midfield: hit 9th and dropped to rr: wl outpcd 12th: plugged on fr 2 out but n.d* **28/1**

133/ **6** *6* **Wishfull Thinking**[182] 5575 10-11-10 **160**........................(t) RichardJohnson 147
(Philip Hobbs) *in rr: j.rt 4th: mstke 7th: sme hdwy whn hmpd 4 out: u.p and no imp 2 out: no ch after* **7/1**[3]

364/ **7** *1* **Edgardo Sol (FR)**[192] 5352 6-11-5 **155**........................ NickScholfield 139
(Paul Nicholls) *nt jump wl in rr: sme hdwy appr 3 out: no imp on ldrs: no ch fr 2 out* **7/1**[3]

000/ **8** *5* **Saint Are (FR)**[182] 5576 7-10-4 **140** oh4........................ DougieCostello 118
(Tim Vaughan) *prom: blnd 5th and lost pl: towards rr whn rdn after 8th: u.p whn mstke 12th: n.d after* **10/1**

P16/ **9** *1 1/4* **Carrickboy (IRE)**[192] 5353 9-10-8 **147** ow3........................ JoshuaMoore(3) 125
(Venetia Williams) *chsd ldrs: effrt in 4th 4 out: rdn appr 2 out: sn wknd* **20/1**

510- **10** *3 1/2* **Pure Faith (IRE)**[8] 1956 9-10-4 **140** oh2........................(tp) BrianHughes 114
(Peter Bowen) *midfield: mstke 11th: sn u.p and wknd* **25/1**

P52/ **U** **Walkon (FR)**[204] 5160 8-11-1 **151**........................(p) RobertThornton
(Alan King) *sn in midfield: trckd ldrs bef 8th: rdn after 12th: 5th abt 4 l down blnd and uns rdr 4 out* **7/2**[1]

4m 50.3s (-13.70) **Going Correction** -0.30s/f (Good) **11** Ran SP% **115.9**
Speed ratings (Par 115): **115,114,114,112,107 105,104,102,102,101**
toteswingers 1&2 £3.80, 1&3 £27.90, 2&3 £35.60 CSF £42.01 CT £539.61 TOTE £9.20: £2.40, £2.00, £5.30; EX 41.60 Trifecta £431.80 Pool: £1,475.21 - 2.56 winning units..
Owner P J Martin **Bred** Bricklow Ltd **Trained** Scamblesby, Lincs

FOCUS
The feature race and for the second year running it looked wide open. There was a solid pace on, but it still paid to race handily.

2072 BETFRED MOBILE LOTTO H'CAP CHASE (16 fncs) 2m 4f
3:40 (3:40) (Class 3) (0-135,135) 4-Y-**£8,790** (£2,619; £1,326; £679; £355)

Form RPR

/51- **1** **Rossini's Dancer**[14] 1872 8-10-9 **125**........................(v) MrKitAlexander(7) 134+
(N W Alexander) *chsd ldr tl mstke 10th: outpcd after 4 out: wnt 2nd appr 2 out where abt 5 l down: clsd last: styd on to ld fnl 150yds: won gng away* **10/1**

15F/ **2** *2 1/4* **Saved By John (IRE)**[228] 4724 8-11-7 **130**........................(t) RichardJohnson 137
(Tim Vaughan) *led: blnd 9th: abt 5 l clr 2 out: rdn bef last: hdd fnl 150yds: no ex cl home* **11/4**[2]

4PP/ **3** *16* **Carlito Brigante (IRE)**[84] 1198 7-11-12 **135**........................(p) BrianHughes 127
(Karen McLintock) *in tch: prom 7th: effrt appr 4 out: rdn and outpcd bef 3 out: kpt on to take 3rd bef last: no ch w front two* **10/1**

2/4- **4** *3 3/4* **Kruzhlinin (GER)**[162] 366 6-11-9 **132**........................ JasonMaguire 120
(Donald McCain) *trckd ldrs: pushed along bef 10th: rdn and wknd after 12th* **2/1**[1]

2P0/ **5** *16* **Gansey (IRE)**[190] 5369 11-11-11 **134**........................ RyanMania 112
(Sue Smith) *in tch: wnt 2nd 10th: nt fluent 4 out: rdn and lost 2nd appr 2 out: wknd on long run bef last* **13/2**[3]

/60- **P** **Falcon Island**[22] 1746 8-11-7 **130**........................(tp) JoeTizzard
(Colin Tizzard) *towards rr: rdn after 3rd: lost tch bef 5th: mstke 6th: p.u sn after* **12/1**

1PP/ **P** **Howard's Legacy (IRE)**[198] 5242 7-11-6 **129**........................ LiamTreadwell
(Venetia Williams) *blnd 1st: sn wl bhd: j. slowly 2nd: lost tch bef 5th: t.o whn p.u after 8th* **7/1**

4m 57.3s (-6.70) **Going Correction** -0.30s/f (Good) **7** Ran SP% **111.7**
Speed ratings (Par 107): **101,100,93,92,85 ,**
toteswingers 1&2 £3.40, 1&3 not won, 2&3 £10.00 CSF £36.99 TOTE £8.80: £2.70, £1.60; EX 31.50 Trifecta £186.40 Pool: £502.65 - 2.02 winning units..
Owner Turcan Barber Fletcher Dunning **Bred** Heather Raw **Trained** Kinneston, Perth & Kinross

FOCUS
A fair handicap, run at a solid gallop.

2073 BETFRED MOBILE CASINO NOVICES' H'CAP HURDLE (13 hdls) 3m 110y
4:15 (4:15) (Class 4) (0-120,120) 4-Y-0+ **£4,548** (£1,335; £667; £333)

Form RPR

6/0- **1** **Josies Orders (IRE)**[34] 1634 5-10-13 **107**........................ APMcCoy 115+
(Jonjo O'Neill) *hld up in rr: tried to make hdwy 8th: nt fluent 9th: rdn and outpcd bef 3 out: rallied and swtchd appr last: led 1f out on run-in: drew clr fnl 100yds* **7/2**[1]

520/ **2** *3 1/4* **Sin Bin (IRE)**[202] 5200 7-11-9 **117**........................(t) NickScholfield 119
(Paul Nicholls) *in tch: wnt 2nd after 7th: chalng fr 3 out: rdn run-in: unable to go w wnr fnl 100yds* **9/2**[3]

P/2- **3** *1 3/4* **Milano Magic (IRE)**[14] 1875 7-11-2 **110**........................(p) LucyAlexander 111
(N W Alexander) *led: pressed fr 3 out: rdn appr last: hdd 1f out on run-in: no ex fnl 75yds* **10/1**

221- **4** *2 1/4* **Cruising Bye**[16] 1829 7-10-0 **94** oh1........................ DougieCostello 92
(Peter Bowen) *hld up: hit 7th: hdwy 9th: trckd ldrs after 10th: outpcd 2 out: styd on run-in but n.d* **4/1**[2]

424- **5** *2 1/4* **Dazinski**[29] 1672 7-11-7 **115**........................ WillKennedy 112
(Sarah-Jayne Davies) *handy: ev ch whn hit 3 out: stl chalng 2 out: rdn and nt qckn appr last: one pce run-in* **16/1**

400/ **6** *5* **Karinga Dandy (IRE)**[190] 5372 7-11-2 **110**........................ RyanMania 101
(Sue Smith) *chsd ldr tl after 7th: remained handy: rdn appr 3 out: wknd bef 2 out* **7/2**[1]

5/F- **7** *10* **Shouldavboughtgold (IRE)**[149] 556 6-10-12 **106**........................ CharlieHuxley 88
(William Kinsey) *nvr gng wl in rr: nvr on terms* **14/1**

225- **8** *52* **Swing Hard (IRE)**[22] 1752 5-10-11 **110**........................ JonathanEngland(5) 46
(Sue Smith) *trckd ldrs: mstke 3rd: dropped to rr 8th: sn bhd: t.o* **9/1**

6m 14.0s (-2.30) **Going Correction** +0.05s/f (Yiel) **8** Ran SP% **114.3**
Speed ratings (Par 105): **105,103,103,102,101 100,97,80**
toteswingers 1&2 £6.00, 1&3 £9.60, 2&3 £10.00 CSF £19.91 CT £141.69 TOTE £4.60: £1.70, £2.00, £2.30; EX 23.80 Trifecta £121.40 Pool: £534.92 - 3.30 winning units..
Owner John P McManus **Bred** Mrs E Moore **Trained** Cheltenham, Gloucs

FOCUS
The winner took a big step over this longer trip.

2074 BETFRED BINGO NOVICES' CHASE (16 fncs) 2m 4f
4:50 (4:50) (Class 3) 4-Y-0+ **£7,507** (£2,217; £1,108; £554)

Form RPR

114/ **1** **Shutthefrontdoor (IRE)**[226] 4747 6-11-3 0........................ APMcCoy 137+
(Jonjo O'Neill) *hld up: wnt 3rd appr 5th: wnt 2nd on bit bef 2 out: rdn to chal last: styd on to ld fnl 75yds* **4/5**[1]

4/1- **2** *1/2* **Beeves (IRE)**[15] 1851 6-11-8 140........................ JasonMaguire 138
(Donald McCain) *led: pushed along appr 3 out: rdn whn pressed last: hdd fnl 75yds: styd on u.p: hld cl home* **7/2**[3]

051- **3** *8* **Bar De Ligne (FR)**[127] 786 7-11-8 128........................(p) RichardJohnson 130
(Steve Gollings) *chsd ldr: rdn and lost 2nd appr 2 out: one pce u.p bef last* **10/1**

010/ **4** *10* **Yesyoucan (IRE)**[204] 5161 8-11-3 0........................ DannyCook 118
(Brian Ellison) *nt jump wl: racd in 3rd pl tl dropped to rr appr 5th: lft bhd after 2 out* **3/1**[2]

4m 58.8s (-5.20) **Going Correction** -0.30s/f (Good) **4** Ran SP% **111.9**
Speed ratings (Par 107): **98,97,94,90**
CSF £4.23 TOTE £1.80; EX 3.50 Trifecta £8.30 Pool: £592.76 - 53.20 winning units..
Owner John P McManus **Bred** Ms Deirdre Connolly **Trained** Cheltenham, Gloucs

FOCUS
A decent novice chase and the winner looked to have a bit in hand.

2075 BETFRED "RACING'S BIGGEST SUPPORTER" MAIDEN HURDLE (9 hdls) 2m 110y
5:20 (5:21) (Class 4) 4-Y-0+ **£4,548** (£1,335; £667; £333)

Form RPR

1/ **1** **Garde La Victoire (FR)**[368] 1977 4-11-0 0........................ RichardJohnson 125+
(Philip Hobbs) *prom: chsd ldr 2nd: led appr 6th: nt fluent 2 out: hit last: drvn out and r.o wl* **7/1**

112/ **2** *2 1/4* **Regal Encore (IRE)**[227] 4738 5-11-0 0........................ APMcCoy 123+
(Anthony Honeyball) *in rr: hdwy appr 3 out: wnt 2nd after last: kpt on but no imp on wnr* **8/15**[1]

3 *4 1/2* **Pulpitarian (USA)**[133] 5-11-0 0........................ PeterBuchanan 116
(Lucinda Russell) *midfield: hdwy to chse ldrs 3 out: rdn and nt qckn after last: kpt on: no imp fnl 150yds* **33/1**

4 *2* **Silsol (GER)**[339] 4-11-0 0........................ NickScholfield 114
(Paul Nicholls) *chsd ldrs: prom 5th: ch 3 out: stl wl there last: rdn run-in: kpt on same pce* **13/2**[3]

5 *6* **Getabuzz**[34] 5-11-0 0........................ HarryHaynes 108
(Tim Easterby) *chsd ldr to 2nd: remained prom: chal 3 out: rdn whn nt fluent 2 out: one pce fr last* **16/1**

221/ **6** *2 1/4* **Salto Chisco (IRE)**[210] 5018 5-11-0 0........................ JasonMaguire 106
(Donald McCain) *t.k.h: hld up in midfield: trckd ldrs after 6th: tried to chal 2 out: rdn bef last: wknd early on run-in* **9/2**[2]

/36- **7** *18* **Call Of Duty (IRE)**[22] 1754 8-11-0 113........................ JamesReveley 93+
(Dianne Sayer) *led: j. bit 1st: nt fluent 2nd: remained handy tl wknd after 2 out* **20/1**

64/ **8** *16* **Blackmore**[385] 1737 6-11-0 0........................ LucyAlexander 72
(N W Alexander) *hld up: struggling after 6th: nvr on terms* **33/1**

9 *56* **Brasingaman Espee**[29] 4-11-0 0........................ BarryKeniry 16
(George Moore) *midfield: nt fluent 1st and 2nd: j. slowly and lost pl 3rd: lost tch bef 3 out: t.o* **66/1**

4m 3.8s (-2.40) **Going Correction** +0.05s/f (Yiel)
WFA 4 from 5yo+ 9lb **9** Ran SP% **127.3**
Speed ratings (Par 105): **107,105,103,102,100 99,90,83,56**
toteswingers 1&2 £2.60, 1&3 £27.00, 2&3 £27.00 CSF £12.64 TOTE £9.30: £2.70, £1.10, £7.20; EX 21.60 Trifecta £983.90 Part won. Pool: £1,311.98 - 0.66 winning units..
Owner Mrs Diana L Whateley **Bred** Mlle Laure Godet **Trained** Withycombe, Somerset

FOCUS
Solid novice form.
T/Plt: £353.60 to a £1 stake. Pool: £109,173.82 - 225.36 winning units T/Qpdt: £35.50 to a £1 stake. Pool: £5,452.40 - 113.40 winning units DO

1862 CHEPSTOW (L-H)
Saturday, October 26

OFFICIAL GOING: Soft (heavy in places; chs 6.0, hdl 5.5)
Wind: quite strong breeze half against Weather: overcast

2076 TOTEJACKPOT MAIDEN HURDLE (12 hdls) 3m
1:50 (1:51) (Class 5) 4-Y-0+ **£1,949** (£572; £286; £143)

Form RPR

5/2- **1** **Kaki De La Pree (FR)**[22] 1749 6-11-0 0........................ FelixDeGiles 127+
(Tom Symonds) *in tch: wnt 3rd bef 6th: mounting chal whn hit 4 out: rdn whn hit 2 out: narrow advantage last: styd on wl to assert run-in* **1/1**[1]

3/ **2** *2* **Closing Ceremony (IRE)**[233] 4621 4-10-13 0........................ DarylJacob 123+
(Emma Lavelle) *hld up in tch: hdwy 8th: led after 4 out: hrd pressed and rdn fr next: hit 2 out: wnt sltly rt whn hdd last: kpt on but no ex* **10/3**[2]

2- **3** *21* **Doing Fine (IRE)**[21] 1770 5-11-0 0 TomScudamore 107
(Rebecca Curtis) *nvr fluent: trckd ldrs: pushed up to chal 8th: qcknd pce to ld bef next: rdn and hdd bef next: sn one pce: blnd last* **7/2**[3]

0/ **4** *16* **Blazing Bouncer**[924] 8-11-0 0 TomO'Brien 86
(Richard Woollacott) *t.k.h: hld up: plld way through to trck ldrs 3rd: rdn after 8th: lost pl qckly bef 4 out: snatched modest 4th fnl stride* **33/1**

5 *shd* **Hurricane Ivan (IRE)**[188] 5-10-7 0 (t) MissAEStirling(7) 86
(Fergal O'Brien) *trckd ldrs: in front whn hit 5th: hdd bef next: styd prom tl rdn appr 4 out: sn wknd* **50/1**

452- **6** *1 1/4* **Midnight Mustang**[20] 1784 6-10-7 83 MrJMartin(7) 85
(Andrew J Martin) *t.k.h: w ldr: hit 4th: led after 5th: rdn and hdd bef 4 out: sn btn: wknd 3 out* **12/1**

0- **7** *4 1/2* **You Too Pet (IRE)**[14] 1869 5-11-0 0 PaddyBrennan 80
(Fergal O'Brien) *led tl 5th: trckd ldrs: rdn appr 4 out: sn wknd* **20/1**

8 *21* **Ask The Boss**[1049] 8-11-0 0 ConorO'Farrell 59
(Tim Dennis) *hld up but wl in tch: rdn whn pce qcknd after 8th: wknd bef 4 out: t.o* **28/1**

6m 16.8s (14.60) **Going Correction** +0.175s/f (Yiel)
WFA 4 from 5yo+ 11lb 8 Ran SP% **116.1**
Speed ratings (Par 103): **82,81,74,69,68 68,67,60**
toteswingers 1&2 £2.90, 1&3 £2.00, 2&3 £1.10 CSF £4.60 TOTE £1.90: £1.10, £1.60, £1.60; EX 5.80 Trifecta £11.10 Pool: £523.61 - 35.10winning units..
Owner Thomas R Symonds **Bred** Michel Froissard **Trained** Harewood End, H'fords

FOCUS
Punters were only interested in three of these prior to the off, and the early gallop was really slow before developing into a sprint to the line

2077 TOTESCOOP6 NOVICES' CHASE (18 fncs) 3m
2:25 (2:25) (Class 4) 4-Y-0+ **£4,548** (£1,335; £667; £333)

Form RPR

233/ **1** **Shotgun Paddy (IRE)**[252] 4250 6-11-4 0 LeightonAspell 148+
(Emma Lavelle) *j. cleverly: trckd ldrs: led 9th: pushed along fr after 4 out: sn in command: quite impressive* **7/2**[2]

22/ **2** *13* **Just A Par (IRE)**[204] 5161 6-11-4 0 DarylJacob 136+
(Paul Nicholls) *j.w: trckd ldrs: wnt 2nd 5 out: rdn after 4 out: hld fr next: styd on same pce* **4/7**[1]

0/3- **3** *9* **Boyfromnowhere (IRE)**[23] 1728 6-11-4 0 (p) TomScudamore 123
(Rebecca Curtis) *disp ld: clr ldr but jumping rt fr 5th: hdd 9th: pressed wnr tl 5 out: sn rdn: outpcd after next* **14/1**

32P/ **4** *7* **Arthurian Legend**[268] 3964 8-11-4 132 TomO'Brien 117
(Philip Hobbs) *hld up 5th: nudged aong after 3rd: reminders whn nt fluent 8th: wnt cl enough 4th 11th: rdn after 5 out: wknd 3 out* **8/1**[3]

212/ **5** *32* **Rev It Up (IRE)**[364] 2045 7-11-1 129 MichaelByrne(3) 88
(Tim Vaughan) *disp ld tl nt fluent 4th: dropped to last and struggling 11th: bk disputing cl 4th 5 out: wknd next: t.o* **10/1**

6m 12.6s (-9.40) **Going Correction** -0.325s/f (Good) 5 Ran SP% **112.7**
Speed ratings (Par 105): **102,97,94,92,81**
CSF £6.49 TOTE £4.80: £2.90, £1.02; EX 6.10 Trifecta £40.10 Pool: £739.91 - 18.32 winning units..
Owner Axom (XXXVI) **Bred** Mrs Richella Rohan **Trained** Hatherden, Hants

FOCUS
This had a competitive look to it and appeared to be run at a sound gallop. The winner looks smart.

2078 TOTEQUADPOT H'CAP CHASE (16 fncs) 2m 3f 110y
3:00 (3:00) (Class 4) (0-120,118) 4-Y-0+ **£3,898** (£1,144; £572; £286)

Form RPR

524/ **1** **Get It On (IRE)**[240] 4480 8-11-0 **113** ConorRing(7) 135+
(Evan Williams) *travelled wl thrght: hit 11th: chal 5 out: slt ld whn hit 2 out: qcknd readily clr: v easily* **6/1**[3]

2/4- **2** *35* **Ballinvarrig (IRE)**[20] 1796 6-11-11 **117** PaddyBrennan 124+
(Tom George) *j.rt at times: trckd ldrs: wnt 2nd 6th: led 5 out: sn jnd by wnr: rdn and hdd 2 out: sn outpcd: wnt rt and blnd last: wl clr of remainder whn heavily eased run-in* **7/4**[1]

0U1/ **3** *12* **Topaze Collonges (FR)**[230] 4681 6-11-4 **110** (b) TomScudamore 84
(Charlie Longsdon) *led: jnd 11th: hdd 5 out: sn rdn: wknd 3 out: t.o* **11/4**[2]

3P0/ **4** *6* **Lough Coi (IRE)**[196] 5286 7-10-3 **100** (tp) JamesBanks(5) 64
(Anthony Middleton) *in last pair: lost tch 10th: wnt poor 4th run-in* **8/1**

0P5- **5** *6* **Takeroc (FR)**[29] 1670 10-11-12 **118** (t) PaulMoloney 76
(Sophie Leech) *in last pair: wnt 4th 11th: nvr thretaned to get on terms w ldrs: wknd 4 out: lost poor 4th run-in* **16/1**

/22- **P** **Ski Sunday**[22] 1744 8-11-11 **117** (t) TomO'Brien
(Tim Vaughan) *trckd ldr tl 6th: rdn after next: sn dropped to 4th: wknd after 11th: t.o whn p.u bef 4 out* **6/1**[3]

5m 2.1s (-9.20) **Going Correction** -0.325s/f (Good) 6 Ran SP% **108.6**
Speed ratings (Par 105): **105,91,86,83,81**
toteswingers 1&2 £3.10, 1&3 £2.40, 2&3 £1.70 CSF £16.54 CT £30.49 TOTE £6.50: £2.30, £1.90; EX 20.40 Trifecta £88.60 Pool: £933.02 - 7.89 winning units..
Owner John Lee Jones **Bred** G Martin **Trained** Llancarfan, Vale Of Glamorgan

FOCUS
Just a modest event for some mainly exposed chasers. Only two counted from some way out and the winner did it easily.

2079 TOTEPOOL MOBILE PERSIAN WAR NOVICES' HURDLE (GRADE 2) (11 hdls) 2m 4f
3:35 (3:36) (Class 1) 4-Y-0+
£17,085 (£6,411; £3,210; £1,599; £804; £402)

Form RPR

1- **1** **Timesremembered (IRE)**[20] 1795 5-11-0 0 LeightonAspell 139+
(Emma Lavelle) *travelled wl: trckd ldr: led bef 4 out: comf asserting whn mstke 3 out: nt fluent 2 out: easily* **9/1**

3- **2** *6* **Potters Cross**[14] 1864 6-11-0 0 TomScudamore 130+
(Rebecca Curtis) *led: nt fluent 7th: hdd and rdn in disp 2nd fr 4 out: styd on but no ch w wnr fr next* **12/1**

21F/ **3** *7* **Lienosus (IRE)**[205] 5141 7-11-0 131 PaulMoloney 126+
(Evan Williams) *trckd ldrs: pckd bdly 5th: blnd next: rdn in disp 2nd 4 out: no ch w wnr fr next: no ex fr last* **9/4**[2]

1/2- **4** *1 1/4* **Berkeley Barron (IRE)**[14] 1864 5-11-4 130 (t) TomO'Brien 125
(Philip Hobbs) *trckd ldrs: pushed along fr 6th: struggling in last trio after next: outpcd 4 out: styd on again fr 3 out: wnt 4th next but no ch w ldrs* **9/2**[3]

42/ **5** *13* **Tinker Time (IRE)**[195] 5310 5-11-0 0 LiamHeard 107
(Bob Buckler) *hld up in last pair: hdwy after 6th: rdn and lost pl after next: outpcd and no threat after* **50/1**

/60- **6** *3* **Johnny Og**[25] 1712 4-11-0 0 IanPopham 107
(Martin Keighley) *a in last pair: effrt after 7th: outpcd 4 out: wknd next* **33/1**

1/ **7** *35* **Ceasar Milan (IRE)**[231] 4654 5-11-0 0 DarylJacob 94+
(Paul Nicholls) *trckd ldrs: travelling wl in disp 2nd 4 out: sn rdn: wknd tamely after next: virtually p.u run-in: bled post r* **11/8**[1]

4m 59.8s (-2.00) **Going Correction** +0.175s/f (Yiel)
WFA 4 from 5yo+ 10lb 7 Ran SP% **113.7**
Speed ratings (Par 115): **111,108,105,105,100 98,84**
toteswingers 1&2 £4.10, 2&3 £5.10, 1&3 £6.10 CSF £97.32 TOTE £9.50: £4.70, £2.00; EX 55.90 Trifecta £281.30 Pool: £26785.61 - 71.39 winning units..
Owner Tim Syder & Sarah Prior **Bred** Jarlath Glynn **Trained** Hatherden, Hants

FOCUS
Winners of this are always worth noting for the future, with Wonderful Charm, Fingal Bay, Silviniaco Conti and Reve De Sivola taking the last four renewals.

2080 TOTEQUICKPICK SILVER TROPHY H'CAP HURDLE (GRADE 3) (11 hdls) 2m 4f
4:10 (4:11) (Class 1) 4-Y-0+
£22,780 (£8,548; £4,280; £2,132; £1,072; £536)

Form RPR

5/0- **1** **Shammick Boy (IRE)**[170] 176 8-10-13 **128** JackDoyle 128
(Victor Dartnall) *mid-div: hdwy 6th: rdn to chse ldrs after 4 out: str run to ld sn after last: drvn out* **20/1**

10P/ **2** *2* **Lamb Or Cod (IRE)**[287] 3612 6-11-1 **130** (t) TomO'Brien 130
(Philip Hobbs) *racd wd: prom: led 6th tl appr 4 out: rdn and styd chalng tl mstke 3 out: swtchd lft next: r.o fr last: wnt 2nd nring fin* **9/2**[2]

315/ **3** *1 1/4* **Kaylif Aramis**[218] 4905 6-11-4 **133** DaveCrosse 132
(Nigel Twiston-Davies) *mid-div: hit 6th: hdwy after next: rdn to chse ldr after 4 out: chalng whn mstke 2 out: ev ch sn after last: kpt on but no ex whn lost 2nd nring fin* **7/1**[3]

110/ **4** *shd* **Broadway Buffalo (IRE)**[204] 5162 5-11-11 **140** TomScudamore 139+
(David Pipe) *trckd ldrs: jnd ldrs 6th: led bef 4 out: rdn after 2 out: hit last: sn hdd: no ex* **9/4**[1]

1/4- **5** *4 1/2* **Araldur (FR)**[168] 215 9-11-12 **141** WayneHutchinson 135
(Alan King) *mid-div: rdn bef 4 out: chsng ldrs whn nt fluent 3 out: styng on at same pce whn awkward last* **7/1**[3]

0/3- **6** *3 1/2* **Quaddick Lake (IRE)**[6] 1989 10-10-5 **130** [1] ChrisMeehan(10) 119
(Jeremy Scott) *hld up towards rr: hdwy on outer aftert 7th: rdn to chse ldrs after next: hung lft: kpt on but nt gng pce to chal* **20/1**

F/6- **7** *1/2* **Peckhamecho (IRE)**[21] 1766 7-11-1 **140** PaulO'Brien(10) 128
(Rebecca Curtis) *racd keenly: trckd ldrs: rdn after 4 out: kpt on but nt gng pce to chal* **9/1**

652/ **8** *8* **Hold Court (IRE)**[197] 5264 6-10-9 **127** AdamWedge(3) 107
(Evan Williams) *umped sltly rt at times: hld up bhd: rdn after 4 out: no imp: wknd 2 out* **8/1**

2F2/ **9** *8* **Makethe Mostofnow (IRE)**[195] 5308 8-10-13 **128** PaulMoloney 100
(Evan Williams) *led tl 6th: prom: rdn 4 out: wknd next* **20/1**

3FP/ **10** *shd* **Notus De La Tour (FR)**[315] 3054 7-11-6 **135** ConorO'Farrell 107
(David Pipe) *struggling after 7th: a in rr* **16/1**

1/ **11** *28* **Virak (FR)**[210] 5021 4-11-7 **136** (t) DarylJacob 80
(Paul Nicholls) *trckd ldrs: rdn after 4 out: wknd qckly: t.o* **11/1**

5m 0.3s (-1.50) **Going Correction** +0.175s/f (Yiel)
WFA 4 from 5yo+ 10lb 11 Ran SP% **123.6**
Speed ratings (Par 113): **110,109,108,108,106 105,105,102,98,98 87**
toteswingers 1&2 £31.00, 1&3 £26.90, 2&3 £6.90 CSF £111.94 CT £705.32 TOTE £24.00: £6.30, £2.00, £2.20; EX 181.50 Trifecta £898.00 Part won. Pool: £1197.42 - 0.01 winning units..
Owner First Brayford Partnership **Bred** Miss D Flanagan **Trained** Brayford, Devon

FOCUS
This is thoroughly unreliable form as they went no pace for much of the contest and plenty had some sort of chance off the final bend.

2081 TOTEPOOL.COM HOME OF KING SIZE POOLS H'CAP CHASE (12 fncs) 2m 110y
4:45 (4:45) (Class 2) 4-Y-0+ **£16,245** (£4,770; £2,385; £1,192)

Form RPR

411/ **1** **Sire De Grugy (FR)**[182] 5575 7-11-12 **161** JamieMoore 170+
(Gary Moore) *travelled strly thrght: last but in tch: hdwy 5th: jnd ldr after 4 out: led after 3 out: qcknd readily clr after next: mstke last: impressive* **7/2**[3]

161/ **2** *11* **Majala (FR)**[192] 5357 7-11-1 **150** (t) PaddyBrennan 146+
(Tom George) *led at gd pce: jnd after 4 out: blnd 3 out: sn hdd: readily outpcd by wnr after next* **5/2**[2]

1/0- **3** *2 1/2* **Theatrical Star**[14] 1868 7-10-2 **137** BrendanPowell 126
(Colin Tizzard) *trckd ldr: wnt rt 1st: rdn after 5 out: sn hld: kpt on same pce* **5/1**

/P5- **4** *12* **Cornas (NZ)**[43] 1583 11-10-0 **135** PaulMoloney 112
(Nick Williams) *trckd ldr tl rdn after 5 out: grad fdd* **14/1**

P24/ **5** *6* **Rebel Rebellion (IRE)**[189] 5401 8-10-5 **140** (t) DarylJacob 111
(Paul Nicholls) *trckd ldrs: hmpd 1st: nt fluent 7th: sn struggling in last pair: no ch fr next* **7/4**[1]

365- **6** *54* **Mister Matt (IRE)**[22] 1746 10-10-0 **135** oh11 GerardTumelty 52
(Bob Buckler) *trckd ldrs: struggling in last but stl in tch 7th: wknd bef 5 out: t.o* **33/1**

4m 5.2s (-11.90) **Going Correction** -0.325s/f (Good) 6 Ran SP% **113.4**
Speed ratings (Par 109): **115,109,108,103,100 74**
toteswingers 1&2 £1.02, 2&3 £3.50, 1&3 £3.10 CSF £13.32 TOTE £3.40: £1.90, £1.80; EX 12.30 Trifecta £53.70 Pool: £1299.71 - 18.11 winning units..
Owner The Preston Family & Friends Ltd **Bred** La Grugerie **Trained** Lower Beeding, W Sussex

FOCUS
A fine weight-carrying performance by the winner.

2082 COLLECT TOTEPOOL WINNINGS AT BETFRED SHOPS CONDITIONAL JOCKEYS' H'CAP CHASE (18 fncs) 3m
5:15 (5:15) (Class 5) (0-95,89) 4-Y-0+ **£2,599** (£763; £381; £190)

Form RPR

3P4/ **1** **Somerby (IRE)**[195] 5319 10-11-6 **83** (t) AdamWedge 94+
(Richenda Ford) *led tl jnd after 7th: rdn after 4 out: outrt ld 2 out: styd on gamely* **11/4**[2]

5/P- **2** *9* **Flugzeug**[167] 242 5-11-0 **85** KevinJones(8) 87
(Seamus Mullins) *racd keenly: disp ld most of way fr after 7th: rdn after 3 out: hdd 2 out: styd on same pce* **11/2**

5/0- **3** *24* **Notabotheronme (IRE)**[155] 461 11-11-4 **81** (p) RobertWilliams 59
(Dai Burchell) *chsd ldrs: nudged along and nt that fluent at times: rdn after 13th: no ch w ldng pair fr next: t.o* **7/2**[3]

351- 4 *8* **Volio Vincente (FR)**[26] 1701 6-10-4 **72**.................... JonPark(5) 42
(Carroll Gray) *nt a fluent: hld up bhd ldrs: rdn and no imp after 13th: no ch fr next: t.o* **2/1**[1]
554- P **Upper Deck (IRE)**[26] 1701 8-9-8 **65**.................... DanielHiskett(8)
(Richard Phillips) *chsd ldrs: rdn after 13th: sn wknd: t.o whn p.u after 3 out* **8/1**
6m 40.4s (18.40) **Going Correction** -0.325s/f (Good) **5** Ran SP% **108.7**
Speed ratings (Par 103): **56,53,45,42,**
CSF £16.30 TOTE £3.00: £2.50, £3.30; EX 16.20 Trifecta £125.10 Pool: £641.12 - 3.84 winning units..
Owner K Snook **Bred** King Bloodstock **Trained** Brockhampton Green, Dorset
FOCUS
A moderate contest that only concerned the two who shared the lead.
T/Plt: £171.00 to a £1 stake. Pool of £58931.64 - 251.50 winning tickets. T/Qpdt: £109.00 to a £1 stake. Pool of £2828.60 - 19.20 winning tickets. TM

1594 STRATFORD (L-H)
Saturday, October 26

OFFICIAL GOING: Soft (good to soft in places; 7.8) changing to good to soft (soft in places) after race 5 (3.55)
Wind: Light; against Weather: Dry

2083 EXCLUSIVE TICKET GIVEAWAYS AT TOTEPOOL TWITTER MAIDEN HURDLE (DIV I) (6 hdls 2 omitted) 2m 110y
1:35 (1:35) (Class 4) 4-Y-0+ **£3,249** (£954; £477; £238)

Form RPR
6/ 1 **King Rolfe (IRE)**[202] 5208 5-11-0 0.................... AidanColeman 109+
(Tim Vaughan) *hld up in tch in midfield: rdn and effrt to chse ldr on long run between last 2: clsd to chal last: sn led and r.o strly: readily* **13/2**[3]
2 *2 1/4* **Sir Valentino (FR)**[516] 4-10-9 0.................... AodhaganConlon(5) 106
(Tom George) *led: kicked clr 2 out: 4 l clr on long run between last 2: jnd and outj. last: sn hdd and styd on same pce flat* **4/1**[1]
34/- 3 *6* **Edmaaj (IRE)**[261] 4078 5-10-9 0.................... MauriceLinehan(5) 101
(Jonjo O'Neill) *t.k.h: chsd ldrs: effrt to chse clr ldr sn after 2 out: 3rd and unable qck bnd bef last: wknd last: jst hld on to 3rd* **4/1**[1]
40/- 4 *nk* **Whispering Bob (IRE)**[350] 2334 6-11-0 0.................... NoelFehily 100
(Charlie Longsdon) *in tch: rdn and effrt to chse ldng trio on long run after 2 out: styd on same pce fr bnd bef last* **4/1**[1]
46/ 5 *6* **Saffron Prince**[238] 4514 5-11-0 0.................... TomCannon 94
(David Bridgwater) *j. novicey: hld up in last quartet: stl towards rr 2 out: rdn and gd hdwy on long run between last 2: wnt modest 5th and no treat to ldrs whn mstke last* **33/1**
600- 6 *11* **Cool Fantasy (IRE)**[32] 1643 4-10-11 65.................... JamesBest(3) 83
(Caroline Keevil) *chsd ldr tl 2nd: styd chsng ldrs tl rdn after 2 out: sn struggling and wknd on long run to last* **200/1**
50/ 7 *6* **Bayley's Dream**[189] 5407 4-11-0 0.................... DenisO'Regan 77
(Paul Webber) *t.k.h: chsd ldrs: chsd ldr 2nd tl after 2 out: sn rdn and struggling: wknd on long run to last* **14/1**
0- 8 *nk* **Qasser (IRE)**[43] 1578 4-11-0 0.................... JamesDavies 76
(Harry Whittington) *t.k.h: hld up in tch in midfield: hdwy 2 out: 5th and no imp u.p bnd bef last: sn wknd* **40/1**
6/4- 9 *2 1/4* **Even If**[15] 1856 5-11-0 0.................... RichieMcLernon 74
(Jonjo O'Neill) *hld up in rr: stdy hdwy on outer on long run after 4th: struggling jst bef 2 out: wknd on long run between last 2* **9/2**[2]
5- 10 *6* **Forget And Forgive (IRE)**[115] 874 5-10-11 0.................... KielanWoods(3) 68
(Anthony Middleton) *in tch in midfield: rdn and struggling 2 out: sn wknd: t.o* **16/1**
11 *13* **Spunky**[48] 148 4-11-0 0.................... DonalDevereux 55
(Marc Barber) *hld up in rr: mstke 1st: rdn and struggling whn hit 2 out: sn lost tch: t.o* **100/1**
P5/ 12 *25* **Errol Flynn (IRE)**[1476] 1601 7-11-0 0.................... LeeEdwards 30
(Tony Carroll) *in tch in midfield: mstke: reminders and lost pl 4th: lost tch 2 out: t.o* **200/1**
6- 13 *1 1/4* **Tweedle Dee**[20] 1795 4-10-4 0.................... JackQuinlan(3) 22
(Noel Quinlan) *hld up in rr: sltly hmpd 4th: rdn and wkng whn mstke next: t.o* **25/1**
4m 1.2s (5.20) **Going Correction** +0.30s/f (Yiel)
WFA 4 from 5yo+ 9lb **13** Ran SP% **115.3**
Speed ratings (Par 105): **99,97,95,94,92 86,84,84,82,80 74,62,61**
toteswingers 1&2 £16.70, 1&3 £5.70, 2&3 £2.80 CSF £31.24 TOTE £7.60: £3.00, £1.50, £1.60; EX 45.80 Trifecta £123.10 Pool: £412.84 - 2.51 winning units..
Owner Four Corners Syndicate **Bred** Cathal Ennis **Trained** Aberthin, Vale of Glamorgan
FOCUS
The first race on a bumper eight-race card was a modest maiden hurdle in which they went a sensible, even gallop on ground officially described as Soft, good to soft in places. The jockeys felt it was riding more like good to soft ground.

2084 BIG MONEY TOTEJACKPOT POOLS AT TOTEPOOL.COM MARES' H'CAP HURDLE (6 hdls 2 omitted) 2m 110y
2:10 (2:12) (Class 3) (0-130,124) 4-Y-0 **£6,330** (£1,870; £935; £468; £234)

Form RPR
211- 1 **Rosie Probert**[89] 1132 4-11-5 **116**.................... AndrewTinkler 124+
(Nicky Henderson) *chsd ldr tl led bef 2 out: rdn and 3 l clr bef last: r.o strly flat: readily* **5/1**[2]
3/2- 2 *2 3/4* **Phase Shift**[152] 506 5-10-12 **116**.................... (t) CraigGallagher(7) 118
(Brian Ellison) *hld up in tch in last quartet: hdwy bef 2 out: chsd wnr u.p bef last: pressed wnr briefly sn after last: no ex and outpcd fnl 150yds* **17/2**
251- 3 *5* **Top Totti**[32] 1639 5-10-8 **108**.................... JakeGreenall(3) 106
(Henry Daly) *wl in tch in midfield: effrt and chsd wnr on long run between last 2: 3rd and no ex in st: hld whn mstke last* **9/2**[1]
/36- 4 *1 1/2* **Flying Phoenix**[86] 1173 5-10-6 **106**.................... RobertDunne(3) 102
(Dai Burchell) *hld up wl in tch in midfield: rdn and effrt in cl 4th on long run between last 2: outpcd and btn in st: plugged on* **16/1**
4/3- 5 *3 1/2* **Loyaute (FR)**[162] 353 6-11-13 **124** ow11.................... JamesDavies 116
(Chris Down) *wl in tch in midfield: hdwy to chse ldrs 4th: rdn bef 2 out: 5th and outpcd on long run between last 2: wknd in st* **7/1**
3/4- 6 *26* **Lindsay's Dream**[123] 384 7-10-5 **102**.................... (p) DaveCrosse 68
(Zoe Davison) *hld up in tch in last quartet: rdn and effrt 2 out: sn struggling and wknd on long run between last 2: t.o* **25/1**
1U5- 7 *3 1/4* **Faith Jicaro (IRE)**[23] 1729 6-11-2 **113**.................... DonalDevereux 76
(James Unett) *chsd ldrs: drvn and lost pl 4th: wknd and bhd next: lost tch on long run between last 2: t.o* **40/1**
101/ P **Golden Gael**[611] 4469 7-11-12 **123**.................... TimmyMurphy
(Jeremy Scott) *hld up in tch in last trio: effrt and no hdwy on long run after 4th: wl bhd whn p.u between last 2* **6/1**[3]
5/6- P **Dreambrook Lady (IRE)**[170] 176 7-11-11 **122**.................... RichieMcLernon
(Jonjo O'Neill) *t.k.h: hld up in tch in last trio: short-lived effrt on long run after 4th: no imp: t.o whn p.u between last 2* **7/1**
/41- F **Mini Muck**[23] 1731 7-10-1 **105**.................... RyanHatch(7)
(Nigel Twiston-Davies) *chsd ldrs: rdn and lost pl qckly after 2 out: sn wknd and wl btn whn fell last* **7/1**
323- P **Definitely Glad (IRE)**[137] 717 6-10-13 **110**.................... DenisO'Regan
(Paul Webber) *led tl hdd bef 2 out: rdn and wknd qckly on long run between last 2: wl bhd whn p.u bef last* **18/1**
3m 57.5s (1.50) **Going Correction** +0.30s/f (Yiel)
WFA 4 from 5yo+ 9lb **11** Ran SP% **114.6**
Speed ratings (Par 107): **108,106,104,103,102 89,88, , ,**
toteswingers 1&2 £5.60, 1&3 £4.50, 2&3 £10.30 CSF £46.00 CT £204.18 TOTE £3.10: £1.80, £2.60, £1.10; EX 36.50 Trifecta £88.20 Pool: £392.83 - 3.33 winning units..
Owner Seasons Holidays **Bred** Seasons Holidays **Trained** Upper Lambourn, Berks
FOCUS
A fairly decent mares' handicap hurdle in which they went an honest gallop. The winner showed a good attitude and is the type to rate higher.

2085 BET TOTESCOOP6 AT TOTEPOOL.COM (S) HURDLE (6 hdls 2 omitted) 2m 110y
2:45 (2:45) (Class 5) 4-6-Y-0 **£1,949** (£572; £286; £143)

Form RPR
343- 1 **Imperial Stargazer**[34] 1625 4-10-12 105.................... MarcGoldstein 104
(Sheena West) *mde all and sn clr: rdn and drew further clr bnd bef last: easily* **4/1**[3]
441/ 2 *10* **Rowlestone Lad**[44] 4777 6-11-10 120.................... RhysFlint 105
(John Flint) *racd off the pce in last quartet: clsd and in tch on long run after 4th: rdn and chsd clr wnr on long run between last 2: no imp* **5/2**[2]
5/0- 3 *2 1/2* **Waving**[20] 1779 4-10-7 0.................... (tp) JoshHamer(5) 92
(Tony Carroll) *hld up off the pce in last pair: clsd and in tch on long run after 4th: effrt to chal for 2nd but no threat to ldr bef last: blnd last and lost any ch of 2nd: one pce* **20/1**
F/0- 4 *2 1/4* **Langley**[65] 1342 6-11-3 104.................... (vt) AidanColeman 93
(Tim Vaughan) *chsd clr ldr but racd clr of field tl after 5th: rdn and no imp sn after 2 out: 4th and wl hld st* **9/1**
/06- 5 *3/4* **Kyles Faith (IRE)**[29] 1672 5-10-12 0.................... TomSiddall 87
(Martin Keighley) *racd off the pce in last quartet: clsd and in tch on long run after 4th: 5th and struggling u.p after 2 out: n.d after: plugged on flat* **15/2**
0/1- 6 *67* **Formal Bid (IRE)**[31] 1656 6-11-10 120.................... (bt) TimmyMurphy 32
(Gordon Elliott, Ire) *racd wd: hld up off the pce in last pair: clsd and in tch on long run after 4th: rdn and fnd nil 2 out: sn lost tch and t.o bef last* **7/4**[1]
4m 1.55s (5.55) **Going Correction** +0.30s/f (Yiel)
WFA 4 from 5yo+ 9lb **6** Ran SP% **111.5**
Speed ratings: **98,93,92,91,90 59**
toteswingers 1&2 £2.30, 1&3 £7.90, 2&3 £7.60 CSF £14.50 TOTE £7.30: £3.30, £2.00; EX 13.20 Trifecta £196.10 Pool: £469.92 - 1.79 winning units..The winner was bought in for 5,700gns
Owner Tapestry Partnership **Bred** Peter Taplin **Trained** Falmer, E Sussex
FOCUS
A fair selling hurdle in which the winner made all at a decent tempo.

2086 TOTEQUADPOT FOUR PLACES IN FOUR RACES H'CAP CHASE (FOR THE JOHN H KENNY MEMORIAL CUP) (12 fncs 2 omitted) 2m 4f
3:20 (3:20) (Class 3) (0-135,133) 4-Y-**£9,495** (£2,805; £1,402; £702; £351)

Form RPR
400/ 1 **Ikorodu Road**[182] 5576 10-11-5 **133**.................... (p) MrJMRidley(7) 143
(Matt Sheppard) *in tch in midfield: pushed along and hdwy to chse ldrs 8th: 3rd and outpcd bypassing 10th: 6 l down 2 out: styd on to chal last: sn in command and styd on strly* **12/1**
0P0- 2 *4 1/2* **Passato (GER)**[22] 1746 9-10-13 **120**.................... (t) DominicElsworth 127
(Jo Davis) *chsd ldr: pushed along to join ldr and wnt clr bypassing 10th: rdn and led bnd bef last: pressed wnr: sn hdd and styd on same pce flat* **25/1**
/1U- 3 *10* **Al Alfa**[9] 1944 6-10-9 **119**.................... JamesBest(3) 117
(Philip Hobbs) *led and set str gallop: jnd and wnt clr w rival bypassing 10th: rdn and hdd bnd bef last: 3rd and btn last: wknd last: tired flat but hld on for 3rd* **6/5**[1]
0P5/ 4 *1 1/2* **All For Free (IRE)**[337] 2595 7-11-2 **123**.................... AidanColeman 118
(David Bridgwater) *in tch in midfield: dropped to last pair 5th: rdn and effrt 3 out: 4th and no imp whn mstke last: plugged on* **18/1**
1P6/ 5 *3/4* **Sir Du Bearn (FR)**[294] 3501 7-11-12 **133**.................... CharliePoste 127
(Robin Dickin) *hld up in last pair: rdn and no hdwy after 9th: 7th and no imp 3 out: plugged on flat* **12/1**
P/P- 6 *nk* **Havingotascoobydo (IRE)**[21] 1766 8-11-8 **129**.................... TomSiddall 122
(Martin Keighley) *chsd ldrs: rdn and outpcd after 9th: wl hld between last 2: plugged on flat* **10/1**
3/0- 7 *23* **The Chazer (IRE)**[147] 587 8-11-3 **127**.................... MichealNolan(3) 107
(Richard Lee) *t.k.h: hld up towards rr: hdwy 5th: mstke 9th: 6th and no imp whn blnd 2 out: n.d after: eased flat: t.o* **9/1**[3]
1P3/ P **Arthur's Pass**[191] 5365 9-11-12 **133**.................... NoelFehily
(Tom George) *in tch in midfield: mstke 5th: rdn and struggling bypassing 10th: wknd 3 out: t.o whn p.u last* **3/1**[2]
4m 55.8s (5.80) **Going Correction** +0.525s/f (Soft) **8** Ran SP% **114.0**
Speed ratings (Par 107): **109,107,103,102,102 102,92,**
toteswingers 1&2 not won, 1&3 £3.90, 2&3 £22.00 CSF £212.30 CT £622.17 TOTE £11.70: £1.70, £5.10, £1.10; EX 148.50 Trifecta £339.20 Part won. Pool: £452.32 - 0.20 winning units..
Owner W J Odell **Bred** R W Huggins **Trained** Eastnor, H'fords
FOCUS
A decent handicap chase in which they went a particularly searching gallop.

2087 LIVE POOL INFORMATION AT TOTEPOOL.COM H'CAP HURDLE (7 hdls 2 omitted) 2m 3f
3:55 (3:55) (Class 3) (0-130,130) 4-Y-0 **£6,330** (£1,870; £935; £468; £234)

Form RPR
130/ 1 **Magnifique Etoile**[589] 4882 6-11-12 **130**.................... NoelFehily 152+
(Charlie Longsdon) *hld up wl in tch in midfield: clsd to trck ldrs bef 2 out: led wl bef last and sn readily racd clr: r.o v strly: impressive* **2/1**[1]
1/2- 2 *12* **Dolatulo (FR)**[147] 591 6-11-5 **126**.................... GavinSheehan(3) 131+
(Warren Greatrex) *chsd ldr tl led 5th: rdn and hit 2 out: drvn and hdd wl bef last: immediately brushed aside by wnr but kpt on for clr 2nd* **6/1**[2]

332/ **3** *3* **Kilmurvy (IRE)**[183] 5537 5-11-4 **125**....(p) MattGriffiths(3) 125
(Jeremy Scott) *hld up in tch in midfield: rdn and effrt jst bef 2 out: chsd ldng pair on long run between last 2: styd on same pce* **10/1**

3/0- **4** *7* **Who's Cross (IRE)**[170] 176 5-11-5 **123**.... AndrewTinkler 116
(Nicky Henderson) *in tch in midfield: effrt but outpcd by wnr on long run between last 2: plugged on to go modest 4th bef last* **10/1**

346/ **5** *2 1/4* **No Duffer**[196] 5293 6-10-4 **111**.... JakeGreenall(3) 102
(Henry Daly) *chsd ldrs: rdn and outpcd sn after 2 out: 4th and wl hld on long run between last 2: wknd bef last* **14/1**

310/ **6** *1* **Dollar Bill**[202] 5197 4-10-13 **117**....(t) TomCannon 107
(Nick Gifford) *in tch in midfield: hdwy to chse ldrs 5th: chsd ldr and rdn bef 2 out: 3rd and outpcd jst after 2 out: wknd bef last* **40/1**

042- **7** *5* **Escort'men (FR)**[13] 1889 7-10-5 **109**....(t) AidanColeman 94
(Anthony Middleton) *t.k.h: hld up in midfield: hdwy bef 2 out: rdn and no ex on long run between last 2: wknd bef last* **11/1**

411- **8** *1/2* **Alwaystheoptimist**[9] 1943 10-10-12 **123**.... RyanHatch(7) 107
(Phil Middleton) *hld up wl off the pce towards rr: clsd on long run after 5th: rdn and no hdwy on long run between last 2: wknd bef last* **10/1**

056/ **9** *16* **Touch Back (IRE)**[506] 644 7-11-11 **129**.... RichieMcLernon 97
(Jonjo O'Neill) *hld up off the pce in rr: clsd 5th: rdn and btn bef 2 out: wknd wl bef last: t.o* **25/1**

403- **10** *1* **Toubab (FR)**[13] 1889 7-11-9 **127**....[1] HarrySkelton 95
(Dan Skelton) *led tl hit 5th and hdd: lost pl qckly jst bef 2 out: sn wknd and wl bhd on long run between last 2: t.o* **22/1**

00/- **11** *1/2* **Lac Sacre (FR)**[28] 5573 4-10-8 **117**....(p) JoshHamer(5) 84
(Tony Carroll) *hld up in tch in midfield: rdn and struggling jst bef 2 out: sn btn: wknd wl bef last: t.o* **50/1**

5/5- **12** *2 1/4* **Veauce De Sivola (FR)**[138] 703 4-10-13 **117**....(t) DavidBass 82
(Nick Williams) *chsd ldrs: losing pl u.p whn mstke 2 out: wknd and bhd on long run between last 2: t.o* **12/1**

3/F- **13** *23* **Kartanian (IRE)**[3] 2020 7-9-13 **113**.... ThomasCheesman(10) 55
(Philip Hobbs) *wl in tch in midfield: pushed along and lost pl 4th: bhd bef 2 out: t.o* **7/1[3]**

14 *12* **Heurtevent (FR)**[31] 4-11-3 **121**.... LeeEdwards 51
(Tony Carroll) *in tch in midfield on outer: rdn and struggling sn after 5th: bhd next: t.o* **66/1**

5/6- **15** *60* **Captain Cardington (IRE)**[74] 1268 4-10-4 **115**.... CiaranMckee(7)
(John O'Shea) *a wl off pce in last: losing tch and appeared to p.u after 5th: continued wl t.o* **50/1**

264/ **P** **Colebrooke**[270] 3925 5-11-4 **122**....(b[1]) DominicElsworth
(Renee Robeson) *chsd ldrs: blnd 4th: lost pl jst bef 2 out: t.o and p.u last* **20/1**

4m 33.4s (1.90) **Going Correction** +0.30s/f (Yiel)
WFA 4 from 5yo+ 9lb **16** Ran SP% **130.9**
Speed ratings (Par 107): **108,102,101,98,97 97,95,95,88,87 87,86,77,72,46**
toteswingers 1&2 £4.30, 1&3 £13.80, 2&3 £17.70 CSF £14.52 CT £109.49 TOTE £3.20: £1.40, £1.90, £2.00, £2.50; EX 21.90 Trifecta £80.70 Pool: £264.62 - 2.45 winning units..
Owner Magnifique Etoile Partnership **Bred** R C Douglas And C A Vernon **Trained** Over Norton, Oxon

FOCUS
A decent handicap hurdle which produced a winner to follow closely.

2088 PLAY CAPTAIN AMERICA SLOT AT TOTEPOOL.COM NOVICES' H'CAP CHASE (15 fncs 2 omitted) 2m 7f
4:30 (4:30) (Class 5) (0-100,100) 4-Y-0+ **£2,599** (£763; £381; £190)

Form RPR

033- **1** **What A Good Night (IRE)**[29] 1675 5-10-10 **91**.... RyanHatch(7) 111+
(Nigel Twiston-Davies) *in tch in midfield: cl 5th whn mstke 12th: wnt clr w runner-up after 3 out: led wl bef last and sn drew wl clr: easily* **7/1**

P51- **2** *31* **Artic Night (FR)**[29] 1673 7-11-2 **90**....(bt) DavidEngland 78
(Nigel Twiston-Davies) *in tch in last trio: rdn and struggling after 10th: lost tch u.p on long run after next: plugged on past btn horses to go poor 2nd flat* **8/1**

0/0- **3** *2 1/4* **Pod**[179] 42 5-9-12 **75** oh2 ow1.... JamesBest(3) 61
(Caroline Keevil) *w ldrs tl dropped into midfield 5th: clsd and pressed ldrs again 11th: led after 3 out: rdn and hdd wl bef last: sn btn and tired whn j.rt and mstke last: lost 2nd flat* **25/1**

05P/ **4** *7* **Further More (IRE)**[208] 5085 6-11-2 **90**.... AidanColeman 69
(Emma Lavelle) *in tch in midfield: hdwy to join ldr and travelling strly 10th: stl upsides whn blnd bdly 3 out: nt rcvr and btn next: wknd: t.o* **6/1[3]**

3F5- **F** **Bobbisox (IRE)**[9] 1936 8-9-12 **77**.... KillianMoore(5)
(Alex Hales) *pressed ldr: mstke 7th: fell 9th* **11/1**

0/0- **P** **Bens Moor (IRE)**[29] 1672 8-10-13 **90**.... MichaelByrne(3)
(Tim Vaughan) *led: jnd and reminders 10th: drvn and hdd after 3 out: sn struggling and wknd next: t.o whn p.u last* **4/1[2]**

/33- **P** **The Goldmeister (IRE)**[26] 1701 6-10-11 **85**....(p) NoelFehily
(Charlie Longsdon) *in tch in last trio: rdn and struggling bef 10th: wknd 3 out: t.o whn p.u last* **10/3[1]**

330/ **P** **Bincombe**[230] 4683 5-11-9 **100**.... MichealNolan(3)
(Philip Hobbs) *t.k.h: chsd ldrs: clr in ldng quintet 12th: wknd rapidly bef next: t.o whn p.u bef last* **13/2**

5F4- **P** **Lucky To Be Alive (IRE)**[11] 1917 6-11-0 **88**....(p) DonalDevereux
(Peter Bowen) *nt jump wl: a in rr: in tch: lost tch u.p 10th: tailing off whn p.u 12th* **10/1**

5m 48.65s (9.45) **Going Correction** +0.525s/f (Soft) **9** Ran SP% **115.6**
Speed ratings (Par 103): **104,93,92,90, , , ,**
toteswingers 1&2 £2.30, 1&3 £13.80, 2&3 £23.10 CSF £60.88 CT £1320.74 TOTE £6.10: £1.90, £3.00, £8.00; EX 21.70 Trifecta £269.90 Part won. Pool: £359.88 - 0.10 winning units..
Owner Mr & Mrs Gordon Pink **Bred** Miss Jane Mangan **Trained** Naunton, Gloucs

FOCUS
A modest novices' handicap chase in which they went quite steadily early on. The winner was taking a big step up on his hurdling form.

2089 EXCLUSIVE TICKET GIVEAWAYS AT TOTEPOOL TWITTER MAIDEN HURDLE (DIV II) (6 hdls 2 omitted) 2m 110y
5:05 (5:05) (Class 4) 4-Y-0+ **£3,249** (£954; £477; £238)

Form RPR

4/2- **1** **Purple Bay (IRE)**[11] 1919 4-11-0 0.... DenisO'Regan 120+
(John Ferguson) *a travelling wl: hld up in tch in midfield: clsd to trck ldrs bef 2 out: led bef last: pushed along and readily asserted after last: eased cl home: comf* **15/8[1]**

5/3- **2** *1* **Dakar Run**[20] 1795 4-11-0 0.... RichieMcLernon 117+
(Jonjo O'Neill) *t.k.h: hld up in tch in midfield: clsd and chsd ldrs 2 out: drvn and effrt on long run between last 2: kpt on u.p and chsd wnr last: r.o but a hld* **7/2[3]**

3 *3 1/2* **Memory Cloth**[17] 6-10-7 0.... CraigGallagher(7) 113+
(Brian Ellison) *t.k.h: hld up in midfield: hdwy on long run after 5th: rdn to press wnr bef last: mstke last: outpcd flat* **8/1**

4 *2 1/4* **Madame De Guise (FR)**[207] 4-10-7 0.... DavidBass 104
(Nicky Henderson) *chsd ldrs tl led bef 2 out: drvn and hdd on long run between last 2: drvn and no ex bef last: plugged on same pce flat* **10/3[2]**

4/1- **5** *2 1/2* **Mrs Jordan (IRE)**[39] 1599 5-10-7 0.... AidanColeman 101
(Venetia Williams) *chsd ldrs: cl up 2 out: rdn and unable qck bnd between last 2: wknd bef last* **6/1**

0- **6** *36* **Keen Eye (IRE)**[9] 1935 4-10-9 0.... MauriceLinehan(5) 72
(Jonjo O'Neill) *chsd ldr tl bef 2 out: 6th and wknd rapidly on long run between last 2: t.o* **50/1**

335/ **7** *24* **Duke's Affair**[188] 5444 5-10-11 0.... MattGriffiths(3) 48
(Jeremy Scott) *t.k.h: hld up in rr: blnd 2nd: effrt on long run after 4th: lost tch bef next: t.o btwen last 2* **33/1**

0/ **8** *26* **Kill Van Kull (IRE)**[290] 3579 4-11-0 0.... RhysFlint 22
(Marc Barber) *hld up in last pair: rdn and hdwy to chse ldrs on long run after 5th: btn next and sn dropped out: wl t.o and mstke last* **150/1**

45- **9** *7* **Seamus Rua (IRE)**[17] 1826 5-11-0 0.... NoelFehily 15
(Charlie Longsdon) *nt a fluent: led tl bef 2 out: sn dropped out and bhd: wl t.o between last 2* **25/1**

0- **10** *18* **My Best Man**[20] 1779 7-11-0 0....(t) LeeEdwards
(Tony Carroll) *hld up in tch in last trio: rdn and struggling 4th: sn lost tch: wl t.o whn blnd last* **200/1**

4m 4.7s (8.70) **Going Correction** +0.30s/f (Yiel)
WFA 4 from 5yo+ 9lb **10** Ran SP% **115.4**
Speed ratings (Par 105): **91,90,88,87,86 69,58,46,42,34**
toteswingers 1&2 £2.30, 1&3 £2.60, 2&3 £2.60 CSF £8.51 TOTE £2.80: £1.10, £1.80, £2.30; EX 9.00 Trifecta £38.70 Pool: £1,013.29 - 19.58 winning units..
Owner Bloomfields **Bred** Darley **Trained** Cowlinge, Suffolk

FOCUS
The second division of the maiden hurdle looked the stronger of the pair on paper, but the jury is still out afterwards, although the winner looks a progressive type.

2090 FANTASY FOOTBALL BETTING AT TOTEPOOL.COM LADY RIDERS' H'CAP HURDLE (6 hdls 2 omitted) 2m 110y
5:35 (5:37) (Class 5) (0-95,95) 4-Y-0+ **£1,949** (£572; £286; £143)

Form RPR

/50- **1** **Whispering Harry**[20] 1799 4-10-4 **80**.... MissJBuck(7) 82
(Henry Oliver) *in tch in midfield: 6th and rdn and hdwy on long run between last 2: chal whn j.rt and mstke last: sn led and styd on: rdn out* **8/1[3]**

/20- **2** *2* **Lordship (IRE)**[34] 1633 9-10-7 **83**.... MissBAndrews(7) 82
(Tom Gretton) *t.k.h: hld up in rr: clsd to trck ldrs on long run after 4th: jnd ldr on long run between last 2: drvn st: led jst bef last: hdd sn after last: drvn and one pce after* **14/1**

/34- **3** *2 1/4* **Ratify**[153] 485 9-10-10 **86**.... MrsAlexDunn(7) 83
(Dai Burchell) *led: j.rt 2nd: jnd bef 2 out: clr w rival and rdn st: hdd jst bef last: wknd fnl 100yds* **7/2[2]**

454- **4** *2 3/4* **Thomas Bell (IRE)**[16] 1837 9-9-12 **70**....(p) RachaelGreen(3) 65
(John O'Shea) *hld up in tch towards rr: hdwy 4th: ev ch 2 out: drvn and outpcd on long run between last 2: hld and one pce last* **7/4[1]**

1/0- **5** *3 3/4* **Rock Peak (IRE)**[26] 1700 8-10-4 **80**....(b) MissJodieHughes(7) 70
(Bernard Llewellyn) *chsd ldrs: rdn and ev ch 2 out: no ex on long run between last: wknd bef last* **12/1**

/F4- **6** *6* **Rigid**[97] 1058 6-11-6 **94**.... MissGAndrews(5) 78
(Tony Carroll) *plld hrd early: chsd ldrs: rdn and struggling bef 2 out: wknd on long run between last 2* **12/1**

0/6- **7** *94* **Just Beware**[167] 243 11-10-8 **84**....(p) MissTWorsley(7)
(Zoe Davison) *in tch in midfield: dropped to rr and struggling after 3rd: lost tch next: t.o 2 out* **20/1**

026- **P** **Bazart**[16] 1833 11-10-13 **89**....(tp) MissLBrooke(7)
(Bernard Llewellyn) *in tch in midfield: hit 3rd: rdn and lost tch on long run after 4th: t.o whn p.u last* **9/1**

P05- **P** **Tara Warrior (IRE)**[20] 1799 7-11-4 **94**....(b) MissRPLeyshon(7)
(Tim Vaughan) *w ldr: ev ch 2 out: sn rdn and wknd on long run between last 2: wl bhd whn p.u last* **8/1[3]**

4m 9.7s (13.70) **Going Correction** +0.30s/f (Yiel)
WFA 4 from 6yo+ 9lb **9** Ran SP% **117.6**
Speed ratings (Par 103): **79,78,77,75,73 71,26, ,**
CSF £109.08 CT £466.12 TOTE £11.40: £2.40, £2.50, £1.10; EX 77.40 Trifecta £600.70 Part won. Pool: £801.00 - 0.76 winning units..
Owner R G Whitehead **Bred** S A Brookshaw **Trained** Broomhall, Worcs

FOCUS
A moderate handicap hurdle restricted to lady riders concluded proceedings, in which they went quite a steady gallop until after three out. The winner was taking a big step up.
T/Plt: £63.30 to a £1 stake. Pool: £63,296.22 - 728.96 winning units T/Qpdt: £24.40 to a £1 stake. Pool: £3,501.50 - 106.10 winning units SP

2069 AINTREE (L-H)
Sunday, October 27

OFFICIAL GOING: Good (good to soft in places on hurdle course; mildmay 6.8, hdl 6.7)
Wind: Fairly strong, half against Weather: Fine

2098 DORNAN ENGINEERING LTD INTRODUCTORY JUVENILE HURDLE (THE SUNDAY £5K BONUS RACE) (9 hdls) 2m 1f
1:00 (1:00) (Class 4) 3-Y-O **£4,548** (£1,335; £667; £333)

Form RPR

1 **Hawk High (IRE)**[30] 3-11-0 0.... DannyCook 111+
(Tim Easterby) *racd keenly: trckd ldrs: effrt 2 out: led appr last: edgd lft and drew clr run-in: r.o wl* **5/2[2]**

1- **2** *9* **Halling's Wish**[23] 1743 3-11-2 0.... JoshuaMoore(3) 107
(Gary Moore) *prom: wnt cl 2nd appr 3 out: ch whn hit 2 out: sn lost 2nd: outpcd bef last: kpt on u.p run-in: styd on to take 2nd fnl stride: no ch w wnr* **6/1[3]**

3- **3** *hd* **Sleepy Haven (IRE)**[136] 725 3-11-0 0.... SeanQuinlan 100
(Jennie Candlish) *chsd ldr: led appr 3 out: rdn and hdd bef last: outpcd by wnr early on run-in: sn no ch: ct for 2nd fnl stride* **40/1**

4- **4** *44* **Green And White (ITY)**[10] 1934 3-11-0 0.... LeeEdwards 60
(Frank Sheridan) *hld up in rr: pushed along after 6th: outpcd bef 3 out: lost tch w ldrs 2 out: t.o* **150/1**

P **Rich Forever (IRE)**[20] 3-10-11 0 JohnKington(3)
(James Bethell) *hld up: reminder after 5th: struggling after next: lost tch bef 3 out: t.o whn p.u bef last* **33/1**

P **Memberof (FR)**[45] 3-11-5 0 RobertThornton
(Alan King) *led: pushed along and hdd appr 3 out: wknd bef 2 out: eased and tailing off whn p.u bef last* **4/6**[1]

4m 14.8s (1.10) **Going Correction** +0.10s/f (Yiel) **6** Ran SP% **108.9**
Speed ratings (Par 103): **101,96,96,75,**
Tote Swingers: 1&2 £1.60, 1&3 £3.10, 2&3 £7.10 CSF £15.36 TOTE £2.80: £1.60, £2.00; EX 12.80 Trifecta £67.30 Pool: £1,545.59 - 17.21 winning units..
Owner Trevor Hemmings **Bred** Gleadhill House Stud Ltd **Trained** Great Habton, N Yorks

FOCUS
All Bends moved out 2yds from yesterday and hurdles re-sited. A modest juvenile hurdler, rated around the second.

2099 WARWICK BIFOLDING DOORS NOVICES' LIMITED H'CAP CHASE (19 fncs) 3m 1f
1:30 (1:31) (Class 3) (0-125,120) 5-Y-0+ **£6,564** (£2,104; £1,169)

Form RPR

/50- **1** **Samingarry (FR)**[14] 1887 6-10-2 106 oh1 MarkQuinlan(3) 114+
(Nigel Hawke) *hld up in tch: wnt 2nd 14th: rdn and chalng whn rdr lost iron briefly appr 3 out where j.rt: led bef 2 out where j.rt again: drew clr bef last where j.rt: styd on wl* **11/1**

0/P- **2** *10* **Abbey Storm (IRE)**[30] 1669 7-11-5 120 JasonMaguire 120
(Donald McCain) *led: nt fluent 3rd: hdd appr 2 out: rdn and unable to go w wnr bef last: no ch after* **14/1**

/21- **3** *14* **Susquehanna River (IRE)**[11] 1925 6-11-0 115 SamTwiston-Davies 106
(Nigel Twiston-Davies) *w ldr: blnd 9th: dropped off ldr sltly bef 12th: hit 13th: lost 2nd next: u.p after 15th: stl there jst bhd ldrs 3 out: wknd after 2 out: sn lft mod 3rd* **11/4**[2]

153/ **P** **Matrow's Lady (IRE)**[221] 4876 6-11-2 117 (t) NoelFehily
(Neil Mulholland) *hld up: trying to cl whn blnd 13th: bhd after: lost tch 15th: t.o whn p.u bef 3 out* **13/2**

251/ **U** **Powerful Ambition (IRE)**[203] 5205 7-11-1 116 (t) DannyCook
(Brian Ellison) *trckd ldrs tl blnd and uns rdr 6th* **3/1**[3]

442- **P** **My Mate Vinnie (IRE)**[56] 1486 6-10-11 112 (t) APMcCoy
(Jonjo O'Neill) *hld up in rr: sltly hmpd 6th: clsd 13th: trckd ldrs appr 3 out: effrt bef 2 out: hld in 3rd and outpcd by ldrs whn eased and p.u qckly on long run to last* **5/2**[1]

6m 32.0s (2.00) **Going Correction** +0.15s/f (Yiel) **6** Ran SP% **108.6**
Speed ratings: **102,98,94, ,**
Tote Swingers: 1&2 £22.30, 1&3 £22.30, 2&3 £4.60 CSF £110.57 TOTE £14.20: £4.10, £3.10; EX 147.00 Trifecta £511.60 Pool: £717.48 - 1.05 winning units..
Owner Pearce Bros 1 **Bred** Isabelle Garcon & Jean-Pierre Garcon **Trained** Stoodleigh, Devon

FOCUS
This staying novice handicap served up a proper test.

2100 PERTEMPS NETWORK H'CAP HURDLE (SERIES QUALIFIER) (7 hdls 6 omitted) 3m 110y
2:05 (2:10) (Class 2) 4-Y-0+
£11,573 (£3,418; £1,709; £854; £427; £214)

Form RPR

160/ **1** **Ely Brown (IRE)**[206] 5141 8-10-1 135 (p) CharlieDeutsch(10) 144+
(Charlie Longsdon) *mde all: mstke 4th: pushed along over 2f out on extended run-in: clr over 1f out: styd on wl* **6/5**[1]

/04- **2** *8* **Gauvain (GER)**[15] 1867 11-10-13 137 (t) RichardJohnson 138
(Philip Hobbs) *hld up in tch: wnt 2nd 5th (2 out): nt fluent 6th (last): sn w wnr: rdn and nt qckn 3f out on extended run-in: one pce after: no ch fnl f* **10/1**

640/ **3** *13* **Lovcen (GER)**[274] 3861 8-11-7 145 RobertThornton 134
(Alan King) *trckd ldrs: rdn appr 5th (2 out): sn outpcd: kpt on to take 3rd ins fnl f on extended run-in: no ch w front two* **5/1**[2]

1/0- **4** *16* **Orsippus (USA)**[126] 215 7-10-9 133 DannyCook 115+
(Michael Smith) *racd in cl 2nd: mstke and lost pl 5th (2 out): outpcd 5f out on extended run-in: no real imp after: lost 3rd ins fnl f: wknd* **10/1**

242/ **5** *33* **Burton Port (IRE)**[563] 5376 9-11-12 150 APMcCoy 95
(Jonjo O'Neill) *hld up in rr: niggled along appr 6th: outpcd after: eased whn wl btn over 2f out: t.o* **8/1**[3]

3/0- **6** *16* **First Fandango**[169] 215 6-11-1 142 (t) MichaelByrne(3) 73
(Tim Vaughan) *hld up in tch: j. slowly 2nd: pushed along and struggling bef 4th: losing tch whn blnd 6th (last): t.o after* **17/2**

543- **P** **Malin Bay (IRE)**[32] 1660 8-10-3 127 BrianHarding
(Nicky Richards) *trckd ldrs: lost pl on long run between 3rd and 4th: rdn and bhd bef 4th: t.o whn p.u bef 6th (last)* **10/1**

6m 6.8s (-9.50) **Going Correction** -0.375s/f (Good) **7** Ran SP% **111.0**
Speed ratings (Par 109): **100,97,93,88,77 72,**
Tote Swingers: 1&2 £3.10, 1&3 £2.40, 2&3 £8.70 CSF £12.78 CT £42.50 TOTE £2.20: £1.70, £4.60; EX 13.90 Trifecta £61.00 Pool: £2,553.87 - 31.38 winning tickets..
Owner Countrywide Vehicle Rentals Taxi Hire **Bred** James Meagher **Trained** Over Norton, Oxon

FOCUS
This Pertemps qualifier proved a strange event as the three hurdles in the home straight were dolled off due to low sun which meant for a very long run-in.

2101 WEATHERBYS HAMILTON INSURANCE H'CAP CHASE (FOR THE JOHN PARRETT MEMORIAL TROPHY) (12 fncs) 2m
2:40 (2:42) (Class 2) (0-145,139) 4-Y-0+
£13,763 (£4,065; £2,032; £1,016; £508; £255)

Form RPR

113/ **1** **Eastlake (IRE)**[191] 5370 7-11-8 135 APMcCoy 141+
(Jonjo O'Neill) *hld up: nt fluent 6th: hdwy after 8th: wnt 2nd 3 out: led between last 2: styd on wl and in command run-in* **11/4**[1]

125- **2** *3 1/4* **Anay Turge (FR)**[9] 1960 8-10-11 127 (t) MarkQuinlan(3) 128
(Nigel Hawke) *hld up: mstke 4th: shkn up after 7th: rdn and outpcd after 4 out: rallied between last 2: styd on run-in: tk 2nd towards fin: nt trble wnr* **9/2**[3]

/16- **3** *1/2* **Kings Grey (IRE)**[168] 249 9-11-12 139 JamesReveley 139
(Keith Reveley) *trckd ldrs: effrt to take 2nd appr last: no imp on wnr run-in: no ex and lost 2nd towards fin* **10/1**

/44- **4** *7* **Boxer Beat (IRE)**[21] 1804 6-11-5 132 (t) JamieMoore 128
(Paul W Flynn, Ire) *w ldr: led 5th: tried to slip field on bnd bef 3 out: rdn and hdd between last 2: sn btn* **12/1**

F/1- **5** *17* **Ballybriggan (IRE)**[178] 78 9-10-9 122 JasonMaguire 100
(Donald McCain) *hld up in rr: carried hd to one side: shkn up after 3 out: rdn and fnd nil after 2 out* **9/2**[3]

123- **6** *3* **Great Oak (IRE)**[24] 1731 7-11-0 127 RichardJohnson 103
(Tim Vaughan) *prom: led 4th: mstke and hdd 5th: ev ch 4 out: mstke and lost 2nd 3 out: wknd bef next* **14/1**

5/2- **7** *nk* **Stagecoach Pearl**[11] 1921 9-11-5 137 JonathanEngland(5) 112
(Sue Smith) *led: hdd 4th: remained prom: shkn up appr 8th: stmbld 4 out: wknd bef next* **3/1**[2]

3m 58.3s (-1.70) **Going Correction** +0.15s/f (Yiel) **7** Ran SP% **111.5**
Speed ratings (Par 109): **110,108,108,104,96 94,94**
Tote Swingers: 1&2 £4.40, 1&3 £4.10, 2&3 £5.50 CSF £14.96 CT £101.71 TOTE £2.90: £1.70, £2.50; EX 17.40 Trifecta £86.30 Pool: £2,664.07 - 23.14 winning tickets..
Owner John P McManus **Bred** Mrs Eleanor Hadden **Trained** Cheltenham, Gloucs

FOCUS
A fair handicap and the form should work out.

2102 MAXILEAD METALS H'CAP HURDLE (11 hdls) 2m 4f
3:15 (3:18) (Class 2) (0-145,145) 4-Y-0+
£10,635 (£3,141; £1,570; £785; £392; £197)

Form RPR

212/ **1** **Crowning Jewel**[209] 5076 7-11-1 134 JamesReveley 137
(Keith Reveley) *chsd ldr: led bef 3 out: rdn after last: hrd pressed fnl 100yds: all out* **8/1**

/14- **2** *hd* **Drum Valley**[163] 356 5-10-11 130 LeightonAspell 131
(Oliver Sherwood) *trckd ldrs: effrt appr 2 out: wnt 2nd run-in 1f out: str chal fnl 100yds: r.o: jst hld* **8/1**

1/2- **3** *1 1/2* **Uncle Jimmy (IRE)**[16] 1858 6-10-9 128 RichardJohnson 128
(Philip Hobbs) *prom: str chal fr 3 out: nt qckn run-in: styd on u.p: hld fnl 100yds* **5/1**[2]

0/ **4** *2 1/2* **Scots Gaelic (IRE)**[15] 2775 6-10-6 125 DougieCostello 123
(John Quinn) *midfield: effrt bhd ldrs 3 out: styd on u.p after last: kpt on same pce fnl 100yds* **13/2**[3]

006/ **5** *2 3/4* **Munsaab (IRE)**[153] 3882 7-10-8 127 NoelFehily 122
(Charlie Longsdon) *hld up: hdwy 8th: chsd ldrs after: rdn appr last: no ex fnl 100yds* **9/2**[1]

235- **6** *1 1/4* **Ruler Of All (IRE)**[119] 850 7-10-4 130 MrRWinks(7) 126+
(Peter Winks) *hld up: trying to make hdwy whn bmpd last: hung bdly lft fnl 150yds: kpt on: nt trble ldrs* **16/1**

1/1- **7** *6* **Party Rock (IRE)**[163] 356 6-11-12 145 SeanQuinlan 136
(Jennie Candlish) *in tch: rdn bef 2 out: no imp appr last: wl btn run-in* **10/1**

0/4- **8** *2* **Moon Dice (IRE)**[21] 1801 8-11-4 137 APMcCoy 124
(Paul W Flynn, Ire) *hld up: pushed along and wanted to lugg lft after 2 out: nt fluent last: nvr a threat* **14/1**

240- **9** *3 3/4* **Get Home Now**[8] 1972 5-10-8 127 (tp) JamieMoore 111
(Peter Bowen) *midfield: pushed along and lost pl after 8th: rdn bef 2 out: one pce bef last: no imp after* **25/1**

214- **10** *30* **Bright Abbey**[21] 1788 5-10-3 122 LucyAlexander 79
(Dianne Sayer) *led: rdn and hdd bef 3 out: wkng whn mstke 2 out* **20/1**

306/ **11** *6* **Ruacana**[206] 5135 4-11-6 139 DenisO'Regan 90
(John Ferguson) *hld up: plld to outer appr 3 out: failed to pick up: nt fluent 2 out: eased whn wl btn bef last* **9/2**[1]

4m 56.9s (-3.80) **Going Correction** +0.10s/f (Yiel)
WFA 4 from 5yo+ 10lb **11** Ran SP% **118.8**
Speed ratings (Par 109): **111,110,110,109,108 107,105,104,103,91 88**
Tote Swingers: 1&2 £10.20, 1&3 £8.30, 2&3 £12.50 CSF £71.44 CT £357.66 TOTE £10.60: £3.00, £3.10, £2.10; EX 91.60 Trifecta £1745.00 Part won. Pool: £2,326.69 - 0.75 winning units..
Owner Sir Ian Good **Bred** J Good, C Anderson And K G Reveley **Trained** Lingdale, Redcar & Cleveland

FOCUS
This was competitive and there was a cracking finish.

2103 EBF STALLIONS MATALAN "NATIONAL HUNT" NOVICES' HURDLE (QUALIFIER) (5 hdls 6 omitted) 2m 4f
3:50 (3:55) (Class 4) 4-6-Y-0 **£5,198** (£1,526; £763; £381)

Form RPR

1/ **1** **Royal Regatta (IRE)**[221] 4864 5-10-12 0 RichardJohnson 129+
(Philip Hobbs) *led after 1st: mde rest: rdn ins fnl f on extended run-in: kpt on wl towards fin* **11/4**[2]

2/1- **2** *1 1/2* **Spirit Of Shankly**[29] 1688 5-11-4 125 NoelFehily 134+
(Charlie Longsdon) *hld up: hdwy after 5th (last): wnt 2nd over 2f out on extended run-in: rdn over 1f out: kpt on and tried to chal ins fnl f: edgd lft fnl 75yds: styd on same pce cl home* **9/4**[1]

3/1- **3** *21* **Revocation**[23] 1754 5-11-4 0 PeterBuchanan 115
(Lucinda Russell) *trckd ldrs: wnt 2nd over 3f out on extended run-in: rdn and lost 2nd over 2f out: wknd over 1f out* **11/1**

115- **4** *19* **Rolling Maul (IRE)**[15] 1863 5-10-12 0 JamieMoore 92
(Peter Bowen) *in tch: rdn and outpcd after 5th (last): no imp after* **7/1**

6/3- **5** *14* **Dundee**[177] 91 5-10-12 0 RobertThornton 79
(Alan King) *hld up: rdn after 5th (last): nvr able to get on terms w ldrs: wl btn* **16/1**

102/ **6** *5* **Hellorboston (IRE)**[191] 5373 5-10-12 0 JasonMaguire 75
(Donald McCain) *led tl after 1st: remained in tch: j. slowly 3rd: sn in rr: struggling after 5th (last): wl btn* **7/2**[3]

2- **7** *13* **Wakanda (IRE)**[26] 1713 4-11-4 122 RyanMania 69
(Sue Smith) *chsd ldr: rdn and lost 2nd over 3f out on extended run-in: wknd over 2f out* **16/1**

4m 49.6s (-11.10) **Going Correction** -0.375s/f (Good) **7** Ran SP% **112.3**
Speed ratings: **107,106,98,90,84 82,77**
Tote Swingers: 1&2 £1.80, 1&3 £6.60, 2&3 £4.80 CSF £9.30 TOTE £3.50: £2.10, £1.90; EX 10.10 Trifecta £39.90 Pool: £3,717.99 - 69.73 winning units..
Owner J C Murphy & Mrs L Field **Bred** W B Mactaggart **Trained** Withycombe, Somerset

FOCUS
A good novice hurdle and it saw two useful novices come well clear on the extended run-in, in play again due to the three hurdles in the home straight being omitted due to low sun.

2104 MATALAN.CO.UK STANDARD OPEN NATIONAL HUNT FLAT RACE 2m 1f
4:20 (4:23) (Class 5) 4-6-Y-0 **£2,599** (£763; £381; £190)

Form RPR

2/ **1** **Deadly Sting (IRE)**[198] 5279 4-11-0 0 APMcCoy 115+
(Jonjo O'Neill) *in tch: rdn briefly after 6f: wnt 2nd over 5f out: led narrowly over 2f out: rdn and hdd narrowly over 1f out: carried lft ent fnl f: bmpd rival more than once clsng stages: regained ld and edgd rt towards fin* **11/8**[1]

2 *hd* **Bally Braes (IRE)**[183] 5-11-0 0 .... SamTwiston-Davies 115+
(Nigel Twiston-Davies) *in tch: travelling wl whn wnt 2nd upsides over 2f out: tk narrow ld over 1f out: edgd lft ent fnl f whn strly pressed: bmpd rival more than once clsng stages: carried rt and hdd narrowly towards fin* **10/1**

3 *38* **Sir Mangan (IRE)**[231] 5-11-0 0 .... JasonMaguire 81
(Donald McCain) *led: rdn and hdd over 2f out: wknd over 1f out* **11/2**

21/ 4 *23* **Pair Of Jacks (IRE)**[313] [3126] 5-11-7 0 .... BrianHughes 67
(Malcolm Jefferson) *racd keenly: prom: chsd ldr after 4f tl 6f out: rdn and wknd 4f out* **7/2**[2]

214- 5 *2 ¾* **Factor Fifty (IRE)**[21] [1792] 4-11-2 0 .... AdamNicol(5) 64
(Philip Kirby) *chsd ldr tl after 4f: remained prom: rdn over 4f out: sn outpcd: wknd 2f out* **5/1**[3]

64/ 6 *58* **Hope For Glory**[237] [4572] 4-11-0 0 .... RobertThornton 5
(Jason Ward) *hld up: pushed along over 6f out: lost tch 5f out: eased over 2f out: t.o* **66/1**

7 *67* **The Perfect Crime (IRE)** 4-11-0 0 .... RichardJohnson
(Ian Williams) *hld up: pushed along 8f out: lost tch 6f out: t.o* **16/1**

4m 7.4s **Going Correction** +0.10s/f (Yiel)
WFA 4 from 5yo+ 9lb **7** Ran SP% **112.8**
Speed ratings: **104,103,86,75,73 46,15**
Tote Swingers: 1&2 £4.30, 1&3 £3.10, 2&3 £7.20 CSF £16.25 TOTE £2.10: £1.40, £3.20; EX 15.20 Trifecta £76.80 Pool: £1,875.07 - 18.30 winning units..
Owner Maxilead Limited **Bred** Michael Shanahan **Trained** Cheltenham, Gloucs

FOCUS
The front pair dominated the business end of this interesting bumper and it saw another thrilling finish.
T/Plt: £1,540.30 to a £1 stake. Pool: £97,271.03 - 46.10 winning tickets. T/Qpdt: £13.40 to a £1 stake. Pool: £10,069.85 - 555.31 winning tickets. DO

1941 WINCANTON (R-H)

Sunday, October 27

OFFICIAL GOING: Good (good to soft in places; chs 8.1, hdl 8.3)
Wind: very strong against Weather: overcast

2105 BLACKMORE BUILDING CONTRACTORS H'CAP HURDLE (11 hdls) 2m 6f
1:15 (1:15) (Class 4) (0-110,110) 4-Y-0+ **£3,249** (£954; £477; £238)

Form RPR

/6F- 1 **Invicta Lake (IRE)**[23] [1745] 6-11-7 **105** ....(p) PaddyBrennan 111+
(Suzy Smith) *hld up towards rr: hdwy after 3 out to trck ldrs next: led last: kpt on wl: rdn out* **10/1**

310- 2 *1 ½* **Bold Raider (IRE)**[26] [1707] 6-10-11 **105** .... TommieMO'Brien(10) 110
(Jonjo O'Neill) *mid-div: hdwy 3 out: led 2 out: sn rdn: hdd last: kpt on but no ex* **10/1**

0/3- 3 *5* **Call A Truce (IRE)**[165] [318] 5-11-7 **105** .... DarylJacob 105
(Ben Case) *mid-div: hdwy after 7th: chal 2 out: sn rdn: styd on same pce* **8/1**[3]

40F/ 4 *1* **Young Hurricane (IRE)**[250] [4301] 7-11-5 **110** .... ChristopherWard(7) 109
(Dr Richard Newland) *mid-div: hdwy after 3 out: rdn bef next: styd on to go 4th run-in* **17/2**

P/0- 5 *4* **Rigolo Ville (FR)**[44] [1580] 8-10-13 **97** .... JackDoyle 94
(Richard Hobson) *mid-div: rdn after 8th: styd on same pce fr 2 out* **14/1**

414- 6 *2* **Amuse Me**[29] [1687] 7-11-9 **107** .... RichieMcLernon 101
(Jonjo O'Neill) *prom: mstke 3 out: ev ch 2 out: sn rdn: wknd last* **20/1**

060/ 7 *¾* **Regal Flow**[369] [1974] 6-11-0 **105** .... MrLDrowne(7) 98
(Caroline Keevil) *trckd ldrs: prom 5th: rdn and ev ch 2 out: fdd appr last* **25/1**

515/ 8 *2* **Torrential Raine**[189] [5440] 5-11-7 **105** .... NickScholfield 98
(Michael Blake) *trckd ldrs tl after 5th: struggling towards rr after: wnt lft 2 out: styng on but no ch whn blnd last* **20/1**

530/ 9 *5* **American Life (FR)**[194] [5328] 6-11-2 **105** ....(tp) JamesBanks(5) 93
(Anthony Middleton) *mid-div tl after 6th: struggling after: nvr bk on terms* **14/1**

040- 10 *6* **Sonoftheking (IRE)**[17] [1828] 5-11-2 **100** .... TomO'Brien 81
(Philip Hobbs) *towards rr: reminders after 4th: nvr a factor* **20/1**

000- 11 *17* **Until The Man (IRE)**[110] [927] 6-10-0 **84** oh7 ....(v¹) MarcGoldstein 50
(Natalie Lloyd-Beavis) *hld up towards rr: hdwy after 5th: rdn after 3 out: wknd 2 out: t.o* **100/1**

3/5- 12 *hd* **Brockwell Park**[171] [179] 6-11-5 **103** .... LiamHeard 69
(Jeremy Scott) *trckd ldrs: led 6th: rdn and hdd appr 2 out: wknd qckly: t.o* **25/1**

F/2- 13 *1* **Key To Milan**[17] [1833] 7-10-11 **98** ....(tp) GilesHawkins(3) 63
(Chris Down) *led tl nt fluent 6th: chsd ldrs tl wknd appr 2 out where hmpd: t.o* **7/1**[2]

536/ 14 *10* **Bois Des Aigles (FR)**[196] [5317] 4-11-7 **105** .... TomScudamore 61
(David Pipe) *trckd ldrs: rdn 2 out: qckly btn: blnd last: eased* **6/1**[1]

3/1- 15 *2 ¾* **Kentford Legend**[173] [156] 6-11-6 **104** .... AndrewThornton 57
(Seamus Mullins) *mid-div: pushed along after 6th: wknd after 3 out: t.o* **12/1**

U0P- 16 *67* **Kilcolman Wizard (IRE)**[18] [1824] 7-10-7 **91** .... ConorO'Farrell
(Liam Corcoran) *a bhd: t.o fr 3 out* **66/1**

544/ U **Old Way (IRE)**[196] [5321] 7-11-2 **100** .... AidanColeman
(Venetia Williams) *mid-div tl blnd and uns rdr 3 out* **10/1**

5m 6.6s (-19.90) **Going Correction** -0.80s/f (Firm)
WFA 4 from 5yo+ 10lb **17** Ran SP% **121.2**
Speed ratings (Par 105): **104,103,101,101,99 99,98,98,96,94 87,87,87,83,82 58,**
Tote Swingers: 1&2 £19.10, 1&3 £16.50, 2&3 £29.90 CSF £96.38 CT £852.82 TOTE £12.70: £3.40, £2.70, £3.10, £1.70; EX 119.80 Trifecta £405.40 Part won. Pool: £540.56 - 0.34 winning units..
Owner Bernard & Jan Wolford **Bred** Patrick Doyle **Trained** Lewes, E Sussex

FOCUS
All Bends in normal position.After 14mm of overnight rain the ground had eased to good, good to soft in places. The general opinion after riding in the opener was that the conditions were riding on the easy side of good. A modest handicap hurdle run at a solid pace and they finished well strung out.

2106 COUNTRYSIDE ALLIANCE NOVICES' HURDLE (11 hdls) 2m 6f
1:45 (1:45) (Class 4) 4-Y-0+ **£3,249** (£954; £477; £238)

Form RPR

311/ 1 **Southfield Theatre (IRE)**[196] [5318] 5-11-7 132 .... HarryDerham(5) 142+
(Paul Nicholls) *trckd ldrs: pressed ldr 3 out: led 2 out: rdn clr: mstke last: comf* **4/5**[1]

2 *5* **Padre Tito (IRE)**[287] 5-10-9 0 .... GavinSheehan(3) 120+
(Emma Lavelle) *trckd ldr: j.lft thrght: blnd 6th: ch 2 out: sn rdn and hld by wnr: styd on same pce* **5/1**[2]

133/ 3 *18* **Ballyallia Man (IRE)**[232] [4668] 8-10-12 0 ....(t) PaddyBrennan 107
(Tom George) *led: rdn whn pressed 3 out: hdd next: styd on same pce* **6/1**[3]

1/2- 4 *7* **Forresters Folly**[178] [80] 7-11-5 124 ....(p) WayneHutchinson 106
(Alan King) *trckd ldrs: blnd 7th: rdn after 3 out: grad fdd fr next: nt fluent last* **6/1**[3]

0/0- 5 *4 ½* **Merchant Of Milan**[26] [1712] 5-10-12 0 .... BrendanPowell 92
(Brendan Powell) *trckd ldr tl after 6th: rdn after 3 out: wknd bef next* **66/1**

0/ 6 *12* **Gilanto (IRE)**[199] [5263] 6-10-12 0 .... ConorO'Farrell 81
(Michael Blake) *nvr travelling and rarely fluent in rr: wknd after 3 out* **100/1**

7 *47* **Tresor De La Vie (FR)**[147] 6-10-12 0 .... JackDoyle 39
(Victor Dartnall) *trckd ldrs: rdn after 8th: wknd after 3 out: t.o* **16/1**

5m 5.1s (-21.40) **Going Correction** -0.80s/f (Firm) **7** Ran SP% **109.2**
Speed ratings (Par 105): **106,104,97,95,93 89,72**
Tote Swingers: 1&2 £1.10, 1&3 £1.10, 2&3 £2.60 CSF £4.77 TOTE £2.00: £1.60, £2.50; EX 4.90 Trifecta £21.80 Pool: £848.11 - 29.09 winning units..
Owner Mrs Angela Yeoman **Bred** Mrs Angela Yeoman **Trained** Ditcheat, Somerset

FOCUS
Little depth to this novices' hurdle and the odds-on favourite made the most of a good opportunity.

2107 SUPPORT WORLD HORSE WELFARE BY REHOMING NOVICES' LIMITED H'CAP CHASE (16 fncs 1 omitted) 2m 5f
2:20 (2:20) (Class 3) (0-125,124) 4-Y-0+ **£6,498** (£1,908; £954; £477)

Form RPR

22/- 1 **Deciding Moment (IRE)**[226] [4775] 7-10-7 **112** ....(t) MarkGrant 120+
(Ben De Haan) *hld up towards rr: stdy prog fr 9th: chal 3 out: rdn to ld whn wnt sltly rt 2 out: styd on strly* **25/1**

110- 2 *5* **Cinevator (IRE)**[26] [1709] 6-11-2 **124** ....(p) JamesBest(3) 127
(Caroline Keevil) *led tl 3rd: chsd ldrs: lft disputing whn hmpd 11th: rdn and ev ch fr 3 out tl bef last: styd on same pce* **50/1**

/22- 3 *2* **Silver Commander**[17] [1831] 6-11-5 **124** ....(t) JackDoyle 126
(Victor Dartnall) *mid-div: hdwy after 11th: led 3 out: rdn and hdd 2 out: sn hld: styd on same pce* **12/1**

0- 4 *18* **Ultragold (FR)**[9] [1957] 5-11-3 **122** .... JoeTizzard 107
(Colin Tizzard) *hld up towards rr: hdwy after 6th: lft disputing ld whn v bdly hmpd 11th: hdd by-passing omitted next: wknd 3 out: no ch whn lft 5th 2 out: wnt modest 4th towards fin* **12/1**

03/ 5 *½* **Mister Snowball (FR)**[379] [1836] 6-10-12 **117** .... TomScudamore 101
(Chris Down) *mid-div: hmpd 4th: hdwy fr 6th: lft disputing ld 11th: rdn and hdd whn hit 3 out: wknd after 2 out: lost modest 4th nring fin* **16/1**

U/1- 6 *16* **Kings Lodge**[23] [1744] 7-11-5 **124** .... AndrewTinkler 99
(Nicky Henderson) *trckd ldr tl 3rd: mid-div whn hmpd 4th: reminders after next: towards rr whn hmpd on bnd bef 9th: sn bhd: t.o* **8/1**

5/2- 7 *3 ½* **Phone Home (IRE)**[180] [38] 6-10-10 **118** .... GavinSheehan(3) 85
(Nick Mitchell) *sn detached: a bhd: t.o* **25/1**

142- F **Compton Blue**[53] [1498] 7-11-1 **120** ....(b) GerardTumelty
(Alan King) *mid-div whn fell 5th* **33/1**

/20- F **Coole River (IRE)**[148] [587] 9-11-4 **123** .... AidanColeman
(Emma Lavelle) *mid-div whn fell 4th* **6/1**[2]

415/ S **Sergeant Dick (IRE)**[193] [5354] 8-11-3 **122** ....(t) FelixDeGiles
(Barry Brennan) *prom: led 5th tl slipped up on bnd bef 9th* **25/1**

00P- P **Captain Sully (IRE)**[21] [1783] 8-10-5 **110** oh1 .... LiamTreadwell
(Jim Wilson) *hld up towards rr: hmpd 5th: hdwy 13th: rdn whn mstke 4 out: sn wknd: t.o whn p.u bef last* **100/1**

/04- F **Polisky (FR)**[26] [1709] 6-11-1 **120** ....(tp) DarylJacob 114
(Paul Nicholls) *mid-div: wnt bdly lft and hmpd 4th: trckd ldrs 9th tl v bdly hmpd and lost pl 11th: rdn after 4 out: styng on at same pce in disp 4th whn fell 2 out* **7/1**[3]

211/ P **Decimus (IRE)**[211] [5019] 6-11-0 **119** .... NickScholfield
(Jeremy Scott) *a bhd: t.o 4 out: p.u bef last* **12/1**

315/ U **Midnight Oscar (IRE)**[262] [4076] 6-11-3 **122** .... TimmyMurphy
(Kim Bailey) *hld up bhd: veered v bdly lft and uns rdr 5th* **5/1**[1]

430/ U **Hot Whiskey (IRE)**[249] [4319] 5-10-8 **113** .... WayneHutchinson
(Alan King) *prom: led 3rd tl 5th: prom: lft in ld on bnd bef 9th: blnd bdly and uns rdr 11th* **5/1**[1]

/00- P **Darkestbeforedawn (IRE)**[16] [1857] 6-10-6 **111** .... IanPopham
(Caroline Keevil) *mid-div: towards rr and struggling 7th: wkng whn p.u bef 3 out* **25/1**

5m 10.9s (-14.30) **Going Correction** -0.675s/f (Firm) **16** Ran SP% **121.5**
Speed ratings (Par 107): **100,98,97,90,90 84,82,, , ,,,,**
Tote Swingers: 1&2 £43.90 CSF £870.77 CT £14638.18 TOTE £34.60: £6.20, £7.60, £2.70, £3.30; EX 1494.10 TRIFECTA Not won..
Owner William A Tyrer **Bred** John O'Brien **Trained** Lambourn, Berks

FOCUS
A competitive novices' handicap chase in which several lost their chance with jumping errors, and in a dramatic race only seven runners finished.

2108 F J CHALKE DESERT ORCHID H'CAP CHASE (FOR THE DESERT ORCHID SILVER CUP) (SUNDAY £5K BONUS RACE) (22 fncs) 3m 3f 110y
2:55 (2:56) (Class 3) (0-140,136) 4-Y-0+ **£9,495** (£2,805; £1,402; £702; £351)

F11- 1 **Standing Ovation (IRE)**[10] [1942] 6-10-0 **110** oh2 ....(tp) ConorO'Farrell 127+
(David Pipe) *j.w: trckd ldr: led 18th: rdn after 4 out: jnd next: styd on strly fr last: asserting nr fin: drvn out* **5/1**[2]

356/ 2 *1 ¾* **Highland Lodge (IRE)**[228] [4732] 7-11-12 **136** .... AidanColeman 150+
(Emma Lavelle) *led tl 18th: sn rdn to press wnr: bk upsides 3 out but hung bdly lft after: ev ch last: styd on but no ex* **6/4**[1]

/23- 3 *28* **Inside Dealer (IRE)**[18] [1815] 9-11-0 **124** ....(tp) JoeTizzard 112
(Colin Tizzard) *trckd ldrs: lft 3rd 17th: sn rdn: one pce and no ch w ldng pair fr after 4 out* **20/1**

/12- 4 *2 ¼* **Seven Woods (IRE)**[150] [553] 7-11-5 **129** ....(t) PaddyBrennan 117
(Tom George) *mid-div: hit 12th: lft disputing 4th 17th: sn rdn: wl hld fr after 4 out* **6/1**[3]

0/P- 5 *2 ½* **Any Currency (IRE)**[165] [317] 10-11-6 **130** ....(e) IanPopham 114
(Martin Keighley) *chsd ldr tl 9th: sn pushed along to hold pl: rdn after 14th: plugged on but no ch fr after 4 out* **14/1**

F/1- 6 *43* **Top Smart**[180] [39] 7-11-2 **126** .... DominicElsworth 71
(Seamus Mullins) *nt fluent 9th: struggling 15th: a towards rr: t.o after 4 out* **16/1**

151/ P **Clash Duff (IRE)**[600] [4685] 8-11-4 **128** ....(p) NickScholfield
(Jeremy Scott) *a towards rr: struggling and reminders 13th: lost tch after next: p.u bef 17th* **33/1**

6/5- P **Brackloon High (IRE)**[23] [1747] 8-11-9 **133** .... BrendanPowell
(Brendan Powell) *mid-div: rdn after 15th: wknd 4 out: p.u bef last* **14/1**

211/ **P** **The Clyda Rover (IRE)**[194] 5329 9-10-1 **111** PaulMoloney
(Helen Nelmes) *hld up towards rr: stmbld bdly 1st: detached 6th: t.o 13th: p.u bef 17th* **25/1**

P02/ **U** **Swincombe Rock**[355] 2249 8-11-9 **133** TomScudamore
(David Bridgwater) *hld up towards rr: rdn along and no imp whn blnd and uns rdr 18th* **22/1**

1/F- **F** **Buck's Bond (FR)**[171] 190 7-10-13 **123** (tp) RyanMahon
(Paul Nicholls) *trckd ldrs: blnd 2nd: pckd 11th: 3rd whn fell 17th* **14/1**

1/4- **P** **Savant Bleu (FR)**[18] 1815 7-11-3 **127** TimmyMurphy
(Kim Bailey) *hld up towards rr: stmbld 1st: hdwy after 13th: lft disputing 4th 17th: rdn after 3 out: sn hld: lost action whn p.u bef 2 out: dismntd* **20/1**

6m 42.8s (-25.40) **Going Correction** -0.675s/f (Firm) **12** Ran SP% **117.5**
Speed ratings (Par 107): **109,108,100,99,99 86,,,,,**
Tote Swingers: 1&2 £1.90, 1&3 £55.00, 2&3 £39.30 CSF £12.26 CT £139.89 TOTE £6.40: £2.00, £1.60, £3.80; EX 15.20 Trifecta £959.90 Part won. Pool: £1,279.88 - 0.61 winning units..
Owner The Bravo Partnership **Bred** Patrick McGrath **Trained** Nicholashayne, Devon

FOCUS
What had looked a competitive staying chase on paper developed into a two-horse race before the home turn, but it still proved a terrific spectacle with the first two giving their all.

2109 DOMINIC BAKER MEMORIAL "NATIONAL HUNT" NOVICES' HURDLE (8 hdls) 2m
3:30 (3:32) (Class 4) 4-Y-0+ **£5,198** (£1,526; £763; £381)

Form RPR

60/ **1** **Minellaforleisure (IRE)**[197] 5287 5-10-12 0 PaddyBrennan 118+
(Alex Hales) *trckd ldrs: nt fluent 2 out: rdn to ld bef last: r.o strly to draw readily clr* **17/2**[3]

0/ **2** *7* **Toowoomba (IRE)**[234] 4621 5-10-12 0 TomO'Brien 108
(Philip Hobbs) *trckd ldrs: pushed along in 4th 2 out: swtchd rt bef last: rdn and styd on to go 2nd run-in: no ch w wnr* **7/1**[2]

246/ **3** *1* **Berkeley Avenue**[201] 5230 4-10-9 0 GavinSheehan(3) 107
(Warren Greatrex) *led tl 2nd: disp fr next: rdn appr 2 out: hdd between last 2: sn outpcd by wnr: no ex whn lost 2nd run-in* **33/1**

4 *1 ½* **Vicente (FR)**[231] 4-10-12 0 RyanMahon 106
(Paul Nicholls) *awkward: j.lft thrght: led 2nd: disp fr next: rdn after 2 out: sn hdd: sn outpcd by wnr: no ex run-in* **1/3**[1]

0/0- **5** *10* **Rule Of Thumb**[23] 1749 5-10-12 0 (t) NickScholfield 95
(Paul Henderson) *hld up last: rdn in tch bef 2 out: nvr gng pce to threaten: wknd jst bef last* **16/1**

0- **6** *2 ¾* **Henwood (IRE)**[151] 544 5-10-12 0 JoeTizzard 92
(Colin Tizzard) *in tch: rdn after 5th: nvr gng pce to get on terms: wknd after 2 out* **12/1**

3m 43.1s (-5.80) **Going Correction** -0.80s/f (Firm)
WFA 4 from 5yo 9lb **6** Ran SP% **114.6**
Speed ratings (Par 105): **82,78,78,77,72 70**
Tote Swingers: 1&2 £3.50, 1&3 £2.10, 2&3 £7.50 CSF £62.25 TOTE £8.60: £3.10, £2.60; EX 67.80 Trifecta £280.40 Pool: £2,553.97 - 6.83 winning units..
Owner The Patient Partnership **Bred** Ballina Stud Ltd **Trained** Edgcote, Northants

FOCUS
An interesting novice event in which the gallop was steady and it turned into a sprint up the home straight. The favourite disappointed, but nothing can be taken away from the winner who looks a good prospect.

2110 COUNTRYSIDE ALLIANCE H'CAP CHASE (21 fncs) 3m 1f 110y
4:05 (4:05) (Class 4) (0-110,109) 4-Y-0+ **£3,898** (£1,144; £572; £286)

Form RPR

5/1- **1** **Franklin Roosevelt (IRE)**[168] 242 7-11-12 **109** (b) TomScudamore 127+
(David Pipe) *trckd ldrs: jnd ldrs 15th: led after next: drawing clr whn clever 4 out: in command after: comf* **7/2**[3]

1F2- **2** *6* **Jayandbee (IRE)**[16] 1859 6-11-2 **99** (p) TomO'Brien 105
(Philip Hobbs) *disp ld tl outrt ldr after 13th: hdd after 16th: rdn to chse wnr after next: hld fr 4 out: styd on same pce* **5/2**[2]

PUP/ **3** *1 ¼* **Global Warming (IRE)**[208] 5104 9-10-12 **98** GavinSheehan(3) 104
(Emma Lavelle) *j.lft at times: prom on outer: trckd ldrs fr 4th: slipped on bnd bef 13th: rdn to dispute 2nd after 17th: hld fr 4 out: styd on same pce* **2/1**[1]

/PP- **4** *19* **Hinton Indiana**[12] 1914 8-9-11 **85** (tp) NicodeBoinville(5) 73
(Adrian Wintle) *trckd ldrs: rdn after 17th: sn btn* **12/1**

12/- **5** *65* **Royal Chatelier (FR)**[189] 5443 8-11-2 **102** MichealNolan(3) 31
(Michael Blake) *disp ld tl pushed along after 13th: sn rdn in last pair: mstke 16th: sn wknd: t.o 4 out* **10/1**

643- **P** **Redlynch Rock (IRE)**[17] 1831 5-11-1 **98** SamJones
(Bob Buckler) *trckd ldrs: nt fluent 7th: pushed along fr 11th: hit 16th: awkward next: sn wknd: t.o whn p.u bef 3 out* **9/1**

6m 30.4s (-9.10) **Going Correction** -0.675s/f (Firm) **6** Ran SP% **110.9**
Speed ratings (Par 105): **87,85,84,78,58**
Tote Swingers: 1&2 £1.40, 1&3 £2.00, 2&3 £1.00 CSF £12.75 CT £19.89 TOTE £2.90: £1.50, £2.20; EX 12.60 Trifecta £32.20 Pool: £1,750.88 - 40.67 winning units..
Owner Malcolm C Denmark **Bred** Kenneth Parkhill **Trained** Nicholashayne, Devon

FOCUS
A fair handicap chase that was dominated by the winner.

2111 COUNTRYSIDE ALLIANCE H'CAP HURDLE (8 hdls) 2m
4:35 (4:40) (Class 4) (0-120,120) 4-Y-0+ **£3,898** (£1,144; £572; £286)

Form RPR

001- **1** **Theatrelands**[18] 1822 5-10-12 **106** (p) AidanColeman 110
(Charlie Longsdon) *mid-div: pushed along and hdwy after 3 out: rdn upsides last: edgd ahd run-in: hld on: all out* **9/2**[1]

2P/ **2** *hd* **Maxi Chop (FR)**[253] 4259 5-11-7 **120** HarryDerham(5) 124
(Paul Nicholls) *trckd ldr: led 5th: jnd 3 out: sltly hmpd whn jst clr again after 3 out: rdn 2 out: narrowly hdd run-in: kpt on wl* **7/1**

U16/ **3** *2 ¼* **Chemistry Master**[208] 5103 5-11-2 **120** (t) MartinMcIntyre(10) 122
(Harry Fry) *trckd ldr tl 3 out: rdn to chse ldrs bef 2 out: kpt on same pce* **8/1**

322/ **4** *8* **Umberto D'Olivate (FR)**[196] 5320 5-11-2 **110** FelixDeGiles 107
(Robert Walford) *trckd ldrs: disputing whn slipped on bnd after 3 out: rdn to chse ldrs bef next: sn outpcd* **11/2**[2]

/04- **5** *¾* **Ladies Dancing**[17] 1828 7-11-4 **112** JamesDavies 106
(Chris Down) *mid-div: hdwy 5th: disp 3rd after next: rdn bef 2 out: sn outpcd* **14/1**

/63- **6** *2 ¾* **Bold Cuffs**[17] 1829 4-10-8 **102** JoeTizzard 96
(Colin Tizzard) *hld up towards rr: hdwy whn pckd 4th: rdn after 3 out: nvr gng pce to get involved* **8/1**

P/F- **7** *nk* **Sleeping City (FR)**[176] 116 6-11-5 **113** JackDoyle 104
(Victor Dartnall) *hld up towards rr: smooth hdwy after 3 out: ev ch 2 out: sn rdn: fnd nil: wknd last* **13/2**[3]

355/ **8** *11* **Ultravox (USA)**[424] 1410 6-11-2 **110** (t) NickScholfield 91
(Jeremy Scott) *led tl 5th: sn rdn: wknd after 3 out* **18/1**

P14/ **9** *8* **Beside The Fire**[356] 2234 8-11-5 **120** MrMLegg(7) 94
(Colin Tizzard) *sn outpcd in rr: nvr any danger* **10/1**

0/0- **10** *11* **Soliwery (FR)**[21] 1794 5-11-10 **118** TomScudamore 82
(David Pipe) *hld up towards rr of mid-div: rdn after 3 out: sn wknd* **16/1**

3m 36.4s (-12.50) **Going Correction** -0.80s/f (Firm)
WFA 4 from 5yo+ 9lb **10** Ran SP% **108.5**
Speed ratings (Par 105): **99,98,97,93,93 92,91,86,82,76**
Tote Swingers: 1&2 £5.00, 1&3 £6.30, 2&3 £10.60 CSF £30.81 CT £180.89 TOTE £4.10: £1.40, £2.70, £3.00; EX 30.40 Trifecta £182.90 Pool: £1,390.69 - 5.70 winning units..
Owner N Davies & S Crowley **Bred** Juddmonte Farms Ltd **Trained** Over Norton, Oxon
■ Looking Hopeful was withdrawn. Rule 4 applies to all bets. Deduction - 10p in the pound.

FOCUS
This looked a fair handicap hurdle.
T/Jkpt: Not won. T/Plt: £970.00 to a £1 stake. Pool: £82,172.05 - 61.84 winning tickets. T/Qpdt: £179.90 to a £1 stake. Pool: £7,029.42 - 28.90 winning tickets. TM

2112 - 2115a (Foreign Racing) - See Raceform Interactive

1568 GALWAY (R-H)
Sunday, October 27

OFFICIAL GOING: Heavy

2116a FABER AUDIOVISUALS BALLYBRIT NOVICE CHASE (GRADE 3) (12 fncs) 2m 1f
3:35 (3:35) 4-Y-0+ **£15,853** (£4,634; £2,195; £731)

RPR

1 **Shrapnel (IRE)**[15] 1879 7-11-1 (t) DavyRussell 140+
(Gordon Elliott, Ire) *trckd ldr tl disp fr 5th: hdd fr next tl led after 8th: brought to nrside into st gng best and kpt on wl under hands and heels: comf* **5/4**[1]

2 *2 ½* **Clar Na Mionn (IRE)**[21] 1804 6-11-1 APHeskin 136
(V T O'Brien, Ire) *chsd ldrs in 3rd: tk clsr order fr 9th: rdn in 3rd fr last and kpt on wl u.p into 2nd nr fin: nt trble wnr* **11/4**[2]

3 *4* **Six Stone Ned (IRE)**[10] 1950 7-11-1 130 (t) BryanCooper 132
(Noel Meade, Ire) *led tl jnd fr 5th: regained advantage fr next tl hdd after 8th and dropped to 3rd: rdn in 2nd fr last and no imp on wnr u.p into st: dropped to 3rd nr fin* **4/1**[3]

4 *37* **Shadow Eile (IRE)**[27] 1702 8-10-8 AndrewJMcNamara 88
(Mrs D A Love, Ire) *w.w in rr: tk clsr order in 4th fr last: sn pushed along and no imp on ldrs into st: wknd* **5/1**

5 *47* **Ted Dolly (IRE)**[21] 1803 9-11-1 121 DJCasey 48
(Edward U Hales, Ire) *chsd ldrs in 4th: stl in tch whn pckd bdly last: no ex after and sn eased* **20/1**

(24.50) **5** Ran SP% **112.5**
CSF £5.42 TOTE £1.90: £1.10, £1.90; DF 4.00 Trifecta £9.40.
Owner Gigginstown House Stud **Bred** Aaron Metcalfe **Trained** Trim, Co Meath

FOCUS
The winner improved from his winning chasing debut.

2117 - 2122a (Foreign Racing) - See Raceform Interactive

2091 WEXFORD (R-H)
Sunday, October 27

OFFICIAL GOING: Soft (yielding in places)

2123a M.W. HICKEY MEMORIAL CHASE (LISTED RACE) (13 fncs) 2m 6f
3:20 (3:20) 5-Y-0+ **£13,739** (£4,016; £1,902; £634)

RPR

1 **Double Seven (IRE)**[14] 1897 7-11-5 146 (tp) MarkWalsh 135+
(Martin Brassil, Ire) *chsd ldrs in 3rd tl tk clsr order 6 out: prog into 2nd after 2 out: sn pressed ldr and led appr last: pushed clr run-in* **5/4**[1]

2 *5 ½* **Ballinahow Lady (IRE)**[184] 5560 8-11-3 118 JohnCullen 129
(David M O'Brien, Ire) *led and clr tl advantage reduced 5 out: pressed after 2 out and hdd appr last where mstke: sn no ex w wnr* **16/1**

3 *3 ¾* **Sweeney Tunes**[181] 5559 7-11-10 140 ACLynch 130
(Paul Nolan, Ire) *chsd ldr in 2nd: clsd 5 out: pressed ldr whn mstke 2 out: sn pushed along and no imp on principals bef last* **5/2**[2]

4 *2 ½* **Laganbank (IRE)**[22] 1776 7-11-10 143 RWalsh 128
(W P Mullins, Ire) *hld up in rr tl prog 5 out into 4th: no imp on ldrs after 2 out: kpt on one pce* **4/1**[3]

5 *21* **Theroadtocroker (IRE)**[103] 1004 9-11-1 (t) MPFogarty 98
(Denis Paul Murphy, Ire) *a towards rr: no threat bef 3 out* **50/1**

6 *18* **Carrig Millie (IRE)**[183] 5579 8-11-3 124 BarryGeraghty 82
(Michael Cullen, Ire) *w.w: no imp bef 4 out and dropped to rr* **5/1**

5m 48.4s (348.40) **6** Ran SP% **117.5**
CSF £20.14 TOTE £1.70: £1.10, £4.20; DF 30.70 Trifecta £58.60.
Owner John P McManus **Bred** M Doran **Trained** Dunmurray, Co Kildare

FOCUS
This was quite an interesting chase in which the winner tried to avoid the worst of the ground. He didn't have to be at his best to win.

2124 - 2125a (Foreign Racing) - See Raceform Interactive

1727 BANGOR-ON-DEE (L-H)
Monday, October 28

2126 Meeting Abandoned - Waterlogged

2136 - 2140a (Foreign Racing) - See Raceform Interactive

[1999]NAAS (L-H)
Monday, October 28

OFFICIAL GOING: Yielding to soft

2141a POPLAR SQUARE CHASE (GRADE 3) (10 fncs) 2m
1:45 (1:45) 5-Y-O+ **£14,532** (£4,247; £2,012; £670)

RPR
1 **Twinlight (FR)**[186] 5527 6-11-10 153 .... RWalsh 159+
(W P Mullins, Ire) *sn pressed ldr in 2nd: kpt wd and crossed to stands' side bef 2 out: sn led: readily drew clr run-in* **11/4**[2]
2 *7* **Oscars Well (IRE)**[186] 5531 8-11-5 148 .... BarryGeraghty 146
(Mrs John Harrington, Ire) *chsd ldrs in 3rd: almost on terms appr 2 out: sn wnt 2nd: no match for wnr run-in* **11/8**[1]
3 *6* **Realt Mor (IRE)**[186] 5531 8-11-12 150 .... DavyRussell 147
(Gordon Elliott, Ire) *lft in front at 1st: led tl pressed after 3 out: hdd and dropped to 3rd after next: no ex and wknd run-in* **5/1**[3]
4 *19* **Alderwood (IRE)**[186] 5531 9-11-5 149 .... MarkWalsh 125
(Thomas Mullins, Ire) *hld up in rr whn mstke 1st: j.big 2nd and nt fluent 3rd: pushed along after 3 out: no imp whn lft 4th and hmpd 2 out* **6/1**
U **Dylan Ross (IRE)**[78] 1244 7-11-1 136 .... RobbiePower
(Noel Meade, Ire) *w.w: travelled wl to cl on ldrs in 4th whn blnd bdly and uns rdr 2 out* **25/1**
U **Special Tiara**[186] 5531 6-11-12 149 .... BryanCooper
(Henry De Bromhead, Ire) *led whn blnd: uns rdr 1st* **7/1**

4m 2.5s (-20.80) **6 Ran SP% 116.1**
CSF £7.68 TOTE £3.60: £2.50, £1.02; DF 7.40 Trifecta £45.30.
Owner M L Bloodstock Ltd **Bred** M L Bloodstock Limited **Trained** Muine Beag, Co Carlow

FOCUS
Not many runners, but an interesting edition of this Grade 3 chase which has produced some useful winners in recent years. With five of the six appearing for the first time since Punchestown in April it did not look a race to be dogmatic about beforehand. The winner rates a fair personal best.

[1885]FFOS LAS (L-H)
Tuesday, October 29

OFFICIAL GOING: Heavy (5.5)
Wind: moderate across Weather: sunny spells

2147 RACING POST WEEKENDER OUT EVERY WEDNESDAY MAIDEN HURDLE (10 hdls) 2m 4f
1:30 (1:30) (Class 5) 4-Y-O+ **£1,949** (£572; £286; £143)

Form RPR
/05- 1 **Berea Boru (IRE)**[32] 1672 5-11-0 0 .... (t) DonalDevereux 118+
(Peter Bowen) *hld up in mod 4th: t.k.h early: wnt 12 l 3rd 3 out: sn rdn: chsd ldr appr last where nt fluent: r.o u.p to ld last strides* **16/1**
2- 2 *hd* **Gate Please (IRE)**[24] 1764 8-11-0 0 .... APMcCoy 117+
(Rebecca Curtis) *disp slow pce tl def ld 4th: increased pce next: rdn along fr 3 out: edgd rt appr last: kpt on: hdd last strides* **15/8**[2]
P- 3 *6* **Batu Ferringhi (FR)**[181] 60 7-11-0 0 .... BrendanPowell 112
(Jamie Snowden) *disp slow pce tl hdd 4th: lost 2nd 6th: chsd wnr again after next tl wknd appr last* **10/1**[3]
220/ 4 *9* **Copper Birch (IRE)**[255] 4240 5-11-0 128 .... PaulMoloney 102
(Evan Williams) *trckd ldrs: wnt 2nd 6th tl after next: sn rdn and wknd: plugged on for 4th* **4/5**[1]
5 *12* **Millenary Magic (IRE)**[144] 667 6-10-11 0 .... AdamWedge[(3)] 90
(David Rees) *t.k.h: hld up in mid-div: hit 6th: sn lost tch: t.o* **66/1**
PF2/ 6 *10* **Mezzanisi (IRE)**[431] 1351 8-11-0 0 .... TomO'Brien 80
(Peter Bowen) *hld up in rr trio: lost tch 6th: t.o* **12/1**
50- 7 *54* **Wynn Darwi (IRE)**[17] 1863 8-10-9 0 .... AodhaganConlon[(5)] 26
(Debra Hamer) *hld up in rr trio: lost tch 6th: t.o* **66/1**
/00- 8 *27* **Home Girl (IRE)**[16] 1885 5-10-7 0 .... RichardJohnson
(Susan Johnson) *hld up in mid-div: lost pl 5th: t.o fr next* **100/1**
0/ 9 *¾* **Hunky Dorey**[164] 7-11-0 0 .... NickScholfield
(Marc Barber) *hld up in rr trio: lost tch fr 5th: t.o* **25/1**

5m 25.1s (34.20) **Going Correction** +0.825s/f (Soft) 9 Ran SP% **120.8**
Speed ratings (Par 103): **64,63,61,57,53 49,27,16,16**
toteswingers 1&2 £2.40, 1&3 £22.00, 2&3 £3.90 CSF £49.75 TOTE £13.80: £2.90, £1.10, £2.60; EX 40.40 Trifecta £1311.40 Pool: £1945.16 - 1.11 winning units..
Owner Ashley Hart **Bred** Mrs E Thompson **Trained** Little Newcastle, Pembrokes

FOCUS
A modest maiden hurdle in which the very steady pace lifted going out onto the final circuit. The winner is rated up a stone, the second in line with his recent win.

2148 RACING POST WEEKENDER OUT TOMORROW H'CAP HURDLE (11 hdls) 2m 6f
2:00 (2:00) (Class 5) (0-95,95) 4-Y-O+ **£1,949** (£572; £286; £143)

Form RPR
040/ 1 **Brave Buck**[224] 4857 5-11-3 89 .... JakeGreenall[(3)] 101+
(Henry Daly) *cl up: led 4th: nt fluent 3 out: rdn clr appr last: styd on wl* **8/1**
000- 2 *11* **Landenstown Star (IRE)**[35] 1645 8-10-8 77 .... (tp) TommyPhelan 78
(Mark Gillard) *led narrowly to 4th: styd cl up: nt fluent 7th: rdn after next: no ex appr last: kpt on to hold 2nd* **9/2**[3]
0/2- 3 *3 ½* **Captain Moonman (IRE)**[16] 1890 8-11-10 93 .... (p) APMcCoy 91
(Rebecca Curtis) *in tch: clsd to trck ldrs 4th: rdn after 8th: kpt on same pce fr next* **10/3**[2]
/00- 4 *1 ½* **Go Annie**[28] 1711 5-11-2 85 .... (bt) DominicElsworth 81
(Jo Davis) *hld up in rr gp: hdwy 8th: one pce fr next: btn whn mstke 2 out* **14/1**
050- 5 *12* **Bob Will (IRE)**[117] 881 8-9-7 69 .... JPKiely[(7)] 52
(Tim Vaughan) *tk keene hold early: hld up in rr gp: lost tch after 8th: passed btn rivals latter stages* **6/1**
031/ 6 *1* **Direct Flo (IRE)**[461] 1077 6-11-2 90 .... JoshHamer[(5)] 72
(Tony Carroll) *hld up in rr gp: hdwy to trck ldrs 8th: nt fluent 3 out: sn rdn and wknd* **16/1**
340- 7 *29* **Kimora (IRE)**[16] 1885 7-11-5 95 .... (t) MrMatthewBarber[(7)] 48
(Marc Barber) *in tch in 5th: hit 2nd and 6th: wknd appr 3 out: t.o* **28/1**
112/ 8 *1* **The Last Bridge**[234] 4661 6-10-9 78 .... RichardJohnson 30
(Susan Johnson) *disp ld to 1st: trckd ldng pair: pushed along and lost pl 6th: wknd 8th: t.o* **9/4**[1]
50/- 9 *32* **Macra Na Feirme (IRE)**[439] 1247 10-10-5 79 .... (t) AodhaganConlon[(5)]
(Debra Hamer) *hld up in rr gp: rdn 8th: sn wknd: t.o* **25/1**

5m 58.8s (38.80) **Going Correction** +0.825s/f (Soft) 9 Ran SP% **117.3**
Speed ratings (Par 103): **62,58,56,56,51 51,40,40,28**
toteswingers 1&2 £10.40, 1&3 £5.30, 2&3 £4.70 CSF £45.17 CT £145.60 TOTE £11.20: £3.40, £1.30, £1.20; EX 76.50 Trifecta £278.00 Pool: £2025.52 - 5.46 winning units..
Owner P E Truscott **Bred** Mr & Mrs P E Truscott **Trained** Stanton Lacy, Shropshire

FOCUS
A moderate staying handicap hurdle in which they went a respectable gallop considering the stamina-sapping conditions. A massive step up from the winner, the form rated around the third.

2149 AVA SECURITY H'CAP CHASE (15 fncs) 2m 3f 110y
2:30 (2:30) (Class 4) (0-120,120) 4-Y-O+ **£3,768** (£1,106; £553; £276)

Form RPR
4/1- 1 **Get It On (IRE)**[3] 2078 8-11-5 120 7ex .... ConorRing[(7)] 135+
(Evan Williams) *hld up last but wl in tch: sltly hmpd 4th: clsd 4 out: led next: drew clr fr 2 out: eased nr fin* **1/1**[1]
533- 2 *5* **Hodgson (IRE)**[31] 1687 8-11-4 112 .... (tp) JamieMoore 117
(Peter Bowen) *trckd ldr: led appr 4 out tl slow jump and relegated to 3rd next: wnt 2nd again 2 out: kpt on but no ch w easy wnr* **5/1**[3]
662- 3 *1 ¾* **Royal Riviera**[10] 1981 7-10-13 107 .... (t) SamTwiston-Davies 111+
(Nigel Twiston-Davies) *in tch in 3rd: j.rt at times: nt fluent 3 out where wnt 2nd: mstke and lost 2nd next: one pce* **2/1**[2]
224- 4 *33* **Qoubilai (FR)**[19] 1840 9-11-12 120 .... (t) RichardJohnson 97
(Tim Vaughan) *led: mstke 7th: nt fluent 9th: hdd appr 4 out: wknd qckly: t.o whn j.rt 2 out* **9/1**

5m 12.9s (11.80) **Going Correction** +0.75s/f (Soft) 4 Ran SP% **110.0**
Speed ratings (Par 105): **106,104,103,90**
CSF £6.12 TOTE £2.10; EX 7.80 Trifecta £15.00 Pool: £1263.36 - 62.93 winning units..
Owner John Lee Jones **Bred** G Martin **Trained** Llancarfan, Vale Of Glamorgan

FOCUS
A modest handicap chase. The easy winner comfirmed the merit of his easy recent win.

2150 O'BRIEN & PARTNERS H'CAP HURDLE (12 hdls) 3m
3:00 (3:00) (Class 4) (0-120,119) 4-Y-O+ **£3,119** (£915; £457; £228)

Form RPR
202- 1 **Minella For Steak (IRE)**[14] 1917 6-11-4 111 .... (tp) APMcCoy 118
(Jonjo O'Neill) *tended to r wd: hld up in tch: clsd 7th: rdn to chse ldr appr 3 out: led appr last: edgd rt flat: drvn out* **7/4**[1]
5/P- 2 *1 ¾* **Ifyouthinkso**[19] 1829 6-10-6 99 .... (p) WillKennedy 104
(Lucy Jones) *led: pressed on after 9th: 4 l up whn mstke 3 out: sn rdn: hdd appr last: kpt on same pce* **11/1**
525/ 3 *20* **Water Wagtail**[248] 4378 6-11-2 112 .... GavinSheehan[(3)] 100
(Emma Lavelle) *racd in 3rd: hit 8th: chsd ldr briefly after next: wknd 3 out* **15/8**[2]
4P5/ 4 *59* **Leeroar (IRE)**[201] 5245 5-10-7 100 .... (t) DominicElsworth 24
(Jo Davis) *hld up in tch: hdwy to trck ldr after 4th: wknd after 9th: tk poor 4th flat: t.o* **11/1**
512- 5 *8* **Ajman (IRE)**[61] 1443 8-10-5 105 .... (t) ConorRing[(7)] 21
(Evan Williams) *hld up in rr: wknd and lost tch after 9th: t.o whn mstke 2 out: lost poor 4th flat* **15/2**[3]
146- P **My Lucky Flame (IRE)**[20] 1818 6-11-2 119 .... MikeyHamill[(10)]
(Sean Curran) *trckd ldr: hit 1st: lost pl 5th: dropped to rr after next: t.o whn p.u bef 8th: lame* **17/2**

6m 21.5s (32.50) **Going Correction** +0.825s/f (Soft) 6 Ran SP% **110.1**
Speed ratings (Par 105): **78,77,70,51,48**
toteswingers 1&2 £12.00, 1&3 £1.50, 2&3 £3.70 CSF £18.56 TOTE £2.50: £1.40, £3.80; EX 16.90 Trifecta £46.70 Pool: £1584.53 - 25.40 winning units..
Owner Mrs Gay Smith & Mrs John Magnier **Bred** D Harnett **Trained** Cheltenham, Gloucs

FOCUS
A modest staying handicap hurdle. The first two ran pretty much to their marks.

2151 STRADEY PARK NOVICES' CHASE (13 fncs) 2m
3:30 (3:31) (Class 4) 4-Y-O+ **£4,548** (£1,335; £667; £333)

Form RPR
16/- 1 **Taquin Du Seuil (FR)**[230] 4733 6-11-2 0 .... APMcCoy 148+
(Jonjo O'Neill) *hld up in 3rd: couple of sticky jumps early: clsd after 9th: sn wnt 2nd: chal 3 out: led on bit appr last: v easily* **4/9**[1]
113/ 2 *2* **Bob Ford (IRE)**[195] 5350 6-11-2 128 .... TomScudamore 133+
(Rebecca Curtis) *t.k.h: tended to jump lft: chsd clr ldr: clsd after 9th: led appr next: stmbld 3 out: rchd for next: sn hdd and no ch w easy wnr* **4/1**[2]
533- 3 *24* **Zarzal (IRE)**[29] 1698 5-11-2 0 .... PaulMoloney 107
(Evan Williams) *hld up in last: nt fluent 4th: mstke 8th: sme hdwy after next: sn lost tch w ldng pair: shkn up to take remote 3rd flat: improve* **12/1**
125/ 4 *11* **Westward Point**[189] 5463 6-10-13 0 .... GavinSheehan[(3)] 99
(Warren Greatrex) *led: clr fr 2nd: mstke 6th: reduced ld fr 9th: hdd appr next: sn wknd: lost poor 3rd flat: t.o* **7/1**[3]

4m 9.8s (10.40) **Going Correction** +0.75s/f (Soft) 4 Ran SP% **109.4**
Speed ratings (Par 105): **104,103,91,85**
CSF £2.81 TOTE £1.50; EX 2.80 Trifecta £3.50 Pool: £1912.77 - 404.29 winning units..
Owner Martin Broughton & Friends 1 **Bred** Marc Boudot **Trained** Cheltenham, Gloucs

FOCUS
An interesting novice chase in which Westward Point, the last horse home, set a searching gallop. The facile winner was value for a lot further and should better his 150+ hurdle rating over fences.

2152 32RED H'CAP CHASE (18 fncs) 3m
4:00 (4:00) (Class 5) (0-95,91) 4-Y-O+ **£2,144** (£629; £314; £157)

Form RPR
P/P- 1 **Tom Bach (IRE)**[18] 1859 9-10-0 65 oh1 .... (b) LiamTreadwell 81+
(Hywel Evans) *tended to jump rt: trckd ldr to 10th: dropped to last 12th: rallied to chse ldr after 14th: led 3 out: gng clr whn j.rt 2 out: styd on wl* **10/1**
422/ 2 *7* **Billybo**[198] 5309 10-11-2 91 .... AlanJohns[(10)] 97
(Tim Vaughan) *racd in share of cl 3rd: trckd ldr 10th: mstke 13th: lost 2nd after next: chsd wnr 2 out: kpt on one pce* **6/4**[1]
513- 3 *½* **Kilvergan Boy (IRE)**[18] 1859 9-10-11 76 .... (p) SamTwiston-Davies 80
(Nigel Twiston-Davies) *led at stdy pce: mstke 1st: shkn up appr 4 out: hdd 3 out: no ex fr 2 out* **13/8**[2]
626- 4 *3* **Mr Robinson (FR)**[113] 926 6-10-7 72 .... AndrewTinkler 73
(Tony Carroll) *racd in share of cl 3rd: nt fluent 8th: rdn 4 out: one pce fr next* **7/2**[3]

6m 53.4s (36.00) **Going Correction** +0.75s/f (Soft) 4 Ran SP% **109.4**
Speed ratings (Par 103): **70,67,67,66**
CSF £25.64 TOTE £9.20; EX 32.30 Trifecta £140.50 Pool: £1896.46 - 10.11 winning units..
Owner Hywel Evans **Bred** Carthage Molloy **Trained** Kidwelly, Carmarthens
■ The first winner under rules for permit holder Hywel Evans.

FOCUS
A weak staying handicap chase which took place in gruelling underfoot conditions. The winner can take another of these.

2153 32RED.COM STANDARD OPEN NATIONAL HUNT FLAT RACE 2m
4:30 (4:30) (Class 6) 4-6-Y-0 £1,559 (£457; £228; £114)

Form RPR
1 **Capilla (IRE)**[261] 5-10-11 0 AdamWedge(3) 116+
(Evan Williams) *trckd ldr: led gng wl over 1f out: sn clr: r.o wl fnl f* 6/1[3]
2 4 **Red Devil Lads (IRE)**[205] 4-11-0 0 APMcCoy 112+
(Rebecca Curtis) *led at stdy pce: rdn 2f out: sn hdd: hung rt and outpcd by wnr: kpt on same pce* 5/6[1]
64- 3 7 **Little Jon**[28] 1712 5-11-0 0 SamTwiston-Davies 105
(Nigel Twiston-Davies) *hld up in rr: clsd after 7f: wnt 3rd 6f out: rdn 2f out: sn outpcd by ldng pair: kpt on* 5/1[2]
1- 4 7 **Squeeze Me**[118] 874 6-11-0 0 TomO'Brien 98
(Peter Bowen) *hld up in tch: rdn over 3f out: one pce fnl 2f* 14/1
5 2 **Uncle Tone (IRE)**[185] 5583 4-11-0 0 RichardJohnson 96
(David A Kiely, Ire) *t.k.h: trckd ldrs: drvn over 3f out: one pce fnl 2f* 5/1[2]
4- 6 dist **Iouascore (IRE)**[16] 1891 6-10-7 0 MissLBrooke(7)
(Lady Susan Brooke) *racd on ins: hld up in tch: wknd over 3f out: t.o* 100/1
7 7 **Carpies Boy** 4-10-11 0 GavinSheehan(3)
(Warren Greatrex) *in rr: struggling 6f out: lost tch 4f out: t.o* 25/1
8 2 **Anglo Paddy (IRE)** 4-10-7 0 JamesDavies
(Sean Curran) *hld up towards rr: drvn 6f out: wknd over 4f out: t.o* 28/1

3m 55.6s (12.70) **Going Correction** +0.825s/f (Soft)
WFA 4 from 5yo+ 9lb 8 Ran SP% **117.1**
Speed ratings: **101,99,95,92,91** , ,
toteswingers 1&2 £2.00, 1&3 £5.00, 2&3 £2.90 CSF £11.63 TOTE £7.70: £1.90, £1.10, £1.80; EX 14.70 Trifecta £54.10 Pool: £3892.51 - 53.92 winning units..
Owner Mrs Janet Davies **Bred** Sean Kinsella **Trained** Llancarfan, Vale Of Glamorgan

FOCUS
A fair bumper and the first two look above average.
T/Plt: £347.40. Pool: £67,839.69 - 142.52 winning units. T/Qpdt: £189.30. Pool: £5296.15 - 20.70 winning units. RL

2030 CARLISLE (R-H)
Wednesday, October 30

OFFICIAL GOING: Soft (chs 6.4, hdl 6.3)
Meeting switched from Haydock. Hurdle races run on Flat track.
Wind: fresh 1/2 against Weather: overcast, breezy, showers race 3, rain after race 6

2154 COMPARE BOOKMAKERS WITH BOOKMAKERS.CO.UK JUVENILE HURDLE (8 hdls) 2m 1f
1:10 (1:20) (Class 4) 3-Y-0 £3,898 (£1,144; £572; £286)

Form RPR
1 **Azza (FR)**[54] 3-10-12 0 TomScudamore 103+
(David Pipe) *led 1st: nt fluent 4th: clr whn nt fluent last: easily* 1/6[1]
4- 2 6 **Most Honourable**[35] 1658 3-10-12 0 DannyCook 92
(Michael Smith) *led to 1st: chsd ldrs: clr 2nd bef 3 out: no ch w wnr* 7/1[2]
0- 3 12 **Multilicious**[14] 1920 3-10-5 0 (t) DougieCostello 73
(Tim Easterby) *chsd ldrs: clr 3rd bef 3 out: wknd 2 out* 25/1
6- 4 8 **Major Parkes**[21] 1813 3-10-12 0 JasonMaguire 72
(Donald McCain) *hld up in rr: t.k.h: sme hdwy 6th: lost pl next* 33/1
5 16 **Banreenahreenkah (IRE)**[22] 3-10-5 0 SeanQuinlan 53
(Jennie Candlish) *t.k.h: nt fluent: trckd ldrs: j. slowly and blnd 1st: wknd 3 out* 14/1[3]
0- 6 49 **Jebulani**[24] 1786 3-10-12 0 BrianHughes 7
(Barry Murtagh) *chsd ldrs: drvn 6th: sn lost pl and bhd: t.o next: j. bdly rt last 2* 25/1
P **Everreadyneddy**[180] 3-10-5 0 (t) StephenMulqueen(7)
(Maurice Barnes) *nt fluent in rr: lost pl and bhd 4th: t.o whn p.u after next* 100/1

4m 26.5s (-2.70) **Going Correction** -0.40s/f (Good) 7 Ran SP% **116.5**
Speed ratings (Par 103): **90,87,81,77,70 47,**
toteswingers 1&2 £1.40, 1&3 £3.30, 2&3 £9.10 CSF £2.12 TOTE £1.20: £1.10, £1.60; EX 2.90 Trifecta £17.60 Pool: £1808.09 - 77.01 winning units..
Owner Prof Caroline Tisdall **Bred** Francois Marie Cottin **Trained** Nicholashayne, Devon

FOCUS
All hurdles races run on Flat course. Apart from the winner, this was only modest fare. The winner is rated well below her French form.

2155 BOOKMAKERS ON YOUR MOBILE AT BOOKMAKERS.CO.UK NOVICES' H'CAP CHASE (16 fncs) 2m 4f
1:40 (1:50) (Class 4) (0-110,110) 4-Y-0+ £4,873 (£1,431; £715; £357)

Form RPR
060/ 1 **Hollow Blue Sky (FR)**[621] 4371 6-11-2 100 SamTwiston-Davies 114+
(Nigel Twiston-Davies) *prom: wnt 2nd 2 out: led last: drvn and jst hld on* 7/2[1]
113- 2 nk **The Nephew (IRE)**[29] 1710 5-11-10 108 (t) RichieMcLernon 122+
(Jonjo O'Neill) *stdd s: hld up in rr: nt fluent 4th: hdwy11th: chsng ldrs 4 out: 4th whn pckd next: swtchd lft run-in and chsd wnr last 100yds: kpt on: jst hld* 6/1[3]
UF5/ 3 2 3/4 **Russe Blanc (FR)**[193] 5412 6-10-11 95 (p) CharliePoste 104
(Richard Lee) *chsd ldrs: stmbld on landing 3rd: led 4 out: hdd last: kpt on same pce* 7/1
40P/ 4 2 1/2 **Samstown**[308] 3229 6-11-6 107 EwanWhillans(3) 114
(Alistair Whillans) *chsd ldrs: one pce fr 2 out* 25/1
040/ 5 18 **Newspage (IRE)**[524] 423 7-10-0 84 oh20 BrianHughes 75
(John Wade) *w ldrs: led 5th: hdd 4 out: wknd 2 out* 66/1
0/P- 6 32 **Trouble In Paris (IRE)**[175] 168 6-10-11 95 LucyAlexander 51
(Barry Murtagh) *in rr: bhd fr 8th: t.o 11th* 40/1
4/0- 7 10 **Fozy Moss**[168] 316 7-10-0 84 oh13 BrianHarding 30
(Stuart Coltherd) *hld up in rr: bhd fr 8th: t.o 11th* 100/1
/PF- 8 1 **Stagecoach Jasper**[172] 224 7-11-7 105 RyanMania 50
(Sue Smith) *chsd ldrs: lost pl and blnd 4 out: bhd whn eased 2 out: t.o* 9/2[2]
2/U- P **Forgotten Symphony (IRE)**[6] 2046 9-11-12 110 DannyCook
(Brian Ellison) *w ldrs: led 2nd to 5th: blnd 8th: wknd after 12th: sn bhd: t.o whn p.u bef 2 out* 7/1
345- P **Terfel's Toscar (IRE)**[24] 1798 8-11-3 101 (t) RichardJohnson
(Tim Vaughan) *led to 2nd: chsd ldrs: wknd 3 out: eased and bhd whn p.u bef next* 10/1
/30- U **Jukebox Melody (IRE)**[152] 563 7-11-4 109 JohnDawson(7)
(John Wade) *in rr: bhd whn blnd and uns rdr 10th* 20/1
0/F- P **Snowed In (IRE)**[13] 1939 4-10-11 105 (p) SeanQuinlan
(Jennie Candlish) *mid-div: blnd 6th and 8th: sn lost pl and bhd: t.o 4 out* 40/1
110/ F **Gwladys Street (IRE)**[214] 5009 6-11-11 109 CharlieHuxley
(William Kinsey) *mstke 1st: mid-div whn fell 8th* 20/1
2/P- P **On Broadway (IRE)**[172] 224 7-11-5 110 (p) CraigNichol(7)
(Lucinda Russell) *in rr: drvn 7th: bhd fr 9th: t.o whn p.u bef 2 out* 12/1

5m 16.3s (-11.10) **Going Correction** -0.40s/f (Good)
WFA 4 from 5yo+ 10lb 14 Ran SP% **117.2**
Speed ratings (Par 105): **106,105,104,103,96 83,79,79,** , , ,
toteswingers 1&2 £4.80, 1&3 £6.80, 2&3 £9.20 CSF £22.79 CT £140.54 TOTE £4.40: £1.70, £2.00, £2.90; EX 34.00 Trifecta £271.10 Pool: £759.21 - 2.09 winning units..
Owner The Hollow Partnership **Bred** E A R L Elevage Des Loges **Trained** Naunton, Gloucs

FOCUS
Probably a decent race of its type, and future winners should emerge from it. The form looks pretty solid.

2156 GET FREE BETS WITH BOOKMAKERS.CO.UK NOVICES' HURDLE (8 hdls) 2m 1f
2:10 (2:20) (Class 4) 4-Y-0+ £3,898 (£1,144; £572; £286)

Form RPR
141/ 1 **The Liquidator**[189] 5516 5-10-12 0 TomScudamore 127+
(David Pipe) *trckd ldrs: upsides 3 out: led on bit next: wnt clr run-in: v easily* 2/7[1]
3- 2 11 **Knightly Escapade**[12] 1415 5-10-12 0 (p) DannyCook 107+
(Brian Ellison) *chsd ldrs: wnt 2nd 2 out: no ch w wnr* 33/1
/0U- 3 3 1/2 **Quick Brew**[11] 1975 5-10-5 0 (t) StephenMulqueen(7) 102
(Maurice Barnes) *in rr: hdwy 6th: chsng ldrs next: modest 3rd between last 2: kpt on same pce* 200/1
5- 4 1 3/4 **Spookydooky (IRE)**[18] 1864 5-10-12 0 (t) APMcCoy 100
(Jonjo O'Neill) *led: j.lft 5th: hdd bef 3 out: kpt on one pce* 9/2[2]
0/0- 5 7 **Vinstar (FR)**[24] 1793 4-10-12 0 JasonMaguire 92
(Donald McCain) *trckd ldrs: led bef 3 out: hdd 2 out: wknd between last 2* 25/1
2/1- 6 nse **Damascus Steel (IRE)**[172] 218 5-11-5 114 BrianHarding 99
(Alison Hamilton) *chsd ldrs: effrt 3 out: wknd between last 2* 20/1[3]
0- 7 1 1/4 **Cloudy Deal (IRE)**[19] 1850 6-10-12 0 (t) WilsonRenwick 90
(Martin Todhunter) *hld up towards rr: hdwy 5th: wknd appr 2 out* 200/1
04/ 8 4 1/2 **Coquet Head**[172] 7-10-7 0 MissCWalton(5) 86
(James Walton) *in rr: sme hdwy appr 3 out: sn lost pl* 66/1
3- 9 4 **Tourtiere**[19] 1853 5-10-12 0 BarryKeniry 82
(George Moore) *hld up towards rr: hdwy to chse ldrs 4th: lost pl bef 2 out* 50/1
0/ 10 2 3/4 **Next Hight (IRE)**[708] 2689 6-10-7 0 JonathanEngland(5) 79
(Sue Smith) *chsd ldrs 3rd: drvn 6th: lost pl bef next* 33/1
0/0- 11 2 **Amethyst Rose (IRE)**[168] 313 6-10-5 0 RichieMcGrath 70
(Stuart Coltherd) *in rr: bhd fr 6th: t.o 3 out: plugged on* 100/1
500/ 12 25 **Irish By Name (IRE)**[265] 4074 7-10-5 0 JohnDawson(7) 52
(John Wade) *w ldrs: drvn 6th: sn lost pl: t.o 2 out* 150/1

4m 23.6s (-5.60) **Going Correction** -0.40s/f (Good)
WFA 4 from 5yo+ 9lb 12 Ran SP% **116.5**
Speed ratings (Par 105): **97,91,90,89,86 86,85,83,81,80 79,67**
toteswingers 1&2 £6.00, 1&3 £55.60, 2&3 £57.80 CSF £18.66 TOTE £1.50: £1.02, £5.30, £31.10; EX 14.80 Trifecta £340.20 Pool: £1447.17 - 3.18 winning units..
Owner R S Brookhouse **Bred** Ms E L White **Trained** Nicholashayne, Devon

FOCUS
A lot of these were still close up heading into the home straight for the final time, which suggests they didn't go that quick early on. The easy winner looks a smart prospect, sure to rate higher. The third to fifth help with the level.

2157 LIVE FOOTBALL SCORES WITH SCORES.CO.UK H'CAP CHASE (18 fncs) 3m 110y
2:40 (2:50) (Class 3) (0-125,124) 4-Y-0+ £8,122 (£2,385; £1,192; £596)

Form RPR
31P/ 1 **Papamoa**[187] 5548 8-10-8 106 LucyAlexander 110
(N W Alexander) *w ldr: drvn whn lft in ld 10th: jnd 14th: styd on u.p: hld on towards fin* 5/1[3]
U46/ 2 1/2 **My Boy Paddy (IRE)**[199] 5306 9-11-0 112 SamTwiston-Davies 116
(Nigel Twiston-Davies) *trckd ldrs: upsides 14th: drvn after last: styd on same pce: no ex clsng stages* 7/2[1]
2/5- 3 29 **Incentivise (IRE)**[156] 509 10-11-4 119 MichealNolan(3) 93
(Richard Lee) *pckd 1st: in tch: drvn 10th: outpcd and lft modest 4th 4 out: sn bhd: j. bdly rt last: tk poor 3rd nr fin* 8/1
216- 4 4 1/2 **Full Of Joy (IRE)**[29] 1709 8-11-12 124 (tp) APMcCoy 94
(Jonjo O'Neill) *chsd ldrs: upsides 14th: sn drvn in 3rd: wknd next: j. bdly lft last 2: demotaed and eased towards fin* 6/1
1/4- F **Mohi Rahrere (IRE)**[168] 321 10-10-13 111 (b[1]) LiamHeard
(Barry Leavy) *in rr: fell 5th* 22/1
316/ P **Dusky Bob (IRE)**[196] 5351 8-11-6 118 (p) DannyCook
(Brian Ellison) *in rr: bdly hmpd and lost pl 10th: t.o whn hit 13th: p.u bef 4 out* 9/2[2]
216/ F **Chac Du Cadran (FR)**[228] 4797 7-11-12 124 (p) TomMessenger
(Chris Bealby) *led: hit 1st: fell 10th* 7/1
/U0- F **Sun Cloud (IRE)**[35] 1660 6-11-4 116 BrianHughes
(Malcolm Jefferson) *in rr: mstke 4th: hdwy 14th: 5 l down in 4th whn fell 4 out* 16/1
/34- U **Ultra Du Chatelet (FR)**[18] 1872 5-11-0 112 (t) PeterBuchanan
(Lucinda Russell) *trckd ldrs: cl 3rd whn pckd bdly landing: hmpd and uns rdr 10th* 9/1

6m 33.5s (-9.10) **Going Correction** -0.40s/f (Good) 9 Ran SP% **115.2**
Speed ratings (Par 107): **98,97,88,87,** , , ,
toteswingers 1&2 £3.30, 1&3 £9.40, 2&3 £7.60 CSF £23.57 CT £137.62 TOTE £5.30: £1.90, £1.30, £2.60; EX 25.80 Trifecta £164.30 Pool: £1314.37 - 5.99 winning units..
Owner The Papamoans **Bred** Miss Deborah J Baker **Trained** Kinneston, Perth & Kinross

FOCUS
This only concerned two from a long way out, but it didn't produce the result that seemed likely for much of the final stages. The first two were well handicapped and ran close to their marks.

2158 BOOKMAKERS.CO.UK H'CAP HURDLE (11 hdls) 2m 4f
3:15 (3:25) (Class 4) (0-120,120) 4-Y-0+ **£3,898** (£1,144; £572; £286)

Form RPR
2/3- **1** **Big Casino**174 174 7-11-1 **109**................................ SamTwiston-Davies 123+
(Nigel Twiston-Davies) *trckd ldrs 3rd: led 3 out: styd on to forge clr run-in: eased towards fin* **9/5**1
20/ **2** *3 ½* **Talkin Sence (IRE)**234 4679 8-10-11 **115**.................... DaraghBourke(10) 122
(Stuart Coltherd) *trckd ldrs: upsides 3 out: edgd rt between last 2: kpt on same pce* **10/1**
2P1- **3** *8* **Ballyben (IRE)**18 1875 5-10-12 **113**.................................. CraigNichol(7) 113
(Lucinda Russell) *chsd ldrs: modest 3rd bef 2 out: one pce* **15/2**
3/3- **4** *18* **Houston Dynimo (IRE)**137 752 8-11-0 **115**............ MissJRRichards(7) 96
(Nicky Richards) *chsd ldr: led 5th: hit next: hdd 3 out: wknd bef next* **18/1**
00F/ **5** *11* **Kent Street (IRE)**184 24 8-10-13 **112**.................... JonathanEngland(5) 82
(Sue Smith) *in rr: reminders after 4th: bhd fr 6th* **12/1**
0/2- **6** *3* **Knockraheen (IRE)**169 289 5-11-9 **117**........................ RichieMcLernon 84
(Jonjo O'Neill) *in rr: hdwy 5th: wknd appr 3 out: bhd whn j.rt last 2* **7/2**2
UU1- **7** *6* **Border Phoenix**143 676 6-11-4 **112**.. AdrianLane 73
(Sandy Forster) *in rr: lost pl 6th: nvr a factor after* **66/1**
F/2- **8** *22* **Purcell's Bridge (FR)**14 1926 6-11-2 **120**.................. ShaunDobbin(10) 59
(Rose Dobbin) *hit 1st: in rr: drvn8th: sn bhd: eased run-in: t.o* **13/2**3
P/0- **P** **Makhzoon (USA)**35 1656 9-11-1 **116**........................(v) MrKitAlexander(7)
(N W Alexander) *led to 5th: reminders next: wknd appr 3 out: bhd whn p.u between last 2* **33/1**
/11- **P** **Rattlin**148 626 5-11-0 **108**.. RyanMania
(Sue Smith) *in rr: chsd ldrs 3rd: drvn and lost pl 7th: sn bhd: t.o whn p.u bef 2 out* **16/1**

5m 11.8s (-11.00) **Going Correction** -0.40s/f (Good) **10 Ran SP% 115.4**
Speed ratings (Par 105): **106,104,101,94,89 88,86,77, ,**
toteswingers 1&2 £6.10, 1&3 £4.80, 2&3 £13.20 CSF £20.47 CT £110.55 TOTE £3.30: £2.10, £3.00, £2.00; EX 25.00 Trifecta £190.60 Pool: £1781.38 - 7.00 winning units..
Owner R Jukes **Bred** Mrs M A Jukes **Trained** Naunton, Gloucs

FOCUS
An open handicap won by the least-exposed runner, who produced a big step up. The next two were close to their marks.

2159 DONATE TO EDEN VALLEY HOSPICE NOVICES' LIMITED H'CAP CHASE (11 fncs 1 omitted) 2m
3:50 (3:55) (Class 3) (0-125,122) 4-Y-0+ **£6,498** (£1,908; £954; £477)

Form RPR
302/ **1** **Definite Dream (IRE)**199 5304 6-10-10 **113**...................... PaulMoloney 125+
(Evan Williams) *w ldrs: led 3 out: jnd last: hld on wl towards fin* **10/3**2
265/ **2** *1* **Firth Of The Clyde**217 4971 8-10-12 **115**.......................... BrianHughes 125
(Malcolm Jefferson) *hld up in rr: gd hdwy 7th: 3rd 3 out: styd on and upsides last: no ex clsng stages* **10/1**
1/F- **3** *14* **Kykate**174 181 7-11-4 **121**..(t) CharlieHuxley 118
(William Kinsey) *chsd ldrs: one pce fr 2 out* **14/1**
F/0- **4** *6* **Blackwater King (IRE)**14 1922 5-10-13 **116**.................. JasonMaguire 107
(Donald McCain) *nt fluent in rr: bhd whn mstke 5th: gd hdwy after 4 out: one pce fr 2 out: modest 4th last* **10/3**2
P24/ **5** *5* **Rupert Bear**214 5005 7-10-7 **115**.................................. MissCWalton(5) 99
(James Walton) *mde most to 4th: led 6th: hdd 3 out: wknd next* **17/2**3
0/0- **6** *nk* **Leroy Parker (IRE)**34 1665 5-10-7 **110**.........................(b) LucyAlexander 94
(Barry Murtagh) *hld up in mid-div: outpcd appr 4 out: 6th whn hit 2 out* **50/1**
332- **7** *6* **Swaledale Lad (IRE)**19 1849 6-11-0 **122**.................. HarryChalloner(5) 104
(Richard Ford) *w ldrs: led 4th: hdd and hit 6th: lost pl appr 4 out* **5/2**1
8 *13* **Champagne Agent (IRE)**129 814 7-11-3 **120**..........(p) PeterBuchanan 85
(Lucinda Russell) *chsd ldrs: lost pl appr 4 out: sn bhd* **16/1**

4m 9.6s (-6.50) **Going Correction** -0.40s/f (Good) **8 Ran SP% 108.9**
Speed ratings (Par 107): **100,99,92,89,87 86,83,77**
toteswingers 1&2 £5.90, 1&3 £7.00, 2&3 £7.10 CSF £31.60 CT £363.91 TOTE £4.60: £1.40, £2.50, £2.60; EX 36.20 Trifecta £430.00 Pool: £2530.94 - 4.41 winning units..
Owner R J H Geffen **Bred** Andrew Dunne **Trained** Llancarfan, Vale Of Glamorgan

FOCUS
The first fence on the final circuit was omitted due to slippery ground. There's a case for rating this form up to 7lb higher.

2160 BOOKMAKERS.CO.UK "JUNIOR" STANDARD OPEN NATIONAL HUNT FLAT RACE 1m 6f
4:20 (4:27) (Class 5) 3-Y-0 **£1,949** (£572; £286; £143)

Form RPR
1 **Hurricane Hollow** 3-10-12 0.. WilsonRenwick 105+
(Keith Dalgleish) *hld up in rr: trckd ldrs 6f out: swtchd lft and led 2f out: forged clr* **4/1**3
2 *9* **Lebanna** 3-10-5 0.. DougieCostello 84
(Tim Easterby) *trckd ldrs: upsides 7f out: kpt on same pce fnl 2f* **8/1**
3 *nk* **Gone Forever** 3-10-5 0...................................... NathanMoscrop(7) 91
(Brian Ellison) *set stdy pce: qcknd pce over 5f out: hdd 2f out: kpt on one pce* **3/1**1
4 *hd* **River Bollin** 3-10-12 0.. HarryHaynes 91
(Tim Easterby) *trckd ldrs: upsides 6f out: kpt on one pce fnl 2f* **9/1**
5 *6* **Albatros Tresor (FR)** 3-10-5 0............................ GrantCockburn(7) 83
(Lucinda Russell) *hld up in mid-div: trckd ldrs 4f out: wknd 2f out* **7/2**2
6 *8* **Diego Suarez (FR)** 3-10-12 0.. TomMessenger 74
(Chris Bealby) *sn trcking ldrs: drvn over 4f out: lost pl over 2f out* **9/2**
7 *1 ½* **Dermo's Dilemma** 3-10-5 0.................................... DiarmuidO'Regan(7) 72
(Chris Grant) *unruly: uns rdr and rn loose bef s: hld up in rr: hdwy to trck ldrs 9f out: drvn 4f out: lost pl over 2f out* **14/1**
8 *shd* **Falcon's Ginger** 3-10-5 0.. RichieMcGrath 65
(John Weymes) *hld up in rr: hdwy 9f out: outpcd over 5f out: lost pl over 3f out* **28/1**

4m 1.7s (241.70) **8 Ran SP% 116.6**
toteswingers 1&2 £5.30, 1&3 £3.30, 2&3 £5.20 CSF £36.41 TOTE £4.60: £1.40, £2.00, £1.60; EX 24.00 Trifecta £69.50 Pool: £3227.01 - 34.80 winning units..
Owner Equus Syndicate **Bred** Wood Hall Stud **Trained** Carluke, S Lanarks
■ The first winner under jumps rules for trainer Keith Dalgleish.

FOCUS
Quite what this form is worth is anyone's guess considering none of these young horses had run before and were still in a pack heading to the 2f marker.
T/Plt: £22.30 to a £1 stake. Pool: £69784.45 - 2274.36 winning tickets T/Qpdt: £14.40 to a £1 stake. Pool: £5983.60 - 307.40 winning tickets WG

1713 SEDGEFIELD (L-H)
Thursday, October 31

OFFICIAL GOING: Good to soft (good in places; 6.7)
Wind: fairly strong behind Weather: shower before first then fine

2168 TODDS HIRE SPECIALIST VEHICLE HIRE JUVENILE HURDLE (PAXTONS HURDLE SERIES QUALIFIER) (8 hdls) 2m 1f
1:00 (1:00) (Class 4) 3-Y-0 **£3,119** (£915; £457; £228)

Form RPR
3- **1** **War Lord (IRE)**14 1934 3-10-12 0.. BarryKeniry 99
(Philip Kirby) *w ldr: led narrowly 3 out: rdn bef 2 out: mstke last: hld on wl flat* **8/1**3
1- **2** *¾* **Dispour (IRE)**28 1727 3-11-5 0...................................... JasonMaguire 105
(Donald McCain) *led narrowly: hdd narrowly 3 out: rdn 2 out: nt fluent last: kpt on but a jst hld* **11/10**1
3 *1 ¼* **Erica Starprincess**23 3-10-0 0...................................... JoeColliver(5) 90
(George Moore) *hld up: stl wl bhd 3 out: hdwy appr 2 out: styd on wl flat: wnt 3rd post* **100/1**
4 *shd* **Nautical Twilight**42 3-10-5 0.. BrianHughes 89
(Malcolm Jefferson) *in tch: rdn bef 2 out: wnt 3rd appr last: one pce: lost 3rd post* **50/1**
5 *7* **Marlborough House**86 3-10-12 0.................................... DenisO'Regan 93
(Chris Grant) *hld up: hdwy appr 2 out: hit last: no further imp* **28/1**
6 *nk* **Innsbruck**42 3-10-12 0.. DougieCostello 93+
(John Quinn) *nt fluent: trckd ldrs: rdn bef 2 out: lost 3rd appr last: wknd* **6/4**2
7 *17* **Baraboy (IRE)**21 3-10-12 0.. LucyAlexander 80
(Barry Murtagh) *midfield: hdwy to dispute 4th whn hit 3 out: sn btn* **25/1**
8 *6* **Roycano**70 3-10-5 0.. MrHAABannister(7) 69
(Michael Easterby) *hld up in rr: a bhd* **100/1**
9 *28* **Special Report (IRE)**45 3-10-9 0................................ MichaelByrne(3) 43
(Neil Mulholland) *hld up: bhd after 5th: t.o* **28/1**
0- **U** **Attansky (IRE)**15 1920 3-10-12 0.. HarryHaynes
(Tim Easterby) *trckd ldrs: wknd after 5th: t.o whn abt to be p.u jinked rt: hit rail and uns rdr jst bef 2 out* **20/1**

4m 8.0s (1.10) **Going Correction** -0.05s/f (Good) **10 Ran SP% 118.2**
Speed ratings (Par 103): **95,94,94,94,90 90,82,79,66,**
toteswingers 1&2 £2.90, 2&3 £73.60, 1&3 £26.60 CSF £17.46 TOTE £12.70: £2.10, £1.10, £22.30; EX 22.80 Trifecta £789.30 Pool: £1743.71 - 1.65 winning units..
Owner Geoff & Sandra Turnbull **Bred** Mrs Brid Cosgrove **Trained** Middleham, N Yorks

FOCUS
Divided bends on fresh ground. Chases on inside, hurdles moved in. This opening juvenile hurdle was a modest contest in which they went an honest gallop, on ground officially described as good to soft, good in places. A step up from the winner and there's a case for rating the form a bit higher through the second.

2169 WITCHES OF NORTONTHORPE H'CAP HURDLE (8 hdls) 2m 1f
1:30 (1:30) (Class 5) (0-100,100) 4-Y-0+ **£1,949** (£572; £286; £143)

Form RPR
0U3- **1** **Dynamic Drive (IRE)**25 1790 6-10-3 **84**..............(t) StephenMulqueen(7) 95+
(Maurice Barnes) *hld up: smooth hdwy fr appr 3 out: trckd ldr 2 out: pushed along to ld appr last: kpt on* **8/1**
035/ **2** *4 ½* **Sam Lord**185 27 9-11-12 **100**.. DenisO'Regan 105
(James Moffatt) *trckd ldr: led after 3 out: rdn bef 2 out: hdd appr last: hit last: one pce* **6/1**2
661- **3** *1 ¼* **Honourable Gent**25 1790 5-10-6 **80**.............................. WilsonRenwick 83
(Rose Dobbin) *hld up: stdy hdwy fr 3 out: wnt 3rd 2 out: sn rdn: kpt on: nt fluent last* **11/2**1
060/ **4** *6* **Lysino (GER)**228 4815 4-11-12 **100**.................................... BrianHarding 96
(Chris Grant) *midfield: rdn bef 2 out: kpt on one pce: wnt 4th last* **18/1**
153- **5** *7* **Logical Approach (IRE)**93 1143 6-11-7 **100**..................(p) TonyKelly(5) 91
(David Thompson) *prom: rdn bef 2 out: grad wknd* **11/1**
/60- **6** *7* **Garth Mountain**132 788 6-10-7 **81**.................................... BrianHughes 67
(Hugh Burns) *trckd ldrs: rdn whn hit 2 out: sn wknd* **7/1**3
364/ **7** *1 ½* **Operateur (IRE)**12 1706 5-11-0 **88**.............................. AndrewTinkler 71
(Ben Haslam) *midfield: rdn bef 2 out: wknd after 2 out* **16/1**
/00- **8** *1 ¾* **Strandfield Bay (IRE)**17 1908 7-10-4 **78**....................(p) DougieCostello 59
(Michael O'Hare, Ire) *led: hdd after 3 out: wknd appr 2 out* **16/1**
055/ **9** *6* **Kathlatino**12 2479 6-10-9 **88**.. JoeColliver(5) 64
(Micky Hammond) *midfield: rdn bef 2 out: sn btn* **33/1**
P26- **10** *2 ¼* **Mr Mistopheles (IRE)**25 1790 5-10-5 **79**......................(bt) HenryBrooke 53
(Philip Kirby) *hld up: nvr threatened* **10/1**
6/1- **11** *¾* **Iktiview**12 75 5-11-3 **94**...(p) KyleJames(3) 67
(Philip Kirby) *midfield: wknd after 3 out* **8/1**
300- **12** *8* **Optical High**149 629 4-10-7 **86**.................................. JonathanEngland(5) 52
(Sue Smith) *midfield: lost pl 5th: sn btn* **20/1**
040/ **13** *6* **Dan's Heir**12 4115 11-11-2 **90**.......................................(b1) BarryKeniry 50
(Wilf Storey) *hld up in rr: a bhd* **80/1**
/40- **14** *5* **El Toreros (USA)**123 854 5-11-5 **96**..........................(vt1) MichaelByrne(3) 52
(Tim Vaughan) *chsd ldrs: rdn bef 3 out: sn wknd* **12/1**

4m 4.8s (-2.10) **Going Correction** -0.05s/f (Good) **14 Ran SP% 115.5**
Speed ratings (Par 103): **102,99,99,96,93 89,89,88,85,84 84,80,77,75**
toteswingers 1&2 £12.70, 2&3 £5.20, 1&3 £7.40 CSF £52.86 CT £288.39 TOTE £10.70: £3.20, £1.40, £2.60; EX 69.80 Trifecta £296.30 Pool: £1005.30 - 2.54 winning units..
Owner Ring Of Fire **Bred** Pendley Farm **Trained** Farlam, Cumbria

FOCUS
A modest handicap hurdle. A big step up from the cosy winner in a fair time for the grade.

2170 SPOOKIE BROOKIE NORTONTHORPE H'CAP HURDLE (13 hdls) 3m 3f 110y
2:00 (2:00) (Class 3) (0-135,129) 4-Y-0 **£5,253** (£1,552; £776; £388; £194)

Form RPR
P/P- **1** **Abnaki (IRE)**7 2033 8-11-1 **123**..............................(b1) MauriceLinehan(5) 131+
(Jonjo O'Neill) *trckd ldr: upsides 3 out: led 2 out: styd on wl: firmly in command whn hit last* **17/2**
/60- **2** *8* **Jeu De Roseau (IRE)**36 1660 9-11-0 **117**........................ DenisO'Regan 117
(Chris Grant) *hld up: hdwy to trck ldng pair 3 out: rdn bef 2 out: sn one pce: nt fluent 2nd run-in: no threat wnr* **10/1**
1/2- **3** *4 ½* **Night In Milan (IRE)**167 355 7-11-9 **126**........................ JamesReveley 124
(Keith Reveley) *led: jnd 3 out: hdd 2 out: grad wknd: lost 2nd run-in* **9/4**1
006- **4** *8* **Bourne**15 1926 7-11-12 **129**.. JasonMaguire 118
(Donald McCain) *hld up in rr: rdn after 3 out: sn btn* **15/2**
230- **5** *7* **Howizee**15 1926 7-11-4 **128**......................................(t) StephenMulqueen(7) 113
(Maurice Barnes) *trckd ldr: lost pl appr 3 out: wknd bef 2 out* **4/1**3

The Form Book Jumps, Raceform Ltd, Compton, RG20 6NL.

123/ **F** **One In A Milan (IRE)**[229] 4797 8-11-5 **122**........................ PaulMoloney
(Evan Williams) *hld up: fell 2nd* **11/4**[2]
6m 52.9s (0.90) **Going Correction** -0.05s/f (Good) **6** Ran SP% **108.8**
Speed ratings (Par 107): **96,93,92,90,88**
toteswingers 1&2 £14.60, 2&3 £4.20, 1&3 £6.80 CSF £72.88 TOTE £9.80: £5.30, £5.20; EX 126.70 Trifecta £245.50 Pool: £1807.62 - 5.52 winning units..
Owner G & P Barker Ltd/globe Engineering **Bred** Robert McCarthy & Nicholas W Alexander' **Trained** Cheltenham, Gloucs

FOCUS
A fairly decent handicap hurdle over a marathon trip in which jockey Maurice Linehan made his first ride on this track a winning one. A small personal best from the winner, with the next two setting the level.

2171 COMPARE BOOKMAKERS AT BOOKMAKERS.CO.UK NOVICES' LIMITED H'CAP CHASE (16 fncs) 2m 4f
2:30 (2:30) (Class 3) (0-125,125) 4-Y-0 **£6,279** (£1,871; £947; £485; £254)

Form RPR
2P3/ **1** **King Of The Wolds (IRE)**[195] 5366 6-11-3 **123**................ BrianHughes 133+
(Malcolm Jefferson) *prom: led 4th: clr 7th: briefly hung rt on bnd after 8th: pushed along and dwindling advantage appr last: rdn and edgd lft after last: sn pressed: jst hld on* **11/2**[3]
4/0- **2** *nk* **Deise Dynamo (IRE)**[180] 121 5-10-9 **115**....................... JasonMaguire 123+
(Donald McCain) *chsd ldrs: rdn to go 2nd after 3 out: clsd on ldr appr last: ev ch whn short of room on rail 75yds out: jst hld* **14/1**
22F/ **3** *10* **See What Happens (IRE)**[237] 4634 7-11-0 **120**.............. DenisO'Regan 119
(Martin Todhunter) *hld up in rr: sme hdwy after 3 out: rdn and one pce after 2 out: lft 3rd last: no threat to ldng pair* **17/2**
0/3- **4** *9* **Timesawastin (IRE)**[175] 182 7-11-5 **125**........................ PaulMoloney 117
(Evan Williams) *led: hdd 4th: trckd ldr: rdn after 3 out: wknd between last 2* **11/2**[3]
10P/ **5** *14* **Herdsman (IRE)**[195] 5368 8-10-12 **118**.................................. RyanMania 100
(Sue Smith) *hld up: pushed along after 10th: sn struggling* **11/1**
115/ **U** **Porgy**[127] 2024 8-10-11 **117**.. DannyCook 120
(Brian Ellison) *hld up: hit 8th: rdn and hdwy after 3 out: wnt 3rd between last 2: 4 l down whn blnd and uns last* **16/1**
0P6/ **P** **Knight Pass (IRE)**[253] 4319 7-11-5 **125**........................ TomScudamore
(David Pipe) *in tch: slow 6th and sn lost pl: p.u after 9th* **11/5**[1]
424- **P** **Balding Banker (IRE)**[12] 1976 7-11-0 **125**........................ TonyKelly(5) 107
(Rebecca Menzies) *midfield: rdn bef 3 out: btn whn hit 2 out: sn eased and p.u bef last* **9/2**[2]
4m 51.5s (-11.50) **Going Correction** -0.40s/f (Good) **8** Ran SP% **111.6**
Speed ratings (Par 107): **107,106,102,99,93 , ,**
toteswingers 1&2 £12.90, 2&3 £6.20, 1&3 £6.50 CSF £67.91 CT £632.53 TOTE £7.60: £3.30, £2.40, £1.40; EX 77.90 Trifecta £455.90 Pool: £1780.16 - 2.92 winning units..
Owner Mr & Mrs G Calder **Bred** Miss Mary O'Sullivan **Trained** Norton, N Yorks
■ Stewards' Enquiry : Brian Hughes one-day ban: careless riding (Nov 14)

FOCUS
A fair novices' handicap chase. The first two are up 5lb on the best of their hurdle form.

2172 FREE BETS ON YOUR MOBILE AT BOOKMAKERS.CO.UK NOVICES' H'CAP HURDLE (10 hdls) 2m 4f
3:00 (3:00) (Class 4) (0-115,115) 3-Y-0+ **£3,119** (£915; £457; £228)

Form RPR
221- **1** **Carlton Jack**[25] 1794 6-11-7 **115**........................ MauriceLinehan(5) 127+
(Jonjo O'Neill) *trckd ldng pair: led gng wl 3 out: pushed along to assert between last 2: in command tl jinked rt 150yds out and lost momentum: sn firmly drvn: hld on nr fin* **13/8**[1]
2 *nk* **Mr Utah**[41] 1615 6-11-1 **109**.. TonyKelly(5) 117
(Rebecca Menzies) *in tch: trckd ldr 3 out: rdn after 2 out: 3 l down whn hit last: given ch by errnt ldr run-in: kpt on: jst hld* **7/1**[3]
11- **3** *4* **Ballyglasheen (IRE)**[7] 2038 3-10-8 **115** 7ex...................... PaulMoloney 101
(Evan Williams) *midfield: hdwy to trck ldr 3 out: rdn 2 out: sn one pce in 3rd: nt fluent last* **9/4**[2]
360- **4** *27* **Monbeg (IRE)**[19] 1873 6-10-0 **89** oh2..............................(p) WilsonRenwick 68
(Martin Todhunter) *w ldr: rdn after 6th: wknd after 3 out* **16/1**
155- **5** *14* **Granaruid (IRE)**[109] 958 10-10-12 **108**....................(p) GrantCockburn(7) 74
(Alison Hamilton) *hld up: bhd after 6th* **28/1**
2P6/ **6** *18* **Mr Bolt (IRE)**[17] 1909 8-10-0 **89** oh1..................................(p) BrianHarding 39
(Michael O'Hare, Ire) *led narrowly: hdd 3 out: sn wknd* **10/1**
0/4- **P** **Herostatus**[15] 1924 6-11-5 **108**..(p) BrianHughes
(Jason Ward) *hld up in rr: looked reluctant and p.u bef 6th* **8/1**
4m 52.3s (-0.40) **Going Correction** -0.05s/f (Good)
WFA 3 from 5yo+ 18lb **7** Ran SP% **110.9**
Speed ratings (Par 105): **98,97,96,85,79 72,**
toteswingers 1&2 £3.30, 2&3 £2.90, 1&3 £1.10 CSF £12.63 CT £23.65 TOTE £2.80: £1.40, £6.20; EX 18.60 Trifecta £40.20 Pool: £1810.66 - 33.72 winning units..
Owner John P McManus **Bred** A J Wall **Trained** Cheltenham, Gloucs

FOCUS
A modest novices' handicap hurdle. The wayward winner was value for further and there's probably more to come.

2173 TODDS HIGHWAY MAINTENANCE NORTH EAST NOVICES' H'CAP CHASE (12 fncs 1 omitted) 2m 110y
3:30 (3:30) (Class 4) (0-110,110) 4-Y-0+ **£3,768** (£1,106; £553; £276)

Form RPR
55U- **1** **Cavite Eta (IRE)**[12] 1981 6-11-4 **102**........................ HenryBrooke 110
(Barry Murtagh) *hld up in rr: tk clsr order 4 out: gd hdwy after 3 out: led jst after 2 out: sn rdn: hld on wl run-in* **25/1**
6/2- **2** *½* **Think Its All Over (USA)**[7] 2039 6-10-6 **90**........................ AdamWedge 98
(Evan Williams) *midfield: hdwy to trck ldrs after 4 out: rdn and ev ch after 2 out: kpt on but a jst hld* **5/2**[1]
5/6- **3** *½* **Talkin Thomas (IRE)**[25] 1785 7-11-10 **108**........................ BrianHarding 116+
(Nicky Richards) *in tch: blnd 8th: drvn to chse ldr between last 2: ev ch last: one pce run-in* **11/4**[2]
2/5- **4** *7* **Bocamix (FR)**[176] 167 7-10-13 **100**.................................. JohnKington(3) 102
(Andrew Crook) *midfield: nt fluent 4th: chsd ldrs 3 out: rdn 2 out: wknd appr last* **50/1**
122- **5** *6* **Alderbrook Lad (IRE)**[39] 1629 7-11-4 **105**................... MichaelByrne(3) 100
(Neil Mulholland) *chsd ldr: led 7th: rdn whn hdd jst after 2 out: wknd* **8/1**
U32- **6** *13* **Turf Trivia**[7] 2048 6-10-11 **95**..(b) BarryKeniry 84
(George Moore) *midfield: in tch 3 out: sn rdn: wkng whn hmpd by faller 2 out* **12/1**
221- **7** *6* **Muwalla**[56] 1503 6-11-10 **108**..(tp) DenisO'Regan 86
(Chris Grant) *hld up: nvr threatened* **12/1**
456- **8** *4½* **Reef Dancer (IRE)**[20] 1851 10-10-9 **93**........................(tp) KennyJohnson 67
(Robert Johnson) *hld up in rr: a bhd* **40/1**
046- **P** **Toledo Gold (IRE)**[20] 1849 7-11-5 **110**..................(t) StephenMulqueen(7)
(Maurice Barnes) *led: clr 2nd tl 5th: hdd 7th: wknd after 4 out: p.u bef last* **50/1**
55P/ **P** **Accordion To Paddy (IRE)**[570] 5365 9-10-12 **96**.......... DougieCostello
(Michael O'Hare, Ire) *hld up in rr: a bhd: p.u bef 4 out* **20/1**
121- **F** **Sendiym (FR)**[12] 1981 6-10-9 **93**...(b) BrianHughes 88
(Dianne Sayer) *chsd ldrs: rdn after 3 out: wkng whn fell 2 out* **7/1**[3]
25P- **U** **Brady (IRE)**[16] 1916 7-11-11 **109**..(b[1]) JasonMaguire
(Donald McCain) *trckd ldrs: uns rdr 1st* **11/1**
4m 6.1s (-2.50) **Going Correction** -0.40s/f (Good) **12** Ran SP% **117.5**
Speed ratings (Par 105): **89,88,88,85,82 76,73,71, , ,**
toteswingers 1&2 £18.50, 2&3 £3.20, 1&3 £22.40 CSF £87.01 CT £237.20 TOTE £40.20: £9.20, £1.70, £1.80; EX 131.70 Trifecta £2142.80 Part won. Pool: £2857.08 - 0.94 winning units..
Owner Don't Tell Henry **Bred** Michael Keane **Trained** Low Braithwaite, Cumbria

FOCUS
A modest novices' handicap chase which produced a thrilling finish with any number in there pitching at the top of the hill. The winner is rated to the best of his hurdles form with the second similar to his recent win.

2174 HORSE RACING FREE BETS AT BOOKMAKERS.CO.UK MAIDEN OPEN NATIONAL HUNT FLAT RACE 2m 1f
4:00 (4:01) (Class 6) 4-6-Y-0 **£1,559** (£457; £228; £114)

Form RPR
3/ **1** **Classic Move (IRE)**[191] 5488 4-11-2 0.............................. JasonMaguire 106+
(Donald McCain) *mde all: pushed clr 2f out: rdn and idled ins fnl f: eased nr fin* **8/13**[1]
4/ **2** *2* **Serenity Now (IRE)**[254] 4306 5-11-2 0.................................. DannyCook 101
(Brian Ellison) *trckd ldr: rdn over 2f out: kpt on but a hld by idling wnr* **11/2**[2]
0- **3** *3½* **Bellorophon (IRE)**[182] 76 4-11-2 0............................... WilsonRenwick 98
(Tim Vaughan) *hld up: hdwy over 4f out: rdn over 2f out: wnt 3rd over 1f out: kpt on* **25/1**
4 *6* **Palmarrick (IRE)** 6-11-2 0.. HarryHaynes 92
(Nick Kent) *in tch: rdn over 2f out: one pce in 4th fr over 1f out* **80/1**
3/0- **5** *7* **Our Boy Ben**[44] 1599 4-11-2 0...[1] BrianHughes 86
(Malcolm Jefferson) *in tch: rdn over 2f out: wknd over 1f out* **10/1**[3]
6 *25* **Reggie Parrot** 6-10-9 0.. CallumBewley(7) 64
(Sue Smith) *trckd ldrs: wknd over 3f out* **25/1**
7 *7* **Blondinabar** 4-10-6 0.. KyleJames(3) 50
(Philip Kirby) *midfield: rdn over 5f out: sn struggling* **25/1**
8 *4* **Keep Hope Alive** 4-11-2 0.. BrianHarding 54
(Michael O'Hare, Ire) *midfield: rdn over 4f out: sn wknd* **12/1**
9 *nk* **Samtomjones (IRE)**[157] 5-10-9 0.............................. MissJRRichards(7) 53
(John Norton) *hld up in rr: a bhd* **100/1**
0/ **10** *21* **Banderitos**[193] 5429 4-11-2 0.. DougieCostello 34
(Tim Easterby) *midfield: rdn 6f out: sn wknd* **25/1**
26- **11** *30* **Abel J Tasman (IRE)**[19] 1877 5-11-2 0......................(tp) DenisO'Regan 7
(James Moffatt) *hld up: reminders 1/2-way: sn t.o* **14/1**
4m 1.8s (0.50) **Going Correction** -0.05s/f (Good) **11** Ran SP% **118.4**
Speed ratings: **96,95,93,90,87 75,72,70,70,60 46**
toteswingers 1&2 £1.20, 2&3 £12.90, 1&3 £8.60 CSF £3.73 TOTE £1.50: £1.10, £2.10, £6.30; EX 5.20 Trifecta £58.80 Pool: £3281.87 - 41.83 winning units..
Owner T G Leslie **Bred** Jim Mernagh **Trained** Cholmondeley, Cheshire

FOCUS
A fair bumper in which the stand-out horse on form duly obliged. He's rated in line with his Punchestown run.
T/Plt: £404.50 to a £1 stake. Pool of £63202.73 - 114.04 winning tickets. T/Qpdt: £156.20 to a £1 stake. Pool of £4941.40 - 23.40 winning tickets. AS

2083 STRATFORD (L-H)
Thursday, October 31

OFFICIAL GOING: Soft (good to soft in places) changing to soft after race 3 (2.10) changing to soft (heavy in places) on the hurdle course after race 4 (2.55)
The first fence in the back straight, and the first hurdle in the back straight, were omitted on all circuits.
Wind: Light across Weather: Overcast

2175 AJA FEGENTRI AMATEUR RIDERS' H'CAP HURDLE (FOR GENTLEMEN AMATEUR RIDERS) (9 hdls 2 omitted) 2m 6f 110y
1:10 (1:10) (Class 5) (0-95,90) 4-Y-0+ **£1,975** (£607; £303)

Form RPR
300- **1** **Brass Monkey (IRE)**[39] 1630 6-11-5 **83**.............................. MrCSmith 104+
(Neil King) *a.p: chsd ldr 4th: led next: drvn along after 2 out: styd on u.p* **11/2**[2]
0/1- **2** *1¾* **Easy Beesy**[8] 2016 5-11-5 **83**.. MrMLegg 101
(Charles Egerton) *chsd ldrs: wnt 2nd 6th: rdn after 2 out: styd on* **2/7**[1]
63/- **3** *35* **Hector's House**[250] 4383 7-11-7 **85**.................................. MrKevinTobin 68
(Nikki Evans) *hld up: hdwy appr 2 out: rdn and wknd wl bef last* **13/2**[3]
/PP- **4** *nk* **Caught By Witness (IRE)**[128] 833 8-11-12 **90**..............(t) MrFMitchell 73
(Anthony Middleton) *hld up: hdwy 6th: rdn and wknd wl bef last* **12/1**
P/P- **5** *3* **Laughing Game**[8] 2023 9-10-0 **64** oh3..................................(t[1]) MrPJohn 44
(Laura Hurley) *led: hit 4th: hdd next: wknd after 7th* **25/1**
0/U- **6** *34* **Best Bette**[160] 461 8-10-10 **74**.. MrLKilgarriff 20
(Clarissa Caroe) *bhd fr 3rd* **20/1**
PF0- **P** **Guns Of Love (IRE)**[7] 2044 11-10-1 **65**......................(b[1]) MrTWWheeler
(Robin Dickin) *plld hrd: trckd ldr to 4th: pushed along whn mstke next: wknd after 6th: bhd whn p.u bef 2 out* **20/1**
446- **F** **Trakeur (FR)**[21] 1834 6-11-6 **84**.............................. MrAlexandreLemarie
(Simon Hodgson) *prom: pushed along and wkng whn fell 2 out* **25/1**
5m 52.06s (23.96) **Going Correction** +1.00s/f (Soft) **8** Ran SP% **131.4**
Speed ratings (Par 103): **98,97,85,85,84 72, ,**
toteswingers 1&2 £1.40, 2&3 £1.80, 1&3 £1.70 CSF £8.77 CT £14.86 TOTE £6.80: £1.30, £1.02, £1.60; EX 16.30 Trifecta £58.50 Pool: £2998.35 - 38.42 winning units..
Owner The St Gatien Racing For Fun Partnership **Bred** Oliver McDonnell **Trained** Newmarket, Suffolk

FOCUS
Bends moved where necessary. A very weak affair. A big step up from the winner but it looks believable with the second probably running at least as well as his recent win.

2176 STRATFORD-ON-AVON RACECOURSE RACING EXCELLENCE "HANDS & HEELS" (S) HURDLE (CONDITIONAL/AMATEURS) (7 hdls 2 omitted) 2m 3f
1:40 (1:40) (Class 5) 4-7-Y-0 **£1,949** (£572; £286; £143)

Form RPR
056- 1 **Stadium Of Light (IRE)**[6] 1791 6-10-9 77 WilliamFeatherstone(3) 94
(Shaun Harris) *chsd ldr tl led 2nd: pushed along and hdd 2 out: hmpd bnd appr last: styd on to ld towards fin* **17/2**
/42- 2 ¾ **Isola Bella**[54] 1517 4-10-2 93 (b[1]) MrJHarding(3) 87
(Jonathan Portman) *a.p: chsd ldr 3rd: led and hit 2 out: pushed along and edgd lft bnd appr last: hung rt and hdd towards fin* **5/2[1]**
301- 3 shd **Persian Herald**[6] 2062 5-11-5 89 (bt) MissBAndrews 99
(Neil King) *led to 2nd: chsd ldr to next: outpcd after 3 out: rallied appr last: styd on* **3/1[2]**
000- 4 10 **Cash For Steel (IRE)**[13] 1958 6-10-5 0 DanielHiskett 74
(Richard Phillips) *mid-div: j.rt 1st: pushed along after 3 out: nvr trbld ldrs* **9/1**
6/P- 5 2 ¾ **Edlomond (IRE)**[8] 2021 7-11-5 0 (t) JackSherwood 86
(Bill Turner) *prom: pushed along appr 2 out: wknd bef last* **16/1**
/40- 6 22 **Haling Park (UAE)**[142] 711 7-10-2 64 OllieGarner(3) 49
(Clarissa Caroe) *in rr: pushed along after 3rd: wknd next* **33/1**
250/ 7 2 ½ **Ponte Di Rosa**[37] 2265 5-10-12 96 CiaranMckee 54
(Simon Hodgson) *mid-div: hmpd 1st: pushed along and wknd after 3 out* **14/1**
615- 8 24 **Advisor (FR)**[29] 1171 7-11-5 109 JakeHodson 37
(Mark Gillard) *in rr: pushed along after 2nd: bhd fr 4th* **6/1[3]**
550- 9 16 **Little Bit Lively (IRE)**[26] 1770 4-10-12 0 JosephAkehurst 14
(Sarah Humphrey) *prom: mstke 4th: wknd after 3 out* **66/1**
14F/ U **Mister Fantastic**[57] 2871 7-10-7 0 MissSLewis(5)
(Dai Burchell) *uns rdr 1st* **11/1**
660/ P **Lara Dora (IRE)**[369] 2057 7-10-5 0 KieronEdgar
(Laura Hurley) *bhd fr 3rd: p.u bef last* **100/1**

5m 1.5s (30.00) **Going Correction** +1.15s/f (Heavy)
WFA 4 from 5yo+ 9lb **11 Ran SP% 114.7**
Speed ratings: **82,81,81,77,76 67,65,55,49,**
toteswingers 1&2 £5.40, 2&3 £2.00, 1&3 £5.70 CSF £29.88 TOTE £8.10: £2.10, £1.50, £1.40; EX 34.80 Trifecta £99.60 Pool: £2376.82 - 17.89 winning units..There was no bid for the winner.
Owner Nick Blencowe Mark Lenton S HarrisRacing **Bred** Rabbah Bloodstock Limited **Trained** Carburton, Notts

FOCUS
A weak seller in which a lot were beaten with a circuit remaining. The form makes sense.

2177 WALLS AND CEILINGS INTERNATIONAL NOVICES' LIMITED H'CAP CHASE (15 fncs 2 omitted) 2m 7f
2:10 (2:10) (Class 3) (0-125,125) 4-Y-0 **£6,330** (£1,870; £935; £468; £234)

Form RPR
1/6- 1 **Midnight Prayer**[167] 358 8-11-3 123 WayneHutchinson 139+
(Alan King) *hld up: hdwy 9th: chsd ldr after 12th: rdn to chal whn lft clr last* **11/4[1]**
151- 2 19 **Adrenalin Flight (IRE)**[73] 1316 7-10-7 113 AndrewThornton 110
(Seamus Mullins) *chsd ldrs: mstke 10th: rdn and wknd after 2 out* **14/1**
030/ 3 hd **Castle Conflict (IRE)**[599] 4799 8-10-8 114 RichardJohnson 111
(Henry Daly) *chsd ldrs: outpcd 12th: rallied 3 out: mstke and wknd next* **8/1[2]**
03P/ 4 11 **Toby Lerone (IRE)**[197] 5354 6-10-9 115 HarrySkelton 100
(Dan Skelton) *hld up: hdwy appr 3 out: sn rdn: wknd next* **10/1[3]**
015- 5 15 **Fearless Leader**[26] 1767 6-10-5 111 oh3 (p) SeanQuinlan 81
(David Bridgwater) *hld up: nt fluent 4th: rdn and wknd 3 out* **50/1**
3P0/ 6 ¾ **Who Owns Me (IRE)**[207] 5200 7-11-3 123 NickScholfield 92
(Charlie Mann) *led 2nd to 6th: chsd ldr tl after 12th: wknd 3 out* **16/1**
31P- 7 29 **Connectivity (IRE)**[12] 1971 9-11-5 125 (b) SamTwiston-Davies 65
(Dr Richard Newland) *chsd ldrs tl rdn and wknd appr 3 out* **8/1[2]**
P23- P **What An Oscar (IRE)**[18] 1888 8-10-4 117 (p) RyanHatch(7)
(Nigel Twiston-Davies) *led to 2nd: chsd ldrs: lost pl 7th: reminders after next: rdn and wknd 11th: bhd whn p.u bef 3 out* **10/1[3]**
0/U- U **Hayjack**[8] 2020 8-10-13 119 AidanColeman 132
(Charlie Longsdon) *trckd ldrs: led 6th: rdn and jnd whn mstke and uns rdr last* **11/4[1]**
2/1- F **Financial Climate (IRE)**[170] 294 6-10-12 118 LeightonAspell
(Oliver Sherwood) *prom tl fell 6th* **10/1[3]**

5m 50.8s (11.60) **Going Correction** +0.70s/f (Soft) **10 Ran SP% 117.3**
Speed ratings (Par 107): **107,100,100,96,91 91,80, , ,**
toteswingers 1&2 £10.00, 2&3 £27.40, 1&3 £8.90 CSF £40.15 CT £279.78 TOTE £4.70: £1.70, £4.00, £3.40; EX 45.90 Trifecta £558.90 Pool: £2284.59 - 3.06 winning units..
Owner The Legends Partnership **Bred** J P L Reynolds **Trained** Barbury Castle, Wilts

FOCUS
A dramatic novice handicap. The winner is rated up a stone on the best of his hurdle form and the unseater was heading for a personal best. The time compared favourably with the later handicap.

2178 EBF STALLIONS "NATIONAL HUNT" NOVICES' HURDLE (QUALIFIER) (6 hdls 2 omitted) 2m 110y
2:40 (2:40) (Class 3) 4-6-Y-0 **£6,330** (£1,870; £935; £468; £234)

Form RPR
5/1- 1 **Irish Cavalier (IRE)**[162] 433 4-10-12 0 RichardJohnson 122+
(Rebecca Curtis) *chsd ldrs: led after 3 out: pushed clr whn nt fluent last: comf* **7/2[2]**
66/ 2 4 **Strollawaynow (IRE)**[298] 3533 6-10-12 0 TomCannon 116
(David Arbuthnot) *hld up: hdwy after 3 out: outpcd bef next: rallied appr last: styd on* **20/1**
53/- 3 2 **Fergal Mael Duin**[214] 5039 5-10-12 0 SeanQuinlan 115
(David Bridgwater) *hld up in tch: ev ch 2 out: sn rdn: styd on same pce appr last* **9/1**
324/ 4 8 **Snake Eyes (IRE)**[253] 4318 5-10-12 0 APMcCoy 107
(Nicky Henderson) *hld up: racd keenly: hdwy 3 out: rdn after next: wknd bef last* **2/5[1]**
/05- 5 8 **West End (IRE)**[14] 1935 6-10-12 0 NickScholfield 98
(Kim Bailey) *prom: chsd ldr appr 3rd tl next: rdn and wknd appr 2 out* **14/1**
0- 6 36 **No Routine (IRE)**[14] 1935 4-10-12 0 RichieMcLernon 62
(Jonjo O'Neill) *chsd ldr to appr 3rd: wknd next* **50/1**
/50- 7 nk **Saudi Pearl (IRE)**[9] 2011 5-10-5 0 RyanHatch(7) 62
(Nigel Twiston-Davies) *in rr whn blnd 1st: bhd fr 3rd* **33/1**
6/U- 8 12 **Over My Head**[166] 367 5-10-5 0 GeraldQuinn(7) 50
(Claire Dyson) *hld up: rdn and wknd after 3 out* **100/1**
3- P **Mission To Mars (IRE)**[18] 1891 4-10-12 0 SamTwiston-Davies
(Nigel Twiston-Davies) *led tl after 3 out: rdn and wknd bef next: bhd whn p.u bef last* **8/1[3]**

4m 14.0s (18.00) **Going Correction** +1.30s/f (Heav) **9 Ran SP% 132.1**
Speed ratings: **109,107,106,102,98 81,81,75,**
toteswingers 1&2 £13.10, 2&3 £24.00, 1&3 £4.00 CSF £65.90 TOTE £4.10: £1.10, £4.00, £2.70; EX 110.90 Trifecta £433.00 Pool: £2719.72 - 4.70 winning units..
Owner A McIver **Bred** Limetree Stud **Trained** Newport, Dyfed

FOCUS
An ordinary novice hurdle. The winner is rated in line with his bumper form but can rate higher.

2179 JOHN SMITH'S H'CAP CHASE (FOR THE J H ROWE CHALLENGE TROPHY) (15 fncs 2 omitted) 2m 7f
3:10 (3:10) (Class 4) (0-120,120) 4-Y-0+ **£4,548** (£1,335; £667; £333)

Form RPR
10P- 1 **Danandy (IRE)**[7] 2041 6-10-12 106 TomO'Brien 125+
(Philip Hobbs) *a.p: led 3 out: clr bef last: eased flat* **5/1[3]**
0/4- 2 9 **Cornish Ice**[15] 1925 9-10-8 102 CharliePoste 106
(Robin Dickin) *prom: lost pl 8th: sn drvn along: rallied after 12th: rdn and wknd bef 2 out: wnt mod 2nd last* **16/1**
441/ 3 1 ¼ **Listen Boy (IRE)**[307] 3314 7-11-12 120 SamTwiston-Davies 125
(Nigel Twiston-Davies) *hld up: hdwy 7th: rdn and wknd appr last* **6/4[1]**
226/ 4 1 ¼ **Desperate Dex (IRE)**[243] 4523 13-11-10 118 PaddyBrennan 119
(Tom George) *led to 3rd: led 7th: hdd 3 out: rdn and wknd appr last* **12/1**
313/ 5 8 **Milo Milan (IRE)**[246] 4449 8-11-7 118 (p) MichealNolan(3) 113
(Richard Lee) *prom: mstke 2nd (water): nt fluent next: lost pl after 5th: wknd 9th* **4/1[2]**
05P- 6 44 **Very Stylish (IRE)**[109] 972 9-11-4 112 (p) APMcCoy 61
(Jonjo O'Neill) *chsd ldrs: lost pl after 10th: wknd after 12th* **15/2**
250/ 7 4 ½ **Circus Of Dreams**[215] 5012 10-11-5 113 (v) LeightonAspell 57
(Oliver Sherwood) *chsd ldr tl led 3rd: hdd 7th: wknd 3 out* **14/1**
552/ P **Thats Ben (IRE)**[172] 8-11-0 108 FelixDeGiles
(Tom Gretton) *a in rr: bhd fr 9th: p.u after 12th* **18/1**

5m 59.7s (20.50) **Going Correction** +0.85s/f (Soft) **8 Ran SP% 113.9**
Speed ratings (Par 105): **98,94,94,94,91 75,74,**
toteswingers 1&2 £10.00, 2&3 £7.70, 1&3 £3.40 CSF £70.87 CT £174.54 TOTE £7.20: £1.80, £3.60, £1.20; EX 107.60 Trifecta £930.10 Pool: £2353.47 - 1.89 winning units..
Owner Michelle Ryan **Bred** Mrs Mary Motherway **Trained** Withycombe, Somerset

FOCUS
A modest handicap with a progressive winner who improved to the level of his best hurdle form. The next three were close to their marks.

2180 GEORGE PRAGNELL H'CAP CHASE (12 fncs 2 omitted) 2m 4f
3:40 (3:40) (Class 3) (0-140,137) 4-Y-0+ **£6,498** (£1,908; £954; £477)

Form RPR
166/ 1 **Mart Lane (IRE)**[178] 152 8-11-3 128 SamTwiston-Davies 133
(Dr Richard Newland) *chsd ldr to 6th: wnt 2nd again next: rdn appr 3 out: led last: styd on wl* **5/1[2]**
123/ 2 3 **Simply Wings (IRE)**[225] 4862 9-11-4 132 MichealNolan(3) 134
(Richard Lee) *hld up: hdwy 6th: led 3 out: rdn and hdd last: styd on same pce flat* **10/1**
213- 3 2 ½ **Harry Hunt**[18] 603 6-11-3 128 WayneHutchinson 128
(Graeme McPherson) *hld up: nt fluent 5th: drvn along 9th: hdwy 3 out: rdn appr last: no ex flat* **15/2[3]**
166/ 4 3 ½ **The Druids Nephew (IRE)**[194] 5406 6-11-2 132 JamesBanks(5) 130
(Andy Turnell) *prom: lost pl whn blnd 4th: hdwy appr 3 out: styd on same pce appr last* **13/8[1]**
410/ 5 shd **Arctic Ben (IRE)**[209] 5160 9-10-11 125 JakeGreenall(3) 122
(Henry Daly) *led to 3m out: sn rdn: mstke and wknd last* **10/1**
F1P/ 6 46 **Bennys Mist (IRE)**[209] 5160 7-11-7 132 AidanColeman 98
(Venetia Williams) *prom: nt fluent 2nd: chsd ldr 6th to next: wnt 2nd again 2 out: sn rdn: wknd appr last* **16/1**
131/ 7 14 **Amigo (FR)**[195] 5372 6-11-12 137 (t) ConorO'Farrell 73
(David Pipe) *hld up and a in rr: bhd fr 8th* **5/1[2]**
00/- P **Overclear**[1234] 756 11-11-0 125 JackDoyle
(Victor Dartnall) *chsd ldrs: lost pl 7th: wknd after 9th: p.u bef next* **28/1**
P6U/ P **Rouge Et Blanc (FR)**[188] 5547 8-11-5 130 LeightonAspell
(Oliver Sherwood) *hld up: hdwy 7th: wknd 2 out: bhd whn p.u bef last* **25/1**

5m 5.6s (15.60) **Going Correction** +1.00s/f (Soft) **9 Ran SP% 114.6**
Speed ratings (Par 107): **108,106,105,104,104 85,80, ,**
toteswingers 1&2 £5.70, 2&3 £5.60, 1&3 £8.90 CSF £51.97 CT £371.06 TOTE £5.90: £1.70, £3.40, £1.50; EX 60.10 Trifecta £355.50 Pool: £3421.73 - 7.21 winning units..
Owner Jim Stewart **Bred** Ronnie O'Neill **Trained** Claines, Worcs

FOCUS
Virtually all of these were returning from a long absence, so improvement can be expected from most, although some are on fairly high official ratings. Straightforward form.

2181 JENKINSONS CATERERS MAIDEN HURDLE (9 hdls 2 omitted) 2m 6f 110y
4:10 (4:10) (Class 4) 4-Y-0+ **£3,249** (£954; £477; £238)

Form RPR
4- 1 **Andy Kelly (IRE)**[11] 1991 4-10-10 0 GavinSheehan(3) 123+
(Emma Lavelle) *a.p: led 2 out: hung rt bnd sn after: pushed clr appr last: eased flat* **9/4[1]**
030- 2 22 **Lost Arca (FR)**[66] 1405 7-10-9 72 (t) EdCookson(5) 95
(Robin Mathew) *chsd ldr: nt fluent 2nd: led 3rd tl after 3 out: sn rdn: wknd after next* **125/1**
0- 3 5 **Flintham**[171] 270 4-10-8 0 NicodeBoinville(5) 89
(Mark Bradstock) *chsd ldrs: led after 3 out: sn rdn: hdd next: sn wknd* **40/1**
4 1 ½ **Bob Keown (IRE)**[201] 5-11-0 0 APMcCoy 89
(Rebecca Curtis) *hld up: hdwy 4th: pushed along after 3 out: wknd after next* **7/2[2]**
5 3 ½ **Shinooki (IRE)**[242] 6-11-0 0 PaddyBrennan 87
(Alex Hales) *hld up: j.rt 7th: hdwy sn after: chsd wnr after 2 out: wkng whn blnd last* **50/1**
0/ 6 hd **Drumgooland (IRE)**[195] 5392 6-11-0 109 SamTwiston-Davies 85
(Dr Richard Newland) *hld up: mstke 5th: sn pushed along: hdwy 7th: rdn and wknd after 2 out* **9/1**
7 12 **Many Stars (IRE)**[228] 5-11-0 0 (t) HarrySkelton 74
(Dan Skelton) *prom: racd keenly: rdn and wknd after 2 out* **10/1**

5/6- **8** *1 ½* **Degenerate (FR)**[9] 2009 6-11-0 0 NickScholfield 71
(Jeremy Scott) *hld up: hdwy appr 2 out: wknd sn after* **28/1**

6/2- **9** *23* **Fond Memory (IRE)**[170] 291 5-10-7 0 RyanHatch(7) 48
(Nigel Twiston-Davies) *prom: lost pl after 4th: bhd fr 6th* **16/1**

10 *¾* **Area Access (IRE)**[207] 5-11-0 0 DaveCrosse 48
(Charlie Mann) *prom: mstke 4th: rdn and wknd after 2 out* **50/1**

11 *shd* **Billy Biscuit (IRE)**[270] 5-11-0 0 WayneHutchinson 47
(Alan King) *hld up: hdwy after 6th: mstke next: rdn and wknd bef 2 out* **7/1**[3]

4- **12** *2 ¼* **Badger Wood**[26] 1771 4-10-13 0 DavidEngland 44
(Giles Smyly) *mid-div: lost pl appr 6th: sn bhd* **33/1**

P **Georgie Lad (IRE)**[165] 5-11-0 0 RichardJohnson
(Philip Hobbs) *plld hrd: led to 3rd: trckd ldrs: nt fluent 6th: rdn and wknd after 2 out: p.u bef last* **7/1**[3]

P **Redoubtablefighter (IRE)**[172] 7-11-0 0 (t) AidanColeman
(Anthony Middleton) *hld up: bhd fr 6th: p.u bef last* **100/1**

5m 58.2s (30.10) **Going Correction** +1.45s/f (Heav)
WFA 4 from 5yo+ 10lb **14** Ran SP% **117.5**
Speed ratings (Par 105): **105,97,95,95,93 93,89,89,81,80 80,80, ,**
toteswingers 1&2 £41.60, 2&3 £194.70, 1&3 £17.80 CSF £352.69 TOTE £3.70: £1.60, £9.00, £9.00; EX 227.40 Trifecta £2021.50 Pool: £2695.37 - 0.77 winning units..
Owner The Optimists **Bred** Grace Leahy **Trained** Hatherden, Hants

FOCUS
A modest maiden hurdle and one-way traffic for the winner, who built on his recent run.
T/Plt: £111.90 to £1 stake. Pool of £68362.51 - 445.76 winning tickets. T/Qpdt: £71.90 to £1 stake. Pool of £5460.65 - 56.20 winning tickets. CR

1934 UTTOXETER (L-H)

Friday, November 1

OFFICIAL GOING: Chase course - soft; hurdle course - soft (good to soft in places in the home straight) changing to soft after race 1 (12.50); heavy in 2m start chute
Wind: moderate across Weather: overcast, raining race 1 onwards

2189 BREEDERS' CUP LIVE ONLY ON ATR NOVICES' HURDLE (10 hdls) 2m 4f 110y
12:50 (12:50) (Class 4) 4-Y-0+ **£3,249** (£954; £477; £238)

Form RPR

1 **Carraig Mor (IRE)**[334] 5-10-12 0 RobertThornton 145+
(Alan King) *trckd ldrs: led after 3rd: j.rt: wnt clr appr 2 out: v easily* **9/4**[1]

4/F- **2** *25* **Milord (GER)**[26] 1793 4-10-12 125 TomScudamore 115
(Kim Bailey) *hld up in rr: hdwy to chse wnr 4th: kpt on same pce fr 3 out* **11/4**[2]

5/4- **3** *17* **I Am Colin**[20] 1863 4-10-5 0 RyanHatch(7) 101
(Nigel Twiston-Davies) *chsd ldrs: hmpd and mstke 2nd: hdwy 6th: modest 3rd appr 3 out: one pce* **6/1**

34/ **4** *9* **Royal Palladium (FR)**[235] 4718 5-10-12 0 LiamTreadwell 89
(Venetia Williams) *in rr: hdwy 7th: wnt poor 4th sn after 3 out* **33/1**

06/ **5** *14* **Western Movie**[463] 1089 5-10-12 0 TomO'Brien 75
(Philip Hobbs) *prom: wknd 7th* **20/1**

5- **6** *¾* **Gonalston Cloud (IRE)**[29] 1732 6-10-12 0 HarryHaynes 74
(Nick Kent) *chsd ldrs: lost pl 5th: sn bhd* **100/1**

0- **7** *21* **Oak Wood (IRE)**[15] 1937 5-10-12 0 LeeEdwards 53
(John Upson) *t.k.h: trckd ldrs: lost pl 5th: bhd fr 7th* **100/1**

3- **8** *½* **Vujiyama (FR)**[26] 1793 4-10-12 0 RichieMcLernon 61
(Jonjo O'Neill) *hld up in rr: hdwy 5th: modest 3rd 7th: 4th and weakning whn mstke next: sn heavily eased* **14/1**

200- **9** *¾* **Straits Of Messina (IRE)**[8] 2040 4-10-12 0 FelixDeGiles 52
(Tom Symonds) *mid-div: lost pl 6th: sn bhd* **100/1**

0- **10** *31* **Rocky Island (IRE)**[16] 1924 5-10-12 0 SeanQuinlan 21
(Jennie Candlish) *j. slowly: led hdd after 3rd: sn drvn: lost pl 6th: sn bhd: t.o 3 out* **100/1**

P **Murtys Delight (IRE)**[229] 4827 6-10-12 0 JamieMoore
(Dr Richard Newland) *mid-div: j.rt 3rd: bhd and drvn 5th: sn t.o: p.u bef 3 out* **10/3**[3]

P **Leap In The Dark** 7-10-5 0 DonalDevereux
(John Mackie) *chsd ldrs: lost pl after 4th: sn bhd: t.o whn p.u bef 6th* **100/1**

5m 1.3s (2.30) **Going Correction** +0.55s/f (Soft) **12** Ran SP% **114.1**
Speed ratings (Par 105): **117,107,101,97,92 91,83,83,83,71 ,**
toteswingers 1&2 £1.40, 1&3 £3.40, 2&3 £2.10 CSF £8.17 TOTE £3.60: £1.20, £1.30, £2.70; EX 8.80 Trifecta £50.40 Pool: £872.06 - 12.96 winning units..
Owner Masterson Holdings Limited **Bred** G T Greene **Trained** Barbury Castle, Wilts

FOCUS
Divided bends on fresh ground. Hurdles sited 10-12yds off inside. The first hurdle in the 2m chute was left out and the first fence in the back straight was omitted in all chases. This wasn't a bad novice hurdle and the impressive winner looks a top-class prospect.

2190 GET IN! ATR BREEDERS' CUP SPECIAL TONIGHT MARES' MAIDEN HURDLE (8 hdls 1 omitted) 2m
1:20 (1:20) (Class 5) 3-Y-0+ **£2,209** (£648; £324; £162)

Form RPR

154/ **1** **Centasia**[210] 5163 6-11-4 0 (t) TomScudamore 120+
(David Pipe) *trckd ldrs: led after 5th: styd on wl between last 2: drvn out* **2/1**[1]

5/1- **2** *4 ½* **The Pirate's Queen (IRE)**[183] 85 4-11-4 0 RobertThornton 113+
(Alan King) *mid-div: hdwy 4th: jnd wnr 3 out: swtchd lft between last 2: styd on same pce* **9/4**[2]

0- **3** *9* **Born To Benefit (IRE)**[15] 1938 7-11-4 92 (t) AlainCawley 105
(Fergal O'Brien) *chsd ldrs: 4th and outpcd whn mstke 2 out: lft modest 3rd last* **50/1**

2/5- **4** *10* **August Hill (IRE)**[21] 1861 5-11-4 0 (t) TomO'Brien 95
(Philip Hobbs) *hld up: hdwy 3rd: sn trcking ldrs: one pce fr 3 out: lft modest 4th last* **10/1**

330- **5** *4 ½* **Hopeand**[65] 1428 8-11-4 81 (t) AdamPogson 90
(Charles Pogson) *t.k.h: w ldrs whn mstke 2nd: led 4th: hdd after next: wknd bef 2 out* **66/1**

P/0- **6** *8* **Buxom (IRE)**[162] 450 6-11-4 108 BrendanPowell 81
(Jamie Snowden) *hld up in rr: hdwy 5th: wknd 3 out* **6/1**[3]

P/ **7** *1 ¾* **Tribu D'Estruval (FR)**[540] 257 6-11-4 0 PaddyBrennan 79
(Tom George) *mid-div: hdwy 4th: sn chsng ldrs: wknd bef 3 out* **20/1**

0/3- **8** *7* **Tenmoku**[19] 1885 4-11-4 0 RichieMcLernon 72
(Jonjo O'Neill) *hld up in mid-div: hdwy 5th: wknd appr next* **10/1**

0/ **9** *18* **Un Jour D Ete (FR)**[197] 5364 5-11-4 0 JamieMoore 57
(Nick Littmoden) *chsd ldrs: lost pl 5th* **50/1**

00/ **10** *1* **Rightonthyme**[288] 3698 6-11-4 0 FelixDeGiles 53
(Tom Symonds) *in rr: hdwy whn mstke 5th: sn wknd* **100/1**

P5- **11** *4 ½* **Astrogold**[26] 1793 4-11-4 0 ColinBolger 49
(Mark H Tompkins) *chsd ldrs: lost pl 5th: sn bhd* **100/1**

12 *31* **Choral Bee**[399] 4-11-4 0 DavidBass 18
(Alan Jessop) *in rr: bhd fr 5th: t.o 3 out* **100/1**

0/0- **13** *3 ¾* **Ticket**[167] 372 4-11-4 0 [1] SeanQuinlan 14
(Jennie Candlish) *led: hit 2nd: hdd 4th: lost pl next: sn bhd: t.o 2 out* **100/1**

P **Hittin'The Skids (IRE)**[14] 5-11-4 0 TomMessenger
(Mandy Rowland) *stdd s: hld up in rr: bhd fr 5th: t.o whn p.u bef 3 out* **100/1**

0/ **F** **Cantony**[192] 5479 4-11-4 0 HarrySkelton
(Henry Daly) *mid-div whn fell 4th* **66/1**

16- **R** **Tara Muck**[19] 1885 6-10-11 0 RyanHatch(7) 98
(Nigel Twiston-Davies) *chsd ldrs: 3rd 5th: one pce fr 3 out: rn out and crashed through wing and fell last* **11/1**

3m 59.7s (7.70) **Going Correction** +0.70s/f (Soft) **16** Ran SP% **121.5**
Speed ratings (Par 103): **108,105,101,96,94 90,89,85,76,76 73,58,56, ,**
toteswingers 1&2 £1.10, 1&3 £30.10, 2&3 £17.60 CSF £6.46 TOTE £3.00: £1.30, £1.20, £12.50; EX 7.40 Trifecta £138.40 Pool: £992.34 - 5.37 winning units..
Owner R S Brookhouse **Bred** Fawley House Stud **Trained** Nicholashayne, Devon

FOCUS
Not nearly as competitive as the numbers might have suggested and the two market leaders dominated, but the form ought to work out. The winner can rate higher.

2191 BREEDERS' CUP ON ATR SKY 415 H'CAP HURDLE (8 hdls 1 omitted) 2m
1:50 (1:50) (Class 5) (0-100,98) 4-Y-0+ **£2,209** (£648; £324; £162)

Form RPR

P/0- **1** **Blake Dean**[15] 1938 5-9-9 74 CallumBewley(7) 97+
(Sue Smith) *mde all: mstkes: lft clr 3 out: drvn out* **7/2**[1]

0/U- **2** *15* **My Nosy Rosy**[15] 1938 5-10-11 88 (t) KillianMoore(5) 92
(Ben Case) *hld up in rr: hdwy 4th: lft modest 2nd 3 out: one pce* **6/1**[3]

/60- **3** *8* **Katnapping**[146] 669 5-11-1 92 MrSWaley-Cohen(5) 88
(Robert Waley-Cohen) *chsd ldrs: lost pl 3rd: sn drvn: hdwy appr 3 out: modest 3rd 2 out* **6/1**[3]

30F- **4** *½* **Lost In Newyork (IRE)**[23] 1820 6-10-10 82 (t) HarryHaynes 78
(Nick Kent) *chsd ldrs: blnd 2nd: lost pl 5th: kpt on fr next: modest 4th 2 out* **6/1**[3]

/00- **5** *4 ½* **Prince Freddie**[73] 1331 5-10-5 77 JamieMoore 71
(Roy Brotherton) *prom: lost pl 3rd: sme hdwy whn bdly hmpd 3 out: no ch after* **20/1**

P60/ **6** *16* **Oriental Cat**[375] 1961 6-10-7 86 MrJHamilton(7) 61
(Venetia Williams) *chsd ldrs: drvn 5th: wknd 2 out* **7/1**

0BF/ **7** *1 ¼* **Lilac Belle**[202] 5290 7-11-6 92 (t) WillKennedy 66
(Alex Hales) *hld up in rr: hdwy 4th: drvn 3 out: wknd appr next* **14/1**

342- **F** **Another Flutter (IRE)**[9] 2025 9-11-12 98 (tp) CharliePoste
(Matt Sheppard) *chsd ldr: t.k.h: drvn whn fell 3 out* **5/1**[2]

005/ **B** **Peqeno Diablo (IRE)**[498] 780 8-9-11 76 (tp) GeraldQuinn(7)
(Claire Dyson) *trckd ldrs: drvn and outpcd whn b.d 3 out* **12/1**

4m 5.4s (13.40) **Going Correction** +0.85s/f (Soft) **9** Ran SP% **113.4**
Speed ratings (Par 103): **100,92,88,88,86 78,77, ,**
toteswingers 1&2 £8.30, 1&3 £6.50, 2&3 £32.10 CSF £24.57 CT £120.14 TOTE £5.70: £1.70, £2.40, £2.90; EX 24.80 Trifecta £109.90 Pool: £633.50 - 4.32 winning units..
Owner Widdop Wanderers **Bred** Lordship Stud **Trained** High Eldwick, W Yorks

FOCUS
A moderate handicap, run at a fair gallop. The winner was well in on old form and should still be competitive when reassessed.

2192 VISIT ATTHERACES.COM/BREEDERSCUP BEGINNERS' CHASE (11 fncs 1 omitted) 2m
2:20 (2:20) (Class 4) 4-Y-0+ **£4,431** (£1,309; £654)

Form RPR

25F/ **1** **Raya Star (IRE)**[211] 5137 7-11-2 0 RobertThornton 135+
(Alan King) *trckd ldr: led 3rd: drvn 3 out: jnd next: hld on towards fin* **1/1**[1]

325/ **2** *½* **Tanerko Emery (FR)**[231] 4768 7-11-2 0 (t) ConorO'Farrell 135+
(David Pipe) *hld up: wnt 2nd 7th: effrt 4 out: upsides 2 out: stmbld on landing last: styd on towards fin* **11/10**[2]

3 *25* **Carli King (IRE)**[229] 7-11-2 0 TomMessenger 110
(Caroline Bailey) *led to 3rd: outpcd appr 4 out: bhd fr next* **14/1**[3]

4m 10.5s (15.50) **Going Correction** +1.00s/f (Soft) **3** Ran SP% **104.3**
Speed ratings (Par 105): **101,100,88**
CSF £2.41 TOTE £1.80; EX 1.90 Trifecta £1.80 Pool: £733.39 - 290.69 winning units..
Owner Simon Munir **Bred** Patrick Fennessy **Trained** Barbury Castle, Wilts

FOCUS
After the defection of Colour Squadron this was essentially a match, but a fascinating one at that and so it played out in the home straight. The first two are both potential 150+ chasers.

2193 $26M BREEDERS' CUP STARTS TONIGHT ON ATR MARES' H'CAP HURDLE (12 hdls) 3m
2:55 (2:55) (Class 4) (0-120,117) 4-Y-0+ **£3,249** (£954; £477; £238)

Form RPR

321/ **1** **Upbeat Cobbler (FR)**[192] 5466 5-10-10 101 TomO'Brien 102
(Henry Daly) *trckd ldrs: led after 4th: qcknd pce 8th: narrowly hdd 3 out: regained narrow advantage next: kpt on run-in: all out* **7/2**[1]

605/ **2** *hd* **Silver Wren**[611] 4580 6-10-12 103 SamJones 105
(Renee Robeson) *trckd ldrs: clr 2nd after 9th: narrow ld 3 out: hdd next: kpt on wl run-in: jst hld* **12/1**

6/2- **3** *5* **Vinnieslittle Lamb (IRE)**[15] 1935 5-11-0 105 AlainCawley 102
(David Bridgwater) *set v stdy pce tl after 4th: outpcd 9th: rallied and 3rd 3 out: one pce* **7/2**[1]

5/F- **4** *1 ¼* **Micro Mission (IRE)**[13] 1978 7-11-5 117 DiarmuidO'Regan(7) 113
(Chris Grant) *chsd ldrs: outpcd 3 out: 4th last: kpt on* **6/1**[3]

600- **5** *2 ½* **Carhue Princess (IRE)**[26] 1799 7-9-9 91 oh9 BenPoste(5) 83
(Tom Symonds) *trckd ldrs: hit 5th: drvn and outpcd appr 3 out: fdd last* **6/1**[3]

0/4- **6** *17* **Bebinn (IRE)**[172] 268 6-10-7 103 KillianMoore(5) 81
(Ben Case) *t.k.h in last: drvn 9th: lost pl bef next: bhd 2 out: eased clsng stages* **7/1**

10/ **7** *12* **Lastchanceforlisa (IRE)**[197] 5360 7-11-4 **109** .... RhysFlint 72
(John Flint) *chsd ldrs: drvn 9th: lost pl appr 3 out: bhd whn eased 2 out* **4/1**[2]

6m 32.1s (42.10) **Going Correction** +1.00s/f (Soft) **7** Ran SP% **113.2**
Speed ratings (Par 105): **69,68,67,66,66 60,56**
toteswingers 1&2 £6.50, 1&3 £1.70, 2&3 £8.50 CSF £39.89 CT £155.59 TOTE £2.90: £1.60, £5.50; EX 46.80 Trifecta £135.70 Pool: £1778.27 - 9.82 winning units..
Owner Mrs A Timpson **Bred** Daniel & Mme Jeannine Laupretre **Trained** Stanton Lacy, Shropshire
■ Stewards' Enquiry : Sam Jones two-day ban: used whip above permitted level (Nov 15-16)

FOCUS
A modest staying handicap hurdle for mares, run at a steady gallop until around five out. Ordinary form with a small step up from the winner.

2194 BUICK'S BREEDERS' CUP BLOG ON ATTHERACES.COM H'CAP CHASE (14 fncs 1 omitted) 2m 4f

3:30 (3:30) (Class 4) (0-120,115) 4-Y-0 **£3,798** (£1,122; £561; £280; £140)

Form RPR
1/0- **1** **Forest Walker (IRE)**[184] 58 6-11-12 **115** .... HarrySkelton 131+
(Dan Skelton) *hld up: trckd ldrs 8th: led appr 4 out: sn clr: 12 l ahd last: heavily eased clsng stages* **11/4**[1]
0/4- **2** *7* **Lough Coi (IRE)**[6] 2078 7-10-6 **100** ....(tp) JamesBanks(5) 101
(Anthony Middleton) *chsd ldrs: drvn 8th: outpcd appr 4 out: kpt on to take modest 2nd appr 2 out* **5/1**[2]
500- **3** *2 1/2* **Hollins**[15] 1939 9-10-0 **96** .... JoshWall(7) 94
(Tony Forbes) *in rr: hdwy 8th: outpcd appr 4 out: tk modest 3rd appr 2 out: one pce* **10/1**
0/0- **4** *7* **Mallusk (IRE)**[26] 1797 8-11-3 **106** .... RichieMcLernon 97
(Shaun Lycett) *chsd ldrs: outpcd 9th: one pce appr next* **7/1**
/P3- **5** *7* **Ring Bo Ree (IRE)**[19] 1886 10-11-4 **107** ....(p) PaddyBrennan 93
(Tom George) *led: hdd after 10th: wknd 3 out: 4th whn mstke next* **6/1**[3]
460/ **6** *24* **Camden George (IRE)**[239] 4610 12-11-2 **105** .... TomMessenger 65
(Sue Smith) *chsd ldr: reminders 8th: lost pl next: bhd fr 4 out: t.o 2 out* **20/1**
11F/ **P** **Marie Des Anges (FR)**[197] 5359 5-11-7 **113** .... RachaelGreen(3)
(Anthony Honeyball) *hld up: jnd ldrs 9th: led after next: hdd appr 4 out: hit 4 out: wknd qckly: wl bhd whn p.u bef 2 out* **11/4**[1]

5m 25.5s (20.00) **Going Correction** +1.15s/f (Heav) **7** Ran SP% **110.6**
Speed ratings (Par 105): **106,103,102,99,96 87,**
toteswingers 1&2 £7.30, 1&3 £5.70, 2&3 £13.10 CSF £15.89 TOTE £4.80: £2.60, £2.60; EX 19.70 Trifecta £127.70 Pool: £2652.16 - 15.56 winning units..
Owner Ken Price **Bred** Andrew Pierce **Trained** Alcester, Warwicks

FOCUS
Not a bad handicap for the class. The easy winner should go in again.

2195 BREEDERS' CUP ON ATR VIRGIN 534 STANDARD OPEN NATIONAL HUNT FLAT RACE 2m

4:05 (4:05) (Class 6) 4-6-Y-0 **£1,559** (£457; £228; £114)

Form RPR
20/ **1** **Wilde Blue Yonder (IRE)**[209] 5179 4-11-4 0 .... RobertThornton 122+
(Alan King) *trckd ldrs: led 3f out: drew wl clr over 1f out: eased clsng stages* **2/1**[1]
2 *13* **At Reception (IRE)**[182] 108 6-10-8 0 .... TommieMO'Brien(10) 107
(Jonjo O'Neill) *hld up in rr: hdwy 7f out: sn w ldrs: 2nd over 2f out: no ch w wnr: wknd clsng stages* **5/1**[3]
2/ **3** *shd* **Theatrebar**[199] 5334 5-11-4 0 .... FelixDeGiles 107
(Tom Symonds) *hdwy to trck ldrs after 6f: outpcd over 2f out: kpt on fnl f* **5/1**[3]
4 *4 1/2* **Smiles For Miles (IRE)**[229] 5-11-4 0 .... TomScudamore 104+
(David Pipe) *led: hdd 3f out: sn wknd* **5/2**[2]
6- **5** *27* **Cusheen Bridge (IRE)**[17] 1919 5-11-4 0 .... AdamPogson 76
(Charles Pogson) *racd wd 3f: jnd ldrs after 4f: wknd 3f out* **25/1**
0/ **6** *2 3/4* **Royal Macnab (IRE)**[187] 4 5-11-4 0 ....(t) BrendanPowell 73
(Jamie Snowden) *trckd ldrs: drvn 6f out: lost pl over 4f out* **16/1**
7 *29* **Presenting Pricila (IRE)** 4-10-8 0 .... KielanWoods(3) 37
(Charlie Longsdon) *in rr: drvn 7f out: sn lost tch: t.o* **12/1**
8 *67* **Tea In Marrakech (IRE)** 5-11-4 0 .... CharlieHuxley
(William Kinsey) *chsd ldrs: drvn and lost pl over 5f out: sn t.o: virtually p.u: eventually completed* **33/1**

4m 3.7s (17.30) **Going Correction** +1.15s/f (Heav)
WFA 4 from 5yo+ 7lb **8** Ran SP% **115.6**
Speed ratings: **102,95,95,93,79 78,63,30**
toteswingers 1&2 £2.50, 1&3 £3.10, 2&3 £2.70 CSF £12.71 TOTE £3.20: £1.50, £1.40, £1.80; EX 10.40 Trifecta £41.00 Pool: £2453.22 - 44.78 winning units..
Owner Maybe Only Fools Have Horses **Bred** Edmond Kent **Trained** Barbury Castle, Wilts

FOCUS
There were four abreast 2f out in this interesting bumper, but the winner ultimately drew right away. He looks a decent prospect.
T/Plt: £34.30. Pool: £68,133.51 - 1449.06 winning units. T/Qpdt: £23.90. Pool: £4254.70 - 131.50 winning units. WG

1920 WETHERBY (L-H)

Friday, November 1

OFFICIAL GOING: Good to soft changing to good to soft (soft in places) after race 4 (2.10)
Wind: Light across Weather: Rain

2196 WATCH RACING UK ON SKY 432 "NATIONAL HUNT" NOVICES' HURDLE (DIV I) (11 hdls) 2m 4f

12:40 (12:40) (Class 4) 4-Y-0+ **£3,422** (£997; £499)

Form RPR
211/ **1** **Oscar Rock (IRE)**[265] 4127 5-10-12 0 .... BrianHughes 141+
(Malcolm Jefferson) *t.k.h: w ldr: led on bit appr 3 out: sn clr: hit last: impressive* **8/15**[1]
3/2- **2** *19* **Run Ructions Run (IRE)**[170] 324 4-10-5 0 .... DannyCook 109
(Tim Easterby) *midfield: hdwy appr 3 out: wnt 2nd 2 out: hit last: no ch w wnr* **12/1**
1/ **3** *8* **Zermatt (IRE)**[193] 5454 4-10-12 0 .... DougieCostello 107
(John Quinn) *midfield: styd on after 3 out: wnt modest 3rd last* **10/1**
4 *3 1/4* **Straidnahanna (IRE)**[188] 4-10-12 0 .... RyanMania 106
(Sue Smith) *led narrowly: rdn whn hdd appr 3 out: mstke 2 out and lost 2nd: wknd: lost 3rd last* **25/1**
321/ **5** *14* **Sealous Scout (IRE)**[247] 4452 5-10-12 0 .... JasonMaguire 94
(Donald McCain) *chsd ldng pair: mstkes 4th: rdn bef 3 out: sn btn* **15/2**[3]
6 *6* **Vide Cave (FR)**[176] 4-11-5 0 .... NickScholfield 93
(Paul Nicholls) *chsd clr ldng pair: rdn appr 3 out: hit 3 out: sn wknd* **9/2**[2]
0/ **7** *37* **Solstice Dawn**[193] 5452 5-9-12 0 .... MrRWinks(7) 45
(Peter Winks) *hld up: a bhd* **125/1**
6/U- **8** *1 3/4* **Cinnomhor**[20] 1871 5-10-5 0 .... HenryBrooke 44
(Chris Grant) *hld up: mstke 7th: a bhd* **125/1**
0- **9** *5* **Mr Kealshore**[20] 1877 4-10-12 0 .... BarryKeniry 46
(George Moore) *hld up: hit 5th and 6th: a towards rr* **100/1**
FP- **10** *33* **Gloshen (IRE)**[13] 1975 7-10-12 0 .... RichieMcGrath 17
(Philip Kirby) *hld up: a bhd* **150/1**

4m 52.2s (-7.30) **Going Correction** -0.075s/f (Good) **10** Ran SP% **119.0**
Speed ratings (Par 105): **111,103,100,98,93 90,76,75,73,60**
toteswingers 1&2 £3.90, 2&3 £7.40, 1&3 £2.90 CSF £9.08 TOTE £1.80: £1.10, £2.80, £3.10; EX 7.40 Trifecta £42.50 Pool: £1252.47 - 22.05 winning units..
Owner Mr & Mrs G Calder **Bred** Alice Kehoe **Trained** Norton, N Yorks

FOCUS
A fair start to the Charlie Hall meeting, despite the miserable weather, and a much to like about the performance of Oscar Rock, who was opening his account over hurdles at the first time of asking for new connections. He'a a potential 150+ novice hurdler this season.

2197 WATCH RACING UK ON SKY 432 "NATIONAL HUNT" NOVICES' HURDLE (DIV II) (11 hdls) 2m 4f

1:10 (1:11) (Class 4) 4-Y-0+ **£3,422** (£997; £499)

Form RPR
5- **1** **Rally**[26] 1794 4-10-12 0 ....(p) BarryGeraghty 120+
(Nicky Henderson) *trckd ldr: led after 4 out: rdn 3 out: kpt on: idled run-in* **4/1**[3]
2 *2* **Vivaldi Collonges (FR)** 4-10-12 0 .... NickScholfield 117+
(Paul Nicholls) *midfield: hdwy to trck ldr after 4 out: rdn after 3 out: kpt on but a hld by idling wnr* **12/1**
113- **3** *26* **Fairwood Massini (IRE)**[40] 1636 8-10-9 0 ....(vt) MichaelByrne(3) 92
(Tim Vaughan) *trckd ldr: rdn appr 3 out: sn btn in 3rd: wnt lft last* **13/2**
0/ **4** *3 1/4* **Famousandfearless (IRE)**[212] 5125 5-10-12 0 .... TimmyMurphy 89
(David Pipe) *hld up in rr: hdwy into 4th appr 3 out: no further imp after 3 out* **3/1**[2]
3- **5** *4* **Lakefield Rebel (IRE)**[21] 1850 7-10-12 0 .... RichieMcGrath 85
(Henry Hogarth) *in tch: lost pl 6th: no threat after* **28/1**
121/ **6** *15* **Master Rajeem (USA)**[206] 5230 4-10-12 0 .... SamTwiston-Davies 72
(Nigel Twiston-Davies) *midfield: rdn after 6th: wknd after 4 out* **11/4**[1]
5/6- **7** *3 1/2* **Lord Brendy**[13] 1975 5-10-12 0 .... KennyJohnson 70
(Robert Johnson) *t.k.h: midfield: hit 4th: rdn after 7th: sn wknd* **33/1**
8 *4* **Unknown Legend (IRE)**[169] 352 6-10-12 0 .... WayneHutchinson 65
(Alan King) *led: hdd after 4 out: wknd* **7/1**
/35- **9** *14* **Rene Le Roi (FR)**[154] 560 4-10-12 0 .... DannyCook 52
(Tim Easterby) *hld up: rdn after 7th: wknd after 4 out* **66/1**
0/5- **P** **Alaplee**[16] 1924 5-10-12 0 .... HenryBrooke
(Chris Grant) *hld up in rr: mstke 5th: sn wl bhd: p.u after 6th* **100/1**

4m 54.2s (-5.30) **Going Correction** -0.075s/f (Good) **10** Ran SP% **114.1**
Speed ratings (Par 105): **107,106,95,94,92 86,85,83,78,**
toteswingers 1&2 £4.60, 1&3 £1.90, 2&3 £26.10 CSF £46.34 TOTE £4.50: £1.40, £3.30, £1.50; EX 46.90 Trifecta £187.30 Pool: £646.43 - 2.58 winning units..
Owner Walters Plant Hire Ltd **Bred** Juddmonte Farms Ltd **Trained** Upper Lambourn, Berks

FOCUS
It's unlikely that this took as much winning as the first division, but the principals pulled a long way clear and appear to have bright futures ahead of them. The winner improved to the level expected from his bumper form.

2198 BET365.COM H'CAP HURDLE (9 hdls) 2m 110y

1:40 (1:45) (Class 3) (0-125,125) 4-Y-0+ **£5,523** (£1,621; £810; £405)

Form RPR
/04- **1** **Hartside (GER)**[17] 1913 4-10-3 **109** .... MrRWinks(7) 116+
(Peter Winks) *midfield: stdy prog to chse ldrs bef 2 out: sn rdn: upsides whn nt fluent last: kpt on: led towards fin* **16/1**
423/ **2** *3/4* **Pertuis (IRE)**[14] 3624 7-9-10 **100** oh3 ow1 .... JoeColliver(5) 105+
(Micky Hammond) *hld up: stdy hdwy after 4 out: rdn to chse ldrs 2 out: hit last but stl led narrowly: one pce: hdd towards fin* **15/2**
430- **3** *3 1/4* **Lifetime (IRE)**[16] 1922 5-9-12 **104** .... CraigGallagher(7) 105
(Brian Ellison) *hld up: stl plenty to do 2 out: r.o wl: wnt 3rd towards fin* **14/1**
1/4- **4** *1* **Mojolika**[65] 901 5-11-5 **118** .... BrianHarding 119
(Tim Easterby) *midfield: rdn 3 out: kpt on* **22/1**
/01- **5** *3/4* **Tidal Way (IRE)**[29] 1729 4-11-12 **125** ....(p) AidanColeman 126
(Charlie Longsdon) *racd keenly: trckd ldrs: rdn 3 out: led bef 2 out: hdd last: wknd* **7/1**[3]
60/- **6** *1 1/2* **Zafranagar (IRE)**[188] 4524 8-10-3 **107** .... RobertMcCarth(5) 105
(Ian Williams) *trckd ldrs: nt fluent 4th: rdn and ev ch 2 out: wknd last* **9/2**[1]
2/3- **7** *1 1/4* **Travis County (IRE)**[7] 475 4-10-8 **107** .... DannyCook 105
(Brian Ellison) *racd keenly: trckd ldrs: moved upsides after 3rd: rdn 3 out: wknd appr last* **8/1**
201- **8** *2* **Glencree (IRE)**[26] 1785 9-11-5 **118** ....(p) BrianHughes 115
(John Wade) *led narrowly: nt fluent 3 out: hdd bef 2 out: grad wknd* **16/1**
U21/ **9** *2 1/4* **Shadows Lengthen**[195] 5409 7-11-8 **124** .... JakeGreenall(3) 118
(Michael Easterby) *midfield: rdn 3 out: wknd last* **16/1**
1/4- **10** *2 1/4* **Pippa Greene**[29] 1729 9-11-4 **117** .... BarryGeraghty 109
(Nicky Henderson) *hld up: rdn after 3 out: sn no imp* **5/1**[2]
F60/ **11** *3/4* **Beat The Shower**[24] 2975 7-10-6 **105** .... WilsonRenwick 96
(Peter Niven) *hld up: nvr threatened* **16/1**
0/4- **12** *8* **King Zeal (IRE)**[17] 505 9-10-6 **105** ....(t) LiamHeard 89
(Barry Leavy) *prom: rdn bef 3 out* **40/1**
006- **13** *35* **Hi Dancer**[57] 1504 10-11-4 **117** .... AndrewTinkler 69
(Ben Haslam) *midfield: pushed along after 5th: wknd after 4 out: t.o* **20/1**
00/ **14** *3 3/4* **Air Chief**[93] 1166 8-10-10 **112** ....(t) JohnKington(3) 61
(Andrew Crook) *midfield: wknd after 4 out: t.o* **50/1**
246- **15** *2 1/2* **Tinseltown**[16] 1922 7-11-0 **113** .... DougieCostello 60
(Brian Rothwell) *midfield: wknd after 4 out: t.o* **14/1**

3m 59.3s (3.50) **Going Correction** -0.075s/f (Good) **15** Ran SP% **120.6**
Speed ratings (Par 107): **88,87,86,85,85 84,84,83,82,80 80,76,60,58,57**
toteswingers 1&2 £43.00, 1&3 £43.00, 2&3 £43.00 CSF £126.97 CT £1745.29 TOTE £16.00: £3.00, £3.80, £5.10; EX 180.80 Trifecta £846.80 Part won. Pool: £1129.19 - 0.31 winning units..
Owner P Winks **Bred** Gestut Ammerland **Trained** Little Houghton, S Yorks

FOCUS
This was every bit as competitive as the market suggested and it served up a good finish, although they finished in a bit of a heap. The winner was nicely in on the best of his Irish form and ran to a similar level.

2199 BET365 H'CAP CHASE (LISTED RACE) (16 fncs) 2m 4f 110y
2:10 (2:12) (Class 1) (0-155,145) 4-Y-O+

£14,237 (£5,342; £2,675; £1,332; £670; £335)

Form RPR

0/2- **1** **Ultimate**[13] 677 7-11-2 **135**.................... DannyCook 144+
(Brian Ellison) *mde most: hit 10th: rdn 2 out: drvn out run-in* **25/1**

1/5- **2** *1 ½* **Humbie (IRE)**[158] 512 9-10-4 **123**.................... WilsonRenwick 130
(Pauline Robson) *midfield: hdwy to chse ldrs 4 out: rdn 3 out: wnt 2nd last: kpt on but a hld by wnr* **14/1**

424/ **3** *6* **Mac Aeda**[190] 5523 9-10-6 **125**.................... BrianHughes 128
(Malcolm Jefferson) *midfield: hdwy to trck ldr appr 4 out: chal whn hit 3 out: sn rdn: jst lost 2nd whn mstke last: wknd* **5/1**[1]

P24/ **4** *7* **Triptico (FR)**[216] 5014 7-10-10 **129**.................... PaulMoloney 124
(Evan Williams) *hld up: hit 7th: rdn after 5 out: plugged on: wnt modest 4th run-in: nvr threatened ldrs* **9/1**

111- **5** *1 ¾* **Green Wizard (IRE)**[155] 553 7-10-13 **132**.................... RyanMania 126
(Sue Smith) *trckd ldrs: hit 11th: rdn 4 out: sn one pce: wknd run-in* **16/1**

133/ **6** *2* **Frontier Spirit (IRE)**[190] 5523 9-11-2 **135**.................... SamTwiston-Davies 130
(Nigel Twiston-Davies) *hld up: mstke 3rd: rdn 4 out: nvr threatened* **12/1**

213- **7** *1 ¼* **Sergeant Pink (IRE)**[21] 1852 7-10-5 **124**.................... LucyAlexander 114
(Dianne Sayer) *hld up: reminder after 2nd: rdn 5 out: nvr threatened* **28/1**

4/P- **8** *¾* **Easter Meteor**[13] 1969 7-11-9 **142**.................... DominicElsworth 133
(Emma Lavelle) *trckd ldr: hit 1st: led briefly 3rd: prom: rdn 4 out: hit 3 out: wknd* **8/1**

110/ **9** *1 ¼* **Cantlow (IRE)**[209] 5176 8-11-8 **141**.................... BarryGeraghty 131
(Paul Webber) *hld up in rr: pushed along after 7th: minor hdwy whn sltly hmpd 4 out: nvr threatened* **11/2**[2]

0/6- **10** *14* **Duke Of Lucca (IRE)**[20] 1868 8-11-3 **136**....................(t) RichardJohnson 114
(Philip Hobbs) *midfield: nt fluent: rdn after 5 out: mstke 4 out: wknd* **6/1**[3]

311/ **11** *9* **Noble Legend**[216] 5015 6-11-0 **133**.................... AndrewThornton 101
(Caroline Bailey) *trckd ldrs: mstke 4 out: wknd* **7/1**

034/ **P** **Mon Parrain (FR)**[587] 5066 7-11-12 **145**.................... NickScholfield
(Paul Nicholls) *in tch on outer: awkward 9th: wknd bef 4 out: p.u bef last* **9/1**

5m 0.2s (-7.60) **Going Correction** -0.075s/f (Good) **12** Ran SP% **117.5**
Speed ratings (Par 111): **111,110,108,105,104 104,103,103,102,97 94,**
toteswingers 1&2 £33.80, 1&3 £33.80, 2&3 £28.60 CSF £326.36 CT £2041.86 TOTE £23.60: £5.60, £3.60, £2.00; EX 642.10 Trifecta £765.60 Part won. Pool: £1020.89 - 0.21 winning units..
Owner Dan Gilbert **Bred** Avington Manor Stud **Trained** Norton, N Yorks

FOCUS
A good renewal of this feature chase and it certainly lived up to expectations as the versatile Ultimate saw off a host of challengers under a fine front-running ride. Solid handicap form, the winner rated back to his best.

2200 WEATHERBYS HAMILTON INSURANCE WENSLEYDALE JUVENILE HURDLE (LISTED RACE) (9 hdls) 2m 110y
2:45 (2:45) (Class 1) 3-Y-O

£9,681 (£3,632; £1,819; £906; £455; £227)

Form RPR

1- **1** **Royal Irish Hussar (IRE)**[34] 1684 3-11-6 0.................... BarryGeraghty 136+
(Nicky Henderson) *mde all: pushed clr after 3 out: nt fluent last: comf* **5/2**[1]

2 *14* **Cadoudoff (FR)**[139] 3-11-6 0.................... AidanColeman 119
(Charlie Longsdon) *in tch: rdn to chse ldr 3 out: sn one pce: wnt 2nd run-in last: no ch w wnr* **4/1**[2]

3 *1 ¾* **Zamoyski**[114] 3-10-12 0.................... RichardJohnson 110
(Steve Gollings) *in tch: wnt 2nd 3 out: sn outpcd by wnr: hit last: no ex and lost 2nd run-in* **12/1**

1- **4** *5* **Keltus (FR)**[20] 1862 3-11-4 125.................... NickScholfield 113
(Paul Nicholls) *w ldr: rdn whn nt fluent 3 out: sn wknd* **5/1**[3]

5 *3* **Ainsi Fideles (FR)**[188] 3-11-6 0.................... TomScudamore 112
(David Pipe) *trckd ldng pair: wknd after 3 out* **5/2**[1]

351- **6** *32* **Kitchapoly (FR)**[26] 1786 3-11-6 130.................... JasonMaguire 81
(Donald McCain) *hld up in tch: pushed along after 4 out: sn wknd* **12/1**

64- **7** *14* **Hazza The Jazza**[16] 1920 3-10-12 0....................(p) WilsonRenwick 61
(Richard Guest) *hld up in rr: a bhd* **66/1**

3m 56.2s (0.40) **Going Correction** -0.075s/f (Good) **7** Ran SP% **110.7**
Speed ratings (Par 110): **96,89,88,86,84 69,63**
toteswingers 1&2 £2.70, 1&3 £6.40, 2&3 £12.90 CSF £12.14 TOTE £3.10: £1.80, £2.40; EX 13.10 Trifecta £98.40 Pool: £2251.04 - 17.14 winning units..
Owner Triermore Stud **Bred** Adjalisa Syndicate **Trained** Upper Lambourn, Berks

FOCUS
Arguably the best juvenile hurdle race of the season so far. The winner looks decent and the second probably stepped up on his French form.

2201 BET365.COM H'CAP CHASE (18 fncs) 3m 1f
3:20 (3:20) (Class 4) (0-110,110) 4-Y-O+ **£3,898** (£1,144; £572; £286)

Form RPR

6/1- **1** **Orange Nassau (FR)**[21] 1859 7-11-12 **110**.................... AidanColeman 115
(Charlie Longsdon) *trckd ldr: rdn to ld appr 4 out: hdd 3 out: 3 l down whn lft in front again 2 out: drvn out* **7/4**[1]

16P/ **2** *1 ½* **Beau Dandy (IRE)**[189] 5548 8-11-1 **99**....................(b) WilsonRenwick 103
(John Wade) *hld up: tk clsr order 8th: rdn to chal 4 out: sn one pce: lft 2nd 2 out: plugged on but a jst hld* **11/2**[3]

U/0- **3** *30* **Palos Conti (FR)**[37] 1659 10-11-12 **110**.................... DannyCook 92
(Brian Ellison) *led: rdn whn hdd appr 4 out: wknd* **5/2**[2]

P/5- **4** *17* **Mannered**[155] 555 8-10-10 **101**.................... JohnDawson[(7)] 62
(John Wade) *hld up: rdn 5 out: a towards rr* **20/1**

PP2/ **5** *2 ¼* **Boris The Blade**[203] 5276 11-10-10 **99**....................(b) SamanthaDrake[(5)] 58
(Tina Jackson) *trckd ldr: pushed along and lost pl 1/2-way: sn struggling* **14/1**

/PP- **6** *17* **Acrai Rua (IRE)**[135] 766 10-11-9 **107**....................(b) BrianHughes 51
(Tim Fitzgerald) *midfield: reminders and dropped to rr 1/2-way: sn t.o* **28/1**

642- **P** **Baltic Pathfinder (IRE)**[28] 1756 9-10-11 **100**.................... JonathanEngland[(5)]
(Sue Smith) *hld up: reminder after 5th: mstke 6th: lost tch 1/2-way: t.o whn p.u bef 5 out* **12/1**

136- **F** **Polarbrook (IRE)**[28] 1750 6-11-12 **110**....................(b) JasonMaguire 120+
(Donald McCain) *midfield: mstke 11th: nt flunt 12th: hdwy to trck ldrs bef 4 out: hdd gng wl 3 out: rdn 3 l clr whn fell 2 out* **9/1**

6m 11.4s (2.00) **Going Correction** -0.075s/f (Good) **8** Ran SP% **112.9**
Speed ratings (Par 105): **93,92,82,77,76 71,,**
toteswingers 1&2 £2.60, 1&3 £2.00, 2&3 £4.10 CSF £11.92 CT £22.97 TOTE £3.00: £1.30, £1.70, £1.80; EX 14.90 Trifecta £53.80 Pool: £1679.99 - 23.39 winning units..
Owner The Ferandlin Peaches **Bred** E A R L La Dariole **Trained** Over Norton, Oxon

FOCUS
Any softening of the ground was a major concern for recent Newton Abbot winner Orange Nassau, but those who kept the faith with Charlie Longsdon's grey were rewarded as he was handed victory by the fall of Polarbrook. The winner is rated to his mark.

2202 BOOK TICKETS ON-LINE @ WETHERBYRACING.CO.UK CONDITIONAL JOCKEYS' NOVICES' H'CAP HURDLE (11 hdls 1 omitted) 2m 6f
3:55 (3:55) (Class 4) (0-105,104) 3-Y-O+ **£3,422** (£997; £499)

Form RPR

0/0- **1** **Cyrien Star**[181] 121 6-11-5 **100**.................... JakeGreenall[(3)] 110+
(Henry Daly) *trckd ldrs: rdn to chal 3 out: briefly outpcd by ldr 2 out: j. to front last: kpt on* **4/1**[2]

511- **2** *6* **My Oh Mount Brown (IRE)**[23] 1820 6-11-8 **103**.......... MichaelByrne[(3)] 111+
(Tim Vaughan) *led: rdn 3 out: 2 l up 2 out: jnd whn blnd last: nt rcvr* **11/1**

421- **3** *2 ½* **Silver Dragon**[15] 1940 5-11-0 **92**.................... JackQuinlan 98+
(Tony Coyle) *hld up in tch: hdwy to trck ldrs 4 out: nt fluent 3 out: sn rdn and one pce in 3rd: hit last* **11/4**[1]

0/4- **4** *6* **Lookout Mountain (IRE)**[67] 1388 5-11-8 **103**......(vt[1]) MauriceLinehan[(3)] 101
(Jonjo O'Neill) *trckd ldng pair: rdn appr 3 out: grad wknd* **5/1**[3]

400/ **5** *8* **Heron's Mill (IRE)**[194] 5423 5-11-4 **104**.................... DaleIrving[(8)] 93
(James Ewart) *hld up in tch: rdn bef 3 out: sn imp* **10/1**

3/4- **6** *45* **Cleve Cottage**[26] 1794 5-11-9 **104**.................... AdamNicol[(3)] 53
(Philip Kirby) *trckd ldrs: lost pl 1/2-way: wknd 4 out* **4/1**[2]

6/6- **7** *33* **Bold Slasher (IRE)**[8] 2035 5-10-9 **90**.................... JonathanEngland[(3)] 9
(Sue Smith) *w ldr: rdn and lost pl qckly 1/2-way: t.o* **16/1**

0/ **P** **Macklycuddy (USA)**[342] 2637 7-11-0 **95**....................(t) TonyKelly[(3)]
(Rebecca Menzies) *hld up in rr: a bhd: p.u bef last* **25/1**

6P0/ **P** **Stitched In Time (IRE)**[194] 5423 6-10-9 **95**.................... ShaunDobbin[(8)]
(Rose Dobbin) *midfield: hit 4 out: sn wknd: p.u bef 3 out* **20/1**

/00- **P** **Just Tyn (IRE)**[21] 1853 6-10-0 **76**.................... HarryChalloner
(Martin Todhunter) *hld up in rr: rdn 1/2-way: t.o whn p.u bef 4 out* **40/1**

5m 23.8s (-3.00) **Going Correction** -0.075s/f (Good) **10** Ran SP% **117.7**
Speed ratings (Par 105): **102,99,98,96,93 77,65,,,**
toteswingers 1&2 £16.30, 1&3 £2.50, 2&3 £1.70 CSF £45.62 CT £141.74 TOTE £5.70: £1.70, £1.60, £1.70; EX 65.00 Trifecta £252.20 Pool: £1562.93 - 4.64 winning units..
Owner Puteus Profundus **Bred** Wood Farm Stud **Trained** Stanton Lacy, Shropshire

FOCUS
Another slow-motion finish, despite the steady early pace, and stamina appeared to win the day. The winner probably has more to offer.
T/Jkpt: £40,445.00. Pool: £56,964.92 - 1 winning unit. T/Plt: £688.20. Pool: £73,540.18 - 78 winning units. T/Qpdt: £145.80. Pool: £6858.00 - 34.80 winning units. AS

2203 - 2204a (Foreign Racing) - See Raceform Interactive

1450 DOWN ROYAL (R-H)
Friday, November 1

OFFICIAL GOING: Hurdle course - good to yielding (yielding in places); chase course - yielding (good to yielding in places)

2205a EUROPEAN BREEDERS FUND LOUGH CONSTRUCTION LTD. MARES NOVICE HURDLE (GRADE 3) (9 hdls) 2m
2:05 (2:05) 4-Y-O+ **£18,495** (£5,406; £2,560; £853)

RPR

1 **Gambling Girl (IRE)**[28] 1757 4-10-7 .... RobbiePower 125+
(Mrs John Harrington, Ire) *chsd ldrs: sltly hmpd on inner 1st: 5th 1/2-way: tk clsr order gng wl bef 3 out: led fr next and wnt clr bef last where bad mstke: kpt on wl u.p run-in* **11/4**[2]

2 *8* **Roja Dove (IRE)**[19] 1892 4-10-11 118.................... EddieO'Connell 118
(K J Condon, Ire) *attempted to make all: nt fluent 4th: strly pressed into st and hdd fr 2 out: sn no imp on wnr u.p: kpt on same pce fr last* **10/1**

3 *2 ¼* **The Cookie Jar (IRE)**[5] 2122 6-10-10 105.................... JodyMcGarvey 115
(C A Murphy, Ire) *w.w towards rr: 7th 1/2-way: rdn in 6th after 3 out and no imp on ldrs next: kpt on wl u.p fr last into nvr threatening 3rd fnl strides* **25/1**

4 *nk* **Little King Robin (IRE)**[15] 1948 5-10-10 116....................(t) MarkWalsh 114
(Colin Bowe, Ire) *chsd ldrs: nt fluent 3rd: pushed along in 4th after 3 out and no imp on ldrs into st: mod 5th between last 2: kpt on fr last: jst denied 3rd* **8/1**

5 *2 ¼* **Que Pasa (IRE)**[26] 1802 5-11-3 131.................... BryanCooper 119
(David Harry Kelly, Ire) *chsd ldrs: sltly hmpd between horses 1st: slt mstke 4th: wnt mod 3rd after 2 out and no imp on wnr whn mstke last: wknd run-in* **9/4**[1]

6 *3 ¾* **Honey Bach (IRE)**[26] 1802 6-10-10 114.................... RWalsh 108
(B R Hamilton, Ire) *chsd ldrs: 4th 1/2-way: tk clsr order on outer 3 out: rdn in 3rd 2 out and sn no ex u.p in 4th: one pce run-in* **6/1**

7 *¾* **Sultana Belle (IRE)**[20] 1871 5-10-10 92.................... PeterBuchanan 108
(S R B Crawford, Ire) *trckd ldr: 2nd 1/2-way pushed along and lost pl bef 3 out where slt mstke: no imp in 7th bef st next: one pce after* **33/1**

8 *6 ½* **Only Exception (IRE)**[5] 2114 4-10-7 109.................... DannyMullins 98
(M C Grassick, Ire) *chsd ldrs: j.rt 1st: 8th 1/2-way: rdn and no imp fr 3 out* **33/1**

9 *24* **Kilbarry Beauty (IRE)**[173] 256 6-10-10 128.................... PaulTownend 77
(John E Kiely, Ire) *towards rr: rdn and no imp fr 3 out: wknd and eased: t.o: lame* **9/2**[3]

10 *40* **Revolution (FR)**[14] 1961 4-10-7 .... LiamMcKenna 34
(J J Lambe, Ire) *towards rr thrght: nt fluent 2nd: pushed along bef 4 out and no imp: wknd: completely t.o* **50/1**

3m 55.2s (-8.10)
WFA 4 from 5yo+ 7lb **10** Ran SP% **121.8**
CSF £30.11 TOTE £3.40: £1.70, £2.00, £4.20; DF 53.70.
Owner River Racing Partnership **Bred** Ardmulchan Stud **Trained** Moone, Co Kildare

FOCUS
This looked an up-to-scratch renewal. Last year's winner Top Madam was rated 117 on arrival so the presence of Que Pasa, with a mark of 131, suggested this was a better affair. The early gallop was reasonably generous and it produced a winner that has the potential to go very far in the game. The second and third help with the standard.

2206a WKD HURDLE (GRADE 2) (9 hdls) 2m
2:35 (2:35) 4-Y-0+ £26,422 (£7,723; £3,658; £1,219)

RPR
1 **Jezki (IRE)**[192] 5485 5-11-10 161 APMcCoy 155+
(Mrs John Harrington, Ire) *led at slow pce: t.k.h early: over 1 l clr at 1/2-way: jnd 3 out: pushed along w narrow advantage gng best between last 2: kpt on wl towards fin: comf* **2/9**[1]
2 3 ¼ **Caid Du Berlais (FR)**[233] 4737 4-10-13 142 RWalsh 141
(Paul Nicholls) *trckd ldrs in 3rd at slow pce: pushed along fr 3 out and clsd after next to chal between horses: nt fluent last and no imp on wnr in 2nd run-in: kpt on same pce* **7/1**[3]
3 2 ¼ **Flaxen Flare (IRE)**[55] 1380 4-11-2 140 (b) DavyRussell 142
(Gordon Elliott, Ire) *trckd ldr in 2nd at slow pce: nt fluent 2nd: slt mstkes 4th and next: on terms 3 out: rdn in cl 2nd between last 2 and sn no ex u.p: kpt on same pce in 3rd fr last* **6/1**[2]
4 ½ **Massini's Trap (IRE)**[19] 1892 4-10-9 134 DJCasey 134
(J A Nash, Ire) *w.w in rr at slow pce: stl gng wl after 3 out: wnt 4th between last 2: kpt on wl run-in wout ever threatening principals* **25/1**
5 18 **Courtly Conduct (IRE)**[309] 3301 8-11-2 118 MichaelDarcy 124
(W M Roper, Ire) *w.w towards rr at slow pce: tk clsr order on outer bef 4th: pushed along in 4th fr 3 out and sn no ex u.p: wknd* **33/1**

4m 18.9s (15.60)
WFA 4 from 5yo+ 7lb 5 Ran SP% 115.4
CSF £3.02 TOTE £1.20: £1.02, £1.90; DF 2.20 Trifecta £4.90.
Owner John P McManus **Bred** Gerard M McGrath **Trained** Moone, Co Kildare

FOCUS
This contest is confined to second-season novices and the presence of last year's Supreme Novices' Hurdle third as well as the first two home in the Fred Winter ensured it was an intriguing renewal. The worry beforehand was where the early pace would come from and they dawdled for the first mile, with the long odds-on favourite having to do his own donkey work. Not form to set too much store by given the lack of a gallop.

2207 - 2209a (Foreign Racing) - See Raceform Interactive

ASCOT (R-H)
Saturday, November 2

OFFICIAL GOING: Good to soft changing to good to soft (soft in places) after race 3 (2:10)
Wind: Fresh, half against Weather: Changeable with showers

2210 GARDINER & THEOBALD NOVICES' H'CAP HURDLE (11 hdls) 2m 3f 110y
1:00 (1:00) (Class 4) (0-120,118) 3-Y-0+
£5,630 (£1,663; £831; £415; £207; £104)

Form RPR
52P/ 1 **Willow's Saviour**[199] 5354 6-11-9 115 HarrySkelton 135+
(Dan Skelton) *t.k.h: cl up: trckd ldr 6th to 8th and again after 3 out: led bef 2 out: drew rt away: eased nr fin* **9/1**
5/4- 2 8 **Coup De Grace (IRE)**[12] 2004 4-10-5 100 JoshuaMoore(3) 103
(Pat Phelan) *wl in tch in midfield: rdn and prog fr 3 out to chse wnr sn after 2 out: styd on but no ch* **14/1**
/41- 3 5 **Letemgo (IRE)**[16] 1941 5-11-7 113 DavidEngland 112
(Giles Smyly) *prom: chsd ldr 8th to sn after 3 out: sn rdn and lost pl: kpt on again to take 3rd after 2 out* **6/1**[1]
6U2- 4 5 **Sedgemoor Express (IRE)**[9] 2045 5-10-12 107 (t[1]) MarkQuinlan(3) 101
(Nigel Hawke) *hld up in last: pushed along and prog fr 3 out into midfield 2 out: rdn and kpt on to take 4th after last: no hope of threatening ldrs* **9/1**
223- 5 3 ½ **Kalmbeforethestorm**[23] 1828 5-11-9 115 PaulMoloney 105
(Helen Nelmes) *trckd ldrs on inner: blnd 6th: lost pl and pushed along after 8th: kpt on bef 2 out* **16/1**
430- 6 6 **Sterling Gent (IRE)**[99] 1118 6-10-11 103 ConorO'Farrell 92
(Liam Corcoran) *led: rdn bef 2 out where blnd: wknd qckly* **40/1**
4F6/ 7 2 ¼ **Ourmanmassini (IRE)**[197] 5376 5-11-9 118 (t) GavinSheehan(3) 101
(Suzy Smith) *racd wd: in rr fr 4th: rdn after 7th: sme prog 3 out: no hdwy bef next* **6/1**[1]
8 3 **Vedani (IRE)**[71] 1366 4-11-6 112 (t) LeeEdwards 92
(Tony Carroll) *mstkes in rr: struggling fr 8th: plugged on past btn horses fr 2 out* **20/1**
/33- 9 6 **Agincourt Reef (IRE)**[144] 706 4-11-8 114 JamieMoore 89
(Gary Moore) *nt jump wl: wl in rr: struggling after 8th: nvr on terms after* **16/1**
006/ 10 nk **Hand On Bach (IRE)**[195] 5440 5-10-13 105 NoelFehily 80
(Warren Greatrex) *cl up: jnd ldrs 3 out: wknd bef next* **7/1**[3]
3P- 11 nk **Dance Floor King (IRE)**[136] 764 6-10-13 105 WayneHutchinson 79
(Nick Mitchell) *trckd ldrs: gng strly bef 8th: wknd sn after 3 out* **20/1**
5S6- 12 2 ¾ **Minellaforlunch (IRE)**[16] 1937 6-11-6 112 DenisO'Regan 84
(Henry Oliver) *w.w in rr: n.m.r bnd after 7th: no prog 3 out: wl btn after* **13/2**[2]
6/6- 13 11 **Was My Valentine**[144] 717 6-10-0 102 JackSavage(10) 64
(Jo Davis) *racd wd: mostly trckd ldr to 6th: wknd fr 8th* **20/1**
P21/ 14 2 ¼ **Ballybach (IRE)**[1035] 3339 9-11-9 115 TomCannon 75
(Nick Gifford) *mstkes: a in rr: t.o after 3 out* **16/1**
000/ 15 20 **Waldorf Salad**[204] 5264 5-10-13 105 AidanColeman 47
(Venetia Williams) *chsd ldrs to 5th: sn dropped to rr and struggling: t.o after 8th* **25/1**

4m 48.2s (3.50) **Going Correction** +0.25s/f (Yiel)
WFA 4 from 5yo+ 7lb 15 Ran SP% 119.3
Speed ratings (Par 105): **103,99,97,95,94 92,91,89,87,87 87,86,81,80,72**
toteswingers 1&2 £44.70, 1&3 £12.50, 2&3 £19.00 CSF £115.03 CT £824.56 TOTE £12.10: £3.80, £6.50, £2.40; EX 182.30 Trifecta £1113.90 Pool: £ - winning units..
Owner Triple F Partnership **Bred** Mrs M Cuff **Trained** Alcester, Warwicks

FOCUS
There was 2mm of rain overnight, but despite the official ground description, it looked quite hard work. What had looked a wide-open handicap hurdle was won in dominant fashion by Willow's Saviour, who produced a massive step up.

2211 ASCOT UNDERWRITING NOVICES' LIMITED H'CAP CHASE (16 fncs) 2m 3f
1:35 (1:36) (Class 3) (0-140,137) 4-Y-0+
£6,881 (£2,032; £1,016; £508; £254; £127)

Form RPR
/14- 1 **Ivor's King (IRE)**[22] 1857 6-10-11 129 JoeTizzard 134
(Colin Tizzard) *led at str pce and sn 5 l clr: c bk to two rivals 12th: hdd bef 2 out: rallied last: kpt on bravely to ld fnl strides* **5/1**[2]
1/1- 2 nk **Up To Something (FR)**[22] 1849 5-11-5 137 (p) NoelFehily 142
(Charlie Longsdon) *chsd clr ldr: clsd but lost 2nd and nt fluent 4 out: rallied u.p 2 out: led sn after last: hung lft and hdd fnl strides* **5/2**[1]
30P/ 3 2 ¼ **Persian Snow (IRE)**[329] 2910 7-10-11 129 (t) RichardJohnson 133+
(Philip Hobbs) *hld up: trckd ldng pair 7th: clsd 12th: wnt 2nd 3 out: led bef 2 out and looked sure to win: idled after and stuttered into last: sn hdd and nt qckn* **7/1**[3]
0P0/ 4 9 **Lyvius**[210] 5178 5-10-10 128 BarryGeraghty 125+
(Nicky Henderson) *sketchy jumping in rr early: hmpd 3rd: blnd 10th: nt on terms fr 12th: wnt 4th and threatened to cl after 3 out: 8 l down next: sn rdn and no hdwy* **5/2**[1]
114/ 5 16 **Thunderstorm (IRE)**[227] 4859 8-10-13 131 TomO'Brien 113+
(Philip Hobbs) *nt fluent: hld up and last early: mstke and sltly hmpd 9th: lost tch fr 11th: nvr involved after: light reminder after 2 out* **10/1**
0/1- 6 13 **Le Bacardy (FR)**[174] 234 7-10-12 130 (p) LeeEdwards 98
(Tony Carroll) *chsd ldrs: no imp fr 12th: wknd fr 4 out* **16/1**
2/U- 7 32 **Orzare (IRE)**[10] 2019 7-10-2 123 oh1 JoshuaMoore(3) 62
(Philip Hide) *blnd bdly 3rd: sn last and toiling: continued wl t.o fr 10th* **10/1**
10/- F **Minella Definitely (IRE)**[238] 4665 6-10-9 130 (p) MichaelByrne(3)
(Neil Mulholland) *chsd ldrs: 4th whn fell 9th* **20/1**

4m 44.2s (-2.20) **Going Correction** +0.075s/f (Yiel) 8 Ran SP% 115.1
Speed ratings (Par 107): **107,106,105,102,95 89,76,**
toteswingers 1&2 £3.40, 1&3 £6.80, 2&3 £5.60 CSF £18.82 CT £87.21 TOTE £7.10: £1.90, £1.40, £2.30; EX 20.40 Trifecta £146.00 Pool: £2666.02 - 13.69 winning units..
Owner W I M Perry **Bred** W Bourke **Trained** Milborne Port, Dorset

FOCUS
Run at a good gallop, there was some ragged jumping early and the field was soon quite well strung out. Little got into it, though, and they finished tired. The winner was back to form with the second building on his recent win.

2212 BYRNE GROUP H'CAP CHASE (LISTED RACE) (13 fncs) 2m 1f
2:10 (2:10) (Class 1) (0-150,146) 4-Y-0+
£28,475 (£10,685; £5,350; £2,665; £1,340; £670)

Form RPR
245/ 1 **Drumshambo (USA)**[196] 5401 7-11-4 138 AidanColeman 150+
(Venetia Williams) *tended to jump rt: trckd ldng pair: wnt 2nd 9th: led sn after 3 out: rdn 5 l clr bef last: styd on* **16/1**
3/0- 2 2 ½ **Lancetto (FR)**[15] 1960 8-10-11 131 PaulMoloney 138
(Evan Williams) *nt a fluent and j. sltly lft: w.w in rr: prog fr 9th: rdn to chse clr wnr bef last: styd on but unable to chal* **20/1**
112/ 3 7 **Greywell Boy**[209] 5198 6-10-7 127 DavidBass 130
(Nick Williams) *trckd ldrs: lunged at 6th: clsd and mstke 9th: rdn after 3 out: one pce bef next* **7/1**[2]
014/ 4 nk **Filbert (IRE)**[252] 4385 7-10-7 127 RichardJohnson 130
(Philip Hobbs) *mstke 1st: hld up in rr: gd prog fr 9th to chse wnr bef 2 out where mstke: lost 2nd bef last: fdd* **9/1**
0/4- 5 2 ½ **Gus Macrae (IRE)**[30] 1730 9-10-2 127 (tp) PatrickCorbett(5) 125
(Rebecca Curtis) *mostly in midfield: tried to cl on ldrs 3 out: one pce and no imp fr 2 out* **12/1**
1/2- 6 12 **King Edmund**[29] 1746 10-11-6 140 (t) TomCannon 128
(Chris Gordon) *chsd ldr: clsd to chal 6th: led 8th: hdd sn after 3 out: wknd* **14/1**
210/ 7 ½ **Consigliere (FR)**[273] 3986 10-11-4 145 (p) TomBellamy(7) 133
(David Pipe) *a towards rr: struggling and no ch whn mstke 3 out: passed a few late on* **33/1**
233- 8 4 ½ **Temple Lord (FR)**[17] 1921 7-10-3 123 (bt) RichieMcLernon 108
(Jonjo O'Neill) *sltly hmpd 1st: hld up wl in rr: prog bef 8th: chsd ldrs 3 out: no hdwy and btn whn blnd 2 out: wknd* **16/1**
1PU/ 9 1 ¾ **Ulck Du Lin (FR)**[217] 5022 5-11-7 146 HarryDerham(5) 128
(Paul Nicholls) *trckd ldrs: mstke 5th: wnt 3rd briefly 3 out: rdn and wknd bef next* **7/1**[2]
331- 10 7 **Notarfbad (IRE)**[22] 1857 7-10-7 127 NoelFehily 104
(Jeremy Scott) *racd wd: in tch: nt fluent 6th: chsd ldrs 3 out: losing pl whn hmpd bnd bef next* **8/1**[3]
4/1- 11 6 **Avoca Promise (IRE)**[18] 1916 8-10-7 127 FelixDeGiles 101
(Tom Symonds) *mstke 1st: a in rr: blnd 7th: toiling fr next* **8/1**[3]
300/ 12 16 **Dan Breen (IRE)**[189] 5575 8-11-4 145 (p) KieronEdgar(7) 103
(David Pipe) *mstke 1st: a in rr: blnd 7th: no ch fr 9th: t.o* **14/1**
512- 13 2 **My Brother Sylvest**[16] 1943 7-11-6 140 (b) TomScudamore 94
(David Pipe) *led at str pce: hdd and nt fluent 8th: wknd rapidly: t.o* **20/1**
/24- 14 1 ¾ **Olympian Boy (IRE)**[29] 1746 9-9-11 120 oh5 JamesBest(3) 72
(Sophie Leech) *hld up in last: blnd 3rd: mstkes after: t.o* **33/1**
1/1- F **Fairy Rath (IRE)**[175] 217 7-10-12 132 (t) BarryGeraghty
(Nick Gifford) *trckd ldrs: lost pl fr 8th: wkng whn mstke 3 out: 12th whn fell last* **6/1**[1]

4m 9.7s (-4.90) **Going Correction** +0.075s/f (Yiel) 15 Ran SP% 119.7
Speed ratings (Par 111): **114,112,109,109,108 102,102,100,99,96 93,85,84,83,**
toteswingers 1&2 £131.10, 1&3 £10.90, 2&3 £82.10 CSF £298.03 CT £2436.76 TOTE £17.00: £3.50, £8.20, £2.50; EX 539.80 Trifecta £1382.50 Part won. Pool: £1843.40 - 0.72 winning units..
Owner The Grouse Partnership **Bred** Airlie Stud **Trained** Kings Caple, H'fords

FOCUS
A good, competitive chase that was run at a decent gallop. Solid form. The winner was up 8lb on the best of last season's form and there's probably more to come.

2213 WILLIAM HILL H'CAP HURDLE (LISTED RACE) (9 hdls) 2m
2:45 (2:45) (Class 1) 4-Y-0+

£28,135 (£10,600; £5,305; £2,650; £1,330; £665)

Form RPR
115/ **1** **Pine Creek**[238] 4665 5-10-4 **130**.. DenisO'Regan 139+
(John Ferguson) *trckd ldng pair: nt fluent 5th and mstke next: gng strly whn led 2 out: drvn and pressed after last: kpt on wl* **11/2**[2]
160/ **2** *3/4* **Chris Pea Green**[232] 4767 4-10-7 **136**........................ JoshuaMoore(3) 142
(Gary Moore) *trckd ldrs: mstke 4th: prog after 3 out: mstke 2 out: sn chsd wnr: nt fluent last: chal flat: styd on but a hld* **8/1**
325/ **3** *3 3/4* **Dildar (IRE)**[280] 3862 5-9-13 **130**........................ HarryDerham(5) 133
(Paul Nicholls) *hld up in midfield: prog after 3 out: rdn to chse ldng pair bef last: styd on but unable to chal* **8/1**
P64/ **4** *5* **Dunraven Storm (IRE)**[623] 4377 8-10-6 **132**................. RichardJohnson 131
(Philip Hobbs) *hld up in rr: pushed along and sme prog after 3 out: stl pushed along fr 2 out: outpcd but kpt on to take 4th after last* **14/1**
231/ **5** *1 3/4* **Gibb River (IRE)**[553] 5650 7-11-4 **144**.......................... BarryGeraghty 141
(Nicky Henderson) *w.w in midfield: dropped to rr 6th: sme hdwy after 3 out: jst pushed along and no imp on ldrs fr 2 out* **9/1**
/21- **6** *2* **Rayvin Black**[23] 1832 4-9-9 **126** oh7.......................... ThomasGarner(5) 122
(Oliver Sherwood) *tk fierece hold: led after 2nd: hdd and nt fluent 2 out: wknd and nt fluent last* **20/1**
/11- **7** *4 1/2* **Makari**[9] 2045 6-10-6 **132**.. AndrewTinkler 124
(Nicky Henderson) *hld up in rr: hit 5th: shkn up after 3 out: no real hdwy bef next and sn btn* **7/1**[3]
411/ **8** *2 1/2* **Court Minstrel (IRE)**[196] 5402 6-11-9 **149**.......................... PaulMoloney 138
(Evan Williams) *t.k.h: hld up wl in rr: mstke 4th: shkn up and no prog 3 out: nvr on terms after* **5/1**[1]
110/ **9** *nk* **Shotavodka (IRE)**[210] 5178 7-11-0 **140**.......................... TomScudamore 131
(David Pipe) *allowed easy ld but hdd after 2nd: pressed ldr tl nt fluent 3 out: wknd bef next* **9/1**
16/- **10** *3/4* **Jumps Road**[210] 5178 6-10-1 **127**.............................. BrendanPowell 117
(Colin Tizzard) *nvr bttr than midfield: struggling after 3 out: wl btn next: mstke last* **25/1**
2/F- **11** *1 1/2* **Specialagent Alfie**[175] 216 7-10-2 **128**............................(t) TomCannon 115
(Nick Gifford) *prom: disputing 3rd whn hit 6th: wknd qckly after 3 out* **10/1**
PP0/ **12** *1 3/4* **Get Me Out Of Here (IRE)**[211] 5162 9-11-7 **152**....(t) MauriceLinehan(5) 137
(Jonjo O'Neill) *hld up in last pair: urged along and struggling after 6th: no hdwy* **16/1**

3m 47.6s (0.20) **Going Correction** +0.25s/f (Yiel)
WFA 4 from 5yo+ 7lb 12 Ran SP% **117.0**
Speed ratings (Par 111): **109,108,106,104,103 102,100,98,98,98 97,96**
toteswingers 1&2 £11.00, 1&3 £8.20, 2&3 £14.10 CSF £48.79 CT £353.25 TOTE £5.70: £2.20, £2.70, £3.50; EX 49.10 Trifecta £574.50 Pool: £1791.48 - 2.33 winning units..
Owner Bloomfields **Bred** Darley **Trained** Cowlinge, Suffolk

FOCUS
The right horses came to the fore and the form looks solid. The first two are on the upgrade and both should rate higher.

2214 UNITED HOUSE GOLD CUP H'CAP CHASE (GRADE 3) (20 fncs) 3m
3:20 (3:20) (Class 1) 4-Y-0+

£56,270 (£21,200; £10,610; £5,300; £2,660; £1,330)

Form RPR
204/ **1** **Houblon Des Obeaux (FR)**[199] 5355 6-11-3 **144**........... AidanColeman 158+
(Venetia Williams) *prom: trckd ldr 10th: mstke next: led 16th: clr after 3 out: in n.d whn mstke last* **12/1**
220/ **2** *6* **Merry King (IRE)**[235] 4721 6-10-10 **137**........................ RichieMcLernon 144
(Jonjo O'Neill) *hld up in rr: stdy prog fr 14th: rdn 3 out: styd on to take 2nd sn after last: no ch w wnr* **8/1**[3]
011/ **3** *3* **Triolo D'Alene (FR)**[188] 6 6-11-6 **147**.......................... BarryGeraghty 151
(Nicky Henderson) *awkward 1st: t.k.h towards rr: prog 14th: rdn 3 out: kpt on to chse clr wnr briefly last: one pce flat* **7/1**[2]
55U/ **4** *nse* **Roberto Goldback (IRE)**[210] 5177 11-11-5 **151**........ NicodeBoinville(5) 156
(Nicky Henderson) *w.w in midfield: hmpd 4th: clsd on ldrs fr 15th: rdn 4 out: last of 6 w any ch after 3 out: keeping on at one pce whn stmbld last* **14/1**
0/1- **5** *2 3/4* **Bouggler**[35] 1686 8-11-3 **147**..(p) GavinSheehan(3) 150
(Emma Lavelle) *trckd ldrs: j.lft 4th: moved out wd bef 1/2-way: prom fr 14th: drvn to chse clr wnr 2 out to last: wknd* **14/1**
10P/ **6** *1 3/4* **Bless The Wings (IRE)**[233] 4750 8-11-6 **147**............ WayneHutchinson 147
(Alan King) *trckd ldrs on inner: moved to chse wnr 16th: drvn 3 out: wknd 2 out* **20/1**
501- **7** *8* **Twirling Magnet (IRE)**[15] 1957 7-10-11 **143**.........(tp) MauriceLinehan(5) 136
(Jonjo O'Neill) *j.lft: hld up in last pair: sme prog fr 15th: rchd 7th bef 2 out but no ch* **20/1**
1P0/ **8** *1/2* **On Trend (IRE)**[189] 5576 7-10-9 **136**.............................. TomCannon 128
(Nick Gifford) *prom: lost pl fr 12th: in midfield whn blnd 16th: no ch 3 out* **33/1**
103/ **9** *7* **Wyck Hill (IRE)**[189] 5579 9-11-0 **141**.............................. DenisO'Regan 126
(David Bridgwater) *sltly hmpd 3rd: nvr on terms: no real prog fr 15th: no ch after 3 out* **8/1**[3]
351- **10** *1* **Al Co (FR)**[21] 1868 8-10-13 **140**.. TomO'Brien 126
(Peter Bowen) *a in rr: no prog fr 15th: wl bhd 3 out* **20/1**
612/ **11** *5* **Same Difference (IRE)**[189] 5576 7-11-0 **148**..................(v) RyanHatch(7) 131
(Nigel Twiston-Davies) *trckd ldrs: mstke 12th and 14th: wknd 4 out* **9/1**
2U5/ **12** *24* **Big Fella Thanks**[199] 5353 11-11-12 **153**..........................(t) AlainCawley 111
(Tom George) *led to 8th: lost pl fr next: in rr whn mstke 13th: t.o* **33/1**
2B6/ **P** **There's No Panic (IRE)**[189] 5576 8-10-1 **133**.......... HarryDerham(5)
(Paul Nicholls) *wl in rr: hmpd 3rd: stl in rr whn blnd 13th and qckly p.u* **14/1**
PP4/ **P** **Quinz (FR)**[252] 4389 9-11-1 **142**...................................... RichardJohnson
(Philip Hobbs) *pressed ldr: mstke 4th: led 8th: hdd & wknd 16th: wl bhd whn p.u bef last* **14/1**
11P/ **P** **Opening Batsman (IRE)**[210] 5176 7-11-7 **148**...................... NoelFehily
(Harry Fry) *sketchy jumping in rr: nvr a factor: t.o in last whn p.u bef 2 out* **8/1**[3]
114/ **F** **Buddy Bolero (IRE)**[234] 4732 7-11-0 **141**........................ TomScudamore
(David Pipe) *chsng ldrs whn fell 3rd* **13/2**[1]

6m 3.2s (-0.30) **Going Correction** +0.075s/f (Yiel) 16 Ran SP% **123.7**
Speed ratings (Par 113): **103,101,100,99,99 98,95,95,93,92 91,83,,,**
toteswingers: 1&2 £29.30, 2&3 £35.50, 1&3 £35.40 CSF £99.70 CT £737.47 TOTE £15.00: £3.10, £2.90, £1.90, £2.70; EX 147.70 Trifecta £1479.60 Pool: £56777.20 - 28.77 winning units..
Owner Mrs Julian Blackwell **Bred** Mme Marie Devilder & Benjamin Devilder **Trained** Kings Caple, H'fords

FOCUS
Pleasing to see a few of the second-season chasers come to the fore in this, a valuable handicap chase, and again it turned into a thorough test. Very solid form, with a step up from the impressive winner who looks obvious Hennessy material.

2215 GL EVENTS OWEN BROWN NOVICES' HURDLE (9 hdls) 2m
3:50 (3:53) (Class 3) 4-Y-0+

£7,507 (£2,217; £1,108; £554; £277; £139)

Form RPR
200/ **1** **Zamdy Man**[212] 5135 4-10-12 127.. AidanColeman 132+
(Venetia Williams) *mde all: clr 2nd to 5th: rdn clr again bef 2 out: styd on wl* **7/4**[1]
312- **2** *11* **Beachfire**[18] 1915 6-11-4 128.. DenisO'Regan 126
(John Ferguson) *hld up in 4th: hit 5th: effrt to dispute 2nd after 3 out: chsd wnr last: no imp* **15/8**[2]
1/2- **3** *3/4* **No No Mac (IRE)**[27] 1795 4-10-12 0...................................... NoelFehily 119
(Charlie Longsdon) *chsd wnr: hit 5th: no imp 3 out: sn lost 2nd: kpt on fr next* **3/1**[3]
21/ **4** *3 1/4* **Couldhavehaditall (IRE)**[213] 5125 5-10-12 0...................... TomO'Brien 118+
(Paul Webber) *trckd ldng pair: chsd wnr after 3 out: no imp: lost 2nd and stmbld last: wknd* **11/1**
566- **5** *46* **Mount Odell**[10] 2018 5-10-12 0.. JamieMoore 74
(Gary Moore) *hld up: detached fr ldrs after 4th: wknd 3 out: t.o* **40/1**
6- **6** *2 3/4* **Uramazin (IRE)**[27] 1779 7-10-12 0.................................. WayneHutchinson 72
(Philip Hide) *hld up: mstke 2nd: detached fr 4th: pushed along and no imp on ldng quartet 3 out: wknd bef next: t.o* **33/1**
\- **7** *29* **Moratab (IRE)**[502] 4-10-12 0.. FelixDeGiles 45
(Keiran Burke) *mstke 1st: nt jump wl after: a in rr: t.o bef 3 out* **40/1**

3m 53.4s (6.00) **Going Correction** +0.25s/f (Yiel)
WFA 4 from 5yo+ 7lb 7 Ran SP% **112.3**
Speed ratings (Par 107): **95,89,89,87,64 63,48**
toteswingers 1&2 £1.10, 1&3 £1.90, 2&3 £1.30 CSF £5.33 TOTE £2.60: £1.60, £1.80; EX 5.80 Trifecta £11.70 Pool: £3568.20 - 228.63 winning units..
Owner Muhammad Nadeem Khan **Bred** The Kathryn Stud **Trained** Kings Caple, H'fords

FOCUS
A fair novice hurdle that saw Venetia Williams gain a third success on the card. The winner improved to the level of his Flat form.

2216 CHILDREN'S TRUST STANDARD OPEN NATIONAL HUNT FLAT RACE 2m
4:20 (4:21) (Class 4) 4-6-Y-0

£3,128 (£924; £462; £231; £115; £58)

Form RPR
1 **Pleasant Company (IRE)**[181] 5-11-0 0........................ TomScudamore 118+
(David Pipe) *mde all: grad increased pce fr 1/2-way: kicked for home over 2f out: drvn clr over 1f out* **11/4**[1]
3/ **2** *8* **Rhapando**[215] 5070 4-11-0 0.. DenisO'Regan 109
(Paul Webber) *chsd wnr: reminder 1/2-way: pushed along after: drvn to try to mount a chal 2f out: one pce after* **16/1**
3 *2 1/4* **Ebony Empress (IRE)** 4-10-4 0...................................... MichaelByrne(3) 100
(Neil Mulholland) *trckd ldrs: sltly outpcd fr 4 out: kpt on fr 2f out to take 3rd last 100yds* **50/1**
1/ **4** *nk* **Robinsfirth (IRE)**[205] 5263 4-11-7 0.. JoeTizzard 114
(Colin Tizzard) *trckd ldrs: pushed along to chse ldng pair 3f out: no imp: one pce and lost 3rd fnl 100yds* **8/1**
2/ **5** *6* **Boogie In The Barn (IRE)**[200] 5333 5-11-0 0............. RichardJohnson 102
(Jeremy Scott) *t.k.h: hld up: outpcd by ldrs fr 4f out: nvr on terms after* **4/1**[3]
6 *2 3/4* **Hunters Hoof (IRE)** 4-11-0 0.. BarryGeraghty 99
(Nicky Henderson) *hld up in rr: effrt over 4f out but sn outpcd by ldrs: pushed along and no hdwy fnl 2f* **7/2**[2]
2/1- **7** *1 1/2* **Solstice Son**[20] 1891 4-11-4 0...................................(t) RachaelGreen(3) 105
(Anthony Honeyball) *hld up in last pair: effrt over 4f out but sn outpcd by ldrs: no hdwy fnl 2f* **8/1**
8 *1/2* **Aces Over Kings (IRE)** 6-10-9 0.................................. PatrickCorbett(5) 97
(Rebecca Curtis) *chsd ldng pair to 3f out: wknd* **12/1**
9 *1 1/4* **Polamco (IRE)** 4-11-0 0.. NoelFehily 96
(Harry Fry) *a in last trio: outpcd 4f out: nvr on terms after* **10/1**
4- **10** *5* **Vikekhal (FR)**[28] 1770 4-11-0 0.. JamieMoore 92
(Gary Moore) *chsd ldrs tl wknd 4f out* **33/1**

3m 50.3s (9.50) **Going Correction** +0.25s/f (Yiel) 10 Ran SP% **118.7**
Speed ratings: **86,82,80,80,77 76,75,75,74,72**
toteswingers 1&2 £20.50, 1&3 £27.60, 2&3 £74.80 CSF £50.53 TOTE £3.70: £1.70, £4.20, £7.10; EX 51.20 Trifecta £1564.20 Part won. Pool: £2085.66 - 0.44 winning units..
Owner Malcolm C Denmark **Bred** Susan Bredin **Trained** Nicholashayne, Devon
■ Stewards' Enquiry : Patrick Corbett one-day ban: careless riding (Nov 16)

FOCUS
Little got into what looked a decent bumper. The winner appears a smart prospect.
T/Jkpt: Not won. T/Plt: £333.00 to a £1 stake. Pool: £143787.42 - 315.12 winning tickets T/Qpdt: £71.20 to a £1 stake. Pool: £11223.81 - 116.50 winning tickets JN

AYR (L-H)
Saturday, November 2

OFFICIAL GOING: Soft changing to soft (heavy in places) after race 5 (3.10)
Wind: Fairly strong, half behind Weather: Overcast, showers

2217 JOHN SMITH'S MAIDEN HURDLE (9 hdls) 2m
12:55 (12:55) (Class 5) 4-Y-0+ £2,599 (£763; £381; £190)

Form RPR
4- **1** **Redpender (IRE)**[21] 1875 7-11-0 0.. DannyCook 114+
(James Moffatt) *cl up: led bef 3 out: pushed clr after next* **6/1**
4/0- **2** *4* **Silverton**[171] 316 6-10-7 94.. AdrianLane 101
(Lucy Normile) *t.k.h: led to bef 3 out: rallied: kpt on same pce fr next* **40/1**

1/U- **3** 1 ½ **Frankie's Promise (IRE)**[14] 1975 5-11-0 0 LucyAlexander 109+
(N W Alexander) *nt fluent: midfield: mstke 4th: hdwy to chse ldrs bef 3 out: nt fluent next: kpt on fr last* **4/1[2]**

5- **4** ¾ **Final Assault (IRE)**[27] 1792 4-11-0 0 PeterBuchanan 103
(Lucinda Russell) *hld up: stdy hdwy and in tch bef 3 out: effrt and pushed along next: one pce fr last* **14/1**

04/ **5** 13 **Scorpions Sting (IRE)**[195] 5429 4-11-0 0 BrianHughes 90
(James Ewart) *prom tl rdn and wknd fr 3 out* **28/1**

500/ **6** 1 ¾ **Finaghy Ayr (IRE)**[190] 5550 5-10-7 0 GrahamWatters(7) 88
(Ian Duncan) *hld up in midfield: stdy hdwy 4 out: outpcd whn nt fluent next: sn n.d* **100/1**

/44- **7** ½ **Hallmark Star**[14] 1979 4-10-7 112 CraigNichol(7) 88
(Lucinda Russell) *prom: rdn bef 3 out: wknd bef next* **2/1[1]**

33- **8** nk **Apollo Eleven (IRE)**[15] 1958 4-11-0 114 HenryBrooke 87
(Donald McCain) *prom tl rdn and wknd appr 3 out* **9/2[3]**

0- **9** 11 **Brighton Road (IRE)**[14] 1977 6-10-7 0 CallumBewley(7) 76
(R Mike Smith) *midfield: rdn 1/2-way: rallied: wknd bef 3 out* **66/1**

405/ **10** 2 ¼ **Danehills Well (IRE)**[239] 4629 5-11-0 0 BrianHarding 74
(Alison Hamilton) *hld up on ins: outpcd after 4 out: btn next* **100/1**

11 hd **Spring Over (IRE)** 7-10-2 0 AdamNicol(5) 67
(Ian Duncan) *nt fluent in rr: struggling fnl circ: nvr on terms* **100/1**

12 1 ½ **Inniscastle Boy**[19] 4-11-0 0 HarryHaynes 72
(Jim Goldie) *hld up: stdy hdwy appr 4 out: pushed along and wknd bef next* **66/1**

04- **13** 5 **Dunkirk's First (IRE)**[21] 1877 5-11-0 0 RichieMcGrath 67
(Rose Dobbin) *nt fluent in rr: mstke 4th: sn struggling: nvr on terms* **50/1**

46/ **14** 6 **Molly Milan**[197] 5373 5-10-7 0 [1] GaryBartley 54
(Jim Goldie) *nt fluent on occasions in rr: struggling bef 4 out: sn btn* **16/1**

4F6- **15** 11 **Tim's Approach (IRE)**[32] 1718 8-10-9 68 (t) TonyKelly(5) 50
(William Young Jnr) *prom to 4 out: sn rdn and lost pl* **200/1**

/10- **16** ½ **On The Buckle**[37] 1661 5-11-0 0 [1] WilsonRenwick 50
(Rose Dobbin) *nt fluent on occasions: bhd: struggling fr 4th: nvr on terms* **20/1**

6- **17** 15 **Military Call**[23] 1661 6-10-9 0 (p) CallumWhillans(5) 35
(R Mike Smith) *t.k.h early: in tch to 4 out: sn wknd* **80/1**

0/ **P** **Knockcairn (IRE)**[190] 5550 6-10-0 0 GrantCockburn(7)
(Ian Duncan) *nt fluent in rr: struggling fnl circ: t.o whn p.u after 4 out* **100/1**

3m 54.1s (-9.00) **Going Correction** -0.15s/f (Good)
WFA 4 from 5yo+ 7lb **18** Ran SP% **119.6**
Speed ratings (Par 103): **112,110,109,108,102 101,101,101,95,94 94,93,91,88,82 82,74,**
Tote Swingers: 1&2 £2.50, 1&3 £1.10, 2&3 £3.10 CSF £220.79 TOTE £6.60: £1.90, £9.70, £2.10; EX 178.80 Trifecta £312.80 Part won. Pool: £417.16 - 0.02 winning units..
Owner K Bowron **Bred** Andrew Murphy **Trained** Cartmel, Cumbria

FOCUS
Both tracks on innermost line and distances as advertised. After 0.5mm of rain overnight the going remained as soft. All but two of the field had run before for this modest maiden hurdle which was run at an honest pace in the conditions. It paid to race handy, with the field well strung out at the line. After riding in the first jockeys described it as "sloppy, wet, soft ground". The first two are on the upgrade.

2218 PLUMBSTORE H'CAP HURDLE (12 hdls) 3m 110y
1:25 (1:29) (Class 4) (0-110,110) 4-Y-0+ **£3,898** (£1,144; £572; £286)

Form RPR

3/4- **1** **Amore Mio (GER)**[21] 1873 8-11-0 98 (tp) PeterBuchanan 107+
(Lucinda Russell) *pressed ldr: led 7th to bef 2 out: rdn and rallied: regained ld run-in: styd on gamely* **4/1[1]**

0/1- **2** 4 ½ **Hartforth**[21] 1873 5-9-12 87 CallumWhillans(5) 90
(Donald Whillans) *t.k.h: hld up in tch: stdy hdwy to chse wnr 8th: led bef 2 out: sn rdn: hdd run-in: kpt on same pce* **11/2[3]**

5U5- **3** 14 **Solway Sam**[38] 1660 10-10-7 98 CraigGallagher(7) 87
(Lisa Harrison) *t.k.h: hld up: hdwy to chse ldrs 1/2-way: outpcd after 4 out: plugged on fr 2 out: no ch w first two* **11/2[3]**

443- **4** nk **Auberge (IRE)**[9] 2035 9-10-9 100 CallumBewley(7) 89
(Evelyn Slack) *hld up in tch: stdy hdwy to chse clr ldng pair after 4 out: rdn and wknd fr 2 out* **16/1**

65/- **5** 39 **Plus Jamais (FR)**[187] 22 6-11-7 105 GaryBartley 55
(Jim Goldie) *t.k.h early: hld up: rdn along bef 4 out: sn btn: t.o* **9/2[2]**

P14/ **6** 21 **Daasij (IRE)**[190] 5549 8-11-7 105 LucyAlexander 34
(N W Alexander) *chsd clr ldrs to 1/2-way: sn drvn along and lost pl: lost tch after 4 out: t.o* **13/2**

163/ **P** **Aggie's Lad (IRE)**[572] 11-11-12 110 PaddyBrennan
(Alison Hamilton) *hld up: mstke and struggling 7th: sn lost tch: t.o whn p.u bef 4 out* **33/1**

604- **P** **Almutaham (USA)**[21] 1874 6-10-0 84 oh1 (p) BrianHarding
(Nicky Richards) *led to 7th: chsd wnr to next: struggling after 4 out: sn lost tch: p.u bef next* **6/1**

0/1- **P** **The Flaming Matron (IRE)**[157] 532 7-10-10 101 MrKitAlexander(7)
(N W Alexander) *in tch: outpcd 8th: struggling next: no ch whn blnd bdly 3 out: p.u bef next* **17/2**

6m 25.1s (-6.70) **Going Correction** -0.15s/f (Good) **9** Ran SP% **115.9**
Speed ratings (Par 105): **104,102,98,97,85 78, , ,**
Tote Swingers: 1&2 £4.40, 1&3 £6.00, 2&3 £6.50 CSF £26.71 CT £121.40 TOTE £5.80: £1.60, £2.60, £1.90; EX 30.20 Trifecta £107.40 Pool: £563.70 - 3.93 winning units..
Owner CMC - W & P Marzouk & Team Kirkton **Bred** Gestut Hof Ittlingen **Trained** Arlary, Perth & Kinross

FOCUS
An open handicap run at a sensible pace. It was slow motion stuff up the straight with few ever getting competitive. The winner was on a good mark and is rated to the level of his 2011 form.

2219 TOPSTAFF EMPLOYMENT H'CAP CHASE (17 fncs) 2m 4f
2:00 (2:01) (Class 5) (0-100,97) 4-Y-0+ **£3,249** (£954; £477; £238)

Form RPR

0/6- **1** **Tresor De L'Isle (FR)**[156] 555 6-11-4 89 (p) BrianHughes 103+
(James Ewart) *cl up: led bef 9th: mde rest: nt fluent next: kpt on wl u.p fr 2 out* **15/2**

4P0/ **2** 3 **Shoal Bay Dreamer**[262] 4185 7-9-12 74 (p) TonyKelly(5) 83
(Dianne Sayer) *cl up: drvn along 12th: outpcd next: rallied bef 2 out: styd on to go 2nd towards fin: no ch w wnr* **15/2**

5/0- **3** 1 ¾ **Milan Royale**[21] 1870 8-11-2 87 HarryHaynes 95
(Kevin Hunter) *in tch: stdy hdwy 1/2-way: effrt whn lft 2nd 4 out: hit next: one pce last: no ex and lost 2nd towards fin* **11/1**

2/4- **4** 14 **Alexander Oats**[171] 311 10-11-3 88 (p) DannyCook 81
(Robert Goldie) *prom: rdn along and effrt bef 4 out: outpcd whn hit next: lft modest 4th last* **7/2[1]**

4/F- **5** ½ **Acordingtoscript (IRE)**[21] 1870 7-11-7 92 WilsonRenwick 86
(Martin Todhunter) *hld up in tch: mstke 12th: stdy hdwy on outside bef 4 out: edgd lft and wknd after next* **10/1**

P55- **F** **Laybach (IRE)**[27] 1791 9-10-8 79 LucyAlexander
(Jim Goldie) *led to 9th: chsd wnr: 2 l down and rdn along whn fell 4 out* **10/1**

/U5- **U** **Ballycool (IRE)**[21] 1870 6-11-5 97 (t) MrSFox(7) 93
(Lucinda Russell) *t.k.h: hld up: stdy hdwy on ins bef 4 out: effrt and rdn 2 out: sn btn: 11 l 4th whn nt fluent and uns rdr last* **9/2[3]**

304- **U** **Spitfire Ace (IRE)**[21] 1870 5-11-6 91 HenryBrooke
(Donald McCain) *prom: hit and uns rdr 1st* **4/1[2]**

5m 29.1s (6.20) **Going Correction** -0.15s/f (Good) **8** Ran SP% **110.4**
Speed ratings (Par 103): **81,79,79,73,73 , ,**
Tote Swingers: 1&2 £17.90, 1&3 £11.10, 2&3 £7.80 CSF £56.73 CT £583.28 TOTE £10.30: £2.60, £1.80, £2.90; EX 47.80 Trifecta £320.80 Part won. Pool: £427.82 - 0.04 winning units..
Owner Miss Anna Bramall **Bred** Mme Pierre Sayet **Trained** Langholm, Dumfries & G'way

FOCUS
A modest handicap run at a steady pace. A massive step up from the winner with the second close to his mark.

2220 JOHN SMITH'S NOVICES' LIMITED H'CAP CHASE (19 fncs) 3m 1f
2:35 (2:37) (Class 3) (0-140,136) 4-Y-0+ **£7,988** (£2,480; £1,335)

Form RPR

2/1- **1** **Green Flag (IRE)**[14] 1976 6-11-1 132 PeterBuchanan 144+
(Lucinda Russell) *hld up: nt fluent 7th: stdy hdwy 5 out: led bef 3 out: asserting whn lft jst over 4 l clr last: styd on wl* **10/11[1]**

465- **2** 7 **Scotswell**[68] 1398 7-10-7 124 BrianHughes 128
(Harriet Graham) *cl up: led 3rd: hdd after 5 out: rdn next: one pce fr 3 out: jst over 4 l down and hld whn lft 2nd last* **16/1**

211- **3** 19 **Sivola De Sivola (FR)**[20] 1888 7-11-5 136 PaddyBrennan 131+
(Tom George) *trckd ldrs: wnt 2nd 9th: chal 12th to next: sn pushed along: rdn and wknd 4 out: no ch whn lft modest 3rd last: eased run-in* **3/1[2]**

440/ **F** **Pause And Clause (IRE)**[243] 4562 9-10-5 122 oh8 (p) LucyAlexander
(N W Alexander) *hld up: mstke 6th: last and outpcd whn fell 12th* **12/1**

/P1- **F** **Streams Of Whiskey (IRE)**[21] 1870 6-10-5 122 oh3 BrianHarding 130
(Nicky Richards) *t.k.h: nt fluent: led to 3rd: pressed ldr to 9th: hit 13th: rallied and led after 5 out: hit next: sn hdd: rdn bef 2 out: nrly 3 l down and one pce whn fell last* **9/2[3]**

6m 39.2s (-10.70) **Going Correction** -0.15s/f (Good) **5** Ran SP% **109.1**
Speed ratings (Par 107): **111,108,102, ,**
CSF £12.53 TOTE £1.90: £1.10, £4.80; EX 12.80 Trifecta £67.00 Pool: £746.39 - 8.35 winning units..
Owner John R Adam **Bred** L M Walshe **Trained** Arlary, Perth & Kinross

FOCUS
A decent contest run at a sound pace in the testing conditions. A small step up from the winner with the second rated to his hurdles mark.

2221 JOHN SMITH'S EXTRA SMOOTH H'CAP HURDLE (9 hdls) 2m
3:10 (3:10) (Class 3) (0-140,126) 4-Y-0+ **£6,498** (£1,908; £954; £477)

Form RPR

404- **1** **Trucking Along (IRE)**[17] 1926 7-11-6 120 WilsonRenwick 126
(S R B Crawford, Ire) *t.k.h: hld up: hdwy and prom 4th: effrt after 2 out: led run-in: drvn and hld on wl* **11/1**

335/ **2** nk **Morning Royalty (IRE)**[210] 5173 6-11-12 126 BrianHughes 133
(James Moffatt) *led: rdn whn hit 2 out: hdd run-in: rallied: hld nr fin* **8/1**

353/ **3** 4 ½ **Titus Bolt (IRE)**[19] 4629 4-10-10 110 GaryBartley 112
(Jim Goldie) *t.k.h: cl up: effrt and ev ch whn hit 2 out: edgd lft and outpcd after last* **18/1**

120- **4** 16 **Cool Baranca (GER)**[7] 2069 7-11-1 120 EmmaSayer(5) 105
(Dianne Sayer) *prom: lost pl 3rd: struggling next: plugged on fr 2 out: nvr able to chal* **14/1**

0/0- **5** 3 ¼ **Saphir River (FR)**[169] 356 7-11-5 126 GrantCockburn(7) 107
(Lucinda Russell) *hld up: rdn and hdwy after 4 out: outpcd fr next* **11/4[2]**

513- **6** ½ **Call Box (IRE)**[29] 1752 8-11-4 118 PeterBuchanan 101
(S R B Crawford, Ire) *cl up: mstke 4 out: rdn and wknd after next* **15/2[3]**

425- **7** 14 **Outrageous Request**[22] 1849 7-10-12 119 CraigNichol(7) 86
(Lucinda Russell) *hld up: pushed along 1/2-way: struggling fr 4 out* **16/1**

1/5- **8** 6 **Big Water (IRE)**[17] 1922 5-11-10 124 PaddyBrennan 91
(Alan Swinbank) *prom: hit 5th: rdn and wknd bef 3 out* **5/2[1]**

/52- **P** **Ubaltique (FR)**[157] 534 5-11-11 125 HenryBrooke
(Donald McCain) *nt fluent in rr: struggling 1/2-way: t.o whn p.u bef 2 out* **12/1**

4m 3.2s (0.10) **Going Correction** -0.15s/f (Good)
WFA 4 from 5yo+ 7lb **9** Ran SP% **112.0**
Speed ratings (Par 107): **89,88,86,78,76 76,69,66,**
Tote Swingers: 1&2 £15.70, 1&3 £10.90, 2&3 £10.40 CSF £90.87 CT £1556.71 TOTE £10.40: £2.30, £2.00, £4.40; EX 110.60 Trifecta £748.40 Pool: £1,842.36 - 1.84 winning units..
Owner Mrs Denise Bailey **Bred** Michael Doyle **Trained** Larne, Co Antrim

FOCUS
The pace was solid for this competitive handicap with the front two fighting out an exciting finish. The winner is rated 4lb off his best.

2222 JOHN SMITH'S NO NONSENSE H'CAP CHASE (12 fncs) 2m
3:45 (3:48) (Class 3) (0-135,130) 4-Y-0+ **£7,797** (£2,289; £1,144; £572)

Form RPR

P/F- **1** **Simply Ned (IRE)**[22] 1849 6-11-12 130 BrianHarding 143+
(Nicky Richards) *t.k.h: hld up: nt fluent 5 out: smooth hdwy bef next: led and edgd lft between last 2: drvn clr run-in* **11/4[1]**

004/ **2** 3 ½ **Stormin Exit (IRE)**[187] 24 10-11-1 119 WilsonRenwick 129
(Jim Goldie) *in tch on outside: hdwy to ld 4 out: rdn and hdd between last 2: hit last: kpt on same pce* **9/1**

F24/ **3** 7 **Un Guet Apens (FR)**[283] 3788 5-11-1 119 BrianHughes 120
(James Ewart) *chsd ldrs: nt fluent 4th: rdn and outpcd bef 3 out: plugged on fr last: no ch w first two* **9/2[2]**

061- **4** 7 **Catch Tammy (IRE)**[46] 1596 7-11-2 120 PaddyBrennan 115
(Tom George) *cl up: led 5 out to next: rdn and wknd bef 2 out* **11/2[3]**

4/6- **5** 3 **Kealigolane (IRE)**[17] 1921 9-11-6 124 [1] LucyAlexander 118
(Barry Murtagh) *led to 5 out: rdn whn blnd next: sn wknd* **6/1**

143/ **6** 3 ½ **Prosecco (IRE)**[283] 3790 11-11-5 123 PeterBuchanan 112
(Lucinda Russell) *in tch: nt fluent and pushed along 3rd: rallied next: outpcd bef 5 out: n.d after* **11/2[3]**

33P- **7** 1 ¼ **Endeavor**[14] 1979 8-10-0 109 TonyKelly(5) 97
(Dianne Sayer) *hld up: mstke 5th: nt fluent next: shortlived effrt after 5 out: wknd fr next* **12/1**

605/ **P** **Mister Stickler (IRE)**[588] 5067 9-10-10 114 .... HenryBrooke
(Chris Grant) *t.k.h early: hld up in tch: blnd 7th: sn struggling: t.o whn p.u bef next* **14/1**

4m 10.1s (-0.60) **Going Correction** -0.15s/f (Good) 8 Ran SP% **114.3**
Speed ratings (Par 107): **95,93,89,86,84 83,82,**
Tote Swingers: 1&2 £6.40, 1&3 £3.00, 2&3 £6.60 CSF £26.99 CT £107.34 TOTE £3.40: £1.20, £2.60, £2.30; EX 26.90 Trifecta £123.60 Pool: £1,359.41 - 8.24 winning units..
Owner David & Nicky Robinson **Bred** Miss Irene Hatton **Trained** Greystoke, Cumbria

FOCUS
The going was eased to soft, heavy in places after the fifth race. A decent contest run at a fair pace, and the winner looks a pretty good novice.

2223 ODDS & EVENS BOOKMAKERS CATRINE "NEWCOMERS" STANDARD OPEN NATIONAL HUNT FLAT RACE 1m 6f
4:15 (4:16) (Class 5) 3-5-Y-O **£2,053** (£598; £299)

Form RPR
1 **Fly Home Harry** 4-11-9 0 .... PaddyBrennan 104+
(Alan Swinbank) *t.k.h: hld up: hdwy on outside 1/2-way: led and rn green over 2f out: drvn and hld on wl fnl f* **9/2**[3]
2 *1* **Warriors Tale** 4-11-9 0 .... BrianHarding 103+
(Nicky Richards) *in tch: smooth hdwy over 5f out: ev ch over 1f out: sn rdn: kpt on ins fnl f: hld nr fin* **6/4**[1]
3 *8* **The Squinty Bridge** 5-11-2 0 .... CraigNichol(7) 93
(Lucinda Russell) *pressed ldr: led over 5f out to over 2f out: sn outpcd by ldng pair* **11/4**[2]
4 *7* **Gilnockie** 5-11-9 0 .... BrianHughes 85
(James Ewart) *t.k.h: led to over 5d out: stv... outpcd over 2f out: n.d after* **8/1**
5 *1 1/4* **Shanroe Boru (IRE)** 4-11-2 0 ... GrahamWatters(7) 83
(J J Lambe, Ire) *prom: drvn ... n.d after* **8/1**
6 *61* **Macgillycuddy** 4-11 ... LucyAlexander 10
(Harriet Graham) ... *out: t.o* **20/1**

3m 31.5s (211.50) ... % **111.8**
Tote Swingers: 1&2 ... £1.60; EX 12.10 Trifecta ...
Owner Pan...
FOCU...
Not a ...
T/Plt: ... to a £1 stake. ...

OFFI...
Wind...

22...

Form RPR
F/ **1** ... (5) 128+
(Ha... *out: wn...* ... *led 3* **7/4**[2]
414- **2** *12* **Bracken H**... ....(tp) JasonMaguire 120
(Graeme McPhe... *reminders bef next: hld and mstke 3 out: fin t...* **16/1**
520- **3** *4 1/2* **Attycran (IRE)**[21] 1872 ... 103 ....(tp) StephenMulqueen(7) 107
(Maurice Barnes) *chsd ldng pair: 2nd 13th: one pce fr 4 out* **33/1**
3/ **4** *10* **Royal Sam (IRE)**[64] 1454 8-10-12 0 .... HarryChalloner(5) 101
(Martin Todhunter) *chsd ldrs: mstke 3rd: outpcd and lost pl 14th* **12/1**[3]
416/ **F** **Sixty Something (FR)**[212] 5141 7-11-3 135 .... APMcCoy
(Paul Webber) *in rr: blnd bdly and almost fell 3rd: j.lft next: mstke 4th: hdwy and in tch 6th: fell next* **4/5**[1]
P **Grey Shadow (IRE)** 7-11-3 0 .... RyanMania
(John Wade) *in rr: wl outpcd whn mstke 12th: sn bhd: t.o whn p.u bef 4 out* **66/1**

6m 16.6s (7.20) **Going Correction** +0.10s/f (Yiel) 6 Ran SP% **109.9**
Speed ratings (Par 105): **92,88,86,83,**
Tote Swingers: 1&2 £3.70, 1&3 £7.70, 2&3 £23.30 CSF £23.22 TOTE £2.60: £1.60, £4.20; EX 21.70 Trifecta £63.50 Pool: £696.19 - 8.21 winning units..
Owner The Mendip Syndicate **Bred** Miss E Hamilton **Trained** Seaborough, Dorset

FOCUS
This novice chase looked a two-horse race according to the betting. The winner can rate higher and the next two were close to their marks.

2225 BET365 NOVICES' HURDLE (9 hdls) 2m 110y
1:15 (1:15) (Class 3) 4-Y-O+ **£5,523** (£1,621; £810; £405)

Form RPR
2/1- **1** **Gone Too Far**[174] 239 5-11-0 0 .... APMcCoy 120+
(Alan King) *t.k.h: trckd ldrs: led appr 3 out: drvn to forge clr run-in* **4/6**[1]
3/ **2** *2 1/4* **Varom (FR)**[344] 2610 4-11-0 0 .... SamTwiston-Davies 115
(Paul Nicholls) *hld up in mid-div: hdwy to trck ldrs 4th: disputing 2nd and rdn between last 2: kpt on: no real imp* **13/2**[3]
/34- **3** *1* **Gassin Golf**[14] 1970 4-10-11 125 .... MichealNolan(3) 115
(Richard Lee) *chsd ldrs: drvn appr 2 out: one pce and lft 3rd last* **5/2**[2]
30- **4** *4* **Rock A Doodle Doo (IRE)**[17] 1924 6-11-0 0 .... AndrewThornton 113+
(Sally Hall) *sn mid-div: hdwy to trck ldrs 5th: outpcd next: rallied and upsides 3 out: disputing 2nd whn blnd last: nt rcvr* **25/1**
4- **5** *4* **Satanic Beat (IRE)**[32] 1713 4-10-9 0 .... JoeColliver(5) 107
(Jedd O'Keeffe) *t.k.h: led 1st: increased pce 6th: hdd appr next: wknd appr 2 out* **25/1**
1/1- **6** *19* **Lemony Bay**[170] 338 4-11-0 0 .... LeightonAspell 90
(Oliver Sherwood) *trckd ldrs: upsides 5th: wknd 3 out* **8/1**
7 *11* **Light The City (IRE)**[23] 6-10-11 0 .... JakeGreenall(3) 80
(Ruth Carr) *in rr: sme hdwy 6th: lost pl bef next* **100/1**
0/0- **8** *5* **Next Hight (IRE)**[3] 2156 6-10-9 0 .... JonathanEngland(5) 75
(Sue Smith) *led to 1st: riodden and lost pl 6th: sn bhd* **66/1**
9 *11* **Durham Express (IRE)**[38] 6-10-9 0 .... SamanthaDrake(5) 65
(Tina Jackson) *t.k.h in rr: mstke 2nd: lost pl after 5th: sn bhd* **200/1**

10 *15* **Narcissist (IRE)**[8] 4-11-0 0 .... DougieCostello 52
(Michael Easterby) *t.k.h in rr: nt fluent 2nd: bhd fr 5th* **50/1**

3m 59.3s (3.50) **Going Correction** +0.10s/f (Yiel)
WFA 4 from 5yo+ 7lb 10 Ran SP% **125.6**
Speed ratings (Par 107): **95,93,93,91,89 80,75,73,68,61**
Tote Swingers: 1&2 £2.50, 1&3 £1.10, 2&3 £3.10 CSF £6.70 TOTE £1.70: £1.10, £1.80, £1.10; EX 9.00 Trifecta £17.20 Pool: £1,478.92 - 64.29 winning units..
Owner John P McManus **Bred** Richard Evans Bloodstock **Trained** Barbury Castle, Wilts

FOCUS
Plenty of interest in this novice hurdle featuring recruits from the Flat and bumpers. The form would be rated lower on time but the first two were decent in bumpers.

2226 OLBG.COM MARES' HURDLE (LISTED RACE) (9 hdls) 2m 110y
1:50 (1:51) (Class 1) 4-Y-O+
£12,813 (£4,808; £2,407; £1,199; £603; £301)

Form RPR
211/ **1** **Cockney Sparrow**[42] 5178 4-10-12 141 .... DougieCostello 141+
(John Quinn) *trckd ldrs: hdwy to ld 2 out: styd on strly: readily* **3/1**[2]
160/ **2** *1 1/4* **Prima Porta**[198] 5360 7-10-12 132 .... AdamWedge 137
(Evan Williams) *chsd ldrs: wnt 2nd between last 2: styd on run-in: no real imp* **11/1**
106/ **3** *7* **Alasi**[212] 5144 9-10-12 137 .... DominicElsworth 131
(Paul Webber) *trckd ldrs: led briefly appr 2 out: wknd towards fin* **10/1**[3]
211/ **4** *hd* **Mischievous Milly (IRE)**[307] 3379 5-11-6 137 .... LeightonAspell 139
(Oliver Sherwood) *t.k.h towards rr: hdwy 6th: chsng ldrs whn swtchd lft appr 2 out: disp 4th last: styd on same pce* **12/1**
331/ **5** *nk* **Doyly Carte**[198] 5358 5-11-6 131 .... JasonMaguire 139
(Donald McCain) *hld up in rr: hdwy and swtchd lft appr 3 out: kpt on and disp 4th last: styd on same pce* **16/1**
131/ **6** *3 1/2* **L'Unique (FR)**[212] 5135 4-11-6 142 .... RobertThornton 138+
(Alan King) *trckd ldrs: drvn upsides whn mstke 3 out: wknd last* **5/2**[1]
10P/ **7** *1/2* **Une Artiste (FR)**[196] 5402 5-11-6 141 .... APMcCoy 135
(Nicky Henderson) *led: hdd appr 2 out: wknd last* **3/1**[2]
454- **8** *18* **Ixora (IRE)**[14] 1972 7-10-12 119 ....(v) IanPopham 111
(Jamie Snowden) *chsd ldrs: lost pl bef 2 out: sn bhd* **66/1**
4F5- **9** *36* **Exclusive Dancer**[32] 1713 4-10-12 0 ....[1] BarryKeniry 78
(George Moore) *in rr: lost pl after 6th: sn bhd: t.o* **200/1**

3m 55.2s (-0.60) **Going Correction** +0.10s/f (Yiel) 9 Ran SP% **111.6**
Speed ratings (Par 111): **105,104,101,101,100 99,99,90,73**
Tote Swingers: 1&2 £7.30, 1&3 £5.90, 2&3 £14.60 CSF £33.52 TOTE £3.70: £1.40, £3.50, £2.90; EX 33.60 Trifecta £365.00 Pool: £1,815.41 - 3.72 winning units..
Owner Mr & Mrs Paul Gaffney **Bred** P Cunningham **Trained** Settrington, N Yorks

FOCUS
...od, competitive renewal of this Listed mares' hurdle, which featured the two previous winners ...race. The winner is improving in line with her Flat form and the second posted a personal ...too.

2227 BET365.COM NOVICES' LIMITED H'CAP CHASE (13 fncs) 2m
2:25 (2:25) (Class 3) (0-140,140) 4-Y-O+ **£6,945** (£2,385)

Form RPR
3/2- **1** **Valco De Touzaine (FR)**[33] 1698 4-10-6 135 ....(t) SamTwiston-Davies 130+
(Paul Nicholls) *mde all: sn clr: styd on fr 4 out: drvn clr run-in* **6/4**[1]
2PP/ **2** *12* **It's A Gimme (IRE)**[232] 4768 6-11-2 137 .... APMcCoy 132+
(Jonjo O'Neill) *chsd wnr: drvn 4 out: 5 l down and no imp last* **6/4**[1]
U/1- **U** **Fair Trade**[125] 235 6-10-8 129 .... RobertThornton
(Alan King) *racd in ldrs: mstke 1st: drvn 8th: lost tch and blnd bdly 9th: t.o whn blnd bdly and uns rdr next* **3/1**[2]

3m 51.8s (-4.00) **Going Correction** +0.10s/f (Yiel)
WFA 4 from 6yo 7lb 3 Ran SP% **105.0**
Speed ratings (Par 107): **114,108,**
CSF £3.92 TOTE £2.50; EX 3.00 Trifecta £4.00 Pool: £889.83 - 163.15 winning units..
Owner The Gi Gi Syndicate **Bred** Daniel Jandard & Mme Andree Jandard **Trained** Ditcheat, Somerset

FOCUS
A decent limited novice handicap chase despite the small field. A step up from the winner and there's a case for rating the form 7lb+ higher through the third.

2228 BET365 HURDLE (REGISTERED AS THE WEST YORKSHIRE HURDLE RACE) (GRADE 2) (13 hdls) 3m 1f
3:00 (3:00) (Class 1) 4-Y-O+ **£20,884** (£7,897; £4,003; £2,043; £1,076)

Form RPR
121/ **1** **Tidal Bay (IRE)**[309] 3325 12-11-8 160 .... SamTwiston-Davies 156
(Paul Nicholls) *trckd ldrs: pushed along and 2nd between last 2: nt fluent last: styd on run-in: led towards fin* **11/4**[2]
11P/ **2** *1* **Medinas (FR)**[210] 5175 6-11-4 154 .... RobertThornton 150
(Alan King) *trckd ldrs: shkn up 10th: led appr next: 1 1/2 l ahd last: edgd lft: hdd towards fin* **9/4**[1]
2/0- **3** *4* **Captain Sunshine**[15] 1956 7-11-0 140 ....(p) DominicElsworth 142
(Emma Lavelle) *chsd ldrs: reminders 8th: drvn and outpcd appr 3 out: kpt on and 3rd between last 2: styd on same pce* **6/1**[3]
132/ **4** *11* **Trustan Times (IRE)**[259] 4248 7-11-4 149 .... DougieCostello 136
(Tim Easterby) *hld up: trckd ldrs 9th: effrt and almost upsides 3 out: sn drvn: hung lft and wknd between last 2* **9/4**[1]
010/ **5** *20* **Across The Bay (IRE)**[210] 5177 9-11-8 146 ....(tp) JasonMaguire 125
(Donald McCain) *led: hdd appr 3 out: 5th and btn whnhit 2 out: bhd whn hung rt run-in* **16/1**
F63/ **P** **The Knoxs (IRE)**[236] 4715 10-11-0 143 .... RyanMania
(Sue Smith) *w ldr: lost pl after 10th: sn bhd: t.o whn p.u bef next* **28/1**

6m 17.4s (0.90) **Going Correction** +0.10s/f (Yiel) 6 Ran SP% **111.8**
Speed ratings (Par 115): **102,101,100,96,90**
Tote Swingers: 1&2 £1.60, 1&3 £4.40, 2&3 £2.20 CSF £9.56 TOTE £2.50: £2.60, £1.90; EX 9.20 Trifecta £30.50 Pool: £2,441.08 - 59.88 winning units..
Owner Andrea & Graham Wylie **Bred** John Dorgan **Trained** Ditcheat, Somerset

■ Stewards' Enquiry : Dominic Elsworth two-day ban: used whip above permitted level (Nov 16-17)

FOCUS
Tiday Bay was bidding to follow up last year's success in this high-class staying hurdle and did so by coming out best in a terrific finish. The winner is rated similarly to last year's win in the race, with the second 5lb off and the third to his mark.

2229 BET365 CHARLIE HALL CHASE (GRADE 2) (18 fncs) 3m 1f
3:35 (3:38) (Class 1) 5-Y-0+ £57,218 (£21,638; £10,968; £5,598; £2,948)

Form RPR
1UB/ **1** **Harry Topper**[193] 5489 6-11-6 152 .... JasonMaguire 154+
(Kim Bailey) *nt fluent 1st: in rr whn hit 2nd: reminders after 4th: chsd ldrs 10th: upsides 4 out: led appr last: all out* **5/1**[2]
6/5- **2** *nk* **Wayward Prince**[22] 1858 9-11-10 147 .... (t) JackDoyle 156
(Hilary Parrott) *trckd ldrs: led narrowly appr 3 out: hdd appr last: no ex nr fin* **50/1**
114/ **3** *4* **Unioniste (FR)**[234] 4734 5-11-6 153 .... SamTwiston-Davies 148
(Paul Nicholls) *trckd ldrs: pushed along 12th: upsides 4 out: wknd fnl 75yds* **13/2**[3]
1P/- **4** *32* **Beneficient (IRE)**[42] 5531 7-11-5 157 .... APMcCoy 118
(A J Martin, Ire) *led to 13th: rallied and upsides appr 4 out: wknd appr 2 out: t.o* **17/2**
132/ **5** *5* **Long Run (FR)**[192] 5515 8-11-10 171 .... (p) MrSWaley-Cohen 118
(Nicky Henderson) *trckd ldrs: blnd11th: drvn and lost pl appr 4 out: sn bhd: t.o* **4/5**[1]
155/ **P** **Cape Tribulation**[212] 5136 9-11-10 160 .... DougieCostello
(Malcolm Jefferson) *in rr: drvn and wknd 14th: bhd whn p.u bef next* **15/2**
656/ **F** **Master Of The Hall (IRE)**[266] 4123 9-11-0 148 .... DominicElsworth
(Micky Hammond) *trckd ldrs: led 13th: hdd and 4th whn fell heavily 3 out* **66/1**

6m 4.2s (-5.20) **Going Correction** +0.10s/f (Yiel) 7 Ran SP% **111.3**
Speed ratings: **112,111,110,100,98** ,
Tote Swingers: 1&2 £17.20, 1&3 £4.40, 2&3 £8.90 CSF £116.03 TOTE £6.20: £2.20, £8.90; EX 170.40 Trifecta £1069.50 Pool: £4,197.43 - 2.94 winning units..
Owner D J Keyte **Bred** The Round Oak Partnership **Trained** Andoversford, Gloucs

FOCUS
A very interesting renewal of this important early-season staying chase. Harry Topper was below the best of his heavy-ground form, with the second probably the best guide. Unioniste will need to improve to win off his current mark.

2230 WATCH RACING UK ON FREEVIEW 231 H'CAP HURDLE (11 hdls) 2m 4f
4:05 (4:08) (Class 3) (0-135,131) 4-Y-0+ £5,523 (£1,621; £810; £405)

Form RPR
1/ **1** **More Of That (IRE)**[333] 2834 5-11-11 **130** .... APMcCoy 143
(Jonjo O'Neill) *hld up in rr: hdwy 7th: handy 3rd sn after next: 2nd 2 out: 1 l down last: styd on to ld clsng stages* **3/1**[1]
/12- **2** *1* **Twelve Roses**[23] 1828 5-11-5 **124** .... JasonMaguire 136
(Kim Bailey) *hld up in rr: hdwy 6th: handy 2nd 8th: led 2 out: hdd and no ex clsng stages* **7/2**[3]
P03- **3** *24* **Cloudy Bob (IRE)**[21] 1867 6-11-0 **119** .... ColinBolger 111
(Pat Murphy) *chsd ldrs: drvn 8th: outpcd next: kpt on to take poor 3rd last* **5/1**
16P/ **4** *4 ½* **Vasco D'Ycy (FR)**[210] 5173 4-11-4 **126** .... JackQuinlan(3) 114
(Sarah Humphrey) *w ldr: led 3rd: qcknd pce 5th: hdd 2 out: wknd* **33/1**
120/ **P** **Rock Relief (IRE)**[128] 5405 7-10-13 **125** .... DiarmuidO'Regan(7)
(Chris Grant) *chsd ldrs: lost pl and mstke 6th: bhd 8th: distant 5th whn p.u bef next* **16/1**
02F/ **P** **Great Value (IRE)**[400] 1661 8-10-10 **120** .... KillianMoore(5)
(Graeme McPherson) *prom: lost pl after 6th: bhd 8th: t.o whn p.u bef next* **25/1**
350/ **P** **Ardlui (IRE)**[95] 3854 5-11-9 **128** .... RobertThornton
(Alan King) *chsd ldrs: reminders 4th: drvn 6th: lost pl next: bhd 8th: t.o whn p.u bef next* **10/3**[2]
4/4- **P** **Pas Trop Tard (FR)**[17] 1922 6-11-5 **131** .... (t) StephenMulqueen(7)
(Maurice Barnes) *led to 3rd: chsd ldr: wknd qckly 8th: sn bhd: p.u bef next* **8/1**
3/0- **P** **Northern Oscar (IRE)**[182] 116 5-10-5 **110** .... DougieCostello
(Tim Walford) *in rr: bhd fr 7th: t.o whn p.u bef 3 out* **25/1**

4m 56.5s (-3.00) **Going Correction** +0.10s/f (Yiel)
WFA 4 from 5yo+ 8lb 9 Ran SP% **114.6**
Speed ratings (Par 107): **110,109,100,98**, , , ,
Tote Swingers: 1&2 £1.90, 2&3 £2.40 CSF £13.84 CT £49.64 TOTE £3.20: £1.50, £1.70, £1.80; EX 11.40 Trifecta £41.90 Pool: £1,811.43 - 32.39 winning units..
Owner John P McManus **Bred** Mrs Eleanor Hadden **Trained** Cheltenham, Gloucs

FOCUS
Quite a competitive handicap hurdle but they got well strung out and only the first four mattered in the straight. The winner was potentially well in but this rates a step up, and the form could be rated up to 7lb higher through the third and fourth.
T/Plt: £229.30 to a £1 stake. Pool: £75,495.06 - 240.30 winning tickets. T/Qpdt: £152.40 to a £1 stake. Pool: £6,529.56 - 31.70 winning tickets. WG

2231 - 2233a (Foreign Racing) - See Raceform Interactive

2203 DOWN ROYAL (R-H)
Saturday, November 2

OFFICIAL GOING: Yielding to soft (soft in places on chase course) changing to soft after race 4 (2:30)

2234a JNWINE.COM CHAMPION CHASE (GRADE 1) (15 fncs) 3m
2:30 (2:30) 5-Y-0+ £68,292 (£21,626; £10,243; £3,414; £1,707)

RPR
1 **Roi Du Mee (FR)**[16] 1951 8-11-10 154 .... (t) BryanCooper 164+
(Gordon Elliott, Ire) *mde virtually all: disp early bef led narrowly after 1st: stl gng wl into st and extended advantage fr 3 out: sn clr: eased cl home* **12/1**
2 *13* **Sizing Europe (IRE)**[28] 1776 11-11-10 169 .... AELynch 154+
(Henry De Bromhead, Ire) *chsd ldrs: slt mstke 4th: pushed along in cl 2nd after 4 out: mstke next and no imp on wnr u.p: dropped to mod 2nd whn mstke last: kpt on same pce* **9/4**[1]
3 *10* **Prince De Beauchene (FR)**[252] 4402 10-11-10 155 .... RWalsh 141+
(W P Mullins, Ire) *led and disp early: settled bhd ldr after 1st: dropped towards rr fr 10th: no imp on wnr in 4th bef 3 out where slt mstke: wnt mod 3rd after next and kpt on one pce* **7/1**
4 *2 ½* **First Lieutenant (IRE)**[16] 1951 8-11-10 170 .... (p) DavyRussell 139+
(M F Morris, Ire) *trckd ldrs: clsr in 2nd bef 9th: rdn in 3rd after 4 out and no imp on wnr whn slt mstke next: kpt on one pce* **9/4**[1]
5 *2 ½* **Kauto Stone (FR)**[192] 5515 7-11-10 158 .... NickScholfield 136+
(Paul Nicholls) *w.w in rr: nt fluent 3rd and 5th: niggled along fr 9th and wnt 4th next: rdn bef 3 out and sn no imp: kpt on one pce* **6/1**[3]
U **Mount Benbulben (IRE)**[193] 5489 8-11-10 160 .... DannyMullins
(Gordon Elliott, Ire) *chsd ldrs: j. sltly rt 4th and 6th: dropped towards rr 8th: tk clsr order in 4th bef 4 out where bad mstke and uns rdr* **9/2**[2]

6m 10.3s (-7.90) 6 Ran SP% **114.2**
CSF £41.24 TOTE £16.00: £3.00, £1.60; DF 47.70 Trifecta £209.60.
Owner Gigginstown House Stud **Bred** Jacques Hersent & Mrs Jacqueline Hersent **Trained** Trim, Co Meath

FOCUS
A quality renewal wion by the outsider of the sextet. The pace, set throughout by the winner, was sensible given the conditions but it nonetheless developed into a true test. Roi Du Mee rates a personal best but the next four were all below par.

2235a POWERS IRISH WHISKEY CHASE (GRADE 2) (13 fncs) 2m 4f
3:05 (3:05) 5-Y-0+ £26,422 (£7,723; £3,658; £1,219)

RPR
1 **Rolling Aces (IRE)**[252] 4389 7-11-5 153 .... NickScholfield 156+
(Paul Nicholls) *trckd ldr tl led 5th: strly pressed fr 3 out and jnd next: sn rdn and disp u.p whn lft clr last: eased cl home* **9/4**[1]
2 *2* **Toner D'Oudairies (FR)**[16] 1951 6-11-8 149 .... (tp) BryanCooper 154
(Gordon Elliott, Ire) *w.w: 6th 1/2-way: hdwy on outer to chse ldrs bef 2 out: sn rdn in 3rd and lft 2nd at last where hmpd: kpt on wl towards fin: nt trble wnr* **6/1**
3 *1 ¾* **Texas Jack (IRE)**[233] 4746 7-11-10 149 .... RWalsh 154
(Noel Meade, Ire) *hld up in rr: tk clsr order 3 out: rdn in 4th between last 2 and no ex u.p whn lft 3rd and sltly hmpd last: kpt on same pce* **4/1**[3]
4 *2 ¼* **Oscars Well (IRE)**[5] 2141 8-11-5 148 .... DJCasey 147
(Mrs John Harrington, Ire) *w.w: 5th 1/2-way: pushed along fr 3 out and n.m.r between horses and lost pl: swtchd lft bef next in 5th: no imp on ldrs whn lft 4th last: kpt on same pce* **11/4**[2]
5 *21* **Buckers Bridge (IRE)**[94] 1168 7-11-10 140 .... AELynch 135
(Henry De Bromhead, Ire) *chsd ldrs: j.big 1st and next: 4th 1/2-way: dropped towards rr after 3 out and no imp on ldrs whn lft 5th and hmpd next: wknd* **14/1**
F **Tofino Bay (IRE)**[193] 5489 10-11-10 149 .... (p) DavyRussell 142
(D T Hughes, Ire) *led: slow 5th and hdd: niggled along in cl 3rd bef 3 out: sn no ex u.p and dropped to mod 6th whn fell 2 out* **7/1**
F **Argocat (IRE)**[193] 5489 5-11-9 143 .... PaulTownend 158+
(T J Taaffe, Ire) *chsd ldrs in 3rd: t.k.h: tk clsr order in 2nd 3 out: got on terms next and ev ch whn fell last* **20/1**

4m 59.7s (299.70) 7 Ran SP% **115.7**
CSF £16.66 TOTE £3.60: £2.90, £1.30; DF 12.20 Trifecta £48.30.
Owner Paul Barber, Ian Fogg & David Martin **Bred** Michael Daly **Trained** Ditcheat, Somerset
■ A sixth consecutive win in this Grade 2 event for Paul Nicholls.

FOCUS
An eventful race in which the outcome was in the balance at the final fence where Argocat, the youngest horse in the line-up, fell when upsides Rolling Aces, who went on to credit trainer with a sixth consecutive win in this Grade 2 event. The second and third set a modest standard and the winner didn't need to be at his best.

2236 - 2239a (Foreign Racing) - See Raceform Interactive

1983 AUTEUIL (L-H)
Saturday, November 2

OFFICIAL GOING: Turf: heavy

2240a GRAND PRIX D'AUTOMNE (HURDLE) (GRADE 1) (5YO+) (TURF) 3m
2:40 (12:00) 5-Y-0+
£135,365 (£66,178; £39,105; £27,073; £15,040; £10,528)

RPR
1 **Reve De Sivola (FR)**[146] 685 8-10-8 0 .... JamesReveley 143+
(Nick Williams) *trckd ldng pair: sltly outpcd 6 out and dropped to 5th: reminders after 3 out: 8th and plenty to do 2 out: 10 l to find but styng on appr last: r.o u.p run-in: chal between horses to ld fnl strides* **36/1**
2 *1* **Lord Prestige (FR)**[20] 1901 6-10-8 0 .... JonathanPlouganou 142+
(M Rolland, France) *midfield wl in tch: prom on inner 8th: led 10th and sn clr: hdd between last 2 flights: rdn and rallied run-in: styd on to go 2nd fnl strides* **17/1**
3 *snk* **Gemix (FR)**[45] 1608 5-10-6 0 ow3 .... DavidCottin 140+
(N Bertran De Balanda, France) *led: wnt rt 1st: hdd 10th: chsd ldrs: rallied u.p to regain to ld between last 2 flight: hrd rdn and r.o: wandered u.p 100yds out: hdd and dropped to 3rd fnl strides* **9/5**[2]
4 *shd* **Lamego (FR)**[20] 1901 6-10-8 0 .... Jean-LucBeaunez 142
(Mme P Butel, France) *w.w in rr: stdy hdwy fr 3 out: 4th and styng on whn hmpd by faller last: kpt on gamely u.p run-in* **95/1**
5 *1* **Saint Du Chenet (FR)**[20] 1901 7-10-8 0 .... (b) RegisSchmidlin 141
(M Rolland, France) *prom: lost pl bef 4 out: hdwy 2 out: chsd ldng quartet appr last: one pce u.p run-in* **63/10**[3]
6 *4* **Prince Oui Oui (FR)**[20] 1901 7-10-8 0 .... JacquesRicou 137
(P Peltier, France) *midfield wl in tch: lost pl 4 out: kpt on at same pce fr 2 out* **10/1**
7 *¾* **Dulce Leo (FR)**[20] 1901 7-10-8 0 .... (p) JonathanNattiez 136
(J-P Gallorini, France) *towards rr: sme late prog: nvr on terms w ldrs* **45/1**
F **Ceasar's Palace (FR)**[20] 1901 6-10-8 0 .... ChristopheSoumillon
(J-P Gallorini, France) *trckd ldr: pckd 4 out: rdn and no immediate imp after 2 out: cl 3rd and styng on whn fell last* **13/10**[1]
P **Thyflori (FR)**[39] 5-9-13 0 .... (p) FredericDitta
(R Le Gal, France) *towards rr: wl bhd bef 3 out: p.u bef 2 out* **29/1**

6m 0.82s (360.82) 9 Ran SP% **116.8**
PARI-MUTUEL (all including 1 euro stake): WIN 37.10; PLACE 4.30, 2.80, 1.50; DF 119.00; SF 318.90.
Owner Paul Duffy Diamond Partnership **Bred** Gilles Trapenard & Thomas Trapenard **Trained** George Nympton, Devon

FOCUS
They finished in a bunch and the first three are all capable of better.

[2154]CARLISLE (R-H)

Sunday, November 3

OFFICIAL GOING: Heavy (chs 5.7; hdl 5.7)

Wind: Fairly strong, half against Weather: Cloudy, bright

2241 NORTHERN RACING CLUB "SATURDAY NAPS CHALLENGE" NOVICES' H'CAP HURDLE (THE SUNDAY £5K BONUS RACE) (8 hdls) 2m 1f

1:00 (1:02) (Class 4) (0-110,108) 3-Y-O+ **£3,249** (£954; £477; £238)

Form				RPR
501-	1		**Turtle Watch**[15] 1979 5-11-6 **102** WilsonRenwick (Jim Goldie) *hld up: smooth hdwy 3 out: led gng wl bef last: drvn clr run-in* **7/2**[3]	116+
6/2-	2	12	**Bernardelli (IRE)**[15] 1975 5-11-12 **108** APMcCoy (Nicky Richards) *in tch: smooth hdwy bef 3 out: led gng wl bef next: rdn and hdd bef last: kpt on same pce run-in* **4/1**	111+
315-	3	10	**Frontier Vic**[21] 1887 6-10-11 **93** SamTwiston-Davies (Nigel Twiston-Davies) *led to bef 2nd: chsd clr ldr: drvn and outpcd 3 out: rallied whn nt fluent next: sn no ch w first two* **5/2**[1]	85
5/5-	4	5	**Yorkist (IRE)**[10] 2032 5-11-2 **105** NathanMoscrop(7) (Brian Ellison) *cl up chsng gp: hit 4 out: chal bef 2 out: rdn and wknd between last 2* **3/1**[2]	92
0/0-	5	2	**Bollin Julie**[15] 1979 6-9-10 **83** CallumWhillans(5) (Donald Whillans) *nt fluent on occasions: hld up: drvn and outpcd after 3 out: no imp bef next* **28/1**	68
/FP-	6	34	**Snowed In (IRE)**[4] 2155 4-11-2 **105** (p) ConorRing(7) (Jennie Candlish) *hld up: struggling bef 3 out: sn btn* **12/1**	56
625/	7	nk	**Circus Star (USA)**[214] 5121 5-11-1 **104** MrJDixon(7) (John Dixon) *plld hrd: led bef 2nd and sn clr: hdd bef 2 out: sn wknd: btn whn nt fluent last* **20/1**	55

4m 19.5s (-9.70) **Going Correction** -0.625s/f (Firm)

WFA 4 from 5yo+ 7lb 7 Ran SP% **111.7**

Speed ratings (Par 105): **97,91,86,84,83 67,67**

toteswingers 1&2 £2.20, 1&3 £1.60, 2&3 £5.10 CSF £17.22 CT £38.92 TOTE £4.70: £2.00, £2.40; EX 16.50 Trifecta £36.70 Pool: £769.75 - 15.69 winning units..

Owner Mr & Mrs Raymond Anderson Green **Bred** Design And Planning Consultants Ltd **Trained** Uplawmoor, E Renfrews

FOCUS

After 10mm rain in the previous 24 hours conditions were very testing. The hurdle races were run on the new inner track for the first time this season. They ignored the tearaway leader and just the first two seriously involved at the business end. Ordinary form with the first two on the upgrade.

2242 BOOKMAKERS.CO.UK BEGINNERS' CHASE (15 fncs 1 omitted) 2m 4f

1:30 (1:30) (Class 4) 4-Y-O+ **£6,498** (£1,908; £954; £477)

Form				RPR
12P/	1		**Many Clouds (IRE)**[213] 5141 6-11-2 0 LeightonAspell (Oliver Sherwood) *t.k.h: chsd ldrs: led 3rd: hesitated 5th: rdn after 2 out: edgd lft run-in: styd on strly* **5/2**[2]	141+
502/	2	2 1/4	**Knock A Hand (IRE)**[260] 4252 8-11-2 0 (b) RichardJohnson (Richard Lee) *led to 3rd: chsd wnr to 10th: sn drvn along: rallied and regained 2nd 2 out: kpt on fr last: nt rch wnr* **5/1**[3]	139
124/	3	7	**Holywell (IRE)**[192] 5529 6-11-2 0 (p) APMcCoy (Jonjo O'Neill) *nt fluent: cl up: j.lft and hit 2nd: lost pl after next: nt fluent and drvn 8th: rallied 10th: outpcd after next: plugged on fr 2 out: nvr rchd ldrs* **4/5**[1]	134
114/	4	5	**Walkabout Creek (IRE)**[198] 5368 6-11-2 0 SamTwiston-Davies (Steve Gollings) *prom: clsd 4th: chsd wnr 10th to 2 out: sn rdn: 3rd and outpcd whn mstke last: wknd* **14/1**	130

5m 11.1s (-16.30) **Going Correction** -1.075s/f (Hard) 4 Ran SP% **107.5**

Speed ratings (Par 105): **89,88,85,83**

CSF £12.91 TOTE £3.80; EX 10.50 Trifecta £19.60 Pool: £794.02 - 30.38 winning units..

Owner Trevor Hemmings **Bred** Aidan Aherne **Trained** Upper Lambourn, Berks

FOCUS

The first fence after the stands was again omitted after giving problems here four days earlier. A high-class beginners' chase. The first two are rated in line with their hurdle form.

2243 MR & MRS HANDLEY RUBY WEDDING NOVICES' HURDLE (10 hdls) 2m 3f 110y

2:05 (2:05) (Class 4) 4-Y-O+ **£3,898** (£1,144; £572; £286)

Form				RPR
1/1-	1		**Oscar Fortune (IRE)**[19] 1915 5-11-5 0 APMcCoy (Jonjo O'Neill) *chsd ldr to 5th: pushed along 4 out: hdwy to ld appr 2 out: kpt on strly fr last: veered lft nr fin* **5/4**[1]	129+
311/	2	1 3/4	**Deputy Dan (IRE)**[201] 5333 5-10-12 0 LeightonAspell (Oliver Sherwood) *t.k.h: prom: hdwy and ev ch appr 2 out: rdn and sltly outpcd last: kpt on wl to take 2nd nr fin: nt rch wnr* **9/4**[2]	117
4-	3	1/2	**Glowinginthedark (IRE)**[23] 1861 5-10-12 0 JasonMaguire (Charlie Longsdon) *chsd ldrs: wnt 2nd 5th: effrt and ev ch appr 2 out: kpt on fr last: lost 2nd nr fin* **12/1**	117
/42-	4	24	**Splash Of Ginge**[33] 1706 5-10-12 127 SamTwiston-Davies (Nigel Twiston-Davies) *led: rdn and hdd appr 2 out: hung rt and wknd bef last* **3/1**[3]	100
0/4-	5	30	**Ellistrin Belle**[15] 1975 5-10-0 0 CallumWhillans(5) (Donald Whillans) *hld up: struggling 3 out: sn lost tch: t.o* **50/1**	56
460-	P		**Bertielicious**[23] 1853 5-10-9 62 JohnKington(3) (Jonathan Haynes) *nt fluent: hld up: struggling 6th: t.o whn p.u after 3 out* **200/1**	

4m 57.0s (-11.80) **Going Correction** -0.625s/f (Firm)

WFA 4 from 5yo+ 7lb 6 Ran SP% **110.4**

Speed ratings (Par 105): **98,97,97,87,75**

toteswingers 1&2 £1.60, 1&3 £2.30, 2&3 £4.00 CSF £4.34 TOTE £1.70: £1.60, £1.60; EX 5.10 Trifecta £16.60 Pool: £1315.61 - 59.21 winning units..

Owner The Jackdaws Strangers **Bred** John Hennessy **Trained** Cheltenham, Gloucs

FOCUS

An interesting novices' hurdle run at a sound pace in the testing conditions. Four in a line two out. The winner is on the upgrade.

2244 COLIN PARKER MEMORIAL INTERMEDIATE CHASE (LISTED RACE) (15 fncs 1 omitted) 2m 4f

2:40 (2:40) (Class 1) 4-Y-O+ **£14,860** (£5,565; £2,780; £1,387)

Form				RPR
103/	1		**Cloudy Too (IRE)**[218] 5014 7-11-6 147 JonathanEngland (Sue Smith) *chsd ldrs: hdwy to ld 5 out: rdn and styd on strly to draw clr fr 3 out* **4/1**[2]	154+
522/	2	8	**Tap Night (USA)**[197] 5401 6-11-2 152 APMcCoy (Lucinda Russell) *hld up in tch: pushed along 10th: hdwy bef 4 out: rdn next: chsd (clr) wnr run-in: no imp* **11/8**[1]	141+
411/	3	3 3/4	**Grey Gold (IRE)**[190] 5578 8-11-6 137 JamieMoore (Richard Lee) *hld up in tch: hdwy to chse wnr bef 4 out: rdn and edgd rt after 2 out: sn one pce: lost 2nd run-in: improve* **9/2**[3]	143
115/	4	21	**Violin Davis (FR)**[199] 5359 7-10-9 133 (t) NickScholfield (Harry Fry) *chsd ldr to 10th: rdn after next: wknd bef 4 out: t.o* **11/1**	109
F/1-	5	13	**Hazy Tom (IRE)**[31] 1730 7-11-6 142 JasonMaguire (Charlie Longsdon) *led to 5 out: sn drvn: lost pl bef next: sn struggling: t.o* **9/2**[3]	107

5m 5.6s (-21.80) **Going Correction** -1.075s/f (Hard) 5 Ran SP% **106.8**

Speed ratings (Par 111): **100,96,95,86,81**

CSF £9.77 TOTE £5.60: £2.50, £1.30; EX 12.10 Trifecta £31.20 Pool: £1885.05 - 45.28 winning units..

Owner Formulated Polymer Products Ltd **Bred** E J O'Sullivan **Trained** High Eldwick, W Yorks

FOCUS

A high-class renewal of what is now a Listed race, which has thrown up some smart chasers over the years. The form is rated around the first two.

2245 GEOFFREY MCLEAN IS SIXTY H'CAP HURDLE (10 hdls) 2m 3f 110y

3:10 (3:10) (Class 4) (0-110,110) 4-Y-O+ **£3,249** (£954; £477; £238)

Form				RPR
06/-	1		**Beauboreen (IRE)**[220] 4989 6-11-12 **110** SeanQuinlan (Jennie Candlish) *hld up: smooth hdwy 3 out: chsd ldr bef next: sn rdn: 5 l down last: styd on wl to ld nr fin* **3/1**[2]	115
450/	2	nk	**Funky Munky**[15] 5217 8-10-11 **98** (p) EwanWhillans(3) (Alistair Whillans) *w ldr: led bef 6th: rdn bef 2 out: 5 l clr last: idled run-in: hdd towards fin* **11/4**[1]	103
4P0/	3	22	**Nodda High Kid**[209] 5222 7-10-9 **98** CallumWhillans(5) (Donald Whillans) *rn in snatches: in tch: hit 5th: drvn and outpcd bef 2 out: plugged on fr last: no ch w first two* **13/2**	81
U03-	4	shd	**The Weatherman (IRE)**[31] 1729 6-11-7 **105** JasonMaguire (Donald McCain) *t.k.h: prom: outpcd 6th: rallied bef 2 out: sn no imp* **7/2**[3]	88
5/P-	5	1/2	**Markem (IRE)**[10] 2035 6-11-4 **102** (t) WilsonRenwick (Rose Dobbin) *prom: hdwy 3 out: rdn and outpcd after next: btn last* **9/1**	84
44-	6	62	**Mister D (IRE)**[15] 1980 7-10-8 **99** JonathonBewley(7) (George Bewley) *led to bef 6th: cl up tl rdn and wknd bef 2 out: t.o* **11/2**	19

5m 2.4s (-6.40) **Going Correction** -0.625s/f (Firm)

WFA 4 from 5yo+ 7lb 6 Ran SP% **112.6**

Speed ratings (Par 105): **87,86,78,78,77 53**

toteswingers 1&2 £2.40, 1&3 £4.00, 2&3 £7.20 CSF £12.00 CT £47.36 TOTE £3.50: £1.60, £2.00; EX 12.70 Trifecta £88.20 Pool: £2051.73 - 17.43 winning units..

Owner Mrs Hall & Exors of the Late Hall **Bred** Richard Hall **Trained** Basford Green, Staffs

■ Stewards' Enquiry : Sean Quinlan two-day ban: used whip above permitted level (Nov 17-18)

FOCUS

A depleted field and the complexion of the race changed dramatically late on. The winner ran to the level of last season's Bangor debut.

2246 CUMBERLAND H'CAP CHASE (17 fncs 2 omitted) 3m 2f

3:45 (3:45) (Class 3) (0-135,132) 4-Y-O+ **£16,245** (£4,770; £2,385; £1,192)

Form				RPR
342/	1		**Global Power (IRE)**[201] 5329 7-11-1 **121** LeightonAspell (Oliver Sherwood) *hld up: hdwy to dispute 2nd pl 5 out: hit and rdn 5 out: rallied to ld after next: drvn out run-in* **3/1**[1]	131+
F43/	2	1 3/4	**Mister Marker (IRE)**[197] 5404 9-11-12 **132** BrianHarding (Nicky Richards) *chsd ldr: effrt and rdn 4 out: chal briefly 2 out: kpt on fr last: nt pce of wnr* **8/1**	139
423-	3	6	**Kris Cross (IRE)**[28] 1787 6-10-10 **116** (t) PeterBuchanan (Lucinda Russell) *prom: hdwy and cl up whn hit 3 out: sn rdn: styd on fr last: nt pce of first two* **5/1**[2]	118
32U-	4	2	**Rhum (FR)**[30] 1748 8-10-7 **120** (vt) RyanHatch(7) (Nigel Twiston-Davies) *led: rdn 4 out: hdd jst after 2 out: outpcd run-in* **9/1**	119
/1B-	5	4 1/2	**Jaunty Journey**[160] 509 10-10-11 **117** SamTwiston-Davies (Nigel Twiston-Davies) *chsd ldrs: drvn and outpcd after 5 out: plugged on fr 2 out: no imp* **13/2**[3]	112
322-	6	3/4	**Bescot Springs (IRE)**[15] 1978 8-10-11 **117** (v) APMcCoy (Lucinda Russell) *prom: pushed along 10th: hdwy and cl up 4 out: wknd bef 2 out* **5/1**[2]	111
P/2-	7	14	**Lively Baron (IRE)**[23] 1852 8-11-7 **127** (tp) JasonMaguire (Donald McCain) *t.k.h: hld up in tch: outpcd 11th: struggling fr 4 out* **13/2**[3]	107
31P/	8	27	**Monsieur Cadou (FR)**[197] 5404 8-11-6 **126** PaddyBrennan (Tom George) *hld up: stdy hdwy whn mstke 12th: rdn and wknd after next* **12/1**	79

6m 50.4s (-16.80) **Going Correction** -1.075s/f (Hard) 8 Ran SP% **113.8**

Speed ratings (Par 107): **82,81,79,79,77 77,73,64**

toteswingers 1&2 £4.20, 1&3 £6.30, 2&3 £5.80 CSF £26.52 CT £115.03 TOTE £4.90: £1.70, £1.60, £2.10; EX 41.70 Trifecta £179.60 Pool: £1841.13 - 7.68 winning units..

Owner It Wasn't Us **Bred** R J Whitford **Trained** Upper Lambourn, Berks

FOCUS

An open-looking handicap chase that carried £35,000 guaranteed prize-money. Half a dozen were in with a shout four out and four were almost in a line two out. A chase best from the winner.

2247 RATTEN ROW "JUNIOR" STANDARD OPEN NATIONAL HUNT FLAT RACE 1m 6f

4:15 (4:15) (Class 6) 3-Y-O **£1,559** (£457; £228; £114)

Form				RPR
	1		**Red Lion Rock (IRE)** 3-10-12 0 APMcCoy (J J Lambe, Ire) *t.k.h: prom: smooth hdwy to ld over 1f out: shkn up and kpt on strly fnl f* **11/8**[1]	105+
	2	1 3/4	**Chesbey Beau** 3-10-12 0 DougieCostello (John Quinn) *prom: rdn and outpcd over 3f out: rallied over 2f out: drvn over 1f out: chsd wnr ins fnl f: kpt on* **85/40**[2]	98

3 4 ½ **Innis Shannon (IRE)** 3-9-12 0 JonathonBewley(7) 86
(George Bewley) *t.k.h: w ldr: led over 3f out: rdn and hdd over 1f out: outpcd ins fnl f* **7/2**3

4 40 **Teide Mistress (USA)** 3-10-2 0 EwanWhillans(3) 38
(Alistair Whillans) *hld up: struggling over 4f out: lost tch over 3f out: t.o* **18/1**

5 42 **Ski Guide** 3-10-5 0 GrahamWatters(7)
(Lucinda Russell) *led at stdy pce: rdn and hdd over 3f out: wknd qckly over 2f out: t.o* **12/1**

3m 37.4s (217.40) 5 Ran SP% **109.3**
CSF £4.48 TOTE £2.20: £1.30, £1.90; EX 5.40 Trifecta £11.50 Pool: £1263.88 - 82.26 winning units..
Owner Patrick Joseph McCann **Bred** Bakewell Bloodstock **Trained** Kilmore, Co Armagh

FOCUS
Five unraced three-year-olds lined up for this bumper and the first three finished a long way clear. What the form is worth is suspect but the winner was by far the best in the line-up.
T/Jkpt: £5,517.40 to a £1 stake. Pool: £27198.89 - 3.50 winning tickets T/Plt: £61.60 to a £1 stake. Pool: £70991.40 - 840.81 winning tickets T/Qpdt: £5.70 to a £1 stake. Pool: £6854.46 - 878.90 winning tickets RY

1913 HUNTINGDON (R-H)

Sunday, November 3

OFFICIAL GOING: Good to soft (soft in places; chs 5.9, hdl 6.5)
Wind: strong, across Weather: dry, windy

2248 ERS MEDICAL JUVENILE HURDLE (8 hdls) 2m 110y
12:45 (12:45) (Class 4) 3-Y-O **£4,548** (£1,335; £667; £333)

Form RPR

132- **1** **Town Mouse**14 [1985] 3-11-2 127 TrevorWhelan(3) 111
(Neil King) *taken down early: t.k.h: chsd ldr tl 2nd: chsd ldrs after: rdn and effrt to ld 2 out: wandering between last 2: a finding enough whn pressed fnl 50yds: rdn out* **5/4**1

- **2** ½ **Brave Helios**79 3-10-9 0 GavinSheehan(3) 104
(Jonathan Portman) *t.k.h: hld up in tch in midfield: effrt in cl 4th after 3 out: styd on to chse wnr flat: pressing wnr fnl 50yds: a hld* **28/1**

3 2 ¾ **Andi'Amu (FR)**148 3-10-12 0 (t) NoelFehily 101
(Warren Greatrex) *t.k.h: led: hdd bef 2 out: rdn and no real rspnse between last 2: styd on same pce flat* **7/2**2

3- **4** ½ **Keychain (IRE)**23 [1855] 3-10-12 106 BrendanPowell 101
(Brendan Powell) *chsd ldr 2nd tl rdn to ld bef 2 out: hdd 2 out and sn drvn: styd on same pce fr between last 2* **5/1**3

5- **5** 42 **Eton Rambler (USA)**18 [1920] 3-10-12 0 (p) AndrewTinkler 63
(George Baker) *mstkes: hld up in tch in last pair: rdn and effrt after 5th: struggling whn hit 3 out: sn dropped out: t.o* **7/2**2

P5P- **6** 46 **Double Jeopardy**36 [1684] 3-10-9 0 (p) JackQuinlan(3) 21
(Dr Jon Scargill) *hld up in tch in rr: rdn and btn sn after 3 out: lost tch bef next: t.o* **100/1**

4m 2.8s (7.90) **Going Correction** +0.375s/f (Yiel) 6 Ran SP% **110.0**
Speed ratings (Par 104): **96,95,94,94,74 52**
toteswingers 1&2 £9.00, 1&3 £1.10, 2&3 £32.80 CSF £29.50 TOTE £2.20: £1.10, £8.40; EX 29.30 Trifecta £242.60 Pool: £1223.28 - 3.78 winning units..
Owner Brian Bell & John Smith **Bred** Bishop Wilton Stud **Trained** Newmarket, Suffolk

FOCUS
Jockeys reported the ground to be riding beautifully, and just on the soft side. Ordinary juvenile hurdle form, the winner and fourth pretty much to their marks.

2249 32RED NOVICES' CHASE (THE SUNDAY £5K BONUS RACE) (16 fncs) 2m 4f 110y
1:15 (1:15) (Class 4) 4-Y-0+ **£5,198** (£1,526; £763; £381)

Form RPR

1/U- **1** **Le Reve (IRE)**9 [2063] 5-11-2 0 AidanColeman 129
(Lucy Wadham) *in tch in last pair: reminder and outpcd 13th: 12 l 4th and looked wl hld 2 out: lft 3 l 2nd last: styd on to chal idling ldr flat: led towards fin* **10/1**3

522- **2** nk **Hi Note**29 [1766] 5-10-9 0 MarcGoldstein 121
(Sheena West) *chsd ldng pair: rdn and outpcd after 13th: wnt 2nd but no threat to wnr 2 out: 12 l down whn lft in 3 l ld last: idling u.p and pressed flat: hdd towards fin* **16/1**

320- **3** 16 **Asian Prince (IRE)**40 [844] 4-10-7 98 (bt) WillKennedy 105
(Alastair Lidderdale) *j.w: led: hdd 3 out: btn on long run to next: lost 2nd 2 out: wl btn whn lft 5 l 3rd last: wknd flat* **100/1**

P/2- **4** 21 **Superior Quality (IRE)**23 [1851] 8-11-2 136 (t) NoelFehily 95
(Charlie Longsdon) *in tch in rr: effrt and hdwy 11th: struggling 13th: dropped to last and pckd 3 out: lost tch bef next: lft poor 4th last: t.o* **11/4**2

233/ **U** **Smad Place (FR)**211 [5175] 6-11-2 0 RobertThornton 147+
(Alan King) *chsd ldr tl j. into ld 3 out: drew clr bef next: 12 l ld and in command whn blnd and uns rdr last* **1/2**1

5m 3.6s (-1.70) **Going Correction** +0.15s/f (Yiel)
WFA 4 from 5yo+ 8lb 5 Ran SP% **109.3**
Speed ratings (Par 105): **109,108,102,94,**
CSF £97.24 TOTE £9.30: £3.10, £3.80; EX 79.50 Trifecta £68.50 Pool: £693.20 - 7.58 winning units..
Owner P H Betts **Bred** J D Flood **Trained** Newmarket, Suffolk

FOCUS
With Superior Quality running poorly, red-hot favourite and high-class hurdler Smad Place looked to be cruising to victory on this first start over fences, but there was high drama at the last. The first two and the faller did 10lb+ figures over hurdles but the third was plenty close enough.

2250 32RED.COM CLAIMING HURDLE (8 hdls) 2m 110y
1:45 (1:48) (Class 5) 4-Y-0+ **£2,274** (£667; £333; £166)

Form RPR

110- **1** **Belle De Fontenay (FR)**16 [1960] 8-10-0 120 (p) TrevorWhelan(3) 109+
(George Baker) *j.lft: led tl 3rd: chsd ldr tl led again and hit next: clr and travelling strly 3 out: j. bdly lft next: idling u.p between last 2: drvn and pressed flat: fnd enough and holding rival towards fin* **6/5**1

3P5- **2** ½ **Not Til Monday (IRE)**19 [1913] 7-10-10 113 AidanColeman 114
(J R Jenkins) *hld up in tch in rr: hdwy after 5th: rdn to chse clr wnr bef 2 out: clsd on idling wnr between last 2: upsides flat: no ex and hld towards fin* **15/8**2

0/0- **3** 11 **Bin End**10 [2045] 7-10-10 105 (p) FelixDeGiles 104
(Barry Brennan) *t.k.h: chsd ldrs: rdn to chse wnr after 5th tl bef 2 out: wknd between last 2* **20/1**

204/ **4** 19 **A Little Bit Dusty**8 [1783] 5-11-2 0 (p) AndrewThornton 93
(Conor Dore) *mstkes: a in rr: rdn after 5th: sn lost tch: plugged on past btn horses between last 2: n.d* **33/1**

005- **5** 2 ¼ **Vexillum (IRE)**19 [1429] 4-10-1 104 (t) CiaranMckee(7) 83
(Simon Hodgson) *t.k.h: chsd ldr tl led 3rd tl next: chsd ldr tl after 5th: wknd qckly u.p bef 2 out* **16/1**

6 11 **Johnnys Legacy (IRE)**52 [2150] 6-10-12 108 (p) DaveCrosse 77
(Conor Dore) *hld up in tch in midfield: rdn and struggling after 5th: wknd rapidly next: t.o* **66/1**

P- **P** **Seattle Drive (IRE)**15 [1979] 5-10-10 110 (t) TomScudamore
(David Pipe) *t.k.h: hld up in tch in midfield: rdn and btn 3 out: fdd rapidly and wl btn whn p.u next* **6/1**3

3m 59.35s (4.45) **Going Correction** +0.375s/f (Yiel) 7 Ran SP% **109.6**
Speed ratings (Par 103): **104,103,98,89,88 83,**
toteswingers 1&2 £1.02, 1&3 £5.90, 2&3 £14.70 CSF £3.40 TOTE £2.20: £1.30, £2.30; EX 4.30 Trifecta £14.70 Pool: £1761.63 - 89.66 winning units..
Owner George Baker & Partners **Bred** E A R L Elevage Des Loges **Trained** Manton, Wilts

FOCUS
The two at the head of the market dominated this ordinary claiming hurdle. The winner is rated 10lb off his best.

2251 MACER GIFFORD H'CAP CHASE (11 fncs 1 omitted) 2m 110y
2:20 (2:21) (Class 4) (0-105,103) 4-Y-0+ **£6,498** (£1,908; £954; £477)

Form RPR

3/4- **1** **Gandalfe (FR)**175 [245] 8-11-12 103 (b) AndrewThornton 114+
(David Arbuthnot) *chsd ldrs: wnt 2nd 5th tl led wl bef 2 out: sn pushed clr: wl in command bypassing last: comf* **8/1**

P3- **2** 10 **Un Anjou (FR)**13 [2007] 5-11-12 103 NoelFehily 105
(David Dennis) *hld up in tch towards rr: effrt and rdn after 3 out: no imp and btn whn mstke 2 out (actual last): plugged on to go 2nd towards fin: no ch w wnr* **12/1**

025- **3** 1 ¼ **Benny The Swinger (IRE)**13 [2004] 8-11-4 95 TomCannon 97
(Chris Gordon) *hld up in tch in midfield: hmpd and mstke 3rd: effrt to chse clr wnr bef 2 out (actual last): no imp and wl hld bypassing last: lost 2nd towards fin* **6/1**2

6/3- **4** ½ **Strawberry Hill (IRE)**17 [1939] 7-11-12 103 IanPopham 103
(Caroline Keevil) *hld up in midfield: hdwy to chse ldrs 4th: 3rd and drvn after 3 out: outpcd and btn next: plugged on same pce after* **13/2**3

53S- **5** 9 **Julie Prince (IRE)**10 [2039] 7-11-8 99 (t) BrendanPowell 94
(Brendan Powell) *led tl after 1st: led again 4th: mstke 8th: j.lft and mstke next: hdd wl bef 3 out: lost 2nd and btn bnd bef next: wknd bypassing last* **10/1**

233/ **6** 39 **Bobby Dove**224 [4945] 6-10-10 90 RobertDunne(3) 47
(Andrew Price) *hld up in tch towards rr: hdwy into midfield and j. slowly 6th: rdn and struggling whn mstke 3 out: wknd bef next: t.o* **7/1**

P23/ **P** **Zen Factor**235 [4744] 8-10-5 85 GavinSheehan(3)
(Jonathan Portman) *j. bdly lft thrght: led after 1st tl 4th: styd chsng ldrs tl wknd 3 out: t.o whn p.u next* **9/1**

/54- **F** **Topthorn**148 [674] 7-11-10 101 WayneHutchinson 86
(Martin Bosley) *hld up in tch in midfield: distracted, sltly hmpd and fell heavily 3rd* **20/1**

P63- **P** **Outback (IRE)**9 [2067] 4-10-2 90 (bt) TrevorWhelan(3)
(Neil King) *chsd ldrs but sn niggled along: j.lft 2nd and 3rd: dropped to last and drvn after 5th: losing tch whn p.u 3 out* **9/1**

5- **U** **Troufion (FR)**11 [2028] 4-11-3 102 (t) HarrySkelton
(Dan Skelton) *hld up in tch: j.lft and mstke 9th: rdn after next: hung lft and sn btn: bhd whn mstke: wnt lft on landing and uns rdr 2 out (actual last)* **7/2**1

4m 10.8s (0.60) **Going Correction** +0.15s/f (Yiel)
WFA 4 from 5yo+ 7lb 10 Ran SP% **115.0**
Speed ratings (Par 105): **104,99,98,98,94 75, , , ,**
toteswingers 1&2 £14.10, 1&3 £45.10, 2&3 £23.20 CSF £94.87 CT £617.33 TOTE £10.80: £3.10, £4.80, £2.70; EX 111.60 Trifecta £600.20 Part won. Pool: £800.27 - 0.01 winning units..
Owner A T A Wates **Bred** Jean-Marie & Mlle Nathalie Callier **Trained** Beare Green, Surrey

FOCUS
The final fence had to be bypassed after it was damaged. A modest handicap chase. The winner is rated in line with the best of last year's form, with the next three pretty much to their marks.

2252 MICHAEL QUINLAN MEMORIAL NOVICES' HURDLE (10 hdls) 2m 4f 110y
2:55 (2:59) (Class 4) 4-Y-0+ **£4,548** (£1,335; £667; £333)

Form RPR

0/3- **1** **Chase The Spud**19 [1919] 5-10-12 0 TimmyMurphy 118+
(Fergal O'Brien) *led and set stdy gallop: hdd after 7th: j.lft: lft in ld and hmpd next: rdn and drew clr bef 2 out: styd on: comf* **16/1**

35/ **2** 17 **Yabadabadoo**268 [4113] 5-10-12 0 AidanColeman 103
(Emma Lavelle) *t.k.h: hld up in tch in rr of main gp: clsd and rdn whn lft 3rd and hmpd 3 out: drvn and chsd wnr bnd bef next: btn whn mstke next: wknd but hld on to 2nd flat* **6/1**3

3 1 ½ **Paladin (IRE)**571 4-10-9 0 JackQuinlan(3) 102
(John Ferguson) *t.k.h: hld up in tch in midfield: mstke 6th: effrt after next: lft 2nd and wnt lft 3 out: drvn and btn 3rd whn j.lft 2 out: j.lft again last: wknd flat* **16/1**

/U0- **4** 70 **Over My Head**3 [2178] 5-10-5 0 GeraldQuinn(7) 39
(Claire Dyson) *mstke 1st: chsd ldr tl after 6th: j. slowly and losing pl next: sn wl bhd: t.o whn lft 4th last* **150/1**

/50- **P** **Guest Of Honour (FR)**29 [1771] 5-10-9 0 JoshuaMoore(3)
(Renee Robeson) *in tch in midfield: mstke 4th: rdn and mstke 6th: sn dropped out and t.o whn p.u 3 out* **50/1**

/21- **F** **Hannibal The Great (IRE)**29 [1764] 5-11-5 0 (t) NoelFehily
(Charlie Longsdon) *chsd ldrs tl led after 7th: travelling strly whn stmbld on landing and fell 3 out* **4/7**1

B **Sego Success (IRE)**252 5-10-12 0 WayneHutchinson
(Alan King) *t.k.h: hld up in tch in midfield: mstke 4th: clsd to trck ldng pair after 7th: cl 3rd whn b.d next* **7/2**2

2/5- **P** **Operatic Heights (IRE)**36 [1690] 4-10-9 0 MichaelByrne(3)
(Tim Vaughan) *chsd ldrs: rdn after 7th: struggling whn lft 4th and v bdly hmpd next: nt rcvr and p.u bef next* **40/1**

52- **F** **Full Throttle (IRE)**137 [768] 4-10-12 0 RichieMcLernon 103
(Jonjo O'Neill) *t.k.h: hld up in tch in rr of main goup: effrt and n.m.r on inner after 7th: lft 4th and hmpd next: btn next: no ch w wnr but ev ch of 2nd whn fell last* **8/1**

P0- P **Flamin June**[77] 1305 7-10-5 0....................(p) AdamWedge
(Kevin Morgan) *w.r.s and slowly away: a in rr: j. 2nd: rdn and lost tch after 5th: t.o whn p.u bef next* **100/1**

5m 7.0s (8.00) **Going Correction** +0.375s/f (Yiel)
WFA 4 from 5yo+ 8lb **10** Ran SP% **129.1**
Speed ratings (Par 105): **99,92,91,65, , , , ,**
toteswingers 1&2 £15.80, 1&3 £7.40, 2&3 £16.00 CSF £117.90 TOTE £19.10: £3.20, £2.60, £4.10; EX 223.20 Trifecta £1442.40 Part won. Pool: £1923.26 - 0.02 winning units..
Owner Mrs C Banks **Bred** Mrs C J Banks **Trained** Coln St. Dennis, Gloucs

FOCUS

More drama here, with red-hot favourite Hannibal The Great falling when in front at the third from home, and bringing down the chasing Sego Success, who would most likely have gone on to win had he been able to sidestep him. The winner looked fortunate and the second is rated in line with his bumper form.

2253 32RED CASINO H'CAP HURDLE (12 hdls) 3m 2f

3:30 (3:30) (Class 4) (0-105,105) 4-Y-0+ **£4,548** (£1,335; £667; £333)

Form RPR

/44- **1** **Lookout Mountain (IRE)**[2] 2202 5-11-5 **103**........(vt) MauriceLinehan(5) 118+
(Jonjo O'Neill) *hld up in tch in rr of main gp: clsd to chse ldrs and travelling strly after 8th: upsides ldr and drew clr after 3 out: led gng best bef last: readily asserted sn after last: v easily* **5/1**[2]

4/6- **2** *7* **Flemi Two Toes (IRE)**[19] 1917 7-11-6 **102**..................(p) JackQuinlan(3) 104
(Sarah Humphrey) *wl in tch in midfield: rdn and effrt to chse ldng pair bef 2 out: no ch w wnr but kpt on flat to go 2nd cl home* **20/1**

P/6- **3** *½* **Night Alliance (IRE)**[21] 1887 8-11-10 **103**..................(b) TomO'Brien 105
(Dr Richard Newland) *wl in tch in midfield: clsd to ld and gng wl 3 out: sn drew clr w wnr: rdn and hdd bef last: brushed aside by wnr sn after last: wknd fnl 100yds and lost 2nd cl home* **9/1**

45P- **4** *5* **Elegant Olive**[19] 1917 10-11-2 **95**.............................. HaddenFrost 93
(Roger Curtis) *in tch in rr: rdn along briefly after 7th: hdwy 3 out: chsd ldng trio and rdn bef 2 out: no imp and one pce last* **16/1**

505- **5** *13* **Xenophon**[9] 2062 5-9-9 **79**.............................. JoeCornwall(5) 64
(Michael Chapman) *in tch towards rr: rdn and hdwy into midfield after 7th: chsd ldrs and drvn 3 out: wknd 2 out: wl hld whn j.rt and mstke last* **66/1**

2/P- **6** *2* **Iconic Rose**[183] 122 6-10-13 **95**.............................. KielanWoods(3) 79
(Pam Sly) *chsd ldrs tl led 9th: hdd and mstke next: wknd bef 2 out* **16/1**

016- **7** *27* **Award Winner**[17] 1940 10-11-3 **96**..............................(v) BrendanPowell 55
(Brendan Powell) *pressed ldr fr after 2nd tl mstke 3 out: sn wknd: t.o last* **16/1**

35P/ **8** *22* **Musical Wedge**[200] 5351 9-11-5 **105**.............................. GeraldQuinn(7) 44
(Claire Dyson) *chsd ldrs on outer: rdn and struggling 9th: lost tch next: t.o* **50/1**

113- **P** **Go Amwell**[19] 1917 10-11-8 **101**..............................(v) AidanColeman
(J R Jenkins) *wl in tch in midfield: dropped to rr but stl in tch whn rdn and mstke 8th: wknd next: t.o whn p.u 3 out* **8/1**

F5F- **P** **Bobbisox (IRE)**[8] 2088 8-10-0 **79**.............................. RichieMcLernon
(Alex Hales) *in tch towards rr: rdn and struggling 9th: sn lost tch: t.o whn p.u 2 out* **28/1**

/00- **P** **Lombardy Boy (IRE)**[19] 1917 8-10-8 **90**.............................. TrevorWhelan(3)
(Michael Banks) *in tch towards rr: losing tch whn eased and p.u bef 8th* **20/1**

UP5- **P** **Almadan (IRE)**[17] 1940 5-10-7 **91**..............................(t) EdCookson(5)
(Kim Bailey) *chsd ldrs: mstke 9th: sn rdn and dropped out: t.o whn p.u 2 out* **7/1**[3]

F31- **P** **Dom Lukka (FR)**[19] 1917 5-11-4 **104**.............................. CharlieDeutsch(7)
(Charlie Longsdon) *led tl hdd and mstke 9th: rdn and wknd bef next: t.o whn p.u 2 out* **2/1**[1]

6m 28.45s (5.55) **Going Correction** +0.375s/f (Yiel) **13** Ran SP% **117.7**
Speed ratings (Par 105): **106,103,103,102,98 97,89,82, , , ,**
toteswingers 1&2 £19.00, 1&3 £6.80, 2&3 £18.10 CSF £102.90 CT £881.26 TOTE £7.60: £2.30, £4.70, £4.00; EX 72.90 Trifecta £724.20 Part won. Pool: £965.69 - 0.66 winning units..
Owner Mrs J Magnier, D Smith & M Tabor **Bred** Larry Mealiffe **Trained** Cheltenham, Gloucs

FOCUS

What had looked quite an open handicap was turned into a rout, the winner producing a big step up. A fair race of its type.

2254 CONNOLLY'S RED MILLS BUMPER CHALLENGE STANDARD OPEN NATIONAL HUNT FLAT RACE 2m 110y

4:00 (4:01) (Class 6) 4-6-Y-0 **£1,624** (£477; £238; £119)

Form RPR

1 **Urban Hymn (FR)**[218] 5-11-2 0.............................. BrianHughes 120+
(Malcolm Jefferson) *mde all: c readily clr over 2f out: pushed out: easily* **11/4**[2]

2- **2** *7* **Mr Cardle (IRE)**[185] 76 4-10-11 0.............................. ThomasGarner(5) 108
(Oliver Sherwood) *in tch towards rr: rdn and effrt 4f out: chsd ldng pair over 1f out: styd on to go 2nd fnl 100yds: no threat to wnr* **8/1**

3 *2* **In The Rough (IRE)** 4-11-2 0.............................. RichieMcLernon 106
(Jonjo O'Neill) *hld up in tch in rr: hdwy 5f out: rdn to chse ldng pair over 2f out: chsd clr wnr wl over 1f out: no imp and lost 2nd fnl 100yds* **16/1**

2/ **4** *20* **Presenting The Way**[194] 5475 6-11-2 0.............................. NoelFehily 86
(Harry Fry) *chsd wnr tl 4f out: sn rdn: 4th and wknd over 2f out* **9/2**[3]

5 *½* **Flashyfrank** 4-10-9 0.............................. MissLAllan(7) 86
(David Elsworth) *t.k.h: hld up wl in tch towards rr: rdn and outpcd 4f out: 8th and wl hld over 2f out: plugged on fnl f: pressing for modest 4th cl home* **33/1**

1- **6** *4½* **Father Edward (IRE)**[158] 544 4-11-9 0.............................. DenisO'Regan 88
(John Ferguson) *hld up wl in tch in midfield: hdwy to chse wnr 4f out: btn jst over 2f out and nt pushed: 4th and wl btn 1f out* **5/2**[1]

6/ **7** *10* **Yes I Will**[268] 4113 4-10-13 0..............................(t) KielanWoods(3) 71
(Charlie Longsdon) *chsd ldrs: rdn over 4f out: outpcd and btn 3f out: sn wknd: t.o* **14/1**

/4- **8** *¾* **Arakelton**[64] 1472 5-10-9 0.............................. ColinBolger 63
(Mark H Tompkins) *in tch towards rr: rdn and struggling 5f out: wknd 4f out: t.o* **66/1**

9 *1¾* **Untilla Legend** 5-11-2 0.............................. WillKennedy 69
(Alex Hales) *chsd ldrs: rdn over 4f out: sn struggling and wknd 4f out: wl bhd whn swtchd rt 1f out: t.o* **40/1**

10 *3½* **Tashkaldou (FR)** 4-11-2 0.............................. HarrySkelton 65
(Dan Skelton) *t.k.h: hld up in tch towards rr: rdn 3f out: sn btn: wknd over 2f out: t.o* **15/2**

11 *62* **Top Show** 4-11-2 0.............................. PaulMoloney 3
(Dean Ivory) *chsd ldrs tl lost pl qckly 6f out: t.o fnl 4f* **33/1**

3m 55.2s (6.10) **Going Correction** +0.375s/f (Yiel) **11** Ran SP% **118.7**
Speed ratings: **100,96,95,86,86 84,79,78,78,76 47**
toteswingers 1&2 £6.50, 1&3 £9.80, 2&3 £15.50 CSF £24.80 TOTE £5.70: £1.90, £1.30, £5.40; EX 32.40 Trifecta £355.10 Pool: £2242.66 - 4.73 winning units..
Owner Mr & Mrs G Calder **Bred** Jean-Jacques Augier **Trained** Norton, N Yorks

FOCUS

Probably quite a decent bumper and it's likely we saw a smart performer in Urban Hymn. There's a case for rating the form higher.
T/Plt: £8,731.60 to a £1 stake. Pool: £54423.02 - 4.55 winning tickets T/Qpdt: £201.20 to a £1 stake. Pool: £8241.10 -0 30.30 winning tickets SP

2255 - (Foreign Racing) - See Raceform Interactive

1992 CORK (R-H)

Sunday, November 3

OFFICIAL GOING: Soft (yielding in places) changing to soft (soft to heavy in places) after race 3 (2:15)

2256a PADDY POWER COLLECT WINNING BETS IN ANY SHOP EUROPEAN BREEDERS FUND NOVICE HURDLE (GRADE 3) (13 hdls) 3m

1:40 (1:41) 4-Y-0+ **£18,495** (£5,406; £2,560; £853)

RPR

1 **Lots Of Memories (IRE)**[21] 1893 6-11-0.............................. ShaneButler 144+
(P G Fahey, Ire) *trckd ldr in 2nd: t.k.h and led w a circ to r: clr 5 out: wandered appr 2 out and last: styd on wl: easily* **7/4**[2]

2 *10* **Horendus Hulabaloo (IRE)**[7] 2119 4-10-9....................[1] DavyRussell 127+
(M F Morris, Ire) *chsd ldrs in 3rd: dropped to 4th 5 out: no imp on ldr whn lft 3rd 3 out: kpt on into 2nd at next: no threat to wnr* **16/1**

3 *4* **Courtncatcher (IRE)**[6] 2144 6-11-6 128.................. AndrewJMcNamara 134
(Patrick J Duffy, Ire) *hld up in rr tl prog 2 out: kpt on wl into 3rd appr last: nvr nrr* **7/1**[3]

4 *2¼* **Silver Tassie (IRE)**[21] 1893 5-11-3 126.............................. BarryGeraghty 129
(Noel Meade, Ire) *w.w in 5th: pushed along after 4 out: no imp whn lft 4th 3 out: sn one pce* **8/1**

5 *19* **Old Kilcash (IRE)**[16] 1962 5-11-0 120.............................. DannyMullins 107
(John Joseph Hanlon, Ire) *led tl hdd w a circ to r: chsd clr ldr in 2nd tl wknd appr 2 out* **8/1**

F **Indevan**[21] 1893 5-11-6 133.............................. RWalsh
(W P Mullins, Ire) *chsd ldrs in 4th tl prog into 3rd bef 5 out where nt fluent: sn pushed along: kpt on same pce in 3rd whn fell 3 out* **13/8**[1]

6m 20.8s (-11.30)
WFA 4 from 5yo+ 9lb **6** Ran SP% **115.1**
CSF £25.75 TOTE £3.90: £1.60, £4.40; DF 25.30 Trifecta £184.40.
Owner Mrs Siobhain Fahey & John A Breen **Bred** Mary Lett **Trained** Nurney, Co. Kildare

FOCUS

When Indevan beat two of these recently at Limerick, the gallop rendered the race a bit of a farce. They were never going hard here either but it was a truer-run race; however, Indevan running so flat takes away from the form. The first two still ran personal bests.

2258a PADDY POWER WE PAY UP TO 1MILLION EURO ON WINNING BETS EUROPEAN BREEDERS FUND NOVICE CHASE (GRADE 3) (14 fncs) 2m 4f

2:50 (2:51) 5-Y-0+ **£18,495** (£5,406; £2,560; £853)

RPR

1 **Sizing Rio (IRE)**[171] 348 5-10-13.............................. AELynch 148+
(Henry De Bromhead, Ire) *mde all: j.w: stl travelled wl appr 2 out and sn extended advantage: easily* **13/8**[1]

2 *10* **Clar Na Mionn (IRE)**[7] 2116 6-11-0.............................. APHeskin 135
(V T O'Brien, Ire) *sn chsd ldr in 2nd: pushed along after 3 out: no imp on wnr next: kpt on one pce* **6/1**[3]

3 *2½* **Rogue Angel (IRE)**[18] 1933 5-10-13..............................(t) DavyRussell 132
(M F Morris, Ire) *chsd ldrs in 4th: pushed along after 3 out and sn 3rd: no imp bef next: kpt on one pce* **11/4**[2]

4 *12* **Darroun (IRE)**[14] 1996 5-10-13..............................(b[1]) RWalsh 125
(W P Mullins, Ire) *hld up in rr and adrift of rivals after bad blunder 3rd: reminders w a circ to r: no imp 3 out: kpt on one pce whn mstke last* **8/1**

5 *1* **Golden Wonder (IRE)**[14] 1996 7-11-0 134.............................. BryanCooper 124
(D T Hughes, Ire) *sn chsd ldr in 3rd: pushed along after 3 out and sn no imp in 4th: wknd* **11/4**[2]

5m 13.9s (313.90) **5** Ran SP% **116.8**
CSF £11.94 TOTE £2.60: £1.40, £2.80; DF 16.80 Trifecta £44.60.
Owner Ann & Alan Potts Partnership **Bred** Jimmy Finn **Trained** Knockeen, Co Waterford

FOCUS

This race cut up badly. While the field was still strong, what a race it would have been if they all partook. A personal best from the winner, with the second helping the standard.

2259 - 2261a (Foreign Racing) - See Raceform Interactive

2238 AUTEUIL (L-H)

Sunday, November 3

OFFICIAL GOING: Turf: heavy

2262a RMC PRIX CAMBACERES (GRANDE COURSE DE HAIES DES 3 ANS) (HURDLE) (GRADE 1) (3YO) (TURF) 2m 2f

1:00 (12:00) 3-Y-0

£98,780 (£48,292; £28,536; £19,756; £10,975; £7,682)

RPR

1 **Hippomene (FR)**[21] 1899 3-10-6 0....................(p) ChristopheSoumillon 132
(J-P Gallorini, France) *towards rr: tk clsr order 6 out: sn trcking ldrs: 2nd and gng wl 2 out: led last: rdn clr: comf* **2/1**[1]

2 *3* **Alabama Le Dun (FR)**[21] 1899 3-10-6 0.............................. JonathanNattiez 129
(J-P Gallorini, France) *towards rr: prog into midfield and wl in tch 3 out: led on landing 2 out: hdd last: kpt on u.p: nt pce of wnr* **16/1**

3 *1½* **Roll On Has (FR)**[25] 3-10-1 0.............................. VincentCheminaud 123
(J-P Gallorini, France) *midfield: rdn to chse ldrs 2 out: 3rd and ev ch between last 2: one pce u.p run-in* **4/1**[3]

4 *nk* **Hilton Du Berlais (FR)**[21] 1899 3-10-1 0.............................. FrancoisPamart 122
(A Chaille-Chaille, France) *towards rr: stdy hdwy after 3 out: 5th and styng on between last 2 flights: kpt on wout qckning u.p run-in* **6/1**

5 *10* **Street Name (FR)**[21] 1899 3-10-6 0.............................. CyrilleGombeau 117
(G Cherel, France) *hld up in rr: hdwy 6 out: trcking ldrs on inner 3 out: rdn and nt qckn after 2 out: wknd u.p run-in* **11/4**[2]

6 *1* **Attila De Sivola (FR)**[21] 3-10-6 0.............................. GaelBarbedette 116
(Y-M Porzier, France) *a.p: led briefly appr 2 out: hdd on landing: rdn and edgd lft: sn outpcd by ldrs: wknd u.p run-in* **16/1**

7 4 **Le Rocher (FR)**[31] 1741 3-10-6 0 ..... JamesReveley 112
(Nick Williams) *led: hdd appr 2 out: sn outpcd and grad lft bhd* **10/1**

8 1 **Red Name (FR)**[21] 1899 3-10-6 0 ..... OlivierJouin 111
(P Peltier, France) *trckd ldr: rdn and outpcd on fnl bnd bef 2 out: sn wknd* **16/1**

P **Positano Sud (FR)**[21] 1899 3-10-6 0 ..... RegisSchmidlin
(M Rolland, France) *midfield: dropped toward rr bef 1/2-way: lost tch appr 3 out: p.u bef 2 out* **33/1**

4m 26.8s (266.80) **9** Ran SP% **124.0**
PARI-MUTUEL (all including 1 euro stake): WIN 2.90; PLACE 1.40, 2.40, 1.50; DF 16.70; SF 26.70.
Owner Ecurie Zingaro **Bred** R Monnier **Trained** France

2263a PARIS-TURF PRIX MAURICE GILLOIS (GRAND STEEPLE-CHASE DES 4 ANS) (CHASE) (GRADE 1) (4YO) (TURF) 2m 6f

1:30 (12:00) 4-Y-O

£128,048 (£62,601; £36,991; £25,609; £14,227; £9,959)

RPR

1 **Milord Thomas (FR)**[31] 1742 4-10-8 0 ..... JacquesRicou 127
(D Bressou, France) *a.p in main gp on inner: rdn and chsd clr ldr fr 2 out: lft in front rnk last: drvn out* **10/1**[3]

2 2 **Polidam (FR)**[21] 1900 4-10-8 0 ..... MathieuCarroux 125
(A Chaille-Chaille, France) *midfield: tk clsr order 12th: chsd clr ldr appr 2 out: lft in front rnk last: kpt on at same pce u.p run-in* **16/1**

3 3/4 **Square Beaujon (FR)**[21] 1900 4-10-8 0 ..... (p) AnthonyLecordier 124
(D Windrif, France) *midfield: prog to be prom in main gp bhd clr ldr fr 4 out: chsd clr ldr fr 2 out: lft in front rnk last: one pce u.p run-in* **11/1**

4 2 1/2 **Monsamou (IRE)**[7] 4-10-8 0 ..... (p) JoAudon 122
(P Chevillard, France) *hld up towards rr: hdwy 5 out: styd on u.p fr 2 out: nrest at fin* **33/1**

5 7 **Chardonnay (FR)**[21] 1900 4-10-8 0 ..... (p) AlainDeChitray 115
(G Cherel, France) *towards rr: sme late prog: nvr in contention* **25/1**

6 8 **Vieux Morvan (FR)**[21] 1900 4-10-8 0 ..... (p) CyrilleGombeau 107
(G Cherel, France) *a.p: chsd ldr between last 2 fences: sn rdn and wknd run-in* **6/1**[2]

7 6 **La Garde Royale (FR)**[46] 1607 4-10-3 0 ..... MorganRegairaz 96
(J Ortet, France) *led: sn clr: mstke 5 out: hdd on fnl bnd bef 2 out: plugged on but sn wl btn* **16/1**

8 20 **Plougala (FR)**[10] 4-10-8 0 ..... RaymondO'Brien 81
(Y-M Porzier, France) *prom in main gp: lost pl bef 3 out: bhd and btn 2 out: t.o but completed* **25/1**

F **Storm Of Saintly (FR)**[21] 1900 4-10-8 0 ..... VincentCheminaud
(G Macaire, France) *a.p in main gp: led on fnl bnd appr 2 out: 3 l clr and travelling wl enough whn fell last* **4/6**[1]

P **Saint Firmin (FR)**[21] 1900 4-10-8 0 ..... KevinNabet
(Robert Collet, France) *in rr detached fr rest of field fr s: rdn and no imp 4 out: bhd whn p.u bef 2 out* **33/1**

P **Votez Pour Moi (FR)**[10] 4-10-8 0 ..... JonathanPlouganou
(G Macaire, France) *a.p in main gp bhd clr ldr: wknd bef 3 out: bhd whn p.u bef 2 out* **20/1**

P **Peti Kap (FR)**[21] 1900 4-10-8 0 ..... AngeloGasnier
(L Viel, France) *a in fnl 3rd: bad mstke 5 out and dropped to last: p.u bef 3 out* **32/1**

5m 50.27s (6.27) **12** Ran SP% **124.8**
PARI-MUTUEL (all including 1 euro stake): WIN 6.60 (coupled with La Garde Royale); PLACE 3.00, 5.40, 3.40; DF 70.50; SF 137.90.
Owner Mme Magalen Bryant **Bred** S Boucheron **Trained** France

2264a PRIX LA HAYE JOUSSELIN (CHASE) (GRADE 1) (5YO+) (TURF) 3m 3f 110y

2:08 (12:00) 5-Y-O+

£201,219 (£98,373; £58,130; £40,243; £22,357; £15,650)

RPR

1 **Shannon Rock (FR)**[21] 1902 7-10-8 0 ..... (p) DavidCottin 143
(J-P Gallorini, France) *hld up in midfield: in tch fr 9th: hdwy fr 5 out: gng best in cl 2nd appr last: rdn to chal on landing and sn led: styd on wl* **5/2**[1]

2 3/4 **Saint Palois (FR)**[21] 1902 5-10-3 0 ..... JamesReveley 137
(J Ortet, France) *trckd ldrs: w ldrs 12th to 15th then trckd ldr again tl led 4 out: rdn after 2 out: untidy last and strly pressed on landing: sn hdd: styd on wl but hld* **5/1**[2]

3 3 **Quart Monde (FR)**[21] 1902 9-10-8 0 ..... GaetanOlivier 139
(F Nicolle, France) *sn w ldrs: hdd after 14th and chsd ldrs: rdn 2 out: cl 3rd and ev ch jumping last: styd on wl wout matching front pair flat* **7/1**

4 dist **River Choice (FR)**[15] 1984 10-10-8 0 ..... (b) GeoffreyRe
(Yannick Fouin, France) *midfield in tch: prom 10th: led after 15th: hdd whn bad mstke 4 out: outpcd by ldng trio fr bef 2 out: plugged on for mod 4th* **20/1**

5 20 **Pibrac (FR)**[25] 9-10-8 0 ..... RegisSchmidlin
(F-M Cottin, France) *hld up in midfield: clsd 15th: rdn in 4th 2 out: sn outpcd by ldng trio and dropped to 5th: t.o but plugged on to complete* **12/1**

6 20 **Join Together (IRE)**[22] 1868 8-10-8 0 ..... (p) RyanMahon
(Paul Nicholls) *midfield: mstke 4th: towards rr and reminders 11th: hdwy and in tch 14th: lost pl again after 17th: rdn in rr and struggling whn slow 5 out: tailed rt off but completed* **6/1**[3]

P **Remember Rose (IRE)**[21] 1902 10-10-8 0 ..... (p) BertrandBourez
(Y-M Porzier, France) *w ldrs tl 12th: lost pl and in rr whn slow 14th: bhd whn p.u bef 16th* **33/1**

U **Reglis Brunel (FR)**[21] 1902 8-10-8 0 ..... ThierryMajorcryk
(E Lecoiffier, France) *hld up towards rr: in tch fr 10th: cl up and stl ev ch whn slt mstke and uns rdr 4 out* **12/1**

P **Halley (FR)**[21] 1902 6-10-8 0 ..... (b[1]) AlainCawley
(Tom George) *w ldrs to 5th: lost pl and reminders after 6th: towards rr whn mstke 11th: sn drvn and no imp: bhd whn p.u* **20/1**

U **Parigny (FR)**[21] 1902 7-10-8 0 ..... (p) MlleNathalieDesoutter
(F-M Cottin, France) *midfield: reminders after 4th: hdwy to trck ldrs after next: cl up and disputing 4th whn blnd and uns rdr 9th* **25/1**

P **Ozamo (FR)**[21] 1902 6-10-8 0 ..... JonathanPlouganou
(P Peltier, France) *hld up in rr: slow 9th: rdn and reminders 12th: bhd and p.u bef 14th* **9/1**

P **Le Bel Anjou (FR)**[10] 5-10-3 0 ..... KevinNabet
(F-M Cottin, France) *mstkes: hld up and a towards rr: stmbld on landing and almost uns rdr 2nd: wl bhd whn p.u bef 16th* **10/1**

P **Kotkieglote (FR)**[33] 6-10-3 0 ..... (p) VincentCheminaud
(J-P Gallorini, France) *w ldrs to 4th: sn midfield: dropped to rr 15th: sn bhd and p.u bef next* **10/1**

7m 19.86s (439.86) **13** Ran SP% **131.9**
PARI-MUTUEL (all including 1 euro stake): WIN 3.40; PLACE 1.60, 1.90, 2.30; DF 6.30; SF 12.00.
Owner Mme Henri Devin **Bred** Mme H Devin **Trained** France

1985 KEMPTON (R-H)

Monday, November 4

OFFICIAL GOING: Good to soft (chs 6.4, hdl 6.3)
Wind: Fresh, half against Weather: Fine

2265 WEATHERBYS BANK NOVICES' HURDLE (8 hdls) 2m

1:05 (1:05) (Class 4) 4-Y-O+ **£3,898** (£1,144; £572; £286)

Form RPR

1 **Volnay De Thaix (FR)**[139] 4-11-5 0 ..... BarryGeraghty 137+
(Nicky Henderson) *trckd ldr: led after 3 out: drew clr fr 2 out: easily* **15/8**[1]

10/ 2 11 **Devon Drum**[25] 5408 5-10-12 0 ..... LiamTreadwell 109+
(Paul Webber) *t.k.h: trckd ldrs: gng strly after 3 out: chsd wnr 2 out: pushed along and kpt on but no ch* **11/4**[2]

4/0- 3 1 3/4 **Cape Breton**[176] 235 7-10-7 0 ..... NicodeBoinville[(5)] 107
(Patrick Chamings) *chsd ldrs: shkn up bef 2 out: styd on bef last and rdn to take 3rd flat* **50/1**

4 2 3/4 **Bugler's Dream (USA)**[886] 5-10-12 0 ..... DenisO'Regan 105
(John Ferguson) *chsd ldng pair: shkn up and on terms bef 2 out: one pce after* **12/1**

/04- 5 shd **Ballygrooby Bertie (IRE)**[11] 2040 5-10-12 0 ..... (t) PaddyBrennan 105
(Fergal O'Brien) *hld up in midfield: prog to trck ldrs 3 out: shkn up 2 out: wnt 3rd briefly last: one pce flat* **25/1**

144- 6 4 1/2 **Chalk It Down (IRE)**[18] 1935 4-10-12 0 ..... APMcCoy 104
(Warren Greatrex) *awkward to post and kpt away fr others at s: t.k.h: led: clr whn j. slowly 5th: hdd after 3 out: pushed along and wknd 2 out* **8/1**

7 3/4 **Mr Fickle (IRE)**[27] 4-10-9 0 ..... JoshuaMoore[(3)] 99
(Gary Moore) *racd on outer towards rr: prog 3 out: gng bttr than several bef 2 out but outpcd: one pce after: nt wout promise* **33/1**

- 8 1 3/4 **Norfolk Sky**[41] 4-9-9 0 ..... NathanAdams[(10)] 92
(Laura Mongan) *chsd ldrs: j.rt and mstke 5th: rdn after 3 out: steadily fdd* **20/1**

330- 9 3 **Grand March**[18] 1935 4-10-12 0 ..... JasonMaguire 94
(Kim Bailey) *hld up in midfield: reminders after 3 out whn in tch: steadily fdd* **50/1**

2/1- 10 1 1/4 **Seedling**[30] 1770 4-10-12 0 ..... SamTwiston-Davies 94
(Charles Egerton) *hld up wl in rr: prog fr 5th: blnd next: sn drvn: no hdwy 2 out* **9/2**[3]

06- 11 4 1/2 **No Routine (IRE)**[4] 2178 4-10-12 0 ..... DougieCostello 89
(Jonjo O'Neill) *chsd ldrs to 4th: lost pl bef next: wl in rr after 3 out* **66/1**

12 2 1/2 **Mariet**[27] 4-10-2 0 ..... WayneKavanagh[(3)] 79
(Suzy Smith) *a wl in rr: no ch after 3 out* **66/1**

0U6/ 13 1 **Dan's Wee Man**[190] 4 4-10-7 0 ..... JamesBanks[(5)] 85
(Andy Turnell) *j.rt 1st: a in rr: mstkes 5th and 3 out: wl bhd after* **66/1**

00- 14 13 **Qasser (IRE)**[9] 2083 4-10-12 0 ..... JamesDavies 72
(Harry Whittington) *j. slowly 2nd: wl in rr: 11th after 3 out and clr of remainder: v awkward 2 out and rdr nrly off: wknd* **66/1**

15 8 **Join The Clan (IRE)**[177] 226 4-10-12 0 ..... RichieMcLernon 64
(Jonjo O'Neill) *nvr bttr than midfield: hmpd 5th: wknd next: t.o* **40/1**

30- 16 29 **Iguacu**[29] 1795 9-10-12 0 ..... RichardJohnson 35
(Richard Price) *j. bdly lft 1st and j.lft 2nd: a wl in rr: wl t.o* **66/1**

R **Sister Guru**[165] 4-10-0 0 ..... CharlieWallis[(5)]
(Peter Hedger) *j. bdly: t.o whn ref 4th* **66/1**

3m 57.4s (-0.70) **Going Correction** +0.075s/f (Yiel) **17** Ran SP% **125.3**
Speed ratings (Par 105): **104,98,97,96,96 93,93,92,91,90 88,87,86,80,76 61,**
toteswingers 1&2 £2.30, 1&3 £27.40, 2&3 £34.00 CSF £6.56 TOTE £2.30: £1.60, £2.00, £8.30; EX 9.50 Trifecta £358.70 Pool: £2303.96 - 4.81 winning units..
Owner Mrs Judy Wilson **Bred** Michel Bourgneuf **Trained** Upper Lambourn, Berks

FOCUS
A fair novice hurdler and won by a smart prospect. The race should produce a few winners.

2266 WEATHERBYS BANK FOREIGN EXCHANGE "NATIONAL HUNT" NOVICES' HURDLE (10 hdls) 2m 5f

1:35 (1:35) (Class 4) 4-Y-O+ **£3,898** (£1,144; £572; £286)

Form RPR

132/ 1 **Captain Cutter (IRE)**[193] 5533 6-10-12 0 ..... APMcCoy 130+
(Nicky Henderson) *hld up: trckd ldrs 6th: stmbld quite bdly next: wnt 2nd 3 out: led bef next: easily drew clr* **4/11**[1]

04/ 2 10 **Fine Words**[217] 5070 5-10-12 0 ..... RobertThornton 109+
(Alan King) *chsd ldng trio: cl up fr 6th: rdn 3 out: wnt 2nd jst bef 2 out: styd on but no ch w wnr* **10/1**[3]

/15- 3 12 **Jack By The Hedge**[13] 2011 4-11-5 0 ..... IanPopham 106
(Caroline Keevil) *led: nt fluent 5th: hdd 7th: outpcd 3 out: kpt on again to take 3rd after last* **14/1**

/34- 4 1 **Reverb**[147] 699 4-10-12 0 ..... BarryGeraghty 95+
(Nicky Henderson) *hld up in rr: already lost tch whn mstke 6th: bhd fr next: lost no further grnd fr 3 out: pushed along fr last and fin w plenty of gusto* **9/2**[2]

5 4 **Always Smiling (IRE)**[330] 6-9-12 0 ..... (t) MrHAABannister[(7)] 84
(Charlie Mann) *mstke 1st: hld up in rr: lost tch after 5th: tried to cl on ldng quintet fr 7th: no imp bef 2 out: hung lft after last* **25/1**

6 2 3/4 **Mr Grey (IRE)**[217] 5-10-12 0 ..... SamTwiston-Davies 88
(Ben Case) *trckd ldr: led 7th: gng wl enough 3 out: hdd bef 2 out: wknd rapidly* **16/1**

0/ 7 94 **Nash Point (IRE)**[221] 4982 4-10-12 0 ..... RichardJohnson
(Tim Vaughan) *a in rr: hopelessly t.o after 6th: eventually fin* **50/1**

P **Here I Am (IRE)**[175] 271 6-10-12 0 ..... SamThomas
(Diana Grissell) *chsd ldng pair to 7th: sn rdn and wknd: t.o in 7th whn p.u bef last* **33/1**

210/ P **Ifits A Fiddle**[247] 4528 4-10-5 0 ..... (t) WayneHutchinson
(Richard Phillips) *hld up: lost tch after 5th: tried to make sme inroads on ldrs fr 7th: mstke 3 out and wknd qckly: t.o in 8th whn p.u bef 2 out* **20/1**

5m 21.5s (4.00) **Going Correction** +0.075s/f (Yiel) **9** Ran SP% **126.6**
Speed ratings (Par 105): **95,91,86,86,84 83,47,,**
toteswingers 1&2 £2.30, 1&3 £2.40, 2&3 £8.70 CSF £6.21 TOTE £1.30: £1.10, £2.00, £3.40; EX 6.30 Trifecta £30.50 Pool: £3200.77 - 78.65 winning units..
Owner John P McManus **Bred** Mrs S Brennan **Trained** Upper Lambourn, Berks

The Form Book Jumps, Raceform Ltd, Compton, RG20 6NL.

FOCUS
One-way traffic for the winner, who looks a smart prospect and is a potential 145+ novice.

2267 WEATHERBYS HAMILTON INSURANCE NOVICES' LIMITED H'CAP CHASE (18 fncs) 3m
2:05 (2:06) (Class 3) (0-125,124) 4-Y-0+ **£6,657** (£2,067; £1,113)

Form RPR

/55- **1** **Annacotty (IRE)**[13] [2012] 5-11-4 **123** IanPopham 139
(Martin Keighley) *cl up: led 5th: mde most after: rdn and narrowly hdd fr 3 out tl rallied to ld bef last: drvn clr* **8/1**

2/3- **2** *5* **Present View**[20] [1915] 5-10-13 **118** BrendanPowell 129
(Jamie Snowden) *hld up in tch: impeded 5th: prog 12th: jnd ldng pair 4 out: narrow ld fr 3 out tl hdd bef last: fdd* **9/2**[2]

46P/ **3** *11* **Off The Ground (IRE)**[247] [4522] 7-11-2 **121** AidanColeman 125+
(Emma Lavelle) *wl in tch: cl up in ldng gp fr 12th: nt fluent 4 out: rdn and hld sn after: j.lft last 3: lft 3rd last* **7/2**[1]

200/ **U** **Badgers Cove (IRE)**[201] [5351] 9-10-6 **111** CharliePoste 114
(Robin Dickin) *mde most to 5th: pressed ldr after tl drvn and lost pl 13th: u.p but kpt on after: 10 l bhd in 5th whn bdly hmpd and uns rdr last* **16/1**

1/0- **P** **Super Villan**[171] [358] 8-10-10 **120** NicodeBoinville[(5)]
(Mark Bradstock) *chsd ldrs: rdn fr 1/2-way: lost tch after slow jump 11th: t.o whn p.u bef 14th* **12/1**

031/ **F** **Billy Dutton**[202] [5328] 7-11-1 **120** JamesDavies
(Chris Down) *stmbld and fell 1st* **20/1**

43P/ **P** **Duke Of Monmouth (IRE)**[240] [4657] 6-11-1 **120** SamTwiston-Davies
(Charlie Mann) *cl up tl wknd 13th: t.o whn p.u bef 3 out* **15/2**

102- **P** **Cinevator (IRE)**[8] [2107] 6-11-2 **124** (p) JamesBest[(3)]
(Caroline Keevil) *chsd ldr to 4th: lost pl and mstke next: mstke 6th and sn in rr: t.o whn p.u bef 12th* **10/1**

5/U- **F** **Midnight Oscar (IRE)**[8] [2107] 6-11-3 **122** JasonMaguire
(Kim Bailey) *jumping lacked conviction: mostly in last tl fell 9th* **5/1**[3]

26/ **F** **Via Sundown (FR)**[211] [5195] 5-10-4 **112** JoshuaMoore[(3)] 120
(Gary Moore) *hld up in tch: prog to join ldrs 12th: w wnr fr next tl rdn after 4 out: 6 l down in 3rd and hld whn fell last* **9/1**

6m 12.0s (-3.40) **Going Correction** +0.075s/f (Yiel) **10** Ran SP% **117.4**
Speed ratings (Par 107): **108,106,102,, , , , ,**
toteswingers 1&2 £9.50, 1&3 £7.60, 2&3 £4.60 CSF £45.31 CT £151.26 TOTE £10.30: £2.80, £2.00, £1.50; EX 55.40 Trifecta £313.70 Pool: £2622.55 - 6.26 winning units..
Owner Mrs Peter Prowting **Bred** Patrick Crotty Jnr **Trained** Condicote, Gloucs

FOCUS
This staying novice handicap looked wide open. It was run at an average gallop and the first two fought it out in the home straight. A big step up from the winner on his previous chase form.

2268 PERTEMPS NETWORK H'CAP HURDLE (SERIES QUALIFIER) (10 hdls) 2m 5f
2:40 (2:40) (Class 2) 4-Y-0+
£11,573 (£3,418; £1,709; £854; £427; £214)

Form RPR

3/U- **1** **God's Own (IRE)**[23] [1867] 5-10-0 **129** oh1 PaddyBrennan 135+
(Tom George) *trckd ldrs: wnt 2nd 7th: j.rt 3 out: led and j.rt 2 out: clr whn j.rt last: rdn out* **11/4**[2]

334/ **2** *6* **Like Minded**[428] [1476] 9-10-0 **129** oh2 (t) HarrySkelton 126
(Dan Skelton) *hld up in last pair: lost tch after 4th: wl bhd 6th: pushed along and kpt on fr 3 out: rdn next: styd on to take 2nd last stride* **11/1**

025- **3** *nk* **Pateese (FR)**[10] [1594] 8-10-5 **134** (p) RichardJohnson 133
(Philip Hobbs) *led tl bef 5th: lost 2nd 7th: nt fluent 3 out whn rdn: outpcd bef next: kpt on to chse wnr sn after last: no imp and lost 2nd fnl stride* **20/1**

P21/ **4** *3/4* **Seventh Sign**[192] [5537] 4-10-3 **132** (p) WayneHutchinson 129
(Alan King) *chsd ldr tl after 4th: nt fluent next 2: rdn after 7th and struggling: wl btn after 3 out: kpt on again bef last* **7/1**[3]

3P0/ **5** *1 3/4* **Grands Crus (FR)**[212] [5175] 8-11-12 **155** (t) TomScudamore 152+
(David Pipe) *t.k.h: hld up in last pair tl prog 4th: led bef next: hdd and carried rt 2 out: whn rdn last and lost 3 pls flat* **9/4**[1]

53/ **6** *24* **The Crafty Butcher (IRE)**[30] [1775] 6-10-10 **139** (t) BarryGeraghty 112
(Michael Hourigan, Ire) *hld up: in last pair fr 4th: lost tch next: nvr remotely involved after: mstke last* **11/4**[2]

5m 15.3s (-2.20) **Going Correction** +0.075s/f (Yiel)
WFA 4 from 5yo+ 8lb **6** Ran SP% **109.7**
Speed ratings (Par 109): **107,104,104,104,103 94**
toteswingers 1&2 £6.50, 1&3 £4.50, 2&3 £11.10 CSF £27.55 TOTE £3.70: £1.90, £3.60; EX 31.90 Trifecta £309.00 Pool: £2659.20 - 6.45 winning units..
Owner Crossed Fingers Partnership **Bred** Mrs Caroline O'Driscoll **Trained** Slad, Gloucs

FOCUS
A good-quality handicap, run at a fair gallop. The winner is rated back to the level of his Musselburgh win.

2269 WEATHERBYS HAMILTON INSURANCE GRADUATION CHASE (16 fncs) 2m 4f 110y
3:10 (3:10) (Class 2) 4-Y-0+ **£12,627** (£3,811; £1,963; £1,039)

Form RPR

523/ **1** **Bury Parade (IRE)**[216] [5105] 7-11-2 139 SamTwiston-Davies 150+
(Paul Nicholls) *mde all: j. bttr than rivals: looked in command whn blnd 3 out: sn shkn up: 4 l clr next: hrd pressed after last: jst prevailed* **5/2**[2]

235/ **2** *nse* **Hadrian's Approach (IRE)**[191] [5576] 6-11-6 146 BarryGeraghty 154+
(Nicky Henderson) *trckd wnr: hit 7th: nt fluent 4 out and dropped to 3rd: rdn to chse wnr again 3 out: rallied last: upsides nr fin: jst denied* **11/10**[1]

FP1/ **3** *9* **Theatre Guide (IRE)**[195] [5472] 6-11-9 147 (t) JoeTizzard 148
(Colin Tizzard) *trckd ldng pair: nt fluent 10th: effrt to press wnr 4 out: lost 2nd and shkn up 3 out: steadily fdd* **3/1**[3]

F/0- **4** *23* **Solix (FR)**[22] [1901] 7-11-9 0 JasonMaguire 128
(Ian Williams) *nt a fluent: a in last pair: lost tch 11th: lft poor 4th last* **18/1**

6/5- **U** **Sir Du Bearn (FR)**[9] [2086] 7-11-9 132 CharliePoste 137
(Robin Dickin) *tended to jump lft: a in last pair: lft bhd fr 11th: 18 l down in 4th whn mstke and uns rdr last* **50/1**

5m 11.5s (-5.10) **Going Correction** +0.075s/f (Yiel) **5** Ran SP% **108.4**
Speed ratings (Par 109): **112,111,108,99,**
CSF £5.77 TOTE £2.70: £1.80, £1.10; EX 5.80 Trifecta £9.90 Pool: £2785.10 - 209.36 winning units..
Owner HighclereThoroughbredRacing- Bury Parade **Bred** J R Weston **Trained** Ditcheat, Somerset

FOCUS
There was a cracking finish to this decent little graduation chase. The winner is rated to the best of last season's form, in a good time compared with the later handicap.

2270 WEATHERBYS BANK FOREIGN EXCHANGE H'CAP CHASE (16 fncs) 2m 4f 110y
3:45 (3:45) (Class 4) (0-120,114) 4-Y-0+ **£4,548** (£1,335; £667; £333)

Form RPR

0/2- **1** **Foundation Man (IRE)**[18] [1939] 6-11-12 **114** APMcCoy 125+
(Jonjo O'Neill) *disp ld: reminders after 10th: def advantage 3 out: cajoled along after: pressed last: shkn up but wl in command flat* **11/10**[1]

2P1- **2** *2 3/4* **Upton Mead (IRE)**[14] [2003] 6-11-0 **102** (b) RichardJohnson 106
(Kevin Tork) *mostly chsd ldng pair: rdn after 4 out: wnt 2nd after 3 out: drvn to chal last: kpt on but readily hld flat* **13/2**[3]

346- **3** *34* **Violets Boy (IRE)**[25] [1830] 6-11-12 **114** (t) AndrewTinkler 87
(Brendan Powell) *mostly in last trio: struggling to stay in tch fr 10th: j.lft next: sn no ch: tk remote 3rd after last* **8/1**

4/1- **4** *3 1/4* **Lemon's Gent**[184] [117] 6-11-3 **105** (p) SamJones 78+
(Paul Webber) *disp ld: looked to be gng bttr than wnr fr 10th: hdd 3 out and wknd rapidly* **4/1**[2]

/P0- **5** *6* **Porters War (IRE)**[15] [1988] 11-10-12 **103** MattGriffiths[(3)] 68
(Jeremy Scott) *chsd ldng trio: jst in tch whn lunged at 12th: rdn and wknd next* **16/1**

432- **6** *31* **Synthe Davis (FR)**[30] [1767] 8-11-12 **114** (p) HarrySkelton 51
(Laura Mongan) *a in last trio: struggling to stay in tch fr 10th: sn wknd: t.o* **11/1**

354- **P** **Lucy's Legend (IRE)**[30] [1767] 7-10-10 **98** (tp) PaddyBrennan
(Paul Henderson) *mostly in last trio: struggling to stay in tch fr 10th: sn no ch: wl bhd whn p.u bef 2 out* **12/1**

5m 19.8s (3.20) **Going Correction** +0.075s/f (Yiel) **7** Ran SP% **114.0**
Speed ratings (Par 105): **96,94,82,80,78 66,**
toteswingers 1&2 £2.50, 1&3 £2.60, 2&3 £9.40 CSF £9.07 CT £38.39 TOTE £2.00: £1.10, £1.90; EX 7.60 Trifecta £43.30 Pool: £3775.16 - 65.31 winning units..
Owner P Hickey **Bred** Headfield Farm Ltd **Trained** Cheltenham, Gloucs

FOCUS
A modest handicap in which only three mattered from five out. A step up for the winner with a personal best in defeat from the second.

2271 WEATHERBYS VAT SERVICES CONDITIONAL JOCKEYS' H'CAP HURDLE (8 hdls) 2m
4:15 (4:15) (Class 4) (0-115,115) 4-Y-0+ **£3,249** (£954; £477; £238)

Form RPR

/12- **1** **Bollin Judith**[54] [1562] 7-11-9 **112** (t) TrevorWhelan 116+
(Jim Best) *hld up in tch: pushed along after 3 out: chsd ldng trio bef next: rdn to chal last: led fnl 150yds: styd on* **10/1**

4/2- **2** *1 1/4* **Uriah Heep (FR)**[29] [1779] 4-11-7 **113** TomBellamy[(3)] 116+
(Alan King) *t.k.h: hld up in tch: trckd ldng pair 4th: cl up after 3 out: rdn to ld after 2 out: hdd and one pce last 150yds* **5/2**[1]

250/ **3** *4* **Headly's Bridge (IRE)**[202] [5340] 7-11-7 **115** RyanHatch[(5)] 115
(Simon Earle) *hld up in last pair: prog fr 5th to trck ldrs 3 out: rdn to ld 2 out where nt fluent: sn hdd: one pce after* **5/2**[1]

464- **4** *3 3/4* **Flashy Star**[43] [1630] 4-10-0 **89** oh1 JamesBest 85
(Paul Henderson) *hld up in tch: rdn towards rr of ldng gp on long run after 3 out: lft bhd fr 2 out: plugged on* **9/1**[3]

6PP- **5** *1* **Rachael's Ruby**[14] [2004] 6-10-1 **95** (p) NathanAdams[(5)] 92+
(Roger Teal) *led and mostly 4 l clr: c bk to rivals after 3 out: hdd and nt fluent 2 out: fading whn mstke last* **25/1**

0/6- **6** *hd* **Reggie Perrin**[100] [304] 5-10-8 **105** PaddyBradley[(8)] 101
(Pat Phelan) *hld up in last: lost tch w ldng gp fr 5th and sn wl adrift: pushed along and latched on to gp bef 2 out: one pce after: nvr involved* **12/1**

0/0- **7** *hd* **Looks Like Slim**[46] [251] 6-11-4 **107** GavinSheehan 101
(Ben De Haan) *trckd ldrs: wl on terms after 3 out: shkn up and fdd fr 2 out* **9/2**[2]

005- **8** *9* **Khazium (IRE)**[70] [1402] 4-10-2 **97** (tp) GeraldQuinn[(6)] 85
(Claire Dyson) *mostly chsd ldr tl after 3 out: wkng whn rdr dropped whip after 2 out* **25/1**

3/4- **9** *40* **Sash Of Honour (IRE)**[30] [1764] 4-11-9 **115** (v) MichaelByrne[(3)] 65
(Tim Vaughan) *prom: j. sloppily fr 3rd and sn dropped to rr: wknd 5th: t.o* **10/1**

3m 59.9s (1.80) **Going Correction** +0.075s/f (Yiel) **9** Ran SP% **118.9**
Speed ratings (Par 105): **98,97,95,93,93 92,92,88,68**
toteswingers 1&2 £3.50, 1&3 £10.10, 2&3 £3.10 CSF £37.31 CT £83.46 TOTE £8.10: £3.10, £1.70, £1.10; EX 21.00 Trifecta £119.00 Pool: £2380.73 - 14.99 winning units..
Owner Jack Callaghan **Bred** Sir Neil & Exors Of Late Lady Westbrook **Trained** Lewes, E Sussex

FOCUS
A moderate handicap, confined to conditional riders, but solid form at the level. It saw plenty in with a chance at the top of the home straight, but the principals dominated from two out.
T/Plt: £11.40 to a £1 stake. Pool: £74854.24 - 4787.71 winning tickets T/Qpdt: £9.40 to a £1 stake. Pool: £4909.28 - 382.65 winning tickets JN

[2002] PLUMPTON (L-H)
Monday, November 4

OFFICIAL GOING: Heavy (soft in places) changing to soft (heavy in places) after race 2 (1:20)
Wind: Light, across Weather: Sunny

2272 AT THE RACES SKY 415 MAIDEN HURDLE (9 hdls) 2m
12:50 (12:53) (Class 5) 4-Y-0+ **£2,053** (£598; £299)

Form RPR

52- **1** **Ashdown Lad**[11] [2040] 4-11-0 FelixDeGiles 111+
(Tom Symonds) *prom: wnt 2nd appr 3 out: drvn to ld run-in* **3/1**[2]

02- **2** *1 1/2* **Auld Sthock (IRE)**[14] [2002] 5-11-0 117 JamieMoore 108
(Gary Moore) *chsd ldr: led 4th tl run-in: hrd rdn: r.o* **6/4**[1]

14/ **3** *1 1/4* **Unowhatimeanharry**[223] [4970] 5-11-0 PaulMoloney 107
(Helen Nelmes) *chsd ldrs: wnt 3rd at 6th: one pce appr last* **6/1**[3]

/40- **4** *7* **Even If**[9] [2083] 5-11-0 DominicElsworth 100
(Jonjo O'Neill) *mid-div: hdwy 6th: shkn up and no imp fr 2 out* **7/1**

5/4- **5** *17* **Noble Friend (IRE)**[14] [2002] 5-11-0 GerardTumelty 83
(Chris Gordon) *bhd: hdwy and in tch 5th: outpcd fr 3 out* **10/1**

545- **6** *1 1/4* **Snapchat (IRE)**[14] [2002] 6-11-0 ConorO'Farrell 82
(Seamus Durack) *outpcd: nvr trbld ldrs* **20/1**

5/0- **7** *15* **Lightentertainment (IRE)**[23] 1864 5-11-0 .... TomCannon 67
(Chris Gordon) *mstke 6th: a bhd* **33/1**
8 *4* **Silver Marizah (IRE)**[49] 4-10-7 .... MattieBatchelor 56
(Roger Ingram) *led: j.lft 3rd: hdd next: wknd 6th* **100/1**
9 *9* **Two Sugars**[35] 5-11-0 .... DavidBass 54
(Laura Mongan) *chsd ldrs tl wknd 6th* **66/1**
0- **10** *nk* **Into The Wind**[17] 1958 6-10-0 .... MrTAddis(7) 46
(Jim Best) *s.s: a wl bhd* **100/1**
0- **11** *16* **Heading To First**[14] 2002 6-10-11 ....(p) KielanWoods(3) 37
(Paddy Butler) *in tch tl wknd 6th: bhd whn blnd 3 out* **100/1**
P **Finlodex**[18] 6-11-0 .... AndrewThornton
(Murty McGrath) *a bhd: t.o whn p.u after 3 out* **100/1**
450- **R** **Slaney Star (IRE)**[14] 2002 5-10-8 ow1 .... JamesO'Neill(7)
(Jim Best) *s.s: wl bhd tl rn out 2nd* **50/1**

4m 4.2s (3.40) **Going Correction** +0.275s/f (Yiel)
WFA 4 from 5yo+ 7lb 13 Ran SP% **116.0**
Speed ratings (Par 103): **102,101,100,97,88 88,80,78,74,73 65,,**
toteswingers 1&2 £1.10, 1&3 £4.40, 2&3 £2.50 CSF £7.57 TOTE £2.40: £1.40, £1.10, £2.30; EX 8.50 Trifecta £31.70 Pool: £1675.70 - 39.63 winning units..
Owner Foster, Coe, Stagg, Rowlinson **Bred** Mr & Mrs A E Pakenham **Trained** Harewood End, H'fords
■ Stewards' Enquiry : Mr T Addis fourteen-day ban: failed to obtain the best position (18, 24, 28, 29 Nov, 1, 6, 17, 19 Dec)

FOCUS
A modest maiden in which they were well strung out from an early stage. A small personal best from the winner with the second to his mark.

2273 FOLLOW AT THE RACES ON TWITTER MARES' NOVICES' HURDLE (12 hdls) 2m 5f
1:20 (1:21) (Class 4) 4-Y-0+ **£3,249** (£954; £477; £238)

Form RPR
123/ **1** **Carole's Spirit**[213] 5163 5-10-10 0 .... FelixDeGiles 120+
(Robert Walford) *trckd ldrs: mstke 9th: chal gng wl 2 out: led on bit last: hrd hld* **2/5**[1]
146/ **2** *nk* **Fountains Mary**[205] 5287 5-10-7 0 .... RachaelGreen(3) 105
(Anthony Honeyball) *hld up in tch: hdwy and gng wl 9th: led appr 2 out: rdn and hdd run-in: kpt on: no ch w wnr: flattered by margin* **7/1**[3]
022/ **3** *17* **Brantingham Breeze**[269] 4105 5-10-7 0 .... GavinSheehan(3) 88
(Emma Lavelle) *led tl 3rd: led 5th tl appr 2 out: sn wknd* **7/2**[2]
/56- **4** *79* **Lacunae (IRE)**[26] 1823 5-10-10 0 .... RyanMahon 9
(Seamus Mullins) *led 3rd tl 5th: j. slowly and lost tch 9th* **33/1**
0/- **P** **Misty Mornin**[205] 5295 5-10-10 0 .... DaveCrosse
(Zoe Davison) *chsd ldrs: rdn and wknd 8th: sn bhd: mstke 3 out: p.u bef 2 out* **100/1**

5m 24.0s (7.00) **Going Correction** +0.275s/f (Yiel) 5 Ran SP% **110.1**
Speed ratings (Par 105): **97,96,90,60,**
CSF £4.06 TOTE £1.50: £1.10, £2.90; EX 3.40 Trifecta £4.80 Pool: £2122.44 - 326.08 winning units..
Owner Paul Murphy **Bred** Paul Murphy **Trained** Child Okeford, Dorset

FOCUS
A mare's contest with little depth. The facile winner was value for a lot further and is rated in line with her bumper form.

2274 AT THE RACES VIRGIN 534 H'CAP HURDLE (9 hdls) 2m
1:50 (1:50) (Class 4) (0-105,105) 3-Y-0+ **£3,249** (£954; £477; £238)

Form RPR
22- **1** **Raven's Tower (USA)**[26] 1813 3-10-13 105 .... DavidBass 100+
(Ben Pauling) *hld up in last: smooth hdwy on outer fr 3 out: led after 2 out: sn clr: easily* **3/1**[3]
040/ **2** *7* **Hold The Bucks (USA)**[697] 3018 7-10-4 80 .... JamieMoore 80
(Daniel Steele) *hld up: hdwy and drvn to ld 2 out: sn hdd and unable qck: no ch w wnr* **14/1**
2/0- **3** *4* **Kalamill (IRE)**[38] 1674 6-11-12 102 ....(t) DominicElsworth 97
(Shaun Lycett) *led tl 6th: outpcd and btn 2 out* **9/4**[1]
655- **4** *4* **Delphi Mountain (IRE)**[35] 1699 8-11-10 100 ....(t) TomO'Brien 92
(Richard Woollacott) *cl up tl wknd 2 out* **11/4**[2]
/60- **5** *3 ½* **Just Beware**[9] 2090 11-10-4 80 ....(p) DaveCrosse 68
(Zoe Davison) *chsd ldr: led 6th tl wknd 2 out* **12/1**
31- **6** *12* **Border Station (IRE)**[146] 708 7-11-12 102 .... LeightonAspell 82
(Alison Batchelor) *chsd ldrs tl wknd appr 2 out* **6/1**

4m 4.1s (3.30) **Going Correction** +0.275s/f (Yiel)
WFA 3 from 6yo+ 15lb 6 Ran SP% **111.1**
Speed ratings (Par 105): **102,98,96,94,92 86**
CSF £35.83 TOTE £3.50: £2.20, £4.90; EX 43.50 Trifecta £213.50 Pool: £1364.50 - 4.79 winning units..
Owner Faithful Friends **Bred** Darley **Trained** Bourton-On-The-Water, Gloucs
■ The first winner for Ben Pauling, a former assistant to Nicky Henderson.

FOCUS
A moderate handicap. The easy winner was well in on his recent run and is rated to a similar level.

2275 JOIN AT THE RACES ON FACEBOOK NOVICES' H'CAP CHASE (18 fncs) 3m 2f
2:25 (2:26) (Class 4) (0-110,112) 4-Y-0+ **£3,898** (£1,144; £572; £286)

Form RPR
P61- **1** **Days Of Pleasure (IRE)**[12] 2023 8-10-5 84 ....(b) TomCannon 92
(Chris Gordon) *led: wnt 5 l clr at 14th: hdd 2 out: led again last: drvn clr: gamely* **7/2**[2]
063/ **2** *4* **Smart Exit (IRE)**[207] 5242 6-11-10 103 ....(p) JamieMoore 110+
(Renee Robeson) *disp 2nd: chsd wnr 12th: led and blnd 2 out: hdd and no ex last* **9/2**[3]
501- **3** *7* **Samingarry (FR)**[8] 2099 6-12-2 112 7ex .... MarkQuinlan(3) 112
(Nigel Hawke) *hld up in rr: hdwy 14th: one pce fr 3 out* **5/1**
562- **4** *23* **Always Bold (IRE)**[18] 1936 8-11-7 100 ....(v) TomSiddall 74
(Martin Keighley) *disp 2nd tl 12th: rdn and lost pl next: sn bhd* **3/1**[1]
PP/- **P** **Orvita (FR)**[195] 5474 11-10-4 83 ....(p) PaulMoloney
(Helen Nelmes) *a in rr: mstke 2nd: often j.rt: wl bhd whn p.u bef 14th* **16/1**
56P/ **P** **Gospel Preacher**[182] 8-11-8 104 ....(p) MichealNolan(3)
(Richard Woollacott) *hld up in 5th: sme hdwy 13th: 4th and btn whn mstke 3 out: bhd whn p.u bef next* **8/1**
0/5- **P** **The Informant**[185] 95 7-11-4 97 .... AndrewThornton
(Seamus Mullins) *chsd ldrs: mstke 10th: blnd and lost tch next: bhd whn p.u bef 13th* **6/1**

7m 1.7s (11.00) **Going Correction** +0.50s/f (Soft) 7 Ran SP% **113.3**
Speed ratings (Par 105): **103,101,99,92,**
CSF £19.43 TOTE £4.40: £2.40, £2.10; EX 22.00 Trifecta £141.20 Pool: £1464.27 - 7.77 winning units..
Owner E J Farrant **Bred** Shay White **Trained** Morestead, Hants

FOCUS
A modest novice handicap and the winner stepped up only slightly on his recent win.

2276 ATTHERACES.COM EXCLUSIVE BARRY GERAGHTY BLOG JUVENILE HURDLE (9 hdls) 2m
3:00 (3:00) (Class 4) 3-Y-0 **£3,119** (£915; £457; £228)

Form RPR
1 **Violet Dancer**[140] 3-10-12 .... JamieMoore 122+
(Gary Moore) *t.k.h in 4th: clsd on ldrs 3 out: led next: clr whn hit last: easily* **7/2**[2]
3- **2** *10* **Aldopicgros (FR)**[15] 1985 3-10-12 .... NickScholfield 107
(Paul Nicholls) *cl up in 2nd: jnd ldr and mstke 5th: led 3 out tl 2 out: sn outpcd* **8/15**[1]
33- **3** *35* **Unidexter (IRE)**[31] 1743 3-10-12 .... MarcGoldstein 75
(Sheena West) *led: mstke 3rd: hdd 3 out: wknd appr next* **5/1**[3]
254- **4** *12* **Karl Marx (IRE)**[24] 1855 3-10-12 94 .... TommyPhelan 58
(Mark Gillard) *prom: rdn 5th: wknd 3 out* **33/1**
46P- **5** *11* **Complexity**[15] 1985 3-10-12 .... AndrewThornton 47
(Seamus Mullins) *a bhd* **50/1**
6- **6** *8* **Herbalist**[11] 2038 3-10-12 .... DavidBass 39
(Ben Pauling) *bhd: rdn 6th: no ch after* **33/1**
U- **P** **Mighty Thor**[31] 1743 3-10-12 .... LeightonAspell
(Lydia Richards) *in tch tl wknd 6th: wl bhd whn p.u bef last* **66/1**

4m 0.6s (-0.20) **Going Correction** +0.275s/f (Yiel) 7 Ran SP% **113.5**
Speed ratings (Par 104): **111,106,88,82,77 73,**
CSF £5.97 TOTE £4.90: £2.00, £1.10; EX 9.60 Trifecta £19.50 Pool: £4470.49 - 171.28 winning units..
Owner D Bessell & Galloping On The South Downs **Bred** Jeremy Hinds **Trained** Lower Beeding, W Sussex

FOCUS
A weak affair.

2277 VISIT ATTHERACES.COM/JUMPS H'CAP CHASE (13 fncs 1 omitted) 2m 4f
3:30 (3:30) (Class 5) (0-95,84) 4-Y-0+ **£2,329** (£723; £389)

Form RPR
/42- **1** **Croco Mister (IRE)**[29] 1800 6-11-4 81 .... BenPoste(5) 92+
(Rosemary Gasson) *in tch: wnt 2nd at 9th: led after bypassing omitted 3 out: sn clr* **6/4**[1]
3P2- **2** *6* **Mister Wiseman**[12] 2021 11-11-9 84 ....(bt) MarkQuinlan(3) 87
(Nigel Hawke) *led: nt fluent 10th: hrd rdn and hdd after bypassing omitted 3 out: one pce* **3/1**[2]
322/ **3** *16* **Ballyman (IRE)**[218] 5029 12-11-11 83 ....(v) PaulMoloney 79
(Jonathan Geake) *cl up: wnt 2nd at 5th: lost pl 9th: hld fr next: eased whn wl btn run-in* **9/2**[3]
PP6- **C** **Bobbits Way**[48] 1596 8-11-9 81 ....(p) TomO'Brien 89
(Alan Jones) *hld up: hdwy to join ldrs whn carried out at omitted 3 out* **7/1**
5/P- **F** **Kevin Fancy (IRE)**[26] 1825 7-9-7 58 oh10 .... MrFTett(7)
(John Upson) *chsd ldr tl 5th: cl 3rd whn fell next* **25/1**
F/4- **B** **Carbis Bay**[176] 234 7-11-3 75 ....(p) DaveCrosse
(Zoe Davison) *hld up in rr: b.d 6th: fatally injured* **8/1**

5m 30.4s (23.10) **Going Correction** +0.50s/f (Soft) 6 Ran SP% **110.6**
Speed ratings (Par 103): **90,87,81,,**
CSF £6.50 TOTE £2.40: £1.10, £2.40; EX 7.10 Trifecta £14.90 Pool: £2823.89 - 141.89 winning units..
Owner Mrs Rosemary Gasson **Bred** Corbally Stud **Trained** Balscote, Oxon

FOCUS
An eventful handicap chase. The third-last was bypassed due to a stricken horse. The winner was probably in front earlier than ideal and the second is rated in line with his recent form.

2278 MELBOURNE CUP LIVE ON AT THE RACES CONDITIONAL JOCKEYS' H'CAP HURDLE (12 hdls) 2m 5f
4:05 (4:05) (Class 5) (0-95,89) 4-Y-0+ **£2,053** (£598; £299)

Form RPR
3/0- **1** **Proud Times (USA)**[5] 141 7-11-10 87 ....(p) AdamWedge 96+
(Ali Brewer) *hld up towards rr: blnd bdly 6th: sn bhd: styd on strly fr 2 out: led fnl 50yds* **10/1**
505- **2** *1* **Phar Away Island (IRE)**[12] 2016 5-10-13 76 ....(p) KillianMoore 82+
(Charlie Brooks) *towards rr: blnd 8th: sme hdwy and rdn next: chsd clr ldr 2 out: swtchd lft run-in: styd on* **7/1**
002- **3** *nk* **Landenstown Star (IRE)**[6] 2148 8-10-11 77 ....(tp) PatrickCorbett(3) 81
(Mark Gillard) *in tch: chsd clr ldr 9th tl 2 out: kpt on run-in* **5/2**[1]
053- **4** *1 ¼* **Osmosia (FR)**[14] 2003 8-10-5 78 ....(tp) LouisMuspratt(10) 82+
(Chris Gordon) *trckd ldrs: led 7th: wnt 7 l clr 3 out: rdn and wknd run-in: hdd fnl 50yds* **8/1**
4F4- **5** *17* **Bold Tara**[14] 2008 6-10-6 77 ....(tp) OllieGarner(8) 65
(Martin Keighley) *chsd ldr tl 9th: wknd 3 out* **4/1**[3]
/64- **6** *48* **Actodos (IRE)**[152] 633 9-11-6 83 .... MichealNolan 21
(Richard Woollacott) *bhd: modest effrt 9th: wknd 3 out* **20/1**
633- **P** **Morestead (IRE)**[12] 2021 8-11-0 82 ....(p) MikeyHamill(5)
(Brendan Powell) *led: nt fluent and drvn along 5th: hdd and lost pl 7th: sn wl bhd: p.u bef 2 out* **16/1**
0/6- **P** **Regal Park (IRE)**[12] 2016 6-11-9 89 ....(p) JoshuaMoore(3)
(Gary Moore) *bhd: mod hdwy 9th: wknd 3 out: bhd whn p.u bef next* **7/2**[2]
040- **P** **Shot In The Dark (IRE)**[19] 946 4-11-10 87 ....(tp) HarryDerham
(Jonathan Geake) *prom tl 8th: bhd whn p.u bef 2 out* **33/1**

5m 26.2s (9.20) **Going Correction** +0.275s/f (Yiel) 9 Ran SP% **117.1**
Speed ratings (Par 103): **93,92,92,92,85 67,,,**
toteswingers 1&2 £3.10, 1&3 £1.20, 2&3 £5.90 CSF £78.63 CT £231.52 TOTE £8.90: £2.00, £2.30, £1.70; EX 97.00 Trifecta £451.70 Pool: £2645.29 - 4.39 winning units..
Owner Miss Ali Brewer **Bred** Timothy Thornton & Meg & Mike Buckley **Trained** Eastbury, Berks
■ Stewards' Enquiry : Killian Moore two day ban: careless riding (

FOCUS
A modest handicap for conditional jockeys and a thrilling finish. The first four were all well in on their best form.

T/Plt: £20.00 to a £1 stake. Pool: £58659.55 - 2136.38 winning tickets T/Qpdt: £19.20 to a £1 stake. Pool: £4249.55 - 163.10 winning tickets LM

2009EXETER (R-H)

Tuesday, November 5

OFFICIAL GOING: Good to soft (soft in places on hurdle course; chs 6.8; hdl 6.5)

Hurdle on bend after winning post moved to back straight.

Wind: quite strong across Weather: sunny with cloudy periods

2279 BATHWICK TYRES & FESTIVAL RACING SUPPORTS RACING "NATIONAL HUNT" NOVICES' HURDLE (11 hdls) 2m 5f 110y

1:50 (1:55) (Class 3) 4-Y-0+ £5,523 (£1,621; £810; £405)

Form RPR

22F/ 1 **Rydon Pynes**249 4502 5-10-12 0 HaddenFrost 127+
(Martin Hill) *hld up towards rr: stdy prog fr 6th: narrow ld whn hit 3 out: sn rdn: narrowly hdd next: hmpd by loose horse and swtchd lft bef last: r.o wl whn clr of loose horse to ld fnl 100yds: rdn out* 7/1

1- 2 1 **Flemenson (IRE)**19 1937 4-11-4 0 APMcCoy 132+
(Jonjo O'Neill) *trckd ldrs: chal 3 out: led narrowly 2 out: sn rdn: kpt on but no ex whn hdd fnl 100yds* 2/11

5/ 3 6 **Junction Fourteen (IRE)**208 5262 4-10-12 0 AidanColeman 120
(Emma Lavelle) *mid-div: hdwy after 6th: rdn to chse ldng pair after 3 out: styd on same pce* 12/1

/31- 4 11 **Billy No Name (IRE)**19 1946 5-11-4 121 JoeTizzard 118
(Colin Tizzard) *disp ld: j.lft at imes: rdn and hdd jst bef 3 out: sn one pce* 4/13

5 26 **The Wealerdealer (IRE)**170 6-10-12 0 TomScudamore 93
(David Pipe) *mid-div: effrt appr 3 out: nvr threatened ldrs: wkng whn mstke and hung lft after 2 out: t.o* 50/1

3- 6 7 **Master Butcher (IRE)**35 1712 6-10-12 0 RobertThornton 80
(Rebecca Curtis) *disp ld: hmpd by loose horse after 1st: nt fluent 8th: sn rdn and hdd: wknd 3 out: t.o* 20/1

4/ 7 7 **Sea Wall (FR)**208 5263 5-10-12 0 NickScholfield 77
(Paul Nicholls) *hmpd 5th: a towards rr: wknd 3 out: t.o* 16/1

50/ 8 15 **Milanese (IRE)**268 4156 5-10-9 0 GavinSheehan(3) 67
(Emma Lavelle) *mid-div: awkward 1st: hdwy whn bdly hmpd 7th and lost pl: bhd and no ch after: t.o* 100/1

2/ 9 16 **Champagne West (IRE)**234 4786 5-10-12 0 RichardJohnson 46
(Philip Hobbs) *trckd ldrs: nt fluent 3rd: sltly hmpd by loose horse whn hit 5th and sprawled on landing: sn bhd: nvr rcvrd: t.o* 9/42

46/ 10 shd **Stoney Silence**196 5469 5-10-12 0 NoelFehily 46
(Charlie Mann) *struggling after 4th: a towards rr: t.o fr after 8th* 100/1

P00/ U **Cool George**302 3547 5-10-9 0 JamesBest(3)
(Jackie Du Plessis) *trckd ldrs: prom whn bdly hmpd by loose horse and uns rdr jst bef 7th* 50/1

13- U **Beau De Tabel (FR)**25 1856 5-10-12 0 DavidBass
(Nick Williams) *awkward whn wnt lft and uns rdr 1st* 25/1

5m 17.0s (-16.00) **Going Correction** -0.65s/f (Firm) 12 Ran SP% **124.7**

Speed ratings (Par 107): **103,102,100,96,87 84,81,76,70,70** ,

toteswingers 1&2 £5.60, 1&3 £14.20, 2&3 £10.20 CSF £22.43 TOTE £8.10: £2.30, £1.60, £3.30; EX 30.90 Trifecta £469.80 Pool: £3147.17 - 5.02 winning units..

Owner The Rydon Pynes Partnership **Bred** Jamie Donovan **Trained** Littlehempston, Devon

FOCUS

Chase course out wide on fresh ground. The ground on the hurdles course appeared to be riding slower than on the chase track. Fair novice form, with them going a steady early gallop, and the race should still produce winners. The first two are on the upgrade. It proved an eventful race, mainly due to the loose horse, Beau De Tabel, who unseated at the first and proved a nuisance throughout, getting in the way of Champagne West as that one sprawled on landing, veering left towards the end of the back straight and causing Cool George to unseat and hampering Milanese, and then getting in the way of both the first two on the run-in.

2280 BATHWICK TYRES PLYMOUTH NOVICES' HURDLE (8 hdls) 2m 1f

2:20 (2:25) (Class 3) 4-Y-0+ £5,523 (£1,621; £810; £405)

Form RPR

10/- 1 **Doctor Harper (IRE)**237 4738 5-10-12 0 TimmyMurphy 129+
(David Pipe) *trckd ldrs: led 3 out: sn in command: impressive* 8/111

56/ 2 8 **Leave It Be (IRE)**213 5187 6-10-12 0 BrendanPowell 113
(Johnny Farrelly) *hld up towards rr of mid-div: stdy prog fr 2nd: rdn whn lft 4th and hmpd 3 out: mstke 2 out: styd on to go 2nd run-in: no ch w easy wnr* 33/1

324/ 3 4 **Broomfield**711 2768 6-10-12 0 NickScholfield 110+
(Paul Nicholls) *trckd ldrs: ev ch bef 3 out tl rdn bef 2 out: sn outpcd by wnr: no ex whn lost 2nd run-in* 9/22

P/6- 4 ½ **Gallic Warrior (FR)**21 1915 6-10-12 0 PaddyBrennan 108
(Fergal O'Brien) *in tch: trckd ldrs 5th: rdn after 3 out: styd on same pce* 22/1

5 8 **Attimo (GER)**482 4-10-12 0 NoelFehily 102
(Charlie Mann) *mid-div: rdn whn hmpd 3 out: styd on same pce wout threatening to get involved* 25/1

6 4½ **Neighbourhood (USA)**26 5-10-12 0 LiamTreadwell 99
(James Evans) *hld up towards rr: stdy prog after 5th: midfield 3 out: blnd next: no further imp* 50/1

06- 7 14 **Keen Eye (IRE)**10 2089 4-10-12 0 APMcCoy 84
(Jonjo O'Neill) *in tch: nudged along fr 4th: rdn after next: wknd bef 3 out* 16/1

5/0- 8 ¾ **Duke's Affair**10 2089 5-10-9 0 1 MattGriffiths(3) 83
(Jeremy Scott) *mid-div tl wknd after 5th* 100/1

6- 9 1¼ **Here's Herbie**13 2028 5-10-7 0 MissLucyGardner(5) 82
(Sue Gardner) *mid-div tl wknd after 5th* 80/1

1/0- 10 1¼ **Chill Factor (IRE)**17 1974 4-10-9 0 RachaelGreen(3) 81
(Anthony Honeyball) *struggling 3rd: a towards rr* 10/13

400- 11 nk **Brians Well (IRE)**13 2018 6-10-12 0 AndrewTinkler 81
(Brendan Powell) *mid-div tl wknd 5th* 100/1

/00- 12 9 **Puerto Azul (IRE)**14 2011 9-10-9 97 MichealNolan(3) 73
(Bernard Scriven) *mid-div: rdn after 5th: sn wknd* 200/1

U3/ F **New Christmas (USA)**614 4601 6-10-12 0 JamesDavies
(Chris Down) *mid-div: hdwy after 6th: rdn to chse ldrs in disp 4th whn fell 3 out* 25/1

0/ P **Village Secret**531 409 7-10-9 0 GavinSheehan(3)
(Brian Barr) *led tl 5th: sn riodden: wknd qckly: p.u bef next* 200/1

0- F **Ernest Speak (IRE)**14 2011 4-10-12 0 HaddenFrost
(Martin Hill) *mid-div: untidy 1st: blnd 4th: wknd 3 out: fell next* 100/1

- P **Shakespeare Dancer**162 4-10-2 0 MarkQuinlan(3)
(James Evans) *a towards rr: t.o whn p.u bef 3 out* 200/1

U- P **Luckwell Bridge**14 2011 8-10-2 0 JonPark(10)
(Kevin Bishop) *racd green: a in rr: t.o whn p.u bef 3 out* 200/1

R2- F **Sea Island Pearl**26 1832 4-10-5 0 TomO'Brien
(Philip Hobbs) *t.k.h: trckd ldr: led 5th: rdn and hdd in 3rd whn fell 3 out* 10/13

4m 1.0s (-14.50) **Going Correction** -0.65s/f (Firm) 18 Ran SP% **123.3**

Speed ratings (Par 107): **108,104,102,102,98 96,89,89,88,88 87,83,** , , , ,

toteswingers 1&2 £12.30, 1&3 £1.10, 2&3 £30.70 CSF £39.84 TOTE £1.70: £1.10, £6.20, £2.00; EX 38.80 Trifecta £221.20 Pool: £2665.40 - 9.03 winning units..

Owner The Johnson Family **Bred** Stephen O'Flynn **Trained** Nicholashayne, Devon

FOCUS

There was little depth to this novice hurdle and they were soon strung out. Although impressive enough, the winner beat little. He can rate a fair bit higher.

2281 BETVICTOR HALDON GOLD CUP CHASE (LIMITED H'CAP) GRADE 2 (12 fncs) 2m 1f 110y

2:50 (2:55) (Class 1) 4-Y-0+

£35,593 (£13,356; £6,687; £3,331; £1,675; £837)

Form RPR

34U/ 1 **Somersby (IRE)**237 4735 9-10-7 155 DominicElsworth 158
(Mick Channon) *trckd ldrs: t.k.h: mounting chal whn squeezed out appr 4 out: swtchd lft: chal again 2 out: more fluent jump to ld sn after last: jst hld on: all out* 9/23

114/ 2 hd **Module (FR)**236 4746 6-10-4 152 PaddyBrennan 158+
(Tom George) *trckd ldrs: hit 4th: pressed ldrs 6th tl rdn after 8th: chal again 4 out: led 3 out: nt as fluent as wnr and hdd sn after last: rallied run-in: jst failed* 8/1

112/ 3 6 **Cue Card**214 5159 7-11-10 172 JoeTizzard 172+
(Colin Tizzard) *led: slipped whn rching for 4th where rdr lost iron briefly: hdd 8th: sn bk upsides: led next: rdn whn hdd 3 out: styd on same pce tl no ex fnl 75yds* 11/101

F/0- 4 ¾ **Kumbeshwar**17 1969 6-10-4 152 oh4 (p) WayneHutchinson 149
(Alan King) *hld up bhd ldrs: pushed along to hold pl fr after 6th: drvn whn outpcd bef 4 out: mstke 3 out: styd on fr after next: fin wl to go 4th run-in: nrly rchd 3rd* 25/1

111/ 5 4 **William's Wishes (IRE)**304 3514 8-10-5 153 PaulMoloney 145
(Evan Williams) *trckd ldrs: led 8th tl rdn bef next: styd on same pce fr 3 out tl fdd run-in* 4/12

F25/ 6 27 **Fago (FR)**215 5140 5-10-4 152 NickScholfield 127
(Paul Nicholls) *travelled wl trcking ldrs: effrt 4 out: qckly btn: t.o* 9/1

4m 11.1s (-7.90) **Going Correction** -0.275s/f (Good) 6 Ran SP% **110.8**

Speed ratings (Par 115): **106,105,103,102,101 89**

toteswingers 1&2 £4.60, 1&3 £1.50, 2&3 £2.70 CSF £35.02 TOTE £5.30: £1.40, £3.80; EX 34.00 Trifecta £72.10 Pool: £3781.67 - 39.32 winning units..

Owner Mrs T P Radford **Bred** Miss Nicola Ann Adams **Trained** West Ilsley, Berks

FOCUS

A good-looking edition of a race that is traditionally one of the early-season highlights and is often used as a stepping stone to greater things. They went just a steady gallop, resulting in most of them taking a keen hold, and that may explain why they appeared to finish quite tired. The front pair drew clear late on. Somersby is rated in line with his reappearances the last two years, with Module still on the upgrade and Cue Card to a similar level as this race last year.

2282 BATHWICK TYRES NOVICES' CHASE (11 fncs 1 omitted) 2m 1f 110y

3:20 (3:25) (Class 2) 4-Y-0+ £12,627 (£3,811; £1,963; £1,039)

Form RPR

034/ 1 **Manyriverstocross (IRE)**192 5162 8-11-1 0 RobertThornton 143+
(Alan King) *disp ld tl clr ldr after 3rd: pushed along appr 4 out: narrowly hdd 2 out: sn rdn: kpt on gamely to regain narrow advantage nring fin: all out* 9/23

1/1- 2 nse **Claret Cloak (IRE)**27 1821 6-11-6 140 AidanColeman 149+
(Emma Lavelle) *trckd ldrs: nudged along at times fr 5th: travelling wl whn chalng after 4 out: led narrowly 2 out: rdn whn nt as fluent as wnr last: kpt on: hdd nring fin* 1/11

160/ 3 77 **Lord Of House (GER)**262 4243 5-11-1 0 (t) NoelFehily 74
(Charlie Mann) *disp ld tl after 3rd: trcking wnr whn slipped on take off and virtually fell 6th: nt rcvr and sn t.o: mstke last* 16/1

1P6/ 4 110 **Reverend Green (IRE)**741 3478 7-11-1 0 JamesDavies
(Chris Down) *trckd ldrs tl rdn after 7th: sn lost tch: t.o* 100/1

3/1- F **Dark Lover (GER)**17 1973 8-11-9 0 NickScholfield 140
(Paul Nicholls) *trckd ldrs: wnt 2nd after 6th tl rdn appr 4 out: 3rd and hld whn fell 2 out* 2/12

4m 13.4s (-5.60) **Going Correction** -0.275s/f (Good) 5 Ran SP% **108.4**

Speed ratings (Par 109): **101,100,66,** ,

CSF £9.69 TOTE £5.40: £2.80, £1.10; EX 9.70 Trifecta £53.70 Pool: £3490.42 - 48.68 winning units..

Owner Mrs M C Sweeney **Bred** Crone Stud Farms Ltd **Trained** Barbury Castle, Wilts

FOCUS

A fair novice chase, although there was no future stars on show. The winner is rated in line with the best of last season's hurdle form.

2283 SMITH & WILLIAMSON H'CAP CHASE (17 fncs 1 omitted) 3m

3:50 (3:55) (Class 3) (0-130,130) 4-Y-£7,912 (£2,337; £1,168; £585; £292)

Form RPR

0/3- 1 **Gas Line Boy (IRE)**35 1709 7-11-9 127 RichardJohnson 137+
(Philip Hobbs) *hld up towards rr: hdwy after 11th: jnd ldrs after 13th: rdn and 2 l down 2 out: looking hld fr next: styd on to ld sn after last: drvn out* 11/41

5FP/ 2 3½ **Rydalis (FR)**220 5015 8-10-11 115 AidanColeman 123+
(Venetia Williams) *trckd ldr: led 6th: jnd after 13th tl rdn 2 l clr 4 out: wnt rt and slow last: sn hdd: no ex* 15/2

453/ 3 14 **Arkose (IRE)**193 5549 9-11-2 120 (p) LeightonAspell 112
(Oliver Sherwood) *nt a fluent: hld up: pushed along after 10th: rdn and hdwy 4 out: wnt 3rd next: nvr threatened ldng pair: styd on same pce* 5/13

0/3- 4 8 **Regal Presence (IRE)**168 422 6-11-0 118 (p) JackDoyle 104
(Victor Dartnall) *trckd ldrs tl rdn and outpcd after 13th: plugged on fr 3 out: wnt 4th run-in* 12/1

/1F- 5 1½ **Well Hello There (IRE)**23 1888 7-11-11 129 (tp) APMcCoy 115
(Jonjo O'Neill) *in tch: taking clsr order whn blnd bdly 10th: upsides ldrs after 13th tl rdn bef next: grad fdd* 4/12

4F/- 6 hd **Mr Gardner (IRE)**212 5199 10-11-7 130 MrSWaley-Cohen(5) 116
(Polly Gundry) *t.k.h: led tl 6th: w ldr tl after 10th: rdn after 13th: sn outpcd: plugged on fr 3 out* 14/1

U14/ 7 1 1/4 **Alderluck (IRE)**[251] 4457 10-11-10 **128**......................(p) TomScudamore 112
(David Pipe) *in tch: struggling after 12th and lost pl: styd on again fr after 4 out: hit 2 out: no ex fr last* **14/1**

U/1- 8 15 **Kind Of Easy (IRE)**[13] 2017 7-11-4 **125**......................(p) GavinSheehan(3) 102
(Emma Lavelle) *trckd ldrs: nt a fluent: lost pl and struggling 12th: wknd 4 out: mstke next* **4/1**[2]

6m 14.5s (5.20) **Going Correction** -0.275s/f (Good) **8** Ran SP% **116.1**
Speed ratings (Par 107): **80,78,74,71,71 70,70,65**
toteswingers 1&2 £5.30, 1&3 £2.70, 2&3 £1.50 CSF £23.95 CT £98.54 TOTE £4.00: £1.30, £2.60, £1.80; EX 24.80 Trifecta £140.60 Pool: £3599.33 - 19.19 winning units..
Owner Mick Fitzgerald Racing Club **Bred** Mrs Mary Fouhy **Trained** Withycombe, Somerset
■ Bendant was withdrawn. Price at time of withdrawal 14-1. Rule 4 does not apply.

FOCUS
This proved a thorough test at the distance and the front pair, although tired, ended up well clear. The winner builto on his good recent chase debut.

2284 CHRISTMAS PARTIES HERE H'CAP HURDLE (12 hdls) 2m 7f 110y
4:20 (4:25) (Class 4) (0-115,115) 4-Y-0+ **£3,249** (£954; £477; £238)

Form RPR

2/2- 1 **Royal Native (IRE)**[32] 1747 5-11-6 **112**......................(t) RachaelGreen(3) 116
(Anthony Honeyball) *pressed ldr: drew clr w ldr after 7th tl after 10th: led 3 out: sn rdn: styd on wl: rdn out* **8/1**

312- 2 1 **Tarvini (IRE)**[35] 1707 8-10-13 **112**......................(p) PatrickCowley(10) 115
(Jonjo O'Neill) *mid-div: hdwy after 10th: wnt 2nd 3 out: chalng whn mstke 2 out: hld after: kpt on same pce* **10/1**

132/ 3 2 1/4 **Storm Alert**[231] 4857 6-11-1 **109**...................... MissLucyGardner(5) 111
(Sue Gardner) *hld up in mid-div: hdwy after 10th: rdn to chse ldrs after 3 out: styd on to go 3rd at the last: fin wl* **7/1**

545- 4 5 **Cute Court (IRE)**[35] 1706 6-10-6 **95**...................... ConorO'Farrell 91
(Liam Corcoran) *hld up bhd: hdwy after 10th: rdn bef 3 out: styd on wl fr 2 out but nvr rching ldrs* **50/1**

616/ 5 3/4 **Cloudingstar (IRE)**[220] 5021 6-11-5 **108**...................... RichieMcLernon 106+
(Jonjo O'Neill) *hld up in last trio: hdwy after 8th: trckd ldrs after 10th: rdn bef 3 out: sn one pce* **12/1**

3/3- 6 hd **Fix It Right (IRE)**[35] 1707 5-11-5 **111**...................... GavinSheehan(3) 106
(Emma Lavelle) *trckd ldrs: led 6th: drew clr w one other after 7th tl after 10th: rdn and hdd bef 3 out: lost 3rd at the last: wknd* **7/2**[1]

/56- 7 20 **Bygones Sovereign (IRE)**[17] 1972 7-11-12 **115**.......(p) TomScudamore 92
(David Pipe) *led tl 6th: chsd ldrs tl rdn after 10th: sn wknd: t.o* **11/2**[3]

F/0- 8 1 1/2 **Thedeboftheyear**[21] 1917 9-10-9 **98**......................(t) JamesDavies 73
(Chris Down) *mid-div: trckd ldrs 6th: rdn after 10th: wknd 3 out: t.o* **16/1**

4PP/ 9 1/2 **Gran Torino (IRE)**[234] 4782 8-11-10 **113**...................... PaulMoloney 88
(Evan Williams) *hld up and a in rr: t.o* **20/1**

/35- 10 1/2 **Barton Jubilee**[19] 1941 5-11-8 **111**......................(t) NoelFehily 85
(Neil Mulholland) *mid-div: rdn after 10th: wknd 3 out: t.o* **10/1**

514/ 11 36 **Tolkeins Tango (IRE)**[220] 5019 5-11-10 **113**...................... JackDoyle 55
(Victor Dartnall) *trckd ldrs: rdn after 9th: sn btn: t.o* **9/2**[2]

440- F **Mixed Meaning (IRE)**[169] 407 5-10-0 **89** oh25..........(p) BrendanPowell
(Stuart Howe) *mid-div: rdn in last trio 7th: fell 9th* **100/1**

5m 52.4s (-6.60) **Going Correction** -0.65s/f (Firm) **12** Ran SP% **118.9**
Speed ratings (Par 105): **85,84,83,82,82 81,75,74,74,74 62,**
toteswingers 1&2 £9.90, 1&3 £5.80, 2&3 £3.40 CSF £84.10 CT £594.42 TOTE £10.00: £3.00, £2.60, £2.10; EX 65.50 Trifecta £157.00 Pool: £3052.29 - 14.57 winning units..
Owner Michael & Angela Bone **Bred** Paul Gibbons **Trained** Mosterton, Dorset

FOCUS
They got racing a fair way out here and it was yet another race in which they finished tired. The first two are rated prety much to their marks.
T/Plt: £153.20. Pool: £122,342.10 - 582.65 winning units. T/Qpdt: £33.40. Pool: £7933.20 - 175.50 winning units. TM

2076 CHEPSTOW (L-H)
Wednesday, November 6

OFFICIAL GOING: Heavy (soft in places; chs 5.7; hdl 5.1)
Wind: Brisk across Weather: Rain Rails: This is a test

2285 R.A.B.I. GATEWAY PROJECT MAIDEN HURDLE (11 hdls) 2m 4f
1:10 (1:11) (Class 5) 4-Y-0+ **£1,949** (£572; £286; £143)

Form RPR

32/ 1 **Jean De Florette (IRE)**[221] 5018 6-11-0 0............. SamTwiston-Davies 115+
(Nigel Twiston-Davies) *t.k.h: hit 1st: trckd ldrs: hit 4 out: styng on strly whn hit 2 out: led last: readily* **3/1**[2]

606- 2 3 **Johnny Og**[11] 2079 4-11-0 0...................... IanPopham 110
(Martin Keighley) *t.k.h: led to 3rd: styd chsng ldr tl led appr 4 out: hit 2 out: hdd last: sn outpcd by wnr but kpt on wl for 2nd* **11/4**[1]

154- 3 2 1/4 **Man Of Steel (IRE)**[13] 2049 4-11-0 0......................(p) DonalDevereux 107
(Peter Bowen) *chsd ldrs: rdn 3 out: kpt on u.p fr 2 out but no imp on ldng duo run-in* **12/1**

0- 4 1/2 **Filatore (IRE)**[12] 1793 4-10-9 0......................(p) RobertWilliams(5) 106
(Bernard Llewellyn) *t.k.h: chsd ldrs: wnt 2nd briefly and rdn 3 out: styd on same pce after 2 out* **20/1**

- 5 13 **El Macca (IRE)** 4-11-0 0...................... APMcCoy 101+
(Rebecca Curtis) *in tch: hdwy and nt fluent 4 out: wknd and j. slowly 2 out: wl hld whn nt fluent last* **7/2**[3]

/U0- 6 29 **Echoes Of Joy**[14] 2028 4-11-0 0...................... SeanQuinlan 64
(David Evans) *in rr: blnd 4th: mod prgress past btn horses fr 2 out: t.o* **100/1**

46/ 7 2 **Wing Mira (IRE)**[219] 5070 5-11-0 0...................... AidanColeman 62
(Venetia Williams) *hit 2nd: in tch: sme hdwy whn j. slowly 4 out: sn wknd: t.o* **8/1**

0/ 8 3 1/2 **Lucas Pitt**[442] 1315 6-11-0 0...................... LiamTreadwell 59
(Michael Scudamore) *a in rr: t.o* **100/1**

0- 9 11 **Alwayslookback (IRE)**[28] 1826 4-10-9 0...................... BenPoste(5) 48
(Rosemary Gasson) *blnd 1st: rdr lost irons: rcvrd and led 3rd: hdd & wknd qckly appr 4 out* **100/1**

10 20 **Elysian Heights (IRE)**[347] 5-11-0 0...................... TomCannon 28
(David Bridgwater) *j. modly in rr: sme hdwy appr 4 out: sn btn* **66/1**

245- F **Dazinski**[11] 2073 7-11-0 114...................... WillKennedy 83
(Sarah-Jayne Davies) *chsd ldrs: wknd bef 3 out: no ch whn fell last* **6/1**

5m 15.35s (13.55) **Going Correction** +0.525s/f (Soft) **11** Ran SP% **116.2**
Speed ratings (Par 103): **93,91,90,90,85 73,73,71,67,59**
toteswingers 1&2 £3.70, 1&3 £7.40, 2&3 £5.10 CSF £11.65 TOTE £4.10: £1.40, £1.70, £2.80; EX 17.00 Trifecta £85.90 Pool: £1234.35 - 10.75 winning units..
Owner Alan Parker **Bred** A Parker **Trained** Naunton, Gloucs

FOCUS
The jockeys reported the ground was heavy but they were getting through it, with the hurdles down the back straight on fresh ground before it got heavier in the straight. The time for the opener, an ordinary maiden hurdle run at a pretty steady pace, was no less than 41sec slower than the RP standard. The winner built on his bumper form.

2286 R.A.B.I. MANSON HOUSE "NATIONAL HUNT" MAIDEN HURDLE (8 hdls) 2m 110y
1:40 (1:42) (Class 5) 4-Y-0+ **£1,949** (£572; £286; £143)

Form RPR

12/ 1 **Vice Et Vertu (FR)**[197] 5469 4-11-0 0...................... RichardJohnson 115+
(Henry Daly) *trckd ldr to 4 out: chal fr 3 out tl led last: sn rdn: edgd rt: styd on strly* **5/2**[2]

/16- 2 1 1/4 **Regal Diamond (IRE)**[18] 1974 5-11-0 0...................... TomO'Brien 114+
(Peter Bowen) *chsd ldrs: wnt 2nd 4 out: chal fr next tl slt ld but hrd pressed after 2 out: hdd last: styd on same pce* **7/4**[1]

245- 3 1 1/4 **Never Says Never**[20] 1946 5-11-0 100...................... SamJones 110
(Bob Buckler) *chsd ldrs: outpcd 3 out: styd on again after 2 out: kpt on clsng stages but nt trble ldng duo* **14/1**

4 nk **Tribulation (IRE)** 5-11-0 0...................... DougieCostello 110
(Robert Walford) *in rr: stdy hdwy fr 2 out: kpt on run-in: gng on clsng stages* **50/1**

20/ 5 9 **Expanding Universe (IRE)**[213] 5195 6-11-0 122... SamTwiston-Davies 101
(Tony Carroll) *led: narrowly hdd 3 out: sn outpcd but kpt on again appr last* **11/4**[3]

0- 6 4 **Midnight Request**[20] 1935 4-10-9 0...................... BenPoste(5) 97
(Tom Symonds) *hit 1st: in tch: rdn 3 out and no prog* **100/1**

7 nk **Bajan Blu**[592] 5-11-0 0...................... DonalDevereux 96
(David Brace) *chsd ldrs: slt ld but hrd pressed fr 3 out tl hdd & wknd sn after 2 out* **50/1**

0/0- 8 6 **Ghost Of A Smile (IRE)**[31] 1795 5-11-0 0...................... WillKennedy 90
(Ian Williams) *t.k.h: sme hdwy 4 out: wknd sn after* **20/1**

40/- 9 3 3/4 **Two Mile Bridge (IRE)**[459] 1179 7-10-7 0...................... NickScholfield 80
(Paul Henderson) *bhd most of way* **33/1**

0/0- 10 19 **Kill Van Kull (IRE)**[11] 2089 4-10-7 0...................... MrMatthewBarber(7) 68
(Marc Barber) *hit 4 out: a in rr* **100/1**

066/ 11 1 1/4 **Aldeburgh**[199] 5441 4-11-0 0...................... MarkGrant 66
(Jim Old) *in tch tl wknd 4 out* **66/1**

4/3- 12 9 **Indiefront**[166] 462 4-10-7 0...................... DominicElsworth 50
(Jo Davis) *a in rr* **40/1**

064/ 13 nse **Miss Tilly Dove**[315] 3208 5-10-4 0...................... RobertDunne(3) 50
(Andrew Price) *hit 2nd: chsd ldrs tl wknd 4 out* **66/1**

0/0- 14 2 1/4 **Hunky Dorey**[8] 2147 7-11-0 0...................... AidanColeman 55
(Marc Barber) *a in rr* **100/1**

4m 18.24s (7.64) **Going Correction** +0.525s/f (Soft)
WFA 4 from 5yo+ 7lb **14** Ran SP% **118.3**
Speed ratings (Par 103): **103,102,101,101,97 95,95,92,90,81 81,77,77,75**
toteswingers 1&2 £1.70, 1&3 £9.10, 2&3 £5.50 CSF £6.94 TOTE £2.90: £1.40, £1.10, £2.40; EX 9.10 Trifecta £44.10 Pool: £1317.70 - 22.39 winning units..
Owner Neville Statham & Family **Bred** R Reveillere Et Al **Trained** Stanton Lacy, Shropshire

FOCUS
Another steadily run race, but one that should produce winners. A step up from the winner on his bumper form.

2287 OVERLEC LTD SUPPORTS R.A.B.I. NOVICES' LIMITED H'CAP CHASE (12 fncs) 2m 110y
2:10 (2:11) (Class 3) (0-125,125) 4-Y-0+ **£6,498** (£1,908; £954; £477)

Form RPR

0/F- 1 **Flaming Charmer (IRE)**[15] 2012 5-10-9 **115**.................. BrendanPowell 128+
(Colin Tizzard) *in tch: hit 6th and lost position: hdwy 8th: chsd ldr 4 out: chal 2 out: sn led: c clr run-in: easily* **5/1**[3]

0/P- 2 9 **Un Bon P'Tit Gars (FR)**[167] 455 5-11-5 **125**............... RichardJohnson 128+
(Nick Williams) *led: hit 3 out: jnd next: sn hdd: no ch w wnr last but styd on wl for clr 2nd* **9/2**[2]

3 6 **Sands Cove (IRE)**[104] 1115 6-11-2 **122**...................... MarkGrant 115
(Charlie Mann) *chsd ldr 5th to 8th: rdn 4 out: styd on same pce fr next* **5/1**[3]

546/ 4 1/2 **Regal One (IRE)**[272] 4089 5-10-8 **114**...................... SeanQuinlan 109
(David Bridgwater) *in rr: hdwy 8th: slipped and mstke 4 out: hit 2 out: styd on wl run-in: gng on clsng stages* **20/1**

412- 5 2 3/4 **Roger Beantown (IRE)**[109] 1049 8-11-5 **125**...................... DaveCrosse 118
(Zoe Davison) *chsd ldr 4th: blnd next: mstke and rdn 8th: sn outpcd: kpt on again run-in* **14/1**

6- 6 1 **Vesperal Dream (FR)**[26] 1857 4-10-8 **122**...................... NickScholfield 103
(Paul Nicholls) *chsd ldrs: lost pl 4 out: styd on again last* **4/1**[1]

121- 7 3 **Red Riverman**[15] 2012 5-11-5 **125**...................... SamTwiston-Davies 113
(Nigel Twiston-Davies) *in rr: rdn 4 out: sme hdwy 3 out: nvr rchd ldrs and no ch fr 2 out* **4/1**[1]

344- 8 42 **Grey Soldier (IRE)**[13] 2041 8-10-6 **112**......................(t) PaulMoloney 56
(Sophie Leech) *sn bhd: t.o fr 7th* **9/1**

4m 22.77s (5.67) **Going Correction** +0.525s/f (Soft)
WFA 4 from 5yo+ 7lb **8** Ran SP% **112.9**
Speed ratings (Par 107): **107,102,99,99,98 97,96,76**
toteswingers 1&2 £4.30, 1&3 £11.00, 2&3 £18.60 CSF £27.50 CT £116.66 TOTE £6.20: £1.70, £1.90, £1.80; EX 25.50 Trifecta £257.40 Pool: £1297.70 - 3.78 winning units..
Owner Tom Chadney & Peter Green **Bred** Mrs Brid McCrea **Trained** Milborne Port, Dorset

FOCUS
A fair race of its type. Big steps up from the first two on their hurdles form.

2288 NFU MUTUAL SUPPORTS R.A.B.I. H'CAP HURDLE (THE £5K BONUS RACE) (12 hdls) 3m
2:40 (2:42) (Class 3) (0-125,125) 4-Y-0+ **£5,393** (£1,583; £791; £395)

Form RPR

021- 1 **Minella For Steak (IRE)**[8] 2150 6-11-5 **118** 7ex.................(tp) APMcCoy 125+
(Jonjo O'Neill) *trckd ldr: hit 6th: slt ld fr 4 out: hrd pressed tl drvn to assert after 2 out: jnd again last: rdn and fnd ex run-in* **3/1**[1]

11U/ 2 3/4 **Heronshaw (IRE)**[257] 4371 6-11-5 **118**...................... TomO'Brien 124+
(Henry Daly) *chsd ldrs: blnd and lost position 4 out: hdwy fr 2 out: rdn to chal last: no ex and one pce run-in* **9/2**[2]

120/ 3 15 **Qalinas (FR)**[203] 5354 6-11-0 **123**......................(bt) AnthonyFox(10) 113
(David Pipe) *chsd ldrs: led 3rd: narrowly hdd 8th but styd upsides and ev ch fr 4 out to 2 out: one pce into 3rd sn after* **20/1**

01/ 4 9 **Manballandall (IRE)**[229] 4901 5-11-12 **125**..................(t) TimmyMurphy 107
(Fergal O'Brien) *in rr: hdwy after 8th: styd far side: rdn 3 out and no ch w ldrs after* **16/1**

0/5- **5** *2* **Alberobello (IRE)**[14] 2020 5-10-12 **118**..........................(t) MissVWade[7] 96
(Jeremy Scott) *chsd ldrs tl dropped to rr 8th: styd on again after 3 out and kpt on run-in but nvr any ch* **14/1**

1/ **6** *13* **Minellahalfcentury (IRE)**[263] 4257 5-11-7 **120**............... NickScholfield 88
(Paul Nicholls) *chsd ldrs: hit 6th: chal 4 out: wknd next* **11/2**[3]

/UP- **7** *3 ½* **Virginia Ash (IRE)**[27] 1831 5-11-3 **116**..........................(b) BrendanPowell 78
(Colin Tizzard) *in rr: hit 3rd: hdwy 5th: hit 8th and sn btn* **33/1**

133- **8** *6* **Cardigan Island (IRE)**[20] 1944 8-10-10 **112**..............(tp) RobertDunne[3] 68
(Dai Burchell) *in tch: wknd 4 out: hit next* **25/1**

212/ **9** *10* **Promised Wings (GER)**[213] 5200 6-11-9 **122**..................(v) TomCannon 68
(Chris Gordon) *chsd ldrs: narrow ld 8th: hdd 4 out and sn wknd* **16/1**

P04/ **10** *9* **Mic's Delight (IRE)**[206] 5308 9-11-8 **121**................................ JackDoyle 58
(Victor Dartnall) *in rr: hdwy 8th: chsd ldrs 4 out: wknd sn after* **10/1**

650/ **11** *2 ¼* **Old Tricks (IRE)**[193] 5574 6-11-9 **122**....................................(t) JoeTizzard 56
(Colin Tizzard) *bhd most of way* **12/1**

/00- **12** *4* **Mauricetheathlete (IRE)**[31] 1797 10-10-12 **118**................ NickSlatter[7] 48
(Martin Keighley) *led to 3rd: styd pressing ldr to 5th: wknd after 8th* **14/1**

15/ **13** *16* **Woodford County**[241] 4685 6-11-8 **121**........................ RichardJohnson 35
(Philip Hobbs) *in tch: hit 5th and 7th: wknd 8th* **16/1**

6m 24.56s (22.36) **Going Correction** +0.825s/f (Soft) **13** Ran SP% **117.9**
Speed ratings (Par 107): **95,94,89,86,86 81,80,78,75,72 71,70,64**
toteswingers 1&2 £4.30, 1&3 £11.00, 2&3 £18.60 CSF £16.23 CT £230.48 TOTE £3.70: £1.40, £2.20, £8.40; EX 18.60 Trifecta £329.40 Pool: £1330.64 - 3.02 winning units..
Owner Mrs Gay Smith & Mrs John Magnier **Bred** D Harnett **Trained** Cheltenham, Gloucs

FOCUS
Quite a competitive handicap hurdle, in which the first two drew clear over the final three flights. They're both on the upgrade.

2289 FARMERS' UNION OF WALES SUPPORT R.A.B.I. H'CAP HURDLE (11 hdls) 2m 4f
3:15 (3:15) (Class 5) (0-95,96) 4-Y-0+ **£1,949** (£572; £286; £143)

Form RPR

0/1- **1** **Brave Buck**[8] 2148 5-12-2 **96** 7ex.................................. RichardJohnson 104+
(Henry Daly) *mde all: drvn 2 out: forged clr run-in: styd on strly* **5/4**[1]

554- **2** *6* **Pirans Car**[15] 2013 7-11-7 **87**..................................(t) SamTwiston-Davies 88
(Nigel Hawke) *in tch: hit 3rd: hdwy 5th: chsd wnr 3 out: effrt to chal after 2 out: imp and one pce run-in* **8/1**

/02- **3** *9* **Jeanry (FR)**[54] 1582 10-11-1 **88**.. JoshWall[7] 81
(Arthur Whitehead) *chsd ldrs: wnt 2nd after 7th: sn rdn and no imp on wnr: wknd into 3rd fr 2 out* **6/1**[3]

000/ **4** *29* **Radical Impact (IRE)**[231] 4873 5-10-8 **74**........................ AidanColeman 41
(Venetia Williams) *in tch tl j. slowly and bhd 7th: sn drvn: styd on u.p for mod 4th cl home* **11/4**[2]

0/U- **5** *¾* **Salut L'As (FR)**[15] 2011 7-11-10 **90**.................................... WillKennedy 52
(Sue Gardner) *t.k.h: chsd ldr to 7th: wknd bef 4 out* **33/1**

460- **6** *nk* **Bolberry Springs**[20] 1941 6-11-6 **86**.. JoeTizzard 48
(Colin Tizzard) *in rr but in tch: j. slowly 6th: sme hdwy 7th: wknd bef 4 out* **8/1**

001/ **P** **Flora Lea**[230] 4880 6-11-9 **92**.. RobertDunne[3]
(Andrew Price) *chsd ldrs: wknd after 7th: t.o whn p.u after 2 out* **20/1**

5m 17.77s (15.97) **Going Correction** +0.825s/f (Soft) **7** Ran SP% **115.3**
Speed ratings (Par 103): **101,98,95,83,83 82,**
CSF £12.20 TOTE £2.40: £2.00, £3.60; EX 13.00 Trifecta £31.30 Pool: £2097.53 - 50.14 winning units..
Owner P E Truscott **Bred** Mr & Mrs P E Truscott **Trained** Stanton Lacy, Shropshire

FOCUS
Not much depth to this handicap hurdle. The winner can rate higher.

2290 HSBC AGRICULTURE SUPPORTS R.A.B.I. H'CAP CHASE (18 fncs) 3m
3:50 (3:50) (Class 4) (0-105,102) 4-Y-0+ **£3,768** (£1,106; £553; £276)

Form RPR

003- **1** **Stormyisland Ahead**[76] 1344 8-11-6 **96**...........................(t) PaulMoloney 105+
(Evan Williams) *in rr: hit 4th: hdwy 13th: chsd ldr 4 out: chal last: led sn after: drvn out* **14/1**

4/2- **2** *1 ¼* **Merlin's Wish**[175] 321 8-11-10 **100**...................................... IanPopham 108+
(Martin Keighley) *led 3rd tl appr 8th: led 9th: hdd next: blnd and lost pl 4 out: rallied fr 2 out: styd on run-in to go 2nd clsng stages: nt rch wnr* **5/1**[1]

121/ **3** *2 ¼* **Loughalder (IRE)**[208] 5270 7-11-10 **100**..........................(tp) CharliePoste 104
(Matt Sheppard) *chsd ldrs: led appr 14th: rdn 3 out: jnd last: sn hdd: no ex and lost 2nd clsng stages* **7/1**[2]

2/5- **4** *2 ½* **Royal Chatelier (FR)**[10] 2110 8-11-9 **102**.................... MichealNolan[3] 103
(Michael Blake) *led to 3rd: chsd ldrs: rdn appr 14th: styd on again fr 2 out: kpt on same pce run-in* **20/1**

P06- **5** *40* **River D'Or (FR)**[19] 1959 8-11-4 **99**.................................. CharlieWallis[5] 59
(Sophie Leech) *bhd fr 10th: t.o* **5/1**[1]

/P2- **6** *½* **Flugzeug**[11] 2082 5-10-0 **83**.. KevinJones[7] 43
(Seamus Mullins) *chsd ldrs: led 10th: hdd appr 14th: sn wknd* **10/1**

6/6- **P** **Lupita (IRE)**[166] 461 9-10-0 **76** oh8..................................(t) BrendanPowell
(Derrick Scott) *a in rr: t.o whn p.u bef 4 out* **50/1**

P30/ **P** **Peut Etre Sivola (FR)**[201] 5377 10-11-5 **102**........(bt) MrRobertHawker[7]
(Johnny Farrelly) *blnd 1st: chsd ldrs: rdn 11ith: sn bhd: t.o whn p.u bef 3 out* **7/1**[2]

/03- **P** **Notabotheronme (IRE)**[11] 2082 11-9-12 **77**...............(p) RobertDunne[3]
(Dai Burchell) *hit 7th: bhd fr 10th: t.o whn p.u bef 3 out* **16/1**

066/ **P** **Elite Beneficial (IRE)**[237] 4761 8-10-3 **84**........................ BenPoste[5]
(Rosemary Gasson) *in rr: sme hdwy 10th: wknd 13th: t.o whn p.u bef 2 out* **8/1**[3]

/0P- **P** **Sandynow (IRE)**[108] 1055 8-11-7 **97**..................................(p) TomO'Brien
(Peter Bowen) *chsd ldrs: led appr 8th to 9th: chal after 13th tl wknd 14th: tailed fof whn p.u bef 2 out* **5/1**[1]

P5P- **P** **Thehorsemaytalk (IRE)**[37] 1701 8-9-11 **76** oh6..........(v) MarkQuinlan[3]
(Mark Shears) *j. bdly in rr tl p.u after 7th* **25/1**

6m 43.09s (21.09) **Going Correction** +0.825s/f (Soft) **12** Ran SP% **118.3**
Speed ratings (Par 105): **97,96,95,95,81 81, , , ,**
CSF £82.70 CT £544.22 TOTE £18.60: £5.40, £2.30, £3.70; EX 86.20 Trifecta £554.50 Pool: £2508.87 - 3.39 winning units..
Owner David M Williams **Bred** R D And Mrs J S Chugg **Trained** Llancarfan, Vale Of Glamorgan

FOCUS
A modest handicap chase in which the emphasis was firmly on stamina. The first four finished clear. The winner was on a good mark and is rated back to form.

2291 R.A.B.I. BEAUFORT HOUSE H'CAP HURDLE (8 hdls) 2m 110y
4:20 (4:22) (Class 5) (0-95,95) 4-Y-0+ **£1,949** (£572; £286; £143)

Form RPR

243/ **1** **Bathwick Junior**[240] 4704 6-11-1 **84**................................. NickScholfield 93+
(Michael Blake) *chsd ldrs: wnt 2nd after 4 out: led after 2 out: drvn run-in: readily* **9/1**

640- **2** *2 ½* **Pagham Belle**[31] 1799 5-10-9 **81**....................................(t) MarkQuinlan[3] 85
(Nigel Hawke) *chsd ldr fr 3rd: led 4 out but hrd pressed: hdd after 2 out: styd on but nt pce of wnr* **8/1**

013- **3** *1* **Ivebeenthinking**[16] 2004 5-10-6 **80**....................................... BenPoste[5] 82
(Tom Symonds) *in rr but in tch: hdwy appr 4 out: chsd ldrs fr next: kpt on u.p run-in but nt gng pce of ldng duo* **5/1**[2]

2/2- **4** *1 ¾* **Meirig's Dream (IRE)**[16] 2004 7-10-8 **77**............................ JamesDavies 78
(Philip Hobbs) *in tch chsd ldrs fr 4 out: styd on fr 2 out: kpt on run-in but nvr gng pce to rch ldrs* **6/1**[3]

/05- **5** *3 ¾* **Old Magic (IRE)**[13] 2045 8-11-4 **87**...................................... PaulMoloney 86
(Sophie Leech) *led: hdd 4 out: blnd next: kpt on but no ch after* **9/2**[1]

004- **6** *2 ¼* **No Ifs No Buts**[14] 2016 4-10-6 **82**..................................(p) JakeHodson[7] 76
(David Bridgwater) *sn in tch: chsd ldrs 4 out: wknd fr 2 out* **20/1**

200- **7** *4 ½* **Chankillo**[14] 2016 4-11-5 **88**.. SamTwiston-Davies 78
(Sarah-Jayne Davies) *in tch but rdn along 2nd: sn wl in tch: rdn 4 out and no ch after* **16/1**

F44- **8** *6* **Cash Injection**[27] 1833 4-11-1 **91**...................................(t) TomBellamy[7] 75
(Richard Woollacott) *chsd ldrs to 4 out* **20/1**

400- **9** *2* **Kimora (IRE)**[8] 2148 7-11-5 **95**.................................. MrMatthewBarber[7] 77
(Marc Barber) *in rr: mod prog 4 out: no ch after* **50/1**

103/ **10** *4 ½* **Todareistodo**[208] 5268 7-11-9 **92**.. MarkGrant 69
(Jim Old) *in rr: hdwy 4 out: sn wknd* **10/1**

F46- **11** *11* **Rigid**[11] 2090 6-11-8 **91**... LeeEdwards 57
(Tony Carroll) *bhd fr 4th* **33/1**

F50- **12** *12* **Clear Mix**[14] 2027 5-10-11 **80**.. WillKennedy 34
(Sue Gardner) *bhd most of way* **33/1**

0- **13** *12* **Spunky**[11] 2083 4-11-7 **90**.. AidanColeman 32
(Marc Barber) *a in rr* **50/1**

060- **14** *12* **Dont Call Me Oscar (IRE)**[25] 1863 6-10-12 **86**.........(t) PatrickCorbett[5] 16
(Mark Gillard) *in rr: hdwy 4th: sn wknd* **16/1**

344/ **P** **Out Of Nothing**[381] 847 10-11-5 **91**................................ RobertDunne[3]
(Dai Burchell) *hit 2nd: chsd ldrs: wknd after 4th: t.o whn p.u bef last* **20/1**

212/ **P** **Admiral Blake**[201] 5381 6-10-6 **75**...................................... DougieCostello
(Laura Young) *sn bhd: t.o whn p.u after 3 out* **7/1**

4m 23.91s (13.31) **Going Correction** +0.825s/f (Soft)
WFA 4 from 5yo+ 7lb **16** Ran SP% **127.7**
Speed ratings (Par 103): **101,99,99,98,96 95,93,90,89,87 82,76,71,65,**
CSF £77.10 CT £412.84 TOTE £9.10: £2.60, £4.30, £1.70, £2.60; EX 143.80 Trifecta £664.90 Pool: £1752.18 - 1.97 winning units..
Owner Wayne Clifford **Bred** Mrs S Clifford **Trained** Trowbridge, Wilts

FOCUS
This moderate handicap was run in decidedly gloomy conditions, but the form seems sound enough. Steps up from the first two.
T/Plt: £43.60 to a £1 stake. Pool: £91571.28 - 1529.99 winning tickets T/Qpdt: £23.70 to a £1 stake. Pool: £6474.30 - 201.90 winning tickets ST

WARWICK (L-H)
Wednesday, November 6

OFFICIAL GOING: Good changing to good to soft after race 1 (12:50)
Wind: Light behind Weather: Light rain

2292 FOLLOW US ON TWITTER @WARWICKRACES H'CAP HURDLE (8 hdls) 2m
12:50 (12:51) (Class 4) (0-110,110) 4-Y-0+ **£3,119** (£915; £457; £228)

Form RPR

233- **1** **Keel Haul (IRE)**[85] 1256 5-10-9 **100**......................... ChristopherWard[7] 110+
(Henry Oliver) *mid-div: hdwy 5th: rdn and mstke 2 out: lft 2nd last: str run to ld towards fin* **4/1**[1]

/44- **2** *1 ¼* **Shady Lane**[173] 353 6-11-1 **99**.. RobertThornton 108+
(Alan King) *hld up: hdwy 5th: rdn and hit 2 out: 2 l down whn lft in ld last: hdd towards fin* **13/2**[2]

P40- **3** *9* **Court In Session (IRE)**[18] 1972 8-11-12 **110**.................. JasonMaguire 109
(Martin Keighley) *chsd ldr tl led 3 out: rdn and hdd bef next: lft 3rd and wknd last* **15/2**

/2F- **4** *2* **Who's Jeff (IRE)**[28] 1816 5-10-13 **107**......................[1] JonathanMoore[10] 104
(Philip Hobbs) *hld up: racd keenly: hdwy after 2nd: rdn and wknd after 3 out* **8/1**

F/0- **5** *10* **Nether Stream (IRE)**[13] 2045 9-11-10 **108**...................... TomMessenger 96
(David Dennis) *hld up: nt fluent 3 out: sn rdn: nvr nrr* **100/1**

146- **6** *shd* **Ironical (IRE)**[50] 1597 9-11-3 **101**.................................(t) TomScudamore 89
(Shaun Lycett) *prom tl rdn and wknd after 3 out* **8/1**

060/ **7** *2 ¾* **Graylyn Ruby (FR)**[27] 2637 8-9-4 **84** oh3............. JosephPalmowski[10] 70
(Robin Dickin) *chsd ldrs: rdn 5th: wknd after 3 out* **100/1**

160/ **8** *¾* **Minneapolis**[24] 5455 8-11-7 **105**...................................(t) LeightonAspell 90
(Alison Batchelor) *hld up: rdn appr 3 out: n.d* **66/1**

406- **9** *½* **Laurens Ruby (IRE)**[28] 1814 4-11-2 **100**................................ RhysFlint 84
(John Flint) *chsd ldrs: ev ch 3 out: sn rdn and wknd* **50/1**

265- **10** *1 ½* **Taroum (IRE)**[27] 1840 6-11-3 **101**.. LeeEdwards 84
(Tony Carroll) *mid-div: rdn after 5th: wknd 3 out* **7/1**[3]

2/1- **11** *1 ¾* **Pret A Thou (FR)**[161] 537 10-11-5 **108**.........................(p) HarryChalloner[5] 89
(John Bryan Groucott) *led to 3 out: wknd bef next* **16/1**

/00- **12** *7* **Dealing River**[22] 1913 6-11-12 **110**...................................... AndrewThornton 85
(Caroline Bailey) *in rr and pushed along after 3rd: bhd fr next* **20/1**

/PP- **13** *¾* **Cape Schanck**[22] 1915 9-10-4 **88**......................................(t) JamesDavies 62
(Alan Coogan) *prom to 5th* **100/1**

4UP/ **14** *12* **Arte Del Calcio**[50] 4662 4-10-11 **100**.................................. JoshHamer[5] 64
(Tony Carroll) *hld up and a in rr* **33/1**

5/0- **F** **Luggers Hall (IRE)**[33] 1378 5-11-6 **104**................................... NoelFehily
(Tony Carroll) *hld up: pushed along in rr whn stmbld and fell bef 5th: fatally injured* **8/1**

3/0- **F** **Watt Broderick (IRE)**[26] 1319 4-10-5 **94**..................(t) RobertMcCarth(5) 104
(Ian Williams) *hld up: racd keenly: hdwy 5th: led appr 2 out: shkn up and 2 l ahd whn slipped and fell last* **10/1**

3m 39.2s (-17.30) **Going Correction** -0.975s/f (Hard)
WFA 4 from 5yo+ 7lb **16** Ran SP% **120.0**
Speed ratings (Par 105): **104,103,98,97,92 92,91,91,90,90 89,85,85,79,**
toteswingers 1&2 £4.60, 1&3 £5.90, 2&3 £14.30 CSF £28.49 CT £189.86 TOTE £5.60: £1.50, £1.70, £2.20, £2.70; EX 27.00 Trifecta £57.40 Pool: £669.71 - 8.74 winning units..
Owner R G Whitehead **Bred** Aaron Stronge **Trained** Broomhall, Worcs

FOCUS
This competitive, if only moderate handicap hurdle, was run in steady rain on deteriorating ground. The market, albeit wide open, was headed by a couple of handicap debutants and the race planned out exactly to plan for punters. A personal best from the winner under a claimer.

2293 STRIDE INSURANCE GROUP H'CAP CHASE (17 fncs) 2m 4f 110y
1:20 (1:20) (Class 4) (0-120,122) 4-Y-0+ **£3,833** (£1,125; £562; £281)

Form RPR
/40- **1** **Rockchasebullett (IRE)**[20] 1939 5-10-6 **99**..................... PaddyBrennan 115+
(Fergal O'Brien) *mde all: shkn up appr 2 out: clr last: styd on wl* **17/2**

/41- **2** *10* **The Potting Shed (IRE)**[27] 1834 6-11-5 **115**............(p) GavinSheehan(3) 121
(Emma Lavelle) *hld up in tch: hmpd 2nd: rdn 14th: wnt 2nd last: no ex flat* **5/2**[2]

2/3- **3** *¾* **Ballywatt (IRE)**[187] 92 7-11-12 **119**..........................(tp) JasonMaguire 124
(Kim Bailey) *hld up: mstke 7th: hdwy after 3 out: chsd wnr next: sn rdn: no ex last* **5/1**[3]

/01- **4** *1* **Forest Walker (IRE)**[5] 2194 6-12-1 **122** 7ex....................... HarrySkelton 124
(Dan Skelton) *prom: lost pl appr 11th: hdwy 14th: rdn appr 2 out: styd on same pce* **15/8**[1]

623- **5** *3* **Tony Dinozzo (FR)**[43] 1645 6-10-10 **103**.........................(p) JamieMoore 105
(Peter Bowen) *chsd wnr: mstke 1st: blnd next: sn lost pl: wnt 2nd again 5th tl rdn appr 2 out: wknd bef last* **8/1**

505- **6** *4 ½* **George Nympton (IRE)**[14] 2025 7-11-10 **117**...................... NoelFehily 112
(Nick Williams) *prom: chsd wnr 3nd to 5th: remained handy tl rdn and wknd 2 out* **16/1**

4P1- **7** *2* **Balinroab (IRE)**[72] 1403 6-11-10 **117**............................... DenisO'Regan 111
(Richard Guest) *hld up: wknd after 3 out* **16/1**

244- **8** *1* **Trooper Clarence**[37] 1696 9-11-6 **113**................................ AdamWedge 106
(Evan Williams) *hld up: hdwy 11th: wknd after 3 out* **50/1**

5m 6.6s (-14.40) **Going Correction** -0.75s/f (Firm) **8** Ran SP% **115.4**
Speed ratings (Par 105): **97,93,92,91 89,88,88**
toteswingers 1&2 £3.40, 1&3 £6.30, 2&3 £1.90 CSF £31.57 CT £119.82 TOTE £10.60: £2.50, £1.20, £1.90; EX 37.60 Trifecta £225.70 Pool: £1153.02 - 3.83 winning units..
Owner The Yes No Wait Sorries **Bred** Patrick Kelly **Trained** Coln St. Dennis, Gloucs

FOCUS
The going was officially changed from good, to good to soft after the running of the opening handicap hurdle. This fair handicap chase included three last time out winners. A step up from the winner on the best of his hurdles form.

2294 ANIXTER PARTNERS TECHNOLOGY JUVENILE HURDLE (8 hdls) 2m
1:50 (1:52) (Class 4) 3-Y-O **£3,249** (£954; £477; £238)

Form RPR
21- **1** **Herod The Great**[20] 1934 3-11-5 122.............................. RobertThornton 125+
(Alan King) *mde all: set stdy pce tl qcknd appr 4th: pushed clr bef 2 out: j.lft last: styd on* **5/2**[2]

2 *6* **Cafe Au Lait (GER)**[17] 3-10-12 0.................................... TomScudamore 111
(C Von Der Recke, Germany) *racd keenly: hdwy to trck wnr and mstke 2nd: rdn whn j.lft and mstke 2 out: styd on same pce* **11/4**[3]

1- **3** *6* **Harristown**[26] 1855 3-11-5 0.. NoelFehily 114
(Charlie Longsdon) *chsd ldrs: pushed along after 5th: styd on same pce appr 2 out: mstke last* **11/8**[1]

4- **4** *10* **Handsome Stranger (IRE)**[17] 1985 3-10-12 0................ JamesDavies 97
(Alan Bailey) *hld up: hdwy after 3rd: rdn and wknd after 3 out* **16/1**

5 *35* **Collingbourneducis (IRE)**[22] 3-10-12 0........................... AdamWedge 65
(Michael Gates) *racd keenly: trckd wnr to 2nd: dropped to rr after next: rdn 5th: wknd bef 3 out* **50/1**

6 *55* **Caramack**[111] 3-10-12 0... JamieMoore 15
(Richard Lee) *hld up: wkng whn mstke 3 out* **16/1**

3m 43.1s (-13.40) **Going Correction** -0.75s/f (Firm) **6** Ran SP% **111.1**
Speed ratings (Par 104): **103,100,97,92,74 47**
toteswingers 1&2 £2.00, 1&3 £1.10, 2&3 £1.60 CSF £9.81 TOTE £2.50: £1.10, £1.70; EX 13.50 Trifecta £15.00 Pool: £1938.40 - 96.48 winning units..
Owner S M Smith & D Minton **Bred** Whitsbury Manor Stud **Trained** Barbury Castle, Wilts

FOCUS
An intriguing juvenile hurdle. A big step forward from the winner towards the level expected from the best of his Flat form.

2295 ANIXTER'S PARTNER DAY NOVICES' CHASE (12 fncs) 2m
2:20 (2:20) (Class 3) 4-Y-0+ **£7,147** (£2,098; £1,049; £524)

Form RPR
/1F- **1** **Balder Succes (FR)**[18] 1973 5-11-8 145........................ RobertThornton 153+
(Alan King) *trckd ldr tl led 6th: pushed clr appr 2 out: easily* **8/15**[1]

012- **2** *11* **Baby Mix (FR)**[134] 830 5-11-8 132.. NoelFehily 143+
(Warren Greatrex) *chsd ldrs: blnd 7th: wnt 2nd 4 out: outpcd appr 2 out* **9/2**[2]

3F2/ **3** *12* **Roc D'Apsis (FR)**[257] 4375 4-10-7 113............................. PaddyBrennan 114
(Tom George) *hld up: pushed along 6th: wknd after 3 out: wnt mod 3rd next* **8/1**

510/ **4** *4* **Buthelezi (USA)**[216] 5141 5-11-1 0..................................... DenisO'Regan 120
(John Ferguson) *led to 6th: mstke 9th: wknd after 3 out* **6/1**[3]

4/4- **5** *68* **Rebel High (IRE)**[177] 269 9-11-1 90..................................... DavidBass 57
(Derek Frankland) *in rr: nt fluent 2nd: bhd fr 5th* **100/1**

3m 49.2s (-16.40) **Going Correction** -0.75s/f (Firm)
WFA 4 from 5yo+ 7lb **5** Ran SP% **109.8**
Speed ratings (Par 107): **111,105,99,97,63**
CSF £3.55 TOTE £1.40: £1.10, £2.00; EX 3.60 Trifecta £6.80 Pool: £2176.89 - 239.93 winning units..
Owner Masterson Holdings Limited **Bred** Damien Bellanger Et Al **Trained** Barbury Castle, Wilts

2296 RACINGUK.COM NOVICES' HURDLE (12 hdls) 3m 1f
2:50 (2:50) (Class 4) 4-Y-0+ **£3,249** (£954; £477; £238)

Form RPR
4/1- **1** **Willoughby Hedge**[160] 554 6-11-5 125..................... WayneHutchinson 124+
(Alan King) *hld up: hdwy to ld 3 out: drvn out* **7/4**[1]

4- **2** *1 ½* **Patsys Castle (IRE)**[22] 1915 6-10-12 0............................. JasonMaguire 117+
(Kim Bailey) *trckd ldrs: wnt 2nd 7th: ev ch fr 3 out: sn rdn: nt fluent last: unable qck towards fin* **11/4**[2]

065- **3** *22* **Kyles Faith (IRE)**[11] 2085 5-10-12 0...................................... TomSiddall 97
(Martin Keighley) *hld up: hdwy 3 out: rdn and wknd bef next* **20/1**[3]

5- **4** *4* **Golden Calf (IRE)**[26] 1854 6-10-12 0.................................. JamieMoore 93
(Peter Bowen) *prom tl rdn and wknd appr 2 out* **20/1**[3]

322- **5** *4* **Keltic Rhythm (IRE)**[31] 1794 6-10-9 114....................... TrevorWhelan(3) 93
(Neil King) *hld up: hdwy 3 out: sn rdn and wknd* **7/4**[1]

0- **6** *14* **Grilyne (FR)**[14] 2026 4-10-12 0... FelixDeGiles 76
(Tom Symonds) *led: pushed along 8th: hdd & wknd next* **50/1**

P- **7** *5* **Stickers**[14] 2028 6-10-12 0.. AndrewTinkler 74
(Alan Jessop) *chsd ldr: hit 6th and next: lost pl bef next: wknd 3 out* **100/1**

543/ **8** *55* **Special Vintage**[769] 1775 7-10-7 0....................................... KillianMoore(5) 22
(Graeme McPherson) *hld up: bhd fr 8th* **66/1**

6m 11.3s (-3.70) **Going Correction** -0.75s/f (Firm)
WFA 4 from 5yo+ 9lb **8** Ran SP% **113.4**
Speed ratings (Par 105): **75,74,67,66,64 60,58,41**
toteswingers 1&2 £1.60, 1&3 £7.10, 2&3 £8.80 CSF £6.71 TOTE £2.30: £1.10, £1.20, £4.80; EX 6.30 Trifecta £40.10 Pool: £1110.48 - 20.74 winning units..
Owner Trevor Hemmings **Bred** East Burrow Farm **Trained** Barbury Castle, Wilts

FOCUS
Worsening conditions ahead of this novice hurdle and that appeared to impact on the race as they went very steadily in the early stages.

2297 RACING UK CONDITIONAL JOCKEYS' H'CAP CHASE (19 fncs 1 omitted) 3m 2f
3:25 (3:25) (Class 4) (0-120,119) 4-Y-0+ **£3,768** (£1,106; £553; £276)

Form RPR
133/ **1** **Guess Again (IRE)**[303] 3546 8-11-6 119.......................(t) KieronEdgar(6) 129+
(David Pipe) *hld up: hdwy 5th: chsd ldr 13th: led 3 out: drvn out: edgd lft towards fin* **7/2**[1]

123- **2** *¾* **Whistling Senator (IRE)**[27] 1830 6-11-5 115.........(v) MauriceLinehan(3) 121
(Jonjo O'Neill) *hld up: hdwy 10th: rdn appr 2 out: r.o wl u.p flat: n.m.r towards fin* **7/1**

062- **3** *2 ¼* **Double Chocolate**[14] 2017 10-10-1 100......................(p) CiaranMckee(6) 105
(John O'Shea) *chsd ldr tl led 12th: rdn and hdd 3 out: ev ch next: no ex flat* **8/1**

431/ **4** *22* **Top Dancer (FR)**[203] 5351 6-11-6 116........................... GavinSheehan(3) 103
(Warren Greatrex) *hld up: hdwy 13th: rdn and wknd appr 2 out* **4/1**[2]

2/2- **5** *7* **Timpo (FR)**[166] 461 10-10-2 98...................................(p) JakeGreenall(3) 76
(Henry Daly) *prom: mstke 12th: rdn and wknd 3 out* **6/1**[3]

566- **6** *14* **Lord Lescribaa (FR)**[14] 2017 10-9-10 97..........(tp) ThomasCheesman(8) 62
(Philip Hobbs) *led to 12th: rdn and wknd appr 14th* **40/1**

134/ **P** **One More Dinar**[191] 32 10-10-1 94.. JoshHamer
(John Bryan Groucott) *hld up: a in rr: wknd appr 14th: bhd whn p.u bef 2 out* **33/1**

5/0- **U** **Bally Sands (IRE)**[17] 1988 9-11-0 107................................(p) EdCookson
(Robin Mathew) *blnd and uns rdr 1st* **6/1**[3]

065/ **P** **Tim The Chair (IRE)**[258] 4352 8-10-12 105....................(p) JoshuaMoore
(Emma Lavelle) *prom: rdn after 13th: wknd bef next: bhd whn p.u bef 2 out* **6/1**[3]

6m 35.9s (-16.80) **Going Correction** -0.75s/f (Firm) **9** Ran SP% **114.1**
Speed ratings (Par 105): **95,94,94,87,85 80,,,**
toteswingers 1&2 £5.20, 1&3 £8.20, 2&3 £7.30 CSF £28.02 CT £181.36 TOTE £6.60: £2.30, £1.20, £1.60; EX 25.00 Trifecta £137.40 Pool: £1621.17 - 8.84 winning units..
Owner Malcolm C Denmark **Bred** T McKeever **Trained** Nicholashayne, Devon
■ Stewards' Enquiry : Kieron Edgar two-day ban: careless riding (Nov 20-21)

FOCUS
This race was all about stamina. Small personal bests from the first two.

2298 WHITSON BLOODSTOCK GEORGE MERNAGH MEMORIAL MARES' STANDARD OPEN NATIONAL HUNT FLAT RACE 2m
4:00 (4:00) (Class 6) 4-6-Y-O **£1,559** (£457; £228; £114)

Form RPR
36/ **1** **Kayfleur**[215] 5163 4-10-9 0.. JakeGreenall(3) 104
(Henry Daly) *a.p: led over 1f out: rdn ins fnl f: jst hld on* **5/2**[1]

2 *hd* **Makadamia** 4-10-7 0... MrSWaley-Cohen(5) 104
(David Pipe) *hld up in tch: chsd ldr over 5f out: rdn and ev ch fr over 1f out: r.o* **7/1**

31- **3** *3 ¾* **Balmusette**[100] 1138 4-11-5 0... JamesReveley 107
(Keith Reveley) *led after 1f: rdn and hdd over 1f out: styd on same pce ins fnl f* **6/1**[3]

4 *½* **Avispa** 4-10-12 0.. RobertThornton 100
(Alan King) *chsd ldrs: rdn over 2f out: styd on same pce fnl f* **11/2**[2]

01/ **5** *11* **Land Of Vic**[209] 5255 5-11-5 0... DonalDevereux 97
(Peter Bowen) *plld hrd: trckd ldr after 1f tl over 5f out: rdn and wknd over 2f out* **12/1**

45/ **6** *6* **Definitely Better (IRE)**[207] 5295 5-10-12 0...................... PaddyBrennan 85
(Tom George) *plld hrd: racd wd and led 1f: trckd ldrs: rdn and wknd over 2f out* **12/1**

3/ **7** *4 ½* **Dunmallet Belle**[235] 4786 4-10-12 0...................................... FelixDeGiles 81
(Tom Symonds) *hld up: hdwy 1/2-way: rdn over 3f out: sn wknd* **20/1**

8 *4 ½* **Leith Hill Legasi** 4-10-9 0.. KielanWoods(3) 77
(Charlie Longsdon) *hld up: hdwy over 5f out: rdn over 3f out: sn wknd* **25/1**

9 *½* **Present Trend (IRE)** 4-10-12 0... NoelFehily 76
(Charlie Longsdon) *hld up: sme hdwy 5f out: rdn and wknd over 3f out* **8/1**

10 *3* **Pattara** 4-10-12 0.. WayneHutchinson 73
(Noel Williams) *hld up: hdwy u.p over 4f out: wknd 3f out* **16/1**

11 *2 ¾* **Always Managing** 4-10-12 0... AndrewTinkler 71
(Brendan Powell) *hld up: drvn along over 6f out: wknd over 3f out* **20/1**

12 *9* **Delineate (IRE)** 4-10-12 0.. GerardTumelty 63
(G C Maundrell) *chsd ldrs: lost pl after 4f: bhd fr 1/2-way* **50/1**

13 *11* **Gaye Memories** 5-10-12 0.. HarrySkelton 53
(Dan Skelton) *hld up: pushed along 1/2-way: sn wknd* **33/1**

14 *12* **Clyffe Dancer** 5-10-9 0.. GavinSheehan(3) 42
(Emma Lavelle) *mid-div: hdwy over 6f out: rdn and wknd over 3f out* **33/1**

15 *21* **Materiana (IRE)** 5-10-5 0.. JamesCowley(7) 23
(Andrew Hollinshead) *s.s: a bhd* **66/1**

16 *nk* **Leahnor (IRE)** 4-10-12 0.. RhysFlint 23
(John Flint) *hld up: bhd fnl 6f* **50/1**

The Form Book Jumps, Raceform Ltd, Compton, RG20 6NL.

17 34 **Tambalong** 5-10-9 0 .... JamesBest(3)
(Caroline Keevil) *hld up: drvn along 1/2-way: sn bhd* 80/1

3m 37.3s (-13.60) **Going Correction** -0.75s/f (Firm) **17** Ran SP% **129.0**
Speed ratings: **104,103,102,101,96 93,91,88,88,87 85,81,75,69,59 59,42**
toteswingers 1&2 £6.90, 1&3 £5.50, 2&3 £10.00 CSF £18.66 TOTE £3.30: £1.50, £3.60, £2.70; EX 23.00 Trifecta £105.50 Pool: £1382.44 - 9.82 winning units..
Owner B G Hellyer **Bred** B G Hellyer & H D J Daly **Trained** Stanton Lacy, Shropshire
■ Stewards' Enquiry : Mr S Waley-Cohen two-day ban: used whip in incorrect place (Nov 24,28)

FOCUS
There was plenty of pace on in this bumper and that sorted the wheat from the chaff as four of them broke clear in a race that looks almost certain to work out. The form is rated around the winner, third and fifth.
T/Plt: £21.50 to a £1 stake. Pool: £55634.50 - 1885.73 winning tickets T/Qpdt: £5.00 to a £1 stake. Pool: £4081.90 - 596.90 winning tickets CR

2299 - 2305a (Foreign Racing) - See Raceform Interactive

MUSSELBURGH (R-H)
Thursday, November 7

OFFICIAL GOING: Good (good to firm in places; 7.6)
Wind: Fairly strong, half against Weather: Cloudy, bright

2306 NORTHERN HOTEL BRECHIN CONDITIONAL JOCKEYS' H'CAP HURDLE (9 hdls) 2m
1:00 (1:01) (Class 5) (0-100,100) 4-Y-0+ **£3,249** (£954; £477; £238)

Form RPR
441- 1 **Civil Unrest (IRE)**[37] 1715 7-10-11 **93** .... (b) DaleIrving(8) 109+
(James Ewart) *mde all: clr 4th: given breather after 4 out: qcknd clr fr next: easily* **11/2**[2]
410- 2 17 **Cadore (IRE)**[42] 1665 5-11-9 **100** .... (p) GrantCockburn(3) 101
(Lucy Normile) *hld up: hit 3rd: stdy hdwy 4 out: effrt bef next: hit 2 out: chsd (clr) wnr run-in: no imp* **7/1**[3]
P03/ 3 2 ¾ **Shan Valley (IRE)**[588] 5149 7-10-0 **82** ow1 .... DaraghBourke(8) 81
(Stuart Coltherd) *t.k.h: hld up in tch: stdy hdwy to chse (clr) wnr 4 out: effrt bef next: edgd rt appr 2 out: no ex and lost 2nd run-in: bttr for r* **10/1**
401- 4 4 ½ **Tweedo Paradiso (NZ)**[27] 1848 6-10-11 **93** .... ShaunDobbin(8) 86
(Rose Dobbin) *t.k.h: in tch: rdn along after 3 out: kpt on same pce fr next* **11/4**[1]
3U4- 5 15 **Claude Carter**[57] 1567 9-11-11 **99** .... CallumWhillans 82
(Alistair Whillans) *prom: blkd 3rd: wnt 2nd 5th to next: drvn and wknd after 3 out* **9/1**
/60- 6 13 **Lillioftheballet (IRE)**[32] 1785 6-10-12 **89** .... GrahamWatters(3) 57
(Jim Goldie) *hld up in tch: drvn and outpcd 1/2-way: n.d after* **7/1**[3]
46F- 7 1 ½ **Newdane Dancer (IRE)**[14] 2035 6-10-6 **80** .... (b[1]) TonyKelly 47
(Dianne Sayer) *chsd wnr to 5th: rdn next: wknd bef 3 out* **28/1**
446- 8 14 **The Lodge Road (IRE)**[37] 1713 5-11-7 **95** .... (t) HarryChalloner 49
(Martin Todhunter) *sn towards rr: struggling 4th: nvr on terms* **20/1**
/02- 9 12 **Schinken Otto (IRE)**[46] 1638 12-9-13 **78** .... DeanPratt(5) 22
(Malcolm Jefferson) *prom to 1/2-way: sn lost pl: btn bef 3 out* **7/1**[3]
206/ 10 12 **Good Boy Jackson**[38] 2528 5-11-7 **100** .... CallumBewley(5) 33
(R Mike Smith) *hld up: struggling 1/2-way: sn btn* **14/1**

3m 40.1s (-8.30) **Going Correction** -0.225s/f (Good) **10** Ran SP% **113.5**
Speed ratings (Par 103): **111,102,101,98,91 84,84,77,71,65**
toteswingers 1&2 £6.00, 2&3 £10.90, 1&3 £7.30 CSF £42.75 CT £372.49 TOTE £6.60: £1.80, £2.80, £2.70; EX 43.90 Trifecta £186.80 Part won. Pool: £249.09 - 0.69 winning units..
Owner The Ancrum Pointer 1 **Bred** D And Mrs Noonan **Trained** Langholm, Dumfries & G'way

FOCUS
Hurdles and chases used common bend. A moderate contest that's unlikely to produce many winners in the short term. The easy winner is rated similar to his old hurdle best.

2307 ARCHFIELD JUVENILE HURDLE (9 hdls) 2m
1:30 (1:33) (Class 4) 3-Y-0 **£3,249** (£954; £477; £238)

Form RPR
323- 1 **Akdam (IRE)**[26] 1862 3-11-0 119 .... (p) JoshHamer(5) 103+
(Tony Carroll) *led: rdn 3 out: hdd briefly run-in: kpt on gamely towards fin* **10/11**[1]
2 ½ **Gold Chain (IRE)**[54] 3-10-5 0 .... BrianHughes 89
(Dianne Sayer) *nt fluent on occasions: sn chsng wnr: gng wl 2 out: rdn to ld briefly run-in: kpt on: hld cl home* **12/5**[2]
3 20 **Seaside Rock (IRE)**[14] 3-10-12 0 .... WilsonRenwick 78
(Keith Dalgleish) *mstkes: prom: effrt whn hit 3 out: rdn and wknd after next* **9/2**[3]
435- 4 28 **Wild Diamond (IRE)**[78] 1335 3-10-5 98 .... (t) RichardJohnson 45
(Tim Vaughan) *chsd ldrs: drvn 4 out: wknd bef next: t.o* **12/1**

3m 52.9s (4.50) **Going Correction** -0.225s/f (Good) **4** Ran SP% **107.7**
Speed ratings (Par 104): **79,78,68,54**
CSF £3.42 TOTE £1.80; EX 3.60 Trifecta £7.60 Pool. £473.15 - 40.17 winning units..
Owner Stephen Louch **Bred** His Highness The Aga Khan's Studs S C **Trained** Cropthorne, Worcs

FOCUS
A very weak juvenile event. It was steadily run and has been given a token rating through the winner.

2308 WILLIAM HILL - SUPPORTING MUSSELBURGH'S FREE RACEDAY NOVICES' H'CAP CHASE (16 fncs) 2m 4f
2:00 (2:01) (Class 4) (0-110,107) 4-Y-0 **£3,798** (£1,122; £561; £280; £140)

Form RPR
422- 1 **Cloudy Joker (IRE)**[37] 1714 5-11-12 **107** .... HenryBrooke 113+
(Donald McCain) *chsd ldr: led appr 4 out: drvn out fr last* **17/2**
/33- 2 2 ¼ **Ballymoat**[33] 1765 6-11-12 **107** .... (t) RichardJohnson 111
(Tim Vaughan) *hld up towards rr: mstke 9th: stdy hdwy to chse wnr after 4 out: kpt on u.p fr last* **6/1**[2]
50P- 3 6 **Forestside (IRE)**[14] 2036 8-10-7 **88** .... DenisO'Regan 90+
(Barry Murtagh) *hld up: mstke 10th: effrt and pushed along 3 out: one pce after next* **12/1**
5/6- 4 1 **Clondaw Flicka (IRE)**[19] 1979 5-11-9 **104** .... PeterBuchanan 101
(Lucinda Russell) *nt fluent on occasions: in tch: outpcd 1/2-way: styd on fr 2 out: nvr able to chal* **17/2**
300/ 5 9 **Get The Papers**[313] 3341 6-10-5 **86** .... (t) BarryKeniry 78
(Pauline Robson) *led: j.w tl mstke whn jst hdd 4 out: wknd qckly* **11/8**[1]
223- F **Agricultural**[26] 1870 7-11-1 **96** .... WilsonRenwick
(Lucy Normile) *hmpd 1st: chsd ldrs: disputing 3rd pl and drvn along whn fell 4 out* **13/2**[3]
330/ F **Teo Vivo (FR)**[207] 5313 6-11-9 **104** .... BrianHughes
(James Ewart) *chsng ldrs whn fell 1st* **13/2**[3]
0/5- F **Ben Akram (IRE)**[19] 1981 5-10-8 **96** .... GrahamWatters(7)
(Lucinda Russell) *chsd ldrs: fell 1st* **25/1**

4m 59.5s (-1.70) **Going Correction** 0.0s/f (Good) **8** Ran SP% **115.6**
Speed ratings (Par 105): **103,102,99,99,95 , ,**
toteswingers 1&2 £1.80, 2&3 £15.50, 1&3 £15.50 CSF £58.70 CT £615.64 TOTE £5.30: £2.30, £1.70, £3.70; EX 18.10 Trifecta £580.50 Part won. Pool of £774.12 - 0.65 winning units..
Owner D McCain Jnr **Bred** Miss Penny Downes **Trained** Cholmondeley, Cheshire

FOCUS
A moderate novice handicap. The winner is up 6lb on the best of his hurdle form.

2309 DON KING AND NEVILLE PORTER BOOKMAKER MARES' MAIDEN HURDLE (8 hdls 1 omitted) 2m
2:30 (2:31) (Class 5) 4-Y-0+ **£3,249** (£954; £477; £238)

Form RPR
210/ 1 **Brijomi Queen (IRE)**[216] 5163 6-10-12 0 .... DenisO'Regan 101+
(Nicky Richards) *hld up: smooth hdwy to ld after 2 out (usual 3 out): drvn out fr last* **6/5**[1]
0/2- 2 2 **Rathvawn Belle (IRE)**[26] 1871 6-10-12 0 .... WilsonRenwick 98
(Lucinda Russell) *chsd ldrs: hit 1st: effrt and chsd wnr after 2 out (usual 3 out): swtchd lft run-in: kpt on fin* **5/2**[2]
252- 3 7 **Retrieve The Stick**[68] 1472 4-10-12 0 .... BrianHughes 92
(Malcolm Jefferson) *t.k.h: cl up: led briefly 2 out (usual 3 out): outpcd fr last* **6/1**[3]
42/ 4 1 ½ **Hellesbelles (IRE)**[222] 5011 5-10-12 0 .... RichardJohnson 91
(Tim Vaughan) *hld up: rdn and effrt bef 2 out (usual 3 out): no imp fr last* **8/1**
30/ 5 11 **Geanie Mac (IRE)**[6] 2279 4-10-12 0 .... (p) HenryBrooke 81
(Linda Perratt) *nt fluent on occasions: hld up: stdy hdwy 3 out (usual 4 out): rdn and wknd after next* **40/1**
6 1 ¼ **Voice From Above (IRE)**[45] 4-10-7 0 .... JoeColliver(5) 80
(Patrick Holmes) *t.k.h: prom tl rdn and wknd bef 2 out (usual 3 out)* **33/1**
005/ 7 24 **Just Stripe**[584] 5208 6-10-12 73 .... JamesReveley 58
(Rayson Nixon) *w ldr: led after 3rd to 2 out (usual 3 out): sn struggling* **66/1**
/05- 8 24 **Mieuxmix (IRE)**[37] 1719 4-10-12 0 .... DannyCook 36
(Peter Niven) *led to after 3rd: hung bdly lft bnd bef next: lost pl qckly 5th: sn lost tch* **50/1**
2PP- 9 21 **Lady Gargoyle**[28] 1664 5-10-12 88 .... GaryBartley 18
(Jim Goldie) *t.k.h: trckd ldrs to 3 out (usual 4 out): sn struggling* **16/1**
/P3- F **Jordans Day**[26] 1871 8-10-2 0 .... JamesCorbett(10)
(Susan Corbett) *hld up: fell heavily 2nd* **200/1**

3m 47.6s (-0.80) **Going Correction** -0.225s/f (Good) **10** Ran SP% **114.6**
Speed ratings (Par 103): **93,92,88,87,82 81,69,57,47,**
toteswingers 1&2 £1.10, 2&3 £1.30, 1&3 £2.70 CSF £4.21 TOTE £2.10: £1.10, £1.50, £3.00; EX 5.60 Trifecta £12.90 Pool: £887.86 - 51.53 winning units..
Owner M S Borders Racing Club & Partners **Bred** Aidan Aherne **Trained** Greystoke, Cumbria

FOCUS
An ordinary mares' maiden. The winner should rate higher and win again.

2310 LYN'S SAHARA WALK: RESPONSIBLE GAMBLING TRUST H'CAP CHASE (18 fncs) 3m
3:00 (3:03) (Class 4) (0-110,108) 4-Y-0+ **£3,898** (£1,144; £572; £286)

Form RPR
143- 1 **More Equity**[19] 1978 11-11-12 **108** .... RyanMania 112
(Dianne Sayer) *prom: hdwy to ld 4 out: drvn and styd on wl fr 2 out* **5/1**
342- 2 1 ¼ **Dukeofchesterwood**[22] 1925 11-10-4 **86** .... (p) BrianHughes 88
(Karen McLintock) *led to 3rd: cl up: effrt and led briefly appr 4 out: kpt on fr 2 out: nt rch wnr* **7/2**[2]
656- 3 3 ¼ **Knight Woodsman**[32] 1789 9-9-13 **88** .... (p) CallumBewley(7) 87
(R Mike Smith) *in tch: hdwy to ld 5th: hdd bef 11th: cl up: rdn bef 4 out: kpt on same pce after 2 out* **4/1**[3]
/12- 4 40 **Foot The Bill**[139] 789 8-11-6 **102** .... BrianHarding 65
(Patrick Holmes) *chsd ldrs: hit 1st: lost pl 5th: struggling fr 13th: t.o* **5/2**[1]
026- 5 2 **Quinder Spring (FR)**[21] 1936 9-10-8 **97** .... (v) GrantCockburn(7) 58
(Lucinda Russell) *cl up: led 3rd to 5th: led bef 11th to appr 4 out: wknd qckly bef next: t.o* **15/2**
0FP/ P **Jan Jandura (IRE)**[334] 2931 8-10-0 **82** oh4 .... (t) HenryBrooke
(William Amos) *t.k.h: nt fluent on occasions in rr: stdy hdwy 5 out: wknd bef next: t.o whn p.u bef 2 out* **7/1**

6m 0.9s (-2.50) **Going Correction** 0.0s/f (Good) **6** Ran SP% **111.7**
Speed ratings (Par 105): **104,103,102,89,88**
toteswingers 1&2 £2.40, 2&3 £3.50, 1&3 £5.40 CSF £22.61 TOTE £3.80: £2.10, £1.70; EX 13.70 Trifecta £85.80 Pool: £696.77 - 6.08 winning units..
Owner Mrs Margaret Coppola **Bred** Mrs A F Tullie **Trained** Hackthorpe, Cumbria

FOCUS
A moderate handicap. The first two are rated pretty much to their marks.

2311 LOGANBET THE BRECHIN SPECIAL BOOKMAKER H'CAP HURDLE (12 hdls) 2m 4f
3:30 (3:32) (Class 4) (0-120,116) 4-Y-0+ **£4,548** (£1,335; £667; £333)

Form RPR
2/2- 1 **Ueueteotl (FR)**[19] 1977 5-11-12 **116** .... BrianHughes 125+
(James Ewart) *chsd ldrs: hdwy to ld 2 out: styd on strly fr last* **5/1**[3]
23/ 2 8 **Merchant Of Dubai**[26] 3226 8-11-7 **111** .... DenisO'Regan 113
(Jim Goldie) *hld up: stdy hdwy bef 3 out: effrt and chsd (clr) wnr last: kpt on: no imp* **15/2**
/22- 3 5 **Any Given Moment (IRE)**[166] 476 7-11-3 **107** .... RyanMania 105
(Sandy Thomson) *led: rdn and hdd 2 out: sn rdn: outpcd fr last* **8/1**
3/3- 4 2 ½ **Bogside (IRE)**[19] 1979 9-11-5 **109** .... LucyAlexander 105
(George Charlton) *t.k.h: hld up: mstke 7th: drvn and outpcd bef 3 out: kpt on fr last: no imp* **9/2**[2]
313- 5 3 ¼ **Weybridge Light**[14] 2051 8-10-7 **102** .... (b) TonyKelly(5) 94
(David Thompson) *in tch: effrt 3 out: hung rt bef next: sn outpcd* **17/2**
/ 6 4 ½ **Easy Reach (IRE)**[409] 1627 5-11-7 **114** .... (bt[1]) KeithDonoghue(3) 106
(Mrs Gillian Callaghan, Ire) *prom: effrt and rdn bef 3 out: one pce fr next: 5th and btn whn blnd last* **13/2**
316- 7 4 ½ **Red Eyes**[30] 1654 5-10-13 **110** .... DiarmuidO'Regan(7) 94
(Chris Grant) *w ldr tl rdn and wknd appr 2 out* **18/1**
P- 8 67 **Ballyreesode (IRE)**[14] 2034 8-10-12 **102** .... RichardJohnson 26
(Susan Corbett) *bhd: struggling bef 8th: t.o* **40/1**
/P4- 9 27 **Abbey Garth (IRE)**[32] 1785 6-11-1 **105** .... BrianHarding 5
(Nicky Richards) *hld up: pushed along after 4 out: wknd qckly next: eased whn no ch run-in* **11/4**[1]

4m 46.7s (-4.80) **Going Correction** -0.225s/f (Good) **9** Ran SP% **116.0**
Speed ratings (Par 105): **100,96,94,93,92 90,88,62,51**
toteswingers 1&2 £2.20, 2&3 £13.10, 1&3 £3.50 CSF £42.21 CT £296.32 TOTE £4.90: £2.30, £1.70, £2.30; EX 27.60 Trifecta £28.50 Pool: £883.26 - 23.18 winning units..

Owner Going Grey **Bred** William Ewart **Trained** Langholm, Dumfries & G'way
FOCUS
A modest handicap. the winner is the type to rate higher and the second ran to his mark.
T/Plt: £36.90 to a £1 stake. Pool of £51,567.19 - 1,018.94 winning units. T/Qpdt: £6.10 to a £1 stake. Pool of £4199.40 - 503.90 winning units. RY

1820 TOWCESTER (R-H)
Thursday, November 7

OFFICIAL GOING: Good to soft (soft in places; 8.1)
Wind: light, against Weather: dry

2312 HAYGAIN HAY STEAMERS CLEAN HEALTHY FORAGE MARES' H'CAP HURDLE (11 hdls) 2m 5f
1:10 (1:11) (Class 5) (0-100,100) 4-Y-0+ **£1,949** (£572; £286; £143)

Form RPR
005- 1 **Carhue Princess (IRE)**[6] 2193 7-10-8 **82** FelixDeGiles 87
(Tom Symonds) *chsd ldrs: wnt 2nd 5th: led and lft 2 l clr 3 out: styd on wl* **6/1**[2]
252- 2 4 **Je T'Aime (IRE)**[75] 1373 4-11-6 **94** (p) JasonMaguire 95
(Donald McCain) *hld up in tch in midfield: chsd ldng pair after 8th: lft 2nd next: rdn and no ex between last 2: styd on same pce flat* **11/1**
440- 3 3 **Night Of Passion (IRE)**[17] 2004 5-10-0 **74** oh1 (p) TomScudamore 74
(Jeremy Scott) *wl in tch in midfield: rdn and cl enough whn lft 6th and hmpd 3 out: outpcd bef next: rallied and styd on flat* **7/2**[1]
0/1- 4 ½ **Realta Mo Croi (IRE)**[149] 710 5-11-2 **90** DougieCostello 88
(Neil Mulholland) *hld up in tch in midfield: rdn and effrt 3 out: hld and disputing 3rd whn blnd last: one pce flat* **8/1**[3]
441/ 5 ½ **Lansdowne Princess**[473] 1034 11-10-6 **80** (t) BrendanPowell 77
(Johnny Farrelly) *hld up in rr: prog on outer jst bef 3 out: rdn and effrt to chse ldng pair bef 2 out: no imp and hit last: one pce flat* **12/1**
440- 6 5 **Marie Deja La (FR)**[21] 1945 7-10-13 **97** (b) LouisMuspratt(10) 90
(Chris Gordon) *chsd ldrs: 3rd and no ex whn rdn after 3 out: wknd between last 2* **14/1**
444- 7 ½ **Sapphire Rouge (IRE)**[33] 1768 7-11-2 **97** (p) KevinJones(7) 89
(Seamus Mullins) *chsd ldrs: shuffled bk into midfield but stl wl in tch 6th: rdn and effrt bef 3 out: no imp and mstke 2 out: wknd between last 2* **10/1**
35F- 8 3¼ **June French (FR)**[121] 932 5-10-0 **74** oh2 DavidEngland 64
(Giles Smyly) *t.k.h: hld up in tch in midfield: hdwy bef 3 out: no ex 2 out: sn rdn and wknd* **8/1**[3]
6/0- 9 3¾ **Young Lou**[14] 2040 4-10-13 **92** BenPoste(5) 78
(Robin Dickin) *hld up wl in tch in midfield: rdn and effrt jst bef 3 out: outpcd and btn bef 2 out: wknd between last 2* **50/1**
/U6- 10 13 **Best Bette**[7] 2175 8-9-7 **74** MrLKilgarriff(7) 48
(Clarissa Caroe) *in tch in midfield: rdn and dropped to rr after 3rd: nvr travelling wl after: wknd u.p 3 out* **80/1**
/64- 11 14 **Niki Royal (FR)**[15] 2021 8-11-5 **100** (v[1]) MikeyHamill(7) 62
(Jamie Snowden) *hld up in tch in last pair: rdn and effrt on outer after 8th: btn next: wknd bef 2 out: t.o* **14/1**
/06- 12 6 **Roseini (IRE)**[55] 1582 7-10-7 **81** [1] AndrewTinkler 37
(Tony Carroll) *in tch towards rr: mstke and rdn 8th: sn struggling: wknd next: t.o* **16/1**
/40- 13 6 **Romney Marsh**[17] 2008 12-11-6 **94** HaddenFrost 45
(Roger Curtis) *in tch towards rr: rdn and no hdwy 8th: wknd next: t.o* **50/1**
060/ P **Cruise In Luxury (IRE)**[337] 2856 8-9-13 **83** JonPark(10)
(Kevin Bishop) *in tch in midfield: rdn and struggling 8th: lost tch next: wl bhd whn p.u 2 out* **50/1**
464- F **Possibly Flora**[35] 1731 8-11-6 **94** (t) AidanColeman
(Richard Woollacott) *w ldr tl led 2nd: hdd jst bef 3 out: 1 l 2nd whn stmbld on landing and fell 3 out* **40/1**
00- P **Maxi's Lady (IRE)**[25] 1885 6-10-0 **74** oh4 (p) DonalDevereux
(David Rees) *led tl 2nd: chsd ldr tl 5th: rdn and lost pl 7th: wl bhd whn p.u 2 out* **11/1**

5m 23.9s (-3.30) **Going Correction** -0.10s/f (Good) **16** Ran SP% **121.0**
Speed ratings (Par 103): **102,100,99,99,98 97,96,95,94,89 83,81,79, ,**
toteswingers 1&2 £18.20, 2&3 £13.00, 1&3 £5.90 CSF £68.40 CT £270.73 TOTE £5.90: £1.60, £1.50, £1.40, £2.40; EX 71.20 Trifecta £928.80 Pool: £ 1813.87 - 1.46 winning units..
Owner The Ever Hopeful Partnership **Bred** Patrick F Kelly **Trained** Harewood End, H'fords
■ Amazingreyce was withdrawn. Price at time of withdrawal 66/1. Rule 4 does not apply.
FOCUS
Chases and hurdles were on shared bends with hurdles course on inside line. The going was good to soft, soft in places and the hurdle and chase courses were on shared bends. They went a steady pace in this mares' handicap but the well handicapped winner scored with authority and the market leader finished third. The form is sound with the winner 5lb off her best.

2313 NASMYTH 10TH ANNIVERSARY H'CAP CHASE (16 fncs) 2m 6f
1:40 (1:41) (Class 5) (0-100,99) 4-Y-0+ **£2,144** (£629; £314; £157)

Form RPR
P/4- 1 **Salut Honore (FR)**[166] 472 7-11-2 **89** WillKennedy 102+
(Alex Hales) *hld up towards rr: stdy hdwy 8th: chsd ldrs 12th: led 3 out: forged clr next: drew wl clr and in n.d between last 2: eased flat* **20/1**
6P4- 2 12 **Ballyvoneen (IRE)**[14] 2047 8-11-6 **93** (b) DougieCostello 94
(Neil King) *in tch in midfield: clsd to chse ldrs and hmpd after 9th: 3rd whn hit next: rdn and pressing ldrs whn racd awkwardly 3 out: no ex and j. slowly next: chsd clr wnr between last 2: no imp* **6/1**[3]
/43- 3 4 **Glenwood Prince (IRE)**[21] 1942 7-11-8 **95** (t) NickScholfield 94
(Jeremy Scott) *nt fluent: in rr: pushed along and struggling after 7th: mstke last: wl bhd 13th: styd on past btn horses 2 out: wnt 3rd flat: no ch w wnr* **2/1**[1]
0/6- 4 2¼ **Overton Lad**[29] 1825 12-10-0 **73** oh7 (bt) HarrySkelton 68
(Peter Pritchard) *chsd ldr tl after 7th: rdn after: drvn and outpcd 3 out: wl hld on uphill run to next: plugged on past btn horses between last 2: no ch w wnr* **50/1**
500- 5 11 **Ifonlyalfie**[21] 1936 8-10-13 **86** (bt) TomMessenger 71
(Chris Bealby) *chsd ldrs: mstke and pckd 1st: chsd ldr after 7th: led and hmpd bef 10th: hdd 3 out: 4th and btn next: wknd* **20/1**
PP5- 6 6 **Top Benefit (IRE)**[14] 2044 11-10-9 **87** JamesBanks(5) 69
(Richard Harper) *in tch in midfield: drvn after 13th: 5th and outpcd next: wl hld whn mstke and nrly uns rdr last: t.o* **20/1**
443- 7 15 **Henry Hurst (IRE)**[80] 1320 7-11-7 **94** AndrewThornton 67
(Jimmy Fox) *hld up in rr: mstke 7th: hdwy and hit 10th: jnd ldrs after 13th: drew clr w wnr on uphill run bef 2 out: no ex and btn 2 out: 3rd and tired whn blnd last: fdd flat: t.o* **9/1**
210/ 8 9 **Bravo Riquet (FR)**[204] 5354 7-11-12 **99** (vt) LeeEdwards 57
(Robin Mathew) *j.lft and mstkes: in tch in midfield: lost pl and bhd whn mstke 8th: struggling 10th: wl bhd after 3 out: t.o* **11/2**[2]
/P1- P **Von Galen (IRE)**[29] 1825 12-10-8 **81** (p) TomScudamore
(Michael Scudamore) *in tch in midfield: mstke 10th: rdn whn blnd bdly next: wknd 13th: wl bhd whn p.u 3 out* **10/1**
PPP- P **Autumm Spirit**[23] 1914 9-11-2 **89** (bt) CharliePoste
(Robin Dickin) *j.lft and racd wd: led tl after 9th: chsd ldrs tl lost pl 13th: wl bhd whn p.u 3 out* **25/1**
432/ P **Endofdiscusion (IRE)**[198] 5481 6-11-10 **97** (p) TomO'Brien
(Paul Webber) *in tch in midfield: hdwy to chse ldrs and mstke 12th: drvn and effrt after 13th: wknd on uphill run to 2 out: wl bhd whn p.u last* **7/1**
4/P- P **Dramatic Victory (IRE)**[170] 422 6-9-11 **73** oh14 GavinSheehan(3)
(John Upson) *a in rr: in last and lost tch after 7th: tailing off whn blnd bdly 10th: p.u next* **100/1**

5m 39.5s (-13.50) **Going Correction** -0.575s/f (Firm) **12** Ran SP% **115.7**
Speed ratings (Par 103): **101,96,95,94,90 88,82,79, , ,**
toteswingers 1&2 £16.40, 2&3 £4.40, 1&3 £8.00 CSF £125.26 CT £352.83 TOTE £27.30: £5.20, £2.60, £1.30; EX 219.00 Trifecta £1269.10 Pool: £2046.29 - 1.20 winning units..
Owner The Hexagon Racing Partnership **Bred** Ecurie Pegase **Trained** Edgcote, Northants
FOCUS
They went a good pace in this minor handicap. The two market leaders were never involved but the winner scored in good style and the form looks solid enough. The winner is rated back to the level of his last couple of wins.

2314 AGETUR UK H'CAP HURDLE (11 hdls) 2m 5f
2:10 (2:11) (Class 4) (0-120,120) 4-Y-0+ **£3,119** (£915; £457; £228)

Form RPR
450/ 1 **Valid Point (IRE)**[203] 5362 7-11-9 **117** (t) JasonMaguire 121
(Jim Old) *hld up in tch in rr: hdwy on uphill run after 3 out: sltly hmpd 2 out: styd on to chse ldr last: r.o u.p to ld last strides* **7/1**[3]
004/ 2 hd **Squire Trelawney**[208] 5280 7-10-11 **105** (t) HarrySkelton 109
(Dan Skelton) *hld up in tch towards rr: hdwy to chse ldrs 3 out: rdn to ld next: drvn and forged ahd between last 2: kpt on flat tl hdd and no ex last strides* **20/1**
/66- 3 2¼ **Rior (IRE)**[21] 1941 6-10-4 **98** TomO'Brien 100
(Paul Henderson) *hld up in tch towards rr: clsd bef 3 out: chsd ldrs and rdn whn j.lft 2 out: unable qck between last 2: one pce flat* **8/1**
14P- 4 1½ **Halucha (IRE)**[29] 1825 8-10-1 **98** (p) JakeGreenall(3) 97
(Paul Webber) *led and set stdy gallop: rdn and hrd pressed on uphill run after 3 out: hdd next: no ex u.p and one pce between last 2* **40/1**
100- 5 4½ **Church Field (IRE)**[19] 1972 5-11-10 **118** APMcCoy 115
(Jonjo O'Neill) *in tch in midfield: nt fluent 3rd: effrt and chsd ldrs whn mstke 8th: drvn bef 2 out: no ex and btn between last 2: wknd flat* **3/1**[1]
/10- 6 1¾ **Thoresby (IRE)**[57] 1565 7-10-13 **107** (p) SamTwiston-Davies 101
(Ben Case) *in tch in midfield: effrt and clsd on uphill run after 3 out: hrd drvn and unable qck between last 2: wknd last* **16/1**
3/U- 7 5 **Hollow Penny**[14] 2050 5-11-10 **118** RobertThornton 109
(Alan King) *in tch in midfield and travelled wl: clsng whn mstke 7th: chsd ldrs and fnd little whn rdn on uphill run after 3 out: wknd between last 2* **7/2**[2]
/56- 8 2¾ **Phare Isle (IRE)**[149] 718 8-11-5 **120** (t) MrMJPKendrick(7) 107
(Ben Case) *in tch in midfield: effrt and n.m.r on inner bef 2 out: outpcd and btn 2 out: plugged on* **33/1**
/26- 9 ½ **Murcar**[141] 767 8-11-2 **110** ConorO'Farrell 96
(Liam Corcoran) *hld up in tch in midfield: rdn and effrt on outer 3 out: no ex on uphill run to next: wknd sn after 2 out* **40/1**
001- 10 1½ **Scales (IRE)**[25] 1887 7-10-9 **106** MichealNolan(3) 92
(Richard Lee) *hld up in tch in rr: clsd and wl in tch in midfield 3 out: rdn and no ex bef next: wknd between last 2* **20/1**
/40- 11 2¼ **Earcomesthedream (IRE)**[172] 393 10-10-1 **100** (b) NicodeBoinville(5) 83
(Peter Pritchard) *chsd ldrs: wnt 2nd after 4th tl 3 out: wkng whn mstke next* **40/1**
205/ 12 ½ **Moscow Presents (IRE)**[199] 5449 5-11-9 **117** RichieMcGrath 100
(Philip Kirby) *hld up in tch in midfield: rdn and effrt on uphill run after 3 out: sn struggling and wknd bef next* **25/1**
24/- 13 nse **Reyno**[202] 5376 5-10-10 **107** JoshuaMoore(3) 90
(Renee Robeson) *chsd ldrs: rdn 8th: wknd on uphill run bef 2 out: bhd between last 2* **16/1**
U51/ 14 13 **Market Option (IRE)**[224] 4989 7-11-1 **109** AidanColeman 80
(Venetia Williams) *chsd ldrs: rdn and lost pl after 8th: bhd next* **7/1**[3]
5U/- 15 5 **Crystal Swing**[201] 5400 6-11-6 **114** WayneHutchinson 80
(Richard Phillips) *hld up in tch towards rr: rdn and short-lived effrt sn after 3 out: wknd on uphill run to next: t.o* **33/1**
1P/ 16 18 **Thinger Licht (FR)**[194] 5573 4-11-12 **120** LeeEdwards 70
(Tony Carroll) *chsd ldrs tl 6th: lost pl after next: bhd 3 out: sn lost tch: t.o* **50/1**

5m 26.6s (-0.60) **Going Correction** -0.10s/f (Good) **16** Ran SP% **123.6**
Speed ratings (Par 105): **97,96,96,95,93 93,91,90,89,89 88,88,88,83,81 74**
toteswingers 1&2 £49.30, 2&3 £52.80, 1&3 £13.20 CSF £141.26 CT £1162.87 TOTE £10.80: £1.90, £5.50, £2.20, £7.60; EX 243.80 Trifecta £1529.20 Part won. Pool: £2038.98 - 0.48 winning units..
Owner W E Sturt **Bred** Pier House Stud **Trained** Barbury Castle, Wilts
FOCUS
They were tightly bunched for a long way in this fair, steadily run handicap, and there was an exciting finish. The form is rated around the first four.

2315 WEATHERBYS NOVICES' H'CAP CHASE (12 fncs) 2m 110y
2:40 (2:40) (Class 4) (0-110,110) 4-Y-0+ **£3,768** (£1,106; £553; £276)

Form RPR
0/5- 1 **Arkaim**[151] 384 5-11-0 **101** KielanWoods(3) 110+
(Pam Sly) *t.k.h: j.rt: chsd ldrs: mstke 2nd: led sn after next and mde rest: drvn and j.rt 2 out: hrd pressed but keeping on whn lft 4 l clr last: being clsd down fnl 100yds but a lasting home* **25/1**
0/1- 2 ½ **Beforeall (IRE)**[173] 368 5-11-7 **105** LeightonAspell 113+
(Oliver Sherwood) *led: mstke 2nd: hdd sn after next: chsd wnr after tl 4th and sltly outpcd on uphill run after 3 out: lft 4 l 2nd and hmpd last: kpt on gamely u.p and clsng on wnr fnl 100yds* **4/1**[2]
640- 3 11 **Brassbound (USA)**[58] 1551 5-11-9 **107** RobertThornton 112+
(Caroline Bailey) *chsd ldrs: j.rt and mstke 4th: drvn and 3rd on uphill run after 3 out: chsd wnr 2 out: chalng whn mstke and slipped on landing last: nt rcvr and wknd flat* **20/1**
4/3- 4 nk **Minella For Party (IRE)**[179] 237 6-11-12 **110** HarrySkelton 106
(Dan Skelton) *t.k.h: hld up wl in tch in midfield: chsd ldrs 5th: pressing ldr and looked to travelling best 3 out: rdn and no rspnse on uphill run bef next: 4th and wkng whn hung lft between last 2: j.rt last* **3/1**[1]

The Form Book Jumps, Raceform Ltd, Compton, RG20 6NL.

0/4- **5** *15* **Chicklemix**[29] [1821] 7-11-6 **109**.......................... MissGAndrews(5) 92
(Pam Sly) *t.k.h: hld up in midfield on outer: dropped to rr bnd after 3rd: pushed rt by loose horse and hmpd next: sn lost tch and j.rt after: virtually t.o fr 6th and n.d after: mstke 2 out* **10/1**

/44- **6** *hd* **Gizzit (IRE)**[37] [1710] 7-10-13 **97**.......................... AndrewThornton 81
(Karen George) *chsd ldrs: cl 4th whn mstke 3 out: sn rdn and wknd on uphill run to next: wl bhd between last 2* **6/1**

0/6- **7** *38* **Tyrur Ted**[21] [1938] 8-10-12 **96**..........................(t) LeeEdwards 45
(Dave Roberts) *chsd ldrs: 6th and struggling u.p after 8th: lost tch next: t.o 3 out* **25/1**

603/ **U** **Swincombe Stone**[210] [5240] 6-11-10 **108**.......................... RyanMahon
(Anthony Honeyball) *hld up in tch in rr: mstke and slipped on landing 2nd: j.lft and uns rdr next* **13/2**

4/0- **P** **Best Boy Barney (IRE)**[21] [1941] 7-11-10 **108**................(t) NickScholfield
(Jeremy Scott) *in tch towards rr: bdly hmpd and dropped to rr 4th: wl bhd next: t.o fr 6th: j. slowly next: p.u 9th* **16/1**

P/P- **U** **Goodtoknow**[177] [289] 5-11-4 **105**.......................... JakeGreenall(3)
(Richard Lee) *hld up in tch in midfield: bdly hmpd and uns rdr 4th* **11/2**[3]

4m 8.1s (-8.00) **Going Correction** -0.575s/f (Firm) **10** Ran SP% **115.4**
Speed ratings (Par 105): **95,94,89,89,82 82,64,,,**
toteswingers 1&2 £10.50, 2&3 £26.00, 1&3 £57.10 CSF £122.05 CT £2057.16 TOTE £21.70: £4.10, £1.30, £4.60; EX 114.60 Trifecta £813.70 Part won. Pool: £1084.96 - 0.02 winning units..
Owner G A Libson D L Bayliss G Taylor P M Sly **Bred** Harton Limited **Trained** Thorney, Cambs

FOCUS
The winner scored under a positive ride in this novice handicap and the third ran much better than his finishing position. The first two are seemingly better chasers than hurdlers.

2316 WEATHERBYS NOVICES' HURDLE (11 hdls) 2m 5f
3:10 (3:11) (Class 4) 4-Y-O+ **£3,119** (£915; £457; £228)

Form RPR

1 **Mountain Tunes (IRE)**[250] 4-10-12 0.......................... APMcCoy 125+
(Jonjo O'Neill) *nt a fluent: hld up in tch in rr: hdwy bef 3 out: rdn to chse ldng trio bnd bef 2 out: 5 l down and j. awkwardly 2 out: kpt on to go 2nd whn j.lft and bmpd rival last: led fnl 50yds: styd on wl* **6/4**[1]

042/ **2** *½* **Kris Spin (IRE)**[201] [5408] 5-10-12 125.......................... JamieMoore 123+
(Richard Lee) *chsd ldrs: mstke 7th: rdn to ld on uphill run after 3 out: hdd next: sn drvn to ld again: kpt on tl hdd and no ex fnl 50yds* **7/1**[3]

3/ **3** *7* **Panama Petrus (IRE)**[358] [2416] 5-10-12 0.......................... AidanColeman 116+
(Venetia Williams) *wl in tch in midfield: hdwy on outer to join ldrs on outer on uphill run after 3 out: led and j.rt next: sn hdd and drvn: 3rd and keeping on same pce whn bmpd last: wknd flat* **20/1**

1- **4** *15* **Premier Portrait (IRE)**[15] [2028] 6-11-5 0.......................... JasonMaguire 108
(Kim Bailey) *wl in tch in midfield: clsd to chse ldr 3 out: rdn and ev ch on uphill run bef next: 4th and btn 2 out: wknd* **8/1**

5 *¾* **Walk On Al (IRE)**[225] 5-10-12 0.......................... HarrySkelton 100
(Dan Skelton) *hld up wl in tch in midfield: rdn and effrt on uphill run after 3 out: btn bnd befroe 2 out and sn wknd* **33/1**

1- **6** *25* **Prideofthecastle (IRE)**[172] [395] 6-10-12 0.......................... TomScudamore 78
(David Pipe) *w ldr tl led after 6th: rdn and hdd on uphill run after 3 out: sn btn: fdd 2 out: eased flat: t.o* **15/8**[2]

5- **7** *5* **Hurricane Ivan (IRE)**[12] [2076] 5-10-5 0.......................... ConorShoemark(7) 73
(Fergal O'Brien) *chsd ldrs: rdn 7th: ev ch 3 out: btn on uphill run to next and sn dropped out: fdd bef 2 out: t.o* **100/1**

6/3- **P** **Westaway (IRE)**[162] [538] 6-10-12 115.......................... TomCannon
(David Arbuthnot) *t.k.h: hld up in wl in tch in midfield: sddle slipped after 1st: p.u 3rd* **10/1**

06/ **P** **Scuderia (IRE)**[552] [75] 6-10-12 0.......................... BrendanPowell
(Jamie Snowden) *led tl after 6th: chsd ldr tl jst bef 3 out: losing pl whn mstke 3 out: sn dropped out and t.o whn p.u 2 out* **100/1**

5/0- **U** **Major Martin (IRE)**[37] [1712] 4-10-12 0.......................... SamTwiston-Davies
(Charlie Brooks) *hld up in lst pair: blnd bdly and uns rdr 1st* **100/1**

/P0- **P** **Rose Of Marron (IRE)**[32] [1794] 6-10-9 0.......................... GavinSheehan(3)
(John Upson) *racd wd and j.lft: bhd and rdn 5th: lost tch 6th: t.o next tl p.u 2 out* **125/1**

5m 23.1s (-4.10) **Going Correction** -0.10s/f (Good)
WFA 4 from 5yo+ 8lb **11** Ran SP% **119.0**
Speed ratings (Par 105): **103,102,100,94,94 84,82,,,**
toteswingers 1&2 £4.30, 2&3 £22.50, 1&3 £16.40 CSF £12.78 TOTE £2.50: £1.10, £2.50, £5.50; EX 12.10 Trifecta £143.80 Pool: £2028.57 - 10.58 winning units..
Owner John P McManus **Bred** Neil R Tector **Trained** Cheltenham, Gloucs
■ Tony McCoy's 4,000th winner under jumps rules in Britain and Ireland.
■ Stewards' Enquiry : Jason Maguire one-day ban: careless riding (Nov 21)

FOCUS
Plenty had chances around the final turn in this decent novice hurdle. The winner is above average and can rate higher. The second set a fair standard.

2317 WEATHERBYS MARES' "NATIONAL HUNT" MAIDEN HURDLE (8 hdls) 2m
3:40 (3:43) (Class 5) 4-Y-O+ **£1,949** (£572; £286; £143)

Form RPR

1/1- **1** **Down Ace (IRE)**[173] [372] 6-11-0 0.......................... TimmyMurphy 110+
(Fergal O'Brien) *hld up wl in tch and a travelling wl: drew clr w ldr on uphill run after 3 out: led between last: in command whn wnt lft last: pushed along and readily asserted flat: comf* **4/5**[1]

12- **2** *1 ¼* **Reves D'Amour (IRE)**[29] [1823] 4-11-0 0.......................... BrendanPowell 103
(Jamie Snowden) *chsd ldrs: rdn and effrt to ld on uphill run after 3 out: clr w wnr bef next: hdd and no ex between last 2: lft pressing wnr again last: sn brushed aside and one pce flat* **6/1**[2]

150/ **3** *4 ½* **My Miss Lucy**[607] [4780] 7-11-0 0.......................... NoelFehily 99
(Charlie Longsdon) *w ldr tl led jst bef 3 out: rdn and hdd on uphill run wl bef 2 out: 3rd and hld whn j. slowly 2 out: kpt on same pce after* **15/2**[3]

200/ **4** *4 ½* **Rising Teal**[192] [35] 4-11-0 0.......................... LeightonAspell 95
(Lucy Wadham) *mstkes: hld up in rr: rdn and hdwy on uphill run after 3 out: wnt 4th between last 2: kpt on but no threat to ldrs* **50/1**

63/ **5** *6* **Lady Charisma**[198] [5469] 4-11-0 0.......................... TomO'Brien 90
(Philip Hobbs) *t.k.h: wl in tch in midfield: rdn and outpcd on uphill run after 3 out: wl hld and one pce fr next* **12/1**

240/ **6** *2 ¼* **Queen Olivia**[311] [3389] 5-11-0 0.......................... AndrewThornton 88
(Caroline Bailey) *t.k.h: hld up in tch in midfield: hdwy to chse ldrs after 3rd: 3rd and rdn on uphill run after 3 out: 4th and btn 2 out: wknd bef last* **40/1**

6/- **7** *hd* **Armedandbeautiful**[198] [5479] 5-11-0 0.......................... DougieCostello 87
(Tom Gretton) *chsd ldrs: lost pl and towards rr whn rdn after 4th: outpcd 3 out: rallied 2 out: swtchd rt between last 2: styd on but no threat to ldrs* **40/1**

342/ **8** *1 ¼* **Bonnet's Vino**[192] [36] 5-10-11 0.......................... KielanWoods(3) 86
(Pam Sly) *led: hit 4th: hdd jst bef 3 out: btn on uphill run wl bef 2 out: wknd 2 out* **20/1**

0/ **9** *¾* **Lady Fingers**[544] [221] 5-11-0 0.......................... SamTwiston-Davies 86
(Nigel Twiston-Davies) *in tch in midfield: effrt and mstke 3 out: no imp on uphill ruin to next: wknd 2 out* **28/1**

4/4- **10** *½* **Siksika (IRE)**[15] [2027] 5-11-0 0.......................... HarrySkelton 85
(Dan Skelton) *in tch in midfield: hdwy bef 3 out: 6th and btn on uphill run bef 2 out: wknd u.p between last 2* **33/1**

40- **11** *1* **Amber Flush**[15] [2022] 4-11-0 0.......................... FelixDeGiles 84
(Tom Symonds) *hld up in tch in rr of main gp: mstke 5th: rdn and no hdwy 3 out: wknd on uphill run to next* **66/1**

605- **12** *18* **Katie's Massini (IRE)**[29] [1823] 5-11-0 0.......................... RobertThornton 68
(Henry Oliver) *hld up in tch towards rr of main gp: rdn and btn 3 out: wknd on uphill run to next: wl bhd and blnd last: t.o* **66/1**

06- **13** *33* **Langarve Lady (IRE)**[14] [2053] 5-10-11 0.......................... MichaelByrne(3) 38
(Neil Mulholland) *mstkes and sn bhd: t.o fr 4th* **100/1**

60- **14** *15* **Fairy Bay**[41] [1671] 6-10-7 0.......................... MrRJarrett(7) 25
(Pam Ford) *mstkes: sn bhd in last pair: t.o after 4th* **200/1**

2/3- **15** *2 ¼* **Amazing D'Azy (IRE)**[29] [1823] 5-11-0 0.......................... JasonMaguire 23
(Kim Bailey) *chsd ldrs: ev ch 3 out: sn btn and dropped out on uphill run to next: eased bef 2 out: t.o* **14/1**

4m 2.2s (-5.70) **Going Correction** -0.10s/f (Good)
WFA 4 from 5yo+ 7lb **15** Ran SP% **118.4**
Speed ratings (Par 103): **110,109,107,104,101 100,100,100,99,99 98,89,73,65,64**
toteswingers 1&2 £1.70, 2&3 £3.50, 1&3 £3.30 CSF £4.94 TOTE £2.00: £1.20, £1.50, £2.30; EX 6.10 Trifecta £24.20 Pool: £1852.20 - 57.27 winning units..
Owner Paul Sullivan **Bred** Mrs C J Berry **Trained** Coln St. Dennis, Gloucs

FOCUS
The two market leaders pulled clear in this modest mares' maiden hurdle and the winner scored with more in hand than the winning margin. She should rate higher.

2318 AGETUR UK "JUNIOR" FILLIES' STANDARD OPEN NATIONAL HUNT FLAT RACE 1m 5f 110y
4:10 (4:10) (Class 6) 3-Y-O **£1,559** (£457; £228; £114)

Form RPR

1 **Pitter Patter** 3-11-0 0.......................... PaddyBrennan 93+
(Fergal O'Brien) *chsd ldrs: wnt 2nd and travelling wl over 3f out: clr w ldr 2f out: rdn to ld ent fnl f: rn green and edgd rt: styd on* **6/1**[2]

2 *2 ½* **Puzzle Time** 3-10-11 0.......................... JackQuinlan(3) 90
(Giles Bravery) *t.k.h: led and rn green: rdn and clr w wnr 2f out: hdd ent fnl f: swtchd lft and styd on same pce fnl 100yds* **14/1**

3 *2 ½* **May Hay** 3-11-0 0.......................... RobertThornton 87
(Anthony Carson) *in tch in midfield: effrt to chse ldng pair 3f: rdn and sltly outpcd over 2f out: kpt on u.p fnl f* **10/1**[3]

4 *9* **Anda De Grissay (FR)** 3-10-11 0..........................(t) RachaelGreen(3) 76
(Anthony Honeyball) *hld up in tch in last trio: hdwy whn swtchd ins and hit rail on uphill run 3f out: 4th and no imp fnl 2f* **10/3**[1]

5 *11* **Todoistodare** 3-11-0 0.......................... BrendanPowell 63
(Brendan Powell) *chsd ldr tl over 3f out: 4th and drvn over 2f out: sn btn: wknd 2f out* **10/3**[1]

6 *nk* **Instagramher** 3-11-0 0.......................... SamTwiston-Davies 63
(Charlie Brooks) *in tch in midfield: lost pl and rdn 6f out: sme hdwy on uphill run 3f out but no threat to ldrs: no imp fnl 2f* **10/1**[3]

7 *13* **Bally Broadwell** 3-11-0 0.......................... MarcGoldstein 47
(Michael Madgwick) *in tch in midfield: rdn over 3f out: sn struggling on uphill run: wknd over 2f out: t.o* **25/1**

8 *hd* **Tina's Gift** 3-10-11 0.......................... WayneKavanagh(3) 47
(Seamus Mullins) *in tch in last trio: rdn and effrt 4f out: sn struggling on uhill run: wknd over 2f out: t.o* **6/1**[2]

9 *11* **Seven Belle** 3-10-11 0.......................... RobertDunne(3) 34
(Dai Burchell) *t.k.h: chsd ldrs tl lost pl 4f out: wknd on uphill run over 3f out and sn bhd: t.o* **40/1**

10 *2* **Gilly's Filly** 3-10-7 0.......................... RyanWhile(7) 31
(Bill Turner) *chsd ldrs: rdn 4f out: wknd on uphill run over 3f out: bhd fnl 2f: t.o* **22/1**

11 *13* **Life In Bars** 3-10-7 0.......................... MrAlexEdwards(7) 16
(Dave Roberts) *in tch in last trio: rdn 4f out: sn dropped out: wl bhd 2f out: t.o* **50/1**

3m 27.5s (-13.10) **11** Ran SP% **112.2**
toteswingers 1&2 £34.30, 2&3 £3.40, 1&3 £9.30 CSF £78.01 TOTE £2.40: £1.10, £4.60, £4.80; EX 89.80 Trifecta £787.10 Pool: £2008.76 - 1.91 winning units..
Owner Nicholas Jones **Bred** Coln Valley Stud **Trained** Coln St. Dennis, Gloucs

FOCUS
Eleven newcomers lined-up in this junior fillies' bumper. The pace was steady but the winner scored in smooth style and the first three finished clear of the rest.
T/Jkpt: Not won. T/Plt: £92.40 to a £1 stake. Pool of £95673.62 - 755.78 winning tickets. T/Qpdt: £46.20 to a £1 stake. Pool of £6738.55 - 107.90 winning tickets. SP

2319 - 2325a (Foreign Racing) - See Raceform Interactive

2016 FONTWELL (L-H)
Friday, November 8
2326 Meeting Abandoned - Waterlogged

1870 HEXHAM (L-H)
Friday, November 8

OFFICIAL GOING: Soft (4.8)
Wind: light 1/2 behind Weather: fine, becoming overcast, light showers race 4

2333 HEXHAM H'CAP HURDLE (12 hdls) 3m
12:50 (12:50) (Class 5) (0-100,99) 4-Y-O+ **£2,053** (£598; £299)

Form RPR

/40- **1** **Charlie Bucket**[167] [471] 10-10-4 **82**.......................... CallumWhillans(5) 87
(Donald Whillans) *hdwy to chse ldrs 6th: drvn 9th: led between last 2: all out* **5/1**[3]

500- **2** *hd* **Brae On (IRE)**[33] [1791] 5-10-3 **83**.......................... JonathonBewley(7) 89
(George Bewley) *hld up in rr: hdwy 9th: modest 4th 2 out: styd on and cl 3rd last: no ex nr fin* **10/1**

3/0- 3 1 3/4 **Lady Of Verona (IRE)**[43] 1664 6-10-9 89 CraigNichol(7) 92
(Lucinda Russell) *hdwy to trck ldrs 6th: upsides last: kpt on same pce* 10/3[1]

/34- 4 21 **Bob's Ticket (IRE)**[157] 628 8-10-8 86 AdamNicol(5) 74
(Philip Kirby) *led: hdd between last 2: wknd appr last* 9/2[2]

663- P **Flying Doctor**[27] 1874 10-11-8 98 EwanWhillans(3)
(Alistair Whillans) *chsd ldrs: wknd 3 out: t.o whn p.u bef last* 15/2

230- P **Oh Right (IRE)**[33] 1800 9-9-13 77 (p) EmmaSayer(5)
(Dianne Sayer) *t.k.h: trckd ldr: lost pl 8th: sn bhd: t.o whn p.u bef 2 out* 17/2

0/0- P **Morello Mist**[27] 1874 8-9-9 66 SamanthaDrake(5)
(Richard Drake) *chsd ldrs: wknd 3 out: t.o whn p.u bef last* 14/1

0/P- P **Macklycuddy (USA)**[7] 2202 7-11-3 95 (t) TonyKelly(5)
(Rebecca Menzies) *chsd ldrs: pushed along 7th: lost pl 8th: sn bhd: t.o whn p.u bef last* 12/1

650- P **Silver Sophfire**[157] 629 7-11-12 99 RyanMania
(Sue Smith) *mid-div: lost pl 5th: bhd and reminders 7th: t.o whn p.u bef next* 16/1

PPF- P **Two Oscars (IRE)**[81] 1320 7-10-2 78 JohnKington(3)
(Andrew Crook) *in rr: sme hdwy 8th: lost pl 3 out: sn bhd: t.o whn p.u bef last* 66/1

6m 22.0s (13.00) **Going Correction** +0.525s/f (Soft) **10 Ran SP% 111.0**
Speed ratings (Par 103): **99,98,98,91, , , , ,**
toteswingers 1&2 £11.90, 2&3 £5.00, 1&3 £7.90 CSF £50.70 CT £181.83 TOTE £4.00: £1.90, £1.80, £1.60; EX 55.10 Trifecta £531.00 Part won. Pool: £708.03 - 0.86 winning units..
Owner D W Whillans **Bred** S W And J R Knowles **Trained** Hawick, Borders

FOCUS
Fresh ground on bends, back straight and all but one hurdle site. Very little in the way of recent form to go on in this weak staying handicap hurdle and it's hard to get excited about the form. The first three were close to their marks.

2334 WEATHERBYS HAMILTON INSURANCE NOVICES' H'CAP CHASE (19 fncs) 3m 1f
1:20 (1:21) (Class 4) (0-110,110) 4-Y-0 **£3,671** (£1,084; £542; £271; £135)

Form RPR

/33- 1 **The Friary (IRE)**[15] 2033 6-11-7 110 (tp) DerekFox(5) 117
(Lucinda Russell) *chsd ldrs: nt fluent 1st: sn lost pl: last and drvn 6th: hdwy 3 out: 3rd next: styd on to ld last 75yds: kpt on* 9/4[1]

2/P- 2 1 1/4 **Moyode Wood**[15] 2033 8-11-9 107 (p) DannyCook 112
(Brian Ellison) *led to 9th: led 12th: j.rt 4 out: hdd appr last: rallied to chse wnr last 75yds* 6/1

3/1- 3 4 1/2 **Capital Venture (IRE)**[20] 1982 7-11-4 102 LucyAlexander 104
(N W Alexander) *hld up: hdwy to trck ldrs 8th: led appr last: stmbld landing: hdd & wknd fnl 75yds* 5/2[2]

/1P- 4 19 **Lukey Luke**[162] 555 10-11-2 100 BrianHarding 85
(James Turner) *in rr: hdwy to trck ldrs 8th: handy 3rd 15th: wknd between last 2* 14/1

PF0- 5 23 **Stagecoach Jasper**[9] 2155 7-11-7 105 RyanMania 75
(Sue Smith) *w ldr: led 9th: hit 11th: hdd next: 5th and wkng whn hit 2 out: sn bhd and eased* 5/1[3]

420/ P **Notonebuttwo (IRE)**[221] 5078 6-10-7 91 BarryKeniry
(Chris Grant) *in rr: sme hdwy 8th: lost pl 11th: sn bhd: t.o whn p.u after 2 out* 10/1

0/0- P **Darlington County (IRE)**[23] 1924 5-11-5 103 (p) AdrianLane
(Donald McCain) *chsd ldrs: hit 5th and reminders: reminders and lost pl 15th: sn bhd: t.o whn p.u bef last* 25/1

6m 53.3s (21.10) **Going Correction** +0.775s/f (Soft) **7 Ran SP% 109.9**
Speed ratings (Par 105): **97,96,95,89,81 ,**
toteswingers 1&2 £2.70, 2&3 £1.90, 1&3 £1.40 CSF £14.85 TOTE £3.00: £1.70, £3.70; EX 17.40 Trifecta £54.90 Pool: £1621.73 - 22.13 winning units..
Owner Mrs S Russell & A M Russell **Bred** Michael And Fiona O'Connor **Trained** Arlary, Perth & Kinross

FOCUS
Testing ground for this moderate novices' handicap chase and it required a dour staying effort from the winner.

2335 WEATHERBYS HAMILTON INSURANCE CONDITIONAL JOCKEYS' H'CAP CHASE (15 fncs) 2m 4f 110y
1:50 (1:50) (Class 5) (0-100,93) 4-Y-0+ **£2,144** (£629; £314; £157)

Form RPR

153- 1 **Settledoutofcourt (IRE)**[23] 1925 7-11-6 93 CraigNichol(6) 114+
(Lucinda Russell) *chsd clr ldr 5th: led 12th: drew clr appr last: eased towards fin* 5/2[2]

P54- 2 12 **Fitandproperjob**[15] 2044 7-10-11 78 (tp) KielanWoods 83
(Anthony Middleton) *last whn hit 1st: hdwy to chse ldrs 8th: cl 2nd 3 out: kpt on same pce appr last* 8/1

020- 3 nk **Discoverie**[20] 1982 5-10-3 75 DiarmuidO'Regan(5) 80
(Dianne Sayer) *chsd ldrs to 3rd: reminders 9th: outpcd and lost pl 11th: kpt on to take modest 3rd bef last: styd on* 10/1

P/3- 4 24 **Twice Lucky**[15] 2036 9-10-13 83 JonathanEngland(3) 64
(Sue Smith) *led: wnt clr 4th: jnd 8th: hdd 12th: wknd qckly between last 2: sn bhd* 9/4[1]

5/0- 5 32 **Samson Collonges (FR)**[167] 473 7-10-0 67 HarryChalloner 16
(Rebecca Menzies) *chsd ldrs to 3rd: j. slowly and lost pl 7th: bhd fr 10th: t.o 3 out* 10/3[3]

0PF- P **King's Chorister**[27] 1870 7-11-10 91 (t) TonyKelly
(Barry Murtagh) *in rr 4th: drvn 10th: sn bhd: t.o whn p.u bef last* 18/1

5m 31.9s (18.40) **Going Correction** +0.775s/f (Soft) **6 Ran SP% 107.9**
Speed ratings (Par 103): **95,90,90,81,68**
toteswingers 1&2 £4.60, 1&3 £5.40, 2&3 Not won CSF £19.35 TOTE £3.10: £1.80, £3.00; EX 15.90 Trifecta £79.60 Pool: £1302.56 - 12.26 winning units..
Owner Andrew McAllister **Bred** Sean Naughton **Trained** Arlary, Perth & Kinross

FOCUS
They went a good clip given the conditions. A big step up from the easy winner with the next two setting the level.

2336 ROWLANDS CHARTERED ACCOUNTANTS H'CAP HURDLE (8 hdls) 2m 110y
2:25 (2:26) (Class 5) (0-95,95) 4-Y-0+ **£2,874** (£837; £419)

Form RPR

203- 1 **Morning Time (IRE)**[27] 1876 7-11-5 95 (p) GrantCockburn(7) 103+
(Lucinda Russell) *trckd ldrs: cl 2nd 2 out: led bef last: drvn out* 5/1[2]

/01- 2 5 **Blake Dean**[7] 2191 5-10-7 81 7ex JonathanEngland(5) 87
(Sue Smith) *w ldr: led 3rd: hdd appr last: styd on same pce* 8/11[1]

550- 3 13 **Mrs Grass**[33] 1790 6-10-10 82 JohnKington(3) 72
(Jonathan Haynes) *hld up in rr: chsd ldrs 5th: one pce fr 2 out* 100/1

00/- 4 8 **Master Murphy (IRE)**[201] 5423 8-11-5 95 AlistairFindlay(7) 77
(Jane Walton) *in rr: hdwy to chse ldrs after 4th: lost pl next: kpt on to take poor 4th appr last* 10/1

/60- 5 32 **Wave Breaker (IRE)**[157] 628 6-10-7 76 (p) KennyJohnson 26
(Robert Johnson) *led to 3rd: drvn next: lost pl 3 out: sn bhd: t.o between last 2* 13/2[3]

500- 6 31 **Ancient Times (USA)**[146] 749 6-11-3 89 KyleJames(3) 8
(Philip Kirby) *chsd ldrs: drvn 3rd: sn lost pl: bhd whn hit 5th: t.o next* 10/1

016- P **Ravi River (IRE)**[24] 1575 9-10-7 79 (p) EwanWhillans(3)
(Alistair Whillans) *chsd ldrs: 2nd whn hit 3 out: sn wknd: t.o whn p.u bef last* 16/1

/00- P **Rayadour (IRE)**[15] 2030 4-11-7 90 (t) BrianHarding
(Micky Hammond) *in rr: bhd and drvn 4th: t.o whn p.u bef 3 out* 20/1

4m 25.7s (8.30) **Going Correction** +0.525s/f (Soft) **8 Ran SP% 117.7**
Speed ratings (Par 103): **101,98,92,88,73 59, ,**
toteswingers 1&2 £1.10, 1&3 £21.50, 2&3 £5.00 CSF £9.67 CT £329.14 TOTE £5.30: £1.60, £1.10, £7.40; EX 10.50 Trifecta £177.40 Pool: £1602.51 - 6.77 winning units..
Owner Bill Forrester **Bred** Joe O'Flaherty **Trained** Arlary, Perth & Kinross

FOCUS
A fair race for the grade. A step up from the winner on his recent form, and similar to his old best.

2337 HAPPY BIRTHDAY RON WOODMAN NOVICES' HURDLE (10 hdls) 2m 4f 110y
2:55 (2:55) (Class 4) 4-Y-0+ **£3,119** (£915; £457; £228)

Form RPR

32- 1 **Kilbree Chief (IRE)**[23] 1924 5-10-5 0 CraigNichol(7) 116+
(Lucinda Russell) *mde all: j. soundly: jnd 3 out: drvn and kpt on wl between last 2: hld on wl* 13/8[1]

2/4- 2 1 3/4 **Romany Ryme**[15] 2034 7-10-5 104 JonathonBewley(7) 111
(George Bewley) *jnd ldrs 3rd: outpcd appr 2 out: rallied: swtchd lft and chsd wnr appr last: nt fluent: kpt on wl* 15/2

132- 3 11 **Ocean Club**[43] 1662 6-11-5 120 DannyCook 107
(Brian Ellison) *chsd ldrs: outpcd 3rd and drvn 2 out: one pce* 2/1[2]

4- 4 8 **Uppercut De L'Orne (FR)**[176] 345 5-10-12 0 AdrianLane 92
(Donald McCain) *chsd ldrs: outpcd 7th: one pce fr 2 out* 12/1

P/6- 5 2 1/4 **Danebrook Lad (IRE)**[27] 1875 7-10-12 0 RyanMania 89
(Sandy Thomson) *in rr: reminders 6th: sn bhd: kpt on between last 2: nvr on terms* 100/1

6- 6 6 **Milan Flyer (IRE)**[20] 1977 7-10-7 0 DerekFox(5) 83
(Noel C Kelly, Ire) *chsd ldrs: lost pl 7th: sn bhd* 33/1

3- 7 18 **You'resomedreamer (IRE)**[27] 1877 5-10-5 0 GrantCockburn(7) 73
(Lucinda Russell) *trckd ldrs 3rd: 2nd 6th: upsides 3 out: wknd between last 2: 4th whn eased last: virtually p.u clsng stages* 40/1

00- 8 16 **Marlee Massie (IRE)**[15] 2037 4-10-12 0 LucyAlexander 49
(N W Alexander) *nt jump wl in last: in rr: bhd fr 7th: t.o 2 out* 150/1

6- F **Ballinalacken (IRE)**[19] 1991 5-10-9 0 MarkMarris(10) 96
(Anthony Middleton) *trckd ldrs: mstke 3 out: 4th and wkng whn fell 2 out* 5/1[3]

5m 30.5s (18.00) **Going Correction** +0.525s/f (Soft)
WFA 4 from 5yo+ 8lb **9 Ran SP% 114.6**
Speed ratings (Par 105): **86,85,81,78,77 74,68,62,**
toteswingers 1&2 £1.30, 1&3 £1.02, 2&3 £7.60 CSF £14.38 TOTE £2.60: £1.30, £1.50, £1.10; EX 13.50 Trifecta £36.10 Pool: £1760.58 - 36.47 winning units..
Owner John R Adam **Bred** James Griffin **Trained** Arlary, Perth & Kinross
■ A 178-1 four-timer for Lucinda Russell.

FOCUS
Ocean Club set a decent standard on paper and the way in which he was brushed aside suggests the winner could be useful. The first two rate on the upgrade under claimers, with the third a stone+ off.

2338 SIS H'CAP CHASE (12 fncs) 2m 110y
3:25 (3:25) (Class 5) (0-95,95) 4-Y-0+ **£2,258** (£658; £329)

Form RPR

6P0- 1 **Have You Had Yours (IRE)**[28] 1851 7-9-11 73 ow2 AlistairFindlay(7) 84
(Jane Walton) *chsd ldrs 2nd: outpcd after 9th: styd on and modest 3rd between last 2: chsd ldr sn after last: styd on to ld towards fin* 9/2[2]

336/ 2 nk **Pamak D'Airy (FR)**[243] 4681 10-11-7 95 (p) TonyKelly(5) 107
(Henry Hogarth) *trckd ldrs: 2nd 9th: led 2 out: 4 l ahd last: hdd and no ex clsng stages* 13/2[3]

6P0- 3 2 3/4 **Panthers Run**[27] 1876 13-9-11 69 oh4 (t) JohnKington(3) 77
(Jonathan Haynes) *led to 2 out: kpt on one pce appr last* 18/1

0/0- 4 13 **Prince Blackthorn (IRE)**[178] 279 7-10-5 74 BrianHarding 69
(William Amos) *in rr: hdwy to chse ldrs 4th: outpcd 7th: hdwy 9th: outpcd and modest 5th whn hit next* 7/2[1]

3/4- 5 19 **Crackerjack Lad (IRE)**[177] 314 10-10-13 82 PeterBuchanan 58
(Lucinda Russell) *trckd ldrs: 3rd 9th: outpcd after next: wknd qckly between last 2* 7/2[1]

/0P- 6 14 **Vardas Supreme (IRE)**[15] 2048 10-11-1 89 (vt[1]) SamanthaDrake(5) 58
(Richard Drake) *chsd ldrs: drvn 6th: lost pl next: bhd fr 3 out* 14/1

4/1- P **Local Present (IRE)**[27] 1876 10-10-13 82 BarryKeniry
(James Turner) *rn in snatches: chsd ldrs 7th: lost pl and j.lft 9th: sn bhd: t.o 2 out: p.u bef last* 7/2[1]

4m 23.3s (13.50) **Going Correction** +0.775s/f (Soft) **7 Ran SP% 110.1**
Speed ratings (Par 103): **99,98,97,91,82 75,**
toteswingers 1&2 £21.40, 1&3 £18.20, 2&3 £14.20 CSF £30.27 TOTE £4.40: £2.20, £2.40; EX 36.80 Trifecta £328.00 Pool: £1347.97 - 3.08 winning units..
Owner Highly Recommended Partnership **Bred** Margaret McKenna **Trained** Otterburn, Northumberland

FOCUS
It was hard to be confident about any of these beforehand and, with the ground going against Local Present, it remains to be seen how well the form holds up.

2339 RAMSIDE EVENT CATERING H'CAP CHASE (19 fncs) 3m 1f
3:55 (3:56) (Class 5) (0-95,95) 4-Y-0+ **£2,144** (£629; £314; £157)

Form RPR

310/ 1 **Matmata De Tendron (FR)**[200] 5450 13-10-6 78 (p) JohnKington(3) 87
(Andrew Crook) *w ldrs: hit 4th: led 6th to 9th: led 13th: drvn 3 out: styd on gamely* 14/1

3PP/ 2 11 **Presented (IRE)**[240] 4741 6-11-12 95 DannyCook 94
(Brian Ellison) *chsd ldrs: hdwy and 15th: rdn 2 out: kpt on one pce* 9/4[1]

406- 3 11 **Cilliseal (IRE)**[27] 1873 8-11-5 93 (bt[1]) DerekFox(5) 80
(Noel C Kelly, Ire) *in rr: hdwy 15th: 3rd 2 out: one pce* 11/2[3]

0/P- 4 shd **Stormion (IRE)**[27] 1874 8-11-4 94 (v) MrSFox(7) 81
(Lucinda Russell) *in rr: bhd fr 7th: kpt on fr 2 out: styng on at fin* 22/1

021- 5 28 **Bennys Well (IRE)**[22] 1936 7-10-7 81 JonathanEngland(5) 40
(Sue Smith) *chsd ldrs: wknd 4 out: wl bhd 2 out* 3/1[2]

The Form Book Jumps, Raceform Ltd, Compton, RG20 6NL.

0/5- P Great Ocean Road (IRE)[177] 311 10-9-9 69 oh2............ AdamNicol(5)
(David Thompson) *led to 2nd: led 9th to 13th: blnd next: sn lost pl: bhd 4 out: t.o whn p.u bef 2 out* 33/1

5/0- P Runswick Relax[167] 473 7-11-9 92.................................. BrianHarding
(John Wade) *in rr: bhd fr 7th: t.o 4 out: p.u bef 2 out* 10/1

0/0- P The Shrimp (IRE)[27] 1870 6-10-6 75.................................(p) RyanMania
(Sandy Thomson) *chsd ldrs: outpcd 12th: lost pl bef 14th: t.o whn p.u bef next* 18/1

5- P Terry Tibbs (IRE)[36] 1728 8-11-12 95............................. RichieMcGrath
(J T R Dreaper, Ire) *hld up in rr: hdwy 7th: chsng ldrs after 13th: weakend qckly appr 2 out: t.o 6th whn p.u bef last* 6/1

6m 55.4s (23.20) **Going Correction** +0.825s/f (Soft) **9** Ran SP% **113.7**
Speed ratings (Par 103): **95,91,87,87,78** , , ,
toteswingers 1&2 £5.20, 1&3 £17.40, 2&3 £2.50 CSF £47.01 CT £200.01 TOTE £8.20: £2.80, £1.30, £1.80; EX 49.70 Trifecta £646.20 Pool: £1482.92 - 1.72 winning units..
Owner Lucky Catch Partnership **Bred** Gerard Mercier **Trained** Middleham Moor, N Yorks

FOCUS
A real slog and a brave front-running effort from the winner. He's rated in line with best of form from last year.
T/Plt: £66.90 to a £1 stake. Pool: £73455.82 - 801.16 winning tickets T/Qpdt: £15.80 to a £1 stake. Pool: £6566.48 - 305.77 winning tickets WG

2306 MUSSELBURGH (R-H)
Friday, November 8

OFFICIAL GOING: Good (good to soft in places; 6.8)
Wind: Fresh, half against Weather: Cloudy

2340 DALHOUSIE BONNYRIGG NOVICES' HURDLE (DIV I) (9 hdls) 2m
12:30 (12:30) (Class 4) 4-Y-0+ **£3,898** (£1,144; £572; £286)

Form RPR
/21- 1 Purple Bay (IRE)[13] 2089 4-11-5 0.................................. DenisO'Regan 126+
(John Ferguson) *t.k.h early: prom: hit 1st: wnt 2nd next: led gng wl 2 out: clr whn nt fluent last: easily* 1/3[1]

/25- 2 7 Biggar (IRE)[28] 1853 5-10-5 0...................................... GrahamWatters(7) 105
(Lucinda Russell) *led: rdn and hdd 2 out: kpt on same pce fr last* 12/1

3- 3 11 Downtown Boy (IRE)[38] 1713 5-10-12 0............................ AidanColeman 99
(Chris Grant) *in tch: pushed along and no imp whn lft 6 l 3rd and hmpd 2 out: one pce* 8/1[3]

4 16 May's Boy[49] 5-10-12 0.. BrianHughes 81
(James Moffatt) *hld up: struggling 1/2-way: no imp whn lft 4th 2 out* 33/1

5 32 Ferney Boy[20] 7-10-12 0.. JamesReveley 52
(Chris Fairhurst) *mstkes: chsd ldr to 2nd: struggling fr 4th: t.o* 100/1

0/P- 6 2 Tchatchaco Ya Ya[20] 1977 6-10-12 0............................... JasonMaguire 50
(Nicky Richards) *nt fluent in rr: struggling fr 4th: t.o* 50/1

3- F Memory Cloth[13] 2089 6-10-5 0.................................. CraigGallagher(7) 105+
(Brian Ellison) *plld hrd early and sddle sn slipped forward: trckd ldrs: hit 4th: effrt 3 out: nrly 3 l down and disputing 3rd whn fell next* 4/1[2]

50- F Trois Vallees (USA)[21] 1958 4-10-12 0............................. PeterBuchanan 105
(Lucinda Russell) *hld up in tch: effrt and rdn bef 3 out: nrly three l down and disputing 3rd whn fell next* 16/1

3m 46.3s (-2.10) **Going Correction** -0.30s/f (Good) **8** Ran SP% **125.6**
Speed ratings (Par 105): **93,89,84,76,60 59**, ,
toteswingers 1&2 £3.80, 2&3 £7.30, 1&3 £1.80 CSF £7.63 TOTE £1.60: £1.02, £3.50, £2.60; EX 9.40 Trifecta £40.00 Pool: £2438.84 - 45.64 winning units..
Owner Bloomfields **Bred** Darley **Trained** Cowlinge, Suffolk

FOCUS
Hurdles and chases used common bend. A steadily run novice hurdle. The easy winner was value for further and should go on to rate higher, while the third helps set the level.

2341 DALHOUSIE BONNYRIGG NOVICES' HURDLE (DIV II) (9 hdls) 2m
1:00 (1:00) (Class 4) 4-Y-0+ **£3,898** (£1,144; £572; £286)

Form RPR
1- 1 Franciscan[74] 1389 5-11-5 0... JasonMaguire 125+
(Donald McCain) *trckd ldrs: hdwy to ld bef 2 out: drvn clr fr last* 7/4[1]

1/1- 2 6 Clever Cookie[140] 790 5-10-12 0................................... WilsonRenwick 106
(Peter Niven) *t.k.h: hld up in tch: mstke 2nd: stdy hdwy after 4 out: drvn and outpcd briefly bef 2 out: rallied to chse (clr) wnr run-in: no imp* 3/1[2]

/14- 3 1 Bellgrove (IRE)[43] 1667 5-10-12 0................................. DougieCostello 107+
(Ian Semple) *led: rdn and hdd whn mstke 2 out: lost 2nd run-in: no imp* 12/1

30- 4 2 3/4 Tourtiere[9] 2156 5-10-12 0... HarrySkelton 103
(George Moore) *t.k.h: hld up: stdy hdwy after 4 out: effrt whn hit 2 out: kpt on same pce* 66/1

P/ 5 1 Figaro[252] 4498 5-10-12 0..(t) RichardJohnson 102
(Tim Vaughan) *chsd ldr: rdn bef 2 out: outpcd bef last* 9/1[3]

3- 6 11 Pulpitarian (USA)[13] 2075 5-10-12 0............................... PeterBuchanan 94
(Lucinda Russell) *t.k.h: in tch: rdn and outpcd whn nt fluent 3 out: sn btn* 3/1[2]

0/ 7 3 1/4 Thorlak (FR)[593] 5089 6-10-12 0.................................... BrianHughes 88
(James Ewart) *chsd ldrs: lost pl 5th: struggling fr next* 16/1

0- 8 1 3/4 Inniscastle Boy[6] 2217 4-10-12 0..................................... GaryBartley 87
(Jim Goldie) *t.k.h: hld up: rdn and outpcd after 4 out: btn next* 80/1

333/ 9 48 New Academy[200] 5454 5-10-5 0................................... JohnDawson(7) 44
(John Wade) *prom: nt fluent and lost pl 5th: lost tch after next: t.o* 33/1

3m 46.3s (-2.10) **Going Correction** -0.30s/f (Good)
WFA 4 from 5yo+ 7lb **9** Ran SP% **115.6**
Speed ratings (Par 105): **93,90,89,88,87 82,80,79,55**
toteswingers 1&2 £2.80, 2&3 £7.30, 1&3 £6.00 CSF £7.31 TOTE £2.40: £1.10, £1.90, £2.20; EX 8.20 Trifecta £26.40 Pool: £2412.75 - 68.41 winning units..
Owner T G Leslie **Bred** Fittocks Stud **Trained** Cholmondeley, Cheshire

FOCUS
The second division of the novice hurdle and there was another routine gallop on. The easy winner is on the upgrade and there should be more to come, while the next two were close to their bumper marks.

2342 TURFTV HELPING VICTIM SUPPORT SCOTLAND MAIDEN HURDLE (14 hdls) 3m 110y
1:30 (1:30) (Class 4) 4-Y-0+ **£3,249** (£954; £477; £238)

Form RPR
12P- 1 Clondaw Hero (IRE)[65] 1497 5-11-0 0............................... JasonMaguire 122+
(Donald McCain) *mde all: rdn bef 3 out: styd on strly to go clr fr last* 7/2[3]

2/2- 2 10 Desgrey[28] 1850 5-11-0 114.. WilsonRenwick 111
(Peter Niven) *nt fluent: chsd ldrs: effrt whn hit 2 out: chsd (clr) wnr last: no imp* 7/4[1]

3 7 Masterleaderman (IRE)[391] 5-11-0 0........................... TomScudamore 105
(Michael Smith) *chsd wnr: hit 8th and next: drvn along bef 3 out: one pce next: lost 2nd last* 3/1[2]

336- 4 14 Twill Stand To Us (IRE)[43] 1666 6-10-7 107.........(t[1]) NathanMoscrop(7) 89
(Brian Ellison) *nt fluent on occasions: t.k.h: hld up: stdy hdwy whn hit 4 out: wkng whn nt fluent next* 4/1

5/4- 5 22 Knockturnal (IRE)[152] 682 5-10-7 0................................. BrianHughes 62
(Malcolm Jefferson) *hld up in tch: nt fluent 6th: rdn and wknd bef 3 out: t.o* 12/1

645- P Mo Rouge (IRE)[20] 1980 5-11-0 0.................................. DenisO'Regan
(Mrs Jackie Stephen) *in tch: outpcd 7th: lost tch fr next: t.o whn p.u bef 3 out* 40/1

5m 45.9s (-10.80) **Going Correction** -0.30s/f (Good) **6** Ran SP% **113.7**
Speed ratings (Par 105): **105,101,99,95,88**
toteswingers 1&2 £1.90, 2&3 £2.50, 1&3 £2.00 CSF £10.63 TOTE £3.70: £2.10, £1.50; EX 10.10 Trifecta £39.20 Pool: £1324.17 - 25.29 winning units..
Owner D McCain Jnr **Bred** P J Fortune **Trained** Cholmondeley, Cheshire

FOCUS
A modest staying maiden, run at a solid gallop. The winner looks a fair recruit and the form has been given a token rating through the second.

2343 SCOBAN NOVICES' LIMITED H'CAP CHASE (16 fncs) 2m 4f
2:00 (2:00) (Class 3) (0-140,138) 4-Y-0+ **£6,797** (£2,337)

Form RPR
/31- 1 Robbie[170] 425 9-10-13 132.. JamesReveley 125+
(Keith Reveley) *chsd ldr: hit 9th: nt fluent next: wnt 2nd and effrt bef 4 out: hit 2 out: shkn up and disputing ld whn lft 24 l clr last* 2/1[2]

40/ 2 21 Katys Girl (IRE)[15] 2054 7-10-5 124 oh3.........................(bt) BrianHughes 98
(Mrs Gillian Callaghan, Ire) *nt fluent: led to 5 out: rdn and wknd fr next: no ch whn lft 24 l 2nd last* 3/1[3]

/13- F Princely Player (IRE)[20] 1972 6-11-5 138..................... RichardJohnson 131
(Philip Hobbs) *t.k.h: nt fluent: chsd ldrs: mstke 4th: hit 6th: wnt 2nd 10th: led 5 out: rdn whn pckd 2 out: jnd whn fell last* 11/10[1]

4m 57.2s (-4.00) **Going Correction** -0.125s/f (Good) **3** Ran SP% **106.0**
Speed ratings (Par 107): **103,94,**
CSF £6.85 TOTE £2.60; EX 7.50 Trifecta £10.80 Pool: £1270.14 - 88.15 winning units..
Owner Mrs Susan McDonald **Bred** Mrs Susan McDonald **Trained** Lingdale, Redcar & Cleveland

FOCUS
An eventful novice handicap and dubious form with the time very slow. The winenr and faller are rated in line with their hurdles form.

2344 FERGUSSON COAL H'CAP HURDLE (9 hdls) 2m
2:35 (2:35) (Class 2) 4-Y-0+ **£12,996** (£3,816; £1,908; £954)

Form RPR
P/1- 1 Willow's Saviour[6] 2210 6-10-2 121 6ex............................. HarrySkelton 130+
(Dan Skelton) *pressed ldr: led appr 3 out: clr bef last: rdn and r.o wl* 11/8[1]

2/2- 2 3 1/2 Discovery Bay[20] 531 5-10-8 127.................................... AidanColeman 130
(Brian Ellison) *t.k.h: hld up: hdwy bef 3 out: effrt and chsd (clr) wnr bef last: kpt on run-in: no imp* 8/1[3]

P23/ 3 2 3/4 Population[276] 4040 6-10-4 123 ow1..............................(p) DenisO'Regan 124
(John Ferguson) *in tch: outpcd and hung rt bef 3 out: rallied bef last: kpt on: nt rch first two* 5/2[2]

100- 4 3/4 Australia Day (IRE)[61] 1046 10-11-4 137........................ LiamTreadwell 138
(Paul Webber) *led: rdn and hdd appr 3 out: one pce whn mstke last* 12/1

310- 5 1 Solaras Exhibition (IRE)[41] 1685 5-10-11 130............ RichardJohnson 131
(Tim Vaughan) *t.k.h: hld up in tch: mstke 5th: effrt whn hmpd 3 out: sn rdn: one pce whn mstke last* 28/1

112/ 6 hd Runswick Royal (IRE)[218] 5135 4-11-12 145.................... WilsonRenwick 144
(Ann Hamilton) *t.k.h in midfield: effrt and rdn after 3 out: one pce fr last* 14/1

/13- 7 11 Dhaular Dhar (IRE)[43] 1665 11-10-0 119 oh13.................. GaryBartley 112
(Jim Goldie) *hld up: rdn and outpcd bef 3 out: btn fr next* 66/1

211- 8 4 1/2 Saint Thomas (IRE)[38] 1713 6-10-6 125............................. BrianHughes 113
(John Mackie) *trckd ldrs: hit 2nd: rdn 3 out: wknd fr next* 10/1

061/ 9 10 Nine Stories (IRE)[364] 2317 8-10-8 127...........................(p) HenryBrooke 103
(Chris Grant) *bhd: outpcd bef 4th: sn struggling: nvr on terms* 28/1

112- U Smart Ruler (IRE)[60] 1540 7-10-0 119 oh2........................ DougieCostello
(James Moffatt) *t.k.h: trckd ldrs: cl 4th and stl gng wl whn stmbld and uns rdr 3 out* 16/1

3m 39.0s (-9.40) **Going Correction** -0.30s/f (Good) **10** Ran SP% **119.5**
Speed ratings (Par 109): **111,109,107,107,107 106,101,99,94,**
toteswingers 1&2 £4.50, 1&3 £2.60, 2&3 £4.90 CSF £13.64 CT £26.88 TOTE £2.80: £1.10, £2.10, £1.40; EX 15.70 Trifecta £47.20 Pool: £2832.42 - 44.98 winning units..
Owner Triple F Partnership **Bred** Mrs M Cuff **Trained** Alcester, Warwicks

FOCUS
A fair handicap. The winner was well in on his recent win and is rated a bit below that level.

2345 I & H BROWN H'CAP HURDLE (14 hdls) 3m 110y
3:05 (3:05) (Class 2) 4-Y-0+ **£12,996** (£3,816; £1,908; £954)

Form RPR
1/6- 1 Arctic Court (IRE)[175] 356 9-10-12 121............................. DenisO'Regan 120+
(Jim Goldie) *hld up on ins: stdy hdwy bef 3 out: led last: drvn out* 7/2[3]

0/1- 2 1/2 Capellanus (IRE)[15] 2050 7-10-11 127......................... CraigGallagher(7) 126
(Brian Ellison) *hld up: hdwy to chse ldrs 8th: rdn and outpcd bef 3 out: rallied next: chsd wnr last: kpt on u.p* 11/2

/00- 3 1 Monetary Fund (USA)[21] 1956 7-11-6 129......................... AidanColeman 126
(Venetia Williams) *chsd ldrs: effrt and rdn bef 3 out: kpt on fr last: hld nr fin* 12/5[1]

/44- 4 nk Los Nadis (GER)[27] 1541 9-10-7 116................................. HenryBrooke 114
(Jim Goldie) *led: rdn 3 out: hdd last: rallied: hld nr fin* 14/1

101- 5 12 Marmas[41] 1689 4-10-5 114... BrianHughes 104
(John Mackie) *cl up: nt fluent 6th: rdn and ev ch bef 3 out: wknd after next* 12/1

41/- 6 26 Golden Sparkle (IRE)[198] 5492 7-10-6 122................ GrahamWatters(7) 85
(Ian Duncan) *hld up in tch: hdwy on outside 8th: outpcd after next: struggling fr 3 out* 20/1

413- 7 7 So Fine (IRE)[21] 1956 7-11-9 132.................................... RichardJohnson 88
(Philip Hobbs) *prom: reminders 8th: rallied next: outpcd after 4 out: wknd bef next* 10/3[2]

141/ **P** **Ongenstown Lad (IRE)**[97] 1198 9-11-9 **135**............... KeithDonoghue[(3)]
(Mrs Gillian Callaghan, Ire) *nt fluent in rr: struggling 8th: losing tch whn p.u bef 4 out* **20/1**

5m 41.9s (-14.80) **Going Correction** -0.30s/f (Good)
WFA 4 from 7yo+ 9lb **8** Ran SP% **114.0**
Speed ratings (Par 109): **111,110,110,110,106 98,96,**
toteswingers 1&2 £5.20, 1&3 £3.10, 2&3 £4.10 CSF £23.07 CT £52.94 TOTE £5.50: £2.40, £1.10, £1.90; EX 28.20 Trifecta £123.30 Pool: £3062.01 - 18.61 winning units..
Owner Mr & Mrs Raymond Anderson Green **Bred** Paul Doyle **Trained** Uplawmoor, E Renfrews
■ Stewards' Enquiry : Henry Brooke two-day ban: used whip above permitted level (Nov 22,24)
Craig Gallagher four-day ban: used whip above permitted level (Nov 22,24-26)

FOCUS
An open handicap and sound form. The winner was a 129 horse at his peak and may still be capable of matching that.

2346 LAWRENCE SMITH AND SON H'CAP CHASE (16 fncs) 2m 4f
3:35 (3:35) (Class 3) (0-125,122) 4-Y-O+ **£6,498** (£1,908; £954; £477)

Form RPR
340- **1** **Quito Du Tresor (FR)**[44] 1659 9-11-7 **117**..................(p) TomScudamore 131+
(Lucinda Russell) *trckd ldrs: hdwy to ld 10th: clr fr 5 out: easily* **85/40**[2]

F4B- **2** *3* **Father Shine (IRE)**[10] 1636 10-10-12 **108**...................... WilsonRenwick 110
(Shaun Harris) *hld up: blnd 9th: hdwy to chse (clr) wnr 5 out: rdn whn hit 3 out: kpt on: flattered by proximity to easy wnr* **9/1**

P16- **3** *16* **Strobe**[27] 1872 9-10-11 **107**..(p) DougieCostello 94
(Lucy Normile) *nt fluent on occasions: prom: outpcd 11th: rallied bef 4 out: sn no imp* **11/2**[3]

/00- **4** *¾* **Diamond Frontier (IRE)**[23] 1921 10-11-2 **119**.............. JohnDawson[(7)] 105
(John Wade) *cl up: led 6th to bef 9th: outpcd bef 5 out: btn fr next* **6/1**

233/ **5** *25* **Aikman (IRE)**[625] 4445 9-11-12 **122**................................(b[1]) BrianHughes 91
(James Ewart) *nt jump wl: t.k.h: led to 6th: led bef 9th to next: struggling fr 5 out: t.o* **7/4**[1]

4m 55.2s (-6.00) **Going Correction** -0.125s/f (Good) **5** Ran SP% **108.0**
Speed ratings (Par 107): **107,105,99,99,89**
CSF £17.38 TOTE £2.80: £1.40, £2.70; EX 19.30 Trifecta £43.10 Pool: £2275.23 - 39.50 winning units..
Owner Mrs Sandra Giles **Bred** Mme Claude Menard & Jacques Cherel **Trained** Arlary, Perth & Kinross

FOCUS
This was run at a frantic gallop. The easy winner is rated in line with the best of his 2012 form.

2347 SHEPHERD AND WEDDERBURN STANDARD OPEN NATIONAL HUNT FLAT RACE 2m
4:05 (4:05) (Class 5) 4-6-Y-O **£1,949** (£572; £286; £143)

Form RPR
1 **Theatrical Style (IRE)**[160] 4-11-2 0................................ JasonMaguire 106+
(Donald McCain) *led 1f: chsd ldrs: rdn over 3f out: led over 1f out: drvn and hld on wl* **13/2**

2 *½* **It's High Time (IRE)**[213] 5238 5-11-2 0......................... WilsonRenwick 106+
(Lucinda Russell) *cl up: led and rdn wl over 2f out: hdd over 1f out: rallied: kpt on fnl f: hld nr fin* **9/2**[3]

3 *5* **Ronnie Lawson (IRE)** 4-11-2 0..................................... DenisO'Regan 102+
(John Ferguson) *t.k.h: hld up towards rr: hdwy 3f out: sn pushed along: edgd lft 2f out: outpcd by first two fr over 1f out* **10/3**[1]

4 *hd* **Chieftain's Choice (IRE)** 4-11-2 0................................ DougieCostello 100+
(John Quinn) *t.k.h: hld up towards rr: rdn over 5f out: hdwy over 3f out: edgd rt over 1f out: kpt on ins fnl f* **4/1**[2]

5 *2¼* **Coozan George** 4-11-2 0... BrianHughes 98
(Malcolm Jefferson) *t.k.h early: prom: effrt and rdn over 2f out: one pce whn checked over 1f out* **9/1**

453- **6** *3¼* **Dalstontosiloth (IRE)**[73] 1420 5-10-9 0...................... CraigGallagher[(7)] 95
(Barry Murtagh) *hld up towards rr: stdy hdwy over 4f out: rdn and no imp fr over 2f out* **22/1**

7 *1¼* **Lucky Cody (IRE)**[40] 4-10-9 0..................................... NathanMoscrop[(7)] 95
(Brian Ellison) *hld up on outside: stdy hdwy and in tch after 5f: rdn and outpcd over 3f out: btn over 1f out* **18/1**

3/ **8** *1½* **Favourable Fellow (IRE)**[217] 5168 4-11-2 0................ RichardJohnson 92
(Geoffrey Harker) *t.k.h: led after 1f: rdn and hdd wl over 2f out: rallied: wknd over 1f out* **11/2**

9 *1¼* **Revanna** 4-10-2 0... MrJHamilton[(7)] 84
(Peter Niven) *hld up: drvn and outpcd over 5f out: n.d after* **12/1**

00/ **10** *3½* **Kastela Stari**[226] 4976 6-10-2 0.................................. GrahamWatters[(7)] 80
(Tim Fitzgerald) *hld up on outside: struggling over 3f out: sn btn* **80/1**

0- **11** *7* **Zuileka**[184] 173 4-10-9 0.. AidanColeman 73
(James Moffatt) *hld up: stdy hdwy over 6f out: rdn and wknd over 3f out* **50/1**

12 *5* **Indigo Island (IRE)**[159] 4-11-2 0.................................... HenryBrooke 75
(Robert Bewley) *midfield on ins: lost pl bef 1/2-way: rallied 5f out: wknd 3f out* **40/1**

3m 47.6s (4.80) **Going Correction** -0.30s/f (Good) **12** Ran SP% **122.9**
Speed ratings: **76,75,73,73,72 70,69,69,68,66 63,60**
toteswingers 1&2 £8.10, 1&3 £7.00, 2&3 £1.10 CSF £36.47 TOTE £6.20: £2.20, £1.90, £1.80; EX 28.60 Trifecta £71.40 Pool: £1047.01 - 10.99 winning units..
Owner Deva Racing Palladium Partnership **Bred** Spratstown Bloodstock Ltd **Trained** Cholmondeley, Cheshire
■ Stewards' Enquiry : Dougie Costello caution: careless riding.

FOCUS
The first pair came nicely clear and the runner-up sets the level.A fair bumper for the track.
T/Plt: £12.30 to a £1 stake. Pool: £59780.55 - 3545.00 winning tickets T/Qpdt: £8.80 to a £1 stake. Pool: £3480.10 - 291.90 winning tickets RY

[2046]SOUTHWELL (L-H)
Friday, November 8

OFFICIAL GOING: Soft (heavy in places; 5.8)
A replacement fixture for Fontwell's abandoned meeting.
Wind: light to medium, across Weather: dry, overcast

2348 32RED.COM MARES' NOVICES' H'CAP CHASE (19 fncs) 3m 110y
12:40 (12:40) (Class 4) (0-110,105) 4-Y-O+ **£3,768** (£1,106; £553; £276)

Form RPR
6/5- **1** **Dancing Daffodil**[26] 1890 8-10-9 88...................................... CharliePoste 92+
(Robin Dickin) *in tch: mstke 7th and 8th: clsd to chse ldr 13th: led bef next: hdd and rdn bef 3 out: led again 2 out: sn drvn: styd on wl and forged clr flat* **5/2**[2]

/54- **2** *3* **Tea Caddy**[155] 645 7-11-12 105.. TomO'Brien 106+
(Jamie Snowden) *in tch in rr: mstke 2nd: chsd ldng pair 15th: rdn and effrt 3 out: wnt 2nd and pressing wnr whn j.lft last: no ex flat* **5/1**

134- **3** *2½* **Glen Countess (IRE)**[114] 1015 6-11-11 104.................(t) BrendanPowell 101
(Brendan Powell) *led tl after 2nd: chsd ldr: nt fluent 12th: dropped to 4th bef next: chsd wnr again after 14th: rdn to ld bef 3 out: hdd 2 out: no ex: 3rd and btn last* **2/1**[1]

004- **4** *46* **Go Annie**[10] 2148 5-10-5 84...(tp) DominicElsworth 51
(Jo Davis) *chsd ldrs: mstke 2nd: hdwy to chsd ldr after 12th tl 13th: in 4th and struggling 15th: wknd 3 out: heavily eased flat: t.o* **8/1**

/0F- **F** **Quantique (FR)**[15] 2039 9-10-0 82................................. RobertDunne[(3)]
(Venetia Williams) *racd wd: chsd ldr tl led after 2nd: hdd after 13th: qckly dropped to last whn fell heavily next* **4/1**[3]

6m 45.1s (22.10) **Going Correction** +0.875s/f (Soft) **5** Ran SP% **109.7**
Speed ratings (Par 105): **99,98,97,82,**
CSF £14.32 TOTE £2.50: £1.60, £5.50; EX 15.80 Trifecta £17.80 Pool: £871.08 - 36.52 winning units..
Owner Mr & Mrs Cooper And Mrs C Dickin **Bred** Mrs C M Dickin **Trained** Alcester, Warwicks

FOCUS
Golf Club bend inside the line and bend into home straight outside the lines used on October 24th. The ground was pretty testing and the time for the opener was 41 seconds outside standard, although they went what appeared a fair pace. The first two were held up in this weak event for mares, which saw a 1-2 for recently deceased stallion Kadastrof. The first two are rated in line with their hurdles form.

2349 32RED CASINO H'CAP CHASE (12 fncs 1 omitted) 2m
1:10 (1:10) (Class 5) (0-95,95) 4-Y-O+ **£2,144** (£629; £314; £157)

Form RPR
305- **1** **Hopeand**[7] 2190 8-11-2 85...(t) AdamPogson 107+
(Charles Pogson) *mde all and racd wd in the sts: drew clr wl bef 3 out: in n.d after: eased flat* **3/1**[1]

362- **2** *28* **Finch Flyer (IRE)**[15] 2044 6-9-13 75.........................(p) MrAlexEdwards[(7)] 67
(Aytach Sadik) *chsd ldrs: dropped to last pair after 6th: rdn after next: 4th and wl btn bypassing 4 out: plugged on to go modest 2nd and pckd 2 out: no imp* **3/1**[1]

0F6- **3** *5* **The Absent Mare**[15] 2039 5-10-11 80................................... CharliePoste 68
(Robin Dickin) *in tch in rr: mstke 2nd: hdwy to chse wnr and j.lft 2 out: rdn and btn wl bef 3 out: wknd and lost modest 2nd 2 out* **10/1**

026- **4** *1¾* **Mad Professor (IRE)**[101] 1149 10-9-11 71...................(b) JoeCornwall[(5)] 55
(John Cornwall) *chsd wnr tl 2nd: dropped to last and rdn after 5th: struggling u.p 7th: lost tch and virtually t.o bypassing 4 out* **8/1**[3]

0/0- **F** **Swiss Art (IRE)**[15] 2051 7-11-5 95.................................... CallumBewley[(7)] 87
(Sue Smith) *t.k.h: chsd ldrs: chsd wnr 2nd tl 6th: 3rd and rdn bypassing 4 out: sn wl btn: disputing modest 2nd whn fell 2 out* **3/1**[1]

0P4- **F** **Peaks Of Fire (IRE)**[20] 1981 6-11-10 93.....................(p) TomMessenger
(Joanne Foster) *rel to r and lost many l s: detached in last tl dived and fell 3rd* **5/1**[2]

4m 16.6s (14.60) **Going Correction** +0.875s/f (Soft) **6** Ran SP% **111.9**
Speed ratings (Par 103): **98,84,81,80,**
toteswingers 1&2 £3.60, 2&3 £2.50, 1&3 £19.70 CSF £12.63 TOTE £2.90: £1.20, £2.00; EX 11.90 Trifecta £90.40 Pool: £1334.84 - 11.06 winning units..
Owner C T Pogson **Bred** Stewart Pike **Trained** Farnsfield, Notts

FOCUS
A weak, low-grade handicap chase. The winner is seemingly a better chaser than hurdler and could be rated higher but this is probably not one to get carried away with.

2350 32RED H'CAP CHASE (16 fncs) 2m 4f 110y
1:40 (1:40) (Class 4) (0-115,113) 4-Y-O+ **£3,768** (£1,106; £553; £276)

Form RPR
P/4- **1** **Toby Lerone (IRE)**[8] 2177 6-11-12 113................................ IanPopham 130+
(Dan Skelton) *mde all: rdn and drew clr bef 2 out: wl in command between last 2: styd on strly* **5/2**[3]

236/ **2** *17* **Trojan Sun**[199] 5467 7-11-9 110...(t) FelixDeGiles 110
(Tom Symonds) *mounted on crse: chsd wnr thrght: rdn and effrt 13th: 2 l down bef next: btn bef 2 out: wknd between last 2* **2/1**[2]

600/ **3** *50* **Inoogoo (IRE)**[214] 5219 8-11-11 112.................................(t) WillKennedy 62
(Brian Ellison) *t.k.h: hld up in tch in last pair: wnt 3rd after 9th: mstke 11th: rdn 13th: sn btn and lost tch: j.lft 3 out: t.o and tired whn blnd last* **7/4**[1]

45F- **4** *2¾* **That's The Deal (IRE)**[14] 2065 9-11-2 108...................... JoeCornwall[(5)] 55
(John Cornwall) *in tch in last pair: dropped to last and rdn after 9th: sn struggling: t.o 13th* **8/1**

5m 32.4s (15.40) **Going Correction** +0.875s/f (Soft) **4** Ran SP% **109.4**
Speed ratings (Par 105): **105,98,79,78**
CSF £7.96 TOTE £3.40; EX 11.30 Trifecta £16.10 Pool: £1005.13 - 46.64 winning units..
Owner Regan, Dunning, Pettey & Morgan **Bred** M J Halligan **Trained** Alcester, Warwicks

FOCUS
A very ordinary handicap chase. Toby Lerone should win more chases.

2351 32RED CASINO CONDITIONAL JOCKEYS' NOVICES' HURDLE (9 hdls) 2m
2:15 (2:17) (Class 4) 4-Y-O+ **£3,119** (£915; £457; £228)

Form RPR
0/F- **1** **Key To The West (IRE)**[15] 2049 6-10-12 123.................. MichealNolan 120
(David Dennis) *t.k.h: hld up in tch: hdwy to chse ldrs 5th: led and travelling best bef 2 out: drvn between last 2: styd on wl u.p flat* **5/2**[2]

The Form Book Jumps, Raceform Ltd, Compton, RG20 6NL.

2/0- **2** *1 ¾* **Cloud Creeper (IRE)**[188] 116 6-10-9 120........................ JamesBest(3) 118
(Philip Hobbs) *hld up in rr: clsd and wl in tch after 4th: effrt to chse wnr bef 2 out: drvn between last 2: unable qck and j.lft last: one pce flat* **3/1**[3]

1- **3** *1 ¼* **Call The Cops (IRE)**[178] 291 4-10-9 0........................ PeterCarberry(3) 119
(Nicky Henderson) *nt jump wl: in tch: rdn and mstke 3 out: rallied to chse ldng pair next: drvn and styd on to press ldrs whn anther mstke last: one pce flat* **7/4**[1]

4 *18* **Brunello**[32] 5-10-12 0........................(p) JoeColliver 99
(Philip Kirby) *chsd ldr: mstke 5th: lost 2nd and mstke next: sn rdn and dropped to last pair: wknd 2 out* **50/1**

000- **5** *8* **Straits Of Messina (IRE)**[7] 2189 4-10-9 0........................ BenPoste(3) 91
(Tom Symonds) *chsd ldrs: lost pl and last whn rdn bef 3 out: wknd 2 out* **100/1**

21- **6** *15* **Curzon Line**[15] 2040 4-10-11 118........................ JosephAkehurst(8) 88
(John Ferguson) *t.k.h led and racd wd in sts: rdn and hdd after 3 out: wkng whn mstke next: sn bhd: t.o* **3/1**[3]

4m 5.8s (8.80) **Going Correction** +0.875s/f (Soft)
WFA 4 from 5yo+ 7lb **6** Ran SP% **117.9**
Speed ratings (Par 105): **113,112,111,102,98 91**
toteswingers 1&2 £2.50, 1&3 £3.60, 2&3 £19.70 CSF £11.36 TOTE £3.00: £1.70, £2.80; EX 9.40 Trifecta £20.40 Pool: £2717.78 - 99.70 winning units..
Owner Favourites Racing **Bred** Paddy Behan **Trained** Hanley Swan, Worcestershire
■ David Dennis's first jumps winner as a trainer.

FOCUS
This ordinary novice hurdle was run at a solid pace in the conditions. The winner is rated to the level of his best form over this trip.

2352 32RED MARES' H'CAP HURDLE (11 hdls) 2m 4f 110y
2:45 (2:45) (Class 3) (0-130,127) 4-Y-0+ **£5,523** (£1,621; £810; £405)

Form RPR

5/1- **1** **Midnight Belle**[16] 2029 6-10-13 114........................ FelixDeGiles 119+
(Tom Symonds) *hld up in tch in last pair: effrt to join ldrs sn after 3 out: rdn to ld 2 out: drvn and forged ahd flat: styd on wl* **2/1**[1]

3/1- **2** *2 ¼* **In By Midnight**[16] 2027 5-10-4 105........................ PaddyBrennan 108+
(Tom George) *racd wd: chsd ldr tl after 6th: styd prom: rdn to ld after 3 out: hdd next: stl ev ch whn mstke last: wknd fnl 100yds* **5/2**[2]

11P- **3** *¾* **Rattlin**[9] 2158 5-9-13 107........................ CallumBewley(7) 108
(Sue Smith) *t.k.h: chsd ldrs: wnt 2nd after 6th: upsides ldr 8th: rdn and outpcd in 4th after 3 out: rallied u.p to chse ldng pair bef last: styd on flat* **6/1**

123/ **4** *17* **Alder Mairi (IRE)**[204] 5358 6-11-12 127........................ AndrewThornton 117
(Seamus Mullins) *racd wd: led tl rdn and hdd after 3 out: 3rd and outpcd after 2 out: wknd jst bef last* **4/1**[3]

010/ **5** *16* **A Little Swifter (IRE)**[303] 3576 7-10-11 115........................ TrevorWhelan(3) 82
(Neil King) *in tch in midfield: nt fluent 5th and 6th: rdn 3 out: sn struggling and wknd bef next* **12/1**

/6P- **P** **Dreambrook Lady (IRE)**[13] 2084 7-11-4 119.............1 RichieMcLernon
(Jonjo O'Neill) *racd wd: hld up in tch in rr: effrt and little rspnse sn after 3 out: wknd bef next: t.o whn p.u last* **10/1**

5m 27.6s (14.60) **Going Correction** +0.875s/f (Soft) **6** Ran SP% **113.0**
Speed ratings (Par 107): **107,106,105,99,93**
toteswingers 1&2 £1.10, 1&3 £1.40, 2&3 £6.90 CSF £7.78 TOTE £3.60: £1.10, £1.40; EX 7.00 Trifecta £24.70 Pool: £1726.78 - 52.22 winning units..
Owner Mrs Patricia Holtorp **Bred** Mrs Patricia Ellen Holtorp **Trained** Harewood End, H'fords

FOCUS
A fair handicap for mares, in which the first two home were daughters of Midnight Legend who'd both won at Worcester a fortnight ago. They're both on the upgrade.

2353 32RED ON THE APP STORE NOVICES' H'CAP HURDLE (11 hdls) 2m 4f 110y
3:15 (3:15) (Class 5) (0-100,98) 4-Y-0+ **£1,949** (£572; £286; £143)

Form RPR

001- **1** **Brass Monkey (IRE)**[8] 2175 6-11-1 90........................ TrevorWhelan(3) 100+
(Neil King) *chsd ldr: rdn and ev ch 2 out: forged ahd between last 2: styd on wl flat: rdn out* **5/2**[1]

P/0- **2** *3* **The Young Master**[38] 1711 4-11-8 94........................(p) NoelFehily 99
(Neil Mulholland) *t.k.h: chsd ldrs: mstke 3 out: 3rd and outpcd 2 out: rallied u.p flat to go 2nd cl home* **16/1**

200- **3** *nk* **Finmerello**[81] 1321 7-11-4 90........................ NickScholfield 95
(Kim Bailey) *led: mstke 3rd and 7th: rdn and hdd between last 2: no ex and mstke last: one pce and lost 2nd cl home* **4/1**[2]

/05- **4** *20* **Rigolo Ville (FR)**[12] 2105 8-11-6 95........................ GilesHawkins(3) 79
(Richard Hobson) *in tch: 4th and rdn sn after 3 out: wknd bef next* **4/1**[2]

534/ **5** *38* **Blue Top**[29] 5164 4-11-9 98........................(p) JakeGreenall(3) 44
(Tim Walford) *in tch in last pair: rdn 7th: 5th and cl enough 3 out: wknd wl bef next: t.o between last 2* **4/1**[2]

640/ **P** **Teenage Dream (IRE)**[246] 4611 5-11-3 96........................ OllieGarner(7)
(Derek Shaw) *in tch in rr: mstke 2nd: rdn 7th: lost tch next: t.o whn p.u last* **8/1**[2]

4/5- **P** **Nurse Brace**[159] 4-11-2 88........................ DonalDevereux
(David Brace) *in tch in midfield: rdn and dropped to rr 8th: sn lost tch: t.o whn p.u 2 out* **33/1**

5m 31.05s (18.05) **Going Correction** +0.875s/f (Soft) **7** Ran SP% **108.5**
Speed ratings (Par 103): **100,98,98,91,76** ,
toteswingers 1&2 £12.50, 1&3 £2.40, 2&3 £9.60 CSF £33.17 TOTE £2.80: £3.20, £10.00; EX 46.40 Trifecta £75.30 Pool: £2628.23 - 26.16 winning units..
Owner The St Gatien Racing For Fun Partnership **Bred** Oliver McDonnell **Trained** Newmarket, Suffolk

FOCUS
They went a steady gallop in this decidedly ordinary race, and nothing got into it from the rear. The winner rates a bit below his Stratford form.

2354 32RED.COM STANDARD OPEN NATIONAL HUNT FLAT RACE 2m
3:45 (3:47) (Class 6) 4-6-Y-0 **£1,642** (£478; £239)

Form RPR

2- **1** **No No Romeo (IRE)**[180] 250 4-11-2 0........................ NoelFehily 110+
(Charlie Longsdon) *chsd ldrs: led over 2f out: sn rdn and c clr w runner-up: r.o strly and drew clr fnl f: readily* **9/4**[2]

2 *3* **Forthefunofit (IRE)** 4-11-2 0........................ APMcCoy 105+
(Jonjo O'Neill) *hld up in tch in midfield: clsd to chse ldrs 5f out: rdn to go 2nd and clr w wnr 2f out: drvn: no ex and btn 1f out: one pce* **2/1**[1]

3 *9* **Powerstown Dreams (IRE)**[202] 4-10-9 0........................ PaulBohan(7) 95
(Steve Gollings) *in tch in midfield: clsd to chse ldrs 5f out: rdn and outpcd over 2f out: no threat to ldng pair but kpt on to go 3rd ins fnl f* **10/1**

4 *½* **Clubs Are Trumps (IRE)** 4-11-2 0........................ RichieMcLernon 95
(Jonjo O'Neill) *t.k.h: chsd ldrs: rdn and effrt over 3f out: outpcd and btn over 2f out: no threat to ldng pair but kpt on and battling for 3rd ins fnl f* **10/1**

1- **5** *2 ¾* **Viacometti (FR)**[176] 345 4-11-4 0........................ AodhaganConlon(5) 99
(Tom George) *led tl hdd 10f out: chsd ldr tl led again over 3f out: rdn and hdd over 2f out: 3rd and btn 2f out: wknd and lost 2 pls fnl f* **6/1**[3]

6 *6* **Hurricane's Girl** 4-10-4 0........................ MauriceLinehan(5) 79
(Jonjo O'Neill) *t.k.h: chsd ldrs: rdn and struggling 3f out: sn outpcd: wknd 2f out* **25/1**

0/5- **7** *3 ¾* **Camptown Lady**[174] 380 4-10-9 0........................ GerardTumelty 75
(Laura Young) *t.k.h: hld up in midfield: hdwy to chse ldr after 4f tl led 10f out: hdd over 3f out: rdn and btn over 2f out: sn wknd* **100/1**

8 *1 ½* **Paddy Mulligan (IRE)** 4-10-13 0........................ JackQuinlan(3) 81
(John Ferguson) *t.k.h: hld up in tch in last trio: shkn up and hdwy 5f out: drvn and btn 3f out: wknd 2f out* **8/1**

4/ **9** *8* **Secure Investment**[202] 5413 5-10-11 0........................ ThomasGarner(5) 73
(Oliver Sherwood) *t.k.h: hld up in midfield: stdd bk to rr but stl in tch 10f out: rdn 4f out: wknd 3f out* **22/1**

10 *4* **Nearly Normal (IRE)**[229] 4-11-2 0........................ WayneHutchinson 69
(David Dennis) *t.k.h: chsd ldrs: rdn and effrt 4f out: sn struggling and btn 3f out: no ch fnl 2f: t.o* **33/1**

6- **11** *6* **Island Whisper (IRE)**[15] 2052 6-10-0 0 ow1........................ RyanLynam(10) 57
(Ben Case) *t.k.h: hld up in tch in rr: sme hdwy 7f out: rdn and wknd 4f out: t.o 2f out* **100/1**

0- **12** *7* **Torrington Deal**[41] 1690 5-10-9 0........................ HarryHaynes 49
(Malcolm Jefferson) *styd on inner thrght: in tch in midfield: dropped to rr but stl in tch 10f out: rdn 6f out: sn bhd: t.o fnl 3f* **50/1**

4m 10.5s (19.10) **Going Correction** +0.875s/f (Soft) **12** Ran SP% **122.8**
Speed ratings: **87,85,81,80,79 76,74,73,69,67 64,61**
toteswingers 1&2 £2.10, 1&3 £8.40, 2&3 £6.00 CSF £7.07 TOTE £3.00: £1.10, £1.10, £4.20; EX 10.20 Trifecta £74.40 Pool: £3259.74 - 32.85 winning units..
Owner R Jenner & J Green **Bred** J D Flood **Trained** Over Norton, Oxon

FOCUS
A modest bumper, with improved form from the winner.
T/Plt: £273.90 to a £1 stake. Pool: £50984.97 - 135.85 winning tickets T/Qpdt: £56.10 to a £1 stake. Pool: £4717.50 - 62.20 winning tickets SP

1975 KELSO (L-H)
Saturday, November 9

OFFICIAL GOING: Good to soft (6.6)
Wind: Fresh; half against Weather: Cloudy, bright

2355 JANE MEDD "NATIONAL HUNT" NOVICES' HURDLE (11 hdls) 2m 6f 110y
12:30 (12:30) (Class 4) 4-Y-0+ **£3,898** (£1,144; £572; £286)

Form RPR

2- **1** **The Last Samuri (IRE)**[16] 2037 5-10-12 0........................ JasonMaguire 125+
(Donald McCain) *hld up in tch: smooth hdwy and cl up 4 out: led 2 out: sn rdn: drvn clr next to stands' rail fr last* **5/2**[1]

/12- **2** *6* **Mysteree (IRE)**[21] 1980 5-11-5 120........................ PeterBuchanan 124
(Lucinda Russell) *cl up: drvn and ev ch bef 2 out: hung rt between last 2: styd on same pce against far rail run-in* **7/2**[2]

1- **3** *4* **Kilgefin Star (IRE)**[21] 1980 5-11-5 0........................ DannyCook 122
(Michael Smith) *led: hit 4 out: rdn and hdd 2 out: outpcd by first two after last* **7/2**[2]

0/5- **4** *27* **Heart Dancer (FR)**[21] 1977 7-10-12 0........................ BarryKeniry 89
(Simon Shirley-Beavan) *hld up towards rr: stdy hdwy and in tch bef 3 out: shkn up and wknd bef next* **28/1**

/14- **5** *½* **Magic Present**[141] 790 6-10-12 0........................ BrianHughes 88
(Malcolm Jefferson) *hld up in tch: outpcd and pushed along 4 out: rallied bef 2 out: sn no imp* **9/1**

6 *2 ¼* **Volo Mio**[202] 6-10-5 0........................ DiarmuidO'Regan(7) 88
(Chris Grant) *hld up towards rr: hdwy and prom 8th: hit and outpcd 3 out: wknd bef next* **20/1**

325/ **7** *13* **Mr Syntax (IRE)**[234] 4862 9-10-12 0........................(t) BrianHarding 75
(Tim Fitzgerald) *hld up on ins: stdy hdwy 8th: wknd after 3 out* **15/2**[3]

5/0- **8** *13* **Ultiep (FR)**[16] 2037 5-10-12 0........................ TomSiddall 63
(Karen McLintock) *mstkes in rr: struggling fnl circ: nvr on terms* **100/1**

333/ **9** *nk* **L'Eminence Grise (IRE)**[365] 2316 6-10-5 97.......(t) StephenMulqueen(7) 63
(Maurice Barnes) *chsd ldrs tl drvn and wknd fr 4 out* **12/1**

00- **10** *44* **Amilliontimes (IRE)**[28] 1875 5-10-12 0........................ HenryBrooke 23
(Mrs Jackie Stephen) *chsd ldr to 8th: rdn and wknd after next: t.o* **200/1**

000/ **P** **Native Optimist (IRE)**[632] 4344 6-10-12 0........................ RichieMcGrath
(Sheena Walton) *nt fluent: a bhd: struggling fnl circ: t.o whn p.u bef last* **250/1**

0- **P** **Print Shiraz (IRE)**[28] 1875 5-10-12 0........................1 WilsonRenwick
(Rose Dobbin) *midfield: drvn and outpcd bef 8th: t.o whn p.u bef 3 out* **66/1**

00- **P** **Wind Echo**[16] 2037 5-10-5 0........................ DaraghBourke(7)
(Rayson Nixon) *in tch to 1/2-way: struggling fnl circ: t.o whn p.u bef 3 out* **250/1**

P **Allforthelove** 5-10-12 0........................ LucyAlexander
(N W Alexander) *nt fluent in rr: lost tch and p.u bef 7th* **50/1**

5m 34.4s (-6.60) **Going Correction** -0.20s/f (Good) **14** Ran SP% **116.4**
Speed ratings (Par 105): **103,100,99,90,89 89,84,80,80,64** , , ,
toteswingers 1&2 £3.70, 1&3 £2.50, 2&3 £1.50 CSF £10.58 TOTE £3.50: £1.70, £2.10, £1.10; EX 13.80 Trifecta £30.80 Pool: £601.55 - 14.63 winning units..
Owner Paul & Clare Rooney **Bred** Edmond Coleman **Trained** Cholmondeley, Cheshire

FOCUS
Fresh ground on all bends on both courses. A modest staying novices' hurdle in which they went an honest gallop on ground officially described as good to soft. The winenr can probably rate higher.

2356 THE SHIP INN, DALKEITH NOVICES' H'CAP CHASE (12 fncs) 2m 1f
1:05 (1:05) (Class 4) (0-110,110) 4-Y-0+ **£3,898** (£1,144; £572; £286)

Form RPR

3/3- **1** **Clondaw Knight (IRE)**[178] 313 5-11-12 110........................ PeterBuchanan 132+
(Lucinda Russell) *j.w: in tch: hdwy to chse ldr 5 out: led after 3 out: rdn and r.o strly fr next* **2/1**[1]

/16- **2** *4* **Suprise Vendor (IRE)**[135] 493 7-10-7 101........................ DaraghBourke(10) 116
(Stuart Coltherd) *cl up: slipped bnd bef 6th: rdn and outpcd briefly 3 out: rallied to chse wnr appr next: kpt on same pce fr last* **12/1**

250- **3** 4 ½ **Swing Hard (IRE)**[14] 2073 5-11-7 **105** .... RyanMania 116
(Sue Smith) *nt fluent on occasions: hld up: rdn along 5 out: hdwy after 3 out: kpt on fr next: nt pce of first two* **14/1**

600/ **4** 12 **Coax**[39] 3442 5-10-11 **95** .... RichieMcGrath 95
(Patrick Holmes) *t.k.h: cl up: led 5th to after 3 out: rdn and outpcd fr next* **80/1**

0/0- **5** 1 ¾ **Robin's Command (IRE)**[21] 1982 6-10-0 **84** oh5 .... WilsonRenwick 85
(Rose Dobbin) *hld up in midfield on outside: hdwy and prom 6th: effrt and rdn after 3 out: 4th and hld whn mstke last* **12/1**

235- **6** 2 ¾ **My Idea**[16] 2031 7-10-11 **102** ....(t) StephenMulqueen(7) 103
(Maurice Barnes) *nt fluent on occasions: towards rr: pushed along whn hmpd bnd bef 6th: struggling fr next* **5/1**[3]

P5/- **7** 4 **Brieryhill Boy**[216] 5204 6-10-11 **95** .... BrianHarding 88
(William Amos) *led to 5th: cl up tl rdn and wknd qckly after 2 out* **14/1**

001/ **8** 43 **Jimmie Brown (USA)**[211] 5273 5-11-9 **110** .... JohnKington(3) 94
(Andrew Crook) *hld up: reminders 4th: struggling bef 4 out: virtually p.u run-in* **20/1**

/06- **P** **Leroy Parker (IRE)**[10] 2159 5-11-3 **108** ....(b) GrahamWatters(7)
(Barry Murtagh) *t.k.h: in tch: hmpd and lost pl bnd bef 6th: struggling fr next: t.o whn p.u bef 2 out* **33/1**

3F6/ **S** **Alfred Oats**[247] 4608 9-11-2 **100** .... DannyCook
(Robert Goldie) *prom whn slipped and fell bnd bef 6th* **11/1**

0/F- **P** **Teo Vivo (FR)**[2] 2308 6-11-6 **104** ....(p) BrianHughes
(James Ewart) *trckd ldrs: slipped and lost pl bnd bef 6th: sn struggling: t.o whn p.u bef 2 out* **9/2**[2]

4m 15.6s (-2.40) **Going Correction** -0.325s/f (Good) **11** Ran SP% **114.2**
Speed ratings (Par 105): **92,90,88,82,81 80,78,58, ,**
toteswingers 1&2 £5.10, 1&3 £9.80, 2&3 £17.20 CSF £24.96 CT £265.13 TOTE £2.90: £1.40, £3.10, £3.10; EX 25.30 Trifecta £214.20 Pool: £782.40 - 2.73 winning units..
Owner Sandy Seymour **Bred** Patrick G J Murphy **Trained** Arlary, Perth & Kinross

FOCUS
A modest novices' handicap chase in which they went a stronger gallop than the opening hurdle, and the ground appeared to be riding slightly better on the chase course. A massive step up on the winner's hurdle form and he's the type to win more races.

2357 GRAEME TODD HAULAGE AND FRIENDS H'CAP HURDLE (13 hdls) 3m 3f
1:40 (1:41) (Class 3) (0-135,135) 4-Y-0+ **£5,393** (£1,583; £791; £395)

Form RPR

0/2- **1** **Talkin Sence (IRE)**[10] 2158 8-10-1 **120** .... DaraghBourke(10) 123+
(Stuart Coltherd) *t.k.h: cl up: led gng wl bef 2 out: rdn and r.o wl fr last* **15/8**[1]

124/ **2** 1 ¼ **Bishops Heir**[586] 5206 8-10-5 **114** .... BrianHughes 113
(James Ewart) *hld up in tch: stdy hdwy 4 out: effrt and chsd wnr 2 out: rdn and kpt on run-in* **13/2**[3]

0/6- **3** 2 ¾ **Karinga Dandy (IRE)**[14] 2073 7-9-9 **109** oh1 .... JonathanEngland(5) 108
(Sue Smith) *nt fluent: prom: rdn and outpcd 3 out: rallied next: one pce whn nt fluent last* **85/40**[2]

0R/- **4** 13 **Alpha Victor (IRE)**[278] 4027 8-11-7 **135** .... HarryChalloner(5) 123
(William Kinsey) *led: rdn and hdd bef 2 out: wkng whn mstke last* **20/1**

5/3- **5** 19 **Devotion To Duty (IRE)**[24] 1926 7-11-0 **123** .... RichieMcGrath 91
(Philip Kirby) *hld up: drvn and outpcd 4 out: btn bef 2 out* **15/2**

/F4- **6** 10 **Micro Mission (IRE)**[8] 2193 7-10-2 **116** .... SamanthaDrake(5) 75
(Chris Grant) *prom: drvn and outpcd after 9th: struggling fr next* **7/1**

6m 36.5s (-3.50) **Going Correction** -0.20s/f (Good) **6** Ran SP% **109.1**
Speed ratings (Par 107): **109,108,107,103,98 95**
toteswingers 1&2 £1.10, 1&3 £1.10, 2&3 £5.20 CSF £13.26 TOTE £3.20: £2.40, £2.90; EX 12.20 Trifecta £36.40 Pool: £791.66 - 16.27 winning units..
Owner Gunning, Conchar, Hancock **Bred** Mrs Christine Wilson **Trained** Selkirk, Borders

FOCUS
A decent long-distance handicap hurdle in which they went a respectable gallop. The winner confirmed the merit of his good recent run, with the next two close to their marks.

2358 FLANNIGAN SKIP HIRE H'CAP CHASE (17 fncs) 2m 7f 110y
2:15 (2:15) (Class 3) (0-140,138) 4-Y-0+ **£7,147** (£2,098; £1,049; £524)

Form RPR

/44- **1** **Kruzhlinin (GER)**[14] 2072 6-11-4 **130** .... JasonMaguire 149+
(Donald McCain) *t.k.h: cl up: blnd 4 out: sn rcvrd: led appr 2 out: drvn and kpt on wl fnl f* **5/1**[3]

541- **2** 2 ¼ **Maggio (FR)**[34] 1788 8-10-12 **129** ....(t) DerekFox(5) 141
(Patrick Griffin, Ire) *cl up: smooth hdwy and ev ch 2 out: sn rdn and edgd lft: one pce fr last* **9/2**[2]

P3F- **3** 16 **Aneyeforaneye (IRE)**[15] 2065 7-11-4 **130** .... BrianHughes 130
(Malcolm Jefferson) *hld up in tch: effrt after 3 out: outpcd by first two fr next* **11/2**

402/ **4** 1 ½ **Sa Suffit (FR)**[630] 4384 10-11-12 **138** .... WilsonRenwick 135
(Jim Goldie) *prom: effrt and rdn whn mstke 2 out: sn btn* **7/1**

/60- **5** ½ **Rolecarr (IRE)**[170] 448 10-10-10 **129** .... GrahamWatters(7) 127
(Ann Hamilton) *nt fluent in rr: bhd: hdwy u.p bef 3 out: no imp fr next* **16/1**

4P6- **6** 11 **Garleton (IRE)**[21] 1978 12-10-13 **132** ....(t) StephenMulqueen(7) 124
(Maurice Barnes) *early mstkes: led: rdn and hdd appr 2 out: sn btn* **7/1**

5PP/ **P** **Blenheim Brook (IRE)**[199] 5496 8-10-13 **125** .... PeterBuchanan
(Lucinda Russell) *hld up: rdn bef 5 out: struggling 3 out: t.o whn p.u bef last* **9/4**[1]

5m 54.0s (-14.00) **Going Correction** -0.325s/f (Good) **7** Ran SP% **111.9**
Speed ratings (Par 107): **110,109,103,103,99 99,**
toteswingers 1&2 £3.00, 1&3 £3.90, 2&3 £26.60 CSF £26.55 TOTE £4.60: £2.80, £4.10; EX 16.40 Trifecta £46.90 Pool: £1,132.29 - 18.08 winning units..
Owner Paul & Clare Rooney **Bred** Gestut Kussaburg **Trained** Cholmondeley, Cheshire

FOCUS
A good quality staying handicap chase The winner can rate higher and the second ran to his mark.

2359 MAYFIELD RESTAURANT H'CAP CHASE (12 fncs) 2m 1f
2:50 (2:50) (Class 3) (0-140,136) 4-Y-0+ **£9,747** (£2,862; £1,431; £715)

Form RPR

3/4- **1** **Swift Arrow (IRE)**[29] 1850 7-11-4 **128** .... JasonMaguire 136+
(Donald McCain) *hld up: rdn and outpcd bef 4 out: rallied bef 2 out: led last: drvn out* **5/1**[3]

/UU- **2** ¾ **Jet Master (IRE)**[16] 2031 7-11-1 **125** ....(t) LucyAlexander 133+
(N W Alexander) *t.k.h: hld up in tch: smooth hdwy to ld bef 2 out: rdn and hdd whn hit last: rallied run-in* **7/1**

212/ **3** hd **Upsilon Bleu (FR)**[199] 5494 5-11-12 **136** .... WilsonRenwick 141
(Pauline Robson) *trckd ldrs: hdwy to ld after 4 out: rdn and hdd bef 2 out: rallied run-in: kpt on fin* **5/2**[2]

U33- **4** 5 **Rhymers Ha**[36] 1753 6-10-7 **117** .... PeterBuchanan 119
(Lucinda Russell) *trckd ldrs: nt fluent 5th: rdn after 3 out: outpcd next: no imp run-in* **13/2**

2/4- **5** 10 **Mr Moonshine (IRE)**[14] 2071 9-11-11 **135** .... RyanMania 129
(Sue Smith) *w ldr to 4 out: rdn next: wknd fr 2 out* **9/4**[1]

115/ **6** 11 **Wilde Pastures (IRE)**[222] 5075 8-11-8 **132** ....(p) BrianHughes 119
(James Ewart) *led tl blnd and hdd 4 out: rdn and wknd fr next* **9/1**

4m 13.4s (-4.60) **Going Correction** -0.325s/f (Good) **6** Ran SP% **111.8**
Speed ratings (Par 107): **97,96,96,94,89 84**
toteswingers 1&2 £13.40, 1&3 £2.00, 2&3 £7.90 CSF £36.03 TOTE £5.70: £2.80, £4.80; EX 56.70 Trifecta £270.80 Pool: £1,853.53 - 5.13 winning units..
Owner Mrs C Strang Steel **Bred** Paul Stacey **Trained** Cholmondeley, Cheshire

FOCUS
A decent handicap chase in which there was a contested gallop. The winner is rated to his best, with the second in line with his hurdles mark.

2360 DAVID MCLEAN (DM27) 7/7 MEMORIAL NOVICES' H'CAP HURDLE (6 hdls 4 omitted) 2m 2f
3:25 (3:27) (Class 5) (0-100,100) 4-Y-0+ **£2,599** (£763; £381; £190)

Form RPR

411- **1** **Civil Unrest (IRE)**[2] 2306 7-10-9 **93** ....(b) DaleIrving(10) 101
(James Ewart) *mde all: rdn after bypassed 2 out: hld on wl towards fin* **5/6**[1]

/43- **2** ¾ **Trust Thomas**[39] 1717 5-11-5 **100** .... GrahamWatters(7) 107
(Ann Hamilton) *hld up: blnd 2 out (usual 4 out): effrt and chsd wnr bef omitted last: kpt on: hld nr fin* **18/1**

0/5- **3** hd **Rhymers Stone**[34] 1790 5-10-13 **94** .... CraigNichol(7) 100
(Lucinda Russell) *prom: effrt and chsd wnr bef bypassed 2 out to bef omitted last: kpt on u.p run-in* **11/1**

0/4- **4** 7 **Blue Sea Of Ibrox (IRE)**[29] 1848 5-9-9 **74** .... HarryChalloner(5) 74
(Alan Brown) *hld up in tch: hdwy after 2 out (usual 4 out): rdn bef bypassed 2 out: sn one pce* **33/1**

/34- **5** 4 **Tiny Dancer (IRE)**[16] 2030 5-11-12 **100** .... BrianHughes 97
(Alan Swinbank) *chsd ldrs: nt fluent 2 out (usual 4 out): rdn and outpcd passing bypassed 2 out* **12/1**

302/ **6** 3 ½ **Vittachi**[21] 2325 6-9-9 **74** oh2 ....(p) CallumWhillans(5) 67
(Alistair Whillans) *chsd ldrs: drvn and outpcd after last (usual 3 out): no imp fr bypassed 2 out* **5/1**[2]

/34- **7** 4 ½ **Vodka Red (IRE)**[34] 1790 5-10-12 **86** ....(t) KennyJohnson 79
(Robert Johnson) *t.k.h: hld up: smooth hdwy to chse wnr 2 out (usual 4 out) to after next: wknd bef omitted last* **10/1**[3]

30P/ **8** 39 **Jan Smuts (IRE)**[54] 4545 5-10-0 **74** oh5 ....(tp) BarryKeniry 28
(Wilf Storey) *hld up: struggling 2 out (usual 4 out): btn bef bypassed 2 out: tailed off* **14/1**

04F/ **9** nk **Young Sparky (IRE)**[197] 5546 6-10-5 **79** ....(t[1]) WilsonRenwick 33
(Pauline Robson) *hld up: struggling after 2 out (usual 4 out): sn btn: t.o* **20/1**

000- **10** 26 **Optical High**[9] 2169 4-10-3 **82** .... JonathanEngland(5) 12
(Sue Smith) *chsd ldrs: drvn after 3rd: wknd after 2 out (usual 4 out): t.o* **66/1**

4m 26.0s (-1.00) **Going Correction** -0.20s/f (Good)
WFA 4 from 5yo+ 7lb **10** Ran SP% **117.5**
Speed ratings (Par 103): **94,93,93,90,88 87,85,67,67,56**
toteswingers 1&2 £4.20, 1&3 £3.90, 2&3 £13.40 CSF £17.00 CT £109.85 TOTE £1.80: £1.10, £3.30, £2.70; EX 18.90 Trifecta £111.10 Pool: £1,774.30 - 11.97 winning units..
Owner The Ancrum Pointer 1 **Bred** D And Mrs Noonan **Trained** Langholm, Dumfries & G'way

FOCUS
A moderate novices' handicap hurdle in which the last two obstacles in the home straight were omitted on both circuits due to a low sun, leaving just six to jump, and a run-in of about half-a-mile. The winner is rated well below the form of his recent win.

2361 GEORGE HARROW MEMORIAL H'CAP CHASE (12 fncs) 2m 1f
4:00 (4:00) (Class 5) (0-100,96) 4-Y-0+ **£2,924** (£858; £429; £214)

Form RPR

056- **1** **Jim Tango (FR)**[28] 1876 9-10-9 **79** ....(p) TomSiddall 90
(Karen McLintock) *prom: hdwy to ld 2 out: kpt on strly fr last* **6/1**[3]

/5F- **2** 1 ¾ **Ben Akram (IRE)**[2] 2308 5-11-12 **96** .... PeterBuchanan 106
(Lucinda Russell) *nt fluent on occasions: hld up: rdn and hdwy 4 out: effrt and drvn bef 2 out: styd on run-in: nt rch wnr* **6/1**[3]

0/P- **3** ¾ **Bob's Dream (IRE)**[179] 281 11-11-7 **91** ....(t) BrianHarding 99
(William Amos) *prom: effrt and drvn bef 2 out: wnt 2nd between last 2 to run-in: kpt on same pce* **14/1**

U5U- **4** 8 **Ballycool (IRE)**[7] 2219 6-11-3 **94** ....(t) MrSFox(7) 98
(Lucinda Russell) *nt fluent in rr: rdn bef 4 out: styd on fr 2 out: nvr rchd ldrs* **5/2**[2]

21F- **5** 3 ¼ **Sendiym (FR)**[9] 2173 6-11-9 **93** ....(b) BrianHughes 96
(Dianne Sayer) *mstkes: led to 2nd: ev ch tl wknd after 2 out* **9/4**[1]

250/ **6** 3 ¾ **Overlaw**[201] 5448 11-10-11 **91** .... DaraghBourke(10) 88
(Stuart Coltherd) *t.k.h: cl up: led 2nd to 2 out: sn wknd* **11/1**

030- **7** 12 **Breeze With Ease (IRE)**[29] 1848 9-11-2 **93** ....(t) GrahamWatters(7) 80
(Barry Murtagh) *nt fluent on occasions: prom to 1/2-way: struggling fr 4 out* **25/1**

55F- **U** **Laybach (IRE)**[7] 2219 9-10-9 **79** .... LucyAlexander
(Jim Goldie) *t.k.h: w ldr: sddle slipped and uns rdr 1st* **14/1**

4m 20.5s (2.50) **Going Correction** -0.325s/f (Good) **8** Ran SP% **113.4**
Speed ratings (Par 103): **81,80,79,76,74 72,67,**
toteswingers 1&2 £6.60, 1&3 £8.70, 2&3 £12.50 CSF £40.86 CT £479.70 TOTE £9.20: £2.30, £1.80, £3.70; EX 55.60 Trifecta £568.20 Pool: £2,424.31 - 3.19 winning units..
Owner Mrs C J Todd **Bred** Mme Laurence Gagneux **Trained** Ingoe, Northumberland

FOCUS
A weak handicap chase. The winner was well in on his best form.
T/Plt: £35.80 to a £1 stake. Pool: £62,872.97 - 1,278.81 winning units T/Qpdt: £16.90 to a £1 stake. Pool: £3,743.33 - 163.77 winning units RY

SANDOWN (R-H)

Saturday, November 9

OFFICIAL GOING: Chase course - soft (good to soft in places; 5.9); hurdle course - heavy (4.9)

Wind: Almost nil Weather: Rain before racing; very overcast

2362 HINCHLEY WOOD CONDITIONAL JOCKEYS' H'CAP HURDLE (8 hdls 1 omitted) 2m 4f

12:45 (12:47) (Class 3) (0-130,126) 4-Y-0+ **£6,498** (£1,908; £954; £477)

Form RPR

/00- **1** **Gores Island (IRE)**[34] 1783 7-10-12 **115**....................... JoshuaMoore(3) 115
(Gary Moore) *t.k.h: trckd ldrs: cl up after 3 out: rdn to ld sn after 2 out: hrd pressed after last: hld on* **25/1**

436/ **2** ¾ **Dawn Twister (GER)**[244] 4679 6-11-2 **119**...................... MattCrawley(3) 118
(Lucy Wadham) *hld up in tch: prog whn nt fluent 2 out: rdn to chal sn after last: kpt on but jst hld* **5/1**[3]

P55/ **3** 6 **The Bear Trap (IRE)**[210] 5281 6-11-3 **123**.................... PatrickCorbett(6) 116
(Rebecca Curtis) *trckd ldng pair: chal gng wl bef 2 out: upsides between last 2: wknd flat* **11/2**

/60- **4** ¾ **Captain Cardington (IRE)**[14] 2087 4-10-6 **112**.........(v) CiaranMckee(6) 106
(John O'Shea) *led at mod pce: had to be rdn gng out on fnl circ: hrd pressed whn mstke 2 out: sn hdd: no ex u.p* **33/1**

41/- **5** 2½ **Doctor Foxtrot (IRE)**[262] 4319 8-11-5 **122**.................(b) MichealNolan(3) 113
(Philip Hobbs) *wl in tch: rdn bef 2 out: no imp on ldrs after* **17/2**

6/0- **6** 2½ **Touch Back (IRE)**[14] 2087 7-11-4 **126**......................... JamesHuxham(8) 113
(Jonjo O'Neill) *racd wd: hld up in tch: nt fluent 3 out: wd bnd bef 2 out: urged along and fdd* **6/1**

531/ **7** 3¼ **Frizzo (FR)**[580] 5305 6-11-7 **124**... TomBellamy(3) 110
(Alan King) *hld up in tch: rdn and making no imp on ldrs whn mstke 2 out: fdd* **14/1**

/25- **8** 9 **Occasionally Yours (IRE)**[15] 2064 9-11-0 **114**................. JackQuinlan 89
(Alan Blackmore) *pressed ldr tl wknd bef 2 out* **20/1**

321/ **P** **Merehead (FR)**[742] 2192 7-10-12 **115**............................. HarryDerham(3)
(Paul Nicholls) *t.k.h: hld up in last: brief effrt after 3 out: sn wknd: bhd whn p.u bef last* **9/2**[2]

2/3- **R** **Kilmurvy (IRE)**[14] 2087 5-11-8 **125**...............................(p) MattGriffiths(3)
(Jeremy Scott) *in tch: shkn up 3 out: sn lost pl: 8th and struggling whn ducked out 2 out* **3/1**[1]

5m 22.9s (23.30) **Going Correction** +0.65s/f (Soft)
WFA 4 from 5yo+ 8lb **10** Ran SP% **118.3**
Speed ratings (Par 107): **79,78,76,76,75 74,72,69, ,**
toteswingers 1&2 £33.30, 1&3 £44.90, 2&3 £3.20 CSF £146.49 CT £808.16 TOTE £38.50: £6.20, £2.10, £3.10; EX 233.20 Trifecta £600.80 Part won. Pool: £801.10 - 0.10 winning units..

Owner Collins, Horsfall, Michael & O'Sullivan **Bred** Michael Byrnes **Trained** Lower Beeding, W Sussex

FOCUS
This handicap, confined to conditional riders, was understandably run at a steady early gallop. That saw most of the field in with a chance at the top of the home straight, but they got sorted out in between the final two. The first two are rated pretty much to their marks.

2363 CREW CLOTHING CO. BEGINNERS' CHASE (13 fncs) 2m

1:20 (1:20) (Class 3) 4-Y-0+ **£6,657** (£2,067; £1,113)

Form RPR

222/ **1** **Hinterland (FR)**[286] 3905 5-11-1 0....................................... RyanMahon 142+
(Paul Nicholls) *hld up in last pair: nt fluent 10th: clsd to chal 3 out: led and pckd sltly 2 out: a l up whn blnd and lft clr last: rdn out* **11/4**[2]

/02- **2** 5 **Turn Over Sivola (FR)**[20] 1986 6-11-1 132.................... RobertThornton 137
(Alan King) *jumping smetimes lacked zip: hld up in last pair: wnt 3rd after 3 out: no imp whn lft 2nd last* **11/1**[3]

2/3- **3** 13 **Elsafeer (IRE)**[42] 1689 8-11-1 118.................................. RichardJohnson 123
(Tim Vaughan) *led: set slow pce to 4th: hdd 3 out: sn wknd* **66/1**

2F6/ **U** **Grandouet (FR)**[219] 5137 6-11-1 0.................................... BarryGeraghty 141+
(Nicky Henderson) *j.big 1st: trckd ldr: led 3 out: shkn up and hdd next: a l down whn blnd last and uns rdr* **4/11**[1]

4m 15.4s (13.60) **Going Correction** +0.45s/f (Soft) **4** Ran SP% **109.8**
Speed ratings (Par 107): **84,81,75,**
CSF £21.06 TOTE £3.90; EX 11.50 Trifecta £24.40 Pool: £1,279.80 - 39.19 winning units..

Owner Chris Giles **Bred** E Aubree & C Bresson **Trained** Ditcheat, Somerset

FOCUS
An intriguing beginners' chase which proved dramatic late on. A step up from the winner on his previous C&D form. Grandouet was heading for a figure 20lb+ off his hurdle mark.

2364 MOVEMBER SPITFIRE ALE JUVENILE HURDLE (7 hdls 1 omitted) 2m 110y

1:55 (1:55) (Class 3) 3-Y-0 **£6,498** (£1,908; £954; £477)

Form RPR

1 **Kentucky Hyden (IRE)**[174] 3-10-12 0................................ BarryGeraghty 120+
(Nicky Henderson) *hld up: clsd to ld wl bef 2 out: sauntered clr: v easily* **1/3**[1]

00- **2** 33 **Dude Alert (IRE)**[36] 1743 3-10-12 0.................................... AdamWedge 85
(Anna Newton-Smith) *pressed ldr: upsides wl bef 2 out: no ch w wnr after: j.lft 2 out: mstke last* **66/1**

5- **3** 16 **Innoko (FR)**[23] 1934 3-10-7 0... JoshHamer(5) 69
(Tony Carroll) *hld up: in tch after 3 out: sn wknd: t.o whn blnd last* **16/1**

6- **4** 19 **Dark Emerald (IRE)**[20] 1985 3-10-12 0.......................(tp) BrendanPowell 50
(Brendan Powell) *mde most at fair pce: hdd & wknd wl bef 2 out: hmpd after 2 out: blnd last: v tired* **8/1**[3]

U **Shalianzi (IRE)**[24] 3-10-12 0... JamieMoore
(Gary Moore) *hld up in last: clsd after 3 out: drvn to dispute 2nd whn bmpd 2 out: swvd rt u.p sn after and uns rdr* **4/1**[2]

4m 16.1s (8.90) **Going Correction** +0.65s/f (Soft) **5** Ran SP% **113.5**
Speed ratings (Par 106): **105,89,81,73,**
CSF £16.99 TOTE £1.30: £1.10, £6.80; EX 19.40 Trifecta £127.30 Pool: £1,446.53 - 8.52 winning units..

Owner Simon Munir & Isaac Souede **Bred** Haras De Manneville **Trained** Upper Lambourn, Berks

FOCUS
There was a fair gallop set in this modest juvenile contest and the winner impressed, but the oppostion was not up to much.

2365 LITTLEWORTH H'CAP CHASE (17 fncs) 2m 4f 110y

2:30 (2:30) (Class 2) (0-150,147) 4-Y-0+ **£25,024** (£7,392; £3,696; £1,848; £924; £464)

Form RPR

1PB/ **1** **Kapga De Cerisy (FR)**[200] 5472 5-11-4 **139**.................... AidanColeman 152+
(Venetia Williams) *prom: led 4th: mde rest and mostly 4 l clr: mstke 10th: rdn 3 out: drew clr fr last* **4/1**[2]

521/ **2** 12 **Ackertac (IRE)**[206] 5355 8-11-12 **147**...........................(b) RichardJohnson 147
(Tim Vaughan) *prom: chsd wnr and mstke 7th: rdn 3 out: keeping on but hld whn j.big last: wknd flat: fin tired* **14/1**

101- **3** 1½ **Grandads Horse**[24] 1923 7-11-5 **140**.............................(p) BarryGeraghty 137
(Charlie Longsdon) *nt a fluent: dropped to last pair 7th: struggling fr 10th: wl bhd 4 out: styd on fr 2 out to take 3rd nr fin* **9/2**[3]

4/5- **4** ¾ **Rebel Rebellion (IRE)**[14] 2081 8-11-5 **140**.......................(t) RyanMahon 136
(Paul Nicholls) *led to 4th: lost pl and in midfield by 7th: lost tch w ldrs fr 12th: kpt on again fr 2 out* **10/1**

335/ **5** hd **Domtaline (FR)**[219] 5144 6-10-12 **138**............................ HarryDerham(5) 136
(Paul Nicholls) *hld up towards rr: prog 12th: chsd ldng pair bef 3 out: sn rdn: no imp after 2 out: wknd bdly flat* **7/1**

6/1- **6** 12 **Mart Lane (IRE)**[9] 2180 8-10-11 **135**............................ JoshuaMoore(3) 119
(Dr Richard Newland) *chsd ldrs: rdn and no imp in 4th after 4 out: wknd 2 out* **6/1**

060/ **7** 12 **Hector's Choice (FR)**[218] 5160 9-11-2 **137**........................ JamieMoore 111
(Richard Lee) *prom: disp 2nd pl fr 6th to 10th: wknd qckly 12th* **10/1**

14- **8** 10 **Mister Grez (FR)**[21] 1971 7-10-6 **127**................................. HarrySkelton 89
(Dan Skelton) *hld up: prog 7th: prom next: wknd qckly after 4 out* **3/1**[1]

P/0- **P** **Nozic (FR)**[181] 236 12-9-11 **123**...............................(bt) NicodeBoinville(5)
(Zoe Davison) *a in rr: j. slowly 7th: sn lost tch: t.o whn p.u bef 11th* **25/1**

5m 22.0s (3.60) **Going Correction** +0.45s/f (Soft) **9** Ran SP% **118.7**
Speed ratings (Par 109): **111,106,105,105,105 100,96,92,**
toteswingers 1&2 £48.00, 1&3 £4.30, 2&3 £11.20 CSF £56.33 CT £265.64 TOTE £5.30: £1.80, £3.50, £1.90; EX 84.60 Trifecta £410.50 Pool: £964.07 - 1.76 winning units..

Owner A Brooks **Bred** Olivier Varin **Trained** Kings Caple, H'fords

FOCUS
This was a good-quality handicap. They went an average gallop until leaving the back straight and most were caught out at that stage. Another step up from the winner, who looks a high-class prospect.

2366 SIGN 2000 CELEBRATORY H'CAP HURDLE (7 hdls 1 omitted) 2m 110y

3:05 (3:05) (Class 3) (0-130,130) 4-Y-0+ **£12,512** (£3,696; £1,848; £924; £462; £232)

Form RPR

200- **1** **Hawkhill (IRE)**[42] 1685 7-11-7 **125**...............................(t) RichardJohnson 132
(Tim Vaughan) *mde all at decent pce: shkn up and drew clr bef 2 out: in n.d after: drvn out* **25/1**

24P/ **2** 6 **Valid Reason**[28] 3227 6-11-7 **125**.......................................[1] BarryGeraghty 126
(Dean Ivory) *trckd ldrs: rdn bef 2 out: no ch w wnr but kpt on to take 2nd after last* **13/2**[3]

040/ **3** 2 **Mcvicar**[15] 5573 4-11-6 **124**... RobertThornton 124
(Alan King) *mostly chsd wnr: rdn and no imp whn mstke 2 out: no ch after: one pce and lost 2nd flat* **10/1**

/05- **4** ¾ **Oscar Prairie (IRE)**[23] 1943 8-11-5 **126**........................ GavinSheehan(3) 124
(Warren Greatrex) *racd on outer in midfield: lost pl 4th: detached last after next: kpt on fr 2 out: stl only 10th last: r.o to take 4th nr fin* **33/1**

10/- **5** 2¾ **Saphir Du Rheu (FR)**[241] 4737 4-11-7 **130**...................... HarryDerham(5) 127
(Paul Nicholls) *hld up in midfield: rdn to chse ldrs bef 2 out: sn no imp: wl btn bef last* **6/1**[2]

0/0- **6** ½ **Kingcora (FR)**[36] 1745 5-10-11 **115**................................. AidanColeman 110
(Venetia Williams) *chsd ldng pair: drvn and lost pl wl bef 2 out: struggling after: kpt on again after last* **6/1**[2]

4/2- **7** 1¾ **Crafty Roberto**[183] 202 5-11-1 **119**..................................(t) WillKennedy 112
(Alex Hales) *in tch towards rr: sme prog on inner after 3 out: no hdwy 2 out: wl hld after* **20/1**

205/ **8** 1¼ **Ut Majeur Aulmes (FR)**[262] 4318 5-10-10 **114**...................... JackDoyle 107
(Victor Dartnall) *hld up in rr: prog after 3 out to chse ldrs bef 2 out: sn rdn: wknd last* **12/1**

420- **9** ½ **Escort'men (FR)**[14] 2087 7-10-1 **108**............................(t) KielanWoods(3) 100
(Anthony Middleton) *hld up in last: mstke 2nd: modest prog after 3 out: no hdwy fr 2 out* **14/1**

1/ **10** 1¾ **Chat Room**[316] 3310 5-11-3 **124**....................................... JackQuinlan(3) 115
(John Ferguson) *trckd ldng trio: rdn to take 3rd bef 2 out: no imp whn blnd last: wknd* **7/2**[1]

240/ **11** 10 **Whipcrackaway (IRE)**[20] 5573 4-10-9 **120**..................(p) TomBellamy(7) 100
(Peter Hedger) *hld up and a wl in rr: rdn sn after 3 out: wknd* **25/1**

222/ **12** 5 **Ubaldo Des Menhies (FR)**[222] 5065 5-11-9 **127**......... RichieMcLernon 102
(Jonjo O'Neill) *hld up wl in rr: pushed along and no prog on long run bef 2 out: sn wknd* **12/1**

/34- **13** 40 **Swampfire (IRE)**[112] 1045 5-11-1 **122**............................ JoshuaMoore(3) 57
(Gary Moore) *t.k.h in midfield: wknd sn after 3 out: wl t.o* **8/1**

4m 14.5s (7.30) **Going Correction** +0.65s/f (Soft)
WFA 4 from 5yo+ 7lb **13** Ran SP% **121.8**
Speed ratings (Par 107): **108,105,104,103,102 102,101,100,100,99 95,92,74**
toteswingers 1&2 £52.10, 1&3 £52.10, 2&3 £10.90 CSF £178.52 CT £1769.13 TOTE £30.40: £8.80, £2.70, £2.10; EX 182.40 Trifecta £558.20 Pool: £899.98 - 1.20 winning units..

Owner Exors of the Late R H D Smith **Bred** Bernard Cooke **Trained** Aberthin, Vale of Glamorgan

FOCUS
This fair handicap looked competitive, but the winner bolted up from the front. Straightforward form.

2367 ORIGINAL SPACEMAN H'CAP CHASE (22 fncs) 3m 110y

3:40 (3:40) (Class 3) (0-125,125) 4-Y-0+ **£12,512** (£3,696; £1,848; £924; £462; £232)

Form RPR

3/1- **1** **Fine Parchment (IRE)**[166] 508 10-11-5 **125**.......(tp) MrHAABannister(7) 133
(Charlie Mann) *j.w: led 5th: mde rest: drew clr 3 out: j.lft 2 out: 8 l ahd last: tired flat: hld on* **14/1**

14P/ **2** 1¼ **Gorgehous Lliege (FR)**[236] 4838 7-10-4 **103**.................. AidanColeman 110
(Venetia Williams) *led to 5th: chsd wnr to 14th: rdn and no imp whn mstke 3 out: kpt on to take 2nd again last: clsd on tiring wnr fin* **11/4**[1]

/11- **3** 2 1/4 **Franklin Roosevelt (IRE)**[13] 2110 7-10-13 **119**...........(b) KieronEdgar(7) 124
(David Pipe) *nt a fluent towards rr: rdn after 12th and struggling in last: wl bhd 4 out: styd on fr 2 out: fin wl* **7/2**[2]

221- **4** 6 **Firm Order (IRE)**[20] 1988 8-11-12 **125**.......................(p) RichieMcLernon 125
(Paul Webber) *hld up in rr: prog 12th: chsd wnr 14th: mstkes 4 out and 3 out whn no imp: wknd and lost 2nd last* **8/1**

4/5- **5** 1/2 **Shuil Royale (IRE)**[23] 1944 8-11-6 **119**.....................(p) AndrewThornton 115
(David Arbuthnot) *in tch: rdn fr 13th: no prog: wl btn after 4 out* **6/1**[3]

/42- **6** 4 1/2 **Lough Coi (IRE)**[8] 2194 7-10-1 **100**.................................(tp) JamieMoore 94
(Anthony Middleton) *in tch: rdn fr 13th: struggling fr 17th: wl btn bef 3 out* **8/1**

6/4- **P** **Time For Spring (IRE)**[29] 1852 9-11-9 **122**..............(p) RichardJohnson
(Charlie Longsdon) *hld up: prog into 4th at 17th: no hdwy after: wknd 3 out: t.o whn p.u bef last* **7/2**[2]

6m 44.7s (16.90) **Going Correction** +0.45s/f (Soft) 7 Ran SP% **114.3**
Speed ratings (Par 107): **90,89,88,86,86 85,**
toteswingers 1&2 £11.90, 1&3 £2.90, 2&3 £1.70 CSF £53.77 CT £168.75 TOTE £13.80: £3.80, £2.00; EX 47.00 Trifecta £106.90 Pool: £1,153.16 - 8.08 winning units..
Owner N W A Bannister **Bred** Timothy Considine **Trained** Upper Lambourn, Berks

FOCUS
A modest staying handicap, run at a routine gallop. Probably not form to get carried away with.

2368 RICHARD STONE 40TH BIRTHDAY CELEBRATION STANDARD OPEN NATIONAL HUNT FLAT RACE 2m 110y
4:10 (4:15) (Class 5) 4-6-Y-O **£3,249** (£954; £477; £238)

Form RPR

/32- **1** **Hello George (IRE)**[28] 1869 4-11-0 0........................... RichardJohnson 116
(Philip Hobbs) *hld up in rr: prog over 4f out: rdn to cl on ldrs fr 3f out: led jst ins fnl f but jnd: gained upper hand last 50yds* **6/4**[1]

2- **2** 1/2 **Flying Eagle (IRE)**[31] 1819 5-11-0 0.................................. JamieMoore 116
(Peter Bowen) *in tch: prog 4f out: rdn to chal wl over 2f out: kpt on and upsides again ins fnl f: no ex nr fin* **8/1**

3 1 1/4 **Tara Road**[230] 5-11-0 0... BarryGeraghty 114
(Rebecca Curtis) *hld up in tch: smooth prog to ld wl over 2f out: shkn up wl over 1f out: hdd and one pce jst ins fnl f* **15/8**[2]

4/3- **4** 12 **Trevaylor Boy (IRE)**[28] 1869 6-11-0 0............................... WillKennedy 102
(Sue Gardner) *t.k.h: cl up: led over 3f out to wl over 2f out: steadily wknd* **5/1**[3]

0- **5** 5 **Mr Shantu (IRE)**[180] 270 4-11-0 0............................... RichieMcLernon 97
(Jonjo O'Neill) *led to over 3f out: sn wknd u.p* **25/1**

5/ **6** 1/2 **Kaki Island (IRE)**[316] 3333 5-11-0 0.................................. TomCannon 97
(Chris Gordon) *hld up in last: rdn 4f out: lft bhd fr 3f out* **40/1**

0- **7** 10 **Viking Mistress**[169] 462 5-10-7 0... IanPopham 80
(Martin Keighley) *in tch in rr: n.m.r on inner 5f out: rdn over 3f out: steadily wknd* **33/1**

1- **8** 14 **Lemons Ground**[178] 309 4-11-4 0............................... GavinSheehan(3) 80
(Jamie Snowden) *prom tl wknd u.p over 4f out: wl bhd fnl 2f* **16/1**

9 30 **Wunfurlez** 5-11-0 0... SamThomas 43
(Diana Grissell) *prom tl wknd over 5f out: wl t.o* **20/1**

4m 10.7s (9.10) **Going Correction** +0.65s/f (Soft) 9 Ran SP% **122.4**
Speed ratings: **104,103,103,97,95 94,90,83,69**
toteswingers 1&2 £5.20, 1&3 £1.10, 2&3 £6.70 CSF £15.00 TOTE £2.20: £1.30, £2.70, £1.50; EX 11.30 Trifecta £36.30 Pool: £2,173.88 - 44.85 winning units..
Owner M St Quinton/ C Hellyer/ M Strong **Bred** George Ward **Trained** Withycombe, Somerset

FOCUS
Not a bad bumper. A step up from the winner on his Chepstow form with the fourth.
T/Plt: £724.00 to a £1 stake. Pool: £82,423.45 - 83.10 winning units T/Qpdt: £43.00 to a £1 stake. Pool: £6,603.05 - 113.55 winning units JN

2105 WINCANTON (R-H)
Saturday, November 9

OFFICIAL GOING: Good to soft (good in places; chs 7.8; hdl 7.9)
Wind: Mild breeze; across Weather: Showers

2369 TOTEPLACEPOT ON ALL UK MEETINGS E B F STALLIONS "NATIONAL HUNT NOVICES" HURDLE (QUALIFIER) (8 hdls) 2m
12:20 (12:21) (Class 3) 4-6-Y-O **£6,498** (£1,908; £954; £477)

Form RPR

1/4- **1** **Amore Alato**[28] 1864 4-10-12 0.. APMcCoy 121+
(Nick Williams) *mde all: kpt on strly fr 2 out: rdn out* **11/4**[2]

1/ **2** 4 **Heath Hunter (IRE)**[280] 3988 6-10-12 0........................ TomScudamore 117+
(David Pipe) *trckd ldrs: wnt 2nd after 3 out: rdn bef next: kpt on but nt pce to chal* **15/8**[1]

100/ **3** 1 1/4 **Sgt Reckless**[217] 5179 6-10-12 0................................. DominicElsworth 115
(Mick Channon) *hld up towards rr: nt that fluent early: smooth hdwy 3 out: wnt 3rd gng to 2 out: sn rdn: styd on same pce* **11/4**[2]

02/ **4** 7 **Money For Nothing**[209] 5323 4-10-12 0.................... WayneHutchinson 108
(Alan King) *mid-div: hdwy into 4th gng to 2 out: sn rdn: styd on same pce* **16/1**

/30- **5** 1 3/4 **Very Noble (FR)**[28] 1869 4-10-12 0.................................(t) NickScholfield 107
(Paul Nicholls) *hld up: stdy hdwy after 3 out: rdn into disp 4th after 2 out: styd on same pce fr last* **20/1**

453- **6** 1 1/2 **Beaujolais (IRE)**[15] 2068 5-10-12 0................................ DenisO'Regan 105
(John Ferguson) *trckd wnr tl rdn after 3 out: one pce fr next* **20/1**

456/ **7** 3/4 **Lamblord (IRE)**[627] 4430 6-10-12 101.................................... IanPopham 104
(Carroll Gray) *mid-div: rdn after 3 out: nvr any imp* **100/1**

0/4- **8** 7 **Whispering Bob (IRE)**[14] 2083 6-10-12 0.............................. NoelFehily 97
(Charlie Longsdon) *in tch: rdn appr 2 out: grad fdd* **14/1**[3]

06- **9** 9 **Henwood (IRE)**[13] 2109 5-10-12 0.. JoeTizzard 88
(Colin Tizzard) *t.k.h: in mid-div tl dropped to rr 3 out: sn struggling: nvr bk on terms* **50/1**

440/ **10** 8 **Downtown Manhattan (IRE)**[615] 4655 6-10-7 0....... MauriceLinehan(5) 80
(Jonjo O'Neill) *trckd ldrs: nt fluent 1st: rdn and wknd after 3 out* **50/1**

50- **11** 55 **Forget And Forgive (IRE)**[14] 2083 5-10-12 0.................. PaulMoloney 25
(Anthony Middleton) *trckd ldrs: rdn after 3 out: sn wknd: t.o* **100/1**

3m 42.5s (-6.40) **Going Correction** -0.60s/f (Firm)
WFA 4 from 5yo+ 7lb 11 Ran SP% **116.1**
Speed ratings: **92,90,89,85,85 84,83,80,75,71 44**
toteswingers 1&2 £1.30, 1&3 £1.60, 2&3 £2.10 CSF £8.00 TOTE £3.80: £1.40, £1.30, £1.50; EX 8.20 Trifecta £23.80 Pool: £888.99 - 27.96 winning units..
Owner Mrs Sarah Faulks **Bred** Mr And Mrs N Faulks **Trained** George Nympton, Devon

FOCUS
All bends moved out, fences and hurdles moved out 4yds on to better ground. Probably a fair contest and the form looks believable despite a relatively slow time.

2370 BET TOTESCOOP6 AT TOTEPOOL.COM H'CAP CHASE (17 fncs) 2m 5f
12:55 (12:55) (Class 4) (0-120,119)
4-Y-0+ **£9,495** (£2,805; £1,402; £702; £351)

Form RPR

3/4- **1** **Plein Pouvoir (FR)**[179] 294 10-11-12 **119**...................... LiamTreadwell 131+
(Venetia Williams) *in tch: tk clsr order 8th: led 13th: styd on wl and in command fr 3 out but j.rt: cosily* **17/2**

P/4- **2** 6 **Be Definite (IRE)**[20] 1988 9-11-5 **112**..........................(p) PaddyBrennan 119+
(Tom George) *j.rt: disp fr after 4th: lft in ld 8th: jnd 10th: hdd 13th: rdn to chse wnr after 4 out: styd on same pce* **5/1**[3]

P12- **3** 1 3/4 **Upton Mead (IRE)**[5] 2270 6-10-9 **102**...............................(b) TomCannon 104
(Kevin Tork) *trckd ldrs: disp fr 10th tl 13th: rdn after 4 out: styd on same pce fr next* **5/1**[3]

3/2- **4** 10 **Taffy Thomas**[27] 1886 9-11-0 **107**.......................................(t) TomO'Brien 101
(Peter Bowen) *hld up in tch: pushed along fr after 9th: rdn into 4th after 4 out: sn hld: hit 2 out: styd on same pce* **9/2**[2]

5/3- **5** 6 **O'Callaghan Strand (AUS)**[18] 2014 7-11-11 **118**...............(p) APMcCoy 106
(Jonjo O'Neill) *trckd ldrs: hmpd 8th: rdn after 4 out: sn hld: wknd 2 out* **7/1**

3/5- **6** 1 3/4 **Mister Snowball (FR)**[13] 2107 6-11-8 **115**..................... TomScudamore 103
(Chris Down) *j.lft: disp tl 3rd: trckd ldrs: disp 11th tl next: rdn after 13th: sn btn* **4/1**[1]

4/0- **F** **Beside The Fire**[13] 2111 8-11-8 **115**... JoeTizzard
(Colin Tizzard) *disp ld tl clr ldr 3rd: jnd after next: fell 8th* **25/1**

1PF- **P** **Next Oasis (IRE)**[48] 1636 7-11-6 **113**................................. NickScholfield
(Paul Henderson) *disp ld tl after 3rd: trckd ldrs tl lost pl 8th: lost tch qckly after 9th: p.u bef 12th* **6/1**

5m 19.9s (-5.30) **Going Correction** -0.10s/f (Good) 8 Ran SP% **112.7**
Speed ratings (Par 105): **106,103,103,99,96 96, ,**
toteswingers 1&2 £11.70, 1&3 £3.50, 2&3 £5.00 CSF £49.36 CT £235.03 TOTE £7.60: £2.10, £1.80, £1.80; EX 52.60 Trifecta £474.90 Part won. Pool: £633.30 - 0.30 winning units..
Owner Dr Moira Hamlin **Bred** Mme Jean-Marc & Jean-Marc Baudrelle **Trained** Kings Caple, H'fords

FOCUS
A fair event. The winner is rated to his best and the second is on a mark he can win off.

2371 YOUR FAVOURITE POOL BETS AT TOTEPOOL.COM MARES' H'CAP HURDLE (11 hdls) 2m 6f
1:30 (1:31) (Class 2) 4-Y-0+
£15,640 (£4,620; £2,310; £1,155; £577; £290)

Form RPR

313/ **1** **Highland Retreat**[207] 5328 6-11-0 **125**....................................... NoelFehily 131
(Harry Fry) *trckd ldrs: jnd ldr 3 out: led 2 out: sn rdn: kpt on wl whn chal after last: drvn rt out* **13/2**[3]

141- **2** 3/4 **Mrs Peachey (IRE)**[34] 1783 6-10-12 **123**......................... NickScholfield 128
(Kim Bailey) *mid-div: hdwy after 3 out: rdn into 4th between last 2: styd on wl to press wnr run-in: hld nring fin* **17/2**

111- **3** 3 1/4 **As I Am (IRE)**[82] 1321 5-11-0 **132**.............................. ConorShoemark(7) 134
(Don Cantillon) *led: rdn and hdd 2 out: rallied gamely and ev ch last: no ex and hung rt run-in* **9/1**

521/ **4** 6 **Utopie Des Bordes (FR)**[199] 5493 5-11-12 **137**.................... DavidBass 134
(Nicky Henderson) *in tch: trckd ldrs 4th: rdn to chse ldng pair appr 2 out: styd on same pce fr last* **8/1**

P/U- **5** 2 3/4 **Mickie**[21] 1972 5-11-1 **129**.. JakeGreenall(3) 125
(Henry Daly) *trckd ldrs tl outpcd after 3 out: styd on between last 2 but no ch w ldrs* **9/2**[1]

113- **6** 3 1/4 **Emily's Flyer (IRE)**[31] 1818 6-10-9 **120**.......................(t) PaddyBrennan 112
(Fergal O'Brien) *prom tl pushed along after 7th: chsd ldrs tl outpcd after 3 out: styd on again between last 2* **16/1**

/35- **7** 8 **Loyaute (FR)**[14] 2084 6-10-2 **113**.. JamesDavies 98
(Chris Down) *trckd ldrs: rdn appr 2 out: sn wknd* **9/1**

1/2- **8** 4 1/2 **Tara Rose**[24] 1923 8-11-1 **126**................................(t) SamTwiston-Davies 106
(Nigel Twiston-Davies) *mid-div: rdn after 3 out: wknd next* **7/1**

212/ **9** 3 1/2 **Call Me A Star**[207] 5339 6-11-11 **136**.......................... WayneHutchinson 113
(Alan King) *mid-div: hdwy 3 out to trck ldrs: rdn appr 2 out: wknd qckly* **6/1**[2]

232- **10** 2 1/2 **Emerald Rose**[31] 1818 6-10-0 **111** oh1................................(p) MarkGrant 86
(Julian Smith) *mid-div: pushed along after 5th: sn in rr* **25/1**

6/1- **11** 6 **Blase Chevalier (IRE)**[31] 1823 7-9-11 **111** oh4........ WayneKavanagh(3) 81
(Seamus Mullins) *hit 8th: wnt lft 2 out: mstke last: a towards rr* **66/1**

540- **12** 42 **Va'Vite (IRE)**[22] 1956 6-11-0 **125**....................................(p) PaulMoloney 57
(Anthony Middleton) *pushed along after 6th: a towards rr: t.o after 3 out* **50/1**

1/P- **13** 66 **Kim Tian Road (IRE)**[152] 688 7-10-3 **117**............. JeremiahMcGrath(3)
(Martin Hill) *a towards rr: t.o fr 3 out* **10/1**

5m 9.5s (-17.00) **Going Correction** -0.60s/f (Firm) 13 Ran SP% **122.2**
Speed ratings (Par 109): **106,105,104,102,101 100,97,95,94,93 91,76,52**
toteswingers 1&2 £10.40, 1&3 £5.20, 2&3 £7.50 CSF £61.88 CT £509.69 TOTE £7.00: £2.40, £3.30, £2.70; EX 66.50 Trifecta £887.40 Part won..
Owner Richard Barber **Bred** Richard Bridges **Trained** Seaborough, Dorset

FOCUS
An open contest as the betting suggested, but the winner and third were always prominent, suggesting it was an advanatge to race handy. The third and fourth set the level and the form should work out.

2372 TOTEPOOL ENTER THE TEN TO FOLLOW ELITE HURDLE (LIMITED H'CAP) GRADE 2 (8 hdls) 2m
2:05 (2:05) (Class 1) 4-Y-0+
£34,170 (£12,822; £6,420; £3,198; £1,608; £804)

Form RPR

111/ **1** **Melodic Rendezvous**[272] 4152 7-11-10 **150**..................... NickScholfield 157+
(Jeremy Scott) *trckd ldrs: slipped on bnd turning in: disputing 2nd whn hit 2 out: sn rdn: chal last: led sn after: r.o wl: rdn out* **9/2**

112/ **2** 1 3/4 **Far West (FR)**[239] 4767 4-11-6 **146**........................ SamTwiston-Davies 149
(Paul Nicholls) *trckd ldr: led jst bef 2 out: sn rdn: hdd after last: kpt on but no ex* **5/2**[1]

/41- **3** 3 **Ahyaknowyerself (IRE)**[42] 1685 7-11-7 **147**.......................(b) APMcCoy 148
(Dr Richard Newland) *led: mstke 5th: rdn and hdd jst bef 2 out: lost 2nd between last 2: kpt on same pce run-in* **10/1**

2F0/ **4** 3 1/2 **Cotton Mill**[218] 5162 6-11-8 **148**...................................... DenisO'Regan 145
(John Ferguson) *trckd ldr: hit 5th: rdn to chse ldng pair appr 2 out: hld between last 2: kpt on same pce* **10/3**[3]

1/1- **5** 2 ¾ **Karinga Dancer**[14] 2069 7-11-7 **147**.....................................(t) NoelFehily 142
(Harry Fry) *hld up bhd ldrs: nudged along after 3 out: effrt bef 2 out but nvr finding pce to get on terms* **11/4**[2]

356- **6** 1 ¾ **Ruler Of All (IRE)**[13] 2102 7-9-11 **130**.................................. MrRWinks[(7)] 125
(Peter Winks) *hld up bhd ldrs: j.lft at times: pushed along after 4th: stl in tch whn rdn after 3 out: hung lft between last 2 and run-in: kpt on but nvr finding pce to get involved* **20/1**

3m 34.1s (-14.80) **Going Correction** -0.60s/f (Firm)
WFA 4 from 6yo+ 7lb **6** Ran SP% **110.4**
Speed ratings (Par 115): **113,112,110,108,107 106**
toteswingers 1&2 £1.10, 1&3 £8.70, 2&3 £4.20 CSF £15.90 TOTE £6.00: £2.60, £1.80; EX 12.50 Trifecta £44.80 Pool: £1,732.15 - 28.97 winning units..
Owner Cash For Honours **Bred** Mrs N A Ward **Trained** Brompton Regis, Somerset

FOCUS
A strong-looking renewal of this long-established contest, with quite a few appearing to hold realistic chances of success. The winner is a potential 160 horse but still a way shy of Champion Hurdle class.

2373 BADGER ALES TROPHY (HANDICAP CHASE) (LISTED RACE) (18 fncs 3 omitted) 3m 1f 110y
2:40 (2:40) (Class 1) 4-Y-0+
£34,170 (£12,822; £6,420; £3,198; £1,608; £804)

Form RPR

111- **1** **Standing Ovation (IRE)**[13] 2108 6-10-2 **120**................(tp) ConorO'Farrell 136+
(David Pipe) *travelled wl through out: trckd ldrs: jnd ldr 12th: led 15th: pushed clr after 3 out: styd on strly: readily* **5/2**[1]

/60- **2** 5 **Alfie Spinner (IRE)**[28] 1868 8-10-8 **126**.......................... TomScudamore 130
(Nick Williams) *led tl 15th: rdn to chse wnr after 3 out: styd on but a being readily hld by wnr* **16/1**

0/3- **3** 3 ¼ **Court By Surprise (IRE)**[28] 1868 8-10-13 **131**....................... NoelFehily 135+
(Emma Lavelle) *mid-div: slipped on bnd after 7th: rdn and clsng on ldrs but short of room whn stmbld bdly 3 out: wnt 3rd after 2 out: styd on* **5/1**[2]

521/ **4** 2 **Poungach (FR)**[238] 4788 7-11-12 **144**...................(b) SamTwiston-Davies 144
(Paul Nicholls) *mid-div: pushed along after 12th: rdn after 15th: styd on wl fr last: wnt 4th by-passing omitted last* **13/2**[3]

02/- **5** 2 ½ **Ballyoliver**[205] 5361 9-10-13 **131**....................................... LiamTreadwell 128
(Venetia Williams) *mid-div: nt fluent 3rd (water): hdwy 12th: nt fluent 15th: sn rdn: styd on same pce fr 3 out* **16/1**

244- **6** 2 ¼ **Billie Magern**[70] 1476 9-11-3 **142**....................................(v) RyanHatch[(7)] 138
(Nigel Twiston-Davies) *trckd ldrs: w ldr fr 5th tl trckd ldrs after 8th: rdn after 14th: styd on same pce tl no ex on long run-in* **50/1**

021/ **7** 10 **De La Bech**[249] 4576 6-10-9 **127**.. TomO'Brien 114
(Philip Hobbs) *towards rr of mid-div: blnd 5th: pushed along fr10th: hdwy 12th: rdn in tch after 15th: wknd bef 2 out* **7/1**

/22- **8** ¾ **Lamboro Lad (IRE)**[37] 1730 8-10-5 **123**......................(tp) DonalDevereux 109
(Peter Bowen) *towards rr of mid-div: squeezed up on bnd after 7th: hdwy 12th: rdn after 15th: wknd after next* **25/1**

305- **9** 19 **Owen Glendower (IRE)**[24] 1923 8-10-11 **129**.................(t) PaulMoloney 97
(Sophie Leech) *stmbld 8th: hit next: a towards rr: wknd 3 out: t.o* **40/1**

3/3- **10** 7 **Ballyallia Man (IRE)**[13] 2106 8-10-9 **127**........................(t) PaddyBrennan 89
(Tom George) *trckd ldr tl after 8th: chsd ldrs: rdn after 14th: wknd after next: t.o* **14/1**

200/ **P** **Aiteen Thirtythree (IRE)**[651] 3967 9-11-12 **144**.............. NickScholfield
(Paul Nicholls) *hld up towards rr: rdn after 14th: wknd after 3 out: p.u bef last* **16/1**

P/1- **P** **Masters Hill (IRE)**[18] 2009 7-11-5 **137**.................................... JoeTizzard
(Colin Tizzard) *mid-div: pckd 1st: blnd 10th: lost pl tamely 11th: sn bhd: p.u bef 13th* **10/1**

112- **P** **Pantxoa (FR)**[22] 1957 6-11-9 **141**.......................... WayneHutchinson
(Alan King) *trckd ldrs: nt fluent 2nd: struggling whn pckd 13th: sn btn: p.u 3 out* **10/1**

6m 29.3s (-10.20) **Going Correction** -0.10s/f (Good) **13** Ran SP% **121.8**
Speed ratings (Par 111): **111,109,108,107,107 106,103,103,97,95 ,,**
toteswingers 1&2 £15.10, 1&3 £3.20, 2&3 £28.30 CSF £42.30 CT £195.84 TOTE £3.10: £2.20, £6.40, £2.40; EX 57.70 Trifecta £1428.70 Part won. Pool: £1,905.01 - 0.73 winning units..
Owner The Bravo Partnership **Bred** Patrick McGrath **Trained** Nicholashayne, Devon

FOCUS
The last fence was omitted due to the ground on the chase course on stable bend being slippery, which meant three fences in all were omitted. The hurdle course was used on the stable bend. The cosy winner was well in and this was another step forward.

2374 CONGRATULATIONS A. P. MCCOY RISING STARS NOVICES' CHASE (GRADE 2) (15 fncs 2 omitted) 2m 5f
3:15 (3:15) (Class 1) 4-Y-0+ **£17,911** (£7,059; £3,805)

Form RPR

0/1- **1** **Wonderful Charm (FR)**[15] 2063 5-11-8 0.......................(t) NickScholfield 159+
(Paul Nicholls) *trckd ldr: disputing ld whn nt fluent and hdd 2 out: 3 l down u.p last: r.o strly to ld fnl 100yds: drvn rt out* **11/8**[1]

/52- **2** 1 **Fox Appeal (IRE)**[17] 2019 6-11-2 0.................................... LeightonAspell 150
(Emma Lavelle) *trckd ldr: blnd 10th: didn't appear to handle bnd whn swtchd out after 12th: disputing ld whn lft clr 2 out: 3 l up last: sn rdn: kpt on but no ex whn hdd fnl 100yds* **6/1**

2/1- **3** 10 **Third Intention (IRE)**[22] 1955 6-11-8 151...........................(t) JoeTizzard 147
(Colin Tizzard) *led: j.lft at times: rchd for 10th: rdn and hdd appr 2 out: kpt on same pce fr last* **3/1**[3]

223/ **P** **Meister Eckhart (IRE)**[218] 5162 7-11-2 0.................. WayneHutchinson 139
(Alan King) *trckd ldng trio: carried wd on bnd after 12th: rdn after next whn looking to be hanging lft: struggling to find pce to get on terms but stl cl up 4th whn virtually fell 2 out: immediately p.u* **11/4**[2]

5m 19.4s (-5.80) **Going Correction** -0.10s/f (Good) **4** Ran SP% **108.1**
Speed ratings (Par 115): **107,106,102,**
CSF £8.67 TOTE £2.30; EX 11.40 Trifecta £20.70 Pool: £1,075.00 - 38.91 winning units..
Owner R J H Geffen **Bred** Jean-Philippe Dubois **Trained** Ditcheat, Somerset

FOCUS
Some really good horses have taken this race down the years, including Silviniaco Conti (2011), Wishfull Thinking (2010) and Comply Or Die (2004). The pace appeared steady early. The winner is a smart novice and is rated similar to his Fakenham form.

2375 COLLECT TOTEPOOL WINNINGS AT BETFRED SHOPS INTERMEDIATE OPEN NATIONAL HUNT FLAT RACE 2m
3:50 (3:51) (Class 6) 4-6-Y-0 **£1,624** (£477; £238; £119)

Form RPR

6/2- **1** **Zulu Oscar**[179] 298 4-11-4 0.. NoelFehily 118+
(Harry Fry) *trckd ldrs: led 5f out: drew clr w runner-up fr 2f out: rdn ent fnl f: styd on wl to assert sn after: rdn out* **5/1**[3]

2 2 **Inner Drive (IRE)**[216] 5-10-11 0................................ ConorShoemark[(7)] 114+
(Don Cantillon) *hld up towards rr: hdwy fr over 5f out: chal over 2f out: sn rdn: ev ch jst over 1f out: kpt on but hld by wnr ins fnl f: wl clr of remainder* **12/1**

/ **3** 14 **River Deep (IRE)** 4-11-4 0... TomO'Brien 101
(Philip Hobbs) *mid-div: rdn 3f out: hdwy 2f out: styd on but nvr any ch w ldng pair* **16/1**

3- **4** 3 ½ **Vazaro Delafayette (FR)**[21] 1974 4-11-4 0.................. TomScudamore 98
(David Pipe) *trckd ldrs: rdn over 2f out: sn outpcd by front 2: no ex whn lost 3rd ent fnl f* **6/4**[1]

0/ **5** 1 ¼ **Morning Reggie**[211] 5279 4-11-4 0................................. LeightonAspell 97
(Oliver Sherwood) *hld up towards rr: struggling 5f out: styd on fnl 2f: nvr trbld ldrs* **25/1**

1- **6** 3 ¾ **Ulzana's Raid (IRE)**[180] 270 4-11-11 0..................... WayneHutchinson 101
(Alan King) *pushed along 5f out: rdn 3f out: nvr bttr than mid-div* **14/1**

2- **7** 5 **Royal Ripple (IRE)**[28] 1877 5-11-4 0................................ PaddyBrennan 89
(Paul Henderson) *hld up towards rr: sme prog u.p on outer over 2f out: nvr trbld ldrs* **40/1**

8 1 ¾ **Now Ben (IRE)**[251] 5-11-4 0... AndrewTinkler 87
(Nicky Henderson) *trckd ldrs: rdn 3f out: wknd over 1f out* **5/2**[2]

3- **9** 2 **Definite Future (IRE)**[152] 699 4-10-11 0.................. MrAlexEdwards[(7)] 86
(Dave Roberts) *t.k.h: racd wd: hld up towards rr of mid-div: sme prog on outer 4f out: sn rdn: wknd 2f out* **40/1**

0- **10** nk **Spending Time**[28] 1869 4-11-4 0... JoeTizzard 85
(Colin Tizzard) *racd keenly: trckd ldrs: prom over 5f out: rdn over 2f out: sn wknd* **20/1**

0/ **11** 4 **Beat The Bounds**[238] 4793 4-11-4 0.................................. HaddenFrost 82
(Martin Hill) *mid-div: hdwy to trck ldrs 4f out: rdn over 2f out: sn wknd* **66/1**

0/ **12** 17 **Starship Trouper**[381] 1993 5-11-1 0.............................. MichaelByrne[(3)] 66
(Neil Mulholland) *chsd ldrs tl 6f out: sn bhd: t.o* **100/1**

20/ **13** 6 **Beaujolais Bob**[305] 3558 5-10-11 0.........................(t) MrRobertHawker[(7)] 61
(Richard Hawker) *led tl 5f out: chsd ldrs tl rn wd on bnd and slipped turning in: sn wknd: t.o* **50/1**

/43- **14** 9 **Bandol (IRE)**[154] 675 5-11-4 0.. DougieCostello 53
(Laura Young) *mid-div tl 4f out: sn bhd: t.o* **100/1**

3m 34.9s (-8.40) **Going Correction** -0.60s/f (Firm) **14** Ran SP% **124.4**
Speed ratings: **97,96,89,87,86 84,82,81,80,80 78,69,66,62**
toteswingers 1&2 £5.50, 1&3 £23.90, 2&3 £38.90 CSF £61.66 TOTE £8.00: £2.00, £3.70, £5.40; EX 84.80 Trifecta £903.70 Part won. Pool: £1,204.97 - 0.69 winning units..
Owner Caroline Fry & Susie Dilhorne **Bred** R Robinson **Trained** Seaborough, Dorset

FOCUS
It's a difficult to know what to make of this form quite yet, but two came miles clear in the final stages. A literal interpretation would suggest that the pair are above-average performers. There's a case for rating the form a lot higher through the fourth.
T/Plt: £56.70 to a £1 stake. Pool: £108,363.92 - 1,393.95 winning units T/Qpdt: £26.70 to a £1 stake. Pool: £7,011.14 - 194.12 winning units TM

2376 - (Foreign Racing) - See Raceform Interactive

2140 NAAS (L-H)
Saturday, November 9

OFFICIAL GOING: Yielding to soft (soft in places)

2377a FISHERY LANE HURDLE (GRADE 3) (8 hdls) 2m
12:50 (12:50) 4-Y-0 **£14,532** (£4,247; £2,012; £670)

RPR

1 **Diakali (FR)**[153] 683 4-11-10 145.. RWalsh 145+
(W P Mullins, Ire) *mde all: nt fluent 3rd: over 2 l clr at 1/2-way: reduced advantage bef 4 out: stl gng wl 2 out and kpt on wl under hands and heels fr last: comf* **4/6**[1]

2 2 ¼ **Mr Fiftyone (IRE)**[3] 2300 4-10-13 .... RobbiePower 132+
(Mrs John Harrington, Ire) *trckd ldr in 3rd: tk clsr order 3 out: swtchd rt briefly bef next and nt clr run: clsd on far side into 2nd bef last: n.m.r on inner and swtchd rt fr last: kpt on same pce wout troubling wnr* **5/2**[2]

3 6 **Dalasiri (IRE)**[153] 683 4-11-3 134.. AELynch 130+
(Sabrina J Harty, Ire) *trckd ldr: nt fluent 3rd and next: tk clsr order bef 4 out: rdn fr 2 out and no imp on wnr in 3rd bef last where slt mstke: kpt on one pce* **8/1**[3]

4 2 ¾ **Art Of Payroll (GER)**[20] 1992 4-10-13 .... BryanCooper 123+
(D T Hughes, Ire) *hld up in rr of quartet: nt fluent 3rd: cl up in rr appr st: bmpd sltly bef 2 out: sn rdn and no imp on wnr between last 2: kpt on one pce* **9/1**

3m 48.4s (-15.10) **4** Ran SP% **109.7**
CSF £2.77 TOTE £1.30; DF 1.60 Trifecta £1.90.
Owner Wicklow Bloodstock Limited **Bred** Haras De Son Altesse L'Aga Khan S C E A **Trained** Muine Beag, Co Carlow
■ Stewards' Enquiry : Robbie Power severe caution: careless riding

FOCUS
The winner was a small improver on last year's best.

559 COMPIEGNE (L-H)
Saturday, November 9

OFFICIAL GOING: Turf: heavy

2384a GRAND STEEPLE CHASE-CROSS-COUNTRY DE COMPIEGNE (CROSS-COUNTRY CHASE) (CONDITIONS) (5YO+) (TURF) 3m 3f
2:25 (12:00) 5-Y-0+ **£15,609** (£7,804; £4,552; £3,089; £1,463)

RPR

1 **Maljimar (IRE)**[43] 1683 13-11-3 0.. JamesReveley 121
(Nick Williams) *trckd ldrs: chsd ldr fr 18th: led 4 out: rdn and r.o run-in: a holding runner-up* **19/5**[1]

2 2 ½ **Sarika (FR)**[27] 1904 7-10-12 0.......................................(b) AlainDeChitray 114
(Nick Williams) *settled in midfield: dropped into fnl 3rd 13th: hdwy 6 out: 4th and styng on 3 out: rdn to chse ldr appr last: kpt on u.p: nvr able to chal wnr* **21/1**

3 10 **Lady De Crusse (FR)** 8-10-10 0.................................... WilfridDenuault 102
(E Leenders, France) **73/10**

4 10 **Roselaine (FR)**[358] 2464 8-10-1 0...............................(p) RaphaelDelozier 83
(G Chaignon, France) **26/1**

5 dist **Buffalo Pile (FR)**[83] 5-10-10 0... AlbanDesvaux
(Patrice Quinton, France) **25/1**

P **Quick Gold (FR)**293 9-10-10 0 Marc-AntoineDragon
(E Leray, France) **17/1**
F **Dumorazy (FR)**209 5325 10-10-12 0 (b) GaetanOlivier
(J-L Guillochon, France) **7/1**3
P **Roi Du Tango (FR)**37 1740 7-10-6 0 BertrandBourez
(J Bigot, France) **52/1**
P **Major Dolois (FR)**27 7-11-0 0 (b) JeromeZuliani
(Patrice Quinton, France) **11/2**2
F **Yanky Sundown (FR)**27 8-11-7 0 MrChristopheCorduan
(M Nicolau, France) **10/1**
F **Majaresca (FR)**584 5249 8-10-8 0 JonathanPlouganou
(E Lecoiffier, France) **15/1**
F **Shalimar Fromentro (FR)**27 1905 7-10-12 0 StephanePaillard
(Nick Williams) *towards rr early: midfield fr 5th: in tch whn fell 18th* **19/1**
F **Taupin Rochelais (FR)**13 6-11-3 0 SebastienZuliani
(Patrice Quinton, France) **16/1**
U **Quercy Du Manoir (FR)**27 9-11-0 0 (b) AngeloGasnier
(Jean-Paul Gasnier, France) **20/1**
F **Rebel Brunel (FR)** 8-11-0 0 ThomasBeaurain
(J-L Guillochon, France) **14/1**

4m 35.0s (275.00) **15** Ran SP% **118.0**
PARI-MUTUEL (all including 1 euro stake): WIN 3.30 (combined with Sarika and Shalimar Fromentro); PLACE 2.80, 5.10, 3.00; DF 30.00; SF 38.30.
Owner Mrs Jane Williams **Bred** Robert B Hodgins **Trained** George Nympton, Devon

FOCUS
A 1-2 for Nick Williams means he has al but wrapped up the Crystal Cup series.

2147 FFOS LAS (L-H)

Sunday, November 10

OFFICIAL GOING: Heavy (5.3)
Wind: almost nil Weather: fine

2385 INTEGRAL GEOTECHNIQUE NOVICES' HURDLE (8 hdls) 2m
12:55 (12:55) (Class 4) 4-Y-0+ **£3,119** (£915; £457; £228)

Form RPR
P3- **1** **Batu Ferringhi (FR)**12 2147 7-10-12 0 (p) BrendanPowell 115+
(Jamie Snowden) *led to 4th: lft in narrow ld next: jnd 3 out: styd on to go 2 l ahd last: drvn out* **4/1**3
154- **2** *1* **Rolling Maul (IRE)**14 2103 5-10-12 0 JamieMoore 113
(Peter Bowen) *hld up in tch: clsd 3rd: j.rt next: jnd ldr 3 out: one pce appr last: kpt on flat* **5/4**1
2/6- **3** *17* **Mezzanisi (IRE)**12 2147 8-10-12 100 TomO'Brien 98
(Peter Bowen) *hld up in tch: rdn to chse ldng pair after 3 out: sn no imp: wl hld in 3rd whn nt fluent last* **20/1**
/00- **4** *4 ½* **Chill Factor (IRE)**5 2280 4-10-9 0 RachaelGreen(3) 92
(Anthony Honeyball) *hld up in rr: clsd to trck ldrs after 5th: pushed along next: wknd 2 out* **15/2**
00- **5** *9* **Stag Hill (IRE)**17 2040 4-10-7 0 RobertWilliams(5) 85
(Bernard Llewellyn) *in tch: mstke 2nd: hdwy 5th: outpcd by ldrs 3 out: wkng whn j.lft next* **66/1**
34/ **6** *14* **Going Concern (IRE)**213 5254 6-10-12 0 PaulMoloney 71
(Evan Williams) *t.k.h early: hld up in rr: hmpd 5th: sn pushed along: clsd to chse ldrs 3 out: wknd 2 out: t.o* **5/2**2
00- **7** *9* **Drummond**19 2011 4-10-7 0 AodhaganConlon(5) 60
(Bernard Llewellyn) *prom tl lost pl 4th: bdly hmpd next and sn lost tch: t.o* **100/1**
000/ **F** **Genuine Art**234 4880 6-10-5 0 WillKennedy
(Lucy Jones) *racd keenly: in tch: hdwy to ld 4th: narrowly ahd whn fell next* **100/1**

4m 11.1s (22.60) **Going Correction** +1.55s/f (Heav)
WFA 4 from 5yo+ 7lb **8** Ran SP% **113.0**
Speed ratings (Par 105): **105,104,96,93,89 82,77,**
Tote Swingers: 1&2 £1.70, 1&3 £10.10, 2&3 £4.30 CSF £9.55 TOTE £6.00: £2.00, £1.10, £3.20; EX 12.40 Trifecta £83.60 Pool: £1,796.58 - 16.11 winning units..
Owner R M E Wright **Bred** J P Dubois **Trained** Lambourn, Berks

FOCUS
Jamie Moore described the ground as "heavy and hard work". They finished tired in what was an ordinary novice hurdle.

2386 ARUP NOVICES' HURDLE (12 hdls) 3m
1:25 (1:25) (Class 4) 4-Y-0+ **£3,119** (£915; £457; £228)

Form RPR
051- **1** **Berea Boru (IRE)**12 2147 5-11-5 122 (t) DonalDevereux 135+
(Peter Bowen) *racd in 3rd: jnd ldng pair next: nt fluent 8th: briefly relegated to 4th after next: led appr 2 out: styd on strly to draw clr bef last: eased nr fin* **3/1**3
- **2** *18* **Champagne Rian (IRE)**224 5048 5-10-7 0 PatrickCorbett(5) 110
(Rebecca Curtis) *cl up: led narrowly 4th to 6th: led again and pckd bdly next: rdn 3 out: sn hdd: wandered and j.lft 2 out: sn no ch w wnr: mstke last* **2/1**2
3 *2 ¾* **El Indio (IRE)**364 6-10-2 0 PaulO'Brien(10) 106
(Rebecca Curtis) *in tch in 4th: clsd 8th: shkn up after next: chal 3 out: sn drvn: one pce fr 2 out* **10/1**
5- **4** *15* **Millenary Magic (IRE)**12 2147 6-10-5 0 MissJodieHughes(7) 90
(David Rees) *hld up in last: pushed along and lost tch w other 4 after 9th: plugged on to go poor 4th post* **66/1**
2/5- **5** *nk* **Tinker Time (IRE)**15 2079 5-10-12 0 LiamHeard 94
(Bob Buckler) *led narrowly at slow pce tl hdd 4th: remained cl up: stl ev ch 3 out: wknd 2 out: eased flat and ct for poor 4th post* **11/8**1

6m 55.3s (66.30) **Going Correction** +1.55s/f (Heav) **5** Ran SP% **111.0**
Speed ratings (Par 105): **51,45,44,39,38**
CSF £9.73 TOTE £3.00: £1.60, £1.80; EX 10.90 Trifecta £17.80 Pool: £1,321.10 - 55.66 winning units..
Owner Ashley Hart **Bred** Mrs E Thompson **Trained** Little Newcastle, Pembrokes
■ Stewards' Enquiry : Liam Heard four-day ban: failed to ride out for 4th (Nov 24-27)

FOCUS
This was run at a slow early gallop.

2387 BAYLISS METALS H'CAP CHASE (12 fncs 1 omitted) 2m
2:00 (2:00) (Class 4) (0-105,103) 4-Y-0+ **£3,861** (£1,198; £645)

Form RPR
4/1- **1** **Take Of Shoc'S (IRE)**40 1710 9-11-12 103 (t) PaulMoloney 107+
(Sophie Leech) *mde all: jnd and nt fluent 3 out (usual 4 out): shkn up after 2 out and qcknd clr: easily* **15/8**1
040- **2** *10* **Amaury De Lusignan (IRE)**36 1767 7-11-5 96 (tp) TomO'Brien 87
(Paul Henderson) *trckd wnr 2nd to 8th: reminder after next and sn in 2nd again: chal 3 out (normal 4 out): outpcd by easy wnr appr last: kpt on to hold 2nd* **5/1**
/24- **3** *5* **Brousse En Feux (FR)**24 1936 10-11-2 93 (vt) SamTwiston-Davies 82
(Nigel Twiston-Davies) *trckd wnr to 2nd: nt fluent 5th and 6th: wnt 2nd again 8th tl after 9th: rdn to chal whn mstke 3 out (normal 4 out): disputing 2nd whn blnd 2 out: no ex* **11/4**3
P01- **F** **Walcot Lathyrus**31 1835 8-11-12 103 JamieMoore
(Richard Lee) *hld up in last: hit 1st: fell heavily 2nd* **5/2**2

4m 22.9s (23.50) **Going Correction** +1.175s/f (Heav) **4** Ran SP% **106.7**
Speed ratings (Par 105): **88,83,80,**
CSF £9.94 TOTE £2.70; EX 19.80 Trifecta £22.40 Pool: £750.76 - 25.11 winning units..
Owner C J Leech **Bred** Frank Ryan **Trained** Elton, Gloucs

FOCUS
This had looked quite a tight handicap chase.

2388 POTTER GROUP WALES H'CAP HURDLE (12 hdls) 3m
2:30 (2:30) (Class 3) (0-135,130) 4-Y-0+ **£6,108** (£1,793; £896; £448)

Form RPR
0/1- **1** **Pension Plan**188 144 9-11-10 128 (p) TomO'Brien 140+
(Peter Bowen) *hld up in tch: wnt 2nd after 9th: led 3 out: hit next: styd on strly to draw clr between last 2: easily* **7/2**2
11P/ **2** *19* **Victors Serenade (IRE)**393 1837 8-11-9 130 RachaelGreen(3) 121
(Anthony Honeyball) *t.k.h: trckd ldrs: led 6th to 3 out: j.lft and lost 2nd 2 out: sn one pce: kpt on to go 2nd again nr fin* **3/1**1
51/ **3** *½* **Still Believing (IRE)**239 4780 5-9-13 110 ConorRing(7) 103
(Evan Williams) *hld up in tch in last pair: clsd into 3rd appr 3 out: wnt 2nd 2 out: sn no ch w easy wnr: stmbld last: lost 2nd cl home* **10/1**
632- **4** *2* **Nicky Nutjob (GER)**18 2020 7-9-7 104 (p) CiaranMckee(7) 95
(John O'Shea) *hld up in tch in last pair: clsng whn blnd 9th: sn struggling: plugged on into mod 4th 2 out* **10/1**
/P1- **5** *25* **Abnaki (IRE)**10 2170 8-11-7 130 (b) MauriceLinehan(5) 101
(Jonjo O'Neill) *hit 1st: mainly trckd ldr to 6th: styd prom tl hrd rdn and wknd after 9th: t.o* **4/1**3
P21/ **6** *56* **Firebird Flyer (IRE)**227 4980 6-11-9 127 PaulMoloney 35
(Evan Williams) *led at stdy pce tl hdd 6th: styd cl up tl rdn and wknd appr 3 out: t.o* **3/1**1

6m 39.5s (50.50) **Going Correction** +1.55s/f (Heav) **6** Ran SP% **110.4**
Speed ratings (Par 107): **77,70,70,69,61 42**
Tote Swingers: 1&2 £2.30, 1&3 £6.80, 2&3 £8.10 CSF £14.10 TOTE £3.60: £1.60, £2.60; EX 12.70 Trifecta £89.50 Pool: £2,098.18 - 17.56 winning units..
Owner The Loppington Five **Bred** Roy David Burden **Trained** Little Newcastle, Pembrokes

FOCUS
This was always likely to prove a thorough test in the conditions.

2389 COOLMORE NATIONAL HUNT SIRES NOVICES' LIMITED H'CAP CHASE (15 fncs) 2m 3f 110y
3:05 (3:05) (Class 3) (0-125,125) 4-Y-0+ **£7,797** (£2,289; £1,144; £572)

Form RPR
5/S- **1** **Sergeant Dick (IRE)**14 2107 8-11-2 122 (t) FelixDeGiles 125
(Barry Brennan) *j.w: cl up tl led 3rd: rdn fr 3 out: styd on bravely u.p* **12/1**
200/ **2** *1 ½* **Wychwoods Brook**253 4526 7-10-12 118 AdamWedge 120
(Evan Williams) *trckd ldrs: lft 2nd 4 out: rdn next: 1 l down whn stmbld 2 out: kpt on: no ex fnl 50yds* **10/3**2
/U2- **3** *1* **Hansupfordetroit (IRE)**28 1888 8-11-0 125 RobertWilliams(5) 133+
(Bernard Llewellyn) *t.k.h: prom: trckd wnr fr 5th: half-l 2nd whn blnd bdly and knocked bk to 8 l 3rd 4 out: rallied appr last: styd on flat* **4/1**3
130/ **4** *20* **Xaarcet (IRE)**222 5103 6-10-13 119 JoeTizzard 102
(Colin Tizzard) *hld up in tch: clsd after 11th: 2 l down in 4th whn bdly hmpd 4 out: nt rcvr: mstke 2 out: t.o* **5/1**
142/ **5** *nse* **Speed Master (IRE)**574 5428 7-11-5 125 SamTwiston-Davies 108
(Nigel Twiston-Davies) *hld up: mstke 5th: nt fluent 9th and sn rdn along: struggling and no ch w ldrs fr 11th: t.o* **11/4**1
133- **P** **Fairwood Massini (IRE)**9 2197 8-10-12 121 (vt) MichaelByrne(3)
(Tim Vaughan) *chsd ldrs: mstke 8th: rdn after 11th: wknd 4 out: wl bhd whn p.u bef 2 out* **12/1**
0/5- **P** **Book'Em Danno (IRE)**30 1851 7-10-5 111 oh2 JamieMoore
(Peter Bowen) *led to 3rd: blnd bdly and lost pl 5th: mstke 8th: lost tch after 11th: t.o whn p.u bef 3 out* **10/1**
/00- **P** **Celtic Fella (IRE)**29 1864 6-10-5 111 oh44 DonalDevereux
(Debra Hamer) *in rr: rdn along fr 7th: lost tch after 11th: t.o whn p.u bef 3 out* **100/1**

5m 21.1s (20.00) **Going Correction** +1.175s/f (Heav) **8** Ran SP% **111.9**
Speed ratings (Par 107): **107,106,106,98,97 , ,**
Tote Swingers: 1&2 £9.90, 1&3 £14.20, 2&3 £5.60 CSF £51.01 CT £189.42 TOTE £16.50: £3.50, £2.70, £1.60; EX 79.80 Trifecta £402.40 Pool: £2,732.23 - 5.09 winning units..
Owner Connect Eight **Bred** David Cotter **Trained** Upper Lambourn, Berks

FOCUS
This looked quite a decent race. Hansupfordetroit looked an unlucky loser.

2390 PINSENT MASONS H'CAP CHASE (THE SUNDAY £5K BONUS RACE) (18 fncs) 3m
3:35 (3:36) (Class 4) (0-115,115) 4-Y-0+ **£3,768** (£1,106; £553; £276)

Form RPR
/63- **1** **Night Alliance (IRE)**7 2253 8-11-1 104 (b) TomO'Brien 124+
(Dr Richard Newland) *trckd ldr: mstke 2nd: led 13th: 4 l up whn lft 15 l clr 3 out: unchal after* **2/1**1
240- **2** *15* **Chasers Chance (IRE)**23 1959 10-10-13 102 NickScholfield 98
(Paul Henderson) *hld up in tch: j. slowly 2nd: dropped to rr 12th: lost tch w ldrs after 14th: plugged on to take mod 2nd last: no ch w wnr* **14/1**
/63- **3** *10* **Miss Saffron**18 2029 10-10-10 104 MissLucyGardner(5) 90
(Sue Gardner) *hld up in rr: sme hdwy 14th: wknd and lost tch 4 out: plugged on to take poor 3rd flat* **16/1**
004/ **4** *12* **Ravens Brook (IRE)**204 5409 7-11-2 105 JamieMoore 87
(Richard Lee) *in tch: mstke 8th: clsd 13th: sltly hmpd and lft 15 l 2nd 3 out: no imp on wnr: lost 2nd last: wknd bdly flat* **7/1**3
F/2- **F** **Bendant**19 2014 8-11-12 115 RobertThornton
(Debra Hamer) *hld up: hdwy after 9th: 4 l 2nd and rdn whn fell 3 out* **8/1**
/10- **P** **Power Pack Jack (IRE)**112 1060 10-11-10 113 (v) SamTwiston-Davies
(Nigel Twiston-Davies) *led: rdn along whn hit 11th: hdd 13th: mstke next: sn wknd: t.o whn p.u bef 3 out* **8/1**

The Form Book Jumps, Raceform Ltd, Compton, RG20 6NL.

P/0- **P** **Whiskey And Red (IRE)**^{50} [1618] 8-10-8 **97**..................(t) JasonMaguire
(Colin Bowe, Ire) *trckd ldrs: mstke and rdn along 13th: wknd 4 out: t.o whn p.u bef last* **9/4**^{2}

6m 47.5s (30.10) **Going Correction** +1.175s/f (Heav) **7** Ran SP% **111.4**
Speed ratings (Par 105): **96,91,87,83,** ,
Tote Swingers: 1&2 £4.40, 1&3 £7.60, 2&3 £31.10 CSF £25.48 TOTE £2.90: £1.70, £6.40; EX 27.50 Trifecta £180.40 Pool: £2,788.20 - 11.59 winning units..
Owner Dr R D P Newland **Bred** Mrs Mary Doyle And Peter Sherry **Trained** Claines, Worcs

FOCUS
No real depth to this modest handicap.

2391 INTEGRAL GEOTECHNIQUE "JUNIOR" STANDARD OPEN NATIONAL HUNT FLAT RACE 1m 6f
4:10 (4:11) (Class 6) 3-Y-O **£1,559** (£457; £228; £114)

Form RPR
- **1** **Coyaba** 3-10-12 0.. IanPopham 99+
(Martin Keighley) *cl up in v slowly run r: led after 6f: qcknd tempo 4f out: pushed along 2f out: sn drew clr: easily* **5/1**^{3}
2 *7* **Princess Tara (IRE)** 3-10-5 0.. DonalDevereux 80
(Peter Bowen) *in tch in 4th in slowly run r: rdn over 2f out: sn outpcd by wnr: kpt on to go 2nd 100yds out* **2/1**^{2}
4- **3** *nk* **Leviche**^{19} [2015] 3-10-12 0...(t) RobertThornton 87
(Alan King) *hld up in last in v slowly run r: hdwy to go 2nd over 3f out: sn rdn: outpcd by wnr fr 2f out: lost 2nd 100yds out* **1/1**^{1}
0- **4** *14* **Alfa Red**^{19} [2015] 3-10-2 0.. MikeyHamill$^{(10)}$ 70
(Sean Curran) *led at v slow pce tl hdd after 6f: lost 2nd over 3f out: wknd over 2f out* **25/1**
5 *18* **Spin The Beat** 3-10-12 0... SamTwiston-Davies 49
(Marc Barber) *mainly in 3rd in slowly run r tl outpcd whn tempo qckned 4f out: wknd 2f out: t.o* **20/1**

3m 59.5s (239.50) **5** Ran SP% **108.6**
CSF £14.96 TOTE £7.00: £2.10, £1.50; EX 15.80 Trifecta £22.40 Pool: £2,996.26 - 100.15 winning units..
Owner Mrs Peter Prowting **Bred** Mrs E A Prowting **Trained** Condicote, Gloucs

FOCUS
They dawdled in this junior bumper.
T/Plt: £50.00 to a £1 stake. Pool: £91,217.08 - 1,331.30 winning tickets. T/Qpdt: £19.00 to a £1 stake. Pool: £6,229.30 - 241.70 winning tickets. RL

1684 MARKET RASEN (R-H)
Sunday, November 10

OFFICIAL GOING: Soft (good to soft in places; chs 5.3, hdl 5.7)
Wind: almost nil Weather: fine and sunny, cold

2392 1STSECURITYSOLUTIONS JUVENILE HURDLE (8 hdls) 2m 1f
1:10 (1:10) (Class 4) 3-Y-O **£3,898** (£1,144; £572; £286)

Form RPR
1 **Tiger Roll (IRE)** 3-10-9 0... MarkQuinlan$^{(3)}$ 95+
(Nigel Hawke) *trckd ldrs: led appr 2 out: hung lft and wandered last 100yds: drvn out* **12/1**^{3}
2 *3 3/4* **Nonotnow**^{34} 3-10-12 0... HarryHaynes 90
(Tim Easterby) *nt fluent: trckd ldr: 3 l 2nd and drvn whn mstke 2 out: kpt on same pce run-in* **7/1**^{2}
3- **3** *8* **Zamoyski**^{9} [2200] 3-10-12 0... RichardJohnson 81
(Steve Gollings) *led: j.lft 1st 2: hit 5th: drvn and hdd appr 2 out: sn btn* **2/11**^{1}
4 *1 3/4* **Last Chance Ranch**^{9} 3-10-5 0.. OllieGarner$^{(7)}$ 80
(Derek Shaw) *hld up in rr: drvn 4th: lost pl appr 2 out* **66/1**
5 *2 1/4* **Dennis**^{61} 3-10-12 0.. DannyCook 78
(Tim Easterby) *hld up in rr: pushed along 4th: lost pl bef 2 out: j.rt and mstke last* **12/1**^{3}

4m 29.0s (22.30) **Going Correction** +1.275s/f (Heav) **5** Ran SP% **114.0**
Speed ratings (Par 104): **98,96,92,91,90**
CSF £79.97 TOTE £16.00: £5.80, £2.60; EX 41.60 Trifecta £74.20 Pool: £1,560.68 - 15.76 winning units..
Owner Mrs K Wetherall **Bred** G O'Brien **Trained** Stoodleigh, Devon

FOCUS
There was a right turn up this seemingly uncompetitive juvenile contest as long odds-on Zamoyski flopped.

2393 BDN CONSTRUCTION NOVICES' HURDLE (10 hdls) 2m 3f
1:40 (1:40) (Class 4) 4-Y-O+ **£4,548** (£1,335; £667; £333)

Form RPR
4/1- **1** **Shantou Magic (IRE)**^{18} [2018] 6-11-5 0................................ NoelFehily 137+
(Charlie Longsdon) *hld up: hdwy to chse ldr bef 6th: led 3 out: wnt clr next: heavily eased run-in* **1/2**^{1}
326/ **2** *12* **Rossoneri (IRE)**^{637} [4268] 6-10-5 0.................................... RyanHatch$^{(7)}$ 108
(Nigel Twiston-Davies) *hld up: hdwy to chse 2 ldrs 7th: 2nd after 3 out: 10 l down whn blnd 2 out: no ch w wnr* **25/1**
2/3- **3** *7* **Comeback Colin**^{17} [2049] 5-10-12 0...................................... RyanMania 101
(Sue Smith) *mid-div: hit 4th: blnd next: hdwy 7th: modest 4th 2 out: 3rd last* **9/1**
2/4- **4** *10* **Gold Futures (IRE)**^{22} [1977] 4-10-12 0............................... BrianHarding 90
(Nicky Richards) *hld up in rr: mstke 3rd: hdwy 7th: modest 2nd 2 out: wknd last* **6/1**^{3}
5 *2* **Danby's Legend** 6-10-12 0.. BrianHughes 87
(Malcolm Jefferson) *in rr: sme hdwy 3 out: modest 5th whn mstke last* **40/1**
0- **6** *1/2* **Light The City (IRE)**^{8} [2225] 6-10-9 0............................ JakeGreenall$^{(3)}$ 87
(Ruth Carr) *in rr: nvr on terms* **66/1**
/03- **7** *4* **Stella's Fella**^{36} [1770] 5-10-12 0.. DavidEngland 85
(Giles Smyly) *chsd ldr: mstke 1st: hit 5th: lost pl 7th: b.b.v* **80/1**
03/ **8** *51* **Theology**^{9} [4410] 6-10-12 0.. TomScudamore 32
(Steve Gollings) *led: blnd 6th: hdd 3 out: wknd qckly: t.o whn blnd last: virtually p.u* **11/2**^{2}
P/ **9** *10* **Lecale Lad (IRE)**^{266} [4267] 6-10-12 0.............................. RichardJohnson 22
(Tim Vaughan) *t.k.h: trckd ldrs: lost pl 6th: t.o 3 out* **16/1**
0/0- **10** *1/2* **Lucanor (IRE)**^{185} [185] 5-10-12 0...................................... CharliePoste 21
(Paul Webber) *chsd ldrs: drvn and lost pl 5th: sn bhd: t.o 3 out* **66/1**

4m 58.8s (19.40) **Going Correction** +1.275s/f (Heav)
WFA 4 from 5yo+ 7lb **10** Ran SP% **122.7**
Speed ratings (Par 105): **110,104,102,97,96 96,95,73,69,69**
Tote Swingers: 1&2 £11.50, 1&3 £2.00, 2&3 £13.10 CSF £21.57 TOTE £1.60: £1.10, £7.10, £2.00; EX 18.80 Trifecta £103.30 Pool: £1,790.10 - 12.98 winning units..
Owner Owners For Owners: Shantou Magic **Bred** Daniel Fogarty **Trained** Over Norton, Oxon

FOCUS
There was no hanging about in this novice hurdle thanks to front-running Theology and it saw a very impressive display from Shantou Magic, who shrugged off his penalty with ease.

2394 BDN CONSTRUCTION H'CAP CHASE (17 fncs) 3m 1f
2:15 (2:16) (Class 4) (0-120,120) 4-Y-O+ **£5,198** (£1,526; £763; £381)

Form RPR
4/3- **1** **Italian Master (IRE)**^{172} [431] 7-11-12 **120**........................ HarrySkelton 135+
(Dan Skelton) *led to 2nd: trckd ldrs: led between last 2: drvn out* **11/1**
6/0- **2** *3 3/4* **The Magic Bishop**^{186} [169] 8-10-13 **107**............................ BrianHughes 115
(Malcolm Jefferson) *hld up towards rr: stdy hdwy 4 out: styd on run-in: tk 2nd clsng stages* **8/1**
P22/ **3** *1 1/2* **Balbriggan (IRE)**^{201} [5474] 6-11-7 **115**............................ DominicElsworth 124
(Mick Channon) *j. boldly: led 2nd: hdd 10th: led 4 out: hmpd by loose horse and mstke next: hdd between last 2: kpt on same pce* **3/1**^{2}
/13- **4** *2 1/2* **Little Chip (IRE)**^{37} [1748] 6-11-11 **119**.................................. NoelFehily 123
(Charlie Longsdon) *chsd ldrs: hrd drvn appr 3 out: one pce fr 2 out* **11/4**^{1}
1F5- **5** *18* **Tregaro (FR)**^{29} [1872] 7-10-4 **98**.......................................(t) AidanColeman 84
(Mike Sowersby) *in rr: sme hdwy 4 out: wknd 2 out* **20/1**
P/5- **6** *12* **Ringa Bay**^{17} [2041] 8-11-9 **117**.. TomScudamore 103
(David Bridgwater) *unruly and tk long way to s: w ldrs: led 10th: hdd 4 out: 5th last: sn heavily eased* **15/2**
506/ **7** *7* **Noakarad De Verzee (FR)**^{210} 12-11-4 **119**.................. MrDMaxwell$^{(7)}$ 86
(Giles Smyly) *chsd ldrs: outpcd 4 out: lost pl and 7th whn mstke 2 out* **22/1**
/42- **8** *9* **Call Me Mulligan (IRE)**^{144} [766] 9-10-0 **101**................. JohnDawson$^{(7)}$ 59
(John Wade) *chsd ldrs: reminders 5th: drvn 7th: lost pl 9th: t.o 4 out* **14/1**
5P6- **9** *1 3/4* **Very Stylish (IRE)**^{10} [2179] 9-11-2 **110**........................(p) RichieMcLernon 66
(Jonjo O'Neill) *in rr: hdwy to chse ldrs 4th: drvn and lost pl 12th: sme hdwy 4 out: sn lost pl and bhd* **33/1**
65P/ **U** **Honest John**^{199} [5521] 9-11-0 **115**.. PaulBohan$^{(7)}$
(Steve Gollings) *in rr: outpcd whn blnd and uns rdr 12th* **6/1**^{3}

6m 35.9s (4.60) **Going Correction** +0.325s/f (Yiel) **10** Ran SP% **115.9**
Speed ratings (Par 105): **105,103,103,102,96 92,90,87,87,**
Tote Swingers: 1&2 £39.60, 1&3 £4.00, 2&3 £30.50 CSF £91.47 CT £333.26 TOTE £6.70: £3.00, £2.20, £2.30; EX 85.40 Trifecta £864.40 Part won. Pool: £1,152.65 - 0.08 winning units..
Owner The Bevy Syndicate **Bred** Terence O'Donnell **Trained** Alcester, Warwicks

FOCUS
A modest staying handicap with an open look about it. It was run at an average gallop and the third sets the level.

2395 JOHN LUCAS MEMORIAL NOVICES' LIMITED H'CAP CHASE (14 fncs) 2m 6f 110y
2:45 (2:47) (Class 3) (0-140,138) 4-Y-O+ **£9,747** (£2,862; £1,431; £715)

Form RPR
52F/ **1** **Gullinbursti (IRE)**^{288} [3856] 7-11-1 **134**............................ AidanColeman 150+
(Emma Lavelle) *trckd ldrs: cl 2nd 8th: led appr 3 out: wnt clr: heavily eased run-in* **10/11**^{1}
513- **2** *27* **Bar De Ligne (FR)**^{15} [2074] 7-10-9 **128**......................(p) TomScudamore 115
(Steve Gollings) *led: hit 2nd: hdd bef 3 out: 15 l 2nd whn mstke last: fin tired* **13/2**^{3}
240/ **3** *2* **Greenlaw**^{276} [4076] 7-10-5 **124** oh4..................................... NoelFehily 107
(Charlie Longsdon) *in rr: hdwy 8th: 4 l down in 3rd whn blnd 3 out: 8 l down in 3rd last: kpt on* **12/1**
022/ **4** *39* **Rick (FR)**^{345} [2737] 9-10-10 **129**... DenisO'Regan 71
(John Ferguson) *trckd ldrs: drvn 4 out: lost pl bef next: sn heavily eased: t.o* **14/1**
431/ **5** *12* **Dunlough Bay (IRE)**^{227} [4986] 7-10-10 **132**..................... JakeGreenall$^{(3)}$ 62
(Paul Webber) *chsd ldr: mstke 2nd: blnd 9th: sn wknd: t.o 4 out* **20/1**
115- **P** **Green Wizard (IRE)**^{9} [2199] 7-10-11 **130**................................ RyanMania
(Sue Smith) *chsd ldrs: blnd bdly and lost pl 6th: bhd 8th: t.o whn p.u bef 10th* **14/1**
P/1- **U** **Dursey Sound (IRE)**^{38} [1728] 5-11-5 **138**........................ RichieMcLernon
(Jonjo O'Neill) *hld up: hdwy to trck ldrs 7th: blnd and uns rdr 10th* **7/2**^{2}

5m 47.4s (1.40) **Going Correction** +0.325s/f (Yiel) **7** Ran SP% **113.7**
Speed ratings (Par 107): **110,100,99,86,82** ,
Tote Swingers: 1&2 £1.90, 1&3 £3.70, 2&3 £13.00 CSF £7.68 CT £42.38 TOTE £1.90: £1.10, £3.30; EX 7.30 Trifecta £50.30 Pool: £2,205.59 - 32.85 winning units..
Owner Nicholas Mustoe **Bred** Gerard Kelleher **Trained** Hatherden, Hants

FOCUS
A good-quality novice handicap, run at a solid gallop and they finished strung out.

2396 1STSECURITYSOLUTIONS H'CAP CHASE (14 fncs) 2m 4f
3:20 (3:21) (Class 5) (0-95,93) 4-Y-O+ **£2,599** (£763; £381; £190)

Form RPR
463/ **1** **Legendary Hop**^{363} [2384] 7-11-12 **93**................................ TomMessenger 104+
(Chris Bealby) *hld up: wnt 3rd 7th: cl 2nd 4 out: sn lft in ld: kpt on fr 2 out: drvn out* **3/1**^{2}
/01- **2** *3 1/4* **Molko Jack (FR)**^{17} [2048] 9-10-13 **83**.............................. KielanWoods$^{(3)}$ 91
(Michael Mullineaux) *in rr: hdwy and handy 3rd 4 out: lft cl 2nd: almost upsides 3 out: kpt on same pce fr next* **6/1**^{3}
U55- **3** *11* **Peak Seasons (IRE)**^{16} [2067] 10-10-9 **81**........................ JoeCornwall$^{(5)}$ 77
(Michael Chapman) *in rr: pushed along 5th: detached last and reminders 7th: kpt on to take15 l 3rd 3 out: one pce* **20/1**
PP4- **4** *16* **Sycho Fred (IRE)**^{40} [1715] 12-10-8 **75**.................................(t) BrianHughes 60
(Mike Sowersby) *chsd ldng pair to 7th: lost pl 4 out: sn bhd* **8/1**
65F/ **P** **Irish Guard**^{201} [5481] 12-10-12 **79**.................................(p) AndrewThornton
(John O'Neill) *chsd ldr: wknd 4 out: last and bhd whn p.u bef next* **7/1**
P22- **S** **Mister Wiseman**^{6} [2277] 11-11-0 **84**...............................(vt^{1}) MarkQuinlan$^{(3)}$
(Nigel Hawke) *led: reminders 10th: slipped and fell bnd between 4 out and 3 out* **11/8**^{1}

5m 23.2s (17.50) **Going Correction** +0.325s/f (Yiel) **6** Ran SP% **109.8**
Speed ratings (Par 103): **78,76,72,65,**
Tote Swingers: 1&2 £5.70, 1&3 £14.90, 2&3 £10.70 CSF £19.44 CT £274.19 TOTE £5.00: £2.60, £2.60; EX 16.70 Trifecta £103.40 Pool: £1,104.92 - 8.00 winning units..
Owner Messrs Duke,Umpleby,Holmes & Bealby **Bred** B G Duke **Trained** Barrowby, Lincs

FOCUS
A weak handicap, run at a fair gallop.

2397 BDN CONSTRUCTION "HANDS AND HEELS" H'CAP HURDLE (SUNDAY £5K BONUS RACE) (CONDITIONALS & AMATEURS) (10 hdls) 2m 3f
3:50 (3:51) (Class 4) (0-115,115) 4-Y-0+ **£3,249** (£954; £477; £238)

Form RPR
310/ **1** **Wily Fox**[59] 4907 6-11-8 **111** KieronEdgar 117+
(James Eustace) *trckd ldrs: cl 2nd 3 out: led appr next: drvn out* **4/1**[1]
320/ **2** *6* **Favorite Girl (GER)**[223] 5058 5-10-11 **100** JackSherwood 99
(Michael Appleby) *trckd ldrs: t.k.h: cl 2nd appr 2 out: styd on same pce between last 2* **12/1**
146- **3** *2 ¾* **Amuse Me**[14] 2105 7-10-12 **104** MrDLevey(3) 100
(Jonjo O'Neill) *in rr: hdwy 5th: outpcd 3 out: kpt on to take modest 4th between last 2: 3rd clsng stages* **8/1**
/21- **4** *2 ¼* **Bowie (IRE)**[163] 560 6-11-9 **115** CharlieDeutsch(3) 110
(Nick Kent) *chsd ldrs: led after 5th: hdd and 3rd whn mstke 3 out: wknd last 100yds* **9/2**[2]
1/6- **5** *8* **Pudsey House**[186] 168 6-10-8 **100** (b) DiarmuidO'Regan(3) 86
(John Wade) *led: hit 3rd: hdd next: outpcd and lost pl 3 out* **14/1**
144/ **6** *19* **Benmadigan (IRE)**[310] 3495 11-9-12 **92** MrJNuttall(5) 59
(Nicky Richards) *towards rr: hdwy 4th: lost pl 3 out: sn bhd* **12/1**
424- **7** *½* **Dormouse**[152] 719 8-11-9 **115** (p) MrOJMurphy(3) 93
(Anabel K Murphy) *in rr: hdwy 3 out: modest 4th whn mstke 2 out: sn wknd: heavily eased clsng stages* **13/2**[3]
/05- **8** *1 ½* **Souter Point (USA)**[30] 1848 7-10-11 **100** RyanHatch 65
(William Kinsey) *chsd ldrs: lost pl bef 2 out* **16/1**
223- **9** *18* **Wom**[24] 1938 5-10-9 **101** (b) MrCSmith(3) 48
(Neil King) *prom: nt fluent and lost pl 7th: sn wl bhd* **9/2**[2]
050- **10** *3 ½* **Phoenix Eye**[43] 1689 12-10-0 **89** oh17 StephenMulqueen 32
(Michael Mullineaux) *hld up in rr: sme hdwy 3 out: sn wknd* **80/1**
P/P- **11** *6* **Icy Colt (ARG)**[43] 1687 7-10-10 **104** (b) LukeWatson(5) 41
(Paul Webber) *trckd ldrs: led 4th: hdd after next: wknd 3 out: sn wl bhd* **33/1**

5m 0.9s (21.50) **Going Correction** +1.275s/f (Heav) **11 Ran SP% 112.9**
Speed ratings (Par 105): **105,102,101,100,97 89,88,88,80,79 76**
Tote Swingers: 1&2 £10.40, 1&3 £3.40, 2&3 £23.40 CSF £48.89 CT £362.84 TOTE £4.30: £1.70, £4.00, £2.90; EX 43.50 Trifecta £319.50 Pool: £1,352.16 - 3.17 winning units..
Owner Blue Peter Racing 10 **Bred** Juddmonte Farms Ltd **Trained** Newmarket, Suffolk
■ Stewards' Enquiry : Mr O J Murphy seven-day ban: used whip contrary to race conditions (Nov 24,28,29, Dec 1,6,17,19)
FOCUS
A typically moderate handicap of its type.
T/Jkpt: Not won. T/Plt: £289.80 to a £1 stake. Pool: £84,748.9 - 213.44 winning tickets. T/Qpdt: £18.80 to a £1 stake. Pool: £10,03044 - 392.77 winning tickets. WG

2398 - 2406a (Foreign Racing) - See Raceform Interactive

1691 NAVAN (L-H)
Sunday, November 10

OFFICIAL GOING: Yielding

2407a BOYLESPORTS.COM QUICK BET RACING 'FOR AUCTION' NOVICE HURDLE (GRADE 3) (10 hdls) 2m
1:20 (1:21) 4-Y-0+ **£15,325** (£4,479; £2,121; £707)

RPR
1 **Minella Foru (IRE)**[50] 1619 4-10-12 APMcCoy 136+
(Edward P Harty, Ire) *trckd ldr at slow early pce: tk clsr order fr 4 out: rdn fr 2 out on far side and styd on wl fr last to ld ins fnl 100yds* **11/8**[2]
2 *1 ½* **Very Wood (FR)**[14] 2112 4-10-13 ow1 DavyRussell 136+
(Noel Meade, Ire) *led at slow early pce: j.rt thrght: mstke 2nd and nt fluent 5th: 2 l clr at 1/2-way: reduced advantage fr 4 out: stl gng wl 2 out: rdn fr last and hdd u.p ins fnl 100yds: no ex* **4/5**[1]
3 *6 ½* **King Of The Picts (IRE)**[35] 1802 4-11-5 134 AndrewJMcNamara 133
(John Patrick Shanahan, Ire) *settled bhd principals in 3rd at slow early pce: stl in tch bef 3 out: rdn fr next and sn no imp on ldrs: kpt on same pce* **7/1**[3]
4 *12* **Definite Elegance (IRE)**[10] 2182 6-10-8 106 APHeskin 110
(Denis Gerard Hogan, Ire) *w.w in rr of quartet: stl in tch appr st: niggled along 3 out where nt fluent and sn no ex u.p: kpt on one pce* **100/1**

4m 14.4s (6.40) **4 Ran SP% 111.2**
CSF £3.06 TOTE £2.60; DF 4.20 Trifecta £4.90.
Owner John P McManus **Bred** Louis G Vambeck **Trained** Curragh, Co Kildare
FOCUS
A fascinating contest rendered something of a farce because of the pace set. It might be said that the winner has now won a point-to-point, maiden hurdle and a sprint.

2408a BOYLESPORTS.COM DOWNLOAD OUR APP LISMULLEN HURDLE (GRADE 2) (11 hdls) 2m 4f
1:50 (1:52) 4-Y-0+ **£21,138** (£6,178; £2,926; £975)

RPR
1 **Dedigout (IRE)**[182] 259 7-11-12 146 (t) DavyRussell 155+
(A J Martin, Ire) *hld up in tch: niggled along bef st: rdn in 4th fr 2 out and sn clsd to chal last: styd on wl to ld fnl 150yds and extended advantage towards fin* **9/2**[3]
2 *1 ¾* **Mala Beach (IRE)**[224] 5051 5-11-7 148 RobbieColgan 148+
(Gordon Elliott, Ire) *trckd ldr: almost on terms on outer 3 out: sn clsd to ld after slt mstke next: strly pressed fr last and hdd fnl 150yds: kpt on wl towards fin wout matching wnr* **5/2**[2]
3 *16* **Captain Cee Bee (IRE)**[35] 1801 12-11-10 150 APMcCoy 137
(Edward P Harty, Ire) *hld up in tch: slt mstkes 1st and 4th: tk clsr order in 3rd bef 6th: niggled along bef st and wnt cl 3rd whn mstke 2 out: no ex u.p fr last: wknd and eased run-in* **15/8**[1]
4 *6 ½* **Un Beau Matin (IRE)**[197] 5582 5-11-5 136 AELynch 126
(Gordon Elliott, Ire) *led: j. sltly rt at times: j.rt 8th and next: jnd fr 3 out and mstke next and hdd: no ex u.p in 4th bef last: wknd* **10/1**
5 *35* **Jetson (IRE)**[153] 701 8-11-5 143 BarryGeraghty 89
(Mrs John Harrington, Ire) *chsd ldrs: slt mstkes 2nd and 4th: pushed along in rr fr 8th and sn no imp on ldrs: detached after next: nt fluent 3 out: one pce after* **9/2**[3]

5m 3.9s (2.10) **5 Ran SP% 108.8**
CSF £15.78 TOTE £4.10: £2.40, £1.70; DF 14.90 Trifecta £45.10.
Owner Gigginstown House Stud **Bred** Stone Electrical Ltd **Trained** Summerhill, Co. Meath

FOCUS
A slowly run race.

2410a BOYLESPORTS.COM FORTRIA CHASE (GRADE 2) (11 fncs) 2m
2:50 (2:51) 5-Y-0+ **£21,138** (£6,178; £2,926; £975)

RPR
1 **Flemenstar (IRE)**[219] 5159 8-11-12 169 AELynch 164+
(A J Martin, Ire) *settled bhd ldr in 2nd: j.big at times: nt fluent 4th: clsd to ld fr 3 out: sn clr: idled bef last where j.big again: sn pressed and rdn out towards fin* **1/4**[1]
2 *1 ¼* **Days Hotel (IRE)**[201] 5487 8-11-10 153 BryanCooper 157
(Henry De Bromhead, Ire) *settled bhd ldr in 3rd: slt mstke 2nd: pushed along bef 3 out: clsd u.p fr next into 2nd bef last: pressed wnr towards fin: a hld* **13/2**[2]
3 *11* **Realt Mor (IRE)**[13] 2141 8-11-9 150 DavyRussell 147
(Gordon Elliott, Ire) *led: nt fluent 3rd: 5 l clr at 1/2-way: j. sltly rt 7th where reduced advantage: got in cl next: mstke 3 out and hdd: dropped to 3rd bef last: one pce run-in* **13/2**[2]
4 *29* **Rubert (IRE)**[50] 1617 10-11-4 116 RobbiePower 111
(Denis W Cullen, Ire) *racd in rr thrght: detached bef 7th: nvr a factor* **100/1**[3]

4m 1.9s (-8.60) **4 Ran SP% 107.7**
CSF £2.51 TOTE £1.70; DF 2.70 Trifecta £2.60.
Owner Stephen Curran **Bred** Donal Barnwell **Trained** Summerhill, Co. Meath
FOCUS
A winning start for a class horse on his debut for Tony Martin

2409 - 2413a (Foreign Racing) - See Raceform Interactive

2262 AUTEUIL (L-H)
Sunday, November 10

OFFICIAL GOING: Turf: heavy

2414a PRIX RENAUD DU VIVIER (GRANDE COURSE DE HAIES DES 4 ANS) (HURDLE) (GRADE 1) (4YO) (TURF) 2m 3f 110y
2:40 (12:00) 4-Y-0

£98,780 (£48,292; £28,536; £19,756; £10,975; £7,682)

RPR
1 **Ptit Zig (FR)**[154] 683 4-10-8 0 DavidCottin 153
(Paul Nicholls) *led to 1st: a.p: cl 2nd fnl bnd after 3 out: c stands' side st: one of three ldrs jumping 2 out: sn led and rdn appr last: drvn out run-in: won gng away* **3/1**[2]
2 *2* **Le Grand Luce (FR)**[22] 1983 4-10-8 0 BertrandLestrade 151
(J-P Gallorini, France) *towards rr: prog 1/2-way: trckd ldr fr 4 out: c down centre of trck ent st: one of three ldrs jumping 2 out: edgd towards stands' side to chse ldr appr last: r.o u.p run-in: no imp on wnr* **3/1**[2]
3 *5* **Un Temps Pour Tout (IRE)**[43] 4-10-8 0 BenoitGicquel 146
(F Nicolle, France) *a.p: rdn and slighly outpcd fnl bnd after 3 out: drvn to chse ldrs 2 out: styd on fr last: nt pce to chal* **5/2**[1]
4 *10* **Singapore Sling (FR)**[22] 1983 4-10-8 0 KevinNabet 136
(A Bonin, France) *led 1st: hdd 4 out: led again 3 out: one of three ldrs jumping 2 out: sn hdd: wknd run-in* **16/1**
5 *nk* **My Maj (FR)**[22] 1983 4-10-8 0 GeoffreyRe 136
(Yannick Fouin, France) *trckd ldrs: led 4 out: hdd 3 out: styd prom: chsd ldr stands' side ent st: sn hrd rdn and no imp: grad lft bhd by ldrs: one pce run-in* **15/2**[3]
6 *6* **Saint Firmin (FR)**[7] 2263 4-10-8 0 JacquesRicou 130
(Robert Collet, France) *towards rr: midfield fr 4 out: chsd ldrs stands' side appr 2 out: sn rdn and no imp: fdd run-in* **25/1**
7 *nk* **Storminator (FR)**[22] 1983 4-10-8 0 JonathanNattiez 129
(J-P Gallorini, France) *w.w towards rr: rdn and effrt fnl bnd after 3 out: sltly hmpd bef 2 out: sn hrd rdn and btn* **9/1**
8 *½* **Voiladenuo (FR)**[22] 1983 4-10-8 0 JonathanPlouganou 129
(Guy Denuault, France) *hld up towards rr: effrt fnl bnd: hrd rdn and no further imp fr 2 out: sn wknd* **40/1**
9 *20* **Kemaliste (FR)**[22] 1983 4-10-8 0 BertrandBourez 109
(Y-M Porzier, France) *midfield: towards rr but in tch 4 out: rdn and lost tch fnl bnd bef 2 out: nvr in contention* **33/1**
P **Extreme Cara (FR)**[22] 1983 4-10-8 0 (p) BertrandThelier
(G Cherel, France) *trckd ldng pair: reminders 4 out: rdn and lost pl after 3 out: wl bhd whn p.u bef last* **16/1**
P **Wanaba (FR)**[43] 4-10-8 0 (p) Jean-LucBeaunez
(Mme P Butel, France) *towards rr: nt fluent 3 out: lost tch: wl bhd and p.u bef 2 out* **33/1**

4m 55.93s (0.93) **11 Ran SP% 124.3**
PARI-MUTUEL (all including 1 euro stake): WIN 5.10; PLACES 1.70, 1.30, 1.50; DF 7.90; SF 17.60.
Owner Barry Fulton, Chris Giles & Richard Webb **Bred** Jean-Francois Vermand **Trained** Ditcheat, Somerset

2415a PRIX GENERAL DONNIO (CHASE) (LISTED RACE) (5YO+) (TURF) 2m 5f 110y
3:15 (12:00) 5-Y-0+ **£37,073** (£18,536; £10,813; £7,337; £3,475)

RPR
1 **Tiot Cas (FR)**[15] 6-10-6 0 ChristopheHerpin 128
(P Chemin, France) **41/1**
2 *2 ½* **Parigny (FR)**[7] 2264 7-10-12 0 (p) JacquesRicou 132
(F-M Cottin, France) **17/1**
3 *6* **Cokydal (FR)**[15] 8-10-10 0 (p) AlainDeChitray 124
(G Cherel, France) **41/1**
4 *3* **Mail De Bievre (FR)**[214] 5239 8-10-3 0 PaddyBrennan 114
(Tom George) *tk str hold: led 1st: hdd 8th and trckd ldr: led again after 11th: hdd fnl bnd bef 2 out: rdn and no imp on ldr appr last: wknd run-in* **15/2**[3]
5 *7* **Oculi (FR)**[22] 9-10-3 0 (p) StevenColas 107
(A Adeline De Boisbrunet, France) **12/1**
6 *5* **Nom De D'La (FR)**[22] 1984 7-10-6 0 (b) JonathanNattiez 105
(J-P Gallorini, France) **10/1**
P **Dragon Mask (FR)**[28] 1902 7-10-12 0 (b) BertrandLestrade
(J-P Gallorini, France) **9/2**[2]
P **Dolcetto (FR)**[252] 6-10-10 0 (p) BertrandThelier
(G Cherel, France) **17/1**

The Form Book Jumps, Raceform Ltd, Compton, RG20 6NL.

P **Kotkieglote (FR)**[7] 2264 6-10-10 0....................................(p) DavidCottin
(J-P Gallorini, France) 9/2[2]
P **Sundahia (FR)**[22] 1984 6-11-3 0..(b) KevinNabet
(J-D Marion, France) 9/1
P **Sadyjaune (FR)**[22] 1984 7-9-13 0................................. ThierryMajorcryk
(E Lecoiffier, France) 28/1
P **United Park (FR)**[22] 1984 5-11-3 0................................... JamesReveley
(G Macaire, France) 7/2[1]

6m 1.32s (14.32) **12** Ran SP% **116.5**
PARI-MUTUEL (all including 1 euro stake): WIN 41.60; PLACES 7.90, 4.70, 10.40; DF 151.90; SF 511.10.
Owner Mme Philippe Chemin **Bred** Mme C Winkel **Trained** France

2241 CARLISLE (R-H)

Monday, November 11

OFFICIAL GOING: Heavy (chs 5.7, hdl 5.4)
First fence down the hill omitted in all chases.
Wind: Breezy, half against Weather: Overcast, light rain

2416 WATCH RACING UK ON SKY432 H'CAP CHASE (17 fncs 2 omitted) 3m 2f

12:45 (12:45) (Class 4) (0-105,105) 4-Y-0+ **£4,873** (£1,431; £715; £357)

Form RPR
/22- **1** **Snuker**[169] 492 6-10-0 **79**.. BrianHughes 95+
(James Ewart) *cl up: chalng whn nt fluent 3 out: led gng wl bef next: kpt on strly run-in* **2/1**[1]
0/2- **2** *4 1/2* **Shoal Bay Dreamer**[9] 2219 7-9-9 **79** oh3.........................(p) TonyKelly(5) 87
(Dianne Sayer) *in tch: rdn and outpcd 1/2-way: rallied after 5 out: chsd wnr 2 out: rdn and kpt on run-in* **18/1**
/53- **3** *21* **Etxalar (FR)**[30] 1872 10-11-12 **105**..................................(t) PeterBuchanan 92
(Lucinda Russell) *nt fluent on occasions: in tch: rdn and outpcd whn nt fluent 5 out: rallied 3 out: sn no imp* **10/3**[2]
0/6- **4** *1* **Camden George (IRE)**[10] 2194 12-11-7 **100**....................... RyanMania 86
(Sue Smith) *cl up: led 10th to 12th: drvn 4 out: outpcd after next* **40/1**
/22- **5** *12* **Bertie Milan (IRE)**[18] 2036 8-11-12 **105**.......................... LucyAlexander 79
(N W Alexander) *hld up: rdn 11th: hdwy u.p after 5 out: btn fnl 3* **9/2**[3]
/2P- **6** *1 1/2* **Bollin Fiona**[170] 473 9-10-8 **92**.................................. CallumWhillans(5) 65
(Donald Whillans) *hld up in tch: outpcd 9th: rallied next: struggling 12th: n.d after* **16/1**
/P6- **7** *21* **Trouble In Paris (IRE)**[12] 2155 6-10-13 **92**....................... HenryBrooke 44
(Barry Murtagh) *hld up: hdwy bef 10th: struggling fr next: t.o* **20/1**
03P/ **8** *32* **Billsgrey (IRE)**[276] 4115 11-10-0 **79** oh6............................ BrianHarding
(William Amos) *led to 10th: sn drvn along: struggling fr next: t.o* **12/1**
PP6- **P** **One For The Boss (IRE)**[18] 2044 6-10-0 **82** ow3......(tp) RobertDunne(3)
(Dai Burchell) *hld up in tch: stdy hdwy 5th: led 12th: nt fluent 4 out: rdn and hdd bef 2 out: wkng whn blnd last: sn p.u* **8/1**

6m 57.3s (-9.90) **Going Correction** -0.45s/f (Good) **9** Ran SP% **111.7**
Speed ratings (Par 105): **97,95,89,88,85 84,78,68,**
toteswingers 1&2 £5.50, 1&3 £1.30, 2&3 £10.70 CSF £33.77 CT £112.64 TOTE £2.40: £1.50, £4.10, £1.50; EX 31.70 Trifecta £131.90 Pool: £1201.55 - 6.83 winning units..
Owner Mrs Percy, Mr Down & Mr Boyd **Bred** Mr And Mrs N M L Ewart **Trained** Langholm, Dumfries & G'way

FOCUS
Hurdle races on Inner Hurdles track and all bends moved out. Gruelling conditions for this opener. The winner is rated similar to his Kelso run.

2417 DURDAR NOVICES' H'CAP HURDLE (10 hdls) 2m 3f 110y

1:15 (1:15) (Class 4) (0-110,105) 3-Y-0+ **£3,898** (£1,144; £572; £286)

Form RPR
/5F- **1** **Dickie Henderhoop (IRE)**[18] 2034 8-10-9 **95**......(b1) GrantCockburn(7) 101
(Lucy Normile) *t.k.h: cl up on outside: led 6th: mde rest: drvn and hld on wl fr last* **3/1**[2]
415- **2** *hd* **Aficionado**[47] 1658 3-10-7 **103**......................................(p) WilsonRenwick 92
(Chris Grant) *hld up in tch: smooth hdwy to chse ldrs bef 2 out: effrt and wnt 2nd last: drvn and kpt on: hld nr fin* **9/1**
000/ **3** *6* **Goodacres Garden (IRE)**[225] 5039 6-10-8 **87**.................... AdrianLane 87
(Donald McCain) *w ldr: rdn and outpcd 4 out: rallied bef 2 out: plugged on fr last: nt pce of first two* **7/1**
0/6- **4** *3/4* **Oscar Lateen (IRE)**[23] 1980 5-11-0 **93**............................... RyanMania 92
(Sandy Thomson) *prom: smooth hdwy and ev ch 3 out to next: sn drvn: wknd fr last* **20/1**
436/ **5** *3* **Captain Clayton (IRE)**[200] 5522 6-11-12 **105**................(t) HenryBrooke 101
(Simon West) *hld up in tch: drvn along after 3 out: rallied after next: wknd fr last* **15/2**
0/0- **6** *21* **Radio Nowhere (IRE)**[25] 1937 5-11-12 **105**...................... JasonMaguire 80
(Donald McCain) *led: reminders after 5th: hdd whn hit next: rdn and wknd 3 out* **4/1**[3]
042- **7** *18* **Top Billing**[23] 1982 4-10-11 **90**..(p) BrianHarding 47
(Nicky Richards) *t.k.h: chsd ldrs: rdn 4 out: rallied: wknd bef 2 out* **5/2**[1]

5m 4.7s (-4.10) **Going Correction** -0.125s/f (Good)
WFA 3 from 4yo 15lb 4 from 5yo+ 7lb **7** Ran SP% **112.6**
Speed ratings (Par 105): **103,102,100,100,99 90,83**
toteswingers 1&2 £2.70, 1&3 £8.20, 2&3 £6.70 CSF £27.70 TOTE £3.80: £1.70, £4.40; EX 25.20 Trifecta £26.30 Pool: £1457.60 - 41.49 winning units..
Owner L B N Racing Club **Bred** Mrs Maureen Ring **Trained** Duncrievie, Perth & Kinross

FOCUS
This fair handicap hurdle produced an exciting finish. The winner was heading for this sort of figure when falling here last time.

2418 JOIN NOW AT REWARDS4RACING.COM NOVICES' LIMITED H'CAP CHASE (11 fncs 1 omitted) 2m

1:50 (1:50) (Class 3) (0-125,123) 4-Y-0+ **£6,498** (£1,908; £954)

Form RPR
260/ **1** **Rockawango (FR)**[21] 4861 7-11-5 **123**...........................(tp) BrianHughes 130+
(James Ewart) *chsd ldr to 3rd: prom: wnt 2nd gng wl 5 out: shkn up to ld run-in: qcknd clr: readily* **11/8**[2]
113/ **2** *6* **Little Glenshee (IRE)**[247] 4650 7-11-2 **120**..................... LucyAlexander 115
(N W Alexander) *nt fluent on occasions: led: rdn whn hit 2 out: hdd run-in: nt pce of wnr* **5/6**[1]
06P- **3** *56* **Leroy Parker (IRE)**[2] 2356 5-10-5 **109** oh1.....................(bt) HenryBrooke 48
(Barry Murtagh) *chsd ldrs: nt fluent and reminder after 2nd: wnt 2nd next to 5 out: sn rdn and lost tch next* **9/1**[3]

4m 11.7s (-4.40) **Going Correction** -0.45s/f (Good) **3** Ran SP% **106.7**
Speed ratings (Par 107): **93,90,62**
CSF £2.95 TOTE £2.30; EX 2.40 Trifecta £3.10 Pool: £663.72 - 155.76 winning units..
Owner M Tedham **Bred** E A R L Haras Du Camp Benard **Trained** Langholm, Dumfries & G'way

FOCUS
A disappointing turnout for this, but the winner could be decent.

2419 WEATHERBYS HAMILTON INSURANCE GRADUATION CHASE (16 fncs 2 omitted) 3m 110y

2:25 (2:25) (Class 2) 4-Y-0+ **£12,512** (£3,696; £1,848; £924; £462)

Form RPR
12P/ **1** **Vintage Star (IRE)**[243] 4734 7-11-3 137................................ RyanMania 146+
(Sue Smith) *pressed ldr: led 5th to 8th: chalng whn nt fluent and pckd 5 out: led bef next: rdn 3 out: hit last: styd on gamely run-in* **13/2**[3]
4/F- **2** *nk* **Buddy Bolero (IRE)**[9] 2214 7-11-10 141.................. TomScudamore 152
(David Pipe) *t.k.h early: hld up: hdwy to chse ldng pair 5th: nt fluent 10th: effrt and wnt 2nd after 3 out: effrt whn nt fluent last: kpt on: hld nr fin* **13/8**[2]
/12- **3** *3/4* **Imperial Vic (IRE)**[23] 1976 8-10-13 137................................ DannyCook 140
(Michael Smith) *led to 5th: led 8th: drvn and hdd bef 4 out: outpcd next: rallied bef last: kpt on run-in: hld nr fin* **6/5**[1]
222/ **4** *24* **Cappa Bleu (IRE)**[219] 5177 11-11-10 147........................(t) PaulMoloney 133
(Evan Williams) *chsd clr ldng pair to 5th: in tch: outpcd 10th: struggling fr 5 out: bttr for r* **11/1**
0/0- **5** *13* **Rebeccas Choice (IRE)**[30] 1868 10-11-10 123............(p) RobertDunne 118
(Dai Burchell) *hld up in tch: outpcd whn hit 9th: struggling fr next: t.o* **40/1**

6m 28.7s (-13.90) **Going Correction** -0.45s/f (Good) **5** Ran SP% **107.7**
Speed ratings (Par 109): **104,103,103,95,91**
CSF £17.33 TOTE £10.40: £3.10, £1.50; EX 14.60 Trifecta £36.00 Pool: £1469.19 - 30.58 winning units..
Owner Trevor Hemmings **Bred** Gleadhill House Stud Ltd **Trained** High Eldwick, W Yorks

FOCUS
An intriguing renewal of this graduation chase but it's fair to say that the form shouldn't be taken too literally. A small step up from the winner on the best of his novice form.

2420 CHRISTMAS PARTIES AT CARLISLE RACECOURSE NOVICES' HURDLE (8 hdls) 2m 1f

3:00 (3:00) (Class 4) 4-Y-0+ **£3,898** (£1,144; £572; £286)

Form RPR
10/ **1** **Milo Man (IRE)**[243] 4738 5-10-12 0...................................... PaulMoloney 127+
(Evan Williams) *mde all at ordinary gallop: qcknd clr 2 out: hit last: unchal* **4/5**[1]
232/ **2** *5* **Greensalt (IRE)**[199] 5550 5-10-12 0.................................. JasonMaguire 118+
(Donald McCain) *chsd wnr: nt fluent 3 out: effrt and drvn after next: lost 2nd bef last: rallied and regained 2nd post: no ch w wnr* **3/1**[2]
222/ **3** *shd* **Maybe I Wont**[330] 3092 8-10-12 0.. BrianHughes 117
(James Moffatt) *chsd ldrs: drvn and outpcd bef 2 out: rallied to chse (clr) wnr bef last: one pce run-in* **5/1**[3]
5- **4** *dist* **Shine A Diamond (IRE)**[30] 1877 5-10-12 0.................... PeterBuchanan 82
(Lucinda Russell) *prom: drvn along bef 2 out: wknd between last 2* **16/1**
5 *4* **Courtown Oscar (IRE)**[191] 4-10-12 0............................. RichieMcGrath 78
(Philip Kirby) *hld up: pushed along 2nd: struggling bef 4 out: nvr on terms* **25/1**
6- **6** *3 1/4* **Cockney Lacey**[31] 1854 4-10-5 0.................................... GrantCockburn(7) 75
(Lucinda Russell) *hld up on outside: stdy hdwy 4th: rdn and wknd bef 2 out* **50/1**
3/4- **7** *20* **Politeness (FR)**[31] 1853 4-10-12 0................................... WilsonRenwick 65
(Rose Dobbin) *t.k.h early: hld up: stdy hdwy 1/2-way: rdn and wknd bef 2 out: t.o* **12/1**
FP0- **8** *3 1/4* **Gloshen (IRE)**[10] 2196 7-10-9 0.. KyleJames(3) 52
(Philip Kirby) *hld up: rdn and outpcd after 4 out: btn after next: t.o* **100/1**
F- **U** **Shirls Son Sam**[38] 1754 5-10-12 0.. BarryKeniry
(Chris Fairhurst) *hld up: jinked lft and uns rdr 1st* **50/1**
0P/ **P** **Running Brook (IRE)**[204] 6-10-5 0............................. CallumBewley(7)
(R Mike Smith) *hld up in tch: mstke and outpcd 4 out: struggling fr next: t.o whn p.u run-in* **100/1**

4m 27.3s (-1.90) **Going Correction** -0.125s/f (Good)
WFA 4 from 5yo+ 7lb **10** Ran SP% **120.5**
Speed ratings (Par 105): **99,96,96,80,78 76,67,65,,**
toteswingers 1&2 £1.20, 1&3 £1.80, 2&3 £1.80 CSF £3.60 TOTE £1.70: £1.10, £1.60, £1.60; EX 4.60 Trifecta £8.00 Pool: £2613.02 - 242.23 winning units..
Owner Mr & Mrs William Rucker **Bred** S G Deacon **Trained** Llancarfan, Vale Of Glamorgan

FOCUS
A modest event. The winner should go on to rate higher.

2421 BORDER CITY H'CAP CHASE (15 fncs 1 omitted) 2m 4f

3:30 (3:30) (Class 4) (0-120,120) 4-Y-0+ **£6,498** (£1,908; £954; £477)

Form RPR
/61- **1** **Tutchec (FR)**[18] 2036 6-10-12 **106**.. BrianHarding 118+
(Nicky Richards) *mde virtually all: rdn bef 2 out: styd on wl fr last* **4/1**[2]
252/ **2** *4* **Ros Castle (IRE)**[263] 4338 7-11-11 **119**........................... WilsonRenwick 125
(Rose Dobbin) *hld up: smooth hdwy and in tch 5 out: effrt bef 2 out: chsd wnr last: kpt on same pce run* **5/1**[3]
2/P- **3** *nk* **Wicklow Lad**[23] 1978 9-11-6 **114**....................................(v1) LucyAlexander 121
(N W Alexander) *hld up: hdwy and prom after 7th: rdn and outpcd after 3 out: kpt on fr last: no imp* **8/1**
603/ **4** *5* **Whats Up Woody (IRE)**[201] 5502 8-11-3 **118**................ JohnDawson(7) 120
(John Wade) *w wnr: rdn 3 out: outpcd fr last* **15/2**
0/5- **5** *3* **Oil Burner**[191] 113 8-10-8 **102**.. HenryBrooke 101
(William Amos) *hld up in tch: rdn and outpcd 5 out: rallied after 2 out: no imp fr last* **8/1**
1FF/ **6** *1 1/4* **Zaru (FR)**[236] 4858 7-11-12 **120**.. BrianHughes 118
(James Ewart) *cl up: hit 2nd: chal 8th: nt fluent next: outpcd 5 out: no imp fr 3 out* **3/1**[1]
3/0- **7** *7* **Riguez Dancer**[26] 1923 9-11-10 **118**..............................(b1) JasonMaguire 110
(Donald McCain) *prom: effrt and rdn 4 out: wknd between last 2* **6/1**
460- **P** **Fred Bojangals (IRE)**[130] 879 11-11-2 **110**........................ SeanQuinlan
(Barbara Butterworth) *t.k.h: prom: lost pl whn mstke 9th: sn struggling: t.o whn p.u 3 out* **66/1**

5m 15.0s (-12.40) **Going Correction** -0.45s/f (Good) **8** Ran SP% **111.4**
Speed ratings (Par 105): **106,104,104,102,101 100,97,**
toteswingers 1&2 £3.10, 1&3 £4.30, 2&3 £2.40 CSF £23.35 CT £146.32 TOTE £3.50: £1.20, £2.20, £2.30; EX 24.50 Trifecta £152.60 Pool: £2397.58 - 11.78 winning units..
Owner Club 4 Racing **Bred** William Ewart **Trained** Greystoke, Cumbria

FOCUS
The winner built on his recent win and the form should work out.

2422 CONNOLLY'S RED MILLS BUMPER CHALLENGE A STANDARD OPEN NATIONAL HUNT FLAT RACE 2m 1f
4:00 (4:00) (Class 6) 4-6-Y-0 **£1,949** (£572; £286; £143)

Form RPR
1 **Stonebrook (IRE)**[184] 232 5-11-0 0 JasonMaguire 117+
(Donald McCain) *chsd ldrs: smooth hdwy to ld over 1f out: shkn up last 100yds: sn clr: readily* **4/5**[1]
2 *7* **Leney Cottage (IRE)**[176] 6-11-0 0 BrianHarding 104
(Alison Hamilton) *t.k.h: chsd ldrs: led over 2f out to over 1f out: outpcd last 150yds* **20/1**
5- 3 *2 ½* **Kilkenny Kim (IRE)**[27] 1919 4-10-2 0 KillianMoore[(5)] 93
(Jennie Candlish) *hld up: stdy hdwy over 4f out: drvn and outpcd over 2f out: rallied over 1f out: kpt on: no imp* **4/1**[2]
4 *11* **Katies Choice (IRE)**[176] 5-11-0 0 WilsonRenwick 89
(R Mike Smith) *prom: drvn and outpcd over 3f out: plugged on fnl f: no ch w first three* **33/1**
2/U- 5 *3 ¾* **Marrakech Trader (NZ)**[18] 2037 6-10-7 0 TomBellamy[(7)] 85
(Rose Dobbin) *t.k.h: hld up in tch: hdwy and cl up over 3f out: wknd wl over 1f out* **5/1**[3]
6 *18* **Rocky Stone (IRE)**[229] 5-11-0 0 HenryBrooke 67
(Donald McCain) *led: rdn and hdd over 2f out: sn wknd* **8/1**
0/ 7 *21* **Jon (IRE)**[265] 4306 5-10-11 0 EwanWhillans[(3)] 46
(Alistair Whillans) *hld up: rdn over 4f out: struggling fnl 3f* **66/1**
8 *16* **Miss Twiggy** 5-10-7 0 DannyCook 23
(Brian Ellison) *in tch on ins: drvn along fr 1/2-way: lost tch fr 4f out* **16/1**

4m 26.5s (2.30) **Going Correction** -0.125s/f (Good)
WFA 4 from 5yo+ 7lb **8** Ran SP% **118.4**
Speed ratings: **89,85,84,79,77 69,59,51**
CSF £23.45 TOTE £1.30: £1.10, £5.60, £1.80; EX 22.80 Trifecta £62.50 Pool: £2542.68 - 30.48 winning units..
Owner Roger O'Byrne **Bred** George Ward **Trained** Cholmondeley, Cheshire

FOCUS
It's unlikely this was anything other than an ordinary bumper. The easy winner stood out on his Irish run and should rate higher.
T/Plt: £70.90 to a £1 stake. Pool: £63664.02 - 654.73 winning tickets T/Qpdt: £10.90 to a £1 stake. Pool: £6555.76 - 442.07 winning tickets RY

2348 SOUTHWELL (L-H)
Monday, November 11

OFFICIAL GOING: Soft (6.4)
Wind: light across Weather: overcast, damp

2423 £32 BONUS AT 32RED.COM H'CAP CHASE (16 fncs) 2m 4f 110y
12:30 (12:30) (Class 5) (0-100,96) 4-Y-0+ **£2,144** (£629; £314; £157)

Form RPR
123- 1 **Shalamiyr (FR)**[18] 2039 8-11-12 **96** WillKennedy 103
(Sarah-Jayne Davies) *led 2nd to 9th: led 4 out: hit last: hld on gamely* **3/1**[2]
4/P- 2 *1 ½* **Jim Job Jones**[173] 431 9-9-7 **70** oh8 (tp) ConorRing[(7)] 75
(Neil Mulholland) *chsd ldrs: 2nd 3 out: kpt on same pce fr next* **12/1**
433- 3 *1* **Cloudy Dawn**[18] 2047 8-9-11 **72** JonathanEngland[(5)] 77
(Sue Smith) *led to 2nd: reminders 6th: drvn 11th: kpt on one pce fr 2 out* **11/10**[1]
06F- 4 *27* **Wheelavher**[162] 601 7-9-10 **73** (t) GeraldQuinn[(7)] 55
(Claire Dyson) *w ldrs: led 9th: blnd 12th: hdd next: sn lost pl and bhd* **6/1**[3]
400- 5 *25* **Checkmate**[45] 1668 8-10-0 **70** MarkGrant 22
(Christopher Kellett) *in tch: pushed along 8th: outpcd 10th: bhd fr 4 out: sn t.o* **28/1**
36P- P **Petrarchick (USA)**[146] 759 6-9-9 **70** oh10 MauriceLinehan[(5)]
(Emma Baker) *in tch: drvn 6th: lost pl next: bhd 10th: sn t.o: p.u bef 4 out* **7/1**

5m 42.2s (25.20) **Going Correction** +1.125s/f (Heav) **6** Ran SP% **110.5**
Speed ratings (Par 103): **97,96,96,85,76**
toteswingers 1&2 £7.60, 1&3 £1.10, 2&3 £3.80 CSF £31.31 TOTE £4.20: £1.60, £7.70; EX 27.80 Trifecta £79.50 Pool: £2345.62 - 22.12 winning units..
Owner Miss Sarah-Jayne Davies **Bred** H H The Aga Khan's Studs Sc **Trained** Leominster, H'fords

FOCUS
Fences moved 5yds inside line utilised on November 8th and both bends moved to fresh ground where possible. The gallop was steady for this weak handicap. The winner was a class above these and is rated to his mark.

2424 32RED MARES' H'CAP CHASE (16 fncs) 2m 4f 110y
1:00 (1:00) (Class 4) (0-120,110) 4-Y-0+ **£3,768** (£1,106; £553; £276)

Form RPR
153- 1 **Midnight Macarena**[154] 693 8-11-0 **103** (p) MattCrawley[(5)] 110+
(Lucy Wadham) *trckd ldrs: upsides 4 out: led appr next: drvn out* **6/5**[1]
2 *2 ¾* **Rossa Parks (IRE)**[85] 1313 7-11-12 **110** NoelFehily 110
(Neil Mulholland) *chsd ldr to 12th: 3rd and drvn next: chsd wnr appr last: kpt on same pce* **5/2**[2]
/36- 3 *4 ½* **Fair Bramble**[21] 2007 7-11-5 **103** LeightonAspell 102+
(Oliver Sherwood) *j.rt: led: increased pce 10th: hdd appr 3 out: wknd appr last* **3/1**[3]
245- 4 *7* **Ninfea (IRE)**[12] 1192 5-11-2 **103** (p) TrevorWhelan[(3)] 94
(Neil King) *t.k.h: trckd ldrs: drvn 11th: rdn and wl outpcd 4 out* **10/1**

5m 52.3s (35.30) **Going Correction** +1.125s/f (Heav) **4** Ran SP% **108.1**
Speed ratings (Par 105): **77,75,74,71**
CSF £4.62 TOTE £1.80; EX 3.70 Trifecta £4.60 Pool: £1282.48 - 205.61 winning units..
Owner The Bees **Bred** Mrs Elizabeth Gordon Lennox **Trained** Newmarket, Suffolk

FOCUS
A tight mares' contest run at a steady pace. Modest form, the idling winner value for further.

2425 32REDPOKER.COM H'CAP CHASE (19 fncs) 3m 110y
1:35 (1:35) (Class 5) (0-100,93) 4-Y-0+ **£2,423** (£823)

Form RPR
236- 1 **Waltzing Tornado (IRE)**[153] 713 9-11-8 **89** (p) NoelFehily 111
(Neil Mulholland) *trckd ldrs: cl 2nd 15th: led 3 out: lft wl clr next* **7/4**[1]
P42- 2 *43* **Ballyvoneen (IRE)**[4] 2313 8-11-12 **93** (v[1]) TomMessenger 72
(Neil King) *chsd ldr: nt fluent 12th: drvn 15th: lost pl and hit 4 out: sn bhd: lft distant 2nd 2 out* **9/4**[3]
P2P- P **Flichity (IRE)**[162] 597 8-10-1 **73** JoeCornwall[(5)]
(John Cornwall) *last but in tch: pushed along 6th: detached 12th: t.o whn p.u bef 15th* **14/1**
/PF- U **Kevin Fancy (IRE)**[7] 2277 7-9-7 **67** oh19 MrFTett[(7)]
(John Upson) *w ldrs whn blnd and uns rdr 1st* **50/1**
0F1- F **Inandover**[18] 2047 8-10-10 **77** (t) DonalDevereux 84
(John Mackie) *led: hdd 3 out: 6 l down and tired whn fell next* **2/1**[2]

6m 55.0s (32.00) **Going Correction** +1.125s/f (Heav) **5** Ran SP% **109.1**
Speed ratings (Par 103): **93,79, , ,**
CSF £6.19 TOTE £2.70: £1.40, £1.60; EX 6.50 Trifecta £7.50 Pool: £2431.73 - 240.57 winning units..
Owner John Hobbs **Bred** Miss Anne Heaney **Trained** Limpley Stoke, Wilts

FOCUS
The pace was honest for this moderate handicap, with only two finishing. A step up from the winner for his new yard.

2426 32RED.COM "NATIONAL HUNT" NOVICES' HURDLE (9 hdls) 2m
2:05 (2:06) (Class 4) 4-Y-0+ **£3,119** (£915; £457; £228)

Form RPR
2/3- 1 **John Reel (FR)**[25] 1935 4-10-12 0 HarrySkelton 123+
(Dan Skelton) *trckd ldrs: hit 3rd: led 2 out: qcknd clr: j.rt last: v easily* **2/1**[1]
14- 2 *9* **Make Me A Fortune (IRE)**[27] 1919 5-10-12 0 APMcCoy 107
(Steve Gollings) *w ldr: upsides and drvn 2 out: kpt on: no ch w wnr* **7/2**[3]
3 *1 ½* **Spiculas (IRE)** 4-10-12 0 JamesReveley 106+
(Keith Reveley) *hld up in rr: hdwy to trck ldrs 5th: cl 4th whn mstke 2 out: 3rd between last 2: kpt on same pce* **16/1**
200/ 4 *5* **Lotus Pond (IRE)**[257] 4452 5-10-12 0 RobertThornton 100
(Alan King) *trckd ldrs: lft cl 3rd 2 out: one pce* **14/1**
01/ 5 *9* **Ballyhooley Boy (IRE)**[252] 4577 6-10-12 0 CharliePoste 94
(Robin Dickin) *trckd ldrs: upsides 6th: led briefly appr 2 out: mstke: sn lost pl* **25/1**
3/0- 6 *15* **No No Charlie (IRE)**[27] 1915 6-10-12 0 (t) NoelFehily 83
(Charlie Longsdon) *led tl hdd appr 2 out: sn wknd* **9/4**[2]
3- 7 *2 ½* **Emral Silk**[18] 2037 5-10-7 0 JonathanEngland[(5)] 84
(Sue Smith) *j.lft and nt fluent: t.k.h: trckd ldrs: dropped bk 6th: reminder and eased after next* **12/1**
/36- 8 *34* **Milan Of Hope (IRE)**[163] 584 6-10-12 0 (t) AdamPogson 40
(Charles Pogson) *in last: nt fluent 4th: sn bhd: t.o 6th* **100/1**

4m 13.8s (16.80) **Going Correction** +1.125s/f (Heav) **8** Ran SP% **111.4**
Speed ratings (Par 105): **103,98,97,95,90 83,82,65**
toteswingers 1&2 £1.70, 1&3 £6.50, 2&3 £8.50 CSF £9.08 TOTE £2.80: £1.10, £1.40, £3.70; EX 8.90 Trifecta £158.60 Pool: £4107.02 - 19.41 winning units..
Owner Walters Plant Hire Ltd **Bred** Ecurie Biraben **Trained** Alcester, Warwicks

FOCUS
A fair novice hurdle. The easy winner built on his recent run.

2427 32REDBET.COM H'CAP HURDLE (11 hdls) 2m 4f 110y
2:40 (2:40) (Class 5) (0-100,100) 4-Y-0+ **£1,949** (£572; £286; £143)

Form RPR
322/ 1 **Motou (FR)**[438] 1419 8-11-5 **100** DanielHiskett[(7)] 107+
(Richard Phillips) *hld up in rr: hdwy 8th: modest 4th next: 3rd appr 2 out: hung lft and led appr last: drvn out* **7/2**[2]
20P/ 2 *2 ½* **Lord Landen (IRE)**[347] 2721 8-11-6 **94** (t) PaddyBrennan 98+
(Fergal O'Brien) *t.k.h: led: drvn between last 2: edgd rt: hdd appr last: styd on same pce* **11/8**[1]
0/P- 3 *shd* **Midnight Choice**[153] 710 8-9-11 **74** oh1 MarkQuinlan[(3)] 77
(James Evans) *hld up towards rr: hdwy and 3rd whn hit 7th: wnt 2nd after 3 out: upsides between last 2: styd on same pce* **5/1**[3]
5/B- 4 *34* **Peqeno Diablo (IRE)**[10] 2191 8-9-8 **75** (tp) GeraldQuinn[(7)] 49
(Claire Dyson) *trckd ldr 3rd: upsides 7th: drvn 3 out: sn wknd: t.o* **14/1**
P00- P **Gainsborough's Art (IRE)**[18] 2051 8-9-9 **74** oh19 MauriceLinehan[(5)]
(Harry Chisman) *chsd ldrs: nt fluent 3rd: drvn next: reminders and lost pl 5th: t.o whn p.u bef 7th* **50/1**
561- P **Stadium Of Light (IRE)**[11] 2176 6-10-11 **90** BenPoste[(5)]
(Shaun Harris) *trckd ldrs 4th: drvn 8th: rdn and wknd next: sn bhd: t.o whn p.u bef last* **7/2**[2]

5m 35.2s (22.20) **Going Correction** +1.125s/f (Heav) **6** Ran SP% **111.8**
Speed ratings (Par 103): **102,101,101,88,**
toteswingers 1&2 £1.60, 1&3 £3.20, 2&3 £1.70 CSF £9.01 TOTE £5.50: £1.60, £1.60; EX 14.60 Trifecta £48.90 Pool: £3271.74 - 50.10 winning units..
Owner The Summer Club **Bred** Earl Haras De La Croix Sonnet **Trained** Adlestrop, Gloucs

FOCUS
A fair gallop on in this handicap with the winner coming from the rear. He's rated to form and the second should win off his current mark.

2428 32REDBINGO.COM CLAIMING HURDLE 5 (13 hdls) 3m 110y
3:10 (3:10) (Class 5) 4-Y-0+ **£1,949** (£572; £286; £143)

Form RPR
1P0- 1 **Connectivity (IRE)**[11] 2177 9-11-4 0 (b) APMcCoy 134+
(Dr Richard Newland) *racd wd: trckd ldrs: led 9th: wnt clr between last 2: easily* **6/5**[1]
P/3- 2 *15* **Neptune Equester**[168] 509 10-11-8 126 AidanColeman 116
(Brian Ellison) *in rr: wnt prom 4th: drvn 9th: 3rd and outpcd after 3 out: kpt on to take 13 l 2nd appr last* **15/8**[2]
060/ 3 *8* **Corkage (IRE)**[196] 24 10-11-12 125 (b) JamesReveley 112
(Keith Reveley) *chsd ldr to 4th: 2nd 3 out: wknd appr last* **5/1**[3]
640- 4 *23* **Noble Witness (IRE)**[27] 1917 10-11-2 99 (b) AdamPogson 79
(Charles Pogson) *led: hdd 9th: wknd after 3 out: bhd next: t.o* **33/1**
2/0- 5 *18* **Kauto The Roc (FR)**[164] 566 9-11-2 0 (t) TomMessenger 61
(Anabel K Murphy) *t.k.h in rr: wnt prom 4th: drvn 9th: sn lost pl: t.o 2 out* **50/1**
660- P **Nomadic Dreamer**[41] 1709 10-10-12 106 (t) RichieMcLernon
(Sophie Leech) *hld up in rr: prom 4th: drvn 9th: sn lost pl: bhd whn p.u bef 3 out* **20/1**

6m 44.0s (29.00) **Going Correction** +1.125s/f (Heav) **6** Ran SP% **106.6**
Speed ratings (Par 103): **98,93,90,83,77**
toteswingers 1&2 £1.10, 1&3 £1.50, 2&3 £2.00 CSF £3.35 TOTE £2.60: £1.10, £1.70; EX 3.80 Trifecta £7.40 Pool: £2792.21 - 279.48 winning units..
Owner Paul L Drinkwater **Bred** Mrs K Healy **Trained** Claines, Worcs

The Form Book Jumps, Raceform Ltd, Compton, RG20 6NL.

FOCUS
Not a bad contest for the grade, run at a steady pace. The easy winner was back to form.

2429 32RED CASINO NOVICES' HURDLE (11 hdls) 2m 4f 110y
3:40 (3:40) (Class 4) 4-Y-0+ **£3,195** (£992; £534)

Form RPR
2/6- **1** **Houndscourt (IRE)**[189] [140] 6-10-12 124..............(t) SamTwiston-Davies 100
(Jamie Snowden) *w ldrs: led 7th: drvn 2 out: hdd between last 2: lft clr last: hmpd by loose horse and eased nr fin* **4/7**[1]

2 *13* **Speckled Door**[204] 5-10-12 0.. AndrewThornton 85
(Caroline Bailey) *hld up wl in tch: trckd ldrs 6th: hit 3 out: sn drvn to chse ldr: wknd 2 out: lft modest 2nd last* **4/1**[2]

534- **3** *31* **Balinderry (IRE)**[164] [560] 6-10-12 0.. APMcCoy 67
(Steve Gollings) *led 2nd to 7th: rdn appr 2 out: sn wknd: lft poor 3rd and eased last* **9/2**[3]

603- **U** **Church Hall (IRE)**[25] [1946] 5-10-7 0.......................... AodhaganConlon(5) 107+
(Emma Baker) *trckd ldrs: upsides 2 out: led between last 2: 4 l ahd whn blnd and eventually uns rdr last* **14/1**

P- **P** **Leap In The Dark**[10] [2189] 7-10-5 0..................................(t) DonalDevereux
(John Mackie) *led to 2nd: drvn and lost pl 6th: sn bhd: t.o whn p.u after 7th* **100/1**

5m 49.1s (36.10) **Going Correction** +1.125s/f (Heav) 5 Ran SP% **109.5**
Speed ratings (Par 105): **76,71,59,** ,
CSF £3.33 TOTE £1.50: £1.10, £1.90; EX 3.70 Trifecta £5.70 Pool: £2239.58 - 291.69 winning units..
Owner Owners For Owners: Houndscourt **Bred** Ian Downey **Trained** Lambourn, Berks

FOCUS
This moderate novice event changed complexion at the final flight. The lucky winner was again well below his best, and the time was slow.
T/Plt: £26.00 to a £1 stake. Pool: £65001.78 - 1818.48 winning tickets T/Qpdt: £3.00 to a £1 stake. Pool: £8228.93 - 1967.85 winning tickets WG

2248 HUNTINGDON (R-H)
Tuesday, November 12

OFFICIAL GOING: Hurdle course - soft (heavy in places); chase course - soft changing to soft (heavy in places) after race 2 (1.10)
Wind: Fresh behind Weather: Cloudy with sunny spells

2430 WILLIAM HILL THE JUMPS WIN £100,000 H'CAP HURDLE (10 hdls) 2m 5f 110y
12:40 (12:41) (Class 4) (0-105,105) 4-Y-0+ **£3,119** (£915; £457; £228)

Form RPR
0/6- **1** **Tigresse Bleue**[178] [379] 5-11-12 105.. APMcCoy 120+
(Jonjo O'Neill) *hld up: hdwy appr 6th: wnt 2nd after next: jnd ldr 2 out: led on bit flat: easily* **5/1**[2]

/13- **2** *1 ¼* **Just Cloudy**[22] [2008] 9-11-3 96..(t) FelixDeGiles 100
(Robert Walford) *trckd ldr tl led after 6th: drvn along appr 2 out: hdd flat: styd on same pce* **9/2**[1]

434- **3** *17* **Commitment**[26] [1945] 4-11-5 101.................................. MichaelByrne(3) 92
(Neil Mulholland) *hld up: hit 5th: hdwy next: rdn after 3 out: wknd next* **11/2**[3]

/P0- **4** *7* **Admiral Boom (IRE)**[26] [1945] 7-11-2 95.................................. TomO'Brien 75
(Paul Henderson) *hld up: hdwy 7th: rdn and wknd after 3 out* **12/1**

2/4- **5** *15* **Boss In Boots (IRE)**[193] [95] 5-11-7 100...................[1] AndrewThornton 70
(Seamus Mullins) *hld up: hdwy 6th: rdn and wknd after 3 out: blnd next* **11/2**[3]

4/U- **6** *3 ¼* **Old Way (IRE)**[16] [2105] 7-11-7 100..................................(b[1]) LiamTreadwell 62
(Venetia Williams) *led: j.lft 5th: pushed along and hdd after next: wknd appr 3 out* **11/2**[3]

100/ **7** *15* **Lisdonagh House (IRE)**[268] [4275] 11-10-11 90.................................. TomSiddall 37
(Lynn Siddall) *hld up: drvn along after 5th: sn lost tch: blnd next* **22/1**

432- **P** **Royal Defence (IRE)**[14] [1913] 7-11-6 99.. RyanMahon
(Mick Quinn) *prom: rdn and lost pl appr 6th: sn bhd: p.u bef 2 out* **16/1**

0/5- **P** **Zelos Diktator**[174] [436] 7-10-1 90.. MikeyHamill(10)
(Sean Curran) *chsd ldrs tl pushed along and wknd appr 6th: bhd whn p.u bef 3 out* **20/1**

055- **P** **Xenophon**[9] [2253] 5-9-9 79.. JoeCornwall(5)
(Michael Chapman) *chsd ldrs: rdn appr 6th: wknd bef next: bhd whn p.u bef 3 out* **50/1**

032/ **P** **Marble Walk (IRE)**[310] [3534] 8-11-2 95.. LeightonAspell
(Richard Rowe) *hld up: wknd 6th: bhd whn blnd next: p.u bef 3 out* **12/1**

5m 30.1s (19.50) **Going Correction** +0.775s/f (Soft)
WFA 4 from 5yo+ 8lb 11 Ran SP% **113.3**
Speed ratings (Par 105): **95,94,88,85,80 79,73,** , ,
toteswingers 1&2 £2.60, 1&3 £3.60, 2&3 £3.00 CSF £26.49 CT £126.65 TOTE £6.10: £1.60, £1.80, £2.80; EX 30.80 Trifecta £38.70 Pool: £1273.85 - 24.65 winning units..
Owner Mrs Felicity Loudon **Bred** Dayton Investments Ltd **Trained** Cheltenham, Gloucs

FOCUS
Tony McCoy said after winning the first "It's proper soft ground, very hard work". They went a solid gallop in this very ordinary handicap and only the first two, who finished clear, truly saw it out. The asy winner finally built on the promise of her Towcester run.

2431 REWARDS4RACING.COM NOVICES' H'CAP CHASE (19 fncs) 3m
1:10 (1:10) (Class 4) (0-110,106) 4-Y-0+ **£3,768** (£1,106; £553; £276)

Form RPR
522- **1** **Suburban Bay**[23] [1988] 8-11-9 103.. WayneHutchinson 123+
(Alan King) *t.k.h: led 2nd: clr 9th to 3 out: clr again next: hit last: unchal* **10/3**[2]

41F- **2** *26* **Riddlestown (IRE)**[18] [2067] 6-11-12 106..................................(p) HarrySkelton 101
(Caroline Fryer) *hld up: hdwy 10th: chsd wnr 3 out: rdn and wkng whn mstke next: nt fluent last* **9/1**

6/5- **3** *11* **Tickatack (IRE)**[19] [2046] 8-11-11 105.. RobertThornton 86
(Graeme McPherson) *prom: nt fluent 3rd: rdn and wknd appr 2 out* **8/1**

133- **4** *1 ¾* **Long Wave (IRE)**[19] [2046] 6-11-11 105..................................(p) RichardJohnson 86
(Charlie Longsdon) *chsd wnr tl mstke 3 out: rdn and wknd bef next* **3/1**[1]

2/2- **5** *4 ½* **Barton Gift**[193] [89] 6-11-1 95.. LiamTreadwell 69
(John Spearing) *chsd ldrs: lost pl 14th: wknd after next* **7/2**[3]

010- **6** *28* **Divine Folly (IRE)**[85] [1320] 8-11-0 94.. DavidBass 40
(Lawney Hill) *prom: lost pl 6th: pushed along after 8th: wknd 13th* **20/1**

P/U- **P** **Ballyhilty Bridge**[26] [1942] 7-11-4 98.. TomO'Brien
(Paul Henderson) *hld up: pushed along after 12th: wknd bef next: bhd whn p.u bef 2 out* **7/1**

6m 26.1s (15.80) **Going Correction** +0.775s/f (Soft) 7 Ran SP% **108.7**
Speed ratings (Par 105): **104,95,91,91,89 80,**
toteswingers 1&2 £7.60, 1&3 £7.10, 2&3 £11.40 CSF £28.12 TOTE £3.30: £1.70, £3.80; EX 23.50 Trifecta £124.30 Pool: £1557.82 - 9.39 winning units..
Owner Simon Bullimore **Bred** S Bullimore **Trained** Barbury Castle, Wilts

FOCUS
Just a fair novices' handicap. The winner is rated back to his best though there's a case for rating the form up to 5lb higher.

2432 WEATHERBYS HAMILTON INSURANCE NOVICES' HURDLE (8 hdls) 2m 110y
1:40 (1:41) (Class 4) 4-Y-0+ **£3,768** (£1,106; £553; £276)

Form RPR
5- **1** **Prince Siegfried (FR)**[18] [2068] 7-10-12 0.. DenisO'Regan 117+
(John Ferguson) *trckd ldrs: chal and mstke 2 out: rdn flat: edgd lft flat: styd on to ld nr fin* **9/2**[2]

/34- **2** *hd* **My Wigwam Or Yours (IRE)**[24] [1974] 4-10-12 0.................. APMcCoy 116
(Nicky Henderson) *trckd ldr tl led appr 3 out: rdn and hit next: hdd nr fin* **4/5**[1]

1/0- **3** *1* **Werenearlyoutofit (IRE)**[24] [1974] 5-10-12 0............. WayneHutchinson 115
(Graeme McPherson) *hld up: reminders after 3rd: hdwy 5th: rdn appr 2 out: styd on* **5/1**[3]

4 *16* **Know No Fear**[22] 8-10-12 0.. WillKennedy 100
(Alastair Lidderdale) *hld up: hdwy appr 3 out: rdn and wknd after next: mstke last* **100/1**

450/ **5** *2 ¼* **Tender Surprise**[213] [5295] 4-10-2 0.................................. TrevorWhelan(3) 90
(Neil King) *hld up: hdwy appr 3 out: rdn and wknd next* **100/1**

04/ **6** *9* **St Ignatius**[29] [2736] 6-10-12 0.. JamesDavies 88
(Alan Bailey) *chsd ldrs tl rdn and wknd appr 2 out* **16/1**

0/6- **7** *8* **Wah Wah Taysee (IRE)**[22] [2002] 6-10-12 0.......................... TomScudamore 80
(David Bridgwater) *led: hdd appr 3 out: rdn and wknd bef next* **25/1**

526/ **8** *3* **La Belle Sauvage**[682] [3473] 6-10-5 0.......................... SamTwiston-Davies 70
(Kim Bailey) *prom: rdn after 5th: wknd after next* **20/1**

0/6- **9** *1 ¾* **Allez Zane**[20] [2027] 4-10-5 0..................................(t) DavidEngland 68
(Giles Smyly) *hld up: hdwy appr 3 out: sn rdn and wknd* **50/1**

00/ **10** *19* **Bill The Lad (IRE)**[611] [4799] 6-10-12 0.. SamThomas 56
(Paul Cowley) *hld up: bhd fr 4th* **100/1**

600/ **11** *14* **Father Arthur**[210] [5335] 5-10-12 0.. LeightonAspell 42
(Richard Rowe) *hld up: hdwy 5th: rdn and wknd next* **150/1**

/45- **12** *25* **Agent Fedora**[20] [2027] 5-10-5 0..................................(t) NickScholfield 10
(Kim Bailey) *prom: pushed along and lost pl after 4th: sn bhd* **16/1**

P **Lennoxwood (IRE)**[664] 5-10-12 0.. DaveCrosse
(Mark Usher) *hld up: t.k.h: wknd after 4th: bhd whn p.u bef 3 out* **150/1**

356- **P** **Volcanic Jack (IRE)**[25] [1958] 5-10-7 91.. JoeCornwall(5)
(Michael Chapman) *prom tl wknd after 5th: p.u bef next* **100/1**

P **Running On Faith**[56] 5-10-12 0..................................(t) AdamPogson
(Garry Woodward) *hld up: bhd fr 4th: p.u bef 3 out* **125/1**

P00- **P** **Daizy (IRE)**[19] [2040] 4-10-12 87.. FelixDeGiles
(Hilary Parrott) *trckd ldrs tl p.u after 4th* **100/1**

4m 5.0s (10.10) **Going Correction** +0.775s/f (Soft) 16 Ran SP% **119.8**
Speed ratings (Par 105): **107,106,106,98,97 93,89,88,87,78 72,60,** , ,
toteswingers 1&2 £1.80, 1&3 £3.00, 2&3 £1.60 CSF £8.27 TOTE £4.20: £1.90, £1.20, £1.70; EX 9.80 Trifecta £26.20 Pool: £2100.96 - 59.93 winning units..
Owner Bloomfields **Bred** Haras Saint Pair Du Mont **Trained** Cowlinge, Suffolk

FOCUS
The official going was changed to soft, heavy in places on both the chase and hurdles courses before this race. Not a great deal of depth to this novice hurdle, and ordinary form.

2433 WILLIAM HILL THE JUMPS MICHAELMAS HURDLE (H'CAP) (10 hdls) 2m 4f 110y
2:10 (2:11) (Class 2) (0-150,142) 4-Y-0+
£15,640 (£4,620; £2,310; £1,155; £577; £290)

Form RPR
0/1- **1** **Hidden Identity (IRE)**[31] [1867] 7-10-11 127.......................... RichardJohnson 139+
(Tim Vaughan) *hld up: hdwy and mstke 3 out: led bef next: wnt lft and hit last: drvn out* **10/1**

213/ **2** *2 ¾* **Zuider Zee (GER)**[221] [5157] 6-11-3 133.. DenisO'Regan 140
(John Ferguson) *hld up: hdwy 7th: led briefly appr 2 out: sn rdn: styd on same pce flat* **11/4**[2]

040/ **3** *16* **Baile Anrai (IRE)**[277] [4112] 9-10-9 125.. HarrySkelton 116
(Dan Skelton) *chsd ldrs: rdn after 7th: wkd appr 2 out* **5/1**[3]

0/4- **4** *1 ¼* **Broadway Buffalo (IRE)**[17] [2080] 5-11-11 141.......................... TomScudamore 131
(David Pipe) *led and sn clr: rdn after 7th: hdd & wknd after 3 out* **9/4**[1]

0/0- **5** *17* **Vulcanite (IRE)**[24] [1969] 6-11-12 142.. APMcCoy 120
(Charlie Longsdon) *chsd clr ldr tl led after 3 out: sn rdn and hdd: wkng whn blnd next: j.lft last* **8/1**

U26- **6** *6* **Man Of Leisure**[25] [1954] 9-11-6 139..................................(t) RachaelGreen(3) 108
(Anthony Honeyball) *hld up: hdwy 7th: wknd after 3 out* **28/1**

412/ **P** **Salmanazar**[210] [5337] 5-11-3 133.. RobertThornton
(Alan King) *hld up: blnd 6th: hdwy next: mstke and slipped 3 out: sn wknd and p.u* **13/2**

5m 9.1s (10.10) **Going Correction** +0.775s/f (Soft) 7 Ran SP% **111.1**
Speed ratings (Par 109): **111,109,103,103,96 94,**
toteswingers 1&2 £10.70, 1&3 £6.40, 2&3 £5.30 CSF £36.24 TOTE £10.20: £4.90, £2.70; EX 38.80 Trifecta £411.30 Pool: £1922.73 - 3.50 winning units..
Owner Paul Bowtell **Bred** J P Kiely **Trained** Aberthin, Vale of Glamorgan

FOCUS
A valuable handicap hurdle, and although it wasn't the strongest line-up for the grade this is still decent form. The pace was sound and it proved quite a test in the ground. The winner is on the upgrade.

2434 WEATHERBYS AND NORTHAMPTON TOWN FOOTBALL CLUB NOVICES' LIMITED H'CAP CHASE (12 fncs) 2m 110y
2:40 (2:41) (Class 3) (0-140,125) 4-Y-0+ **£7,797** (£2,289; £1,144; £572)

Form RPR
3/0- **1** **Tempest River (IRE)**[179] [358] 7-11-5 125.......................... WayneHutchinson 130+
(Ben Case) *bhd and nt fluent: hdwy appr 2 out: rdn bef last: led flat: sn drvn clr* **9/2**[3]

541/ **2** *10* **Royal Guardsman (IRE)**[203] [5470] 6-11-4 124........ SamTwiston-Davies 121
(Ali Brewer) *led and sn clr: mstke 2nd: nt fluent next: stl 11 l clr 3 out: pushed along bef next: nt fluent last: wknd and hdd flat* **1/1**[1]

110- 3 2 1/4 **Alwaystheoptimist**[17] 2087 10-11-2 **125** KielanWoods(3) 123
(Phil Middleton) *chsd clr ldrs: rdn to go 2nd after 3 out: mstke next: 3 l down whn stmbld on landing last: sn wknd* **9/1**

/32- 4 46 **Able Deputy**[23] 1990 6-11-2 **122** (t) NickScholfield 90
(Kim Bailey) *chsd clr ldr: nt fluent 2nd: 11 l down and no imp whn blnd 3 out: sn wknd* **2/1**[2]

4m 25.3s (15.10) **Going Correction** +0.775s/f (Soft) 4 Ran SP% **111.5**
Speed ratings (Par 107): **95,90,89,67**
CSF £10.13 TOTE £6.10; EX 9.40 Trifecta £36.00 Pool: £1401.85 - 29.18 winning units..
Owner Fly Like The Wind Partnership **Bred** Eileen, Countess of Mount Charles **Trained** Edgcote, Northants

FOCUS
There was no shortage of incident in this fair novice handicap. The runners stood still for a long time after the tape was raised - not reflected in the official time for the race. Suspect form with the winner given a token rating to her mark.

2435 ENTER THE JUMPS FOR £2 MARES' H'CAP HURDLE (8 hdls) 2m 110y
3:10 (3:10) (Class 4) (0-120,114) 4-Y-0+ **£3,119** (£915; £457; £228)

Form RPR
/06- 1 **Buxom (IRE)**[11] 2190 6-11-2 **104** (v[1]) BrendanPowell 105
(Jamie Snowden) *trckd ldr tl led 5th: rdn appr last: all out* **3/1**[3]

1/6- 2 1 **Definite Ruby (IRE)**[163] 604 5-11-12 **114** DavidBass 114
(Nicky Henderson) *chsd ldrs: pushed along after 3rd: wnt 2nd after 3 out: rdn appr last: styd on u.p* **11/4**[2]

023/ 3 4 1/2 **Mistral Reine**[207] 5374 4-10-13 **101** LeightonAspell 99
(Lucy Wadham) *hld up: pushed along after 5th: hdwy u.p appr last: styd on same pce flat* **5/1**

/46- 4 4 1/2 **Lindsay's Dream**[17] 2084 7-10-12 **100** (p) DaveCrosse 92
(Zoe Davison) *hld up: hdwy 5th: rdn after 3 out: hit last: wknd flat* **16/1**

441/ 5 2 3/4 **Iron Butterfly**[14] 4968 4-11-4 **106** PaulMoloney 96
(James Eustace) *led to 5th: pushed along and swtchd lft whn mstke 2 out: wknd bef last* **15/8**[1]

4m 11.8s (16.90) **Going Correction** +0.775s/f (Soft)
WFA 4 from 5yo+ 7lb 5 Ran SP% **109.0**
Speed ratings (Par 105): **91,90,88,86,85**
CSF £11.43 TOTE £3.40: £2.80, £1.30; EX 13.80 Trifecta £57.80 Pool: £2365.88 - 30.65 winning units..
Owner Ward, Smith & Harper Families **Bred** Michael Lee **Trained** Lambourn, Berks

FOCUS
A weak handicap confined to mares and not a race to have much confidence in.

2436 HUNTINGDON RACECOURSE "JUNIOR" STANDARD OPEN NATIONAL HUNT FLAT RACE 1m 6f
3:40 (3:40) (Class 6) 3-Y-0 **£1,559** (£457; £228; £114)

Form RPR
1 **Two Jabs** 3-10-12 [0] LiamTreadwell 98+
(Mark Brisbourne) *mde all: shkn up and clr fnl 2f: eased towards fin: unchal* **25/1**

2 12 **Mad Jack Mytton (IRE)** 3-10-12 [0] APMcCoy 84
(Jonjo O'Neill) *trckd wnr: shkn up over 2f out: wknd over 1f out* **3/1**[2]

3 2 1/4 **Kibo** 3-10-12 [0] NickScholfield 81
(Kim Bailey) *hld up: hdwy over 5f out: rdn over 2f out: sn wknd* **9/2**[3]

4 2 **Ronnie Rockcake** 3-10-12 [0] DavidBass 79
(Ben Pauling) *chsd ldrs: rdn over 2f out: sn wknd* **22/1**

5 2 **Smart Motive** 3-10-12 [0] RobertThornton 76
(Alan King) *hld up: hdwy over 5f out: rdn and wknd over 2f out* **15/8**[1]

6 22 **Dorton (IRE)** 3-10-5 [0] MrDGannon(7) 50
(Phil Middleton) *mid-div: lost pl 1/2-way: wknd over 4f out* **33/1**

7 2 1/4 **Coffers** 3-10-12 [0] TomO'Brien 47
(Renee Robeson) *trckd ldrs: pushed along over 4f out: wknd over 3f out* **20/1**

8 shd **Kentford Heiress** 3-10-2 [0] WayneKavanagh(3) 40
(Seamus Mullins) *hld up: hdwy over 4f out: rdn and wknd 3f out* **10/1**

9 77 **Thyne Gale (IRE)** 3-10-5 [0] WayneHutchinson
(Graeme McPherson) *hld up: pushed along over 5f out: wknd over 3f out: bhd whn swvd lft over 2f out* **12/1**

10 1 **Invisible Touch** 3-10-5 [0] [1] LeightonAspell
(Martin Smith) *mid-div: pushed along 1/2-way: wknd 5f out* **33/1**

3m 28.5s (8.50) 10 Ran SP% **113.6**
toteswingers 1&2 £21.30, 1&3 £7.40, 2&3 £2.00 CSF £91.91 TOTE £15.60: £5.90, £1.20, £2.80; EX 78.90 Trifecta £540.80 Pool: £1050.12 - 1.45 winning units..
Owner Mark Brisbourne **Bred** Paramount Bloodstock **Trained** Great Ness, Shropshire

FOCUS
The very useful Chris Pea Green took this newcomers' bumper last season. The winner did it well.
T/Jkpt: £33,897.90. Pool: £143,230.59 - 3 winning units. T/Plt: £187.40. Pool: £69,682.51 - 271.43 winning units. T/Qpdt: £31.50. Pool: £4016.40 - 94.30 wining units. CR

LINGFIELD (L-H)
Tuesday, November 12

OFFICIAL GOING: Chase course - heavy (5.2); all-weather - standard
The scheduled hurdle races were abandoned due to waterlogging.
Wind: medium, against Weather: dry, bright spells

2437 AT THE RACES NOVICES' H'CAP CHASE (14 fncs) 2m 4f
1:30 (1:30) (Class 4) (0-110,110) 4-Y-0+ **£3,768** (£1,106; £553; £276)

Form RPR
3P3/ 1 **Richmond (FR)**[279] 4067 8-11-12 **110** AidanColeman 129+
(Venetia Williams) *j. accurately: w ldr tl led 5th: mde rest: readily c clr 3 out: wl in command next: eased flat* **11/8**[1]

636/ 2 12 **Farbreaga (IRE)**[197] 31 7-11-4 **105** JeremiahMcGrath(3) 106
(Jamie Poulton) *j.lft at times: chsd ldrs: mstke 8th: drvn after 11th: btn whn j.lft 3 out: plugged on to go 2nd flat: no ch w wnr* **7/2**[2]

453/ 3 2 1/4 **Cody Wyoming**[684] 3413 7-11-9 **107** NoelFehily 105
(Heather Main) *t.k.h: hld up in tch in rr: j.big 2nd: stdy prog 9th: trckd ldrs after 11th: chsd wnr and j.lft 3 out: no hdwy and btn next: lost 2nd fnl 100yds* **16/1**

236/ 4 4 **Itoldyou (IRE)**[198] 5 7-11-2 **100** TomCannon 94
(Linda Jewell) *led tl 5th: chsd wnr after: drvn after 11th: 4th and btn whn mstke next: plugged on* **6/1**[3]

/14- 5 49 **Bit Of A Clown (IRE)**[20] 2017 7-10-9 **100** MrJSole(7) 44
(Nick Gifford) *chsd ldrs on outer: lost pl 7th: mstke next: blnd and rdn 9th: sn toiling: t.o 11th* **8/1**

6/P- 6 1/2 **Barenger (IRE)**[192] 121 6-11-11 **109** JackDoyle 53
(Ali Brewer) *hld up wl in tch: mstke 1st: hdwy to chse ldrs 8th: rdn and btn after 11th: wknd on long run to next: t.o bef 2 out: eased flat* **16/1**

6/0- 7 23 **Hand On Bach (IRE)**[10] 2210 5-11-0 **101** (p) GavinSheehan(3) 22
(Warren Greatrex) *wl in tch in midfield: j.lft 1st: struggling 8th: sn lost tch: t.o 11th* **10/1**

03/- P **Lord Kennedy (IRE)**[212] 5319 8-11-4 **102** PaddyBrennan
(Alex Hales) *t.k.h: wl in tch in midfield: trckd ldrs after 5th: rdn and wknd on long run after 11th: t.o whn p.u 3 out* **14/1**

5m 30.2s (19.80) **Going Correction** +1.025s/f (Soft) 8 Ran SP% **117.2**
Speed ratings (Par 105): **101,96,95,93,74 73,64,**
toteswingers 1&2 £1.90, 1&3 £3.10, 2&3 £9.20 CSF £7.32 CT £52.55 TOTE £2.30: £1.10, £1.70, £3.50; EX 5.60 Trifecta £41.60 Pool: £1634.15 - 29.39 winning units..
Owner Hills Of Ledbury (Aga) **Bred** Mme Arlette Guyennot **Trained** Kings Caple, H'fords

FOCUS
A modest handicap that was won in dominant fashion. This rates a step up from the winner.

2438 RACINGPROFITSGUIDES.COM H'CAP CHASE (14 fncs) 2m 4f
2:00 (2:00) (Class 3) (0-130,129) 4-Y-0+ **£6,498** (£1,908; £954; £477)

Form RPR
/41- 1 **Toby Lerone (IRE)**[4] 2350 6-11-3 120 7ex IanPopham 130+
(Dan Skelton) *j.rt: mde all: rdn bef 2 out: styd on gamely u.p to forge ahd flat* **5/4**[1]

P/P- 2 1 3/4 **Howard's Legacy (IRE)**[17] 2072 7-11-12 129 AidanColeman 136
(Venetia Williams) *hld up wl in tch in last pair: mstke 7th: trcking ldrs and mstke 11th: chsd wnr bef 3 out: pressing wnr and rdn 2 out: styd on same pce u.p flat* **8/1**

124- 3 8 **Seven Woods (IRE)**[16] 2108 7-11-10 127 (t) PaddyBrennan 128
(Tom George) *nt fluent and nvr travelling wl: chsd ldr: j.big 1st: swtchd lft after 3rd: mstke and dropped to last 7th: hit next and rdn: stl cl 4th bef 3 out: 3rd and btn 2 out: mstke last: plugged on same pce flat* **11/4**[2]

F/2- 4 5 **De Blacksmith (IRE)**[22] 2005 5-11-6 123 JamieMoore 119
(Gary Moore) *chsd ldng pair: wnt 2nd 7th tl bef 3 out: rdn but stl cl 3rd 3 out: btn next: mstke last: wknd flat* **7/2**[3]

441/ P **Red Anchor (IRE)**[207] 5380 9-9-9 105 oh7 ow2 ConorShoemark(7)
(Linda Jewell) *in tch in last pair: gd jump and hdwy to chse ldrs 7th: blnd 10th: drvn next: sn dropped out and t.o whn p.u 3 out* **16/1**

5m 26.65s (16.25) **Going Correction** +1.025s/f (Soft) 5 Ran SP% **110.3**
Speed ratings (Par 107): **108,107,104,102,**
CSF £10.72 TOTE £2.40: £1.60, £2.40; EX 12.80 Trifecta £33.60 Pool: £1926.15 - 42.95 winning units..
Owner Regan, Dunning, Pettey & Morgan **Bred** M J Halligan **Trained** Alcester, Warwicks

FOCUS
The front pair drew clear and the form looks sound for the level. The winner ran to a similar mark as at Southwell.

2439 LINGFIELD STANDARD OPEN NATIONAL HUNT FLAT RACE 1m 7f 169y
2:30 (2:30) (Class 6) 4-6-Y-0 **£1,642** (£478; £239)

Form RPR
04/ 1 **Prouts Pub (IRE)**[203] 5483 4-11-0 [0] ColinBolger 101
(Pat Phelan) *in tch in last pair: hdwy to chse ldr 4f out: drvn and ev ch over 1f out: drvn to ld fnl 150yds: r.o wl* **10/1**

\- 2 1 **Rendezvous Peak** 4-10-9 [0] [1] MattCrawley(5) 100
(Lucy Wadham) *hld up in tch in last: wnt 4th 3f out: rdn and unable qck 2f out: hdwy and forced to switch rt 1f out: styd on wl to go 2nd fnl 50yds* **6/1**[3]

3/2- 3 3/4 **Masquerade (IRE)**[19] 2053 4-11-0 [0] NoelFehily 100
(Warren Greatrex) *t.k.h: chsd ldr tl led 6f out: rdn and qcknd over 2f out: drvn and hrd pressed over 1f out: hdd fnl 150yds: one pce after* **10/11**[1]

6/6- 4 1/2 **Vodka 'n Tonic (IRE)**[186] 207 4-11-0 [0] AndrewTinkler 99
(Nicky Henderson) *t.k.h: chsd ldng pair: rdn and effrt on inner wl over 1f out: styd on same pce fnl f* **2/1**[2]

5 12 **Dark Mix** 5-10-4 [0] PaddyBradley(10) 87
(Pat Phelan) *led and set stdy gallop: hdd and rdn 6f out: dropped to rr and btn 3f out: hit rail and wknd over 2f out* **33/1**

3m 38.8s (0.80) 5 Ran SP% **112.0**
CSF £62.86 TOTE £8.00: £4.90, £4.40; EX 46.80 Trifecta £151.10 Pool: £2179.60 - 10.81 winning units..
Owner Edward Gleeson **Bred** Edward Gleeson **Trained** Epsom, Surrey
■ Sirrah Star was withdrawn. Price at time of withdrawal 14-1. Rule 4 applies to all bets - deduction 5p in the pound.

FOCUS
These Polytrack bumpers are never races to take much notice of going forward. They went a steady gallop and it produced a surprise result. The form is given a token rating around the third and fourth.

2440 WORLD HORSE WELFARE H'CAP CHASE (12 fncs) 2m
3:00 (3:00) (Class 4) (0-120,118) 4-Y-0+ **£3,768** (£1,106; £553; £276)

Form RPR
441- 1 **Be All Man (IRE)**[19] 2042 6-11-11 **117** JamieMoore 125+
(Gary Moore) *chsd ldrs: wnt 2nd 7th tl led bef 3 out: mstke 3 out: kpt on wl and a holding rival flat: rdn out* **3/1**[2]

P55- 2 1 1/4 **Takeroc (FR)**[17] 2078 10-11-8 **117** (t) JamesBest(3) 122
(Sophie Leech) *hld up in tch in rr: cl 4th and mstke 9th: chsd wnr 2 out: kpt on u.p flat but a hld* **12/1**

212- 3 16 **Chestnut Ben (IRE)**[42] 1710 8-11-1 **107** (t) AndrewThornton 96
(Gary Brown) *chsd ldrs on outer: mstke 6th: ev ch 9th: rdn bef next: wknd 2 out: battling for modest 3rd flat: wnt 3rd last strides* **7/2**[3]

304/ 4 hd **Mam Ratagan**[943] 5305 12-11-9 **115** DominicElsworth 104
(Heather Main) *led tl hdd bef 3 out: no ex and btn 2 out: wl hld and battling for modest 3rd flat: lost 3rd last strides* **16/1**

1/3- 5 17 **Topaze Collonges (FR)**[17] 2078 6-11-3 **109** (b) NoelFehily 81
(Charlie Longsdon) *chsd ldr tl dropped to last and j. awkwardly 7th: detached and nvr gng after: wknd 3 out: wl hld whn j.lft and mstke last* **11/10**[1]

4m 23.3s (15.50) **Going Correction** +1.025s/f (Soft) 5 Ran SP% **108.4**
Speed ratings (Par 105): **102,101,93,93,84**
CSF £27.92 TOTE £3.60: £1.10, £5.60; EX 27.40 Trifecta £97.30 Pool: £1759.03 - 13.55 winning units..
Owner A Head, R Lockwood & M Burne **Bred** Howard Barton Stud **Trained** Lower Beeding, W Sussex

The Form Book Jumps, Raceform Ltd, Compton, RG20 6NL.

FOCUS
Modest handicap chase form, with the favourite failing to perform, and the first two drew clear. The winner built on his recent victory.

2441 YOUR EXPERT GUIDE TO LINGFIELD LINGFIELDRACECOURSETIPS.CO.UK H'CAP CHASE (14 fncs) 2m 4f
3:30 (3:32) (Class 5) (0-95,92) 4-Y-0+ **£2,258** (£658; £329)

Form RPR
3P5/ **1** **Seventh Hussar**[207] [5380] 7-11-2 **85** JoshuaMoore[(3)] 98+
(Alison Batchelor) *hld up in last pair: clsd to press ldrs after 9th: drew clr w rival and travelling best after 11th: led bef 3 out: clr and in command 2 out: pushed out* **14/1**
2U4/ **2** *13* **Goring Two (IRE)**[200] [5552] 8-11-8 **88** (p) AndrewThornton 88
(Anna Newton-Smith) *chsd ldrs: wnt 2nd after 2nd tl bef 9th: 5th and wl outpcd 11th: rallied to chse clr ldng pair bef 3 out: plugged on to go 2nd flat: no ch w wnr* **6/1**
4/1- **3** *3 ½* **Somerby (IRE)**[17] [2082] 10-11-10 **90** (t) NoelFehily 87
(Richenda Ford) *chsd ldr tl after 2nd: dropped to rr and rdn after 5th: nvr travelling after: struggling u.p after 9th: wnt modest 4th bef 3 out: plugged on to snatch 3rd cl home: no ch w wnr* **2/1**[1]
602- **4** *½* **Rusty Nail (IRE)**[49] [1644] 8-10-6 **72** TomCannon 69
(James Frost) *in tch in midfield: clsd to chse ldr after 9th: led 11th: and sn drew clr w wnr: hdd and rdn bef 3 out: sn btn and wknd 2 out: lost 2 pls flat* **4/1**[2]
243/ **5** *8* **Tchang Goon (FR)**[215] [5246] 9-9-10 **67** (p) NicodeBoinville[(5)] 56
(Zoe Davison) *in tch in midfield: mstke 3rd: rdn and struggling after 9th: wknd wl bef 3 out* **6/1**
45P- **P** **She's Humble (IRE)**[22] [2003] 11-10-2 **68** (p) GerardTumelty
(Linda Jewell) *reluctant to line up: bhd: hdwy to chse ldrs after 5th: dropping herself out and j. slowly next: lost tch 8th: t.o whn p.u 11th* **33/1**
PP2/ **P** **According To Them (IRE)**[610] [4813] 9-10-6 **72** JamieMoore
(Daniel Steele) *chsd ldrs: rdn after 10th: 3rd and wknd u.p sn after 11th: last and t.o next: p.u last* **16/1**
0P0- **F** **Officially Modern (IRE)**[86] [1306] 6-11-5 **92** ConorShoemark[(7)]
(Fergal O'Brien) *t.k.h: led: stmbld bdly on landing 7th: hdd 11th: sn rdn and wknd: t.o 6th whn fell 2 out: winded* **5/1**[3]

5m 33.2s (22.80) **Going Correction** +1.025s/f (Soft) **8** Ran SP% **114.1**
Speed ratings (Par 103): **95,89,88,88,85** , ,
toteswingers 1&2 £5.90, 1&3 £3.50, 2&3 £5.40 CSF £93.67 CT £241.93 TOTE £12.90: £1.90, £2.70, £1.10; EX 83.60 Trifecta £460.80 Pool: £1167.50 - 1.90 winning units..
Owner Mrs Alison Batchelor **Bred** M E R Allsopp **Trained** Petworth, W Sussex

FOCUS
A moderate handicap chase. The form is rated around the first two.

2442 SIS MARES' INTERMEDIATE OPEN NATIONAL HUNT FLAT RACE 1m 7f 169y
4:05 (4:05) (Class 6) 4-6-Y-0 **£1,642** (£478; £239)

Form RPR
1- **1** **Hannah's Princess (IRE)**[73] [1472] 4-11-5 0 NoelFehily 106+
(Warren Greatrex) *hld up in tch in rr: clsd to trck ldrs over 2f out: rdn and qcknd to ld over 1f out: r.o wl: readily* **10/11**[1]
0- **2** *4* **Playhara (IRE)**[178] [372] 4-10-12 0 AndrewTinkler 92
(Nicky Henderson) *chsd ldrs: hdwy to press ldr 3f out: rdn and ev ch ent fnl 2f: unable qck w wnr over 1f out: one pce fnl f* **11/4**[2]
0- **3** *1* **The Selector**[139] [842] 4-10-12 0 TomCannon 91
(Chris Gordon) *mde most in narrow ld: rdn over 2f out: hdd and drvn over 1f out: styd on same pce after* **50/1**
36- **4** *2 ¾* **Georgea (IRE)**[20] [2022] 4-10-9 0 [1] JoshuaMoore[(3)] 88
(Gary Moore) *t.k.h: hld up in tch in last trio: clsd and rdn ent fnl 2f: unable qck and hung rt bnd wl over 1f out: kpt on but no threat to ldrs after* **9/2**[3]
5 *3 ½* **Greatday Allweek (IRE)** 4-10-5 0 KevinJones[(7)] 85
(Seamus Mullins) *hld up in tch in last trio: hdwy on outer over 3f out: wd bnd and lost pl bnd wl over 1f out: 5th and wl hld after: wknd fnl f* **16/1**
0/ **6** *5* **Do Be Dashing**[202] [5511] 5-10-7 0 KillianMoore[(5)] 80
(Graeme McPherson) *chsd ldrs: shuffled bk to rr and swtchd rt over 2f out: sn rdn and unable qck: wknd over 1f out* **25/1**
0/ **7** *6* **Just Satisfaction**[328] [3147] 4-10-12 0 GerardTumelty 74
(Nick Lampard) *w ldr tl rdn and lost pl wl over 2f out: bhd over 1f out* **25/1**

3m 35.0s (-3.00) **7** Ran SP% **112.8**
toteswingers 1&2 £1.10, 1&3 £8.20, 2&3 £17.20 CSF £3.42 TOTE £1.60: £1.10, £1.70; EX 4.10 Trifecta £56.10 Pool: £3754.51 - 50.13 winning units..
Owner Warren Greatrex **Bred** Gary Adams **Trained** Upper Lambourn, Berks

FOCUS
An uncompetitive bumper. A step forward from the winner with the fourth and sixth seting the level.
T/Plt: £224.00. Pool: £65,494.40 - 213.35 wining units. T/Qpdt: £121.80. Pool: £3670.91 - 22.30 winning units. SP

[2168] SEDGEFIELD (L-H)
Tuesday, November 12

OFFICIAL GOING: Chase course - soft (good to soft in places; 6.0); hurdle course - good to soft (soft in places; 6.9)
Wind: Fresh behind Weather: Sunny

2443 BRITISH STALLION STUDS E B F "NATIONAL HUNT" NOVICES' HURDLE (QUALIFIER) (8 hdls) 2m 1f
12:50 (12:50) (Class 4) 4-6-Y-0 **£3,443** (£1,011; £505; £252)

Form RPR
122- **1** **Another Hero (IRE)**[31] [1866] 4-11-8 127 RichieMcLernon 128+
(Jonjo O'Neill) *hld up: tk clsr order after 3rd: upsides 3 out: led 2 out: sn rdn: kpt on* **Evs**[1]
1/6- **2** *4 ½* **Salto Chisco (IRE)**[17] [2075] 5-10-12 0 JasonMaguire 115+
(Donald McCain) *in tch: trckd ldr after 2nd: led 3 out: hit 2 out and hdd: stl ev ch whn nt fluent last: drvn and one pce: eased towards fin* **Evs**[1]
040- **3** *35* **Dunkirk's First (IRE)**[10] [2217] 5-10-12 0 WilsonRenwick 78
(Rose Dobbin) *hld up: nvr threatened: wnt remote 3rd bef 2 out: wnt lft 2 out* **100/1**[3]
0- **4** *27* **Not Another Monday (IRE)**[144] [790] 5-10-12 0 BarryKeniry 51
(George Moore) *led: hdd 3 out: wknd* **25/1**[2]
00- **5** *34* **Lordenshaws (IRE)**[164] [584] 6-10-12 0 KennyJohnson 17
(Robert Johnson) *hld up: a bhd* **150/1**
/P0- **U** **Northern Warrior**[170] [494] 5-10-12 0 HenryBrooke
(Hugh Burns) *trckd ldr: lost pl qckly after 3rd and sn in rr: blnd and uns rdr 3 out* **100/1**[3]

4m 11.8s (4.90) **Going Correction** +0.325s/f (Yiel) **6** Ran SP% **106.5**
Speed ratings: **101,98,82,69,53**
toteswingers 1&2 £1.10, 1&3 £4.60, 2&3 £2.40 CSF £2.08 TOTE £2.00: £1.10, £1.10; EX 2.10 Trifecta £8.00 Pool: £1335.78 - 125.09 winning units..
Owner John P McManus **Bred** Miss Noreen Hayes **Trained** Cheltenham, Gloucs

FOCUS
Divided bends moved on to fresher ground, hurdles on outside. After winning the first race Richie McLernon described the conditions as "a little bit dead, but nice ground." The opener was a match and predictably the two principals pulled well clear. The pace was steady. The winner is rated to his mark.

2444 CIU NOVICES' HURDLE (PAXTONS HURDLE SERIES QUALIFIER) (10 hdls) 2m 4f
1:20 (1:20) (Class 4) 4-Y-0+ **£3,119** (£915; £457; £228)

Form RPR
421/ **1** **Ivan Boru (IRE)**[197] [22] 5-11-5 120 JamesReveley 124+
(Keith Reveley) *led: hdd 3rd: trckd ldr: led again between last 2: wnt lft last: hung rt u.p run-in: jinked bdly rt and nrly collided w rail 50yds out: stened out nr fin* **11/4**[2]
3- **2** *1 ¾* **Kodicil (IRE)**[28] [1754] 5-10-12 0 PeterBuchanan 110
(Tim Walford) *trckd ldr: led after 3 out: rdn whn jnd next: hdd between last 2: one pce: a hld run-in despite wayward wnr* **5/1**[3]
2/0- **3** *25* **Halo Moon**[26] [1937] 5-10-12 0 JasonMaguire 92
(Donald McCain) *trckd ldr: led 3rd: hdd after 3 out: wknd bef next* **11/10**[1]
/06- **4** *19* **Omid**[19] [2030] 5-10-12 0 HenryBrooke 66
(Evelyn Slack) *hld up: a bhd* **100/1**
5 *27* **Clues And Arrows (IRE)**[198] 5-10-12 0 RichieMcLernon 39
(Jonjo O'Neill) *in tch: rdn after 3 out: sn wknd* **6/1**
05P/ **P** **Rosquero (FR)**[583] [5305] 8-10-12 88 KennyJohnson
(Robert Johnson) *hld up: a bhd: p.u bef 2 out* **150/1**
0/6- **F** **Fairweather Friend**[26] [1935] 4-10-5 0 SeanQuinlan
(Jennie Candlish) *hld up: fell 4th* **20/1**
U **Allez Cool (IRE)** 4-10-5 0 JohnDawson[(7)]
(John Wade) *midfield: stmbld and uns rdr 2nd* **40/1**

5m 1.2s (8.50) **Going Correction** +0.325s/f (Yiel)
WFA 4 from 5yo+ 8lb **8** Ran SP% **114.1**
Speed ratings (Par 105): **96,95,85,77,66** , ,
toteswingers 1&2 £2.80, 1&3 £1.50, 2&3 £2.30 CSF £16.32 TOTE £2.40: £1.10, £1.80, £1.10; EX 10.20 Trifecta £17.20 Pool: £1970.29 - 85.89 winning units..
Owner Thwaites Furness & Zetland **Bred** Miss Ann Twomey **Trained** Lingdale, Redcar & Cleveland

FOCUS
The pace was steady in this fair novices' hurdle, in which the winner nearly threw it away on the run-in. The winner is on the upgrade and there's probably more to come.

2445 NEWCASTLE FLOORING H'CAP CHASE (16 fncs) 2m 4f
1:50 (1:50) (Class 5) (0-100,99) 4-Y-0+ **£2,209** (£648; £324; £162)

Form RPR
/3P- **1** **Pistol Basc (FR)**[86] [1300] 9-10-0 **78** [1] TonyKelly[(5)] 92+
(Rebecca Menzies) *trckd ldr: pressed ldr after 9th: led 5 out: clr 3 out: rdn between last 2: kpt on* **7/2**[1]
130/ **2** *5* **Sambelucky (IRE)**[546] [280] 8-10-7 **80** JamesReveley 88
(Keith Reveley) *midfield: wnt 2nd 4 out: rdn bef 3 out: one pce and nvr threatened wnr* **7/2**[1]
/54- **3** *5* **Bocamix (FR)**[12] [2173] 7-11-9 **99** JohnKington[(3)] 102
(Andrew Crook) *hld up: tk clsr order 1/2-way: disp 2nd after 4 out tl wknd appr last* **15/2**[3]
30P- **4** *3* **Oh Right (IRE)**[4] [2333] 9-10-4 **77** (p) LucyAlexander 77
(Dianne Sayer) *hld up: reminders after 7th: wnt poor 4th between last 2: nvr threatened* **4/1**[2]
/00- **5** *4* **Fozy Moss**[13] [2155] 7-9-7 **73** oh2 CallumBewley[(7)] 69
(Stuart Coltherd) *hld up: rdn after 5 out: nvr threatened* **10/1**
215- **6** *8* **Chicago Outfit (IRE)**[19] [2036] 8-11-11 **98** (b[1]) BrianHughes 88
(John Wade) *w ldr: slow 8th and lost pl: hit 10th: sn dropped to rr: no threat after* **7/2**[1]
SP5/ **P** **Ravensbill (IRE)**[356] [2553] 11-10-0 **73** oh12 (t) BrianHarding
(William Amos) *hld up: hmpd 1st: sn bhd: p.u bef 9th* **66/1**
50P- **P** **Over And Above (IRE)**[19] [2047] 7-10-0 **73** oh8 (b[1]) RichieMcGrath
(Henry Hogarth) *led narrowly: hdd 5 out: wknd after 4 out: p.u bef last* **20/1**

4m 59.5s (-3.50) **Going Correction** -0.225s/f (Good) **8** Ran SP% **113.8**
Speed ratings (Par 103): **98,96,94,92,91 88**, ,
toteswingers 1&2 £3.80, 1&3 £5.50, 2&3 £3.20 CSF £16.55 CT £84.38 TOTE £4.10: £1.10, £1.60, £2.30; EX 22.00 Trifecta £151.60 Pool: £2337.10 - 11.55 winning units..
Owner Panther Racing Ltd **Bred** Sebastien & Alain Dufrancatel **Trained** Stearsby, N Yorks
■ Rebecca Menzies' first winner under rules.

FOCUS
Nothing more than an ordinary handicap chase, but the time was fair and the form makes sense.

2446 JOHN SMITH'S NOVICES' LIMITED H'CAP CHASE (16 fncs) 2m 4f
2:20 (2:20) (Class 3) (0-125,124) 4-Y-0+ **£6,342** (£1,934; £1,010; £548)

Form RPR
/02- **1** **Coverholder (IRE)**[19] [2032] 6-10-6 **116** JonathanEngland[(5)] 131+
(Sue Smith) *trckd ldr: led 5 out: rdn clr after 3 out: eased nr fin* **3/1**[2]
2P2- **2** *8* **Atlanta Falcon (IRE)**[37] [1787] 8-11-4 **123** (t) JasonMaguire 127
(Donald McCain) *led narrowly: hdd 5 out: rdn bef 3 out: sn one pce and no ch w wnr* **10/3**[3]
U0F- **3** *8* **Sun Cloud (IRE)**[13] [2157] 6-10-11 **116** BrianHughes 112
(Malcolm Jefferson) *hld up: hit 1st: nt fluent 9th: nvr threatened: lft poor 3rd last* **16/1**
0/0- **4** *17* **Kilmacowen (IRE)**[25] [1956] 7-11-5 **124** AlainCawley 103
(Fergal O'Brien) *trckd ldr: sltly hmpd 6th and lost pl: mstke 9th: sn struggling* **8/1**
F/2- **F** **Rocking Blues (FR)**[19] [2034] 8-10-7 **112** WilsonRenwick 114
(Rose Dobbin) *hld up in tch: tk clsr order after 7th: upsides 9th: rdn and one pce in 3rd after 3 out: fell last* **11/2**
03/- **P** **Seedsman**[213] [5281] 6-11-5 **124** MarkGrant
(Charles Egerton) *in tch: wnt prom after 4th: slow 6th: lost pl 5 out: wknd after 3 out: p.u bef last* **5/2**[1]

(-3.00) **Going Correction** -0.225s/f (Good) **6** Ran SP% **109.0**
Speed ratings (Par 107): **97,93,90,83,**
toteswingers 1&2 £2.60, 1&3 £8.20, 2&3 £8.80 CSF £12.82 TOTE £4.10: £2.10, £2.00; EX 10.50 Trifecta £54.50 Pool: £2422.95 - 33.30 winning units..
Owner Mrs S Smith **Bred** T Duggan And P McCarthy **Trained** High Eldwick, W Yorks

FOCUS
An interesting limited novices' handicap, won by one of the three chasing newcomers. The winner stepped up on his hurdles form.

2447 QUICKSILVERSLOTS GET UP TO £200 FREEPLAY H'CAP HURDLE (10 hdls) 2m 4f

2:50 (2:50) (Class 4) (0-120,117) 4-Y-0+ **£3,119** (£915; £457; £228)

Form RPR
325- **1** **Waltz Darling (IRE)**[25] 1289 5-11-5 **110**........................ JamesReveley 121+
(Keith Reveley) *hld up in rr: stdy hdwy fr bef 3 out: led after 2 out: pushed along to assert: rdn out run-in* **10/1**
5/2- **2** *4* **Sam Lord**[12] 2169 9-10-11 **102**........................ DannyCook 106
(James Moffatt) *trckd ldr: led 3rd: hdd after 2 out: nt fluent last: kpt on but a hld by wnr* **4/1**[2]
45P/ **3** *1 1/4* **Embsay Crag**[28] 27 7-11-0 **105**........................ RichieMcGrath 109+
(Philip Kirby) *trckd ldrs: rdn 2 out: kpt on* **7/2**[1]
P/3- **4** *6* **One For Harry (IRE)**[19] 2032 5-11-12 **117**........................ BrianHarding 116
(Nicky Richards) *nt a fluent: hld up: hdwy appr 3 out: rdn to chse ldrs bef 2 out: wknd last* **7/2**[1]
/41- **5** *27* **Big Sound**[142] 804 6-10-11 **102**........................ PeterBuchanan 72
(Tim Walford) *in tch: rdn 3 out: wknd bef 2 out* **8/1**
220/ **6** *4 1/2* **Mary Milan (IRE)**[227] 5009 6-11-1 **106**........................ BrianHughes 71
(Malcolm Jefferson) *midfield: wknd bef 3 out* **13/2**[3]
05F- **7** *1 1/4* **Total Assets**[42] 1717 5-10-8 **102**........................ JohnKington(3) 66
(Simon Waugh) *trckd ldrs: wknd after 3 out* **100/1**
150- **8** *27* **Surf And Turf (IRE)**[21] 2013 7-11-7 **112**..................(p) RichieMcLernon 49
(Jonjo O'Neill) *in tch: wknd after 3 out* **20/1**
4/U- **9** *1 1/2* **Call It On (IRE)**[185] 224 7-11-9 **117**........................ KyleJames(3) 53
(Philip Kirby) *led: hdd 3rd: trckd ldr: wknd appr 3 out* **25/1**
0P/- **10** *2* **Another Dimension (IRE)**[630] 4439 7-10-9 **100**.............. HenryBrooke 34
(Rose Dobbin) *hld up: a towards rr* **33/1**
22P/ **P** **Caerlaverock (IRE)**[738] 2322 8-10-9 **110**........................ ShaunDobbin(10)
(Rose Dobbin) *hld up: struggling fr 1/2-way: p.u bef last* **25/1**

4m 56.5s (3.80) **Going Correction** +0.325s/f (Yiel) **11 Ran SP% 114.4**
Speed ratings (Par 105): **105,103,102,100,89 87,87,76,76,75**
toteswingers 1&2 £7.50, 1&3 £6.80, 2&3 £4.20 CSF £46.40 CT £169.78 TOTE £9.00: £2.60, £2.20, £2.10; EX 39.80 Trifecta £319.90 Pool: £2329.92 - 5.46 winning units..
Owner Mrs M B Thwaites & M E Foxton **Bred** Ms Natalie Cleary **Trained** Lingdale, Redcar & Cleveland

FOCUS
They went a steady pace in this fair handicap hurdle. The winner is on the upgrade and the type to win more races.

2448 #SPIRIT OF TEESSIDE H'CAP CHASE (16 fncs) 2m 4f

3:20 (3:20) (Class 3) (0-140,135) 4-Y-0+
£6,256 (£1,848; £924; £462; £231; £116)

Form RPR
00/- **1** **Silver Roque (FR)**[201] 5523 7-11-9 **132**..................(t) TimmyMurphy 148+
(Fergal O'Brien) *hld up: stdy hdwy after 9th: trckd ldr gng wl 4 out: led 2 out: sn clr: easily* **3/1**[1]
1/4- **2** *16* **Tahiti Pearl (IRE)**[194] 77 9-10-13 **122**........................ RyanMania 118
(Sue Smith) *trckd ldrs: led 5 out: rdn whn hdd 2 out: sn no ch w wnr* **8/1**
3/4- **3** *10* **Granville Island (IRE)**[27] 1921 6-10-13 **122**........................ SeanQuinlan 111
(Jennie Candlish) *hld up: tk clsr order after 1/2-way: wnt 3rd 4 out: rdn bef 2 out: sn btn* **4/1**[2]
/3P- **4** *12* **Sublime Talent (IRE)**[58] 411 7-10-9 **118**..................(t) AdamWedge 95
(Evan Williams) *hld up: mstke 7th: wnt poor 4th bef 3 out: nvr threatened* **20/1**
/20- **5** *11* **Stagecoach Pearl**[16] 2101 9-11-7 **135**........................ JonathanEngland(5) 101
(Sue Smith) *led: clr 6th tl 9th: hdd 5 out: sn btn* **11/1**
/11- **6** *3* **Riskier**[39] 1753 8-11-4 **127**........................ BrianHughes 87
(John Wade) *trckd ldr: hit 5 out: sn wknd* **9/2**[3]
200- **P** **Finger Onthe Pulse (IRE)**[24] 1969 12-11-6 **129**........(t) RichieMcLernon
(Jonjo O'Neill) *in tch: wknd after 11th: t.o whn p.u bef 2 out* **11/1**
300/ **P** **Divers (FR)**[215] 5251 9-11-7 **130**........................ JasonMaguire
(Donald McCain) *hld up: nt fluent 3rd and reminder: a bhd: t.o whn p.u bef 2 out* **9/2**[3]

4m 53.9s (-9.10) **Going Correction** -0.225s/f (Good) **8 Ran SP% 113.9**
Speed ratings (Par 107): **109,102,98,93,89 88, ,**
toteswingers 1&2 £7.50, 1&3 £3.60, 2&3 £4.50 CSF £26.57 CT £95.93 TOTE £4.80: £1.30, £2.80, £1.70; EX 32.40 Trifecta £134.00 Pool: £2186.75 - 12.23 winning units..
Owner Lord Vestey **Bred** Mme Genevieve Mongin **Trained** Coln St. Dennis, Gloucs

FOCUS
The gallop was strong from the outset and they finished well strung out. The easy winner took a big step forward.

2449 QUICKSILVERSLOTS PLAY £500 ROULETTE H'CAP HURDLE (8 hdls) 2m 1f

3:50 (3:50) (Class 5) (0-100,100) 4-Y-0+ **£1,949** (£572; £286; £143)

Form RPR
34P/ **1** **Amir Pasha (UAE)**[24] 4161 8-11-2 **90**..................(v) JasonMaguire 96
(Micky Hammond) *trckd ldr: led narrowly 2 out: sn drvn: kpt on wl: asserted nr fin* **14/1**
1/0- **2** *1 1/4* **Broctune Papa Gio**[25] 605 6-11-9 **97**........................ JamesReveley 103+
(Keith Reveley) *trckd ldrs: rdn 2 out: upsides whn hit last: stl chalng strly 100yds out: hld nr fin* **3/1**[2]
0/4- **3** *6* **Lysino (GER)**[12] 2169 4-11-11 **99**........................ BrianHarding 97
(Chris Grant) *midfield: hdwy to chse ldrs bef 2 out: one pce: wnt 3rd nr fin* **6/1**
4/0- **4** *1/2* **Queen Of Epirus**[89] 932 5-11-3 **91**........................ HarryHaynes 89
(Brian Rothwell) *led narrowly: hdd 2 out: stl ev ch last: wknd fnl 100yds: lost 3rd nr fin* **40/1**
U31- **5** *3/4* **Dynamic Drive (IRE)**[12] 2169 6-10-10 **91**............(t) StephenMulqueen(7) 90+
(Maurice Barnes) *midfield: hdwy to trck ldrs appr 2 out: sn rdn: wknd fnl 100yds* **5/2**[1]
562- **6** *1 3/4* **Kayalar (IRE)**[58] 1487 5-11-5 **100**........................ ConorRing(7) 95
(Evan Williams) *in tch: rdn bef 2 out: wknd last* **5/1**[3]
0P6/ **7** *9* **Freedom Flying**[1022] 3728 10-10-0 **74**..................(t) RichieMcGrath 60
(Lee James) *midfield: wknd bef 2 out* **40/1**
5/0- **8** *11* **Kathlatino**[12] 2169 6-10-5 **84**........................ JoeColliver(5) 59
(Micky Hammond) *hld up: hit 3 out: nvr threatened* **40/1**
9 *9* **Monthly Medal**[18] 810 10-11-5 **93**..................(t) BarryKeniry 59
(Wilf Storey) *hld up: hit 3 out: nvr threatened* **33/1**
4/0- **10** *8* **Operateur (IRE)**[12] 2169 5-10-11 **85**........................ DougieCostello 43
(Ben Haslam) *hld up on outside: nvr threatened* **16/1**
/10- **11** *19* **Iktiview**[12] 2169 5-11-3 **94**..................(p) KyleJames(3) 33
(Philip Kirby) *midfield: lost pl after 4th: sn struggling: t.o* **16/1**
F60- **F** **Tim's Approach (IRE)**[10] 2217 8-9-9 **74** oh8..................(t) TonyKelly(5)
(William Young Jnr) *w ldr: fell 2nd* **100/1**
60P- **P** **Bertielicious**[9] 2243 5-10-0 **74** oh12..................(p) HenryBrooke
(Jonathan Haynes) *a in rr: p.u bef 2 out* **100/1**
655- **P** **Aw Ripe China (IRE)**[24] 1975 5-11-6 **97**........................ JohnKington(3)
(Simon Waugh) *trckd ldrs: wknd bef 3 out: p.u bef 2 out; dead* **25/1**

4m 16.3s (9.40) **Going Correction** +0.325s/f (Yiel) **14 Ran SP% 119.0**
Speed ratings (Par 103): **90,89,86,86,86 85,80,75,71,67 58, , ,**
toteswingers 1&2 £8.80, 1&3 £15.80, 2&3 £5.10 CSF £54.55 CT £289.68 TOTE £10.20: £4.10, £1.10, £2.80; EX 51.00 Trifecta £649.20 Pool: £2438.42 - 2.81 winning units..
Owner M H O G **Bred** Darley **Trained** Middleham Moor, N Yorks

FOCUS
A modest handicap hurdle. The winner was well in on old form and the second is on the upgrade.
T/Plt: £10.30. Pool: £74,999.22 - 5291.41 winning units. T/Qpdt: £9.80. Pool: £5603.60 - 421.80 winning units. AS

1727 BANGOR-ON-DEE (L-H)

Wednesday, November 13

OFFICIAL GOING: Soft changing to heavy on chase course after race 1 (12.50)
Wind: Light, half against Weather: Fine

2450 REA VALLEY TRACTORS H'CAP CHASE (15 fncs) 2m 4f 110y

12:50 (12:51) (Class 4) (0-120,119) 4-Y-0+ **£3,898** (£1,144; £572; £286)

Form RPR
2/3- **1** **Allerton (IRE)**[29] 1914 6-10-1 **101**..................(t) ConorShoemark(7) 108
(Fergal O'Brien) *a.p: led appr 11th: rdn and hdd bef 2 out: 2nd abt 4 l down and no imp last: r.o cl home to catch tiring rival* **9/2**[2]
3/3- **2** *3/4* **Ballylifen (IRE)**[128] 921 6-11-11 **118**..................(t) APMcCoy 124
(Jonjo O'Neill) *midfield: hdwy 5th: w ldr 11th: ev ch appr 2 out: sltly outpcd in 3rd bef last: swtchd rt run-in: sn rallied: r.o cl home: fin wl to take 2nd* **4/1**[1]
124/ **3** *hd* **Opera Og (IRE)**[201] 5545 7-11-10 **117**........................ AidanColeman 123
(Venetia Williams) *trckd ldrs: led appr 2 out: abt 4 l clr last: drvn run-in: tired cl home: sn hdd and no ex* **6/1**
0/U- **4** *8* **Hot Whiskey (IRE)**[17] 2107 5-11-6 **113**..................(b[1]) WayneHutchinson 111
(Alan King) *in tch: reminder after 9th: rdn whn chsng ldrs but unable qck appr 2 out: kpt on same pce after* **9/2**[2]
511/ **5** *4* **Morgan's Bay**[242] 4790 8-11-4 **111**........................ PaddyBrennan 106
(Tom George) *towards rr: hdwy whn nt fluent 11th: trckd ldrs 4 out: one pce bef last* **14/1**
0/4- **6** *5* **Good Egg (IRE)**[48] 1666 10-11-7 **114**........................ WilsonRenwick 104
(Mrs Lorna Fowler, Ire) *hld up: hdwy 9th: prom next: u.p and outpcd after 3 out: no imp after* **20/1**
/26- **7** *7* **Achimota (IRE)**[21] 2024 7-11-4 **118**..................(t) MrJMRidley(7) 101
(Matt Sheppard) *prom: pushed along and lost pl after 9th: wknd 4 out* **12/1**
F/3- **8** *10* **See What Happens (IRE)**[13] 2171 7-11-12 **119**.............. DenisO'Regan 93
(Martin Todhunter) *bhd: blnd 7th: hdwy 10th: prom 4 out: ev ch 3 out: pushed along and wknd bef 2 out* **5/1**[3]
605/ **P** **Got Attitude (IRE)**[364] 2411 10-11-1 **108**........................ AndrewTinkler
(Tony Carroll) *led: hdd appr 11th: wknd qckly: t.o whn p.u bef 3 out* **20/1**

5m 42.6s (33.50) **Going Correction** +1.125s/f (Heav) **9 Ran SP% 111.2**
Speed ratings (Par 105): **81,80,80,77,76 74,71,67,**
toteswingers 1&2 £2.30, 2&3 £3.80, 1&3 £7.50 CSF £22.24 CT £103.45 TOTE £3.40: £1.10, £2.70, £3.60; EX 23.70 Trifecta £86.50 Pool: £1216.81 - 10.54 winning units..
Owner Terry Evans **Bred** Michael Fox & Ms Alison Hayden **Trained** Coln St. Dennis, Gloucs
■ Stewards' Enquiry : Conor Shoemark two-day ban: used whip above permitted level (Nov 27-28)

FOCUS
The ground was changed to soft, heavy in places (from soft) after the first. An ordinary handicap with the first two to their marks.

2451 MONEY ADVICE GROUP SIR JOHN HANMER NOVICES' LIMITED H'CAP CHASE (18 fncs) 3m 110y

1:20 (1:21) (Class 3) (0-125,123) 4-Y-0+ **£6,498** (£1,908; £954; £477)

Form RPR
P/5- **1** **Herdsman (IRE)**[13] 2171 8-10-11 **115**........................ RyanMania 125
(Sue Smith) *trckd ldrs: reminder after 9th: lost pl 11th: reminder sn after: nt fluent 4 out: sn outpcd: rallied to chse ldr appr 2 out: styd on to ld run-in: in command towards fin* **10/1**
/04- **2** *3* **Tullyraine (IRE)**[21] 2024 9-11-2 **120**........................ SamTwiston-Davies 126+
(Nigel Twiston-Davies) *led: clr 3 out: sn at least 12 l ahd: reduced advantage 2 out: rdn bef last: hdd run-in: no ex* **5/2**[1]
P42/ **3** *20* **Black Is Beautiful (FR)**[230] 4978 5-10-5 **109**........................ JamieMoore 100
(Richard Lee) *trckd ldrs: u.p and lost pl after 13th: sn outpcd: rallied appr 2 out: one pce and no further imp bef last* **9/1**
146/ **4** *26* **Ifyousayso (IRE)**[258] 4477 6-10-11 **115**..................(t) PaddyBrennan 75
(Tom George) *hld up in rr: nt fluent 6th: hdwy on wd outside to take 2nd 12th: lost grnd on wnr 3 out: lost 2nd bef 2 out: wknd qckly: eased bef last* **9/2**[3]
500/ **5** *40* **Cheat The Cheater (IRE)**[207] 5410 6-10-4 **115**..........(p) GeraldQuinn(7) 35
(Claire Dyson) *in tch: prom 9th: stmbld 14th: sn bhd: hit 3 out: t.o* **50/1**
164- **P** **Full Of Joy (IRE)**[14] 2157 8-11-4 **122**..................(tp) APMcCoy
(Jonjo O'Neill) *hld up: nt fluent 10th: hit 13th: sn struggling: p.u bef next* **5/1**
P/2- **P** **Winds And Waves (IRE)**[21] 2024 7-11-2 **123**................ JakeGreenall(3)
(Henry Daly) *chsd ldr to 11th: losing pl whn hit 12th: sn bhd: p.u bef next* **3/1**[2]

6m 48.2s (28.40) **Going Correction** +1.125s/f (Heav) **7 Ran SP% 109.5**
Speed ratings (Par 107): **99,98,91,83,70 ,**
toteswingers 1&2 £5.20, 2&3 £5.50, 1&3 £20.00 CSF £33.40 CT £216.09 TOTE £23.60: £9.50, £1.70; EX 37.90 Trifecta £328.60 Pool: £1336.55 - 3.05 winning units..
Owner Trevor Hemmings **Bred** Eddie Flavin **Trained** High Eldwick, W Yorks

FOCUS

The Form Book Jumps, Raceform Ltd, Compton, RG20 6NL.

Hardly anything got into this thanks to the front-running tactics employed on the runner-up. The winner improved to the \n\x\x level of his best bumper/hurdle form.

2452 ANNE DUCHESS OF WESTMINSTER MEMORIAL H'CAP CHASE (18 fncs) 3m 110y
1:50 (1:53) (Class 2) (0-150,148) 4-Y£02,660 (£3,740; £1,870; £936; £468)

Form RPR
1/0- **1** **Midnight Appeal**[186] 215 8-10-10 **132**...................(b) WayneHutchinson 143+
(Alan King) *trckd ldrs: led 12th: rdn bef last: styd on wl: wl in comand towards fin* **25/1**

1U5/ **2** *4 ½* **Loch Ba (IRE)**[221] 5176 7-10-11 **133**.......................... DominicElsworth 140+
(Mick Channon) *sweating: hld up: hdwy 12th: chsd ldrs: mstke 4 out: sltly outpcd after 3 out: rallied to take 2nd for press appr last: one pce fnl 100yds* **10/3**[1]

241/ **3** *9* **Mountainous (IRE)**[242] 4784 8-10-11 **133**........................ JamieMoore 129
(Richard Lee) *in tch: wnt 2nd 4 out: rdn and ev ch appr 2 out: lost 2nd bef last: no ex and wl btn run-in* **11/1**

6/2- **4** *6* **What A Warrior (IRE)**[32] 1868 6-11-0 **136**.............. SamTwiston-Davies 126
(Nigel Twiston-Davies) *prom: lost pl 9th: rdn 14th: outpcd after 4 out: no imp after* **12/1**

F0P/ **5** *13* **Quartz De Thaix (FR)**[246] 4721 9-11-12 **148**.................. AidanColeman 125
(Venetia Williams) *hld up in rr: pushed along 13th: effrt 14th but unable to get to ldrs: outpcd after 4 out: n.d after* **10/1**

0/F- **P** **Pete The Feat (IRE)**[32] 1868 9-11-1 **137**........................... NoelFehily
(Charlie Longsdon) *prom: led 5th: j.rt fnl circ: hdd 12th: wkng whn blnd 4 out: t.o whn p.u bef last* **5/1**[3]

1/6- **P** **Golden Call (IRE)**[28] 1923 9-10-8 **130**............................ PaddyBrennan
(Tom George) *led: hdd 5th: remained prom: wknd 14th: t.o whn p.u bef 2 out* **11/2**

U2P/ **P** **Our Mick**[207] 5404 7-11-9 **145**.. JasonMaguire
(Donald McCain) *in tch: lost pl 3rd: in rr 5th: rdn after 7th: wl bhd whn p.u bef 14th* **4/1**[2]

0/0- **P** **Malt Master (IRE)**[25] 1969 6-11-1 **137**..................................... APMcCoy
(Nicky Henderson) *hld up: nt fluent 6th: rdn bef 12th: wl bhd whn p.u bef 14th* **10/1**

6m 40.9s (21.10) **Going Correction** +1.125s/f (Heav) **9** Ran SP% **113.2**
Speed ratings (Par 109): **111,109,106,104,100 , , ,**
toteswingers 1&2 £29.00, 2&3 £11.20, 1&3 £6.00 CSF £108.11 CT £991.53 TOTE £22.40: £6.70, £2.70, £3.30; EX 105.00 Trifecta £554.60 Pool: £1968.87 - 2.66 winning units..
Owner David Sewell **Bred** William Wilkinson **Trained** Barbury Castle, Wilts

FOCUS
The leaders probably went too hard early, and they dropped away some way from home. Solid handicap form.

2453 MONEY ADVICE GROUP NOVICES' HURDLE (9 hdls) 2m 1f
2:20 (2:25) (Class 4) 4-Y-0+ **£3,249** (£954; £477; £238)

Form RPR
/11- **1** **Irish Cavalier (IRE)**[13] 2178 4-11-5 0................................... APMcCoy 130+
(Rebecca Curtis) *mde all: rdn appr 2 out: styd on wl to draw clr run-in: comf* **8/11**[1]

121/ **2** *7* **Master Red (IRE)**[222] 5168 4-10-12 0.............................. JasonMaguire 115+
(Donald McCain) *trckd ldrs: hit 4th: nt fluent 4 out: stl travelling str on inner appr 2 out: sltly short of room bef taking 2nd between last 2: abt 3 l down whn j.lft and mstke last: no ch w wnr after* **7/4**[2]

43/ **3** *2 ¾* **Goohar (IRE)**[238] 4864 4-10-9 0.. JakeGreenall(3) 109
(Henry Daly) *racd w wnr most of way tl rdn appr 2 out: lost 2nd between last 2: one pce after* **15/2**[3]

00- **4** *27* **Cloudy Deal (IRE)**[14] 2156 6-10-12 0............................ WilsonRenwick 82
(Martin Todhunter) *hld up in rr: plugged on fr bef 2 out: nvr a threat* **66/1**

0/6- **5** *8* **Six One Away (IRE)**[20] 2040 4-10-12 0................................ DenisO'Regan 74
(Paul Webber) *racd keenly: j.lft 1st: in tch: wknd after 3 out* **33/1**

0- **6** *24* **Modeligo (IRE)**[21] 2026 4-10-12 0.. CharliePoste 50
(Matt Sheppard) *hld up in rr: rdn after 4 out: dropped away after next: t.o* **200/1**

000- **7** *13* **Home Girl (IRE)**[15] 2147 5-10-5 0.. TomSiddall 30
(Susan Johnson) *j.lft 1st: in tch: dropped to rr after 3rd: struggling 4th: t.o 3 out* **200/1**

4m 26.7s (15.80) **Going Correction** +1.125s/f (Heav) **7** Ran SP% **111.5**
Speed ratings (Par 105): **107,103,102,89,85 74,68**
toteswingers 1&2 £1.10, 2&3 £1.20, 1&3 £1.70 CSF £2.22 TOTE £1.80: £1.10, £1.50; EX 2.60 Trifecta £5.80 Pool: £3091.11 - 394.92 winning units..
Owner A McIver **Bred** Limetree Stud **Trained** Newport, Dyfed

FOCUS
This only looked to concern three prior to the off and that proved to be the case. The winner is the type to rate higher.

2454 ROOFING CONSULTANTS GROUP H'CAP HURDLE (11 hdls) 2m 4f
2:50 (2:50) (Class 2) 4-Y-0+ **£12,996** (£3,816; £1,908; £954)

Form RPR
151/ **1** **Stopped Out**[26] 5574 8-11-10 **139**...............................(p) RichieMcGrath 144+
(Philip Kirby) *mde all: pushed along appr 2 out: styd on wl run-in and a in control* **13/2**

0/0- **2** *1 ¾* **Shotavodka (IRE)**[11] 2213 7-11-9 **138**....................................... APMcCoy 139
(David Pipe) *prom: chsd wnr fr 6th: tried to chal approachng 2 out: rdn bef last: kpt on but no imp after* **3/1**[1]

064- **3** *2 ¼* **Bourne**[13] 2170 7-10-10 **125**.......................................(b) JasonMaguire 125
(Donald McCain) *chsd wnr to 6th: pushed along appr 3 out: outpcd bef next: tk 3rd last: kpt on run-in but n.d* **9/2**[2]

3/0- **4** *2 ¾* **Native Gallery (IRE)**[180] 356 8-11-12 **141**................ WayneHutchinson 139+
(Ben De Haan) *in tch: effrt whn chsng ldrs appr 2 out: j.lft last: one pce after* **6/1**[3]

113- **5** *3 ¾* **Azure Fly (IRE)**[24] 1987 5-11-3 **132**...................................(tp) NoelFehily 125
(Charlie Longsdon) *hld up: pushed along appr 2 out: nvr able to trble ldrs* **13/2**

0/2- **6** *7* **Hada Men (USA)**[187] 205 8-11-3 **132**................................ AidanColeman 118
(Venetia Williams) *in tch: rdn appr 4 out: wknd bef next* **9/2**[2]

2/0- **7** *3 ½* **Bob's World**[18] 2069 4-10-5 **120**.. SeanQuinlan 102
(Jennie Candlish) *hld up in rr: pushed along appr 3 out: rdn whn hit 2 out: nvr a threat* **16/1**

1/6- **U** **Phoenix Returns (IRE)**[20] 2032 5-10-4 **119**.......................... PaddyBrennan
(Alan Swinbank) *hld up in rr: stmbld and uns rdr 7th* **33/1**

5m 14.3s (22.30) **Going Correction** +1.125s/f (Heav)
WFA 4 from 5yo+ 8lb **8** Ran SP% **111.1**
Speed ratings (Par 109): **100,99,98,97,95 93,91,**
toteswingers 1&2 £5.00, 2&3 £4.10, 1&3 £9.10 CSF £25.40 CT £92.92 TOTE £9.90: £2.20, £2.00, £1.60; EX 28.40 Trifecta £430.90 Pool: £1516.83 - 2.64 winning units..
Owner The Well Oiled Partnership **Bred** J And T Shally **Trained** Middleham, N Yorks

The Form Book Jumps, Raceform Ltd, Compton, RG20 6NL

FOCUS
Plenty of these could be given some sort of chance but the winner had the run of things. Another step forward from the winner, with the second to his mark.

2455 EPDS RACING BTO SERIES FINALE JUVENILE MAIDEN HURDLE (9 hdls) 2m 1f
3:20 (3:21) (Class 5) 3-Y-0 **£3,249** (£954; £477; £238)

Form RPR
33- **1** **Sleepy Haven (IRE)**[17] 2098 3-10-12 114............................ SeanQuinlan 100+
(Jennie Candlish) *racd in cl 2nd pl: led 4 out: rdn between last 2: hit last: sn drew clr and styd on wl* **11/4**[3]

44- **2** *6* **Green And White (ITY)**[17] 2098 3-10-12 103......... SamTwiston-Davies 93
(Dave Roberts) *chsd ldrs: stl wl there 2 out: rdn and nt qckn appr last: kpt on u.p run-in to take 2nd towards fin: no ch w wnr* **28/1**

3 *hd* **Rayak (IRE)**[143] 3-10-12 0.. APMcCoy 93
(Jonjo O'Neill) *hld up: blnd 1st: mstke 5th: hdwy 3 out: wnt 2nd 2 out: rdn appr last where j.lft: sn unable to go w wnr and no ch: lost 2nd towards fin* **7/4**[1]

4 *2* **Marju's Quest (IRE)**[46] 3-10-12 0.............................. WayneHutchinson 91
(David Dennis) *hld up in rr and racd keenly: hdwy appr 2 out and jst off ldrs: rdn and one pce whn mstke last: no imp after* **5/2**[2]

0- **5** *11* **Henri De Boistron (FR)**[22] 2015 3-10-12 0.................. PaddyBrennan 81
(Tom George) *led: hdd 4 out: stl ev ch next: u.p and wkng whn j.flt 2 out* **11/1**

4- **6** *4 ½* **Moaning Butcher**[41] 1727 3-10-5 0..........................(v) MrAlexEdwards(7) 74
(Dave Roberts) *chsd ldrs: mstke 5th: rdn and wknd 3 out* **50/1**

4m 33.9s (23.00) **Going Correction** +1.125s/f (Heav) **6** Ran SP% **105.3**
Speed ratings (Par 102): **90,87,87,86,80 78**
toteswingers 1&2 £10.20, 2&3 £8.20, 1&3 £1.10 CSF £45.60 TOTE £4.00: £1.60, £3.70; EX 44.60 Trifecta £123.00 Pool: £1472.23 - 8.97 winning units..
Owner Alan Baxter **Bred** Equine Associates Fr **Trained** Basford Green, Staffs

FOCUS
This doesn't seem particularly strong form considering the pace was moderate. Modest form, the winner rated to his mark.

2456 KNIGHTS SOLICITORS LLP "NEWCOMERS" STANDARD OPEN NATIONAL HUNT FLAT RACE 2m 1f
3:50 (3:50) (Class 6) 3-5-Y-0 **£1,642** (£478; £239)

Form RPR
1 **A Vos Gardes (FR)** 3-10-7 0.. NoelFehily 98
(Charlie Longsdon) *hld up in rr: trcking ldrs in cl 3rd after 1/2-way: wnt 2nd and rdn over 2f out: swtchd lft 1f out: styd on to chal strly ins fnl f: nosed ahd fnl 50yds* **9/4**[2]

2 *hd* **Foryourinformation** 4-11-9 0.. APMcCoy 114
(Rebecca Curtis) *w ldr: led over 4f out: rdn over 1f out: hrd pressed ins fnl f: styd on u.p: hdd narrowly fnl 50yds* **5/6**[1]

3 *8* **Howaboutnever (IRE)** 5-11-9 0.. JasonMaguire 106
(Donald McCain) *led: rdn 6f out: hdd over 4f out: lost 2nd u.p over 2f out: wknd over 1f out* **4/1**[3]

- **4** *38* **Queenys King (IRE)** 5-11-9 0.................................. WayneHutchinson 68
(David Dennis) *trckd ldrs: pushed along 5f out: wknd 4f out: eased whn wl btn over 2f out: t.o* **25/1**

4m 20.4s (15.10) **Going Correction** +1.125s/f (Heav)
WFA 3 from 4yo 15lb 4 from 5yo 7lb **4** Ran SP% **109.2**
Speed ratings (Par 101): **109,108,105,87**
CSF £4.61 TOTE £4.90; EX 4.70 Trifecta £7.10 Pool: £1181.76 - 124.46 winning units..
Owner The Rollright Stones **Bred** U J And B Lenouvel De Vulpian **Trained** Over Norton, Oxon

FOCUS
It's unlikely that this form means a lot in the grand scheme of things, because it contained four newcomers. However the first three showed promise.
T/Plt: £64.30 to a £1 stake. Pool of £65617.63 - 743.84 winning tickets. T/Qpdt: £14.00 to a £1 stake. Pool of £5242.90 - 276.90 winning tickets. DO

2279 EXETER (R-H)
Wednesday, November 13

OFFICIAL GOING: Chase course - good to soft; hurdle course - soft (good to soft in places)
Wind: mild breeze against Weather: sunny

2457 EQUINE INVESTMENTS - A DECADE OF PROFITABLE TIPPING NOVICES' HURDLE (11 hdls) 2m 5f 110y
1:10 (1:11) (Class 4) 4-Y-0+ **£4,548** (£1,335; £667; £333)

Form RPR
1 **Mosspark (IRE)**[361] 5-10-12 0.. LeightonAspell 123+
(Emma Lavelle) *mid-div: pushed along and hdwy after 8th: led sn after 2 out: running green but styd on nicely fr last: rdn out* **4/1**[2]

2 *2* **Ned Stark (IRE)**[240] 5-10-12 0.................................... RobertThornton 119+
(Alan King) *in tch: tk clsr order 8th: rdn after 3 out: wnt 2nd at the last: styd on* **7/1**[3]

2- **3** *1 ¾* **Minella Friend (IRE)**[22] 2011 4-10-12 0............................ PaulMoloney 118+
(Evan Williams) *led: rdn whn blnd 2 out: sn hdd: styd on same pce* **4/5**[1]

0/U- **4** *8* **Cool George**[8] 2279 5-10-9 0.. JamesBest(3) 108
(Jackie Du Plessis) *pressed ldr: rdn and ev ch appr 3 out tl bef 2 out: styd on same pce* **20/1**

4/0- **5** *3 ¾* **Gentleman Jon**[25] 1974 5-10-12 0.. JoeTizzard 105
(Colin Tizzard) *trckd ldrs: rdn appr 3 out: sn one pce* **14/1**

13U- **6** *14* **Beau De Tabel (FR)**[8] 2279 5-10-12 0............................ TomScudamore 90
(Nick Williams) *trckd ldrs: nt fluent 4th: rdn after 8th: wknd bef next* **18/1**

0/P- **7** *1* **Shipton**[27] 1937 4-10-12 0.. AlainCawley 89
(Brendan Powell) *hld up towards rr: rdn into midfield after 8th: nvr rchd ldrs and no further imp fr 3 out* **150/1**

5- **8** *4 ½* **Cadeau George**[20] 2053 4-10-12 0.. DavidBass 85
(Ben Pauling) *mid-div: rdn after 8th: wknd bef next* **80/1**

/05- **9** *3 ¼* **Merchant Of Milan**[17] 2106 5-10-12 0.......................... BrendanPowell 82
(Brendan Powell) *mid-div: awkward 1st: nt fluent 4th: rdn after 8th: wknd bef next* **100/1**

/60- **10** *2 ¼* **Degenerate (FR)**[13] 2181 6-10-12 0............................ NickScholfield 79
(Jeremy Scott) *mid-div: nt fluent 7th: wknd after next* **66/1**

0/6- **11** *18* **Gilanto (IRE)**[17] 2106 6-10-12 0...................................... DougieCostello 61
(Michael Blake) *mid-div: mstke 3rd: nt fluent 7th: wknd after next: t.o whn mstke 2 out* **100/1**

0- **12** *hd* **Ask The Boss**[18] 2076 8-10-12 0..................................... ConorO'Farrell 61
(Tim Dennis) *a towards rr: t.o* **200/1**

13 ½ **Castarnie** 5-10-12 0 FelixDeGiles 61
(Robert Walford) *j.rt 6th: a towards rr: t.o* **100/1**

0- 14 hd **Sedgemoor Top Bid (IRE)**141 828 5-10-9 0 MarkQuinlan(3) 60
(Nigel Hawke) *a towards rr: t.o* **150/1**

0- 15 21 **Bonds Conquest**21 2026 4-10-12 0 AndrewThornton 39
(Seamus Mullins) *t.k.h: trckd ldrs tl 5th: sn wknd: t.o* **100/1**

0/P- P **Village Secret**8 2280 7-10-9 0 GavinSheehan(3)
(Brian Barr) *a towards rr: t.o whn p.u after 2 out* **250/1**

13- F **Neville**21 2028 5-10-12 0 RichardJohnson
(Philip Hobbs) *mid-div: rdn after 8th: styng on at same pce in hld 6th whn crumpled on landing and fell 3 out* **12/1**

5m 22.9s (-10.10) **Going Correction** -0.60s/f (Firm)
WFA 4 from 5yo+ 8lb **17** Ran SP% **121.3**
Speed ratings (Par 105): **94,93,92,89,88 83,82,81,80,79 72,72,72,72,64 ,**
toteswingers 1&2 £4.10, 2&3 £2.70, 1&3 £1.80 CSF £31.78 TOTE £5.30: £2.50, £4.60, £1.02; EX 33.40 Trifecta £39.60 Pool: £1360.97 - 25.72 winning units..
Owner N Mustoe & Tim Syder **Bred** Mrs Anthea Smyth **Trained** Hatherden, Hants

FOCUS
Chase course out wide on fresh ground. Leighton Aspell described the ground as "good to soft and soft in places". Probably quite a decent novice hurdle, with a pair of promising rules debutants proving too strong for the favourite, who had already shown a fair level of form. The winner looks a fair recruit.

2458 VISIT THE NEW AP BAR AT EXETER RACECOURSE H'CAP HURDLE (12 hdls) 2m 7f 110y
1:40 (1:40) (Class 4) (0-120,120) 4-Y-0+ **£3,898** (£1,144; £572; £286)

Form RPR

1/3- 1 **Ballyculla (IRE)**23 2006 6-11-8 **119** GavinSheehan(3) 132+
(Warren Greatrex) *in tch: tk clsr order 7th: led appr 3 out: pushed clr after 2 out: readily* **12/1**

0/3- 2 5 **Nicene Creed**27 1940 8-10-6 **100** (tp) PaulMoloney 107+
(Sophie Leech) *mid-div: struggling towards rr whn hmpd 8th: drvn and hdwy appr 3 out: styd on: str run fr last to snatch 2nd nring fin: nvr any ch w wnr* **20/1**

/65- 3 nk **Sir Frank (IRE)**38 1797 8-11-5 **113** ConorO'Farrell 117
(David Pipe) *hld up towards rr on outer: hdwy fr 7th: cl up whn it 3 out: sn rdn: styd on fr last: wnt 3rd nr fin* **33/1**

213/ 4 nk **Moorlands Mist**210 5354 6-11-2 **120** ThomasCheesman(10) 124
(Philip Hobbs) *hld up towards rr: hdwy fr 6th: rdn to chal 3 out: hit 2 out: sn hld by wnr: lost 2 pls nring fin* **5/1**2

/20- 5 2 **Buckhorn Tom**27 1941 5-11-6 **114** JoeTizzard 116
(Colin Tizzard) *in tch: rdn after 9th: styd on same pce fr 3 out* **14/1**

031- 6 10 **Bob Tucker (IRE)**34 1838 6-11-9 **117** AlainCawley 108
(Brendan Powell) *trckd ldrs: lft 2nd at the 8th: rdn and ev ch briefly appr 3 out: wknd 2 out* **25/1**

UP0- 7 8 **Virginia Ash (IRE)**7 2288 5-11-8 **116** (b) BrendanPowell 99
(Colin Tizzard) *mid-div tl struggling towards rr after 7th: sme late prog but no threat after* **40/1**

230/ 8 4 **Bladoun (FR)**216 5257 5-11-8 **116** (t) TomScudamore 95
(David Pipe) *trckd ldrs: disputing 3rd whn bdly hmpd and lost pl 8th: nt a threat after* **7/1**3

220- 9 ¾ **Royale Knight**79 1396 7-10-11 **112** ChristopherWard(7) 91
(Dr Richard Newland) *hld up towards rr: midfield 9th: sn rdn: wknd next* **10/1**

005/ 10 3½ **Count Vettori (IRE)**613 4771 7-10-1 **105** JonPark(10) 80
(Kevin Bishop) *mid-div: rdn after 9th: wknd next* **66/1**

221/ 11 10 **Armenian Boy (FR)**399 1780 10-11-9 **120** (p) JamesBest(3) 85
(Jackie Du Plessis) *led: rdn and hdd appr 3 out: sn wknd: t.o* **33/1**

/00- 12 2¼ **Pyleigh Lass**22 2013 7-11-5 **113** (t) IanPopham 76
(Jeremy Scott) *mid-div whn bdly hmpd 1st: nvr travelling in rr after: t.o* **14/1**

0PP- 13 3½ **Sandynow (IRE)**7 2290 8-10-10 **104** (p) TomO'Brien 63
(Peter Bowen) *mid-div whn bdly hmpd 1st: in rr: struggling 6th: t.o after 9th* **25/1**

3- 14 5 **Twice Returned (IRE)**32 1863 7-11-9 **117** HarrySkelton 71
(Dan Skelton) *mid-div: hmpd 1st: wknd after 9th: blnd 3 out: t.o* **9/2**1

114/ 15 2 **Wood Yer (IRE)**601 5009 7-10-11 **112** (t) RyanHatch(7) 64
(Nigel Twiston-Davies) *mid-div: mstke 4th: wknd after 7th: t.o whn looked to be pulling up bef 3 out: continued* **14/1**

214- U **Cruising Bye**18 2073 7-10-0 **94** oh1 DonalDevereux
(Peter Bowen) *mid-div whn blnd and uns rdr 1st* **14/1**

/21- F **Royal Native (IRE)**8 2284 5-11-8 **119** 7ex (t) RachaelGreen(3)
(Anthony Honeyball) *trckd ldr: upsides travelling wl whn fell 8th* **7/1**3

5m 43.3s (-15.70) **Going Correction** -0.60s/f (Firm) **17** Ran SP% **125.6**
Speed ratings (Par 105): **102,100,100,100,99 96,93,92,91,90 87,86,85,83,83 ,**
toteswingers 1&2 £61.90, 2&3 £73.70, 1&3 £73.70 CSF £235.48 CT £7523.84 TOTE £10.20: £3.80, £4.40, £7.30, £2.40; EX 213.80 Trifecta £794.50 Part won. Pool: £1059.40 - 0.01 winning units..
Owner No Dramas Partnership **Bred** J Mangan **Trained** Upper Lambourn, Berks

FOCUS
A fair staying handicap. The winner is on the upgrade and there's probably more to come, and this form looks solid enough.

2459 RNLI NOVICES' CHASE (18 fncs) 3m
2:10 (2:10) (Class 3) 4-Y-0+ **£6,330** (£1,870; £935; £468; £234)

Form RPR

3/U- 1 **Smad Place (FR)**10 2249 6-11-3 0 RobertThornton 139+
(Alan King) *j.w: trckd ldrs: wnt 2nd after 5th: led after 10th: pushed along whn pressed appr 4 out: styd on wl and in command last: pushed out* **4/11**1

220/ 2 7 **Ardkilly Witness (IRE)**244 4747 7-11-3 0 TomO'Brien 130
(Dr Richard Newland) *trckd ldrs: jnd ldrs 14th: rdn and ev ch 4 out: nt fluent 3 out: cl 2nd but hld fr next: styd on same pce* **5/1**2

131/ 3 4 **Seymour Eric**208 5368 8-11-3 0 (p) IanPopham 126
(Martin Keighley) *disp tl clr ldr 4th: hdd after 10th: rdn and ev ch appr 4 out: styd on same pce and j.rt fr 3 out* **6/1**3

240/ 4 3¾ **Counting House (IRE)**334 3048 10-11-3 0 MarkGrant 122
(Jim Old) *hld up bhd ldrs: rdn bef 4 out: styd on into 4th 3 out: blnd next: kpt on but nvr gng pce to get on terms w ldrs* **33/1**

/20- 5 15 **Phone Home (IRE)**17 2107 6-11-3 115 NickScholfield 108
(Nick Mitchell) *disp tl 4th: nt fluent 8th (water): sn lost pl: bk trcking ldrs after next: outpcd 4 out: lost 4th 3 out: fading whn mstke next* **50/1**

P- 6 42 **Typical Oscar (IRE)**21 2028 6-11-3 0 TomCannon 64
(Michael Blake) *hld up bhd ldrs: lost tch fr 12th: t.o* **100/1**

6m 11.8s (2.50) **Going Correction** -0.275s/f (Good) **6** Ran SP% **110.2**
Speed ratings (Par 107): **84,81,80,79,74 60**
toteswingers 1&2 £1.10, 2&3 £1.50, 1&3 £1.10 CSF £2.69 TOTE £1.40: £1.10, £1.80; EX 2.60 Trifecta £6.60 Pool: £4281.77 - 483.48 winning units..
Owner Mrs Peter Andrews **Bred** Eric Aubree & Mme Maryse Aubree **Trained** Barbury Castle, Wilts

FOCUS
They went steady here and a couple of them, including the winner, weren't seen to best effect. The winner didn't need to be at his best to land this fair novice. The fourth was close enough and the time was ordinary.

2460 JACK FLETCHER BEGINNERS' CHASE (12 fncs) 2m 1f 110y
2:40 (2:40) (Class 4) 4-Y-0+ **£4,548** (£1,335; £667; £333)

Form RPR

302/ 1 **Valdez**210 5350 6-11-1 135 RobertThornton 141+
(Alan King) *trckd ldrs: wnt 2nd after 4th: led 8th: j.rt but in command fr 4 out: rchd for 3 out: comf* **7/4**1

6/2- 2 6 **The Italian Yob (IRE)**22 2012 5-11-1 125 RichardJohnson 133+
(Nick Williams) *led tl 8th: sn rdn: j.rt fr 4 out: styd on but a being hld* **5/2**3

1/F- 3 24 **Billy Dutton**9 2267 7-11-1 120 JamesDavies 107
(Chris Down) *in tch: rdn after 8th: styd on into 3rd but no ch w ldng fr pair 3 out: nvr gng pce to threaten* **12/1**

P/3- 4 13 **Ohio Gold (IRE)**21 2019 7-11-1 134 JoeTizzard 99
(Colin Tizzard) *trckd ldrs: tended to jump lft fr 5th: mstke 8th: sn rdn and wl hld: wkng whn lost 3rd 3 out* **2/1**2

400/ 5 21 **Gingers Reflection**191 7-10-8 0 (t) JonPark(7) 73
(Carroll Gray) *in tch: struggling 8th: sn lost tch: t.o* **50/1**

F/2- 6 8 **Wise Hawk**168 540 8-10-12 0 JamesBest(3) 65
(Jackie Du Plessis) *hld up: nt fluent early: struggling 7th: lost tch after 8th: t.o* **66/1**

3UP/ P **Roman Conquest**269 4269 9-11-1 115 AndrewThornton
(Seamus Mullins) *trckd ldr tl after 4th: lost action whn p.u bef 5th* **33/1**

/20- P **Key To Milan**17 2105 7-10-12 0 (tp) GilesHawkins(3)
(Chris Down) *hld up: mstke 4th: sn struggling in rr: blnd 6th: p.u bef next* **50/1**

4m 14.2s (-4.80) **Going Correction** -0.275s/f (Good) **8** Ran SP% **114.3**
Speed ratings (Par 105): **99,96,85,79,70 67, ,**
toteswingers 1&2 £1.10, 2&3 £3.40, 1&3 £3.90 CSF £6.72 TOTE £2.20: £1.10, £1.60, £2.80; EX 7.60 Trifecta £31.60 Pool: £2195.10 - 51.93 winning units..
Owner Riverdee Stable **Bred** David & Julie Andrews **Trained** Barbury Castle, Wilts

FOCUS
An ordinary novice chase. The winner looks a fair recruit and should go on to rate higher.

2461 THANK YOU SUE TUCKER H'CAP HURDLE (8 hdls) 2m 1f
3:10 (3:10) (Class 3) (0-135,130) 4-Y-0 **£6,330** (£1,870; £935; £468; £234)

Form RPR

146- 1 **Waterunder (IRE)**115 1054 6-11-12 **130** (t) TomScudamore 134
(David Pipe) *mid-div: hdwy on outer after 5th: led next: sn rdn and hrd pressed: styd on wl to assert run-in: drvn out* **14/1**

2/1- 2 2 **Horizontal Speed (IRE)**22 2011 5-11-7 **125** RichardJohnson 127
(Philip Hobbs) *mid-div: hdwy after 3rd to trck ldrs: nt clr run and swtchd lft appr 3 out: str chal 2 out: rdn and ev ch last: nt qckn* **9/4**1

323- 3 ½ **Highway Code (USA)**18 1425 7-11-1 **122** MichealNolan(3) 125+
(Richard Lee) *mid-div: hdwy after 3rd: chal bef 3 out where mstke: sn rdn: ev ch whn hit last: drifted rt: kpt on same pce* **7/2**2

030- 4 4 **Dragon's Den (IRE)**25 1972 6-10-7 **111** LeightonAspell 108
(Chris Down) *hld up: hdwy after 5th: rdn to chse ldrs after 3 out: styd on same pce: wnt 4th run-in* **9/1**

6/3- 5 1½ **Chemistry Master**17 2111 5-10-9 **123** (t) MartinMcIntyre(10) 119
(Harry Fry) *trckd ldrs: jnd ldrs 5th: rdn 3 out: kpt on same pce fr next* **7/1**

002- 6 2¼ **Royale's Charter**47 1670 7-11-6 **124** LiamTreadwell 119
(Nick Williams) *led: tended to jump sltly lft at times: rdn and hdd 2 out: kpt on same pce* **14/1**

/36- 7 ½ **Quaddick Lake (IRE)**18 2080 10-11-10 **128** NickScholfield 121
(Jeremy Scott) *hld up: hdwy after 5th: rdn to chse ldrs after 3 out: nt pce to get on terms* **13/2**3

/20- 8 1 **Dark And Dangerous (IRE)**172 480 5-10-13 **117** BrendanPowell 109
(Brendan Powell) *prom: rdn to chse ldrs after 3 out: no ex appr last* **14/1**

416- 9 40 **Multitude Of Sins**27 1943 6-11-5 **123** (p) JoeTizzard 75
(Colin Tizzard) *trckd ldrs tl dropped in rr rapidly u.p after 4th: t.o* **25/1**

/F0- P **Train Of Thought (IRE)**32 1867 5-11-3 **121** PaulMoloney
(Evan Williams) *trckd ldrs tl dropped in rr tamely after 3rd: t.o whn p.u bef last* **50/1**

4m 1.5s (-14.00) **Going Correction** -0.60s/f (Firm) **10** Ran SP% **114.6**
Speed ratings (Par 107): **108,107,106,104,104 103,102,102,83,**
toteswingers 1&2 £12.50, 2&3 £1.90, 1&3 £2.20 CSF £46.16 CT £139.09 TOTE £15.20: £3.10, £1.10, £2.50; EX 64.30 Trifecta £254.40 Pool: £2055.74 - 6.05 winning units..
Owner Mrs S Clifford **Bred** Charles Clarke **Trained** Nicholashayne, Devon

FOCUS
A few of these raced keenly, with them going just a steady gallop early, and it developed into a bit of a dash in the straight. The first two are on the upgrade.

2462 RACING UK PROFITS RETURNED TO RACING H'CAP CHASE (15 fncs) 2m 3f 110y
3:40 (3:40) (Class 4) (0-110,110) 4-Y-0+ **£3,898** (£1,144; £572; £286)

Form RPR

4/4- 1 **Last Shot (FR)**179 370 6-11-11 **109** LiamTreadwell 121+
(Venetia Williams) *disp ld tl appr 8th: trckd ldrs: chal 4 out: led bef 2 out: styd on wl: rdn out* **5/1**3

4/3- 2 2 **Moleskin (IRE)**24 1988 10-11-10 **108** (bt) JackDoyle 116
(Victor Dartnall) *trckd ldrs: hit 7th: jnd ldrs next: led 9th: rdn whn hrd pressed appr 4 out: hdd bef 2 out: styd on same pce* **11/4**1

1U2- 3 2¼ **Moorlands Jack**23 2007 8-11-4 **102** (p) NickScholfield 108
(Jeremy Scott) *trckd ldrs: nt fluent 7th: swtchd lft after 4 out: rdn after next: styd on same pce* **7/2**2

051- 4 5 **Midnight Lira**39 1769 6-10-9 **96** JamesBest(3) 98
(Caroline Keevil) *disp ld: hdd 9th: pressed ldr: rdn and ev ch 4 out tl 3 out: styd on same pce* **15/2**

14P- 5 43 **Chase Gate**83 1349 8-10-11 **95** (p) HaddenFrost 52
(James Frost) *hld up bhd ldrs: pckd 6th: rdn after 11th: sn wknd: t.o* **28/1**

61P/ 6 25 **Thedreamstillalive (IRE)**349 2722 13-10-0 **84** oh2 (t) MarkGrant 16
(Jim Old) *racd keenly: trckd ldrs: disp ld after 7th tl nt fluent 9th: rdn after 11th: sn wknd: t.o* **25/1**

The Form Book Jumps, Raceform Ltd, Compton, RG20 6NL.

P/2- 7 7 **Moorland Sunset**[20] 2046 6-11-12 110 .... IanPopham 35
(Caroline Keevil) *hld up bhd ldrs: nt fluent 3rd: struggling after 8th: sn bhd: t.o* **7/2**[2]

/50- P **Brockwell Park**[17] 2105 6-11-2 100 .... LiamHeard
(Jeremy Scott) *j.lft and bmpd 1st: hld up bhd ldrs: lost tch fr 11th: t.o whn p.u bef 4 out* **14/1**

4m 49.8s (-7.50) **Going Correction** -0.275s/f (Good) **8** Ran SP% **113.5**
Speed ratings (Par 105): **104,103,102,100,83 73,70,**
toteswingers 1&2 £5.40, 2&3 £3.10, 1&3 £3.70 CSF £19.60 CT £53.40 TOTE £6.80: £2.20, £1.50, £1.70; EX 20.90 Trifecta £54.40 Pool: £2139.59 - 29.45 winning units..
Owner Basil Richards & Lady Bolton **Bred** Guy-Roger Petit **Trained** Kings Caple, H'fords

FOCUS
This was quite competitive and any one of four was in with a chance down the straight. A step up from the winner for an in-form yard.

2463 CHRISTMAS PARTIES AT EXETER RACECOURSE MARES' NOVICES' HURDLE (10 hdls) 2m 3f
4:10 (4:10) (Class 4) 4-Y-0+ **£3,249** (£954; £477; £238)

Form RPR

1/1- 1 **Joanne One (IRE)**[31] 1885 5-11-2 0 .... (t) BrendanPowell 116+
(Jamie Snowden) *trckd ldrs: prom whn hmpd by loose horse after 3rd: led after next: drew clr fr 3 out: hit last: unextended* **4/5**[1]

252/ 2 9 **Ruby Glow**[373] 2239 5-10-10 0 .... AndrewThornton 96
(Seamus Mullins) *t.k.h: trckd ldrs: wnt 2nd 3 out: sn rdn: kpt on but nvr any ch w wnr* **5/1**[3]

000/ 3 2 ¼ **Just Fee**[664] 3821 6-10-10 0 .... DaveCrosse 93
(Nick Mitchell) *bdly hmpd 1st: in tch: hdwy after 5th: rdn to chse wnr appr 3 out tl bef 2 out: styd on same pce* **100/1**

4 4 ½ **Big Night Out** 7-10-7 0 .... MarkQuinlan(3) 89
(Nigel Hawke) *hmpd 1st: towards rr after: mstke 5th: rdn into 4th 3 out: no further imp* **50/1**

0/4- 5 4 ½ **Summertime Lady**[195] 85 5-10-10 0 .... JoeTizzard 85
(Colin Tizzard) *trckd ldrs: hmpd 1st: in tch whn rdn appr 3 out: sn one pce: hit 2 out* **20/1**

60/ 6 14 **Its April**[251] 4621 5-10-10 0 .... FelixDeGiles 69
(Robert Walford) *lft trcking ldrs 1st: rdn appr 3 out: sn wknd* **100/1**

05P/ 7 8 **Affiliate**[306] 3598 5-10-10 0 .... MarkGrant 61
(Geoffrey Deacon) *hld up: hmpd 1st: rdn appr 3 out: nvr a threat: wknd 3 out* **100/1**

FF5- 8 5 **Lily Potts**[34] 1832 4-10-10 0 .... (p) JamesDavies 56
(Chris Down) *trcking ldrs whn bdly hmpd 1st: mid-div tl after 4th: sn struggling: wknd bef 3 out* **40/1**

006/ 9 22 **Forgotten Promise**[373] 2239 6-10-7 0 .... GavinSheehan(3) 34
(Brian Barr) *hld up: hdwy on long run after 3rd to sit prom next: blnd 7th: sn wknd: t.o* **200/1**

UF- 10 4 ½ **Lady Oaksey**[22] 2009 7-10-10 0 .... GerardTumelty 30
(Bob Buckler) *nt fluent: led tl after 4th: wknd 7th: t.o* **200/1**

/02- U **Unefille De Guye (FR)**[21] 2022 5-10-10 0 .... JackDoyle
(Victor Dartnall) *veered bdly rt and uns rdr 1st* **9/1**

2/4- F **Blue Buttons (IRE)**[179] 372 5-10-10 0 .... (t) RyanMahon
(Harry Fry) *bdly hmpd whn fell 1st* **7/2**[2]

4m 41.7s (-1.00) **Going Correction** -0.60s/f (Firm)
WFA 4 from 5yo+ 7lb **12** Ran SP% **117.6**
Speed ratings (Par 105): **78,74,73,71,69 63,60,58,48,46 ,**
toteswingers 1&2 £1.90, 2&3 £81.70, 1&3 £26.00 CSF £5.22 TOTE £2.00: £1.10, £1.70, £6.70; EX 5.80 Trifecta £508.50 Pool: £2953.80 - 4.35 winning units..
Owner Sir Chips Keswick **Bred** Gerry Burke **Trained** Lambourn, Berks

FOCUS
The easy winner built on her recent win and the second is rated below her best.
T/Plt: £18.60 to a £1 stake. Pool: £74425.43 - 2908.25 winning tickets. T/Qpdt: £2.40 to £1 stake. Pool of £4860.60 - 1439.65 winning tickets. TM

1583 ENGHIEN (L-H)
Wednesday, November 13

OFFICIAL GOING: Turf: heavy

2464a PRIX BISON FUTE (CHASE) (CLAIMER) (4YO) (TURF) 2m 1f 110y
1:35 (12:00) 4-Y-0 **£8,975** (£4,487; £2,617; £1,776; £841)

RPR

1 **Tell Everyone (FR)**[41] 1742 4-10-6 0 .... AlexisPoirier(8) 96
(G Cherel, France) **68/10**

2 5 **Vauban Laugil (FR)**[20] 4-10-6 0 .... ThomasGillet(8) 91
(C Aubert, France) **15/1**

3 1 ½ **Yoneti (FR)**[71] 4-10-3 0 .... (p) DavyDelalande(9) 88
(E Leenders, France) **5/1**[3]

4 3 **Rubis Du Rheu (FR)**[20] 4-10-1 0 .... (p) YoannMichaux(6) 83
(T Trapenard, France) **38/1**

5 ½ **Milton D'Or (FR)**[17] 4-10-1 0 .... (b) HugoLucas(9) 82
(E Leray, France) **24/1**

6 2 **Kamiro D'Or (FR)**[238] 4-10-10 0 .... (b) StephanePaillard 80
(E Leray, France) **9/1**

7 1 ¼ **Rubayat (IRE)**[18] 4-9-11 0 .... (b) GeoffreyRe(9) 75
(Yannick Fouin, France) **3/1**[1]

8 dist **Thinger Licht (FR)**[6] 2314 4-11-3 0 .... LeeEdwards
(Tony Carroll) *tk a t.k.h: wl in tch on outer: mstke 6th: reminders 8th: nt fluent 9th: rdn to hold pl 3 out: wkng whn mstke 3 out: sn bhd: t.o* **11/2**

P **Volcan D'Oudairies (FR)**[35] 4-10-3 0 .... MllePaolaBeacco(9)
(G Cherel, France) **33/1**

F **Tweety Kash (FR)** 4-9-11 0 .... DamienMescam(9)
(F-M Cottin, France) **7/2**[2]

4m 41.93s (281.93) **10** Ran SP% **117.8**
PARI-MUTUEL (all including 1 euro stake): WIN 6.30 (coupled with Volcan d'Oudairies); PLACE 2.70, 4.20, 2.30; DF 38.80; SF 73.20.
Owner M L Bloodstock Ltd **Bred** M.L. Bloodstock Ltd **Trained** France

2465a PRIX DES COUDRAIES (CHASE) (CONDITIONS) (5YO+) (TURF) 2m 2f 110y
2:35 (12:00) 5-Y-0+ **£21,463** (£10,731; £6,260; £4,247; £2,012)

RPR

1 **Taikun Tino (FR)**[43] 6-10-6 0 .... MorganRegairaz 123
(Yannick Fouin, France) **12/5**[1]

2 1 ¼ **Sable Des Ongrais (FR)**[11] 9-10-8 0 .... ChristopheHerpin 124
(P Chemin, France) **11/1**

3 4 **Serienschock (GER)**[56] 1608 5-10-10 0 .... RegisSchmidlin 122
(F-M Cottin, France) **33/10**[2]

4 4 **Bournie (FR)**[46] 5-10-12 0 .... (b) VincentCheminaud 120
(J-P Gallorini, France) **9/1**

5 2 **Oklahoma Seven (FR)**[10] 6-10-1 0 .... ThierryMajorcryk 107
(J-L Gay, France) **17/1**

6 5 **Montpellier (FR)**[13] 7-11-0 0 .... JoAudon 115
(Mme L Audon, France) **78/10**

7 1 ¼ **Rafale Precieux (FR)**[43] 8-11-3 0 .... AlbanDesvaux 117
(Mme M Desvaux, France) **32/1**

8 1 ¼ **Super De Sivola (FR)**[13] 7-11-0 0 .... AlainDeChitray 113
(T Trapenard, France) **24/1**

9 ½ **Trempolin (FR)**[517] 6-10-12 0 .... DavidCottin 110
(F-M Cottin, France) **11/2**[3]

10 hd **Le Bacardy (FR)**[11] 2211 7-10-8 0 .... (p) LeeEdwards 106
(Tony Carroll) *hld up towards rr: nt fluent 5th: briefly outpcd 6 out: sn rcvrd into midfield: chsd ldrs 3 out: sn rdn and lost pl: hrd rdn and no imp fr 2 out* **17/1**

11 18 **Kotmaille (FR)**[684] 8-10-6 0 .... RaphaelDelozier 86
(F Leralle, France) **114/1**

4m 52.34s (292.34) **11** Ran SP% **116.8**
PARI-MUTUEL (all including 1 euro stake): WIN 3.40; PLACE 1.60, 2.70, 1.80; DF 13.80; SF 20.90.
Owner Mme Magalen Bryant **Bred** Mme Magalen Bryant, Eurl Du Chene & Denis Baer **Trained** France

2038 LUDLOW (R-H)
Thursday, November 14

OFFICIAL GOING: Good (good to soft in places; 7.6) changing to good to soft after after race 4 (2.30)
Wind: Mdoerate, half against Weather: showers

2466 WATCH ON 3 DEVICES RACINGUK.COM/ANYWHERE JUVENILE HURDLE (9 hdls) 2m
1:00 (1:00) (Class 4) 3-Y-0 **£3,249** (£954; £477; £238)

Form RPR

3- 1 **Saint Jerome (IRE)**[36] 1813 3-10-12 0 .... RobertThornton 111
(Jamie Osborne) *mde all: clr early on: pressed fr 3 out: sn rdn: kpt on wl towards fin* **11/2**[3]

2- 2 1 ¾ **Aglaophonos**[21] 2038 3-10-12 0 .... (p) AidanColeman 110
(Ian Williams) *sn chsd wnr: upsides whn mstke 3 out: sn rdn and continued to chal: swtchd rt fnl 75yds: one pce cl home* **13/8**[1]

113- 3 9 **Ballyglasheen (IRE)**[14] 2172 3-11-12 120 .... PaulMoloney 115
(Evan Williams) *handy in chsng gp: niggled along appr 6th: styd on same pce fr 3 out: no imp on front two* **11/4**[2]

4 2 ¾ **Ivanhoe**[50] 3-10-12 0 .... MarkGrant 99
(Michael Blanshard) *in rr: hdwy 5th: rdn whn chsng ldrs bef 3 out: no imp: kpt on same pce* **18/1**

124- 5 38 **Refer**[33] 1862 3-11-5 115 .... (p) SamTwiston-Davies 81
(Phil Middleton) *midfield: impr to chse ldrs after 5th: blnd 6th: sn lost pl and wknd* **10/1**

6 5 **Misteray**[23] 3-10-9 0 .... (t) JakeGreenall(3) 65
(Bill Turner) *in rr: niggled along after 4th: nvr on terms* **200/1**

P0- 7 23 **Big John Cannon (IRE)**[21] 2038 3-10-5 0 .... (p) MrPJohn(7) 39
(Sarah-Jayne Davies) *midfield: pushed along after 4th: lost pl bef next: toiling 6th: lost tch* **150/1**

8 13 **Clement (IRE)**[58] 3-10-5 0 .... CiaranMckee(7) 27
(John O'Shea) *in tch: hdwy to chse ldrs after 3rd: wknd after 5th: toiling 6th: t.o* **40/1**

4- 9 3 ¼ **Maxi Mac (IRE)**[36] 1813 3-10-5 0 .... JoshWall(7) 25
(Trevor Wall) *midfield: u.p and lost pl 5th: bhd after: toiling 6th: t.o* **50/1**

0- P **Minister Of Mayhem**[25] 1985 3-10-5 0 ....[1] TomBellamy(7)
(Nick Mitchell) *handy: wknd appr 5th: t.o whn p.u bef 3 out* **100/1**

2- F **Brave Helios**[11] 2248 3-10-9 0 .... GavinSheehan(3) 98
(Jonathan Portman) *hld up: hdwy appr 5th: pushed along whn chsng ldrs bef 3 out: sn no imp: 5th abt 10 l off pce and wl hld whn fell last* **8/1**

3m 55.8s (6.30) **Going Correction** +0.40s/f (Soft) **11** Ran SP% **112.2**
Speed ratings (Par 104): **100,99,94,93,74 71,60,53,52,**
toteswingers 1&2 £4.00, 2&3 £1.80, 1&3 £2.60 CSF £14.58 TOTE £7.30: £2.20, £1.10, £1.50; EX 17.80 Trifecta £71.70 Pool: £1079.11 - 11.28 winning units..
Owner Mrs F Walwyn **Bred** P Turley **Trained** Upper Lambourn, Berks

FOCUS
All bends moved since last meeting and false wings in all fences. The ground appeared to be riding on the slow side of good and the runners had to contend with a blustery wind. This was a pretty moderate juvenile hurdle. A big step up from the winner with the next two to their marks.

2467 BET WITH THE LUDLOW ON COURSE BOOKMAKERS MAIDEN HURDLE (9 hdls) 2m
1:30 (1:30) (Class 5) 4-Y-0+ **£3,249** (£954; £477; £238)

Form RPR

130/ 1 **Free Thinking**[223] 5163 5-10-2 0 .... MrSWaley-Cohen(5) 122+
(Nicky Henderson) *trckd ldrs: led 6th: clr fr 2 out: easily* **1/1**[1]

15/ 2 13 **Koolala (IRE)**[210] 5364 5-10-7 0 .... DenisO'Regan 104
(Paul Webber) *prom: hit 1st: chsd ldr 4th: pushed along whn mstke 3 out: outpcd fr next: nt fluent last* **13/2**[2]

3 1 ¾ **Nesterenko (GER)**[117] 4-11-0 0 ....[1] AndrewTinkler 108
(Nicky Henderson) *hld up in tch: mstke 5th: rdn appr 3 out: hit next: styd on same pce* **8/1**

0/5- 4 1 ¾ **Pembroke House**[179] 395 6-11-0 0 .... WillKennedy 106
(Sarah-Jayne Davies) *prom: mstke 1st: rdn appr 3 out: styd on same pce* **100/1**

5 4 ½ **Broadway Symphony (IRE)**[114] 1102 6-11-0 0 .... MarkGrant 103
(Tracey L Bailey) *hld up in tch: racd keenly: mstke 2nd: rdn and hit 3 out: styd on same pce* **12/1**

6/2- 6 ¾ **Strollawaynow (IRE)**[14] 2178 6-11-0 0 .... TomCannon 100
(David Arbuthnot) *chsd ldr tl after 3rd: rdn and outpcd appr 3 out: styd on flat* **9/1**

06/ 7 nk **Torgamah Lad (IRE)**[268] 4299 5-11-0 0 .... AidanColeman 100
(Venetia Williams) *mid-div: rdn appr 3 out: nt trble ldrs* **50/1**

8 ½ **Peak Storm**[51] 4-10-7 0 .... CiaranMckee(7) 99
(John O'Shea) *hld up: racd keenly: rdn appr 3 out: n.d* **66/1**

350/ **9** 1 ¾ **Freckle Face**[269] 4289 6-11-0 99 .... PaddyBrennan 99
(Bill Turner) *led to 6th: pushed along appr 3 out: wkng whn nt fluent last* **66/1**

233- **10** 3 ½ **Macarthur**[21] 2045 9-11-0 111 .... (v) PaulMoloney 94
(David Rees) *prom: rdn appr 3 out: wknd next* **7/1**[3]

0/5- **11** 7 **The Master Remover (IRE)**[40] 1770 4-11-0 0 .... MarcGoldstein 87
(Chris Gordon) *hld up: rdn and wknd appr 3 out* **100/1**

0/6- **12** 35 **Drumgooland (IRE)**[14] 2181 6-10-7 109 .... (p) ChristopherWard(7) 52
(Dr Richard Newland) *hld up: a in rr: bhd fr 5th* **20/1**

5/0- **13** 15 **Errol Flynn (IRE)**[19] 2083 7-11-0 0 .... LeeEdwards 37
(Tony Carroll) *hld up: a in rr: bhd fr 5th* **150/1**

14 2 **Dune Island**[602] 5-10-4 0 .... GavinSheehan(3) 28
(John Upson) *a in rr: bhd whn hmpd 4th* **100/1**

F **Supreme Luxury (IRE)**[133] 4-10-7 0 .... HarrySkelton
(Dan Skelton) *prom tl hmpd and fell 4th* **25/1**

3m 52.4s (2.90) **Going Correction** +0.40s/f (Soft) **15** Ran SP% **121.8**
Speed ratings (Par 103): **108,101,100,99,97 97,96,96,95,94 90,73,65,64,**
toteswingers 1&2 £5.40, 2&3 £13.60, 1&3 £2.40 CSF £7.47 TOTE £1.90: £1.10, £2.70, £2.40; EX 12.20 Trifecta £82.90 Pool: £829.77 - 7.50 winning units..
Owner Robert Waley-Cohen **Bred** Upton Viva Stud **Trained** Upper Lambourn, Berks
■ Roxy Beat was withdrawn. Price at time of withdrawal 100/1. Rule 4 does not apply.

FOCUS
An ordinary race, the winner excepted, and they didn't go a great pace. The winner looks decent and can rate higher.

2468 WEATHERBYS 2014 POINT-TO-POINT ANNUAL H'CAP CHASE (22 fncs) 3m 1f 110y
2:00 (2:02) (Class 3) (0-125,125) 4-Y-£9,495 (£2,805; £1,402; £702; £351)

Form RPR

F22- **1** **Jayandbee (IRE)**[18] 2110 6-10-0 99 .... (p) JamesDavies 108
(Philip Hobbs) *in tch: clsd to go 2nd and w ldr 15th: chal 4 out: sn rdn: over 2 l down last: styd on to ld fnl 100yds: on top cl home* **4/1**[2]

P/2- **2** 1 ¼ **Rydalis (FR)**[9] 2283 8-11-2 115 .... AidanColeman 123
(Venetia Williams) *prom: led 3rd: rdn appr 3 out: over 2 l clr last: hdd fnl 100yds: one pce and hld cl home* **9/4**[1]

535- **3** 3 ½ **Cootehill (IRE)**[36] 1815 9-11-12 125 .... SamTwiston-Davies 130
(Nigel Twiston-Davies) *hld up: hdwy appr 15th: trckd ldrs bef 4 out: rdn bef 2 out and no imp: chal for 3rd run-in: styd on towards fin but no ch* **7/1**[3]

/12- **4** ½ **Raduis Bleu (FR)**[21] 2041 8-10-9 115 .... MissLBrooke(7) 119
(Lady Susan Brooke) *trckd ldrs: pushed along and no imp appr 2 out: chal for 3rd run-in: styd on same pce and no ch w front two* **12/1**

/16- **5** 13 **Kings Lodge**[18] 2107 7-11-9 122 .... AndrewTinkler 115
(Nicky Henderson) *in tch: wnt prom 4th: rdn and wknd after 18th: wl hld whn stmbld 3 out* **9/1**

233- **6** 3 ¼ **Inside Dealer (IRE)**[18] 2108 9-11-10 123 .... (tp) JoeTizzard 113
(Colin Tizzard) *led to 3rd: remained prom: lost pl bef 15th: u.p after: plugged on but n.d fr 4 out* **8/1**

030/ **7** 1 ¼ **Present To You (IRE)**[246] 4732 8-10-9 115 .... JakeHodson(7) 104
(David Bridgwater) *midfield: lost pl and towards rr 7th: pushed along after 14th (water): bhd 18th* **12/1**

031- **P** **Lava Lamp (GER)**[36] 1817 6-11-8 121 .... AdamWedge
(Evan Williams) *in rr: pushed along 18th and gng nowhere: wl bhd whn p.u bef 3 out* **12/1**

1FF/ **P** **Low Gales (IRE)**[365] 2419 7-11-2 115 .... (t) MarkGrant
(Charlie Mann) *in rr: slipped on bnd after 9th: rdn after 10th: detached 13th: t.o whn p.u after 18th* **25/1**

6m 52.3s (17.00) **Going Correction** +0.75s/f (Soft) **9** Ran SP% **111.3**
Speed ratings (Par 107): **103,102,101,101,97 96,96, ,**
toteswingers 1&2 £2.20, 2&3 £6.30, 1&3 £9.60 CSF £13.26 CT £56.91 TOTE £4.90: £1.80, £1.10, £2.90; EX 12.60 Trifecta £140.60 Pool: £1170.31 - 6.24 winning units..
Owner J & B Gibbs & Sons Ltd **Bred** Miss E Violet Sweeney **Trained** Withycombe, Somerset

FOCUS
A fair handicap chase in which the emphasis was on stamina. The winner is rated similar to his recent best.

2469 VERA DAVIES CUP NOVICES' LIMITED H'CAP CHASE (13 fncs) 2m
2:30 (2:31) (Class 3) (0-125,124) 4-Y-0+ £6,498 (£1,908; £954; £477)

Form RPR

323- **1** **Oyster Shell**[21] 2042 6-10-13 121 .... JakeGreenall(3) 132+
(Henry Daly) *mde all: clr 6th: hmpd by loose horse flat: pushed out* **5/1**[3]

00/- **2** ¾ **Daymar Bay (IRE)**[380] 2118 7-10-2 110 oh8 .... GavinSheehan(3) 119+
(Emma Lavelle) *hld up and bhd: nt fluent 5th (water): plenty to do 9th: r.o appr last: wnt 2nd flat: nt quite rch wnr* **7/2**[1]

2/6- **3** 4 ½ **Pearls Legend**[196] 82 6-10-13 118 .... JamieMoore 122
(John Spearing) *plld hrd and sn prom: chsd wnr 9th: rdn 4 out: styd on same pce fr 2 out: lost 2nd flat* **8/1**

2/6- **4** 1 ¾ **Bullet Street (IRE)**[186] 251 5-10-11 116 .... PaulMoloney 118
(Evan Williams) *hld up: hdwy after 9th: rdn appr 2 out: styd on* **9/2**[2]

/31- **5** nk **Drumlang (IRE)**[21] 2039 7-10-0 110 oh3 .... RobertMcCarth(5) 112
(Ian Williams) *trckd ldrs: wnt 2nd 7th to 9th: rdn and mstke 2 out: kpt on* **9/1**

/13- **6** 6 **Suerte Al Salto (IRE)**[34] 1857 6-11-0 119 .... TomCannon 116
(Chris Gordon) *chsd wnr to 6th: remained handy: rdn appr 4 out: wknd appr last* **7/1**

043/ **7** 2 ¾ **Mount Gunnery**[214] 5317 5-10-5 110 oh2 .... PaddyBrennan 106
(Robert Walford) *mid-div: racd keenly: hmpd 1st: lost pl 5th: in rr whn blnd 7th: n.d after* **12/1**

0/0- **8** 6 **Rocky Elsom (USA)**[24] 2007 6-10-0 110 oh5 .... (t) NicodeBoinville(5) 99
(David Arbuthnot) *hld up: hdwy 8th: pushed along whn pckd 4 out: sn wknd* **50/1**

/51- **9** 37 **Christopher Wren (USA)**[22] 2025 6-10-8 118 .... MauriceLinehan(5) 74
(Nick Gifford) *hld up: a in rr: rdn and wknd after 9th* **11/1**

16/- **U** **Kings Flagship**[343] 2882 8-10-13 118 .... JamesDavies
(Chris Down) *mstke and uns rdr 1st* **20/1**

210- **P** **Strongly Suggested**[29] 1922 6-11-5 124 .... (t) RichieMcLernon
(Jonjo O'Neill) *hld up: a in rr: pushed along 7th: bhd whn blnd 9th: p.u bef next* **28/1**

4m 7.5s (9.00) **Going Correction** +0.75s/f (Soft) **11** Ran SP% **116.9**
Speed ratings (Par 107): **107,106,104,103,103 100,98,95,77,**
toteswingers 1&2 £5.60, 2&3 £9.50, 1&3 £12.70 CSF £23.03 CT £138.96 TOTE £5.60: £2.30, £2.30, £4.00; EX 29.70 Trifecta £461.20 Pool: £2070.90 - 3.36 winning units..
Owner The Glazeley Partnership 2 **Bred** W P Jenks **Trained** Stanton Lacy, Shropshire

FOCUS
They went a decent pace in this fair event, which should produce winners. The winner is on the upgrade and the form looks solid.

2470 AJA AMATEUR RIDERS' H'CAP HURDLE (11 hdls) 2m 5f
3:00 (3:01) (Class 5) (0-95,95) 4-Y-0+ £3,119 (£967; £483; £242)

Form RPR

300/ **1** **Kings Apollo**[193] 4-10-1 77 .... MrJNixon(7) 82
(Tom Symonds) *hld up: swtchd lft and hdwy after 8th: led appr 3 out: hit last: rdn out and styd on* **7/1**[2]

013- **2** 2 ¾ **Tribal Dance (IRE)**[32] 1890 7-11-7 95 .... MissSMDoolan(5) 97
(John O'Shea) *prom: led after 2nd: hdd 4th: led after 5th: hdd 8th: remained prom: ev ch 3 out: kpt on u.p run-in but hld* **8/1**[3]

660- **3** ½ **Queen Spud**[36] 1824 4-10-9 85 .... MrPJohn(7) 87
(Henry Daly) *hld up: hdwy appr 7th: rdn to chse ldrs after 8th: styd on u.p: kpt on same pce towards fin* **20/1**

526- **4** 10 **Midnight Mustang**[19] 2076 6-10-9 83 .... MrJMartin(5) 76
(Andrew J Martin) *prom: lost pl and in tch after 2nd: led 8th: hdd appr 3 out: one pce fr 2 out* **8/1**[3]

045/ **5** hd **Free Falling**[227] 5084 7-10-11 85 .... (v) MissCBoxall(5) 78
(Alastair Lidderdale) *hld up in midfield: effrt to chse ldrs appr 2 out: one pce* **25/1**

/0P- **6** 4 **Original Star (IRE)**[186] 254 8-11-2 90 .... MrJMRidley(5) 79
(Derek Frankland) *midfield: effrt appr 3 out: nvr able to trble ldrs* **14/1**

F00- **7** 14 **Tisfreetdream (IRE)**[135] 860 12-11-3 93 .... (p) MissCVHart(7) 70
(Peter Pritchard) *chsd ldrs: pushed along appr 2 out: sn btn* **22/1**

230- **8** 4 ½ **Master Cardor Visa (IRE)**[28] 1945 8-11-5 95 .... MrHBeswick(7) 68
(Emma Baker) *towards rr: plugged on fr 3 out: nvr a threat* **11/1**

/51- **9** 9 **Dancing Daffodil**[6] 2348 8-10-12 88 .... MrTWWheeler(7) 52
(Robin Dickin) *hld up: u.p after 8th: nvr on terms* **4/1**[1]

4U2/ **10** 2 ½ **Cool Bob (IRE)**[1099] 2327 10-10-7 83 .... (t[1]) MrStanSheppard(7) 45
(Matt Sheppard) *hld up: hdwy appr 8th: sn chsd ldrs: wknd bef 3 out* **16/1**

05P- **11** 5 **Tara Warrior (IRE)**[19] 2090 7-11-4 92 .... (b) MrBGibbs(5) 50
(Tim Vaughan) *led to 2nd: trckd ldrs after: rdn and wknd appr 3 out* **22/1**

0P0- **12** 84 **Kilcolman Wizard (IRE)**[18] 2105 7-10-9 85 .... (b[1]) MrTSquire(7)
(Liam Corcoran) *prom tl j. slowly 1st: sn dropped to midfield: rdn and bhd bef 7th: t.o* **50/1**

5/4- **P** **Best Lover (FR)**[174] 457 11-11-5 95 .... MrJBargary(7)
(Laura Hurley) *in tch: lost pl and rdn 4th: u.p and bhd 6th: t.o whn p.u bef last* **25/1**

023/ **P** **Miss Tilly Oscar (IRE)**[448] 1330 7-11-9 95 .... MrFMitchell(3)
(David Evans) *racd keenly: prom: led 2nd: sn hdd: led again 4th: hdd after 5th: remained handy tl rdn and lost pl bef 7th: wknd appr 8th: wl bhd whn p.u bef 3 out* **14/1**

65P/ **P** **Shades Of Autumn (IRE)**[522] 682 8-11-0 90 .... MrCSmith(7)
(Linda Blackford) *in tch: pushed along appr 8th: wknd sn after: t.o whn p.u bef 3 out* **33/1**

422- **P** **Isola Bella**[14] 2176 4-11-3 93 .... (b) MrJHarding(7)
(Jonathan Portman) *hld up in rr: hdwy appr 7th into midfield: wknd 8th: t.o whn p.u bef 3 out* **10/1**

603- **P** **Katnapping**[13] 2191 5-11-6 89 .... MrSWaley-Cohen
(Robert Waley-Cohen) *hld up: mstke 5th: hdwy to go prom sn after: pushed along and wknd after 8th: bhd whn p.u bef 3 out* **10/1**

5m 22.2s (7.40) **Going Correction** +0.40s/f (Soft)
WFA 4 from 5yo+ 8lb **17** Ran SP% **126.5**
Speed ratings (Par 103): **101,99,99,95,95 94,89,87,83,82 81,49, , ,**
toteswingers 1&2 £13.10, 2&3 £34.90, 1&3 £30.90 CSF £58.70 CT £1102.29 TOTE £11.00: £2.60, £2.20, £5.40, £2.90; EX 95.80 Trifecta £1122.00 Part won. Pool: £1496.01 - 0.32 winning units..
Owner G&M Roberts Churchward Frost Green W-Williams **Bred** M Watt & Exors Of The Late Miss J John **Trained** Harewood End, H'fords
■ Stewards' Enquiry : Mr J Bargary three-day ban: used whip without giving gelding time to respond (Nov 28,29,Dec 1)

FOCUS
The official going description was amended before this event, a weak handicap confined to amateur riders. It was well run and the winner produced a step up.

2471 NOVEMBER INTRODUCTORY HURDLE (11 hdls) 2m 5f
3:30 (3:32) (Class 3) 4-Y-0+ £5,523 (£1,621; £810; £405)

Form RPR

0- **1** **Gallery Exhibition (IRE)**[25] 1991 6-11-0 0 .... SamThomas 100
(Kim Bailey) *trckd ldrs: led appr 3 out: drvn out* **14/1**

1/6- **2** 1 **Master Rajeem (USA)**[13] 2197 4-11-0 0 .... SamTwiston-Davies 99
(Nigel Twiston-Davies) *plld hrd and prom: pushed along after 3 out: rdn and hung rt flat: styd on* **16/1**

20- **3** 6 **Owen Na View (IRE)**[25] 1991 5-11-0 0 .... PaddyBrennan 93
(Fergal O'Brien) *hld up: hdwy appr 3 out: rdn after next: no ex flat* **11/1**

1/3- **4** 1 ½ **Anteros (IRE)**[22] 2018 5-11-0 0 .... PaulMoloney 94
(Sophie Leech) *hld up: hdwy and blnd 3 out: sn rdn: styd on same pce fr next* **3/1**[1]

/32- **5** 3 **Simply A Legend**[22] 2018 4-11-0 0 .... RobertThornton 89
(Alan King) *hld up in tch: racd keenly: chsd ldr appr 3 out: wknd last* **3/1**[1]

0/0- **6** 5 **Bayley's Dream**[19] 2083 4-11-0 0 .... DenisO'Regan 85
(Paul Webber) *hld up: hdwy appr 3 out: hit next: sn wknd* **66/1**

P- **7** 6 **Murtys Delight (IRE)**[13] 2189 6-11-0 0 .... AndrewTinkler 78
(Dr Richard Newland) *hld up: rdn appr 3 out: nvr on terms* **20/1**

2- **8** ¾ **Forgivienne**[21] 2043 6-10-7 0 .... AdamWedge 70
(Evan Williams) *trckd ldrs: racd keenly: mstke 5th: rdn and mstke 3 out: sn wknd* **10/1**[3]

/05- **9** 4 **Hare In A Round (IRE)**[23] 2009 5-10-9 0 .... PatrickCorbett(5) 73
(Rebecca Curtis) *led and nt fluent 1st: rdn and hdd appr 3 out: hit next: sn wknd* **25/1**

200/ **10** 14 **Willpower (IRE)**[231] 4991 4-11-0 0 .... DavidBass 59
(Nicky Henderson) *hld up: a in rr: rdn and wknd appr 3 out* **20/1**

0/0- **11** 15 **Nash Point (IRE)**[10] 2266 4-11-0 0 .... AidanColeman 44
(Tim Vaughan) *racd keenly: trckd ldr to 2nd: remained handy: pushed along after 8th: wknd bef next* **100/1**

0/2- **12** 15 **Dreams And Songs**[36] 1814 5-10-7 0 .... RichardJohnson 22
(Philip Hobbs) *hld up: hdwy after 8th: rdn and wknd 3 out* **7/2**[2]

P- **13** dist **Just Lewis**[32] 1891 6-10-11 0 .... RobertDunne(3)
(Nikki Evans) *prom: hit 2nd: chsd ldr and mstke 4th: lost 2nd 6th: sn wknd* **200/1**

5m 25.1s (10.30) **Going Correction** +0.40s/f (Soft) **13** Ran SP% **118.5**
Speed ratings (Par 107): **96,95,93,92,91 89,87,87,85,80 74,68,**
toteswingers 1&2 £12.30, 2&3 £11.30, 1&3 £14.40 CSF £192.07 TOTE £14.00: £4.10, £3.50, £3.10; EX 176.80 Trifecta £1613.80 Pool: £2528.01 - 1.17 winning units..
Owner The GFH Partnership **Bred** Joe Fogarty **Trained** Andoversford, Gloucs

The Form Book Jumps, Raceform Ltd, Compton, RG20 6NL.

FOCUS
An interesting race, but one run at a fairly steady gallop and the form may not prove wholly reliable. The form is rated through the winner and third.

2472 CHRISTMAS PARTIES ON 18 DECEMBER INTERMEDIATE OPEN NATIONAL HUNT FLAT RACE — 2m
4:00 (4:00) (Class 5) 4-6-Y-O — **£2,599** (£763; £381; £190)

Form — RPR

4- **1** **Sign Of A Victory (IRE)**[181] [359] 4-11-2 0 ... AndrewTinkler 116+
(Nicky Henderson) *midfield: hdwy 6f out: led gng wl 3f out: shkn up over 1f out: drew clr ins fnl f: easily* **6/5**[1]

1- **2** *8* **On Tour (IRE)**[36] [1819] 5-11-9 0 ... PaulMoloney 111
(Evan Williams) *chsd ldrs: rdn and ev ch over 2f out: wnt 2nd over 1f out: no ch w wnr fnl f* **9/2**[3]

3 *2 ¾* **Monbeg Theatre (IRE)**[186] 4-11-2 0 ... SamTwiston-Davies 101
(Jamie Snowden) *in tch: rdn and ev ch over 2f out: one pce fr over 1f out* **7/2**[2]

4 *4* **Letterofthelaw (IRE)**[179] 4-11-2 0 ... JamieMoore 97
(Rebecca Curtis) *led: rdn and hdd 3f out: no ex fr 2f out* **14/1**

5 *29* **Bellucia** 4-10-9 0 ... LeightonAspell 61
(Oliver Sherwood) *midfield: hdwy to chse ldrs 5f out: no imp and btn 2f out* **14/1**

6- **6** *1 ½* **Retroson (IRE)**[36] [1819] 5-11-2 0 ... AdamWedge 67
(Michael Scudamore) *hld up: hdwy to chse ldrs 5f out: no imp and btn 2f out* **100/1**

0- **7** *14* **Back By Midnight**[33] [1869] 4-10-11 0 ... AodhaganConlon(5) 53
(Emma Baker) *hld up: hdwy into midfield 6f out: rdn and wknd over 3f out* **100/1**

U- **8** *11* **Dorton Lad (IRE)**[30] [1919] 4-10-9 0 ... MrDGannon(7) 42
(Phil Middleton) *plld hrd: hld up: sme hdwy 1/2-way: pushed and bhd 5f out* **100/1**

9 *shd* **Monart Diamond**[187] 4-11-2 0 ... RichardJohnson 42
(Tim Vaughan) *chsd ldr to 1/2-way: wknd 5f out* **18/1**

26/ **10** *1 ½* **When Ben When (IRE)**[208] [5413] 4-11-2 0 ... JoeTizzard 40
(Colin Tizzard) *racd keenly: chsd ldrs tl rdn and wknd over 4f out* **16/1**

11 *15* **Castanum (IRE)** 4-11-2 0 ... TomCannon 25
(Laura Young) *hld up: pushed along 1/2-way: wl bhd whn hung lft 6f out and again bdly 3f out: t.o* **100/1**

12 *2 ¼* **Sonic Weld** 4-10-4 0 ow2 ... MrJMartin(7) 18
(Andrew J Martin) *in tch: lost pl 1/2-way: bhd 6f out: t.o* **66/1**

3m 55.9s (12.00) **Going Correction** +0.40s/f (Soft)
WFA 4 from 5yo 7lb — **12** Ran SP% **115.8**
Speed ratings: **86,82,80,78,64 63,56,50,50,50 42,41**
toteswingers 1&2 £2.40, 2&3 £2.70, 1&3 £1.70 CSF £6.45 TOTE £2.40: £1.10, £1.60, £1.80; EX 7.70 Trifecta £23.80 Pool: £1521.24 - 47.83 winning units..
Owner Matt & Lauren Morgan **Bred** John Hore **Trained** Upper Lambourn, Berks

FOCUS
A fair bumper. The impressive winner was the form pick but this rates a step up.
T/Jkpt: Not won. T/Plt: £192.90 to a £1 stake. Pool of £64797.99 - 245.10 winning tickets.
T/Qpdt: £190.90 to a £1 stake. Pool of £5830.83 - 22.60 winning tickets. DO

[79]TAUNTON (R-H)
Thursday, November 14

OFFICIAL GOING: Good (good to firm in places; 6.2)
Wind: strong across Weather: light showers

2473 DEBUT RMB CHIVENOR H'CAP HURDLE (12 hdls) — 3m 110y
1:10 (1:10) (Class 5) (0-100,100) 4-Y-0+ — **£2,737** (£798; £399)

Form — RPR

4P4- **1** **Halucha (IRE)**[7] [2314] 8-11-10 **98** ... (p) LiamTreadwell 103+
(Paul Webber) *j.rt: mde all: clr at times: pushed along and wl in command fr 2 out: styd on wl* **13/2**

0/0- **2** *7* **Regal Flow**[18] [2105] 6-11-5 **100** ... MrLDrowne(7) 98
(Caroline Keevil) *trckd wnr: rdn after 3 out: hld fr next: styd on same pce* **7/2**[2]

512- **3** *6* **Artic Night (FR)**[19] [2088] 7-11-2 **90** ... (bt) DavidEngland 83
(Nigel Twiston-Davies) *hld up towards rr: pushed along after 8th: rdn and stdy prog after 3 out: wnt 3rd next: styd on same pce fr last* **5/1**[3]

P/0- **4** *9* **Typhon De Guye (FR)**[186] [254] 6-11-9 **97** ... IanPopham 83
(Martin Keighley) *mid-div: tk clsr order 4th: rdn in 3rd after 3 out: lost 2nd 2 out: fdd* **11/4**[1]

6FP/ **5** *8* **Saint Peray (FR)**[635] [4393] 7-11-7 **95** ... SamJones 72
(Bob Buckler) *hld up towards rr on outer: hdwy after 4th: rdn after 8th: 4th 3 out but nvr threatened to get on terms: wknd 2 out* **40/1**

241- **6** *2* **Southway Queen**[39] [1784] 9-10-13 **94** ... (tp) NathanAdams(7) 70
(Sue Gardner) *trckd ldrs: struggling after 8th: wknd bef 3 out* **9/1**

0/6- **7** *14* **Wychwoods Mist**[22] [2029] 6-10-12 **93** ... (tp) GoraldQuinn(7) 56
(Claire Dyson) *in tch: chsd wnr after 8th tl wknd qckly after 3 out* **33/1**

0P4- **8** *¾* **Tang Royal (FR)**[156] [706] 6-11-4 **95** ... JeremiahMcGrath(3) 57
(Richard Rowe) *mid-div: rdn after 3 out: sn wknd* **40/1**

P/0- **9** *46* **Madam Noso**[195] [99] 9-11-4 **95** ... JamesBest(3) 16
(Richard King) *chsd wnr tl rdn after 8th: sn wknd: t.o* **28/1**

0/0- **10** *¾* **Ponte Di Rosa**[14] [2176] 5-11-2 **90** ... NickScholfield 10
(Simon Hodgson) *mid-div tl 7th: sn in rr: t.o* **50/1**

341- **B** **Transfer**[35] [1837] 8-11-4 **92** ... APMcCoy
(Richard Price) *hld up towards rr: being pushed along whn b.d between 8th and 9th* **6/1**

000- **F** **Puerto Azul (IRE)**[9] [2280] 9-11-6 **97** ... MichealNolan(3)
(Bernard Scriven) *hld up towards rr: hdwy after 7th: chsng wnr whn stmbld and fell after path between 8th and 9th* **50/1**

6m 1.9s (-2.10) **Going Correction** -0.25s/f (Good) — **12** Ran SP% **118.4**
Speed ratings (Par 103): **93,90,88,85,83 82,78,78,63,63 ,**
toteswingers 1&2 £5.10, 2&3 £3.30, 1&3 £7.10 CSF £28.63 CT £124.49 TOTE £7.90: £2.70, £1.80, £2.20; EX 30.30 Trifecta £241.40 Pool: £1007.43 - 3.12 winning units..
Owner R W Barnett **Bred** Mrs Mai O'Sullivan **Trained** Mollington, Oxon

FOCUS
Chases and Hurdles on shared bends. Suspect form but the winner is rated to his best.

2474 KAY HILL BIRTHDAY CELEBRATION H'CAP HURDLE (9 hdls) — 2m 1f
1:40 (1:40) (Class 4) (0-115,115) 4-Y-0+ — **£4,106** (£1,197; £598)

Form — RPR

4/4- **1** **Brinestine (USA)**[23] [2011] 4-11-11 **114** ... NickScholfield 122+
(Paul Nicholls) *trckd ldrs: gd run on inner to ld after 3 out: pckd last: sn rdn: edgd lft: r.o wl* **13/2**[3]

3FF/ **2** *6* **Don Pooleoni (IRE)**[216] [5268] 8-11-4 **107** ... NoelFehily 107
(Harry Fry) *mid-div: smooth hdwy appr 3 out: upsides on home bnd: rdn to chse wnr after 2 out: kpt on same pce* **3/1**[2]

316- **3** *2 ½* **Border Station (IRE)**[10] [2274] 7-10-10 **102** ... JoshuaMoore(3) 100
(Alison Batchelor) *hld up towards rr: stdy prog fr 6th: drvn after 3 out: lft 4th 2 out: styd on fr last: wnt 3rd fnl 75yds* **18/1**

315- **4** *2* **Cruise In Style (IRE)**[28] [1939] 7-10-7 **99** ... (bt) JamesBest(3) 94
(Kevin Bishop) *hld up towards rr: smooth hdwy 3 out: rdn whn lft 3rd 2 out: no ex whn lost 3rd fnl 75yds* **20/1**

/14- **5** *3* **To The Sky (IRE)**[45] [1697] 5-11-1 **109** ... HarryDerham(5) 102
(John O'Shea) *trckd ldrs: ev ch 3 out: sn rdn: sn one pce: lft 5th next* **25/1**

260/ **6** *6* **Going Nowhere Fast (IRE)**[336] [3026] 8-9-13 **93** ... RobertWilliams(5) 80
(Bernard Llewellyn) *mid-div: lost pl and pushed along after 5th: plugged on again after 3 out: nvr a threat* **33/1**

045- **7** *¾* **Ladies Dancing**[18] [2111] 7-11-4 **110** ... GilesHawkins(3) 97
(Chris Down) *trckd ldrs: wnt lft and led 6th: wnt lft next: sn rdn and hdd: wknd bef 2 out* **9/1**

4P5- **8** *7* **Bedouin Bay**[35] [1833] 6-10-5 **101** ow1 ... MrRobertHawker(7) 81
(Johnny Farrelly) *mid-div: rdn after 3 out: wknd next* **20/1**

/U4- **9** *19* **Backhomeinderry (IRE)**[172] [484] 8-10-10 **99** ... (t) LiamTreadwell 62
(Kate Buckett) *led 2nd tl 6th: wknd after 3 out: t.o* **14/1**

33/- **10** *10* **Enchanting Smile (FR)**[229] [5025] 6-10-1 **90** ... (t) TommyPhelan 44
(Mark Gillard) *led tl 2nd: chsd ldrs tl wknd after 6th: t.o* **66/1**

/55- **11** *49* **In The Crowd (IRE)**[26] [1970] 4-11-9 **112** ... (t) ConorO'Farrell 22
(Richard Price) *struggling after 4th: a towards rr: t.o* **66/1**

/36- **12** *½* **Exemplary**[33] [1864] 6-11-1 **104** ... TomO'Brien 13
(Marc Barber) *sn struggling: a towards rr: t.o bef 3 out* **14/1**

564/ **P** **Shivsingh**[214] [5317] 4-11-4 **107** ... HaddenFrost
(Martin Hill) *mid-div tl stmbld v bdly 4th: sn p.u* **33/1**

/22- **P** **Uriah Heep (FR)**[10] [2271] 4-11-10 **113** ... WayneHutchinson 112
(Alan King) *mid-div: hdwy 3 out: rdn in 4th and styng on at same pce whn slipped on landing and virtually fell 2 out: immediately p.u* **11/4**[1]

P/2- **P** **Foxes Bridge**[183] [306] 5-11-1 **104** ... BrendanPowell
(Colin Tizzard) *j.lft and nvr fluent: in tch tl wknd appr 3 out: t.o whn p.u bef 2 out* **14/1**

4m 0.9s (-7.10) **Going Correction** -0.25s/f (Good)
WFA 4 from 5yo+ 7lb — **15** Ran SP% **122.5**
Speed ratings (Par 105): **106,103,102,101,99 96,96,93,84,79 56,56, , ,**
toteswingers 1&2 £3.00, 2&3 £35.50, 1&3 £8.10 CSF £25.18 CT £346.06 TOTE £8.60: £2.40, £1.50, £4.40; EX 31.20 Trifecta £692.50 Part won. Pool: £923.39 - 0.24 winning units..
Owner The Johnson & Stewart Families **Bred** Joe Murphy **Trained** Ditcheat, Somerset

FOCUS
This looked quite a competitive event, and it was run at a reasonable gallop. The winner is entitled to rate higher on Flat form and this looks form to be positive about.

2475 SIS LIVE NOVICES' LIMITED H'CAP CHASE (17 fncs) — 2m 7f 110y
2:10 (2:10) (Class 3) (0-125,124) 4-Y-0+ — **£6,844** (£1,995; £998)

Form — RPR

20F- **1** **Coole River (IRE)**[18] [2107] 9-11-4 **123** ... NoelFehily 133+
(Emma Lavelle) *trckd ldrs: jnd ldr 4th: upsides travelling strly 4 out: w.w: led after 2 out: styd on wl: rdn out run-in* **8/1**

5/2- **2** *2* **Bertie Boru (IRE)**[39] [1797] 6-11-1 **120** ... TomO'Brien 127+
(Philip Hobbs) *hld up bhd ldrs: j.lft at times: disputing cl 4th 4 out: rdn after 3 out: disputing 2nd jst bef last: edgd rt run-in: kpt on but hld by wnr* **14/1**

0/6- **3** *1* **The Mumper (IRE)**[184] [289] 6-10-5 **110** ... GerardTumelty 114
(Alan King) *in tch: hit 10th: cl up after 4 out: rdn whn pckd 2 out: disputing cl 2nd last: kpt on but no ex* **20/1**

231/ **4** *2 ½* **Hatters River (IRE)**[207] [5440] 6-10-13 **118** ... JackDoyle 121
(Ali Brewer) *hld up bhd ldrs: disputing cl 5th 3 out: sn rdn: kpt on but nt gng pce to get on terms* **14/1**

131- **5** *3 ¼* **Western King (IRE)**[21] [2041] 6-11-4 **123** ... (tp) APMcCoy 122
(Charlie Mann) *led: rchd for 3rd: rdn whn jnd by str travelling wnr after 4 out: kpt holding narrow advantage: hdd after 2 out: sn no ex* **5/1**[3]

3/1- **6** *4* **Guess Again (IRE)**[8] [2297] 8-11-0 **119** ... (t) TomScudamore 118+
(David Pipe) *trckd ldrs: mstke 6th: rdn after 13th: remained cl up tl fdd appr last* **13/8**[1]

0/2- **P** **Sin Bin (IRE)**[19] [2073] 7-11-0 **119** ... (t) NickScholfield
(Paul Nicholls) *in tch: rdn after 12th: wknd after 4 out: p.u after next* **4/1**[2]

/24- **F** **Forresters Folly**[18] [2106] 7-11-5 **124** ... (p) WayneHutchinson 116
(Alan King) *in tch: mstke 12th: rdn after 4 out: disp 3rd next: hld in 6th whn fell 2 out* **16/1**

6m 5.4s (-10.60) **Going Correction** -0.25s/f (Good) — **8** Ran SP% **109.9**
Speed ratings (Par 107): **107,106,106,105,104 102, ,**
toteswingers 1&2 £9.60, 2&3 £0.00, 1&3 £29.90 CSF £93.90 CT £1997.31 TOTE £11.10: £2.30, £1.60, £5.00; EX 95.20 Trifecta £535.40 Part won. Pool: £713.87 - 0.02 winning units..
Owner Queens' Prices Syndicate **Bred** Seamus Larkin **Trained** Hatherden, Hants

FOCUS
A modest novice handicap. A chase best from the winner but there should be more to come from him.

2476 "DAVID HALL...BEEN TO 'EM ALL" NOVICES' HURDLE (9 hdls) — 2m 1f
2:40 (2:40) (Class 3) 4-Y-0+ — **£5,848** (£1,717; £858; £429)

Form — RPR

1 **Irving**[76] 5-10-12 0 ... NickScholfield 120+
(Paul Nicholls) *trckd ldrs: mstke 3rd: travelling best whn chalng appr 2 out: w.w: hit last: sn led: qcknd clr: easily* **11/4**[2]

4/ **2** *4* **Cup Final (IRE)**[207] [5444] 4-10-12 0 ... APMcCoy 111+
(Nicky Henderson) *trckd ldrs: rdn to chal appr 2 out: led narrowly on landing: hdd sn after last: nt pce of easy wnr: returned w nasty cut on hind leg* **10/11**[1]

/51- **3** *3 ¾* **Magic Money**[36] [1814] 5-10-4 0 ... JackSherwood(7) 102
(Kim Bailey) *led: veered rt 4th: rdn and hdd on landing 2 out: kpt on same pce* **6/1**[3]

06/ **4** *1 ¼* **Barista (IRE)**[24] [5143] 5-10-9 0 ... WayneKavanagh(3) 101
(Brian Forsey) *mid-div: hdwy 3 out: sn rdn: styd on into 4th sn after 2 out but nt gng pce to get on terms w ldrs* **66/1**

5 *3 ¾* **Red Seventy**[110] 4-10-5 0 ... (b) MikeyEnnis(7) 99
(David Pipe) *mid-div: hdwy after 6th: rdn in cl 4th appr 2 out: kpt on same pce* **40/1**

2/0- **6** *3 ¼* **The Kvilleken**[26] [1974] 5-10-12 0 ... IanPopham 94
(Martin Keighley) *trckd ldrs: mstke 5th: rdn whn outpcd after 3 out: nt a threat after* **33/1**

5- **7** *1 ½* **The Wealerdealer (IRE)**[9] [2279] 6-10-12 0 ... TomScudamore 92
(David Pipe) *hld up towards rr: rdn after 3 out: kpt on but no real imp on ldrs* **28/1**

U00- **8** 3 3/4 **Wicklewood**^{28} [1940] 7-10-12 76 ....(t^{1}) TommyPhelan 89
(Mark Gillard) *chsd ldrs tl lost pl appr 3 out: nt a danger after* **200/1**

6- **9** 5 **Frozen Over**^{35} [1832] 5-10-9 0 .... GilesHawkins$^{(3)}$ 84
(Chris Down) *mid-div: hdwy 6th: hit 3 out: sn rdn: wknd bef next* **40/1**

10 11 **Hint Of Mint**^{483} 4-10-12 0 .... NoelFehily 73
(Nick Williams) *mid-div tl wknd 3 out* **33/1**

0/4- **11** 2 1/4 **Famousandfearless (IRE)**^{13} [2197] 5-10-12 0 .... TimmyMurphy 70
(David Pipe) *hld up towards rr: sme prog 5th: wknd 3 out* **11/1**

04/- **12** 18 **Watchmetail (IRE)**^{267} [4331] 7-10-12 0 .... ConorO'Farrell 52
(John Panvert) *a bhd: t.o bef 3 out* **200/1**

0- **13** 47 **Arcas (IRE)**^{39} [1793] 4-10-12 0 .... TomO'Brien 5
(Alan Jones) *a in rr: t.o fr 6th* **200/1**

4m 6.4s (-1.60) **Going Correction** -0.25s/f (Good) **13** Ran SP% **118.9**
Speed ratings (Par 107): **93,91,89,88,87 85,84,83,80,75 74,65,43**
toteswingers 1&2 £1.10, 2&3 £1.30, 1&3 £2.60 CSF £5.53 TOTE £4.20: £1.40, £1.10, £2.10; EX 8.10 Trifecta £12.70 Pool: £1126.65 - 66.23 winning units..
Owner Axom XLIX **Bred** Gestut Schlenderhan **Trained** Ditcheat, Somerset

FOCUS
A fair novice hurdle run at a slow pace. The winner should go on to rate higher.

2477 JEREMY PARSONS 50TH BIRTHDAY CELEBRATION MARES' H'CAP HURDLE (10 hdls) 2m 3f 110y
3:10 (3:10) (Class 4) (0-120,119) 4-Y-0+ **£4,106** (£1,197; £598)

Form RPR

1/0- **1** **Weather Babe**^{185} [267] 5-10-13 **106** .... TomScudamore 112
(David Pipe) *trckd ldrs: nt fluent 5th: prom next: led after 3 out: styd on: rdn out* **4/1**^{2}

/53- **2** 1 1/4 **Pass The Time**^{111} [1084] 4-11-2 **109** ....(p) NoelFehily 114
(Neil Mulholland) *hung lft most of way: led: wnt lft and hit 1st: hdd 4th: trckd ldrs: rdn after 3 out: wnt 2nd between last 2: styd on run-in* **20/1**

/46- **3** 1 **Russie With Love**^{144} [811] 7-10-9 **105** .... GilesHawkins$^{(3)}$ 108
(Chris Down) *trckd ldrs: led 4th: rdn and hdd sn after 3 out: nt fluent next: styd on again fr last* **16/1**

121- **4** 3/4 **Bollin Judith**^{10} [2271] 7-11-2 **112** ....(t) TrevorWhelan$^{(3)}$ 114
(Jim Best) *hld up in tch: sltly outpcd after 3 out: hdwy last: styd on into 4th run-in* **4/1**^{2}

4/3- **5** 4 1/2 **Springinherstep (IRE)**^{184} [292] 6-11-12 **119** .... APMcCoy 120
(Nicky Henderson) *hld up bhd: hdwy after 6th and sed to take t.k.h: upsides whn hit 3 out: rdn bef 2 out: fnd little: snatched up whn disputing 2nd jst bef 2 out: wknd whn hit last* **11/10**^{1}

320/ **6** 13 **September Blaze**^{217} [5252] 6-11-6 **113** .... LiamTreadwell 101
(Paul Webber) *hld up in tch: effrt sn after 3 out: wknd next* **25/1**

P/4- **7** 1 1/4 **Combustible Lady (IRE)**^{22} [2029] 8-10-13 **106** .... AndrewThornton 91
(Seamus Mullins) *trckd ldrs: rdn after 3 out: wknd bef next* **12/1**^{3}

4m 45.0s (-1.00) **Going Correction** -0.25s/f (Good)
WFA 4 from 5yo+ 7lb **7** Ran SP% **109.8**
Speed ratings (Par 105): **92,91,91,90,89 83,83**
toteswingers 1&2 £15.00, 2&3 £27.90, 1&3 £8.20 CSF £60.62 TOTE £8.90: £4.00, £3.70; EX 68.00 Trifecta £320.40 Pool: £1733.22 - 4.05 winning units..
Owner Wayne Clifford **Bred** Mrs S Clifford **Trained** Nicholashayne, Devon

FOCUS
A modest mares' contest. Steps up from the first two.

2478 BJ DIXON WALSH H'CAP CHASE (17 fncs) 2m 7f 110y
3:40 (3:40) (Class 5) (0-95,87) 4-Y-0+ **£3,422** (£997; £499)

Form RPR

/4P- **1** **Milosam (IRE)**^{28} [1942] 6-10-12 **73** ....(p) TomO'Brien 83+
(Philip Hobbs) *trckd ldrs: disp ld most of way fr 6th: pckd 8th: rdn and strly pressed after 4 out: won on nod: all out* **15/8**^{1}

/03- **2** shd **Pod**^{19} [2088] 5-10-8 **72** .... JamesBest$^{(3)}$ 80
(Caroline Keevil) *trckd ldrs: pushed along after 10th: disp w wnr fr 12th: rdn after 4 out: styd on: lost on nod* **5/1**^{3}

016- **3** 1 1/4 **Isthereadifference (IRE)**^{24} [2008] 6-11-12 **87** ....(tp) NoelFehily 95
(Neil Mulholland) *hld up: hdwy after 11th: sn nudged along: wnt 3rd after 4 out: 2 l down next: sn rdn: styd on same pce* **4/1**^{2}

3P3- **4** 13 **Quayside Court (IRE)**^{36} [1825] 9-10-2 **70** ....(vt) GeraldQuinn$^{(7)}$ 69
(Claire Dyson) *disp ld tl 3rd: chsd ldr and lost pl 5th: hdwy to dispute after 7th tl rdn jst bef 4 out: hld fr next: plugged on* **4/1**^{2}

555- **5** 21 **Time Book (IRE)**^{24} [2007] 7-11-5 **80** ....(bt^{1}) BrendanPowell 56
(Colin Tizzard) *chsd ldrs: reminders after 7th: lost tch fr 12th: t.o* **25/1**

545- **P** **Might As Well**^{21} [2047] 10-11-8 **83** ....(b) AndrewThornton
(Seamus Mullins) *bmpd 1st: disp ld tl 4th: chsd ldrs: sn pushed along: lost tch fr after 11th: t.o whn p.u after 4 out* **12/1**

/P2- **P** **Doheny Bar (IRE)**^{24} [2003] 10-11-2 **77** ....(t) NickScholfield
(Paul Henderson) *disp ld: wnt lft and bmpd 1st: hdd 13th: lost tch qckly: p.u after 4 out* **12/1**

3/P- **P** **Roybuoy**^{189} [175] 6-11-11 **86** ....(t) LiamTreadwell
(Derrick Scott) *sn struggling in rr: tailing off whn p.u after 10th* **22/1**

6m 10.4s (-5.60) **Going Correction** -0.25s/f (Good) **8** Ran SP% **115.0**
Speed ratings (Par 103): **99,98,98,94,87 , ,**
toteswingers 1&2 £4.70, 2&3 £4.00, 1&3 £3.30 CSF £12.26 CT £33.25 TOTE £2.90: £1.10, £2.90, £2.90; EX 15.10 Trifecta £86.80 Pool: £1761.79 - 15.22 winning units..
Owner Rob Croker **Bred** James Canty **Trained** Withycombe, Somerset

FOCUS
A weak handicap. The winner is rated up 5lb on his best hurdles form.

2479 AT THE RACES SKY 415 MAIDEN OPEN NATIONAL HUNT FLAT RACE 2m 1f
4:10 (4:10) (Class 5) 4-6-Y-0 **£2,053** (£598; £299)

Form RPR

3/2- **1** **Assam Black (IRE)**^{34} [1861] 5-11-2 0 .... NoelFehily 114+
(Harry Fry) *led for 2f: prom: led 8f out: qcknd clr 3f out: in command after: comf* **10/11**^{1}

2 6 **Ivor's Queen (IRE)** 4-10-9 0 .... BrendanPowell 98+
(Colin Tizzard) *hld up: gd hdwy 3f out: sn chsng wnr and rdn: kpt on but nvr gng pce to get on terms* **12/1**

6- **3** 10 **Minella Scamp (IRE)**^{33} [1869] 4-11-2 0 .... TomScudamore 96
(David Pipe) *hld up towards rr: gd hdwy on inner 8f out: squeezed out on bnd over 4f out: rdn into 2nd briefly wl over 2f out: styd on same pce* **4/1**^{2}

0/- **4** 3/4 **Mr Bridger**^{217} [5262] 4-11-2 0 .... DarylJacob 94
(Paul Nicholls) *in tch: trckd ldrs 8f out: pushed along and short of room on bnd 4f out: rdn to chse wnr briefly 3f out: styd on same pce* **7/1**^{3}

5 2 3/4 **Turkey Creek (IRE)** 4-11-2 0 .... APMcCoy 92
(Paul Webber) *hld up: nudged along and hdwy over 3f out: sn rdn: one pce fnl 2f* **7/1**^{3}

0/ **6** 2 **The Sweetener (IRE)**^{200} [14] 4-11-2 0 ....(t) TomO'Brien 90
(Richard Woollacott) *mid-div: rdn 3f out: sn btn* **16/1**

7 8 **War Treaty (IRE)** 5-10-13 0 .... MarkQuinlan$^{(3)}$ 82
(Mark Shears) *trckd ldrs: trckd wnr over 7f out tl rdn over 3f out: wknd 2f out* **100/1**

8 10 **Proper Job** 5-10-9 0 .... MrJoshuaNewman$^{(7)}$ 72
(Polly Gundry) *mid-div: rdn 3f out: sn wknd* **50/1**

9 7 **Spirit Minded** 5-10-9 0 .... DavidEngland 58
(Giles Smyly) *led after 2f tl 8f out: wknd 4f out* **100/1**

0- **S** **Sutes**^{34} [1861] 5-10-13 0 .... MichaelByrne$^{(3)}$
(Alan Jones) *trcking ldrs whn slipped up on bnd after 7f* **100/1**

4m 4.3s (1.90) **Going Correction** -0.25s/f (Good) **10** Ran SP% **115.9**
Speed ratings: **85,82,77,77,75 74,71,66,63,**
toteswingers 1&2 £2.60, 2&3 £6.90, 1&3 £2.10 CSF £14.01 TOTE £1.70: £1.60, £3.30, £1.50; EX 14.60 Trifecta £49.40 Pool: £2234.14 - 33.90 winning units..
Owner The Tea Party Syndicate **Bred** L McCabe **Trained** Seaborough, Dorset

FOCUS
An average bumper. The easy winner is rated in line with his previous run.
T/Plt: £344.70 to a £1 stake. Pool of £80140.80 - 169.68 winning tickets. T/Qpdt: £127.30 to a £1 stake. Pool of £6729.63 - 39.10 winning tickets. TM

2480 - 2482a (Foreign Racing) - See Raceform Interactive

2182 CLONMEL (R-H)
Thursday, November 14

OFFICIAL GOING: Hurdle course - yielding to soft; chase course - yielding (good in places)

2483a CLONMEL OIL CHASE (GRADE 2) (13 fncs) 2m 4f
2:25 (2:25) 5-Y-0+ **£23,780** (£6,951; £3,292; £1,097)

RPR

1 **Arvika Ligeonniere (FR)**^{203} [5531] 8-11-8 160 .... RWalsh 158+
(W P Mullins, Ire) *trckd ldr in 2nd: bad mstke 5th: mstke 4 out: led into st gng best: pushed clr fr 2 out and drvn out towards fin: comf* **4/5**^{1}

2 3 1/2 **Toner D'Oudairies (FR)**^{12} [2235] 6-11-4 152 ....(tp) DavyRussell 149
(Gordon Elliott, Ire) *hld up in tch: niggled along after 4th: tk clsr order bef st and chal 2 out: no imp on wnr in 2nd whn slt mstke last: kpt on same pce* **13/2**

3 1 1/2 **Texas Jack (IRE)**^{12} [2235] 7-11-6 152 .... BarryGeraghty 150
(Noel Meade, Ire) *chsd ldrs: slow in 4th at 3rd: pushed along briefly after 4th: slow again 5th and 4 out: pushed along and wnt cl 2nd bef 2 out: sn no imp on wnr in 3rd: kpt on same pce fr last: jst hld 3rd* **5/1**^{2}

4 nk **Foildubh (IRE)**^{12} [2233] 9-11-10 150 .... BryanCooper 152+
(John Patrick Ryan, Ire) *chsd ldrs: mstke in 3rd at 6th: slt mstke 2 out: pushed along and no imp on wnr in 5th between last 2: kpt on wl fr last: jst failed for 3rd* **20/1**

5 1 **Mikael D'Haguenet (FR)**^{201} [5578] 9-11-1 147 .... PaulTownend 145
(W P Mullins, Ire) *w.w in rr: mstke 8th and sn detached: tk clsr order in rr into st: pushed along in 4th between last 2: no imp whn mstke last and sn dropped to 5th: kpt on same pce* **8/1**

6 16 **Rubi Light (FR)**^{40} [1776] 8-11-12 158 .... AELynch 137
(Robert Alan Hennessy, Ire) *led: pushed along and hdd into st: sn no ex u.p: wknd and eased* **6/1**^{3}

4m 54.8s (-22.80) **6** Ran SP% **115.7**
CSF £7.18 TOTE £1.60: £1.60, £1.60; DF 5.50 Trifecta £18.30.
Owner Mrs S Ricci **Bred** Yves Lepage **Trained** Muine Beag, Co Carlow

FOCUS
A tight finish and the fourth sets the standard back to his best.

2484a EUROPEAN BREEDERS FUND T.A. MORRIS MEMORIAL MARES CHASE (GRADE 3) (13 fncs) 2m 4f
2:55 (2:55) 5-Y-0+ **£18,495** (£5,406; £2,560; £853)

RPR

1 **Ballinahow Lady (IRE)**^{18} [2123] 8-11-0 121 .... JohnCullen 129
(David M O'Brien, Ire) *sn disp tl hdd bef 2nd: mod 2nd 1/2-way: tk clsr order 4 out and led narrowly bef st: hdd bef 2 out where mstke: kpt on wl u.p to regain advantage fr last: gng away at fin* **16/1**

2 2 1/4 **Backinthere (IRE)**^{14} [2187] 8-10-7 126 .... APHeskin 122
(Eamonn Francis Gallagher, Ire) *disp early tl settled bhd ldrs fr 1st: mstke next and lost pl: last 1/2-way: pushed along and prog fr 3 out into 3rd bef next: kpt on wl fr last into 2nd fnl stride: nt trble wnr* **3/1**^{2}

3 hd **Avondhu Lady (IRE)**^{21} [2054] 8-11-0 133 .... MarkEnright 126
(David Fenton, Ire) *chsd ldrs: 5th 1/2-way: tk clsr order in 3rd 3 out: sn pushed along and clsd to chal into st: led narrowly bef 2 out: rdn and hdd fr last: no ex cl home and dropped to 3rd fnl stride* **7/2**^{3}

4 3/4 **Caheronaun (IRE)**^{179} [400] 7-11-0 123 .... BryanCooper 125
(D T Hughes, Ire) *chsd ldrs: 3rd 1/2-way: slow 4 out and lost pl: pushed along in 6th after 3 out and no imp on ldrs bef next where lft 4th: kpt on wl fr last: nt trble wnr* **11/2**

5 6 1/2 **Kalico Kim (IRE)**^{14} [2187] 9-10-7 100 ....(t) MPFogarty 112
(John Patrick Ryan, Ire) *w.w: clsr in 5th at 1/2-way: outpcd fr 4 out: mod 7th appr st: lft mod 6th 2 out and kpt on wl fr last* **25/1**

6 13 **Dazzling Susie (IRE)**^{56} [1610] 8-11-0 134 .... BrianO'Connell 106
(John F Phelan, Ire) *chsd ldrs tl hdwy to ld bef 2nd: 12 l clr at 6th where slow: reduced advantage 4 out and hdd bef st: wknd* **8/1**

P **Caoimhe's Delight (IRE)**^{21} [2054] 7-10-7 124 .... BarryGeraghty
(Sean O'Brien, Ire) *chsd ldrs: niggled along fr 3rd: 7th 1/2-way: wknd fr 8th and p.u bef next* **9/4**^{1}

F **Liz's D'Estruval (IRE)**^{164} [621] 5-10-6 107 .... DavidSplaine 117
(John Joseph Murphy, Ire) *chsd ldrs: 4th 1/2-way: stl in tch in 4th whn fell 2 out* **20/1**

4m 57.2s (-20.40) **8** Ran SP% **119.0**
CSF £68.24 TOTE £18.90: £3.50, £1.20, £1.90; DF 56.10 Trifecta £400.20.
Owner MC Syndicate **Bred** Roger McLoughlin **Trained** Piltown, Co. Kilkenny

FOCUS
Not a strong renewal of this race but a good game winner. She, and the fourth, help the standard.

2485 - 2486a (Foreign Racing) - See Raceform Interactive

[1968]CHELTENHAM (L-H)

Friday, November 15

OFFICIAL GOING: Good (good to soft in places on chase & hurdle courses; chs 7.5, hdl 7.5, cross country 7.7)

Wind: Virtually nil Weather: Overcast

2487 OPUS ENERGY AMATEUR RIDERS' H'CAP CHASE (19 fncs) 3m 110y

1:05 (1:05) (Class 3) (0-140,139) 4-Y-0+

£11,992 (£3,746; £1,872; £936; £468; £236)

Form				RPR
0/4-	**1**		**Handy Andy (IRE)**[28] 1959 7-10-5 **123**..............................(t) MrMLegg(5) (Colin Tizzard) *hit 1st: trckd ldrs: wnt 2nd 3 out: chal fr 2 out tl slt ld after last: styd on wl* **15/2**	132+
20P/	**2**	*2 ½*	**Charingworth (IRE)**[240] 4862 10-10-9 **127**............... MrHAABannister(5) (Kim Bailey) *pressed ldrs: led 5th to 8th: led 9th: rdn and jnd fr 2 out: narrowly hdd after last: styd on same pce* **50/1**	135
641-	**3**	*1 ¾*	**Hunters Lodge (IRE)**[28] 1959 7-10-6 **126**......................(p) MrJBargary(7) (Nigel Twiston-Davies) *slt ld to 3rd to 5th: styd pressing ldrs tl rdn and outpcd 4 out: rallied under pressed fr next and chsd ldrs sn after: styd on run-in but no imp on ldng duo* **7/1**[3]	131
2/0-	**4**	*½*	**Victrix Gale (IRE)**[57] 1611 7-10-12 **125**.................................. MrJJCodd (A J Martin, Ire) *hit 1st: hld up in rr: hdwy 3 out: rdn 2 out: styd on u.p run-in but nt rch ldng trio* **6/1**[2]	130
P/5-	**5**	*11*	**Mr Moss (IRE)**[26] 1991 8-11-11 **138**.............................. MrPWMullins (Evan Williams) *in rr: hit 3 out and hdwy sn after: styd on same pce fr next* **18/1**	134
3/5-	**6**	*1 ½*	**Fredo (IRE)**[28] 1959 9-10-7 **120**.................................. MrSWaley-Cohen (Ian Williams) *chsd ldrs: hit 5th: rdn and outpcd fr 3 out: styd on u.p run-in* **7/1**[3]	113
111-	**7**	*hd*	**Standing Ovation (IRE)**[6] 2373 6-11-0 **127** 7ex...........(tp) MrSClements (David Pipe) *lw: led 3rd to 5th: styd chsng ldrs: led 8th: hdd next: wknd after 2 out* **15/8**[1]	124
5/1-	**8**	*13*	**Imperial Circus (IRE)**[37] 1815 7-10-5 **125**..................(p) MrCGethings(7) (Philip Hobbs) *chsd ldrs: rdn 4 out and sn btn: mstke next* **14/1**	108
01F/	**9**	*2 ¾*	**Ruben Cotter (IRE)**[253] 4615 7-11-12 **139**...................... MrWBiddick (Paul Nicholls) *lw: in rr: hdwy to cl on ldrs 4 out: wknd bef 2 out* **10/1**	120
/5F-	**10**	*10*	**Major Malarkey (IRE)**[172] 509 10-10-6 **126**...................... MrCSmith(7) (Nigel Twiston-Davies) *chsd ldrs: hit 10th: j. slowly 13th (water) and sn rdn: wknd 14th* **16/1**	96

6m 27.76s (9.46) **Going Correction** +0.275s/f (Yiel) **10** Ran SP% **114.7**

Speed ratings (Par 107): **95,94,93,93,89 89,89,85,84,81**

toteswingers 1&2 £47.80, 1&3 £5.30, 2&3 £155.10 CSF £236.27 CT £2707.03 TOTE £8.70: £2.50, £10.70, £1.90; EX 395.70 Trifecta £1661.90 Part won. Pool: £2215.95 - 0.01 winning units..

Owner Brocade Racing **Bred** John Connolly **Trained** Milborne Port, Dorset

■ Stewards' Enquiry : Mr S Clements two-day ban: failed to ride out for 6th (Nov 29,Dec 1)

FOCUS

All races on Old Course except for Race 5: Cross Country. This competitive amateur riders' handicap was run at an ordinary gallop until the runners went out on to the final lap, but despite that the form looks sound enough. The first three are rated to their marks.

2488 PADDY POWER H'CAP CHASE (13 fncs) 2m

1:35 (1:38) (Class 2) (0-145,143) 4-Y-0+

£28,152 (£8,316; £4,158; £2,079; £1,039; £522)

Form				RPR
252-	**1**		**Anay Turge (FR)**[19] 2101 8-10-7 **127**...........................(tp) MarkQuinlan(3) (Nigel Hawke) *lw: mid-div: hdwy after 10th: led 2 out: r.o wl fr last: rdn out* **9/1**	138
/23-	**2**	*2 ¾*	**Sew On Target (IRE)**[27] 1969 8-10-10 **127**............................... JoeTizzard (Colin Tizzard) *prom most of way: rdn and ev ch 2 out and last: kpt on but no ex* **12/1**	136
3/1-	**3**	*2 ½*	**Eastlake (IRE)**[19] 2101 7-11-9 **140**.................................... APMcCoy (Jonjo O'Neill) *mid-div: hdwy after 3 out: rdn after 2 out: wnt 3rd at the last: kpt on same pce* **7/1**[2]	147
115/	**4**	*nk*	**Ballygarvey (FR)**[222] 5198 7-11-7 **138**.................................. TomO'Brien (Philip Hobbs) *trckd ldrs: wnt 3rd after 9th: rdn after 3 out: nt quite pce to chal: lost 3rd at the last: kpt on* **20/1**	144
2/0-	**5**	*3 ¼*	**Elenika (FR)**[188] 217 5-10-12 **129**.................................... AidanColeman (Venetia Williams) *hld up towards rr: stdy prog fr 9th: rdn to chse ldrs appr 2 out: styd on fr last but nvr finding pce to get on terms* **8/1**[3]	133
012-	**6**	*3*	**De Faoithesdream (IRE)**[37] 1817 7-10-13 **130**.................. PaulMoloney (Evan Williams) *trckd ldrs: hit 4th: led next: nt fluent 10th: mstke 3 out: rdn and hdd 2 out: no ex fr last* **25/1**	134+
/46	**7**	*3*	**Gus Macrae (IRE)**[13] 2212 9-10-4 **126**......................(tp) PatrickCorbett(5) (Rebecca Curtis) *hld up towards rr of midfield: effrt to cl 3 out: styd on but nvr gng pce to get involved* **20/1**	124
6/0-	**8**	*¾*	**Renard (FR)**[27] 1969 8-10-12 **129**.................................. LiamTreadwell (Venetia Williams) *lw: hld up towards rr: pushed along in midfield after 8th: styd on but nvr gng pce to get involved* **11/2**[1]	127
/03-	**9**	*½*	**Theatrical Star**[20] 2081 7-11-4 **135**.................................. BrendanPowell (Colin Tizzard) *mid-div: rdn after 4 out: nvr finding pce to get involved* **16/1**	134
0/1-	**10**	*6*	**Parsnip Pete**[22] 2049 7-11-2 **133**....................................... PaddyBrennan (Tom George) *in tch: hit 2nd: 3rd whn blnd 9th: rdn after 3 out: wknd between last 2* **17/2**	129
/P6-	**11**	*4 ½*	**Havingotascoobydo (IRE)**[20] 2086 8-10-10 **127**................. TomSiddall (Martin Keighley) *struggling 7th: a in rr* **16/1**	115
1/0-	**12**	*4 ½*	**Shadows Lengthen**[14] 2198 7-10-12 **132**......................... JakeGreenall(3) (Michael Easterby) *a towards rr* **25/1**	117
4/5-	**13**	*nk*	**Oh Crick (FR)**[26] 1990 10-10-6 **130**............................. MrJoshuaNewman(7) (Alan King) *mid-div: rdn after 8th: wknd sn after 3 out* **14/1**	113
0/0-	**14**	*16*	**Consigliere (FR)**[13] 2212 10-11-12 **143**..........................(p) ConorO'Farrell (David Pipe) *mid-div tl 5th: sn towards rr: nvr bk on terms: t.o fr 3 out* **50/1**	112
3F4/	**15**	*2*	**Ballyadam Brook (IRE)**[13] 2233 9-11-1 **132**.................... PaulTownend (Terence O'Brien, Ire) *prom whn stmbld bdly 1st: chsd ldrs tl lost pl appr 6th: sn in rr: t.o* **33/1**	101
3/3-	**16**	*6*	**Have You Seen Me (IRE)**[167] 587 10-10-10 **127**(t) SamTwiston-Davies (Nigel Twiston-Davies) *led tl 5th: trckd ldrs: rdn after 10th: wknd after 3 out: t.o* **9/1**	89
221-	**P**		**Tindaro (FR)**[42] 1746 6-11-7 **138**..................................(t) RichieMcLernon (Paul Webber) *hit 3rd: a in rr: t.o whn p.u bef 3 out* **25/1**	

3m 57.8s (-0.20) **Going Correction** +0.275s/f (Yiel) **17** Ran SP% **121.6**

Speed ratings (Par 109): **111,109,108,108,106 105,103,103,102,99 97,95,95,87,86 83,**

toteswingers 1&2 £19.20, 1&3 £10.60, 2&3 £4.70 CSF £100.86 CT £812.59 TOTE £9.70: £2.70, £2.50, £2.30, £5.50; EX 92.90 Trifecta £738.10 Pool: £4465.61 - 4.53 winning units..

Owner Mrs K Wetherall **Bred** Mme Annick Penouilh **Trained** Stoodleigh, Devon

FOCUS

Highly competitive stuff. There was a sound gallop on, but not that many got seriously involved from off the pace and the first five were clear at the finish. Steps up from the winner and third.

2489 STEEL PLATE AND SECTIONS NOVICES' CHASE (16 fncs) 2m 4f 110y

2:05 (2:06) (Class 2) 4-Y-0+ **£12,512** (£3,696; £1,848; £924)

Form				RPR
6/1-	**1**		**Taquin Du Seuil (FR)**[17] 2151 6-11-7 0.................................. APMcCoy (Jonjo O'Neill) *j. slowly 1st: trckd ldr at modest pce: hit 3 out: qcknd to chal and hit 2 out: narrow advantage last: kpt on wl whn hrd pressed thrght run-in: drvn out* **3/1**[2]	150+
2P4/	**2**	*nk*	**Oscar Whisky (IRE)**[225] 5137 8-11-2 0.............................. BarryGeraghty (Nicky Henderson) *blnd 1st: led next at mod pce: jnd 2 out: narrowly hdd last: str chal u.p run-in: jst failed* **4/6**[1]	145+
0/2-	**3**	*3 ¾*	**The Romford Pele (IRE)**[34] 1865 6-11-2 134........................ NoelFehily (Rebecca Curtis) *lw: disp 3rd off mod pce: blnd 6th: hit 3 out: hdwy to cl on ldng duo sn after: wnt clr 3rd after 2 out: kpt on but nvr gng pce to chal* **9/2**[3]	141
22F-	**4**	*12*	**The Cockney Mackem (IRE)**[27] 1973 7-11-7 132(t) SamTwiston-Davies (Nigel Twiston-Davies) *led and blnd 1st: racd in disp 3rd off mod pce: j.big 7th: hdwy to cl on ldng duo after 3 out: mstke and wknd next* **33/1**	136

5m 28.84s (17.84) **Going Correction** +0.275s/f (Yiel) **4** Ran SP% **106.1**

Speed ratings (Par 109): **77,76,75,70**

CSF £5.55 TOTE £3.30; EX 5.30 Trifecta £8.10 Pool: £2402.05 - 220.91 winning units..

Owner Martin Broughton & Friends 1 **Bred** Marc Boudot **Trained** Cheltenham, Gloucs

FOCUS

A farcial early gallop rather spoilt this fascinating novice chase, that has been won by some top-notchers in the past. The first three are all capable of better than the bare form.

2490 DAVID JOHNSON MEMORIAL INTERMEDIATE H'CAP HURDLE (10 hdls) 2m 5f

2:40 (2:40) (Class 3) (0-140,137) 4-Y-0+

£12,512 (£3,696; £1,848; £924; £462; £232)

Form				RPR
P/1-	**1**		**Thomas Crapper**[27] 1972 6-11-3 **128**.................................. CharliePoste (Robin Dickin) *hld up in rr tl stdy hdwy fr 5th to trck ldrs 4 out: wnt 2nd next: chal 2 out: sn led: styd on wl run-in and a doing enough* **16/1**	137+
6/1-	**2**	*¾*	**Angles Hill (IRE)**[52] 1641 6-10-9 **120**................................. TomO'Brien (Richard Woollacott) *chsd ldrs: wnt 2nd appr last: styd on wl u.p run-in but a hld by wnr* **33/1**	126
141/	**3**	*2 ½*	**Whisper (FR)**[212] 5350 5-11-12 **137**................................ BarryGeraghty (Nicky Henderson) *lw: in tch: hdwy 3 out: styng on whn blnd 2 out: rallied last and kpt on run-in to take 3rd cl home but no imp on ldng duo* **11/2**[3]	144+
/23-	**4**	*nk*	**Uncle Jimmy (IRE)**[19] 2102 6-11-5 **130**......................... RichardJohnson (Philip Hobbs) *in tch: hdwy to cl on ldrs whn blnd 3 out: styd on u.p to take 3rd after last: no imp and dropped to 4th cl home* **25/1**	134
4U5/	**5**	*5*	**Free To Dream (IRE)**[228] 5095 6-11-5 **130**..................... AidanColeman (Venetia Williams) *chsd ldrs: rdn and slt ld fr 3 out: jnd next: sn hdd: wknd run-in* **33/1**	130
1/1-	**6**	*1 ½*	**Upswing (IRE)**[22] 2032 5-10-13 **124**................................. APMcCoy (Jonjo O'Neill) *lw: in rr: rdn along fr 4 out: styd on u.p appr last but nvr any ch* **5/1**[2]	123+
/11-	**7**	*4*	**Killala Quay**[34] 1863 6-11-7 **132**.. NoelFehily (Charlie Longsdon) *in rr: hdwy 3 out: styng on: stl a fair bit to do but lost any ch whn hmpd 2 out: kpt on again run-in* **11/1**	129+
2/1-	**8**	*½*	**Warden Hill (IRE)**[26] 1991 5-10-13 **124**.......................... DominicElsworth (Mick Channon) *in rr: hdwy 6th: sn rdn: wl bhd whn hmpd 2 out: styd on appr last* **12/1**	118
211/	**9**	*2*	**Top Gamble (IRE)**[286] 3982 5-11-8 **133**.............................. ConorO'Farrell (David Pipe) *lw: led: narrowly hdd 3 out: wknd after next* **9/2**[1]	127
10/-	**10**	*26*	**Scarlet Fire (IRE)**[221] 5216 6-10-13 **124**.............................. DavyRussell (Nicky Richards) *a towards rr* **40/1**	92
221/	**11**	*3 ¼*	**Atlantic Roller (IRE)**[374] 2245 6-11-5 **130**............................ DarylJacob (Paul Nicholls) *lw: in tch: chsd ldrs 6th: wknd after 4 out* **16/1**	95
	12	*½*	**Milborough (IRE)**[302] 3716 7-11-7 **135**.............................. MichaelByrne(3) (Tim Vaughan) *b.bkwd: hit 1st: towards rr most of way* **66/1**	100
/63-	**13**	*/*	**Kellys Brow (IRE)**[170] 631 6-11-2 **127**.................................. DavidBass (Ben Pauling) *in tch: hit 5th: sn bhd* **100/1**	86
/U1-	**14**	*nk*	**God's Own (IRE)**[11] 2268 5-11-10 **135** 7ex........................ PaddyBrennan (Tom George) *chsd ldrs: rdn after 4 out: sn wknd* **12/1**	93
/13-	**15**	*8*	**Handazan (IRE)**[27] 1970 4-11-9 **134**............................(p) RobertThornton (Alan King) *chsd ldrs: rdn 6th: wknd 4 out* **25/1**	85
1/P-	**16**	*11*	**Decimus (IRE)**[19] 2107 6-10-8 **119**..................................... NickScholfield (Jeremy Scott) *a towards rr* **40/1**	60
1/0-	**17**	*32*	**Watered Silk**[48] 1685 5-10-10 **121**.................................... LeightonAspell (Lucy Wadham) *in rr: hdwy 5th: wknd 4 out* **66/1**	34
2/0-	**18**	*1*	**Hold Court (IRE)**[20] 2080 6-11-0 **125**................................... PaulMoloney (Evan Williams) *a in rr: lost tch fr 6th* **16/1**	37
5/3-	**F**		**Kaylif Aramis**[20] 2080 6-11-9 **134**............................. SamTwiston-Davies (Nigel Twiston-Davies) *in rr: hdwy 4 out: stl a bit to do but styng on wl enough whn fell 2 out* **14/1**	134
126/	**F**		**One Conemara (IRE)**[216] 5289 5-10-12 **123**..................... AndrewTinkler (Nicky Henderson) *chsd ldrs: rdn and fading whn fell 3 out* **14/1**	

5m 8.02s (-5.38) **Going Correction** 0.0s/f (Good)

WFA 4 from 5yo+ 8lb **20** Ran SP% **127.4**

Speed ratings (Par 107): **110,109,108,108,106 106,104,104,103,93 92,92,89,89,86 82,70,69, ,**

toteswingers 1&2 £106.20, 1&3 £18.60, 2&3 £53.10 CSF £482.41 CT £3278.81 TOTE £16.90: £3.20, £7.60, £2.00, £5.30; EX 524.50 Trifecta £1926.10 Pool: £4428.95 - 1.64 winning units..

Owner apis.uk.com **Bred** Mrs J A Carr-Evans **Trained** Alcester, Warwicks

FOCUS
A solid-looking handicap with another step forward from the winner.

2491 GLENFARCLAS CROSS COUNTRY CHASE (32 fncs) 3m 7f
3:15 (3:15) (Class 2) 5-Y-0+

£15,640 (£4,620; £2,310; £1,155; £577; £290)

Form RPR

/11- **1** **Balthazar King (IRE)**[27] 1971 9-11-8 150 RichardJohnson 150+
(Philip Hobbs) *sn trcking ldrs: blnd bdly 3rd: wnt lft next: disp fr 10th: outrt ldr 21st: jnd 27th tl next: shkn up whn nt fluent last: styd on v gamely: drvn out* **5/4**[1]

04P/ **2** *1* **Uncle Junior (IRE)**[202] 5577 12-11-8 149 MrPWMullins 148+
(W P Mullins, Ire) *hld up: struggling in rr 26th: rapid hdwy appr 2 out: ¾ l down whn hit last: styd on but no ex* **8/1**

/P5- **3** *5* **Any Currency (IRE)**[19] 2108 10-11-5 127 (p[1]) IanPopham 139
(Martin Keighley) *trckd ldr: rdn after 25th: chal 27th tl next: rallied briefly whn nt clr run on bnd appr last: styd on but no ex run-in* **28/1**

/43- **4** *4 ½* **Diamond Harry**[158] 704 10-10-10 137 JamesReveley 126
(Nick Williams) *trckd ldrs: wnt 3rd 25th: pushed along whn slipped on bnd bef 2 out: lost 3rd next: styd on same pce: jst hld on for 4th* **11/2**[2]

1PP/ **5** *shd* **Chicago Grey (IRE)**[205] 5515 10-11-8 149 (t) DavyRussell 139+
(Gordon Elliott, Ire) *cl up tl blnd bdly 21st: towards rr: struggling and gng nowhere detached 3 out: gd hdwy after 2 out: styd on wl fr last: jst failed to snatch 4th* **15/2**[3]

3/0- **6** *1* **Sire Collonges (FR)**[27] 1971 7-11-8 140 RyanMahon 137
(Paul Nicholls) *hld up: squeezed up and hit rails after 22nd: hdwy to dispute 3rd 27th tl after 3 out: looked btn sn after tl styd on again appr last* **9/1**

/15- **7** *11* **Theroadtocroker (IRE)**[19] 2123 9-11-5 101 (t) MrPaulGahan 122
(Denis Paul Murphy, Ire) *hld up: j.lft 10th: hdwy 21st: rdn in 4th after 3 out: 5th whn pckd 2 out: wknd bef last* **100/1**

U/U- **8** *19* **Zest For Life (IRE)**[33] 1905 9-11-5 133 MsNCarberry 103
(E Bolger, Ire) *led: jnd 10th: nt fluent 19th: hdd 21st: wknd 3 out: t.o* **20/1**

00F/ **9** *23* **Quiscover Fontaine (FR)**[19] 9-10-10 133 RichieMcLernon 71
(E Bolger, Ire) *a last: t.o fr 26th* **12/1**

110- **F** **Gullible Gordon (IRE)**[84] 1362 10-11-5 135 (tp) DonalDevereux
(Peter Bowen) *trckd ldrs tl 7th: mid-div: fell on bank between hedges 18th* **33/1**

P/0- **U** **Viking Blond (FR)**[28] 1956 8-11-2 130 (v) SamTwiston-Davies
(Nigel Twiston-Davies) *pushed along in rr fr 9th: blnd and uns rdr 12th* **20/1**

8m 16.1s (-21.90) **Going Correction** -0.375s/f (Good) 11 Ran SP% **117.3**
Speed ratings: **113,112,111,110,110 110,107,102,96,**
toteswingers 1&2 £3.00, 1&3 £10.30, 2&3 £33.00 CSF £11.01 TOTE £2.30: £1.20, £2.70, £7.20; EX 14.90 Trifecta £216.60 Pool: £5772.76 - 19.98 winning units..
Owner The Brushmakers **Bred** Sunnyhill Stud **Trained** Withycombe, Somerset

FOCUS
A decent renewal of this Cross Country chase, the sole conditions event of its type here during the season, and it's solid form for the discipline, despite the proximity of the third. The first two are rated below their best.

2492 COUNTRYSIDE RACEDAY NOVICES' H'CAP HURDLE (8 hdls) 2m 110y
3:50 (3:51) (Class 3) (0-125,125) 3-Y-0+

£7,507 (£2,217; £1,108; £554; £277; £139)

Form RPR

1 **Quick Jack (IRE)**[12] 1620 4-11-0 **113** RWalsh 127+
(A J Martin, Ire) *hld up in rr: stdy hdwy on outside fr 3 out to ld last: drvn and styd on strly run-in* **15/8**[1]

212- **2** *2 ¼* **Deep Trouble (IRE)**[22] 2049 6-11-5 **118** WayneHutchinson 126+
(Ben Case) *in rr: hdwy whn hmpd and nt clr run 2 out: gd hdwy again sn after to chse wnr after last: kpt on but a hld* **20/1**

0/1- **3** *2 ¼* **Three Kingdoms (IRE)**[30] 1924 4-11-11 **124** DenisO'Regan 130+
(John Ferguson) *lw: trckd ldrs: drvn to chal whn hit last: kpt on but nt gng pce of ldng duo* **16/1**

P/2- **4** *4 ½* **Maxi Chop (FR)**[19] 2111 5-11-7 **125** HarryDerham[(5)] 125
(Paul Nicholls) *chsd ldrs: chal 2 out: led sn after: narrowly hdd an hit last: one pce into 4th fnl 150yds* **25/1**

3/2- **5** *2 ½* **Vibrato Valtat (FR)**[190] 174 4-11-8 **121** DarylJacob 119
(Paul Nicholls) *in rr: hdwy fr 3f out: chsd ldrs and rdn appr last: one pce run-in* **16/1**

43/ **6** *½* **Roberto Pegasus (USA)**[312] 2440 7-11-4 **117** RobertThornton 114
(Alan King) *chsd ldrs: rdn after 2 out: no ex run-in* **12/1**

4/3- **7** *3 ¾* **Edmaaj (IRE)**[20] 2083 5-10-6 **105** APMcCoy 98
(Jonjo O'Neill) *lw: hld up in rr: stdy hdwy appr 2 out: styd on but nvr gng pce to rch ldrs* **9/2**[2]

0- **8** *nk* **Vedani (IRE)**[13] 2210 4-10-10 **109** (t) LeeEdwards 102
(Tony Carroll) *in rr: styd on fr 2 out: nvr rchd ldrs* **100/1**

111- **9** *2 ½* **Rosie Probert**[20] 2084 4-11-12 **125** BarryGeraghty 119+
(Nicky Henderson) *chsd ldrs: outpcd 4 out: rallied next: wknd after 2 out* **7/1**[3]

323- **10** *½* **Daliance (IRE)**[31] 1913 4-10-4 **108** MattCrawley[(5)] 98
(Lucy Wadham) *in rr: sme late hdwy* **25/1**

11 *2 ¼* **Noche De Reyes (FR)**[154] 4-10-13 **112** PaddyBrennan 102
(Tom George) *t.k.h: chsd ldrs: wknd after 2 out* **20/1**

/51- **12** *4* **Just When**[25] 2004 4-11-2 **120** (v) NicodeBoinville[(5)] 104
(Patrick Chamings) *chsd ldrs to 3 out* **33/1**

141- **13** *4 ½* **Dresden (IRE)**[150] 756 5-11-12 **125** WillKennedy 104
(Sarah-Jayne Davies) *chsd ldrs: led 3 out to next: sn wknd* **50/1**

5/0- **14** *1* **Mister Bricolage (IRE)**[30] 1924 6-10-13 **112** AlainCawley 90
(Fergal O'Brien) *towards rr most of way* **100/1**

323- **15** *3 ½* **Quite By Chance**[24] 2011 4-11-7 **120** JoeTizzard 95
(Colin Tizzard) *in tch to 4 out* **33/1**

0/5- **16** *2 ¾* **Expanding Universe (IRE)**[9] 2286 6-11-9 **122** NoelFehily 95
(Tony Carroll) *chsd ldrs early: bhd fr 4 out* **50/1**

/21- **17** *22* **Little Pop**[29] 1935 5-11-2 **115** SamTwiston-Davies 65
(Nigel Twiston-Davies) *led: hdd 3 out: wkng mstke 2 out* **12/1**

5/0- **18** *25* **Lone Ranger (FR)**[22] 2040 5-10-10 **109** AidanColeman 34
(Venetia Williams) *a in rr* **20/1**

110- **P** **Falcarragh (IRE)**[48] 1685 6-11-7 **120** (p) RichardJohnson
(Tim Vaughan) *a in rr: t.o whn p.u after 4 out* **33/1**

4m 0.73s (-1.27) **Going Correction** 0.0s/f (Good)
WFA 4 from 5yo+ 7lb 19 Ran SP% **129.3**
Speed ratings (Par 107): **102,100,99,97,96 96,94,94,93,93 91,90,87,87,85 84,74,62,**
toteswingers 1&2 £16.30, 1&3 £10.00, 2&3 £40.70 CSF £47.53 CT £516.52 TOTE £2.90: £1.50, £4.10, £4.00, £4.40; EX 40.20 Trifecta £626.40 Pool: £4679.58 - 5.60 winning units..
Owner John Breslin **Bred** Newtown Anner Stud **Trained** Summerhill, Co. Meath

FOCUS
Another highly competitive-looking handicap, this time for novices. They went a sound enough gallop and the form should work out fine. The winner can rate higher yet on his Flat form.
T/Jkpt: Not won. T/Plt: £589.10 to a £1 stake. Pool: £244851.44 - 303.36 winning tickets T/Qpdt: £50.50 to a £1 stake. Pool: £16675.85 - 244.27 winning tickets ST

NEWCASTLE (L-H)
Friday, November 15

OFFICIAL GOING: Good (good to firm in places in home straight; 7.4)
Wind: Almost nil Weather: Breezy, half against

2493 VIRGIN MEDIA BUSINESS NOVICES' HURDLE (9 hdls) 2m
12:10 (12:10) (Class 4) 4-Y-0+ £3,119 (£915; £457; £228)

Form RPR

30/ **1** **Moss Cloud (IRE)**[240] 4863 6-10-12 0 JasonMaguire 113+
(Donald McCain) *trckd ldrs: led bef 3 out: drvn clr fr last* **22/1**

32- **2** *3 ¾* **Knightly Escapade**[16] 2156 5-10-12 108 (p) DannyCook 107
(Brian Ellison) *hld up in midfield: rdn bef 3 out: rallied to chse (clr) wnr appr last: kpt on: no imp* **15/2**

5/0- **3** *nk* **Danehills Well (IRE)**[13] 2217 5-10-12 0 LucyAlexander 106
(Alison Hamilton) *t.k.h: prom: rdn and outpcd 3 out: rallied bef last: kpt on wl run-in* **150/1**

210/ **4** *4* **Avidity**[223] 5179 4-10-12 0 (t) BrianHughes 104
(James Ewart) *trckd ldrs: smooth hdwy and ev ch bef 3 out: pushed along and lost 2nd last: sn outpcd* **3/1**[2]

04/- **5** *2 ¼* **Regal Swain (IRE)**[59] 3186 5-10-12 0 TomScudamore 99
(Alan Swinbank) *hld up: stdy hdwy 3 out: rdn last: nvr nr to chal* **66/1**

21/ **6** *1* **Mister Nibbles (IRE)**[208] 5428 5-10-9 0 MrSCrawford[(3)] 98
(S R B Crawford, Ire) *plld hrd: hld up: hdwy and prom after 3rd: rdn and hung lft after 3 out: kpt on same pce fr next* **9/4**[1]

7 *hd* **Gold Show**[28] 4-10-0 0 TonyKelly[(5)] 92
(Edwin Tuer) *nt fluent in rr: hdwy whn mstke 4 out: sn drvn along: kpt on fr 2 out: no imp* **66/1**

5- **8** *½* **Getabuzz**[20] 2075 5-10-12 0 HarryHaynes 98
(Tim Easterby) *cl up: ev ch and rdn bef 3 out: no ex between last 2* **12/1**

45- **9** *1 ¼* **Satanic Beat (IRE)**[13] 2225 4-10-12 0 BrianHarding 97
(Jedd O'Keeffe) *midfield: rdn and outpcd 4 out: plugged on fr 2 out: nvr rchd ldrs* **20/1**

/03- **10** *2 ¼* **Orchard Road (USA)**[27] 1977 6-10-12 0 (t) PeterBuchanan 94
(Lucinda Russell) *midfield: hit 4th: effrt and rdn bef 3 out: wknd bef next* **7/1**[3]

00- **11** *6* **Rocky Island (IRE)**[14] 2189 5-10-12 0 SeanQuinlan 88
(Jennie Candlish) *t.k.h: led to bef 3 out: wknd bef next: no ch whn hit last* **80/1**

12 *hd* **Choisan (IRE)**[9] 4-10-12 0 DougieCostello 88
(Tim Easterby) *in tch on outside: outpcd bef 1/2-way: n.d after* **25/1**

450/ **13** *3* **Tough Trade**[222] 5208 4-10-12 0 HenryBrooke 85
(Chris Grant) *nt fluent in rr: struggling after 4 out: nvr on terms* **125/1**

14 *3 ½* **Kiwayu**[21] 4-10-12 0 (p) RichieMcGrath 82
(Philip Kirby) *nt fluent in midfield: effrt and rdn bef 3 out: wknd bef next* **8/1**

0- **15** *10* **Durham Express (IRE)**[13] 2225 6-10-7 0 SamanthaDrake[(5)] 72
(Tina Jackson) *towards rr: struggling after 4 out: btn next* **250/1**

334/ **16** *6* **Thurnham**[653] 4047 7-10-7 0 ColmMcCormack[(5)] 66
(Keith Reveley) *hld up: rdn along bef 4 out: btn bef next* **80/1**

3m 53.0s (-17.00) **Going Correction** -0.925s/f (Hard)
WFA 4 from 5yo+ 7lb 16 Ran SP% **119.1**
Speed ratings (Par 105): **105,103,102,100,99 99,99,99,98,97 94,94,92,90,85 82**
toteswingers 1&2 £56.40, 1&3 Not won, 2&3 £10.00 CSF £171.18 TOTE £27.80: £6.50, £3.00, £17.20; EX 188.30 TRIFECTA Not won..
Owner Trevor Hemmings **Bred** Miss Catherine O'Donovan **Trained** Cholmondeley, Cheshire

FOCUS
No dividing rails apart from run-in from final obstacles. Jason Maguire, who won the opener, said: "It's good ground for jumping." Brian Hughes described it as "Nice ground, good with no firm in it." They went no real gallop in this fair novice hurdle and the form should not be taken too literally, but a few winners ought to emerge from the race. The form has been given a token rating through the runner-up.

2494 CELLULAR SOLUTIONS NOVICES' CHASE (16 fncs) 2m 4f
12:40 (12:40) (Class 4) 4-Y-0+ £4,548 (£1,335; £667; £333)

Form RPR

0/4- **1** **Yesyoucan (IRE)**[20] 2074 8-11-2 0 DannyCook 141+
(Brian Ellison) *led to 2nd: led next to 5th: regained ld 9th: nt fluent 5 out: drew clr after next: easily* **10/11**[1]

443/ **2** *9* **Bit Of A Jig (IRE)**[216] 5289 6-11-2 122 JasonMaguire 122
(Donald McCain) *cl up: led 2nd to next: chsd ldrs: outpcd 8th: rallied bef 3 out: chsd (clr) wnr between last 2: no imp* **15/8**[2]

P/4- **3** *6* **War On (IRE)**[169] 553 6-11-2 110 HenryBrooke 116
(Chris Grant) *in tch: drvn and outpcd 1/2-way: styd on fr 2 out: no imp* **33/1**

213- **4** *1 ½* **Indigo Rock (IRE)**[42] 1755 7-11-2 120 RyanMania 116+
(Michael Smith) *chsd ldrs: hdwy to ld 5th: hdd 9th: upsides to 4 out: sn outpcd: wknd fr 2 out* **4/1**[3]

5m 1.7s (-25.50) **Going Correction** -1.00s/f (Hard) 4 Ran SP% **110.1**
Speed ratings (Par 105): **111,107,105,104**
CSF £3.18 TOTE £1.80; EX 3.10 Trifecta £9.60 Pool: £1267.56 - 98.17 winning units..
Owner Prism Bloodstock **Bred** Thomas Steele **Trained** Norton, N Yorks

FOCUS
Not a great turnout for this novice chase. The easy winner was still well below his hurdle mark and there should be more to come. The next two were close to their marks.

2495 HUAWEI ENTERPRISE MARES' MAIDEN HURDLE (11 hdls) 2m 4f
1:15 (1:15) (Class 5) 4-Y-0+ £1,949 (£572; £286; £143)

Form RPR

000- **1** **Rev Up Ruby**[27] 1975 5-10-5 0 [1] JonathonBewley[(7)] 102+
(George Bewley) *hld up: smooth hdwy to ld 4 out: drvn along 2 out: kpt on wl fr last* **18/1**

23- **2** *5* **Texas Rose (IRE)**[27] 1982 6-10-7 105 TonyKelly[(5)] 99
(Rebecca Menzies) *t.k.h: prom: hdwy to chse wnr bef 3 out: rdn next: one pce whn nt fluent last* **5/2**[3]

0- **3** *1* **Spring Over (IRE)**[13] 2217 7-10-5 0 GrahamWatters[(7)] 97
(Ian Duncan) *nt fluent on occasions: hld up in tch: effrt bef 3 out: kpt on same pce after next* **100/1**

The Form Book Jumps, Raceform Ltd, Compton, RG20 6NL.

6/0- 4 9 **Molly Milan**[13] 2217 5-10-12 0 GaryBartley 90
(Jim Goldie) *t.k.h: cl up: wnt 2nd after 4 out to bef next: sn outpcd* **16/1**

1- 5 ¾ **Monita Bonita**[124] 970 4-10-12 0 DannyCook 88
(Tim Easterby) *nt fluent on occasions: hld up towards rr: drvn after 4 out: hung lft and no imp fr next* **15/8**[1]

5- 6 41 **Aintnosanityclause (IRE)**[26] 1999 5-10-9 93 MrSCrawford(3) 52
(S R B Crawford, Ire) *t.k.h: led: hit 4th: hdd 4 out: wknd appr next: t.o* **14/1**

/U0- 7 22 **Cinnomhor**[14] 2196 5-10-12 0 HenryBrooke 31
(Chris Grant) *nt fluent towards rr: struggling bef 4 out: t.o* **100/1**

P **Johanna Fosie (IRE)**[515] 4-10-12 0 PeterBuchanan
(W T Reed) *bhd: struggling 1/2-way: t.o whn p.u bef 3 out* **100/1**

530/ P **Supreme Present**[224] 5163 5-10-12 0 (t) JasonMaguire
(Kim Bailey) *cl up: nt fluent 7th: rdn after 4 out: wknd and p.u bef next* **9/4**[2]

00P/ P **Olive Grove**[222] 5205 7-10-12 0 (p) BrianHarding
(Alan Mactaggart) *cl up whn p.u bef 4th* **100/1**

5m 0.8s (-20.30) **Going Correction** -0.925s/f (Hard) **10** Ran SP% **115.9**
Speed ratings (Par 103): **103,101,100,97,96 80,71, , ,**
toteswingers 1&2 £7.90, 1&3 Not won, 2&3 Not won CSF £64.86 TOTE £20.90: £3.60, £1.10, £6.70; EX 80.40 Trifecta £989.70 Part won. Pool: £1315.67 - 0.01 winning units..
Owner R Fisher,Fools With Horses&Twentyman **Bred** Mrs J A Niven **Trained** Bonchester Bridge, Borders

FOCUS
A modest event for mares, run at a steady gallop, and there are doubts over the form. The winner and fourth improved to the level of their best bumper runs.

2496 QUICKSILVERSLOTS GET UP TO £200 FREEPLAYS H'CAP CHASE (13 fncs) 2m 110y
1:45 (1:45) (Class 4) (0-120,120) 4-Y-0+ **£3,768** (£1,106; £553; £276)

Form RPR

/31- 1 **Next Sensation (IRE)**[25] 2007 6-11-10 **118** (t) TomScudamore 141+
(Michael Scudamore) *j.w: mde all: drew clr 4 out: easily* **15/8**[1]

/42- 2 14 **Prince Tam**[34] 1876 9-9-9 **94** oh2 JonathanEngland(5) 96
(Harriet Graham) *prom: lft 3rd 7th: effrt 3 out: chsd (clr) wnr bef next: no imp* **12/1**

635/ 3 2 **Shadrack (IRE)**[574] 5480 9-11-12 **120** RichieMcGrath 121
(Keith Reveley) *prom: lft 2nd 7th: mstke next: rdn and lost 2nd bef 2 out: sn no ex* **12/1**

232- 4 14 **Mulligan's Man (IRE)**[42] 1753 6-11-6 **114** JasonMaguire 104
(Donald McCain) *nt fluent on occasions: hld up: lft 4th and hmpd 7th: effrt bef 3 out: no imp fr next* **4/1**[2]

5/U- 5 4 **Porgy**[15] 2171 8-11-10 **118** DannyCook 100
(Brian Ellison) *bhd: shortlived effrt bef 5 out: sn btn* **9/2**[3]

/65- B **Alpha One (IRE)**[174] 470 7-10-13 **107** BrianHughes
(Chris Grant) *chsd ldrs: b.d 7th* **11/1**

230- F **Castlelawn (IRE)**[30] 1921 6-11-10 **118** PeterBuchanan
(Lucinda Russell) *chsd wnr: fell 7th* **7/1**

4m 1.2s (-19.90) **Going Correction** -1.00s/f (Hard) **7** Ran SP% **109.2**
Speed ratings (Par 105): **106,99,98,91,90 ,**
toteswingers 1&2 £3.70, 1&3 £7.30, 2&3 £11.60 CSF £20.69 TOTE £3.00: £1.60, £2.10; EX 18.70 Trifecta £98.20 Pool: £1330.32 - 10.15 winning units..
Owner Mark Blandford **Bred** Mrs Regina McAuliffe **Trained** Bromsash, H'fords

FOCUS
An ordinary handicap chase but another big step forward from the impressive winner who looks set to compete at a higher level. Solid form.

2497 QUICKSILVERSLOTS PLAY £500 ROULETTE H'CAP HURDLE (13 hdls) 3m
2:15 (2:15) (Class 5) (0-100,100) 4-Y-0+ **£1,949** (£572; £286; £143)

Form RPR

0/0- 1 **Maggie Blue (IRE)**[40] 1790 5-10-5 **86** CallumBewley(7) 99+
(Harriet Graham) *in tch: hdwy to ld bef 3 out: clr next: kpt on wl* **14/1**

/P0- 2 9 **St Gregory (IRE)**[34] 1873 5-10-0 **74** oh1 BrianHarding 72
(Nicky Richards) *prom: rdn bef 3 out: rallied next: chsd (clr) wnr run-in: no imp* **12/1**

5/F- 3 ¾ **Heez A Steel (IRE)**[167] 580 12-11-0 **95** AlistairFindlay(7) 92
(Jane Walton) *mde most to bef 3 out: kpt on same pce fr next: no imp whn lost 2nd run-in* **16/1**

6PP- 4 2½ **Shooting Times**[40] 1789 8-10-13 **94** (b[1]) GrahamWatters(7) 89
(Lucinda Russell) *chsd ldrs on outside: hit 2nd: disp ld 4 out: outpcd next: n.d after* **11/1**

0/5- 5 3 **Heron's Mill (IRE)**[14] 2202 5-11-5 **100** DaleIrving(7) 92
(James Ewart) *cl up: disp ld 6th to 4 out: outpcd bef next: no imp fnl 2* **4/1**[1]

5/5- 6 nse **Northern Acres**[22] 2034 7-11-7 **95** LucyAlexander 87
(N W Alexander) *hld up: hdwy whn mstke 9th: effrt and rdn bef 3 out: kpt on same pce* **9/2**[2]

/P5- 7 1¼ **Delightfully (FR)**[34] 1873 9-11-0 **95** (vt) GrantCockburn(7) 86
(Lucinda Russell) *hld up towards rr: hdwy whn bmpd bnd bef 3 out: sn rdn and outpcd* **9/2**[2]

63P- 8 13 **Flying Doctor**[7] 2333 10-11-7 **98** EwanWhillans(3) 84
(Alistair Whillans) *in tch tl rdn and wknd fr 3 out: eased whn no ch fr last* **9/1**

260- 9 72 **Mr Mistopheles (IRE)**[15] 2169 5-10-4 **78** (v[1]) HenryBrooke
(Philip Kirby) *hld up in tch: drvn and outpcd after 4 out: lost tch fr next: t.o* **7/1**[3]

043- 10 2 **Western Bound (IRE)**[40] 1789 12-10-0 **74** oh10 (t) SeanQuinlan
(Barbara Butterworth) *hld up: mstke 2nd: struggling fr 4 out: t.o* **25/1**

U46- P **Cumbrian Farmer**[35] 1850 6-10-11 **92** JonathonBewley(7)
(George Bewley) *a bhd: struggling fnl circ: t.o whn p.u bef 3 out* **22/1**

5m 50.3s (-23.70) **Going Correction** -0.925s/f (Hard) **11** Ran SP% **115.6**
Speed ratings (Par 103): **102,99,98,97,96 96,96,92,68,67**
toteswingers 1&2 £34.90, 1&3 £34.90, 2&3 Not won CSF £165.64 CT £2700.72 TOTE £19.10: £4.30, £5.10, £4.30; EX 370.90 TRIFECTA Not won..
Owner Exors of the Late Sam Hamilton **Bred** George Ward **Trained** Philip Law, Borders

FOCUS
A weak handicap lacking obvious progressive types, but the easy winner was value for further and this rates a big step up.

2498 NEWCASTLE FLOORING COMPANY H'CAP CHASE (19 fncs) 3m
2:50 (2:50) (Class 4) (0-110,108) 4-Y-0+ **£3,768** (£1,106; £553; £276)

Form RPR

531- 1 **Settledoutofcourt (IRE)**[7] 2335 7-10-11 **93** TomScudamore 117+
(Lucinda Russell) *mde all: rdn and styng on wl whn lft 10 l clr 2 out: kpt on* **4/6**[1]

P/4- 2 14 **Frank The Slink**[22] 2036 7-11-11 **107** WilsonRenwick 113
(Micky Hammond) *hld up in tch: stdy hdwy whn hit 10th: effrt after 5 out: outpcd after next: no imp whn lft 10 l 2nd 2 out* **16/1**

32U/ 3 14 **Mr Supreme (IRE)**[350] 2737 8-11-12 **108** RichieMcGrath 103
(Keith Reveley) *nt fluent in rr: outpcd 1/2-way: stdy hdwy after 5 out: no imp whn lft modest 3rd 2 out* **9/1**

124- 4 24 **Foot The Bill**[8] 2310 8-11-6 **102** (v[1]) BrianHarding 83
(Patrick Holmes) *chsd ldrs: hit 10th and 12th: wknd fr 5 out: t.o* **20/1**

325- P **Bishophill Jack (IRE)**[36] 1830 7-11-12 **108** (p) JasonMaguire
(Kim Bailey) *chsd ldrs tl lost pl 6th: struggling fr 9th: t.o whn p.u bef 11th* **8/1**[3]

114/ F **Dingo Bay**[228] 5077 7-10-0 **82** oh3 BrianHughes 96
(John Wade) *chsd wnr: effrt and rdn 3 out: jst over two l down and one pce whn fell heavily next* **9/2**[2]

6m 1.9s (-20.60) **Going Correction** -1.00s/f (Hard) **6** Ran SP% **109.9**
Speed ratings (Par 105): **94,89,84,76,**
toteswingers 1&2 £5.90, 1&3 £5.40, 2&3 £8.70 CSF £10.73 TOTE £1.70: £1.20, £5.40; EX 15.20 Trifecta £95.20 Pool: £1907.54 - 15.02 winning units..
Owner Andrew McAllister **Bred** Sean Naughton **Trained** Arlary, Perth & Kinross

FOCUS
An ordinary handicap chase. The easy winner stood out on his recent win and probably ran to a similar level.

2499 ITPS MAIDEN OPEN NATIONAL HUNT FLAT RACE 2m
3:25 (3:29) (Class 6) 4-6-Y-0 **£1,559** (£457; £228; £114)

Form RPR

1 **Chidswell (IRE)** 4-11-2 0 BrianHarding 109+
(Nicky Richards) *hld up: stdy hdwy over 6f out: effrt and rdn over 2f out: led ins fnl f: keeping on wl whn drifted lft towards fin* **9/1**

2 ½ **Degooch (IRE)**[195] 4-11-2 0 JasonMaguire 107
(Donald McCain) *t.k.h: w ldrs: led after 2f: rdn over 2f out: hdd ins fnl f: kpt on: hld nr fin* **4/1**[2]

3 2½ **Surging Seas (IRE)** 4-11-2 0 DougieCostello 105
(Tony Coyle) *prom: effrt and chsd ldr over 2f out: rn green: lost 2nd ins fnl f: one pce* **13/2**[3]

3/ 4 2¾ **Gurkha Brave (IRE)**[341] 2953 5-11-2 0 BrianHughes 103
(Karen McLintock) *t.k.h: cl up: effrt and rdn over 2f out: one pce fr over 1f out* **10/1**

5 ¾ **Ride The Range (IRE)** 4-11-2 0 HenryBrooke 101
(Chris Grant) *t.k.h: hld up: rdn and hdwy over 3f out: kpt on fr 2f out: nvr able to chal* **40/1**

4/2- 6 1½ **Serenity Now (IRE)**[15] 2174 5-11-2 0 DannyCook 101
(Brian Ellison) *hld up in tch: effrt and rdn 3f out: no imp fr over 1f out* **7/2**[1]

0- 7 9 **Thatildee (IRE)**[34] 1877 5-10-9 0 DiarmuidO'Regan(7) 91
(Chris Grant) *bhd: outpcd 7f out: rdn and kpt on fr 2f out: nvr able to chal* **50/1**

8 ¾ **Res Ipsa Loquitur (IRE)**[29] 1953 5-10-2 0 MrPPower(7) 83
(J F Levins, Ire) *hld up in midfield: hdwy over 3f out: rdn and outpcd wl over 1f out* **7/1**

4- 9 1¾ **Utopian**[35] 1854 4-11-2 0 WilsonRenwick 88
(Rose Dobbin) *midfield: effrt and rdn over 3f out: wknd wl over 1f out* **22/1**

10 9 **Got The Nac (IRE)**[13] 2237 4-10-13 0 MrSCrawford(3) 79
(S R B Crawford, Ire) *t.k.h: hld up: rdn and hdwy over 3f out: outpcd fnl 2f* **10/1**

11 nk **Kilquiggan (IRE)**[220] 5238 5-11-2 0 RyanMania 79
(Sandy Thomson) *prom tl rdn and outpcd over 3f out: sn btn* **50/1**

12 2¾ **Wildest Dreams (IRE)** 4-10-9 0 AlistairFindlay(7) 76
(Jane Walton) *t.k.h: led 2f: cl up: outpcd whn stmbld and nrly uns rdr over 2f out: wknd* **16/1**

13 36 **Caldew Lad (IRE)** 5-10-9 0 CallumBewley(7) 40
(Barry Murtagh) *bhd: lost tch fr over 4f out: t.o* **100/1**

56- 14 2¼ **Chester Legend**[159] 682 6-10-9 0 JohnDawson(7) 38
(Sue Taylor) *hld up towards rr: struggling 1/2-way: t.o* **100/1**

3m 51.1s (-13.30) **Going Correction** -0.925s/f (Hard) **14** Ran SP% **114.8**
Speed ratings: **96,95,94,93,92 92,87,87,86,81 81,80,62,61**
toteswingers 1&2 £17.10, 1&3 £36.10, 2&3 £10.00 CSF £37.65 TOTE £10.90: £4.50, £1.80, £2.50; EX 54.30 Trifecta £1132.70 Pool: £1668.10 - 1.10 winning units..
Owner Langdale Bloodstock **Bred** Victor Dunne **Trained** Greystoke, Cumbria
■ Wolf Sword was withdrawn. Price at time of withdrawal 8-1. Rule 4 applies to all bets - deduction 10p in the pound.

FOCUS
A fair bumper which should produce a few winners. It has been rated around the sixth and eighth.
T/Plt: £3,120.20 to a £1 stake. Pool: £56635.01 - 13.25 winning tickets T/Qpdt: £319.80 to a £1 stake. Pool: £6354.63 - 14.70 winning tickets RY

2487 CHELTENHAM (L-H)
Saturday, November 16

OFFICIAL GOING: Good (good to soft in places; 7.5)
Wind: Virtually nil Weather: Overcast

2500 JCB TRIUMPH HURDLE TRIAL (REGISTERED AS THE PRESTBURY JUVENILE HURDLE RACE) (GRADE 2) (8 hdls) 2m 110y
12:40 (12:40) (Class 1) 3-Y-O
£17,085 (£6,411; £3,210; £1,599; £804; £402)

Form RPR

11- 1 **Royal Irish Hussar (IRE)**[15] 2200 3-11-6 142 BarryGeraghty 138+
(Nicky Henderson) *lw: neat: athletic: led to 2nd: styd pressing ldr: nt fluent 4 out: led 3 out: drvn and nt fluent last: styd on strly* **10/11**[1]

2 3¾ **Guitar Pete (IRE)**[14] 2231 3-11-6 130 (v) BryanCooper 133
(D T Hughes, Ire) *trckd ldrs: chsd wnr sn after 2 out: drvn and effrt appr last whn nt fluent: kpt on but no imp run-in* **15/2**

1- 3 15 **Azza (FR)**[17] 2154 3-10-13 135 (t) TomScudamore 112
(David Pipe) *w ldr: led 2nd: hdd 3 out: wknd into wl hld 3rd after 2 out* **7/1**[3]

231- 4 4½ **Akdam (IRE)**[9] 2307 3-11-2 119 (p) JoshHamer 111
(Tony Carroll) *rdn along and dropped to rr 3rd: wl bhd after 4 out: styd on u.p fr 2 out to take wl-hld 4th nr fin* **66/1**

2- 5 ½ **Abracadabra Sivola (FR)**[36] 1855 3-10-12 0 RichardJohnson 108
(Nick Williams) *hit 1st: chsd ldrs: hit 4th: lost pl and bhd after 4 out: styd on again after 2 out* **33/1**

211- 6 1¼ **Herod The Great**[10] 2294 3-11-2 130 RobertThornton 111
(Alan King) *chsd ldrs: rdn 3 out: wknd and hit 2 out: no ch whn hit last* **14/1**

7 82 **Art Mauresque (FR)**[74] 3-11-6 0 .... DarylJacob 39
(Paul Nicholls) *unf: chsd ldrs: rdn 4 out: sn wknd: no ch whn mstke 3 out: t.o* 7/2[2]

4m 0.27s (-1.73) **Going Correction** +0.20s/f (Yiel) 7 Ran SP% **110.0**
Speed ratings (Par 114): **112,110,103,101,100 100,61**
toteswingers 1&2 £2.70, 1&3 £2.20, 2&3 £3.90 CSF £7.91 TOTE £1.90: £1.30, £2.60; EX 6.90 Trifecta £37.50 Pool: £2557.36 - 51.01 winning units..

Owner Triermore Stud **Bred** Adjalisa Syndicate **Trained** Upper Lambourn, Berks

FOCUS
All races on Old Course and track configured same as previous day. Undoubtedly the best juvenile heat of the current campaign. It was run at an ordinary gallop and the first pair had it to themselves in the home straight. Royal Irish Hussar was the form pick but this rates another step up and he's a smart juvenile. A step up from the second on his Irish form.

2501 ROY BLANDFORD 65 YEARS AT CHELTENHAM NOVICES' CHASE (19 fncs) 3m 110y
1:15 (1:15) (Class 2) 5-Y-0+

£12,512 (£3,696; £1,848; £924; £462; £232)

Form RPR

4/1- **1** **Le Bec (FR)**[41] 1796 5-11-4 142 .... NoelFehily 155+
(Emma Lavelle) *lw: trckd ldr: mstke 12th: led after 4 out: reminders after 3 out: drvn and kpt on finding run-in* 3/1[2]

4/1- **2** ¾ **Shutthefrontdoor (IRE)**[21] 2074 6-11-4 0 .... APMcCoy 154+
(Jonjo O'Neill) *lw: hld up towards rr but in tch: disp 3rd fr 15th: disp 2nd fr 3 out tl chsd wnr appr last: kpt on u.p but a hld* 9/4[1]

103/ **3** 2½ **Sam Winner (FR)**[212] 5362 6-10-13 0 .... DarylJacob 148
(Paul Nicholls) *b.bkwd: in rr but in tch: hdwy to cl on ldrs fr 12th: disputed 2nd fr 3 out: rdn bef next: one pce into 3rd appr last* 10/1

125/ **4** 23 **African Gold (IRE)**[224] 5175 5-10-13 0 ....(t) SamTwiston-Davies 132+
(Nigel Twiston-Davies) *trckd ldrs: nt fluent 7th: wl there on inner whn bmpd and mstke 3 out: wknd sn after* 9/4[1]

3/2- **5** 1¾ **Bob Ford (IRE)**[18] 2151 6-10-13 128 .... TomScudamore 129
(Rebecca Curtis) *led: nt fluent 14th: mstke and hdd 4 out: stl chalng whn blnd 3 out: sn wknd: no ch whn blnd last* 25/1

3/1- **6** 7 **White Star Line (IRE)**[16] 2186 9-11-7 143 .... BryanCooper 126
(D T Hughes, Ire) *hld up in rr: nt fluent 10th: hdwy after 4 out to cl on ldrs next whn nt fluent: sn btn* 8/1[3]

6m 16.17s (-2.13) **Going Correction** +0.20s/f (Yiel) 6 Ran SP% **110.6**
Speed ratings: **111,110,109,102,102 99**
toteswingers 1&2 £2.40, 1&3 £4.00, 2&3 £3.90 CSF £10.25 TOTE £3.60: £2.10, £2.10; EX 12.20 Trifecta £54.80 Pool: £3012.52 - 41.17 winning units..

Owner Tim Syder **Bred** N Madamet, I Kellitt & D Thomlinson **Trained** Hatherden, Hants

FOCUS
A warm staying novice chase and they went a sound gallop. The principals dominated from the third-last fence. The first two should end up being two of the better staying novices and this form looks very solid.

2502 MURPHY GROUP H'CAP CHASE (GRADE 3) (22 fncs) 3m 3f 110y
1:50 (1:53) (Class 1) 4-Y-0+

£28,475 (£10,685; £5,350; £2,665; £1,340; £670)

Form RPR

3/5- **1** **Alvarado (IRE)**[35] 1868 8-10-0 132 oh3 .... PaulMoloney 140+
(Fergal O'Brien) *lw: hld up towards rr: smooth hdwy after 4 out: trcking ldrs whn coming wd on home turn: rdn after next: styd on v strly after last: led fnl 120yds: rdn out* 12/1

/51- **2** 2 **Knockara Beau (IRE)**[28] 1978 10-10-13 145 .... JanFaltejsek 152+
(George Charlton) *trckd ldrs tl mstke and lost pl 4 out: sn rdn: gd hdwy after 3 out: styd on strly fr last to go 2nd towards fin* 25/1

/05- **3** 1¾ **Bradley**[28] 1971 9-10-0 132 oh4 .... PaddyBrennan 137+
(Fergal O'Brien) *j.rt at times smetimes bdly: mid-div: wnt rt 11th: rdn after 4 out: styd on after next: disputing 3rd whn wnt rt last: flattered briefly whn coming w str run w wnr after last tl no ex fnl 75yds* 5/1[2]

P/3- **4** ½ **Monbeg Dude (IRE)**[28] 1968 8-10-6 138 .... RichardJohnson 142
(Michael Scudamore) *hld up towards rr: awkward 1st: hdwy after 18th: mounting chal whn hmpd on bnd after 3 out: led sn after next: hdd fnl 120yds: no ex and lost 2 pls nring fin* 10/1

131/ **5** nk **Godsmejudge (IRE)**[210] 5404 7-11-2 148 .... WayneHutchinson 151
(Alan King) *lw: trckd ldr: led 3 out: plld wd on bnd: rdn whn hit 2 out: sn hdd: ev ch after last: no ex fnl 120yds* 8/1

4/2- **6** 6 **Tour Des Champs (FR)**[28] 1971 6-10-1 133 .... SamTwiston-Davies 133+
(Nigel Twiston-Davies) *mid-div: rdn after 18th: styd on between last 2: nvr rchd ldrs* 9/2[1]

0/0- **7** 13 **On Trend (IRE)**[14] 2214 7-10-3 135 .... TomCannon 120
(Nick Gifford) *mid-div: pushed along fr 12th: rdn after 4 out: nvr threatened ldrs* 40/1

/32- **8** 2½ **Spring Heeled (IRE)**[34] 1897 6-10-10 142 ....(p) BarryGeraghty 126
(J H Culloty, Ire) *hld up bhd: nudged along at times: hdwy on outer 17th: rdn and ev ch whn carried wd on bnd after 3 out: wknd between last 2* 7/1

112- **9** 3¾ **Ballybough Gorta (IRE)**[64] 1579 6-10-0 132 ....(v) JamieMoore 111
(Peter Bowen) *trckd ldrs tl 11th: sn struggling towards rr: nvr bk on terms* 25/1

162/ **10** 7 **Goulanes (IRE)**[213] 5355 7-11-0 146 .... TomScudamore 119
(David Pipe) *mid-div: nt fluent 10th: hmpd 11th: rdn after 18th: sn btn* 11/2[3]

/00- **11** 15 **Becauseicouldntsee (IRE)**[16] 2186 10-10-0 132 ....(v) BrendanPowell 91
(N F Glynn, Ire) *led tl 3 out: sn rdn and wknd: t.o* 33/1

2/5- **12** 15 **Burton Port (IRE)**[20] 2100 9-11-12 158 .... APMcCoy 104
(Jonjo O'Neill) *hld up bhd: nudged along fr 8th: rdn after 4 out: nvr threatened: wknd 2 out: t.o* 16/1

011/ **U** **Quentin Collonges (FR)**[203] 5576 9-10-11 143 ....(t) AndrewTinkler 141
(Henry Daly) *mid-div: hdwy after 15th: disputing 3rd whn nt fluent 17th: rdn and ev ch whn carried sltly wd on home bnd: hld next: 6th whn blnd and uns rdr last* 9/1

7m 11.3s (1.90) **Going Correction** +0.20s/f (Yiel) 13 Ran SP% **119.6**
Speed ratings (Par 113): **105,104,103,103,103 101,98,97,96,94 90,85,**
toteswingers 1&2 £62.80, 1&3 £15.10, 2&3 £25.80 CSF £269.32 CT £1701.13 TOTE £16.10: £4.80, £6.30, £2.00; EX 376.30 Trifecta £1556.70 Pool: £6125.83 - 2.95 winning units..

Owner Mr & Mrs William Rucker **Bred** P R Joyce **Trained** Coln St. Dennis, Gloucs

FOCUS
Competitive stuff, they went a solid gallop, and there were seven in with a chance jumping the second-last. The winner looked to have a bit in hand but plenty of others made costly mistakes.

2503 PADDY POWER GOLD CUP CHASE (H'CAP) (GRADE 3) (16 fncs) 2m 4f 110y
2:30 (2:32) (Class 1) 4-Y-0+

£91,120 (£34,192; £17,120; £8,528; £4,288; £2,144)

Form RPR

3/1- **1** **Johns Spirit (IRE)**[28] 1969 6-10-2 139 .... RichieMcLernon 150+
(Jonjo O'Neill) *hld up towards rr: impr fr 11th: chsd ldrs fr 4 out: led sn after 2 out: rdn run-in: idled clsng stages: hld on wl* 7/1[2]

25/- **2** ¾ **Colour Squadron (IRE)**[249] 4724 7-10-2 139 .... TomO'Brien 148+
(Philip Hobbs) *in rr: hdwy 12th: chsd ldrs 4 out: disp 2nd next: chsng ldr whn mstke and hmpd 2 out and lost 6 l on wnr: rallied run-in: styd on to take 2nd cl home: a jst hld* 12/1

/21- **3** 1½ **Hidden Cyclone (IRE)**[57] 1613 8-11-1 152 ....(p) AndrewJMcNamara 158
(John Joseph Hanlon, Ire) *led to 10th: styd chsng ldr tl lft disputing ld 2 out: styd chsng wnr but no imp run-in: lost 2nd cl home* 20/1

/P2- **4** 3¾ **Attaglance**[51] 1663 7-10-0 137 oh6 ....(t) BrianHughes 141
(Malcolm Jefferson) *chsd ldrs: lost pl and rdn 4 out: rallied u.p after 3 out: mstke last: kpt on wl run-in* 16/1

011/ **5** 2½ **Rajdhani Express**[210] 5401 6-10-13 155 .... MrSWaley-Cohen[(5)] 156
(Nicky Henderson) *chsd ldrs: rdn after 3 out: styd on same pce fr 2 out* 8/1[3]

3/6- **6** 4 **Wishfull Thinking**[21] 2071 10-11-7 158 ....(t) RichardJohnson 157
(Philip Hobbs) *chsd ldrs: mstke 2nd: blnd 4 out: wknd 3 out* 33/1

251/ **7** 7 **Champion Court (IRE)**[213] 5353 8-11-6 157 .... IanPopham 149
(Martin Keighley) *lw: chsd ldrs: rdn and blnd 3 out: wknd bef 2 out: mstke last* 6/1[1]

2/2- **8** 1 **Tap Night (USA)**[13] 2244 6-10-12 149 .... APMcCoy 140
(Lucinda Russell) *in rr: hdwy 11th: bhd whn mstke 3 out: kpt on again fr 2 out: nvr a threat* 16/1

23G- **9** 1¾ **Woolcombe Folly (IRE)**[28] 1969 10-10-8 150 .... HarryDerham[(5)] 141
(Paul Nicholls) *in rr: blnd 3rd: mstke 6th: wl bhd whn hmpd 3 out: kpt on wl fr 2 out but nvr any ch* 28/1

/04- **10** ¾ **Kumbeshwar**[11] 2281 6-10-11 148 ....(p) WayneHutchinson 136
(Alan King) *in rr: blnd 9th: rdn 12th: sme prog u.p after 3 out* 40/1

452- **11** 6 **Astracad (FR)**[21] 2071 7-10-5 142 ....(v[1]) SamTwiston-Davies 126
(Nigel Twiston-Davies) *in tch: chsd ldrs fr 9th: wknd 3 out* 20/1

6/0- **12** 29 **Carrickboy (IRE)**[21] 2071 9-10-7 144 .... AidanColeman 100
(Venetia Williams) *lw: chsd ldrs to 8th: wknd 10th* 33/1

P15/ **13** ¾ **Nadiya De La Vega (FR)**[206] 5517 7-10-3 140 ....(p) AndrewTinkler 95
(Nicky Henderson) *swtg: chsd ldrs: rdn and wknd 12th: no ch whn hmpd 3 out* 12/1

/21- **14** 12 **Conquisto**[21] 2071 8-11-3 154 .... PaulTownend 98
(Steve Gollings) *chsd ldrs: hit 6th: rdn and rr fr 12th* 28/1

642/ **P** **Finian's Rainbow (IRE)**[203] 5575 10-11-12 163 .... BarryGeraghty
(Nicky Henderson) *mstke 1st: mid-div: in tch whn hit 9th: wknd qckly bef 4 out: t.o whn p.u bef next* 14/1

5/U- **F** **Vino Griego (FR)**[28] 1969 8-11-0 151 ....(v) JamieMoore
(Gary Moore) *towards rr tl fell 3 out* 25/1

1/1- **P** **Battle Group**[189] 215 8-10-13 150 ....(p[1]) BrendanPowell
(Johnny Farrelly) *blnd 1st: in rr tl wknd and p.u bef 11th* 14/1

F/6- **P** **Gift Of Dgab (IRE)**[19] 2144 9-10-1 138 .... BryanCooper
(A J Martin, Ire) *in rr: hit 3rd: mstke 8th: blnd 9th: t.o whn p.u after 4 out* 20/1

/P0- **F** **Easter Meteor**[15] 2199 7-10-3 140 .... LeightonAspell 144
(Emma Lavelle) *lw: chsd ldr: led 10th: l ldr and styng on strly whn fell 2 out* 20/1

110/ **P** **Ballynagour (IRE)**[247] 4750 7-10-6 143 .... TomScudamore
(David Pipe) *in tch 8th: hdwy 12th: wknd qckly after 4 out: t.o whn p.u bef 2 out* 8/1[3]

5m 7.02s (-3.98) **Going Correction** +0.20s/f (Yiel) 20 Ran SP% **127.6**
Speed ratings (Par 113): **115,114,114,112,111 110,107,107,106,106 103,92,92,88, , , , ,**
toteswingers 1&2 £25.10, 1&3 £58.10, 2&3 £86.10 CSF £77.48 CT £1644.31 TOTE £7.30: £2.40, £4.30, £4.60, £4.90; EX 102.50 Trifecta £3711.10 Pool: £140,022.87 - 28.29 winning units..

Owner Christopher W T Johnston **Bred** Arctic Tack Stud & Crossogue Stud **Trained** Cheltenham, Gloucs

■ Stewards' Enquiry : Tom O'Brien one-day ban: careless riding (Dec 1)

FOCUS
The feature race this year had a classy look about it. They went a proper gallop and it saw a cracking finish, with the novice handicap chase over C&D at last season's festival proving the key form race. The second was arguably unlucky but the idling winner would probably have won anyway.

2504 ULTIMA BUSINESS SOLUTIONS H'CAP HURDLE (LISTED RACE) (13 hdls) 3m 1f 110y
3:00 (3:05) (Class 1) 4-Y-0+

£15,376 (£5,769; £2,889; £1,439; £723; £361)

Form RPR

4P2/ **1** **Return Spring (IRE)**[214] 5327 6-9-13 125 .... JamesBest[(3)] 133+
(Philip Hobbs) *mid-div: pushed along after 3 out: rdn and hdwy after 2 out: disputing 3rd whn hmpd last: styd on strly fnl 120yds: led fnl stride* 20/1

115/ **2** shd **Salubrious (IRE)**[225] 5162 6-11-7 149 .... HarryDerham[(5)] 155
(Paul Nicholls) *hld up towards rr: hdwy after 10th: rdn to chal after 2 out: narrow advantage sn after last: kpt on: hdd fnl stride* 16/1

1/1- **3** nse **Southfield Theatre (IRE)**[20] 2106 5-11-3 140 .... DarylJacob 147
(Paul Nicholls) *lw: mid-div: hdwy after 10th: led after 2 out: sn rdn and strly pressed: narrowly hdd after last: kpt on w ev ch: lost 2nd on nod* 5/1[1]

/30- **4** 3½ **Cross Kennon (IRE)**[29] 1956 9-11-2 139 ....(v) SeanQuinlan 143
(Jennie Candlish) *led: j.rt: rdn and hdd after 2 out: hld in 3rd whn wnt rt and bmpd chalrs last: kpt on same pce* 12/1

023- **5** nk **Pineau De Re (FR)**[85] 1362 10-10-12 135 .... SamTwiston-Davies 138
(Dr Richard Newland) *hld up towards rr: hdwy after 2 out: sn rdn: styd on fr last but nvr rching ldrs* 33/1

042- **6** 4½ **Gauvain (GER)**[20] 2100 11-11-0 137 ....(t) RichardJohnson 138+
(Philip Hobbs) *mid-div: hdwy after 10th: rdn after 3 out: styng on at same pce in 5th whn hmpd last: no ex flat* 25/1

003- **7** 4 **Monetary Fund (USA)**[8] 2345 7-10-7 130 .... AidanColeman 125
(Venetia Williams) *mid-div: rdn after 2 out: wknd last* 11/1[3]

340- **8** *4* **Red Not Blue (IRE)**[28] 1972 10-10-7 **130** PaddyBrennan 121
(Simon Earle) *hld up bhd and kpt wd: nudged along after 7th: stdyu prog after 3 out: sn rdn: styd on but nvr threatening to get involved* **66/1**

100/ **9** *1 3/4* **Close House**[212] 5362 6-11-4 **141** TomScudamore 132
(David Pipe) *swtg: mid-div: hdwy 10th: rdn and ev ch after 2 out tl bef last: wknd* **16/1**

5PU/ **10** *3/4* **Sunnyhillboy (IRE)**[224] 5177 10-10-7 **130** APMcCoy 119
(Jonjo O'Neill) *hld up towards rr: struggling 3 out: sme late prog: nvr a danger* **7/1**[2]

/12- **11** *1* **Silver Eagle (IRE)**[28] 1972 5-10-11 **134** (t) SamThomas 122
(Kim Bailey) *mid-div tl dropped to rr tamely bef 10th: sn struggling: sme late prog past wkng horses but nt a danger after* **5/1**[1]

115/ **12** *1 3/4* **Recession Proof (FR)**[35] 4788 7-10-13 **136** BryanCooper 123
(John Quinn) *in tch: rdn after 2 out: sn wknd* **14/1**

P/2- **13** *1 3/4* **Lamb Or Cod (IRE)**[21] 2080 6-10-10 **133** (t) TomO'Brien 118
(Philip Hobbs) *trckd ldrs: rdn after 3 out: wknd last* **11/1**[3]

6/1- **14** *nse* **Bally Legend**[24] 2020 8-11-2 **139** IanPopham 124
(Caroline Keevil) *trckd ldrs: rdn appr 3 out: wknd 2 out* **25/1**

/45- **15** *2* **Araldur (FR)**[21] 2080 9-11-3 **140** RobertThornton 124
(Alan King) *lw: mid-div tl wknd 3 out* **16/1**

113/ **16** *51* **Edmund Kean (IRE)**[252] 4663 6-10-9 **132** ConorO'Farrell 69
(David Pipe) *t.k.h: hld up towards rr: hdwy into midfield after 9th: rdn after 3 out: wknd qckly next: t.o* **7/1**[2]

02P- **17** *49* **Cinevator (IRE)**[12] 2267 6-10-7 **130** (p) BrendanPowell 23
(Caroline Keevil) *trckd ldrs tl rdn after 10th: sn wknd: t.o* **50/1**

6m 32.2s (6.10) **Going Correction** +0.20s/f (Yiel) **17** Ran SP% **125.9**
Speed ratings (Par 111): **98,97,97,96,96 95,94,92,92,92 91,91,90,90,90 74,59**
toteswingers 1&2 £45.30, 1&3 £28.30, 2&3 £18.50 CSF £297.61 CT £1869.27 TOTE £32.50: £6.60, £4.40, £1.80, £2.80; EX 517.60 Trifecta £4882.00 Part won. Pool: £6,509.45 - 0.80 winning units..
Owner D J Jones **Bred** A V Bloodstock **Trained** Withycombe, Somerset

FOCUS
A thrilling finish to this staying handicap. Solid form. A step up from the winenr under a claimer with the second close to his festival win.

2505 NEPTUNE INVESTMENT MANAGEMENT NOVICES' HURDLE (REGISTERED AS THE HYDE NOVICES' HURDLE) (GRADE 2) (10 hdls) 2m 5f
3:35 (3:38) (Class 1) 4-Y-0+
£17,085 (£6,411; £3,210; £1,599; £804; £402)

Form RPR

/12- **1** **Creepy (IRE)**[28] 1968 5-11-0 131 IanPopham 137+
(Martin Keighley) *trckd ldrs: led 4 out: drvn wl bef last and qckdn: kpt finding u.p run-in* **9/2**[3]

11- **2** *1* **Timesremembered (IRE)**[21] 2079 5-11-7 143 LeightonAspell 144
(Emma Lavelle) *hld up towards rr: hdwy 4 out: clsd on ldrs 2 out: rdn to go 2nd wl bef last: kpt on u.p run-in but a hld* **9/4**[1]

3 *4* **Port Melon (IRE)**[203] 5-11-0 0 DarylJacob 134+
(Paul Nicholls) *strong: lengthy: lw: in tch: trckd ldrs travelling wl 2 out whn disputing 2nd: rdn sn after: one pce into 3rd wl bef last* **7/2**[2]

1F- **4** *5* **Indevan**[13] 2256 5-11-7 137 PaulTownend 137
(W P Mullins, Ire) *lw: strong: hld up in rr: travelling wl after 3 out: rdn after 2 out and sn fnd no ex* **15/2**

5/4- **5** *5* **Pure Science (IRE)**[29] 1954 5-11-0 0 SamTwiston-Davies 124
(Nigel Twiston-Davies) *chsd ldrs: blnd 3 out: wknd u.p 2 out* **11/1**

/11- **6** *6* **Drop Out Joe**[36] 1850 5-11-4 129 NoelFehily 122
(Charlie Longsdon) *led to 4 out: styd chsng wnr to next: wknd sn after* **22/1**

1/1- **7** *19* **Toubeera**[182] 374 7-10-11 135 AidanColeman 98
(Venetia Williams) *chsd ldrs: rdn appr 3 out: wknd sn after* **8/1**

51- **8** *6* **Rally**[15] 2197 4-11-4 0 (p) BarryGeraghty 100
(Nicky Henderson) *hit 1st: chsd ldrs: rdn 5th: wknd qckly 4 out* **12/1**

5m 11.71s (-1.69) **Going Correction** +0.20s/f (Yiel)
WFA 4 from 5yo+ 8lb **8** Ran SP% **114.4**
Speed ratings (Par 115): **111,110,109,107,105 103,95,93**
toteswingers 1&2 £2.70, 1&3 £3.90, 2&3 £3.10 CSF £15.53 TOTE £5.40: £1.90, £1.20, £1.80; EX 15.30 Trifecta £75.90 Pool: £5201.24 - 51.35 winning units..
Owner M Boothright, T Hanlon, S Harman **Bred** Gareth Metcalfe **Trained** Condicote, Gloucs

FOCUS
This is always a decent novice hurdle. It was run at a solid gallop and the winner is on the upgrade.

2506 UKASH MARES' STANDARD OPEN NATIONAL HUNT FLAT RACE (LISTED RACE) 2m 110y
4:05 (4:06) (Class 1) 4-6-Y-0
£11,390 (£4,274; £2,140; £1,066; £536; £268)

Form RPR

1/5- **1** **The Govaness**[28] 1974 4-11-0 0 PaddyBrennan 116+
(Fergal O'Brien) *strong: hld up in rr: gd hdwy over 3f out: drvn to chal appr fnl f: led sn after: r.o wl* **28/1**

/21- **2** *1 1/2* **Lily Waugh (IRE)**[42] 1771 6-10-11 0 RachaelGreen(3) 114
(Anthony Honeyball) *chsd ldrs: chal fr 3f out tl led appr fnl f but hrd pressed and sn hdd: nt pce of wnr but kpt on wl for 2nd* **14/1**

111/ **3** *2* **Legacy Gold (IRE)**[225] 5163 5-11-4 0 TomScudamore 116
(David Pipe) *in tch: chsd ldrs 6f out: led ins fnl 3f: hdd u.p appr fnl f: styd on same pce* **3/1**[2]

310/ **4** *5* **Cabaret Girl**[280] 4127 6-11-0 0 RobertThornton 108
(John O'Neill) *led: rdn and hdd ins fnl 3f: wknd over 1f out* **40/1**

1/ **5** *1/2* **Mayfair Music (IRE)**[229] 5062 4-11-0 0 BarryGeraghty 108
(Nicky Henderson) *lengthy: lw: in tch: chsd ldrs 6f out: rdn 3f out: styd on same pce fnl 2f* **9/2**[3]

6 *2 1/2* **Supreme Bailerina (IRE)**[113] 1128 5-11-0 0 PaulTownend 105
(W P Mullins, Ire) *w'like: stdd in rr: rdn along 7f out: hdwy to cl on ldrs over 3f out: one pce u.p and wknd ins fnl 2f* **15/8**[1]

2/ **7** *nse* **Bull And Bush (IRE)**[212] 5364 4-11-0 0 WayneHutchinson 105
(Alan King) *strong: towards rr 1/2-way: drvn and hdwy over 2f out: styd on clsng stages* **12/1**

0/1- **8** *1 1/4* **Wyfield Rose**[38] 1826 4-11-0 0 NoelFehily 104
(Jamie Snowden) *chsd ldrs: ev ch 3f out: wknd 2f out* **33/1**

0/ **9** *shd* **Sunday Serenade (IRE)**[122] 1025 5-11-0 0 APMcCoy 104
(Peter Fahey, Ire) *strong: chal 3f out: wknd 2f out* **10/1**

3/3- **10** *1/2* **Welcometothejungle**[198] 85 5-11-0 0 SamTwiston-Davies 104
(Keiran Burke) *in tch: rdn over 3f out: sn btn* **50/1**

1/5- **11** *1 1/2* **Land Of Vic**[10] 2298 5-11-0 0 DonalDevereux 102
(Peter Bowen) *chsd ldrs tl wknd 3f out* **50/1**

3/ **12** *2 1/4* **Fairytale Theatre (IRE)**[212] 5364 6-11-0 0 DarylJacob 100
(Paul Nicholls) *unf: chsd ldrs: wknd 3f out* **20/1**

13 *5* **Vilja (IRE)**[204] 4-11-0 0 ConorO'Farrell 96
(David Pipe) *in rr: effrt and nt clr run over 3f out: sn wknd* **25/1**

2/4- **14** *hd* **A Shade Of Bay**[24] 2022 5-11-0 0 SamThomas 95
(Kim Bailey) *in rr: sme hdwy 4f out: sn wknd* **50/1**

212- **15** *20* **Handmaid**[68] 1539 4-11-0 0 JamieMoore 77
(Peter Bowen) *prom to 1/2-way* **40/1**

3m 56.82s (0.42) **Going Correction** +0.20s/f (Yiel)
WFA 4 from 5yo+ 7lb **15** Ran SP% **127.2**
Speed ratings: **107,106,105,103,102 101,101,100,100,100 99,98,96,96,87**
toteswingers 1&2 £67.90, 1&3 £25.10, 2&3 £14.80 CSF £366.99 TOTE £40.30: £6.70, £3.10, £2.10; EX 416.20 Trifecta £2596.20 Part won. Pool: £3,461.72 - 0.19 winning units..
Owner C B Brookes **Bred** C B Brookes **Trained** Coln St. Dennis, Gloucs

FOCUS
A solid Listed bumper for mares with the first three all above average. The third was below the level of her Aintree run.
T/Jkpt: Not won. T/Plt: £149.40. Pool: £324,052.70 - 1582.51 winning units. T/Qpdt: £55.30. pool: £24,092.62 - 321.90 winning units. ST

2189 UTTOXETER (L-H)
Saturday, November 16

OFFICIAL GOING: Soft (good to soft in places in straight on hurdle course; heavy in chute; chs 5.8; hdl 6.6)
First hurdle in 2m races omitted; bad ground. First fence in back straight omitted; false patch of ground.
Wind: light 1/2 against Weather: overcast

2507 MARSTON'S PEDIGREE NOVICES' HURDLE (8 hdls 1 omitted) 2m
12:35 (12:35) (Class 4) 4-Y-0+ **£3,798** (£1,122; £561; £280; £140)

Form RPR

1/ **1** **Oscars Den (IRE)**[291] 3927 5-10-9 0 MichaelByrne(3) 127+
(Tim Vaughan) *trckd ldrs: 2nd appr 3 out: led appr 2 out: clr whn j.lft last: v comf* **11/4**[1]

/31- **2** *6* **Chase The Spud**[13] 2252 5-11-5 0 TimmyMurphy 122
(Fergal O'Brien) *t.k.h: trckd ldrs: led appr 3 out: hdd appr 2 out: styd on same pce* **11/4**[1]

3 *1* **It's A Doddle (IRE)**[209] 5-10-12 0 DominicElsworth 114+
(Jonjo O'Neill) *hld up in rr: hdwy after 5th: 3rd 2 out: kpt on* **7/2**[2]

4 *13* **After The Storm**[26] 4-10-5 0 CiaranMckee(7) 100
(John O'Shea) *hld up in rr: hdwy appr 3 out: kpt on one pce to take modest 4th last* **66/1**

0/ **5** *2 1/2* **Flemensmix**[210] 5413 5-10-12 0 NickScholfield 98
(Kim Bailey) *chsd ldrs: drvn appr 3 out: wknd 2 out* **17/2**[3]

46/ **6** *2 3/4* **Un Bleu A L'Aam (FR)**[235] 4970 5-10-12 0 JackDoyle 95
(Victor Dartnall) *j.lft 1st: chsd ldrs 3rd: wknd last* **14/1**

56- **7** *21* **Gonalston Cloud (IRE)**[15] 2189 6-10-12 0 HarryHaynes 74
(Nick Kent) *chsd ldrs: reminders and lost pl 4th: t.o 3 out* **100/1**

1- **8** *3 1/2* **Crookstown (IRE)**[135] 880 6-11-0 0 KillianMoore(5) 77
(Ben Case) *chsd ldr 2nd: led 4th: mstke next: hdd appr 3 out: sn wknd: t.o* **9/1**

9 *nk* **Baile Atha Cliath (IRE)**[11] 4-10-12 0 TomSiddall 70
(Declan Carroll) *hld up in rr: bhd and drvn 3rd: t.o 5th* **50/1**

0/0- **10** *3 3/4* **Veratan (FR)**[23] 2040 6-10-7 0 HarryChalloner(5) 66
(Venetia Williams) *in rr: bhd fr 4th: t.o next* **33/1**

00/ **11** *5* **Watts Up Son**[32] 2865 5-10-12 0 [1] TommyPhelan 61
(Declan Carroll) *led to 4th: lost plbef 3 out: sn bhd: t.o* **33/1**

6- **12** *56* **Ll Cool Horse**[181] 395 4-10-12 0 DavidEngland
(Tom Gretton) *bhd fr 4th: t.o next: eventually completed* **66/1**

2/ **U** **Clara Peggotty**[552] 242 6-10-5 0 FelixDeGiles
(Tom Gretton) *mid-div whn hmpd and uns rdr 1st* **40/1**

4m 0.4s (8.40) **Going Correction** +0.75s/f (Soft)
WFA 4 from 5yo+ 7lb **13** Ran SP% **117.0**
Speed ratings (Par 105): **109,106,105,99,97 96,85,84,83,82 79,51,**
toteswingers 1&2 £2.50, 1&3 £3.40, 2&3 £2.90 CSF £9.79 TOTE £4.20: £1.70, £1.40, £1.80; EX 16.20 Trifecta £46.20 Pool: £743.44 - 12.05 winning units..
Owner Mrs Z Wentworth **Bred** Paul Gibbons **Trained** Aberthin, Vale of Glamorgan

FOCUS
Hurdles moved out on to fresher ground. Divided bends and hurdle in Chute omitted in 2m race. The ground had dried a little from the overnight description. An ordinary novice hurdle run at a fair gallop. The time was 18sec slower than standard, relatively quick for the day. The impressive winner looks a smart recruit, and can rate higher.

2508 WYCHWOOD HOBGOBLIN NOVICES' LIMITED H'CAP CHASE (14 fncs 1 omitted) 2m 4f
1:05 (1:11) (Class 3) (0-125,124) 4-Y-0+
£6,256 (£1,848; £924; £462; £231; £116)

Form RPR

424/ **1** **Renard D'Irlande (FR)**[281] 4112 8-11-3 **122** LiamTreadwell 131+
(Venetia Williams) *t.k.h: trckd ldrs: 1 1/2 l down whn lft in ld last: idled: drvn rt out* **11/4**[1]

4/2- **2** *1 1/4* **No Buts**[193] 163 5-10-1 **113** JakeHodson(7) 119
(David Bridgwater) *chsd ldrs: 3rd 6th: 2 1/2 l down in 3rd whn hmpd last: styd on to take 2nd last 50yds* **16/1**

10F/ **3** *2 1/4* **Henry King (IRE)**[228] 5103 9-10-9 **114** (t) JackDoyle 123+
(Victor Dartnall) *led: 1 1/2 l ahd whn stmbld bdly landing last: sn hdd: wknd and lost 2nd last 50yds* **15/2**

351- **4** *12* **Special Account (IRE)**[25] 2014 8-11-2 **121** NickScholfield 114
(Jeremy Scott) *in rr: hdwy 9th: modest 4th 3 out: nvr on terms* **9/2**[3]

0/3- **5** *1 1/2* **Cocacobana (IRE)**[24] 2020 8-10-11 **121** KillianMoore(5) 111
(Graeme McPherson) *in rr: sme hdwy 9th: lost pl after next: kpt on fr 2 out* **7/1**

241/ **6** *1 3/4* **Viva Steve (IRE)**[253] 4647 5-11-5 **124** DominicElsworth 112
(Mick Channon) *chsd ldrs: reminders after 10th: lost pl bef next* **3/1**[2]

3/5- **7** *8* **Jat Punjabi**[196] 114 9-10-13 **118** MarkGrant 99
(Jo Hughes) *nt fluent: chsd ldrs: drvn 9th: lost pl after next: sn bhd: t.o 2 out* **25/1**

3/4- **8** *7* **San Telm (IRE)**[24] 2020 8-11-2 **124** JoshuaMoore(3) 97
(Renee Robeson) *in rr: outpcd 9th: bhd fr 4 out: t.o 2 out* **6/1**

5m 16.9s (11.40) **Going Correction** +0.75s/f (Soft) **8** Ran SP% **118.1**
Speed ratings (Par 107): **107,106,105,100,100 99,96,93**
toteswingers 1&2 £11.00, 1&3 £6.80, 2&3 £36.70 CSF £42.71 CT £303.61 TOTE £3.20: £1.30, £2.80, £2.50; EX 54.50 Trifecta £730.10 Pool: £1549.58 - 1.59 winning units..
Owner Hills Of Ledbury (Aga) **Bred** Mlle Marie Drion At Al **Trained** Kings Caple, H'fords

FOCUS
Another interesting race of its type. It was run at a solid gallop and the first three finished clear. The winner is rated to form but it would have been close but for the third's last-fence error.

2509 MARSTON'S EPA MAIDEN HURDLE (10 hdls) 2m 4f 110y
1:40 (1:42) (Class 5) 4-Y-O+ **£2,599** (£763; £381; £190)

Form RPR

P/2- **1** **Ashes House (IRE)**[30] [1937] 7-11-0 0 NickScholfield 117+
(Rebecca Curtis) *t.k.h: led 1st: jnd 3 out: narrowly hdd next: j.rt and led last: sn hdd: styd on wl to regain ld nr fin* **4/7**[1]

22- **2** *1* **A Tail Of Intrigue (IRE)**[44] [1732] 5-11-0 0 WillKennedy 114+
(Ian Williams) *mid-div: chsd ldrs 6th: clr 2nd sn after next: led narrowly 2 out: hdd last: sn regain ld: hdd and no ex clsng stages* **7/1**

12/ **3** *28* **Rugged Jack (FR)**[659] [3950] 6-11-0 0 JackDoyle 86
(Victor Dartnall) *in rr: hdwy 6th: distant 3rd appr 2 out* **9/2**[2]

00- **4** *11* **Oak Wood (IRE)**[15] [2189] 5-10-11 0 GavinSheehan(3) 75
(John Upson) *t.k.h: led to 1st: chsd ldrs: outpcd sn after 7th: lost pl appr next: distant 4th appr 2 out* **100/1**

4/4- **5** *8* **Royal Palladium (FR)**[15] [2189] 5-11-0 0 LiamTreadwell 67
(Venetia Williams) *trckd ldrs: outpcd sn after 7th: wknd appr next* **11/2**[3]

6 *9* **High Aspirations (IRE)**[244] 5-10-11 0 MichealNolan(3) 58
(Michael Blake) *chsd ldrs: outpcd 7th: sn lost pl* **10/1**

U04- **7** *1* **Over My Head**[13] [2252] 5-10-7 0 GeraldQuinn(7) 57
(Claire Dyson) *trckd ldrs: t.k.h: wknd appr 3 out* **100/1**

60- **8** *7* **Anchoretta Eyre (IRE)**[25] [2009] 7-10-7 0 TimmyMurphy 43
(Fergal O'Brien) *mid-div: hdwy 5th: lost pl 7th* **40/1**

0/6- **9** *½* **Blue Cove**[197] [89] 8-11-0 75 TomSiddall 50
(Lynn Siddall) *hld up in rr: drvn and bhd 6th: t.o after next* **100/1**

00/ **10** *36* **Dee Ayes Delight**[258] [4542] 6-10-7 0 JakeHodson(7) 14
(David Bridgwater) *prom: lost pl 5th: bhd fr 7th: sn t.o: ventually completed* **40/1**

0/ **11** *18* **Honour The King (IRE)**[1282] [319] 7-10-9 0 HarryChalloner(5)
(John Bryan Groucott) *last whn blnd bdly 6th: lost tch and mstke 6th: sn hopelessly t.o: eventually completed* **80/1**

5m 12.4s (13.40) **Going Correction** +0.75s/f (Soft) **11 Ran SP% 127.9**
Speed ratings (Par 103): **104,103,92,88,85 82,81,79,79,65 58**
toteswingers 1&2 £1.80, 1&3 £1.40, 2&3 £2.60 CSF £6.57 TOTE £1.60: £1.10, £2.50, £2.00; EX 6.50 Trifecta £17.40 Pool: £1862.16 - 80.13 winning units..
Owner Diamond Racing Ltd **Bred** J Roberts **Trained** Newport, Dyfed

FOCUS
Little depth to this maiden hurdle, in which the first two drew a long way clear as they fought out a fine battle over the last three flights. The winner is rated to the level of his recent run.

2510 BANKS'S BITTER H'CAP HURDLE (10 hdls) 2m 4f 110y
2:15 (2:17) (Class 4) (0-115,115) 4-Y-O **£3,798** (£1,122; £561; £280; £140)

Form RPR

/64- **1** **Red Admirable (IRE)**[155] [737] 7-11-6 114 KillianMoore(5) 119+
(Graeme McPherson) *chsd ldrs: cl 2nd appr 3 out: led 2 out: drvn rt out* **14/1**

150- **2** *1¼* **Di Kaprio (FR)**[55] [1634] 7-11-7 110 LiamHeard 114+
(Barry Leavy) *led: hdd and hit 2 out: rallied run-in: a jst hld* **25/1**

621- **3** *1¾* **Finding Your Feet (IRE)**[23] [2034] 5-10-10 109 (p) JamesHuxham(10) 110
(Jonjo O'Neill) *in rr: hdwy to chse ldrs 4th: 3rd bef 2 out: styd on same pce* **5/2**[1]

05P/ **4** *3¼* **Wellforth (IRE)**[308] [3620] 9-11-12 115 (p) DavidEngland 113
(Barry Brennan) *chsd ldrs: lost pl 4th: hdwy after 7th: 4th appr 2 out: hit last: one pce* **33/1**

6/P- **5** *nk* **The Jugopolist (IRE)**[174] [500] 6-10-13 112 PaulO'Brien(10) 108
(Rebecca Curtis) *mid-div: reminders and lost pl after 5th: hdwy after 7th: kpt on fr 2 out: tk 5th last 50yds* **4/1**[2]

124- **6** *2¼* **The Road Ahead**[38] [1814] 6-10-12 101 NickScholfield 95
(Peter Bowen) *chsd ldrs: drvn 7th: one pce fr next* **7/1**[3]

004/ **7** *36* **Take The Mick**[233] [4989] 6-10-12 101 LiamTreadwell 59
(Venetia Williams) *chsd ldrs: wknd bef 2 out: distant 7th whn blnd last: t.o* **7/1**[3]

055/ **8** *6* **I Know The Code (IRE)**[217] [5293] 8-10-8 97 TomSiddall 49
(Lynn Siddall) *in rr: sme hdwy 6th: lost pl appr 3 out: t.o* **16/1**

630/ **9** *4½* **Tokyo Javilex (FR)**[204] [5546] 6-10-7 99 (t) MarkQuinlan(3) 47
(Nigel Hawke) *mid-div: hdwy 6th: chsng ldrs next: lost pl bef 3 out: sn bhd: t.o* **8/1**

P20/ **10** *3¼* **Heavenstown (IRE)**[202] [12] 7-11-9 112 RhysFlint 56
(John Spearing) *chsd ldrs: lost pl after 7th: sn bhd: t.o* **20/1**

6- **11** *14* **Johnnys Legacy (IRE)**[13] [2250] 6-11-0 103 (p) DaveCrosse 33
(Conor Dore) *hld up in rr: drvn 7th: sn bhd: t.o next* **50/1**

630/ **12** *4* **Ctappers**[37] [4238] 4-11-7 110 WillKennedy 36
(Mick Channon) *in rr: drvn 6th: sn bhd: t.o 3 out* **33/1**

P **Kilflora**[482] [1041] 10-11-4 114 (t) GeraldQuinn(7)
(Claire Dyson) *chsd ldrs: lost pl 7th: sn bhd: t.o next: p.u bef last* **33/1**

30F/ **P** **Basford Bob (IRE)**[602] [5075] 8-11-2 112 ConorRing(7)
(Jennie Candlish) *mstkes: chsd ldrs: lost pl and blnd 7th: sn bhd: t.o 3 out: p.u bef last* **14/1**

5m 14.5s (15.50) **Going Correction** +0.75s/f (Soft)
WFA 4 from 5yo+ 8lb **14 Ran SP% 123.3**
Speed ratings (Par 105): **100,99,98,97,97 96,82,80,78,77 72,70, ,**
toteswingers 1&2 £0.00, 1&3 £18.50, 2&3 £12.20 CSF £325.59 CT £1175.25 TOTE £20.40: £5.00, £6.70, £1.60; EX 377.00 Trifecta £527.30 Part won Pool: £703.19 - 0.90 winning units..
Owner Wildcat Syndicate **Bred** Sean Duggan **Trained** Upper Oddington, Gloucs

FOCUS
A modest handicap run in a time two seconds slower than the preceding maiden hurdle. A step up from the winner and there's a case for rating the form a bit higher.

2511 JENNINGS CUMBERLAND ALE H'CAP HURDLE (8 hdls 1 omitted) 2m
2:50 (2:52) (Class 5) (0-100,99) 4-Y-O+ **£2,339** (£686; £343; £171)

Form RPR

6F0- **1** **Poetic Power (IRE)**[41] [1799] 4-10-7 87 GeraldQuinn(7) 92+
(Claire Dyson) *hld up towards rr: hdwy to trck ldrs 4th: led appr 3 out: rdn between last 2: styd on* **16/1**

005- **2** *3¾* **Prince Freddie**[15] [2191] 5-9-10 76 RyanHatch(7) 75
(Roy Brotherton) *chsd ldrs: 2nd appr 3 out: styd on same pce between last 2* **16/1**

535- **3** *2¼* **Logical Approach (IRE)**[16] [2169] 6-11-6 98 (p) TonyKelly(5) 95
(David Thompson) *t.k.h: led: hdd appr 3 out: kpt on one pce* **17/2**

4/0- **4** *3¾* **Lean Burn (USA)**[174] [503] 7-10-10 83 LiamHeard 76
(Barry Leavy) *in rr: hdwy 4th: modest 4th appr 2 out: kpt on* **8/1**

320- **5** *17* **Rose Red**[66] [1567] 6-10-10 90 JakeHodson(7) 66
(Rob Summers) *chsd ldrs 2nd: drvn 5th: outpcd bef next: wknd bef 2 out* **15/2**[3]

000/ **6** *4* **Adili (IRE)**[26] [1676] 4-10-2 85 GLavery(10) 57
(Brian Ellison) *in rr: drvn 2nd: bhd fr 5th: t.o 3 out* **16/1**

501- **7** *12* **Whispering Harry**[21] [2090] 4-10-5 85 ChristopherWard(7) 45
(Henry Oliver) *chsd ldrs to 2nd: drvn and reminders 4th: sn lost pl: t.o 3 out: struck into* **5/1**[2]

000/ **8** *1¾* **On The Record (IRE)**[304] [3680] 5-11-2 99 TommieMO'Brien(10) 58
(Jonjo O'Neill) *chsd ldrs: lost pl 3rd: bhd fr 5th: t.o next* **7/2**[1]

006- **9** *1¾* **Ancient Times (USA)**[8] [2336] 6-10-11 87 KyleJames(3) 44
(Philip Kirby) *chsd ldr: lost pl 5th: sn bhd: t.o next* **20/1**

402- **F** **Pagham Belle**[10] [2291] 5-10-8 84 (t) MarkQuinlan(3) 77
(Nigel Hawke) *chsd ldrs: handy 4th but drvn whn fell 3 out* **7/2**[1]

4m 8.9s (16.90) **Going Correction** +0.75s/f (Soft)
WFA 4 from 5yo+ 7lb **10 Ran SP% 116.9**
Speed ratings (Par 103): **87,85,84,82,73 71,65,64,63,**
toteswingers 1&2 £20.20, 1&3 £20.60, 2&3 £26.30 CSF £235.30 CT £2319.29 TOTE £25.10: £6.70, £4.30, £2.60; EX 254.20 Trifecta £909.60 Part won Pool: £1,212.91 - 0.14 winning units..
Owner Miss C Dyson **Bred** Paget Bloodstock **Trained** Cleeve Prior, Worcs

FOCUS
They went a sound pace in this very modest contest. The first two were well in on the best of their old form.

2512 RINGWOOD OLD THUMPER H'CAP CHASE (14 fncs 2 omitted) 2m 6f 110y
3:25 (3:27) (Class 4) (0-120,120) 4-Y-O+
£6,256 (£1,848; £924; £462; £231; £116)

Form RPR

P/P- **1** **Duke Of Monmouth (IRE)**[12] [2267] 6-11-4 112 DominicElsworth 122+
(Charlie Mann) *chsd ldrs: upsides whn hit 3 out: led next: kpt on run-in: all out* **7/2**[2]

003- **2** *nk* **Hollins**[15] [2194] 9-9-7 94 JoshWall(7) 103+
(Tony Forbes) *hld up in rr: stdy hdwy whn hit 6th: drvn appr 4 out: 2nd appr last: sn upsides on run-in: no ex clsng stages* **11/2**

/56- **3** *4½* **Ringa Bay**[6] [2394] 8-11-2 117 (p) JakeHodson(7) 120
(David Bridgwater) *chsd ldrs: 2nd 4th: drvn appr 4 out: kpt on same pce appr last* **9/2**[3]

/36- **4** *2¼* **The Thirsty Bricky (IRE)**[185] [312] 11-11-1 114 TonyKelly(5) 114
(David Thompson) *hld up off pce: pushed along 8th: hdwy 4 out: 5th between last 2: kpt on to take n.d 4th nr fin* **16/1**

1/P- **5** *nk* **Pensnett Bay**[196] [113] 8-11-7 115 (p) MarkGrant 115
(Jo Hughes) *led: hit 3rd: drvn 10th: hung rt appr 3 out: hdd 2 out: one pce* **11/2**

123/ **6** *15* **Dancing Art (IRE)**[379] [2161] 7-11-4 112 JamesReveley 107+
(Keith Reveley) *hld up in tch: modest 5th and effrt appr 4 out: rdn appr 2 out: wknd between last 2: eased clsng stages* **9/4**[1]

4/0- **P** **Stow**[24] [2024] 8-11-12 120 (p) NickScholfield
(Michael Blake) *nt fluent in rr: reminders 3erd: bhd fr 8th: t.o 10th: p.u bef 3 out* **18/1**

6m 5.4s (16.90) **Going Correction** +0.75s/f (Soft) **7 Ran SP% 113.1**
Speed ratings (Par 105): **100,99,98,97,97 92,**
toteswingers 1&2 £4.30, 1&3 £6.00, 2&3 £5.70 CSF £22.34 TOTE £4.80: £3.00, £3.20; EX 27.20 Trifecta £110.30 Pool: £2429.63 - 16.51 winning units..
Owner Bryan & Philippa Burrough **Bred** Mrs C Sutton **Trained** Upper Lambourn, Berks

FOCUS
They went a good pace in this fair handicap chase, in which six still held some sort of chance heading to the final fence. The winner is rated in line with his hurdles form.

2513 OXFORD GOLD STANDARD OPEN NATIONAL HUNT FLAT RACE 2m
4:00 (4:00) (Class 6) 4-6-Y-O **£1,559** (£457; £228; £114)

Form RPR

1 **Gunner Fifteen (IRE)**[234] 5-11-0 0 TimmyMurphy 122+
(Fergal O'Brien) *mde all: wnt clr over 1f out: pushed out: v readily* **6/4**[1]

2 *10* **I Need Gold (IRE)**[230] 5-11-0 0 AdrianLane 107+
(Donald McCain) *trckd wnr: drvn and upsides over 3f out: hung lft and wknd over 1f out* **5/1**[3]

14- **3** *5* **Squeeze Me**[18] [2153] 6-10-11 0 JoshuaMoore(3) 101
(Peter Bowen) *mid-div: drvn 7f out: outpcd over 4f out: kpt on to take modest 3rd over 1f out* **15/2**

- **4** *8* **Clancy's Cross (IRE)** 4-11-0 0 NickScholfield 93
(Rebecca Curtis) *trckd ldrs: 3rd over 4f out: wknd over 1f out* **4/1**[2]

6/ **5** *3¼* **Rosa Fleet (IRE)**[217] [5295] 5-10-7 0 LiamTreadwell 83
(Venetia Williams) *chsd ldrs: t.k.h: outpcd over 4f out: kpt on one pce fnl 2f* **12/1**

6 *17* **Greybougg** 4-10-11 0 MarkQuinlan(3) 73
(Nigel Hawke) *t.k.h in mid-div: drvn 6f out: wknd 3f out* **33/1**

7 *1¼* **Pandy Wells** 4-10-7 0 CharliePoste 65
(Graeme McPherson) *mid-div: drvn 7f out: lost pl 7f out* **25/1**

5- **8** *7* **Billy The Bandit (IRE)**[23] [2052] 5-10-9 0 KillianMoore(5) 65
(Jennie Candlish) *t.k.h in rr: lost pl 7f out: sn bhd* **22/1**

4- **9** *11* **Kilfinichen Bay (IRE)**[182] [380] 5-11-0 0 WillKennedy 54
(Violet M Jordan) *chsd ldrs: drvn and lost pl over 4f out* **40/1**

0- **10** *6* **Castanum (IRE)**[2] [2472] 4-11-0 0 RhysFlint 48
(Laura Young) *hld up in rr: hdwy 9f out: drvn 7f out: sn lost pl* **100/1**

0- **11** *hd* **Alfie Moone**[182] [380] 5-11-0 0 LiamHeard 47
(Barry Leavy) *hld up in rr: bhd fnl 6f* **25/1**

12 *31* **Echo Foxtrot** 4-10-7 0 GeraldQuinn(7) 16
(Claire Dyson) *hld up in mid-div: lost pl 6f out: sn bhd: t.o 4f out: eventually completed* **25/1**

40/ **P** **Fine Moment**[309] [3600] 5-10-7 0 DominicElsworth
(Kevin Frost) *in rr: drvn and lost pl 9f out: t.o 7f out: p.u over 4f out* **22/1**

4m 1.4s (15.00) **Going Correction** +0.75s/f (Soft) **13 Ran SP% 122.7**
Speed ratings: **92,87,84,80,78 70,69,66,60,57 57,42,**
toteswingers 1&2 £2.40, 1&3 £4.80, 2&3 £4.90 CSF £8.10 TOTE £2.90: £1.50, £2.50, £1.80; EX 10.50 Trifecta £51.00 Pool: £1417.11 - 20.81 winning units..
Owner Masterson Holdings Limited **Bred** Mrs Eleanor Lane **Trained** Coln St. Dennis, Gloucs

FOCUS
An ordinary bumper overall but a potentially smart winner who looks sure to win more races.
T/Plt: £476.50 to a £1 stake. Pool: £90607.17 - 138.80 winning tickets T/Qpdt: £200.20 to a £1 stake. Pool: £6574.40 - 24.30 winning tickets WG

2224 WETHERBY (L-H)

Saturday, November 16

OFFICIAL GOING: Good to soft (6.7)

Wind: Fresh, half behind Weather: Cloudy

2514 COLIN BALDWIN 82ND BIRTHDAY MARES' NOVICES' HURDLE (9 hdls) 2m 110y

12:25 (12:25) (Class 4) 4-Y-0+ £3,573 (£1,049; £524; £262)

Form RPR

/22- 1 **Run Ructions Run (IRE)**15 2196 4-10-10 0 DougieCostello 109+
(Tim Easterby) cl up: chal 1/2-way: led after 3 out: drifted rt and drvn out fr last 7/4[1]

03- 2 2½ **Born To Benefit (IRE)**15 2190 7-10-10 98 (t) AlainCawley 105
(Fergal O'Brien) hld up: stdy hdwy after 4 out: effrt and chsd wnr between last 2: kpt on run-in 5/1[3]

3 4 **Dewala**29 4-10-10 0 RyanMahon 101+
(Michael Appleby) t.k.h early: chsd ldrs: mstke 1st: effrt and rdn bef 2 out: kpt on same pce between last 2 9/1

F50- 4 6 **Exclusive Dancer**14 2226 4-10-10 102 BarryKeniry 96
(George Moore) led: rdn whn hit and hdd 3 out: outpcd fr next 33/1

5 4½ **Princess Caetani (IRE)**33 4-10-10 0 JasonMaguire 91
(David Dennis) hmpd 1st: hld up: stdy hdwy bef 3 out: wknd next 11/2

6 1¼ **Villa Royale**18 4-10-10 0 DenisO'Regan 93+
(David O'Meara) hmpd 1st: hld up: stdy hdwy after 4 out: shkn up bef 2 out: sn wknd 7/2[2]

/U5- 7 1¼ **Captive Moment**170 552 7-10-3 0 StephenMulqueen(7) 89
(John Norton) hld up: rdn and outpcd 4 out: styd on fr 2 out: nvr able to chal 100/1

6- 8 5 **Voice From Above (IRE)**9 2309 4-10-5 0 JoeColliver(5) 84
(Patrick Holmes) midfield: drvn and outpcd 4 out: n.d after 50/1

/60- 9 2¾ **Innocent Girl (IRE)**28 1974 4-10-10 0 WilsonRenwick 82
(Lucinda Russell) in tch tl rdn and wknd appr 3 out 33/1

0/0- 10 1 **Solstice Dawn**15 2196 5-10-3 0 MrRWinks(7) 82
(Peter Winks) chsd ldrs: outpcd whn blnd 4 out: sn wknd 100/1

11 1¾ **Langham Lily (USA)**129 4-10-7 0 JackQuinlan(3) 79
(Sarah Humphrey) in tch tl rdn and wknd bef 3 out 20/1

P/5- P **Alistorm**154 748 7-10-5 0 SamanthaDrake(5)
(Mark Campion) a bhd: lost tch 1/2-way: t.o whn p.u bef 3 out 200/1

3m 57.6s (1.80) **Going Correction** +0.225s/f (Yiel) 12 Ran SP% **115.7**

Speed ratings (Par 105): **104,102,100,98,96 95,94,92,91,90 89,**

toteswingers 1&2 £4.00, 1&3 £9.00, 2&3 £11.00 CSF £10.19 TOTE £3.20: £1.30, £2.40, £2.10; EX 8.60 Trifecta £49.00 Pool: £618.46 - 9.45 winning units..

Owner Tom Ford **Bred** Minch Bloodstock & AV Bloodstock **Trained** Great Habton, N Yorks

FOCUS

After riding in the opener Alain Cawley said: "I thought the ground was dead" and Dougie Costello said: "It is good - on a quick-ground horse you would call it good to soft." This looked an ordinary novice hurdle for mares. The fourth and eighth help set the level.

2515 RACINGUK.COM/FREETRIAL NOVICES' CHASE (13 fncs) 2m

12:55 (12:55) (Class 4) 4-Y-0+ £4,790 (£1,396; £698)

Form RPR

1/0- 1 **Mwaleshi**21 2069 8-10-9 0 JonathanEngland(5) 131+
(Sue Smith) led to 3rd: chsd ldrs: effrt and wnt 2nd bef 2 out: drvn to ld run-in: styd on wl 11/8[1]

123/ 2 2¼ **Imjoeking (IRE)**209 5425 6-10-7 0 GrahamWatters(7) 130+
(Lucinda Russell) t.k.h early: cl up: led bef 4 out: nrly 4 l clr 2 out: rdn: hung lft and hdd run-in: one pce 11/4[2]

13/- 3 23 **Supreme Asset (IRE)**207 5463 5-11-0 0 JasonMaguire 109
(Donald McCain) cl up: led 3rd to bef 4 out: sn pushed along: wknd appr 2 out 11/4[2]

/22- 4 5 **Phase Shift**21 2084 5-10-7 0 (t) RyanMania 100
(Brian Ellison) hld up in tch: nt fluent 3rd: clsd after next: 4th and drvn along whn blnd 4 out: sn wknd 15/2[3]

1/0- 5 36 **Jimmie Brown (USA)**7 2356 5-10-11 107 JohnKington(3) 76
(Andrew Crook) hld up in tch: pushed along fr 5th: nt fluent and struggling 5 out: lost tch bef next: t.o 40/1

3m 43.3s (-12.50) **Going Correction** -0.525s/f (Firm) 5 Ran SP% **109.6**

Speed ratings (Par 105): **110,108,97,94,76**

toteswingers 1&2 £1.50, 1&3 £7.60, 2&3 £4.30 CSF £5.67 TOTE £2.40: £1.70, £1.50; EX 7.40 Trifecta £14.70 Pool: £1236.96 - 62.95 winning units..

Owner Mrs S Smith **Bred** Helshaw Grange Stud Ltd **Trained** High Eldwick, W Yorks

FOCUS

This novice chase was run at a good gallop and the first two pulled well clear. The form is rated around the hurdles marks of the first two.

2516 BRANSFIELDS CIU CHARITY RACEDAY H'CAP HURDLE (13 hdls) 3m 1f

1:30 (1:30) (Class 4) (0-120,120) 4-Y-0+ £3,249 (£954; £477; £238)

Form RPR

/11- 1 **Flicka Williams (IRE)**41 1797 6-11-12 120 DougieCostello 127+
(Tony Coyle) t.k.h: hld up: smooth hdwy bef 3 out: effrt and rdn next: led appr last: drvn out run-in 3/1[2]

441- 2 1½ **Lookout Mountain (IRE)**13 2253 5-11-5 118 (vt) MauriceLinehan(5) 125+
(Jonjo O'Neill) hld up: smooth hdwy to chse ldr 3 out: effrt whn hit next: ev ch whn hit last: kpt on run-in 9/4[1]

313- 3 nk **Wayward Glance**11 1708 5-11-8 116 (p) WilsonRenwick 120
(Keith Dalgleish) led: rdn and qcknd bef 3 out: hdd appr last: kpt on same pce run-in 12/1

3/0- 4 13 **Joseph Mercer (IRE)**196 121 6-11-5 113 BrianHarding 106
(Tina Jackson) hld up on ins: rdn after 4 out: sn outpcd: rallied whn flattened 2 out: kpt on: nvr able to chal 28/1

144/ 5 ¾ **Forty Crown (IRE)**209 5423 7-10-11 112 JohnDawson(7) 104
(John Wade) in tch: effrt and drvn bef 3 out: wknd fr next 7/1[3]

PF5- 6 1¾ **Danceintothelight**31 1926 6-10-3 104 MissBeckySmith(7) 94
(Micky Hammond) t.k.h: hld up: rdn bef 3 out: no imp bef next 25/1

F/5- 7 3 **Kent Street (IRE)**17 2158 8-10-9 108 JonathanEngland(5) 95
(Sue Smith) prom: rdn and chsd wnr briefly whn j.rt 3 out: outpcd whn j.rt next: wknd 10/1

61U/ 8 31 **Outlaw Tom (IRE)**568 5624 9-10-9 110 GrantCockburn(7) 69
(Lucinda Russell) chsd ldr to 4th: drvn and lost pl 8th: struggling fr 4 out 16/1

265- 9 10 **Wolf Shield (IRE)**23 2050 6-11-9 117 BarryKeniry 67
(George Moore) chsd ldrs: wnt 2nd 4th tl rdn and wknd bef 3 out 9/1

13P/ F **Madam Lilibet (IRE)**26 4630 4-10-4 105 JosephPalmowski(7)
(Sharon Watt) hld up in midfield: drvn and outpcd after 7th: rallied 9th: struggling after 4 out: seventh and wkng whn fell next 11/1

6m 18.8s (2.30) **Going Correction** +0.225s/f (Yiel)

WFA 4 from 5yo+ 9lb 10 Ran SP% **116.6**

Speed ratings (Par 105): **105,104,104,100,100 99,98,88,85,**

toteswingers 1&2 £1.50, 1&3 £7.60, 2&3 £4.30 CSF £10.47 CT £69.22 TOTE £3.70: £1.50, £1.80, £2.30; EX 6.90 Trifecta £34.90 Pool: £929.06 - 19.96 winning units..

Owner Twenty Four Seven Recruitment **Bred** Tony Hickey **Trained** Norton, N Yorks

FOCUS

A handicap hurdle with little depth but it produced a thrilling finish. Another step up from the winner.

2517 BET TOTESCOOP6 AT TOTEPOOL.COM H'CAP CHASE (18 fncs) 3m 1f

2:05 (2:08) (Class 3) (0-130,130) 4-Y-0+ £8,122 (£2,385; £1,192; £596)

Form RPR

F/3- 1 **No Planning**31 1923 6-11-9 127 RyanMania 134+
(Sue Smith) chsd ldrs: led 10th: mde rest: mstke and rdn 3 out: hld on wl fr next 15/8[1]

111/ 2 1¼ **Denali Highway (IRE)**241 4877 6-11-10 128 AndrewThornton 133
(Caroline Bailey) in tch: drvn and hdwy to chse wnr 4 out: edgd lft and kpt on fr last 7/2[3]

652- 3 9 **Scotswell**14 2220 7-11-5 123 LucyAlexander 121
(Harriet Graham) led: hit 8th: hdd 10th: drvn and outpcd bef 4 out: rallied 2 out: no ch w first two 9/2

3/4- 4 ½ **Royal Sam (IRE)**14 2224 8-11-0 118 DenisO'Regan 116
(Martin Todhunter) nt fluent on occasions: chsd ldrs: lost pl 2nd: pushed along fr 1/2-way: shortlived effrt whn hit 4 out: sn no imp 14/1

131/ 5 12 **Grouse Lodge (IRE)**212 5365 7-11-12 130 (p) JasonMaguire 119
(Donald McCain) pressed ldr: rdn bef 4 out: wknd fr next 5/2[2]

6m 0.6s (-8.80) **Going Correction** -0.525s/f (Firm) 5 Ran SP% **110.4**

Speed ratings (Par 107): **93,92,89,89,85**

CSF £8.90 TOTE £2.90: £1.50, £1.90; EX 11.80 Trifecta £23.20 Pool: £1780.91 - 57.44 winning units..

Owner Mrs Jacqueline Conroy **Bred** Mrs S Johnson **Trained** High Eldwick, W Yorks

FOCUS

A competitive handicap chase run at an even tempo, until the pace quickened after the fifth-last. Fair form with a small step up from the winner.

2518 ROB SELDON RETIREMENT H'CAP CHASE (16 fncs) 2m 4f 110y

2:40 (2:42) (Class 4) (0-105,105) 4-Y-0+ £3,898 (£1,144; £572; £286)

Form RPR

4/5- 1 **Badger Foot (IRE)**43 1756 8-10-12 98 (t) GrahamWatters(7) 113+
(Lucinda Russell) prom: smooth hdwy to chse ldr 5 out: ev ch fr next: led 2 out: rdn and hld on wl fr last 9/2[3]

/PU- 2 ¾ **Goodtoknow**9 2315 5-11-9 105 JakeGreenall(3) 117
(Richard Lee) in tch: rdn and effrt bef 4 out: rallied bef 2 out: chsd wnr last: kpt on: hld nr fin 8/1

311- 3 9 **Midnight Charmer**22 2067 7-10-5 89 JamesBanks(5) 94
(Emma Baker) hld up in tch: rdn and outpcd bef 4 out: rallied 2 out: kpt on fr last: no ch w first two 3/1[1]

04U- 4 3¼ **Spitfire Ace (IRE)**14 2219 5-10-12 91 JasonMaguire 94
(Donald McCain) led: jnd bef 4 out: nt fluent and hdd 2 out: 3rd and hld whn mstke last 6/1

/34- 5 4½ **Twice Lucky**8 2335 9-9-12 82 JonathanEngland(5) 79
(Sue Smith) hld up: pushed along 10th: sn outpcd: no imp fr 4 out 7/1

0P6- 6 20 **Vardas Supreme (IRE)**8 2338 10-10-1 85 (bt) SamanthaDrake(5) 69
(Richard Drake) hld up in tch: hdwy 4th: chsd ldr 8th to 5 out: rdn and outpcd whn hit next: sn btn 50/1

/61- F **Tresor De L'Isle (FR)**14 2219 6-11-3 96 (p) BrianHarding
(James Ewart) trckd ldr: hit 5th: lost 2nd 8th: drvn 10th: struggling fr 5 out: last and no ch whn fell 4 out 7/2[2]

/F5- P **Acordingtoscript (IRE)**14 2219 7-10-9 88 DenisO'Regan
(Martin Todhunter) nt fluent in rr: blnd and lost tch 5th: p.u after 7th 12/1

5m 2.5s (-5.30) **Going Correction** -0.525s/f (Firm) 8 Ran SP% **113.0**

Speed ratings (Par 105): **89,88,85,84,82 74, ,**

toteswingers 1&2 £12.40, 1&3 £5.60, 2&3 £4.90 CSF £38.19 CT £123.00 TOTE £6.40: £2.40, £2.20, £1.20; EX 45.90 Trifecta £224.60 Pool: £639.93 - 2.13 winning units..

Owner Peter J S Russell **Bred** J Moran **Trained** Arlary, Perth & Kinross

FOCUS

Only a modest handicap chase. The winner may still be capable of better than this.

2519 YOUR FAVOURITE POOL BETS AT TOTEPOOL.COM H'CAP HURDLE (9 hdls) 2m 110y

3:15 (3:15) (Class 3) (0-130,129) 4-Y-0+ £6,498 (£1,908; £954; £477)

Form RPR

136/ 1 **Zaplamation (IRE)**29 2164 8-10-4 114 DeanPratt(7) 120+
(John Quinn) plld hrd in midfield: effrt bef 2 out: chsd ldr between last 2: styd on wl run-in: led nr fin 14/1

0/6- 2 shd **Zafranagar (IRE)**15 2198 8-9-12 106 RobertMcCarth(5) 112+
(Ian Williams) t.k.h: hld up: smooth hdwy on outside to ld bef 3 out: rdn and nrly 3 l clr last: kpt on: hdd nr fin 11/2[1]

303- 3 3¼ **Lifetime (IRE)**15 2198 5-9-10 106 CraigGallagher(7) 110+
(Brian Ellison) hld up: hdwy and in tch whn nt fluent 3 out: sn rdn: kpt on fr last: nt rch first two 15/2[3]

220/ 4 ½ **Doynosaur**399 1839 6-10-10 113 HenryBrooke 115
(K R Burke) hld up: effrt and hdwy bef 3 out: chsd ldr briefly after next: one pce fr last 25/1

041- 5 1 **Hartside (GER)**15 2198 4-10-4 114 MrRWinks(7) 116
(Peter Winks) hld up in tch: rdn outpcd after 3 out: edgd lft: kpt on fr last: no imp 8/1

3/2- 6 ½ **Pertuis (IRE)**15 2198 7-9-10 104 JoeColliver(5) 105
(Micky Hammond) hld up: rdn bef 3 out: kpt on fr next: nvr able to chal 8/1

/34- 7 shd **The Bull Hayes (IRE)**22 2064 7-10-11 114 (p) RyanMahon 115
(Michael Appleby) led to bef 3 out: rdn and outpcd after next 22/1

/44- 8 ½ **Mojolika**15 2198 5-11-1 118 BrianHarding 118
(Tim Easterby) chsd ldrs: drvn along bef 3 out: rallied: no ex fr next 8/1

403- 9 1½ **Dumbarton (IRE)**31 1922 5-11-10 127 DenisO'Regan 126
(James Moffatt) hld up: rdn bef 3 out: nvr able to chal 17/2

1/6- 10 2½ **Lightening Rod**22 2064 8-11-5 125 JakeGreenall(3) 122
(Michael Easterby) taken early to post: midfield: smooth hdwy to chal bef 3 out: rdn and wknd next 20/1

50P/ 11 9 **Golden Future**83 2317 10-10-0 103 oh1 WilsonRenwick 91
(Peter Niven) t.k.h: chsd ldr: chal 4th: rdn and wknd fr 3 out 40/1

/1U- **12** *41* **Fair Trade**[14] 2227 6-11-5 **129** ... TomBellamy(7) 81
(Alan King) *t.k.h: in tch tl rdn and wknd bef 3 out: t.o* **7/1**[2]

412/ **13** *1 ¾* **Mitchell's Way**[244] 4817 6-11-6 **123** ... JasonMaguire 73
(Alan Swinbank) *nt fluent on occasions: t.k.h: prom: lost pl bef 3 out: sn struggling: t.o* **9/1**

3m 56.2s (0.40) **Going Correction** +0.225s/f (Yiel)
WFA 4 from 5yo+ 7lb **13** Ran SP% **115.6**
Speed ratings (Par 107): **108,107,106,106,105 105,105,105,104,103 99,79,78**
toteswingers 1&2 £28.90, 1&3 £39.40, 2&3 £14.20 CSF £83.34 CT £630.31 TOTE £17.40: £4.50, £2.60, £2.70; EX 103.80 Trifecta £354.10 Part won. Pool: £472.26 - 0.10 winning units..
Owner Andrew Turton & David Barker **Bred** Mesnil Investments Ltd And Deerpark Stud **Trained** Settrington, N Yorks
■ Stewards' Enquiry : Robert McCarth three-day ban: used whip without giving gelding time to respond (Dec 1-3)

FOCUS
A competitive handicap and straightforward form which will probably be reliable.

2520 NEW RACING UK ANYWHERE AVAILABLE NOW NOVICES' HURDLE (11 hdls) 2m 4f
3:50 (3:50) (Class 4) 4-Y-0+ **£3,422** (£997; £499)

Form RPR

3- **1** **Blakemount (IRE)**[23] 2030 5-10-12 0 ... RyanMania 123+
(Sue Smith) *mde all: drew clr fr 3 out: easily* **4/7**[1]

3- **2** *7* **Sir Mangan (IRE)**[20] 2104 5-10-12 0 ... JasonMaguire 109+
(Donald McCain) *cl up: effrt and ev ch bef 3 out: one pce whn hit next* **5/2**[2]

0- **3** *4* **Narcissist (IRE)**[14] 2225 4-10-5 0 ... MrHAABannister(7) 104
(Michael Easterby) *hld up: hdwy to chse clr ldng pair 3 out: no imp whn hit last* **33/1**

4 *13* **Rozener (IRE)** 7-10-12 0 ... RichieMcGrath 91
(Henry Hogarth) *hld up: outpcd 4 out: sme late hdwy: nvr rchd ldrs* **33/1**

06- **5** *½* **Light The City (IRE)**[6] 2393 6-10-9 0 ... JakeGreenall(3) 92
(Ruth Carr) *t.k.h: nt fluent on occasions: chsd ldrs tl wknd fr 3 out* **25/1**

/0U- **6** *4* **Major Martin (IRE)**[9] 2316 4-10-9 0 ... PeterCarberry(3) 89
(Charlie Brooks) *nt fluent on occasions: in tch tl rdn and wknd bef 3 out* **28/1**

0/6- **7** *1 ¾* **Jokers And Rogues (IRE)**[31] 1924 5-10-5 0 ... JohnDawson(7) 88
(John Wade) *mstkes: hld up in tch: struggling bef 3 out: sn btn* **9/1**

5/4- **8** *49* **King Kurt (IRE)**[35] 1540 5-10-12 0 ... DougieCostello 42
(Kevin Ryan) *nt fluent on occasions: t.k.h: sn cl up: drvn after 4 out: sn lost tch: t.o* **8/1**[3]

4m 57.0s (-2.50) **Going Correction** +0.225s/f (Yiel)
WFA 4 from 5yo+ 8lb **8** Ran SP% **126.5**
Speed ratings (Par 105): **114,111,109,104,104 102,101,82**
toteswingers 1&2 £1.10, 1&3 £9.20, 2&3 £3.60 CSF £2.70 TOTE £1.80: £1.10, £1.20, £4.20; EX 3.80 Trifecta £44.20 Pool: £1944.33 - 32.95 winning units..
Owner Mrs Jacqueline Conroy **Bred** T Horgan **Trained** High Eldwick, W Yorks

FOCUS
A weak novice hurdle dominated by the two market leaders. The easy winner was the form pick on his recent run but this looks a step up.
T/Plt: £13.40. Pool: £72,933.52 - 3966.62 winning units. T/Qpdt: £9.20. Pool: £5046.26 - 402.40 winning units. RY

2521 - 2528a (Foreign Racing) - See Raceform Interactive

2500 CHELTENHAM (L-H)
Sunday, November 17

OFFICIAL GOING: Good (good to soft in places; 7.6)
Wind: Virtually nil Weather: Misty and overcast

2529 MALLARD PAWNBROKERS AND FAMILY JEWELLERS CONDITIONAL JOCKEYS' H'CAP HURDLE (10 hdls) 2m 5f
1:00 (1:01) (Class 3) (0-125,125) 4-Y-0+
£7,507 (£2,217; £1,108; £554; £277; £139)

Form RPR

0/0- **1** **Home Run (GER)**[159] 718 5-11-1 **120** ... (b) KieronEdgar(6) 128+
(David Pipe) *chsd ldrs: rdn to ld last: wandered u.p run-in but kpt on wl* **40/1**

F1/ **2** *3* **Western Warhorse (IRE)**[219] 5264 5-11-12 **125** ... MauriceLinehan 130
(David Pipe) *led narrowly: rdn whn hdd last: kpt on but a hld run-in* **14/1**

223/ **3** *1 ¼* **Sausalito Sunrise (IRE)**[274] 4240 5-11-1 **117** ... MichealNolan(3) 121
(Philip Hobbs) *midfield: rdn and in tch 2 out: wnt 3rd jst after last: styd on wl* **9/2**[2]

P22/ **4** *5* **Lieutenant Miller**[36] 2971 7-11-4 **120** ... JeremiahMcGrath(3) 120
(Nicky Henderson) *trckd ldrs: briefly pushed along bef 3 out: rdn after 2 out: 3 l down in 3rd last: grad wknd* **7/2**[1]

33/ **5** *nk* **Pay The King (IRE)**[240] 4901 6-11-0 **116** ... HarryDerham(3) 116
(Paul Nicholls) *hld up in rr towards outer: stdy hdwy after 4 out: rdn to chse ldrs appr last: no further imp run-in* **7/1**

P/0- **6** *hd* **Kingsmere**[29] 1969 8-11-2 **118** ... JakeGreenall(3) 118
(Henry Daly) *hld up in midfield on inner: hdwy and in tch whn stmbld 2 out: sn rdn: one pce run-in* **25/1**

2/3- **7** *8* **Amok (IRE)**[26] 2013 5-10-12 **114** ... (t) MichaelByrne(3) 106
(Tim Vaughan) *midfield: hdwy to chse ldr on outside 3 out: sn rdn: wknd appr last* **33/1**

1/ **8** *1 ½* **Undertheboardwalk (IRE)**[16] 2208 7-11-4 **125** ... SAShortall(8) 115
(A J Martin, Ire) *midfield: lost pl and dropped towards rr 4 out: plugged on after 2 out: nvr threatened* **16/1**

143/ **9** *½* **Timesishard (IRE)**[205] 5537 6-11-9 **125** ... KillianMoore(3) 115
(Graeme McPherson) *prom: rdn 3 out: wknd appr last* **33/1**

/31- **10** *2 ¼* **Big Casino**[18] 2158 7-11-4 **125** ... RyanHatch(8) 113
(Nigel Twiston-Davies) *hld up: rdn bef 6th: nvr threatened* **11/2**[3]

F/4- **11** *5* **King Helissio (IRE)**[24] 2050 5-11-2 **115** ... JamesBest 98
(Neil Mulholland) *hld up: nvr threatened* **20/1**

/00- **12** *1 ½* **The Chazer (IRE)**[22] 2086 8-11-10 **123** ... JackQuinlan 105
(Richard Lee) *midfield: rdn after 4 out: sn btn* **100/1**

120- **13** *1 ¼* **Della Sun (FR)**[30] 1960 7-11-5 **123** ... JoshWall(5) 104
(Arthur Whitehead) *a towards rr* **33/1**

/06- **14** *3* **Kingcora (FR)**[8] 2366 5-10-11 **113** ... CallumWhillans(3) 91
(Venetia Williams) *trckd ldrs: nt fluent 4th: rdn after 4 out: wknd after 2 out* **16/1**

560- **15** *1* **Phare Isle (IRE)**[10] 2314 8-11-4 **117** ... (tp) BenPoste 94
(Ben Case) *hld up: nvr threatened* **40/1**

0/4- **16** *3* **Copper Birch (IRE)**[19] 2147 5-11-6 **122** ... AdamWedge(3) 97
(Evan Williams) *midfield: rdn after 4 out: sn struggling: bhd whn hit 2 out* **20/1**

536/ **17** *11* **Becausewecan (USA)**[13] 4145 7-10-2 **107** ... CraigGallagher(6) 72
(Brian Ellison) *sn w ldr: rdn bef 3 out: sn wknd* **20/1**

403- **18** *10* **Court In Session (IRE)**[11] 2292 8-10-3 **110** ... (t) OllieGarner(8) 66
(Martin Keighley) *slowly away: hld up: hdwy on outer to trck ldrs bef 3rd: lost pl 4 out: wknd 3 out* **33/1**

/1L- **R** **Toughness Danon**[19] 1634 7-10-13 **112** ... KielanWoods
(Ian Williams) *Refused to r* **33/1**

5m 18.4s (5.00) **Going Correction** +0.20s/f (Yiel) **19** Ran SP% **125.4**
Speed ratings (Par 107): **98,96,96,94,94 94,91,90,90,89 87,87,86,85,85 84,79,76,**
toteswingers 1&2 £46.60, 1&3 £18.50, 2&3 £14.40 CSF £467.19 CT £3030.20 TOTE £46.20: £6.60, £2.70, £1.50, £1.70; EX 260.60 TRIFECTA Not won..
Owner W Frewen **Bred** Gestut Ammerland **Trained** Nicholashayne, Devon

FOCUS
All races on Old Course and hurdle rail moved out 2yds from Saturday, adding 12yds to a circuit. This handicap for conditional riders usually brings the curtain down on the opening day. In its new slot this year, it was very competitive event and they went a sound gallop. Sound form, the winner rated to a similar level to last year.

2530 SKY BET SUPREME TRIAL NOVICES' HURDLE (REGISTERED AS THE SHARP NOVICES' HURDLE) (GRADE 2) (8 hdls) 2m 110y
1:35 (1:36) (Class 1) 4-Y-0+ **£17,085** (£6,411; £3,210; £1,599)

Form RPR

1/1- **1** **The Liquidator**[18] 2156 5-11-4 0 ... TomScudamore 143+
(David Pipe) *mde all: qcknd pce 4th: clr 3 out: unchal* **6/4**[2]

111- **2** *15* **Sea Lord (IRE)**[28] 1987 6-11-7 150 ... DenisO'Regan 132
(John Ferguson) *disp 2nd to 3rd: shkn up as pce qcknd fr 4th: rdn 4 out and outpcd: rallied and styng on to press for 2nd whn blnd 3 out: styd on appr last and kpt on wl run-in to take 2nd cl home: no ch w wnr* **1/1**[1]

0/1- **3** *½* **Minellaforleisure (IRE)**[21] 2109 5-11-4 0 ... PaddyBrennan 126
(Alex Hales) *racd wd thrght in 4th tl hdwy to chse wnr 3 out but nvr any ch: rdn 2 out: no ex run-in and lost 2nd cl home* **28/1**

0/1- **4** *18* **Lac Fontana (FR)**[30] 1958 4-11-7 130 ... DarylJacob 117
(Paul Nicholls) *disp 2nd tl chsd wnr fr 4th to 3 out: sn rdn and btn* **7/1**[3]

4m 1.52s (-0.48) **Going Correction** +0.20s/f (Yiel) **4** Ran SP% **105.9**
Speed ratings (Par 115): **109,101,101,93**
CSF £3.36 TOTE £2.30; EX 3.00 Trifecta £20.70 Pool: £4,013.93 - 144.97 winning units..
Owner R S Brookhouse **Bred** Ms E L White **Trained** Nicholashayne, Devon

FOCUS
A new title for this race but an event that has had a limited impact on the Supreme Novices' Hurdle at the festival. Five winners of this have run in the big one in the past decade, with fourths from Cue Card and Steps To Freedom the best they could achieve, while a couple of runners-up in this went on to finish third in March. The field rather cut up and with a couple of runners seemingly well below par, it's debatable what exactly The Liquidator achieved, for all that he ran out an impressive winner.

2531 RACING POST ARKLE TROPHY TRIAL NOVICES' CHASE (REGISTERED AS THE NOVEMBER NOVICES' CHASE) (GRADE 2) (13 fncs) 2m
2:10 (2:10) (Class 1) 4-Y-0+ **£18,224** (£6,838; £3,424; £1,705; £857)

Form RPR

0/1- **1** **Dodging Bullets**[28] 1986 5-11-2 0 ... DarylJacob 146+
(Paul Nicholls) *t.k.h early: trckd ldrs in 3rd: hdwy 3 out: chal 2 out: sn led: rdn and styd on wl run-in* **2/1**[2]

F/1- **2** *5* **Raya Star (IRE)**[16] 2192 7-11-2 0 ... RobertThornton 140
(Alan King) *chsd ldr: blnd 4th: led 4 out: rdn after 3 out: hrd pressed whn hit next: outpcd run-in but kpt on wl for 2nd* **15/8**[1]

312/ **3** *3 ¼* **Ted Veale (IRE)**[85] 1180 6-11-2 146 ... BarryGeraghty 136+
(A J Martin, Ire) *trckd ldrs in 4th: outpcd 4 out and shkn up: hdwy next: styd on same pce fr 2 out to hold 3rd run-in but no imp on ldng duo* **2/1**[2]

2F4- **4** *½* **The Cockney Mackem (IRE)**[2] 2489 7-11-2 132(t) SamTwiston-Davies 136
(Nigel Twiston-Davies) *towards rr but in tch: hdwy to cl on ldrs 3 out: styd on same pce fr 2 out* **28/1**

120- **5** *16* **My Brother Sylvest**[15] 2212 7-11-8 139 ... (b) TomScudamore 130
(David Pipe) *led: hdd 4 out: wknd bef 2 out* **20/1**[3]

4m 0.81s (2.81) **Going Correction** +0.20s/f (Yiel) **5** Ran SP% **109.7**
Speed ratings (Par 115): **100,97,95,95,87**
CSF £6.36 TOTE £2.90: £1.70, £1.30; EX 6.20 Trifecta £10.10 Pool: £3,616.11 - 266.10 winning units..
Owner Martin Broughton & Friends **Bred** L Dettori **Trained** Ditcheat, Somerset

FOCUS
Although this well established Arkle trial looked to lack a star name this year, the form does look strong. However the winner was a stone+ shy of a typical Arkle winner. The second was a stone off his best hurdles mark.

2532 SHLOER CHASE (LISTED RACE) (13 fncs) 2m
2:40 (2:43) (Class 1) 5-Y-0+
£39,865 (£14,959; £7,490; £3,731; £1,876; £938)

Form RPR

520/ **1** **Kid Cassidy (IRE)**[227] 5139 7-11-0 150 ... APMcCoy 162+
(Nicky Henderson) *hld up in rr and patiently rdn: stdy hdwy to take 3rd after 3 out: trckd ldr sn after last: qcknd run-in to ld fnl 50yds: comf* **4/1**[2]

1/1- **2** *3 ¼* **Sire De Grugy (FR)**[22] 2081 7-11-10 169 ... JamieMoore 170
(Gary Moore) *trckd ldrs: stmbld bdly 4th: nt fluent 6th: wnt 2nd 8th: led 2 out: rdn after last: hdd and outpcd fnl 50yds* **5/6**[1]

3/U- **3** *3* **Special Tiara**[20] 2141 6-11-5 157 ... NoelFehily 161
(Henry De Bromhead, Ire) *j.big 1st: led: hdd 2 out: outpcd by ldng duo run-in but kpt on for 3rd* **7/1**[3]

4/5- **4** *7* **Oiseau De Nuit (FR)**[22] 2071 11-11-6 157 ... (t) BrendanPowell 155
(Colin Tizzard) *chsd ldr to 7th: wknd after 3 out* **12/1**

05F/ **5** *10* **Tataniano (FR)**[204] 5575 9-11-0 155 ... DarylJacob 140
(Richard Rowe) *trckd ldrs: dropped to rr 7th: wknd bef 3 out* **25/1**

RR/- **6** *13* **Mad Moose (IRE)**[148] 5159 9-11-0 143 ... (v[1]) SamTwiston-Davies 133+
(Nigel Twiston-Davies) *rel to r and lost all ch w v slow s: blnd 3rd and 3 out: styd on past btn horse after 2 out* **25/1**

F42/ **7** *9* **His Excellency (IRE)**[211] 5403 5-11-3 148 ... (b) TomScudamore 123
(David Pipe) *j. slowly 5th: a in rr* **11/1**

3m 56.44s (-1.56) **Going Correction** +0.20s/f (Yiel) **7** Ran SP% **110.8**
Speed ratings: **111,109,107,104,99 92,88**
toteswingers 1&2 £1.70, 1&3 £1.80, 2&3 £2.20 CSF £7.66 TOTE £4.10: £2.10, £1.20; EX 8.50 Trifecta £34.50 Pool: £3,404.16 - 73.87 winning units..
Owner John P McManus **Bred** Greenville House Stud And M Morgan **Trained** Upper Lambourn, Berks

FOCUS
There was no hanging about here and the race saw changing fortunes after the final fence. A step up from the winner in a good time compared with the earlier novice, and a solid renewal.

2533 STANJAMES.COM GREATWOOD HURDLE (H'CAP) (GRADE 3) (8 hdls) 2m 110y

3:15 (3:17) (Class 1) 4-Y-O+

£56,950 (£21,370; £10,700; £5,330; £2,680; £1,340)

Form				RPR
1		**Dell' Arca (IRE)**[157] 4-10-5 **128** TomScudamore	134+
		(David Pipe) *towards rr: hdwy 3 out: chsd ldrs after 2 out: big jump to take slt ld last: sn narrowly hdd: styd upsides and led again fnl 150yds: rdn out* **12/1**
2/1-	**2**	½	**Sametegal (FR)**[29] 1970 4-11-7 **144** DarylJacob	149+
		(Paul Nicholls) *chsd ldrs: wnt 2nd 2 out: chal last: slt ld sn after: hdd fnl 150yds: styd chalng: no ex clsng stages* **8/1**[2]
0/	**3**	1¼	**Rawnaq (IRE)**[14] 1180 6-10-8 **138** KMSmith(7)	143+
		(Matthew J Smith, Ire) *chsd ldr 2nd: chalng whn lft in ld 4th: rdn 2 out: narrowly hdd last: chal between horses run-in: n.m.r: swtchd lft and outpcd fnl 75yds* **20/1**
4/3-	**4**	4½	**Flaxen Flare (IRE)**[16] 2206 4-11-4 **141** (b) JasonMaguire	141
		(Gordon Elliott, Ire) *chsd ldrs: rdn appr last: outpcd by ldng trio run-in* **8/1**[2]
5/2-	**5**	¾	**Tanerko Emery (FR)**[16] 2192 7-11-10 **147** (t) ConorO'Farrell	148+
		(David Pipe) *in tch whn hmpd 4th: hdwy 2 out: styd on to cl on 4th run-in but no imp on ldrs* **22/1**
5/1-	**6**	nk	**Pine Creek**[15] 2213 5-11-0 **137** DenisO'Regan	139+
		(John Ferguson) *chsd ldrs: lft 2nd 4th: hit 4 out and 3 out: outpcd u.p appr last* **6/1**[1]
1/0-	**7**	nse	**Court Minstrel (IRE)**[15] 2213 6-11-12 **149** PaulMoloney	148
		(Evan Williams) *in rr: hdwy 2 out: styd on run-in: nt rch ldrs* **14/1**
0/0-	**8**	hd	**Get Me Out Of Here (IRE)**[15] 2213 9-11-7 **149** (t) MauriceLinehan(5)	150
		(Jonjo O'Neill) *chsd ldrs: hmpd 4th: styd wl there: rdn and swtchd lft appr last: styd on same pce run-in* **33/1**
116/	**9**	2¼	**Calculated Risk**[34] 5573 4-10-6 **129** RichardJohnson	127
		(John Quinn) *in rr whn hmpd 4th: hdwy after 2 out: styd on run-in: nt rch ldrs* **25/1**
F/3-	**10**	nk	**Ifandbutwhynot (IRE)**[22] 2069 7-10-10 **133** TimmyMurphy	131
		(David O'Meara) *hmpd in rr 4th: styd on fr 2 out* **9/1**[3]
00/-	**11**	4	**Redera (IRE)**[71] 1180 7-10-3 **133** SAShortall(7)	126
		(A J Martin, Ire) *led tl after 1st: chsd ldrs: rdn 2 out: wknd bef last* **25/1**
1/6-	**12**	3¼	**L'Unique (FR)**[15] 2226 4-11-3 **140** RobertThornton	131
		(Alan King) *in tch: rdn and sme hdwy appr 2 out: nvr rchd ldrs* **20/1**
520/	**13**	1¾	**Kalann (IRE)**[23] 4836 6-11-0 **137** PaddyBrennan	125
		(Sabrina J Harty, Ire) *in rr: hdwy after 2 out: kpt on run-in* **22/1**
3/	**14**	5	**Enchanted Forest (IRE)**[15] 2232 5-10-2 **125** WayneHutchinson	109
		(Michael Hourigan, Ire) *towards rr most of way* **50/1**
1U0/	**15**	¾	**Kashmir Peak (IRE)**[22] 4767 4-10-12 **135** DougieCostello	120
		(John Quinn) *chsd ldrs tl after 3 out* **12/1**
U00/	**16**	7	**Cash And Go (IRE)**[249] 4736 6-11-4 **141** BarryGeraghty	118
		(Nicky Henderson) *in tch tl wknd 3 out* **6/1**[1]
413-	**F**		**Ahyaknowyerself (IRE)**[8] 2372 7-11-10 **147** (b) SamTwiston-Davies
		(Dr Richard Newland) *led: jnd whn fell 4th* **33/1**
00B/	**B**		**Thomas Edison (IRE)**[15] 2233 6-11-1 **138** (t) APMcCoy
		(A J Martin, Ire) *in rr tl hmpd and b.d 4th* **10/1**

3m 59.7s (-2.30) **Going Correction** +0.20s/f (Yiel)
WFA 4 from 5yo+ 7lb **18** Ran SP% **125.7**
Speed ratings (Par 113): **113,112,112,110,109 109,109,109,108,108 106,104,104,101,101 98,,**
toteswingers 1&2 £19.90, 1&3 £60.90, 2&3 £17.60 CSF £93.01 CT £1942.10 TOTE £12.10: £3.50, £2.70, £5.70, £2.70; EX 163.60 Trifecta £5745.70 Pool: £9,240.92 - 1.20 winning units..
Owner Prof Caroline Tisdall **Bred** Bernhard & Brigitta Matusche **Trained** Nicholashayne, Devon
■ Stewards' Enquiry : Tom Scudamore two-day ban: careless riding (Dec 1-2)
FOCUS
Backed by the Racing Post last year, this event has reverted to its former title. It has held Grade 3 status since 2004 and this was another classy and competitive edition. It's a race that has had quite a bearing on the Champion Hurdle in the past decade or so with Rooster Booster winning both races in 2002-3, Khyber Kim finishing runner-up in the Champion after winning this and Osana finishing second in both races, while Sizing Europe and Detroit City were both beaten favourite in March. The first two are on the upgrade with the next half dozen close to their marks.

2534 FAIRLAWNE - FESTIVAL JOCKEY CLUB FINE DINING BUMPER (STANDARD OPEN NH FLAT RACE) (LISTED RACE) 2m 110y

3:50 (3:51) (Class 1) 4-6-Y-O

£11,390 (£4,274; £2,140; £1,066; £536; £268)

Form				RPR
11/	**1**		**Red Sherlock**[274] 4246 4-11-0 0 TimmyMurphy	124+
		(David Pipe) *trckd ldng pair: kpt frmly to ins fr 10f out. racd isolated on occasions: led narrowly 1/2-way: rdn 2f out: drvn ent fnl f: styd on wl* **7/2**[1]
1/1-	**2**	1½	**Carningli (IRE)**[29] 1974 4-11-0 0 BarryGeraghty	123
		(Rebecca Curtis) *led narrowly: hdd 1/2-way but remained pressing ldr: rdn over 2f out: kpt on but a hld ins fnl f* **7/2**[1]
1-	**3**	hd	**Our Kaempfer (IRE)**[38] 1836 4-10-11 0 KielanWoods(3)	123
		(Charlie Longsdon) *midfield: hdwy to chse ldng pair over 2f out: sn rdn: kpt on wl* **25/1**
1-	**4**	4	**Champagne At Tara**[37] 1861 4-11-0 0 APMcCoy	119
		(Jonjo O'Neill) *hld up: stdy hdwy 4f out: rdn to chse ldrs 2f out: one pce fnl f* **9/2**[2]
1/2-	**5**	3¾	**Southfield Vic (IRE)**[47] 1712 4-11-0 0 DarylJacob	116
		(Paul Nicholls) *w ldr: rdn 3f out: sn outpcd by ldrs* **10/1**
1-	**6**	nse	**Cogry**[24] 2053 4-11-0 0 SamTwiston-Davies	116
		(Nigel Twiston-Davies) *midfield: hdwy and in tch whn rdn over 2f out: sn outpcd by ldrs* **20/1**
4/1-	**7**	2	**Wadswick Court (IRE)**[33] 1919 5-11-0 0 NoelFehily	114
		(Charlie Longsdon) *midfield: rdn 3f out: one pce and nvr threatened ldrs* **8/1**[3]
8	shd	**Neck Or Nothing (GER)**[31] 1953 4-11-0 0 DenisO'Regan	117+
		(T Hogan, Ire) *hld up: stl gng wl whn j. path and stmbld over 2f out: no ch after* **10/1**
9	20	**Storm Of Swords (IRE)**[215] 5349 5-11-0 0 HarrySkelton	96
		(Dan Skelton) *trckd ldrs: wknd over 2f out* **11/1**
/11-	**10**	1¼	**It's All An Act (IRE)**[52] 1667 5-11-0 0 AndrewJMcNamara	95
		(John Joseph Hanlon, Ire) *racd keenly: trckd ldrs: rdn over 3f out: sn wknd* **33/1**
11	8	**Count Danilo (IRE)**[204] 4-11-0 0 TomScudamore	87
		(David Pipe) *midfield: wknd over 3f out* **20/1**
0/	**12**	32	**Pink Gin**[217] 5324 5-11-0 0 (t) JasonMaguire	59
		(Jim Old) *hld up: a towards rr: t.o* **100/1**
13	8	**Foolsandorses (IRE)** 5-10-9 0 JamesBanks(5)	51
		(W De Best-Turner) *hld up: t.o 1/2-way* **150/1**

3m 58.8s (2.40) **Going Correction** +0.20s/f (Yiel) **13** Ran SP% **118.2**
Speed ratings: **102,101,101,99,97 97,96,96,87,86 82,67,63**
toteswingers 1&2 £3.40, 1&3 £11.70, 2&3 £23.20 CSF £13.88 TOTE £4.80: £2.30, £1.70, £5.80; EX 13.10 Trifecta £1093.10 Pool: £4,219.53 - 2.89 winning units..
Owner The Johnson Family **Bred** David Johnson **Trained** Nicholashayne, Devon
FOCUS
This Listed bumper has been won by horses of the calibre of Best Mate, Rhinestone Cowboy (who beat Champion Bumper winner Liberman) and Rock On Ruby over the years, and this looked a good-quality edition. It was dominated by 4-y-os and the winner gave David Pipe a four-timer on the card. The second, fourth and fifth help set the level.
T/Jkpt: Not won. T/Plt: £39.10 to a £1 stake. Pool: £199,028.57 - 3,713.76 winning units T/Qpdt: £6.60 to a £1 stake. Pool: £17,526.48 - 1,958.51 winning units ST

2016 FONTWELL (L-H)

Sunday, November 17

OFFICIAL GOING: Heavy (soft in places; 6.3)
Second last fence omitted in all chases.
Wind: Light; half against Weather: Overcast, dry

2535 BET TOTEJACKPOT WITH TOTEPOOL NOVICES' H'CAP HURDLE (11 hdls) 2m 6f 110y

12:45 (12:45) (Class 5) (0-95,95) 3-Y-O+ **£1,949** (£572; £286; £143)

Form				RPR
/02-	**1**		**The Young Master**[9] 2353 4-11-4 **94** (p) ConorShoemark(7)	101
		(Neil Mulholland) *led tl after 3rd: styd chsng ldr tl led after 7th: hdd next: 4th and drvn bef 3 out: rallied to chse ldr bef 2 out: swtchd lft and drvn to chal last: led fnl 100yds: styd on* **4/1**[2]
011-	**2**	1¼	**Brass Monkey (IRE)**[9] 2353 6-11-9 **95** TrevorWhelan(3)	100
		(Neil King) *chsd ldrs tl led 8th: rdn and sn after 2 out: hrd pressed and drvn last: hdd fnl 100yds: no ex* **7/2**[1]
024/	**3**	4	**Bredon Hill Lad**[207] 5495 6-10-13 **82** WillKennedy	83
		(Sue Gardner) *hld up in rr: stdy prog 7th: chsd ldrs 3 out: rdn bef next: 3rd and kpt on same pce between last 2* **4/1**[2]
052-	**4**	20	**Phar Away Island (IRE)**[13] 2278 5-10-2 **78** MrFMitchell(7)	59
		(Charlie Brooks) *in tch in midfield: hdwy to chse ldr after 8th: lost 2nd and sltly hmpd bnd after 3 out: 4th and btn between last 2: wkng whn j.rt last* **4/1**[2]
656/	**5**	2½	**Head Spin (IRE)**[225] 5184 5-10-13 **82** AndrewThornton	61
		(Seamus Mullins) *hld up in tch in midfield: chsd ldrs after 7th: rdn and btn after 3 out: hit next: wknd* **17/2**[3]
/6B-	**6**	10	**Millenarys Lady (IRE)**[71] 1517 6-10-13 **82** NickScholfield	51
		(David Rees) *t.k.h: hld up in rr: hdwy to ld after 3rd: hdd after 7th: rdn and wknd after 3 out: t.o* **16/1**
406-	**7**	44	**Haling Park (UAE)**[17] 2176 7-10-1 **70** oh5 ow1 TomMessenger
		(Clarissa Caroe) *in tch towards rr: rdn after 5th: lost tch after 7th: t.o next* **40/1**
P06/	**8**	10	**Boy Of Boru (IRE)**[256] 4593 6-11-1 **84** (t) SamThomas
		(Diana Grissell) *in tch in midfield: dropped to rr after 6th: rdn and lost tch after next: j.lft 8th: t.o after* **10/1**
/05-	**F**		**Peter Muck**[37] 1860 10-10-9 **78** DaveCrosse
		(Nigel Twiston-Davies) *chsd ldrs: rdn after 7th: struggling next: wl hld and wkng whn fell 3 out* **25/1**
0/P-	**P**		**Lara Dora (IRE)**[17] 2176 7-9-7 **69** oh7 MrPJohn(7)
		(Laura Hurley) *t.k.h: chsd ldrs: mstke 4th: lost pl after next: tailing off whn p.u after 7th* **100/1**

5m 59.6s (17.10) **Going Correction** +0.775s/f (Soft)
WFA 4 from 5yo+ 8lb **10** Ran SP% **115.0**
Speed ratings (Par 103): **101,100,99,92,91 87,72,69,,**
toteswingers 1&2 £2.80, 1&3 £1.50, 2&3 £2.90 CSF £18.35 CT £58.80 TOTE £5.30: £1.60, £1.50, £1.90; EX 14.90 Trifecta £50.60 Pool: £1,173.94 - 17.38 winning units..
Owner Dajam Ltd **Bred** Brendan Boyle **Trained** Limpley Stoke, Wilts
■ Stewards' Enquiry : Trevor Whelan two-day ban: used whip above permitted level (Dec 1-2)
FOCUS
Fences down back straight jumped on inside line and the rest on outside line. Top bend and bottom hurdle bend out at minimum width. Bottom chase bend 3yds off inner line. This modest novice handicap was understandably run at a modest pace in the conditions and, with the jockeys describing the ground as "very soft", the winning time was nearly 48sec outside standard. It resulted in a thrilling finish between two old rivals who were always close to the pace. They are rated close to their recent run.

2536 BET TOTETRIFECTA WITH TOTEPOOL MAIDEN HURDLE (10 hdls) 2m 4f

1:15 (1:16) (Class 4) 4-Y-O+ **£3,119** (£915; £457; £228)

Form				RPR
/14-	**1**		**Cole Harden (IRE)**[25] 2018 4-10-11 0 (t) GavinSheehan(3)	122+
		(Warren Greatrex) *j.lft: led 1st: mde rest: clr w runner-up and gng best bef 2 out: rdn between last 2: styd on wl and drew clr flat* **9/4**[1]
/3P-	**2**	4	**Westaway (IRE)**[10] 2316 6-11-0 115 TomCannon	116
		(David Arbuthnot) *chsd wnr after 2nd: clr w wnr and rdn to chal after 3 out: ev ch and hit next: no ex last: outpcd flat* **11/2**
13/	**3**	10	**Harry's Farewell**[215] 5333 6-11-0 0 TomO'Brien	107
		(Polly Gundry) *t.k.h: chsd ldrs: j.lft 2nd: mstke 5th and 6th: wnt 2nd 4th tl after 6th: 3rd and rdn after 3 out: no ex next: wknd last* **7/2**[3]
5/3-	**4**	46	**Dougalstar (FR)**[186] 307 4-10-4 100 MikeyHamill(10)	59
		(Sean Curran) *in tch in midfield: hdwy to chse ldrs after 6th: struggling whn j.lft and bmpd rival 3 out: wknd and wl hld whn hit next: t.o whn mstke last: tired flat* **20/1**
60-	**5**	8	**Here's Herbie**[12] 2280 5-10-9 0 MissLucyGardner(5)	51
		(Sue Gardner) *wl off the pce in last trio: pushed along and passed btn horses fr 7th: nvr on terms and poor 5th between last 2: t.o* **50/1**
1/F-	**6**	35	**Court Appeal (IRE)**[38] 1838 6-11-0 0 AidanColeman	16
		(Charlie Longsdon) *in tch in midfield: 6th and rdn whn mstke 7th: wl btn next: wknd and t.o bef 2 out* **3/1**[2]
006/	**7**	3¾	**Landerbee (IRE)**[541] 430 6-10-7 0 KevinJones(7)	12
		(Seamus Mullins) *hld up in tch in midfield: hdwy to chse ldrs and travelling wl after 6th: disputing 4th whn bmpd and nrly uns rdr 3 out: sn wl btn and wknd qckly bef next: t.o 2 out* **100/1**
0/0-	**8**	3¾	**Rightonthyme**[16] 2190 6-10-7 0 AlainCawley
		(Tom Symonds) *a wl bhd in rr: n.d: t.o after 6th* **100/1**

P/ **9** 3/4 **Steepleofcopper (IRE)**[215] 5327 7-10-7 0................ JosephAkehurst(7) 8
(Alan Jessop) *racd in midfield: mstke 5th: rdn and lost tch after next: t.o after 3 out* **200/1**

40P- **10** shd **Money Money Money**[33] 1915 7-10-7 0........................ MattieBatchelor
(Jim Best) *mstkes: a wl bhd in last pair: t.o after 6th* **66/1**

54- **11** 3 1/4 **Micquus (IRE)**[31] 1946 4-11-0 0.. MarkGrant
(Jonathan Geake) *nt fluent: led tl 1st: chsd ldr tl 4th: lost pl 6th: bhd after next: t.o bef 2 out* **50/1**

400/ **S** **Ballycassel (IRE)**[224] 5195 8-11-0 115...............................[1] FelixDeGiles
(Tom Symonds) *racd in midfield: 7th and struggling u.p after 7th: wkng whn slipped up bnd after 3 out* **12/1**

P **Arcayo (IRE)**[195] 4-10-11 0.. JoshuaMoore(3)
(Gary Moore) *racd in midfield: rdn and lost pl after 6th: t.o after next tl p.u bef 2 out* **22/1**

5m 18.6s (19.20) **Going Correction** +0.875s/f (Soft)
WFA 4 from 5yo+ 8lb **13** Ran SP% **118.1**
Speed ratings (Par 105): **96,94,90,72,68 54,53,51,51,51 50, ,**
toteswingers 1&2 £3.30, 1&3 £2.70, 2&3 £4.10 CSF £14.45 TOTE £3.20: £1.40, £1.90, £1.90; EX 13.10 Trifecta £58.00 Pool: £1,799.92 - 23.24 winning units..
Owner Mrs Jill Eynon & Robin Eynon **Bred** Mrs J O'Callaghan **Trained** Upper Lambourn, Berks

FOCUS
An interesting maiden hurdle featuring a few bumper/point winners, but again the conditions took their toll and, in a race run at a sensible gallop, it paid to be handy. There should be more to come from the winner.

2537 TOTEPOOL SOUTHERN NATIONAL H'CAP CHASE (17 fncs 4 omitted) 3m 4f

1:50 (1:50) (Class 3) (0-135,134) 4-Y-0+ **£12,660** (£3,740; £1,870; £936; £468)

Form RPR

/33- **1** **Boyfromnowhere (IRE)**[22] 2077 6-10-12 **125**...........(p) PatrickCorbett(5) 134+
(Rebecca Curtis) *a w ldrs: led 15th: gng best bef 2 out: rdn and asserted on long run to 2 out: kpt on and a in command flat* **9/2**[2]

512- **2** 1 3/4 **Adrenalin Flight (IRE)**[17] 2177 7-10-5 **113**.............. AndrewThornton 119
(Seamus Mullins) *hld up wl in tch: hdwy to trck ldrs 15th: reminder and effrt to chse wnr 2 out: drvn on long run between last 2: styd on same pce flat* **25/1**

2/U- **3** nk **Swincombe Rock**[21] 2108 8-11-4 **133**........................(b[1]) JakeHodson(7) 139
(David Bridgwater) *t.k.h: hld up wl in tch in midfield: rdn and effrt after 15th: chsd ldng pair on long run between last 2: mstke last: styd on same pce flat* **16/1**

4/0- **4** 5 **Alderluck (IRE)**[12] 2283 10-10-11 **126**.....................(b) MikeyEnnis(7) 127
(David Pipe) *t.k.h: hld up wl in tch: rdn and effrt after 15th: 4th and plugged on same pce flat* **8/1**

/FF- **5** 9 **Buck's Bond (FR)**[21] 2108 7-11-1 **123**.........................(bt[1]) NickScholfield 114
(Paul Nicholls) *w ldr tl 15th: rdn bef next: wknd u.p on long run between last 2: edgd rt flat* **8/1**

110/ **6** 1 **Emperor's Choice (IRE)**[249] 4732 6-11-12 **134**.............. AidanColeman 128+
(Venetia Williams) *w ldrs tl led after 2nd: hdd and mstke 15th: mstke next: wknd on long run between last 2* **4/1**[1]

261/ **7** 36 **Flying Award (IRE)**[205] 5548 9-10-9 **122**................ MissLucyGardner(5) 76
(Sue Gardner) *in tch towards rr: pushed along and outpcd 13th: wknd bef 2 out* **10/1**

6/4- **8** 23 **Pettifour (IRE)**[29] 1978 11-10-4 **112**.. DaveCrosse 43
(Nigel Twiston-Davies) *in tch in midfield: mstke and reminders 11th: drvn after next: wknd 2 out* **7/1**

1/P- **P** **The Clyda Rover (IRE)**[21] 2108 9-10-3 **111**.............(p) RichieMcLernon
(Helen Nelmes) *in tch in rr: rdn and lost tch after 12th: t.o whn p.u 15th* **14/1**

1P2/ **P** **Camden (IRE)**[220] 5242 7-11-5 **127**.................................... LeightonAspell
(Oliver Sherwood) *nvr travelling: in tch towards rr: reminder after 5th: lost tch 13th: t.o whn p.u last* **5/1**[3]

7m 45.6s (18.30) **Going Correction** +0.55s/f (Soft) **10** Ran SP% **115.1**
Speed ratings (Par 107): **95,94,94,92,90 90,79,73, ,**
toteswingers 1&2 £28.70, 1&3 £11.30, 2&3 £85.00 CSF £95.79 CT £1643.12 TOTE £5.20: £1.90, £3.50, £5.80; EX 107.00 Trifecta £1294.60 Part won. Pool: £1,726.18 - 0.44 winning units..
Owner A J Rhead & G B Williams **Bred** James Murtagh **Trained** Newport, Dyfed

FOCUS
This was a real stamina test in the conditions with three horses, including the winner, disputing the advantage for much of the journey. The first two are on the upgrade.

2538 TOTEEXACTA SALMON SPRAY H'CAP HURDLE (FOR THE SALMON SPRAY CHALLENGE TROPHY) (9 hdls) 2m 2f 110y

2:25 (2:25) (Class 3) (0-135,134) 4-Y-0 **£6,330** (£1,870; £935; £468; £234)

Form RPR

406/ **1** **Knight Of Pleasure**[224] 5197 4-10-13 **124**.............. JoshuaMoore(3) 134+
(Gary Moore) *t.k.h: hld up wl in tch in last pair: clsd and stl travelling strly 3 out: nt handle bnd and outpcd bef next: rallied u.p to chse ldr between last 2: led flat: styd on strly: rdn out* **5/2**[2]

/22- **2** 3 1/2 **Dolatulo (FR)**[22] 2087 6-11-2 **127**.................................. GavinSheehan(3) 131
(Warren Greatrex) *j.lft: chsd ldr tl led 2nd: hdd 5th: led again after 3 out: gd jump and wnt 2 l clr 2 out: hrd pressed and j.lft last: hdd and no ex flat* **9/4**[1]

6/5- **3** 7 **Munsaab (IRE)**[21] 2102 7-11-4 **126**.................................. AidanColeman 122
(Charlie Longsdon) *hld up wl in tch: trckd ldrs 5th: ev ch after 3 out: outj. and 2 l down next: 3rd and btn last: plugged on flat* **7/2**[3]

431- **4** 4 1/2 **Imperial Stargazer**[22] 2085 4-10-4 **112**.......................... MarcGoldstein 104
(Sheena West) *led tl hit 2nd: chsd ldr tl led again 5th: hdd sn after 3 out: 4th and btn next: wknd between last 2* **9/1**

/U0- **5** 6 **Orzare (IRE)**[15] 2211 7-10-13 **121**.................................... LeightonAspell 107
(Philip Hide) *t.k.h: hld up wl in tch in midfield: mstke 6th: rdn and btn bef 2 out: wknd between last 2* **16/1**

1F3/ **6** 40 **Orabora**[314] 3547 7-11-1 **123**... TomO'Brien 69
(Philip Hobbs) *t.k.h: hld up in tch in last pair: mstke 1st: clsd and wl in tch after 6th: rdn and btn after next: wknd between last 2: eased flat: t.o* **7/1**

5/6- **7** 20 **Maller Tree**[61] 1594 6-11-5 **134**.............................. ChristopherWard(7) 60
(David Dennis) *chsd ldrs: mstke 4th: lost pl and rdn next: lost tch u.p 6th: t.o after 3 out* **25/1**

4m 48.5s (14.20) **Going Correction** +0.975s/f (Soft)
WFA 4 from 5yo+ 7lb **7** Ran SP% **113.8**
Speed ratings (Par 107): **109,107,104,102,100 83,74**
toteswingers 1&2 £2.10, 1&3 £2.80, 2&3 £2.30 CSF £8.76 CT £18.34 TOTE £3.70: £2.40, £1.60; EX 8.90 Trifecta £27.50 Pool: £1,454.92 - 39.66 winning units..
Owner The Knights Of Pleasure **Bred** Bryan Fry **Trained** Lower Beeding, W Sussex

FOCUS
A decent handicap hurdle. A big step up from the winner to beat the well treated second.

2539 JOHN ROGERSON MEMORIAL NOVICES' LIMITED H'CAP CHASE (THE SUNDAY £5K BONUS RACE) (11 fncs 5 omitted) 2m 6f

2:55 (2:56) (Class 3) (0-140,135) 5-Y-0+ **£8,305** (£2,507; £1,291; £684)

Form RPR

4/P- **1** **Colebrooke**[22] 2087 5-10-2 **121** oh1...........................(p) JoshuaMoore(3) 130+
(Renee Robeson) *lft 4th and hmpd 1st: in tch: rdn to chse ldr and clsng on long run after 10th: j. into ld 2 out: sn clr: kpt on: rdn out* **10/1**

0/3- **2** 7 **Loose Chips**[27] 2005 7-11-5 **135**....................................(b) AidanColeman 136
(Charlie Longsdon) *led: rdn bypassing 11th: outj. and hdd 2 out: racing awkwardly u.p and no ex on long run between last 2: plugged on to hold 2nd flat* **7/2**[2]

0/6- **3** 4 **Who Owns Me (IRE)**[17] 2177 7-10-5 **121** oh1......................... MarkGrant 119
(Charlie Mann) *lft 3rd 1st: chsd ldr bef next tl 7th: rdn after 8th: 4th and struggling u.p bef 2 out: wnt 3rd on long run between last 2: no imp* **9/2**[3]

P/F- **4** 32 **Rendl Beach (IRE)**[26] 2010 6-10-0 **126**........................... PaulO'Brien(10) 90
(Rebecca Curtis) *t.k.h: lft 2nd 1st: sn 3rd and stl keen: wnt 2nd again 7th: rdn bypassing 11th: 3rd and btn whn mstke 2 out: sn wknd: t.o* **7/2**[2]

3F0/ **U** **Curtain Razer (IRE)**[304] 3706 7-10-5 **121** oh1...................... TomCannon
(Chris Gordon) *hmpd 1st: hld up in last tl blnd bdly and uns rdr 2nd* **10/1**

311/ **F** **Benvolio (IRE)**[274] 4256 6-11-3 **133**.................................. NickScholfield
(Paul Nicholls) *chsd ldr tl fell 1st* **2/1**[1]

5m 52.25s (9.25) **Going Correction** +0.65s/f (Soft) **6** Ran SP% **114.1**
Speed ratings: **109,106,105,93,**
toteswingers 1&2 £3.90, 1&3 £10.60, 2&3 £2.20 CSF £45.51 TOTE £12.40: £2.00, £2.60; EX 70.00 Trifecta £280.70 Pool: £2,195.91 - 5.86 winning units..
Owner TMT Grand **Bred** Rabbah Bloodstock Limited **Trained** Tyringham, Bucks

FOCUS
This novices' handicap became a lot less competitive when the favourite Benvolio fell at the first fence and Curtain Razer unseated his rider at the second. The rider of the former Nick Scholfield required medical attention, which meant that fence was omitted on the final two circuits. A step up from the winner on his best hurdles form.

2540 FOLLOW TOTEPOOL ON TWITTER CONDITIONAL JOCKEYS' H'CAP CHASE (13 fncs 3 omitted) 2m 6f

3:30 (3:30) (Class 5) (0-100,100) 4-Y-0+ **£2,664** (£782; £391; £195)

Form RPR

361- **1** **Waltzing Tornado (IRE)**[6] 2425 9-11-5 **96** 7ex......(p) ConorShoemark(3) 107+
(Neil Mulholland) *hld up in tch in last pair: clsd to trck ldrs after 8th: mstke and wnt lft 9th: chsd wnr next: lft in ld 11th: mstke last and sn jnd: drvn and forged ahd fnl 100yds* **6/4**[1]

33P- **2** 2 **Morestead (IRE)**[13] 2278 8-10-13 **87**.................................. JoshuaMoore 93
(Brendan Powell) *led tl hdd 9th: drvn and lft 2nd whn sltly hmpd 11th: kpt on u.p and str chal sn after last: no ex and btn fnl 100yds* **18/1**

235- **3** 17 **Princely Hero (IRE)**[25] 2017 9-10-5 **89**...................(tp) LouisMuspratt(10) 78
(Chris Gordon) *chsd ldrs: dropped to last and drvn after 8th: lft 3rd and sltly hmpd 11th: no ex next: wknd on long run between last 2* **16/1**

623- **4** 8 **Double Chocolate**[11] 2297 10-11-6 **100**.....................(p) CiaranMckee(6) 86
(John O'Shea) *chsd ldr: mstke 4th: blnd 10th: lost pl and rdn after 8th: cl 4th whn bmpd next: wknd 2 out* **11/4**[2]

5/6- **F** **Rozolenn (FR)**[31] 1939 8-11-3 **94**..................................... HarryChalloner(3)
(Venetia Williams) *chsd ldrs tl led after 8th: stl travelling wl whn overj. and fell 11th* **7/2**[3]

P26- **F** **Flugzeug**[11] 2290 5-9-10 **78** ow2.. KevinJones(8)
(Seamus Mullins) *hld up in tch in last pair tl fell 7th* **8/1**

6m 3.5s (20.50) **Going Correction** +0.75s/f (Soft) **6** Ran SP% **111.1**
Speed ratings (Par 103): **92,91,85,82,**
toteswingers 1&2 £4.20, 1&3 £4.70, 2&3 £6.80 CSF £22.46 TOTE £2.30: £1.40, £5.60; EX 30.00 Trifecta £129.70 Pool: £2,316.90 - 13.39 winning units..
Owner John Hobbs **Bred** Miss Anne Heaney **Trained** Limpley Stoke, Wilts

FOCUS
A modest conditional jockeys' chase and another race notable for jumping errors. The winner is rated below the level of his recent win.

2541 COLLECT TOTEPOOL WINNINGS IN BETFRED SHOPS H'CAP HURDLE (13 hdls) 3m 3f

4:00 (4:00) (Class 5) (0-100,92) 4-Y-0+ **£1,949** (£572; £286; £143)

Form RPR

P/P- **1** **Orvita (FR)**[13] 2275 11-11-9 **89**.....................................(p) RichieMcLernon 97+
(Helen Nelmes) *hld up in tch in last pair: clsd after 9th: jnd ldr and stl on bit after 3 out: led next: sn rdn clr and in command last: comf* **16/1**

064- **2** 6 **Changing Lanes**[35] 1890 10-11-7 **87**...........................(tp) AidanColeman 87
(David Rees) *wl in tch in midfield: chsd ldrs and drvn after 3 out: outpcd bef nxt: plugged on to chse wnr last: styd on but no imp flat* **11/2**[3]

011- **3** 9 **Absolute Shambles**[43] 1768 9-11-12 **92**..........................(p) TomCannon 84
(Chris Gordon) *chsd ldrs: lft in 2nd at 2nd: led after 9th: jnd and drvn after 3 out: hdd 2 out and brushed aside by wnr bef last: lost 2nd last: wknd flat* **4/1**[2]

/53- **4** 4 **Miss Mayfair (IRE)**[68] 1552 6-11-10 **90**.................................. DavidBass 77
(Lawney Hill) *hld up wl in tch: hdwy to chse ldrs 10th: wnt 2nd next tl bef 2 out: sn drvn and no ex: wknd between last 2* **9/1**

044- **5** 32 **Spanish Fork (IRE)**[42] 1784 4-11-7 **87**............................ MarcGoldstein 42
(Sheena West) *rn in snatches: wl in tch in midfield: drvn and effrt to chse ldrs 10th: wknd wl bef 2 out: fdd between last 2: t.o* **7/2**[1]

U60- **6** 22 **Best Bette**[10] 2312 8-9-10 **69**... MrLKilgarriff(7)
(Clarissa Caroe) *in tch in last pair: rdn after 5th: styd in tch: drvn after 9th: toiling next and sn lost tch: t.o sn after 3 out* **20/1**

/P5- **7** 16 **Laughing Game**[17] 2175 9-9-7 **66** oh5.................................... MrPJohn(7)
(Laura Hurley) *j.rt at times: led: mstke 4th and 5th: mstke 8th: hdd next and sn lost pl u.p: lost tch next: t.o 3 out* **20/1**

/P3- **8** 10 **Brunette'Sonly (IRE)**[177] 460 8-11-9 **89**........................ AndrewThornton
(Seamus Mullins) *chsd ldr tl j.big and pitched on landing 2nd: chsd ldrs after: cl 5th and rdn after 3 out: wknd bef next: eased after 2 out: t.o and virtually p.u flat* **7/2**[1]

PF0- **P** **Une Des Bieffes (FR)**[90] 1320 5-10-10 **76**....................(v) LiamTreadwell
(Michael Scudamore) *wl in tch in midfield: hdwy to join ldr after 9th: rdn and hit 3 out: sn dropped out: wl btn 6th whn eased p.u next* **10/1**

7m 22.6s (29.80) **Going Correction** +1.075s/f (Soft)
WFA 4 from 5yo+ 9lb **9** Ran SP% **114.3**
Speed ratings (Par 103): **98,96,93,92,82 76,71,68,**
toteswingers 1&2 £16.10, 1&3 £14.60, 2&3 £4.40 CSF £100.85 CT £423.45 TOTE £16.00: £4.70, £2.00, £2.30; EX 104.40 Trifecta £1072.00 Part won. Pool: £1,429.41 - 0.78 winning units..
Owner K A Nelmes **Bred** Serge Troadec, Luc Troadec & J-P Tanguy **Trained** Warmwell, Dorset

FOCUS
This was still a real test of stamina despite a sedate pace. The easy winner is rated in line with his course form from 2012.
T/Plt: £124.40 to a £1 stake. Pool: £116,326.26 - 682.21 winning units T/Qpdt: £67.70 to a £1 stake. Pool: £6,925.98 - 75.60 winning units SP

2542 - 2549a (Foreign Racing) - See Raceform Interactive

2521 PUNCHESTOWN (R-H)
Sunday, November 17

OFFICIAL GOING: Yielding

2550a MADIGANS BARS CRADDOCKSTOWN NOVICE CHASE (GRADE 2) (11 fncs) 2m
1:05 (1:05) 4-Y-0+ £20,873 (£6,101; £2,890; £963)

RPR
1 **Felix Yonger (IRE)**[190] 230 7-11-4 ... RWalsh 156+
(W P Mullins, Ire) *w.w towards inner tl tk clsr order in 3rd appr 5th: pressed ldr after 3 out: led next and styd on wl run-in* **9/4**[2]
2 2 ½ **Defy Logic (IRE)**[20] 2143 6-11-4 ... MarkWalsh 152
(Paul Nolan, Ire) *attempted to make all: strly pressed after 3 out: hdd 2 out and no imp on wnr whn mstke last: kpt on same pce* **10/11**[1]
3 18 **Passage Vendome (FR)**[38] 1844 7-11-4 135 ... DJCasey 135
(W P Mullins, Ire) *hld up in rr tl tk clsr order to chse ldrs in modest 3rd after 3 out: sn no imp: kpt on one pce fr bef last* **20/1**
4 4 ¾ **Shrapnel (IRE)**[21] 2116 7-11-7 140 ...(t) BryanCooper 133
(Gordon Elliott, Ire) *chsd ldrs: pushed along and nt qckn after 3 out: kpt on one pce fr bef last* **7/1**[3]
5 5 **Balnaslow (IRE)**[24] 2055 6-11-4 133 ... MsKWalsh 126
(W P Mullins, Ire) *w.w tl prog to briefly 3 out into 3rd: sn pushed along and wknd bef next* **20/1**
6 14 **Sizing Machine (IRE)**[80] 1447 5-11-4 130 ... AELynch 110
(Henry De Bromhead, Ire) *chsd ldrs tl nt qckn after 3 out: sn dropped towards rr* **16/1**
7 24 **Six Stone Ned (IRE)**[21] 2116 7-11-4 130 ...(t) NiallPMadden 86
(Noel Meade, Ire) *trckd ldr whn mstke 1st: remained cl up tl nt qckn appr 3 out where nt fluent: sn wknd* **33/1**
P **Jim Will Fix It (IRE)**[18] 2164 8-11-4 128 ...(t) MarkEnright
(Seamus Roche, Ire) *trckd ldrs: collided w ldr 2nd: awkward at 3rd and nt fluent thereafter: dropped to rr after 5th and detached 4 out: p.u bef next* **20/1**

4m 2.2s (-16.40) **8 Ran SP% 118.8**
CSF £4.88 TOTE £2.80: £1.40, £1.02, £3.30; DF 5.20 Trifecta £45.10.
Owner Andrea & Graham Wylie **Bred** J Brophy **Trained** Muine Beag, Co Carlow

FOCUS
Eight runners for this Grade 2 event and a decent field on paper, but it boiled down to a match. The winner produced a very smart performance. The runner-up has been rated to his chase debut winning mark.

2551a DOBBINS OUTDOOR CATERING FLORIDA PEARL NOVICE CHASE (GRADE 2) (15 fncs) 2m 6f
1:40 (1:40) 5-Y-0+ £20,873 (£6,101; £2,890; £963)

RPR
1 **Morning Assembly (IRE)**[18] 2165 6-11-3 ... RWalsh 151+
(P A Fahy, Ire) *disp tl hdd 4th: bk on terms 7th: pressed after 3 out and hdd next: rallied wl run-in to ld again clsng stages* **6/4**[2]
2 ½ **Don Cossack (GER)**[20] 2136 6-11-3 ... BryanCooper 150+
(Gordon Elliott, Ire) *trckd ldrs in 3rd tl travelled wl to dispute after 3 out: led next: kpt on wl run-in but hdd clsng stages* **4/5**[1]
3 12 **Clonbanan Lad (IRE)**[18] 2165 7-11-3 133 ... AELynch 139
(Henry De Bromhead, Ire) *w.w last of 4: prog into 3rd 3 out: nt qckn w principals after next: kpt on one pce* **20/1**
4 9 ½ **Si C'Etait Vrai (FR)**[18] 2165 7-11-3 ... MarkEnright 132
(D T Hughes, Ire) *disp tl led 4th: jnd again 7th: nt qckn and dropped to rr 3 out: sn detached* **12/1**[3]

5m 47.9s (-15.10) **4 Ran SP% 108.0**
CSF £3.21 TOTE £1.90; DF 2.70 Trifecta £9.30.
Owner Clipper Logistics Group Ltd **Bred** J J Brennan **Trained** Leighlinbridge, Co Carlow

FOCUS
Only four runners, and none for Willie Mullins, who had plundered the first two here and at Cork, but this produced a cracking race between two high-class staying novices. The second and third set the standard.

2552a STANJAMES.COM MORGIANA HURDLE (GRADE 1) (9 hdls) 2m
2:15 (2:17) 4-Y-0+ £39,024 (£12,357; £5,853; £1,951; £1,300)

RPR
1 **Hurricane Fly (IRE)**[205] 5561 9-11-10 175 ... RWalsh 154+
(W P Mullins, Ire) *trckd ldr in 2nd tl clsd bef 2 out: led appr last and rdn clr run-in: advantage reduced cl home* **1/16**[1]
2 1 ¼ **Marito (GER)**[206] 5526 7-11-10 138 ... MsKWalsh 153+
(W P Mullins, Ire) *chsd ldrs in 3rd: pushed along bef last where awkward: styd on wl run-in into 2nd clsng stages* **14/1**[2]
3 ¾ **Mikael D'Haguenet (FR)**[3] 2483 9-11-10 147 ... DJCasey 152
(W P Mullins, Ire) *led: pressed after 2 out and hdd appr last: kpt on same pce run-in: dropped to 3rd clsng stages* **16/1**[3]
4 5 **Midnight Game**[42] 1801 6-11-10 141 ... BryanCooper 147
(W P Mullins, Ire) *racd in 4th thrght: no imp bef last: kpt on one pce* **14/1**[2]
5 7 **Akatara (IRE)**[128] 950 6-11-3 106 ... BrianHayes 133?
(Michael J Bowe, Ire) *a in rr: detached 2 out* **50/1**

3m 56.3s (-8.70) **5 Ran SP% 115.2**
CSF £3.05 TOTE £1.10: £1.02, £1.70; DF 2.90 Trifecta £8.20.
Owner George Creighton & Mrs Rose Boyd **Bred** Agricola Del Parco **Trained** Muine Beag, Co Carlow
■ Hurricane Fly's 17th Grade 1 win, a new world record, Flat or jumps.

FOCUS
The fifth limits the form and the standard is set around the fourth. Hurricane Fly, who beat a trio of stablemates, did not need to be anywhere near his best.

2553 - 2556a (Foreign Racing) - See Raceform Interactive

LEICESTER (R-H)
Monday, November 18

OFFICIAL GOING: Chase course - good to firm (good in places, good to soft on flat course crossings; 7.9); hurdle course - good to soft (soft in places; 6.8)
Wind: virtually nil Weather: dull and drizzly

2557 YOUR EXPERT GUIDE TO LEICESTER LEICESTERRACECOURSETIPS.CO.UK JUVENILE FILLIES' HURDLE (7 hdls 1 omitted) 2m
12:35 (12:35) (Class 4) 3-Y-0 £3,898 (£1,144; £572; £286)

Form RPR
1 **Mystery Drama**[23] 3-10-8 0 ... RobertThornton 105+
(Alan King) *hld up in tch towards rr: hdwy bef 3 out: ev ch 2 out (actual last): led u.p bypassing last: styd on to forge ahd fnl 100yds: rdn out* **7/4**[1]
2 ¾ **Poetic Verse**[40] 3-10-8 0 ... DougieCostello 104+
(John Quinn) *in tch in midfield: mstke 2nd: hdwy to chse ldrs 3 out: ev ch next (actual last): drvn and sn led: hdd bypassing last: no ex and btn fnl 100yds* **9/4**[2]
3 10 **Maypole Lass**[117] 3-10-8 0 ... PaddyBrennan 94
(Renee Robeson) *in tch in midfield: hdwy to chse ldrs and mstke 5th: led after 3 out (actual last): hdd sn after 2 out (actual last): 3rd and wknd on long run-in* **6/1**[3]
4 7 **Magic Skyline (IRE)**[59] 3-10-8 0 ... AidanColeman 90
(Brian Ellison) *j.rt and mstkes: in tch towards rr: rdn and effrt after mstke 3 out: 4th and no imp next (actual last): wknd on long run-in* **7/1**
5 shd **Uganda Glory (USA)**[70] 3-10-8 0 ...(p) AndrewTinkler 88
(George Baker) *chsd ldrs: mstke 2nd: rdn after 3 out: 5th and no ex next (actual last): wknd on long run-in* **10/1**
6 4 **Youmaysee**[116] 3-10-8 0 ... DominicElsworth 84
(Mick Channon) *t.k.h: hld up in rr: j.rt 2nd: rdn and struggling bef 3 out: no ch but plugged on past btn horses on long run-in* **100/1**
5- 7 10 **Banreenahreenkah (IRE)**[19] 2154 3-10-8 0 ... SeanQuinlan 75
(Jennie Candlish) *t.k.h: led: wandering at sme hurdles: rdn and hdd after 3 out: sn btn: wknd next (actual last)* **20/1**
4- 8 14 **Taming The Tweet**[24] 2066 3-9-12 0 ... StevieSanders[(10)] 63
(J R Jenkins) *t.k.h: chsd ldrs: rdn and lost pl after 5th: wknd next: t.o on long run-in* **40/1**
9 20 **Sweet Louise (IRE)**[46] 3-10-8 0 ...(t) FelixDeGiles 45
(Barry Brennan) *chsd ldr tl 3 out: sn wknd: t.o on long run-in* **100/1**

3m 48.5s (-12.50) **Going Correction** -0.725s/f (Firm) **9 Ran SP% 112.2**
Speed ratings (Par 101): **102,101,96,93,93 91,86,79,69**
toteswingers 1&2 £1.80, 1&3 £3.00, 2&3 £3.50 CSF £5.68 TOTE £2.90: £1.20, £1.10, £2.50; EX 6.50 Trifecta £20.80 Pool: £1618.46 - 58.08 winning units..
Owner Incipe Partnership **Bred** Barbury Castle Stud **Trained** Barbury Castle, Wilts

FOCUS
Fairly useful efforts from the leading pair, who came well clear despite the pace appearing on the steady side for a long way. Not form to be too confident about.

2558 JOHN O'GAUNT NOVICES' CHASE (12 fncs) 2m
1:05 (1:05) (Class 3) 4-Y-0+ £6,388 (£1,928; £993; £526)

Form RPR
/21- 1 **Valco De Touzaine (FR)**[16] 2227 4-11-0 142 ...(t) SamTwiston-Davies 135+
(Paul Nicholls) *tendency to jump lft: chsd ldr tl led 3rd: mde rest: mistske 2 out: nt fluent last: rdn flat: fnd ex to assert fnl 100yds: styd on* **4/9**[1]
0/4- 2 2 ¼ **Buthelezi (USA)**[12] 2295 5-11-0 0 ... DenisO'Regan 130
(John Ferguson) *led tl 3rd: chsd wnr after and tendency to jump lft: rdn and effrt to press wnr last: drvn and no ex fnl 100yds: hld whn eased cl home* **5/2**[2]
3- 3 44 **Carli King (IRE)**[17] 2192 7-11-0 0 ... TomMessenger 90
(Caroline Bailey) *lft chsng ldng pair 1st: steadily lost tch: t.o fr 6th* **33/1**
- 4 62 **Force Of Habit**[125] 1004 7-10-9 97 ...(p) SamanthaDrake[(5)] 35
(Joanne Foster) *lft 4th 1st: steadily lost tch: t.o fr 5th* **50/1**
403- U **Akula (IRE)**[40] 1821 6-11-0 114 ... ColinBolger
(Mark H Tompkins) *t.k.h: hld up in 3rd tl blnd and uns rdr 1st* **14/1**[3]

3m 57.1s (-11.10) **Going Correction** -0.40s/f (Good) **5 Ran SP% 109.4**
Speed ratings (Par 107): **111,109,87,56,**
CSF £2.01 TOTE £1.80: £1.10, £1.40; EX 2.00 Trifecta £6.80 Pool: £2956.40 - 322.07 winning units..
Owner The Gi Gi Syndicate **Bred** Daniel Jandard & Mme Andree Jandard **Trained** Ditcheat, Somerset

FOCUS
Effectively a match between two useful novices. The winner is rated to his mark with the second improving to the level of his hurdle form.

2559 EASTWELL (S) HURDLE (8 hdls) 2m
1:35 (1:35) (Class 5) 3-5-Y-0 £1,949 (£572; £286; £143)

Form RPR
013- 1 **Persian Herald**[18] 2176 5-11-5 96 ...(bt) TrevorWhelan[(3)] 100+
(Neil King) *led tl hdd 5th: drvn and outpcd by ldr bef next: rallied u.p to chal last: sn lft in ld: clr and in command but idling bdly flat: pulling himself up and slowing towards fin: a gng to last home* **11/4**[1]
0/0- 2 ½ **Lac Sacre (FR)**[23] 2087 4-11-12 113 ...(tp) LeeEdwards 100+
(Tony Carroll) *chsd ldrs: clsd and j. into ld 5th: wnt clr bef next: rdn between last 2: jnd whn mstke: landed awkwardly and hdd last: styd on same pce flat: clsng on slowing wnr towards fin* **7/2**[2]
000- 3 ½ **Chankillo**[12] 2291 4-11-8 87 ... SamTwiston-Davies 92
(Sarah-Jayne Davies) *w ldr tl 3rd and outpcd after 5th: drvn next: no imp whn mstke flat: kpt on fnl 100yds and clsng on slowing wnr towards fin* **5/1**
4/4- 4 hd **A Little Bit Dusty**[15] 2250 5-11-12 102 ...(p) AndrewThornton 98
(Conor Dore) *in tch in midfield: j. bdly rt 1st: 4th and outpcd after 5th: drvn after next: mstke 2 out: kpt on u.p fnl 100yds: clsng on slowing wnr towards fin* **16/1**
P00- 5 10 **Big John Cannon (IRE)**[4] 2466 3-10-0 0 ... MrPJohn[(7)] 70
(Sarah-Jayne Davies) *hld up in last trio: outpcd 5th: rdn and sme hdwy after next: no imp whn mstke last: nvr trbld ldrs* **100/1**
55- 6 10 **I Told You So (IRE)**[46] 1731 4-11-1 0 ... JasonMaguire 67
(Donald McCain) *in tch towards rr: bmpd 1st: rdn and struggling after 5th: wknd next* **6/1**
44- 7 7 **Eyeline**[25] 2038 3-10-0 0 ...(tp) JamesCowley[(7)] 55
(Andrew Hollinshead) *in tch in midfield: bmpd 1st: j. slowly and lost pl 3rd: rdn and wknd after 5th: wl btn next* **9/2**[3]

5/4- **8** 9 **Makellys Blackpool**173 531 4-10-10 0 HarryChalloner(5) 52
(Richard Ford) *in tch in rr: mstke 3rd: rdn and lost tch after 5th: no ch next: t.o* **14/1**

3m 54.7s (-6.30) **Going Correction** -0.725s/f (Firm)
WFA 3 from 4yo+ 15lb **8** Ran SP% **111.6**
Speed ratings (Par 103): **86,85,85,85,80 75,71,67**
toteswingers 1&2 £3.80, 1&3 £3.70, 2&3 £4.00 CSF £12.13 TOTE £3.10: £1.30, £1.60, £1.80; EX 13.50 Trifecta £30.80 Pool: £2414.16 - 58.68 winning units..There was no bid for the winner.
Owner The St Gatien Racing For Fun Partnership **Bred** J W P Clark **Trained** Newmarket, Suffolk

FOCUS
A modest seller. The winner idled and the third and fourth may be a bit flattered.

2560 KATHERINE SWYNFORD H'CAP CHASE (18 fncs) 2m 7f 110y
2:10 (2:10) (Class 4) (0-105,105) 4-Y-0+ **£3,898** (£1,144; £572; £286)

Form RPR
000- **1** **Smart Catch (IRE)**32 1939 7-11-0 **93** LeeEdwards 100+
(Tony Carroll) *j.lft: hld up wl in tch in last: effrt to chse ldr and swtchd lft bef 2 out: chal and slt mstke last: led flat: hld on wl u.p towards fin* **8/1**
2F/- **2** *nk* **Nom De Guerre (IRE)**265 4441 11-11-12 **105** (p) JackDoyle 111
(Ben De Haan) *chsd ldrs: wnt 2nd 9th tl after 14th: led sn after3 out: rdn and drew clr w rival between last 2: hdd flat: battled on gamely u.p: hld towards fin* **7/4**2
P16/ **3** *23* **Doubletoilntrouble (IRE)**213 5377 7-11-8 **101** (t) PaddyBrennan 90
(Fergal O'Brien) *wl in tch in 4th: rdn and effrt bef 3 out: wknd between last 2: eased towards fin* **5/4**1
/0P- **4** *22* **Phoenix Des Mottes (FR)**127 969 10-9-9 **79** oh9 JoeCornwall(5) 44
(John Cornwall) *chsd ldr tl 9th: rdn 12h: styd pressing ldrs: chsd ldr again after 14th tl next: btn 2 out: sn wknd: t.o* **50/1**
2/P- **5** *39* **Thats Ben (IRE)**18 2179 8-11-7 **100** (t) FelixDeGiles 29
(Tom Gretton) *led: rdn after 14th: mstke 3 out and sn hdd: immediately btn and bhd: t.o and eased flat* **6/1**3

5m 52.25s (-11.75) **Going Correction** -0.40s/f (Good) **5** Ran SP% **108.2**
Speed ratings (Par 105): **103,102,95,87,74**
CSF £22.20 TOTE £11.30: £3.60, £1.60; EX 25.10 Trifecta £47.30 Pool: £2300.47 - 36.42 winning units..
Owner Cover Point Racing **Bred** His Highness The Aga Khan's Studs S C **Trained** Cropthorne, Worcs

FOCUS
A weak handicap. The winner was a 115+ hurdler at best and there may be more to come.

2561 WEATHERBYS HAMILTON INSURANCE H'CAP HURDLE (8 hdls) 2m
2:40 (2:40) (Class 3) (0-125,122) 4-Y-0+ **£6,498** (£1,908; £954; £477)

Form RPR
/62- **1** **Zafranagar (IRE)**2 2519 8-10-5 **106** RobertMcCarth(5) 114+
(Ian Williams) *hld up wl in tch in last trio: smooth hdwy to trck ldrs 2 out: shkn up to chse ldr last: drvn fnl 100yds: r.o to ld fnl 50yds: rdn out* **9/4**1
P02- **2** ½ **Canadian Diamond (IRE)**31 1960 6-11-9 **122** (p) MichealNolan(3) 128
(Brendan Powell) *chsd ldrs tl led 3rd: rdn bef 2 out: drvn last: kpt on wl tl hdd and no ex fnl 50yds* **6/1**3
0/6- **3** 3½ **Tealissio**25 2050 7-10-4 **105** MattCrawley(5) 109
(Lucy Wadham) *in tch in midfield: hdwy to trck ldrs after 5th: wnt 2nd next: mstke and pckd 2 out: lost 2nd last and styd on same pce flat* **8/1**
6/0- **4** *9* **Ourmanmassini (IRE)**16 2210 5-11-5 **115** (t) PaddyBrennan 110
(Suzy Smith) *wl in tch in midfield: rdn bef 3 out: outpcd bef 2 out: plugged on to go 4th last: no threat to ldrs* **10/1**
/30- **5** *6* **Travis County (IRE)**17 2198 4-10-9 **105** JasonMaguire 96
(Brian Ellison) *led tl 3rd: chsd ldr after 4th tl bef 3 out: drvn and no ex bef 2 out: wknd bef last* **4/1**2
/60- **6** ½ **Drussell (IRE)**28 486 7-10-7 **108** ThomasGarner(5) 97
(Martin Bosley) *hld up wl in tch in last trio: effrt u.p and sme hdwy after 3 out: no ex 2 out: wknd bef last* **33/1**
05F- **7** 3¾ **Bathcounty (IRE)**32 1938 6-10-8 **104** SamTwiston-Davies 90
(Barry Brennan) *chsd ldr tl after 4th: drvn and struggling bef 3 out: wknd bef 2 out* **10/1**
/40- **8** 1¼ **King Zeal (IRE)**17 2198 9-10-6 **102** (t) LiamHeard 86
(Barry Leavy) *in tch in midfield: effrt u.p 3 out: sn no imp: wknd next* **80/1**
P1/- **9** *16* **Santo Thomas (FR)**553 262 7-11-0 **110** AidanColeman 80
(Venetia Williams) *chsd ldrs: rdn and no rspnse 3 out: sn wknd: bhd and eased flat: t.o* **16/1**
0- **10** 1¼ **Heurtevent (FR)**23 2087 4-11-6 **116** LeeEdwards 85
(Tony Carroll) *hld up wl in tch towards rr: hdwy to chse ldrs 4th: wnt 2nd after 5th tl mstke 3 out: sn wknd: t.o* **100/1**
521- **11** ¾ **Ashdown Lad**14 2272 4-11-10 **120** FelixDeGiles 88
(Tom Symonds) *wl in tch: dropped to rr and nt fluent 4th: hit next and sn rdn: wknd bef 2 out: t.o* **10/1**

3m 46.25s (-14.75) **Going Correction** -0.725s/f (Firm) **11** Ran SP% **114.5**
Speed ratings (Par 107): **107,106,105,100,97 97,95,94,86,86 85**
toteswingers 1&2 £3.40, 1&3 £4.90, 2&3 £8.80 CSF £15.94 CT £90.78 TOTE £3.80: £1.10, £1.80, £3.30; EX 16.20 Trifecta £152.70 Pool: £3245.37 - 15.93 winning units..
Owner Paul Downing **Bred** His Highness The Aga Khan's Studs S C **Trained** Portway, Worcs
■ Stewards' Enquiry : Robert McCarth three-day ban: used whip without giving gelding time to respond (Dec 4-6)

FOCUS
A fair handicap. The pace didn't look that strong until past halfway but it was much the fastest of the hurdle races. The winner was on a good mark and there is probably a bit more to come.

2562 CASTLE CONDITIONAL JOCKEYS' H'CAP CHASE (15 fncs) 2m 4f 110y
3:10 (3:10) (Class 5) (0-95,94) 4-Y-0+ **£2,599** (£763; £381; £190)

Form RPR
621- **1** **Mr Bachster (IRE)**25 2044 8-10-10 **78** JakeGreenall 93+
(Richard Lee) *chsd ldng trio tl led after 11th: mde rest: rdn after 2 out: kpt on and a holding rival flat: rdn out* **3/1**2
434- **2** *1* **Tinelyra (IRE)**25 2039 7-10-10 **84** (t¹) ConorShoemark(6) 97
(Fergal O'Brien) *in tch in rr: hdwy 9th: rdn after 11th: chsd wnr bef next: drvn and pressing wnr 2 out: kpt on same pce and a hld flat* **5/4**1
/45- **3** *26* **Rebel High (IRE)**12 2295 9-11-8 **90** NicodeBoinville 80
(Derek Frankland) *chsd ldrs: rdn and outpcd bef 12th: chsd ldng pair 3 out: no imp: wknd and wl btn whn j.lft last* **12/1**
02U- **4** 2¼ **Cara Court (IRE)**25 2047 7-11-2 **89** (p) CallumBewley(5) 77
(Joanne Foster) *led after 1st tl 10th: drvn and struggling bef 12th: wknd after 3 out: wl hld but plugged on flat* **6/1**3
P40- **5** *25* **Vertueux (FR)**25 2039 8-10-13 **84** (p) JoshHamer(3) 49
(Tony Carroll) *nt fluent: hld up in last trio: reminder after 3rd: hdwy 9th: chsd ldrs whn j. awkwardly 11th: sn rdn and wknd: eased briefly after 2 out: t.o* **16/1**
553- **6** 2½ **Peak Seasons (IRE)**8 2396 10-10-13 **81** JoeCornwall 44
(Michael Chapman) *a last trio: rdn after 5th: lost tch bef 12th: no ch fr 3 out: t.o* **20/1**
00S- **7** ¾ **Prickles**25 2039 8-11-12 **94** (p) MichealNolan 56
(Richard Woollacott) *t.k.h: led tl after 1st: styd pressing ldr tl led 10th: hdd after next and sn rdn: btn bef 3 out: fdd fr 2 out: t.o* **33/1**
622- **8** *7* **Finch Flyer (IRE)**10 2349 6-10-7 **75** (p) HarryDerham 31
(Aytach Sadik) *racd in midfield: rdn and struggling whn j. slowly 10th: lost tch bef next: t.o* **10/1**

5m 8.5s (-10.40) **Going Correction** -0.40s/f (Good) course record **8** Ran SP% **114.1**
Speed ratings (Par 103): **103,102,92,91,82 81,81,78**
toteswingers 1&2 £1.30, 1&3 £6.80, 2&3 £3.50 CSF £7.49 CT £35.75 TOTE £4.40: £2.40, £1.10, £2.10; EX 9.80 Trifecta £42.20 Pool: £3203.26 - 56.83 winning units..
Owner Richard Lee **Bred** Mrs Anne Caplice **Trained** Byton, H'fords

FOCUS
Ordinary fare, though worth viewing the performances of the leading pair, who pulled well clear, in a positive light. The winner improved to the level of his old hurdle form.

2563 BURTON OVERY NOVICES' HURDLE (8 hdls) 2m
3:40 (3:40) (Class 4) 4-Y-0+ **£3,898** (£1,144; £572; £286)

Form RPR
1 **Dubai Prince (IRE)**451 5-10-12 0 DenisO'Regan 125+
(John Ferguson) *hld up wl in tch: hdwy to trck ldrs on bit after 5th: led 2 out and sn wnt clr on bit: nt extended: v easily* **8/11**1
3/3- **2** *6* **Algernon Pazham (IRE)**183 395 4-10-12 0 SamTwiston-Davies 110
(Nigel Twiston-Davies) *t.k.h: hld up wl in tch in midfield: pckd 2nd: hdwy to join ldrs 5th: led next but jnd by wnr: hdd 2 out and sn brushed aside by wnr: mstke last: kpt on for 2nd flat* **6/1**3
045- **3** 3¾ **Ballygrooby Bertie (IRE)**14 2265 5-10-12 0 (t) PaddyBrennan 105
(Fergal O'Brien) *t.k.h: chsd ldrs: rdn and effrt to chse ldrs 2 out: no threat to wnr and styd on same pce after: mstke last* **4/1**2
0- **4** *2* **Join The Clan (IRE)**14 2265 4-10-7 0 MauriceLinehan(5) 104+
(Jonjo O'Neill) *wl in tch in last quartet: j. slowly 5th: rdn and sme hdwy bef 2 out: wnt 4th between last 2: kpt on: nvr trbld ldrs* **50/1**
0- **5** *7* **Great Link**34 1915 4-11-0 115 (t) JoshHamer(5) 105+
(Tony Carroll) *t.k.h: chsd ldrs: rdn 3 out: btn whn mstke next: wknd between last 2* **33/1**
500/ **6** 1¾ **Whileaway (USA)**218 5317 4-10-7 0 (t) JamesBanks(5) 94
(Andy Turnell) *t.k.h: w ldr tl led 5th: hdd next: rdn and btn whn mstke 2 out: sn wknd* **100/1**
P/ **7** *8* **Catching On (IRE)**345 2926 5-10-12 0 RichieMcLernon 86
(Jonjo O'Neill) *led and set stdy gallop tl hdd 5th: sn rdn and lost pl: wknd after next* **13/2**
0/0- **8** *12* **Elixir Du Lac**163 671 6-10-5 0 DominicElsworth 67
(Jo Davis) *wl in tch in midfield on outer: j. slowly 5th: rdn and wknd 3 out: t.o* **100/1**
0- **9** *hd* **Brasingaman Espee**23 2075 4-10-12 0 BarryKeniry 74
(George Moore) *t.k.h: hld up wl in tch in midfield: rdn 3 out: sn btn and wknd bef next: t.o* **100/1**
10 *19* **Grandad Mac**459 5-10-12 0 JamesDavies 55
(Alan Coogan) *t.k.h: hld up wl in tch in midfield: sltly hmpd 1st: rdn and struggling bef 3 out: sn wknd: t.o* **50/1**
6U0/ **11** 4½ **Midnight Return (IRE)**628 4572 7-10-0 0 HarryChalloner(5) 44
(Richard Ford) *wl in tch in midfield: dropped to rr 5th: rdn and lost tch bef next: t.o* **200/1**
U **The Yank**74 4-10-12 0 LeeEdwards
(Tony Carroll) *t.k.h: hld up wl in tch in rr tl blnd and uns rdr 4th* **66/1**

3m 54.4s (-6.60) **Going Correction** -0.725s/f (Firm) **12** Ran SP% **117.3**
Speed ratings (Par 105): **87,84,82,81,77 76,72,66,66,57 54,**
toteswingers 1&2 £2.20, 1&3 £1.40, 2&3 £3.10 CSF £5.71 TOTE £2.00: £1.10, £2.20, £1.40; EX 7.20 Trifecta £13.00 Pool: £4093.77 - 234.51 winning units..
Owner Bloomfields **Bred** Mrs Eithne Hamilton **Trained** Cowlinge, Suffolk
■ Stewards' Enquiry : Maurice Linehan 14-day ban: failed to take all reasonable and permissable measures to obtain best possible placing (Dec 2-15)

FOCUS
No depth to this novice but the winner looks a smart recruit. The time was slow and a few may have been flattered.
T/Plt: £4.70 to a £1 stake. Pool: £64805.73 - 9978.80 winning tickets T/Qpdt: £4.90 to a £1 stake. Pool: £5221.10 - 775.50 winning tickets SP

2272 PLUMPTON (L-H)
Monday, November 18

OFFICIAL GOING: Good to soft (soft in places; hdl 6.4, chs 6.5)
Wind: Almost nil Weather: Very overcast

2564 CALL STAR SPORTS 08000 521 321 NOVICES' HURDLE (9 hdls) 2m
12:50 (12:51) (Class 4) 4-Y-0+ **£3,249** (£954; £477; £238)

Form RPR
2/2- **1** **Regal Encore (IRE)**23 2075 5-10-12 0 APMcCoy 127+
(Anthony Honeyball) *hld up in rr early: prog 5th: trckd clr ldr bef 3 out: clsd and on terms 2 out: led last: nt extended* **1/9**1
6/5- **2** 1¾ **Saffron Prince**23 2083 5-10-12 0 TomScudamore 108
(David Bridgwater) *led: drew clr 6th: 10 l up 3 out: c bk to wnr 2 out: hdd and blnd last: kpt on but no ch* **7/1**2
3 *9* **Mr Spiggott (IRE)**28 4-10-9 0 JoshuaMoore(3) 96
(Gary Moore) *hld up: prog fr 6th: chsd clr ldng pair after 3 out: shkn up and kpt on same pce* **8/1**3
4 *2* **Sudden Wish (IRE)**41 4-10-5 0 JamieMoore 89
(Gary Moore) *in rr whn blnd 5th: prog 3 out: kpt on to take 4th and mstke 2 out: n.d* **10/1**
0- **5** 1½ **Mariet**14 2265 4-10-2 0 WayneKavanagh(3) 87
(Suzy Smith) *mstkes: hld up in rr: prog after 6th: j.rt 3 out: rdn and no imp on ldrs bef next* **28/1**
500- **6** *7* **Slaney Star (IRE)**14 2272 5-10-12 0 MattieBatchelor 89+
(Jim Best) *nt fluent: dropped to last and mstke 4th: light reminders after next: lost tch 6th: passed wkng rivals after 3 out: nvr involved* **33/1**
600- **7** *13* **Top Chief**28 2002 5-10-12 0 ConorO'Farrell 73
(Mark Rimell) *chsd ldrs to 6th: wknd 3 out* **33/1**
000/ **8** *2* **Sweet Boy Vic (IRE)**218 5317 5-10-12 0 MarcGoldstein 71
(Chris Gordon) *chsd ldrs to 5th: wknd and bhd fr next* **50/1**
500- **9** 2¾ **Forget And Forgive (IRE)**9 2369 5-10-12 0 PaulMoloney 68
(Anthony Middleton) *j. slowly 1st: prom in chsng gp: wknd qckly after 3 out* **40/1**

0- 10 *nk* **Two Sugars**[14] 2272 5-10-12 0 .... TomCannon 69
(Laura Mongan) *chsd ldr tl after 6th: wknd qckly* **40/1**
4m 3.5s (2.70) **Going Correction** +0.30s/f (Yiel)
WFA 4 from 5yo 7lb **10** Ran SP% **138.9**
Speed ratings (Par 105): **105,104,99,98,97 94,87,86,85,85**
toteswingers 1&2 £1.10, 1&3 £1.10, 2&3 £4.10 CSF £2.97 TOTE £1.10: £1.02, £1.60, £1.80; EX 2.50 Trifecta £6.50 Pool: £1742.31 - 198.22 winning units..
Owner John P McManus **Bred** John Browne **Trained** Mosterton, Dorset

FOCUS
An effortless win for Regal Encore, who was value for a lot further and is a potential 140+ novice hurdler.

2565 SIS LIVE NOVICES' CHASE (14 fncs) 2m 4f
1:20 (1:20) (Class 3) 4-Y-O+ **£6,498** (£1,908; £954; £477)

Form RPR
5/1- 1 **Uxizandre (FR)**[28] 2005 5-11-8 142 .... APMcCoy 153+
(Alan King) *mde most: j.lft 5th: drew clr after 3 out: nt fluent 2 out: easily* **8/11**[1]

0/3- 2 *17* **Funny Star (FR)**[27] 2012 5-11-1 132 .... (t) DarylJacob 128
(Paul Nicholls) *cl up: pressed wnr fr 9th tl rdn and one pce after 3 out* **2/1**[2]

222- 3 *34* **Hi Note**[15] 2249 5-10-8 0 .... MarcGoldstein 100
(Sheena West) *cl up: mstke 8th and reminders: rdn after next: wknd bef 4 out: lft poor 3rd and hmpd 2 out* **8/1**[3]

201/ 4 *18* **Bangkok Pete (IRE)**[1309] 5287 8-10-12 0 .... JeremiahMcGrath(3) 82
(Jamie Poulton) *a in last pair: rdn and lost tch after 8th: mstke 10th: lft remote 4th 2 out* **50/1**

0/F- F **Minella Definitely (IRE)**[16] 2211 6-10-12 128 .... (p) MichaelByrne(3) 116
(Neil Mulholland) *pressed wnr: led briefly 3rd: on terms whn mstke 9th: rdn and lft bhd fr next: plugging on in 12 l 3rd whn fell 2 out* **16/1**

5m 5.2s (-2.10) **Going Correction** +0.175s/f (Yiel) **5** Ran SP% **110.2**
Speed ratings (Par 107): **111,104,90,83,**
CSF £2.68 TOTE £1.60: £1.30, £1.50; EX 2.50 Trifecta £3.70 Pool: £2040.11 - 412.49 winning units..
Owner John P McManus **Bred** Frederic Aimez **Trained** Barbury Castle, Wilts

FOCUS
A fair novice chase and an impressive winner, who looks a smart novice.

2566 FOLLOW US ON TWITTER @STARSPORTS_BET "NATIONAL HUNT" NOVICES' HURDLE (12 hdls) 2m 5f
1:50 (1:50) (Class 4) 4-Y-O+ **£3,249** (£954; £477; £238)

Form RPR
3- 1 **Wither Yenot (IRE)**[27] 2009 6-10-5 0 .... MrMJPKendrick(7) 114+
(Ben Case) *cl up: nt fluent 8th: chsd ldr after 3 out: hld whn lft in ld 2 out: hung rt flat: urged along and hld on* **12/1**[3]

2 *3/4* **V Neck (IRE)**[183] 4-10-12 0 .... APMcCoy 112+
(Paul Nicholls) *tk fierce hold early: hld up: clsd up 9th: trckd ldr briefly 3 out: sn pushed along: hld whn lft in 2nd 2 out: chal and mstke last: hung lft flat: nt qckn* **6/4**[2]

23P/ 3 *4* **Grace And Fortune**[231] 5081 6-10-5 110 .... LeightonAspell 101
(Richard Rowe) *tended to jump rt: w ldr to 3 out: sn outpcd and dropped to 5th: lft modest 3rd 2 out: styd on quite wl after* **25/1**

30- 4 *19* **Blue Bear (IRE)**[28] 2002 4-10-12 0 .... MarcGoldstein 89
(Diana Grissell) *cl up: nt fluent 5th: stl wl there 3 out: wknd rapidly* **66/1**

0/2- F **Carole's Destrier**[29] 1991 5-10-12 0 .... NoelFehily 120+
(Neil Mulholland) *mde most at mod pce: asserted after 3 out: 4 l up and in command whn fell heavily 2 out* **5/6**[1]

/35- P **Tigridia (IRE)**[160] 706 6-10-5 0 .... GerardTumelty
(Sarah Wall) *hld up: mstkes 2nd and 6th: lost tch 9th: wl bhd whn p.u bef 2 out* **100/1**

P **Oh So High (IRE)** 4-10-5 0 .... ConorO'Farrell
(Liam Corcoran) *a in rr: mstke 7th and reminders: sn bhd: t.o whn p.u bef 2 out* **100/1**

5m 27.8s (10.80) **Going Correction** +0.30s/f (Yiel) **7** Ran SP% **109.6**
Speed ratings (Par 105): **91,90,89,81, ,**
toteswingers 1&2 £2.30, 1&3 £3.20, 2&3 £4.00 CSF £28.87 TOTE £16.30: £3.30, £1.30; EX 41.10 Trifecta £124.70 Pool: £2559.90 - 15.39 winning units..
Owner Mrs Carolyn Kendrick **Bred** Mrs Gillian Vaughan **Trained** Edgcote, Northants
■ Max Kendrick's first winner under rules.

FOCUS
A dramatic novice event and a fortunate winner as Carole's Destrier was heading for a comfortable win.

2567 RON RUDOLPH 70TH BIRTHDAY H'CAP CHASE (14 fncs) 2m 4f
2:20 (2:20) (Class 4) (0-120,120) 4-Y-O+ **£5,523** (£1,621; £810; £405)

Form RPR
/12- 1 **Beforeall (IRE)**[11] 2315 5-11-1 109 .... LeightonAspell 115+
(Oliver Sherwood) *chsd ldr: chal 3 out: rdn to ld bef 2 out: drew clr fr last* **5/2**[1]

UP3- 2 *7* **Venetian Lad**[26] 2017 8-10-13 107 .... MarcGoldstein 106
(Lydia Richards) *hld up in tch: trckd ldng pair 9th: rdn 3 out: wnt 2nd 2 out: one pce after* **16/1**

P06/ 3 *3 1/4* **Carpincho (FR)**[212] 5411 9-11-0 111 .... JackQuinlan(3) 108+
(Sarah Humphrey) *j.w: led: pressed 3 out: hdd and shkn up bef 2 out: nt qckn and sn wl hld in 3rd* **9/2**[3]

123- 4 *26* **Upton Mead (IRE)**[9] 2370 6-10-9 103 .... (b) RichardJohnson 76
(Kevin Tork) *in tch: chsd ldng trio after 9th: sn drvn: no imp 4 out: wknd next: fin tired* **5/1**

/22- 5 *14* **Plum Pudding (FR)**[24] 2067 10-10-11 105 .... (b[1]) TomScudamore 65
(David Bridgwater) *prom: mstke 8th: wknd fr next: t.o* **11/4**[2]

OPP/ 6 *3 1/2* **Reblis (FR)**[216] 5329 8-11-0 111 .... JoshuaMoore(3) 68
(Gary Moore) *j. stickily: in tch: drvn and struggling after 8th: bhd fr 4 out: t.o* **8/1**

/0P- P **Nozic (FR)**[9] 2365 12-11-12 120 .... (p) LiamTreadwell
(Zoe Davison) *a in rr: drvn and struggling after 8th: t.o whn p.u after 10th* **20/1**

5m 10.0s (2.70) **Going Correction** +0.175s/f (Yiel) **7** Ran SP% **111.8**
Speed ratings (Par 105): **101,98,96,86,80 79,**
toteswingers 1&2 £4.20, 1&3 £3.40, 2&3 £12.50 CSF £34.26 TOTE £3.50: £1.50, £4.60; EX 42.50 Trifecta £347.90 Pool: £1531.62 - 3.30 winning units..
Owner Beforeall Partnership **Bred** Ms Barbara Johnston **Trained** Upper Lambourn, Berks

FOCUS
Fair form for the class and the winner is on the upgrade.

2568 ANISE CATERING H'CAP HURDLE (10 hdls) 2m 2f
2:50 (2:52) (Class 5) (0-100,100) 4-Y-O+ **£2,053** (£598; £299)

Form RPR
0/0- 1 **The Game Is A Foot (IRE)**[176] 488 6-11-4 95 .... JoshuaMoore(3) 107+
(Gary Moore) *hld up in rr: stdy prog after 6th: led sn after 3 out and rdn clr: drvn out* **4/1**[1]

4/3- 2 *10* **Superciliary**[23] 1711 4-11-10 98 .... TomCannon 102
(Chris Gordon) *hld up towards rr: stdy prog after 6th: rdn and outpcd sn after 3 out: wnt 2nd bef 2 out: styd on and clr of rest but no ch w wnr* **8/1**[3]

4F5/ 3 *13* **Our Phylli Vera (IRE)**[24] 5119 4-11-4 92 .... WayneHutchinson 83
(Alan King) *hld up in rr: stdy prog after 6th: rdn and outpcd after 3 out: kpt on to take 3rd 2 out: n.d* **4/1**[1]

4/3- 4 *6* **Mighty Mambo**[26] 2016 6-11-5 93 .... DavidBass 79
(Lawney Hill) *wl plcd: trckd ldng pair 6th: on terms after 3 out: wknd bef next* **9/2**[2]

200- 5 *2 3/4* **Ashcott Boy**[28] 2004 5-11-6 94 .... (b[1]) NoelFehily 78
(Neil Mulholland) *w ldr: led briefly 3 out: sn lft bhd: fdd fr 2 out* **11/1**

4/0- 6 *1* **Rosoff (IRE)**[176] 489 11-9-9 79 .... (p) NathanAdams(10) 62
(Laura Mongan) *in tch: lost pl qckly u.p bef 7th: sn no ch: plugged on again fr 2 out* **20/1**

/02- 7 *26* **Definite Lady (IRE)**[157] 738 7-11-8 96 .... TomScudamore 55
(Mark Rimell) *mstke 2nd: a in rr: lost tch after 6th: t.o fr next* **12/1**

/64- 8 *1 1/2* **Ibiza Sunset (IRE)**[55] 1641 5-11-1 89 .... (t) BrendanPowell 47
(Brendan Powell) *racd wd: hld up in rr: sme prog and in tch w ldrs after 7th: shkn up and wknd qckly after 3 out: t.o* **8/1**[3]

006- 9 *2* **Cool Fantasy (IRE)**[23] 2083 4-10-6 80 .... IanPopham 36
(Caroline Keevil) *dropped to rr 3rd: rdn and struggling after 5th: t.o fr 7th* **16/1**

35P- 10 *6* **Airedale Lad (IRE)**[81] 1438 12-9-7 74 oh9 .... (p) MrJoshuaNewman(7) 25
(Zoe Davison) *chsd ldrs to 4th: sn wknd u.p: t.o fr 7th* **66/1**

231/ 11 *33* **Goochypoochyprader**[221] 5243 6-11-12 100 .... (t) GerardTumelty 21
(Nick Lampard) *reluctant to line up: led in s and rel to r: prog fr last to chse ldng pair 3rd: lost pl 6th: wknd after next: t.o* **10/1**

353- P **Illegale (IRE)**[19] 1479 7-10-0 77 oh3 ow3 .... (t) RobertDunne(3)
(Nikki Evans) *mde most to 3 out: sn btn: 6th and wkng whn p.u bef 2 out* **25/1**

4m 35.4s (4.50) **Going Correction** +0.30s/f (Yiel)
WFA 4 from 5yo+ 7lb **12** Ran SP% **121.5**
Speed ratings (Par 103): **102,97,91,89,87 87,75,75,74,71 57,**
toteswingers 1&2 £9.30, 1&3 £5.50, 2&3 £10.10 CSF £36.63 CT £139.77 TOTE £5.10: £2.40, £2.80, £2.00; EX 46.50 Trifecta £263.30 Pool: £1483.10 - 4.22 winning units..
Owner G L Moore **Bred** Fintina Kealey & Irene Giles **Trained** Lower Beeding, W Sussex

FOCUS
A moderate handicap won by a progressive sort, who took a big step forward.

2569 SICAME UK AMATEUR RIDERS' H'CAP HURDLE (12 hdls) 2m 5f
3:20 (3:20) (Class 4) (0-120,118) 4-Y-O+ **£3,743** (£1,161; £580; £290)

Form RPR
6F1- 1 **Invicta Lake (IRE)**[22] 2105 6-11-3 114 .... (p) MrHAABannister(5) 117+
(Suzy Smith) *hld up in 5th: prog to trck ldr 3 out: led bef 2 out: rdn and styd on wl fr last* **11/4**[1]

612/ 2 *3* **Henryville**[211] 5438 5-11-12 118 .... MrWBiddick 119
(Harry Fry) *hld up in last in slowly run event: prog 3 out: chsd wnr 2 out: cl enough whn hit last: nt qckn* **11/4**[1]

022- 3 *1 1/4* **Auld Sthock (IRE)**[14] 2272 5-11-4 117 .... MrGGorman(7) 117
(Gary Moore) *trcked ldr 3rd to 5th: lost pl 3 out but stl gng wl: wnt 3rd 2 out: cl enough whn mstke last and rdr clinging on: nt qckn* **7/2**[2]

0/P- 4 *13* **King Ozzy (IRE)**[43] 1783 9-11-3 109 .... (tp) MissGAndrews 97
(Lawney Hill) *led at sedate pce: fnlly kicked on fr 9th: hdd & wknd bef 2 out* **25/1**

5 *7* **Cru Classe (FR)**[31] 7-10-3 95 ow3 .... (t) MrCCoste 74
(F Lagarde, France) *trckd ldr to 3rd: outpcd and struggling in last 3 out: no ch after* **7/2**[2]

4/0- 6 *13* **Arrayan**[202] 48 8-11-0 113 .... MrGBall(7) 79
(Alexandra Dunn) *t.k.h: clattered into many hurdles w rdr unbalanced: hld up tl trckd ldr 5th: lost pl and wknd 3 out* **10/1**[3]

5m 39.1s (22.10) **Going Correction** +0.30s/f (Yiel) **6** Ran SP% **110.7**
Speed ratings (Par 105): **69,67,67,62,59 54**
toteswingers 1&2 £1.90, 1&3 £2.10, 2&3 £2.60 CSF £10.65 TOTE £3.20: £1.50, £1.80; EX 11.50 Trifecta £21.00 Pool: £2144.93 - 76.55 winning units..
Owner Bernard & Jan Wolford **Bred** Patrick Doyle **Trained** Lewes, E Sussex

FOCUS
A modest handicap, confined to amateur riders. It was a very steadily run affair, and the form is suspect.

2570 SW CATERING STANDARD OPEN NATIONAL HUNT FLAT RACE 2m 2f
3:50 (3:50) (Class 6) 4-6-Y-O **£1,711** (£498; £249)

Form RPR
1 **Tullyesker Hill (IRE)**[196] 4-11-2 0 .... TomScudamore 120+
(David Pipe) *mde all: stepped on it fr 7f out: shkn up and drew rt away fr 3f out* **11/8**[1]

43- 2 *15* **Another Brandy (IRE)**[38] 1861 5-11-2 0 .... NoelFehily 103
(Neil Mulholland) *cl up: chsd wnr 8f out: rdn 3f out: sn lft bhd* **2/1**[2]

10/ 3 *2* **Come On Laurie (IRE)**[260] 4542 5-11-9 0 .... DavidBass 108
(Lawney Hill) *prom: chsd wnr after 8f to 8f out: shoved along and outpcd over 6f out: kpt on to take 3rd 3f out: one pce after* **7/1**[3]

4 *7* **Snippetydoodah** 5-10-9 0 .... TomO'Brien 88
(Michael Roberts) *in tch: chsd ldng pair 6f out to 3f out: wknd* **22/1**

5 *7* **Double U Dot Ede'S** 4-10-6 0 .... PaddyBradley(10) 89
(Pat Phelan) *hld up in last trio: rn green and lost tch 7f out: sn bhd: plugged on fnl 2f* **8/1**

5- 6 *1* **Frank N Fair**[26] 2022 5-10-9 0 .... DaveCrosse 81
(Zoe Davison) *t.k.h: hld up in last trio: prog to dispute 3rd 6f out: wknd over 3f out* **33/1**

5- 7 *19* **Buckboru (IRE)**[26] 2026 5-10-9 0 .... TomCannon 64
(Laura Young) *hld up in last trio: shkn up and lost tch 6f out: sn bhd* **50/1**

6- 8 *51* **Larks Rising**[170] 588 5-11-2 0 .... IanPopham 25
(Caroline Keevil) *t.k.h: hld up: in tch 6f out: sn wknd rapidly: t.o* **14/1**

9 *99* **Catch The Katt** 6-10-9 0 .... GerardTumelty
(Richard Mitchell) *chsd wnr 8f: wknd rapidly u.p and sn wl t.o: eventually completed* **50/1**

4m 32.4s (7.10) **Going Correction** +0.30s/f (Yiel)
WFA 4 from 5yo+ 7lb **9** Ran SP% **116.9**
Speed ratings: **96,89,88,85,82 81,73,50,6**
toteswingers 1&2 £1.10, 1&3 £2.40, 2&3 £3.30 CSF £4.16 TOTE £1.80: £1.10, £1.20, £1.90; EX 5.50 Trifecta £9.40 Pool: £3664.86 - 289.57 winning units..
Owner Bryan Drew **Bred** Miss Patricia McGlynn **Trained** Nicholashayne, Devon

FOCUS
A fair little bumper for the track and the impressive winner looks a smart prospect.
T/Plt: £18.50 to a £1 stake. Pool: £73408.31 - 2886.10 winning tickets T/Qpdt: £15.80 to a £1 stake. Pool: £4912.10 - 229.15 winning tickets JN

2062 FAKENHAM (L-H)
Tuesday, November 19

OFFICIAL GOING: Good to soft (6.7) changing to good to soft (soft in places) after race 5 (3.00)
Wind: medium, against Weather: showers, chilly

2571 BET TOTEJACKPOT (S) H'CAP HURDLE (11 hdls) 2m 4f
1:00 (1:00) (Class 5) (0-95,95) 3-Y-0+ **£2,053** (£598; £299)

Form RPR

003- **1** **Ruby Valentine (FR)**[39] 1860 10-10-1 **70** .... LiamTreadwell 77
(Jim Wilson) *in tch in midfield: hdwy to chse ldr 7th: ev ch 3 out: led bef next and sn clr: pushed out: comf* **10/1**[3]

FF4- **2** *6* **Monroe Park (IRE)**[25] 2062 8-10-1 **77** ow3 .... (p) JosephAkehurst[(7)] 77
(Alan Blackmore) *chsd ldrs tl led 6th: clr w wnr bef 3 out: hdd bef 2 out and sn brushed aside by wnr: kpt on for clr 2nd* **25/1**

P05- **3** *7* **Pennant Dancer**[40] 1837 6-9-11 **69** oh10 .... (tp) TrevorWhelan[(3)] 64
(Debra Hamer) *hld up in last pair: mstke 4th and 7th: rdn 8th: modest 4th next: chsd ldng pair 2 out: no imp* **16/1**

P60- **4** *12* **Arguidos (IRE)**[37] 1887 9-11-2 **90** .... AodhaganConlon[(5)] 73
(Debra Hamer) *chsd ldr tl 8th: sn u.p and flashed tail: 3rd and outpcd bef 3 out: wknd bef 2 out* **16/1**

132- **5** *5* **Tribal Dance (IRE)**[5] 2470 7-11-5 **95** .... CiaranMckee[(7)] 73
(John O'Shea) *led tl mstke and hdd 5th: nvr gng wl after: rdn and lost tch 8th: wl bhd next* **1/1**[1]

PP4- **6** *26* **Caught By Witness (IRE)**[19] 2175 8-11-2 **85** .... (t) PaulMoloney 40
(Anthony Middleton) *hld up in tch in rr: short-lived effrt after 7th: sn struggling and wl btn 3 out: t.o and eased flat* **3/1**[2]

/06- **7** *36* **Mon Homme**[142] 847 6-11-6 **89** .... RichardJohnson 11
(Mark Rimell) *in tch in midfield: dropped to last after 6th: rdn bef 8th and sn lost tch: t.o 3 out* **10/1**[3]

5m 27.9s (15.30) **Going Correction** +0.80s/f (Soft) **7** Ran SP% **108.8**
Speed ratings (Par 103): **101,98,95,91,89 78,64**
toteswingers 1&2 £16.20, 2&3 £18.20, 1&3 £18.20 CSF £159.61 TOTE £7.40: £3.40, £6.20; EX 152.10 Trifecta £833.50 Part won. Pool of £1111.37 - 0.12 winning units..There was no bid for the winner.
Owner The Winbledon Partnership **Bred** Earl Elevage De La Source **Trained** Ham, Gloucs

FOCUS
A weak handicap.

2572 SIS MARES' H'CAP CHASE (18 fncs) 3m 110y
1:30 (1:30) (Class 4) (0-120,110) 4-Y-0+ **£4,533** (£1,550)

Form RPR

542- **1** **Tea Caddy**[11] 2348 7-11-7 **105** .... TomO'Brien 106+
(Jamie Snowden) *j.rt: led: mstke 2 out: sn rdn: hdd and briefly outpcd: rallied u.p to ld again last: gng clr whn hung rt and idled fnl 100yds: pushed out* **11/10**[1]

0/5- **2** *5* **A Little Swifter (IRE)**[11] 2352 7-11-9 **110** .... TrevorWhelan[(3)] 107
(Neil King) *lft chsng wnr and hmpd 2nd: mstke 6th: pressed wnr 12th: led and rdn 2 l clr after 2 out: hdd last: no ex and wknd fnl 100yds* **4/1**[3]

531- **F** **Midnight Macarena**[8] 2424 8-11-7 **110** 7ex .... (p) MattCrawley[(5)]
(Lucy Wadham) *chsd wnr tl fell 2nd* **6/4**[2]

6m 49.5s (13.80) **Going Correction** +0.225s/f (Yiel) **3** Ran SP% **107.6**
Speed ratings (Par 105): **86,84,**
CSF £4.89 TOTE £2.00; EX 3.10 Trifecta £4.80 Pool: £408.00 - 63.59 winning units..
Owner R Matthews **Bred** Richard Matthews **Trained** Lambourn, Berks

FOCUS
This was reduced to a match when recent scorer Midnight Macarena came down at the second, and after a prolonged tussle, it was Tea Caddy who came out on top.

2573 YOKOHAMA TYRES NOVICES' H'CAP HURDLE (9 hdls) 2m
2:00 (2:01) (Class 4) (0-105,104) 3-Y-0+ **£3,249** (£954; £477; £238)

Form RPR

131- **1** **Persian Herald**[1] 2559 5-11-8 **103** 7ex .... (bt) TrevorWhelan[(3)] 108
(Neil King) *led tl hdd sn after 5th sn u.p and dropped to last but stl wl in tch next: rallied to go 3rd 2 out: led jst bef last: gd jump to go clr: styd on: rdn out* **2/1**[2]

/0F- **2** *2 ¼* **Watt Broderick (IRE)**[13] 2292 4-11-4 **101** .... (t) RobertMcCarth[(5)] 105
(Ian Williams) *t.k.h: hld up off the pce in last: clsd and in tch 4th: trckd ldr after 3 out tl led between last 2: rdn and hdd jst bef last: outj. last and sn btn: one pce* **7/4**[1]

56P- **3** *10* **Volcanic Jack (IRE)**[7] 2432 5-10-8 **91** .... JoeCornwall[(5)] 85
(Michael Chapman) *hld up off the pce in 3rd: clsd to chse ldrs 4th: led on inner after 6th: rdn bef 2 out: hdd between last 2: wknd qckly last* **14/1**

/05- **4** *3 ¼* **Rule Of Thumb**[23] 2109 5-11-12 **104** .... (t) TomO'Brien 95
(Paul Henderson) *hld up off the pce in last trio: clsd and in tch 4th: chsd ldrs and rdn after 3 out: outpcd and btn next: wknd between last 2* **9/4**[3]

000- **5** *14* **Mac's Grey (IRE)**[29] 2008 6-10-0 **78** oh2 .... (t[1]) GerardTumelty 58
(Zoe Davison) *chsd ldr: blnd 3 out: rdn and btn bef next: wknd sn after 2 out* **25/1**

4m 21.0s (15.60) **Going Correction** +0.80s/f (Soft)
WFA 4 from 5yo+ 7lb **5** Ran SP% **111.0**
Speed ratings (Par 105): **93,91,86,85,78**
CSF £6.17 TOTE £3.00: £1.90, £1.10; EX 6.80 Trifecta £11.80 Pool: £1463.12 - 92.64 winning units..
Owner The St Gatien Racing For Fun Partnership **Bred** J W P Clark **Trained** Newmarket, Suffolk
■ Stewards' Enquiry : Robert McCarth one-day ban: careless riding (Dec 8)

FOCUS
Changing fortunes late on in this uncompetitive handicap, with Watt Broderick, who went on looking certain to score (hit 1.13 on Betfair) being run down in the straight by rallying early leader Persian Herald.

2574 AT THE RACES NOVICES' LIMITED H'CAP CHASE (16 fncs) 2m 5f 110y
2:30 (2:30) (Class 3) (0-140,138) 4-Y-0+ **£7,322** (£2,273; £1,224)

Form RPR

3/1- **1** **King Of The Wolds (IRE)**[19] 2171 6-10-11 **130** .... BrianHughes 136+
(Malcolm Jefferson) *j.w: mde all: pressed 2 out: rdn and wnt 2 l clr between last 2: pressed again whn mstke: rdr lost iron and lft wl clr last* **5/4**[2]

2PP- **2** *64* **Flichity (IRE)**[8] 2425 8-10-0 **124** oh51 .... JoeCornwall[(5)] 72
(John Cornwall) *a bhd: j. slowly 1st: rdn and lost tch after 11th: t.o 13th: lft poor 2nd last* **100/1**

223- **3** *20* **Hunting Tower**[39] 1851 9-10-13 **132** .... (t) RichardJohnson 62
(Tim Vaughan) *nt a fluent: chsd wnr tl 4th: mstke 10th: hit next: rdn and losing tch whn mstke 13th: t.o bef 2 out: lft poor 3rd last* **8/1**[3]

250- **F** **Occasionally Yours (IRE)**[10] 2362 9-10-5 **124** oh13 .... DavidBass
(Alan Blackmore) *hld up in last pair: in tch tl fell 10th* **33/1**

/1U- **U** **Dursey Sound (IRE)**[9] 2395 5-11-5 **138** .... (p) APMcCoy 144+
(Jonjo O'Neill) *chsd wnr 4th: drvn to press wnr 2 out: sltly outpcd 2 l down beween last 2: swtchd rt and rallied to chal whn blnd and uns rdr last* **10/11**[1]

5m 41.15s (-0.65) **Going Correction** +0.225s/f (Yiel) **5** Ran SP% **111.9**
Speed ratings (Par 107): **110,86,79,,**
CSF £31.91 TOTE £2.70: £1.90, £4.80; EX 49.30 Trifecta £80.80 Pool: £1435.58 - 13.31 winning units..
Owner Mr & Mrs G Calder **Bred** Miss Mary O'Sullivan **Trained** Norton, N Yorks

FOCUS
A straight match between the big two in the market and the pair were clear from a long way out. There was last-fence drama, with Dursey Sound, who was finding plenty for pressure and looked set to come win the race, blundering badly and getting rid of McCoy, gifting it on a plate for King Of The Wolds.

2575 GEOFFREY HEWETSON MEMORIAL NOVICES' H'CAP HURDLE (13 hdls) 2m 7f 110y
3:00 (3:00) (Class 5) (0-100,95) 3-Y-0+ **£2,053** (£598; £299)

Form RPR

510- **1** **Safferano (IRE)**[27] 2016 7-11-10 **93** .... RichardJohnson 91
(Tim Vaughan) *t.k.h: hld up wl in tch in last: hdwy to press ldr 3 out: rdn and hit next: sltly hmpd bnd bef last: led fnl 100yds: styd on* **7/4**[1]

212- **2** *½* **Burns Night**[36] 1673 7-11-7 **95** .... (p) AdamNicol[(5)] 93
(Philip Kirby) *chsd ldr tl led 10th: looked to be gng best after 3 out: shkn up bef last: drvn: fnd litte and hdd fnl 100yds: a hld after* **7/4**[1]

\- **3** *1 ½* **Killegney**[135] 909 9-11-5 **95** .... (b[1]) CraigNichol[(7)] 90
(Michael Gates) *wl in tch in 4th: drvn and chse ldng pair after 3 out: styd on same pce u.p flat* **20/1**

P4U- **4** *13* **Minella Ranger (IRE)**[80] 1474 7-11-12 **95** .... TomO'Brien 79
(Paul Henderson) *chsd ldng pair tl dropped to last and outpcd bef 3 out: chsd ldng trio u.p bef 2 out: no imp and wknd between last 2* **8/1**[3]

P/6- **5** *28* **Why Always Me (IRE)**[26] 2049 5-10-0 **69** .... TomMessenger 27
(Chris Bealby) *led and set stdy gallop: rdn and qcknd after 9th: mstke and hdd next: dropped to last and btn after 3 out: mstke and wknd next: t.o* **3/1**[2]

6m 49.0s (42.60) **Going Correction** +0.80s/f (Soft) **5** Ran SP% **113.6**
Speed ratings (Par 103): **61,60,60,56,46**
CSF £5.63 TOTE £2.70: £1.40, £1.50; EX 10.40 Trifecta £41.90 Pool: £1828.23 - 32.71 winning units..
Owner Exors of the Late R H D Smith **Bred** John Irish **Trained** Aberthin, Vale of Glamorgan

FOCUS
The ground looked to have softened further by this point and the runners finished tired.

2576 COLLECT TOTEPOOL WINNINGS AT BETFRED SHOPS CONDITIONAL JOCKEYS' H'CAP CHASE (12 fncs) 2m 110y
3:30 (3:32) (Class 5) (0-95,87) 4-Y-0+ **£2,599** (£763; £381; £190)

Form RPR

P05- **1** **Carobello (IRE)**[26] 2039 6-11-3 **78** .... (bt[1]) NicodeBoinville 86
(Martin Bosley) *j.w: mde all: rdn and wnt clr between last 2: styd on: rdn out* **3/1**[3]

046- **2** *3* **Full Ov Beans**[27] 2025 9-11-9 **87** .... CraigNichol[(3)] 93
(Michael Gates) *in tch in last pair: mstake 2nd and 3rd: cl 3rd and mstke 2 out: chsd wnr between last 2: kpt on same pce flat* **11/4**[2]

542- **3** *½* **Fitandproperjob**[11] 2335 7-11-3 **78** .... (tp) KielanWoods 82
(Anthony Middleton) *hld up in tch in last pair: mstke 2nd: chsd wnr after 8th: rdn: unable qck and dropped to 3rd between last 2: one pce after* **11/10**[1]

264- **4** *38* **Mad Professor (IRE)**[11] 2349 10-10-4 **68** .... (b) JoeCornwall[(3)] 40
(John Cornwall) *chsd wnr tl after 8th: mstke and dropped to last next: wknd 2 out: eased flat: t.o* **7/1**

4m 30.0s (13.40) **Going Correction** +0.225s/f (Yiel) **4** Ran SP% **111.8**
Speed ratings (Par 103): **77,75,75,57**
CSF £11.38 TOTE £4.80; EX 18.10 Trifecta £20.70 Pool: £899.56 - 32.49 winning units..
Owner Ian J Herbert **Bred** John J Slattery **Trained** Chalfont St Giles, Bucks

FOCUS
Weak form.
T/Plt: £810.70 to a £1 stake. Pool of £57937.46 - 52.17 winning tickets. T/Qpdt: £25.20 to a £1 stake. Pool of £4870.60 - 142.80 winning tickets. SP

2437 LINGFIELD (L-H)
Tuesday, November 19

OFFICIAL GOING: Chase course - heavy; all-weather - standard
Wind: Moderate, against Weather: Fine, crisp

2577 QUICKSILVERSLOTS GET UP TO £200 FREEPLAYS JUVENILE MAIDEN HURDLE (8 hdls) 2m
12:50 (12:50) (Class 5) 3-Y-0 **£2,053** (£598; £299)

Form RPR

34- **1** **Keychain (IRE)**[16] 2248 3-10-12 **106** .... BrendanPowell 101
(Brendan Powell) *trckd ldr: chalng whn mstke 5th: rdn 2 out: 2 l down after tl lft upsides after last: sn led and drvn out* **6/4**[1]

The Form Book Jumps, Raceform Ltd, Compton, RG20 6NL.

2 1 3/4 **Ninepointsixthree**[63] 3-10-7 0.. JamesBanks(5) 101+
(John O'Shea) *racd on inner: led: pressed fr 5th: abt 2 l up fr 2 out tl blnd last: sn hdd and nt rcvr* **50/1**
3 7 **Slipper Satin (IRE)**[31] 3-10-2 0.. JackQuinlan(3) 85
(Noel Quinlan) *trckd ldng pair: nt fluent 3 out: cl enough bef next: sn rdn: one pce* **14/1**
0- 4 5 **Special Report (IRE)**[19] 2168 3-10-12 0.. NoelFehily 87
(Neil Mulholland) *hld up: nudged along and lost tch in 7th after 3 out: styd on steadily bef last: tk 4th fnl strides: nt disgracd* **14/1**
5 1 **Hermosa Vaquera (IRE)**[20] 3-10-5 0.. AndrewThornton 80
(Anna Newton-Smith) *hld up in last pair: nt fluent 5th: modest prog after 3 out: kpt on same pce fr 2 out* **33/1**
333- 6 1/2 **Unidexter (IRE)**[15] 2276 3-10-12 103.. MarcGoldstein 86
(Sheena West) *chsd ldng trio: rdn after 3 out: no imp 2 out: sn wknd* **9/2[3]**
0- 7 22 **Couloir Extreme (IRE)**[52] 1684 3-10-12 0.. JamieMoore 64
(Gary Moore) *t.k.h: hld up: wl in tch whn mstke 4th: struggling in 5th after 3 out: wknd after 2 out* **7/4[2]**
8 5 **Sporting Club Girl**[19] 3-10-5 0..(b) MattieBatchelor 52
(Jim Best) *hld up: mstke 4th: sn rdn and struggling: wl bhd after 3 out* **100/1**

4m 20.5s (14.10) **Going Correction** +0.525s/f (Soft) **8 Ran SP% 113.8**
Speed ratings (Par 102): **85,84,80,78,77 77,66,63**
toteswingers 1&2 £20.80, 2&3 £20.80, 1&3 £1.90 CSF £64.58 TOTE £2.70: £1.50, £8.80, £2.40; EX 72.70 Trifecta £297.80 Pool: £1110.02 - 2.79 winning units..
Owner T H Chadney **Bred** Castlemartin Sky & Skymarc Farm **Trained** Upper Lambourn, Berks

FOCUS
A weak maiden hurdle and they went a steady gallop, with the jockeys reporting afterwards that the ground road "heavy" and "testing". Suspect form, the winner rated close to his mark.

2578 GREAT POINT MEDIA INVESTMENTS H'CAP CHASE (18 fncs) 3m
1:20 (1:20) (Class 4) (0-105,102) 4-Y-0+ **£3,768** (£1,106; £553; £276)

Form RPR
/54- 1 **Royal Chatelier (FR)**[13] 2290 8-11-9 102.. MichealNolan(3) 115+
(Michael Blake) *led to 4th: led again 11th: mde rest: shkn up and drew clr after 2 out: rdn out* **6/1**
1/3- 2 12 **Loughalder (IRE)**[13] 2290 7-11-12 102..(tp) CharliePoste 104
(Matt Sheppard) *in tch: shoved along fr 1/2-way: u.p fr 13th: wnt 3rd next: kpt on to take 2nd after last: no ch w wnr* **3/1[2]**
051- 3 11 **Roseneath (IRE)**[118] 1103 9-11-8 98..(tp) PaddyBrennan 95+
(Alex Hales) *in tch: prog to trck wnr 13th: cl enough fr 3 out tl wknd after 2 out: lost 2nd after last: eased to a walk nr fin* **6/1**
/PU- 4 23 **Tarraco (FR)**[46] 1748 6-11-5 95.. AidanColeman 62
(Venetia Williams) *prom: pressed ldr 12th to next: wknd qckly after 14th: t.o 3 out* **7/2[3]**
PB0/ 5 32 **Abbey Dore (IRE)**[238] 4967 10-10-10 86.. MarkGrant 21
(Jonathan Geake) *led 4th to 11th: wknd rapidly after 13th: t.o* **33/1**
P/3- P **Global Warming (IRE)**[23] 2110 9-11-4 97..(p) GavinSheehan(3)
(Emma Lavelle) *in tch: urged along after 9th: sn struggling: lost tch 12th: t.o whn p.u after 15th* **5/2[1]**
P1P/ P **Dermatologiste**[217] 5329 10-11-11 101..(p) AndrewThornton
(Caroline Bailey) *prom early: in rr whn j. slowly 5th and 6th: sn btn: t.o whn p.u bef 10th* **14/1**

6m 34.4s (10.70) **Going Correction** +0.525s/f (Soft) **7 Ran SP% 114.0**
Speed ratings (Par 105): **103,99,95,87,77 ,**
toteswingers 1&2 £4.00, 2&3 £2.50, 1&3 £10.20 CSF £24.81 TOTE £7.50: £4.10, £2.20; EX 15.90 Trifecta £62.20 Pool: £1611.96 - 19.41 winning units..
Owner The Moonlighters **Bred** Marc Trinquet And Olivier Trinquet **Trained** Trowbridge, Wilts

FOCUS
A moderate staying handicap, run at a solid enough pace and they finished well strung out. A personal best from the winner with the second to his mark.

2579 QUICKSILVERSLOTS PLAY £500 ROULETTE MARES' MAIDEN HURDLE (10 hdls) 2m 3f 110y
1:50 (1:50) (Class 5) 4-Y-0+ **£2,053** (£598; £299)

Form RPR
1 **Spirit Oscar (IRE)**[310] 5-10-12 0.. LeightonAspell 112+
(Oliver Sherwood) *mde all: hit 3 out: pushed along bef next: kpt on wl fr last: drvn out* **1/1[1]**
5- 2 3 1/4 **Comedinewithme**[92] 1318 5-10-12 0.. BrendanPowell 109
(Jamie Snowden) *in tch: trckd wnr 3 out: rdn and nt qckn sn after 2 out: sltly awkward last: one pce flat* **6/1[3]**
6/ 3 43 **Lady Boru (IRE)**[234] 5-10-12 0.. HarrySkelton 79
(Dan Skelton) *chsd wnr to 3 out: sn rdn but clr of rest in 3rd: wknd and blnd 2 out* **3/1[2]**
0- 4 5 **Flemengo (IRE)**[38] 1863 4-10-12 0.. RichieMcLernon 61
(Jonjo O'Neill) *in tch: drvn after 6th: sn dropped to last and btn: t.o* **10/1**
0/P- 5 5 **Misty Mornin**[15] 2273 5-10-12 0.. MarkGrant 56
(Zoe Davison) *in tch in rr to 6th: sn wknd and t.o* **100/1**
3/0 6 18 **Chambray Dancer (IRE)**[27] 2027 5-10-12 0.. AndrewThornton 38
(Seamus Mullins) *in tch to 6th: sn wknd and t.o: blnd bdly last* **16/1**
P **Zaffaran Rain (IRE)**[172] 4-10-12 0.. DaveCrosse
(K F Clutterbuck) *chsd ldr to 6th: wknd rapidly next: t.o after 3 out: p.u bef last* **20/1**

5m 17.1s (10.40) **Going Correction** +0.525s/f (Soft) **7 Ran SP% 110.0**
Speed ratings (Par 103): **100,98,81,79,77 70,**
toteswingers 1&2 £2.10, 2&3 £3.60, 1&3 £2.20 CSF £7.10 TOTE £2.30: £1.40, £3.40; EX 9.10 Trifecta £27.40 Pool: £1694.77 - 46.36 winning units..
Owner Million In Mind Partnership **Bred** Martin C Fleming **Trained** Upper Lambourn, Berks

FOCUS
A modest mares' maiden hurdle lacking depth. They went a steady gallop, but finished very tired with the front two pulling well clear. Not much rules form to go on.

2580 QUICKSILVERSLOTS £1 TO WIN £500 H'CAP CHASE (14 fncs) 2m 4f
2:20 (2:21) (Class 5) (0-95,95) 4-Y-0+ **£2,423** (£823)

Form RPR
5/1- 1 **Seventh Hussar**[7] 2441 7-11-6 92 7ex.. JoshuaMoore(3) 98+
(Alison Batchelor) *trckd ldr: pckd 1st: mstke 4th: led 8th: jnd whn lft clr 3 out: mstke last* **1/2[1]**
/04- 2 35 **Budsson**[174] 543 7-10-0 69 oh13.. AdamWedge 40
(Anna Newton-Smith) *led: awkward 6th: hdd 8th and sn dropped to last: lost tch after slow jump 11th: lft remote 2nd 3 out* **12/1[3]**
414/ U **Join The Navy**[214] 5380 8-11-12 95..(b[1]) MarkGrant
(Kate Buckett) *hld up: trckd wnr 9th: drew alongside whn almost fell 3 out and uns rdr* **2/1[2]**

5m 38.9s (28.50) **Going Correction** +0.525s/f (Soft) **3 Ran SP% 107.7**
Speed ratings (Par 103): **64,50,**
CSF £4.65 TOTE £1.50; EX 5.10 Trifecta £7.90 Pool: £1157.86 - 108.70 winning units..
Owner Mrs Alison Batchelor **Bred** M E R Allsopp **Trained** Petworth, W Sussex

FOCUS
Much of the interest in this handicap chase was lost after the withdrawal of Further More and it turned into a procession for the winner. He's been given a token rating to his mark.

2581 GREAT POINT MEDIA H'CAP HURDLE (8 hdls) 2m
2:50 (2:51) (Class 5) (0-100,99) 4-Y-0+ **£2,053** (£598; £299)

Form RPR
/01- 1 **Proud Times (USA)**[15] 2278 7-11-3 90..(p) JackDoyle 103+
(Ali Brewer) *prom: w ldng pair fr 4th: led after 3 out: jnd and rdn 2 out: kpt on wl and asserted bef last* **7/1**
450/ 2 4 **Voltchesko (FR)**[219] 5317 4-11-8 95.. DarylJacob 104
(Robert Walford) *hld up in tch: trckd ldng trio after 4th: wnt 2nd after 3 out: chal and upsides 2 out: one pce u.p bef last* **11/4[1]**
534- 3 19 **Osmosia (FR)**[15] 2278 8-10-6 79..(p) TomCannon 69
(Chris Gordon) *mde most tl hdd after 3 out: sn btn in 3rd: fdd* **9/2[3]**
342/ 4 8 **Little Roxy (IRE)**[253] 4704 8-10-6 79.. AdamWedge 61
(Anna Newton-Smith) *pressed ldr: upsides 3 out: rdn and wknd on long run bef next* **12/1**
112/ 5 19 **Beau Lake (IRE)**[976] 4874 9-11-12 99.. PaddyBrennan 62
(Suzy Smith) *t.k.h early: racd wd: j.rt: w ldrs to 3rd: lost pl qckly: wl in rr after next: t.o* **7/1**
B5/- 6 9 **Maccabees**[173] 5379 4-11-4 91.. JamieMoore 45
(Gary Moore) *hld up in last: lost tch w ldrs bef 5th: modest prog next: sn t.o* **20/1**
32P- 7 39 **Royal Defence (IRE)**[7] 2430 7-11-12 99.. DougieCostello 14
(Mick Quinn) *trckd ldrs to 4th: wknd next: wl t.o after 3 out* **20/1**
605- 8 16 **Just Beware**[15] 2274 11-10-5 78..(p) DaveCrosse
(Zoe Davison) *a in rr: struggling fr 4th: t.o after next* **25/1**
3/1- P **Bathwick Junior**[13] 2291 6-11-4 91.. TomScudamore
(Michael Blake) *dropped to rr and reminder after 2nd: lost tch bef 5th: wl t.o in 8th whn p.u bef 2 out* **7/2[2]**

4m 14.5s (8.10) **Going Correction** +0.525s/f (Soft)
WFA 4 from 6yo+ 7lb **9 Ran SP% 113.1**
Speed ratings (Par 103): **100,98,88,84,75 70,51,43,**
toteswingers 1&2 £2.90, 2&3 £4.40, 1&3 £4.70 CSF £25.89 CT £95.93 TOTE £6.90: £2.00, £1.80, £1.80; EX 28.60 Trifecta £152.70 Pool: £2752.34 - 13.51 winning units..
Owner Miss Ali Brewer **Bred** Timothy Thornton & Meg & Mike Buckley **Trained** Eastbury, Berks

FOCUS
A moderate handicap but the time was reasonable. The winner should still be competitive when reassessed.

2582 GREAT POINT MEDIA INVESTMENTS NOVICES' H'CAP CHASE (18 fncs) 3m
3:20 (3:22) (Class 4) (0-110,110) 4-Y-0+ **£3,768** (£1,106; £553; £276)

Form RPR
F/4- 1 **Young Hurricane (IRE)**[23] 2105 7-11-12 110.. SamTwiston-Davies 119+
(Dr Richard Newland) *cl up: mostly pressed ldr fr 14th: shkn up 2 out: led last: bttr spd flat: rdn out* **9/4[1]**
/42- 2 1 1/4 **Cornish Ice**[19] 2179 9-11-4 102..(p) CharliePoste 106
(Robin Dickin) *pressed ldr: led 4th and maintained v stdy pce: hrd pressed 3 out: hdd last: styd on but nt gng pce of wnr* **4/1[3]**
0/4- 3 3 1/4 **Kastani Beach (IRE)**[28] 2009 7-10-12 103.. KevinJones(7) 105
(Seamus Mullins) *w.w in last pair: wl in tch on run to 3 out: tried to cl bef 2 out: one pce* **9/2**
0/U- 4 2 1/2 **Roparta Avenue**[188] 308 6-10-4 88.. MarcGoldstein 88
(Diana Grissell) *hld up in last pair: mstke 4th: prog after 15th to chal 3 out: no ex 2 out: fdd* **25/1**
/15- 5 4 1/2 **Kilrush (IRE)**[35] 1917 7-11-7 108.. MichaelByrne(3) 105
(Neil Mulholland) *led to 4th: awkward jump 8th: prom whn j. awkwardly 14th and next: dropped to last and rdn: fdd fr 3 out* **8/1**
002/ 6 3/4 **Guanciale**[222] 5241 6-11-4 102.. BrendanPowell 95
(Brendan Powell) *prom: pressed ldr 8th to 14th: rdn and cl up 3 out: wknd next* **5/2[2]**

6m 48.9s (25.20) **Going Correction** +0.525s/f (Soft) **6 Ran SP% 112.5**
Speed ratings (Par 105): **79,78,77,76,75 74**
toteswingers 1&2 £1.40, 2&3 £4.20, 1&3 £1.90 CSF £11.87 TOTE £3.20: £1.80, £1.70; EX 9.60 Trifecta £39.30 Pool: £2121.58 - 40.41 winning units..
Owner Paul Jenkins **Bred** Cleaboy Stud **Trained** Claines, Worcs

FOCUS
A moderate staying novices' handicap without much form over fences on the table beforehand. The pace was steady and all six were still tightly grouped entering the home straight. Not form to be confident about.

2583 JOIN OUR YOUNG HOOVES CLUB MARES' STANDARD OPEN NATIONAL HUNT FLAT RACE 1m 7f 169y
3:50 (3:54) (Class 6) 4-6-Y-0 **£1,642** (£478; £239)

Form RPR
1 **Plum Stone** 4-10-12 0.. NoelFehily 111+
(Charlie Mann) *hld up in last pair: prog 5f out: clsd to ld over 2f out: rn green and shkn up: drew away over 1f out* **3/1[2]**
02- 2 6 **Playhara (IRE)**[7] 2442 4-10-12 0.. AndrewTinkler 102
(Nicky Henderson) *trckd ldr: rdn to chal over 4f out: upsides as wnr wnt by over 2f out: chsd her after: no ch over 1f out* **7/2[3]**
632- 3 4 1/2 **Lola Galli**[82] 1445 5-10-12 0..(b[1]) TomScudamore 97
(David Pipe) *led: set decent pce after 3f: rdn over 4f out: hdd over 2f out: wknd over 1f out* **11/4[1]**
4 shd **Holy Veil** 4-10-5 0.. MrsAlexDunn(7) 97
(Alexandra Dunn) *racd wd: in tch: pushed along and outpcd by ldng trio 3f out: kpt on to press for 3rd nr fin* **33/1**
3/0- 5 4 1/2 **Move Along**[45] 1770 6-10-9 0.. RachaelGreen(3) 92
(Anthony Honeyball) *chsd ldrs: rdn over 4f out: lft bhd over 3f out: no ch after* **10/1**
2- 6 7 **Lilywhite Gesture (IRE)**[49] 1719 4-10-12 0.. PaddyBrennan 85
(Fergal O'Brien) *chsd ldrs: rdn 5f out: wknd over 3f out* **7/2[3]**
0- 7 3/4 **Anglo Paddy (IRE)**[21] 2153 4-10-2 0.. MikeyHamill(10) 85
(Sean Curran) *chsd ldrs: rdn and wknd 5f out: sn struggling* **66/1**
8 57 **Sisterbrooke (IRE)** 4-10-12 0.. ConorO'Farrell 28
(John Panvert) *a in last: struggling bef 1/2-way: t.o* **50/1**

3m 28.6s (-9.40) **8 Ran SP% 111.6**
toteswingers 1&2 £3.90, 2&3 £2.80, 1&3 £1.80 CSF £13.16 TOTE £7.00: £1.80, £1.40, £1.10; EX 15.70 Trifecta £56.20 Pool: £2634.81 - 35.12 winning units..
Owner The Top Cats II **Bred** Mrs S C Welch **Trained** Upper Lambourn, Berks

FOCUS
They went an honest enough pace in this mares' AW bumper and it saw an impressive performance from the winner. The third sets the level.

T/Plt: £30.90 to a £1 stake. Pool of £58747.52 - 1385.74 winning tickets. T/Qpdt: £5.40 to a £1 stake. Pool of £4393.60 - 595.35 winning tickets. JN

2333 HEXHAM (L-H)

Wednesday, November 20

OFFICIAL GOING: Heavy (soft in places; 4.3)

The first fence in the back straight was omitted on all circuits of all chases.
Wind: Fairly strong, half against Weather: Overcast

2591 AT THE RACES NOVICES' H'CAP CHASE (14 fncs 1 omitted) 2m 4f 110y

12:40 (12:40) (Class 5) (0-100,100) 4-Y-0+ **£2,144** (£629; £314; £157)

Form RPR

221- **1** **Snuker**[9] 2416 6-10-12 **86** 7ex.. BrianHughes 103+
(James Ewart) *pressed ldr: led 8th to between last 2: rallied u.p and regained ld last: styd on strly run-in* **11/8**[1]

005- **2** 4 ½ **Fozy Moss**[8] 2445 7-9-7 **74** oh3.................................. CallumBewley(7) 83
(Stuart Coltherd) *chsd ldrs: wnt 2nd 1/2-way: rdn and led between last 2: hdd last: kpt on same pce run-in* **33/1**

P/4- **3** 4 ½ **Farm Pixie (IRE)**[196] 168 7-10-10 **91**...................... GrahamWatters(7) 95
(Ann Hamilton) *t.k.h: hld up towards rr: effrt bef 3 out: drvn and chsd clr ldng pair last: kpt on: no imp* **12/1**

P01- **4** ¾ **Have You Had Yours (IRE)**[12] 2338 7-9-11 **78**........... AlistairFindlay(7) 82
(Jane Walton) *prom: rdn and outpcd whn hit 2 out: rallied appr last: kpt on same pce run-in* **6/1**[3]

P/5- **5** 3 ½ **Decent Lord (IRE)**[175] 536 9-10-6 **80**.......................... DougieCostello 81
(Jennie Candlish) *hld up: smooth hdwy to chse ldrs bef 3 out: rdn between last 2: outpcd fr last* **22/1**

414- **6** 16 **Mia's Anthem (IRE)**[32] 1982 5-10-13 **92**.......................... DerekFox(5) 78
(Noel C Kelly, Ire) *bhd: detached 1/2-way: hdwy 3 out: rdn and wknd between last 2* **11/1**

0/5- **7** 11 **Jack Albert (IRE)**[200] 117 6-10-2 **76**............................ BrianHarding 51
(Dianne Sayer) *hld up bhd ldng gp: drvn and outpcd after 4 out: btn fr next* **9/2**[2]

604- **8** 2 ¾ **Monbeg (IRE)**[20] 2172 6-10-11 **85**..............................(p) WilsonRenwick 55
(Martin Todhunter) *t.k.h: nt fluent early: led: hit 7th: hdd next: cl up tl rdn and wknd bef 3 out* **22/1**

324/ **9** 22 **Samtheman**[232] 5102 8-11-7 **100**...................................... JoeColliver(5) 48
(Micky Hammond) *chsd ldrs tl rdn and wknd bef 3 out* **12/1**

5m 35.6s (22.10) **Going Correction** +0.65s/f (Soft) 9 Ran SP% **109.9**
Speed ratings (Par 103): **83,81,79,79,77 71,67,66,58**
toteswingers 1&2 £28.60, 2&3 £31.20, 1&3 £3.90 CSF £45.06 CT £361.05 TOTE £1.90: £1.30, £7.40, £2.50; EX 44.80 Trifecta £424.50 Part won. Pool: £566.11 - 0.31 winning units..
Owner Mrs Percy, Mr Down & Mr Boyd **Bred** Mr And Mrs N M L Ewart **Trained** Langholm, Dumfries & G'way

FOCUS
Bends moved onto fresh ground and hurdles sited in best available positions. There was a strong wind blowing against the runners up the home straight. Due to waterlogged ground on the approach, the first fence in the back straight was omitted in all chases. Brian Hughes, who won the first three races, stated it was "heavy, proper winter jumping ground." With a few of these making their debut over fences this didn't look to be the strongest of races. They didn't go a great pace, which was probably sensible considering the conditions. The decisive winner is on the upgrade and can win more races.

2592 RAMSIDE EVENT CATERING JUVENILE MAIDEN HURDLE (8 hdls) 2m 110y

1:10 (1:11) (Class 5) 3-Y-0 **£2,053** (£598; £299)

Form RPR

1 **Forced Family Fun**[33] 3-10-12 0... BrianHughes 92+
(John Quinn) *t.k.h: cl up: lft chsng clr ldr 3 out: led gng wl bef last: sn clr: easily* **11/10**[1]

0- **2** 9 **Roycano**[20] 2168 3-10-12 0.. WilsonRenwick 78
(Michael Easterby) *t.k.h: in tch: stdy hdwy bef 2 out: effrt and chsd (clr) wnr last: kpt on: no imp* **100/1**

0- **3** 9 **Baraboy (IRE)**[20] 2168 3-10-12 0.................................... LucyAlexander 71
(Barry Murtagh) *t.k.h: in tch: hdwy to ld bef 3rd: clr next to 2 out: rdn and hdd bef last: one pce* **25/1**

4 5 **Vicky Valentine**[15] 3-10-2 0.. EwanWhillans(3) 61
(Alistair Whillans) *prom: stdy hdwy 3 out: outpcd whn hit next: wknd bef last* **10/1**[3]

0- **5** 39 **Dermo's Dilemma**[21] 2160 3-10-5 0........................ DiarmuidO'Regan(7) 25
(Chris Grant) *hld up: rdn and outpcd after 3 out: btn next: t.o* **125/1**

03- **6** 23 **Multilicious**[21] 2154 3-10-5 0.. DougieCostello
(Tim Walford) *t.k.h: led at stdy pce: hesitated 1st: hdd bef 3rd: rdn and wknd fr 3 out: t.o* **22/1**

42- **U** **Most Honourable**[21] 2154 3-10-12 116.................................. RyanMania
(Michael Smith) *cl up: j.rt 2nd: chsng clr ldr whn j.rt and uns rdr 4 out* **11/8**[2]

4m 35.9s (18.50) **Going Correction** +1.00s/f (Soft) 7 Ran SP% **108.8**
Speed ratings (Par 102): **96,91,87,85,66 56,**
toteswingers 1&2 £5.50, 2&3 £10.70, 1&3 £13.90 CSF £93.84 TOTE £1.70: £1.10, £14.60; EX 70.40 Trifecta £643.80 Pool: £1199.62 - 1.39 winning units..
Owner The Top Silk Syndicate **Bred** M B Hawtin **Trained** Settrington, N Yorks

FOCUS
Tough conditions for these juvenile hurdlers. They went no pace initially and even when the hard-pulling Baraboy went to the front the field ignored him and continued to go a more sedate pace. The form means little.

2593 E B F STALLIONS/AT THE RACES "NATIONAL HUNT" NOVICES' HURDLE (QUALIFIER) (8 hdls) 2m 110y

1:40 (1:40) (Class 4) 4-6-Y-0 **£3,443** (£1,011; £505; £252)

Form RPR

/05- **1** **Our Boy Ben**[20] 2174 4-10-12 0.. BrianHughes 110+
(Malcolm Jefferson) *hld up in tch: stdy hdwy 3 out: led bef last: sn shkn up and kpt on strly run-in* **5/1**[2]

/60- **2** 4 **Lord Brendy**[19] 2197 5-10-12 0.. KennyJohnson 102
(Robert Johnson) *chsd ldrs: wnt 2nd 4 out: led after 2 out to bef last: nt fluent last: kpt on same pce run-in* **14/1**

U- **3** 9 **Allez Cool (IRE)**[8] 2444 4-10-5 0.................................... JohnDawson(7) 93
(John Wade) *hld up in tch: outpcd after 3 out: rallied after next: no imp bef last* **50/1**

505- **4** 24 **Beyondtemptation**[85] 1415 5-10-2 0.............................. JohnKington(3) 62
(Jonathan Haynes) *hld up: rdn and outpcd after 3 out: rallied next: sn no imp* **125/1**

0- **5** ¾ **Westend Theatre (IRE)**[40] 1854 4-10-5 0...................... AlistairFindlay(7) 70
(Jane Walton) *pressed ldr to 4 out: nt fluent next: rdn and wknd 2 out* **66/1**

062- **6** 9 **Johnny Og**[14] 2285 4-10-12 0.. IanPopham 59
(Martin Keighley) *led: clr 3 out to bef next: hdd after 2 out: wknd qckly bef last* **2/5**[1]

30- **7** 36 **You'resomedreamer (IRE)**[12] 2337 5-10-12 0............. PeterBuchanan 23
(Lucinda Russell) *in tch: drvn and outpcd after 3 out: sn wknd: t.o* **7/1**[3]

4m 29.0s (11.60) **Going Correction** +1.00s/f (Soft)
WFA 4 from 5yo+ 7lb 7 Ran SP% **111.5**
Speed ratings: **112,110,105,94,94 90,73**
toteswingers 1&2 £5.50, 2&3 £4.00, 1&3 £16.00 CSF £55.51 TOTE £5.40: £2.80, £3.40; EX 52.10 Trifecta £789.60 Pool: £1831.96 - 1.74 winning units..
Owner P Nelson **Bred** P Nelson **Trained** Norton, N Yorks

FOCUS
A novice event in which the odds-on favourite was comprehensively turned over. A big step up from the winner on his bumper form.

2594 SOLAR SIGNS H'CAP CHASE (23 fncs 2 omitted) 4m

2:10 (2:10) (Class 4) (0-120,110) 4-Y-0 **£3,641** (£1,085; £549; £281; £147)

Form RPR

/22- **1** **Merlin's Wish**[14] 2290 8-11-6 **104**...................................... IanPopham 118+
(Martin Keighley) *a cl up: led 4 out to next: regained ld bef 2 out: drvn and styd on strly fr last* **9/4**[1]

/PP- **2** 4 ½ **On Broadway (IRE)**[21] 2155 7-11-10 **108**....................(p) PeterBuchanan 114
(Lucinda Russell) *chsd ldrs: lost pl 7th: pushed along 1/2-way: rallied bef 3 out: chsd wnr bef last: kpt on same pce run-in* **14/1**

0/1- **3** 18 **Matmata De Tendron (FR)**[12] 2339 13-10-2 **89**.........(p) JohnKington(3) 82
(Andrew Crook) *led to 4th: cl up: rdn after 18th: rallied after 3 out: effrt and drvn after next: dropped by first two fr last* **10/1**

/64- **4** 8 **Camden George (IRE)**[9] 2416 12-11-2 **100**............................ RyanMania 80
(Sue Smith) *in tch: nt fluent 14th: hdwy to ld 18th: hdd 4 out: rallied and regained ld next: hdd bef 2 out: wknd last* **12/1**

063- **5** 12 **Cilliseal (IRE)**[12] 2339 8-10-1 **90**..................................(bt) DerekFox(5) 58
(Noel C Kelly, Ire) *chsd ldrs: outpcd 19th: rallied after 3 out: wknd appr last* **9/2**[3]

P/2- **P** **Beau Dandy (IRE)**[19] 2201 8-10-8 **99**..........................(b) JohnDawson(7)
(John Wade) *t.k.h: cl up: led 4th to 18th: ev ch next: rdn and wknd bef 3 out: t.o whn p.u bef last* **3/1**[2]

4/0- **P** **The Big Freeze (IRE)**[33] 1959 7-11-6 **104**......................(t) DougieCostello
(Tim Vaughan) *hld up: outpcd 17th: losing tch whn p.u after next* **10/1**

114- **F** **Pyjama Game (IRE)**[27] 2033 7-11-12 **110**......................... WilsonRenwick
(Rose Dobbin) *hld up: racd wd fr 10th to 13th: struggling fr next: t.o whn fell 4 out* **20/1**

9m 11.0s (15.60) **Going Correction** +0.65s/f (Soft) 8 Ran SP% **111.3**
Speed ratings (Par 105): **106,104,100,98,95 , ,**
toteswingers 1&2 £7.50, 2&3 £37.70, 1&3 £3.60 CSF £29.64 CT £252.08 TOTE £2.80: £1.30, £4.50, £2.40; EX 36.00 Trifecta £388.00 Pool: £1588.58 - 3.07 winning units..
Owner Miss R Toppin **Bred** Mrs J M Bailey **Trained** Condicote, Gloucs

FOCUS
A stamina-sapping test in these conditions. The winner up was up 10lb for the marathon trip and there is probably more to come, while the second ran to his mark.

2595 DR HOWARD SCOTT MEMORIAL NOVICES' H'CAP CHASE (11 fncs 1 omitted) 2m 110y

2:40 (2:40) (Class 4) (0-110,108) 4-Y-0+ **£3,768** (£1,106; £553; £276)

Form RPR

162- **1** **Suprise Vendor (IRE)**[11] 2356 7-10-10 **102**................ DaraghBourke(10) 125+
(Stuart Coltherd) *t.k.h early: mde all: drew clr fr 2 out: easily* **11/4**[2]

5U1- **2** 17 **Cavite Eta (IRE)**[20] 2173 6-11-12 **108**............................... HenryBrooke 106
(Barry Murtagh) *chsd ldrs: drvn and outpcd after 3 out: rallied to take 2nd nr fin: no ch w easy wnr* **9/2**

255/ **3** nk **Dotties Dilema (IRE)**[248] 4817 5-11-12 **108**..................... PeterBuchanan 106
(Lucinda Russell) *chsd wnr: effrt and ev ch 3 out: hit and outpcd next: one pce fr last: lost 2nd nr fin* **13/8**[1]

0/5- **4** 1 ¾ **Dorlesh Way (IRE)**[174] 558 6-10-0 **82** oh16.................. RichieMcGrath 78
(Patrick Holmes) *bhd: outpcd after 4 out: plugged on fr last: no imp* **50/1**

2/4- **P** **Gleann Na Ndochais (IRE)**[188] 341 7-11-3 **102**........ EwanWhillans(3)
(Alistair Whillans) *in tch tl outpcd after 3 out: last and btn whn p.u bef last* **10/3**[3]

4m 24.8s (15.00) **Going Correction** +0.65s/f (Soft) 5 Ran SP% **108.0**
Speed ratings (Par 105): **90,82,81,81,**
CSF £14.15 TOTE £2.90: £1.10, £3.80; EX 13.80 Trifecta £25.40 Pool: £1502.99 - 44.30 winning units..
Owner Aidan Gunning **Bred** P Travers **Trained** Selkirk, Borders

FOCUS
They went a fair enough gallop considering the conditions and the winner made every yard for a facile win. This rates a big step forward.

2596 NORTHUMBRIA H'CAP HURDLE (10 hdls) 2m 4f 110y

3:10 (3:10) (Class 5) (0-100,100) 4-Y-0+ **£1,949** (£572; £286; £143)

Form RPR

/00- **1** **Amethyst Rose (IRE)**[21] 2156 6-10-0 **84**.................. DaraghBourke(10) 89
(Stuart Coltherd) *chsd ldrs: chal bef 4 out: led bef last: rdn and edgd lft run-in: kpt on wl* **11/2**[1]

302- **2** 3 ½ **Saddlers Mot**[39] 1874 9-11-3 **98**...................................(b) JohnDawson(7) 100
(Karen Tutty) *in tch: hdwy to ld bef 4 out: sn jnd: rdn and hdd bef last: kpt on same pce run-in* **10/1**

435/ **3** 13 **Stickleback**[22] 3969 4-10-7 **86**.. JoeColliver(5) 74
(Micky Hammond) *hld up: drvn along after 3 out: plugged on fr next: nt gng pce of first two* **15/2**[3]

0/5- **4** 16 **Willie Hall**[202] 77 9-11-0 **88**.. BrianHarding 63
(William Amos) *midfield: stdy hdwy and in tch 4 out: rdn whn lft 3rd 2 out: wknd bef last* **25/1**

/P3- **5** 3 ¼ **Lucky Sun**[45] 1791 7-10-8 **87**.......................................(p) AdamNicol(5) 56
(Philip Kirby) *prom: drvn and outpcd bef 2 out: btn bef last* **11/2**[1]

/PP- **6** 21 **Macklycuddy (USA)**[12] 2333 7-10-7 **86**..........................(p) TonyKelly(5) 34
(Rebecca Menzies) *chsd ldrs: drvn and outpcd whn lft 4th 2 out: sn btn: t.o* **40/1**

033- **7** 21 **Symphonick (FR)**[27] 2034 7-11-12 **100**........................(p) BrianHughes 27
(Tim Fitzgerald) *w ldr: struggling bef 4 out: btn after next: t.o* **8/1**

004/ **P** **Sea Cliff (IRE)**[197] 4590 9-10-7 **81**...................................... RyanMania
(Andrew Crook) *a bhd: struggling 4 out: t.o whn p.u bef 2 out* **50/1**

3P3/ **P** **Wee Giant (USA)**[22] 633 7-11-8 **96**................................. DougieCostello
(Tony Coyle) *hld up: blnd 3rd: struggling bef 3 out: t.o whn p.u bef last* **6/1**[2]

5/0- **P** **Native Court (IRE)**[33] 1963 7-11-3 **94**....(t) RobertDunne(3)
(Mark Michael McNiff, Ire) *nt fluent in rr: drvn and outpcd bef 4 out: sn btn: t.o whn p.u bef 2 out* **12/1**

P24/ **P** **Luctor Emergo (IRE)**[183] 5426 4-11-12 **100**....(p) WilsonRenwick
(Keith Dalgleish) *a bhd: struggling bef 4 out: t.o whn p.u bef 2 out* **20/1**

0PP- **P** **Bertielicious**[8] 2449 5-9-11 **74** oh14....(v[1]) JohnKington(3)
(Jonathan Haynes) *mde most to bef 4 out: qckly lost pl and p.u* **150/1**

4/4- **U** **Doyenthedecenthing**[202] 75 5-10-0 **74**.... AdrianLane 64
(John Davies) *prom: cl 3rd and stl gng wl whn hit and uns rdr 2 out* **16/1**

0/6- **P** **First Of Never (IRE)**[193] 223 7-10-7 **81**.... TomSiddall
(Lynn Siddall) *a bhd: lost tch and p.u bef 4 out* **100/1**

500/ **F** **W Six Times**[511] 839 7-9-9 **74** oh2.... CallumWhillans(5)
(Alistair Whillans) *in tch whn fell 6th* **25/1**

000/ **P** **Highlander Ted**[273] 4318 5-11-7 **95**.... PeterBuchanan
(Tim Walford) *hld up on ins: struggling bef 4 out: t.o whn p.u bef last* **16/1**

000- **B** **Optical High**[11] 2360 4-9-12 **77**.... JonathanEngland(5)
(Sue Smith) *hld up: pushed along whn b.d 6th* **40/1**

5m 32.1s (19.60) **Going Correction** +1.00s/f (Soft) **17** Ran SP% **117.4**
Speed ratings (Par 103): **102,100,95,89,88 80,72,, , ,,,, ,**
toteswingers 1&2 £36.90, 2&3 £8.00, 1&3 £39.20 CSF £52.72 CT £417.34 TOTE £9.20: £3.20, £2.80, £1.40, £5.50; EX 87.50 Trifecta £777.00 Part won. Pool: £1036.02 - 0.21 winning units..
Owner Whyte Binnie Macdonald Coltherd **Bred** Sean Kinsella **Trained** Selkirk, Borders

FOCUS
Despite the big field this didn't look to be the most competitive. Those that finished were well strung out in the testing conditions. A big step up from the winner with the second setting the level.

2597 WELL DONE DURHAM CCC CHAMPIONS AGAIN H'CAP HURDLE (8 hdls) 2m 110y
3:40 (3:40) (Class 4) (0-120,114) 4-Y-0+ **£3,285** (£957; £479)

Form RPR

425/ **1** **Tikkandemickey (IRE)**[281] 4172 7-11-1 **110**.... CallumBewley(7) 115+
(Raymond Shiels) *t.k.h: hld up: gd hdwy bef last: led run-in: drifted lft: kpt on wl* **11/1**

253/ **2** *7* **Walser (IRE)**[262] 4543 6-11-12 **114**....(b[1]) BrianHughes 112
(John Wade) *chsd ldrs: effrt and ch last: kpt on run-in: nt gng pce of wnr* **15/2**

P/0- **3** *1* **Formulation (IRE)**[40] 1848 6-10-9 **102**....(p) TonyKelly(5) 99
(Rebecca Menzies) *trckd ldrs: smooth hdwy to ld bef last: rdn and hdd run-in: sn outpcd* **13/2**

0/2- **4** *2 ½* **Funky Munky**[17] 2245 8-10-13 **104**....(p) EwanWhillans(3) 98
(Alistair Whillans) *cl up: led 2 out to bef last: rdn and outpcd run-in* **7/2**[2]

031- **5** *hd* **Morning Time (IRE)**[12] 2336 7-10-12 **107**....(p) GrantCockburn(7) 103
(Lucinda Russell) *in tch: effrt and drvn bef last: no ex run-in* **3/1**[1]

5/0- **6** *3 ¼* **Circus Star (USA)**[17] 2241 5-10-5 **100**.... MrJDixon(7) 91
(John Dixon) *t.k.h in rr: nt fluent 2nd: gd hdwy to ld next: rdn and hdd 2 out: wknd appr last* **22/1**

5/6- **7** *3* **Saddle Pack (IRE)**[172] 583 10-10-7 **100**.... MissCWalton(5) 88
(James Walton) *cl up tl lost pl 1/2-way: rallied bef last: nt gng pce to chal* **33/1**

200- **8** *6* **Stanley Bridge**[32] 1979 6-10-12 **100**.... LucyAlexander 82
(Barry Murtagh) *t.k.h: hld up: rdn along bef 2 out: sn outpcd* **16/1**

3F3/ **9** *9* **Bonnie Burnett (IRE)**[213] 5426 6-11-1 **103**.... HarryHaynes 76
(Brian Rothwell) *hld up: stdy hdwy after 3 out: rdn and wknd next* **9/2**[3]

060- **10** *27* **Hi Dancer**[19] 2198 10-11-4 **113**.... MrRyanClark(7) 59
(Ben Haslam) *t.k.h: hld up on outside: stdy hdwy 3 out: wknd bef next: t.o* **40/1**

4m 34.9s (17.50) **Going Correction** +1.00s/f (Soft) **10** Ran SP% **114.4**
Speed ratings (Par 105): **98,94,94,93,92 91,90,87,82,70**
toteswingers 1&2 £8.60, 2&3 £11.70, 1&3 £21.90 CSF £86.85 CT £583.35 TOTE £14.70: £3.00, £1.30, £2.70; EX 112.70 Trifecta £297.40 Pool: £2145.31 - 5.41 winning units..
Owner R Shiels **Bred** Alistair Thompson **Trained** Jedburgh, Borders
■ The first winner under rules for Raymond Shiels since March 1994.

FOCUS
A few in with a chance off the final bend and the complexion of the race changed dramatically in the final couple of furlongs. A step up from the winner.
T/Plt: £655.40 to a £1 stake. Pool of £66258.37 - 73.80 winning tickets. T/Qpdt: £97.20 to a £1 stake. Pool of £5203.0 - 39.60 winning tickets. RY

2292 WARWICK (L-H)
Wednesday, November 20

OFFICIAL GOING: Good to soft (chs 6.3, hdl 6.7)
Wind: Strong across Weather: Blustery showers

2598 32RED.COM H'CAP HURDLE (9 hdls) 2m 3f
12:50 (12:51) (Class 4) (0-115,115) 4-Y-0+ **£3,119** (£915; £457; £228)

Form RPR

465/ **1** **Swinging Hawk (GER)**[39] 3977 7-10-11 **105**.... RobertMcCarth(5) 112+
(Ian Williams) *hld up: hdwy 3 out: rdn to ld flat: r.o* **8/1**

365/ **2** *nk* **Presence Felt (IRE)**[221] 5292 5-11-7 **110**.... RichieMcLernon 116+
(Jonjo O'Neill) *hld up: hdwy appr 5th: chsd ldr 3 out: led next: rdn and hdd flat: r.o* **5/1**[2]

240- **3** *3 ½* **Dormouse**[10] 2397 8-11-9 **115**....(p) MichealNolan(3) 118
(Anabel K Murphy) *hld up: hdwy 6th: styd on same pce flat* **16/1**

F/2- **4** *8* **Don Pooleoni (IRE)**[6] 2474 8-11-4 **107**.... NoelFehily 106
(Harry Fry) *led: rdn and hdd 2 out: wknd flat* **9/4**[1]

1/ **5** *5* **Supreme Bob (IRE)**[243] 4907 7-11-1 **111**.... TomBellamy(7) 102
(Lucy Jones) *chsd ldrs: rdn appr 3 out: wknd next* **16/1**

442- **6** *1 ¼* **Shady Lane**[14] 2292 6-11-0 **103**.... RobertThornton 93
(Alan King) *hld up in tch: pushed along 6th: wknd after 3 out: hit next* **8/1**

7 *11* **Goodtime Boy (IRE)**[136] 914 5-11-7 **110**.... WillKennedy 90
(Alex Hales) *mid-div: drvn along 6th: wknd after 3 out* **50/1**

/05- **8** *¾* **Nether Stream (IRE)**[14] 2292 9-10-11 **107**.... MikeyEnnis(7) 87
(David Dennis) *hld up: rdn after 6th: wknd next* **50/1**

403/ **9** *hd* **Lisheen Hill (IRE)**[275] 4291 7-11-3 **106**.... RichardJohnson 85
(Richard Phillips) *hld up: pushed along 5th: wknd next* **7/1**[3]

/00- **10** *7* **Young Lou**[13] 2312 4-10-0 **89**.... CharliePoste 62
(Robin Dickin) *hld up: a in rr: wknd 5th* **66/1**

466- **11** *7* **Ironical (IRE)**[14] 2292 9-10-11 **100**....(t) TomScudamore 67
(Shaun Lycett) *chsd ldrs tl rdn and wknd appr 3 out* **25/1**

504/ **12** *26* **Rasheed**[206] 3 5-11-7 **110**.... LeightonAspell 53
(Lucy Wadham) *chsd ldr tl rdn appr 3 out: sn wknd* **25/1**

44P- **13** *15* **Trumix**[38] 1887 5-11-2 **105**.... JasonMaguire 35
(Kim Bailey) *hld up: a in rr: bhd fr 4th* **20/1**

P/0- **14** *7* **Gran Torino (IRE)**[15] 2284 8-11-10 **113**.... PaulMoloney 37
(Evan Williams) *prom to 5th* **33/1**

4m 22.8s (-19.90) **Going Correction** -0.90s/f (Hard)
WFA 4 from 5yo+ 7lb **14** Ran SP% **114.7**
Speed ratings (Par 105): **105,104,103,100,97 97,92,92,92,89 86,75,69,66**
toteswingers 1&2 £11.80, 2&3 £21.50, 1&3 £26.30 CSF £42.91 CT £626.77 TOTE £8.80: £3.30, £2.10, £3.00; EX 67.40 Trifecta £261.80 Part won. Pool: £349.07 - 0.43 winning units..
Owner Jamie Roberts & Jack Turton **Bred** Gestut Wittekindshof **Trained** Portway, Worcs

FOCUS
This looked quite competitive. The winner has the potential to rate higher on his flat form.

2599 32RED CASINO NOVICES' H'CAP CHASE (17 fncs) 2m 4f 110y
1:20 (1:24) (Class 4) (0-110,110) 4-Y-0+ **£3,768** (£1,106; £553; £276)

Form RPR

606/ **1** **Alpancho**[260] 4576 7-11-12 **110**....(t) DarylJacob 123+
(Ben Case) *chsd ldr tl led 6th: hdd 9th: led again 11th: rdn flat: all out* **25/1**

314- **2** *3* **Sonofagun (FR)**[122] 1062 7-11-7 **105**.... WillKennedy 115
(Ian Williams) *a.p: mstke 3 out: sn chsng wnr: rdn bef next: nt fluent last: no ex flat* **10/1**

/05- **3** *12* **Louis Phillipe (IRE)**[179] 479 6-10-3 **90**.... MichealNolan(3) 88
(Linda Blackford) *mid-div: hdwy 9th: rdn 13th: wknd next: wnt 3rd nr fin* **33/1**

401- **4** *nk* **Rockchasebullett (IRE)**[14] 2293 5-11-12 **110**.... PaddyBrennan 112+
(Fergal O'Brien) *sn led: blnd 2nd: hdd 6th: led again 9th: hdd 11th: ev ch whn mstke 3 out: sn rdn: nt fluent last: wknd flat* **3/1**[1]

0/3- **5** *8* **Bally Lagan (IRE)**[42] 1820 5-10-1 **85**....(t) CharliePoste 78
(Robin Dickin) *chsd ldrs tl rdn and wknd appr 3 out* **14/1**

314/ **6** *5* **Omaruru (IRE)**[609] 4989 6-11-7 **108**.... JoshuaMoore(3) 94
(Renee Robeson) *mid-div: rdn and wknd 11th* **20/1**

7 *10* **Sir Lynx (IRE)**[120] 1099 6-11-9 **107**.... TomMessenger 84
(Chris Bealby) *hld up: mstke 6th: rdn and wknd 11th* **33/1**

/34- **8** *43* **Minella For Party (IRE)**[13] 2315 6-11-12 **110**....(t[1]) HarrySkelton 48
(Dan Skelton) *chsd ldrs tl wknd 13th* **9/2**[2]

3/3- **P** **Scampi Boy (IRE)**[190] 286 9-11-11 **109**.... LiamTreadwell
(Paul Webber) *hld up: rdn and wknd appr 11th: bhd whn p.u bef 13th* **7/1**[3]

235- **P** **Tony Dinozzo (FR)**[14] 2293 6-11-2 **100**....(tp) JamieMoore
(Peter Bowen) *hld up: bhd and pushed along after 10th: p.u bef 2 out* **8/1**

3P0/ **P** **Malibu Sun**[482] 1088 6-11-2 **100**.... DavidBass
(Ben Pauling) *mid-div whn blnd 3rd: bhd fr 6th: p.u bef 9th* **50/1**

6/5- **P** **No Duffer**[25] 2087 6-11-8 **109**.... JakeGreenall(3)
(Henry Daly) *prom: lost pl 4th: bhd fr 10th: p.u bef next* **9/2**[2]

5m 10.8s (-10.20) **Going Correction** -0.375s/f (Good) **12** Ran SP% **117.2**
Speed ratings (Par 105): **104,102,98,98,95 93,89,73, , ,**
toteswingers 1&2 £44.60, 2&3 £41.30, 1&3 £44.60 CSF £237.52 CT £8026.40 TOTE £19.60: £4.40, £3.60, £8.10; EX 188.20 TRIFECTA Not won..
Owner Apple Pie Partnership **Bred** Mrs S C Welch **Trained** Edgcote, Northants

FOCUS
The front pair drew clear in what was just a modest handicap chase. The winner improed to the level of his best hurdle form.

2600 THOROUGHBRED BREEDERS' ASSOCIATION MARES' NOVICES' HURDLE (11 hdls) 2m 5f
1:50 (1:53) (Class 4) 4-Y-0+ **£3,898** (£1,144; £572; £286)

Form RPR

0/1- **1** **Keshi Pearl**[189] 324 5-10-12 0.... RichardJohnson 121+
(Henry Daly) *chsd ldrs: led appr 7th: clr appr last: easily* **7/2**[2]

00/ **2** *9* **Our Pollyanna (IRE)**[229] 5163 6-10-12 0.... RobertThornton 108
(Alan King) *hld up: hdwy 7th: rdn to chse wnr after 3 out: styd on same pce fr next* **10/1**

/4F- **3** *6* **Blue Buttons (IRE)**[7] 2463 5-10-12 0....(t) NoelFehily 103
(Harry Fry) *chsd ldrs: led 6th tl appr next: ev ch 3 out: sn rdn: wkng whn hit last* **8/1**

/6F- **4** *2 ½* **Fairweather Friend**[8] 2444 4-10-12 0.... SeanQuinlan 101
(Jennie Candlish) *hld up: hdwy after 3 out: sn rdn: wknd bef next* **66/1**

/15- **5** *8* **Mrs Jordan (IRE)**[25] 2089 5-10-12 0.... AidanColeman 93
(Venetia Williams) *mid-div: hdwy 6th: rdn and wknd after 3 out* **8/1**

/30- **6** *7* **Tenmoku**[19] 2190 4-10-12 0.... RichieMcLernon 86
(Jonjo O'Neill) *hld up: hdwy after 6th: rdn and wknd after 3 out* **25/1**

4- **7** *½* **Madame De Guise (FR)**[25] 2089 4-10-12 0.... DavidBass 86
(Nicky Henderson) *prom tl rdn and wknd after 3 out* **5/1**[3]

6/ **8** *1 ¾* **Ereyna**[205] 36 4-10-12 0.... BrendanPowell 84
(Renee Robeson) *hld up: mstke 5th: hdwy 7th: wknd 3 out* **80/1**

110/ **9** *15* **Molly's A Diva**[229] 5163 6-10-12 0.... JasonMaguire 71
(Kim Bailey) *w ldrs tl rdn appr 8th: wknd next* **13/8**[1]

600- **10** *10* **Anchoretta Eyre (IRE)**[4] 2509 7-10-12 0.... PaddyBrennan 62
(Fergal O'Brien) *hld up: wknd after 7th* **100/1**

0- **11** *2 ¾* **Gaye Memories**[14] 2298 5-10-12 0.... HarrySkelton 59
(Dan Skelton) *hld up: a in rr: bhd fr 7th: hit last* **66/1**

400- **12** *12* **Amber Flush**[13] 2317 4-10-12 0.... FelixDeGiles 48
(Tom Symonds) *mde most tl 6th: wknd bef next* **80/1**

13 *1 ¾* **Miss Biscotti** 5-10-12 0.... JamesDavies 47
(Martin Bosley) *hld up: rdn and wknd appr 7th* **100/1**

4m 58.9s (-16.10) **Going Correction** -0.90s/f (Hard)
WFA 4 from 5yo+ 8lb **13** Ran SP% **119.6**
Speed ratings (Par 105): **94,90,88,87,84 81,81,80,75,71 70,65,64**
toteswingers 1&2 £7.20, 2&3 £10.50, 1&3 £5.60 CSF £37.22 TOTE £5.60: £1.50, £2.80, £3.30; EX 42.90 Trifecta £216.70 Pool: £1219.83 - 4.22 winning units..
Owner The Wadeley Partnership **Bred** W P Jenks **Trained** Stanton Lacy, Shropshire

FOCUS
This looked quite a strong mares' hurdle. The impressie winner looks quite decent.

2601 MILLION IN MIND/HIGHFLYER 4YO CHASE (12 fncs) 2m
2:20 (2:20) (Class 3) 4-Y-0 **£7,507** (£2,217; £1,108; £554)

Form RPR

/50- **1** **Rio De Sivola (FR)**[48] 1742 4-10-12 115.... RichardJohnson 119+
(Nick Williams) *mde all: nt fluent 8th: drvn out* **8/1**

2/3- **2** *8* **Roc D'Apsis (FR)**[14] 2295 4-10-12 113.... PaddyBrennan 116+
(Tom George) *a.p: chsd wnr 4th to 6th: wnt 2nd again after 3 out: blnd next: sn rdn: no ex flat* **11/4**[3]

1/0- **3** *7* **Virak (FR)**[25] 2080 4-10-12 0.... DarylJacob 107
(Paul Nicholls) *chsd wnr to 4th: wnt 2nd again 6th: mstke 3 out: sn rdn and lost 2nd: wknd appr last* **2/1**[2]

252- **4** *31* **Dont Take Me Alive**[42] 1821 4-10-12 118..........................(tp) NoelFehily 83
(Charlie Longsdon) *hld up: bhd fr 6th* **15/8**[1]

3m 55.0s (-10.60) **Going Correction** -0.375s/f (Good) **4** Ran SP% **105.9**
Speed ratings: **111,107,103,88**
CSF £26.91 TOTE £8.20; EX 12.50 Trifecta £45.40 Pool: £311.54 - 5.14 winning units..
Owner Forty Winks Syndicate **Bred** Giles Trapenard Et Al **Trained** George Nympton, Devon

FOCUS
These 4yo chases are often fascinating contests and this one saw a nice performance by the winner, who produced a big step up on his recent efforts.

2602 I'M A CELEB SLOT ONLY AT 32RED.COM "NATIONAL HUNT" NOVICES' HURDLE (8 hdls) 2m
2:50 (2:51) (Class 4) 4-Y-0+ **£3,898** (£1,144; £572; £286)

Form RPR
1/1- **1** **Garde La Victoire (FR)**[25] 2075 4-11-5 0.................... RichardJohnson 132+
(Philip Hobbs) *racd keenly: trckd ldrs: wnt 2nd after 3rd: led 3 out: hit next: clr last: easily* **15/8**[2]
/11- **2** *11* **Gone Too Far**[18] 2225 5-11-5 0.. RobertThornton 117
(Alan King) *a.p: rdn to chse wnr appr 2 out: no ex last* **5/6**[1]
/45- **3** *2* **Mystifiable**[33] 1958 5-10-12 0..(t) PaddyBrennan 108
(Fergal O'Brien) *led to 3 out: sn rdn: styd on same pce fr next* **14/1**[3]
/02- **4** *½* **Benefique Royale**[28] 2027 5-10-5 0...................................... DarylJacob 101
(Nick Williams) *hld up: hdwy 3 out: sn rdn: styd on same pce fr next* **20/1**
6/0- **5** *16* **Yes I Will**[17] 2254 4-10-12 0..(t) NoelFehily 93
(Charlie Longsdon) *hld up: racd keenly: hdwy 3 out: mstke last: nvr trbld ldrs* **50/1**
6 *¾* **Highpower (IRE)** 4-10-12 0... DominicElsworth 91
(Jonjo O'Neill) *hld up: pushed along after 5th: nvr nrr* **50/1**
3- **7** *7* **Ronnie Lawson (IRE)**[12] 2347 4-10-12 0.......................... DenisO'Regan 84
(John Ferguson) *chsd ldrs tl wknd appr 3 out* **20/1**
3- **8** *1* **According To Sarah (IRE)**[93] 1318 5-10-2 0.................. JamesBest(3) 76
(Philip Hobbs) *hld up: nvr on terms* **40/1**
353/ **9** *2 ¼* **Etania**[340] 3070 5-10-5 0.. WillKennedy 74
(Ian Williams) *hld up: plld hrd: wknd after 5th* **50/1**
0/ **10** *nk* **Royalracket (IRE)**[375] 2333 5-10-12 0............................ LiamTreadwell 80
(Paul Webber) *prom: plld hrd: rdn and wknd after 3 out* **100/1**
400/ **11** *½* **Table Bluff (IRE)**[233] 5070 4-10-12 0................................... JamieMoore 80
(John Spearing) *hld up: plld hrd: wknd 3 out* **150/1**
0/0- **12** *¾* **Grand Gigolo (FR)**[36] 1919 4-10-7 0........................ RobertMcCarth(5) 79
(Ian Williams) *hld up: a in rr* **100/1**
/10- **13** *nk* **Solstice Son**[18] 2216 4-10-9 0...................................... RachaelGreen(3) 79
(Anthony Honeyball) *hld up: plld hrd: a in rr* **33/1**
6/ **14** *nk* **Spagetti Western (IRE)**[325] 6-10-12 0.......................... TomScudamore 78
(David Bridgwater) *chsd ldrs tl rdn and wknd after 3 out* **100/1**
0- **15** *3 ¼* **Joe Bugg (IRE)**[39] 1869 4-10-5 0.. RyanHatch(7) 75
(Roy Brotherton) *hld up: a in rr: bhd fr 4th* **100/1**
16 *17* **There You Are** 4-10-12 0... RichieMcLernon 58
(Jonjo O'Neill) *hld up: pushed along 4th: a in rr* **50/1**
/40- **17** *27* **Siksika (IRE)**[13] 2317 5-10-5 0.. HarrySkelton 24
(Dan Skelton) *chsd ldr tl after 3rd: sn pushed along: wknd appr 3 out* **100/1**
00/ **18** *9* **Mackeson**[252] 4745 4-10-12 0..[1] TomMessenger 22
(Chris Bealby) *hld up: a in rr: bhd fr 4th* **100/1**

3m 42.2s (-14.30) **Going Correction** -0.90s/f (Hard)
WFA 4 from 5yo+ 7lb **18** Ran SP% **125.4**
Speed ratings (Par 105): **99,93,92,92,84 83,80,79,78,78 78,77,77,77,76 67,54,49**
toteswingers 1&2 £1.10, 2&3 £2.10, 1&3 £6.90 CSF £3.55 TOTE £4.40: £1.10, £1.10, £4.40; EX 4.10 Trifecta £25.30 Pool: £1301.36 - 38.45 winning units..
Owner Mrs Diana L Whateley **Bred** Mlle Laure Godet **Trained** Withycombe, Somerset

FOCUS
A pair of potentially very useful novices faced off in what looked a fair event. The smart winner is open to further improvment.

2603 32RED ON THE APP STORE H'CAP CHASE (20 fncs) 3m 2f
3:20 (3:24) (Class 5) (0-95,89) 4-Y-0+ **£2,144** (£629; £314; £157)

Form RPR
353- **1** **Princely Hero (IRE)**[3] 2540 9-11-12 **89**..........................(tp) TomCannon 100
(Chris Gordon) *chsd ldr tl led 7th: hdd 9th: pushed along appr 14th: nt fluent 16th: sn drvn along: styd on wl to ld towards fin* **9/2**[3]
6/P- **2** *½* **Elite Beneficial (IRE)**[14] 2290 8-10-11 **79**..........................(p) BenPoste(5) 90
(Rosemary Gasson) *chsd ldrs: wnt 2nd 14th tl led 17th: rdn flat: hdd towards fin* **5/2**[1]
/64- **3** *4 ½* **Overton Lad**[13] 2313 12-10-3 **66**......................................(bt) HarrySkelton 73
(Peter Pritchard) *led to 7th: led again 9th: hdd 17th: sn rdn: styd on same pce flat* **8/1**
133- **4** *3 ¼* **Kilvergan Boy (IRE)**[22] 2152 9-10-13 **76**............(p) SamTwiston-Davies 82
(Nigel Twiston-Davies) *hld up: hdwy 3 out: sn rdn: blnd last: no ex* **3/1**[2]
514- **5** *6* **Volio Vincente (FR)**[25] 2082 6-10-1 **71**.. JonPark(7) 72
(Carroll Gray) *prom: pushed along 13th: rdn 15th: wknd appr 2 out* **3/1**[2]
/PP- **P** **Dramatic Victory (IRE)**[13] 2313 6-9-11 **63** oh18............. GavinSheehan(3)
(John Upson) *hld up: hdwy 6th: rdn and wknd appr 14th: bhd whn p.u bef 2 out* **20/1**

6m 53.4s (0.70) **Going Correction** -0.375s/f (Good) **6** Ran SP% **112.6**
Speed ratings (Par 103): **83,82,81,80,78**
toteswingers 1&2 £2.00, 2&3 £3.90, 1&3 £3.30 CSF £16.73 TOTE £4.60: £1.80, £2.50; EX 21.40 Trifecta £82.60 Pool: £1729.12 - 15.69 winning units..
Owner L Gilbert **Bred** Morristown Lattin Stud **Trained** Morestead, Hants

FOCUS
Moderate handicap form. The first two ran pretty much to their marks.

2604 DAVID NICHOLSON MEMORIAL FILLIES' "JUNIOR" STANDARD OPEN NATIONAL HUNT FLAT RACE 1m 6f
3:50 (3:50) (Class 6) 3-Y-0 **£1,819** (£534; £267; £133)

Form RPR
2- **1** **Puzzle Time**[13] 2318 3-10-9 0.. JackQuinlan(3) 94+
(Giles Bravery) *plld hrd: w ldr tl led 1/2-way: pushed clr 1f out: styd on* **9/2**[2]
4- **2** *1 ½* **Anda De Grissay (FR)**[13] 2318 3-10-9 0...................(t) RachaelGreen(3) 92
(Anthony Honeyball) *led at stdy pce tl hdd 1/2-way: chsd wnr tl pushed along over 3f out: wnt 2nd again over 1f out: rdn and hung rt ins fnl f: styd on* **9/2**[2]
3 *2 ¾* **Montana Belle (IRE)** 3-10-12 0.. RichieMcLernon 88
(John Butler) *hld up: hdwy over 4f out: rdn over 1f out: styd on same pce fnl f* **6/1**
2- **4** *1* **Lebanna**[21] 2160 3-10-12 0.. TomScudamore 87
(Tim Easterby) *a.p: chsd wnr over 3f out: sn pushed along: no ex fnl f* **7/1**
5 *½* **Tree Of Life** 3-10-12 0...(t) RichardJohnson 86
(Paul Fitzsimons) *chsd ldrs: rdn over 3f out: styd on same pce fnl 2f* **11/2**[3]
6 *33* **Wojciech** 3-10-12 0... NoelFehily 47
(Warren Greatrex) *hld up in tch: racd keenly: rdn and wknd over 3f out* **9/4**[1]
6- **P** **Instagramher**[13] 2318 3-10-12 0.............................. SamTwiston-Davies
(Charlie Brooks) *lost many l s: p.u after 1f* **33/1**

3m 24.1s (5.00) **7** Ran SP% **112.2**
toteswingers 1&2 £4.00, 2&3 £3.70, 1&3 £3.90 CSF £23.90 TOTE £4.60: £1.60, £3.60; EX 34.20 Trifecta £123.50 Pool: £959.99 - 5.82 winning units..
Owner J J May **Bred** Plantation Stud **Trained** Newmarket, Suffolk

FOCUS
A modest-looking junior bumper, predictably run at a steady pace. The winner and fourth set the level.
T/Jkpt: Not won. T/Plt: £4,232.00 to a £1 stake. Pool of £61915.28 - 10.68 winning tickets. T/Qpdt: £57.80 to a £1 stake. Pool of £4353.60 - 55.65 winning tickets. CR

2285 CHEPSTOW (L-H)
Thursday, November 21

OFFICIAL GOING: Heavy (chs 5.5; hdl 5.6)
Wind: Strong behind, easing after 3rd Weather: Sunny periods, windy

2614 P. C. AIR CONDITIONING SUPPORTING PAUL'S PLACE NOVICES' HURDLE (8 hdls) 2m 110y
12:40 (12:40) (Class 4) 4-Y-0+ **£3,119** (£915; £457; £228)

Form RPR
4/6- **1** **Going Concern (IRE)**[11] 2385 6-10-12 0........................... PaulMoloney 112+
(Evan Williams) *mde virtually all: hrd pressed tl asserted after 2 out: drvn and styd on strly run-in* **10/1**
344- **2** *2 ½* **Reverb**[17] 2266 4-10-9 0..................................... JeremiahMcGrath(3) 109
(Nicky Henderson) *trckd ldrs: swtchd rt appr last and qcknd to chse wnr: kpt on but no imp run-in* **5/1**[2]
4/6- **3** *2 ¼* **Dream Deal**[30] 2011 5-10-12 0... NickScholfield 106
(Jeremy Scott) *chsd ldrs: drvn along 3 out: kpt on to take 3rd run-in but no imp on ldng duo* **5/1**[2]
30- **4** *1 ¾* **Vujiyama (FR)**[20] 2189 4-10-12 0.. APMcCoy 106
(Jonjo O'Neill) *pressed wnr and stl upsides whn rdn 2 out: outpcd last: wknd into 4th run-in* **5/2**[1]
F/ **5** *7* **Buywise (IRE)**[227] 5221 6-10-12 0.. AdamWedge 97
(Evan Williams) *in rr: pushed along and styd on wl fr 2 out: nt rch ldrs* **14/1**
0- **6** *4 ½* **Bajan Blu**[15] 2286 5-10-12 0.. JamieMoore 93
(David Brace) *chsd ldrs: rdn 4 out: wknd after 2 out* **8/1**[3]
0- **7** *10* **Peak Storm**[7] 2467 4-10-5 0.. CiaranMckee(7) 83
(John O'Shea) *in rr: styd on fr 2 out: nvr any ch* **14/1**
/00- **8** *7* **Duke's Affair**[16] 2280 5-10-9 0.. MattGriffiths(3) 76
(Jeremy Scott) *t.k.h: chsd ldrs to 4 out* **50/1**
0/ **9** *2* **Forrardon Xmoor**[221] 5324 4-10-12 0..................................... WillKennedy 74
(Miss Jessica Westwood) *towards rr most of way* **100/1**
/00- **10** *½* **Veratan (FR)**[5] 2507 6-10-5 0.. MrJHamilton(7) 73
(Venetia Williams) *in tch to 4 out: no ch whn hmpd last* **50/1**
06- **11** *¾* **Midnight Request**[15] 2286 4-10-12 0....................................... FelixDeGiles 73
(Tom Symonds) *in tch: chsd ldrs 4th: wknd 4 out* **16/1**
0- **12** *16* **Elysian Heights (IRE)**[15] 2285 5-10-9 0......................... MichaelByrne(3) 57
(David Brace) *nt fluent in rr thrght* **100/1**
0/0- **13** *15* **Lucas Pitt**[15] 2285 6-10-12 0.. ConorO'Farrell 42
(Michael Scudamore) *a in rr* **100/1**
F **Hendry Trigger**[66] 4-10-7 0.. RobertWilliams(5)
(Bernard Llewellyn) *in rr whn fell 1st* **100/1**
/U2- **F** **Powderonthebonnet (IRE)**[179] 498 5-10-5 0............. DanielHiskett(7) 73
(Richard Phillips) *chsd ldrs to 4 out: bhd whn fell last* **17/2**
/50- **U** **Camptown Lady**[13] 2354 4-10-2 0.. RobertDunne(3) 73
(Laura Young) *in tch 4 out: wknd after 3 out: no ch whn mstke and uns rdr last* **100/1**

4m 10.34s (-0.26) **Going Correction** +0.225s/f (Yiel) **16** Ran SP% **120.7**
Speed ratings (Par 105): **109,107,106,105,102 100,95,92,91,91 91,83,76, ,**
toteswingers 1&2 £13.50, 1&3 £8.90, 2&3 £5.50 CSF £59.54 TOTE £14.50: £3.60, £1.90, £1.90; EX 82.10 Trifecta £675.70 Pool: £1580.92 - 1.75 winning units..
Owner Paul Langford **Bred** Miss Jenny Hunt **Trained** Llancarfan, Vale Of Glamorgan

FOCUS
A meeting that was formerly held at Hereford. Mixed opinions on the ground after the first, winning rider Paul Moloney calling it good to soft and soft" but Nick Scholfield considering it "hard work and heavy in places". They went a steady pace in this ordinary novice hurdle, and when it lifted off the home turn a group of five were quickly clear. The winner threatened this sort of rating in bumpers.

2615 MCPHERSON RACING SUPPORTING PAUL'S PLACE H'CAP CHASE (12 fncs) 2m 110y
1:10 (1:10) (Class 5) (0-100,103) 4-Y-0+ **£2,196** (£682; £367)

Form RPR
200/ **1** **Riddleofthesands (IRE)**[450] 1398 9-11-8 **92**.......... SamTwiston-Davies 107+
(Nigel Twiston-Davies) *mde all: travelling wl whn lft wl clr 2 out: eased to a walk at line* **15/2**
3/3- **2** *12* **Hector's House**[21] 2175 7-10-0 **73**...................................... RobertDunne(3) 69
(Nikki Evans) *chsd wnr fr 5th tl wknd 4 out: lft poor 2nd 2 out: clsd run-in as wnr eased to a walk at line* **3/1**[2]
P6C- **3** *15* **Bobbits Way**[17] 2277 8-10-11 **81**..(p) WillKennedy 62
(Alan Jones) *a in rr: t.o whn lft poor 3rd 2 out* **13/2**
231- **P** **Shalamiyr (FR)**[10] 2423 8-12-0 **103** 7ex...................... ConorShoemark(5)
(Sarah-Jayne Davies) *chsd wnr to 5th: sn drvn along: wknd after 8th: t.o whn p.u bef 3 out* **11/4**[1]
/44- **F** **Missionaire (USA)**[35] 1939 6-11-3 **92**.................................. JoshHamer(5) 98
(Tony Carroll) *in tch: hdwy to take 3rd whn hit 8th: chsd wnr 4 out: rdn next: 4 l down and styng on same pce whn fell 2 out* **6/1**
003- **P** **Le Grand Chene (FR)**[120] 1104 7-11-9 **93**.....................(bt) PaulMoloney
(Sophie Leech) *chsd ldrs: wknd 8th: t.o whn p.u bef 4 out* **9/2**[3]

4m 15.12s (-1.98) **Going Correction** 0.0s/f (Good) **6** Ran SP% **109.2**
Speed ratings (Par 103): **104,98,91, ,**
toteswingers 1&2 £4.70, 1&3 £6.50, 2&3 £3.60 CSF £28.91 TOTE £8.90: £3.70, £2.00; EX 31.80 Trifecta £803.60 Part won. Pool: £1071.57 - 0.98 winning units..
Owner N A Twiston-Davies **Bred** Terence Kelly **Trained** Naunton, Gloucs

FOCUS
A weak handicap chase with an all-the-way winner. He was a 112 horse in the past and can probably match that, while the faller was heading for a personal best.

2616 DALEPAK LTD SUPPORTING PAUL'S PLACE NOVICES' H'CAP HURDLE (11 hdls) 2m 4f
1:40 (1:40) (Class 4) (0-115,112) 4-Y-O+ **£3,119** (£915; £457; £228)

Form RPR
/61- **1** **Tigresse Bleue**[9] 2430 5-11-13 **112** 7ex................................ APMcCoy 125+
(Jonjo O'Neill) *trckd ldr 3rd: chal after 7th: led wl bef 4 out: shkn up: clr last: comf* **8/13**[1]
5/0- **2** *7* **He's The Daddy**[186] 393 6-11-6 **105**...................... SamTwiston-Davies 107
(Nigel Twiston-Davies) *chsd ldr to 3rd: chsd wnr 4 out: rdn and effrt 2 out: nvr quite on terms: outpcd appr last* **7/2**[2]
/05- **3** *10* **Nail 'M (IRE)**[173] 592 5-11-5 **107**.................................. MarkQuinlan(3) 99
(Nigel Hawke) *towards rr but in tch: styd on to take wl-hld 3rd fr 2 out: no ch whn mstke last* **16/1**
114- **4** *5* **Sugar Hiccup (IRE)**[35] 1941 5-11-12 **111**.......................... MattieBatchelor 98
(Jim Best) *led: jnd after 7th: hdd wl bef 4 out whn mstke: dropped to 3rd sn after and wknd into 4th 2 out* **14/1**
/03- **5** *15* **Kalamill (IRE)**[17] 2274 6-11-3 **102**..............................(t) DominicElsworth 77
(Shaun Lycett) *in tch: sme hdwy appr 4 out: sn wknd* **8/1**[3]
U06- **6** *59* **Echoes Of Joy**[15] 2285 4-10-9 **97**................................ MichaelByrne(3) 8
(David Evans) *j. slowly 6th: a bhd: t.o bef 4 out* **66/1**
5m 5.15s (3.35) **Going Correction** +0.225s/f (Yiel)
WFA 4 from 5yo+ 8lb **6** Ran SP% **109.3**
Speed ratings (Par 105): **102,99,95,93,87 63**
toteswingers 1&2 £1.20, 1&3 £3.30, 2&3 £5.20 CSF £3.16 TOTE £1.50: £1.10, £2.20; EX 4.00 Trifecta £19.40 Pool: £1660.72 - 63.95 winning units..
Owner Mrs Felicity Loudon **Bred** Dayton Investments Ltd **Trained** Cheltenham, Gloucs

FOCUS
An uncompetitive novices' handicap. The easy winner confirmed the merit of her improved recent win.

2617 PP ELECTRICAL SYSTEMS SUPPORTING PAUL'S PLACE H'CAP HURDLE (8 hdls) 2m 110y
2:15 (2:15) (Class 4) (0-120,120) 4-Y-O+ **£3,119** (£915; £457; £228)

Form RPR
6/1- **1** **Radmores Revenge**[194] 219 10-11-12 **120**...................... PaulMoloney 122+
(Sophie Leech) *hld up in rr: hdwy appr 4 out: trckd ldr 3 out: qcknd to ld last: easily* **5/1**[2]
161/ **2** *4* **Boston Blue**[15] 4499 6-11-5 **118**...................................... JoshHamer(5) 113
(Tony Carroll) *in rr: hdwy 4th: chal 4 out: sn led: drvn 2 out: hdd last: sn outpcd by wnr but hld on wl for 2nd* **14/1**
0/0- **3** *4* **Islandmagee (IRE)**[180] 480 6-10-4 **105**............................ ConorRing(7) 94
(Evan Williams) *led and j. slowly 1st: sn clr tl j. slowly 2nd: jnd 4 out and sn hdd: styd on same pce u.p fr 2 out* **2/1**[1]
162/ **4** *5* **Thundering Home**[157] 5330 6-10-7 **108**......................... TomBellamy(7) 95
(Richard Mitchell) *in rr: hdwy 4 out: styng on but nt gng pce of ldng duo whn blnd 2 out: no ch after* **7/1**
650- **5** *2 ½* **Taroum (IRE)**[15] 2292 6-10-5 **99**.. LeeEdwards 81
(Tony Carroll) *chsd ldr 2nd: rdn after 4th: wknd 3 out* **8/1**
036- **P** **Captain Sharpe**[129] 995 5-9-12 **97**.........................(bt) RobertWilliams(5)
(Bernard Llewellyn) *chsd ldrs: wknd qckly appr 4 out: t.o whn p.u bef 2 out* **6/1**[3]
31/- **P** **Alborz (IRE)**[37] 3106 4-11-4 **115**..................................... MichaelByrne(3)
(Tim Vaughan) *mstke 1st: chsd ldr and mstke 2nd: hit 3rd: blnd 4th: wknd 4 out: t.o whn p.u bef 2 out* **5/1**[2]
4m 11.46s (0.86) **Going Correction** +0.225s/f (Yiel)
WFA 4 from 5yo+ 7lb **7** Ran SP% **111.2**
Speed ratings (Par 105): **106,104,102,99,98 ,**
toteswingers 1&2 £4.00, 1&3 £3.10, 2&3 £6.40 CSF £59.88 CT £177.59 TOTE £5.30: £2.10, £4.60; EX 31.50 Trifecta £276.30 Pool: £1900.49 - 5.15 winning units..
Owner C J Leech **Bred** J R Salter **Trained** Elton, Gloucs

FOCUS
Modest handicap form. The winner was well in on the best of his form over further.

2618 LOCAL PARKING SECURITIES SUPPORTING PAUL'S PLACE H'CAP CHASE (16 fncs) 2m 3f 110y
2:50 (2:50) (Class 4) (0-120,120) 4-Y-O+ **£3,768** (£1,106; £553; £276)

Form RPR
2/4- **1** **Umberto D'Olivate (FR)**[25] 2111 5-11-2 **110**.................... FelixDeGiles 120+
(Robert Walford) *blnd 1st: chsd ldrs: chal 4 out: led next: drvn out run-in* **9/4**[1]
U/3- **2** *1 ½* **Overnight Fame (IRE)**[187] 370 9-10-3 **102**.........(p) AodhaganConlon(5) 109
(Tom George) *led to 2nd: styd chsng ldrs: chal 8th and again 4 out: chsd wnr fr next: styd on u.p run-in but no imp on run-in* **10/1**
3/0- **3** *1 ½* **Todareistodo**[15] 2291 7-10-3 **97**................................ MarkGrant 106+
(Jim Old) *in rr: hdwy to cl on ldrs 12th: chal and blnd 4 out: rallied fr 2 out: kpt on run-in but nt pce to trble ldng duo* **10/1**
/10- **4** *1 ¾* **Pret A Thou (FR)**[15] 2292 10-11-7 **120**.....................(p) HarryChalloner(5) 123
(John Bryan Groucott) *led 2nd: jnd 4 out: hdd next: styd on same pce fr 2 out* **25/1**
/13- **5** *18* **Captain Paulie (IRE)**[46] 1780 10-10-13 **114**...................... ConorRing(7) 102
(Evan Williams) *blnd 1st: in rr: hit 10th: blnd 11th: hdwy 12th: wknd 3 out* **8/1**
P32- **6** *2 ½* **Un Anjou (FR)**[18] 2251 5-10-9 **103**......................... SamTwiston-Davies 85
(David Dennis) *in tch: hdwy to chse ldrs 12th: hit 4 out and wknd* **3/1**[2]
24- **P** **Woody Waller**[30] 2014 8-11-5 **113**...................................(tp) PaulMoloney
(Sophie Leech) *chsd ldrs: blnd and wknd 12th: t.o whn p.u bef 3 out* **14/1**
035- **P** **Humbel Ben (IRE)**[30] 2014 10-10-9 **103**............................ WillKennedy
(Alan Jones) *a in rr: t.o 12th: p.u bef 4 out* **33/1**
440- **P** **Grey Soldier (IRE)**[15] 2287 8-10-10 **109**......................(t) CharlieWallis(5)
(Sophie Leech) *chsd ldrs 4th: wknd 9th: t.o whn p.u bef 4 out* **20/1**
225- **F** **Another Kate (IRE)**[40] 1865 9-10-13 **107**.............................. APMcCoy
(David Richards) *chsd ldrs: lost position 7th: hdwy to chse ldrs again 9th: wknd after 11th: wl bhd whn fell next* **7/1**[3]
5m 10.91s (-0.39) **Going Correction** 0.0s/f (Good) **10** Ran SP% **115.8**
Speed ratings (Par 105): **100,99,98,98,90 89, , , ,**
toteswingers 1&2 £5.30, 1&3 £8.60, 2&3 £24.20 CSF £24.09 CT £189.21 TOTE £3.80: £1.30, £2.70, £2.40; EX 36.90 Trifecta £613.20 Pool: £1961.12 - 2.39 winning units..
Owner Mrs S De Wilde **Bred** J P Rivoire **Trained** Child Okeford, Dorset

FOCUS
An ordinary handicap chase in which the first four finished clear. The second to fourth set the level.

2619 DALEPAK LTD SUPPORTING PAUL'S PLACE H'CAP CHASE (18 fncs) 3m
3:20 (3:21) (Class 5) (0-95,95) 4-Y-O+ **£2,144** (£629; £314; £157)

Form RPR
433- **1** **Glenwood Prince (IRE)**[14] 2313 7-11-9 **95**..................(t) MattGriffiths(3) 104+
(Jeremy Scott) *chsd ldrs tl j. slowly and in rr 8th: hdwy 13th: hit 14th: lft 3rd 4 out: drvn to ld 2 out: hld on all out* **3/1**[2]
062- **2** *1* **Tin Pot Man (IRE)**[42] 1837 7-11-9 **92**...............................(t) PaulMoloney 100
(Evan Williams) *in rr: hdwy 14th: styng on whn mstke 3 out: rallied to chse wnr last: kpt on u.p run-in: nt rch wnr* **8/1**
2PP/ **3** *27* **Mansonien L'As (FR)**[213] 5450 7-11-0 **83**.......................... AdrianLane 74
(Donald McCain) *pressed ldr: hit 3rd: rdn appr 14th: 4 l down and rdn whn hit 4 out and lft in ld: hdd 2 out: btn in 3rd whn hit last* **11/4**[1]
15/- **4** *67* **Tara Tavey (IRE)**[223] 5270 8-10-10 **89**................................ JonPark(10)
(Kevin Bishop) *a in rr: t.o* **9/1**
PP- **F** **Roisini Bay (IRE)**[52] 1701 9-10-13 **82**..............................(p) AdamWedge
(Richenda Ford) *towards rr whn fell 4th* **66/1**
/P1- **U** **Tom Bach (IRE)**[23] 2152 9-10-5 **74**.................................(b) JamieMoore 81
(Hywel Evans) *mde most: stl 4 l clr and gng ok whn mstke and uns rdr 4 out* **7/1**
P/5- **P** **Ballyegan (IRE)**[41] 1859 8-11-8 **91**................................. GerardTumelty
(Bob Buckler) *chsd ldrs: hit 6th: in rr 8th: t.o whn p.u bef 14th* **12/1**
/P2- **F** **Jim Job Jones**[10] 2423 9-9-7 **69** oh7...........................(tp) ConorRing(7) 65
(Neil Mulholland) *hit 1st and 5th: sn chsng ldrs: wnt 3rd 13th: keeping on u.p and 2 l down whn fell 2 out* **13/2**[3]
/5P- **P** **The Informant**[17] 2275 7-11-6 **89**..............................(v[1]) AndrewThornton
(Seamus Mullins) *chsd ldrs tl blnd 13th: wknd bef next: t.o whn p.u bef 4 out* **14/1**
6m 35.09s (13.09) **Going Correction** 0.0s/f (Good) **9** Ran SP% **114.5**
Speed ratings (Par 103): **78,77,68,46, , , ,**
toteswingers 1&2 £4.60, 1&3 £2.50, 2&3 £7.60 CSF £27.02 CT £72.21 TOTE £3.70: £1.10, £2.30, £1.40; EX 20.80 Trifecta £93.10 Pool: £1770.28 - 14.24 winning units..
Owner Gale Force Seven **Bred** Colin Motherway **Trained** Brompton Regis, Somerset
■ Stewards' Enquiry : Matt Griffiths four-day ban: used whip above permitted level (Dec 5-8)

FOCUS
A weak handicap chase which was thrown wide open when leader Tom Bach exited four from home. A small step up from the winner with the second to his mark.

2620 PAUL'S PLACE H'CAP HURDLE (12 hdls) 3m
3:50 (3:52) (Class 5) (0-100,100) 4-Y-O+ **£1,949** (£572; £286; £143)

Form RPR
P/1- **1** **Hopatina (IRE)**[31] 2008 7-11-9 **100**................................ MichaelByrne(3) 107+
(Neil Mulholland) *hit 1st and 2nd: hld up in rr: hdwy 4 out: chsd ldr next: rdn 2 out: hung lft u.p appr last and on run-in: led fnl 25yds: drvn out* **8/1**[3]
/P2- **2** *1* **Ifyouthinkso**[23] 2150 6-11-12 **100**.................................(p) WillKennedy 104
(Lucy Jones) *led but hrd pressed fr 3rd tl hdd 7th: led again appr 4 out: rdn and styd on fr 2 out: hdd and no ex fnl 25yds* **9/4**[1]
642- **3** *1 ½* **Changing Lanes**[4] 2541 10-10-13 **87**..............................(tp) PaulMoloney 89
(David Rees) *in tch: dropped to rr after 7th: hdwy next: chsd ldrs 4 out: styd on fr 2 out and kpt on run-in but no imp on ldng duo* **3/1**[2]
132- **4** *26* **Just Cloudy**[9] 2430 9-11-8 **96**...(t) FelixDeGiles 72
(Robert Walford) *chsd ldrs: chal fr 5th tl led 7th: hdd and rdn appr 4 out: sn btn* **9/4**[1]
00P- **5** *hd* **Maxi's Lady (IRE)**[14] 2312 6-9-7 **74** oh4..............(p) MissJodieHughes(7) 49
(David Rees) *in rr: hdwy 7th: rdn next: sn wknd* **33/1**
6P4/ **6** *9* **Waywood Princess**[257] 4656 8-10-1 **80**...................... HarryChalloner(5) 46
(John Bryan Groucott) *pressed ldr and chal fr 3rd to 7th: wknd 4 out* **16/1**
6m 25.87s (23.67) **Going Correction** +0.225s/f (Yiel)
WFA 4 from 5yo+ 9lb **6** Ran SP% **106.5**
Speed ratings (Par 103): **69,68,68,59,59 56**
toteswingers 1&2 £2.30, 1&3 £3.10, 2&3 £1.90 CSF £24.20 CT £54.61 TOTE £5.30: £2.00, £1.40; EX 16.20 Trifecta £48.20 Pool: £2342.48 - 36.38 winning units..
Owner J R Baigent **Bred** Avon Thoroughbreds **Trained** Limpley Stoke, Wilts

FOCUS
A moderate handicap hurdle which was hit by five non-runners. The winner building on her recent victory and may be capable of a bit better yet, while the second and third ran pretty much to marks.
T/Plt: £129.50. Pool: £71,685.36 - 403.88 winning units. T/Qpdt: £13.50. Pool: £6857.10 - 374.30 winning units. ST

2392 MARKET RASEN (R-H)
Thursday, November 21

OFFICIAL GOING: Soft (good to soft in places) changing to soft after race 1 (12.30)
Wind: light across Weather: fine and sunny, cold

2621 PHS BESAFE SPECIALIST PROTECTIVE WORKWEAR "NATIONAL HUNT" NOVICES' HURDLE (10 hdls) 2m 3f
12:30 (12:30) (Class 4) 4-Y-O+ **£3,898** (£1,144; £572; £286)

Form RPR
210/ **1** **Howaboutnow (IRE)**[586] 5408 6-10-12 0.......................... HenryBrooke 114+
(Donald McCain) *nt fluent: chsd ldrs: 3rd whn hit 3 out: led appr next: nt fluent last: drvn out* **3/1**[2]
52F- **2** *3 ¼* **Full Throttle (IRE)**[18] 2252 4-10-12 0........................... RichieMcLernon 109
(Jonjo O'Neill) *chsd ldr: upsides whn 7th: 2nd appr 2 out: kpt on same pce run-in* **8/1**
2/0- **3** *2 ½* **Bonnet's Vino**[14] 2317 5-10-2 0....................................... KielanWoods(3) 98+
(Pam Sly) *mid-div: hdwy 3 out: kpt on to take 3rd last: one pce whn eased nr fin* **16/1**
0- **4** *8* **Lucky Cody (IRE)**[13] 2347 4-10-12 0........................... WayneHutchinson 97
(Brian Ellison) *chsd ldrs: drvn 5th: outpcd 3 out: kpt on to take modest 4th sn after last* **33/1**
65- **5** *6* **Cusheen Bridge (IRE)**[20] 2195 5-10-12 0........................... AdamPogson 95
(Charles Pogson) *led: hdd appr 2 out: sn wknd* **100/1**
343- **6** *7* **Balinderry (IRE)**[10] 2429 6-10-5 95..................................... PaulBohan(7) 89
(Steve Gollings) *mid-div: hdwy 6th: outpcd 3 out: wknd next: eased towards fin* **33/1**
142- **7** *1 ½* **Make Me A Fortune (IRE)**[10] 2426 5-10-12 0................. JamesReveley 93
(Steve Gollings) *nt fluent and j.lft: chsd ldrs: hrd drvn 3 out: 3rd next: j.lft and wknd last: bhd whn eased towards fin* **7/4**[1]

35- **8** *16* **Lakefield Rebel (IRE)**[20] 2197 7-10-12 0 RichieMcGrath 67
(Henry Hogarth) *in rr: bhd and drvn 5th: t.o 7th: kpt on fr 2 out: nvr on terms* **50/1**

3/ **9** *1* **In The Gate (IRE)**[238] 4982 5-10-12 0 NoelFehily 67
(Charlie Longsdon) *in rr: mstke 3rd: sme hdwy 7th: wknd appr 2 out* **9/2**[3]

350- **10** *10* **Rene Le Roi (FR)**[20] 2197 4-10-12 0 WilsonRenwick 56
(Tim Easterby) *in rr: bhd whn blnd 3 out* **150/1**

0/0- **11** *2 1/2* **Banderitos**[21] 2174 4-10-12 0 HarryHaynes 53
(Tim Easterby) *chsd ldrs: lost pl after 7th: sn bhd* **125/1**

0- **12** *9* **Area Access (IRE)**[21] 2181 5-10-7 0 ThomasGarner(5) 44
(Charlie Mann) *in rr: wl bhd fr 3 out* **100/1**

5- **13** *13* **Danby's Legend**[11] 2393 6-10-12 0 BrianHughes 31
(Malcolm Jefferson) *rr-div: wl bhd fr 3 out* **16/1**

14 *44* **Think Out Loud** 4-10-12 0 DougieCostello
(Jonjo O'Neill) *nt jump wl in rr: bhd and reminders 3rd: t.o 3 out: eventually fin* **50/1**

0/ **15** *1 3/4* **Dream Mistress**[206] 36 4-10-5 0 TomMessenger
(Chris Bealby) *chsd ldrs: lost pl and hit 6th: sn bhd: t.o 3 out: eventually completed* **150/1**

4m 57.1s (17.70) **Going Correction** +1.20s/f (Heav) 15 Ran SP% **116.3**
Speed ratings (Par 105): **110,108,107,104,101 98,98,91,90,86 85,81,76,57,57**
toteswingers 1&2 £5.50, 1&3 £13.40, 2&3 £29.30 CSF £25.34 TOTE £4.50: £1.30, £3.10, £5.60; EX 38.00 Trifecta £245.20 Pool: £1430.32 - 4.37 winning units..
Owner Brannon, Dick, Hernon & Holden **Bred** Mrs A Connolly **Trained** Cholmondeley, Cheshire

FOCUS
Rail moved in 3m to provide fresh ground on bends. A big field lined up for this ordinary novice hurdle but there really weren't too many with realistic chances. The winner ran to 120+ figures in bumpers and there should be more to come.

2622 RCJ ASSOCIATES BEGINNERS' CHASE (14 fncs) 2m 6f 110y
1:00 (1:02) (Class 4) 4-Y-0+ **£6,498** (£1,908; £954; £477)

Form RPR

332/ **1** **Corrin Wood (IRE)**[267] 4448 6-11-2 0 HenryBrooke 141+
(Donald McCain) *mde all: drvn 4 out: hit next: styd on wl fr 2 out: rdr dropped whip between last 2: drvn out* **2/1**[2]

5/F- **2** *4* **Baby Shine (IRE)**[29] 2019 7-10-9 132 LeightonAspell 127
(Lucy Wadham) *chsd wnr: drvn and 3 l down whn nt fluent 2 out: kpt on same pce* **7/4**[1]

4/4- **3** *55* **Walkabout Creek (IRE)**[18] 2242 6-11-2 0 JamesReveley 79
(Steve Gollings) *trckd ldrs: hit 7th: lost pl 9th: sn bhd: distant 3rd 3 out: t.o* **9/4**[3]

4 *20* **Benevolent (IRE)**[189] 348 6-11-2 0 TomMessenger 59
(Chris Bealby) *trckd ldrs: hit 4th: modest 3rd 8th: drvn and outpcd 10th: sn lost pl: disputing distant 3rd whn mstke 3 out: sn wknd: hopelessly t.o whn eased run-in* **12/1**

5m 49.0s (3.00) **Going Correction** +0.05s/f (Yiel) 4 Ran SP% **108.2**
Speed ratings (Par 105): **96,94,75,68**
CSF £5.99 TOTE £2.40; EX 4.80 Trifecta £12.40 Pool: £1289.77 - 77.57 winning units..
Owner Dermot Hanafin **Bred** Margaret Nevin **Trained** Cholmondeley, Cheshire

FOCUS
The official going description was changed to soft following the opening novice hurdle. An intriguing beginners' chase despite the small field. The form is rated using the hurdles figures of the first two.

2623 PHS BESAFE WORKWEAR LAUNDERING H'CAP CHASE (JOCKEY CLUB GRASSROOTS JUMPS SERIES QUALIFIER) (14 fncs) 2m 6f 110y
1:30 (1:31) (Class 3) (0-125,122) 4-Y-0+ **£9,747** (£2,862; £1,431; £715)

Form RPR

/32- **1** **Present View**[17] 2267 5-11-8 118 BrendanPowell 135+
(Jamie Snowden) *trckd ldrs: cl 2nd after 7th: j.rt and led 10th: styd on wl fr 2 out: eased clsng stages* **13/8**[1]

P10- **2** *5* **Balinroab (IRE)**[15] 2293 6-11-4 117 [1] JackQuinlan(3) 124
(Richard Guest) *hld up: wnt prom 8th: drvn to chse wnr appr 3 out: 5 l down and wl hld whn hit last* **33/1**

/02- **3** *18* **The Magic Bishop**[11] 2394 8-10-11 107 BrianHughes 94
(Malcolm Jefferson) *hld up: hdwy 7th: outpcd and lost pl next: tk distant 4th after 11th: kpt on and modest 3rd last* **8/1**

0/3- **4** *3* **Spanish Arch (IRE)**[29] 2024 6-11-7 117 (p) NoelFehily 101
(Charlie Longsdon) *chsd ldrs: 2nd after 8th: wknd 3 out* **7/2**[3]

221- **P** **Suburban Bay**[9] 2431 8-11-0 110 7ex WayneHutchinson
(Alan King) *led 1st: hit 2nd: hdd and hmpd 10th: lost pl and 4th whn blnd bdly next: sn t.o: 5th whn p.u bef 3 out* **3/1**[2]

516- **P** **Strumble Head (IRE)**[58] 1642 8-11-6 116 (v) DonalDevereux
(Peter Bowen) *led to 1st: drvn 7th: sn lost pl: bhd 9th: t.o 11th: last whn p.u bef next* **20/1**

/63- **P** **Talkin Thomas (IRE)**[21] 2173 7-11-2 112 BrianHarding
(Nicky Richards) *in rr: lost pl 4th: t.o 9th: p.u bef next* **11/1**

5m 47.8s (1.80) **Going Correction** +0.25s/f (Yiel) 7 Ran SP% **112.5**
Speed ratings (Par 107): **106,104,98,96,** ,
toteswingers 1&2 £12.30, 1&3 £4.00, 2&3 £24.40 CSF £37.71 CT £337.01 TOTE £3.00: £1.60, £8.70; EX 51.50 Trifecta £401.40 Pool: £1327.46 - 2.47 winning units..
Owner Sir Chips Keswick **Bred** Richard Mathias **Trained** Lambourn, Berks

FOCUS
Jamie Snowden can do little wrong at present and his excellent recent run of form continued. A big step up from the impressive winner, who should win more chases.

2624 PHS BESAFE BRIGHT GEAR WORKWEAR H'CAP HURDLE (12 hdls) 3m
2:05 (2:07) (Class 2) 4-Y-0+ **£16,245** (£4,770; £2,385; £1,192)

Form RPR

5/5- **1** **Free To Dream (IRE)**[6] 2490 6-11-8 130 LiamTreadwell 140+
(Venetia Williams) *trckd ldrs: led after 3 out: wnt clr appr next: heavily eased clsng stages* **9/4**[1]

510- **2** *7* **Al Co (FR)**[19] 2214 8-11-12 134 TomO'Brien 130
(Peter Bowen) *hld up: trckd ldrs 5th: outpcd and 3rd bef 2 out: kpt on to take 2nd run-in* **13/2**

/56- **3** *4* **Act Of Kalanisi (IRE)**[34] 1956 7-10-12 127 (bt) ChristopherWard(7) 120
(Dr Richard Newland) *hld up in rr: hdwy 3 out: sn rdn and chsng wnr: drvn appr next: no imp in 10 l 2nd whn hit last* **7/2**[2]

116- **4** *3 1/2* **Koultas King (IRE)**[31] 2006 6-10-2 110 (t) DougieCostello 98
(Tim Vaughan) *led: qcknd pce 8th: hdd after 3 out: one pce* **15/2**

P56/ **5** *14* **Going Wrong**[264] 4519 10-11-3 125 (t) IanPopham 99
(Dan Skelton) *trckd ldrs: drvn 8th: sn lost pl and bhd* **16/1**

2/4- **6** *23* **Kaysersberg (FR)**[188] 358 6-11-3 125 LeightonAspell 87
(Neil King) *chsd ldrs: 2nd 9th: lost pl bef 2 out: sn bhd: t.o* **4/1**[3]

41/- **P** **Greyfriars Drummer**[473] 1191 5-11-7 129 (t) NoelFehily
(Charlie Mann) *racd wd: trckd ldrs 3rd: dropped bk 6th: drvn 8th: sn lost pl: t.o 3 out: p.u bef next* **12/1**

6m 18.6s (28.10) **Going Correction** +1.40s/f (Heav) 7 Ran SP% **111.7**
Speed ratings (Par 109): **109,106,105,104,99 91,**
toteswingers 1&2 £2.90, 1&3 £2.60, 2&3 £3.90 CSF £16.32 CT £47.64 TOTE £3.10: £1.40, £4.20; EX 15.80 Trifecta £40.60 Pool: £1815.37 - 33.45 winning units..
Owner Mrs Vida Bingham **Bred** Neil R Tector **Trained** Kings Caple, H'fords

FOCUS
Not the strongest of races for the grade but it's hard to criticise the performance of the winner, who's on the upgrade. The form could be rated a few pounds higher.

2625 PHS BESAFE FLAME GEAR WORKWEAR H'CAP HURDLE (JOCKEY CLUB GRASSROOTS JUMPS SERIES QUALIFIER) (10 hdls) 2m 5f
2:40 (2:42) (Class 4) (0-120,120) 4-Y-0+ **£3,898** (£1,144; £572; £286)

Form RPR

033- **1** **Cloudy Bob (IRE)**[19] 2230 6-11-10 118 ColinBolger 125+
(Pat Murphy) *trckd ldrs: led appr 2 out: hung lft and drvn clr run-in* **5/2**[2]

140- **2** *11* **Andreo Bambaleo**[151] 801 9-10-12 113 (p) NathanMoscrop(7) 109
(Brian Ellison) *hld up in rr: hdwy 3 out: modest 3rd next: kpt on to take 2nd fnl strides* **17/2**

0/1- **3** *shd* **Wily Fox**[11] 2397 6-11-0 111 JackQuinlan(3) 107
(James Eustace) *trckd ldrs: led after 3 out: hdd appr 2 out: one pce* **6/4**[1]

235- **4** *10* **Oneofapear (IRE)**[40] 1875 7-11-2 110 BrianHughes 96
(Mike Sowersby) *chsd ldrs: hit 7th: outpcd after next: wknd last* **28/1**

0/0- **5** *14* **Beat The Shower**[20] 2198 7-10-8 102 WilsonRenwick 74
(Peter Niven) *in rr: outpcd 7th: drvn next: tk poor 5th last* **12/1**

42F- **6** *10* **Compton Blue**[25] 2107 7-11-5 120 (b) StephenO'Donovan(7) 90
(Alan King) *chsd ldrs: reminders 7th: lost pl bef 2 out: eased clsng stages* **16/1**

6/0- **7** *3 1/4* **Becausewecan (USA)**[4] 2529 7-10-13 107 (p) WayneHutchinson 78
(Brian Ellison) *led: clr 4th: hit 7th and next: sn hdd: lost pl bef 2 out: bhd whn eased between last 2* **6/1**[3]

5m 39.1s (30.30) **Going Correction** +1.60s/f (Heav) 7 Ran SP% **110.4**
Speed ratings (Par 105): **106,101,101,97,92 88,87**
toteswingers 1&2 £3.60, 1&3 £1.40, 2&3 £4.90 CSF £21.52 TOTE £3.30: £2.10, £4.20; EX 26.40 Trifecta £78.60 Pool: £2669.38 - 25.44 winning units..
Owner Men Of Stone **Bred** P Shanahan & R Fitzgearld **Trained** East Garston, Berks

FOCUS
They went plenty quick enough in this. The winner was on a good mark and is rated back to his best.

2626 PHS BESAFE ARC GEAR WORKWEAR H'CAP CHASE (14 fncs) 2m 4f
3:10 (3:13) (Class 5) (0-100,100) 4-Y-0+ **£3,249** (£954; £477; £238)

Form RPR

012- **1** **Molko Jack (FR)**[11] 2396 9-10-6 83 KielanWoods(3) 100+
(Michael Mullineaux) *hld up: hdwy to chse ldrs 5th: cl 2nd 10th: led appr 3 out: drvn clr run-in* **4/1**[2]

051- **2** *11* **Hopeand**[13] 2349 8-11-12 100 (t) AdamPogson 107
(Charles Pogson) *led: hdd appr 3 out: rallied between last 2: 3 l down last: kpt on same pce* **7/1**[3]

346- **3** *8* **Detour Ahead**[28] 2036 5-11-9 97 (p) SeanQuinlan 95
(Jennie Candlish) *chsd ldrs: reminders and outpcd 11th: j.rt and one pce last 3* **4/1**[2]

421- **4** *29* **Croco Mister (IRE)**[17] 2277 6-10-8 87 BenPoste(5) 64
(Rosemary Gasson) *chsd ldrs: outpcd 11th: poor 4th whn mstke 3 out: t.o next* **11/4**[1]

45/- **P** **Gorey Lane (IRE)**[288] 4063 7-11-5 93 FearghalDavis
(John Norton) *nvr travelling: j. poorly: bhd whn hit 4th: drvn and in tch next: j.rt and lost pl 7th: sn bhd: t.o whn p.u bef 10th* **11/4**[1]

62P/ **P** **Weston Lodge (IRE)**[235] 5030 7-11-11 99 RichieMcGrath
(Christopher Kellett) *trckd ldrs: j.lft and lost pl 6th: bhd and reminders next: t.o 8th: p.u bef next* **28/1**

5m 17.4s (11.70) **Going Correction** +0.45s/f (Soft) 6 Ran SP% **109.3**
Speed ratings (Par 103): **94,89,86,74,**
toteswingers 1&2 £4.50, 1&3 £5.00, 2&3 £7.50 CSF £27.97 TOTE £4.80: £3.50, £3.50; EX 19.90 Trifecta £136.20 Pool: £1447.92 - 7.96 winning units..
Owner David Ashbrook **Bred** Mme Jacqueline Vuillard **Trained** Alpraham, Cheshire

FOCUS
It was evident that conditions were testing enough for many of these. The winner was well treated on old form and the second was a bit below her recent form over shorter.

2627 CONNOLLY'S RED MILLS BUMPER CHALLENGE STANDARD OPEN NATIONAL HUNT FLAT RACE 2m 1f
3:40 (3:40) (Class 6) 4-6-Y-0 **£1,642** (£478; £239)

Form RPR

2- **1** **Kilcooley (IRE)**[41] 1854 4-11-2 0 NoelFehily 118+
(Charlie Longsdon) *t.k.h: trckd ldrs: led over 4f out: styd on strly to forge clr fnl f* **5/4**[1]

4- **2** *6* **Uppingham**[161] 731 4-11-2 0 BrianHughes 112+
(Malcolm Jefferson) *stdd s: t.k.h in rr: hdwy 6f out: 2nd over 2f out: sn drvn and edgd rt: kpt on same pce over 1f out* **14/1**

3- **3** *7* **In The Rough (IRE)**[18] 2254 4-11-2 0 RichieMcLernon 106
(Jonjo O'Neill) *stdd s: hld up in rr: hdwy over 4f out: drvn over 3f out: modest 3rd over 2f out: one pce* **5/1**[3]

40/ **4** *13* **Dunluce Castle (IRE)**[234] 5070 5-10-9 0 PaulBohan(7) 92
(Steve Gollings) *hld up in mid-div: drvn over 4f out: sn wl outpcd: tk modest 4th over 1f out* **8/1**

5 *1 1/2* **The Backup Plan (IRE)**[187] 4-11-2 0 HenryBrooke 91
(Donald McCain) *led: hdd 5f out: hung lft and lost pl over 3f out: sn bhd* **8/1**

4- **6** *18* **Palmarrick (IRE)**[21] 2174 6-11-2 0 HarryHaynes 73
(Nick Kent) *chsd ldrs: drvn over 5f out: lost pl over 4f out: hung lft and sn bhd* **50/1**

7 *12* **Jac The Legend**[207] 4-11-2 0 JamesReveley 73
(Steve Gollings) *trckd ldr: led briefly 5f out: drvn and outpcd over 2f out: wknd and eased over 1f out: virtually p.u* **7/2**[2]

4m 29.7s (28.60) **Going Correction** +1.80s/f (Heav) 7 Ran SP% **114.2**
Speed ratings: **104,101,97,91,91 82,76**
toteswingers 1&2 £3.20, 1&3 £1.10, 2&3 £15.00 CSF £21.25 TOTE £2.20: £1.60, £8.20; EX 18.70 Trifecta £54.60 Pool: £1272.24 - 17.47 winning units..
Owner J H & S M Wall **Bred** Fergal O'Mahoney **Trained** Over Norton, Oxon

FOCUS
Fair bumper form, with a big step up from the winner on his debut effort.

T/Plt: £443.00. Pool: £51,203.89 - 84.37 winning units. T/Qpdt: £35.00. Pool: £4030.68 - 85.20 winning units. WG

[2369]WINCANTON (R-H)

Thursday, November 21

OFFICIAL GOING: Good (good to soft in places; chs 7.9; hdl 8.2)

Wind: quite strong half across Weather: overcast

2628 RACING EXCELLENCE "HANDS AND HEELS" NOVICES' H'CAP HURDLE (CONDITIONAL JOCKEYS/AMATEUR RIDERS) (8 hdls) 2m

12:50 (12:51) (Class 4) (0-105,105) 3-Y-O+ **£3,898** (£1,144; £572; £286)

Form RPR

4/4- **1** **Massena (IRE)**[162] 247 6-11-6 **104**.................... MrJSKnox(5) 114+
(Venetia Williams) *trckd ldrs: led 2nd tl next: led 5th: clr 2 out: comf* **9/2**[3]

U40- **2** *5* **Backhomeinderry (IRE)**[7] 2474 8-11-6 **99**....................(t) KieronEdgar 98
(Kate Buckett) *mid-div: rdn and stdy hdwy after 3 out: styd on to go 2nd at the last: no ch w wnr* **4/1**[2]

000- **3** *2 ¼* **Native Brian (IRE)**[30] 2009 7-11-7 **100**....................(t) MrJBarber 97
(Alexandra Dunn) *trckd ldrs: stmbld 2nd: rdn after 3 out: styd on same pce* **14/1**

055- **4** *17* **Vexillum (IRE)**[18] 2250 4-11-7 **100**....................(t) MrFMitchell 84
(Simon Hodgson) *hld up towards rr: rdn after 3 out: wnt lft 2 out: nvr any danger: wnt modest 4th fnl strides* **25/1**

453- **5** *hd* **Tempuran**[28] 2040 4-11-12 **105**.................... JakeHodson 86
(David Bridgwater) *mid-div: rdn after 3 out: nvr any imp on ldrs* **5/2**[1]

600- **6** *8* **Dont Call Me Oscar (IRE)**[15] 2291 6-10-4 **83**..........(bt[1]) JackSherwood 57
(Mark Gillard) *in tch: rdn after 3 out: wnt bdly lft and slipped 2 out: wknd* **16/1**

024/ **7** *10* **While You Wait (IRE)**[10] 3349 4-11-7 **100**.................... MissHayleyMoore 65
(Gary Moore) *mid-div tl 4th: sn bhd* **8/1**

P- **8** *3* **Coin River (IRE)**[181] 459 7-10-7 **89**....................(t) GaryDerwin(3) 52
(Bob Buckler) *mid-div: hdwy 5th: rdn to chse wnr after 3 out tl wknd qckly next: t.o* **25/1**

0/P- **R** **Cruise In Luxury (IRE)**[14] 2312 8-9-11 **79** oh2..... ThomasCheesman(3)
(Kevin Bishop) *bhd: nt fluent: rn out 4th* **50/1**

044/ **U** **Withy Mills**[222] 5286 8-10-6 **88**....................(tp) JonPark(3)
(Kevin Bishop) *trcking ldrs whn blnd and uns rdr 2nd* **10/1**

22P- **P** **Isola Bella**[7] 2470 4-10-11 **93**....................(b) MrJHarding(3)
(Jonathan Portman) *t.k.h: led after 2nd: mstke 5th sn hdd: wknd after 3 out: t.o whn p.u bef last* **14/1**

0/0- **R** **Ricketyrock**[202] 95 7-10-1 **80**.................... KevinJones
(Nick Mitchell) *led tl 2nd: trckd ldrs: hung bdly lft fr 5th: sddle slipped and rn out on bnd bef 2 out* **50/1**

3m 41.7s (-7.20) **Going Correction** -0.325s/f (Good) **12** Ran SP% **117.8**
Speed ratings (Par 105): **105,102,101,92,92 88,83,82,** ,
toteswingers 1&2 £4.70, 1&3 £13.20, 2&3 £14.80 CSF £22.41 CT £232.92 TOTE £5.60: £2.30, £1.70, £4.60; EX 29.10 Trifecta £686.90 Part won. Pool: £915.89 - 0.67 winning units..
Owner Miss V M Williams **Bred** Frank Dunne **Trained** Kings Caple, H'fords
■ A winner on his first ride under rules for Joe Knox. He is the son of former jump jockey Wayne Knox.

FOCUS
There was 1mm of rain overnight and the going was good, good to soft in places on a blustery day. There was a clear-cut winner in this novices' handicap and not many got involved from off the pace. The form is rated around the second and third.

2629 BATHWICK TYRES H'CAP CHASE (13 fncs) 2m

1:20 (1:20) (Class 4) (0-120,117) 4-Y-O+ **£5,198** (£1,526; £763; £381)

Form RPR

/13- **1** **Miss Tenacious**[185] 411 6-11-10 **115**.................... JackDoyle 125+
(Ron Hodges) *mde all: j. sltly lft: kpt on wl and in command fr 3 out* **7/1**

253- **2** *9* **Benny The Swinger (IRE)**[18] 2251 8-10-3 **94**.................... TomCannon 96
(Chris Gordon) *j.rt: hld up bhd ldrs: hdwy 9th: rdn to chse wnr after 4 out: hit 3 out: styd on same pce* **5/2**[1]

343/ **3** *9* **Mon Chevalier (IRE)**[230] 5169 10-11-3 **111**.................... MichealNolan(3) 104
(Carroll Gray) *chsd ldrs: pushed along fr 8th: styd on same pce fr 3 out* **8/1**

154- **4** *6* **Cruise In Style (IRE)**[7] 2474 7-10-5 **99**....................(bt) JamesBest(3) 89
(Kevin Bishop) *j.lft at times: chsd ldrs: hit 2nd: rdn after 9th: hld in 4th fr next: wknd 2 out* **9/2**[3]

54P- **5** *20* **Lucy's Legend (IRE)**[17] 2270 7-10-5 **96**....................(bt[1]) PaddyBrennan 70
(Paul Henderson) *chsd wnr: hit 7th: wknd after 9th: t.o* **10/1**

3P6/ **F** **Coolbeg (IRE)**[219] 5338 7-11-1 **106**....................(t) DarylJacob
(Heather Main) *fell 1st* **16/1**

0/0- **P** **Old Tricks (IRE)**[15] 2288 6-11-10 **115**....................[1] JoeTizzard
(Colin Tizzard) *nvr fluent: trcking ldr whn slow 1st: sn in last: struggling 5th: tailing off whn p.u after 6th* **3/1**[2]

3m 58.1s (-1.80) **Going Correction** +0.05s/f (Yiel) **7** Ran SP% **110.3**
Speed ratings (Par 105): **106,101,97,94,84** ,
toteswingers 1&2 £3.70, 1&3 £13.10, 2&3 £9.00 CSF £23.93 CT £134.07 TOTE £4.90: £1.60, £1.80; EX 16.10 Trifecta £53.30 Pool: £1105.07 - 15.52 winning units..
Owner John Frampton & Paul Frampton **Bred** Frampton Farms & Widdin Stud **Trained** Charlton Mackrell, Somerset

FOCUS
Not a strong race for the grade and one of the market leaders was disappointing but the winner delivered in decent style under a front-running ride. The form is rated around the second.

2630 BATHWICK TYRES H'CAP HURDLE (10 hdls) 2m 4f

1:50 (1:50) (Class 3) (0-135,132) 4-Y-O+ **£7,797** (£2,289; £1,144; £572)

Form RPR

F/6- **1** **Carrigmorna King (IRE)**[40] 1867 7-11-5 **125**..........(t) RichardJohnson 130+
(Philip Hobbs) *in tch: hmpd 4th: trckd ldrs 3 out: rdn to chse ldr bef next: looking hld in 3 l 2nd whn lft clr last* **4/1**[1]

560- **2** *7* **Bygones Sovereign (IRE)**[16] 2284 7-10-6 **112**.........(p) TomScudamore 109
(David Pipe) *led: rdn after 3 out: hdd bef next: styng on at same pce whn lft 2nd at the last* **5/1**[2]

002/ **3** *7* **Balzaccio (FR)**[599] 5196 8-11-2 **122**.................... PaddyBrennan 112
(Fergal O'Brien) *mid-div: hdwy after 3 out: rdn to chse ldrs bef next: styd on same pce: lft 3rd at the last* **10/1**

4/0- **4** *2 ½* **Jetnova (IRE)**[201] 119 8-11-5 **125**.................... RobertThornton 115
(Alan King) *in tch: mstke 7th: sn rdn: styd on same pce fr 2 out: lft 5th at the last: wnt 4th fnl strides* **10/1**

151/ **5** *½* **Sound Investment (IRE)**[214] 5438 5-11-8 **128**....................(t) DarylJacob 118
(Paul Nicholls) *trckd ldrs: rdn bef 2 out: sn hld: lft 4th at the last: no ex whn dropped to 5th fnl strides* **5/1**[2]

214- **6** *7* **Halifax (IRE)**[182] 449 5-11-0 **120**.................... AndrewTinkler 101
(Tony Newcombe) *mid-div: rdn after 3 out: nvr any imp on ldrs* **50/1**

122- **7** *19* **Beachfire**[19] 2215 6-11-8 **128**.................... DenisO'Regan 102
(John Ferguson) *mid-div: pushed along after 3 out: rdn bef next: nvr any imp: wknd between last 2* **5/1**[2]

026- **8** *3 ¼* **Decoy (FR)**[29] 2020 7-11-0 **127**....................(p) MikeyEnnis(7) 88
(David Pipe) *a towards rr: t.o* **20/1**

132/ **9** *¾* **Look For Love**[210] 5522 5-10-7 **118**.................... MissLucyGardner(5) 84
(Sue Gardner) *hld up: nt a fluent: wknd after 3 out* **33/1**

124- **10** *¾* **Union Saint (FR)**[110] 1195 5-11-9 **129**.................... HaddenFrost 89
(James Frost) *hld up towards rr: hdwy whn mstke 7th: wknd after 3 out* **14/1**

2B3/ **11** *51* **Bathwick Brave (IRE)**[236] 5016 6-11-12 **132**..........(t) TimmyMurphy 46
(Johnny Farrelly) *hld up bhd: hmpd on bnd after 5th: struggling fr next: wknd after 3 out: t.o* **12/1**

313- **F** **Foxcub (IRE)**[34] 1960 5-10-13 **119**.................... DaveCrosse 128+
(Tom Symonds) *trckd ldrs: wnt rt 4th: led after 3 out: j.rt next: rdn and styng on wl whn wnt rt and fell last* **8/1**[3]

4m 45.7s (-11.10) **Going Correction** -0.325s/f (Good) **12** Ran SP% **123.3**
Speed ratings (Par 107): **109,106,103,102,102 99,91,90,90,89 69,**
toteswingers 1&2 £11.20, 1&3 £7.60, 2&3 £47.80 CSF £25.31 CT £194.12 TOTE £7.10: £2.00, £2.70, £4.40; EX 36.00 Trifecta £370.90 Pool: £1279.40 - 2.58 winning units..
Owner Robert & Janet Gibbs **Bred** Tom McCarthy **Trained** Withycombe, Somerset

FOCUS
The two unexposed runners who were prominent in the market were well held in this competitive handicap and there was a dramatic incident at the last hurdle when the leader Foxcub took a nasty fall. He was set for a big personal best. The form is rated around the runner-up.

2631 LENNY ROBERTS MEMORIAL TROPHY NOVICES' HURDLE (11 hdls) 2m 6f

2:25 (2:25) (Class 4) 4-Y-O+ **£4,548** (£1,335; £667; £333)

Form RPR

3- **1** **Swallowshide**[193] 239 4-10-12 0.................... AidanColeman 127+
(Emma Lavelle) *hld up in tch: hdwy 3 out: sn rdn to chse ldng pair: wnt cl 2nd 2 out: led between last 2: wnt lft last: styd on wl: readily* **11/4**[2]

2- **2** *8* **Lumpys Gold**[30] 2009 5-10-12 0....................(t) DarylJacob 116
(Paul Nicholls) *t.k.h: led 2nd: jnd after 3 out: rdn and hdd between last 2: styd on same pce* **11/10**[1]

0P/ **3** *31* **Stage King**[284] 4151 7-10-9 0.................... GavinSheehan(3) 97
(Warren Greatrex) *hld up: stmbld bdly 4th: rdn after 3 out: nvr any imp on ldrs: lft 4th 2 out: wkng whn lft modest 3rd at the last* **12/1**

000/ **4** *3 ½* **Uncle Pettit (IRE)**[223] 5264 5-10-12 0.................... TimmyMurphy 83
(Jonathan Portman) *led tl 2nd: trckd ldrs: losing pl whn wnt bdly lft 3 out: sn wknd: lft modest 4th at the last* **100/1**

P **Already Basking (CAN)**[1137] 5-10-5 0.................... MissAliceMills(7)
(Simon Earle) *hld up: struggling 8th: t.o after 3 out: p.u bef next* **200/1**

5/0- **F** **Somerset Lias (IRE)**[30] 2011 5-10-12 0.................... SamJones 108
(Bob Buckler) *trckd ldrs: rdn after 8th: styng on at same pce in hld 4th whn lft 3rd 2 out: fell last* **25/1**

2- **F** **Knight Of Noir (IRE)**[192] 270 4-10-12 0.................... TomScudamore 97
(David Pipe) *trckd ldr fr after 3rd: rchd for 8th: chal after 3 out: sn rdn: cl 3rd but hld whn fell 2 out* **3/1**[3]

5m 16.3s (-10.20) **Going Correction** -0.325s/f (Good) **7** Ran SP% **112.3**
Speed ratings (Par 105): **105,102,90,89,** ,
toteswingers 1&2 £1.90, 1&3 £10.00, 2&3 £8.60 CSF £6.18 TOTE £3.30: £1.70, £1.10; EX 9.70 Trifecta £44.60 Pool: £2640.13 - 44.34 winning units..
Owner D I Bare **Bred** D I Bare **Trained** Hatherden, Hants

FOCUS
An interesting novice hurdle. The strong favourite was turned over but the well-related winner scored in decent style on his hurdling debut and the first two were a long way clear. The form is rated through the second.

2632 EBF & TBA MARES' NOVICES' LIMITED H'CAP CHASE (17 fncs) 2m 5f

3:00 (3:00) (Class 3) (0-125,124) 4-Y-O+ **£9,837**

Form RPR

2- **1** **Rossa Parks (IRE)**[10] 2424 7-10-5 **110**.................... RichardJohnson 113+
(Neil Mulholland) *lft in ld 2nd tl after 4th: chsd clr ldr: clsd on ldr 10th: lft in clr ld 12th: in command after 2 out: lft to fin alone last* **3/1**[2]

454- **U** **Ninfea (IRE)**[10] 2424 5-10-2 **110** oh7....................(p) TrevorWhelan(3)
(Neil King) *led: j.lft 1st: wnt bdly lft whn nt fluent and uns rdr 2nd* **25/1**

06P/ **P** **Tante Sissi (FR)**[250] 4791 6-11-5 **124**.................... RobertThornton
(Alan King) *t.k.h: led after 4th: clr 6th tl 10th: jnd whn hit 12th: slipped and virtually fell and hdd: dropped to 4th: nt rcvr: p.u bef 4 out* **11/4**[1]

1/P- **P** **Golden Gael**[26] 2084 7-11-4 **123**.................... NickScholfield
(Jeremy Scott) *trckd ldrs tl mstke and stmbld v bdly 8th: nt rcvr: p.u bef 8th* **9/2**[3]

23/ **F** **Steady Girlfriend**[631] 4580 8-10-5 **110** oh7....................(t) RyanMahon 106
(Anthony Honeyball) *hld up bhd ldrs: stmbld 5th: hmpd next: nt fluent 7th: lft 3rd 12th: stmbld bdly 4 out: rdn to chse wnr sn after: 3 l down whn mstke 2 out: sn hld: fell last* **8/1**

303- **F** **Kindly Note**[65] 1594 6-10-10 **115**.................... AidanColeman 102
(Emma Lavelle) *chsd ldrs: reminder after 9th and 11th: lft 2nd next: rdn in 3rd after 4 out: hit 3 out: styd on same pce fr next: fell last* **11/4**[1]

5m 22.2s (-3.00) **Going Correction** +0.05s/f (Yiel) **6** Ran SP% **111.5**
Speed ratings (Par 107): **107,** , , ,
TOTE £4.70: £3.90; EX 2.80 Trifecta £2.90 Pool: £2129.23 - 539.70 winning units..
Owner Mrs P L Bridel **Bred** G Aherne **Trained** Limpley Stoke, Wilts

FOCUS
There was only one finisher in this mares' handicap chase but the winner put in a professional display and deserved the victory. She is rated to a similar level as Southwell.

2633 CLIFF PAYNE & ALFIE SMITH MEMORIAL H'CAP CHASE (17 fncs) 2m 5f

3:30 (3:30) (Class 4) (0-110,117) 4-Y-O+ **£5,749** (£1,735; £894; £473)

Form RPR

/52- **1** **Highbury High (IRE)**[40] 1870 6-10-7 **91**.................... PaddyBrennan 110+
(Paul Henderson) *disp 3rd fr 2nd: pckd 2nd: wnt 2nd after 4 out: chal after next gng best: slt ld whn stmbld bdly last and nrly uns rdr: rcvrd qckly to run on strly and regain ld towards fin* **6/1**[3]

3/1- **2** *1* **Richmond (FR)**[9] 2437 8-12-5 **117** 7ex.................... AidanColeman 127
(Venetia Williams) *trckd ldr: led 13th: pckd 4 out: rdn whn jnd after 3 out: narrowly hdd whn lft in 2 l ld last: outpcd and hdd towards fin* **8/13**[1]

45P/ **3** *28* **Kirbys Glen (IRE)**[484] 1076 11-10-3 **87**............................ AndrewTinkler 70
(Johnny Farrelly) *disp 3rd fr 2nd tl 12th: wnt 3rd after 4 out: sn rdn: wknd 2 out* **33/1**

6/4- **4** *8* **Material Boy**[39] 1886 6-11-9 **107**..............................(vt) DarylJacob 83
(Nick Williams) *j. sltly lft: led: slow 9th (water): hdd 13th: sn rdn: wknd bef 3 out* **4/1**[2]

3/U- **U** **Swincombe Stone**[14] 2315 6-11-10 **108**.............................. RyanMahon
(Anthony Honeyball) *hld up bhd ldrs: blnd and uns rdr 2nd* **10/1**

5m 23.8s (-1.40) **Going Correction** +0.05s/f (Yiel) **5** Ran SP% **108.2**
Speed ratings (Par 105): **104,103,92,89,**
CSF £10.53 TOTE £4.50: £2.50, £1.10; EX 10.90 Trifecta £52.00 Pool: £1720.09 - 24.79 winning units..
Owner The Affordable Partnership **Bred** Sean Deu Burca **Trained** Whitsbury, Hants

FOCUS
There was a dramatic finish in this handicap chase. The winner nearly threw it away when making a bad mistake at the last but he rallied well to score and was value for much more than the winning margin. This was a big step up on his previous form.

2634 MARY WILLIAMS OF BRIDGWATER "NEWCOMERS" STANDARD OPEN NATIONAL HUNT FLAT RACE 1m 6f 110y

4:00 (4:00) (Class 6) 3-5-Y-O **£1,624** (£477; £238; £119)

Form RPR

1 **Bjornlucky (IRE)** 3-10-7 0.................................... HarrySkelton 88+
(Dan Skelton) *trckd ldrs: wnt 2nd 2f out: sn rdn: styd on to ld wl ins fnl f: rdn out* **3/1**[2]

- **2** *¾* **Sirrah Star (IRE)** 5-11-1 0.................................... RichardJohnson 95+
(Neil Mulholland) *hld up in tch: gd hdwy to ld over 2f out: rdn over 1f out: no ex whn hdd wl ins fnl f* **5/1**

3 *3 ¼* **Swincombe Star** 4-11-8 0.................................... DarylJacob 98
(Robert Walford) *prom: rdn over 2f out: sn sltly outpcd: styd on again to go 3rd ent fnl f* **5/2**[1]

4 *1 ½* **The Snappy Poet** 4-11-8 0.................................... NickScholfield 96
(Jeremy Scott) *hld up in tch: effrt over 2f out: wnt 4th ent fnl f: styd on same pce* **8/1**

5 *5* **Gotham City (IRE)** 4-11-8 0.................................... TomScudamore 90
(David Pipe) *led: rdn over 2f out: sn hdd: kpt on same pce tl no ex and lost 2 pls ent fnl f* **7/2**[3]

6 *10* **Dream Destiny** 4-11-1 0....................................(t) TommyPhelan 71
(Mark Gillard) *prom tl rn sltly wd on bnd after winning post: chsd ldrs tl outpcd over 2f out* **14/1**

7 *41* **Ellymac** 5-11-1 0.................................... RobertThornton 22
(Richard Mitchell) *chsd ldrs: drvn along after 4f: wknd over 3f out: eased fnl 2f: t.o* **100/1**

3m 17.8s (197.80) **7** Ran SP% **111.2**
toteswingers 1&2 £4.90, 1&3 £2.70, 2&3 £3.20 CSF £17.23 TOTE £3.70: £2.10, £2.60; EX 18.30 Trifecta £55.90 Pool: £1024.10 - 13.73 winning units..
Owner Donlon, Doyle & MacDonald **Bred** Austin Lyons **Trained** Alcester, Warwicks

FOCUS
They went a reasonable pace in this newcomers' bumper and the winner rallied well to snatch the prize.
T/Plt: £123.90. Pool: £56,126.14 - 330.65 winning units. T/Qpdt: £15.50. Pool: £4503.00 - 214.00 winning units. TM

2635 - 2641a (Foreign Racing) - See Raceform Interactive

2210 ASCOT (R-H)

Friday, November 22

OFFICIAL GOING: Good to soft (chs 7.4, hdl 7.9)
Wind: Moderate, across Weather: Fine

2642 GEOTECH SOLUTIONS "NATIONAL HUNT" MAIDEN HURDLE (11 hdls) 2m 3f 110y

1:00 (1:00) (Class 3) 4-Y-0+ **£5,630** (£1,663; £831; £415; £207; £104)

Form RPR

26/ **1** **Beat That (IRE)**[212] 5518 5-11-0 0.................................... BarryGeraghty 138+
(Nicky Henderson) *trckd ldng pair: pushed along to cl after 3 out: led 2 out: sn drew rt away: eased nr fin* **5/4**[1]

2/0- **2** *10* **Champagne West (IRE)**[17] 2279 5-11-0 0.................. RichardJohnson 123+
(Philip Hobbs) *tended to jump lft: led: nt fluent 5th and 6th: rdn and hdd 2 out: no ch w wnr sn after: kpt on* **3/1**[2]

61/ **3** *½* **Knock House (IRE)**[208] 4 4-11-0 0.................. DominicElsworth 121
(Mick Channon) *trckd ldr: rdn to chal 2 out: sn outpcd: nt fluent last: kpt on nr fin* **12/1**

1/ **4** *5* **Bodega**[283] 4184 5-11-0 0.................................... WillKennedy 117
(Ian Williams) *chsd ldng trio: outpcd fr 3 out: n.d after: one pce* **33/1**

2/0- **5** *3* **Brother Brian (IRE)**[34] 1974 5-11-0 0.................. NickScholfield 115
(Hughie Morrison) *t.k.h: hld up in last and detached early: prog on inner bef 2 out: shkn up briefly and kpt on: shaped w sme promise* **12/1**

652/ **6** *4* **Sybarite (FR)**[216] 7-11-0 0.................. SamTwiston-Davies 111
(Nigel Twiston-Davies) *wl in tch: pushed along after 7th: no rspnse and lost pl after next: wl btn 3 out* **7/2**[3]

40- **7** *9* **Vikekhal (FR)**[20] 2216 4-10-11 0.................. JoshuaMoore(3) 102
(Gary Moore) *t.k.h: hld up towards rr: sme prog 3 out: shkn up and wknd 2 out* **66/1**

1/5- **8** *3* **Ballyhooley Boy (IRE)**[11] 2426 6-11-0 0.................. CharliePoste 99
(Robin Dickin) *in tch in midfield: shkn up after 3 out: wknd 2 out* **50/1**

/45- **9** *36* **Noble Friend (IRE)**[18] 2272 5-11-0 0.................. TomCannon 67
(Chris Gordon) *hld up: jst in tch whn mstke 8th: wknd rapidly: t.o* **40/1**

4m 41.3s (-3.40) **Going Correction** +0.025s/f (Yiel)
WFA 4 from 5yo+ 7lb **9** Ran SP% **115.9**
Speed ratings (Par 107): **107,103,102,100,99 98,94,93,78**
toteswingers 1&2 £1.70, 2&3 £6.30, 1&3 £5.10 CSF £5.22 TOTE £2.60: £1.10, £1.30, £2.30; EX 5.60 Trifecta £29.00 Pool: £2079.17 - 53.64 winning units..
Owner Michael Buckley **Bred** John O'Brien **Trained** Upper Lambourn, Berks

FOCUS
This wasn't a novice event without depth and it saw a promising winner who looks a smart prospect. The overall form isn't great for the track.

2643 DAVID & TONI EYLES BEGINNERS' CHASE (16 fncs) 2m 3f

1:30 (1:30) (Class 3) 4-Y-0+ **£7,507** (£2,217; £1,108; £554)

Form RPR

105/ **1** **Top Of The Range (IRE)**[219] 5352 6-11-1 138.................. BarryGeraghty 131+
(Nicky Henderson) *j.lft: trckd ldr: awkward 3rd and rdr airborne briefly: led next tl after 6th: led again 4 out: pressed fr 2 out: drvn out* **4/7**[1]

501/ **2** *1 ¼* **Titchwood (IRE)**[277] 4289 5-11-1 0.................. RichieMcLernon 130+
(Jonjo O'Neill) *hld up in 3rd: blnd 4th: mstke 7th: clsd 4 out: chsd wnr next: tried to chal fr 2 out: ch last: hung lft flat: kpt on* **4/1**[2]

3 *20* **My Dads Horse**[615] 7-11-1 0.................................... PaulMoloney 113
(Evan Williams) *hld up in last: lost tch 11th though stl gng wl enough: nudged along and tk modest 3rd after 2 out: rn down the last: eased flat* **12/1**

0/3- **4** *11* **Lord Of House (GER)**[17] 2282 5-11-1 0..............................(t) MarkGrant 106
(Charlie Mann) *led to 4th: led again after 6th tl 4 out: mstke next and wknd: lost modest 3rd after 2 out* **5/1**[3]

4m 47.4s (1.00) **Going Correction** +0.25s/f (Yiel) **4** Ran SP% **108.0**
Speed ratings (Par 107): **107,106,98,93**
CSF £3.32 TOTE £1.50; EX 3.10 Trifecta £6.60 Pool: £1638.68 - 184.29 winning units..
Owner Walters Plant Hire Ltd **Bred** Kevin Foley **Trained** Upper Lambourn, Berks

FOCUS
An interesting beginners' chase, but the first pair dominated from four out and the form is worth treating with a little caution. The winner is rated 10lb off his best hurdles mark, with the second stepping up on his hurdles figure.

2644 ROBERT GILES AGENCIES INTRODUCTORY HURDLE (9 hdls) 2m

2:05 (2:05) (Class 3) 4-Y-0+ **£6,881** (£2,032; £1,016; £508; £254; £127)

Form RPR

1- **1** **Irving**[8] 2476 5-11-5 0.................................... NickScholfield 122+
(Paul Nicholls) *trckd ldng pair: nt fluent 5th: clsd to ld bef 2 out: sn drew clr: eased nr fin* **8/11**[1]

2 *4* **A Hare Breath (IRE)**[271] 5-11-0 0.................................... TomCannon 107+
(Nick Gifford) *j.lft: trckd ldr: chal after 3 out: chsd wnr bef next: no ch but kpt on* **25/1**[3]

012/ **3** *2 ¾* **Tradewinds (FR)**[216] 5407 5-11-0 0.................................... BarryGeraghty 105+
(Nicky Henderson) *hld up: trckd ldng trip 5th: mstke 3 out: pushed along and outpcd sn after: shkn up after 2 out: styd on to take 3rd after last: nrst fin* **5/4**[2]

/20- **4** *1 ¼* **Fond Memory (IRE)**[22] 2181 5-11-0 0.................. SamTwiston-Davies 105
(Nigel Twiston-Davies) *hld up: outpcd and pushed along 3 out: reminders and prog 2 out: tk 3rd briefly last: kpt on same pce* **33/1**

P/ **5** *3 ¼* **Hung Parliament (FR)**[331] 3222 5-11-0 0.................. RobertThornton 100
(Alan King) *t.k.h: hld up in rr: outpcd 3 out: fdd fr 2 out* **50/1**

6 *4 ½* **Freddy Q (IRE)**[40] 4-11-0 0.................................... RichieMcLernon 95
(Roger Teal) *led at v stdy pce: nt fluent 5th: hdd & wknd bef 2 out* **50/1**

0/0- **F** **Pullmen**[48] 1764 5-11-0 0.................................... RichardJohnson
(Paul Henderson) *t.k.h: hld up in last: abt 6 l down and sing to be outpcd whn fell 3 out* **100/1**

3m 54.2s (6.80) **Going Correction** +0.025s/f (Yiel)
WFA 4 from 5yo 7lb **7** Ran SP% **114.0**
Speed ratings (Par 107): **84,82,80,80,78 76,**
toteswingers 1&2 £3.00, 2&3 £3.60, 1&3 £1.02 CSF £16.33 TOTE £2.00: £1.20, £5.10; EX 15.20 Trifecta £26.60 Pool: £3154.95 - 88.91 winning units..
Owner Axom XLIX **Bred** Gestut Schlenderhan **Trained** Ditcheat, Somerset

FOCUS
A tricky race to assess, as it was steadily run, but the winner remains an exciting prospect. He was value for further.

2645 WINKWORTH H'CAP CHASE (16 fncs) 2m 3f

2:40 (2:40) (Class 3) (0-135,134) 4-Y-0+ **£12,512** (£3,696; £1,848; £924; £462; £232)

Form RPR

525/ **1** **Niceonefrankie**[208] 6 7-11-7 **129**.................................... LiamTreadwell 150+
(Venetia Williams) *hld up in tch: clsd on ldrs fr 11th: wnt 2nd bef 3 out: led bef 2 out: readily drew clr: comf* **8/1**

613- **2** *13* **Double Ross (IRE)**[41] 1865 7-11-11 **133**.................. SamTwiston-Davies 142+
(Nigel Twiston-Davies) *chsd ldrs: mstke 2nd: lft in ld 4th: jnd 7th: drvn and hdd bef 2 out: one pce and no ch w wnr* **15/8**[1]

3/2- **3** *13* **Simply Wings (IRE)**[22] 2180 9-11-9 **134**.................. MichealNolan(3) 134
(Richard Lee) *smetimes j.rt: cl up: squeezed for room 4th: trckd ldng pair 6th: mstke 9th: chal and on terms 4 out: mstke next: wknd tamely* **8/1**

/51- **4** *11* **Gallox Bridge**[33] 1990 8-11-11 **133**..............................(t) BarryGeraghty 120
(Tim Vaughan) *hld up and last tl 6th: lft bhd and pushed along fr 11th: no ch after: tk remote 4th after 2 out: mstke last* **12/1**

1U3- **5** *22* **Al Alfa**[27] 2086 6-10-11 **119**.................................... RichardJohnson 96
(Philip Hobbs) *led: terrible blunder 4th and hdd: jnd ldr 7th tl wknd qckly after 4 out: t.o* **6/1**[3]

2/3- **6** *26* **Greywell Boy**[20] 2212 6-11-5 **127**.................................... DavidBass 68
(Nick Williams) *chsd ldrs: mstke 5th and lost pl: nt fluent and dropped to last next: nvr gng wl after: wl t.o* **11/4**[2]

464- **F** **Donnas Palm (IRE)**[97] 1283 9-11-0 **125**.................. JoshuaMoore(3)
(Gary Moore) *chsd ldrs: lost pl 8th: lost tch w ldrs 11th: abt 8 l down in 5th and making no imp whn fell 3 out* **16/1**

4m 41.7s (-4.70) **Going Correction** +0.25s/f (Yiel) **7** Ran SP% **111.5**
Speed ratings (Par 107): **119,113,108,103,94 83,**
toteswingers 1&2 £2.60, 1&3 £7.80, 2&3 £1.70 CSF £23.29 TOTE £6.00: £2.80, £2.10; EX 18.80 Trifecta £328.20 Pool: £2001.93 - 4.57 winning units..
Owner Old Carthusian Racing Society **Bred** Mrs M E Jones **Trained** Kings Caple, H'fords

FOCUS
This was always going to be a truly run handicap and they finished very well strung out. Solid form, with the winner making a big step up. The second ran to form.

2646 BROWN ADVISORY H'CAP CHASE (20 fncs) 3m

3:15 (3:15) (Class 3) (0-135,135) 4-Y-0+ **£12,512** (£3,696; £1,848; £924; £462; £232)

Form RPR

631- **1** **Night Alliance (IRE)**[12] 2390 8-10-2 **111** 7ex..................(b) PaulMoloney 127+
(Dr Richard Newland) *wl plcd bhd ldrs: j. slowly 1st: crept into 3rd 3 out: clsd fr next: led and lft in command last: sn clr: comf* **5/1**[3]

/60- **2** *4 ½* **Duke Of Lucca (IRE)**[21] 2199 8-11-12 **135**..............(bt[1]) RichardJohnson 140
(Philip Hobbs) *hld up early: stdy prog fr 9th: jnd ldrs 14th: wnt 2nd 16th: led bef 2 out: drvn and hdd whn mstke last: immediately btn* **15/2**

P/1- **3** *½* **Goring One (IRE)**[36] 1944 8-10-6 **115**.................................... AndrewThornton 120
(Anna Newton-Smith) *chsd ldng pair to 10th: styd prom: wnt 2nd after 14th: lft in ld 16th: drvn and hdd 2 out: kpt trying and on terms whn mstke last: no ex* **20/1**

1/U- **4** *2 ¾* **Ballypatrick (IRE)**[38] 1918 7-11-4 **127**.................................... DominicElsworth 130
(Mick Channon) *prom: trckd ldng pair 10th to 14th: lost pl: rdn to go 4th after 3 out: fnd little and nvr threatened* **10/1**

6/P- **5** *1 1/4* **There's No Panic (IRE)**[20] 2214 8-11-9 **132** .... NickScholfield 133
(Paul Nicholls) *mostly in last quartet: mstke 9th: tried to make prog fr 15th: nt on terms fr 4 out: kpt on fr 2 out* **12/1**
551- **6** *18* **Annacotty (IRE)**[18] 2267 5-11-7 **130** .... IanPopham 122+
(Martin Keighley) *wl plcd: mstke 7th: pushed along fr 13th: no prog 15th: wl btn after next* **5/2**[1]
P23/ **7** *17* **Grove Pride**[222] 5314 8-11-8 **131** .... RobertThornton 112
(Henry Daly) *w ldr: led 11th: mstke 14th: blnd and hdd 16th: mstke 3 out and wknd: t.o* **9/2**[2]
U/0- **F** **Mahogany Blaze (FR)**[187] 392 11-11-12 **135** ....(t) SamTwiston-Davies
(Nigel Twiston-Davies) *towards rr: in tch fr 11th: pushed along in 6th and 6 l down whn fell heavily 4 out* **28/1**
/UR- **P** **Sarando**[16] 158 8-11-0 **123** .... WillKennedy
(Alex Hales) *a in rr: wkng whn j. slowly 14th: t.o after: p.u bef 2 out* **50/1**
30F/ **P** **Summery Justice (IRE)**[255] 4721 9-11-9 **132** .... LiamTreadwell
(Venetia Williams) *a in rr: mstke 8th: blnd 11th: lost tch whn mstke 13th: p.u bef next* **12/1**
/5P- **U** **Brackloon High (IRE)**[26] 2108 8-11-7 **130** ....(p) BrendanPowell
(Brendan Powell) *led: mstke 4th and reminders: hdd 11th: w ldr whn mstke 14th and rdn: j.v.slowly next and dropped to rr: 9th whn blnd and uns rdr 4 out* **25/1**
101- **P** **Wiesentraum (GER)**[28] 2065 7-11-7 **130** .... BarryGeraghty
(Lucy Wadham) *j. both lft and bdly in rr: last whn p.u bef 11th* **16/1**

6m 3.8s (0.30) **Going Correction** +0.25s/f (Yiel) 12 Ran SP% **119.6**
Speed ratings (Par 107): **109,107,107,106,106 100,94,,,**
CSF £41.11 CT £700.40 TOTE £5.20: £2.10, £2.80, £4.60; EX 33.90 Trifecta £1262.80 Pool: £3643.76 - 2.16 winning units..
Owner Dr R D P Newland **Bred** Mrs Mary Doyle And Peter Sherry **Trained** Claines, Worcs
■ Stewards' Enquiry : Andrew Thornton four-day ban: used whip above permitted level (Dec 6,8-10)

FOCUS
A fair staying handicap run at a solid gallop, and only three mattered from the penultimate fence. The winner was well in but this rates a step up and the second ran his best race since February.

2647 CANACCORD GENUITY H'CAP HURDLE (9 hdls) 2m
3:50 (3:50) (Class 2) (0-145,137) 4-Y-0+
£9,384 (£2,772; £1,386; £693; £346; £174)

Form RPR
4/4- **1** **Dunraven Storm (IRE)**[20] 2213 8-11-7 **132** .... RichardJohnson 134+
(Philip Hobbs) *mde all: allowed to set stdy pce: flattened 4th and 5th: set alight fr 3 out: 2 l clr 2 out: styd on and nvr seriously threatened* **3/1**[1]
/F0- **2** *1 1/2* **Specialagent Alfie**[20] 2213 7-11-1 **126** ....(t) TomCannon 127
(Nick Gifford) *chsd wnr to 3rd: styd prom: rdn bef 2 out: kpt on to take 2nd again last: unable to chal* **16/1**
/F2- **3** *1/2* **Milord (GER)**[21] 2189 4-11-0 **125** .... SamThomas 125
(Kim Bailey) *hld up in last: stl there 2 out: pushed along and prog jst bef last: rdn and r.o flat to take 3rd last strides* **16/1**
3/3- **4** *nse* **Population**[14] 2344 6-10-9 **123** ....(v[1]) JackQuinlan[(3)] 123
(John Ferguson) *trckd ldrs: lost pl sltly fr 6th: pushed along after 3 out: rdn and styd on fr last: nrly snatched 3rd* **9/2**[3]
/41- **5** *1 1/4* **Brinestine (USA)**[8] 2474 4-10-10 **121** 7ex .... NickScholfield 121
(Paul Nicholls) *hld up tl plld way through to trck wnr 3rd: distracted and mstke next: rdn whn mstke 2 out: nt qckn and lost 2nd last: fdd* **10/3**[2]
6/0- **6** *1 3/4* **Jumps Road**[20] 2213 6-11-0 **125** .... BrendanPowell 122
(Colin Tizzard) *hld up in 6th: prog to trck ldrs 3 out: cl enough 2 out: fdd last* **20/1**
/22- **7** *3 1/4* **Discovery Bay**[14] 2344 5-11-5 **130** .... WillKennedy 124
(Brian Ellison) *hld up in last trio in slowly run event: prog on outer 6th: no hdwy after 3 out: fdd fr 2 out* **12/1**
2P6/ **8** *nk* **Whitby Jack**[245] 4905 6-10-11 **125** .... JoshuaMoore[(3)] 119
(Gary Moore) *hld up in last trio in slowly run event: same pl but cl up 2 out: rdn and no prog whn nt fluent last: fdd* **12/1**
F **Hammersly Lake (FR)**[795] 5-11-12 **137** .... BarryGeraghty 133
(Nicky Henderson) *trckd ldrs: lost pl fr 6th: in last trio and pushed along after 3 out: prog on inner and cl 5th whn fell heavily 2 out* **9/2**[3]

3m 51.3s (3.90) **Going Correction** +0.025s/f (Yiel)
WFA 4 from 5yo+ 7lb 9 Ran SP% **116.4**
Speed ratings (Par 109): **91,90,90,89,89 88,86,86,**
toteswingers 1&2 £12.00, 1&3 £10.80, 2&3 £24.70 CSF £47.93 CT £664.95 TOTE £3.90: £1.80, £4.00, £3.60; EX 45.60 Trifecta £322.60 Pool: £3992.66 - 9.28 winning units..
Owner Mrs Karola Vann **Bred** Miss Violet Sweeney **Trained** Withycombe, Somerset

FOCUS
A good-quality handicap. All of the runners held a chance of sorts at the top of the straight. The winner may still be capable of a bit better.
T/Jkpt: £1,382.00 to a £1 stake. Pool: £81424.46 - 41.83 winning tickets T/Plt: £58.10 to a £1 stake. Pool: £107623.60 - 1351.25 winning tickets T/Qpdt: £29.40 to a £1 stake. Pool: £8096.49 - 203.13 winning tickets JN

2385 FFOS LAS (L-H)
Friday, November 22

OFFICIAL GOING: Soft (heavy in places; 6.1)
Wind: almost nil Weather: fine

2648 GLYN ABBEY MAIDEN HURDLE (10 hdls) 2m 4f
12:40 (12:40) (Class 5) 4-Y-0+ **£1,949** (£572; £286; £143)

Form RPR
15- **1** **Cloud Brook (IRE)**[35] 1954 5-11-0 0 .... APMcCoy 130+
(Rebecca Curtis) *cl up: jnd ldr 4th: led after 7th: drew clr fr 3 out: v easily* **4/6**[1]
2- **2** *7* **Padre Tito (IRE)**[26] 2106 5-10-11 0 .... GavinSheehan[(3)] 115
(Emma Lavelle) *trckd ldrs: rdn in 4th appr 3 out: wnt 2nd 2 out: kpt on same pce and no imp on easy wnr* **9/4**[2]
543- **3** *7* **Man Of Steel (IRE)**[16] 2285 4-11-0 110 ....(p) DonalDevereux 107
(Peter Bowen) *led: jnd 4th: hdd after 7th: styd cl up tl outpcd by wnr 3 out: lost 2nd next: one pce* **7/1**[3]
25/ **4** *nk* **Spencer Lea**[222] 5310 5-10-11 0 .... RobertDunne[(3)] 107
(Andrew Price) *hld up towards rr: hdwy after 4th: chsd ldrs 7th: wknd 2 out: plugged on to chal for 3rd flat* **20/1**
220/ **5** *43* **Kayf Moss**[254] 4738 5-11-0 0 .... RhysFlint 76
(John Flint) *wl in tch in midfield: pushed along 5th: rdn and wknd appr 3 out: poor 5th whn blnd last: t.o* **10/1**
6 *14* **Twopoundsofbutter (IRE)**[201] 6-10-7 0 .... JPKiely[(7)] 49
(Tim Vaughan) *wl in tch in midfield tl rdn and wknd after 7th: t.o whn hit 3 out* **50/1**
/00- **7** *hd* **Kill Van Kull (IRE)**[16] 2286 4-10-8 0 ow1 .... MrMatthewBarber[(7)] 50
(Marc Barber) *hld up in rr: wknd 7th: t.o* **100/1**
0/F- **8** *16* **Genuine Art**[12] 2385 6-10-7 0 .... DaveCrosse 26
(Lucy Jones) *towards rr: sme hdwy 7th: wknd appr next: t.o* **66/1**
500- **9** *16* **Wynn Darwi (IRE)**[24] 2147 8-10-9 0 .... AodhaganConlon[(5)] 17
(Debra Hamer) *t.k.h early: hld up in rr: wknd 7th: t.o* **66/1**
54- **P** **Millenary Magic (IRE)**[12] 2386 6-10-7 100 .... MissJodieHughes[(7)]
(David Rees) *prom tl wknd 6th: lost tch after next: t.o whn p.u bef 3 out* **66/1**

5m 22.9s (32.00) **Going Correction** +1.85s/f (Heav)
WFA 4 from 5yo+ 8lb 10 Ran SP% **124.5**
Speed ratings (Par 103): **110,107,104,104,87 81,81,75,68,**
toteswingers 1&2 £1.10, 2&3 £2.80, 1&3 £1.80 CSF £2.67 TOTE £1.60: £1.10, £1.20, £1.60; EX 2.70 Trifecta £8.80 Pool: £3706.96 - 314.48 winning units..
Owner R J H Geffen **Bred** Edward & Mrs Bernadette Walsh **Trained** Newport, Dyfed

FOCUS
Tony McCoy described the ground as "heavy". Little depth to this contest, but the easy winner is on the upgrade and there should be more to come.

2649 IWEC ELECTRICAL "NATIONAL HUNT" NOVICES' HURDLE (12 hdls) 3m
1:10 (1:11) (Class 4) 4-Y-0+ **£3,119** (£915; £457; £228)

Form RPR
32- **1** **Potters Cross**[27] 2079 6-10-12 134 .... APMcCoy 130+
(Rebecca Curtis) *mde all: hit 3 out: sn shkn up: 4 l up and rdn whn mstke last: styd on to draw clr flat* **8/13**[1]
511- **2** *9* **Berea Boru (IRE)**[12] 2386 5-11-12 122 ....(t) DonalDevereux 136
(Peter Bowen) *chsd ldrs: rdn after 9th: wnt 2nd after 2 out: 4 l down whn mstke last: no ex* **8/1**[3]
3/2- **3** *6* **Closing Ceremony (IRE)**[27] 2076 4-10-9 0 .... GavinSheehan[(3)] 117
(Emma Lavelle) *racd wd in bk st on first circ: chsd ldrs: rdn along after 6th: j. slowly 8th: chsd wnr 9th tl after 2 out: 3rd and one pce whn j.rt last* **9/4**[2]
0/4- **4** *72* **Blazing Bouncer**[27] 2076 8-10-12 0 .... RhysFlint 40
(Richard Woollacott) *chsd ldr to 9th: wknd qckly: t.o* **66/1**
53- **5** *82* **Lord Fox (IRE)**[176] 554 6-10-7 0 .... BenPoste[(5)]
(Shaun Harris) *nt fluent: hld up in last: struggling 7th: t.o fr next: eventually completed* **50/1**

6m 32.6s (43.60) **Going Correction** +1.85s/f (Heav)
WFA 4 from 5yo+ 9lb 5 Ran SP% **107.3**
Speed ratings (Par 105): **101,98,96,72,44**
CSF £5.99 TOTE £1.50: £1.10, £2.20; EX 3.90 Trifecta £6.30 Pool: £4017.75 - 473.47 winning units..
Owner Conyers, O'Reilly, Roddis, Zeffman **Bred** Shade Oak Stud **Trained** Newport, Dyfed

FOCUS
A fair novice hurdle that proved a thorough test of stamina in the conditions.

2650 SHUFFLEBOTTOM LTD H'CAP CHASE (18 fncs) 3m
1:40 (1:40) (Class 4) (0-120,119) 4-Y-0+ **£3,861** (£1,198; £645)

Form RPR
/2F- **1** **Bendant**[12] 2390 8-11-8 **115** .... TomO'Brien 122+
(Debra Hamer) *racd in 3rd tl trckd ldr 6th: led 14th: drew clr appr last: comf* **11/4**[2]
110/ **2** *8* **Armedanddangerous (IRE)**[277] 4285 8-11-5 **112** .... JamesReveley 109
(Tom Gretton) *trckd ldr tl relegated to 3rd at 6th: pushed along 10th: rdn after 14th: wnt 2nd 4 out: one pce and no imp on wnr: wkng whn blnd last* **5/2**[1]
124- **3** *29* **Raduis Bleu (FR)**[8] 2468 8-11-1 **115** .... MissLBrooke[(7)] 92
(Lady Susan Brooke) *led: hit 1st: tended to jump rt: hdd 14th: lost 2nd next: sn wknd: t.o* **11/4**[2]
/U0- **F** **Robin Will (FR)**[35] 1959 8-11-12 **119** .... AlainCawley
(Richard Woollacott) *hld up in last tl fell heavily 7th* **11/4**[2]

6m 53.1s (35.70) **Going Correction** +1.30s/f (Heav) 4 Ran SP% **108.6**
Speed ratings (Par 105): **92,89,79,**
CSF £9.71 TOTE £2.70; EX 8.00 Trifecta £20.40 Pool: £1209.14 - 44.40 winning units..
Owner Les Cooper **Bred** T L Cooper **Trained** Nantycaws, Carmarthens

FOCUS
With Robin Will coming down relatively early and Raduis Bleu making mistakes out in front, it was left to Bendant to run out quite a ready winner. The form is rated around the first two.

2651 WYG GROUP NOVICES' LIMITED H'CAP CHASE (17 fncs) 2m 5f
2:15 (2:15) (Class 3) (0-125,125) 4-Y-0+ **£7,213** (£2,623)

Form RPR
/0P- **1** **Super Villan**[18] 2267 8-10-1 **112** ....(b[1]) NicodeBoinville[(5)] 123+
(Mark Bradstock) *led to 13th: hrd rdn to ld appr next: styd on to draw clr fr 2 out: idled flat: drvn out* **3/1**[2]
U23- **2** *1 3/4* **Hansupfordetroit (IRE)**[12] 2389 8-11-0 **125** .... RobertWilliams[(5)] 129
(Bernard Llewellyn) *racd keenly early: trckd ldr: mstke 2nd: led 13th tl appr next: sn hrd rdn and one pce: clsd on wnr flat but a being hld* **3/1**[2]
0/0- **F** **Vintage Tea**[156] 767 6-10-5 **111** oh1 ....(t) JamieMoore
(Richard Woollacott) *in rr tl fell heavily 2nd* **33/1**
0P1- **F** **Danandy (IRE)**[22] 2179 6-11-0 **120** .... TomO'Brien
(Philip Hobbs) *lft last of 3 remaining 2nd: j. slowly 10th: pushed along in cl 3rd whn fell 4 out* **5/1**[3]
6/F- **U** **Big Society (IRE)**[30] 2024 7-10-9 **120** .... AodhaganConlon[(5)]
(Tom George) *prom tl blnd and uns rdr 2nd* **13/2**
0/2- **F** **Wychwoods Brook**[12] 2389 7-10-12 **118** .... AdamWedge
(Evan Williams) *in rr: mstke 1st: fell heavily next* **5/2**[1]

5m 53.1s (24.50) **Going Correction** +1.35s/f (Heav) 6 Ran SP% **111.5**
Speed ratings (Par 107): **107,106,,,**
CSF £12.54 TOTE £4.70: £2.30, £1.60; EX 14.70 Trifecta £16.80 Pool: £2061.89 - 92.02 winning units..
Owner Mark Tamburro **Bred** Shade Oak Stud **Trained** Letcombe Bassett, Oxon
■ Stewards' Enquiry : Nico de Boinville two-day ban: used whip above permitted level (Dec 6,8)

FOCUS
Early drama with Big Society, Wychwoods Brook and Vintage Tea all coming down independently at the second, and only two were left standing after Danandy departed early in the straight. The idling winner was value for further.

2652 32RED H'CAP HURDLE (11 hdls) 2m 6f
2:50 (2:50) (Class 3) (0-130,127) 4-Y-0+ **£5,393** (£1,583; £791; £395)

Form RPR
/31- **1** **Ballyculla (IRE)**[9] 2458 6-11-8 **126** 7ex .... GavinSheehan[(3)] 136+
(Warren Greatrex) *hld up in tch: hdwy 5th: mstke next: chal briefly 8th: sn pushed along in 4th: disp ld 3 out: led and mstke next: styd on to draw away flat* **6/4**[1]

402- 2 3 ¾ **Awaywiththegreys (IRE)**[115] 1150 6-11-12 127................ JamieMoore 132
(Peter Bowen) *trckd ldrs: wnt 2nd after 8th: tk slt ld 3 out: hit next and sn narrowly hdd: ev ch last: no ex flat* **8/1**

3/F- 3 20 **One In A Milan (IRE)**[22] 2170 8-11-0 122.......................... ConorRing(7) 107
(Evan Williams) *hld up last but in tch: rdn after 8th: outpcd by ldrs bef next: mstke 2 out but sn wnt remote 3rd: no imp* **4/1[3]**

2/0- 4 14 **Makethe Mostofnow (IRE)**[27] 2080 8-11-11 126............. AdamWedge 97
(Evan Williams) *cl up: disp ld 3rd to 4th: led 7th tl after next: wknd after 3 out* **8/1**

604- 5 27 **Captain Cardington (IRE)**[13] 2362 4-10-2 110..........(v) CiaranMckee(7) 54
(John O'Shea) *mde most to 7th: drvn to ld again after 8th: hdd 3 out: wknd 2 out: t.o* **18/1**

0/3- 6 63 **Qalinas (FR)**[16] 2288 6-10-12 123.................................(bt) AnthonyFox(10) 4
(David Pipe) *hld up in tch: hdwy to join ldrs 4th: rdn 8th: wknd qckly: t.o* **7/2[2]**

6m 0.2s (40.20) **Going Correction** +1.85s/f (Heav)
WFA 4 from 6yo+ 8lb **6** Ran SP% **109.7**
Speed ratings (Par 107): **100,98,91,86,76 53**
CSF £12.78 TOTE £2.40: £1.60, £3.20; EX 9.80 Trifecta £27.40 Pool: £2726.30 - 74.50 winning units..
Owner No Dramas Partnership **Bred** J Mangan **Trained** Upper Lambourn, Berks

FOCUS
The front pair drew clear. Another step forward from the progressive winner with the second back to something like his best.

2653 32RED.COM H'CAP CHASE (15 fncs) 2m 3f 110y
3:25 (3:25) (Class 5) (0-95,95) 4-Y-0+ **£2,144** (£629; £314; £157)

Form RPR
1P6/ 1 **Lamb's Cross**[43] 1846 7-11-7 95....................................[1] PatrickCorbett(5) 112+
(Mark Gillard) *trckd ldr: led 4 out: drawing clr whn blnd bdly 2 out: easily* **4/1[3]**

2/2- 2 21 **Billybo**[24] 2152 10-10-12 91.. AlanJohns(10) 85
(Tim Vaughan) *led to 4 out: sn one pce u.p: no ch w wnr fr 2 out: wknd flat: jst hld 2nd* **6/5[1]**

3/6- 3 hd **Bobby Dove**[19] 2251 6-11-3 89.. RobertDunne(3) 87
(Andrew Price) *a in 3rd: blnd bdly 6th and jumping lacked fluency after: no ch fr 3 out: r.o flat and nrly snatched 2nd* **5/2[2]**

1/6- 4 17 **Direct Flo (IRE)**[24] 2148 6-11-4 92.................................... JoshHamer(5) 68
(Tony Carroll) *hld up in last: blnd 1st: clsd 11th: wknd 4 out: t.o* **6/1**

5m 36.2s (35.10) **Going Correction** +1.35s/f (Heav) **4** Ran SP% **108.3**
Speed ratings (Par 103): **83,74,74,67**
CSF £9.52 TOTE £4.20; EX 11.60 Trifecta £12.40 Pool: £1545.24 - 93.07 winning units..
Owner Out Of Bounds Racing Club **Bred** Shade Oak Stud **Trained** Holwell, Dorset

FOCUS
Moderate form, with jumping letting down a couple of the runners. The winner did it well and could go in again.

2654 WALTERS UK LTD STANDARD OPEN NATIONAL HUNT FLAT RACE 2m
4:00 (4:00) (Class 6) 4-5-Y-0 **£1,642** (£478; £239)

Form RPR
22- 1 **Flying Eagle (IRE)**[13] 2368 5-11-0 0.................................... JamieMoore 110
(Peter Bowen) *t.k.h early: racd in 3rd tl trckd ldr 6f out: chal 3f out: led 2f out: drvn and hld on wl* **11/8[1]**

1- 2 1 ¼ **Capilla (IRE)**[24] 2153 5-11-7 0... AdamWedge 116
(Evan Williams) *led to 2f out: sn rdn: dropped bk to cl 3rd over 1f out: n.m.r and swtchd lft ins fnl f: r.o to take 2nd nr fin* **9/4[2]**

2/ 3 shd **Thomas Junior (FR)**[239] 4982 4-11-0 0.......................... ConorO'Farrell 109
(David Pipe) *hld up: rdn along 5f out: chsd ldng pair over 3f out: wnt 2nd over 1f out: unable qck u.p: no ex and lost 2nd nr fin* **11/4[3]**

4 3 **Gorsky Island**[208] 5-10-9 0....................................... AodhaganConlon(5) 106
(Tom George) *trckd ldr tl 6f out: rdn 4f out and sn outpcd by ldng trio: styd on fnl f* **10/1**

2- 5 76 **Jazz Thyme (IRE)**[95] 1318 4-10-2 0............................ RobertWilliams(5) 23
(Bernard Llewellyn) *t.k.h: hld up in rr: wknd over 4f out: t.o* **20/1**

4m 14.5s (31.60) **Going Correction** +1.85s/f (Heav)
WFA 4 from 5yo 7lb **5** Ran SP% **113.4**
Speed ratings: **95,94,94,92,54**
CSF £4.97 TOTE £2.30: £1.50, £1.30; EX 4.40 Trifecta £6.50 Pool: £2491.50 - 286.31 winning units..
Owner West Coast Haulage Limited **Bred** Dion Egan **Trained** Little Newcastle, Pembrokes

FOCUS
A fair bumper that saw the three market leaders battling it out for much of the straight. The form is rated around the first three.
T/Plt: £92.10 to a £1 stake. Pool: £59228.18 - 468.99 winning tickets T/Qpdt: £87.20 to a £1 stake. Pool: £2748.10 - 23.30 winning tickets RL

[215]HAYDOCK (L-H)
Friday, November 22

OFFICIAL GOING: Soft (good to soft in places) changing to soft after race 2 (1:20)
Wind: light 1/2 against Weather: fine

2655 POLYFLOR AT HOME H'CAP HURDLE 3m
12:50 (12:51) (Class 3) (0-130,128) 4-Y-0+ **£9,747** (£2,862; £1,431; £715)

Form RPR
/01- 1 **Cyrien Star**[21] 2202 6-10-2 107....................................... JakeGreenall(3) 119+
(Henry Daly) *w ldrs: led 6th: wnt clr appr 3 out: drvn out: readily* **4/1[1]**

115- 2 3 ¼ **Fighter Jet**[41] 1867 5-11-7 123.................................(v) WayneHutchinson 128
(Alan King) *in rr: drvn 6th: hdwy to chse ldrs 9th: 3rd 3 out: chsd wnr and nt fluent last: kpt on: no imp* **20/1**

/52- 3 1 ¾ **Abruzzi**[32] 2006 5-11-4 120... FelixDeGiles 122
(Tom Symonds) *chsd ldrs: nt fluent 2nd: drvn 7th: 2nd 3 out: styd on same pce* **9/1**

3/2- 4 2 ¼ **Our Joey (IRE)**[47] 1788 5-10-11 120......................... JonathonBewley(7) 120
(George Bewley) *hld up in rr: hdwy 8th: chsng ldrs next: 3rd 2 out: hung rt and one pce run-in* **5/1[3]**

/13- 5 4 ½ **Revocation**[26] 2103 5-11-3 119.. PeterBuchanan 115
(Lucinda Russell) *chsd ldrs: one pce fr 3 out* **14/1**

2/3- 6 10 **Storm Alert**[17] 2284 6-10-4 111............................... MissLucyGardner(5) 97
(Sue Gardner) *in rr: hung rt and reminders bnd after 6th: drvn next: hdwy 8th: lost pl appr 3 out* **9/1**

0/4- 7 nk **Scots Gaelic (IRE)**[26] 2102 6-11-9 125............................ DenisO'Regan 110
(John Quinn) *chsd ldrs: dropped in rr 7th: chsng ldrs 9th: sn drvn: lost pl bef next* **9/2[2]**

220/ 8 1 **Beyeh (IRE)**[185] 4512 5-11-0 121............................. JonathanEngland(5) 105
(Michael Appleby) *t.k.h in rr: hdwy to trck ldrs 3rd: wknd 3 out* **33/1**

/F0- 9 ½ **Shouldavboughtgold (IRE)**[27] 2073 6-9-10 103.....(t) HarryChalloner(5) 87
(William Kinsey) *chsd ldrs: drvn 8th: lost pl next: sn bhd* **25/1**

/23- 10 7 **Milano Magic (IRE)**[27] 2073 7-10-8 110.........................(p) LucyAlexander 87
(N W Alexander) *led to 6th: rdn and lost pl 9th: sn bhd: hmpd last* **16/1**

244/ 11 1 **Talkonthestreet (IRE)**[275] 4315 6-11-2 128......... ThomasCheesman(10) 104
(Philip Hobbs) *hld up in rr: hdwy 7th: chsng ldrs 9th: drvn and lost pl bef next: bhd whn hmpd last* **15/2**

120- 12 ¾ **Mission Complete (IRE)**[35] 1956 7-11-1 122............ MauriceLinehan(5) 97
(Jonjo O'Neill) *in rr: drvn 3rd: bhd fr 7th* **16/1**

U10- 13 1 ½ **Border Phoenix**[23] 2158 6-10-8 110... AdrianLane 83
(Sandy Forster) *a in rr: j.rt 1st: bhd fr 9th: j.lft last: struck into* **66/1**

5m 43.1s (-16.90) **13** Ran SP% **118.1**
toteswingers 1&2 £18.50, 2&3 £11.10, 1&3 £7.70 CSF £84.02 CT £687.30 TOTE £5.20: £2.20, £4.60, £3.30; EX 76.30 Trifecta £687.90 Part won. Pool: £917.20 - 0.12 winning units..
Owner Puteus Profundus **Bred** Wood Farm Stud **Trained** Stanton Lacy, Shropshire

FOCUS
The chases were run on the inner Flat Course, adding half a furlong per circuit compared to the normal configuration. The hurdle races were run on what is normally the Chase Course and there was a long run-in of around 2f. Due to the unusual configuration of the two tracks, no speed figures are possible for this meeting. This was a decent test of stamina in the conditions and they finished well spread out. The well treated winner is on the upgrade, and the form looks sound.

2656 WINGATE SIGNS & GRAPHICS GRADUATION CHASE 2m 1f
1:20 (1:20) (Class 2) 4-Y-0+ **£16,245** (£4,770; £2,385; £1,192)

Form RPR
5/6- 1 **Fago (FR)**[17] 2281 5-11-7 152... DarylJacob 155+
(Paul Nicholls) *t.k.h: led 1st: j.w: wnt clr between last 2: styd on wl* **9/4[1]**

/F1- 2 3 ¼ **Simply Ned (IRE)**[20] 2222 6-11-0 138................................. BrianHarding 143
(Nicky Richards) *hld up in last: hit 2nd: trckd ldrs 7th: 2nd 4 out: effrt next: over 2 l down and drvn whn stmbld on landing 2 out: sn rdn and no imp* **9/4[1]**

420/ 3 20 **Shangani (USA)**[210] 5559 7-11-7 137................................ AidanColeman 131
(Venetia Williams) *trckd ldrs: 2nd 6th: rdn and wknd 4 out* **9/4[1]**

0/0- 4 28 **Dan Breen (IRE)**[20] 2212 8-11-7 142...........................(p) TomScudamore 110
(David Pipe) *led to 1st: chsd ldrs: pushed along 8th: outpcd next: lost pl appr 4 out: sn bhd* **6/1[2]**

4m 12.0s (252.00) **4** Ran SP% **106.6**
CSF £7.43 TOTE £2.80; EX 5.70 Trifecta £14.20 Pool: £660.57 - 34.67 winning units..
Owner Andrea & Graham Wylie **Bred** Gildas Blain **Trained** Ditcheat, Somerset

FOCUS
Just the four runners for this graduation chase, but an interesting race nonetheless and the winner made sure it was run at a fair pace. He's rated in line with the best of his novice form.

2657 READ NICHOLLS & MCCAIN EXCLUSIVELY ON BETFAIR NOVICES' HURDLE (LISTED RACE) 2m
1:55 (1:55) (Class 1) 4-Y-0+ **£11,888** (£4,452; £2,224; £1,110)

Form RPR
0/1- 1 **Zamdy Man**[20] 2215 4-11-8 132.. AidanColeman 138+
(Venetia Williams) *mde all: clr tl after 5th: nt fluent 4th and next: edgd lft run-in: styd on wl* **15/8[1]**

131/ 2 1 ½ **Oscar Hoof (IRE)**[209] 5572 5-11-0 0................................ AndrewTinkler 129+
(Nicky Henderson) *nt fluent 3rd: hdwy 5th: sn chsng ldrs: effrt 3 out: styd on and 2nd last: swtchd rt last 100yds: kpt on wl* **3/1[3]**

11- 3 3 ¼ **Franciscan**[14] 2341 5-11-6 127... JasonMaguire 130
(Donald McCain) *chsd wnr: drvn 3 out: outpcd between last 2: rallied run-in: tk 3rd nr fin* **7/1**

211- 4 nse **Purple Bay (IRE)**[14] 2340 4-11-6 130.............................. DenisO'Regan 129
(John Ferguson) *hld up: taken wd bef 4th: chsng ldrs after 5th: 2nd 3 out: kpt on same pce between last 2* **9/4[2]**

6/1- 5 60 **King Rolfe (IRE)**[27] 2083 5-11-6 0..................................... MichaelByrne 89
(Tim Vaughan) *t.k.h: trckd ldrs 3rd: drvn 6th: sn lost pl and bhd: t.o bef 2 out: virtually p.u* **20/1**

3m 51.5s (-12.70) **5** Ran SP% **107.8**
CSF £7.58 TOTE £3.10: £1.10, £2.80; EX 7.20 Trifecta £38.50 Pool: £1969.22 - 38.32 winning units..
Owner Muhammad Nadeem Khan **Bred** The Kathryn Stud **Trained** Kings Caple, H'fords

FOCUS
Some interesting novices lined up for this Listed hurdle and it saw a brave front-running performance from the winner, who stepped up on his recent win. The third and fourth set the level.

2658 BETFAIR CASH OUT NOVICES' CHASE 2m 7f
2:30 (2:30) (Class 2) 4-Y-0+ **£16,245** (£4,770; £2,385; £1,192)

Form RPR
/01- 1 **Black Thunder (FR)**[30] 2019 6-11-7 146................................ DarylJacob 157+
(Paul Nicholls) *hld up: travelled strly: jnd ldrs 12th: led gng wl appr 3 out: drvn out run-in* **11/4[2]**

P/1- 2 2 ¼ **Many Clouds (IRE)**[19] 2242 6-11-7 0.............................. LeightonAspell 154
(Oliver Sherwood) *trckd ldrs: t.k.h: j.rt: bmpd 11th: effrt 4 out: clr 2nd appr 2 out: kpt on wl run-in* **10/3**

3/1- 3 14 **Shotgun Paddy (IRE)**[27] 2077 6-11-7 0.................................. NoelFehily 144
(Emma Lavelle) *chsd ldrs: hit 1st: bmpd 11th: upsides 14th: sn pushed along: lost pl bef 3 out: modest 3rd appr 2 out* **15/8[1]**

116/ 4 41 **Up And Go (FR)**[230] 5173 5-11-2 0.................................... JasonMaguire 114
(Donald McCain) *led: j. slowly 12th: jnd 14th: hrd drvn appr next: hdd 3 out: lost pl and bhd whn blnd 2 out: t.o whn eased run-in* **3/1[3]**

5m 53.1s (353.10) **4** Ran SP% **109.5**
CSF £11.45 TOTE £3.10; EX 10.70 Trifecta £10.20 Pool: £1712.17 - 125.76 winning units..
Owner Donlon, MacDonald, Fulton & Webb **Bred** Mickael Keane **Trained** Ditcheat, Somerset

FOCUS
A decent novices' chase containing three who had won their only previous start over fences. The pace wasn't strong, though, and there was barely a length covering the quartet jumping four out. Steps up from the first two.

2659 BROWN SHIPLEY WEALTH WELL MANAGED "FIXED BRUSH" "NATIONAL HUNT" NOVICES' HURDLE 2m 4f
3:05 (3:06) (Class 3) 4-7-Y-0 **£6,498** (£1,908; £954; £477)

Form RPR
/12- 1 **Spirit Of Shankly**[26] 2103 5-11-4 133......................................(t) NoelFehily 138+
(Charlie Longsdon) *hld up: trckd ldrs 5th: 2nd 2 out: plld wd after last: styd on strly to ld and forge clr last 100yds* **7/2[2]**

1- **2** 5 **Urban Hymn (FR)**[19] 2254 5-10-12 0 BrianHughes 126+
(Malcolm Jefferson) *led: hit 6th: jnd 3 out: hdd and no ex last 100yds* **11/8**[1]
3/1- **3** 6 **Classic Move (IRE)**[22] 2174 4-10-12 0 JasonMaguire 120+
(Donald McCain) *t.k.h: trckd ldrs: upsides 3 out: sn rdn: outpcd between last 2: styd on run-in* **15/2**[3]
4- **4** 2 1/2 **Straidnahanna (IRE)**[21] 2196 4-10-12 0 RyanMania 117
(Sue Smith) *chsd ldrs: drvn 7th: outpcd 2 out: kpt on run-in* **12/1**
3/2- **5** 12 **Varom (FR)**[20] 2225 4-10-12 0 DarylJacob 108
(Paul Nicholls) *hld up: hdwy 4th: sn trcking ldrs: drvn 7th: lost pl bef next* **7/2**[2]
/60- **6** 11 **Agesilas (FR)**[37] 1924 5-10-9 0 JohnKington(3) 94
(Andrew Crook) *in rr: j.rt: bhd fr 4th* **150/1**
0- **7** 10 **Unknown Legend (IRE)**[21] 2197 6-10-12 0 WayneHutchinson 84
(Alan King) *in rr: bhd fr 4th* **66/1**
41/ **8** 35 **Rafafie**[223] 5287 5-10-7 0 MissLucyGardner(5) 49
(Sue Gardner) *j. bdly in rr: bhd fr 4th: t.o whn blnd last: sn virtually p.u* **40/1**
P **Up The Ante (IRE)**[272] 5-10-12 0 PaddyBrennan
(Fergal O'Brien) *t.k.h: trckd ldrs: drvn 6th: sn weakaned: bhd and eased after next: t.o whn p.u bef 3 out* **16/1**

4m 41.5s (-11.50)
WFA 4 from 5yo+ 8lb **9** Ran SP% **116.5**
toteswingers 1&2 £1.40, 1&3 £4.00, 2&3 £2.90 CSF £9.10 TOTE £4.20: £1.30, £1.30, £2.20; EX 9.40 Trifecta £39.70 Pool: £4761.58 - 89.89 winning units..
Owner Alan Halsall **Bred** Mrs S M Newell **Trained** Over Norton, Oxon

FOCUS
A fascinating "fixed brush" novices' hurdle featuring a previous hurdles winner, a few bumper winners and five winning pointers. The winner is rated in line with his Aintree run.

2660 POLYFLOR EXPONA STANDARD OPEN NATIONAL HUNT FLAT RACE 2m
3:40 (3:40) (Class 4) 4-6-Y-0 **£3,249** (£954; £477; £238)

Form RPR
1 **Desoto County**[236] 4-11-0 0 JasonMaguire 111+
(Donald McCain) *hld up: stdy hdwy over 3f out: 2nd over 1f out: drvn and qcknd to ld last 150yds: styd on wl* **10/3**[2]
2 1 1/4 **Wuff (IRE)**[327] 5-11-0 0 PaddyBrennan 106
(Tom George) *sn led: drvn 3f out: hdd and no ex ins fnl f* **4/1**[3]
3 5 **Battle Born**[216] 4-11-0 0 NoelFehily 101
(Charlie Longsdon) *mid-div: effrt 3f out: kpt on to take 3rd nr fin* **13/8**[1]
\- **4** nk **Wolf Sword (IRE)** 4-11-0 0 BarryKeniry 101
(George Moore) *sn trcking ldrs: 2nd over 3f out: sn rdn: kpt on one pce over 1f out* **10/1**
1/ **5** 3 **King Of Strings (IRE)**[278] 4280 4-11-7 0 DougieCostello 105
(Tim Walford) *hld up in rr: hdwy over 3f out: nvr trbld ldrs* **20/1**
6 6 **Nimbus Gale (IRE)** 4-11-0 0 LeightonAspell 93
(Oliver Sherwood) *uns rdr and rn loose to s: in rr: drvn over 5f out: sn bhd: last 3f out: kpt on* **10/1**
\- **7** 6 **Brave Encounter (IRE)** 5-10-9 0 MissLucyGardner(5) 86
(Sue Gardner) *led early: chsd ldr: drvn 4f out: sn wl outpcd* **100/1**
8 4 **Presentings Return (IRE)** 4-10-9 0 MauriceLinehan(5) 82
(Jonjo O'Neill) *mid-div: lost pl over 3f out* **18/1**
9 11 **Ceilidh (IRE)** 5-10-7 0 LucyAlexander 64
(N W Alexander) *in rr: drvn over 5f out: lost pl 4f out* **66/1**
10 25 **Mr Lennygreengrass (IRE)** 6-10-9 0 ConorShoemark(5) 46
(Fergal O'Brien) *chsd ldrs: pushed along 7f out: lost pl over 3f out: sn bhd: t.o* **25/1**

3m 53.2s (-5.40) **10** Ran SP% **115.7**
toteswingers 1&2 £3.60, 1&3 £1.80, 2&3 £2.20 CSF £16.42 TOTE £4.60: £1.40, £1.90, £1.20; EX 17.20 Trifecta £43.80 Pool: £4562.54 - 78.12 winning units..
Owner Paul & Clare Rooney **Bred** Miss K Rausing **Trained** Cholmondeley, Cheshire

FOCUS
An interesting bumper containing a previous winner in this sphere plus two winning pointers and another that had finished second in a point. The pointers filled the first three places and, although typically for a race of this type the pace wasn't strong, this may still be form to take a positive view of.
T/Plt: £71.30 to a £1 stake. Pool: £75485.19 - 772.08 winning tickets T/Qpdt: £11.00 to a £1 stake. Pool: £5064.90 - 337.80 winning tickets WG

2642 ASCOT (R-H)
Saturday, November 23

OFFICIAL GOING: Good to soft (chs 7.2; hdl 7.5)
Wind: Virtually nil Weather: Sunny spells

2661 PLAYBOY CLUB LONDON NOVICES' HURDLE (12 hdls) 2m 6f
12:25 (12:25) (Class 2) 4-Y-0+ **£10,009** (£2,956; £1,478; £739; £369)

Form RPR
23- **1** **Doing Fine (IRE)**[28] 2076 5-10-12 0 JamieMoore 117
(Rebecca Curtis) *chsd ldrs: wnt 2nd 4 out: led whn ldr blnd 3 out: hrd drvn bef next: styd on wl u.p* **10/1**[3]
1- **2** 1 **Carraig Mor (IRE)**[22] 2189 5-11-3 0 RobertThornton 128+
(Alan King) *led tl blnd, hdd and dropped to 3rd 3 out: rallied u.p to chse wnr sn after: chal 2 out to last: no ex run-in* **1/8**[1]
4- **3** 1 1/4 **By The Boardwalk (IRE)**[37] 1937 5-10-12 0 SamThomas 115
(Kim Bailey) *hld up in rr: outpcd 4 out: hdwy to trck ldrs after 3 out: rdn 2 out: styd on same pce run-in* **8/1**[2]
/55- **4** 16 **Tinker Time (IRE)**[13] 2386 5-10-12 0 RichardJohnson 103
(Bob Buckler) *j. slowly 1st: in tch: chsd ldrs 7th: wknd bef 2 out* **14/1**
5- **5** 32 **Attimo (GER)**[18] 2280 4-10-12 0 MarkGrant 77
(Charlie Mann) *chsd ldr to 4 out: wknd after 3 out* **25/1**

5m 17.68s (-8.32) **Going Correction** -0.20s/f (Good)
WFA 4 from 5yo 8lb **5** Ran SP% **119.6**
Speed ratings (Par 109): **107,106,106,100,88**
CSF £13.80 TOTE £11.70: £3.70, £1.02; EX 20.00 Trifecta £39.70 Pool: £1751.77 - 33.07 winning units..
Owner Carl Hinchy **Bred** Steven Vaughan **Trained** Newport, Dyfed

FOCUS
Jockeys reported the ground to be riding as advertised. There was little obvious depth to this novice hurdle and it produced a shock result, with 1-8 favourite Carraig Mor being turned over. He was well belowe his debut level even allowing for the error, with a step up from the winner.

2662 BAM CONSTRUCT UK NOVICES' LIMITED H'CAP CHASE (20 fncs) 3m
1:00 (1:00) (Class 3) (0-125,124) 4-Y-£6,907 (£2,058; £1,041; £533; £279)

Form RPR
233- **1** **Kris Cross (IRE)**[20] 2246 6-10-3 **115** (t) GrantCockburn(7) 123+
(Lucinda Russell) *chsd ldrs: hit 9th: blnd 12th: led 13th: jnd fr 15th and again 2 out whn mstke: sn hdd: 3 l down after last: rallied as ldr fnd little and led last strides* **11/2**[3]
04F- **2** hd **Polisky (FR)**[27] 2107 6-11-1 **120** (tp) DarylJacob 128+
(Paul Nicholls) *hld up in rr: hdwy 14th: trckd ldrs 4 out: chal travelling wl next: sn led: 3 l clr after last: rdn: fnd little: hdd last strides* **8/1**
/32- **3** 12 **Ballylifen (IRE)**[10] 2450 6-11-0 **119** (t) RichieMcLernon 114
(Jonjo O'Neill) *in rr: hdwy 7th: lost pl 15th: rallied to take 3rd after 3 out: no ch w ldng duo* **8/1**
/55- **4** 1 1/2 **Comeonginger (IRE)**[31] 2024 6-10-9 **114** (t) TomCannon 109
(Chris Gordon) *in tch: chsd ldrs 8th: hit 13th: wknd after 4 out* **25/1**
/23- **5** 12 **Civil Disobedience**[36] 1959 9-10-11 **116** AidanColeman 101
(Richard Woollacott) *led 4th: rdn and lost pl 14th: rallied to chal next: wknd after 3 out* **15/2**
2/F- **F** **Oscar Davy (IRE)**[36] 1959 7-10-13 **118** RichardJohnson
(Philip Hobbs) *in rr whn fell 4th* **7/2**[1]
3/1- **U** **Shockingtimes (IRE)**[30] 2046 6-11-1 **120** MarkGrant
(Charlie Mann) *in rr whn bdly hmpd and uns rdr 4th* **11/1**
522/ **P** **Fiddlers Bid**[258] 4685 6-11-0 **124** ConorShoemark(5)
(Fergal O'Brien) *led: blnd 2nd: hdd 4th: chsd ldrs: wknd 4 out: hit next: t.o whn p.u bef 2 out* **5/1**[2]
21P/ **U** **Count Guido Deiro (IRE)**[221] 5328 6-11-2 **121** AdamWedge
(Nigel Twiston-Davies) *in tch: chsd ldrs fr 9th tl blnd and uns rdr 13th* **16/1**
/02- **F** **Deise Dynamo (IRE)**[23] 2171 5-11-1 **120** HenryBrooke 105
(Donald McCain) *chsd ldrs but rn in snatches: hit 12th and sn rr: t.o whn fell last* **10/1**

6m 4.74s (1.24) **Going Correction** +0.15s/f (Yiel) **10** Ran SP% **115.4**
Speed ratings (Par 107): **103,102,98,98,94** , , , ,
toteswingers 1&2 £9.30, 2&3 £16.90, 1&3 £9.00 CSF £48.46 CT £351.08 TOTE £6.50: £2.50, £3.60, £2.60; EX 56.30 Trifecta £359.70 Pool: £1435.14 - 2.99 winning units..
Owner Ms Deborah Thomson **Bred** Richard Healy **Trained** Arlary, Perth & Kinross

FOCUS
Quite a messy race, littered by jumping errors. The first two were on decent marks but neither was that convincing.

2663 TRISOFT MARES' H'CAP HURDLE (12 hdls) 2m 6f
1:30 (1:32) (Class 3) (0-125,124) 4-Y-0+ **£5,630** (£1,663; £831; £415; £207; £104)

Form RPR
20/- **1** **Scholastica**[219] 5360 6-11-5 **117** FelixDeGiles 126+
(Tom Symonds) *trckd ldrs: wnt 2nd travelling wl 2 out: chal last and sn led: rdn and hung lft run-in: kpt on wl* **4/1**[1]
513- **2** 1 **Top Totti**[28] 2084 5-10-10 **108** AndrewTinkler 114
(Henry Daly) *chsd ldrs: rdn to ld bef 2 out: jnd last and sn hdd: styng on whn carried lft run-in: kpt on cl home* **9/2**[2]
5P0/ **3** 9 **Florafern**[218] 5371 8-11-7 **124** [1] ThomasGarner(5) 123
(Oliver Sherwood) *in rr: rdn 7th: hdwy after 3 out to chse ldrs and hit 2 out: styd on same pce* **7/1**[3]
200/ **4** 1 3/4 **Lady Kathleen**[256] 4723 6-11-2 **114** DominicElsworth 110
(Paul Webber) *chsd ldrs: lost pl 7th: hdwy after 3 out: one pce sn after* **8/1**
3/3- **5** 10 **Mistral Reine**[11] 2435 4-9-12 **101** ConorShoemark(5) 90
(Lucy Wadham) *chsd ldrs: hit 4 out: j. slowly next: wknd 2 out* **10/1**
41F- **6** shd **Chilworth Screamer**[37] 1941 5-10-13 **111** TomCannon 98
(Chris Gordon) *in rr but in tch: chsd ldrs 3 out: sn rdn: wknd 2 out* **9/1**
1/1- **7** 4 **Upbeat Cobbler (FR)**[22] 2193 5-10-9 **107** RichardJohnson 92
(Henry Daly) *led: jnd fr 4 out tl hdd & wknd bef 2 out* **4/1**[1]
U43/ **8** 16 **Lights Of Broadway (IRE)**[379] 2300 7-9-13 **100** MarkQuinlan(3) 75
(Bernard Llewellyn) *j.big 1st and 2nd and sn towards rr: hdwy 5th: hit next: wknd 3 out* **25/1**
023/ **9** 19 **Fashion Faux Pas (IRE)**[447] 1473 6-10-7 **105** IanPopham 57
(Paul Henderson) *a towards rr: no ch whn hit 2 out* **50/1**
F52- **10** 13 **Venceremos**[31] 2028 6-10-8 **106** (p) AidanColeman 46
(Charlie Longsdon) *chsd ldrs: rdn 6th: drvn to chal 4 out to next: wknd 2 out* **9/1**

5m 17.23s (-8.77) **Going Correction** -0.20s/f (Good)
WFA 4 from 5yo+ 8lb **10** Ran SP% **116.7**
Speed ratings (Par 107): **107,106,103,102,99 99,97,91,84,80**
toteswingers 1&2 £4.00, 2&3 £8.90, 1&3 £5.30 CSF £22.83 CT £122.60 TOTE £5.20: £1.60, £1.90, £3.00; EX 29.50 Trifecta £217.50 Pool: £1389.04 - 4.78 winning units..
Owner Dominic Burke & Jonathan Palmer-Brown **Bred** Dr B Mayoh **Trained** Harewood End, H'fords
■ Stewards' Enquiry : Felix De Giles three-day ban: careless riding (Dec 8-10)
Andrew Tinkler two-day ban: used whip above permitted level (Dec 8-9)

FOCUS
The front pair drew clear in this mares' hurdle. A step up from the winner for an in-form yard, with the second to her best.

2664 AMLIN 1965 CHASE GRADE 2 (16 fncs) 2m 3f
2:05 (2:05) (Class 1) 4-Y-0+ **£28,475** (£10,685)

Form RPR
431/ **1** **Al Ferof (FR)**[371] 2468 8-11-7 0 DarylJacob 168+
(Paul Nicholls) *travelled wl: mde all: j.big 2 out and last: easily* **1/5**[1]
205/ **2** 8 **French Opera**[210] 5575 10-11-1 150 AndrewTinkler 151
(Nicky Henderson) *chsd wnr but nvr any ch: tendancy to jump lft: mstke 11th: rdn and no prog fr 4 out: wl-hld whn mstke last* **7/2**[2]

4m 44.99s (-1.41) **Going Correction** +0.15s/f (Yiel) **2** Ran SP% **105.6**
Speed ratings (Par 115): **108,104**
TOTE £1.10.
Owner J Hales **Bred** J Rauch & G Chenu **Trained** Ditcheat, Somerset

FOCUS
This was a disappointing numerical turnout for the prize, even before the defection of last year's winner Captain Chris through lameness, and Al Ferof enjoyed what was little more than a vigorous schooling session. He didn't need to be at his best.

2665 CORAL HURDLE (REGISTERED AS THE ASCOT HURDLE RACE) GRADE 2 (11 hdls) 2m 3f 110y
2:40 (2:40) (Class 1) 4-Y-O+ **£52,233** (£20,670; £11,139)

Form RPR
11/ **1** **Annie Power (IRE)**[237] 5050 5-10-11 155 RWalsh 161+
(W P Mullins, Ire) *hld up in last pl: hdwy to trck ldr and nt fluent 4 out: pushed along to chal 2 out: slt ld last and sn hrd rdn: styd on strly fnl 100yds* **8/13**[1]
141/ **2** *5* **Zarkandar (IRE)**[233] 5137 6-11-8 167 DarylJacob 165
(Paul Nicholls) *w ldr: slt ld 2nd: sn narrowly hdd: styd chalng tl led 6th: rdn appr 2 out and sn jnd: narrowly hdd last: styd on same pce u.p fnl 100yds* **15/8**[2]
3R2- **3** *80* **Bygones Of Brid (IRE)**[28] 2069 10-11-0 129 (p) RichardJohnson 110
(Karen McLintock) *led to 2nd: sn slt ld again but hrd pressed tl hdd 6th: lost 2nd 4 out: sn btn* **100/1**
0/1- **F** **Magnifique Etoile**[28] 2087 6-11-0 148 AidanColeman
(Charlie Longsdon) *trcking ldrs in 3rd whn fell 4th* **10/1**[3]

4m 34.47s (-10.23) **Going Correction** -0.20s/f (Good) **4** Ran SP% **106.8**
Speed ratings (Par 115): **112,110,78,**
CSF £2.08 TOTE £1.30; EX 1.70 Trifecta £8.00 Pool: £2069.31 - 192.79 winning units..
Owner Mrs S Ricci **Bred** Eamon Cleary **Trained** Muine Beag, Co Carlow

FOCUS
Just the four runners, reduced to three after Magnifique Etoile fell with a circuit to race, but the duel between the big two in the market, both top hurdlers, developed nicely with the pair still neck-and-neck at the last. Annie Power should still have more to offer.

2666 CAREY GROUP H'CAP CHASE (13 fncs) 2m 1f
3:15 (3:18) (Class 2) 4-Y-O+
£30,950 (£9,190; £4,595; £2,290; £1,150; £580)

Form RPR
6/3- **1** **Alasi**[21] 2226 9-11-0 135 DominicElsworth 140
(Paul Webber) *towards rr but in tch: wnt 3rd 7th: chsd ldr 4 out: chal 2 out: led last: hrd rdn run-in: all out* **5/1**[3]
F/2- **2** *nk* **Saved By John (IRE)**[28] 2072 8-10-12 133 (t) RichardJohnson 138
(Tim Vaughan) *led: rdn and hrd pressed 2 out: sn rdn: narrowly hdd last: rallied gamely u.str.p to cl on wnr nr fin: jst hld* **7/1**
5/1- **3** *2 ¼* **Drumshambo (USA)**[21] 2212 7-11-12 147 AidanColeman 152+
(Venetia Williams) *in tch: rdn along 9th: styd on to chse ldrs 2 out: swtchd rt and effrt whn blnd last: one pce* **5/2**[1]
/02- **4** *2 ½* **Lancetto (FR)**[21] 2212 8-11-0 135 PaulMoloney 137
(Evan Williams) *chsd ldrs: lost position and rdn along 9th: hdwy to cl on ldrs 2 out: sn one pce: kpt on again run-in to take 4th clsng stages* **4/1**[2]
/26- **5** *½* **King Edmund**[21] 2212 10-11-4 139 (t) TomCannon 142
(Chris Gordon) *in rr: hit 4th and 7th: sme hdwy whn blnd 4 out: chsd ldrs u.p 2 out: styd on same pce* **11/1**
/03- **6** *2 ¼* **Viva Colonia (IRE)**[28] 2071 8-11-5 140 DarylJacob 139
(Brian Ellison) *in rr: hdwy 8th: disp 2nd after 3 out: chal 2 out: swtiched lft u.p and wknd last* **13/2**
321/ **7** *24* **Kie (IRE)**[213] 5494 5-11-0 135 HenryBrooke 118
(Donald McCain) *pressed ldr tl blnd bdly 5th and rdr had both legs one side of sddle: rcvrd to chal next: hit 9th: wknd 3 out* **8/1**

4m 12.31s (-2.29) **Going Correction** +0.15s/f (Yiel) **7** Ran SP% **110.5**
Speed ratings (Par 109): **111,110,109,108,108 107,96**
toteswingers 1&2 £3.70, 2&3 £2.70, 1&3 £3.40 CSF £35.54 TOTE £5.50: £2.90, £2.50; EX 27.80 Trifecta £199.50 Pool: £3689.27 - 13.86 winning units..
Owner Swanbridge Bloodstock Limited **Bred** Mrs Claire Massey **Trained** Mollington, Oxon

FOCUS
No hanging around here, with a good gallop being set by the duelling leaders, yet the field bunched right up in the straight and any one of five still had a chance two out. Solid handicap form.

2667 HARRIET ROBERTS MEMORIAL STANDARD OPEN NATIONAL HUNT FLAT RACE 2m
3:50 (3:50) (Class 5) 4-6-Y-O
£2,283 (£674; £337; £168; £84; £42)

Form RPR
- **1** **Josses Hill (IRE)**[196] 232 5-11-0 0 AndrewTinkler 112+
(Nicky Henderson) *trckd ldrs: wnt 2nd 3f out: led 2f out: pushed clr and green fnl f: comf* **8/11**[1]
1- **2** *4* **Sidbury Hill**[31] 2026 5-11-0 0 KevinJones(7) 112
(Seamus Mullins) *towards rr but in tch: hdwy 4f out: chsd ldrs 3f out: styd on to chse wnr fnl f but no imp and hung lft sn after* **20/1**
5- **3** *2* **Minella On Line (IRE)**[42] 1869 4-11-0 0 RWalsh 103
(Rebecca Curtis) *chsd ldrs: rdn over 2f out: edging rt and styd on same pce fr over 1f out* **7/2**[2]
1/ **4** *1* **Volt Face (FR)**[272] 4418 4-11-7 0 ConorO'Farrell 109
(David Pipe) *led: t.k.h: hdd 2f out: one pce fr over 1f out* **8/1**[3]
5 *2 ¼* **Saddlers Encore (IRE)** 4-11-0 0 RichardJohnson 100
(Philip Hobbs) *in tch: pushed along 4f out: one pce fnl 3f* **12/1**
5- **6** *11* **Flashyfrank**[20] 2254 4-10-7 0 MissLAllan(7) 89
(David Elsworth) *t.k.h towards rr but in tch tl drvn 3f out and sn wknd* **50/1**
7 *½* **Kotkiri (FR)** 4-11-0 0 RobertThornton 88
(Alan King) *chsd ldrs: wknd 3f out* **12/1**
35/ **8** *7* **Jammy (IRE)**[272] 4412 4-11-0 0 DavidBass 81
(Lawney Hill) *in rr but in tch tl wknd fr 4f out* **40/1**
9 *9* **Head Rush** 5-10-11 0 GavinSheehan(3) 72
(Warren Greatrex) *t.k.h in rr tl hdwy to pressed ldr 1/2-way: wknd 4f out* **14/1**

3m 44.11s (3.31) **Going Correction** -0.20s/f (Good) **9** Ran SP% **122.5**
Speed ratings: **83,81,80,79,78 72,72,69,64**
toteswingers 1&2 £7.20, 1&3 £1.10, 2&3 £9.20 CSF £23.43 TOTE £1.80: £1.10, £3.80, £1.70; EX 17.20 Trifecta £73.40 Pool: £1837.67 - 18.75 winning units..
Owner A D Spence **Bred** I W Moore **Trained** Upper Lambourn, Berks

FOCUS
Run at a stop-start gallop, this looked just an ordinary bumper for Ascot.
T/Plt: £48.40. Pool: £111,486.38 - 1678.84 winning units. T/Qpdt: £12.10. Pool: 6486.85 - 394.00 winning units. ST

2655 HAYDOCK (L-H)
Saturday, November 23

OFFICIAL GOING: Soft (chs 5.2; hdl 4.6)
Wind: Nil Weather: Fine

2668 CASH OUT YOUR SATURDAY MULTIPLES WITH BETFAIR H'CAP HURDLE 2m
12:10 (12:10) (Class 3) (0-135,133)
4-Y-O+ **£12,996** (£3,816; £1,908; £954)

Form RPR
50/ **1** **Moujik Borget (FR)**[619] 4852 5-11-1 122 LiamTreadwell 125
(Venetia Williams) *hld up in midfield: hdwy 6th: led 2 out: wanted to lug lft sn after: jnd and hrd pressed last: r.o for press run-in: plld out a little more fnl strides* **12/1**
566- **2** *½* **Ruler Of All (IRE)**[14] 2372 7-10-13 127 MrRWinks(7) 129
(Peter Winks) *midfield: hdwy 3 out: upsides and str chal fr last: r.o for press and hung lft run-in: no ex fnl strides* **8/1**
464- **3** *2 ½* **Smadynium (FR)**[30] 2032 5-10-3 110 (b[1]) AdrianLane 110
(Donald McCain) *a.p: led jst bef 3 out: hdd 2 out: stl wl there last: kpt on u.p run-in: no imp fnl 150yds* **20/1**
/00- **4** *¾* **Bob's World**[10] 2454 4-10-10 117 (p) SeanQuinlan 119
(Jennie Candlish) *midfield: mstke 5th: rdn and outpcd appr 2 out: rallied and swtchd rt after last: styd on towards fin: nt rch ldrs* **16/1**
015- **5** *2 ¼* **Tidal Way (IRE)**[22] 2198 4-11-4 125 (p) NoelFehily 122
(Charlie Longsdon) *hld up: hdwy 6th: effrt and abt 5 l off pce whn mstke 3 out: rdn bef next: nt qckn appr last: styd on same pce run-in* **12/1**
/05- **6** *shd* **Deepsand (IRE)**[28] 2069 4-11-9 130 (p) DougieCostello 127
(Tim Easterby) *midfield: mstke 2nd: nt fluent 4th: hdwy 3 out: effrt to chse ldrs bef 2 out: one pce appr last: no imp run-in* **12/1**
4F2- **7** *6* **Captain Brown**[35] 1979 5-10-12 119 BrianHughes 109
(James Moffatt) *led: hdd jst bef 3 out: wknd appr last* **33/1**
/U1- **8** *9* **Honour System (IRE)**[179] 517 6-11-4 125 DenisO'Regan 106
(John Ferguson) *hld up in rr: sme hdwy after 6th: shkn up bef 2 out: sn wl btn* **8/1**
131/ **9** *¾* **Quick Decisson (IRE)**[244] 4944 5-10-11 118 TomO'Brien 101
(Philip Hobbs) *chsd ldrs: pushed along appr 3 out: wknd bef 2 out* **3/1**[1]
2/0- **10** *16* **Ubaldo Des Menhies (FR)**[14] 2366 5-11-4 125 APMcCoy 90
(Jonjo O'Neill) *hld up: struggling after 6th: sn wl btn* **15/2**[3]
1P2/ **11** *2 ½* **Golden Hoof (IRE)**[210] 5566 5-11-9 130 BarryGeraghty 92
(Nicky Henderson) *hld up: niggled along appr 6th: lft bhd and toiling after 6th: t.o* **9/2**[2]
001- **S** **Hawkhill (IRE)**[14] 2366 7-11-9 133 (t) MichaelByrne(3)
(Tim Vaughan) *chsd ldrs: mstke 6th: sn rdn and lost pl: wkng and bhd whn slipped up on bnd bef 3 out* **16/1**

3m 51.7s (-12.50)
WFA 4 from 5yo+ 7lb **12** Ran SP% **119.7**
toteswingers 1&2 £29.60, 2&3 £48.60, 1&3 £48.60 CSF £106.13 CT £1920.11 TOTE £15.00: £4.50, £2.60, £6.50; EX 138.10 Trifecta £735.30 Part won. Pool: £980.50 - 0.01 winning units..
Owner Sunday Lunch Partnership **Bred** Elevage Borget, J Flottes & T Robert **Trained** Kings Caple, H'fords

FOCUS
Due to the unusual configuration of the two tracks, no speed figures are possible for this meeting. This competitive handicap was run at a decent gallop and they got sorted out from the third-last flight. A big step up on previous efforts from the winner, and sound form.

2669 READ NICHOLLS AND MCCAIN EXCLUSIVELY ON BETFAIR HURDLE (AN INTERMEDIATE HURDLE) 2m
12:45 (12:45) (Class 2) 4-Y-O+ **£25,024** (£7,392; £3,696; £1,848; £924)

Form RPR
165/ **1** **Rolling Star (FR)**[233] 5135 4-11-6 143 BarryGeraghty 153+
(Nicky Henderson) *hld up: effrt after 2 out: led run-in: sn edgd lft: styd on to draw clr ins fnl 100yds* **5/2**[2]
1/5- **2** *2 ¾* **Doyly Carte**[21] 2226 5-10-13 137 JasonMaguire 141+
(Donald McCain) *racd in cl 2nd: led 2 out: rdn whn hit last: hdd run-in: one pce and unable to go w wnr ins fnl 100yds* **16/1**
2/6- **3** *5* **Runswick Royal (IRE)**[15] 2344 4-10-12 145 WilsonRenwick 135
(Ann Hamilton) *hld up: shkn up after 6th: rdn appr last: styd on to take 3rd fnl 200yds: no imp on front two* **7/2**[3]
2/2- **4** *1 ½* **Far West (FR)**[14] 2372 4-11-6 148 NickScholfield 141
(Paul Nicholls) *trckd ldrs: rdn and nt qckn after 2 out: one pce run-in* **11/10**[1]
5/2- **5** *nk* **Morning Royalty (IRE)**[21] 2221 6-10-12 130 BrianHughes 132
(James Moffatt) *led: hdd 2 out: stl cl up bef last: rdn run-in: sn btn* **25/1**

3m 52.2s (-12.00) **5** Ran SP% **108.1**
CSF £28.60 TOTE £3.00: £2.00, £2.50; EX 30.70 Trifecta £148.50 Pool: £1446.93 - 7.30 winning units..
Owner Michael Buckley & The Vestey Family **Bred** Laurent Deniel **Trained** Upper Lambourn, Berks

FOCUS
A decent affair and a classy winner, but a race that became something of a sprint. The winner can rate higher without looking obvious Champion Hurdle material.

2670 BETFAIR COMMITS £40 MILLION TO BRITISH RACING H'CAP CHASE 3m 5f
1:15 (1:15) (Class 3) (0-135,132) 4-Y-O+ **£16,245** (£4,770; £2,385; £1,192)

Form RPR
16P/ **1** **Nuts N Bolts**[217] 5404 7-11-11 131 (t) PeterBuchanan 145+
(Lucinda Russell) *hld up: hdwy 8th: sn trckd ldrs: wnt 2nd after 18th: mstke 4 out: led next: mstke 2 out: drew clr after last: styd on wl* **8/1**
114/ **2** *6* **Red Rocco (IRE)**[294] 3984 6-11-9 129 SamTwiston-Davies 134
(Nigel Twiston-Davies) *in tch: rdn after 9th: styd on to cl appr 4 out: rdn and outpcd by ldrs bef 2 out: kpt on to take 2nd run-in: nt trble wnr* **6/1**[3]
P/0- **3** *1 ½* **Ace High**[35] 1971 9-11-12 132 TomScudamore 136
(David Pipe) *led to 4th: remained w ldr: led again 10th: hdd 12th: regained ld 18th: hdd 3 out: rdn appr last: lost 2nd run-in: kpt on same pce* **5/1**[2]
/53- **4** *15* **Incentivise (IRE)**[24] 2157 10-10-10 119 MichealNolan(3) 110
(Richard Lee) *in tch: rdn after 13th: outpcd 14th: plugged on for press fr 4 out: no imp* **25/1**
5/0- **5** *11* **Our Island (IRE)**[36] 1959 8-11-2 122 (b[1]) DougieCostello 103
(Tim Vaughan) *in rr: u.p after 4th: blnd whn toiling 14th: plugged on u.p fr 18th wout threatening* **6/1**[3]

/20- **6** *13* **Lively Baron (IRE)**[20] 2246 8-11-6 **126**..........................(bt) JasonMaguire 91
(Donald McCain) *in tch: prom after 4th: rdn and wknd 17th* **12/1**
6/P- **7** *10* **Dusky Bob (IRE)**[24] 2157 8-10-9 **118**..............................(p) JamesBest(3) 73
(Brian Ellison) *trckd ldrs: rdn and lost pl 11th: nt fluent 12th: struggling bef 14th: n.d after* **16/1**
1B5- **8** *hd* **Jaunty Journey**[20] 2246 10-10-8 **114**.................................. BrianHughes 68
(Nigel Twiston-Davies) *midfield: mstke 5th: lost pl and towards rr bef 9th: toiling bef 14th* **14/1**
P/2- **9** *2 1/4* **Gorgehous Lliege (FR)**[14] 2367 7-10-0 **106** oh1........... LiamTreadwell 58
(Venetia Williams) *t.k.h: prom: rdr lost iron briefly 1st: led 4th to 10th: led again 12th: hdd 18th: sn rdn: wknd bef 4 out* **4/1[1]**
21/ **P** **Mister Philson (IRE)**[230] 5203 8-10-4 **110**...................(p) WilsonRenwick
(S R B Crawford, Ire) *a bhd: hit 6th: toiling bef 14th: t.o whn p.u bef 4 out* **14/1**
6/F- **P** **Chac Du Cadran (FR)**[24] 2157 7-11-4 **124**.................(p) TomMessenger
(Chris Bealby) *midfield early: bhd 9th: struggling whn mstke 14th: t.o whn p.u bef 15th* **10/1**

7m 40.1s (8.50) **11** Ran SP% **116.2**
toteswingers 1&2 £1.50, 2&3 £10.40, 1&3 £3.50 CSF £55.69 CT £266.87 TOTE £9.20: £3.00, £2.50, £2.10; EX 55.70 Trifecta £536.70 Pool: £1023.75 - 1.43 winning units..
Owner The County Set **Bred** R J Cornelius **Trained** Arlary, Perth & Kinross

FOCUS
A fair marathon handicap, run at an average gallop. Most were done with prior to the home straight and the principals came well clear. A step up from the winner with the second to his mark.

2671 BEST ODDS WITH BETFAIR SPORTSBOOK H'CAP HURDLE 2m 4f
1:50 (1:50) (Class 2) 4-Y-0+ **£24,692** (£7,250; £3,625; £1,812)

Form RPR
1/1- **1** **More Of That (IRE)**[21] 2230 5-11-2 **137**.................................. APMcCoy 150+
(Jonjo O'Neill) *midfield: nt fluent 4th: on heels of ldrs appr 3 out: rdn and outpcd bef last where in 6th pl: styd on run-in: led ins fnl 150yds: sn in command* **3/1[1]**
4- **2** *2* **Blue Fashion (IRE)**[167] 683 4-11-8 **143**........................... BarryGeraghty 150+
(Nicky Henderson) *chsd ldrs: ev ch 2 out: rdn after last: ch 150yds out: sn unable to go w wnr* **9/1**
5/4- **3** *1 1/4* **Special Catch (IRE)**[28] 2069 6-10-4 **125**........................ JamesReveley 131
(Keith Reveley) *a.p: ev ch 2 out: rdn after last: ch 150yds out: nt qckn: styd on same pce towards fin* **8/1**
/01- **4** *3/4* **Home Run (GER)**[6] 2529 5-9-7 **121** oh1.......................(b) KieronEdgar(7) 127
(David Pipe) *midfield: hdwy appr 3 out: led 2 out: rdn bef last: hdd fnl 150yds: one pce cl home* **9/2[3]**
114/ **5** *5* **Mcmurrough (IRE)**[218] 5369 9-10-9 **130**.........................(b) BrianHughes 131
(Malcolm Jefferson) *chsd ldr: led after 3 out: hdd next: 4th and u.p whn mstke last: one pce run-in* **33/1**
4/0- **6** *nk* **Edgardo Sol (FR)**[28] 2071 6-11-7 **147**............................ HarryDerham(5) 148
(Paul Nicholls) *midfield: effrt appr 3 out: outpcd and lost pl bef 2 out: styd on run-in: no imp on ldrs* **22/1**
/10- **7** *2 1/2* **Party Rock (IRE)**[27] 2102 6-11-8 **143**................................. SeanQuinlan 140
(Jennie Candlish) *in tch: ev ch 2 out: rdn appr last: wknd run-in* **25/1**
041- **8** *1/2* **Trucking Along (IRE)**[21] 2221 7-10-4 **125**...................... WilsonRenwick 122
(S R B Crawford, Ire) *hld up: pushed along appr last: nvr able to trble ldrs* **40/1**
11P/ **9** *nk* **Clondaw Kaempfer (IRE)**[329] 3352 5-11-1 **136**............. JasonMaguire 133
(Donald McCain) *hld up: nt fluent 6th: sme hdwy appr 2 out: nvr trbld ldrs: wl hld bef last* **4/1[2]**
215/ **10** *3/4* **Matthew Riley (IRE)**[212] 5525 6-10-5 **126**...................... RichieMcGrath 122
(Philip Kirby) *hld up: pushed along after 7th: nvr threatened* **16/1**
3/2- **11** *4* **Zuider Zee (GER)**[11] 2433 6-11-5 **140**............................ DenisO'Regan 134
(John Ferguson) *midfield: pushed along and outpcd bef 2 out: sn btn* **9/1**
P/4- **12** *1* **Vasco D'Ycy (FR)**[21] 2230 4-9-13 **123**............................ JackQuinlan(3) 114
(Sarah Humphrey) *led: rdn and hdd after 3 out: sn wknd* **50/1**

4m 42.2s (-10.80) **12** Ran SP% **115.7**
toteswingers 1&2 £2.50, 1&3 £50.00, 2&3 £22.90 CSF £27.55 CT £196.72 TOTE £3.60: £1.80, £3.20, £2.20; EX 35.80 Trifecta £441.20 Pool: £2095.55 - 3.56 winning units..
Owner John P McManus **Bred** Mrs Eleanor Hadden **Trained** Cheltenham, Gloucs
■ Stewards' Enquiry : Kieron Edgar two-day ban: used whip above permitted level (Dec 8-9)

FOCUS
A decent handicap but it was steadily run. The first two are improvers who can rate higher, and the next four were pretty much to their marks.

2672 BETFAIR CASH OUT "FIXED BRUSH" H'CAP HURDLE (GRADE 3) 3m
2:25 (2:25) (Class 1) 4-Y-0+
£45,560 (£17,096; £8,560; £4,264; £2,144; £1,072)

Form RPR
1P6/ **1** **Gevrey Chambertin (FR)**[232] 5161 5-11-7 **143**.........(p) TomScudamore 149+
(David Pipe) *prom: led 4th: mde rest travelling strly: tried to go clr bef 3 out: rdn after last: all out* **6/1[2]**
1/4- **2** *1/2* **Utopie Des Bordes (FR)**[14] 2371 5-11-0 **136**................. BarryGeraghty 141
(Nicky Henderson) *hld up: hdwy 8th: rdn to take 2nd last: styd on run-in: pressed wnr cl home* **14/1**
P/1- **3** *1 1/2* **Lie Forrit (IRE)**[38] 1926 9-11-2 **138**.................................. PeterBuchanan 141
(Lucinda Russell) *midfield: niggled along and hdwy appr 7th: chsd ldrs 3 out: rdn bef next: styd on run-in: clsd towards fin* **10/1**
304/ **4** *2 3/4* **Alfie Sherrin**[254] 4751 10-10-12 **134**................................... APMcCoy 134
(Jonjo O'Neill) *midfield: hdwy appr 3 out: styd on fr 2 out: kpt on run-in: nt quite able to chal* **20/1**
F/1- **5** *4 1/2* **Gullinbursti (IRE)**[13] 2395 7-11-7 **143**................................. NoelFehily 140
(Emma Lavelle) *midfield: hdwy to take 2nd 9th: lost 2nd last: sn rdn: no ex fnl 150yds* **11/2[1]**
2/1- **6** *3 1/2* **Crowning Jewel**[27] 2102 7-11-2 **138**................................... JamesReveley 130
(Keith Reveley) *trckd ldrs: lost pl bef 7th: plugged on in midfield fr 3 out: kpt on wout troubling ldrs run-in* **14/1**
030- **7** *1 3/4* **Monetary Fund (USA)**[7] 2504 7-10-8 **130**........................ LiamTreadwell 122
(Venetia Williams) *hld up: plugged on fr 3 out: nvr a threat* **20/1**
2/4- **8** *1/2* **Trustan Times (IRE)**[21] 2228 7-11-12 **148**....................... DougieCostello 138
(Tim Easterby) *hld up: stmbld 4th: hdwy after 7th: wknd 3 out* **9/1**
110/ **9** *1* **Two Rockers (IRE)**[255] 4733 6-11-8 **144**....................... WayneHutchinson 134
(Alan King) *hld up: hdwy 7th: effrt whn chsng ldrs appr 3 out: wknd bef last* **6/1[2]**
P/0- **10** *2 1/4* **Restless Harry**[36] 1956 9-10-6 **128**.................................... CharliePoste 116
(Robin Dickin) *hld up: rdn in midfield after 9th: rdn and outpcd bef 3 out* **33/1**
2/2- **11** *12* **Knock A Hand (IRE)**[20] 2242 8-10-13 **138**................(b) MichealNolan(3) 115
(Richard Lee) *in tch: rdn and wknd appr 3 out* **25/1**
0/3- **12** *6* **Lovcen (GER)**[27] 2100 8-11-4 **140**.................................(p) WillKennedy 109
(Alan King) *prom: reminders appr 7th: rdn and wknd bef 3 out* **25/1**
6/F- **13** *2 1/4* **Sixty Something (FR)**[21] 2224 7-10-10 **135**.................... JakeGreenall(3) 103
(Paul Webber) *hld up: reminders after 6th: struggling after: n.d* **25/1**
/23- **14** *1 3/4* **Night In Milan (IRE)**[23] 2170 7-10-3 **125**.........................(b) BrianHughes 90
(Keith Reveley) *led: hdd 4th: wknd 8th* **20/1**
0/1- **15** *4 1/2* **Ely Brown (IRE)**[27] 2100 8-10-13 **142**......................(p) CharlieDeutsch(7) 104
(Charlie Longsdon) *nt jump wl: prom: rdn after 9th: wknd bef 3 out* **14/1**
3/P- **P** **The Knoxs (IRE)**[21] 2228 10-11-2 **138**................................... RyanMania
(Sue Smith) *in tch: rdn whn blnd 3 out: sn eased: p.u bef next* **50/1**
144/ **P** **Master Of The Sea (IRE)**[232] 5161 6-11-7 **143**....(t) SamTwiston-Davies
(Nigel Twiston-Davies) *hld up: wnt wrong after 6th: sn p.u: fatally injured* **8/1[3]**

5m 42.5s (-17.50) **17** Ran SP% **124.9**
toteswingers 1&2 £21.50, 1&3 £19.40, 2&3 £29.20 CSF £77.04 CT £847.84 TOTE £6.00: £2.00, £2.90, £2.60, £3.50; EX 103.80 Trifecta £1685.60 Pool: £94,680.17 - 42.12 winning units..
Owner Roger Stanley & Yvonne Reynolds III **Bred** M Jean-Marie Prost Alamartine **Trained** Nicholashayne, Devon

FOCUS
A cracking edition of this well-established handicap and it served up a proper test. The winner was up 4lb on the best of his novice form with the second another on the upgade.

2673 BETFAIR CHASE (REGISTERED AS THE LANCASHIRE CHASE) GRADE 1 3m 1f
3:00 (3:00) (Class 1) 5-Y-0+
£112,637 (£42,497; £21,317; £10,697; £5,417; £2,757)

Form RPR
2/3- **1** **Cue Card**[18] 2281 7-11-7 172.. JoeTizzard 180+
(Colin Tizzard) *t.k.h early on: w ldr: led 4th: mde rest: rdn after last: styd on to draw clr fnl 110yds* **9/1**
121/ **2** *4 1/2* **Dynaste (FR)**[232] 5158 7-11-7 159................................... TomScudamore 175
(David Pipe) *hld up: hdwy 14th: trckd ldrs 4 out: wnt 2nd and chal wnr 2 out: rdn and nt qckn run-in: one pce and hld fnl 110yds* **11/2[3]**
1F3/ **3** *1 1/4* **Silviniaco Conti (FR)**[233] 5136 7-11-7 173............................. NoelFehily 173
(Paul Nicholls) *in tch: impr 10th: wnt 2nd after 11th: ev ch 3 out: rdn and lost 2nd 2 out: nt qckn bef last: kpt on u.p towards fin* **7/2[2]**
2/5- **4** *15* **Long Run (FR)**[21] 2229 8-11-7 171............................(p) MrSWaley-Cohen 161
(Nicky Henderson) *trckd ldrs: wnt 2nd 7th: lost 2nd after 9th: remained prom: wknd 3 out* **7/1**
1/1- **5** *9* **Tidal Bay (IRE)**[21] 2228 12-11-7 171........................ SamTwiston-Davies 152
(Paul Nicholls) *hld up: struggling bef 12th: tried to get into it after 14th but no imp on ldrs: wl btn bef 2 out* **17/2**
111/ **6** *10* **Bobs Worth (IRE)**[253] 4770 8-11-7 180.............................. BarryGeraghty 142
(Nicky Henderson) *in tch: nt fluent 14th: sn lost pl: wknd 4 out: nt fluent 3 out: sn eased whn wl btn* **15/8[1]**
240/ **7** *4* **The Giant Bolster**[233] 5136 8-11-7 164..........................(p) DenisO'Regan 137
(David Bridgwater) *hld up in rr: outpcd after 14th: swtchd rt appr 4 out: nvr a threat* **28/1**
F21- **P** **Roi Du Mee (FR)**[21] 2234 8-11-7 168...............................(t) JasonMaguire
(Gordon Elliott, Ire) *led to 4th: nt fluent and lost 2nd 7th: regained 2nd after 9th: rdn and lost 2nd after 11th: wknd 14th: t.o whn p.u bef 4 out* **25/1**

6m 10.1s (-20.40) **8** Ran SP% **112.7**
toteswingers 1&2 £10.60, 1&3 £9.50, 2&3 £4.60 CSF £55.97 CT £206.38 TOTE £9.80: £3.00, £2.00, £1.60; EX 51.30 Trifecta £200.00 Pool: £6776.25 - 25.40 winning units..
Owner Mrs Jean R Bishop **Bred** R T Crellin **Trained** Milborne Port, Dorset

FOCUS
With the steeplechase fences at this meeting on the Flat course, this race was run over a furlong further than in previous years. This was a real early-season treat and by far the most competitive running of this Grade 1 prize. Predictably they went a solid gallop and it saw a cracking three-way finish. The impressive Cue Card is rated to a small step up on his Aintree second, with Dynaste up 7lb on his best novice form. Silviniaco Conti is rated to the level of his win in this last year, but Bobs Worth was a long way below his best.

2674 UNBEATABLE IN-RUNNING VALUE WITH BETFAIR EXCHANGE H'CAP CHASE 3m 1f
3:35 (3:35) (Class 2) (0-145,145) 4-Y-0+
£21,896 (£6,468; £3,234; £1,617; £808; £406)

Form RPR
105/ **1** **Sydney Paget (IRE)**[217] 5406 6-10-13 **132**.......................... JasonMaguire 149+
(Donald McCain) *w ldr: led 3rd: mde rest: easily drew clr fr 3 out: eased down run-in* **5/1[1]**
0P4/ **2** *2 3/4* **Silver By Nature**[211] 5560 11-11-12 **145**......................... PeterBuchanan 152
(Lucinda Russell) *midfield: hdwy after 14th: pushed along appr 4 out: no imp: styd on to take 2nd fnl 110yds: clsd on eased down wnr fin: flattered* **14/1**
/31- **3** *5* **Gas Line Boy (IRE)**[18] 2283 7-11-1 **134**................................ TomO'Brien 137
(Philip Hobbs) *hld up: sme hdwy into midfield 8th: blnd 9th: stdy prog fr 13th: wnt 2nd last whn no ch w wnr: lost 2nd fnl 110yds: one pce* **6/1[2]**
0/0- **4** *3/4* **Saint Are (FR)**[28] 2071 7-11-3 **136**...............................(v[1]) DougieCostello 138
(Tim Vaughan) *trckd ldrs: niggled along after 9th: wnt 2nd appr 4 out: no imp on wnr: lost 2nd last: one pce run-in* **20/1**
302- **5** *1* **Pigeon Island**[28] 2070 10-11-2 **135**.......................(vt) SamTwiston-Davies 135
(Nigel Twiston-Davies) *hld up: pushed along appr 4 out: kpt on u.p after but n.d* **16/1**
P/2- **6** *24* **The Rainbow Hunter**[29] 2065 9-11-4 **137**.......................(t) NickScholfield 113
(Kim Bailey) *hld up bhd: struggling bef 4 out: nvr a threat* **14/1**
/45- **7** *13* **Mr Moonshine (IRE)**[14] 2359 9-11-2 **135**................................ RyanMania 98
(Sue Smith) *sn chsd ldrs: outpcd 13th: rallied briefly bef 4 out: wknd bef 3 out* **12/1[3]**
1/0- **P** **Noble Legend**[22] 2199 6-11-0 **133**....................................... AndrewThornton
(Caroline Bailey) *trckd ldrs: lost pl 7th: struggling after 9th: bhd whn hmpd 11th: p.u bef 12th* **6/1[2]**
621/ **U** **Quincy Des Pictons (FR)**[212] 5523 9-11-4 **140**................ JamesBest(3)
(Alan Jones) *in tch: dropped to midfield whn landed awkwardly and uns rdr 10th* **25/1**
4/3- **F** **Mac Aeda**[22] 2199 9-10-6 **125**..(bt[1]) BrianHughes
(Malcolm Jefferson) *midfield: mstke 7th: impr to chse ldrs 9th: fell 11th* **5/1[1]**
2PP/ **P** **Relax (FR)**[217] 5404 8-10-10 **129**.. LiamTreadwell
(Venetia Williams) *led: mstke 2nd: hdd 3rd: remained in 2nd pl: j.rt fnl circ: wknd appr 4 out: bhd whn p.u bef 3 out* **5/1[1]**
100- **P** **Problema Tic (FR)**[126] 1047 7-11-5 **138**....................(bt) TomScudamore
(David Pipe) *bhd fr 3rd: reminders after 5th: p.u bef 11th* **20/1**

6m 20.2s (-10.30) **12** Ran SP% **118.8**
toteswingers 1&2 £19.90, 1&3 £8.60, 2&3 £8.90 CSF £68.87 CT £434.54 TOTE £6.50: £2.40, £4.70, £2.50; EX 105.10 Trifecta £839.70 Pool: £3063.42 - 2.73 winning units..
Owner Roger O'Byrne **Bred** Mrs P Kiely **Trained** Cholmondeley, Cheshire

FOCUS
There was no hanging around in this fair staying handicap and the form, which can be rated around the third, should work out. The easy winner is rated back to his Carlisle level.
T/Jkpt: Not won. T/Plt: £1069.40. Pool: £168,014.61 - 114.69 winning units. T/Qpdt: £50.50. Pool: £14,227.19 - 208.15 winning units. DO

^{2430}HUNTINGDON (R-H)

Saturday, November 23

OFFICIAL GOING: Soft (6.7)
Wind: light, half behind Weather: cloudy, dry

2675 MARK AND ROSANNA SERGEANT WEDDING DAY MARES' "NATIONAL HUNT" NOVICES' HURDLE (10 hdls) 2m 4f 110y
12:00 (12:00) (Class 4) 4-Y-0+ **£3,119** (£915; £457; £228)

Form RPR
220/ 1 **Woodland Walk**^{267} 4507 5-10-7 0 GavinSheehan(3) 113+
(Emma Lavelle) *j.lft at times: chsd ldr: mstke 1st: led sn after 7th: hdd and pushed along after 3 out: stl ev ch whn j.lft and slt mstke 2 out: rallied u.p to jump ahd last: styd on strly flat: rdn out* **3/1**^{3}

6/1- 2 5 **Kayfleur**^{17} 2298 4-10-7 0 JakeGreenall(3) 107
(Henry Daly) *chsd ldng pair: wnt 2nd sn after 7th: led and looked to be travelling best after 3 out: mstke 2 out: rdn whn outj. and hdd last: outpcd flat* **5/4**^{1}

212- 3 14 **Luci Di Mezzanotte**^{165} 706 5-11-2 0 LeightonAspell 101
(Oliver Sherwood) *t.k.h: hld up in tch in last pair: mstke 6th: rdn and effrt next: chsd clr ldng pair sn after 3 out: no imp: wknd between last 2* **5/2**^{2}

/34- 4 25 **Dahteste**^{170} 644 5-10-5 0 NicodeBoinville(5) 68
(Mark Bradstock) *led: mstke 7th: immediately hdd and drvn: wknd next: t.o between last 2* **25/1**

530/ 5 2 ½ **Taffy Dare (IRE)**^{224} 5295 4-10-10 0 GerardTumelty 68
(Alan King) *t.k.h: hld up in tch in midfield: hdwy to chse ldng pair after 7th: mstke next and immediately btn: wl bhd next: t.o* **20/1**

/45- 6 33 **Knockturnal (IRE)**^{15} 2342 5-10-10 0 HarryHaynes 33
(Malcolm Jefferson) *wl in tch in midfield: lost pl and rdn 7th: sn bhd: mstke 3 out: t.o next* **33/1**

0- 7 8 **Scolt Head Island**^{45} 1823 7-10-10 0 AndrewThornton 25
(Caroline Bailey) *t.k.h early: a last: struggling 7th: sn lost tch: t.o bef 2 out* **150/1**

5m 10.65s (11.65) **Going Correction** +0.575s/f (Soft)
WFA 4 from 5yo+ 8lb 7 Ran SP% **110.2**
Speed ratings (Par 105): **100,98,92,83,82 69,66**
toteswingers 1&2 £1.10, 2&3 £1.02, 1&3 £1.20 CSF £6.84 TOTE £4.80: £2.20, £1.40; EX 9.50 Trifecta £16.90 Pool: £1049.48 - 46.30 winning units..
Owner Cottage Stables Racing Club **Bred** Jethro Bloodstock **Trained** Hatherden, Hants

FOCUS
A modest mares' novices' hurdle in terms of prior form, but a few nice sorts took part at the fledgling stage of their careers, and they went an even gallop on soft ground. A step up from the winner on her bumper form.

2676 WHITTLEBURY HALL "NATIONAL HUNT" NOVICES' H'CAP HURDLE (8 hdls) 2m 110y
12:35 (12:35) (Class 4) (0-120,112) 4-Y-0+ **£3,119** (£915; £457; £228)

Form RPR
/22- 1 **Bernardelli (IRE)**^{20} 2241 5-11-8 108 BrianHarding 112+
(Nicky Richards) *wl in tch in midfield: clsd on outer and barging match w rival after 3 out: jnd ldrs next: sn led and rdn: drvn flat: styd on wl and a jst hoding rival flat: drvn out* **4/1**^{3}

4P3/ 2 nk **Ballincurrig (IRE)**^{321} 3531 7-11-3 108 (t) MissGAndrews(5) 112+
(Dan Skelton) *hld up wl in tch in last pair: switching to inner after 5th: hdwy to join ldrs after 3 out: ev ch next: rdn between last 2: drvn and kpt on wl flat: a jst hld* **6/1**

531- 3 5 **The Stig (FR)**^{29} 2068 5-11-12 112 PaddyBrennan 110
(Nick Littmoden) *w ldr tl led 3 out: rdn and hit next: sn hdd: no ex u.p last: one pce flat* **8/1**

330- 4 2 ¼ **Agincourt Reef (IRE)**^{21} 2210 4-11-9 112 JoshuaMoore(3) 109
(Gary Moore) *chsd ldng pair: ev ch whn mstke 3 out tl unable qck bef next: wknd flat* **14/1**

011- 5 1 ¼ **Theatrelands**^{27} 2111 5-11-9 112 (p) KielanWoods(3) 106
(Charlie Longsdon) *wl in tch in midfield: short of room and barging match w rival after 3 out: drvn and unable qck bef next: wknd flat* **11/4**^{2}

611- 6 1 ½ **Moscow Me (IRE)**^{30} 2051 6-11-6 106 PaulMoloney 99
(Henry Oliver) *mde most tl mstke and hdd 3 out: sn outpcd and dropped to last bef next: wl hld but edgd rt and kpt on again flat* **5/2**^{1}

0/P- P **Teenage Dream (IRE)**^{15} 2353 5-10-3 96 OllieGarner(7)
(Derek Shaw) *hld up wl tch in last pair: hdwy 5th: rdn and struggling 3 out: bhd whn eased and p.u next* **25/1**

4m 1.85s (6.95) **Going Correction** +0.575s/f (Soft)
WFA 4 from 5yo+ 7lb 7 Ran SP% **111.1**
Speed ratings (Par 105): **106,105,103,102,101 101,**
toteswingers 1&2 £5.20, 2&3 £2.80, 1&3 £8.60 CSF £26.08 TOTE £5.20: £2.50, £3.70; EX 33.70 Trifecta £92.20 Pool: £995.73 - 8.09 winning units..
Owner Henriques & LLoyd-Bakers **Bred** Minch Bloodstock **Trained** Greystoke, Cumbria

FOCUS
A modest novices' handicap hurdle. A small step up from the winner, the form rated through the third.

2677 BOONGATE KIA "POWER TO SURPRISE" NOVICES' H'CAP CHASE (12 fncs) 2m 110y
1:10 (1:10) (Class 4) (0-110,110) 4-Y-0+ **£3,768** (£1,106; £553; £276)

Form RPR
/51- 1 **Arkaim**^{16} 2315 5-11-5 106 KielanWoods(3) 117+
(Pam Sly) *t.k.h: chsd ldrs tl dashed into ld after 1st: clr next: c bk to field 3 out: jnd 2 out: rdn and asserted last: in command and idling fnl 100yds: rdn out* **10/3**^{2}

/53- 2 1 ¼ **Bertie's Desire**^{44} 1834 5-10-4 88 LeightonAspell 97+
(Oliver Sherwood) *led tl after 1st: chsd wnr: blnd 6th: lost 2nd and rdn sn after 3 out: 3rd and trying to rally whn mstke 2 out: styng on whn mstke last: chsd wnr again fnl 100yds: styd on but a hld* **13/8**^{1}

/00- 3 2 ¼ **Twoways (IRE)**^{39} 1913 7-11-1 104 (t) KillianMoore(5) 109
(Mark Rimell) *racd in midfield: clsd and wl in tch 9th: rdn and outpcd after 3 out: rallied between last 2: styd on u.p flat to go 3rd towards fin* **10/1**

/00- 4 1 ½ **Looks Like Slim**^{19} 2271 6-11-7 105 (p) JackDoyle 108
(Ben De Haan) *racd in midfield: hdwy to chse ldrs 4th: rdn and chal 2 out: no ex last: lost 2nd fnl 100yds: wknd towards fin* **14/1**

202- 5 19 **Lordship (IRE)**^{24} 2090 9-9-10 85 NicodeBoinville(5) 71
(Tom Gretton) *hld up in last pair: hdwy 8th: wl in tch and rdn after 3 out: sn struggling: wknd next* **9/1**

664- 6 hd **Eightfold**^{30} 2045 4-11-0 105 (t) ConorO'Farrell 88
(Seamus Durack) *hld up in last piar: clsd and wl in tch 9th: 4th and unable qck bef 2 out: wknd between last 2* **17/2**

403- 7 30 **Brassbound (USA)**^{16} 2315 5-11-12 110 (p) AdamPogson 64
(Caroline Bailey) *racd in midfield: lost pl and dropped to rr 4th: nvr gng wl after: lost tch 3 out: t.o next* **11/2**^{3}

4m 19.4s (9.20) **Going Correction** +0.575s/f (Soft)
WFA 4 from 5yo+ 7lb 7 Ran SP% **112.8**
Speed ratings (Par 105): **101,100,99,98,89 89,75**
toteswingers 1&2 £1.30, 2&3 £8.30, 1&3 £16.10 CSF £9.39 TOTE £3.90: £2.40, £1.80; EX 13.10 Trifecta £124.40 Pool: £1433.18 - 6.83 winning units..
Owner G A Libson D L Bayliss G Taylor P M Sly **Bred** Harton Limited **Trained** Thorney, Cambs

FOCUS
A modest novices' handicap chase in which the winner built on his recent victory.

2678 BOONGATE KIA PETERBOROUGH CAMBRIDGESHIRE NATIONAL H'CAP CHASE (25 fncs) 3m 6f 110y
1:40 (1:42) (Class 4) (0-120,118) 5-Y-0+ **£6,498** (£1,908; £954; £477)

Form RPR
213/ 1 **Soudain (FR)**^{211} 5548 7-10-13 112 PaulBohan(7) 129+
(Steve Gollings) *j.w and a travelling wl: chsd ldrs: mostly 2nd fr 4th: led 17th: pushed along and readily asserted 2 out: styd on strly: comf* **9/4**^{1}

3/3- 2 15 **Arkose (IRE)**^{18} 2283 9-11-8 114 (p) LeightonAspell 118+
(Oliver Sherwood) *in tch towards rr: on and off the bridle fr 4th: hdwy u.p to chse ldrs 17th: j.rt next: chsd wnr 22nd: clr w wnr after next: btn 2 out: wknd flat* **3/1**^{2}

3/2- 3 6 **Smart Exit (IRE)**^{19} 2275 6-10-8 103 (p) JoshuaMoore(3) 95
(Renee Robeson) *hld up in tch in last trio: rdn and effrt 19th: no ch w ldrs but battling for 3rd 2 out: plugged on to go 3rd cl home* **7/2**^{3}

2U4- 4 1 **Rhum (FR)**^{20} 2246 8-11-5 118 (vt) RyanHatch(7) 110
(Nigel Twiston-Davies) *led: out j. and hdd 17th: chsd wnr tl 22nd: 3rd and wknd bef next: plugged on but lost 3rd cl home* **8/1**

6/4- 5 13 **Desperate Dex (IRE)**^{23} 2179 13-11-10 116 PaddyBrennan 94
(Tom George) *a in rr: rdn and struggling 19th: wl bhd 3 out: n.d* **14/1**

/0U- 6 23 **Bally Sands (IRE)**^{17} 2297 9-11-1 107 LeeEdwards 62
(Robin Mathew) *chsd ldr tl 4th: styd chsng ldrs: 4th and mstke 21st: sn struggling: lost tch after 3 out: t.o* **12/1**

4/P- P **One More Dinar**^{17} 2297 10-9-9 92 JoshHamer(5)
(John Bryan Groucott) *j.lft and nvr fluent or travelling wl: a detached in last: blnd 13th: p.u next* **33/1**

422- P **Ballyvoneen (IRE)**^{12} 2425 8-9-11 92 oh2 (b) TrevorWhelan(3)
(Neil King) *chsd ldrs tl lost pl and mstke 19th: wknd 21st: t.o whn p.u after 3 out* **14/1**

8m 25.8s (13.00) **Going Correction** +0.575s/f (Soft) 8 Ran SP% **113.1**
Speed ratings: **106,102,100,100,96 91, ,**
toteswingers 1&2 £1.90, 2&3 £2.90, 1&3 £2.40 CSF £9.65 CT £21.58 TOTE £3.40: £1.20, £1.40, £2.20; EX 11.50 Trifecta £30.50 Pool: £1185.35 - 29.09 winning units..
Owner P J Martin **Bred** Marc Trinquet & Oliver Trinquet **Trained** Scamblesby, Lincs

FOCUS
The inaugural running of the Cambridgeshire National, a fair handicap chase over a marathon trip, and they went a decent gallop. A step up from the easy winner.

2679 BOONGATE KIA PICANTO CITY CONDITIONAL JOCKEYS' H'CAP HURDLE (8 hdls) 2m 110y
2:15 (2:15) (Class 5) (0-95,102) 4-Y-0+ **£1,949** (£572; £286; £143)

Form RPR
260- 1 **Dalrymple (IRE)**^{53} 1711 7-10-6 80 (t) OllieGarner(5) 94+
(Nick Ayliffe) *off the pce in last trio: hdwy to go prom in chsng gp after 3rd: chsd ldrs 4th: led bef 3 out: drew readily clr 2 out: r.o wl* **33/1**

F01- 2 21 **Poetic Power (IRE)**^{7} 2511 4-11-5 94 GeraldQuinn(6) 92
(Claire Dyson) *t.k.h: hld up off the pce in rr: clsd on ldrs 4th: hdwy on outer to join wnr bef 3 out: clr w wnr and rdn after 3 out: btn next: wknd last* **8/1**

603- 3 8 **Fair Breeze**^{54} 1700 6-9-13 76 DanielHiskett(8) 60
(Richard Phillips) *racd off the pce in midfield: dropped to last pair 4th: styd on past btn horses u.p fr 5th: lft modest 3rd and hmpd 2 out: plugged on* **16/1**

/05- 4 14 **Ivans Back (IRE)**^{120} 1120 8-11-2 88 (t) NickSlatter(3) 58
(Nick Kent) *racd freely: led and sn clr w rival tl 4th: hdd next: wknd qckly 3 out: lft poor 4th next: t.o* **33/1**

003- 5 5 **Finmerello**^{15} 2353 7-11-2 90 (p) JackSherwood(5) 55
(Kim Bailey) *t.k.h: w ldr and clr tl 4th: led and hit next: rdn and hdd bef next: mstke 3 out and sn wknd: lft poor 5th 2 out: t.o* **4/1**^{2}

F/0- 6 10 **Lilac Belle**^{22} 2191 7-11-5 88 (t) PeterCarberry 43
(Alex Hales) *racd off the pce in midfield: clsd on ldrs 4th: struggling and lost pl u.p next: t.o after 3 out* **33/1**

/20- 7 22 **So Cheeky**^{77} 1400 4-11-12 95 JonathanEngland 28
(Richard Guest) *nt a fluent: a in rr: n.d: t.o 3 out* **25/1**

U0P- P **Samizdat (FR)**^{37} 1940 10-10-2 71 oh3 ow2 KielanWoods
(John Upson) *prom in chsng gp: lost pl and rdn after 3rd: lost tch 5th: t.o whn p.u after 3 out* **66/1**

450- F **Maxdelas (FR)**^{37} 1938 7-11-3 91 ^{1} RyanHatch(5)
(Roy Brotherton) *prom in chsng gp: clsd and pressing ldrs 5th: short of room and lost pl bnd bef next: 7th and wkng whn fell 3 out* **16/1**

445/ P **Mytara**^{602} 5174 8-11-6 89 TrevorWhelan
(Clive Drew) *chsd clr ldng pair: clsd 4th: lost 3rd and qckly dropped out jst bef next: bhd whn p.u 3 out* **25/1**

/U2- B **My Nosy Rosy**^{22} 2191 5-11-4 87 (t) KillianMoore 85
(Ben Case) *prom in chsng gp: clsd on ldrs 4th: chsd ldrs after next: drvn and btn after 3 out: wl hld 4th whn b.d next* **7/1**^{3}

/01- F **The Game Is A Foot (IRE)**^{5} 2568 6-12-2 102 7ex JoshuaMoore(3) 100
(Gary Moore) *racd off the pce in midfield: clsd but rdn 4th: hdwy and chsd ldrs after next: drvn and btn after 3 out: 3rd and no ch w whn fell 2 out* **11/10**^{1}

4m 2.8s (7.90) **Going Correction** +0.575s/f (Soft)
WFA 4 from 5yo+ 7lb 12 Ran SP% **121.0**
Speed ratings (Par 103): **104,94,90,83,81 76,66, , ,**
toteswingers 1&2 £19.40, 2&3 £17.00, 1&3 £0.00 CSF £266.40 CT £4386.68 TOTE £23.60: £4.50, £3.00, £4.60; EX 356.80 Trifecta £1139.50 Part won. Pool: £1519.34 - 0.01 winning units..
Owner Michael J Hayes **Bred** Darley **Trained** Winsford, Somerset

The Form Book Jumps, Raceform Ltd, Compton, RG20 6NL.

FOCUS
A modest conditional jockeys' handicap hurdle in which they went an honest gallop. A surprise step up from the easy winner.

2680 BOONGATE KIA 7 YEAR WARRANTY H'CAP HURDLE (12 hdls) 3m 2f
2:50 (2:50) (Class 5) (0-100,100) 4-Y-0+ **£1,949** (£572; £286; £143)

Form RPR
5P4- **1** **Elegant Olive**[20] 2253 10-11-5 **93**........ HaddenFrost 100
(Roger Curtis) *racd in midfield: dropped to last and niggled along after 7th: hdwy to chse ldrs 9th: rdn and effrt to chal whn wnt rt 2 out: sn led: drvn and hld on gamely flat* **5/1**[3]
/P6- **2** *hd* **Iconic Rose**[20] 2253 6-10-13 **90**........ KielanWoods(3) 96
(Pam Sly) *chsd ldr and clr in ldng trio tl 8th: rdn to ld 3 out: drvn and hdd sn after 2 out: battled on gamely u.p and sustained duel w wnr after: jst hld* **4/1**[1]
0/0- **3** *9* **Crushed Ice**[204] 91 7-10-8 **82**........ HarryHaynes 80
(Malcolm Jefferson) *chsd clr ldng trio: clsd and chsng ldrs 8th: cl 3rd and rdn after 3 out: no ex between last 2: wknd flat* **9/1**
454- **4** *9* **Cute Court (IRE)**[18] 2284 6-11-6 **94**........ TimmyMurphy 82
(Liam Corcoran) *racd wd: hld up in rr: clsd on ldrs after 7th: hdwy to chse ldrs 9th: wnt 2nd and rdn bnd bef 2 out: unable qck and sltly hmpd next: sn wknd* **9/2**[2]
026/ **5** *2 1/4* **Acosta**[236] 5085 9-9-11 **74** oh2........(b) WayneKavanagh(3) 60
(Dr Jeremy Naylor) *chsd ldng pair and clr in ldng trio: wnt 2nd 7th tl rdn to ld after 9th: hdd next: wknd u.p bef 2 out* **25/1**
123- **6** *9* **Artic Night (FR)**[9] 2473 7-11-0 **88**........(bt) DavidEngland 65
(Nigel Twiston-Davies) *hld up off the pce in last trio: clsd on ldrs after 7th: wl in tch and rdn after 9th: little rspnse and btn next: wknd 3 out* **4/1**[1]
13P- **7** *41* **Go Amwell**[20] 2253 10-11-12 **100**........(v) LeightonAspell 36
(J R Jenkins) *t.k.h: hld up off the pce in last trio: clsd on ldrs after 7th: in tch and rdn after next: wknd bef 3 out: t.o between last 2* **6/1**
04P- **P** **Almutaham (USA)**[21] 2218 6-10-0 **81**........(v[1]) MissJRRichards(7)
(Nicky Richards) *led and clr w 2 rivals tl 8th: hdd and rdn bef 3 out: sn dropped out: t.o whn p.u 2 out* **17/2**
0/0- **P** **Bravo Riquet (FR)**[16] 2313 7-11-11 **99**........(vt) LeeEdwards
(Robin Mathew) *racd in midfield: clsd on ldrs after 7th: struggling and mstke next: wknd bef next: t.o whn p.u 2 out* **14/1**

6m 39.4s (16.50) **Going Correction** +0.575s/f (Soft) **9** Ran SP% **120.2**
Speed ratings (Par 103): **97,96,94,91,90 87,75, ,**
toteswingers 1&2 £3.60, 2&3 £8.60, 1&3 £26.50 CSF £26.94 CT £179.44 TOTE £6.20: £2.30, £1.60, £2.80; EX 39.30 Trifecta £380.10 Pool: £1446.34 - 2.85 winning units..
Owner Collective Dreamers **Bred** Edward Crow **Trained** Lambourn, Berks

FOCUS
An ordinary staying handicap hurdle. The winner is rated to something like her best.

2681 BOONGATE KIA COMPETITIVE CONTRACT HIRE MAIDEN OPEN NATIONAL HUNT FLAT RACE 1m 6f
3:25 (3:25) (Class 6) 4-6-Y-0 **£1,559** (£457; £228; £114)

Form RPR
1 **Fort Worth (IRE)**[217] 4-11-4 0........ RichieMcLernon 114+
(Jonjo O'Neill) *a travelling wl: hld up in midfield: hdwy to trck ldr 4f out: pushed into ld ins fnl f: sn in command: easily* **4/6**[1]
3/4- **2** *3 1/4* **Newforge House (IRE)**[45] 1826 5-11-4 0........ BrendanPowell 100
(Brendan Powell) *led: clr w wnr over 2f out: drvn and wandered over 1f out: hdd ins fnl f and sn brushed aside: kpt on for clr 2nd* **6/1**[3]
3 *19* **Abijoe** 4-10-8 0........ KielanWoods(3) 70
(Pam Sly) *in tch in midfield: pushed along briefly 10f out: rdn and effrt 4f out: chsd clr ldng pair 3f out: no imp* **17/2**
4- **4** *5* **Closest Friend**[31] 2026 4-10-8 0........ StevieSanders(10) 72
(J R Jenkins) *in tch in last trio: hdwy 1/2-way: rdn 5f out: wnt 3rd briefly 4f out: 4th and wl hld fnl 2f* **4/1**[2]
0- **5** *19* **Roxy Madam**[176] 567 4-10-11 0........ AdamPogson 41
(Mandy Rowland) *chsd ldr tl 4f out: rdn and wknd over 3f out: 5th and wl btn fnl 3f: t.o* **66/1**
6 *6* **Flash Tommie (IRE)** 5-10-13 0........ NicodeBoinville(5) 41
(Martin Bosley) *chsd ldrs: rdn and lost pl over 5f out: sn bhd: t.o fnl 3f* **25/1**
U0- **7** *2 1/2* **Dorton Lad (IRE)**[9] 2472 4-10-11 0........ MrDGannon(7) 38
(Phil Middleton) *hld up in tch in last trio: rdn and lost tch qckly 5f out: t.o fnl 3f* **66/1**
8 *19* **Crowd Control (IRE)** 4-11-4 0........ LeightonAspell 15
(Martin Smith) *rn green: a in rr: rdn and lost tch 9f out: t.o fr 1/2-way: hung lft bnd over 2f out* **10/1**

3m 27.0s (7.00) **8** Ran SP% **120.7**
toteswingers 1&2 £1.10, 2&3 £3.20, 1&3 £2.60 CSF £5.86 TOTE £1.90: £1.10, £1.70, £2.30; EX 7.60 Trifecta £28.20 Pool: £1360.06 - 36.12 winning units..
Owner Mrs J Magnier, D Smith & M Tabor **Bred** Kenneth Parkhill **Trained** Cheltenham, Gloucs

FOCUS
An ordinary maiden bumper in which they went an, at best, even gallop. The easy winner was value for further and looks a decent prospect.
T/Plt: £203.00 to a £1 stake. Pool of £52401.73 - 185.15 winning tickets. T/Qpdt: £77.00 to a £1 stake. Pool of £4542.40 - 43.20 winning tickets. SP

2682 - 2688a (Foreign Racing) - See Raceform Interactive

2457 EXETER (R-H)
Sunday, November 24

OFFICIAL GOING: Good (good to soft in places on hurdle course; chs 7.3 hdl 7.1)
Hurdle on bend after winning post moved to back straight.
Wind: mild breeze half behind Weather: overcast

2689 BATHWICK TYRES BRIDGWATER NOVICES' HURDLE (DIV I) (8 hdls) 2m 1f
12:35 (12:35) (Class 4) 4-Y-0+ **£3,249** (£954; £477; £238)

Form RPR
0/1- **1** **Doctor Harper (IRE)**[19] 2280 5-11-5 0........ TimmyMurphy 132+
(David Pipe) *mde all: wl in command fr 3 out: wnt rt 2 out: v easily* **1/5**[1]
045/ **2** *3 1/2* **Sky Watch (IRE)**[222] 5337 6-10-9 0........ GavinSheehan(3) 109
(Warren Greatrex) *mid-div: hdwy after 5th: rdn after 3 out: wnt 2nd between last 2: styd on but no ch w easy wnr* **7/1**[2]
404- **3** *10* **Even If**[20] 2272 5-10-12 0........ RichieMcLernon 99
(Jonjo O'Neill) *trckd ldrs: wnt 2nd after 3rd: rdn bef 3 out: kpt on same pce fr 2 out* **7/1**[2]
4 *1 1/2* **All But Grey**[196] 7-10-9 0........ MichealNolan(3) 99
(Carroll Gray) *trckd ldrs: pckd 1st: mstke 2nd: rdn to dispute 2nd 3 out tl after 2 out: kpt on same pce* **33/1**
00- **5** *7* **Sedgemoor Top Bid (IRE)**[11] 2457 5-10-9 0........ MarkQuinlan(3) 91
(Nigel Hawke) *trckd wnr tl after 3rd: chsd ldrs: rdn appr 3 out: sn one pce: fdd bef last* **66/1**
1/ **6** *3 3/4* **Chapter Five**[53] 4547 6-10-0 0........(p) RobertMcCarth(5) 83
(Ian Williams) *mid-div: making hdwy whn blnd 3 out: sn rdn: nt a danger after: wknd bef last* **7/1**[2]
02U- **7** *1* **Unefille De Guye (FR)**[11] 2463 5-10-2 0........[1] GilesHawkins(3) 79
(Victor Dartnall) *a towards rr* **11/1**[3]
520/ **8** *2 1/4* **Miles Of Sunshine**[23] 4097 8-10-12 0........ PaulMoloney 86
(Ron Hodges) *hld up towards rr: rdn and sme prog after 5th: no further imp fr next: wkng whn blnd last* **100/1**
00- **9** *4 1/2* **Ask The Boss**[11] 2457 8-10-12 0........ NickScholfield 79
(Tim Dennis) *mid-div: rdn after 5th: wknd next* **100/1**
60/- **10** *27* **Follow The Master**[327] 3424 7-10-9 0........ WayneKavanagh(3) 52
(Brian Forsey) *mid-div: struggling after 4th: sn in rr: t.o* **100/1**

4m 9.0s (-6.50) **Going Correction** -0.55s/f (Firm) **10** Ran SP% **136.6**
Speed ratings (Par 105): **93,91,86,85,82 80,80,79,77,64**
Tote Swingers: 1&2 £1.60, 1&3 £2.00, 2&3 £5.20 CSF £4.10 TOTE £1.40: £1.02, £2.70, £1.20; EX 3.40 Trifecta £16.20 Pool: £3,888.41 - 179.83 winning units..
Owner The Johnson Family **Bred** Stephen O'Flynn **Trained** Nicholashayne, Devon

FOCUS
Timmy Murphy described the ground as "beautiful". The facile winner stood out in this steadily run novice, which is rated through the second.

2690 BATHWICK TYRES H'CAP HURDLE (11 hdls) 2m 5f 110y
1:05 (1:05) (Class 5) (0-95,101) 4-Y-0+ **£2,274** (£667; £333; £166)

Form RPR
054- **1** **Rigolo Ville (FR)**[16] 2353 8-11-6 **92**........(p) GilesHawkins(3) 101+
(Richard Hobson) *mid-div tl dropped to rr 6th: hdwy on outer after 8th: led appr 2 out: styd on wl: rdn out* **14/1**
403- **2** *2* **Night Of Passion (IRE)**[17] 2312 5-10-6 **75**........(p) NickScholfield 81
(Jeremy Scott) *trckd ldrs tl dropped to midfield and reminder after 3rd: rdn after 7th: hdwy appr 3 out: styd on to go 2nd run-in* **5/1**[1]
/00- **3** *3 3/4* **Matako (FR)**[38] 1940 10-11-10 **93**........ IanPopham 96
(Caroline Keevil) *mid-div: hdwy after 8th: rdn to chse ldrs after 3 out: styd on same pce* **20/1**
440- **4** *nk* **Cash Injection**[18] 2291 4-10-12 **88**........(t) TomBellamy(7) 91
(Richard Woollacott) *trckd ldrs: rdn to ld 3 out: hdd bef 2 out: styd chsng wnr tl no ex and lost 2 pls run-in* **25/1**
1/5- **5** *4 1/2* **Lansdowne Princess**[17] 2312 11-10-11 **80**........(t) BrendanPowell 78
(Johnny Farrelly) *mid-div: hdwy after 8th: sn rdn to chse ldrs: styd on same pce fr 2 out* **11/2**[2]
5/5- **6** *11* **Free Falling**[10] 2470 7-11-1 **84**........(v) AidanColeman 72
(Alastair Lidderdale) *prom: led after 5th tl rdn after 8th: wknd next* **12/1**
264- **7** *4 1/2* **Midnight Mustang**[10] 2470 6-10-6 **82**........ MrJMartin(7) 66
(Andrew J Martin) *mid-div: rdn and hdwy appr 3 out: wknd after 2 out* **10/1**
14U- **8** *1* **Cruising Bye**[11] 2458 7-11-10 **93**........ TomO'Brien 76
(Peter Bowen) *trckd ldrs tl 4th: midfield: rdn after 8th: nvr any imp* **11/2**[2]
400/ **9** *nk* **Pearl (IRE)**[23] 4027 9-10-5 **74**........ PaulMoloney 57
(Ron Hodges) *hld up towards rr: sme prog after 8th: no further imp fr next* **20/1**
300- **10** *4 1/2* **Master Cardor Visa (IRE)**[10] 2470 8-11-5 **93**........ JamesBanks(5) 72
(Emma Baker) *chsd ldrs tl after 5th: struggling in rr fr next* **25/1**
6PP- **11** *2 1/2* **Petrarchick (USA)**[13] 2423 6-10-1 **75**........(b[1]) AodhaganConlon(5) 52
(Emma Baker) *prom: rdn to dispute after 8th tl hdd bef 3 out: wkng whn hmpd 2 out* **80/1**
46F- **12** *5* **Trakeur (FR)**[24] 2175 6-10-9 **78**........(p) JamesDavies 50
(Simon Hodgson) *trckd ldrs: rdn after 8th: sn wknd* **80/1**
P/1- **13** *3 1/4* **North London**[55] 1700 6-11-0 **83**........ HaddenFrost 52
(James Frost) *a towards rr* **12/1**
400- **14** *10* **Sonoftheking (IRE)**[28] 2105 5-11-12 **95**........(p) RichardJohnson 55
(Philip Hobbs) *trckd ldrs: nt fluent 7th: rdn after next: wknd bef 3 out* **8/1**[3]
021- **F** **The Young Master**[7] 2535 4-11-13 **101** 7ex........(p) ConorShoemark(5) 103
(Neil Mulholland) *led tl 4th: prom: rdn to dispute ld after 8th: styng on at same pce in disp 2nd whn fell 2 out* **8/1**[3]

5m 19.0s (-14.00) **Going Correction** -0.55s/f (Firm) **15** Ran SP% **120.5**
Speed ratings (Par 103): **103,102,100,100,99 95,93,93,93,91 90,88,87,83,**
Tote Swingers: 1&2 £27.00, 1&3 £19.90, 2&3 £65.50 CSF £77.40 CT £1425.88 TOTE £20.30: £4.10, £2.20, £6.50; EX 118.00 Trifecta £1120.30 Part won. Pool: £1,493.79 - 0.19 winning units..
Owner Richard Hobson **Bred** J Poumaillou, & E Poumaillou **Trained** Barnstaple, Devon
■ The first winner as a trainer for former jump jockey Richard Hobson.
■ Stewards' Enquiry : Tom Bellamy two-day ban: used whip above permitted level (Dec 8-9)

FOCUS
A moderate handicap run at a strong pace. The winner was well in on his best form.

2691 BATHWICK TYRES PLYMOUTH H'CAP HURDLE (12 hdls) 2m 7f 110y
1:35 (1:35) (Class 4) (0-115,115) 4-Y-0+ **£3,249** (£954; £477; £238)

Form RPR
653- **1** **Sir Frank (IRE)**[11] 2458 8-11-11 **114**........(p) ConorO'Farrell 121
(David Pipe) *hld up towards rr: nudged along for stdy prog fr after 6th: led 3 out: sn rdn and strly chal: drifted sltly rt run-in: won on nod: all out* **7/1**[3]
440/ **2** *nse* **Georgian King**[734] 2677 10-11-2 **105**........ IanPopham 112
(Martin Keighley) *racd keenly: trckd ldrs: str chal fr 3 out: sn rdn: ev ch fr last: kpt on: jst failed on nod* **8/1**
205- **3** *9* **Buckhorn Tom**[11] 2458 5-11-4 **114**........(p) MrMLegg(7) 114
(Colin Tizzard) *trckd ldrs: rdn whn outpcd appr 3 out: styd on again fr 2 out: wnt 3rd at the last* **6/1**[2]
5/3- **4** *4* **Water Wagtail**[26] 2150 6-11-4 **110**........ GavinSheehan(3) 105
(Emma Lavelle) *trckd ldrs: rdn appr 3 out: styd on same pce* **5/1**[1]
100/ **5** *2 1/4* **Kayef (GER)**[36] 2453 6-11-7 **110**........(v) LiamTreadwell 104
(Michael Scudamore) *hld up towards rr: hdwy fr 9th: rdn to chse ldrs 3 out: styd on same pce fr 2 out* **50/1**
6/6- **6** *5* **Rocky Bender (IRE)**[31] 2041 8-11-5 **108**........ AidanColeman 96
(Venetia Williams) *mid-div: rdn after 9th: mstke 3 out: nvr threatened* **14/1**
452/ **7** *2 1/2* **Long John**[215] 5470 6-10-13 **105**........ JamesBest(3) 93+
(Jackie Du Plessis) *plld hrd: mid-div: hdwy after 5th: led 7th tl rdn appr 3 out: sn hld: fdd appr last* **8/1**
P/1- **8** *1 1/4* **Jump Up**[42] 1890 7-10-11 **100**........ TomO'Brien 85
(Peter Bowen) *led tl 7th: chsd ldrs: rdn appr 3 out: grad fdd* **15/2**
230/ **9** *1/2* **Canadian Dreamer (IRE)**[346] 3023 6-11-7 **110**........ WayneHutchinson 95
(Graeme McPherson) *mid-div: rdn after 9th: nvr any imp* **33/1**

241/ **10** *nk* **Genstone Trail**[404] 1880 7-10-12 **101** RobertThornton 86
(Alan King) *mid-div: hdwy 8th: rdn bef 3 out: wknd bef 2 out* **7/1**[3]

50P- **11** *6* **Brockwell Park**[11] 2462 6-10-4 **100** (p) MissVWade[(7)] 79
(Jeremy Scott) *mid-div: nt fluent 4th: wknd bef 3 out* **40/1**

653- **12** *2 1/4* **Kyles Faith (IRE)**[18] 2296 5-11-3 **106** TomSiddall 83
(Martin Keighley) *trckd ldrs: rdn appr 3 out: sn wknd* **33/1**

3/0- **13** *hd* **Petit Fleur**[163] 738 11-10-12 **101** SamTwiston-Davies 78
(Julian Smith) *a towards rr* **66/1**

60/- **14** *9* **Nutin Fancy (IRE)**[260] 4655 7-11-12 **115** RichardJohnson 84
(Philip Hobbs) *mid-div tl rdn after 7th: sn towards rr: wknd 3 out* **12/1**

6/0- **15** *28* **Bois Des Aigles (FR)**[28] 2105 4-11-2 **105** (p) TomScudamore 48
(David Pipe) *hld up towards rr: sme prog 9th: wknd bef 3 out: t.o* **16/1**

5m 51.0s (-8.00) **Going Correction** -0.55s/f (Firm)
WFA 4 from 5yo+ 8lb **15** Ran SP% **122.0**
Speed ratings (Par 105): **91,90,87,86,85 84,83,82,82,82 80,79,79,76,67**
Tote Swingers: 1&2 £1.10, 1&3 £2.20, 2&3 £1.80 CSF £60.84 CT £364.21 TOTE £6.60: £2.40, £4.10, £2.70; EX 74.70 Trifecta £205.70 Pool: £1,876.90 - 46.00 winning units..
Owner R Wilkin And The Frankophiles **Bred** Mrs G Galvin **Trained** Nicholashayne, Devon
■ Stewards' Enquiry : Conor O'Farrell caution: careless riding.

FOCUS
The front pair managed to draw right away despite them going a steady gallop and there was Stewards' enquiry after they made contact, but the result was left alone. The winner is on the upgrade and rated in line with the best of his chase form.

2692 BATHWICK TYRES TAUNTON NOVICES' LIMITED H'CAP CHASE (18 fncs) 3m
2:05 (2:05) (Class 3) (0-140,140) 4-Y-0+ **£9,495** (£2,805; £1,402; £702)

Form RPR

252/ **1** **Kasbadali (FR)**[351] 2921 8-10-8 **129** LeightonAspell 134
(Oliver Sherwood) *disp ld tl 4th: trckd ldr: disp again 12th: rdn and ev ch 4 out: sn led: hdd after 3 out: looked hld at the last: styd on gamely to ld run-in: drvn rt out* **5/1**[3]

P/0- **2** *nk* **Ballytober**[191] 358 7-10-6 **127** (t) TomO'Brien 132
(Philip Hobbs) *travelled wl most of way: trckd ldrs: chal 4 out: rdn to ld after next: drifted lft run-in: kpt on whn hdd towards fin* **11/2**

113- **3** *13* **According To Trev (IRE)**[37] 1957 7-11-1 **136** (t) SamTwiston-Davies 130
(Nigel Twiston-Davies) *trckd ldrs: pushed along briefly after 6th: struggling to hold pl after 12th: disputing cl 3rd after 14th but u.str.p: styd on same pce fr 4 out* **3/1**[2]

F/1- **4** *5* **Sonofvic (IRE)**[33] 2010 8-11-5 **140** DarylJacob 135
(Paul Nicholls) *disp ld: pckd 2nd: clr ldr 4th tl 12th where jnd: rdn and hdd whn rchd for 4 out: ev ch whn nt fluent next: btn whn mstke 2 out* **1/1**[1]

6m 2.1s (-7.20) **Going Correction** -0.125s/f (Good) **4** Ran SP% **107.1**
Speed ratings (Par 107): **107,106,102,100**
CSF £25.28 TOTE £4.20; EX 24.10 Trifecta £47.20 Pool: £2,297.87 - 1.02 winning units..
Owner Tim Syder **Bred** Olivier Delegue **Trained** Upper Lambourn, Berks

FOCUS
The two outsiders came clear in what had looked a fair novice handicap. Not form to be confident about with the two market leaders underperforming.

2693 BATHWICK TYRES BARNSTAPLE H'CAP CHASE (18 fncs) 3m
2:35 (2:35) (Class 3) (0-125,125) 4-Y-0£7,912 (£2,337; £1,168; £585; £292)

Form RPR

013- **1** **Samingarry (FR)**[20] 2275 6-10-13 **115** MarkQuinlan[(3)] 126+
(Nigel Hawke) *mid-div: in last trio whn pushed along after 12th: rdn and hdwy to chal 4 out: led 2 out: 2 l clr last: hung lft: styd on wl: rdn out* **17/2**

04- **2** *2 1/2* **Ultragold (FR)**[28] 2107 5-11-7 **120** (t) JoeTizzard 127
(Colin Tizzard) *travelled wl in tch: trckd ldrs 11th: rdn bef 4 out: styd on wl fr last to snatch 2nd fnl stride* **13/2**

/34- **3** *hd* **Barlow (IRE)**[34] 2005 6-11-8 **121** NoelFehily 129
(Warren Greatrex) *trckd ldr: led after 11th: rdn whn strly pressed fr 4 out: hdd 2 out: sn hld: styd on same pce* **7/2**[2]

0FR- **4** *2 1/2* **Triggerman**[29] 2070 11-11-6 **119** (b[1]) RichardJohnson 126+
(Philip Hobbs) *sn trcking ldrs: rdn to chal 4 out: styng on at same pce in 3rd fr next: disputing 2nd whn blnd bdly last: no ex: fin lame* **10/1**

1/1- **5** *3/4* **Trafalgar (FR)**[32] 2024 6-11-11 **124** SamTwiston-Davies 130
(Nigel Twiston-Davies) *trckd ldrs: pushed along after 11th: rdn and ev ch appr 4 out: styd on same pce fr 3 out* **3/1**[1]

/1F- **6** *31* **Dorset Naga**[39] 1923 7-11-9 **122** (t) AidanColeman 98
(Anthony Honeyball) *hld up but in tch: rdn after 14th: wknd after 4 out: t.o* **8/1**

3P2- **7** *15* **Qianshan Leader (IRE)**[45] 1830 9-11-9 **125** (p) GavinSheehan[(3)] 87
(Emma Lavelle) *led: hit 5th: rdn and hdd after 11th: mstke 14th: sn wknd: tailing off whn mstke 4 out* **9/2**[3]

/P3- **P** **No Principles**[151] 845 10-11-7 **120** WayneHutchinson
(Julian Smith) *a towards rr: struggling fr 10th: t.o whn p.u bef 4 out* **25/1**

U/P- **P** **Addiction**[194] 294 8-11-4 **117** (tp) NickScholfield
(Jeremy Scott) *reminders after 10th: sn in rr: t.o whn p.u bef 4 out* **16/1**

6m 4.0s (-5.30) **Going Correction** -0.125s/f (Good) **9** Ran SP% **119.2**
Speed ratings (Par 107): **103,102,102,101,101 90,85, ,**
Tote Swingers: 1&2 £9.70, 1&3 £7.80, 2&3 £6.30 CSF £64.53 CT £233.60 TOTE £9.30: £2.70, £2.60, £1.90; EX 72.90 Trifecta £352.50 Pool: £3,015.39 - 6.41 winning units..
Owner Pearce Bros 1 **Bred** Isabelle Garcon & Jean-Pierre Garcon **Trained** Stoodleigh, Devon

FOCUS
Ordinary form for the grade, but sound enough.

2694 BATHWICK TYRES H'CAP CHASE (THE SUNDAY £5K BONUS RACE) (12 fncs) 2m 1f 110y
3:05 (3:05) (Class 3) (0-130,128) 4-Y-0£7,912 (£2,337; £1,168; £585; £292)

Form RPR

/04- **1** **Oscar Hill (IRE)**[35] 1990 7-11-12 **128** TomO'Brien 141+
(David Bridgwater) *mde all: clr after 2nd tl 4 out: pushed clr again appr last: r.o wl: pushed out* **8/1**

U/P- **2** *19* **Rouge Et Blanc (FR)**[24] 2180 8-11-6 **127** ThomasGarner[(5)] 124
(Oliver Sherwood) *hld up in tch: hdwy appr 4 out: disp 2nd 4 out: sn rdn: nt fluent next: lft in hld 2nd 2 out: wnt rt last: a holding on for 2nd* **20/1**

310- **3** *1/2* **Notarfbad (IRE)**[22] 2212 7-11-11 **127** RichardJohnson 123
(Jeremy Scott) *chsd clr ldr in clr 2nd: rdn after 4 out: hld whn lft 4th and hmpd 2 out: styd on again fr last* **3/1**[2]

/50- **4** *2 1/4* **Oh Crick (FR)**[9] 2488 10-11-11 **127** RobertThornton 118
(Alan King) *racd in 3rd fr 4th: struggling to hold pl after 6th: sn lost pl hld fr 4 out: rallied briefly after 2 out: no ex fr last* **9/1**

210- **5** *3 1/2* **Red Riverman**[18] 2287 5-11-9 **125** (p) SamTwiston-Davies 113
(Nigel Twiston-Davies) *hld up but in tch: rdn appr 4 out: nvr gng pce to get involved* **17/2**

P02- **6** *55* **Passato (GER)**[29] 2086 9-11-6 **122** (t) DominicElsworth 61
(Jo Davis) *chsd ldrs tl lost pl after 4th: struggling fr next: no ch fr 8th: t.o* **7/1**

3- **F** **Sands Cove (IRE)**[18] 2287 6-11-6 **122** (t) NoelFehily 128+
(Charlie Mann) *hld up in tch: creot clsr fr 4 out: wnt 2nd 2 out: travelling wl enough in 3 l 2nd whn fell 2 out* **6/1**[3]

0- **P** **Vif Argent (FR)**[36] 1971 4-11-4 **127** TomScudamore
(David Pipe) *chsd ldrs tl after 4th: blnd 5th: sn lost tch: t.o whn p.u bef 4 out* **11/4**[1]

4m 13.0s (-6.00) **Going Correction** -0.125s/f (Good)
WFA 4 from 5yo+ 7lb **8** Ran SP% **114.9**
Speed ratings (Par 107): **108,99,99,98,96 72, ,**
Tote Swingers: 1&2 £9.50, 1&3 £6.80, 2&3 £18.90 CSF £128.41 CT £587.21 TOTE £10.40: £3.00, £6.00, £1.40; EX 144.60 Trifecta £371.50 Pool: £1,762.57 - 3.55 winning units..
Owner K W Bradley **Bred** Elizabeth Tudor Syndicate **Trained** Icomb, Gloucs

FOCUS
Little got into this. A small personal best from the winner.

2695 BATHWICK TYRES BRIDGWATER NOVICES' HURDLE (DIV II) (8 hdls) 2m 1f
3:35 (3:35) (Class 4) 4-Y-0+ **£3,249** (£954; £477; £238)

Form RPR

130- **1** **Neston Grace**[38] 1941 5-10-12 104 [1] JamesDavies 111
(Simon Hodgson) *trckd ldrs: rdn appr 3 out: chal last: styd on to ld towards fin: drvn out* **14/1**

2 *nk* **Madness Light (FR)**[150] 4-10-12 0 NoelFehily 110+
(Warren Greatrex) *led tl after 1st: prom: led after 3 out: rdn after 2 out: no ex whn hdd towards fin* **5/4**[1]

3 *4 1/2* **Benbecula**[63] 4-10-12 0 RobertThornton 108+
(Richard Mitchell) *racd freely: nvr fluent: led after 1st: mstke 3 out: sn hdd: rdn and kpt on to regain 3rd nring fin* **14/1**

/64- **4** *1/2* **Gallic Warrior (FR)**[19] 2280 6-10-12 0 PaddyBrennan 107
(Fergal O'Brien) *trckd ldrs: bmpd 1st: rdn after 3 out: kpt on same pce fr next: lost 3rd nring fin* **3/1**[2]

3/0- **5** *2 3/4* **Trillerin Minella (IRE)**[43] 1869 5-10-12 0 WayneHutchinson 105
(Graeme McPherson) *hmpd 1st: trckd ldrs: rdn after 5th: kpt on same pce fr 3 out: mstke last* **25/1**

5/0- **6** *5* **Absolutely Bygones (IRE)**[33] 2011 5-10-9 0 JamesBest[(3)] 99
(Jackie Du Plessis) *hld up in tch: effrt 3 out: kpt on but nvr gng pce to threaten* **16/1**

652/ **7** *23* **Sammyman**[86] 4762 6-10-12 0 NickScholfield 83
(Michael Blanshard) *hld up in tch: rdn whn nt fluent 3 out: sn wknd: t.o* **40/1**

R2F- **8** *14* **Sea Island Pearl**[19] 2280 4-10-5 0 TomO'Brien 59
(Philip Hobbs) *hld up in tch: short-lived effrt 3 out: sn wknd: t.o* **12/1**

4- **9** *20* **Clubs Are Trumps (IRE)**[16] 2354 4-10-12 0 RichieMcLernon 48
(Jonjo O'Neill) *sn trcking ldrs: lost tch qckly after 3rd: t.o* **7/1**[3]

4m 4.5s (-11.00) **Going Correction** -0.55s/f (Firm) **9** Ran SP% **115.1**
Speed ratings (Par 105): **103,102,100,100,99 96,86,79,70**
Tote Swingers: 1&2 £6.30, 1&3 £8.60, 2&3 £4.50 CSF £33.00 TOTE £12.10: £3.40, £1.50, £2.40; EX 45.00 Trifecta £296.30 Pool: £2,637.63 - 6.67 winning units..
Owner Dr Nigel Knott **Bred** Dr N J Knott **Trained** Yeovil, Somerset

FOCUS
The lesser of the two divisions and there was a bit of a turn-up. The fourth and sixth help set the level.

2696 BATHWICK TYRES CONDITIONAL JOCKEYS' H'CAP HURDLE (8 hdls) 2m 1f
4:05 (4:05) (Class 4) (0-105,105) 4-Y-0+ **£3,249** (£954; £477; £238)

Form RPR

6/0- **1** **Lamblord (IRE)**[15] 2369 6-11-8 **101** JamesBest 105
(Carroll Gray) *mid-div: hdwy 4th: lft in narrow ld 2 out: hld on gamely: asserting nr fin: drvn out* **9/1**[3]

/63- **2** *1* **Mezzanisi (IRE)**[14] 2385 8-11-7 **100** MichaelByrne 103
(Peter Bowen) *mid-div: hdwy 5th: trcking ldr 3 out: lft w ev ch 2 out: rdn and hung lft after last: kpt on tl no ex nring fin: dismntd* **6/1**[2]

046/ **3** *7* **Togiak (IRE)**[60] 854 6-11-4 **103** (b[1]) TomBellamy[(6)] 101
(David Pipe) *mid-div: hdwy 5th: rdn after 3 out: lft 3rd whn hmpd next: styd on same pce* **4/1**[1]

/S0- **4** *4* **Oscar Jane (IRE)**[33] 2013 6-11-3 **96** MattGriffiths 90
(Johnny Farrelly) *hld up towards rr: struggling 5th: styd on fr 3 out: hmpd 2 out: snatched 4th fnl strides* **14/1**

F45- **5** *1/2* **Bold Tara**[20] 2278 6-9-6 **79** oh2 (tp) OllieGarner[(8)] 72
(Martin Keighley) *led tl after 1st: prom: rdn appr 3 out: sltly hmpd 2 out: styd on same pce: no ex whn lost 4th fnl strides* **9/1**[3]

446- **6** *11* **Gizzit (IRE)**[17] 2315 7-11-1 **94** (p) PeterCarberry 78
(Karen George) *hld up towards rr: struggling 5th: sme late prog: nvr threatened ldrs* **6/1**[2]

/23- **7** *1 1/2* **Lady Bridget**[163] 293 5-10-5 **84** (bt) PatrickCorbett 65
(Mark Gillard) *trckd ldrs: rdn appr 3 out: sn one pce* **16/1**

P50- **8** *nk* **Bedouin Bay**[10] 2474 6-11-0 **98** ThomasCheesman[(5)] 80
(Johnny Farrelly) *hld up towards rr: struggling 5th: nvr threatened* **16/1**

665- **9** *4 1/2* **Mount Odell**[22] 2215 5-11-9 **105** JoshuaMoore[(3)] 82
(Gary Moore) *hld up towards rr: rdn after 5th: nvr threatened* **6/1**[2]

050- **10** *12* **Khazium (IRE)**[20] 2271 4-10-8 **93** (tp) GeraldQuinn[(6)] 64
(Claire Dyson) *trckd ldrs tl rdn after 5th: sn wknd: bhd whn blnd last* **50/1**

/6S- **11** *hd* **Residence And Spa (IRE)**[45] 1833 5-10-1 **80** (bt) JackQuinlan 46
(Helen Rees) *slowly away: in rr: hdwy to trck ldrs bef 2nd: wknd after 5th* **16/1**

060- **12** *7* **Keen Eye (IRE)**[19] 2280 4-11-2 **103** TommieMO'Brien[(8)] 63
(Jonjo O'Neill) *mid-div: rdn after 4th: sn bhd: t.o* **12/1**

646- **P** **Actodos (IRE)**[20] 2278 9-9-11 **79** oh3 (tp) KieronEdgar[(3)]
(Richard Woollacott) *nt jump wl: led after mstke 1st: blnd 4th and 5th where hdd: sn wknd: bdly hmpd 2 out: sn p.u* **50/1**

554- **F** **Delphi Mountain (IRE)**[20] 2274 8-11-7 **100** (bt) MichealNolan 98
(Richard Woollacott) *in tch: hdwy 5th: led sn after: stl travelling wl enough whn fell 2 out* **16/1**

4m 5.5s (-10.00) **Going Correction** -0.55s/f (Firm)
WFA 4 from 5yo+ 7lb **14** Ran SP% **124.7**
Speed ratings (Par 105): **101,100,97,95,95 89,89,89,86,81 81,77, ,**
Tote Swingers: 1&2 £12.30, 1&3 £9.60, 2&3 £4.00 CSF £65.24 CT £257.59 TOTE £15.10: £4.80, £3.00, £2.30; EX 86.00 Trifecta £382.40 Pool: £3,277.91 - 6.42 winning units..
Owner The Lamb Inn - Pethy **Bred** John Mc Cann **Trained** Moorland, Somerset

FOCUS
Modest form, and not a race to get carried away with.
T/Jkpt: Not won. T/Plt: £544.50 to a £1 stake. Pool: £110,853.73 - 148.60 winning tickets. T/Qpdt: £135.00 to a £1 stake. Pool: £6,696.40 - 36.70 winning tickets. TM

The Form Book Jumps, Raceform Ltd, Compton, RG20 6NL.

2312 TOWCESTER (R-H)

Sunday, November 24

OFFICIAL GOING: Good to soft (8.6)

Wind: Fresh across Weather: Overcast

2697 HAYGAIN HAY STEAMERS CLEAN HEALTHY FORAGE MARES' NOVICES' HURDLE (11 hdls) 2m 5f

12:45 (12:47) (Class 4) 4-Y-O+ **£3,119** (£915; £457; £228)

Form				RPR
154-	1		**Dardanella**[42] 1885 6-10-10 0 JamieMoore (Richard Lee) *a.p: chsd ldr 8th: led appr 2 out: rdn clr whn hit last: styd on* **13/2**[3]	104+
0/4-	2	6	**Rising Teal**[17] 2317 4-10-10 0 DougieCostello (Lucy Wadham) *hld up: mstke 5th: hdwy 7th: rdn to chse wnr last: no imp* **9/1**	100
/23-	3	5	**Vinnieslittle Lamb (IRE)**[23] 2193 5-10-10 105 DenisO'Regan (David Bridgwater) *chsd ldr tl led 7th: rdn and hdd appr 2 out: wknd last* **11/8**[1]	96
6/2-	4	7	**Fountains Mary**[20] 2273 5-10-7 0 RachaelGreen(3) (Anthony Honeyball) *hld up: nt fluent: hdwy after 5th: wknd appr 2 out* **9/4**[2]	91
5-	5	1 ½	**Always Smiling (IRE)**[20] 2266 6-10-3 0 (t) MrHAABannister(7) (Charlie Mann) *prom: lost p[lace 6th: rdn and wknd appr 2 out* **7/1**	87
0/0-	P		**Cayetina**[190] 372 4-10-10 0 JackDoyle (Ali Brewer) *hld up: mstke 3rd: pushed along appr 7th: sn wknd: bhd whn p.u after 3 out* **100/1**	
/00-	P		**Ticket**[23] 2190 4-10-10 0 SeanQuinlan (Jennie Candlish) *led: j.lft 6th: hdd next: rdn and wknd appr 8th: bhd whn p.u bef last* **100/1**	

5m 27.5s (0.30) **Going Correction** -0.775s/f (Firm)

WFA 4 from 5yo+ 8lb **7** Ran SP% **110.7**

Speed ratings (Par 105): **68,65,63,61,60**

Tote Swingers: 1&2 £3.10, 1&3 £7.30, 2&3 £2.50 CSF £55.43 TOTE £7.70: £3.40, £3.00; EX 37.70 Trifecta £219.40 Pool: £2,231.74 - 7.62 winning units..

Owner Ray Bailey **Bred** Ray Bailey **Trained** Byton, H'fords

FOCUS

A modest mares' novice event. A big step up from the winner, and a smaller one from the second.

2698 BEST RACING BLOGS ON GG.COM CLAIMING HURDLE (8 hdls) 2m

1:15 (1:15) (Class 5) 4-Y-O+ **£1,949** (£572; £286; £143)

Form				RPR
/P5-	1		**Edlomond (IRE)**[24] 2176 7-10-4 107 (t) RyanWhile(7) (Bill Turner) *a.p: chsd ldr 2 out: shkn up to ld appr last: styd on wl* **33/1**	118+
364-	2	3	**Flying Phoenix**[29] 2084 5-10-2 105 ow1 RobertDunne(3) (Dai Burchell) *hld up: hit 4th: hdwy 3 out: led appr next: rdn and hdd bef last: styd on same pce flat* **3/1**[1]	108
1/2-	3	14	**Rowlestone Lad**[29] 2085 6-11-3 117 RhysFlint (John Flint) *trckd ldrs: racd keenly: ev ch appr 2 out: sn rdn: wkng whn mstke last* **9/2**[3]	108
101-	4	7	**Belle De Fontenay (FR)**[21] 2250 8-10-13 120 (p) AndrewThornton (Conor Dore) *led: hit 4th: pushed along after 3 out: hdd & wknd bef next* **7/2**[2]	99
640-	5	1 ½	**Niki Royal (FR)**[17] 2312 8-10-10 95 (p) AndrewTinkler (Jamie Snowden) *chsd ldr: mstke 3rd: rdn and wknd appr 2 out* **5/1**	93
104-	6	15	**James Pollard (IRE)**[42] 1889 8-11-1 113 (t) RobertWilliams(5) (Bernard Llewellyn) *hld up: hit 3 out: sn rdn and wknd* **14/1**	89
/04-	7	3 ¼	**Langley**[29] 2085 6-10-1 104 (vt) AlanJohns(10) (Tim Vaughan) *hld up: rdn and wknd after 3 out* **10/1**	77
022-	8	nk	**Kayfton Pete**[31] 2051 7-11-9 104 (t) AdamPogson (Charles Pogson) *plld hrd and prom: rdn and wknd appr 2 out* **8/1**	89
000/	P		**My Silver Lilly**[276] 4347 6-10-7 79 TrevorWhelan(3) (Clive Drew) *hld up: bhd fr 3rd: p.u bef 2 out* **100/1**	

3m 53.1s (-14.80) **Going Correction** -0.775s/f (Firm) **9** Ran SP% **112.9**

Speed ratings (Par 103): **106,104,97,94,93 85,84,83,**

Tote Swingers: 1&2 £33.30, 1&3 £33.30, 2&3 £2.40 CSF £130.27 TOTE £20.70: £5.80, £1.50, £1.70; EX 145.90 Trifecta £589.10 Pool: £1,415.73 - 1.80 winning units..Flying Phoenix claimed by Mr Michael Blake £5,000.

Owner Mrs Tracy Turner **Bred** Bernard Flynn **Trained** Sigwells, Somerset

FOCUS

They went a fair gallop in this claimer and the placed horses set the level. The winner was back to the boot of lact yoar'c form.

2699 BRIAN O'REILLY H'CAP CHASE (14 fncs) 2m 3f 110y

1:45 (1:46) (Class 5) (0-95,99) 4-Y-O+ **£2,144** (£629; £314; £157)

Form				RPR
343-	1		**Ratify**[29] 2090 9-11-0 86 RobertDunne(3) (Dai Burchell) *a.p: chsd ldr 7th: led 11th: clr after 3 out: easily* **11/4**[2]	116+
0/1-	2	10	**Riddleofthesands (IRE)**[3] 2615 9-11-9 99 7ex RyanHatch(7) (Nigel Twiston-Davies) *led tl hdd and mstke 11th: styd on same pce fr 3 out* **5/4**[1]	108
060-	3	25	**Roseini (IRE)**[17] 2312 7-10-13 82 AndrewTinkler (Tony Carroll) *hld up: bhd fr 6th: mstke 8th: j.rt last* **8/1**[3]	69
/05-	4	19	**Kauto The Roc (FR)**[13] 2428 9-11-7 95 (t) JoshHamer(5) (Anabel K Murphy) *s.s: hld up: in rr whn blnd 6th: sme hdwy 8th: wknd after 10th: j. slowly 2 out* **9/1**	64
F/P-	P		**Irish Guard**[14] 2396 12-10-7 76 (t) AndrewThornton (John O'Neill) *prom: mstke 5th: lost pl whn blnd next: sn bhd: p.u bef 3 out* **8/1**[3]	
066-	R		**Red Rosso**[45] 1835 8-10-10 86 JakeHodson(7) (Rob Summers) *racd keenly: trckd ldr to 7th: wknd 11th: bhd whn ref last* **14/1**	

5m 11.1s (-7.10) **Going Correction** -0.35s/f (Good) **6** Ran SP% **110.0**

Speed ratings (Par 103): **100,96,86,78,**

Tote Swingers: 1&2 £1.10, 1&3 £2.20, 2&3 £1.80 CSF £6.67 TOTE £3.20: £1.90, £1.20; EX 6.60 Trifecta £30.50 Pool: £1,578.49 - 5.75 winning units..

Owner J J King **Bred** Mrs R Lyon **Trained** Briery Hill, Blaenau Gwent

FOCUS

A weak little handicap in which only two mattered from the fifth-last fence. The winner was well in on the best of his old form over further and is rated back to that level, with the second similar to his recent win.

2700 MIKE AND FREDA CLAYTON MEMORIAL H'CAP CHASE (THE SUNDAY £5K BONUS RACE) (18 fncs) 3m 110y

2:15 (2:15) (Class 4) (0-120,120) 4-Y-O+ **£3,768** (£1,106; £553; £276)

Form				RPR
P/0-	1		**Musical Wedge**[21] 2253 9-11-2 110 JamieMoore (Claire Dyson) *a.p: chsd ldr 11th: ev ch fr 3 out: sn rdn: hit last: led fnl 100yds: styd on* **16/1**	116+
0/0-	2	2 ½	**Present To You (IRE)**[10] 2468 8-10-10 111 JakeHodson(7) (David Bridgwater) *led: rdn appr 2 out: hdd and unable qck fnl 100yds* **14/1**	113
633-	3	4 ½	**Miss Saffron**[14] 2390 10-9-12 97 MissLucyGardner(5) (Sue Gardner) *hld up: hdwy 13th: rdn appr 2 out: styd on* **7/1**[3]	95
0/U-	4	15	**Badgers Cove (IRE)**[20] 2267 9-11-0 108 (p) CharliePoste (Robin Dickin) *chsd ldr to 11th: sn pushed along: rdn and wknd after 14th* **2/1**[1]	95
/41-	5	3 ½	**Salut Honore (FR)**[17] 2313 7-10-6 100 WillKennedy (Alex Hales) *hld up: hdwy 12th: blnd next: rdn and wknd appr 2 out* **11/2**[2]	84
235-	6	27	**High Ron**[90] 1403 8-10-13 107 AndrewThornton (Caroline Bailey) *prom: mstke 10th: blnd next: rdn and wknd after 15th: bhd whn mstke last* **20/1**	69
UPP/	U		**Jolly Boys Outing (IRE)**[209] 32 10-9-13 98 BenPoste(5) (Rosemary Gasson) *hld up: blnd and uns rdr 11th* **16/1**	
/04-	P		**Mallusk (IRE)**[23] 2194 8-10-9 103 JasonMaguire (Shaun Lycett) *hld up: a in rr: bhd whn hmpd 12th: sn p.u* **14/1**	
/24-	F		**The Musical Guy (IRE)**[163] 733 7-11-5 120 (v1) RyanHatch(7) (Nigel Twiston-Davies) *hld up: hdwy whn fell 12th* **11/2**[2]	
25P-	P		**Bishophill Jack (IRE)**[9] 2498 7-10-11 105 (p) SamThomas (Kim Bailey) *chsd ldrs: lost pl 12th: sn bhd: p.u bef last* **10/1**	

6m 24.2s (-12.70) **Going Correction** -0.35s/f (Good) **10** Ran SP% **115.6**

Speed ratings (Par 105): **106,105,103,98,97 89,,,,**

Tote Swingers: 1&2 £17.30, 1&3 £12.90, 2&3 £11.60 CSF £206.88 CT £1712.51 TOTE £10.30: £3.40, £4.60, £1.90; EX 224.30 Trifecta £1680.20 Pool: £2,097.83 - 33.31 winning units..

Owner D J Dyson **Bred** Wood Farm Stud **Trained** Cleeve Prior, Worcs

FOCUS

Not a bad handicap for the class and it proved an eventful heat. The form is rated around the second and third.

2701 VISIT FORUM AT GG.COM H'CAP HURDLE (11 hdls) 2m 5f

2:45 (2:47) (Class 5) (0-100,99) 4-Y-O+ **£1,949** (£572; £286; £143)

Form				RPR
5/4-	1		**Monderon (FR)**[194] 293 6-11-3 97 [1] MrRobertHawker(7) (Richard Hawker) *hld up: hdwy 3 out: led next: shkn up appr last: styd on* **16/1**	101+
0/1-	2	1 ¼	**Kings Apollo**[10] 2470 4-11-1 88 FelixDeGiles (Tom Symonds) *hld up in tch: nt clr run and lost pl bnd after 3 out: rallied after next: wnt 2nd last: r.o: nt rch wnr* **10/3**[2]	93+
400-	3	6	**Earcomesthedream (IRE)**[17] 2314 10-11-7 99 (b) NicodeBoinville(5) (Peter Pritchard) *chsd ldr tl led appr 2 out: sn hdd: no ex last* **7/1**[3]	95
604/	4	3 ¼	**Faith Keeper (IRE)**[739] 2557 8-11-4 91 JasonMaguire (Fergal O'Brien) *chsd ldrs: shkn up after 3 out: wknd appr last* **3/1**[1]	85
440-	5	4	**Sapphire Rouge (IRE)**[17] 2312 7-11-1 95 (p) KevinJones(7) (Seamus Mullins) *led: rdn and hdd appr 2 out: wknd bef last* **8/1**	85
/44-	6	3 ¼	**Blue Sea Of Ibrox (IRE)**[15] 2360 5-9-9 73 oh1 HarryChalloner(5) (Alan Brown) *trckd ldrs: rdn after 3 out: wknd 2 out* **15/2**	60
3PP-	7	1 ½	**Terntheothercheek**[115] 1169 4-10-3 76 [1] SeanQuinlan (Jennie Candlish) *hld up: sme hdwy appr 3 out: sn rdn: wknd bef next* **33/1**	62
/6P-	8	4 ½	**First Of Never (IRE)**[4] 2596 7-10-8 81 AndrewThornton (Lynn Siddall) *hld up: hdwy appr 3 out: rdn and wknd bef next* **66/1**	64
560-	9	2 ¾	**Drombeg West**[117] 1152 6-10-5 78 AndrewTinkler (Anna Brooks) *trckd ldrs: racd keenly: rdn and wknd appr 2 out* **17/2**	57
6/0-	10	14	**Amazingreyce**[190] 376 8-10-0 73 oh2 MarkGrant (Christopher Kellett) *hld up: rdn after 8th: wknd bef 3 out* **50/1**	40
405-	11	½	**Thefriendlygremlin**[46] 1820 5-10-5 85 (p) MrFTett(7) (John Upson) *hld up: plld hrd: pushed along 8th: wknd bef next* **25/1**	51
050/	P		**Vintage Vixon (IRE)**[253] 4780 6-11-1 95 JPKiely(7) (Tim Vaughan) *hld up: bhd fr 7th: p.u bef 3 out* **16/1**	

5m 34.3s (7.10) **Going Correction** -0.775s/f (Firm)

WFA 4 from 5yo+ 8lb **12** Ran SP% **116.0**

Speed ratings (Par 103): **55,54,52,51,49 48,47,45,44,39 39,**

Tote Swingers: 1&2 £12.40, 1&3 £21.00, 2&3 £5.70 CSF £67.38 CT £419.11 TOTE £21.50: £5.10, £1.60, £2.60; EX 73.70 Trifecta £1203.00 Pool: £2,706.35 - 1.68 winning units..

Owner Mrs G Morgan **Bred** Sci La Viguerie **Trained** Rode, Somerset

FOCUS

An ordinary handicap in which the first pair drew clear in between the final two hurdles.

2702 AJA INSURE THEIR MEMBERS AMATEUR RIDERS' H'CAP CHASE (16 fncs) 2m 6f

3:15 (3:15) (Class 5) (0-95,96) 4-Y-O+ **£2,058** (£638; £319; £159)

Form				RPR
611-	1		**Waltzing Tornado (IRE)**[7] 2540 9-11-13 96 (p) MrWBiddick (Neil Mulholland) *chsd ldrs: lost pl 5th: hdwy 13th: led on bit 2 out: hdd flat: led again towards fin: easily* **5/6**[1]	111+
P1P-	2	1 ¼	**Von Galen (IRE)**[17] 2313 12-10-7 81 MrJMRidley(5) (Michael Scudamore) *chsd ldrs: led 12th: rdn and hdd 2 out: led again flat: hdd and no ex towards fin* **7/1**[3]	85
262-	3	6	**Rifleman (IRE)**[46] 1825 13-10-2 76 (tp) MissLBrooke(5) (Richard Lee) *hld up: mstke 8th: hdwy 12th: pushed along and hmpd bnd after 3 out: styd on same pce fr next* **15/2**	75
P/0-	4	76	**Cash In Hand (IRE)**[75] 1547 13-9-9 69 oh10 MrHAABannister(5) (Christopher Kellett) *led to 8th: hmpd and lft in ld agin after next: hdd 12th: sn rdn: wknd appr 3 out* **50/1**	
P45-	P		**Curragh Dancer (FR)**[34] 2003 10-9-11 69 oh5 (b) MrFMitchell(3) (Paddy Butler) *prom: j. slowly 2nd: lost pl after 10th: wknd 12th: bhd whn p.u bef 2 out* **33/1**	
P56-	R		**Top Benefit (IRE)**[17] 2313 11-10-10 86 MrJBargary(7) (Richard Harper) *chsd ldr tl led 8th: tk wrong crse after next* **16/1**	

03P- F Notabotheronme (IRE)[18] 2290 11-9-11 69 oh1.......(b) MrsAlexDunn(3)
(Dai Burchell) *fell 1st* 9/2[2]
5m 51.3s (-1.70) **Going Correction** -0.35s/f (Good) 7 Ran SP% **107.8**
Speed ratings (Par 103): **89,88,86,58,** ,
Tote Swingers: 1&2 £1.90, 1&3 £2.30, 2&3 £3.00 CSF £6.53 TOTE £1.90: £1.30, £2.40; EX 6.50 Trifecta £22.00 Pool: £3,819.26 - 130.16 winning units..
Owner John Hobbs **Bred** Miss Anne Heaney **Trained** Limpley Stoke, Wilts
■ Stewards' Enquiry : Mr J Bargary twelve-day ban: took wrong course (Dec 17,19 and others tbn); three-day ban: failed to pull up after taking wrong course (tbn)
FOCUS
There was real drama in this moderate amateur riders' handicap when Top Benefit took the wrong course going out onto the far side. The in-form winner rates value for a deal further and is rated to his mark.

2703 FREE TIPS EVERY DAY ON GG.COM INTERMEDIATE OPEN NATIONAL HUNT FLAT RACE 2m
3:45 (3:45) (Class 6) 4-6-Y-O £1,559 (£457; £228; £114)

Form RPR
1 So Oscar (IRE)[105] 1249 5-11-0 0.........(t) DavidBass 95+
(Lawney Hill) *hld up: hdwy 10f out: trckd ldr 4f out: led over 1f out: edgd rt: drvn clr* 3/1[2]
2 6 Trapper Peak (IRE) 4-11-0 0......... AndrewThornton 89
(Caroline Bailey) *hld up: hdwy over 4f out: rdn to chse wnr ins fnl f: styd on same pce* 9/2[3]
3 8 Grey Earl 6-11-0 0......... JamieMoore 82
(Richard Lee) *plld hrd and prom: led over 4f out: rdn and hdd over 1f out: wknd ins fnl f* 12/1
4 5 Chicoria (IRE) 4-10-11 0......... JakeGreenall(3) 76
(Henry Daly) *hld up: pushed along 1/2-way: rdn over 4f out: nvr trbld ldrs* 13/8[1]
0- 5 3 3/4 Venez Horace (FR)[32] 2026 4-11-0 0......... DavidEngland 72
(Giles Smyly) *prom: rdn over 4f out: wknd over 2f out* 25/1
2- 6 14 Driving Well (IRE)[42] 1891 5-11-0 0......... AndrewTinkler 58
(Arthur Whiting) *chsd ldrs: drvn along over 6f out: wknd over 2f out* 10/1
7 nk Ding Dong Dennis (IRE) 6-11-0 0......... DougieCostello 58
(Laura Young) *hld up: rdn over 5f out: sn wknd* 25/1
0- 8 20 Revouge[190] 380 4-11-0 0......... MarkGrant 38
(Jim Old) *led: hit rails 10f out: rdn and hdd over 4f out: wknd 3f out* 16/1
9 dist Tikketoride 5-11-0 0......... CharliePoste
(Peter Pritchard) *chsd ldrs: lost pl over 7f out: wknd over 5f out* 33/1
3m 56.5s (-5.80) **Going Correction** -0.775s/f (Firm)
WFA 4 from 5yo+ 7lb 9 Ran SP% **114.6**
Speed ratings: **83,80,76,73,71 64,64,54,4**
Tote Swingers: 1&2 £3.50, 1&3 £4.90, 2&3 £9.90 CSF £16.39 TOTE £3.90: £1.10, £2.50, £3.20; EX 18.10 Trifecta £120.60 Pool: £3,177.26 - 19.75 winning units..
Owner Mrs K Exall & R Lee **Bred** Peter Magnier & Ms Margaret Mullins **Trained** Aston Rowant, Oxon
FOCUS
They came home strung out in this modest bumper and the form ought to work out. The winner ran similar to his Irish level.
T/Plt: £200.00 to a £1 stake. Pool: £106,092.14 - 387.23 winning tickets. T/Qpdt: £14.60 to a £1 stake. Pool: £9,819.21 - 494.64 winning tickets. CR

2406 NAVAN (L-H)
Sunday, November 24
OFFICIAL GOING: Good to yielding (yielding in places)

2706a "MONKSFIELD" NOVICE HURDLE (GRADE 2) (11 hdls) 2m 4f
1:25 (1:27) 4-Y-0+ £19,817 (£5,792; £2,743; £914)

RPR
1 Apache Stronghold (IRE)[39] 1929 5-11-3......... PCarberry 149+
(Noel Meade, Ire) *chsd ldrs: 4th 1/2-way: awkward at 7th: gng v wl in 3rd fr 3 out: eased into ld next: hit last: sn rcvrd and nudged clr run-in: easily* 9/2[3]
2 3 Azorian (IRE)[21] 2257 5-11-3......... DavyRussell 143
(Eoin Griffin, Ire) *attempted to make all: hit 4th: rdn whn pressed for ld after 3 out: hdd next: kpt on wl u.p but no imp on wnr fr last* 2/1[1]
3 6 1/2 Carriganog (IRE)[28] 2122 4-10-13 138......... APMcCoy 134
(A P O'Brien, Ire) *mid-div: 5th 1/2-way: prog to go 2nd 3 out: relegated to 3rd next: styd on same pce fr last* 7/2[2]
4 2 1/2 Lots Of Memories (IRE)[21] 2256 6-11-6 132......... ShaneButler 137
(P G Fahey, Ire) *hld up towards rr: mstke 4th: 6th 1/2-way: rdn and no ex appr 3 out: styd on same pce fr next* 9/2[3]
5 1/2 Empire Of Dirt (IRE)[25] 2161 6-11-3......... BryanCooper 134
(C A Murphy, Ire) *trckd ldr: 2nd 1/2-way: rdn appr 3 out where dropped to 4th: no ex and kpt on same pce* 16/1
6 13 Mrs Mac Veale (IRE)[15] 2381 8-10-13 115......... AndrewJMcNamara 117
(Robert Murphy, Ire) *hld up in rr: 8th 1/2-way: rdn in 7th fr 4 out and sn no imp* 33/1
7 1 Alelchi Inois (FR)[18] 2299 5-11-3......... RWalsh 120
(W P Mullins, Ire) *chsd ldrs: slt mstke 5th: 3rd 1/2-way: rdn fr 4 out and sn no imp on principals* 7/1
P Devils Bride (IRE)[41] 1906 6-11-3......... PaulTownend
(W P Mullins, Ire) *hld up towards rr: 7th 1/2-way: rdn and wknd fr 4 out: p.u bef 2 out: lame* 20/1
4m 59.1s (-2.70)
WFA 4 from 5yo+ 8lb 8 Ran SP% **118.0**
CSF £14.90 TOTE £6.00: £1.70, £1.30, £1.50; DF 18.50 Trifecta £79.30.
Owner Mrs Patricia Hunt **Bred** James Robinson **Trained** Castletown, Co Meath
FOCUS
On paper this appeared a competitive race, but Apache Stronghold, whose trainer has a good recent record in this race, made it look easy. He looks top-class.

2708a LADBROKES TROYTOWN H'CAP CHASE (GRADE B) (17 fncs) 3m
2:25 (2:25) (0-150,147) 4-Y-0+
£48,780 (£15,447; £7,317; £2,439; £1,626; £813)

RPR
1 Cootamundra (IRE)[35] 1996 10-10-3 125 ow1......... RobbieMoran 141+
(J A Berry, Ire) *in rr of mid-div: hdwy into 8th 4 out: gd prog to go 3rd 2 out: gng wl and rdn to chal last where on terms: kpt on wl u.p run-in* 25/1
2 1/2 Mad Brian (IRE)[23] 2208 7-10-12 135......... MsNCarberry 150+
(Mrs Gillian Callaghan, Ire) *mid-div: 11th at 8th: smooth hdwy fr 4 out: rdn into 2nd 2 out: kpt on wl to dispute at last: styd on wl u.p run-in* 7/1[3]
3 2 3/4 Colbert Station (IRE)[27] 2144 9-11-10 147.........(t) APMcCoy 159
(T M Walsh, Ire) *mid-div: tk clsr order after 1/2-way: prog to go 3rd 3 out: led appr next: sn rdn and jnd at last: no ex in 3rd run-in* 10/1
4 1 Rockyaboya (IRE)[21] 2259 9-9-13 122......... PaulTownend 133+
(W P Mullins, Ire) *mid-div: wnt 7th 3 out: sn rdn and 5th appr last: lft 4th run-in: styd on same pce* 7/1[3]
5 2 1/2 Goonyella (IRE)[27] 2137 6-10-13 136......... AELynch 144
(J T R Dreaper, Ire) *prom: in 5th at 8th: mstke 10th: rdn after 4 out: sn no ex and styd on same pce fr 2 out* 5/1[1]
6 6 1/2 Pass The Hat[27] 2144 6-9-11 120.........(t) DJCasey 122
(A L T Moore, Ire) *towards rr: rdn and sme prog fr 4 out: kpt on same pce fr 2 out* 6/1[2]
7 1 1/4 Sole Witness (IRE)[23] 2204 9-10-0 126......... BenDalton(3) 127
(C A McBratney, Ire) *cl up: collided in air w rival 1st: sn led: hdd bef 4th: led again at 8th: hdd 3 out: sn rdn and no ex* 33/1
8 nse Panther Claw (IRE)[212] 5560 7-10-7 130......... MPFogarty 130
(Paul Nolan, Ire) *cl up: 4th at 8th: rdn and no ex fr 4 out* 14/1
9 1 1/4 Cross Appeal (IRE)[211] 5579 7-10-4 127.........(t) RobbieColgan 126
(Noel Meade, Ire) *chsd ldrs: 2nd at 8th: prog to ld 3 out: sn rdn and hdd next: sn no ex* 33/1
10 1 1/4 Jamsie Hall (IRE)[29] 2070 10-11-1 138.........(tp) RPMcNally 136
(Gordon Elliott, Ire) *towards rr: rdn and styd on same pce fr 4 out: no threat to principals* 25/1
11 4 Glenquest (IRE)[27] 2137 10-9-10 124.........(b) KevinSexton(5) 118
(Terence O'Brien, Ire) *prom: cl 5th at 8th: rdn appr 4 out and sn no imp* 20/1
12 27 Tom Horn (IRE)[21] 2259 7-10-6 129......... PCarberry 96
(Noel Meade, Ire) *cl up: collided in air w rival 1st: mstke next and lost few pls: mstke 10th: rdn and wknd fr 4 out* 12/1
13 2 Shot From The Hip (GER)[42] 1897 9-11-0 137.........(vt[1]) MarkWalsh 102
(E J O'Grady, Ire) *mid-div: 11th at 8th: rdn and no imp fr 4 out* 20/1
P Muirhead (IRE)[42] 1897 10-11-0 137.........(b[1]) BarryGeraghty
(Noel Meade, Ire) *in rr: nvr in contention: p.u after 5 out* 20/1
P Tofino Bay (IRE)[22] 2235 10-11-10 147.........(p) DavyRussell
(D T Hughes, Ire) *prom: led bef 4th: hdd again at 8th: styd cl up: rdn in 3rd 4 out: sn wknd: p.u after next* 12/1
P Please Talk (IRE)[251] 4849 7-9-10 119......... NiallPMadden
(Noel Meade, Ire) *in rr: nvr in contention: p.u bef 4 out* 25/1
P Sweet My Lord (FR)[31] 2057 7-10-7 130......... RWalsh
(W P Mullins, Ire) *towards rr: p.u after 3 out* 14/1
P Raz De Maree (FR)[385] 2223 8-11-5 142......... BryanCooper
(D T Hughes, Ire) *towards rr: no imp fr 5 out: p.u bef 3 out* 16/1
P Carrig Millie (IRE)[28] 2123 8-10-1 124......... MarkEnright
(Michael Cullen, Ire) *towards rr: rdn and no imp fr 1/2-way: p.u after 5 out* 20/1
F Living Next Door (IRE)[27] 2137 7-9-10 119 oh2......... PhillipEnright 130+
(A J Martin, Ire) *in rr: gd prog fr 4 out to go 4th 2 out: sn rdn and running on whn fell last* 12/1
6m 13.4s (-15.90) 20 Ran SP% **143.8**
CSF £199.18 CT £1945.19 TOTE £38.90: £5.30, £1.40, £3.50, £2.60; DF 363.40 Trifecta £1596.70.
Owner Turbine Syndicate **Bred** Suzanne Moran **Trained** Blackwater, Co Wexford
FOCUS
A fiercely competitive handicap. The first three all posted personal bests.

2265 KEMPTON (R-H)
Monday, November 25
OFFICIAL GOING: Good (good to soft on bend adjacent to lake; chs 7.5, hdl 7.2)
Wind: Light, against Weather: Fine but cloudy

2711 OPENWORK FOUNDATION BRITISH STALLION STUDS EBF "NATIONAL HUNT" NOVICES' HURDLE (QUALIFIER) (8 hdls) 2m
12:30 (12:30) (Class 4) 4-6-Y-O £3,898 (£1,144; £572; £286)

Form RPR
0/3- 1 Sgt Reckless[16] 2369 6-10-12 0......... DominicElsworth 140+
(Mick Channon) *trckd ldng pair: clsd to ld after 3 out: wl in command fr 2 out: pushed out nr fin* 7/2[2]
1/ 2 5 West Wizard (FR)[254] 4793 4-10-12 0......... BarryGeraghty 134+
(Nicky Henderson) *t.k.h: hld up in tch: trckd wnr after 3 out: sn pushed along: no imp and wl hld fr 2 out* 1/6[1]
2/4- 3 38 Hawaii Five Nil (IRE)[38] 1958 5-10-12 0......... APMcCoy 105+
(Jonjo O'Neill) *hld up: j.lft fr 3rd: lost tch w ldrs 5th: chalng for 3rd whn wnt bdly lft last: nudged along to take remote 3rd nr fin* 6/1[3]
5/6- 4 1 Kaki Island (IRE)[16] 2368 5-10-12 0......... TomCannon 100
(Chris Gordon) *fast away: led at gd pce: mstke 3 out: sn hdd & wknd: lost remote 3rd nr fin* 33/1
6/5- 5 14 Western Movie[24] 2189 5-10-12 0......... TomO'Brien 87
(Philip Hobbs) *t.k.h: chsd ldr: mstke 5th: wkng whn nt fluent 3 out: sn bhd* 20/1
/00- 6 1 Lightentertainment (IRE)[21] 2272 5-10-12 0......... MarcGoldstein 86
(Chris Gordon) *hld up: lost tch w ldrs 5th: wknd after 3 out* 33/1
6/0- R Ma'Ire Rua (IRE)[37] 1974 6-10-12 0......... DenisO'Regan
(Alan Jones) *hld up in last: bhd whn rn out bnd after 2nd and j. rail* 40/1
F Mojeek (IRE) 5-10-9 0......... JoshuaMoore(3)
(Gary Moore) *hld up: mstke 3rd: wknd 5th: wl t.o whn fell heavily 2 out: winded* 25/1
3m 48.8s (-9.30) **Going Correction** -0.275s/f (Good) 8 Ran SP% **139.1**
Speed ratings: **112,109,90,90,83 82,** ,
CSF £5.67 TOTE £7.20: £1.10, £1.02, £1.50; EX 12.90 Trifecta £20.60 Pool: £3065.81 - 111.27 winning units..
Owner Mrs T P Radford **Bred** Miss Bridget Coyle **Trained** West Ilsley, Berks

The Form Book Jumps, Raceform Ltd, Compton, RG20 6NL.

FOCUS
Dual bend configuration after winning post. Fresh ground on all bends and distances as advertised. The pace was not strong in this intriguing novice event and the first two finished some way clear. A big step forward from the impressive winner, who looks decent.

2712 HALCYON GALLERY BEGINNERS' CHASE (18 fncs) 3m
1:00 (1:00) (Class 4) 4-Y-0+ **£5,198** (£1,526; £763; £381)

Form RPR
/22- **1** **Bear's Affair (IRE)**[31] 2063 7-11-2 138 BarryGeraghty 134+
(Nicky Henderson) *tended to jump sltly lft: cl up: trckd ldr 4 out: narrow ld next: in command fr 2 out: easily* **30/100**[1]
1/5- **2** 3 ¾ **Dunlough Bay (IRE)**[15] 2395 7-11-2 128 (p) DenisO'Regan 126
(Paul Webber) *w ldr: led briefly and nt fluent 7th: led 13th: narrowly hdd 3 out: shkn up bef next: kpt on but no threat to wnr* **3/1**[2]
/10- **3** 39 **Kentford Legend**[29] 2105 6-11-2 0 AndrewThornton 99
(Seamus Mullins) *mde most to 13th: wknd after 4 out: t.o* **20/1**[3]
0/0- **4** 27 **Oscar Baby (IRE)**[35] 2008 7-10-9 91 MarcGoldstein 60
(Diana Grissell) *cl up: mstke 13th: sn lost tch: wknd after 4 out: wl t.o* **66/1**

6m 18.3s (2.90) **Going Correction** -0.275s/f (Good) **4** Ran SP% **108.2**
Speed ratings (Par 105): **84,82,69,60**
CSF £1.69 TOTE £1.30; EX 1.50 Trifecta £2.20 Pool: £2535.33 - 847.23 winning units..
Owner G B Barlow **Bred** T J Whitley **Trained** Upper Lambourn, Berks

FOCUS
A one-sided beginners chase, run at a very steady place until the final mile. The easy winner didn't need to be near his best.

2713 OLBG MARES' HURDLE (LISTED RACE) (12 hdls) 3m 110y
1:30 (1:30) (Class 1) 4-Y-0+ **£14,405** (£5,510; £2,842; £1,500)

Form RPR
3/1- **1** **Highland Retreat**[16] 2371 6-10-12 130 NoelFehily 122+
(Harry Fry) *mde all: pushed along 2 out: at least 2 l up whn blnd last: drvn out and hld on* **4/7**[1]
/01- **2** 1 **Weather Babe**[11] 2477 5-10-12 110 ConorO'Farrell 119
(David Pipe) *sn trckd ldng pair: lost tch briefly after 8th: cl up 3 out: drvn to try to chal 2 out: kpt on to take 2nd flat: a hld* **12/1**[3]
102/ **3** ½ **Ma Filleule (FR)**[221] 5358 5-11-6 134 BarryGeraghty 127
(Nicky Henderson) *sn trcked wnr: rdn 2 out: nt qckn bef last: kpt on but lost 2nd flat* **2/1**[2]
0/0- **4** 10 **Tweedledrum**[38] 1956 6-11-6 115 (p) BenPoste 117
(Tom Symonds) *hld up in last pair: outpcd and pushed along after 8th: clsd next: rdn and lft bhd bef 2 out: plugged on again flat* **25/1**
23P- **P** **Definitely Glad (IRE)**[30] 2084 6-10-12 110 DenisO'Regan
(Paul Webber) *hld up in last pair: lost tch after 8th: no prog next: wl bhd whn p.u bef 2 out* **66/1**

6m 10.1s (-5.90) **Going Correction** -0.275s/f (Good) **5** Ran SP% **110.0**
Speed ratings (Par 111): **98,97,97,94,**
CSF £8.35 TOTE £1.70: £1.10, £3.00; EX 6.30 Trifecta £11.50 Pool: £2819.31 - 182.88 winning units..
Owner Richard Barber **Bred** Richard Bridges **Trained** Seaborough, Dorset

FOCUS
A Listed mares' hurdle that was run at a sound pace. The time and the fourth limit the ratings.

2714 PERTEMPS NETWORK H'CAP CHASE (JOCKEY CLUB GRASSROOTS JUMPS SERIES QUALIFIER) (16 fncs) 2m 4f 110y
2:05 (2:05) (Class 3) (0-135,134) 4-Y-0+ **£9,747** (£2,862; £1,431; £715)

Form RPR
0/3- **1** **Giorgio Quercus (FR)**[193] 334 8-11-7 129 BarryGeraghty 141+
(Nicky Henderson) *trckd ldrs: rt on terms after 13th: led next: sltly awkward 2 out and sn jnd: drvn and styd on wl flat* **9/2**[3]
/10- **2** ¾ **Bally Legend**[9] 2504 8-11-12 134 IanPopham 143
(Caroline Keevil) *mde most: rdn and hdd 3 out: rallied wl and upsides after 2 out: styd on but jst hld last 50yds* **5/1**
3/1- **3** 5 **Jump City (FR)**[39] 1944 7-11-5 132 (b[1]) MrWBiddick[(5)] 139
(Paul Nicholls) *tried to dispute ld but nt slick enough over the fences: cl up: rdn to chal and upsides 3 out: one pce bef next* **7/2**[2]
U16- **4** 16 **Lost Legend (IRE)**[73] 1581 6-11-7 129 (p) APMcCoy 122
(Jonjo O'Neill) *hld up: last to 9th: wl in tch fr next: cl 5th whn mstke 13th: shuffled along and steadily outpcd* **12/1**
P/3- **5** 8 **Persian Snow (IRE)**[23] 2211 7-11-8 130 TomO'Brien 114
(Philip Hobbs) *cl up: lost pl 8th: nt gng wl fr 10th: toiling in rr after 13th: no ch after* **3/1**[1]
P5/- **6** 2 ¾ **Midnight Sail**[226] 5282 10-11-10 132 RobertThornton 114
(Alan King) *prom: trckd ldr 7th: rt on terms after 13th: wknd qckly bef next (3 out)* **9/1**
351/ **P** **Mentalist (FR)**[252] 4839 5-10-8 116 LiamTreadwell
(Venetia Williams) *wl there: j.lft 9th and scrubbed along: blnd next and wknd: t.o whn p.u after 13th: bttr for r* **7/1**

5m 8.45s (-8.15) **Going Correction** -0.275s/f (Good) **7** Ran SP% **112.3**
Speed ratings (Par 107): **104,103,101,95,92 91,**
toteswingers 1&2 £4.20, 1&3 £4.20, 2&3 £4.80 CSF £26.06 TOTE £5.00: £2.70, £3.20; EX 30.00 Trifecta £169.40 Pool: £2634.60 - 11.66 winning units..
Owner Seasons Holidays **Bred** Daniel Chassagneux Et Al **Trained** Upper Lambourn, Berks

FOCUS
An open-looking handicap chase. Three in a line two out and a tight two-way battle on the run-in. The winner is a 152 chaser at best and is probably still capable of a bit better.

2715 BRADLEY PARTNERSHIP H'CAP HURDLE (12 hdls) 3m 110y
2:40 (2:40) (Class 4) (0-120,120) 4-Y-0+ **£3,898** (£1,144; £572; £286)

Form RPR
11P- **1** **Dreamsoftheatre (IRE)**[52] 1747 5-11-9 117 (t) APMcCoy 126+
(Jonjo O'Neill) *v prom: pressed ldr after 8th: pushed into narrow ld 2 out: shkn up after last: readily* **7/2**[1]
/55- **2** 2 ¼ **Alberobello (IRE)**[19] 2288 5-11-7 115 (t) NickScholfield 118+
(Jeremy Scott) *pressed ldr: led 3rd: mde rest tl rdn and hdd 2 out: kpt on but no threat to wnr after last* **5/1**[3]
406- **3** 1 ¼ **Marie Deja La (FR)**[18] 2312 7-9-6 96 (b) LouisMuspratt[(10)] 97
(Chris Gordon) *hld up in last trio: prog to trck ldrs 3 out: rdn bef next: kpt on but nvr able to chal* **14/1**
/55- **4** nk **Rich Buddy**[176] 606 7-11-9 117 IanPopham 119
(Richard Phillips) *cl up: rdn after 3 out: awkward 2 out: kpt on same pce u.p: nvr able to chal* **10/1**
5/0- **5** 36 **Woodford County**[19] 2288 6-11-12 120 TomO'Brien 88
(Philip Hobbs) *cl up: mstke 2nd: stl rt there whn mstke 3 out: rdn and wknd bef 2 out: t.o* **20/1**
/4P- **6** 11 **Time For Spring (IRE)**[16] 2367 9-11-6 114 (b[1]) NoelFehily 72
(Charlie Longsdon) *wl in tch: shkn up and wknd rapidly after 3 out: t.o* **8/1**
P41- **7** 15 **Halucha (IRE)**[11] 2473 8-10-13 107 (p) LiamTreadwell 52
(Paul Webber) *led to 3rd: nvr gng as sweetly once hdd: rdn 9th: wknd bef 3 out: t.o and eased* **6/1**
122- **8** 1 **Tarvini (IRE)**[20] 2284 8-10-12 116 (p) PatrickCowley[(10)] 60
(Jonjo O'Neill) *hld up in last: cajoled along fr 5th: nvr any rspnse: lost tch after 8th: t.o* **9/2**[2]
241/ **9** ¾ **Barton Stacey (IRE)**[552] 394 8-11-6 114 ConorO'Farrell 57
(David Pipe) *hld up in last pair: nt fluent 6th: mstke next: pushed along and lost tch 3 out: eased bef next: t.o* **7/1**

6m 6.5s (-9.50) **Going Correction** -0.275s/f (Good) **9** Ran SP% **115.5**
Speed ratings (Par 105): **104,103,102,102,91 87,82,82,82**
toteswingers 1&2 £4.10, 1&3 £10.60, 2&3 £12.90 CSF £21.75 CT £216.77 TOTE £3.10: £1.60, £1.70, £4.30; EX 26.50 Trifecta £940.40 Pool: £2793.77 - 2.22 winning units..
Owner John P McManus **Bred** Kieran Gleeson **Trained** Cheltenham, Gloucs

FOCUS
An open-looking handicap and good recent form was thin on the ground. The pace was sound and the first four finished well clear of the remainder. The winner is back on the upgrade.

2716 COOLMORE NOVICES' LIMITED H'CAP CHASE (16 fncs) 2m 4f 110y
3:10 (3:10) (Class 3) (0-140,133) 4-Y-0+ **£6,410** (£2,002; £1,078)

Form RPR
122- **1** **Baby Mix (FR)**[19] 2295 5-11-4 132 NoelFehily 143+
(Warren Greatrex) *mde virtually all: drew clr bef 3 out: easily* **5/2**[2]
022- **2** 18 **Turn Over Sivola (FR)**[16] 2363 6-11-4 132 RobertThornton 130
(Alan King) *mstke 1st: cl up: nt fluent 7th: shkn up to go 2nd 3 out: sn lft wl bhd by wnr* **7/2**[3]
23/ **3** 26 **Royal Boy (FR)**[324] 3515 6-11-5 133 BarryGeraghty 111+
(Nicky Henderson) *hld up in cl tch: mstke 8th and j. slowly next: nvr gng wl after: wknd 13th: wl bhd whn hmpd next (3 out)* **10/11**[1]
/14- **F** **Jimbill (IRE)**[53] 1728 7-10-13 130 MichaelByrne[(3)] 124
(Tim Vaughan) *w wnr: nt fluent 4th: rdn after 13th: lost 2nd and wkng whn fell 3 out* **16/1**

5m 5.7s (-10.90) **Going Correction** -0.275s/f (Good) **4** Ran SP% **109.1**
Speed ratings (Par 107): **109,102,92,**
CSF £10.76 TOTE £3.30; EX 6.50 Trifecta £11.00 Pool: £1909.15 - 129.12 winning units..
Owner Gdm Partnership **Bred** Henrietta Charlet & Danny Charlesworth **Trained** Upper Lambourn, Berks

FOCUS
The first running of of a novices' limited handicap chase replacing at the behest of the trainers a 0-120 handicap hurdle. Just a 3lb weight range. Another step up from the winner.

2717 STARLIGHT CHILDREN'S FOUNDATION CONDITIONAL JOCKEYS' H'CAP HURDLE (8 hdls) 2m
3:40 (3:40) (Class 3) (0-130,130) 3-Y-0+ **£5,393** (£1,583; £791; £395)

Form RPR
000/ **1** **Ranjaan (FR)**[212] 5574 5-11-9 130 (p) HarryDerham[(3)] 133+
(Paul Nicholls) *hld up in cl tch: brought to chal 2 out in tightly packed field: narrow ld last: edgd rt flat: r.o* **4/1**[2]
114/ **2** nk **Fourth Estate (IRE)**[597] 5282 7-11-0 121 JeremiahMcGrath[(3)] 124+
(Nicky Henderson) *trckd ldrs: produced gng strly to ld 2 out: sn jnd in dash for the fin: narrowly hdd last: edgd rt flat and r.o: jst hld* **4/1**[2]
5/3- **3** ¾ **Roman Flight (IRE)**[128] 1046 5-11-4 125 KieronEdgar[(3)] 127+
(David Dennis) *hld up in rr: cl up 2 out but looking for room: drvn to take 3rd bef last: r.o flat but jst unable to catch ldng pair* **13/2**[3]
/40- **4** 3 ½ **Pippa Greene**[24] 2198 9-10-8 115 NicodeBoinville[(3)] 114
(Nicky Henderson) *t.k.h: hld up in cl tch: lost pl after 1st: mstke 5th: stl last and rdn after 2 out: kpt on to take 4th last: nt pce to threaten* **17/2**
140- **5** 3 ½ **Taaresh (IRE)**[40] 1922 8-10-9 113 (p) AdamWedge 108
(Kevin Morgan) *hld up in tch: trckd ldrs bef 2 out and stl gng wl: nt qckn after 2 out: outpcd after* **20/1**
0/6- **6** hd **Dollar Bill**[30] 2087 4-10-10 114 (tp) JoshuaMoore 109
(Nick Gifford) *cl up to 2 out: outpcd sn after* **20/1**
145- **7** 7 **To The Sky (IRE)**[11] 2474 5-9-10 106 CiaranMckee[(6)] 95
(John O'Shea) *led at mod pce: hdd whn blnd 2 out: wknd* **16/1**
16/ **8** 1 ¼ **Poet**[324] 3515 8-11-10 128 TrevorWhelan 116
(Clive Cox) *trckd ldr tl wknd jst bef 2 out* **11/4**[1]
/04- **9** 1 **Who's Cross (IRE)**[30] 2087 5-11-1 122 PeterCarberry[(3)] 108
(Nicky Henderson) *trckd ldrs: shoved along after 3 out: wkng whn mstke 2 out* **10/1**

3m 57.2s (-0.90) **Going Correction** -0.275s/f (Good)
WFA 4 from 5yo+ 7lb **9** Ran SP% **115.0**
Speed ratings (Par 107): **91,90,90,88,86 86,83,82,82**
toteswingers 1&2 £3.80, 1&3 £4.70, 2&3 £4.30 CSF £20.73 CT £98.98 TOTE £5.20: £1.90, £1.70, £2.00; EX 20.70 Trifecta £115.20 Pool: £3127.06 - 20.34 winning units..
Owner Highclere Thoroughbred Racing - Ranjaan **Bred** H H The Aga Khan's Studs Sc **Trained** Ditcheat, Somerset

FOCUS
This conditional jockeys' handicap hurdle has been upgraded having been a 0-100 previously. As a result the top yards were represented. After a very steady gallop, there was little to choose between them all two out. The first two were well in on the best of their form and to their marks, but this is not a race to be confident about.
T/Plt: £113.50 to a £1 stake. Pool: £58415.21 - 375.66 winning tickets T/Qpdt: £97.00 to a £1 stake. Pool: £3726.39 - 28.40 winning tickets JN

[2466]LUDLOW (R-H)
Monday, November 25

OFFICIAL GOING: Good to soft (7.5)
Wind: Light across Weather: Fine

2718 ALAN & HILARY RIMMER MAIDEN HURDLE (9 hdls) 2m
12:45 (12:45) (Class 4) 4-Y-0+ **£3,249** (£954; £477; £238)

Form RPR
4/4- **1** **My Guardian Angel**[31] 2068 4-11-0 107 ColinBolger 120+
(Mark H Tompkins) *mde all: shkn up and clr last: comf* **33/1**
4/2- **2** 9 **Spin Cast**[30] 1754 5-10-7 110 MissHBethell[(7)] 111
(Brian Ellison) *a.p: chsd wnr 2 out: sn rdn: no ex flat* **4/1**[2]
0/2- **3** 5 **Toowoomba (IRE)**[29] 2109 5-11-0 0 RichardJohnson 106
(Philip Hobbs) *mid-div: hdwy 6th: chsd wnr 3 out to next: wknd last* **6/1**[3]
3F- **4** 2 **Memory Cloth**[17] 2340 6-11-0 0 AidanColeman 104
(Brian Ellison) *hld up: mstke 3rd: hdwy appr 3 out: mstke next: wknd last* **7/1**

6/3- **5** *hd* **Berkeley Avenue**[29] 2109 4-10-11 0 .... GavinSheehan(3) 105
(Warren Greatrex) *chsd ldrs: rdn appr 3 out: mstke next: wknd last* **20/1**

4- **6** *1* **Know No Fear**[13] 2432 8-11-0 0 .... (t) WillKennedy 103
(Alastair Lidderdale) *hld up: hdwy appr 3 out: wknd next* **20/1**

40/ **7** *4 ½* **Admirable Duque (IRE)**[43] 2960 7-11-0 0 .... MarkGrant 98
(Dominic Ffrench Davis) *hld up: hdwy and hit 3 out: wknd next* **100/1**

3/5- **8** *nk* **Devil's Dyke (USA)**[32] 2040 5-11-0 0 .... PaulMoloney 98
(Evan Williams) *hld up: hdwy after 6th: wknd 2 out* **6/1**[3]

9 *¾* **Santayana (GER)**[52] 4-10-7 0 .... SamTwiston-Davies 92
(David Evans) *prom: rdn appr 3 out: wknd next* **100/1**

0P0- **10** *10* **Kims Firebud**[69] 1595 6-10-9 0 .... CharlieWallis(5) 87
(Debra Hamer) *hld up: mstke 2nd: a in rr* **200/1**

1/4- **11** *9* **Couldhavehaditall (IRE)**[23] 2215 5-11-0 0 .... RichieMcLernon 86
(Paul Webber) *prom: mstke 4th: nt fluent and lost pl 6th: wknd bef 3 out* **2/1**[1]

456- **12** *6* **Snapchat (IRE)**[21] 2272 6-11-0 0 .... DougieCostello 72
(Seamus Durack) *hld up: mstke 5th: a in rr* **25/1**

0- **13** *9* **Tashkaldou (FR)**[22] 2254 4-11-0 0 .... HarrySkelton 63
(Dan Skelton) *prom: mstke 2nd: rdn and wknd appr 3 out* **20/1**

5/ **14** *5* **Scribe (IRE)**[20] 1169 5-11-0 0 .... (vt) SeanQuinlan 58
(David Evans) *prom: mstke 3rd: rdn and wknd bef 3 out* **50/1**

P/ **15** *34* **Berties Coin**[521] 782 4-11-0 0 .... JackDoyle 24
(Hilary Parrott) *chsd ldr tl after 6th: rdn and wknd bef next* **100/1**

060- **P** **Langarve Lady (IRE)**[18] 2317 5-10-2 0 .... ConorShoemark(5)
(Neil Mulholland) *hld up: a in rr: bhd whn p.u bef 3 out* **100/1**

3m 45.2s (-4.30) **Going Correction** -0.15s/f (Good) **16** Ran SP% **121.9**
Speed ratings (Par 105): **104,99,97,96,95 95,93,93,92,87 83,80,75,73,56**
toteswingers 1&2 £71.10, 1&3 £28.90, 2&3 £6.10 CSF £155.12 TOTE £29.90: £6.70, £2.20, £2.20; EX 396.50 Trifecta £948.10 Part won. Pool: £1264.26 - 0.33 winning units..
Owner Sarabex **Bred** Dullingham Park **Trained** Newmarket, Suffolk

FOCUS
False wings on all fences. Hurdles sited outside in straight and on inside on back straight. All bends moved onto fresh ground and stable bend divided. Little got into this modest maiden hurdle. A big step up from the surprise winner but he is entitled to be this good on Flat form.

2719 DOWNLOAD THE TOTEPOOL MOBILE APP BEGINNERS' CHASE (17 fncs) 2m 4f
1:15 (1:15) (Class 4) 4-Y-0+ **£5,198** (£1,526; £763; £381)

Form RPR

13F- **1** **Princely Player (IRE)**[17] 2343 6-11-2 138 .... RichardJohnson 123+
(Philip Hobbs) *mde all: clr fr 5th: hit 12th: rdn out* **10/11**[1]

2/0- **2** *6* **Cloudy Spirit**[114] 1195 8-10-9 0 .... PaulMoloney 110+
(Andrew Hollinshead) *prom: chsd wnr who was clr 5th: tk clsr order appr 4 out: styd on same pce fr last* **9/4**[2]

0/0- **3** *19* **Freckle Face**[11] 2467 6-11-2 0 .... TommyPhelan 100
(Bill Turner) *hld up: hdwy 9th: mstke 4 out: wknd 2 out* **50/1**

520/ **4** *16* **Duaiseoir (IRE)**[149] 5405 7-10-13 0 .... RobertDunne(3) 94
(Venetia Williams) *hld up: mstke 6th: hdwy 12th: j.lft next: wnt 3rd briefly 4 out: wknd 2 out* **4/1**[3]

50/ **5** *2 ¾* **Simply Charles (IRE)**[589] 5430 6-11-2 0 .... JackDoyle 82
(Hilary Parrott) *prom to 8th: bhd fr 10th* **50/1**

0/0- **6** *12* **Bill The Lad (IRE)**[13] 2432 6-11-2 0 .... SamThomas 70
(Paul Cowley) *chsd wnr to 5th: bhd fr 10th* **100/1**

5m 0.9s (-3.50) **Going Correction** 0.0s/f (Good) **6** Ran SP% **108.1**
Speed ratings (Par 105): **107,104,97,90,89 84**
toteswingers 1&2 £1.10, 1&3 £17.70, 2&3 £12.70 CSF £3.15 TOTE £1.70: £1.10, £1.20; EX 3.20 Trifecta £24.70 Pool: £2189.81 - 66.25 winning units..
Owner Thurloe 52 **Bred** Patrick Burling Developments Ltd **Trained** Withycombe, Somerset

FOCUS
An ordinary beginners' chase. The winner is rated 10lb off his hurdles mark.

2720 BET TOTEJACKPOT WITH TOTEPOOL EBF STALLIONS "NATIONAL HUNT" NOVICES' HURDLE (QUALIFIER) (11 hdls) 2m 5f
1:45 (1:45) (Class 4) 4-6-Y-0 **£3,898** (£1,144; £572; £286)

Form RPR

2/3- **1** **Theatrebar**[24] 2195 5-10-12 0 .... FelixDeGiles 112+
(Tom Symonds) *mde all: mstke 4th: shkn up appr 3 out: rdn out* **9/2**[3]

513/ **2** *3* **Forever Present (IRE)**[376] 2422 6-10-5 0 .... DavidBass 103
(Nicky Henderson) *a.p: pushed along after 7th: rdn and ev ch 3 out: hit next: styd on same pce last* **7/2**[2]

400/ **3** *7* **Westerly Breeze (IRE)**[223] 5333 5-10-12 0 .... TomSiddall 105
(Martin Keighley) *chsd ldrs: rdn appr 3 out: hit next: styd on same pce* **50/1**

22- **4** *2 ¼* **Mr Cardle (IRE)**[22] 2254 4-10-12 0 .... LeightonAspell 102+
(Oliver Sherwood) *hld up: mstke 5th: hdwy appr 3 out: sn rdn: styd on same pce* **3/1**[1]

305/ **5** *nse* **Moss On The Mill**[252] 4844 5-10-12 0 .... [1] DarylJacob 102
(Ben Case) *hld up: hdwy appr 3 out: hit next: styd on same pce* **16/1**

655/ **6** *13* **Winged Crusader (IRE)**[213] 5550 5-10-12 0 .... SamTwiston-Davies 92
(Nigel Twiston-Davies) *hld up: hdwy 7th: rdn appr 3 out: sn wknd* **10/1**

4/4- **7** *20* **Audacious Plan (IRE)**[33] 2028 4-10-12 0 .... JamieMoore 71
(Rebecca Curtis) *chsd ldrs: rdn after 8th: wknd bef next* **12/1**

/54- **8** *1* **Pembroke House**[11] 2467 6-10-12 0 .... WillKennedy 70
(Sarah-Jayne Davies) *hld up: hdwy 7th: rdn and wknd appr 3 out* **14/1**

9 *nk* **Sand Artist (IRE)** 5-10-12 0 .... AidanColeman 70
(Venetia Williams) *hld up: nt fluent 2nd: hdwy 7th: rdn appr 3 out: sn wknd* **25/1**

03U- **10** *1 ¼* **Church Hall (IRE)**[14] 2429 5-10-7 0 .... JamesBanks(5) 69
(Emma Baker) *hld up: hdwy and nt fluent 8th: rdn and wknd bef next* **8/1**

050- **11** *9* **Hare In A Round (IRE)**[11] 2471 5-10-7 0 .... PatrickCorbett(5) 61
(Rebecca Curtis) *chsd wnr tl rdn and wknd after 8th* **25/1**

5/ **12** *99* **Wheelavim**[299] 3947 5-10-5 0 .... GeraldQuinn(7)
(Claire Dyson) *a in rr: bhd fr 6th* **200/1**

50P- **P** **Guest Of Honour (FR)**[22] 2252 5-10-12 0 .... (b[1]) BrendanPowell
(Renee Robeson) *prom: rdn after 6th: sn wknd: bhd whn p.u bef next* **66/1**

200- **P** **Radharc Nahabhainn (IRE)**[37] 1974 5-10-12 0 .... (t) PaddyBrennan
(Fergal O'Brien) *prom: pushed along 7th: wknd next: bhd whn p.u bef 3 out* **25/1**

5m 6.4s (-8.40) **Going Correction** -0.15s/f (Good)
WFA 4 from 5yo+ 8lb **14** Ran SP% **121.3**
Speed ratings: **110,108,106,105,105 100,92,92,92,91 88,50, ,**
toteswingers 1&2 £2.70, 1&3 £77.80, 2&3 £77.80 CSF £20.15 TOTE £5.20: £2.10, £1.80, £8.30; EX 20.30 Trifecta £1143.80 Part won. Pool: £1525.10 - 0.70 winning units..
Owner Exors of the Late T J Wyatt **Bred** T J Wyatt **Trained** Harewood End, H'fords

FOCUS
Another race in which the winner made all. Ordinary mares' form.

2721 TRY A TOTETRIFECTA H'CAP CHASE (13 fncs) 2m
2:15 (2:15) (Class 3) (0-125,123) 4-Y-**£9,495** (£2,805; £1,402; £702; £351)

Form RPR

333- **1** **Zarzal (IRE)**[27] 2151 5-11-11 **122** .... PaulMoloney 132
(Evan Williams) *trckd ldrs: wnt 2nd after 9th: led appr last: drvn out* **2/1**[1]

/41- **2** *shd* **Last Shot (FR)**[12] 2462 6-11-4 **115** .... AidanColeman 125
(Venetia Williams) *led 2nd to 4th: led 6th: rdn and hdd appr last: r.o: rdr unbalanced last strides* **11/4**[2]

552- **3** *14* **Takeroc (FR)**[13] 2440 10-11-5 **119** .... (t) JamesBest(3) 118
(Sophie Leech) *chsd ldrs: hit 4 out: rdn and wknd appr last* **8/1**

/34- **4** *14* **Free World (FR)**[148] 853 9-10-3 **107** .... MissLBrooke(7) 92
(Lady Susan Brooke) *chsd ldrs: led 5th to next: remained handy: tl wknd 4 out* **10/1**

03U- **5** *3 ½* **Akula (IRE)**[7] 2558 6-11-3 **114** .... ColinBolger 96
(Mark H Tompkins) *led to 2nd: led 4th to next: lost pl 7th: hdwy appr 4 out: sn wknd: j.lft 2 out* **14/1**

440/ **6** *13* **Save My Blushes**[42] 1907 7-11-8 **119** .... PaddyBrennan 89
(Denis Gerard Hogan, Ire) *hld up: a in rr: rdn and wknd appr 4 out* **14/1**

54F- **7** *7* **Topthorn**[22] 2251 7-10-4 **101** .... WayneHutchinson 65
(Martin Bosley) *hld up: hdwy appr 4 out: sn wknd* **7/1**[3]

205- **8** *16* **Nez Rouge (FR)**[43] 1886 12-10-10 **107** .... SamTwiston-Davies 56
(Nigel Twiston-Davies) *chsd ldrs: wnt 2nd 6th tl rdn after 9th: wknd bef next* **16/1**

3m 55.5s (-3.00) **Going Correction** 0.0s/f (Good) **8** Ran SP% **111.9**
Speed ratings (Par 107): **107,106,99,92,91 84,81,73**
toteswingers 1&2 £1.50, 1&3 £6.20, 2&3 £1.60 CSF £7.95 CT £32.91 TOTE £3.40: £1.10, £1.40, £2.70; EX 7.70 Trifecta £40.80 Pool: £1482.79 - 27.23 winning units..
Owner Mrs Janet Davies **Bred** His Highness The Aga Khan's Studs S C **Trained** Llancarfan, Vale Of Glamorgan

FOCUS
The front pair pulled clear.

2722 CONCHA Y TORO NOVICES' H'CAP CHASE (19 fncs) 3m
2:50 (2:50) (Class 4) (0-110,110) 4-Y-0+ **£4,659** (£1,446; £779)

Form RPR

63/- **1** **King Massini (IRE)**[254] 4794 7-11-9 **107** .... PaulMoloney 115+
(Evan Williams) *mde all: clr last: shkn up and edgd rt flat: styd on: comf* **11/4**[1]

/62- **2** *2 ¾* **Flemi Two Toes (IRE)**[22] 2253 7-10-10 **97** .... (p) JackQuinlan(3) 99
(Sarah Humphrey) *prom: lost pl 8th: rallied and lft 3rd 4 out: styd on* **11/4**[1]

334- **3** *nk* **Long Wave (IRE)**[13] 2431 6-10-11 **98** .... (p) KielanWoods(3) 100
(Charlie Longsdon) *chsd wnr to 15th: rdn whn lft 2nd 4 out: styd on u.p* **9/2**[3]

135/ **F** **Keltic Crisis (IRE)**[440] 1546 9-11-6 **104** .... RichieMcLernon
(Sophie Leech) *hld up: fell 7th* **25/1**

/55- **U** **Genny Wren**[51] 1768 7-10-13 **97** .... SamJones 99+
(Renee Robeson) *chsd ldrs: pushed along 13th: cl 3rd whn hmpd and uns rdr 4 out* **12/1**

P/P- **P** **Wolf Hall (IRE)**[35] 2006 6-11-12 **110** .... WillKennedy
(Violet M Jordan) *hld up: hit 1st: bhd fr 12th: p.u bef 4 out* **50/1**

331- **F** **What A Good Night (IRE)**[30] 2088 5-11-9 **107** .... SamTwiston-Davies 111+
(Nigel Twiston-Davies) *hld up: hdwy 8th: chsd wnr 15th: ev ch whn fell next* **3/1**[2]

6m 9.6s (1.30) **Going Correction** 0.0s/f (Good) **7** Ran SP% **110.0**
Speed ratings (Par 105): **97,96,95, , ,**
toteswingers 1&2 £2.00, 1&3 £2.30, 2&3 £2.70 CSF £10.30 TOTE £3.80: £2.00, £2.40; EX 12.80 Trifecta £48.00 Pool: £2524.11 - 39.38 winning units..
Owner Border Pointers **Bred** Tim Jones **Trained** Llancarfan, Vale Of Glamorgan

FOCUS
Continuing the theme set earlier in the afternoon, there was another all-the-way winner. He's rated up a stone on the bset of his hurdles form.

2723 COLLECT TOTEPOOL WINS FROM BETFRED SHOPS CONDITIONAL JOCKEYS' H'CAP HURDLE (12 hdls) 3m
3:20 (3:20) (Class 5) (0-95,91) 4-Y-0+ **£3,249** (£954; £477; £238)

Form RPR

053- **1** **Princesse Katie (IRE)**[50] 1784 7-10-4 **69** .... (t) ThomasGarner 76+
(James Bennett) *hld up: hdwy after 7th: chsd ldr appr 3 out: rdn to ld bef last: styd on* **7/1**[3]

153- **2** *4* **Frontier Vic**[22] 2241 6-11-4 **91** .... RyanHatch(8) 93
(Nigel Twiston-Davies) *a.p: led after 6th: rdn and hdd appr last: styd on same pce flat* **11/8**[1]

/14- **3** *4* **Realta Mo Croi (IRE)**[18] 2312 5-11-11 **90** .... ConorShoemark 88
(Neil Mulholland) *hld up in tch: chsd ldr after 9th tl rdn appr 3 out: styng on same pce whn hit last* **5/2**[2]

021/ **4** *86* **Boosha**[969] 5103 8-11-8 **90** .... NickSlatter(3) 10
(John Bryan Groucott) *prom: chsd ldr 6th tl after 9th: wknd bef 3 out* **20/1**

/P0- **5** *1 ½* **Flexi Time (IRE)**[55] 1706 9-11-6 **90** .... JPKiely(5) 9
(Stephen Hughes) *led tl after 1st: chsd ldrs: hit 6th: wknd 8th* **33/1**

/P0- **6** *17* **Cowbridge (IRE)**[177] 590 7-10-7 **72** .... (b[1]) MauriceLinehan
(Peter Pritchard) *sn given reminders: led after 1st: j.lft: hdd after 6th: wknd 8th* **8/1**

/60- **7** *30* **Wychwoods Mist**[11] 2473 6-11-5 **90** .... (tp) GeraldQuinn(6)
(Claire Dyson) *hld up: a in rr: blnd 4th: wknd after 7th* **8/1**

6m 1.3s (9.00) **Going Correction** -0.15s/f (Good)
WFA 4 from 5yo+ 9lb **7** Ran SP% **113.1**
Speed ratings (Par 103): **79,77,76,47,47 41,31**
toteswingers 1&2 £3.10, 1&3 £2.60, 2&3 £1.70 CSF £17.33 CT £30.59 TOTE £4.50: £2.40, £1.80; EX 17.90 Trifecta £43.70 Pool: £2676.18 - 45.88 winning units..
Owner Miss J C Blackwell **Bred** M W And Mrs M Doran **Trained** Letcombe Bassett, Oxon

FOCUS
A weak handicap rated around the second and third.

2724 MILLION IN MIND MAIDEN OPEN NATIONAL HUNT FLAT RACE 1m 6f
3:50 (3:50) (Class 5) 4-6-Y-0 **£2,599** (£763; £381; £190)

Form RPR

320/ **1** **Bobble Boru (IRE)**[221] 5364 5-10-9 0 .... AidanColeman 93
(Venetia Williams) *mde virtually all: rdn over 1f out: jst hld on* **9/2**[1]

2 *½* **Blue Heron (IRE)** 5-11-2 0 .... HarrySkelton 99
(Dan Skelton) *hld up: hdwy over 5f out: rdn over 1f out: r.o* **6/1**

3 *1 ½* **Rough Fighter (USA)** 4-10-11 0 .... [1] JamesBanks(5) 98
(Andy Turnell) *hld up: hdwy over 5f out: chsd wnr 2f out: rdn over 1f out: styd on same pce ins fnl f* **16/1**

4 *5* **Canicallyouback** 5-11-2 0 PaulMoloney 92
(Evan Williams) *hld up: hdwy over 3f out: rdn over 1f out: no ex ins fnl f* **8/1**

6- 5 *1 1/4* **Shantou Tiger (IRE)**[53] 1732 4-11-2 0 JasonMaguire 90
(Donald McCain) *w wnr tl rdn over 2f out: styd on same pce fr over 1f out* **10/1**

03- 6 *1 1/4* **Bellorophon (IRE)**[25] 2174 4-11-2 0 WilsonRenwick 89
(Tim Vaughan) *chsd ldrs: rdn and hung lft 2f out: styd on same pce* **5/1**[2]

7 *17* **Master Wickham (IRE)** 4-11-2 0 RichieMcLernon 68
(Paul Webber) *prom: rdn over 3f out: wknd over 2f out* **8/1**

0- 8 *nk* **Carpies Boy**[27] 2153 4-10-13 0 GavinSheehan(3) 68
(Warren Greatrex) *chsd ldrs: rdn over 4f out: wknd over 3f out* **16/1**

9 *11* **Eastern Calm** 4-10-9 0 LeightonAspell 48
(Oliver Sherwood) *hld up: pushed along over 6f out: wknd over 4f out* **11/2**[3]

0- 10 *22* **Materiana (IRE)**[19] 2298 5-10-2 0 JamesCowley(7) 21
(Andrew Hollinshead) *hld up: pushed along after 4f: bhd fnl 6f* **100/1**

11 *16* **Conquering Spirit** 5-11-2 0 SamTwiston-Davies 9
(David Evans) *prom: pushed along 1/2-way: wknd over 4f out* **10/1**

3m 18.2s (5.20) **11** Ran SP% **117.7**
toteswingers 1&2 £5.60, 1&3 £14.20, 2&3 £16.00 CSF £31.32 TOTE £4.00: £1.50, £1.50, £5.40; EX 26.30 Trifecta £398.90 Pool: £2622.11 - 4.92 winning units..
Owner Mrs B Grainger **Bred** Jimmy Coffey **Trained** Kings Caple, H'fords

FOCUS
An ordinary bumper that was predictably run at a steady gallop.
T/Jkpt: Not won. T/Plt: £34.70 to a £1 stake. Pool: £77184.39 - 1619.33 winning tickets T/Qpdt: £7.40 to a £1 stake. Pool: £6953.65 - 689.36 winning tickets CR

2577 LINGFIELD (L-H)
Tuesday, November 26

OFFICIAL GOING: Heavy (chs 4.9; hdl 5.2)
Wind: Light, against Weather: Fine, crisp

2725 WORLD HORSE WELFARE MARES' NOVICES' HURDLE (8 hdls) 2m
12:30 (12:30) (Class 4) 4-Y-0+ **£3,285** (£957; £479)

Form RPR

/11- 1 **Down Ace (IRE)**[19] 2317 6-11-3 0 TimmyMurphy 110+
(Fergal O'Brien) *mde all: nt fluent 3 out: 3 l clr and wl in command fr 2 out: comf* **1/3**[1]

2 *2* **Truckers Darling (IRE)**[292] 4094 6-10-10 0 LeightonAspell 93
(Don Cantillon) *j. sltly rt: hld up in last: prog to trck ldng trio after 3 out: pushed along firmly and kpt on wl to take 2nd nr fin: no ch w wnr* **8/1**[3]

4- 3 *1 1/4* **Sudden Wish (IRE)**[8] 2564 4-10-10 0 JamieMoore 92
(Gary Moore) *t.k.h: cl up: chsd wnr 3 out: shkn up and no imp after 2 out: kpt on but lost 2nd nr fin* **7/1**[2]

4 *1 3/4* **Bermacha**[1470] 8-10-10 0 MattieBatchelor 90
(John E Long) *t.k.h early: hld up in 5th: prog to trck ldng pair after 3 out: rdn and nt qckn after 2 out: one pce after* **100/1**

/25- 5 *12* **Revaader**[174] 631 5-10-10 95 TommyPhelan 78
(Mark Gillard) *cl up: mstke 3 out: sn rdn: steadily fdd* **10/1**

/P5- 6 *35* **Misty Mornin**[7] 2579 5-10-10 0 MarkGrant 43
(Zoe Davison) *pressed wnr to 3 out: wknd qckly: t.o* **100/1**

4m 17.5s (11.10) **Going Correction** +0.60s/f (Soft)
WFA 4 from 5yo+ 7lb **6** Ran SP% **109.7**
Speed ratings (Par 105): **96,95,94,93,87 70**
toteswingers 1&2 £1.30, 1&3 £1.30, 2&3 £2.50 CSF £3.66 TOTE £1.40: £1.02, £8.10; EX 3.40 Trifecta £9.50 Pool: £1658.20 - 129.67 winning units..
Owner Paul Sullivan **Bred** Mrs C J Berry **Trained** Coln St. Dennis, Gloucs

FOCUS
Jamie Moore described the ground as "soft, heavy in places" and "hard work". A straightforward opportunity for the favourite, who stood out in this weak race. The form is given a token rating through the third.

2726 LINGFIELDPARK.CO.UK NOVICES' CHASE (12 fncs) 2m
1:00 (1:00) (Class 4) 4-Y-0+ **£3,768** (£1,106; £553; £276)

Form RPR

0/1- 1 **Pendra (IRE)**[33] 2031 5-11-7 139 APMcCoy 140+
(Charlie Longsdon) *j.lft 1st: trckd ldr: led 4th: mde rest: nt extended* **1/6**[1]

316- 2 *2 1/2* **Marcus Antonius**[61] 1665 6-11-0 0 LeightonAspell 118
(Jim Boyle) *in tch: trckd wnr 8th: nrly upsides 3 out: styd on but no ch fr last* **7/1**[2]

U- 3 *24* **Ruapehu (IRE)**[209] 58 7-11-0 0 NickScholfield 94
(Charles Whittaker) *led to 4th: chsd wnr to 8th: sn pushed along: lft bhd by ldng pair after next* **8/1**[3]

/6P- 4 *9* **Regal Park (IRE)**[22] 2278 6-10-11 85 JoshuaMoore(3) 85
(Gary Moore) *hld up in last: in tch 4 out: lft bhd bef next* **16/1**

3/0- 5 *15* **Enchanting Smile (FR)**[12] 2474 6-10-7 0 (t) TommyPhelan 63
(Mark Gillard) *hmpd 1st: in tch: mstke 4 out and wknd: wl bhd next* **28/1**

4m 15.6s (7.80) **Going Correction** +0.675s/f (Soft) **5** Ran SP% **118.6**
Speed ratings (Par 105): **107,105,93,89,81**
CSF £2.88 TOTE £1.10: £1.10, £2.50; EX 3.00 Trifecta £5.80 Pool: £1979.20 - 253.54 winning units..
Owner John P McManus **Bred** P Murphy **Trained** Over Norton, Oxon

FOCUS
This was all about Pendra, who won readily. He was value for further and looks a smart prospect.

2727 AT THE RACES H'CAP CHASE (12 fncs) 2m
1:30 (1:30) (Class 5) (0-100,99) 4-Y-0+ **£2,258** (£658; £329)

Form RPR

0/P- 1 **Sablazo (FR)**[123] 1121 7-10-0 73 oh5 LiamTreadwell 82
(Andy Turnell) *prom: j.lft 4th: led 7th: jnd next: drvn to ld last: hld on u.p* **16/1**

3P2- 2 *1/2* **Morestead (IRE)**[9] 2540 8-11-0 87 APMcCoy 94
(Brendan Powell) *led to 7th: sn urged along: dropped to 4th pl after 9th and looked wl btn: rallied u.p after 3 out: kpt on to take 2nd nr fin: jst hld* **11/4**[1]

3/P- 3 *nk* **Zen Factor**[23] 2251 8-10-10 83 JamieMoore 91
(Jonathan Portman) *a in ldng trio: w wnr fr 8th: rdn after next: upsides tl j.lft last: kpt on flat but lost 2nd nr fin* **14/1**

12/- 4 *11* **Little Jimmy**[247] 4945 6-11-2 89 FelixDeGiles 86
(Tom Gretton) *hld up: nt fluent 2nd: prog 7th: trckd ldng pair after 9th and gng wl: rdn after 3 out: wknd 2 out* **7/2**[2]

/06- 5 *15* **Rosoff (IRE)**[8] 2568 11-10-10 83 (p) TomCannon 63
(Laura Mongan) *mstke 3rd: prog fr rr to chse ldrs 7th: on terms next: drvn and wknd after 9th* **10/1**

426- 6 *2 3/4* **Lough Coi (IRE)**[17] 2367 7-11-7 99 (tp) JamesBanks(5) 76
(Anthony Middleton) *wl in rr and nt gng wl: lost tch w ldrs 6th: no ch after: plugged on* **9/2**[3]

3/5- 7 *13* **Tchang Goon (FR)**[14] 2441 9-10-0 73 oh8 (p) DaveCrosse 37
(Zoe Davison) *prom: hmpd 4th: sn dropped to rr: lost tch 7th: wl bhd next* **25/1**

64/- 8 *3/4* **Zhukov (IRE)**[452] 1438 11-11-3 97 (b) MrGGorman(7) 61
(Kevin Tork) *in tch in midfield to 6th: struggling in rr after next: no ch after* **33/1**

402- 9 *39* **Amaury De Lusignan (IRE)**[16] 2387 7-11-8 95 (tp) RichardJohnson 20
(Paul Henderson) *rdn in last pl 4th: sn t.o* **8/1**

0/ P **Autumn Day (IRE)**[496] 1001 8-11-1 88 LeightonAspell
(Alison Batchelor) *sn in rr: wknd 7th: t.o whn p.u bef 3 out* **8/1**

4m 17.8s (10.00) **Going Correction** +0.675s/f (Soft) **10** Ran SP% **117.7**
Speed ratings (Par 103): **102,101,101,96,88 87,80,80,60,**
toteswingers 1&2 £14.40, 1&3 £31.80, 2&3 £10.60 CSF £62.81 CT £655.59 TOTE £21.70: £5.20, £2.10, £4.60; EX 89.90 Trifecta £1292.20 Part won. Pool: £1723.05 - 0.89 winning units..
Owner Miss S Douglas-Pennant **Bred** Denis Fontaine **Trained** Broad Hinton, Wilts

FOCUS
This looked quite hard work. The surprise winner was rated back to the level of his 2011 form, with the next two to their marks.

2728 ARC SUPPORTS RETRAINING OF RACEHORSES NOVICES' HURDLE (10 hdls) 2m 3f 110y
2:00 (2:00) (Class 4) 4-Y-0+ **£3,285** (£957; £479)

Form RPR

/F1- 1 **Key To The West (IRE)**[18] 2351 6-10-12 125 NoelFehily 112+
(David Dennis) *hld up in tch: nt fluent 3 out: hanging sltly bnd on downhill run: clsd to ld 2 out: sn rdn clr: mstke last: pushed out* **8/11**[1]

34/ 2 *2 1/2* **Major Milborne**[251] 4878 5-10-12 0 BrendanPowell 104
(Jamie Snowden) *cl up: nt fluent 6th: jnd ldrs and nt fluent next: led 3 out: shkn up and hdd 2 out: styd on* **20/1**[3]

0- 3 *87* **Grandad Mac**[8] 2563 5-10-12 0 JamesDavies 17
(Alan Coogan) *led to 4th: w ldrs tl wknd rapidly and mstke 3 out: sn t.o* **100/1**

2/1- P **Jean De Florette (IRE)**[20] 2285 6-11-5 0 SamTwiston-Davies
(Nigel Twiston-Davies) *trckd ldr: led 4th to 3 out: cl 3rd whn p.u bef 2 out: fatally injured* **5/4**[2]

5m 16.1s (9.40) **Going Correction** +0.60s/f (Soft) **4** Ran SP% **108.1**
Speed ratings (Par 105): **105,104,69,**
CSF £10.79 TOTE £2.30; EX 7.30 Trifecta £23.50 Pool: £1289.90 - 41.07 winning units..
Owner Favourites Racing **Bred** Paddy Behan **Trained** Hanley Swan, Worcestershire

FOCUS
Ordinary novice form.

2729 DELIA AND KENNY 40TH ANNIVERSARY H'CAP HURDLE (8 hdls) 2m
2:30 (2:30) (Class 4) (0-120,115) 4-Y-0+ **£3,285** (£957; £479)

Form RPR

/63- 1 **Tealissio**[8] 2561 7-11-2 105 (t) LeightonAspell 110+
(Lucy Wadham) *hld up in tch: prog to trck ldng pair 3 out: rdn to go 2nd next: styd on to ld after last: drvn out* **11/4**[2]

2 *2 3/4* **Smart Money (IRE)**[240] 5053 6-11-7 110 AidanColeman 111+
(Venetia Williams) *t.k.h: sn prom: led 3rd: rdn after 2 out: hdd and no ex after last* **5/2**[1]

313- 3 *2 1/4* **Golanova**[40] 1941 5-11-9 112 JamieMoore 112
(Gary Moore) *in tch: trckd ldr 5th: mstke next: rdn and lost 2nd 2 out: one pce after* **4/1**[3]

200- 4 *18* **Dark And Dangerous (IRE)**[13] 2461 5-11-12 115 BrendanPowell 96
(Brendan Powell) *led: hdd 3rd and pushed along: lost pl u.p after 5th: kpt on to take modest 4th bef 2 out* **6/1**

340- 5 *20* **The Bull Hayes (IRE)**[10] 2519 7-11-11 114 (p) RichardJohnson 75
(Michael Appleby) *in tch: u.p fr 4th: lost tch 3 out: t.o* **6/1**

/40- 6 *7* **Comedy House**[71] 809 5-10-3 92 MarcGoldstein 46
(Michael Madgwick) *in tch: hrd rdn 5th: stl there after 3 out: wknd rapidly bef next: t.o* **33/1**

7 *1 1/4* **Paddy The Stout (IRE)**[224] 5346 8-11-7 110 TomO'Brien 63
(Paul Henderson) *in tch: gng bttr than sme whn nt fluent 3 out: wknd qckly sn after: t.o* **12/1**

4m 13.8s (7.40) **Going Correction** +0.60s/f (Soft) **7** Ran SP% **114.4**
Speed ratings (Par 105): **105,103,102,93,83 80,79**
toteswingers 1&2 £1.30, 1&3 £1.90, 2&3 £5.00 CSF £10.41 CT £26.04 TOTE £3.60: £2.20, £2.60; EX 11.30 Trifecta £42.70 Pool: £1792.85 - 31.43 winning units..
Owner The Dyball Partnership **Bred** The Dyball Partnership **Trained** Newmarket, Suffolk

FOCUS
Average form for the grade. The winner should still be competitive when reassessed.

2730 WEATHERBYS BANK FOREIGN EXCHANGE H'CAP CHASE (18 fncs) 3m
3:00 (3:00) (Class 4) (0-115,114) 4-Y-0+ **£3,768** (£1,106; £553; £276)

Form RPR

6/F- 1 **Via Sundown (FR)**[22] 2267 5-11-7 112 JoshuaMoore(3) 133+
(Gary Moore) *hld up in last: prog to join ldrs 12th: led 14th: mde most after: readily drew clr fr 3 out: pushed out* **5/4**[1]

623- 2 *9* **Royal Riviera**[28] 2149 7-11-3 105 (t) SamTwiston-Davies 111
(Nigel Twiston-Davies) *cl up: wl there after 15th: rdn 3 out: tk 2nd next: no ch w wnr* **9/2**[3]

20U/ 3 *7* **Samurai Way**[672] 3901 11-11-8 110 AidanColeman 109
(Venetia Williams) *cl up: mstke 6th: wl on terms after 15th: rdn and one pce fr 3 out* **6/1**

402- 4 *2 1/2* **Chasers Chance (IRE)**[16] 2390 10-10-13 101 RichardJohnson 99
(Paul Henderson) *cl up: rdn fr 13th: drvn to ld on suffernce briefly after 15th: lost 2nd and wknd 2 out: mstke last* **4/1**[2]

/0P- 5 *8* **Best Boy Barney (IRE)**[19] 2315 7-11-5 107 (t) NickScholfield 95
(Jeremy Scott) *w ldr: mstke 4th: led 6th tl after 9th: on terms after 15th: wknd jst bef 3 out* **10/1**

6/0- 6 *11* **Noakarad De Verzee (FR)**[16] 2394 12-11-5 114 MrDMaxwell(7) 91
(Giles Smyly) *led to 6th: led after 9th to 14th: wknd and last after next* **14/1**

6m 40.1s (16.40) **Going Correction** +0.675s/f (Soft) **6** Ran SP% **112.7**
Speed ratings (Par 105): **99,96,93,92,90 86**
toteswingers 1&2 £1.90, 1&3 £1.30, 2&3 £2.00 CSF £7.65 TOTE £3.00: £2.00, £2.80; EX 7.10 Trifecta £35.80 Pool: £1988.47 - 41.57 winning units..
Owner The Old Brokers **Bred** Elevage Avicole Lozach Le Yan Et Al **Trained** Lower Beeding, W Sussex

FOCUS
A modest handicap, run at a steady gallop. A big step up from the easy winner with the second to his mark.

2731 THE GREYHOUND PUB LINGFIELD "JUNIOR" STANDARD OPEN NATIONAL HUNT FLAT RACE 1m 5f
3:30 (3:30) (Class 6) 3-Y-O **£1,642** (£478; £239)

Form RPR
1 **Uncle Muf (USA)** 3-10-12 0 NoelFehily 97+
(Ali Brewer) *hld up in tch: prog on inner to chal wl over 1f out: pressed ldr after: looked hld tl rallied to ld last strides* **3/1**[3]
2 *hd* **Arctic Chief** 3-10-12 0 RichardJohnson 97+
(Richard Phillips) *hld up in tch: prog on wd outside over 2f out: led wl over 1f out and qcknd: sn pressed: r.o but hdd last strides* **11/4**[2]
- 3 *6* **Bigindie (IRE)** 3-10-12 0 AidanColeman 89
(John Weymes) *hld up in last pair: shkn up over 2f out: sn outpcd: rdn and kpt on fr over 1f out to take 3rd last strides* **14/1**
- 4 *½* **Silver Songstress** 3-10-5 0 SamTwiston-Davies 82
(John Weymes) *cl up: pushed along 5f out: rdn to ld briefly 2f out: sn easily outpcd: lost 3rd nr fin* **10/1**
43- 5 *4* **Leviche**[16] 2391 3-10-12 0 (t) RobertThornton 83
(Alan King) *w ldr: led 5f out to over 3f out: sn rdn: easily outpcd wl over 1f out* **7/4**[1]
6- 6 *2¼* **Dorton (IRE)**[14] 2436 3-10-5 0 MrDGannon(7) 80
(Phil Middleton) *w ldng pair after 4f: led over 3f out to 2f out: wknd* **33/1**
0- 7 *5* **Gilly's Filly**[19] 2318 3-9-12 0 RyanWhile(7) 67
(Bill Turner) *hld up in last pair: in tch on inner over 2f out: wknd over 1f out* **33/1**
04- 8 *5* **Alfa Red**[16] 2391 3-10-2 0 MikeyHamill(10) 67
(Sean Curran) *narrow ldr at mod pce to 5f out: wknd qckly and hanging over 2f out* **20/1**

3m 53.7s (233.70) **8 Ran SP% 114.4**
toteswingers 1&2 £2.10, 1&3 £3.70, 2&3 £3.80 CSF £11.45 TOTE £3.90: £1.10, £1.30, £4.10; EX 14.90 Trifecta £90.40 Pool: £3008.16 - 24.94 winning units..
Owner Miss Ali Brewer **Bred** Fares Farm Llc **Trained** Eastbury, Berks

FOCUS
A modest junior bumper that saw the front pair pull clear in the straight. Little form to go on.
T/Plt: £12.10. Pool: £54,270.37 - 3255.28 winning units. T/Qpdt: £10.40. Pool: £4262.40 - 302.85 winning units. JN

2443 SEDGEFIELD (L-H)
Tuesday, November 26

OFFICIAL GOING: Soft (good to soft in places; 5.9)
Wind: light behind Weather: Sunny

2732 CROWN, WHICKHAM @ WEAR INNS CONDITIONAL JOCKEYS' NOVICES' HURDLE (PAXTONS HURDLE SERIES QUALIFIER) (10 hdls) 2m 4f
12:20 (12:20) (Class 4) 4-Y-O+ **£3,119** (£915; £457; £228)

Form RPR
1/2- 1 **Heath Hunter (IRE)**[17] 2369 6-10-6 0 TomBellamy(6) 121+
(David Pipe) *mde all: pushed clr appr 2 out: 6 l up last: diminishing advantage run-in but a holding on* **1/3**[1]
33- 2 *1¼* **Downtown Boy (IRE)**[18] 2340 5-10-4 107 DiarmuidO'Regan(8) 116+
(Chris Grant) *hld up: hit 3 out: rdn and hdwy appr 2 out: wnt 2nd between last 2: styd on wl* **20/1**
/13- 3 *10* **Oscar Tanner (IRE)**[164] 747 5-11-5 120 HarryChalloner 114
(Martin Todhunter) *midfield: rdn and hdwy whn hit 2 out: nt fluent again last but sn 3rd: kpt on* **13/2**[2]
4- 4 *3½* **Brunello**[18] 2351 5-10-9 0 (p) AdamNicol(3) 102
(Philip Kirby) *trckd ldr: rdn after 3 out: one pce* **28/1**
0U3- 5 *6* **Quick Brew**[27] 2156 5-10-6 0 (t) StephenMulqueen(6) 97
(Maurice Barnes) *hld up: hit 4th: sn midfield: hdwy into 2nd 3 out: rdn bef next: lost 2nd between last 2: wknd and lost 2 more pls fr last* **33/1**
10- 6 *8* **Minella Hero (IRE)**[51] 1794 5-10-12 0 JackQuinlan 88
(Sarah Humphrey) *trckd ldr: rdn after 3 out: wknd bef 2 out* **8/1**[3]
44- 7 *16* **Uppercut De L'Orne (FR)**[18] 2337 5-10-4 0 JamesCowley(8) 72
(Donald McCain) *midfield: wknd after 3 out* **12/1**
03- 8 *21* **Narcissist (IRE)**[10] 2520 4-10-12 0 JakeGreenall 51
(Michael Easterby) *hld up: a bhd* **16/1**
00- 9 *1¾* **Dancing Lancer**[40] 1937 4-10-9 0 JohnDawson(3) 49
(Tim Walford) *trckd ldrs: reminders after 3rd and sn lost pl: bhd after 6th* **150/1**
5- 10 *28* **Ferney Boy**[18] 2340 7-10-12 0 JoeColliver 21
(Chris Fairhurst) *in tch: rdn after 4 out: sn wknd* **200/1**
0- S **Indigo Island (IRE)**[18] 2347 4-10-9 0 CallumBewley(3)
(Robert Bewley) *hld up: bhd whn slipped up on bnd bef 2 out* **100/1**

5m 4.1s (11.40) **Going Correction** +0.875s/f (Soft)
WFA 4 from 5yo+ 8lb **11 Ran SP% 126.3**
Speed ratings (Par 105): **112,111,107,106,103 100,94,85,85,73**
toteswingers 1&2 £3.50, 1&3 £1.40, 2&3 £4.60 CSF £15.51 TOTE £1.40: £1.02, £4.60, £1.70; EX 16.90 Trifecta £27.50 Pool: £1287.24 - 35.06 winning units..
Owner The Heath Hunter Partnership **Bred** Pat And Oliver McCarthy **Trained** Nicholashayne, Devon

FOCUS
Chases stepped off inner rail, Hurdles on outside and divided bends. After the first jockeys described the ground as "tacky". The market suggested there was only one horse that mattered, and it panned out as expected. A decent novice for the track with the winner better than the bare result.

2733 NEWTON AYCLIFFE WORKING MENS CLUB JUVENILE HURDLE (PAXTONS HURDLE SERIES QUALIFIER) (8 hdls) 2m 1f
12:50 (12:50) (Class 4) 3-Y-O **£3,119** (£915; £457; £228)

Form RPR
4- 1 **Magic Skyline (IRE)**[8] 2557 3-10-5 0 (t) JamesReveley 104+
(Brian Ellison) *in tch: led bef 2nd: hit 4th: hdd next: rdn and 3 l down whn lft in front 2 out: kpt on* **14/1**[2]
1- 2 *3¼* **Hawk High (IRE)**[30] 2098 3-11-5 0 DougieCostello 115+
(Tim Easterby) *in tch: wnt a little in snatches: nt fluent 5th: sn trckd ldr: rdn after 3 out: lft cl 2nd 2 out: hung lft between last 2: one pce and a hld run-in* **11/10**[1]
4- 3 *16* **Nautical Twilight**[26] 2168 3-10-5 0 BrianHughes 83
(Malcolm Jefferson) *trckd ldrs: rdn after 3 out: sn btn: lft poor 3rd 2 out* **25/1**[3]
06- 4 *7* **Jebulani**[27] 2154 3-10-12 0 BrianHarding 83
(Barry Murtagh) *hld up: rdn after 3 out: nvr threatened* **100/1**
P- P **Everreadyneddy**[27] 2154 3-10-5 0 (t) StephenMulqueen(7)
(Maurice Barnes) *hld up: a bhd: p.u bef 3 out* **200/1**
5- F **Ainsi Fideles (FR)**[25] 2200 3-11-5 0 (t) TomScudamore 119+
(David Pipe) *led tl bef 2nd: trckd ldr: led again 5th: 3 l up and gng wl whn fell 2 out* **11/10**[1]

4m 22.5s (15.60) **Going Correction** +0.875s/f (Soft) **6 Ran SP% 107.2**
Speed ratings (Par 104): **98,96,88,85,**
toteswingers 1&2 £4.60, 1&3 £2.50, 2&3 £4.00 CSF £28.64 TOTE £14.90: £3.70, £1.10; EX 40.50 Trifecta £147.00 Pool: £2144.42 - 10.93 winning units..
Owner Mike And Eileen Newbould **Bred** Rabbah Bloodstock Limited **Trained** Norton, N Yorks

FOCUS
This was run at an early crawl, and neither of the joint-favourites were able to capitalise for different reasons. A step up from the winner, but the faller was unlucky.

2734 WHIZZ KIDZ NOVICES' H'CAP CHASE (16 fncs) 2m 4f
1:20 (1:20) (Class 4) (0-110,108) 4-Y-O+ **£3,768** (£1,106; £553; £276)

Form RPR
040- 1 **Monbeg (IRE)**[6] 2591 6-10-3 **85** (p) WilsonRenwick 90+
(Martin Todhunter) *hld up: tk clsr order after 1/2-way: rdn to chse ldng pair after 2 out: upsides whn bmpd and pckd last: gathered up qckly and styd on to ld towards fin* **7/1**
543- 2 *1¾* **Bocamix (FR)**[14] 2445 7-11-0 **99** JohnKington(3) 102
(Andrew Crook) *chsd ldrs: led 3 out: sn rdn: hdd last: hld towards fin* **4/1**[3]
5/0- 3 *nk* **Brieryhill Boy**[17] 2356 6-10-10 **92** BrianHarding 94
(William Amos) *led: hdd 3 out: remained cl up: led again last: hdd towards fin* **4/1**[3]
U12- 4 *hd* **Cavite Eta (IRE)**[6] 2595 6-11-12 **108** HenryBrooke 110
(Barry Murtagh) *hld up: hdwy to trck ldr after 4th: rdn and outpcd bef 2 out: kpt on run-in* **7/2**[2]
1P3- 5 *28* **Rattlin**[18] 2352 5-11-12 **108** RyanMania 81
(Sue Smith) *trckd ldr: hit 4th: jnd ldr 5 out: rdn after next: wknd after 3 out* **2/1**[1]
/0P- P **Morello Mist**[18] 2333 8-9-9 **82** oh16 (t) SamanthaDrake(5)
(Richard Drake) *hld up: bhd 1/2-way: p.u after 11th* **50/1**

5m 5.5s (2.50) **Going Correction** +0.225s/f (Yiel) **6 Ran SP% 110.0**
Speed ratings (Par 105): **104,103,103,103,91**
toteswingers 1&2 £10.50, 1&3 £12.00, 2&3 £3.80 CSF £33.11 TOTE £5.50: £4.20, £1.50; EX 30.50 Trifecta £176.00 Pool: £1572.82 - 6.70 winning units..
Owner Island Intermodal Services **Bred** Peter O'Keeffe **Trained** Orton, Cumbria

FOCUS
This was run at a reasonable pace and it produced an exciting finish with three in a line at the last. An ordinary handicap but the form makes sense.

2735 BEECHWOOD & EASTERSIDE SOCIAL CLUB H'CAP CHASE (21 fncs) 3m 3f
1:50 (1:50) (Class 5) (0-100,97) 4-Y-O+ **£2,209** (£648; £324; £162)

Form RPR
/5P- 1 **Great Ocean Road (IRE)**[18] 2339 10-9-9 **71** oh6 AdamNicol(5) 79+
(David Thompson) *trckd ldrs: upsides 5 out: led 3 out: stl on bit in narrow ld between last 2: rdn out after last* **25/1**
/F3- 2 *2* **Heez A Steel (IRE)**[11] 2497 12-11-2 **94** AlistairFindlay(7) 99
(Jane Walton) *w ldr: led 5th: hdd 3 out: remained cl up but wnr a gng bttr: nt fluent last: hld run-in* **13/2**
422- 3 *1¾* **Dukeofchesterwood**[19] 2310 11-11-1 **86** (p) BrianHughes 88
(Karen McLintock) *trckd ldrs: rdn after 3 out: kpt on* **7/2**[2]
0/P- 4 *7* **Esme Rides A Gaine**[208] 74 11-9-13 **77** StephenMulqueen(7) 72
(Christopher Wilson) *hld up: rdn after 3 out: plugged on to go modest 4th last: nvr threatened* **18/1**
420- 5 *3* **Call Me Mulligan (IRE)**[16] 2394 9-11-5 **97** (p) JohnDawson(7) 90
(John Wade) *led narrowly tl 5th: remained cl up tl pushed along and outpcd 15th: wknd after 2 out* **13/2**
333- 6 *½* **Cloudy Dawn**[15] 2423 8-10-1 **72** DougieCostello 65
(Sue Smith) *in tch: rdn after 4 out: wknd after 2 out* **9/4**[1]
0PP- 7 *21* **Over And Above (IRE)**[14] 2445 7-10-0 **71** oh6 (bt) RichieMcGrath 42
(Henry Hogarth) *hld up in tch: rdn after 4 out: sn struggling* **14/1**
/05- 8 *3¾* **Samson Collonges (FR)**[18] 2335 7-9-11 **73** oh7 ow2.. MissCWalton(5) 40
(Rebecca Menzies) *hld up: a towards rr* **9/2**[3]

7m 10.3s (21.30) **Going Correction** +0.225s/f (Yiel) **8 Ran SP% 113.6**
Speed ratings (Par 103): **77,76,75,73,72 72,66,65**
toteswingers 1&2 £6.60, 1&3 £28.70, 2&3 £1.10 CSF £172.67 CT £717.69 TOTE £20.30: £4.60, £1.50, £1.70; EX 181.10 Trifecta £392.70 Pool: £1676.77 - 3.20 winning units..
Owner J A Moore **Bred** Michael Conroy **Trained** Bolam, Co Durham

FOCUS
An open-looking handicap with the oldest competitors filling the first four places. The winner is rated back to something like his best.

2736 O'GRADY'S REDCAR H'CAP HURDLE (8 hdls) 2m 1f
2:20 (2:20) (Class 5) (0-100,99) 4-Y-O+ **£1,949** (£572; £286; £143)

Form RPR
P/1- 1 **Amir Pasha (UAE)**[14] 2449 8-11-11 **98** (v) JasonMaguire 102+
(Micky Hammond) *in tch: rdn to chse ldr bef 3 out: led appr 2 out: kpt on* **2/1**[1]
/04- 2 *4½* **Queen Of Epirus**[14] 2449 5-11-4 **91** HarryHaynes 89+
(Brian Rothwell) *led narrowly: hdd 4 out: outpcd by ldng pair after 5th: rallied to go 2nd bef 2 out: hit 2 out: kpt on but a hld by wnr* **5/1**[3]
503- 3 *11* **Mrs Grass**[18] 2336 6-10-6 **82** JohnKington(3) 66
(Jonathan Haynes) *hld up: rdn 3 out: plugged on to go poor 3rd last: no threat to ldng pair* **14/1**
060- 4 *1½* **Ancient Times (USA)**[10] 2511 6-10-9 **85** (p) KyleJames(3) 68
(Philip Kirby) *w ldr: lost pl after 4th: dropped to rr bef 3 out: plugged on again after 2 out* **6/1**
/00- 5 *6* **Kathlatino**[14] 2449 6-10-1 **79** JoeColliver(5) 56
(Micky Hammond) *hld up: nvr threatened* **7/1**
360/ 6 *3* **High Hoylander**[674] 3875 7-11-12 **99** RyanMania 76+
(Sue Smith) *trckd ldr: led 4th: rdn whn hdd appr 2 out: wknd* **10/3**[2]
P/P- 7 *1¾* **Rosquero (FR)**[14] 2444 8-10-11 **84** KennyJohnson 56
(Robert Johnson) *trckd ldrs: wknd bef 3 out* **33/1**

4m 20.8s (13.90) **Going Correction** +0.875s/f (Soft) **7 Ran SP% 109.5**
Speed ratings (Par 103): **102,99,94,94,91 89,88**
toteswingers 1&2 £2.40, 1&3 £8.30, 2&3 £9.40 CSF £11.47 CT £95.23 TOTE £2.80: £1.10, £2.20; EX 10.90 Trifecta £34.60 Pool: £1825.20 - 39.49 winning units..
Owner M H O G **Bred** Darley **Trained** Middleham Moor, N Yorks

The Form Book Jumps, Raceform Ltd, Compton, RG20 6NL.

FOCUS
C&D form of two weeks ago played out as the winner and second did battle once again. The winner was well in on the best of his form but is getting close to that level.

2737 CHAMPIONS LEAGUE ODDS AT BOOKMAKERS.CO.UK H'CAP CHASE (13 fncs) **2m 110y**
2:50 (2:50) (Class 5) (0-100,98) 4-Y-0+ **£2,209** (£648; £324; £162)

Form RPR
/P3- 1 **Bob's Dream (IRE)**17 2361 11-11-8 **94**..........(t) BrianHarding 103
(William Amos) *trckd ldr on inner: upsides 3 out: rdn 2 out: led appr last: drvn out* **13/2**
561- 2 ½ **Jim Tango (FR)**17 2361 9-11-0 **86**..........(p) TomSiddall 94
(Karen McLintock) *trckd ldrs towards outer: chal 2 out: upsides last: rdn and one pce run-in* **6/1**
6/2- 3 1¼ **Pamak D'Airy (FR)**18 2338 10-11-7 **98**..........(p) TonyKelly(5) 105
(Henry Hogarth) *trckd ldrs: rdn after 3 out: ev ch appr last: one pce and hld run-in* **9/2**2
0/6- 4 6 **Overlaw**17 2361 11-10-10 **89**.......... DaraghBourke(7) 90
(Stuart Coltherd) *led: rdn whn hdd appr last: wknd* **5/1**3
/05- 5 2½ **Robin's Command (IRE)**17 2356 6-10-7 **79**.......... WilsonRenwick 78
(Rose Dobbin) *t.k.h: hld up: in tch after 3 out: rdn 2 out: sn btn* **15/8**1
326- 6 6 **Turf Trivia**26 2173 6-11-9 **95**..........(b) BarryKeniry 87
(George Moore) *trckd ldrs: lost pl 7th: mstke 8th: wknd after 2 out* **7/1**
400- 7 10 **Strathaird (IRE)**45 1876 9-9-11 **72** oh25..........(p) JohnKington(3) 54
(Andrew Crook) *hld up: nvr threatened* **66/1**

4m 22.8s (14.20) **Going Correction** +0.225s/f (Yiel) **7 Ran SP% 111.2**
Speed ratings (Par 103): **75,74,74,71,70 67,62**
toteswingers 1&2 £4.20, 1&3 £3.20, 2&3 £2.50 CSF £41.43 CT £187.08 TOTE £10.40: £5.40, £3.10; EX 22.40 Trifecta £113.70 Pool: £2044.61 - 13.47 winning units..
Owner Bonney, Elliot & Crook **Bred** Shane A Moran **Trained** Rochester, Northumberland
FOCUS
A tactical affair that did not heat up until the home turn. The second and third look the best guides.

2738 BOOKMAKERS FREE BETS AT BOOKMAKERS.CO.UK STANDARD OPEN NATIONAL HUNT FLAT RACE **2m 1f**
3:20 (3:20) (Class 6) 4-6-Y-0 **£1,559** (£457; £228; £114)

Form RPR
1 **Mystical Dreamer (IRE)** 4-11-2 0.......... DougieCostello 110+
(Ronald O'Leary, Ire) *midfield: smooth hdwy to trck ldr 5f out: led on bit 2f out: rdn out fnl f* **5/4**1
2 2½ **Hitman Harry** 5-11-2 0.......... BrianHarding 104
(Tina Jackson) *hld up: smooth hdwy over 4f out: rdn to chse ldrs over 2f out: kpt on to go 2nd ins fnl f* **25/1**
3 2 **Carrybridge (IRE)**178 6-10-6 0.......... MrSCrawford(3) 95
(S R B Crawford, Ire) *led for 3f: trckd ldr: led again 4f out: rdn whn hdd 2f out: one pce and lost 2nd ins fnl f* **11/4**2
41- 4 7 **Mister Jones**178 584 5-11-9 0.......... RyanMania 102
(Sue Smith) *trckd ldrs: rdn over 3f out: one pce in 4th fnl 2f* **4/1**3
5 8 **Spring Back** 5-10-4 0.......... TonyKelly(5) 80
(Edwin Tuer) *trckd ldrs: rdn over 3f out: grad wknd* **33/1**
6 15 **Lachlan Mor** 4-10-9 0.......... DaraghBourke(7) 72
(Stuart Coltherd) *midfield: wknd over 3f out* **14/1**
7 3¾ **Fev Rover (IRE)** 6-11-2 0.......... TomSiddall 68
(Simon West) *trckd ldrs: wknd over 3f out* **66/1**
8 1 **Camden Vine** 5-10-2 0.......... MrJDixon(7) 60
(Victor Thompson) *hld up: rdn 1/2-way: nvr threatened* **100/1**
9 9 **Escape To The West** 5-10-11 0.......... SamanthaDrake(5) 58
(Joanne Foster) *t.k.h: hld up: rdn over 6f out: sn btn* **16/1**
00/ 10 6 **Precentors Court (IRE)**237 5125 6-11-2 0.......... HarryHaynes 52
(Brian Rothwell) *led after 3f: hdd 4f out: sn wknd* **125/1**
11 13 **Harleys Max** 4-10-9 0.......... StephenMulqueen(7) 39
(Susan Corbett) *hld up: rdn over 5f out: sn wknd* **40/1**

4m 16.3s (15.00) **Going Correction** +0.875s/f (Soft)
WFA 4 from 5yo+ 7lb **11 Ran SP% 116.2**
Speed ratings: **99,97,96,93,89 82,81,80,76,73 67**
toteswingers 1&2 £4.20, 1&3 £3.20, 2&3 £2.50 CSF £43.22 TOTE £2.70: £1.40, £3.40, £1.60; EX 48.20 Trifecta £80.60 Pool: £1853.83 - 17.23 winning units..
Owner Mrs Ronald O'Leary **Bred** Edward Devereux **Trained** Killaloe, Co. Clare
FOCUS
The main contenders began to pull clear from the home turn. The third and fourth give the race a bit of substance.
T/Plt: £56.00. Pool: £65,238.93 - 850.38 winning units. T/Qpdt: £31.60. Pool: 5423.00 - 126.60 winning units. AS

2535 FONTWELL (L-H)
Wednesday, November 27

OFFICIAL GOING: Good to soft (soft in places; 6.5)
Wind: virtually nil Weather: overcast

2739 QUICKSILVERSLOTS GET UP TO £200 FREEPLAYS CONDITIONAL JOCKEYS' TRAINING SERIES H'CAP CHASE (15 fncs) **2m 4f**
12:40 (12:40) (Class 5) (0-95,95) 4-Y-0+ **£2,144** (£629; £314; £157)

Form RPR
22S- 1 **Mister Wiseman**17 2396 11-10-10 **84**..........(vt) ThomasCheesman(5) 92
(Nigel Hawke) *led tl 7th: trckd ldrs: led after 4 out: styd on wl: rdn out* **3/1**3
2/P- 2 5 **According To Them (IRE)**15 2441 9-10-0 **69** oh5..........(t) PatrickCorbett 73
(Daniel Steele) *hld up bhd ldrs: wnt 3rd after 11th: rdn after 3 out: styd on to go 2nd run-in: a being hld* **16/1**
4/U- 3 1 **Join The Navy**8 2580 8-11-12 **95**..........(b) KieronEdgar 98
(Kate Buckett) *t.k.h: trckd wnr: led bef 7th: hdd after 4 out: rdn after next: styd on same pce: lost 2nd run-in* **5/4**1
45P- 4 19 **Curragh Dancer (FR)**3 2702 10-9-7 **69** oh5..........(tp) LouisMuspratt(7) 55
(Paddy Butler) *trckd ldrs: nt fluent 9th: sn pushed along: rdn and wl hld fr after 4 out* **33/1**
01P/ P **Frosty Lad (IRE)**603 5222 9-11-6 **89**..........(t) ConorShoemark
(Lawney Hill) *j.rt: hld up 4th: hit 5th: pushed along after 9th: wknd 11th: t.o whn p.u bef 3 out* **11/4**2
462- U **Full Ov Beans**8 2576 9-11-4 **87**.......... CiaranMckee
(Michael Gates) *hld up bhd ldrs: cl 4th whn stmbld bdly and uns rdr 10th* **10/1**

5m 7.6s (0.30) **Going Correction** 0.0s/f (Good) **6 Ran SP% 114.0**
Speed ratings (Par 103): **99,97,96,89,**
toteswingers: 1&2 £9.40, 1&3 £1.02, 2&3 £6.60. CSF £39.13 TOTE £4.90: £3.10, £8.00; EX 41.80 Trifecta £295.40 Pool: £1032.08 - 2.62 winning units..
Owner Thorne Farm Racing Partnership **Bred** Mrs D Thomson **Trained** Stoodleigh, Devon
FOCUS
Top bend and bottom Hurdle bend on inside line. Bottom Chase bend dolled out 6yds adding 15yds per circuit to Chase course. Jockeys reported it to be "good to soft, lovely jumping ground" and "good to soft jumping ground with soft patches". A very weak handicap chase, run at a fair gallop. The first three are rated pretty much to their marks.

2740 QUICKSILVER SLOTS PLAY £500 ROULETTE NOVICES' HURDLE (10 hdls) **2m 4f**
1:10 (1:10) (Class 4) 4-Y-0+ **£3,898** (£1,144; £572; £286)

Form RPR
5/3- 1 **Junction Fourteen (IRE)**22 2279 4-10-12 0.......... AidanColeman 122
(Emma Lavelle) *racd keenly: trckd ldrs: rn sltly wd on bnd after 3 out whn rdn to chse ldr: jst over a l down at the last: styd on strly fnl 75yds: led fnl stride* **9/4**1
/02- 2 hd **Cloud Creeper (IRE)**19 2351 6-10-12 120.......... RichardJohnson 123
(Philip Hobbs) *hld up but in tch: smooth hdwy to ld after 3 out: hit 2 out: jst over a l up at the last: sn rdn: hdd fnl stride* **5/2**2
4/3- 3 15 **Unowhatimeanharry**23 2272 5-10-12 0.......... PaulMoloney 113
(Helen Nelmes) *in tch: sltly outpcd 7th: hdwy to chse ldng pair after 3 out: styd on same pce fr next* **8/1**
22- 4 13 **Gate Please (IRE)**29 2147 8-10-12 124.......... APMcCoy 97
(Rebecca Curtis) *trckd ldr: led 7th tl rdn after 3 out: sn outpcd: wknd last* **11/4**3
0/U- 5 4 **Curtain Razer (IRE)**10 2539 7-10-12 120..........1 TomCannon 93
(Chris Gordon) *led tl 7th: sn pushed along: rdn after 3 out: wknd bef next* **50/1**
63/ 6 10 **Horace**396 2056 5-10-12 0.......... NoelFehily 84
(Harry Fry) *hld up in tch: jnd ldrs after 6th tl next: sn pushed along: rdn after 3 out: wknd next* **7/1**
0/0- 7 ¾ **Two Mile Bridge (IRE)**21 2286 7-10-5 0.......... TomO'Brien 77
(Paul Henderson) *hld up: struggling 7th: sn bhd* **100/1**
006- 8 30 **Slaney Star (IRE)**9 2564 5-10-12 0.......... MattieBatchelor 57
(Jim Best) *trckd ldrs: losing pl whn hit 6th: reminders: wknd after 3 out: t.o* **100/1**

4m 54.0s (-5.40) **Going Correction** +0.125s/f (Yiel) **8 Ran SP% 113.6**
Speed ratings (Par 105): **115,114,108,103,102 98,97,85**
toteswingers: 1&2 £2.20, 1&3 £3.50, 2&3 £6.60. CSF £8.32 TOTE £3.20: £1.10, £1.30, £2.60; EX 10.10 Trifecta £50.70 Pool: £2326.56 - 34.35 winning units..
Owner M St Quinton & T Syder **Bred** John And Iris Lunny **Trained** Hatherden, Hants
FOCUS
An ordinary novice hurdle. The pace lifted appreciably on the final circuit and the first two contested a tight finish, clear of the rest. The winner is on the upgrade and the second is rated back to last season's best.

2741 QUICKSILVER £1 TO WIN £500 NOVICES' H'CAP CHASE (13 fncs) **2m 2f**
1:40 (1:40) (Class 4) (0-110,103) 4-Y-0+ **£3,768** (£1,106; £553; £276)

Form RPR
/34- 1 **Strawberry Hill (IRE)**24 2251 7-11-8 **102**.......... JamesBest(3) 114+
(Caroline Keevil) *j.w: trckd ldr: chal briefly 4 out: sn rdn: chal again 2 out: led sn after last: styd on strly to assert towards fin* **5/2**2
351- 2 7 **Red Rock (FR)**35 2021 8-11-9 **103**.......... GavinSheehan(3) 110
(Emma Lavelle) *led: hit 3rd and 8th: jnd briefly 4 out: rdn after 2 out: jnd again last: sn hdd: no ex* **1/1**1
2/P- 3 45 **Marble Walk (IRE)**15 2430 8-11-1 **92**.......... LeightonAspell 58
(Richard Rowe) *trckd ldng pair most of way: lost tch w principles fr bef 4 out: hld on for modest 3rd: t.o* **12/1**
300- 4 1¾ **Unsist (FR)**37 2008 5-10-0 **77** oh8..........(tp) TomCannon 41
(Nick Gifford) *racd in 5th tl disp 3rd 6th: j.rt fr 8th: no ch w front pair fr bef 4 out: t.o* **8/1**3
6B6- 5 12 **Millenarys Lady (IRE)**10 2535 6-10-1 **78** oh1 ow1.......... PaulMoloney 31
(David Rees) *racd in 4th tl 5th: struggling to hold pl 7th: lost tch bef 4 out: t.o* **8/1**3

4m 33.3s (-1.40) **Going Correction** 0.0s/f (Good) **5 Ran SP% 108.5**
Speed ratings (Par 105): **103,99,79,79,73**
CSF £5.53 TOTE £2.70: £1.60, £1.10; EX 5.20 Trifecta £15.30 Pool: £2024.94 - 99.01 winning units..
Owner K S B Bloodstock **Bred** Mrs Patricia Doran **Trained** Motcombe, Dorset
FOCUS
A weakly contested event that concerned just two from a long way out. A step up from the winner with the second probably running at least as well as when winning last time.

2742 32RED CASINO H'CAP HURDLE (10 hdls) **2m 4f**
2:10 (2:10) (Class 3) (0-130,125) 4-Y-0+ **£5,393** (£1,583; £791; £395)

Form RPR
11/- 1 **Seebright**216 5522 6-11-12 **125**.......... JackDoyle 129+
(Victor Dartnall) *in tch: rdn to chal after 3 out: led after next: strly chal last: styd on wl to assert fnl 75yds: drvn out* **7/4**1
511/ 2 ¾ **Smart Freddy**871 1061 7-11-6 **119**.......... DavidBass 121+
(Ben Pauling) *trckd ldrs: led 3 out: rdn and hdd after next: rallied gamely to hold ev ch last tl fnl 75yds: no ex* **25/1**
001- 3 4 **Gores Island (IRE)**18 2362 7-11-4 **120**.......... JoshuaMoore(3) 120
(Gary Moore) *hld up but in tch: mstke 1st: tk clsr order 6th: rdn after 3 out: wnt 3rd next: styd on same pce fr last* **2/1**2
0/0- 4 11 **Whipcrackaway (IRE)**18 2366 4-11-2 **115**..........(v1) LeightonAspell 104
(Peter Hedger) *hld up but in tch: tk clsr order 6th: rdn after 3 out: wnt 4th next: nt pce to get involved* **8/1**
2/0- 5 14 **Promised Wings (GER)**21 2288 6-11-9 **122**..........(b) TomCannon 98
(Chris Gordon) *trckd ldr: led 5th: nt fluent and hdd 3 out: sn rdn: wknd qckly* **6/1**3
044/ 6 2 **The Pier (IRE)**265 4616 7-11-8 **121**..........(t) AndrewTinkler 95
(Anna Brooks) *trckd ldrs: rdn in cl 3rd after 3 out tl bef next: wknd between last 2* **25/1**
/41- 7 48 **Tijori (IRE)**33 1864 5-11-2 **120**.......... RobertWilliams(5) 51
(Bernard Llewellyn) *hld up but in tch: slipped on bnd bef 3rd: struggling and detached after 4th: t.o fr bef 7th* **12/1**
0/F- P **Shannon Spirit (IRE)**202 179 8-11-5 **118**..........(b) RichardJohnson
(Paul Henderson) *led tl reminders and hdd 5th: dropped out v qckly: p.u after next* **25/1**

4m 58.4s (-1.00) **Going Correction** +0.125s/f (Yiel)
WFA 4 from 5yo+ 8lb **8 Ran SP% 114.3**
Speed ratings (Par 107): **107,106,105,100,95 94,75,**
toteswingers 1&2 £21.70, 1&3 £2.20, 2&3 £17.10 CSF £43.01 CT £92.83 TOTE £2.50: £1.10, £5.10, £1.10; EX 37.20 Trifecta £174.90 Pool: £1726.05 - 7.40 winning units..
Owner Mrs D J Fleming **Bred** R Johnson **Trained** Brayford, Devon

FOCUS
A fair handicap hurdle, and sound form despite a fairly steady pace. There should be more to come from the winner.

2743 32RED.COM H'CAP CHASE (19 fncs) 3m 2f 110y
2:45 (2:45) (Class 5) (0-95,82) 4-Y-0+ **£2,380** (£865)

Form RPR
145- **1** **Volio Vincente (FR)**[7] 2603 6-10-12 **71** JamesBest(3) 78
(Carroll Gray) *j.w: mde all: rdn whn idling between last 2: strly pressed fr last: styd on wl: drvn out* **9/4**[2]
6/3- **2** *nk* **Alteranthela (IRE)**[169] 712 9-11-12 **82** (p) LeightonAspell 89
(Richard Rowe) *trckd wnr thrght: rdn after 4 out: chal last: ev ch run-in: styd on: hld nring fin* **7/4**[1]
53U/ **U** **Poppy Gregg**[241] 5033 8-11-2 **75** WayneKavanagh(3)
(Dr Jeremy Naylor) *chsd ldng pair: struggling 12th: clsng on ldng pair whn blnd bdly and uns rdr 14th* **7/1**
2/P- **R** **Cool Cascade**[182] 541 7-11-12 **82** DavidBass
(Lawney Hill) *ref to r: tk no part* **11/4**[3]
7m 9.2s (8.10) **Going Correction** 0.0s/f (Good) 4 Ran SP% **106.3**
Speed ratings (Par 103): **88,87, ,**
CSF £6.48 TOTE £3.70; EX 6.60 Trifecta £6.50 Pool: £1002.97 - 115.00 winning units..
Owner optimumracing.co.uk **Bred** Classic Breeding Sarl Et Al **Trained** Moorland, Somerset
FOCUS
A very weak handicap chase.

2744 32RED ON THE APP STORE H'CAP HURDLE (13 hdls) 3m 3f
3:20 (3:20) (Class 4) (0-110,108) 4-Y-0+ **£3,119** (£915; £457; £228)

Form RPR
155- **1** **Kilrush (IRE)**[8] 2582 7-11-9 **108** MichaelByrne(3) 109+
(Neil Mulholland) *hld up bhd: hdwy 3 out: sn rdn: chsng wnr whn nt fluent 2 out: styng on at same pce in 2 l 2nd whn lft in ld last: rdn out* **7/1**
113- **2** *3 ¼* **Absolute Shambles**[10] 2541 9-10-10 **92** (p) TomCannon 87
(Chris Gordon) *trckd ldrs: rdn after 3 out: styng on at same pce whn lft 2nd at the last* **4/1**[2]
302- **3** *2 ¾* **Sea Cadet**[53] 1768 11-9-4 **82** oh2 NathanAdams(10) 78
(Laura Mongan) *hld up in tch: blnd bdly and gd rcvry by rdr 8th: hdwy after next: rdn bef 3 out and lost pl: styd on again after 2 out: wnt 3rd sn after last: kpt on* **5/1**[3]
3- **4** *3* **Killegney**[8] 2575 9-10-8 **95** (b) ConorShoemark(5) 85
(Michael Gates) *hld up: hdwy 10th: rdn after 3 out: styng on at same pce whn lft 3rd briefly last: no ex* **12/1**
40/- **5** *12* **Strange Bird (IRE)**[222] 5381 8-10-3 **88** JeremiahMcGrath(3) 72
(Richard Rowe) *disp ld: mstke 2nd: hit 10th: mstke 3 out: sn rdn and hdd: hld next: wknd bef last* **25/1**
1/5- **6** *24* **Dunkelly Castle (IRE)**[197] 294 9-10-10 **97** (t) ThomasGarner(5) 66
(Brendan Powell) *trckd ldrs tl rdn 3 out: sn wknd* **7/1**
31P- **F** **Dom Lukka (FR)**[24] 2253 5-11-8 **104** NoelFehily 106
(Charlie Longsdon) *disp ld tl outrt ldr after 3 out: wnt rt next: sn rdn: 2 l up and styng on whn fell last* **6/4**[1]
7m 0.1s (7.30) **Going Correction** +0.125s/f (Yiel) 7 Ran SP% **113.2**
Speed ratings (Par 105): **94,93,92,91,87 80,**
toteswingers 1&2 £15.40, 1&3 £8.40, 2&3 £6.40 CSF £34.45 TOTE £6.90: £2.50, £3.00; EX 48.80 Trifecta £148.00 Pool: £1983.71 - 10.05 winning units..
Owner Six Shades Of Grey **Bred** J P And Miss M Mangan **Trained** Limpley Stoke, Wilts
FOCUS
A modest marathon handicap, run at a steady pace. The winner and the faller are rated pretty much to their marks.

2745 32RED STANDARD OPEN NATIONAL HUNT FLAT RACE 1m 6f
3:50 (3:52) (Class 6) 4-6-Y-O **£1,559** (£457; £228; £114)

Form RPR
60- **1** **Larks Rising**[9] 2570 5-11-2 0 TomO'Brien 110+
(Caroline Keevil) *mde all: sn best part of 30 l clr: nvr in any danger: unchal* **16/1**
/1- **2** *17* **Rouquine Sauvage**[35] 2022 5-11-2 0 (t) APMcCoy 102+
(Anthony Honeyball) *trckd ldrs in chsng gp: wnt 25 l 2nd over 6f out: shkn up over 3f out: fnd little and hrdly any imp* **1/5**[1]
2- **3** *8* **Lucky Thirteen**[133] 1016 5-11-2 0 RichardJohnson 90
(Richard Phillips) *chsd clr wnr tl over 6f out: styd on same pce fnl 3f* **5/1**[3]
56- **4** *shd* **Frank N Fair**[9] 2570 5-10-9 0 DaveCrosse 83
(Zoe Davison) *trckd ldrs in chsng gp: no ch w front pair but chal for wl-hld 3rd fr over 3f out: styd on same pce fnl 2f* **33/1**
/ **5** *23* **Cut'N'Shut** 6-11-2 0 [1] GerardTumelty 62
(Zoe Davison) *a in rr: t.o* **66/1**
0- **6** *1 ¼* **Tambalong**[21] 2298 5-10-6 0 (t) JamesBest(3) 54
(Caroline Keevil) *a towards rr: nvr any danger: t.o* **66/1**
7 *4 ½* **Pure Poteen (IRE)**[17] 5-11-2 0 (t) NoelFehily 55
(Neil Mulholland) *trckd ldr in chsng gp tl over 3f out: wknd: t.o* **9/2**[2]
/0- **8** *15* **Goodgoshmsmolly**[199] 239 4-10-9 0 PaulMoloney 30
(Helen Nelmes) *a towards rr: t.o* **25/1**
3m 31.1s 8 Ran SP% **133.8**
toteswingers 1&2 £4.90, 1&3 £4.20, 2&3 £1.60 CSF £23.49 TOTE £27.90: £3.90, £1.02, £1.40; EX 83.10 Trifecta £301.70 Pool: £3282.87 - 8.15 winning units..
Owner Mrs L R Lovell **Bred** Mrs Jane Wood **Trained** Motcombe, Dorset
FOCUS
Something of a farce, with the winner stealing it at the start. Very difficult form to assess, but the runner-up failed to match her debut effort.
T/Plt: £73.30. Pool: £68,436.41 - 680.76 winning units. T/Qpdt: £11.00. Pool: £5270.10 - 351.60 winning units. TM

2514 WETHERBY (L-H)
Wednesday, November 27

OFFICIAL GOING: Good to soft (6.5)
Wind: almost nil Weather: fine

2746 NEW RACING UK ANYWHERE AVAILABLE NOW CONDITIONAL JOCKEYS' CLAIMING HURDLE (12 hdls) 2m 6f
12:15 (12:15) (Class 5) 4-Y-0+ **£2,053** (£598; £299)

Form RPR
/0P- **1** **Makhzoon (USA)**[28] 2158 9-10-7 110 (v) DiarmuidO'Regan(5) 114
(N W Alexander) *w ldr: led sn after 9th: forged clr between last 2: rdn out* **14/1**
/32- **2** *13* **Neptune Equester**[16] 2428 10-10-12 125 NathanMoscrop(6) 108
(Brian Ellison) *chsd ldrs: drvn after 6th: lost pl 8th: hdwy and 3rd 3 out: kpt on to take 2nd clsng stages* **85/40**[2]
P01- **3** *1 ½* **Connectivity (IRE)**[16] 2428 9-11-6 135 (b) ChristopherWard(6) 116
(Dr Richard Newland) *trckd ldrs: rdn to chse wnr appr 3 out: one pce between last 2: fin lame* **1/1**[1]
/60- **4** *11* **Bold Slasher (IRE)**[26] 2202 5-10-3 82 DaraghBourke(5) 87
(Sue Smith) *led tl after 9th: wknd 3 out* **100/1**
0/4- **5** *shd* **Dooney Rock (IRE)**[30] 2135 9-11-0 119 (p) JackQuinlan 95
(John Butler) *in rr: hdwy 7th: 5th and wl outpcd whn mstke 3 out* **9/2**[3]
/4P- **6** *47* **Herostatus**[27] 2172 6-11-9 108 CraigNichol(3) 75
(Jason Ward) *chsd ldrs: nt fluent and lost pl 7th: sn bhd: t.o 3 out: eventually completed* **50/1**
3/P- **U** **Aggie's Lad (IRE)**[25] 2218 11-10-9 105 GrantCockburn(3)
(Alison Hamilton) *chsd ldrs: pushed along 4th: lost pl 6th: last whn stmbld bdly landing 8th and uns rdr* **66/1**
5m 25.1s (-1.70) **Going Correction** +0.15s/f (Yiel) 7 Ran SP% **111.3**
Speed ratings (Par 103): **109,104,103,99,99 82,**
toteswingers: 1&2 £3.30, 1&3 £2.10, 2&3 £1.10. CSF £42.66 TOTE £10.20: £4.80, £1.90; EX 39.90 Trifecta £89.80 Pool: £1461.77 - 12.20 winning units..
Owner The Ladies Who **Bred** Vision Bloodstock Et Al **Trained** Kinneston, Perth & Kinross
FOCUS
A moderate contest. The winner is rated 4lb off the best of his 2013 figures.

2747 WATCH ON 3 DEVICES RACINGUK.COM/ANYWHERE BEGINNERS' CHASE (18 fncs) 3m 1f
12:50 (12:50) (Class 4) 4-Y-0+ **£3,898** (£1,144; £572; £286)

Form RPR
2/1- **1** **Indian Castle (IRE)**[195] 339 5-11-2 129 JasonMaguire 132+
(Donald McCain) *trckd ldr: led 13th: shkn up 3 out: rdn between last 2: styd on strly: eased nr fin* **6/4**[2]
1/3- **2** *2* **Seymour Eric**[14] 2459 8-11-2 133 (p) IanPopham 124
(Martin Keighley) *led: reminder after 9th: j.rt 12th: blnd and hdd next: upsides 4 out: kpt on same pce fr 2 out* **5/6**[1]
203- **3** *16* **Attycran (IRE)**[25] 2224 8-10-9 103 (tp) StephenMulqueen(7) 107
(Maurice Barnes) *chsd ldrs 6th: drvn and outpcd bef 4 out: wknd 2 out* **33/1**
2/ **4** *29* **Cottiers Den (IRE)**[326] 3506 6-11-2 0 WilsonRenwick 85
(Martin Todhunter) *chsd ldrs: pushed along 6th: hit 11th: bhd fr 13th: t.o 4 out* **50/1**
/63- **F** **Karinga Dandy (IRE)**[18] 2357 7-11-2 0 RyanMania
(Sue Smith) *trckd ldrs: 4th whn fell 10th* **12/1**[3]
6m 13.5s (4.10) **Going Correction** -0.075s/f (Good) 5 Ran SP% **107.1**
Speed ratings (Par 105): **90,89,84,74,**
CSF £3.07 TOTE £2.90: £1.20, £1.10; EX 3.50 Trifecta £15.50 Pool: £1358.73 - 65.32 winning units..
Owner Askew Dick Hernon Reynard **Bred** Robert McCarthy **Trained** Cholmondeley, Cheshire
FOCUS
A race that lacked depth. The winner was value for further and is a potential 140+ novice.

2748 THECONISTONHOTEL.COM IDEAL FOR BUSINESS & PLEASURE "NATIONAL HUNT" NOVICES' HURDLE (9 hdls) 2m 110y
1:20 (1:22) (Class 4) 4-Y-0+ **£3,422** (£997; £499)

Form RPR
11/ **1** **Diamond King (IRE)**[221] 5413 5-10-12 0 JasonMaguire 125+
(Donald McCain) *trckd ldrs: led 3 out: shkn up and wnt clr run-in: v readily* **30/100**[1]
/15- **2** *4 ½* **Secrete Stream (IRE)**[62] 1667 4-10-12 0 BrianHughes 111+
(Malcolm Jefferson) *mid-div: hdwy to trck ldrs 3rd: outpcd 3 out: 3rd and styng on whn nt fluent last: kpt on to take 2nd nr fin* **17/2**[3]
/4P- **3** *nk* **Another Mattie (IRE)**[39] 1977 6-10-12 110 (t) LucyAlexander 110
(N W Alexander) *in rr: hdwy to chse ldrs 6th: sn outpcd: hdwy appr 2 out: chsd wnr appr last: kpt on same pce* **16/1**
536- **4** *9* **Beaujolais (IRE)**[18] 2369 5-10-12 0 DenisO'Regan 101
(John Ferguson) *rn wout declared tongue strap: led: drvn: hung rt and hdd 5th: reminders and led again after next: hdd 3 out: wknd between last 2* **6/1**[2]
P0- **5** *1 ¼* **Murtys Delight (IRE)**[13] 2471 6-10-12 0 (t) SamTwiston-Davies 102
(Dr Richard Newland) *mid-div: mstke 3rd: chsd ldrs 6th: wknd last* **14/1**
3/1- **6** *3 ¼* **Clan William (IRE)**[196] 318 5-11-5 0 RyanMania 106
(Sue Smith) *chsd ldrs: wknd between last 2* **10/1**
5/0- **7** *5* **Spanish Fleet**[46] 1875 5-10-5 0 JohnDawson(7) 92
(John Wade) *mid-div: hdwy 6th: outpcd and lost pl appr next* **100/1**
4- **8** *1 ¼* **Rozener (IRE)**[11] 2520 7-10-12 0 RichieMcGrath 92
(Henry Hogarth) *trckd ldrs: led 5th: hdd after next: one pce whn blnd 2 out: sn wknd* **50/1**
54- **9** *14* **Shine A Diamond (IRE)**[16] 2420 5-10-12 0 PeterBuchanan 76
(Lucinda Russell) *hld up towards rr: hdwy 6th: outpcd and lost pl next* **50/1**
560- **10** *9* **Gonalston Cloud (IRE)**[11] 2507 6-10-12 0 HarryHaynes 67
(Nick Kent) *prom: lost pl after 5th: sn bhd* **150/1**
0- **11** *hd* **Boric**[39] 1980 5-10-9 0 JohnKington(3) 67
(Simon Waugh) *sn prom: drvn 6th: sn lost pl and bhd* **100/1**
0/6- **12** *2* **Bobs Lady Tamure**[34] 2037 6-9-12 0 (t) StephenMulqueen(7) 58
(Maurice Barnes) *nt fluent in rr: stmbld on landing 1st: bhd fr 6th* **66/1**
3m 58.4s (2.60) **Going Correction** +0.15s/f (Yiel)
WFA 4 from 5yo+ 7lb 12 Ran SP% **131.4**
Speed ratings (Par 105): **99,96,96,92,91 90,88,87,80,76 76,75**
toteswingers: 1&2 £2.50, 1&3 £8.10, 2&3 £16.00. CSF £5.21 TOTE £1.30: £1.10, £2.40, £3.40; EX 4.90 Trifecta £46.10 Pool: £1840.96 - 29.93 winning units..
Owner Mrs Diana L Whateley **Bred** Cleaboy Stud **Trained** Cholmondeley, Cheshire
FOCUS
There were plenty involved off the home bend, so this probably isn't strong form, although it was run in a time much quicker than the juvenile hurdle over the same trip later on the card. The impressive winner confirmed the merit of his bumper form.

2749 STOWFORD PRESS CIDER H'CAP CHASE (18 fncs) 2m 6f 110y
1:50 (1:50) (Class 4) (0-115,112) 4-Y-0+ **£3,898** (£1,144; £572; £286)

Form RPR
343- **1** **Glen Countess (IRE)**[19] 2348 6-11-3 **103** (t) BrendanPowell 114+
(Brendan Powell) *trckd ldrs: upsides whn lft 3 l clr 3 out: kpt on run-in: jst hld on* **9/1**[3]
PU2- **2** *hd* **Goodtoknow**[11] 2518 5-11-7 **110** JakeGreenall(3) 118
(Richard Lee) *w ldr: led 2nd to 10th: drvn 14th: sn wl outpcd: hdwy and lft 4th 3 out: styd on wl run-in: jst hld* **7/2**[1]

The Form Book Jumps, Raceform Ltd, Compton, RG20 6NL.

364- 3 1 1/4 **The Thirsty Bricky (IRE)**[11] 2512 11-11-7 112.................. TonyKelly(5) 121
(David Thompson) *in rr: hdwy 10th: drvn and outpcd after 14th: hdwy and lft 4th 2 out: styd on run-in* **14/1**

0/1- 4 1 **Hollow Blue Sky (FR)**[28] 2155 6-11-7 107............. SamTwiston-Davies 117+
(Nigel Twiston-Davies) *chsd ldrs: mstke 11th: outpcd 4 out: hdwy next: chsd wnr last: one pce* **4/1**[2]

34U- 5 17 **Ultra Du Chatelet (FR)**[28] 2157 5-11-12 112................(t) PeterBuchanan 108
(Lucinda Russell) *trckd ldrs: led briefly 14th: drvn next: lft 2nd whn hmpd 3 out: wknd next* **4/1**[2]

P/2- 6 22 **Allanard (IRE)**[46] 1872 9-11-11 111..............................(v) LucyAlexander 82
(Martin Todhunter) *nt fluent and j.rt: in rr: wnt prom 10th: lost pl 13th: sn bhd* **12/1**

505- 7 3/4 **Jewel In The Sun (IRE)**[93] 1397 8-11-5 105.............(t) RichieMcLernon 75
(Ben Haslam) *chsd ldrs: lost pl 10th: sn bhd* **25/1**

/21- F **Whiskey Ridge (IRE)**[181] 555 7-10-11 97.......................... RyanMania
(Sue Smith) *led to 2nd: w ldr: led 10th: jnd whn fell 3 out* **7/2**[1]

5m 39.5s (2.50) **Going Correction** -0.075s/f (Good) **8 Ran SP% 112.6**
Speed ratings (Par 105): **92,91,91,91,85 77,77,**
toteswingers 1&2 £4.90, 1&3 £10.60, 2&3 £11.20 CSF £40.37 CT £438.43 TOTE £12.00: £2.60, £1.80, £4.80; EX 53.20 Trifecta £194.40 Pool: £1990.46 - 7.67 winning units..
Owner The Naughty Partnership **Bred** David Pim **Trained** Upper Lambourn, Berks

FOCUS
A modest but competitive handicap. The winneris rated back to her best, with a step up from the second.

2750 HARROGATE POLO CLUB JUVENILE MAIDEN HURDLE (9 hdls) 2m 110y
2:25 (2:25) (Class 5) 3-Y-O **£2,053** (£598; £299)

Form RPR

1 **Rutherglen**[40] 3-10-12 0.. JasonMaguire 109+
(John Quinn) *trckd ldrs: effrt and upsides 3 out: led last: drvn and styd on wl* **8/11**[1]

2 1 1/4 **Stephen Hero (IRE)**[43] 3-10-12 0...................................... HarrySkelton 105+
(Dan Skelton) *hld up: trckd ldrs 6th: led narrowly between last 2: hdd last: styd on same pce* **9/2**[2]

6- 3 8 **Bugsy**[41] 1934 3-10-12 0..(t) ConorO'Farrell 96
(Seamus Durack) *led to 5th: led after next: drvn 3 out: hdd between last 2: fdd* **22/1**

- 4 3 1/4 **Mandy's Boy (IRE)**[64] 3-10-12 0..................................... WillKennedy 93
(Ian Williams) *in rr: hdwy 6th: outpcd and swtchd rt appr next: styd on fr 2 out: tk modest 4th sn after last* **16/1**

5 6 **Super Cookie**[36] 3-10-2 0.. JackQuinlan(3) 80
(Noel Quinlan) *t.k.h: trckd ldrs 6th: wknd appr last* **33/1**

4- 6 4 **Marju's Quest (IRE)**[14] 2455 3-10-12 0...................... WayneHutchinson 83
(David Dennis) *t.k.h: trckd ldrs 3rd: upsides next: led 5th tl after next: wknd between last 2* **5/1**[3]

5- 7 8 **Marlborough House**[27] 2168 3-10-12 0............................ DenisO'Regan 80
(Chris Grant) *trckd ldrs 2nd: wknd 2 out* **12/1**

05- 8 2 3/4 **Henri De Boistron (FR)**[14] 2455 3-10-12 0...................... PaddyBrennan 75
(Tom George) *t.k.h: trckd ldrs: mstke and lost pl 4th: drvn 6th: sn bhd* **20/1**

4m 6.1s (10.30) **Going Correction** +0.15s/f (Yiel) **8 Ran SP% 118.4**
Speed ratings (Par 102): **81,80,76,75,72 70,66,65**
toteswingers 1&2 £1.50, 1&3 £8.20, 2&3 £12.20 CSF £4.57 TOTE £1.50: £1.02, £1.90, £5.00; EX 4.40 Trifecta £55.60 Pool: £2678.48 - 36.06 winning units..
Owner The Beer Swigging Strangers **Bred** Frank Brady **Trained** Settrington, N Yorks

FOCUS
Probably just a fair juvenile event, in which two drew clear, in a slow time.

2751 WILLIAM HILL YORKSHIRE WINTER FESTIVAL H'CAP CHASE (13 fncs) 2m
3:00 (3:00) (Class 3) (0-125,125) 4-Y-0+ **£6,498** (£1,908; £954; £477)

Form RPR

5/2- 1 **Firth Of The Clyde**[28] 2159 8-11-7 120.............................. BrianHughes 126+
(Malcolm Jefferson) *hld up: hdwy appr 4 out: upsides 2 out: lft in ld last: hrd drvn and hld on* **9/5**[1]

/42- 2 1 **Tahiti Pearl (IRE)**[15] 2448 9-11-9 122............................... RyanMania 127+
(Sue Smith) *led: qcknd pce 9th: jnd 2 out: stmbld on landing and hdd last: kpt on wl* **7/1**

65B- 3 3 1/4 **Alpha One (IRE)**[12] 2496 7-10-8 107.............................. DenisO'Regan 109
(Chris Grant) *chsd ldrs: 2nd and drvn appr 4 out: one pce fr 2 out* **16/1**

116/ 4 3 1/2 **Sacre Toi (FR)**[221] 5403 7-11-5 125..............................(p) DaleIrving(7) 123
(James Ewart) *w ldrs: hit 3rd: outpcd 3 out: kpt on run-in* **5/1**[3]

/43- 5 3/4 **Granville Island (IRE)**[15] 2448 6-11-7 120......................... SeanQuinlan 118
(Jennie Candlish) *t.k.h: trckd ldrs: drvn 4 out: one pce* **11/4**[2]

334- 6 3 1/4 **Rhymers Ha'**[18] 2359 6-11-4 117...................................... PeterBuchanan 112
(Lucinda Russell) *in tch in rr: drvn 8th: sn wl outpcd: nvr a factor* **6/1**

3m 51.7s (-4.10) **Going Correction** -0.075s/f (Good) **6 Ran SP% 111.7**
Speed ratings (Par 107): **107,106,104,103,102 101**
toteswingers 1&2 £4.20, 1&3 £7.70, 2&3 £0.90 CSF £14.13 TOTE £2.40: £1.00, £3.40; EX 15.00 Trifecta £184.70 Pool: £2556.36 - 10.37 winning units..
Owner Robert H Goldie **Bred** Robert H Goldie **Trained** Norton, N Yorks

FOCUS
Most of these had something to prove for one reason or another, so this isn't strong form. Steps up from the first two.

2752 EBF MARES' STANDARD OPEN NATIONAL HUNT FLAT RACE 2m 110y
3:30 (3:30) (Class 6) 4-6-Y-O **£1,711** (£498; £249)

Form RPR

1 **Star Lily (IRE)** 4-10-12 0.. JamesReveley 102+
(Keith Reveley) *hld up in rr: stdy hdwy 6f out: led gng wl over 2f out: r.o wl: comf* **13/2**[3]

2 3 **Shanendou (IRE)**[186] 4-10-12 0.. PaddyBrennan 99+
(Tom George) *hld up in mid-div: hdwy 6f out: chsng wnr over 1f out: hung lft: no imp* **6/1**[2]

3 3 1/2 **Conjola** 6-10-12 0.. RichieMcGrath 93
(Geoffrey Harker) *in rr: hdwy 8f out: outpcd over 3f out: styd on: tk 3rd over 1f out: kpt on* **40/1**

4/6- 4 2 **Shankhouse Wells (IRE)**[203] 173 5-10-12 0......................... RyanMania 91
(George Charlton) *rr-div: hdwy 6f out: sn drvn and wl outpcd: hdwy over 2f out: styd on wl to take 4th nr fin* **33/1**

5 3/4 **Sheilas Lady** 5-10-9 0.. JohnKington(3) 90
(Andrew Crook) *chsd ldrs: drvn and lost pl 7f out: styd on u.p fnl 2f* **100/1**

00- 6 2 1/4 **Viking Mistress**[18] 2368 5-10-12 0.. TomSiddall 88
(Martin Keighley) *hld up in mid-div: hdwy to trck ldrs7f out: drvn over 4f out: wknd 2f out* **40/1**

0/- 7 1 1/2 **Spinning Away**[308] 3792 5-10-12 0................................... LucyAlexander 89
(N W Alexander) *chsd ldr: upsides after 6f: led over 3f out: hdd over 2f out: wknd over 1f out: eased towards fin* **40/1**

2- 8 8 **Makadamia**[21] 2298 4-10-12 0.. TomScudamore 84+
(David Pipe) *trckd ldrs: upsides 3f out: sn rdn: wknd over 1f out* **8/11**[1]

535- 9 3 3/4 **Lacocodanza**[34] 2037 4-10-7 0.. JoeColliver(5) 75
(George Moore) *led: hdd over 3f out: sn wknd* **22/1**

10 5 **Silver Storm** 5-10-9 0... EwanWhillans(3) 70
(Tristan Davidson) *chsd ldrs: lost pl over 5f out* **20/1**

0- 11 8 **Lymm Grey**[46] 1869 4-10-12 0... DominicElsworth 62
(Jo Davis) *chsd ldrs: lost pl 6f out* **66/1**

12 13 **Cashed That** 4-10-12 0... HarrySkelton 49
(Dan Skelton) *chsd ldrs: pushed along 6f out: lost pl over 4f out* **16/1**

13 1/2 **Just Chilly** 4-10-5 0... CraigNichol(7) 48
(Lucinda Russell) *mid-div: lost pl over 5f out: sn bhd* **14/1**

5/ 14 72 **Annie's Daughter**[279] 4354 6-10-12 0............................. AndrewThornton
(Lynn Siddall) *chsd ldrs: lost pl 9f out: sn wl bhd: t.o 6f out: eventually completed* **150/1**

3m 56.6s (6.40) **Going Correction** +0.15s/f (Yiel) **14 Ran SP% 120.6**
Speed ratings: **90,88,86,86,85 84,83,80,78,76 72,66,65,32**
toteswingers 1&2 £6.00, 1&3 £48.10, 2&3 £49.70 CSF £41.79 TOTE £10.30: £2.50, £2.60, £9.70; EX 36.20 Trifecta £1532.60 Part won. Pool: £2043.51 - 0.46 winning units..
Owner I Valentine **Bred** Mr And Mrs R A St George **Trained** Lingdale, Redcar & Cleveland

FOCUS
It's hard to know what to make of this form, although it was run at a sound gallop. The fourth and sixth are the best guides.
T/Plt: £17.90. Pool: £53,900.88 - 2190.77 winning units. T/Qpdt: £6.60. Pool: £4770.05 - 530.20 winning units. WG

NEWBURY (L-H)
Thursday, November 28

OFFICIAL GOING: Good to soft (soft in places on hurdle course; good in places on chase course)
Wind: Virtually nil Weather: Overcast

2753 BET365 NOVICES' HURDLE (8 hdls) 2m 110y
12:25 (12:25) (Class 3) 4-Y-0+ **£6,256** (£1,848; £924; £462)

Form RPR

1- 1 **Volnay De Thaix (FR)**[24] 2265 4-11-8 0......................... BarryGeraghty 123+
(Nicky Henderson) *mde all: clr fr 3 out: nvr off bridle* **1/16**[1]

/50- 2 7 **The Master Remover (IRE)**[14] 2467 4-11-0 0............... MarcGoldstein 94
(Chris Gordon) *chsd wnr thrght: nvr any ch and rdn fr 3 out: hit last: styd on u.p for wl hld 2nd* **100/1**

00- 3 2 1/2 **Peak Storm**[7] 2614 4-10-7 0.. CiaranMckee(7) 93
(John O'Shea) *chsd ldrs in 4th: rdn and hit 3 out: nvr nr: blnd 2 out and sn tk 3rd: nvr any ch w v easy wnr and no imp on 2nd run-in* **33/1**[3]

4 23 **Pelmanism**[30] 6-11-0 0... DougieCostello 78
(Brian Ellison) *racd in 3rd: rdn 3 out and nvr nr v easy wnr: blnd 2 out and sn wknd into 4th* **14/1**[2]

4m 11.44s (1.44) **Going Correction** -0.275s/f (Good) **4 Ran SP% 104.7**
Speed ratings (Par 107): **85,81,80,69**
CSF £6.68 TOTE £1.10; EX 8.60 Trifecta £16.10 Pool: £2381.11 - 110.32 winning units..
Owner Mrs Judy Wilson **Bred** Michel Bourgneuf **Trained** Upper Lambourn, Berks

FOCUS
Bends set out wide on both tracks. Finian's Rainbow and Prospect Wells have taken this contest in recent times, so the winner is entitled to respect when tried in better company. He had little to beat in what was a weak novice for the track.

2754 BURGES SALMON AMATEUR RIDERS' H'CAP CHASE (21 fncs) 3m 2f 110y
12:55 (12:55) (Class 3) (0-125,125) 4-Y-0+
£5,996 (£1,873; £936; £468; £234; £118)

Form RPR

1/4- 1 **Top Dancer (FR)**[22] 2297 6-11-1 114..................................... MrJJCodd 126+
(Warren Greatrex) *trckd ldrs wnt 2nd after 17th: led appr 2 out: pushed along and styd on strly run-in* **15/8**[1]

213- 2 3 **Susquehanna River (IRE)**[32] 2099 6-10-10 114............... MrBGibbs(5) 120
(Nigel Twiston-Davies) *j. to rt at times: led to 5th: led again 6th to 10th: led next: hit 13th: jnd 15th to 16th: rdn 4 out: hdd appr 2 out: sn outpcd by wnr: wl hld whn hit last* **11/2**

4F2- 3 6 **Polisky (FR)**[5] 2662 6-11-7 120..(bt[1]) MrWBiddick 122
(Paul Nicholls) *t.k.h: hld up towards rr but in tch: hdwy to cl on ldrs 17th: tk 3rd 4 out: rdn next: no imp whn j. slowly 2 out and styd on same pce* **9/4**[2]

P/0- 4 12 **Cnoc Seoda (IRE)**[55] 1745 8-11-5 125............................(t) MrGBranton(7) 115
(Paul Henderson) *in rr: hit 9th: hdwy 15th: hit 17th and lost pl: styd on 3 out but nvr nr ldrs: no ch fr 2 out* **33/1**

F/6- 5 3 **Milarrow (IRE)**[37] 2014 6-10-11 115.................................. MrMLegg(5) 103
(Colin Tizzard) *j.rt: mstke 1st: in rr: hdwy 12th: j. slowly next: blnd 15th: hit 4 out and wl bhd: no ch fr 2 out but kpt on run-in* **5/1**[3]

6/3- 6 1 **Doubletoilntrouble (IRE)**[10] 2560 7-9-9 101............(bt) MrHBeswick(7) 85
(Fergal O'Brien) *tendency to jump rt: pressed ldr: led 5th to next: led 10th to 11th: chal 15th to 16th: wknd 4 out: no ch whn hit last* **10/1**

6m 47.48s (1.48) **Going Correction** -0.075s/f (Good) **6 Ran SP% 109.6**
Speed ratings (Par 107): **94,93,91,87,86 86**
toteswingers 1&2 £1.90, 2&3 £1.80, 1&3 £1.40 CSF £11.87 TOTE £2.70: £1.60, £2.50; EX 8.30 Trifecta £20.10 Pool: £2013.34 - 74.92 winning units..
Owner The Lone Star Partnership **Bred** E R Hanbury **Trained** Upper Lambourn, Berks

FOCUS
Most of these had something to prove, so this isn't likely to be strong form, although the pace seemed decent for a small field. A big step up from the decisive winner and there should be more to come.

2755 BET365.COM NOVICES' H'CAP HURDLE (10 hdls) 2m 5f
1:30 (1:32) (Class 4) (0-120,120) 3-Y-0+ **£6,498** (£1,908; £954; £477)

Form RPR

5/1- 1 **Swinging Hawk (GER)**[8] 2598 7-10-13 112 7ex......... RobertMcCarth(5) 121+
(Ian Williams) *hld up in rr: stdy hdwy appr 2 out: wnt 3rd and rdn last: chsd ldr sn after: led fnl 150yds: drvn out* **8/1**

050/ 2 2 1/4 **Bohemian Rhapsody (IRE)**[19] 5197 4-11-2 110............ ConorO'Farrell 118
(Seamus Durack) *hld up in rr: hdwy 3 out: trckd ldrs and hit 2 out: led sn after: mstke last: hdd and no ex fnl 150yds* **7/1**[3]

4/3- **3** 2 ½ **Broomfield**[23] 2280 6-11-12 **120** DarylJacob 126
(Paul Nicholls) *hld up in rr: hdwy on bit 3 out: chal gng wl 2 out: chsd ldr sn after and rdn: sn no imp: outpce into 3rd sn after last* **16/1**

41- **4** 1 ¾ **Andy Kelly (IRE)**[28] 2181 4-11-9 **120** GavinSheehan(3) 125
(Emma Lavelle) *chsd ldrs: hit 5th: rdn and wl there 3 out: slt ld 2 out: hdd sn after: kpt on same pce* **5/1**[2]

4/2- **5** 4 **Squire Trelawney**[21] 2314 7-11-1 **109** (tp) HarrySkelton 109
(Dan Skelton) *narrow ldr at mod pce tl hdd appr 4th: styd upsides: led 6th tl after 4 out: chal 3 out to next: wknd bef last* **12/1**

/41- **6** 5 **Jojabean (IRE)**[183] 538 6-11-9 **117** RobertThornton 113
(Alan King) *chsd ldrs: chal out to next: wknd bef last* **18/1**

636- **7** ¾ **Bold Cuffs**[32] 2111 4-10-8 **102** JoeTizzard 97
(Colin Tizzard) *in rr: hdwy after 3 out: hit next: styd on but nvr gng pce to rch ldrs* **20/1**

230- **8** 2 **Daliance (IRE)**[13] 2492 4-10-13 **107** LeightonAspell 100
(Lucy Wadham) *in rr but in tch: hdwy 5th: chsd ldrs 4 out: lost pl appr 3 out: kpt on again run-in* **25/1**

453- **9** ½ **Never Says Never**[22] 2286 5-11-2 **110** SamJones 103
(Bob Buckler) *in tch: hdwy to chse ldrs 4 out: wknd 2 out* **40/1**

3F4/ **10** 3 ½ **Vico (IRE)**[606] 5197 9-11-7 **115** AidanColeman 104
(Ali Brewer) *in tch: rdn 3 out: sn btn* **100/1**

5/2- **11** 7 **Presence Felt (IRE)**[8] 2598 5-11-2 **110** (p) RichieMcLernon 93
(Jonjo O'Neill) *chsd ldrs to 3 out* **11/4**[1]

3/5- **12** 3 **Union Du Chenet (FR)**[191] 417 5-11-7 **115** (p) BarryGeraghty 95
(Nicky Henderson) *chsd ldrs: drvn to hold position after 5th: wknd 3 out* **14/1**

/43- **13** 1 ½ **I Am Colin**[27] 2189 4-11-3 **111** SamTwiston-Davies 94
(Nigel Twiston-Davies) *pressed ldr: led appr 4th: hdd and hit 6th: hit 4 out: led sn after: hdd & wknd bef 2 out* **25/1**

/33- **14** 1 ¼ **Call A Truce (IRE)**[32] 2105 5-10-11 **105** NoelFehily 83
(Ben Case) *in rr: hdwy 5th: chsd ldrs 6th: wknd bef 3 out* **7/1**[3]

5m 18.12s (-0.88) **Going Correction** -0.275s/f (Good)
WFA 4 from 5yo+ 8lb **14** Ran SP% **120.8**
Speed ratings (Par 105): **90,89,88,87,86 84,83,83,82,81 78,77,77,76**
toteswingers 1&2 £12.90, 2&3 £24.00, 1&3 £32.30 CSF £60.38 CT £890.63 TOTE £10.20: £3.10, £2.50, £5.00; EX 96.70 Trifecta £1430.90 Pool: £4384.38 - 2.29 winning units..
Owner Jamie Roberts & Jack Turton **Bred** Gestut Wittekindshof **Trained** Portway, Worcs
■ Stewards' Enquiry : Robert McCarth four-day ban: used whip above permitted level (Dec 12-15)

FOCUS
A competitive handicap, full of interesting types. The early gallop was slow, so it was a little surprising that horses who were held up dominated. The winner is rated in line with his old best.

2756 RSA WORCESTER NOVICES' CHASE (GRADE 2) (18 fncs) 3m
2:05 (2:05) (Class 1) 4-Y-O+ **£18,184** (£7,332; £4,077)

Form RPR

2/2- **1** **Just A Par (IRE)**[33] 2077 6-11-2 0 DarylJacob 155+
(Paul Nicholls) *led: jnd fr 9th tl narrowly hdd appr 14th: led again 4 out: forged clr after 2 out and r.o strly* **5/4**[1]

/13- **2** 14 **Third Intention (IRE)**[19] 2374 6-11-9 151 (t) JoeTizzard 144
(Colin Tizzard) *chsd ldrs: disputing 2nd whn n.m.r 4 out: chsd wnr next: sn rdn: chal next: no ch u.p sn after but wl clr of 3rd* **11/8**[2]

0/2- **3** 16 **Ardkilly Witness (IRE)**[15] 2459 7-11-2 134 SamTwiston-Davies 129
(Dr Richard Newland) *chsd: chal fr 9th: j.rt fr next: led appr 14th: hdd 4 out and veered rt: btn in 3rd whn j. bdly rt and collided w opponent 3 out* **6/1**[3]

/U1- **U** **Le Reve (IRE)**[25] 2249 5-11-6 134 LeightonAspell 133
(Lucy Wadham) *in tch: chsd ldrs fr 14th and wl there 4 out: rdn and one pce in 3 l 3rd whn bdly bmpd in mid-air and uns rdr 3 out* **14/1**

P6- **U** **Typical Oscar (IRE)**[15] 2459 6-11-2 0 ConorO'Farrell
(Michael Blake) *chsng ldrs whn blnd and uns rdr 2nd* **150/1**

5m 54.39s (-11.61) **Going Correction** -0.075s/f (Good) **5** Ran SP% **108.2**
Speed ratings (Par 115): **116,111,106, ,**
CSF £3.36 TOTE £2.00: £1.50, £1.40; EX 3.30 Trifecta £6.00 Pool: £2160.20 - 266.09 winning units..
Owner C G Roach & Paul K Barber **Bred** Sean Whelan **Trained** Ditcheat, Somerset

FOCUS
Not a great deal happened before the fourth-last, where the remaining four runners jumped it in unison. A big step up from the winner on his Chepstow run and he looks a smart novice.

2757 BET365 NOVICES' LIMITED H'CAP CHASE (17 fncs) 2m 6f 110y
2:40 (2:40) (Class 3) (0-140,140) 4-Y-£7,507 (£2,217; £1,108; £554; £277)

Form RPR

0/4- **1** **Easter Day (FR)**[47] 1865 5-11-0 **135** DarylJacob 147+
(Paul Nicholls) *trckd ldr: slt ld 4th to next: styd cl 2nd: chalng whn stmbld 3 out: chal again next: led bef last: drvn clr: readily* **5/4**[1]

0/ **2** 6 **Whats Happening (IRE)**[144] 915 6-11-2 **137** (t) PaddyBrennan 141+
(Tom George) *blnd 2nd: chsd ldrs: hit 11th and 13th: styd on u.p in 3rd fr 4 out: tk 2nd fnl 25yds but no ch w wnr* **11/2**[3]

/S1- **3** nk **Sergeant Dick (IRE)**[18] 2389 8-10-5 **126** (t) SamTwiston-Davies 128
(Barry Brennan) *j.rt early: led to 4th: led again 5th: jnd 3 out tl hdd bef last: no ch w wnr and lost 2nd fnl 25yds* **6/1**

4/1- **4** 6 **Renard D'Irlande (FR)**[12] 2508 8-10-6 **127** AidanColeman 128
(Venetia Williams) *in tch: hdwy 13th: rdn appr 4 out and mstke: wknd fr 3 out* **11/4**[2]

133- **5** 52 **Harry Hunt**[28] 2180 6-10-7 **128** RobertThornton 93
(Graeme McPherson) *chsd ldrs: j.rt: rdn and blnd 12th: wl btn whn veered bdly rt and mstkes fnl 4 fences* **8/1**

5m 39.93s (-7.07) **Going Correction** -0.075s/f (Good) **5** Ran SP% **111.9**
Speed ratings (Par 107): **109,106,106,104,86**
CSF £8.53 TOTE £2.10: £1.40, £1.80; EX 9.60 Trifecta £37.40 Pool: £2483.13 - 49.68 winning units..
Owner B Fulton, Broughton Thermal Insulation **Bred** Pierre De Maleissye Melun **Trained** Ditcheat, Somerset

FOCUS
A decent novices' handicap chase. A big step up from the winner on the form of his chase debut and there should be more to come.

2758 BET365 INTERMEDIATE HURDLE (LIMITED H'CAP) (REGISTERED AS THE GERRY FEILDEN HURDLE) (LISTED RACE) (8 hdls) 2m 110y
3:15 (3:15) (Class 1) (0-155,146)£20,026 (£7,573; £3,838; £1,959; £1,031)

/30- **1** **Ifandbutwhynot (IRE)**[11] 2533 7-10-11 **133** TimmyMurphy 139+
(David O'Meara) *mde all: rdn and styd on strly after 2 out: kpt on wl run-in* **8/1**[3]

114/ **2** 4 ½ **Chatterbox (IRE)**[260] 4733 5-11-7 **143** BarryGeraghty 144
(Nicky Henderson) *chsd ldrs: disp 2nd 3 out tl chsd wnr fr next: no imp but styd on wl to hold 2nd cl home* **5/2**[1]

0/2- **3** shd **Chris Pea Green**[26] 2213 4-11-3 **142** JoshuaMoore(3) 144
(Gary Moore) *in tch: hdwy to chse ldrs fr 3f out: kpt on u.p run-in to press for 2nd in clsng stages but nvr any ch w wnr* **9/2**[2]

241/ **4** 6 **Fleet Dawn**[243] 5013 7-10-7 **129** (t) DougieCostello 126
(Brian Ellison) *in tch rdn 3 out: styd on same pce fr next* **25/1**

255/ **5** 3 ½ **Puffin Billy (IRE)**[225] 5350 5-11-10 **146** LeightonAspell 139
(Oliver Sherwood) *chsd wnr: rdn after 3 out: wknd 2 out* **5/2**[1]

P/R- **P** **Lordofthehouse (IRE)**[46] 1889 5-10-7 **129** PaddyBrennan
(Tom George) *rel to r: sn t.o: p.u bef 3rd* **40/1**

213/ **F** **Irish Saint (FR)**[238] 5135 4-11-7 **143** DarylJacob 140
(Paul Nicholls) *in tch: hdwy to chse ldrs 3 out: rdn and one pce next: hld disputing 8 l 4th whn fell last* **8/1**[3]

21/ **U** **Get Back In Line (IRE)**[300] 3972 5-10-5 **127** RichieMcLernon 121
(Jonjo O'Neill) *hld up in rr: sme hdwy whn blnd and uns rdr 2 out* **8/1**[3]

4m 0.42s (-9.58) **Going Correction** -0.275s/f (Good)
WFA 4 from 5yo+ 7lb **8** Ran SP% **114.9**
Speed ratings (Par 111): **111,108,108,106,104 , ,**
toteswingers 1&2 £5.50, 2&3 £3.60, 1&3 £6.30 CSF £29.27 CT £102.44 TOTE £10.00: £2.60, £1.50, £1.50; EX 38.70 Trifecta £192.30 Pool: £4441.47 - 17.31 winning units..
Owner Claire Hollowood & Henry Dean **Bred** John Weld And Mrs Gay Veitch **Trained** Nawton, N Yorks

FOCUS
This is historically a decent contest, but it appeared to be run at an ordinary gallop. The winner and third set the level.

2759 BET365.COM STANDARD OPEN NATIONAL HUNT FLAT RACE 2m 110y
3:45 (3:45) (Class 4) 4-6-Y-O **£3,249** (£954; £477; £238)

Form RPR

4- **1** **Thomas Brown**[47] 1869 4-11-0 0 NoelFehily 119+
(Harry Fry) *chsd ldrs in 3rd: wnt 2nd 4f out: led ins fnl 3f: rdn and styd on strly fnl 2f* **15/8**[1]

2 11 **Maestro Royal** 4-11-0 0 BarryGeraghty 109+
(Nicky Henderson) *t.k.h early: hdwy 4f out: drvn to chse wnr fnl 2f but no imp: styd on same pce for 2nd* **9/4**[2]

5/4- **3** 1 ¾ **Fred Le Macon (FR)**[202] 207 4-11-0 0 RobertThornton 106
(Alan King) *in rr: rdn over 2f out: styd on to take 3rd ins fnl f: clsng on wnr fnl 100yds but nvr any ch w wnr* **14/1**

2- **4** 7 **Red Devil Lads (IRE)**[30] 2153 4-11-0 0 NickScholfield 104
(Rebecca Curtis) *led: clr whn hung rt on bnd after 2f and jnd: clr again 10f out: rdn 4f out: hdd ins fnl 3f: wknd 2f out* **3/1**[3]

4/- **5** 3 ¼ **Arthur Mc Bride (IRE)**[231] 5262 4-11-0 0 PaddyBrennan 98
(Fergal O'Brien) *in tch: hdwy to chse ldrs 5f out: disp 2nd over 3f out: wknd over 1f out* **10/1**

6 7 **Run On Sterling** 4-11-0 0 RichieMcLernon 89
(Paul Webber) *disp ld whn ldr hung rt after 2f: styd in 2nd to 4f out: sn btn* **20/1**

3m 57.0s (-7.30) **Going Correction** -0.275s/f (Good) **6** Ran SP% **111.1**
Speed ratings: **106,100,100,96,95 91**
toteswingers 1&2 £1.30, 2&3 £4.00, 1&3 £2.60 CSF £6.22 TOTE £3.10: £1.30, £1.50; EX 6.60 Trifecta £42.80 Pool: £3245.83 - 56.84 winning units..
Owner The Corse Lawners **Bred** Elms Stud Co Ltd **Trained** Seaborough, Dorset

FOCUS
Some nice horses have taken this in the past, and Harry Fry took it for the second year in a row. A big step up from the impressive winner, who looks decent.
T/Plt: £33.10 to a £1 stake. Pool of £65191.63 - 1435.23 winning tickets. T/Qpdt: £24.10 to a £1 stake.Pool of £4602.20 - 141.30 winning tickets. ST

2473 TAUNTON (R-H)
Thursday, November 28

OFFICIAL GOING: Good
Wind: virtually nil Weather: overcast

2760 FOLLOW TAUNTON RACECOURSE ON FACEBOOK (S) HURDLE (9 hdls) 2m 1f
12:35 (12:35) (Class 5) 4-Y-O+ **£2,053** (£598; £299)

Form RPR

035- **1** **Gigondas**[38] 2006 4-10-12 105 (b[1]) JamieMoore 104
(Gary Moore) *j.w: mde all: rdn appr 2 out: kpt on strly fr last: drvn out* **7/1**[3]

046- **2** 2 ¾ **James Pollard (IRE)**[4] 2698 8-11-0 113 (tp) RobertWilliams(5) 109
(Bernard Llewellyn) *trckd wnr: rdn to chal whn nt so fluent as wnr 2 out: kpt on same pce fr last* **16/1**

214- **3** 4 **Bollin Judith**[14] 2477 7-10-12 118 (t) RichardJohnson 99
(Jim Best) *mid-div: hdwy 3 out: rdn to chse wnr briefly bef next: sn hld in 3rd: kpt on same pce* **8/11**[1]

0/0- **4** 1 ¾ **Pearl (IRE)**[4] 2690 9-10-5 74 ColinBolger 90
(Ron Hodges) *mid-div: rdn after 3 out: wnt 4th between last 2: styd on but nt gng pce to rch ldrs* **20/1**

36P- **5** 20 **Captain Sharpe**[7] 2617 5-10-9 97 (t) MarkQuinlan(3) 87
(Bernard Llewellyn) *trckd wnr: mstke 6th: sn rdn: wkng whn lost 4th between last 2* **20/1**

150- **6** 8 **Advisor (FR)**[28] 2176 7-11-5 106 TommyPhelan 79
(Mark Gillard) *in tch: trckd ldr 3rd tl rdn after 5th: wknd after 3 out* **40/1**

/P4- **7** shd **King Ozzy (IRE)**[10] 2569 9-10-5 109 (tp) CharlieDeutsch(7) 72
(Lawney Hill) *trckd ldrs tl 3rd: in tch: rdn after 5th: wknd bef 2 out* **12/1**

256- **8** 34 **Spice Hill (IRE)**[67] 1635 7-10-7 83 CharlieWallis(5) 41
(Nick Ayliffe) *struggling 4th: a bhd: t.o* **100/1**

125- **9** 7 **Ajman (IRE)**[30] 2150 8-10-5 105 (t) ConorRing(7) 35
(Evan Williams) *mid-div tl wknd 3 out: t.o* **7/2**[2]

4m 0.1s (-7.90) **Going Correction** -0.175s/f (Good)
WFA 4 from 5yo+ 7lb **9** Ran SP% **119.2**
Speed ratings (Par 103): **111,109,107,107,97 93,93,77,74**
toteswingers 1&2 £14.60, 2&3 £5.30, 1&3 £1.90 CSF £94.87 TOTE £7.10: £2.50, £4.30, £1.10; EX 75.70 Trifecta £182.30 Pool: £2241.28 - 9.10 winning units..There was no bid for the winner.
Owner C E Stedman **Bred** C E Stedman **Trained** Lower Beeding, W Sussex
■ Lady Oaksey was withdrawn. Price at time of withdrawal 100/1. Rule 4 does not apply.
■ Stewards' Enquiry : Robert Williams two-day ban: used whip above permitted level (Dec 12-13)

The Form Book Jumps, Raceform Ltd, Compton, RG20 6NL.

FOCUS
Both bends moved out by 3-4m and hurdles moved out by two sections. Few got into this ordinary seller. The first two set the level with the third a stone+ off.

2761 WRAXALL VINEYARD "NATIONAL HUNT" NOVICES' HURDLE (10 hdls) 2m 3f 110y
1:05 (1:08) (Class 4) 4-Y-0+ **£4,106** (£1,197; £598)

Form				RPR
1/1-	**1**		**The Skyfarmer**[48] 1856 5-11-5 0 RichardJohnson (Philip Hobbs) *trckd ldr: shkn up to chal 2 out: slt ld last: styd on strly: rdn out* **8/11**[1]	118+
40-	**2**	2	**Badger Wood**[28] 2181 4-10-12 0 DavidEngland (Giles Smyly) *led at stdy pce: qcknd after 5th: hrd pressed 2 out: sn rdn: narrowly hdd last: kpt on but no ex* **66/1**	108
24/	**3**	1 1/4	**Elmore Back (IRE)**[223] 5388 4-10-12 0 MarkGrant (Charlie Mann) *trckd ldrs: rdn to chal 2 out: ev ch whn nodded last: kpt on same pce* **14/1**	107
2/4-	**4**	9	**Presenting The Way**[25] 2254 6-10-12 0 RyanMahon (Harry Fry) *trckd ldrs: rdn after 3 out: kpt on same pce fr next* **6/1**[3]	98
6/	**5**	nk	**Prasina Russata (IRE)**[703] 3317 6-10-12 0 TomScudamore (David Pipe) *mid-div: rdn after 3 out: styd on same pce fr next* **25/1**	98
50-	**6**	3/4	**The Wealerdealer (IRE)**[14] 2476 6-10-5 0 MrMHeard(7) (David Pipe) *mid-div: rdn after 3 out: styd on same pce* **16/1**	98
305-	**7**	2 1/4	**Very Noble (FR)**[19] 2369 4-10-12 0 (t) NickScholfield (Paul Nicholls) *mid-div: rdn to dispute 4th appr 2 out: wknd run-in* **7/2**[2]	96
/40-	**8**	6	**Famousandfearless (IRE)**[14] 2476 5-10-5 0 MikeyEnnis(7) (David Pipe) *mid-div: hit 6th: rdn after 3 out: sn outpcd* **25/1**	89
0/0-	**9**	20	**Forrardon Xmoor**[7] 2614 4-10-12 0 WillKennedy (Miss Jessica Westwood) *mid-div tl wknd after 3 out* **100/1**	69
0-	**10**	2 1/2	**Baksheesh**[180] 589 4-10-9 0 JamesBest(3) (Sue Gardner) *struggling 7th: a towards rr: t.o* **100/1**	66
430-	**11**	12	**Bandol (IRE)**[19] 2375 5-10-12 0 TomCannon (Laura Young) *a towards rr: t.o* **100/1**	54
3/0-	**U**		**Party Girls (FR)**[36] 2022 5-9-12 0 (t) KieronEdgar(7) (David Pipe) *t.k.h: hld up in last: nt a fluent: blnd and uns rdr 7th* **50/1**	

4m 49.8s (3.80) **Going Correction** -0.175s/f (Good)
WFA 4 from 5yo+ 7lb 12 Ran SP% **121.1**
Speed ratings (Par 105): **85,84,83,80,79 79,78,76,68,67 62,**
toteswingers 1&2 £16.30, 2&3 £35.20, 1&3 £4.00 CSF £85.62 TOTE £1.80: £1.10, £9.10, £2.30; EX 56.60 Trifecta £421.60 Pool: £3278.81 - 5.83 winning units..
Owner Mrs Joanna Peppiatt **Bred** Barkfold Manor Stud **Trained** Withycombe, Somerset

FOCUS
An uncompetitive novice hurdle run at a steady pace. The form is suspect with the winner below his best.

2762 TAUNTON RACECOURSE OWNERS CLUB NOVICES' LIMITED H'CAP CHASE (11 fncs 1 omitted) 2m 110y
1:40 (1:42) (Class 3) (0-125,123) 4-Y-0+ **£6,498** (£1,908; £954; £477)

Form				RPR
200/	**1**		**Workbench (FR)**[236] 5185 5-10-9 **113** (t) RyanMahon (Dan Skelton) *mde all: pushed along and in command fr 2 out (usual 3 out): kpt on wl* **10/1**	126+
411-	**2**	8	**Be All Man (IRE)**[16] 2440 6-11-4 **122** JamieMoore (Gary Moore) *chsd wnr: bmpd 3 out: sn rdn: kpt on but a being hld fr next* **9/2**[2]	128
/64-	**3**	1	**Bullet Street (IRE)**[14] 2469 5-10-11 **115** PaulMoloney (Evan Williams) *trckd ldrs: hit 5th: disputing 2nd whn j.rt and bmpd 3 out (usual 4 out): sn rdn: kpt on same pce fr next tl no ex run-in* **2/1**[1]	118
103-	**4**	10	**Alwaystheoptimist**[16] 2434 10-10-12 **123** RyanHatch(7) (Phil Middleton) *hld up: rdn after 7th: hit next: wnt 4th 2 out (usual 3 out) but no ch w ldrs* **13/2**	120
/41-	**5**	18	**Gandalfe (FR)**[25] 2251 8-10-10 **114** (b) AndrewThornton (David Arbuthnot) *trckd wnr: nt fluent 3rd: hit 7th: rdn after 3 out (usual 4 out): wknd next: t.o* **7/1**	92
463-	**6**	14	**Violets Boy (IRE)**[24] 2270 6-10-8 **112** AndrewTinkler (Brendan Powell) *hld up: hmpd 4th: detached and nvr travelling after: t.o* **8/1**	77
/33-	**U**		**Elsafeer (IRE)**[19] 2363 8-11-0 **118** RichardJohnson (Tim Vaughan) *hld up: blnd bdly and uns rdr 4th* **11/2**[3]	

4m 7.9s (-6.10) **Going Correction** -0.175s/f (Good) 7 Ran SP% **112.9**
Speed ratings (Par 107): **107,103,102,98,89 83,**
toteswingers 1&2 £8.60, 2&3 £2.50, 1&3 £7.30 CSF £52.79 TOTE £18.20: £6.30, £1.80; EX 59.00 Trifecta £772.60 Pool: £2319.94 - 2.25 winning units..
Owner N W Lake **Bred** M Bernard Le Roux **Trained** Alcester, Warwicks

FOCUS
The second-last fence was bypassed. A modest novice handicap. The winner is rated up a stone on the best of his hurdle figures.

2763 MICHAEL SPIERS JEWELLERS MARES' H'CAP HURDLE (9 hdls) 2m 1f
2:15 (2:16) (Class 3) (0-135,135) 3-Y-0+ **£5,848** (£1,717; £858; £429)

Form				RPR
532-	**1**		**Pass The Time**[14] 2477 4-10-2 **111** (p) RichardJohnson (Neil Mulholland) *trckd ldrs: squeezed through gap to ld and wandered appr 2 out: in command whn wnt lft last: r.o wl: rdn out* **9/2**	120+
120/	**2**	11	**She Ranks Me (IRE)**[261] 4723 6-11-12 **135** (p) JasonMaguire (Donald McCain) *nvr travelling bhd ldrs: hdwy after 5th: hrd rdn after 3 out: led briefly bef next: hld bef last: kpt on same pce* **11/4**[2]	133
00/	**3**	1	**Stone Light (FR)**[242] 5031 5-10-9 **118** LiamTreadwell (Venetia Williams) *led tl 6th: kpt pressing ldr: rdn and v ch bef 2 out: sn hld: kpt on same pce* **15/8**[1]	114
12P-	**4**	10	**Fairyinthewind (IRE)**[28] 1697 4-10-11 **120** AndrewTinkler (Brendan Powell) *trckd ldr: led 6th: rdn and hdd appr 2 out: wknd last* **10/1**	109
6/6-	**5**	14	**Western Approaches**[35] 2045 6-10-0 **109** oh2 (t) TomScudamore (Ian Williams) *trckd ldr tl pushed along after 5th: rdn after next: sn btn* **4/1**[3]	84

4m 1.1s (-6.90) **Going Correction** -0.175s/f (Good)
WFA 4 from 5yo+ 7lb 5 Ran SP% **108.7**
Speed ratings (Par 107): **109,103,103,98,92**
CSF £16.70 TOTE £4.90: £2.70, £1.10; EX 10.30 Trifecta £23.80 Pool: £2822.99 - 88.77 winning units..
Owner Dajam Ltd **Bred** M Burbidge **Trained** Limpley Stoke, Wilts

FOCUS
A fair mares' handicap run in a slower time than the seller. The winner probably didn't need to improve on her recent course run with nothing else really performing.

2764 FOLLOW TAUNTON RACECOURSE ON TWITTER NOVICES' H'CAP HURDLE (12 hdls) 3m 110y
2:50 (2:53) (Class 4) (0-115,115) 4-Y-0+ **£4,106** (£1,197; £598)

Form				RPR
423-	**1**		**King Boru (IRE)**[53] 1797 5-11-12 **115** RichardJohnson (Emma Lavelle) *hld up in tch: hdwy 3 out: str chal fr 2 out: rdn whn nt fluent last: kpt on but looking to edge rt: won on nod* **7/2**[2]	123+
213-	**2**	shd	**Listen And Learn (IRE)**[35] 2050 5-11-6 **114** (p) MauriceLinehan(5) (Jonjo O'Neill) *trckd ldrs: tk narrow advantage bef 2 out: rdn and strly pressed sn after: nt fluent last: edgd lft briefly fnl 75yds: kpt on: lost on nod* **11/4**[1]	121+
413-	**3**	13	**Letemgo (IRE)**[26] 2210 5-11-10 **113** DavidEngland (Giles Smyly) *disp tl 5th: trckd ldrs: rdn after 3 out: wnt 3rd bef last: styd on same pce* **13/2**	107
133/	**4**	6	**Airmen's Friend (IRE)**[480] 1193 7-10-11 **100** (tp) MarkGrant (Charlie Mann) *hld up: hdwy appr 3 out: rdn to chse ldrs bef 2 out: styd on same pce* **20/1**	89
626-	**5**	2 1/2	**Kayalar (IRE)**[16] 2449 5-10-9 **98** PaulMoloney (Evan Williams) *hld up in tch: trcking ldrs whn hit 3 out: sn rdn: nvr threatened: kpt on same pce* **10/1**	86
0/0-	**6**	6	**Bladoun (FR)**[15] 2458 5-11-12 **115** (tp) TomScudamore (David Pipe) *trckd ldrs: disp fr 6th: rdn after 3 out: hdd bef next: wknd bef last* **11/2**	97
00F-	**7**	34	**Puerto Azul (IRE)**[14] 2473 9-9-13 **91** JamesBest(3) (Bernard Scriven) *taken to s early: hld up towards rr: rdn after 8th: nt fluent next: wknd after 3 out: t.o* **33/1**	42
513-	**P**		**Magic Money**[14] 2476 5-11-3 **106** JasonMaguire (Kim Bailey) *trckd ldrs: hit 6th: wknd qckly after 3 out: p.u bef next* **5/1**[3]	
1/0-	**P**		**Ballybach (IRE)**[26] 2210 9-11-9 **112** TomCannon (Nick Gifford) *disp ld tl rdn and hdd after 3 out: wkng whn eased and p.u bef next* **28/1**	

5m 59.6s (-4.40) **Going Correction** -0.175s/f (Good) 9 Ran SP% **114.5**
Speed ratings (Par 105): **100,99,95,93,93 91,80, ,**
toteswingers 1&2 £2.60, 2&3 £4.60, 1&3 £5.00 CSF £13.47 CT £58.45 TOTE £4.30: £1.50, £1.30, £1.90; EX 14.60 Trifecta £85.90 Pool: £3552.17 - 30.99 winning units..
Owner Lavelle Wallis Farrington **Bred** John O'Mahony **Trained** Hatherden, Hants
■ Stewards' Enquiry : Mark Grant one-day ban: careless riding (Dec 12)
Maurice Linehan one-day ban: careless riding (Dec 16)

FOCUS
A moderate staying handicap in which the first two are on the upgrade.

2765 XMAS FAIR 12TH DECEMBER H'CAP CHASE (THE £5K BONUS RACE) (17 fncs) 2m 7f 110y
3:25 (3:25) (Class 5) (0-100,100) 4-Y-0+ **£3,422** (£997; £499)

Form				RPR
4P1-	**1**		**Milosam (IRE)**[14] 2478 6-9-12 **75** (b1) JamesBest(3) (Philip Hobbs) *disp ld: clr ldr whn nt fluent and wnt lft 7th: rdn and hrd pressed fr after 4 out: sticking to task whn lft wl clr 2 out: mstke last* **2/1**[1]	90+
26F-	**2**	28	**Flugzeug**[11] 2540 5-9-9 **76** KevinJones(7) (Seamus Mullins) *hld up: hdwy into 4th after 13th: sn rdn: no ch after 4 out: wnt 3rd whn lft modest 2nd 2 out* **10/1**	64
250/	**3**	2 1/4	**Brandon Thomas (IRE)**[321] 3599 7-11-12 **100** TomCannon (Nick Gifford) *hld up in tch: trckd ldrs: wnt 3rd 12th: rdn after 4 out: sn hld by front pair: jst dropped to 4th whn lft 3rd 2 out: styd on same pce* **12/1**	86
/6F-	**4**	20	**Rozolenn (FR)**[11] 2540 8-11-1 **94** HarryChalloner(5) (Venetia Williams) *hld up in tch: nt fluent 4th: rdn after 11th: blnd next: wknd after 4 out: lft poor 4th 2 out* **9/4**[2]	62
23-	**5**	5	**Landenstown Star (IRE)**[24] 2278 8-11-7 **95** (tp) TommyPhelan (Mark Gillard) *trckd ldrs: nt fluent 1st: struggling 13th: wknd after 4 out: t.o* **20/1**	58
0/5-	**6**	2 3/4	**Gingers Reflection**[15] 2460 7-10-11 **92** (t) JonPark(7) (Carroll Gray) *nt a fluent: chsd ldrs tl 7th: pushed along after 10th: rdn after next: wknd after 12th: t.o* **10/1**	53
514-	**F**		**Midnight Lira**[15] 2462 6-11-7 **95** IanPopham (Caroline Keevil) *disp tl 7th: trckd wnr: chal again 4 out: nudged along but gng sltly bttr than wnr whn fell 2 out* **5/1**[3]	107

6m 6.6s (-9.40) **Going Correction** -0.175s/f (Good) 7 Ran SP% **111.4**
Speed ratings (Par 103): **108,98,97,91,89 88,**
toteswingers 1&2 £4.80, 2&3 £14.00, 1&3 £4.90 CSF £20.04 TOTE £2.80: £1.80, £5.90; EX 14.90 Trifecta £190.70 Pool: £2431.47 - 9.56 winning units..
Owner Rob Croker **Bred** James Canty **Trained** Withycombe, Somerset

FOCUS
A weak handicap with a dramatic conclusion. The winner would probably have won anyway although the faller looked to be heading for a personal best.

2766 INDEPENDENT RACECOURSES LTD H'CAP HURDLE (10 hdls) 2m 3f 110y
3:55 (3:58) (Class 5) (0-95,102) 4-Y-0+ **£2,737** (£798; £399)

Form				RPR
0/0-	**1**		**Sylvan Legend**[54] 1764 5-10-5 **74** IanPopham (Caroline Keevil) *trckd ldrs: rdn after 3 out: led last: kpt on: drvn out* **4/1**[2]	81
601-	**2**	3/4	**Dalrymple (IRE)**[5] 2679 7-10-6 **80** (t) CharlieWallis(5) (Nick Ayliffe) *mid-div: rdn along fr 7th: hdwy after 3 out: styd on fr next: fin wl to go 2nd towards fin but nvr quite reeling in wnr* **11/8**[1]	87+
003-	**3**	1	**Chankillo**[10] 2559 4-11-4 **87** WillKennedy (Sarah-Jayne Davies) *led tl 5th: prom: rdn after 3 out: led bef next: hdd last: kpt on but no ex: lost 2nd towards fin* **12/1**	92
01F-	**4**	1/2	**The Game Is A Foot (IRE)**[5] 2679 6-11-9 **102** 7ex LeeOswin(10) (Gary Moore) *hld up towards rr: hdwy after 3 out: rdn to chse ldrs bef next: styd on same pce* **5/1**[3]	107
/P3-	**5**	4	**Midnight Choice**[17] 2427 8-10-5 **74** LiamTreadwell (James Evans) *mid-div: pushed along after 5th: rdn after 7th: styd on fr 2 out: nvr trbld ldrs* **10/1**	75
P/P-	**6**	1 1/2	**Shades Of Autumn (IRE)**[14] 2470 8-10-9 **85** (v1) MrCSmith(7) (Linda Blackford) *prom: led 5th: rdn and hdd bef 2 out: sn one pce* **40/1**	86
555-	**7**	4	**Time Book (IRE)**[14] 2478 7-10-8 **77** (bt) DaveCrosse (Colin Tizzard) *trckd ldrs: prom tl nt fluent 7th: sn rdn: one pce fr after 3 out* **20/1**	75
5/4-	**8**	15	**Leeroar (IRE)**[30] 2150 5-11-12 **95** SamJones (Jo Davis) *a towards rr* **25/1**	78
4/U-	**9**	hd	**Withy Mills**[7] 2628 8-11-2 **88** (tp) JamesBest(3) (Kevin Bishop) *trckd ldrs: rdn after 3 out: sn wknd* **18/1**	70

0/6- **10** *2 ¾* **Going Nowhere Fast (IRE)**[14] 2474 8-11-4 **92**.......... RobertWilliams(5) 72
(Bernard Llewellyn) *in tch: pushed along after 6th: rdn after next: wknd after 3 out* **10/1**

4/0- **11** *11* **Watchmetail (IRE)**[14] 2476 7-10-9 **78**................................ PaulMoloney 48
(John Panvert) *hld up towards rr: stdy prog fr after 5th: nvr rchd ldrs: rdn after 7th: sn wknd: t.o* **66/1**

26P- **12** *¾* **Bazart**[33] 2090 11-11-3 **89**..(tp) MarkQuinlan(3) 58
(Bernard Llewellyn) *mid-div: pckd bdly 6th: sn struggling: wknd bef 3 out: t.o* **33/1**

0/0- **13** *13* **Behtarini (IRE)**[199] 264 6-10-13 **82**...............................(tp) AdamWedge 40
(Richenda Ford) *mid-div tl wknd after 3 out: t.o* **25/1**

6/0- **14** *5* **Forgotten Promise**[15] 2463 6-10-5 **77**........................(t[1]) KielanWoods(3) 30
(Brian Barr) *a towards rr: t.o* **50/1**

4m 46.7s (0.70) **Going Correction** -0.175s/f (Good)
WFA 4 from 5yo+ 7lb **14** Ran SP% **131.2**
Speed ratings (Par 103): **91,90,90,90,88 87,86,80,80,79 74,74,69,67**
toteswingers 1&2 £3.60, 2&3 £6.50, 1&3 £13.70 CSF £10.49 CT £68.89 TOTE £9.30: £2.50, £1.20, £3.40; EX 18.80 Trifecta £211.60 Pool: £3541.02 - 12.55 winning units..
Owner Brian Derrick **Bred** Larkinglass Ltd **Trained** Motcombe, Dorset
■ Stewards' Enquiry : Charlie Wallis two-day ban: used whip above permitted level (Dec 12-13)

FOCUS
Not much pace on early in this moderate handicap. The winner is rated up 7lb with the third to fifth setting the level.
T/Plt: £14.40 to a £1 stake. Pool of £63940.86 - 3226.12 winning tickets. T/Qpdt: £9.90 to a £1 stake. Pool of £4432.65, 329.15 winning tickets. TM

[2507]UTTOXETER (L-H)
Thursday, November 28

OFFICIAL GOING: Chase course - soft; hurdle course - good to soft (soft in places; heavy in the chute in 2m hurdle races)
Wind: almost nil Weather: overcast

2767 TBA MARES' NOVICES' HURDLE (9 hdls) 2m
12:15 (12:15) (Class 4) 4-Y-0+ **£3,508** (£1,030; £515; £257)

Form RPR

5/2- **1** **Koolala (IRE)**[14] 2467 5-10-12 0.. DenisO'Regan 112+
(Paul Webber) *w ldrs: led 3 out: styd on wl run-in* **5/2[1]**

5- **2** *3 ¾* **Princess Caetani (IRE)**[12] 2514 4-10-12 0........................ BrianHughes 107
(David Dennis) *trckd ldrs: 2nd 3 out: 2 l down whn hit last: styd on same pce* **16/1**

3- **3** *3* **Dewala**[12] 2514 4-10-12 0.. APMcCoy 104
(Michael Appleby) *led to 3rd: chsd ldrs: 3rd appr 2 out: kpt on same pce* **11/4[2]**

12/ **4** *7* **Tickity Bleue**[588] 5470 5-10-12 0................................ WayneHutchinson 97
(Alan King) *hld up in rr: hdwy 5th: one pce and 4th 2 out* **4/1[3]**

6/0- **5** *2 ¼* **La Belle Sauvage**[16] 2432 6-10-5 0.............................. JackSherwood(7) 94
(Kim Bailey) *mid-div: hdwy 6th: sn chsng ldrs: 5th and one pce 2 out* **66/1**

0/0- **6** *2 ½* **Lady Fingers**[21] 2317 5-10-12 0... DaveCrosse 91
(Nigel Twiston-Davies) *chsd ldrs: drvn 6th: one pce next* **50/1**

/54- **7** *6* **August Hill (IRE)**[27] 2190 5-10-12 0..................................(t) TomO'Brien 86
(Philip Hobbs) *stdd s: t.k.h: jnd ldrs 2nd: led next: hdd 3 out: sn wknd* **6/1**

P/0- **8** *8* **Tribu D'Estruval (FR)**[27] 2190 6-10-7 0.................(t) AodhaganConlon(5) 77
(Tom George) *in rr: bhd 6th: nvr on terms* **33/1**

0/5- **9** *1* **Barton Rose**[49] 1836 4-10-12 0.. BrendanPowell 76
(Neil Mulholland) *mid-div: lost pl 6th* **100/1**

3/0- **10** *9* **Dunmallet Belle**[22] 2298 4-10-12 0...................................... FelixDeGiles 67
(Tom Symonds) *mid-div: chsd ldrs 6th: lost pl appr next: sn bhd* **20/1**

34- **11** *6* **Barton Heather**[49] 1836 4-10-9 0...............................(t) MichaelByrne(3) 61
(Neil Mulholland) *chsd ldrs: lost pl after 6th: sn bhd* **100/1**

/40- **12** *6* **Makellys Blackpool**[10] 2559 4-10-12 0.......................... RichieMcGrath 55
(Richard Ford) *mid-div: chsd ldrs 5th: lost pl after next: sn bhd* **200/1**

4/0- **13** *31* **Miss Tilly Dove**[22] 2286 5-10-9 0................................. RobertDunne(3) 24
(Andrew Price) *in rr: bhd fr 5th: t.o whn hung rt bnd bef 3 out* **200/1**

6- **U** **Villa Royale**[12] 2514 4-10-12 0... FearghalDavis
(David O'Meara) *hld up in rr: nt fluent: last whn blnd and uns rdr 3rd* **20/1**

3m 54.8s (2.80) **Going Correction** +0.20s/f (Yiel) **14** Ran SP% **114.3**
Speed ratings (Par 105): **101,99,97,94,93 91,88,84,84,79 76,73,58,**
toteswingers 1&2 £5.80, 2&3 £7.50, 1&3 £1.90 CSF £36.60 TOTE £2.80: £1.10, £3.20, £1.20; EX 28.10 Trifecta £124.00 Pool: £1751.48 - 10.58 winning units..
Owner Lady Richard Wellesley **Bred** Marston Stud **Trained** Mollington, Oxon

FOCUS
Hurdles on inside, divided bends and fences reduced in width from outside. The going was soft on the chase course and good to soft, soft in places on the hurdles course. The pace was honest for this novices' hurdle with the prominent runners dominating. The winner was the form pick on her recent run but is on the upgrade.

2768 32RED CASINO NOVICES' HURDLE (12 hdls) 3m
12:45 (12:45) (Class 4) 4-Y-0+ **£3,249** (£954; £477; £238)

Form RPR

1- **1** **Milan Bound (IRE)**[35] 2030 5-11-5 0.. APMcCoy 132+
(Jonjo O'Neill) *trckd ldrs: 2nd appr 3 out: upsides on bit whn lft in ld 2 out: 10 l ahd last: eased: v easily* **1/2[1]**

2/3- **2** *7* **Rio Milan (IRE)**[42] 1937 7-10-12 0.........................(t) WayneHutchinson 108
(Fergal O'Brien) *chsd ldrs: drvn 9th: 3rd appr next: lft 4 l 2nd and hmpd 2 out: no ch w wnr* **9/4[2]**

03- **3** *34* **Flintham**[28] 2181 4-10-7 0.. NicodeBoinville(5) 84
(Mark Bradstock) *led: drvn 9th: hdd appr next and 4th and wkng whn blnd: sn bhd: lft poor 3rd 2 out* **20/1**

0/0- **4** *69* **Honour The King (IRE)**[12] 2509 7-10-5 0......................... NickSlatter(7) 5
(John Bryan Groucott) *in last: pushed along 6th: lost tch bef 8th: t.o next: lft distant 4th 2 out: eventually completed* **100/1**

143- **F** **Squeeze Me**[12] 2513 6-10-5 0.. TomO'Brien 101
(Peter Bowen) *w ldr: led bef 3 out: jnd and rdn whn fell 2 out* **14/1[3]**

6m 3.4s (13.40) **Going Correction** +0.20s/f (Yiel)
WFA 4 from 5yo+ 9lb **5** Ran SP% **109.9**
Speed ratings (Par 105): **85,82,71,48,**
CSF £1.99 TOTE £1.40: £1.10, £1.10; EX 2.40 Trifecta £5.30 Pool: £2025.40 - 284.18 winning units..
Owner John P McManus **Bred** T J Nagle **Trained** Cheltenham, Gloucs

FOCUS
This novices' hurdle looked a match on the book and it was the well-backed favourite who ran out an impressive winner. He looks decent.

2769 32RED.COM MARES' BEGINNERS' CHASE (18 fncs) 3m
1:20 (1:21) (Class 4) 4-Y-0+ **£4,431** (£1,309; £654; £327; £163)

Form RPR

411/ **1** **Definite Memories (IRE)**[623] 4874 6-11-2 0.................... DenisO'Regan 124+
(David Bridgwater) *t.k.h: j.rt 1st: trckd ldrs: 2nd 6th: led 4 out: 1 l ahd last: drvn and hld on* **10/1**

0/1- **2** *¾* **Ballinahow Star (IRE)**[194] 379 7-10-13 0.....................(t) MattGriffiths(3) 124+
(Jeremy Scott) *hld up wl in tch: nt fluent 12th: effrt and chsng ldrs 4 out: swtchd lft bef next: sn chalng: styd on same pce in clsng stages* **5/2[2]**

2/2- **3** *9* **Jean Fleming (IRE)**[36] 2029 6-11-2 118.......................... BrendanPowell 115
(Jamie Snowden) *led: j.rt 2nd and 4th: hdd 4 out: outpcd next: modest 4th whn mstke 3 out: hung rt and kpt on run-in to take 3rd nr fin* **10/3[3]**

3/2- **4** *hd* **Kentford Grey Lady**[37] 2010 7-11-2 0.......................... DominicElsworth 114
(Emma Lavelle) *j.big: trckd ldrs 4th: effrt 4 out: outpcd next: fdd run-in and lost modest 3rd nr fin* **5/4[1]**

5FP- **5** *28* **Bobbisox (IRE)**[25] 2253 8-11-2 74.......................................(t) FelixDeGiles 89
(Alex Hales) *chsd ldr to 6th: outpcd and lost pl 13th: bhd whn eased run-in: t.o* **100/1**

6m 27.0s (11.90) **Going Correction** +0.40s/f (Soft) **5** Ran SP% **106.2**
Speed ratings (Par 105): **96,95,92,92,83**
CSF £32.68 TOTE £8.30: £3.30, £1.30; EX 23.30 Trifecta £76.50 Pool: £2933.56 - 28.73 winning units..
Owner David A Hunt **Bred** Marjorie Gibbons & Penny Sheehy **Trained** Icomb, Gloucs
■ Stewards' Enquiry : Matt Griffiths three-day ban: used whip without giving mare time to respond (Dec 12-14)

FOCUS
An interesting mares' beginners' chase despite the small field size, with the front two fighting out an exciting finish. The winner is rated up a stone on the best of his hurdle figures, with the second similar to her hurdles mark.

2770 DRAINCARE H'CAP HURDLE (9 hdls) 2m
1:55 (1:59) (Class 5) (0-100,99) 4-Y-0+ **£2,079** (£610; £305; £152)

Form RPR

011- **1** **Proud Times (USA)**[9] 2581 7-11-10 **97** 7ex.......................(p) JackDoyle 118+
(Ali Brewer) *trckd ldrs: led 6th: mstke next: wnt clr between last 2: 14 l ahd whn mstke last: heavily eased* **2/1[1]**

052- **2** *14* **Prince Freddie**[12] 2511 5-10-5 **78**...................................... RichieMcGrath 78
(Roy Brotherton) *mid-div: drvn after 4th: chsd wnr appr 3 out: styd on same pce* **9/1**

/B4- **3** *6* **Peqeno Diablo (IRE)**[17] 2427 8-9-7 **73** oh4.................(tp) GeraldQuinn(7) 66
(Claire Dyson) *led to 2nd: led 4th to 6th: one pce fr 3 out* **9/1**

60- **4** *7* **Johnnys Legacy (IRE)**[12] 2510 6-11-9 **96**........................(p) BarryKeniry 81
(Conor Dore) *in rr: sme hdwy 6th: modest 4th sn after 2 out: nvr a threat: mstke last* **25/1**

F50/ **5** *10* **Crackerjack**[236] 5180 6-10-12 **90**................................. JamesBanks(5) 65
(Emma Baker) *t.k.h to post: hld up in rr: nt fluent 1st: sme hdwy appr 3 out: nvr on terms* **28/1**

5/0- **6** *4 ½* **Cane Cat (IRE)**[35] 2040 6-11-1 **88**.....................................(t) LeeEdwards 59
(Tony Carroll) *in rr: bhd fr 6th: poor 9th whn blnd 2 out* **25/1**

1/P- **7** *3 ¼* **Flora Lea**[22] 2289 6-11-0 **90**...................................... RobertDunne(3) 57
(Andrew Price) *trckd ldrs: drvn appr 3 out: sn lost pl* **40/1**

6/6- **8** *½* **Mr Bolt (IRE)**[28] 2172 8-10-12 **85**....................................... HenryBrooke 54
(Michael O'Hare, Ire) *led 2nd: blnd next: hdd 3rd: modest 4th and wkng whn blnd 2 out* **10/1**

060- **9** *3* **No Routine (IRE)**[24] 2265 4-11-12 **99**...................................... APMcCoy 63
(Jonjo O'Neill) *sn bhd: hdwy 4th: drvn and lost pl after next: sn bhd* **9/2[2]**

0/0- **10** *¾* **Lisdonagh House (IRE)**[16] 2430 11-11-0 **87**....................... TomSiddall 50
(Lynn Siddall) *in rr: detached last whn j.rt and reminders 3rd: t.o 5th* **20/1**

/00- **11** *26* **Errol Flynn (IRE)**[14] 2467 7-9-11 **75** ow1........................ JoshHamer(5) 12
(Tony Carroll) *chsd ldrs: drvn 6th: lost pl appr next: sn bhd: eased run-in: t.o* **33/1**

0/2- **P** **Hold The Bucks (USA)**[24] 2274 7-10-8 **81**...................... BrendanPowell
(Daniel Steele) *chsd ldrs: hit 5th: drvn and lost pl next: sn bhd: t.o whn p.u bef 3 out* **6/1[3]**

3m 57.2s (5.20) **Going Correction** +0.20s/f (Yiel) **12** Ran SP% **116.2**
Speed ratings (Par 103): **95,88,85,81,76 74,72,72,70,70 57,**
toteswingers 1&2 £2.70, 2&3 £11.80, 1&3 £3.70 CSF £17.74 CT £134.07 TOTE £2.80: £1.40, £2.60, £3.20; EX 18.60 Trifecta £120.20 Pool: £2633.93 - 16.43 winning units..
Owner Miss Ali Brewer **Bred** Timothy Thornton & Meg & Mike Buckley **Trained** Eastbury, Berks

FOCUS
A moderate handicap run at a steady pace. Another step forward from the winner, in line with his old hurdles mark.

2771 £32 BONUS AT 32RED.COM H'CAP HURDLE (10 hdls) 2m 4f 110y
2:30 (2:31) (Class 4) (0-110,110) 4-Y-0+ **£3,249** (£954; £477; £238)

Form RPR

112- **1** **My Oh Mount Brown (IRE)**[27] 2202 6-11-6 **107**........... MichaelByrne(3) 119+
(Tim Vaughan) *led to 2nd: chsd ldrs: hit 6th: led bef 3 out: wnt clr between last 2: drvn out* **10/3[2]**

304- **2** *8* **Larteta (FR)**[58] 1714 4-11-3 **104**.. JackQuinlan(3) 104
(Sarah Humphrey) *trckd ldrs: 2nd 3 out: styd on same pce fr next* **14/1**

U/0- **3** *9* **Crystal Swing**[21] 2314 6-11-12 **110**.............................. WayneHutchinson 102
(Richard Phillips) *in rr: reminders and hdwy 7th: modest 3rd 2 out: one pce* **9/1**

6/5- **4** *2* **Cloudingstar (IRE)**[23] 2284 6-11-9 **107**.................................. APMcCoy 96
(Jonjo O'Neill) *chsd ldrs: hrd drvn 7th: one pce appr next* **13/8[1]**

5/0- **5** *nk* **I Know The Code (IRE)**[12] 2510 8-10-11 **95**........................ TomSiddall 84
(Lynn Siddall) *in rr: j.rt 2nd: sme hdwy 7th: kpt on fr next: nvr on terms* **18/1**

5F0- **6** *21* **Bathcounty (IRE)**[10] 2561 6-11-6 **104**............................ BrendanPowell 72
(Barry Brennan) *chsd ldrs: lost pl appr 3 out: sn bhd* **14/1**

01P/ **7** *2 ½* **Boomtown**[331] 3427 8-10-9 **100**...................................(t) GeraldQuinn(7) 65
(Claire Dyson) *w ldrs: led after 6th: hdd appr 3 out: sn wknd* **20/1**

3F4/ **8** *17* **Sunshine Buddy**[603] 5236 6-10-10 **94**.................................. JamesDavies 42
(Chris Down) *prom: lost pl 7th: bhd whn eased 2 out: t.o* **66/1**

051- **9** *10* **Carhue Princess (IRE)**[21] 2312 7-10-6 **90**........................ FelixDeGiles 28
(Tom Symonds) *t.k.h: led 2nd: hdd after 6th: sn lost pl and bhd: eased 3 out: t.o* **11/2[3]**

0/0- 10 7 **Heavenstown (IRE)**[12] 2510 7-11-12 **110**................................ RhysFlint 41
(John Spearing) *chsd ldrs: drvn 5th: sn lost pl: wl bhd 7th: t.o next* **33/1**

5m 1.1s (2.10) **Going Correction** +0.20s/f (Yiel)
WFA 4 from 6yo+ 8lb **10** Ran SP% **114.4**
Speed ratings (Par 105): **104,100,97,96,96 88,87,81,77,74**
toteswingers 1&2 £8.80, 2&3 £20.90, 1&3 £6.70 CSF £45.42 CT £383.32 TOTE £3.60: £1.30, £4.00, £2.90; EX 45.50 Trifecta £330.40 Pool: £4084.44 -9.27 winning units..
Owner Craig and Maureen Buckingham **Bred** James Dillon **Trained** Aberthin, Vale of Glamorgan

FOCUS
They went a fair gallop in this handicap. Another step up from the winner, with the second to his mark.

2772 CLAIM YOUR FREE BETS AT WELOVEFREEBETS.CO.UK H'CAP CHASE (15 fncs) 2m 4f
3:05 (3:05) (Class 5) (0-100,98) 4-Y-0+ **£2,599** (£763; £381; £190)

Form RPR
5/3- 1 **Russe Blanc (FR)**[29] 2155 6-11-11 **97**.............................(p) CharliePoste 110+
(Richard Lee) *chsd ldr: led 8th: nt fluent 3 out: j.rt next: drvn out* **2/1**[2]
032- 2 1 ½ **Hollins**[12] 2512 9-11-5 **98**.. JoshWall(7) 108
(Tony Forbes) *hld up in rr: hdwy to chse ldrs 6th: effrt 4 out: 2 1/2 l 2nd last: kpt on same pce* **9/2**[3]
P6P- 3 1 ½ **One For The Boss (IRE)**[17] 2416 6-10-0 **75** oh1 ow3(t) RobertDunne(3) 84
(Dai Burchell) *chsd ldrs: 2nd 11th: kpt on one pce run-in* **15/8**[1]
23/- 4 21 **Thorncliffer**[242] 5036 9-9-12 **77**..(t) OllieGarner(7) 64
(Derek Shaw) *led: drvn and hdd 8th: outpcd 4 out: bhd whn j.rt 2 out* **7/1**
0P4- 5 41 **Phoenix Des Mottes (FR)**[10] 2560 10-9-13 **72** oh2.......... JoeCornwall(5) 18
(John Cornwall) *rn in snatches: pushed along 2nd: outpcd next: lost pl 10th: bhd fr 4 out: t.o whn eased run-in* **28/1**
P/P- P **Accordion To Paddy (IRE)**[28] 2173 9-11-4 **90**................ HenryBrooke
(Michael O'Hare, Ire) *chsd ldrs: drvn 9th: sn wknd: t.o whn p.u bef 4 out* **14/1**

5m 12.2s (6.70) **Going Correction** +0.40s/f (Soft) **6** Ran SP% **108.9**
Speed ratings (Par 103): **102,101,100,92,76**
toteswingers 1&2 £1.80, 2&3 £3.20, 1&3 £1.10 CSF £10.77 TOTE £2.60: £1.60, £1.90; EX 8.20 Trifecta £28.40 Pool: £2703.99 - 71.21 winning units..
Owner Mark Jackson **Bred** B De La Motte Saint-Pierre & Jean-Francois Lambert **Trained** Byton, H'fords

FOCUS
The pace was sound for this weak contest. The winner is on the upgrade and the next two were close to their marks.

2773 32RED INTERMEDIATE OPEN NATIONAL HUNT FLAT RACE 2m
3:35 (3:35) (Class 6) 4-6-Y-0 **£1,559** (£457; £228; £114)

Form RPR
1 **Hot Whiskey N Ice (IRE)**[193] 4-11-0 0..................... WayneHutchinson 106+
(Noel Williams) *w ldr: drvn to ld 3f out: rdn and styd on wl fnl f* **16/1**
2- 2 1 ¼ **Forthefunofit (IRE)**[20] 2354 4-11-0 0..................................... APMcCoy 105
(Jonjo O'Neill) *hld up in rr: t.k.h: hdwy to trck ldrs after 5f: effrt and upsides 3f out: rdn over 1f out: kpt on same pce last 100yds* **8/11**[1]
5- 3 2 **Son Of Suzie**[199] 270 5-11-0 0.............................. DominicElsworth 103
(Fergal O'Brien) *led: hdd 7f out: outpcd over 3f out: rallied over 2f out: kpt on to take 3rd last 100yds* **8/1**[3]
35- 4 5 **Grape Tree Flame**[122] 1138 5-10-7 0.................................. TomO'Brien 92
(Peter Bowen) *sn trcking ldrs: led 7f out: hdd 3f out: wknd fnl 150yds* **10/1**
5 13 **Veyranno (FR)** 4-10-9 0... AodhaganConlon(5) 85
(Tom George) *hld up in rr: hdwy after 5f: trckd ldrs 5f out: lost pl over 2f out* **20/1**
6 11 **Kings River (FR)** 4-10-11 0...................................... RobertDunne(3) 74
(Venetia Williams) *hld up in rr: hdwy 9f out: drvn over 6f out: lost pl over 3f out* **4/1**[2]

3m 59.2s (12.80) **Going Correction** +0.20s/f (Yiel) **6** Ran SP% **108.8**
Speed ratings: **76,75,74,71,65 59**
CSF £26.93 TOTE £11.10: £2.70, £1.60; EX 24.60 Trifecta £120.40 Pool: £3045.63 - 18.96 winning units..
Owner Whitehorsemen **Bred** G Durrheim & Mrs Maria Mulcahy Durrheim **Trained** Blewbury, Oxon
■ The first winner for Noel Williams, a former assistant to Alan King.

FOCUS
Not a bad bumper run at a steady pace. The first two home came widest into the straight and the form is rated through the second.
T/Plt: £21.40 to a £1 stake. Pool of £63561.26 - 2162.24 winning tickets. T/Qpdt: £14.70 to a £1 stake. Pool of £4034.57 - 202.0 winning tickets. WG

2774 - 2780a (Foreign Racing) - See Raceform Interactive

FONTAINEBLEAU
Thursday, November 28

OFFICIAL GOING: Turf: very soft

2781a PRIX DE MACHERIN (DIV II) (HURDLE) (CONDITIONS) (3YO FILLIES) (TURF) 2m 1f 165y
12:00 (12:00) 3-Y-0 **£8,975** (£4,487; £2,617; £1,776; £841)

RPR
1 **Ahkel Vie (FR)**[22] 3-10-6 0.. HakimTabet(4)
(Yannick Fouin, France) **1/1**[1]
2 4 **Moonlit Bay**[131] 3-10-7 0 ow1.. DavidCottin
(Venetia Williams) *restrained and hld up towards rr: hdwy fr 4 out: rdn in 2nd jst after 2 out: styd on and chsd wnr flat but readily outpcd towards fin* **44/5**
3 5 **Dence (FR)**[51] 3-10-0 0 ow1.............................. Marc-AntoineBillard(4)
(Mlle C Comte, France) **76/1**
4 12 **Poligrouas (FR)**[33] 3-11-0 0.......................................(p) OlivierJouin
(P Peltier, France) **4/1**[2]
5 1 ½ **Agent Mimi (FR)**[29] 3-9-13 0....................................... BenoitClaudic(4)
(M Seror, France) **13/1**
6 3 ½ **Pas De Blabla (FR)** 3-10-3 0.................................... MathieuDelage
(A Lefeuvre, France) **20/1**
P **Lucax (FR)**[36] 3-10-8 0 ow5.............................. JonathanPlouganou
(M Seror, France) **25/1**
P **Oriental Love (GER)**[15] 3-10-8 0.................................... JacquesRicou
(F-X De Chevigny, France) **15/2**[3]
P **City Nebula (FR)**[28] 3-10-6 0...................................... GaetanMasure
(J Bertran De Balanda, France) **18/1**
P **Khahyalista (FR)** 3-10-3 0......................................(p) LaurentBouldoires
(Mlle N Pfohl, France) **98/1**
P **Top Lune (FR)** 3-10-3 0...(p) RaphaelDelozier
(J Delaunay, France) **94/1**

4m 20.1s (260.10) **11** Ran SP% **116.3**
PARI-MUTUEL (all including 1 euro stake): WIN 2.00; PLACE 1.40, 2.60, 9.80; DF 9.10; SF 10.00.
Owner Scea Haras D'Orfausse **Bred** Mme M Dutertre **Trained** France

DONCASTER (L-H)
Friday, November 29

OFFICIAL GOING: Good (good to firm in places on hurdle course; chs 7.5, hdl 8.0)
Wind: fresh 1/2 against Weather: fine but windy

2782 KELLY'S SCOOPING ICE CREAM NOVICES' CHASE (15 fncs) 2m 3f
12:20 (12:20) (Class 4) 4-Y-0+ **£4,548** (£1,335; £667; £333)

Form RPR
/32- 1 **Funny Star (FR)**[11] 2565 5-11-1 132...............................(t) NickScholfield 141+
(Paul Nicholls) *trckd ldr: upsides 6th: led 10th: drvn out: hld on towards fin* **13/8**[1]
150/ 2 ½ **Ericht (IRE)**[239] 5141 7-11-1 0.. AndrewTinkler 141+
(Nicky Henderson) *hld up: trckd ldrs 8th: pushed along and 2nd appr 4 out: styd on and 2 1/2 l down last: kpt on wl clsng stages* **13/8**[1]
132- 3 35 **Bar De Ligne (FR)**[19] 2395 7-11-8 126................................ DenisO'Regan 116
(Steve Gollings) *nt fluent in last: drvn 7th: wnt modest 3rd 4 out: no ch w 1st 2* **3/1**[2]
33- 4 2 **Carli King (IRE)**[11] 2558 7-11-1 0.................................. TomMessenger 107
(Caroline Bailey) *chsd ldrs: one pce fr 4 out* **40/1**
0/P- 5 17 **Big George**[41] 1976 6-11-1 0.. RyanMania 92
(Simon Waugh) *chsd ldrs: outpcd appr 4 out: wl bhd fr 2 out* **125/1**
3U5- U **Akula (IRE)**[4] 2721 6-11-1 114.. ColinBolger
(Mark H Tompkins) *led: hit 3rd: nt fluent and hdd 10th: outpcd whn blnd and uns rdr next* **28/1**[3]

4m 38.3s (-10.70) **Going Correction** -0.425s/f (Good) **6** Ran SP% **107.9**
Speed ratings (Par 105): **105,104,90,89,82**
toteswingers 1&2 £1.02, 1&3 £1.20, 2&3 £1.30 CSF £4.39 TOTE £3.40: £1.10, £1.50; EX 6.00 Trifecta £11.60 Pool: £1283.99 - 82.87 winning units..
Owner Mr And Mrs J D Cotton **Bred** Suc Jean-Pierre Villey **Trained** Ditcheat, Somerset

FOCUS
The two market leaders pulled well clear in this novices' chase, which was run at a reasonable gallop. The winner is rated back to form on better ground.

2783 ALLIED MASSARELLAS BENTLEY CASH & CARRY NOVICES' HURDLE (8 hdls) 2m 110y
12:50 (12:50) (Class 4) 4-Y-0+ **£3,898** (£1,144; £572; £286)

Form RPR
1 **Mijhaar**[55] 5-10-12 0.. DenisO'Regan 134+
(John Ferguson) *trckd ldr: led 5th: wnt clr after 2 out: eased run-in: impressive* **2/1**[1]
/16- 2 7 **Lemony Bay**[27] 2225 4-10-12 0.. LeightonAspell 117
(Oliver Sherwood) *trckd ldrs: 2nd 3 out: kpt on: no ch w wnr* **7/1**
163- 3 9 **Kings Grey (IRE)**[33] 2101 9-10-12 0................................... JamesReveley 108
(Keith Reveley) *chsd ldrs: clr 3rd 2 out: one pce* **9/4**[2]
/05- 4 1 ¼ **Vinstar (FR)**[30] 2156 4-10-12 0...(t) HenryBrooke 108
(Donald McCain) *nt fluent in rr: hit 4th: reminders and hdwy appr 3 out: 6th last: kpt on* **20/1**
5 6 **Dark Dune (IRE)**[105] 5-10-12 0.. HarryHaynes 102
(Tim Easterby) *blnd 1st: mid-div: hdwy 4th: 5th and one pce whn blnd 2 out: fdd run-in* **33/1**
0/2- 6 3 ¼ **Devon Drum**[25] 2265 5-10-12 0.. LiamTreadwell 100+
(Paul Webber) *mid-div: hdwy 4th: sn chsng ldrs: wknd last* **3/1**[3]
7 nk **Canuspotit** 6-10-9 0.. JackQuinlan(3) 97
(Lucy Wadham) *stdd s: t.k.h in rr: sme hdwy 5th: nvr nr ldrs* **66/1**
5/ 8 11 **Like Clockwork**[10] 2068 4-10-12 0.. ColinBolger 86
(Mark H Tompkins) *chsd ldrs: wknd 3 out* **100/1**
100- 9 9 **On The Buckle**[27] 2217 5-10-12 0..................................... RichieMcGrath 77
(Rose Dobbin) *in rr: sme hdwy appr 3 out: sn wknd* **80/1**
00- 10 5 **Durham Express (IRE)**[14] 2493 6-10-7 0...................... SamanthaDrake(5) 72
(Tina Jackson) *t.k.h: trckd ldrs after 1st: lost pl after 4th: bhd and reminders appr 3 out* **200/1**
04- 11 37 **Not Another Monday (IRE)**[17] 2443 5-10-12 0.................. BarryKeniry 35
(George Moore) *mid-div: reminders 5th: sn lost pl and bhd: t.o 2 out* **150/1**
12 18 **Hollywood All Star (IRE)**[203] 4-10-12 0............................ CharliePoste 17
(Graeme McPherson) *in rr-div: in rr whn blnd 5th: sn bhd: t.o 2 out* **150/1**
/00- P **Audacious**[102] 560 5-10-12 0.. AdamPogson
(Charles Pogson) *t.k.h: led: hdd 5th: lost pl and bhd whn p.u bef next* **150/1**
P **Mahab El Shamaal**[795] 5-10-5 0................................ JosephAkehurst(7)
(Alan Jessop) *wl bhd 4th: t.o next: p.u bef 3 out* **150/1**

3m 54.0s (-10.70) **Going Correction** -0.675s/f (Firm)
WFA 4 from 5yo+ 7lb **14** Ran SP% **116.2**
Speed ratings (Par 105): **98,94,90,89,87 85,85,80,75,73 56,47, ,**
toteswingers 1&2 £5.50, 1&3 £1.40, 2&3 £1.40 CSF £16.07 TOTE £2.90: £1.20, £1.80, £1.60; EX 17.20 Trifecta £50.40 Pool: £1389.98 - 20.66 winning units..
Owner Bloomfields **Bred** Darley **Trained** Cowlinge, Suffolk

FOCUS
There was little depth to this novices' hurdle and the winning debutant proved far too good. He's a potential 150+ hurdler if translating the best of his Flat form. The race should produce winners.

2784 CADBURY FLAKE "99" NOVICES' H'CAP CHASE (18 fncs) 3m
1:20 (1:20) (Class 4) (0-110,110) 4-Y-0+ **£3,898** (£1,144; £572; £286)

Form RPR
/64- 1 **Clondaw Flicka (IRE)**[22] 2308 5-11-5 **103**...................... PeterBuchanan 114+
(Lucinda Russell) *j. boldly: w ldr: led 4th: jnd whn mstke last: rallied to ld last 150yds: styd on gamely* **5/2**[2]
/53- 2 2 ¼ **Tickatack (IRE)**[17] 2431 8-11-4 **102**............................ RichieMcLernon 108
(Graeme McPherson) *chsd ldrs: 2nd 13th: upsides 3 out: hit 2 out: upsides last: sn led briefly: kpt on same pce* **11/2**
1P4- 3 2 ¼ **Lukey Luke**[21] 2334 10-10-13 **97**.. BrianHarding 100
(James Turner) *hld up in rr: hdwy 7th: trcking ldrs 11th: 3rd and effrt appr 3 out: upsides whn stmbld on landing last: one pce last 150yds* **14/1**

/63- **4** *36* **The Mumper (IRE)**[15] [2475] 6-11-12 **110**.......................... GerardTumelty 80
(Alan King) *nt fluent: hdwy to chse ldrs 7th: mstke 13th: sn drvn: wknd next: bhd fr 4 out: t.o* **4/1**[3]
P/P- **5** *3* **Weston Lodge (IRE)**[8] [2626] 7-11-1 **99**.......................... RichieMcGrath 66
(Christopher Kellett) *led to 4th: pushed along 9th: reminders 10th: wknd 4 out: t.o* [illegible] **80/1**
[illegible] **U** **Highbury High (IRE)**[illegible] [2633] 6-11-11 98 7ex PaddyBrennan
(Paul Henderson) *hld up: [illegible] in tch whn blnd and uns rdr next* **7/4**[1]
5m 2.1s (-9.90) **Going Correction** -0.425s/f (Good) 6 Ran SP% 108.5
Speed ratings (Par 105): **98,90,87,85,84**
toteswingers 1&2 [illegible] CSF [illegible] TOTE [illegible] EX 18.00 Trifecta £107.20 Pool: £2154.67 - 15.06 winning units..
Owner Dan & Michelle Macdonald, Mackie, Levein **Bred** Fergal O'Mahoney **Trained** Arlary, Perth & Kinross

FOCUS
A moderate novice handicap chase in which much of the interest was lost when the favourite unseated his rider at halfway. The winner is rated up 12lb on the best of his hurdles form over shorter.

2785 NATIONAL ICE CREAM WHOLESALERS H'CAP CHASE (15 fncs) 2m 3f
1:55 (1:55) (Class 3) (0-130,130) 4-Y-O+ **£6,498** (£1,908; £954; £477)

Form RPR
P/3- **1** **Off The Ground (IRE)**[25] [2267] 7-11-0 **118**.......................... LeightonAspell 143+
(Emma Lavelle) *trckd ldrs 4th: led appr 4 out: clr next: eased run-in: v comf* **13/8**[1]
/U2- **2** *7* **Woodbank**[36] [2042] 6-11-2 **120**.......................... AndrewTinkler 133+
(Nicky Henderson) *prom: chsd wnr 3 out: kpt on same pce: no imp* **11/2**[2]
/65- **3** *14* **Marley Roca (IRE)**[194] [392] 9-11-7 **125**.......................... LiamTreadwell 123
(Paul Webber) *prom: outpcd 9th: hdwy 11th: kpt on one pce to take 4th 3 out: 3rd nr fin* **20/1**
4/0- **4** *1 1/4* **Galway Jack (IRE)**[194] [392] 8-11-12 **130**.......................... AndrewThornton 131
(Caroline Bailey) *mstkes: led: hit 2nd: hdd appr 4 out: 3rd whn mstke 3 out: wknd run-in* **20/1**
5P0- **5** *15* **Jack The Gent (IRE)**[44] [1921] 9-11-8 **126**.......................... BarryKeniry 110
(George Moore) *chsd ldrs: outpcd after 11th: sn wknd* **50/1**
/6P- **6** *4 1/2* **Golden Call (IRE)**[16] [2452] 9-11-10 **128**..........................(p) PaddyBrennan 111
(Tom George) *chsd ldrs: mstke 1st: 3rd whn mstke 10th: wknd next* **9/1**
7 *1* **Bellenos (FR)**[383] 5-11-6 **124**.......................... HarrySkelton 103
(Dan Skelton) *hld up in rr: hdwy 4th: sn trcking ldrs: 2nd 10th: wknd appr 4 out* **6/1**[3]
0/5- **8** *26* **Arctic Ben (IRE)**[29] [2180] 9-11-6 **124**.......................... NickScholfield 79
(Henry Daly) *trckd ldrs: lost pl 9th: bhd next: t.o 11th* **8/1**
335- **9** *4* **Be My Deputy (IRE)**[104] [1291] 8-10-13 **117**..........................(t) PeterBuchanan 69
(Lucinda Russell) *sn drvn along in rr: wl bhd 6th: t.o 9th* **25/1**
0/3- **10** *44* **Corkage (IRE)**[18] [2428] 10-11-12 **130**..........................(b) JamesReveley 42
(Keith Reveley) *in rr: last whn blnd bdly 4th: t.o 6th: eventually completed* **11/1**
00P- **P** **Finger Onthe Pulse (IRE)**[17] [2448] 12-11-9 **127**........(t) RichieMcLernon
(Jonjo O'Neill) *prom 4th: lost pl and hit 11th: sn bhd: t.o whn p.u bef 3 out* **28/1**
4m 36.9s (-12.10) **Going Correction** -0.425s/f (Good) **11** Ran SP% **116.0**
Speed ratings (Par 107): **108,105,99,98,92 90,90,79,77,58**
toteswingers 1&2 £1.10, 1&3 £23.40, 2&3 £18.50 CSF £10.22 CT £129.63 TOTE £3.20: £1.40, £1.90, £4.70; EX 15.20 Trifecta £429.20 Pool: £1227.40 - 2.14 winning units..
Owner Axom (XXVI) **Bred** Mrs Kay Devereux **Trained** Hatherden, Hants

FOCUS
This looked a competitive handicap chase on paper, but the well-backed favourite turned it into a procession. The time was good compared with the novice event.

2786 WALLS ICE CREAM H'CAP HURDLE (11 hdls) 3m 110y
2:30 (2:30) (Class 4) (0-120,117) 3-Y-O+ **£3,249** (£954; £477; £238)

Form RPR
/36- **1** **Fix It Right (IRE)**[24] [2284] 5-11-5 **110**.......................... LeightonAspell 116+
(Emma Lavelle) *hld up: trckd ldrs 4th: pushed along and dropped bk 8th: hdwy to ld next: drvn rt out* **2/1**[1]
223- **2** *1 1/4* **Any Given Moment (IRE)**[22] [2311] 7-11-2 **107**.......................... RyanMania 108
(Sandy Thomson) *chsd ldrs: upsides 3 out: chsd wnrappr next: styd on same pce run-in* **8/1**
102- **3** *2 1/4* **Bold Raider (IRE)**[33] [2105] 6-10-9 **110**.......................... TommieMO'Brien(10) 110+
(Jonjo O'Neill) *hld up: trckd ldrs 4th: outpcd 2 out: rallied and 3rd last: kpt on same pce* **3/1**[2]
F/P- **4** *8* **Low Gales (IRE)**[15] [2468] 7-11-8 **113**..........................(t) MarkGrant 105
(Charlie Mann) *hld up in rr: hdwy 7th: sn chsng ldrs: outpcd appr 3 out: j.lft 2 out: kpt on to take modest 4th last 50yds* **33/1**
/U0- **5** *5* **Call It On (IRE)**[17] [2447] 7-11-7 **115**..........................(p) KyleJames(3) 105
(Philip Kirby) *chsd ldr: drvn to ld briefly bef 3 out: 4th and one pce whn blnd last: wknd last 100yds* **25/1**
212- **6** *nk* **Granwood**[167] [751] 7-10-12 **103**..........................(p) PeterBuchanan 90
(Tim Walford) *led: hit 6th: hdd appr 3 out: wknd 2 out* **9/1**
/46- **7** *2 1/4* **Cleve Cottage**[28] [2202] 5-10-13 **104**.......................... RichieMcGrath 89
(Philip Kirby) *chsd ldr: drvn 8th: lost pl and hit next* **11/2**[3]
251- **P** **Waltz Darling (IRE)**[17] [2447] 5-11-12 **117**.......................... JamesReveley
(Keith Reveley) *nt fluent in last: lost tch 5th: t.o whn p.u bef 7th* **13/2**
5m 56.9s (-2.10) **Going Correction** -0.675s/f (Firm) **8** Ran SP% **114.9**
Speed ratings (Par 105): **76,75,74,72,70 70,69,**
toteswingers 1&2 £3.00, 1&3 £1.50, 2&3 £3.50 CSF £18.64 CT £47.03 TOTE £3.50: £1.40, £1.90, £1.20; EX 21.60 Trifecta £75.40 Pool: £2176.56 - 21.63 winning units..
Owner The Hawk Inn Syndicate **Bred** Tim O'Connell **Trained** Hatherden, Hants

FOCUS
Not the strongest handicap hurdle for the grade. The idling winner was value for a bit further and is rated to his mark.

2787 FREE BETS FREEBETS.CO.UK NOVICES' H'CAP HURDLE (10 hdls) 2m 3f 110y
3:05 (3:06) (Class 5) (0-100,100) 3-Y-O+ **£2,599** (£763; £381; £190)

Form RPR
56- **1** **Portway Flyer (IRE)**[68] [1632] 5-11-11 **99**.......................... WillKennedy 124+
(Ian Williams) *trckd ldrs: led 7th: wnt clr bef 2 out: 15 l ahd whn heavily eased run-in* **6/1**[3]
446- **2** *9* **Wintered Well (IRE)**[119] [1183] 5-10-8 **82**.......................... SeanQuinlan 89+
(Jennie Candlish) *chsd ldrs 3rd: 2nd appr 3 out: 5 l down whn j.lft and mstke 2 out: no ch w wnr* **11/4**[1]
5/3- **3** *1 1/2* **Reyes Magos (IRE)**[50] [1832] 7-11-12 **100**..........................(t) LeightonAspell 106
(Seamus Durack) *in tch: wnt 3rd 3 out: kpt on one pce* **9/2**[2]
/06- **4** *4 1/2* **Radio Nowhere (IRE)**[18] [2417] 5-11-5 **100**..........................(b[1]) NickSlatter(7) 100
(Donald McCain) *led: hdd 7th: 4th and rdn 3 out: one pce* **16/1**
00F- **5** *15* **River Purple**[36] [2046] 6-10-9 **83**..........................(t) DonalDevereux 69
(John Mackie) *prom: outpcd 3 out: no ch after* **16/1**
014- **6** *5* **Tweedo Paradiso (NZ)**[22] [2306] 6-11-4 **92**.......................... RichieMcGrath 74
(Rose Dobbin) *mid-div: hmpd 5th: lost pl after next: kpt on fr 2 out* **10/1**
205 **7** *1* **Rose Red**[13] [2611] 6-10-12 **89**..........................(p) JamesBest(3) 70
(Rob Summers) [illegible] **10/1**
[illegible] **8** *2 1/4* **Inside Knowledge (USA)**[illegible] [illegible] 7-11-5 [illegible]..........................(p) AdamPogson 72
(Garry Woodward) [illegible] **8/1**
0F4- **9** *1* **Lost In Newyork (IRE)**[28] [2191] 6-10-5 **79**..........................(tp) HarryHaynes 57
(Nick Kent) *w ldrs: lost pl appr 3 out* **20/1**
/PP- **10** *6* **Teenage Dream (IRE)**[6] [2676] 5-11-0 **96**..........................(t) CharliePoste 70
(Derek Shaw) [illegible] **80/1**
01P- **11** *nk* **Stadium Of Light (IRE)**[illegible] [illegible] 6-10-11 **90**.......................... BenPoste(3) 60
(Shaun Harris) *mid-div: hdwy 6th: chsng ldrs appr 3 out: sn wknd* **22/1**
0/0- **12** *nk* **Graylyn Ruby (FR)**[20] [2292] 8-10-4 **81**.......................... WayneKavanagh(3) 57
(Robin Dickin) *chsd ldrs: 6th and mstke 3 out: hung lft and wknd next* **20/1**
3/5- **13** *1 1/2* **Desert Nova (IRE)**[195] [368] 11-9-9 **76**.......................... GLavery(7) 50
(Mark Campion) *mid-div: drvn 6th: bhd fr next* **33/1**
6/0- **14** *1 3/4* **Think**[41] [558] 6-10-11 **85**..........................(t) DenisO'Regan 58
(Clive Mulhall) *nt fluent in rr: hdwy 3 out: modest 5th whn eased between last 2: virtually p.u run-in* **25/1**
554- **P** **Snow Alert**[68] [1635] 7-10-2 **83**.......................... JamesCowley(7)
(John Norton) *mid-div: drvn 5th: lost pl next: sn bhd: t.o whn p.u bef 3 out* **16/1**
630- **P** **Precision Strike**[15] [1790] 3-9-11 **90** oh9..........................(p) JackQuinlan(3)
(Richard Guest) *in rr: j. violently lft fr 4th: t.o next: p.u after 7th* **40/1**
4m 36.5s (-14.80) **Going Correction** -0.675s/f (Firm)
WFA 3 from 5yo+ 15lb **16** Ran SP% **130.7**
Speed ratings (Par 103): **102,98,97,96,90 88,87,86,86,85 85,85,84,83,**
toteswingers 1&2 £6.10, 1&3 £11.60, 2&3 £4.60 CSF £22.67 CT £88.28 TOTE £8.80: £2.50, £1.20, £1.70, £3.70; EX 41.40 Trifecta £126.30 Pool: £1417.96 - 8.41 winning units..
Owner Patrick Kelly **Bred** DDE Syndicate **Trained** Portway, Worcs

FOCUS
An ordinary novice handicap hurdle, but it was hard not to be impressed with the very easy winner. A massive step up from the facile winner for an in-form yard and he should win again.

2788 MOBILE BETTING FREEBETS.CO.UK NATIONAL HUNT FLAT RACE (CONDITIONALS & AMATEURS) 2m 110y
3:35 (3:36) (Class 6) 4-6-Y-O **£1,624** (£477; £238; £119)

Form RPR
3- **1** **Powerstown Dreams (IRE)**[21] [2354] 4-10-11 0.......................... PaulBohan(7) 113+
(Steve Gollings) *led 3f: chsd ldrs: led over 2f out: kpt on fnl f: jst hld on* **6/1**
6- **2** *shd* **Hunters Hoof (IRE)**[27] [2216] 4-10-11 0.......................... MrFMitchell(7) 113+
(Nicky Henderson) *chsd ldrs: drvn 6f out: styd on and 2nd over 1f out: sn upsides: styd on towards fin: jst failed* **9/2**[3]
0/3- **3** *11* **Black Cow (IRE)**[199] [298] 5-10-11 0.......................... MissMNicholls(7) 105+
(Paul Nicholls) *uns rdr and rn loose in paddock: t.k.h: w ldr: led after 3f: hdd over 2f out: hung lft and wknd 1f out* **7/2**[2]
20- **4** *4* **Royal Ripple (IRE)**[20] [2375] 5-10-11 0.......................... MrGBranton(7) 99
(Paul Henderson) *trckd ldrs: t.k.h: drvn 5f out: wknd over 3f out* **16/1**
5 *1 3/4* **Whichwaytobougie** 4-10-13 0.......................... ColmMcCormack(5) 98
(Keith Reveley) *in rr: drvn along after 6f: lost pl 7f out: kpt on fnl 2f* **10/1**
2- **6** *4* **Rendezvous Peak**[17] [2439] 4-10-13 0.......................... MattCrawley(5) 94
(Lucy Wadham) *hld up: hdwy to chse ldrs after 5f: drvn 7f out: sn outpcd: wknd 3f out* **7/1**
7 *8* **Foxtail Hill (IRE)** 4-10-8 0.......................... PaulO'Brien(10) 87
(Rebecca Curtis) *trckd ldrs: reminders over 3f out: hung lft and lost pl over 3f out* **2/1**[1]
6- **8** *54* **Rossington**[62] [1690] 4-10-11 0.......................... GLavery(7) 38
(John Wainwright) *hdwy to chse ldrs after 4f: drvn and lost pl 7f out: t.o 4f out: eventually completed* **100/1**
3m 45.0s (-14.10) **Going Correction** -0.675s/f (Firm) **8** Ran SP% **116.5**
Speed ratings: **106,105,100,98,98 96,92,67**
toteswingers 1&2 £7.00, 1&3 £3.40, 2&3 £2.00 CSF £33.74 TOTE £5.80: £1.70, £1.40, £1.70; EX 30.80 Trifecta £181.40 Pool: £2738.57 - 11.31 winning units..
Owner P J Martin **Bred** M F Condon **Trained** Scamblesby, Lincs

FOCUS
The first two pulled clear in just an ordinary bumper. The form looks believable.
T/Plt: £22.50 to a £1 stake. Pool: £77413.47 - 2508.24 winning tickets T/Qpdt: £22.20 to a £1 stake. Pool: £5019.91 - 166.90 winning tickets WG

2340 MUSSELBURGH (R-H)
Friday, November 29

OFFICIAL GOING: Good (good to firm in places; 7.3)
Wind: Fresh, half against Weather: Cloudy, bright

2789 SALTIRE CONDITIONAL JOCKEYS' H'CAP HURDLE (14 hdls) 3m 110y
12:10 (12:10) (Class 5) (0-100,99) 4-Y-O+ **£3,249** (£954; £477; £238)

Form RPR
0/P- **1** **Stitched In Time (IRE)**[28] [2202] 6-10-9 **90**.......................... ShaunDobbin(8) 96+
(Rose Dobbin) *cl up: led 2nd: mde rest: pushed along and clr between last 2: styd on strly* **33/1**
434- **2** *6* **Auberge (IRE)**[27] [2218] 9-11-11 **98**.......................... EmmaSayer 100+
(Evelyn Slack) *hld up: pushed along whn hmpd 6th: hdwy bef 3 out: chsd (clr) wnr run-in: no imp* **11/1**
/65- **3** *3 3/4* **Pudsey House**[19] [2397] 6-11-6 **99**..........................(b) JohnDawson(6) 98
(John Wade) *nt fluent on occasions: led to 2nd: chsd wnr: effrt and cl 2nd appr 3 out: one pce whn j.rt last* **8/1**
/P6- **4** *8* **Vallani (IRE)**[48] [1874] 8-10-4 **83**.......................... GrantCockburn(6) 73
(Lucinda Russell) *bhd: pushed along 1/2-way: hdwy bef 2 out: no imp fr last* **10/1**
41F/ **5** *11* **Tears From Heaven (USA)**[547] [513] 7-9-11 **78**..(p) DiarmuidO'Regan(8) 58
(Chris Grant) *midfield on ins: drvn and outpcd 4 out: n.d after* **8/1**
4/6- **6** *nk* **Benmadigan (IRE)**[19] [2397] 11-11-0 **90**.......................... GrahamWatters(3) 69
(Nicky Richards) *hld up: pushed along 9th: drvn after next: no imp fr 3 out* **7/2**[2]
122- **7** *2 1/4* **Burns Night**[10] [2575] 7-11-5 **95**..........................(p) AdamNicol(3) 72
(Philip Kirby) *hld up: shortlived effrt bef 3 out: sn rdn: wknd next* **3/1**[1]
563- **8** *7* **Knight Woodsman**[22] [2310] 9-10-13 **86**..........................(p) TonyKelly 57
(R Mike Smith) *in tch tl rdn and wknd after 3 out* **11/1**

P44- 9 2 1/4 **Harrys Whim**[128] 1104 8-9-9 **74** oh4 ow1................. StephenMulqueen(6) 43
(Maurice Barnes) *chsd ldrs: rdn 4 out: wknd fr next* **6/1**[3]

3PO- F **Flying Doctor**[14] 2497 10-11-8 **95**.................................... CallumWhillans
(Alistair Whillans) *chsd ldrs tl fell 6th* **20/1**

5m 52.0s (-4.70) **Going Correction** -0.125s/f (Good) **10** Ran SP% **117.2**
Speed ratings (Par 103): **102,100,98,96,92 92,91,89,89,**
toteswingers 1&2 £23.70, 1&3 £23.70, 2&3 £6.50 CSF £351.30 CT £3186.57 TOTE £19.00: £6.10, £3.10, £2.40; EX 469.60 Trifecta £617.40 Pool: £1045.49 - 1.27 winning units..

Owner Mr & Mrs Duncan Davidson **Bred** Mrs Mary Doyle **Trained** South Hazelrigg, Northumbria

FOCUS
Hurdles and Chases used common bends. Jockeys riding in the opener reckoned the ground was softer than the official description, backed up by the official time which was 26secs over the Racing Post standard. This was a moderate handicap hurdle, run at a modest pace until the winner rider quickened things up on the final circuit. A small step up from the winner with the next two to their marks.

2790 BAM CONSTRUCTION JUVENILE HURDLE (9 hdls) 2m
12:40 (12:40) (Class 4) 3-Y-O **£3,249** (£954; £477)

Form RPR

12- 1 **Dispour (IRE)**[29] 2168 3-11-5 122.................................. JasonMaguire 120+
(Donald McCain) *mde all: j.lft 4 out and 2 out: pushed along whn j. bdly lft last: rdn and qcknd clr run-in* **30/100**[1]

2 4 **Thorpe (IRE)**[44] 3-10-7 0.. DerekFox(5) 106+
(Lucinda Russell) *nt fluent: t.k.h: pressed wnr: effrt and pushed along 2 out: cl 2nd whn carried lft last: n.m.r and brushed plastic rail run-in: no imp* **3/1**[2]

3- 3 49 **Seaside Rock (IRE)**[22] 2307 3-10-12 0........................ WilsonRenwick 62
(Keith Dalgleish) *t.k.h: chsd ldrs tl wknd fr 3 out* **20/1**[3]

3m 53.3s (4.90) **Going Correction** -0.125s/f (Good) **3** Ran SP% **106.7**
Speed ratings (Par 104): **82,80,55**
CSF £1.59 TOTE £1.50; EX 1.40 Trifecta £1.80 Pool: £989.47 - 339.38 winning units..

Owner Paul & Clare Rooney **Bred** His Highness The Aga Khan's Studs S C **Trained** Cholmondeley, Cheshire

■ Stewards' Enquiry : Jason Maguire two-day ban: careless riding (13-14 Dec)

FOCUS
A disappointing turnout for this event, which was won by the smart Carlito Brigante in 2009. The McCain yard won this with another odds-on shot, Kie, when it was last run two years ago. That horse went on to finish second in the Scottish Triumph Hurdle back at Musselburgh in the February, as did the 2010 winner of this, The Starboard Bow. The pace was slow and the order was the same throughout. Not form to be confident about.

2791 SEMICHEM NOVICES' H'CAP CHASE (16 fncs) 2m 4f
1:10 (1:10) (Class 4) (0-110,108) 4-Y-O+ **£3,898** (£1,144; £572; £286)

Form RPR

356- 1 **My Idea**[20] 2356 7-10-11 **100**..................................(t) StephenMulqueen(7) 109+
(Maurice Barnes) *prom: hdwy to chal 4 out: led next: hung rt fr 2 out: kpt on strly to draw clr run-in* **9/2**

/FP- 2 5 **Teo Vivo (FR)**[20] 2356 6-11-5 **101**.. BrianHughes 107
(James Ewart) *nt fluent: prom: hdwy to ld appr 4 out: hdd next: upsides whn pckd next: one pce fr last* **7/2**[3]

23F- 3 13 **Agricultural**[22] 2308 7-11-0 **96**.. WilsonRenwick 92
(Lucy Normile) *led: clr 7th to 9th: hdd next: led 5 out to appr next: outpcd whn hit 3 out: sn no ch w first two* **10/3**[2]

210- 4 26 **Muwalla**[29] 2173 6-11-12 **108**..(tp) JasonMaguire 77
(Chris Grant) *sn chsng ldr: led 10th to 5 out: lost tch after next: t.o* **13/2**

PFP- U **King's Chorister**[21] 2335 7-9-12 **85**..................................(t) TonyKelly(5)
(Barry Murtagh) *hld up in tch: stdy hdwy 9th: hit and uns rdr 11th* **12/1**

5F2- U **Ben Akram (IRE)**[20] 2361 5-10-13 **100**................................ DerekFox(5)
(Lucinda Russell) *chsng ldrs whn distracted by rival: j.rt and uns rdr 2nd* **3/1**[1]

5m 3.6s (2.40) **Going Correction** +0.125s/f (Yiel) **6** Ran SP% **109.5**
Speed ratings (Par 105): **100,98,92,82,**
toteswingers 1&2 £3.80, 1&3 £2.80, 2&3 £2.10 CSF £19.64 TOTE £7.20: £3.50, £2.90; EX 25.10 Trifecta £84.00 Pool: £1641.71 - 14.65 winning units..

Owner The Whisperers **Bred** Mrs P M Grainger **Trained** Farlam, Cumbria

FOCUS
A pretty modest event. The winner had long been on a good mark but was left with little to beat.

2792 CORNHILL BUILDING SERVICES LTD MAIDEN HURDLE (12 hdls) 2m 4f
1:45 (1:45) (Class 4) 4-Y-O+ **£3,249** (£954; £477; £238)

Form RPR

/22- 1 **Mandarin Sunset (IRE)**[173] 676 6-11-0 110..................... BrianHughes 112+
(James Ewart) *trckd ldrs gng wl: wnt 2nd bef 3 out: led last: sn drvn along: kpt on wl* **4/1**[3]

143- 2 2 1/2 **Bellgrove (IRE)**[21] 2341 5-11-0 0.................................. DougieCostello 110+
(Ian Semple) *t.k.h: w ldr: led 4th: rdn 2 out: hit and hdd last: rallied run-in: one pce towards fin* **13/8**[1]

3 13 **Yourholidayisover (IRE)**[66] 733 6-10-9 0...................... JoeColliver(5) 96
(Patrick Holmes) *hld up: hdwy to chse ldrs appr 3 out: rdn and outpcd by first two fr next* **50/1**

252- 4 10 **Biggar (IRE)**[21] 2340 5-10-7 0................................... GrahamWatters(7) 87
(Lucinda Russell) *led to 4th: w ldr to 4 out: drvn and wknd after next* **7/4**[2]

504/ 5 21 **Dissidancer (IRE)**[276] 4436 5-10-7 0................................ JohnDawson(7) 68
(John Wade) *prom tl rdn and wknd appr 3 out* **16/1**

00- 6 17 **Inniscastle Boy**[21] 2341 4-11-0 0.. GaryBartley 53
(Jim Goldie) *nt fluent on occasions: hld up: rdn 4 out: btn next* **66/1**

/26- 7 10 **Azerodegree (IRE)**[6] 313 4-11-0 109.................................(v1) AdrianLane 44
(Iain Jardine) *hld up bhd ldng gp: hit and rdn 7th: wknd fr 4 out* **18/1**

PP4- P **Askalott (IRE)**[138] 959 8-10-7 0................................ MissAMcGregor(7)
(Jean McGregor) *hld up: mstke and lost tch 7th: p.u next* **100/1**

0/5- P **Geanie Mac (IRE)**[22] 2309 4-10-7 95.............................(p) LucyAlexander
(Linda Perratt) *nt fluent in rr: rdn 9th: wknd after next: no ch whn p.u bef last* **20/1**

4m 53.2s (1.70) **Going Correction** -0.125s/f (Good)
WFA 4 from 5yo+ 8lb **9** Ran SP% **114.8**
Speed ratings (Par 105): **91,90,84,80,72 65,61,,**
toteswingers 1&2 £1.50, 1&3 £4.60, 2&3 £5.20 CSF £11.04 TOTE £4.20: £1.60, £1.10, £7.00; EX 12.50 Trifecta £195.50 Pool: £2557.74 - 9.80 winning units..

Owner The Sunsets **Bred** John Studd **Trained** Langholm, Dumfries & G'way

FOCUS
No depth to this maiden hurdle, which was run at a modest pace. The winner was the form pick on and is rated to a similar level.

2793 WEATHERBYS PRINTING SERVICES ST ANDREW'S DAY H'CAP CHASE (12 fncs) 2m
2:20 (2:20) (Class 3) (0-135,132) 4-Y-O+ **£7,797** (£2,289; £1,144; £572)

Form RPR

1 **Claragh Native (IRE)**[42] 1966 8-10-4 **110**...................(tp) LucyAlexander 123+
(Martin Todhunter) *cl up: effrt and led 3 out: hung rt after next: drvn clr fr last* **20/1**

3PO- 2 6 **Endeavor**[27] 2222 8-9-10 **107**... TonyKelly(5) 113
(Dianne Sayer) *in tch: hdwy to ld 4 out: hdd next: effrt and ev ch 2 out: outpcd appr last* **12/1**

401- 3 1 1/2 **Quito Du Tresor (FR)**[21] 2346 9-10-12 **125**....................(p) CraigNichol(7) 131
(Lucinda Russell) *prom: hdwy to ld 6th: rdn and hdd 4 out: kpt on same pce bef 2 out* **11/4**[2]

0/3- 4 29 **Inoogoo (IRE)**[21] 2350 8-10-3 **109**...............................(t) DougieCostello 94
(Brian Ellison) *j.lft: led to 6th: cl up tl rdn and wknd fr 3 out* **15/8**[1]

1/0- P **Nine Stories (IRE)**[21] 2344 8-11-2 **122**.......................(b1) WilsonRenwick
(Chris Grant) *mstkes in rr: outpcd whn hmpd 5th: t.o whn p.u after 5 out* **12/1**

/14- F **Sleep In First (FR)**[173] 678 7-11-7 **127**............................... BrianHughes
(James Ewart) *in tch whn fell 5th* **7/1**

/41- P **Swift Arrow (IRE)**[20] 2359 7-11-12 **132**............................ JasonMaguire
(Donald McCain) *bhd: rdn and outpcd after 4th: nvr on terms: t.o whn p.u bef 4 out* **4/1**[3]

3m 50.8s (-1.60) **Going Correction** +0.125s/f (Yiel) **7** Ran SP% **114.1**
Speed ratings (Par 107): **109,106,105,90, ,**
toteswingers 1&2 £17.40, 1&3 £13.40, 2&3 £17.00 CSF £203.27 TOTE £17.00: £7.60, £5.90; EX 174.40 Trifecta £620.00 Pool: £2371.73 - 2.86 winning units..

Owner Mrs S J Matthews **Bred** B Mellon **Trained** Orton, Cumbria

FOCUS
Not a strong handicap chase for the grade, and there are doubts over the form, but the time was decent. The winner is rated up a stone on the best of his Irish chase form.

2794 BORDER SAFEGUARD H'CAP HURDLE (9 hdls) 2m
2:55 (2:55) (Class 5) (0-100,100) 4-Y-O+ **£3,249** (£954; £477; £238)

Form RPR

006/ 1 **Pass Muster**[270] 4571 6-10-8 **87**.. AdamNicol(5) 109+
(Philip Kirby) *cl up: chal 1/2-way: led gng wl 3 out: clr whn hit next: nt fluent last: easily* **7/1**

102- 2 11 **Cadore (IRE)**[22] 2306 5-11-5 **100**..............................(p) GrantCockburn(7) 105
(Lucy Normile) *hld up: rdn along 4 out: hdwy next: chsd (clr) wnr run-in: no imp* **11/2**[3]

2/6- 3 6 **Vittachi**[20] 2360 6-9-9 **74** oh2.....................................(p) CallumWhillans(5) 76
(Alistair Whillans) *led: rdn 1/2-way: hdd 3 out: nt fluent next: outpcd and lost 2nd run-in* **12/1**

/10- 4 3/4 **Push Me (IRE)**[15] 1979 6-11-0 **95**.. DaleIrving(7) 95
(Iain Jardine) *hld up: rdn and hdwy bef 3 out: edgd rt and no imp fr next* **16/1**

/43- 5 6 **Lysino (GER)**[17] 2449 4-11-11 **99**.................................... WilsonRenwick 93
(Chris Grant) *hld up in midfield: effrt and rdn after 4 out: outpcd fr next* **10/1**

606- 6 8 **Lillioftheballet (IRE)**[22] 2306 6-10-11 **85**...................(v1) LucyAlexander 71
(Jim Goldie) *in tch tl rdn and wknd fr 3 out* **18/1**

P/0- 7 3 1/2 **Golden Future**[13] 2519 10-11-10 **98**..................................... BrianHughes 81
(Peter Niven) *chsd ldrs: drvn after 4 out: wknd after next* **20/1**

5FU- P **Laybach (IRE)**[20] 2361 9-10-0 **74** oh3....................................... GaryBartley
(Jim Goldie) *cl up: struggling 4 out: t.o whn p.u next* **40/1**

400/ P **Destiny Blue (IRE)**[17] 1188 6-11-2 **90**..........................(t) DougieCostello
(Brian Ellison) *in tch: rdn after 4 out: wknd bef next: p.u bef 2 out* **10/1**

450- P **Palus San Marco (IRE)**[36] 2051 4-11-12 **100**.................. JasonMaguire
(Charlie Longsdon) *towards rr: early reminders: hdwy on outside 4th: wknd next: t.o whn p.u 3 out* **3/1**[1]

/53- P **Rhymers Stone**[20] 2360 5-11-3 **98**...................................... CraigNichol(7)
(Lucinda Russell) *bhd: outpcd after 3rd: nvr on terms: no ch whn p.u 3 out* **7/2**[2]

3m 46.8s (-1.60) **Going Correction** -0.125s/f (Good) **11** Ran SP% **119.3**
Speed ratings (Par 103): **99,93,90,90,87 83,81,,,**
toteswingers 1&2 £11.80, 1&3 £39.70, 2&3 £15.90 CSF £46.62 CT £462.87 TOTE £11.10: £4.30, £2.60, £4.70; EX 64.20 Trifecta £794.60 Pool: £1910.12 - 1.80 winning units..

Owner C B Construction (Cleveland) Limited **Bred** Darley **Trained** Middleham, N Yorks

FOCUS
An ordinary handicap hurdle run at a good gallop. A couple of the market leaders under-performed. A big step up from the easy winner but he is entitled to be better than this on Flat form.

2795 32REDPOKER.COM MAIDEN OPEN NATIONAL HUNT FLAT RACE 2m
3:25 (3:25) (Class 5) 4-6-Y-O **£1,949** (£572; £286; £143)

Form RPR

1 **Wilcos Mo Chara (IRE)**[207] 5-11-2 0.................................. JasonMaguire 115+
(Donald McCain) *mde all: shkn up and qcknd clr 2f out: easily* **11/10**[1]

3- 2 11 **Ollie G**[205] 173 5-11-2 0.. WilsonRenwick 100
(Chris Grant) *hld up in tch: hdwy 5f out: outpcd over 3f out: rallied to chse (clr) wnr over 1f out: no imp* **5/1**[3]

3 6 **Varene De Vauzelle (FR)**[173] 4-11-2 0................................. BrianHughes 95
(James Ewart) *t.k.h: cl up: wnt 2nd over 5f out: rdn over 2f out: edgd rt and one pce over 1f out* **3/1**[2]

4 1 **Calton Entry (IRE)** 4-11-2 0... DougieCostello 94
(Ian Semple) *hld up in tch: drvn and outpcd 6f out: rallied 4f out: outpcd fnl 2f* **14/1**

5 1 **Trackanais (FR)** 6-11-2 0...(t) LucyAlexander 93
(Simon Shirley-Beavan) *t.k.h: trckd ldrs: hdwy to chal after 4f to 1/2-way: outpcd over 3f out: n.d after* **14/1**

5/ 6 40 **Horton**[551] 457 5-10-9 0... GrahamWatters(7) 57
(Barry Murtagh) *prom: pushed along over 4f out: wknd over 3f out: t.o* **25/1**

7 14 **Waterside Road** 4-11-2 0.. AdrianLane 44
(Iain Jardine) *t.k.h: in tch on ins: outpcd 6f out: struggling fnl 3f: t.o* **20/1**

3m 43.24s (0.44) **Going Correction** -0.125s/f (Good) **7** Ran SP% **111.2**
Speed ratings: **93,87,84,84,83 63,56**
toteswingers 1&2 £1.70, 1&3 £1.10, 2&3 £4.30 CSF £6.58 TOTE £2.10: £2.20, £1.90; EX 5.50 Trifecta £11.20 Pool: £1745.12 - 116.34 winning units..

Owner A&K Ecofilm Ltd **Bred** Michael Crean **Trained** Cholmondeley, Cheshire

FOCUS
Subsequent Cheltenham festival winner Brindisi Breeze was runner-up in this race two years ago. A moderate bumper overall but the winner looks well above aerage.

T/Plt: £2,929.50 to a £1 stake. Pool: £48156.48 - 12.00 winning tickets T/Qpdt: £400.80 to a £1 stake. Pool: £4279.06 - 7.90 winning tickets RY

[illegible] NEWBURY (L-H)
Friday November 29

OFFICIAL GOING: [illegible]

Wind: Moderate ahead Weather: Overcast, some sunny periods

2796 [illegible] ASSOCIATES JUVENILE HURDLE ([illegible]) 2m 110y
[illegible] (Class 3) 3-Y-O £6,498 (£1,908; £954; £477)

Form				RPR
	1		**Calipto (FR)**[78] 3-10-12 0 .... DarylJacob (Paul Nicholls) *hld up in tch: hdwy to trck ldrs in 3rd appr 3 out: travelling best whn tk slt ld and nt fluent last: drvn and styd on strly sn after* **5/2**[1]	126+
	2	3 1/4	**Activial (FR)**[75] 3-10-12 0 .... NoelFehily (Harry Fry) *trckd ldr: upsides fr 3rd and styd chalng fr 3 out: rdn 2 out: chsd wnr last: styd on but no imp run-in* **8/1**[3]	121+
	3	5	**Chocala (IRE)**[46] 3-10-12 0 .... RobertThornton (Alan King) *led after 1st and jnd fr 3rd: stl hrd pressed whn rdn 2 out: hdd last and dropped to 3rd: no ch w ldng duo after* **5/2**[1]	118+
	4	5	**Dawalan (FR)**[147] 3-10-12 0 .... BarryGeraghty (Nicky Henderson) *led tl after 1st: chsd ldrs tl rdn appr 3 out: outpcd 2 out and no ch after but kpt on run-in* **5/1**[2]	112+
3-	5	8	**Andi'Amu (FR)**[26] 2248 3-10-9 0 ....(t) GavinSheehan(3) (Warren Greatrex) *in rr: rdn after 3 out: kpt on same pce fr 2 out* **20/1**	105
	6	7	**Baradari (IRE)**[168] 3-10-12 0 .... AidanColeman (Venetia Williams) *chsd ldrs: hit 3 out: wknd next* **5/1**[2]	100
U-	7	8	**Shalianzi (IRE)**[20] 2364 3-10-9 0 ....(b[1]) JoshuaMoore(3) (Gary Moore) *j. slowly 3rd: a towards rr: no ch fr 3 out* **33/1**	93
	8	7	**Star Of Mayfair (USA)**[38] 3-10-12 0 .... SamTwiston-Davies (Alan Jarvis) *chsd ldrs to 4 out: wknd bef next* **100/1**	87
6-	9	35	**Youmaysee**[11] 2557 3-10-5 0 .... DominicElsworth (Mick Channon) *a in rr: lost tch after 4 out: t.o whn blnd 2 out* **66/1**	62

4m 5.7s (-4.30) **Going Correction** -0.275s/f (Good) 9 Ran SP% 111.8
Speed ratings (Par 106): **99,97,95,92,89 85,81,78,62**
toteswingers 1&2 £5.10, 1&3 £1.70, 2&3 £3.90 CSF £22.11 TOTE £3.60: £1.40, £2.20, £1.30; EX 19.40 Trifecta £87.90 Pool: £2260.13 - 19.27 winning units..
Owner Ian Fogg & Chris Giles **Bred** Andre Priolet **Trained** Ditcheat, Somerset

FOCUS
Bends moved in from Thursday. It was dry overnight and underfoot conditions were expected to be very close to the previous day's going on both courses. Although this juvenile event has not produced a Triumph Hurdle winner in the past decade, it's always informative and this year's edition was an absorbing affair. There was a solid early gallop and two leaders went some way clear leaving the back straight, so it was a proper test. The form looks good and the race should produce winners.

2797 BET365 CONDITIONAL JOCKEYS' H'CAP CHASE (15 fncs) 2m 2f 110y
1:00 (1:00) (Class 3) (0-125,125) 4-Y-O+ **£6,498** (£1,908; £954; £477)

Form				RPR
233-	1		**Highway Code (USA)**[16] 2461 7-11-9 **122** ....(t) JoshuaMoore (Richard Lee) *in tch: hdwy to trck ldrs 11th: slt ld appr 4 out: drvn to assert after 3 out: kpt on strly run-in* **5/1**[3]	133+
/41-	2	2 1/2	**Massena (IRE)**[8] 2628 6-10-2 **104** .... HarryChalloner(3) (Venetia Williams) *chsd ldr: chal fr 11th and upsides 4 out: sn rdn: chsd wnr fr next: kpt on but a hld run-in* **4/1**[2]	112
/33-	3	2 1/4	**Ballywatt (IRE)**[23] 2293 7-11-3 **119** ....(tp) TomBellamy(3) (Kim Bailey) *in rr but in tch: hdwy appr 4 out: tk 3rd and rdn 2 out: kpt on run-in but no imp on ldng duo* **6/1**	125
3/4-	4	14	**Wings Of Smoke (IRE)**[63] 1670 8-11-9 **125** ....(t) MichaelByrne(3) (Tim Vaughan) *in rr: blnd 8th: hdwy 4 out: tk 3rd and rdn 3 out: wknd sn after* **7/1**	120
2/1-	5	1/2	**Definite Dream (IRE)**[30] 2159 6-11-4 **120** .... AdamWedge(3) (Evan Williams) *chsd ldrs to 4 out whn mstke: sn wknd* **11/4**[1]	115
3/0-	6	8	**Wessex King (IRE)**[191] 432 9-11-4 **120** .... JakeGreenall(3) (Henry Daly) *led tl hdd & wknd appr 4 out* **20/1**	106
1/F-	7	nk	**Majorica King (FR)**[195] 369 7-11-2 **118** .... ThomasGarner(3) (Oliver Sherwood) *in rr but in tch: hdwy and mstke 11th: wknd 4 out* **12/1**	104
2/5-	8	41	**Speed Master (IRE)**[19] 2389 7-11-2 **123** .... RyanHatch(8) (Nigel Twiston-Davies) *dropped in rr and rdn 5th: no ch fr 7th: t.o fr 9th* **7/1**	72

4m 31.87s (1.87) **Going Correction** -0.075s/f (Good) 8 Ran SP% 115.1
Speed ratings (Par 107): **93,91,91,85,84 81,81,64**
toteswingers 1&2 £5.20, 1&3 £3.90, 2&3 £5.50 CSF £26.08 CT £122.31 TOTE £5.60: £1.70, £1.60, £2.10; EX 15.60 Trifecta £159.30 Pool: £2474.12 - 11.64 winning units..
Owner D E Edwards **Bred** T Leung **Trained** Byton, H'fords

FOCUS
This modest handicap for conditional riders was run at a sound gallop and it saw plenty holding a chance turning for home, but they got sorted out from the third-last fence. The winner is rated in line with the best of his hurdles form.

2798 PERTEMPS NETWORK H'CAP HURDLE SERIES (QUALIFIER) (12 hdls) 3m 110y
1:30 (1:31) (Class 3) (0-140,137) 4-Y-O+
£8,758 (£2,587; £1,293; £646; £323; £162)

Form				RPR
/U5-	1		**Mickie**[20] 2371 5-11-3 **128** .... JakeGreenall(3) (Henry Daly) *in tch: rdn and one pce after 3 out: styd on wl fr 2 out: str run after last to ld fnl 150yds: kpt on wl* **9/1**	137
253-	2	1 1/2	**Pateese (FR)**[25] 2268 8-11-2 **134** ....(p) ThomasCheesman(10) (Philip Hobbs) *in rr: hdwy after 4 out: slt ld 2 out: hrd pressed and nt fluent last: hdd and no ex fnl 150yds* **33/1**	144+
400-	3	8	**Red Not Blue (IRE)**[13] 2504 10-11-5 **127** .... DominicElsworth (Simon Earle) *in rr: hdwy appr 3 out: styd on wl fr 2 out: blnd last: styd on wl clsng stages to take 3rd but no ch w ldng duo* **66/1**	129
122-	4	1	**Twelve Roses**[27] 2230 5-11-8 **130** .... SamTwiston-Davies (Kim Bailey) *in tch chsd ldrs fr 4 out: chsd ldr after 2 out: chal and nt fluent last: no ex run-in* **6/1**[2]	131+
/30-	5	1/2	**Kilmurvy (IRE)**[20] 2362 5-10-12 **123** ....(p) MattGriffiths(3) (Jeremy Scott) *chsd ldrs: rdn 3 out: hit 2 out: no ex whn hit last* **20/1**	123
1/2-	6	7	**Western Warhorse (IRE)**[12] 2529 5-11-3 **125** .... TomScudamore (David Pipe) *led: drvn 4 l clr appr 3 out: hdd 2 out: sn wknd* **9/2**[1]	120+
F11-	7	4	**Invicta Lake (IRE)**[11] 2569 6-10-6 **121** 7ex........(p) MrHAABannister(7) (Suzy Smith) *in rr: hdwy fr 3 out: styd on appr last: nt rch ldrs* **33/1**	111
211-	8	1	**Minella For Steak (IRE)**[23] 2288 6-11-4 **126** ....(b) APMcCoy (Jonjo O'Neill) *chsd ldrs to 3 out: sn btn* **8/1**	115
112/	9	2 1/4	**Fourovakind**[227] 5328 8-11-6 **131** .... JeremiahMcGrath(3) (Harry Whittington) [illegible] **16/1**	118
000	10	1 1/4	**Virginia Ash (IRE)**[10] 2430 5-10-4 **112** ....(b) BrendanPowell (Colin Tizzard) *chsd ldr: drvn along fr 8th: wknd 3 out* [illegible]	97
1/2	11	1 1/2	[illegible] [illegible] **20/1**	110
615/	12	20	**Chiberta King**[48] 4141 7-11-6 **128** .... TomO'Brien (Andrew Balding) *chsd ldrs to 3 out* **6/1**[2]	93
/51-	13	9	**Free To Dream (IRE)**[8] [illegible] .... AidanColeman (Venetia Williams) *chsd ldrs to 4 out: wknd bef next* **13/2**[3]	94
1/0-	14	1 1/2	**Amigo (FR)**[29] 2180 6-11-11 **133** ....(tp) ConorO'Farrell (David Pipe) *chsd ldrs to 4 out: wknd next* **25/1**	89
416/	15	22	**Upham Atom**[227] 5329 10-10-11 **119** .... TomSiddall (Kate Buckett) *rdn 5th: a in rr* **100/1**	55
1/4-	16	13	**Seventh Sign**[25] 2268 4-11-10 **132** ....(p) RobertThornton (Alan King) *chsd ldrs tl 4 out: wknd bef next* **33/1**	56
6/2-	17	8	**Dawn Twister (GER)**[20] 2362 6-11-1 **123** .... NoelFehily (Lucy Wadham) *towards rr most of way* **25/1**	40
P/4-	18	68	**Arthurian Legend**[34] 2077 8-11-12 **134** ....(b[1]) RichardJohnson (Philip Hobbs) *prom early: bhd fr 5th: t.o* **25/1**	
1/6-	19	5	**Firebird Flyer (IRE)**[19] 2388 6-11-3 **125** .... PaulMoloney (Evan Williams) *a bhd: t.o* **66/1**	
0/P-	P		**Aiteen Thirtythree (IRE)**[20] 2373 9-11-10 **132** ....(p) DarylJacob (Paul Nicholls) *a towards rr: t.o after 4 out: p.u bef last* **25/1**	
020/	P		**Rangitoto (IRE)**[293] 4122 8-11-1 **130** .... MissAliceMills(7) (Charles Whittaker) *a in rr: t.o 4 out p.u bef last* **100/1**	

6m 0.27s (-8.03) **Going Correction** -0.275s/f (Good)
WFA 4 from 5yo+ 9lb 21 Ran SP% 128.1
Speed ratings (Par 107): **101,100,97,97,97 95,93,93,92,92 91,85,82,81,74 70,68,46,44,**
toteswingers 1&2 £49.90, 1&3 Not won, 2&3 Not won CSF £279.20 CT £17041.22 TOTE £11.10: £2.60, £7.00, £13.60, £1.90; EX 399.10 TRIFECTA Not won..
Owner Ludlow Racing Partnership **Bred** J B Sumner **Trained** Stanton Lacy, Shropshire

FOCUS
A highly competitive staying handicap and it was run at a generous gallop. Under new rules this season, the first eight home qualify for the final of this series at the Cheltenham Festival in March. The time was good and the first two ran personal bests.

2799 FULLER'S LONDON PRIDE NOVICES' CHASE (REGISTERED AS BERKSHIRE NOVICES' CHASE) (GRADE 2) (16 fncs) 2m 4f
2:05 (2:07) (Class 1) 4-Y-O+ **£17,911** (£7,059; £3,805)

Form				RPR
/11-	1		**Wonderful Charm (FR)**[20] 2374 5-11-8 152 ....(t) DarylJacob (Paul Nicholls) *trckd ldr: nt fluent 9th: slt ld fr 2 out tl qcknd to assert run-in: readily* **8/11**[1]	152+
/12-	2	6	**Up To Something (FR)**[27] 2211 5-11-8 140 ....(tp) NoelFehily (Charlie Longsdon) *j.w: led tl narrowly hdd 2 out: styd upsides to last: outpcd by wnr run-in but styd on wl for 2bnd* **14/1**	142
/23-	3	3 3/4	**The Romford Pele (IRE)**[14] 2489 6-11-1 134 .... APMcCoy (Rebecca Curtis) *r in 4th: mistale 2: 3rd and 4th: j. slowly 6th (water): lft 3rd 8th: mstke 4 out: drvn to press ldrs next: btn after 2 out* **6/1**[3]	135
/25-	F		**Tanerko Emery (FR)**[12] 2533 7-11-1 0 ....(t) ConorO'Farrell (David Pipe) *chsd ldrs in 3rd tl fell 8th* **5/2**[2]	

5m 0.69s (-2.31) **Going Correction** -0.075s/f (Good) 4 Ran SP% 107.4
Speed ratings (Par 115): **101,98,97,**
CSF £8.46 TOTE £1.80; EX 6.80 Trifecta £15.20 Pool: £3364.68 - 165.78 winning units..
Owner R J H Geffen **Bred** Jean-Philippe Dubois **Trained** Ditcheat, Somerset

FOCUS
This usually goes the way of a top-notcher and had been won by the likes of Bobs Worth, Denman and Dynaste in recent years. There was no hanging about. The winner didn't need to improve and is a potential 160 novice chaser in a stronger race.

2800 BET365 OPEN H'CAP CHASE (16 fncs) 2m 4f
2:40 (2:41) (Class 2) 4-Y-O+
£31,280 (£9,240; £4,620; £2,310; £1,155; £580)

Form				RPR
0/0-	1		**Cantlow (IRE)**[28] 2199 8-11-5 **140** .... APMcCoy (Paul Webber) *in rr but in tch: hdwy 8th: chsng ldrs whn blnd 4 out: nt fluent next: styd on wl fr 2 out to take slt ld last but hrd pressed tl asserted u.p fnl 150yds* **6/1**[3]	152+
P0F-	2	1 3/4	**Easter Meteor**[13] 2503 7-11-8 **143** .... DominicElsworth (Emma Lavelle) *hit 2nd: chsd ldrs tl led 11th: hdd next: led again 4 out: rdn appr last and narrowly hdd: stl chalng run-in tl outpcd fnl 150yds* **5/1**[2]	151
211/	3	3 1/2	**Grandioso (IRE)**[279] 4387 6-11-10 **145** ....(t) RyanMahon (Paul Nicholls) *chsd ldrs: rdn to take 3rd after 3 out: styd on u.p rn-in but no imp on ldng duo* **14/1**	150
2/3-	4	8	**Upsilon Bleu (FR)**[20] 2359 5-11-3 **138** .... TimmyMurphy (Pauline Robson) *hld up in rr: hdwy 10th: chsd ldr next: led 12th: hdd 4 out: wknd u.p bef last* **9/1**	137
5/1-	5	2	**Niceonefrankie**[7] 2645 7-11-0 **135** 6ex .... AidanColeman (Venetia Williams) *in tch: chsd ldrs 12th: rdn 4 out: btn after 3 out* **9/4**[1]	131
1/2-	6	3/4	**Ackertac (IRE)**[20] 2365 8-11-9 **147** ....(b) MichaelByrne(3) (Tim Vaughan) *chsd ldrs: rdn 4 out: u.p and one pce whn hmpd 3 out: no ch after* **20/1**	141
F14/	7	3/4	**Cedre Bleu (FR)**[225] 5361 6-11-4 **139** ....(bt) DarylJacob (Paul Nicholls) *in tch: hdwy and sltly hmpd 3 out: styng on same pce whn blnd 2 out and no ch after* **9/1**	133
4/P-	8	28	**Quinz (FR)**[27] 2214 9-11-5 **140** .... RichardJohnson (Philip Hobbs) *led3rd: hit 10th: hdd next: wknd 12th* **20/1**	108
33-	9	3/4	**Full Jack (FR)**[41] 1976 6-11-2 **137** .... AlainCawley (Pauline Robson) *a in rr* **66/1**	105
030-	U		**Theatrical Star**[14] 2488 7-10-12 **133** .... JoeTizzard (Colin Tizzard) *led to 3rd: wknd 11th: t.o whn blnd bdly and uns rdr 3 out* **7/1**	
/15-	U		**Hazy Tom (IRE)**[26] 2244 7-11-7 **142** .... NoelFehily (Charlie Longsdon) *in tch: hit 7th: chsd ldrs 12th: wnt lft u.p 3 out: btn whn blnd bdly and uns rdr next* **16/1**	137

4m 55.43s (-7.57) **Going Correction** -0.075s/f (Good) 11 Ran SP% 117.8
Speed ratings (Par 109): **112,111,109,106,105 105,105,94,93,**
toteswingers 1&2 £6.40, 1&3 £10.20, 2&3 £11.80 CSF £36.15 CT £407.45 TOTE £5.60: £2.00, £2.60, £3.60; EX 33.00 Trifecta £623.00 Pool: £2902.52 - 3.49 winning units..
Owner John P McManus **Bred** Mrs Ann Jenkins **Trained** Mollington, Oxon

FOCUS
A decent prize and a good-quality field. There was no more than a fair early gallop on and it saw the principals fight it out from the second-last. The first three are rated in line with the best of last season's form.

2801 INKERMAN E B F MARES' "NATIONAL HUNT" NOVICES' HURDLE (10 hdls) 2m 5f
3:15 (3:17) (Class 3) 4-Y-0+ **£6,498** (£1,908; £954; £477)

Form RPR
3/1- **1** **Carole's Spirit**[25] 2273 5-11-2 0 NoelFehily 132+
(Robert Walford) *trckd ldr after 3rd: chal 4 out: led 3 out: hrd pressed and rdn last: kpt on wl to go clr run-in* **11/8**[1]
214/ **2** *6* **Fabrika**[225] 5364 5-10-10 0 BarryGeraghty 121+
(Nicky Henderson) *in tch: mstke 5th: hdwy to trck ldrs 3 out: wnt 2nd sn after travelling ok and chalng whn mstke last: no ex and outpcd* **11/4**[2]
3 *8* **Tagrita (IRE)**[201] 5-10-10 0 DarylJacob 113+
(Paul Nicholls) *hld up in rr but in tch: shkn up after 4 out: drvn to take 3rd 2 out: styd on same pce* **11/2**[3]
/10- **4** *3* **Toubeera**[13] 2505 7-11-6 133 AidanColeman 119
(Venetia Williams) *led tl hdd 3 out: wknd 2 out* **8/1**
/41- **5** *5* **Midnight Cataria**[36] 2043 4-11-2 0 WayneHutchinson 111
(Alan King) *chsd ldrs: rdn 3 out: wknd next* **28/1**
543- **6** *22* **Oscar's Pet (IRE)**[37] 2027 5-10-10 0 FelixDeGiles 88
(Tom Symonds) *hit 1st: in rr: wknd 3 out* **66/1**
5- **P** **Tropical Three (IRE)**[47] 1893 5-11-6 122 APMcCoy
(Michael Hourigan, Ire) *chsd ldr to 3rd: chal 6th to 4 out: wknd 3 out: p.u bef next* **8/1**
5m 10.58s (-8.42) **Going Correction** -0.275s/f (Good)
WFA 4 from 5yo+ 8lb 7 Ran SP% **111.3**
Speed ratings (Par 107): **105,102,99,98,96 88,**
toteswingers 1&2 £1.10, 1&3 £2.60, 2&3 £2.40 CSF £5.15 TOTE £2.50: £1.70, £1.90; EX 5.90 Trifecta £25.00 Pool: £2970.13 - 88.86 winning units..
Owner Paul Murphy **Bred** Paul Murphy **Trained** Child Okeford, Dorset
FOCUS
This was a decent little mares' event. It turned into something of a speed test from the fourth-last, but the form still looks strong for the division. The winner is a decent mare and there is probably more to come.

2802 BET365 "NATIONAL HUNT" MAIDEN HURDLE (8 hdls) 2m 110y
3:45 (3:48) (Class 3) 4-Y-0+ **£6,498** (£1,908; £954; £477)

Form RPR
0/1- **1** **Wilde Blue Yonder (IRE)**[28] 2195 4-11-0 0 RobertThornton 127+
(Alan King) *chsd ldrs: wnt 2nd 2 out: rdn to chal whn hit last: led sn after: drvn out* **7/2**[2]
/10- **2** *1* **Seedling**[25] 2265 4-11-0 0 SamTwiston-Davies 125
(Charles Egerton) *chsd ldrs: rdn to take 3rd after 2 out: styd on u.p run-in to take 2nd last strides: no imp on wnr* **33/1**
232/ **3** *hd* **Tiqris**[324] 3573 5-11-0 0 (t) RichardJohnson 124
(Philip Hobbs) *mstke 1st: chsd ldr to next: led bef 2 out: jnd last: hdd sn after: kpt on u.p: one pce fnl 150yds and lost 2nd last strides* **7/1**[3]
41- **4** *6* **Sign Of A Victory (IRE)**[15] 2472 4-11-0 0 BarryGeraghty 121+
(Nicky Henderson) *trckd ldrs: rdn after 2 out: wknd last* **5/4**[1]
140/ **5** *13* **Fascino Rustico**[261] 4738 5-11-0 0 (t) RyanMahon 107
(Paul Nicholls) *in tch: hdwy appr 3 out: wknd bef next* **11/1**
4- **6** *8* **In Fairness (IRE)**[201] 239 4-11-0 0 DavidBass 100
(Nicky Henderson) *chsd ldrs to 3 out* **25/1**
/00- **7** *hd* **Ghost Of A Smile (IRE)**[23] 2286 5-10-9 0 RobertMcCarth(5) 100
(Ian Williams) *in rr: sme hdwy appr 3 out: no ch after* **100/1**
3P- **8** *4* **Mission To Mars (IRE)**[29] 2178 4-11-0 0 DaveCrosse 99
(Nigel Twiston-Davies) *led: hit 3 out: hdd bef 2 out and wkng whn blnd* **100/1**
34- **9** *nk* **Vazaro Delafayette (FR)**[20] 2375 4-11-0 0 TomScudamore 96
(David Pipe) *towards rr most of way* **25/1**
2/2- **10** *13* **Chase The Wind (IRE)**[41] 1974 4-11-0 0 NoelFehily 89
(Warren Greatrex) *in rr: sme hdwy after 4 out: sn wknd* **15/2**
6/0- **11** *3 ½* **Aldeburgh**[23] 2286 4-11-0 0 AlainCawley 81
(Jim Old) *mstke 1st and 4th: a in rr* **125/1**
0/1- **12** *2 ½* **Amazing Scenes (IRE)**[211] 76 4-11-0 0 BrendanPowell 79
(Brendan Powell) *chsd ldrs to 4th* **50/1**
402- **13** *3 ½* **Backhomeinderry (IRE)**[8] 2628 8-10-7 97 KieronEdgar(7) 76
(Kate Buckett) *a in rr* **66/1**
004- **14** *hd* **Chill Factor (IRE)**[19] 2385 4-10-11 0 RachaelGreen(3) 76
(Anthony Honeyball) *a in rr* **66/1**
4m 0.63s (-9.37) **Going Correction** -0.275s/f (Good) 14 Ran SP% **117.6**
Speed ratings (Par 107): **111,110,110,107,101 97,97,95,95,89 87,86,85,84**
toteswingers 1&2 £17.90, 1&3 £4.90, 2&3 £23.60 CSF £110.78 TOTE £4.50: £1.70, £6.10, £1.90; EX 112.40 Trifecta £985.80 Pool: £6118.30 - 4.65 winning units..
Owner Maybe Only Fools Have Horses **Bred** Edmond Kent **Trained** Barbury Castle, Wilts
FOCUS
This is always a strong maiden. Despite the fact they were fairly strung out early, the majority took a keen grip and the first four dominated from two out. The winner is rated in line with his recent winning mark along with the fourth.
T/Jkpt: £17,994.30 to a £1 stake. Pool: £25344.15 - 1.00 winning tickets T/Plt: £81.60 to a £1 stake. Pool: £84655.81 - 756.71 winning tickets T/Qpdt: £37.10 to a £1 stake. Pool: £6972.07 - 139.05 winning tickets ST

2450 BANGOR-ON-DEE (L-H)
Saturday, November 30

OFFICIAL GOING: Soft
Wind: Nil Weather: Fine

2803 GINGER MCCAIN MEMORIAL NOVICES' CHASE (18 fncs) 3m 110y
12:30 (12:30) (Class 3) 4-Y-0+ **£6,498** (£1,908; £954; £477)

Form RPR
F/1- **1** **Mendip Express (IRE)**[28] 2224 7-11-4 0 (t) MrWBiddick(5) 145+
(Harry Fry) *hld up: tk clsr order 9th: wnt 2nd 14th: travelling wl whn led bef 2 out: shkn up whn mstke last: sn rdn: pressed briefly run-in: styd on wl and in control towards fin* **3/1**[3]
/25- **2** *2* **Bob Ford (IRE)**[14] 2501 6-10-11 128 PatrickCorbett(5) 131
(Rebecca Curtis) *led: rdn and hdd bef 2 out: rallied to try and chal briefly run-in: one pce and hld towards fin* **15/8**[1]
111/ **3** *2 ¼* **Swatow Typhoon (IRE)**[266] 4648 6-11-2 132 HenryBrooke 130
(Donald McCain) *chsd ldrs: reminders after 6th: sn lost pl: hrd at work in rr fr 10th: outpcd 4 out: wnt 3rd 2 out: styd on u.p run-in but unable to get to front two* **5/2**[2]
231- **4** *15* **Buachaill Alainn (IRE)**[157] 839 6-11-9 134 (v) TomO'Brien 124
(Peter Bowen) *chsd ldr tl appr 7th: reminders sn after: hrd at work fr 10th in rr: wl outpcd 4 out: no imp after: wl btn whn mstke last* **13/2**
0/3- **5** *30* **Chestertern**[37] 2031 6-11-2 118 SeanQuinlan 96
(Jennie Candlish) *hld up: impr to chse ldr appr 7th: lost 2nd and mstke 14th: outpcd whn j.lft 4 out and 3 out: wl btn bef 2 out* **14/1**
6m 39.1s (19.30) **Going Correction** +1.00s/f (Soft) 5 Ran SP% **108.4**
Speed ratings (Par 107): **109,108,107,102,93**
CSF £9.05 TOTE £2.70: £2.40, £1.40; EX 7.60 Trifecta £27.10 Pool: £1,022.42 - 28.26 winning units..
Owner The Mendip Syndicate **Bred** Miss E Hamilton **Trained** Seaborough, Dorset
FOCUS
Will Biddick described the ground as "soft and softer in places", and Patrick Corbett said it was "soft and hard work". A good novice chase in which the runner-up set a sound gallop. The winner looks smart.

2804 AMI SYSTEMS H'CAP CHASE (8 fncs 4 omitted) 2m 1f 110y
1:00 (1:03) (Class 4) (0-115,115) 4-Y-0+ **£3,898** (£1,144; £572; £286)

Form RPR
621- **1** **Suprise Vendor (IRE)**[10] 2595 7-11-1 111 DaraghBourke(7) 122+
(Stuart Coltherd) *chsd ldr: led 2nd: mde rest: clr on long run to 2 out: advantage reduced at 2 out: nrly 4 l clr last: pushed clr run-in: styd on wl* **7/4**[2]
463- **2** *6* **Detour Ahead**[9] 2626 5-10-5 94 (v[1]) SeanQuinlan 98
(Jennie Candlish) *led to 2nd: chsd ldr: mstke 3rd: reminders after: lost 2nd after 5th: pushed along after: outpcd after 6th: rallied to cl 2 out: nrly 4 l down last: one pce and no further imp run-in* **5/1**[3]
0/0- **3** *26* **Air Chief**[29] 2198 8-11-6 112 JohnKington(3) 90
(Andrew Crook) *hld up: pushed along after 5th: sn outpcd: plugged on wout troubling ldrs fr 2 out* **28/1**
/04- **4** *nk* **Blackwater King (IRE)**[31] 2159 5-11-12 115 HenryBrooke 93
(Donald McCain) *racd keenly: prom: wnt 2nd after 5th: upsides after next: rdn on long run to 2 out: sn wknd* **11/8**[1]
266- **P** **Lough Coi (IRE)**[4] 2727 7-10-10 99 (bt[1]) JamesDavies
(Anthony Middleton) *hld up in rr: struggling after 3rd: t.o 6th: p.u bef 2 out* **15/2**
4m 40.8s (18.70) **Going Correction** +1.00s/f (Soft) 5 Ran SP% **110.3**
Speed ratings (Par 105): **98,95,83,83,**
CSF £10.53 TOTE £2.40: £1.50, £2.70; EX 4.70 Trifecta £77.20 Pool: £1,250.70 - 12.14 winning units..
Owner Aidan Gunning **Bred** P Travers **Trained** Selkirk, Borders
FOCUS
The chases were scheduled for the start of the card to try and avoid potential problems with a low sun, but three obstacles had to be omitted in this ordinary handicap. The winner was thrown in on his recent win and is rated to a similar level.

2805 CORBETTSPORTS H'CAP CHASE (12 fncs 6 omitted) 3m 110y
1:30 (1:31) (Class 3) (0-125,125) 4-Y-0+ **£6,498** (£1,908; £954; £477)

Form RPR
0/3- **1** **Castle Conflict (IRE)**[30] 2177 8-11-1 114 TomO'Brien 125+
(Henry Daly) *sn w ldr: led 9th: drew clr appr 2 out: idled run-in whn in command* **9/4**[1]
0/F- **2** *5* **Gwladys Street (IRE)**[31] 2155 6-10-10 109 RyanMahon 107
(William Kinsey) *chsd ldrs: pushed along appr 5th: lost pl and rdn after 6th: in rr 7th: struggling to keep up and almost losing tch 9th: wnt poor 3rd bef 2 out: tk 2nd last: kpt on wout troubling wnr* **9/1**
36F- **3** *7* **Polarbrook (IRE)**[29] 2201 6-11-2 115 (b) HenryBrooke 107
(Donald McCain) *hld up: mstke 2nd: wnt 3rd at 8th: chsd wnr 10th: rdn appr 2 out: sn btn* **6/1**
6/3- **4** *24* **Carpincho (FR)**[12] 2567 9-10-8 110 JackQuinlan(3) 77
(Sarah Humphrey) *led: hdd 9th: sn pushed along: wknd after 10th* **11/4**[3]
132/ **P** **Fentara**[224] 5406 8-11-7 125 (p) MrWBiddick(5)
(Tim Walford) *chsd ldrs: pushed along appr 9th: rallied whn mstke 10th: wknd on long run between 3 out and 2 out: t.o whn p.u bef 2 out* **5/2**[2]
6m 43.5s (23.70) **Going Correction** +1.00s/f (Soft) 5 Ran SP% **110.3**
Speed ratings (Par 107): **102,100,98,90,**
CSF £18.98 TOTE £2.80: £1.70, £4.30; EX 31.20 Trifecta £117.20 Pool: £971.56 - 6.21 winning units..
Owner Strachan,Clarke,Gabb,Corbett & Salwey **Bred** B S T Syndicate **Trained** Stanton Lacy, Shropshire
FOCUS
A fair handicap chase. Again three fences were omitted, placing less emphasis on jumping. The idling winner was value for further and is on the upgrade.

2806 RAY WILLIAMSON "NATIONAL HUNT" NOVICES' HURDLE (5 hdls 4 omitted) 2m 1f
2:00 (2:05) (Class 4) 4-Y-0+ **£3,249** (£954; £477; £238)

Form RPR
F11- **1** **Key To The West (IRE)**[4] 2728 6-10-12 125 JakeHodson(7) 127
(David Dennis) *chsd ldrs: moved into 2nd appr 2 out where jst over 1 l down whn lft in ld: sn clr: styd on wl* **5/2**[2]
542- **2** *12* **Rolling Maul (IRE)**[20] 2385 5-10-12 117 TomO'Brien 109
(Peter Bowen) *chsd ldr tl rdn appr 2 out where lft 2nd: no imp on wnr after* **7/4**[1]
3- **3** *25* **It's A Doddle (IRE)**[14] 2507 5-10-7 0 MauriceLinehan(5) 88
(Jonjo O'Neill) *hld up in rr: pushed along after 3rd: outpcd on long run to 2 out: sn btn* **3/1**[3]
6/0- **4** *78* **Wing Mira (IRE)**[24] 2285 5-10-7 0 HarryChalloner(5) 5
(Venetia Williams) *hld up in rr: struggling 3rd: sn lost tch: t.o* **50/1**
1/2- **F** **Master Red (IRE)**[17] 2453 4-10-12 0 HenryBrooke 118
(Donald McCain) *led: over 3 l clr on long run to 2 out: rdn and over 1 l up whn fell 2 out* **9/2**
4m 19.2s (8.30) **Going Correction** +0.675s/f (Soft) 5 Ran SP% **110.1**
Speed ratings (Par 105): **107,101,89,52,**
CSF £7.51 TOTE £4.30: £2.00, £1.10; EX 6.20 Trifecta £17.40 Pool: £1,671.81 - 71.72 winning units..
Owner Favourites Racing **Bred** Paddy Behan **Trained** Hanley Swan, Worcestershire

FOCUS
An interesting novice hurdle. They jumped only five flights but the penultimate of those caught out Master Red, who was still in front when coming down. He was heading for a step up, and the winner arguably rates a personal best.

2807 RACING UK H'CAP HURDLE ([illegible] hdls [illegible] omitted) 3m
[illegible] ([illegible]) (Class [illegible]) (0-[illegible]) 4-Y-O+ £[illegible] (£1,900; £954; £477)

Form RPR
F52/ 1 Alderley Rover (IRE)[illegible] [4626] 9-11-13 119 HenryBrooke 124+
(Donald McCain) [illegible]
[illegible] [illegible]/1
0/1- 2 [illegible] [illegible] (IRE)[27] [illegible] 9-10-11 117 [illegible] 119
(Jennie Candlish) hld up: hdwy on long run to 3 out: chsd wnr between last 2: hit last: styd towards fin 9/1
U/0- 3 [illegible] [illegible] (IRE)[24] [illegible] [illegible] RyanMahon 121
([illegible]) [illegible]
15/8[1]
305- 4 2 ½ **Howizee**[30] [2170] 7-10-12 **125**.................................(t) StephenMulqueen[(7)] 123
(Maurice Barnes) *hld up: pushed along and effrt appr 2 out: one pce bef last* **16/1**
0/0- 5 1 ½ **American Life (FR)**[34] [2105] 6-9-9 **106** oh4............(bt) MauriceLinehan[(5)] 101
(Anthony Middleton) *in tch: lost pl 4th: rdn and swtchd rt bef 2 out: tried to rally: one pce sn after* **6/1**[3]
P/4- 6 ½ **Wellforth (IRE)**[14] [2510] 9-10-9 **115**..................................(p) DavidEngland 110
(Barry Brennan) *w ldr tl rdn and wknd on long run to 2 out* **12/1**
/26- 7 36 **Hada Men (USA)**[17] [2454] 8-11-7 **132**........................... HarryChalloner[(5)] 102
(Venetia Williams) *in rr: niggled along bef 3rd: struggling bef 4th: sn detached: n.d after* **17/2**
PP1/ P **Shalone**[231] [5293] 9-11-4 **124**...(p) GerardTumelty
(Adrian Wintle) *in tch: losing pl whn n.m.r 4f out on long run to 2 out: sn wknd: p.u bef 2 out* **33/1**
311/ P **Western Jo (IRE)**[232] [5265] 5-11-3 **123**................................ TomO'Brien
(Philip Hobbs) *prom: ev ch 3f out on long run to 2 out: sn wknd: bhd whn p.u bef last* **4/1**[2]

6m 18.3s (27.30) **Going Correction** +0.675s/f (Soft) **9** Ran SP% **112.0**
Speed ratings (Par 107): **81,80,79,78,78 78,66, ,**
toteswingers: 1&2 £9.50, 1&3 £14.90, 2&3 £3.80. CSF £162.19 CT £445.72 TOTE £21.50: £4.80, £1.70, £1.10; EX 137.50 Trifecta £520.70 Pool: £1,541.52 - 2.22 winning units..
Owner Alec Craig & Andrew Dick **Bred** Miss Kitty O'Connor **Trained** Cholmondeley, Cheshire
■ Stewards' Enquiry : Sean Quinlan four-day ban: use whip (14-17 Dec)

FOCUS
A fair handicap hurdle run at a steady pace. With the omitted hurdles the form should be taken with a pinch of salt. The winner was well in on old hurdles form.

2808 FANWAZE NOVICES' HURDLE (11 hdls) 2m 4f
3:10 (3:11) (Class 4) 4-Y-O+ **£3,249** (£954; £477; £238)

Form RPR
21- 1 **The Last Samuri (IRE)**[21] [2355] 5-11-5 0.......................... HenryBrooke 132+
(Donald McCain) *prom: chal fr 3 out: rdn bef next: abt 1 l down whn lft in ld and hmpd last: styd on* **7/2**[3]
/12- 2 2 ¾ **Horizontal Speed (IRE)**[17] [2461] 5-11-5 128....................... TomO'Brien 127+
(Philip Hobbs) *prom: w ldr 6th: led 7th: hdd 4 out: outpcd after 3 out: lft 2nd last: kpt on: no real imp on wnr* **11/10**[1]
36- 3 3 ½ **Master Butcher (IRE)**[25] [2279] 6-10-7 0........................ PatrickCorbett[(5)] 112
(Rebecca Curtis) *in tch: rdn appr 3 out: sn outpcd: no imp after* **25/1**
/45- 4 10 **Royal Palladium (FR)**[14] [2509] 5-10-7 0................... HarryChalloner[(5)] 102
(Venetia Williams) *hld up: rdn and lft bhd after 3 out* **33/1**
/P0- 5 40 **Shipton**[17] [2457] 4-10-12 0... AlainCawley 62
(Brendan Powell) *a bhd: struggling 7th: t.o* **100/1**
5/3- P **Miss Duffy**[184] [552] 5-10-5 0.. RyanMahon
(William Kinsey) *hld up: lost tch after 4 out: t.o whn p.u bef last* **66/1**
342- F **My Wigwam Or Yours (IRE)**[18] [2432] 4-10-9 0...... JeremiahMcGrath[(3)] 127+
(Nicky Henderson) *racd keenly: led: hdd 7th: led again 4 out: nt fluent 2 out: shkn up abt 1 l ahd whn fell last* **2/1**[2]

5m 26.6s (34.60) **Going Correction** +0.675s/f (Soft)
WFA 4 from 5yo+ 8lb **7** Ran SP% **112.4**
Speed ratings (Par 105): **57,55,54,50,34 ,**
toteswingers: 1&2 £1.30, 1&3 £11.20, 2&3 £11.20. CSF £7.82 TOTE £6.60: £3.60, £1.10; EX 10.80 Trifecta £52.90 Pool: £1,662.84 - 23.55 winning units..
Owner Paul & Clare Rooney **Bred** Edmond Coleman **Trained** Cholmondeley, Cheshire

FOCUS
They went a steady pace in this fair novice hurdle, which was decided at the final flight. A step up from the fortunate winner.

2809 GOLDFORD STUD MARES' STANDARD OPEN NATIONAL HUNT FLAT RACE 2m 1f
3:45 (3:45) (Class 6) 4-6-Y-O **£2,053** (£598; £299)

Form RPR
1 **Bitofapuzzle**[294] 5-10-12 0...(t) RyanMahon 109+
(Harry Fry) *mde all: drew clr 1f out: styd on wl: comf* **5/2**[2]
2 8 **Mighty Minnie** 4-10-12 0.. TomO'Brien 98
(Henry Daly) *hld up: shkn up whn struggling to go pce 6f out: styd on fnl 2f: tk 2nd fnl 150yds: no ch w wnr* **4/1**[3]
43/ 3 1 ¾ **Jessica Valentine (IRE)**[360] [2851] 6-10-7 0........... ColmMcCormack[(5)] 96
(Keith Reveley) *chsd wnr for 4f: remained cl up: lft 2nd over 2f out: no imp on wnr: lost 2nd fnl 150yds: kpt on same pce* **13/2**
02/ 4 2 **Pandy**[224] [5413] 4-10-9 0..(t) TrevorWhelan[(3)] 94
(George Baker) *in tch: pushed along and outpcd 6f out: kpt on fnl 2f but no real imp* **14/1**
53- 5 17 **Kilkenny Kim (IRE)**[19] [2422] 4-10-5 0.............................. ConorRing[(7)] 80
(Jennie Candlish) *hld up: hdwy to chse ldrs 5f out: wknd wl over 1f out* **12/1**
6 99 **Radmores Surprise** 4-10-5 0.. CiaranMckee[(7)]
(John O'Shea) *hld up in rr: struggling 7f out: lost tch 5f out: t.o* **25/1**
7 20 **Sunsational Girl** 4-10-9 0.. PeterCarberry[(3)]
(Brian Eckley) *midfield: rdn and wknd 6f out: t.o* **50/1**
P **Mona Agnes (IRE)**[268] [4628] 5-10-12 0.................................. AlainCawley
(Fergal O'Brien) *racd keenly: chsd ldrs: wnt 2nd after 4f: chal 3f out: sn wnt bdly wrong and p.u* **9/4**[1]

4m 26.2s (20.90) **Going Correction** +0.675s/f (Soft) **8** Ran SP% **112.8**
Speed ratings: **77,73,72,71,63 16,7,**
toteswingers: 1&2 £1.70, 1&3 £6.00, 2&3 £13.40. CSF £12.62 TOTE £3.70: £1.10, £2.30, £2.10; EX 15.80 Trifecta £46.80 Pool: £1,741.76 - 27.86 winning units..
Owner Richard Barber **Bred** R J & S A Carter **Trained** Seaborough, Dorset

FOCUS
A fair race of its type. The winner looks a decent mare and should win more races.

T/Plt: £47.10 to a £1 stake. Pool: £45,554.41 - 720.48 winning tickets. T/Qpdt: £9.60 to a £1 stake. Pool: £2,270.55 - 174.05 winning tickets. DO

2796 NEWBURY (L-H)
Saturday, November 30

OFFICIAL GOING: Hurdle course - soft (good to soft in places), chase course - good (good to soft in places)
Wind: Virtually nil Weather: Sunny spells

2810 THOROUGHBRED BREEDERS ASSOCIATION MARES' NOVICES' HURDLE (LISTED RACE) (8 hdls) 2m 110y
12:20 (12:20) (Class 1) 4-Y-O+ **£11,888** (£4,452; £2,224; £1,110)

Form RPR
113- 1 **As I Am (IRE)**[21] [2371] 5-11-0 133.................................... ConorShoemark 132+
(Don Cantillon) *mde all: 8 l clr 2nd: drvn whn packed clsd 2 out: forged clr again bef last: unchal* **11/2**[3]
/12- 2 9 **The Pirate's Queen (IRE)**[29] [2190] 4-11-0 0................. RobertThornton 126+
(Alan King) *hld up in rr but in tch: hdwy 3 out: disp 2nd next: rdn and styng on same pce whn blnd last: no ch w wnr but kpt on wl for 2nd* **12/1**
3 1 ¼ **Vicky De L'Oasis (FR)**[35] [2092] 4-11-0 0................................... RWalsh 123
(W P Mullins, Ire) *hld up in rr but in tch: stdy hdwy to dispute 2nd 2 out: rdn sn after: styng on one pce whn hit last: no ex run-in* **1/1**[1]
110- 4 2 ¾ **Rosie Probert**[15] [2492] 4-11-0 124....................................... BarryGeraghty 121
(Nicky Henderson) *chsd ldr to 4th: styd wl there: rdn after 3 out and edgd lft bef 2 out: styd on same pce appr last* **8/1**
0/1- 5 11 **Brijomi Queen (IRE)**[23] [2309] 6-11-0 0....................................... NoelFehily 111
(Nicky Richards) *in rr but in tch: hdwy to cl on ldrs after 4 out: wknd 2 out* **33/1**
0/1- 6 7 **Free Thinking**[16] [2467] 5-11-0 0.................................... MrSWaley-Cohen 107
(Nicky Henderson) *racd in 3rd: hit 2nd: chsd ldr fr 4th to 3 out: wknd qckly and hit 2 out* **7/2**[2]

3m 54.0s (-16.00) **Going Correction** -0.575s/f (Firm)
WFA 4 from 5yo+ 7lb **6** Ran SP% **109.4**
Speed ratings (Par 111): **114,109,109,107,102 99**
toteswingers 1&2 £2.90, 2&3 £3.30, 1&3 £1.30 CSF £54.91 TOTE £5.70: £2.30, £3.70; EX 41.60 Trifecta £128.50 Pool: £784.32 - 4.57 winning units..
Owner Don Cantillon **Bred** Don Cantillon **Trained** Newmarket, Suffolk

FOCUS
Bends moved in from Friday. The going was officially described as Good to soft, soft in places on the hurdles track and Good, good to soft in places on the chase track. Only the second running of this Listed mares' novices' hurdle. The winner set a consistent pace from the start and was particularly impressive. She's rated to her best minus her rider's claim.

2811 BET365.COM NOVICES' LIMITED H'CAP CHASE (13 fncs) 2m 1f
12:50 (12:50) (Class 3) (0-140,135) 4-Y-O+ **£9,470** (£2,858; £1,472; £779)

Form RPR
2/1- 1 **Valdez**[17] [2460] 6-11-5 **135**.. RobertThornton 159+
(Alan King) *in rr but in tch: hdwy and mstke 6th: led 9th: gng clr whn j.rt 3 out: v easily* **2/1**[2]
/P2- 2 24 **Un Bon P'Tit Gars (FR)**[24] [2287] 5-10-9 **125**................ RichardJohnson 123
(Nick Williams) *led: hdd 9th: no ch w wnr after 4 out but styd on for clr 2nd* **11/2**[3]
/F1- 3 9 **Flaming Charmer (IRE)**[24] [2287] 5-10-10 **126**....................... JoeTizzard 116
(Colin Tizzard) *in rr but in tch: hit 5th: lost pl 4 out: blnd 2 out: styd of for mod 3rd fnl 150yds* **11/2**[3]
F/3- 4 3 ¾ **Earls Quarter (IRE)**[41] [1986] 7-11-0 **130**.........................(t) AidanColeman 118
(Ian Williams) *chsd ldr: mstke 2nd: hit 5th: btn into 3rd after 9th: no ch w wnr fr 4 out: dropped to mod 4th fnl 150yds* **25/1**
F **Black River (FR)**[265] 4-10-11 **134**.. DarylJacob
(Paul Nicholls) *trckd ldrs: travelling wl to dispute 2 l 2nd whn fell 8th* **5/4**[1]

3m 57.34s (-10.66) **Going Correction** -0.40s/f (Good) course record
WFA 4 from 5yo+ 7lb **5** Ran SP% **112.4**
Speed ratings (Par 107): **109,97,93,91,**
CSF £12.85 TOTE £2.90: £1.40, £2.40; EX 11.30 Trifecta £45.30 Pool: £1043.93 - 17.27 winning units..
Owner Riverdee Stable **Bred** David & Julie Andrews **Trained** Barbury Castle, Wilts

FOCUS
This looked an interesting small-field contest, but the fall of the favourite some way out probably robbed the race of an exciting climax. The leader went a generous gallop and the winner set a new course record, but it's worth remembering that the way times are taken was changed at the start of this season (April 28th), as timing doesn't commence until the field has passed the starter. The winner looks a high-class novice.

2812 BET365 H'CAP CHASE (FOR THE FULKE WALWYN TROPHY) (17 fncs) 2m 6f 110y
1:20 (1:22) (Class 3) (0-135,135) 4-Y-O+
£9,384 (£2,772; £1,386; £693; £346; £174)

Form RPR
6F0/ 1 **Tatenen (FR)**[217] [5576] 9-11-5 **128**....................................... LeightonAspell 141+
(Richard Rowe) *hld up in rr: hdwy and n.m.r on inner after 12th: chsd ldrs 4 out: chal 2 out: pushed along sn after to ld: c readily clr run-in* **14/1**
/61- 2 8 **Carrigmorna King (IRE)**[9] [2630] 7-11-6 **129**.............(t) RichardJohnson 135+
(Philip Hobbs) *in rr and hmpd 1st: hit 2nd and 3rd: blnd 11th: hdwy 12th: mstke 4 out: chal and hit 3 out: upsides next: chsd wnr fr last but no ch* **9/2**[1]
F/0- 3 2 ½ **Ruben Cotter (IRE)**[15] [2487] 7-11-11 **134**.............................. DarylJacob 136
(Paul Nicholls) *in tch: hdwy 4 out: disp 2nd fr 3 out: styd on to take 3rd fnl 150yds but no ch w ldng duo* **10/1**
11P/ 4 1 ¾ **No Secrets (IRE)**[261] [4751] 9-11-6 **129**...........................(t) TomScudamore 129
(David Pipe) *led 2nd to 5th: led 12th to 4 out: styd chalng: led 2 out: hdd sn after: no ex run-in* **14/1**
FU1/ 5 ¾ **Valoroso**[259] [4782] 8-11-2 **125**...(t) ConorO'Farrell 125
(Richard Woollacott) *in rr tl hdwy 4 out and mstke: drvn to chse ldrs 2 out: styd on same pce appr last* **25/1**
/04- 6 1 ¼ **Solix (FR)**[26] [2269] 7-11-12 **135**..(p) JasonMaguire 133
(Ian Williams) *chsd ldrs: lost position bnd after 12th: bhd whn mstke 3 out: rallied fr 2 out: kpt on again run-in: fin wl* **33/1**
/24- 7 1 **What A Warrior (IRE)**[17] [2452] 6-11-11 **134**............ SamTwiston-Davies 130
(Nigel Twiston-Davies) *chsd ldrs: rdn and lost position 4 out: styd on again fr last* **20/1**

The Form Book Jumps, Raceform Ltd, Compton, RG20 6NL.

5/4- **8** *nk* **Violin Davis (FR)**[27] 2244 7-11-10 **133**..............................(tp) NoelFehily 130
(Harry Fry) *mstke 2nd: in rr: hdwy 12th: chsd ldrs 4 out: ev ch 2 out: wknd bef last* **14/1**

F/6- **9** *2 ¾* **Mr Gardner (IRE)**[25] 2283 10-10-12 **126**................ MrSWaley-Cohen(5) 120
(Polly Gundry) *led to 2nd: styd pressing tl led again 5th: hdd 9th: styd chalng next: led 11th: hdd 12th: wknd 2 out* **20/1**

450- **10** *½* **Gus Macrae (IRE)**[15] 2488 9-10-4 **123**..........................(tp) PaulO'Brien(10) 116
(Rebecca Curtis) *chsd ldrs: chal fr 12th tl slt ld 4 out: narrowly hdd 2 out: wknd sn after* **20/1**

/5U- **11** *½* **Sir Du Bearn (FR)**[26] 2269 7-11-9 **132**.......................... DonalDevereux 128
(Peter Bowen) *in tch: hit 9th and lost pl: blnd 4 out and 2 out: styd on again run-in* **33/1**

0/0- **12** *7* **Hector's Choice (FR)**[21] 2365 9-11-11 **134**...................... JamieMoore 123
(Richard Lee) *chsd ldrs: wknd 4 out* **12/1**

3/0- **13** *36* **Kilcrea Asla (IRE)**[187] 508 12-11-0 **123**.......................... RobertThornton 77
(Graeme McPherson) *mstke 9th: a in rr* **66/1**

4/3- **F** **Opera Og (IRE)**[17] 2450 7-10-8 **117**................................ AidanColeman
(Venetia Williams) *fell 1st* **7/1**

3/P- **P** **Arthur's Pass**[35] 2086 9-11-9 **132**.. RhysFlint
(Tom George) *chsd ldrs to 12th: t.o whn p.u bef last* **33/1**

/41- **P** **Handy Andy (IRE)**[15] 2487 7-11-8 **131**..........................(t) JoeTizzard
(Colin Tizzard) *chsd ldrs: led 9th to 11th: wknd and hit 13th: t.o whn p.u bef 2 out* **6/1[3]**

/F4- **P** **Rendl Beach (IRE)**[13] 2539 6-10-11 **120**...................(p) RichieMcLernon
(Rebecca Curtis) *blnd 4th: a in rr: t.o whn p.u bef last* **33/1**

6/4- **F** **The Druids Nephew (IRE)**[30] 2180 6-11-4 **132**.........(p) JamesBanks(5)
(Andy Turnell) *fell 1st* **5/1[2]**

5m 31.4s (-15.60) **Going Correction** -0.40s/f (Good) **18** Ran SP% **129.8**
Speed ratings (Par 107): **111,108,107,106,106 106,105,105,104,104 104,101,89, , , ,**
toteswingers 1&2 £20.60, 2&3 £15.10, 1&3 £34.50 CSF £72.82 CT £693.78 TOTE £21.40: £5.50, £1.70, £3.10, £2.80; EX 135.60 Trifecta £1360.10 Pool: £2445.46 - 1.34 winning units..

Owner The Stewart Family **Bred** Olivier Tricot **Trained** Sullington, W Sussex

FOCUS
A fiercely competitive handicap chase, though made a little less so when the fancied pair The Druids Nephew and Opera Og both departed at the first. Solid handicap form. The winner may still be capable of a bit better than this.

2813 BET365 H'CAP HURDLE (10 hdls) 2m 3f
1:50 (1:54) (Class 2) (0-150,144) 4-Y-O+**£19,494** (£5,724; £2,862; £1,431)

Form RPR

U/0- **1** **Vendor (FR)**[197] 356 5-10-12 **130**.. JackDoyle 138+
(Alan King) *hld up bhd: smooth prog fr 3 out: chal last: sn rdn to ld: r.o strly: rdn out* **16/1**

/02- **2** *2 ½* **Shotavodka (IRE)**[17] 2454 7-11-1 **140**.......................... KieronEdgar(7) 144
(David Pipe) *led: rdn after 3 out: jnd last: sn hdd: kpt on gamely but sn hld by wnr: jst hld on for 2nd* **12/1**

121- **3** *shd* **Don't Be Late (IRE)**[109] 1268 5-10-9 **127**...................(p) RichieMcLernon 131
(Jonjo O'Neill) *hld up towards rr: rdn after 3 out: hdwy after 2 out: styd on wl fr last: nrly snatched 2nd fnl stride* **20/1**

0/5- **4** *2 ¾* **Saphir Du Rheu (FR)**[21] 2366 4-10-6 **129**...................... HarryDerham(5) 131+
(Paul Nicholls) *mid-div tl outpcd appr 3 out: styd on wl fr last: wnt 4th run-in: clsng on ldrs at fin* **14/1**

343- **5** *5* **Gassin Golf**[28] 2225 4-10-4 **122**.. JamieMoore 120
(Richard Lee) *mid-div: smooth hdwy 3 out: disp 2nd next: rdn bef last: nt gng pce to chal: no ex run-in* **8/1[2]**

1/4- **6** *3* **Mischievous Milly (IRE)**[28] 2226 5-11-5 **137**................ LeightonAspell 131
(Oliver Sherwood) *hld up towards rr: hdwy on outer home turn: rdn to dispute 2nd 2 out: fdd fr last* **6/1[1]**

321/ **7** *1 ¼* **Batonnier (FR)**[672] 3961 7-11-1 **133**................................ RobertThornton 126
(Alan King) *mid-div: effrt 2 out: nvr gng pce to get involved w ldrs: styd on nicely fr last* **10/1[3]**

00P/ **8** *hd* **Punjabi**[239] 5162 10-10-12 **130**.. TomScudamore 123
(David Pipe) *mid-div: rdn after 2 out: styd on same pce fr last* **16/1**

1/5- **9** *½* **Gibb River (IRE)**[28] 2213 7-11-12 **144**............................ BarryGeraghty 137
(Nicky Henderson) *trckd ldrs: rdn to dispute 2nd 2 out: fdd run-in* **8/1[2]**

10F/ **10** *2* **Aegean Dawn**[385] 2337 8-11-5 **137**...................................... DavidBass 128
(Robert Walford) *mid-div: rdn appr 3 out: nt gng pce to get involved: wknd last* **14/1**

5/3- **11** *1 ½* **The Bear Trap (IRE)**[21] 2362 6-10-5 **123**...................(p) NoelFehily 114
(Rebecca Curtis) *hld up towards rr: hdwy after 7th: rdn to chse ldrs 2 out: fdd run-in* **10/1[3]**

/04- **12** *1 ¾* **Native Gallery (IRE)**[17] 2454 8-11-8 **140**...................... JasonMaguire 128
(Ben De Haan) *trckd ldr: rdn after 3 out: sn wknd* **14/1**

430/ **13** *2 ¼* **Imperial Leader (IRE)**[266] 4663 5-10-13 **131**.......(t) SamTwiston-Davies 119
(Nigel Twiston-Davies) *hld up towards rr early: trckd ldrs after 5th: jnd ldrs 7th tl rdn 3 out: hld whn blnd 2 out: wknd* **8/1[2]**

135- **14** *4* **Azure Fly (IRE)**[17] 2454 5-10-13 **131**.........................(tp) RichardJohnson 113
(Charlie Longsdon) *mid-div: rdn after 7th: wknd 3 out* **20/1**

500/ **15** *7* **Citizenship**[221] 5486 7-10-12 **130**...................................... AidanColeman 106
(Venetia Williams) *trckd ldr: rdn 3 out: wknd qckly* **16/1**

P/0- **16** *5* **Notus De La Tour (FR)**[35] 2080 7-10-13 **131**................... ConorO'Farrell 102
(David Pipe) *trckd ldrs tl after 5th: rdn after 7th: wknd bef 3 out* **16/1**

133/ **17** *31* **Master Of The Game (IRE)**[228] 5337 7-10-8 **126**.......... AndrewTinkler 70
(Nicky Henderson) *in tch: tk clsr order 5th: rdn after 3 out: sn wknd: t.o* **16/1**

4m 36.7s (-11.30) **Going Correction** -0.575s/f (Firm)
WFA 4 from 5yo+ 7lb **17** Ran SP% **132.4**
Speed ratings (Par 109): **100,98,98,97,95 94,93,93,93,92 92,91,90,88,85 83,70**
toteswingers 1&2 £78.60, 2&3 £62.10, 1&3 £113.30 CSF £210.73 CT £3872.67 TOTE £23.90: £4.60, £3.60, £2.40, £4.70; EX 370.40 Trifecta £15900.40 Pool: £71044.72 - 3.35 winning units..

Owner Thurloe 52 **Bred** Mme Marie-Therese Caron **Trained** Barbury Castle, Wilts

FOCUS
A really competitive event, but the early gallop was modest to say the least, meaning plenty took strong holds under restraint. The winner is rated back to the level of his juvenile form but it is not a race to be that confident about.

2814 BET365 LONG DISTANCE HURDLE (GRADE 2) (12 hdls) 3m 110y
2:25 (2:25) (Class 1) 4-Y-O+ **£23,048** (£8,816; £4,548; £2,400)

Form RPR

/16- **1** **Celestial Halo (IRE)**[174] 685 9-11-8 **161**......................(bt) DarylJacob 165+
(Paul Nicholls) *mde all: travelling wl whn lft w clr advantage 2 out: unchal* **7/2[2]**

P/2- **2** *17* **Medinas (FR)**[28] 2228 6-11-4 154.................................. RobertT[illegible]
(Alan King) *screwed 1st: in rr but in tch: drvn 6th: rdn after 4 out: sty[illegible] fr 2 out: nt fluent last and tk wl hld 2nd: all out to hold that position cl home* **1[illegible]**

/01- **3** *nk* **Reve De Sivola (FR)**[28] 2240 8-11-8 162...................... RichardJohn[illegible]
(Nick Williams) *chsd wnr to 2 out whn wl hld: sn lft disputing that positi[illegible] tl dropped to 3rd sn after last: rallied to press for that position cl home but no ch w unchal wnr* **7/2[illegible]**

11/- **4** *5* **At Fishers Cross (IRE)**[239] 5161 6-11-4 157.................. BarryGeraghty
(Rebecca Curtis) *nvr really jumping fluently: hit 2nd: trckd ldrs in 3rd: hdwy to trck wnr: 1 l down and pushed along whn screwed 2 out and stmbld bdly on landing: nt rcvr* **10/11[1]**

/1P- **R** **Battle Group**[14] 2503 8-11-4 150...................................(p) JasonMaguire
(Johnny Farrelly) *ref to r* **25/1**

5m 48.35s (-19.95) **Going Correction** -0.575s/f (Firm) **5** Ran SP% **112.4**
Speed ratings (Par 115): **108,102,102,100,**
CSF £26.04 TOTE £4.90: £2.40, £2.60; EX 22.70 Trifecta £79.80 Pool: £3391.15 - 31.84 winning units..

Owner The Stewart Family **Bred** Roncon Churchtown Bloodstock & Lane Ltd **Trained** Ditcheat, Somerset

FOCUS
Only four horses had won this Grade 2 staying hurdle in the previous ten years and there was no Big Buck's this time (who had taken the previous four runnings), but it was business as usual for that star hurdler's owner and trainer. Celestial Halo is rated to his best, with Medinas similar to Wetherby. At Fishers Cross looked to be heading for his mark.

2815 HENNESSY GOLD CUP CHASE (H'CAP) (GRADE 3) (21 fncs) 3m 2f 110y
3:00 (3:03) (Class 1) 4-Y-O+
£99,662 (£37,397; £18,725; £9,327; £4,690; £2,345)

Form RPR

1/3- **1** **Triolo D'Alene (FR)**[28] 2214 6-11-1 **147**.......................... BarryGeraghty 164+
(Nicky Henderson) *trckd ldrs: chal 4 out: slt ld fr 3 out: drvn: hit last and jnd: rallied wl u.p and sn asserted: styd on strly* **20/1**

113/ **2** *2 ¾* **Rocky Creek (IRE)**[239] 5158 7-11-5 **151**................................ DarylJacob 164
(Paul Nicholls) *chsd ldrs: str chal fr 3 out and upsides last: rdn sn after: kpt on same pce* **8/1**

1/3- **3** *1 ¾* **Theatre Guide (IRE)**[26] 2269 6-10-13 **145**.........................(t) JoeTizzard 156
(Colin Tizzard) *in rr: hdwy 12th: chsd ldrs fr 17th: kpt on to dispute 3rd 2 out: kpt on same pce u.p run-in* **33/1**

6/2- **4** *9* **Highland Lodge (IRE)**[34] 2108 7-10-11 **143**................. LeightonAspell 147
(Emma Lavelle) *led 2nd: kpt slt ld but a hrd pressed tl narrwly hdd 4 out: stl chalng 3 out: wknd last* **6/1[2]**

0/2- **5** *4 ½* **Merry King (IRE)**[28] 2214 6-10-8 **140**.......................... RichieMcLernon 140
(Jonjo O'Neill) *in rr: hdwy to cl on ldrs 17th: rdn 4 out: styd on fr 2 out: no imp on ldrs* **12/1**

4/1- **6** *shd* **Houblon Des Obeaux (FR)**[28] 2214 6-11-8 **154**............ LiamTreadwell 153
(Venetia Williams) *in rr hit 14th: rdn 17th: stl plenty to do u.p 2 out: styd on run-in but nvr a threat* **25/1**

124/ **7** *1 ¾* **Our Father (IRE)**[294] 4126 7-11-1 **147**........................(t) ConorO'Farrell 144
(David Pipe) *in rr: rdn 11th: hdwy 17th: styd on same pce u.p fr 4 out* **11/2[1]**

231/ **8** *2 ½* **Lord Windermere (IRE)**[262] 4734 7-11-8 **154**................. DougieCostello 152+
(J H Culloty, Ire) *towards rr whn hmpd 14th: hdwy next: chsd ldrs and rdn 4 out: wknd after 3 out* **7/1[3]**

/0P- **9** *nk* **Terminal (FR)**[73] 1604 6-10-12 **144**.............................. TomScudamore 139
(W P Mullins, Ire) *in rr: hmpd 14th: rdn 4 out: kpt on fr 2 out: nvr a threat* **33/1**

2/0- **10** *½* **Same Difference (IRE)**[28] 2214 7-11-1 **147**.........(v) SamTwiston-Davies 142
(Nigel Twiston-Davies) *in tch: hdwy 12th: hit 15th and 4 out: sn btn* **33/1**

131/ **11** *3 ¾* **Invictus (IRE)**[651] 4374 7-10-13 **145**.............................. RobertThornton 139+
(Alan King) *towards rr: hdwy 13th: chsd ldrs fr 17th: pressed ldrs 3 out: wknd sn after next: fin lame* **8/1**

3/1- **12** *1 ¼* **Cloudy Too (IRE)**[27] 2244 7-11-4 **150**.......................... RichardJohnson 141
(Sue Smith) *chsd ldrs: mstke 14th: wnt 2nd 17th: slt ld 4 out: narrowly hdd and hit next: sn wknd* **20/1**

2/3- **13** *2 ¼* **Prince De Beauchene (FR)**[28] 2234 10-11-9 **155**..................... RWalsh 143
(W P Mullins, Ire) *mstke 3rd: chsd ldrs: rdn 4 out: wknd next* **16/1**

5/2- **14** *8* **Loch Ba (IRE)**[17] 2452 7-10-1 **133**............................ DominicElsworth 115
(Mick Channon) *in rr: sme hdwy 17th: sn btn: blnd 2 out* **16/1**

P/0- **15** *36* **Whodoyouthink (IRE)**[33] 2137 8-9-11 **132**..............(p) PatrickMangan(3) 79
(Oliver McKiernan, Ire) *chsd ldrs: hit 10th: sn bhd* **100/1**

5/P- **16** *7* **Cape Tribulation**[28] 2229 9-11-12 **158**................................ JackDoyle 99
(Malcolm Jefferson) *rdn 16th: a in rr* **50/1**

P2P/ **P** **Imperial Commander (IRE)**[238] 5177 12-11-7 **153**.....(t) PaddyBrennan
(Nigel Twiston-Davies) *pressed ldr to 16th: wknd qckly next and p.u bef 4 out* **20/1**

211/ **F** **Katenko (FR)**[308] 3857 7-11-11 **157**.................................. AidanColeman
(Venetia Williams) *pressed ldrs: stl wl there and travelling ok whn fell 14th* **20/1**

P/P- **F** **Opening Batsman (IRE)**[28] 2214 7-11-0 **146**...................(tp) NoelFehily
(Harry Fry) *towards rr tl fell 5th* **25/1**

224/ **P** **Super Duty (IRE)**[239] 5158 7-11-2 **148**................................ JasonMaguire
(Donald McCain) *led first: sn hdd: chsd ldrs: bhd fr 11th: t.o whn p.u bef 17th* **14/1**

5/2- **U** **Hadrian's Approach (IRE)**[26] 2269 6-10-9 **146**......(p) NicodeBoinville(5)
(Nicky Henderson) *in tch tl mstke and uns rdr 5th* **12/1**

6m 25.94s (-20.06) **Going Correction** -0.40s/f (Good) **21** Ran SP% **136.7**
Speed ratings (Par 113): **113,112,111,109,107 107,107,106,106,106 105,104,103,101,90 88, , , ,**
toteswingers 1&2 £31.30, 2&3 £77.10, 1&3 £249.70 CSF £170.65 CT £5310.51 TOTE £26.30: £5.10, £2.80, £7.20, £2.80; EX 287.40 Trifecta £8676.40 Part won. Pool: £11568.59 - 0.30 winning units..

Owner Mr & Mrs Sandy Orr **Bred** Louis Couteaudier **Trained** Upper Lambourn, Berks

FOCUS
Some iconic horses have taken this contest down the years and it has produced a lot of tremendous finishes, but this renewal, while very open, didn't appear to contain any obvious potential Gold Cup winners. The gallop was predictably quick from the outset for such a competitive event, and it proved beneficial to race close to the pace. Triolo D'Alene seemed to win with a bit in hand and the second and third both posted personal bests. The winner is well up to the race standard.

2816 BET365 H'CAP CHASE (FOR THE JIM JOEL MEMORIAL TROPHY) (13 fncs) 2m 1f
3:35 (3:36) (Class 2) (0-145,145) 4-Y-O+
£18,768 (£5,544; £2,772; £1,386; £693; £348)

Form — RPR
4/4- **1** **Filbert (IRE)**[28] 2212 7-10-8 **127**........ RichardJohnson 138+
(Philip Hobbs) *hld up: hdwy after 9th: chal 3 out: shkn up whn 1 l down last: sn drvn: r.o wl to ld fnl 120yds: rdn out* **6/1**[3]
/10- **2** *3* **Parsnip Pete**[15] 2488 7-10-13 **132**........ PaddyBrennan 140+
(Tom George) *trckd ldrs: hmpd 8th: led after next: rdn after 4 out: 1 l up last: kpt on but no ex whn hdd fnl 120yds* **12/1**
/36- **3** *7* **Greywell Boy**[8] 2645 6-10-6 **125**........ SamTwiston-Davies 125
(Nick Williams) *prom: lft in ld 8th tl after next: rdn and ev ch 3 out: hld and kpt on same pce fr next* **7/1**
01P/ **4** *2 3/4* **Rody (FR)**[219] 5523 8-11-7 **145**........(t) AodhaganConlon(5) 143
(Tom George) *mid-div: pushed along after 8th: hdwy appr 4 out: sn rdn: styd on same pce fr 3 out* **33/1**
/05- **5** *1 1/4* **Elenika (FR)**[15] 2488 5-10-9 **128**........ AidanColeman 125
(Venetia Williams) *hld up: hdwy after 8th: rdn to chse ldrs after 4 out: styd on but nvr gng pce to get on terms* **6/1**[3]
/00- **6** *3 3/4* **Consigliere (FR)**[15] 2488 10-11-0 **140**........(p) KieronEdgar(7) 133
(David Pipe) *hld up towards rr: struggling 7th: sme late prog fr last: nvr trbld ldrs* **33/1**
/1F- **7** *nk* **Fairy Rath (IRE)**[28] 2212 7-10-13 **132**........(t) TomCannon 124
(Nick Gifford) *trckd ldrs: nt fluent 4th: rdn to chal 4 out: ev ch next tl hld 2 out: fdd run-in* **25/1**
U/0- **8** *2 1/4* **Ulck Du Lin (FR)**[28] 2212 5-11-11 **144**........ DarylJacob 136
(Paul Nicholls) *blnd 1st: towards rr: hmpd on bnd by loose horse after 8th: rdn appr 4 out: sme prog 2 out: wknd flat* **9/1**
1F0/ **9** *7* **Tetlami (IRE)**[237] 5198 7-11-5 **138**........ BarryGeraghty 122
(Nicky Henderson) *mid-div: in tch whn hmpd 8th: short-lived effrt 4 out: grad fdd* **9/2**[2]
521- **U** **Anay Turge (FR)**[15] 2488 8-10-12 **134**........(tp) MarkQuinlan(3)
(Nigel Hawke) *mid-div whn mstke: stmbld v bdly and uns rdr 8th* **8/1**
311- **U** **Next Sensation (IRE)**[15] 2496 6-11-0 **133**........(t) TomScudamore
(Michael Scudamore) *led tl blnd and uns rdr 8th* **7/2**[1]

3m 59.5s (-8.50) **Going Correction** -0.40s/f (Good) **11** Ran SP% **120.0**
Speed ratings (Par 109): **104,102,99,98,97 95,95,94,91,**
toteswingers 1&2 £18.50, 2&3 £12.80, 1&3 £6.20 CSF £73.35 CT £518.05 TOTE £5.90: £2.40, £2.30, £2.60; EX 55.70 Trifecta £498.00 Pool: £3213.68 - 4.83 winning units..
Owner R Triple H **Bred** Micheal Woodlock **Trained** Withycombe, Somerset

FOCUS
A competitive handicap chase to end the card. A big step up from the winner with the second in line with last year's C&D win.
T/Jkpt: Not won. T/Plt: £3,628.70 to a £1 stake. Pool of £202316.99 - 40.70 winning tickets.
T/Qpdt: £220.00 to a £1 stake. Pool of £21137.45 - 71.09 winning tickets. ST

2493 NEWCASTLE (L-H)
Saturday, November 30

OFFICIAL GOING: Good (good to soft in places; 7.3)
Wind: Fresh, half against Weather: Race 1 sunny, remainder cloudy

2817 PIN POINT RECRUITMENT NOVICES' LIMITED H'CAP CHASE (18 fncs 1 omitted) 3m
12:05 (12:05) (Class 3) (0-140,138) 4-Y-O+ **£6,498** (£1,908; £954; £477)

Form — RPR
/11- **1** **Green Flag (IRE)**[28] 2220 6-11-5 **138**........ PeterBuchanan 147+
(Lucinda Russell) *chsd ldrs: niggled along 1/2-way: clsd 5 out: led next: jst in front and shkn up whn lft nrly 13 l clr 2 out* **5/6**[1]
15P- **2** *9* **Green Wizard (IRE)**[20] 2395 7-10-9 **128**........ RyanMania 125
(Sue Smith) *chsd ldrs: nt fluent 4th: rdn and outpcd 6 out: rallied 4 out: lft 13 l 2nd 2 out: no ch w wnr* **5/1**[3]
523- **3** *7* **Scotswell**[14] 2517 7-9-12 **124** oh3........ MrJHamilton(7) 116
(Harriet Graham) *slt ld to 5 out: rdn and outpcd next: lft disputing 13 l 2nd 2 out: no ex* **6/1**
323- **4** *42* **Ocean Club**[22] 2337 6-10-5 **124** oh9........ JamesReveley 75
(Brian Ellison) *hld up last but in tch: drvn outpcd 6 out: no ch whn lft 4th 2 out* **22/1**
P1F- **F** **Streams Of Whiskey (IRE)**[28] 2220 6-10-5 **124** oh2........ BrianHarding 130
(Nicky Richards) *nt fluent on occasions: w ldr tl hit 11th: led 5 out to next: sn rdn: rallied and ev ch whn fell 2 out* **4/1**[2]

5m 51.5s (-31.00) **Going Correction** -1.025s/f (Hard) **5** Ran SP% **109.9**
Speed ratings (Par 107): **110,107,104,90,**
CSF £5.54 TOTE £1.80: £1.40, £2.10; EX 5.20 Trifecta £13.80 Pool: £ 1298.22 - 70.09 winning units..
Owner John R Adam **Bred** L M Walshe **Trained** Arlary, Perth & Kinross

FOCUS
Both bends moved and divided. Hurdles sited on fresh ground. After a dry spell the ground was reckoned only just on the slow side of good. Due to the low sun the first fence going away from the stands had to be omitted. Despite there being just five runners in this novices' limited handicap chase the pace was very sound with the two leaders taking each other on. The winner is a smart novice with the potential to rate higher.

2818 COOPERS' MARQUEES H'CAP CHASE (19 fncs) 3m
12:35 (12:37) (Class 5) (0-100,98) 4-Y-O+ **£2,144** (£629; £314; £157)

Form — RPR
P/2- **1** **Presented (IRE)**[22] 2339 6-11-9 **95**........ JamesReveley 111+
(Brian Ellison) *prom: stdy hdwy 5 out: led 2 out: drvn out* **9/4**[1]
345- **2** *3* **Twice Lucky**[14] 2518 9-10-8 **80**........ RyanMania 92
(Sue Smith) *hld up in midfield: stdy hdwy and cl up 13th: led bef 4 out to 2 out: rallied: kpt on same pce run-in* **10/1**
/22- **3** *13* **Shoal Bay Dreamer**[19] 2416 7-10-3 **80**........(p) TonyKelly(5) 80
(Dianne Sayer) *rn in snatches: midfield: drvn and outpcd 1/2-way: rallied u.p 6 out: outpcd after next: plugged on fr 3 out: no ch w first two* **8/1**[3]
/44- **4** *1/2* **Alexander Oats**[28] 2219 10-10-12 **84**........(p) BrianHughes 84
(Robert Goldie) *prom: rdn along 6 out: outpcd after next: kpt on fr 2 out: no imp* **16/1**
U3P/ **5** *nk* **Soul Angel**[222] 5450 9-10-7 **79**........(v) AdrianLane 78
(Sandy Forster) *in tch: hdwy to ld 12th: nt fluent 5 out: hdd bef next: sn drvn: wknd after 2 out* **33/1**
2/5- **6** *2* **Boris The Blade**[29] 2201 11-11-7 **98**........(b) SamanthaDrake(5) 96
(Tina Jackson) *led: mstke 11th: hdd next: rallied: outpcd whn nt fluent 4 out and next* **14/1**
265- **7** *36* **Quinder Spring (FR)**[23] 2310 9-11-3 **96**........(p) GrantCockburn(7) 61
(Lucinda Russell) *bmpd 1st: hld up: hdwy u.p after 13th: wknd 5 out* **25/1**
0/5- **8** *3/4* **Newspage (IRE)**[31] 2155 7-10-0 **72** oh6........ WilsonRenwick 36
(John Wade) *cl up: chal 6th: hit 13th and next: rdn and wknd bef 4 out* **4/1**[2]
300- **P** **Breeze With Ease (IRE)**[21] 2361 9-11-1 **87**........(tp) LucyAlexander
(Barry Murtagh) *hld up: hdwy into midfield after 9th: wknd fr 11th: t.o whn p.u bef 4 out* **66/1**
5/P- **F** **Gorey Lane (IRE)**[9] 2626 7-11-7 **93**........(v1) FearghalDavis
(John Norton) *hld up: j.rt: bmpd rival and fell 1st* **16/1**
46P/ **P** **Barnevelder (IRE)**[222] 5450 8-10-12 **84**........(tp) TomMessenger
(Sandy Forster) *nt jump wl: in tch: struggling fr 10th: t.o whn p.u 6 out* **16/1**
F05- **F** **Stagecoach Jasper**[22] 2334 7-11-11 **97**........ ShaneByrne
(Sue Smith) *nt fluent in rr: outpcd whn fell 13th* **10/1**
0/P- **P** **Notonebuttwo (IRE)**[22] 2334 6-10-11 **83**........ BarryKeniry
(Chris Grant) *nt fluent: a bhd: lost tch and p.u 6 out* **10/1**

6m 1.8s (-20.70) **Going Correction** -1.025s/f (Hard) **13** Ran SP% **121.7**
Speed ratings (Par 103): **93,92,87,87,87 86,74,74, , ,**
toteswingers 1&2 £15.60, 2&3 £9.00, 1&3 £15.30 CSF £25.96 CT £161.62 TOTE £3.20: £1.80, £2.80, £2.50; EX 26.20 Trifecta £129.40 Pool: £357.04 - 2.06 winning units..
Owner Miss C A Carr **Bred** Miss Catherine M Walsh **Trained** Norton, N Yorks

FOCUS
All the fences were jumped this time and again the pace was sound with the first two having it to themselves over the final three fences. There's a case for rating the form a bit higher through the beaten horses.

2819 STRAIGHTLINE CONSTRUCTION "THE FRENCH FURZE" NOVICES' HURDLE (13 hdls) 2m 6f
1:05 (1:08) (Class 2) 4-Y-O+
£9,384 (£2,772; £1,386; £693; £346; £174)

Form — RPR
2/1- **1** **Ballyalton (IRE)**[55] 1793 6-11-3 130........ APMcCoy 134+
(Ian Williams) *t.k.h: hld up: smooth hdwy to trck ldrs 4 out: plld out and led 2 out: edgd lft run-in: drvn out* **3/1**[2]
1/1- **2** *1/2* **Oscar Rock (IRE)**[29] 2196 5-11-3 0........ BrianHughes 133+
(Malcolm Jefferson) *trckd ldrs: wnt 2nd 8th: led gng wl 3 out: hdd next: sn drvn and edgd lft: rallied: kpt on u.p fr last: hld nr fin* **4/9**[1]
31- **3** *3 1/4* **Blakemount (IRE)**[14] 2520 5-11-3 0........ RyanMania 130+
(Sue Smith) *cl up: led 4 out: rdn and hdd next: nt fluent last: kpt on: nt gng pce of first two* **20/1**
1- **4** *8* **Five In A Row (IRE)**[37] 2037 5-10-12 0........ JamesReveley 119+
(Brian Ellison) *in tch: nt fluent 8th: rallied 4 out: drvn and outpcd next: no imp whn nt fluent last* **14/1**[3]
321- **5** *10* **Kilbree Chief (IRE)**[22] 2337 5-11-3 119........ PeterBuchanan 112
(Lucinda Russell) *led at stdy pce tl hdd 4 out: rdn and wknd fr next* **33/1**
0/4- **6** *13* **Master Murphy (IRE)**[22] 2336 8-10-12 93........ AlistairFindlay 94
(Jane Walton) *chsd ldr to 8th: sn pushed along: wknd after 4 out* **150/1**
303/ **7** *nk* **Caledonia**[49] 5179 6-10-12 0........ DenisO'Regan 95
(Jim Goldie) *t.k.h: hld up: stdy hdwy but stl in last pl whn hit and sprawled bdly 4 out: nt rcvr* **25/1**

5m 28.9s (-7.10) **Going Correction** -0.70s/f (Firm) **7** Ran SP% **113.1**
Speed ratings (Par 103): **84,83,82,79,76 71,71**
toteswingers 1&2 £1.02, 2&3 £3.40, 1&3 £5.60 CSF £4.80 TOTE £3.70: £1.70, £1.30; EX 6.30 Trifecta £23.50 Pool: £1615.58 - 51.55 winning units..
Owner John Westwood **Bred** P Doyle **Trained** Portway, Worcs

FOCUS
A high-class renewal of a 2m6f novices' hurdle that went the way of Green Flag a year ago. The pace was just steady until the final three-quarters of a mile. The winner and third are on the upgrade amd the second is rated below the level of his recent win.

2820 ANGLO SCOTTISH H'CAP CHASE (16 fncs) 2m 4f
1:35 (1:37) (Class 4) (0-115,115) 4-Y-O+ **£3,768** (£1,106; £553; £276)

Form — RPR
503- **1** **Swing Hard (IRE)**[21] 2356 5-11-2 **105**........ RyanMania 120+
(Sue Smith) *hld up in tch: stdy hdwy 1/2-way: led bef 4 out: rdn bef 2 out: styd on strly fr last* **5/1**[3]
/03- **2** *5* **Palos Conti (FR)**[29] 2201 10-11-5 **108**........ JamesReveley 119+
(Brian Ellison) *led to 8th: rallied and led after 5 out to bef next: chsd wnr: 2 l down and styng on whn blnd 2 out: one pce whn mstke last* **5/1**[3]
535- **3** *9* **Peachey Moment (USA)**[130] 1085 8-11-9 **112**........ DenisO'Regan 112
(Nicky Richards) *hld up: stdy hdwy after 5 out: effrt and rdn bef 3 out: outpcd fr next* **9/2**[2]
/30- **4** *hd* **See What Happens (IRE)**[17] 2450 7-11-12 **115**........(p) WilsonRenwick 116
(Martin Todhunter) *hld up: stdy hdwy and prom bef 4 out: effrt and rdn bef next: sn outpcd* **7/2**[1]
/51- **5** *2 1/2* **Badger Foot (IRE)**[14] 2518 8-10-9 **105**........(t) GrahamWatters(7) 103
(Lucinda Russell) *in tch: nt fluent 6 out: rdn and outpcd whn nt fluent 4 out: n.d after* **11/2**
/00- **6** *nk* **Riguez Dancer**[19] 2421 9-11-12 **115**........(b) WayneHutchinson 114
(Donald McCain) *cl up: led 8th: hit and hdd 5 out: rallied: wknd after next* **8/1**
/P2- **P** **Moyode Wood**[22] 2334 8-11-6 **109**........(tp) HarryHaynes
(Brian Ellison) *chsd ldrs: mstke and lost pl 7th: struggling fr next: lost tch and p.u 10th* **8/1**
6/S- **P** **Alfred Oats**[21] 2356 9-10-11 **100**........ BrianHughes
(Robert Goldie) *chsd ldrs: hit 7th: hit and outpcd 9th: wknd fr next: t.o whn p.u bef 4 out* **16/1**

5m 3.1s (-24.10) **Going Correction** -1.025s/f (Hard) **8** Ran SP% **117.2**
Speed ratings (Par 105): **107,105,101,101,100 100, ,**
toteswingers 1&2 £4.80, 2&3 £2.30, 1&3 £3.70 CSF £31.28 CT £121.50 TOTE £4.40: £1.60, £2.20, £1.80; EX 16.10 Trifecta £199.00 Pool: £734.30 - 2.76 winning units..
Owner DP van der Hoeven, DG Pryde & J Beaumont **Bred** Paddy Kinsella **Trained** High Eldwick, W Yorks

FOCUS
The pace was sound but still half a dozen were in with a shout turning for home. It soon only seriously involved only the first two. A step up from the winner and there should be more to come.

2821 STANJAMES.COM FIGHTING FIFTH HURDLE (GRADE 1) (9 hdls) 2m
2:05 (2:11) (Class 1) 4-Y-0+

£56,270 (£21,200; £10,610; £5,300; £2,660; £1,330)

Form RPR
121/ **1** **My Tent Or Yours (IRE)**[239] 5157 6-11-7 160 APMcCoy 155+
(Nicky Henderson) *t.k.h: hld up towards rr: hit 5th: nt fluent next: smooth hdwy to ld 2 out: shkn up and qcknd after last: comf* **8/11**[1]
1/1- **2** *3* **Cockney Sparrow**[28] 2226 4-11-0 141 BrianHughes 141+
(John Quinn) *chsd ldrs: wnt 2nd 5th: smooth hdwy and ev ch 3 out: sn rdn: wnt 2nd run-in: kpt on: nt gng pce of wnr* **6/1**[3]
314/ **3** *2½* **Grumeti**[224] 5402 5-11-7 151 WayneHutchinson 147
(Alan King) *t.k.h: prom: smooth hdwy to ld 3 out: rdn and hdd next: one pce fr last* **9/1**
0/4- **4** *1* **Cotton Mill**[21] 2372 6-11-7 147 (b[1]) DenisO'Regan 146
(John Ferguson) *led: nt fluent 3rd: qcknd clr next: rdn and hdd 3 out: kpt on same pce fr next* **16/1**
1/1- **5** *½* **Melodic Rendezvous**[21] 2372 7-11-7 155 NickScholfield 144
(Jeremy Scott) *prom: effrt and rdn appr 3 out: plugged on fr last: no imp* **5/2**[2]
411/ **6** *7* **Duke Of Navan (IRE)**[289] 4209 5-11-7 148 BrianHarding 137
(Nicky Richards) *t.k.h: hld up: stdy hdwy after 4 out: rdn and wknd after next* **20/1**
361- **7** *8* **Stormy Weather (FR)**[45] 1922 7-11-7 129 (p) JamesReveley 129
(Brian Ellison) *hld up in last pl: drvn and outpcd bef 4 out: nvr on terms* **100/1**
0/P- **8** *5* **Rock Relief (IRE)**[28] 2230 7-11-7 123 PeterBuchanan 124
(Chris Grant) *chsd ldr to 5th: rdn and wknd after next* **200/1**

3m 51.7s (-18.30) **Going Correction** -0.70s/f (Firm)
WFA 4 from 5yo+ 7lb **8** Ran SP% **122.9**
Speed ratings (Par 117): **117,115,114,113,113 110,106,103**
toteswingers 1&2 £2.10, 2&3 £10.00, 1&3 £5.90 CSF £6.89 TOTE £1.60: £1.02, £2.10, £2.10; EX 6.00 Trifecta £32.60 Pool: £3570.43 - 81.98 winning units..
Owner John P McManus **Bred** F Dunne **Trained** Upper Lambourn, Berks

FOCUS
The first Grade 1 of the jump season with many of the big name post-war hurdlers on the roll of honour. A strong renewal and an impeccable return to action for the winner. My Tent Or Yours didn't need to be at his best.

2822 AT THE RACES REHEARSAL CHASE (H'CAP) (LISTED RACE) (19 fncs) 3m
2:40 (2:42) (Class 1) 4-Y-0+

£22,780 (£8,548; £4,280; £2,132; £1,072; £536)

Form RPR
P/4- **1** **Hey Big Spender (IRE)**[35] 2070 10-11-4 **140** (t) BrendanPowell 149+
(Colin Tizzard) *hld up: hdwy and cl up 8th: led bef 4 out: rdn and edgd lft after 2 out: hrd pressed fr last: kpt on gamely u.p* **5/1**[2]
P/1- **2** *nk* **Vintage Star (IRE)**[19] 2419 7-11-1 **137** RyanMania 148+
(Sue Smith) *chsd ldrs: blnd 5th: hit 8th: effrt on outside and ev ch whn nt fluent 4 out: sn drvn: edgd lft after next: rallied to chal last: kpt on: hld nr fin* **9/4**[1]
0/3- **3** *9* **Baile Anrai (IRE)**[18] 2433 9-10-3 **125** (b[1]) HarrySkelton 125
(Dan Skelton) *led to 4th: led 7th to bef 4 out: rdn and outpcd by first two fr 2 out* **5/1**[2]
/21- **4** *3* **Ultimate**[29] 2199 7-11-7 **143** JamesReveley 141
(Brian Ellison) *pressed ldr: led 4th to 7th: cl up tl outpcd bef 4 out: rallied next: no imp* **16/1**
1/P- **5** *6* **Netminder (IRE)**[42] 1976 7-10-3 **125** PeterBuchanan 119
(Sandy Thomson) *chsd ldrs: blnd 13th: rdn and outpcd bef 4 out: n.d after* **6/1**[3]
/55- **6** *7* **Mr Moss (IRE)**[15] 2487 8-11-0 **136** PaulMoloney 123
(Evan Williams) *hld up: rdn along after 6 out: nvr able to chal* **9/1**
220/ **7** *35* **Tarquinius (FR)**[20] 2412 10-10-6 **128** (bt) WilsonRenwick 82
(Gordon Elliott, Ire) *hld up: outpcd whn blnd 10th: struggling fr 5 out* **20/1**
6/F- **8** *12* **Master Of The Hall (IRE)**[28] 2229 9-11-12 **148** DenisO'Regan 91
(Micky Hammond) *nt fluent: bhd: outpcd 12th: no ch whn mstke last* **22/1**
3/2- **P** **Mister Marker (IRE)**[27] 2246 9-10-13 **135** BrianHarding
(Nicky Richards) *in tch: rdn bef 6 out: wknd after next: t.o whn p.u bef last* **13/2**

5m 54.0s (-28.50) **Going Correction** -1.025s/f (Hard) **9** Ran SP% **116.7**
Speed ratings (Par 111): **106,105,102,101,99 97,85,81,**
toteswingers 1&2 £1.10, 2&3 £5.80, 1&3 £6.30 CSF £17.62 CT £59.52 TOTE £3.80: £1.90, £1.50, £2.20; EX 13.60 Trifecta £65.80 Pool: £1082.26 - 12.32 winning units..
Owner Brocade Racing **Bred** Oliver Brennan **Trained** Milborne Port, Dorset

FOCUS
The seventh renewal of this race at Gosforth Park having previously been staged at Chepstow. The pace was sound and the first two fought it out, literally, in the home straight. The winner is rated to the level of last season's Newbury second.

2823 EBF STALLIONS "NATIONAL HUNT" MAIDEN HURDLE (QUALIFIER) (9 hdls) 2m
3:15 (3:16) (Class 5) 4-6-Y-0 **£3,119** (£915; £457; £228)

Form RPR
\- **1** **Full Shift (FR)**[300] 4-11-0 0 APMcCoy 121+
(Nicky Henderson) *t.k.h early: trckd ldrs: wnt 2nd bef 3 out: led and hit next: sn rdn: hld on wl towards fin* **8/13**[1]
/12- **2** *½* **Clever Cookie**[22] 2341 5-11-0 0 WilsonRenwick 118
(Peter Niven) *t.k.h: hld up in midfield: stdy hdwy bef 3 out: effrt after next: wnt 2nd last 125yds: kpt on: hld cl home* **7/2**[2]
1/4- **3** *2½* **Pair Of Jacks (IRE)**[34] 2104 5-11-0 0 BrianHughes 115
(Malcolm Jefferson) *t.k.h: led and clr to after 2nd: rdn and hdd 2 out: kpt on same pce after last* **8/1**[3]
54- **4** *2½* **Final Assault (IRE)**[28] 2217 4-11-0 0 PeterBuchanan 113
(Lucinda Russell) *t.k.h: in tch: effrt 2 out: rdn and one pce fr last* **9/1**
4- **5** *7* **Landecker (IRE)**[37] 2037 5-11-0 0 LucyAlexander 106
(N W Alexander) *hld up: hdwy and shkn up bef 3 out: 5th and styng on but no imp whn blnd last* **33/1**
62/ **6** *14* **Pierrers Bounty (IRE)**[248] 4971 6-11-0 0 RichieMcGrath 92
(Henry Hogarth) *chsd ldr: rdn and wknd 3 out: btn whn blnd last* **10/1**
000- **7** *11* **Runswick Days (IRE)**[37] 2030 6-10-7 0 JohnDawson[(7)] 81
(John Wade) *prom: hit 4th: rdn and wknd after 4 out* **100/1**
536- **8** *15* **Dalstontosiloth (IRE)**[22] 2347 5-11-0 0 DenisO'Regan 66
(Barry Murtagh) *nt fluent in rr: struggling 4 out: nvr on terms* **66/1**
403- **9** *3* **Dunkirk's First (IRE)**[18] 2443 5-11-0 0 BrianHarding 63
(Rose Dobbin) *mstkes in rr: no ch fr 4 out* **66/1**
5P6/ **10** *34* **Teaatreids (IRE)**[292] 4163 5-10-7 0 JamesReveley 22
(Brian Ellison) *hld up in tch: hit 3rd: rdn and wknd after 4 out: t.o* **100/1**

4m 0.4s (-9.60) **Going Correction** -0.70s/f (Firm)
WFA 4 from 5yo+ 7lb **10** Ran SP% **122.3**
Speed ratings: **96,95,94,93,89 82,77,69,68,51**
toteswingers 1&2 £1.10, 2&3 £3.20, 1&3 £3.30 CSF £3.39 TOTE £1.60: £1.10, £1.40, £2.00; EX 3.50 Trifecta £13.20 Pool: £1405.79 - 79.51 winning units..
Owner John P McManus **Bred** Mme Catherine Niederhauser Dietrich **Trained** Upper Lambourn, Berks

FOCUS
An interesting and almost certainly above-average maiden hurdle. They finished in a heap off a steady pace and the second and fourth set the level.
T/Plt: £6.70 to a £1 stake. Pool of £99253.95 - 10692.54 winning tickets. T/Qpdt: £4.50 to a £1 stake. Pool of £5462.25 - 889.60 winning tickets. RY

2697 TOWCESTER (R-H)
Saturday, November 30

OFFICIAL GOING: Good to soft (8.9)
Wind: Medium, against Weather: Dry and bright

2824 PRINT DATA SOLUTIONS LTD MARES' "NATIONAL HUNT" NOVICES' HURDLE (8 hdls) 2m
12:15 (12:17) (Class 4) 3-Y-0+ **£3,119** (£915; £457; £228)

Form RPR
3/5- **1** **Lady Charisma**[23] 2317 4-10-12 0 JamesBest[(3)] 106+
(Philip Hobbs) *reluctant to line up: t.k.h: hld up in midfield: clsd and wl in tch 5th: rdn and effrt after next: chsd wnr 2 out: styd on to ld last: blnd bdly and hdd: rallied gamely u.p to ld again on post* **4/1**[2]
032- **2** *nse* **Born To Benefit (IRE)**[14] 2514 7-11-1 104 (t) PaddyBrennan 105+
(Fergal O'Brien) *nt fluent: chsd ldrs: clsd to press ldr 5th: ev ch and mstke next: sn led: wnt lft and mstke 2 out: rdn and hdd last: sn lft in ld and hrd drvn: hdd on post* **4/5**[1]
160- **3** *2* **Tara Muck**[29] 2190 6-10-8 0 RyanHatch[(7)] 102
(Nigel Twiston-Davies) *racd in midfield: clsd and in tch 5th: rdn and effrt after 3 out: pressing ldng pair whn nt clr run and swtchd lft jst bef last: kpt on same pce flat* **9/1**[3]
0/0- **4** *15* **Honour A Promise**[37] 2053 5-11-1 0 LiamHeard 89
(Paul Webber) *hld up towards rr: hmpd 1st: clsd and in tch 5th: rdn and btn after next: plugged on to go modest 4th nr fin* **66/1**
0/6- **5** *½* **Queen Olivia**[23] 2317 5-11-1 0 AndrewThornton 88
(Caroline Bailey) *t.k.h: chsd ldr tl after 4th: pressing ldr next: led 3 out: sn hdd: rdn and btn bef next: wknd between last 2* **14/1**
364- **6** *11* **Georgea (IRE)**[18] 2442 4-10-12 0 JoshuaMoore[(3)] 78
(Gary Moore) *taken down early: nt a fluent: handed clr ld s: c bk to field 5th: hdd next: rdn and wknd bef 2 out* **20/1**
43/ **7** *9* **Seas Of Green**[257] 4844 6-11-1 0 SamThomas 70
(Paul Cowley) *hld up in midfield: j.lft 1st: clsd and in tch 5th: rdn and struggling whn bdly hmpd next: lost tch bef 2 out: t.o* **28/1**
3/0- **F** **Etania**[10] 2602 5-10-10 0 RobertMcCarth[(5)]
(Ian Williams) *hld up in rr: mstke 2nd: clsd on ldrs 5th: wl in tch whn fell next* **9/1**[3]
2/U- **P** **Clara Peggotty**[14] 2507 6-11-1 0 FelixDeGiles
(Tom Gretton) *hld up in last trio: dropped to last and struggling bef 4th: sn lost tch and t.o whn p.u bef 3 out* **50/1**
0/F- **F** **Cantony**[29] 2190 4-10-12 0 JakeGreenall[(3)]
(Henry Daly) *hld up in midfield: clsd on ldr and wl in tch whn j.lft and fell 5th* **50/1**

3m 59.8s (-8.10) **Going Correction** -0.55s/f (Firm)
WFA 4 from 5yo+ 7lb **10** Ran SP% **115.8**
Speed ratings (Par 105): **98,97,96,89,89 83,79, , ,**
toteswingers: 1&2 £1.20, 1&3 £15.90, 2&3 £2.50. CSF £7.51 TOTE £6.40: £1.70, £1.10, £2.00; EX 10.90 Trifecta £77.40 Pool: £1,317.18 - 12.76 winning units..
Owner Owners For Owners: Lady Charisma **Bred** R T Crellin **Trained** Withycombe, Somerset

FOCUS
Chasers and hurdlers on separate bends and Hurdles course dolled out to middle position. Plenty of pace on for this weak mares novices' hurdle. The second set a decent standard.

2825 PDS LTD "DEVELOPING IDEAS, SURPASSING EXPECTATIONS" NOVICES' H'CAP CHASE (14 fncs) 2m 3f 110y
12:45 (12:49) (Class 5) (0-100,97)
4-Y-0+ **£2,144** (£629; £314; £157)

Form RPR
5/0- **1** **Classic Case (IRE)**[44] 1939 6-11-0 **85** WillKennedy 96+
(Ian Williams) *chsd ldr tl led 3rd: mde rest: rdn bef 2 out: kpt on wl u.p between last 2: rdn out* **3/1**[2]
2/P- **2** *2¾* **Endofdiscusion (IRE)**[23] 2313 6-11-12 **97** (p) SamJones 105
(Paul Webber) *chsd ldrs: chsd wnr after 3 out and sn drvn: edgd lft u.p between last 2: kpt on same pce flat* **7/1**
P/2- **3** *7* **Lord Landen (IRE)**[19] 2427 8-11-9 **94** (t) PaddyBrennan 99+
(Fergal O'Brien) *t.k.h: hld up towards rr: mstke 2nd: hdwy to chse ldng trio 3 out: rdn and chsd ldng pair bef 2 out: swtchd rt between last 2: no imp whn j. slowly last* **7/2**[3]
3/P- **4** *17* **Lord Kennedy (IRE)**[18] 2437 8-11-7 **97** KillianMoore[(5)] 85
(Alex Hales) *hld up in rr: clsd and in midfield after 7th: mstke 9th: rdn after next: drvn and btn 3 out: plugged on into modest 4th between last 2* **12/1**
64P/ **5** *13* **Moonlight Maggie**[243] 5083 6-10-0 **76** AodhaganConlon[(5)] 54
(Tom George) *in tch in midfield: mstke 2nd: chsd ldrs 6th: wnt 2nd 11th tl sn after 3 out: wknd u.p bef next: fdd between last 2: t.o* **25/1**
020/ **P** **Graylyn Amber**[967] 5191 8-10-13 **84** CharliePoste
(Robin Dickin) *taken down early: t.k.h: led tl 3rd: chsd ldr tl next: sn lost pl: bhd 7th: j. slowly 9th and t.o next: p.u 3 out* **25/1**
500- **F** **Saudi Pearl (IRE)**[30] 2178 5-11-7 **92** (v[1]) DaveCrosse
(Nigel Twiston-Davies) *chsd ldrs: j.lft 5th: wnt 2nd bef next tl 11th: 7th and wkng whn fell 3 out* **25/1**
032- **P** **Pod**[16] 2478 5-9-13 **73** JamesBest[(3)]
(Caroline Keevil) *chsd ldrs: wnt 2nd 4th tl after next: styd chsng ldrs: rdn: mstke and lost pl 11th: wknd next: wl bhd whn p.u 2 out* **11/4**[1]

0/0- F **Gorhams Gift**[211] 95 5-10-9 **83**.............................. WayneKavanagh(3)
(Jamie Poulton) *hld up in tch towards rr tl fell 6th* **28/1**
5m 6.0s (-12.20) **Going Correction** -0.55s/f (Firm) **9** Ran SP% **114.3**
Speed ratings (Par 103): **102,100,98,91,86** , , ,
toteswingers: 1&2 £6.80, 1&3 £10.90, 2&3 £2.70. CSF £23.38 CT £75.58 TOTE £4.70: £1.70, £2.20, £1.50; EX 34.00 Trifecta £401.80 Pool: £753.05 - 1.40 winning units..
Owner The Three Graces **Bred** William Kinsella **Trained** Portway, Worcs

FOCUS
A modest handicap run at an honest pace. Solid enough form at its level.

2826 PDS LTD "DESIGN STUDIO" EBF STALLIONS "NATIONAL HUNT" NOVICES' HURDLE (QUALIFIER) (11 hdls) 2m 5f
1:15 (1:18) (Class 4) 4-6-Y-O **£3,249** (£954; £477; £238)

Form RPR

1 **Knockanrawley (IRE)**[195] 5-10-5 0.............................. TomBellamy(7) 125+
(Kim Bailey) *wl in tch in last pair: hdwy to chse ldrs 3 out: squeezed for room, bdly hmpd and lost pl bef 2 out: rallied and rdn to ld between last 2: rn green: wnt lft and blnd last: styd on wl flat: rdn out* **14/1**

120- 2 2 ½ **Silver Eagle (IRE)**[14] 2504 5-11-8 134..............................(t) SamThomas 129
(Kim Bailey) *led tl after 6th: chsd ldr tl led again and dived 3 out: drvn and hdd between last 2: lft w ch last: no ex and outpcd flat* **10/11**[1]

4- 3 2 ¼ **Garrahalish (IRE)**[37] 2052 5-10-12 0.............................. CharliePoste 116
(Robin Dickin) *chsd ldrs: rdn to chal and clr w ldr bef 2 out: 3rd and unable qck between last 2: one pce and hld whn j.lft last* **100/1**

43- 4 13 **Glowinginthedark (IRE)**[27] 2243 5-10-9 0.................... KielanWoods(3) 104
(Charlie Longsdon) *hld up wl in tch in midfield: rdn and effrt bef 3 out: drvn and chsd ldng pair briefly bef 2 out: 4th and btn 2 out: wknd between last 2* **11/4**[2]

222- 5 3 **A Tail Of Intrigue (IRE)**[14] 2509 5-10-12 0.......................... WillKennedy 102
(Ian Williams) *t.k.h: hld up wl in tch in last pair: hdwy after 6th: pressed ldrs 8th tl rdn and no ex after 3 out: btn whn hmpd bnd bef 2 out: wknd* **5/1**[3]

0U6- 6 9 **Major Martin (IRE)**[14] 2520 4 10 9 0.............................. JoshuaMoore(3) 93
(Charlie Brooks) *t.k.h: wl in tch in midfield: rdn and struggling bef 3 out: wknd bef 2 out* **100/1**

10- 7 47 **Crookstown (IRE)**[14] 2507 6-10-13 0.............................. KillianMoore(5) 57
(Ben Case) *t.k.h: wl in tch in midfield: hdwy to chse ldr and mstke 5th: led after 6th tl 3 out: sn wknd: t.o between last 2* **25/1**

0/0- P **Beaujolais Bob**[21] 2375 5-10-5 0..........................(t) MrRobertHawker(7)
(Richard Hawker) *chsd ldr tl 5th: wl in tch tl lost pl and mstke 7th: sn lost tch: t.o whn p.u next* **66/1**

2- P **Speckled Door**[19] 2429 5-10-12 0.............................. AndrewThornton
(Caroline Bailey) *chsd ldrs: lost pl and pushed along briefly after 5th: dropped to last 7th: lost tch next: wl t.o whn p.u bef 2 out* **16/1**

5m 18.5s (-8.70) **Going Correction** -0.55s/f (Firm)
WFA 4 from 5yo+ 8lb **9** Ran SP% **115.6**
Speed ratings: **94,93,92,87,86 82,64**, ,
toteswingers: 1&2 £6.60, 1&3 £19.00, 2&3 £20.30. CSF £28.46 TOTE £15.60: £3.50, £1.40, £9.50; EX 28.50 Trifecta £949.90 Part won. Pool: £1,266.63 - 0.04 winning units..
Owner Kim Bailey Racing Partnership VIII **Bred** Joe Fogarty **Trained** Andoversford, Gloucs
■ Stewards' Enquiry : Mr Robert Hawker £290 fine: wore a modified vest

FOCUS
The gallop was steady for this novices' hurdle. The winner overcame trouble and is probably capable of better, and there's a case for rating the form 10lb+ higher.

2827 PDS LTD "PRINT MANAGEMENT TEAM" H'CAP HURDLE (12 hdls) 3m
1:45 (1:46) (Class 5) (0-100,104) 4-Y-O+ **£1,949** (£572; £286; £143)

Form RPR

/12- 1 **Kings Apollo**[6] 2701 4-10-9 **88**.............................. BenPoste(5) 95+
(Tom Symonds) *wl in tch in midfield: effrt and rdn to chse ldr whn swtchd lft bef 2 out: led and mstke last: styd on wl flat: rdn out* **9/4**[1]

423- 2 1 ¼ **Changing Lanes**[9] 2620 10-10-10 **91** ow1.....................(tp) MrBGibbs(7) 95
(David Rees) *in tch towards rr: mstke 2nd: hdwy to chse ldrs 5th tl led and j.rt 3 out: drvn bef next: hdd and mstke last: one pce flat* **14/1**

/60- 3 1 ½ **Blue Cove**[14] 2509 8-10-1 **75**.............................. TomSiddall 78
(Lynn Siddall) *in tch in last trio: rdn after 8th: styd on and hdwy bef 2 out: wnt 3rd and hung rt between last 2: swtchd lft and kpt on same pce flat* **66/1**

00P- 4 3 ½ **Burnthill (IRE)**[55] 1784 8-9-7 **74**..............................(tp) GeraldQuinn(7) 75
(Claire Dyson) *chsd ldrs: rdn after 9th: 3rd and drvn bef 2 out: keeping on same pce whn sltly hmpd between last 2: wknd flat* **20/1**

0/6- 5 4 ½ **Adili (IRE)**[14] 2511 4-10-7 **81**..............................(p) FelixDeGiles 77
(Brian Ellison) *in tch in rr: reminder after 2nd: hdwy after 7th: rdn and struggling bef 3 out: no threat to ldrs but plugged on between last 2* **20/1**

534- 6 hd **Miss Mayfair (IRE)**[13] 2541 6-10-13 **87**.............................. TomCannon 83
(Lawney Hill) *hld up in tch in last trio: hdwy 8th: rdn and outpcd after 3 out: wknd between last 2* **25/1**

P22- 7 20 **Ifyouthinkso**[9] 2620 6-11-9 **104**..............................(p) TomBellamy(7) 82
(Lucy Jones) *chsd ldr tl bmpd 3 out: rdn and btn bef next: wknd sn after 2 out* **4/1**[2]

/02- 8 5 **Regal Flow**[16] 2473 6-11-5 **100**.............................. MrLDrowne(7) 73
(Caroline Keevil) *chsd ldrs tl led 5th: hdd 3 out: rdn and btn bef next: wknd 2 out: t.o* **11/2**[3]

003- 9 9 **Earcomesthedream (IRE)**[6] 2701 10-11-4 **99**..............(b) RyanHatch(7) 64
(Peter Pritchard) *wl in tch in midfield: rdn after 9th: wknd wl bef 2 out: t.o between last 2* **9/1**

P06- P **Cowbridge (IRE)**[5] 2723 7-9-7 **74** oh2.............................. CharlieDeutsch(7)
(Peter Pritchard) *midfield: rdn after 3rd: dropped to rr and no rspnse to press 5th: tailing off whn p.u 7th* **50/1**

0/6- P **D'Argent Cloud**[211] 91 5-10-8 **89**.............................. CraigGallagher(7)
(Brian Ellison) *wl in tch in midfield: lost pl and rdn 8th: tailing off whn p.u next* **13/2**

0/0- P **Alfie Alexander (IRE)**[193] 417 5-10-9 **83**..........................(p) ColinBolger
(Mark Hoad) *midfield tl lost pl and reminders 4th: bhd after: rdn and lost tch after 7th: t.o next tl p.u 3 out* **40/1**

004- P **Oak Wood (IRE)**[14] 2509 5-11-4 **95**.............................. GavinSheehan(3)
(John Upson) *led tl 5th: sn drvn and lost pl: t.o 8th tl p.u 3 out* **50/1**

6m 8.2s (-6.80) **Going Correction** -0.55s/f (Firm)
WFA 4 from 5yo+ 9lb **13** Ran SP% **117.4**
Speed ratings (Par 103): **89,88,88,86,85 85,78,77,74**, , ,
toteswingers: 1&2 £6.50, 1&3 £24.40, 2&3 £24.40. CSF £30.26 CT £1630.88 TOTE £3.50: £1.70, £2.80, £7.20; EX 22.00 Trifecta £735.40 Part won. Pool: £980.58 - 0.11 winning units..
Owner G&M Roberts Churchward Frost Green W-Williams **Bred** M Watt & Exors Of The Late Miss J John **Trained** Harewood End, H'fords

FOCUS
Not a strong handicap, run at a steady pace. The second and third help with the level.

2828 PDS LTD "PROMOTIONAL GIFTS & MERCHANDISE" H'CAP HURDLE (10 hdls) 2m 3f 110y
2:15 (2:19) (Class 3) (0-125,125) 4-Y-O **£5,253** (£1,552; £776; £388; £194)

Form

163/ 1 **If In Doubt (IRE)**[230] 5308 5-11-8 **124**.............................. JamesBest(3) 136+
(Philip Hobbs) *hld up in tch in last trio: rapid hdwy to join ldrs on bit 3 out: led bef 2 out: in command and rdn between last 2: r.o: rdn out* **3/1**[1]

031- 2 5 **Ray Diamond**[39] 2013 8-10-3 **102**.............................. MarcGoldstein 105
(Jackie Du Plessis) *chsd ldrs: wnt 2nd after 6th tl rdn to ld after 3 out: sn hdd and outpcd by wnr: kpt on for clr 2nd but no threat to wnr* **10/1**

214- 3 7 **Bowie (IRE)**[20] 2397 6-10-9 **115**.............................. CharlieDeutsch(7) 112
(Nick Kent) *t.k.h: chsd ldr tl after 6th: styd chsng ldrs: rdn and outpcd bef 2 out: 3rd and wl hld whn j.rt last* **8/1**[3]

/62- 4 nk **All That Remains (IRE)**[36] 2064 8-11-8 **121**....................(t) WillKennedy 117
(Brian Ellison) *wl in tch in midfield: j.rt 3 out: sn rdn and no imp: kpt on same pce fr next* **12/1**

1U0/ 5 5 **Saroque (IRE)**[225] 5376 6-10-10 **112**.............................. RobertDunne(3) 105
(Venetia Williams) *led: hit 4th: rdn and hdd after 3 out: sn btn: wknd and wl btn 5th whn mstke last* **10/1**

00P- 6 5 **Darkestbeforedawn (IRE)**[34] 2107 6-11-2 **115**.................... IanPopham 102
(Caroline Keevil) *chsd ldrs: rdn after 3 out: sn struggling: 6th and wkng next* **12/1**

/06- 7 1 ¾ **Touch Back (IRE)**[21] 2362 7-11-1 **124**.............................. JamesHuxham(10) 110
(Jonjo O'Neill) *in tch in midfield: lost pl and towards rr: rdn and btn after 3 out: sn wknd* **12/1**

1/F- 8 4 ½ **Urcalin (FR)**[212] 82 5-11-6 **119**..............................[1] AndrewThornton 101
(David Arbuthnot) *hld up in tch in last trio: mstke 7th: rdn and short-lived effrt jst bef next: wknd bef 2 out* **14/1**

005- 9 1 ¼ **Church Field (IRE)**[23] 2314 5-10-8 **117**.................... TommieMO'Brien(10) 98
(Jonjo O'Neill) *wl in tch in last trio: rdn and effrt bef 3 out: no imp: wknd bef 2 out* **9/2**[2]

0/0- 10 1 ¼ **Minneapolis**[24] 2292 8-10-1 **103** ow3..............................(t) JoshuaMoore(3) 83
(Alison Batchelor) *wl in tch in midfield: rdn and lost pl after 7th: struggling bef next: wknd bef 2 out* **33/1**

641- 11 5 **Red Admirable (IRE)**[14] 2510 7-11-2 **120**.............................. KillianMoore(5) 97
(Graeme McPherson) *wl in tch in midfield: rdn after 2 out: sn btn and wknd bef next: bhd and eased flat: t.o* **8/1**[3]

4m 55.0s (-14.60) **Going Correction** -0.55s/f (Firm) **11** Ran SP% **116.3**
Speed ratings (Par 107): **107,105,102,102,100 98,97,95,95,94 92**
toteswingers: 1&2 £22.20, 1&3 £8.80, 2&3 £8.30. CSF £33.01 CT £219.54 TOTE £3.60: £1.80, £3.30, £3.10; EX 38.90 Trifecta £203.70 Pool: £1,088.25 - 4.00 winning units..
Owner John P McManus **Bred** James Browne **Trained** Withycombe, Somerset

FOCUS
The pace was honest for this fair contest, with the field finishing strung out. A big step forward from the impressive winner.

2829 PDS LTD "FOLLOW US ON FACEBOOK" CONDITIONAL JOCKEYS' H'CAP CHASE (13 fncs 5 omitted) 3m 110y
2:50 (2:53) (Class 5) (0-95,91) 4-Y-O+ **£2,144** (£629; £314; £157)

Form RPR

P34- 1 **Quayside Court (IRE)**[16] 2478 9-9-10 **67**....................(vt) GeraldQuinn(6) 81+
(Claire Dyson) *mde most tl 11th: chsd ldr after tl rdn to ld 3 out (actual last): plugged on u.p and looked in command tl idled in bhd loose horse fnl 100yds: jnd towards fin: fnd enough to prevail cl home* **7/2**[2]

106- 2 hd **Divine Folly (IRE)**[18] 2431 8-11-10 **89**.............................. JoshuaMoore 103+
(Lawney Hill) *in tch in midfield: chsd ldrs after 11th: drvn after 15th (actual 2 out): hrd drvn and chsd wnr bypassing 2 out: kpt on and str chal fnl 50yds: hmpd by loose horse and btn cl home* **12/1**

643- 3 7 **Overton Lad**[10] 2603 12-10-0 **65** oh1..............................(bt) GavinSheehan 73
(Peter Pritchard) *chsd ldrs: mstke 4th: rdn 1/2-way: 4th whn blnd 3 out (actual last): wnt 3rd over 1f out: no imp after* **14/1**

P1U- 4 7 **Tom Bach (IRE)**[9] 2619 9-10-9 **74**..............................(b) JamesBest 74
(Hywel Evans) *w ldr tl led 11th: drvn and hdd 3 out (actual last): 4th and wknd over 1f out* **3/1**[1]

1P2- 5 15 **Von Galen (IRE)**[6] 2702 12-10-13 **81**....................(p) ChristopherWard(3) 67
(Michael Scudamore) *hld up towards rr: hdwy into midfield 1/2-way: 5th and rdn 15th (actual 2 out): no imp bef next: wknd on uphill run after 3 out (actual last)* **8/1**

/43- 6 1 ½ **Kilcascan**[44] 1936 9-11-8 **87**.............................. BenPoste 72
(Rosemary Gasson) *bhd: bdly hmpd 2nd and detached in last next: clsd and in tch 1/2-way: struggling after 11th: n.d after* **8/1**

560- 7 16 **Top Benefit (IRE)**[6] 2702 11-11-2 **86**.............................. OllieGarner(5) 56
(Richard Harper) *in tch in midfield: lost pl 1/2-way: no prog whn rdn 13th: wknd bef 3 out (actual last): t.o* **25/1**

32P- 8 79 **Annie Confidential (IRE)**[37] 2044 10-10-4 **74**.................... KevinJones(5)
(Pam Ford) *midfield: hmpd 2nd: hdwy to chse ldrs 1/2-way: lost pl and bhd 13th: t.o 15th (actual 2 out)* **20/1**

334- B **Kilvergan Boy (IRE)**[10] 2603 9-10-1 **74**..........................(p) RyanHatch(8)
(Nigel Twiston-Davies) *chsd ldrs tl b.d 2nd* **15/2**

5/3- F **Royaume Bleu (FR)**[38] 2023 8-11-12 **91**....................(b[1]) KillianMoore
(Alex Hales) *t.k.h: w wnr tl fell 2nd* **7/1**[3]

6m 24.1s (-12.80) **Going Correction** -0.55s/f (Firm) **10** Ran SP% **116.7**
Speed ratings (Par 103): **98,97,95,93,88 88,83,57**, ,
toteswingers: 1&2 £35.30, 1&3 £3.80, 2&3 £36.80. CSF £44.10 CT £527.12 TOTE £5.40: £2.20, £4.30, £4.20; EX 80.20 Trifecta £958.20 Part won. Pool: £1,277.68 - 0.35 winning units..
Owner Guy Sainsbury & Carl Mason **Bred** Miss Catherine M Walsh **Trained** Cleeve Prior, Worcs

FOCUS
The three fences in the home straight were omitted due to the low sun. They went a sound gallop for this open handicap which saw plenty of incident. The winner was well treated on the best of his course form.

2830 MARTYN BATLEY "BACK" TO WORK AT LAST "JUNIOR" STANDARD OPEN NATIONAL HUNT FLAT RACE 1m 5f 110y
3:25 (3:26) (Class 6) 3-Y-O **£1,559** (£457; £228; £114)

Form RPR

1- 1 **Coyaba**[20] 2391 3-11-5 0.............................. IanPopham 111+
(Martin Keighley) *hld up wl in tch: clsd to press ldr over 3f out: travelling best after: led wl over 1f out: rdn and asserted 1f out: r.o: readily* **3/1**[1]

3- 2 4 ½ **Gone Forever**[31] 2160 3-10-5 0.............................. CraigGallagher(7) 96
(Brian Ellison) *chsd ldrs: wnt clr in ldng trio 3f out: sn rdn and outpcd 2f out: no threat to wnr but kpt on to go 2nd ins fnl f* **6/1**[2]

1- **3** 1 1/2 **Two Jabs**[18] 2436 3-11-5 0 .... AndrewThornton 101
(Mark Brisbourne) *racd wd: chsd ldr tl led over 3f out: rdn and hdd wl over 1f out: brushed aside by wnr 1f out: one pce and lost 2nd ins fnl f* **3/1**[1]

- **4** 35 **Nightline** 3-10-9 0 .... JakeGreenall(3) 52
(Henry Daly) *chsd ldrs: lost pl but stl in tch 5f out: rdn and wknd 3f out: wl hld but plugged on fnl f to snatch 4th last stride: t.o* **13/2**[3]

5 shd **Bouggietopieces** 3-10-9 0 .... KielanWoods(3) 52
(Pam Sly) *in tch in midfield: rdn and outpcd 3f out: sn wknd and wl btn whn wnt 4th 2f out: tired and lost 4th last stride: t.o* **12/1**

6 1 1/4 **Simmi's Tiger** 3-10-9 0 .... (t) JoshuaMoore(3) 50
(Anthony Carson) *rn green: in tch in rr: sme hdwy but outpcd by ldrs 3f out: 5th and wl hld 2f out: wknd: t.o* **9/1**

4- **7** 7 **Ronnie Rockcake**[18] 2436 3-10-12 0 .... DavidBass 42
(Ben Pauling) *chsd ldrs tl 4th and btn over 2f out: lost 4th 2f out and wknd qckly: t.o* **16/1**

8 10 **Dan's Quest** 3-10-12 0 .... CharliePoste 30
(Robin Dickin) *in tch in midfield tl 4f out: sn outpcd and bhd: t.o fnl 2f* **10/1**

0- **9** 5 **Seven Belle**[23] 2318 3-10-2 0 .... RobertDunne(3) 17
(Dai Burchell) *led tl over 3f out: sn bhd: t.o fnl 2f* **100/1**

0- **10** 33 **Thyne Gale (IRE)**[18] 2436 3-10-0 0 .... KillianMoore(5)
(Graeme McPherson) *in tch in rr tl 5f out: sn struggling: t.o fnl 3f* **50/1**

11 43 **Mister Carrot** 3-10-12 0 .... MattieBatchelor
(George Baker) *in tch in rr tl 5f out: sn btn: t.o fnl 3f* **20/1**

3m 15.3s (-25.30) **11 Ran SP% 118.0**
toteswingers: 1&2 £2.10, 1&3 £1.40, 2&3 £3.00. CSF £20.90 TOTE £4.20: £1.30, £2.10, £1.90; EX 19.50 Trifecta £38.30 Pool: £1,706.12 - 33.35 winning units..
Owner Mrs Peter Prowting **Bred** Mrs E A Prowting **Trained** Condicote, Gloucs

FOCUS
This bumper was run at a decent gallop, with the winner looking above average. The front three finished a long way clear, all building on their debut runs.
T/Plt: £76.70 to a £1 stake. Pool: £78,799.00 - 760.08 winning tickets. T/Qpdt: £59.90 to a £1 stake. Pool: £4,409.05 - 54.56 winning tickets. SP

2416 CARLISLE (R-H)
Sunday, December 1

OFFICIAL GOING: Chase course - good to soft (soft in places; 6.4); hurdle course - soft (5.3)
Wind: Almost nil Weather: Cloudy, bright

2838 32RED.COM EBF "NATIONAL HUNT" NOVICES' HURDLE (QUALIFIER) (10 hdls) 2m 3f 110y
12:20 (12:23) (Class 4) 4-6-Y-0 **£4,386** (£1,287; £643; £321)

Form RPR

1- **1** **Vinny Gambini (IRE)**[43] 1977 6-11-5 0 .... WilsonRenwick 117+
(Rose Dobbin) *trckd ldrs: hdwy to ld 2 out: drvn out fr last* **4/1**[3]

/U3- **2** 2 1/4 **Frankie's Promise (IRE)**[29] 2217 5-10-12 0 ....[1] LucyAlexander 109+
(N W Alexander) *nt fluent: in tch: rdn and outpcd after 4 out: rallied u.p bef 2 out: effrt and pressed wnr last: kpt on same pce run-in* **2/1**[2]

3/0- **3** 6 **L'Eminence Grise (IRE)**[22] 2355 6-10-5 97 ....(t) StephenMulqueen(7) 101
(Maurice Barnes) *w ldr: rdn and ev ch 2 out: outpcd by first two fr last* **7/1**

0/1- **4** 2 **Moss Cloud (IRE)**[16] 2493 6-11-5 0 .... JasonMaguire 107
(Donald McCain) *led: rdn and hdd 2 out: outpcd fr last* **7/4**[1]

5 11 **Prairie Lad** 5-10-12 0 .... RyanMania 88
(Sandy Thomson) *bhd: outpcd whn j.lft 6th: sn struggling: sme late hdwy: nvr on terms* **50/1**

0/P- **6** 5 **Native Optimist (IRE)**[22] 2355 6-10-7 0 .... MissCWalton(5) 83
(Sheena Walton) *hld up: rdn and outpcd bef 3 out: btn next* **200/1**

30- **7** nk **Crown And Glory (IRE)**[38] 2037 6-10-12 0 .... PeterBuchanan 83
(Karen Tutty) *hld up: outpcd whn nt fluent 4 out: wknd bef 2 out* **25/1**

00- **8** dist **Brighton Road (IRE)**[29] 2217 6-10-12 0 .... BrianHarding 48
(R Mike Smith) *uns rdr and loose bef s: in tch: drvn and outpcd 4 out: lost tch bef 2 out* **25/1**

0- **P** **Caldew Lad (IRE)**[16] 2499 5-10-12 0 .... HenryBrooke
(Barry Murtagh) *nt fluent in rr: struggling bef 3rd: t.o whn p.u after 5th* **100/1**

4m 53.7s (-15.10) **Going Correction** -0.575s/f (Firm) **9 Ran SP% 113.3**
Speed ratings: **107,106,103,102,98 96,96,82,**
toteswingers 1&2 £2.10, 1&3 £3.90, 2&3 £3.50 CSF £12.24 TOTE £4.20: £1.70, £1.20, £1.70; EX 13.80 Trifecta £77.60 Pool: £3057.65 - 29.54 winning units..
Owner Mr & Mrs Duncan Davidson **Bred** Brian Mulcahy **Trained** South Hazelrigg, Northumbria

FOCUS
Chase bends moved out. Hurdles on New course and inside rail moved out 3yds. A modest event but the winner looks a fair novice.

2839 HAPPY BIRTHDAY COURTNEY WALTON NOVICES' CHASE (11 fncs 1 omitted) 2m
12:50 (12:50) (Class 3) 4-Y-0+ **£7,147** (£2,098; £1,049; £524)

Form RPR

4/2- **1** **Eduard (IRE)**[38] 2031 5-11-0 0 .... BrianHarding 138+
(Nicky Richards) *trckd ldrs: hit 6th: nt fluent next: effrt and wnt 2nd appr 3 out: led next: rdn and edgd rt after last: styd on strly* **4/7**[1]

/01- **2** 5 **Mwaleshi**[15] 2515 8-11-6 0 .... RyanMania 136
(Sue Smith) *t.k.h early: led: rdn and hdd 2 out: rallied and ch last: outpcd by wnr run-in* **3/1**[2]

/41- **3** 8 **Yesyoucan (IRE)**[16] 2494 8-11-6 0 .... JamesReveley 131
(Brian Ellison) *trckd ldr: hit 1st: mstke 4th: rdn and lost 2nd bef 3 out: outpcd fr next* **11/2**[3]

360- **4** 12 **Call Of Duty (IRE)**[8] 2075 8-10-9 0 .... ColmMcCormack(5) 110
(Dianne Sayer) *hld up: nt fluent 3rd: rdn and outpcd bef 5 out: n.d after* **200/1**

0/6- **5** 10 **Hunters Belt (IRE)**[60] 1378 9-11-0 0 .... HenryBrooke 101
(Barry Murtagh) *in tch: outpcd after 4th: short-lived effrt bef 4 out: sn n.d: btn next* **50/1**

4m 3.6s (-12.50) **Going Correction** -0.575s/f (Firm) **5 Ran SP% 106.5**
Speed ratings (Par 107): **108,105,101,95,90**
CSF £2.57 TOTE £1.70: £1.30, £1.20; EX 2.60 Trifecta £4.80 Pool: £2273.22 - 352.73 winning units..
Owner Kingdom Taverns Ltd **Bred** Cecil And Martin McCracken **Trained** Greystoke, Cumbria

FOCUS
A fair novice chase. The winner rates a decent northern novice, and the second was 6lb off his best hurdles figure.

2840 JOHN MCARTHUR EDMUNDSON'S RETIREMENT NOVICES' HURDLE (8 hdls) 2m 1f
1:20 (1:20) (Class 4) 4-Y-0+ **£4,386** (£1,287; £643; £321)

Form RPR

11/ **1** **Meadowcroft Boy**[225] 5407 4-10-9 0 .... EwanWhillans(3) 122+
(Alistair Whillans) *t.k.h early: led 1st: mde rest: drew clr after 2 out: easily* **7/4**[1]

/54- **2** 21 **Heart Dancer (FR)**[22] 2355 7-10-12 0 .... BarryKeniry 97
(Simon Shirley-Beavan) *hld up towards rr: nt fluent 2nd: effrt and hdwy bef 2 out: chsd (clr) wnr run-in: no imp* **9/1**

0- **3** 3 1/4 **Choisan (IRE)**[16] 2493 4-10-12 0 .... DougieCostello 92
(Tim Easterby) *nt fluent on occasions: chsd ldrs: effrt and disp 2nd pl briefly bef 2 out: outpcd fr last* **14/1**

3/2- **4** 2 1/4 **Blades Lad**[51] 1853 4-10-12 120 .... WilsonRenwick 91
(Peter Niven) *trckd ldrs: stmbld appr 4th: effrt and wnt 2nd 3 out: rdn and edgd lft after next: one pce and lost 2nd run-in* **5/1**[3]

322- **5** 4 **Knightly Escapade**[16] 2493 5-10-12 115 ....(p) JamesReveley 86
(Brian Ellison) *midfield on outside: stdy hdwy on outside 4th: effrt and rdn bef 2 out: sn no imp* **2/1**[2]

/60- **6** 3/4 **Gilanto (IRE)**[18] 2457 6-10-12 0 .... NickScholfield 85
(Michael Blake) *led to 1st: cl up: drvn and outpcd bef 3 out: sme late hdwy: nvr rchd ldrs* **100/1**

0/0- **7** 1/2 **Moheebb (IRE)**[58] 1754 9-10-12 0 ....(p) KennyJohnson 85
(Robert Johnson) *plld hrd: cl up: wnt 2nd 4th to 3 out: rdn and weakened after next* **125/1**

8 15 **Badea**[71] 4-10-12 0 .... DenisO'Regan 70
(Martin Todhunter) *hld up: outpcd 4th: btn bef 2 out* **33/1**

/P6- **P** **Tchatchaco Ya Ya**[23] 2340 6-10-12 0 .... JasonMaguire
(Nicky Richards) *t.k.h: hld up: struggling bef 3 out: t.o whn p.u after next* **100/1**

0- **P** **Mr Selby**[56] 1792 4-10-12 0 .... BrianHarding
(Nicky Richards) *t.k.h in rr: blkd 4th: sn struggling: t.o whn p.u bef 2 out* **40/1**

4m 19.3s (-9.90) **Going Correction** -0.575s/f (Firm) **10 Ran SP% 111.2**
Speed ratings (Par 105): **100,90,88,87,85 85,85,78, ,**
toteswingers 1&2 £3.20, 1&3 £5.30, 2&3 £11.30 CSF £16.82 TOTE £3.30: £1.10, £2.20, £4.00; EX 19.10 Trifecta £175.20 Pool: £1615.50 - 6.91 winning units..
Owner W J E Scott & Mrs M A Scott **Bred** Simon And Helen Plumbly **Trained** Newmill-On-Slitrig, Borders

FOCUS
A weak novice hurdle, with plenty of dead wood behind a very impressive winner who looks a decent prospect and can rate higher.

2841 CARLISLE RACECOURSE ANNUAL MEMBERS H'CAP CHASE (THE SUNDAY £5K BONUS RACE) (17 fncs 2 omitted) 3m 2f
1:55 (1:57) (Class 3) (0-135,130) 4-Y-0+ **£8,122** (£2,385; £1,192; £596)

Form RPR

611- **1** **Tutchec (FR)**[20] 2421 6-10-10 114 .... BrianHarding 126+
(Nicky Richards) *mainly j.w: mde all: nt fluent 11th: clr bef 4 out: styd on wl u.p fr last: unchal* **4/1**[2]

/51- **2** 2 **Herdsman (IRE)**[18] 2451 8-11-5 123 .... RyanMania 132
(Sue Smith) *chsd ldrs: rdn 11th: rallied to chse wnr 4 out: kpt on fr last: nt pce to chal* **11/2**[3]

11P/ **3** 14 **Safran De Cotte (FR)**[256] 4862 7-11-9 130 .... JakeGreenall(3) 127
(Henry Daly) *chsd wnr to 4 out: sn drvn and outpcd by first two fr 2 out* **2/1**[1]

/42- **4** 3/4 **Frank The Slink**[16] 2498 7-10-3 107 .... WilsonRenwick 102
(Micky Hammond) *hld up: outpcd 10th: rallied bef 4 out: plugged on fr last: no imp* **17/2**

1/3- **5** shd **Fiddlers Reel**[199] 340 10-10-13 117 .... DenisO'Regan 114+
(Jane Clark) *hld up in tch: stdy hdwy bef 5 out: rdn and no imp fr next: hld whn mstke last* **6/1**

P/1- **6** 5 **Harouet (FR)**[51] 1852 8-11-12 130 ....(p) JamieMoore 120
(Peter Bowen) *chsd ldrs: outpcd 11th: n.d after* **15/2**

F2/- **7** 2 **Isla Pearl Fisher**[238] 5205 10-11-6 124 ....[1] LucyAlexander 115
(N W Alexander) *hld up: shortlived effrt after 5 out: nvr able to chal* **20/1**

6m 46.8s (-20.40) **Going Correction** -0.575s/f (Firm) **7 Ran SP% 110.1**
Speed ratings (Par 107): **108,107,103,102,102 101,100**
toteswingers 1&2 £4.10, 1&3 £2.10, 2&3 £3.20 CSF £23.97 TOTE £3.50: £2.10, £2.90; EX 21.00 Trifecta £63.70 Pool: £2212.42 - 26.03 winning units..
Owner Club 4 Racing **Bred** William Ewart **Trained** Greystoke, Cumbria

FOCUS
A fair staying handicap. The first two are on the on upgrade.

2842 PPM THE PROPERTY MAINTENANCE PEOPLE H'CAP HURDLE (DIV I) (12 hdls) 3m 1f
2:25 (2:25) (Class 4) (0-105,105) 4-Y-0+ **£3,038** (£897; £448; £224; £112)

Form RPR

064- **1** **Omid**[19] 2444 5-10-6 85 ....(p) HenryBrooke 96+
(Evelyn Slack) *hld up: pushed along bef 4 out: gd hdwy bef 2 out: led appr last: drew clr run-in* **12/1**

/12- **2** 6 **Hartforth**[29] 2218 5-10-5 89 .... CallumWhillans(5) 92
(Donald Whillans) *t.k.h: trckd ldrs: rdn and outpcd appr 3 out: rallied next: styd on to take 2nd towards fin: no ch w wnr* **9/2**[3]

/01- **3** 3/4 **Maggie Blue (IRE)**[16] 2497 5-10-11 97 .... MrJHamilton(7) 99
(Harriet Graham) *trckd ldrs: effrt and ev ch 2 out to bef last: kpt on same pce run-in* **9/1**

/32- **4** 1/2 **Nicene Creed**[18] 2458 8-11-8 101 ....(tp) JasonMaguire 105
(Sophie Leech) *in tch: hdwy on outside bef 8th: rdn whn mstke 3 out: rallied and led next to appr last: one pce run-in* **10/3**[2]

5/0- **5** 2 **Torrential Raine**[35] 2105 5-11-9 102 .... NickScholfield 102
(Michael Blake) *disp ld: led 4 out to 2 out: drvn and outpcd fr last* **11/2**

002- **6** 9 **Brae On (IRE)**[23] 2333 5-10-1 87 .... JonathonBewley(7) 81
(George Bewley) *in tch on ins: drvn and outpcd bef 3 out: n.d after* **3/1**[1]

P/F- **7** 12 **Madam Lilibet (IRE)**[15] 2516 4-11-3 103 .... JosephPalmowski(7) 82
(Sharon Watt) *prom: rdn and outpcd bef 3 out: btn next* **20/1**

P0- **P** **Ballyreesode (IRE)**[24] 2311 8-10-12 98 .... StephenMulqueen(7)
(Susan Corbett) *nt fluent on occasions: bhd: struggling 8th: t.o whn p.u bef 2 out* **33/1**

634- **P** **Reckless Romeo (IRE)**[97] 1405 4-9-7 79 .... MrTGreenwood(7)
(Richard Ford) *slt ld to 4 out: rdn and wknd appr next: p.u 2 out* **18/1**

6m 32.4s (-6.60) **Going Correction** -0.575s/f (Firm)
WFA 4 from 5yo+ 7lb 9 Ran SP% 112.3
Speed ratings (Par 105): **87,85,84,84,84 81,77, ,**
toteswingers 1&2 £8.20, 1&3 £14.80, 2&3 £8.80 CSF £63.89 CT £511.57 TOTE £11.20: £2.00, £1.70, £3.80; EX 78.20 Trifecta £1374.20 Part won. Pool: £1832.32 - 0.76 winning units..
Owner Mrs Evelyn Slack **Bred** Silfield Bloodstock **Trained** Hilton, Cumbria

FOCUS
Not for the first time, the Carlisle hill caused fortunes to change. There were four in a line approaching the final flight but stamina proved vital in the first division of this modest handicap hurdle. A big step up from the winner on his hurdles form.

2843 PPM THE PROPERTY MAINTENANCE PEOPLE H'CAP HURDLE (DIV II) (12 hdls) 3m 1f
3:00 (3:00) (Class 4) (0-105,105) 4-Y-0+ **£3,038** (£897; £448; £224; £112)

Form RPR
620- **1** **Gulf Punch**[53] 1818 6-11-9 102 ....(p) JasonMaguire 112+
(Donald McCain) *hld up: stdy hdwy after 8th: led gng wl between last 2: drvn clr fr last* **9/1**
345- **2** *6* **Tiny Dancer (IRE)**[22] 2360 5-11-4 97 .... BrianHughes 100
(Alan Swinbank) *hld up in tch: hdwy and lft 3rd 4th: wnt 2nd 4 out: effrt and rdn 2 out: sn kpt on same pce fr last* **15/2**[3]
/41- **3** *8* **Amore Mio (GER)**[29] 2218 8-11-12 105 ....(tp) PeterBuchanan 101
(Lucinda Russell) *led: rdn and hdd between last 2: outpcd fr last* **11/8**[1]
322/ **4** *43* **See The Legend**[268] 4630 8-10-8 87 .... AdrianLane 39
(Sandy Forster) *hld up: stdy hdwy and prom 4 out: rdn and wknd appr 2 out: t.o* **22/1**
0/4- **5** *7* **Yukon Delta (IRE)**[185] 554 6-10-12 91 .... KennyJohnson 36
(Robert Johnson) *hld up: stdy hdwy bef 6th: outpcd whn nt fluent 4 out: sn struggling: t.o* **33/1**
/65- **6** *22* **Danebrook Lad (IRE)**[23] 2337 7-10-10 89 .... RyanMania 12
(Sandy Thomson) *prom: rdn and outpcd 4 out: struggling fr next: t.o* **8/1**
200/ **7** *9* **Mini The Minx (IRE)**[244] 5078 7-9-10 80 .... CallumWhillans(5)
(Donald Whillans) *chsd ldrs to 3rd: sn drvn and lost pl: lost tch fr 4 out: t.o* **12/1**
2P1- **U** **I'Ll Be Frank**[50] 1874 8-11-1 101 ....(t) StephenMulqueen(7)
(Maurice Barnes) *t.k.h: prom: hdwy to chse ldr 3rd: mstke and uns rdr next* **12/1**
415- **P** **Big Sound**[19] 2447 6-11-9 102 ....(p) DougieCostello
(Tim Walford) *chsd ldr to 3rd: lft 2nd next: drvn and lost 2nd 4 out: wknd qckly and p.u bef 2 out* **6/1**[2]

6m 32.8s (-6.20) **Going Correction** -0.575s/f (Firm) 9 Ran SP% 111.9
Speed ratings (Par 105): **86,84,81,67,65 58,55, ,**
toteswingers 1&2 £7.80, 1&3 £3.80, 2&3 £3.60 CSF £71.11 CT £147.81 TOTE £8.90: £3.00, £2.00, £1.30; EX 48.00 Trifecta £150.30 Pool: £1641.72 - 8.18 winning units..
Owner John Gwynne **Bred** Brook Stud Bloodstock Ltd **Trained** Cholmondeley, Cheshire

FOCUS
There was plenty of pace in the second division of the 3m1f handicap hurdle, which looked an equally modest event to the first. The winner was back to the level of her 2011 course form.

2844 32RED CASINO AMATEUR RIDERS' H'CAP HURDLE (JOCKEY CLUB GRASSROOTS JUMPS SERIES QUALIFIER) (10 hdls) 2m 3f 110y
3:30 (3:30) (Class 4) (0-120,115) 4-Y-0+ **£3,119** (£967; £483; £242)

Form RPR
555- **1** **Granaruid (IRE)**[31] 2172 10-10-10 **106** ....(p) MrTHamilton(7) 112+
(Alison Hamilton) *cl up: hdwy to ld bef 2 out: clr last: idled run-in: drvn out* **25/1**
5F1- **2** *1 1/4* **Dickie Henderhoop (IRE)**[20] 2417 8-10-5 **101** ....(b) MrRWilson(7) 104
(Lucy Normile) *hld up bhd ldng gp: effrt and hdwy after 3 out: chsd (clr) wnr last: kpt on towards fin* **5/1**[3]
0/F- **3** *7* **Knight Valliant**[192] 444 10-9-13 **95** .... MissEButterworth(7) 92
(Barbara Butterworth) *hld up and bhd: smooth hdwy bef 2 out: shkn up and no imp appr last* **10/1**
0P1- **4** *1/2* **Makhzoon (USA)**[4] 2746 9-11-2 **110** ....(v) MrKitAlexander(5) 105
(N W Alexander) *cl up: chal 3 out to bef next: outpcd fr last* **2/1**[1]
/22- **5** *6* **Desgrey**[23] 2342 5-11-8 **114** .... MrJHamilton(3) 105
(Peter Niven) *t.k.h early: cl up: drvn and outpcd bef 2 out: n.d after* **7/2**[2]
5/0- **6** *1 3/4* **Moscow Presents (IRE)**[24] 2314 5-11-5 **115** .... MrPDennis(7) 103
(Philip Kirby) *prom tl rdn and outpcd bef 2 out: btn last* **7/1**
540- **7** *23* **Cigalas**[99] 1374 8-9-7 **89** oh24 .... MissAMcGregor(7) 54
(Jean McGregor) *in tch on outside: hdwy to ld bef 6th: hdd bef 2 out: wknd qckly* **100/1**
F56- **8** *20* **Danceintothelight**[15] 2516 6-10-6 **100** .... MissBeckySmith(5) 45
(Micky Hammond) *bhd: outpcd after 4 out: lost tch fr next* **8/1**
/00- **P** **Hobsons Bay (IRE)**[180] 630 8-10-0 **89** oh2 .... MissCWalton
(Sheena Walton) *led to bef 6th: wknd next: lost tch and p.u bef 3 out* **40/1**

5m 2.1s (-6.70) **Going Correction** -0.575s/f (Firm) 9 Ran SP% 112.2
Speed ratings (Par 105): **90,89,86,86,84 83,74,66,**
toteswingers 1&2 £15.50, 1&3 £19.70, 2&3 £12.20 CSF £141.55 CT £1346.67 TOTE £15.90: £5.20, £1.60, £2.00; EX 125.60 Trifecta £1142.20 Pool: £2138.35 - 1.40 winning units..
Owner J P G Hamilton **Bred** S Donohoe And R Donohoe **Trained** Denholm, Borders

FOCUS
A decent amateur riders' handicap hurdle run at a true pace. They finished strung out with the first two well clear of the remainder. The winner is rated back to the level of his Hexham win in the summer.

T/Plt: £104.70. Pool: £90,371.79 - 629.78 winning units. T/Qpdt: £34.50. Pool: £34.50 - 149.80 winning units. RY

[2557] LEICESTER (R-H)
Sunday, December 1

OFFICIAL GOING: Chase course - good to firm (good in places; 8.3); hurdle course - good to soft (good in places; 7.4)
Wind: Almost nil Weather: Fine

2845 PAT, KEN AND TOM MEMORIAL NOVICES' LIMITED H'CAP CHASE (THE SUNDAY £5K BONUS RACE) (12 fncs) 2m
1:00 (1:00) (Class 3) (0-125,129) 4-Y-0+ **£6,342** (£1,934; £1,010; £548)

Form RPR
510- **1** **Christopher Wren (USA)**[17] 2469 6-10-11 **117** ....(p) TomCannon 129+
(Nick Gifford) *chsd ldr tl led 2nd: hdd 4th: led again 4 out: clr last: pushed out* **16/1**
0/2- **2** *9* **Daymar Bay (IRE)**[17] 2469 7-10-6 **115** .... GavinSheehan(3) 121
(Emma Lavelle) *hld up: mstke 1st: nt fluent after: mstke 3rd (water): j.lft next: hdwy after 3 out: lft 3rd last: styd on to go 2nd nr fin: nvr nrr* **6/4**[1]
315- **3** *1* **Drumlang (IRE)**[17] 2469 7-10-5 **111** oh3 ....(p) WillKennedy 112
(Ian Williams) *led to 2nd: led again 4th: hdd 4 out: sn rdn: styd on same pce appr last* **7/1**
160- **4** *47* **Le Bacardy (FR)**[18] 2465 7-11-5 **125** ....(p) LeeEdwards 94
(Tony Carroll) *prom: lost pl and mstke 4th: wknd 7th* **8/1**
50/ **P** **Ironic (FR)**[338] 3310 5-10-6 **112** .... PaddyBrennan
(Tom George) *chsd ldrs: rdn appr 3 out: wknd next: bhd whn p.u bef last* **7/2**[2]
6/4- **F** **Regal One (IRE)**[25] 2287 5-10-8 **114** .... SeanQuinlan 115
(David Bridgwater) *hld up: hdwy 4th: rdn appr 2 out: disputing 7 l 2nd and btn whn fell last* **9/2**[3]

3m 55.1s (-13.10) **Going Correction** -0.625s/f (Firm) 6 Ran SP% 109.9
Speed ratings (Par 107): **107,102,102,78,**
toteswingers 1&2 £3.70, 1&3 £11.10, 2&3 £3.00 CSF £40.70 CT £177.01 TOTE £6.60: £2.90, £2.00; EX 25.30 Trifecta £107.80 Pool: £1501.69 - 10.44 winning units..
Owner John P McManus **Bred** Rod D'Elia **Trained** Findon, W Sussex

FOCUS
The ground was riding quicker on the chase course than the hurdles track. A fair event won by the outsider of six. The form looks believable.

2846 EAST FARNDON (S) HURDLE (8 hdls) 2m
1:30 (1:30) (Class 5) 4-7-Y-0 **£1,949** (£572; £286; £143)

Form RPR
250- **1** **Outrageous Request**[29] 2221 7-10-13 117 .... ConorShoemark(5) 120+
(William Stone) *hld up: hdwy after 5th: led appr 2 out: rdn out* **3/1**[1]
/44- **2** *9* **A Little Bit Dusty**[13] 2559 5-10-12 100 ....(p) AndrewThornton 108
(Conor Dore) *prom: chsd ldr 5th: led 3 out: rdn and hdd bef next: no ex last* **10/1**
/02- **3** *3 1/2* **Lac Sacre (FR)**[13] 2559 4-11-8 109 ....(tp) LeeEdwards 113
(Tony Carroll) *pushed along in rr early: hdwy 5th: rdn appr 2 out: styd on same pce* **9/2**
311- **4** *16* **Persian Herald**[12] 2573 5-11-5 106 ....(bt) TrevorWhelan(3) 100
(Neil King) *led: pushed along after 4th: hdd 3 out: sn rdn and wknd* **6/1**
000- **5** *2* **Dealing River**[25] 2292 6-10-12 104 ....(p) RobertThornton 92
(Caroline Bailey) *chsd ldrs tl rdn and wknd 3 out* **4/1**[3]
/60- **6** *7* **Drumgooland (IRE)**[17] 2467 6-10-12 102 ....(b) SamTwiston-Davies 80
(Dr Richard Newland) *prom: jnd ldrs 4th tl rdn appr next: wknd bef 3 out* **7/2**[2]
0/0- **P** **Watts Up Son**[15] 2507 5-10-12 0 ....(b) TommyPhelan
(Declan Carroll) *chsd ldr tl rdn appr 5th: wknd and p.u bef next* **33/1**
0- **P** **Dune Island**[17] 2467 5-10-2 0 .... GavinSheehan(3)
(John Upson) *hld up: blnd 2nd: bhd and drvn along 4th: p.u bef 3 out* **150/1**

3m 47.7s (-13.30) **Going Correction** -0.625s/f (Firm) 8 Ran SP% 112.4
Speed ratings: **108,103,101,93,92 89, ,**
toteswingers 1&2 £9.00, 1&3 £3.60, 2&3 £5.60 CSF £31.79 TOTE £4.70: £1.10, £2.10, £1.40; EX 39.50 Trifecta £100.50 Pool: £1547.39 - 11.53 winning units..There was no bid for the winner.
Owner Miss Caroline Scott **Bred** Patrick Eddery Ltd **Trained** West Wickham, Cambs

FOCUS
An ordinary selling hurdle run at a strong pace. The winner is rated below his best.

2847 JAYNE FERGUSON MEMORIAL H'CAP CHASE (18 fncs) 2m 7f 110y
2:05 (2:05) (Class 4) (0-115,115) 4-Y-0 **£6,330** (£1,870; £935; £468; £234)

Form RPR
2/3- **1** **Balbriggan (IRE)**[21] 2394 6-11-12 **115** .... DominicElsworth 126+
(Mick Channon) *w ldr tl led 3rd: mstke 11th: hdd 4 out: rallied to ld appr last: drvn out* **5/2**[2]
412- **2** *1 1/4* **The Potting Shed (IRE)**[25] 2293 6-11-9 **115** ....(p) GavinSheehan(3) 124
(Emma Lavelle) *trckd ldrs: mstke 5th: wnt 2nd 10th: led 4 out: rdn and hdd appr last: hung rt flat: styd on same pce* **9/4**[1]
F/2- **3** *6* **Nom De Guerre (IRE)**[13] 2560 11-11-4 **107** ....(b[1]) JackDoyle 111
(Ben De Haan) *led to 3rd: chsd wnr to 10th: remained handy: rdn and no ex flat* **10/1**
/42- **4** *23* **Be Definite (IRE)**[22] 2370 9-11-9 **112** ....(p) PaddyBrennan 99
(Tom George) *prom: mstke 1st: pushed along 10th: mstke and wknd 4 out* **10/1**
4/P- **5** *5* **Tafika**[200] 321 9-11-10 **113** ....(p) LiamTreadwell 93
(Paul Webber) *chsd ldrs: pushed along 10th: rdn and wknd 3 out* **9/2**[3]
/U4- **P** **Hot Whiskey (IRE)**[18] 2450 5-11-9 **112** ....(b) WayneHutchinson
(Alan King) *hld up: reminders after 7th: bhd fr 10th: p.u bef 4 out* **5/1**

5m 46.7s (-17.30) **Going Correction** -0.625s/f (Firm) 6 Ran SP% 112.4
Speed ratings (Par 105): **103,102,100,92,91**
toteswingers 1&2 £2.10, 1&3 £2.50, 2&3 £5.90 CSF £8.94 TOTE £3.90: £1.60, £1.90; EX 9.00 Trifecta £48.50 Pool: £1037.79 - 16.04 winning units..
Owner Mrs T P Radford **Bred** Ronan Tynan **Trained** West Ilsley, Berks

FOCUS
An ordinary handicap chase, but the form seems sound enough rated around the front three.

2848 BILLY BEIGHTON LOVED RACING MEMORIAL H'CAP HURDLE (8 hdls) 2m
2:35 (2:36) (Class 4) (0-120,120) 4-Y-0 **£6,330** (£1,870; £935; £468; £234)

Form RPR
0/2- **1** **Favorite Girl (GER)**[21] 2397 5-10-7 **101** .... RyanMahon 106+
(Michael Appleby) *hld up: hdwy appr 5th: outpcd bef next: rallied and hung rt bef last: r.o u.p to ld fnl 50yds: sn clr* **6/1**[3]
F/P- **2** *2* **Great Value (IRE)**[29] 2230 8-11-10 **118** ....(t) WayneHutchinson 120
(Graeme McPherson) *a.p: led appr 2 out: rdn and wnt rt last: hdd fnl 50yds* **20/1**
415- **3** *nk* **Hartside (GER)**[15] 2519 4-10-13 **114** .... MrRWinks(7) 116
(Peter Winks) *chsd ldrs: lost pl after 4th: hdwy appr 2 out: sn rdn: styd on* **7/1**
0- **4** *2* **Noche De Reyes (FR)**[16] 2492 4-11-4 **112** .... PaddyBrennan 113
(Tom George) *hld up: hdwy after 3 out: chsd ldr and hit next: sn rdn: wnt rt last: styd on same pce flat* **3/1**[1]
250/ **5** *1* **Bold Adventure**[158] 4540 9-10-5 **99** .... LeightonAspell 98
(Willie Musson) *hld up: hdwy u.p appr last: nt rch ldrs* **25/1**
241/ **6** *6* **Grate Fella (IRE)**[383] 2403 5-11-2 **110** .... SamTwiston-Davies 103
(Sue Smith) *set stdy pce tl hdd 4th: chsd ldr tl rdn appr 2 out: wknd bef last* **9/2**[2]
5/0- **7** *3/4* **Star Presenter (IRE)**[56] 1783 5-10-6 **100** .... PaulMoloney 93
(Paul Webber) *hld up: hdwy 3 out: rdn and wknd after next* **8/1**

2F4- **8** *2 ¼* **Who's Jeff (IRE)**[25] 2292 5-10-13 **107** TomO'Brien 100
(Philip Hobbs) *hld up: plld hrd: pckd 2nd: hdwy to ld 4th: hdd whn hit 2 out: wkng whn blnd last* **9/2**[2]

143/ **9** *7* **Dovils Date**[337] 3349 4-11-12 **120** RichardJohnson 105
(Tim Vaughan) *chsd ldr to 4th: rdn and wknd appr 2 out* **14/1**

00- **10** *5* **Heurtevent (FR)**[13] 2561 4-11-3 **111** LeeEdwards 94
(Tony Carroll) *prom: t.k.h: rdn and wknd appr 3 out* **33/1**

3m 49.5s (-11.50) **Going Correction** -0.625s/f (Firm) **10** Ran SP% **117.5**
Speed ratings (Par 105): **103,102,101,100,100 97,96,95,92,89**
toteswingers 1&2 £23.20, 1&3 £6.30, 2&3 £18.80 CSF £112.13 CT £862.30 TOTE £4.90: £2.30, £6.30, £2.30; EX 124.40 Trifecta £152.10 Pool: £1956.90 - 9.64 winning units..
Owner Terry Pryke **Bred** Gestut Gorlsdorf **Trained** Danethorpe, Notts

FOCUS
They went a steady initial pace in this modest handicap hurdle and there were plenty still in with chances two from home. The second and third set the level.

2849 CLIPSTON H'CAP CHASE (15 fncs) 2m 4f 110y
3:10 (3:10) (Class 5) (0-100,94) 4-Y-0+ **£3,249** (£954; £477; £238)

Form RPR

33U- **1** **Crescent Beach (IRE)**[83] 1534 6-11-3 **85** PaddyBrennan 90+
(Henry Oliver) *hld up: t.k.h: hdwy 7th: hmpd bnd appr 4 out: led 2 out: drvn out* **9/4**[2]

330- **2** *3 ¼* **Lodgician (IRE)**[45] 1939 11-11-12 **94** (vt) SamTwiston-Davies 95
(Nigel Twiston-Davies) *chsd ldr tl hung rt and led appr 4 out: hdd 2 out: sn rdn: hung rt flat: styd on same pce* **9/2**[3]

/35- **3** *nk* **Bally Lagan (IRE)**[11] 2599 5-11-0 **82** (t) CharliePoste 83
(Robin Dickin) *chsd ldrs: rdn appr last: styd on same pce flat* **6/5**[1]

0/6- **4** *36* **Badb Catha (IRE)**[41] 2003 7-10-0 **68** oh2 (t) DaveCrosse 43
(Roger Curtis) *hld up: reminders after 2nd: hdwy 9th: rdn 11th: wkng whn mstke 2 out* **14/1**

644- **5** *25* **Mad Professor (IRE)**[12] 2576 10-9-9 **68** oh3 (b) JoeCornwall(5) 13
(John Cornwall) *bhd fr 4th* **16/1**

PFU- **6** *9* **Kevin Fancy (IRE)**[20] 2425 7-9-11 **68** oh20 GavinSheehan(3) 5
(John Upson) *led: rdn: hdd & wknd 4 out* **40/1**

5m 13.1s (-5.80) **Going Correction** -0.625s/f (Firm) course record **6** Ran SP% **109.4**
Speed ratings (Par 103): **86,84,84,70,61 57**
toteswingers 1&2 £1.50, 1&3 £1.80, 2&3 £1.10 CSF £12.12 CT £14.55 TOTE £4.20: £1.60, £1.60; EX 11.70 Trifecta £20.10 Pool: £2118.31 - 78.98 winning units..
Owner R G Whitehead **Bred** John Mounsey **Trained** Broomhall, Worcs

FOCUS
A really weak handicap chase. The first two ran pretty much to their marks.

2850 FERNIE NOVICES' HURDLE (10 hdls) 2m 4f 110y
3:40 (3:40) (Class 4) 4-Y-0+ **£4,548** (£1,335; £667; £333)

Form RPR

1/1- **1** **Royal Regatta (IRE)**[35] 2103 5-11-5 0 RichardJohnson 130+
(Philip Hobbs) *trckd ldrs: plld hrd: wnt 2nd 3rd: led 5th: mstke 3 out: rdn clr flat* **1/1**[1]

5/ **2** *9* **Allow Dallow (IRE)**[281] 4384 6-10-12 0 RichieMcLernon 110+
(Jonjo O'Neill) *hld up: hdwy 6th: chsd wnr appr 2 out: wnt rt last: no ex flat* **25/1**

/45- **3** *1 ¼* **Pure Science (IRE)**[15] 2505 5-10-12 0 SamTwiston-Davies 109
(Nigel Twiston-Davies) *led to 5th: chsd wnr tl rdn appr 2 out: no ex last* **9/4**[2]

1- **4** *4 ½* **Take A Bow**[61] 1712 4-10-12 0 AndrewTinkler 103
(Nicky Henderson) *chsd ldr to 3rd: remained handy: reminders 5th: rdn and wknd 2 out* **4/1**[3]

/00- **5** *2 ¾* **Solstice Dawn**[15] 2514 5-9-12 0 MrRWinks(7) 93
(Peter Winks) *prom: lost pl 6th: rallied appr 3 out: sn rdn: wknd bef next* **100/1**

3/0- **6** *nk* **In The Gate (IRE)**[10] 2621 5-10-9 0 KielanWoods(3) 102
(Charlie Longsdon) *hld up: hmpd 1st: hdwy after 6th: rdn and wknd appr 2 out* **40/1**

5- **7** *27* **Shinooki (IRE)**[31] 2181 6-10-12 0 PaddyBrennan 73
(Alex Hales) *hld up: hdwy appr 3 out: sn rdn and wknd* **50/1**

/0P- **8** *hd* **Jazz Man (IRE)**[47] 1915 6-10-12 0 ConorO'Farrell 73
(Mark Rimell) *prom: reminders after 4th: outpcd after 6th: rallied appr 3 out: sn wknd* **100/1**

3/ **F** **Anshantor (IRE)**[603] 7-10-12 0 TomO'Brien
(Henry Daly) *fell 1st* **50/1**

P0P- **P** **Rose Of Marron (IRE)**[24] 2316 6-10-9 0 (p) GavinSheehan(3)
(John Upson) *prom: j.flt 3rd: wknd 6th: bhd whn p.u bef 3 out* **200/1**

5m 6.6s (-18.10) **Going Correction** -0.625s/f (Firm)
WFA 4 from 5yo+ 6lb **10** Ran SP% **113.5**
Speed ratings (Par 105): **109,105,105,103,102 102,91,91, ,**
toteswingers 1&2 £7.10, 1&3 £1.20, 2&3 £8.10 CSF £25.49 TOTE £1.80: £1.10, £3.40, £1.20; EX 25.70 Trifecta £77.20 Pool: £4568.59 - 44.34 winning units..
Owner J C Murphy & Mrs L Field **Bred** W B Mactaggart **Trained** Withycombe, Somerset

FOCUS
An ordinary novice hurdle run at a steady gallop. The easy winner was value for further but the third was a stone+ off.
T/Jkpt: £5257.00. Pool: £25,915.24 - 3.50 winning units. T/Plt: £35.10. Pool: £103,576.50 - 2149.31 winning units. T/Qpdt: £11.10. Pool: £6993.16 - 149.80 winning units. CR

2831 FAIRYHOUSE (R-H)
Sunday, December 1

OFFICIAL GOING: Good to yielding

2851a BAR ONE RACING JUVENILE 3-Y-O HURDLE (GRADE 3) (10 hdls) 2m
12:10 (12:10) 3-Y-0 **£14,532** (£4,247; £2,012; £670)

RPR

1 **Analifet (FR)**[15] 2521 3-10-6 RWalsh 137+
(W P Mullins, Ire) *cl up early and led bef 2nd: slt mstke next and nt fluent 4th: over 1 l clr 1/2-way: extended advantage bef 4 out: travelling wl into st and clr fr 2 out: v easily* **30/100**[1]

2 *6 ½* **Noble Inn (FR)**[15] 2521 3-10-9 PaulTownend 130
(W P Mullins, Ire) *hld up: 7th 1/2-way: hit 3 out: sn clsd in 5th bef st and wnt mod 2nd between last 2: kpt on same pce run-in: nt trble easy wnr* **10/1**

3 *6* **Clarcam (FR)**[38] 2056 3-10-9 (t) DavyRussell 124
(Gordon Elliott, Ire) *chsd ldrs: slt mstke 2nd: 5th 1/2-way: nt fluent 4 out: sme hdwy between horses bef 2 out: no imp on easy wnr in 3rd between last 2: kpt on same pce* **7/1**[2]

4 *9 ½* **Gerdago (IRE)**[21] 2406 3-10-9 (t) BryanCooper 115
(K J Condon, Ire) *sn trckd ldr: 2nd 1/2-way: rdn into st and no imp on easy wnr: dropped to mod 4th after 2 out: one pce after* **8/1**[3]

5 *11* **Sin Miedo (IRE)**[8] 2682 3-10-9 (p) RobbiePower 104
(Mrs John Harrington, Ire) *chsd ldrs: mstke 3rd: clsr in 3rd 1/2-way: pushed along fr 3 out and no imp on easy wnr: n.m.r on inner bef 2 out: sn dropped to 5th and no ex: wknd* **16/1**

6 *15* **Elishpour (IRE)**[121] 3-10-9 DannyMullins 89
(A J Martin, Ire) *chsd ldrs: nt fluent 1st: 6th 1/2-way: pushed along and no imp fr 3 out: one pce after* **20/1**

7 *35* **Authorative (IRE)**[2] 2521 3-10-9 AELynch 54
(Patrick O Brady, Ire) *led early: j.flt 1st and hdd bef next where mstke: 3rd bef 1/2-way: niggled along and wknd fr 5th: no imp towards rr fr 4 out: wknd: completely t.o* **100/1**

8 *5 ½* **Diesel Ten (IRE)**[21] 2406 3-10-9 MarkBolger 48
(Patrick O Brady, Ire) *racd in rr thrght: j.big 1st: struggling after 1/2-way: completely t.o* **100/1**

3m 52.7s (-19.30) **8** Ran SP% **122.2**
CSF £5.44 TOTE £1.20: £1.02, £2.20, £1.70; DF 4.10 Trifecta £25.00.
Owner Gigginstown House Stud **Bred** Jacques-Emmanuel Cherel **Trained** Muine Beag, Co Carlow

FOCUS
Unusually quick ground for this meeting, described as being just on the slow side of good. All the talk was about the odds-on favourite and she lived up to the pre-race hype. She set a brisk tempo throughout and had plenty in trouble with three to jump. The form fits the race averages.

2852a BAR ONE RACING ROYAL BOND NOVICE HURDLE (GRADE 1) (10 hdls) 2m
12:40 (12:40) 4-Y-0+ **£39,634** (£11,585; £5,487; £1,829)

RPR

1 **The Tullow Tank (IRE)**[22] 2378 5-11-10 135 DannyMullins 146
(Philip Fenton, Ire) *chsd ldrs: nt fluent 2nd: 5th 1/2-way: pushed along fr 3 out and wnt 4th bef st: clsd on outer to chal in 2nd 2 out: kpt on best fr last to ld nr fin* **5/1**[3]

2 *½* **Renneti (FR)**[44] 1961 4-11-7 PaulTownend 142
(W P Mullins, Ire) *attempted to make all: 2 l clr 1/2-way: stl gng wl into st: sn pushed along and strly pressed bef last where nt fluent: rdn and hdd nr fin: no ex* **14/1**

3 *1* **Arctic Fire (GER)**[8] 2683 4-11-7 135 DJCasey 144+
(W P Mullins, Ire) *w.w in rr: tk clsr order bhd ldrs in 8th bef 2 out: n.m.r between last 2: qcknd into 4th bef last and styd on wl u.p run-in: nrst fin* **16/1**

4 *3 ¾* **Alonso (SPA)**[36] 2091 4-11-7 RWalsh 137
(W P Mullins, Ire) *hld up towards rr: 8th 1/2-way: hdwy into 5th after 3 out: wnt 3rd u.p after next: no imp on ldrs at last where nt fluent: dropped to 4th run-in: kpt on same pce* **11/4**[1]

5 *1 ¾* **Very Wood (FR)**[21] 2407 4-11-7 135 DavyRussell 136
(Noel Meade, Ire) *hld up: 7th 1/2-way: cl 6th after 3 out: rdn bef next and no imp on ldrs in 5th bef last: kpt on same pce* **11/2**

6 *6* **Mr Fiftyone (IRE)**[22] 2377 4-11-7 132 BarryGeraghty 130
(Mrs John Harrington, Ire) *trckd ldr: 3rd 1/2-way: rdn into st and sn no ex u.p: dropped to mod 6th bef last: kpt on one pce* **11/1**

7 *1 ¾* **Minella Foru (IRE)**[21] 2407 4-11-7 135 APMcCoy 128
(Edward P Harty, Ire) *w.w: j. sltly lft 4th: 6th 1/2-way: pushed along fr 3 out and no imp on ldrs bef next where j. sltly lft: no ex* **7/1**

8 *6 ½* **Gilt Shadow (IRE)**[29] 2232 5-11-10 MrSCrawford 124
(S R B Crawford, Ire) *chsd ldrs: slt mstke 2nd: clsr in 2nd bef 4th: rdn bef 2 out and sn no ex u.p: wknd* **9/2**[2]

9 *nse* **Somethingwonderful (IRE)**[25] 2299 5-11-10 116 BryanCooper 124
(D T Hughes, Ire) *hld up towards rr: slt mstke 2nd: 9th 1/2-way: pushed along fr 3 out and no imp bef next* **66/1**

10 *32* **Gambling Girl (IRE)**[30] 2205 4-11-0 133 RobbiePower 82
(Mrs John Harrington, Ire) *chsd ldrs: 4th 1/2-way: niggled along fr 3 out and sn dropped towards rr: wknd: t.o* **8/1**

3m 53.6s (-18.40)
WFA 4 from 5yo 5lb **10** Ran SP% **122.9**
CSF £74.15 TOTE £6.90: £2.30, £3.30, £5.90; DF 110.80 Trifecta £1167.90.
Owner Barry Connell **Bred** Aidan Aherne **Trained** Carrick-On-Suir, Co Tipperary

FOCUS
Not a lot between a few of these at the end. The fifth and ninth help with the standard.

2853a BAR ONE RACING DRINMORE NOVICE CHASE (GRADE 1) (16 fncs) 2m 4f
1:10 (1:11) 4-Y-0+ **£39,634** (£11,585; £5,487; £1,829)

RPR

1 **Don Cossack (GER)**[14] 2551 6-11-10 147 DavyRussell 152+
(Gordon Elliott, Ire) *hld up: j. sltly lft at times: clsr in 4th at 7th: niggled along fr 9th and wnt 2nd on outer bef st: j. sltly lft again 2 out: sn swtchd u.p in 3rd: gd jump last and sn led: styd on wl* **13/8**[1]

2 *1 ¾* **Carlingford Lough (IRE)**[74] 1604 7-11-10 150 APMcCoy 151
(John E Kiely, Ire) *trckd ldrs: j. sltly lft at times: rdn fr 4 out and clsr in 3rd bef st: led u.p between last 2: strly pressed fr last and sn hdd: no ex cl home* **4/1**[3]

3 *2 ½* **Road To Riches (IRE)**[22] 2379 6-11-10 PCarberry 148
(Noel Meade, Ire) *led tl hdd 3rd: regained advantage fr 6th: strly pressed 2 out where j.lft: hdd between last 2: no ex u.p in 3rd fr last: kpt on same pce* **8/1**

4 *7 ½* **Sizing Rio (IRE)**[28] 2258 5-11-10 145 AELynch 140
(Henry De Bromhead, Ire) *trckd ldr tl led 3rd: hdd fr 6th: remained prom tl pushed along fr 4 out: edgd rt briefly bef next where dropped to 5th: no imp on ldrs 2 out: kpt on same pce* **3/1**[2]

5 *1 ¾* **Art Of Logistics (IRE)**[45] 1950 5-11-10 138 BryanCooper 138
(D T Hughes, Ire) *w.w: niggled along briefly in rr fr 6th: no imp on ldrs into st: kpt on same pce fr 2 out* **9/2**

6 *4 ¾* **Clar Na Mionn (IRE)**[28] 2258 6-11-10 131 APHeskin 135
(V T O'Brien, Ire) *trckd ldrs: pushed along in 4th after 3 out and no imp on ldrs u.p into st: wknd fr 2 out* **50/1**

4m 53.1s (-30.90) **6** Ran SP% **114.3**
CSF £9.05 TOTE £2.60: £1.60, £1.90; DF 9.00 Trifecta £60.80.
Owner Gigginstown House Stud **Bred** Gestut Etzean **Trained** Trim, Co Meath

FOCUS
Given some of the novices that could have attended, there was a rather disappointing feel to this year's Drinmore. Despite the small field, it was run a good clip and the entire field was niggled along at various stages before the home turn. The performance of the winner went a long way to answering his critics. The form fits the race averages with the standard around the second and fifth.

2855a BAR ONE RACING HATTON'S GRACE HURDLE (GRADE 1) (12 hdls) 2m 4f
2:15 (2:18) 4-Y-0+ **£42,276** (£12,357; £5,853; £1,951)

RPR

1 **Jezki (IRE)**[30] 2206 5-11-10 161 .... APMcCoy 163+
(Mrs John Harrington, Ire) *hld up: nt fluent 2nd: mod 4th bef 7th: tk clsr order fr 4 out and hdwy between horses fr next travelling wl: j.lft 2 out and sn led: j.lft again and mstke last: rdn and kpt on wl run-in* **4/6**[1]

2 1 ¾ **Zaidpour (FR)**[175] 685 7-11-10 155 .... (p) RWalsh 160+
(W P Mullins, Ire) *settled bhd ldr: slt mstkes 4th and next: mod 2nd at 7th: tk clsr order fr next: nt fluent 3 out: rdn in 3rd fr next: nt fluent last and wnt 2nd u.p: kpt on same pce: nt rch wnr* **9/1**

3 ½ **Diakali (FR)**[22] 2377 4-11-6 145 .... PaulTownend 156
(W P Mullins, Ire) *led: nt fluent 2nd: sn clr: j.lft 6th: reduced advantage fr 4 out: strly pressed into st and hdd after 2 out: no imp on wnr bef last and sn dropped to 3rd: kpt on same pce* **6/1**[3]

4 13 **Rule The World**[34] 2142 6-11-10 152 .... DavyRussell 148
(M F Morris, Ire) *settled bhd ldrs: mod 3rd 1/2-way: tk clsr order bef 3 out: pushed along in 4th bef st and no imp on ldrs: kpt on one pce* **10/3**[2]

5 6 **Dedigout (IRE)**[21] 2408 7-11-10 150 .... (t) BryanCooper 142
(A J Martin, Ire) *w.w in rr: pushed along bef 4 out and no imp u.p fr next: slt mstke 2 out: kpt on one pce* **14/1**

4m 50.5s (-32.50)
WFA 4 from 5yo+ 6lb 5 Ran SP% **114.0**
CSF £7.77 TOTE £1.60: £1.10, £2.30; DF 5.30 Trifecta £14.40.
Owner John P McManus **Bred** Gerard M McGrath **Trained** Moone, Co Kildare

FOCUS
The third ran a personal best from the front. The form is rated around the first and second and fits the race averages.

2854 - 2857a (Foreign Racing) - See Raceform Interactive

[2564] PLUMPTON (L-H)
Monday, December 2

OFFICIAL GOING: Good (good to soft in places; hdl 6.9, chs 7.3)
Wind: Almost nil Weather: Overcast

2858 ATTHERACES.COM EXCLUSIVE BARRY GERAGHTY BLOG NOVICES' HURDLE (9 hdls) 2m
12:40 (12:40) (Class 4) 4-Y-0+ **£3,898** (£1,144; £572; £286)

Form RPR

P/ 1 **Electrolyser (IRE)**[337] 3376 8-10-12 0 .... DavidBass 123+
(Nicky Henderson) *hld up towards rr: mstke 4th: prog next: trckd ldr after 3 out: led next: r.o wl: comf* **11/4**[1]

0/3- 2 2 ¼ **Come On Laurie (IRE)**[14] 2570 5-10-12 0 .... AidanColeman 118+
(Lawney Hill) *hld up in last trio: gd prog fr 3 out: shkn up to chse wnr after 2 out: styd on but no imp* **8/1**

/52- 3 11 **Saffron Prince**[14] 2564 5-10-12 0 .... TomScudamore 108
(David Bridgwater) *mstke 1st: trckd ldng pair: led 4th: shkn up and hdd 2 out: wknd last* **7/2**[2]

3- 4 1 **Nesterenko (GER)**[18] 2467 4-10-12 0 .... AndrewTinkler 106
(Nicky Henderson) *hld up in last trio: j. bdly rt 2nd: pushed along and sme prog bef 3 out: rdn and kpt on fr next: n.d* **4/1**[3]

04- 5 1 ½ **Join The Clan (IRE)**[14] 2563 4-10-12 0 .... (p) APMcCoy 104
(Jonjo O'Neill) *racd wd: hld up in last quartet: prog 6th: pushed along bef 3 out: reminder bef 2 out: kpt on one pce* **6/1**

6 9 **Sadma**[793] 4-10-12 0 .... DenisO'Regan 95
(John Ferguson) *wl in tch: pushed along to chse ldng pair after 3 out tl bef next: lost pl and eased* **16/1**

7 4 **Torero**[55] 4-10-12 0 .... MarcGoldstein 91
(Diana Grissell) *nvr beyond midfield: dropped to rr 6th: brief hdwy after 3 out: nvr on terms* **33/1**

05- 8 2 **Mariet**[14] 2564 4-10-2 0 .... WayneKavanagh(3) 82
(Suzy Smith) *plld hrd: in tch to 3 out: wknd bef next* **50/1**

9 7 **Spartilla**[570] 4-10-12 0 .... TomCannon 82
(Daniel O'Brien) *trckd ldrs: stl in tch 3 out: fdd and eased bef 2 out* **66/1**

/05- 10 2 ¾ **Yes I Will**[12] 2602 4-10-12 0 .... (t) NoelFehily 80
(Charlie Longsdon) *trckd ldrs: wl there after 3 out: lost pl and eased bef next* **14/1**

0/0- 11 13 **Father Arthur**[20] 2432 5-10-12 0 .... LeightonAspell 67
(Richard Rowe) *racd in ldng trio tl lost pl rapidly bef 3 out: bhd fr next* **100/1**

0/ 12 33 **Querido (GER)**[188] 4288 9-10-9 0 .... (t) KielanWoods(3) 34
(Paddy Butler) *in tch to 6th: sn wknd: t.o* **200/1**

13 42 **Meadstown (IRE)**[197] 5-10-9 0 .... (t) MarkQuinlan(3)
(Mark Shears) *led to 4th: wknd rapidly and last after next: sn wl t.o* **200/1**

3- P **Mr Spiggott (IRE)**[14] 2564 4-10-9 0 .... JoshuaMoore(3)
(Gary Moore) *prom: trckd ldr 6th tl p.u sn after 3 out: fatally injured* **12/1**

4m 0.15s (-0.65) **Going Correction** -0.075s/f (Good) 14 Ran SP% **122.9**
Speed ratings (Par 105): **98,96,91,90,90 85,83,82,79,77 71,54,33,**
toteswingers 1&2 £6.10, 1&3 £3.20, 2&3 £7.60 CSF £26.34 TOTE £4.10: £1.60, £3.30, £1.70; EX 32.00 Trifecta £158.60 Pool: £3042.00 - 14.37 winning units..
Owner Mr And Mrs P Hargreaves **Bred** Darley **Trained** Upper Lambourn, Berks

FOCUS
A modest novice hurdle. The winner can rate higher.

2859 AUTUMN GALA NOVICES' LIMITED H'CAP CHASE (14 fncs) 2m 4f
1:10 (1:10) (Class 3) (0-140,140) 4-Y-0+ **£7,797** (£2,289; £1,144)

Form RPR

/42- 1 **Buthelezi (USA)**[14] 2558 5-10-12 133 .... DenisO'Regan 130+
(John Ferguson) *j.w: mde all: drew 4 l clr 3 out: pressed fr next: urged along but wout recrse to whip: hld on wl* **2/1**[2]

P/0- 2 ¾ **Une Artiste (FR)**[30] 2226 5-11-5 140 .... APMcCoy 137+
(Nicky Henderson) *hld up in 3rd tl trckd wnr 9th: pushed along after next: drvn to chal 2 out: upsides last: styd on but hld nr fin* **4/5**[1]

314- 3 18 **Billy No Name (IRE)**[27] 2279 5-10-5 126 oh5 .... BrendanPowell 114
(Colin Tizzard) *pressed wnr tl mstke and stmbld bdly 8th: last fr next: outpcd 4 out: 7 l down whn blnd 2 out: wknd* **9/2**[3]

5m 1.6s (-5.70) **Going Correction** -0.075s/f (Good) 3 Ran SP% **107.1**
Speed ratings (Par 107): **108,107,100**
CSF £4.06 TOTE £2.70; EX 4.90 Trifecta £3.60 Pool: £1187.87 - 242.35 winning units..
Owner Bloomfields **Bred** Dr John A Chandler **Trained** Cowlinge, Suffolk

FOCUS
It was clear from an early stage this was going to be a match, with Billy No Name jumping ponderously, and it was the only runner with previous experience of fences, Buthelezi, who came out on top. He's rated in line with his upgraded Leicester run.

2860 FOLLOW @ATTHERACES ON TWITTER MARES' H'CAP HURDLE (14 hdls) 3m 1f 110y
1:40 (1:41) (Class 3) (0-125,119) 4-Y-0+ **£8,122** (£2,385; £1,192; £596)

Form RPR

/04- 1 **Tweedledrum**[7] 2713 6-11-3 115 .... (p) BenPoste(5) 122+
(Tom Symonds) *trckd ldng pair: rdn to chse ldr after 3 out: clsd last: styd on wl to ld fnl 100yds* **15/8**[1]

131- 2 1 ¼ **Cannon Fodder**[42] 2006 6-11-7 114 .... MarcGoldstein 120
(Sheena West) *trckd ldr: chal 11th: led 3 out: sn rdn: hit 2 out: hdd and one pce last 100yds* **11/4**[2]

/P1- 3 18 **Aimigayle**[71] 1628 10-11-12 119 .... ColinBolger 109
(Suzy Smith) *led at fair pce: hdd 3 out: wknd bef next* **3/1**[3]

246- 4 ¾ **The Road Ahead**[16] 2510 6-10-7 100 .... TomO'Brien 91
(Peter Bowen) *hld up in last: chsd ldng trio 11th and cl enough: mstke 3 out and wknd* **5/1**

P/3- 5 11 **Grace And Fortune**[14] 2566 6-10-12 105 .... LeightonAspell 88
(Richard Rowe) *chsd ldng trio: pushed along fr 9th: mstke 11th and dropped to last: sn btn* **12/1**

6m 30.0s (5.00) **Going Correction** -0.075s/f (Good) 5 Ran SP% **110.8**
Speed ratings (Par 107): **89,88,83,82,79**
CSF £7.62 TOTE £2.80: £1.90, £1.30; EX 8.40 Trifecta £18.30 Pool: £1886.22 - 76.91 winning units..
Owner Wainwright,Hill,Atkin,Cheshire & Rowlinson **Bred** Kingsclere Stud **Trained** Harewood End, H'fords

FOCUS
The front pair drew right away in this staying hurdle. The winner is rated in line with her Kempton run allowing for the jockey's claim.

2861 AT THE RACES SKY 415 H'CAP CHASE (14 fncs) 2m 4f
2:10 (2:11) (Class 5) (0-100,100) 4-Y-0+ **£2,274** (£667; £333; £166)

Form RPR

P05- 1 **Porters War (IRE)**[28] 2270 11-11-12 100 .... NickScholfield 112+
(Jeremy Scott) *w.w: trckd ldrs 8th: clsd fr 4 out: rdn to ld 2 out: drvn clr* **7/1**[3]

2S1- 2 12 **Mister Wiseman**[5] 2739 11-10-3 84 .... (vt) ThomasCheesman(7) 87
(Nigel Hawke) *chsd ldr to 4th: mstke next: chsd ldr again 9th: tried to chal after 3 out: no ex after 2 out: plugged on to snatch 2nd last strides* **2/1**[2]

2/3- 3 ½ **Ballyman (IRE)**[28] 2277 12-10-7 81 .... (v) MarkGrant 84
(Jonathan Geake) *led: rdn and hdd whn nt fluent 2 out: btn whn blnd last: wknd and lost 2nd last strides* **8/1**

P/4- 4 4 **Further More (IRE)**[37] 2088 6-10-13 87 .... AidanColeman 84
(Emma Lavelle) *prom: chsd ldr 4th to 9th: cl up tl wknd 3 out* **15/8**[1]

042- 5 6 **Budsson**[13] 2580 7-10-0 74 oh18 .... AdamWedge 66
(Anna Newton-Smith) *a in rr: nudged along and lost tch 8th: abt 20 l bhd 4 out: lost little further grnd* **50/1**

P2P- P **Doheny Bar (IRE)**[18] 2478 10-10-3 77 .... (t) TomO'Brien
(Paul Henderson) *prom early: lost tch fr 5th: t.o whn p.u bef 7th* **7/1**[3]

1/P- P **Red Anchor (IRE)**[20] 2438 9-11-8 96 .... AndrewThornton
(Linda Jewell) *a in rr: reminders after 6th: struggling fr 8th: t.o 10th: p.u bef 2 out* **16/1**

5m 7.6s (0.30) **Going Correction** -0.075s/f (Good) 7 Ran SP% **112.1**
Speed ratings (Par 103): **96,91,91,89,87 ,**
toteswingers 1&2 £4.10, 1&3 £6.70, 2&3 £2.20 CSF £21.46 TOTE £8.90: £4.20, £1.60; EX 28.70 Trifecta £141.60 Pool: £2882.85 - 15.26 winning units..
Owner Sarah Waugh & Paul Porter **Bred** Mrs Edith Mulcahy **Trained** Brompton Regis, Somerset

FOCUS
Moderate chase form. The winner's best figure since 2009.

2862 AT THE RACES VIRGIN 534 H'CAP HURDLE (9 hdls) 2m
2:40 (2:40) (Class 5) (0-95,95) 4-Y-0+ **£2,053** (£598; £299)

Form RPR

/04- 1 **Shadarpour (IRE)**[19] 1822 4-11-12 95 .... (b) JamieMoore 104+
(Gary Moore) *prom: trckd ldr 5th: led next: sent for home 3 out: 5 l clr 2 out: drvn out* **4/1**[2]

60P/ 2 1 ½ **Agapanthus (GER)**[405] 1976 8-10-12 81 .... (p) NoelFehily 85
(Neil Mulholland) *racd wd: hld up in rr: stdy prog fr 6th: wnt 2nd bef 2 out: clsd on wnr after last: nvr quite able to chal* **4/1**[2]

/U0- 3 11 **Celtic Charlie (FR)**[71] 1630 8-10-7 76 .... (t) ColinBolger 70
(Pat Phelan) *trckd ldrs: prog 6th: chsd wnr 3 out to bef next: fdd but hld on for 3rd* **50/1**

/00- 4 2 ¼ **Tom Sang (FR)**[179] 640 6-10-10 79 .... TomO'Brien 73
(Jamie Snowden) *hld up wl in rr: prog fr 6th: trckd ldrs after 3 out: no imp next: wl hld in 4th whn blnd last* **7/2**[1]

30P- 5 1 ¾ **Conigre**[174] 708 6-11-12 95 .... JackDoyle 87
(Ali Brewer) *hld up wl in rr: stl there whn blnd 6th: only 11th 3 out: kpt on to pass wkng rivals bef next: no threat* **14/1**

531/ 6 10 **Golden Games (IRE)**[182] 5557 7-11-4 92 .... BenPoste(5) 76
(Daniel O'Brien) *hld up wl in rr: pushed along and prog 3 out: nt on terms but keeping on in 5th whn blnd last* **20/1**

050- 7 1 **Just Beware**[13] 2581 11-9-11 73 .... (p) MrGGorman(7) 54
(Zoe Davison) *wl in rr: urged along 3 out: nvr on terms w ldrs* **20/1**

046- 8 ½ **No Ifs No Buts**[26] 2291 4-10-3 79 .... (t) JakeHodson(7) 59
(David Bridgwater) *chsd ldrs: drvn and wknd fr 3 out* **16/1**

/00- 9 nse **Ricketyrock**[11] 2628 7-10-4 80 .... TomBellamy(7) 61
(Nick Mitchell) *chsd ldr to 5th: steadily wknd after 3 out* **50/1**

/4P- 10 5 **Clonusker (IRE)**[174] 708 5-10-0 69 oh1 .... GerardTumelty 45
(Linda Jewell) *settled towards rr: in tch and gng reasonably whn nt fluent 3 out: steadily wknd and eased* **66/1**

P66- 11 52 **Petrocelli**[42] 2004 6-10-5 74 .... (v[1]) RichardJohnson
(Tim Vaughan) *in tch: dropped to rr 5th: sn struggling: t.o after 3 out: eased* **10/1**

055- 12 ½ **Old Magic (IRE)**[26] 2291 8-11-2 85 .... PaulMoloney 13
(Sophie Leech) *wl in tch: lost pl 5th: struggling in rr next: t.o after 3 out: eased* **8/1**

/34- **13** *13* **Mighty Mambo**[14] 2568 6-11-7 **90**..(v[1]) DavidBass 7
(Lawney Hill) *led to 6th: sn rdn: wknd rapidly 3 out: t.o and eased* **6/1**[3]
3m 59.1s (-1.70) **Going Correction** -0.075s/f (Good) **13** Ran SP% **124.2**
Speed ratings (Par 103): **101,100,94,93,92 87,87,87,86,84 58,58,51**
toteswingers 1&2 £7.90, 1&3 £51.00, 2&3 £68.00 CSF £20.70 CT £723.01 TOTE £5.40: £2.30, £2.10, £9.10; EX 37.40 Trifecta £1186.90 Part won. Pool: £1582.55 - 0.02 winning units..
Owner G L Porter **Bred** His Highness The Aga Khan's Studs S C **Trained** Lower Beeding, W Sussex
FOCUS
A moderate handicap. The winner is on the upgrade.

2863 TYSERS H'CAP CHASE (18 fncs) 3m 2f
3:10 (3:11) (Class 5) (0-100,100) 4-Y-0+ **£2,274** (£667; £333; £166)

Form RPR
6/4- **1** **Itoldyou (IRE)**[20] 2437 7-11-9 **97**.. AndrewThornton 107+
(Linda Jewell) *patiently rdn: trckd ldng pair fr 9th: nipped through on inner to ld 2 out: sn clr: comf* **7/4**[1]
125/ **2** *4 ½* **Beware Chalk Pit (IRE)**[266] 4703 9-11-6 **94**.............................. MarkGrant 95
(Jonathan Geake) *blnd 1st: trckd ldr 3rd: led 8th: rdn and hdd 2 out: sn outpcd* **11/4**[3]
P1P/ **3** *9* **Ballinhassig (IRE)**[293] 4181 8-10-4 **78**................................ MarcGoldstein 75
(Sarah Wall) *led: nt fluent 8th and hdd: chsd ldr: upsides whn mstke 3 out: wknd next* **5/2**[2]
405- **4** *80* **Sapphire Rouge (IRE)**[8] 2701 7-10-11 **92**........................(p) KevinJones[(7)] 13
(Seamus Mullins) *trckd ldr to 3rd: mstke 9th and dropped to last: rdn next: wknd 12th: hopelessly t.o* **5/1**
6m 56.9s (6.20) **Going Correction** -0.075s/f (Good) **4** Ran SP% **108.3**
Speed ratings (Par 103): **87,85,82,58**
CSF £6.80 TOTE £2.50; EX 6.90 Trifecta £9.30 Pool: £1773.68 - 142.94 winning units..
Owner Valence Racing **Bred** James O'Leary **Trained** Sutton Valence, Kent
FOCUS
With the second and third making their reappearance and the other runner proving laboured, the race-fit Itoldyou ran out a ready winner. He's rated to the best of last season's heavy-ground form.

2864 ANISE CATERING INTERMEDIATE OPEN NATIONAL HUNT FLAT RACE 2m 2f
3:40 (3:41) (Class 6) 4-5-Y-0 **£1,711** (£498; £249)

Form RPR
2/5- **1** **Boogie In The Barn (IRE)**[30] 2216 5-11-2 0.................... NickScholfield 117+
(Jeremy Scott) *tok t.k.h: hld up tl prog to ld after 5f: mde most after: shkn up and drew clr wl over 1f out: comf* **10/11**[1]
0- **2** *11* **Leith Hill Legasi**[26] 2298 4-10-9 0... NoelFehily 96
(Charlie Longsdon) *disp ld 5f: cl up tl outpcd and pushed along 3f out: rdn and kpt on to take 2nd nr fin* **17/2**
5/2- **3** *nk* **Robbers Roost (IRE)**[202] 284 5-11-2 0........................ RichardJohnson 103
(Tim Vaughan) *cl up: chsd wnr 3f out: sn rdn and no imp: one pce and lost 2nd nr fin* **7/2**[2]
2/ **4** *28* **Malibu Rock**[281] 4418 5-11-2 0... APMcCoy 78
(Anna Newton-Smith) *disp ld 5f: pressed wnr to 4f out: hanging rt and wknd 3f out: t.o* **5/1**[3]
5 *24* **Kikili** 5-11-2 0.. TomCannon 56
(Nick Gifford) *in tch: rdn 4f out: sn wknd and bhd: wl t.o* **10/1**
0- **6** *78* **War Treaty (IRE)**[18] 2479 5-10-13 0................................ MarkQuinlan[(3)]
(Mark Shears) *disp ld 5f: rdn after 6f: sn wknd: hopelessly t.o* **66/1**
4m 29.6s (4.30) **Going Correction** -0.075s/f (Good)
WFA 4 from 5yo 5lb **6** Ran SP% **112.4**
Speed ratings: **87,82,81,69,58 24**
toteswingers 1&2 £2.60, 1&3 £1.40, 2&3 £4.00 CSF £9.76 TOTE £2.00: £1.30, £3.80; EX 8.10 Trifecta £38.40 Pool: £4144.09 - 80.81 winning units..
Owner Bradley Partnership **Bred** Patrick Gardiner **Trained** Brompton Regis, Somerset
FOCUS
Little depth to this bumper. The easy winner was the form pick but this looks a step up.
T/Plt: £285.60 to a £1 stake Pool: £86254.12 - 220.43 winning tickets T/Qpdt: £48.30 to a £1 stake. Pool: £7774.24 - 119.01 winning tickets JN

[2732] SEDGEFIELD (L-H)
Tuesday, December 3

OFFICIAL GOING: Good to soft (good in places; 6.2)
Wind: Almost nil Weather: Overcast, dry

2865 HORSE RACING FREE BETS WITH BOOKMAKERS.CO.UK CONDITIONAL JOCKEYS' MARES' "NH" NOVICES' HURDLE (10 hdls) 2m 4f
12:30 (12:30) (Class 4) 4-Y-0+ **£3,119** (£915; £457; £228)

Form RPR
122- **1** **Reves D'Amour (IRE)**[26] 2317 4-10-12 0............................ GavinSheehan 103+
(Jamie Snowden) *j.w: mde all: qcknd clr on bridle 2 out: v easily* **8/15**[1]
15- **2** *3* **Monita Donita**[18] 2406 4-10-12 0... JoshuaMoore 85
(Tim Easterby) *prom: hdwy to press wnr bef 2 out: sn pushed along: kpt on fr last: flattered by proximity to wnr* **11/4**[2]
U00- **3** *nse* **Cinnomhor**[18] 2495 5-10-4 0............................... DiarmuidO'Regan[(8)] 85
(Chris Grant) *chsd wnr tl rdn and outpcd bef 3 out: styd on fr last* **150/1**
2/4- **4** *32* **Hellesbelles (IRE)**[26] 2309 5-10-9 0........................... MichaelByrne[(3)] 66
(Tim Vaughan) *t.k.h: prom: outpcd bef 3 out: btn next: t.o* **8/1**[3]
456- **5** *11* **Knockturnal (IRE)**[10] 2675 5-10-2 0.............................. JakeHolliday[(10)] 46
(Malcolm Jefferson) *in tch: nt fluent 2nd: drvn and struggling 6th: lost tch after next: t.o* **80/1**
5m 8.3s (15.60) **Going Correction** +0.60s/f (Soft) **5** Ran SP% **104.9**
Speed ratings (Par 105): **92,90,90,77,73**
CSF £2.07 TOTE £1.40: £1.10, £1.40; EX 2.20 Trifecta £17.70 Pool: £3788.67 - 159.70 winning units..
Owner The TTF Partnership **Bred** Paul Keane **Trained** Lambourn, Berks
FOCUS
Chases dolled off inner, hurdles on outside and divided bends to provide fresh ground where possible. This mares' novice hurdle, confined to conditional riders, proved a stroll in the park for the odds-on favourite, who was value for much further.

2866 NO DEPOSIT FREE BETS WITH BOOKMAKERS.CO.UK MAIDEN HURDLE (10 hdls) 2m 5f 110y
1:00 (1:00) (Class 5) 4-Y-0+ **£2,053** (£598; £299)

Form RPR
2- **1** **Mr Utah**[33] 2172 6-10-9 113... TonyKelly[(5)] 107+
(Rebecca Menzies) *mde all: hrd pressed bef 2 out: sn rdn: edgd rt bef last: styd on wl run-in* **4/7**[1]
145- **2** *2* **Magic Present**[24] 2355 6-11-0 0.. BrianHughes 104+
(Malcolm Jefferson) *pressed wnr: effrt and disputing ld whn nt fluent 2 out: sn rdn and edgd lft: nt fluent last: one pce run-in* **2/1**[2]
6- **3** *22* **Rocky Stone (IRE)**[22] 2422 5-11-0 0.................................. JasonMaguire 84
(Donald McCain) *chsd ldrs: drvn 3 out: wknd fr next* **8/1**[3]
0S- **4** *3* **Indigo Island (IRE)**[7] 2732 4-10-7 0........................ GrantCockburn[(7)] 80
(Robert Bewley) *chsd ldrs: nt fluent 6th: drvn after 3 out: wknd bef next* **100/1**
5m 32.0s (17.40) **Going Correction** +0.60s/f (Soft)
WFA 4 from 5yo+ 6lb **4** Ran SP% **109.1**
Speed ratings (Par 103): **92,91,83,82**
CSF £2.13 TOTE £1.80; EX 2.10 Trifecta £3.10 Pool: £2976.00 - 706.69 winning units..
Owner Premier Racing Partnerships **Bred** Dr B Mayoh **Trained** Stearsby, N Yorks
FOCUS
An uncompetitive maiden. The field went a routine gallop and the first pair fought it out down the home straight. The winner is rated below his best.

2867 GET BOOKMAKERS FREE BETS WITH BOOKMAKERS.CO.UK NOVICES' CHASE (21 fncs) 3m 3f
1:30 (1:30) (Class 4) 5-Y-0+ **£4,431** (£1,309; £654)

Form RPR
3/2- **1** **Bit Of A Jig (IRE)**[18] 2494 6-11-0 122............................. JasonMaguire 128+
(Donald McCain) *chsd ldr: rdn and sltly outpcd 3 out: rallied u.p to ld between last 2: nt fluent last: edgd lft: styd on wl* **5/6**[1]
2/5- **2** *2* **Rev It Up (IRE)**[38] 2077 7-11-0 127.............................(v[1]) RichardJohnson 126+
(Tim Vaughan) *nt fluent on occasions: led: rdn bef 2 out: hdd between last 2: kpt on same pce run-in* **6/4**[2]
000- **3** *33* **Mauricetheathlete (IRE)**[27] 2288 10-10-7 0..................... NickSlatter[(7)] 97
(Martin Keighley) *chsd ldrs: drvn and outpcd bef 4 out: lost tch after next* **7/1**[3]
7m 13.0s (24.00) **Going Correction** +0.25s/f (Yiel) **3** Ran SP% **107.1**
Speed ratings: **74,73,63**
CSF £2.46 TOTE £1.50; EX 2.60 Trifecta £2.40 Pool: £2070.27 - 625.68 winning units..
Owner Let's Live Racing **Bred** W Henry **Trained** Cholmondeley, Cheshire
FOCUS
Predictably this marathon novice chase proved a tactical affair, but the form still ought to work out.

2868 COMPARE BOOKMAKERS WITH BOOKMAKERS.CO.UK H'CAP HURDLE (8 hdls) 2m 1f
2:00 (2:00) (Class 4) (0-120,112) 3-Y-0+ **£3,119** (£915; £457; £228)

Form RPR
305- **1** **Travis County (IRE)**[15] 2561 4-11-3 **103**................................. APMcCoy 110+
(Brian Ellison) *mde all: rdn bef 2 out: nt fluent last: styd on wl run-in* **5/2**[1]
450- **2** *nk* **Satanic Beat (IRE)**[18] 2493 4-11-9 **109**........................... BrianHarding 115+
(Jedd O'Keeffe) *chsd ldr: rdn after 3 out: rallied whn hit next: kpt on fr last: hld nr fin* **11/1**
0/2- **3** *9* **Bright Applause**[58] 1785 5-11-3 **103**............................... RichardJohnson 100
(Tracy Waggott) *hld up bhd ldng gp: effrt and rdn after 3 out: kpt on same pce fr next* **9/2**[3]
20P/ **4** *4 ½* **Pinerolo**[271] 4607 7-11-12 **112**.. RyanMania 105
(Sue Smith) *chsd ldrs: lost pl after 3rd: sn rdn: styd on fr 2 out: nvr able to chal* **17/2**
432- **5** *3 ½* **Trust Thomas**[24] 2360 5-11-4 **104**.. BrianHughes 96
(Ann Hamilton) *prom: rdn and outpcd after 3 out: no imp fr next* **3/1**[2]
600- **6** *9* **Hi Dancer**[13] 2597 10-11-1 **108**.. MrRyanClark[(7)] 89
(Ben Haslam) *hld up in tch: drvn along and outpcd 3 out: btn bef next* **33/1**
60P- **7** *shd* **Fred Bojangals (IRE)**[22] 2421 11-10-2 **95**............. MissEButterworth[(7)] 77
(Barbara Butterworth) *bhd: outpcd 4th: sme late hdwy: nvr on terms* **40/1**
0/0- **8** *11* **Celtic Abbey**[47] 1935 6-11-12 **112**..[1] JasonMaguire 83
(Donald McCain) *t.k.h: hld up: hdwy after 4 out: wknd fr next* **17/2**
3/0- **9** *35* **Bonnie Burnett (IRE)**[13] 2597 6-11-0 **100**........................... HarryHaynes 40
(Brian Rothwell) *t.k.h: hld up: hdwy and cl up after 3rd: rdn and wknd bef 3 out: eased whn no ch appr next* **12/1**
4m 14.7s (7.80) **Going Correction** +0.60s/f (Soft)
WFA 4 from 5yo+ 5lb **9** Ran SP% **114.2**
Speed ratings (Par 105): **105,104,100,98,96 92,92,87,70**
toteswingers 1&2 £6.20, 1&3 £2.50, 2&3 £6.00 CSF £29.44 CT £117.20 TOTE £3.30: £1.30, £4.00, £1.70; EX 34.60 Trifecta £111.70 Pool: £3570.36 - 23.96 winning units..
Owner D Gilbert, M Lawrence, A Bruce **Bred** Loughbrown Stud **Trained** Norton, N Yorks
FOCUS
A modest handicap, run at a fair gallop. Few held a serious chance turning for home and the form can be rated around the first two.

2869 COMPARE BOOKMAKERS WITH BOOKMAKERS.CO.UK NOVICES' H'CAP HURDLE (8 hdls) 2m 1f
2:30 (2:30) (Class 5) (0-100,100) 4-Y-0+ **£1,949** (£572; £286; £143)

Form RPR
065- **1** **Light The City (IRE)**[17] 2520 6-11-5 **96**........................... JakeGreenall[(3)] 106+
(Ruth Carr) *prom: led 4 out: mde rest: hrd pressed fr 2 out: styd on strly fr last* **20/1**
/00- **2** *5* **Next Hight (IRE)**[31] 2225 6-10-13 **87**...................................... RyanMania 93
(Sue Smith) *nt fluent on occasions: hld up towards rr: reminder 2nd: hdwy 1/2-way: effrt and rdn bef2 out: wnt 2nd run-in: styd on: nt rch wnr* **15/2**[3]
060/ **3** *1 ¾* **Beaumont's Party (IRE)**[27] 5057 6-11-12 **100**........................ APMcCoy 103
(Brian Ellison) *plld hrd: hld up bhd ldng gp: stdy hdwy bef 3 out: chsd wnr bef next: effrt and ev ch after 2 out: sn rdn and edgd lft: one pce fr last* **2/5**[1]
/36- **4** *16* **Sohcahtoa (IRE)**[40] 2034 7-10-9 **86**............................(p) JohnKington[(3)] 75
(Andrew Crook) *bhd: pushed along and hdwy bef 3 out: rdn and no imp bef next* **12/1**
16P- **5** *2 ¼* **Ravi River (IRE)**[25] 2336 9-10-2 **79**..........................(v) EwanWhillans[(3)] 66
(Alistair Whillans) *cl up tl rdn and wknd bef 2 out* **16/1**
/P0- **6** *13* **Rosquero (FR)**[7] 2736 8-10-10 **84**.................................(p) KennyJohnson 59
(Robert Johnson) *chsd ldrs: lost pl 4 out: n.d after* **33/1**
054- **7** *6* **Beyondtemptation**[13] 2593 5-10-0 **79**................................ TonyKelly[(5)] 48
(Jonathan Haynes) *bhd: struggling 1/2-way: nvr on terms* **33/1**
/0P- **8** *23* **Pampanito**[47] 1940 7-11-4 **92**.. JasonMaguire 41
(Donald McCain) *prom: led after 3rd to 4 out: rdn and wknd qckly after 3 out* **5/1**[2]

00P- **P** **Hobsons Bay (IRE)**[2] 2844 8-10-8 **87**.........................(t) MissCWalton(5)
(Sheena Walton) *led to after 3rd: lost pl 4 out: struggling whn p.u next* **33/1**

4m 15.8s (8.90) **Going Correction** +0.60s/f (Soft) **9** Ran SP% **127.0**
Speed ratings (Par 103): **103,100,99,92,91 85,82,71,**
toteswingers 1&2 £10.10, 1&3 £5.20, 2&3 £2.00 CSF £165.94 CT £207.25 TOTE £22.70: £4.00, £2.10, £1.10; EX 164.40 Trifecta £475.00 Pool: £4575.74 - 7.22 winning units..
Owner Dogberry Racing & Mrs Ruth Carr **Bred** Rabbah Bloodstock Limited **Trained** Huby, N Yorks

FOCUS
This moderate novice handicap was run at a solid gallop and only three mattered in the home straight. Big steps up from the first two.

2870 SIS LIVE H'CAP CHASE (16 fncs) 2m 4f
3:00 (3:00) (Class 5) (0-100,91) 4-Y-0+ **£2,209** (£648; £324; £162)

Form RPR
/04- **1** **Prince Blackthorn (IRE)**[25] 2338 7-10-4 **69**...................... BrianHarding 85+
(William Amos) *hld up in tch: smooth hdwy 4 out: led bef 2 out: shkn up and clr last: kpt on wl* **5/1**[2]

/43- **2** *4* **Farm Pixie (IRE)**[13] 2591 7-11-5 **91**........................... GrahamWatters(7) 103+
(Ann Hamilton) *nt fluent on occasions: in tch: outpcd 4 out: rallied bef 2 out: edgd lft and chsd (clr) wnr bef last: no imp* **13/2**[3]

3P1- **3** *6* **Pistol Basc (FR)**[21] 2445 9-11-3 **87**................................. TonyKelly(5) 92
(Rebecca Menzies) *t.k.h: trckd ldrs: effrt and drvn bef 2 out: one pce between last 2* **3/1**[1]

0P4- **4** *2 ½* **Oh Right (IRE)**[21] 2445 9-10-9 **74**.................................(p) LucyAlexander 76
(Dianne Sayer) *led to 6th: cl up: led 4 out to bef 2 out: outpcd between last 2* **5/1**[2]

P/P- **5** *18* **Jan Jandura (IRE)**[26] 2310 8-10-5 **70**...............................(t) BrianHughes 59
(William Amos) *cl up: led 6th to 4 out: hung lft and wknd after 2 out* **9/1**

401- **6** *23* **Monbeg (IRE)**[7] 2734 6-11-9 **88** 7ex............................(p) WilsonRenwick 61
(Martin Todhunter) *hld up: pushed along 1/2-way: struggling fr 4 out: t.o* **3/1**[1]

430- **F** **Western Bound (IRE)**[18] 2497 12-10-4 **69**.......................(t) SeanQuinlan
(Barbara Butterworth) *prom: fell 7th* **33/1**

5m 7.3s (4.30) **Going Correction** +0.25s/f (Yiel) **7** Ran SP% **109.6**
Speed ratings (Par 103): **101,99,97,96,88 79,**
toteswingers 1&2 £6.40, 1&3 £4.10, 2&3 £3.70 CSF £33.16 TOTE £3.90: £2.50, £3.70; EX 39.80 Trifecta £125.20 Pool: £3218.55 - 19.26 winning units..
Owner J M Stenhouse **Bred** Miss Carmel McGinn **Trained** Rochester, Northumberland

FOCUS
A weak handicap. The first two improved in line with last season's hurdle marks.

2871 FREE BETS WITH BOOKMAKERS.CO.UK STANDARD OPEN NATIONAL HUNT FLAT RACE 2m 1f
3:30 (3:30) (Class 6) 4-6-Y-0 **£1,642** (£478; £239)

Form RPR
1- **1** **Fly Home Harry**[31] 2223 4-11-9 0... APMcCoy 106+
(Alan Swinbank) *w ldrs: led over 3f out: rdn and edgd lft fr 2 out: styd on wl fnl f* **9/4**[2]

33- **2** *1 ¾* **Cousin Guillaume (FR)**[40] 2052 4-11-2 0......................... BrianHughes 97
(Karen McLintock) *led to 1/2-way: effrt and ev ch over 2f out: kpt on same pce ins fnl f* **7/2**[3]

2- **3** *3 ¾* **Vasco Pierji (FR)**[177] 682 4-11-2 0.................................. JasonMaguire 95
(Donald McCain) *w ldrs: led 1/2-way to over 3f out: rallied: one pce fr 2f out* **6/4**[1]

3/0- **4** *36* **Favourable Fellow (IRE)**[25] 2347 4-11-2 0..................[1] RichieMcGrath 62
(Geoffrey Harker) *hld up: stdy hdwy 1/2-way: rdn and outpcd fr over 5f out* **8/1**

5 *23* **Madame Flirt** 4-10-9 0.. LucyAlexander 34
(Dianne Sayer) *in tch to 1/2-way: sn struggling: t.o* **25/1**

0/0- **6** *31* **Precentors Court (IRE)**[7] 2738 6-11-2 0............................ HarryHaynes 13
(Brian Rothwell) *bhd: lost tch 1/2-way: t.o* **125/1**

4m 14.9s (13.60) **Going Correction** +0.60s/f (Soft) **6** Ran SP% **108.7**
Speed ratings: **92,91,89,72,61 47**
toteswingers 1&2 £1.90, 1&3 £1.50, 2&3 £1.40 CSF £9.80 TOTE £2.80: £1.50, £1.10; EX 7.50 Trifecta £18.30 Pool: £4249.54 - 174.08 winning units..
Owner Panther Racing Ltd **Bred** Miss S R Haynes **Trained** Melsonby, N Yorks
■ Stewards' Enquiry : Brian Hughes four-day ban: used whip above permitted level (Dec 17-20)

FOCUS
The market principals set the gallop in this modest little bumper and fought out a tight finish. A step up from the winner.
T/Plt: £22.70. Pool: £60,185.07 - 1933.51 winning units. T/Qpdt: £10.30. Pool: £4600.42 - 328.90 winning units. RY

2423 SOUTHWELL (L-H)
Tuesday, December 3

OFFICIAL GOING: Good (good to soft in places; 7.1)
Wind: light across Weather: overcast, dull and cold

2872 £32 FREE BET AT 32RED.COM H'CAP CHASE (17 fncs 2 omitted) 3m 110y
12:15 (12:15) (Class 5) (0-95,89) 4-Y-0+ **£2,258** (£658; £329)

Form RPR
341- **1** **Quayside Court (IRE)**[3] 2829 9-9-11 **67**.......................(vt) GeraldQuinn(7) 82+
(Claire Dyson) *chsd ldrs 5th: pushed along 6th: led 3 out (normal 4 out): wnt clr next: drvn rt out* **6/4**[1]

215- **2** *4* **Bennys Well (IRE)**[25] 2339 7-11-2 **79**..................... SamTwiston-Davies 87
(Sue Smith) *chsd ldrs: drvn 9th: hit 6 out: wnt modest 2nd 2 out (normal 3 out): styd on same pce appr last* **11/4**[2]

P45- **3** *11* **Phoenix Des Mottes (FR)**[5] 2772 10-10-2 **70**................ JoeCornwall(5) 70
(John Cornwall) *chsd ldr: led 3rd: j.rt fr 6th: hdd 3 out (normal 4 out): wknd bef last* **33/1**

460/ **4** *28* **Bringewood Belle**[264] 4761 10-10-5 **68**.........................(t) TommyPhelan 40
(John Needham) *chsd ldrs 5th: reminders 7 out: outpcd 5 out: sn bhd: distant 4th appr 2 out (normal 3 out)* **14/1**

P44- **P** **Sycho Fred (IRE)**[23] 2396 12-10-10 **73**.........................(t) AidanColeman
(Mike Sowersby) *chsd ldrs: 2nd 6th: lost pl 4 out (normal 5 out): t.o whn p.u bef 2 out (normal 3 out)* **10/1**

/PP- **P** **One More Dinar**[10] 2678 10-11-7 **89**................................ JoshHamer(5)
(John Bryan Groucott) *nt fluent in rr: hdwy 6th: chsng ldrs 9th: drvn 6 out: lost pl next: sn bhd: t.o whn p.u sn after 2 out (normal 3 out)* **14/1**

001/ **P** **How's D Strawboss (IRE)**[428] 1700 8-10-9 **72**.................. LeeEdwards
(Aytach Sadik) *led to 3rd: p.u bef next; fatally injured* **9/2**[3]

6m 33.7s (10.70) **Going Correction** +0.525s/f (Soft) **7** Ran SP% **110.2**
Speed ratings (Par 103): **103,101,98,89, ,**
toteswingers 1&2 £1.10, 1&3 £6.20, 2&3 £9.00 CSF £5.87 TOTE £2.10: £1.60, £1.90; EX 5.50 Trifecta £59.50 Pool: £2598.47 - 32.71 winning units..
Owner Guy Sainsbury & Carl Mason **Bred** Miss Catherine M Walsh **Trained** Cleeve Prior, Worcs

FOCUS
Fences about 4yds inside the line utilised on November 11th, both bends moved to fresh ground. Sam Twiston-Davies described the ground as "a bit dead". The usual second-last had to be omitted the second and third time around. A moderate handicap chase. The winner was idling but is rated in line with his recent win.

2873 32RED H'CAP CHASE (16 fncs) 2m 4f 110y
12:45 (12:45) (Class 4) (0-120,115) 4-Y-0+ **£3,768** (£1,106; £553; £276)

Form RPR
P/0- **1** **Billy Cuckoo (IRE)**[40] 2035 7-11-11 **114**........................(b) DougieCostello 123+
(Tony Coyle) *drvn after s to ld: drvn along 9th: hdd appr 3 out: led 2 out: edgd lft run-in: all out* **12/1**

4B2- **2** *½* **Father Shine (IRE)**[25] 2346 10-11-0 **108**............................. BenPoste(5) 115
(Shaun Harris) *chsd ldrs 9th: rdn appr 2 out: lft handy 3rd next: rallied run-in: styd on to take 2nd last 50yds: jst hld* **12/1**

F55- **3** *2* **Tregaro (FR)**[23] 2394 7-10-7 **96**.............................(t) SamTwiston-Davies 103
(Mike Sowersby) *hld up in last: hdwy 4 out: lft handy 2nd 2 out: 1 l down and styng on same pce whn hmpd run-in: lost 2nd clsng stages* **10/1**

332- **4** *14* **Hodgson (IRE)**[35] 2149 8-11-6 **112**...............................(tp) JackQuinlan(3) 109
(Sarah Humphrey) *chsd ldrs 9th: drvn and outpcd 4 out: modest 5th whn hit next: sn bhd* **13/2**[3]

412- **5** *10* **Last Shot (FR)**[8] 2721 6-11-12 **115**.................................. AidanColeman 105
(Venetia Williams) *chsd ldr: reminders 12th: lost pl next: bhd fr 2 out* **2/1**[2]

5F4- **P** **That's The Deal (IRE)**[25] 2350 9 10 12 **106**.................... JoeCornwall(5)
(John Cornwall) *in tch: drvn 6th: lost pl 10th: sn bhd: p.u bef 12th* **20/1**

U23- **F** **Moorlands Jack**[20] 2462 8-10-13 **102**..........................(p) NickScholfield 107
(Jeremy Scott) *mstke 4 out: led appr next: hdd and fell 2 out* **15/8**[1]

5m 25.4s (8.40) **Going Correction** +0.525s/f (Soft) **7** Ran SP% **110.7**
Speed ratings (Par 105): **105,104,104,98,94 ,**
toteswingers 1&2 £10.10, 1&3 £14.00, 2&3 £9.60 CSF £118.94 TOTE £9.20: £3.30, £2.90; EX 111.70 Trifecta £741.00 Pool: £4563.36 - 4.61 winning units..
Owner Gary Dewhurst & Tony Coyle **Bred** James Robinson **Trained** Norton, N Yorks
■ Stewards' Enquiry : Dougie Costello caution: careless riding

FOCUS
Ordinary form for the grade. The winner is rated back to the best of last season's form.

2874 32RED.COM NOVICES' HURDLE (13 hdls) 3m 110y
1:15 (1:15) (Class 4) 4-Y-0+ **£3,119** (£915; £457; £228)

Form RPR
B- **1** **Sego Success (IRE)**[30] 2252 5-10-12 0.................... WayneHutchinson 115+
(Alan King) *hld up: trckd ldrs 6th: mstke 3 out: 2nd appr next: led after 2 out: styd on wl* **11/8**[1]

0- **2** *2 ½* **Many Stars (IRE)**[33] 2181 5-10-12 0.................................(t) HarrySkelton 108+
(Dan Skelton) *chsd ldrs: outpcd 3 out: rallied next: chsd wnr between last 2: kpt on same pce run-in* **15/2**

050- **3** *10* **Merchant Of Milan**[20] 2457 5-10-12 0............................ BrendanPowell 100
(Brendan Powell) *led: hdd sn after 2 out: wknd bef last* **50/1**

54- **4** *15* **Golden Calf (IRE)**[27] 2296 6-10-12 0................................ JamieMoore 87
(Peter Bowen) *mid-div: chsd ldrs 9th: rdn and hit 2 out: hung lft and sn wknd* **20/1**

360- **5** *½* **Milan Of Hope (IRE)**[22] 2426 6-10-12 0........................... AdamPogson 84
(Charles Pogson) *trckd ldrs: t.k.h: wknd appr 2 out* **100/1**

6 *6* **My Destination (IRE)**[19] 4-10-12 0................................... BarryKeniry 78
(Declan Carroll) *in rr: hdwy 9th: chsng ldrs 3 out: wknd next* **28/1**

/62- **7** *13* **Master Rajeem (USA)**[19] 2471 4-10-12 0............... SamTwiston-Davies 67
(Nigel Twiston-Davies) *in rr: shkn up 4th: hdwy 8th: chsng ldrs whn hit next: rdn and lost pl appr 2 out* **3/1**[2]

31F- **8** *5* **Midnight Macarena**[14] 2572 8-10-7 0...........................(p) MattCrawley(5) 62
(Lucy Wadham) *chsd ldrs: drvn 3 out: sn lost pl and bhd* **11/2**[3]

1F6- **9** *64* **Ziggie (IRE)**[152] 880 6-10-12 0... HenryBrooke 5
(Donald McCain) *racd wd: w ldrs: blnd 4th: lost pl 9th: sn bhd: t.o 3 out: blnd last: virtually p.u* **14/1**

6m 18.4s (3.40) **Going Correction** +0.15s/f (Yiel)
WFA 4 from 5yo+ 7lb **9** Ran SP% **112.1**
Speed ratings (Par 105): **100,99,96,91,91 89,84,83,62**
toteswingers 1&2 £3.60, 1&3 £12.30, 2&3 £24.60 CSF £11.68 TOTE £2.50: £1.10, £2.70, £5.70; EX 13.40 Trifecta £358.80 Pool: £6594.49 - 13.78 winning units..
Owner Tim Leadbeater **Bred** Brendan Noone **Trained** Barbury Castle, Wilts

FOCUS
Little depth to this staying novice hurdle. The winner should go on to rate higher.

2875 32RED CASINO CONDITIONAL JOCKEYS' NOVICES' HURDLE (11 hdls) 2m 4f 110y
1:50 (1:50) (Class 4) 4-Y-0+ **£3,119** (£915; £457; £228)

Form RPR
21F- **1** **Hannibal The Great (IRE)**[30] 2252 5-11-2 0...............(t) KielanWoods(3) 134+
(Charlie Longsdon) *trckd ldr: stdd 7th: 2nd 8th: led 2 out: easily* **4/6**[1]

643- **2** *5* **Little Jon**[35] 2153 5-10-4 0.. RyanHatch(8) 116
(Nigel Twiston-Davies) *trckd ldng pair: t.k.h: led 7th: hdd and pckd landing 2 out: kpt on: no ch w wnr* **10/1**[3]

2/P- **3** *9* **Fiddlers Bid**[10] 2662 6-10-9 124................................. ConorShoemark(3) 109
(Fergal O'Brien) *led: hdd 7th: drvn 3 out: one pce appr next* **7/4**[2]

50- **4** *27* **Hurricane Ivan (IRE)**[26] 2316 5-10-12 0.................................(t) JamesBest 83
(Fergal O'Brien) *in rr: outpcd 4th: modest 4th 8th: sn bhd: t.o* **66/1**

4/0- **5** *12* **Thurnham**[18] 2493 7-10-9 0....................................... ColmMcCormack(3) 72
(Keith Reveley) *in rr: drvn 4th: bhd fr 8th: t.o* **50/1**

5m 17.4s (4.40) **Going Correction** +0.15s/f (Yiel) **5** Ran SP% **108.9**
Speed ratings (Par 105): **97,95,91,81,76**
CSF £7.92 TOTE £1.70: £1.10, £1.90; EX 5.00 Trifecta £12.60 Pool: £6607.32 - 391.00 winning units..
Owner The Pantechnicons **Bred** Mrs Mary Gallagher **Trained** Over Norton, Oxon

The Form Book Jumps, Raceform Ltd, Compton, RG20 6NL.

FOCUS
This looked a good opportunity for the favourite and he duly obliged. There's a case for rating the form 10lb+ higher through the third.

2876 32REDPOKER.COM MAIDEN HURDLE (9 hdls) 2m
2:20 (2:21) (Class 5) 4-Y-0+ **£1,949** (£572; £286; £143)

Form RPR
1 **No Such Number**[39] 5-10-11 0 TrevorWhelan(3) 115+
(Julia Feilden) *trckd ldrs: 3rd 2 out: led appr last: drvn out* **50/1**
/34- 2 1 3/4 **Anteros (IRE)**[19] 2471 5-11-0 120 PaulMoloney 113
(Sophie Leech) *chsd ldrs: effrt appr 2 out: styd on to take 2nd run-in* **9/4**[1]
2- 3 1 3/4 **Sir Valentino (FR)**[38] 2083 4-11-0 0 PaddyBrennan 111
(Tom George) *led: hdd appr last: kpt on one pce* **7/2**[2]
4 1 **Stephanie Frances (IRE)**[188] 551 5-10-7 0 (t) HarrySkelton 105+
(Dan Skelton) *chsd ldrs: 2nd appr 2 out: one pce between last 2* **9/4**[1]
30- 5 17 **Muckle Roe (IRE)**[45] 1974 4-11-0 0 SamTwiston-Davies 95
(Nigel Twiston-Davies) *in rr: hdwy 6th: lost pl after 3 out* **28/1**
0/4- 6 7 **Lotus Pond (IRE)**[22] 2426 5-11-0 0 RobertThornton 91
(Alan King) *hld up in rr: t.k.h: hdwy 6th: wknd bef 2 out* **16/1**
4- 7 7 **Bugler's Dream (USA)**[29] 2265 5-11-0 0 DenisO'Regan 91
(John Ferguson) *trckd ldrs: lost pl bef 2 out: sn bhd and eased* **15/2**[3]
/ 8 5 **Layline (IRE)**[8] 6-11-0 0 JamieMoore 78
(Gay Kelleway) *t.k.h: mid-div: hdwy 5th: rdn and lost pl bef 3 out* **16/1**
9 10 **Invincible Hero (IRE)**[34] 6-11-0 0 BarryKeniry 69
(Declan Carroll) *trckd ldrs: t.k.h: lost pl after 6th: sn bhd* **28/1**
0/ 10 13 **Femme D'Espere**[349] 274 7-10-0 0 JoshWall(7) 50
(Trevor Wall) *mid-div: lost pl after 6th: sn bhd* **200/1**
0- 11 8 **Echo Foxtrot**[17] 2513 4-10-7 0 GeraldQuinn(7) 50
(Claire Dyson) *prom: lost pl 6th: sn bhd: t.o 2 out* **200/1**
00- 12 25 **Alwayslookback (IRE)**[27] 2285 4-10-9 0 BenPoste(5) 28
(Rosemary Gasson) *j. bdly in rr: bhd fr 3rd: t.o 5th: eventually completed* **200/1**
U0P- P **Audacious**[4] 2783 5-11-0 0 [1] AdamPogson
(Charles Pogson) *t.k.h: trckd ldrs: lost pl 6th: sn bhd: t.o whn p.u bef 2 out* **100/1**
0/ P **Kingscombe (USA)**[21] 1244 4-11-0 0 TomCannon
(Linda Jewell) *in rr: reminders 4th: bhd next: t.o whn p.u bef 2 out* **100/1**

3m 56.8s (-0.20) **Going Correction** +0.15s/f (Yiel) **14** Ran SP% **119.6**
Speed ratings (Par 103): **106,105,104,103,95 91,88,85,80,74 70,57, ,**
toteswingers 1&2 £24.60, 1&3 £18.20, 2&3 £3.00 CSF £165.58 TOTE £59.60: £6.50, £1.30, £2.50; EX 354.10 Trifecta £2086.40 Pool: £6213.13 - 2.23 winning units..
Owner Good Company Partnership **Bred** Juddmonte Farms Ltd **Trained** Exning, Suffolk

FOCUS
The front four drew well clear in this ordinary maiden hurdle, and they included the first three in the market. The form looks believable.

2877 32REDBINGO.COM H'CAP HURDLE (11 hdls) 2m 4f 110y
2:50 (2:51) (Class 5) (0-95,95) 4-Y-0+ **£2,053** (£598; £299)

Form RPR
/06- 1 **Homer Run (IRE)**[156] 852 6-11-9 92 PaddyBrennan 92+
(Simon Earle) *in rr: hdwy 8th: styd on to ld last: drvn out* **7/1**[3]
462/ 2 1 1/4 **Ruby Bay (IRE)**[675] 3975 8-11-6 89 PeterBuchanan 87
(Tim Walford) *in tch: chsd ldrs 3 out: 4th last: styd on to take 2nd clsng stages* **14/1**
000- 3 nk **Tisfreetdream (IRE)**[19] 2470 12-11-7 90 (p) JackDoyle 89
(Peter Pritchard) *chsd ldrs: led briefly appr last: kpt on same pce* **14/1**
00B- 4 2 **Optical High**[13] 2596 4-10-8 77 SamTwiston-Davies 73
(Sue Smith) *chsd ldr: led 7th: hdd appr last: one pce* **18/1**
664- 5 3 1/4 **Seaside Shuffle (IRE)**[47] 1938 8-11-4 87 (tp) PaulMoloney 80
(Sophie Leech) *hld up in rr: hdwy 6th: trcking ldrs next: effrt appr 2 out: fdd appr last* **5/1**[1]
41B- 6 2 1/4 **Transfer**[19] 2473 8-11-9 92 DavidBass 83
(Richard Price) *chsd ldrs: wknd appr last* **20/1**
7 1 **Cooldine Run (IRE)**[199] 9-11-4 94 (t) MrJarrett(7) 84
(John Needham) *hld up in rr: hdwy 2 out: styd on: nt rch ldrs* **33/1**
006/ 8 7 **Max Laurie (FR)**[364] 2841 8-10-12 84 TrevorWhelan(3) 68
(Michael Banks) *mid-div: hdwy 8th: lost pl bef 2 out* **25/1**
P/0- 9 2 3/4 **Light The World (FR)**[42] 2013 5-11-1 91 JakeHodson(7) 73
(Kevin Frost) *in rr: sme hdwy 2 out: nvr on terms* **16/1**
000- 10 3 1/4 **Gilded Age**[55] 1824 7-11-10 93 (tp) TomMessenger 72
(Mandy Rowland) *led: j.rt: hdd 7th: lost pl after 3 out* **66/1**
3/P- 11 3/4 **Wee Giant (USA)**[13] 2596 7-11-12 95 DougieCostello 73
(Tony Coyle) *prom: rdn 3 out: wknd between last 2* **17/2**
U40- 12 11 **Whatsupjack (IRE)**[153] 876 6-11-3 91 BenPoste(5) 59
(Shaun Harris) *in rr: bhd fr 3 out* **20/1**
010- 13 1 1/2 **Whispering Harry**[17] 2511 4-10-9 85 ChristopherWard(7) 52
(Henry Oliver) *chsd ldrs: lost pl appr 3 out* **10/1**
342- 14 2 1/2 **Chapelle du Roi (USA)**[41] 2016 4-11-10 93 (v[1]) TomO'Brien 57
(Robert Stephens) *in rr: mstke 7th: bhd fr next* **6/1**[2]
200- 15 15 **So Cheeky**[10] 2679 4-11-4 90 JackQuinlan(3) 41
(Richard Guest) *hld up in rr: bhd fr 3 out* **50/1**
6/5- F **Head Spin (IRE)**[16] 2535 5-10-11 80 (p) AndrewThornton
(Seamus Mullins) *trckd ldrs: wkng whn fell 8th* **15/2**

5m 30.4s (17.40) **Going Correction** +0.15s/f (Yiel)
WFA 4 from 5yo+ 6lb **16** Ran SP% **119.1**
Speed ratings (Par 103): **72,71,71,70,69 68,68,65,64,63 62,58,58,57,51**
toteswingers 1&2 £16.30, 1&3 £31.20, 2&3 £39.10 CSF £89.57 CT £1343.27 TOTE £9.50: £2.60, £2.60, £1.70, £6.50; EX 124.20 Trifecta £2757.60 Pool: £4878.52 - 1.32 winning units..
Owner EPDS Racing Partnership 3 **Bred** Charlie Harnett **Trained** Tytherington, Wilts

FOCUS
Low-grade stuff. The winner and third set the level.

2878 32REDBET.COM STANDARD OPEN NATIONAL HUNT FLAT RACE 2m
3:20 (3:20) (Class 6) 4-6-Y-0 **£1,642** (£478; £239)

Form RPR
1 **Ballybolley (IRE)**[185] 4-11-0 0 SamTwiston-Davies 105+
(Nigel Twiston-Davies) *trckd ldrs: t.k.h: hung lft over 1f out: chal jst ins fnl f: styd on to ld nr fin* **7/4**[2]
0- 2 nk **Jac The Legend**[12] 2627 4-10-7 0 PaulBohan(7) 105
(Steve Gollings) *led: edgd lft jst ins fnl f: hdd and no ex nr fin* **12/1**
21/ 3 4 1/2 **Delta Forty**[234] 5295 5-11-0 0 JamesReveley 101
(Keith Reveley) *trckd ldrs: effrt 3f out: edgd rt 2f out: one pce* **5/4**[1]
33- 4 9 **Di's Gift**[40] 2053 4-11-0 0 [1] DenisO'Regan 93
(Richard Guest) *hld up in rr: racd wd: hdwy 5f out: sn chsng ldrs: wknd 2f out* **8/1**[3]
5 5 **Tanner Hill (IRE)**[227] 5-11-0 0 LiamTreadwell 88
(James Evans) *hld up in rr: drvn over 6f out: chsd ldrs over 4f out: lost pl 3f out* **33/1**
0- 6 6 **Say When**[198] 389 5-11-0 0 RobertThornton 83
(Alan King) *hld up in mid-div: drvn over 3f out: wknd over 2f out* **14/1**
7 22 **Miss Bella Rose** 6-10-4 0 JackQuinlan(3) 56
(Richard Guest) *chsd ldr: drvn 6f out: lost pl over 4f out: sn bhd: t.o* **66/1**

3m 57.8s (6.40) **Going Correction** +0.15s/f (Yiel) **7** Ran SP% **110.7**
Speed ratings: **90,89,87,83,80 77,66**
toteswingers 1&2 £4.60, 1&3 £1.30, 2&3 £4.40 CSF £21.06 TOTE £2.30: £1.10, £4.90; EX 23.30 Trifecta £58.40 Pool: £5339.63 - 68.54 winning units..
Owner N A Twiston-Davies **Bred** The Red Marble Syndicate **Trained** Naunton, Gloucs

FOCUS
More pace on than is often the case in bumpers and the front pair, both ex-pointers, drew clear of the favourite. The form is rated through the third and sixth.
T/Jkpt: Not won. T/Plt: £395.70. Pool: £71435.46 131.78 winning units. T/Qpdt: £35.50. Pool: £7331.15 - 152.80 winning units. WG

CATTERICK (L-H)
Wednesday, December 4

OFFICIAL GOING: Good (chs 8.0, hdl 8.1)
Wind: moderate 1/2 against Weather: fine and sunny, cold

2879 RICHMONDSHIRE CONDITIONAL JOCKEYS' H'CAP HURDLE (10 hdls) 2m 3f
12:20 (12:20) (Class 4) (0-110,110) 3-Y-0+ **£3,249** (£954; £477; £238)

Form RPR
643- 1 **Smadynium (FR)**[11] 2668 5-11-6 110 (b) NickSlatter(6) 119
(Donald McCain) *w ldr: led 3rd: jnd last: all out* **4/1**[2]
152- 2 nk **Aficionado**[23] 2417 3-10-1 108 (p) DiarmuidO'Regan(8) 103
(Chris Grant) *trckd ldrs: clr 2nd sn after 3 out: hit next: upsides last: no ex nr fin* **7/2**[1]
P/0- 3 19 **Another Dimension (IRE)**[22] 2447 7-10-6 96 ow2 ShaunDobbin(8) 91
(Rose Dobbin) *chsd ldrs: pushed along 5th: outpcd after 7th: modest 3rd appr 2 out: one pce* **10/1**[3]
111- 4 10 **Civil Unrest (IRE)**[25] 2360 7-11-1 107 (p) DaleIrving(8) 91
(James Ewart) *led to 3rd: chsd wnr: outpcd sn after 3 out: wknd bef next* **7/2**[1]
/24- 5 nk **Funky Munky**[14] 2597 8-11-6 104 (p) CallumWhillans 87
(Alistair Whillans) *chsd ldrs: drvn 4th: reminders after next: outpcd 7th: wknd next* **10/1**[3]
0/2- 6 5 **Spiekeroog**[12] 1751 7-11-7 105 ConorShoemark 83
(David O'Meara) *in rr: mstke 2nd: drvn to chse ldrs 6th: lost pl 3 out* **10/1**[3]
/11- 7 8 **Amir Pasha (UAE)**[8] 2736 8-11-4 105 7ex (v) JoeColliver(3) 76
(Micky Hammond) *in tch: drvn 6th: lost pl after 7th: modest 5th whn mstke 2 out* **14/1**
P/0- 8 23 **Sparkling Hand**[183] 626 7-11-2 100 (p) TonyKelly 50
(Peter Atkinson) *in rr: bhd 3rd: t.o 7th* **25/1**
304- P **Tourtiere**[26] 2341 5-11-6 107 CraigNichol(3)
(George Moore) *in rr: hit 5th: drvn and lost pl 6th: bhd whn mstke 3 out: t.o whn p.u bef next* **10/1**[3]

4m 31.5s (-4.60) **Going Correction** -0.125s/f (Good) course record
WFA 3 from 5yo+ 13lb **9** Ran SP% **111.3**
Speed ratings (Par 105): **104,103,95,91,91 89,86,76,**
toteswingers 1&2 £1.70, 1&3 £24.30, 2&3 £9.80 CSF £17.81 CT £123.70 TOTE £4.40: £1.70, £1.80, £4.00; EX 23.50 Trifecta £140.80 Pool: £1107.02 - 5.89 winning units..
Owner The Vacuum Pouch Company Limited **Bred** Jerome Herisson & Catherine Herisson **Trained** Cholmondeley, Cheshire
■ Stewards' Enquiry : Shaun Dobbin three-day ban: weighed in 2lb heavy (Dec 18-20)
Nick Slatter two-day ban: used whip above permitted level (Dec 18-19)

FOCUS
A low-grade handicap run at a decent gallop. The winner was on a good mark and is rated to his best.

2880 CATTERICKBRIDGE.CO.UK H'CAP CHASE (15 fncs) 2m 3f
12:50 (12:51) (Class 5) (0-100,88) 4-Y-0+ **£3,422** (£997; £499)

Form RPR
/03- 1 **Milan Royale**[32] 2219 8-11-11 87 HarryHaynes 98
(Kevin Hunter) *w ldrs: drvn 8th: led 4 out: jnd last: crowded run-in: all out* **5/1**[3]
203- 2 shd **Discoverie**[26] 2335 5-10-13 75 (p) RyanMania 87
(Dianne Sayer) *chsd ldrs: hit 7th and sn given reminders: upsides 4 out and last: hrd drvn and edgd lft run-in: jst failed* **7/2**[2]
0P3- 3 17 **Forestside (IRE)**[27] 2308 8-11-12 88 DenisO'Regan 86
(Barry Murtagh) *in rr: hdwy to chse ldrs 8th: outpcd 4 out: lft modest 3rd 2 out: one pce* **15/2**
0/2- 4 12 **Sambelucky (IRE)**[22] 2445 8-11-7 83 (b) JamesReveley 70
(Keith Reveley) *prom: reminders 9th: drvn and lost pl 11th: kpt on fr 2 out to take poor 4th last: b.b.v* **9/4**[1]
0/0- 5 1 3/4 **Dan's Heir**[34] 2169 11-11-8 84 (v) BarryKeniry 67
(Wilf Storey) *chsd ldrs: hit 2nd: sn lost pl: detached last whn blnd 4th: kpt on fr 2 out* **66/1**
/54- 6 nk **Dorlesh Way (IRE)**[14] 2595 6-10-4 66 RichieMcGrath 52
(Patrick Holmes) *hld up in rr: hdwy to chse ldrs 8th: outpcd 4 out: lft modest 5th and hmpd 2 out: sn wknd* **7/1**
350/ 7 4 1/2 **Ballybanks (IRE)**[224] 5495 9-11-0 83 MrTSpeke(7) 62
(Robert Johnson) *led to 4 out: sn lost pl: lft modest 4th 2 out: sn wknd* **8/1**
4- F **Force Of Habit**[16] 2558 7-11-4 87 (p) JohnDawson(7) 85
(Joanne Foster) *chsd ldrs: blnd 2nd: mstke 10th: 7 l 3rd whn fell 2 out* **14/1**

4m 43.1s (-5.70) **Going Correction** -0.35s/f (Good) **8** Ran SP% **113.2**
Speed ratings (Par 103): **98,97,90,85,85 84,82,**
toteswingers 1&2 £1.60, 1&3 £1.50, 2&3 £7.30 CSF £23.04 CT £128.42 TOTE £5.50: £1.60, £1.50, £2.60; EX 29.80 Trifecta £69.80 Pool: £1396.72 - 14.99 winning units..
Owner K Hunter **Bred** R D And Mrs J S Chugg **Trained** Natland, Cumbria
■ Stewards' Enquiry : Harry Haynes one-day ban: careless riding (Dec 18)

FOCUS
The front pair drew clear in what was a moderate handicap chase. A small personal best from the winner with a big step up from the second.

2881 BHEST RACING TO SCHOOL JUVENILE HURDLE (8 hdls) 2m
1:20 (1:21) (Class 4) 3-Y-O **£3,249** (£954; £477; £238)

Form RPR

42U- 1 **Most Honourable**[14] 2592 3-10-12 116 RyanMania 104
(Michael Smith) *chsd ldrs: effrt appr 2 out: cl 2nd and mstke last: styd on to ld towards fin* **5/1**[3]

2 *shd* **Morning With Ivan (IRE)**[108] 3-10-5 0 WilsonRenwick 96
(Martin Todhunter) *t.k.h: trckd ldrs: upsides 4th: led narrowly 2 out: sn rdn: hdd and no ex nr fin* **4/1**[2]

3 *14* **Like A Diamond (IRE)**[18] 3-10-12 0 PaulMoloney 93
(Evan Williams) *led: t.k.h: nt fluent: clr whn mstke 2nd: jnd 4th: hdd 2 out: 3rd whn wandered and mstke last: wknd* **7/1**

03- 4 *10* **Baraboy (IRE)**[14] 2592 3-10-12 0 LucyAlexander 80
(Barry Murtagh) *sn detached in last: t.k.h: sme hdwy 5th: kpt on fr 2 out: tk poor 4th clsng stages* **25/1**

5 *shd* **Ground Ginger**[18] 3-10-9 0 JohnKington(3) 80
(James Bethell) *chsd ldrs 4th: mstke and lost pl next: reminders to chse ldrs after 3 out: wknd appr next* **100/1**

6 *37* **Mitchell**[20] 3-10-7 0 AdamNicol(5) 47
(David Thompson) *chsd ldr: j.lft and bmpd 1st: hit 3rd: drvn and lost pl after 3rd: t.o 3 out: eventually completed* **40/1**

1- U **Forced Family Fun**[14] 2592 3-10-12 0 DeanPratt(7)
(John Quinn) *chsd ldr: j.rt: bmpd and uns rdr 1st* **5/6**[1]

3m 48.8s (-3.70) **Going Correction** -0.125s/f (Good) 7 Ran SP% **111.0**
Speed ratings (Par 104): **104,103,96,91,91 73,**
CSF £23.46 TOTE £5.10: £2.00, £2.00; EX 29.80 Trifecta £158.20 Pool: £1852.83 - 8.77 winning units..
Owner Mrs Sandra Smith **Bred** Darley **Trained** Kirkheaton, Northumberland

FOCUS
Early drama in this juvenile hurdle, with red-hot favourite Forced Family Fun getting a bump mid-air at the first and parting ways with his rider. This blew the race wide open. A step up from the winner.

2882 RACINGUK.COM BEGINNERS' CHASE (15 fncs) 2m 3f
1:50 (1:50) (Class 4) 4-Y-0+ **£4,548** (£1,335; £667; £333)

Form RPR

/43- 1 **Hi George**[164] 801 5-11-0 0 BrianHughes 134
(Malcolm Jefferson) *w ldr: led 8th: 3 l clr last: rdn and hld on clsng stages* **12/1**[3]

4/3- 2 *hd* **Holywell (IRE)**[31] 2242 6-11-0 0 (p) APMcCoy 134+
(Jonjo O'Neill) *chsd ldrs: drvn to chse wnr appr 3 out: styd on run-in: jst hld* **6/4**[1]

P/4- 3 *4* **Barrakilla (IRE)**[43] 2012 6-11-0 129 PaulMoloney 132
(Evan Williams) *chsd ldrs: drvn: outpcd and hit 4 out: 3rd next: styd on same pce between last 2* **6/4**[1]

0/P- 4 *14* **Son Of Flicka**[62] 1728 9-11-0 0 DougieCostello 124
(Tony Coyle) *chsd ldrs: nt fluent 9th: lost pl 4 out: kpt on and modest 4th bef 2 out: eased run-in* **25/1**

21P- 5 *15* **Croco Bay (IRE)**[173] 737 6-11-0 0 RichieMcGrath 104
(Peter Atkinson) *chsd ldrs: outpcd 8th: lost pl and mstke 4 out: bhd whn hit next* **33/1**

1/4- 6 *6* **Star In Flight**[54] 1849 6-11-0 122 JasonMaguire 103
(Donald McCain) *led: blnd 3rd: hdd 8th: wknd 3 out: mstke next* **13/2**[2]

30U- 7 *17* **Jukebox Melody (IRE)**[35] 2155 7-10-7 109 JohnDawson(7) 84
(John Wade) *in rr: bhd whn blnd 5th: t.o 4 out* **66/1**

4/5- 8 *3/4* **Forty Crown (IRE)**[18] 2516 7-11-0 0 WilsonRenwick 83
(John Wade) *sn in rr: bhd fr 8th: t.o 4 out* **33/1**

0/0- 9 *7* **Scarlet Fire (IRE)**[19] 2490 6-11-0 0 BrianHarding 77
(Nicky Richards) *in rr: drvn after 7th: sn bhd: t.o 4 out* **20/1**

4m 38.5s (-10.30) **Going Correction** -0.35s/f (Good) 9 Ran SP% **117.0**
Speed ratings (Par 105): **107,106,105,99,93 90,83,83,80**
CSF £31.07 TOTE £9.50: £1.60, £1.10, £1.30; EX 24.50 Trifecta £63.30 Pool: £2464.92 - 29.16 winning units..
Owner Mr & Mrs H Young **Bred** H Young **Trained** Norton, N Yorks

FOCUS
A fair beginners' chase for the track and the front trio drew right away. The winner was up 11lb on the best of his hurdles book.

2883 YORKSHIRE-OUTDOORS.CO.UK MARES' NOVICES' HURDLE (10 hdls) 2m 3f
2:20 (2:20) (Class 4) 4-Y-0+ **£3,898** (£1,144; £572; £286)

Form RPR

/03- 1 **Bonnet's Vino**[13] 2621 5-10-7 0 KielanWoods(3) 103
(Pam Sly) *trckd ldrs: effrt appr 2 out: 2nd appr last: styd on to ld post* **4/1**[3]

221- 2 *nse* **Run Ructions Run (IRE)**[18] 2514 4-11-3 110 DougieCostello 111
(Tim Easterby) *chsd ldrs: drvn 7th: led 2 out: edgd rt run-in: hdd post* **11/8**[1]

0- 3 *1* **Gold Show**[19] 2493 4-10-5 0 TonyKelly(5) 102
(Edwin Tuer) *hld up in rr: hdwy 6th: effrt appr 2 out: cl 3rd last: upsides and edgd lft run-in: no ex last 50yds* **20/1**

310- 4 *8* **Sultana Belle (IRE)**[15] 2586 5-11-0 116 MrSCrawford(3) 103
(S R B Crawford, Ire) *trckd ldrs: led after 7th: hdd 2 out: wknd last* **8/1**

523- 5 *9* **Retrieve The Stick**[27] 2309 4-10-10 0 BrianHughes 87
(Malcolm Jefferson) *chsd ldrs: drvn appr 2 out: wknd bef last* **8/1**

323/ 6 *nk* **Maison De Ville (GER)**[333] 3511 5-10-10 0 APMcCoy 88
(David O'Meara) *chsd ldrs: drvn 2 out: hung lft: 5th and wkng whn mstke last* **7/2**[2]

00- 7 *32* **Torrington Deal**[26] 2354 5-10-10 0 HarryHaynes 58
(Malcolm Jefferson) *in rr: drvn 5th: bhd whn mstke next: t.o 2 out* **200/1**

60- 8 *6* **Voice From Above (IRE)**[18] 2514 4-10-5 0 JoeColliver(5) 52
(Patrick Holmes) *trckd ldrs: drvn 3 out: sn wknd: t.o* **100/1**

P50- 9 *27* **Rearrange**[48] 1938 4-10-10 71 (b[1]) TomMessenger 28
(Chris Bealby) *nt fluent: j.rt: led: hdd after 7th: sn lost pl: t.o 2 out* **150/1**

P **Amy Farah Fowler (IRE)**[64] 4-10-10 0 WilsonRenwick
(Martin Todhunter) *in rr: hit 5th: bhd next: blnd 3 out: t.o whn p.u bef next* **100/1**

4m 35.9s (-0.20) **Going Correction** -0.125s/f (Good) 10 Ran SP% **114.5**
Speed ratings (Par 105): **95,94,94,91,87 87,73,71,59,**
CSF £10.01 TOTE £5.80: £1.60, £1.40, £5.70; EX 12.80 Trifecta £255.30 Pool: £1974.58 - 5.79 winning units..
Owner Mrs P M Sly **Bred** Mrs P Sly **Trained** Thorney, Cambs

FOCUS
An ordinary mares' hurdle rated around the second.

2884 BOOK NOW FOR 28TH DECEMBER H'CAP CHASE (19 fncs) 3m 1f 110y
2:50 (2:50) (Class 4) (0-120,118) 4-Y-0+ **£5,198** (£1,526; £763; £381)

Form RPR

6/0- 1 **Nodform Richard**[192] 495 7-11-11 117 (b) JasonMaguire 126+
(Donald McCain) *blnd 1st: in rr whn nt fluent 7th: hdwy to chse ldrs 12th: upsides 15th: led next: drvn out* **15/8**[1]

/35- 2 *3 1/2* **O'Callaghan Strand (AUS)**[25] 2370 7-11-12 118 (p) APMcCoy 122
(Jonjo O'Neill) *chsd ldrs: drvn to chse wnr after 4 out: styd on same pce fr 2 out* **7/2**[3]

/53- 3 *3 1/4* **Categorical**[39] 2070 10-11-10 116 JamesReveley 119
(Keith Reveley) *hld up in rr: hdwy to chse ldrs 5th: hit 14th: outpcd next: kpt on and 3rd appr 3 out: one pce* **11/4**[2]

404- 4 *13* **Noble Witness (IRE)**[23] 2428 10-11-2 108 (p) AdamPogson 97
(Charles Pogson) *mde most to 4 out: lost pl appr next* **11/1**

4/P- 5 *2 1/2* **Everaard (USA)**[143] 958 7-11-3 109 (tp) RichieMcGrath 98
(Philip Kirby) *rn in snatches: w ldr: hit 3rd and 12th: sn drvn: lost pl 4 out* **5/1**

6m 28.8s (-13.20) **Going Correction** -0.35s/f (Good) 5 Ran SP% **108.7**
Speed ratings (Par 105): **106,104,103,99,99**
CSF £8.61 TOTE £2.70: £2.20, £1.50; EX 7.40 Trifecta £24.70 Pool: £2166.65 - 65.60 winning units..
Owner D Gorton **Bred** Peter E Clinton **Trained** Cholmondeley, Cheshire

FOCUS
An ordinary staying chase. The first two are rated to his best.

2885 GO RACING AT WETHERBY THIS SATURDAY INTERMEDIATE OPEN NATIONAL HUNT FLAT RACE 2m
3:20 (3:20) (Class 6) 4-6-Y-0 **£1,642** (£478; £239)

Form RPR

12- 1 **On Tour (IRE)**[20] 2472 5-11-11 0 PaulMoloney 116+
(Evan Williams) *hld up: hdwy 9f out: cl 2nd over 2f out: drvn to ld jst ins fnl f: styd on strly clsng stages* **11/8**[1]

05- 2 *2 1/2* **Mr Shantu (IRE)**[25] 2368 4-11-4 0 APMcCoy 104
(Jonjo O'Neill) *trckd ldrs: 2nd over 6f out: led over 2f out: sn hrd drvn: hdd jst ins fnl f: kpt on same pce* **4/1**[2]

3 *2 3/4* **Beatu (IRE)**[24] 4-11-1 0 MrSCrawford(3) 102
(S R B Crawford, Ire) *hld up: hdwy 7f out: handy 3rd 2f out: kpt on same pce over 1f out* **12/1**

3- 4 *7* **Donna's Pride**[109] 1292 4-10-11 0 JamesReveley 88
(Keith Reveley) *hld up in rr: hdwy 4f out: effrt 3f out: 4th and one pce over 1f out* **4/1**[2]

6/1- 5 *14* **Falcon's Present**[209] 187 5-11-4 0 RichieMcGrath 83
(John Weymes) *w ldr: led after 5f: drvn 6f out: hdd over 2f out: wknd over 1f out* **14/1**

6 *19* **Eternal Vine** 4-10-11 0 BrianHughes 59
(Malcolm Jefferson) *chsd ldrs: pushed along over 7f out: lost pl over 5f out: sn bhd* **6/1**[3]

7 *14* **Manyshadesofblack (IRE)** 5-10-11 0 BrianHarding 46
(Tina Jackson) *chsd ldrs: pushed along over 7f out: lost pl over 5f out: sn bhd* **50/1**

8 *47* **Fireside Dreams** 4-11-4 0 HarryHaynes 11
(Geoffrey Harker) *w ldr: drvn over 5f out: lost pl over 4f out: sn bhd: t.o whn eased over 1f out: eventually completed* **25/1**

3m 47.7s (0.80) **Going Correction** -0.125s/f (Good)
WFA 4 from 5yo 5lb 8 Ran SP% **116.6**
Speed ratings: **93,91,90,86,79 70,63,39**
CSF £7.22 TOTE £2.10: £1.20, £1.20, £3.00; EX 7.10 Trifecta £70.10 Pool: £1916.01 - 20.47 winning units..
Owner T Hywel Jones **Bred** Mrs Meliosa Walshe **Trained** Llancarfan, Vale Of Glamorgan
■ Stewards' Enquiry : Mr S Crawford two-day ban: used whip above permitted level (Dec 19, Jan 1)

FOCUS
Not an overly competitive bumper. The cosy winner was the form pick and is rated to his mark.
T/Plt: £65.30 to a £1 stake. Pool: £57580.44 - 643.35 winning tickets T/Qpdt: £11.00 to a £1 stake. Pool: £5347.05 - 356.60 winning tickets WG

2718 LUDLOW (R-H)
Wednesday, December 4
OFFICIAL GOING: Good (good to soft in places; 7.9)
Wind: Light across Weather: Fine

2886 FINGERS & FORKS CATERING NOVICES' CLAIMING HURDLE (9 hdls) 2m
12:40 (12:40) (Class 4) 4-Y-0+ **£3,249** (£954; £477; £238)

Form RPR

05- 1 **Great Link**[16] 2563 4-11-3 112 (t) JoshHamer(5) 102+
(Tony Carroll) *a.p: led appr 3 out: shkn up after next: styd on wl: comf* **7/2**[2]

60P- 2 *2 3/4* **Rolling Dough (IRE)**[62] 1731 5-10-1 0 (p) RichieMcLernon 77
(Sophie Leech) *hld up: hdwy appr 3 out: chsd wnr and hit next: rdn and edgd rt flat: styd on same pce* **25/1**

053- 3 *1 1/2* **Pennant Dancer**[15] 2571 6-10-5 63 (vt) AodhaganConlon(5) 86
(Debra Hamer) *chsd ldr tl rdn and mstke 3 out: styd on same pce last* **66/1**

300- 4 *1 1/4* **Iguacu**[30] 2265 9-10-10 95 WayneHutchinson 84
(Richard Price) *hld up: hdwy appr 3 out: rdn and hung rt bef next: no ex flat* **14/1**

005- 5 *1 3/4* **Stag Hill (IRE)**[24] 2385 4-10-9 97 (t) RobertWilliams(5) 88
(Bernard Llewellyn) *hld up: hdwy after 6th: rdn after 2 out: no ex last* **7/1**[3]

450- 6 *6* **To The Sky (IRE)**[9] 2717 5-10-7 106 CiaranMckee(7) 82
(John O'Shea) *led: clr 3rd tl after 6th: hdd and hit next: wknd appr last* **6/5**[1]

000- 7 *10* **Home Girl (IRE)**[21] 2453 5-10-3 0 RichardJohnson 64
(Susan Johnson) *chsd ldrs: pushed along after 6th: wknd 2 out* **10/1**

0/P- 8 *17* **Jawahal Du Mathan (FR)**[65] 1700 5-10-9 69 (tp) JoshWall(7) 58
(Arthur Whitehead) *hld up: hdwy 6th: wknd 3 out* **100/1**

9 *40* **Diamond Pro (IRE)**[110] 2368 4-10-10 0 (t) JamesDavies 16
(Christopher Kellett) *mid-div: rdn and wknd after 6th* **25/1**

0/0- 10 *shd* **Miles Of Sunshine**[10] 2689 8-11-0 0 NickScholfield 20
(Ron Hodges) *bhd whn mstke 3rd: nvr on terms* **20/1**

11 *6* **Emiratesdotcom**[15] 7-10-13 0 ....(tp) CharlieWallis(5) 19
(Milton Bradley) *hld up in tch: rdn and wknd appr 3 out* **25/1**
3m 51.1s (1.60) **Going Correction** +0.175s/f (Yiel) **11** Ran SP% **114.7**
Speed ratings (Par 105): **103,101,100,100,99 96,91,82,62,62 59**
toteswingers 1&2 £28.60, 1&3 £18.50, 2&3 £28.60 CSF £86.52 TOTE £4.40: £1.30, £6.20, £4.40; EX 110.30 Trifecta £1156.60 Part won. Pool: £1542.15 - 0.02 winning units..
Owner Carl Hodgson **Bred** Granham Farm And P Hearson Bloodstock **Trained** Cropthorne, Worcs

FOCUS
False wings on all fences. Hurdles sited outside in straight and on inside on back straight. All bends moved onto fresh ground and stable bend divided. Just a modest claiming hurdle, with the fourth and fifth helping set the level.

2887 SHUKERS LANDROVER OF LUDLOW NOVICES' H'CAP CHASE (17 fncs) 2m 4f
1:10 (1:10) (Class 4) (0-110,114) 4-Y-0+ **£4,223** (£1,240; £620; £310)

Form RPR
3F0/ 1 **Bobcatbilly (IRE)**[362] 2904 7-11-5 **103** .... TomScudamore 118+
(Ian Williams) *a.p: jnd ldr 3 out: nt fluent next: r.o u.p to ld nr fin* **7/2**[2]
3/1- 2 *hd* **King Massini (IRE)**[9] 2722 7-11-9 **114** 7ex .... ConorRing(7) 127
(Evan Williams) *led: jnd fr 4 out: shkn up appr last: rdn flat: hdd nr fin* **6/4**[1]
F35- 3 *6* **Spoil Me (IRE)**[68] 1674 6-11-4 **102** .... RichieMcLernon 111
(Jonjo O'Neill) *hld up: hdwy 9th: rdn appr last: no ex flat* **7/1**[3]
0/ 4 *6* **Ultimatum Du Roy (FR)**[77] 5-11-12 **110** .... PaddyBrennan 115+
(Alex Hales) *prom: chsd ldr 9th: ev ch whn mstke 4 out: rdn and wknd appr last* **8/1**
/03- 5 *19* **Freckle Face**[9] 2719 6-11-1 **99** .... LiamTreadwell 90
(Bill Turner) *hld up: blnd 13th: rdn and wknd bef next* **17/2**
/03- 6 *32* **Bin End**[31] 2250 7-11-7 **105** ....(p) FelixDeGiles 61
(Barry Brennan) *prom: rdn after 12th: wknd next* **25/1**
/5P- 7 *13* **Book'Em Danno (IRE)**[24] 2389 7-11-11 **109** .... JamieMoore 54
(Peter Bowen) *chsd ldr to 9th: rdn and wknd 13th* **8/1**
0/0- P **Macra Na Feirme (IRE)**[36] 2148 10-10-1 **85** ....(t) DonalDevereux
(Debra Hamer) *hld up in tch: mstke 6th: pushed along and lost pl 9th: rdn and wknd bef next: bhd whn p.u bef 4 out* **50/1**
006- P **Dont Call Me Oscar (IRE)**[13] 2628 6-10-0 **84** oh4.......(t) TommyPhelan
(Mark Gillard) *hld up: a in rr: bhd whn j.lft 12th: p.u bef 2 out* **66/1**
4m 59.1s (-5.30) **Going Correction** -0.125s/f (Good) **9** Ran SP% **114.8**
Speed ratings (Par 105): **105,104,102,100,92 79,74, ,**
toteswingers 1&2 £1.40, 1&3 £4.40, 2&3 £3.40 CSF £9.47 CT £33.23 TOTE £4.10: £1.90, £1.10, £3.20; EX 11.60 Trifecta £50.70 Pool: £1641.95 - 24.24 winning units..
Owner P J Vogt **Bred** Con Troy **Trained** Portway, Worcs

FOCUS
No more than a fair event of its type, but the pace was decent. There should bemore to come from the winner.

2888 RACING UK MARES' H'CAP HURDLE (9 hdls) 2m
1:40 (1:40) (Class 4) (0-120,118) 3-Y-0+ **£4,548** (£1,335; £667; £333)

Form RPR
642- 1 **Flying Phoenix**[10] 2698 5-10-13 **105** .... JoshWall(7) 112+
(Michael Blake) *a.p: chsd ldr 3 out: led next: styd on wl: comf* **6/4**[1]
/65- 2 *6* **Western Approaches**[6] 2763 6-11-8 **107** ....(t) WillKennedy 108
(Ian Williams) *led: rdn and hdd 2 out: styd on same pce last* **6/1**
3/P- 3 *6* **Miss Tilly Oscar (IRE)**[5] 2470 7-10-9 **94** .... SamTwiston-Davies 89
(David Evans) *hld up: hdwy appr 3 out: rdn and wknd bef last* **9/2**[3]
061- 4 *7* **Buxom (IRE)**[22] 2435 6-11-11 **110** ....(v) BrendanPowell 100
(Jamie Snowden) *chsd ldr tl pushed along and mstke 3 out: wknd next* **10/3**[2]
U50- 5 *5* **Faith Jicaro (IRE)**[39] 2084 6-11-12 **111** .... DonalDevereux 96
(James Unett) *prom: pushed along after 6th: wknd bef next* **10/1**
6 *39* **Faustina Pius (IRE)**[51] 1908 5-11-3 **102** ....(b) CharliePoste 51
(Matt Sheppard) *hld up: hdwy 6th: rdn and wknd bef next* **14/1**
3m 50.4s (0.90) **Going Correction** +0.175s/f (Yiel) **6** Ran SP% **111.3**
Speed ratings (Par 105): **104,101,98,94,92 72**
toteswingers 1&2 £2.40, 1&3 £1.30, 2&3 £2.90 CSF £10.70 TOTE £2.90: £1.50, £3.00; EX 11.60 Trifecta £48.70 Pool: £2326.87 - 35.82 winning units..
Owner Francise Tieman **Bred** Winterbeck Manor Stud **Trained** Trowbridge, Wilts

FOCUS
A modest race for mares, run in a time only slightly quicker than the earlier claimer. Arguably a step up from the winner.

2889 BOYNE CUP (HANDICAP CHASE) (22 fncs) 3m 1f 110y
2:10 (2:10) (Class 3) (0-130,130) 4-Y-0+ **£12,660** (£3,740; £1,870; £936; £468)

Form RPR
1/0- 1 **Pickamus (FR)**[46] 1971 10-11-12 **130** .... AndrewTinkler 139+
(Henry Daly) *led to 17th: led again 4 out: nt fluent next: sn rdn: styd on gamely u.p: jst hld on* **10/1**
353- 2 *hd* **Cootehill (IRE)**[20] 2468 9-11-7 **125** .... SamTwiston-Davies 133
(Nigel Twiston-Davies) *hld up: hdwy 17th: chsd wnr and hit 3 out: rdn and ev ch last: styd on u.p* **7/1**[3]
P/2- 3 *12* **Charingworth (IRE)**[19] 2487 10-11-12 **130** .... SamThomas 128
(Kim Bailey) *prom: chsd wnr 5th: led 17th: hdd and blnd 4 out: wknd 2 out* **12/1**
4/0- 4 *nk* **Talkonthestreet (IRE)**[12] 2655 6-11-2 **120** .... RichardJohnson 117
(Philip Hobbs) *prom: rdn 17th: wknd appr 2 out* **5/2**[1]
243- 5 *1 1/4* **Raduis Bleu (FR)**[12] 2650 8-10-3 **114** .... MissLBrooke(7) 108
(Lady Susan Brooke) *hld up: hdwy 11th: styd on same pce fr 4 out* **16/1**
/F3- P **One In A Milan (IRE)**[12] 2652 8-11-8 **126** .... AdamWedge
(Evan Williams) *hld up: hit 2nd: bhd fr 15th: p.u bef 4 out* **8/1**
316- P **Faultless Feelings (IRE)**[47] 1957 7-11-9 **127** .... IanPopham
(Martin Keighley) *chsd wnr: blnd 2nd: lost 2nd 5th: lost pl 12th: mstke 14th (water): bhd fr next: p.u bef 18th* **3/1**[2]
1F5- P **Well Hello There (IRE)**[29] 2283 7-11-9 **127** ....(tp) RichieMcLernon
(Jonjo O'Neill) *prom: rdn 17th: wknd and p.u bef 4 out* **14/1**
3/ P **Union Jack D'Ycy (FR)**[381] 5-11-1 **119** .... AidanColeman
(Venetia Williams) *prom: lost pl 6th: rdn 17th: sn wknd: bhd whn p.u bef 2 out* **12/1**
6m 33.1s (-2.20) **Going Correction** -0.125s/f (Good) **9** Ran SP% **114.2**
Speed ratings (Par 107): **98,97,94,94,93 , , ,**
toteswingers 1&2 £10.70, 1&3 £22.80, 2&3 £10.20 CSF £76.69 CT £850.79 TOTE £5.50: £2.90, £2.10, £3.00; EX 64.00 Trifecta £499.50 Pool: £2088.70 - 3.13 winning units..
Owner Neville Statham & Family **Bred** Regis Reveillere **Trained** Stanton Lacy, Shropshire

FOCUS
A decent handicap chase, as befits the healthy prize money, and a stirring finish between two who pulled clear. The winner should still be competitive when reassessed.

2890 PERROTT PROPERTIES H'CAP CHASE (13 fncs) 2m
2:40 (2:40) (Class 3) (0-140,138) 4-Y-0 **£6,330** (£1,870; £935; £468; £234)

Form RPR
041- 1 **Oscar Hill (IRE)**[10] 2694 7-11-9 **135** 7ex .... TomO'Brien 147+
(David Bridgwater) *mde all: nt fluent 3 out: shkn up appr last: pushed out* **13/8**[1]
024- 2 *1 3/4* **Lancetto (FR)**[11] 2666 8-11-8 **134** ....(p) AdamWedge 141
(Evan Williams) *chsd wnr: rdn and edgd rt flat: styd on* **4/1**[3]
265- 3 *11* **King Edmund**[11] 2666 10-11-12 **138** ....(t) TomCannon 137
(Chris Gordon) *chsd ldrs: lost pl 2nd: hdwy 9th: sn rdn and no imp* **7/1**
21P- 4 *hd* **Tindaro (FR)**[19] 2488 6-11-11 **137** ....(t) RichieMcLernon 135
(Paul Webber) *in rr: sme hdwy 9th: nvr on terms* **16/1**
344- 5 *14* **Free World (FR)**[9] 2721 9-9-7 **112** oh5.......................... MissLBrooke(7) 102
(Lady Susan Brooke) *sn prom: outpcd 7th: effrt 9th: mstke and rdr lost iron 4 out: mstke and wknd next* **33/1**
21U- P **Anay Turge (FR)**[4] 2816 8-11-5 **134** ....(tp) MarkQuinlan(3)
(Nigel Hawke) *chsd ldrs: pushed along 6th: sn wknd: bhd whn p.u bef 9th* **3/1**[2]
214- U **Gud Day (IRE)**[46] 1973 5-10-6 **118** ....(tp) PaddyBrennan
(Fergal O'Brien) *blnd and uns rdr 2nd* **12/1**
3m 57.1s (-1.40) **Going Correction** -0.125s/f (Good) **7** Ran SP% **112.1**
Speed ratings (Par 107): **98,97,91,91,84 ,**
CSF £8.57 TOTE £2.30: £1.30, £3.20; EX 9.10 Trifecta £49.60 Pool: £2376.03 - 35.85 winning units..
Owner K W Bradley **Bred** Elizabeth Tudor Syndicate **Trained** Icomb, Gloucs

FOCUS
They went a good lick in this decent handicap chase and only the first two were ever seriously involved. The winner confirmed the merit of his recent win.

2891 LUDLOW CONDITIONAL JOCKEYS' NOVICES' H'CAP HURDLE (11 hdls) 2m 5f
3:10 (3:10) (Class 4) (0-105,106) 3-Y-0+ **£3,249** (£954; £477; £238)

Form RPR
61- 1 **Portway Flyer (IRE)**[5] 2787 5-11-13 **106** 7ex.......................... GavinSheehan 124+
(Ian Williams) *trckd ldrs: a gng wl: led on bit appr 3 out: clr next: easily* **4/9**[1]
2/1- 2 *7* **Motou (FR)**[23] 2427 8-11-2 **103** .... DanielHiskett(8) 107
(Richard Phillips) *hld up: hdwy u.p and hung lft whn hit 3 out: styd on same pce fr next* **8/1**[2]
116- 3 *4* **Moscow Me (IRE)**[11] 2676 6-11-9 **105** .... ConorRing(3) 107
(Henry Oliver) *led to 2nd: remained w ldr: ev ch after 8th: blnd 3 out: rdn whn hit next: wkng whn mstke last* **8/1**[2]
4/0- 4 *6* **Take The Mick**[18] 2510 6-11-3 **99** .... HarryChalloner(3) 92
(Venetia Williams) *hld up in tch: rdn after 8th: wknd bef 3 out* **16/1**
603- 5 *hd* **Queen Spud**[20] 2470 4-10-8 **90** .... JakeGreenall(3) 83
(Henry Daly) *chsd ldr tl led 2nd: rdn and hdd appr 3 out: sn wknd* **10/1**[3]
000- 6 *9* **Errol Flynn (IRE)**[6] 2770 7-9-11 **79** oh5..........................(t) JoshHamer(3) 67
(Tony Carroll) *prom: pushed along after 6th: rdn and wknd appr 3 out: bhd whn hit next* **100/1**
105- P **Bells Of Berlin**[162] 833 4-11-2 **98** ....(vt) MichaelByrne(3)
(Tim Vaughan) *chsd ldrs tl p.u after 7th* **40/1**
5m 17.0s (2.20) **Going Correction** +0.175s/f (Yiel)
WFA 4 from 5yo+ 6lb **7** Ran SP% **109.9**
Speed ratings (Par 105): **102,99,97,95,95 92,**
CSF £4.52 TOTE £1.70: £1.40, £1.90; EX 5.10 Trifecta £15.90 Pool: £2957.58 - 138.66 winning units..
Owner Patrick Kelly **Bred** DDE Syndicate **Trained** Portway, Worcs

FOCUS
A modest event for conditional riders. The easy winner was value for further.

2892 EBF STALLIONS MARES' STANDARD OPEN NATIONAL HUNT FLAT RACE 2m
3:40 (3:40) (Class 5) 4-6-Y-0 **£2,599** (£763; £381; £190)

Form RPR
1 **Tara Mist** 4-10-12 0 .... RichardJohnson 104+
(Henry Daly) *mid-div: hdwy over 6f out: shkn up to ld over 1f out: rdn out* **4/1**[3]
5- 2 *3* **Ballyhollow**[203] 324 6-10-7 0 .... PatrickCorbett(5) 101
(Rebecca Curtis) *led: clr 13f out tl over 5f out: rdn and hdd over 1f out: edgd rt and styd on same pce ins fnl f* **12/1**
3 *2 3/4* **Side Step** 4-10-12 0 .... AndrewTinkler 98
(Nicky Henderson) *a.p: chsd ldr over 3f out tl rdn over 1f out: styd on same pce fnl f* **2/1**[1]
0- 4 *2 3/4* **Always Managing**[28] 2298 4-10-12 0 .... LeightonAspell 96
(Brendan Powell) *chsd clr ldr tl pushed along over 3f out: styd on same pce fnl 2f* **40/1**
5 *12* **Nordic Nymph** 4-10-9 0 .... JakeGreenall(3) 85
(Henry Daly) *prom: pushed along over 7f out: sn lost pl: styd on again fr over 1f out* **25/1**
25- 6 *3/4* **Jazz Thyme (IRE)**[12] 2654 4-10-12 0 .... JamesDavies 85
(Bernard Llewellyn) *hld up: hdwy over 7f out: rdn over 3f out: sn wknd* **40/1**
4- 7 *10* **Fire Tower**[203] 324 5-10-12 0 .... WayneHutchinson 76
(Richard Phillips) *hld up: nvr on terms* **7/1**
- 8 *3 1/4* **Main Reason (IRE)** 5-10-12 0 .... AdamWedge 73
(Evan Williams) *hld up: pushed along over 4f out: wknd over 3f out* **16/1**
9 *nk* **Miss Lamorna (IRE)** 4-10-12 0 .... WillKennedy 72
(Sue Gardner) *chsd ldrs tl rdn and wknd over 3f out* **33/1**
13- 10 *17* **Centoria (IRE)**[42] 2022 5-10-12 0 .... BrendanPowell 57
(Jamie Snowden) *hld up: hdwy over 6f out: rdn and wknd over 3f out* **3/1**[2]
11 *81* **Peggy's Legend** 5-10-12 0 .... LeeEdwards
(Tony Carroll) *sn pushed along in rr: bhd fnl 12f* **66/1**
3m 42.7s (-1.20) **Going Correction** +0.175s/f (Yiel)
WFA 4 from 5yo+ 5lb **11** Ran SP% **117.6**
Speed ratings: **110,108,107,105,99 99,94,92,92,84 43**
CSF £47.97 TOTE £6.10: £1.90, £3.60, £1.10; EX 51.40 Trifecta £207.50 Pool: £1690.43 - 6.10 winning units..
Owner Strachan,Mangnall,Gabb,Griffith,Graham **Bred** J B Sumner **Trained** Stanton Lacy, Shropshire

FOCUS
An interesting mares' bumper. There's a case for rating the form a fair bit higher.
T/Plt: £33.50 to a £1 stake. Pool: £64837.67 - 1412.10 winning tickets T/Qpdt: £7.50 to a £1 stake. Pool: £4809.50 - 471.95 winning tickets CR

2845 LEICESTER (R-H)

Thursday, December 5

OFFICIAL GOING: Chase course - good to firm (good in places, good to soft on the flat course crossings; 8.3); hurdle course - good to soft (good in places; 7.4)

Wind: Blustery Weather: Overcast

2893 KNIGHTON NOVICES' HURDLE (8 hdls) 2m

1:00 (1:00) (Class 4) 4-Y-O+ **£3,898** (£1,144; £572; £286)

Form RPR

/13- **1** **Three Kingdoms (IRE)**[20] 2492 4-11-5 129 DenisO'Regan 125+
(John Ferguson) *a.p: chsd ldr appr 5th: led bef next: clr last: easily* **4/6**[1]

/31- **2** *20* **John Reel (FR)**[24] 2426 4-11-5 125 HarrySkelton 113+
(Dan Skelton) *chsd ldrs: chal 3 out: sn rdn: wknd and eased flat* **7/4**[2]

0/0- **3** *16* **Table Bluff (IRE)**[15] 2602 4-10-12 0 JamieMoore 77
(John Spearing) *hld up: hdwy whn mstke 3 out: sn rdn and wknd* **80/1**

/60- **4** *1 ½* **Wah Wah Taysee (IRE)**[23] 2432 6-10-12 0 SeanQuinlan 75
(David Bridgwater) *hld up: rdn after 3 out: n.d* **28/1**

P/0- **5** *8* **Ergo Sum**[46] 1991 6-10-9 0 RobertDunne(3) 69
(Robin Mathew) *led: clr whn blnd 3rd: hdd appr 3 out: sn wknd* **66/1**

6P- **6** *nk* **Gravitate**[24] 857 4-10-12 0 (t) PaulMoloney 67
(Paul Webber) *prom tl rdn and wknd after 3 out* **25/1**

00- **7** *11* **Into The Wind**[31] 2272 6-10-5 0 BarryKeniry 49
(Jim Best) *hld up: a in rr: rdn after 5th: sn wknd* **33/1**

P/0- **8** *3 ½* **Catching On (IRE)**[17] 2563 5-10-12 0 RichieMcLernon 52
(Jonjo O'Neill) *chsd ldr tl pushed along appr 5th: wknd sn after* **12/1**[3]

344- **9** *36* **Howlett (IRE)**[136] 1081 5-10-12 0 DavidBass 16
(Derek Frankland) *hld up: pushed along appr 5th: wknd bef next* **66/1**

0- **10** *1 ½* **There You Are**[15] 2602 4-10-12 0 WillKennedy 15
(Jonjo O'Neill) *hld up: pushed along 4th: wknd next* **50/1**

11 *2 ¼* **Action Front (USA)**[8] 5-10-12 0 JamesDavies 12
(Derek Shaw) *hld up: hdwy appr 5th: rdn and wknd bef next* **80/1**

3m 45.7s (-15.30) **Going Correction** -0.75s/f (Firm) **11** Ran SP% **121.7**
Speed ratings (Par 105): **108,98,90,89,85 85,79,77,59,59 57**
toteswingers 1&2 £1.02, 1&3 £15.80, 2&3 £19.30 CSF £2.09 TOTE £1.50: £1.10, £1.10, £17.60; EX 2.30 Trifecta £73.80 Pool: £1604.68 - 16.30 winning units..
Owner Bloomfields **Bred** Darley **Trained** Cowlinge, Suffolk

FOCUS
Not much depth to this novice hurdle, with the two horses carrying a penalty setting a clear standard, and they had it between them from the top of the straight. Both the first two are rated below their best.

2894 BARKBY CONDITIONAL JOCKEYS' (S) HURDLE (10 hdls) 2m 4f 110y

1:30 (1:30) (Class 5) 4-Y-O+ **£1,949** (£572; £286; £143)

Form RPR

014- **1** **Belle De Fontenay (FR)**[11] 2698 8-11-5 120 (p) ConorShoemark 113
(Conor Dore) *hld up: hdwy 6th: chsd ldr after 2 out: styd on u.p to ld towards fin* **9/1**

/0P- **2** *1* **Stow**[19] 2512 8-11-3 0 (p) JoshWall(5) 116
(Michael Blake) *led to 2nd: chsd ldr who wnt clr after 4th: hdwy u.p to ld appr 2 out: j. slowly last: hdd towards fin* **16/1**

/0P- **3** *11* **Nine Stories (IRE)**[6] 2793 8-10-10 124 (v) DiarmuidO'Regan(8) 101
(Chris Grant) *hld up: hit 6th: styd on u.p fr 2 out: mstke last: nvr trbld ldrs* **7/1**

045- **4** *8* **Captain Cardington (IRE)**[13] 2652 4-10-12 108 (v) CiaranMckee(6) 93
(John O'Shea) *hld up: drvn along after 6th: sme hdwy appr 2 out: sn wknd* **14/1**

/P5- **5** *1* **The Jugopolist (IRE)**[19] 2510 6-10-10 112 (b[1]) PaulO'Brien(8) 93+
(Rebecca Curtis) *w ldr tl led 2nd: clr after 4th tl rdn and hdd appr 2 out: wknd bef last* **10/3**[1]

143- **6** *30* **Bollin Judith**[7] 2760 7-11-5 118 (t) NicodeBoinville 71
(Jim Best) *hld up: hdwy appr 3 out: rdn and wknd bef next* **4/1**[3]

541/ **7** *3* **Cygnet**[473] 1278 7-11-4 117 RobertWilliams 62
(Peter Bowen) *mid-div: lost pl after 4th: bhd fr next* **7/2**[2]

F42- **8** *5* **Monroe Park (IRE)**[16] 2571 8-10-7 77 (p) JosephAkehurst(5) 52
(Alan Blackmore) *chsd ldrs tl rdn and wknd appr 7th* **100/1**

060- **P** **Haling Park (UAE)**[18] 2535 7-10-5 64 (v[1]) PeterCarberry
(Clarissa Caroe) *mid-div: lost pl after 3rd: bhd fr 6th: p.u bef 3 out* **100/1**

0/0- **S** **Lastchanceforlisa (IRE)**[34] 2193 7-10-11 105 AdamWedge
(John Flint) *hld up: slipped up bnd bef 5th: fatally injured* **7/1**

5m 16.1s (-8.60) **Going Correction** -0.75s/f (Firm)
WFA 4 from 6yo+ 6lb **10** Ran SP% **114.8**
Speed ratings (Par 103): **86,85,81,78,78 66,65,63, ,**
toteswingers 1&2 £9.10, 1&3 £8.80, 2&3 £15.10 CSF £134.53 TOTE £4.40: £1.30, £4.20, £3.00; EX 57.30 Trifecta £722.50 Part won. Pool: £963.41 - 0.63 winning units..There was no bid for the winner
Owner Boston Park Racing Club **Bred** E A R L Elevage Des Loges **Trained** Hubbert's Bridge, Lincs

FOCUS
A reasonably competitive selling hurdle, with several having a chance at the weights. They were strung out down the back straight having gone a searching gallop. Not form to be confident about.

2895 VALE OF BELVOIR H'CAP CHASE (15 fncs) 2m 4f 110y

2:00 (2:00) (Class 4) (0-115,115) 4-Y-O+ **£4,548** (£1,335; £667; £333)

Form RPR

153- **1** **Drumlang (IRE)**[4] 2845 7-11-5 108 (p) WillKennedy 123+
(Ian Williams) *trckd ldrs: lft 2nd 3 out: led next: clr last: easily* **7/2**[2]

114- **2** *11* **Roc De Guye (FR)**[41] 2067 8-10-10 99 (p) LiamTreadwell 100
(James Evans) *hld up: hdwy 8th: rdn 3 out: styd on same pce appr last* **10/1**

453- **3** *4* **Rebel High (IRE)**[17] 2562 9-10-0 89 oh1 (p) JamieMoore 87
(Derek Frankland) *led to 2nd: led again 4th: hdd 8th: led 4 out: rdn and hdd 2 out: wknd last* **10/1**

/45- **4** *3 ½* **Chicklemix**[28] 2315 7-10-13 107 MissGAndrews(5) 103
(Pam Sly) *chsd ldrs: mstke and lost pl 7th: hdwy appr 4 out: sn wknd* **9/1**

6/F- **5** *4* **Coolbeg (IRE)**[14] 2629 7-11-3 106 (t) FelixDeGiles 99
(Heather Main) *hld up: hdwy 8th: rdn and wknd 2 out* **33/1**

42P- **P** **Points Of View**[68] 1687 8-11-6 109 (tp) SamThomas
(Kim Bailey) *hld up: pushed along 5th: bhd fr 8th: p.u bef 4 out* **20/1**

23P- **U** **What An Oscar (IRE)**[35] 2177 8-11-12 115 (v) SamTwiston-Davies
(Nigel Twiston-Davies) *w ldrs whn blnd bdly and uns rdr 1st* **8/1**

1/5- **P** **Morgan's Bay**[22] 2450 8-11-7 110 PaddyBrennan 106
(Tom George) *hld up: nt fluent: mstke 3rd: hdwy and hit 4 out: hmpd next: looked hld whn slipped shortly after landing over 2 out: sn p.u* **5/1**[3]

/14- **F** **Lemon's Gent**[31] 2270 6-11-0 103 (tp) SamJones
(Paul Webber) *led 2nd to 4th: led again 8th: hdd 4 out: ev ch whn fell next* **11/4**[1]

5m 5.8s (-13.10) **Going Correction** -0.475s/f (Good) course record **9** Ran SP% **112.6**
Speed ratings (Par 105): **105,100,99,97,96 , , ,**
toteswingers 1&2 £6.40, 1&3 £16.60, 2&3 £18.80 CSF £36.35 CT £315.06 TOTE £3.80: £1.50, £1.90, £3.70; EX 21.80 Trifecta £468.20 Pool: £1189.74 - 1.90 winning units..
Owner M Roberts J O'Shea S Hunt R Stearman **Bred** Sandra Hodgins **Trained** Portway, Worcs

FOCUS
A moderate handicap chase.

2896 STONESBY MARES' H'CAP HURDLE (10 hdls) 2m 4f 110y

2:30 (2:30) (Class 4) (0-105,103) 3-Y-O+ **£3,249** (£954; £477; £238)

Form RPR

41F- **1** **Mini Muck**[40] 2084 7-11-12 103 SamTwiston-Davies 115+
(Nigel Twiston-Davies) *a.p: racd wd: led appr 2 out: styd on wl* **9/2**[2]

3/0- **2** *3* **Lights Of Broadway (IRE)**[12] 2663 7-11-2 96 MarkQuinlan(3) 102
(Bernard Llewellyn) *a.p: rdn to chse wnr appr last: styd on same pce flat* **14/1**

510- **3** *16* **Carhue Princess (IRE)**[7] 2771 7-10-13 90 FelixDeGiles 82
(Tom Symonds) *prom: jnd ldr 3rd tl led appr 7th: rdn and hdd bef 2 out: wknd last* **7/2**[1]

54U- **4** *10* **Ninfea (IRE)**[14] 2632 5-11-9 103 JackQuinlan(3) 86
(Neil King) *hld up: hdwy u.p appr 3 out: wknd bef next* **20/1**

400- **5** *4* **Romney Marsh**[28] 2312 12-11-1 92 HaddenFrost 71
(Roger Curtis) *prom tl rdn and wknd 2 out* **33/1**

PP0- **6** *4* **Terntheothercheek**[11] 2701 4-10-0 77 oh1 SeanQuinlan 52
(Jennie Candlish) *chsd ldrs: pushed along 5th: rdn and wknd appr 3 out* **14/1**

1/0- **7** *3 ½* **Goochypoochyprader**[17] 2568 6-11-9 100 (t) GerardTumelty 72
(Nick Lampard) *w ldr tl led and mstke 2nd: hdd appr 7th: rdn and wknd after 3 out* **10/1**

/64- **8** *7* **Direct Flo (IRE)**[13] 2653 6-10-7 89 JoshHamer(5) 55
(Tony Carroll) *hld up: plld hrd hit 6th: rdn and wknd appr 3 out* **12/1**

1/4- **9** *15* **Boosha**[10] 2723 8-10-6 90 NickSlatter(7) 42
(John Bryan Groucott) *hld up: hdwy appr 7th: rdn and wknd bef next* **25/1**

450- **10** *½* **Agent Fedora**[23] 2432 5-10-12 89 (t) SamThomas 41
(Kim Bailey) *hld up: rdn and wknd appr 3 out* **7/1**

/46- **11** *32* **Bebinn (IRE)**[34] 2193 6-11-6 102 (p) KillianMoore(5) 25
(Ben Case) *led to 2nd: chsd ldrs: rdn and wknd 7th* **11/2**[3]

/P0- **P** **Madeira Girl (IRE)**[21] 391 4-11-2 93 RichieMcLernon
(Jonjo O'Neill) *hld up: rdn and wknd after 7th: bhd whn p.u bef next* **16/1**

5m 12.1s (-12.60) **Going Correction** -0.75s/f (Firm)
WFA 4 from 5yo+ 6lb **12** Ran SP% **115.8**
Speed ratings (Par 105): **94,92,86,82,81 79,78,75,70,70 57,**
toteswingers 1&2 £18.90, 1&3 £5.70, 2&3 £27.00 CSF £61.59 CT £245.63 TOTE £5.10: £2.50, £5.50, £1.40; EX 90.90 Trifecta £526.50 Pool: £1339.62 - 1.90 winning units..
Owner N A Twiston-Davies **Bred** N A Twiston-Davies **Trained** Naunton, Gloucs

FOCUS
A competitive mares' handicap hurdle. A big step up from the cosy winner.

2897 MOUNTSORREL NOVICES' H'CAP CHASE (18 fncs) 2m 7f 110y

3:00 (3:01) (Class 4) (0-110,114) 4-Y-O+ **£3,798** (£1,122; £561; £280; £140)

Form RPR

6/4- **1** **Ifyousayso (IRE)**[22] 2451 6-11-11 107 (t) PaddyBrennan 116
(Tom George) *disp ld to 5th: chsd ldr: led 13th to next: rdn to ld appr last: styd on u.p* **5/1**[2]

P/5- **2** *3 ½* **Dark Glacier (IRE)**[50] 1925 8-11-7 103 (v[1]) JamieMoore 108
(Peter Bowen) *disp ld tl led 5th: hdd 13th: led again next: rdn and hdd appr last: styd on same pce flat* **7/1**[3]

1F2- **3** *6* **Riddlestown (IRE)**[23] 2431 6-11-10 106 (p) HarrySkelton 106
(Caroline Fryer) *chsd ldrs: rdn 3 out: no ex last* **12/1**

055- **4** *9* **West End (IRE)**[35] 2178 6-11-7 103 NickScholfield 96
(Kim Bailey) *prom: rdn appr 2 out: wknd last* **7/1**[3]

/25- **5** *2 ½* **Barton Gift**[23] 2431 6-10-5 87 PaulMoloney 77
(John Spearing) *hld up: reminder 6th: hdwy 14th: wknd next* **9/4**[1]

S60- **6** *1 ¼* **Minellaforlunch (IRE)**[33] 2210 6-11-12 108 DenisO'Regan 99
(Henry Oliver) *hld up: hdwy appr 5th: hit next: rdn and wknd after 3 out* **10/1**

0P6- **7** *24* **Original Star (IRE)**[21] 2470 8-10-5 87 DavidBass 54
(Derek Frankland) *prom tl wknd after 14th* **16/1**

8 *1 ¼* **Caspian Piper (IRE)**[193] 6-11-2 105 (b) MikeyEnnis(7) 71
(Hugo Froud) *hld up: rdn and wknd after 14th* **20/1**

001- **U** **Smart Catch (IRE)**[17] 2560 7-11-0 96 LeeEdwards 87
(Tony Carroll) *in rr: j.lft 2nd and 3rd: sn pushed along: hdwy u.p appr 4 out: wknd bef next: bhd whn j.lft and uns rdr last* **5/1**[2]

5m 53.2s (-10.80) **Going Correction** -0.475s/f (Good) **9** Ran SP% **116.5**
Speed ratings (Par 105): **99,97,95,92,92 91,83,83,**
toteswingers 1&2 £7.00, 1&3 £7.80, 2&3 £13.90 CSF £40.18 CT £400.27 TOTE £7.00: £2.30, £2.40, £2.90; EX 44.10 Trifecta £296.60 Pool: £1687.27 - 4.26 winning units..
Owner The Joaly Partnership **Bred** S Delaney **Trained** Slad, Gloucs

FOCUS
A moderate handicap chase and they didn't appear to go particularly quick early on, with the first two filling those positions throughout. The winner improved on line with the bset of his hurdle/bumper form.

2898 WALTHAM ON THE WOLDS H'CAP HURDLE (8 hdls) 2m

3:30 (3:30) (Class 5) (0-100,100) 4-Y-O+ **£3,249** (£954; £477; £238)

Form RPR

F40- **1** **Lost In Newyork (IRE)**[6] 2787 6-9-12 79 CharlieDeutsch(7) 89+
(Nick Kent) *hld up: hdwy appr 3 out: sn chsng ldr: led bef last: drvn out* **7/1**[3]

0/2- **2** *1 ¼* **Voltchesko (FR)**[16] 2581 4-11-7 100 ConorShoemark(5) 109
(Robert Walford) *hld up: nt fluent 2nd: hdwy appr 3 out: rdn bef next: hmpd last: styd on u.p to go 2nd towards fin: nt rch wnr* **4/5**[1]

442- **3** *1* **A Little Bit Dusty**[4] 2846 5-11-12 100 (p) PaddyBrennan 108
(Conor Dore) *chsd ldrs: led 3 out: rdn and hdd whn blnd last: styd on same pce* **4/1**[2]

6P5- **4** *16* **Captain Sharpe**[7] 2760 5-11-2 93 (t) MarkQuinlan(3) 86
(Bernard Llewellyn) *chsd ldrs: pushed along after 5th: rdn and wknd 2 out* **14/1**

000- **5** *7* **Drummond**[25] 2385 4-10-6 85 (tp) RobertWilliams(5) 71
(Bernard Llewellyn) *chsd ldrs: pushed along 4th: wknd appr 3 out* **33/1**

405- **6** 7 **Vertueux (FR)**[17] 2562 8-11-2 **90**........(p) LeeEdwards 70
(Tony Carroll) *led: rdn and hdd 3 out: sn wknd* **16/1**
05- **7** 3 **Powertakeoff (IRE)**[136] 1080 5-10-13 **87**........ HenryOliver 64
(Henry Oliver) *hld up: rdn and wknd appr 3 out* **20/1**
460- **8** 15 **Rigid**[29] 2291 6-10-8 **87**........ JoshHamer(5) 51
(Tony Carroll) *hld up: hdwy after 5th: rdn and wkng whn blnd 3 out* **20/1**
430/ **9** 30 **Kozmina Bay**[188] 5183 4-10-8 **82**........(p) JamesDavies 19
(Bernard Llewellyn) *chsd ldrs tl rdn and wknd after 5th* **33/1**

3m 48.1s (-12.90) **Going Correction** -0.75s/f (Firm)
WFA 4 from 5yo+ 5lb **9** Ran SP% **116.0**
Speed ratings (Par 103): **102,101,100,92,89 85,84,76,61**
toteswingers 1&2 £2.10, 1&3 £3.40, 2&3 £1.30 CSF £13.07 CT £25.49 TOTE £6.10: £1.40, £1.10, £1.70; EX 18.40 Trifecta £70.40 Pool: £2966.42 - 31.60 winning units..
Owner Timbercare Racing Partnership **Bred** J C Fagan **Trained** Brigg, Lincs

FOCUS
Little depth to this handicap hurdle. The first three home copied the tactics Sam Twiston-Davies had successfully implemented earlier in the card by going wide down the back straight, but they were the first three in the market and, given the distance back to the third, would likely have finished in front regardless. The winner's best run for nearly a year.
T/Plt: £88.00. Pool: £70,907.34 - 587.61 winning units. T/Qpdt: £18.50. Pool: £5229.00 - 208.75 winning units. CR

2621 MARKET RASEN (R-H)

Thursday, December 5

OFFICIAL GOING: Hurdle course - good to soft (7.1); chase course - soft (6.2)
Wind: very strong, 1/2 against Weather: rain 1st 2, very windy

2899 32RED CASINO JUVENILE HURDLE (8 hdls) 2m 1f
12:20 (12:21) (Class 4) 3-Y-O **£3,898** (£1,144; £572; £286)

Form RPR
1 **Handiwork**[51] 3-10-12 0........ APMcCoy 117+
(Steve Gollings) *trckd ldrs: t.k.h: wnt cl 2nd last: styd on to ld last 50yds* **11/2**
2 1 3/4 **Aalim**[31] 3-10-9 0........ JackQuinlan(3) 115
(John Ferguson) *trckd ldrs: upsides 2 out: led appr last: hdd and no ex last 50yds* **9/4**[1]
13- **3** 5 **Harristown**[29] 2294 3-11-5 122........(p) NoelFehily 118
(Charlie Longsdon) *led: hdd appr last: kpt on same pce* **5/2**[2]
6- **4** 19 **Innsbruck**[35] 2168 3-10-12 0........ BrianHughes 96
(John Quinn) *chsd ldrs: nt fluent 2nd and next: wknd 2 out: mstke last* **3/1**[3]
5 39 **Spithead**[184] 3-10-12 0........ BrianHarding 58
(Mike Sowersby) *hld up in rr: j.rt 3rd: bhd fr next: mstke 5th: t.o next* **66/1**
4- **6** shd **Last Chance Ranch**[25] 2392 3-10-5 0........ OllieGarner(7) 58
(Derek Shaw) *hld up in rr: bhd fr 4th: t.o whn hit 3 out* **100/1**
7 3/4 **Kalimantan (IRE)**[159] 3-10-9 0........ MichaelByrne(3) 57
(Tim Vaughan) *in rr: bhd fr 4th: t.o 3 out* **9/1**
8 4 1/2 **Bold And Free**[21] 3-10-7 0........ TonyKelly(5) 53
(David Thompson) *mid-div: wkng whn nt fluent 5th: sn bhd: t.o 2 out: b.b.v* **33/1**

4m 11.4s (4.70) **Going Correction** +0.15s/f (Yiel) **8** Ran SP% **115.1**
Speed ratings (Par 104): **94,93,90,81,63 63,63,61**
toteswingers 1&2 £3.80, 1&3 £3.20, 2&3 £2.20 CSF £18.92 TOTE £7.30: £2.10, £1.50, £1.10; EX 26.40 Trifecta £60.30 Pool: £2573.11 - 31.97 winning units..
Owner C Johnstone **Bred** The Queen **Trained** Scamblesby, Lincs

FOCUS
All hurdles and fences sited on fresh ground on winter lines. A very windy day, and an inspection was needed before racing. The runners faced a strong headwind up the home straight. This was a fair juvenile event, rated through the third. As soon as the pace lifted down the back straight the first four left the others way behind.

2900 EXPERT GUIDE AT MARKETRASENRACECOURSETIPS.CO.UK NOVICES' HURDLE (10 hdls) 2m 3f
12:50 (12:51) (Class 4) 4-Y-O+ **£3,898** (£1,144; £572; £286)

Form RPR
2/1- **1** **Captain Cutter (IRE)**[31] 2266 6-11-5 0........ APMcCoy 129+
(Nicky Henderson) *trckd ldrs: nt fluent 2nd and 7th: upsides appr 2 out: styd on to ld run-in: readily* **1/7**[1]
P/5- **2** 2 1/2 **Figaro**[27] 2341 5-10-9 0........(t) MichaelByrne(3) 115+
(Tim Vaughan) *led: hit 3 out: jnd appr next: hdd and no ex run-in* **4/1**[2]
0/6- **3** 7 **Royal Macnab (IRE)**[34] 2195 5-10-12 0........(t) AndrewTinkler 108
(Jamie Snowden) *hld up in rr: hdwy 6th: 3rd 3 out: one pce appr 2 out: hit last* **25/1**
4 13 **Vermouth Bleu (FR)** 4-10-2 0........ TommieMO'Brien(10) 97
(Jonjo O'Neill) *t.k.h towards rr: hdwy 3 out: sn hrd drvn and outpcd: kpt on to take modest 4th last* **8/1**[3]
5 6 **Princeofthedesert**[16] 7-10-12 0........ AdamPogson 91
(Garry Woodward) *chsd ldrs: hit 3rd: wknd appr 2 out* **20/1**
6/0- **6** 8 **Stoney Silence**[30] 2279 5-10-12 0........(p) NoelFehily 85
(Charlie Mann) *w ldrs: nt fluent 6th: drvn and wknd sn after 3 out* **12/1**
7 12 **Auto Mac**[61] 5-10-12 0........ BrianHughes 73
(Mike Sowersby) *in rr: sme hdwy 3 out: sn wknd* **16/1**
/5P- **8** 36 **Alistorm**[19] 2514 7-9-12 0........ GLavery(7) 33
(Mark Campion) *chsd ldrs: drvn 6th: sn lost pl and bhd: t.o 3 out* **66/1**

4m 37.0s (-2.40) **Going Correction** +0.15s/f (Yiel)
WFA 4 from 5yo+ 5lb **8** Ran SP% **142.3**
Speed ratings (Par 105): **111,109,107,101,99 95,90,75**
toteswingers 1&2 £1.50, 1&3 £5.30, 2&3 £10.50 CSF £2.47 TOTE £1.10: £1.02, £1.50, £4.10; EX 2.10 Trifecta £30.20 Pool: £1454.76 - 36.06 winning units..
Owner John P McManus **Bred** Mrs S Brennan **Trained** Upper Lambourn, Berks

FOCUS
There was heavy rain by this stage to accompany the wind, and they took things steadily. The winner is rated below his Kempton mark.

2901 EMERALD GREEN FEEDS NOVICES' LIMITED H'CAP CHASE (17 fncs) 3m 1f
1:20 (1:21) (Class 3) (0-125,120) 4-Y-O+ **£7,988** (£2,480; £1,335)

Form RPR
P/4- **1** **Samstown**[36] 2155 6-10-3 **107**........ EwanWhillans(3) 119
(Alistair Whillans) *trckd ldrs: led 3 out: drvn clr run-in* **9/2**[3]
502/ **2** 7 **Distime (IRE)**[404] 2042 7-11-0 **115**........ BrianHughes 121
(John Quinn) *trckd ldrs: effrt appr 3 out: chsd wnr between last 2: no imp* **7/4**[1]
/41- **3** 4 **Young Hurricane (IRE)**[16] 2582 7-11-1 **116**........ APMcCoy 119
(Dr Richard Newland) *jnd ldrs 7th: led 13th: hdd 3 out: drvn and sn wandered: hung lft and one pce run-in* **4/1**[2]
234- **P** **Ocean Club**[5] 2817 6-11-0 **115**........ DougieCostello
(Brian Ellison) *w ldrs: drvn after 10th: lost pl next and sn p.u* **16/1**
1/6- **P** **Spanish Optimist (IRE)**[60] 1796 7-10-11 **115**........(v[1]) MichaelByrne(3)
(Tim Vaughan) *led: drvn 11th: reminders next: hdd 13th: wknd qckly and p.u after next* **25/1**
/P1- **P** **Duke Of Monmouth (IRE)**[19] 2512 6-11-2 **117**........ NoelFehily
(Charlie Mann) *chsd ldrs: lost pl 7th: sn bhd: reminders 10th: sn t.o and p.u* **4/1**[2]
02F- **P** **Deise Dynamo (IRE)**[12] 2662 5-11-5 **120**........ JasonMaguire
(Donald McCain) *chsd ldrs: lost pl and reminders 3rd: j. poorly in last after: t.o 9th: p.u after next* **9/1**

6m 25.0s (-6.30) **Going Correction** -0.10s/f (Good) **7** Ran SP% **114.3**
Speed ratings (Par 107): **106,103,102, ,**
toteswingers 1&2 £2.60, 1&3 £4.70, 2&3 £3.10 CSF £13.43 TOTE £7.00: £4.10, £1.30; EX 20.40 Trifecta £107.70 Pool: £1197.34 - 8.33 winning units..
Owner Mrs Elizabeth Ferguson **Bred** Cheveley Park Stud Ltd **Trained** Newmill-On-Slitrig, Borders

FOCUS
The rain had stopped prior to this fair novice handicap. It proved a gruelling test and only three completed. The winner built on his solid recent run.

2902 32RED H'CAP CHASE (19 fncs) 3m 5f
1:50 (1:51) (Class 4) (0-105,105) 4-Y-O+ **£4,659** (£1,446; £779)

Form RPR
PP6- **1** **Acrai Rua (IRE)**[34] 2201 10-11-12 **105**........(tp) BrianHughes 112
(Tim Fitzgerald) *chsd ldrs: led 10th to 13th: led appr 3 out: drvn rt out* **9/1**
513- **2** 7 **Roseneath (IRE)**[16] 2578 9-11-4 **97**........(tp) NoelFehily 100
(Alex Hales) *trckd ldrs: hit 4 out: chsd wnr next: kpt on same pce* **2/1**[1]
205- **3** 15 **Moon Melody (GER)**[54] 1874 10-9-10 **80**........(bt) SamanthaDrake(5) 68
(Mike Sowersby) *led to 10th: led 13th tl appr 3 out: sn wknd* **10/1**
650/ **P** **Riptide**[59] 3502 7-11-10 **103**........(v) AndrewTinkler
(Michael Scudamore) *reluctant and j.v.slowly: drvn 2nd: sn bhd: t.o 9th: p.u bef next* **15/2**
P60- **P** **Very Stylish (IRE)**[25] 2394 9-11-11 **104**........(p) APMcCoy
(Jonjo O'Neill) *in rr: hit 6th: drvn 9th: lost pl 12th: sn bhd: t.o whn p.u after 13th* **7/2**[3]
3/4- **P** **Thorncliffer**[7] 2772 9-9-7 **79** oh2........(t) OllieGarner(7)
(Derek Shaw) *chsd ldrs: hit 5th: mstke 11th: lost pl after next: t.o 14th: p.u bef 4 out* **11/4**[2]

7m 40.5s (6.50) **Going Correction** -0.10s/f (Good) **6** Ran SP% **113.1**
Speed ratings (Par 105): **87,85,80, ,**
toteswingers 1&2 £3.80, 1&3 £11.40, 2&3 £2.80 CSF £28.76 TOTE £11.50: £4.90, £1.40; EX 31.20 Trifecta £227.60 Pool: £1468.56 - 4.83 winning units..
Owner Grange Park Racing **Bred** Miss Margaret Wall **Trained** Norton, N Yorks

FOCUS
A very modest marathon handicap, with doubts over all six going into the race, and a stern stamina test in the conditions. All in all, not form to treat positively. The winner is rated back to the level of his Carlisle win.

2903 32RED.COM H'CAP HURDLE (10 hdls) 2m 5f
2:20 (2:21) (Class 4) (0-115,115) 4-Y-O+ **£3,898** (£1,144; £572; £286)

Form RPR
4/3- **1** **Shimla Dawn (IRE)**[54] 1875 5-11-9 **112**........ PeterBuchanan 122+
(Tim Walford) *hld up: hit 3rd: hdwy to trck ldrs 6th: led appr 2 out: 3 l clr last: pushed wl clr run-in: comf* **9/2**
600- **2** 10 **Phare Isle (IRE)**[18] 2529 8-11-12 **115**........(tp) APMcCoy 114
(Ben Case) *trckd ldrs 3rd: 2nd appr 2 out: kpt on same pce appr last* **15/8**[1]
P- **3** 22 **Kilflora**[19] 2510 10-11-0 **110**........ GeraldQuinn(7) 89
(Claire Dyson) *led: hdd appr 2 out: sn wknd* **10/1**
55P- **4** 4 1/2 **Xenophon**[23] 2430 5-9-9 **89** oh15........ JoeCornwall(5) 64
(Michael Chapman) *lost pl 1st: sn in rr and drvn along: j. slowly: t.o 3 out: kpt on fr next: tk distant 4th nr fin* **50/1**
354- **5** nk **Oneofapear (IRE)**[14] 2625 7-11-2 **105**........ BrianHughes 80
(Mike Sowersby) *chsd ldrs: wknd after 3 out: hit next: blnd last: fin tired* **14/1**
PP/- **6** 26 **Russian George (IRE)**[77] 3009 7-11-2 **112**........(tp) PaulBohan(7) 63
(Steve Gollings) *chsd ldrs: drvn 6th: sn lost pl: t.o 3 out* **20/1**
402- **U** **Andreo Bambaleo**[14] 2625 9-11-3 **113**........(p) NathanMoscrop(7)
(Brian Ellison) *in rr: outpcd whn hit 6th: bhd whn hmpd and uns rdr next* **4/1**[3]
/30- **F** **Amok (IRE)**[18] 2529 5-11-7 **113**........(t) MichaelByrne(3)
(Tim Vaughan) *w ldrs: mstke 4th: fell 7th: rn loose: fatally injured* **7/2**[2]

5m 10.8s (2.00) **Going Correction** +0.15s/f (Yiel) **8** Ran SP% **117.7**
Speed ratings (Par 105): **102,98,89,88,87 78, ,**
toteswingers 1&2 £3.20, 1&3 £10.10, 2&3 £7.50 CSF £14.26 CT £80.85 TOTE £5.30: £1.30, £1.10, £3.80; EX 19.60 Trifecta £132.20 Pool: £1924.49 - 10.91 winning units..
Owner Mrs M Cooper **Bred** James Barry **Trained** Sheriff Hutton, N Yorks

FOCUS
Modest handicap form, with a step up from the winner.

2904 32RED ON THE APP STORE CONDITIONAL JOCKEYS' H'CAP HURDLE (8 hdls) 2m 1f
2:50 (2:51) (Class 4) (0-110,110) 4-Y-O+ **£3,119** (£915; £457; £228)

Form RPR
400- **1** **King Zeal (IRE)**[17] 2561 9-11-2 **100**........(t) HarryChalloner 99+
(Barry Leavy) *chsd ldrs: hit 2 out: led last: drvn out* **6/1**
4/0- **2** 2 1/4 **Rasheed**[15] 2598 5-11-6 **107**........(b) MattCrawley(3) 103
(Lucy Wadham) *mid-div: hdwy to chse ldrs 3 out: upsides last: kpt on same pce: tk 2nd last 150yds* **11/1**
FP6- **3** 5 **Snowed In (IRE)**[32] 2241 4-10-8 **97**........(p) RyanHatch(5) 88
(Jennie Candlish) *led tl after 1st: w ldr: led after 3 out: hdd last: one pce* **4/1**[2]
6P3- **4** 1 1/4 **Volcanic Jack (IRE)**[16] 2573 5-10-4 **88**........ JoeCornwall 80
(Michael Chapman) *in rr: hdwy to chse ldrs 4th: hit 3 out: cl 4th whn hit last: one pce* **14/1**
/03- **5** 10 **Formulation (IRE)**[15] 2597 6-11-1 **102**........(p) TonyKelly(3) 83
(Rebecca Menzies) *chsd ldng pair: lost pl after 3 out: sn bhd: tk poor 5th nr fin* **15/8**[1]
50/- **6** 3/4 **Pinotage**[58] 2315 5-11-3 **104**........ CraigNichol(3) 85
(Peter Niven) *chsd ldrs: hit 3rd: wknd 2 out* **12/1**
/40- **7** 11 **Sash Of Honour (IRE)**[31] 2271 4-11-9 **110**........(v) MichaelByrne(3) 81
(Tim Vaughan) *in rr: bhd and reminders 5th: t.o next* **12/1**

533/ **8** *19* **Short Takes (USA)**^{465} [1379] 5-11-2 **108** JamesCowley$^{(8)}$ 62
(Donald McCain) *w ldr: led after 1st: hdd after 3 out: sn lost pl and bhd* **9/2**^{3}

4m 7.2s (0.50) **Going Correction** +0.15s/f (Yiel) **8** Ran SP% **117.6**
Speed ratings (Par 105): **104,102,100,100,95 94,89,80**
toteswingers 1&2 £9.60, 1&3 £10.30, 2&3 £13.90 CSF £67.77 CT £297.71 TOTE £7.90: £2.80, £3.50, £1.80; EX 117.70 Trifecta £1328.90 Pool: £1821.75 - 1.02 winning units..
Owner Deborah Hart & Alan Jackson **Bred** Janus Bloodstock **Trained** Forsbrook, Staffs

FOCUS
A very modest event in which the two leaders, who were clear for a time, set a brisk pace. The winner is rated back to the best of last season's form.

2905 32REDPOKER.COM STANDARD OPEN NATIONAL HUNT FLAT RACE — 2m 1f
3:20 (3:20) (Class 6) 4-6-Y-O **£1,642** (£478; £239)

Form RPR

1 **Bandit Country (IRE)** 4-11-0 0 APMcCoy 119+
(Jonjo O'Neill) *trckd ldrs: effrt over 2f out: led jst ins fnl f: hung lft and drvn out* **6/4**^{1}

2- **2** *4 ½* **Degooch (IRE)**^{20} [2499] 4-11-0 0 JasonMaguire 110
(Donald McCain) *w ldr: led after 2f: increased pce 7f out: drvn over 2f out: hdd jst ins fnl f: styd on same pce* **6/4**^{1}

3 *3* **Frampton (IRE)**^{42} [2061] 4-11-0 0 NoelFehily 107
(Charlie Longsdon) *trckd ldrs: shkn up over 6f out: reminders and 2nd 5f out: one pce fnl 2f* **11/4**^{2}

3/4- **4** *10* **Midnight Chorister**^{200} [395] 5-11-0 0 (t) PeterBuchanan 97
(Alex Hales) *hld up in last: pushed along over 4f out: chsd ldrs 3f out: lost pl wl over 1f out* **16/1**^{3}

666/ **5** *32* **Lapworth (IRE)**^{222} [5572] 6-11-0 0 RyanMahon 65
(Michael Appleby) *set stdy pce 2f: w ldr: drvn 6f out: sn lost pl: t.o 3f out* **50/1**

4m 7.1s (6.00) **Going Correction** +0.15s/f (Yiel) **5** Ran SP% **114.5**
Speed ratings: **91,88,87,82,67**
CSF £4.24 TOTE £2.20: £1.10, £1.90; EX 5.00 Trifecta £5.80 Pool: £1349.03 - 172.21 winning units..
Owner Mrs J Magnier, D Smith & M Tabor **Bred** David Reynolds & Edward Spellman **Trained** Cheltenham, Gloucs

FOCUS
Conditions had calmed by now. The runner-up set a steady pace in this fair bumper until quickening it up down the back. The winner looks potentially decent.
T/Plt: £144.80. Pool: £45,449.39 - 229.01 winning units. T/Qpdt: £146.20. Pool: £1975.80 - 10.00 winning units. WG

2628 WINCANTON (R-H)
Thursday, December 5

OFFICIAL GOING: Good (good to firm in places down the back straight; chs 8.5, hdl 8.6)
Wind: strong behind Weather: overcast

2906 REWARDS4RACING.COM MAIDEN HURDLE (8 hdls) — 2m
12:40 (12:41) (Class 5) 4-Y-O+ **£1,949** (£572; £286; £143)

Form RPR

1 **Stand To Reason (IRE)**^{414} 5-11-0 0 BarryGeraghty 120+
(Nicky Henderson) *mid-div: pushed along and hdwy after 3 out: chal between last 2: nodded last: sn led: nudged out: cosily* **8/11**^{1}

5- **2** *2* **Red Seventy**^{21} [2476] 4-10-7 0 (p) TomBellamy$^{(7)}$ 113
(David Pipe) *t.k.h: sn trcking ldrs: led 4th: clr after 3 out: rdn bef next: jnd between last 2: hdd sn after last: kpt on same pce* **14/1**^{3}

0- **3** *1 ½* **Hint Of Mint**^{21} [2476] 4-11-0 0 WayneHutchinson 112
(Nick Williams) *mid-div: hdwy 5th: rdn and ch between last 2: kpt on same pce fr last* **50/1**

4 *11* **Shareni (IRE)**^{441} 4-11-0 0 (t) DarylJacob 106+
(Paul Nicholls) *mid-div: hdwy 3 out: sn pushed along: 4th whn mstke 2 out: one pce whn mstke last* **3/1**^{2}

3/0- **5** *6* **River Dancing (IRE)**^{183} [631] 6-11-0 94 AidanColeman 95
(Andy Turnell) *mid-div: rdn after 3 out: styd on between last 2 but nvr gng pce to get involved* **20/1**

222/ **6** *1 ½* **Chance Encounter (IRE)**^{620} [5090] 7-11-0 0 IanPopham 93
(Linda Blackford) *disp ld tl after 3rd: trckd ldr: rdn appr 2 out: sn one pce* **25/1**

6/5- **7** *3 ½* **Prasina Russata (IRE)**^{7} [2761] 6-11-0 0 TomScudamore 90
(David Pipe) *t.k.h: hld up towards rr: hdwy to trck ldrs after 2nd: rdn after 3 out: sn outpcd* **18/1**

0- **8** *2 ¾* **Mr Fickle (IRE)**^{31} [2265] 4-10-11 0 JoshuaMoore$^{(3)}$ 87
(Gary Moore) *hld up towards rr: rdn after 3 out: sme prog into midfield next: no further imp whn mstke last* **14/1**^{3}

2U0- **9** *½* **Unefille De Guye (FR)**^{11} [2689] 5-10-4 0 GilesHawkins$^{(3)}$ 79
(Victor Dartnall) *mstke 2 out: nvr bttr than mid-div* **50/1**

P- **10** *5* **Already Basking (CAN)**^{14} [2631] 5-11-0 0 AndrewThornton 81
(Simon Earle) *disp ld tl 3rd: trckd ldrs: rdn after 3 out: wknd between last 2* **200/1**

/00- **11** *8* **Ma'Ire Rua (IRE)**^{10} [2711] 6-11-0 0 JackDoyle 73
(Alan Jones) *a towards rr* **200/1**

000- **12** *6* **Forget And Forgive (IRE)**^{17} [2564] 5-10-9 0 (t) JamesBanks$^{(5)}$ 67
(Anthony Middleton) *trckd ldrs tl 5th: sn towards rr* **200/1**

13 *6* **Strategic Exit**^{222} 5-11-0 0 TomO'Brien 61
(James Frost) *a towards rr* **200/1**

03- **14** *12* **The Selector**^{23} [2442] 4-10-7 0 TomCannon 42
(Chris Gordon) *trckd ldrs tl 5th: wknd after 3 out* **80/1**

/0U- **15** *3 ¾* **Party Girls (FR)**^{7} [2761] 5-10-0 0 (t) KieronEdgar$^{(7)}$ 39
(David Pipe) *nvr fluent: a bhd* **100/1**

233/ **U** **Dance**^{174} [5511] 4-10-7 0 ConorO'Farrell
(Rod Millman) *nt fluent: towards rr whn veered lft and uns rdr 4th* **66/1**

3m 42.1s (-6.80) **Going Correction** -0.70s/f (Firm) **16** Ran SP% **119.7**
WFA 4 from 5yo+ 5lb
Speed ratings (Par 103): **89,88,87,81,78 78,76,74,74,72 68,65,62,56,54**
toteswingers 1&2 £7.00, 1&3 £16.20, 2&3 £33.00 CSF £12.77 TOTE £1.70: £1.10, £3.60, £7.50; EX 18.20 Trifecta £341.50 Pool: £1659.7 - 3.64 winning units..
Owner Seasons Holidays **Bred** Coleman Bloodstock Limited **Trained** Upper Lambourn, Berks

FOCUS
The early pace was really moderate and, despite the big field, this is very unreliable form. The winner looks a decent recruit and should go on to rate higher.

2907 NEW RACING UK ANYWHERE AVAILABLE NOW MARES' MAIDEN HURDLE (11 hdls) — 2m 6f
1:10 (1:10) (Class 4) 4-Y-O+ **£3,249** (£954; £477; £238)

Form RPR

1/5- **1** **Mayfair Music (IRE)**^{19} [2506] 4-10-12 0 BarryGeraghty 117+
(Nicky Henderson) *racd wd: mid-div: nt fluent 4th: stdy prog fr 7th: led gng to 2 out: shkn up whn awkward last: rdn clr: styd on strly* **11/10**^{1}

3/0- **2** *7* **Fairytale Theatre (IRE)**^{19} [2506] 6-10-12 0 (t) DarylJacob 108
(Paul Nicholls) *mid-div: hdwy 3 out: pushed along to chse ldrs bef 2 out: rdn and edgd rt bef last: styd on to go 2nd run-in: no ch w wnr* **7/2**^{2}

/ **3** *3 ½* **Bilidn**^{71} 5-10-12 0 JackDoyle 107
(Ben De Haan) *in tch: tk clsr order 3 out: rdn and ev ch between last 2: mstke last: kpt on but no ex whn lost 2nd run-in* **25/1**

0- **4** *11* **Vilja (IRE)**^{19} [2506] 4-10-12 0 TomScudamore 98
(David Pipe) *trckd ldrs: nt fluent 3rd: led 7th: rdn and hdd appr 2 out: kpt on same pce tl no ex fr last* **10/1**

/50- **5** *10* **Land Of Vic**^{19} [2506] 5-10-12 0 DonalDevereux 88
(Peter Bowen) *mid-div tl outpcd 3 out: styd on fr next but nvr any threat* **14/1**

050- **6** *1* **Superstición**^{43} [2016] 4-10-12 84 MarcGoldstein 85
(Michael Madgwick) *mid-div: rdn after 3 out: styd on same pce wout ever threatening to get on terms* **100/1**

0- **7** *3 ¼* **Swincomb Silvalady**^{144} [970] 5-10-12 0 WayneHutchinson 83
(Robert Walford) *w ldrs: nt fluent 3 out: sn rdn: wknd next* **100/1**

/20- **8** *5* **Dreams And Songs**^{21} [2471] 5-10-12 0 (t) RichardJohnson 78
(Philip Hobbs) *hld up towards rr: pushed along and hdwy after 3 out: wnt 5th next: sn rdn: wkng whn mstke last* **7/1**^{3}

/45- **9** *2 ¼* **Summertime Lady**^{22} [2463] 5-10-12 0 JoeTizzard 79
(Colin Tizzard) *in tch: pushed along whn hmpd on bnd after 3 out: sn rdn: wknd between last 2* **22/1**

0/6- **10** *5* **Its April**^{22} [2463] 5-10-12 0 DaveCrosse 71
(Robert Walford) *hld up towards rr: hdwy appr 3 out: sn rdn: wknd next* **100/1**

5/6- **11** *18* **Definitely Better (IRE)**^{29} [2298] 5-10-12 0 AlainCawley 55
(Tom George) *j.rt 4th: mstke next: a bhd: t.o* **33/1**

12 *13* **Reillys Daughter**^{29} 5-10-5 0 (b^{1}) TomBellamy$^{(7)}$ 43
(Richard Mitchell) *j. sltly lft: led tl 5th: w ldr tl rdn after 3 out: sn wknd: t.o* **100/1**

4- **13** *49* **Miss Probus**^{162} [841] 4-10-12 0 (t) AidanColeman
(Nick Williams) *in tch tl rdn and wknd sn after 3 out: t.o* **33/1**

5- **P** **Greatday Allweek (IRE)**^{23} [2442] 4-10-5 0 KevinJones$^{(7)}$
(Seamus Mullins) *nt fluent 5th: sn struggling: a towards rr: t.o whn p.u bef 2 out* **100/1**

5m 11.1s (-15.40) **Going Correction** -0.70s/f (Firm) **14** Ran SP% **117.1**
Speed ratings (Par 105): **100,97,96,92,88 88,87,85,84,82 76,71,53,**
toteswingers 1&2 £1.80, 1&3 £12.50, 2&3 £31.10 CSF £4.29 TOTE £2.10: £1.10, £1.70, £5.10; EX 5.40 Trifecta £89.70 Pool: £1327.19 - 11.09 winning units..
Owner Mrs E Roberts **Bred** Mrs Marilyn Syme **Trained** Upper Lambourn, Berks

FOCUS
An uncompetitive mares' maiden.

2908 YEOVIL TOWN FOOTBALL CLUB "NATIONAL HUNT" NOVICES' H'CAP HURDLE (11 hdls) — 2m 6f
1:40 (1:40) (Class 4) (0-115,115) 3-Y-O+ **£3,249** (£954; £477; £238)

Form RPR

663- **1** **Rior (IRE)**^{28} [2314] 6-10-11 **100** TomO'Brien 105
(Paul Henderson) *hld up but wl in tch: hdwy after 8th: rdn to callenge between last 2: styd on gamely to ld run-in: asserted nr fin* **10/1**

22- **2** *¾* **Lumpys Gold**^{14} [2631] 5-11-7 **110** (t) DarylJacob 114
(Paul Nicholls) *t.k.h: in tch: trckd ldrs after 5th: nt fluent 3 out: led narrowly 2 out: sn rdn and strly pressed: hdd run-in: no ex towards fin* **9/5**^{1}

225- **3** *9* **Keltic Rhythm (IRE)**^{29} [2296] 6-11-7 **113** TrevorWhelan$^{(3)}$ 111
(Neil King) *in tch: trckd ldrs 5th: rdn in cl 3rd bef 2 out: no ex fr last* **7/1**^{3}

133- **4** *1 ¾* **Letemgo (IRE)**^{7} [2764] 5-11-10 **113** DavidEngland 107
(Giles Smyly) *trckd ldrs tl outpcd after 3 out: styd on again to go 4th between last 2: nvr a threat to ldrs* **9/2**^{2}

10F/ **5** *8* **Pertinent (FR)**^{236} 10-10-4 **100** MissAliceMills$^{(7)}$ 88
(Charles Whittaker) *led tl rdn and hdd appr 2 out: grad fdd* **66/1**

316- **6** *2 ¾* **Bob Tucker (IRE)**^{22} [2458] 6-11-7 **115** JamesBanks$^{(5)}$ 100
(Brendan Powell) *hld up but in tch: pushed along after 5th: effrt after 3 out: wknd bef last* **14/1**

4/0- **7** *¾* **Marmalade Man**^{206} [264] 7-10-5 **97** WayneKavanagh$^{(3)}$ 81
(Seamus Mullins) *in tch: rdn after 6th: nvr really threatened: wknd bef last* **33/1**

/F0- **8** *38* **Kartanian (IRE)**^{40} [2087] 7-11-7 **110** RichardJohnson 85
(Philip Hobbs) *hld up but in tch: rdn after 3 out: wknd next: t.o* **9/2**^{2}

306- **9** *20* **Sterling Gent (IRE)**^{33} [2210] 6-10-12 **101** ConorO'Farrell 33
(Liam Corcoran) *trckd ldr: disp 7th tl 3 out: wknd qckly: t.o* **20/1**

003- **F** **Native Brian (IRE)**^{14} [2628] 7-10-11 **100** (t) AndrewThornton
(Alexandra Dunn) *racd wd: in tch: fell 6th* **25/1**

5m 8.1s (-18.40) **Going Correction** -0.70s/f (Firm) **10** Ran SP% **113.4**
Speed ratings (Par 105): **105,104,101,100,97 96,96,82,75,**
toteswingers 1&2 £4.20, 1&3 £5.40, 2&3 £4.00 CSF £27.52 CT £137.02 TOTE £10.20: £2.10, £1.90, £2.30; EX 19.50 Trifecta £149.00 Pool: £1609.04 - 8.09 winning units..
Owner The Paul Henderson Racing Club **Bred** Glebe House Stud Ltd **Trained** Whitsbury, Hants

FOCUS
A modest novice handicap, but solid enough form.

2909 WEATHERBYS HAMILTON INSURANCE SILVER BUCK H'CAP CHASE (JOCKEY CLUB GRASSROOTS SERIES QUALIFIER) (21 fncs) — 3m 1f 110y
2:10 (2:11) (Class 3) (0-125,125) 4-Y-O+ **£9,582** (£2,892; £1,490; £789)

Form RPR

FF5- **1** **Buck's Bond (FR)**^{18} [2537] 7-11-6 **119** (bt) DarylJacob 132+
(Paul Nicholls) *led 3rd: hdd 12th tl led after 14th: rdn after 3 out: 2 l up whn lft clr 2 out* **10/3**^{2}

32F/ **2** *9* **Allthekingshorses (IRE)**^{323} [3681] 7-11-12 **125** (tp) RichardJohnson 127
(Philip Hobbs) *hld up bhd ldrs: pushed along fr 11th: rdn bef 4 out: wnt hld 3rd bef 3 out: lft 2nd whn hmpd 2 out* **15/8**^{1}

The Form Book Jumps, Raceform Ltd, Compton, RG20 6NL.

336- **3** *6* **Inside Dealer (IRE)**[21] 2468 9-11-6 **119**............................(bt[1]) JoeTizzard 114
(Colin Tizzard) *disp ld tl 3rd: trckd ldr: remained prom tl lost pl and drvn in last after 14th: lft hld 4th 2 out: wnt 3rd at the last* **9/1**

/13- **4** *½* **Goring One (IRE)**[13] 2646 8-11-2 **115**........................ AndrewThornton 110
(Anna Newton-Smith) *j.lft: disp tl after 3rd: remained prom tl rdn after 16th: lft 3rd whn hmpd 4 out: hld after: lost 3rd at the last* **5/1**[3]

6/0- **F** **Upham Atom**[6] 2798 10-11-3 **123**...................................(p) KieronEdgar[(7)] 131
(Kate Buckett) *trckd ldrs: jnd ldrs 16th tl after next: rdn to chse wnr after 4 out: styng on but 2 l down whn fell heavily 2 out* **16/1**

P60- **F** **Havingotascoobydo (IRE)**[20] 2488 8-11-10 **123**................ TomSiddall
(Martin Keighley) *hld up bhd ldrs: fell 3rd* **9/1**

/1U- **F** **Shockingtimes (IRE)**[12] 2662 6-11-7 **120**.............................. MarkGrant
(Charlie Mann) *hld up bhd ldrs: travelling wl in clly disp 2nd whn fell 4 out* **8/1**

6m 28.5s (-11.00) **Going Correction** -0.225s/f (Good) **7** Ran SP% **111.5**
Speed ratings (Par 107): **107,104,102,102, ,**
toteswingers 1&2 £2.30, 1&3 £17.00, 2&3 £4.70 CSF £9.96 TOTE £3.50: £1.90, £1.70; EX 10.10 Trifecta £54.70 Pool: £1937.50 - 26.53 winning units..
Owner Mrs Catherine Penny **Bred** Henri Poulat **Trained** Ditcheat, Somerset

FOCUS
Not form to dwell on, but a step up from the winner.

2910 WEATHERBYS HAMILTON INSURANCE H'CAP HURDLE (8 hdls) 2m
2:40 (2:41) (Class 3) (0-125,125) 4-Y-0**+** **£9,495** (£2,805; £1,402; £702; £351)

Form RPR

/06- **1** **Jumps Road**[13] 2647 6-11-11 **124**.................................... BrendanPowell 130
(Colin Tizzard) *disp ld at modest pce: qcknd into outrt ld appr 2 out: rdn whn strly pressed between last 2: kpt on wl to assert fnl 100yds* **7/2**[2]

2/3- **2** *1* **Prompter**[23] 1685 6-11-9 **122**.................................... DominicElsworth 127+
(Jonjo O'Neill) *hld up: smooth hdwy after 3 out: chal travelling strly between last 2: rdn after last: nt qckn: no ex fnl 100yds* **6/1**[3]

260- **3** *12* **Decoy (FR)**[14] 2630 7-11-5 **125**..(p) MrEBarrett[(7)] 118
(David Pipe) *trckd ldrs: rdn after 3 out: nvr gng pce to chal but kpt on fr next* **10/1**

0/3- **4** *1* **Mcvicar**[26] 2366 4-11-11 **124**.. RobertThornton 116
(Alan King) *disp ld: rdn after 3 out: hdd bef next: kpt on but sn outpcd by ldng pair* **7/1**

/F0- **5** *4 ½* **Sleeping City (FR)**[39] 2111 6-10-12 **111**................................ JackDoyle 100
(Victor Dartnall) *hld up in last: hdwy after 3 out: rdn into 4th between last 2: no ex fr last* **7/1**

6/4- **6** *½* **Barista (IRE)**[21] 2476 5-10-3 **105**.............................. WayneKavanagh[(3)] 92
(Brian Forsey) *trckd ldrs: rdn after 3 out: outpcd bef next* **28/1**

/02- **7** *31* **Kilrye (IRE)**[158] 852 6-9-7 **99** oh13...................................(t) MrMHeard[(7)] 55
(David Pipe) *hld up: rdn after 3 out: nvr gng pce to get on terms: wknd next: t.o* **25/1**

2/4- **8** *76* **Thundering Home**[14] 2617 6-10-1 **107**............................ TomBellamy[(7)]
(Richard Mitchell) *hld up: outpcd after 3 out: virtually p.u whn btn between last 2: t.o* **12/1**

/33- **F** **Roman Flight (IRE)**[10] 2717 5-11-12 **125**...................... RichardJohnson
(David Dennis) *mid-div whn fell 5th* **5/2**[1]

3m 41.5s (-7.40) **Going Correction** -0.70s/f (Firm)
WFA 4 from 5yo+ 5lb **9** Ran SP% **114.2**
Speed ratings (Par 107): **90,89,83,83,80 80,65,27,**
toteswingers 1&2 £4.40, 1&3 £0.00, 2&3 £26.10 CSF £24.76 CT £189.68 TOTE £5.80: £1.60, £1.80, £3.60; EX 22.70 Trifecta £263.80 Pool: £1769.06 - 5.02 winning units..
Owner Chasing Gold Racing Club **Bred** T H Chadney **Trained** Milborne Port, Dorset

FOCUS
A fait handicap, but few got in a blow. It probably didn't take that much winning.

2911 REWARDS4RACING.COM CONDITIONAL JOCKEYS' H'CAP CHASE (17 fncs) 2m 5f
3:10 (3:10) (Class 4) (0-105,104) 4-Y-0+ **£3,898** (£1,144; £572; £286)

Form RPR

0/P- **1** **Bincombe**[40] 2088 5-11-0 **95**... JamesBest[(3)] 110+
(Philip Hobbs) *travelled wl: trckd ldrs: chal appr 3 out: led bef 2 out: sn in command: styd on wl: pushed out* **11/8**[1]

P35- **2** *7* **Ring Bo Ree (IRE)**[34] 2194 10-11-11 **103**......................(p) GavinSheehan 109
(Tom George) *led 2nd: rdn after 4 out: hdd sn after 3 out: hld next: styd on same pce* **9/2**[3]

225- **3** *12* **Plum Pudding (FR)**[17] 2567 10-11-4 **104**......................(p) JakeHodson[(8)] 99
(David Bridgwater) *prom early: dropped to 5th but in tch 7th: wnt 4th 10th: trckd ldng pair 13th: rdn after 4 out: sn one pce* **5/2**[2]

05P/ **4** *29* **Starburst Diamond (IRE)**[192] 11-10-12 **95**................(b) KevinJones[(5)] 64
(Charles Whittaker) *led tl 2nd: trckd ldr tl nudged along after 10th: rdn after next: sn last: wknd after 13th: t.o* **14/1**

234- **5** *6* **Upton Mead (IRE)**[17] 2567 6-11-9 **101**...........................(b) JoshuaMoore 64
(Kevin Tork) *trckd ldrs: pushed along after 8th: rdn after 12th: btn after next: t.o* **6/1**

5m 19.4s (-5.80) **Going Correction** -0.225s/f (Good) **5** Ran SP% **109.0**
Speed ratings (Par 105): **102,99,94,83,81**
CSF £7.89 TOTE £3.10: £1.30, £2.40; EX 9.10 Trifecta £41.60 Pool: £1294.34 - 23.33 winning units..
Owner Martin Short **Bred** R D And Mrs J S Chugg **Trained** Withycombe, Somerset

FOCUS
A moderate handicap, confined to conditional riders. Not a race to be confident about.

2912 NEW RACING UK ANYWHERE AVAILABLE NOW MAIDEN OPEN NATIONAL HUNT FLAT RACE 2m
3:40 (3:40) (Class 6) 4-6-Y-0 **£1,624** (£477; £238; £119)

Form RPR

00/ **1** **Fair Dreamer**[273] 4621 5-10-8 0.................................... MartinMcIntyre[(10)] 99+
(Harry Fry) *hld up in mid-div: smooth hdwy fr 4f out: led over 2f out: sn in command: styd on wl* **11/4**[1]

56- **2** *4* **Flashyfrank**[12] 2667 4-10-11 0.. MissLAllan[(7)] 92
(David Elsworth) *trckd ldrs: rdn 3f out: styd on to go 2nd over 1f out: nvr rching wnr* **11/4**[1]

3 *8* **Thats Yer Man (IRE)** 5-11-4 0... IanPopham 85
(Linda Blackford) *mid-div: hdwy 1/2-way: rdn to ld briefly over 2f out: lost 2nd over 1f out: styd on same pce* **17/2**[3]

4 *1 ¼* **Hill Forts Harry** 4-10-11 0.. KevinJones[(7)] 84
(Seamus Mullins) *hld up towards rr: stdy prog fr 4f out: rdn and styd on fnl 2f: wnt 4th ent fnl f: nvr rchd ldrs* **7/1**[2]

5 *12* **Bostin (IRE)**[213] 5-11-1 0.. GavinSheehan[(3)] 73
(Brian Barr) *trckd ldr: led 1/2-way: hung bdly rt on bnd 4f out: rdn and hdd over 2f out: wknd ent fnl f* **7/1**[2]

0- **6** *7* **Foolsandorses (IRE)**[18] 2534 5-10-13 0......................... JamesBanks[(5)] 67
(W De Best-Turner) *trckd ldrs tl wknd 4f out* **20/1**

0- **7** *6* **Proper Job**[21] 2479 5-10-11 0................................... MrJoshuaNewman[(7)] 61
(Polly Gundry) *mid-div: hdwy 5f out: wknd over 2f out* **20/1**

0S- **8** *3* **Sutes**[21] 2479 5-11-4 0.. JackDoyle 58
(Alan Jones) *trckd ldrs tl dropped to rr tamely 1/2-way: nvr a danger after* **16/1**

0- **9** *19* **Ding Dong Dennis (IRE)**[11] 2703 6-11-4 0.......................... TomCannon 41
(Laura Young) *led tl 1/2-way: sn rdn: wknd over 3f out: t.o* **25/1**

10 *54* **Blackdown Babe** 5-10-11 0.. AndrewThornton
(Alexandra Dunn) *mid-div tl over 4f out: t.o* **25/1**

11 *62* **Hi Bronco** 6-11-4 0.. DaveCrosse
(John Ryall) *dwlt: bhd: reminders on stable bnd after 3f: t.o fr 1/2-way* **12/1**

3m 37.4s (-5.90) **Going Correction** -0.70s/f (Firm)
WFA 4 from 5yo+ 5lb **11** Ran SP% **119.7**
Speed ratings: **86,84,80,79,73 69,66,65,55,28**
toteswingers 1&2 £2.40, 1&3 £7.00, 2&3 £3.40 CSF £8.85 TOTE £3.50: £1.20, £1.70, £2.20; EX 9.10 Trifecta £31.10 Pool: £1904.93 - 45.82 winning units..
Owner J P Blakeney **Bred** Fifehead Farms & J P Blakeney **Trained** Seaborough, Dorset
■ Martin McIntyre's first winner since turning conditional.

FOCUS
A modest bumper. A big step forward from the winner.
T/Jkpt: £11,453.10. Pool: £16,131.15 - 1.00 winning units. T/Plt: £22.80. Pool: £63,661.58 - 2033.08 winning units. T/Qpdt: £16.60. Pool: £3059.46 - 135.70 winning units. TM

2689 EXETER (R-H)
Friday, December 6

OFFICIAL GOING: Good (good to firm in places; 7.9)
Wind: Mild breeze; across Weather: Sunny

2920 FORUM FOR THE BUILT ENVIRONMENT (FBE) CONDITIONAL JOCKEYS' NOVICES' H'CAP HURDLE (10 hdls) 2m 3f
12:25 (12:25) (Class 5) (0-100,98) 3-Y-0+ **£2,274** (£667; £333; £166)

Form RPR

/45- **1** **Boss In Boots (IRE)**[24] 2430 5-11-4 **98**.............................. KevinJones[(8)] 109+
(Seamus Mullins) *trckd ldrs: rdn to chal 3 out: led sn after last: kpt on: drvn out* **9/2**[2]

600- **2** *¾* **Tomibola (IRE)**[44] 2018 5-10-9 **86**.................................... RyanHatch[(5)] 95+
(Harry Whittington) *led tl 2nd: prom: led 5th: rdn whn hrd pressed 3 out: nt fluent last: sn hdd: kpt on: hld towards fin* **6/1**

460- **3** *21* **The Happy Warrior**[50] 1945 5-10-3 **80**........................ GaryDerwin[(5)] 70
(Bob Buckler) *hld up but wl in tch: rdn and hdwy to chse ldrs after 7th: wnt 3rd next: wl hld whn rchd for 2 out* **12/1**

0/0- **4** *4 ½* **Tokyo Javilex (FR)**[20] 2510 6-11-5 **96**................(t) ThomasCheesman[(5)] 82
(Nigel Hawke) *trckd ldrs: rdn after 7th: one pce and hld fr next* **11/2**[3]

6S0- **5** *6* **Residence And Spa (IRE)**[12] 2696 5-10-8 **80**.................. JackQuinlan 60
(Helen Rees) *trckd ldrs: rdn after 6th: hld fr after next: plugged on* **20/1**

336/ **6** *1 ¾* **Cuckoo Rock (IRE)**[30] 4486 6-10-11 **83**.......................(p) GavinSheehan 61
(Jonathan Portman) *led 2nd tl 4th: trckd ldrs: rdn appr 3 out: sn one pce: wknd last* **9/1**

/01- **7** *½* **Sylvan Legend**[8] 2766 5-10-9 **81** 7ex.. JamesBest 59
(Caroline Keevil) *prom: led 4th tl next: rdn appr 3 out: sn one pce: wknd last* **2/1**[1]

544- **8** *41* **Karl Marx (IRE)**[32] 2276 3-10-7 **94**.................................... PatrickCorbett 20
(Mark Gillard) *last but in tch: struggling bef 4th: nvr a danger: wknd 3 out: t.o* **14/1**

0PP/ **9** *23* **Just Watch Ollie (IRE)**[404] 2074 7-9-9 **72** oh3.................. OllieGarner[(5)]
(John Coombe) *trckd ldrs: rdn after 4th: sn lost pl: wknd after 7th: t.o* **80/1**

0F0- **P** **Puerto Azul (IRE)**[8] 2764 9-11-5 **91**................................ ThomasGarner
(Bernard Scriven) *prom: awkward 3rd: rdn after 6th: wknd after next: bhd whn p.u bef 2 out* **50/1**

4m 33.1s (-9.60) **Going Correction** -0.45s/f (Good)
WFA 3 from 5yo+ 13lb **10** Ran SP% **113.5**
Speed ratings (Par 103): **102,101,92,90,88 87,87,70,60,**
toteswingers 1&2 £8.20, 1&3 £14.50, 2&3 £10.20 CSF £30.54 CT £299.76 TOTE £4.00: £1.30, £2.00, £2.40; EX 43.60 Trifecta £124.40 Pool: £861.36 - 5.19 winning units..
Owner Mark Adams **Bred** Fred Mackey **Trained** Wilsford-Cum-Lake, Wilts

FOCUS
The ground was reported to have been riding "dead". The runners took the far bend into the home straight in the hurdle races. A very ordinary event run at a modest pace. Last year's edition was won by Home Run, who has made great strides since. A step up from the winner and the second is on the upgrade.

2921 FOOT ANSTEY H'CAP HURDLE (8 hdls) 2m 1f
12:55 (12:55) (Class 4) (0-105,106) 4-Y-0+ **£3,249** (£954; £477; £238)

Form RPR

11- **1** **Portway Flyer (IRE)**[2] 2891 5-11-12 **106** 7ex................ GavinSheehan[(3)] 124+
(Ian Williams) *trckd ldrs: hmpd by loose horse after 1st: wnt 2nd after 5th: rdn to ld after 3 out: sn in command: kpt on strly* **1/2**[1]

6/1- **2** *5* **Pass Muster**[7] 2794 6-10-12 **94** 7ex................................ AdamNicol[(5)] 106
(Philip Kirby) *prom: led 2nd: rdn whn hdd after 3 out: styd on same pce* **2/1**[2]

500- **3** *7* **Bedouin Bay**[12] 2696 6-11-0 **98**.. JonPark[(7)] 104
(Johnny Farrelly) *hld up bhd ldrs: hdwy into 3rd after 5th: rdn whn hit 3 out: styd on same pce fr next* **40/1**

4 *30* **Railway Vic (IRE)**[174] 6-11-4 **95**.. HaddenFrost 74
(James Frost) *trckd ldrs: nudged along whn slow 4th: wnt 4th but no ch w ldrs whn outpcd bef 3 out* **33/1**

604- **5** *3 ½* **Arguidos (IRE)**[17] 2571 9-10-4 **86**........................(t) AodhaganConlon[(5)] 62
(Debra Hamer) *sn pushed along: led tl 2nd: chsd ldr tl rdn after 5th: wknd next* **50/1**

02F- **U** **Pagham Belle**[20] 2511 5-10-4 **84**....................................(t) MarkQuinlan[(3)]
(Nigel Hawke) *prom whn blnd and uns rdr 1st* **16/1**[3]

4m 10.0s (-5.50) **Going Correction** -0.45s/f (Good) **6** Ran SP% **113.2**
Speed ratings (Par 105): **94,91,88,74,72**
toteswingers 1&2 £1.02, 1&3 £5.80, 2&3 £6.10 CSF £1.99 TOTE £1.60: £1.10, £1.40; EX 1.90 Trifecta £10.50 Pool: £2,041.35 - 145.61 winning units..
Owner Patrick Kelly **Bred** DDE Syndicate **Trained** Portway, Worcs

FOCUS
An interesting clash between two recent winners who were both a long way ahead of the handicapper. Both are rated a bit below their best.

2922 HARRY DUTFIELD MEMORIAL NOVICES' CHASE (14 fncs 1 omitted) 2m 3f 110y
1:30 (1:31) (Class 2) 4-Y-0+ **£12,974** (£4,158; £2,310)

Form				RPR
2/2-	1		**Caid Du Berlais (FR)**[35] 2206 4-10-7 0 NickScholfield (Paul Nicholls) *j.w: mde all: clr after 11th: easily* **4/11**[1]	132+
P00/	2	13	**Farmer Matt (IRE)**[251] 5013 7-11-0 114 (t) PaddyBrennan (Fergal O'Brien) *trckd ldrs: nudged along fr 9th: rdn after 11th: wnt 2nd sn after 3 out (usual 4 out): kpt on but no ch w easy wnr* **8/1**[3]	111
P/4-	3	9	**Pistol (IRE)**[35] 1866 4-10-7 130 (b[1]) TomO'Brien (Philip Hobbs) *trckd wnr: rdn after 10th: hld in disp 2nd whn blnd 3 out (usual 4 out): one pce after* **4/1**[2]	99
/U5-	P		**Salut L'As (FR)**[30] 2289 7-11-0 87 JamesBest (Sue Gardner) *hld up: lft in 4th at 2nd: nt fluent 5th (water): awkward next: struggling fr 9th: wknd after 11th: t.o whn p.u after 2 out* **100/1**	
053-	U		**Nail 'M (IRE)**[15] 2616 5-11-0 105 MarkQuinlan (Nigel Hawke) *blnd v bdly and uns rdr 2nd* **16/1**	

4m 47.2s (-10.10) **Going Correction** -0.45s/f (Good)
WFA 4 from 5yo+ 5lb **5** Ran SP% **111.3**
Speed ratings (Par 109): **102,96,93, ,**
CSF £4.26 TOTE £1.40: £1.10, £2.70; EX 4.00 Trifecta £8.80 Pool: £3,020.18 - 256.87 winning units.
Owner Donlon, Doyle, MacDonald & C Barber **Bred** Jean-Marc Lucas **Trained** Ditcheat, Somerset

FOCUS
The third-last fence was bypassed. A disappointing turnout for the generous prize money on offer, but it's a race that has thrown up some very useful winners over the years and the winner is another who fits that description. He has the potential to rated 140+ over fences.

2923 DEVON MARATHON H'CAP CHASE (22 fncs) 4m
2:05 (2:05) (Class 3) (0-125,125) 4-Y-0+
£12,512 (£3,696; £1,848; £924; £462; £232)

Form				RPR
5F0-	1		**Major Malarkey (IRE)**[21] 2487 10-11-5 118 (v[1]) SamTwiston-Davies (Nigel Twiston-Davies) *mid-div: trckd ldrs 9th: led appr 4 out: rdn and hdd 3 out: rallied to chal appr last: led run-in: drvn out* **10/1**	130+
232-	2	1 ¼	**Whistling Senator (IRE)**[30] 2297 6-11-4 117 (v) RichieMcLernon (Jonjo O'Neill) *mid-div: trckd ldrs after 6th: rdn to ld 3 out: narrow advantage last: sn hdd: no ex* **15/2**	127
221-	3	½	**Jayandbee (IRE)**[22] 2468 6-10-7 106 (p) TomO'Brien (Philip Hobbs) *mid-div: nt fluent 2nd: pushed along fr 13th: hdwy after 17th: rdn in cl 4th bef 4 out: styd on to hold ch last: no ex run-in* **9/2**[1]	116
/04-	4	15	**Alderluck (IRE)**[19] 2537 10-11-4 124 (b) MikeyEnnis[(7)] (David Pipe) *hld up towards rr: stdy prog fr 16th: rdn in 5th appr 4 out: nvr got on terms w ldrs: wnt hld 4th 3 out* **9/1**	120
P/U-	5	44	**Jolly Boys Outing (IRE)**[12] 2700 10-9-9 99 oh1 BenPoste[(5)] (Rosemary Gasson) *a in rr: t.o fr 16th* **33/1**	55
534-	6	shd	**Incentivise (IRE)**[13] 2670 10-11-1 117 JakeGreenall[(3)] (Richard Lee) *a towards rr: struggling 15th: wknd after 17th: t.o* **11/1**	73
/U4-	P		**Ballypatrick (IRE)**[14] 2646 7-11-11 124 DominicElsworth (Mick Channon) *hld up towards rr: pushed along in midfield fr 12th: wknd after 17th: t.o whn p.u bef 4 out* **7/1**[3]	
P20-	U		**Qianshan Leader (IRE)**[12] 2693 9-11-12 125 (v) LeightonAspell (Emma Lavelle) *led 3rd: awkward next: nt fluent 14th: rdn and hdd bef 4 out: grad fdd: stmbld 3 out: tired in 5th whn stmbld bdly and uns rdr last* **18/1**	83
234-	P		**Double Chocolate**[19] 2540 10-9-12 100 JamesBest[(3)] (John O'Shea) *trckd ldrs: rdn and losing pl whn nt fluent 16th: sn wknd: t.o whn p.u bef 4 out* **12/1**	
235-	P		**Civil Disobedience**[13] 2662 9-11-2 115 ConorO'Farrell (Richard Woollacott) *a in last pair: struggling 12th: lost tch fr 15th: t.o whn p.u bef 4 out* **17/2**	
U44-	P		**Rhum (FR)**[13] 2678 8-10-11 117 (vt) RyanHatch[(7)] (Nigel Twiston-Davies) *trckd ldrs: grad lost pl fr 14th: wknd 17th: t.o whn p.u bef 4 out* **16/1**	
065-	P		**River D'Or (FR)**[30] 2290 8-10-1 100 oh3 ow1 PaulMoloney (Sophie Leech) *led tl 3rd: trckd ldrs: losing pl whn reminders after 10th: sn towards rr: t.o whn p.u bef 3 out* **11/2**[2]	

8m 9.3s (-19.40) **Going Correction** -0.45s/f (Good) course record **12** Ran SP% **117.6**
Speed ratings (Par 107): **106,105,105,101,90 90, , , ,**
toteswingers 1&2 £26.90, 1&3 £16.70, 2&3 £2.60 CSF £83.17 CT £389.71 TOTE £11.30: £3.70, £1.60, £2.30; EX 69.50 Trifecta £474.70 Pool: £1,516.24 - 2.39 winning units.
Owner Baker Dodd & Cooke **Bred** Bill Ronayne **Trained** Naunton, Gloucs

FOCUS
A fair long-distance handicap chase, and a proper test at the trip. Only five were still in contention over the last half-dozen fences. The winner is rated back to something like her best.

2924 EBF STALLIONS "NATIONAL HUNT" NOVICES' HURDLE (QUALIFIER) (8 hdls) 2m 1f
2:40 (2:40) (Class 4) 4-6-Y-0 **£3,249** (£954; £477; £238)

Form				RPR
16-	1		**Prideofthecastle (IRE)**[29] 2316 6-10-12 0 TomScudamore (David Pipe) *mde all: rdn whn chal 3 out: hit last: r.o wl to assert run-in: rdn out* **6/4**[2]	111+
341/	2	1 ½	**Steel City**[253] 4982 5-10-12 0 RyanMahon (Seamus Mullins) *trckd ldrs: bmpd 1st: rdn after 3 out: styd on to have ev ch last: kpt on but nt pce of wnr* **5/1**[3]	110+
411/	3	3 ¾	**Foggy's Wall (IRE)**[236] 5323 5-10-12 0 NickScholfield (Paul Nicholls) *trckd wnr: racd keenly: chal 3 out: wnt lft and nt fluent 2 out: sn rdn and hld: kpt on same pce* **10/11**[1]	107+
6/0-	4	¾	**Dan's Wee Man**[32] 2265 4-10-7 0 JamesBanks[(5)] (Andy Turnell) *trckd ldrs: wnt lft 1st: hit 4th: pushed along fr next: rdn bef 3 out: kpt on but nt pce to chal* **50/1**	105

4m 11.7s (-3.80) **Going Correction** -0.45s/f (Good)
WFA 4 from 5yo+ 5lb **4** Ran SP% **111.0**
Speed ratings: **90,89,87,87**
CSF £8.65 TOTE £2.30; EX 7.60 Trifecta £12.80 Pool: £1,775.25 - 103.49 winning units.
Owner Bryan Drew **Bred** Patrick Cronin **Trained** Nicholashayne, Devon

FOCUS
This cut up badly from an entry of 30. It was run at a dawdle, so the form should not be taken at face value. The first three can all do better on their bumper form.

2925 BREWIN DOLPHIN TROPHY H'CAP CHASE (15 fncs) 2m 3f 110y
3:15 (3:15) (Class 3) (0-140,137) 4-Y-0+
£15,640 (£4,620; £2,310; £1,155; £577; £290)

Form				RPR
102-	1		**Bally Legend**[11] 2714 8-11-9 134 IanPopham (Caroline Keevil) *mde all: pushed along bef 4 out: nt fluent 3 out: sn rdn: hrd pressed 2 out: bttr jump last: hld on: all out* **2/1**[1]	143+
5/5-	2	nk	**Domtaline (FR)**[27] 2365 6-11-7 137 HarryDerham[(5)] (Paul Nicholls) *trckd ldrs: nt fluent 2nd: mounting chal whn pckd sltly 2 out: sn rdn: ch whn got tight to last: swtchd rt and kpt on towards fin: jst being hld* **3/1**[2]	146+
/22-	3	¾	**Bertie Boru (IRE)**[22] 2475 6-10-10 121 TomO'Brien (Philip Hobbs) *hld up: looked to be struggling to hold pl 8th: hdwy into 4th appr 4 out: rdn whn hit 3 out: r.o wl fr last but a being hld* **8/1**	129+
/13-	4	2 ¼	**Jump City (FR)**[11] 2714 7-11-7 132 (b) NickScholfield (Paul Nicholls) *trckd ldrs: prom after 4th tl rdn after 4 out: kpt on same pce fr next* **11/2**	137
60P-	5	17	**Falcon Island**[41] 2072 8-11-5 130 JoeTizzard (Colin Tizzard) *disp ld tl 5th: trckd ldrs: pushed along fr 10th: rdn bef 4 out: sn one pce: wknd after 2 out* **25/1**	119
/20-	6	¾	**Tara Rose**[27] 2371 8-11-1 126 SamTwiston-Davies (Nigel Twiston-Davies) *hld up bhd ldrs: rdn appr 4 out: sn one pce: wknd after 2 out* **5/1**[3]	114
P54-	7	47	**Cornas (NZ)**[41] 2081 11-11-7 132 LeightonAspell (Nick Williams) *reluctant to go to s: prom: pushed along to chse ldrs after 11th: fdd fr 4 out: virtually p.u flat* **14/1**	78

4m 43.9s (-13.40) **Going Correction** -0.45s/f (Good) **7** Ran SP% **112.0**
Speed ratings (Par 107): **108,107,107,106,99 99,80**
toteswingers 1&2 £1.90, 1&3 £3.30, 2&3 £4.90 CSF £8.44 TOTE £2.90: £1.40, £2.70; EX 10.60 Trifecta £48.50 Pool: £4,398.02 - 67.88 winning units.
Owner Brian Derrick **Bred** V Thorne, B Derrick And P R Rodford **Trained** Motcombe, Dorset

FOCUS
Quite a valuable race, and sound handicap chase form. The first two are rated to their best.

2926 BILL BRENNAN IS 80 "JUNIOR" STANDARD OPEN NATIONAL HUNT FLAT RACE 1m 5f
3:45 (3:45) (Class 6) 3-Y-0 **£1,624** (£477; £238; £119)

Form				RPR
	1		**Adeupas D'Ycy (FR)**[91] 3-10-12 0 DavidBass (Nicky Henderson) *trckd ldrs: pushed along over 2f out: squeezed up inner to ld ins fnl f: r.o: shade cosily* **10/11**[1]	103+
2-	2	1 ¼	**Flamenco Lad**[45] 2015 3-10-12 0 HaddenFrost (Martin Hill) *racd keenly: led after 2f: pushed along over 1f out: hdd ins fnl f: kpt on but no ex* **14/1**	98
	3	5	**Kingfisher Creek** 3-10-12 0 JoeTizzard (Colin Tizzard) *trckd ldrs: rdn to chal over 2f out: kpt on same pce fr over 1f out* **12/1**	92
	4	6	**Sea Tiger** 3-10-12 0 RobertThornton (Alan King) *in tch: rdn over 2f out: kpt on same pce* **15/2**[3]	84
	5	1	**Alto Des Mottes (FR)**[187] 3-11-0 HarryDerham[(5)] (Paul Nicholls) *in tch: rdn to chse ldrs over 2f out: nt quite pce to mount chal: no ex fnl f* **3/1**[2]	89
3-	6	3 ¼	**Kibo**[24] 2436 3-10-12 0 NickScholfield (Kim Bailey) *led for 2f: trckd ldr: rdn over 2f out: wknd fnl f* **16/1**	78
	7	5	**L Stig** 3-10-9 0 JakeGreenall[(3)] (Henry Daly) *hld up but wl in tch: rdn over 2f out: nt pce to get on terms: wknd ent fnl f* **16/1**	72

3m 8.0s (-8.70) **7** Ran SP% **115.3**
toteswingers 1&2 £4.20, 1&3 £5.00, 2&3 £11.70 CSF £16.42 TOTE £1.80: £1.30, £5.50; EX 16.10 Trifecta £88.60 Pool: £3,631.72 - 30.71 winning units.
Owner Simon Munir & Isaac Souede **Bred** Mlle Anne Vallee **Trained** Upper Lambourn, Berks

FOCUS
There was no pace on in this fair juvenile bumper and it became a sprint up the home straight. The winner could be decent.
T/Plt: £54.90 to a £1 stake. Pool: £50,484.13 - 671.05 winning units T/Qpdt: £13.20 to a £1 stake. Pool: £3,836.10 - 213.50 winning units TM

2362 SANDOWN (R-H)
Friday, December 6

OFFICIAL GOING: Chase course - good (good to soft in places; 7.2) hurdle course - good to soft (good in places in back straight; 6.8)
Wind: Brisk; half against Weather: Fine; crisp

2927 HEADMASTERS JUVENILE HURDLE (8 hdls) 2m 110y
12:35 (12:35) (Class 3) 3-Y-0 **£6,498** (£1,908; £954; £477)

Form				RPR
1-	1		**Violet Dancer**[32] 2276 3-11-4 0 JamieMoore (Gary Moore) *ath: lw: t.k.h: hld up tl trckd ldrs after 3 out: chal and pckd 2 out: led last: drvn clr* **9/4**[2]	124+
331-	2	4	**Sleepy Haven (IRE)**[23] 2455 3-11-4 114 SeanQuinlan (Jennie Candlish) *prom: trckd ldr 3rd: led 2 out but hrd pressed: hdd last: one pce flat* **20/1**	112
25-	3	1 ¾	**Abracadabra Sivola (FR)**[20] 2500 3-10-12 0 RichardJohnson (Nick Williams) *led 2nd: mde most after tl rdn and hdd 2 out: nt qckn bef last: kpt on flat* **3/1**[3]	105
	4	4 ½	**Sweet Deal (IRE)**[50] 3-10-12 0 BarryGeraghty (Nicky Henderson) *lw: hld up: trckd ldrs 3 out: rdn bef next: no imp after 2 out: one pce* **6/4**[1]	102+
412-	5	2	**Sirop De Menthe (FR)**[126] 1182 3-11-4 119 WillKennedy (Miss Jessica Westwood) *cl up: rdn and outpcd bef 2 out: plugged on fr last* **16/1**	104
4-	6	16	**Mandy's Boy (IRE)**[9] 2750 3-10-12 0 JasonMaguire (Ian Williams) *in tch: disp 2nd pl fr 4th tl wknd qckly jst bef 2 out* **14/1**	82
	7	6	**Classic Art**[159] 3-10-12 0 ColinBolger (Roger Teal) *hld up in detached last: nt fluent 3rd: in tch after 3 out: sn rdn and btn: blnd last* **100/1**	79

The Form Book Jumps, Raceform Ltd, Compton, RG20 6NL.

002- P Dude Alert (IRE)[27] 2364 3-10-12 98 .... AdamWedge
(Anna Newton-Smith) *led to 2nd: mstkes 3rd and 4th: wknd qckly: t.o whn p.u bef 2 out* **66/1**

4m 1.2s (-6.00) **Going Correction** -0.325s/f (Good) 8 Ran SP% **115.6**
Speed ratings (Par 106): **101,99,98,96,95 87,84,**
toteswingers 1&2 £3.50, 1&3 £2.20, 2&3 £8.60 CSF £37.87 TOTE £3.60: £1.10, £4.50, £1.30; EX 27.90 Trifecta £130.80 Pool: £1,982.62 - 11.36 winning units.
Owner D Bessell & Galloping On The South Downs **Bred** Jeremy Hinds **Trained** Lower Beeding, W Sussex

FOCUS
They went a fair enough gallop in this fair 3yo event and they got sorted out from the penultimate flight. The winner looked to have a bit in hand and rates a decent propsect.

2928 CLOSE BROTHERS PROPERTY FINANCE NOVICES' LIMITED H'CAP CHASE (17 fncs) 2m 4f 110y

1:10 (1:10) (Class 3) (0-125,125) 4-Y-0+ **£6,498** (£1,908; £954; £477)

Form				RPR
/22-	1		**The Italian Yob (IRE)**[23] 2460 5-11-5 **125** .... DarylJacob (Nick Williams) *lw: mde most and j. proficiently: narrowly hdd 3 out: shkn up to ld again last: drvn and styd on wl* **11/4**[1]	139+
125-	2	2 1/4	**Roger Beantown (IRE)**[30] 2287 8-11-3 **123** ....(p) DaveCrosse (Zoe Davison) *trckd ldrs: wnt 2nd 12th: narrow ld 3 out gng strly: rdn and hdd last: kpt on same pce flat* **20/1**	133
/21-	3	12	**Foundation Man (IRE)**[32] 2270 6-11-0 **120** .... APMcCoy (Jonjo O'Neill) *lw: w wnr to 6th: pushed along 8th: lost 2nd 11th: lost pl 3 out: n.d after: kpt on to take modest 3rd last* **11/4**[1]	121
1/2-	4	2 1/2	**Royal Guardsman (IRE)**[24] 2434 6-11-4 **124** .... NoelFehily (Ali Brewer) *hld up: nt fluent 6th: prog 11th: chsd ldng pair 3 out: abt 3 l down and gng wl enough whn nt fluent 2 out and slithered on landing: lost all ch* **17/2**	126+
223-	5	4 1/2	**Silver Commander**[40] 2107 6-11-3 **123** ....(t) JackDoyle (Victor Dartnall) *prom: nt fluent 9th: chsd wnr 11th tl blnd next: in tch 3 out: sn btn* **6/1**[2]	118
3/2-	6	1 1/2	**Ballincurrig (IRE)**[13] 2676 7-10-2 **113** ....(t) MissGAndrews[(5)] (Dan Skelton) *lw: hld up in last: stmbld bdly 1st: prog after 14th: brought wdst of all and tried to cl on ldrs 3 out: outpcd but disp 3rd after 2 out: wknd* **8/1**	108+
213/	7	11	**Miss Ballantyne**[234] 5339 6-11-1 **121** .... BarryGeraghty (Nicky Henderson) *in tch: rdn whn mstker 14th: sn struggling: tried to rally 3 out: wknd after* **13/2**[3]	104
0/4-	8	1/2	**Xaarcet (IRE)**[26] 2389 6-10-12 **118** .... BrendanPowell (Colin Tizzard) *often nt fluent: in tch: rdn and struggling fr 12th: no ch after 3 out* **20/1**	100
1/5-	9	7	**Doctor Foxtrot (IRE)**[27] 2362 8-11-1 **121** ....(b) RichardJohnson (Philip Hobbs) *in tch: nt fluent 8th: sn dropped to last and struggling: nvr a factor after* **16/1**	101

5m 7.9s (-10.50) **Going Correction** -0.325s/f (Good) 9 Ran SP% **118.0**
Speed ratings (Par 107): **107,106,101,100,98 98,94,93,91**
toteswingers 1&2 £11.90, 1&3 £3.10, 2&3 £15.50 CSF £51.87 CT £163.03 TOTE £3.70: £1.50, £3.80, £1.50; EX 58.50 Trifecta £230.00 Pool: £2,739.30 - 8.93 winning units.
Owner The Macaroni Beach Society **Bred** John Sweeney **Trained** George Nympton, Devon

FOCUS
Not a bad novice handicap for the grade and the first pair dominated from three out. Sound form, with the winner on the upgrade.

2929 NEPTUNE INVESTMENT MANAGEMENT NOVICES' HURDLE (REGISTERED AS THE WINTER NOVICES' HURDLE) (GRADE 2) (9 hdls) 2m 4f

1:45 (1:45) (Class 1) 4-Y-0+ **£15,946** (£5,983; £2,996; £1,492; £750)

Form				RPR
110-	1		**Killala Quay**[21] 2490 6-11-4 132 .... RichardJohnson (Charlie Longsdon) *lw: trckd ldng trio: rdn to chal whn mstke 2 out: swtchd lft after: rallied and best jump last: sn led and drvn out* **5/1**	147+
6/1-	2	2 1/2	**Beat That (IRE)**[14] 2642 5-11-7 0 .... BarryGeraghty (Nicky Henderson) *lw: trckd ldng pair: gng best whn led narrowly 2 out: sn rdn: mstke last and immediately hdd: kpt on flat* **9/4**[2]	149+
111-	3	6	**Saint Roque (FR)**[49] 1954 7-11-7 146 ....(t) DarylJacob (Paul Nicholls) *led: rdn and narrowly hdd 2 out: stl upsides whn nt fluent last: wknd flat* **5/4**[1]	139
/11-	4	8	**Oscar Fortune (IRE)**[33] 2243 5-11-4 131 .... APMcCoy (Jonjo O'Neill) *trckd ldr: hit 3rd: rdn on long run after 3 out: dropped bk to 4th and wl btn 2 out* **9/2**[3]	129
2-	5	46	**Back In June**[56] 1856 5-11-0 0 .... NoelFehily (Paul Henderson) *a last: lost tch 4th: sn t.o* **100/1**	84

4m 58.2s (-1.40) **Going Correction** -0.325s/f (Good) 5 Ran SP% **111.1**
Speed ratings (Par 115): **89,88,85,82,64**
CSF £16.93 TOTE £6.70: £2.50, £2.20; EX 18.40 Trifecta £29.60 Pool: £4,051.83 - 102.42 winning units.
Owner Richard & Mrs Susan Perkins **Bred** N Franklin **Trained** Over Norton, Oxon

FOCUS
A Grade 2 novice hurdle with a rich tradition. It proved a tactical affair this year and saw changing fortunes up the home straight. Big steps up from the first two, and there's a case for rating the form up to 7lb higher through the third.

2930 FUTURE STARS CHASE (INTERMEDIATE RACE) (LISTED RACE) (22 fncs) 3m 110y

2:20 (2:20) (Class 1) 4-Y-0+ **£17,085** (£6,411; £3,210)

Form				RPR
/UF-	1		**Vino Griego (FR)**[20] 2503 8-11-7 149 ....(v) JamieMoore (Gary Moore) *mstke 1st: hld up in last: mostly trckd ldr fr 15th: mstke 3 out: clsd to ld last: drvn and bounded clr* **9/1**[3]	158+
2/1-	2	7	**Rolling Aces (IRE)**[34] 2235 7-11-11 156 .... DarylJacob (Paul Nicholls) *j. bttr than rivals: led: 3 l clr after 2 out and rdn: hdd last: easily outpcd* **8/13**[1]	153
B/1-	3	7	**Harry Topper**[34] 2229 6-11-11 153 .... JasonMaguire (Kim Bailey) *lw: pressed ldr: several ponderous jumps fr 1/2-way: dropped to last and urged along 15th: drvn after 4 out: lft bhd fr next* **15/8**[2]	150+

6m 15.95s (-11.85) **Going Correction** -0.325s/f (Good) 3 Ran SP% **106.7**
Speed ratings (Par 111): **105,102,100**
CSF £15.23 TOTE £5.60; EX 12.40 Trifecta £6.50 Pool: £3,279.10 - 373.98 winning units.
Owner C E Stedman **Bred** Francis Montauban **Trained** Lower Beeding, W Sussex

FOCUS
A tight affair, run at a sound gallop. Vino Griego had a big chance at the weights on his form over shorter.

2931 COLDUNELL AMATEUR JOCKEYS ASSOCIATION AMATEUR RIDERS' H'CAP CHASE (JOHN DUNSDON MEMORIAL CUP) (22 fncs) 3m 110y

2:55 (2:55) (Class 3) (0-130,130) 4-Y-0+ **£7,486** (£2,322; £1,160; £580)

Form				RPR
/11-	1		**Fine Parchment (IRE)**[27] 2367 10-11-7 **130** ....(tp) MrHAABannister[(5)] (Charlie Mann) *j.w: mde virtually all: set mod pce: dashed for home fr 3 out: jnd last: urged along and battled on wl to hold narrow advantage flat* **10/1**	137+
130-	2	nk	**Merrion Square (IRE)**[55] 1868 7-11-6 **129** ....(t) MrADoyle[(5)] (Paul Nicholls) *hld up in midfield: nt fluent 14th: prog after 3 out to chse wnr after 2 out: upsides last: r.o flat but couldn't get past* **13/2**[3]	137+
0F1-	3	6	**Coole River (IRE)**[22] 2475 9-11-10 **128** .... MrBO'Neill (Emma Lavelle) *lw: mostly trckd wnr: mstke 13th: wl plcd whn sprint sed after 3 out: cl enough last: fdd flat but hld on for 3rd* **10/3**[2]	131+
4/0-	4	1/2	**Monkerty Tunkerty**[159] 851 10-11-5 **130** .... MrCGethings[(7)] (Miss Jessica Westwood) *mostly trckd wnr: outpcd whn sprint for home sed after 3 out: plugged on flat* **15/2**	130
/41-	5	1/2	**Top Dancer (FR)**[8] 2754 6-11-3 **121** 7ex .... MrJJCodd (Warren Greatrex) *lw: nt a fluent: hld up in tch: nt wl plcd on inner whn dash for home sed after 3 out: sn outpcd: plugged on flat* **15/8**[1]	124+
/4P-	6	1 1/4	**Savant Bleu (FR)**[40] 2108 7-11-6 **127** .... MrFMitchell[(3)] (Kim Bailey) *trckd ldrs: in tch after 3 out: awkward next and outpcd: plugged on flat* **16/1**	126
4/0-	7	1/2	**Wood Yer (IRE)**[23] 2458 7-10-1 **112** ....(tp) MrJBargary[(7)] (Nigel Twiston-Davies) *mstkes: hld up in rr: rdn bef 3 out: outpcd sn after it* **12/1**	111
/65-	F		**Milarrow (IRE)**[8] 2754 6-10-6 **115** ....(p) MrMLegg[(5)] (Colin Tizzard) *many sloppy jumps in rr: last but in tch though r yet to s in earnest whn fell 18th* **12/1**	

6m 35.8s (8.00) **Going Correction** -0.325s/f (Good) 8 Ran SP% **113.3**
Speed ratings (Par 107): **74,73,71,71,71 71,71,**
toteswingers 1&2 £6.50, 1&3 £5.30, 2&3 £6.50 CSF £70.79 CT £263.51 TOTE £7.50: £2.40, £1.90, £1.80; EX 31.60 Trifecta £220.50 Pool: £4,687.98 - 15.93 winning units.
Owner N W A Bannister **Bred** Timothy Considine **Trained** Upper Lambourn, Berks

FOCUS
This competitive handicap, confined to amateur riders, was a steadily run affair and it turned into a dash for home around the third-last. Not a race to take too seriously.

2932 S CREATIVE PR AND TALENT MANAGEMENT NOVICES' H'CAP HURDLE (GRASSROOTS JUMPS SERIES QUALIFIER) (8 hdls) 2m 110y

3:25 (3:26) (Class 4) (0-120,120) 3-Y-0+ **£6,498** (£1,908; £954; £477)

Form				RPR
620/	1		**Lord Protector (IRE)**[248] 5103 6-11-2 **110** .... RichardJohnson (Philip Hobbs) *hld up towards rr: blnd 2nd: prog fr 4th to trck ldrs 3 out: rdn to ld 2 out: drvn and hld on wl flat* **5/1**[2]	118+
4/1-	2	1	**Uhlan Bute (FR)**[206] 290 5-11-12 **120** .... AidanColeman (Venetia Williams) *hld up wl in rr: gd prog fr 3 out to chse ldrs next: clsng whn nt fluent last: styd on to take 2nd flat: a jst hld* **20/1**	127+
442-	3	1 1/2	**Reverb**[15] 2614 4-11-4 **112** .... BarryGeraghty (Nicky Henderson) *lw: mstke 1st: prom: drvn to try to chal bef 2 out: chsd wnr after: hld and lost 2nd after last: kpt on* **11/2**[3]	117
/23-	4	4 1/2	**No No Mac (IRE)**[34] 2215 4-11-12 **120** .... NoelFehily (Charlie Longsdon) *lw: trckd ldrs: rdn and n.m.r after 3 out: no imp whn mstke 2 out: kpt on after to take 4th nr fin* **8/1**	121
245-	5	1/2	**Refer**[22] 2466 3-10-1 **112** ....(p) KielanWoods[(3)] (Phil Middleton) *settled in midfield: rdn and prog to chse ldrs after 3 out: no imp u.p 2 out: kpt on fr last* **25/1**	100
/41-	6	2 1/4	**My Guardian Angel**[11] 2718 4-11-6 **114** 7ex .... ColinBolger (Mark H Tompkins) *mde most at str pce: drvn and hdd 2 out: btn whn nt fluent last: wknd* **14/1**	115+
111-	7	hd	**Proud Times (USA)**[8] 2770 7-10-13 **107** 7ex ....(p) JackDoyle (Ali Brewer) *w ldr after 2nd: nt fluent 5th: lost pl and btn whn mstke 2 out: fdd* **9/2**[1]	107+
330-	8	9	**Apollo Eleven (IRE)**[34] 2217 4-11-4 **112** .... JasonMaguire (Donald McCain) *in tch in midfield: lost pl and wl in rr 3 out: rdn and sme prog after: no hdwy 2 out* **16/1**	102
301-	9	2 1/2	**Neston Grace**[12] 2695 5-11-3 **111** 7ex .... JamesDavies (Simon Hodgson) *mstke 1st: in rr whn mstke 3rd: drvn and struggling 3 out: nvr on terms after* **20/1**	100
341-	10	2 1/4	**Keychain (IRE)**[17] 2577 3-10-6 **114** .... BrendanPowell (Brendan Powell) *in tch in midfield: rdn to chse ldrs after 3 out: no imp bef next: wl btn whn mstke last* **25/1**	86
4/	11	2	**Admiral Hawke (IRE)**[110] 1308 7-11-6 **114** .... DougieCostello (Brian Ellison) *mstke 1st: in tch in midfield: pushed along and no prog after 3 out: wl btn next* **8/1**	98
033-	12	3	**Lifetime (IRE)**[20] 2519 5-10-13 **107** .... FelixDeGiles (Brian Ellison) *hld up in last: drvn and struggling after 5th: nvr a factor* **12/1**	88
163-	13	7	**Border Station (IRE)**[22] 2474 7-10-5 **102** .... JoshuaMoore[(3)] (Alison Batchelor) *hld up wl in rr: sme prog fr 3 out: no imp on ldrs 2 out: wknd* **25/1**	77
314-	14	2 3/4	**Imperial Stargazer**[19] 2538 4-11-4 **112** .... MarcGoldstein (Sheena West) *a in rr: wl bhd in last pair after 3 out* **25/1**	86
413-	15	37	**Hanga Roa (IRE)**[43] 2038 3-10-11 **119** .... JamieMoore (Gary Moore) *t.k.h: w ldr tl after 2nd: lost pl fr 4th: wl bhd in last pair after 3 out: t.o and eased* **25/1**	44

3m 59.55s (-7.65) **Going Correction** -0.325s/f (Good)
WFA 3 from 4yo+ 13lb 15 Ran SP% **121.5**
Speed ratings (Par 105): **105,104,103,101,101 100,100,96,94,93 92,91,88,86,69**
toteswingers 1&2 £22.00, 1&3 £8.90, 2&3 £13.50 CSF £103.56 CT £562.55 TOTE £5.10: £2.10, £5.30, £2.80; EX 113.40 Trifecta £1341.20 Pool: £3,683.05 - 2.05 winning units.
Owner Louisville Syndicate **Bred** Joan And John Ronayne **Trained** Withycombe, Somerset

FOCUS
There was no hanging about in this competitive novice handicap and the form looks solid. The first three are all on the upgrade.

T/Jkpt: Not won. T/Plt: £176.30 to a £1 stake. Pool: £80,937.45 - 335.09 winning units T/Qpdt: £69.00 to £1 stake. Pool: £5,552.01 - 59.53 winning units JN

2098 AINTREE (L-H)

Saturday, December 7

OFFICIAL GOING: Mildmay course - good to soft (soft in places); hurdle course - soft (good to soft in places); national course - soft (goingstick: hurdle 5.5, mildmay 5.9, national 5.2)

Wind: Moderate, half-behind.

2933 BETFRED "FUN AND FRIENDLY" MAIDEN HURDLE (9 hdls) 2m 1f

12:00 (12:01) (Class 4) 3-Y-O+ **£5,198** (£1,526; £763; £381)

Form RPR

424- **1** **Splash Of Ginge**[34] 2243 5-11-7 127........................ SamTwiston-Davies 139+
(Nigel Twiston-Davies) *mde all: drew clr appr 2 out: eased down fnl 100yds* **3/1**[3]

2 *20* **Gabrial The Great (IRE)**[70] 4-11-7 0.............................. JasonMaguire 114+
(Donald McCain) *tk str hold: hld up: tk clsr order 4th: wnt 2nd 3 out: sn no ch w wnr* **11/4**[2]

3 *7* **Villoresi (IRE)**[59] 4-11-7 0.. BrianHughes 104
(John Quinn) *chsd ldrs: wnt 2nd briefly appr 3 out: rdn and btn bef 2 out* **4/1**

162- **4** *8* **Regal Diamond (IRE)**[31] 2286 5-11-7 0.............................. TomO'Brien 101
(Peter Bowen) *chsd wnr tl rdn bef 3 out: wknd bef 2 out: 4th and wl btn whn blnd last* **2/1**[1]

5- **5** *25* **Clues And Arrows (IRE)**[25] 2444 5-11-7 0......................... WillKennedy 71
(Jonjo O'Neill) *hld up: pushed along appr 5th: lost tch u.p after next: t.o* **66/1**

15- **6** *29* **Viacometti (FR)**[29] 2354 4-11-7 0...................................... PaddyBrennan 42
(Tom George) *nt fluent: a bhd: lost tch 6th: t.o* **18/1**

0- **F** **Presentings Return (IRE)**[15] 2660 4-11-7 0............... RichieMcLernon
(Jonjo O'Neill) *hld up: fell 1st* **50/1**

4m 25.2s (11.50) **Going Correction** +0.925s/f (Soft) **7** Ran SP% **113.7**
Speed ratings (Par 105): **109,99,96,92,80 67,**
toteswingers 1&2 £3.40, 1&3 £4.30, 2&3 £1.90 CSF £11.88 TOTE £4.40: £1.60, £2.40; EX 16.60 Trifecta £72.30 Pool: £1168.55 - 12.10 winning units..
Owner J D Neild **Bred** Stewart Pike **Trained** Naunton, Gloucs

FOCUS
Inside Rail on National Course (Races 5 &7) moved out. Mildmay Course on outermost line adding 55yds per circuit to race distances. Hurdle course on outermost line with hurdles on outside adding 95yds per circuit to distances. A fair maiden. The winner was back to the level promised by his Chepstow run.

2934 BETFRED "DOUBLE DELIGHT" FILLIES' JUVENILE HURDLE (LISTED RACE) (9 hdls) 2m 1f

12:30 (12:31) (Class 1) 3-Y-O **£11,390** (£4,274; £2,140; £1,066; £536)

Form RPR

1 **Gitane Du Berlais (FR)**[35] 2231 3-11-3 0......................... PaulTownend 130+
(W P Mullins, Ire) *mde all: a travelling strly: drew clr bef 4th: reduced advantage 3 out but stl wl in command: clr again after 2 out: easily* **5/4**[1]

1- **2** *8* **Mystery Drama**[19] 2557 3-10-12 0............................ WayneHutchinson 113
(Alan King) *hld up: wnt 3rd at 3rd: clsd briefly 3 out: rdn to take 2nd 2 out but no imp on wnr: edgd lft u.p whn no ch run-in* **6/4**[2]

2- **3** *8* **Poetic Verse**[19] 2557 3-10-12 0.. BrianHughes 106
(John Quinn) *chsd wnr: clsd briefly 3 out: lost 2nd whn stmbld on landing 2 out: wl btn bef last* **9/2**[3]

3- **4** *36* **Maypole Lass**[19] 2557 3-10-12 0.................................... PaddyBrennan 68
(Renee Robeson) *bhd: outpcd after 6th: nvr on terms* **20/1**

5 *6* **Aminah**[65] 3-10-12 0.. AidanColeman 62
(Venetia Williams) *chsd ldrs: outpcd after 6th: bhd after* **25/1**

4m 24.0s (10.30) **Going Correction** +0.925s/f (Soft) **5** Ran SP% **111.2**
Speed ratings (Par 107): **112,108,104,87,84**
CSF £3.63 TOTE £1.90: £1.30, £1.40; EX 3.80 Trifecta £5.20 Pool: £833.74 - 118.95 winning units..
Owner Simon Munir & Isaac Souede **Bred** J M Lucas, L Collet & C Collet **Trained** Muine Beag, Co Carlow

FOCUS
This Listed event for fillies was run at a strong gallop. The winner was the form pick but this rates a step up.

2935 BETFRED GOALS GALORE H'CAP HURDLE (11 hdls) 2m 4f

1:00 (1:00) (Class 2) 4-Y-O+

£15,640 (£4,620; £2,310; £1,155; £577; £290)

Form RPR

4/2- **1** **Like Minded**[33] 2268 9-11-1 129..(t) HarrySkelton 135+
(Dan Skelton) *hld up in midfield: hdwy gng wl 3 out: rdn to chal appr last: led fnl 110yds: styd on gamely* **12/1**

100- **2** *¾* **Party Rock (IRE)**[14] 2671 6-11-5 140................................ ConorRing[(7)] 145
(Jennie Candlish) *midfield: hdwy appr 3 out: rdn to ld 2 out: hrd pressed last: hdd fnl 110yds: kpt on u.p* **7/1**[3]

P/0- **3** *2* **Clondaw Kaempfer (IRE)**[14] 2671 5-11-7 135............... JasonMaguire 139+
(Donald McCain) *chsd ldrs: lost pl and niggled along 7th: rallied 3 out: chsd ldrs u.p bef last: styd on run-in but unable to chal front two* **7/2**[1]

2/4- **4** *1 ½* **Lieutenant Miller**[20] 2529 7-10-6 120............................ AndrewTinkler 122
(Nicky Henderson) *hld up: pushed along after 8th: hdwy u.p 2 out: styd on run-in: unable to chal* **4/1**[2]

/20- **5** *6* **Lamb Or Cod (IRE)**[21] 2504 6-11-5 133..............................(t) TomO'Brien 130
(Philip Hobbs) *chsd ldr to 2nd: remained prom: outpcd appr 3 out: styd on run-in wout troubling ldrs* **8/1**

1/5- **6** *½* **Sound Investment (IRE)**[16] 2630 5-10-12 126....(t) SamTwiston-Davies 121
(Paul Nicholls) *chsd ldrs: wnt 2nd appr 3 out: rdn and stl ev ch 2 out: kpt on same pce fr bef last* **7/1**[3]

/53- **7** *3 ¾* **Munsaab (IRE)**[20] 2538 7-10-7 124...........................(tp) KielanWoods[(3)] 115
(Charlie Longsdon) *midfield: hdwy appr 8th: ev ch 3 out: rdn bef 2 out: nt qckn appr last: one pce run-in* **14/1**

/12- **8** *5* **Capellanus (IRE)**[29] 2345 7-10-7 128...................... CraigGallagher[(7)] 116
(Brian Ellison) *hld up in rr: blnd 3rd: struggling after 8th: nvr able to trble ldrs* **12/1**

R23- **9** *8* **Bygones Of Brid (IRE)**[14] 2665 10-11-1 129.................(p) BrianHughes 112
(Karen McLintock) *led: mstke and hdd 2 out: wknd last* **25/1**

1/0- **10** *42* **Whisky Yankee (IRE)**[210] 215 6-11-4 132..................... RichieMcLernon 68
(Jonjo O'Neill) *racd keenly: hld up: pushed along after 8th: eased bef last: nvr a threat* **12/1**

213/ **11** *10* **Woodpole Academy (IRE)**[328] 3643 6-11-6 134............ JamesReveley 60
(Philip Kirby) *chsd ldr fr 2nd to 7th: mstke whn losing grnd 8th: wknd after: eased bef last* **25/1**

5m 15.2s (14.50) **Going Correction** +0.925s/f (Soft) **11** Ran SP% **115.8**
Speed ratings (Par 109): **108,107,106,106,103 103,102,100,97,80 76**
toteswingers 1&2 £23.30, 1&3 £6.90, 2&3 £17.40 CSF £92.60 CT £356.83 TOTE £8.80: £2.40, £2.90, £1.50; EX 109.60 Trifecta £576.90 Part won. Pool: £769.25 - 0.15 winning units..
Owner D J Coles **Bred** Ian Low **Trained** Alcester, Warwicks

FOCUS
A competitive handicap, run at a decent gallop and the field got sorted out from the second-last. Solid form, the winner rated in line with his 2012 best.

2936 YOU'LL LOVE A BIT OF BETFRED NOVICES' H'CAP HURDLE (11 hdls) 2m 4f

1:30 (1:30) (Class 3) (0-125,120) 3-Y-O+ **£5,848** (£1,717; £858; £429)

Form RPR

132- **1** **Tantamount**[72] 1664 4-10-12 106.................................... TomScudamore 121+
(Lucinda Russell) *hld up: hdwy appr 3 out: led bef 2 out where mstke: styd on wl to draw clr run-in: comf* **9/1**

/35- **2** *9* **Dundee**[41] 2103 5-11-2 110... WayneHutchinson 113+
(Alan King) *hld up in midfield: hdwy appr 3 out: ev ch 2 out: sn in 2nd: no ch w wnr run-in* **8/1**

331- **3** *1 ¾* **Keel Haul (IRE)**[31] 2292 5-10-5 106......................... ChristopherWard[(7)] 108
(Henry Oliver) *in tch: impr to go prom 6th: led 3 out: hdd bef 2 out where hmpd: kpt on same pce run-in* **3/1**[1]

/25- **4** *nk* **Squire Trelawney**[9] 2755 7-11-1 109..............................(tp) HarrySkelton 110
(Dan Skelton) *hld up: hdwy appr 6th: pushed along to chse ldrs 3 out: one pce fr 2 out* **13/2**

/26- **5** *1 ¼* **Knockraheen (IRE)**[38] 2158 5-11-9 117....................(v[1]) RichieMcLernon 117
(Jonjo O'Neill) *hld up: hdwy to chse ldrs appr 3 out: rdn and no imp bef 2 out: one pce* **6/1**[3]

5/5- **6** *9* **Plus Jamais (FR)**[35] 2218 6-10-11 105.............................. PaddyBrennan 96
(Jim Goldie) *led: hdd 3 out: wknd 2 out* **10/1**

0/1- **7** *9* **Unex Canaletto**[213] 168 4-10-13 107................................. BrianHughes 88
(James Ewart) *chsd ldrs tl wknd after 8th* **12/1**

45F- **8** *17* **Dazinski**[31] 2285 7-11-3 111.. WillKennedy 75
(Sarah-Jayne Davies) *chsd ldrs: wnt prom 4th: rn in snatches fr 6th: rdn and wknd appr 3 out* **18/1**

1/1- **9** *4 ½* **Ivan Boru (IRE)**[25] 2444 5-11-12 120................................. JamesReveley 82
(Keith Reveley) *chsd ldr to 8th: wknd appr 3 out: eased whn wl btn bef last* **9/2**[2]

5m 16.7s (16.00) **Going Correction** +0.925s/f (Soft)
WFA 4 from 5yo+ 6lb **9** Ran SP% **114.0**
Speed ratings (Par 107): **105,101,100,100,100 96,92,86,84**
toteswingers 1&2 £23.30, 1&3 £6.90, 2&3 £17.40 CSF £76.80 CT £267.33 TOTE £8.60: £1.90, £1.90, £2.00; EX 62.30 Trifecta £235.80 Pool: £683.05 - 2.17 winning units..
Owner Mutual Friends **Bred** Juddmonte Farms Ltd **Trained** Arlary, Perth & Kinross

FOCUS
A modest handicap. A big step up from the impressive winner with the next three all close to their marks.

2937 BETFRED BECHER H'CAP CHASE (GRADE 3) (21 fncs) 3m 2f

2:05 (2:05) (Class 1) 6-Y-O+

£84,405 (£31,800; £15,915; £7,950; £3,990; £1,995)

Form RPR

400/ **1** **Chance Du Roy (FR)**[233] 5361 9-10-6 135.......................... TomO'Brien 148+
(Philip Hobbs) *sn trcking ldrs: led 2 out: 3 l down sn after last: drvn rt out* **14/1**

U13/ **2** *1* **Baby Run (FR)**[959] 5443 13-10-7 136..................... SamTwiston-Davies 148+
(Nigel Twiston-Davies) *led: blnd 2nd: blnd 4 out: hdd 2 out: rallied run-in: no ex clsng stages* **12/1**

450- **3** *1 ¾* **Mr Moonshine (IRE)**[14] 2674 9-10-4 133............................. RyanMania 142
(Sue Smith) *chsd ldrs: outpcd between last 2: styd on wl fr elbow* **25/1**

120- **4** *4 ½* **Ballybough Gorta (IRE)**[21] 2502 6-9-11 129..............(p) RobertDunne[(3)] 135
(Peter Bowen) *mid-div: hdwy 12th: chsng ldrs 14th (Foinavon): outpcd after 3 out: styd on appr last* **33/1**

406/ **5** *8* **Swing Bill (FR)**[245] 5177 12-10-11 140............................ ConorO'Farrell 137
(David Pipe) *mid-div: trckd ldrs 5th: 2nd 16th (Valentine's): wknd last* **10/1**[3]

5/0- **6** *3* **On His Own (IRE)**[40] 2142 9-11-1 144............................... PaulTownend 137
(W P Mullins, Ire) *mid-div: lost pl 5th: sn bhd: kpt on fr 3 out: styd on wl run-in: gng on at fin* **7/1**[1]

5/0- **7** *2 ½* **Big Fella Thanks**[35] 2214 11-11-8 151..............................(t) PaddyBrennan 142
(Tom George) *hld up towards rr: stdy hdwy 12th: chsng ldrs 4 out: 4th sn after last: fdd* **25/1**

0/5- **8** *½* **Across The Bay (IRE)**[35] 2228 9-11-3 146.................(tp) JasonMaguire 138
(Donald McCain) *chsd ldrs: outpcd 17th: kpt on fr 2 out* **11/1**

3/0- **9** *½* **Wyck Hill (IRE)**[35] 2214 9-10-11 140................................ AndrewTinkler 131
(David Bridgwater) *mid-div: lost pl and hit 9th: hdwy 3 out: styng on at fin* **12/1**

14P/ **10** *hd* **Rose Of The Moon (IRE)**[269] 4732 8-10-3 135............ JakeGreenall[(3)] 124
(David O'Meara) *rr-div: hdwy 12th: one pce fr 3 out* **11/1**

P/6- **11** *2 ½* **Bennys Mist (IRE)**[37] 2180 7-10-1 130.......................... AidanColeman 119
(Venetia Williams) *mid-div: hdwy 6th: mstke 12th: fdd fr 4 out* **20/1**

U/4- **12** *25* **Roberto Goldback (IRE)**[35] 2214 11-11-8 151.................. DavidBass 112
(Nicky Henderson) *mid-div: lost pl 5th: bhd and drvn 8th: sme hdwy 12th: lost pl 17th: tailed off 2 out* **16/1**

10F- **13** *4* **Gullible Gordon (IRE)**[22] 2491 10-10-6 135..............(vt) DonalDevereux 92
(Peter Bowen) *in rr: bhd and drvn after 7th (water): nvr a factor* **28/1**

/06- **14** *20* **Join Together (IRE)**[34] 2264 8-11-3 146.........................(b[1]) RyanMahon 83
(Paul Nicholls) *chsd ldrs: lost pl bef 12th: bhd fr 4 out: t.o* **16/1**

2/0- **15** *23* **Chartreux (FR)**[80] 1604 8-10-5 134..................................(tp) AlainCawley 48
(Tom George) *chsd ldrs: lost pl after 3rd: bhd fr 14th (Foinavon): t.o* **33/1**

0/1- **16** *26* **Ikorodu Road**[42] 2086 10-10-11 140.................................(p) CharliePoste 28
(Matt Sheppard) *in rr: blnd 5th: sn bhd: t.o 4 out* **33/1**

6F5/ **U** **Sizing Australia (IRE)**[21] 2526 11-10-8 137..........................(p) AELynch
(Henry De Bromhead, Ire) *mid-div: blnd and uns rdr 10th* **22/1**

2/5- **P** **Junior**[168] 448 10-11-12 155...(b) LiamHeard
(David Pipe) *prom: blnd and lost pl 6th (Chair): nt jump wl after and sn lost pl: t.o 10th: p.u bef 13th (Becher's)* **50/1**

235- **F** **Pineau De Re (FR)**[21] 2504 10-10-6 135............................. BrianHughes
(Dr Richard Newland) *in rr: sme hdwy whn fell 8th* **14/1**

4/P- **P** **Bostons Angel (IRE)**[212] 199 9-10-13 142.............(bt) TomScudamore
(David Pipe) *chsd ldrs: lost pl 8th: t.o whn p.u bef 13th (Becher's)* **20/1**

313- **F** **Storm Survivor (IRE)**[56] 1868 7-10-5 134...................(v) RichieMcLernon
(Jonjo O'Neill) *in rr: fell 1st* **12/1**

The Form Book Jumps, Raceform Ltd, Compton, RG20 6NL.

302/ F **Vesper Bell (IRE)**[225] 5560 7-10-13 **142**.................................. DJCasey
(W P Mullins, Ire) *in rr whn fell 1st* **9/1**[2]

6m 56.3s (9.30) **Going Correction** +0.50s/f (Soft) **22** Ran SP% **132.2**
Speed ratings: **105,104,104,102,100 99,98,98,98,98 97,89,88,82,75 67,,,, ,**
CSF £159.72 CT £4189.09 TOTE £19.80: £4.40, £2.90, £6.40, £9.10; EX 271.10 Trifecta £2687.10 Part won. Pool: £3224.62 - 0.10 winning units..
Owner Miss I D Du Pre **Bred** Jean, Raymond And Jean-Claude Campos **Trained** Withycombe, Somerset

■ This race has been promoted to Grade 3 status.
■ Stewards' Enquiry : Sam Twiston-Davies two-day ban: used whip above permitted level (Dec 22,27)

FOCUS
A big field for this year's edition of the Becher Chase. It was run at a sound gallop and racing handily proved to be a big asset as few managed to get in a serious blow. Solid form.

2938 BETFRED GOALS GALORE CHASE (LISTED RACE) (19 fncs) 3m 1f
2:40 (2:40) (Class 1) 4-Y-0+ **£17,386** (£6,712; £3,511; £1,900)

Form RPR
4/3- **1** **Unioniste (FR)**[35] 2229 5-11-6 152............................ SamTwiston-Davies 161+
(Paul Nicholls) *hld up in tch: wnt 2nd 15th: nt fluent 3 out: rdn to ld appr last: drvn out and styd on wl to draw clr run-in* **5/2**[1]
/66- **2** *7* **Wishfull Thinking**[21] 2503 10-11-10 156.....................(t) RichardJohnson 157
(Philip Hobbs) *hld up: hdwy 4th to go prom and jumping wl: led 13th: rdn and hdd appr last: kpt on same pce run-in whn unable to go w wnr* **9/1**[3]
P/P- **3** *18* **Our Mick**[24] 2452 7-11-0 142...(p) JasonMaguire 135
(Donald McCain) *mstkes: led: reminders after 11th: hdd 13th: toiling in 4th bef 4 out: plugged on to take poor 3rd appr last* **14/1**
1/F- **4** *16* **Katenko (FR)**[7] 2815 7-11-6 157....................................... AidanColeman 132
(Venetia Williams) *prom: nt fluent 13th: rdn and outpcd appr 3 out: wknd after 2 out: dropped to rr bef last* **11/4**[2]
0/0- **U** **The Giant Bolster**[14] 2673 8-11-0 159........................... TomScudamore
(David Bridgwater) *chsd ldr to 6th: lost pl 7th: in rr but stl in tch whn blnd and uns rdr 12th* **5/2**[1]
/52- **P** **Wayward Prince**[35] 2229 9-11-10 155...............................(t) JackDoyle
(Hilary Parrott) *hld up: sprawled on landing 1st: nt fluent 3rd: wl bhd 7th: t.o whn p.u bef 9th* **9/1**[3]

6m 38.4s (8.40) **Going Correction** +0.675s/f (Soft) **6** Ran SP% **110.5**
Speed ratings (Par 111): **113,110,105,99,**
CSF £22.17 TOTE £3.20: £1.90, £2.20; EX 15.20 Trifecta £83.70 Pool: £1361.76 - 12.19 winning units..
Owner J Hales **Bred** Haras De Saint-Voir Et Al **Trained** Ditcheat, Somerset

FOCUS
They went a solid gallop in this decent Listed event and the form ought to work out. A big step up from the winner but he's still 10lb+ off the top level.

2939 BETFRED GRAND SEFTON H'CAP CHASE (18 fncs) 2m 5f 110y
3:15 (3:16) (Class 2) 6-Y-0+
£43,792 (£12,936; £6,468; £3,234; £1,617; £812)

Form RPR
/54- **1** **Rebel Rebellion (IRE)**[28] 2365 8-11-11 **139**...................(tp) RyanMahon 150+
(Paul Nicholls) *sn chsngd ldrs: hung lft and led appr elbow: hld on towards fin* **16/1**
416- **2** *1/2* **Your Busy (IRE)**[42] 2070 10-10-11 **125**..................................(t) DJCasey 132
(J A Nash, Ire) *chsd ldrs: led sn after 3 out: hdd bef next: led last: short of room: hdd and swtchd rt elbow: sn 3 l down: styd on towards fin: jst hld* **33/1**
2P5/ **3** *3 1/4* **You Must Know Me (IRE)**[28] 2379 7-11-10 **138**..................... AELynch 145
(Henry De Bromhead, Ire) *hld up in rr-div: mstke 6th: stdy hdwy 4 out: trcking ldrs gng to 2 out: 4th last: styd on same pce* **14/1**
0/5- **4** *2 1/2* **Gansey (IRE)**[42] 2072 11-11-2 **130**..................................... RyanMania 132
(Sue Smith) *trckd ldrs: led bef 2 out: hdd and outpcd last: kpt on fr elbow* **8/1**[2]
4/2- **5** *14* **Stormin Exit (IRE)**[35] 2222 10-10-8 **122**.......................... JamesReveley 111
(Jim Goldie) *hld up in rr: stdy hdwy 9th: chsng ldrs 3 out: fdd appr next* **10/1**
313- **6** *23* **Current Event (FR)**[43] 2065 6-11-6 **139**.........................(p) MrWBiddick[(5)] 113
(Paul Nicholls) *mid-div: chsng ldrs 8th: wknd appr 2 out* **25/1**
0/4- **7** *1 1/2* **Poole Master**[210] 217 8-11-4 **132**................................. TomScudamore 95
(David Pipe) *prom: outpcd 11th (Foinavon): bhd fr 15th* **10/1**
1/U- **8** *35* **Forgotten Gold (IRE)**[43] 2065 7-11-7 **135**........................ PaddyBrennan 63
(Tom George) *chsd ldrs: wknd 14th t.o 3 out* **10/1**
130- **9** *2 1/2* **Sergeant Pink (IRE)**[14] 2199 7-10-8 **122**.......................... BrianHughes 48
(Dianne Sayer) *nt fluent: mid-div: lost pl 5th: bhd whn mstke 9th: t.o 3 out* **33/1**
/01- **10** *20* **Midnight Appeal**[24] 2452 8-11-11 **139**.....................(b) WayneHutchinson 45
(Alan King) *mstkes: in rr: blnd 5th: hdwy 9th: lost pl and blnd 14th: bhd whn hit next: sn t.o* **9/1**[3]
/41- **F** **Plein Pouvoir (FR)**[28] 2370 10-10-8 **127**...................... HarryChalloner[(5)]
(Venetia Williams) *in rr: mstke 12th (Bechers): bhd fr 13th (Valentines): t.o whn fell 4 out: fatally injured* **12/1**
1/U- **F** **Quincy Des Pictons (FR)**[14] 2674 9-11-12 **140**.................. TomO'Brien
(Alan Jones) *in rr: last whn mstke 6th: bhd whn fell 8th* **33/1**
0/3- **P** **Shangani (USA)**[15] 2656 7-11-9 **137**................................ AidanColeman
(Venetia Williams) *nt fluent towards rr: mstke 5th: bhd fr 7th: t.o whn p.u bef 10th (Bechers)* **11/1**
3/6- **P** **Frontier Spirit (IRE)**[36] 2199 9-11-6 **134**................ SamTwiston-Davies
(Nigel Twiston-Davies) *mid-div: hit 9th: lost pl 11th (Foinavon): bhd 4 out: t.o whn p.u bef 2 out* **16/1**
204/ **P** **Dunowen Point (IRE)**[246] 5160 7-11-10 **138**.................... JasonMaguire
(Donald McCain) *led to 3 out: sn lost pl: t.o whn p.u bef next* **11/2**[1]
411- **F** **Toby Lerone (IRE)**[25] 2438 6-10-10 **124**............................ HarrySkelton
(Dan Skelton) *inn tch: prom whn fell 8th* **8/1**[2]

5m 42.2s (5.20) **Going Correction** +0.50s/f (Soft) **16** Ran SP% **122.0**
Speed ratings: **110,109,108,107,102 94,93,81,80,72 ,,,,**
CSF £462.61 CT £7325.09 TOTE £17.80: £3.50, £6.20, £3.90, £2.20; EX 810.10 Trifecta £13668.70 Pool: £65294.16 - 3.58 winning units..
Owner Mr & Mrs M Woodhouse & Miss R Dobson **Bred** Frances Galloway **Trained** Ditcheat, Somerset

FOCUS
A typically well-contested Grand Sefton. Again it was an advantage to race handily as those held up struggled. A step up from the winner in first-time headgear, with the next two to their marks.
T/Jkpt: Not won. T/Plt: £363.30 to a £1 stake. Pool: £127717.59 - 256.60 winning tickets T/Qpdt: £168.70 to a £1 stake. Pool: £9990.35 - 43.80 winning tickets DO

[2614]CHEPSTOW (L-H)
Saturday, December 7

OFFICIAL GOING: Good to soft (good in places; chs 6.1, hdl 6.8)
Wind: Virtually nil Weather: Overcast

2940 BUILDING MANAGEMENT SOLUTIONS LTD "NATIONAL HUNT" NOVICES' HURDLE (11 hdls) 2m 4f
12:25 (12:26) (Class 4) 4-Y-0+ **£3,119** (£915; £457; £228)

Form RPR
0- **1** **Aubusson (FR)**[126] 1199 4-10-5 0.................................. MissEKelly[(7)] 129+
(Nick Williams) *chsd ldrs: drvn appr 3 out: chsd ldr after 2 out: chal and hit last: sn led: kpt on wl* **33/1**
/2F- **2** *3 1/4* **Carole's Destrier**[19] 2566 5-10-9 0................................ MichaelByrne[(3)] 124+
(Neil Mulholland) *w ldr fr 5th tl led 3 out: rdn 2 out: jnd last: sn hdd and outpcd but wl clr of 3rd* **7/2**[2]
1- **3** *21* **Gunner Fifteen (IRE)**[21] 2513 5-10-12 0.................................. NoelFehily 110+
(Fergal O'Brien) *led and t.k.h: nt fluent 4th: jnd fr 5th: narrowly hdd 3 out: hit 2 out and wknd qckly* **8/11**[1]
213/ **4** *8* **Roudoudou Ville (FR)**[728] 3056 8-10-9 0...................... GilesHawkins[(3)] 99
(Victor Dartnall) *prom: styd on one pce fr 4 out* **12/1**
33/ **5** *hd* **Morito Du Berlais (FR)**[235] 5334 4-10-12 0.................... NickScholfield 100+
(Paul Nicholls) *in tch: pushed along and outpcd 4 out: styd on again appr last* **11/1**[3]
0- **6** *1* **Midnight Thunder (IRE)**[49] 1974 4-10-12 0.......................... JoeTizzard 102+
(Colin Tizzard) *in rr whn blnd 2nd and rdr lost irons tl 4th: hdwy and wl in tch 7th: wknd after 4 out* **12/1**
6- **7** *1* **Twopoundsofbutter (IRE)**[15] 2648 6-10-5 0...................... MrEDavid[(7)] 96
(Tim Vaughan) *in tch: hit 6th: dropped towards rr 4 out: sme prog again appr last* **100/1**
5/ **8** *3 1/4* **Exmoor Mist**[235] 5333 5-10-12 0.. IanPopham 93
(Victor Dartnall) *mid-div: no ch fr 4 out* **33/1**
4- **9** *11* **Tribulation (IRE)**[31] 2286 5-10-12 0.. TomSiddall 83
(Robert Walford) *hit 4th: chsd ldrs to 4 out* **20/1**
0/0- **10** *15* **Pink Gin**[20] 2534 5-10-12 0...(t) RhysFlint 70
(Jim Old) *sn bhd: t.o* **100/1**
2/0- **11** *10* **Be Bop Boru (IRE)**[50] 1958 6-10-5 0.. JPKiely[(7)] 61
(Tim Vaughan) *bhd fr 4 out: t.o* **33/1**
30/ **12** *12* **Zayfire Aramis**[280] 4528 4-10-5 0.. RyanHatch[(7)] 50
(Nigel Twiston-Davies) *hit 3rd: a bhd: t.o* **66/1**
1/0- **13** *5* **Rafafie**[15] 2659 5-10-7 0.. MissLucyGardner[(5)] 45
(Sue Gardner) *j. slowly 1st: a wl bhd: t.o* **66/1**
4- **14** *9* **Queenys King (IRE)**[24] 2456 5-10-12 0.......................(t) TomMessenger 37
(David Dennis) *sn bhd: t.o* **100/1**
4- **P** **Big Night Out**[24] 2463 7-10-5 0.. PaulMoloney
(Nigel Hawke) *in rr: sme hdwy 4th: sn wknd: t.o whn p.u after 4 out* **66/1**

4m 46.6s (-15.20) **Going Correction** -0.475s/f (Good)
WFA 4 from 5yo+ 6lb **15** Ran SP% **124.9**
Speed ratings (Par 105): **111,109,101,98,98 97,97,95,91,85 81,76,74,71,**
toteswingers 1&2 £10.00, 1&3 £14.50, 2&3 £1.40 CSF £149.47 TOTE £32.70: £6.20, £1.50, £1.30; EX 126.20 Trifecta £406.00 Part won. Pool: £541.43 - 0.11 winning units..
Owner Mrs Jane Williams **Bred** Serge Dubois **Trained** George Nympton, Devon

FOCUS
The opening race was a fair novices' hurdle in which they went an even gallop on ground officially described as good to soft, good in places. A race that should produce a few winners.

2941 BETVICTOR NON-RUNNER FREE BET CHELTENHAM 2014 NOVICES' LIMITED H'CAP CHASE (18 fncs) 3m
12:55 (12:57) (Class 3) (0-140,134)
4-Y-0+ **£6,498** (£1,908; £954; £477)

Form RPR
131- **1** **Samingarry (FR)**[13] 2693 6-10-6 **121**.................................... PaulMoloney 133+
(Nigel Hawke) *chsd ldrs tl pushed along and dropped to rr 9th: hdwy and hmpd 14th: sn hanging lft and drvn: styd on wl fr 2 out: kpt on u.p to ld fnl 75yds* **17/2**
516- **2** *1 3/4* **Annacotty (IRE)**[15] 2646 5-11-1 **130**.. IanPopham 140+
(Martin Keighley) *led: jnd fr 5th and nt fluent: narrowly hdd 7th: rdn after 13th: chsng ldr whn lft in ld 14th: jnd fr 3 out tl narrowly hdd last: styd chalng tl outpcd by wnr fnl 75yds* **7/2**[2]
/02- **3** *3 1/4* **Ballytober**[13] 2692 7-10-9 **127**...(t) JamesBest[(3)] 132
(Philip Hobbs) *blnd 2nd: in rr but in tch: hdwy 10th: lft chsng ldr 14th: chal fr 3 out tl slt ld last: sn jnd: wknd into 3rd fnl 75yds* **4/1**[3]
0/4- **4** *9* **Counting House (IRE)**[24] 2459 10-10-10 **125**.......................... RhysFlint 121
(Jim Old) *in rr but in tch: hdwy 12th: wknd 4 out* **25/1**
/FF- **5** *9* **Minella Definitely (IRE)**[19] 2565 6-10-9 **124**.........................(p) NoelFehily 116
(Neil Mulholland) *chsd ldrs: wknd fr 12th* **7/1**
/61- **U** **Midnight Prayer**[37] 2177 8-11-1 **130**.................................. GerardTumelty
(Alan King) *in rr but in tch: hdwy 7th: disputing l 2nd and travelling wl whn mstke 14th: then hmpd and uns rdr sn after* **2/1**[1]
0/U- **P** **Wilton Milan (IRE)**[57] 1858 5-11-5 **134**.............................. NickScholfield
(Paul Nicholls) *chsd ldr: chal 5th tl slt ld 7th: stl 1 l in ld and gng ok whn sprawled bdly 14th: nt rcvr and p.u bef 4 out* **8/1**

6m 3.4s (-18.60) **Going Correction** -0.475s/f (Good) **7** Ran SP% **113.5**
Speed ratings (Par 107): **112,111,110,107,104 ,**
toteswingers 1&2 £10.00, 2&3 £3.80, 1&3 £3.90 CSF £38.30 CT £137.94 TOTE £5.50: £2.10, £2.70; EX 40.40 Trifecta £127.30 Pool: £473.63 - 2.78 winning units..
Owner Pearce Bros 1 **Bred** Isabelle Garcon & Jean-Pierre Garcon **Trained** Stoodleigh, Devon

FOCUS
A quite good staying novices' handicap chase in which they went a decent gallop. A small step up from the winner with the second back to the level of his recent win.

2942 BETVICTOR.COM NOVICES' HURDLE (12 hdls) 3m
1:25 (1:27) (Class 4) 4-Y-0+ **£3,119** (£915; £457; £228)

Form RPR
3/3- **1** **Sausalito Sunrise (IRE)**[20] 2529 5-10-9 120...................... JamesBest[(3)] 126+
(Philip Hobbs) *trckd ldrs: wnt 2nd 4 out: led and hit 2 out: drvn run-in and styd on wl* **8/11**[1]
2/2- **2** *3* **Kris Spin (IRE)**[30] 2316 5-10-12 125.................................... PaulMoloney 121
(Richard Lee) *t.k.h: in tch: j. slowly l7th: hdwy 4 out: outpcd next: j. slowly 2 out and hdwy sn after: styd on to take 2nd fnl 150yds: no imp on wnr* **9/2**[3]
2- **3** *3/4* **Champagne Rian (IRE)**[27] 2386 5-10-7 0.................... PatrickCorbett[(5)] 122
(Rebecca Curtis) *led but pressed to 8th: hdd and hit 2 out: sn no ch w wnr: outpcd into 3rd fnl 150yds* **12/1**

4- **4** *31* **Bob Keown (IRE)**[37] 2181 5-10-12 0 NickScholfield 92
(Rebecca Curtis) *pressed ldr to 8th: wknd bef 4 out* **25/1**

5 *22* **Kaikias (IRE)**[189] 6-10-2 0 TommieMO'Brien(10) 72
(Jonjo O'Neill) *in rr: j. slowly 4th: t.o 7th* **25/1**

0/0- **F** **Milanese (IRE)**[32] 2279 5-10-9 0 MichaelByrne(3) 115
(Emma Lavelle) *blnd 1st: in tch: hdwy 4 out: 3 l 3rd and travelling ok whn fell 3 out* **66/1**

P **Pamplona Run (IRE)**[215] 5-10-12 0 NoelFehily
(Harry Fry) *in tch: hdwy 5th: trcking ldrs whn wknd: p.u and dismntd after 8th* **4/1**[2]

6m 5.44s (3.24) **Going Correction** -0.475s/f (Good) 7 Ran SP% **113.0**
Speed ratings (Par 105): **75,74,73,63,56** ,
toteswingers 1&2 £2.00, 2&3 £4.30, 1&3 £2.90 CSF £4.37 TOTE £1.70: £1.10, £2.60; EX 4.90 Trifecta £12.60 Pool: £813.16 - 48.06 winning units..
Owner Mrs Diana L Whateley **Bred** Thomas Corish **Trained** Withycombe, Somerset

FOCUS
A fair staying novices' hurdle in which they went an, at best, even gallop. The first three are all rated withina a few pounds of their pre-race marks.

2943 RHYS HOWELLS MEMORIAL H'CAP CHASE (18 fncs) 3m
2:00 (2:00) (Class 2) (0-145,145) 4-Y-O+ **£12,996** (£3,816; £1,908; £954)

Form RPR

1/0- **1** **De La Bech**[28] 2373 6-10-2 **124** JamesBest(3) 136
(Philip Hobbs) *led 2nd to 8th: styd chalng tl led again 12th: drvn fr 4 out: styd on wl u.p fr 2 out: r.o gamely clsng stages* **4/1**[2]

/4F- **2** *½* **The Druids Nephew (IRE)**[7] 2812 6-10-8 **132** (p) JamesBanks(5) 143
(Andy Turnell) *t.k.h: chsd ldrs: hit 10th: chsd wnr fr 2 out: kpt on wl u.p run-in: styd on clsng stages but a jst hld* **6/1**

1/3- **3** *6* **Mountainous (IRE)**[24] 2452 8-10-13 **132** NoelFehily 137
(Richard Lee) *in rr: hdwy fr 13th: styd on u.p fr 2 out: tk 3rd nr fin but no ch w ldng duo* **5/2**[1]

12P/ **4** *hd* **Hawkes Point**[269] 4732 8-11-4 **137** NickScholfield 142
(Paul Nicholls) *chsd ldrs: disp 2nd 11th tl chsd wnr 14th: rdn and no imp whn dropped to 3rd 2 out: wknd run-in and dropped to 4th nr fin* **6/1**

4/4- **5** *24* **Triptico (FR)**[36] 2199 7-10-9 **128** PaulMoloney 111
(Evan Williams) *chsd ldrs: hit 11th: mstke and wknd 14th* **9/2**[3]

/0U- **6** *3¼* **Viking Blond (FR)**[22] 2491 8-10-4 **130** RyanHatch(7) 110
(Nigel Twiston-Davies) *led to 2nd: hdd 4th: styd upsides: led 8th but hrd pressed tl hdd 12th: wknd bef 14th* **16/1**

P/5- **P** **Quartz De Thaix (FR)**[24] 2452 9-11-12 **145** LiamTreadwell
(Venetia Williams) *in rr: pushed along and sme hdwy 8th: wknd 10th: blnd 13th: t.o whn p.u bef next* **16/1**

60F- **P** **Havingotascoobydo (IRE)**[2] 2909 8-10-4 **123** TomSiddall
(Martin Keighley) *in rr: hit 3rd: blnd 9th: t.o whn p.u bef 2 out* **20/1**

6m 4.0s (-18.00) **Going Correction** -0.475s/f (Good) 8 Ran SP% **111.9**
Speed ratings (Par 109): **111,110,108,108,100 99**, ,
toteswingers 1&2 £6.70, 2&3 £7.20, 1&3 £2.20 CSF £26.97 CT £69.47 TOTE £5.20: £1.60, £2.30, £1.40; EX 26.00 Trifecta £110.70 Pool: £1137.21 - 7.69 winning units..
Owner B K Peppiatt **Bred** R D M Sharp **Trained** Withycombe, Somerset

FOCUS
A good-quality staying handicap chase, with a step up from the winner.

2944 MARDEN ROOFING CELEBRATION H'CAP HURDLE (12 hdls) 3m
2:35 (2:35) (Class 3) (0-130,130) 4-Y-O+ **£5,393** (£1,583; £791; £395)

Form RPR

3/4- **1** **Moorlands Mist**[24] 2458 6-10-8 **122** ThomasCheesman(10) 136+
(Philip Hobbs) *hld up in rr: impr after 8th: hdwy to take 3rd 3 out: pushed along to chal last: sn led: drvn clr* **7/2**[1]

5PU- **2** *9* **Brackloon High (IRE)**[15] 2646 8-10-11 **120** JamesBanks(5) 123
(Brendan Powell) *in rr and rdn fr 6th: styd on u.p fr 8th to chal 4 out and sn slt ld: nt fluent 2 out and hrd pressed: narrowly hdd last: styd on for 2nd but no ch w wnr* **20/1**

/02- **3** *¾* **He's The Daddy**[16] 2616 6-9-9 **106** ow1 (t) RyanHatch(7) 108
(Nigel Twiston-Davies) *chsd ldrs: chal fr 4 out tl slt ld last: sn hdd: no ex and kpt on one pce into 3rd* **8/1**

412- **4** *1½* **Lookout Mountain (IRE)**[21] 2516 5-11-6 **124** (vt) NoelFehily 125
(Jonjo O'Neill) *in rr: hdwy appr 4 out: styd on fr 2 out but nvr any ch w wnr* **11/2**[3]

21F- **5** *11* **Royal Native (IRE)**[24] 2458 5-10-9 **116** (t) RachaelGreen(3) 106
(Anthony Honeyball) *chsd ldrs: chal 5th to 6th: wknd after 4 out* **4/1**[2]

P14/ **6** *6* **Ugly Bug**[225] 5537 7-10-10 **121** KevinJones(7) 105
(Seamus Mullins) *chsd ldrs to 4 out* **16/1**

000- **7** *6* **Virginia Ash (IRE)**[8] 2798 5-10-6 **110** (p) JamesDavies 89
(Colin Tizzard) *chsd ldrs: rdn 7th: wknd 4 out* **20/1**

URP- **8** *5* **Sarando**[15] 2646 8-10-12 **119** (p) TrevorWhelan(3) 93
(Alex Hales) *mde most tl hdd after 4 out: sn wknd* **66/1**

/FU- **9** *6* **Big Society (IRE)**[15] 2651 7-10-13 **122** (p) AodhaganConlon(5) 92
(Tom George) *hit 3rd: rdn 7th: wknd 4 out* **12/1**

/60- **10** *16* **Maller Tree**[20] 2538 6-11-5 **130** (v[1]) JakeHodson(7) 85
(David Dennis) *pressed ldr to 4 out: wknd qckly: t.o* **66/1**

3/0- **11** *24* **Timesishard (IRE)**[20] 2529 6-11-2 **125** KillianMoore(5) 58
(Graeme McPherson) *in tch: hit 7th: wknd 8th: t.o* **10/1**

3P2- **12** *40* **Westaway (IRE)**[20] 2536 6-10-11 **115** NickScholfield 12
(David Arbuthnot) *hit 1st: sn bhd: t.o* **12/1**

/00- **13** *5* **Hold Court (IRE)**[22] 2490 6-11-4 **122** PaulMoloney 15
(Evan Williams) *a in rr: t.o* **16/1**

5m 54.5s (-7.70) **Going Correction** -0.475s/f (Good) 13 Ran SP% **117.5**
Speed ratings (Par 107): **93,90,89,89,85 83,81,79,77,72 64,51,49**
toteswingers 1&2 £21.20, 2&3 £35.00, 1&3 £8.70 CSF £74.42 CT £526.48 TOTE £4.80: £1.80, £6.40, £1.60; EX 122.50 Trifecta £694.60 Part won. Pool: £826.23 - 0.12 winning units..
Owner Terry Warner **Bred** Mrs L M Williams **Trained** Withycombe, Somerset

FOCUS
A decent staying handicap hurdle. The winner is on the upgrade and should win again.

2945 CHELTENHAM 14 NRFB AT BETVICTOR.COM H'CAP CHASE (16 fncs) 2m 3f 110y
3:10 (3:11) (Class 3) (0-130,129) 4-Y-O+ **£6,498** (£1,908; £954; £477)

Form RPR

/00- **1** **Renard (FR)**[22] 2488 8-11-10 **127** LiamTreadwell 137
(Venetia Williams) *chsd ldrs: lft cl 2nd 11th: chal and hit 12th: led 3 out: rdn out run-in* **7/4**[1]

/34- **2** *1½* **Timesawastin (IRE)**[37] 2171 7-11-6 **123** PaulMoloney 131
(Evan Williams) *led but hrd pressed fr 7th to 11th: rdn 12th: hdd 3 out: rallied u.p run-in but a hld* **11/2**[2]

4/5- **3** *12* **Thunderstorm (IRE)**[35] 2211 8-11-9 **129** JamesBest(3) 126
(Philip Hobbs) *in tch: hdwy 10th: chsd ldrs fr 12th: mstke 3 out and no ch w ldng duo after* **8/1**

000- **4** *hd* **The Chazer (IRE)**[20] 2529 8-11-8 **125** IanPopham 124
(Richard Lee) *in rr: hdwy 9th: styng on in 4th whn blnd 4 out: so ch w ldrs after but styd on to press for 3rd clsng stages* **20/1**

514- **5** *18* **Special Account (IRE)**[21] 2508 8-11-3 **120** NickScholfield 101
(Jeremy Scott) *in rr whn blnd 4th: sme hdwy appr 12th: sn wknd* **13/2**[3]

60/ **6** *5* **Smoking Aces (IRE)**[577] 166 9-11-6 **123** NoelFehily 98
(Jonjo O'Neill) *screwed 4th: mstkes 5th and 7th: hit 8th: a bhd* **8/1**

50P- **7** *13* **Whispering Jack**[152] 923 8-10-7 **117** ow2 (p) MrDIJAndrews(7) 80
(Keiran Burke) *chsd ldrs: wknd after 11th: mstke next* **25/1**

/0F- **P** **Beside The Fire**[28] 2370 8-10-12 **115** JoeTizzard
(Colin Tizzard) *chsd ldrs: hit 6th: wknd 8th: t.o whn p.u bef 4 out* **12/1**

126/ **F** **Big News**[250] 5066 7-11-6 **123** (t) TomMessenger
(Richard Lee) *chsd ldr fr 4th: chal fr 7th tl fell 11th* **10/1**

4m 59.0s (-12.30) **Going Correction** -0.475s/f (Good) 9 Ran SP% **112.7**
Speed ratings (Par 107): **105,104,99,99,92 90,85**, ,
toteswingers 1&2 £2.70, 2&3 £6.50, 1&3 £4.50 CSF £11.97 CT £58.92 TOTE £2.70: £1.10, £2.70, £3.20; EX 12.40 Trifecta £58.50 Pool: £2136.58 - 27.35 winning units..
Owner Roa Arkle Partnership **Bred** Guillaume Moinon & Pierre Julienne **Trained** Kings Caple, H'fords

FOCUS
A fairly good handicap chase. The winner was on a good mark and is back to something like his best.

2946 BACK OF THE NET AT BETVICTOR.COM STANDARD OPEN NATIONAL HUNT FLAT RACE 2m 110y
3:45 (3:46) (Class 6) 4-6-Y-O **£1,559** (£457; £228; £114)

Form RPR

3- **1** **Tara Road**[28] 2368 5-10-11 0 PatrickCorbett(5) 109+
(Rebecca Curtis) *chsd ldrs: chal fr over 2f out tl led over 1f out: drvn out* **4/6**[1]

3- **2** *2* **Ebony Empress (IRE)**[35] 2216 4-10-9 0 NoelFehily 99
(Neil Mulholland) *chsd ldrs: led over 3f out: jnd over 2f out: hdd over 1f out: kpt on same pce ins fnl f* **7/1**[3]

1- **3** *1¼* **Henllan Harri (IRE)**[146] 962 5-11-6 0 MichaelByrne(3) 112
(Peter Bowen) *chsd ldrs: rdn over 3f out: kpt on same pce fnl 2f* **7/2**[2]

4 *2½* **St Dominick (IRE)** 6-10-13 0 JamesBest(3) 103
(Jackie Du Plessis) *in tch: hdwy over 3f out: pressed ldrs over 2f out: sn one pce* **16/1**

4/ **5** *2½* **Know More Oats (IRE)**[235] 5334 5-10-13 0 GilesHawkins(3) 100
(Victor Dartnall) *in tch: hdwy 6f out: styd on same pce fnl 3f* **11/1**

4- **6** *1* **The Snappy Poet**[16] 2634 4-11-2 0 NickScholfield 99
(Jeremy Scott) *towards rr but in tch: sme hdwy 4f out: one pce fnl 2f* **14/1**

20/ **7** *13* **Morebutwhen**[256] 4970 6-10-9 0 IanPopham 79
(Richard King) *led tl hdd over 3f out: sn btn* **25/1**

0- **8** *½* **Pattara**[31] 2298 4-10-9 0 GerardTumelty 79
(Noel Williams) *in rr but in tch tl wknd 3f out* **33/1**

4m 8.3s (3.30) **Going Correction** -0.475s/f (Good)
WFA 4 from 5yo+ 5lb 8 Ran SP% **122.4**
Speed ratings: **73,72,71,70,69 68,62,62**
toteswingers 1&2 £1.40, 2&3 £2.60, 1&3 £1.10 CSF £7.05 TOTE £1.60: £1.10, £1.70, £1.10; EX 5.20 Trifecta £11.40 Pool: £1875.84 - 123.02 winning units..
Owner Nigel Morris **Bred** G A Bosley **Trained** Newport, Dyfed

FOCUS
A fair bumper in which they didn't go much of a gallop. The form makes sense.
T/Plt: £39.10 to a £1 stake. Pool: £79,056.26 - 1473.61 winning tickets. T/Qpdt: £6.10 to a £1 stake. Pool: £5,459.84 - 656.35 winning tickets. ST

2927 SANDOWN (R-H)
Saturday, December 7

OFFICIAL GOING: Chase course - good; hurdle course - good to soft (good in places in back straight; goingstick: chs 7.3, hdl 6.9)
Wind: Light, against Weather: Cloudy

2947 DAVID JOHNSON "NATIONAL HUNT" NOVICES' HURDLE (8 hdls) 2m 110y
12:20 (12:20) (Class 3) 4-Y-O+ **£6,498** (£1,908; £954; £477)

Form RPR

1 **Vaniteux (FR)**[251] 4-10-12 0 BarryGeraghty 129+
(Nicky Henderson) *str: hld up in tch: trckd ldrs: 5th: led and mstke 2 out: sn hdd and rdn: responded wl fr last and surged into the ld fnl 100yds* **7/2**[3]

/25- **2** *1½* **Vibrato Valtat (FR)**[22] 2492 4-10-12 121 DarylJacob 125+
(Paul Nicholls) *lw: hld up in rr: gd prog to ld sn after 2 out and gng strly: rdn after last: hdd and outpcd fnl 100yds* **6/4**[1]

14- **3** *6* **Champagne At Tara**[20] 2534 4-10-12 0 APMcCoy 120+
(Jonjo O'Neill) *patiently rdn: hld up and last tl 3rd: stl last of those w a ch bef 2 out: prog to chse ldng pair after 2 out: shuffled along and outpcd fr last: do bttr* **2/1**[2]

3/2- **4** *10* **Rhapando**[35] 2216 4-10-12 0 DominicElsworth 109
(Paul Webber) *disp ld to 2 out: sn fdd* **16/1**

0/5- **5** *1¾* **Morning Reggie**[28] 2375 4-10-12 0 LeightonAspell 107
(Oliver Sherwood) *trckd ldrs: rdn and stl cl enough whn slithered on landing 2 out: no ch after: plugged on* **33/1**

1/0- **6** *10* **Comte D'Anjou**[56] 1869 4-10-12 0 BrendanPowell 99
(Nick Williams) *disp ld: jinked and hdd whn mstke 2 out: wknd* **25/1**

2/4- **7** *22* **Money For Nothing**[28] 2369 4-10-12 0 RobertThornton 80
(Alan King) *prom: nt fluent 3rd and 4th: rdn and wknd wl bef 2 out: t.o* **9/1**

00- **8** *32* **Area Access (IRE)**[16] 2621 5-10-12 0 DaveCrosse 43
(Charlie Mann) *chsd ldrs to 5th: wknd 3 out: wl t.o* **66/1**

0/0- **U** **Sweet Boy Vic (IRE)**[19] 2564 5-10-12 0 TomCannon
(Chris Gordon) *prom to 2nd: last fr next: lost tch after 4th: bhd whn uns rdr 3 out* **100/1**

3m 56.6s (-10.60) **Going Correction** -0.25s/f (Good) 9 Ran SP% **120.7**
Speed ratings (Par 107): **114,113,110,105,104 100,89,74**,
toteswingers 1&2 £1.70, 1&3 £3.30, 2&3 £1.90 CSF £9.85 TOTE £5.20: £1.90, £1.10, £1.30; EX 12.90 Trifecta £26.00 Pool: £1250.11 - 35.93 winning units..
Owner Mr & Mrs R Kelvin-Hughes **Bred** Jacques Cypres **Trained** Upper Lambourn, Berks

The Form Book Jumps, Raceform Ltd, Compton, RG20 6NL.

FOCUS
The ground appeared to have dried out a little from the previous day. A fair novice hurdle, with the runner-up used as a reliable guide to the form, and the market principals came to the fore. The winner quickened up well and looks a decent prospect.

2948 "HUTCH" ANNIVERSARY ANNE BOLEYN MARES' H'CAP HURDLE (9 hdls) 2m 4f
12:50 (12:51) (Class 3) (0-135,130) 4-Y-O+

£9,384 (£2,772; £1,386; £693; £346; £174)

Form RPR

024- **1** **Benefique Royale**[17] 2602 5-10-0 **104** oh1 BrendanPowell 107+
(Nick Williams) *hld up towards rr: smooth prog fr 3 out: narrow ld 2 out: rdn and styd on wl fr last* **12/1**

5/5- **2** *2 ¼* **Teochew (IRE)**[45] 2029 5-10-11 **115** DarylJacob 117
(Warren Greatrex) *pressed ldr: led 6th: jnd after next: hdd 2 out: stl nrly upsides whn nt fluent last: one pce* **16/1**

0/1- **3** *1 ½* **Scholastica**[14] 2663 6-11-7 **125** FelixDeGiles 126
(Tom Symonds) *lw: hld up in tch: rdn sn after 3 out: prog to chse ldrs 2 out: kpt on u.p to take 3rd nr fin* **11/2[3]**

412- **4** *shd* **Mrs Peachey (IRE)**[28] 2371 6-11-5 **130** TomBellamy(7) 132
(Kim Bailey) *lw: hld up in last pair: pushed along and prog after 3 out: chsd ldng pair and blnd 2 out: kpt on but lost 3rd nr fin* **4/1[1]**

0/4- **5** *6* **Lady Kathleen**[14] 2663 6-10-9 **113** DominicElsworth 108
(Paul Webber) *led: set mod pce tl upped the tempo fr 5th: hdd next: upsides after 3 out tl fdd fr next* **12/1**

132- **6** *¾* **Top Totti**[14] 2663 5-10-10 **114** BarryGeraghty 108
(Henry Daly) *hld up in tch: dropped to last after 5th and nt gng wl: virtually t.o after 3 out: consented to stay on again fr 2 out* **9/2[2]**

3/4- **7** *2 ½* **Alder Mairi (IRE)**[29] 2352 6-11-9 **127** AndrewThornton 119
(Seamus Mullins) *prom: jnd ldng pair after 3 out: wknd jst bef 2 out* **25/1**

P/P- **8** *2* **Tante Sissi (FR)**[16] 2632 6-11-6 **124** RobertThornton 116
(Alan King) *hld up in last pair: prog gng wl after 3 out: rdn and nt qckn bef 2 out: mstke 2 out: wknd* **16/1**

/12- **9** *¾* **In By Midnight**[29] 2352 5-9-13 **108** ConorShoemark(5) 97
(Tom George) *chsd ldrs on outer: rdn 3 out: lost pl and btn wl bef 2 out* **9/1**

326- **10** *4 ½* **Synthe Davis (FR)**[33] 2270 8-10-9 **113** TomCannon 98
(Laura Mongan) *in tch: rdn after 3 out: sn struggling: no ch fr 2 out* **50/1**

/PP- **11** *47* **Golden Gael**[16] 2632 7-11-2 **123** MattGriffiths(3) 66
(Jeremy Scott) *chsd ldrs: rdn after 3 out: sn lost pl and btn: t.o and virtually p.u nr fin* **25/1**

611- **P** **Tigresse Bleue**[16] 2616 5-11-3 **121** APMcCoy
(Jonjo O'Neill) *trckd ldng pair: nt fluent 3rd: nt fluent next and qckly p.u: dismntd* **4/1[1]**

5m 4.6s (5.00) **Going Correction** -0.25s/f (Good) **12** Ran SP% **120.4**
Speed ratings (Par 107): **80,79,78,78,76 75,74,73,73,71 53,**
toteswingers 1&2 £49.70, 2&3 £19.80, 1&3 £11.80 CSF £182.32 CT £1186.58 TOTE £17.60: £3.50, £5.20, £3.00; EX 277.00 Trifecta £1060.60 Part won. Pool: £1414.26 - 0.02 winning units..
Owner Len,Davies,Downes,Hewlett,White,Booth **Bred** Len Jakeman, J Davies And R Downes **Trained** George Nympton, Devon

FOCUS
A decent mares' hurdle, certainly competitive, and the form looks solid, despite them having gone just a modest pace. The second to fourth set the level.

2949 PERTEMPS NETWORK H'CAP HURDLE (SERIES QUALIFIER) (11 hdls) 2m 6f
1:20 (1:22) (Class 2) 4-Y-O+

£12,512 (£3,696; £1,848; £924; £462; £232)

Form RPR

/54- **1** **Saphir Du Rheu (FR)**[7] 2813 4-11-0 **130** DarylJacob 145+
(Paul Nicholls) *hld up in midfield: smooth prog bef 2 out: led bef last: cruised clr: impressive* **8/1[3]**

014- **2** *8* **Home Run (GER)**[14] 2671 5-10-6 **129** (b) KieronEdgar(7) 135
(David Pipe) *mstke 1st: hld up in last pair: mstke 7th: coaxed along and gd prog on inner bef 2 out: brought to chal last: no ch w wnr and fnd little u.p: hld on for 2nd* **16/1**

1/3- **3** *1 ¼* **Whisper (FR)**[22] 2490 5-11-10 **140** BarryGeraghty 146
(Nicky Henderson) *lw: trckd ldrs: mstke 3rd: wnt 4th after 3 out: trying to chal whn mstke 2 out: upsides between last 2: one pce after* **5/2[1]**

/16- **4** *1 ¼* **Upswing (IRE)**[22] 2490 5-10-7 **123** APMcCoy 126
(Jonjo O'Neill) *lw: hld up wl in rr: tried to make prog on outer after 3 out: clsd on ldrs u.p 2 out: hanging rt but kpt on to take 4th after last* **7/2[2]**

/42- **5** *1 ¾* **Utopie Des Bordes (FR)**[14] 2672 5-11-7 **142** NicodeBoinville(5) 143
(Nicky Henderson) *trckd ldrs: rdn 3 out whn others gng much bttr: prog and tried to chal 2 out: fdd bef last* **8/1[3]**

142- **6** *2 ¾* **Drum Valley**[41] 2102 5-11-3 **133** LeightonAspell 132
(Oliver Sherwood) *hld up in rr: prog into midfield 3 out: tried to cl on ldrs u.p 2 out: one pce after* **14/1**

/1P- **7** *½* **Oscar Magic (IRE)**[49] 1968 6-10-13 **129** (t) JamieMoore 129
(Nigel Twiston-Davies) *led 2nd: hit 3 out: hdd 2 out: steadily fdd* **16/1**

643- **8** *¾* **Bourne**[24] 2454 7-10-9 **125** (b) AdrianLane 124
(Donald McCain) *led to 2nd: pressed ldr: led 2 out: hdd & wknd bef last* **10/1**

054- **9** *7* **Oscar Prairie (IRE)**[28] 2366 8-10-0 **126** (p) WilliamFeatherstone(10) 118
(Warren Greatrex) *racd wd: in tch: trckd ldrs 3 out: sn rdn: fnd little and wl btn bef 2 out* **20/1**

/0P- **10** *½* **Malt Master (IRE)**[24] 2452 6-11-2 **135** PeterCarberry(3) 126
(Nicky Henderson) *nvr bttr than midfield: pushed along 6th: dropped to rr and drvn sn after 3 out: modest prog bef 2 out: sn wknd* **25/1**

124- **11** *¾* **Experimentalist**[63] 1766 5-9-8 **120** (t) AlanJohns(10) 110
(Tim Vaughan) *hld up towards rr: rchd midfield after 3 out but drvn: wknd bef 2 out* **25/1**

563- **12** *1 ¼* **Act Of Kalanisi (IRE)**[16] 2624 7-10-7 **126** (bt) JoshuaMoore(3) 115
(Dr Richard Newland) *nt a fluent: prom: cl 3rd after 3 out tl wknd qckly bef 2 out* **10/1**

2/P- **13** *9* **Salmanazar**[25] 2433 5-11-3 **133** RobertThornton 114
(Alan King) *trckd ldrs on inner: drvn 3 out: wknd bef next* **25/1**

00P- **14** *3 ½* **Problema Tic (FR)**[14] 2674 7-10-6 **129** (tp) MikeyEnnis(7) 107
(David Pipe) *prom: lost pl qckly and drvn after 5th: brief rally 7th: sn wknd* **50/1**

320/ **15** *31* **Liberty Court (IRE)**[252] 5016 6-10-7 **123** (t) DougieCostello 73
(Tim Vaughan) *hld up in rr: prog into midfield and gng bttr than many after 3 out: rdn and wknd qckly bef 2 out: t.o* **25/1**

4/4- **P** **Darroun (IRE)**[34] 2258 5-11-5 **135** DominicElsworth
(Shaun Lycett) *mstke 1st: sn last and nt gng wl: prog to trck ldrs 5th: dropped away again qckly bef next: sn t.o: p.u bef 2 out* **50/1**

5m 18.0s (-12.00) **Going Correction** -0.25s/f (Good)
WFA 4 from 5yo+ 6lb **16** Ran SP% **133.7**
Speed ratings (Par 109): **111,108,107,107,106 105,105,105,102,102 102,101,98,97,85**
toteswingers 1&2 £26.00, 2&3 £12.50, 1&3 £6.50 CSF £128.38 CT £426.30 TOTE £12.00: £2.30, £3.30, £1.50, £1.50; EX 198.50 Trifecta £2106.70 Pool: £3974.41 - 1.41 winning units..
Owner The Stewart Family **Bred** Claude Duval **Trained** Ditcheat, Somerset

FOCUS
These Pertemps qualifiers are often competitive and this race looked no different beforehand, but the winner bolted up. Solid form.

2950 RACING POST HENRY VIII NOVICES' CHASE (GRADE 1) (13 fncs) 2m
1:50 (1:54) (Class 1) 4-Y-O+

£22,780 (£8,548; £4,280; £2,132; £1,072; £536)

Form RPR

2/1- **1** **Hinterland (FR)**[28] 2363 5-11-2 148 DarylJacob 157+
(Paul Nicholls) *hld up in last pair: trckd ldng trio 4 out: smooth prog after next: led between fnl 2 and gd jump last: 2 l clr flat: drvn and hld on* **13/2**

6/U- **2** *nk* **Grandouet (FR)**[28] 2363 6-11-2 0 BarryGeraghty 157+
(Nicky Henderson) *trckd ldrs: wnt 2nd 4 out: poised to chal 3 out: rdn sn after 2 out as wnr swept by: rallied wl flat and clsng at fin* **11/4[2]**

/11- **3** *8* **Taquin Du Seuil (FR)**[22] 2489 6-11-2 147 APMcCoy 152+
(Jonjo O'Neill) *t.k.h: several sketchy jumps: trckd ldrs: pckd bdly 9th and dropped to 5th: struggling after: styd on fr 2 out to take 3rd flat* **9/4[1]**

/12- **4** *2* **Claret Cloak (IRE)**[32] 2282 6-11-2 142 LeightonAspell 147
(Emma Lavelle) *led to after 2nd: led again 4th: hdd between last 2: wknd flat* **7/1**

1F1- **5** *12* **Balder Succes (FR)**[31] 2295 5-11-2 145 RobertThornton 137
(Alan King) *lw: led after 2nd tl 4th: chsd ldr tl nt fluent 4 out: wknd fr 3 out* **7/2[3]**

4/1- **6** *8* **Manyriverstocross (IRE)**[32] 2282 8-11-2 138 DominicElsworth 129
(Alan King) *a in last pair: mstke 8th: sn bhd and no ch* **14/1**

3m 48.9s (-12.90) **Going Correction** -0.25s/f (Good) **6** Ran SP% **112.2**
Speed ratings (Par 117): **122,121,117,116,110 106**
toteswingers 1&2 £3.30, 2&3 £1.80, 1&3 £3.20 CSF £25.08 TOTE £6.40: £2.40, £2.20; EX 28.90 Trifecta £77.50 Pool: £4271.05 - 41.28 winning units..
Owner Chris Giles **Bred** E Aubree & C Bresson **Trained** Ditcheat, Somerset

FOCUS
A race that has proven a rich source of top chasers in the past and a pair of high-class prospects pulled nicely clear. Having gone slow early, Claret Cloak and Balder Succes upped the tempo down the back and it was clear from before the Pond Fence that the race was between old rivals Hinterland and Grandouet. A solid renewal run in a quicker time than the Tongle Creek. The first two are rated up a stone on their recent C&D form.

2951 JUMEIRAH HOTELS & RESORTS DECEMBER H'CAP HURDLE (LISTED RACE) (8 hdls) 2m 110y
2:25 (2:25) (Class 1) (0-150,140) 4-Y-O+

£28,475 (£10,685; £5,350; £2,665; £1,340; £670)

Form RPR

122- **1** **Deep Trouble (IRE)**[22] 2492 6-10-11 **125** LeightonAspell 131+
(Ben Case) *hld up in last: gd prog bef 2 out: led sn after 2 out: in command whn jinked rt last: veered rt to far rail after last and jockey lost both irons: urged along and hld on* **7/1[3]**

000/ **2** *1* **Urbain De Sivola (FR)**[269] 4736 5-11-4 **132** DarylJacob 133
(Paul Nicholls) *hld up in midfield: smooth prog to ld immediately after 2 out: wnr sn swept by: drvn and lft w ch after last: styd on but a hld* **9/2[2]**

120/ **3** *1 ¼* **River Maigue (IRE)**[270] 4719 6-11-12 **140** BarryGeraghty 140
(Nicky Henderson) *lw: hld up towards rr: pushed along after 3 out: rdn and prog bef 2 out: styd on after last: nvr quite able to chal* **10/3[1]**

6/0- **4** *shd* **Ruacana**[41] 2102 4-11-8 **139** JackQuinlan(3) 139
(John Ferguson) *hld up in midfield: prog to chal and upsides 2 out: nt qckn in 3rd whn mstke last: styd on* **25/1**

461- **5** *½* **Waterunder (IRE)**[24] 2461 6-11-1 **136** (t) KieronEdgar(7) 135
(David Pipe) *hld up in rr: rdn wl bef 2 out: kpt on after but nvr gng pce to chal: nrst fin* **12/1**

6/0- **6** *1 ½* **Calculated Risk**[20] 2533 4-11-1 **129** DougieCostello 127
(John Quinn) *trckd ldrs: mstke 3 out: rdn and cl up bhd ldrs 2 out: kpt on same pce* **8/1**

F02- **7** *½* **Specialagent Alfie**[15] 2647 7-10-13 **127** (t) TomCannon 125
(Nick Gifford) *led at mod pce: nt fluent 2nd: nt fluent 3 out and sn hdd: on terms 2 out: no ex last* **14/1**

F23- **8** *4* **Milord (GER)**[16] 2647 4-10-11 **125** SamThomas 119
(Kim Bailey) *hld up in last trio: rdn after 3 out: making sme prog u.p whn mstke 2 out: no hdwy after* **8/1**

P03/ **9** *1 ¼* **Ronaldo Des Mottes (FR)**[251] 5031 8-11-5 **140** TomBellamy(7) 133
(David Pipe) *hld up in midfield on outer: rdn wl bef 2 out and no prog: one pce after* **16/1**

4/2- **10** *7* **Seventh Sky (GER)**[209] 235 6-11-0 **128** (t) MarkGrant 115
(Charlie Mann) *prom: led after 3 out: hdd immediately after 2 out and wknd* **25/1**

/11- **11** *1 ¼* **Radmores Revenge**[16] 2617 10-10-13 **127** HaddenFrost 113
(Sophie Leech) *hld up in last pair: rdn wl bef 2 out and no prog: wl btn after* **33/1**

6/0- **12** *1 ¼* **Whitby Jack**[15] 2647 6-10-9 **123** JamieMoore 107
(Gary Moore) *prom tl wknd u.p 2 out* **9/1**

/05- **13** *27* **Vulcanite (IRE)**[25] 2433 6-11-11 **139** APMcCoy 99
(Charlie Longsdon) *pressed ldr to 3 out: wknd qckly and eased: t.o* **10/1**

4m 0.9s (-6.30) **Going Correction** -0.25s/f (Good)
WFA 4 from 5yo+ 5lb **13** Ran SP% **125.9**
Speed ratings (Par 111): **104,103,102,102,102 101,101,99,99,95 95,94,82**
toteswingers 1&2 £8.40, 2&3 £4.50, 1&3 £7.30 CSF £40.61 CT £129.84 TOTE £7.70: £2.60, £1.80, £1.50; EX 47.30 Trifecta £252.80 Pool: £3859.88 - 11.45 winning units..
Owner Lady Jane Grosvenor **Bred** Paraig O'Rourke **Trained** Edgcote, Northants

■ Stewards' Enquiry : Daryl Jacob two-day ban: used whip above permitted level (Dec 22,27)

Leighton Aspell caution: used whip in incorrect place.

FOCUS
This didn't look a strong race for the grade, with none of the runners rated higher than 140, and just went fairly steady. The winner overcame his late waywardness to score. Not form to be too confident about.

2952 BETVICTOR TINGLE CREEK CHASE (GRADE 1) (13 fncs) 2m
3:00 (3:00) (Class 1) 4-Y-0+
£76,882 (£28,849; £14,445; £7,195; £3,618; £1,809)

Form RPR

/12- **1** **Sire De Grugy (FR)**[20] 2532 7-11-7 169 .... JamieMoore 171+
(Gary Moore) *hld up in midfield: trckd ldng trio and mstke 9th: clsng whn nt clr run on inner after 3 out and swtchd lft: sn chsd ldr: clsd to ld bef last: drvn clr* **7/4[1]**

U/1- **2** *4* **Somersby (IRE)**[32] 2281 9-11-7 161 .... DominicElsworth 167+
(Mick Channon) *lw: hld up in midfield: nt on terms w ldrs and pushed along in 5th 4 out: drvn 3 out: styd on after and tk 2nd last 100yds: no threat to wnr* **4/1[2]**

151/ **3** *3 1/4* **Captain Conan (FR)**[247] 5140 6-11-7 159 .... BarryGeraghty 162
(Nicky Henderson) *lw: trckd ldr fr 2nd: led after 3 out: drvn and hdd bef last: fdd and lost 2nd fnl 100yds* **7/4[1]**

/54- **4** *9* **Oiseau De Nuit (FR)**[20] 2532 11-11-7 154 ....(t) BrendanPowell 155
(Colin Tizzard) *trckd ldng pair after 2nd: wl on terms after 4 out: wknd sn after 3 out* **20/1**

P/5- **5** *1* **Kauto Stone (FR)**[35] 2234 7-11-7 153 ....(b[1]) DarylJacob 156+
(Paul Nicholls) *led and set str pce early: nt fluent 7th: hdd sn after 3 out: mstke 2 out and wknd* **11/1[3]**

036- **6** *14* **Viva Colonia (IRE)**[14] 2666 8-11-7 139 .... LeightonAspell 141
(Brian Ellison) *hld up in last: nvr a factor: tk modest 6th 3 out: no prog after* **66/1**

F/5- **7** *9* **Tataniano (FR)**[20] 2532 9-11-7 147 .... AndrewThornton 133
(Richard Rowe) *chsd ldr to 2nd: mstke next and sn dropped to rr: wl bhd after 4 out* **40/1**

2/0- **8** *1/2* **His Excellency (IRE)**[20] 2532 5-11-7 148 ....(b) APMcCoy 137
(David Pipe) *nvr on terms w ldrs: struggling whn mstke 9th: wl bhd after next* **25/1**

R/6- **P** **Mad Moose (IRE)**[20] 2532 9-11-7 143 ....[1] DaveCrosse
(Nigel Twiston-Davies) *kpt away fr others at s: set off on terms but ref to r properly and plld himself up bef 1st* **40/1**

3m 51.4s (-10.40) **Going Correction** -0.25s/f (Good) **9** Ran SP% **116.0**
Speed ratings (Par 117): **116,114,112,107,107 100,95,95,**
toteswingers 1&2 £2.10, 2&3 £2.40, 1&3 £1.40 CSF £9.01 CT £13.35 TOTE £2.50: £1.10, £1.50, £1.50; EX 8.50 Trifecta £14.30 Pool: £5717.72 - 299.18 winning units..
Owner The Preston Family & Friends Ltd **Bred** La Grugerie **Trained** Lower Beeding, W Sussex
■ The first Grade 1 winner for father and son Gary and Jamie Moore.

FOCUS
No Sprinter Sacre, so hard not to think this was a substandard edition of the race, and the form is a good bit short of the level that will be needed to topple the Champion chaser at next year's festival. The pace was a good one, though, and it was still a high-class performance from Sire De Grugy, who is rated to his mark. Somersby's best figure since his 2012 Victor Chandler win.

2953 LDS LEAK DETECTION SPECIALISTS LONDON NATIONAL (A H'CAP CHASE) (24 fncs) 3m 5f 110y
3:35 (3:35) (Class 2) (0-150,148) 5-Y-0+
£25,024 (£7,392; £3,696; £1,848; £924; £464)

Form RPR

/P5- **1** **There's No Panic (IRE)**[15] 2646 8-10-7 **129** .... DarylJacob 133
(Paul Nicholls) *hld up in rr: mstke 17th: prog fr 19th: rdn after 4 out: chsd ldrs next: wnt 2nd after 2 out: qckly clsd to ld bef last: drvn and all out flat* **9/1**

/33- **2** *3/4* **Court By Surprise (IRE)**[28] 2373 8-10-8 **130** .... BarryGeraghty 135+
(Emma Lavelle) *lw: wl in tch: blnd 8th: trckd ldrs and mstke 17th: prog to ld 3 out gng strly: rdn 3 l clr after 2 out: hdd last: kpt on but a jst hld* **5/1[2]**

P/0- **3** *1 1/2* **Well Refreshed**[49] 1971 9-11-0 **139** .... JoshuaMoore[(3)] 144+
(Gary Moore) *hld up in rr: blnd 16th: prog and mstke 19th: trckd ldrs 4 out: chal next: cl 2nd whn nt fluent 2 out: sn outpcd: kpt on fr last* **25/1**

602- **4** *1/2* **Alfie Spinner (IRE)**[28] 2373 8-10-5 **127** .... BrendanPowell 127
(Nick Williams) *mde most to 15th and set hot pce early: rdn 18th: lost pl 3 out: kpt on again fr last* **7/1**

010/ **5** *2* **Soll**[245] 5177 8-11-3 **139** .... MarkGrant 138
(Jo Hughes) *trckd ldrs: mstke 14th: clsd to ld 4 out: hdd next: sn drvn and nt qckn: plugged on* **16/1**

413- **6** *3 1/2* **Hunters Lodge (IRE)**[22] 2487 7-10-5 **127** ....(p) DaveCrosse 122
(Nigel Twiston-Davies) *tried to contest ld but couldn't: mstke 3rd: steadily lost pl fr 1/2-way: urged along 14th: poor 11th bef 3 out: stormed up run-in after r was over* **25/1**

/F2- **7** *hd* **Buddy Bolero (IRE)**[26] 2419 7-11-8 **144** ....(p) APMcCoy 139
(David Pipe) *lw: wl plcd bhd ldrs on inner: rdn 19th: no hdwy u.p after 4 out: plugged on* **10/3[1]**

113- **8** *nse* **Franklin Roosevelt (IRE)**[28] 2367 7-9-7 **122** oh3........(b) KieronEdgar[(7)] 119
(David Pipe) *in tch in midfield: lost pl 19th and sn rdn: struggling in rr after 4 out: n.d after: styd on wl fr last* **12/1**

053- **9** *7* **Bradley**[21] 2502 9-10-6 **133** .... ConorShoemark[(5)] 124
(Fergal O'Brien) *smetimes j.rt and nvr that fluent: shoved along in midfield sn after 1/2-way: nt on terms after 4 out: no hdwy after* **11/2[3]**

315- **10** *7* **American Spin**[59] 1821 9-10-6 **128** ....(p) JamieMoore 111
(Luke Dace) *w ldr fr 2nd: led 15th: rdn 18th: hdd 4 out: wknd qckly next* **25/1**

/16- **11** *shd* **Top Smart**[41] 2108 7-10-3 **125** .... DominicElsworth 108
(Seamus Mullins) *immediately detached in last: blnd 14th: nvr mde any real prog* **20/1**

P10/ **P** **Michel Le Bon (FR)**[224] 5576 10-11-10 **146** ....(p) TomCannon
(Chris Gordon) *a in rr: blnd 12th: landed on top of next and qckly p.u: dismntd* **40/1**

1/5- **P** **Godsmejudge (IRE)**[21] 2502 7-11-12 **148** .... RobertThornton
(Alan King) *tried to ld but awkward jump 1st and had to trck ldrs: lost pl fr 19th: wknd rapidly 4 out: p.u bef next* **13/2**

7m 30.8s (-13.20) **Going Correction** -0.25s/f (Good) **13** Ran SP% **123.3**
Speed ratings: **107,106,106,106,105 104,104,104,102,101 100,,**
toteswingers 1&2 £11.90, 2&3 £44.60, 1&3 £27.00 CSF £52.87 CT £1117.55 TOTE £11.30: £3.60, £2.20, £7.20; EX 49.60 Trifecta £3714.60 Pool: £5118.95 - 1.03 winning units..
Owner The Stewart Family **Bred** J R Weston **Trained** Ditcheat, Somerset

FOCUS
A good-quality marathon handicap, which produced a bigger field than is normally the case, and there was any number in with a chance coming to the Railway fences. The winner is rated to his best.
T/Plt: £52.80 to a £1 stake. Pool: £117,113.15 - 1617.42 winning tickets. T/Qpdt: £6.70 to a £1 stake. Pool: £10,749.59 - 1180.85 winning tickets. JN

[2746] WETHERBY (L-H)
Saturday, December 7

OFFICIAL GOING: Good to soft (6.5)
Wind: Breezy, half behind Weather: Cloudy

2954 PLACE YOUR TOTESCOOP6 BETS NOW NOVICES' HURDLE (12 hdls) 2m 6f
12:10 (12:10) (Class 4) 4-Y-0+ **£3,249** (£954; £477; £238)

Form RPR

1 **Dream Flyer (IRE)**[69] 6-10-7 0 .... AdamNicol[(5)] 112+
(Michael Smith) *prom: hdwy to chal 3 out: mstke next led bef last: rdn and edgd lft run-in: styd on wl* **20/1**

1/6- **2** *1/2* **Bhakti (IRE)**[212] 185 6-10-12 0 .... WilsonRenwick 111
(Mark Rimell) *in tch: drvn and outpcd after 4 out: rallied to chse ldrs next: styd on wl fr last to take 2nd cl home* **28/1**

2- **3** *nk* **I Need Gold (IRE)**[21] 2513 5-10-12 0 .... HenryBrooke 110
(Donald McCain) *prom rdn after 4 out: rallied and led next: hdd bef last: kpt on run-in: hld and lost 2nd cl home* **3/1[2]**

122- **4** *10* **Mysteree (IRE)**[28] 2355 5-11-5 129 .... PeterBuchanan 109
(Lucinda Russell) *prom: drvn and outpcd after 4 out: rallied whn hit 3 out: no ex fr next* **11/8[1]**

/20- **5** *3* **Mister Newby (IRE)**[49] 1972 7-10-12 117 .... SeanQuinlan 100
(Richard Phillips) *hld up: hdwy on outside bef 3 out: rdn and hung lft after next: sn outpcd* **5/1[3]**

0P0- **6** *8* **Jazz Man (IRE)**[6] 2850 6-10-12 0 ....(p) BrianHarding 92
(Mark Rimell) *led to 3 out: rdn and sn wknd* **66/1**

000- **7** *6* **Top Chief**[19] 2564 5-10-9 0 .... GavinSheehan[(3)] 89
(Mark Rimell) *hld up: rdn and outpcd bef 3 out: nt fluent next: sn n.d* **100/1**

606- **8** *12* **Agesilas (FR)**[15] 2659 5-10-9 0 .... JohnKington[(3)] 80
(Andrew Crook) *midfield: struggling after 4 out: btn after next* **66/1**

/P0- **9** *22* **Moneymix**[157] 878 6-10-12 0 ....(p) BarryKeniry 55
(Ali Brewer) *hld up: smooth hdwy and in tch after 4 out: rdn and wknd bef next* **200/1**

0- **10** *45* **Sir Harry Hotspur**[189] 589 5-10-12 0 .... HarryHaynes 15
(John Mackie) *nt fluent on occasions: t.k.h: w ldr to 4 out: rdn and wknd next* **66/1**

00/ **P** **Battledancer**[417] 1881 7-10-12 0 .... TommyPhelan
(Peter Maddison) *nt fluent in rr: lost tch and p.u bef 8th* **66/1**

/15- **F** **Just Cameron**[176] 737 6-11-5 0 .... RichieMcGrath
(Philip Kirby) *t.k.h: cl up whn fell 2nd* **8/1**

04- **P** **Lucky Cody (IRE)**[16] 2621 4-10-12 0 .... DenisO'Regan
(Brian Ellison) *hld up towards rr: nt fluent and reminders 4th: struggling 8th: lost tch and p.u after next* **12/1**

5m 21.5s (-5.30) **Going Correction** -0.10s/f (Good)
WFA 4 from 5yo+ 6lb **13** Ran SP% **118.2**
Speed ratings (Par 105): **105,104,104,101,99 97,94,90,82,66 ,,**
toteswingers 1&2 £42.60, 1&3 £26.40, 2&3 £28.90 CSF £393.64 TOTE £27.00: £4.20, £6.80, £1.60; EX 249.60 TRIFECTA Not won..
Owner J Stephenson **Bred** Patrick Hennessy **Trained** Kirkheaton, Northumberland

FOCUS
Following a minimal amount of rain overnight, the going remained good to soft (GoingStick 6.5). The bend away from the stands was operated as a single bend and the hurdles were placed on the innermost line down the back straight. This was an ordinary staying novice hurdle. The early pace didn't look that strong and it became a bit of a sprint from the home bend. The form could be rated a lot higher through the fourth and fifth but both have been assessed as a stone+ off.

2955 CONSTANT SECURITY NOVICES' LIMITED H'CAP CHASE (16 fncs) 2m 4f 110y
12:40 (12:40) (Class 3) (0-125,125)
4-Y-0+ **£6,279** (£1,871; £947; £485; £254)

Form RPR

5/4- **1** **Westward Point**[39] 2151 6-11-1 **124** .... GavinSheehan[(3)] 129+
(Warren Greatrex) *t.k.h early: cl up: led after 3rd to 8th: styd upsides: led 4 out: clr whn nt fluent 2 out: styd on strly* **9/2**

512/ **2** *8* **Dreams Of Milan (IRE)**[232] 5368 5-11-3 **123** .... HenryBrooke 118
(Donald McCain) *hld up in tch on outside: hdwy to chse clr ldrs 10th: rdn after 5 out: styng on whn mstke 3 out: chsd (clr) wnr last: no imp* **10/3[1]**

2/4- **3** *4* **Rick (FR)**[27] 2395 9-11-5 **125** ....(b[1]) DenisO'Regan 117
(John Ferguson) *nt fluent on occasions: led to after 3rd: led 8th to 4 out: rdn and outpcd fr 2 out* **7/2[2]**

/61- **4** *16* **Houndscourt (IRE)**[26] 2429 6-10-13 **124** .... HarryDerham[(5)] 106
(Jamie Snowden) *in tch: rdn and outpcd 10th: 4th and hld whn mstkes 3 out and next* **8/1**

115- **5** *14* **Dartford Warbler (IRE)**[62] 1796 6-11-5 **125** .... BrianHarding 88
(Sue Smith) *prom: hdwy bef 8th: pushed along and outpcd fr 10th: hld whn nt fluent 3 out* **9/1**

1/4- **F** **Hatters River (IRE)**[23] 2475 6-10-12 **118** .... SeanQuinlan
(Ali Brewer) *prom: gng wl whn fell 9th* **4/1[3]**

/20- **P** **Purcell's Bridge (FR)**[38] 2158 6-11-0 **120** .... WilsonRenwick
(Rose Dobbin) *t.k.h: hld up: lost tch and p.u after 7th* **12/1**

/05- **P** **Jimmie Brown (USA)**[21] 2515 5-10-2 **111** oh6........ JohnKington[(3)]
(Andrew Crook) *hld up: outpcd whn hmpd 9th: sn lost tch: t.o whn p.u bef 4 out* **50/1**

5m 4.3s (-3.50) **Going Correction** -0.10s/f (Good) **8** Ran SP% **114.2**
Speed ratings (Par 107): **102,98,97,91,86 ,,**
toteswingers 1&2 £3.20, 1&3 £3.10, 2&3 £4.20 CSF £20.51 CT £57.60 TOTE £8.90: £2.70, £1.50, £1.50; EX 32.60 Trifecta £135.80 Pool: £1283.97 - 7.09 winning units..
Owner J F F White **Bred** J F F White **Trained** Upper Lambourn, Berks

FOCUS
Despite a contested lead, the pace was far from strong in this fair novices' handicap chase. The winner and third quickened the tempo jumping the last on the far side, which caught out a few. The winner improved in line with the best of his hurdle form.

2956 BET TOTEQUADPOT WITH TOTEPOOL H'CAP HURDLE (13 hdls) 3m 1f
1:10 (1:10) (Class 4) (0-120,120) 3-Y-0+ **£3,422** (£997; £499)

Form RPR

P35- **1** **Rattlin**[11] 2734 5-10-7 **108** .... CallumBewley[(7)] 119+
(Sue Smith) *trckd ldrs: led 9th: drew clr on bridle after next: hit last: unchal* **9/1**

P13- **2** *8* **Ballyben (IRE)**[38] 2158 5-10-11 **112** .... CraigNichol[(7)] 113
(Lucinda Russell) *chsd ldrs: drvn and outpcd after 4 out: rallied next: chsd (clr) wnr bef last: no imp* **11/4[2]**

The Form Book Jumps, Raceform Ltd, Compton, RG20 6NL.

/01- **3** *9* **Josies Orders (IRE)**[42] 2073 5-11-6 **114**........................ RichieMcGrath 112
(Jonjo O'Neill) *hld up in tch: hdwy to chse (clr) wnr after 4 out: rdn and no imp whn hit 2 out: one pce* **9/4**[1]

/04- **4** *27* **Joseph Mercer (IRE)**[21] 2516 6-11-3 **111**........................ BrianHarding 80
(Tina Jackson) *led to 9th: drvn and outpcd after next: sme late hdwy: no ch w first three* **11/1**

F/P- **5** *4 ½* **Basford Bob (IRE)**[21] 2510 8-11-2 **110**........................ SeanQuinlan 79
(Jennie Candlish) *t.k.h: hld up: stdy hdwy 1/2-way: outpcd whn mstke 3 out: sn btn* **20/1**

P14- **6** *5* **Carmela Maria**[94] 1498 8-9-10 **95**........................(b) JoeColliver(5) 55
(Mike Sowersby) *hld up: struggling 8th: no ch after* **25/1**

P/P- **7** *3 ¾* **Caerlaverock (IRE)**[25] 2447 8-10-5 **106**........................ ShaunDobbin(7) 63
(Rose Dobbin) *hld up rdn and outpcd 8th: btn bef 3 out* **33/1**

32- **8** *1 ½* **Kodicil (IRE)**[25] 2444 5-11-3 **111**........................ PeterBuchanan 66
(Tim Walford) *t.k.h: w ldr to 4 out: rdn and wknd bef next: btn whn blnd 2 out* **6/1**[3]

6/5- **P** **Going Wrong**[16] 2624 10-11-5 **120**........................(t) MrTEllis(7)
(Dan Skelton) *t.k.h: chsd ldrs: lost pl whn nt fluent 6th: p.u bef next* **15/2**

6m 12.2s (-4.30) **Going Correction** -0.10s/f (Good) **9** Ran SP% **113.4**
Speed ratings (Par 105): **102,99,96,87,86 84,83,83,**
toteswingers 1&2 £9.00, 1&3 £5.20, 2&3 £1.02 CSF £33.42 CT £75.17 TOTE £12.20: £2.80, £1.40, £1.40; EX 35.10 Trifecta £137.00 Pool: £1251.64 - 6.84 winning units..
Owner Broadband Partnership **Bred** R F Broad **Trained** High Eldwick, W Yorks

FOCUS
They didn't appear to go that quickly for the first circuit of this staying handicap hurdle, but they still finished well spread out. The form looks solid enough.

2957 DOWNLOAD THE TOTEPOOL APP H'CAP CHASE (13 fncs) 2m
1:40 (1:41) (Class 3) (0-140,138) 4-Y-0+ **£6,498** (£1,908; £954; £477)

Form RPR

126- **1** **De Boitron (FR)**[181] 680 9-11-12 **138**........................ BrianHarding 148+
(Sue Smith) *hld up in last pl: stdy hdwy 1/2-way: led gng wl 2 out: shkn up appr last: kpt on strly run-in* **8/1**[3]

1- **2** *3 ½* **Claragh Native (IRE)**[8] 2793 8-10-6 **118**........................(p) LucyAlexander 125
(Martin Todhunter) *in tch: hdwy and ev ch 3 out to next: sn rdn: wnt 2nd run-in: nt pce of wnr* **9/1**

/P2- **3** *1 ½* **Rouge Et Blanc (FR)**[13] 2694 8-10-10 **127**........................ ThomasGarner(5) 133
(Oliver Sherwood) *w ldr: led 6th: rdn and hdd 2 out: rallied: kpt on same pce fr last* **8/1**[3]

/64- **4** *16* **Tour D'Argent (FR)**[44] 2031 6-11-2 **128**........................ HenryBrooke 119
(Donald McCain) *t.k.h: trckd ldrs: effrt 4 out: outpcd whn blnd next: sn btn* **11/2**[2]

205- **5** *1* **Stagecoach Pearl**[25] 2448 9-11-7 **133**........................ ShaneByrne 124
(Sue Smith) *slt ld tl nt fluent and hdd 6th: 2nd and pushed along whn mstke and outpcd 5 out: n.d after* **11/2**[2]

3/2- **6** *14* **Imjoeking (IRE)**[21] 2515 6-11-2 **128**........................ PeterBuchanan 109
(Lucinda Russell) *trckd ldrs: wnt 2nd 5 out: hit: rdn and wknd next* **6/5**[1]

3m 50.2s (-5.60) **Going Correction** -0.10s/f (Good) **6** Ran SP% **108.4**
Speed ratings (Par 107): **110,108,107,99,99 92**
toteswingers 1&2 £14.60, 1&3 £13.30, 2&3 £5.20 CSF £62.54 TOTE £9.20: £3.60, £3.40; EX 69.30 Trifecta £115.50 Pool: £1987.95 - 12.89 winning units..
Owner Mrs J Morgan & Mrs Lindsey J Shaw **Bred** Mme Isabelle Reverseau **Trained** High Eldwick, W Yorks

FOCUS
Thanks to a disputed lead they went a decent pace in this useful handicap chase. A personal best from the winner.

2958 COLLECT TOTEPOOL WINNINGS AT BETFRED SHOPS H'CAP HURDLE (9 hdls) 2m 110y
2:15 (2:15) (Class 3) (0-140,137) 3-Y-0+ **£5,523** (£1,621; £810; £405)

Form RPR

6/1- **1** **Zaplamation (IRE)**[21] 2519 8-10-1 **119**........................ DeanPratt(7) 121+
(John Quinn) *hld up in midfield: effrt and pushed along 2 out: pckd last: styd on wl to ld nr fin* **3/1**[1]

/4P- **2** *½* **Pas Trop Tard (FR)**[35] 2230 6-10-13 **131**........................(t) StephenMulqueen(7) 132
(Maurice Barnes) *led: rdn 3 out: styd on wl fr last: hdd towards fin* **11/1**

226- **3** *2 ½* **Skint**[111] 1302 7-10-7 **118**........................(p) DenisO'Regan 117
(Ali Brewer) *in tch: stdy hdwy bef 3 out: effrt and hung lft bef last: one pce run-in* **9/2**[2]

056- **4** *¾* **Deepsand (IRE)**[14] 2668 4-11-4 **129**........................(p) HarryHaynes 129
(Tim Easterby) *midfield: hdwy and ev ch 2 out: rdn and kpt on same pce run-in* **9/2**[2]

/60- **5** *4* **Lightening Rod**[21] 2519 8-10-6 **124**........................ MrHAABannister(7) 120
(Michael Easterby) *nt fluent on occasions: hld up and bhd: stdy hdwy bef 3 out: pushed along and no imp fr next* **5/1**[3]

2/3- **6** *4* **Maybe I Wont**[26] 2420 8-10-7 **118**........................ LucyAlexander 110
(James Moffatt) *chsd ldrs: rdn and outpcd 4 out: rallied after 3 out: no imp whn blnd last* **14/1**

11B/ **7** *2 ¼* **Lexi's Boy (IRE)**[492] 1165 5-11-12 **137**........................ HenryBrooke 129
(Donald McCain) *chsd ldr: rdn and ev ch whn nt fluent 3 out: wknd fr next* **8/1**

365/ **8** *2* **Alaivan (IRE)**[946] 278 7-11-12 **137**........................ RichieMcGrath 124
(Jonjo O'Neill) *hld up: stdy hdwy after 4 out: rdn and wknd next* **16/1**

2F4/ **9** *37* **Pertemps Networks**[126] 3181 9-10-9 **120**........................ WilsonRenwick 74
(Michael Easterby) *towards rr: stmbld bdly and nrly uns rdr 3rd: lost tch fr 4 out: t.o* **33/1**

3m 50.9s (-4.90) **Going Correction** -0.10s/f (Good)
WFA 4 from 5yo+ 5lb **9** Ran SP% **113.0**
Speed ratings (Par 107): **107,106,105,105,103 101,100,99,82**
toteswingers 1&2 £25.50, 1&3 £21.60, 2&3 £25.50 CSF £34.43 CT £144.85 TOTE £3.60: £1.60, £3.30, £1.90; EX 50.10 Trifecta £229.00 Pool: £1002.53 - 3.28 winning units..
Owner Andrew Turton & David Barker **Bred** Mesnil Investments Ltd And Deerpark Stud **Trained** Settrington, N Yorks

FOCUS
An interesting handicap hurdle and truly run thanks to the runner-up. Solid-looking form.

2959 KNAGGSY BOY 48TH BIRTHDAY NOVICES' H'CAP CHASE (18 fncs) 3m 1f
2:50 (2:50) (Class 4) (0-110,110) 4-Y-0+ **£3,768** (£1,106; £553; £276)

Form RPR

B43- **1** **Basford Ben**[128] 1172 5-10-7 **91**........................(p) SeanQuinlan 100
(Jennie Candlish) *t.k.h: hld up in tch: stdy hdwy 6 out: effrt whn nt fluent 4 out: edgd lft after next: led last: pushed out* **9/2**[2]

F00- **2** *2* **Shouldavboughtgold (IRE)**[15] 2655 6-10-13 **100**........(t) JohnKington(3) 106
(William Kinsey) *in tch: drvn and outpcd after 5 out: lft 4th next: hdwy 2 out: styd on to chse wnr run-in: no imp* **17/2**

311- **3** *2 ¾* **Settledoutofcourt (IRE)**[22] 2498 7-11-12 **110**........................ PeterBuchanan 116
(Lucinda Russell) *led: rdn 3 out: hdd last: kpt on same pce* **11/4**[1]

535- **4** *5* **Lord Fox (IRE)**[15] 2649 6-9-9 **84** oh5........................ BenPoste(5) 88
(Shaun Harris) *sn chsng ldr: ev ch and hung lft bef 3 out: outpcd bef last* **11/1**

156- **5** *37* **Chicago Outfit (IRE)**[25] 2445 8-10-6 **97**........................(p) JohnDawson(7) 63
(John Wade) *chsd ldrs tl drvn and outpcd fr 10th: lost tch fr 5 out: t.o* **9/1**

21F- **P** **Whiskey Ridge (IRE)**[10] 2749 7-10-13 **97**........................ BrianHarding
(Sue Smith) *chsd ldrs: outpcd whn nt fluent 5 out: sn btn: t.o whn p.u bef next* **11/4**[1]

/50- **F** **Forty Crown (IRE)**[3] 2882 7-11-12 **110**........................ WilsonRenwick
(John Wade) *hld up: stdy hdwy and prom after 5 out: 8 l 4th and outpcd whn fell next* **8/1**[3]

6m 15.1s (5.70) **Going Correction** -0.10s/f (Good) **7** Ran SP% **111.5**
Speed ratings (Par 105): **86,85,84,82,71 ,**
toteswingers 1&2 £5.70, 1&3 £4.10, 2&3 £4.70 CSF £37.60 CT £120.05 TOTE £4.40: £2.20, £4.10; EX 46.70 Trifecta £334.00 Pool: £1492.93 - 3.35 winning units..
Owner The Best Club In The World **Bred** Carmel Stud **Trained** Basford Green, Staffs

FOCUS
An ordinary novices' handicap chase. The winner is rated to his mark.

2960 WATCH RACING UK ON FREEVIEW 231 "JUNIOR" STANDARD OPEN NATIONAL HUNT FLAT RACE 1m 5f
3:25 (3:25) (Class 6) 3-Y-O **£1,711** (£498; £249)

Form RPR

1 **Lady Buttons** 3-10-0 0........................ AdamNicol(5) 104+
(Philip Kirby) *in tch: smooth hdwy to press ldr over 2f out: led over 1f out: drifted lft: kpt on strly* **17/2**

2 *1 ¾* **Diaktoros (IRE)** 3-10-12 0........................ BarryKeniry 108+
(Ben Haslam) *prom: hdwy to ld over 2f out: rdn and hdd over 1f out: kpt on fnl f: nt pce of wnr* **8/1**[3]

3 *8* **Doktor Glaz (FR)** 3-10-12 0........................ WilsonRenwick 98+
(Rose Dobbin) *hld up towards rr: drvn and outpcd over 6f out: rallied over 2f out: styd on fnl f: nt rch first two* **4/1**[1]

2- **4** *3 ¼* **Chebsey Beau**[34] 2247 3-10-12 0........................ RichieMcGrath 94
(John Quinn) *hld up in tch on outside: rdn along over 4f out: kpt on same pce fr 2f out* **4/1**[1]

4- **5** *2 ¼* **River Bollin**[38] 2160 3-10-5 0........................ MrWEasterby(7) 91
(Tim Easterby) *chsd ldrs: drvn and outpcd 3f out: plugged on fnl 2f: no imp* **12/1**

24- **6** *1 ¼* **Lebanna**[17] 2604 3-10-5 0........................ LucyAlexander 82
(Tim Easterby) *led to over 2f out: sn rdn and outpcd* **14/1**

7 *1 ¾* **Bulas Belle** 3-10-0 0........................ TonyKelly(5) 80
(Edwin Tuer) *t.k.h: chsd ldrs: drvn and outpcd over 2f out: n.d after* **25/1**

8 *4 ½* **Lola** 3-10-5 0........................ HenryBrooke 74
(Michael Dods) *hld up on ins: drvn and outpcd over 5f out: n.d after* **16/1**

9 *¾* **Clarence Beeks (IRE)** 3-10-5 0........................ NathanMoscrop(7) 80
(Brian Ellison) *w ldrs tl rdn and wknd over 2f out* **10/1**

10 *7* **Robin The Rich (IRE)** 3-10-12 0........................ HarryHaynes 71
(Richard Guest) *hld up: outpcd over 4f out: btn fnl 2f* **12/1**

11 *1 ¾* **Taraakum (FR)** 3-10-9 0........................(be[1]) JohnKington(3) 69
(Andrew Crook) *hld up: shortlived effrt over 4f out: wknd over 2f out* **12/1**

12 *16* **Amour Collonges (FR)**[83] 3-10-12 0........................ DenisO'Regan 48
(Chris Grant) *in tch tl rdn and wknd over 3f out* **7/1**[2]

13 *15* **Faolan (IRE)** 3-10-12 0........................ BrianHarding 28
(Robin Bastiman) *hld up: struggling over 5f out: sn btn* **33/1**

3m 6.0s (186.00) **13** Ran SP% **125.6**
toteswingers 1&2 £36.00, 2&3 £3.10, 1&3 £32.10 CSF £78.99 TOTE £7.30: £2.90, £2.90, £1.90; EX 124.70 Trifecta £608.50 Part won. Pool: £811.39 - 0.21 winning units..
Owner Mrs Jayne Sivills **Bred** Keith Sivills **Trained** Middleham, N Yorks

FOCUS
A modest junior bumper run at an ordinary pace, but two previously unraced performers pulled a long way clear of the rest, so both should have futures. The form is rated around the fourth to the sixth.
T/Plt: £1,177.20 to a £1 stake. Pool: £57812.96 - 35.85 winning tickets T/Qpdt: £152.40 to a £1 stake. Pool: £4574.45 - 22.20 winning tickets RY

2961 - 2967a (Foreign Racing) - See Raceform Interactive

2355 KELSO (L-H)
Sunday, December 8

OFFICIAL GOING: Good to soft (6.9)
Wind: Fresh, half against Weather: Overcast

2968 BORDER FACILITIES NOVICES' HURDLE (8 hdls) 2m 110y
12:25 (12:26) (Class 4) 4-Y-0+ **£3,249** (£954; £477; £238)

Form RPR

0/0- **1** **Tough Trade**[23] 2493 4-10-12 0........................ HenryBrooke 108+
(Chris Grant) *hld up: stdy hdwy 4 out: swtchd rt bef 2 out: led bef last: styd on strly* **80/1**

1/5- **2** *3* **King Of Strings (IRE)**[16] 2660 4-10-12 0........................ DougieCostello 105+
(Tim Walford) *t.k.h: chsd ldr: effrt and ev ch between last 2: kpt on fr last: nt pce of wnr* **9/2**[2]

36- **3** *2 ¼* **Pulpitarian (USA)**[30] 2341 5-10-12 0........................ PeterBuchanan 104
(Lucinda Russell) *hld up in midfield: effrt bef 2 out: ev ch between last 2: one pce run-in* **7/2**[1]

4 *nk* **Muharrer**[74] 4-10-12 0........................ BarryKeniry 105+
(Michael Dods) *t.k.h early: cl up: hit 4 out: effrt and rdn 2 out: one pce fr last* **9/2**[2]

4/5- **5** *1* **Regal Swain (IRE)**[23] 2493 5-10-12 0........................ PaddyBrennan 102
(Alan Swinbank) *hld up in tch: effrt and pushed along bef 2 out: outpcd fr last* **5/1**[3]

0- **6** *11* **Badea**[7] 2840 4-10-12 0........................ WilsonRenwick 92
(Martin Todhunter) *towards rr: pushed along after 4 out: effrt bef 2 out: nvr rchd ldrs* **40/1**

1- **7** *2* **Roc De Prince**[177] 732 4-11-5 0........................(t) BrianHughes 97
(James Ewart) *led: hit and rdn 2 out: hdd bef last: sn wknd* **7/2**[1]

360- **8** *1 ¼* **Dalstontosiloth (IRE)**[8] 2823 5-10-5 0........................ CallumBewley(7) 89
(Barry Murtagh) *nt fluent on occasions: in rr: rdn bef 3 out: nvr able to chal* **100/1**

9 *5* **Bassett Road (IRE)**[30] 5-10-9 0........................ EwanWhillans(3) 84
(Keith Dalgleish) *nt fluent in rr: rdn 3 out: nvr on terms* **33/1**

65/ **10** *5* **Marlee Mourinho (IRE)**[954] 154 7-10-12 0........................ LucyAlexander 80
(N W Alexander) *in tch tl rdn and wknd after 3 out* **33/1**

260- **11** *1 ¾* **Abel J Tasman (IRE)**[38] 2174 5-10-7 0........................ TonyKelly(5) 78
(James Moffatt) *midfield: hit 1st: struggling 3 out: btn next* **50/1**

4/4- **12** *24* **Benefitofhindsight**[200] 433 4-10-12 0 .... DavidBass 57
(Ben Pauling) *hld up: blnd 4th: struggling fr next: t.o* **33/1**
P **Five To Five**[1270] 5-10-12 0 .... HarryHaynes
(Lynsey Kendall) *in tch to 4th: wknd next: t.o whn p.u bef 2 out* **150/1**
00P- **P** **Wind Echo**[29] 2355 5-10-5 0 .... (b[1]) DaraghBourke(7)
(Rayson Nixon) *cl up: stmbld bdly 2nd: lost pl qckly after next: t.o whn p.u bef 4th* **250/1**

3m 53.7s (-8.10) **Going Correction** -0.60s/f (Firm) **14** Ran SP% **114.0**
Speed ratings (Par 105): **95,93,92,92,91 86,85,85,82,80 79,68, ,**
toteswingers 1&2 £43.40, 2&3 £4.30, 1&3 £43.40 CSF £394.66 TOTE £40.80: £10.10, £2.00, £1.30; EX 906.10 TRIFECTA Not won..
Owner D & D Armstrong Ltd & Nigel E M Jones **Bred** Redvers, Dwyer & Holland **Trained** Newton Bewley, Co Durham

FOCUS
All rails on innermost line on both tracks, reducing distances by between 10-15yds per circuit. Ordinary novice form.

2969 SCOTTY BRAND PARIS PIKE NOVICES' CHASE (17 fncs) 2m 7f 110y
12:55 (12:55) (Class 3) 4-Y-0+ £9,811 (£2,898; £1,449; £725; £362)

Form RPR

021- **1** **Coverholder (IRE)**[26] 2446 6-11-6 127 .... RyanMania 143+
(Sue Smith) *chsd ldrs: wnt 2nd 12th: led 4 out: clr after next: easily* **5/1**[3]
3/2- **2** *9* **Little Glenshee (IRE)**[27] 2418 7-10-8 120 .... LucyAlexander 118
(N W Alexander) *t.k.h early: cl up: led 3rd to 4 out: sn rdn: kpt on same pce fr 2 out* **7/2**[2]
/12- **3** *5* **Beeves (IRE)**[43] 2074 6-11-6 140 .... JasonMaguire 132+
(Donald McCain) *nt fluent on occasions: led to 3rd: nt fluent and outpcd 12th: rallied 3 out: nrly 7 l 3rd and no imp whn blnd next* **5/4**[1]
/21- **4** *34* **Talkin Sence (IRE)**[29] 2357 8-10-8 0 .... DaraghBourke(7) 110
(Stuart Coltherd) *trckd ldrs: drvn after 3 out: wknd next* **5/1**[3]
1/5- **5** *2 1/4* **Standintheband (IRE)**[58] 1850 6-11-1 119 .... PeterBuchanan 88
(N W Alexander) *nt fluent: sn bhd: struggling fnl circ: nvr on terms* **22/1**
033- **6** *19* **Attycran (IRE)**[11] 2747 8-10-8 103 .... (tp) StephenMulqueen(7) 73
(Maurice Barnes) *sn bhd: mstke and struggling 7th: no ch fnl circ* **50/1**

5m 49.4s (-18.60) **Going Correction** -0.60s/f (Firm) **6** Ran SP% **106.3**
Speed ratings (Par 107): **107,104,102,91,90 83**
toteswingers 1&2 £3.40, 2&3 £1.40, 1&3 £1.20 CSF £20.47 TOTE £4.50: £2.00, £2.50; EX 19.40 Trifecta £31.80 Pool: £1,919.47 - 45.25 winning tickets..
Owner Mrs S Smith **Bred** T Duggan And P McCarthy **Trained** High Eldwick, W Yorks

FOCUS
A fair novice chase that was won in dominant fashion. The winner looks like being a much better chaser than hurdler.

2970 KEVIN OLIVER CHRISTMAS H'CAP HURDLE (8 hdls) 2m 110y
1:25 (1:27) (Class 4) (0-120,119) 3-Y-0+ £3,249 (£954; £477; £238)

Form RPR

/34- **1** **Bogside (IRE)**[31] 2311 9-11-0 107 .... LucyAlexander 110
(George Charlton) *hld up: stdy hdwy bef 2 out: hung lft and led last: drvn out* **7/1**[3]
3/3- **2** *1 1/2* **Titus Bolt (IRE)**[36] 2221 4-11-3 110 .... HenryBrooke 112
(Jim Goldie) *led: rdn 2 out: hdd last: kpt on u.p: hld nr fin* **12/1**
430- **3** *1 3/4* **Sud Pacifique (IRE)**[51] 1960 5-11-11 118 .... (b) JasonMaguire 118
(Donald McCain) *trckd ldrs: effrt and rdn bef 2 out: one pce after last* **7/1**[3]
03/ **4** *1 1/4* **Streets Of Newyork**[37] 2204 6-11-2 109 .... BarryKeniry 108
(Brian Ellison) *hld up: rdn and outpcd after 3 out: rallied next: kpt on fr last: nvr able to chal* **17/2**
41- **5** *5* **Redpender (IRE)**[36] 2217 7-11-5 112 .... BrianHughes 107
(James Moffatt) *pressed ldr: effrt and rdn bef 2 out: outpcd bef last* **6/1**[2]
204- **6** *7* **Cool Baranca (GER)**[36] 2221 7-11-6 118 .... EmmaSayer(5) 108
(Dianne Sayer) *hld up: rdn after 3 out: keeping on whn checked last: nvr able to chal* **33/1**
14F- **7** *8* **Sleep In First (FR)**[9] 2793 7-10-12 112 .... DaleIrving(7) 101+
(James Ewart) *prom: blnd 3rd: cl up tl rdn and wknd bef 2 out* **16/1**
/6U- **8** *2* **Phoenix Returns (IRE)**[25] 2454 5-11-12 119 .... PaddyBrennan 98
(Alan Swinbank) *in tch on outside: rdn after 3 out: wknd bef next* **20/1**
9 *19* **Gunner Lindley (IRE)**[35] 1807 6-10-2 102 .... DaraghBourke(7) 74
(Stuart Coltherd) *nt fluent: cl up: rdn and wkng whn blnd 2 out* **5/2**[1]
130- **P** **Dhaular Dhar (IRE)**[30] 2344 11-11-0 107 .... GaryBartley
(Jim Goldie) *bhd: struggling after 3 out: p.u bef last* **33/1**
/U3- **F** **Lone Foot Laddie (IRE)**[196] 494 4-10-12 112 .... GrahamWatters(7) 104
(Lucinda Russell) *midfield: effrt bef 2 out: 8 l sixth and no imp whn fell last* **25/1**
/16- **P** **Damascus Steel (IRE)**[39] 2156 5-11-5 112 .... BrianHarding
(Alison Hamilton) *in tch: rdn bef 2 out: sn wknd: p.u bef last* **18/1**
221- **F** **Raven's Tower (USA)**[34] 2274 3-10-10 117 .... DavidBass 104+
(Ben Pauling) *hld up: hdwy on outside bef 2 out: 3 l down and disputing 3rd pl whn fell heavily last* **15/2**

3m 51.8s (-10.00) **Going Correction** -0.60s/f (Firm)
WFA 3 from 4yo 13lb 4 from 5yo+ 5lb **13** Ran SP% **123.5**
Speed ratings (Par 105): **99,98,97,96,94 91,87,86,77, ,**
toteswingers 1&2 £11.50, 2&3 £12.30, 1&3 £13.20 CSF £86.01 CT £619.11 TOTE £8.70: £2.60, £4.40, £2.80; EX 72.30 Trifecta £1101.30 Part won. Pool: £1,468.46 - 0.10 winning tickets..
Owner Mrs A R Wood **Bred** Pat O'Donovan **Trained** Stocksfield, Northumberland

FOCUS
A modest handicap hurdle, in which the first two are rated to their marks.

2971 PERSIMMON HOMES SCOTTISH BORDERS NATIONAL (HANDICAP CHASE) (24 fncs) 4m
1:55 (1:55) (Class 2) (0-145,135) 5-Y-0+ £16,325 (£4,865; £2,462; £1,261; £660)

Form RPR

200- **1** **Royale Knight**[25] 2458 7-10-3 112 .... SamTwiston-Davies 129+
(Dr Richard Newland) *t.k.h early: cl up: wnt 2nd 20th: led gng wl 2 out: sn clr: rdn and r.o wl run-in* **6/1**[3]
233- **2** *6* **Scotswell**[8] 2817 7-10-12 121 .... JamesReveley 130
(Harriet Graham) *led: hit 15th: rdn and hdd 2 out: plugged on fr last: nt rch wnr* **15/2**
123- **3** *9* **Imperial Vic (IRE)**[27] 2419 8-11-12 135 .... RyanMania 136
(Michael Smith) *cl up: hit 11th: wnt 2nd 18th to 20th: rdn and outpcd by first two after 3 out* **85/40**[1]
431- **4** *6* **More Equity**[31] 2310 11-9-11 111 .... HarryChalloner(5) 105
(Dianne Sayer) *hld up: rdn and outpcd 5 out: rallied bef 2 out: styd on: nvr able to chal* **28/1**
2/2- **5** *20* **Ros Castle (IRE)**[27] 2421 7-10-11 120 .... WilsonRenwick 103
(Rose Dobbin) *hld up: outpcd whn blnd 19th: rallied after 3 out: wknd fr next* **11/1**
4/2- **P** **Bishops Heir**[29] 2357 8-10-10 119 .... (p) BrianHughes
(James Ewart) *chsd ldrs: pushed along 17th: outpcd fr 4 out: no ch whn p.u and dismntd bef last* **7/1**
226- **P** **Bescot Springs (IRE)**[35] 2246 8-9-12 114 .... (v) CraigNichol(7)
(Lucinda Russell) *nt fluent on occasions: in tch: outpcd 9th: struggling fr 18th: t.o whn p.u bef 2 out* **17/2**
/44- **P** **Royal Sam (IRE)**[22] 2517 8-10-6 115 .... LucyAlexander
(Martin Todhunter) *hld up: stdy hdwy 15th: lost pl after 17th: struggling fr next: t.o whn p.u bef 2 out* **22/1**
3/1- **P** **Soudain (FR)**[15] 2678 7-10-12 128 .... PaulBohan(7)
(Steve Gollings) *chsd ldr to 18th: outpcd 20th: blnd and wknd next: p.u bef 2 out* **5/1**[2]

8m 21.3s (-26.70) **Going Correction** -0.60s/f (Firm) **9** Ran SP% **113.9**
Speed ratings: **109,107,105,103,98 , , ,**
toteswingers 1&2 £6.00, 2&3 £4.10, 1&3 £6.40 CSF £49.27 CT £125.37 TOTE £6.80: £2.40, £2.70, £1.20; EX 63.50 Trifecta £216.50 Pool: £1,665.95 - 5.76 winning tickets..
Owner C E Stedman & R J Corsan **Bred** R D And Mrs J S Chugg **Trained** Claines, Worcs

FOCUS
They went steady early and this didn't turn into the slog one would perhaps have imagined, given the distance. The easy winner improved for the marathon trip.

2972 JOHN WADE ALWAYS RIGHT CHAMPION CHASE (HANDICAP CHASE) (THE SUNDAY £5K BONUS RACE) (17 fncs) 2m 7f 110y
2:25 (2:29) (Class 2) 4-Y-0+ £12,027 (£3,553; £1,776; £889; £444)

Form RPR

441- **1** **Kruzhlinin (GER)**[29] 2358 6-11-12 138 .... JasonMaguire 153+
(Donald McCain) *trckd ldrs: mstke 12th: led gng wl after 2 out: rdn out fr last* **4/1**[3]
/31- **2** *5* **No Planning**[22] 2517 6-11-5 131 .... RyanMania 136
(Sue Smith) *chsd ldr: chal 4 out: led briefly 2 out: kpt on fr last: no ch w wnr* **9/4**[2]
605- **3** *9* **Rolecarr (IRE)**[29] 2358 10-10-8 127 .... GrahamWatters(7) 125
(Ann Hamilton) *nt fluent on occasions: in tch: rdn and outpcd bef 4 out: rallied and lft 4th last: kpt on: no ch w first two* **10/1**
P66- **4** *3 3/4* **Garleton (IRE)**[29] 2358 12-10-9 128 .... (t) StephenMulqueen(7) 121
(Maurice Barnes) *led: rdn and hdd 2 out: outpcd whn lft 3rd last: no ex* **14/1**
116- **5** *11* **Riskier**[26] 2448 8-11-1 127 .... BrianHughes 115
(John Wade) *trckd ldrs tl rdn and wknd bef 2 out: lft mod 5th last* **20/1**
511- **6** *64* **Rossini's Dancer**[43] 2072 8-11-0 133 .... (v) MrKitAlexander(7) 58
(N W Alexander) *reluctant to line up: in tch on outside: outpcd 1/2-way: lost tch fr 4 out: virtually p.u run-in* **16/1**
311- **F** **Night Alliance (IRE)**[16] 2646 8-10-9 121 .... (b) SamTwiston-Davies 127+
(Dr Richard Newland) *mstkes in rr: hld up: smooth hdwy after 3 out: effrt next: 4 l down and one pce whn fell heavily last* **2/1**[1]
4/1- **U** **Sean Airgead (IRE)**[18] 2609 8-11-4 130 .... (t) PeterBuchanan
(Mark Michael McNiff, Ire) *hld up last: mstke 1st: pushed along and stdy hdwy bef 4 out: wknd after next: no ch whn hit and uns rdr 2 out* **28/1**

5m 53.5s (-14.50) **Going Correction** -0.60s/f (Firm) **8** Ran SP% **114.0**
Speed ratings (Par 109): **100,98,95,94,90 69, ,**
toteswingers 1&2 £2.00, 2&3 £2.40, 1&3 £8.90 CSF £13.95 CT £81.70 TOTE £4.20: £1.40, £1.20, £2.90; EX 15.00 Trifecta £87.80 Pool: £1,373.47 - 11.72 winning tickets..
Owner Paul & Clare Rooney **Bred** Gestut Kussaburg **Trained** Cholmondeley, Cheshire

FOCUS
A decent handicap and the form looks solid, with the right horses coming to the fore. The winner has developed into a smart handicapper.

2973 MCMILLANFINEART.COM & JAMES EWART RACING MARES' NOVICES' HURDLE (11 hdls) 2m 6f 110y
2:55 (2:57) (Class 4) 4-Y-0+ £3,249 (£954; £477; £238)

Form RPR

141/ **1** **Tonvadosa**[262] 4885 5-10-10 0 .... JasonMaguire 110+
(Donald McCain) *trckd ldr: led 3 out: clr whn wandered between last 2: kpt on strly* **15/8**[1]
2 *5* **Dominetta Vitali (IRE)**[107] 1369 7-10-10 105 .... PaddyBrennan 101
(M P Sunderland, Ire) *in tch: hdwy to chse wnr bef 2 out: one pce bef last* **6/1**
001- **3** *1 1/4* **Rev Up Ruby**[23] 2495 5-10-10 108 .... JonathonBewley(7) 107
(George Bewley) *mstkes in rr: hdwy bef 3 out: styd on fr next: nvr able to chal* **5/1**[3]
03- **4** *3 1/4* **Spring Over (IRE)**[23] 2495 7-10-3 0 .... GrahamWatters(7) 97
(Ian Duncan) *in tch: effrt and rdn along after 3 out: no imp fr next* **14/1**
/1P- **5** *3* **The Flaming Matron (IRE)**[36] 2218 7-11-3 100 .... (t) LucyAlexander 100
(N W Alexander) *led to 3 out: sn rdn: hung lft and wknd after next* **10/1**
/22- **6** *16* **Rathvawn Belle (IRE)**[31] 2309 6-10-10 110 .... WilsonRenwick 79
(Lucinda Russell) *t.k.h: hld up bhd ldng gp: mstke 4 out: rdn and wknd bef 2 out* **5/2**[2]
7 *50* **Ma Cranky (IRE)**[597] 5-10-10 0 .... HenryBrooke 34
(Chris Grant) *chsd ldrs tl wknd bef 3 out: t.o* **16/1**

5m 36.1s (-4.90) **Going Correction** -0.60s/f (Firm) **7** Ran SP% **115.9**
Speed ratings (Par 105): **84,82,81,80,79 74,56**
toteswingers 1&2 £1.30, 2&3 £6.10, 1&3 £4.00 CSF £14.24 TOTE £3.40: £2.10, £2.80; EX 13.90 Trifecta £81.60 Pool: £770.58 - 7.07 winning tickets..
Owner T Meehan & D J Burke **Bred** Whitley Stud **Trained** Cholmondeley, Cheshire

FOCUS
A modest mares' novice but the easy winner is probably capable of better.

2974 LAZY GRACE "NATIONAL HUNT" NOVICES' H'CAP HURDLE (13 hdls) 3m 3f
3:25 (3:26) (Class 5) (0-100,99) 3-Y-0+ £2,599 (£763; £381; £190)

Form RPR

026- **1** **Brae On (IRE)**[7] 2842 5-10-7 87 .... JonathonBewley(7) 95
(George Bewley) *hld up: pushed along after 4 out: hdwy bef 2 out: led between last 2: styd on strly run-in* **14/1**
P02- **2** *3 1/4* **St Gregory (IRE)**[23] 2497 5-10-0 73 .... BrianHarding 78
(Nicky Richards) *prom: drvn and outpcd 3 out: rallied next: chsd wnr run-in: kpt on: no imp* **11/2**[3]
211- **3** *1 1/2* **Snuker**[18] 2591 6-10-1 74 .... (p) BrianHughes 80+
(James Ewart) *mstkes: led to 3rd: led 7th: rdn whn hit 2 out: sn hdd: one pce fr last* **6/4**[1]
/03- **4** *4 1/2* **Lady Of Verona (IRE)**[30] 2333 6-10-11 91 .... CraigNichol(7) 91
(Lucinda Russell) *in tch: hdwy to chse ldr bef 2 out: sn rdn: outpcd fr last* **10/1**
350- **5** *27* **Lakefield Rebel (IRE)**[17] 2621 7-11-12 99 .... RichieMcGrath 74
(Henry Hogarth) *t.k.h: hld up: outpcd bef 3 out: n.d after* **25/1**

The Form Book Jumps, Raceform Ltd, Compton, RG20 6NL.

013- **6** *2 1/4* **Maggie Blue (IRE)**[7] 2842 5-11-3 **97** CallumBewley(7) 70
(Harriet Graham) *cl up: hit 4 out: rdn and wknd fr 2 out* **10/1**

0PP- **7** *11* **Morello Mist**[12] 2734 8-9-9 **73** oh7 (t) SamanthaDrake(5) 36
(Richard Drake) *in tch: hdwy to chse ldrs whn hit 8th: rdn and wknd fr 3 out* **80/1**

001- **8** *9* **Amethyst Rose (IRE)**[18] 2596 6-11-1 **95** DaraghBourke(7) 50
(Stuart Coltherd) *t.k.h: cl up: led 3rd to 7th: hit 4 out: rdn and wknd next* **5/1**[2]

P35- **9** *17* **Lucky Sun**[18] 2596 7-10-5 **83** (p) AdamNicol(5) 23
(Philip Kirby) *hld up bhd ldng gp: struggling appr 3 out: sn btn* **10/1**

146- **10** *13* **Mia's Anthem (IRE)**[18] 2591 5-11-0 **92** DerekFox(5) 20
(Noel C Kelly, Ire) *mstkes: bhd and sn detached: no ch fnl circ* **20/1**

6m 29.0s (-11.00) **Going Correction** -0.60s/f (Firm) **10** Ran SP% **115.8**
Speed ratings (Par 103): **104,103,102,101,93 92,89,86,81,77**
toteswingers 1&2 £21.20, 2&3 £3.00, 1&3 £9.90 CSF £87.45 CT £185.90 TOTE £18.80: £4.30, £2.20, £1.10; EX 92.50 Trifecta £814.10 Part won. Pool: £1,085.49 - 0.73 winning tickets..
Owner West Coast Racing Partnership **Bred** Pat Moore **Trained** Bonchester Bridge, Borders

FOCUS
This proved a decent test of stamina. The winner improved in line with the best of his bumper figures.
T/Jkpt: Not won. T/Plt: £106.40 to a £1 stake. Pool: £90,348.84 - 619.65 winning tickets. T/Qpdt: £19.10 to a £1 stake. Pool: £8,992.76 - 347.75 winning tickets. RY

2598 WARWICK (L-H)
Sunday, December 8

OFFICIAL GOING: Good to soft (good in places; chs 6.5, hdl 6.3)
Wind: Light behind Weather: Cloudy

2975 MAYOR OF SOLIHULL CHARITY FUND JUVENILE HURDLE (8 hdls) 2m
12:40 (12:40) (Class 4) 3-Y-O **£3,768** (£1,106; £553; £276)

Form RPR

1 **Mahican (IRE)**[53] 3-10-12 0 DenisO'Regan 104+
(John Ferguson) *trckd ldr tl led and mstke 3rd: sn hdd: nt fluent 5th: led 3 out: shkn up and hdd appr last: rallied u.p to ld towards fin* **7/4**[1]

46- **2** *1* **Mandy's Boy (IRE)**[2] 2927 3-10-12 0 WillKennedy 100
(Ian Williams) *hld up: hdwy after 5th: led and hung rt appr last: rdn flat: hdd towards fin* **11/1**

3 *9* **Haatefina**[90] 3-10-5 0 DaveCrosse 85
(Mark Usher) *chsd ldrs: rdn appr 2 out: styng on same pce whn mstke last* **50/1**

4 *3/4* **Santo De Lune (FR)** 3-10-12 0 HarrySkelton 93
(Dan Skelton) *prom: j. slowly 3rd: ev ch 3 out: rdn whn stmbld last: wknd flat* **7/1**

50- **5** *1* **Banreenahreenkah (IRE)**[9] 2557 3-10-5 0 [1] SeanQuinlan 83
(Jennie Candlish) *hld up: plld hrd: hdwy 3 out: nt fluent last: nvr nr to chal* **50/1**

6 *1 1/4* **Warrant Officer**[258] 3-10-12 0 MarcGoldstein 90
(Sheena West) *trckd ldrs: plld hrd: rdn appr 2 out: wknd bef last* **50/1**

3- **7** *3* **Rayak (IRE)**[25] 2455 3-10-12 0 APMcCoy 90
(Jonjo O'Neill) *plld hrd: led to 3rd: sn led again: hdd 3 out: wkng whn blnd last* **6/1**[3]

41- **8** *12* **Duroble Man**[49] 1985 3-11-5 0 RobertThornton 88
(Alan King) *prom: mstke 5th: rdn and wknd next* **2/1**[2]

53- **9** *8* **Innoko (FR)**[29] 2364 3-10-7 0 JoshHamer(5) 69
(Tony Carroll) *hld up: rdn and wknd appr 3 out* **25/1**

0- **10** *9* **Coffers**[26] 2436 3-10-12 0 TomO'Brien 60
(Renee Robeson) *hld up: mstke 5th: wknd bef next* **50/1**

11 *17* **Alberto**[54] 3-10-7 0 JamesBanks(5) 45
(Alastair Lidderdale) *hld up: wknd 5th* **100/1**

3m 47.7s (-8.80) **Going Correction** -0.80s/f (Firm) **11** Ran SP% **117.5**
Speed ratings (Par 104): **90,89,85,84,84 83,82,76,72,67 59**
toteswingers 1&2 £5.30, 2&3 £44.40, 1&3 £28.10 CSF £20.51 TOTE £2.40: £1.10, £3.50, £11.30; EX 19.80 Trifecta £1665.90 Part won. Pool: £2,221.31 - 0.92 winning tickets..
Owner Bloomfields **Bred** Ken Lynch **Trained** Cowlinge, Suffolk

FOCUS
A modest juvenile event. which was steadily run. It's rated around the second and fifth.

2976 AGE UK SOLIHULL BEGINNERS' CHASE (THE SUNDAY £5K BONUS RACE) (12 fncs) 2m
1:10 (1:10) (Class 4) 4-Y-0+ **£5,198** (£1,526; £763; £381)

Form RPR

3/2- **1** **Mr Mole (IRE)**[211] 216 5-11-0 0 (t) APMcCoy 133+
(Paul Nicholls) *trckd ldrs: wnt 2nd 3 out: shkn up and qcknd to ld fnl 100yds: readily* **13/8**[2]

2 *1 1/4* **Vukovar (FR)**[178] 4-10-8 0 NoelFehily 123+
(Harry Fry) *led: clr fr 3rd tl rdn flat: hdd and unable qck fnl 100yds* **4/6**[1]

/63- **3** *10* **Pearls Legend**[24] 2469 6-11-0 118 JamieMoore 122
(John Spearing) *trckd wnr tl 3 out: sn pushed along: styd on same pce fr next* **14/1**[3]

/43- **4** *21* **Mr Watson (IRE)**[50] 1973 6-11-0 0 (b) RichieMcLernon 105
(Jonjo O'Neill) *hld up: wknd 9th* **20/1**

PP0- **5** *4 1/2* **Teenage Dream (IRE)**[9] 2787 5-11-0 0 (tp) CharliePoste 100
(Derek Shaw) *hld up: bhd fr 6th: blnd 2 out* **100/1**

3m 51.1s (-14.50) **Going Correction** -0.80s/f (Firm)
WFA 4 from 5yo+ 5lb **5** Ran SP% **110.5**
Speed ratings (Par 105): **104,103,98,87,85**
CSF £3.25 TOTE £2.30: £1.10, £1.10; EX 3.70 Trifecta £7.90 Pool: £1,887.10 - 176.93 winning tickets..
Owner John P McManus **Bred** Mrs Hugh Baird **Trained** Ditcheat, Somerset

FOCUS
A fair little beginners' chase. The winner was a 145 hurdler and was entitled to beat the second on hurdles form.

2977 CITIZENS ADVICE SOLIHULL H'CAP CHASE (12 fncs) 2m
1:40 (1:40) (Class 4) (0-120,118) 4-Y-0+ **£5,848** (£1,717; £858; £429)

Form RPR

326- **1** **Un Anjou (FR)**[17] 2618 5-10-9 **101** (p) AidanColeman 116+
(David Dennis) *hld up: hdwy appr 6th: chsd ldr 9th: led appr 2 out: drvn out* **11/2**[3]

061/ **2** *1* **Mr Muddle**[272] 4701 6-11-5 **111** MarcGoldstein 124
(Sheena West) *sn prom: led 6th: rdn and hdd appr 2 out: styd on* **12/1**

136- **3** *7* **Suerte Al Salto (IRE)**[24] 2469 6-11-12 **118** TomCannon 124
(Chris Gordon) *hld up: hdwy 7th: rdn appr last: styd on same pce* **6/1**

056- **4** *12* **George Nympton (IRE)**[32] 2293 7-11-9 **115** NoelFehily 112
(Nick Williams) *led to 2nd: chsd ldrs tl rdn and wknd appr 2 out* **3/1**[1]

003- **5** *1/2* **Twoways (IRE)**[15] 2677 7-10-13 **105** (t) TomScudamore 103
(Mark Rimell) *prom: lost pl and mstke 2nd: in rr and rdn appr 6th: n.d after* **10/1**

3P4- **6** *9* **Sublime Talent (IRE)**[26] 2448 7-11-10 **116** (t) AdamWedge 103
(Evan Williams) *hld up: bhd fr 7th* **12/1**

4/4- **7** *3 1/2* **Mam Ratagan**[26] 2440 12-11-7 **113** (t) DominicElsworth 100
(Heather Main) *chsd ldrs: led 2nd: sn hdd: led again briefly 5th: rdn after 3 out: wknd next* **16/1**

/11- **8** *3 1/4* **Take Of Shoc'S (IRE)**[28] 2387 9-11-4 **110** (t) PaulMoloney 91
(Sophie Leech) *led after 2nd: hdd 5th: sn led again: hdd next: rdn and wknd 9th* **8/1**

4F0- **9** *38* **Topthorn**[13] 2721 7-10-8 **100** JamesDavies 46
(Martin Bosley) *chsd ldrs tl rdn and wknd 7th* **25/1**

P31- **U** **Batu Ferringhi (FR)**[28] 2385 7-11-11 **117** (v[1]) BrendanPowell
(Jamie Snowden) *blnd and uns rdr 1st* **5/1**[2]

3m 50.1s (-15.50) **Going Correction** -0.80s/f (Firm) **10** Ran SP% **116.7**
Speed ratings (Par 105): **106,105,102,96,95 91,89,87,68,**
toteswingers 1&2 £9.90, 2&3 £20.90, 1&3 £7.50 CSF £67.36 CT £411.24 TOTE £6.90: £2.00, £3.50, £1.70; EX 93.30 Trifecta £421.70 Pool: £1,515.20 - 2.69 winning tickets..
Owner Superdream **Bred** Gildas Vaillant **Trained** Hanley Swan, Worcestershire

FOCUS
A modest handicap. The first two should still be competitive when reassessed.

2978 SOLIHULL - TOWN IN THE COUNTRY MAIDEN HURDLE (11 hdls) 2m 5f
2:10 (2:13) (Class 4) 4-Y-0+ **£3,768** (£1,106; £553; £276)

Form RPR

/02- **1** **Champagne West (IRE)**[16] 2642 5-11-0 0 RichardJohnson 139+
(Philip Hobbs) *chsd ldrs: led and mstke 8th: hdd 2 out: rallied to ld flat: drvn out* **3/1**[2]

1/2- **2** *1* **Deputy Dan (IRE)**[35] 2243 5-11-0 0 LeightonAspell 137+
(Oliver Sherwood) *a.p: jnd wnr 3 out: led next: shkn up appr last: rdn and hdd flat: edgd rt: styd on same pce* **5/2**[1]

16- **3** *22* **Ulzana's Raid (IRE)**[29] 2375 4-11-0 0 RobertThornton 115+
(Alan King) *mid-div: hdwy after 6th: rdn and wknd after 3 out: wnt 3rd next* **33/1**

1- **4** *8* **Tullyesker Hill (IRE)**[20] 2570 4-11-0 0 TomScudamore 110+
(David Pipe) *chsd ldr tl led 7th: rdn and hdd next: wknd appr 2 out* **5/2**[1]

5 *5* **Ampleforth**[20] 5-11-0 0 (p) AidanColeman 102
(Ian Williams) *hld up: hdwy appr 7th: rdn and wknd after 3 out* **33/1**

540- **6** *1/2* **Pembroke House**[13] 2720 6-11-0 0 LiamTreadwell 102
(Sarah-Jayne Davies) *hld up: sme hdwy 8th: wknd after 3 out* **66/1**

1/4- **7** *2 1/4* **Bodega**[16] 2642 5-11-0 0 WillKennedy 99
(Ian Williams) *prom: rdn and mstke 3 out: sn wknd* **16/1**

3/F- **8** *2 1/2* **Anshantor (IRE)**[7] 2850 7-10-11 0 JakeGreenall(3) 97
(Henry Daly) *led to 7th: wknd 3 out* **66/1**

2- **9** *6* **Bally Braes (IRE)**[42] 2104 5-10-7 0 RyanHatch(7) 91
(Nigel Twiston-Davies) *mid-div: rdn appr 7th: sn wknd* **10/1**[3]

P/3- **10** *nk* **Stage King**[17] 2631 7-10-11 0 (t) GavinSheehan(3) 90
(Warren Greatrex) *hld up: a in rr: wknd appr 7th* **66/1**

5- **11** *9* **Powerful Action (IRE)**[68] 1712 5-11-0 0 TomO'Brien 81
(Philip Hobbs) *hld up: hdwy appr 7th: wknd after next* **50/1**

4- **12** *hd* **Letterofthelaw (IRE)**[24] 2472 4-11-0 0 APMcCoy 81
(Rebecca Curtis) *prom tl rdn and wknd 3 out* **20/1**

/22- **13** *16* **Oscars Way (IRE)**[185] 644 5-10-9 0 ConorShoemark(5) 65
(Don Cantillon) *hld up: drvn along 6th: hdwy u.p bef next: wknd 8th* **20/1**

4/0- **14** *18* **Secure Investment**[30] 2354 5-10-9 0 ThomasGarner(5) 47
(Oliver Sherwood) *hld up: a in rr: bhd fr 7th* **100/1**

0- **15** *1 1/4* **Nearly Normal (IRE)**[30] 2354 4-11-0 0 WayneHutchinson 46
(David Dennis) *hld up: a in rr: bhd fr 7th* **100/1**

P **Simmons**[1133] 5-10-2 0 JamesBanks(5)
(Alastair Lidderdale) *hld up: a in rr: lost tch appr 7th: bhd whn p.u bef 2 out* **100/1**

0/0- **P** **Un Jour D Ete (FR)**[37] 2190 5-10-7 0 PaulMoloney
(Nick Littmoden) *hld up: a in rr: bhd fr 7th: p.u bef 2 out* **100/1**

F **Incher Rose (IRE)**[243] 5238 5-10-7 0 BrendanPowell
(Johnny Farrelly) *hld up: rdn and wknd appr 7th: bhd whn fell next* **100/1**

4m 49.1s (-25.90) **Going Correction** -0.80s/f (Firm)
WFA 4 from 5yo+ 6lb **18** Ran SP% **123.9**
Speed ratings (Par 105): **117,116,108,105,103 103,102,101,99,98 95,95,89,82,81 , ,**
toteswingers 1&2 £2.80, 2&3 £20.20, 1&3 £12.50 CSF £10.35 TOTE £4.50: £2.20, £1.30, £6.40; EX 14.90 Trifecta £306.70 Pool: £2,633.86 - 6.44 winning tickets..
Owner R S Brookhouse **Bred** Peter Byrne **Trained** Withycombe, Somerset

FOCUS
A fair maiden, run at a decent gallop and the first pair came right away from the third-last flight. They both look on the upgrade.

2979 CELEBRATING SOLIHULL H'CAP CHASE (22 fncs) 3m 5f
2:40 (2:43) (Class 4) (0-120,118) 4-Y-0+ **£5,848** (£1,717; £858; £429)

Form RPR

/25- **1** **Leg Iron (IRE)**[180] 712 8-11-3 **109** MarcGoldstein 118+
(Sheena West) *chsd ldrs: rdn appr 16th: nt clr run and swtchd rt flat: styd on u.p to ld post* **12/1**

/11- **2** *nse* **Orange Nassau (FR)**[37] 2201 7-11-6 **112** NoelFehily 120
(Charlie Longsdon) *w ldr tl led 4th: hdd appr 6th: led again 17th: rdn appr last: hdd post* **4/1**[1]

/05- **3** *3* **Rebeccas Choice (IRE)**[27] 2419 10-11-9 **118** (p) RobertDunne(3) 123
(Dai Burchell) *hld up: hdwy 12th: rdn appr 2 out: styd on same pce flat* **9/1**

/P2- **4** *nk* **Elite Beneficial (IRE)**[18] 2603 8-9-9 **92** oh11 (p) BenPoste(5) 97
(Rosemary Gasson) *hld up: hdwy 15th: chsd ldr 17th: ev ch fr 3 out tl no ex flat* **33/1**

422- **5** *18* **Cornish Ice**[19] 2582 9-10-13 **105** (p) CharliePoste 96
(Robin Dickin) *prom: drvn along appr 16th: wknd after 3 out* **20/1**

/32- **6** *29* **Loughalder (IRE)**[19] 2578 7-10-3 **102** (tp) MrJMRidley(7) 64
(Matt Sheppard) *hld up: hdwy 7th: rdn after 15th: wknd 17th* **6/1**[3]

/56- **7** *16* **Fredo (IRE)**[23] 2487 9-11-7 **118** (p) RobertMcCarth(5) 66
(Ian Williams) *hld up: rdn and wknd 16th* **4/1**[1]

0P1- **P** **Super Villan**[16] 2651 8-11-9 **115** (b) APMcCoy
(Mark Bradstock) *led to 4th: led again bef 6th: rdn and hdd 17th: wknd next: bhd whn p.u bef 2 out* **5/1**[2]

541- **P** **Royal Chatelier (FR)**[19] 2578 8-11-4 **110** TomCannon
(Michael Blake) *prom: lost pl 7th: in rr and drvn along 11th: wknd 15th: bhd whn p.u bef 4 out* **16/1**

/44- **P** **Material Boy**[17] 2633 6-10-12 **104**..(t) DarylJacob
(Nick Williams) *prom: nt fluent 8th and next: sn given reminders and lost pl: bhd fr 11th: j.lft 13th: p.u bef 15th* **8/1**

7m 15.7s (-25.30) **Going Correction** -0.80s/f (Firm) **10** Ran SP% **113.3**
Speed ratings (Par 105): **102,101,101,101,96 88,83, , ,**
toteswingers 1&2 £10.30, 2&3 £7.00, 1&3 £15.20 CSF £59.57 CT £457.06 TOTE £16.80: £4.00, £1.80, £4.20; EX 102.60 Trifecta £1476.20 Pool: £2,042.30 - 1.03 winning tickets..
Owner Michael Moriarty **Bred** Miss Jane Mangan **Trained** Falmer, E Sussex

FOCUS
A competitive staying handicap for the grade. The winner is rated to his mark.

2980 MAYOR'S CHARITY FUND SUPPORTING SOLIHULL CHARITIES H'CAP HURDLE (11 hdls) 2m 5f
3:10 (3:14) (Class 4) (0-105,110) 3-Y-0+ **£3,768** (£1,106; £553; £276)

Form RPR

1F1- **1** **Mini Muck**[3] 2896 7-11-11 **110** 7ex.. RyanHatch(7) 118+
(Nigel Twiston-Davies) *chsd ldrs: led after 3 out: clr last: rdn and edgd rt flat: styd on* **9/4**[1]

020- **2** 3 1/2 **Definite Lady (IRE)**[20] 2568 7-11-3 **95**........................(b) TomScudamore 97
(Mark Rimell) *chsd ldr: ev ch whn hit 3 out: sn rdn: styd on same pce appr last* **22/1**

/46- **3** 1/2 **Icanmotor**[172] 765 6-10-0 **78** oh2..(tp) JamieMoore 80
(Claire Dyson) *a.p: rdn after 3 out: styd on same pce appr last* **12/1**

613- **4** 3 1/4 **Portofino Wasp (IRE)**[137] 1107 4-11-6 **98**.................. RichieMcLernon 97
(Jonjo O'Neill) *hld up: hdwy 8th: shkn up appr 2 out: styd on same pce* **12/1**

003- **5** 1/2 **Matako (FR)**[14] 2690 10-11-1 **93**.. IanPopham 91
(Caroline Keevil) *prom: rdn after 3 out: styd on same pce fr next: hit last* **6/1**[3]

500- **6** 3 1/4 **Khazium (IRE)**[14] 2696 4-10-5 **90**................................(tp) GeraldQuinn(7) 84
(Claire Dyson) *led to 3 out: sn rdn: wknd last* **50/1**

/41- **7** nk **Monderon (FR)**[14] 2701 6-11-5 **104**.......................... MrRobertHawker(7) 98
(Richard Hawker) *hld up: sme hdwy after 3 out: sn rdn: wknd after next* **14/1**

541- **8** nk **Rigolo Ville (FR)**[14] 2690 8-11-3 **98**............................(p) GilesHawkins(3) 91+
(Richard Hobson) *hld up: pushed along 7th: hdwy next: mstke 3 out: sn rdn and wknd* **5/1**[2]

035- **9** 4 1/2 **Yazdi (IRE)**[104] 1388 4-11-8 **100**.. RobertThornton 91
(Henry Oliver) *prom: hit 5th: pushed along 8th: rdn and wknd appr 2 out* **50/1**

225/ **10** 10 **Craiglands (IRE)**[556] 513 11-10-9 **92**......................(p) RobertMcCarth(5) 71
(Ian Williams) *chsd ldrs tl rdn and wknd after 3 out* **16/1**

P04- **11** 1/2 **Admiral Boom (IRE)**[26] 2430 7-11-1 **93**.............................. TomO'Brien 71
(Paul Henderson) *hld up: bhd fr 7th* **14/1**

S04- **12** 1 1/4 **Oscar Jane (IRE)**[14] 2696 6-11-4 **96**.......................... BrendanPowell 73
(Johnny Farrelly) *mid-div: rdn and wknd after 7th* **10/1**

640- **13** 48 **Ibiza Sunset (IRE)**[20] 2568 5-10-8 **86**............................(t) AndrewTinkler 15
(Brendan Powell) *hld up: reminders after 6th: wknd next* **16/1**

5m 1.8s (-13.20) **Going Correction** -0.80s/f (Firm)
WFA 4 from 5yo+ 6lb **13** Ran SP% **119.6**
Speed ratings (Par 105): **93,91,91,90,90 88,88,88,86,83 82,82,64**
toteswingers 1&2 £6.90, 2&3 £35.70, 1&3 £10.40 CSF £54.38 CT £502.31 TOTE £2.50: £1.10, £3.60, £5.80; EX 40.00 Trifecta £511.70 Pool: £1,960.47 - 2.87 winning tickets..
Owner N A Twiston-Davies **Bred** N A Twiston-Davies **Trained** Naunton, Gloucs

FOCUS
This moderate handicap was run at just an ordinary gallop.

2981 RESORT WORLD SUPPORTING MAYOR OF SOLIHULL STANDARD OPEN NATIONAL HUNT FLAT RACE 2m
3:40 (3:43) (Class 6) 4-6-Y-O **£1,689** (£496; £248; £124)

Form RPR

1 **Mountain King**[210] 261 4-11-2 0.. RichardJohnson 105+
(Philip Hobbs) *hld up in tch: racd keenly: trckd ldr over 3f out: shkn up to ld over 1f out: rdn out* **6/4**[1]

03/ **2** 1 **Delgany Demon**[229] 5483 5-10-13 0.............................. TrevorWhelan(3) 104
(Neil King) *a.p: chsd ldr 9f out: led over 4f out: rdn and hdd over 1f out: styd on* **4/1**[2]

0/P- **3** 2 1/2 **Fine Moment**[22] 2513 5-10-9 0..(t) RobertThornton 95
(Kevin Frost) *chsd ldrs: rdn over 1f out: styd on same pce ins fnl f* **20/1**

10/ **4** 15 **Troyan (IRE)**[233] 5388 6-11-9 0.. CharliePoste 97
(Robin Dickin) *hld up: hdwy over 4f out: rdn over 2f out: sn wknd* **16/1**

0- **5** 18 **Aces Over Kings (IRE)**[36] 2216 6-11-2 0.............................. APMcCoy 76
(Rebecca Curtis) *plld hrd: trckd ldr 3f: remained handy: drvn along over 5f out: wknd over 2f out* **11/2**

601- **6** 7 **Larks Rising**[11] 2745 5-11-9 0.. TomO'Brien 73
(Caroline Keevil) *prom: chsd ldr 13f out tl led 9f out: hdd over 4f out: rdn and wknd over 2f out* **5/1**[3]

7 19 **Ruby Mac (IRE)** 5-10-9 0.. NoelFehily 42
(Tony Carroll) *hld up: bhd fnl 7f* **10/1**

00/ **8** 1 **Lord Westhead (IRE)**[263] 4864 4-11-2 0.............................. AdrianLane 48
(Danielle McCormick) *hld up: bhd fnl 7f* **100/1**

0- **9** 28 **Game Dorabella**[183] 675 5-10-2 0.. MrPJohn(7) 16
(Laura Hurley) *sn pushed along in rr: bhd fr 1/2-way* **100/1**

0/ **10** 74 **Ebony Storm**[424] 1784 6-10-9 0.. MrFMitchell(7)
(H Edward Haynes) *racd keenly: led and racd wd: hdd 9f out: rdn and wknd 7f out* **100/1**

3m 36.1s (-14.80) **Going Correction** -0.80s/f (Firm)
WFA 4 from 5yo+ 5lb **10** Ran SP% **114.8**
Speed ratings: **105,104,103,95,86 83,73,73,59,22**
toteswingers 1&2 £2.60, 2&3 £11.30, 1&3 £6.10 CSF £7.18 TOTE £2.60: £1.80, £1.40, £2.90; EX 10.60 Trifecta £126.60 Pool: £2,057.53 - 12.18 winning tickets..
Owner Mrs Diana L Whateley **Bred** R D Chugg And J R H Fowler **Trained** Withycombe, Somerset

FOCUS
Not a bad bumper. The runner-up sets the level.

T/Plt: £159.20 to a £1 stake. Pool: £82,860.98 - 379.81 winning tickets. T/Qpdt: £42.10 to a £1 stake. Pool: £8,337.21 - 146.2 winning tickets. CR

2982 - (Foreign Racing) - See Raceform Interactive

2542 CORK (R-H)
Sunday, December 8

OFFICIAL GOING: Soft (yielding in places)

2983a KERRY GROUP STAYERS NOVICE HURDLE (GRADE 3) (13 hdls) 3m
1:15 (1:15) 4-Y-0+ **£15,853** (£4,634; £2,195; £731)

RPR

1 **The Job Is Right**[24] 2480 5-11-0 119..(b) APHeskin 135+
(Michael Hourigan, Ire) *chsd ldrs: 3rd 1/2-way: wnt 2nd after 4 out: prog to dispute ld next: r.o gamely u.p to ld after last: on top cl home* **6/1**[3]

2 3 1/4 **Band Of Blood (IRE)**[21] 2545 5-11-3 124........................ BrianO'Connell 135
(Philip Fenton, Ire) *chsd ldrs: cl 4th 1/2-way: prog to dispute ld 3 out: sn rdn and r.o wl: hdd and no ex u.p after last* **8/1**

3 2 **Lots Of Memories (IRE)**[14] 2706 6-11-6 132...................... ShaneButler 136
(P G Fahey, Ire) *hld up towards rr: cl 7th 1/2-way: prog to go cl 3rd 3 out: rdn and rn abt appr next: sn no ex and styd on same pce fr bef last* **11/8**[1]

4 2 1/2 **Alelchi Inois (FR)**[14] 2706 5-11-3 126.............................. PaulTownend 131
(W P Mullins, Ire) *settled bhd ldrs: mstke 6th: 5th 1/2-way: rdn appr 3 out: sn no ex and styd on same pce* **4/1**[2]

5 6 1/2 **Ballyroe Rambler (IRE)**[18] 2606 6-11-0 112........................ MPFogarty 121
(J A Berry, Ire) *nt fluent at times: hld up: 8th 1/2-way: rdn to cl up after 4 out: sn no ex and styd on same pce* **14/1**

6 21 **Oscar Chimes (IRE)**[10] 2780 6-11-0 111................ AndrewJMcNamara 100
(M T O'Donovan, Ire) *led and disp at times: rdn whn pressed for ld after 4 out: sn hdd and no ex: wknd* **12/1**

7 4 1/2 **Some Officer (IRE)**[17] 2638 6-11-0 120.............................. RobbiePower 96
(T Hogan, Ire) *led and disp at times: relegated to 3rd after 4 out: no ex fr next and sn bhd* **13/2**

8 24 **Tullintain (IRE)**[28] 2404 10-11-0..(t) PhillipEnright 72
(Robert Tyner, Ire) *towards rr: 6th 1/2-way: rdn after 4 out and sn bhd: sn eased: t.o* **33/1**

6m 4.4s (-27.70) **8** Ran SP% **118.1**
CSF £53.45 TOTE £7.10: £2.30, £2.80, £1.02; DF 57.00 Trifecta £466.80.
Owner Mrs Mary Devine **Bred** Miss K Rausing **Trained** Patrickswell, Co Limerick

FOCUS
The Job is Right had proved himself tough even in defeat in maiden hurdle; on this occasion he was very tough and relished the step up in trip. The form fits the race averages.

2985a KERRY GROUP HILLY WAY CHASE (GRADE 2) (11 fncs) 2m
2:20 (2:21) 5-Y-0+ **£23,780** (£6,951; £3,292; £1,097)

RPR

1 **Twinlight (FR)**[41] 2141 6-11-10 157.............................. PaulTownend 161+
(W P Mullins, Ire) *cl up: j. sltly to rt at times: slt mstke 4th: prog to be on terms 6th: led appr 3 out where lft clr: j. to rt next and again last: styd on strly: comf* **9/10**[1]

2 6 **Lead Kindly Light (IRE)**[8] 2833 9-11-0 125..................(tp) AndrewLeigh 137
(Sean Byrne, Ire) *hld up towards rr: clsr in 4th 4 out: lft modest 2nd fr 3 out: kpt on but no ch w wnr* **66/1**

3 8 1/2 **Days Hotel (IRE)**[28] 2410 8-11-10 153.............................. PhillipEnright 144
(Henry De Bromhead, Ire) *chsd ldrs: mstke 5 out and lost grnd: modest 5th appr 3 out where lft 3rd: kpt on same pce but no ch w wnr* **11/4**[2]

4 10 **Savello (IRE)**[15] 2686 7-11-4 144.............................. BrianO'Connell 128
(A J Martin, Ire) *cl up: disp at times: 3rd 4 out: sn rdn: u.p whn hmpd next: sn no ex: one pce* **12/1**

5 1 3/4 **Realt Dubh (IRE)**[31] 2320 9-11-4 153..............................(t) RobbieColgan 123
(Noel Meade, Ire) *chsd ldrs: mstke 5th: rdn fr 5 out and sn no imp* **7/1**[3]

F **Foildubh (IRE)**[10] 2778 9-11-10 151.. MPFogarty
(John Patrick Ryan, Ire) *led and disp: jnd fr 6th: rdn and hdd appr 3 out where fell* **11/1**

F **Dylan Ross (IRE)**[29] 2376 7-11-4 138.............................. RobbiePower
(Noel Meade, Ire) *hld up: in rr: clsd in 5th whn fell 4 out* **14/1**

4m 6.0s (246.00) **7** Ran SP% **116.0**
CSF £39.79 TOTE £1.90: £1.20, £8.30; DF 37.40 Trifecta £77.70.
Owner M L Bloodstock Ltd **Bred** M L Bloodstock Limited **Trained** Muine Beag, Co Carlow

FOCUS
This turned into a non-event. The form is rated around the runner-up.

2986a KERRY GROUP EUROPEAN BREEDERS FUND MARES NOVICE CHASE (GRADE 3) (12 fncs) 2m 1f
2:50 (2:52) 4-Y-0+ **£19,552** (£5,715; £2,707; £902)

RPR

1 **Dressedtothenines (IRE)**[41] 2136 6-10-11 .... NiallPMadden 131+
(Edward P Harty, Ire) *chsd ldrs: 4th 1/2-way: prog to go 2nd 3 out: sn chal and rdn: r.o wl to ld narrowly at last: kpt on wl u.p run-in* **2/1**[1]

2 1 **Kates Benefit (IRE)**[17] 2635 7-10-11 .... DannyMullins 130
(David Kenneth Budds, Ire) *sn led: hdd bef 4th: styd 2nd: led again 5 out: rdn whn pressed for ld after 3 out: j. to lft next and again at last where hdd narrowly: r.o wl but no ex cl home* **13/2**

3 13 **Caoimhe's Delight (IRE)**[24] 2484 7-10-11 123........................ JohnAllen 117
(Sean O'Brien, Ire) *settled in mid-div: 5th 1/2-way: rdn and reminders after 5 out: kpt on same pce to go 4th 2 out: one pce and no imp on front pair* **8/1**

4 4 1/2 **Backinthere (IRE)**[24] 2484 8-10-11 126.............................. APHeskin 113
(Eamonn Francis Gallagher, Ire) *settled towards rr: 6th 1/2-way: rdn and reminders appr 4 out: stl cl 7th appr next: sn no ex and styd on same pce* **5/1**[3]

5 6 1/2 **Back In A Tic (IRE)**[38] 2187 7-10-11 123.......................... PaulTownend 106
(Colin Kidd, Ire) *chsd ldrs: 3rd 1/2-way: rdn in 4th 3 out: sn no imp* **7/1**

6 1/2 **Curvacious (IRE)**[154] 916 7-10-11 .... DavidSplaine 106
(Edward Stanners, Ire) *chsd ldrs: led bef 4th: hdd 5 out: wknd fr next: sn no imp* **16/1**

7 1 1/4 **Way Up In The Air (IRE)**[39] 2164 6-10-11 .... PhillipEnright 104
(Robert Tyner, Ire) *hld up in rr: 7th 1/2-way: prog to go 3rd 3 out: rdn and wknd fr next* **5/2**[2]

P **Kalico Kim (IRE)**[7] 2856 9-10-11 101..............................(bt1) MPFogarty
(John Patrick Ryan, Ire) *in rr: bhd fr 1/2-way: p.u bef 3 out* **50/1**

4m 19.4s (259.40) **8** Ran SP% **123.4**
CSF £17.39 TOTE £3.00: £1.02, £3.00, £3.10; DF 18.30 Trifecta £121.50.
Owner John P McManus **Bred** B Walsh **Trained** Curragh, Co Kildare

FOCUS
The winner was still a long way short of her hurdles best.

The Form Book Jumps, Raceform Ltd, Compton, RG20 6NL.

2987 - 2990a (Foreign Racing) - See Raceform Interactive

2549 PUNCHESTOWN (R-H)

Sunday, December 8

OFFICIAL GOING: Good to yielding

2991a JOHN DURKAN MEMORIAL PUNCHESTOWN CHASE (GRADE 1) (15 fncs) 2m 4f

1:35 (1:36) 5-Y-0+ **£42,276** (£12,357)

RPR

1 **Arvika Ligeonniere (FR)**[24] 2483 8-11-10 161 RWalsh 165+
(W P Mullins, Ire) *trckd ldr tl disp fr 2nd and sn led: j.w: in command 2 out: easily* **4/7**[1]

2 9 **Rubi Light (FR)**[24] 2483 8-11-10 152 BarryGeraghty 154
(Robert Alan Hennessy, Ire) *hld up 3rd whn lft 2nd at 3rd: niggled along to cl on wnr 3 out: no imp fr next: mstke last* **16/1**[3]

F **Sir Des Champs (FR)**[228] 5515 7-11-10 173 DavyRussell
(W P Mullins, Ire) *led tl jnd 2nd and sn hdd: fell next* **7/4**[2]

5m 1.9s (-22.10) **3** Ran SP% **105.9**
CSF £5.48 TOTE £1.40; DF 7.70 Trifecta £5.30.
Owner Mrs S Ricci **Bred** Yves Lepage **Trained** Muine Beag, Co Carlow

FOCUS
While the winner is clearly a genuine Grade 1 performer, this year's John Durkan proved the dampest of squibs. After last year's winner Flemenstar was withdrawn through injury on Saturday, at least we were still hoping to see a duel between stablemates Arvika Ligeonniere and Sir Des Champs, but we were even deprived of that after the latter crashed into the third fence and fell. Difficult form to rate.

2995a OLD HOUSE, KILL (PRO/AM) INH FLAT RACE 2m

3:35 (3:38) 4-Y-0 **£4,768** (£1,105; £483; £276)

RPR

1 **Black Hercules (IRE)**[231] 4-11-9 MrPWMullins 120+
(W P Mullins, Ire) *led: jnd 1/2-way tl advantage again 3f out: strly pressed under 2f out: drvn clr ins fnl f and kpt on wl* **4/7**[1]

2 2 ½ **Cillian's Return (IRE)**[280] 4556 4-11-4 MrJJKing(5) 116
(W T Farrell, Ire) *w.w in mid-div tl tk clsr order in 3rd 4f out: pressed ldr in 3rd under 2f out: wnt 2nd 1f out but no imp on wnr: kpt on same pce* **10/1**[3]

3 3 ¾ **Princely Conn (IRE)**[250] 5114 4-11-2 MrDJMullins(7) 112
(Thomas Mullins, Ire) *hld up towards rr tl tk clsr order under 4f out towards outer: pressed ldr in 2nd under 2f out tl no ex and dropped to 3rd 1f out: kpt on one pce* **20/1**

4 6 ½ **Lean Araig (IRE)** 4-11-6 MrRPQuinlan(3) 106
(Oliver McKiernan, Ire) *trckd ldr in 2nd tl on terms bef 1/2-way: dropped to 4th under 2f out: sn one pce* **20/1**

5 4 **Flame And Flower (IRE)** 4-11-2 MrPAKing(7) 102
(Conor O'Dwyer, Ire) *chsd ldrs tl nt qckn over 2f out: kpt on one pce* **14/1**

6 1 **Sucker Punch (IRE)**[252] 4-11-9 MsNCarberry 101
(Noel Meade, Ire) *a mid-div: no threat over 2f out: kpt on one pce* **5/2**[2]

7 5 ½ **Cappacurry Zak (IRE)**[217] 4-11-2 MartinBurke(7) 95
(L Young, Ire) *nvr bttr than mid-div: no threat over 2f out* **66/1**

8 3 ¾ **A Pint Ahead (IRE)**[56] 4-11-6 MrSCrawford(3) 92
(Donal Hassett, Ire) *chsd ldrs: 3rd 1/2-way: wknd under 3f out* **33/1**

9 8 **Drive The Bus (IRE)**[21] 2555 4-11-2 MrPJCawley(7) 84
(Denis Gerard Hogan, Ire) *chsd ldrs in 3rd tl dropped to mid-div 1/2-way: no imp fr 4f out* **25/1**

10 7 ½ **My Dancing Angel (IRE)**[31] 2322 4-10-9 AFO'Neill(7) 69
(Mrs Rosemary Rooney, Ire) *sn towards rr and no threat over 4f out* **66/1**

11 90 **Captain Blonde (IRE)** 4-11-2 MissPElvin(7)
(Gerard O'Leary, Ire) *a towards rr: nvr a factor: t.o* **50/1**

S **Therealmick (IRE)** 4-11-2 BrianCawley(7)
(Martin J Hogan, Ire) *hld up towards rr tl hdwy under 3f out: pushed along and no imp in 5th whn slipped up under 2f out* **50/1**

3m 49.5s (-9.90) **12** Ran SP% **131.2**
Pick Six: 1,000euro. CSF £8.86 TOTE £1.70: £1.02, £1.40, £4.40; DF 7.70 Trifecta £56.60.
Owner Andrea & Graham Wylie **Bred** Spencer Hawkins **Trained** Muine Beag, Co Carlow

FOCUS
The betting made this a match between two impressive point-to-point winners. The winner made virtually all but needed to battle.
T/Jkpt: @45.40. Pool of @4334.00 - 77 winning tickets. T/Plt: @15.40. Pool of @33091.86 - 1494.55 winning tickets. AH

2992 - 2995a (Foreign Racing) - See Raceform Interactive

2789 MUSSELBURGH (R-H)

Monday, December 9

OFFICIAL GOING: Good (good to soft in places; 7.1)
Wind: Breezy, half behind Weather: Overcast

2996 32RED CONDITIONAL JOCKEYS' H'CAP CHASE (16 fncs) 2m 4f

12:15 (12:15) (Class 4) (0-120,111) 4-Y-0+ **£5,198** (£1,526; £763; £381)

Form RPR

123- 1 **Lord Of Drums (IRE)**[114] 1287 7-10-12 **103** CraigNichol(6) 112+
(Lucinda Russell) *mde all: qcknd 9th: effrt and drvn 2 out: sn jnd: lft 4 l clr last: kpt on wl* **5/2**[1]

5B3- 2 5 **Alpha One (IRE)**[12] 2751 7-11-0 **107** DiarmuidO'Regan(8) 116+
(Chris Grant) *chsd ldrs: wnt 2nd 7th: effrt 4 out: nt fluent next: chal between last 2: mstke and lost all ch last: hung rt and no imp run-in* **7/2**[2]

561- 3 10 **My Idea**[10] 2791 7-11-2 **107** (t) StephenMulqueen(6) 104
(Maurice Barnes) *in tch: nt fluent 10th and next: sn outpcd: rallied 4 out: no imp fr next* **7/2**[2]

444- 4 11 **Los Nadis (GER)**[31] 2345 9-11-9 **111** GrahamWatters(3) 96
(Jim Goldie) *cl up tl lost pl 9th: struggling after next: n.d after* **4/1**[3]

P02- 5 18 **Endeavor**[10] 2793 8-11-9 **108** ColmMcCormack 77
(Dianne Sayer) *hld up in tch: stdy hdwy 10th: rdn 4 out: wknd fr next* **11/1**

143/ 6 35 **Mister Wall Street (FR)**[332] 3606 8-11-7 **109** TonyKelly(3) 46
(Rebecca Menzies) *nt jump wl in rr: blnd 4th: outpcd whn hit 9th: hit and lost tch fr 4 out* **10/1**

4m 57.4s (-3.80) **Going Correction** -0.075s/f (Good) **6** Ran SP% **110.4**
Speed ratings (Par 105): **104,102,98,93,86 72**
toteswingers 1&2 £2.10, 1&3 £2.20, 2&3 £2.40 CSF £11.48 TOTE £2.40: £1.90, £2.10; EX 8.90 Trifecta £29.90 Pool: £1491.00 - 37.28 winning tickets..
Owner The Ormello Way **Bred** Gordon Doyle **Trained** Arlary, Perth & Kinross

FOCUS
Bottom bend on Hurdles track at innermost position and at outermost position on Chase course. Home bend split with a false rail after final fence. A drying day and the surface looked in good nick. This was run at a sound gallop and they began to sort themselves out from the sixth-last fence. A step up from the winner under a claimer.

2997 32RED.COM INTERACTIVE NOVICES' H'CAP HURDLE (12 hdls) 2m 4f

12:45 (12:45) (Class 4) (0-105,105) 4-Y-0+ **£3,249** (£954; £477; £238)

Form RPR

/50- 1 **Jack Albert (IRE)**[19] 2591 6-10-0 79 (b[1]) BrianHarding 83
(Dianne Sayer) *nt fluent early: led to 3rd: disp ld tl outpcd after 4 out: rallied bef 2 out: led last 100yds: styd on gamely* **15/2**

44- 2 2 ¼ **Brunello**[13] 2732 5-11-4 102 (p) AdamNicol(5) 104
(Philip Kirby) *t.k.h: led 3rd to bef 3 out: rallied and regained ld last: hdd last 100yds: kpt on same pce* **11/2**

P6/- 3 2 ½ **Solidago (IRE)**[20] 2587 6-11-6 99 (p) PeterBuchanan 97
(S R B Crawford, Ire) *chsd ldrs: hdwy to ld bef 3 out: sn rdn: hdd last: kpt on same pce* **11/1**

4/0- 4 21 **Blackmore**[44] 2075 6-11-12 105 LucyAlexander 84
(N W Alexander) *hld up: nt fluent and outpcd 6th: struggling fr next: shortlived effrt bef 3 out: no ch whn lft mod 4th last* **18/1**

6/5- 5 26 **Captain Clayton (IRE)**[28] 2417 6-11-10 103 HenryBrooke 58
(Simon West) *towards rr: struggling fr 1/2-way: nvr on terms* **9/2**[3]

332- 6 26 **Momkinzain (USA)**[59] 1848 6-11-3 103 (p) CraigNichol(7) 35
(Lucinda Russell) *in tch: drvn along 1/2-way: rallied 7th: rdn and wknd bef 3 out* **4/1**[2]

/55- U **Heron's Mill (IRE)**[24] 2497 5-10-11 97 DaleIrving(7) 80
(James Ewart) *nt fluent on occasions: in tch: lost pl whn nt fluent 5th: hit and struggling 7th: rallied bef 3 out: 22 l 4th but no imp whn blnd and uns rdr last* **3/1**[1]

5UP- P **Fling Me (IRE)**[51] 1982 6-10-9 88 WilsonRenwick
(Rose Dobbin) *in tch: drvn and outpcd after 4 out: struggling next: t.o whn p.u bef 2 out* **14/1**

4m 41.8s (-9.70) **Going Correction** -0.65s/f (Firm) **8** Ran SP% **110.6**
Speed ratings (Par 105): **93,92,91,82,72 61,,**
toteswingers 1&2 £7.50, 1&3 £14.60, 2&3 £10.30 CSF £45.11 CT £429.70 TOTE £7.80: £2.20, £2.60, £4.20; EX 52.80 Trifecta £879.30 Pool: £2838.53 - 2.42 winning tickets..
Owner E F Sporting **Bred** Miss Marie Harding **Trained** Hackthorpe, Cumbria

FOCUS
A modest handicap. The gallop was a fair one and only three mattered from the top of the home straight. The winner's best figure since his Carlisle debut.

2998 32RED.COM MAIDEN HURDLE (9 hdls) 2m

1:15 (1:15) (Class 4) 4-Y-0+ **£3,249** (£954; £477; £238)

Form RPR

/34- 1 **Population**[17] 2647 6-11-0 123 (b[1]) DenisO'Regan 117+
(John Ferguson) *mde all: drew clr 4: shkn up briefly after 2 out: easily* **1/5**[1]

4- 2 9 **May's Boy**[31] 2340 5-11-0 0 BrianHughes 99
(James Moffatt) *t.k.h early: in tch: hdwy to chse (clr) wnr bef 3 out: effrt and clsd next: drifted lft and outpcd fr last* **25/1**

50- 3 1 **Getabuzz**[24] 2493 5-11-0 0 DougieCostello 97
(Tim Easterby) *t.k.h: hld up in tch: nt fluent 4th: stdy hdwy bef 3 out: shkn up and no imp fr next* **11/2**[2]

600- 4 8 **Innocent Girl (IRE)**[23] 2514 4-10-7 0 PeterBuchanan 82
(Lucinda Russell) *hld up in tch: pushed along bef 3 out: sn outpcd* **16/1**[3]

5 4 ½ **Sudski Star (IRE)**[192] 5-11-0 0 (t) JamesReveley 85
(Patrick Griffin, Ire) *chsd wnr to 3rd: prom: struggling bef 3 out: sn btn* **33/1**

4- 6 16 **Katies Choice (IRE)**[28] 2422 5-10-7 0 CallumBewley(7) 69
(R Mike Smith) *t.k.h: hld up in tch: strrugling after 4 out: sn btn: no ch whn mstke last* **40/1**

60- P **Military Call**[37] 2217 6-10-7 0 GrantCockburn(7)
(R Mike Smith) *prom: wnt 2nd 3rd tl rdn and wknd bef 3 out: p.u next* **40/1**

3m 42.6s (-5.80) **Going Correction** -0.65s/f (Firm)
WFA 4 from 5yo+ 5lb **7** Ran SP% **116.3**
Speed ratings (Par 105): **88,83,83,79,76 68,**
toteswingers 1&2 £2.50, 1&3 £1.10, 2&3 £2.40 CSF £10.67 TOTE £1.10: £1.10, £3.40; EX 7.40 Trifecta £12.80 Pool: £4364.18 - 254.65 winning tickets..
Owner Bloomfields **Bred** Darley **Trained** Cowlinge, Suffolk

FOCUS
An easy win for Population, who had little to beat. A step up from the second.

2999 32REDPOKER.COM H'CAP HURDLE (14 hdls) 3m 110y

1:45 (1:45) (Class 5) (0-100,99) 4-Y-0+ **£3,249** (£954; £477; £238)

Form RPR

4/P- 1 **Luctor Emergo (IRE)**[19] 2606 4-11-10 97 (p) WilsonRenwick 100+
(Keith Dalgleish) *hld up in tch: smooth hdwy to ld 2 out: rdn and r.o wl fr last* **10/1**[3]

5F0- 2 10 **Total Assets**[27] 2447 5-11-12 **99** RyanMania 103
(Simon Waugh) *in tch: hdwy to ld after 3 out: rdn and hdd next: mstke last: one pce* **28/1**

P64- 3 9 **Vallani (IRE)**[10] 2789 8-10-1 **81** GrantCockburn(7) 77
(Lucinda Russell) *towards rr: struggling 1/2-way: rallied u.p 3 out: mstke last: plugged on: nvr able to chal* **7/2**[2]

FPU- 4 3 ½ **King's Chorister**[10] 2791 7-10-10 **88** (t) TonyKelly(5) 80
(Barry Murtagh) *hld up: stdy hdwy and cl up bef 3 out: outpcd fr next* **14/1**

/P1- 5 2 ½ **Stitched In Time (IRE)**[10] 2789 6-11-3 **97** ShaunDobbin(7) 87
(Rose Dobbin) *led: rdn and hdd after 3 out: wknd fr next* **9/4**[1]

0/3- 6 17 **Goodacres Garden (IRE)**[28] 2417 6-11-0 **87** JasonMaguire 61
(Donald McCain) *mstkes: pressed ldr tl hung rt and wknd 3 out* **9/4**[1]

04B- 7 9 **Kukurudu (IRE)**[155] 897 6-11-11 **98** HenryBrooke 64
(Simon West) *bhd: rdn after 4 out: struggling next: no ch whn mstke last* **20/1**

PPP/ P **Rhyton (IRE)**[468] 1395 6-10-12 **85** (b) AdrianLane
(Lucy Normile) *chsd ldrs tl broke down and p.u after 4 out* **28/1**

5m 36.8s (-19.90) **Going Correction** -0.65s/f (Firm)
WFA 4 from 5yo+ 7lb **8** Ran SP% **111.2**
Speed ratings (Par 103): **105,101,98,97,97 91,88,**
toteswingers 1&2 £9.50, 1&3 £5.60, 2&3 £7.60 CSF £212.04 CT £1138.84 TOTE £11.50: £2.40, £4.20, £1.60; EX 97.80 Trifecta £549.20 Pool: £3179.10 - 4.34 winning tickets..
Owner Straightline Construction Ltd **Bred** Kilnamoragh Stud **Trained** Carluke, S Lanarks

FOCUS
An ordinary staying handicap, run to suit the closers and it's form to treat with a degree of caution. Big steps up from the first two.

3000 32RED.COM H'CAP HURDLE (12 hdls) 2m 4f
2:20 (2:20) (Class 3) (0-125,125) 3-Y-0+ **£6,498** (£1,908; £954; £477)

Form RPR
222- 1 **Strongpoint (IRE)**[9] 2836 9-11-7 **120** PeterBuchanan 134+
(S R B Crawford, Ire) *mde all: sn clr: pushed along bef 2 out: kpt on strly: unchal* **7/1**

/50- 2 17 **Big Water (IRE)**[37] 2221 5-11-10 **123** PaddyBrennan 125
(Alan Swinbank) *in tch: hdwy to chse wnr 3 out: edgd rt next: sn no imp* **10/3**[1]

/40- 3 3 ¾ **Scots Gaelic (IRE)**[17] 2655 6-11-5 **125** DeanPratt[(7)] 120
(John Quinn) *bhd: struggling and drvn 1/2-way: styd on fr 2 out: nvr able to chal* **5/1**

3/2- 4 8 **Merchant Of Dubai**[32] 2311 8-10-13 **112** DenisO'Regan 100
(Jim Goldie) *hld up in midfield: stdy hdwy after 4 out: rdn and hung rt next: sn no imp* **4/1**[2]

0/P- 5 1 ½ **Divers (FR)**[27] 2448 9-11-10 **123** (b) JasonMaguire 113
(Donald McCain) *chsd ldrs: wnt 2nd 4th: rdn and outpcd 3 out: wknd fr next* **12/1**

440- 6 5 **Mojolika**[23] 2519 5-11-5 **118** BrianHarding 100
(Tim Easterby) *hld up: stdy hdwy after 4 out: rdn and wknd next* **8/1**

/21- 7 23 **Ueueteotl (FR)**[32] 2311 5-11-5 **125** DaleIrving[(7)] 87
(James Ewart) *chsd ldr to 4th: hit 6th: struggling 4 out: sn btn* **9/2**[3]

0P3- P **Nine Stories (IRE)**[4] 2894 8-11-9 **122** (v) WilsonRenwick
(Chris Grant) *hld up: rdn and outpcd bef 4 out: t.o whn p.u bef 2 out* **25/1**

4m 34.7s (-16.80) **Going Correction** -0.65s/f (Firm) course record
WFA 4 from 5yo+ 6lb **8** Ran SP% **113.1**
Speed ratings (Par 107): **107,100,98,95,94 92,83,**
toteswingers 1&2 £5.50, 1&3 £6.00, 2&3 £3.80 CSF £30.47 CT £126.75 TOTE £7.80: £2.70, £1.60, £2.20; EX 40.10 Trifecta £208.90 Pool: £3026.61 - 10.86 winning tickets..
Owner S McAlister **Bred** Seamus Murphy **Trained** Larne, Co Antrim

FOCUS
There was a strong early gallop in this open-looking handicap, but still those racing handily were at an advantage. The winner is rated up nearly a stone on his previous best hurdle figure.

3001 EASTLOTHIAN.GOV.UK H'CAP CHASE (18 fncs) 3m
2:50 (2:50) (Class 3) (0-135,123) 4-Y-0+ **£6,498** (£1,908; £954; £477)

Form RPR
/65- 1 **Kealigolane (IRE)**[37] 2222 9-11-11 **122** JamesReveley 127+
(Barry Murtagh) *mostly j.w: mde all and clr to 5 out: qcknd next: hld on wl run-in* **6/1**

4/6- 2 3 ¼ **Storming Gale (IRE)**[196] 508 7-11-12 **123** (t) JasonMaguire 126
(Donald McCain) *hld up in tch: mstke 2nd: stdy hdwy 6 out: effrt and chsng wnr whn hit 3 out: kpt on same pce fr last* **15/8**[2]

225- 3 4 ½ **Bertie Milan (IRE)**[28] 2416 8-10-7 **104** (p) LucyAlexander 103
(N W Alexander) *nt fluent: prom: rdn and outpcd 4 out: plugged on fr 2 out: no ch w first two* **13/8**[1]

P/P- 4 10 **Blenheim Brook (IRE)**[30] 2358 8-11-11 **122** PeterBuchanan 115
(Lucinda Russell) *chsd wnr: clsd 5 out: rdn and outpcd whn nt fluent 3 out: 4th and hld whn blnd last* **4/1**[3]

6m 4.7s (1.30) **Going Correction** -0.075s/f (Good) **4** Ran SP% **107.2**
Speed ratings (Par 107): **94,92,91,88**
CSF £17.15 TOTE £4.10; EX 10.90 Trifecta £15.70 Pool: £2138.39 - 101.68 winning tickets..
Owner James Callow **Bred** Colin Hadden **Trained** Low Braithwaite, Cumbria

FOCUS
Despite just the four runners this was a truly run staying handicap and the form makes sense, but it may not be a race to completely trust. The winner had his own way out in front.

3002 32RED CASINO STANDARD OPEN NATIONAL HUNT FLAT RACE 2m
3:20 (3:20) (Class 5) 4-6-Y-0 **£1,949** (£572; £286; £143)

Form RPR
2- 1 **It's High Time (IRE)**[31] 2347 5-11-2 0 WilsonRenwick 107+
(Lucinda Russell) *prom: stdy hdwy 3f out: rdn over 1f out: led ins fnl f: styd on wl* **2/1**[1]

3/4- 2 ½ **Gurkha Brave (IRE)**[24] 2499 5-11-2 0 BrianHughes 106
(Karen McLintock) *led: rdn 2f out: edgd lft and hdd ins fnl f: kpt on: hld cl home* **7/1**

3 5 **Katachenko (IRE)**[56] 1912 4-11-2 0 JasonMaguire 102
(Donald McCain) *trckd ldrs: effrt over 2f out: edgd lft and outpcd by first two over 1f out* **11/4**[2]

4 3 **Coinage (IRE)** 4-11-2 0 DougieCostello 99
(Tony Coyle) *t.k.h: hld up bhd ldng gp: effrt whn rn green over 2f out: no imp over 1f out* **7/2**[3]

5 1 ¾ **Donna's Diamond (IRE)** 4-11-2 0 DenisO'Regan 98+
(Chris Grant) *t.k.h: hld up in tch: stdy hdwy over 4f out: drvn and outpcd over 2f out: sn no imp* **14/1**

0/0- 6 9 **Neville Woods**[206] 359 6-10-9 0 AlistairFindlay[(7)] 92+
(J L Gledson) *hld up: pushed along whn carried wd and outpcd bnd appr st: n.d after* **66/1**

7 7 **Randalls Mill (IRE)** 5-11-2 0 PaddyBrennan 83
(M P Sunderland, Ire) *t.k.h: in tch on ins: effrt over 3f out: wknd 2f out* **12/1**

8 ¾ **Lord Fendale (IRE)** 4-11-2 0 TomO'Brien 85+
(S Donohoe, Ire) *bhd: rdn whn carried wd bnd appr st: sn wknd* **25/1**

0- 9 69 **Fev Rover (IRE)**[13] 2738 6-11-2 0 HenryBrooke 20
(Simon West) *w ldr: lost pl whn rn wd bnd appr st: sn wknd: t.o* **80/1**

3m 38.8s (-4.00) **Going Correction** -0.65s/f (Firm)
WFA 4 from 5yo+ 5lb **9** Ran SP% **115.7**
Speed ratings: **84,83,81,79,78 74,70,70,36**
toteswingers 1&2 £3.60, 1&3 £2.50, 2&3 £3.20 CSF £16.81 TOTE £2.60: £1.40, £1.80, £1.60; EX 11.80 Trifecta £18.30 Pool: £4043.38 - 164.89 winning tickets..
Owner Straightline Construction Ltd **Bred** William Flood **Trained** Arlary, Perth & Kinross

FOCUS
Not a bad bumper and it proved a sufficient test, so it's form to be positive about with two coming clear. The first three are rated pretty much to their marks.
T/Plt: £403.70 to a £1 stake. Pool: £68425.30 - 123.71 winning tickets T/Qpdt: £81.70 to a £1 stake. Pool: £5995.77 - 54.30 winning tickets RY

2739 FONTWELL (L-H)
Tuesday, December 10

OFFICIAL GOING: Good to soft (good in places; 7.2)
Wind: virtually nil Weather: sunny

3003 32RED ON THE APP STORE JUVENILE HURDLE (9 hdls) 2m 2f 110y
12:40 (12:41) (Class 4) 3-Y-0 **£3,119** (£915; £457; £228)

Form RPR
- 1 **Muhtaris (IRE)**[32] 3-10-12 0 DenisO'Regan 114+
(John Ferguson) *nt fluent early: hld up: smooth hdwy after 3 out: wnt 4th next: rdn to chal after last: led fnl 75yds: drvn out* **6/4**[1]

6- 2 ½ **Sun Wild Life (FR)**[194] 3-10-12 117 DougieCostello 108
(Robert Walford) *led: rdn appr 2 out: kpt on gamely u.p but no ex whn hdd fnl 75yds* **14/1**

3 1 ¼ **Vandross (IRE)**[63] 3-10-9 0 TrevorWhelan[(3)] 105
(Neil King) *in tch: tk clsr order 6th: rdn to chse ldr after 3 out tl after next: kpt on same pce fr last* **33/1**

32- 4 hd **Aldopicgros (FR)**[36] 2276 3-10-12 120 (p) DarylJacob 107
(Paul Nicholls) *t.k.h: mid-div: hdwy appr 6th: mounting chal whn pckd 2 out: sn pushed along: slt bump after last: sn drvn and ev ch: no ex fnl 75yds* **13/8**[2]

U0- 5 27 **Shalianzi (IRE)**[11] 2796 3-10-9 0 (b) JoshuaMoore[(3)] 81
(Gary Moore) *hld up towards rr: rdn after 6th: hdwy to dispute 4th after 3 out: nt fluent 2 out: wknd last: t.o* **20/1**

412- 6 2 **Wooly Bully**[59] 1862 3-11-5 120 WayneHutchinson 91
(Alan King) *in tch: hit 4th: trckd ldrs after 6th: mstke 3 out: sn rdn: wknd between last 2: mstke last: t.o* **5/1**[3]

5- 7 3 ¼ **Hermosa Vaquera (IRE)**[21] 2577 3-10-5 0 AdamWedge 69
(Anna Newton-Smith) *hld up towards rr: hdwy appr 6th: rdn to chse ldrs after hitting 3 out: wknd after next: t.o* **100/1**

6- 8 hd **Misteray**[26] 2466 3-10-12 0 (t) TommyPhelan 76
(Bill Turner) *trckd ldr: hit 5th: sn rdn: wknd 3 out: t.o* **100/1**

0- 9 19 **Sporting Club Girl**[21] 2577 3-10-5 0 MattieBatchelor 52
(Jim Best) *prom: rdn after 6th: wknd after 3 out: t.o* **150/1**

04- 10 4 ½ **Special Report (IRE)**[21] 2577 3-10-12 0 NoelFehily 55
(Neil Mulholland) *struggling 5th: a towards rr: t.o* **50/1**

00- 11 1 **Couloir Extreme (IRE)**[21] 2577 3-10-12 0 JamieMoore 54
(Gary Moore) *hld up: hdwy after 5th: rdn after 3 out: sn wknd: t.o* **20/1**

0- P **Bally Broadwell**[33] 2318 3-10-5 0 MarcGoldstein
(Michael Madgwick) *untidy 1st: sn trcking ldrs: hit 4th: wknd after next: t.o whn p.u after 3 out* **150/1**

4m 37.6s (3.30) **Going Correction** +0.375s/f (Yiel) **12** Ran SP% **119.2**
Speed ratings (Par 104): **108,107,107,107,95 94,93,93,85,83 83,**
toteswingers 1&2 £2.90, 2&3 £12.90, 1&3 £12.20 CSF £21.41 TOTE £2.30: £1.10, £3.10, £8.10; EX 21.90 Trifecta £339.70 Pool: £2774.07 - 6.12 winning units..
Owner Bloomfields **Bred** Rabbah Bloodstock Limited **Trained** Cowlinge, Suffolk

FOCUS
Hurdles sited middle to inner and bends moved out since last fixture. A fair juvenile hurdle, run at a steady gallop. The first four home pulled a long way clear. The winner rates better than the bare result.

3004 32RED.COM NOVICES' LIMITED H'CAP CHASE (16 fncs) 2m 6f
1:10 (1:11) (Class 3) (0-125,124) 4-Y-0 **£6,330** (£1,870; £935; £468; £234)

Form RPR
0/4- 1 **Bucking The Trend**[56] 1916 5-11-0 **122** MichaelByrne[(3)] 135+
(Tim Vaughan) *hld up: drvn along fr 8th: hdwy fr 11th: wnt 2nd between last 2: led sn after last: styd on wl* **8/1**

121- 2 3 **Beforeall (IRE)**[22] 2567 5-10-12 **117** LeightonAspell 127
(Oliver Sherwood) *racd keenly: j. sltly rt: led tl 2nd: prom: led 11th: rdn after 3 out: hdd sn after last: styd on same pce* **11/4**[1]

/22- 3 3 **No Buts**[24] 2508 5-10-10 **115** DenisO'Regan 123
(David Bridgwater) *hld up: hdwy fr 7th: trckd ldrs 12th: rdn in cl 3rd after 3 out: no ex fr last* **9/2**[2]

0- 4 15 **Coolking**[47] 2060 6-10-13 **118** DavidBass 112
(Lawney Hill) *towards rr but in tch: rdn after 10th: wl hld fr bef 3 out* **9/1**

P1F- 5 ½ **Danandy (IRE)**[18] 2651 6-11-1 **120** TomO'Brien 125
(Philip Hobbs) *in tch: trckd ldrs 7th: chal 4 out: rdn and ev ch whn stmbld and virtually fell 2 out: nt rcvr* **7/1**

246/ 6 16 **Superman De La Rue (FR)**[493] 1179 7-10-9 **114** (p) PaulMoloney 96
(David Rees) *hld up: hdwy to ld 4th: hdd 11th: rdn after next: wknd 3 out: t.o* **16/1**

1/6- 7 74 **Viva Steve (IRE)**[24] 2508 5-11-3 **122** DominicElsworth 34
(Mick Channon) *hld up in tch: dropped to last pair 9th: rdn and n.d fr 12th: virtually p.u run-in* **6/1**[3]

24F- P **Forresters Folly**[26] 2475 7-11-5 **124** (b[1]) WayneHutchinson
(Alan King) *prom: led 2nd tl 4th: trckd ldrs: lost pl and reminders after 7th: chsd ldrs 10th: mstke next and 12th: losing tch whn p.u after 4 out* **25/1**

205- P **Phone Home (IRE)**[27] 2459 6-10-7 **112** DarylJacob
(Nick Mitchell) *trckd ldrs: hit 4th: hmpd 11th: mstke next and lost pl: mstke 4 out: sn p.u* **15/2**

5m 37.6s (-5.40) **Going Correction** -0.025s/f (Good) **9** Ran SP% **114.2**
Speed ratings (Par 107): **108,106,105,100,100 94,67, ,**
toteswingers 1&2 £8.90, 2&3 £2.50, 1&3 £11.20 CSF £31.13 CT £112.12 TOTE £10.70: £4.00, £1.20, £1.60; EX 35.00 Trifecta £221.10 Pool: £2695.90 - 9.14 winning units..
Owner The Marinades **Bred** Richard Evans **Trained** Aberthin, Vale of Glamorgan

FOCUS
The gallop was sound for this novice handicap. A big step up from the winner but the form looks solid enough.

3005 32RED MARES' NOVICES' HURDLE (10 hdls) 2m 4f
1:40 (1:40) (Class 4) 4-Y-0+ **£3,119** (£915; £457; £228)

Form RPR
0/3- 1 **My Miss Lucy**[33] 2317 7-10-10 0 NoelFehily 108+
(Charlie Longsdon) *disp ld tl 3rd: trckd ldrs: rdn after 3 out: led bef last where awkward on landing: drifted rt: styd on: drvn out* **5/1**[2]

2/0- 2 1 **Bull And Bush (IRE)**[24] 2506 4-10-10 0 WayneHutchinson 106
(Alan King) *hld up towards rr: hdwy into midfield 7th: sn rdn: styd on fr after 3 out: wnt cl 3rd at the last: kpt on run-in* **11/2**[3]

212- 3 1 ¼ **Lily Waugh (IRE)**[24] 2506 6-10-10 0 RobertThornton 104
(Anthony Honeyball) *trckd ldrs: chal 3 out: led next: rdn and hdd bef last: kpt on but no ex whn lost 2nd towards fin* **10/11**[1]

The Form Book Jumps, Raceform Ltd, Compton, RG20 6NL.

3/0- **4** *15* **Seas Of Green**[10] 2824 6-10-10 0 SamThomas 90
(Paul Cowley) *mid-div: rdn after 7th: wnt modest 4th bef last: nvr threatened ldrs* **150/1**

2- **5** *5* **Roja Dove (IRE)**[39] 2205 4-11-7 0 TrevorWhelan(3) 100
(Neil King) *disp tl clr ldr 3rd: rdn and hdd appr 2 out: wknd bef last* **17/2**

6 *11* **Queen's Star**[153] 4-10-10 0 TomO'Brien 76
(Andrew Balding) *mid-div: rdn after 6th: sn lost pl: nvr a threat: wknd bef 2 out* **33/1**

/10- **7** *15* **Wyfield Rose**[24] 2506 4-10-10 0 BrendanPowell 62
(Jamie Snowden) *in tch: pushed along after 7th: wknd after 3 out: t.o* **16/1**

2/3- **8** *3/4* **Brantingham Breeze**[36] 2273 5-10-10 0 LeightonAspell 62
(Emma Lavelle) *hld up towards rr: pushed along after 6th: nvr threatened: wknd after 3 out: t.o* **16/1**

30- **9** *nk* **According To Sarah (IRE)**[20] 2602 5-10-7 0 JamesBest(3) 62
(Philip Hobbs) *mid-div: hdwy after 7th: rdn into 4th briefly after 3 out: wknd next: t.o* **25/1**

110/ **10** *19* **Reach The Beach**[42] 4666 4-10-10 0 TomCannon 44
(Brendan Powell) *trckd ldrs: rdn after 3 out: sn wknd: t.o* **40/1**

60P- **11** *42* **Langarve Lady (IRE)**[15] 2718 5-10-7 0 MichaelByrne(3) 7
(Neil Mulholland) *mid-div tl dropped to last trio 4th: wknd after 6th: t.o* **150/1**

0- **12** *31* **Choral Bee**[39] 2190 4-10-10 0 DougieCostello
(Alan Jessop) *struggling 5th: a in rr: t.o fr after 6th* **150/1**

5- **13** *68* **Canarbino Girl**[209] 309 6-10-3 0 MrLDrowne(7)
(Caroline Keevil) *stmbld bdly 2nd: nvr travelling in rr after: lost tch fr after 4th: t.o* **150/1**

5m 0.4s (1.00) **Going Correction** +0.375s/f (Yiel) **13 Ran SP% 118.6**
Speed ratings (Par 105): **113,112,112,106,104 99,93,93,93,85 68,56,29**
toteswingers 1&2 £4.90, 2&3 £2.40, 1&3 £2.10 CSF £32.10 TOTE £9.00: £2.50, £2.30, £1.10; EX 36.70 Trifecta £77.90 Pool: £4132.06 - 39.74 winning units..
Owner Mrs Susan McDonald **Bred** Mrs Susan McDonald **Trained** Over Norton, Oxon

FOCUS
They went an honest gallop for this mares' hurdle with the front three home pulling clear. Ordinary form rated around the bumper marks of the first four.

3006 32RED CASINO H'CAP CHASE (19 fncs) 3m 2f 110y
2:10 (2:11) (Class 3) (0-135,135) 4-Y-0+ **£6,330** (£1,870; £935; £468; £234)

Form RPR

/FP- **1** **Pete The Feat (IRE)**[27] 2452 9-11-12 135 NoelFehily 148+
(Charlie Longsdon) *j.rt: a.p: led 6th: clr 10th tl after 4 out: rdn whn j.rt last and bmpd runner-up: styd on wl: rdn out* **5/2**[2]

214- **2** *1 3/4* **Firm Order (IRE)**[31] 2367 8-11-1 124 (v[1]) DenisO'Regan 135+
(Paul Webber) *hld up: pckd 4th: wnt 3rd 13th: wnt 2nd 3 out: rdn and ev ch whn hmpd last: styd on but no ex* **6/1**

/1F- **3** *3/4* **Financial Climate (IRE)**[40] 2177 6-10-9 118 LeightonAspell 125
(Oliver Sherwood) *tended to jump rt: trckd ldrs: lft 2nd at the 8th tl rdn gng to 3 out: styd on but a being hld fr 2 out* **2/1**[1]

/00- **4** *46* **On Trend (IRE)**[24] 2502 7-11-10 133 TomCannon 98
(Nick Gifford) *trckd ldrs: nudged along after 7th: lft 3rd at the 8th tl rdn after 13th: hld in 4th fr after next: wknd 3 out* **7/2**[3]

131- **5** *28* **Eleazar (GER)**[67] 1748 12-10-9 123 (p) MattCrawley(5) 63
(Lucy Wadham) *hld up bhd ldrs: struggling in last after 10th: no ch fr 15th: t.o* **10/1**

/U5- **U** **Curtain Razer (IRE)**[13] 2740 7-10-6 115 MarcGoldstein
(Chris Gordon) *led tl 6th: trcking ldr whn blnd and uns rdr 8th* **25/1**

6m 54.2s (-6.90) **Going Correction** -0.025s/f (Good) **6 Ran SP% 111.3**
Speed ratings (Par 107): **109,108,108,94,86**
toteswingers 1&2 £3.40, 2&3 £2.30, 1&3 £2.30 CSF £16.93 TOTE £3.30: £1.60, £3.70; EX 17.70 Trifecta £61.30 Pool: £3109.28 - 38.03 winning units..
Owner G J Larby & P J Smith **Bred** Michael O'Keeffe **Trained** Over Norton, Oxon

FOCUS
A competitive handicap despite the small field size. The winner was well in on the best of last year's form.

3007 GOLDEN WEDDING H'CAP HURDLE (9 hdls) 2m 2f 110y
2:40 (2:40) (Class 4) (0-110,110) 3-Y-0+ **£3,119** (£915; £457; £228)

Form RPR

304- **1** **Agincourt Reef (IRE)**[17] 2676 4-11-12 110 JamieMoore 118
(Gary Moore) *hld up bhd ldrs: hdwy 6th: sn rdn: dipsputed 2nd after 3 out: edging lft fr next: led last: a holding on fnl 120yds: rdn out* **9/2**[3]

313/ **2** *nk* **Mixologist**[269] 4787 6-11-12 110 (t) NoelFehily 118+
(Warren Greatrex) *led: pushed along whn narrowly hdd last: sn rdn: styd on but a being jst hld fnl 120yds* **13/8**[1]

/32- **3** *22* **Superciliary**[22] 2568 4-11-0 98 TomCannon 86
(Chris Gordon) *hld up bhd ldrs: rdn after 6th: styd on same pce fr 2 out: wnt 3rd bef last: no ch w ldrs* **3/1**[2]

4 *4* **Stay In My Heart (IRE)**[86] 1587 4-10-10 104 NathanAdams(10) 88
(Laura Mongan) *trckd ldrs: rdn 3 out: styd on same pce fr next* **16/1**

/UU- **5** *1 1/2* **Swincombe Stone**[19] 2633 6-11-10 108 RobertThornton 91
(Anthony Honeyball) *trckd ldr: rdn after 3 out: hld fr next: no ex whn lost 3rd gng to the last* **11/1**

330- **6** *1 3/4* **Macarthur**[26] 2467 9-11-12 110 (v) TomO'Brien 91
(David Rees) *hld up bhd ldrs: rdn appr 2 out: sn btn* **12/1**

/00- **7** *61* **Gran Torino (IRE)**[20] 2598 8-11-12 110 PaulMoloney 37
(Evan Williams) *trckd ldrs tl dropped to last and struggling after 5th: hdwy 3 out: wknd qckly bef next: t.o* **25/1**

406- **8** *1 1/2* **Comedy House**[14] 2729 5-10-3 87 MarcGoldstein 12
(Michael Madgwick) *trckd ldrs: rdn after 6th: wknd after 3 out: t.o* **14/1**

4m 40.8s (6.50) **Going Correction** +0.375s/f (Yiel) **8 Ran SP% 113.7**
Speed ratings (Par 105): **101,100,91,89,89 88,62,62**
toteswingers 1&2 £2.30, 2&3 £1.50, 1&3 £2.40 CSF £12.50 CT £24.50 TOTE £4.40: £1.70, £1.30, £1.40; EX 13.50 Trifecta £49.20 Pool: £3422.69 - 52.11 winning units..
Owner A Head, R Lockwood & M Burne **Bred** Lar & Fiona Cloke **Trained** Lower Beeding, W Sussex

FOCUS
Not much pace on for this handicap hurdle with the front two fighting out an exciting finish. They might both be capable of better but this not not easy form to be confident about.

3008 32REDPOKER.COM H'CAP CHASE (15 fncs) 2m 4f
3:10 (3:10) (Class 5) (0-95,95) 4-Y-0+ **£2,144** (£629; £314; £157)

Form RPR

113- **1** **Midnight Charmer**[24] 2518 7-11-0 88 JamesBanks(5) 99
(Emma Baker) *trckd ldrs: rdn to chse ldr bef 3 out: led last: sn in command: styd on wl* **9/4**[1]

0/P- **2** *3 1/2* **Malibu Sun**[20] 2599 6-11-12 95 DavidBass 105+
(Ben Pauling) *disp fr after 3rd tl clr ldr 5th: nt fluent whn pushed along fr 3 out: hdd last: sn hld by wnr but wl clr of remainder* **6/1**

P04/ **3** *25* **Cypress Grove (IRE)**[255] 5020 10-11-8 91 (vt) DaveCrosse 82
(John Ryall) *disp tl awkward 5th: trckd ldr: nt fluent 6th and 8th: reminders: rdn after 11th: wl hld fr after next: wnt modest 3rd nring fin* **9/1**

4/P- **4** *1/2* **West Bay Hoolie**[111] 1336 7-10-2 71 oh1 ow2 (p) PaulMoloney 58
(Helen Nelmes) *nt fluent and reminders early: in rr but in tch: hdwy 9th: cl 3rd 4 out: sn rdn: wknd after 2 out: lost modest 3rd towards fin* **5/2**[2]

531- **5** *7* **Princely Hero (IRE)**[20] 2603 9-11-10 93 (tp) TomCannon 72
(Chris Gordon) *disp tl 3rd: chsd ldrs: reminders after 4th: detached in last and drvn after 9th: no ch fr next: r.o again fr after 3 out* **5/1**[3]

4/0- **6** *nk* **Zhukov (IRE)**[14] 2727 11-11-5 95 (b) MrGGorman(7) 73
(Kevin Tork) *trckd ldrs: pckd 11th: rdn after next: wknd after 4 out* **12/1**

5P4- **7** *2 3/4* **Curragh Dancer (FR)**[13] 2739 10-9-7 69 oh9 (tp) LouisMuspratt(7) 45
(Paddy Butler) *a struggling: mainly last but in tch tl lost tch bef 10th: r.o but nvr any ch fr after 3 out* **50/1**

5m 13.8s (6.50) **Going Correction** -0.025s/f (Good) **7 Ran SP% 109.9**
Speed ratings (Par 103): **86,84,74,74,71 71,70**
toteswingers 1&2 £2.90, 2&3 £9.10, 1&3 £6.60 CSF £14.87 TOTE £2.80: £1.40, £3.50; EX 13.90 Trifecta £128.00 Pool: £3280.42 - 19.20 winning units..
Owner Mrs M J Arnold **Bred** Mrs J Hoskins And Brian Wilson **Trained** Naunton, Gloucs

FOCUS
Not a strong handicap run at a sound gallop. Arguably another step up from the winner.

3009 R.D. DECS TOSH AND GO H'CAP HURDLE (10 hdls) 2m 4f
3:40 (3:40) (Class 5) (0-95,93) 4-Y-0+ **£1,949** (£572; £286; £143)

Form RPR

343- **1** **Osmosia (FR)**[21] 2581 8-10-2 79 LouisMuspratt(10) 83
(Chris Gordon) *mid-div: hdwy after 4th: wnt 3rd 3 out: wnt 2nd next: rdn to ld last: styd on wl* **4/1**[1]

/00- **2** *2* **Douchkirk (FR)**[62] 1820 6-11-9 90 (b[1]) WillKennedy 93
(John Berry) *j.rt: led: rdn whn hdd jst bef last: styd on but a being hld* **8/1**

030- **3** *1 3/4* **General Girling**[160] 876 6-10-10 77 TomO'Brien 78
(Caroline Keevil) *trckd ldrs: rdn after 3 out: nvr gng pce to get on terms: styd on fnl 120yds: wnt 3rd towards fin* **7/1**

B43- **4** *3/4* **Peqeno Diablo (IRE)**[12] 2770 8-9-9 69 (tp) GeraldQuinn(7) 68
(Claire Dyson) *trckd ldrs after 2nd: rdn and ev ch after 3 out tl next: sn hld: styd on again fnl 120yds* **9/2**[2]

/56- **5** *5* **Free Falling**[16] 2690 7-11-0 81 (v) NoelFehily 76
(Alastair Lidderdale) *mid-div: trckd ldrs 4th: rdn after 7th: sn lost pl: styd on again appr last* **5/1**[3]

PP0- **6** *12* **Petrarchick (USA)**[16] 2690 6-9-11 69 (b) JamesBanks(5) 53
(Emma Baker) *mid-div: rdn after 6th: nvr any imp* **20/1**

033- **7** *36* **Fair Breeze**[17] 2679 6-10-0 74 DanielHiskett(7) 26
(Richard Phillips) *mid-div: rdn bef 7th: sn btn: t.o* **8/1**

5/6- **8** *3* **Maccabees**[21] 2581 4-11-8 89 (b[1]) JamieMoore 38
(Gary Moore) *hld up towards rr: hdwy whn hit 6th: sn rdn: wknd after 3 out: t.o* **10/1**

4/0- **9** *34* **Witchesintune**[196] 521 6-11-12 93 PaulMoloney 11
(Helen Nelmes) *hit 1st: a bhd: t.o fr after 7th* **16/1**

P40- **10** *10* **Tang Royal (FR)**[26] 2473 6-11-9 90 LeightonAspell
(Richard Rowe) *mid-div tl 4th: sn struggling and bhd: t.o* **33/1**

00P- **P** **What's For Tea**[50] 2003 8-9-11 67 (vt) MarkQuinlan(3)
(Paddy Butler) *trckd ldrs: nudged along after 4th: rdn after next: sn in rr: tailing off whn p.u bef 7th* **50/1**

P0- **P** **Coin River (IRE)**[19] 2628 7-11-4 85 (t) SamJones
(Bob Buckler) *trckd ldr tl rdn bef 7th: wknd bef 3 out: t.o whn p.u bef 2 out* **33/1**

5m 6.4s (7.00) **Going Correction** +0.375s/f (Yiel)
WFA 4 from 6yo+ 6lb **12 Ran SP% 117.1**
Speed ratings (Par 103): **101,100,99,99,97 92,78,76,63,59 ,**
toteswingers 1&2 £7.20, 2&3 £12.60, 1&3 £6.90 CSF £34.34 CT £219.08 TOTE £4.80: £1.90, £3.20, £3.30; EX 32.90 Trifecta £324.00 Pool: £4102.70 - 9.49 winning units..
Owner George Sturt **Bred** Olivier Tricot **Trained** Morestead, Hants
■ Louis Muspratt's first winner.
■ Stewards' Enquiry : Tom O'Brien two-day ban: used whip above permiited level (Dec 27,29)

FOCUS
A weak handicap run at a steady pace. It paid to race handy. The second and third are rated close to their marks.
T/Plt: £17.70 to a £1 stake. Pool of £86037.69 - 3547.68 winning tickets. T/Qpdt: £5.90 to a £1 stake. Pool of £7510.38 - 926.70 winning tickets. TM

2767 UTTOXETER (L-H)
Tuesday, December 10

OFFICIAL GOING: Chase course - soft (good to soft in places); hurdle course - good to soft (soft in places and soft in the chute - 2m races only)
Wind: light 1/2 behind Weather: overcast, cold

3010 QUICKSILVERSLOTS GET UP TO £200 FREEPLAYS MARES' MAIDEN HURDLE (9 hdls) 2m
12:20 (12:20) (Class 5) 4-Y-0+ **£2,339** (£686; £343; £171)

Form RPR

1/3- **1** **Legacy Gold (IRE)**[24] 2506 5-10-12 0 TomScudamore 132+
(David Pipe) *trckd ldrs: upsides 5th: led appr 3 out: shkn up between last 2: styd on strly: eased in clsng stages* **8/13**[1]

16/- **2** *4 1/2* **Flementime (IRE)**[606] 5394 5-10-12 0 IanPopham 125+
(Martin Keighley) *chsd ldrs: hit 3rd: chsd wnr appr 3 out: styd on same pce between last 2* **7/2**[2]

52- **3** *13* **Princess Caetani (IRE)**[12] 2767 4-10-12 0 BrianHughes 113
(David Dennis) *chsd ldrs: drvn and 3rd appr 3 out: kpt on one pce* **6/1**[3]

/FF- **4** *12* **Cantony**[10] 2824 4-10-9 0 JakeGreenall(3) 102+
(Henry Daly) *mid-div: hdwy 6th: one pce fr 3 out* **100/1**

/5- **5** *4* **Kathleen Frances**[62] 1814 6-10-12 114 (t) JackDoyle 100
(Ali Brewer) *hld up in mid-div: hdwy 6th: one pce fr next* **20/1**

233- **6** *3 1/4* **Vinnieslittle Lamb (IRE)**[16] 2697 5-10-12 105 [1] AlainCawley 96
(David Bridgwater) *mid-div: hdwy 5th: outpcd appr 3 out: sn wknd* **12/1**

6/0- **7** *3 3/4* **Armedandbeautiful**[33] 2317 5-10-12 0 JamesReveley 92
(Tom Gretton) *in rr: mstke 1st: t.o 3 out: kpt on between last 2* **100/1**

/06- **8** *2 1/2* **Lady Fingers**[12] 2767 5-10-12 0 SamTwiston-Davies 90
(Nigel Twiston-Davies) *hld up: hdwy 5th: sn drvn: lost pl appr next* **50/1**

6/3- **9** *7* **Lady Boru (IRE)**[21] 2579 5-10-12 0 HarrySkelton 90
(Dan Skelton) *chsd ldrs: the and wkng whn blnd 3 out: sn eased* **50/1**

061- **10** ½ **Wymeswold**[70] 1719 6-10-9 0 .... KielanWoods(3) 83
(Michael Mullineaux) *led: hdd appr 3 out: sn wknd* **50/1**

6/0- **11** 20 **Pennies And Pounds**[209] 324 6-10-12 0 .... MarkGrant 65
(Julian Smith) *mid-div: reminders 5th: sn lost pl: t.o 2 out* **100/1**

6/5- **12** 8 **Rosa Fleet (IRE)**[24] 2513 5-10-12 0 .... AidanColeman 58
(Venetia Williams) *t.k.h: trckd ldrs: mstke 1st: lost pl 5th: sn bhd: t.o 3 out* **66/1**

04- **13** 6 **Flemengo (IRE)**[21] 2579 4-10-12 0 .... RichieMcLernon 52
(Jonjo O'Neill) *chsd ldr: lost pl after 6th: sn bhd: t.o 2 out* **100/1**

4/0- **P** **Salford Lady**[48] 2022 4-10-12 0 .... RichardJohnson
(Philip Hobbs) *t.k.h in rr: mstke 5th: sn bhd: t.o whn p.u between last 2: broke* **50/1**

/40- **P** **A Shade Of Bay**[24] 2506 5-10-12 0 .... JasonMaguire
(Kim Bailey) *in rr: bhd fr 5th: t.o whn p.u bef 3 out* **33/1**

3m 59.6s (7.60) **Going Correction** +0.625s/f (Soft) **15** Ran SP% **127.1**
Speed ratings (Par 103): **106,103,97,91,89 87,85,84,81,80 70,66,63, ,**
toteswingers 1&2 £1.50, 2&3 £3.90, 1&3 £1.40 CSF £3.06 TOTE £1.70: £1.10, £1.80, £1.70; EX 3.80 Trifecta £15.90 Pool: £3609.35 - 169.61 winning units..
Owner R S Brookhouse **Bred** C K Johnson **Trained** Nicholashayne, Devon

FOCUS
Hurdles moved out 406m since last meeting and divided bends. A decent race for the division which ought to produce plenty of future winners, and revolved around useful bumper performer Legacy Gold. She's rated in line with her bumper form. The gallop was understandably steady on ground that rode fairly testing.

3011 QUICKSILVERSLOTS PLAY £500 ROULETTE NOVICES' CHASE (18 fncs) 3m
12:50 (12:50) (Class 4) 4-Y-0+ **£5,064** (£1,496; £748; £374; £187)

Form RPR

0- **1** **Milborough (IRE)**[25] 2490 7-11-1 0 .... RichardJohnson 136+
(Tim Vaughan) *chsd ldr: blnd 3rd: hit next: lft cl 2nd 3 out: upsides next: led narrowly appr last: drvn rt out* **8/1**

/F0- **2** nk **Sixty Something (FR)**[17] 2672 7-10-12 132 .... JakeGreenall(3) 135+
(Paul Webber) *led: narrowly hdd and lft in ld 3 out: jnd next: hdd appr last: styd on: no ex nr fin* **6/1**[3]

/12- **3** 16 **Ballinahow Star (IRE)**[12] 2769 7-10-8 125 ....(t) NickScholfield 115
(Jeremy Scott) *mid-div: chsng ldrs whn mstke 13th: lft handy 3rd 3 out: wknd and j. slowly last* **4/1**[2]

4 ¾ **Colonel Iain**[647] 7-10-12 0 .... JackQuinlan(3) 122+
(John Ferguson) *hld up in rr: hdwy 12th: outpcd and lft modest 4th 3 out: j.lft next: kpt on run-in* **16/1**

0/1- **5** 27 **Valid Point (IRE)**[33] 2314 7-11-1 117 ....(t) JasonMaguire 91
(Jim Old) *nt fluent in rr: drvn and sme hdwy 13th: wknd 4 out* **11/1**

0/5- **6** 10 **Simply Charles (IRE)**[15] 2719 6-11-1 0 .... JackDoyle 81
(Hilary Parrott) *prom: lost pl 6th: outpcd 11th: bhd fr 14th: t.o next* **100/1**

P6U- **7** 1 **Typical Oscar (IRE)**[12] 2756 6-11-1 0 .... LiamTreadwell 80
(Michael Blake) *hld up in rr: bhd fr 11th: t.o 4 out* **100/1**

5/4- **F** **African Gold (IRE)**[24] 2501 5-11-1 0 ....(t) SamTwiston-Davies 140+
(Nigel Twiston-Davies) *trckd ldng pair: shkn up after 14th: cl 2nd whn hit next: led narrowly whn fell 3 out* **1/2**[1]

6m 20.5s (5.40) **Going Correction** +0.375s/f (Yiel) **8** Ran SP% **128.3**
Speed ratings (Par 105): **106,105,100,100,91 87,87,**
toteswingers 1&2 £4.60, 2&3 £2.80, 1&3 £3.10 CSF £60.96 TOTE £11.40: £2.30, £2.20, £1.80; EX 83.20 Trifecta £240.00 Pool: £2562.02 - 8.00 winning units..
Owner Pinehurst Stud **Bred** Mrs K White **Trained** Aberthin, Vale of Glamorgan

FOCUS
A well-contested novice chase, but it left us with more questions than answers. It looked a truly run race, on ground that rode slightly more testing than the hurdles course. The winner and second are rated in line with their hurdles form.

3012 SIS LIVE H'CAP HURDLE (9 hdls) 2m
1:20 (1:20) (Class 4) (0-120,118) 4-Y-0+ **£3,898** (£1,144; £572; £286)

Form RPR

5/0- **1** **Ut Majeur Aulmes (FR)**[31] 2366 5-11-4 110 .... JackDoyle 123+
(Victor Dartnall) *hld up in rr: smooth hdwy 6th: trcking ldrs next: led after 2 out: rdn clr run-in* **11/2**

453- **2** 5 **Mystifiable**[20] 2602 5-11-5 111 ....(t) PaddyBrennan 117
(Fergal O'Brien) *mid-div: trckd ldrs 5th: chal 2 out: styd on same pce run-in* **4/1**[2]

225/ **3** 1¼ **Come On Annie**[240] 5320 7-9-10 95 .... MrsAlexDunn(7) 99
(Alexandra Dunn) *trckd ldrs: effrt appr last: styd on to take 3rd nr fin* **14/1**

0/P- **4** ½ **Leviathan**[53] 1960 6-11-12 118 .... AidanColeman 123
(Venetia Williams) *trckd ldrs: led after 3 out: hdd after 2 out: 3rd whn hit last: wknd towards fin* **10/1**

304- **5** 1¼ **Vujiyama (FR)**[19] 2614 4-11-3 109 .... APMcCoy 112
(Jonjo O'Neill) *hld up in rr: hdwy 6th: chsng ldrs 2 out: one pce* **9/2**[3]

1/5- **6** nk **Iron Butterfly**[28] 2435 4-10-11 106 .... JackQuinlan(3) 109
(James Eustace) *chsd ldrs: outpcd 2 out: kpt on run-in* **25/1**

/22- **7** 3½ **Sam Lord**[28] 2447 9-10-12 104 .... BrianHughes 104
(James Moffatt) *chsd clr ldr: drvn 5th: led after next: hdd after 3 out: wknd appr last* **8/1**

240/ **8** 28 **Allusive Power (IRE)**[367] 2906 4-10-5 97 .... CharliePoste 71
(Anna Brooks) *in rr: hdwy 4th: drvn appr 3 out: sn lost pl and bhd: t.o* **66/1**

/00- **9** 56 **Thinger Licht (FR)**[27] 2464 4-11-9 115 .... LeeEdwards 39
(Tony Carroll) *in rr-div: lost pl 6th: sn bhd: t.o next: virtually p.u: eventually completed* **66/1**

001- **P** **King Zeal (IRE)**[5] 2904 9-10-3 100 ....(t) HarryChalloner(5)
(Barry Leavy) *chsd ldrs: drvn 6th: lost pl 2 out: eased and bhd whn p.u bef last* **7/2**[1]

F/3- **P** **Deia Sunrise (IRE)**[171] 235 4-11-8 114 ....(t) LiamTreadwell
(Paul Webber) *led: j. bdly rt 1st: clr 3rd: hit next: hdd after 6th: lost pl appr 2 out: sn bhd and eased: t.o whn p.u bef last* **14/1**

3m 59.3s (7.30) **Going Correction** +0.625s/f (Soft)
WFA 4 from 5yo+ 5lb **11** Ran SP% **116.2**
Speed ratings (Par 105): **106,103,102,102,102 101,100,86,58,**
toteswingers 1&2 £7.00, 2&3 £11.80, 1&3 £17.30 CSF £27.69 CT £291.53 TOTE £7.40: £2.10, £1.90, £4.10; EX 34.20 Trifecta £273.70 Pool: £1467.99 - 4.02 winning units..
Owner Mrs S De Wilde **Bred** Emmanuel Bodard **Trained** Brayford, Devon

FOCUS
A competitive event for the grade. The easy winner was value for further and is rated up a stone.

3013 32RED CASINO H'CAP HURDLE (10 hdls) 2m 4f 110y
1:50 (1:50) (Class 4) (0-120,120) 3-Y-0+ **£3,898** (£1,144; £572; £286)

Form RPR

502- **1** **Di Kaprio (FR)**[24] 2510 7-11-6 114 .... LiamHeard 120+
(Barry Leavy) *mde all: clr in 2nd to 5th: chal 3 out: kpt on wl run-in* **8/1**

010- **2** 1¾ **Scales (IRE)**[33] 2314 7-10-11 105 .... IanPopham 107+
(Richard Lee) *hld up in rr: hdwy 7th: chsng ldrs next: sn rdn: 5th 2 out: 2nd between last 2: kpt on same pce run-in* **12/1**

4/0- **3** 5 **Tolkeins Tango (IRE)**[35] 2284 5-11-5 113 .... JackDoyle 111
(Victor Dartnall) *hld up in rr: stdy hdwy 6th: chal 3 out: hung lft and kpt on one pce between last 2* **15/2**

P/0- **4** nk **Quel Elite (FR)**[197] 512 9-10-11 105 .... BrianHughes 102
(James Moffatt) *hld up in rr: effrt after 7th: sn drvn and outpcd: styd on fr 2 out: modest 5th last: 4th nr fin* **25/1**

14- **5** nk **Premier Portrait (IRE)**[33] 2316 6-11-6 114 .... JasonMaguire 112
(Kim Bailey) *chsd ldrs: rdn and outpcd bef 3 out: one pce fr 2 out* **10/1**

213- **6** 4½ **Finding Your Feet (IRE)**[24] 2510 5-11-3 111 ....(p) APMcCoy 105
(Jonjo O'Neill) *trckd ldrs: cl 3rd 3 out: sn rdn: wknd appr last* **2/1**[1]

1/0- **7** ¾ **Market Option (IRE)**[33] 2314 7-11-1 109 .... AidanColeman 101
(Venetia Williams) *chsd ldrs: rdn 3 out: wknd between last 2* **6/1**[3]

200- **8** ¾ **Mission Complete (IRE)**[18] 2655 7-11-2 120 .... PatrickCowley(10) 112
(Jonjo O'Neill) *in rr-div: pushed along and mid-div: 6th: reminders after next: lost pl bef 3 out* **12/1**

/06- **9** 14 **Bladoun (FR)**[12] 2764 5-11-2 110 ....(tp) TomScudamore 89
(David Pipe) *nt fluent: chsd ldrs: nt fluent 6th: wknd after 7th: sn bhd* **11/2**[2]

5m 11.0s (12.00) **Going Correction** +0.625s/f (Soft) **9** Ran SP% **114.2**
Speed ratings (Par 105): **102,101,99,99,99 97,97,96,91**
toteswingers 1&2 £15.20, 2&3 £20.30, 1&3 £8.70 CSF £94.33 CT £747.58 TOTE £7.90: £1.60, £3.50, £2.60; EX 132.60 Trifecta £810.90 Pool: £2217.09 - 2.05 winning units..
Owner Cops & Robbers **Bred** Mme Dominique Le Drans **Trained** Forsbrook, Staffs

FOCUS
A reasonable gallop in the conditions. The third to fifth set the level.

3014 32RED.COM NOVICES' H'CAP HURDLE (10 hdls) 2m 4f 110y
2:20 (2:20) (Class 5) (0-95,95) 3-Y-0+ **£2,339** (£686; £343; £171)

Form RPR

62- **1** **Wintered Well (IRE)**[11] 2787 5-11-0 83 .... SeanQuinlan 97+
(Jennie Candlish) *trckd ldrs: led 2 out: drew clr appr last: 7 l clr whn heavily eased in clsng stages* **5/6**[1]

/44- **2** 4 **Blazing Bouncer**[18] 2649 8-11-12 95 ....(tp) RhysFlint 96
(Richard Woollacott) *trckd ldrs: led 3 out: hdd next: kpt on same pce* **25/1**

0F0/ **3** ¾ **Dungeness**[293] 4323 5-11-12 95 .... AidanColeman 95
(Venetia Williams) *hld up towards rr: hit 4th: hdwy 6th: chsng ldrs 3 out: 3rd appr last: kpt on one pce* **14/1**

040- **4** 6 **Over My Head**[24] 2509 5-10-11 80 .... NickScholfield 76
(Claire Dyson) *w ldr: led 7th: hdd next: wknd appr last* **33/1**

505- **5** 8 **Bob Will (IRE)**[42] 2148 8-9-7 69 oh3 .... JPKiely(7) 57
(Tim Vaughan) *chsd ldrs: blnd 5th: wknd fr 3 out* **4/1**[2]

600- **6** 12 **Drombeg West**[16] 2701 6-10-4 73 .... AndrewTinkler 50
(Anna Brooks) *led to 7th: lost pl appr 2 out* **8/1**[3]

440- **7** 28 **Eyeline**[22] 2559 3-10-0 91 ....(vt) JamesCowley(7) 27
(Andrew Hollinshead) *chsd ldrs: mstke 3rd: drvn 7th: lost pl bef next: sn bhd: t.o* **16/1**

6P0- **8** 3¼ **First Of Never (IRE)**[16] 2701 7-10-6 75 .... TomSiddall 23
(Lynn Siddall) *chsd ldrs: lost pl after 7th: sn bhd: t.o 2 out* **25/1**

066- **9** 29 **Echoes Of Joy**[19] 2616 4-11-8 91 .... SamTwiston-Davies 13
(David Evans) *wore net muzzle: in rr: bhd frokm 6th: t.o 3 out* **33/1**

/0F- **U** **Song Of Pride (GER)**[54] 1940 9-10-4 73 .... DonalDevereux
(Mandy Rowland) *prom: 9th and outpcd whn blnd and uns rdr 7th* **33/1**

P/P- **P** **Direct Approach (IRE)**[201] 449 9-10-0 69 oh5 .... GerardTumelty
(Lynn Siddall) *in rr: bhd and drvn 4th: t.o 6th: p.u bef next* **100/1**

U50- **P** **Captive Moment**[24] 2514 7-11-0 90 .... StephenMulqueen(7)
(John Norton) *in rr: drvn 2nd: reminders 4th: bhd fr 6th: sn t.o: next: p.u bef 3 out* **20/1**

0/P- **P** **My Silver Lilly**[16] 2698 6-10-10 79 .... AdamPogson
(Clive Drew) *chsd ldrs: lost pl 6th: bhd next: t.o whn p.u bef 3 out* **100/1**

5m 15.1s (16.10) **Going Correction** +0.625s/f (Soft)
WFA 3 from 4yo 14lb 4 from 5yo+ 6lb **13** Ran SP% **121.5**
Speed ratings (Par 103): **94,92,92,89,86 82,71,70,59, , ,**
toteswingers 1&2 £11.20, 2&3 £31.80, 1&3 £4.20 CSF £30.53 CT £201.52 TOTE £1.80: £1.10, £6.70, £4.00; EX 24.60 Trifecta £415.60 Pool: £2056.86 - 3.71 winning units..
Owner Mrs Kristene Hunter **Bred** Mrs Kathleen Leahy **Trained** Basford Green, Staffs

FOCUS
No great strength in depth to this novice handicap. The winner was thrown in on his bumper form.

3015 32RED NOVICES' H'CAP CHASE (15 fncs) 2m 4f
2:50 (2:50) (Class 5) (0-100,99) 4-Y-0+ **£2,859** (£839; £419; £209)

Form RPR

0F5- **1** **River Purple**[11] 2787 6-10-7 80 ....(t) BrianHughes 93+
(John Mackie) *chsd ldrs: led 4 out: clr whn j.lft last 2: pushed out* **16/1**

/30- **2** 7 **Hero's Call**[199] 482 8-10-0 73 oh3 .... MarkGrant 74
(Julian Smith) *in rr-div: hdwy 10th: chsng ldrs appr 4 out: 3rd 2 out: kpt on and 2nd last 75yds* **33/1**

/24- **3** 1¾ **Meirig's Dream (IRE)**[34] 2291 7-10-4 77 .... JamesDavies 78
(Philip Hobbs) *mid-div: hdwy to chse ldrs 11th: 2nd 3 out: one pce whn j.rt last* **9/2**[1]

4/0- **4** 5 **Samtheman**[20] 2591 8-11-6 98 ....(p) JoeCollier(5) 93
(Micky Hammond) *in rr: sme hdwy 12th: j.rt last 3: tk modest 4th nr fin: nvr nr ldrs* **20/1**

/00- **5** 2 **Hand On Bach (IRE)**[28] 2437 5-11-7 97 ....(b[1]) GavinSheehan(3) 90
(Warren Greatrex) *chsd ldrs: wknd 2 out* **9/1**

0/P- **6** 4½ **Tiquer (FR)**[84] 1598 5-11-12 99 .... JackDoyle 88
(Alan Jones) *in rr: drvn 12th: kpt on run-in: nvr on terms* **33/1**

121- **7** 4½ **Molko Jack (FR)**[19] 2626 9-11-2 92 .... KielanWoods(3) 77
(Michael Mullineaux) *nt fluent: chsd ldrs: rdn 12th: lost pl next* **8/1**[3]

/P4- **8** 7 **Lord Kennedy (IRE)**[10] 2825 8-11-7 94 ....(tp) PaddyBrennan 70
(Alex Hales) *led to 4 out: sn wknd* **12/1**

600- **9** 2¼ **Degenerate (FR)**[27] 2457 6-11-8 95 .... NickScholfield 69
(Jeremy Scott) *in rr: reminders 9th: bhd fr 12th* **9/2**[1]

000/ **10** 13 **Browns Brook (IRE)**[231] 5470 7-10-13 86 .... AidanColeman 47
(Venetia Williams) *nt fluent in rr: mstke 10th: sn bhd* **5/1**[2]

302- **P** **Lodgician (IRE)**[9] 2849 11-11-7 94......................(vt) SamTwiston-Davies
(Nigel Twiston-Davies) *chsd ldrs: hung rt and lost pl appr 9th: sn bhd: t.o whn p.u bef 11th* **12/1**

/50- **U** **Ilewin Kim**[119] 1266 7-10-2 75.. TomScudamore
(Gary Brown) *in rr-div: hdwy 12th: in tch whn blnd and uns rdr 4 out* **17/2**

64F- **P** **Possibly Flora**[33] 2312 8-11-7 94..(t) RhysFlint
(Richard Woollacott) *trckd ldrs: wknd appr 4 out: sn bhd: t.o whn p.u bef last* **16/1**

5m 12.0s (6.50) **Going Correction** +0.375s/f (Yiel) **13** Ran SP% **122.5**
Speed ratings (Par 103): **102,99,98,96,95 93,92,89,88,83 , ,**
toteswingers 1&2 £78.70, 2&3 £39.90, 1&3 £14.90 CSF £446.57 CT £2763.62 TOTE £20.30: £6.00, £13.50, £2.20; EX 884.10 Trifecta £1808.50 Part won. Pool: £2411.38 - 0.28 winning units..
Owner Sotby Farming Company Limited **Bred** Wood Farm Stud **Trained** Church Broughton , Derbys

FOCUS
A low-level novice handicap chase run at a decent gallop on the ground. Not an easy race to put a figure on.

3016 £32 BONUS AT 32RED.COM STANDARD OPEN NATIONAL HUNT FLAT RACE 2m
3:20 (3:20) (Class 6) 4-6-Y-0 **£1,559** (£457; £228; £114)

Form RPR

1 **Askamore Darsi (IRE)**[206] 4-11-2 0.................................. JasonMaguire 112+
(Donald McCain) *mde all: qcknd pce 7f out: drvn over 4f out: drew clr over 1f out: edgd lft and styd on wl* **12/1**

F- **2** *6* **Relentless Dreamer (IRE)**[58] 1891 4-11-2 0................ TomScudamore 106
(Rebecca Curtis) *trckd wnr: upsides over 4f out: rdn 3f out: kpt on same pce fnl 2f* **10/1**

3 *1 1/4* **Onenightinvienna (IRE)**[198] 4-11-2 0........................... RichardJohnson 105
(Philip Hobbs) *sn trcking ldrs: effrt 6f out: rdn 3f out: one pce* **5/6**[1]

4 *17* **Maxilian (IRE)** 4-11-2 0.. AidanColeman 91
(Emma Lavelle) *trckd ldrs: effrt over 3f out: wknd over 1f out* **15/2**[3]

4/ **5** *1* **Lucky Emily**[332] 3628 4-10-9 0.. BrianHughes 82
(John Mackie) *hld up in rr: drvn over 4f out: kpt on fnl 2f: nvr on terms* **25/1**

0/6- **6** *11* **Cadgers Hole**[206] 380 6-11-2 0... TomSiddall 79
(Lynn Siddall) *hld up in rr: t.k.h: drvn 6f out: lost pl over 4f out* **100/1**

7 *4 1/2* **Touch Judge (IRE)** 4-11-2 0.. APMcCoy 85+
(Jonjo O'Neill) *trckd ldrs: effrt over 3f out: sn outpcd: wknd 2f out: sn eased* **11/4**[2]

3m 57.9s (11.50) **Going Correction** +0.625s/f (Soft) **7** Ran SP% **114.6**
Speed ratings: **96,93,92,83,83 77,75**
toteswingers 1&2 £9.80, 2&3 £3.10, 1&3 £3.40 CSF £119.79 TOTE £11.50: £3.90, £6.20; EX 75.00 Trifecta £310.80 Pool: £3440.70 - 8.30 winning units..
Owner Deva Racing Darsi Partnership **Bred** William McGladdery **Trained** Cholmondeley, Cheshire

FOCUS
Unusually for this type of race the gallop looked true enough and with some useful, franked Irish point form boasted, it looked a decent contest. The winner looks above average.
T/Plt: £266.40 to a £1 take. Pool of £71714.99 - 196.45 winning tickets. T/Qpdt: £66.80 to a £1 take. Pool of £6672.39 - 73.90 winning tickets. WG

2591 HEXHAM (L-H)
Wednesday, December 11

OFFICIAL GOING: Soft (good to soft in places; 4.9)
Wind: virtually nil Weather: Fine and sunny

3017 HEXHAM BOOKMAKERS "NATIONAL HUNT" NOVICES' HURDLE (8 hdls) 2m 110y
12:50 (12:50) (Class 4) 4-Y-0+ **£3,119** (£915; £457; £228)

Form RPR

1 **Seeyouatmidnight**[227] 5-10-12 0.................................... RyanMania 117
(Sandy Thomson) *mde all: rdn appr last: styd on wl* **66/1**

/21- **2** *2* **Regal Encore (IRE)**[23] 2564 5-11-5 130............................ APMcCoy 122
(Anthony Honeyball) *hld up in midfield: stl only 6th 2 out: pushed along and hdwy to chse ldr appr last: 2 l down in 2nd last: sn rdn and one pce* **1/4**[1]

5/1- **3** *4 1/2* **Tikkandemickey (IRE)**[21] 2597 7-10-12 119................ CallumBewley(7) 117
(Raymond Shiels) *trckd ldr: rdn after 2 out: one pce* **13/2**[3]

602- **4** *4 1/2* **Lord Brendy**[21] 2593 5-10-12 0.................................... KennyJohnson 106
(Robert Johnson) *trckd ldrs: rdn after 2 out: no ex appr last* **20/1**

U35- **5** *2 3/4* **Quick Brew**[15] 2732 5-10-5 105...............................(t) StephenMulqueen(7) 104
(Maurice Barnes) *hld up: hit 2 out: sn rdn: one pce and nvr threatened* **20/1**

051- **6** *3 3/4* **Our Boy Ben**[21] 2593 4-11-5 0.. BrianHughes 106
(Malcolm Jefferson) *in tch: hit 2 out: sn rdn: wknd appr last* **11/2**[2]

U3- **7** *16* **Allez Cool (IRE)**[21] 2593 4-10-5 0.................................. JohnDawson(7) 83
(John Wade) *midfield: wknd after 2 out* **66/1**

8 *24* **Whinstone Dani (IRE)**[361] 3071 6-10-5 0......................... AELynch 52
(Miss Clare Louise Cannon, Ire) *hld up: a bhd* **22/1**

P/0- **9** *5* **Here's To Harry**[210] 313 6-10-12 0............................. LucyAlexander 54
(N W Alexander) *hld up: a bhd* **100/1**

10 *61* **Marine Band** 7-10-5 0.. DaraghBourke(7)
(Sue Smith) *nt fluent: hld up: a towards rr: t.o after 2 out* **66/1**

0- **P** **Champagne Agent (IRE)**[42] 2159 7-10-12 0..............(p) PeterBuchanan
(Lucinda Russell) *prom: wknd qckly appr 2 out: p.u bef last* **14/1**

4m 21.8s (4.40) **Going Correction** +0.50s/f (Soft) **11** Ran SP% **134.7**
Speed ratings (Par 105): **109,108,105,103,102 100,93,81,79,50**
toteswingers 1&2 £30.60, 2&3 £1.10, 1&3 £30.60 CSF £98.45 TOTE £39.30: £12.00, £1.02, £1.90; EX 101.30 Trifecta £888.60 Pool: £1326.98 -1.12 winning units..
Owner Mrs A M Thomson **Bred** Miss F A Evans **Trained** Lambden, Berwicks

FOCUS
Fresh ground on both bends and in the back straight from top of hill to dip. A shock result, with a heavily odds-on shot beaten.

3018 THANK YOU NOVA INTERNATIONAL MAIDEN HURDLE (12 hdls) 3m
1:20 (1:20) (Class 5) 4-Y-0+ **£1,949** (£572; £286; £143)

Form RPR

/25- **1** **Simarthur**[48] 2030 6-11-0 0..(v[1]) PeterBuchanan 117
(Lucinda Russell) *chsd ldrs: rdn after 2 out: led appr last: styd on* **2/1**[2]

2/6- **2** *2* **Hellorboston (IRE)**[45] 2103 5-11-0 0................................ HenryBrooke 116
(Donald McCain) *w ldr: led 5th: hit 3 out: rdn whn hdd 2 out: dropped to 3rd appr last: plugged on to regain 2nd run-in* **13/8**[1]

/42- **3** *1 3/4* **Romany Ryme**[33] 2337 7-10-7 107............................ JonathonBewley(7) 113
(George Bewley) *trckd: nt fluent 3 out: rdn to ld 2 out: hdd appr last: no ex and lost 2nd run-in* **11/4**[3]

P- **4** *44* **Allforthelove**[32] 2355 5-11-0 0.. LucyAlexander 69
(N W Alexander) *hld up: sltly hmpd by faller 7th: sn struggling: wnt distant 4th last* **66/1**

50- **5** *9* **Whinstone Dee (IRE)**[40] 2204 5-11-0 93..............................(tp) AELynch 60
(Miss Clare Louise Cannon, Ire) *trckd ldrs: wknd after 2 out* **10/1**

/00- **6** *3 1/4* **Ultiep (FR)**[32] 2355 5-11-0 0...(p) BrianHughes 57
(Karen McLintock) *led narrowly tl 5th: remained prom tl wknd 2 out* **25/1**

P **Ruberslaw**[304] 7-11-0 0.. BarryKeniry
(Simon Shirley-Beavan) *hld up: mstke 6th: bhd whn hmpd by faller 7th: p.u after 8th* **80/1**

0- **F** **Generous Chief (IRE)**[53] 1980 5-11-0 0........................ WilsonRenwick
(Chris Grant) *in tch: wnt a little in snatches: fell 7th* **66/1**

6m 25.0s (16.00) **Going Correction** +0.50s/f (Soft) **8** Ran SP% **115.3**
Speed ratings (Par 103): **93,92,91,77,74 73, ,**
toteswingers 1&2 £1.30, 2&3 £1.20, 1&3 £1.10 CSF £5.86 TOTE £2.60: £1.10, £1.10, £1.10; EX 9.00 Trifecta £12.80 Pool: £2289.24 - 133.65 winning units..
Owner R A Bartlett **Bred** Simon Tindall **Trained** Arlary, Perth & Kinross
■ Stewards' Enquiry : Jonathon Bewley one-day ban: careless riding (Dec 27)

FOCUS
A moderate event run at a slow gallop early.

3019 FAREWELL AND THANKS JOHN SUTHERLAND H'CAP CHASE (17 fncs) 2m 7f
1:50 (1:51) (Class 4) (0-120,115) 4-Y-0+ **£3,768** (£1,106; £553; £276)

Form RPR

0F3- **1** **Sun Cloud (IRE)**[29] 2446 6-11-10 113................................ BrianHughes 133+
(Malcolm Jefferson) *hld up: tk clsr order 8th: led gng wl 2 out: rdn clr appr last* **5/1**[2]

643- **2** *7* **The Thirsty Bricky (IRE)**[14] 2749 11-11-4 112................... TonyKelly(5) 121
(David Thompson) *midfield: rdn after 4 out: styd on to go 2nd last: no ch w wnr* **17/2**

42P- **3** *11* **Baltic Pathfinder (IRE)**[40] 2201 9-10-11 100...................... RyanMania 100
(Sue Smith) *trckd ldr: pushed along and lost pl 12th: bk in contention 4 out: wnt 2nd 2 out: jst lost 2nd whn hit last: wknd* **14/1**

1/P- **4** *19* **Mister Philson (IRE)**[18] 2670 8-11-7 110...........................(b[1]) APMcCoy 88
(S R B Crawford, Ire) *led: wnt in snatches: rdn whn hdd 2 out: wknd* **9/2**[1]

0/ **5** *4 1/2* **Knockgraffon King (IRE)**[230] 5526 8-11-12 115................ HenryBrooke 89
(Donald McCain) *trckd ldrs: wknd appr 3 out* **8/1**

P/U- **6** *3 3/4* **Honest John**[31] 2394 9-11-5 115....................................... PaulBohan(7) 85
(Steve Gollings) *hld up: rdn 1/2-way: nvr threatened* **7/1**

26/- **7** *9* **Fog Patches (IRE)**[243] 5276 7-10-8 104..................(p) GrahamWatters(7) 65
(Lucinda Russell) *prom tl wknd after 2 out* **11/2**[3]

U/0- **P** **Outlaw Tom (IRE)**[25] 2516 9-11-7 110..........................(p) PeterBuchanan
(Lucinda Russell) *midfield: nt fluent 5th: sn struggling: t.o whn p.u bef 12th* **12/1**

/55- **P** **Oil Burner**[30] 2421 8-10-11 100.. BrianHarding
(William Amos) *in tch: wknd after 5 out: p.u bef last* **6/1**

0U0- **P** **Jukebox Melody (IRE)**[7] 2882 7-10-13 109...............(p) JohnDawson(7)
(John Wade) *nt fluent: hld up: reminders after 8th: sn bhd: p.u bef 12th* **40/1**

6m 19.9s (19.10) **Going Correction** +0.75s/f (Soft) **10** Ran SP% **115.5**
Speed ratings (Par 105): **96,93,89,83,81 80,77, , ,**
toteswingers 1&2 £13.90, 2&3 £29.10, 1&3 £34.40 CSF £46.44 CT £557.99 TOTE £7.50: £2.70, £2.10, £4.10; EX 52.50 Trifecta £783.80 Part won. Pool: £1045.15 - 0.32 winning units..
Owner Boundary Garage (Bury) Limited **Bred** Mrs Rose & Miss Lucy Barry **Trained** Norton, N Yorks

FOCUS
Modest fare, but the pace seemed sound from the outset, so the form should be reliable.

3020 THANK YOU INTU METROCENTRE H'CAP CHASE (12 fncs) 2m 110y
2:20 (2:20) (Class 5) (0-100,98) 4-Y-0+ **£2,144** (£629; £314; £157)

Form RPR

123- **1** **Cloverhill Lad (IRE)**[190] 627 9-11-2 95...................... DaraghBourke(7) 109+
(Stuart Coltherd) *trckd ldr: led 3rd: mde rest: rdn after 2 out: drvn out run-in* **13/2**

/23- **2** *1 3/4* **Pamak D'Airy (FR)**[15] 2737 10-11-7 98...............................(p) TonyKelly(5) 108
(Henry Hogarth) *trckd ldr: rdn after 2 out: kpt on but a hld by wnr* **17/2**

032- **3** *2 1/4* **Discoverie**[7] 2880 5-10-3 75.. BrianHughes 85
(Dianne Sayer) *trckd ldrs: rdn after 3 out: plugged on* **15/8**[1]

/55- **4** *4* **Decent Lord (IRE)**[21] 2591 9-10-8 80................................ SeanQuinlan 85
(Jennie Candlish) *in tch: rdn after 2 out: sn one pce: no ex after last* **7/2**[2]

055- **5** *13* **Robin's Command (IRE)**[15] 2737 6-10-2 74................. WilsonRenwick 65
(Rose Dobbin) *hld up: briefly wnt 4th 2 out: sn rdn: wknd* **4/1**[3]

P66- **6** *40* **Vardas Supreme (IRE)**[25] 2518 10-10-5 82.........(bt) SamanthaDrake(5) 33
(Richard Drake) *led tl slow 3rd (water): reminders and lost pl after 5th: lost tch after 4 out* **40/1**

/45- **P** **Crackerjack Lad (IRE)**[33] 2338 10-10-7 79.......................... PeterBuchanan
(Lucinda Russell) *midfield: wknd after 3 out: p.u bef last* **11/1**

4m 21.3s (11.50) **Going Correction** +0.75s/f (Soft) **7** Ran SP% **111.6**
Speed ratings (Par 103): **102,101,100,98,92 73,**
toteswingers 1&2 £1.60, 2&3 £1.10, 1&3 £2.40 CSF £53.36 TOTE £9.50: £3.00, £2.80; EX 17.00 Trifecta £50.20 Pool: £1664.34 - 24.81 winning units..
Owner Coltherd Turnbull **Bred** D Lynam **Trained** Selkirk, Borders

FOCUS
Not a strong contest and five of these held some sort of chance rounding the final bend.

3021 THANK YOU INTU ELDON SQUARE H'CAP HURDLE (8 hdls) 2m 110y
2:50 (2:55) (Class 4) (0-115,115) 3-Y-0+ **£3,119** (£915; £457; £228)

Form RPR

/06- **1** **Circus Star (USA)**[21] 2597 5-10-2 98.................................... MrJDixon(7) 106+
(John Dixon) *mde all: rdn 6 l clr 2 out: nt fluent last: dwindling advantage run-in but a holding on* **14/1**

651- **2** *1 1/2* **Light The City (IRE)**[8] 2869 6-10-11 103 7ex.................. JakeGreenall(3) 108
(Ruth Carr) *trckd ldrs: rdn to chse ldr after 2 out: kpt on but a hld* **15/2**

221- **3** *hd* **Bernardelli (IRE)**[18] 2676 5-11-11 114................................ BrianHarding 118
(Nicky Richards) *midfield: rdn and outpcd after 3 out: hdwy into 3rd appr last: styd on wl* **7/2**[2]

035- **4** *18* **Formulation (IRE)**[6] 2904 6-10-8 102.................................(p) TonyKelly(5) 88
(Rebecca Menzies) *midfield: rdn and briefly 3rd after 2 out: wknd appr last* **13/2**

6/4- **5** *7* **Sacre Toi (FR)**[14] 2751 7-11-3 113.......................................(p) DaleIrving(7) 94
(James Ewart) *prom: rdn 3 out: wknd appr next* **6/1**[3]

544/ **6** *5* **Alf The Audacious**[269] 4815 7-11-2 **105**...................... RyanMania 79
(Sue Smith) *trckd ldrs: wknd after 2 out* **13/2**

/03- **7** *1* **Danehills Well (IRE)**[26] 2493 5-11-12 **115**...................... LucyAlexander 88
(Alison Hamilton) *hld up: wknd after 3 out* **22/1**

604- **8** *42* **Call Of Duty (IRE)**[10] 2839 8-11-1 **109**...................... ColmMcCormack(5) 40
(Dianne Sayer) *nt fluent in rr: nvr threatened* **33/1**

0/ **P** **Golden Firth (IRE)**[32] 2381 6-11-2 **105**...................... APMcCoy
(A J Martin, Ire) *hld up: hdwy to trck ldrs 5th: rdn appr 2 out: wknd qckly: p.u bef last* **10/3**[1]

4m 26.0s (8.60) **Going Correction** +0.50s/f (Soft) **9** Ran SP% **112.0**
Speed ratings (Par 105): **99,98,98,89,86 84,83,63,**
toteswingers 1&2 £18.30, 2&3 £6.00, 1&3 £8.70 CSF £109.24 CT £449.71 TOTE £13.50: £3.10, £2.30, £1.50; EX 127.00 Trifecta £743.30 Pool: £2339.03 - 2.36 winning units..
Owner Mrs S F Dixon **Bred** Joseph Clay & Wendy Clay **Trained** Thursby, Cumbria
■ The first winner under rules for amateur John Dixon, son of trainer John Dixon senior.

FOCUS
A solid race for the level.

3022 THANK YOU ARUP H'CAP CHASE (19 fncs) 3m 1f
3:20 (3:27) (Class 5) (0-95,95) 4-Y-0+ **£2,144** (£629; £314; £157)

Form RPR

/P4- **1** **Esme Rides A Gaine**[15] 2735 11-9-10 **72**...................... StephenMulqueen(7) 80
(Christopher Wilson) *hld up: only 6th 2 out: stl 5 l down in 3rd last: styd on to ld post* **20/1**

052- **2** *shd* **Fozy Moss**[21] 2591 7-9-13 **75**...................... DaraghBourke(7) 83
(Stuart Coltherd) *trckd ldrs: hit 4th: led 3 out: strly pressed by eventual 3rd after 2 out: got bttr of that rival last: drvn run-in: no ex and hdd post* **7/2**[1]

PP5/ **3** *1 ¾* **Arc Warrior (FR)**[365] 2992 9-10-2 **71**......................(t) BrianHarding 78
(William Amos) *hld up: stdy hdwy fr 1/2-way: upsides 2 out: sn rdn: no ex fr last* **40/1**

644- **4** *7* **Camden George (IRE)**[21] 2594 12-11-10 **93**......................(p) RyanMania 92
(Sue Smith) *hld up: hdwy after 13th: prom 4 out: outpcd by ldng pair after 2 out: and hld in 4th fr appr last* **13/2**[3]

650/ **5** *5* **Filbert Fox (IRE)**[206] 7-10-7 **79**......................(p) EwanWhillans(3) 74
(Alistair Whillans) *hld up in rr: mstke 2nd: rdn after 4 out: plugged on: nvr threatened ldrs* **40/1**

F32- **6** *7* **Heez A Steel (IRE)**[15] 2735 12-11-4 **94**...................... AlistairFindlay(7) 80
(Jane Walton) *prom: rdn after 3 out: wknd after 2 out* **10/1**

/13- **7** *5* **Matmata De Tendron (FR)**[21] 2594 13-11-2 **88**......(p) JohnKington(3) 71
(Andrew Crook) *in tch: hit 13th: sn lost pl: struggling fr 4 out* **16/1**

/56- **8** *18* **Boris The Blade**[11] 2818 11-11-7 **95**......................(b) SamanthaDrake(5) 58
(Tina Jackson) *led: hdd 14th: led again 4 out: jst hdd whn mstke 3 out: wknd after 2 out* **14/1**

2/4- **P** **Cottiers Den (IRE)**[14] 2747 6-11-10 **93**......................(p) WilsonRenwick
(Martin Todhunter) *midfield: lost pl quicky after 8th: p.u bef 11th* **10/1**

5P1- **P** **Great Ocean Road (IRE)**[15] 2735 10-10-2 **76**...................... AdamNicol(5)
(David Thompson) *midfield: mstke 7th and lost pl: in rr whn blnd 12th: p.u bef next* **12/1**

P21/ **P** **Shadow Boxer**[343] 3463 8-11-2 **90**...................... CallumWhillans(5)
(Donald Whillans) *trckd ldrs: rdn 5 out: wknd after 2 out: p.u bef last* **6/1**[2]

/P4- **P** **Stormion (IRE)**[33] 2339 8-11-1 **91**......................(v) MrSFox(7)
(Lucinda Russell) *hld up on rr: a bhd: t.o whn p.u bef 4 out* **22/1**

050- **P** **Samson Collonges (FR)**[15] 2735 7-10-0 **69** oh10...................... BrianHughes
(Rebecca Menzies) *prom: led 14th to 4 out: blnd 3 out: wknd: p.u bef last* **16/1**

/PP- **P** **Notonebuttwo (IRE)**[11] 2818 6-10-8 **77**......................(p) HenryBrooke
(Chris Grant) *trckd ldrs: lost pl qckly after 9th: p.u bef 13th* **9/1**

7m 1.2s (29.00) **Going Correction** +0.75s/f (Soft) **14** Ran SP% **118.1**
Speed ratings (Par 103): **83,82,82,80,78 76,74,68,, ,,,**
toteswingers 1&2 £31.80, 2&3 £31.80, 1&3 £0.00 CSF £87.43 CT £2813.98 TOTE £11.80: £4.00, £2.00, £8.60; EX 73.30 Trifecta £999.00 Pool: £1754.25 - 1.31 winning units..
Owner Mrs J Wilson (durham) **Bred** Mrs H M Woods **Trained** Manfield, N Yorks
■ Stewards' Enquiry : Daragh Bourke four-day ban: used whip above permitted level (Dec 27,29-31)

FOCUS
This proved to be a thorough test as the early leaders went a generous gallop.
T/Plt: £105.70 to a £1 stake. Pool of £75195.50 - 519.08 winning tickets. T/Qpdt: £63.70 to a £1 stake. Pool of £5213.60 - 60.50 winning tickets. AS

2893 LEICESTER (R-H)
Wednesday, December 11

OFFICIAL GOING: Chase course - good to firm (good in places, good to soft on flat course crossings); hurdle course - good to soft (good in places)
Wind: Light half-behind Weather: Hazy sunshine

3023 RACING EXCELLENCE TRAINING SERIES CONDITIONAL JOCKEYS' NOVICES' HURDLE (10 hdls) 2m 4f 110y
12:40 (12:40) (Class 4) 4-Y-0+ **£3,249** (£954; £477; £238)

Form RPR

/32- **1** **Algernon Pazham (IRE)**[23] 2563 4-10-9 0...................... RyanHatch(3) 129+
(Nigel Twiston-Davies) *a.p: led 2 out: pushed along whn blnd last: styd on* **4/1**[2]

4- **2** *3* **Silsol (GER)**[46] 2075 4-10-9 0...................... JackSherwood(3) 125
(Paul Nicholls) *hld up in tch: hmpd and lost pl 6th: hdwy next: rdn to chse ldr 3 out: ev ch next: sn rdn and hung rt: styd on same pce flat* **11/10**[1]

113/ **3** *53* **Speedy Bruere (FR)**[266] 4877 7-10-9 0...................... JakeHodson(3) 76
(David Bridgwater) *chsd ldrs tl rdn and wknd after 3 out* **12/1**

0/0- **4** *22* **Willpower (IRE)**[27] 2471 4-10-12 0...................... TomBellamy 56
(Nicky Henderson) *hld up: hdwy 6th: blnd and wknd next* **33/1**

203- **F** **Owen Na View (IRE)**[27] 2471 5-10-12 0......................(t) ConorShoemark
(Fergal O'Brien) *led tl after 1st: trckd ldr tl lft in ld 6th: rdn whn hdd and fell 2 out* **9/2**[3]

/F6- **F** **Court Appeal (IRE)**[24] 2536 6-10-9 0...................... CharlieDeutsch(3)
(Charlie Longsdon) *led after 1st tl fell 6th* **16/1**

1- **P** **Vivaccio (FR)**[184] 703 4-11-5 0...................... KieronEdgar
(Venetia Williams) *hld up: sme hdwy 7th: rdn and wknd bef next: bhd whn p.u bef last* **8/1**

5m 3.4s (-21.30) **Going Correction** -0.70s/f (Firm) **7** Ran SP% **113.4**
Speed ratings (Par 105): **112,110,90,82,**
toteswingers 1&2 £1.10, 2&3 £5.60, 1&3 £4.30 CSF £9.00 TOTE £4.20: £3.50, £1.20; EX 11.40 Trifecta £69.10 Pool: £1548.87 - 16.79 winning units..
Owner Graham And Alison Jelley **Bred** Ms Cecily Purcell **Trained** Naunton, Gloucs

FOCUS
The ground was described as "genuine good to soft" by a rider in the first. An ordinary novice hurdle which was littered with poor jumping.

3024 YULETIDE BEGINNERS' CHASE (15 fncs) 2m 4f 110y
1:10 (1:11) (Class 4) 4-Y-0+ **£4,882** (£1,669)

Form RPR

115- **1** **Theatrelands**[18] 2676 5-11-2 0......................(p) NoelFehily 101+
(Charlie Longsdon) *trckd ldr tl 11th: clr fr 3 out: eased flat* **8/11**[1]

P/P- **2** *7* **Minkie Moon (IRE)**[202] 449 5-10-9 0......................(t) GLavery(7) 80
(Mark Campion) *led and mstke 1st: hdd 11th: chsd wnr tl rdn appr 4 out: wnt 2nd again bef 3 out: sn outpcd* **33/1**[3]

20/ **U** **Double Double (FR)**[49] 1446 7-11-2 0...................... JamieMoore
(Peter Bowen) *j. poorly thrght: racd in 3rd pl tl drvn along to go 2nd appr 4 out: wknd after 4 out: uns rdr next* **5/4**[2]

5m 22.6s (3.70) **Going Correction** -0.70s/f (Firm) course record **3** Ran SP% **105.3**
Speed ratings (Par 105): **64,61,**
CSF £7.51 TOTE £1.80; EX 7.60 Trifecta £8.90 Pool: £254.97 - 21.31 winning units..
Owner N Davies & S Crowley **Bred** Juddmonte Farms Ltd **Trained** Over Norton, Oxon

FOCUS
Conditions were quicker on the chase track. This weak and slowly run beginners' chase took very little winning. None of the three had run over fences before.

3025 MISTLETOE (S) HURDLE (8 hdls) 2m
1:40 (1:40) (Class 5) 4-7-Y-0 **£1,949** (£572; £286; £143)

Form RPR

405- **1** **The Bull Hayes (IRE)**[15] 2729 7-10-12 113......................(p) RyanMahon 110+
(Michael Appleby) *w ldr tl after 2nd: remained handy: led appr 5th: clr fr 2 out: mstke last: easily* **10/11**[1]

454- **2** *12* **Captain Cardington (IRE)**[6] 2894 4-10-12 108..........(v) CiaranMckee(7) 106
(John O'Shea) *led tl appr 3rd: sn pushed along: rdn after 5th: styd on same pce fr 3 out: wnt 2nd bef last* **7/1**[3]

351- **3** *14* **Gigondas**[13] 2760 4-11-8 110......................(b) JamieMoore 100
(Gary Moore) *hld up in tch: jnd wnr appr 5th: rdn bef 3 out: wknd appr last* **2/1**[2]

033- **4** *39* **Chankillo**[13] 2766 4-10-12 92...................... WillKennedy 52
(Sarah-Jayne Davies) *sn pushed along to join ldrs: led appr 3rd: hdd bef 5th: rdn and wknd sn after* **10/1**

3m 48.4s (-12.60) **Going Correction** -0.70s/f (Firm) **4** Ran SP% **107.3**
Speed ratings: **103,97,90,70**
CSF £6.97 TOTE £2.30; EX 6.20 Trifecta £9.40 Pool: £1339.42 - 106.46 winning units..The winner was bought in for 8000gns.
Owner John Wholey **Bred** Tower Bloodstock **Trained** Danethorpe, Notts

FOCUS
An ordinary selling hurdle, but the pace was reasonable. They came home at wide margins behind the easy winner.

3026 SIS H'CAP CHASE (18 fncs) 2m 7f 110y
2:10 (2:10) (Class 4) (0-120,122) 4-Y-0+ **£4,548** (£1,335; £667; £333)

Form RPR

134- **1** **Little Chip (IRE)**[31] 2394 6-11-10 **118**...................... NoelFehily 129
(Charlie Longsdon) *hld up in tch: jnd ldrs 11th: rdn after 3 out: led last: drvn out* **7/4**[2]

35P- **2** *3* **Tony Dinozzo (FR)**[21] 2599 6-10-4 **98**......................(p) JamieMoore 107
(Peter Bowen) *a.p: chsd ldr 5th: led 4 out: slipped on landing next: rdn and hdd last: styd on same pce flat* **6/1**

/31- **3** *10* **Balbriggan (IRE)**[10] 2847 6-12-0 **122** 7ex...................... DominicElsworth 124
(Mick Channon) *led: hit 11th: hdd 4 out: rdn and wknd appr last* **6/4**[1]

24F- **4** *4 ½* **The Musical Guy (IRE)**[17] 2700 7-11-12 **120**......(v) SamTwiston-Davies 117
(Nigel Twiston-Davies) *chsd ldr to 5th: remained handy: mstke 11th: sn outpcd: rallied u.p appr 4 out: wknd next* **4/1**[3]

5m 44.8s (-19.20) **Going Correction** -0.70s/f (Firm) **4** Ran SP% **110.6**
Speed ratings (Par 105): **104,103,99,98**
CSF £10.78 TOTE £2.90; EX 12.50 Trifecta £26.40 Pool: £962.25 - 27.29 winning units..
Owner L Dens (Shipbrokers) Limited **Bred** Fintan Kealy **Trained** Over Norton, Oxon

FOCUS
An interesting handicap chase, run at what looked a fair gallop.

3027 IVY NOVICES' H'CAP CHASE (12 fncs) 2m
2:40 (2:40) (Class 4) (0-110,108) 4-Y-0+ **£3,898** (£1,144; £572; £286)

Form RPR

000/ **1** **The Last Night (FR)**[421] 1876 6-11-8 **104**...................... AidanColeman 119+
(Emma Lavelle) *mde all: mstke 1st: rdn flat: edgd lft towards fin: all out* **3/1**[2]

423- **2** *hd* **Fitandproperjob**[22] 2576 7-9-9 **82** oh4......................(vt[1]) JamesBanks(5) 95
(Anthony Middleton) *hld up: hdwy to chse wnr last: rdn and edgd rt flat: r.o* **16/1**

261- **3** *1 ¼* **Un Anjou (FR)**[3] 2977 5-11-12 **108** 7ex......................(p) NoelFehily 120
(David Dennis) *hld up in tch: chsd wnr 8th: rdn appr last: styd on u.p: nt clr run towards fin* **5/4**[1]

532- **4** *nk* **Bertie's Desire**[18] 2677 5-10-10 **92**...................... LeightonAspell 105
(Oliver Sherwood) *trckd ldrs: mstke 6th: blnd 8th: outpcd 2 out: rallied and n.m.r flat: styd on* **3/1**[2]

/00- **5** *21* **Mister Bricolage (IRE)**[26] 2492 6-11-11 **107**......................(t) PaddyBrennan 107
(Fergal O'Brien) *chsd ldr to 8th: rdn and wknd after 3 out* **10/1**[3]

3m 58.5s (-9.70) **Going Correction** -0.70s/f (Firm) **5** Ran SP% **109.4**
Speed ratings (Par 105): **96,95,95,95,84**
CSF £32.94 TOTE £3.80: £1.70, £4.00; EX 11.10 Trifecta £11.00 Pool: £2328.68 - 158.43 winning units..
Owner Tim Syder **Bred** I Kellit, N Madamet & Ann Thomlinson **Trained** Hatherden, Hants

FOCUS
A blanket finish in the end to this novice handicap.

3028 ADVENT H'CAP HURDLE (10 hdls) 2m 4f 110y
3:10 (3:10) (Class 3) (0-130,128) 3-Y-0+ **£5,523** (£1,621; £810; £405)

Form RPR

13F- **1** **Foxcub (IRE)**[20] 2630 5-11-11 **127**...................... FelixDeGiles 134+
(Tom Symonds) *chsd ldrs: led appr 2 out: drvn out* **4/1**[1]

242- **2** *5* **Zalgarry (FR)**[72] 1699 6-10-8 **117**...................... JoshWall(7) 120
(Arthur Whitehead) *hld up in tch: ev ch after 3 out: rdn whn hit next: nt fluent last: styd on same pce flat* **6/1**[3]

331- **3** *6* **Cloudy Bob (IRE)**[20] 2625 6-11-9 **125**...................... ColinBolger 121
(Pat Murphy) *chsd ldrs: pushed along 6th: rdn appr 3 out: wknd after 2 out* **9/2**[2]

153- **4** *4 ½* **Kayaan**[129] 1203 6-11-5 **124**...................... KielanWoods(3) 118
(Pam Sly) *hld up: hit 7th: hdwy appr 3 out: sn rdn: wknd 2 out* **12/1**

1/3- **5** 4 **Billy Twyford (IRE)**[221] 119 6-11-12 **128**............(t) DavidBass 116
(Lawney Hill) *sn led: hdd 6th: led again 3 out: sn rdn and hdd: wknd bef next* **12/1**

1U1/ **6** 9 **Fountains Flypast**[803] 1781 9-11-8 **124**............(t) RobertThornton 104
(Anthony Honeyball) *hld up: hdwy appr 3 out: wknd sn after* **8/1**

1/0- **7** 5 **Frizzo (FR)**[32] 2362 6-11-6 **122**............ WayneHutchinson 97
(Alan King) *prom tl rdn and wknd after 3 out* **12/1**

5- **8** 23 **Garde Ville (FR)**[174] 3-10-6 **123**............(b[1]) TomScudamore 63
(David Pipe) *trckd ldr: mstke 4th: led 6th: hdd appr 3 out: sn rdn and wknd* **9/2[2]**

265/ **9** 31 **Saints And Sinners (IRE)**[296] 4289 5-11-7 **123**......... DominicElsworth 50
(Michael Easterby) *hld up: pushed along and bhd fr 5th* **16/1**

/60- **10** ½ **Firebird Flyer (IRE)**[12] 2798 6-11-6 **122**............ PaulMoloney 48
(Evan Williams) *mid-div: wknd appr 3 out* **20/1**

4/6- **11** 61 **The Pier (IRE)**[14] 2742 7-11-3 **119**............(t) AndrewTinkler
(Anna Brooks) *hld up: rdn and wknd appr 7th* **25/1**

5m 4.9s (-19.80) **Going Correction** -0.70s/f (Firm)
WFA 3 from 5yo+ 14lb **11 Ran SP% 119.3**
Speed ratings (Par 107): **109,107,104,103,101 98,96,87,75,75 52**
toteswingers 1&2 £14.40, 2&3 £17.50, 1&3 £3.00 CSF £29.16 CT £114.15 TOTE £5.20: £2.30, £2.50, £1.80; EX 36.00 Trifecta £178.20 Pool: £1444.68 - 6.07 winning units..
Owner Celia & Michael Baker **Bred** St Clare Hall Stud **Trained** Harewood End, H'fords

FOCUS
An open handicap hurdle, and fair form.

T/Plt: £119.20 to a £1 stake. Pool of £51168.60 - 313.11 winning tickets. T/Qpdt: £45.20 to a £1 stake. Pool of £3373.64 - 55.20 winning tickets. CR

[2675]HUNTINGDON (R-H)
Thursday, December 12

OFFICIAL GOING: Good (good in places; 7.6) changing to good to soft (good in places) after race 1 (12.30)
Wind: virtually nil Weather: dry, light cloud

3029 BETFRED FUN AND FRIENDLY H'CAP HURDLE (10 hdls) 2m 5f 110y
12:30 (12:30) (Class 4) (0-110,110) 4-Y-0+ **£3,898** (£1,144; £572; £286)

Form RPR

054- **1** **Rule Of Thumb**[23] 2573 5-11-2 **100**............(t) TomO'Brien 106+
(Paul Henderson) *hld up in tch: clsd to trck ldrs and travelling wl whn nt fluent 2 out: jnd ldr and pushed rt between last 2: pushed into ld flat: r.o: pushed out* **22/1**

042- **2** 1 ¼ **Larteta (FR)**[14] 2771 4-11-0 **105**............ MikeyEnnis[(7)] 108
(Sarah Humphrey) *chsd ldrs tl led sn after 7th: rdn bef 2 out: drvn and jnd whn wnt rt between last 2: hdd and one pce flat* **5/1[2]**

041- **3** 2 ½ **Shadarpour (IRE)**[10] 2862 4-11-4 **102** 7ex............(b) JamieMoore 104
(Gary Moore) *wl in tch in midfield: hdwy to chse ldrs after 3 out: wnt 2nd and mstke next: rdn and nt qckn whn mstke last: styd on same pce flat* **4/1[1]**

000- **4** 1 ¼ **Brians Well (IRE)**[37] 2280 6-10-11 **95**............ APMcCoy 96
(Brendan Powell) *hld up wl in tch in rr: hdwy after 7th: chsd ldrs and rdn bef 2 out: unable qck between last 2: hung lft and one pce flat* **4/1[1]**

106- **5** 5 **Thoresby (IRE)**[35] 2314 7-11-8 **106**............(p) DarylJacob 101
(Ben Case) *in tch in midfield: rdn after 7th: outpcd next: no threat to ldrs but plugged on u.p flat* **4/1[1]**

632- **6** nk **Zafaraban (IRE)**[136] 1136 6-11-6 **104**............(p) AndrewTinkler 101
(George Baker) *chsd ldrs: mstke 5th: rdn and losing pl whn short of room sn after 3 out: drvn and btn whn j.lft 2 out* **11/1**

4P6- **7** nse **Time For Spring (IRE)**[17] 2715 9-11-12 **110**............(bt) NoelFehily 106
(Charlie Longsdon) *led tl after 3rd: styd upsides ldrs: mstke 3 out: rdn and no rspnse bef next: btn between last 2: wknd flat* **12/1**

530- **8** 5 **Kyles Faith (IRE)**[18] 2691 5-11-5 **103**............(p) TomSiddall 93
(Martin Keighley) *wl in tch in last trio: dropped to rr and pushed along after 5th: struggling u.p 7th: n.d after* **11/1**

P/0- **9** 33 **Boomtown**[14] 2771 8-10-4 **95**............(t) GeraldQuinn[(7)] 56
(Claire Dyson) *chsd ldr tl led bef 3rd: hdd sn after 7th and immediately lost pl: lost tch bef 3 out: t.o* **10/1[3]**

5m 7.75s (-2.85) **Going Correction** -0.30s/f (Good)
WFA 4 from 5yo+ 6lb **9 Ran SP% 114.5**
Speed ratings (Par 105): **93,92,91,91,89 89,89,87,75**
toteswingers 1&2 £23.20, 2&3 £5.20, 1&3 £23.70 CSF £128.23 CT £540.85 TOTE £20.00: £5.50, £2.10, £1.70; EX 253.30 Trifecta £928.20 Part won. Pool: £1237.71 - 0.79 winning units..
Owner GLR Racing **Bred** John Ellis **Trained** Whitsbury, Hants

FOCUS
Tom O'Brien said it was riding "proper good to soft", and the official ground description was amended after the first to Good to soft, good in places. They went a moderate pace in this ordinary handicap hurdle. The winner improved in line with his bumper mark.

3030 BETFRED TV EBF STALLIONS/TBA MARES' NOVICES' CHASE (16 fncs) 2m 4f 110y
1:00 (1:00) (Class 4) 4-Y-0+ **£4,873** (£1,431; £715; £357)

Form RPR

/02- **1** **Une Artiste (FR)**[10] 2859 5-11-0 **140**............ BarryGeraghty 138+
(Nicky Henderson) *mde all: pushed along and qcknd to assert after last: r.o wl: comf* **8/15[1]**

/F2- **2** 2 ½ **Baby Shine (IRE)**[21] 2622 7-11-0 **132**............ LeightonAspell 134+
(Lucy Wadham) *chsd ldrs: wnt 2nd 4th: upside wnr fr 12th: shkn up between last 2: rdn and outpcd by wnr flat: kpt on* **5/2[2]**

/01- **3** 14 **Tempest River (IRE)**[30] 2434 7-11-6 **132**............ DarylJacob 130
(Ben Case) *t.k.h: in tch in last pair: chsd ldng pair fr 7th: 6 l down and rdn after 3 out: no imp and mstke next: wknd last* **8/1[3]**

122- **4** 31 **Me And Ben (IRE)**[70] 1731 6-11-0 **0**............(t) PaddyBrennan 94
(Fergal O'Brien) *hld up in tch in rr: lost tch 10th: t.o 3 out* **33/1**

55- **5** 1 ¼ **Always Smiling (IRE)**[18] 2697 6-10-7 **0**............(t) MrHAABannister[(7)] 92
(Charlie Mann) *nt fluent: chsd ldr tl 4th: steadily lost pl: last and lost tch 11th: t.o 3 out: hung lft flat* **100/1**

5m 6.0s (0.70) **Going Correction** -0.20s/f (Good) **5 Ran SP% 108.8**
Speed ratings (Par 105): **90,89,83,71,71**
CSF £2.29 TOTE £1.60: £1.30, £1.10; EX 2.20 Trifecta £3.60 Pool: £2640.93 - 547.32 winning units..
Owner Simon Munir **Bred** E Clayeux & D Clayeux **Trained** Upper Lambourn, Berks

FOCUS
A decent mares' event but it was steadily run and the winner is rated below her best.

3031 BETFRED "GOALS GALORE" H'CAP HURDLE (8 hdls) 2m 110y
1:30 (1:31) (Class 3) (0-130,129) 3-Y-0+ **£10,009** (£2,956; £1,478; £739; £369; £185)

Form RPR

6/1- **1** **Fergall (IRE)**[217] 174 6-11-4 **124**............ WayneKavanagh[(3)] 134+
(Seamus Mullins) *chsd ldng pair and clr of main field: wnt 2nd and hit 3 out: rdn to ld between last 2: in command whn idled and wnt lft fnl 100yds: rdn out hands and heels and kpt on towards fin* **14/1**

14- **2** ¾ **Keltus (FR)**[41] 2200 3-10-6 **123**............ DarylJacob 117
(Paul Nicholls) *handed clr ld at s: pressed whn j.lft and mstke 2 out: hdd and unable qck u.p between last 2: swtchd rt and rallied to press idling wnr towards fin: a hld* **9/2[3]**

/32- **3** 1 ¼ **Prompter**[7] 2910 6-11-5 **122**............ APMcCoy 128+
(Jonjo O'Neill) *t.k.h: hld up wl off the pce in last pair: grad crept clsr fr 3 out: 6 l 3rd last: rdn mainly hands and heels flat: racd awkwardly but styd on: nt rch ldrs* **4/1[2]**

111/ **4** 8 **Karazhan**[319] 3902 5-11-12 **129**............ DavidBass 129
(Nicky Henderson) *racd wl off the pce in main gp: clsd on ldrs bef 3 out: cl enough in 3rd and rdn bef 2 out: no imp: wknd between last 2* **11/2**

/35- **5** 10 **Springinherstep (IRE)**[28] 2477 6-11-2 **119**............ BarryGeraghty 109
(Nicky Henderson) *hld up wl off the pce in last pair: clsd after 5th: mstke next: rdn and no hdwy bef 2 out: sn wknd* **13/2**

146- **6** ¾ **Halifax (IRE)**[21] 2630 5-11-1 **118**............ AndrewTinkler 107
(Tony Newcombe) *racd wl off the pce in main gp: rdn after 5th: no imp and wl btn after next* **50/1**

3/6- **7** 5 **Roberto Pegasus (USA)**[27] 2492 7-11-0 **117**............ RobertThornton 102
(Alan King) *racd wl off the pce in main gp: rdn and effrt bef 3 out: wknd bef 2 out* **7/2[1]**

530/ **8** 1 **Grams And Ounces**[187] 5284 6-11-3 **120**............(t) RhysFlint 104
(John Flint) *chsd ldr: mstke 2nd: lost 2nd after 5th:3rd and struggling whn mstke next: wknd u.p bef 2 out* **66/1**

405- **9** 14 **Taaresh (IRE)**[17] 2717 8-10-7 **110**............(p) AdamWedge 81
(Kevin Morgan) *racd wl off the pce in midfield: short-lived effrt bef 3 out: wknd bef 2 out: t.o* **33/1**

1/0- **10** 27 **Chat Room**[33] 2366 5-11-7 **124**............ DenisO'Regan 71
(John Ferguson) *racd wl off the pce in main gp: dropped to last and rdn after 4th: lost tch bef 3 out: t.o bef 2 out* **13/2**

3m 46.3s (-8.60) **Going Correction** -0.30s/f (Good)
WFA 3 from 5yo+ 13lb **10 Ran SP% 115.5**
Speed ratings (Par 107): **108,107,107,103,98 98,95,95,88,76**
toteswingers 1&2 £23.90, 2&3 £3.80, 1&3 £4.90 CSF £75.68 CT £304.75 TOTE £13.00: £4.10, £1.90, £1.70; EX 105.30 Trifecta £414.00 Pool: £1713.71 - 3.10 winning units..
Owner Andrew Cocks And Tara Johnson **Bred** Mrs Gail C List **Trained** Wilsford-Cum-Lake, Wilts

FOCUS
Quite a valuable handicap hurdle, but a bit of an unsatisfactory race with a number of them being held up off what didn't look a strong pace. The winner is rated similar to his Newton Abbot run.

3032 BETFRED PETERBOROUGH CHASE GRADE 2 (16 fncs) 2m 4f 110y
2:00 (2:00) (Class 1) 4-Y-0+ **£34,170** (£12,822; £6,420; £3,198; £1,608; £804)

Form RPR

646/ **1** **Riverside Theatre**[232] 5515 9-11-0 **167**............ BarryGeraghty 156+
(Nicky Henderson) *chsd ldr tl 6th: pushed along 8th: cl 4th and mstke 12th: rdn and mstke next: drvn wl bef 2 out: rallied to chse ldrs and sltly hmpd last: sn swtchd rt and led fnl 100yds: styd on: rdn out* **9/4[1]**

1/0- **2** ½ **Champion Court (IRE)**[26] 2503 8-11-6 **157**............ IanPopham 161+
(Martin Keighley) *led: rdn bef 2 out: hrd pressed and mstke 2 out: mstke and wnt rt last: shifted rt and sddle slipped flat: rdr unbalanced and hdd fnl 100yds: rallied gamely towards fin: kpt on: uns rdr after fin* **4/1[3]**

64/- **3** nk **Captain Chris (IRE)**[232] 5515 9-11-10 **169**............(t) RichardJohnson 164
(Philip Hobbs) *hld up in tch in rr: mstke 3rd: hdwy into midfield 5th: clsd to trck ldrs 12th: lft 2nd 3 out: rdn and chal next: slt mstke last: ev ch flat: kpt on same pce fnl 100yds* **7/2[2]**

4/2- **4** 9 **Module (FR)**[37] 2281 6-11-2 **157**............ PaddyBrennan 148
(Tom George) *in tch in midfield: drvn after 3 out: stl cl enough last: chsd ldng trio fnl 100yds: no ex and sn wknd* **7/2[2]**

/31- **5** 1 ¾ **Alasi**[19] 2666 9-10-13 **140**............ DominicElsworth 142
(Paul Webber) *in tch in last trio: rdn bef 3 out: drvn wl bef 2 out: no imp: wknd last* **25/1**

36P/ **6** nse **Ghizao (GER)**[239] 5353 9-11-6 **155**............ DarylJacob 151
(Paul Nicholls) *chsd ldrs: wnt 2nd 6th tl hit 3 out: clsd 3rd and stl travelling wl bef 2 out: rdn and no rspnse between last 2: wknd flat* **10/1**

210- **7** 8 **Conquisto**[26] 2503 8-11-6 **154**............ TomScudamore 148
(Steve Gollings) *midfield whn mstke 1st: nvr j. fluently after: dropped to rr but styd in tch 6th: rdn bef 3 out: sn btn* **20/1**

4m 51.95s (-13.35) **Going Correction** -0.20s/f (Good) **7 Ran SP% 112.9**
Speed ratings (Par 115): **117,116,116,113,112 112,109**
toteswingers 1&2 £2.80, 2&3 £3.20, 1&3 £1.40 CSF £11.63 TOTE £2.90: £2.00, £2.50; EX 13.30 Trifecta £49.80 Pool: £2780.14 - 37.32 winning units..
Owner Jimmy Nesbitt Partnership **Bred** Goldford Stud **Trained** Upper Lambourn, Berks

FOCUS
An excellent renewal of this Grade 2 event, which was run at a sound gallop. Riverside Theatre is rated a stone or more off his old best, with Champion Court to his best. Solid form.

3033 BETFRED MOBILE NOVICES' H'CAP CHASE (19 fncs) 3m
2:30 (2:30) (Class 4) (0-110,110) 4-Y-0+ **£4,548** (£1,335; £667; £333)

Form RPR

4/4- **1** **Faith Keeper (IRE)**[18] 2701 8-10-7 **91**............ PaddyBrennan 110+
(Fergal O'Brien) *led tl 6th: styd pressing ldr tl led and travelling best bef 2 out: cruised clr 2 out: eased flat: v easily* **7/2[3]**

0/2- **2** 9 **Ya Hafed**[197] 538 5-11-10 **108**............ LeightonAspell 108
(Sheena West) *t.k.h: hld up in tch in rr: j.rt 1st: hdwy and pckd 11th: chsd ldrs after next: drvn to chse wnr bef 2 out: brushed aside and wl btn between last 2: battled on to hold 2nd flat* **9/1**

622- **3** 1 **Flemi Two Toes (IRE)**[17] 2722 7-10-13 **97**............(v[1]) JamieMoore 98
(Sarah Humphrey) *several slow jumps: chsd ldrs tl lost pl 4th: rdn along after: rallied to chse ldrs again 11th: 4th and outpcd u.p after 13th: no ch w wnr but styd on after flat: swtchd rt and wnt 3rd nr fin* **5/2[1]**

21- **4** 1 ¼ **Rossa Parks (IRE)**[21] 2632 7-11-12 **110**............ RichardJohnson 110
(Neil Mulholland) *chsd ldr tl led 6th: rdn and hdd bef 2 out: 3rd and no ch w wnr between last 2: plugged on but lost 3rd nr fin* **11/4[2]**

436- **5** *nk* **Balinderry (IRE)**[21] 2621 6-10-9 **93**................................ TomScudamore 96+
(Steve Gollings) *in tch in midfield: rdn and struggling whn hmpd 11th: 5th and wl btn 3 out: no ch w wnr but kpt on u.p flat* **8/1**

PP2- **P** **Flichity (IRE)**[23] 2574 8-9-9 **84** oh16.................... JoeCornwall(5)
(John Cornwall) *in tch in midfield: rdn and lost pl 11th: lost tch 13th: t.o whn p.u 15th* **33/1**

3/0- **P** **Fashion Faux Pas (IRE)**[19] 2663 6-11-2 **100**...................... TomO'Brien
(Paul Henderson) *hld up in tch in last trio: hdwy and cl enough in 4th whn blnd bdly 13th: lost pl and nt rcvr: t.o whn p.u 16th* **16/1**

/0F- **P** **Gorhams Gift**[12] 2825 5-9-11 **84** oh1......................... WayneKavanagh(3)
(Jamie Poulton) *mstkes: in tch in rr: hdwy 11th: rdn and hmpd 11th: sn struggling and btn: wl bhd and blnd 16th: p.u next* **33/1**

6m 6.7s (-3.60) **Going Correction** -0.20s/f (Good) **8** Ran SP% **110.3**
Speed ratings (Par 105): **98,95,94,94,94 , ,**
toteswingers 1&2 £5.50, 2&3 £4.10, 1&3 £1.50 CSF £31.41 CT £85.12 TOTE £5.60: £1.80, £1.80, £1.60; EX 39.70 Trifecta £103.90 Pool: £2604.69 - 18.79 winning units..
Owner North And South Racing Partnership **Bred** P Condon **Trained** Coln St. Dennis, Gloucs

FOCUS
Just a modest novice handicap but an impressive winner who is rated up a stone on his best hurdles form.

3034 BETFRED "HAT TRICK HEAVEN" NOVICES' HURDLE (8 hdls) 2m 110y
3:00 (3:02) (Class 4) 4-Y-0+ **£3,898** (£1,144; £572; £286)

Form RPR

/10- **1** **Wadswick Court (IRE)**[25] 2534 5-10-12 0............................ NoelFehily 116+
(Charlie Longsdon) *t.k.h: chsd ldr tl led jst bef 2 out: hrd pressed last: rdn and r.o wl flat: rdn out* **5/2**[2]

325- **2** ½ **Simply A Legend**[28] 2471 4-10-12 0............................... RobertThornton 114
(Alan King) *t.k.h: hld up in midfield: hdwy bef 3 out: rdn and ev ch bef last: r.o wl but jst outpcd fnl 50yds* **14/1**

3 2½ **Nordic Quest (IRE)**[60] 4-10-12 0.............................. BarryGeraghty 113
(Nicky Henderson) *in tch in midfield: nt fluent 3rd: rdn and effrt to press ldrs whn mstke last: no ex and outpcd fnl 50yds* **8/1**

446- **4** 1½ **Chalk It Down (IRE)**[38] 2265 4-10-12 0............................. APMcCoy 110
(Warren Greatrex) *taken down early: handed clr ld a s: set stdy gallop: hdd and rdn jst bef 2 out: styd on same pce flat* **20/1**

5 1¼ **Focail Maith**[59] 1906 5-10-9 0... TrevorWhelan(3) 109
(Neil King) *hld up in midfield: clsd after 5th: rdn and effrt to chse ldrs 2 out: styd on same pce u.p flat* **12/1**

6 1¾ **May Be Some Time**[36] 5-10-12 0...............................(t) TomScudamore 107
(Stuart Kittow) *hld up towards rr: clsd after 5th: hdwy and chsd ldrs stl travelling wl bef 2 out: rdn and effrt between last 2: no ex and wknd flat* **66/1**

7 4½ **Ever Fortune (USA)**[16] 4-10-12 0.. DarylJacob 103
(Brian Ellison) *t.k.h: chsd ldrs: rdn and unable qck whn hit 2 out: outpcd and btn between last 2: hung rt and wknd flat* **33/1**

8 8 **Namibian (IRE)**[848] 5-10-12 0.. DenisO'Regan 98+
(John Ferguson) *chsd ldrs: shkn up and no rspnse jst bef 2 out: nt given a hrd time after and btn between last 2: wknd flat* **2/1**[1]

453/ **9** 1 **Jolly Valentine**[658] 4479 5-10-12 0................................ DominicElsworth 94
(Neil King) *hld up in midfield: clsd after 5th: rdn and effrt after next: no ex 2 out: wknd bef last* **150/1**

00- **10** 4 **Mr Fickle (IRE)**[7] 2906 4-10-9 0.. JoshuaMoore(3) 90
(Gary Moore) *hld up towards rr: clsd after 5th: rdn and wknd bef 2 out: no ch whn pushed lft between last 2* **66/1**

2- **11** 5 **Truckers Darling (IRE)**[16] 2725 6-10-5 0.......................... LeightonAspell 78
(Don Cantillon) *hld up off the pce in last quartet: clsd after 5th: rdn and btn after 3 out: wknd bef next* **20/1**

233/ **12** ½ **Go West Young Man (IRE)**[240] 5335 5-10-12 0.......... RichardJohnson 84
(Henry Daly) *t.k.h: hld up in rr: sme hdwy on inner whn mstke 3 out: no prog wl bef 2 out and nt given a hrd time after* **6/1**[3]

0- **13** ¾ **Valseur Du Granval (FR)**[49] 2053 4-10-12 0.................. PaddyBrennan 83
(Tom George) *chsd ldrs: rdn and no rspnse bef 2 out: sn wknd: fading whn hung lft between last 2* **50/1**

100- **14** 6 **Solstice Son**[22] 2602 4-10-9 0.. RachaelGreen(3) 77
(Anthony Honeyball) *hld up in rr: pushed along and short-lived effrt after 3 out: no hdwy and nt given a hrd time after* **66/1**

15 8 **Isdaal**[58] 6-10-5 0.. AdamWedge 62
(Kevin Morgan) *hld up towards rr: clsd after 5th: rdn and wknd sn after next: t.o* **100/1**

0- **P** **Action Front (USA)**[7] 2893 5-10-12 0................................. CharliePoste
(Derek Shaw) *mstkes: a in rr: lost tch after 3 out: t.o and p.u last: burst a blood vessel* **200/1**

3m 53.65s (-1.25) **Going Correction** -0.30s/f (Good) **16** Ran SP% **122.7**
Speed ratings (Par 105): **90,89,88,87,87 86,84,80,80,78 75,75,75,72,68**
toteswingers 1&2 £12.10, 2&3 £19.20, 1&3 £5.50 CSF £34.97 TOTE £4.90: £1.70, £3.80, £2.80; EX 49.10 Trifecta £368.50 Pool: £3097.22 - 6.30 winning units..
Owner The Chosen Few **Bred** L W Doran **Trained** Over Norton, Oxon

FOCUS
A fair novice hurdle which should produce winners, but they went just a steady early pace and there were quite a number still in with a chance heading to the second-last. The winner is rated in line with his bumper form.

3035 YOU'LL LOVE A BIT OF BETFRED INTERMEDIATE OPEN NATIONAL HUNT FLAT RACE 2m 110y
3:30 (3:31) (Class 6) 4-6-Y-0 **£1,559** (£457; £228; £114)

Form RPR

1 **Brother Tedd** 4-11-2 0... RichardJohnson 112+
(Philip Hobbs) *hld up wl in tch in midfield: trckd ldr over 3f out: led and rn green wl over 1f out: edging rt but r.o wl fnl f* **10/3**[3]

2 *hd* **Paradise Valley (IRE)** 4-11-2 0.................................. DominicElsworth 112+
(Mick Channon) *hld up in tch in last pair: rdn and effrt 3f out: ev ch 1f out: r.o wl but a jst hld fnl 100yds* **5/4**[1]

3 2¼ **Minella Present (IRE)**[189] 654 4-11-2 0............................... NoelFehily 110
(Neil Mulholland) *led: rdn and hdd wl over 1f out: unable qck and struggling whn short of room 1f out: styd on same pce fnl f* **7/4**[2]

4 14 **Princeton Royale (IRE)**[222] 4-10-13 0............................ TrevorWhelan(3) 96
(Neil King) *t.k.h: chsd ldrs: rdn and over 3f out: 4th and outpcd 2f out: wknd over 1f out* **16/1**

0- **5** 19 **Leahnor (IRE)**[36] 2298 4-10-9 0.. RhysFlint 70
(John Flint) *t.k.h: chsd ldr tl over 3f out: sn wknd: wl bhd over 1f out* **100/1**

/5- **6** 15 **Cut'N'Shut**[15] 2745 6-11-2 0... DaveCrosse 62
(Zoe Davison) *hld up wl in tch in last pair: rdn over 3f out: sn btn: t.o over 1f out* **100/1**

3m 53.7s (4.60) **Going Correction** -0.30s/f (Good) **6** Ran SP% **111.7**
Speed ratings: **77,76,75,69,60 53**
toteswingers 1&2 £1.40, 2&3 £1.40, 1&3 £1.20 CSF £7.86 TOTE £4.20: £2.20, £1.50; EX 10.20 Trifecta £16.10 Pool: £4062.35 - 188.19 winning units..
Owner Scrase Farms **Bred** Mrs J E Scrase **Trained** Withycombe, Somerset

FOCUS
A modest bumper with a tight finish. The initial pace had been very steady but the first three could all be above average.
T/Plt: £50.10 to a £1 stake. Pool of £67459.24 - 981.17 winning tickets. T/Qpdt: £20.50 to a £1 stake. Pool of £5353.10 - 192.98 winning tickets. SP

2817 NEWCASTLE (L-H)
Thursday, December 12

OFFICIAL GOING: Good (good to soft in places; 7.0)
Wind: Breezy, half against Weather: Overcast

3036 S V RUTTER NOVICES' HURDLE (13 hdls) 2m 6f
12:20 (12:20) (Class 4) 4-Y-0+ **£3,119** (£915; £457; £228)

Form RPR

1 **Racing Pulse (IRE)**[45] 2146 4-10-12 0............................ JamesReveley 142+
(John Quinn) *t.k.h: in tch: smooth hdwy to ld 3 out: sn clr: v easily* **8/11**[1]

32- **2** 17 **Sir Mangan (IRE)**[26] 2520 5-10-12 0............................... JasonMaguire 120
(Donald McCain) *led: rdn and hdd whn nt fluent 3 out: plugged on same pce* **11/1**

44- **3** 10 **Straidnahanna (IRE)**[20] 2659 4-10-12 **114**........................... RyanMania 113
(Sue Smith) *trckd ldrs: wnt 2nd 6th: drvn and ev ch bef 3 out: outpcd fr next: 3rd and hld whn mstke last: wknd* **3/1**[2]

13- **4** 8 **Kilgefin Star (IRE)**[33] 2355 5-11-0 **125**............................ AdamNicol(5) 111
(Michael Smith) *nt fluent: chsd ldr tl hit 6th: drvn and outpcd fr 9th: no imp bef 3 out* **6/1**[3]

5/0- **5** ½ **Mr Syntax (IRE)**[33] 2355 9-10-12 **118**..............................(t) BrianHarding 100
(Tim Fitzgerald) *midfield: shkn up after 9th: struggling fr next* **20/1**

0/0- **6** 13 **Thorlak (FR)**[34] 2341 6-10-12 0.. HarryHaynes 91
(James Ewart) *trckd ldrs: outpcd 7th: struggling fr next* **66/1**

4- **7** 66 **Sgt Bull Berry**[142] 1094 6-10-9 0.................................... JakeGreenall(3) 29
(Peter Maddison) *hld up in midfield: dropped in rr 8th: sn struggling: t.o* **66/1**

3/ **P** **Classic Rally (IRE)**[692] 3835 7-10-12 0................................. BrianHughes
(Malcolm Jefferson) *hld up: outpcd whn hit 9th: sn btn: t.o whn p.u bef 3 out* **25/1**

0P- **P** **Print Shiraz (IRE)**[33] 2355 5-10-12 0............................. WilsonRenwick
(Rose Dobbin) *hld up: struggling fr 8th: t.o whn p.u bef 3 out* **100/1**

00- **P** **Thatildee (IRE)**[27] 2499 5-10-12 0..................................... HenryBrooke
(Chris Grant) *hld up: pushed along 4th: struggling 8th: t.o whn p.u bef 3 out* **66/1**

5m 28.6s (-7.40) **Going Correction** -0.775s/f (Firm)
WFA 4 from 5yo+ 6lb **10** Ran SP% **119.6**
Speed ratings (Par 105): **82,75,72,69,69 64,40, , ,**
toteswingers 1&2 £2.60, 2&3 £3.70, 1&3 £1.10 CSF £10.13 TOTE £1.70: £1.10, £2.20, £1.30; EX 11.00 Trifecta £29.90 Pool: £3407.07 - 85.23 winning units..
Owner Carl Hinchy **Bred** Thomas O'Keeffe **Trained** Settrington, N Yorks

FOCUS
Home bend common other bend divided. The opening contest was a fair staying hurdle for novices, in which they went an even gallop. The impressive winner looks a smart recruit.

3037 MALONE NOVICES' CHASE (13 fncs) 2m 110y
12:50 (12:50) (Class 4) 4-Y-0+ **£4,548** (£1,335; £667; £333)

Form RPR

0/4- **1** **Doynosaur**[26] 2519 6-10-7 0.. HenryBrooke 121+
(K R Burke) *hld up: stdy hdwy 1/2-way: led gng wl 3 out: pushed along next: styd on wl run-in* **15/2**[3]

F12- **2** 1¾ **Simply Ned (IRE)**[20] 2656 6-11-7 **138**................................. BrianHarding 134+
(Nicky Richards) *hld up: stdy hdwy 1/2-way: chsng ldrs whn shkn up briefly after 5 out: effrt and chal 3 out to next: kpt on same pce run-in* **1/2**[1]

3/3- **3** 6 **Supreme Asset (IRE)**[26] 2515 5-11-0 0............................. JasonMaguire 120
(Donald McCain) *chsd ldrs: wnt 2nd 4th: clsd 8th: led 4 out to next: outpcd fr 3 out* **7/2**[2]

P/4- **4** ½ **Pinerolo**[9] 2868 7-11-0 0... RyanMania 121+
(Sue Smith) *led and sn clr: jnd 5 out: hdd next: outpcd fr 3 out* **12/1**

P- **5** 67 **Grey Shadow (IRE)**[40] 2224 7-11-0 0.................................. BrianHughes 52
(John Wade) *chsd ldr to 4th: lost pl next: lost tch fr 5 out: t.o* **150/1**

4m 8.0s (-13.10) **Going Correction** -0.425s/f (Good) **5** Ran SP% **109.0**
Speed ratings (Par 105): **113,112,109,109,77**
CSF £12.42 TOTE £7.10: £3.10, £1.02; EX 14.60 Trifecta £28.40 Pool: £1307.02 - 34.43 winning units..
Owner Mrs Elaine M Burke **Bred** J C S Wilson Bloodstock & Mrs E M Burke **Trained** Middleham Moor, N Yorks

FOCUS
A fair chase of its type, in which they went an honest gallop. The winner is the type to rate much higher over fences, and this form could be rated up to 9lb higher.

3038 S T P CONSTRUCTION H'CAP HURDLE (9 hdls) 2m
1:20 (1:22) (Class 5) (0-100,100) 4-Y-0+ **£2,144** (£629; £314; £157)

Form RPR

613- **1** **Honourable Gent**[42] 2169 5-10-7 **81**.................................. WilsonRenwick 91+
(Rose Dobbin) *hld up: smooth hdwy to chse ldrs bef 3 out: led next: nt fluent last: drvn out* **4/1**[2]

423- **2** 7 **A Little Bit Dusty**[7] 2898 5-11-7 **100**........................(p) ConorShoemark(5) 103+
(Conor Dore) *hld up in tch on outside: rdn and outpcd bef 3 out: edgd lft and rallied next: chsd (clr) wnr last 100yds: no imp* **3/1**[1]

/00- **3** 1¼ **Operateur (IRE)**[30] 2449 5-9-12 **79**................................. CraigGallagher(7) 79
(Ben Haslam) *cl up: led bef 3 out: hdd next: kpt on same pce fr last: lost 2nd fnl 100yds* **9/2**[3]

054- **4** 8 **Ivans Back (IRE)**[19] 2679 8-10-11 **85**................................... HarryHaynes 79
(Nick Kent) *t.k.h: led 3rd to 3 out: sn rdn: nt fluent next: sn outpcd* **25/1**

000- **5** ¾ **Stanley Bridge**[22] 2597 6-11-3 **98**................................... GrahamWatters(7) 91
(Barry Murtagh) *chsd ldrs: mstke 4 out: hit and rdn next: outpcd fr 2 out* **10/1**

/05- **6** 3 **Bollin Julie**[39] 2241 6-9-13 **78**.. CallumWhillans(5) 67
(Donald Whillans) *hld up: outpcd 1/2-way: rallied 3 out: nvr able to chal* **12/1**

340- 7 1/2 **Vodka Red (IRE)**[33] 2360 5-10-12 **86**..........................(t) KennyJohnson 75
(Robert Johnson) *hld up in tch: stdy hdwy on outside after 4 out: outpcd fr next* **10/1**

432- 8 15 **Pindar (GER)**[48] 2062 9-10-6 **85**..............................(p) SamanthaDrake(5) 60
(Joanne Foster) *led to 3rd: cl up tl rdn and wknd after 4 out* **12/1**

OOP/ 9 2 1/4 **Mr Mansson (IRE)**[594] 5623 6-10-0 **74** oh1.......................... AdrianLane 47
(Lucy Normile) *hld up bhd ldng gp: struggling after 4 out: wknd fr next* **80/1**

000- 10 2 1/2 **Strandfield Bay (IRE)**[5] 2169 7-10-0 **74**............................ HenryBrooke 45
(Sharon Watt) *in tch: stdy hdwy bef 4th: ev ch and rdn bef 3 out: wknd bef next* **6/1**

3m 59.6s (-10.40) **Going Correction** -0.775s/f (Firm) **10** Ran SP% **116.1**
Speed ratings (Par 103): **95,91,90,86,86 85,84,77,76,74**
toteswingers 1&2 £1.50, 2&3 £5.00, 1&3 £6.10 CSF £16.77 CT £55.76 TOTE £4.50: £1.50, £1.20, £2.60; EX 15.60 Trifecta £130.40 Pool: £1781.88 - 10.24 winning units..
Owner Mr & Mrs Duncan Davidson **Bred** Mrs P Wright **Trained** South Hazelrigg, Northumbria

FOCUS
A modest handicap hurdle. The winner is on the upgrade and there should be more to come.

3039 BARBOUR H'CAP CHASE (13 fncs) 2m 110y
1:50 (1:50) (Class 4) (0-120,119) 4-Y-0+ **£3,768** (£1,106; £553; £276)

Form RPR

F/6- 1 **Zaru (FR)**[31] 2421 7-11-11 **118**.. BrianHughes 135+
(James Ewart) *mde all: pushed along whn nt fluent 3 out: kpt on strly to go clr fr last* **11/2**

5/3- 2 8 **Shadrack (IRE)**[27] 2496 9-11-12 **119**............................ JamesReveley 126
(Keith Reveley) *trckd ldrs: effrt and wnt 2nd whn nt fluent 4 out: rdn next: one pce between last 2* **4/1**[2]

/15- 3 4 1/2 **Ballybriggan (IRE)**[46] 2101 9-11-12 **119**...................... JasonMaguire 122
(Donald McCain) *in tch: stdy hdwy 5 out: effrt next: outpcd fr 2 out* **5/1**[3]

/2F- 4 1 3/4 **Rocking Blues (FR)**[30] 2446 8-11-4 **111**...................... WilsonRenwick 114
(Rose Dobbin) *t.k.h early: in tch: rdn and outpcd 4 out: rallied after 2 out: kpt on: no imp* **7/2**[1]

4/5- 5 2 **Rupert Bear**[43] 2159 7-11-1 **113**.................................. MissCWalton(5) 112
(James Walton) *bhd: outpcd 1/2-way: rallied bef 2 out: kpt on: nvr rchd ldrs* **11/1**

240- 6 1 1/4 **Olympian Boy (IRE)**[40] 2212 9-11-8 **115**........................ PaulMoloney 113
(Sophie Leech) *nt fluent early: hld up bhd ldng gp: outpcd bef 5 out: n.d after* **9/1**

422- 7 3/4 **Prince Tam**[27] 2496 9-9-7 **93** oh1.. CallumBewley(7) 90
(Harriet Graham) *pressed wnr: rdn bef 4 out: wknd fr next* **9/1**

432- U **Bocamix (FR)**[16] 2734 7-10-3 **99**..................................... JohnKington(3)
(Andrew Crook) *hld up in tch: mstke: stmbld and uns rdr 7th* **9/1**

4m 11.1s (-10.00) **Going Correction** -0.425s/f (Good) **8** Ran SP% **112.6**
Speed ratings (Par 105): **106,102,100,99,98 97,97,**
toteswingers 1&2 £4.00, 2&3 £3.00, 1&3 £5.30 CSF £27.50 CT £115.41 TOTE £8.00: £2.00, £1.20, £2.50; EX 37.30 Trifecta £96.90 Pool: £2446.99 - 18.92 winning units..
Owner Humbert, Drew **Bred** James Ewart & Mme Briony Ewart **Trained** Langholm, Dumfries & G'way

FOCUS
A fair handicap chase in which they went an even gallop. The winner was well in on his best form and is rated in line with his course fall over 3m.

3040 COMPLETE BUILDING SERVICES H'CAP HURDLE (11 hdls) 2m 4f
2:20 (2:20) (Class 5) (0-100,93) 3-Y-0+ **£1,949** (£572; £286; £143)

Form RPR

U4/- 1 **Snapping Turtle (IRE)**[249] 5204 8-11-6 **92**................ CallumWhillans(5) 94
(Donald Whillans) *hld up: hdwy u.p and in tch 3 out: styd on wl fr last to ld cl home* **33/1**

2/2- 2 hd **Ruby Bay (IRE)**[9] 2877 8-11-8 **89**.................................... PeterBuchanan 91+
(Tim Walford) *t.k.h: in tch: hdwy to chse clr ldr 6th: led bef 3 out: rdn next: 2 l clr last 100yds: no ex and hdd cl home* **7/1**[3]

/4U- 3 1/2 **Doyenthedecenthing**[22] 2596 5-10-7 **74**............................ BrianHughes 75
(John Davies) *in tch: stdy hdwy 7th: effrt and chsd ldr after 3 out: effrt next: one pce and lost 2nd last 100yds* **14/1**

420- 4 12 **Top Billing**[31] 2417 4-11-2 **90**....................................(p) GrahamWatters(7) 82
(Nicky Richards) *hld up in midfield: stdy hdwy 7th: effrt and drvn along bef 3 out: outpcd between last 2* **12/1**

225/ 5 16 **Hotgrove Boy**[623] 5151 6-10-4 **78**.................................. DaraghBourke(7) 58
(Stuart Coltherd) *t.k.h: cl up: led 4th: sn clr: hdd whn hit 3 out: wknd fr next* **8/1**

/56- 6 9 **Northern Acres**[27] 2497 7-11-12 **93**................................ LucyAlexander 61
(N W Alexander) *midfield: hdwy u.p after 4 out: wknd fr next* **13/2**[2]

/54- 7 9 **Willie Hall**[22] 2596 9-11-4 **85**.. BrianHarding 45
(William Amos) *hld up: rdn along after 4 out: nvr on terms* **9/1**

604- 8 1/2 **Ancient Times (USA)**[16] 2736 6-10-13 **83**.....................(p) KyleJames(3) 42
(Philip Kirby) *towards rr: outpcd 1/2-way: n.d after* **20/1**

446- 9 1/2 **Blue Sea Of Ibrox (IRE)**[18] 2701 5-9-13 **71**............... HarryChalloner(5) 30
(Alan Brown) *in tch: lost pl 6th: sn struggling: n.d after* **20/1**

F5P- 10 3/4 **Acordingtoscript (IRE)**[26] 2518 7-11-8 **89**......................(p) HenryBrooke 47
(Martin Todhunter) *midfield: lost pl 5th: n.d after* **25/1**

002- 11 1 **Next Hight (IRE)**[9] 2869 6-11-6 **87**...................................... RyanMania 44
(Sue Smith) *nt fluent on occasions: in tch: stdy hdwy 6th: rdn and wknd fr 3 out* **9/2**[1]

2U4- 12 13 **Cara Court (IRE)**[24] 2562 7-11-0 **86**......................(v[1]) SamanthaDrake(5) 31
(Joanne Foster) *led to 4th: chsd clr ldr to 6th: wknd fr next* **25/1**

P/0- 13 32 **Jan Smuts (IRE)**[33] 2360 5-10-2 **69**................................(tp) BarryKeniry
(Wilf Storey) *hld up: struggling 7th: nvr on terms* **16/1**

000- P **Durham Express (IRE)**[13] 2783 6-11-4 **85**....................(p) DougieCostello
(Tina Jackson) *hld up: struggling bef 4 out: t.o whn p.u bef next* **100/1**

210/ P **Politelysed**[601] 5495 7-10-9 **76**....................................... KennyJohnson
(Robert Johnson) *hld up: struggling 1/2-way: nvr on terms: p.u bef 3 out* **33/1**

0/5- P **Shady Sadie (IRE)**[218] 168 6-10-13 **87**......................... ShaunDobbin(7)
(Rose Dobbin) *towards rr: struggling 1/2-way: t.o whn p.u bef 3 out* **33/1**

/64- P **Oscar Lateen (IRE)**[31] 2417 5-11-11 **92**.......................... JamesReveley
(Sandy Thomson) *in tch: drvn and outpcd 7th: wknd next: t.o whn p.u bef 3 out* **9/1**

030- P **Dunkirk's First (IRE)**[12] 2823 5-11-1 **82**........................ WilsonRenwick
(Rose Dobbin) *t.k.h early: chsd ldrs to 6th: sn struggling: t.o whn p.u bef 3 out* **40/1**

5m 4.9s (-16.20) **Going Correction** -0.775s/f (Firm)
WFA 4 from 5yo+ 6lb **18** Ran SP% **124.8**
Speed ratings (Par 103): **101,100,100,95,89 85,82,82,81,81 81,76,63, , ,,**
toteswingers 1&2 £28.40, 2&3 £17.40, 1&3 £106.80 CSF £234.81 CT £3429.60 TOTE £40.00: £7.30, £2.00, £4.20, £3.30; EX 369.00 Trifecta £1990.70 Part won. Pool: £2654.28 - 0.30 winning units..
Owner D W Whillans **Bred** Robert McCarthy **Trained** Hawick, Borders

FOCUS
A moderate handicap hurdle. The winner was well in on the best of his 2012 form.

3041 NORTH SEA LOGISTICS NOVICES' H'CAP CHASE (16 fncs) 2m 4f
2:50 (2:51) (Class 4) (0-110,110) 4-Y-0+ **£4,548** (£1,335; £667; £333)

Form RPR

436/ 1 **Sharney Sike**[628] 5059 7-10-2 **93**.................................. DaraghBourke(7) 107+
(Stuart Coltherd) *nt fluent: t.k.h: hld up: hit and stmbld bdly 1st: stdy hdwy bef 5 out: rdn next: rallied bef 2 out: styd on wl fr last to ld cl home* **15/2**

064- 2 hd **Radio Nowhere (IRE)**[13] 2787 5-11-0 **98**......................(b) JasonMaguire 106
(Donald McCain) *led: rdn and hrd pressed 4 out: jst over 3 l in front and rdn 2 out: kpt on run-in: hdd cl home* **3/1**[1]

63P- 3 3 3/4 **Talkin Thomas (IRE)**[21] 2623 7-11-12 **110**..................... BrianHarding 116+
(Nicky Richards) *hld up in tch: stdy hdwy on outside to chse ldrs bef 4 out: rdn next: one pce fr 2 out* **9/2**[3]

F2U- 4 shd **Ben Akram (IRE)**[13] 2791 5-11-2 **100**............................ PeterBuchanan 106
(Lucinda Russell) *cl up: chal 4 out to next: rdn and one pce between last 2* **8/1**

545/ 5 5 **Edmund (IRE)**[398] 2316 6-10-7 **91**..............................(t) WilsonRenwick 91
(Ann Hamilton) *t.k.h: hld up in tch: effrt after 5 out: rdn and no imp fr 3 out* **20/1**

0/5- 6 39 **Get The Papers**[35] 2308 6-10-0 **84** oh1..............................(t) BarryKeniry 48
(Pauline Robson) *hld up in tch: nt fluent 8th: stdy hdwy next: rdn and wknd after 5 out: t.o* **7/2**[2]

FP2- 7 8 **Teo Vivo (FR)**[13] 2791 6-11-4 **102**..................................(p) BrianHughes 59
(James Ewart) *chsd ldr to 8th: nt fluent 6 out: outpacecd whn hit next: wknd bef 4 out* **8/1**

6P3- 8 16 **Leroy Parker (IRE)**[31] 2418 5-11-1 **99**...........................(b) HenryBrooke 42
(Barry Murtagh) *hld up in tch: stdy hdwy after 7th: hit and lost pl 9th: rallied 5 out: wknd next: t.o* **50/1**

230- U **Milano Magic (IRE)**[20] 2655 7-11-11 **109**.....................(p) LucyAlexander
(N W Alexander) *trckd ldrs: blnd and uns rdr 7th* **10/1**

5m 16.5s (-10.70) **Going Correction** -0.425s/f (Good) **9** Ran SP% **115.2**
Speed ratings (Par 105): **104,103,102,102,100 84,81,75,**
toteswingers 1&2 £7.00, 2&3 £3.70, 1&3 £8.70 CSF £31.31 CT £114.28 TOTE £11.80: £4.50, £1.10, £2.10; EX 44.80 Trifecta £232.40 Pool: £2447.92 - 7.89 winning units..
Owner John Hogg **Bred** John Hogg **Trained** Selkirk, Borders

FOCUS
A modest handicap chase for novices. The winner has the potential to rate higher.

3042 SWARLANDFENCE.CO.UK STANDARD OPEN NATIONAL HUNT FLAT RACE 2m
3:20 (3:21) (Class 6) 4-6-Y-0 **£1,559** (£457; £228; £114)

Form RPR

1 **Seldom Inn** 5-11-0 **0**... PeterBuchanan 106+
(Sandy Thomson) *hld up in midfield: pushed along bef 5 out: hdwy to chse (clr) ldr over 1f out: led last 125yds: sn clr* **20/1**

4- 2 3 3/4 **Gilnockie**[40] 2223 5-11-0 **0**... BrianHughes 102+
(James Ewart) *led 5f: chsd ldr: regained ld 5 out: qckned clr wl over 2f out: rdn over 1f out: edgd lft and hdd last 125yds: no ex* **14/1**

3 5 **Redkalani (IRE)** 5-11-0 **0**... JamesReveley 98+
(Keith Reveley) *hld up in midfield on outside: drvn and outpcd 6f out: rallied 2f out: styd on wl fnl f: nt rch first two* **4/1**[1]

5- 4 1 **Ride The Range (IRE)**[27] 2499 4-11-0 **0**.......................... HenryBrooke 97
(Chris Grant) *in tch: effrt and chsd ldr over 3f out to over 2f out: sn rdn and edgd lft: outpcd over 1f out* **9/2**[2]

5/ 5 1/2 **Troubled Waters**[235] 5428 4-10-4 **0**................................ KyleJames(3) 90
(Jason Ward) *t.k.h: prom: effrt and chsd ldr over 2f out to over 1f out: sn outpcd* **16/1**

6 6 **Native Spa (IRE)**[263] 5-11-0 **0**.. RyanMania 92
(Michael Smith) *prom: effrt and rdn 3f out: wknd over 1f out* **5/1**[3]

/ 7 6 **Daylan (IRE)** 5-11-0 **0**... DougieCostello 86
(Tony Coyle) *chsd ldrs tl rdn and wknd over 2f out* **11/2**

0- 8 nk **Silver Storm**[15] 2752 5-10-4 **0**...................................... EwanWhillans(3) 78
(Tristan Davidson) *hld up: stdy hdwy over 5f out: rdn and outpcd fr 3f out* **66/1**

3- 9 7 **Conjola**[15] 2752 6-10-7 **0**.. RichieMcGrath 72
(Geoffrey Harker) *hld up: rdn and outpcd 5f out: n.d after* **13/2**

10 2 1/2 **Bandalero (IRE)** 5-10-9 **0**... AdamNicol(5) 77
(Philip Kirby) *bhd: pushed along after 5f: nvr on terms* **14/1**

11 3 3/4 **Dunleer Dixie** 5-11-0 **0**... AdrianLane 74
(Lucy Normile) *hld up: hdwy and in tch 1/2-way: rdn and wknd over 4f out* **66/1**

0- 12 shd **Bracing**[72] 1719 4-10-0 **0**... GrantCockburn(7) 66
(Susan Corbett) *hld up: struggling 1/2-way: nvr on terms* **200/1**

13 32 **Alwaysrecommended (IRE)** 4-10-7 **0**........................ AlistairFindlay(7) 45
(Jane Walton) *plld hrd: hld up: hdwy to ld after 5f: rdn and hdd 5f out: sn wknd* **11/1**

0- 14 13 **Harleys Max**[16] 2738 4-10-7 **0**.................................... StephenMulqueen(7) 33
(Susan Corbett) *t.k.h: hld up: struggling over 5f out: sn btn* **200/1**

3m 57.7s (-6.70) **Going Correction** -0.775s/f (Firm)
WFA 4 from 5yo+ 5lb **14** Ran SP% **119.9**
Speed ratings: **85,83,80,80,79 76,73,73,70,68 67,67,51,44**
toteswingers 1&2 £15.40, 2&3 £14.30, 1&3 £30.80 CSF £272.20 TOTE £30.10: £9.80, £2.80, £1.70; EX 279.00 Trifecta £833.70 Part won. Pool: £1111.60 - 0.10 winning units..
Owner Bill A Walker **Bred** W A Walker **Trained** Lambden, Berwicks

FOCUS
An ordinary bumper concluded the card, in which they went a steady gallop. Probably not one to be carried away with.

T/Plt: £25.40 to a £1 stake. Pool of £64650.49 - 1857.59 winning tickets. T/Qpdt: £19.60 to a £1 stake. Pool of £4742.90 - 178.40 winning tickets. RY

2760 TAUNTON (R-H)

Thursday, December 12

OFFICIAL GOING: Good (good to firm in places 7.0)

Wind: virtually nil Weather: cloudy with sunny periods

3043 HIGOS INSURANCE SERVICES BRIDGWATER H'CAP HURDLE (10 hdls) 2m 3f 110y

12:40 (12:41) (Class 4) (0-115,115) 3-Y-0+ **£4,106** (£1,197; £598)

Form RPR

652- **1** **Western Approaches**[8] 2888 6-10-13 **102**..........(t) WillKennedy 109+
(Ian Williams) *mde all: styd on strly fr 2 out: pushed out* **11/4**[1]

23P/ **2** *4 ½* **Calaf**[44] 4777 5-11-10 **113**.......... RichieMcLernon 115
(Jonjo O'Neill) *racd keenly: trckd wnr: rdn whn nt fluent 2 out: styd on same pce* **13/2**

/46- **3** *6* **Barista (IRE)**[7] 2910 5-11-2 **105**.......... ConorO'Farrell 101
(Brian Forsey) *hld up towards rr: rdn after 6th: styd on fr 2 out: wnt 3rd run-in: nvr gng to reel in ldrs* **12/1**

450- **4** *2* **Ladies Dancing**[28] 2474 7-11-6 **109**.......... JamesDavies 105
(Chris Down) *trckd ldrs: hit 7th and 3 out: sn rdn: nt gng pce to chal: no ex whn lost 3rd run-in* **11/2**[3]

230- **5** *1* **Lady Bridget**[18] 2696 5-9-7 **89** oh7..........(tp) ThomasCheesman[(7)] 82
(Mark Gillard) *trckd ldrs: rdn after 6th: one pce fr after 3 out* **12/1**

506- **6** *30* **Advisor (FR)**[14] 2760 7-11-1 **104**.......... TommyPhelan 70
(Mark Gillard) *trckd ldrs: pushed along whn lost pl after 3rd: rdn after 5th: wknd after 3 out: t.o* **25/1**

4/P- **7** *9* **Shivsingh**[28] 2474 4-10-13 **107**.......... CharlieWallis[(5)] 65
(Martin Hill) *a towards rr: t.o after 3 out* **16/1**

/P0- **8** *2* **Kim Tian Road (IRE)**[33] 2371 7-11-12 **115**.......... HaddenFrost 71
(Martin Hill) *hld up: a towards rr: t.o after 3 out* **3/1**[2]

200/ **P** **Consulate (IRE)**[390] 2474 9-10-10 **102**.......... JamesBest[(3)]
(Gordon Edwards) *trckd ldrs: rdn after 5th: dropped in rr qckly: t.o whn p.u bef 3 out* **10/1**

4m 39.0s (-7.00) **Going Correction** -0.275s/f (Good)
WFA 4 from 5yo+ 5lb 9 Ran SP% **114.6**
Speed ratings (Par 105): **103,101,98,98,97 85,82,81,**
toteswingers 1&2 £2.90, 2&3 £9.10, 1&3 £7.20 CSF £21.11 CT £182.50 TOTE £4.00: £1.10, £1.90, £4.30; EX 15.70 Trifecta £97.70 Pool: £1220.72 - 9.36 winning units..
Owner Ian Williams **Bred** N J Henderson And Mrs S A Aston **Trained** Portway, Worcs

FOCUS
Both bends moved out 2-3metres and hurdles by 1-2 sections. A fair handicap hurdle, but the order didn't change that much. Straightforward form.

3044 HIGOS THATCH PROPERTY INSURANCE H'CAP HURDLE (12 hdls) 3m 110y

1:10 (1:12) (Class 4) (0-110,110) 4-Y-0+ **£4,106** (£1,197; £598)

Form RPR

/24- **1** **Fountains Mary**[18] 2697 5-11-6 **104**..........(b[1]) AidanColeman 103+
(Anthony Honeyball) *towards rr: hrdly ever travelling: reminders after 5th: in tch after 7th but rdn: dropped to last 3 3 out: drvn and stdy prog appr 2 out: lft 7 1/2 l 4th at the last: str run fnl 120yds: led towards fin* **8/1**

21- **2** *1* **The Rattler Obrien (IRE)**[56] 1945 7-11-4 **102**.......... HaddenFrost 99
(Martin Hill) *mid-div: hdwy after 8th: rdn to chse ldrs appr 2 out: lft 2nd at the last: led fnl 120yds: hdd towards fin* **5/2**[1]

410- **3** *½* **Halucha (IRE)**[17] 2715 8-11-9 **107**..........(p) LiamTreadwell 104
(Paul Webber) *led: rdn and hdd bef 2 out: lft 3rd at the last: styd on same pce* **12/1**

2/2- **4** *1* **Upton Wood**[56] 1941 7-11-8 **106**.......... JamesDavies 105+
(Chris Down) *trckd ldrs: hit 3 out: rdn to ld bef 2 out: narrowly hdd beween last 2: lft in ld last: hung lft and idling whn hdd fnl 120yds: no ex* **6/1**[3]

0P2/ **5** *42* **Only Witness (IRE)**[242] 5305 8-11-7 **105**..........(p) BrendanPowell 63
(Brendan Powell) *prom: rdn after 8th: wknd bef 3 out: t.o* **10/1**

P/5- **6** *½* **Saint Peray (FR)**[28] 2473 7-10-6 **90**.......... SamJones 48
(Bob Buckler) *sn trcking ldrs: rdn upsides 8th tl next: wknd bef 2 out: t.o* **16/1**

/P4- **7** *1 ½* **Low Gales (IRE)**[13] 2786 7-11-12 **110**..........(tp) MarkGrant 66
(Charlie Mann) *trckd ldrs: rdn after 9th: wknd after 3 out: t.o* **9/1**

3P6/ **8** *5* **Briefcase (IRE)**[390] 2473 8-11-0 **98**.......... ConorO'Farrell 50
(Gordon Edwards) *mid-div: rdn after 8th: wknd bef 3 out: t.o* **33/1**

035- **U** **Kalamill (IRE)**[21] 2616 6-10-12 **99**..........(t) PeterCarberry[(3)] 98+
(Shaun Lycett) *hld up towards rr: smooth prog fr 8th: chal gng to 2 out: pushed along in narrow ld whn v awkard: stmbld bdly and uns rdr last* **12/1**

3/0- **P** **Lisheen Hill (IRE)**[22] 2598 7-11-7 **105**.......... WayneHutchinson
(Richard Phillips) *mid-div: rdn after 8th: qckly dropped in rr: p.u bef next* **9/2**[2]

5m 54.6s (-9.40) **Going Correction** -0.275s/f (Good) 10 Ran SP% **115.4**
Speed ratings (Par 105): **104,103,103,103,89 89,89,87, ,**
toteswingers 1&2 £4.80, 2&3 £7.90, 1&3 £14.40 CSF £28.75 CT £242.68 TOTE £7.80: £2.10, £1.20, £4.00; EX 25.20 Trifecta £206.00 Pool: £2085.02 - 7.58 winning units..
Owner Mrs Marion Bowden **Bred** Mrs M H Bowden **Trained** Mosterton, Dorset

FOCUS
No shortage of drama in this fair staying handicap hurdle. Pretty solid form.

3045 HIGOS INSURANCE SERVICES NOVICES' LIMITED H'CAP CHASE (12 fncs) 2m 110y

1:40 (1:42) (Class 3) (0-140,137) 4-Y-0+ **£6,498** (£1,908; £954; £477)

Form RPR

321- **1** **Funny Star (FR)**[13] 2782 5-11-5 **137**..........(t) NickScholfield 144+
(Paul Nicholls) *trckd ldrs: pushed along fr 6th: led after 4 out: sn rdn: nt fluent 3 out: blnd 2 out: lft in command last: rdn out* **9/5**[2]

106/ **2** *1 ¾* **Cape Dutch (IRE)**[608] 5393 6-10-6 **127**.......... JackQuinlan[(3)] 134+
(John Ferguson) *trckd ldng trio: chal 4 out: rdn whn hung lft and hit 3 out and next: stl w ch whn hung lft and hit last: no ex* **5/1**

0/1- **3** *4* **Workbench (FR)**[14] 2762 5-10-5 **123**..........(t) HarrySkelton 126+
(Dan Skelton) *led: mstke 8th: rdn and hdd after 4 out: rallying and 1 l down whn blnd last: hld after* **7/4**[1]

3F- **4** *2 ¼* **Sands Cove (IRE)**[18] 2694 6-10-7 **125**..........(t) MarkGrant 123
(Charlie Mann) *trckd ldr fr 3rd tl rdn after 4 out: styd on same pce fr next* **4/1**[3]

4m 5.2s (-8.80) **Going Correction** -0.275s/f (Good) 4 Ran SP% **108.7**
Speed ratings (Par 107): **109,108,106,105**
CSF £9.82 TOTE £2.20; EX 12.50 Trifecta £18.00 Pool: £1176.24 - 48.78 winning units..
Owner Mr And Mrs J D Cotton **Bred** Suc Jean-Pierre Villey **Trained** Ditcheat, Somerset

FOCUS
Quite a decent contest despite the small field, but some iffy jumping from the principals over the last three fences makes the form rather unreliable. Another step up from the winner.

3046 HIGOS FOR YOUR COMMERCIAL INSURANCE SERVICES NOVICES' HURDLE (12 hdls) 3m 110y

2:10 (2:11) (Class 4) 4-Y-0+ **£4,106** (£1,197; £598)

Form RPR

6/0- **1** **Aerial (FR)**[54] 1968 7-10-12 139.......... NickScholfield 99+
(Paul Nicholls) *mde all: in command fr after 3 out: pushed out after last: eased nring fin* **8/15**[1]

5/6- **2** *6* **Demographic (USA)**[67] 1794 4-10-9 0.......... GavinSheehan[(3)] 88
(Emma Lavelle) *hld up in 4th: nt fluent 3rd and 6th: hit 8th: nt fluent next: sn rdn: wnt 2nd 2 out: styd on but no ch w wnr* **7/2**[2]

/00- **3** *5* **Miles Of Sunshine**[8] 2886 8-10-12 0.......... ConorO'Farrell 84
(Ron Hodges) *trckd ldng pair: rdn to chse wnr after 3 out tl next: kpt pressing for 2nd tl no ex fr last* **50/1**

43/ **4** *25* **Power Of God (IRE)**[276] 4718 5-10-9 0.......... MichaelByrne[(3)] 63
(Tim Vaughan) *j.rt: trckd wnr tl rdn after 3 out: sn wknd: t.o* **9/2**[3]

UF0- **5** *21* **Lady Oaksey**[29] 2463 7-10-5 0.......... GerardTumelty 30
(Bob Buckler) *hld up in last but wl in tch: rdn after 9th: wknd sn after 3 out: t.o* **100/1**

5m 59.0s (-5.00) **Going Correction** -0.275s/f (Good)
WFA 4 from 5yo+ 7lb 5 Ran SP% **108.6**
Speed ratings (Par 105): **97,95,93,85,78**
CSF £2.79 TOTE £1.40: £1.10, £1.50; EX 2.80 Trifecta £14.60 Pool: £2162.59 - 110.91 winning units..
Owner Tony Hayward And Barry Fulton **Bred** Olivier Tricot **Trained** Ditcheat, Somerset

FOCUS
They went no pace in this very one-sided affair, so it was no surprise that the time was 4.4sec slower than the earlier handicap. The easy winner didn't need to be anywhere near his best.

3047 HIGOS MOTOR DEAL H'CAP HURDLE (9 hdls) 2m 1f

2:40 (2:45) (Class 5) (0-95,95) 3-Y-0+ **£2,737** (£798; £399)

Form RPR

645- **1** **Seaside Shuffle (IRE)**[9] 2877 8-11-4 **87**..........(tp) RichieMcLernon 92
(Sophie Leech) *hld up towards rr: hdwy 5th: sn trcking ldrs: rdn to chal 2 out: led fnl 100yds: all out* **6/1**[2]

043- **2** *nk* **Spinning Waters**[114] 1331 7-11-2 **88**..........(p) RobertDunne[(3)] 93
(Dai Burchell) *trckd ldrs: rdn after 3 out: led narrowly next: hdd fnl 100yds: kpt on* **6/1**[2]

0/5- **3** *½* **Crackerjack**[14] 2770 6-10-13 **87**.......... JamesBanks[(5)] 92
(Emma Baker) *mid-div: mstkes 2nd and 3rd: hdwy after 3 out: pushed along to chse ldrs 2 out: rdn in 3rd after last: styd on towards fin* **14/1**

/00- **4** *2 ¼* **Light The World (FR)**[9] 2877 5-11-1 **91**..........(p) JakeHodson[(7)] 94
(Kevin Frost) *in tch: rdn after 3 out: styd on same pce fr next: wnt 4th run-in* **16/1**

0- **5** *2 ¾* **Wicklewood**[28] 2476 7-10-7 **76**..........(t) TommyPhelan 77
(Mark Gillard) *mid-div: rdn whn blnd 2 out: styd on fr last* **7/1**[3]

4/P- **6** *4* **Out Of Nothing**[36] 2291 10-11-0 **88**.......... CharlieWallis[(5)] 84
(Dai Burchell) *led tl 6th: rdn to ld briefly bef 2 out: no ex fr last* **18/1**

005- **7** *2 ¼* **Big John Cannon (IRE)**[24] 2559 3-9-9 **85**.......... MrPJohn[(7)] 66
(Sarah-Jayne Davies) *hld up towards rr: sme late prog u.p: nvr threatened ldrs* **20/1**

/U0- **8** *1 ½* **Withy Mills**[14] 2766 8-10-12 **84**..........(b[1]) JamesBest[(3)] 79
(Kevin Bishop) *trckd ldr: led 6th tl rdn and hdd bef 2 out: grad fdd* **20/1**

0/0- **9** *3 ¼* **Miss Tinks**[190] 637 7-10-11 **80**.......... AidanColeman 70
(Richard Woollacott) *mainly towards rr: nvr any danger* **20/1**

50F- **10** *5* **Maxdelas (FR)**[19] 2679 7-10-11 **87**..........(t) RyanHatch[(7)] 73
(Roy Brotherton) *mid-div tl wknd 3 out* **17/2**

/00- **11** *51* **Watchmetail (IRE)**[14] 2766 7-10-6 **75**.......... ConorO'Farrell 15
(John Panvert) *trckd ldrs tl 6th: sn bhd: t.o* **33/1**

0/5- **12** *1 ¼* **Cantabilly (IRE)**[224] 83 10-11-12 **95**.......... NickScholfield 34
(Ron Hodges) *bhd and struggling fr 4th: t.o* **14/1**

00/- **13** *40* **Ramona Chase**[233] 5470 8-10-0 **69** oh10..........(t) MattieBatchelor
(Jim Best) *wnt to s early: plld hrd: sn trcking ldrs: hung lft on bnd after 4th: pushed along bef next: drvn bef 6th: qckly btn: t.o* **5/2**[1]

000- **P** **Bedibyes**[119] 1270 5-9-11 **69** oh4.......... GavinSheehan[(3)]
(Richard Mitchell) *racd wd: hld up towards rr: sme prog 3 out: sn rdn: p.u bef next: dismntd* **33/1**

4m 1.5s (-6.50) **Going Correction** -0.275s/f (Good)
WFA 3 from 5yo+ 13lb 14 Ran SP% **124.8**
Speed ratings (Par 103): **104,103,103,102,101 99,98,97,96,93 69,69,50,**
toteswingers 1&2 £3.80, 2&3 £12.30, 1&3 £22.90 CSF £40.75 CT £499.67 TOTE £8.20: £2.50, £2.50, £3.80; EX 25.10 Trifecta £61.00 Pool: £551.32 - 6.76 winning units..
Owner Cheltenham Racing Club **Bred** W H Neville **Trained** Elton, Gloucs

FOCUS
A moderate handicap hurdle, but run at a solid pace. The winner was well in on old Irish form and the second sets the level.

3048 STABLES BUSINESS PARK CLIENTS DAY OUT H'CAP CHASE (12 fncs) 2m 110y

3:10 (3:11) (Class 5) (0-95,94) 4-Y-0+ **£3,422** (£997; £499)

Form RPR

P62/ **1** **Capisci (IRE)**[385] 2583 8-10-9 **77**.......... WillKennedy 93+
(Sarah-Jayne Davies) *mde all: clr 3rd tl 6th: drew clr again after 8th: wl in command whn mstke 2 out: unchal* **9/2**[3]

/44- **2** *9* **Further More (IRE)**[10] 2861 6-11-5 **87**.......... AidanColeman 93
(Emma Lavelle) *trckd ldrs: mstke 4th: nt fluent 6th: wnt 2nd after 8th: rdn after 4 out: nvr gng pce to get on terms w wnr* **11/4**[1]

024- **3** *4* **Rusty Nail (IRE)**[30] 2441 8-9-7 **68**.......... MrFTett[(7)] 69
(James Frost) *in tch: rdn after 4 out to dispute 3rd: styd on same pce fr next* **7/2**[2]

03P- **4** *7* **Le Grand Chene (FR)**[21] 2615 7-11-8 **90**..........(t) RichieMcLernon 87
(Sophie Leech) *in tch: rdn into 3rd after 4 out tl after next: fdd last* **12/1**

0S0- **U** **Prickles**[24] 2562 8-11-7 **89**..........(p) LiamTreadwell
(Richard Woollacott) *prom whn wnt lft and uns rdr 1st* **25/1**

466- **F** **Gizzit (IRE)**[18] 2696 7-11-12 **94**..........(p) AndrewThornton 90
(Karen George) *hld up: pushed along and hdwy appr 3 out but no ch w wnr: btn 5th whn fell last* **6/1**

/63- **P** **Bobby Dove**[20] 2653 6-11-2 **87**.......... RobertDunne[(3)]
(Andrew Price) *hld up: rdn after 4 out: wknd next: p.u bef last* **5/1**

The Form Book Jumps, Raceform Ltd, Compton, RG20 6NL.

004- **P** **Unsist (FR)**[15] 2741 5-10-1 **69**..(p) TomCannon
(Nick Gifford) *chsd clr ldr: blnd 3rd: nt fluent 6th: sn struggling: wknd next: p.u bef 4 out* **14/1**

4m 10.4s (-3.60) **Going Correction** -0.275s/f (Good) **8** Ran SP% **116.2**
Speed ratings (Par 103): **97,92,90,87, , ,**
toteswingers 1&2 £4.20, 2&3 £3.20, 1&3 £6.30 CSF £18.31 CT £48.08 TOTE £5.60: £1.20, £1.10, £1.80; EX 22.80 Trifecta £60.80 Pool: £484.34 - 5.97 winning units..
Owner Miss Sarah-Jayne Davies **Bred** Danny Doran **Trained** Leominster, H'fords

FOCUS
A moderate handicap chase and the winner had this won a long way out. The winner may well be capable of better.

3049 HIGOS INSURANCE SERVICES LANGPORT "NEWCOMERS" STANDARD OPEN NATIONAL HUNT FLAT RACE 2m 1f
3:40 (3:42) (Class 5) 3-5-Y-O **£2,053** (£598; £299)

Form RPR
1 **Aqalim** 3-10-4 0.. JackQuinlan(3) 100+
(John Ferguson) *hld up towards rr: smooth hdwy fr 3f out: led wl over 1f out: qcknd up wl whn asked ent fnl f: r.o strly* **10/11**[1]

2 *4 ½* **Go Odee Go (IRE)** 5-11-7 0.. HarrySkelton 108+
(Dan Skelton) *trckd ldrs: led over 4f out: rdn over 2f out: hdd wl over 1f out: kpt on but nt gng pce of wnr* **5/1**[2]

3 *10* **Maldivian Reef (IRE)** 5-11-0 0.............................. StephenO'Donovan(7) 98
(Alan King) *hld up towards rr: hdwy fr 5f out to trck ldrs 3f out: sn rdn: kpt on same pce fnl 2f: snatched 3rd fnl stride* **9/1**[3]

4 *hd* **Knight's Reward** 3-10-4 0... MichaelByrne(3) 83
(Tim Vaughan) *mid-div: hdwy over 4f out: rdn in cl 3rd over 2f out: sn outpcd by ldng pair: no ex whn lost 3rd fnl strides* **5/1**[2]

5 *10* **Knight ofthe Realm** 4-11-0 0.. MrLDrowne(7) 87
(Caroline Keevil) *disp ld for 6f: prom: rdn over 3f out: one pce fnl 2f* **28/1**

6 *4 ½* **Borguy (FR)** 3-10-7 0.. BrendanPowell 69
(Jamie Snowden) *trckd ldrs rdn whn squeezed up 4f out: wknd over 2f out* **12/1**

7 *hd* **Tomorrow Night** 3-10-2 0 ow2... FelixDeGiles 64
(Jennifer Mason) *mid-div: hdwy over 5f out: wknd 2f out* **25/1**

8 *16* **Mrs Winchester (IRE)** 4-10-11 0.. JamesBest(3) 60
(Caroline Keevil) *veered rt s: sn disputing ld: hdd after 6f: led over 6f out: hdd over 4f out: wknd over 2f out: t.o* **33/1**

9 *1* **More Tricks** 5-11-0 0.. HaddenFrost 59
(James Frost) *mid-div tl 6f out: sn bhd: t.o* **50/1**

10 *36* **Sequoia Forest** 4-11-0 0.. OllieGarner(7) 30
(Martin Keighley) *plld hrd: hld up: hdwy after 6f to ld: hdd over 6f out: sn wknd: t.o* **16/1**

11 *103* **Valona Star** 5-10-9 0.. CharlieWallis(5)
(Nick Ayliffe) *a bhd: struggling after 7f: t.o fnl 4f* **80/1**

3m 59.3s (-3.10) **Going Correction** -0.275s/f (Good)
WFA 3 from 4yo 13lb 4 from 5yo 5lb **11** Ran SP% **122.7**
Speed ratings (Par 103): **96,93,89,89,84 82,82,74,74,57**
toteswingers 1&2 £2.30, 2&3 £7.00, 1&3 £2.60 CSF £5.72 TOTE £2.10: £1.30, £1.40, £1.90; EX 7.10 Trifecta £14.30 Pool: £1370.04 - 71.57 winning units..
Owner Bloomfields **Bred** Darley **Trained** Cowlinge, Suffolk

FOCUS
None of these had run before, as the race title suggested. The pace was moderate.
T/Plt: £48.40 to a £1 stake. Pool of £66964.48 - 1008.76 winning tickets. T/Qpdt: £22.70 to a £1 stake. Pool of £4434.10 - 144.30 winning tickets. TM

3050 - 3056a (Foreign Racing) - See Raceform Interactive

2803 BANGOR-ON-DEE (L-H)
Friday, December 13

OFFICIAL GOING: Good to soft (good in places on hurdle course; soft in places on chase course) changing to soft on chase course after race 1 (12:10)
Wind: moderate 1/2 against Weather: overcast, rain after race 1

3057 CHRISTMAS NOVICES' CHASE (12 fncs) 2m 1f 110y
12:10 (12:12) (Class 4) 4-Y-0+ **£3,898** (£1,144; £572; £286)

Form RPR
310/ **1** **Open Hearted**[253] 5141 6-11-0 0.. AndrewTinkler 135+
(Nicky Henderson) *trckd ldrs: 2nd 4th: led 9th: drvn between last 2: 2 l ahd last: styd on wl* **2/1**[2]

13F- **2** *2 ½* **Ahyaknowyerself (IRE)**[26] 2533 7-11-0 0............................ TomO'Brien 132+
(Dr Richard Newland) *in rr: shkn up 3rd: drvn 6th: hdwy 3 out: chsd wnr 2 out: kpt on same pce run-in* **10/3**[3]

/34- **3** *20* **Lord Of House (GER)**[21] 2643 5-11-0 125........................(tp) NoelFehily 114
(Charlie Mann) *chsd ldrs: outpcd 8th: lost pl 3 out: tk modest 3rd sn after last* **14/1**

6/4- **4** *3 ½* **Up And Go (FR)**[21] 2658 5-11-0 0...................................... JasonMaguire 114
(Donald McCain) *led: hdd 9th: drvn 3 out: lost 2nd 2 out: modest 3rd whn blnd last: sn eased* **6/4**[1]

P **Festive Affair (IRE)**[231] 5565 5-11-0 0............................ RichieMcGrath
(Jonjo O'Neill) *t.k.h in rr: hdwy 5th: drvn 9th: wknd next: sn bhd: t.o whn hit 2 out: sn p.u* **22/1**

4m 35.3s (13.20) **Going Correction** +0.775s/f (Soft) **5** Ran SP% **107.4**
Speed ratings (Par 105): **101,99,91,89,**
CSF £8.63 TOTE £2.10: £1.70, £1.90; EX 9.60 Trifecta £38.50 Pool: £2175.05 - 42.26 winning units..
Owner The Queen **Bred** The Queen **Trained** Upper Lambourn, Berks

FOCUS
Jockeys in the first reported the ground to be considerably more testing than the official description, which was amended after the first to soft all over on the chase course. There were some useful prospects on show in this novice chase, which was run at a fair pace. The principals all have the potential to rate higher on hurdle form.

3058 DIRECT MORTGAGES MARES' H'CAP CHASE (15 fncs) 2m 4f 110y
12:45 (12:46) (Class 4) (0-120,120) 4-Y-0+ **£3,898** (£1,144; £572; £286)

Form RPR
431- **1** **Glen Countess (IRE)**[16] 2749 6-10-13 **107**....................(t) BrendanPowell 122+
(Brendan Powell) *w ldrs: led appr 2 out: styd on strly: eased clsng stages* **5/1**[3]

/32- **2** *5* **Overnight Fame (IRE)**[22] 2618 9-10-6 **105**..........(p) AodhaganConlon(5) 111
(Tom George) *led: mstke 7th: drvn after 3 out: hdd appr next: kpt on same pce* **6/1**

632- **3** *3 ¾* **Detour Ahead**[13] 2804 5-10-0 **94**.......................................(v) SeanQuinlan 96
(Jennie Candlish) *chsd ldrs 6th: pckd landing 10th: outpcd and lost pl 11th: j.rt 2 out: kpt on to take 3rd run-in* **9/2**[2]

405- **4** *1 ¼* **Niki Royal (FR)**[19] 2698 8-10-1 **95**..................................(t) AndrewTinkler 96
(Jamie Snowden) *chsd ldrs 6th: lost pl 9th: nt fluent and bhd 10th: modest 5th 2 out: kpt on* **9/1**

/24- **5** *6* **My Flora**[194] 596 9-11-9 **117**.. HarrySkelton 111+
(Dan Skelton) *w ldrs: drvn after 3 out: outpcd appr next: modest 3rd whn hit last: wknd* **7/2**[1]

/52- **6** *17* **A Little Swifter (IRE)**[24] 2572 7-10-10 **107**.................... TrevorWhelan(3) 83
(Neil King) *chsd ldrs: outpcd 9th: sn lost pl: bhd fr 3 out* **17/2**

P/P- **7** *4* **Moulin De La Croix**[61] 1886 9-10-6 **107**....................(t) JackSherwood(7) 79
(Oliver Sherwood) *hld up in rr: hdwy 9th: chsng ldrs next: wknd after 11th: bhd fr 3 out* **20/1**

421- **8** *8* **Tea Caddy**[24] 2572 7-10-13 **107**.. TomO'Brien 71
(Jamie Snowden) *in rr: drvn and lost pl 7th: bhd fr 9th: t.o 2 out* **6/1**

5m 32.5s (23.40) **Going Correction** +0.775s/f (Soft) **8** Ran SP% **110.9**
Speed ratings (Par 105): **86,84,82,82,79 73,71,68**
toteswingers 1&2 £4.60, 1&3 £3.80, 2&3 £4.00 CSF £32.81 CT £137.45 TOTE £4.90: £1.30, £1.70, £2.60; EX 25.30 Trifecta £153.40 Pool: £2150.72 - 10.50 winning units..
Owner The Naughty Partnership **Bred** David Pim **Trained** Upper Lambourn, Berks

FOCUS
Just an ordinary handicap for mares. The winner is on the upgrade and is value for further.

3059 PROACTIVE PERSONNEL H'CAP CHASE (18 fncs) 3m 110y
1:20 (1:22) (Class 3) (0-135,127) 4-Y-0+ **£6,498** (£1,908; £954; £477)

Form RPR
523/ **1** **Railway Dillon (IRE)**[236] 5427 8-11-6 **121**..................(bt) JasonMaguire 131
(Donald McCain) *j.rt: w ldrs: led 7th: hdd 14th: outpcd and lost pl 3 out: rallied and upsides 2 out: narrow ld last: drvn rt out* **9/1**[3]

321- **2** *1 ½* **Present View**[22] 2623 5-11-10 **125**..................................... BrendanPowell 133
(Jamie Snowden) *led 2nd to 7th: w ldrs: led gng best 3 out: jnd next: hdd last: no ex clsng stages* **7/4**[1]

F/P- **3** *hd* **Summery Justice (IRE)**[21] 2646 9-11-12 **127**................ LiamTreadwell 134
(Venetia Williams) *in tch: drvn 10th: chsng ldrs 13th: kpt on and 3rd appr 2 out: 4 l down last: styd on* **16/1**

/4F- **4** *30* **Mohi Rahrere (IRE)**[44] 2157 10-10-10 **111**............................ LiamHeard 93
(Barry Leavy) *sn chsng ldrs: lost pl after 3 out: sn bhd: distant 4th 2 out: t.o* **14/1**

/UU- **5** *3 ¾* **Hayjack**[43] 2177 8-11-10 **125**.. NoelFehily 105
(Charlie Longsdon) *w ldrs: hit 6th: led 14th: hdd next: lost pl bef 2 out: sn bhd: t.o* **9/4**[2]

2/P- **P** **Camden (IRE)**[26] 2537 7-11-9 **124**...............................(b[1]) LeightonAspell
(Oliver Sherwood) *w ldrs: pckd landing 9th: lost pl 11th: sn bhd: t.o 7th whn p.u after 13th* **14/1**

0/5- **P** **Rapidolyte De Ladalka (FR)**[55] 1978 8-11-9 **124**.............. BarryKeniry
(Simon Shirley-Beavan) *in rr: drvn 8th: bhd fr 10th: t.o last whn p.u 13th* **20/1**

/16- **P** **Guess Again (IRE)**[29] 2475 8-11-3 **125**........................(tp) KieronEdgar(7)
(David Pipe) *last whn blnd 2nd: sn detached: t.o 10th: 6th whn p.u after 13th* **9/1**[3]

6m 33.0s (13.20) **Going Correction** +0.775s/f (Soft) **8** Ran SP% **111.1**
Speed ratings (Par 107): **109,108,108,98,97 , ,**
toteswingers 1&2 £3.50, 1&3 £3.60, 2&3 £10.10 CSF £24.93 CT £241.87 TOTE £8.60: £2.50, £1.50, £5.10; EX 31.90 Trifecta £1285.60 Pool: £2819.82 - 1.64 winning units..
Owner T W Johnson & G Maxwell **Bred** Miss Laura Duggan **Trained** Cholmondeley, Cheshire

FOCUS
A fair handicap chase. It was run at a sound gallop and became quite a test in rain-eased conditions. The winner was well in on his best form.

3060 ALFA AGGREGATES H'CAP HURDLE (12 hdls) 3m
1:50 (1:52) (Class 3) (0-135,132) 4-Y-0+ **£5,848** (£1,717; £858; £429)

Form RPR
011- **1** **Cyrien Star**[21] 2655 6-10-9 **115**.. TomO'Brien 128+
(Henry Daly) *mde all: j. boldly: drvn clr between last 2: styd on strly: eased towards fin* **1/1**[1]

/UP- **2** *16* **Heronry (IRE)**[51] 2019 5-11-8 **128**...................................... AndrewTinkler 128
(Nicky Henderson) *chsd ldrs: 2nd 6th: drvn after 3 out: kpt on same pce between last 2* **11/1**

022- **3** *10* **Awaywiththegreys (IRE)**[21] 2652 6-11-12 **132**................(p) JamieMoore 122
(Peter Bowen) *chsd ldrs: 3rd and drvn 8th: one pce fr 3 out* **7/1**[3]

F/3- **4** *20* **Lienosus (IRE)**[48] 2079 7-11-11 **131**...................................... PaulMoloney 108
(Evan Williams) *hld up in tch: hdwy to chse ldrs 8th: 4th and drvn 3 out: sn wknd* **5/2**[2]

324- **5** *8* **Nicky Nutjob (GER)**[33] 2388 7-9-7 **106** oh2................(p) CiaranMckee(7) 71
(John O'Shea) *hld ip in rr: drvn 7th: sn bhd: tk distant 7th run-in* **22/1**

P15- **6** *3* **Abnaki (IRE)**[33] 2388 8-11-0 **130**............................(b) TommieMO'Brien(10) 92
(Jonjo O'Neill) *chsd ldrs: reminders after 6th: lost pl bef next: t.o 9th* **16/1**

13/- **P** **Rapid Heat Lad (IRE)**[21] 2095 4-11-2 **125**..................(tp) RobertDunne(3)
(Andrew Hollinshead) *chsd ldrs: lost pl 7th: bhd whn blnd 9th: t.o next: sn p.u* **33/1**

5m 44.5s (-6.50) **Going Correction** -0.025s/f (Good)
WFA 4 from 5yo+ 7lb **7** Ran SP% **112.6**
Speed ratings (Par 107): **109,103,100,93,91 90,**
toteswingers 1&2 £5.00, 1&3 £1.80, 2&3 £5.40 CSF £12.19 TOTE £2.00: £1.30, £5.40; EX 14.00 Trifecta £50.20 Pool: £3395.50 - 50.69 winning units..
Owner Puteus Profundus **Bred** Wood Farm Stud **Trained** Stanton Lacy, Shropshire

FOCUS
A fair handicap hurdle in which they came home at long intervals behind the winner, who set a reasonable gallop. He's on a steep upward curve and there is probably more to come.

3061 TURFTV "NATIONAL HUNT" NOVICES' HURDLE (9 hdls) 2m 1f
2:20 (2:23) (Class 4) 4-Y-0+ **£3,573** (£1,049; £524; £262)

Form RPR
/23- **1** **Masquerade (IRE)**[31] 2439 4-10-9 0.................................. GavinSheehan(3) 116+
(Warren Greatrex) *led: hdd 2 out: led after last: drvn out* **20/1**

3/3- **2** *2* **Goohar (IRE)**[30] 2453 4-10-12 0.. RobertThornton 113
(Henry Daly) *chsd ldrs: drvn and outpcd 6th: kpt on and handy 3rd 2 out: styd on run-in: tk 2nd nr fin* **10/1**[3]

1/1- **3** *hd* **Diamond King (IRE)**[16] 2748 5-11-5 0................................ JasonMaguire 124+
(Donald McCain) *trckd ldrs: led and hit 2 out: 2 1/2 l ahd whn blnd last: nt rcvr: hdd run-in* **2/7**[1]

4 *23* **Sukiyaki (IRE)**[88] 1593 4-10-12 0..[1] NoelFehily 92
(Charlie Longsdon) *in tch: outpcd 6th: lft poor 4th last* **12/1**

/65- 5 2½ **Six One Away (IRE)**[30] 2453 4-10-12 0 .... LiamHeard 90
(Paul Webber) *mid-div: hdwy 4th: outpcd 6th: no threat after: lft poor 5th last* 100/1

P05- 6 9 **Murtys Delight (IRE)**[16] 2748 6-10-12 0 .... (t) AndrewTinkler 82
(Dr Richard Newland) *in rr: sme hdwy 6th: nvr on terms* 33/1

6- 7 ½ **Highpower (IRE)**[23] 2602 4-10-12 0 .... RichieMcGrath 82
(Jonjo O'Neill) *in rr: drvn after 5th: nvr on terms* 80/1

454- 8 1 **Royal Palladium (FR)**[13] 2808 5-10-9 0 .... RobertDunne(3) 81
(Venetia Williams) *mid-div: outpcd 5th: no ch after* 40/1

63- 9 3¼ **Rocky Stone (IRE)**[10] 2866 5-10-12 0 .... AdrianLane 78
(Donald McCain) *in rr: j.rt 1st: sme hdwy 5th: wknd next* 100/1

40- 10 1¼ **Clubs Are Trumps (IRE)**[19] 2695 4-10-12 0 .... DougieCostello 77
(Jonjo O'Neill) *chsd ldrs: outpcd after 5th: lost pl after next* 100/1

6/0- 11 11 **Torgamah Lad (IRE)**[29] 2467 5-10-12 0 .... LiamTreadwell 67
(Venetia Williams) *mid-div: sme hdwy 4th: lost pl 6th* 40/1

/55- 12 3 **Western Movie**[18] 2711 5-10-12 0 .... TomO'Brien 64
(Philip Hobbs) *in rr: wl bhd fr 5th* 40/1

/00- 13 32 **Grand Gigolo (FR)**[23] 2602 4-10-12 0 .... WayneHutchinson 35
(Ian Williams) *nt jump wl in rr: wl bhd 5th: t.o bef 2 out: virtually p.u* 100/1

/50- 14 20 **Devil's Dyke (USA)**[18] 2718 5-10-12 0 .... PaulMoloney 17
(Evan Williams) *mid-div: drvn 5th: sn lost pl and bhd: t.o bef 2 out: virtually p.u* 33/1

0- F **Storm Of Swords (IRE)**[26] 2534 5-10-12 0 .... HarrySkelton 101
(Dan Skelton) *chsd ldr: drvn 6th: wknd between last 2: modest 4th whn fell heavily last* 8/1[2]

4m 3.7s (-7.20) **Going Correction** -0.025s/f (Good)
WFA 4 from 5yo+ 5lb 15 Ran SP% 128.8
Speed ratings (Par 105): **115,114,113,103,101 97,97,97,95,94 89,88,73,63,**
toteswingers 1&2 £3.40, 1&3 £4.30, 2&3 £1.30 CSF £204.22 TOTE £19.60: £3.70, £2.40, £1.02; EX 82.50 Trifecta £203.70 Pool: £2614.15 - 9.62 winning units..
Owner Mrs Sue Griffiths **Bred** Beech Hill Stud **Trained** Upper Lambourn, Berks

FOCUS
This event has been won by some pretty smart novices in the past decade or so, among them My Way De Solzen, Whiteoak, Peddlers Cross and Backspin. The pace was moderate and only a handful got into this, which saw a dramatic twist as the short-priced Diamond King threw it away at the last. He's rated to his mark, with a big step up from the winner on his bumper form.

3062 RACING UK CONDITIONAL JOCKEYS' H'CAP HURDLE (9 hdls) 2m 1f
2:55 (2:59) (Class 5) (0-100,98) 3-Y-0+ **£2,395** (£698; £349)

Form RPR

303- 1 **Kayfrou**[106] 1433 8-10-5 **85** .... GLavery(8) 90
(Brian Ellison) *hld up in rr: hdwy after 5th: chsng ldrs next: upsides last: led last 50yds: jst hld on* 15/8[1]

232/ 2 shd **The Darling Boy**[510] 1028 8-11-3 **95** .... (tp) KieronEdgar(6) 100
(David Pipe) *led: jnd last: hdd last 50yds: rallied and jst denied* 9/2[3]

036- 3 2¼ **Good Of Luck**[93] 1567 4-11-5 **94** .... (p) GavinSheehan(3) 97
(Warren Greatrex) *chsd ldrs: 2nd 3 out: styd on same pce appr last* 7/1

/60- 4 2 **Going Nowhere Fast (IRE)**[15] 2766 8-11-3 **89** .... KillianMoore 90
(Bernard Llewellyn) *mid-div: chsd ldrs 5th: outpcd appr 2 out: kpt on run-in: tk 4th nr fin* 20/1

012- 5 nk **Poetic Power (IRE)**[20] 2679 4-11-2 **94** .... GeraldQuinn(6) 94
(Claire Dyson) *chsd ldrs: drvn appr 2 out: one pce* 13/2

P06- 6 1¼ **Terntheothercheek**[8] 2896 4-9-11 **72** .... (p) ConorRing(3) 71
(Jennie Candlish) *chsd ldr: drvn 6th: outpcd appr 2 out: one pce* 16/1

/04- 7 3¼ **Lean Burn (USA)**[27] 2511 7-10-9 **81** .... KielanWoods 77
(Barry Leavy) *in rr: drvn to chse ldrs bef 2 out: one pce: fdd run-in* 4/1[2]

/60- 8 14 **Tyrur Ted**[36] 2315 8-11-7 **93** .... (tp) PatrickCorbett 76
(Frank Sheridan) *chsd ldrs: lost pl after 3 out: bhd next* 22/1

600- 9 1¼ **Keen Eye (IRE)**[19] 2696 4-11-4 **98** .... TommieMO'Brien(8) 80
(Jonjo O'Neill) *in rr: bhd and drvn 5th: t.o 2 out* 25/1

06P/ P **Final Flyer (IRE)**[359] 3135 9-9-11 **74** .... OllieGarner(5)
(Nikki Evans) *in rr: drvn 3rd: bhd fr 6th: t.o whn p.u after 3 out* 66/1

4m 11.0s (0.10) **Going Correction** -0.025s/f (Good)
WFA 4 from 7yo+ 5lb 10 Ran SP% 119.1
Speed ratings (Par 103): **98,97,96,95,95 95,93,87,86,**
toteswingers 1&2 £3.20, 1&3 £4.70, 2&3 £6.50 CSF £10.82 CT £49.74 TOTE £4.10: £1.70, £1.50, £2.80; EX 16.30 Trifecta £88.40 Pool: £3106.54 - 26.35 winning units..
Owner Dan Gilbert & Kristian Strangeway **Bred** D J And Mrs Deer **Trained** Norton, N Yorks

FOCUS
An interesting event for conditional jockeys, and form that might be worth treating positively. The first three were all debuting for new yards. The winner is on a good mark and is rated 3lb off best.

3063 MAELOR INTERMEDIATE OPEN NATIONAL HUNT FLAT RACE 2m 1f
3:25 (3:29) (Class 6) 4-6-Y-0 **£2,053** (£598; £299)

Form RPR

1 **Stellar Notion (IRE)**[208] 5-11-2 0 .... PaddyBrennan 115+
(Tom George) *hld up in mid-div: hdwy 6f out: chsng ldr over 4f out: upsides over 3f out: led appr fnl f: styd on wl clsng stages* 4/1[2]

1- 2 2 **Desoto County**[21] 2660 4-11-9 0 .... JasonMaguire 120+
(Donald McCain) *led: jnd over 2f out: hdd appr fnl f: kpt on same pce* 8/11[1]

42- 3 10 **Uppingham**[22] 2627 4-11-2 0 .... BrianHughes 103
(Malcolm Jefferson) *hld up towards rr: hdwy 6f out: modest 3rd 3f out: one pce* 5/1[3]

4 15 **River Clare (IRE)**[61] 5-10-9 0 .... CiaranMckee(7) 89
(John O'Shea) *hld up in rr: hdwy to chse ldr 7f out: wknd over 2f out* 16/1

46- 5 25 **Iouascore (IRE)**[45] 2153 6-10-9 0 .... MissLBrooke(7) 63
(Lady Susan Brooke) *t.k.h: trckd ldrs: lost pl over 4f out: sn bhd* 100/1

5/ 6 ¾ **Brogeen Boy (IRE)**[346] 3430 5-11-2 0 .... JackDoyle 62
(Alan Jones) *chsd ldr: lost pl over 4f out: sn bhd* 50/1

7 11 **Miss Twiggs** 4-10-9 0 .... LiamHeard 44
(Barry Leavy) *gave problems s: in rr: lost tch 6f out* 50/1

8 34 **Moel Famau** 4-10-9 0 .... AndrewTinkler 10
(Nicky Henderson) *chsd ldrs: drvn 6f out: sn lost pl: t.o over 2f out: virtually p.u* 13/2

4m 8.6s (3.30) **Going Correction** -0.025s/f (Good) 8 Ran SP% 118.7
Speed ratings: **91,90,85,78,66 66,61,45**
toteswingers 1&2 £1.70, 1&3 £3.40, 2&3 £1.50 CSF £7.59 TOTE £5.90: £1.30, £1.10, £1.40; EX 10.40 Trifecta £32.20 Pool: £4127.99 - 96.10 winning units..
Owner R S Brookhouse **Bred** Meadhill Stables **Trained** Slad, Gloucs

FOCUS
The first two drew clear off a steady gallop in this bumper, and both look to have plenty of ability.
T/Plt: £12.40 to a £1 stake. Pool: £44094.01 - 2580.85 winning tickets T/Qpdt: £3.70 to a £1 stake. Pool: £3151.04 - 628.30 winning tickets WG

2529 CHELTENHAM (L-H)
Friday, December 13

OFFICIAL GOING: Good (good to firm in places on cross-country course; hdl 7.4, chs 7.4, cross-country 7.6)
Wind: Moderate across Weather: Overcast

3064 RYMAN STATIONERY CHELTENHAM BUSINESS CLUB NOVICES' CHASE (17 fncs) 2m 5f
12:30 (12:30) (Class 2) 4-Y-0+ **£12,627** (£3,811; £1,963; £1,039)

Form RPR

4/2- 1 **Oscar Whisky (IRE)**[28] 2489 8-11-0 0 .... BarryGeraghty 154+
(Nicky Henderson) *mde all: nt fluent 13th and 4 out: rdn after 2 out: jnd last: drvn and styd on strly run-in: a doing enough* 4/5[1]

111- 2 ½ **Wonderful Charm (FR)**[14] 2799 5-11-8 152 .... (t) DarylJacob 159+
(Paul Nicholls) *trckd wnr: qcknd fr 2 out to chal last: kpt on wl run-in but a hld by wnr clsng stages* 5/4[2]

105- 3 76 **Red Riverman**[19] 2694 5-11-8 124 .... SamTwiston-Davies 103
(Nigel Twiston-Davies) *racd in 4th: nt fluent 4th: hit 11th: lft poor 3rd 4 out* 50/1

4 73 **Captain Ocana (IRE)**[83] 1620 8-11-5 114 .... NickScholfield 7
(Paul Henderson) *a in last: t.o fr 7th* 100/1

0/0- F **Close House**[27] 2504 6-11-0 0 .... (t) TomScudamore
(David Pipe) *trckd ldng duo: nt fluent 10th: 5 l off wnr and travelling ok whn fell 4 out* 14/1[3]

5m 14.52s (-4.88) **Going Correction** +0.15s/f (Yiel) 5 Ran SP% 109.6
Speed ratings (Par 109): **115,114,85,58,**
CSF £2.22 TOTE £1.90: £1.10, £1.10; EX 2.40 Trifecta £7.00 Pool: £2481.67 - 263.32 winning units..
Owner Walters Plant Hire Ltd **Bred** Stephanie Hanly **Trained** Upper Lambourn, Berks

FOCUS
All races on New Course except race 5: Cross Country. The course officials had selectively watered twice during the past fortnight to ensure the ground was not quick and got aided by 1mm of overnight rain. The going looked perfectly sound in the opening novice chase. Oscar Whisky stepped up on his chase debut and Wonderful Charm showed smart form in defeat.

3065 CASPIAN CAVIAR CONDITIONAL JOCKEYS' H'CAP CHASE (JOCKEY CLUB GRASSROOTS JUMPS SERIES QUALIFIER) (17 fncs) 2m 5f
1:05 (1:05) (Class 3) (0-125,125) 4-Y-0+
£7,507 (£2,217; £1,108; £554; £277; £139)

12- 1 **King Massini (IRE)**[9] 2887 7-10-12 **114** .... AdamWedge(3) 129+
(Evan Williams) *trckd ldrs: led appr 2 out: rdn last: sn jnd: narrowly hdd fnl 150yds: styd upsides u.p: led again last stride* 5/1[2]

340/ 2 nse **Hit The Headlines (IRE)**[19] 2707 7-11-3 **119** .... KeithDonoghue(3) 133+
(Gordon Elliott, Ire) *mid-div: hdwy 3 out: drvn to chal last: styd upsides tl slt advantage fnl 150yds: remained hrd pressed tl hdd last stride* 9/2[1]

1P5/ 3 13 **Max Bygraves**[734] 3064 10-11-9 **122** .... ConorShoemark 123
(Kim Bailey) *in tch: hmpd 4 out: hdwy and hit 3 out: styd on u.p fr 2 out to take 3rd run-in but no ch w ldng duo* 16/1

U35- 4 ¾ **Al Alfa**[21] 2645 6-11-1 **117** .... JamesBest(3) 120
(Philip Hobbs) *chsd ldrs: hit 7th: rdn to chse wnr 2 out: no imp: outpcd last: lost 3rd run-in* 7/1[3]

0/P- 5 2 **Overclear**[43] 2180 11-11-7 **120** .... [1] GilesHawkins 120
(Victor Dartnall) *chsd ldrs: rdn and hit 3 out: wknd bef last* 25/1

653- 6 2 **Marley Roca (IRE)**[14] 2785 9-11-12 **125** .... (p) JakeGreenall 123
(Paul Webber) *chsd ldrs: hit 8th: wknd bef last* 25/1

7 2¾ **Friendly Society (IRE)**[58] 1932 8-11-2 **115** .... (p) ThomasGarner 110
(Noel Williams) *in rr: sme hdwy whn hmpd 4 out: hit next: styd on fr 2 out but nvr a threat* 20/1

/12- 8 6 **Richmond (FR)**[22] 2633 8-11-7 **123** .... HarryChalloner(3) 116
(Venetia Williams) *mid-div: j. slowly: mstke 13th: hmpd 4 out: mod prog after 3 out* 7/1[3]

64F- 9 2¾ **Donnas Palm (IRE)**[21] 2645 9-11-6 **122** .... (p) JoshuaMoore(3) 109
(Gary Moore) *hit 1st: in rr: hit 7th: rdn 11th: nvr nr ldrs* 20/1

050- 10 2¼ **Owen Glendower (IRE)**[34] 2373 8-11-12 **125** .... (t) HarryDerham 113
(Sophie Leech) *in rr: mstke 8th: stl bhd whn hmpd 4 out: mstke next: n.d* 12/1

/30- 11 ¾ **Have You Seen Me (IRE)**[28] 2488 10-11-6 **125** .... (t) RyanHatch(6) 109
(Nigel Twiston-Davies) *led tl hdd appr 2 out: sn btn* 14/1

0PP- 12 8 **Finger Onthe Pulse (IRE)**[14] 2785 12-11-4 **125** .... (t) JamesHuxham(8) 102
(Jonjo O'Neill) *hit 6th: towards rr most of way* 20/1

004- 13 12 **Diamond Frontier (IRE)**[35] 2346 10-10-12 **117** .... JohnDawson(6) 83
(John Wade) *prom tl lost pl 5th: bhd fr 1/2-way* 40/1

332- 14 nk **Ballymoat**[36] 2308 6-10-8 **110** .... (t) MichaelByrne(3) 80
(Tim Vaughan) *hit 3rd: in rr: blnd and rdr lost iron 8th: hit 10th: bhd whn hmpd 4 out* 14/1

0P- 15 39 **Vif Argent (FR)**[19] 2694 4-10-13 **125** .... TomBellamy(6) 49
(David Pipe) *hmpd 4 out: a towards rr* 12/1

P22- F **Atlanta Falcon (IRE)**[31] 2446 8-11-4 **123** .... (tp) NickSlatter(6)
(Donald McCain) *chsd ldrs: 5 l 5th and gng ok whn fell 4 out* 11/1

5m 18.38s (-1.02) **Going Correction** +0.15s/f (Yiel)
WFA 4 from 6yo+ 6lb 16 Ran SP% 127.2
Speed ratings (Par 107): **107,106,102,101,100 100,99,96,95,94 94,91,87,86,72**
toteswingers 1&2 £5.40, 1&3 £12.90, 2&3 £22.70 CSF £26.77 CT £353.39 TOTE £6.40: £2.00, £1.90, £4.60, £2.30; EX 32.00 Trifecta £1806.30 Pool: £2611.51 - 1.08 winning units..
Owner Border Pointers **Bred** Tim Jones **Trained** Llancarfan, Vale Of Glamorgan

FOCUS
This handicap, confined to conditional riders, was wide open. They went a sound gallop but not for the first time in such contests here it proved an advantage to race handily and there was a cracking two-way finish. The winner was on a good mark but this rates a small step up.

3066 CF ROBERTS ELECTRICAL + MECHANICAL SERVICES H'CAP HURDLE (8 hdls) 2m 1f
1:40 (1:40) (Class 3) (0-135,135) 3-Y-0+
£7,507 (£2,217; £1,108; £554; £277; £139)

Form RPR

/11- 1 **The Skyfarmer**[15] 2761 5-11-0 **123** .... RichardJohnson 138+
(Philip Hobbs) *in tch: hdwy 3 out: chal 2 out: rdr dropped whip bef last: led sn after drvn: fnd plenty fnl 150yds: r.o strly* 4/1[2]

The Form Book Jumps, Raceform Ltd, Compton, RG20 6NL.

0/4- **2** *4* **Lyvius**[41] 2211 5-11-4 **127** BarryGeraghty 138+
(Nicky Henderson) *hld up in rr but in tch: hdwy appr 2 out: chsd wnr wl bef last and sn chal gng ok: no ex u.p and outpcd fnl 150yds* **7/1**[3]

022- **3** *27* **Canadian Diamond (IRE)**[25] 2561 6-10-13 **127**.........(p) JamesBanks(5) 114
(Brendan Powell) *t.k.h: trckd ldrs: chal 3 out: led sn after: jnd 2 out: hdd sn after and dropped to 3rd wl bef last: no ch w ldng duo after but hld on for 3rd run-in* **8/1**

621- **4** *3 1/4* **Zafranagar (IRE)**[25] 2561 8-10-4 **113** TomScudamore 97
(Ian Williams) *hld up in rr: hdwy fr 4 out: chsd ldrs u.p in 4th after 2 out but nvr any ch and sn wl hld* **7/1**[3]

410- **5** *1 3/4* **Dresden (IRE)**[28] 2492 5-11-0 **123** WillKennedy 107
(Sarah-Jayne Davies) *in rr: rdn 3 out: mod prog u.p appr last* **16/1**

/04- **6** *1 1/2* **Dan Breen (IRE)**[21] 2656 8-11-5 **135**.........(p) MikeyEnnis(7) 116
(David Pipe) *chsd ldrs: rdn after 4th and 4 out: dropped to rr 3 out: mod prog again run-in* **20/1**

/12- **7** *7* **Uhlan Bute (FR)**[7] 2932 5-10-11 **120** AidanColeman 96
(Venetia Williams) *chsd ldrs: rdn after 2 out: sn wknd* **7/2**[1]

/24- **8** *1/2* **Maxi Chop (FR)**[28] 2492 5-11-2 **125** DarylJacob 102
(Paul Nicholls) *in rr but in tch: hdwy 3 out: in tch next: wknd sn after* **7/2**[1]

010- **9** *32* **Glencree (IRE)**[42] 2198 9-10-9 **118**.........(p) WilsonRenwick 64
(John Wade) *led: jnd 3 out: sn hdd & wknd* **50/1**

4m 1.31s (-9.99) **Going Correction** -0.05s/f (Good) **9** Ran SP% **113.2**
Speed ratings (Par 107): **121,119,106,104,104 103,100,99,84**
toteswingers 1&2 £8.70, 1&3 £11.60, 2&3 £33.60 CSF £31.47 CT £211.10 TOTE £4.30: £1.50, £2.40, £2.20; EX 31.80 Trifecta £241.10 Pool: £2630.48 - 8.18 winning units..
Owner Mrs Joanna Peppiatt **Bred** Barkfold Manor Stud **Trained** Withycombe, Somerset

FOCUS
A fair handicap. They went an average sort of gallop and, with the field getting sorted out from the penultimate flight, the first pair had it to themselves from the last. A massive step up from the winner and there's a case for rating the form a lot higher.

3067 MAJORDOMO HOSPITALITY H'CAP CHASE (GRADE 3) (21 fncs) 3m 1f 110y
2:10 (2:10) (Class 1) 4-Y-0+

£25,627 (£9,616; £4,815; £2,398; £1,206; £603)

Form RPR

/34- **1** **Monbeg Dude (IRE)**[27] 2502 8-11-0 **138** TomScudamore 151+
(Michael Scudamore) *in rr but in tch: hdwy 11th: chsd ldrs fr 16th: wnt 2nd appr 2 out: chal travelling wl last: pushed along to ld sn after: styd on strly* **6/1**[3]

/33- **2** *1 1/4* **Theatre Guide (IRE)**[13] 2815 6-11-9 **147**.........(t) JoeTizzard 158+
(Colin Tizzard) *in tch: hit 12th: hdwy to chse ldrs 16th: chal fr next tl led bef 2 out travelling wl: drvn and jnd last: hdd sn after: kpt on but nt gng pce of wnr* **7/2**[1]

025- **3** *16* **Pigeon Island**[20] 2674 10-10-10 **134**.........(vt) SamTwiston-Davies 131
(Nigel Twiston-Davies) *in rr: hdwy 15th: rdn 4 out and lostpl: styd on again u.p fr 2 out to take 3rd run-in but nvr any ch w ldng duo* **12/1**

P10/ **4** *1 3/4* **Prince Of Pirates (IRE)**[274] 4751 8-11-0 **138** APMcCoy 133
(Nicky Henderson) *in rr: hdwy 4 out: drvn to cl after 3 out: wnt one pce 3rd 2 out: nvr rchd ldrs: wknd into 4th run-in* **9/2**[2]

512- **5** *1 1/4* **Knockara Beau (IRE)**[27] 2502 10-11-10 **148** JanFaltejsek 144
(George Charlton) *led: hdd 10th: hit 14th and sn rr: wl bhd 3 out: styd on again fr 2 out: kpt on run-in* **9/1**

602- **6** *1 1/4* **Duke Of Lucca (IRE)**[21] 2646 8-10-11 **135**.........(bt) RichardJohnson 132
(Philip Hobbs) *chsd ldrs: hit 8th: blnd 4 out: hit 3 out: btn whn mstke 2 out* **6/1**[3]

1/U- **7** *7* **Quentin Collonges (FR)**[27] 2502 9-11-1 **142**.........(t) JakeGreenall(3) 129
(Henry Daly) *chsd ldr 11th: led appr next: hdd 4 out: mstke 3 out and wknd: bhd whn blnd 2 out* **15/2**

P13- **8** *1/2* **Aimigayle**[11] 2860 10-10-1 **124** oh2 ow1 ColinBolger 111
(Suzy Smith) *chsd ldr: led 10th: hdd appr 12th: chal 15th to 17th: led 4 out: hdd & wknd bef 2 out* **8/1**

/50- **9** *22* **Burton Port (IRE)**[27] 2502 9-11-12 **150** RichieMcLernon 115
(Jonjo O'Neill) *a in rr* **25/1**

6m 34.05s (-4.15) **Going Correction** +0.15s/f (Yiel) **9** Ran SP% **113.4**
Speed ratings (Par 113): **112,111,106,106,105 105,103,103,96**
toteswingers 1&2 £2.20, 1&3 £8.20, 2&3 £5.30 CSF £27.65 CT £242.47 TOTE £6.50: £2.10, £2.00, £2.70; EX 28.90 Trifecta £268.60 Pool: £2790.36 - 7.79 winning units..
Owner Oydunow **Bred** Hilary O'Connor **Trained** Bromsash, H'fords

FOCUS
A good-quality staying handicap, run at a fair gallop, and it proved another race where two came clear late on. Monbeg Dude looks a realistic National contender on this evidence and Theatre Guide confirmed the merit of his Hennessy run.

3068 GLENFARCLAS CROSS COUNTRY H'CAP CHASE (32 fncs) 3m 7f
2:40 (2:42) (Class 2) 5-Y-0+

£21,896 (£6,468; £3,234; £1,617; £808; £406)

Form RPR

/06- **1** **Sire Collonges (FR)**[28] 2491 7-11-10 **139**.........(p) RyanMahon 149
(Paul Nicholls) *led 3rd to 18th: led again 20th: hdd: 22: lost pl 26th: styd on again u.p fr 2 out to ld fnl 175yds: kpt on gamely* **7/1**[3]

P53- **2** *1/2* **Any Currency (IRE)**[28] 2491 10-10-12 **127**.........(p) IanPopham 137
(Martin Keighley) *chsd ldrs: rdn 23rd and lost pl: styd on u.p fr 2 out: kpt on wl run-in to take 2nd clsng stages: nt rch wnr* **9/2**[2]

0/ **3** *2 1/4* **Pasquini Rouge (FR)**[47] 5-10-12 **126** ow1.........(tp) DavidCottin 135
(Patrice Quinton, France) *chsd ldrs: chal fr 14th tl led 18th: hdd 20th: led 4 out: rdn fr 3 out: hdd and no ex fnl 175yds* **16/1**

/10- **4** *hd* **Imperial Circus (IRE)**[28] 2487 7-10-8 **123**.........(p) RichardJohnson 131
(Philip Hobbs) *in rr: hdwy fr 17th: mstke 4 out and 3 out: chsd ldrs fr next: styd on u.p run-in* **8/1**

5UF- **5** *7* **Shalimar Fromentro (FR)**[34] 2384 7-10-11 **126**.........(p) JamesReveley 126
(Nick Williams) *led to 3rd: led again 27th: hdd 4 out: wknd run-in* **8/1**

6 *31* **Keep On Track (IRE)**[27] 2526 6-10-1 **116** MsNCarberry 99
(E Bolger, Ire) *chsd ldrs: led 22nd: hdd 24th: led 25th to 27th: wknd last* **3/1**[1]

P/5- **7** *3 1/4* **Chicago Grey (IRE)**[28] 2491 10-11-12 **141**.........(t) MrJJCodd 120
(Gordon Elliott, Ire) *bhd most of way* **15/2**

4U- **8** *43* **Quercy Du Manoir (FR)**[34] 2384 9-9-7 **115** oh2.........(bt) MrGCottreau(7) 46
(Jean-Paul Gasnier, France) *bhd most of way* **9/1**

/U0- **9** *79* **Zest For Life (IRE)**[28] 2491 9-10-10 **130**.........(p) MrSWaley-Cohen(5)
(E Bolger, Ire) *a towards rr* **33/1**

0/6- **10** *74* **Save My Blushes**[18] 2721 7-9-7 **115** oh1..(p) MissEvannaMcCutcheon(7)
(Denis Gerard Hogan, Ire) *nt jump wl: a in rr* **66/1**

0F0- **P** **Qulinton (FR)**[56] 1956 9-11-3 **132** RhysFlint
(Johnny Farrelly) *chsd ldrs: wknd 19th: blnd and p.u 21st* **33/1**

50F/ **S** **Jacks Island (IRE)**[8] 2915 10-10-8 **123** SamTwiston-Davies
(J P Kenny, Ire) *chsd ldrs: led 24th to next: stl in tch but u.p whn slipped up bnd bef 2 out* **40/1**

P **Taiga Des Chambres (FR)**[47] 6-10-5 **125**.........(bt) ColmMcCormack(5)
(Patrice Quinton, France) *in rr: blnd 4th and 25th: t.o whn p.u bef 27th* **50/1**

8m 17.9s (-20.10) **Going Correction** -0.375s/f (Good) **13** Ran SP% **117.3**
Speed ratings: **110,109,109,109,107 99,98,87,67,48 , ,**
toteswingers 1&2 £6.70, 1&3 £88.90, 2&3 £23.90 CSF £37.59 CT £492.56 TOTE £8.50: £2.60, £2.10, £2.60; EX 38.50 Trifecta £526.10 Pool: £3612.59 - 5.14 winning units..
Owner Mrs Angela Tincknell & W Tincknell **Bred** Gaec Delorme Freres **Trained** Ditcheat, Somerset

FOCUS
This Cross Country handicap, which had an international flavour, was run at a routine gallop until the leaders kicked on around four out. They ultimately went too soon and it saw changing fortunes in the home straight. The first two set the level.

3069 CITIPOST H'CAP HURDLE (12 hdls) 3m
3:15 (3:15) (Class 2) 4-Y-0+

£13,763 (£4,065; £2,032; £1,016; £508; £255)

Form RPR

U/0- **1** **Sunnyhillboy (IRE)**[27] 2504 10-10-8 **128** APMcCoy 132
(Jonjo O'Neill) *in rr: hdwy 8th: chal fr 2 out and stl upsides last: rallied u.p run-in to ld fnl 110yds: rdn out* **10/1**

2/1- **2** *3/4* **Return Spring (IRE)**[27] 2504 6-10-10 **130** RichardJohnson 133
(Philip Hobbs) *chsd ldrs: rdn after 2 out: kpt on u.p run-in to chse wnr clsng stages but a hld* **7/1**[3]

130- **3** *1/2* **So Fine (IRE)**[35] 2345 7-10-9 **132** JamesBest(3) 136
(Philip Hobbs) *chsd ldrs: slt ld and hit 2 out: stl narrow advantage last: hdd sn after: one pce fnl 100yds* **20/1**

/13- **4** *hd* **Southfield Theatre (IRE)**[27] 2504 5-11-10 **144** DarylJacob 146
(Paul Nicholls) *chsd ldrs: led 5th: narrowly hdd 2 out: styd chalng and slt ld again sn after last: hdd and no ex fnl 110yds* **11/4**[1]

/20- **5** *3 1/4* **Mister Dillon**[170] 845 6-10-10 **130** BarryGeraghty 129
(Nicky Henderson) *in tch: hdwy appr 2 out: sn chsng ldrs: styd on same pce u.p run-in* **11/1**

/12- **6** *hd* **Angles Hill (IRE)**[28] 2490 6-10-0 **125** ConorShoemark(5) 124
(Richard Woollacott) *in tch: hdwy 3 out: chsd ldrs and rdn after 2 out: no imp and kpt on same pce run-in* **11/1**

003- **7** *3* **Red Not Blue (IRE)**[14] 2798 10-10-7 **127** DominicElsworth 123
(Simon Earle) *in rr: rdn after 2 out: hdwy u.p appr last: no imp on ldrs* **25/1**

/11- **8** *3 1/4* **Thomas Crapper**[28] 2490 6-11-0 **134** CharliePoste 128
(Robin Dickin) *in rr: hdwy after 4 out: drvn to chal 2 out: wknd appr last* **9/2**[2]

2/0- **9** *2* **Destroyer Deployed**[210] 358 7-10-3 **126**.........(v) MichaelByrne(3) 118
(Tim Vaughan) *chsd ldr to 4th: wknd after 2 out* **14/1**

523- **10** *14* **Abruzzi**[21] 2655 5-9-9 **120** BenPoste(5) 97
(Tom Symonds) *led: hit 4th: hdd 5th: wknd after 3 out* **8/1**

/06- **11** *99* **Edgardo Sol (FR)**[20] 2671 6-11-7 **146** HarryDerham(5) 24
(Paul Nicholls) *a in rr: t.o after 3 out* **16/1**

6m 9.32s (8.32) **Going Correction** -0.05s/f (Good) **11** Ran SP% **115.4**
Speed ratings (Par 109): **84,83,83,83,82 82,81,80,79,74 41**
toteswingers 1&2 £24.30, 1&3 £76.90, 2&3 £27.20 CSF £77.28 CT £1375.33 TOTE £10.00: £2.70, £2.00, £6.20; EX 96.60 Trifecta £2757.20 Pool: £3907.89 - 1.06 winning units..
Owner John P McManus **Bred** J P N Parker **Trained** Cheltenham, Gloucs

FOCUS
They went just an average gallop in this competitive staying handicap and it saw any number in with a chance nearing the last. Perhaps not the most reliable piece of form.

3070 BRITISH STALLION STUDS EBF NATIONAL HUNT NOVICES' HURDLE (QUALIFIER) (8 hdls) 2m 1f
3:45 (3:51) (Class 3) 4-6-Y-0

£7,507 (£2,217; £1,108; £554; £277; £139)

Form RPR

/11- **1** **Ballyalton (IRE)**[13] 2819 6-11-8 140 APMcCoy 136+
(Ian Williams) *trckd ldrs: blnd 4 out: chal 2 out: slt ld sn after: hrd pressed last: drvn run-in: hld on wl* **11/4**[2]

/11- **2** *nk* **Garde La Victoire (FR)**[23] 2602 4-11-8 135 RichardJohnson 135+
(Philip Hobbs) *chsd ldrs: chal fr 2 out and stl upsides fr last: kpt on u.p but nt quite gng pce of wnr clsng stages* **7/4**[1]

4/ **3** *9* **Cocktails At Dawn**[359] 3146 5-10-12 0 BarryGeraghty 116
(Nicky Henderson) *chsd ldrs: drvn to chal 2 out: outpcd by ldng duo appr last* **5/1**[3]

/50- **4** *5* **Ballyhooley Boy (IRE)**[21] 2642 6-10-12 0 CharliePoste 111
(Robin Dickin) *in rr: hdwy to cl on ldrs 2 out: nvr quite on terms and styd on same pce sn after* **66/1**

/11- **5** *1* **Doctor Harper (IRE)**[19] 2689 5-11-8 140 TomScudamore 122
(David Pipe) *led tl after 2nd: led again after 4 out: jnd 2 out: hdd sn after wknd wl bef last* **11/4**[2]

000- **6** *10* **Ghost Of A Smile (IRE)**[14] 2802 5-10-12 0 WillKennedy 101
(Ian Williams) *led after 2nd: wandered 3rd and 4th: mstke 4 out and sn hdd: wknd fr 3 out* **66/1**

204- **7** *9* **Fond Memory (IRE)**[21] 2644 5-10-12 0 SamTwiston-Davies 91
(Nigel Twiston-Davies) *a in rr* **33/1**

/43- **8** *3/4* **Hawaii Five Nil (IRE)**[18] 2711 5-10-12 0 RichieMcLernon 90
(Jonjo O'Neill) *in tch: chsd ldrs 3 out: wknd next* **33/1**

06- **9** *16* **Modeligo (IRE)**[30] 2453 4-10-5 0 MrJMRidley(7) 74
(Matt Sheppard) *screwed 1st: a in rr* **150/1**

4m 12.56s (1.26) **Going Correction** -0.05s/f (Good)
WFA 4 from 5yo+ 5lb **9** Ran SP% **115.9**
Speed ratings: **95,94,90,88,87 83,78,78,70**
toteswingers 1&2 £1.20, 1&3 £2.80, 2&3 £2.50 CSF £8.18 TOTE £4.00: £1.40, £1.10, £1.60; EX 8.00 Trifecta £27.70 Pool: £6402.22 - 173.09 winning units..
Owner John Westwood **Bred** P Doyle **Trained** Portway, Worcs

FOCUS
This was a hot novice hurdle. After the field stood still for around 20 seconds as the tapes went up and set a dawdling early gallop, it proved a tactical race but the first pair both look smart. The first three are rated in line with their previous runs but all should rate higher.

T/Jkpt: Not won. T/Plt: £132.40 to a £1 stake. Pool: £154444.80 - 851.17 winning tickets T/Qpdt: £55.30 to a £1 stake. Pool: £11487.90 - 153.60 winning tickets ST

3071 - 3077a (Foreign Racing) - See Raceform Interactive

[3064]CHELTENHAM (L-H)

Saturday, December 14

OFFICIAL GOING: Good (7.6)

Wind: Brisk across Weather: Sunny spells

3078 JCB TRIUMPH HURDLE TRIAL (A JUVENILE HURDLE) (8 hdls) 2m 1f

12:10 (12:12) (Class 2) 3-Y-O

£12,512 (£3,696; £1,848; £924; £462; £232)

Form RPR

133- 1 **Ballyglasheen (IRE)**[30] 2466 3-11-3 120 PaulMoloney 124
(Evan Williams) *w'like: chunky: disp 2nd tl dropped to 3rd 3 out: hdwy to cl again whn pckd 2 out: drvn to chal last and styd upsides tl narrow ld fnl 150yds: hld on all out* **33/1**

1- 2 *nk* **Kentucky Hyden (IRE)**[35] 2364 3-11-7 135 BarryGeraghty 127
(Nicky Henderson) *tall: disp 2nd tl trckd ldr 3 out: led next: hrd drvn bef last and sn jnd: hdd u.p fnl 150yds: no ex clsng stages* **7/4**[2]

3 *3 ¾* **Commissioned (IRE)**[61] 3-11-0 0 JackQuinlan 118+
(John Ferguson) *hld up in rr: stdy hdwy to trck ldrs 2 out: disp 2nd appr last whn nt fluent: kpt on to hold 3rd run-in but no imp on ldng duo* **9/2**[3]

4 *2* **Vicenzo Mio (FR)**[102] 3-11-7 131 DarylJacob 123
(Paul Nicholls) *hld up in rr but in tch: hdwy to cl on ldrs 2 out: nt mouch room: swtchd lft and nt fluent last: no ex and dropped to 4th run-in* **13/8**[1]

2- 5 *34* **Cadoudoff (FR)**[43] 2200 3-11-7 124 (p) AidanColeman 91
(Charlie Longsdon) *led tl hdd and hit 2 out: sn wknd* **15/2**

6 *99* **Burgoyne (USA)**[33] 3-11-0 0 RobertThornton
(C Von Der Recke, Germany) *in rr: lost tch 3 out: t.o* **40/1**

4m 4.63s (-6.67) **Going Correction** -0.15s/f (Good) **6** Ran SP% **109.8**
Speed ratings (Par 108): **109,108,107,106,90 43**
toteswingers 1&2 £33.20, 1&3 £6.10, 2&3 £2.10 CSF £89.44 TOTE £14.40: £3.90, £1.20; EX 51.00 Trifecta £334.70 Pool: £14452.32 - 32.37 winning units..
Owner R J Gambarini **Bred** Mrs Evie Stockwell **Trained** Llancarfan, Vale Of Glamorgan

FOCUS
All races on New Course. An event that tends to suffer by being run on the same day as the Grade 2 Summit Hurdle at Doncaster. Katchit won this and the Triumph Hurdle itself in 2006-7, and Far West, who beat one other finisher in this race 12 months ago, found only Our Conor too good in the big one in March. . They went a reasonable pace but there were four still fighting it out on the long run to the last. There was a surprise winner but the time was fair and the form looks believable if well below the standard needed to make an impact in the Triumph.

3079 RYMAN STATIONERY NOVICES' CHASE (21 fncs) 3m 1f 110y

12:40 (12:42) (Class 2) 4-Y-O+ **£12,512** (£3,696; £1,848; £924)

Form RPR

3/3- 1 **Sam Winner (FR)**[28] 2501 6-11-1 140 DarylJacob 153+
(Paul Nicholls) *mde virtually all: nt fluent 13th: jnd fr 3 out: bmpd between last two and stl hrd pressed last: styd on gamely u.p to assert run-in* **11/4**[3]

/11- 2 *4* **Le Bec (FR)**[28] 2501 5-11-9 149 AidanColeman 158+
(Emma Lavelle) *lw: chsd wnr: nt fluent 10th: chal fr 3 out: edgd lft and bmpd between last two: stl upsides last: no ex and styd on same pce run-in* **7/4**[2]

U1U- 3 *25* **Le Reve (IRE)**[16] 2756 5-11-6 134 RichardJohnson 135
(Lucy Wadham) *racd in 4th and nt particularly fluent: hit 10th and bhd: sme hdwy 12th: sn bhd again: hit 4 out and 3 out: styd on to take mod 3rd fr 2 out* **16/1**

/12- 4 *6* **Shutthefrontdoor (IRE)**[28] 2501 6-11-6 0 APMcCoy 130
(Jonjo O'Neill) *racd in 3rd: hdwy and hit 17th: styng on same pce whn hit 4 out: sn no ch: hit 3 out: dropped to 4th next* **13/8**[1]

6m 26.45s (-11.75) **Going Correction** +0.05s/f (Yiel) **4** Ran SP% **107.0**
Speed ratings (Par 109): **120,118,111,109**
CSF £7.91 TOTE £3.70; EX 7.80 Trifecta £35.80 Pool: £1575.55 - 33.00 winning units..
Owner Mrs Angela Yeoman **Bred** Ecurie Winning **Trained** Ditcheat, Somerset

FOCUS
This involved three horses who clashed here last month on the Old Course, and they appeared to be potential RSA Chase candidates, but it's fair to say that recent history of this race (last ten years) doesn't suggest the winner holds leading claims for that, as only Darkness (2006) and Cornish Rebel (2007) placed in the staying novice event at the Festival, and none have won. That said, this was run at a sound gallop and gave them all valuable experience at a decent racing pace. The form looks pretty solid.

3080 JENNY MOULD MEMORIAL H'CAP CHASE (14 fncs) 2m 110y

1:15 (1:15) (Class 2) 4-Y-O+

£18,768 (£5,544; £2,772; £1,386; £693; £348)

Form RPR

/13- 1 **Eastlake (IRE)**[29] 2488 7-11-0 **140** APMcCoy 148+
(Jonjo O'Neill) *hld up in tch: gd hdwy 3 out: chsd ldrs next: chal last: drvn to take slt ld sn after: styd on wl u.p* **5/1**[1]

5/2- 2 *1* **French Opera**[21] 2664 10-11-10 **150** RobertThornton 155
(Nicky Henderson) *lw: in tch: chsd ldrs fr 4 out: chal fr 3 out tl drvn to take slt ld last: narrowly hdd sn after: kpt on but no imp on wnr* **16/1**

520- 3 *3 ¼* **Astracad (FR)**[28] 2503 7-11-2 **142** (vt) SamTwiston-Davies 146
(Nigel Twiston-Davies) *lw: chsd ldr: chal 10th: led appr 4 out: jnd next and hrd pressed 2 out and nt fluent: narrowly hdd last: styd on same pce* **6/1**[3]

102- 4 *7* **Parsnip Pete**[14] 2816 7-10-11 **137** PaddyBrennan 135
(Tom George) *blnd 1st: in rr: hdwy 3 out: chsd ldrs next: wknd after last* **12/1**

/22- 5 *1 ½* **Saved By John (IRE)**[21] 2666 8-10-10 **136** (t) RichardJohnson 131
(Tim Vaughan) *in rr: mstke 3rd: hdwy 7th: pressed ldrs 3 out: wknd after next* **10/1**

0/P- 6 *16* **Tanks For That (IRE)**[56] 1969 10-11-7 **147** BarryGeraghty 127
(Nicky Henderson) *chsd ldrs: rdn 3 out: wknd sn after* **7/1**

363- 7 *¾* **Greywell Boy**[14] 2816 6-10-0 **126** oh1 BrendanPowell 105
(Nick Williams) *chsd ldrs: rdn 9th: lost pl 4 out: mod prog again fr 2 out* **8/1**

/13- 8 *23* **Drumshambo (USA)**[21] 2666 7-11-8 **148** AidanColeman 107
(Venetia Williams) *in rr 5th: rdn and no ch fr 8th* **10/1**

55P/ 9 *2 ½* **Petit Robin (FR)**[238] 5403 10-11-7 **152** NicodeBoinville(5) 108
(Nicky Henderson) *hit 3rd: mstke 4th: bhd fr 8th* **11/2**[2]

6P6/ 10 *2 ¾* **Shooters Wood (IRE)**[242] 5335 9-10-13 **139** (t) DarylJacob 93
(Paul Nicholls) *led: jnd 10th: hdd appr 4 out: sn wknd* **17/2**

U55- 11 *73* **Anquetta (IRE)**[133] 1194 9-10-11 **142** MrSWaley-Cohen(5) 30
(Nicky Henderson) *bhd for 8th: no ch fr 10th: t.o* **25/1**

4m 2.53s (-4.17) **Going Correction** +0.05s/f (Yiel) **11** Ran SP% **116.1**
Speed ratings (Par 109): **111,110,109,105,105 97,97,86,85,83 49**
toteswingers 1&2 £23.40, 1&3 £4.70, 2&3 £15.30 CSF £77.54 CT £491.74 TOTE £4.90: £2.20, £4.20, £2.20; EX 110.50 Trifecta £606.30 Pool: £2123.60 - 2.62 winning units..
Owner John P McManus **Bred** Mrs Eleanor Hadden **Trained** Cheltenham, Gloucs

FOCUS
A classy and open handicap chase, run at a sound gallop. The form looks solid and should be relevant to races like the Johnny Henderson Grand Annual and the Red Rum Chase later in the season. The winner has developed into a smart handicapper.

3081 ALBERT BARTLETT NOVICES' HURDLE (REGISTERED AS THE BRISTOL NOVICES' HURDLE) (GRADE 2) (12 hdls) 3m

1:50 (1:50) (Class 1) 4-Y-O+

£17,085 (£6,411; £3,210; £1,599; £804; £402)

Form RPR

/11- 1 **Kings Palace (IRE)**[56] 1968 5-11-7 146 TomScudamore 154+
(David Pipe) *str: lw: mde all: j. fast and accurately: c clr fr readily clr after 2 out: unchal: impressive* **10/11**[1]

/1P- 2 *14* **Masters Hill (IRE)**[35] 2373 7-11-4 0 BrendanPowell 136
(Colin Tizzard) *chsd wnr thrght: outpcd after 2 out and no ch w wnr but wl clr of 3rd* **25/1**

321- 3 *19* **Potters Cross**[22] 2649 6-11-4 134 BarryGeraghty 118
(Rebecca Curtis) *chsd ldrs in 3rd tl after 3 out: wl bhd in 4th whn lft 3rd last* **10/1**

11- 4 *14* **Milan Bound (IRE)**[16] 2768 5-11-4 0 APMcCoy 106
(Jonjo O'Neill) *a bhd: sme hdwy 3 out: nvr nr ldrs and sn wl bhd again* **13/2**[3]

111- 5 *15* **Flicka Williams (IRE)**[28] 2516 6-11-4 130 DougieCostello 97
(Tony Coyle) *in rr: sme hdwy 5th: blnd 7th: no ch fr 3 out* **16/1**

112- 6 *38* **Berea Boru (IRE)**[22] 2649 5-11-4 130 (t) DonalDevereux 58
(Peter Bowen) *in tch tl wknd bef 3 out: t.o* **33/1**

113- F **Saint Roque (FR)**[0] 2929 /-11-/ 144 (t) DarylJacob 121
(Paul Nicholls) *in tch: wnt 3rd 3 out but nvr on terms w ldng duo: no ch in poor 3rd whn fell last* **10/3**[2]

5m 57.31s (-3.69) **Going Correction** -0.15s/f (Good) **7** Ran SP% **110.6**
Speed ratings (Par 115): **100,95,89,84,79 66,**
toteswingers 1&2 £7.70, 1&3 £4.00, 2&3 £23.40 CSF £22.91 TOTE £1.90: £1.10, £9.20; EX 24.80 Trifecta £162.20 Pool: £2995.51 - 13.84 winning units..
Owner Drew, George & Johnson Family **Bred** Kahill Burke Racing **Trained** Nicholashayne, Devon

FOCUS
A particularly interesting renewal of this Grade 2 contest, considering the unexposed nature of some of these, but the early pace wasn't overly strong. This rates another step forward from Kings Palace, to a level expected from a Festival-winning novice.

3082 STEWART FAMILY THANK YOU GOLD CUP (A H'CAP CHASE) (GRADE 3) (17 fncs) 2m 5f

2:25 (2:25) (Class 1) 4-Y-O+

£56,950 (£21,370; £10,700; £5,330; £2,680; £1,340)

Form RPR

132- 1 **Double Ross (IRE)**[22] 2645 7-10-8 **133** SamTwiston-Davies 147+
(Nigel Twiston-Davies) *chsd ldrs: hit 8th: mstke 4 out: drvn to ld gng to 2 out: 5 l clr last: idled u.p run-in: all out* **7/1**[3]

/01- 2 *2* **Cantlow (IRE)**[15] 2800 8-11-9 **148** RobertThornton 158+
(Paul Webber) *lw: towards rr but in tch: mstke and drvn 11th: styd on fr 3 out: kpt on u.p fr next to chse wnr after last: kpt on wl clsng stages but a hld* **14/1**

5/2- 3 *3 ¼* **Colour Squadron (IRE)**[28] 2503 7-11-7 **146** APMcCoy 152+
(Philip Hobbs) *in tch: hdwy 12th: chsd ldrs after 3 out: hit 2 out: wnt 2nd u.p and nt fluent last: no imp on wnr and one pce into 3rd run-in* **9/2**[1]

232- 4 *9* **Sew On Target (IRE)**[29] 2488 8-10-5 **130** BrendanPowell 127
(Colin Tizzard) *slt ld but hrd pressed for ld fr s tl hdd 12th: styd chalng tl appr 2 out: wknd appr last* **14/1**

/11- 5 *nk* **Johns Spirit (IRE)**[28] 2503 6-11-9 **148** RichieMcLernon 145
(Jonjo O'Neill) *lw: in rr: hit 4th: impr fr 12th: rdn and effrt after 3 out but no imp on ldrs: wl hld whn hit last* **11/2**[2]

0F2- 6 *4 ½* **Easter Meteor**[15] 2800 7-11-9 **148** AidanColeman 143
(Emma Lavelle) *duelled for ld tl led 12th: styd hrd pressed: hit 3 out: hdd appr 2 out whn nt fluent sn wknd* **14/1**

426- 7 *10* **Gauvain (GER)**[28] 2504 11-11-12 **151** (t) RichardJohnson 136
(Philip Hobbs) *in rr: hit 6th and 11th: sme prog and mstke 13th: btn whn hit 3 out* **33/1**

/20- 8 *10* **Tap Night (USA)**[28] 2503 6-11-6 **145** PeterBuchanan 119
(Lucinda Russell) *sn struggling to go pce: a bhd* **20/1**

P24- 9 *10* **Attaglance**[28] 2503 7-10-12 **137** (t) BrianHughes 102
(Malcolm Jefferson) *lw: nvr able to go pce and a bhd* **7/1**[3]

201/ P **Salut Flo (FR)**[639] 4865 8-11-5 **144** TomScudamore
(David Pipe) *chsd ldrs: hit 3rd and 5th: blnd and wknd 4 out: t.o whn p.u bef2 out* **8/1**

0/1- P **Silver Roque (FR)**[32] 2448 7-11-4 **143** (t) PaddyBrennan
(Fergal O'Brien) *lw: sn bhd: t.o whn p.u bef 3 out* **16/1**

1/3- P **Grandioso (IRE)**[15] 2800 6-11-8 **147** (t) DarylJacob
(Paul Nicholls) *in tch tl lost position and p.u bef 10th* **8/1**

2/3- P **Ma Filleule (FR)**[19] 2713 5-11-3 **142** BarryGeraghty
(Nicky Henderson) *chsd ldrs wknd 13th: t.o whn p.u bef 2 out* **14/1**

5m 13.39s (-6.01) **Going Correction** +0.05s/f (Yiel) **13** Ran SP% **121.0**
Speed ratings (Par 113): **113,112,111,107,107 105,101,98,94, , ,**
toteswingers 1&2 £15.20, 1&3 £14.50, 2&3 £25.90 CSF £100.66 CT £497.09 TOTE £8.30: £3.00, £4.30, £2.40; EX 122.00 Trifecta £982.60 Pool: £75732.09 - 57.80 winning units..
Owner Options O Syndicate **Bred** T McIlhagga **Trained** Naunton, Gloucs

The Form Book Jumps, Raceform Ltd, Compton, RG20 6NL.

FOCUS
A decent renewal of this high-class handicap, which has been sponsored by the Stewart family for the last three years. Irish fancy Home Farm was a notable absentee, as was Champion Court, whose defection meant the weights were raised 6lb. They went a good pace and a number of these could never get seriously involved. Rock-solid handicap form, and Double Ross should still be competitive when reassessed.

3083 STANJAMES.COM INTERNATIONAL HURDLE (GRADE 2) (8 hdls) 2m 1f
3:00 (3:01) (Class 1) 4-Y-0+
£74,035 (£27,781; £13,910; £6,929; £3,484; £1,742)

Form RPR
2/1- **1** **The New One (IRE)**[55] 1989 5-11-8 167 SamTwiston-Davies 158+
(Nigel Twiston-Davies) *lw: in tch: trckd ldrs 3 out: led wl bef last: rdn sn after: drvn clr fnl 110yds: readily* **2/5**[1]
1/2- **2** *6* **Zarkandar (IRE)**[21] 2665 6-11-8 167 (b) DarylJacob 152+
(Paul Nicholls) *chsd ldr: chal 4th: sn led: rdn and edgd rt whn bmpd wl bef last whn sn hdd: rallied after last to chal but sn outpcd by wnr fnl 110yds* **5/2**[2]
061- **3** *6* **Jumps Road**[9] 2910 6-11-0 131 BrendanPowell 138
(Colin Tizzard) *in tch: impr 4 out: chsd ldrs fr 3 out: wnt for run on rails and rdn whn hmpd wl bef last: styd on same pce au.p* **100/1**
/00- **4** *6* **Court Minstrel (IRE)**[27] 2533 6-11-4 149 PaulMoloney 136
(Evan Williams) *lw: nt fluent 2nd: towards rr: hdwy 2 out: nvr quite gng pce to rch ldrs: no ch whn swtchd rt sn after last* **16/1**[3]
P/ **5** *86* **Albert Hall (USA)**[10] 8-11-4 133 (t[1]) MathieuCarroux 58
(A Chaille-Chaille, France) *in tch: hdwy 4 out to chse ldrs next: wknd sn after: t.o* **40/1**
01S- **6** *16* **Hawkhill (IRE)**[21] 2668 7-11-4 132 (vt[1]) RichardJohnson 43
(Tim Vaughan) *led tl jnd 4th: sn hdd: wknd next: t.o* **100/1**
F **Seabreeze D'Ho (FR)**[27] 2556 7-11-4 140 (t) DavidCottin
(Christian Le Galliard, France) *in rr tl fell 2nd: fatally injured* **40/1**
4m 4.45s (-6.85) **Going Correction** -0.15s/f (Good) 7 Ran SP% **112.7**
Speed ratings (Par 115): **110,107,104,101,61 53,**
toteswingers 1&2 £1.02, 1&3 £8.90, 2&3 £10.40 CSF £1.71 TOTE £1.80: £1.40, £1.70; EX 2.50 Trifecta £41.30 Pool: £37937.19 - 687.63 winning units..
Owner Mrs S Such **Bred** R Brown & Ballylinch Stud **Trained** Naunton, Gloucs
■ Stewards' Enquiry : Brendan Powell three-day ban: careless riding (Dec 29-31)

FOCUS
A classy contest but a messy outcome. However, the winner was clearly the best. Tricky form to rate with the proximity of the third a huge concern.

3084 OSBORNE HOUSE RELKEEL HURDLE (GRADE 2) (10 hdls) 2m 4f 110y
3:35 (3:35) (Class 1) 4-Y-0+ **£22,780** (£8,548; £4,280; £2,132)

Form RPR
/11- **1** **More Of That (IRE)**[21] 2671 5-10-12 145 APMcCoy 161+
(Jonjo O'Neill) *str: lw: disp 3rd tl disp 2nd after 7th: nt fluent 2 out and sn trckd ldr: chal last and shkn up to take slt ld w 1f to run: coaxed along to assert fnl 150yds: cosily* **11/4**[2]
5/2- **2** *2 1/4* **Salubrious (IRE)**[28] 2504 6-10-12 153 DarylJacob 155
(Paul Nicholls) *lw: led but jnd to 4th: qckd pce 6th: rdn after 2 out: jnd last: hdd w 1f to run: outpcd fnl 150yds* **3/1**[3]
121/ **3** *27* **Glens Melody (IRE)**[28] 2522 5-10-13 140 RWalsh 139
(W P Mullins, Ire) *w'like: disp 3rd tl disp 2nd after 7th tl rdn after 2 out: wknd wl bef last* **15/8**[1]
/13- **4** *32* **Gemix (FR)**[42] 2240 5-11-6 165 (t) DavidCottin 110
(N Bertran De Balanda, France) *angular: t.k.h: racd wd and disp ld to 4th: wknd fr 7th* **3/1**[3]
4m 57.87s (-3.13) **Going Correction** -0.15s/f (Good) 4 Ran SP% **111.4**
Speed ratings (Par 115): **99,98,87,75**
CSF £11.01 TOTE £4.30; EX 16.60 Trifecta £30.10 Pool: £12606.28 - 314.10 winning units..
Owner John P McManus **Bred** Mrs Eleanor Hadden **Trained** Cheltenham, Gloucs
■ More Of That is a full brother to Eastlake, who won earlier on the card.

FOCUS
A small field and a couple of disappointments, but the first two home are improving and look nice types. Another step forward from the progressive winner who is developing into a realistic World Hurdle contender.
T/Jkpt: Not won. T/Plt: £96.00 to a £1 stake. Pool: £184736.47 - 1403.36 winning tickets T/Qpdt: £7.40 to a £1 stake. Pool: £15396.59 - 1521.28 winning tickets ST

2782 DONCASTER (L-H)
Saturday, December 14

OFFICIAL GOING: Chase course - good; hurdle course - good (good to firm in places) changing to good after race 1 (11.55) (chs 7.0; hdl 7.6)
Wind: fresh 1/2 against Weather: fine but cold and breezy

3085 BETVICTOR.COM INTERACTIVE H'CAP HURDLE (11 hdls) 3m 110y
11:55 (11:55) (Class 3) (0-125,123)
4-Y-0+ **£5,253** (£1,552; £776; £388; £194)

Form RPR
/00- **1** **Timesishard (IRE)**[7] 2944 6-11-12 123 WayneHutchinson 132+
(Graeme McPherson) *trckd ldrs: led 3 out: drvn clr sn after last: kpt rt up to work* **12/1**
/30- **2** *6* **Corkage (IRE)**[15] 2785 10-11-11 122 (v[1]) JamesReveley 126+
(Keith Reveley) *led to 6th: led 8th: hdd next: 1 l down whn nt fluent last: styd on same pce* **14/1**
232- **3** *1 1/2* **Any Given Moment (IRE)**[15] 2786 7-10-12 109 RyanMania 110
(Sandy Thomson) *hld up in rr: hdwy to trck ldrs 4th: drvn 3 out: 3rd last: kpt on same pce and edgd rt run-in* **7/1**
/UF- **4** *2* **Midnight Oscar (IRE)**[40] 2267 6-11-11 122 (p) SamThomas 121
(Kim Bailey) *mid-div: drvn 8th: chsng ldrs next: 4th and one pce whn swtchd lft last 150yds* **5/1**[3]
650- **5** *21* **Wolf Shield (IRE)**[28] 2516 6-11-3 114 BarryKeniry 94
(George Moore) *chsd ldrs: drvn 8th: sn lost pl and bhd: t.o next* **16/1**
531- **6** *3/4* **Sir Frank (IRE)**[20] 2691 8-11-12 123 (p) ConorO'Farrell 102
(David Pipe) *chsd ldrs to 3rd: drvn and dropped to rr 8th: bhd fr next* **9/1**
361- **7** *1* **Fix It Right (IRE)**[15] 2786 5-11-5 116 LeightonAspell 95
(Emma Lavelle) *in rr: pushed along 6th: sme hdwy appr 3 out: sn lost pl* **7/2**[2]
165- **8** *5* **Kings Lodge**[30] 2468 7-11-8 119 AndrewTinkler 93
(Nicky Henderson) *w ldrs: led 6th to 8th: lost pl appr next* **12/1**
/20- **9** *3 1/4* **Presence Felt (IRE)**[16] 2755 5-11-5 116 (p) NoelFehily 87
(Jonjo O'Neill) *in rr: reminders 4th: sme hdwy 7th: lost pl next: poor 6th whn j.lft last: sn eased* **3/1**[1]
5m 51.0s (-8.00) **Going Correction** -0.45s/f (Good) 9 Ran SP% **114.3**
Speed ratings (Par 107): **94,92,91,90,84 84,83,82,81**
toteswingers: 1&2 £34.40, 1&3 £18.90, 2&3 £13.50. CSF £156.27 CT £1265.24 TOTE £16.40: £4.20, £2.60, £1.90; EX 128.40 Trifecta £711.10 Part won. Pool: £948.23 - 0.10 winning units..
Owner James Chamberlain **Bred** Denis O'Herlihy **Trained** Upper Oddington, Gloucs

FOCUS
A fairly useful handicap, though not as competitive as it looked beforehand, with a few of the market leaders running disappointingly. A step up from the winner in a fair time for the grade.

3086 CROWNHOTEL-BAWTRY.COM NOVICES' HURDLE (11 hdls) 3m 110y
12:25 (12:25) (Class 4) 4-Y-0+ **£3,249** (£954; £477; £238)

Form RPR
/10- **1** **Warden Hill (IRE)**[29] 2490 5-11-4 124 DominicElsworth 124+
(Mick Channon) *trckd ldrs: 2nd fr 2nd: effrt and upside 3 out: styd on run-in: led towards fin* **13/8**[1]
116- **2** *1/2* **Drop Out Joe**[28] 2505 5-11-10 129 NoelFehily 130
(Charlie Longsdon) *set stdy pce: increased gallop bef 3 out: sn jnd: j.lft 2 out: hdd and no ex clsng stages* **8/1**[3]
1/0- **3** *7* **Howlongisafoot (IRE)**[55] 1991 4-10-12 0 RyanMahon 111
(Paul Nicholls) *hld up in rr: hdwy to trck ldrs 5th: drvn appr 3 out: sn outpcd: nt fluent 2 out: kpt on same pce* **13/2**[2]
20- **4** *3* **Wakanda (IRE)**[48] 2103 4-11-4 120 RyanMania 114
(Sue Smith) *hld up in rr: hdwy to trck ldrs 7th: effrt appr 3 out: sn outpcd: kpt on one pce* **14/1**
202- **5** *2 1/4* **Silver Eagle (IRE)**[14] 2826 5-11-3 134 (t) TomBellamy[(7)] 117
(Kim Bailey) *trckd ldrs: effrt appr 3 out: sn outpcd: kpt on one pce* **13/8**[1]
605- **6** *68* **Milan Of Hope (IRE)**[11] 2874 6-10-12 0 AdamPogson 37
(Charles Pogson) *t.k.h: trckd ldrs: nt fluent and reminders 3rd: drvn and lost pl bef 3 out: t.o 2 out: virtually p.u: eventually completed* **100/1**
6m 5.3s (6.30) **Going Correction** -0.45s/f (Good)
WFA 4 from 5yo+ 7lb 6 Ran SP% **108.3**
Speed ratings (Par 105): **71,70,68,67,66 45**
toteswingers: 1&2 £5.20, 1&3 £3.70, 2&3 £13.30. CSF £14.37 TOTE £2.40: £1.40, £2.40; EX 13.10 Trifecta £45.40 Pool: £1176.84 - 19.40 winning units..
Owner Mrs T P Radford **Bred** Aaron Metcalfe **Trained** West Ilsley, Berks

FOCUS
A couple of pretty useful novices fought out the finish. The pace looked steady, the race effectively not beginning in earnest until after four out, and the time was slow compared with the opener. The first two are rated to their marks.

3087 MACMILLAN NOVICES' CHASE (15 fncs) 2m 3f
1:00 (1:00) (Class 4) 4-Y-0+ **£4,659** (£1,446; £779)

Form RPR
/15- **1** **Karinga Dancer**[35] 2372 7-11-0 0 (t) NoelFehily 133+
(Harry Fry) *hld up in last: hdwy to trck ldng pair 11th: upsides whn lft in ld and sltly hmpd 3 out: sn clr: shkn up run-in: v comf* **4/5**[1]
3F1- **2** *3 3/4* **Princely Player (IRE)**[19] 2719 6-11-7 138 TomO'Brien 131
(Philip Hobbs) *led: hit 2nd: hdd 8th: 4th and outpcd whn hit 11th: lft modest 3rd 3 out: 8 l 2nd last: kpt on same pce* **3/1**[2]
644/ **3** *13* **Dreamy George (IRE)**[13] 7-11-0 0 DenisO'Regan 115
(John Ferguson) *hld up in rr: mstke 2nd: chsd ldr next: led 8th: hesitant 10th: hdd sn after 4 out: upsides and lft cl 2nd whn mstke next: wknd last* **16/1**
U22- **F** **Woodbank**[15] 2785 6-11-0 123 AndrewTinkler
(Nicky Henderson) *t.k.h: trckd ldr: upsides 10th: led sn after 4 out: jnd whn fell next* **7/2**[3]
4m 45.1s (-3.90) **Going Correction** -0.45s/f (Good) 4 Ran SP% **108.7**
Speed ratings (Par 105): **90,88,82,**
CSF £3.67 TOTE £1.60; EX 3.30 Trifecta £11.10 Pool: £1171.53 - 78.74 winning units..
Owner H B Geddes **Bred** Mr & Mrs J K S Cresswell **Trained** Seaborough, Dorset

FOCUS
The cosy winner was a stone+ off hurdle mark and is sure to rate higher, but this is probably not a strong piece of form.

3088 DFS SUPPORTS MACMILLAN H'CAP HURDLE (8 hdls) 2m 110y
1:35 (1:35) (Class 2) 3-Y-0+ **£12,021** (£3,529; £1,764; £882)

Form RPR
110- **1** **Makari**[42] 2213 6-11-0 131 AndrewTinkler 136+
(Nicky Henderson) *hld up in rr: stdy hdwy after 5th: effrt after next: chsng ldrs and swtchd lft between last 2: led last 150yds: hld on wl* **8/1**
114- **2** *1* **Purple Bay (IRE)**[22] 2657 4-10-11 128 DenisO'Regan 131
(John Ferguson) *hld up: hdwy to trck ldrs after 4th: upsides 3 out: led last: hdd and no ex run-in* **3/1**[1]
311- **3** *2* **Robbie**[36] 2343 9-11-1 132 JamesReveley 133
(Keith Reveley) *led tl after 1st: chsd ldrs: upsides 3 out: styd on to take 3rd last 150yds* **9/1**
605- **4** *4* **Lightening Rod**[7] 2958 8-10-3 123 JakeGreenall[(3)] 120
(Michael Easterby) *in rr: hdwy appr 3 out: styd on same pce fr 2 out: tk 4th nr fin* **12/1**
0/3- **5** *1* **Ted Spread**[226] 82 6-11-1 132 (t) TomO'Brien 128
(Suzy Smith) *trckd ldrs: led appr 3 out: hdd last: wknd fnl 75yds* **12/1**
0/1- **6** *2 1/4* **Ranjaan (FR)**[19] 2717 5-10-13 135 (p) HarryDerham[(5)] 129
(Paul Nicholls) *trckd ldrs: ev ch 3 out: sn rdn: wknd last 100yds* **4/1**[2]
113- **7** *3 3/4* **Franciscan**[22] 2657 5-10-11 128 HenryBrooke 118
(Donald McCain) *chsd ldrs: drvn and outpcd after 5th: rallied and chsng ldrs whn j.lft 2 out: fdd between last 2* **10/1**
U1F/ **8** *9* **Empire Levant (USA)**[235] 5472 6-11-6 137 RyanMahon 121
(Paul Nicholls) *led after 1st: blnd 2nd: hdd appr 3 out: lost pl bef 2 out* **14/1**
/63- **9** *3 3/4* **Runswick Royal (IRE)**[21] 2669 4-11-12 143 WilsonRenwick 122
(Ann Hamilton) *hld up in rr: outpcd and reminders bef 3 out: sn lost pl* **12/1**
662- **10** *6* **Ruler Of All (IRE)**[21] 2668 7-10-6 130 (v) MrRWinks[(7)] 106
(Peter Winks) *trckd ldrs: t.k.h: effrt 3 out: wknd between last 2: eased run-in: b.b.v* **7/1**[3]
3m 52.2s (-12.50) **Going Correction** -0.45s/f (Good) 10 Ran SP% **117.4**
Speed ratings (Par 109): **111,110,109,107,107 106,104,100,98,95**
toteswingers 1&2 £3.70, 1&3 £12.60, 2&3 £3.10 CSF £33.26 CT £225.54 TOTE £10.40: £3.10, £1.70, £2.00; EX 42.40 Trifecta £536.80 Pool: £1472.12 - 2.05 winning units..
Owner Matt & Lauren Morgan **Bred** Longdon Stud Ltd **Trained** Upper Lambourn, Berks

FOCUS
A useful handicap, the finish fought out by a couple of progressive sorts. The gallop didn't look particularly strong, the tempo not really increasing until approaching the third-last.

3089 BETVICTOR SUMMIT JUVENILE HURDLE (GRADE 2) (8 hdls) 2m 110y
2:05 (2:05) (Class 1) 3-Y-O £15,875 (£5,959; £2,983; £1,487; £745)

Form RPR

/42- 1 **Fox Norton (FR)**[77] [1684] 3-11-5 138........................ NoelFehily 137+
(Nick Williams) *hld up: nt fluent 3rd: hdwy 5th: led narrowly next: drvn 2 l ahd after last: hld on all out nr fin* **5/2**[2]

2 *hd* **Broughton (GER)**[63] 3-10-12 0........................ DenisO'Regan 131+
(John Ferguson) *hld up: stdy hdwy 5th: chsng ldrs and swtchd lft bef 2 out: 2nd 2 out: rallied run-in: styd on towards fin: jst hld* **8/1**[3]

111- 3 *16* **Royal Irish Hussar (IRE)**[28] [2500] 3-11-5 147........................ DavidBass 124
(Nicky Henderson) *led: hdd 3 out: wknd sn after 2 out* **4/6**[1]

121- 4 *1 ½* **Dispour (IRE)**[15] [2790] 3-11-2 122........................ HenryBrooke 118
(Donald McCain) *trckd ldr: drvn appr 3 out: wknd appr 2 out* **16/1**

2- 5 *21* **Cafe Au Lait (GER)**[38] [2294] 3-10-12 0........................ TomO'Brien 94
(C Von Der Recke, Germany) *in rr: pushed along 5th: sn reminders and lost pl: bhd fr next* **25/1**

3m 54.0s (-10.70) **Going Correction** -0.45s/f (Good) **5** Ran SP% **109.4**
Speed ratings (Par 114): **107,106,99,98,88**
CSF £19.41 TOTE £3.70: £1.90, £2.90; EX 18.50 Trifecta £28.80 Pool: £1713.25 - 44.61 winning units..

Owner B Dunn **Bred** Scuderia Del Bargello **Trained** George Nympton, Devon

FOCUS
Not a strong Grade 2, but the winner produced a big step up and the second is a useful recruit. The favourite was a stone+ off his mark.

3090 DOWNLOAD THE FREE BETVICTOR APP H'CAP CHASE (15 fncs) 2m 3f
2:40 (2:40) (Class 3) (0-140,140) 4-Y-0+ £7,147 (£2,098; £1,049; £524)

Form RPR

/31- 1 **Off The Ground (IRE)**[15] [2785] 7-11-5 **133**........................ LeightonAspell 151+
(Emma Lavelle) *hld up: trckd ldrs 7th: cl 2nd 11th: led and j.lft 3 out: 8 l clr whn mstke last: pushed out* **11/8**[1]

422- 2 *9* **Tahiti Pearl (IRE)**[17] [2751] 9-10-11 **125**........................ RyanMania 132
(Sue Smith) *led to 3rd: led after next: mstke 8th: hdd 3 out: one pce* **8/1**

5/0- 3 *3 ½* **Nadiya De La Vega (FR)**[28] [2503] 7-11-10 **138**............(p) AndrewTinkler 141
(Nicky Henderson) *w ldr 2nd: led next: hdd after 4th: drvn 9th: outpcd 11th: kpt on to take modest 3rd appr last* **4/1**[2]

/PP- 4 *nse* **Arthur's Pass**[14] [2812] 9-11-1 **129**........................ RhysFlint 131
(Tom George) *chsd ldrs: outpcd 9th: kpt on fr 4 out: tk modest 4th appr last* **16/1**

633- 5 *22* **Kings Grey (IRE)**[15] [2783] 9-11-11 **139**........................ JamesReveley 126
(Keith Reveley) *chsd ldrs: clr 3rd appr 4 out: wknd between last 2* **8/1**

12- 6 *35* **Claragh Native (IRE)**[7] [2957] 8-10-6 **120**....................(p) WilsonRenwick 71
(Martin Todhunter) *prom 8th: outpcd and hit next: lost pl and hit 5 out: sn bhd: t.o 3 out* **12/1**

15U- 7 *13* **Hazy Tom (IRE)**[15] [2800] 7-11-12 **140**........................ NoelFehily 79
(Charlie Longsdon) *in rr: pckd landing and lost pl 10th: sn bhd: t.o 3 out* **7/1**[3]

4m 39.3s (-9.70) **Going Correction** -0.45s/f (Good) **7** Ran SP% **110.4**
Speed ratings (Par 107): **102,98,96,96,87 72,67**
toteswingers 1&2 £3.40, 1&3 £1.50, 2&3 £6.20 CSF £11.93 TOTE £2.30: £1.30, £2.80; EX 11.30 Trifecta £27.20 Pool: £1989.39 - 54.83 winning units..

Owner Axom (XXVI) **Bred** Mrs Kay Devereux **Trained** Hatherden, Hants

FOCUS
By no means a competitive handicap, with a few of these struggling for form, but the winner is very much going the right way. The winner was on a good mark but this rates another step up.

3091 BETVICTOR H'CAP CHASE (18 fncs) 3m
3:15 (3:15) (Class 2) (0-150,145) 4-Y-0+ £12,996 (£3,816; £1,908; £954)

Form RPR

230- 1 **Night In Milan (IRE)**[21] [2672] 7-10-11 **130**....................(b) JamesReveley 143+
(Keith Reveley) *j. boldly: mde all: jnd 2 out: fnd ex and forged clr run-in* **8/1**

261- 2 *6* **De Boitron (FR)**[7] [2957] 9-11-12 **145**........................ RyanMania 152+
(Sue Smith) *hld up in rr: hdwy to trck ldrs 12th: 3rd 14th: 2nd next: upsides 2 out and last: styd on same pce* **7/1**

/16- 3 *7* **Mart Lane (IRE)**[35] [2365] 8-11-1 **134**........................ WayneHutchinson 133
(Dr Richard Newland) *chsd ldrs: j.rt 1st: drvn and outpcd 13th: kpt on fr 2 out: tk 3rd last 75yds* **10/1**

/33- 4 *1* **Baile Anrai (IRE)**[14] [2822] 9-10-6 **125**....................(b) HarrySkelton 125
(Dan Skelton) *chsd wnr: hit 4 out: fdd and lost 3rd last 75yds* **6/1**

612- 5 *10* **Carrigmorna King (IRE)**[14] [2812] 7-11-0 **133**....................(t) TomO'Brien 127
(Philip Hobbs) *in rr: hdwy 8th: blnd 10th: outpcd 14th: modest 5th whn mstke 3 out* **7/2**[2]

221- 6 *14* **Bear's Affair (IRE)**[19] [2712] 7-11-7 **140**........................ DavidBass 116
(Nicky Henderson) *chsd ldrs: bmpd 1st: drvn 13th: wknd bef 3 out* **5/1**[3]

00P/ 7 *25* **Harry The Viking**[252] [5177] 8-11-1 **134**........................ RyanMahon 88
(Paul Nicholls) *chsd ldrs: bmpd 1st: lost pl and reminders 11th: bhd 13th: t.o 3 out* **10/3**[1]

130- P **Lost Glory (NZ)**[56] [1971] 8-11-9 **142**........................(t) NoelFehily
(Jonjo O'Neill) *nt fluent in last: bhd fr 8th: t.o 12th: p.u bef 4 out* **16/1**

5m 54.4s (-17.60) **Going Correction** -0.45s/f (Good) **8** Ran SP% **114.8**
Speed ratings (Par 109): **111,109,106,106,103 98,90,**
toteswingers 1&2 £3.50, 1&3 £4.50, 2&3 £5.50 CSF £61.61 CT £566.96 TOTE £9.90: £2.90, £2.00, £3.70; EX 67.30 Trifecta £315.50 Pool: £2191.95 - 5.21 winning units..

Owner Richard Collins **Bred** Commandant Brendan Healy **Trained** Lingdale, Redcar & Cleveland

FOCUS
Another decent contest, the leading pair having it between themselves from early in the straight. The winner is still on the upgrade.

T/Plt: £426.60. Pool: £85,714.06 - 146.66 winning units. T/Qpdt: £26.70. Pool: £6635.25 - 183.40 winning units. WG

2725 LINGFIELD (L-H)
Saturday, December 14

OFFICIAL GOING: Jumps courses - soft (heavy in places; good to soft in home straight on chase course); all-weather - standard (chs 5.5, hdl 5.2)
Wind: medium, half behind Weather: dry and bright

3092 LINGFIELDPARK.CO.UK NOVICES' HURDLE (10 hdls) 2m 3f 110y
12:15 (12:17) (Class 4) 4-Y-0+ £3,285 (£957; £479)

Form RPR

2- 1 **Madness Light (FR)**[20] [2695] 4-10-9 115....................(t) GavinSheehan(3) 130+
(Warren Greatrex) *mde all: gng best after 3 out: in command between last 2: easily* **6/4**[1]

/26- 2 *3 ½* **Strollawaynow (IRE)**[30] [2467] 6-10-12 115........................ TomCannon 122
(David Arbuthnot) *chsd ldrs tl lft 2nd 1st: chsd wnr after: rdn after 3 out: no imp and nt fluent last: plugged on same pce flat* **4/1**[2]

2/ 3 *6* **Brave Vic (IRE)**[589] [81] 5-10-9 0........................ JoshuaMoore(3) 115
(Gary Moore) *chsd ldrs: 3rd and rdn bef 2 out: no imp and mstke next: plugged on same pce after* **6/1**[3]

204/ 4 *3 ¾* **The Clock Leary (IRE)**[244] [5323] 5-10-12 0........................ LiamTreadwell 112
(Venetia Williams) *t.k.h: in tch in midfield: clr in ldng quintet 7th: rdn and no ex bef 2 out: wl hld and plugged on same pce fr next* **7/1**

/10- 5 *1 ½* **Kind Of Easy (IRE)**[39] [2283] 7-10-12 0....................(p) JamieMoore 110
(Emma Lavelle) *chsd wnr tl j. slowly 1st: styd chsd ldrs: rdn along after 4th: drvn and struggling after 3 out: 5th and wl hld next* **4/1**[2]

6 *34* **Garde Fou (FR)**[242] [5347] 7-10-12 0........................ NickScholfield 76
(Paul Henderson) *hld up in rr: hmpd 1st: rdn and struggling after 5th: mstke 6th and sn lost tch: t.o 8th* **20/1**

50- 7 *¾* **Cadeau George**[31] [2457] 4-10-12 0........................ FelixDeGiles 75
(Ben Pauling) *in tch in midfield: rdn and struggling after 6th: wknd and t.o 8th* **33/1**

50U- 8 *3 ¼* **Camptown Lady**[23] [2614] 4-10-3 0 ow1........................ RobertDunne(3) 66
(Laura Young) *hld up in last trio: sme hdwy into modest 6th 7th: lost tch after next: t.o 2 out* **100/1**

9 *39* **Solid Concrete (IRE)**[232] 7-9-12 0........................ MrLKilgarriff(7) 26
(Neil Mulholland) *mstkes: in tch in midfield: rdn and dropped to rr 5th: lost tch and t.o after next* **25/1**

10 *30* **Gladstone (IRE)**[24] 5-10-9 0........................ JamesBest(3)
(Polly Gundry) *hld up in rr: hmpd 1st: hdwy into midfield 5th: struggling and lost pl next: t.o after 7th* **66/1**

/00- 11 *30* **Elixir Du Lac**[26] [2563] 6-10-5 0........................ SamJones
(Jo Davis) *chsd ldrs: wnt lft whn blnd v bdly and dropped to last 4th: rdn and rcvrd to tag onto bk of field next: sn toiling: t.o after 6th* **100/1**

0/5- F **Upham Running (IRE)**[214] [298] 5-10-12 0........................ MarkGrant
(Kate Buckett) *midfield whn fell 1st* **100/1**

5m 9.1s (2.40) **Going Correction** +0.25s/f (Yiel)
WFA 4 from 5yo+ 5lb **12** Ran SP% **122.8**
Speed ratings (Par 105): **105,103,101,99,99 85,85,83,68,56 44,**
toteswingers: 1&2 £1.60, 1&3 £4.80, 2&3 £5.90. CSF £7.78 TOTE £2.60: £1.50, £1.80, £2.40; EX 10.40 Trifecta £40.20 Pool: £485.65 - 9.04 winning units..

Owner Mrs T Brown **Bred** Alexa Leherissier & Laurent Baudry **Trained** Upper Lambourn, Berks

FOCUS
There was 2.2mm of rain overnight, and the going, given as soft, heavy in places, good to soft between the final three fences, was described as "attritional" by Liam Treadwell after the first. Just a fair novice hurdle. A step up from the cosy winner.

3093 TOM WHITE H'CAP CHASE (14 fncs) 2m 4f
12:50 (12:50) (Class 4) (0-120,119) 4-Y-0+ £3,768 (£1,106; £553; £276)

Form RPR

/2F- 1 **Wychwoods Brook**[22] [2651] 7-11-12 **119**........................ AdamWedge 137+
(Evan Williams) *hld up off the pce in midfield: stdy prog 8th: chsd ldr bef 2 out: pushed into ld between last 2: readily c clr flat: comf* **4/1**[2]

F/3- 2 *10* **Henry King (IRE)**[28] [2508] 9-11-12 **119**........................(t) JackDoyle 127+
(Victor Dartnall) *chsd ldr and clr of field tl led 11th: rdn and hdd between last 2: no ex and btn last: wknd flat* **7/2**[1]

114/ 3 *7* **Time To Think**[232] [5539] 8-11-6 **113**........................ AndrewThornton 113
(Seamus Mullins) *racd off the pce in midfield: pushed along and struggling 6th: modest 7th and looked wl btn 10th: styd on after next: wnt 3rd 3 out: mstke and no imp next* **10/1**

1/P- 4 *12* **Mentalist (FR)**[19] [2714] 5-11-9 **116**........................ LiamTreadwell 105
(Venetia Williams) *racd off the pce in midfield: clsd and rdn 10th: 3rd and no ex u.p after next: 4th and wknd 3 out* **6/1**[3]

0PP- 5 *18* **Nozic (FR)**[26] [2567] 12-11-8 **115**........................(p) DaveCrosse 84
(Zoe Davison) *led and clr w rival tl hdd 11th: sn drvn and btn bef next: wknd 3 out: t.o* **25/1**

/35- 6 *8* **Topaze Collonges (FR)**[32] [2440] 6-10-11 **107**............(b) KielanWoods(3) 68
(Charlie Longsdon) *chsd clr ldng pair: rdn and losing pl after 8th: t.o bef 3 out* **7/1**

U/6- P **Cranky Corner**[228] [40] 9-10-12 **105**........................ JamieMoore
(Helen Nelmes) *hld up off the pce in rr: hmpd 1st: nvr on terms: t.o whn p.u after 11th* **8/1**

0- P **Paddy The Stout (IRE)**[18] [2729] 8-11-7 **114**........................ NickScholfield
(Paul Henderson) *hld up off the pce in rr: hmpd 1st: hdwy 6th: chsd ldrs after 8th: wknd 11th: t.o whn p.u 2 out* **16/1**

232- P **Marky Bob (IRE)**[190] [655] 8-11-2 **116**........................ MikeyEnnis(7)
(Hugo Froud) *t.k.h: prom in main gp but nvr on terms w ldrs: lost pl and mstke 8th: bhd next: t.o and p.u after 11th* **8/1**

U6P/ P **Sherreb (IRE)**[257] [5080] 7-10-5 **98**........................ TomCannon
(Anna Newton-Smith) *j. slowly 1st: nvr jumping or travelling wl in rr: lost tch after 5th: t.o whn p.u 8th* **12/1**

5m 21.6s (11.20) **Going Correction** +0.475s/f (Soft) **10** Ran SP% **117.7**
Speed ratings (Par 105): **96,92,89,84,77 74, , , ,**
toteswingers: 1&2 £3.00, 1&3 £19.70, 2&3 £19.70. CSF £19.32 CT £131.72 TOTE £5.20: £2.60, £1.90, £2.30; EX 16.30 Trifecta £95.60 Pool: £590.05 - 4.62 winning units..

Owner Kevin & Anne Glastonbury **Bred** D T And A T Goldsworthy **Trained** Llancarfan, Vale Of Glamorgan

FOCUS
There was a disputed lead with Nozic taken on by Henry King and the pair set a strong gallop given the conditions. A big step up from the winner in a relatively good time.

3094 MARSH GREEN H'CAP HURDLE (8 hdls) 2m
1:25 (1:25) (Class 4) (0-120,120) 3-Y-0+ **£3,285** (£957; £479)

Form RPR

2/5- **1** **Beau Lake (IRE)**[25] 2581 9-9-12 **95** GavinSheehan(3) 100+
(Suzy Smith) *in tch in midfield: effrt and squeezed through on inner to chse ldrs bef 2 out: j.rt 2 out and last: styd on wl u.p to ld towards fin* **8/1**

2- **2** *1* **Smart Money (IRE)**[18] 2729 6-11-4 **112** LiamTreadwell 115+
(Venetia Williams) *t.k.h: hld up in midfield: hdwy to chse ldr and nt fluent 2nd: led 3 out: rdn between last 2: drvn flat hdd and no ex towards fin* **6/4**[1]

3/2- **3** *1 ¼* **Phantom Prince (IRE)**[225] 95 4-11-2 **115** ConorShoemark(5) 116
(Brendan Powell) *racd wd: chsd ldr tl 2nd: styd chsd ldrs: j.lft 4th: wnt 2nd again bef 2 out: drvn between last 2: kpt on same pce flat* **8/1**

/66- **4** *2 ¾* **Reggie Perrin**[40] 2271 5-9-13 **103** PaddyBradley(10) 101
(Pat Phelan) *in tch in rr: rdn and sme hdwy in 6th after 3 out: styd on to go 4th flat: steadily clsng flat: nvr rchd ldrs* **14/1**

/60- **5** *7* **Was My Valentine**[42] 2210 6-10-6 **100** (p) MarkGrant 91
(Jo Davis) *hld up in tch: hdwy to chse ldrs 5th: rdn and no imp bef 2 out: wknd last* **25/1**

/06- **6** *6* **Arrayan**[26] 2569 8-11-2 **110** NickScholfield 97
(Alexandra Dunn) *led: mstke 1st: hdd 3 out: sn drvn: no ex and btn whn bmpd bef next: wknd last* **16/1**

043- **7** *10* **Even If**[20] 2689 5-11-3 **111** RichieMcGrath 86
(Jonjo O'Neill) *hld up in tch in midfield: clsd to chse ldrs 5th: rdn and no rspnse after 3 out: wknd next* **7/1**[3]

0/0- **8** *18* **Downtown Manhattan (IRE)**[35] 2369 6-9-13 **103** TommieMO'Brien(10) 60
(Jonjo O'Neill) *hld up in tch: rdn and struggling in last pair 5th: lost tch after next: t.o 2 out* **20/1**

9 *21* **Kilavalley (IRE)**[190] 665 6-11-3 **118** MikeyEnnis(7) 54
(Hugo Froud) *chsd ldrs: rdn and mstke 5th: wknd sn after next: t.o between last 2* **25/1**

340- **10** *12* **Swampfire (IRE)**[35] 2366 5-11-12 **120** JamieMoore 44
(Gary Moore) *in tch in rr: rdn and struggling 5th: lost tch next: t.o 2 out* **9/2**[2]

4m 16.2s (9.80) **Going Correction** +0.25s/f (Yiel)
WFA 4 from 5yo+ 5lb **10** Ran SP% **117.9**
Speed ratings (Par 105): **85,84,83,82,79 76,71,62,51,45**
toteswingers 1&2 £3.10, 1&3 £15.60, 2&3 £1.30. CSF £20.79 CT £100.85 TOTE £8.10: £2.40, £1.20, £2.20; EX 22.50 Trifecta £162.60 Pool: £1129.57 - 5.21 winning units..
Owner Sergio Gordon-Watson & Graham Willetts **Bred** Larry Murphy **Trained** Lewes, E Sussex

FOCUS
An ordinary handicap. The winner should still be competitive when reassessed.

3095 RSA NOVICES' TRIAL CHASE (REGISTERED AS THE DECEMBER NOVICES' CHASE) (GRADE 2) (18 fncs) 3m
1:55 (1:57) (Class 1) 4-Y-0+ **£17,369** (£6,517; £3,263)

Form RPR

011- **1** **Black Thunder (FR)**[22] 2658 6-11-8 **146** NickScholfield 155+
(Paul Nicholls) *chsd ldr: effrt to chal last and sn led: drvn and asserted fnl 100yds: r.o wl* **8/11**[1]

/13- **2** *2 ¾* **Shotgun Paddy (IRE)**[22] 2658 6-11-5 0 GavinSheehan 149+
(Emma Lavelle) *led: rdn and hit 2 out: drvn and jnd last: no ex and btn fnl 100yds* **6/4**[2]

314- **3** *93* **Buachaill Alainn (IRE)**[14] 2803 6-11-5 132 (p) JamieMoore 53
(Peter Bowen) *a 3rd: pushed along after 6th: u.p after 9th: lost tch 14th: wl t.o 3 out* **8/1**[3]

6m 28.2s (4.50) **Going Correction** +0.475s/f (Soft) **3** Ran SP% **109.0**
Speed ratings (Par 115): **111,110,79**
CSF £2.27 TOTE £1.70; EX 1.80 Trifecta £1.90 Pool: £707.95 - 275.41 winning units..
Owner Donlon, MacDonald, Fulton & Webb **Bred** Mickael Keane **Trained** Ditcheat, Somerset

FOCUS
Some good horses have won this in recent times, including Burton Port, who went on to finish runner-up in that season's RSA Chase. While this was a more or less a match, there was quality on show. The winner is steadily progressive.

3096 TANDRIDGE H'CAP HURDLE (10 hdls) 2m 3f 110y
2:30 (2:31) (Class 3) (0-140,131) 4-Y-0+ **£5,393** (£1,583; £791; £395)

Form RPR

222- **1** **Dolatulo (FR)**[27] 2538 6-11-8 **130** (b) GavinSheehan(3) 140+
(Warren Greatrex) *mde all: hit wing and mstke 2nd: drew wl clr bef 2 out: in n.d whn hit last: heavily eased flat* **11/4**[2]

6/1- **2** *18* **Knight Of Pleasure**[27] 2538 4-11-9 **131** JoshuaMoore(3) 105
(Gary Moore) *hld up in tch in rr: hdwy to trck ldrs 6th: chsd ldr next: rdn and btn bef 2 out: tired but hung on to 2nd cl home* **9/4**[1]

U05- **3** *hd* **Orzare (IRE)**[27] 2538 7-10-8 **118** ConorShoemark(5) 92
(Philip Hide) *chsd ldrs: 3rd and struggling u.p after 7th: wl btn bef 2 out: plugged on and battling for 2nd cl home* **7/1**

223- **4** *50* **Hi Note**[26] 2565 5-11-12 **131** MarcGoldstein 55
(Sheena West) *in tch in rr: rdn and struggling 6th: lost tch next: t.o 3 out* **14/1**

0FP- **P** **Beside The Fire**[7] 2945 8-10-12 **117** (t) JoeTizzard
(Colin Tizzard) *chsd ldrs: chsd wnr after 4th tl after next: sn rdn and struggling: lost tch 7th: t.o whn p.u after next* **20/1**

F61/ **U** **Kuilsriver (IRE)**[301] 4243 6-11-2 **126** ThomasGarner(5)
(Nick Gifford) *chsd wnr tl rdn and lost pl after 4th: last but stl wl in tch whn blnd and uns rdr next* **8/1**

111- **P** **Key To The West (IRE)**[14] 2806 6-11-1 **127** JakeHodson(7)
(David Dennis) *in tch in midfield: chsd wnr after 5th tl 7th: sn rdn and wknd: t.o whn p.u after 3 out* **4/1**[3]

5m 12.3s (5.60) **Going Correction** +0.25s/f (Yiel)
WFA 4 from 5yo+ 5lb **7** Ran SP% **112.5**
Speed ratings (Par 107): **98,90,90,70, ,**
toteswingers 1&2 £1.20, 1&3 £3.40, 2&3 £4.60 CSF £9.34 TOTE £3.60: £1.50, £2.40; EX 10.90 Trifecta £60.60 Pool: £1166.66 - 14.41 winning units..
Owner Chasemore Farm **Bred** Claude Michel **Trained** Upper Lambourn, Berks

FOCUS
Not as good a race as the ratings banding would indicate, with the top-weight rated 9lb below the ceiling. The winner was value for a lot further and rates a personal best.

3097 HARTFIELD H'CAP CHASE (18 fncs) 3m
3:05 (3:06) (Class 3) (0-130,128) 4-Y-0+ **£6,498** (£1,908; £954; £477)

Form RPR

/F1- **1** **Via Sundown (FR)**[18] 2730 5-11-6 **125** JoshuaMoore(3) 140+
(Gary Moore) *hld up wl in tch in last pair: hdwy to trck ldrs 14th: led 3 out: in command next: rdn out: comf* **3/1**[2]

/55- **2** *3 ¾* **Shuil Royale (IRE)**[35] 2367 8-11-1 **117**[1] TomCannon 124
(David Arbuthnot) *led tl 15th: drvn and stl pressing ldrs bef next: 3rd and outpcd by wnr 2 out: wnt 2nd again flat: kpt on but no ch w wnr* **7/1**

042- **3** *4* **Ultragold (FR)**[20] 2693 5-11-5 **121** (t) JoeTizzard 125
(Colin Tizzard) *t.k.h: chsd ldrs: mstke 9th: jnd ldr 12th: led 15th: hdd 3 out: sn rdn and no ex: hit last: lost 2nd flat and wknd fnl 100yds* **5/2**[1]

026/ **4** *1 ¼* **Master Neo (FR)**[342] 3535 7-10-11 **116** (t) MarkQuinlan(3) 120
(Nigel Hawke) *w ldr tl 12th: styd chsng ldrs: rdn and cl enough bef 3 out: 4th and btn whn blnd 2 out: plugged on same pce* **9/2**[3]

111- **5** *nse* **Waltzing Tornado (IRE)**[20] 2702 9-9-12 **105** (p) ConorShoemark(5) 109
(Neil Mulholland) *wl in tch in last pair: blnd 13th: chsd ldrs and rdn bef 3 out: outpcd and btn 2 out: plugged on same pce flat* **8/1**

65/ **6** *26* **Yellow Ball (FR)**[205] 5-11-12 **128** LiamTreadwell 103
(Venetia Williams) *wl in tch in midfield: rdn and struggling 14th: wknd sn after next* **10/1**

/P1- **7** *48* **Colebrooke**[27] 2539 5-11-11 **127** (p) JamieMoore 54
(Renee Robeson) *chsd ldrs: mstke 2nd: rdn and lost pl 12th: bhd and lost tch u.p after 14th: t.o 3 out* **16/1**

6m 30.8s (7.10) **Going Correction** +0.475s/f (Soft) **7** Ran SP% **110.3**
Speed ratings (Par 107): **107,105,104,104,103 95,79**
toteswingers 1&2 £8.30, 1&3 £2.60, 2&3 £5.20 CSF £21.91 CT £54.67 TOTE £3.90: £2.70, £2.80; EX 23.90 Trifecta £62.70 Pool: £883.38 - 10.55 winning units..
Owner The Old Brokers **Bred** Elevage Avicole Lozach Le Yan Et Al **Trained** Lower Beeding, W Sussex

FOCUS
A competitive handicap. The cosy winner is on the upgrade and looks a decent prospect.

3098 AT THE RACES MAIDEN OPEN NATIONAL HUNT FLAT RACE 1m 7f 169y
3:40 (3:40) (Class 6) 4-6-Y-0 **£1,642** (£478; £239)

Form RPR

1 **Dog Or Divorce** 4-10-7 0 LiamTreadwell 88
(Paul Webber) *mde all: rdn and qcknd l clr 2f out: drvn fnl f: r.o gamely: jst hld on* **5/1**[3]

022- **2** *shd* **Playhara (IRE)**[25] 2583 4-10-4 0 PeterCarberry(3) 88
(Nicky Henderson) *chsd wnr thrght: rdn and sltly outpcd 2f out: rallied u.p ent fnl f: grad clsng fnl 100yds: jst failed* **3/1**[2]

3 *nk* **Subordinate (GER)** 4-11-0 0 (t) NickScholfield 95
(Andy Turnell) *hld up in tch: rdn and hdwy over 1f out: swtchd rt and chsd ldrs ins fnl f: r.o wl: nt quite rch ldrs* **8/1**

6- **4** *1* **Barton Antix**[52] 2026 4-11-0 0 AndrewThornton 94
(Neil Mulholland) *wl in tch in midfield: hdwy to chse ldrs ent fnl 2f: rdn wl over 1f out: kpt on same pce ins fnl f* **8/1**

5 *1 ¾* **Con Forza (IRE)** 4-10-11 0 GavinSheehan(3) 92
(Warren Greatrex) *chsd ldrs: rdn and unable qck jst over 2f out: kpt on same pce ins fnl f* **7/4**[1]

44- **6** *3* **Closest Friend**[21] 2681 4-10-4 0 StevieSanders(10) 89
(J R Jenkins) *hld up wl in tch in last pair: hdwy into midfield 7f out: rdn 3f out: outpcd and btn over 1f out: wknd ins fnl f* **8/1**

7 *10* **Howlin Moon** 5-10-0 0 NathanAdams(7) 72
(Michael Attwater) *t.k.h: hld up in tch in rr: rdn over 3f out: sn struggling: wknd 2f out* **16/1**

3m 38.0s **7** Ran SP% **117.2**
toteswingers 1&2 £1.80, 1&3 £2.80, 2&3 £3.00 CSF £21.22 TOTE £4.80: £1.80, £2.10; EX 23.90 Trifecta £84.00 Pool: £ - winning units..
Owner Mr & Mrs A D Mitchell **Bred** Mrs D L Mitchell **Trained** Mollington, Oxon

FOCUS
No surprise to see this develop into a tactical affair. Pretty much unrateable form.
T/Plt: £16.30. Pool: £67103.33 - 2998.24 winning units. T/Qpdt: £7.60. Pool £3799.43 - 369.47 winning units.

3099 - 3105a (Foreign Racing) - See Raceform Interactive

2838 CARLISLE (R-H)
Sunday, December 15

OFFICIAL GOING: Heavy (soft in places) changing to soft on hurdle course after race 2 (12.45)
Wind: Fresh, half against Weather: Cloudy

3106 32RED CASINO NOVICES' HURDLE (8 hdls) 2m 1f
12:15 (12:15) (Class 4) 4-Y-0+ **£3,249** (£954; £477; £238)

Form RPR

2/1- **1** **Vice Et Vertu (FR)**[39] 2286 4-11-5 0 RichardJohnson 130+
(Henry Daly) *t.k.h early: led to 3rd: chsd ldr: hit 4 out: shkn up and hdwy to ld bef 2 out: styd on strly fr last* **1/3**[1]

5- **2** *11* **Dark Dune (IRE)**[16] 2783 5-10-12 0 JamesReveley 113
(Tim Easterby) *chsd wnr: hdwy to ld 3rd: nt fluent 3 out: rdn and hdd bef next: outpcd by wnr fr last* **7/2**[2]

/00- **3** *13* **Spanish Fleet**[18] 2748 5-10-5 0 JohnDawson(7) 99
(John Wade) *in tch: rdn and outpcd 4 out: hdwy to chse (clr) ldng pair 2 out: no imp last* **20/1**

06- **4** *5* **Badea**[7] 2968 4-10-12 0 WilsonRenwick 93
(Martin Todhunter) *hld up: nt fluent 3rd: outpcd bef 3 out: n.d after* **12/1**[3]

0S4- **5** *8* **Indigo Island (IRE)**[12] 2866 4-10-5 0 (t) CallumBewley(7) 85
(Robert Bewley) *chsd clr ldng pair: rdn 4 out: no imp whn lost 2nd 2 out: sn btn* **33/1**

P **Benidorm**[69] 5-10-5 0 (p) GLavery(7)
(John Wainwright) *hld up: struggling 4 out: nvr on terms: t.o whn p.u 2 out* **100/1**

4m 25.9s (-3.30) **Going Correction** -0.10s/f (Good) **6** Ran SP% **113.6**
Speed ratings (Par 105): **103,97,91,89,85**
toteswingers 1&2 £1.10, 2&3 £3.30, 1&3 £2.70 CSF £1.99 TOTE £1.20: £1.10, £1.50; EX 2.10 Trifecta £9.30 Pool: £1236.48 - 99.57 winning units..
Owner Neville Statham & Family **Bred** R Reveillere Et Al **Trained** Stanton Lacy, Shropshire

FOCUS
All rails on outermost line on both tracks. An uncompetitive event but the winner is on the upgrade.

3107 32RED.COM H'CAP CHASE (15 fncs 1 omitted) 2m 4f
12:45 (12:45) (Class 4) (0-105,105)
4-Y-0+ £3,898 (£1,144; £572; £286)

Form RPR
533- 1 **Etxalar (FR)**34 2416 10-11-10 103..........(t) PeterBuchanan 119+
(Lucinda Russell) *led: rdn and hdd 2 out: rallied and regained ld bef last: styd on gamely run-in* 10/3[1]
/52- 2 5 **Indian Voyage (IRE)**197 579 5-10-8 94..........(t) StephenMulqueen(7) 105+
(Maurice Barnes) *hld up in tch: hdwy to chse wnr 9th: chal 5 out: led 2 out: hdd whn hit last: kpt on same pce* 7/2[2]
61F- 3 12 **Tresor De L'Isle (FR)**29 2518 6-11-3 96..........(p) BrianHughes 93
(James Ewart) *cl up: rdn and outpcd whn lft 5 l 3rd 3 out: btn next* 4/1[3]
0P0- 4 3 1/4 **Fred Bojangals (IRE)**12 2868 11-11-12 105..........(p) JasonMaguire 100
(Barbara Butterworth) *hld up in tch: rdn after 5 out: outpcd whn lft 4th 3 out: sn btn* 16/1
P/5- 5 19 **Soul Angel**15 2818 9-10-0 79 oh4..........(v) AdrianLane 54
(Sandy Forster) *mstkes: w ldr: j.lft and blkd 8th: hit and struggling fr next* 9/2
P03- 6 5 **Panthers Run**37 2338 13-9-11 79 oh10..........(t) JohnKington(3) 49
(Jonathan Haynes) *chsd ldrs: drvn and outpcd bef 10th: btn 4 out* 25/1
P43- F **Lukey Luke**16 2784 10-11-3 96.......... BrianHarding
(James Turner) *hld up: stdy hdwy to chse ldrs 5 out: 4 l 3rd and outpcd whn fell 3 out* 6/1
5m 24.3s (-3.10) **Going Correction** -0.10s/f (Good) 7 Ran SP% 107.5
Speed ratings (Par 105): **102,100,95,93,86 84,**
toteswingers 1&2 £2.30, 2&3 £2.80, 1&3 £3.70 CSF £13.88 TOTE £3.80: £1.50, £3.10; EX 16.80 Trifecta £66.70 Pool: £1600.41 - 17.98 winning units..
Owner Dig In Racing **Bred** Elie Lellouche And Bertrand Clin **Trained** Arlary, Perth & Kinross
FOCUS
A moderate contest. The winner is rated to the level of last season's course win.

3108 PERTEMPS NETWORK H'CAP HURDLE (SERIES QUALIFIER) (12 hdls) 3m 1f
1:20 (1:20) (Class 2) 4-Y-0+ £12,021 (£3,529; £1,764; £882)

Form RPR
/21- 1 **Kaki De La Pree (FR)**50 2076 6-10-6 127.......... FelixDeGiles 135+
(Tom Symonds) *hld up: smooth hdwy bef 3 out: rdn to ld between last 2: sn hrd pressed: styd on wl run-in* 3/1[1]
35F- 2 2 **Pineau De Re (FR)**8 2937 10-11-1 136.......... RichardJohnson 140+
(Dr Richard Newland) *hld up: smooth hdwy bef 2 out: chal gng wl last: sn rdn: kpt on: nt pce of wnr* 7/1
/40- 3 20 **Trustan Times (IRE)**22 2672 7-11-12 147.......... JamesReveley 130
(Tim Easterby) *hld up in tch: hdwy to chse ldr 4 out: rdn and ev ch bef 2 out: outpcd by first two fr last* 6/1[3]
/24- 4 2 3/4 **Our Joey (IRE)**23 2655 5-9-7 121 oh1.......... JonathonBewley(7) 102
(George Bewley) *led: mstke 4 out: rdn bef 2 out: hdd between last 2: wknd last* 4/1[2]
322- 5 3/4 **Neptune Equester**18 2746 10-10-0 121 oh1.......... AidanColeman 101
(Brian Ellison) *cl up to 7th: drvn and outpcd after next: rallied after 3 out: outpcd fr 2 out* 12/1
/13- 6 11 **Lie Forrit (IRE)**22 2672 9-11-8 143.......... PeterBuchanan 117
(Lucinda Russell) *w ldr to 7th: drvn along after next: wknd bef 2 out* 4/1[2]
/P0- 7 47 **Rock Relief (IRE)**15 2821 7-10-2 123.......... HenryBrooke 45
(Chris Grant) *in tch: rdn bef 4 out: rallied next: wknd bef 2 out* 50/1
R/4- P **Alpha Victor (IRE)**36 2357 8-10-7 133.......... HarryChalloner(5)
(William Kinsey) *prom: drvn and outpcd 3 out: struggling bef next: t.o whn p.u bef last* 20/1
054- P **Howizee**15 2807 7-9-9 123..........(t) StephenMulqueen(7)
(Maurice Barnes) *in tch: drvn and struggling after 4 out: wknd next: t.o whn p.u 2 out* 11/1
6m 29.2s (-9.80) **Going Correction** -0.10s/f (Good) 9 Ran SP% 114.5
Speed ratings (Par 109): **111,110,103,103,102 99,84, ,**
toteswingers 1&2 £5.30, 2&3 £6.90, 1&3 £4.80 CSF £24.30 CT £117.73 TOTE £5.10: £2.00, £2.60, £2.00; EX 27.40 Trifecta £85.50 Pool: £2601.76 - 22.82 winning units..
Owner Sir Peter & Lady Gibbings **Bred** Michel Froissard **Trained** Harewood End, H'fords
FOCUS
A good-quality event, which produced a taking winner, who's on the upgrade.

3109 32RED NOVICES' LIMITED H'CAP CHASE (THE SUNDAY £5K BONUS RACE) (16 fncs 1 omitted) 2m 5f
1:55 (1:55) (Class 3) (0-140,133) 4-Y-0+ £6,498 (£1,908; £954)

Form RPR
/20- 1 **Knock A Hand (IRE)**22 2672 8-11-5 133..........(b) RichardJohnson 143+
(Richard Lee) *j.w: mde all: clr bef last: drvn out* 11/10[1]
/10- 2 12 **Avoca Promise (IRE)**43 2212 8-10-13 127..........(p) FelixDeGiles 123
(Tom Symonds) *t.k.h: chsd wnr to bef 4 out: rallied whn nt fluent next: wnt 2nd and effrt appr 2 out: outpcd fr last* 13/8[2]
UU2- 3 1 1/2 **Jet Master (IRE)**36 2359 7-10-13 127..........(t[1]) PeterBuchanan 122
(N W Alexander) *chsd ldrs: effrt and wnt 2nd bef 4 out to bef 2 out: sn hung rt and outpcd* 4/1[3]
5m 37.8s (-7.30) **Going Correction** -0.10s/f (Good) 3 Ran SP% 105.7
Speed ratings (Par 107): **109,104,103**
CSF £3.15 TOTE £1.80; EX 1.70 Trifecta £4.10 Pool: £1081.39 - 195.52winning units..
Owner Alan Halsall **Bred** Patrick Monahan **Trained** Byton, H'fords
FOCUS
Uncompetitive stuff, the winner improving to the level of his best hurdle form.

3110 32RED "NATIONAL HUNT" NOVICES' HURDLE (10 hdls) 2m 3f 110y
2:25 (2:25) (Class 4) 4-Y-0+ £3,249 (£954; £477; £238)

Form RPR
1/1- 1 **Oscars Den (IRE)**29 2507 5-11-5 0.......... RichardJohnson 126+
(Tim Vaughan) *mstkes: t.k.h early: chsd ldrs: hit 4 out and next: effrt whn nt fluent 2 out: swtchd rt and rallied to ld appr last: wandered u.p: drvn out* 8/15[1]
1/5- 2 3 **Sealous Scout (IRE)**44 2196 5-10-12 0.......... JasonMaguire 111
(Donald McCain) *pressed ldr: rdn and led 2 out: hdd bef last: kpt on same pce run-in* 5/2[2]
15F- 3 5 **Just Cameron**8 2954 6-11-5 0.......... RichieMcGrath 115
(Philip Kirby) *led: rdn and hdd 2 out: outpcd whn nt fluent last* 6/1[3]
600- 4 54 **Dalstontosiloth (IRE)**7 2968 5-10-5 0.......... CallumBewley(7) 52
(Barry Murtagh) *hld up in tch: struggling 4 out: t.o* 50/1
033- 5 36 **Mrs Grass**19 2736 6-10-2 82.......... JohnKington(3) 9
(Jonathan Haynes) *in tch: struggling bef 4 out: t.o* 66/1
0- P **Manyshadesofblack (IRE)**11 2885 5-10-5 0.......... BrianHarding
(Tina Jackson) *bhd: lost tch fr 5th: t.o whn p.u 4 out* 100/1
5m 9.9s (1.10) **Going Correction** -0.10s/f (Good) 6 Ran SP% 112.5
Speed ratings (Par 105): **93,91,89,68,53**
toteswingers 1&2 £1.10, 2&3 £1.40, 1&3 £1.10 CSF £2.31 TOTE £1.60: £1.10, £1.20; EX 2.60 Trifecta £4.50 Pool: £2609.91 - 427.22 winning units..
Owner Mrs Z Wentworth **Bred** Paul Gibbons **Trained** Aberthin, Vale of Glamorgan
FOCUS
Not form to get too excited about, but the pace did seem honest in testing conditions. The winner is rated below the level of his Uttoxeter win.

3111 PPM THE PROPERTY MAINTENANCE PEOPLE H'CAP CHASE (17 fncs 2 omitted) 3m 2f
2:55 (2:55) (Class 4) (0-120,118) 4-Y-0+ £3,898 (£1,144; £572; £286)

Form RPR
133- 1 **Wayward Glance**29 2516 5-11-12 118..........(p) WilsonRenwick 128+
(Keith Dalgleish) *led or disp ld: wnt on 12th: hdd briefly 4 out: styd on strly to go clr fr 2 out* 8/1
P1P/ 2 8 **Emma Soda**240 5377 8-10-8 103.......... PeterCarberry(3) 106+
(Paul Davies) *chsd ldrs: chal 11th: led briefly whn hit 4 out: sn hdd: cl 2nd whn mstke next: rdn and one pce fr 2 out* 12/1
331- 3 5 **The Friary (IRE)**37 2334 6-11-4 115..........(tp) DerekFox(5) 113
(Lucinda Russell) *nt fluent on occasions: in tch: outpcd 1/2-way: rallied 5 out: drvn and outpcd next: styng on whn mstke and stmbld 2 out: kpt on: no ch w first two* 11/4[2]
/35- 4 7 **Fiddlers Reel**14 2841 10-11-11 117.......... DenisO'Regan 109
(Jane Clark) *hld up in tch: stdy hdwy 11th: drvn and reminders next: outpcd fr 4 out* 3/1[3]
P/1- P **Papamoa**46 2157 8-11-7 113.......... BrianHarding
(N W Alexander) *led or disp ld to 12th: rdn and wknd 4 out: sn p.u* 6/4[1]
7m 6.5s (-0.70) **Going Correction** -0.10s/f (Good) 5 Ran SP% 110.5
Speed ratings (Par 105): **97,94,93,90,**
CSF £69.91 TOTE £6.10: £1.90, £3.70; EX 63.70 Trifecta £163.00 Pool: £18108.08 - 8.32 winning units..
Owner Straightline Construction Ltd **Bred** The Queen **Trained** Carluke, S Lanarks
FOCUS
This is fair form, but the winner has more to offer.

3112 32RED CASINO STANDARD OPEN NATIONAL HUNT FLAT RACE 2m 1f
3:25 (3:25) (Class 6) 4-6-Y-0 £1,559 (£457; £228; £114)

Form RPR
1- 1 **Stonebrook (IRE)**34 2422 5-11-7 0.......... JasonMaguire 117+
(Donald McCain) *in tch: smooth hdwy over 4f out: led over 1f out: shkn up and kpt on wl fnl f* 4/9[1]
2 1 3/4 **Hail The Brave (IRE)** 4-10-9 0..........[1] AdamNicol(5) 106
(Philip Kirby) *hld up in tch: smooth hdwy on outside 3f out: rdn and ev ch over 1f out: kpt on fnl f* 10/1[3]
3 3 3/4 **The Orange Rogue (IRE)**49 6-10-7 0.......... MrKitAlexander(7) 102
(N W Alexander) *w ldr: led over 2f out to over 1f out: rdn and one pce fnl f* 9/2[2]
5- 4 1 3/4 **Sheilas Lady**18 2752 5-10-4 0.......... JohnKington(3) 93
(Andrew Crook) *led at stdy pce: rdn and hdd over 2f out: rallied: outpcd over 1f out* 12/1
5 6 **Amazing Eight** 4-10-7 0.......... MrHAABannister(7) 94
(Michael Easterby) *hld up in tch: outpcd over 5f out: sme late hdwy: nvr rchd ldrs* 20/1
6 1/2 **Purple Harry** 5-11-0 0.......... BrianHarding 94
(Tina Jackson) *trckd ldrs: drvn and outpcd over 3f out: n.d after* 33/1
4m 34.6s (10.40) **Going Correction** -0.10s/f (Good)
WFA 4 from 5yo+ 5lb 6 Ran SP% 111.9
Speed ratings: **71,70,68,67,64 64**
toteswingers 1&2 £2.10, 2&3 £2.00, 1&3 £1.10 CSF £5.98 TOTE £1.50: £1.10, £3.60; EX 7.40 Trifecta £17.10 Pool: £1662.08 - 72.51 winning units..
Owner John P McManus **Bred** George Ward **Trained** Cholmondeley, Cheshire
FOCUS
The winner and fourth were close to their marks in this slowly run bumper.
T/Plt: £72.80 to a £1 stake. Pool of £63314.09 - 634.20 winning tickets. T/Qpdt: £29.40 to a £1 stake. Pool of £5495.76 - 138.05 winning tickets. RY

2872 SOUTHWELL (L-H)
Sunday, December 15

OFFICIAL GOING: Good (good to soft in places; 6.1) changing to good to soft after race 3 (1.30)
Wind: moderate 1/2 against Weather: overcast, rain 1st 2

3113 BETFRED FRED'S FESTIVE GIVEAWAY H'CAP CHASE (14 fncs 2 omitted) 2m 4f 110y
12:25 (12:25) (Class 4) (0-115,115)
4-Y-0+ £3,898 (£1,144; £572; £286)

Form RPR
/32- 1 **Roc D'Apsis (FR)**25 2601 4-11-3 113.......... PaddyBrennan 121+
(Tom George) *drvn along 5th: hit 6 out (normal 7 out): sn chsng ldrs: mstke 4 out (normal 5 out): chal 2 out (normal 3 out): led last 150yds: drvn out* 5/2[2]
4/3- 2 3/4 **Entertain Me**184 738 9-11-5 108.......... CharliePoste 118
(Robin Dickin) *chsd ldrs: led appr 2 out (normal 3 out): hdd and no ex last 150yds* 16/1
B22- 3 7 **Father Shine (IRE)**12 2873 10-11-4 110.......... TrevorWhelan(3) 115
(Shaun Harris) *chsd ldrs: hit 3rd: 3rd and drvn whn hit 2 out (normal 3 out): one pce and tk modest 3rd last* 8/1[3]
/P5- 4 7 **Pensnett Bay**29 2512 8-11-10 113..........(b) MarkGrant 114+
(Jo Hughes) *led: clr 2nd: drvn and mstke 6 out (normal 7 out): sn jnd: hit 3 out (normal 4 out): hdd appr next: rallied omitted 2 out: sn wknd* 8/1[3]
035/ P **Reelwill (FR)**301 8-9-7 89 oh22.......... OllieGarner(7)
(Derek Shaw) *j.rt: lft 2nd 1st: hit 6th: drvn and lost pl 6 out (normal 7 out): sn lost pl: t.o 4 out (normal 5 out): p.u bef 2 out (normal 3 out)* 50/1
3PU- U **What An Oscar (IRE)**10 2895 8-11-12 115..........(v) SamTwiston-Davies
(Nigel Twiston-Davies) *w ldrs whn j.lft and uns rdr 1st* 8/1[3]
553- B **Tregaro (FR)**12 2873 7-10-9 98..........(t) RyanMania
(Mike Sowersby) *b.d 1st* 8/1[3]

6/2- F Trojan Sun[37] 2350 7-11-1 109 (t) BenPoste[(5)]
(Tom Symonds) *fell 1st* 9/4[1]

5m 34.8s (17.80) **Going Correction** +0.975s/f (Soft)
WFA 4 from 7yo+ 6lb 8 Ran SP% **111.6**
Speed ratings (Par 105): **105,104,102,99, , ,**
toteswingers 1&2 £7.50, 2&3 £15.30, 1&3 £2.60 CSF £36.19 CT £272.48 TOTE £3.40: £1.90, £4.20, £2.20; EX 40.60 Trifecta £254.50 Pool: £2050.85 - 6.04 winning units..
Owner Muhammad Nadeem Khan **Bred** N Colliere, C Verry et al **Trained** Slad, Gloucs

FOCUS
Both bends moved on to fresh ground with fences and hurdles sited on outside rail. This ordinary handicap chase lost much of its lustre after carnage at the first with the fall of market leader Trojan Sun, who brought down Tregaro and unseated What An Oscar. As a result of an injured rider, they missed out the penultimate fence on both circuits.

3114 BETFRED FUN AND FRIENDLY H'CAP CHASE (21 fncs) 3m 2f
12:55 (12:55) (Class 5) (0-100,94) 4-Y-0+ **£2,274** (£667; £333; £166)

Form RPR
453- 1 **Phoenix Des Mottes (FR)**[12] 2872 10-9-9 68 JoeCornwall[(5)] 74
(John Cornwall) *chsd ldrs: drvn along 7th: 2nd 14th: led next: hdd 5 out: lft in ld next: hdd narrowly last: rallied run-in: led nr fin* 16/1

34B- 2 ½ **Kilvergan Boy (IRE)**[15] 2829 9-10-6 74 (p) SamTwiston-Davies 82
(Nigel Twiston-Davies) *chsd ldrs: lft cl 2nd and hmpd 4 out: upsides 2 out: led narrowly last: hdd and no ex in clsng stages* 7/2[2]

/25- 3 64 **Timpo (FR)**[39] 2297 10-11-9 94 (p) JakeGreenall[(3)] 42
(Henry Daly) *chsd ldrs: pckd landing 2nd: drvn after 14th: wknd 5 out: lft modest 3rd and hmpd next: sn wknd: t.o 3 out* 3/1[1]

053- 4 21 **Moon Melody (GER)**[10] 2902 10-10-4 77 (bt) SamanthaDrake[(5)] 7
(Mike Sowersby) *chsd ldrs: drvn 12th: outpcd next: lost pl 16th: t.o whn lft 4th last* 12/1

433- P **Overton Lad**[15] 2829 12-10-0 68 oh4 (bt) HarrySkelton
(Peter Pritchard) *lost pl 6th: bhd 11th: sme hdwy 15th: sn lost pl: lft poor 4th 4 out: sn t.o whn p.u appr last* 7/1[3]

6/5- P **Acosta**[22] 2680 9-10-1 72 (b) WayneKavanagh[(3)]
(Dr Jeremy Naylor) *sn detached in last: drvn 7th: t.o 11th: p.u after 14th* 25/1

641/ F **Oscar The Myth (IRE)**[565] 469 7-11-6 88 (tp) NickScholfield
(Jeremy Scott) *led: hdd 15th: led 5 out: fell next* 3/1[1]

00P- P **Celtic Fella (IRE)**[35] 2389 6-10-0 68 oh1 (tp) DonalDevereux
(Debra Hamer) *chsd ldrs: drvn 14th: lost pl 16th: t.o 4 out: p.u bef next* 8/1

7m 15.4s (29.40) **Going Correction** +0.975s/f (Soft) 8 Ran SP% **113.3**
Speed ratings (Par 103): **93,92,73,66, , ,**
toteswingers 1&2 £9.60, 2&3 £3.20, 1&3 £9.10 CSF £71.68 CT £217.97 TOTE £15.00: £4.00, £1.90, £1.10; EX 79.20 Trifecta £412.60 Pool: £2071.87 - 3.76 winning units..
Owner J R Cornwall **Bred** Mme Claudie Poirier & Yann Poirier **Trained** Long Clawson, Leics

FOCUS
The rain arrived before the start of this modest staying chase, which was run at a decent clip for the conditions. The complexion of the race changed four out when Oscar The Myth fell.

3115 BETFRED GOALS GALORE MAIDEN HURDLE (11 hdls) 2m 4f 110y
1:30 (1:32) (Class 5) 4-Y-0+ **£1,949** (£572; £286; £143)

Form RPR
1/1- 1 **Red Sherlock**[28] 2534 4-11-0 0 TomScudamore 133+
(David Pipe) *trckd ldr: led appr 2 out: pushed along between last 2: sn clr: eased towards fin* 4/9[1]

0- 2 14 **Canuspotit**[16] 2783 6-10-9 0 MattCrawley[(5)] 116+
(Lucy Wadham) *hld up in rr: hdwy 7th: chsng ldrs 3 out: wnt 2nd between last 2: mstke last: no ch w wnr* 33/1

1- 3 6 **Truckers Steel (IRE)**[52] 2052 5-11-0 0 PaddyBrennan 110+
(Tom George) *led: drvn 3 out: hdd appr next: one pce* 3/1[2]

655- 4 16 **Cusheen Bridge (IRE)**[24] 2621 5-11-0 0 AdamPogson 92
(Charles Pogson) *chsd ldrs: one pce fr 3 out* 25/1

/06- 5 ¾ **In The Gate (IRE)**[14] 2850 5-11-0 0 NoelFehily 91
(Charlie Longsdon) *in rr: hdwy 7th: modest 5th and one pce sn after 3 out* 9/1[3]

402- 6 18 **Badger Wood**[17] 2761 4-11-0 0 DavidEngland 73
(Giles Smyly) *chsd ldrs: drvn 7th: lost pl next* 10/1

P/0- 7 15 **Lecale Lad (IRE)**[35] 2393 6-10-11 0 MichaelByrne[(3)] 58
(Tim Vaughan) *stdd s: in rr: j.rt: bhd fr 7th: t.o* 50/1

46- 8 20 **Palmarrick (IRE)**[24] 2627 6-11-0 0 HarryHaynes 38
(Nick Kent) *t.k.h: trckd ldng pair: wknd 3 out: sn bhd: t.o* 100/1

662/ P **Nowdoro**[30] 4863 4-11-0 116 DougieCostello
(Julie Camacho) *chsd ldrs: drvn 6th: lost pl after next: sn bhd: t.o whn p.u bef 2 out* 20/1

000- P **Amber Flush**[25] 2600 4-10-4 0 TrevorWhelan[(3)]
(Tom Symonds) *mid-div: lost pl 7th: t.o 3 out: p.u bef next* 100/1

66- F **Retroson (IRE)**[31] 2472 5-11-0 0 LiamTreadwell
(Michael Scudamore) *in rr: bhd fr 7th: t.o whn fell 2 out* 66/1

P0- P **Secret Island**[172] 841 4-10-7 0 CharliePoste
(Anthony Day) *in rr: bhd 6th: t.o whn p.u bef next* 100/1

5m 26.0s (13.00) **Going Correction** +0.975s/f (Soft)
WFA 4 from 5yo+ 6lb 12 Ran SP% **131.3**
Speed ratings (Par 103): **114,108,106,100,100 93,87,79, , ,**
toteswingers 1&2 £11.20, 2&3 £18.00, 1&3 £1.10 CSF £31.74 TOTE £1.50: £1.10, £7.20, £1.40; EX 32.70 Trifecta £146.10 Pool: £3351.75 - 17.10 winning units..
Owner The Johnson Family **Bred** David Johnson **Trained** Nicholashayne, Devon

FOCUS
The market suggested this was an easy opportunity for Red Sherlock to maintain his unbeaten status, but this novice hurdle was a little more competitive than his SP implied.

3116 BETFRED TV NOVICES' HURDLE (13 hdls) 3m 110y
2:05 (2:05) (Class 4) 4-Y-0+ **£3,249** (£954; £477; £238)

Form RPR
5- 1 **Walk On Al (IRE)**[38] 2316 5-10-12 0 HarrySkelton 115+
(Dan Skelton) *chsd ldrs: drvn 3 out: led between last 2: kpt rt up to work* 3/1[1]

4- 2 2¾ **Gorsky Island**[23] 2654 5-10-12 0 PaddyBrennan 109
(Tom George) *trckd ldrs: cl 2nd 10th: rallied run-in: no imp* 4/1[3]

4- 3 15 **Smiles For Miles (IRE)**[44] 2195 5-10-12 0 TomScudamore 98
(David Pipe) *led: drvn after 3 out: hdd between last 2: sn wknd* 7/2[2]

43F- 4 59 **Squeeze Me**[17] 2768 6-10-5 0 TomO'Brien 34
(Peter Bowen) *chsd ldr: wknd 10th: t.o 2 out* 4/1[3]

4- 5 27 **Church Bray**[190] 675 5-10-12 0 SamTwiston-Davies 17
(Nigel Twiston-Davies) *chsd ldrs: outpcd whn hit 9th: wknd next: sn bhd: t.o 2 out: virtually p.u run-in* 5/1

0/5- 6 74 **Kayf Moss**[23] 2648 5-10-12 0 RhysFlint
(John Flint) *chsd ldrs: drvn 4th: lost pl 8th: sn bhd: t.o 3 out: eventually completed* 14/1

0P/ P **Silk Sky**[231] 1 7-10-2 0 JackQuinlan[(3)]
(Phil McEntee) *in rr: reminders 4th: sn bhd: t.o whn p.u bef 8th* 100/1

P **Frosty Dawn** 5-10-2 0 GavinSheehan[(3)]
(Mike Sowersby) *in rr: reminders 7th: sn bhd: t.o whn p.u bef 9th* 100/1

6m 43.0s (28.00) **Going Correction** +0.975s/f (Soft) 8 Ran SP% **112.5**
Speed ratings (Par 105): **94,93,88,69,60 37, ,**
toteswingers 1&2 £3.00, 2&3 £3.30, 1&3 £2.30 CSF £15.11 TOTE £4.80: £1.40, £2.20, £1.10; EX 17.00 Trifecta £54.90 Pool: £2678.41 - 36.53 winning units..
Owner Donlon, MacDonald & McGowan **Bred** W Dillon **Trained** Alcester, Warwicks

FOCUS
A relatively competitive novice hurdle for the grade and they went a sensible pace for the conditions. The form looks solid.

3117 COLLECT TOTEPOOL BETS IN ALL BETFRED SHOPS MARES' H'CAP HURDLE (THE SUNDAY £5K BONUS RACE) (11 hdls) 2m 4f 110y
2:35 (2:36) (Class 4) (0-120,120) 3-Y-0+ **£3,249** (£954; £477; £238)

Form RPR
0/0- 1 **Beyeh (IRE)**[23] 2655 5-11-4 117 JonathanEngland[(5)] 127+
(Michael Appleby) *trckd ldrs: led on bit bef 2 out: sn wl clr: heavily eased run-in* 5/1[3]

350- 2 15 **Loyaute (FR)**[36] 2371 6-11-2 110 JamesDavies 105+
(Chris Down) *in rr: hdwy to chse ldrs 6th: outpcd and 4th whn blnd 8th: styd on appr next: 3rd 2 out: tk poor 2nd last* 7/2[2]

/11- 3 1 **Midnight Belle**[37] 2352 6-11-11 119 TomScudamore 109
(Tom Symonds) *led: hdd bef 5th: led again after 3 out: sn hdd: one pce* 3/1[1]

/00- 4 20 **Petit Fleur**[21] 2691 11-10-4 98 SamTwiston-Davies 70
(Julian Smith) *in rr: sme hdwy 6th: lost pl 8th: sn bhd* 33/1

141- 5 nk **Belle De Fontenay (FR)**[10] 2894 8-11-2 115 (p) ConorShoemark[(5)] 86
(Conor Dore) *chsd ldrs: led bef 5th: hdd after 3 out: wknd bef next* 15/2

216/ 6 37 **Adiynara (IRE)**[201] 4107 5-11-5 113 (p) NoelFehily 51
(Neil Mulholland) *hld up in rr: racd wd: hdwy 6th: 4th and outpcd whn mstke 3 out: sn lost pl: t.o next: virtually p.u last: eventually completed* 10/1

/00- P **Tribu D'Estruval (FR)**[17] 2767 6-10-6 100 (t) PaddyBrennan
(Tom George) *chsd ldrs: drvn 6th: lost pl bef 3 out: distant 5th whn p.u between last 2* 16/1

2/2- P **Ruby Glow**[32] 2463 5-11-4 112 AndrewThornton
(Seamus Mullins) *racd wd: sn chsng ldrs: lost pl after 7th: eased and p.u after next* 12/1

/62- P **Definite Ruby (IRE)**[33] 2435 5-11-9 117 DavidBass
(Nicky Henderson) *in rr: pushed along 4th: hdwy 6th: lost pl bef next: sn bhd: t.o whn p.u bef 2 out* 8/1

5m 30.0s (17.00) **Going Correction** +0.975s/f (Soft) 9 Ran SP% **112.4**
Speed ratings (Par 105): **106,100,99,92,92 78, , ,**
toteswingers 1&2 £4.30, 2&3 £2.60, 1&3 £4.60 CSF £22.56 CT £60.14 TOTE £6.10: £2.00, £1.60, £1.60; EX 27.30 Trifecta £90.20 Pool: £2807.22 - 23.32 winning units..
Owner Terry Pryke **Bred** Michael McGlynn **Trained** Danethorpe, Notts

FOCUS
The heavy showers had turned the ground good to soft before the previous race and they finished very tired and well strung-out in this decent mares' handicap hurdle.

3118 BETFRED TREBLE ODDS ON LUCKY 15'S CONDITIONAL JOCKEYS' (S) HURDLE (9 hdls) 2m
3:05 (3:05) (Class 5) 4-7-Y-0 **£1,949** (£572; £286; £143)

Form RPR
023- 1 **Lac Sacre (FR)**[14] 2846 4-10-9 108 (tp) JoshHamer[(3)] 117+
(Tony Carroll) *hld up: trckd ldrs: jnd ldrs 6th: led on bit 2 out: 1 l ahd last: shkn up run-in: pushed out* 6/5[1]

/4F- 2 2½ **Juno The Muffinman (IRE)**[203] 501 4-10-9 117 MichaelByrne[(3)] 110
(Tim Vaughan) *w ldrs: drvn to ld briefly appr 2 out: kpt on same pce run-in: no imp* 2/1[2]

3 13 **Hamble**[25] 4-10-12 0 (t) TrevorWhelan 99
(Julia Feilden) *t.k.h: led: hit 3 out: hdd appr next: wknd between last 2* 4/1[3]

1P0- 4 28 **Stadium Of Light (IRE)**[16] 2787 6-10-13 86 WilliamFeatherstone[(5)] 86
(Shaun Harris) *w ldrs: drvn 6th: sn lost pl and bhd: t.o 2 out* 10/1

4m 14.6s (17.60) **Going Correction** +0.975s/f (Soft)
WFA 4 from 5yo+ 5lb 4 Ran SP% **107.9**
Speed ratings: **95,93,87,73**
CSF £3.96 TOTE £2.50; EX 3.10 Trifecta £5.60 Pool: £1028.96 - 136.29 winning units..There was no bid for the winner.
Owner Stephen Louch **Bred** Mlle Francoise Perree **Trained** Cropthorne, Worcs

FOCUS
A paucity of runners and no great pace.

3119 BETFRED MOBILE LOTTO H'CAP HURDLE (13 hdls) 3m 110y
3:35 (3:36) (Class 5) (0-100,99) 4-Y-0+ **£1,949** (£572; £286; £143)

Form RPR
P62- 1 **Iconic Rose**[22] 2680 6-11-5 95 KielanWoods[(3)] 107+
(Pam Sly) *trckd ldrs: led bef 10th: hrd drvn appr 2 out: kpt on wl run-in* 7/2[2]

455- 2 4 **Bold Tara**[21] 2696 6-9-11 77 (tp) OllieGarner[(7)] 84
(Martin Keighley) *chsd ldrs: upsides 10th: hrd drvn appr 2 out: kpt on same pce run-in* 13/2[3]

/5F- 3 2¾ **Head Spin (IRE)**[12] 2877 5-10-7 80 (p) AndrewThornton 85
(Seamus Mullins) *hld up in mid-div: hdwy 6th: handy 3rd 10th: rdn and hit 2 out: kpt on one pce* 10/1

5P4- 4 27 **Xenophon**[10] 2903 5-9-10 74 JoeCornwall[(5)] 53
(Michael Chapman) *rn in snatches: mid-div: hdwy 6th: lost pl 8th: sme hdwy 3 out: wnt distant 4th between last 2* 28/1

0FU- 5 33 **Song Of Pride (GER)**[5] 3014 9-9-9 73 (b) JonathanEngland[(5)] 23
(Mandy Rowland) *in rr: sme hdwy 10th: wknd after next: sn bhd: t.o* 33/1

/5P- P **Zelos Diktator**[33] 2430 7-10-4 87 MikeyHamill[(10)]
(Sean Curran) *led tl bef 2nd: w ldrs: drvn 8th: wknd next: bhd 3 out: t.o whn p.u bef next* 16/1

PP0- P **Sandynow (IRE)**[32] 2458 8-11-12 99 (p) DonalDevereux
(Peter Bowen) *t.k.h: trckd ldrs: led 3rd: hdd bef 10th: wknd 3 out: t.o 6th whn p.u between last 2* 16/1

60P- P **Haling Park (UAE)**[10] 2894 7-9-11 73 oh9 (v) TrevorWhelan[(3)]
(Clarissa Caroe) *in rr: bhd fr 9th: t.o 3 out: p.u bef next* 100/1

265- P **Kayalar (IRE)**[17] 2764 5-11-9 **96**......................................(p) PaulMoloney
(Evan Williams) *racd wd: chsd ldrs: wknd 9th: bhd 3 out: t.o 7th whn p.u bef next* **8/1**[1]

400- P **Whatsupjack (IRE)**[12] 2877 6-10-9 **85**.............................. JakeGreenall(3)
(Shaun Harris) *chsd ldrs: reminders and lost pl 6th: bhd 9th: t.o whn p.u after 3 out* **12/1**

/65- P **Adili (IRE)**[15] 2827 4-10-6 **79**..(v[1]) HarryHaynes
(Brian Ellison) *w ldrs: led bef 2nd: hdd 3rd: drvn 8th: lost pl next: bhd 3 out: t.o whn p.u bef next* **16/1**

143- P **Realta Mo Croi (IRE)**[20] 2723 5-10-12 **90**..............(p) ConorShoemark(5)
(Neil Mulholland) *in rr: hit 3rd: hdwy 9th: modest 5th 3 out: sn lost pl and bhd: t.o whn p.u bef next* **3/1**[1]

6m 39.5s (24.50) **Going Correction** +0.975s/f (Soft)
WFA 4 from 5yo+ 7lb **12 Ran SP% 113.5**
Speed ratings (Par 103): **99,97,96,88,77 ,,,,,**
toteswingers 1&2 £4.10, 2&3 £10.10, 1&3 £7.90 CSF £25.31 CT £204.86 TOTE £3.70: £1.70, £2.40, £2.80; EX 28.00 Trifecta £250.00 Pool: £3278.20 - 9.83 winning units..
Owner The Stablemates **Bred** The Stablemates **Trained** Thorney, Cambs

FOCUS
A trio drew clear from half a mile out in this modest handicap hurdle and proven staying ability won the day.
T/Jkpt: £7,448.50 to a £1 stake. Pool of £118967.22 - 11.34 winning tickets. T/Plt: £10.40 to a £1 stake. Pool of £75846.53 - 5307.41 winning tickets. T/Qpdt: £3.60 to a £1 stake. Pool of £7576.19 - 1521.34 winning tickets. WG

3120 - 3121a (Foreign Racing) - See Raceform Interactive

2961 NAVAN (L-H)
Sunday, December 15

OFFICIAL GOING: Yielding changing to yielding to soft after race 1 (12.05)

3122a NAVAN NOVICE HURDLE (GRADE 1) (11 hdls) 2m 4f
1:05 (1:06) 4-Y-0+ **£36,991** (£10,813)

RPR

1 **Briar Hill (IRE)**[26] 2584 5-11-10 .... RWalsh 147+
(W P Mullins, Ire) *mde all: nt fluent 3 out and sn niggled along: again nt fluent next but extended advantage appr last where j. much bttr: styd on wl* **1/4**[1]

2 4 ¾ **Azorian (IRE)**[21] 2706 5-11-10 139....................................... DavyRussell 143
(Eoin Griffin, Ire) *chsd sole rival whn rn wd off bnd after 5th: sn regained grnd and clsd to press wnr bef 2 out: no imp appr last: kpt on same pce* **11/4**[2]

5m 4.5s (2.70)
WFA 4 from 5yo 6lb **2 Ran SP% 106.7**
TOTE £1.10; DF 1.10.
Owner Andrea & Graham Wylie **Bred** Victor Connolly **Trained** Muine Beag, Co Carlow

FOCUS
This contest has never had more than six runners since it was promoted to Grade 1 status but the defections of Apache Stronghold due to a foot abscess and Very Wood, who was off his feed, diluted the event both in quantity and quality. The winning time was almost eight seconds slower than the handicap hurdle half an hour later. There are obvious limits to the form, which is rated around the runner-up.

3126a 'FUTURE CHAMPIONS' INH FLAT RACE (GRADE 2) 2m
3:20 (3:21) 4-7-Y-0 **£14,532** (£4,247; £2,012; £670)

RPR

1 2 ¼ **Fine Rightly (IRE)**[240] 5373 5-12-0 .... MrSCrawford 124
(S R B Crawford, Ire) *sn trckd ldr in clr 2nd: on terms 3f out and sn led narrowly: hdd appr fnl f and impeded whn wnr edgd lft fnl 150yds: kpt on same pce and no imp in clsng stages* **5/1**[2]

2 **Royal Caviar (IRE)**[25] 2611 5-12-0 .... MrPWMullins 127+
(W P Mullins, Ire) *led tl jnd 3f out: sn narrowly hdd: led again appr fnl f: edgd lft fnl 150yds and bmpd runner-up: drvn clr in clsng stages* **1/4**[1]

3 24 **Desertmore Stream (IRE)**[28] 2548 5-12-0 ....[1] MrRJKiely 100
(Philip Fenton, Ire) *hld up in rr tl prog into modest 3rd bef 1/2-way: clsd on ldrs under 4f out: no imp 2f out and sn one pce* **6/1**[3]

4 13 **Perfect Promise (IRE)**[239] 5-11-7 .... MissJMMangan 80
(James Joseph Mangan, Ire) *w.w: modest 5th 1/2-way: sn no threat: kpt on one pce in remote 4th fr 2f out* **20/1**

5 33 **Dream Beat**[3] 3056 5-11-7 .... MrJPMcKeown 47
(G A Kingston, Ire) *racd in modest 3rd tl dropped to rr 1/2-way: sn adrift: t.o* **50/1**

6 51 **Dannicourtney (IRE)**[187] 723 5-11-7 .... MrADDoyle
(J A Nash, Ire) *racd in rr tl sme hdwy into remote 4th bef 1/2-way: sn no ex and dropped to rr: t.o* **33/1**

3m 58.5s (-8.30) **6 Ran SP% 120.6**
Pick Six: 12,250.00. Pool of 35,000.00 - 2 winning units. CSF £2.45 TOTE £1.80: £1.02, £2.40; DF 3.20 Trifecta £4.10.
Owner Miss Patricia Duffin **Bred** Miss Patricia Duffin **Trained** Larne, Co Antrim
■ Stewards' Enquiry : Mr P W Mullins five-day ban: careless riding (tbn)

FOCUS
Disappointing to see such a timid resistance to the Willie Mullins bumper brigade. The odds-on favourite won but wasn't impressive in doing so and had to survive a pretty lengthy stewards' enquiry before bringing the winner's cheque home. The winning time was good and only three of the field were able to go the early clip.
T/Jkpt: @341.00. Pool of @5,846.00 - 12 winning units. T/Plt: @35.00. Pool of @34,307.56 - 684.89 winning units. AH

3123 - 3126a (Foreign Racing) - See Raceform Interactive

2648 FFOS LAS (L-H)
Monday, December 16

OFFICIAL GOING: Heavy (5.9)
Third-last fence omitted in all chases. Bends realigned on fresh ground and fences and hurdles also sited on fresh ground.
Wind: almost nil Weather: overcast

3127 DAVIES PHARMACY JUVENILE HURDLE (8 hdls) 2m
12:25 (12:25) (Class 4) 3-Y-0 **£3,119** (£915; £457; £228)

Form RPR

4- 1 **Ivanhoe**[32] 2466 3-10-12 0.. NickScholfield 97+
(Michael Blanshard) *hld up in tch: hdwy to join ldr 5th: rdn to ld appr last: r.o wl* **7/2**[2]

1U- 2 1 ½ **Forced Family Fun**[12] 2881 3-11-5 0................................ BrianHughes 103+
(John Quinn) *t.k.h: trckd ldrs: hit 3 out: rdn and clsd after next: j.lft last: r.o flat but a hld by wnr* **8/13**[1]

314- 3 ½ **Akdam (IRE)**[10] 2500 3-11-7 119...............................(p) JoshHamer(5) 108
(Tony Carroll) *trckd ldr tl lft in ld 3rd: rdn 2 out: sn hdd: n.m.r appr last: kpt on same pce flat* **9/1**[3]

33- 4 3 ½ **Seaside Rock (IRE)**[17] 2790 3-10-12 0............................ WilsonRenwick 90
(Keith Dalgleish) *hld up in rr: nt fluent 3 out: outpcd by ldrs appr next: rdn and styd on flat* **50/1**

0- 5 36 **Kalimantan (IRE)**[11] 2899 3-10-9 0................................ MichaelByrne(3) 54
(Tim Vaughan) *hld up in rr: rdn 3 out: qckly lost tch: t.o* **20/1**

R **Arty Campbell (IRE)**[62] 3-10-12 0.. PaulMoloney
(Bernard Llewellyn) *led at v slow pce tl rn out 3rd* **12/1**

4m 36.8s (48.30) **Going Correction** +1.50s/f (Heav) **6 Ran SP% 108.6**
Speed ratings (Par 104): **39,38,38,36,18**
toteswingers 1&2 £1.10, 1&3 £1.60, 2&3 £2.80 CSF £5.87 TOTE £4.70: £2.20, £1.70; EX 6.40 Trifecta £19.80 Pool: £3496.71 - 132.10 winning units..
Owner The Lansdowners & N Price **Bred** Simon Balding **Trained** Upper Lambourn, Berks

FOCUS
Having ridden in the first Nick Scholfield described it as, "heavy but sloppy and they are going through it". An uncompetitive juvenile hurdle run at a very steady pace. Not form to take seriously.

3128 IWEC ELECTRICAL NOVICES' HURDLE (7 hdls 1 omitted) 2m
12:55 (12:56) (Class 4) 4-Y-0+ **£3,898** (£1,144; £572; £286)

Form RPR

33- 1 **It's A Doddle (IRE)**[16] 2806 5-10-12 0................................ APMcCoy 117+
(Jonjo O'Neill) *cl up: led 4th to 5th: rdn 2 out (usual 3 out): only 5th 1f out: r.o u.p to ld last strides* **7/2**[2]

04- 2 nk **Filatore (IRE)**[40] 2285 4-10-12 0...(p) PaulMoloney 117
(Bernard Llewellyn) *led to 4th: styd prom: rdn 2 out: led again 150yds out tl last strides* **11/1**

124/ 3 ¾ **Baltimore Rock (IRE)**[247] 5287 4-10-12 0...................... TomScudamore 116
(David Pipe) *mid-div: clsd 5th: trcking ldrs whn nt fluent 2 out (usual 3 out): styd on wl u.p extended run-in: jst hld* **4/1**[3]

355/ 4 2 **Sir Pitt**[298] 4346 6-10-12 130... DonalDevereux 114
(Peter Bowen) *in tch: clsd 5th: wnt 2nd 2 out (usual 3 out): rdn to ld 1f out: sn hdd and no ex* **14/1**

5 1 ¾ **Minella Reception (IRE)**[138] 1165 7-10-12 0.............. RichardJohnson 113
(Rebecca Curtis) *t.k.h: trckd ldrs: led 5th: hit last (usual 2 out): sn rdn: hdd 1f out: no ex* **9/4**[1]

036- 6 27 **Bellorophon (IRE)**[21] 2724 4-10-12 0.............................. WilsonRenwick 85
(Tim Vaughan) *hld up towards rr: hdwy 5th: wknd last (usual 2 out): t.o* **40/1**

0- 7 1 **Hollywood All Star (IRE)**[17] 2783 4-10-12 0...................... FelixDeGiles 84
(Graeme McPherson) *mid-div: clsd 5th: rdn 2 out (usual 3 out): wkng whn hit next: t.o* **200/1**

F/5- 8 hd **Buywise (IRE)**[25] 2614 6-10-12 0.. AdamWedge 84
(Evan Williams) *hld up: mstke 4th: pushed along after next: wknd 2 out (usual 3 out): t.o* **5/1**

2/0- 9 1 ¼ **Sammyman**[22] 2695 6-10-12 0.. NickScholfield 83
(Michael Blanshard) *in tch: hit 1st and 2nd: rdn after 5th: sn wknd: t.o* **66/1**

/00- 10 31 **Catching On (IRE)**[11] 2893 5-10-12 0.......................... RichieMcLernon 52
(Jonjo O'Neill) *prom tl lost pl appr 5th: sn wl bhd: t.o* **40/1**

/00- P **Hunky Dorey**[40] 2286 7-10-5 0... MrFMitchell(7)
(Marc Barber) *a in rr: mstke 2nd: rdn 4th: lost tch next: t.o whn p.u bef 2 out (usual 3 out)* **100/1**

/F0- P **Genuine Art**[24] 2648 6-10-5 0.. CharliePoste
(Lucy Jones) *a towards rr: lost tch 5th: t.o whn p.u bef next* **100/1**

0- P **Strategic Exit**[11] 2906 5-10-12 0.. HaddenFrost
(James Frost) *a towards rr: wknd qckly 5th: t.o whn p.u bef next* **200/1**

P **Sarahs Doll** 5-10-2 0.. RobertDunne(3)
(Dai Burchell) *mstke 1st: a in rr: struggling 4th: t.o whn p.u after next* **100/1**

4m 9.1s (20.60) **Going Correction** +1.50s/f (Heav)
WFA 4 from 5yo+ 5lb **14 Ran SP% 115.0**
Speed ratings (Par 105): **108,107,107,106,105 92,91,91,90,75 ,,,**
toteswingers 1&2 £5.90, 1&3 £3.40, 2&3 £7.60 CSF £38.53 TOTE £4.00: £1.90, £2.60, £1.10; EX 33.60 Trifecta £100.80 Pool: £4292.55 - 31.91 winning units..
Owner John P McManus **Bred** C Fenton **Trained** Cheltenham, Gloucs
■ Stewards' Enquiry : Tom Scudamore four-day ban: incorrect use of whip (Dec 30-31, Jan 1-2)

FOCUS
An interesting novice hurdle run at an honest pace in the testing conditions, and wioth a bit of strength in depth. The winner is rated back to the level of his Uttoxeter run. The final flight was bypassed leaving a 2f run-in.

3129 WALTERS LAND NOVICES' H'CAP CHASE (15 fncs 2 omitted) 2m 5f
1:30 (1:30) (Class 4) (0-110,110) 4-Y-0+ **£3,768** (£1,106; £553; £276)

Form RPR

4U0- 1 **Cruising Bye**[22] 2690 7-10-8 **92**... TomO'Brien 100+
(Peter Bowen) *hld up: mstke 10th: hdwy next: rdn 3 out: chsd ldr appr last: r.o to ld fnl 100yds* **10/1**

0/5- 2 2 ½ **Saroque (IRE)**[16] 2828 6-11-12 **110**................................... AidanColeman 119+
(Venetia Williams) *led: hit 7th: nt fluent 9th: rdn after 3 out: mstke next: hdd 100yds out: no ex* **7/2**[2]

034/ 3 4 ½ **Off The Wall (IRE)**[244] 5327 6-11-12 **110**.................(bt[1]) TomScudamore 111
(David Pipe) *hld up in rr: stdy hdwy 9th: wnt 2nd 3 out: rdn and unable qck 2 out: sn lost 2nd and one pce* **6/1**[3]

232- 4 ½ **Royal Riviera**[20] 2730 7-11-7 **105**.........................(t) SamTwiston-Davies 105
(Nigel Twiston-Davies) *prom: chsd ldr 9th to 3 out: sn rdn: wknd appr last* **3/1**[1]

P/P- P **Gospel Preacher**[42] 2275 8-10-12 **96**.................................. AdamWedge
(Richard Woollacott) *towards rr: drvn 12th: sn wknd: t.o whn p.u bef 3 out* **7/1**

0P5- P **Best Boy Barney (IRE)**[20] 2730 7-11-1 **99**...................(p) NickScholfield
(Jeremy Scott) *trckd ldr: blnd bdly 3rd: lost 2nd 9th: wknd 12th: t.o whn p.u bef 3 out* **9/1**

1/3- P **Still Believing (IRE)**[36] 2388 5-11-12 **110**............................ PaulMoloney
(Evan Williams) *towards rr: mstke 8th: struggling next: hit 11th: lost tch after next: t.o whn p.u bef 3 out* **7/2**[2]

5m 59.5s (30.90) **Going Correction** +1.50s/f (Heav) **7 Ran SP% 115.3**
Speed ratings (Par 105): **101,100,98,98,**
toteswingers 1&2 £6.80, 1&3 £5.50, 2&3 £4.90 CSF £46.24 CT £232.33 TOTE £11.20: £5.30, £1.50; EX 49.20 Trifecta £371.90 Pool: £3877.90 - 7.81 winning units..
Owner F Lloyd **Bred** F Lloyd **Trained** Little Newcastle, Pembrokes

The Form Book Jumps, Raceform Ltd, Compton, RG20 6NL.

FOCUS
The third-last fence was omitted for all chases, due to the saturated ground. Not much pace on for this novice handicap. The winner built on the best of his hurdle form.

3130 DJM SOLICITORS H'CAP HURDLE (10 hdls) 2m 4f
2:05 (2:06) (Class 3) (0-130,128) 4-Y-0+ **£5,393** (£1,583; £791; £395)

Form RPR

02P/ **1** **Society Shares (IRE)**[649] 4705 8-10-8 **110**............ SamTwiston-Davies 115+
(Graeme McPherson) *in tch: hdwy 5th: chsd ldr appr 3 out: rdn to ld appr last: r.o wl* **16/1**

360- **2** *4* **Quaddick Lake (IRE)**[33] 2461 10-11-9 **125**...................... NickScholfield 125+
(Jeremy Scott) *t.k.h: hld up in rr: hdwy 7th: rdn appr last: chsd wnr flat: unable qck* **5/1**[2]

/04- **3** *6* **Makethe Mostofnow (IRE)**[24] 2652 8-11-9 **125**............... PaulMoloney 119
(Evan Williams) *chsd ldrs: nt fluent 3 out: sn outpcd by ldrs: styd on appr last: snatched 3rd post* **15/2**

224- **4** *nk* **Gate Please (IRE)**[19] 2740 8-11-6 **122**.............................. APMcCoy 117
(Rebecca Curtis) *trckd ldrs tl led after 4th: rdn and hdd appr last: wknd and lost 2 pls flat* **7/1**[3]

422- **5** *17* **Rolling Maul (IRE)**[16] 2806 5-10-13 **115**...................... RichardJohnson 95
(Peter Bowen) *hld up in tch: hdwy to chse ldrs 6th: one pce fr 2 out* **6/4**[1]

1/0- **6** *10* **Cygnet**[11] 2894 7-10-13 **115**.............................. DonalDevereux 82
(Peter Bowen) *led tl after 4th: mstke 6th: rdn next: wknd 3 out: t.o* **33/1**

6/1- **7** *6* **Cawdor House Bert**[224] 145 6-10-13 **115**........................ TomO'Brien 76
(David Rees) *hld up in tch: hit 4th: wknd after 3 out: t.o* **10/1**

510- **8** *1* **Rally**[30] 2505 4-11-9 **125**..(p) DavidBass 85
(Nicky Henderson) *clsd up: drvn along fr 6th: mstke 3 out: wknd 2 out: t.o* **7/1**[3]

240- **P** **Union Saint (FR)**[25] 2630 5-11-12 **128**............................... HaddenFrost
(James Frost) *hld up in rr: sme hdwy 6th: wknd next: t.o whn p.u bef 3 out* **20/1**

5m 34.3s (43.40) **Going Correction** +1.50s/f (Heav)
WFA 4 from 5yo+ 6lb **9** Ran SP% **116.1**
Speed ratings (Par 107): **73,71,69,68,62 58,55,55,**
toteswingers 1&2 £14.20, 1&3 £15.90, 2&3 £7.50 CSF £95.21 CT £661.43 TOTE £21.60: £5.20, £2.20, £2.70; EX 140.60 Trifecta £1234.90 Pool: £4188.80 - 2.54 winning units..
Owner Arion Racing **Bred** M Conaghan **Trained** Upper Oddington, Gloucs

FOCUS
A competitive handicap run at a sound pace in the conditions. A step up from the winner after a long break.

3131 WALTERS UK LTD H'CAP CHASE (17 fncs 2 omitted) 3m 1f 110y
2:40 (2:41) (Class 3) (0-135,131) 4-Y-0+ **£6,498** (£1,908; £954; £477)

Form RPR

P/P- **1** **Relax (FR)**[23] 2674 8-11-8 **127**.............................. AidanColeman 137+
(Venetia Williams) *j. sltly rt: trckd ldr: led 10th: drvn out* **7/2**[1]

5U0- **2** *2 ½* **Sir Du Bearn (FR)**[16] 2812 7-11-11 **130**........................ DonalDevereux 137+
(Peter Bowen) *towards rr: stdy hdwy 11th: mstke and wnt 2nd 14th: drvn appr 2 out: one pce and hld by wnr whn j.lft and mstke last* **10/1**

/35- **3** *21* **Cocacobana (IRE)**[30] 2508 8-11-0 **119**............................ JasonMaguire 106
(Graeme McPherson) *in tch: chalng for 2nd whn mstke 3 out: sn one pce: wknd appr last* **6/1**[2]

1/2- **4** *hd* **Titchwood (IRE)**[24] 2643 5-11-11 **130**............................ APMcCoy 115
(Jonjo O'Neill) *hld up towards rr: clsd 10th: shkn up 3 out where nt fluent: sn one pce: wknd appr last* **7/2**[1]

11P/ **P** **Shaking Hands (IRE)**[317] 3984 9-11-9 **128**..............(bt) TomScudamore
(David Pipe) *led: reminder after 9th: hdd next: wknd 11th: mstke 13th: p.u bef next* **9/1**

031- **P** **Stormyisland Ahead**[40] 2290 8-10-0 **105**......................(t) PaulMoloney
(Evan Williams) *hld up in last: mstke 9th: sn struggling: t.o whn p.u bef 12th* **13/2**[3]

/32- **P** **Seymour Eric**[19] 2747 8-11-12 **131**.......................................(p) IanPopham
(Martin Keighley) *chsd ldrs: rdn along 9th: lost pl next: wknd 12th: t.o whn p.u bef 2 out* **7/2**[1]

7m 14.1s (33.10) **Going Correction** +1.50s/f (Heav) **7** Ran SP% **113.4**
Speed ratings (Par 107): **109,108,101,101,** ,
toteswingers 1&2 £6.20, 1&3 £3.80, 2&3 £10.00 CSF £34.50 CT £201.51 TOTE £4.30: £2.80, £6.00; EX 34.30 Trifecta £193.60 Pool: £4027.36 - 15.59 winning units..
Owner The Bellamy Partnership **Bred** Marc Trinquet & Mlle Marie Trinquet **Trained** Kings Caple, H'fords

FOCUS
They went a fair pace for this decent handicap.

3132 PENNANT WALTERS H'CAP HURDLE (8 hdls) 2m
3:15 (3:16) (Class 3) (0-125,125) 3-Y-0+ **£5,393** (£1,583; £791; £395)

Form RPR

630- **1** **Act Of Kalanisi (IRE)**[9] 2949 7-11-12 **125**..........(bt) SamTwiston-Davies 136+
(Dr Richard Newland) *mde all: hit 1st: qcknd 3 out: in command whn hit 2 out and last: styd on strly* **11/4**[1]

1/0- **2** *10* **Santo Thomas (FR)**[28] 2561 7-10-8 **107**.......................... AidanColeman 110+
(Venetia Williams) *in tch: hdwy after 5th: wnt 2nd 2 out: rdn and no imp on wnr* **5/1**

/35- **3** *7* **Chemistry Master**[33] 2461 5-11-0 **123**.....................(t) MartinMcIntyre(10) 115
(Harry Fry) *chsd ldr: mstke 2nd: rdn 3 out: lost 2nd next: one pce* **4/1**[2]

331- **4** *32* **Zarzal (IRE)**[21] 2721 5-11-12 **125**.................................... PaulMoloney 85
(Evan Williams) *chsd ldrs tl lost pl 4th: rdn after next: wknd 3 out: t.o* **5/1**

/00- **5** *12* **Ubaldo Des Menhies (FR)**[23] 2668 5-11-12 **125**.................. APMcCoy 73
(Jonjo O'Neill) *hld up in rr: rdn and lost tch after 5th: t.o* **9/2**[3]

5/P- **6** *2 ¼* **Pistolet Noir (FR)**[109] 1436 7-10-3 **102**........................... ConorO'Farrell 48
(Richard Woollacott) *hld up in rr: rdn and wknd appr 3 out: t.o* **22/1**

606- **7** *2 ¼* **Drussell (IRE)**[28] 2561 7-10-2 **106**............................... NicodeBoinville(5) 50
(Martin Bosley) *chsd ldrs tl wknd 3 out: t.o* **10/1**

4m 8.9s (20.40) **Going Correction** +1.50s/f (Heav) **7** Ran SP% **111.6**
Speed ratings (Par 107): **109,104,100,84,78 77,76**
toteswingers 1&2 £3.00, 1&3 £2.00, 2&3 £2.80 CSF £16.13 CT £51.85 TOTE £3.20: £1.60, £2.80; EX 16.50 Trifecta £72.70 Pool: £3841.02 - 39.59 winning units..
Owner C E Stedman,Dr R D P And Mrs L J Newland **Bred** Mrs Joan Keaney **Trained** Claines, Worcs

FOCUS
This handicap was run at a sound pace. The front three finished a long way clear and the impressive winner is rated back to his best.

3133 THREE RIVERS "NEWCOMERS" STANDARD OPEN NATIONAL HUNT FLAT RACE 2m
3:50 (3:50) (Class 6) 3-5-Y-0 **£1,559** (£457; £228; £114)

Form RPR

\- **1** **Imagine The Chat** 4-11-6 0... APMcCoy 100+
(Rebecca Curtis) *a.p: led 3f out: rdn over 1f out: styd on wl* **9/4**[1]

2 *¾* **Rons Dream** 3-10-0 0.. DonalDevereux 77
(Peter Bowen) *hld up in tch: hdwy 6f out: chsd wnr over 2f out: sn rdn: kpt on u.p ins fnl f* **6/1**[3]

3 *5* **Dashaway (IRE)** 4-11-6 0.. NickScholfield 92
(Jeremy Scott) *trckd ldrs tl rdn and lost pl 6f out: styd on again fr 3f out: wnt 3rd 1f out: no further imp* **9/4**[1]

4 *2* **Picodean** 5-11-6 0... TomO'Brien 90
(Robert Stephens) *chsd ldrs: rdn over 2f out: kpt on same pce* **25/1**

5 *7* **Destiny's Gold (IRE)** 3-10-4 0.................................. TrevorWhelan(3) 70
(George Baker) *t.k.h early: hld up in tch: clsd 4f out: rdn 3f out: kpt on same pce* **28/1**

6 *22* **Caldey** 4-10-13 0.. JasonMaguire 54
(Keith Goldsworthy) *narrow ld tl hdd 7f out: sn rdn along: wknd over 3f out: t.o* **14/1**

7 *nk* **Wolfe Mountain (IRE)** 4-11-6 0....................................... IanPopham 61
(Linda Blackford) *cl up: led 7f out tl rdn and hdd 3f out: grad wknd: t.o* **12/1**

8 *1 ¾* **Genson** 4-11-6 0.. ConorO'Farrell 59
(Richard Woollacott) *hld up in tch: wknd 3f out: t.o* **66/1**

9 *8* **Raving Renee** 5-10-13 0.. CharliePoste 44
(Lucy Jones) *hld up in tch: hdwy 6f out: rdn 4f out: wknd over 2f out: t.o* **50/1**

10 *11* **Moncarno** 3-10-7 0.. TomScudamore 27
(David Pipe) *hld up in tch: clsd 5f out: wknd 3f out: t.o* **9/2**[2]

4m 27.7s (44.80) **Going Correction** +1.50s/f (Heav)
WFA 3 from 4yo 13lb 4 from 5yo 5lb **10** Ran SP% **119.1**
Speed ratings (Par 101): **48,47,45,44,40 29,29,28,24,19**
toteswingers 1&2 £4.90, 1&3 £1.60, 2&3 £3.50 CSF £16.64 TOTE £2.50: £1.40, £2.00, £1.50; EX 19.40 Trifecta £57.60 Pool: £3542.85 - 46.07 winning units..
Owner John P McManus **Bred** Northcombe Stud **Trained** Newport, Dyfed

FOCUS
This "newcomers" bumper was run at a sedate pace and the time was very slow.
T/Jkpt: Not won. T/Plt: £561.70 to a £1 stake. Pool: £70414.07, 91.51 winning tickets T/Qpdt: £88.60 to a £1 stake. Pool: £8242.67, 68.8 winning tickets RL

2858 PLUMPTON (L-H)
Monday, December 16

OFFICIAL GOING: Good to soft (soft in places) changing to soft after race 1 (12:10)
Wind: medium to fresh, against Weather: overcast, scattered showers

3134 CALL STAR SPORTS 08000 521 321 NOVICES' HURDLE (9 hdls) 2m
12:10 (12:10) (Class 4) 3-Y-0+ **£3,249** (£954; £477; £238)

Form RPR

400- **1** **Vikekhal (FR)**[24] 2642 4-11-6 0.. JamieMoore 110
(Gary Moore) *racd wd: hld up towards rr: hdwy after 5th: trckd ldrs after 3 out: led next: rn green and wnt rt flat: hrd pressed fnl 50yds: hld on wl* **14/1**

2 *shd* **Minority Interest**[104] 4-11-6 0.. TomCannon 110
(Daniel O'Brien) *hld up in rr: 12th and rdn bef 3 out: wnt 8th and styng on u.p but stl plenty to do bef 2 out: lft 4th last: str chal fnl 50yds: jst hld* **33/1**

0- **3** *2 ½* **Torero**[14] 2858 4-11-3 0... JoshuaMoore(3) 109
(Diana Grissell) *in tch in midfield: mstke hdwy to chse ldrs bef 3 out: drvn and ev ch 2 out: stl pressing wnr last: no ex and outpcd fnl 150yds* **25/1**

/20- **4** *1 ¼* **Chase The Wind (IRE)**[17] 2802 4-11-6 0.............................. NoelFehily 106
(Warren Greatrex) *hld up in rr: stdy hdwy after 4th: chsd ldrs and rdn bef 2 out: kpt on but unable qck: lft cl 3rd last: one pce flat* **7/4**[1]

125- **5** *2 ¾* **Sirop De Menthe (FR)**[10] 2927 3-10-13 119...................... WillKennedy 99
(Miss Jessica Westwood) *hld up in midfield: effrt and hdwy u.p after 3 out: chsng ldrs next: keeping on same pce whn bmpd and pushed lft last: no ex* **11/2**[3]

10- **6** *6* **Lemons Ground**[37] 2368 4-11-6 0................................. BrendanPowell 104+
(Jamie Snowden) *wl in tch in midfield: hdwy to chse ldrs after 6th: blnd and wnt lft 2 out: keeping on same pce whn bdly hmpd last: nt rcvr and wknd flat* **25/1**

0- **7** *18* **Spartilla**[14] 2858 4-10-13 0... MrJPearce(7) 82
(Daniel O'Brien) *t.k.h: hld up in rr: styd on past btn horses after 3 out: n.d* **100/1**

313- **8** *24* **The Stig (FR)**[23] 2676 5-11-12 112.................................. PaddyBrennan 67
(Nick Littmoden) *wl in tch in midfield: rdn and no rspnse bef 3 out: wknd and eased 2 out: t.o* **6/1**

6- **9** *7* **Sadma**[14] 2858 4-11-6 0.. DenisO'Regan 55
(John Ferguson) *chsd ldr tl led and j. clr 6th: rdn and hdd bef 2 out: sn btn and fdd: virtually p.u flat: t.o* **5/1**[2]

/35- **10** *3 ¾* **Berkeley Avenue**[21] 2718 4-11-3 0............................... GavinSheehan(3) 51
(Warren Greatrex) *chsd ldrs: losing pl whn mstke 6th: lost tch next: t.o* **10/1**

P **Beggers Belief**[14] 5-11-6 0...(p) DaveCrosse
(Zoe Davison) *mstkes: dropped to rr after mstke 2nd: lost tch after 6th: t.o whn p.u 2 out* **100/1**

0/ **P** **Le Pergolese (FR)**[721] 3330 7-11-3 0............................. MarkQuinlan(3)
(Nigel Hawke) *rn green: led and wandering at hurdles: hdd and mstke 6th: sn dropped out: bhd and mstke next: t.o whn p.u 2 out* **100/1**

5- **P** **Collingbourneducis (IRE)**[40] 2294 3-10-2 0........... ConorShoemark(5)
(Michael Gates) *in tch in midfield: rdn and struggling whn mstke 6th: sn dropped out: t.o whn p.u 2 out* **100/1**

6- **F** **Warrant Officer**[8] 2975 3-10-7 0.................................. MarcGoldstein 90
(Sheena West) *chsd ldrs: wnt 2nd 6th: rdn to ld after 3 out: hdd 2 out: cl 4th but struggling u.p whn fell last* **25/1**

4m 4.75s (3.95) **Going Correction** +0.55s/f (Soft)
WFA 3 from 4yo 13lb 4 from 5yo+ 5lb **14** Ran SP% **116.9**
Speed ratings (Par 105): **112,111,110,110,108 105,96,84,81,79** , , ,
toteswingers 1&2 £47.40, 1&3 £66.90, 2&3 £60.90 CSF £379.83 TOTE £19.30: £4.90, £11.30, £5.80; EX 678.30 Trifecta £1023.50 Part won. Pool: £1364.76 - 0.07 winning units..
Owner The Old Brokers **Bred** E A R L Guittet-Desbois Et Al **Trained** Lower Beeding, W Sussex

FOCUS
This was a competitive event of its type, with seven in contention in the home straight, and the three who chased home the winner all look well up to winning a similar event. A big step up from the winner.

3135 WINTER GALA NOVICES' CHASE (12 fncs) 2m 1f
12:40 (12:41) (Class 3) 4-Y-0+ **£6,975** (£2,385)

Form RPR
3/2- **1** **Rock On Ruby (IRE)**[57] 1989 8-11-0 0 ....(t) NoelFehily 127+
(Harry Fry) *a travelling strly: chsd ldr tl lft in ld 3rd: jnd next: hdd 8th: hit next: led again 2 out: readily wnt clr flat: v easily* **1/10**[1]

464- **2** *4* **Lindsay's Dream**[34] 2435 7-10-7 0 ....(p) DaveCrosse 100
(Zoe Davison) *t.k.h: hld up in 3rd: lft 2nd 3rd: upsides wnr next tl led 8th: hit next: hdd and rdn 2 out: easily outpcd flat* **25/1**[3]

6/1- **U** **Lamb's Cross**[24] 2653 7-11-2 107 .... PatrickCorbett(5)
(Mark Gillard) *led tl propped bdly: wnt rt and uns rdr 3rd* **10/1**[2]

4m 34.1s (11.10) **Going Correction** +0.55s/f (Soft) **3** Ran SP% **103.8**
Speed ratings (Par 107): **95,93,**
CSF £2.72 TOTE £1.10; EX 3.00 Trifecta £3.70 Pool: £1296.06 - 256.88 winning units..
Owner The Festival Goers **Bred** John O'Dwyer **Trained** Seaborough, Dorset

FOCUS
Facile winner Rock On Ruby was value for furrther, with the second in line with his hurdles form.

3136 J H BUILDERS "NATIONAL HUNT" NOVICES' HURDLE (12 hdls) 2m 5f
1:15 (1:15) (Class 4) 4-Y-0+ **£3,249** (£954; £477; £238)

Form RPR
1/3- **1** **Knock House (IRE)**[24] 2642 4-10-12 0 .... DominicElsworth 131+
(Mick Channon) *racd wd: chsd ldrs: ev ch 3 out: rdn bef next: led between last 2: styd on wl to go clr flat: rdn out* **10/11**[1]

2 *3* **Marcilhac (FR)**[179] 4-10-12 0 .... LiamTreadwell 125+
(Venetia Williams) *chsd ldr: mstke 9th: ev ch and hit next: sn led: rdn bef 2 out: hdd between last 2: no ex and one pce flat* **6/1**

5/2- **3** *9* **Sky Watch (IRE)**[22] 2689 6-10-9 121 .... GavinSheehan(3) 116
(Warren Greatrex) *led: rdn and hdd wl bef 2 out: sn outpcd: 3rd and plugged on same pce fr next* **5/1**[3]

223- **4** *13* **Auld Sthock (IRE)**[28] 2569 5-10-12 117 .... JamieMoore 107
(Gary Moore) *racd wd: hld up in rr: hdwy into midfield after 3rd: hdwy to chse ldng trio after 9th: drvn and no ex after next: wknd between last 2* **4/1**[2]

/10- **5** *20* **Amazing Scenes (IRE)**[17] 2802 4-10-12 0 .... BrendanPowell 82
(Brendan Powell) *chsd ldrs: mstke 8th: rdn and struggling after 9th: wknd next: tired flat: t.o* **50/1**

6/ **6** *7* **She's Noble**[294] 4432 6-10-5 0 .... PaddyBrennan 68
(Suzy Smith) *racd wd: hld up in tch in rr: hdwy bef 9th: rdn and no hdwy bef 3 out: wknd wl bef 2 out* **20/1**

7 *9* **Underwood (FR)** 5-10-12 0 .... TomSiddall 66
(Michael Roberts) *mstke 1st: dropped to rr next and rdn along after: lost tch 9th: t.o after next* **66/1**

00- **8** *10* **Bonds Conquest**[33] 2457 4-10-12 0 .... AndrewThornton 56
(Seamus Mullins) *in tch in rr: mstke 6th: reminders after 8th: lost tch next: t.o after 3 out* **100/1**

/00- **9** *6* **Forrardon Xmoor**[18] 2761 4-10-12 0 .... WillKennedy 50
(Miss Jessica Westwood) *t.k.h: hld up in tch in midfield: lost pl and bhd after 8th: lost tch bef 3 out: t.o wl bef 2 out* **66/1**

0- **10** *15* **Wunfurlez**[37] 2368 5-10-12 0 .... SamThomas 35
(Diana Grissell) *in tch in midfield: rdn and struggling after 9th: sn wknd: t.o 2 out* **50/1**

5m 24.7s (7.70) **Going Correction** +0.55s/f (Soft)
WFA 4 from 5yo+ 6lb **10** Ran SP% **116.0**
Speed ratings (Par 105): **107,105,102,97,89 87,83,79,77,71**
toteswingers 1&2 £2.20, 2&3 £3.40, 1&3 £1.40 CSF £6.76 TOTE £2.00: £1.10, £2.10, £1.60; EX 8.30 Trifecta £24.30 Pool: £2800.32 - 86.07 winning units..
Owner Mrs T P Radford **Bred** P Cashman **Trained** West Ilsley, Berks

FOCUS
The first two were above average for the course and the winner can probably do a bit better yet.

3137 JEAN HORSBURGH MEMORIAL H'CAP CHASE (18 fncs) 3m 2f
1:45 (1:45) (Class 4) (0-115,113) 4-Y-0+ **£3,898** (£1,144; £572; £286)

Form RPR
P/6- **1** **Reblis (FR)**[28] 2567 8-11-6 110 .... JoshuaMoore(3) 127+
(Gary Moore) *a travelling wl: in tch: mstke 9th: trckd ldrs 13th tl led 3 out: rdn and readily drew clr 2 out: easily* **7/1**[3]

331- **2** *10* **Glenwood Prince (IRE)**[25] 2619 7-10-10 100 ....(t) MattGriffiths(3) 106
(Jeremy Scott) *chsd ldrs: mstke 9th: wnt 2nd and bmpd 12th: rdn and ev ch after 3 out: btn and brushed next: wknd flat* **3/1**[1]

/41- **3** *3* **Itoldyou (IRE)**[14] 2863 7-11-3 104 .... AndrewThornton 110+
(Linda Jewell) *hld up in tch in last pair: mstke 9th: clsd to chse ldrs 13th: cl 4th and hit 15th: rdn and no ex after 3 out: 3rd and btn next: plugged on flat* **3/1**[1]

P/3- **4** *21* **Ballinhassig (IRE)**[14] 2863 8-10-0 87 oh12 .... MarcGoldstein 74
(Sarah Wall) *j.rt at times: led tl 3 out: sn drvn and btn: wknd bef next* **8/1**

611- **P** **Days Of Pleasure (IRE)**[42] 2275 8-10-4 91 ....(b) TomCannon
(Chris Gordon) *w ldr: rdn 13th: lost pl next: last and losing tch whn p.u bef 14th: lame* **9/2**[2]

P3P- **P** **No Principles**[22] 2693 10-11-12 113 ....(p) WayneHutchinson
(Julian Smith) *racd wd: chsd ldrs: reminders after 7th: rdn and struggling whn mstke 14th: losing tch whn p.u next* **14/1**

/43- **P** **Kastani Beach (IRE)**[27] 2582 7-10-9 103 .... KevinJones(7)
(Seamus Mullins) *nt a fluent: in tch in last pair: rdn and struggling bef next: lost tch 3 out: t.o whn p.u last* **9/2**[2]

7m 3.2s (12.50) **Going Correction** +0.55s/f (Soft) **7** Ran SP% **116.6**
Speed ratings (Par 105): **102,98,98,91,** ,
toteswingers 1&2 £6.20, 1&3 £6.30, 2&3 £2.70 CSF £29.97 TOTE £8.70: £3.20, £2.00; EX 42.30 Trifecta £298.10 Pool: £2075.30 - 5.15 winning units..
Owner Kingsley, Avery, Farr, Glover, Humphreys **Bred** Robert Adenot **Trained** Lower Beeding, W Sussex

FOCUS
This was a typical Plumpton chase, with two former winners of the race in the line-up. Fair form with the winner back to the best of last season's form.

3138 DEREK HUNNISETT MEMORIAL H'CAP HURDLE (14 hdls) 3m 1f 110y
2:20 (2:20) (Class 5) (0-95,92) 4-Y-0+ **£2,053** (£598; £299)

Form RPR
032- **1** **Night Of Passion (IRE)**[22] 2690 5-10-10 79 ....(p) MattGriffiths(3) 95+
(Jeremy Scott) *hld up in tch: hdwy to trck ldrs 11th: led and gng strly bef 2 out: sn drew clr: r.o wl: easily* **7/4**[1]

132- **2** *10* **Absolute Shambles**[19] 2744 9-11-2 92 ....(p) LouisMuspratt(10) 93
(Chris Gordon) *chsd ldrs: rdn along 8th: 3rd and outpcd u.p after 3 out: no ch w wnr but plugged on to go 2nd again last* **13/2**[2]

0/4- **3** *2 ¾* **Uncle Pettit (IRE)**[25] 2631 5-11-2 85 .... GavinSheehan(3) 86
(Jonathan Portman) *racd wd: hld up in tch towards rr: hdwy to chse ldrs 3 out: sn rdn and no ex: 4th and wl hld next: no ch w wnr but plugged on to go 3rd flat* **20/1**

023- **4** *10* **Sea Cadet**[19] 2744 11-10-4 80 .... NathanAdams(10) 72
(Laura Mongan) *chsd ldrs tl led 7th: mstke 11th: clr w wnr and rdn after 3 out: hdd and btn bef 2 out: wknd between last 2: fdd flat* **17/2**

/0U- **5** *7* **Sweet Boy Vic (IRE)**[9] 2947 5-10-13 79 .... TomCannon 60
(Chris Gordon) *in tch in rr: hdwy after 10th: drvn and btn after 3 out: wknd and wl btn next* **12/1**

P30- **6** *47* **Brunette'Sonly (IRE)**[29] 2541 8-11-7 87 .... AndrewThornton 21
(Seamus Mullins) *racd wd: mde most tl 7th: reminders and lost pl after next: lost tch 3 out: t.o next* **8/1**[3]

056/ **P** **Niceboy (IRE)**[638] 4942 9-9-10 67 oh4 ow1 .... ConorShoemark(5)
(Daniel Steele) *racd wd: a in rr: rdn after 5th: losing tch whn p.u after 10th* **33/1**

62/- **P** **Sudden Light (IRE)**[364] 3117 7-10-9 75 ....(vt) RobertThornton
(Jim Best) *chsd ldrs: rdn and lost pl after 10th: wl bhd 3 out: t.o and p.u next* **9/1**

455/ **P** **Lord Aldervale (IRE)**[234] 5555 6-10-1 67 ....(p) MarcGoldstein
(Steve Woodman) *chsd ldrs tl rdn and lost pl bef 3 out: lost tch and wl bhd whn p.u 2 out* **8/1**[3]

/P3- **P** **Marble Walk (IRE)**[19] 2741 8-11-12 92 .... LeightonAspell
(Richard Rowe) *racd wd: in tch in midfield: rdn and wknd 3 out: t.o whn p.u next* **16/1**

000- **P** **Ricketyrock**[14] 2862 7-10-11 77 .... DarylJacob
(Nick Mitchell) *hld up in tch towards rr: hdwy 11th: rdn and btn sn after next: wl bhd and p.u 2 out* **20/1**

/0P- **P** **Alfie Alexander (IRE)**[16] 2827 5-10-7 78 .... JamesBanks(5)
(Mark Hoad) *a bhd: rdn after 4th and nvr gng wl after: lost tch and p.u 11th* **50/1**

6m 48.5s (23.50) **Going Correction** +0.55s/f (Soft) **12** Ran SP% **120.4**
Speed ratings (Par 103): **85,81,81,78,75 61,** , , ,
toteswingers 1&2 £3.70, 1&3 £15.20, 2&3 £17.60 CSF £13.44 CT £177.50 TOTE £2.60: £1.10, £2.50, £7.20; EX 16.20 Trifecta £301.70 Part won. Pool: £1857.80 - 0.02 winning units..
Owner Mrs Pam Pengelly **Bred** Danny Doran **Trained** Brompton Regis, Somerset

FOCUS
There was a mix of experienced and unexposed types in this stamina test. Modest form but the easy winner is on the upgrade.

3139 J H BUILDERS H'CAP CHASE (13 fncs 1 omitted) 2m 4f
2:55 (2:55) (Class 5) (0-95,95) 4-Y-0+ **£2,274** (£667; £333; £166)

Form RPR
2PP- **1** **Doheny Bar (IRE)**[14] 2861 10-10-8 77 .... PaddyBrennan 91+
(Paul Henderson) *mde all: clr bypassing 11th: in command and rdn hands and heels bef 2 out: mstke last: flashing tail and idling flat: rdn out hands and heels* **14/1**

42F- **2** *6* **Crannaghmore Boy (IRE)**[145] 1103 8-11-12 95 ....(v[1]) RobertThornton 98
(Jim Best) *chsd wnr tl 5th: styd chsng ldrs: wnt 2nd again 9th tl after next: 3rd and no imp u.p after 3 out: chsd clr wnr again after 2 out: no imp tl clsd on idling wnr flat* **5/1**[2]

62U- **3** *3 ½* **Full Ov Beans**[19] 2739 9-11-4 87 .... JamieMoore 88
(Michael Gates) *in tch towards rr: hdwy into midfield and mstke 7th: chsd clr wnr after 10th: rdn and btn after 3 out: mstke 2 out and sn lost 2nd: plugged on* **16/1**

145- **4** *1* **Bit Of A Clown (IRE)**[34] 2437 7-11-12 95 .... TomCannon 93
(Nick Gifford) *racd in midfield: reminders after 8th: sltly hmpd 10th: styd on u.p into modest 4th bef 2 out: kpt on but no ch w wnr* **14/1**

/P2- **5** *14* **According To Them (IRE)**[19] 2739 9-9-11 71 ow2(t) ConorShoemark(5) 55
(Daniel Steele) *hld up in last quartet: hdwy after 8th: rdn and sltly hmpd 10th: no imp and btn bypassing next: wknd after 3 out* **14/1**

/33- **6** *2 ½* **Ballyman (IRE)**[14] 2861 12-10-12 81 ....(v) MarkGrant 62
(Jonathan Geake) *chsd ldrs: wnt 2nd 5th tl 9th: struggling u.p bypassing 11th: wknd wl bef 2 out* **10/1**

/50- **7** *37* **Tchang Goon (FR)**[20] 2727 9-10-0 69 oh4 ....(p) DaveCrosse 13
(Zoe Davison) *a in rr: lost tch after 9th: t.o 3 out* **33/1**

S12- **P** **Mister Wiseman**[14] 2861 11-11-7 90 ....(vt) DarylJacob
(Nigel Hawke) *chsd ldrs tl dropped out qckly u.p after 9th: lost tch after next: t.o whn p.u 2 out* **9/1**

065- **P** **Rosoff (IRE)**[20] 2727 11-10-13 82 ....(p) HarrySkelton
(Laura Mongan) *in tch in midfield: mstke 1st: clsd to chse ldrs 7th: rdn and no rspnse after 9th: sn dropped out: t.o whn p.u 2 out* **25/1**

6C3- **F** **Bobbits Way**[25] 2615 8-10-9 78 ....(p) WillKennedy
(Alan Jones) *hld up in midfield: hdwy 9th: cl 4th and stl travelling wl whn fell 10th* **5/1**[2]

4/2- **P** **Goring Two (IRE)**[34] 2441 8-11-5 88 ....(p) AndrewThornton
(Anna Newton-Smith) *racd wd: in tch in midfield: cl enough and rdn after 9th: struggling after next: lost tch 3 out: t.o and p.u next* **9/2**[1]

630- **P** **Border Station (IRE)**[10] 2932 7-11-4 90 .... JoshuaMoore(3)
(Alison Batchelor) *a in rr: detached last 5th: lost tch after 9th: hmpd next: t.o whn p.u 3 out* **10/1**

5PP- **P** **The Informant**[25] 2619 7-10-5 81 ....[1] KevinJones(7)
(Seamus Mullins) *a in rr: mstke 4th: rdn after 8th: lost tch bef 10th: t.o bypassing 11th tl p.u 2 out* **8/1**[3]

5m 24.1s (16.80) **Going Correction** +0.55s/f (Soft) **13** Ran SP% **123.5**
Speed ratings (Par 103): **88,85,84,83,78 77,62,** , , ,
toteswingers 1&2 £24.50, 1&3 Not won, 2&3 £9.00 CSF £87.40 CT £1167.42 TOTE £17.40: £3.30, £2.60, £5.20; EX 107.10 Trifecta £1393.30 Pool: £2239.97 - 5.63 winning units..
Owner The Rockbourne Partnership **Bred** Martin Brickley **Trained** Whitsbury, Hants

FOCUS
The middle fence in the back straight was bypassed on the final circuit. A lively pace made this a good test in the soft ground. The winner was value for further.

3140 ANISE CATERING H'CAP HURDLE (9 hdls) 2m
3:30 (3:30) (Class 5) (0-100,97) 3-Y-0+ **£2,053** (£598; £299)

Form RPR
5/3- **1** **Our Phylli Vera (IRE)**[28] 2568 4-11-5 90 .... WayneHutchinson 105+
(Alan King) *racd wd: wl in tch in midfield: chsd ldr bef 6th: gng best after 3 out: led 2 out: rdn and asserted flat: r.o wl* **9/2**[2]

4P0- **2** *2 ¾* **Clonusker (IRE)**[14] 2862 5-10-0 71 oh6 ....(t) GerardTumelty 80
(Linda Jewell) *j.lft: led: rdn after 3 out: hdd next: no ex u.p and j.lft last: styd on same pce flat* **66/1**

The Form Book Jumps, Raceform Ltd, Compton, RG20 6NL.

000- **3** *5* **Qasser (IRE)**[42] 2265 4-10-10 **86**.....[1] JamesBanks[(5)] 90
(Harry Whittington) *t.k.h: hld up in tch in last quartet: grad clsd after 3 out: shkn up and wnt 3rd last: rdn: flashed tail and no imp flat* **8/1**

2FU- **4** *3 ¾* **Pagham Belle**[10] 2921 5-10-13 **84**.....(t) DarylJacob 85
(Nigel Hawke) *in tch in midfield: hdwy to chse ldrs after 6th: rdn and unable qck after 3 out: wknd between last 2* **9/2**[2]

/2P- **5** *½* **Hold The Bucks (USA)**[18] 2770 7-10-5 **81**..... ConorShoemark[(5)] 81
(Daniel Steele) *in tch in midfield on inner: hdwy to chse ldrs 6th: rdn and outpcd after next: wknd between last 2* **10/1**

050- **6** *4 ½* **Mariet**[14] 2858 4-11-2 **90**..... WayneKavanagh[(3)] 87
(Suzy Smith) *racd wd: in tch in rr: rdn after 6th: styng on past btn horses and mstke 2 out: hit last: kpt on: nvr trbld ldrs* **20/1**

004- **7** *shd* **Tom Sang (FR)**[14] 2862 6-10-5 **79**..... GavinSheehan[(3)] 75
(Jamie Snowden) *racd wd: t.k.h: hld up in tch towards rr: hdwy into midfield after 6th: rdn and no imp after 3 out: wknd between last 2* **7/2**[1]

333/ **8** *¾* **Galiotto (IRE)**[12] 1609 7-11-9 **97**.....(v) JoshuaMoore[(3)] 92
(Gary Moore) *racd wd: hld up in tch in last trio: rdn and effrt after 6th: no prog after next: wknd 2 out* **7/1**[3]

500- **9** *1 ¾* **Just Beware**[14] 2862 11-9-7 **71** oh1.....(p) MrGGorman[(7)] 66
(Zoe Davison) *in tch in midfield: hdwy to chse ldrs after 6th: rdn and btn after next: wknd next* **14/1**

600- **10** *18* **No Routine (IRE)**[18] 2770 4-11-5 **95**..... MauriceLinehan[(5)] 70
(Jonjo O'Neill) *chsd ldr tl after 5th: sn dropped out u.p: bhd 3 out* **7/1**[3]

5P0- **11** *1 ¾* **Airedale Lad (IRE)**[28] 2568 12-9-7 **71** oh6..... MrJoshuaNewman[(7)] 44
(Zoe Davison) *chsd ldrs: wnt 2nd briefly after 5th: lost pl u.p next: bhd 3 out* **66/1**

4m 9.2s (8.40) **Going Correction** +0.55s/f (Soft)
WFA 4 from 5yo+ 5lb **11** Ran SP% **118.2**
Speed ratings (Par 103): **101,99,97,95,95 92,92,92,91,82 81**
CSF £255.02 CT £2304.80 TOTE £5.50: £2.30, £10.80, £3.10; EX 382.00 Trifecta £1971.00 Part won. Pool: £2628.10 - 0.02 winning units..
Owner Let's Live Racing **Bred** Awbeg Stud **Trained** Barbury Castle, Wilts

FOCUS
This was a modest race, likely to be most relevant to future races at a similar level. The first three are on the upgrade.
T/Plt: £993.80 to a £1 stake. Pool: £76513.15 - 56.20 winning tickets T/Qpdt: £24.20 to a £1 stake. Pool: £12627.54 - 385.90 winning tickets SP

2879 CATTERICK (L-H)

Tuesday, December 17

OFFICIAL GOING: Good (good to soft in places; chs 7.4, hdl 7.6)
Wind: virtually nil Weather: fine and sunny

3141 BOOK NOW FOR NEW YEAR'S DAY AMATEUR RIDERS' H'CAP HURDLE (10 hdls) 2m 3f

12:10 (12:10) (Class 5) (0-100,95) 3-Y-0+ **£2,495** (£774; £386; £193)

Form RPR

46P- **1** **Cumbrian Farmer**[32] 2497 6-10-11 **87**.....(p) MissJWalton[(7)] 91
(George Bewley) *trckd ldrs: led 6th: hit next: hdd last: regained ld last 75yds: hld on towards fin* **40/1**

2 *hd* **Summerlea (IRE)**[92] 2011 7-11-4 **92**..... MissBeckySmith[(5)] 95
(Micky Hammond) *in rr: hdwy 3 out: upsides last: no ex clsng stages* **14/1**

100- **3** *2* **Iktiview**[35] 2449 5-11-2 **92**.....(bt) MrPDennis[(7)] 93
(Philip Kirby) *hld up in mid-div: trcking ldrs 6th: led last: hdd and no ex last 75yds* **11/1**

146- **4** *1 ¾* **Tweedo Paradiso (NZ)**[18] 2787 6-11-0 **90**..... MissHHarper[(7)] 89
(Rose Dobbin) *mid-div: trckd ldrs 3 out: upsides last: kpt on same pce* **9/2**[1]

/F3- **5** *3* **Knight Valliant**[16] 2844 10-11-4 **94**..... MissEButterworth[(7)] 91
(Barbara Butterworth) *hld up in rr: hdwy 3 out: chsng ldrs next: one pce appr last* **9/2**[1]

104- **6** *4* **Push Me (IRE)**[18] 2794 6-11-3 **93**..... MrBCampbell[(7)] 86
(Iain Jardine) *in rr: hdwy 3 out: wknd between last 2* **8/1**

6/0- **7** *4 ½* **Freedom Flying**[35] 2449 10-9-12 **74**.....(t) MrTHamilton[(7)] 63
(Lee James) *mid-div: drvn 5th: hdwy 7th: lost pl bef 2 out* **11/1**

042- **8** *6* **Queen Of Epirus**[21] 2736 5-11-7 **93**..... MrJHamilton[(3)] 77
(Brian Rothwell) *chsd ldrs: mstke 3rd: drvn 6th: wknd 2 out* **17/2**

P04- **9** *5* **Stadium Of Light (IRE)**[2] 3118 6-10-10 **86**.....(t) MrGrahamCarson[(7)] 65
(Shaun Harris) *chsd ldrs: wknd between last 2* **15/2**[3]

/00- **10** *21* **Amazingreyce**[23] 2701 8-9-9 **69**..... MrHAABannister[(5)] 29
(Christopher Kellett) *mid-div: drvn 5th: sme hdwy next: lost pl after 3 out: sn bhd: t.o* **33/1**

/6P- **11** *9* **D'Argent Cloud**[17] 2827 5-10-13 **85**..... MissHBethell[(3)] 42
(Brian Ellison) *chsd ldrs: drvn 3 out: lost pl and blnd next: sn bhd: t.o* **7/1**[2]

036/ **12** *¾* **Next To Nowhere (IRE)**[273] 4852 8-11-5 **95**..... MrDaveWilliams[(7)] 47
(Christopher Kellett) *mid-div: hdwy to chse ldrs 5th: lost pl 3 out: sn bhd: t.o* **50/1**

3/P- **P** **Arizona River**[59] 1977 7-11-5 **95**.....(t) MrMGarnett[(7)]
(Jason Ward) *j.lft: led: hdd and blnd 6th: sn lost pl and bhd: t.o 3 out: p.u bef next* **50/1**

4m 46.5s (10.40) **Going Correction** +0.075s/f (Yiel) **13** Ran SP% **114.9**
Speed ratings (Par 103): **81,80,80,79,78 76,74,71,69,61 57,56,**
toteswingers 1&2 £139.00, 1&3 £109.10, 2&3 £39.50 CSF £492.83 CT £6434.50 TOTE £59.90: £8.10, £6.70, £3.40; EX 499.50 Trifecta £2054.60 Part won. Pool: £2739.51 - 0.16 winning units..
Owner Southdean Racing Club **Bred** E R Hanbury **Trained** Bonchester Bridge, Borders

FOCUS
A moderate handicap hurdle for amateur riders in which they went an honest gallop. The second and fourth set the level.

3142 CATTERICK INTERACTIVE NOVICES' LIMITED H'CAP CHASE (15 fncs) 2m 3f

12:40 (12:40) (Class 3) (0-125,125) 5-Y-0+ **£6,388** (£1,928; £993; £526)

Form RPR

3F5/ **1** **Diocles (IRE)**[232] 26 7-10-12 **118**..... JasonMaguire 132+
(Donald McCain) *trckd ldng pair: j.lft 2nd: wnt cl 2nd after 4 out: led appr next: pckd landing: forged clr run-in* **4/1**

502- **2** *14* **Big Water (IRE)**[8] 3000 5-11-3 **123**..... PaddyBrennan 130+
(Alan Swinbank) *led to 3rd: w ldr: led 3rd: hit 9th: led 4 out: hdd appr next: 3 l down and wl hld whn hit last: sn eased* **11/4**[2]

/43- **3** *26* **Rick (FR)**[10] 2955 9-11-2 **122**.....(b) DenisO'Regan 100
(John Ferguson) *mstke 1st: w ldr: led 3rd: hdd 4 out: lost pl appr next: bhd whn mstke last: sn eased* **2/1**[1]

221- **4** *21* **Mandarin Sunset (IRE)**[18] 2792 6-10-9 **115**..... BrianHarding 74
(James Ewart) *nt fluent: hdwy to chse ldrs 8th: outpcd next: mstke and lost tch 11th* **7/2**[3]

/65- **F** **Hunters Belt (IRE)**[16] 2839 9-11-5 **125**.....(vt) HenryBrooke
(Barry Murtagh) *sn detached in last: hit 5th: sn bhd: fell 10th* **28/1**

4m 42.5s (-6.30) **Going Correction** -0.15s/f (Good) **5** Ran SP% **105.7**
Speed ratings: **107,101,90,81,**
CSF £14.15 TOTE £4.90: £1.80, £1.70; EX 17.40 Trifecta £35.50 Pool: £2210.53 - 46.67 winning units..
Owner L G M Racing **Bred** Eric Watson **Trained** Cholmondeley, Cheshire

FOCUS
A fair novices' handicap chase in which they went a decent gallop. The first two are rated up 10lb on the best of their hurdling form.

3143 GO RACING IN YORKSHIRE WINTER FESTIVAL H'CAP CHASE (12 fncs) 2m

1:10 (1:10) (Class 4) (0-105,103) 4-Y-0+ **£4,548** (£1,335; £667; £333)

Form RPR

0/4- **1** **Coax**[38] 2356 5-11-1 **92**..... RichieMcGrath 105+
(Patrick Holmes) *hld up in rr: hdwy 5th: clr 2nd appr 3 out: led appr 2 out: wnt clr bef last: heavily eased clsng stages* **22/1**

P33- **2** *8* **Forestside (IRE)**[13] 2880 8-10-8 **85**..... JamesReveley 90
(Barry Murtagh) *chsd ldrs: nt fluent 8th: last whn hit 3 out: kpt on fr next: 3rd whn blnd last: tk 2nd last 50yds* **7/1**

231- **3** *nk* **Lord Of Drums (IRE)**[8] 2996 7-11-5 **103**..... CraigNichol[(7)] 107
(Lucinda Russell) *led: blnd and hdd briefly 4th: hdd 7th: drvn 4 out: sn outpcd: kpt on one pce fr 2 out* **5/4**[1]

266- **4** *4 ½* **Turf Trivia**[21] 2737 6-11-2 **93**.....(b) BarryKeniry 91
(George Moore) *jnd ldrs 2nd: led briefly 4th: led 7th: hdd appr 2 out: wknd and lost 2 pls run-in* **18/1**

612- **5** *13* **Jim Tango (FR)**[21] 2737 9-10-10 **87**.....(p) PaddyBrennan 72
(Karen McLintock) *chsd ldrs: drvn 9th: lost pl appr 2 out* **5/1**[3]

P31- **6** *16* **Bob's Dream (IRE)**[21] 2737 11-11-6 **97**.....(t) BrianHarding 83
(William Amos) *in rr: hmpd 1st: nt fluent 3rd: drvn 7th: hdwy appr 3 out: disputing 3rd 2 out: sn wknd: bhd whn eased run-in* **12/1**

225- **F** **Alderbrook Lad (IRE)**[47] 2173 7-11-12 **103**..... JasonMaguire
(Micky Hammond) *w ldrs: fell 1st* **9/2**[2]

4m 0.2s (0.10) **Going Correction** -0.15s/f (Good) **7** Ran SP% **109.1**
Speed ratings (Par 105): **93,89,88,86,80 72,**
toteswingers 1&2 £13.00, 1&3 £5.80, 2&3 £2.00 CSF £144.48 CT £310.41 TOTE £23.60: £7.60, £5.30; EX 178.70 Trifecta £458.70 Pool: £3228.42 - 5.27 winning units..
Owner Di Midwinter Foulrice Park Racing Ltd **Bred** Darley **Trained** Middleham, N Yorks

FOCUS
A modest handicap chase but a step up from the winner.

3144 YORKSHIRE-OUTDOORS.CO.UK NOVICES' HURDLE (10 hdls) 2m 3f

1:40 (1:40) (Class 4) 4-Y-0+ **£3,249** (£954; £477; £238)

Form RPR

22- **1** **Forthefunofit (IRE)**[19] 2773 4-10-12 0..... APMcCoy 121+
(Jonjo O'Neill) *trckd ldrs: upsides 7th: led bef 2 out: drvn and styd on run-in* **11/4**[1]

332- **2** *4* **Downtown Boy (IRE)**[21] 2732 5-10-12 **114**..... PaddyBrennan 116+
(Chris Grant) *hld up in mid-div: hdwy 7th: chsng ldrs after next: 2nd and nt fluent last: edgd lft: styd on same pce* **3/1**[2]

4- **3** *5* **Cool Sky**[113] 1399 4-10-12 0..... JasonMaguire 112+
(Donald McCain) *trckd ldrs: led 3 out: hdd bef next: one pce between last 2* **7/2**[3]

4 *13* **Save The Bees**[57] 5-10-12 0..... DougieCostello 98
(Declan Carroll) *mid-div: hdwy 7th: chsng ldrs next: hung rt and wknd 2 out* **16/1**

414- **5** *½* **Mister Jones**[21] 2738 5-10-12 0..... RyanMania 98
(Sue Smith) *chsd ldrs: 3rd whn hit 2 out: wknd bef last* **7/1**

5/4- **6** *12* **Latest Fashion (IRE)**[201] 552 7-9-12 0..... StephenMulqueen[(7)] 80
(Christopher Wilson) *chsd ldrs: wknd apprloaching 2 out* **66/1**

5- **7** *4* **Whichwaytobougie**[18] 2788 4-10-7 0..... ColmMcCormack[(5)] 83
(Keith Reveley) *in rr: drvn 3 out: kpt on fr next: nvr on terms* **16/1**

0- **8** *8* **Badged**[83] 1654 4-10-5 0..... GrantCockburn[(7)] 76
(Lucy Normile) *mid-div: hdwy 6th: chsng ldrs next: lost pl after 3 out* **100/1**

55- **9** *18* **Clues And Arrows (IRE)**[10] 2933 5-10-12 0..... RichieMcLernon 60
(Jonjo O'Neill) *led to 2nd: lft in ld 6th: hdd 3 out: sn lost pl and bhd* **50/1**

10 *6* **Nexius (IRE)**[114] 4-10-12 0..... WilsonRenwick 54
(Tim Vaughan) *mid-div: hdwy 6th: chsng ldrs next: lost pl bef 2 out* **9/1**

0- **11** *2 ½* **Auto Mac**[12] 2900 5-10-12 0..... BrianHarding 52
(Mike Sowersby) *in rr: bhd fr 3 out* **80/1**

00- **12** *18* **Brasingaman Espee**[29] 2563 4-10-12 0..... BarryKeniry 36
(George Moore) *in rr: bhd fr 3 out: t.o next* **100/1**

/60- **R** **Jokers And Rogues (IRE)**[31] 2520 5-10-5 0..... JohnDawson[(7)]
(John Wade) *w ldr: led 2nd: wnt bdly rt and rn out 6th* **50/1**

0- **P** **Waterside Road**[18] 2795 4-10-12 0..... AdrianLane
(Iain Jardine) *in rr: bhd fr 7th: t.o whn p.u bef 2 out* **150/1**

4m 46.3s (10.20) **Going Correction** +0.075s/f (Yiel) **14** Ran SP% **117.4**
Speed ratings (Par 105): **81,79,77,71,71 66,64,61,53,51 50,42, ,**
toteswingers 1&2 £2.10, 1&3 £3.50, 2&3 £2.90 CSF £10.95 TOTE £2.90: £1.30, £1.60, £1.90; EX 11.10 Trifecta £25.90 Pool: £3210.55 - 92.69 winning units..
Owner John P McManus **Bred** Vincent Finn **Trained** Cheltenham, Gloucs

FOCUS
A decent novices' hurdle for the track in which they went a steady initial gallop. The second sets the level.

3145 WATCH ON 3 DEVICES RACINGUK.COM/ANYWHERE H'CAP HURDLE (12 hdls) 3m 1f 110y

2:10 (2:12) (Class 4) (0-110,110) 4-Y-0+ **£2,101** (£2,101; £477; £238)

Form RPR

201- **1** **Gulf Punch**[16] 2843 6-11-12 **110**.....(p) JasonMaguire 112
(Donald McCain) *in rr: shkn up 7th: hdwy next: drvn 3 out: 3rd last: styd on wl run-in: dead-heated on line* **5/1**[1]

/PP- **1** *dht* **Harris (IRE)**[54] 2035 6-11-8 **106**..... JamesReveley 110
(William Kinsey) *hld up in rr: hdwy 5th: trcking ldrs 8th: drvn 3 out: cl 2nd last: led nr fin: jnd on line* **5/1**[1]

653- **3** *hd* **Pudsey House**[18] 2789 6-10-6 **97**.....(b) JohnDawson[(7)] 99
(John Wade) *led to 3rd: led 5th to 3 out: led appr next: 3 l clr last: hdd nr fin* **6/1**[2]

34- 4 13 **Merrydown Vintage (IRE)**[37] 6-10-10 **94**..........................(p) APMcCoy 84
(S R B Crawford, Ire) *w ldrs: led 3rd: hdd next: hit 6th: led 3 out: hdd appr next: wknd sn after last* **5/1**[1]

146- 5 6 **Carmela Maria**[10] 2956 8-10-4 **93**..................................(b) JoeColliver(5) 78
(Mike Sowersby) *chsd ldrs: reminders after 7th: lost pl next: sn bhd: kpt on fr 2 out* **17/2**

P1U- 6 2 1/4 **I'Ll Be Frank**[16] 2843 8-10-10 **101**..........................(t) StephenMulqueen(7) 87
(Maurice Barnes) *w ldrs: led 4th: hdd next: led 9th: hdd next: wknd and 5th whn blnd last* **10/1**

560- 7 40 **Danceintothelight**[16] 2844 6-10-7 **98**........................ MissBeckySmith(7) 45
(Micky Hammond) *in rr: drvn 7th: bhd fr next: t.o 2 out* **20/1**

364- 8 1 1/4 **Sohcahtoa (IRE)**[14] 2869 7-9-11 **84** oh1........................(p) JohnKington(3) 30
(Andrew Crook) *chsd ldrs: drvn 8th: lost pl next: sn bhd: t.o whn blnd 2 out* **20/1**

463/ P **Wheyaye**[253] 5222 11-10-9 **100**.................................... GrahamWatters(7)
(Valerie Jackson) *chsd ldrs: pushed along 7th: lost pl next: sn bhd: t.o whn p.u bef 2 out* **22/1**

/13- P **Mrs Eff**[206] 476 7-11-9 **110**......................................(t) KyleJames(3)
(Philip Kirby) *mid-div: lost pl sn after 3 out: sn bhd: p.u bef last* **13/2**[3]

6m 26.7s (-0.90) **Going Correction** +0.075s/f (Yiel) **10** Ran SP% **111.1**
Speed ratings (Par 105): **104,104,103,99,98 97,85,84, ,** WIN: Gulf Punch £3.40, Harris £2.30; PL: GP £1.40, H £2.60, Pudsey House £2.40; EX: GP/H £15.10, H/GP £15.80; CSF: £14.01; TC: £73.16; Trifecta: GP/H/PH £105.00, H/GP/PH £119.00; toteswingers GP&H £6.30, GP&PH £6.90, H&PH £6.20 TRIFECTA Pool: £327 Owner.
Owner John Gwynne **Bred** Brook Stud Bloodstock Ltd **Trained** Cholmondeley, Cheshire

FOCUS
A modest staying handicap hurdle which produced the finish of the day. The two dead-heaters and the third were close to their marks.

3146 BUY YOUR 2014 ANNUAL BADGE TODAY NOVICES' LIMITED H'CAP CHASE (19 fncs) 3m 1f 110y
2:40 (2:41) (Class 3) (0-140,140) 4-Y-0+ **£9,747** (£2,862; £1,431)

Form RPR

2/1- 1 **Corrin Wood (IRE)**[26] 2622 6-11-0 **135**.. JasonMaguire 150+
(Donald McCain) *j. boldly: mde all: pushed clr before 17th: coasted home run-in: heavily eased clsng stages* **10/11**[1]

1UU- 2 23 **Dursey Sound (IRE)**[28] 2574 5-11-5 **140**...........................(b[1]) APMcCoy 140+
(Jonjo O'Neill) *trckd wnr fr 3rd: mstke 11th: drvn 4 out: no imp: wl hld whn eased last 100yds* **11/8**[2]

24P- 3 13 **Balding Banker (IRE)**[47] 2171 7-10-0 **126** oh3.................. TonyKelly(5) 102
(Rebecca Menzies) *detached 3rd after 3rd: hit 8th: sme hdwy 14th: outpcd and lost tch 4 out: mstke last* **15/2**[3]

6m 35.3s (-6.70) **Going Correction** -0.15s/f (Good) **3** Ran SP% **106.3**
Speed ratings (Par 107): **104,96,92**
CSF £2.51 TOTE £1.80; EX 2.60 Trifecta £2.70 Pool: £1944.35 - 523.47 winning units..
Owner Dermot Hanafin **Bred** Margaret Nevin **Trained** Cholmondeley, Cheshire

FOCUS
A small field, but quite a decent staying novices' handicap chase in which they went an even gallop. The easy winner built on his Market Rasen win and looks a smart novice.

3147 RACING AGAIN ON SATURDAY 28TH DECEMBER INTERMEDIATE OPEN NATIONAL HUNT FLAT RACE 2m
3:10 (3:10) (Class 6) 4-6-Y-O **£1,642** (£478; £239)

Form RPR

3- 1 **Beatu (IRE)**[13] 2885 4-11-4 0.. APMcCoy 105+
(S R B Crawford, Ire) *sn trcking ldrs: led over 2f out: drvn clr appr fnl f: eased towards fin* **6/1**[3]

2 6 **Master Dee (IRE)**[212] 4-11-4 0.. JasonMaguire 99+
(Donald McCain) *trckd ldrs: led over 2f out: sn drvn: hdd over 2f out: edgd lft: kpt on same pce* **1/1**[1]

5- 3 12 **Trackanais (FR)**[18] 2795 6-11-4 0......................................(t) BarryKeniry 86
(Simon Shirley-Beavan) *hld up in mid-div: trckd ldrs 9f out: outpcd over 2f out: kpt on to take modest 3rd nr fin* **25/1**

02- 4 1/2 **Herecomestrouble**[147] 1094 6-11-4 0........................... DougieCostello 85
(Malcolm Jefferson) *trckd ldrs: led 7f out: hdd over 3f out: outpcd over 2f out: lost 3rd nr fin* **12/1**

0/ 5 19 **Pennine Josie**[239] 5454 4-10-11 0.................................... PaddyBrennan 61
(James Moffatt) *t.k.h in rr: drvn 7f out: sn bhd: kpt on fnl 2f: tk distant 5th clsng stages* **100/1**

2- 6 4 **I Got Power**[223] 173 4-11-4 0.. JamesReveley 65
(Keith Reveley) *hld up in rr: hdwy over 5f out: sn trcking ldrs: wknd over 2f out: eased fnl f* **3/1**[2]

7 10 **Be A Dreamer** 5-10-8 0.............................. Zachery-JamesGaughan(10) 56
(Sue Smith) *chsd ldrs: drvn over 6f out: lost pl 5f out* **33/1**

8 2 1/2 **He's A Gentleman**[233] 6-11-1 0...................................... JakeGreenall(3) 53
(Michael Easterby) *led: hdd 7f out: lost pl over 3f out: sn bhd* **8/1**

06/ 9 19 **Bellingo**[650] 4702 6-10-11 0... KennyJohnson 29
(Robert Johnson) *in rr: drvn over 5f out: sn bhd: t.o whn eased over 1f out* **100/1**

10 25 **Dave The Dauphin** 4-11-4 0.. BrianHarding 14
(Mike Sowersby) *mid-div: drvn 7f out: sn lost pl: t.o 3f out: eased over 1f out: virtually p.u* **100/1**

3m 48.5s (1.60) **Going Correction** +0.075s/f (Yiel) **10** Ran SP% **117.8**
Speed ratings: **99,96,90,89,80 78,73,72,62,50**
toteswingers 1&2 £2.30, 1&3 £19.70, 2&3 £9.50 CSF £12.43 TOTE £5.70: £1.70, £1.10, £4.60; EX 12.60 Trifecta £320.60 Pool: £4470.69 - 10.45 winning units..
Owner Raymond Scullion/Martin McGrogan **Bred** J Travers **Trained** Larne, Co Antrim

FOCUS
An ordinary bumper in which the initial gallop was a steady one. The winner is on the upgrade.
T/Jkpt: Not won. T/Plt: £4462.40. Pool: £68,892.57 - 11.27 winning units. T/Qpdt: £63.70. Pool: £8358.76 - 97.00 winning units. WG

[2571]FAKENHAM (L-H)
Tuesday, December 17

OFFICIAL GOING: Good to soft (soft in places; 6.2)
8ft of fresh ground on hurdles track and 6ft of fresh ground on chase course.
Wind: virtually nil Weather: dry and bright

3148 SIS "NATIONAL HUNT" MAIDEN HURDLE (11 hdls) 2m 4f
12:50 (12:50) (Class 5) 4-Y-0+ **£1,997** (£620; £333)

Form RPR

0- 1 **Count Danilo (IRE)**[30] 2534 4-11-0 0................................ TomScudamore 121+
(David Pipe) *mde all: rdn bef 2 out: forged clr between last 2: in command and gd jump last: styd on wl* **10/11**[1]

0/6- 2 6 **Saffron Wells (IRE)**[73] 1771 5-10-11 0............................ TrevorWhelan(3) 118+
(Neil King) *hld up in 3rd: mstke 7th: wnt 2nd bef 3 out: 2 l down and travelling wl bef 2 out: rdn: hung rt and nt qckn between last 2: hld whn hit last* **6/4**[2]

023- 3 70 **Houseparty**[156] 968 5-11-0 105.. DaveCrosse 53
(Zoe Davison) *chsd wnr: mstke 3rd and 7th: rdn and dropped to 3rd bef 3 out: sn bhd: t.o bef 2 out: hit last* **6/1**[3]

60U- P **Tropical Sky (IRE)**[80] 1690 5-10-9 0.............................(t) JoeCornwall(5)
(Michael Chapman) *j. slowly: bhd: lost tch and rdn after 4th: tailing off and j.v.slowly next: immediately p.u* **100/1**

5m 16.7s (4.10) **Going Correction** +0.40s/f (Soft) **4** Ran SP% **107.7**
Speed ratings (Par 103): **107,104,76,**
CSF £2.66 TOTE £1.60; EX 2.80 Trifecta £4.00 Pool: £1804.43 - 333.68 winning units..
Owner B A Kilpatrick **Bred** B A Kilpatrick **Trained** Nicholashayne, Devon

FOCUS
Conor O'Farrell described the ground as "good to soft", while Trevor Whelan felt it to be riding "dead". Little depth to this modest maiden hurdle, and the level of the form is guessy.

3149 RACING AT FAKENHAM NEW YEAR'S DAY H'CAP HURDLE (6 hdls 3 omitted) 2m
1:20 (1:23) (Class 4) (0-105,105) 3-Y-0+ **£4,873** (£1,431; £715; £357)

Form RPR

5/5- 1 **White Diamond**[54] 2051 6-11-2 **95**.................................... DavidEngland 99+
(Nigel Twiston-Davies) *chsd ldrs tl wnt 2nd bef 6th: led after 3 out (actual 2 out): rdn bnd ent st: hung rt but kpt on wl fnl f* **7/1**

220- 2 1 3/4 **Kayfton Pete**[23] 2698 7-11-11 **104**.................................... AdamPogson 106
(Charles Pogson) *t.k.h: led on long run to 1st: j.rt 6th: j. bdly rt next (actual 2 out): hdd bef next (actual last): 3rd and unable qck on long run: wnt 2nd and one pce fnl f* **10/1**

560- 3 3/4 **Snapchat (IRE)**[22] 2718 6-11-12 **105**................................ ConorO'Farrell 105
(Seamus Durack) *hld up in tch in rr: hdwy after 6th: chsd ldrs bef 2 out (actual last): rdn and chsd wnr on long run-in: lost 2nd bypassing last: kpt on same pce fnl 100yds* **8/1**

114- 4 shd **Persian Herald**[16] 2846 5-11-9 **105**..........................(bt) TrevorWhelan(3) 105
(Neil King) *led early: chsd ldr fr 1st tl rdn and lost 2nd bef 6th: rallied u.p bef 2 out (actual last): clsd and cl 4th bypassing last: hung lft and no imp ins fnl f* **5/1**[2]

/06- 5 7 **Lilac Belle**[24] 2679 7-10-1 **85**.....................................(t) KillianMoore(5) 79
(Alex Hales) *racd in last pair: niggled along after 3rd: rdn and no imp bef 3 out (actual 2 out): styd on past btn horses on long run-in: nvr trbld ldrs* **6/1**[3]

353- 6 4 **Logical Approach (IRE)**[31] 2511 6-11-5 **98**................. TomScudamore 88
(David Thompson) *t.k.h: hld up wl in tch in midfield: rdn and effrt bef 3 out (actual 2 out): wknd on long run-in* **7/1**

036/ 7 10 **Cappielow Park**[233] 3 4-10-10 **89**.............................. LeightonAspell 70
(Fleur Hawes) *t.k.h: hld up in tch in midfield: nt clr run and swtchd rt after 3 out (actual 2 out): sn rdn and no hdwy: wknd next (actual last)* **25/1**

125- 8 1 **Poetic Power (IRE)**[4] 3062 4-10-8 **94**.............................. GeraldQuinn(7) 74
(Claire Dyson) *in tch in midfield: hdwy to chse ldrs bef 3 out (actual 2 out): wknd u.p bef 2 out (actual last)* **11/4**[1]

/23- 9 36 **County Zen (FR)**[208] 445 10-11-2 **102**............................ MissBAndrews(7) 50
(Caroline Fryer) *in tch in midfield: lost pl 3rd: in last trio and rdn after 5th: lost tch bef 3 out (actual 2 out): t.o* **16/1**

4m 13.4s (8.00) **Going Correction** +0.40s/f (Soft)
WFA 4 from 5yo+ 5lb **9** Ran SP% **112.5**
Speed ratings (Par 105): **96,95,94,94,91 89,84,83,65**
toteswingers 1&2 £10.60, 1&3 £10.30, 2&3 £8.40 CSF £70.73 CT £567.69 TOTE £6.90: £1.90, £3.10, £2.50; EX 61.90 Trifecta £349.20 Pool: £2500.43 - 5.37 winning units..
Owner The Atkin Partnership **Bred** Newsells Park Stud **Trained** Naunton, Gloucs

FOCUS
The hurdle in the straight was omitted due to the low sun. Ordinary form for the level but the winner is on the upgrade.

3150 WEATHERBYS HAMILTON INSURANCE H'CAP CHASE (16 fncs) 2m 5f 110y
1:50 (1:52) (Class 3) (0-130,129) 4-Y-0+ **£7,147** (£2,098; £1,049; £524)

Form RPR

/40- 1 **San Telm (IRE)**[31] 2508 8-11-0 **120**................................ JoshuaMoore(3) 130+
(Renee Robeson) *nt fluent: in tch: j. and reminders 8th: 3rd and rdn whn mstke 2 out: qckd u.p to ld between last 2: sn clr in command: comf* **5/2**[1]

F4P- 2 15 **That's The Deal (IRE)**[14] 2873 9-9-10 **104**........................ JoeCornwall(5) 96
(John Cornwall) *chsd ldrs: hdwy on inner after 11th: led 12th: rdn and hdd between last 2: immediately outpcd by wnr: plugged on same pce after* **10/1**

1/4- 3 2 **Flaming Gorge (IRE)**[219] 238 8-11-12 **129**...................... LeightonAspell 123+
(Fleur Hawes) *j.rt: w ldr: rdn and ev ch 3 out tl no ex and outpcd between last 2: plugged on same pce after* **8/1**

525- 4 15 **Epee Celeste (FR)**[91] 1598 7-9-7 **103**........................ MissAliceMills(7) 78
(Michael Chapman) *led tl 12th: dropped to 4th and struggling next: wknd 3 out* **8/1**

432- F **The Thirsty Bricky (IRE)**[6] 3019 11-10-9 **112**............. TomScudamore
(David Thompson) *in tch: hdwy to chse ldrs and hit 5th: fell next* **3/1**[3]

21U- B **Highbury High (IRE)**[18] 2784 6-10-1 **104**........................... IanPopham
(Paul Henderson) *hld up in tch in rr tl b.d 6th* **11/4**[2]

5m 46.0s (4.20) **Going Correction** +0.40s/f (Soft) **6** Ran SP% **111.6**
Speed ratings (Par 107): **108,102,101,96,**
toteswingers 1&2 £5.30, 1&3 £5.80, 2&3 £7.20 CSF £24.06 TOTE £3.20: £2.10, £5.80; EX 26.20 Trifecta £127.40 Pool: £2550.34 - 15.00 winning units..
Owner The Tyringham Partnership **Bred** Miss Kathleen Clinton **Trained** Tyringham, Bucks

The Form Book Jumps, Raceform Ltd, Compton, RG20 6NL.

FOCUS
Modest form but the winner can rate higher if his jumping improves.

3151 CHRISTMAS H'CAP HURDLE (13 hdls) 2m 7f 110y
2:20 (2:20) (Class 4) (0-115,109) 4-Y-0+ **£3,119** (£915; £457; £228)

Form RPR
/35- **1** **Mistral Reine**[24] 2663 4-11-2 **99**........................ LeightonAspell 105+
(Lucy Wadham) *chsd ldrs: mstke 8th: 3rd and rdn after 3 out: led between last 2: drvn clr and j.rt last: styd on* **9/2**[3]
031- **2** *3 ½* **Bonnet's Vino**[13] 2883 5-11-6 **106**........................ KielanWoods(3) 106
(Pam Sly) *t.k.h: chsd ldrs tl wnt 2nd 10th: ev ch next: mstke 2 out: sn led: drvn: hdd and hung rt u.p bef last: kpt on same pce after* **2/1**[1]
31- **3** *6* **Wither Yenot (IRE)**[29] 2566 6-11-5 **109**........................ MrMJPKendrick(7) 109+
(Ben Case) *t.k.h: chsd ldr: mstke 5th: led 9th: rdn and mstke 2 out: sn hdd: 3rd and btn whn j. awkwardly last: rdr unbalanced and wknd flat: jst hld on for 3rd* **9/2**[3]
F23- **4** *hd* **Riddlestown (IRE)**[12] 2897 6-11-0 **104**........................(p) MissBAndrews(7) 98
(Caroline Fryer) *hld up in tch in last pair: rdn after 9th: 5th and outpcd bef 3 out: wnt 4th and drvn wl bef 2 out: kpt on same pce u.p after: jst missed 3rd last strides* **7/2**[2]
P40- **5** *30* **King Ozzy (IRE)**[19] 2760 9-10-7 **97**........................(tp) CharlieDeutsch(7) 64
(Lawney Hill) *in tch in midfield: 4th and rdn after 10th: wknd wl bef 2 out: t.o* **12/1**
3P0- **6** *38* **Go Amwell**[24] 2680 10-11-2 **99**........................(v) BrendanPowell 32
(J R Jenkins) *a in rr: pushed along after 7th: rdn and struggling after 9th: lost tch next: t.o 3 out* **8/1**
200/ **7** *28* **Asker (IRE)**[74] 4597 5-11-11 **108**........................(p) DaveCrosse 15
(Zoe Davison) *led tl 9th: sn rdn and immediately dropped out: t.o bef 3 out* **33/1**

6m 32.4s (26.00) **Going Correction** +0.40s/f (Soft)
WFA 4 from 5yo+ 6lb 7 Ran SP% **113.7**
Speed ratings (Par 105): **72,70,68,68,58 46,36**
toteswingers 1&2 £4.80, 1&3 £3.10, 2&3 £2.80 CSF £14.20 TOTE £4.00: £1.80, £1.50; EX 11.50 Trifecta £67.20 Pool: £1270.10 - 14.16 winning units..
Owner Sara Dennis And Dominic And Sarah Reilly **Bred** Elms Stud Co Ltd & Miss J Winter **Trained** Newmarket, Suffolk
■ Stewards' Enquiry : Kielan Woods two-day ban; used whip above permitted level (31st Dec, 1st Jan).

FOCUS
Sound form, with the right horses coming to the fore. The first two are on the upgrade.

3152 MULLED WINE NOVICES' H'CAP CHASE (12 fncs) 2m 110y
2:50 (2:50) (Class 4) (0-110,105) 4-Y-0+ **£3,768** (£1,106; £553; £276)

Form RPR
512- **1** **Hopeand**[26] 2626 8-11-7 **100**........................(t) AdamPogson 107+
(Charles Pogson) *mde all and j. much bttr than rivals: pressed but stl gng wl whn lft clr 2 out: drvn between last 2: kpt on* **5/1**[3]
004- **2** *10* **Looks Like Slim**[24] 2677 6-11-12 **105**........................(p) JackDoyle 110+
(Ben De Haan) *bhd: mstke 1st: hdwy to chse ldrs 4th: lft 2nd next: mstke 7th: clr w wnr and mstke 9th: rdn and effrt to press wnr whn blnd bdly 2 out: nt rcvr and plugged on same pce after* **9/2**[2]
/FP- **3** *23* **Shannon Spirit (IRE)**[20] 2742 8-11-10 **103**........................ IanPopham 79
(Paul Henderson) *chsd ldr tl 3rd: lost pl next: lft 3rd 5th: sn rdn: mstke 8th: 5th and wl outpcd next: no ch 2 out: lft modest 4th last: wnt 3rd flat* **10/1**
644- **4** *7* **Radsoc De Sivola (FR)**[54] 2048 8-9-9 **79** oh29........................ JoeCornwall(5) 49
(John Cornwall) *racd in midfield: rdn and outpcd after 8th: 4th and wl btn 3 out: lft modest 3rd and j. slowly last: sn lost 3rd and wknd: t.o* **33/1**
F06- **5** *28* **Bathcounty (IRE)**[19] 2771 6-11-7 **100**........................ FelixDeGiles 45
(Barry Brennan) *midfield tl dropped to last pair and blnd 3rd: stl in tch whn mstke 8th: sn rdn and lost tch: j.lft next: t.o 3 out* **7/1**
/00- **P** **Rocky Elsom (USA)**[33] 2469 6-11-10 **103**........................(t) TomCannon
(David Arbuthnot) *hld up in last pair: j. slowly 4th: blnd next and immediately p.u* **7/2**[1]
4U4- **U** **Ninfea (IRE)**[12] 2896 5-11-2 **98**........................ TrevorWhelan(3) 87
(Neil King) *hld up in last pair: hmpd 2nd: hdwy 8th: chsd clr ldng pair bef next: no imp and j. slowly 3 out: keeping on but n.d whn blnd and uns rdr last* **10/1**
051- **U** **Carobello (IRE)**[28] 2576 6-9-13 **83**........................(bt) NicodeBoinville(5)
(Martin Bosley) *chsd ldrs: wnt 2nd 3rd untl blnd and uns rdr 5th* **7/2**[1]

4m 27.75s (11.15) **Going Correction** +0.40s/f (Soft) 8 Ran SP% **112.9**
Speed ratings (Par 105): **89,84,73,70,57 , ,**
toteswingers 1&2 £3.00, 1&3 £12.40, 2&3 £10.50 CSF £27.49 CT £213.77 TOTE £5.80: £2.00, £1.50, £2.80; EX 16.50 Trifecta £218.60 Pool: £2250.87 - 7.71 winning units..
Owner C T Pogson **Bred** Stewart Pike **Trained** Farnsfield, Notts

FOCUS
This was shaping up into an interesting duel until Looks Like Slim blundered badly at the second-last. The winner is rated in line with his recent easy win.

3153 THOROUGHBRED BREEDERS' ASSOCIATION MARES' NOVICES' HURDLE (9 hdls) 2m
3:20 (3:24) (Class 4) 4-Y-0+ **£3,119** (£915; £457; £228)

Form RPR
0- **1** **Miss Biscotti**[27] 2600 5-10-5 0........................ NicodeBoinville(5) 95
(Martin Bosley) *mde all: rdn after 2 out: forged ahd bef last: styd on wl flat: rdn out* **100/1**
43- **2** *3* **Sudden Wish (IRE)**[21] 2725 4-10-10 0........................ JamieMoore 92
(Gary Moore) *in tch in midfield: rdn and effrt after 3 out: mstke 2 out: sn drvn and chsd wnr: pressed wnr briefly bnd bef last: no ex and mstke last: one pce flat* **5/1**[2]
236- **3** *¾* **Great Oak (IRE)**[51] 2101 7-11-3 105........................ TomCannon 98
(Tim Vaughan) *hld up in tch in last pair: rdn and effrt bef 2 out: styd on u.p to chse ldng pair bef last: kpt on same pce flat* **5/4**[1]
0/2- **4** *2 ½* **Java Rose**[94] 101 4-10-10 0........................ NoelFehily 90
(Charlie Longsdon) *chsd wnr: mstke 4th: rdn after 3 out: mstke next: lost 2nd between last 2: 4th and hld whn j. slowly last: wknd flat* **5/4**[1]
/40- **5** *nk* **Resourceful Miss**[18] 1779 4-10-10 0........................(b[1]) PaulMoloney 88
(Paul Webber) *chsd ldrs: rdn and fnd little after 2 out: 5th and hld whn j. slowly last: wknd flat* **25/1**[3]
564- **6** *17* **Frank N Fair**[20] 2745 5-10-10 0........................ DaveCrosse 71
(Zoe Davison) *mstkes: hld up in tch in last pair: rdn after 6th: wknd bef 2 out* **50/1**

4m 23.5s (18.10) **Going Correction** +0.40s/f (Soft)
WFA 4 from 5yo+ 5lb 6 Ran SP% **112.4**
Speed ratings (Par 105): **70,68,68,66,66 58**
toteswingers 1&2 £5.50, 1&3 £18.50, 2&3 £1.50 CSF £514.83 TOTE £23.20: £8.20, £2.50; EX 180.30 Trifecta £672.70 Pool: £4971.76 - 5.54 winning units..
Owner Mrs Carol B Herbert **Bred** D B Dennison **Trained** Chalfont St Giles, Bucks

FOCUS
Each of the market principals appeared to have something to prove and the race went to the complete outsider. The race was slowly run and the form is dubious.
T/Plt: £302.00. Pool: £63,431.79 - 153.29 winning units. T/Qpdt: £72.80. Pool: £6823.37 - 69.30 winning units. SP

2886 LUDLOW (R-H)
Wednesday, December 18

OFFICIAL GOING: Good to soft (good in places; 7.5)
Fresh ground on bends and hurdles out wide.
Wind: Light across Weather: Light rain

3154 TANNERS BURGUNDY JUVENILE CLAIMING HURDLE (9 hdls) 2m
12:20 (12:20) (Class 4) 3-Y-0 **£3,994** (£1,240; £667)

Form RPR
050- **1** **Big John Cannon (IRE)**[6] 3047 3-10-7 85........................ AidanColeman 101+
(Sarah-Jayne Davies) *chsd ldrs: pushed along appr 3 out: led and hit next: rdn out* **25/1**
130- **2** *3* **Hanga Roa (IRE)**[12] 2932 3-11-1 114........................(p) JamieMoore 105
(Gary Moore) *led: clr fr 2nd tl 6th: rdn and hit 3 out: hdd next: ev ch last: styd on same pce flat* **9/4**[2]
23- **3** *4* **Poetic Verse**[11] 2934 3-11-6 122........................ JamesReveley 108
(John Quinn) *chsd ldr: ev ch 3 out: rdn and hit last: no ex* **8/15**[1]
P **Hillbilly Boy (IRE)**[286] 3-10-8 0........................ RyanWhile(7)
(Bill Turner) *hld up: pushed along and wknd after 6th: bhd whn p.u bef next* **14/1**[3]

3m 58.9s (9.40) **Going Correction** +0.70s/f (Soft) 4 Ran SP% **106.5**
Speed ratings (Par 104): **104,102,100,**
CSF £74.31 TOTE £8.30; EX 92.90 Trifecta £48.30 Pool: £1,470.85 - 22.81 winning units..
Owner Miss Sarah-Jayne Davies **Bred** David McGuinness **Trained** Leominster, H'fords

FOCUS
Bends were moved to provide fresh ground and the hurdles were sited on the extreme outside. After the first race Aidan Coleman described the ground as being "on the slow side of good, getting towards soft." A weak contest and, despite the small field, it was run a true enough pace. A big step up from the winner.

3155 ALFA AGGREGATE PRODUCTS NOVICES' LIMITED H'CAP CHASE (17 fncs) 2m 4f
12:50 (12:50) (Class 3) (0-125,125) 4-Y-0+ **£9,495** (£2,805; £1,402; £702; £351)

Form RPR
221- **1** **Cloudy Joker (IRE)**[41] 2308 5-10-8 **114**........................ HenryBrooke 126+
(Donald McCain) *hld up: hdwy 7th: led 13th: rdn and hung rt appr 2 out: jst hld on* **12/1**
216/ **2** *hd* **Benbens (IRE)**[609] 5461 8-10-7 **113**........................ SamTwiston-Davies 130+
(Nigel Twiston-Davies) *hld up: hdwy 10th: pushed along whn hmpd 4 out: mstke 2 out: sn rdn: edgd rt flat: r.o u.p: jst failed* **7/4**[1]
0/1- **3** *1 ¼* **Bobcatbilly (IRE)**[14] 2887 7-10-5 **111**........................ WayneHutchinson 121+
(Ian Williams) *a.p: racd keenly: lft 2nd 4 out: rdn and edgd lft flat: styd on* **9/4**[2]
/40- **4** *9* **Copper Birch (IRE)**[31] 2529 5-10-10 **116**........................ PaulMoloney 118
(Evan Williams) *led to 4th: remained handy: rdn and hung rt appr last: wknd flat* **8/1**
060- **5** *2 ½* **Kingcora (FR)**[31] 2529 5-10-5 **111**........................ AidanColeman 110
(Venetia Williams) *chsd ldrs: led 5th: hdd 13th: rdn appr 2 out: wknd last* **12/1**
112- **P** **Be All Man (IRE)**[20] 2762 6-11-2 **122**........................ JamieMoore
(Gary Moore) *chsd ldr tl led 4th: hdd next: remained handy: w ldrs whn blnd 12th: rdn and wknd bef 4 out: bhd whn p.u bef next* **7/1**[3]
11P- **F** **Lord Grantham (IRE)**[151] 1042 6-11-2 **125**........................ JakeGreenall(3)
(Henry Daly) *hld up: mstke 3rd: hdwy 12th: chsd wnr whn fell 4 out* **12/1**

5m 12.3s (7.90) **Going Correction** +0.55s/f (Soft) 7 Ran SP% **113.8**
Speed ratings (Par 107): **106,105,105,101,100 ,**
Tote Swingers: 1&2 £11.10, 1&3 £2.60, 2&3 £1.50 CSF £34.66 CT £66.39 TOTE £6.50: £3.00, £2.60; EX 48.90 Trifecta £61.30 Pool: £1,538.64 - 18.81 winning units..
Owner D McCain Jnr **Bred** Miss Penny Downes **Trained** Cholmondeley, Cheshire

FOCUS
Little in the way of early pace in this decent handicap chase and a close finish was fought out by three interesting horses. The winner built on his recent win but the second was unlucky.

3156 TANNERS CHAMPAGNE H'CAP CHASE (13 fncs) 2m
1:20 (1:20) (Class 3) (0-125,123) 4-Y-0+**£12,777** (£3,857; £1,987; £1,053)

Form RPR
125- **1** **Last Shot (FR)**[15] 2873 6-11-9 **120**........................ AidanColeman 135+
(Venetia Williams) *w ldr tl led 6th: clr fr 4 out: easily* **6/1**
633- **2** *14* **Pearls Legend**[10] 2976 6-11-7 **118**........................ JamieMoore 122+
(John Spearing) *prom: mstke 8th: chsd wnr next: rdn appr 4 out: blnd next: mstke and wknd 2 out* **9/4**[1]
445- **3** *18* **Free World (FR)**[14] 2890 9-10-1 **105**........................ MissLBrooke(7) 87
(Lady Susan Brooke) *prom tl wknd appr 4 out* **20/1**
/12- **4** *8* **Riddleofthesands (IRE)**[24] 2699 9-10-5 **102**........ SamTwiston-Davies 77
(Nigel Twiston-Davies) *racd keenly: led to 6th: chsd wnr to 9th: rdn and wknd bef next* **3/1**[3]
523- **P** **Takeroc (FR)**[23] 2721 10-11-5 **119**........................(t) JamesBest(3)
(Sophie Leech) *hld up: mstke 2nd: rdn and wknd after 9th: blnd 3 out: p.u bef next* **12/1**
0/4- **F** **Tornado In Milan (IRE)**[55] 2042 7-11-9 **120**........................ PaulMoloney
(Evan Williams) *fell 1st* **5/2**[2]

4m 4.5s (6.00) **Going Correction** +0.55s/f (Soft) 6 Ran SP% **111.1**
Speed ratings (Par 107): **107,100,91,87,**
Tote Swingers: 1&2 £4.80, 1&3 £13.60, 2&3 £9.40 CSF £20.09 TOTE £4.60: £2.90, £1.10; EX 5.40 Trifecta £469.50 Pool: £2147.00 - 3.42 winning units..
Owner Basil Richards & Lady Bolton **Bred** Guy-Roger Petit **Trained** Kings Caple, H'fords

FOCUS
This looked to be a fair race but it lost some of its interest when Tornado in Milan went at the first. Seemingly a big step up from the easy winner.

3157 TANNERS CAVA LADY AMATEUR RIDERS' H'CAP HURDLE (9 hdls) 2m
1:50 (1:50) (Class 4) (0-105,105) 3-Y-0+ **£4,367** (£1,354; £676; £338)

Form RPR
0P2- 1 **Rolling Dough (IRE)**[14] 2886 5-9-11 79 oh4....(p) MissHannahWatson(3) 81
(Sophie Leech) *hld up: hdwy appr 2 out: shkn up and r.o to ld fnl 50yds* **14/1**
102- 2 *nk* **Scales (IRE)**[8] 3013 7-11-7 105........ MissLBrooke(5) 108
(Richard Lee) *hld up: hdwy 6th: n.m.r bnd appr 3 out: rdn flat: r.o* **5/1**[3]
360- 3 *1 1/4* **Exemplary**[34] 2474 6-11-2 100........ MissBAndrews(5) 101
(Marc Barber) *a.p: chsd ldr 4th: ev ch appr 3 out: sn rdn: styd on* **4/1**[2]
/P3- 4 *1* **Miss Tilly Oscar (IRE)**[14] 2888 7-11-0 93........(v[1]) MissGAndrews 93+
(David Evans) *hld up in tch: plld hrd: led appr 3 out: rdn flat: hdd and no ex fnl 50yds* **8/1**
163- 5 *nk* **Moscow Me (IRE)**[14] 2891 6-11-6 104........ MissJBuck(5) 105
(Henry Oliver) *chsd ldrs: rdn appr 3 out: styd on* **3/1**[1]
000- 6 *2 1/2* **Veratan (FR)**[27] 2614 6-10-4 90........ MissLMTurner(7) 88
(Venetia Williams) *sn pushed along in rr: hdwy on outer appr 3 out: styd on same pce fr next* **6/1**
003- 7 *6* **Peak Storm**[20] 2753 4-11-3 101........ MissSMDoolan(5) 92
(John O'Shea) *prom: racd keenly: hit 3 out: wknd appr last* **16/1**
P34- 8 *1/2* **Volcanic Jack (IRE)**[13] 2904 5-10-3 87........ MissAliceMills(5) 79
(Michael Chapman) *hld up: hdwy appr 3 out: wknd after next* **12/1**
P0F- 9 *10* **Officially Modern (IRE)**[36] 2441 6-10-10 94........[1] MissAEStirling(5) 77
(Fergal O'Brien) *led: hdd appr 3 out: wknd bef next* **12/1**
F/U- 10 *26* **Mister Fantastic**[48] 2176 7-10-6 92........ MissSLewis(7) 51
(Dai Burchell) *chsd ldr: mstke 3rd: grad lost pl: wknd after 5th* **25/1**

3m 59.5s (10.00) **Going Correction** +0.70s/f (Soft)
WFA 4 from 5yo+ 5lb **10 Ran SP% 118.8**
Speed ratings (Par 105): **103,102,102,101,101 100,97,97,92,79**
Tote Swingers: 1&2 £14.20, 1&3 £8.20, 2&3 £7.40 CSF £85.13 CT £340.92 TOTE £11.60: £3.70, £2.50, £2.00; EX 40.10 Trifecta £364.50 Pool: £1,224.74 - 2.51 winning units..
Owner C J Leech **Bred** Noel O'Brien **Trained** Elton, Gloucs

FOCUS
Just a modest race but it served up a good finish. The form is believable even though they finished in a heap.

3158 TANNERS WINES H'CAP CHASE (19 fncs) 3m
2:25 (2:25) (Class 3) (0-130,130) 4-Y£12,660 (£3,740; £1,870; £936; £468)

Form RPR
121- 1 **King Massini (IRE)**[5] 3065 7-11-2 120........ AdamWedge 133+
(Evan Williams) *trckd ldrs: wnt 2nd 13th: led 3 out: styd on wl* **7/4**[1]
/22- 2 *7* **Rydalis (FR)**[34] 2468 8-11-0 118........ AidanColeman 126+
(Venetia Williams) *w ldr tl led 3rd: nt fluent 11th (water): hdd 3 out: styd on same pce last* **7/2**[2]
532- 3 *9* **Cootehill (IRE)**[14] 2889 9-11-12 130........ SamTwiston-Davies 128
(Nigel Twiston-Davies) *hld up: hdwy 14th: wknd after 2 out* **9/1**
/4F- 4 *4* **Hatters River (IRE)**[11] 2955 6-11-0 118........ WayneHutchinson 112
(Ali Brewer) *hld up: hdwy 12th: weaekned 2 out* **5/1**[3]
500- 5 *7* **Owen Glendower (IRE)**[5] 3065 8-11-2 125........(tp) CharlieWallis(5) 119
(Sophie Leech) *led to 3rd: chsd ldr: hit 8th: lost 2nd 13th: wknd 4 out: blnd next* **16/1**
/50- P **Doctor Foxtrot (IRE)**[12] 2928 8-10-12 119........(b) JamesBest(3)
(Philip Hobbs) *hit 1st: hld up: hdwy after 6th: hit 10th: pushed along 12th: blnd 14th: sn wknd: bhd whn p.u bef 4 out* **14/1**
6/F- P **Big News**[11] 2945 7-11-5 123........(t) JamieMoore
(Richard Lee) *chsd ldrs: pushed along and lost pl after 6th: mstke next: bhd fr 8th: p.u bef 12th* **6/1**

6m 20.2s (11.90) **Going Correction** +0.55s/f (Soft) **7 Ran SP% 112.1**
Speed ratings (Par 107): **102,99,96,95,93** ,
Tote Swingers: 1&2 £1.60, 1&3 £1.40, 2&3 £2.10 CSF £8.32 CT £39.90 TOTE £2.70: £1.40, £2.00; EX 7.80 Trifecta £15.60 Pool: £1,396.74 - 66.79 winning units..
Owner Border Pointers **Bred** Tim Jones **Trained** Llancarfan, Vale Of Glamorgan

FOCUS
An above-average handicap for the grade and it was taken by a progressive horse in King Massini who produced another step up.

3159 EUROPEAN BREEDERS' FUND & HORSEWEIGH MARES' "NATIONAL HUNT" NOVICES' HURDLE (11 hdls) 2m 5f
3:00 (3:00) (Class 4) 4-Y-0+ **£4,548** (£1,335; £667; £333)

Form RPR
/12- 1 **Kayfleur**[25] 2675 4-10-7 0........ JakeGreenall(3) 116+
(Henry Daly) *hld up: hdwy 7th: led 2 out: styd on wl* **10/11**[1]
20- 2 *7* **Forgivienne**[34] 2471 6-10-10 0........ AdamWedge 107
(Evan Williams) *led: rdn and hdd 2 out: hit last: styd on same pce flat* **12/1**
415- 3 *1 1/2* **Midnight Cataria**[19] 2801 4-11-3 0........ WayneHutchinson 111
(Alan King) *hld up: hdwy 7th: rdn appr last: styd on same pce flat* **9/2**[2]
/30- 4 *1* **Amazing D'Azy (IRE)**[41] 2317 5-10-10 0........ SamThomas 103
(Kim Bailey) *hld up: hdwy appr 3 out: shkn up after next: styd on same pce last* **20/1**
3/0- 5 *nk* **Carolina Wren**[76] 1731 4-10-10 0........ PaulMoloney 104
(Renee Robeson) *prom: rdn whn hit last: styd on same pce* **25/1**
6F4- 6 *8* **Fairweather Friend**[28] 2600 4-10-10 0........ SeanQuinlan 96
(Jennie Candlish) *hld up: hdwy after 8th: rdn and wknd appr last* **8/1**[3]
4- 7 *40* **Beatrix Kiddo (IRE)**[101] 1531 4-10-10 0........ HarrySkelton 59
(Dan Skelton) *hld up: hdwy after 8th: wknd bef next* **14/1**
0/6- 8 *3* **Do Be Dashing**[36] 2442 5-10-10 0........ CharliePoste 57
(Graeme McPherson) *hld up: nt fluent 2nd: sme hdwy appr 3 out: sn wknd* **50/1**
0- 9 *15* **Glacial Roes (IRE)**[56] 2026 5-10-3 0........ MrPJohn(7) 43
(Sarah-Jayne Davies) *chsd ldrs tl rdn and wknd after 8th* **100/1**
00- 10 *nse* **Miss Dimples (IRE)**[175] 841 4-10-10 0........ AidanColeman 43
(Sarah-Jayne Davies) *chsd ldr to 7th: rdn and wknd appr 3 out* **50/1**
/04- 11 *9* **Honour A Promise**[18] 2824 5-10-10 0........ LiamHeard 35
(Paul Webber) *mid-div: rdn and wknd after 8th* **20/1**
12 *4 1/2* **Tirley Bay**[226] 9-10-10 0........ SamTwiston-Davies 31
(Julian Smith) *hld up: sme hdwy appr 6th: wknd after 8th* **66/1**
6/0- 13 *15* **Ereyna**[28] 2600 4-10-10 0........ JamieMoore 17
(Renee Robeson) *mid-div: hdwy 4th: mstke 8th: sn wknd* **33/1**

2/4- P **Pandy**[18] 2809 4-10-10 0........(t) AndrewTinkler
(George Baker) *prom: chsd ldr 7th tl after next: wkng whn stmbld 3 out: sn p.u* **16/1**

5m 31.1s (16.30) **Going Correction** +0.70s/f (Soft) **14 Ran SP% 124.6**
Speed ratings (Par 105): **96,93,92,92,92 89,73,72,67,67 63,61,56,**
Tote Swingers: 1&2 £4.70, 1&3 £1.10, 2&3 £7.90 CSF £12.90 TOTE £1.80: £1.10, £3.70, £1.30; EX 16.30 Trifecta £40.20 Pool: £1,922.85 - 35.81 winning units..
Owner B G Hellyer **Bred** B G Hellyer & H D J Daly **Trained** Stanton Lacy, Shropshire

FOCUS
The front six pulled well clear in this steadily run affair and the winner took it in fair style. She built on her debut run with the next two close to their marks.

3160 TANNERS CLARET STANDARD OPEN NATIONAL HUNT FLAT RACE 1m 6f
3:30 (3:30) (Class 4) 4-5-Y-0 **£3,249** (£954; £477; £238)

Form RPR
2- 1 **Blue Heron (IRE)**[23] 2724 5-11-2 0........ HarrySkelton 99+
(Dan Skelton) *mde all: clr 3f out: rdn over 1f out: swtchd lft ins fnl f: styd on* **4/5**[1]
2 *1* **Hughesie (IRE)** 4-10-9 0........ ConorRing(7) 98+
(Evan Williams) *a.p: chsd wnr 9f out: rdn over 3f out: styng on whn nt clr run and swtchd rt ins fnl f* **9/2**[3]
3 *20* **Paolozzi (IRE)** 4-11-2 0........ ConorO'Farrell 74
(Seamus Durack) *prom: rdn over 3f out: wknd over 2f out* **8/1**
4 *18* **Home For Tea** 4-11-2 0........ FelixDeGiles 52
(Tom Symonds) *hld up: hdwy 8f out: rdn over 4f out: wknd sn after* **4/1**[2]
5 *7* **Hannah Just Hannah** 4-10-9 0........[1] GerardTumelty 37
(Alastair Lidderdale) *hld up: a in rr: bhd fnl 8f* **16/1**
00- 6 *85* **Game Dorabella**[10] 2981 5-10-2 0........(p) MrPJohn(7)
(Laura Hurley) *chsd wnr 5f: sn pushed along: wknd over 7f out* **66/1**

3m 25.4s (12.40) **6 Ran SP% 112.2**
Tote Swingers: 1&2 £3.60, 2&3 £2.20 CSF £4.83 TOTE £1.70: £1.50, £2.30; EX 5.20 Trifecta £16.20 Pool: £5,175.61 - 238.81 winning units..
Owner Horwood Harriers Partnership **Bred** Louise Cooper-Joyce **Trained** Alcester, Warwicks

FOCUS
The front pair pulled clear and the winner is rated to his recent C&D mark.
T/Plt: £2,261.00 to a £1 stake. Pool: £42,743.44 - 13.80 winning tickets. T/Qpdt: £9.00 to a £1 stake. Pool: £6,560.70 - 534.10 winning tickets. CR

2810 NEWBURY (L-H)
Wednesday, December 18

OFFICIAL GOING: Chase course - good to soft; hurdle course - soft (good to soft in places) (chs 6.0, hdl 5.6)
Rails on chase bends moved out and moved in on hurdle bends.
Wind: Brisk across Weather: Overcast

3161 BLACKMORE BUILDING JUVENILE HURDLE (8 hdls) 2m 110y
12:10 (12:10) (Class 4) 3-Y-0 **£3,249** (£954; £477; £238)

Form RPR
4- 1 **Dawalan (FR)**[19] 2796 3-10-12 0........ BarryGeraghty 116+
(Nicky Henderson) *in tch: hdwy 4th: pressed ldrs fr 3 out: chal fr 2 out tl led w 1f to run: forged clr: readily* **4/6**[1]
30- 2 *8* **Rayak (IRE)**[10] 2975 3-10-12 0........ APMcCoy 105
(Jonjo O'Neill) *hld up in rr: stdy hdwy to trck ldrs 3 out: chal 2 out and sn slt ld but hrd pressed last: hdd w 1f to run: sn outpcd by wnr* **20/1**
3 *1 1/2* **Certification (IRE)**[112] 3-10-12 0........ DenisO'Regan 104
(John Ferguson) *hld up towards rr but in tch: hdwy to trck ldrs 3 out: ev ch 2 out: rdn and one pce last: swtchd rt run-in and styd on to cl on 2nd nr fin* **8/1**[3]
4 *1/2* **Alco Sivola (FR)** 3-10-12 0........ DarylJacob 106+
(Nick Williams) *chsd ldrs: mstke 3rd: nt fluent 4 out: blnd 3 out and lost pl: styd on appr last: kpt on clsng stages* **10/1**
63- 5 *5* **Bugsy**[21] 2750 3-10-12 0........(t) ConorO'Farrell 99
(Seamus Durack) *narrow ldr but hrd pressed: kpt advantage but hrd pressed fr 3 out and hdd after 2 out: wknd bef last* **40/1**
2F- 6 *nk* **Brave Helios**[34] 2466 3-10-12 0........ JasonMaguire 98
(Jonathan Portman) *chsd ldrs: one pce after 4 out: styd on fr 2 out: one pce run-in* **33/1**
22- 7 *nk* **Aglaophonos**[34] 2466 3-10-12 114........(v[1]) TomScudamore 98
(Ian Williams) *chsd ldrs: chal 3 out: one pce and hit 2 out* **6/1**[2]
46- 8 *2 1/2* **Marju's Quest (IRE)**[21] 2750 3-10-12 0........[1] NoelFehily 95
(David Dennis) *plld hrd: in rr: hdwy to trck ldrs after 3 out: no ex appr last* **40/1**
9 *5* **Candyman Can (IRE)**[59] 3-10-12 0........ MarkGrant 90
(Dominic Ffrench Davis) *nt fluent towards rr: styd on fr 2 out: nvr a threat* **25/1**
10 *2 1/2* **Mr Fitzroy (IRE)**[65] 3-10-12 0........ DominicElsworth 87
(Jo Davis) *nt fluent: mstke 3 out: a in rr* **50/1**
35- 11 *6* **Andi'Amu (FR)**[19] 2796 3-10-9 0........(t) GavinSheehan(3) 81
(Warren Greatrex) *chsd ldrs: ev ch 3 out: wknd next* **16/1**
050- 12 *8* **Henri De Boistron (FR)**[21] 2750 3-10-12 0........ PaddyBrennan 73
(Tom George) *racd towards outside: chsd ldrs to 4 out: wknd bef next* **100/1**
13 *3 1/4* **The Green Ogre**[177] 3-10-9 0........ JoshuaMoore(3) 70
(Gary Moore) *in rr: hdwy to cl on ldrs 3 out: sn wknd* **50/1**
14 *1 1/4* **Luckster**[47] 3-10-12 0........ RobertThornton 69
(David Evans) *pressed ldr to 3 out: sn wknd* **50/1**

4m 6.57s (-3.43) **Going Correction** -0.30s/f (Good) **14 Ran SP% 123.7**
Speed ratings (Par 104): **96,92,91,91,88 88,88,87,85,83 81,77,75,75**
Tote Swingers: 1&2 £8.10, 1&3 £3.00, 2&3 £6.80 CSF £21.67 TOTE £2.20: £1.40, £2.70, £2.00; EX 26.00 Trifecta £503.30 Pool: £3,199.98 - 4.76 winning units..
Owner Simon Munir & Isaac Souede **Bred** H H The Aga Khan's Studs Sc **Trained** Upper Lambourn, Berks

The Form Book Jumps, Raceform Ltd, Compton, RG20 6NL.

FOCUS
A damp and windy day. The rails had been moved in on the hurdles track, and moved outside for the chases. The ground was reckoned to be soft on the hurdles course. An interesting juvenile hurdle run at a sound pace and the first four finished clear. The winner was close to his debut level but the form is pretty ordinary.

3162 WATCH ON 3 DEVICES RACINGUK.COM/ANYWHERE NOVICES' LIMITED H'CAP CHASE (18 fncs) 3m
12:40 (12:40) (Class 3) (0-140,138) 4-Y-0+ **£6,498** (£1,908; £954; £477)

Form RPR

1/F- **1** **Benvolio (IRE)**[31] 2539 6-11-0 **133**........ DarylJacob 147+
(Paul Nicholls) *pressed ldr tl led 7th: narrowly hdd appr 9th: styd upsides: led 11th: hrd pressed fr 14th and jnd fr 4 out: nt fluent 3 out: stl pressed last: styd on wl u.p run-in* **8/1**

61U- **2** *2* **Midnight Prayer**[11] 2941 8-10-11 **130**........ RobertThornton 143+
(Alan King) *chsd ldrs: pushed along and outpcd 8th: sn chsng ldrs again: chal fr 14th and upsides fr 4 out to last: no ex u.p run-in* **7/4**[1]

/41- **3** *42* **Ace Fighter Pilot**[163] 921 7-10-8 **127**........ TomScudamore 101
(Jim Best) *mde most to 7th: led again appr 9th: hdd 11th: wknd 14th but stage on for poor 3rd run-in* **16/1**

313- **4** *11* **Gas Line Boy (IRE)**[25] 2674 7-11-1 **134**........ RichardJohnson 104
(Philip Hobbs) *mstkes in rr thrght: no ch whn blnd 14th* **5/1**[3]

0/2- **5** *22* **Whats Happening (IRE)**[20] 2757 6-11-5 **138**........(t) PaddyBrennan 83
(Tom George) *hit 1st and 2nd: a in rr: lost tch fr 9th: mstkes 13th and 13th: t.o whn blnd 3 out* **11/2**

133- **F** **According To Trev (IRE)**[24] 2692 7-11-0 **133**........(vt[1]) APMcCoy
(Nigel Twiston-Davies) *chsd ldrs: 2 l 4th whn fell 10th* **7/2**[2]

6/1- **P** **Alpancho**[28] 2599 7-10-0 **124** oh7........(t) KillianMoore[(5)]
(Ben Case) *chsd ldrs: chal 13th: ev ch 14th: wknd sn after: no ch whn blnd 3 out: p.u bef next* **16/1**

5m 52.22s (-13.78) **Going Correction** -0.30s/f (Good) **7** Ran SP% **113.5**
Speed ratings (Par 107): **110,109,95,91,84** ,
Tote Swingers: 1&2 £5.00, 1&3 £32.30, 2&3 £8.30 CSF £23.16 TOTE £9.30: £4.50, £1.70; EX 44.80 Trifecta £242.70 Pool: £4,391.23 - 13.56 winning units..
Owner Dobson, Sutton & Woodhouse **Bred** Mrs Mary And Paul Motherway **Trained** Ditcheat, Somerset

FOCUS
The pace was sound and it only involved the first two up the home straight. They could be rated higher through the beaten horses.

3163 TONY JONES 60TH BIRTHDAY BASH MAIDEN HURDLE (8 hdls) 2m 110y
1:10 (1:13) (Class 4) 4-Y-0+ **£3,898** (£1,144; £572; £286)

Form RPR

1- **1** **Josses Hill (IRE)**[25] 2667 5-11-0 0........ BarryGeraghty 133+
(Nicky Henderson) *trckd ldrs: pushed along to chal last: fnl 200yds: pushed out* **1/1**[1]

2 *3* **Communicator**[39] 5-11-0 0........ TomO'Brien 128
(Andrew Balding) *chsd ldrs: drvn after 2 out: styd on wl rin-in to take 2nd clsng stages but no ch w wnr* **9/1**[3]

2/3- **3** *1* **Tiqris**[19] 2802 5-11-0 0........(t) RichardJohnson 127
(Philip Hobbs) *chsd ldrs: slt ld 3 out: jnd next and hrd pressed last: hdd and no ex fnl 200yds: lost 2nd clsng stages* **7/4**[2]

2- **4** *5* **A Hare Breath (IRE)**[26] 2644 5-11-0 0........ TomCannon 124
(Nick Gifford) *chsd ldrs: jot 3 out: nt fluent and str chal 2 out: no ex and one pce run-in* **12/1**

050- **5** *25* **Yes I Will**[16] 2858 4-11-0 0........(t) NoelFehily 97
(Charlie Longsdon) *towards rr: hdwy appr 3 out: styd on for mod 4th run-in* **66/1**

300- **6** *2 ¾* **Grand March**[44] 2265 4-10-9 0........ EdCookson[(5)] 94
(Kim Bailey) *disp ld to 3 out: wknd next* **66/1**

60- **7** *nk* **Frozen Over**[34] 2476 5-11-0 0........ JamesDavies 94
(Chris Down) *mid-div: sme hdwy 3 out: nvr any ch* **100/1**

6/6- **8** *nk* **Un Bleu A L'Aam (FR)**[32] 2507 5-11-0 0........ JackDoyle 94
(Victor Dartnall) *chsd ldrs to 3 out* **40/1**

46- **9** *9* **Know No Fear**[23] 2718 8-11-0 0........(t) WillKennedy 85
(Alastair Lidderdale) *mde most tl hdd 3 out: sn wknd* **50/1**

4- **10** *4* **All But Grey**[24] 2689 7-11-0 0........ IanPopham 81
(Carroll Gray) *chsd ldrs: rdn appr 3 out and sn btn* **66/1**

32P- **11** *6* **Rosslyn Castle**[169] 856 4-11-0 117........ JasonMaguire 75
(Gary Brown) *in rr: hdwy to trck ldrs after 4 out: wknd next* **33/1**

/0F- **12** *3 ¾* **Etania**[18] 2824 5-10-7 0........ RobertThornton 64
(Ian Williams) *a in rr* **50/1**

0- **13** *5* **Matripajo (IRE)**[67] 1869 4-11-0 0........ APMcCoy 66
(Jonjo O'Neill) *in tch to 4 out* **33/1**

0- **14** *3 ¾* **Moratab (IRE)**[46] 2215 4-11-0 0........ NickScholfield 62
(Keiran Burke) *sn bhd* **100/1**

6/4- **15** *5* **Reverend Green (IRE)**[43] 2282 7-10-11 0........(t) GilesHawkins[(3)] 57
(Chris Down) *in tch to 4 out* **100/1**

P0/ **16** *hd* **Dorry K (IRE)**[237] 3566 4-10-7 0........ MattieBatchelor 50
(Jim Best) *a in rr* **200/1**

156- **17** *10* **Viacometti (FR)**[11] 2933 4-11-0 0........ PaddyBrennan 47
(Tom George) *chsd ldrs to 4th* **100/1**

0F- **18** *22* **Presentings Return (IRE)**[11] 2933 4-11-0 0........ RichieMcLernon 25
(Jonjo O'Neill) *in tch to 4th* **100/1**

/50- **F** **Prasina Russata (IRE)**[13] 2906 6-11-0 0........ TomScudamore 94
(David Pipe) *towards rr: sme hdwy 3 out: nvr any ch and bhd whn fell last* **50/1**

P **Guardi (IRE)**[170] 4-11-0 0........ AlainCawley
(Dean Ivory) *mstke 1st: in rr: t.o whn p.u bef last* **200/1**

000/ **P** **Digger's Mate**[384] 2716 5-11-0 0........ SamJones
(Bob Buckler) *a in rr: t.o whn blnd 3 out: p.u bef last* **200/1**

0/0- **P** **Royalracket (IRE)**[28] 2602 5-11-0 0........ LiamTreadwell
(Paul Webber) *a in rr: t.o whn p.u bef 3 out* **100/1**

4m 1.09s (-8.91) **Going Correction** -0.30s/f (Good) **22** Ran SP% **130.2**
Speed ratings (Par 105): **108,106,106,103,92 90,90,90,86,84 81,79,77,75,73 73,68,58,** , ,
CSF £11.92 TOTE £2.10: £1.70, £2.30, £1.40; EX 11.30 Trifecta £37.10 Pool: £2,573.36 - 51.93 winning units..
Owner A D Spence **Bred** I W Moore **Trained** Upper Lambourn, Berks

FOCUS
Any price bar five with plenty of deadwood in the line-up and they were soon well strung out. The form looks strong by maiden hurdle standards with the first two looking decent recruits.

3164 POWERSOLVE ELECTRONICS GREATWOOD CHARITY H'CAP CHASE (15 fncs) 2m 2f 110y
1:40 (1:42) (Class 4) (0-115,111) 4-Y-0+ **£4,548** (£1,335; £667; £333)

Form RPR

123- **1** **Chestnut Ben (IRE)**[36] 2440 8-11-6 **105**........(t) APMcCoy 113
(Gary Brown) *set mod early pce: pushed along fr 3 out: drvn out clsng stages* **11/2**[3]

431- **2** *1* **Osmosia (FR)**[8] 3009 8-10-0 **95**........(tp) LouisMuspratt[(10)] 101
(Chris Gordon) *hit 1st: in rr: rdn appr 4 out: styd on to chse wnr 2 out: kpt on u.p run-in to cl on wnr but a hld* **8/1**

600- **3** *9* **Fintan**[55] 2051 10-10-13 **98**........ DougieCostello 96
(Laura Young) *in rr: hdwy 11th: hit 4 out: styd on to take 3rd last but no ch w ldng duo* **7/1**

1/2- **4** *6* **Mr Muddle**[10] 2977 6-11-12 **111**........ MarcGoldstein 109+
(Sheena West) *sn chsng wnr at mod pce: t.k.h: blnd 9th: drvn and disputing 2 l 2nd whn blnd 3 out: no ch w wnr after: wknd after 2 out* **5/2**[2]

142- **5** *1 ¼* **Sonofagun (FR)**[28] 2599 7-11-9 **108**........ WillKennedy 104+
(Ian Williams) *chsd ldrs: hit 11th: disputing 2 l 2nd whn blnd 3 out: mstke next and no ch after* **7/4**[1]

5/P- **6** *18* **Got Attitude (IRE)**[35] 2450 10-11-1 **105**........ JoshHamer[(5)] 80
(Tony Carroll) *in tch: hit 9th: hit 4 out and wknd: no ch whn blnd 2 out* **16/1**

4m 51.9s (21.90) **Going Correction** -0.30s/f (Good) **6** Ran SP% **109.8**
Speed ratings (Par 105): **41,40,36,34,33 26**
CSF £41.59 TOTE £4.10: £1.80, £2.80; EX 15.20 Trifecta £96.40 Pool: £3,770.95 - 29.31 winning units..
Owner Russell H Lee **Bred** Sean Deu Burca **Trained** Lambourn, Berks

FOCUS
A weak handicap chase by course standards. The pace was very steady until turning in and the complexion changed dramatically at the third-last, the final ditch. The first two set the level.

3165 COOLMATION GRADUATION CHASE (18 fncs) 3m
2:15 (2:15) (Class 2) 4-Y-0+ **£12,021** (£3,529; £1,764; £882)

Form RPR

/2U- **1** **Hadrian's Approach (IRE)**[18] 2815 6-11-4 146........ BarryGeraghty 153
(Nicky Henderson) *trckd ldrs: wnt 2nd 2 out: drvn after last: styd on wl to ld fnl 150yds: a doing enough* **9/4**[2]

4/P- **2** *1 ¼* **Super Duty (IRE)**[18] 2815 7-11-7 145........ JasonMaguire 155
(Donald McCain) *led: drvn along 4 out: kpt finding but u.p after 2 out: jnd after last: hdd and no ex fnl 150yds* **5/1**[3]

/15- **3** *2 ¼* **Gullinbursti (IRE)**[25] 2672 7-11-0 148........ NoelFehily 146
(Emma Lavelle) *trckd ldrs: disp 2nd 10th to 12th: ev ch 3 out: one pce appr last* **5/4**[1]

1/4- **4** *29* **Poungach (FR)**[39] 2373 7-11-7 143........(b) DarylJacob 144
(Paul Nicholls) *chsd ldr to 10th: rdn after 13th and mstke next: wknd and blnd 4 out* **5/1**[3]

5m 58.94s (-7.06) **Going Correction** -0.05s/f (Good) **4** Ran SP% **108.5**
Speed ratings (Par 109): **109,108,107,98**
CSF £11.88 TOTE £2.90; EX 12.70 Trifecta £23.00 Pool: £1,809.17 - 58.78 winning units..
Owner Mr & Mrs R Kelvin-Hughes **Bred** Marie Gavin **Trained** Upper Lambourn, Berks

FOCUS
A fascinating graduation chase. The rain had arrived and the pace was just sensible in the deteriorating conditions until the final 6f. Sound form in a decent race of its type.

3166 EBF STALLIONS "NATIONAL HUNT" NOVICES' HURDLE (QUALIFIER) (10 hdls) 2m 3f
2:45 (2:47) (Class 4) 4-6-Y-0 **£3,898** (£1,144; £572; £286)

Form RPR

/05- **1** **Brother Brian (IRE)**[26] 2642 5-10-12 0........ TomO'Brien 124+
(Hughie Morrison) *led to 2nd: styd chsng ldr tl appr 3 out: chal again next and upsides whn hit last: rallied wl u.p to ld fnl 120yds: r.o strly* **7/1**[3]

0/1- **2** *1 ¼* **Tistory (FR)**[208] 458 6-11-5 0........ BarryGeraghty 128
(Nicky Henderson) *chsd ldrs: chal 3 out: slt ld fr next and hrd pressed last: hdd and no ex fnl 120yds* **11/4**[2]

24- **3** *12* **Red Devil Lads (IRE)**[20] 2759 4-10-12 0........ APMcCoy 112+
(Rebecca Curtis) *ld 2nd: jnd 3 out: narrowly hdd 2 out: wknd sn after and hld in 3rd whn nt fluent last* **11/1**

0/ **4** *1 ¼* **The Ould Lad (IRE)**[292] 4502 5-10-12 0........ PaddyBrennan 109
(Tom George) *chsd ldrs to 3 out: wknd fr 2 out* **8/1**

2/5- **5** *8* **Generous Ransom (IRE)**[56] 2018 5-10-12 0........ NoelFehily 102
(Nick Gifford) *in tch: hdwy after 4 out: chsd ldrs: next: wknd 2 out* **25/1**

01- **6** *17* **Gallory Exhibition (IRE)**[34] 2471 6-11-5 0........ JasonMaguire 94
(Kim Bailey) *chsd ldrs to 3 out: wknd and mstke next* **20/1**

4/2- **7** *¾* **Fine Words**[44] 2266 5-10-12 0........ RobertThornton 86
(Alan King) *in rr: mstke 3rd: hdwy after 4 out: wknd next* **16/1**

340- **8** *1 ¼* **Vazaro Delafayette (FR)**[19] 2802 4-10-12 0........ TomScudamore 85
(David Pipe) *in rr: sme hdwy after 4 out: nvr rchd ldrs and wknd sn after* **33/1**

46- **9** *14* **In Fairness (IRE)**[19] 2802 4-10-12 0........ DavidBass 72
(Nicky Henderson) *chsd ldrs: wknd bef 3 out* **33/1**

/50- **10** *13* **Vendredi Trois (FR)**[56] 2018 4-10-9 0........ GavinSheehan[(3)] 60
(Emma Lavelle) *a in rr* **80/1**

P05- **11** *shd* **Shipton**[18] 2808 4-10-7 0........ JamesBanks[(5)] 60
(Brendan Powell) *bhd most of way* **200/1**

5- **12** *42* **Veyranno (FR)**[20] 2773 4-10-12 0........ AlainCawley 23
(Tom George) *blnd 4 out: a in rr* **100/1**

3U6- **13** *hd* **Beau De Tabel (FR)**[35] 2457 5-10-12 111........ RichardJohnson 22
(Nick Williams) *chsd ldrs: rdn after 4 out: sn wknd* **33/1**

/33- **P** **Broomfield**[20] 2755 6-10-12 125........ DarylJacob
(Paul Nicholls) *towards rr whn wknd rapidly, p.u and dismntd bnd after 3rd* **15/8**[1]

4m 43.6s (-4.40) **Going Correction** -0.05s/f (Good)
WFA 4 from 5yo+ 5lb **14** Ran SP% **119.4**
Speed ratings: **107,106,101,100,97 90,90,89,83,78 78,60,60,**
CSF £25.39 TOTE £9.00: £2.40, £1.70, £3.30; EX 41.20 Trifecta £529.80 Pool: £3,392.29 - 4.80 winning units..
Owner L A Garfield **Bred** Daniel N O'Donovan **Trained** East Ilsley, Berks

FOCUS
A decent novice hurdle. The winner showed big improvement.

3167 KENTFORD RACING FILLIES' "JUNIOR" STANDARD OPEN NATIONAL HUNT FLAT RACE 1m 4f 110y
3:20 (3:20) (Class 6) 3-Y-O **£1,711** (£498; £249)

Form RPR
3- **1** **Montana Belle (IRE)**[28] 2604 3-10-12 0 .... APMcCoy 91
(John Butler) *mde all: drvn and green wl over 1f out: kpt on wl fnl f* **5/1**[3]
3- **2** *2 ¾* **May Hay**[41] 2318 3-10-12 0 .... RobertThornton 87
(Anthony Carson) *chsd ldrs: wnt 2nd over 4f out: rdn over 2f out: styd on fr over 1f out but no imp on wnr* **8/1**
3 *6* **Morello Royale (IRE)** 3-10-12 0 .... JoeTizzard 78
(Colin Tizzard) *chsd ldrs: rdn and outpcd over 4f out: styd on again fr over 1f to take 3rd cl home but no ch w ldng duo* **14/1**
4 *½* **Montjen (IRE)** 3-10-12 0 .... DenisO'Regan 77
(Karen Tutty) *hld up in rr: hdwy fr 4f out to take 3rd over 3f out: styd on same pce fnl 2f: dropped to 4th cl home* **16/1**
5 *4 ½* **Kentford Myth** 3-10-5 0 .... KevinJones(7) 71
(Seamus Mullins) *in rr: styd on fnl 2f: nt rch ldrs* **20/1**
6P- **6** *2 ¾* **Instagramher**[28] 2604 3-10-9 0 .... PeterCarberry(3) 66
(Charlie Brooks) *towards rr: rdn over 3f out: sme prog fnl 2f* **66/1**
7 *¾* **Midnight Jazz** 3-10-12 0 .... DarylJacob 65
(Ben Case) *in rr: hdwy over 4f out: nvr rchd ldrs: wknd ins fnl 2f* **10/1**
8 *2 ¼* **Attente De Sivola (FR)** 3-10-12 0 .... NoelFehily 62
(Nick Williams) *chsd ldrs: rdn 4f out: wknd over 2f out* **3/1**[1]
9 *4* **Flute Bowl** 3-10-9 0 .... JoshuaMoore(3) 56
(Gary Moore) *chsd ldrs: wknd 2f out* **14/1**
10 *7* **Herecomesthebride** 3-10-12 0 .... RichardJohnson 45
(Philip Hobbs) *in tch: wknd ins fnl 3f* **9/2**[2]
6- **11** *1 ¾* **Wojciech**[28] 2604 3-10-9 0 .... GavinSheehan(3) 43
(Warren Greatrex) *towards rr most of way* **14/1**
5- **12** *shd* **Todoistodare**[41] 2318 3-10-12 0 .... BrendanPowell 43
(Brendan Powell) *chsd wnr tl over 4f out: sn wknd* **25/1**
13 *1 ¾* **Summer Echo** 3-10-9 0 .... JackQuinlan(3) 40
(Andi Brown) *in tch chsd ldrs 5f out: wknd 3f out* **66/1**
14 *99* **Lead The Way** 3-10-12 0 .... JasonMaguire
(Jonathan Portman) *prom early: wknd rapidly and t.o 1/2-way* **25/1**

3m 9.68s (3.88) **14** Ran SP% **121.4**
Tote Swingers: 1&2 £8.10, 1&3 £9.00, 2&3 £3.20 CSF £42.74 TOTE £5.80: £1.90, £2.30, £4.30; EX 23.30 Trifecta £206.30 Pool: £2,894.44 - 10.51 winning units..
Owner J Butler **Bred** Bernard Cooke **Trained** Newmarket, Suffolk

FOCUS
Only five of the runners had run before in this fillies' junior bumper and two of those with previous experience dominated the finish. The form is rated around the first two and the sixth.
T/Plt: £56.00 to a £1 stake. Pool: £56,100.14 - 730.65 winning tickets. T/Qpdt: £21.10 to a £1 stake. Pool: £5,663.65 - 195.50 winning tickets. ST

2920 EXETER (R-H)
Thursday, December 19

OFFICIAL GOING: Soft (6.9)
The hurdle after the winning post was moved into the back straight. Shared bends on the hurdle course as they were moved to fresh ground.
Wind: mild breeze behind becoming stronger from 1.50 Weather: showers, heavy at times

3168 RACING WELFARE MARES' NOVICES' HURDLE (10 hdls) 2m 3f
12:50 (12:51) (Class 4) 4-Y-0+ **£3,249** (£954; £477; £238)

Form RPR
4F3- **1** **Blue Buttons (IRE)**[29] 2600 5-10-10 0 .... (t) NoelFehily 114+
(Harry Fry) *racd keenly: mde virtually all: rdn clr after 2 out: styd on strly* **13/2**
4/1- **2** *4* **Centasia**[48] 2190 6-11-2 0 .... (t) TomScudamore 117+
(David Pipe) *trckd ldrs: chal 3 out: rdn after next: kpt on but sn hld by wnr* **6/5**[1]
155- **3** *9* **Mrs Jordan (IRE)**[29] 2600 5-10-10 0 .... AidanColeman 101
(Venetia Williams) *trckd ldrs: rdn appr 3 out: styd on same pce wout troubling front pair* **14/1**
0/1- **4** *5* **Woodland Walk**[26] 2675 5-10-13 0 .... GavinSheehan(3) 103
(Emma Lavelle) *mid-div: hdwy after 6th: rdn after 3 out: styd on same pce to go 4th between last 2* **5/1**[3]
0/3- **5** *3 ¼* **Just Fee**[36] 2463 6-10-10 0 .... DaveCrosse 94
(Nick Mitchell) *prom: hmpd 1st: rdn appr 3 out: sn one pce* **40/1**
0/ **6** *7* **Aroseforoscar**[252] 5263 4-10-10 0 .... JamesDavies 86
(Chris Down) *mid-div: sme prog u.p appr 3 out: nvr trbld ldrs: wknd 2 out* **100/1**
00- **7** *3 ¼* **Swincomb Silvalady**[14] 2907 5-10-10 0 .... WayneHutchinson 83
(Robert Walford) *prom: rdn after 7th: wknd fr next* **80/1**
/60- **8** *4* **Definitely Better (IRE)**[14] 2907 5-10-10 0 .... PaddyBrennan 79
(Tom George) *mstke 3rd: sme minor late prog but mainly towards rr* **50/1**
0/0- **9** *nk* **Molly's A Diva**[29] 2600 6-10-10 0 .... JasonMaguire 78
(Kim Bailey) *nvr fluent: led tl wnt lft: bmpd and hdd 1st: racd keenly: prom 3rd tl after next: nudged along in midfield 6th: rdn to chse ldrs 3 out: grad fdd* **3/1**[2]
10 *3 ¼* **Landulph Lass**[662] 6-10-7 0 .... JamesBest(3) 75
(Jackie Du Plessis) *mid-div: rdn after 7th: wknd bef next* **100/1**
0U0- **11** *23* **Party Girls (FR)**[14] 2906 5-10-3 0 .... (t) MrEBarrett(7) 52
(David Pipe) *nt a fluent: racd keenly: a in rr: t.o* **100/1**
12 *1 ½* **Peaceful Gardens** 4-10-7 0 .... MattGriffiths(3) 51
(Jeremy Scott) *a towards rr: t.o after 7th* **66/1**
10/ **13** *2 ¼* **Miner Distraction**[245] 5364 5-10-10 0 .... (t) NickScholfield 48
(Jeremy Scott) *mid-div: mstke 2nd: pushed along towards rr 5th: no imp whn rdn after 7th: blnd 3 out: wknd* **33/1**
0- **14** *16* **More Tricks**[7] 3049 5-10-10 0 .... HaddenFrost 32
(James Frost) *a towards rr: t.o after 7th* **200/1**

4m 48.2s (5.50) **Going Correction** +0.275s/f (Yiel)
WFA 4 from 5yo+ 5lb **14** Ran SP% **120.7**
Speed ratings (Par 105): **99,97,93,91,90 87,85,84,83,82 72,72,71,64**
CSF £15.11 TOTE £7.50: £2.10, £1.60, £3.60; EX 25.30 Trifecta £148.30 Pool: £3311.85 - 16.74 winning units..
Owner Richard Barber **Bred** Miss Annette McMahon **Trained** Seaborough, Dorset
■ Stewards' Enquiry : Mr E Barrett ten-day ban: failed to take all reasonable and permissable measures to obtain best possible placing (Jan 6,9,12,15,16,19,22,23,29,30)

FOCUS
Noel Fehily described the ground as "soft and heavy in places". This had the look of a good mares' hurdle, but the very steady pace affected the chances of a couple of the key players. The winner is on the upgrade in a steadily run race.

3169 EXETER RACECOURSE WISHES YOU A HAPPY CHRISTMAS H'CAP HURDLE (JC GRASSROOTS JUMPS SERIES QUAL') (8 hdls) 2m 1f
1:20 (1:20) (Class 3) (0-135,133) 3-Y-O **£5,697** (£1,683; £841; £421; £210)

Form RPR
0/0- **1** **Citizenship**[19] 2813 7-11-6 127 .... AidanColeman 138+
(Venetia Williams) *travelled wl: hld up: smooth hdwy 5th: led after 3 out: rdn between last 2: kpt on wl: eased nring fin* **12/1**
3/2- **2** *2 ¾* **Mixologist**[9] 3007 6-10-0 110 .... (t) GavinSheehan(3) 115
(Warren Greatrex) *j.lft: mde most tl rdn and hdd after 3 out: hld fr after next: kpt on same pce* **6/4**[1]
0/3- **3** *2 ½* **Headly's Bridge (IRE)**[45] 2271 7-10-8 115 .... GerardTumelty 118
(Simon Earle) *hld up: hdwy after 5th: rdn to chse ldng pair after 3 out: 3rd and hld whn nt fluent last: kpt on same pce* **8/1**
/U4- **4** *6* **Cool George**[36] 2457 5-10-7 117 .... JamesBest(3) 112
(Jackie Du Plessis) *trckd ldrs: rdn after 5th: one pce fr next* **13/2**[3]
603- **5** *2 ¼* **Decoy (FR)**[14] 2910 7-10-8 125 .... (p) AnthonyFox(10) 117
(David Pipe) *trckd ldrs: rdn after 5th: one pce and hld fr next* **8/1**
/01- **6** *4 ½* **Shammick Boy (IRE)**[54] 2080 8-11-12 133 .... JackDoyle 121
(Victor Dartnall) *in tch: taken wd in bk st: rdn after 5th: one pce fr next* **5/1**[2]
510- **7** *½* **Just When**[34] 2492 4-10-5 117 .... (v) NicodeBoinville(5) 104
(Patrick Chamings) *w ldr: pushed along after 4th: rdn bef 3 out: sn btn* **10/1**
2/0- **8** *10* **Look For Love**[28] 2630 5-10-6 118 .... MissLucyGardner(5) 95
(Sue Gardner) *hld up in rr: rdn after 7th: nvr any imp: wknd 2 out* **22/1**

4m 16.2s (0.70) **Going Correction** +0.275s/f (Yiel)
WFA 4 from 5yo+ 5lb **8** Ran SP% **113.4**
Speed ratings (Par 107): **109,107,106,103,102 100,100,95**
toteswingers 1&2 £6.10, 2&3 £4.00, 1&3 £9.60 CSF £31.00 CT £157.87 TOTE £10.90: £1.50, £1.30, £2.80; EX 41.50 Trifecta £578.70 Pool: £2212.26 - 2.86 winning units..
Owner The Fizz Fund **Bred** Juddmonte Farms Ltd **Trained** Kings Caple, H'fords

FOCUS
Not a particularly strong race for the grade. The cosy winner has been rated in line with his best Irish form, but there may be more to come.

3170 FREE RACING TIPS GRADUATION CHASE (12 fncs) 2m 1f 110y
1:50 (1:50) (Class 2) 4-Y-0+ **£12,820** (£4,004; £2,156)

Form RPR
3/P- **1** **Desert Cry (IRE)**[222] 217 7-11-7 139 .... JasonMaguire 147+
(Donald McCain) *trckd ldr: chal 4 out: led 2 out: rdn clr run-in* **7/2**[2]
332/ **2** *2 ¾* **Lidar (FR)**[342] 2181 8-11-7 0 .... (b) WayneHutchinson 144
(Alan King) *led: nt fluent 2nd (water): rdn and hdd 2 out: sn hld: kpt on same pce* **6/1**[3]
/1U- **3** *62* **Lamb's Cross**[3] 3135 7-10-10 107 .... PaulMoloney 71
(Mark Gillard) *nt that fluent early: trckd ldng pair tl outpcd after 8th: t.o* **40/1**
3/1- **R** **Bury Parade (IRE)**[45] 2269 7-11-7 143 .... SamTwiston-Davies
(Paul Nicholls) *ref to r: tk no part* **4/9**[1]

4m 33.9s (14.90) **Going Correction** +0.175s/f (Yiel) **4** Ran SP% **108.2**
Speed ratings (Par 109): **73,71,44,**
CSF £19.27 TOTE £3.90; EX 7.40 Trifecta £30.10 Pool: £2857.02 - 71.00 winning units..
Owner N.Y.P.D Racing **Bred** Fin A Co S R L **Trained** Cholmondeley, Cheshire

FOCUS
The winner has been rated to his mark, with the second rated 9lb off on his return, with his yard quiet.

3171 EBF STALLIONS/TBA MARES' NOVICES' LIMITED H'CAP CHASE (15 fncs) 2m 3f 110y
2:20 (2:20) (Class 3) (0-125,125) 4-Y-0+ **£6,388** (£1,928; £993; £526)

Form RPR
14F- **1** **Midnight Lira**[21] 2765 6-10-2 111 oh9 .... JamesBest(3) 108
(Caroline Keevil) *mde all: pushed along whn hit 3 out: rdn after next: gd jump last: styd on v gamely* **7/2**[3]
363- **2** *1 ¾* **Fair Bramble**[38] 2424 7-10-5 111 oh11 .... (v1) LeightonAspell 105
(Oliver Sherwood) *j.rt: trckd wnr: rdn after 3 out: ch 2 out: kpt on same pce* **10/1**
0/3- **3** *5* **Stone Light (FR)**[21] 2763 5-10-11 117 .... AidanColeman 108
(Venetia Williams) *trckd ldrs: rdn after 3 out: chal for 2nd between last 2: no ex fr last* **9/5**[1]
322- **4** *14* **Born To Benefit (IRE)**[19] 2824 7-10-5 111 oh5 .... (t) PaddyBrennan 92
(Fergal O'Brien) *hld up bhd ldng trio: nt fluent 1st: rdn after 3 out: nt pce to get on terms: comf hld in 4th whn awkward last* **11/4**[2]
4/4- **P** **Danvilla**[82] 1689 6-10-6 112 .... (p) DominicElsworth
(Paul Webber) *nvr that fluent: sltly detached last 6th: struggling 9th: tailing off appr 4 out: p.u bef 2 out* **9/2**

5m 9.3s (12.00) **Going Correction** +0.175s/f (Yiel) **5** Ran SP% **111.9**
Speed ratings (Par 107): **83,82,80,74,**
CSF £30.11 TOTE £4.30: £2.60, £3.50; EX 17.80 Trifecta £124.20 Pool: £1521.32 - 9.18 winning units..
Owner Brian Derrick **Bred** B Derrick And P R Rodford **Trained** Motcombe, Dorset

FOCUS
A modest mares' handicap that developed into something of a dash for the line in the straight, with the runners more or less holding their positions throughout. The first two have been rated close to their marks.

3172 REWARDS4RACING - REWARDING YOUR PASSION H'CAP CHASE (JC GRASSROOTS JUMPS SERIES QUALIFIER) (15 fncs) 2m 3f 110y
2:50 (2:50) (Class 4) (0-120,120) 4-Y-0+ **£3,898** (£1,144; £572; £286)

Form RPR
/42- **1** **Ballinvarrig (IRE)**[54] 2078 6-11-9 117 .... PaddyBrennan 130+
(Tom George) *trckd ldrs: rdn after 4 out: chal 2 out: 2 l 3rd jumping last: styd on to ld towards fin: drvn rt out* **5/1**[2]
312- **2** *1 ½* **Ray Diamond**[19] 2828 8-10-0 97 .... JamesBest(3) 109
(Jackie Du Plessis) *led tl 9th: prom: led appr 4 out: rdn after 3 out: 1 1/2 l up whn got cl to last: no ex whn hdd towards fin* **9/2**[1]
/14- **3** *nk* **Hollow Blue Sky (FR)**[22] 2749 6-10-13 107 .... SamTwiston-Davies 117
(Nigel Twiston-Davies) *trckd ldrs: rdn appr 4 out: ev ch 2 out: 1 1/2 l down in 2nd at the last: styd on but no ex* **9/2**[1]

/P1- **4** *6* **Bincombe**[14] 2911 5-10-9 **103**.. RichardJohnson 107
(Philip Hobbs) *trckd ldrs: led 9th tl rdn appr 4 out: kpt chsng ldrs tl wknd appr last* **6/1**
/41- **5** *18* **Umberto D'Olivate (FR)**[28] 2618 5-11-9 **117**........................ FelixDeGiles 106
(Robert Walford) *prom: rdn after 11th: wknd bef next* **11/2**[3]
/32- **6** *21* **Moleskin (IRE)**[36] 2462 10-11-2 **110**..................................(bt) JackDoyle 75
(Victor Dartnall) *trckd ldrs tl lost pl 10th: sn wknd: t.o* **8/1**
P/5- **P** **Knapp Bridge Boy**[233] 40 13-10-0 **94**........................ TomScudamore
(James Payne) *hld up: hit 9th: p.u bef next* **50/1**
35P- **P** **Humbel Ben (IRE)**[28] 2618 10-10-7 **101**..........................(p) WillKennedy
(Alan Jones) *sn struggling in ear: t.o whn p.u bef 10th* **66/1**
4P5/ **P** **Sir Kezbaah (IRE)**[312] 4154 9-11-9 **120**.......................(t) MattGriffiths[(3)]
(Richard Woollacott) *prom: hit 8th: wknd 10th: t.o whn j.rt fr 4 out: stmbld bdly 2 out: p.u bef last* **25/1**
145- **P** **Special Account (IRE)**[12] 2945 8-11-11 **119**.................. NickScholfield
(Jeremy Scott) *hld up: nt that fluent and detched fr 7th: sn struggling: t.o fr after 10th: p.u bef 4 out* **14/1**
333- **P** **Ballywatt (IRE)**[20] 2797 7-11-11 **119**.............................(tp) JasonMaguire
(Kim Bailey) *hld up: lost tch 10th: t.o whn p.u bef 4 out* **9/1**

4m 57.7s (0.40) **Going Correction** +0.175s/f (Yiel) **11** Ran SP% **117.8**
Speed ratings (Par 105): **106,105,105,102,95 87,, , ,**
toteswingers 1&2 £5.50, 2&3 £6.30, 1&3 £6.50 CSF £28.29 CT £109.67 TOTE £6.70: £2.40, £1.90, £2.50; EX 34.60 Trifecta £339.40 Pool: £1097.18 - 2.42 winning units..
Owner Lady Hilda Clarke & S W Clarke **Bred** James Browne **Trained** Slad, Gloucs

FOCUS
Conditions had become really quite testing by this stage. The winner has been rated as stepping up for a right-handed track, and the second and third are on decent marks and have been rated to form.

3173 DOWNLOAD THE FREE RACING UK APP MAIDEN HURDLE (12 hdls) 2m 7f 110y
3:20 (3:21) (Class 4) 4-Y-0+ **£3,249** (£954; £477; £238)

Form RPR
3- **1** **Tagrita (IRE)**[20] 2801 5-10-7 0.. NickScholfield 121+
(Paul Nicholls) *mde all: hit 5th: styd on nicely and in command fr after 3 out: rdn after last: eased nring fin* **11/8**[1]
2- **2** *5* **V Neck (IRE)**[31] 2566 4-11-0 0.. RyanMahon 120+
(Paul Nicholls) *racd keenly early: hld up towards rr: pushed along and hdwy after 7th: wnt 3rd next: sn rdn* **13/2**[3]
3 *1 1/4* **Ivy Gate (IRE)**[92] 1606 5-10-9 0................................ MauriceLinehan[(5)] 117
(Jonjo O'Neill) *trckd wnr: j.rt thrght: rdn appr 3 out: a being hld by wnr: hit last: no ex whn lost 2nd run-in* **16/1**
5/5- **4** *21* **Moss On The Mill**[24] 2720 5-11-0 0.................................. PaddyBrennan 95
(Ben Case) *mid-div: hdwy after 9th: rdn bef next: sn hld: wknd 2 out: wnt modest 4th nring fin* **14/1**
22- **5** *hd* **Padre Tito (IRE)**[27] 2648 5-11-0 **119**................................ LeightonAspell 95
(Emma Lavelle) *j.lft progively worse: mid-div: hdwy 9th: rdn in 4th whn stmbld 3 out: sn hld: wknd 2 out: lost modest 4th nring fin* **5/2**[2]
6 *3* **Eastern Witness (IRE)**[263] 6-11-0 0................................ AidanColeman 94
(Venetia Williams) *trckd ldrs: rdn appr 3 out: wknd 2 out* **18/1**
2/3- **7** *34* **Rugged Jack (FR)**[33] 2509 6-11-0 0.. JackDoyle 58
(Victor Dartnall) *mid-div: trckd ldrs 5th: pushed along after 7th: hit 8th: rdn after next: wknd 3 out: t.o* **8/1**
0- **8** *12* **Brave Encounter (IRE)**[27] 2660 5-11-0 0.......................... WillKennedy 46
(Sue Gardner) *trckd ldrs tl dropped in rr qckly 6th: t.o* **100/1**
9 *23* **Silvergrove**[214] 5-11-0 0......................................(t) PaulMoloney 23
(Richard Woollacott) *hld up towards rr: hdwy 6th: wknd 9th: t.o* **50/1**
10 *21* **Whatwillwedonext (IRE)**[74] 7-11-0 0................................ HaddenFrost
(Martin Hill) *hld up towards rr: wknd after 9th: t.o* **80/1**
00- **P** **Arcas (IRE)**[35] 2476 4-10-9 0.. CharlieWallis[(5)]
(Alan Jones) *trckd ldrs tl 5th: in tch tl wknd after 7th: t.o whn p.u bef 3 out* **200/1**

6m 23.3s (24.30) **Going Correction** +1.15s/f (Heav)
WFA 4 from 5yo+ 6lb **11** Ran SP% **117.6**
Speed ratings (Par 105): **105,103,102,95,95 94,83,79,71,64**
CSF £11.39 TOTE £2.60: £1.10, £1.70, £4.20; EX 14.30 Trifecta £111.40 Pool: £2689.58 - 18.10 winning units..
Owner Axom XLVIII **Bred** John Kidd **Trained** Ditcheat, Somerset

FOCUS
An ordinary maiden hurdle. The easy winner has been rated to her mark.

3174 COME RACING ON NEW YEAR'S DAY AMATEUR RIDERS' H'CAP HURDLE (11 hdls) 2m 5f 110y
3:50 (3:50) (Class 5) (0-100,100) 4-Y-0+ **£2,183** (£677; £338; £169)

Form RPR
404- **1** **Cash Injection**[25] 2690 4-10-7 **88**...................................(t) MrMHeard[(7)] 97
(Richard Woollacott) *trckd ldrs: prom 3rd: led 5th: clr after 8th: rdn after being nt fluent 2 out: hld on: all out* **7/1**[2]
003- **2** *nk* **Bedouin Bay**[17] 2921 6-11-3 **90**................................ MrRobertHawker[(7)] 106
(Johnny Farrelly) *hld up bhd: stdy prog fr after 8th: pushed along to chse wnr gng to 3 out: sn rdn: styd on wl fr last: nvr quite getting to wnr* **8/1**
4- **3** *25* **Railway Vic (IRE)**[13] 2921 6-10-9 **90**................................ MissBFrost[(7)] 74
(James Frost) *in tch: rdn in 3rd briefly after 8th: plugged on to regain modest 3rd between last 2: t.o* **14/1**
121- **4** *4 1/2* **Kings Apollo**[19] 2827 4-11-0 **95**.. MrJNixon[(7)] 76
(Tom Symonds) *hld up towards rr: hdwy fr after 5th: rdn to chse wnr after 8th tl next: grad fdd: lost modest 3rd between last 2: t.o* **13/8**[1]
/UP- **5** *3/4* **Ballyhilty Bridge**[37] 2431 7-11-0 **95**................................ MrGBranton[(7)] 73
(Paul Henderson) *hld up towards rr: nvr any imp on ldrs: t.o* **12/1**
P0P- **6** *11* **Comical Red**[151] 1053 5-9-10 **75**.................................[1] MissAliceMills[(5)] 42
(Mark Gillard) *trckd ldrs: rdn after 8th: wknd bef next: t.o* **14/1**
020- **7** *4 1/2* **Amaury De Lusignan (IRE)**[23] 2727 7-10-11 **92**............. MrGTreacy[(7)] 54
(Paul Henderson) *led tl 5th: wknd after 8th: t.o* **25/1**
400- **8** *1* **Dbanks (IRE)**[71] 1825 10-10-2 **83**.. MrTSquire[(7)] 44
(Liam Corcoran) *mid-div: hdwy 5th: wknd after 8th: t.o* **28/1**
0/0- **P** **Admirable Duque (IRE)**[16] 2718 7-11-5 **100**........... BenFfrenchDavis[(7)]
(Dominic Ffrench Davis) *a bhd: t.o whn p.u bef 3 out* **22/1**
/00- **P** **Madam Noso**[35] 2473 9-10-13 **90**.................................... MrFMitchell[(3)]
(Richard King) *mid-div tl struggling in rr after 4th: t.o whn p.u bef 3 out* **33/1**
6/6- **U** **Cuckoo Rock (IRE)**[13] 2920 6-9-13 **80**............................(p) MrJHarding[(7)]
(Jonathan Portman) *midfield: pushed along after 4th: sn towards rr: awkward whn unseating rdr next* **15/2**[3]
UP0/ **P** **Waldsee (GER)**[12] 1275 8-10-5 **86**............................(p) MissBHampson[(7)]
(Paul Morgan) *prom 3rd: lost pl qckly 5th: towards rr whn hit next: sn p.u* **66/1**
560- **P** **Spice Hill (IRE)**[21] 2760 7-10-2 **83**.................................... MrEBarrett[(7)]
(Nick Ayliffe) *mid-div tl after 4th: t.o whn p.u bef 6th* **40/1**
03F- **P** **Native Brian (IRE)**[14] 2908 7-11-7 **100**.............................. MrJBarber[(5)]
(Alexandra Dunn) *trckd ldrs: prom 3rd tl after 5th: wknd afer 8th: t.o whn p.u bef 2 out* **12/1**

5m 56.7s (23.70) **Going Correction** +1.15s/f (Heav)
WFA 4 from 5yo+ 6lb **14** Ran SP% **120.7**
Speed ratings (Par 103): **102,101,92,91,90 86,85,84, , , , ,**
toteswingers 1&2 £11.50, 2&3 £38.50, 1&3 £16.20 CSF £57.83 CT £776.04 TOTE £9.00: £3.10, £2.20, £4.60; EX 68.40 Trifecta £775.00 Pool: £2284.27 - 2.21 winning units..
Owner Eight Ball Partnership **Bred** C A Green **Trained** South Molton, Devon

FOCUS
The front pair drew right away in what was a weak handicap. The winner has been rated to his mark.
T/Plt: £239.00 to a £1 stake. Pool of £66386.83 - 202.72 winning tickets. T/Qpdt: £56.40 to a £1 stake. Pool of £4102.36 - 53.80 winning tickets. TM

[2824] TOWCESTER (R-H)
Thursday, December 19

OFFICIAL GOING: Soft (good to soft in places; 7.6) changing to soft after race 1 (12.40)
Shared bends and hurdles track at widest configuration.
Wind: medium to fresh against Weather: dry and bright

3175 BEST RACING BLOGS ON GG.COM MAIDEN HURDLE (8 hdls) 2m
12:40 (12:41) (Class 5) 4-Y-0+ **£1,949** (£572; £286; £143)

Form RPR
13- **1** **Call The Cops (IRE)**[41] 2351 4-11-0 0.................................. AndrewTinkler 122+
(Nicky Henderson) *chsd ldrs and a gng wl: led bef 2 out: readily wnt clr 2 out: comf* **7/4**[1]
4/2- **2** *7* **Major Milborne**[23] 2728 5-11-0 0...................................... BrendanPowell 112
(Jamie Snowden) *chsd ldrs: rdn and cl 3rd after 3 out: outpcd by wnr next: chsd clr wnr after 2 out: kpt on but no imp* **15/2**[3]
33- **3** *5* **In The Rough (IRE)**[28] 2627 4-11-0 0.. APMcCoy 108+
(Jonjo O'Neill) *in tch in midfield: mstke 4th: lost pl and in last pair next: modest 9th but keeping on bef 2 out: styd on wl and swtchd rt flat: wnt 3rd cl home* **6/1**[2]
/00- **4** *nk* **Pink Gin**[12] 2940 5-11-0 0..(t) MarkGrant 106
(Jim Old) *in tch in midfield: 7th and outpcd after 3 out: styd on to go 4th and j.rt 2 out: no threat to wnr but kpt on flat* **150/1**
1/4- **5** *1* **Volt Face (FR)**[26] 2667 4-11-0 0.................................... ConorO'Farrell 106
(David Pipe) *t.k.h: w ldr tl led 3rd: rdn and hdd bef 2 out: 3rd and btn sn after 2 out: fdd flat and lost 2 pls cl home* **7/4**[1]
/64- **6** *10* **Kaki Island (IRE)**[24] 2711 5-11-0 0...................................... TomCannon 95
(Chris Gordon) *led tl 3rd: styd w ldr tl rdn and struggling jst bef 3 out: wknd bef 2 out* **66/1**
4- **7** *1 1/2* **Vermouth Bleu (FR)**[14] 2900 4-11-0 0.............................. RichieMcLernon 95
(Jonjo O'Neill) *in tch in midfield: j.big 1st: j.rt 3rd: rdn after 3 out: sn struggling and wknd bef next* **40/1**
00- **8** *4* **Tashkaldou (FR)**[24] 2718 4-11-0 0..................................(t) HarrySkelton 91
(Dan Skelton) *hld up in rr: hdwy 4th: chsd ldrs 3 out: rdn and btn bef next: wknd between last 2* **66/1**
/03- **9** *11* **Table Bluff (IRE)**[14] 2893 4-11-0 0...................................... JamieMoore 78
(John Spearing) *in tch in midfield: rdn and struggling after 3 out: sn btn and wknd bef next: t.o* **66/1**
502- **10** *1/2* **The Master Remover (IRE)**[21] 2753 4-11-0 0............... MarcGoldstein 78
(Chris Gordon) *hld up in midfield: mstke 2nd: rdn and struggling 3 out: sn wknd and bhd next: t.o* **40/1**
/05- **11** *3* **Trillerin Minella (IRE)**[25] 2695 5-11-0 0............................ CharliePoste 75
(Graeme McPherson) *taken down early: hld up in rr: rdn bef 5th: struggling bef next: wknd wl bef 2 out: t.o* **16/1**
000- **12** *3 3/4* **Into The Wind**[14] 2893 6-10-4 0.................................... WayneKavanagh[(3)] 64
(Jim Best) *a bhd: mstke 3rd and 5th: lost tch bef next: t.o* **100/1**
P **Dustland Fairytale (IRE)**[41] 2568 5-10-7 0................... RobertThornton
(Ian Williams) *hld up in rr: j.big 1st: hdwy into midfield 4th: rdn and btn 3 out: sn wknd: t.o whn p.u last* **100/1**
0- **P** **The Perfect Crime (IRE)**[53] 2104 4-10-9 0................ RobertMcCarth[(5)]
(Ian Williams) *hld up in rr: j.lft 1st: rdn and lost tch bef 3 out: t.o whn p.u last* **100/1**

4m 4.05s (-3.85) **Going Correction** +0.05s/f (Yiel) **14** Ran SP% **117.6**
Speed ratings (Par 103): **111,107,105,104,104 99,98,96,91,90 89,87, ,**
CSF £16.46 TOTE £3.00: £1.20, £2.00, £1.90; EX 11.70 Trifecta £21.60 Pool: £1944.12 - 67.24 winning units..
Owner Matt & Lauren Morgan **Bred** Martin Donnellan **Trained** Upper Lambourn, Berks

FOCUS
Not a bad maiden hurdle. It was run at a sensible pace in the conditions. The first two and sixth and seventh help set the level.

3176 "KNOWLEDGE IS THE CURE" SUPPORTING CRUK NOVICES' H'CAP CHASE (16 fncs) 2m 6f
1:10 (1:10) (Class 4) (0-110,110) 4-Y-0+ **£3,768** (£1,106; £553; £276)

Form RPR
454- **1** **Chicklemix**[14] 2895 7-11-0 **103**...................................... MissGAndrews[(5)] 114+
(Pam Sly) *a travelled wl: chsd ldrs tl wnt 2nd after 7th: led and gng best bef 2 out: clr and rdn between last 2: slt mstke last: kpt on: rdn out* **14/1**
605/ **2** *4* **Mighty Mobb (IRE)**[251] 5264 6-11-10 **108**............................ TomO'Brien 115+
(Philip Hobbs) *in tch in midfield: 3rd and rdn after 3 out: chsd clr wnr and mstke last: kpt on but no threat to wnr flat* **8/1**[3]
225- **3** *2 1/2* **Cornish Ice**[11] 2979 9-11-7 **105**..(b[1]) CharliePoste 109
(Robin Dickin) *led: rdn bef 3 out: drvn and hdd bef 2 out: plugged on same pce after: lost 2nd and mstke last* **12/1**
53U- **4** *4 1/2* **Nail 'M (IRE)**[13] 2922 5-11-4 **105**................................ MarkQuinlan[(3)] 105
(Nigel Hawke) *chsd ldrs: drvn bef 3 out: no ex and outpcd 4th bef 2 out: plugged on same pce after* **25/1**
364- **5** *17* **Beaujolais (IRE)**[22] 2748 5-11-12 **110**.........................(b[1]) DenisO'Regan 95
(John Ferguson) *hld up in tch in rr: crept nrr 8th: 5th and rdn after 3 out: btn bef next: wl hld and hung rt between last 2: blnd last: wknd flat* **16/1**
/0F- **6** *3 3/4* **Vintage Tea**[27] 2651 6-11-12 **110**......................................(t) RhysFlint 87
(Richard Woollacott) *in tch in midfield: blnd 6th: mstke 9th: rdn and struggling 12th: wknd sn after 3 out* **50/1**
0/0- **7** *35* **Jigsaw Puzzle (IRE)**[57] 2018 7-11-4 **102**.....................(b[1]) ConorO'Farrell 44
(David Pipe) *in tch towards rr and mstke 6th: sn u.p: hmpd and dropped to last 8th: lost tch 13th: t.o after 3 out* **16/1**

/41- **U** **Faith Keeper (IRE)**[7] 3033 8-10-9 **98** 7ex.................. ConorShoemark(5)
(Fergal O'Brien) *mstkes: chsd ldrs: pushed along after 6th: blnd and uns rdr 8th* **1/1**[1]

6/2- **F** **Farbreaga (IRE)**[37] 2437 7-11-7 **105**................................ DougieCostello
(Jamie Poulton) *racd wd: in tch in midfield: pushed along and mstke 6th: fell 8th* **9/2**[2]

005- **F** **Sedgemoor Top Bid (IRE)**[25] 2689 5-10-11 **102**. ThomasCheesman(7)
(Nigel Hawke) *in tch towards rr whn fell 1st* **66/1**

5m 47.1s (-5.90) **Going Correction** -0.15s/f (Good) **10** Ran SP% **112.7**
Speed ratings (Par 105): **104,102,101,100,93 92,79,,,**
toteswingers 1&2 £12.60, 2&3 £7.80, 1&3 £0.00 CSF £114.13 CT £1382.38 TOTE £12.20: £2.60, £1.90, £2.40; EX 109.80 Trifecta £580.40 Pool: £1699.77 - 2.19 winning units..
Owner Michael H Sly Dr T Davies Mrs Pam Sly **Bred** Mrs P Sly **Trained** Thorney, Cambs

FOCUS

The going was eased to soft This handicap was run at a fair gallop. The winner has been rated as improving to the level of her hurdles form, with the third running a small pb.

3177 HAYGAIN HAY STEAMERS CLEAN HEALTHY FORAGE NOVICES' HURDLE (11 hdls) 2m 5f

1:40 (1:40) (Class 4) 4-Y-0+ **£3,119** (£915; £457; £228)

Form RPR

1- **1** **Mountain Tunes (IRE)**[42] 2316 4-11-5 0.................................. APMcCoy 131+
(Jonjo O'Neill) *in tch in midfield: clsd to trck ldrs 3 out: trckd ldr bef next: rdn to ld bef last: styd on u.p and fnd enough to assert towards fin* **5/4**[1]

1- **2** *nk* **Knockanrawley (IRE)**[19] 2826 5-11-0 0............................ EdCookson(5) 129+
(Kim Bailey) *in tch in midfield: hdwy to chse ldrs 6th: lft in ld sn after 3 out: rdn bef next: hdd and drvn bef last: ev ch and mstke last: battled on gamely u.p: no ex cl home* **9/2**[3]

5- **3** *10* **Broadway Symphony (IRE)**[35] 2467 6-10-12 0.................. MarkGrant 114+
(Tracey L Bailey) *hld up in last trio: hdwy after 5th: chsd ldrs 8th: cl 3rd after 3 out: rdn and no ex sn after 2 out: wknd bef last* **22/1**

4 *15* **Castle Cheetah (IRE)**[354] 5-10-12 0.................................... IanPopham 104+
(Martin Keighley) *racd wd: w ldrs tl led 8th: stl travelling wl enough whn blnd bdly next: sn hdd: nt rcvr: rdn and btn bef next: blnd 2 out: wknd* **15/2**

5/6- **5** *1 ¼* **Winged Crusader (IRE)**[24] 2720 5-10-5 0........................ RyanHatch(7) 96
(Nigel Twiston-Davies) *in tch in midfield: pushed along 6th: stl wl in tch 3 out: wknd u.p bef next* **16/1**

/21- **6** *23* **Ashes House (IRE)**[33] 2509 7-11-5 125.............................. JamieMoore 80
(Rebecca Curtis) *t.k.h: led tl 8th: wknd qckly after next: t.o last* **7/2**[2]

3/0- **P** **Special Vintage**[43] 2296 7-10-7 0.................................... KillianMoore(5)
(Graeme McPherson) *in tch in midfield: mstke 4th: lost pl next: bhd whn p.u 6th* **100/1**

50/ **P** **Island Cruise (IRE)**[611] 5449 5-10-12 0.............................. ColinBolger
(Pat Murphy) *in tch in midfield: rdn and lost pl 7th: sn struggling: lost tch after next: t.o and p.u 2 out* **100/1**

40/ **P** **Weigh It Up (IRE)**[295] 4452 5-10-9 0...........................[1] KielanWoods(3)
(Charlie Longsdon) *chsd ldr tl after 7th: rdn and lost pl qckly bef 3 out: fdd on uphill run bef 2 out: t.o and p.u 2 out* **16/1**

6- **P** **Flash Tommie (IRE)**[26] 2681 5-10-7 0.............................. JamesBanks(5)
(Martin Bosley) *nt a fluent: hld up in rr: rdn and lost tch 6th: t.o next tl p.u 2 out* **150/1**

P **Carrigeen Aspen (IRE)** 6-10-0 0.............................. ThomasGarner(5)
(Oliver Sherwood) *hld up in last pair: hdwy 6th: rdn and wknd jst bef 3 out: fdd on uphill run and t.o whn p.u 2 out* **33/1**

5m 30.95s (3.75) **Going Correction** +0.20s/f (Yiel) **11** Ran SP% **118.3**
Speed ratings (Par 105): **100,99,96,90,89 81,,,,**
toteswingers 1&2 £1.50, 2&3 £11.90, 1&3 £7.90 CSF £7.14 TOTE £2.90: £1.10, £2.10, £3.10; EX 7.00 Trifecta £67.90 Pool: £2365.20 - 26.10 winning units..
Owner John P McManus **Bred** Neil R Tector **Trained** Cheltenham, Gloucs

FOCUS

The gallop was steady for this fair novices' hurdle, with two nice types fighting out an exciting finish. The first two have been rated as building on their recent course wins.

3178 WINVIC CONSTRUCTION H'CAP CHASE (18 fncs) 3m 110y

2:10 (2:10) (Class 4) (0-120,119) 4-Y-0+ **£3,768** (£1,106; £553; £276)

Form RPR

/20- **1** **Gorgehous Lliege (FR)**[26] 2670 7-10-10 **103**.................. LiamTreadwell 117+
(Venetia Williams) *mde virtually all: mstke 13th: rdn and forged clr 2 out:5 l clr and in command last: rdn out* **7/4**[1]

/23- **2** *1 ¼* **Smart Exit (IRE)**[26] 2678 6-10-3 **99**...........................(p) JoshuaMoore(3) 110
(Renee Robeson) *w wnr: rdn after 3 out: 5 l down and hit last: kpt on gamely u.p flat* **9/4**[2]

0/2- **3** *20* **Armedanddangerous (IRE)**[27] 2650 8-11-1 **108**........... JamesReveley 99
(Tom Gretton) *in tch in last pair: mstke and rdn 12th: swtchd lft bef next: rallied bef 3 out: wknd on uphill run to 2 out: kpt on flat to go 3rd last strides* **4/1**[3]

/U5- **4** *½* **Jolly Boys Outing (IRE)**[13] 2923 10-9-9 **93**.................. KillianMoore(5) 85
(Rosemary Gasson) *in tch in last pair: lft 3rd 9th: mstke and rdn 15th: 3rd and btn on uphill run after next: wknd flat and lost 3rd last strides* **16/1**

/63- **F** **Who Owns Me (IRE)**[32] 2539 7-11-4 **118**.................. MrHAABannister(7)
(Charlie Mann) *chsd ldrs tl fell 9th* **6/1**

6m 32.55s (-4.35) **Going Correction** 0.0s/f (Good) **5** Ran SP% **107.3**
Speed ratings (Par 105): **106,105,99,99,**
CSF £5.96 TOTE £2.10: £1.60, £1.30; EX 5.40 Trifecta £12.20 Pool: £1732.42 - 105.86 winning units..
Owner A Brooks **Bred** Mme Bernard Le Gentil **Trained** Kings Caple, H'fords

FOCUS

They went a steady pace in this handicap. The idling winner is value for a bit further, with the second rated as running to his mark.

3179 IN LOVING MEMORY OF CAROLINE BEESLEY H'CAP HURDLE (12 hdls) 3m

2:40 (2:40) (Class 5) (0-100,99) 4-Y-0+ **£1,949** (£572; £286; £143)

Form RPR

/12- **1** **Easy Beesy**[49] 2175 5-11-8 **95**... APMcCoy 101+
(Charles Egerton) *racd wd: w ldr: led 8th tl next: styd upsides ldr: gng best after 3 out: rdn to ld and blnd last: forged ahd fnl 75yds: rdn out* **10/11**[1]

/04- **2** *2* **Typhon De Guye (FR)**[35] 2473 6-11-8 **95**........................ IanPopham 98
(Martin Keighley) *chsd ldrs: jnd wnr 8th: led next: rdn bef 2 out: drvn and hdd whn blnd last: no ex and wknd flat* **9/2**[2]

603- **3** *hd* **Blue Cove**[19] 2827 8-10-5 **78**.. TomSiddall 80
(Lynn Siddall) *t.k.h: hld up in tch: rdn along bef 8th: 3rd 3 out: plugged on u.p and edgd rt flat: pressing for 2nd cl home* **14/1**

232- **4** *2* **Changing Lanes**[19] 2827 10-11-1 **95**..............................(tp) MrBGibbs(7) 94
(David Rees) *in tch towards rr: hdwy 7th: rdn after next: 4th and plugged on same pce u.p fr bef 2 out* **9/1**

030- **P** **Earcomesthedream (IRE)**[19] 2827 10-11-5 **99**...........(b) TomBellamy(7)
(Peter Pritchard) *mde most tl 8th: sn rdn and lost pl bef next: wl btn whn p.u 2 out* **22/1**

U/U- **P** **Poppy Gregg**[22] 2743 8-9-11 **73** oh4.......................(v) WayneKavanagh(3)
(Dr Jeremy Naylor) *chsd ldrs: rdn and lost pl after 6th: lost tch and t.o after next: p.u 2 out* **40/1**

34- **P** **Killegney**[22] 2744 9-11-2 **94**.......................................(b) ConorShoemark(5)
(Michael Gates) *in tch towards rr: dropped to last after 4th: rdn after 6th: lost tch 8th: t.o bef next tl p.u 2 out* **33/1**

442- **P** **Blazing Bouncer**[9] 3014 8-11-8 **95**..(tp) RhysFlint
(Richard Woollacott) *chsd ldrs: rdn and lost pl 8th: lost tch bef 3 out: t.o whn p.u 2 out* **16/1**

460- **P** **No Ifs No Buts**[17] 2862 4-9-12 **78** ow2............................. JakeHodson(7)
(David Bridgwater) *hld up in tch: hdwy into midfield 7th: rdn and no ex 3 out: sn wknd: wl bhd whn p.u next* **8/1**[3]

6m 30.35s (15.35) **Going Correction** +0.35s/f (Yiel) **9** Ran SP% **114.0**
WFA 4 from 5yo+ 7lb
Speed ratings (Par 103): **88,87,87,86,,,,,**
toteswingers 1&2 £1.80, 2&3 £19.40, 1&3 £6.20 CSF £5.53 CT £32.40 TOTE £1.70: £1.10, £2.00, £2.70; EX 5.00 Trifecta £37.40 Pool: £2412.75 - 48.38 winning units..
Owner Mrs Sandra A Roe **Bred** Mrs Sandra A Roe **Trained** Upper Lambourn, Berks

FOCUS

A modest handicap run at a steady pace. The first four have been rated pretty much to their marks.

3180 PATRICIA ATKINSON H'CAP CHASE (14 fncs) 2m 3f 110y

3:10 (3:11) (Class 5) (0-100,100) 4-Y-0+ **£2,144** (£629; £314; £157)

Form RPR

/06- **1** **Bill The Lad (IRE)**[24] 2719 6-10-7 **81**.................................... SamThomas 100+
(Paul Cowley) *hld up in last pair and hugged inner: clsd on ldrs bef 3 out: effrt to chse ldr after 3 out: led 2 out: sn clr and in command whn lft wl clr last: comf* **11/1**

334- **2** *10* **Carli King (IRE)**[20] 2782 7-11-10 **98**........................... RobertThornton 100
(Caroline Bailey) *in tch in midfield: hdwy to chse ldrs and mstke 10th: rdn and mstke next: wknd bef 2 out: lft wl btn 3rd last: kpt on to go 2nd fnl 100yds* **11/8**[1]

5/0- **3** *1 ½* **Witch's Hat (IRE)**[229] 117 10-10-10 **84**.............................(t) MarkGrant 85
(Jim Old) *chsd ldr tl led 7th: outj. and hdd 3 out: 3rd and wknd bef next: lft 15 l 2nd last: lost 2nd fnl 100yds* **9/1**[3]

600- **4** *5* **Top Benefit (IRE)**[19] 2829 11-10-3 **82**.............................. JamesBanks(5) 77
(Richard Harper) *led tl 7th: chsd ldrs after: rdn after 11th: wknd bef 2 out: lft modest 4th last* **22/1**

666- **5** *7* **Vardas Supreme (IRE)**[8] 3020 10-10-3 **82**..........(tp) JonathanEngland(5) 70
(Richard Drake) *chsd ldrs tl wnt 2nd 7th: j. slowly and rdn 11th: losing pl and blnd next: sn wknd* **25/1**

0- **6** *¾* **Caspian Piper (IRE)**[14] 2897 6-11-5 **100**.......................(b) MikeyEnnis(7) 86
(Hugo Froud) *in tch in midfield: losing pl and mstke 9th: lost tch u.p bef 3 out: wl btn bef 2 out* **25/1**

536- **P** **Peak Seasons (IRE)**[31] 2562 10-9-12 **77**........................ JoeCornwall(5)
(Michael Chapman) *bhd: struggling and detached after 7th: wl bhd whn p.u 2 out* **20/1**

035- **U** **Freckle Face**[15] 2887 6-11-9 **97**.................................... TommyPhelan 105
(Bill Turner) *t.k.h: hld up in rr: mstke 1st: hdwy 4th: chsd ldrs 10th: j. into ld and stl travelling strly 3 out: hdd next: sn rdn and btn: 6 l down whn mstke and uns rdr last* **10/1**

353- **P** **Bally Lagan (IRE)**[18] 2849 5-10-8 **82**..............................(tp) CharliePoste
(Robin Dickin) *chsd ldrs: mstke 8th: rdn bef 3 out: wknd wl bef 2 out: t.o whn p.u last* **3/1**[2]

5m 20.9s (2.70) **Going Correction** +0.15s/f (Yiel) **9** Ran SP% **111.3**
Speed ratings (Par 103): **100,96,95,93,90 90,,,**
CSF £25.70 CT £141.60 TOTE £16.50: £2.90, £1.30, £3.00; EX 35.90 Trifecta £393.60 Pool: £2432.94 - 4.63 winning units..
Owner Stan West **Bred** Michael Lenihan **Trained** Culworth, Northants

FOCUS

Not a strong contest run at a fair gallop. This was a big step up from the easy winner, while the second is on a mark he can win off.

3181 HAYGAIN HAY STEAMERS CLEAN HEALTHY FORAGE MARES' STANDARD OPEN NATIONAL HUNT FLAT RACE 2m

3:40 (3:40) (Class 6) 4-6-Y-O **£1,559** (£457; £228; £114)

Form RPR

52- **1** **Ballyhollow**[15] 2892 6-10-12 0... APMcCoy 98
(Rebecca Curtis) *mde all: gng best over 2f out: rdn and asserted jst ins fnl f: r.o wl: rdn out* **11/4**[2]

3/ **2** *1 ½* **No Pushover**[234] 36 4-10-12 0.................................. AndrewTinkler 96
(Nicky Henderson) *chsd ldrs: rdn and clr in ldng trio 3f out: kpt on u.p to go 2nd towards fin* **15/8**[1]

3 *½* **Jennys Surprise (IRE)**[243] 5-10-12 0.............................. AlainCawley 96
(Fergal O'Brien) *chsd wnr: rdn and ev ch jst over 2f out: no ex jst ins fnl f: kpt on same pce fnl 100yds lost 2nd towards fin* **3/1**[3]

0- **4** *11* **Delineate (IRE)**[43] 2298 4-10-7 0................................ JamesBanks(5) 85
(G C Maundrell) *in tch in midfield: effrt and barging match w rival over 3f out: swtchd lft and hdwy 3f out: wnt 4th 1f out: no threat to ldrs* **66/1**

0- **5** *2 ¼* **Present Trend (IRE)**[43] 2298 4-10-9 0............................ KielanWoods(3) 82
(Charlie Longsdon) *in tch in midfield: hdwy to chse ldng trio 4f out: rdn and no ex over 2f out: wknd over 1f out* **16/1**

0- **6** *20* **Pandy Wells**[33] 2513 4-10-12 0.. CharliePoste 62
(Graeme McPherson) *t.k.h: chsd ldrs: rdn and struggling over 3f out: sn btn and wknd over 2f out* **40/1**

\- **7** *½* **The Iron Maiden** 4-10-12 0...[1] SamJones 62
(Jo Davis) *hld up in tch in last trio: sme hdwy 1/2-way: rdn and lost pl 4f out: n.d fnl 3f* **33/1**

\- **8** *2 ¼* **Ella's Promise** 4-10-12 0.. TomO'Brien 60
(Barry Brennan) *in tch in midfield: lost pl but stl in tch 10f out: rdn 4f out: sn wknd: bhd fnl 2f* **25/1**

9 *15* **Rose Pageant** 4-10-12 0... HarrySkelton 45
(Dan Skelton) *in tch in last trio: pushed along 4f out: sn dropped out and bhd 2f out: t.o* **12/1**

10 *4* **Thymeandthymeagain** 4-10-5 0.................................... MikeyEnnis(7) 41
(Hugo Froud) *t.k.h: hld up in tch in rr: sme hdwy 4f out: barging mayh w rival and wknd over 3f out: wl bhd and eased over 1f out: t.o* **50/1**

4m 9.0s (6.70) **Going Correction** +0.50s/f (Soft) **10** Ran SP% **112.7**
Speed ratings: **103,102,102,96,95 85,85,84,76,74**
toteswingers 1&2 £1.02, 2&3 £3.30, 1&3 £9.10 CSF £7.63 TOTE £3.30: £1.10, £1.10, £2.00; EX 5.80 Trifecta £12.70 Pool: £2106.00 - 123.43 winning units..

The Form Book Jumps, Raceform Ltd, Compton, RG20 6NL.

Owner Miss Sarah Gallagher **Bred** Gallagher Enterprises Ltd **Trained** Newport, Dyfed

FOCUS

Not a bad pace in this mares' bumper. The front three in the market dominated and the form looks solid. It's rated around the first two and the fifth and sixth.

T/Plt: £84.60 to a £1 stake. Pool of £81574.99 - 703.09 winning tickets. T/Qpdt: £3.60 to a £1 stake. Pool of £7409.85 - 1487.15 winning tickets. SP

2661 ASCOT (R-H)

Friday, December 20

OFFICIAL GOING: Soft (chs 6.9, hdl 6.8)

Wind: Light, against Weather: Fine

3182 IRON STAND "NATIONAL HUNT" MAIDEN HURDLE (12 hdls) 2m 6f

1:00 (1:00) (Class 3) 4-Y-0+

£5,630 (£1,663; £831; £415; £207; £104)

Form RPR

3/3- **1** **Royal Boy (FR)**[25] 2716 6-11-0 133 BarryGeraghty 141+
(Nicky Henderson) *hld up in tch: prog to trck ldrs 8th: wnt 2nd wl bef 2 out: led on bit bef last: shkn up and drew clr flat: comf* **7/4**[1]

2 *6* **Big Hands Harry**[236] 4-11-0 0 AndrewTinkler 132+
(Nicky Henderson) *hld up in tch: nt fluent 7th: cl up and nt fluent 3 out: sn wnt 2nd: led wl bef 2 out: rdn and hdd bef last: styd on but no ch w wnr* **12/1**

1- **3** *10* **Pleasant Company (IRE)**[48] 2216 5-11-0 0 TomScudamore 120
(David Pipe) *led to 1st and after 2nd: drvn and hdd wl bef 2 out: hld on to 3rd pl fr last* **9/4**[2]

4 *½* **Medieval Chapel (FR)**[277] 5-10-9 0 NicodeBoinville[(5)] 121
(Nicky Henderson) *t.k.h: trckd ldrs: wl in tch 3 out: sn rdn and outpcd: plugged on fr 2 out* **14/1**

31- **5** *29* **Tara Road**[13] 2946 5-11-0 0 APMcCoy 101
(Rebecca Curtis) *cl up: hit 7th: trckd ldr fr next to 3 out: nudged along and sn lost tch w ldrs: eased bef 2 out* **4/1**[3]

6 *16* **Sacramento King (IRE)**[215] 4-11-0 0 GerardTumelty 75
(Jonathan Geake) *hld up in rr: mstke 5th: lost tch w ldrs fr 8th: t.o* **100/1**

41/ **7** *25* **Such A Legend**[300] 4391 5-11-0 0 SamThomas 50
(Kim Bailey) *in tch: mstke 6th: wkng whn j. slowly 8th: t.o after 3 out* **25/1**

0/ **P** **Mac's Return (IRE)**[317] 4072 6-11-0 0 DarylJacob
(Paul Nicholls) *hld up in rr: mstke 6th: wknd and mstke 8th: blnd next: wl t.o whn p.u bef 2 out* **10/1**

0- **P** **Donapollo**[61] 1991 5-11-0 0 WillKennedy
(Ian Williams) *led 1st to after 2nd: chsd ldr tl rdn and wknd 8th: t.o whn p.u bef 2 out* **100/1**

5m 28.7s (2.70) **Going Correction** +0.35s/f (Yiel)
WFA 4 from 5yo+ 6lb 9 Ran SP% **116.4**
Speed ratings (Par 107): **109,106,103,103,92 86,77, ,**
toteswingers 1&2 £4.50, 1&3 £1.50, 2&3 £5.70 CSF £23.91 TOTE £3.00: £1.20, £3.00, £1.30; EX 22.00 Trifecta £73.40 Pool: £3571.27 - 36.46 winning units..
Owner Michael Buckley **Bred** Earl Haras Du Luy **Trained** Upper Lambourn, Berks

FOCUS

A strong maiden hurdle and one which looks almost certain to work out as the season progresses. The easy winner stood out on last season's smart form and has been rated to a similar level. The second should win a similar race, as should the third and fourth., who have been rated close to their bumper marks.

3183 SHOOTING STAR CHASE NOVICES' LIMITED H'CAP CHASE (13 fncs) 2m 1f

1:30 (1:30) (Class 3) (0-125,122) 4-Y-0+

£6,881 (£2,032; £1,016; £508; £254; £127)

Form RPR

0- **1** **Bellenos (FR)**[21] 2785 5-11-5 122 HarrySkelton 136+
(Dan Skelton) *hld up in tch: prog fr 8th: jnd ldng pair 10th: led 2 out gng wl: rdn clr bef last: styd on wl* **9/2**[2]

501- **2** *6* **Rio De Sivola (FR)**[30] 2601 4-11-0 122 APMcCoy 123
(Nick Williams) *not a fluent: led: rdn and hdd 2 out: no ch w wnr fr last: wknd flat but hld on for 2nd* **15/8**[1]

132- **3** *2 ¼* **Double Handful (GER)**[180] 806 7-11-2 119 (t) DavidBass 124
(Lawney Hill) *trckd ldrs: mstke 6th: rdn and no imp 3 out: kpt on after to take 3rd bef last: clsd on tiring runner-up fin* **16/1**

135- **4** *9* **Captain Paulie (IRE)**[29] 2618 10-10-10 113 AdamWedge 107
(Evan Williams) *trckd ldrs: rdn whn j.lft 3 out: no imp on ldrs bef next* **10/1**

3/6- **5** *7* **Orabora**[33] 2538 7-11-3 120 RichardJohnson 113+
(Philip Hobbs) *prom: jnd ldr 8th: wl on terms 3 out: lost 2nd and wknd bef 2 out: wl btn 4th whn blnd bdly last: eased* **11/2**[3]

162- **6** *4* **Marcus Antonius**[24] 2726 6-11-1 118 LeightonAspell 101
(Jim Boyle) *nt a fluent: hld up in last: jst in tch 9th: wknd and mstke 3 out* **16/1**

15P- **P** **Pasture Bay (IRE)**[66] 1916 7-10-4 112 ConorShoemark[(5)]
(Fergal O'Brien) *last fr 6th: lost tch 8th: t.o whn p.u bef 2 out* **25/1**

430/ **P** **Getting Ready (IRE)**[396] 2525 6-10-10 113 SamTwiston-Davies
(Nigel Twiston-Davies) *chsd ldr to 8th: wknd rapidly: j. slowly next and p.u* **9/2**[2]

4m 19.5s (4.90) **Going Correction** +0.475s/f (Soft)
WFA 4 from 5yo+ 5lb 8 Ran SP% **111.2**
Speed ratings (Par 107): **107,104,103,98,95 93, ,**
toteswingers 1&2 £2.50, 1&3 £5.30, 2&3 £3.00 CSF £13.23 CT £115.36 TOTE £5.90: £1.60, £1.30, £2.00; EX 14.20 Trifecta £111.10 Pool: £4383.97 - 29.57 winning units..
Owner Mr And Mrs J D Cotton **Bred** Pierre De Maleissye Melun **Trained** Alcester, Warwicks

FOCUS

This looked a hot race for the grade. The cosy winner looks a fair prospect and can win again.

3184 MITIE KENNEL GATE NOVICES' HURDLE GRADE 2 (9 hdls) 2m

2:00 (2:00) (Class 1) 4-Y-0+ **£17,386** (£6,712; £3,511; £1,900)

Form RPR

11- **1** **Irving**[28] 2644 5-11-7 0 NickScholfield 146+
(Paul Nicholls) *hld up: hit 2nd: last of five remaining after 3 out but cl up: shkn up and prog 2 out: tk narrow ld last where lft clr: r.o wl* **11/4**[2]

11- **2** *6* **Volnay De Thaix (FR)**[22] 2753 4-11-7 138 BarryGeraghty 139+
(Nicky Henderson) *cl up: nt fluent 2nd: rdn and nt qckn 2 out: hmpd last: styd on to snatch 2nd post* **4/5**[1]

241- **3** *shd* **Splash Of Ginge**[13] 2933 5-11-4 135 SamTwiston-Davies 135
(Nigel Twiston-Davies) *led: mstke 1st: j.lft 3rd: nt fluent next: stl in front 2 out but only on suffernce: sn hdd and outpcd: lft chsng wnr last: one pce and lost 2nd post* **6/1**[3]

4- **4** *3* **Massini's Trap (IRE)**[49] 2206 4-11-7 134 APMcCoy 134
(J A Nash, Ire) *wl in tch: nt fluent 4th: cl up bef 2 out: sn shkn up and outpcd: kpt on fr last* **16/1**

51- **F** **Prince Siegfried (FR)**[38] 2432 7-11-4 0 DenisO'Regan 140+
(John Ferguson) *trckd ldr: mstke 4th: led gng strly immediately after 2 out: shkn up and narrowly hdd whn fell heavily last* **18/1**

/11- **F** **Long Lunch**[60] 2002 4-11-0 0 (t) NoelFehily
(Charlie Longsdon) *hld up in tch: cl 4th but r yet to unfold whn fell 3 out* **20/1**

3m 53.3s (5.90) **Going Correction** +0.35s/f (Yiel) 6 Ran SP% **112.4**
Speed ratings (Par 115): **99,96,95,94,**
toteswingers 1&2 £1.10, 1&3 £2.20, 2&3 £1.70 CSF £5.58 TOTE £4.30: £2.80, £1.20; EX 9.10 Trifecta £20.80 Pool: £22259.21 - 798.96 winning units..
Owner Axom XLIX **Bred** Gestut Schlenderhan **Trained** Ditcheat, Somerset

FOCUS

This looked every bit as strong as in recent years. The winner thrived for the better pace and looks a smart novice and obvious Supreme material. The faller, who was high class on the Flat, was heading for a big pb. The second has been rated as running a small pb, with the third to similar and fourth to his best in a solid renewal.

3185 BETFRED NOVICES' CHASE (REGISTERED AS THE NOEL NOVICES' CHASE) GRADE 2 (16 fncs) 2m 3f

2:35 (2:35) (Class 1) 4-Y-0+ **£17,162** (£6,466; £3,236; £1,616)

Form RPR

522- **1** **Fox Appeal (IRE)**[41] 2374 6-11-0 145 AidanColeman 155+
(Emma Lavelle) *trckd ldr: led 10th: drew clr bef 2 out: nt fluent last: easily* **5/4**[1]

/12- **2** *10* **Raya Star (IRE)**[33] 2531 7-11-0 149 RobertThornton 142
(Alan King) *trckd ldng pair: wnt 2nd 12th: easily lft bhd by wnr bef 2 out* **3/1**[3]

/21- **3** *15* **Mr Mole (IRE)**[12] 2976 5-11-0 0 (t) APMcCoy 135+
(Paul Nicholls) *hld up in last: mstke 6th: blnd 9th: mstkes 4 out and next: no ch after tk 3rd 2 out* **11/4**[2]

122- **4** *12* **Up To Something (FR)**[21] 2799 5-11-4 140 (tp) NoelFehily 124
(Charlie Longsdon) *led to 10th: outpcd fr 4 out: last and wl btn 2 out* **13/2**

4m 50.2s (3.80) **Going Correction** +0.475s/f (Soft) 4 Ran SP% **109.4**
Speed ratings (Par 115): **111,106,100,95**
CSF £5.40 TOTE £2.80; EX 5.80 Trifecta £12.50 Pool: £12345.42 - 734.98 winning units..
Owner The Hawk Inn Syndicate 3 **Bred** Sean And Batt Leahy **Trained** Hatherden, Hants

FOCUS

This went to Simonsig a year ago. The winner was the form pick but this rated another step up and he's entitled to run well at the Festival, although he's still around 10lb shy of what is needed to win a typical Arkle. The second took a small step up on his Cheltenaham run, but is still 13lb off his hurdles mark, and the third should do better.

3186 BARCLAYS H'CAP HURDLE (12 hdls) 2m 6f

3:10 (3:10) (Class 3) (0-130,129) 4-Y-0+

£6,256 (£1,848; £924; £462; £231; £116)

Form RPR

602- **1** **Bygones Sovereign (IRE)**[29] 2630 7-10-8 111 (p) TomScudamore 119
(David Pipe) *mde all: kicked on fr 8th: 3 l clr after 3 out: drvn and jnd last: edgd lft flat: hld on wl* **7/1**

414- **2** *nk* **Andy Kelly (IRE)**[22] 2755 4-11-3 123 GavinSheehan[(3)] 132
(Emma Lavelle) *trckd wnr: nt fluent 2nd and 3rd: rdn after 3 out: hanging and 3 l down whn nt fluent 2 out: clsd to chal last: sltly impeded nr fin: jst hld* **7/2**[1]

305- **3** *10* **Kilmurvy (IRE)**[21] 2798 5-11-6 123 (tp) NickScholfield 123
(Jeremy Scott) *towards rr: dropped to last trio 8th: rdn and prog after 3 out: hit 2 out: styd on to take 3rd bef last: no imp* **11/2**[3]

110- **4** *4* **Invicta Lake (IRE)**[21] 2798 6-11-3 120 (p) DarylJacob 114
(Suzy Smith) *hld up in midfield: clsd on ldrs 3 out and looked a threat: rdn and no rspnse 2 out: wl btn after* **16/1**

041/ **5** *2 ½* **Polly Peachum (IRE)**[248] 5339 5-11-0 117 BarryGeraghty 110
(Nicky Henderson) *trckd ldrs: lost pl 7th: effrt again 3 out: no imp whn mstke 2 out: mstke last* **4/1**[2]

350- **6** *3 ¼* **Azure Fly (IRE)**[20] 2813 5-11-11 128 (tp) AidanColeman 117
(Charlie Longsdon) *hld up in midfield: cl up 3 out: sn rdn in 6th: nt qckn and wl btn after 2 out* **25/1**

/00- **7** *7* **Whisky Yankee (IRE)**[13] 2935 6-11-12 129 APMcCoy 110
(Jonjo O'Neill) *t.k.h: hld up in rr: lost tch w main gp after 7th: shkn up after 3 out: nvr on terms* **8/1**

/10- **8** *¾* **Sinbad The Sailor**[63] 1956 8-11-4 121 (t) AndrewTinkler 102
(George Baker) *wl in tch: mstke 6th: rdn after 8th: sn struggling: wknd after 3 out* **25/1**

/20- **9** *22* **Valid Reason**[21] 2798 6-11-9 126 RobertThornton 85
(Dean Ivory) *prom tl wknd rapidly jst bef 3 out: t.o* **14/1**

6PP- **P** **Dreambrook Lady (IRE)**[42] 2352 7-10-8 116 MauriceLinehan[(5)]
(Jonjo O'Neill) *plld hrd: hld up in rr: prog and prom 5th: racd wd and stl pulling after: dropped out rapidly after 7th: p.u bef next* **50/1**

253- **P** **Keltic Rhythm (IRE)**[15] 2908 6-10-10 113 DougieCostello
(Neil King) *prom tl wknd rapidly 8th: t.o whn p.u bef 2 out* **20/1**

631- **F** **Rior (IRE)**[15] 2908 6-10-3 106 RichardJohnson 105
(Paul Henderson) *hld up and last early: mstke 4th: prog fr 7th to trck ldrs 3 out: disp 2nd jst bef 2 out: sn wknd: disputing 4th whn fell heavily last* **8/1**

5m 28.8s (2.80) **Going Correction** +0.35s/f (Yiel)
WFA 4 from 5yo+ 6lb 12 Ran SP% **119.3**
Speed ratings (Par 107): **108,107,104,102,101 100,98,97,89, ,**
toteswingers 1&2 £6.80, 1&3 £7.20, 2&3 £5.10 CSF £31.21 CT £148.43 TOTE £7.40: £2.40, £2.20, £2.00; EX 35.20 Trifecta £243.90 Pool: £4804.45 - 14.76 winning units..
Owner Arnie & Alan Kaplan **Bred** Mrs S Brennan **Trained** Nicholashayne, Devon

■ Stewards' Enquiry : Tom Scudamore two-day ban; careless riding (3rd,5th Jan).

FOCUS

An ultra-competitive handicap hurdle on paper, but it was dominated by those ridden up with the pace. The winner has been rated back to his best, and this was another step up from the second.

3187 RARC 15TH YEAR CELEBRATION CHAMPIONSHIP STANDARD OPEN NATIONAL HUNT FLAT RACE (LISTED RACE) 2m

3:40 (3:41) (Class 1) 4-6-Y-0

£11,390 (£4,274; £2,140; £1,066; £536; £268)

Form RPR

1/ **1** **Seven Nation Army (IRE)**[253] 5247 4-11-4 0 TomScudamore 125
(David Pipe) *trckd ldr 4f and again 5f out: rdn to ld over 2f out: hrd pressed after: hld on wl nr fin* **8/1**[3]

2 nk **Joshua Lane (IRE)**[41] 2383 4-11-4 0 BarryGeraghty 124
(Edward P Harty, Ire) *plld hrd early: hld up in midfield: cl up 4f out: rdn to chal fr 2f out: kpt trying fnl f: jst hld* **8/1**[3]

121- 3 2¼ **On Tour (IRE)**[16] 2885 5-11-4 0 AdamWedge 122
(Evan Williams) *hld up towards rr: prog over 3f out: chal 2f out: n.m.r whn hanging 1f out: nt qckn fnl f* **20/1**

/12- 4 4 **Carningli (IRE)**[33] 2534 4-11-4 0 APMcCoy 118
(Rebecca Curtis) *led 4f: led again over 6f out: drvn and hdd over 2f out: one pce* **11/10**[1]

/21- 5 2 **Oscarteea (IRE)**[69] 1869 4-11-4 0 AidanColeman 116
(Anthony Honeyball) *plld hrd: hld up: dropped to last of main gp 4f out: tried to rally 2f out but racd awkwardly: one pce* **6/1**[2]

6 3 **Themanfrom Minella (IRE)**[257] 4-11-4 0 (t) DarylJacob 113
(Ben Case) *trckd ldrs: rdn over 2f out: steadily outpcd* **20/1**

7 ¾ **Herons Heir (IRE)**[54] 2125 5-11-4 0 HarrySkelton 112
(Dan Skelton) *hld up in last: effrt 4f out: shkn up and no prog over 2f out* **10/1**

8 8 **Nathans Pride (IRE)**[182] 797 5-11-4 0 DougieCostello 104
(Tim Vaughan) *t.k.h: hld up in rr: rdn and outpcd 4f out: no ch over 2f out* **8/1**[3]

9 42 **Parting Way (IRE)**[621] 5-11-4 0 RichardJohnson 62
(Tim Vaughan) *t.k.h: hld up tl plld way through to ld after 4f: hdd over 6f out: wknd rapidly 5f out: t.o* **25/1**

3m 48.6s (7.80) **Going Correction** +0.35s/f (Yiel) **9** Ran SP% **117.7**
Speed ratings: **94,93,92,90,89 88,87,83,62**
CSF £68.76 TOTE £8.90: £2.00, £2.80, £4.50; EX 78.00 Trifecta £1133.90 Pool: £5244.27 - 3.46 winning units..
Owner R S Brookhouse **Bred** New England, Myriad & Watership Down **Trained** Nicholashayne, Devon

FOCUS
One of the strongest bumper races to be run this season and it served up an exhilarating finish. The first three are on the upgrade, while the fourth has been rated 9lb off his Cheltenham mark.
T/Plt: £49.00 to a £1 stake. Pool: £137193.23 - 2042.06 winning tickets T/Qpdt: £34.20 to a £1 stake. Pool: £6826.18 - 147.30 winning tickets JN

3010 UTTOXETER (L-H)
Friday, December 20

OFFICIAL GOING: Heavy (soft in places; heavy with some standing water in chute; chs 4.2, hdl 4.4)
Hurdles moved out a further 4-6m from meeting on Tuesday December 10th. Divided bends moved to outer on fresh ground.
Wind: freesh 1/2 behind Weather: overcast, breezy, cold

3188 BURTON KIA "HANDS AND HEELS" NOVICES' H'CAP HURDLE (CONDITIONALS & AMATEURS) (9 hdls) 2m
12:20 (12:20) (Class 5) (0-100,98) 3-Y-O+ **£2,209** (£648; £324; £162)

Form RPR

0/0- 1 **Kozmina Bay**[15] 2898 4-10-0 **77** (b[1]) MrSPBowen(5) 81+
(Bernard Llewellyn) *chsd ldr: led bef 3 out: styd on wl run-in: eased nr fin* **16/1**

012- 2 6 **Blake Dean**[42] 2336 5-11-2 **88** CallumBewley 86+
(Sue Smith) *led: hdd bef 3 out: styd on to take 2nd last: no imp* **15/8**[1]

/05- 3 1 **La Belle Sauvage**[22] 2767 6-11-12 **98** JackSherwood 95
(Kim Bailey) *chsd ldrs: hit 2nd: 2nd 3 out: 3rd whn hit last: kpt on same pce* **6/1**

055- 4 ¾ **Stag Hill (IRE)**[16] 2886 4-11-6 **95** (t) MrBGibbs(3) 90
(Bernard Llewellyn) *chsd ldrs: outpcd after 3 out: styd on appr last* **20/1**

522- 5 nk **Prince Freddie**[22] 2770 5-10-6 **78** RyanHatch 73
(Roy Brotherton) *sn trcking ldrs: drvn appr 3 out: one pce* **5/1**[3]

060- 6 5 **Midnight Request**[29] 2614 4-11-1 **90** MrJNixon(3) 80
(Tom Symonds) *nt fluent in rr: bhd and drvn 6th: kpt on fr 2 out* **7/2**[2]

2/0- 7 nk **Cool Bob (IRE)**[36] 2470 10-10-5 **82** (t) MrStanSheppard(5) 72
(Matt Sheppard) *mid-div: drvn 6th: sn lost pl: kpt on between last 2* **16/1**

000- 8 ¾ **Young Lou**[30] 2598 4-10-8 **85** MrTWWheeler(5) 74
(Robin Dickin) *chsd ldrs: drvn appr 3 out: wknd 2 out* **25/1**

P45- 9 10 **Photogenique (FR)**[80] 1718 10-9-9 **72** oh8 MissGeorgiaHenderson(5) 51
(Rob Summers) *nt fluent in last: drvn 5th: sn bhd* **50/1**

/34- 10 12 **Ata Boy (IRE)**[192] 716 7-10-11 **83** DanielHiskett 50
(Richard Phillips) *in rr: bhd and drvn 6th* **16/1**

4m 16.6s (24.60) **Going Correction** +1.40s/f (Heav)
WFA 4 from 5yo+ 5lb **10** Ran SP% **116.2**
Speed ratings (Par 103): **94,91,90,90,89 87,87,86,81,75**
toteswingers 1&2 £5.90, 1&3 £25.00, 2&3 £3.00 CSF £46.74 CT £210.97 TOTE £16.50: £3.10, £1.40, £1.60; EX 76.10 Trifecta £569.20 Pool: £1371.17 - 1.80 winning units..
Owner Geraint Anstee **Bred** Hermes Services Ltd **Trained** Fochriw, Caerphilly
■ A winner on his first ride under rules for Sean Bowen.
■ Stewards' Enquiry : Mr B Gibbs seven-day ban; used whip down shoulder (tba).
Mr T W Wheeler seven-day ban; used whip down shoulder (tba).

FOCUS
Plenty of rain in the ten days since the last meeting ensured conditions were extremely testing. The hurdles had been moved a few yards wider to provide better ground. A competitive handicap for the grade and understandably the gallop was steady in the prevailing conditions. A small pb from the winner.

3189 QUICKSILVERSLOTS GET UP TO £200 FREEPLAYS "NATIONAL HUNT" MAIDEN HURDLE (10 hdls) 2m 4f 110y
12:50 (12:50) (Class 5) 4-Y-O+ **£2,209** (£648; £324; £162)

Form RPR

2- 1 **Wuff (IRE)**[28] 2660 5-11-0 0 PaddyBrennan 119+
(Tom George) *trckd ldrs: effrt 3 out: chsd wnr last: styd on to ld clsng stages* **7/4**[1]

5/2- 2 ½ **Allow Dallow (IRE)**[19] 2850 6-11-0 0 RichieMcLernon 118+
(Jonjo O'Neill) *hld up towards rr: smooth hdwy appr 3 out: led appr last: rdn: no ex and hdd nr fin* **11/2**[3]

16- 3 7 **Cogry**[33] 2534 4-10-7 0 RyanHatch(7) 115+
(Nigel Twiston-Davies) *chsd ldrs: hit 1st: drvn 3 out: bmpd next: kpt on one pce* **3/1**[2]

/32- 4 1¼ **Rio Milan (IRE)**[22] 2768 7-11-0 118 (t) AlainCawley 113
(Fergal O'Brien) *led: nt fluent 6th: j.rt 2 out: hdd appr last: one pce* **6/1**

005/ 5 ½ **Dare To Endeavour**[251] 5289 6-10-9 0 AodhaganConlon(5) 110
(Tom George) *in rr: hdwy 7th: kpt on one pce fr 2 out* **40/1**

354- 6 6 **Grape Tree Flame**[22] 2773 5-10-7 0 TomO'Brien 97
(Peter Bowen) *mid-div: hdwy 6th: lost pl appr 2 out* **50/1**

12/ 7 10 **Master Cynk**[625] 5248 6-11-0 0 JasonMaguire 94
(Tom George) *in rr: sme hdwy 3rd: drvn 5th: lost pl after next: sn bhd* **20/1**

2/6- 8 4½ **Pierrers Bounty (IRE)**[20] 2823 6-11-0 0 RichieMcGrath 89
(Henry Hogarth) *chsd ldrs: drvn 6th: reminder after next: lost pl appr 3 out* **16/1**

43/ 9 4½ **Miss Lucky Penny**[252] 5267 7-10-2 0 RobertMcCarth(5) 78
(Ian Williams) *mid-div: hit 6th: hdwy next: lost pl after 3 out* **25/1**

/50- 10 8 **Barton Rose**[22] 2767 4-10-7 0 MattieBatchelor 70
(Neil Mulholland) *nt fluent in rr: nvr on terms* **100/1**

340- 11 1 **Barton Heather**[22] 2767 4-10-4 0 (t) MichaelByrne(3) 69
(Neil Mulholland) *chsd ldrs: lost pl and blnd 3 out: sn bhd* **100/1**

/42- 12 28 **Barney Rubble**[193] 695 4-11-0 0 JamieMoore 48
(Richard Lee) *in rr: bhd fr 6th: t.o 3 out* **25/1**

5m 23.1s (24.10) **Going Correction** +1.40s/f (Heav) **12** Ran SP% **115.8**
Speed ratings (Par 103): **110,109,107,106,106 104,100,98,96,93 93,82**
toteswingers 1&2 £3.10, 1&3 £2.70, 2&3 £2.60 CSF £10.80 TOTE £2.90: £1.50, £1.90, £1.80; EX 14.50 Trifecta £25.20 Pool: £1944.06 - 57.74 winning units..
Owner R S Brookhouse **Bred** Mrs Miriam Tarrant **Trained** Slad, Gloucs

FOCUS
An interesting maiden hurdle, with plenty of fair Irish point form and recent bumper form boasted by the participants. The first two are above average and should go on to rate higher.

3190 QUICKSILVER SLOTS PLAY £500 ROULETTE H'CAP CHASE (15 fncs) 2m 4f
1:20 (1:20) (Class 4) (0-115,115) 4-Y-O **£3,924** (£1,159; £579; £290; £145)

Form RPR

322- 1 **Hollins**[22] 2772 9-10-3 **99** JoshWall(7) 111+
(Tony Forbes) *in rr: hdwy 10th: drvn after next: 3rd 4 out: led appr 2 out: drvn clr last* **6/1**

431- 2 5 **Ratify**[26] 2699 9-10-9 **101** RobertDunne(3) 106
(Dai Burchell) *chsd ldrs: led 4 out: hdd appr 2 out: kpt on same pce* **6/1**

/31- 3 1¼ **Russe Blanc (FR)**[22] 2772 6-10-13 **102** (p) CharliePoste 107
(Richard Lee) *chsd ldrs: hit 5th: drvn 9th: outpcd 4 out: kpt on to take modest 3rd last* **11/4**[1]

411/ 4 3¾ **Stormhoek (IRE)**[491] 1251 8-11-3 **113** (vt[1]) RyanHatch(7) 115+
(Nigel Twiston-Davies) *w ldrs: led 8th: hdd 4 out: wknd last* **5/1**[2]

/50- 5 11 **Jat Punjabi**[34] 2508 9-11-12 **115** MarkGrant 106
(Jo Hughes) *w ldrs: drvn 11th: lost pl appr next* **9/1**

P3- P **Kilflora**[15] 2903 10-11-0 **110** GeraldQuinn(7)
(Claire Dyson) *led: nt fluent and hdd 8th: lost pl after 10th: sn bhd: t.o whn p.u bef 3 out* **10/1**

/3P- P **Scampi Boy (IRE)**[30] 2599 9-11-4 **107** LiamTreadwell
(Paul Webber) *chsd ldrs: wknd 4 out: modest 5th whn p.u bef next: b.b.v* **11/2**[3]

P1P/ P **And The Man**[286] 4651 7-11-11 **114** BrianHarding
(Nicky Richards) *in rr: drvn 8th: bhd fr 10th: t.o whn p.u bef 3 out* **16/1**

5m 23.0s (17.50) **Going Correction** +1.00s/f (Soft) **8** Ran SP% **112.3**
Speed ratings (Par 105): **105,103,102,101,96 , ,**
toteswingers 1&2 £7.00, 1&3 £12.00, 2&3 £6.60 CSF £40.04 CT £119.51 TOTE £6.30: £1.60, £1.70, £1.90; EX 32.50 Trifecta £97.70 Pool: £2143.69 - 16.44 winning units..
Owner Tony Forbes **Bred** Bricklow Ltd And Hyperion Stud Ltd **Trained** Stramshall, Staffs

FOCUS
A tight handicap, but no great strength in depth. The winner was on a decent mark and has been rated in line with his previous best chase run.

3191 MARSTON'S PEDIGREE H'CAP HURDLE (12 hdls) 3m
1:50 (1:50) (Class 4) (0-115,122) 4-Y-O+ **£3,249** (£954; £477; £238)

Form RPR

/05- 1 **Woodford County**[25] 2715 6-11-12 **115** TomO'Brien 123+
(Philip Hobbs) *trckd ldrs: led appr 2 out: jnd run-in: fnd ex towards fin* **14/1**

/34- 2 1 **One For Harry (IRE)**[38] 2447 5-11-12 **115** BrianHarding 124+
(Nicky Richards) *in rr: reminders 4th: hdwy to chse ldrs 8th: 3rd 3 out: cl 2nd next: ev ch last 100yds: no ex* **10/1**[3]

/PP- 3 3 **Halley (FR)**[47] 2264 6-11-12 **115** PaddyBrennan 118
(Tom George) *led: j.lft: hdd appr 2 out: styd on same pce run-in* **20/1**

/05- 4 4 **American Life (FR)**[20] 2807 6-10-8 **102** (bt) JamesBanks(5) 101
(Anthony Middleton) *chsd ldrs: drvn 9th: outpcd appr 3 out: one pce fr 2 out* **10/1**[3]

U0F- 5 2½ **Robin Will (FR)**[28] 2650 8-11-11 **114** ConorO'Farrell 111
(Richard Woollacott) *racd wd: hld up in rr: hdwy 9th: 4th 2 out: one pce* **25/1**

044- 6 11 **Joseph Mercer (IRE)**[13] 2956 6-11-0 **108** SamanthaDrake(5) 94
(Tina Jackson) *drvn and lost pl 2nd: sme hdwy 9th: nvr on terms* **33/1**

0/0- 7 hd **Canadian Dreamer (IRE)**[26] 2691 6-11-3 **106** WayneHutchinson 91
(Graeme McPherson) *chsd ldrs: wknd bef 2 out* **20/1**

/05- 8 19 **I Know The Code (IRE)**[22] 2771 8-10-3 **92** TomSiddall 58
(Lynn Siddall) *chsd ldrs 5th: drvn 9th: lost pl bef next: sn bhd* **16/1**

/12- 9 12 **Motou (FR)**[16] 2891 8-10-7 **103** DanielHiskett(7) 57
(Richard Phillips) *in rr: drvn 8th: lost pl after next: sn bhd* **7/1**[2]

1P5/ P **The Red Laird**[238] 5549 10-11-4 **110** TrevorWhelan(3)
(Neil King) *w ldrs: reminders and lost pl 8th: sn bhd: t.o whn p.u after next* **25/1**

111- P **Cyrien Star**[7] 3060 6-11-12 **122** 7ex JackSherwood(7)
(Henry Daly) *chsd ldrs: drvn 8th: lost pl and hit 3 out: bhd whn p.u bef next* **5/6**[1]

6m 20.4s (30.40) **Going Correction** +1.40s/f (Heav) **11** Ran SP% **117.9**
Speed ratings (Par 105): **105,104,103,102,101 97,97,91,87, ,**
toteswingers 1&2 £3.80, 1&3 £13.00, 2&3 £9.60 CSF £130.02 CT £2793.78 TOTE £12.50: £5.00, £2.90, £6.10; EX 123.50 Trifecta £982.10 Pool: £2849.16 - 2.17 winning units..
Owner E & A England and A & A Heywood **Bred** Wendy Robinson **Trained** Withycombe, Somerset

FOCUS
Modest handicap form. The winner has been rated back to the form of last year's Towcester win.

3192 DOVE VALLEY MARQUEES H'CAP HURDLE (10 hdls) 2m 4f 110y
2:20 (2:20) (Class 5) (0-100,100) 3-Y-O+ **£2,209** (£648; £324; £162)

Form RPR

061- 1 **Homer Run (IRE)**[17] 2877 6-11-9 **97** AndrewThornton 108+
(Simon Earle) *hld up in rr: racd wd thrght: hdwy to trck ldrs 6th: chal 2 out: led appr last: drvn rt out* **8/1**[3]

21- 2 ¾ **Wintered Well (IRE)**[10] 3014 5-11-2 **90** 7ex SeanQuinlan 100+
(Jennie Candlish) *trckd ldrs: hit 6th: led appr 2 out: hdd and hit last: kpt on: no ex clsng stages* **10/11**[1]

/00- 3 15 **Boomtown**[8] 3029 8-11-0 **95**..(t) GeraldQuinn(7) 91
(Claire Dyson) *led: hdd appr 2 out: wknd between last 2* **16/1**
435- 4 nse **Highland River**[49] 1675 7-10-0 **74** oh3..............................(p) LeeEdwards 68
(Dave Roberts) *t.k.h: trckd ldrs: lost pl 6th: last after next: kpt on fr 2 out: tk modest 4th last* **12/1**
/F0- 5 4 **Madam Lilibet (IRE)**[19] 2842 4-11-5 **100**............... JosephPalmowski(7) 90
(Sharon Watt) *in rr: drvn and outpcd 7th: kpt on fr 2 out: tk modest 5th nr fin: nvr a factor* **16/1**
4/0- 6 ¾ **Sunshine Buddy**[22] 2771 6-11-4 **92**.................................. JamesDavies 81
(Chris Down) *in rr: hdwy to chse ldrs 6th: sn lost pl and bhd: kpt on fr 2 out* **33/1**
/00- 7 5 **Lisdonagh House (IRE)**[22] 2770 11-10-8 **82**...................... TomSiddall 66
(Lynn Siddall) *in rr: hdwy to chse ldrs 6th: cl up 2 out: wknd between last 2* **25/1**
463- 8 9 **Icanmotor**[12] 2980 6-10-2 **76**...(tp) JamieMoore 53
(Claire Dyson) *chsd ldrs: lost pl bef 2 out* **6/1**[2]
0/0- 9 37 **Swing State**[75] 1793 8-10-8 **82**.................................. FelixDeGiles 20
(Tom Gretton) *chsd ldrs to 2nd: lost pl 5th: hdwy next: lost pl bef 3 out: sn bhd: t.o* **20/1**
000- P **Dancing Lancer**[24] 2732 4-10-3 **80**...............................(b[1]) JakeGreenall(3)
(Tim Walford) *chsd ldrs: reminders 3rd: lost pl 7th: sn bhd: t.o whn p.u bef next* **16/1**

5m 32.5s (33.50) **Going Correction** +1.40s/f (Heavy)
WFA 4 from 5yo+ 6lb **10** Ran SP% **114.7**
Speed ratings (Par 103): **92,91,86,85,84 84,82,78,64,**
toteswingers 1&2 £1.20, 1&3 £10.80, 2&3 £7.30 CSF £15.56 CT £117.69 TOTE £8.80: £2.60, £1.10, £6.20; EX 18.00 Trifecta £283.70 Pool: £2505.52 - 6.62 winning units..
Owner EPDS Racing Partnership 3 **Bred** Charlie Harnett **Trained** Tytherington, Wilts

FOCUS
A modest handicap and two in-form runners battled out a tight finish. This is a step up from the winner, while the second has been rated in line with his recent course win.

3193 BANK'S BITTER H'CAP CHASE (18 fncs) 3m
2:55 (2:56) (Class 4) (0-110,108) 4-Y-0 **£3,924** (£1,159; £579; £290; £145)

Form RPR
/52- 1 **Dark Glacier (IRE)**[15] 2897 8-11-9 **105**..............................(v) JamieMoore 122+
(Peter Bowen) *chsd ldrs: pushed along 4th: led 4 out: drew clr next: eased clsng stages* **7/1**[3]
152- 2 11 **Bennys Well (IRE)**[17] 2872 7-9-9 **82** oh1................ JonathanEngland(5) 87
(Sue Smith) *chsd ldrs: led 13th: hdd 4 out: styd on same pce fr next* **5/1**[2]
/66- 3 5 **Rocky Bender (IRE)**[26] 2691 8-11-12 **108**.................... LiamTreadwell 107
(Venetia Williams) *in rr: hdwy to chse ldrs 6th: 3rd and one pce fr 4 out* **15/2**
044- 4 9 **Noble Witness (IRE)**[16] 2884 10-11-9 **105**....................(p) AdamPogson 95
(Charles Pogson) *w ldrs: lost pl 12th: hdwy appr 4 out: tk modest 4th after 2 out* **25/1**
0U6- 5 7 **Bally Sands (IRE)**[27] 2678 9-11-7 **103**...............................(p) LeeEdwards 86
(Robin Mathew) *led to 12th: wknd 4 out* **14/1**
436- 6 20 **Kilcascan**[20] 2829 9-9-11 **84**.. KillianMoore(5) 56
(Rosemary Gasson) *chsd ldrs: drvn 6th: lost pl 13th: bhd 4 out: sn t.o* **8/1**
2/3- 7 20 **Black Is Beautiful (FR)**[37] 2451 5-11-5 **101**...................... IanPopham 44
(Richard Lee) *in rr: drvn along 2nd: sme hdwy 11th: nt fluent and lost pl next: sn bhd: t.o 4 out: virtually p.u between last 2* **5/2**[1]
5PP- 8 11 **Bishophill Jack (IRE)**[26] 2700 7-11-0 **101**...................(p) EdCookson(5) 33
(Kim Bailey) *chsd ldrs 3rd: reminders 9th: lost pl 12th: bhd 14th: t.o: virtually p.u between last 2* **16/1**
3PF- P **Notabotheronme (IRE)**[26] 2702 11-10-0 **85** oh14 ow3(p) RobertDunne(3)
(Dai Burchell) *in rr: bhd fr 12th: tailed off whn p.u bef 4 out* **40/1**
31F- U **What A Good Night (IRE)**[25] 2722 5-11-4 **107**................ RyanHatch(7)
(Nigel Twiston-Davies) *in rr: bhd fr 10th: t.o whn virtually p.u: swvd and uns rdr 13th* **5/1**[2]

6m 40.3s (25.20) **Going Correction** +1.00s/f (Soft) **10** Ran SP% **116.1**
Speed ratings (Par 105): **98,94,92,89,87 80,74,70, ,**
toteswingers 1&2 £5.30, 1&3 £9.40, 2&3 £15.40 CSF £42.65 CT £272.35 TOTE £7.00: £2.40, £1.70, £2.00; EX 38.10 Trifecta £325.50 Pool: £2956.31 - 6.81 winning units..
Owner Mrs N Unsworth & R Greenway **Bred** C Kenneally **Trained** Little Newcastle, Pembrokes

FOCUS
A competitive handicap, but a slight question mark about the form as a couple of the market leaders failed to give their running. The winner was building on his recent run, but was a 130+ hurdler at his best and there's probably more to come.

3194 MARSTON'S STANDARD OPEN NATIONAL HUNT FLAT RACE 2m
3:30 (3:31) (Class 6) 4-6-Y-O **£1,559** (£457; £228; £114)

Form RPR
53- 1 **Son Of Suzie**[22] 2773 5-11-4 0... PaddyBrennan 112
(Fergal O'Brien) *in rr: hdwy to chse ldrs after 4f: 2nd over 2f out: mde up 5 l fnl f: led nr fin* **7/2**[2]
2 ¾ **Great Choice (IRE)**[202] 4-11-4 0...................................... ConorO'Farrell 111
(David Pipe) *hld up: jnd ldrs after 4f: led over 4f out: drvn 6 l clr over 2f out: tired and ct nr fin* **6/1**
3 7 **Padge (IRE)**[321] 4-11-4 0... PaulMoloney 105
(Evan Williams) *hld up in mid-div: chsd ldrs after 4f: 2nd over 3f out: one pce* **5/4**[1]
4/ 4 6 **Kings Bandit (IRE)**[290] 4585 5-11-4 0.............................. JasonMaguire 98
(Donald McCain) *t.k.h: led: stdd and hdd after 4f: outpcd and lost pl over 3f out: modest 4th 2f out* **9/2**[3]
2/- 5 10 **Vineman**[633] 5116 6-10-11 0... JakeHodson(7) 88
(David Bridgwater) *chsd ldrs: wknd over 3f out* **33/1**
0/6- 6 2¾ **The Sweetener (IRE)**[36] 2479 4-11-4 0...............................(t) TomO'Brien 85
(Richard Woollacott) *hld up in rr: outpcd and lost pl over 4f out* **50/1**
7 2 **Solitairy Girl** 4-10-11 0.......................................[1] RichieMcLernon 76
(Harry Dunlop) *in rr: hdwy 7f out: outpcd and lost pl over 4f out* **25/1**
8 6 **Mercers Court (IRE)**[55] 5-11-1 0........................ TrevorWhelan(3) 77
(Neil King) *w ldrs: led after 4f: hdd over 4f out: lost pl over 3f out* **14/1**
3- 9 5 **Grey Earl**[26] 2703 6-11-4 0.. JamieMoore 72
(Richard Lee) *t.k.h: sn trcking ldrs: outpcd over 4f out: sn lost pl* **20/1**

4m 3.7s (17.30) **Going Correction** +1.40s/f (Heav)
WFA 4 from 5yo+ 5lb **9** Ran SP% **119.3**
Speed ratings: **112,111,108,105,100 98,97,94,92**
CSF £24.44 TOTE £3.90: £1.10, £2.40, £1.10; EX 20.90 Trifecta £53.30 Pool: £3349.25 - 47.05 winning units..
Owner Mrs R Mackness **Bred** Caroline Mackness **Trained** Coln St. Dennis, Gloucs

FOCUS
An interesting bumper and the early steady gallop increased markedly 6f from home. The winner was the pick of those to have raced but this was still a step up for this stiffer stamina test. The second and third should win similar races.

T/Jkpt: Not won. T/Plt: £72.20 to a £1 stake. Pool: £81654.26 - 824.98 winning tickets T/Qpdt: £33.00 to a £1 stake. Pool: £5991.21 - 134.08 winning tickets WG

3182 ASCOT (R-H)
Saturday, December 21
OFFICIAL GOING: Soft changing to soft (heavy in places) after race 2 (1.15)
Wind: Squally, across Weather: Very overcast with some rain

3195 FOUNDATION DEVELOPMENTS NOVICES' H'CAP HURDLE (13 hdls) 3m
12:45 (12:47) (Class 4) (0-120,120) 4-Y-0+
£6,256 (£1,848; £924; £462; £231; £116)

Form RPR
013- 1 **Josies Orders (IRE)**[14] 2956 5-11-6 **114**..............................(b[1]) APMcCoy 123+
(Jonjo O'Neill) *hld up in rr: prog fr 10th to chse ldrs after 3 out: drvn 2 out: led bef last: styd on wl* **6/1**[3]
2/6- 2 2½ **Sybarite (FR)**[29] 2642 7-11-4 **112**............................. SamTwiston-Davies 119+
(Nigel Twiston-Davies) *hld up wl in rr: prog fr 3 out gng wl: 6th whn checked and had to switch after 2 out: clsd on ldrs bef last but nt qckn: styd on to take 2nd flat* **10/1**
166- 3 3¾ **Bob Tucker (IRE)**[16] 2908 6-10-11 **110**........................... JamesBanks(5) 112
(Brendan Powell) *prom gng wl: j.rt 2nd: led bef 2 out: drvn and hdd bef last where mstke: one pce* **14/1**
/42- 4 nk **Coup De Grace (IRE)**[49] 2210 4-10-5 **102**.................... JoshuaMoore(3) 103
(Pat Phelan) *trckd ldrs: mstke 1st: cl up 3 out: rdn to chal and upsides after 2 out: fdd* **14/1**
P20- 5 11 **Westaway (IRE)**[14] 2944 6-11-7 **115**..................................... TomCannon 105
(David Arbuthnot) *w ldng pair: disp after 9th tl led 3 out: hdd & wknd bef next* **33/1**
300- 6 16 **Daliance (IRE)**[23] 2755 4-10-6 **105**...............................(p) MattCrawley(5) 79
(Lucy Wadham) *chsd ldrs: nt fluent 10th: sn drvn and lost pl: wl btn after 3 out* **20/1**
451- 7 nk **Boss In Boots (IRE)**[15] 2920 5-10-4 **105**.......................... KevinJones(7) 78
(Seamus Mullins) *hld up in midfield: chsd ldrs after 3 out and in tch: wknd qckly jst after 2 out* **10/1**
3/2- 8 1½ **Forever Present (IRE)**[26] 2720 6-10-12 **106**.................... BarryGeraghty 78
(Nicky Henderson) *hld up in midfield: nt fluent 4th: prog to trck ldrs 10th: wknd bef 2 out* **5/1**[2]
003- 9 3¼ **Miles Of Sunshine**[9] 3046 8-10-1 **95**................................ ConorO'Farrell 64
(Ron Hodges) *mstke 1st: hld up in last: rdn 9th: prog and in tch after 3 out: sn wknd* **66/1**
/11- 10 ¾ **Brave Buck**[45] 2289 5-10-10 **104**.................................... RichardJohnson 72
(Henry Daly) *disp ld: mstke 8th: hdd and blnd 3 out: wknd rapidly* **4/1**[1]
326- 11 40 **Zafaraban (IRE)**[9] 3029 6-10-9 **103**..............................(p) TomScudamore 31
(George Baker) *hld up in rr: rdn 9th: no prog and struggling after next: wl t.o* **20/1**
/00- P **Lone Ranger (FR)**[36] 2492 5-10-11 **105**.......................... AidanColeman
(Venetia Williams) *hld up wl in rr: in tch 10th: wknd rapidly 3 out: eased and t.o whn p.u bef next* **6/1**[3]
23P/ F **Knight Flight**[649] 4816 8-10-3 **97**....................................... AdamWedge
(Anna Newton-Smith) *prom on outer: lost pl 7th: in tch in rr whn fell 9th* **50/1**
42- P **Patsys Castle (IRE)**[45] 2296 6-11-7 **120**........................ EdCookson(5)
(Kim Bailey) *disp ld to 9th: lost pl rapidly and last by next: wl bhd in 11th whn p.u bef last* **14/1**

6m 13.3s (17.30) **Going Correction** +0.425s/f (Soft)
WFA 4 from 5yo+ 7lb **14** Ran SP% **119.3**
Speed ratings (Par 105): **88,87,85,85,82 76,76,76,75,74 61, , ,**
toteswingers 1&2 £21.80, 1&3 £16.40, 2&3 £31.70 CSF £60.35 CT £814.60 TOTE £5.20: £2.10, £4.20, £4.30; EX 87.30 Trifecta £1364.30 Part won..
Owner John P McManus **Bred** Mrs E Moore **Trained** Cheltenham, Gloucs

FOCUS
Tony McCoy described the ground as "heavy, very testing", adding "they need to stay, that's for sure". An open handicap that was run at a steady pace, understandably so given the conditions. A step up from the winner in headgear. The third and fourth help set the level.

3196 DAVID JOHNSON MEMORIAL SHAWBROOK GRADUATION CHASE (17 fncs) 2m 5f 110y
1:15 (1:17) (Class 2) 4-Y-0+ **£16,025** (£5,005; £2,695)

Form RPR
/41- 1 **Easter Day (FR)**[23] 2757 5-11-0 144...................................... DarylJacob 147
(Paul Nicholls) *trckd ldr: upsides fr 12th: pushed along after 3 out and nt gng as wl as new ldr: chal again 2 out: narrow ld last: styd on wl to assert flat* **1/1**[1]
14/- 2 2¼ **O'Faolains Boy (IRE)**[281] 4769 6-10-10 0.............................. APMcCoy 140+
(Rebecca Curtis) *hld up in 3rd: clsd to ld 3 out gng wl: jnd and rdn 2 out: kpt on but narrowly hdd last: hld whn rdr dropped whip 100yds out* **2/1**[2]
221- 3 22 **Baby Mix (FR)**[26] 2716 5-11-3 142.. NoelFehily 128
(Warren Greatrex) *led: pckd 10th: nt fluent next: hdd 3 out: wknd bef next* **7/2**[3]
/U3- F **Join The Navy**[24] 2739 8-11-7 94..(b) MarkGrant
(Kate Buckett) *hld up in last: in tch to 9th: sn bhd: fence bhd whn fell heavily 4 out* **100/1**

5m 31.2s (5.20) **Going Correction** +0.50s/f (Soft) **4** Ran SP% **106.5**
Speed ratings (Par 109): **110,109,101,**
CSF £3.37 TOTE £1.80; EX 2.80 Trifecta £5.70 Pool: £2358.13 - 305.10 winning units..
Owner B Fulton, Broughton Thermal Insulation **Bred** Pierre De Maleissye Melun **Trained** Ditcheat, Somerset

FOCUS
The two with proven stamina drew right away. The winner is rated to his mark.

3197 BGC PARTNERS H'CAP CHASE (13 fncs) 2m 1f
1:50 (1:50) (Class 3) (0-140,140) 4-Y-0+
£12,512 (£3,696; £1,848; £924; £462; £232)

Form RPR
242- 1 **Lancetto (FR)**[17] 2890 8-11-7 **135**.................................(p) AdamWedge 147
(Evan Williams) *prom: chal after 3 out: sn rdn: gd jump to ld last: drvn and hld on* **14/1**
500- 2 ½ **Gus Macrae (IRE)**[21] 2812 9-9-12 **122**.........................(tp) PaulO'Brien(10) 135
(Rebecca Curtis) *a in ldng pair: chal fr 9th tl led 3 out: hrd pressed next: hdd last: styd on flat: jst hld* **8/1**

1/3- **3** *4* **Grey Gold (IRE)**[48] 2244 8-11-9 **137**.................................... JamieMoore 146
(Richard Lee) *j.lft 1st and bmpd rival: prom: led 9th to 3 out: drvn and stl upsides after 2 out: no ex fr last* **9/2**[2]

055- **4** *10* **Elenika (FR)**[21] 2816 5-10-12 **126**...................................... AidanColeman 126
(Venetia Williams) *hld up in tch: bad mstke 7th and dropped to last pair: tried to rally 3 out: no imp on ldrs next* **7/1**

/00- **5** *hd* **Ulck Du Lin (FR)**[21] 2816 5-11-12 **140**...............................(p) DarylJacob 137
(Paul Nicholls) *hld up in tch: nt fluent 9th: tried to cl 3 out: sn rdn and no imp on ldrs* **13/2**[3]

006- **6** *2 ¾* **Consigliere (FR)**[21] 2816 10-11-11 **139**......................(p) TomScudamore 134
(David Pipe) *lost pl after 3rd and last fr next: tried to rally 3 out: no hdwy bef next* **16/1**

/11- **7** *hd* **Pendra (IRE)**[25] 2726 5-11-11 **139**.. APMcCoy 133
(Charlie Longsdon) *hld up in last pair: prog 9th: chsd ldng trio 3 out: sn rdn and no imp: wknd after 2 out* **2/1**[1]

653- **8** *36* **King Edmund**[17] 2890 10-11-9 **137**....................................(t) TomCannon 110
(Chris Gordon) *chsd ldrs: rdn after 7th: nt fluent 9th: struggling after: wl btn bef 2 out* **16/1**

60P- **P** **The Sneezer (IRE)**[167] 900 10-9-10 **117**........................ KieronEdgar(7)
(Alexandra Dunn) *nt a fluent: led to 9th: sn wknd: t.o in last whn p.u bef 2 out* **40/1**

F44- **F** **The Cockney Mackem (IRE)**[34] 2531 7-11-4 **132**(vt)
SamTwiston-Davies 107
(Nigel Twiston-Davies) *hld up in rr: prog and cl up whn mstke 4 out: sn btn: 9th whn fell 2 out* **16/1**

4m 18.3s (3.70) **Going Correction** +0.575s/f (Soft) **10** Ran SP% **115.2**
Speed ratings (Par 107): **114,113,111,107,107 105,105,88, ,**
toteswingers 1&2 £49.10, 1&3 £6.50, 2&3 £11.10 CSF £119.06 CT £590.21 TOTE £18.40: £4.60, £2.90, £1.70; EX 206.00 Trifecta £1273.10 Pool: £3386.58 - 1.99 winning units..

Owner R J Gambarini **Bred** Gestut Ittlingen **Trained** Llancarfan, Vale Of Glamorgan

■ Stewards' Enquiry : Paul O'Brien two-day ban; excessive use of whip (5th,6th Jan).

FOCUS
The ground was changed to soft, heavy in places prior to this contest. The field was soon quite well strung out, with them going a good clip, and the front three pulled right away. The winner is progressive, with the second rated back to something like his best.

3198 WESSEX YOUTH TRUST LONG WALK HURDLE (GRADE 1) (14 hdls) 3m 1f

2:25 (2:26) (Class 1) 4-Y-0+ **£42,701** (£16,398; £8,456; £4,473)

Form RPR

013- **1** **Reve De Sivola (FR)**[21] 2814 8-11-7 160....................... RichardJohnson 161
(Nick Williams) *mde all: often j.w: mstke 5th: nt fluent 8th: 5 l clr 3 out: threatened 2 out: rdn and styd on wl to draw away bef last* **9/4**[2]

/22- **2** *10* **Salubrious (IRE)**[7] 3084 6-11-7 153...................................... DarylJacob 156+
(Paul Nicholls) *hld up in last pair: trckd ldrs after 3 out: gng wl whn tk 2nd but slithered on landing 2 out: nt rcvr: lft 2nd again last* **6/1**[3]

041- **3** *37* **Tweedledrum**[19] 2860 6-11-0 123..(p) FelixDeGiles 106
(Tom Symonds) *a in last pair: lost tch after 10th: t.o 3 out: lft poor 3rd last* **100/1**

454/ **4** *3 ¼* **Time For Rupert (IRE)**[413] 2195 9-11-7 154.................... DenisO'Regan 110
(Paul Webber) *chsd wnr to 3 out: wknd v rapidly: t.o* **20/1**

1/4- **U** **At Fishers Cross (IRE)**[21] 2814 6-11-7 161........................... APMcCoy 154
(Rebecca Curtis) *nt fluent 1st and 2nd: trckd ldng pair: chsd wnr and mstke 3 out: tried to cl but dropped to 3rd bef 2 out where lft in 2nd again: 6 l down and no imp whn dived at last: propped bdly and uns rdr* **8/11**[1]

6m 17.6s (6.60) **Going Correction** +0.65s/f (Soft) **5** Ran SP% **108.7**
Speed ratings (Par 117): **115,111,99,98,**
CSF £14.47 TOTE £2.80: £1.20, £2.20; EX 8.00 Trifecta £99.00 Pool: £5116.68 - 38.73 winning units..

Owner Paul Duffy Diamond Partnership **Bred** Gilles Trapenard & Thomas Trapenard **Trained** George Nympton, Devon

FOCUS
No Celestial Halo (foot infection), so this was left looking a match, but the result was never really in much doubt throughout the final third of the race. Reve De Sivola is rated back to something like his best, with Salubrious close to his Cheltenahm run and At Fishers Cross a few punds off his best.

3199 MAPPIN & WEBB SILVER CUP H'CAP CHASE (LISTED RACE) (20 fncs) 3m

3:00 (3:00) (Class 1) 4-Y-0+

£24,525 (£9,269; £4,663; £2,353; £1,204; £626)

Form RPR

/16- **1** **Houblon Des Obeaux (FR)**[21] 2815 6-11-6 **152**............ AidanColeman 161+
(Venetia Williams) *nt a fluent: trckd ldr fr 3rd: clsd to ld 15th: drvn after 2 out: jnd last: battled on wl flat* **6/4**[1]

4/0- **2** *nk* **Cedre Bleu (FR)**[22] 2800 6-10-5 **137**..................................(tp) DarylJacob 144
(Paul Nicholls) *mstke 3rd: wl in tch: clsd fr 15th: wnt 2nd after 3 out: clsd next: coaxed along to chal and upsides last: wouldn't go past flat* **10/3**[2]

240- **3** *3 ½* **What A Warrior (IRE)**[21] 2812 6-10-0 **132**.............. SamTwiston-Davies 136
(Nigel Twiston-Davies) *hld up in last pair: mstke 2nd: stl only 5th after 3 out: prog to take 3rd 2 out: rdn and kpt on but nvr able to threaten ldng pair* **8/1**

P/6- **4** *6* **Bless The Wings (IRE)**[49] 2214 8-11-0 **146**............. WayneHutchinson 143
(Alan King) *hld up in last pair: prog to chse ldrs after 15th: rdn and no imp after 3 out* **13/2**[3]

0P0- **5** *27* **Problema Tic (FR)**[14] 2949 7-10-0 **132**.......................... TomScudamore 102
(David Pipe) *chsd ldr to 3rd: steadily drifted bk through field: last after mstke 11th: urged along 15th: wknd 4 out* **16/1**

13F- **6** *6* **Storm Survivor (IRE)**[14] 2937 7-10-2 **134**.................(v) RichieMcLernon 98
(Jonjo O'Neill) *wl in tch: chsd wnr after 15th tl after 3 out: rdn and wknd rapidly* **7/1**

1PR- **P** **Battle Group**[21] 2814 8-11-4 **150**...................................(b) BrendanPowell
(Johnny Farrelly) *racd freely: led and sn 5 l clr: hdd 15th and immediately dropped rt out: t.o whn p.u bef 2 out* **20/1**

6m 20.2s (16.70) **Going Correction** +0.725s/f (Soft) **7** Ran SP% **110.7**
Speed ratings (Par 111): **101,100,99,97,88 86,**
toteswingers 1&2 £1.10, 1&3 £4.00, 2&3 £6.20 CSF £6.78 CT £25.83 TOTE £2.30: £1.60, £2.10; EX 5.90 Trifecta £38.50 Pool: £2859.97 - 55.61 winning units..

Owner Mrs Julian Blackwell **Bred** Mme Marie Devilder & Benjamin Devilder **Trained** Kings Caple, H'fords

FOCUS
Not many of these could be fancied, with Hennessy winner Triolo D'Alene, one of three in with a serious shout, coming out on account of the ground. The form is sound.

3200 THE LADBROKE (A H'CAP HURDLE) (GRADE 3) (9 hdls) 2m

3:35 (3:35) (Class 1) 4-Y-0+

£84,405 (£31,800; £15,915; £7,950; £3,990; £1,995)

Form RPR

/11- **1** **Willow's Saviour**[43] 2344 6-10-5 **130**.................................. HarrySkelton 142+
(Dan Skelton) *wl plcd bhd ldrs: gng strly whn produced to ld jst bef 2 out: rdn and r.o wl* **10/1**

/21- **2** *4* **Ptit Zig (FR)**[41] 2414 4-11-12 **151**.. DarylJacob 160+
(Paul Nicholls) *trckd ldrs: gng strly whn brought to chal jst bef 2 out: chsd wnr after: r.o and clr of rest but no imp whn nt fluent last* **16/1**

/34- **3** *7* **Flaxen Flare (IRE)**[34] 2533 4-11-2 **141**.......................(b) RichardJohnson 143
(Gordon Elliott, Ire) *hld up in midfield: sltly hmpd 3 out and sn pushed along in 9th: styd on fr 2 out to take 3rd bef last: no ch w ldng pair* **16/1**

/23- **4** *3 ½* **Chris Pea Green**[23] 2758 4-11-0 **142**............................. JoshuaMoore(3) 141
(Gary Moore) *wl in tch: u.p to chse ldrs after 3 out: outpcd fr 2 out: blnd last but kpt on to take 4th flat* **12/1**

3/0- **5** *nk* **Ronaldo Des Mottes (FR)**[14] 2951 8-10-5 **137**...........(p) TomBellamy(7) 134
(David Pipe) *v prom: w ldrs fr 5th: upsides 2 out: sn outpcd: fdd last* **40/1**

/3F- **6** *1 ¾* **Kaylif Aramis**[36] 2490 6-10-9 **134**............................ SamTwiston-Davies 129
(Nigel Twiston-Davies) *wl plcd on inner bhd ldrs: cl up after 3 out: drvn and outpcd fr 2 out* **12/1**

/16- **7** *4 ½* **Pine Creek**[34] 2533 5-10-12 **137**.. DenisO'Regan 128
(John Ferguson) *hld up in last: mstke 3rd: tried to make prog fr 6th: unable to rch ldrs bef 2 out: kpt on* **14/1**

022- **8** *½* **Shotavodka (IRE)**[21] 2813 7-10-12 **144**............................ MikeyEnnis(7) 134
(David Pipe) *mde most tl hdd & wknd jst bef 2 out* **25/1**

046- **9** *2* **Dan Breen (IRE)**[8] 3066 8-10-10 **135**.........................(bt) ConorO'Farrell 123
(David Pipe) *pressed ldrs tl drvn and lost pl after 3 out: steadily fdd* **50/1**

615- **10** *1* **Waterunder (IRE)**[14] 2951 6-10-5 **137**..........................(t) KieronEdgar(7) 124
(David Pipe) *hld up in rr: stl there whn hmpd 3 out: lost tch and no ch after: plugged on fr 2 out* **25/1**

5/1- **11** *1* **Rolling Star (FR)**[28] 2669 4-11-11 **150**............................ BarryGeraghty 136
(Nicky Henderson) *a in midfield towards outer: pushed along after 5th: no prog after 3 out: wl btn next* **15/2**[2]

3/F- **12** *6* **Irish Saint (FR)**[23] 2758 4-11-3 **142**................................... NickScholfield 122
(Paul Nicholls) *hld up towards rr: tried to latch on to ldng gp after 3 out: no prog bef next: wknd* **20/1**

13 *8* **City Slicker (IRE)**[34] 2553 5-10-13 **138**....................................... APMcCoy 110
(W P Mullins, Ire) *v prom: jnd ldr after 5th: stl upsides bef 2 out: sn wknd qckly and heavily eased* **6/1**[1]

5/0- **14** *7* **Alaivan (IRE)**[14] 2958 7-10-9 **134**.................................. RichieMcLernon 99
(Jonjo O'Neill) *a towards rr: pushed along 6th: no prog and wl btn after 3 out* **33/1**

050- **15** *2 ½* **Vulcanite (IRE)**[14] 2951 6-10-9 **134**... NoelFehily 97
(Charlie Longsdon) *hld up in rr: nvr mde any prog: reminder after 3 out* **40/1**

5/0- **F** **Recession Proof (FR)**[35] 2504 7-10-9 **134**.................(b1) BrendanPowell
(John Quinn) *v prom: hit 6th: stl cl up whn fell 3 out* **20/1**

5F3/ **P** **Landscape (FR)**[244] 5430 5-10-11 **136**.............................. AidanColeman
(Venetia Williams) *a in rr: last after 5th: struggling whn hmpd next: t.o whn p.u bef 2 out* **33/1**

115/ **P** **Totalize**[48] 4737 4-10-6 **131**.. WayneHutchinson
(Brian Ellison) *hld up in rr: shkn up after 5th: struggling fr next: t.o whn p.u bef 2 out* **9/1**

4/2- **P** **Chatterbox (IRE)**[23] 2758 5-11-4 **143**...................................... DavidBass
(Nicky Henderson) *wl in tch: pushed along sn after 5th and dropped to rr bef next: t.o whn p.u bef 2 out* **8/1**[3]

1- **U** **Dell' Arca (IRE)**[34] 2533 4-10-11 **136**............................ TomScudamore
(David Pipe) *wl in tch: towards rr of main gp but gng wl enough whn bdly hmpd and uns rdr 3 out* **15/2**[2]

3m 54.3s (6.90) **Going Correction** +0.80s/f (Soft) **20** Ran SP% **131.8**
Speed ratings (Par 113): **114,112,108,106,106 105,103,103,102,101 101,98,94,90,89 , , , ,**
toteswingers 1&2 £35.80, 1&3 £44.20, 2&3 £103.70 CSF £149.47 CT £2585.75 TOTE £12.10: £3.20, £4.60, £4.20, £3.10; EX 172.00 Trifecta £7522.40 Part won..

Owner Triple F Partnership **Bred** Mrs M Cuff **Trained** Alcester, Warwicks

■ Stewards' Enquiry : Harry Skelton two-day ban; used whip above permitted level.

FOCUS
Traditionally a competitive handicap hurdle and it was no different this time around, although being the last race on the card, it was run on the worst of the ground, which was a pity. Still, the front pair, both highly progressive but at different ends of the weights, drew nicely clear and the form looks good. The winner is developing into a smart novice and the second is on the verge of Champion Hurdle class.

T/Jkpt: £22495.30 to a £1 stake. Pool: £95,050.64 - 3.00 winning units. T/Plt: £320.40 to a £1 stake. Pool: £239,852.24 - 546.45 winning units. T/Qpdt: £34.00 to a £1 stake. Pool: £17,671.60 - 384.60 winning units. JN

2668 HAYDOCK (L-H)

Saturday, December 21

OFFICIAL GOING: Soft (good to soft in places on hurdle course; 5.3)
West bend at inner configuration. East bend moved out 3yds increasing distances by 9yds per circuit.
Wind: Moderate to strong against Weather: Cloudy, sunny intervals

3201 TERRY RUGG MEMORIAL H'CAP HURDLE 2m

12:00 (12:00) (Class 3) (0-125,125) 4-Y-0+ **£7,797** (£2,289; £1,144; £572)

Form RPR

/P4- **1** **Leviathan**[11] 3012 6-11-6 **119**.. LiamTreadwell 124+
(Venetia Williams) *nt fluent: trckd ldrs: swtchd rt appr 2 out: rdr dropped whip between last 2: sn led: pressed run-in: styd on gamely towards fin* **3/1**[1]

153- **2** *1* **Hartside (GER)**[20] 2848 4-10-10 **116**.. MrRWinks(7) 118
(Peter Winks) *hld up: effrt appr 2 out: wnt 2nd and chal last: rdn and ev ch run-in: kpt on u.p: one pce and hld towards fin* **15/2**

410- **3** *2 ½* **Trucking Along (IRE)**[28] 2671 7-11-5 **125**.................. MrBGCrawford(7) 125
(S R B Crawford, Ire) *plld hrd early: sn chsd ldr: led 3rd: pressed whn mstke 2 out: rdn and hdd appr last: styd on same pce fnl 100yds* **5/1**[3]

431- **4** *8* **Smadynium (FR)**[17] 2879 5-11-4 **117**..........(b) JasonMaguire 109
(Donald McCain) *led: hdd 3rd: reminder after 4th: lost 2nd appr 6th whn rdn: outpcd bef 3 out: kpt on run-in but no ch* **4/1**[2]

004- **5** *¾* **Bob's World**[28] 2668 4-11-4 **117**..........(p) SeanQuinlan 111
(Jennie Candlish) *prom: wnt 2nd appr 6th: upsides bef 3 out: dropped to 4th whn mstke last: sn wknd* **3/1**[1]

4/0- **6** *16* **Pertemps Networks**[14] 2958 9-10-13 **115**.......... JakeGreenall(3) 94
(Michael Easterby) *hld up: niggled along appr 6th: u.p after: lft bhd bef 2 out* **50/1**

110- **7** *39* **Radmores Revenge**[14] 2951 10-11-12 **125**.......... PaulMoloney 61
(Sophie Leech) *hld up bhd: niggled along after 6th: lost tch bef 2 out: t.o* **12/1**

3m 52.7s (-11.50) **Going Correction** -0.525s/f (Firm)
WFA 4 from 5yo+ 5lb **7** Ran SP% **108.1**
Speed ratings (Par 107): **107,106,105,101,100 92,73**
toteswingers 1&2 £2.20, 1&3 £3.60, 2&3 £8.20 CSF £22.17 CT £92.97 TOTE £3.90: £2.20, £4.10; EX 20.00 Trifecta £93.90 Pool: £1265.75 - 10.10 winning units..
Owner Harry Ansell **Bred** Laundry Cottage Stud Farm **Trained** Kings Caple, H'fords

FOCUS
In contrast to the previous meeting here in late November, when the chases were run on the inner Flat course and the hurdles on the chase course, the correct courses were in use for all events this time around. The course took 3mm of rain overnight. The winner has been rated to a small pb, and the second and third to their marks.

3202 ONESTOPENERGY.CO.UK NOVICES' CHASE 2m
12:30 (12:30) (Class 2) 4-Y-0+ **£12,021** (£3,529; £1,764; £882)

Form RPR

012- **1** **Mwaleshi**[20] 2839 8-11-3 135.......... JonathanEngland 143+
(Sue Smith) *led: hdd 3rd: chsd ldr tl rdn to regain ld jst bef 2 out: styd on gamely to draw clr run-in* **4/1**[3]

211- **2** *5* **Valco De Touzaine (FR)**[33] 2558 4-11-1 144..........(t) RyanMahon 135
(Paul Nicholls) *chsd ldr: led 3rd: abt 5 l clr after 9th: rdn and hdd jst bef 2 out: one pce u.p run-in* **9/4**[2]

3F2- **3** *15* **Ahyaknowyerself (IRE)**[8] 3057 7-10-12 0..........(b) TomO'Brien 121
(Dr Richard Newland) *chsd ldrs: nt fluent 4th: rdn and lost pl after 9th: struggling bef 4 out: plugging on at one pce whn mstke last: tk 3rd run-in but no ch* **15/8**[1]

04- **4** *1¼* **Noche De Reyes (FR)**[20] 2848 4-10-7 112.......... PaddyBrennan 113
(Tom George) *hld up bhd: nt fluent 5th: detached: tk poor 3rd bef last where mstke: lost 3rd run-in* **16/1**

0/1- **5** *13* **Rockawango (FR)**[40] 2418 7-11-3 130..........(p) DominicElsworth 118
(James Ewart) *hld up: pckd 9th: sn wnt 3rd: rdn and no imp on front two fr 2 out: lost 3rd bef mstke last: wknd* **11/2**

4m 1.1s (-9.90) **Going Correction** -0.35s/f (Good)
WFA 4 from 7yo+ 5lb **5** Ran SP% **106.8**
Speed ratings (Par 109): **110,107,100,99,92**
CSF £12.82 TOTE £3.50: £1.20, £1.70; EX 8.90 Trifecta £21.90 Pool: £1601.37 - 54.80 winning units..
Owner Mrs S Smith **Bred** Helshaw Grange Stud Ltd **Trained** High Eldwick, W Yorks

FOCUS
Only 2lb separated the top four in the market on adjusted RPRs, but the race didn't prove anywhere near as competitive as that detail might have promised. The early pace was decent. The winner has been rated as improving to the level of his hurdle form, with the second to his mark.

3203 CALL 08006118377 OSE MARES' NOVICES' HURDLE (REG' AS THE ABRAM MARES' NOVICES' HURDLE) (LISTED RACE) 2m 4f
1:00 (1:00) (Class 1) 4-Y-0+ **£11,888** (£4,452; £2,224; £1,110)

Form RPR

/11- **1** **Carole's Spirit**[22] 2801 5-11-0 130.......... LeightonAspell 139+
(Robert Walford) *handy: chalng 3 out: in 2nd bef 2 out: abt 3 l down last: styd on to ld fnl 120yds: on top cl home* **2/1**[1]

131- **2** *2½* **As I Am (IRE)**[21] 2810 5-11-5 137.......... ConorShoemark 140
(Don Cantillon) *led: hdd after 7th: sn rdn: rallied to ld 3 out: abt 3 l clr last: hdd u.p fnl 120yds: no ex cl home* **11/4**[2]

/11- **3** *21* **Keshi Pearl**[31] 2600 5-11-0 0.......... JakeGreenall 121
(Henry Daly) *prom: mstke 6th: led after 7th: hdd 3 out: 3rd and wkng whn blnd last* **7/1**

4 *16* **Our Katie (IRE)**[30] 2639 6-11-0 0.......... PaulTownend 98
(Garrett Ahern, Ire) *prom: lost pl after 4th: mstke 6th: wknd bef 3 out* **7/2**[3]

104- **5** *6* **Rosie Probert**[21] 2810 4-11-0 124.......... AndrewTinkler 92
(Nicky Henderson) *hld up: rdn after 7th whn toiling: nvr a threat* **14/1**

224- **6** *nk* **Me And Ben (IRE)**[9] 3030 6-11-0 100..........(t) PaddyBrennan 92
(Fergal O'Brien) *in rr: toiling 7th: nvr on terms* **100/1**

1/1- **7** *2¾* **Tonvadosa**[13] 2973 5-11-0 0.......... JasonMaguire 89
(Donald McCain) *prom: rdn after 6th: wknd appr 3 out: n.d whn mstke last* **14/1**

0/4- **P** **Cabaret Girl**[35] 2506 6-11-0 0.......... RobertThornton
(John O'Neill) *hld up in rr: blnd 1st: toiling 7th: t.o whn p.u bef 3 out* **33/1**

4m 37.8s (-15.20) **Going Correction** -0.525s/f (Firm)
WFA 4 from 5yo+ 6lb **8** Ran SP% **112.0**
Speed ratings (Par 111): **109,108,99,93,90 90,89,**
toteswingers 1&2 £1.90, 1&3 £4.50, 2&3 £8.00 CSF £7.52 TOTE £2.90: £1.30, £1.30, £2.00; EX 10.10 Trifecta £36.60 Pool: £1168.94 - 23.89 winning units..
Owner Paul Murphy **Bred** Paul Murphy **Trained** Child Okeford, Dorset

FOCUS
The second running of one of the six Listed mares' novice hurdles added to the fixture list by the BHA in 2012-13, and a deeper-looking renewal compared to the inaugural running, though in the event few got seriously involved. The first two are smart and progressive mares but the third failed to build on her recent win.

3204 SHIRLEY LEIGH MEMORIAL H'CAP CHASE 2m
1:30 (1:30) (Class 3) (0-135,123) 4-Y-0+ **£9,747** (£2,862; £1,431; £715)

Form RPR

435- **1** **Granville Island (IRE)**[24] 2751 6-11-7 **118**.......... SeanQuinlan 131
(Jennie Candlish) *prom: chal fr 3 out: carried sltly lft last: led run-in: styd on gamely* **4/1**[2]

/44- **2** *2* **Wings Of Smoke (IRE)**[22] 2797 8-11-9 **123**..........(vt[1]) MichaelByrne(3) 134
(Tim Vaughan) *hld up: hdwy 7th: led 9th: pressed fr 3 out: j.lft and mstke last: hdd run-in: no ex towards fin* **11/1**

4/3- **3** *2¼* **Un Guet Apens (FR)**[49] 2222 5-11-8 **119**.......... JasonMaguire 128+
(James Ewart) *dropped to rr bef 4th: nvr travelled: toiling bef 4 out: kpt on to take 3rd appr last: styd on run-in: nt rch front two* **4/1**[2]

/50- **4** *19* **Arctic Ben (IRE)**[22] 2785 9-11-8 **122**.......... JakeGreenall(3) 113
(Henry Daly) *led: hdd 9th: mstke 4 out: wknd bef 2 out* **9/2**[3]

/4F- **5** *1¼* **Tornado In Milan (IRE)**[3] 3156 7-11-9 **120**.......... PaulMoloney 108
(Evan Williams) *hld up: hit 1st: wknd bef 4 out* **5/2**[1]

P **Thouva (FR)**[167] 917 6-11-11 **122**.......... JamesReveley
(Tristan Davidson) *chsd ldrs: wkng whn nt fluent 9th: wl bhd whn p.u bef 2 out* **13/2**

4m 6.7s (-4.30) **Going Correction** -0.35s/f (Good) **6** Ran SP% **108.4**
Speed ratings (Par 107): **96,95,93,84,83**
toteswingers 1&2 £2.40, 1&3 £1.10, 2&3 £7.30 CSF £37.11 TOTE £4.30: £2.10, £2.80; EX 40.70 Trifecta £90.80 Pool: £994.69 - 8.21 winning units..
Owner P and Mrs G A Clarke **Bred** Gareth Metcalfe **Trained** Basford Green, Staffs

FOCUS
A tightly knit handicap, with half a stone covering the entire field on both official and RPRs. The early pace looked generous enough in the conditions. The first three have been rated to their marks.

3205 ONE STOP ENERGY TOMMY WHITTLE H'CAP CHASE 3m
2:05 (2:05) (Class 2) (0-145,133) 4-Y-0+**£21,118** (£6,201; £3,100; £1,550)

Form RPR

11F- **1** **Night Alliance (IRE)**[13] 2972 8-11-0 **121**..........(b) LeightonAspell 139+
(Dr Richard Newland) *midfield: hdwy 10th: travelled strly: wnt 2nd 12th: led 3 out: styd on strly to draw clr run-in: eased down cl home* **12/1**

/20- **2** *11* **Loch Ba (IRE)**[21] 2815 7-11-4 **132**.......... MrHAABannister(7) 140
(Mick Channon) *led: hdd 8: remained handy: hit 2 out: mstke last: no ch w wnr after but kpt on to take 2nd fnl stride* **8/1**[2]

312- **3** *hd* **No Planning**[13] 2972 6-11-6 **132**.......... JonathanEngland(5) 138
(Sue Smith) *prom: led 10th: hdd 3 out: unable to go w wnr after last: lost 2nd fnl stride* **8/1**[2]

/41- **4** *6* **Samstown**[16] 2901 6-10-4 **114**.......... EwanWhillans(3) 113
(Alistair Whillans) *in rr: hdwy 13th: styd on fr 4 out: nvr able to chal* **8/1**[2]

046- **5** *10* **Solix (FR)**[21] 2812 7-11-12 **133**..........(p) JasonMaguire 123
(Ian Williams) *midfield: lost pl 10th: hrd at work trying to make grnd 14th: no imp on ldrs after* **20/1**

/P3- **6** *5* **Wicklow Lad**[40] 2421 9-10-1 **115**..........(v) MrKitAlexander(7) 101
(N W Alexander) *prom: led 8th: hdd 10th: wknd 4 out* **9/1**[3]

023- **7** *10* **Ballytober**[14] 2941 7-11-5 **126**..........(tp) TomO'Brien 106
(Philip Hobbs) *hld up: mstke 1st: hdwy 13th: rdn and chsd ldrs appr 4 out: wknd bef 2 out* **8/1**[2]

F/4- **P** **Tartak (FR)**[63] 1969 10-11-9 **130**..........(t) JackDoyle
(Victor Dartnall) *midfield: rdn and lost pl 13th: bhd and struggling after: t.o whn p.u bef 2 out* **10/1**

P/3- **P** **Safran De Cotte (FR)**[20] 2841 7-11-5 **129**.......... JakeGreenall(3)
(Henry Daly) *prom: lost pl 10th: mstke 12th: toiling 13th: mstke 14th: t.o whn p.u bef 2 out* **11/2**[1]

/45- **P** **Triptico (FR)**[14] 2943 7-11-7 **128**.......... PaulMoloney
(Evan Williams) *nt fluent: hld up: nvr on terms: toiling 14th: t.o whn p.u bef 2 out* **11/1**

0/6- **P** **Emperor's Choice (IRE)**[34] 2537 6-11-11 **132**.......... LiamTreadwell
(Venetia Williams) *prom: lost pl 4th: nt fluent 6th: bhd 12th: t.o whn p.u after 14th* **10/1**

102- **P** **Balinroab (IRE)**[30] 2623 6-10-7 **117**.......... JackQuinlan(3)
(Richard Guest) *hld up: toiling 14th: t.o whn p.u bef 2 out* **20/1**

5m 59.9s (-14.10) **Going Correction** -0.35s/f (Good) **12** Ran SP% **113.6**
Speed ratings (Par 109): **109,105,105,103,99 98,94,, , ,**
toteswingers 1&2 £19.10, 1&3 £27.40, 2&3 £1.20 CSF £101.13 CT £813.31 TOTE £15.90: £4.40, £2.30, £3.60; EX 122.40 Trifecta £1128.60 Pool: £71,938.06 - 47.80 winning units..
Owner Dr R D P Newland **Bred** Mrs Mary Doyle And Peter Sherry **Trained** Claines, Worcs

FOCUS
First converted from a Grade 2 to a handicap in 2005, this was the sixth renewal with a ratings ceiling of 145 imposed, although in the event nothing rated within 12lb of that figure took its chance this time. Self-preservation looked the watchword early on, with the field still quite tightly grouped embarking on the final circuit. The winner has been rated as running a pb, with the second and third to their marks.

3206 NATIONWIDEVEHICLECONTRACTS.CO.UK H'CAP HURDLE 2m 4f
2:40 (2:40) (Class 2) 3-Y-0+ **£14,295** (£4,197; £2,098; £1,049)

Form RPR

/43- **1** **Special Catch (IRE)**[28] 2671 6-10-12 **129**.......... JamesReveley 136+
(Keith Reveley) *trckd ldrs: wnt 2nd appr 2 out: sn jnd ldr: led after 2 out: styd on wl to draw abt 5 l clr run-in: kpt up to work towards fin* **11/8**[1]

0/0- **2** *2* **Art Professor (IRE)**[224] 215 9-10-13 **130**.......... LiamTreadwell 132
(Venetia Williams) *nt fluent: in tch: rdn and outpcd appr 3 out: styd on u.p run-in: tk 2nd run-in 1f out: clsd on wnr ins fnl 100yds: hld towards fin* **8/1**

/25- **3** *3¼* **Morning Royalty (IRE)**[28] 2669 6-10-13 **130**.......... PaddyBrennan 129
(James Moffatt) *led: nt fluent 5th: mstke whn jnd 2 out: sn hdd: no unable to go w wnr run-in: lost 2nd 1f out: no ex fnl 100yds* **5/1**[3]

0/2- **4** *6* **She Ranks Me (IRE)**[23] 2763 6-11-4 **135**..........(p) JasonMaguire 127
(Donald McCain) *prom tl rdn and wknd appr 2 out* **11/4**[2]

05P/ **P** **Storm Brig**[790] 2121 8-10-4 **124**.......... EwanWhillans(3)
(Alistair Whillans) *hld up in rr: stl last but in tch whn wnt wrong and p.u qckly appr 3 out: dismntd* **13/2**

4m 40.7s (-12.30) **Going Correction** -0.525s/f (Firm) **5** Ran SP% **109.9**
Speed ratings (Par 109): **103,102,100,98,**
CSF £11.64 TOTE £2.50: £1.50, £2.70; EX 11.10 Trifecta £28.10 Pool: £1404.52 - 37.41 winning units..
Owner Mike Browne & William McKeown **Bred** Thistletown Stud **Trained** Lingdale, Redcar & Cleveland

FOCUS
The latest edition of this useful handicap was robbed of much of its interest when Puffin Billy, so impressive in landing the Kennel Gate at Ascot this race weekend a year earlier, was struck down with a serious bout of colic 20 minutes after final declarations. This was another step forward from the progressive winner and he's the type to rate higher, particularly over fences. The second and third have been rated close to their marks.

3207 ONE STOP ENERGY RACE DAY H'CAP HURDLE 3m
3:15 (3:15) (Class 3) (0-140,140) 4-Y-0+ **£9,495** (£2,805; £1,402; £702; £351)

Form RPR

/31- **1** **Sausalito Sunrise (IRE)**[14] 2942 5-11-1 **129**.......... TomO'Brien 136+
(Philip Hobbs) *hld up: hdwy appr 4 out: led 2 out: styd on to draw clr run-in: comf* **4/1**[2]

5/0- **2** *2¼* **Matthew Riley (IRE)**[28] 2671 6-10-10 **124**.......... RichieMcGrath 126
(Philip Kirby) *in tch: nt fluent 7th: led after 3 out: hdd 2 out: stl cl 3rd whn mstke last: wnt 2nd run-in: styd on towards fin but nt trble wnr* **15/2**

F/0- **3** *4* **Aegean Dawn**[21] 2813 8-11-6 **134**.......... LeightonAspell 132
(Robert Walford) *cl up: wnt 2nd and chal 2 out: stl ev ch last: unable to go w wnr run-in: lost 2nd after: no ex fnl 100yds* **14/1**

311- **4** *18* **Ballyculla (IRE)**[29] 2652 6-11-4 **135**.......... GavinSheehan(3) 117
(Warren Greatrex) *sn prom: led appr 3rd: nt fluent 4th: hdd after 4 out: rdn and swtchd rt bef 2 out: sn wknd* **11/2**[3]

FU0- **5** *5* **Big Society (IRE)**[14] 2944 7-10-6 **120**.............................. PaddyBrennan 94
(Tom George) *nt fluent: prom: led after 4 out: hdd after 3 out: rdn and wknd bef last* **16/1**

260- **6** *1* **Hada Men (USA)**[21] 2807 8-11-2 **130**.............................. LiamTreadwell 103
(Venetia Williams) *midfield: sn niggled along: lost pl after 6th: sn in rr: t.o 4 out: plugged on past btn horses run-in: no ch* **12/1**

5F2- **7** *nk* **Pineau De Re (FR)**[6] 3108 10-11-8 **136**.............................. JasonMaguire 114
(Dr Richard Newland) *hld up: 6th and in tch whn mstke 3 out: sn btn* **11/2**[3]

304- **8** *2 ¾* **Cross Kennon (IRE)**[35] 2504 9-11-5 **140**..............................(v) ConorRing(7) 110
(Jennie Candlish) *led: hdd appr 3rd: remained prom: rdn whn nt fluent 8th: wknd bef 4 out* **11/4**[1]

/11- **P** **Pension Plan**[41] 2388 9-11-12 **140**..............................(p) DonalDevereux
(Peter Bowen) *hld up: struggling after 7th: mstke 8th: t.o whn p.u after 4 out* **14/1**

5m 44.4s (-15.60) **Going Correction** -0.525s/f (Firm) **9** Ran SP% **116.1**
Speed ratings (Par 107): **105,104,102,96,95 94,94,93,**
toteswingers 1&2 £7.20, 1&3 £9.70, 2&3 £8.80 CSF £34.20 CT £382.76 TOTE £4.50: £1.70, £2.60, £4.10; EX 32.70 Trifecta £1225.20 Pool: £1869.01 - 1.14 winning units..
Owner Mrs Diana L Whateley **Bred** Thomas Corish **Trained** Withycombe, Somerset

FOCUS
A fair stayers' handicap hurdle, albeit one that took a little less winning than it might with a few of the market leaders comprehensively failing to give their running. This rates another step up from the winner and there should be more to come from him. The second has been rated to his mark.
T/Plt: £148.20. Pool: £82,780.24 - 407.57 winning units. T/Qpdt: £29.30. Pool: £6364.31 - 160.60 winning units. DO

3036 NEWCASTLE (L-H)
Saturday, December 21

OFFICIAL GOING: Soft (good to soft in places; 5.7) changing to soft after race 1 (12.10)
Rails on common bends moved on to fresh ground and hurdles re-sited.
Wind: Blustery, half against Weather: Overcast

3208 PIN POINT RECRUITMENT PLACING PEOPLE PROFESSIONALLY NOVICES' HURDLE (13 hdls) 2m 6f
12:10 (12:10) (Class 4) 4-Y-0+ **£3,119** (£915; £457; £228)

Form RPR

313- **1** **Blakemount (IRE)**[21] 2819 5-11-5 133.............................. RyanMania 135+
(Sue Smith) *j.w: mde all: drew clr fr 3 out: easily* **1/2**[1]

2/2- **2** *10* **Greensalt (IRE)**[40] 2420 5-10-12 0.............................. HenryBrooke 116+
(Donald McCain) *chsd ldrs: wnt 2nd 8th: drvn after 4 out: no imp whn hit 2 out: hld whn mstke last* **3/1**[2]

452- **3** *11* **Magic Present**[18] 2866 6-10-12 0..............................(b[1]) BrianHughes 104
(Malcolm Jefferson) *chsd wnr: mstke and lost 2nd 8th: hit next: rdn and outpcd after 4 out: no imp fr next* **14/1**

0P/- **4** *2* **Rinnagree Rosie**[342] 3645 7-10-5 0.............................. AdrianLane 93
(Lucy Normile) *nt fluent on occasions: hld up in tch: struggling 4 out: btn next* **100/1**

3/- **P** **Bishops Gate (IRE)**[312] 4171 7-10-12 0.............................. BrianHarding
(Nicky Richards) *hld up in tch: struggling after 4 out: t.o whn p.u 2 out* **9/1**[3]

6- **P** **My Destination (IRE)**[18] 2874 4-10-12 0.............................. DougieCostello
(Declan Carroll) *hld up: hit and outpcd 9th: struggling fr next: t.o whn p.u bef 3 out* **28/1**

40- **P** **Sgt Bull Berry**[9] 3036 6-10-12 0.............................. TomSiddall
(Peter Maddison) *hld up: struggling fr 8th: t.o whn p.u bef 3 out* **100/1**

5m 46.5s (10.50) **Going Correction** +0.075s/f (Yiel)
WFA 4 from 5yo+ 6lb **7** Ran SP% **113.8**
Speed ratings (Par 105): **83,79,75,74, ,**
toteswingers 1&2 £1.02, 1&3 £1.70, 2&3 £1.30 CSF £2.37 TOTE £1.50: £1.20, £1.30; EX 2.50 Trifecta £10.90 Pool: £1995.26 - 136.75 winning units..
Owner Mrs Jacqueline Conroy **Bred** T Horgan **Trained** High Eldwick, W Yorks

FOCUS
A breezy day made conditions quite testing. After finishing runner-up in the opener Henry Brooke reported "it is hard work out there". A sensible gallop the pace increasing in the final mile. The easy winner was the form pick and has the potential to be a 140+ horse. The second and third have been rated pretty much to their marks.

3209 PIN POINT HEALTH & SOCIAL CARE BEGINNERS' CHASE (18 fncs 1 omitted) 3m
12:40 (12:40) (Class 4) 4-Y-0+ **£4,548** (£1,335; £667; £333)

Form RPR

1/3- **1** **Swatow Typhoon (IRE)**[21] 2803 6-11-0 128..............................(p) HenryBrooke 124+
(Donald McCain) *mde all: pushed along after 4 out: clr fr next: nt fluent 3 out: styd on strly* **4/6**[1]

/43- **2** *9* **War On (IRE)**[36] 2494 6-11-0 110.............................. BrianHughes 116
(Chris Grant) *chsd ldrs: pushed along fr 1/2-way: wnt 2nd after 6 out: effrt next: kpt on: no ch w wnr* **10/1**[3]

132- **3** *8* **Ballyben (IRE)**[14] 2956 5-10-7 0.............................. CraigNichol(7) 108
(Lucinda Russell) *trckd ldrs: lft 2nd 12th: rdn 5 out: outpcd fr next* **15/8**[2]

/45- **4** *66* **Yukon Delta (IRE)**[20] 2843 6-11-0 0.............................. KennyJohnson 40
(Robert Johnson) *nt fluent in rr: lost tch 10th: t.o* **50/1**

440- **F** **Harrys Whim**[22] 2789 8-10-0 62..............................(t) StephenMulqueen(7)
(Maurice Barnes) *chsd wnr: cl 2nd whn fell 12th* **40/1**

6m 24.6s (2.10) **Going Correction** -0.325s/f (Good) **5** Ran SP% **108.3**
Speed ratings (Par 105): **83,80,77,55,**
toteswingers 1&2 £1.02, 1&3 £1.70, 2&3 £1.30 CSF £7.36 TOTE £1.60: £1.10, £2.20; EX 6.30 Trifecta £10.40 Pool: £1648.50 - 118.56 winning units..
Owner G E Fitzpatrick **Bred** Glenn Turley **Trained** Cholmondeley, Cheshire

FOCUS
After the opener the ground was changed to soft all round. The first fence going out into the country had to be omitted due to the low sun. The winner has been rated below the level of his recent runs, with a small step up from the second.

3210 PIN POINT INDUSTRIAL NOVICES' H'CAP HURDLE (8 hdls 1 omitted) 2m
1:10 (1:12) (Class 5) (0-100,98) 3-Y-0+ **£1,949** (£572; £286; £143)

Form RPR

53P- **1** **Rhymers Stone**[22] 2794 5-11-4 **97**..............................(p) CraigNichol(7) 103+
(Lucinda Russell) *cl up: led 4 out: drvn bef 2 out: styd on wl u.p fr last* **9/2**[1]

435- **2** *½* **Lysino (GER)**[22] 2794 4-11-12 **98**.............................. WilsonRenwick 103+
(Chris Grant) *hld up in tch: stdy hdwy to chse wnr 3 out: effrt and cl 2nd whn mstke next: rallied last: kpt on run-in* **9/2**[1]

/46- **3** *18* **Master Murphy (IRE)**[21] 2819 8-11-0 **93**.............................. AlistairFindlay(7) 82
(Jane Walton) *chsd ldrs: lost pl and outpcd 1/2-way: rallied bef 3 out: no imp whn lft 12 l 3rd 2 out: one pce* **11/2**[3]

034- **4** *19* **Baraboy (IRE)**[17] 2881 3-10-7 **92**..............................[1] HenryBrooke 51
(Barry Murtagh) *hld up: nt fluent 3rd: hdwy to chse ldrs after 4 out: rdn and wknd next* **9/1**

004- **5** *6* **Cloudy Deal (IRE)**[38] 2453 6-11-2 **95**.............................. GrahamWatters(7) 56
(Martin Todhunter) *hld up bhd ldng gp: effrt bef 4 out: wknd bef next* **14/1**

/02- **6** *hd* **Silverton**[49] 2217 6-11-12 **98**.............................. AdrianLane 59
(Lucy Normile) *led to 5th: rdn and wknd after 4 out* **5/1**[2]

0/F- **7** *1 ½* **W Six Times**[31] 2596 7-10-0 **72**.............................. BrianHarding 31
(Alistair Whillans) *hld up: struggling bef 4 out: sn btn* **22/1**

400- **8** *7* **Vodka Red (IRE)**[9] 3038 5-10-12 **84**..............................(t) KennyJohnson 36
(Robert Johnson) *hld up: outpcd after 5th: struggling fr next: sn btn* **10/1**

003- **F** **Operateur (IRE)**[9] 3038 5-10-1 **80**.............................. CraigGallagher(7) 69
(Ben Haslam) *t.k.h: cl up: led 5th to next: rdn and outpcd fr 3 out: 8 l 3rd and hld whn fell next* **9/2**[1]

4m 9.7s (-0.30) **Going Correction** +0.075s/f (Yiel)
WFA 3 from 4yo 13lb 4 from 5yo+ 5lb **9** Ran SP% **116.7**
Speed ratings (Par 103): **103,102,93,84,81 81,80,76,**
toteswingers 1&2 £7.10, 1&3 £8.60, 2&3 £7.40 CSF £25.79 CT £114.23 TOTE £5.90: £2.30, £1.60, £2.40; EX 28.00 Trifecta £89.80 Pool: £1230.19 - 10.27 winning units..
Owner G Adam **Bred** Miss Carrie Key-Forestal **Trained** Arlary, Perth & Kinross

FOCUS
A low-grade and wide-open novice handicap hurdle and only the first two in serious contention in the home straight. The first two have been rated as stepping up, and there's a case for rating them higher through the third.

3211 PIN POINT TECHNICAL & ME NORTHUMBERLAND CHASE (A H'CAP CHASE) (15 fncs 1 omitted) 2m 4f
1:40 (1:42) (Class 3) (0-135,129) 4-Y-0 **£6,330** (£1,870; £935; £468; £234)

Form RPR

515- **1** **Badger Foot (IRE)**[21] 2820 8-9-11 **105**..............................(t) DerekFox(5) 118+
(Lucinda Russell) *hld up in tch: stdy hdwy after 5 out: led 3 out: drvn next: edgd lft and styd on wl fr last* **11/1**

/61- **2** *2 ½* **Zaru (FR)**[9] 3039 7-11-10 **127**.............................. BrianHughes 137+
(James Ewart) *cl up: hit 2nd: led and nt fluent 5 out and next: hdd 3 out: sn rdn and rallied: kpt on same pce run-in* **3/1**[2]

/01- **3** *28* **Billy Cuckoo (IRE)**[18] 2873 7-11-0 **117**..............................(b) DougieCostello 100
(Tony Coyle) *led to 8th: led 6 out to next: lost 2nd and wknd fr 4 out* **8/1**

031- **4** *½* **Swing Hard (IRE)**[21] 2820 5-10-9 **112**.............................. RyanMania 92
(Sue Smith) *blnd 1st and detached: drvn along on fnl circ: nvr on terms* **7/4**[1]

/04- **5** *36* **Galway Jack (IRE)**[22] 2785 8-11-12 **129**.............................. AndrewThornton 73
(Caroline Bailey) *cl up: led 8th to 6 out: rdn and wknd next: t.o* **5/1**[3]

3/4- **F** **Whats Up Woody (IRE)**[40] 2421 8-11-1 **118**.............................. WilsonRenwick
(John Wade) *chsd ldng gp: drvn along but stl in tch whn fell 10th* **6/1**

5m 19.5s (-7.70) **Going Correction** -0.325s/f (Good) **6** Ran SP% **111.8**
Speed ratings (Par 107): **102,101,89,89,75**
toteswingers 1&2 £18.30, 1&3 £18.30, 2&3 £3.90 CSF £43.87 TOTE £13.20: £4.80, £1.70; EX 48.00 Trifecta £386.40 Pool: £2114.65 - 4.10 winning units..
Owner Peter J S Russell **Bred** J Moran **Trained** Arlary, Perth & Kinross

FOCUS
After a sound gallop it only involved the first two over the final three fences. The winner has been rated back to his best of 2011 form, while the second, who excels at this track, has been rated back to his best.

3212 HAPPY BIRTHDAY GEMMA FINDLAY MARES' H'CAP HURDLE (8 hdls 1 omitted) 2m
2:15 (2:20) (Class 4) (0-120,117) 3-Y-0+ **£3,119** (£915; £457; £228)

Form RPR

/00- **1** **Sparkling Hand**[17] 2879 7-10-6 **97**..............................(p) HenryBrooke 102+
(Peter Atkinson) *chsd ldrs: rdn and hdwy to ld bef 2: styd on gamely u.p fr last* **8/1**

43- **2** *nk* **Nautical Twilight**[25] 2733 3-10-1 **105**.............................. BrianHughes 96
(Malcolm Jefferson) *t.k.h: cl up: smooth hdwy and led briefly bef 2 out: sn rdn: ev ch last: kpt on: hld nr fin* **15/2**

2- **3** *11* **Chasse En Mer (FR)**[57] 2066 3-10-10 **114**.............................. DougieCostello 95
(Caroline Bailey) *hld up: rdn after 4 out: rallied next: kpt on fr 2 out: nt pce of first two* **11/4**[1]

1P5- **4** *1 ½* **The Flaming Matron (IRE)**[13] 2973 7-10-7 **105**...(t) DiarmuidO'Regan(7) 97
(N W Alexander) *chsd ldrs: drvn and outpcd 4 out: rallied after next: kpt on: no imp* **9/2**[3]

/0P- **5** *2* **Flogarose (FR)**[63] 1979 4-9-7 **91** oh5.............................. GrantCockburn(7) 81
(Lucy Normile) *t.k.h: led to bef 2 out: wknd between last 2* **14/1**

31P- **6** *4 ½* **Hi Candy (IRE)**[84] 1684 3-9-7 **104** oh2.............................. MrRyanClark(7) 76
(Ben Haslam) *hld up: drvn and outpcd after 3rd: n.d after* **10/1**

00U- **7** *4* **Overpriced**[58] 2032 7-11-5 **117**..............................(t) StephenMulqueen(7) 98
(Maurice Barnes) *hld up: struggling bef 4 out: sn btn* **15/2**

046- **8** *17* **Cool Baranca (GER)**[13] 2970 7-11-6 **116**.............................. EmmaSayer(5) 80
(Dianne Sayer) *bhd and detached: no ch fr 1/2-way* **7/2**[2]

4m 8.8s (-1.20) **Going Correction** +0.075s/f (Yiel)
WFA 3 from 4yo 13lb 4 from 7yo 5lb **8** Ran SP% **117.5**
Speed ratings (Par 105): **106,105,100,99,98 96,94,85**
toteswingers 1&2 £19.10, 1&3 £27.40, 2&3 £1.20 CSF £66.63 CT £209.01 TOTE £12.00: £3.20, £1.50, £1.30; EX 94.60 Trifecta £246.50 Pool: £1692.64 - 5.15 winning units..
Owner P G Atkinson **Bred** Victor G And Mrs Izabel Palmer **Trained** Yafforth, N Yorks

FOCUS
A modest mares' handicap hurdle and again only two seriously involved at the business end. The first hurdle after the stands was omitted due to the low sun. The winner was on a good mark and has been rated back to something like his best.

3213 HAPPY BIRTHDAY GILLIAN FINDLAY NOVICES' H'CAP CHASE (12 fncs 1 omitted) 2m 110y
2:45 (2:46) (Class 4) (0-110,110) 4-Y-0 **£4,431** (£1,309; £654; £327; £163)

Form RPR

5/5- **1** **Edmund (IRE)**[9] 3041 6-10-6 **90**..............................(t) WilsonRenwick 108+
(Ann Hamilton) *hld up in tch: stdy hdwy bef 4 out: led between last 2: rdn and styd on strly* **5/1**

450- **2** *4 ½* **Mumgos Debut (IRE)**[76] 1791 5-10-1 **85**.............................. PeterBuchanan 99+
(Lucinda Russell) *led: rdn 3 out: hdd between last 2: kpt on same pce run-in* **9/2**[3]

231- **3** *12* **Cloverhill Lad (IRE)**[10] 3020 9-10-10 **101** DaraghBourke(7) 105
(Stuart Coltherd) *chsd ldr: effrt and pushed along bef 4 out: wknd between last 2* **9/4**[1]

4/6- **4** *9* **Daasij (IRE)**[49] 2218 8-11-5 **103** BrianHarding 95
(N W Alexander) *hld up: struggling fr 4th: styd on fr 2 out: nvr on terms* **8/1**

/4P- **5** *5* **Gleann Na Ndochais (IRE)**[31] 2595 7-11-3 **101** BrianHughes 89
(Alistair Whillans) *t.k.h: prom on outside: struggling after 5 out: btn whn lft mod 4th 3 out* **4/1**[2]

542- **F** **Heart Dancer (FR)**[20] 2840 7-11-12 **110** BarryKeniry
(Simon Shirley-Beavan) *t.k.h: hld up in tch: mstke 5 out: rdn bef next: 5 l 4th and hld whn fell heavily 3 out* **7/1**

05P- **P** **Jimmie Brown (USA)**[14] 2955 5-10-13 **100** (p) JohnKington(3)
(Andrew Crook) *chsd ldrs tl rdn and wknd bef 4 out: no ch whn p.u bef 2 out* **25/1**

4m 13.5s (-7.60) **Going Correction** -0.325s/f (Good) **7** Ran SP% **113.1**
Speed ratings (Par 105): **104,101,96,92,89** ,
toteswingers 1&2 £1.50, 1&3 £3.60, 2&3 £3.00 CSF £27.13 TOTE £4.00: £1.90, £4.20; EX 46.90 Trifecta £181.10 Pool: £1276.42 - 5.28 winning units..
Owner Ian Hamilton **Bred** Raymond Murphy **Trained** Great Bavington, Northumbland

FOCUS
Just three in contention after Heart Dancer, who was making his chase and handicap debut and who looked held at the time, came to grief at the third-last. The first two have been rated in line with their best hurdles form.

3214 PIN POINT RECRUITMENT "JUNIOR" STANDARD OPEN NATIONAL HUNT FLAT RACE 1m 6f
3:20 (3:24) (Class 6) 3-Y-O **£1,559** (£457; £228; £114)

Form RPR

1 **Starplex** 3-10-5 0 GrantCockburn(7) 94
(Lucinda Russell) *prom: smooth hdwy to ld over 2f out: sn rdn: edgd rt ins fnl f: kpt on wl: all out* **7/1**

2 *nse* **Rock On Bollinski** 3-10-12 0 BrianHughes 94
(Tim Fitzgerald) *hld up in midfield on outside: stdy hdwy 4f out: effrt 2f out: cl up whn n.m.r and swtchd lft ins fnl f: kpt on wl fin: jst hld* **14/1**

0- **3** *shd* **Bulas Belle**[14] 2960 3-9-12 0 CraigNichol(7) 87
(Edwin Tuer) *t.k.h: midfield on ins: smooth hdwy to chal over 2f out: sn rdn: kpt on on fnl f: jst hld* **10/1**

4 *1 ¾* **Lilly's Legend** 3-10-5 0 DougieCostello 85
(Tim Walford) *prom: drvn and outpcd over 2f out: rallied fnl f: kpt on fin* **11/4**[1]

5 *3 ¼* **Boruma (IRE)** 3-10-7 0 EmmaSayer(5) 88
(Dianne Sayer) *uns rdr at s: hld up: hdwy over 4f out: rdn 2f out: one pce appr fnl f* **14/1**

6 *8* **Spencers Lad** 3-10-12 0 BrianHarding 78
(Michael Easterby) *hld up: hdwy and rn green 3f out: no imp over 1f out* **7/1**

7 *1 ¼* **Vision De La Vie (FR)** 3-10-12 0 WilsonRenwick 77
(Pauline Robson) *hld up in midfield: drvn and outpcd over 4f out: rallied 2f out: sn no imp* **9/2**[3]

8 *10* **Trooper Royal** 3-10-12 0 RyanMania 65
(Sue Smith) *cl up tl rdn and wknd wl over 2f out* **4/1**[2]

0- **9** *9* **Falcon's Ginger**[52] 2160 3-10-5 0 HarryHaynes 47
(John Weymes) *t.k.h: led at stdy pce to over 2f out: sn wknd* **50/1**

10 *2* **New Zafeen (IRE)** 3-10-7 0 TonyKelly(5) 52
(Rebecca Menzies) *chsd ldrs tl rdn and wknd over 3f out* **16/1**

11 *53* **John's Ruby** 3-9-12 0 StephenMulqueen(7)
(William Young Jnr) *bhd: lost tch 5f out: t.o* **80/1**

12 *99* **Castle Eden (IRE)** 3-10-12 0 AdrianLane
(Colin Teague) *bhd: lost tch 1/2-way: t.o* **33/1**

3m 41.3s (221.30) **12** Ran SP% **124.3**
toteswingers 1&2 £29.40, 1&3 £6.00, 2&3 £4.60 CSF £104.86 TOTE £8.40: £3.00, £3.40, £2.60; EX 131.40 Trifecta £475.70 Part won..
Owner G & J Park **Bred** Jill Park **Trained** Arlary, Perth & Kinross

FOCUS
A junior bumper and all but two were making their racecourse debut. The pace was sound and in the end it was a tight three-way photo. The third is the best guide to the level.
T/Plt: £74.00. Pool: £61,459.44 - 606.07 winning units. T/Qpdt: £71.00. Pool: £4178.86 - 43.50 winning units. RY

[3120] NAVAN (L-H)
Saturday, December 21

OFFICIAL GOING: Soft to heavy (heavy in places)

3215a CHRISTMAS NOVICE HURDLE (10 hdls) 2m
12:05 (12:05) 4-Y-0+ **£7,292** (£1,691; £739; £422)

RPR

1 **Valseur Lido (FR)**[34] 2543 4-11-7 DavyRussell 133+
(W P Mullins, Ire) *trckd ldr in cl 2nd tl got on terms at 3rd and led fr next: j. sltly rt 4 out and next: in command travelling wl 2 out: eased clr run-in: v easily* **1/12**[1]

2 *4 ¼* **King William (IRE)**[21] 2835 5-11-10 119 RobbiePower 124
(David Martin Kelly, Ire) *chsd ldrs: 3rd 1/2-way: pushed along into 2nd between last 2: no imp u.p on easy wnr at last: kpt on same pce run-in* **7/1**[2]

3 *4 ½* **Age Of Glory**[28] 2683 4-11-7 114 AELynch 116
(D J Bunyan, Ire) *led: nt fluent 3rd and jnd tl hdd fr next: remained prom tl niggled along fr 2 out and sn dropped to 3rd: no ex u.p: kpt on same pce* **10/1**[3]

4 *42* **Buachaill Tapa (IRE)**[52] 2161 4-10-11 DavidSplaine(3) 67
(H Rogers, Ire) *chsd ldrs: 4th 1/2-way: niggled along into st: sn no ex u.p: wknd* **100/1**

5 *5 ½* **Augher Castle (IRE)**[21] 2831 5-11-3 MartinMooney 65
(Patrick Mooney, Ire) *in rr for most: nt fluent w jumping at times: nvr a factor* **100/1**

6 *8 ½* **Moonunderwater (IRE)**[14] 2967 6-11-3 SeanMcDermott 56
(R Donohoe, Ire) *towards rr thrght: nt fluent w jumping at times: mod 5th 1/2-way: nvr a factor* **25/1**

4m 3.3s (-4.70)
WFA 4 from 5yo+ 5lb **6** Ran SP% **119.8**
CSF £2.05 TOTE £1.10: £1.02, £1.20; DF 2.00 Trifecta £3.30.
Owner Gigginstown House Stud **Bred** M Contignon & Mme N Contignon **Trained** Muine Beag, Co Carlow

FOCUS
This was a good time compared to the handicap.

3216 - 3221a (Foreign Racing) - See Raceform Interactive

[3057] BANGOR-ON-DEE (L-H)
Sunday, December 22

OFFICIAL GOING: Hurdles course - soft (heavy in places); chase course - heavy (hdl 5.9; chs 5.3)
Wind: Light, across Weather: Fine

3222 BANGORBET CONDITIONAL JOCKEYS' H'CAP CHASE (15 fncs) 2m 4f 110y
12:40 (12:44) (Class 5) (0-100,98) 4-Y-O+ **£2,258** (£658; £329)

Form RPR

4/4- **1** **Ravens Brook (IRE)**[42] 2390 7-11-12 **98** (p) JakeGreenall 116+
(Richard Lee) *mde all: abt 3 l up and stl travelling wl whn lft clr 4 out: unchal after* **5/4**[1]

0/4- **2** *35* **Bringewood Belle**[19] 2872 10-10-0 **72** oh12 (t) JamesBest 50
(John Needham) *w wnr tl after 5th: niggled along after next: lost 2nd 7th: u.p and lost grnd on ldrs bef 9th: lft mod 2nd 4 out: toiling and no ch w wnr after* **11/2**[3]

/P5- **3** *21* **Weston Lodge (IRE)**[23] 2784 7-11-8 **94** GavinSheehan 60
(Christopher Kellett) *hld up: bhd whn j.lft 8th: struggling 10th: wnt poor 3rd bef j.lft 2 out: n.d* **25/1**

- **4** *25* **Bishop's Lane (IRE)**[224] 10-11-10 **96** MichaelByrne 42
(Hugo Froud) *nt fluent: hld up: pushed along whn hmpd 4 out: sn lost tch: dropped to last pl bef 2 out: t.o* **8/1**

/22- **F** **Think Its All Over (USA)**[52] 2173 6-11-6 **95** AdamWedge(3)
(Evan Williams) *t.k.h early on: trckd ldrs: wnt 2nd 7th: abt 3 l down and stl gng ok whn fell 4 out: b.b.v* **2/1**[2]

6m 3.7s (54.60) **Going Correction** +1.875s/f (Heav) **5** Ran SP% **108.1**
Speed ratings (Par 103): **71,57,49,40,**
CSF £8.01 TOTE £1.80: £1.10, £3.00; EX 7.10 Trifecta £48.20 Pool: £1159.54 - 18.03 winning units..
Owner Richard Lee **Bred** Michael Keane **Trained** Byton, H'fords

FOCUS
Jake Greenall said after the first: "You need a horse with a soft-ground action - it's very testing." A weakly contested handicap chase. A weak handicap, but seemingly a big step up from the easy winner.

3223 EIGHTH DECADE H'CAP CHASE (18 fncs) 3m 110y
1:10 (1:14) (Class 4) (0-120,125) 5-Y-0+ **£3,768** (£1,106; £553; £276)

Form RPR

U22- **1** **Goodtoknow**[25] 2749 5-11-0 **111** JakeGreenall(3) 126+
(Richard Lee) *hld up in tch: w ldr 13th: led 3 out: blnd 2 out: drew clr after last: styd on wl: comf* **5/2**[1]

U/3- **2** *10* **Samurai Way**[26] 2730 11-10-13 **107** AidanColeman 112
(Venetia Williams) *prom: led 8th: hdd 3 out: rdn after 2 out: 2nd and looking hld whn mstke last: one pce and no ch w wnr after* **15/2**

/F2- **3** *4 ½* **Gwladys Street (IRE)**[22] 2805 6-10-13 **107** RyanMahon 106
(William Kinsey) *led tl hdd 6th: blnd 9th: pushed along and lost pl bef 13th: struggling to keep up wl bhd 14th: tk mod 3rd appr last: plugged on* **5/1**[3]

504/ **4** *7* **Mortimers Cross**[255] 5244 12-11-5 **120** (t) MrJarrett(7) 113
(John Needham) *prom: led 6th: hdd 8th: remained w ldr tl wknd after 3 out* **14/1**

331- **F** **Wayward Glance**[7] 3111 5-12-3 **125** 7ex (p) WilsonRenwick
(Keith Dalgleish) *hld up: mstke 10th: 4th and abt 4 l off the pce whn fell 4 out* **9/2**[2]

/31- **P** **Allerton (IRE)**[39] 2450 6-10-9 **103** (t) PaddyBrennan
(Fergal O'Brien) *in tch: blnd 9th: pushed along and struggling to keep up 13th: p.u bef 4 out* **5/2**[1]

7m 1.9s (42.10) **Going Correction** +1.875s/f (Heav) **6** Ran SP% **110.4**
Speed ratings: **107,103,102,100,**
toteswingers 1&2 £3.80, 1&3 £2.80, 2&3 £5.60 CSF £19.41 TOTE £3.00: £1.30, £2.90; EX 19.30 Trifecta £86.70 Pool: £3399.08 - 29.38 winning units..
Owner Burling Daresbury MacEchern Nolan Potter **Bred** P J Hughes Berkswell **Trained** Byton, H'fords

FOCUS
They went a reasonable gallop in this fair handicap chase. The winner is on the upgrade and looks a nice prosepct. The third has been rated close to his recent C&D mark.

3224 NORTHERN RACING CLUB "SATURDAY NAPS CHALLENGE" JUVENILE HURDLE (9 hdls) 2m 1f
1:40 (1:43) (Class 4) 3-Y-O **£3,285** (£957; £479)

Form RPR

1- **1** **Rutherglen**[25] 2750 3-11-5 0 JasonMaguire 122+
(John Quinn) *j.rt: t.k.h: mde all: wnt clr after 3 out: shkn up appr 2 out: easily* **5/4**[2]

2 *21* **Mr Vendman (IRE)**[46] 3-10-12 0 WillKennedy 89
(Ian Williams) *hld up: wl adrift of front two after 3rd: nt fluent 3 out: kpt on after: tk poor 2nd after 2 out: no ch w wnr* **33/1**[3]

3 *26* **Orgilgo Bay (IRE)**[67] 1928 3-11-2 0 MarkBolger(3) 76
(John C McConnell, Ire) *chsd wnr: hit 4th: pushed along and tried to cl on wnr 3 out: sn rdn and btn: blnd 2 out: sn lost 2nd* **8/11**[1]

46- **4** *45* **Moaning Butcher**[39] 2455 3-10-12 0 (v) LeeEdwards 18
(Dave Roberts) *in rr: mstke 2nd: pushed along after 3rd: sn wl adrift: lost tch after 4th: t.o* **33/1**[3]

4m 16.7s (5.80) **Going Correction** +0.575s/f (Soft) **4** Ran SP% **108.2**
Speed ratings (Par 104): **109,99,86,65**
CSF £17.63 TOTE £1.60; EX 10.60 Trifecta £26.10 Pool: £1949.68 - 55.98 winning units..
Owner The Beer Swigging Strangers **Bred** Frank Brady **Trained** Settrington, N Yorks

FOCUS
This looked an interesting match between a pair who were successful first time out, but the favourite was below par. The easy winner is on the upgrade over hurdles and there should be more to come.

3225 DUNDEE PARTNERSHIP "NATIONAL HUNT" NOVICES' HURDLE (11 hdls) 2m 4f
2:10 (2:12) (Class 4) 4-Y-0+ **£3,119** (£915; £457; £228)

Form RPR

/13- **1** **Classic Move (IRE)**[30] 2659 4-10-12 0 JasonMaguire 123+
(Donald McCain) *mde all: clr to 6th: rdn clr appr last: styd on wl* **4/5**[1]

5/4- 2 10 **Spencer Lea**[30] 2648 5-10-9 0 RobertDunne(3) 113
(Andrew Price) *chsd ldrs: effrt appr 3 out: kpt on to take 2nd after last: no ch w wnr* **14/1**
/31- 3 2 1/4 **Theatrebar**[27] 2720 5-11-5 0 FelixDeGiles 117
(Tom Symonds) *chsd wnr: rdn appr 2 out: no imp between last 2: lost 2nd last: no ex* **3/1**[2]
00- 4 8 **Unknown Legend (IRE)**[30] 2659 6-10-12 0 WayneHutchinson 101
(Alan King) *t.k.h: hld up: sme hdwy after 6th: kpt on appr 2 out: nvr able to get nr ldrs* **25/1**
- 5 20 **Farasi Kubwa** 5-10-12 0 AidanColeman 90
(Venetia Williams) *mstkes: hld up: kpt on appr 2 out but n.d* **25/1**
4- 6 103 **Crazy Chester (IRE)**[173] 862 4-10-9 0 JakeGreenall(3)
(Michael Easterby) *hld up: struggling and t.o after 7th* **50/1**
/61- P **Going Concern (IRE)**[31] 2614 6-11-5 0 PaulMoloney
(Evan Williams) *chsd ldrs: lost pl after 6th: t.o whn p.u bef 3 out* **7/1**[3]

5m 5.6s (13.60) **Going Correction** +0.775s/f (Soft)
WFA 4 from 5yo+ 6lb **7** Ran SP% **109.4**
Speed ratings (Par 105): **103,99,98,94,86 ,**
toteswingers 1&2 £2.90, 1&3 £1.10, 2&3 £4.70 CSF £11.65 TOTE £1.70: £1.20, £3.90; EX 10.70 Trifecta £36.10 Pool: £3193.89 - 66.22 winning units..
Owner T G Leslie **Bred** Jim Mernagh **Trained** Cholmondeley, Cheshire

FOCUS
Quite an interesting novice hurdle. The first three have been rated close to their marks.

3226 LADY MOSTYN MEMORIAL RED CROSS MAIDEN HURDLE (9 hdls) 2m 1f
2:40 (2:42) (Class 5) 4-Y-0+ **£2,053** (£598; £299)

Form RPR
1 **Dubawi Island (FR)**[241] 4-11-0 0 AidanColeman 128+
(Venetia Williams) *trckd ldr tl after 3rd: regained 2nd 3 out: led 2 out: asserted appr last: easily drew clr run-in* **13/2**[3]
225- 2 4 1/2 **A Tail Of Intrigue (IRE)**[22] 2826 5-11-0 0 WillKennedy 118
(Ian Williams) *led: hdd 2 out: no ch w wnr fr last* **13/8**[1]
5- 3 17 **El Macca (IRE)**[46] 2285 4-11-0 0 APMcCoy 101
(Rebecca Curtis) *hld up in rr: hdwy 3 out: sn trckd ldrs: rdn after 2 out: sn btn* **7/4**[2]
/00- 4 12 **Torgamah Lad (IRE)**[9] 3061 5-11-0 0 LiamTreadwell 91
(Venetia Williams) *midfield: hdwy to trck ldrs 4 out: no imp whn nt fluent 2 out: wl btn* **9/1**
000- 5 5 **Solstice Son**[10] 3034 4-10-11 0 RachaelGreen(3) 84
(Anthony Honeyball) *hld up: struggling after 4 out: wl btn* **8/1**
/P0- 6 10 **Jawahal Du Mathan (FR)**[18] 2886 5-10-7 69 (p) JoshWall(7) 74
(Arthur Whitehead) *hld up: rdn and btn after 3 out* **66/1**
00- 7 3 **Echo Foxtrot**[19] 2876 4-11-0 0 NickScholfield 71
(Claire Dyson) *chsd ldrs: wnt 2nd after 3rd: lost 2nd 3 out: sn wknd* **66/1**
P0P- 8 32 **Secret Island**[7] 3115 4-10-7 0 CharliePoste 32
(Anthony Day) *in tch: wknd 4 out: t.o* **100/1**

4m 20.8s (9.90) **Going Correction** +0.775s/f (Soft) **8** Ran SP% **112.9**
Speed ratings (Par 103): **107,104,96,91,88 84,82,67**
toteswingers 1&2 £2.40, 1&3 £2.60, 2&3 £1.50 CSF £17.66 TOTE £7.60: £1.30, £1.10, £1.10; EX 14.00 Trifecta £28.50 Pool: £3342.28 - 87.75 winning units..
Owner Andrew Brooks & Julian Taylor **Bred** Darley Stud Management Co Ltd **Trained** Kings Caple, H'fords

FOCUS
They went steadily in this maiden hurdle. The winner has the potential to rate a lot higher on his Flat form. The second, third and fifth help set the level.

3227 FOURSEASONS MARQUEE HIRE H'CAP HURDLE (THE SUNDAY £5K BONUS RACE) (12 hdls) 3m
3:10 (3:10) (Class 5) (0-100,100) 4-Y-0+ **£2,053** (£598; £299)

Form RPR
321- 1 **Night Of Passion (IRE)**[6] 3138 5-10-12 **86** 7ex (p) NickScholfield 100+
(Jeremy Scott) *trckd ldrs: led 2 out: drew clr appr last: styd on wl* **11/8**[1]
544- 2 11 **Golden Calf (IRE)**[19] 2874 6-11-12 **100** JamieMoore 102+
(Peter Bowen) *in tch: rdn along appr 8th: hrd at work after: chsd ldrs bef 2 out: keeping on for press but hld whn blnd and nrly uns rdr last: gd rcvry but rdr lost irons: tk 2nd cl home: no ch* **12/1**
44- 3 nk **Bob Keown (IRE)**[15] 2942 5-11-0 **98** PaulO'Brien(10) 99
(Rebecca Curtis) *prom: led after 3 out: sn rdn: hdd 2 out: hld whn blnd last: lost 2nd cl home* **9/1**
1/0- 4 7 **Genstone Trail**[28] 2691 7-11-5 **100** StephenO'Donovan(7) 94
(Alan King) *midfield: hdwy whn hit 4 out: chsd ldrs after: rdn appr 2 out: one pce bef last* **10/1**
235- 5 6 **Landenstown Star (IRE)**[24] 2765 8-10-5 **79** (p) TommyPhelan 67
(Mark Gillard) *led: rdn and hdd after 3 out: wknd after 2 out* **25/1**
2/0- 6 9 **The Last Bridge**[54] 2148 6-10-4 **78** RichardJohnson 55
(Susan Johnson) *trckd ldrs: niggled along and lost pl after 7th: u.p after: mstke 8th: no imp after: eased whn btn 2 out* **6/1**[2]
0- 7 7 **Cooldine Run (IRE)**[19] 2877 9-10-13 **94** (t) MrJRJarrett(7) 64
(John Needham) *hld up: hdwy 7th: rdn to chse ldrs appr 2 out: sn wknd* **25/1**
236- 8 3 1/2 **Artic Night (FR)**[29] 2680 7-10-13 **87** (bt) DavidEngland 53
(Nigel Twiston-Davies) *in rr: pushed along after 7th: nvr a threat* **12/1**
/65- P **Ballycracken (IRE)**[206] 553 9-10-5 **84** JoeCornwall(5)
(David Pearson) *in rr: nt travel wl fr after 2nd: t.o whn p.u bef 2 out* **100/1**
4/0- P **Blowing A Hoolie (IRE)**[82] 1707 5-11-12 **100** (p) PaulMoloney
(Sophie Leech) *a bhd: t.o whn p.u bef last* **40/1**
0/4- P **Radical Impact (IRE)**[46] 2289 5-10-0 **74** oh2 AidanColeman
(Venetia Williams) *prom: hit 3rd: reminder sn after: lost pl whn rdn after 6th: bhd after 7th: t.o whn p.u bef 3 out* **7/1**[3]

6m 15.0s (24.00) **Going Correction** +0.975s/f (Soft)
WFA 4 from 5yo+ 7lb **11** Ran SP% **117.3**
Speed ratings (Par 103): **99,95,95,92,90 87,85,84, ,**
toteswingers 1&2 £5.60, 1&3 £4.30, 2&3 £11.00 CSF £18.72 CT £113.87 TOTE £2.10: £1.10, £2.50, £3.30; EX 22.50 Trifecta £206.10 Pool: £1599.11 - 5.81 winning units..
Owner Mrs Pam Pengelly **Bred** Danny Doran **Trained** Brompton Regis, Somerset

FOCUS
A modest handicap hurdle. The winner was well in on her recent win but this was another step up.

3228 SANTA CLAUS MARES' STANDARD OPEN NATIONAL HUNT FLAT RACE 2m 1f
3:40 (3:40) (Class 6) 4-6-Y-0 **£1,642** (£478; £239)

Form RPR
1 **Cloudante (IRE)**[35] 5-10-12 0 JasonMaguire 97+
(Donald McCain) *mde all: rdn over 2f out whn briefly pressed: drew clr over 1f out: styd on wl* **1/1**[1]
2 3 1/4 **Chantara Rose** 4-10-12 0 AidanColeman 93+
(Anthony Honeyball) *hld up in rr: hdwy 5f out: wnt 2nd over 3f out: chal over 2f out: one pce over 1f out: no ch after* **2/1**[2]
00- 3 16 **Lymm Grey**[25] 2752 4-10-2 0 [1] JackSavage(10) 77
(Jo Davis) *w wnr: lost 2nd over 3f out: rdn over 2f out: wknd wl over 1f out* **25/1**
4 29 **Eaton Louie** 4-10-12 0 FelixDeGiles 48
(Tom Symonds) *chsd ldrs: rdn and lost pl over 5f out: bhd fnl 4f* **12/1**
5/U- 5 21 **Princess Bella (IRE)**[234] 85 4-10-12 0 PaddyBrennan 27
(Fergal O'Brien) *racd on wd outside: chsd ldrs tl rdn and wknd over 3f out* **11/2**[3]

4m 19.1s (13.80) **Going Correction** +0.975s/f (Soft) **5** Ran SP% **110.3**
Speed ratings: **106,104,96,83,73**
CSF £3.24 TOTE £1.90: £2.20, £2.10; EX 3.70 Trifecta £17.40 Pool: £3773.81 - 161.80 winning units..
Owner D McCain Jnr **Bred** Martin Allen **Trained** Cholmondeley, Cheshire

FOCUS
A modest mares' bumper run on poached ground. The third helps set the level.
T/Jkpt: £1420.00. Pool: £10,000.00 - 5.00 winning units. T/Plt: £43.30. Pool: £85,955.92 - 1448.39 winning units. T/Qpdt: £6.30. Pool: £7587.07 - 887.50 winning units. DO

3092 LINGFIELD (L-H)
Sunday, December 22

OFFICIAL GOING: Standard
Wind: strong, half behind Weather: dry, breeezy

3229 LADBROKES "JUNIOR" STANDARD OPEN NATIONAL HUNT FLAT RACE (ALL-WEATHER) 1m 5f
12:30 (12:40) (Class 6) 3-Y-0 **£2,053** (£598; £299)

Form RPR
1- 1 **Uncle Muf (USA)**[26] 2731 3-11-5 0 JackDoyle 100+
(Ali Brewer) *hld up wl in tch: hdwy to trck ldr over 3f out: led and gng best ent fnl 2f: a in command after: pushed out towards fin* **7/4**[2]
2 1/2 **Magna Cartor** 3-10-12 0 AndrewTinkler 89
(Nicky Henderson) *chsd ldng pair: wnt 2nd over 4f out: led over 3f out: hdd and rdn ent fnl 2f: kpt on u.p but a comf hld* **5/4**[1]
0- 3 8 **Ceevee**[61] 2015 3-10-2 0 (t) AlanJohns(10) 79
(Tim Vaughan) *hld up wl in tch: rdn and swtchd rt and barging match w rival over 3f out: no ch w ldng pair but kpt on fnl 2f* **20/1**
4 hd **Double Dealites** 3-10-5 0 DougieCostello 72
(Jamie Poulton) *hld up in tch: rdn whn barging match w rival over 3f out: no ch w ldng pair but kpt on same pce fnl 2f* **25/1**
6- 5 24 **Simmi's Tiger**[22] 2830 3-10-12 0 (t) RobertThornton 47
(Anthony Carson) *t.k.h: w ldr tl led over 4f out: hdd and rdn over 3f out: sn dropped out and bhd* **10/1**
6 19 **Molly Beag (IRE)** 3-10-5 0 BrendanPowell 16
(Adrian Maguire, Ire) *led tl over 4f out: sn dropped out u.p: t.o fnl 3f* **7/1**[3]

2m 47.0s (167.00) **6** Ran SP% **111.0**
toteswingers 1&2 £1.10, 1&3 £5.20, 2&3 £5.00 CSF £4.17 TOTE £3.20: £1.70, £1.30; EX 4.80 Trifecta £36.00 Pool: £3850.43 - 80.17 winning units..
Owner Robert Tyrrell **Bred** Fares Farm Llc **Trained** Eastbury, Berks

FOCUS
A waterlogged track meant the scheduled jumps fixture was switched to a mix of AW bumpers and AW Flat. There was a slight delay to the first when an ambulance got stuck in the mud and had to be towed out. This meant the 3yos in the first were kept waiting at the start, and all but previous winner Uncle Muf showed signs of impatience. The cosy winner has been rated to his mark.

3230 LADBROKES STANDARD OPEN NATIONAL HUNT FLAT RACE (ALL-WEATHER) 1m 7f 169y
1:00 (1:01) (Class 6) 4-6-Y-0 **£2,053** (£598; £299)

Form RPR
1 **Mm Dazzler (IRE)**[14] 2988 5-11-4 0 BrendanPowell 114+
(Adrian Maguire, Ire) *trckd ldrs tl wnt 2nd over 3f out: rdn to ld over 1f out: sn in command: comf* **4/6**[1]
13- 2 8 **Bugsy's Girl (IRE)**[179] 841 5-11-4 0 [1] RobertThornton 101
(Jim Best) *hld up in tch in last: hdwy 4f out: 3rd and outpcd u.p 2f out: no ch w wnr after: kpt on to go 2nd fnl 100yds: fin lame* **9/4**[2]
3 1 1/4 **Seas The Moment (IRE)** 4-10-11 0 TomCannon 93
(Chris Gordon) *led for 3f: chsd ldr after tl led again 5f out: rdn and hdd over 1f out: sn btn: wknd and lost 2nd fnl 100yds* **8/1**[3]
0- 4 26 **Howlin Moon**[8] 3098 5-10-4 0 NathanAdams(7) 67
(Michael Attwater) *t.k.h: w ldr tl led after 3f: hdd 5f out: rdn and btn 3f out: sn lost tch: t.o* **25/1**
0- 5 8 **Sonic Weld**[38] 2472 4-10-4 0 MrJMartin(7) 59
(Andrew J Martin) *hld up wl in tch: rdn and dropped to last over 4f out: sn lost tch: t.o* **33/1**

3m 30.9s (-7.10)
WFA 4 from 5yo 5lb **5** Ran SP% **108.7**
CSF £2.29 TOTE £1.80: £1.10, £1.60; EX 2.50 Trifecta £4.40 Pool: £1564.46 - 264.70 winning units..
Owner Mrs S Maguire **Bred** Liam McCarthy **Trained** Lombardstown, Co Cork

FOCUS
This was not a strong contest. The cosy winner was the form pick and the runner-up has been rated to her mark.

3231 - 3237a (Foreign Racing) - See Raceform Interactive

3127 FFOS LAS (L-H)
Thursday, December 26

3238 Meeting Abandoned - waterlogged

[3003] FONTWELL (L-H)

Thursday, December 26

OFFICIAL GOING: Heavy (5.0)

Wind: Almost nil Weather: Sunny

3245 32RED.COM JUVENILE HURDLE (9 hdls) 2m 2f 110y

12:20 (12:20) (Class 4) 3-Y-0 **£3,119** (£915; £457; £228)

Form RPR

3- **1** **Vandross (IRE)**[16] 3003 3-10-9 0 TrevorWhelan(3) 108+
(Neil King) *chsd clr ldrs: clsd at 6th: chal 2 out: drvn to ld run-in: all out* **7/4**[2]

143- **2** ½ **Akdam (IRE)**[10] 3127 3-11-7 119 (p) JoshHamer(5) 119
(Tony Carroll) *chsd clr ldrs: clsd at 6th: led appr 2 out tl run-in: kpt on u.p* **6/1**[3]

U05- **3** 9 **Shalianzi (IRE)**[16] 3003 3-10-9 102 (v[1]) JoshuaMoore(3) 96
(Gary Moore) *hld up: hdwy 5th: one pce appr 2 out* **6/1**[3]

50- **4** shd **Garde Ville (FR)**[15] 3028 3-10-5 123 (bt) KieronEdgar(7) 99
(David Pipe) *hld up: hdwy 6th: led briefly after 3 out: no ex run-in* **6/4**[1]

00- **5** 26 **Sporting Club Girl**[16] 3003 3-10-5 0 MattieBatchelor 63
(Jim Best) *nt a fluent: chsd clr ldr tl 3 out: sn wknd: 5th and no ch whn j.lft last* **100/1**

05- **6** 18 **Kalimantan (IRE)**[10] 3127 3-10-5 0 JPKiely(7) 52
(Tim Vaughan) *a in rr* **25/1**

2- **7** 11 **Ninepointsixthree**[37] 2577 3-10-5 0 CiaranMckee(7) 41
(John O'Shea) *nt fluent: led: sn 10 l clr: hdd & wknd qckly after 3 out* **10/1**

5m 6.3s (32.00) **Going Correction** +1.775s/f (Heav) 7 Ran SP% **118.9**

Speed ratings (Par 104): **103,102,99,98,88 80,75**

Tote Swingers: 1&2 £3.50, 1&3 £21.70, 2&3 £5.10 CSF £13.72 TOTE £2.70: £1.10, £4.60; EX 11.20 Trifecta £28.20 Pool: £482.70 - 12.81 winning units..

Owner D S Lee **Bred** John J Cosgrave **Trained** Newmarket, Suffolk

FOCUS

Fences sited on opposite side from last meeting, hurdles outside. Top and bottom hurdle bend on outer, bottom chases bend moved out from last meeting. Modest juvenile hurdle form. The first three have been rated pretty much to their marks.

3246 32RED CASINO H'CAP CHASE (16 fncs) 2m 6f

12:55 (12:55) (Class 4) (0-120,120) 4-Y-0+ **£3,768** (£1,106; £553; £276)

Form RPR

212- **1** **Beforeall (IRE)**[16] 3004 5-11-12 120 LeightonAspell 132+
(Oliver Sherwood) *led tl 9th: led 11th: drvn along 2 out: j.rt last: styd on* **5/4**[1]

345- **2** 4 **Upton Mead (IRE)**[21] 2911 6-9-13 100 (b) MrPJohn(7) 106
(Kevin Tork) *chsd ldr: led 9th tl 11th: styd on same pce fr 2 out: hld whn rdr dropped whip after last* **12/1**

4F0- **3** 26 **Donnas Palm (IRE)**[13] 3065 9-11-10 118 (p) JamieMoore 98
(Gary Moore) *in tch tl wknd 10th: sn bhd* **11/4**[3]

/11- **4** ½ **Seventh Hussar**[37] 2580 7-10-1 98 ow2 JoshuaMoore(3) 79
(Alison Batchelor) *chsd ldng pair: hrd rdn 4 out: sn wknd* **5/2**[2]

6m 18.7s (35.70) **Going Correction** +1.775s/f (Heav) 4 Ran SP% **107.4**

Speed ratings (Par 105): **106,104,95,94**

CSF £11.47 TOTE £2.00; EX 12.60 Trifecta £33.30 Pool: £135.22 - 3.04 winning units..

Owner Beforeall Partnership **Bred** Ms Barbara Johnston **Trained** Upper Lambourn, Berks

FOCUS

Modest form, but a progressive winner. This was another step forward for the winner, while the second has been rated back to form.

3247 DAVID HAZELDEN 65TH BIRTHDAY MARES' NOVICES' HURDLE (8 hdls 2 omitted) 2m 4f

1:30 (1:30) (Class 4) 4-Y-0+ **£3,119** (£915; £457; £228)

Form RPR

1- **1** **Spirit Oscar (IRE)**[37] 2579 5-11-3 0 LeightonAspell 123+
(Oliver Sherwood) *racd keenly: mde all: drvn clr fr last: styd on wl* **1/1**[1]

52- **2** 9 **Comedinewithme**[37] 2579 5-10-5 0 ThomasGarner(5) 109
(Jamie Snowden) *hld up in 3rd: chsd wnr 3 out: 2nd and hld whn hit last* **11/4**[2]

/42- **3** 30 **Rising Teal**[32] 2697 4-10-5 105 MattCrawley(5) 82
(Lucy Wadham) *chsd wnr tl hit 3 out: sn wknd* **7/2**[3]

313- **4** 10 **When In Roam (IRE)**[84] 1732 4-10-3 0 CiaranMckee(7) 67
(John O'Shea) *stdd s: nt a fluent: hld up in rr: no ch fr 5th* **8/1**

5m 29.5s (30.10) **Going Correction** +1.775s/f (Heav)

WFA 4 from 5yo 6lb 4 Ran SP% **110.0**

Speed ratings (Par 105): **110,106,94,90**

CSF £4.19 TOTE £1.80; EX 3.50 Trifecta £2.90 Pool: £138.51 - 35.41 winning units..

Owner Million In Mind Partnership **Bred** Martin C Fleming **Trained** Upper Lambourn, Berks

FOCUS

Little depth to this mares' hurdle. The time was good, though, and this was a big step up from the winner.

3248 WARD-THOMAS MASTER REMOVERS H'CAP CHASE (13 fncs) 2m 2f

2:05 (2:05) (Class 4) (0-105,100) 4-Y-0+ **£3,861** (£1,198; £645)

Form RPR

/06- **1** **Zhukov (IRE)**[16] 3008 11-10-11 92 (b) MrGGorman(7) 87
(Kevin Tork) *mstke 4th: sn outpcd and wl bhd: poor 4th whn lft 7 l 2nd at last: styd on run-in: led nr fin* **12/1**

P22- **2** 1 **Morestead (IRE)**[30] 2727 8-10-13 90 (p) JoshuaMoore(3) 86
(Brendan Powell) *led: j. slowly 4th: hdd 7th: sn lost pl: 3rd and no ch whn lft in clr ld last: slowed down considerably run-in: ct nr fin* **5/4**[1]

/P0- **3** 17 **Moulin De La Croix**[13] 3058 9-11-5 100 (t) JackSherwood(7) 109+
(Oliver Sherwood) *hld up in 3rd: wnt 2nd at 9th: jnd ldr whn carried rt and n.m.r last: j.v.slowly: nt rcvr* **4/1**[3]

/P1- **U** **Sablazo (FR)**[30] 2727 7-9-13 78 ConorShoemark(5) 87
(Andy Turnell) *chsd ldr: j. slowly 4th: led 7th: jnd whn nrly ref last: uns rdr* **7/4**[2]

5m 23.0s (48.30) **Going Correction** +1.775s/f (Heav) 4 Ran SP% **108.5**

Speed ratings (Par 105): **63,62,55,**

CSF £28.00 TOTE £12.30; EX 24.80 Trifecta £127.30 Pool: £171.96 - 1.01 winning units..

Owner K Tork **Bred** Sweetmans Bloodstock **Trained** Leigh, Surrey

FOCUS

A bizarre finish to this four-runner contest, with clear leaders Sablazo and Moulin De La Croix coming to a virtual standstill at the last, with only the latter making it to the other side, and then Morestead, having been gifted the race on a plate, finding little in front and being claimed on the run to the line by the outsider Zhukov. The winner was probably fourth best on the day.

3249 32RED H'CAP HURDLE (9 hdls) 2m 2f 110y

2:45 (2:45) (Class 4) (0-115,115) 3-Y-0+ **£3,119** (£915; £457; £228)

Form RPR

4/0- **1** **Jeano De Toulouse (FR)**[70] 1941 6-11-0 108 ThomasGarner(5) 117+
(Oliver Sherwood) *in tch: wnt 3rd at 6th: led after 2 out: drvn clr* **8/1**

112- **2** 6 **Brass Monkey (IRE)**[39] 2535 6-10-8 102 ConorShoemark(5) 104
(Neil King) *led tl 2nd: mainly 2nd after: chsd wnr appr last: styd on same pce* **4/1**[2]

664- **3** ½ **Reggie Perrin**[12] 3094 5-10-2 101 PaddyBradley(10) 102
(Pat Phelan) *bhd: hrd rdn and struggling 5th: styd on fr 2 out: nrest at fin* **5/1**

/FP- **4** 7 **Should I Stay (FR)**[64] 2025 5-11-2 108 JoshuaMoore(3) 105
(Gary Moore) *led and j. slowly 2nd: slow again 6th: j.lft 3 out: hdd & wknd after 2 out* **14/1**

2P5- **5** 3 **Hold The Bucks (USA)**[10] 3140 7-9-7 89 oh8 CiaranMckee(7) 80
(Daniel Steele) *bhd: modest hdwy 3 out: nt trble ldrs* **16/1**

631- **6** 7 **Tealissio**[30] 2729 7-11-2 110 (t) MattCrawley(5) 96
(Lucy Wadham) *hld up in 6th: hdwy 3 out: wknd qckly 2 out* **5/2**[1]

/50- **7** 31 **Expanding Universe (IRE)**[41] 2492 6-11-7 115 JoshHamer(5) 68
(Tony Carroll) *prom tl wknd qckly 3 out* **9/2**[3]

P/2- **P** **Explained (IRE)**[228] 251 6-11-4 114 JPKiely(7)
(Tim Vaughan) *chsd ldrs: wknd qckly 3 out: bhd whn p.u bef 2 out* **8/1**

5m 5.7s (31.40) **Going Correction** +1.775s/f (Heav) 8 Ran SP% **118.2**

Speed ratings (Par 105): **104,101,101,98,97 94,81,**

Tote Swingers: 1&2 £8.00, 1&3 £9.30, 2&3 £2.70 CSF £41.88 CT £180.11 TOTE £8.40: £2.50, £2.10, £1.80; EX 47.90 Trifecta £286.50 Part won. Pool: £382.06 - 0.30 winning units..

Owner D P Barrie & D Redhead **Bred** S C I La Viguerie **Trained** Upper Lambourn, Berks

FOCUS

Moderate form. The second and third have been rated pretty much to their marks in a solid enough handicap.

3250 32RED ON THE APP STORE H'CAP CHASE (19 fncs) 3m 2f 110y

3:20 (3:20) (Class 5) (0-95,94) 4-Y-0+ **£2,144** (£629; £314; £157)

Form RPR

/32- **1** **Alteranthela (IRE)**[29] 2743 9-11-0 81 (b) ColinBolger 90
(Richard Rowe) *mde most: hld on gamely u.p fr 2 out* **5/2**[1]

P25- **2** 1 **According To Them (IRE)**[10] 3139 9-9-13 71 ow2(t) ConorShoemark(5) 79
(Daniel Steele) *hld up: smooth hdwy 4 out: chsd wnr 3 out: kpt on run-in: jst hld* **6/1**

4/3- **3** 73 **Cypress Grove (IRE)**[16] 3008 10-11-9 90 (vt) DaveCrosse 25
(John Ryall) *blnd 1st: sn prom: w wnr fr 11th tl wknd 3 out* **8/1**

315- **4** 50 **Princely Hero (IRE)**[16] 3008 9-11-12 93 (tp) MarcGoldstein
(Chris Gordon) *in tch tl 4th: sn last and drvn along: no ch fr 14th* **7/1**

6P4- **P** **Regal Park (IRE)**[30] 2726 6-11-1 85 JoshuaMoore(3)
(Gary Moore) *in tch: wnt 3rd at 12th: wknd 4 out: bhd whn p.u bef 3 out* **4/1**[3]

5/4- **P** **Tara Tavey (IRE)**[35] 2619 8-10-3 80 JonPark(10)
(Kevin Bishop) *prom tl lost pl 12th: wl bhd whn p.u bef last* **11/4**[2]

7m 59.6s (58.50) **Going Correction** +1.775s/f (Heav) 6 Ran SP% **113.1**

Speed ratings (Par 103): **84,83,62,47,**

Tote Swingers: 1&2 £2.40, 1&3 £2.00, 2&3 £6.20 CSF £17.49 CT £102.35 TOTE £2.80: £2.00, £3.00; EX 23.40 Trifecta £140.50 Pool: £336.18 - 1.79 winning units..

Owner Tim Clowes **Bred** Harold McGahern **Trained** Sullington, W Sussex

FOCUS

Moderate form. The winner has been rated similar to his recent win, and the second to his mark.

3251 32REDPOKER.COM CONDITIONAL JOCKEYS' H'CAP HURDLE (10 hdls) 2m 4f

3:50 (3:50) (Class 5) (0-95,95) 3-Y-0+ **£1,949** (£572; £286; £143)

Form RPR

434- **1** **Peqeno Diablo (IRE)**[16] 3009 8-10-3 69 (tp) JoshHamer 70
(Claire Dyson) *sn w ldr: led 6th: hld on wl u.p run-in* **9/4**[1]

346- **2** ½ **Miss Mayfair (IRE)**[26] 2827 6-11-5 85 JoshuaMoore 86
(Lawney Hill) *hld up in rr: j. slowly 3rd: styd on fr 3 out: wnt 2nd and clsd on wnr run-in: jst hld nr fin* **9/4**[1]

0/0- **3** 8 **Juicy Legend**[237] 95 6-10-6 80 LouisMuspratt(8) 73
(Chris Gordon) *chsd ldrs: wnt 2nd at 7th tl no ex run-in* **4/1**[2]

400- **4** 64 **El Toreros (USA)**[56] 2169 5-11-4 92 (vt) JPKiely(8) 65
(Tim Vaughan) *in tch: rdn 3 out: sn outpcd: 4th and btn whn blnd and slipped bdly last* **4/1**[2]

6/P- **P** **Niceboy (IRE)**[10] 3138 9-10-0 66 oh4 (b[1]) ConorShoemark
(Daniel Steele) *racd keenly: led tl 6th: sn bhd: p.u bef 2 out* **10/1**[3]

5m 50.1s (50.70) **Going Correction** +1.775s/f (Heav) 5 Ran SP% **110.6**

Speed ratings (Par 103): **69,68,65,40,**

CSF £7.94 TOTE £2.70: £1.80, £1.50; EX 4.00 Trifecta £14.70 Pool: £255.71 - 13.01 winning units..

Owner FSF Racing **Bred** Noel Finegan **Trained** Cleeve Prior, Worcs

■ Stewards' Enquiry : Joshua Moore two-day ban: use of whip (9-10 Jan)

FOCUS

The front pair drew clear late on. The time was slow and the first two have been rated to their marks.

T/Plt: £748.60 to a £1 stake. Pool: £41,805.99 - 40.76 winning tickets. T/Qpdt: £198.30 to a £1 stake. Pool: £2,224.80 - 8.30 winning tickets. LM

[3029] HUNTINGDON (R-H)

Thursday, December 26

3252 Meeting Abandoned - waterlogged

[2711]KEMPTON (R-H)

Thursday, December 26

OFFICIAL GOING: Soft (heavy on bend alongside lake; chs 5.2 hdl 4.7)
Wind: Light; across Weather: Overcast, becoming brighter

3258 WILLIAM HILL - IN THE APP STORE NOVICES' HURDLE (8 hdls) 2m

12:50 (12:50) (Class 2) 4-Y-0+

£9,384 (£2,772; £1,386; £693; £346; £174)

Form RPR

/41- **1** **Amore Alato**[47] 2369 4-11-8 127 .... RichardJohnson 139+
(Nick Williams) *str: mde all and varied the pce: kicked on after 3 out: rdn bef next where nt fluent: hrd pressed after last: fnd more and gng away at fin* **12/1**

0/5- **2** *1 ½* **Fascino Rustico**[27] 2802 5-11-0 0 ....(t) DarylJacob 129+
(Paul Nicholls) *trckd ldrs: sltly outpcd and lost pl after 3 out: rallied bef next: wnt 2nd last: upsides flat: nt qckn nr fin* **16/1**

/31- **3** *1 ½* **Sgt Reckless**[31] 2711 6-11-5 0 .... DominicElsworth 132
(Mick Channon) *chsd wnr: rdn and tried to chal fr 2 out: lost 2nd but stl cl up last: one pce flat* **10/3**[3]

1- **4** *5* **Vaniteux (FR)**[19] 2947 4-11-8 0 .... BarryGeraghty 135+
(Nicky Henderson) *lw: scruffy rnd of jumping: t.k.h: trckd ldrs: rdn to chse ldng pair bef 2 out: trying to mount a chal whn mstke last and slipped on landing: nt rcvr* **9/4**[1]

143- **5** *14* **Champagne At Tara**[19] 2947 4-11-0 0 .... APMcCoy 113+
(Jonjo O'Neill) *tk v t.k.h: hld up in last pair: outpcd and nudged along after 3 out: nvr involved after* **4/1**

4- **6** *22* **Sukiyaki (IRE)**[13] 3061 4-11-0 0 .... NoelFehily 86
(Charlie Longsdon) *lw: chsd ldrs tl wknd qckly after 3 out: t.o* **100/1**

1- **P** **Dubai Prince (IRE)**[38] 2563 5-11-5 0 .... DenisO'Regan
(John Ferguson) *t.k.h: hld up in last pair: nt fluent 5th: prog to trck ldrs after 3 out: wknd qckly bef 2 out: wl bhd whn p.u bef last* **3/1**[2]

3m 59.9s (1.80) **Going Correction** +0.30s/f (Yiel) **7** Ran SP% **113.4**
Speed ratings (Par 109): **107,106,105,103,96 85,**
toteswingers 1&2 £18.90, 1&3 £7.30, 2&3 £10.80 CSF £154.16 TOTE £15.60: £4.40, £7.20; EX 196.30 Trifecta £661.80 Pool: £2,467.09 - 2.79 winning units..
Owner Mrs Sarah Faulks **Bred** Mr And Mrs N Faulks **Trained** George Nympton, Devon

FOCUS
6yds of fresh ground on both courses and distances as advertised. The riders described the ground as "soft", with Richard Johnson on the winner adding that it was "tiring, and hard work" and Barry Geraghty describing it as "very fresh, but very deep." The opening time was almost 18sec slower than standard. This is usually a warm novice hurdle. Menorah won it in 2009 before taking the Supreme Novices' later in the season. The winner has been rated as taking a big step forward, but still 10lb plus off a typical Supreme winner.

3259 WILLIAM HILL - DOWNLOAD THE APP NOVICES' LIMITED H'CAP CHASE (16 fncs) 2m 4f 110y

1:25 (1:30) (Class 3) (0-140,137) 4-Y-0+

£12,512 (£3,696; £1,848; £924; £462; £232)

Form RPR

/32- **1** **Loose Chips**[39] 2539 7-11-3 **135** ....(b) NoelFehily 142
(Charlie Longsdon) *mde all: blnd 2nd: jnd briefly 11th: rdn 3 out: at least 2 l clr last: jst hld on* **8/1**

/34- **2** *shd* **Ohio Gold (IRE)**[43] 2460 7-10-12 **130** ....(t) JoeTizzard 138
(Colin Tizzard) *occasionally j.lft: trckd ldrs: pushed along bef 3 out to stay in tch: drvn 2 out: wnt 2nd after last: clsd on wnr nr fin: jst failed* **5/1**[3]

0/2- **3** *1 ¾* **Urbain De Sivola (FR)**[19] 2951 5-11-3 **135** .... DarylJacob 142+
(Paul Nicholls) *lw: sn trckd wnr: chal 11th but btn off: tried to chal again but j.lft fr 3 out: lost 2nd after last: one pce* **10/3**[1]

/53- **4** *47* **Thunderstorm (IRE)**[19] 2945 8-10-9 **127** .... APMcCoy 84
(Philip Hobbs) *hld up in last pair: nt fluent 1st: j.lft fr 8th: brief effrt 10th: lft bhd fr next: wl t.o* **8/1**

0/2- **5** *7* **Ericht (IRE)**[27] 2782 7-11-3 **135** .... BarryGeraghty 85
(Nicky Henderson) *lw: hld up in last pair: wknd tamely and j. slowly fr 10th: wl t.o* **7/2**[2]

252- **6** *2 ¼* **Roger Beantown (IRE)**[20] 2928 8-10-9 **127** ....(p) DaveCrosse 75
(Zoe Davison) *chsd ldrs: mstke 5th: blnd 8th: lost tch fr 11th: mstke 4 out: wl t.o* **16/1**

1P0- **P** **Oscar Magic (IRE)**[19] 2949 6-10-10 **128** ....(t) SamTwiston-Davies
(Nigel Twiston-Davies) *lw: set off promly but j. bdly lft and last fr 4th: in tch but hanging lft whn p.u after 7th* **10/1**

5m 17.5s (0.90) **Going Correction** +0.30s/f (Yiel) **7** Ran SP% **99.2**
Speed ratings (Par 107): **110,109,109,91,88 87,**
toteswingers 1&2 £5.80, 1&3 £4.30, 2&3 £4.30 CSF £35.29 CT £103.65 TOTE £7.40: £3.10, £2.40; EX 31.70 Trifecta £92.10 Pool: £1,984.04 - 16.15 winning units..
Owner Barrels Of Courage **Bred** Peter Lamyman **Trained** Over Norton, Oxon
■ Western Warhorse was withdrawn. Price at time of withdrawal 6-1. Rule 4 applies to all bets - deduction 10p in the pound.

FOCUS
The chase track seemed to be riding slightly quicker than the hurdles course. A decent event won 12 months ago by Rajdhani Express, who went on to land the novice handicap at the Cheltenham festival. The race was delayed slightly after Western Warhorse, who was withdrawn, got loose down at the start. The winner has been rated as improving to the level of his best course hurdles win, with the second back to form.

3260 KAUTO STAR NOVICES' CHASE (IN MEMORY OF NIGEL CLARK) (FORMERLY THE FELTHAM NOVICES' CHASE) (GRADE 1) (18 fncs) 3m

2:00 (2:00) (Class 1) 4-Y-0+ **£39,865** (£14,959; £7,490; £3,731; £1,876)

Form RPR

162- **1** **Annacotty (IRE)**[19] 2941 5-11-7 130 ....(b[1]) IanPopham 155+
(Martin Keighley) *mstke 1st: mde all: gng best fr 4 out: drew clr bef next: mstke 2 out: comf* **12/1**

111- **2** *10* **Green Flag (IRE)**[26] 2817 6-11-7 145 .... TomScudamore 144
(Lucinda Russell) *trckd ldrs: rdn 4 out: wnt 2nd next: no imp on wnr after* **7/2**[2]

132- **3** *8* **Third Intention (IRE)**[28] 2756 6-11-7 147 ....(t) JoeTizzard 136
(Colin Tizzard) *trckd ldng pair: dropped to 4th pl after 11th whn rdn w no rspnse: sed jumping lft after: tk modest 3rd bef last* **6/1**[3]

/21- **4** *11* **Just A Par (IRE)**[28] 2756 6-11-7 148 .... DarylJacob 128
(Paul Nicholls) *lw: trckd wnr: chal 1/2-way: rdn 13th: no imp 4 out: lost 2nd and wknd qckly 3 out* **8/13**[1]

143- **5** *61* **Buachaill Alainn (IRE)**[12] 3095 6-11-7 132 ....(p) RichardJohnson 64
(Peter Bowen) *nt fluent: struggling in last pl fr 7th: blnd 11th: t.o after: btn more than a fence* **25/1**

6m 17.1s (1.70) **Going Correction** +0.30s/f (Yiel) **5** Ran SP% **110.0**
Speed ratings (Par 117): **109,105,103,99,79**
CSF £50.81 TOTE £13.10: £4.30, £1.90; EX 52.90 Trifecta £73.10 Pool: £4,514.65 - 46.27 winning units..
Owner Mrs Peter Prowting **Bred** Patrick Crotty Jnr **Trained** Condicote, Gloucs

FOCUS
Long Run won this in 2009, while there was a vintage edition two years ago when Grands Crus beat Silviniaco Conti and Bobs Worth. This was perhaps not a strong renewal of the race previously known as the Feltham, with victory going to the runner with the least chance on official figures. The winner has been rated as taking a big step up in the headgear, with the third and fourth clearly well below their best.

3261 WILLIAMHILL.COM CHRISTMAS HURDLE (GRADE 1) (8 hdls) 2m

2:35 (2:35) (Class 1) 4-Y-0+

£56,950 (£21,370; £10,700; £5,330; £2,680; £1,340)

Form RPR

1/1- **1** **My Tent Or Yours (IRE)**[26] 2821 6-11-7 160 .... APMcCoy 171+
(Nicky Henderson) *lw: hld up in last pair: trckd ldrs and mstke 5th: wnt 2nd after 3 out: rdn after 2 out: lft upsides after last: drvn to ld fnl 100yds: styd on gamely* **11/8**[2]

/11- **2** *½* **The New One (IRE)**[12] 3083 5-11-7 167 .... SamTwiston-Davies 171+
(Nigel Twiston-Davies) *lw: trckd ldr: led 3 out: drvn bef next: abt a l up and keeping on whn blnd last and rdr lost an iron: hdd fnl 100yds: styd on but hld nr fin* **5/6**[1]

/12- **3** *28* **Sametegal (FR)**[39] 2533 4-11-7 150 ....(t) DarylJacob 144
(Paul Nicholls) *trckd ldrs: cl up whn mstke 3 out: sn lft bhd: tk poor 3rd after 2 out* **12/1**[3]

1/6- **4** *6* **Duke Of Navan (IRE)**[26] 2821 5-11-7 145 .... BrianHarding 136
(Nicky Richards) *led to 3 out: sn lft bhd: lost poor 3rd after 2 out* **50/1**

4/3- **5** *8* **Grumeti**[26] 2821 5-11-7 151 .... RobertThornton 131
(Alan King) *trckd ldng pair: cl up 3 out: sn rdn and wknd: eased bef next* **16/1**

PPP- **6** *60* **Chapel House**[78] 1824 10-11-7 74 .... ThomasCheesman 68
(Richard Harper) *a last: in tch to 5th: sn t.o* **100/1**

3m 55.2s (-2.90) **Going Correction** +0.30s/f (Yiel) **6** Ran SP% **113.2**
Speed ratings (Par 117): **119,118,104,101,97 67**
toteswingers 1&2 £1.02, 1&3 £1.70, 2&3 £2.30 CSF £3.02 TOTE £2.20: £1.20, £1.10; EX 3.10 Trifecta £9.10 Pool: £6,965.13 - 568.97 winning units..
Owner John P McManus **Bred** F Dunne **Trained** Upper Lambourn, Berks

FOCUS
This was a compelling clash on paper between two leading Champion Hurdle contenders, and the race didn't disappoint, with both enhancing their credentials for the big race. With no obvious front runner in the field there were doubts over who would make the pace, but Duke Of Navan carried out that role. The early gallop didn't look strong, but the time was good, around five seconds quicker than the novice hurdle, with the first two fairly tanking from the home turn. The first two are on the upgrade, are potential 170+ hurdlers, and there's a case for rating the race 7lb higher through the third.

3262 WILLIAM HILL KING GEORGE VI CHASE (GRADE 1) (18 fncs) 3m

3:10 (3:10) (Class 1) 4-Y-0 **£114,436** (£43,276; £21,936; £11,196; £5,896)

Form RPR

3/3- **1** **Silviniaco Conti (FR)**[33] 2673 7-11-10 173 .... NoelFehily 179
(Paul Nicholls) *lw: mostly trckd ldr: rdn 3 out: styd on powerfully fr 2 out to ld bef last where gd jump: drvn clr* **7/2**[2]

/31- **2** *3 ½* **Cue Card**[33] 2673 7-11-10 174 .... JoeTizzard 176
(Colin Tizzard) *led at gd pce: gng strly fr 4 out: at least 2 l clr 2 out: faltered and hdd bef last: one pce* **10/3**[1]

1/1- **3** *11* **Al Ferof (FR)**[33] 2664 8-11-10 168 .... DarylJacob 165
(Paul Nicholls) *j.lft 1st: wl in tch: chsd ldng pair 13th to 3 out: plugged on to take modest 3rd again bef last* **5/1**[3]

1/U- **4** *2 ¼* **Mount Benbulben (IRE)**[54] 2234 8-11-10 160 .... DannyMullins 165+
(Gordon Elliott, Ire) *hld up in last: in tch whn mstke 12th: prog to dispute 3rd whn mstke 4 out: drvn in 3rd and wl btn 3 out: wknd after 2 out* **20/1**

1/2- **5** *30* **Dynaste (FR)**[33] 2673 7-11-10 169 .... TomScudamore 142
(David Pipe) *wl in tch: rdn and struggling fr 14th: wl bhd bef 3 out: t.o* **10/3**[1]

6/1- **U** **Riverside Theatre**[14] 3032 9-11-10 163 ....(b[1]) BarryGeraghty
(Nicky Henderson) *hld up in rr: 7th whn blnd and uns rdr 5th* **20/1**

/54- **U** **Long Run (FR)**[33] 2673 8-11-10 168 ....(v[1]) MrSWaley-Cohen 162
(Nicky Henderson) *lw: racd wd: pressed ldng pair: mstke 12th and lost pl: trying to rally but btn whn blnd bdly 3 out: 5th whn blnd bdly last and uns rdr* **8/1**

P22/ **P** **Menorah (IRE)**[253] 5353 8-11-10 169 .... RichardJohnson
(Philip Hobbs) *lw: in tch in rr: mstke 8th: rdn after 13th: sn btn: last and wl bhd whn p.u bef 2 out* **16/1**

/02- **U** **Champion Court (IRE)**[14] 3032 8-11-10 157 .... IanPopham
(Martin Keighley) *hld up in rr: hmpd and uns rdr 5th* **33/1**

6m 9.5s (-5.90) **Going Correction** +0.30s/f (Yiel) **9** Ran SP% **114.5**
Speed ratings (Par 117): **121,119,116,115,105 , , ,**
toteswingers 1&2 £3.00, 1&3 £3.50, 2&3 £2.90 CSF £15.55 CT £56.98 TOTE £5.90: £2.40, £1.10, £2.30; EX 17.10 Trifecta £68.50 Pool: £15,261.44 - 166.88 winning units..
Owner Potensis Limited & Chris Giles **Bred** Patrick Joubert **Trained** Ditcheat, Somerset

FOCUS
An up-to-scratch King George, run at a solid pace thanks to the runner-up. The time was 7.6sec quicker than the Grade 1 novice chase. The winner has been rated well up to standard, up 4lb on his previous best, with the second rated 4lb off his Haydock win. The fourth can rate higher if eliminating mistakes.

3263 WILLIAM HILL - BET ON THE MOVE H'CAP HURDLE (10 hdls) 2m 5f

3:45 (3:45) (Class 3) (0-135,131) 3-Y-0+ **£9,747** (£2,862; £1,431; £715)

Form RPR

/31- **1** **Junction Fourteen (IRE)**[29] 2740 4-11-3 **121** .... LeightonAspell 137+
(Emma Lavelle) *wl in tch: clsd on ldrs 3 out: led bef 2 out: pushed clr bef last: easily* **9/2**[2]

0/2- **2** *11* **Georgian King**[32] 2691 10-10-9 **113** .... IanPopham 114
(Martin Keighley) *led to after 2nd: styd prom: rdn sn after 3 out: kpt on to take 2nd 2 out: no ch w wnr* **25/1**

310- **3** *2* **Big Casino**[39] 2529 7-11-7 **125** .... SamTwiston-Davies 123
(Nigel Twiston-Davies) *led after 2nd: rdn and hdd bef 2 out: one pce and sn btn* **13/2**

240- **4** *1 ½* **Experimentalist**[19] 2949 5-11-0 **118** ....(t) RichardJohnson 116
(Tim Vaughan) *wl in tch: on terms w ldrs after 3 out: rdn and one pce fr 2 out* **33/1**

/35- **5** 6 **Billy Twyford (IRE)**[15] 3028 6-11-9 **127**................................(t) JoeTizzard 119
(Lawney Hill) *trckd ldrs: mstke 3 out: sn rdn and lost pl qckly: looked like tailing off on long run bef 2 out: plugged on again after 2 out* **16/1**

1/2- **6** 2½ **McIlhatton (IRE)**[220] 410 5-11-7 **125**.................................... DarylJacob 114
(Paul Nicholls) *lw: hld up in last trio: mstke 5th: prog after 3 out: trckd ldrs on long run bef 2 out and gng bttr than most: sn rdn and wknd* **14/1**

602- **7** nk **Quaddick Lake (IRE)**[10] 3130 10-10-11 **125**............... ChrisMeehan[(10)] 113
(Jeremy Scott) *hld up in last trio: sme prog 3 out: sn rdn and nvr able to rch ldrs bef next* **5/1**[3]

/01- **8** 38 **Beyeh (IRE)**[11] 3117 5-11-6 **124** 7ex...................................... RyanMahon 74
(Michael Appleby) *in tch: rdn after 7th: struggling 3 out: wknd: t.o* **11/1**

224- **9** hd **Twelve Roses**[27] 2798 5-11-12 **130**.. APMcCoy 80
(Kim Bailey) *hld up in last trio: prog to trck ldrs 6th: wl on terms after 3 out: rdn and wknd qckly wl bef 2 out: t.o* **5/2**[1]

210- **10** 31 **Ashdown Lad**[38] 2561 4-10-8 **117**..(p) BenPoste[(5)] 36
(Tom Symonds) *t.k.h: prom: trckd ldr 5th: upsides 3 out: sn wknd v rapidly: t.o* **50/1**

/04- **P** **Whipcrackaway (IRE)**[29] 2742 4-10-9 **113**.................(v) TomScudamore
(Peter Hedger) *prom to 5th: wknd rapidly after next: t.o whn p.u bef 3 out* **25/1**

/04- **P** **Ourmanmassini (IRE)**[38] 2561 5-10-9 **113**................(tp) RobertThornton
(Suzy Smith) *racd wd: hld up in rr: lost tch w main gp and shoved along 7th: nvr on terms after: wknd bef 2 out: t.o whn p.u bef last* **8/1**

5m 23.4s (5.90) **Going Correction** +0.30s/f (Yiel)
WFA 4 from 5yo+ 6lb **12** Ran SP% **121.3**
Speed ratings (Par 107): **100,95,95,94,92 91,91,76,76,64 ,**
toteswingers 1&2 £46.80, 1&3 £10.40, 2&3 £11.60 CSF £113.73 CT £743.88 TOTE £5.80: £2.20, £6.40, £2.10; EX 175.60 Trifecta £2385.30 Part won. Pool: £3,180.40 - 0.30 winning units..
Owner M St Quinton & T Syder **Bred** John And Iris Lunny **Trained** Hatherden, Hants

FOCUS
A fair handicap hurdle. The winner is on a steep upward curve and can rate higher and win again. The second and third set the level.
T/Jkpt: Not won. T/Plt: £2,951.60 to a £1 stake. Pool: £259,645.59 - 64.22 winning units T/Qpdt: £23.00 to a £1 stake. Pool: £19,844.45 - 635.86 winning units JN

2899 MARKET RASEN (R-H)
Thursday, December 26

OFFICIAL GOING: Soft (good to soft in places on hurdle course; chs 6.0, hdl 6.5)
Wind: almost nil Weather: fine and sunny, cold, misty race 3 onwards

3264 32RED.COM (S) H'CAP HURDLE (8 hdls) 2m 1f
12:25 (12:25) (Class 5) (0-100,94) 3-Y-O+ **£2,599** (£763; £381; £190)

Form RPR

/00- **1** **Walter De La Mare (IRE)**[12] 903 6-11-10 **92**.............. TomMessenger 93+
(Anabel K Murphy) *hld up in rr: t.k.h: stdy hdwy on ins bef 2 out: swtchd lft between last 2: led sn after last: kpt on towards fin* **14/1**

000- **2** ¾ **Kimora (IRE)**[50] 2291 7-11-1 **90**...................(p) MrMatthewBarber[(7)] 91+
(Marc Barber) *led: nt fluent 2nd: hdd 4th: drvn 3 out: upsides last: no ex last 75yds* **7/1**

000- **3** hd **Ghaabesh (IRE)**[128] 1331 6-10-11 **79**....................................(t) LiamHeard 78
(Barry Leavy) *chsd ldrs: drvn appr 2 out: upsides last: kpt on towards fin* **13/2**[3]

604- **4** 1½ **Johnnys Legacy (IRE)**[28] 2770 6-11-9 **94**.................(p) PeterCarberry[(3)] 92
(Conor Dore) *w ldr: led 4th: hdd sn after last: kpt on same pce* **7/1**

P46- **5** ½ **Caught By Witness (IRE)**[37] 2571 8-10-5 **80**..........(t) CharlieDeutsch[(7)] 77
(Anthony Middleton) *nt fluent: mid-div: drvn to chse ldrs 3 out: one pce fr next* **7/1**

003- **6** 1 **Iktiview**[9] 3141 5-11-7 **92**..(bt) KyleJames[(3)] 88
(Philip Kirby) *chsd ldrs: drvn bef 2 out: one pce between last 2* **7/2**[2]

113- **7** 1¼ **Hail Tiberius**[78] 1822 6-11-12 **94**..(t) TomSiddall 89
(Martin Keighley) *hld up in rr: t.k.h: hrd drvn 3 out: one pce fr next* **11/4**[1]

000- **P** **So Cheeky**[23] 2877 4-11-3 **85**..(t) SamThomas
(Richard Guest) *mid-div: drvn 3 out: lost pl and p.u bef next* **9/1**

4m 25.9s (19.20) **Going Correction** +0.975s/f (Soft)
WFA 4 from 5yo+ 5lb **8** Ran SP% **116.4**
Speed ratings (Par 103): **93,92,92,91,91 91,90,**
Tote Swingers: 1&2 £18.80, 1&3 £16.30, 2&3 £9.70 CSF £107.54 CT £706.63 TOTE £11.60: £2.70, £2.50, £2.70; EX 181.30 Trifecta £1485.80 Part won. Pool: £1,981.09 - 0.41 winning units..There was no bid for the winner.
Owner Mrs Anabel K Murphy **Bred** Ballinacrow Stud **Trained** Wilmcote, Warwicks

FOCUS
Mostly unreliable types and they finished well grouped, so probably not form to get too excited about. The winner was well in on his novice form and there's a case for rating him higher through the second, but they finished in a heap in a modest time and it's not a race to get carried away with.

3265 LINCS TURKEYS NOVICES' H'CAP HURDLE (10 hdls) 2m 5f
1:00 (1:00) (Class 5) (0-100,98) 3-Y-O+ **£2,599** (£763; £381; £190)

Form RPR

100- **1** **Crookstown (IRE)**[26] 2826 6-11-9 **98**............................ KielanWoods[(3)] 101+
(Ben Case) *hld up: hdwy 6th: trcking ldrs 3 out: led last: hrd rdn and edgd lft: all out* **11/1**

350- **2** nk **Yazdi (IRE)**[18] 2980 4-11-4 **97**....................................... ChristopherWard[(7)] 100+
(Henry Oliver) *chsd ldrs 3rd: mstke 3 out: led next: hdd last: no ex clsng stages* **14/1**

3/4- **3** 3½ **Airmen's Friend (IRE)**[28] 2764 7-11-10 **96**.......................(tp) MarkGrant 95
(Charlie Mann) *in rr: hrd drvn and hdwy 3 out: 4th between last 2: kpt on one pce to take 3rd last 50yds* **9/2**[2]

460- **4** nk **Blue Sea Of Ibrox (IRE)**[14] 3040 5-10-0 **72** oh4..........(b[1]) DavidEngland 71
(Alan Brown) *led early: chsd ldr: mstke 4th: cl 2nd whn mstke 2 out: one pce* **20/1**

544- **5** 6 **Ivans Back (IRE)**[14] 3038 8-10-5 **84**............................ CharlieDeutsch[(7)] 78
(Nick Kent) *sn led: hit 6th: hdd appr 2 out: wknd appr last* **8/1**

444- **6** 28 **Combustible Kate (IRE)**[117] 1468 7-10-12 **91**............. ShaunDobbin[(7)] 55
(Nick Kent) *chsd ldrs: drvn and lost pl after 5th: bhd 3 out: sn t.o* **7/1**[3]

0P5- **P** **Conigre**[24] 2862 6-11-8 **94**..(tp) LiamHeard
(Ali Brewer) *in rr: lost pl after 7th: t.o whn p.u bef 2 out* **9/1**

554- **P** **Exit To Freedom**[95] 1631 7-10-5 **84**.................................(p) MrJHamilton[(7)]
(John Wainwright) *chsd ldrs: drvn 6th: wknd 3 out: t.o whn p.u bef last* **11/1**

P00- **P** **First Of Never (IRE)**[16] 3014 7-9-9 **74** oh3 ow2.............. GeraldQuinn[(7)]
(Lynn Siddall) *chsd ldrs 6th: lost pl after next: sn bhd: t.o whn p.u bef 2 out* **33/1**

/F6- **P** **Nomadic Storm**[222] 374 7-10-12 **84**.................................... SamThomas
(Graeme McPherson) *chsd ldrs: mstke 3rd: drvn 5th: lost pl next: sn bhd: t.o whn p.u bef 3 out* **16/1**

213- **P** **Silver Dragon**[55] 2202 5-11-11 **97**................................... TomMessenger
(Tony Coyle) *nvr travelling: in rr: reminders 3rd: drvn next: bhd 6th: t.o next: p.u bef 3 out* **5/2**[1]

5m 29.2s (20.40) **Going Correction** +0.975s/f (Soft)
WFA 4 from 5yo+ 6lb **11** Ran SP% **117.3**
Speed ratings (Par 103): **100,99,98,98,96 85, , , ,**
Tote Swingers: 1&2 £21.50, 1&3 £10.70, 2&3 £12.00 CSF £150.76 CT £799.34 TOTE £13.70: £3.00, £5.00, £1.80; EX 149.80 Trifecta £626.30 Pool: £2,298.21 - 2.75 winning units..
Owner Case Racing Partnership **Bred** Vincent Walsh **Trained** Edgcote, Northants
■ Stewards' Enquiry : Christopher Ward two-day ban: use of whip (9-10 Jan)

FOCUS
With the favourite running no sort of race, this became wide open. The first four have been rated pretty much to their marks.

3266 32RED CASINO NOVICES' LIMITED H'CAP CHASE (14 fncs) 2m 6f 110y
1:35 (1:36) (Class 3) (0-125,124) 4-Y-O+ **£8,656** (£3,148)

Form RPR

/34- **1** **Spanish Arch (IRE)**[35] 2623 6-10-9 **117**.....................(tp) KielanWoods[(3)] 121+
(Charlie Longsdon) *w ldrs: lft in ld 3rd: hit 7th: hung lft and sn hdd briefly on bnd bef next: drvn 3 out: hung rt appr last: all out* **11/4**[2]

1UF- **2** 1¼ **Shockingtimes (IRE)**[21] 2909 6-11-1 **120**.............................. MarkGrant 121
(Charlie Mann) *lft handy 2nd 3rd: blnd 7th: led briefly bnd after 7th: effrt and hit 3 out: 2 l down last: styd on towards fin* **6/1**

P2P- **U** **Flichity (IRE)**[14] 3033 8-10-0 **110** oh45............................ JoeCornwall[(5)]
(John Cornwall) *chsd ldrs: hit 2nd: hmpd: swvd lft and uns rdr next* **33/1**

2/2- **B** **Distime (IRE)**[21] 2901 7-10-7 **115**................................... PeterCarberry[(3)]
(John Quinn) *chsd ldrs: b.d 3rd* **11/8**[1]

2/2- **F** **Dreams Of Milan (IRE)**[19] 2955 5-11-4 **123**....................... SamThomas
(Donald McCain) *led: fell 3rd* **3/1**[3]

6m 6.1s (20.10) **Going Correction** +0.60s/f (Soft) **5** Ran SP% **111.0**
Speed ratings (Par 107): **89,88, , ,**
CSF £17.79 TOTE £4.30: £2.50, £2.00; EX 17.60 Trifecta £23.80 Pool: £1,143.91 - 33.97 winning units..
Owner Tunnel Vision **Bred** John Boden And Willie Kane **Trained** Over Norton, Oxon

FOCUS
This was carnage. The major incident came at the third where Dreams Of Milan blundered, unseated his rider and also brought down market leader Distime. It concerned only two from a long way out. Not form to take seriously.

3267 CLUGSTON LINCOLNSHIRE NATIONAL (A H'CAP CHASE) (19 fncs) 3m 5f
2:10 (2:10) (Class 4) (0-120,115) 4-Y-O+ **£7,472** (£2,194; £1,097; £548)

Form RPR

221- **1** **Merlin's Wish**[36] 2594 8-11-9 **112**... TomSiddall 132+
(Martin Keighley) *hld up: hit 6th and next: trckd ldrs 9th: led appr 3 out: forged clr between last 2: eased towards fin* **9/4**[1]

/01- **2** 25 **Musical Wedge**[32] 2700 9-11-5 **115**............................... GeraldQuinn[(7)] 109
(Claire Dyson) *led to 5th: w ldr: drvn to ld 14th: hit 4 out: sn hdd: regained 2nd next: kpt on one pce* **9/2**[2]

112- **3** 1¾ **Orange Nassau (FR)**[18] 2979 7-11-9 **115**..................... KielanWoods[(3)] 107
(Charlie Longsdon) *w ldr: led 5th: hdd 14th: led after 3 out: hdd appr next and hit fence: kpt on one pce* **9/4**[1]

4F4- **4** 8 **Mohi Rahrere (IRE)**[13] 3059 10-11-6 **109**............................ LiamHeard 92
(Barry Leavy) *hld up: chsd ldrs 12th: outpcd 14th: no threat after* **9/1**

254- **P** **Epee Celeste (FR)**[9] 3150 7-10-9 **103**............................. JoeCornwall[(5)]
(Michael Chapman) *chsd ldrs: pushed along 5th: lost pl 12th: sn bhd: blnd 15th: sn t.o: p.u bef 3 out* **10/1**

22P- **P** **Ballyvoneen (IRE)**[33] 2678 8-10-0 **89** oh2...................... TomMessenger
(Neil King) *chsd ldrs 7th: lost pl 13th: sn bhd: t.o 5th whn p.u bef 3 out* **7/1**[3]

7m 46.5s (12.50) **Going Correction** +0.60s/f (Soft) **6** Ran SP% **111.3**
Speed ratings (Par 105): **106,99,98,96,**
Tote Swingers: 1&2 £3.00, 1&3 £1.02, 2&3 £1.80 CSF £12.59 CT £23.12 TOTE £3.10: £1.70, £3.00; EX 17.30 Trifecta £28.00 Pool: £1,125.24 - 30.09 winning units..
Owner Miss R Toppin **Bred** Mrs J M Bailey **Trained** Condicote, Gloucs

FOCUS
A real stamina test on the ground and the field had thinned right out by the home turn. The winner isn't fast but seems to be able to maintain the same pace indefinitely and can win more marathons, although he may get too far behind in higher class races. There's a case for rating him 10lb higher through the second and third, but neither got home.

3268 GARTHWEST NOVICES' H'CAP CHASE (12 fncs) 2m 2f
2:45 (2:46) (Class 4) (0-110,110) 4-Y-O+ **£5,198** (£1,526; £763; £381)

Form RPR

/P6- **1** **Barenger (IRE)**[44] 2437 6-11-12 **105**.................................. SamThomas 113+
(Ali Brewer) *hld up: hit 1st: jnd ldrs 7th: swtchd rt between last 2: led appr last: styd on wl* **4/1**[3]

121- **2** 7 **Hopeand**[9] 3152 8-12-0 **107** 7ex.......................................(t) AdamPogson 109
(Charles Pogson) *led: hdd appr last: kpt on same pce* **11/4**[2]

042- **3** 1¾ **Looks Like Slim**[9] 3152 6-11-12 **105**................................(p) MarkGrant 103
(Ben De Haan) *chsd ldrs: lft handy 2nd 7th: upsides 3 out: kpt on same pce between last 2* **11/4**[2]

200- **4** 5 **Around A Pound (IRE)**[144] 1205 8-11-2 **102**........... CharlieDeutsch[(7)] 100
(Nick Kent) *t.k.h: trckd ldrs 2nd: j. slowly: blnd and lost pl 7th: tk modest 4th 3 out* **5/2**[1]

444- **5** 29 **Radsoc De Sivola (FR)**[9] 3152 8-9-9 **79** oh29............... JoeCornwall[(5)] 43
(John Cornwall) *chsd ldrs: reminder after 2nd: sn pushed along: lost pl appr 3 out: bhd whn hit last: virtually p.u: t.o* **9/1**

4m 49.1s (14.10) **Going Correction** +0.60s/f (Soft) **5** Ran SP% **111.9**
Speed ratings (Par 105): **92,88,88,85,73**
CSF £15.62 TOTE £6.50: £2.40, £1.70; EX 20.70 Trifecta £40.20 Pool: £1,440.76 - 26.85 winning units..
Owner Kings Of The Castle **Bred** Roger A Ryan **Trained** Eastbury, Berks

FOCUS
Three broke clear and it was the stalking Barenger who hit the front approaching the last and surged clear to score decisively. The winner has been rated in line with the best of his hurdling form for Nicky Henderson, while the runner-up has been rated as running a small pb.

3269 32RED H'CAP HURDLE (JOCKEY CLUB GRASSROOTS JUMPS SERIES QUALIFIER) (10 hdls) 2m 3f
3:20 (3:20) (Class 4) (0-120,119) 3-Y-0+ **£3,249** (£954; £477; £238)

Form RPR
P3P- **1** **Kilflora**[6] 3190 10-10-5 **105** (p) GeraldQuinn(7) 108+
(Claire Dyson) *best away: led: drvn 3 out: hit next: hdd narrowly and hit last: hrd drvn and styd on to ld nr fin: jst hld on* **14/1**
313- **2** *nse* **Keel Haul (IRE)**[19] 2936 5-10-6 **106** ChristopherWard(7) 110+
(Henry Oliver) *hld up towards rr: hdwy 3 out: chsng ldrs and drvn appr next: sn outpcd: styd on wd outside and 5th appr last: kpt on wl towards fin: jst failed* **3/1**[1]
143- **3** *hd* **Bowie (IRE)**[26] 2828 6-10-13 **113** CharlieDeutsch(7) 114
(Nick Kent) *trckd ldrs: cl 2nd sn after 5th: led narrowly last: hdd and no ex clsng stages* **7/2**[2]
/0P- **4** *½* **Northern Oscar (IRE)**[54] 2230 5-10-12 **105** TomSiddall 106
(Tim Walford) *chsd ldrs: effrt and upsides 2 out: styd on same pce last 50yds* **10/1**
410- **5** *shd* **Red Admirable (IRE)**[26] 2828 7-11-9 **119** KielanWoods(3) 120
(Graeme McPherson) *trckd ldrs: drvn appr 2 out: cl 4th whn j.rt and hit last: kpt on same pce last 50yds* **5/1**[3]
02U- **6** *21* **Andreo Bambaleo**[21] 2903 9-10-10 **113** (p) GLavery(10) 92
(Brian Ellison) *in rr: drvn and lost pl 7th: sn bhd* **7/1**
403- **7** *¾* **Dormouse**[36] 2598 8-11-10 **117** (p) TomMessenger 96
(Anabel K Murphy) *hld up in rr: hdwy 3 out: drvn and hung rt appr next: sn lost pl and bhd* **7/1**
5- **8** *40* **Focail Maith**[14] 3034 5-11-3 **117** MissBAndrews(7) 56
(Neil King) *chsd ldrs: drvn 3 out: lost pl bef next: sn bhd: t.o whn eased run-in* **9/1**

4m 54.9s (15.50) **Going Correction** +0.975s/f (Soft)
WFA 4 from 5yo+ 5lb **8** Ran SP% **114.6**
Speed ratings (Par 105): **106,105,105,105,105 96,96,79**
Tote Swingers: 1&2 £3.50, 1&3 £4.00, 2&3 £2.50 CSF £57.23 CT £183.96 TOTE £19.50: £5.60, £1.50, £1.60; EX 81.00 Trifecta £339.20 Part won. Pool: £452.39 - 0.74 winning units..
Owner Lisa Rogers, B & S Vaughan & Partner **Bred** Mrs J M Bailey **Trained** Cleeve Prior, Worcs

FOCUS
A cracking finish to a wide-open handicap. The winner was a 130+ horse in Ireland and should still be competitive when reassessed, along with the second, who probably should have won.
T/Plt: £863.10 to a £1 stake. Pool: £36,534.77 - 30.90 winning tickets. T/Qpdt: £26.60 to a £1 stake. Pool: £1,927.93 - 53.60 winning tickets. WG

2865 SEDGEFIELD (L-H)
Thursday, December 26

OFFICIAL GOING: Soft (5.0)
Wind: Almost nil Weather: Foggy

3270 COMPARE BOOKMAKERS AT BOOKMAKERS.CO.UK "NATIONAL HUNT" NOVICES' HURDLE (BETFRED HURDLE SERIES) (8 hdls) 2m 1f
12:10 (12:10) (Class 4) 4-Y-0+ **£3,119** (£915; £457; £228)

Form RPR
/21- **1** **Heath Hunter (IRE)**[30] 2732 6-10-5 122 TomBellamy(7) 121+
(David Pipe) *mde all: sn clr: drvn bef 2 out: styd on wl: unchal* **4/11**[1]
420- **2** *10* **Make Me A Fortune (IRE)**[35] 2621 5-10-12 0 (p) DougieCostello 111
(Steve Gollings) *t.k.h: sn chsng wnr: rdn and effrt bef 2 out: kpt on same pce* **9/2**[2]
130/ **3** *10* **Forward Flight (IRE)**[391] 2736 7-10-12 0 BarryKeniry 101
(Sue Smith) *hld up in tch: effrt and drvn after 3 out: no imp bef next* **10/1**
152- **4** *6* **Monita Bonita**[23] 2865 4-10-5 0 HenryBrooke 88
(Tim Easterby) *t.k.h in midfield: drvn and outpcd after 3 out: sn no imp* **6/1**[3]
P06- **5** *15* **Rosquero (FR)**[23] 2869 8-10-12 79 (p) KennyJohnson 80
(Robert Johnson) *prom: drvn and outpcd bef 3 out: btn next* **100/1**
00/- **6** *6* **One For Hocky (IRE)**[322] 4078 5-10-5 0 GrahamWatters(7) 74
(Nicky Richards) *hld up: outpcd bef 3 out: nvr on terms* **22/1**
300- **7** *7* **Crown And Glory (IRE)**[25] 2838 6-10-7 0 SamanthaDrake(5) 67
(Karen Tutty) *towards rr: struggling bef 3 out: sn btn* **28/1**
610- **8** *9* **Wymeswold**[16] 3010 6-10-0 0 HarryChalloner(5) 51
(Michael Mullineaux) *midfield: outpcd 1/2-way: btn 3 out* **40/1**
P50/ **9** *7* **One In A Row (IRE)**[244] 5546 6-10-9 82 JohnKington(3) 51
(Alan Swinbank) *prom to 1/2-way: and wknd bef 3 out* **50/1**
6/0- **P** **Teaatreids (IRE)**[26] 2823 5-10-5 0 HarryHaynes
(Brian Ellison) *bhd: struggling 1/2-way: no ch whn p.u bef 2 out* **66/1**

ms (-246.90)
WFA 4 from 5yo+ 5lb **10** Ran SP% **129.6**
Tote Swingers: 1&2 £1.02, 1&3 £2.50, 2&3 £9.00 CSF £3.06 TOTE £1.20: £1.10, £1.20, £2.70; EX 2.30 Trifecta £10.30 Pool: £412.35 - 29.96 winning units..
Owner The Heath Hunter Partnership **Bred** Pat And Oliver McCarthy **Trained** Nicholashayne, Devon

FOCUS
Common bends hurdles sited in centre. Overnight fog had lifted just enough for the meeting to take place. The ground had turned to Soft (GoingStick 5.0) and rode dead. They went no great early pace for this weak novices' hurdle, with much of the interest lost when Carlisle winner Milo Man was scratched. The winner was the form pick and has been rated to his mark.

3271 FREE BETS ON YOUR MOBILE AT BOOKMAKERS.CO.UK NOVICES' HURDLE (BETFRED HURDLE SERIES) (10 hdls) 2m 4f
12:40 (12:40) (Class 4) 4-Y-0+ **£3,119** (£915; £457; £228)

Form RPR
/36- **1** **Maybe I Wont**[19] 2958 8-10-12 115 BrianHughes 117
(James Moffatt) *cl up: ev ch 3 out: led after next: rdn and styd on wl run-in* **3/1**[2]
322- **2** *3* **Downtown Boy (IRE)**[9] 3144 5-10-5 114 (p) DiarmuidO'Regan(7) 114
(Chris Grant) *trckd ldrs: led 3 out: sn rdn: hdd after next: kpt on same pce fr last* **2/1**[1]
032- **3** *4* **Hit The Top (IRE)**[121] 1418 6-10-5 113 CallumBewley(7) 110
(Sue Smith) *prom: drvn and outpcd 3 out: rallied next: kpt on: nt gng pce to rch first two* **11/2**[3]
02- **4** *10* **Jac The Legend**[23] 2878 4-10-12 0 DougieCostello 101
(Steve Gollings) *led to 3 out: sn drvn and outpcd: no imp fr next* **6/1**
000/ **5** *16* **Grand Vintage (IRE)**[450] 1706 7-10-7 0 ColmMcCormack(5) 84
(Evelyn Slack) *bhd: outpcd 1/2-way: sme late hdwy: nvr on terms* **50/1**
/23- **6** *8* **Robbers Roost (IRE)**[24] 2864 5-10-2 0 AlanJohns(10) 76
(Tim Vaughan) *hld up in tch: outpcd after 4 out: btn bef 2 out* **10/1**
2P6/ **7** *4½* **Three White Socks (IRE)**[30] 4911 6-10-12 112 (p) HarryHaynes 72
(Brian Ellison) *towards rr: reminders and outpcd 1/2-way: nvr on terms* **7/1**
0/ **P** **Bollin Line**[319] 6-10-5 0 NathanMoscrop(7)
(Lucinda Egerton) *t.k.h: chsd ldrs to 1/2-way: sn struggling: t.o whn p.u bef 2 out* **14/1**

5m 0.1s (7.40) **Going Correction** +0.35s/f (Yiel) **8** Ran SP% **118.2**
Speed ratings (Par 105): **99,97,96,92,85 82,80,**
Tote Swingers: 1&2 £6.20, 1&3 £3.30, 2&3 £1.10 CSF £10.15 TOTE £3.20: £1.50, £1.10, £2.00; EX 6.80 Trifecta £23.60 Pool: £99.84 - 3.16 winning units..
Owner The Sheroot Partnership **Bred** Wheelersland Stud **Trained** Cartmel, Cumbria

FOCUS
Heavy fog made life difficult for the riders in this modest novices' hurdle, weakened by five non runners. They went no great pace early and they finished tired. Two drew clear of the remainder from three flights out. It's been rated around the balance of the first three.

3272 COUNTRY HARVEST FARM FOODS H'CAP CHASE (13 fncs) 2m 110y
1:15 (1:15) (Class 4) (0-120,119) 4-Y-0+ **£3,807** (£1,220; £678)

Form RPR
/33- **1** **Un Guet Apens (FR)**[5] 3204 5-11-12 **119** BrianHughes 130+
(James Ewart) *trckd ldrs: led 2nd to 4th: led again 3 out: rdn clr after next* **2/1**[1]
353- **2** *16* **Peachey Moment (USA)**[26] 2820 8-10-9 **109** (p) MissJRRichards(7) 104
(Nicky Richards) *led to 2nd: led 4th to 3 out: sn rdn: j.rt and outpcd fr next* **5/1**
210- **3** *39* **Molko Jack (FR)**[16] 3015 9-9-9 **93** oh2 HarryChalloner(5) 49
(Michael Mullineaux) *chsd ldrs: drvn and outpcd 7th: lost tch fr 4 out* **9/1**
/03- **P** **Air Chief**[26] 2804 8-10-11 **107** (tp) JohnKington(3)
(Andrew Crook) *in tch: blnd and lost tch 4th: struggling fr next: t.o whn p.u bef 3 out* **16/1**
33U- **P** **Elsafeer (IRE)**[28] 2762 8-11-1 **118** AlanJohns(10)
(Tim Vaughan) *chsd ldrs: outpcd 8th: 4th and t.o whn p.u after 2 out* **9/2**[3]
324- **U** **Mulligan's Man (IRE)**[41] 2496 6-11-5 **112** HenryBrooke
(Donald McCain) *nt fluent in rr: hdwy and in tch whn mstke and uns rdr 6th* **11/4**[2]

4m 13.1s (4.50) **Going Correction** +0.35s/f (Yiel) **6** Ran SP% **110.7**
Speed ratings (Par 105): **103,95,77, ,**
Tote Swingers: 1&2 £7.90, 1&3 £4.90, 2&3 £9.10 CSF £12.03 TOTE £2.50: £1.80, £2.10; EX 13.30 Trifecta £136.20 Pool: £190.27 - 1.04 winning units..
Owner Drew, Sperling, Graham, Carruthers **Bred** Pierre De Maleissye Melun **Trained** Langholm, Dumfries & G'way

FOCUS
The fog that had shrouded the track for the first two races had given way to bright sunshine. A paucity of runners for this reasonable handicap, although the pace was true and the trio that finished were very tired. This is a step up from the winner, while the second has slipped to a good mark but needs better ground.

3273 WILLS PROPERTY SERVICES H'CAP HURDLE (10 hdls) 2m 4f
1:55 (1:55) (Class 3) (0-140,134) 3-Y-0 **£5,317** (£1,570; £785; £393; £196)

Form RPR
/06- **1** **Calculated Risk**[19] 2951 4-11-7 **129** DougieCostello 137+
(John Quinn) *hld up in tch: stdy hdwy appr 3 out: led bef last: sn rdn and edgd lft: rdn out towards fin* **5/2**[1]
133- **2** *¾* **Oscar Tanner (IRE)**[30] 2732 5-10-3 **116** HarryChalloner(5) 122
(Martin Todhunter) *chsd ldrs: nt fluent 3rd: led and rdn bef 2 out: hdd bef last: rallied: kpt on: hld nr fin* **7/2**[2]
4P2- **3** *18* **Pas Trop Tard (FR)**[19] 2958 6-11-4 **133** (t) StephenMulqueen(7) 124
(Maurice Barnes) *led: rdn along 3 out: hdd bef next: sn outpcd by first two* **9/2**[3]
/PP- **4** *13* **The Knoxs (IRE)**[33] 2672 10-11-3 **132** CallumBewley(7) 107
(Sue Smith) *prom: drvn and outpcd bef 2 out: 4th and hld whn mstke last* **7/1**
016/ **5** *6* **Allow Me**[663] 4628 8-10-8 **121** ColmMcCormack(5) 90
(Dianne Sayer) *bhd: outpcd bef 4 out: n.d after* **20/1**
3/2- **6** *26* **Walser (IRE)**[36] 2597 6-10-0 **115** (b) JohnDawson(7) 58
(John Wade) *cl up tl rdn and outpcd bef 3 out: btn next* **6/1**
030- **7** *11* **Dumbarton (IRE)**[40] 2519 5-11-5 **127** BrianHughes 59
(James Moffatt) *t.k.h: hld up: rdn and outpcd bef 3 out: sn struggling: btn bef next* **9/1**

4m 54.4s (1.70) **Going Correction** +0.35s/f (Yiel)
WFA 4 from 5yo+ 6lb **7** Ran SP% **110.5**
Speed ratings (Par 107): **110,109,102,97,94 84,80**
Tote Swingers: 1&2 £2.10, 1&3 £3.00, 2&3 £7.20 CSF £11.11 CT £33.35 TOTE £2.70: £1.10, £3.40; EX 12.30 Trifecta £54.40 Pool: £170.46 - 2.34 winning units..
Owner Terry Warner **Bred** Newsells Park Stud **Trained** Settrington, N Yorks

FOCUS
The pace quickened with five to jump in this decent handicap hurdle which went with the script, the market principals drawing clear. The winner is on the upgrade for the step up in trip, while the second is on a decent mark and has been rated to his best.

3274 NO DEPOSIT FREE BETS WITH BOOKMAKERS.CO.UK H'CAP HURDLE (8 hdls) 2m 1f
2:30 (2:31) (Class 4) (0-110,110) 4-Y-0+ **£3,119** (£915; £457; £228)

Form RPR
512- **1** **Light The City (IRE)**[15] 3021 6-11-3 **104** JakeGreenall(3) 111+
(Ruth Carr) *t.k.h: cl up: led 3 out: j.lft last 2: drvn out* **5/2**[2]
220- **2** *3½* **Sam Lord**[16] 3012 9-11-6 **104** BrianHughes 107
(James Moffatt) *led to 3 out: rallied: regained 2nd and drvn whn mstke last: kpt on* **12/5**[1]
3F4- **3** *3¼* **Memory Cloth**[31] 2718 6-11-12 **110** DougieCostello 110
(Brian Ellison) *prom: effrt and chsd wnr 2 out to last: kpt on same pce run-in* **9/2**[3]
625/ **4** *15* **Painted Tail (IRE)**[204] 3601 6-10-5 **96** DaraghBourke(7) 80
(Alan Swinbank) *chsd ldrs on outside: drvn along and outpcd after 3 out: no imp fr next* **10/1**
354- **5** *10* **Formulation (IRE)**[15] 3021 6-10-11 **100** (p) TonyKelly(5) 74
(Rebecca Menzies) *hld up: nt fluent and dropped to rr 4 out: rallied bef 2 out: nvr able to chal* **10/1**
355- **6** *2¼* **Quick Brew**[15] 3017 5-11-0 **105** (t) StephenMulqueen(7) 77
(Maurice Barnes) *hld up: stdy hdwy bef 3 out: rdn and outpcd bef next* **17/2**

/44- 7 3 ½ **Hellesbelles (IRE)**23 2865 5-10-8 **102** AlanJohns(10) 70
(Tim Vaughan) *t.k.h: w ldr: nt fluent 4 out: rdn and wknd fr next* **14/1**
5/P- 8 16 **Needwood Park**173 283 5-10-13 **97** (p) KennyJohnson 49
(Ray Craggs) *hld up: outpcd after 4 out: n.d after* **50/1**
040- 9 7 **Call Of Duty (IRE)**15 3021 8-11-2 **105** ColmMcCormack(5) 50
(Dianne Sayer) *hld up: stdy hdwy 4 out: outpcd bef next: sn btn* **28/1**
4m 11.5s (4.60) **Going Correction** +0.35s/f (Yiel) **9** Ran SP% **116.9**
Speed ratings (Par 105): **103,101,99,92,88 87,85,77,74**
Tote Swingers: 1&2 £1.10, 1&3 £1.70, 2&3 £5.90 CSF £9.38 CT £24.94 TOTE £3.00: £1.10, £2.20, £3.10; EX 10.00 Trifecta £22.00 Pool: £294.63 - 10.00 winning units..
Owner Dogberry Racing & Mrs Ruth Carr **Bred** Rabbah Bloodstock Limited **Trained** Huby, N Yorks
■ Stewards' Enquiry : Colm McCormack caution: careless riding

FOCUS
The pace was solid enough for this ordinary event and a trio drew clear, with the two market leaders fighting out the finish. This was another step forward from the progressive winner, while the second is rock-solid round here and has been rated to his mark.

3275 COMPARE BOOKIES FREE BETS AT BOOKMAKERS.CO.UK H'CAP CHASE (16 fncs) 2m 4f

3:05 (3:05) (Class 4) (0-110,110) 4-Y-0 **£3,671** (£1,084; £542; £271; £135)

Form RPR
P/3- 1 **King's Grace**230 203 7-11-9 **107** HenryBrooke 127
(Donald McCain) *chsd ldr: rdn bef 2 out: edgd lft and rallied bef last: styd on wl to ld towards fin* **7/2**2
/03- 2 1 ¼ **Brieryhill Boy**30 2734 6-10-3 **92** TonyKelly(5) 113+
(William Amos) *led: rdn after 2 out: rdn and 2 l clr whn mstke last: kpt on: hdd towards fin* **5/1**3
/22- 3 14 **Ruby Bay (IRE)**14 3040 8-10-5 **89** (p) DougieCostello 96
(Tim Walford) *t.k.h: hld up in tch: hit 1st: stdy hdwy 4 out: rdn and kpt on fr 2 out: nt rch first two* **7/4**1
2P3- 4 6 **Baltic Pathfinder (IRE)**15 3019 9-11-1 **99** ShaneByrne 98
(Sue Smith) *chsd ldrs: lost pl 3rd: rdn and rallied after 4 out: no imp after next* **10/1**
B32- 5 3 ¼ **Alpha One (IRE)**17 2996 7-11-12 **110** BrianHughes 106
(Chris Grant) *chsd ldrs tl rdn and outpcd fr 3 out* **5/1**3
/50- 6 17 **Newspage (IRE)**26 2818 7-9-8 **85** oh18 ow1 StephenMulqueen(7) 64
(John Wade) *chsd ldrs: lost pl 11th: n.d after* **16/1**
016- 7 8 **Monbeg (IRE)**23 2870 6-10-0 **89** HarryChalloner(5) 60
(Martin Todhunter) *prom: hit 10th: outpcd 12th: btn bef 2 out* **12/1**
5m 8.8s (5.80) **Going Correction** +0.35s/f (Yiel) **7** Ran SP% **114.6**
Speed ratings (Par 105): **102,101,95,93,92 85,82**
Tote Swingers: 1&2 £4.60, 1&3 £1.60, 2&3 £1.40 CSF £21.43 CT £39.53 TOTE £6.20: £2.50, £3.90; EX 38.70 Trifecta £129.40 Pool: £266.39 - 1.54 winning units..
Owner T G Leslie **Bred** R T Crellin **Trained** Cholmondeley, Cheshire

FOCUS
They went no pace in this open-looking handicap chase, which produced last-fence drama. The winner is on a fair mark and has been rated back to his best.

3276 BOOKMAKERS.CO.UK STANDARD OPEN NATIONAL HUNT FLAT RACE 2m 1f

3:35 (3:37) (Class 6) 4-6-Y-0 **£1,559** (£457; £228; £114)

Form RPR
4- 1 **Wolf Sword (IRE)**34 2660 4-11-4 0 BarryKeniry 106+
(George Moore) *t.k.h: in tch: hdwy to ld 2f out: edgd lft ins fnl f: drvn out* **10/3**3
11- 2 2 ¼ **Fly Home Harry**23 2871 4-11-7 0 DaraghBourke(7) 114
(Alan Swinbank) *led at ordinary gallop: rdn and hdd 2f out: kpt on fnl f: nt pce of wnr* **7/4**1
3 2 ¼ **Dreamisi (IRE)** 4-10-11 0 DaleIrving(7) 102
(James Ewart) *chsd ldrs: drvn over 3f out: effrt and cl up wl over 1f out: one pce ins fnl f* **16/1**
4 9 **The Grey Taylor (IRE)**82 4-10-11 0 PaulBohan(7) 95
(Steve Gollings) *t.k.h early: pressed ldr: rdn over 2f out: wknd over 1f out* **2/1**2
5 95 **General Tiberius** 4-11-4 0 HenryBrooke
(K R Burke) *hld up in tch: drvn along after 6f: hung lft and struggling over 6f out: sn btn: t.o* **17/2**
4m 8.0s (6.70) **Going Correction** +0.35s/f (Yiel) **5** Ran SP% **109.2**
Speed ratings: **98,96,95,91,46**
Tote Swingers: 1&2 £1.60, 1&3 £5.20, 2&3 £4.10 CSF £9.44 TOTE £5.90: £4.50, £1.10; EX 9.10 Trifecta £139.90 Pool: £270.63 - 1.45 winning units..
Owner G R Orchard **Bred** Maurice Smiddy **Trained** Middleham Moor, N Yorks

FOCUS
A paucity of runners for a weak bumper which turned into something of sprint. The first two have been rated as improving slightly.
T/Plt: £12.90 to a £1 stake. Pool: £48,674.93 - 2,744.39 winning tickets. T/Qpdt: £11.70 to a £1 stake. Pool: £1,676.50 - 105.50 winning tickets. RY

3175 TOWCESTER (R-H)
Thursday, December 26

OFFICIAL GOING: Heavy (7.3)
Wind: Virtually nil Weather: Low cloud

3277 BET ON TOTEJACKPOT AT KEMPTON H'CAP CHASE (18 fncs) 3m 110y

12:45 (12:45) (Class 5) (0-95,95) 4-Y-0+ **£2,144** (£629; £314; £157)

Form RPR
P/3- 1 **Mansonien L'As (FR)**35 2619 7-10-13 **82** (p) AdrianLane 107+
(Donald McCain) *chsd ldr: chal fr 9th tl led 14th: c clr appr 2 out: styd on wl* **11/2**2
4B2- 2 27 **Kilvergan Boy (IRE)**11 3114 9-9-12 **74** (p) RyanHatch(7) 72
(Nigel Twiston-Davies) *chsd ldrs: rdn along fr 12th: outpcd 4 out: styd on again after 3 out: kpt on run-in to take wl hld 2nd clsng stages* **8/1**
/3F- 3 ½ **Royaume Bleu (FR)**26 2829 8-11-3 **91** KillianMoore(5) 90
(Alex Hales) *led: hit 5th: jnd fr 10th: blnd and hdd 14th and 4 out: rallied 3 out to chse wnr bef 2 out but no ch: lost mod 2nd clsng stages* **17/2**
65P- 4 23 **River D'Or (FR)**20 2923 8-11-6 **94** CharlieWallis(5) 68
(Sophie Leech) *chsd ldrs: outpcd 13th: effrt after 4 out: wknd after next* **11/1**
/04- P **Cash In Hand (IRE)**32 2702 13-9-7 **69** oh14 MrHAABannister(7)
(Christopher Kellett) *in rr tl wknd and p.u bef 9th* **100/1**
U54- P **Jolly Boys Outing (IRE)**7 3178 10-11-5 **93** BenPoste(5)
(Rosemary Gasson) *in tch: wknd after 3 out: t.o whn p.u bef last* **12/1**
/22- P **Billybo**34 2653 10-10-13 **89** MrEDavid(7)
(Tim Vaughan) *in rr: hdwy 11th: chal 13th: blnd and wknd 3 out: t.o whn p.u bef last* **15/2**
FP5- P **Bobbisox (IRE)**28 2769 8-10-5 **74** (t) CharliePoste
(Alex Hales) *blnd 1st: in rr: blnd 6th: in rr: t.o whn p.u bef 3 out* **20/1**
342- F **Tinelyra (IRE)**38 2562 7-11-6 **89** (t) AlainCawley
(Fergal O'Brien) *in rr whn fell 6th* **13/2**3
255- P **Barton Gift**21 2897 6-11-1 **84** LiamTreadwell
(John Spearing) *in tch: pushed alongafter 8th: blnd 9th: wknd 11th: t.o whn p.u bef 2 out* **7/2**1
/0P- P **Atriptomilan (IRE)**162 1010 5-11-2 **95** (bt1) TommieMO'Brien(10)
(Jonjo O'Neill) *in rr: blnd 9th and 10th: t.o whn p.u bef11th* **9/1**
6m 38.84s (1.94) **Going Correction** +0.125s/f (Yiel) **11** Ran SP% **116.1**
Speed ratings (Par 103): **101,92,92,84, , , , ,**
Tote Swingers: 1&2 £6.90, 1&3 £4.90, 2&3 £7.10 CSF £48.74 CT £371.56 TOTE £5.10: £2.70, £2.50, £2.50; EX 58.30 Trifecta £172.20 Part won. Pool: £229.71 - 0.11 winning units..
Owner Let's Live Racing **Bred** Mme Evelyne Van Haaren **Trained** Cholmondeley, Cheshire

FOCUS
Shared bends and hurdles course dolled out wide. All areas of the standing water noted on-course on Christmas Eve had gone, but the ground was heavy. Racing began with a modest handicap chase, in which the top weight was rated 95. The winner has been rated as running a big pb on his second start for his new yard, and there's a case for rating him a stone higher through the placed horses.

3278 TOTEPOOL WISHING RACEGOERS A MERRY CHRISTMAS EBF "NATIONAL HUNT" NOVICES' HURDLE (QUALIFIER) (7 hdls 1 omitted) 2m

1:20 (1:20) (Class 4) 4-6-Y-0 **£3,249** (£954; £477; £238)

Form RPR
43- 1 **Garrahalish (IRE)**26 2826 5-10-12 0 CharliePoste 125
(Robin Dickin) *trckd ldrs: led wl bef 2 out: hrd drvn and kpt on wl run-in* **10/1**
/32- 2 1 ½ **Come On Laurie (IRE)**24 2858 5-10-12 0 LiamTreadwell 123
(Lawney Hill) *in tch: hdwy 4th: drvn to chse wnr bef 2 out: hrd drvn run-in: no imp: jst hld on for 2nd* **4/1**3
42F- 3 shd **My Wigwam Or Yours (IRE)**26 2808 4-10-12 0 DavidBass 124
(Nicky Henderson) *in tch: hdwy to chse ldrs 3 out: rdn bef last: kpt on u.p run-in to cl on 2nd last strides but no imp on wnr* **11/8**1
342- 4 15 **Anteros (IRE)**23 2876 5-10-12 122 AlainCawley 110
(Sophie Leech) *in rr: hdwy and hit 3 out: styd on bef next: wknd: sn wknd* **11/4**2
/42- 5 12 **Newforge House (IRE)**33 2681 5-10-7 0 JamesBanks(5) 96
(Brendan Powell) *led: t.k.h: jnd 3 out: hdd & wknd wl bef 2 out* **25/1**
0/ 6 3 ½ **Ultra Klass (FR)**445 1766 5-10-12 0 AndrewTinkler 92
(Jamie Snowden) *in tch: wknd 3 out* **66/1**
440- 7 nk **Uppercut De L'Orne (FR)**30 2732 5-10-12 0 AdrianLane 92
(Donald McCain) *chsd ldrs to 4th: wknd bef 3 out* **33/1**
400- 8 4 **Clubs Are Trumps (IRE)**13 3061 4-10-2 0 JamesHuxham(10) 88
(Jonjo O'Neill) *chsd ldrs tl wknd appr 3 out* **25/1**
20- 9 9 **Truckers Darling (IRE)**14 3034 6-10-0 0 KillianMoore(5) 72
(Don Cantillon) *in rr: sme hdwy 3 out: sn wknd* **20/1**
/40- 10 22 **Benefitofhindsight**18 2968 4-10-12 0 RhysFlint 57
(Ben Pauling) *bhd most of way* **66/1**
4m 11.45s (3.55) **Going Correction** +0.40s/f (Soft) **10** Ran SP% **116.2**
Speed ratings: **107,106,106,98,92 90,90,88,84,73**
Tote Swingers: 1&2 £13.40, 1&3 £4.60, 2&3 £1.02 CSF £46.03 TOTE £14.20: £3.10, £1.20, £1.30; EX 75.30 Trifecta £137.20 Pool: £223.36 - 1.22 winning units..
Owner Just 4 Fun **Bred** Godfrey Moylan **Trained** Alcester, Warwicks

FOCUS
Few had obvious claims in this run-of-the-mill novices' hurdle. The winner is on the upgrade and the second and fourth help set the level.

3279 BET TOTEQUADPOT WITH TOTEPOOL BEGINNERS' CHASE (16 fncs) 2m 6f

1:55 (1:55) (Class 4) 4-Y-0+ **£4,548** (£1,335; £667; £333)

Form RPR
F22- 1 **Baby Shine (IRE)**14 3030 7-10-7 132 LiamTreadwell 130+
(Lucy Wadham) *chsd ldrs: mstke 3rd: chal 8th tl slt ld fr 4 out: rdn after 3 out: drvn clr 2 out* **11/8**1
/52- 2 10 **Dunlough Bay (IRE)**31 2712 7-11-0 125 (p) CharliePoste 126
(Paul Webber) *chsd ldrs: slt ld fr 8th: hrd pressed tl narrowly hdd 4 out: stl ev ch after 3 out: no ch w wnr fr next but kpt on for clr 2nd* **13/2**3
3 5 **Danners (IRE)**299 7-10-9 0 MrMWall(5) 121
(Giles Smyly) *hit 2nd: chsd ldrs: chal after 9th to 10th: outpcd 4 out: styd on again fr 2 out to take wl hld 3rd run-in* **12/1**
2/0- 4 9 **Fourovakind**27 2798 8-10-9 0 JamesBanks(5) 111
(Harry Whittington) *nt fluent 10th: towards rr most of way: styd on for modest 4th run-in* **5/2**2
3/0 5 2 ¼ **Bathwick Bravo (IRE)**35 2630 6-11-0 0 (t) RhysFlint 111
(Johnny Farrelly) *chsd ldrs: cl 3rd 4 out: wknd fr 3 out: tired and lost 2 pls run-in* **9/1**
5/F- U **Keltic Crisis (IRE)**31 2722 9-10-9 104 CharlieWallis(5)
(Sophie Leech) *uns rdr 1st* **33/1**
F6F- P **Court Appeal (IRE)**15 3023 6-11-0 0 DavidBass
(Charlie Longsdon) *led tl hdd & wknd 8th: t.o whn p.u bef 3 out* **10/1**
5m 52.68s (-0.32) **Going Correction** +0.225s/f (Yiel) **7** Ran SP% **113.7**
Speed ratings (Par 105): **109,105,103,100,99 ,**
Tote Swingers: 1&2 £2.10, 1&3 £3.00, 2&3 £7.20 CSF £11.00 TOTE £2.00: £1.30, £2.20; EX 8.50 Trifecta £37.80 Pool: £122.22 - 2.41 winning units..
Owner P A Philipps,T S Redman & Mrs L Redman **Bred** Kevin Francis O'Donnell **Trained** Newmarket, Suffolk

FOCUS
Just two of these had previous chasing form and they finished first and second. The first two set the level.

3280 TOTEPOOL.COM "NATIONAL HUNT" NOVICES' H'CAP HURDLE (9 hdls 2 omitted) 2m 5f

2:30 (2:30) (Class 4) (0-110,109) 3-Y-0+ **£3,119** (£915; £457; £228)

Form RPR
023- 1 **He's The Daddy**19 2944 6-11-1 **105** RyanHatch(7) 110+
(Nigel Twiston-Davies) *chsd ldrs: rdn and outpcd 6th: rallied u.p to chse ldr 3 out: kpt on to ld after 2 out: hld on all out clsng stages* **5/4**1
460- 2 2 ½ **Bebinn (IRE)**21 2896 6-11-3 **100** (p1) CharliePoste 101
(Ben Case) *chsd ldrs: rdn 5th: lost pl 3 out: rallied appr 2 out to take 2nd after last: kpt on but no imp on wnr cl home* **12/1**

043/ **3** 4 **Trozulon (FR)**[601] 75 6-11-8 **105**.............................. LiamTreadwell 102
(Venetia Williams) *chsd ldrs: led appr 3 out: sn rdn: hdd after 2 out: no ex and lost 2nd after last* **7/2**[2]

503- **4** 24 **Merchant Of Milan**[23] 2874 5-11-7 **109**.......................... JamesBanks(5) 81
(Brendan Powell) *led tl hdd appr 3 out: wknd wl bef 2 out* **9/2**[3]

4/0- **P** **Reyno**[49] 2314 5-11-8 **105**...(p) SamJones
(Renee Robeson) *pressed ldrs: wknd 3 out: t.o whn p.u bef next* **7/1**

000- **P** **Top Chief**[19] 2954 5-10-11 **99**.. KillianMoore(5)
(Mark Rimell) *chsd ldrs: rdn 5th: wknd next: t.o whn p.u bef 2 out* **16/1**

5m 50.73s (23.53) **Going Correction** +0.50s/f (Soft) **6** Ran SP% **110.9**
Speed ratings (Par 105): **75,74,72,63,**
Tote Swingers: 1&2 £7.50, 1&3 £2.00, 2&3 £5.40 CSF £15.03 CT £40.61 TOTE £1.70: £1.10, £5.70; EX 14.00 Trifecta £149.40 Part won. Pool: £199.23 - 0.60 winning units..
Owner Adrian Gillman **Bred** Mrs Susan Orton **Trained** Naunton, Gloucs

FOCUS
A modest novices' handicap hurdle, but competitive on paper. The first three have been rated to their marks.

3281 TOTEPOOL MOBILE H'CAP CHASE (14 fncs) 2m 3f 110y
3:05 (3:09) (Class 5) (0-100,100) 4-Y-0+ **£2,144** (£629; £314; £157)

Form RPR

3P4- **1** **Le Grand Chene (FR)**[14] 3048 7-10-9 **88**......................(t) CharlieWallis(5) 102
(Sophie Leech) *towards rr but in tch: hdwy 3 out: styd on wl fr 2 out to press ldrs last: led sn after: pushed clr* **16/1**

2/6- **2** 6 **Guanciale**[37] 2582 6-11-6 **99**..............................(t) JamesBanks(5) 107
(Brendan Powell) *chsd ldrs: chal 3 out: sn led: kpt slt ld but hrd pressed fr 2 out tl hdd after last: kpt on same pce* **9/2**[2]

061- **3** 1½ **Bill The Lad (IRE)**[7] 3180 6-11-0 **88** 7ex.............................. AdamWedge 98+
(Paul Cowley) *trckd ldrs fr 7th: hit 10th: slt ld 3 out: sn narrowly hdd: chal and hit 2 out: ev ch last: one pce sn after* **6/4**[1]

11/- **4** shd **Tarabela**[305] 4416 10-11-12 **100**...(t) RhysFlint 106
(Johnny Farrelly) *in rr: hdwy fr 9th: chsd ldrs 3 out: styd on fr 2 out: kpt on nr fin but no ch w wnr* **7/1**[3]

415 **5** 8 **Salut Honore (FR)**[32] 2700 7-11-9 **97**................................... WillKennedy 95
(Alex Hales) *led fr 3rd: hrd pressed fr 10th: narrowly hdd 3 out: wknd after 2 out* **15/2**

04P- **6** 14 **Mallusk (IRE)**[32] 2700 8-11-9 **97**..................................(t) DominicElsworth 81
(Shaun Lycett) *led 2nd to 3rd: chsd ldrs to 10th: wknd 4 out* **11/1**

/P2- **7** 2½ **Endofdiscusion (IRE)**[26] 2825 6-11-12 **100**...................(p) CharliePoste 82
(Paul Webber) *chsd ldrs to 3 out: wknd bef next* **15/2**

P/3- **P** **Kirbys Glen (IRE)**[35] 2633 11-10-6 **87** ow3............. MrRobertHawker(7)
(Johnny Farrelly) *led to 2nd: wknd 8th: t.o whn p.u bef2 out* **25/1**

5m 26.82s (8.62) **Going Correction** +0.325s/f (Yiel) **8** Ran SP% **112.3**
Speed ratings (Par 103): **95,92,92,91,88 83,82,**
Tote Swingers: 1&2 £0.00, 1&3 £9.70, 2&3 £2.50 CSF £84.15 CT £173.95 TOTE £21.70: £4.40, £2.20, £1.10; EX 141.60 Trifecta £253.20 Part won. Pool: £337.60 - 0.70 winning units..
Owner T Westmacott & C J Leech **Bred** Joel Degroote **Trained** Elton, Gloucs

FOCUS
A moderate handicap chase, with a top weight rated 100. The winner has been rated back to his best and the second as improving towards his best bumper figure.

3282 COLLECT TOTEPOOL WINNINGS AT BETFRED SHOPS INTERMEDIATE OPEN NATIONAL HUNT FLAT RACE 2m
3:40 (3:40) (Class 6) 4-6-Y-0 **£1,559** (£457; £228; £114)

Form RPR

3/2- **1** **Delgany Demon**[18] 2981 5-10-11 0................................ TrevorWhelan(3) 104+
(Neil King) *chsd ldrs: wnt 2nd ins fnl 2f: styd on u.p to ld ins fnl f: kpt on wl* **5/2**[2]

4- **2** 5 **Coinage (IRE)**[17] 3002 4-11-0 0.. AndrewTinkler 99
(Tony Coyle) *led: rdn 2f out: hdd ins fnl f: kpt on same pce* **7/1**

3 11 **Mistariva (IRE)** 6-11-0 0... LiamTreadwell 90
(Venetia Williams) *in rr but in tch: pushed along 5f out: styd on to take wel-hld 3rd over 1f out* **9/1**

/43- **4** 11 **Fred Le Macon (FR)**[28] 2759 4-11-0 0....................... WayneHutchinson 77
(Alan King) *hdwy to trck ldrs 1/2-way: rdn and one pce in 3rd fr over 2f out: dropped to 4th over 1f out* **15/8**[1]

6/ **5** 47 **Carmino (IRE)**[281] 4878 4-10-9 0.................................[1] NicodeBoinville(5) 30
(Mark Bradstock) *pushed along in rr after 4f: rdn 6f out: sn wknd: t.o* **20/1**

0- **6** 77 **Clyffe Dancer**[50] 2298 5-10-7 0.. DominicElsworth
(Emma Lavelle) *in rr: lost tch fnl 4f: t.o* **25/1**

4/ **U** **Whiskey Chaser (IRE)**[285] 4800 5-11-0 0............................ AdrianLane 90
(Donald McCain) *chsd ldrs: rdn and disputing cl up 3rd whn stmbld and uns rdr ins fnl 2f* **5/1**[3]

4m 9.0s (6.70) **Going Correction** +0.60s/f (Soft)
WFA 4 from 5yo+ 5lb **7** Ran SP% **111.1**
Speed ratings: **107,104,99,93,70 31,**
Tote Swingers: 1&2 £3.20, 1&3 £3.40, 2&3 £4.20 CSF £18.94 TOTE £3.60: £2.00, £2.60; EX 24.00 Trifecta £245.20 Part won. Pool: £326.98 - 0.08 winning units..
Owner C M Wilson **Bred** C M Wilson **Trained** Newmarket, Suffolk

FOCUS
Quite an interesting finale, with a handful of runners boasting encouraging previous form. The first two have been rated to their marks.
T/Plt: £19.60 to a £1 stake. Pool: £50,486.46 - 1871.40 winning tickets. T/Qpdt: £5.10 to a £1 stake. Pool: £2,259.65 - 324.70 winning tickets. ST

2954 WETHERBY (L-H)
Thursday, December 26

OFFICIAL GOING: Soft (good to soft in places; 6.0)
Wind: Virtually nil Weather: Sunny

3283 WILLIAM HILL - DOWNLOAD THE APP NOVICES' H'CAP CHASE (18 fncs) 3m 1f
12:35 (12:35) (Class 4) (0-110,109) 4-Y-0+ **£3,898** (£1,144; £572; £286)

Form RPR

641- **1** **Clondaw Flicka (IRE)**[27] 2784 5-11-12 **109**.................(p) PeterBuchanan 121+
(Lucinda Russell) *trckd ldrs: led 5th: rdn after 4 out: hdd between last 2: nt fluent last: kpt on to ld again towards fin* **7/2**[1]

002- **2** hd **Shouldavboughtgold (IRE)**[19] 2959 6-11-0 **102**..(t) JonathanEngland(5) 116+
(William Kinsey) *led narrowly tl 5th: sn dropped to midfield: outpcd 13th: hdwy after 5 out to chse ldr 4 out: led between last 2: 2 l up tl stopped in front fnl 100yds: hdd towards fin* **8/1**

223- **3** 28 **Dukeofchesterwood**[30] 2735 11-10-3 **86**......................(p) ConorO'Farrell 70
(Karen McLintock) *hld up: nvr threatened: wnt poor 3rd last* **14/1**

44P- **4** 5 **Royal Sam (IRE)**[18] 2971 8-11-6 **108**..............................(t) AdamNicol(5) 87
(Martin Todhunter) *in tch tl grad wknd fr 4 out* **12/1**

1FP- **5** 7 **Whiskey Ridge (IRE)**[19] 2959 7-11-0 **97**................................ RyanMania 69
(Sue Smith) *trckd ldrs: wnt in snatches: nt fluent 8th: wknd 4 out* **8/1**

0/3- **6** 31 **Brandon Thomas (IRE)**[28] 2765 7-10-11 **94**........................ TomCannon 35
(Nick Gifford) *hld up: hdwy 13th: rdn after 5 out and sn wknd* **14/1**

/4P- **F** **Cottiers Den (IRE)**[15] 3022 6-10-2 **85**............................ WilsonRenwick
(Martin Todhunter) *prom: reminder after 4th: drvn bef 4 out: blnd 3 out: ev ch whn fell 2 out* **40/1**

U/3- **P** **Mr Supreme (IRE)**[41] 2498 8-11-11 **108**.......................... RichieMcGrath
(Keith Reveley) *hld up in rr: nt fluent 5 out: sn btn: p.u bef 4 out* **15/2**[3]

365- **P** **Balinderry (IRE)**[14] 3033 6-10-6 **89**..................................... HarrySkelton
(Steve Gollings) *midfield: reminders 1/2-way: wknd after 10th: p.u bef 12th* **14/1**

431- **P** **Basford Ben**[19] 2959 5-10-12 **95**..(p) JasonMaguire
(Jennie Candlish) *midfield: nt fluent 7th and dropped to rr: sn detached: p.u bef 10th* **9/2**[2]

354- **U** **Lord Fox (IRE)**[19] 2959 6-9-9 **83** oh4...................................... JoeColliver(5)
(Shaun Harris) *trckd ldrs: hmpd and uns 8th* **10/1**

6m 20.0s (10.60) **Going Correction** +0.60s/f (Soft) **11** Ran SP% **113.6**
Speed ratings (Par 105): **107,106,97,96,94 84, , ,**
toteswingers 1&2 £5.10, 1&3 £3.90, 2&3 £4.30 CSF £30.94 CT £344.86 TOTE £4.10: £1.40, £2.80, £2.40; EX 40.00 Trifecta £111.60 Pool: £567.75 - 3.81 winning units..
Owner Dan & Michelle Macdonald, Mackie, Levein **Bred** Fergal O'Mahoney **Trained** Arlary, Perth & Kinross

FOCUS
Away bend put back to split chase and hurdles tracks. A moderate staying handicap run at a decent gallop. The first two are on the upgrade.

3284 WILLIAM HILL - IN THE APP STORE NOVICES' H'CAP HURDLE (11 hdls) 2m 4f
1:10 (1:11) (Class 4) (0-110,108) 3-Y-0+ **£3,249** (£954; £477; £238)

Form RPR

606/ **1** **Catcher Star (IRE)**[259] 5240 5-10-3 **85**..............................(p) TomCannon 89+
(Nick Gifford) *midfield: wnt 3rd 7th: chal whn nt fluent 2 out: upsides whn mstke and lost momentum last: rallied to ld post* **11/2**

503- **2** nk **Getabuzz**[17] 2998 5-11-10 **106**.. RichieMcGrath 106
(Tim Easterby) *trckd ldr: jnd ldr after 4th: led appr 3 out: wandered u.p after 2 out: one pce run-in: hdd post* **5/1**[3]

005- **3** 1 **Kathlatino**[30] 2736 6-9-9 **82** oh6.. JoeColliver(5) 81
(Micky Hammond) *midfield: rdn and in tch appr 3 out: wnt 3rd 2 out: kpt on* **33/1**

330- **4** hd **Lifetime (IRE)**[20] 2932 5-11-3 **106**.............................(t) CraigGallagher(7) 105
(Brian Ellison) *hld up in rr: rdn and hdwy 3 out: wnt 4th 2 out: kpt on* **4/1**[2]

0/5- **5** 4½ **Bold Adventure**[25] 2848 9-11-2 **98**...................................... HarrySkelton 92
(Willie Musson) *hld up: rdn after 3 out: sn one pce and no imp on ldrs* **10/1**

442- **6** 12 **Brunello**[17] 2997 5-11-4 **105**...(p) AdamNicol(5) 87
(Philip Kirby) *led: jnd after 4th: rdn whn hdd appr 3 out: sn wknd* **6/1**

440- **P** **Hallmark Star**[54] 2217 4-11-5 **108**..................................(p) CraigNichol(7)
(Lucinda Russell) *hld up in midfield: mstke 7th: sn wknd: p.u bef 3 out* **8/1**

4U3- **U** **Doyenthedecenthing**[14] 3040 5-9-9 **82** oh4............ JonathanEngland(5)
(John Davies) *in tch: 3 l down disputing 4th whn mstke and uns rdr 3 out* **7/2**[1]

P06- **P** **Jazz Man (IRE)**[19] 2954 6-11-8 **104**.............................(p) WilsonRenwick
(Mark Rimell) *prom: wknd fr 6th: t.o whn p.u bef 3 out* **16/1**

5m 13.2s (13.70) **Going Correction** +0.50s/f (Soft)
WFA 4 from 5yo+ 6lb **9** Ran SP% **117.6**
Speed ratings (Par 105): **92,91,91,91,89 84, ,**
toteswingers 1&2 £21.30, 1&3 £43.20, 2&3 £43.20 CSF £34.17 CT £835.46 TOTE £8.10: £2.30, £2.10, £8.30; EX 64.20 Trifecta £751.80 Part won. Pool: £1,002.51 - 0.87 winning units..
Owner Exors of the Late P A Byrne **Bred** K J Duggan **Trained** Findon, W Sussex

FOCUS
Not form to trust, as the gallop increased quite early when two were clear and the winner had shown little previously. The second and third help set the level.

3285 WILLIAM HILL ROWLAND MEYRICK H'CAP CHASE (GRADE 3) (18 fncs) 3m 1f
1:45 (1:45) (Class 1) 4-Y-0+ **£22,887** (£8,655; £4,387; £2,239; £1,179)

Form RPR

/10- **1** **Cloudy Too (IRE)**[26] 2815 7-11-0 **148**.......................... JonathanEngland(5) 161+
(Sue Smith) *hld up: wnt prom 8th: led appr 4 out: sn pushed clr: nt fluent last: rdn out run-in* **11/4**[2]

0/3- **2** 10 **Tullamore Dew (IRE)**[68] 1971 11-10-0 **129** oh3................. TomCannon 132
(Nick Gifford) *in tch: wnt 2nd 4 out: one pce and sn no ch w wnr* **8/1**

/P0- **3** 2¾ **Cape Tribulation**[26] 2815 9-11-10 **153**............................... HarrySkelton 156+
(Malcolm Jefferson) *midfield: rdn in disp 2nd 4 out: sn one pce: hld in 3rd fr 2 out* **6/1**

/5P- **4** 24 **Junior**[19] 2937 10-11-10 **153**...(b) ConorO'Farrell 128
(David Pipe) *w ldr: nt fluent 8th and lost pl: bhd fr 11th* **25/1**

51P/ **5** 1¼ **Auroras Encore (IRE)**[250] 5404 11-11-5 **148**........................ RyanMania 122
(Sue Smith) *midfield: wknd appr 4 out* **20/1**

/F0- **P** **Master Of The Hall (IRE)**[26] 2822 9-10-11 **140**............ WilsonRenwick
(Micky Hammond) *j. slowly towards rr: p.u after 6th* **33/1**

P/1- **P** **Nuts N Bolts**[33] 2670 7-10-11 **140**.................................(t) PeterBuchanan
(Lucinda Russell) *hld up in rr: a bhd: p.u bef 4 out* **4/1**[3]

5/1- **P** **Sydney Paget (IRE)**[33] 2674 6-11-2 **145**.............................. JasonMaguire
(Donald McCain) *led narrowly: nt fluent 3rd: hdd appr 4 out: wknd qckly and p.u bef 3 out* **5/2**[1]

6m 15.8s (6.40) **Going Correction** +0.60s/f (Soft) **8** Ran SP% **112.2**
Speed ratings (Par 113): **113,109,108,101,100 , ,**
toteswingers 1&2 £9.20, 1&3 £5.20, 2&3 £3.10 CSF £22.97 CT £119.40 TOTE £4.10: £1.50, £2.10, £2.10; EX 27.90 Trifecta £80.70 Pool: £1,585.51 - 14.73 winning units..
Owner Formulated Polymer Products Ltd **Bred** E J O'Sullivan **Trained** High Eldwick, W Yorks

The Form Book Jumps, Raceform Ltd, Compton, RG20 6NL.

FOCUS
With two horses towards the head of the betting running badly, this well-established contest may not have taken a lot of winning. The winner was the form pick on his Carlisle win, but this rates a step up with his jockey claiming this time. The second has been rated to his mark.

3286 WILLIAM HILL - IPHONE, IPAD, IPAD MINI H'CAP HURDLE (12 hdls) 2m 6f
2:20 (2:20) (Class 4) (0-130,125) 4-Y-0+ **£5,523** (£1,621; £810; £405)

Form RPR
/05- **1** **Saphir River (FR)**[54] 2221 7-11-4 **124**..........................(tp) CraigNichol[(7)] 127
(Lucinda Russell) *hld up: stdy hdwy after 4 out: chsd ldr 3 out: lft 2nd 2 out: led last: kpt on* **12/1**
351- **2** *3 ¼* **Rattlin**[19] 2956 5-11-0 **118**.. JonathanEngland[(5)] 117
(Sue Smith) *trckd ldr: led bef 7th: rdn 3 out: 4 l up 2 out: hdd last: no ex* **4/1**[2]
430- **3** *1 ½* **Bourne**[19] 2949 7-11-12 **125**..(b) JasonMaguire 125
(Donald McCain) *midfield: reminders and lost pl 1/2-way: stl in rr after 4 out: styd on fr 3 out: 2 l down whn mstke last: nt rcvr* **10/3**[1]
342/ **4** *22* **Awesome Freddie**[986] 5321 8-11-4 **117**.............................. HarrySkelton 93
(Dan Skelton) *in tch: wnt 2nd 7th: rdn appr 3 out: sn wknd* **9/2**[3]
251/ **5** *2 ¾* **Orangeaday**[269] 5063 6-11-0 **113**..................................(t) PeterBuchanan 86
(Ben Case) *midfield: rdn 3 out: wknd 2 out* **12/1**
P/3- **F** **Embsay Crag**[24] 2447 7-10-7 **106**.............................. RichieMcGrath 99
(Philip Kirby) *hld up: hit 5th: hdwy after 4 out to chse ldr 3 out: 4 l down in 2nd whn fell 2 out* **9/1**
11- **P** **Vinny Gambini (IRE)**[25] 2838 6-11-5 **118**...................... WilsonRenwick
(Rose Dobbin) *in tch: lost pl 8th: sn wknd: p.u bef 2 out* **7/1**
121- **P** **My Oh Mount Brown (IRE)**[28] 2771 6-11-4 **120**.......... MichaelByrne[(3)]
(Tim Vaughan) *led: hdd bef 7th: hit 7th: sn struggling: p.u bef 3 out* **6/1**
5m 33.8s (7.00) **Going Correction** +0.50s/f (Soft) **8** Ran SP% **113.4**
Speed ratings (Par 105): **107,105,105,97,96 , ,**
toteswingers 1&2 £7.60, 1&3 £9.20, 2&3 £4.20 CSF £59.21 CT £198.34 TOTE £15.80: £3.80, £2.00, £1.20; EX 77.40 Trifecta £780.50 Pool: £1,529.83 - 1.47 winning units..
Owner Sandy Seymour **Bred** Jean Collet & Mlle Marie-Laure Collet **Trained** Arlary, Perth & Kinross
FOCUS
Plenty of reasons to oppose most of these, so not form to go mad about. The winner was thrown in on his best form and this was more like it, but he's not easy to predict. The second is on the upgrade and put up a good effort to split well-in rivals.

3287 WILLIAM HILL - NO. 1 DOWNLOADED BETTING APP H'CAP CHASE (16 fncs) 2m 4f 110y
2:55 (2:55) (Class 3) (0-135,133) 4-Y-0+ **£6,498** (£1,908; £954; £477)

Form RPR
/0P- **1** **Noble Legend**[33] 2674 6-11-8 **129**.............................. AndrewThornton 139
(Caroline Bailey) *trckd ldrs: rdn after 5 out: led jst after last: styd on* **8/1**
222- **2** *3 ½* **Tahiti Pearl (IRE)**[12] 3090 9-11-6 **127**.................................... RyanMania 134
(Sue Smith) *prom: led 8th: rdn 4 out: hdd jst after last: no ex* **6/1**[3]
1F0- **3** *12* **Fairy Rath (IRE)**[26] 2816 7-11-8 **129**..................................(t) TomCannon 125
(Nick Gifford) *in tch: rdn after 5 out: one pce: wnt 3rd 2 out: no threat to ldng pair* **12/1**
/F3- **4** *¾* **Kykate**[57] 2159 7-11-0 **121**...(t) RichieMcGrath 114
(William Kinsey) *hld up: rdn after 5 out: sn no imp on ldrs: wnt modest 4th appr last* **14/1**
140- **5** *½* **Mister Grez (FR)**[47] 2365 7-11-4 **125**.............................. HarrySkelton 118
(Dan Skelton) *midfield: rdn after 5 out: sn no imp on ldrs* **11/4**[1]
3F3- **6** *5* **Aneyeforaneye (IRE)**[47] 2358 7-11-2 **128**......... JonathanEngland[(5)] 119
(Malcolm Jefferson) *midfield: mstke 10th: wnt 3rd bef 4 out: sn rdn: lost 3rd 2 out: wknd* **15/2**
/00- **F** **Shadows Lengthen**[41] 2488 7-11-9 **130**........................ WilsonRenwick
(Michael Easterby) *hld up: sme hdwy whn hit 5 out: rdn after 4 out: chalng for 3rd whn fell 3 out* **14/1**
1/5- **P** **Grouse Lodge (IRE)**[40] 2517 7-11-7 **128**......................(p) JasonMaguire
(Donald McCain) *led: hdd 8th: wknd after 10th: p.u bef 4 out* **7/2**[2]
424- **P** **Frank The Slink**[25] 2841 7-9-9 **107** oh4.............................. JoeColliver[(5)]
(Micky Hammond) *hld up in rr: a bhd: p.u bef 4 out* **12/1**
5m 15.9s (8.10) **Going Correction** +0.60s/f (Soft) **9** Ran SP% **114.8**
Speed ratings (Par 107): **108,106,102,101,101 99, , ,**
toteswingers 1&2 £42.20, 1&3 £10.20, 2&3 £4.80 CSF £55.24 CT £574.67 TOTE £9.50: £2.80, £2.00, £3.70; EX 85.20 Trifecta £353.00 Pool: £1,498.28 - 3.18 winning units..
Owner P Dixon Smith **Bred** P Dixon Smith **Trained** Holdenby, Northants
FOCUS
Probably just a fair handicap. The winner was on a good mark and has been rated back to his best. The second is on the upgrade and the third built on his recent reappearance but was still rated 7lb off his best.

3288 WILLIAM HILL - BET ON THE MOVE H'CAP HURDLE (9 hdls) 2m 110y
3:30 (3:31) (Class 4) (0-115,115) 3-Y-0+ **£3,249** (£954; £477; £238)

Form RPR
061- **1** **Circus Star (USA)**[15] 3021 5-10-6 **102**.................................. MrJDixon[(7)] 115+
(John Dixon) *mde all: sn clr: rdn after 2 out: kpt on: unchal* **8/1**
225- **2** *12* **Desgrey**[25] 2844 5-11-10 **113**..(p) AndrewThornton 116
(Peter Niven) *chsd clr ldr in 2nd: clr of main gp tl appr 3 out: rdn 3 out: hit 2 out: plugged on: no threat to wnr* **10/1**
/26- **3** *shd* **Pertuis (IRE)**[40] 2519 7-10-10 **104**....................................(p) JoeColliver[(5)] 105
(Micky Hammond) *hld up: hdwy appr 3 out: chalng for 2nd whn hit 2 out: one pce* **13/2**[2]
035- **4** *3 ¾* **Twoways (IRE)**[18] 2977 7-10-10 **104**........................ JonathanEngland[(5)] 101
(Mark Rimell) *midfield: rdn appr 3 out: plugged on: wnt 4th run-in: nvr threatened* **16/1**
0/3- **5** *½* **Beaumont's Party (IRE)**[23] 2869 6-10-11 **100**..................[1] HarrySkelton 99
(Brian Ellison) *racd keenly: hld up: hdwy appr 3 out: hit 3 out: 4th whn nt fluent 2 out: wknd after last* **5/2**[1]
P63- **6** *5* **Snowed In (IRE)**[21] 2904 4-10-8 **97**...............................(p) RichieMcGrath 89
(Jennie Candlish) *prom main gp: rdn appr 3 out: grad wknd* **11/1**
/66- **7** *9* **Dollar Bill**[31] 2717 4-11-8 **111**...(tp) TomCannon 94
(Nick Gifford) *midfield: rdn bef 3 out: sn wknd* **9/1**
020- **8** *8* **Kilrye (IRE)**[21] 2910 6-10-0 **89** oh3..................................(t) ConorO'Farrell 64
(David Pipe) *hld up: sme hdwy appr 3 out: wknd 2 out* **7/1**[3]
230/ **9** *3 ¼* **Amtired**[6] 3441 7-11-9 **115**...(p) KyleJames[(3)] 86
(Marjorie Fife) *midfield: wnt remote 3rd 5th: wknd after 3 out* **10/1**
0F6/ **10** *6* **Right To Rule (IRE)**[245] 5519 4-11-7 **110**........................ JasonMaguire 75
(Donald McCain) *hld up: a towards rr* **14/1**
/24- **11** *46* **Blades Lad**[25] 2840 4-11-10 **113**.. PeterBuchanan 32
(Peter Niven) *prom main gp: wknd after 5th: t.o 3 out* **20/1**
4m 3.3s (7.50) **Going Correction** +0.50s/f (Soft)
WFA 4 from 5yo+ 5lb **11** Ran SP% **119.3**
Speed ratings (Par 105): **102,96,96,94,94 91,87,83,82,79 57**
toteswingers 1&2 £44.00, 1&3 £11.40, 2&3 £44.00 CSF £86.06 CT £558.04 TOTE £9.50: £3.20, £2.00, £2.00; EX 107.80 Trifecta £1090.20 Part won. Pool: £1,453.68 - 0.90 winning units..
Owner Mrs S F Dixon **Bred** Joseph Clay & Wendy Clay **Trained** Thursby, Cumbria
FOCUS
The winner took this easily after holding a very easy lead. The winner was building on his recent win under similar tactics, while the second has been rated as running a small personal best in the headgear.
T/Plt: £258.90 to a £1 stake. Pool: £75,612.82 - 213.17 winning units T/Qpdt: £32.80 to a £1 stake. Pool: £4,368.33 - 98.30 winning units AS

[2906]WINCANTON (R-H)
Thursday, December 26

OFFICIAL GOING: Heavy (soft in places; chs 6.1, hdl 6.2)
Hurdle on stable bend omitted due to bad ground.
Wind: Mild breeze Weather: Sunny

3289 FDB SHIELDACRE LTD MARES' NOVICES' HURDLE (7 hdls 1 omitted) 2m
12:30 (12:31) (Class 4) 4-Y-0+ **£3,249** (£954; £477; £238)

Form RPR
0/1- **1** **Bobble Boru (IRE)**[31] 2724 5-10-10 0.............................. AidanColeman 105+
(Venetia Williams) *j.lft at times: trckd ldrs: awkward whn wnt lft 2nd: led and wnt lft 2 out: jnd last: styd on wl u.p to assert fnl 100yds* **5/2**[1]
540- **2** *1 ¾* **August Hill (IRE)**[28] 2767 5-10-10 0..................................(t) TomO'Brien 102+
(Philip Hobbs) *plld hrd in tch: trckd ldrs after 3 out: mounting chal whn hmpd next: sn rdn: ev ch fr last tl no ex fnl 100yds* **7/2**[2]
255- **3** *2 ¾* **Revaader**[30] 2725 5-10-10 95.. TommyPhelan 99
(Mark Gillard) *led: hit 3 out: rdn and hdd 2 out: stl ev ch last: sn no ex* **8/1**[3]
450- **4** *13* **Summertime Lady**[21] 2907 5-10-10 0.............................. BrendanPowell 85
(Colin Tizzard) *mid-div: rdn after 3 out: wnt 4th next: styd on wout threatening ldrs* **9/1**
0P0- **5** *3* **Langarve Lady (IRE)**[16] 3005 5-10-3 0.............................. MrLKilgarriff[(7)] 82
(Neil Mulholland) *trckd ldrs: rdn appr 2 out: sn one pce* **100/1**
40P- **6** *7* **A Shade Of Bay**[16] 3010 5-10-5 0.............................. EdCookson[(5)] 75
(Kim Bailey) *j.lft at times: in tch: rdn after 3 out: wknd bef next* **16/1**
0/0- **7** *23* **Reach The Beach**[16] 3005 4-10-10 0.............................. RichieMcLernon 52
(Brendan Powell) *trckd ldr: rdn after 3 out: sn wknd: t.o* **12/1**
/60- **8** *20* **Its April**[21] 2907 5-10-10 0.. SeanQuinlan 32
(Robert Walford) *mstke 2nd: a towards rr: t.o after 3 out* **33/1**
/30- **9** *¾* **Welcometothejungle**[40] 2506 5-10-10 0.............................. NickScholfield 31
(Keiran Burke) *mid-div whn blnd and nrly uns rdr 2nd: fine rcvry by rdr but hmpd whn in rr next: horse nvr rcvrd: sn t.o* **7/2**[2]
P **Ice Nelly (IRE)**[57] 5-10-10 0.. PaddyBrennan
(Stuart Kittow) *hld up bhd: rdn after 3 out: no imp and wkng whn p.u bef next* **16/1**
60/ **F** **Rosa Imperialis**[257] 5295 4-10-10 0.............................. FelixDeGiles
(Robert Walford) *hld up towards rr: fell 3rd* **50/1**
0- **R** **Valley Road**[225] 324 5-10-10 0.. JackDoyle
(Tim Dennis) *towards rr: awkward 1st: tailing off whn ref 3rd* **100/1**
3m 44.8s (-4.10) **Going Correction** -0.05s/f (Good)
WFA 4 from 5yo 5lb **12** Ran SP% **120.5**
Speed ratings (Par 105): **108,107,105,99,97 94,82,72,72,**
toteswingers 1&2 £2.00, 1&3 £13.90, 2&3 £8.20 CSF £11.46 TOTE £3.40: £1.50, £1.10, £3.40; EX 10.40 Trifecta £62.80 Pool: £319.88 - 3.81 winning units..
Owner Mrs B Grainger **Bred** Jimmy Coffey **Trained** Kings Caple, H'fords
FOCUS
The form of this modest mares' event, which saw some erratic jumping, is straightforward with the principals dominating from the home turn. It's been rated around the second, third and fourth.

3290 BATHWICK TYRES NOVICES' H'CAP HURDLE (7 hdls 1 omitted) 2m
1:05 (1:05) (Class 5) (0-100,100) 3-Y-0+ **£1,949** (£572; £286; £143)

Form RPR
603- **1** **Exemplary**[8] 3157 6-11-12 **100**.. NickScholfield 107+
(Marc Barber) *in tch: tk clsr order 3 out: led narrowly 2 out: sn rdn: wandered appr last: styd on: drvn out* **4/1**[2]
F/5- **2** *1 ½* **Pertinent (FR)**[21] 2908 10-11-5 **100**..........................(t) MissAliceMills[(7)] 105
(Charles Whittaker) *led: hdd narrowly 2 out: sn rdn for str chal: ev ch fr last tl no ex fnl 100yds* **14/1**
P/2- **3** *14* **Agapanthus (GER)**[24] 2862 8-11-0 **88**........................(p) BrendanPowell 79
(Neil Mulholland) *in tch: struggling after 3 out: stdy prog whn lft 4th 2 out: wnt 3rd bef last but nvr any ch w ldng pair* **7/2**[1]
000- **4** *11* **Duke's Affair**[35] 2614 5-11-9 **100**.. MattGriffiths[(3)] 80
(Jeremy Scott) *hld up in tch: hdwy 3 out: sn rdn: lft btn 3rd briefly next: wknd* **5/1**[3]
/05- **5** *1 ½* **River Dancing (IRE)**[21] 2906 6-11-6 **94**........................ AidanColeman 72
(Andy Turnell) *hld up in tch: hdwy after 3 out: rdn bef next: sn btn* **7/2**[1]
554- **6** *6* **Vexillum (IRE)**[17] 2628 4-11-3 **98**..................................(t) MrFMitchell[(7)] 71
(Simon Hodgson) *trckd ldrs: rdn after 4th: styd in tch tl wknd after 2 out* **25/1**
/00- **7** *30* **Two Mile Bridge (IRE)**[29] 2740 7-11-7 **95**........................ TomO'Brien 37
(Paul Henderson) *hld up: lost tch after 3 out: t.o* **10/1**
2/6- **F** **Chance Encounter (IRE)**[21] 2906 7-11-2 **97**........................ MrCSmith[(7)] 88
(Linda Blackford) *trckd ldr: rdn in cl 3rd whn fell 2 out* **6/1**
3m 47.1s (-1.80) **Going Correction** -0.05s/f (Good)
WFA 4 from 5yo+ 5lb **8** Ran SP% **115.0**
Speed ratings (Par 103): **102,101,94,88,88 85,70,**
toteswingers 1&2 £9.10, 1&3 £1.50, 2&3 £21.70 CSF £54.40 CT £214.00 TOTE £4.80: £1.90, £3.80, £1.80; EX 35.10 Trifecta £163.40 Part won. Pool: £217.91 - 0.19 winning units..
Owner G M Barber **Bred** Darley **Trained** Haverfordwest, Pembrokes

FOCUS
A wide-open handicap, run at an average gallop. The winner recorded a pb and the second, who is well in on his old form, has been rated back to something like that level.

3291 ARMISHAWS REMOVALS HARRY DUFOSEE NOVICES' CHASE (17 fncs) 2m 5f
1:40 (1:40) (Class 3) 4-Y-0+ **£6,564** (£2,104; £1,169)

Form RPR
/23- 1 **Ardkilly Witness (IRE)**[28] 2756 7-10-13 133.................. BrendanPowell 139+
(Dr Richard Newland) *j.rt at times: disp ld: reminders after 4th: clr ldr whn pushed along 9th: travelling best after 13th: rdn and nrly 3 l up whn lft wl clr 2 out* 3/1[3]
205- 2 19 **Lamb Or Cod (IRE)**[19] 2935 6-10-13 132............................(t) TomO'Brien 124
(Philip Hobbs) *j.lft thrght getting progively worse: trckd ldrs: stmbld bdly 6th: nudged along after next: disp 2nd 9th tl rdn after 12th: wknd after 4 out: lft modest 2nd 2 out* 11/4[2]
U3- 3 36 **Ruapehu (IRE)**[30] 2726 7-10-13 0..(t) JackDoyle 82
(Charles Whittaker) *trckd ldrs: nudged along after 8th: steadily lost tch fr 11th: t.o whn lft 3rd 2 out* 25/1
512/ F **Provo (IRE)**[407] 2417 6-10-13 0.. NickScholfield 135
(Paul Nicholls) *nt a fluent: disp ld tl 8th: trckd wnr: pushed along after 4 out: styng on at same pce in nrly 3 l 2nd whn knuckled on landing and fell 2 out* 11/4[2]
/32- U **Holywell (IRE)**[22] 2882 6-10-13 0................................(p) RichieMcLernon
(Jonjo O'Neill) *bdly hmpd whn uns rdr 1st* 5/2[1]
5m 22.9s (-2.30) **Going Correction** +0.125s/f (Yiel) **5 Ran SP% 110.8**
Speed ratings (Par 107): **109,101,88, ,**
CSF £11.81 TOTE £3.70: £1.40, £1.80; EX 17.10 Trifecta £197.50 Pool: £284.95 - 1.08 winning units..
Owner C E Stedman & Dr R D P Newland **Bred** F Tierney **Trained** Claines, Worcs
FOCUS
An eventful novice chase. This was a step up from the winner, while the faller has been rated in line with his best hurdles form.

3292 PERTEMPS NETWORK H'CAP HURDLE (SERIES QUALIFIER) (10 hdls 1 omitted) 2m 6f
2:15 (2:15) (Class 2) 4-Y-0+ **£11,710** (£3,459; £1,729; £865; £432)

Form RPR
021- 1 **Champagne West (IRE)**[18] 2978 5-10-2 123...................... TomO'Brien 138+
(Philip Hobbs) *j.lft progively worse: prom: led 4th: hanging lft whn rdn between last 2: styng on and 1 l up whn lft clr last* 6/4[1]
/0P- 2 10 **Old Tricks (IRE)**[35] 2629 6-10-0 121 oh4......................(p) BrendanPowell 126
(Colin Tizzard) *in tch: hdwy after 3 out: rdn bef next: styd on same pce: lft in hld 2nd whn hmpd at the last* 25/1
134- 3 1 1/4 **Southfield Theatre (IRE)**[13] 3069 5-11-7 147.............. HarryDerham(5) 149
(Paul Nicholls) *hld up: pushed along bef 6th: tk clsr order 3 out: sn rdn: styd on same pce fr next: lft btn 3rd at the last* 7/2[2]
540- 4 32 **Oscar Prairie (IRE)**[19] 2949 8-10-0 124....................(p) GavinSheehan(3) 94
(Warren Greatrex) *hld up last: nudged along after 5th: struggling after next: lost tch u.p after 3 out: wnt modest 4th sn after last: t.o* 16/1
1/1- 5 3 3/4 **Seebright**[29] 2742 6-10-10 131... JackDoyle 97
(Victor Dartnall) *trckd ldrs: rdn sn after 3 out: wknd between last 2: lft 4th briefly at the last: t.o* 6/1
002- 6 2 **Party Rock (IRE)**[19] 2935 6-11-10 145............................... SeanQuinlan 109
(Jennie Candlish) *hld up: struggling 6th: wknd after 3 out: t.o* 14/1
233/ 7 22 **Chesil Beach Boy**[259] 5260 10-10-8 129..........................(t) NickScholfield 71
(John Coombe) *j.rt: led tl 4th: trckd wnr tl after 7th: wknd after 3 out: t.o* 16/1
164- F **Upswing (IRE)**[19] 2949 5-10-2 123................................ RichieMcLernon 133
(Jonjo O'Neill) *trckd ldrs: trckd wnr after 3 out: rdn between last 2: styng on and 1 l down whn fell last* 9/2[3]
5m 22.9s (-3.60) **Going Correction** +0.125s/f (Yiel) **8 Ran SP% 117.0**
Speed ratings (Par 109): **111,107,106,95,93 93,85,**
toteswingers 1&2 £6.40, 1&3 £1.20, 2&3 £11.40 CSF £35.65 CT £120.29 TOTE £2.40: £1.30, £4.10, £1.50; EX 46.40 Trifecta £286.40 Part won. Pool: £381.90 - 0.65 winning units..
Owner R S Brookhouse **Bred** Peter Byrne **Trained** Withycombe, Somerset
FOCUS
Not the most competitive qualifier for the final of this series at the Cheltenham Festival, and under new rules all eight of the runners become eligible for a run in March. They went an ordinary gallop. The winner was on a good mark but is still on the upgrade. The second has been rated as running close to his course run in January.

3293 BATHWICK TYRES LORD STALBRIDGE MEMORIAL CUP (A H'CAP CHASE) (21 fncs) 3m 1f 110y
2:50 (2:51) (Class 3) (0-125,124) 4-Y-**£9,418** (£2,806; £1,420; £727; £381)

Form RPR
P/U- 1 **Count Guido Deiro (IRE)**[33] 2662 6-11-6 121............ GavinSheehan(3) 131+
(Nigel Twiston-Davies) *disp ld most of way tl clr ldr 14th: rdn whn chal appr 3 out: styd on strly: in control after 2 out: rdn out* 16/1
115- 2 2 1/4 **Waltzing Tornado (IRE)**[12] 3097 9-10-0 103............(p) HarryDerham(5) 113
(Neil Mulholland) *hld up: smooth hdwy fr 15th: rdn to chal appr 3 out: kpt pressing wnr tl 2 out: styd on but no ex* 10/1
024- 3 19 **Chasers Chance (IRE)**[30] 2730 10-10-0 98 oh1.......(p) RichieMcLernon 90
(Paul Henderson) *mid-div: pushed along after 8th: trckd ldrs 17th: sn rdn: hld fr after next: plugged on into modest 3rd bef 2 out* 25/1
222- 4 24 **Rydalis (FR)**[8] 3158 8-11-6 118.. AidanColeman 82
(Venetia Williams) *disp ld tl after 13th: trckd wnr: rdn after 4 out: wknd bef 2 out: t.o* 6/1[3]
552- 5 13 **Shuil Royale (IRE)**[12] 3097 8-11-5 117............................ BrendanPowell 68
(David Arbuthnot) *towards rr but in tch: rdn after 14th: wknd 4 out: t.o* 10/3[2]
/30- P **Ballyallia Man (IRE)**[47] 2373 8-11-12 124......................(t) PaddyBrennan
(Tom George) *trckd ldrs: nt fluent 9th or next: struggling 12th: losing tch qckly whn p.u bef 14th* 6/1[3]
F51- P **Buck's Bond (FR)**[21] 2909 7-11-12 124........................(bt) NickScholfield
(Paul Nicholls) *trckd ldrs: rdn after 16th: wknd after 4 out: p.u bef next* 3/1[1]
554- P **Comeonginger (IRE)**[33] 2662 6-10-13 111............................(t) JackDoyle
(Chris Gordon) *mid-div: hdwy to trck ldrs 16th: mstke 4 out: sn rdn and wknd qckly: p.u bef next* 10/1
413- P **Young Hurricane (IRE)**[21] 2901 7-11-3 115.......................(t) TomO'Brien
(Dr Richard Newland) *j.lft progively worse: mid-div tl stmbld bdly 6th: towards rr: losing tch 14th: p.u bef next* 7/1
6m 42.3s (2.80) **Going Correction** +0.30s/f (Yiel) **9 Ran SP% 117.1**
Speed ratings (Par 107): **107,106,100,93,89 , , ,**
toteswingers 1&2 £14.10, 1&3 £23.90, 2&3 £9.40 CSF £160.79 CT £3948.91 TOTE £19.50: £3.90, £3.60, £5.40; EX 214.10 Trifecta £238.40 Part won. Pool: £317.93 - 0.01 winning unit..
Owner R N Bevis **Bred** Raymond McDonnell **Trained** Naunton, Gloucs
FOCUS
This competitive staying handicap served up a real test. This was a big step up by the winner on his hurdles form, while the second has been rated to his mark.

3294 BATHWICK TYRES MID SEASON CHASE (A H'CAP CHASE) (13 fncs) 2m
3:25 (3:26) (Class 3) (0-130,127) 4-Y-0**£6,330** (£1,870; £935; £468; £234)

Form RPR
343- 1 **Lord Of House (GER)**[13] 3057 5-11-4 122.................(t) GavinSheehan(3) 135+
(Charlie Mann) *j.rt at times: trckd ldrs: rdn after 9th: chal 3 out: led 2 out: kpt on: pushed out* 5/2[2]
251- 2 4 1/2 **Last Shot (FR)**[8] 3156 6-11-12 127 7ex............................ AidanColeman 135+
(Venetia Williams) *disp ld tl 7th: bk disputing after 9th: led appr 3 out: sn rdn and hrd pressed: hdd 2 out: kpt on but no ex fr last* 7/4[1]
0P- 3 10 **Paddy The Stout (IRE)**[12] 3093 8-10-9 110..........(t) NickScholfield 108+
(Paul Henderson) *nt fluent 4th: sn struggling in last but kpt jst abt in tch: no imp tl styd on fr after 2 out: wnt 3rd run-in: nvr threatened ldrs* 7/1
0P5- 4 2 1/4 **Falcon Island**[20] 2925 8-11-12 127.................................. BrendanPowell 122
(Colin Tizzard) *trckd ldrs: rdn after 9th: hld fr next: kpt on same pce to go 4th run-in* 5/1[3]
131- 5 4 **Miss Tenacious**[35] 2629 6-11-10 125..................................... JackDoyle 121
(Ron Hodges) *disp ld: hit 6th: blnd 8th: rdn and hdd appr 3 out: sn dropped to hld 3rd: wknd between last 2: lost 2 pls run-in* 5/1[3]
4m 3.7s (3.80) **Going Correction** +0.30s/f (Yiel) **5 Ran SP% 110.8**
Speed ratings (Par 107): **102,99,94,93,91**
CSF £7.65 TOTE £3.30: £2.10, £1.20; EX 8.50 Trifecta £101.10 Pool: £378.87 - 2.80 winning units..
Owner Good Lord Partnership **Bred** R Venn Bloodstock Ltd **Trained** Upper Lambourn, Berks
FOCUS
This looks to be fair form with two coming nicely clear. The winner improved on his hurdles form and the second has been rated close to the level of his recent win.

3295 CONNOLLY'S RED MILLS BUMPER CHALLENGE STANDARD OPEN NATIONAL HUNT FLAT RACE 2m
3:55 (3:55) (Class 6) 4-6-Y-0 **£1,624** (£477; £238; £119)

Form RPR
0/2- 1 **Mountain Of Mourne (IRE)**[218] 433 4-10-9 0................. MrCSmith(7) 108+
(Linda Blackford) *mde all: qcknd up wl over 2f out: clr over 1f out: readily* 3/1[2]
2 8 **Lily Mars (IRE)** 6-10-2 0.. MikeyHamill(7) 91
(Neil Mulholland) *travelled wl on outer most of way: trckd ldrs: chal over 2f out: sn outpcd: kpt on for clr 2nd* 8/1
6- 3 6 **Dream Destiny**[35] 2634 4-10-9 0.. TommyPhelan 84
(Mark Gillard) *trckd ldrs: rdn 3f out: kpt on same pce fnl 2f* 16/1
4 12 **Supari** 4-11-2 0.. AidanColeman 79
(Sarah-Jayne Davies) *t.k.h trcking ldrs: lost pl over 4f out: wnt 4th over 1f out but nvr any danger to ldrs* 10/1
5 2 1/2 **Free Of Charge (IRE)** 4-11-2 0.. TomO'Brien 76
(Philip Hobbs) *trckd ldrs: effrt 3f out: sn outpcd: wknd over 1f out* 7/4[1]
00- 6 7 **Much A Doo**[177] 862 5-10-9 0.. MrGBranton(7) 69
(Paul Henderson) *trckd ldrs tl wknd over 3f out* 12/1
7 1/2 **Gray Beck** 5-10-13 0.. GavinSheehan(3) 69
(Seamus Durack) *hld up bhd ldrs: pushed along 1/2-way: wknd over 3f out* 7/2[3]
3m 46.0s (2.70) **Going Correction** +0.30s/f (Yiel) **7 Ran SP% 117.4**
Speed ratings: **105,101,98,92,90 87,87**
toteswingers 1&2 £8.60, 1&3 £3.20, 2&3 £10.50 CSF £27.86 TOTE £4.10: £2.30, £3.70; EX 25.60 Trifecta £361.30 Pool: £693.57 - 1.43 winning units..
Owner Over de Last Racing **Bred** Lionel Beresford **Trained** Rackenford, Devon
FOCUS
An ordinary bumper, run at a steady gallop. The cosy winner has been rated as stepping up on his previous efforts.
T/Plt: £408.70 to a £1 stake. Pool: £52,012.37 - 92.90 winning units T/Qpdt: £128.10 to a £1 stake. Pool: £1,974.20 - 11.40 winning units TM

3296 - 3304a (Foreign Racing) - See Raceform Interactive

LEOPARDSTOWN (L-H)
Thursday, December 26
OFFICIAL GOING: Soft (yielding in places)

3305a KNIGHT FRANK JUVENILE HURDLE (GRADE 2) (8 hdls) 2m
1:20 (1:20) 3-Y-0 **£21,138** (£6,178; £2,926; £975)

RPR
1 **Guitar Pete (IRE)**[40] 2500 3-10-12 132..............................(v) BryanCooper 140+
(D T Hughes, Ire) *chsd clr ldr in 2nd whn lft in front after 3rd: jnd and hdd 1/2-way: travelled best to ld appr last and sn clr: comf* 9/2[2]
2 7 **Clarcam (FR)**[25] 2851 3-10-12 123.......................................(t) AELynch 131
(Gordon Elliott, Ire) *chsd ldrs whn lft 2nd after 3rd: sn on terms and led 1/2-way tl hdd appr last: sn no match for wnr* 14/1
3 25 **Henry Higgins (IRE)**[196] 3-10-12 .... MarkWalsh 106
(Charles O'Brien, Ire) *w.w in rr tl prog into 3rd after 3 out: nt fluent next and sn no imp on principals* 16/1
4 28 **Arzembouy Premier (FR)**[102] 3-10-12 .... PCarberry 78
(Gordon Elliott, Ire) *w.w whn lft modest 3rd after 3rd: dropped to 4th after 3 out and sn no ex* 10/1[3]
P **Analifet (FR)**[25] 2851 3-10-8 140.. DavyRussell
(W P Mullins, Ire) *t.k.h and sn clr ldr tl p.u qckly after 3rd w suspected pelvic injury* 30/100[1]
3m 55.0s (-12.50) **Going Correction** -0.80s/f (Firm) **5 Ran SP% 116.7**
Speed ratings: **99,95,83,69,**
CSF £47.92 TOTE £4.00: £1.80, £5.10; DF 50.10 Trifecta £125.00.
Owner Mrs P Sloan **Bred** P J Burke **Trained** The Curragh, Co Kildare

The Form Book Jumps, Raceform Ltd, Compton, RG20 6NL.

FOCUS
An unfortunate injury early in the race to Analifet, who was odds-on to make it four from four over hurdles, robbed this Grade 2 contest of much interest as far as the Triumph Hurdle is concerned. The winner has been rated to his mark.

3308a RACING POST NOVICE CHASE (GRADE 1) (11 fncs) 2m 1f
2:55 (2:55) 4-Y-0+ £44,918 (£13,130; £6,219; £2,073)

RPR

1 **Defy Logic (IRE)**[39] 2550 6-11-12 148 MarkWalsh 154+
(Paul Nolan, Ire) *led tl hdd 5th: sn bk on terms: nt fluent 3 out: tk def advantage next and styd on wl fr bef last* **7/2**[2]

2 3 ½ **Trifolium (FR)**[19] 2965 6-11-12 141 (p) DavyRussell 149+
(C Byrnes, Ire) *chsd ldrs in 3rd: nt qckn bef 4 out in remote 3rd tl prog 2 out: chsd wnr in 2nd bef last: kpt on wl wout getting on terms* **8/1**[3]

3 11 **Champagne Fever (IRE)**[40] 2523 6-11-12 RWalsh 142+
(W P Mullins, Ire) *pressed ldr in 2nd tl led 5th: sn rejnd and disp whn bad mstke 2 out: no imp on wnr whn dropped to 3rd bef last: kpt on one pce* **8/15**[1]

4 5 **Art Of Logistics (IRE)**[25] 2853 5-11-12 138 BryanCooper 133
(D T Hughes, Ire) *racd in modest 4th tl sme hdwy whn pckd sltly 2 out: sn pushed along and no imp: kpt on one pce* **20/1**

5 27 **Ted Veale (IRE)**[39] 2531 6-11-12 RobbiePower 106
(A J Martin, Ire) *hld up in rr: j. slow at times: no imp 3 out* **12/1**

P **Road To Riches (IRE)**[25] 2853 6-11-12 147 PCarberry
(Noel Meade, Ire) *w.w: dropped to rr 1/2-way and sn adrift: p.u after 3 out* **12/1**

4m 0.9s (-21.10) **Going Correction** -0.80s/f (Firm) **6** Ran SP% **118.7**
Speed ratings: **117,115,110,107,95**
CSF £30.18 TOTE £4.20: £1.80, £3.20; DF 17.00 Trifecta £68.50.
Owner John P McManus **Bred** William McCarthy **Trained** Enniscorthy, Co. Wexford

FOCUS
A solid-looking renewal of this event. The favourites took each other on in front and put each other's jumping under pressure. The time was good and the first three help set the standard.

3309 - 3313a (Foreign Racing) - See Raceform Interactive

2398 LIMERICK (R-H)
Thursday, December 26

OFFICIAL GOING: Hurdle course - heavy (soft to heavy in places); chase course - soft (heavy in places)

3314a GREENMOUNT PARK NOVICE CHASE (GRADE 2) (14 fncs) 2m 3f 120y
2:45 (2:45) 4-Y-0+ £19,817 (£5,792; £2,743; £914)

RPR

1 **The Paparrazi Kid (IRE)**[19] 2965 6-11-6 133 EmmetMullins 146
(W P Mullins, Ire) *rapid hdwy to ld after 1st: mde rest: clr fr 5 out: reduced advantage appr 2 out: rdn whn chal and kpt on wl u.p fr bef last: styd on strly run-in* **5/1**[2]

2 1 ½ **Felix Yonger (IRE)**[19] 2965 7-11-12 154 PaulTownend 151+
(W P Mullins, Ire) *hld up towards rr: 5th 1/2-way: smooth hdwy to chse wnr after 3 out: slt mstke next: rdn bef last: styd on wl run-in but no ex cl home: hld* **2/5**[1]

3 4 **Balnaslow (IRE)**[39] 2550 6-11-6 132 PatrickMangan 141
(W P Mullins, Ire) *hld up in rr: 7th 1/2-way: gd prog after 3 out to go 3rd appr next: no ex and styd on same pce* **10/1**

4 1 ½ **Clar Na Mionn (IRE)**[25] 2853 6-11-6 131 PhillipEnright 139
(V T O'Brien, Ire) *chsd ldrs: 4th 1/2-way: rdn after 3 out: no ex appr next and styd on same pce* **14/1**

5 7 ½ **Dushybeag (IRE)**[18] 2993 6-11-6 126 APHeskin 132
(Michael Hourigan, Ire) *towards rr: 6th 1/2-way: rdn to cl after 3 out: one pce and no ex fr next* **20/1**

6 44 **Shrapnel (IRE)**[39] 2550 7-11-9 138 (t) KeithDonoghue 91
(Gordon Elliott, Ire) *chsd ldrs: 2nd 1/2-way: slow jump 8th and again at 5 out: rdn and wknd appr 2 out: t.o* **6/1**[3]

U **Jim Will Fix It (IRE)**[39] 2550 8-11-6 128 (t) MarkBolger
(Seamus Roche, Ire) *chsd ldrs: 3rd 1/2-way: hit 9th and uns rdr* **25/1**

5m 17.0s (317.00) **7** Ran SP% **126.7**
CSF £8.93 TOTE £5.60: £1.60, £1.10; DF 10.90 Trifecta £58.20.
Owner Byerley Thoroughbred Racing **Bred** Pat O'Donovan **Trained** Muine Beag, Co Carlow

FOCUS
Fairly or not, it was an outcome more about the runner-up than the winner. The standard is set by the third, fourth and fifth. The runner-up was below his best.

3315 - 3316a (Foreign Racing) - See Raceform Interactive

3258 KEMPTON (R-H)
Friday, December 27

OFFICIAL GOING: Soft (heavy in places; chs 5.4, hdl 4.8)
Wind: Strong; across Weather: Heavy shower before racing, becoming bright

3317 WILLIAM HILL - IPHONE, IPAD, IPAD MINI JUVENILE HURDLE (8 hdls) 2m
1:00 (1:00) (Class 3) 3-Y-O £6,498 (£1,908; £954; £477)

Form RPR

4- 1 **Vicenzo Mio (FR)**[13] 3078 3-11-8 131 DarylJacob 137+
(Paul Nicholls) *lw: trckd ldr: led sn after 3 out: easily drew clr bef next* **1/1**[1]

2- 2 17 **Stephen Hero (IRE)**[30] 2750 3-10-12 0 HarrySkelton 108
(Dan Skelton) *leggy: lw: chsd ldng pair: rdn to go 2nd on long run bef 2 out but easily lft bhd* **10/3**[3]

21F- 3 4 **Raven's Tower (USA)**[19] 2970 3-11-4 119 DavidBass 110
(Ben Pauling) *racd freely: led at gd pce: mstke 3 out: sn hdd and btn: didn't weaken as much as looked likely* **14/1**

4 19 **Astre De La Cour (FR)**[262] 3-10-12 0 SamTwiston-Davies 91
(Robert Walford) *medium-sized: str: a same pl: in tch 3 out: sn rdn: wknd bef 2 out* **11/4**[2]

0- 5 54 **Classic Art**[21] 2927 3-10-12 0 ColinBolger 30
(Roger Teal) *lots of mstkes: a in last pair: lost tch w ldrs 5th: wl t.o* **100/1**

501- P **Big John Cannon (IRE)**[9] 3154 3-11-4 82 AidanColeman
(Sarah-Jayne Davies) *tall: a in last pair: lost tch 5th: wl t.o whn p.u bef 2 out* **33/1**

4m 3.3s (5.20) **Going Correction** +0.625s/f (Soft) **6** Ran SP% **110.3**
Speed ratings (Par 106): **112,103,101,92,65**
toteswingers 1&2 £1.40, 1&3 £1.40, 2&3 £4.00 CSF £4.67 TOTE £1.60: £1.10, £1.80; EX 5.10 Trifecta £13.10 Pool: £3,154.17 - 180.51 winning units..
Owner Mrs Johnny de la Hey **Bred** Raymonde Wingtans **Trained** Ditcheat, Somerset

FOCUS
All rails out 2yds and distances as advertised. Paul Nicholls has dominated this race in recent seasons, being responsible for three of the previous six winners. This was a big step up from the winner, the time was decent and he looks a smart juvenile. The second and third have been rated as improving slightly.

3318 WILLIAMHILL.COM NOVICES' CHASE (REGISTERED AS THE WAYWARD LAD NOVICES' CHASE) (GRADE 2) (12 fncs) 2m
1:30 (1:30) (Class 1) 4-Y-0+ £20,167 (£7,714; £3,979; £2,100)

Form RPR

/11- 1 **Dodging Bullets**[40] 2531 5-11-8 0 DarylJacob 158+
(Paul Nicholls) *lw: j.lft: chsd ldr 2nd: clsd to ld after 4 out: steadily drew clr: rdn out* **7/4**[2]

/U2- 2 10 **Grandouet (FR)**[20] 2950 6-11-2 0 BarryGeraghty 144
(Nicky Henderson) *led at decent pce: hdd after 4 out: no rspnse whn mstke 3 out: wl btn after* **1/2**[1]

036- 3 34 **Bin End**[23] 2887 7-11-2 102 (p) FelixDeGiles 110
(Barry Brennan) *chsd ldr to 2nd: lost tch after 5th: t.o fr next* **100/1**

053- 4 24 **Red Riverman**[14] 3064 5-11-8 124 SamTwiston-Davies 98
(Nigel Twiston-Davies) *a in last pair: lost tch after 5th: t.o fr next: lft poor 4th last* **16/1**[3]

642- U **Lindsay's Dream**[11] 3135 7-10-9 98 (p) DaveCrosse 85
(Zoe Davison) *mostly in last: lost tch 5th: t.o fr next: remote 4th whn blnd and uns rdr last* **66/1**

4m 4.5s (4.20) **Going Correction** +0.625s/f (Soft) **5** Ran SP% **111.4**
Speed ratings (Par 115): **114,109,92,80,**
CSF £3.19 TOTE £2.00: £1.10, £1.10; EX 3.20 Trifecta £30.40 Pool: £4,336.47 - 106.75 winning units..
Owner Martin Broughton & Friends **Bred** L Dettori **Trained** Ditcheat, Somerset

FOCUS
Despite the absence of Valdez, this renewal provided an interesting clash between two former high-class hurdlers and the pair had it between them from very early on. The winner is on the upgrade and closing in on the level one would expect from a serious Arkle contender, although he lost his form in the second half of last season.

3319 WILLIAM HILL - DOWNLOAD THE APP MARES' H'CAP HURDLE (12 hdls) 3m 110y
2:00 (2:00) (Class 2) 4-Y-0+

£12,512 (£3,696; £1,848; £924; £462; £232)

Form RPR

U51- 1 **Mickie**[28] 2798 5-11-5 135 RichardJohnson 146+
(Henry Daly) *hld up: n.m.r bnd after 4th: prog whn awkward jump 9th: led bef 3 out: 3 l up bef 2 out: sn rdn: nrly jnd last: fnd ex flat* **5/2**[1]

312- 2 1 **Cannon Fodder**[25] 2860 6-10-4 120 MarcGoldstein 126
(Sheena West) *w ldrs: chal bef 3 out: rdn to chse wnr after: rallied fr 2 out: nrly upsides last: kpt on but hld nr fin* **12/1**

123- 3 22 **Ballinahow Star (IRE)**[17] 3011 7-10-9 125 (t) NickScholfield 109
(Jeremy Scott) *w ldr: lost pl qckly after 8th and last bef next: plugged on again bef 2 out to take modest 3rd after last* **12/1**

425- 4 1 ½ **Utopie Des Bordes (FR)**[20] 2949 5-11-7 142 NicodeBoinville(5) 125
(Nicky Henderson) *lw: trckd ldrs: cl 3rd 3 out but rdn: wknd bef 2 out* **3/1**[2]

124- 5 nk **Mrs Peachey (IRE)**[20] 2948 6-11-0 130 AidanColeman 112
(Kim Bailey) *lw: hld up in last: prog bef 3 out: pushed along and lft bhd by ldng pair bef 2 out: sn wnt 3rd: rdn and floundering after: wknd last* **6/1**

/13- 6 6 **Scholastica**[20] 2948 6-10-9 125 FelixDeGiles 105
(Tom Symonds) *pckd 2nd: in tch: mstke 4th: rdn fr 1/2-way: kpt chsng ldrs tl steadily wknd after 3 out* **9/2**[3]

/45- P **Lady Kathleen**[20] 2948 6-9-9 116 oh5 MauriceLinehan(5)
(Paul Webber) *mde most to 5th: drvn and wknd rapidly after 9th: t.o whn p.u bef 2 out* **12/1**

/40- P **Alder Mairi (IRE)**[20] 2948 6-10-8 124 AndrewThornton
(Seamus Mullins) *racd wd: prom: led 5th to bef 3 out: wknd rapidly: t.o whn p.u bef 2 out* **16/1**

6m 27.0s (11.00) **Going Correction** +0.625s/f (Soft) **8** Ran SP% **115.0**
Speed ratings (Par 109): **107,106,99,99,99 97, ,**
toteswingers 1&2 £5.60, 1&3 £4.30, 2&3 £3.30 CSF £31.41 CT £304.03 TOTE £3.10: £1.10, £2.70, £2.60; EX 34.90 Trifecta £449.70 Pool: £1,104.35 - 1.84 winning units..
Owner Ludlow Racing Partnership **Bred** J B Sumner **Trained** Stanton Lacy, Shropshire

FOCUS
Traditionally a decent mares' handicap hurdle and two likeable sorts came clear. The winner is on the upgrade and is a bit better than the bare result, while the second recorded a small pb in defeat.

3320 WILLIAMHILL.COM DESERT ORCHID CHASE (GRADE 2) (12 fncs) 2m
2:30 (2:30) (Class 1) 4-Y-0+ £45,774 (£17,310; £8,774; £4,478; £2,358)

Form RPR

121- 1 **Sire De Grugy (FR)**[20] 2952 7-11-10 169 JamieMoore 166+
(Gary Moore) *lw: w.w: trckd ldr after 5th: clsd to ld 4 out: rdn and j.lft last 3: kpt on wl* **4/1**[2]

544- 2 4 **Oiseau De Nuit (FR)**[20] 2952 11-11-6 154 (t) BrendanPowell 155
(Colin Tizzard) *hld up: lft in 3rd pl after 7th: chsd wnr after 4 out: kpt on wl but nvr able to chal* **33/1**

203- 3 26 **Astracad (FR)**[13] 3080 7-11-0 144 (vt) SamTwiston-Davies 131
(Nigel Twiston-Davies) *lw: nt fluent: hld up in last: nvr on terms but plugged on into poor 3rd bef 2 out* **50/1**

/50- 4 10 **Tataniano (FR)**[20] 2952 9-11-0 145 AndrewThornton 113
(Richard Rowe) *chsd clr ldr to 5th: lost pl rapidly and last fr next: sn t.o: passed a toiling rival nr fin* **66/1**

/61- 5 2 ½ **Fago (FR)**[35] 2656 5-11-6 152 DarylJacob 119
(Paul Nicholls) *led and sn clr: lunged at 5th: hdd 4 out: wknd rapidly bef next and sed jumping lft* **14/1**[3]

111/ P **Sprinter Sacre (FR)**[248] 5487 7-11-10 188 BarryGeraghty
(Nicky Henderson) *lw: hld up in 5th: trckd ldng pair after 5th: sing to lose grnd whn nt fluent 7th and qckly p.u* **2/9**[1]

4m 6.5s (6.20) **Going Correction** +0.625s/f (Soft) **6** Ran SP% **114.9**
Speed ratings (Par 115): **109,107,94,89,87**
toteswingers 1&2 £3.30, 1&3 £7.70, 2&3 £18.20 CSF £60.87 TOTE £3.20: £1.40, £5.10; EX 31.50 Trifecta £227.70 Pool: £35,320.81 - 116.30 winning units..
Owner The Preston Family & Friends Ltd **Bred** La Grugerie **Trained** Lower Beeding, W Sussex

FOCUS
Even though the favourite pulled up, the result still makes sense considering the form of the winner. The winner wasn't quite at his best in a messy affair.

3321 WILLIAM HILL - BET ON THE MOVE H'CAP CHASE (18 fncs) 3m
3:05 (3:05) (Class 2) (0-145,140) 4-Y-0+
£25,024 (£7,392; £3,696; £1,848; £924; £464)

Form RPR
/3P- **1** **Ma Filleule (FR)**[13] 3082 5-11-9 **137**................................. BarryGeraghty 145+
(Nicky Henderson) *trckd ldrs: shkn up after 4 out: clsd to ld narrowly 2 out: mstke last: hdd flat: rallied to ld nr fin* **13/2**
1/5- **2** *hd* **Valoroso**[27] 2812 8-10-11 **125**...(t) ConorO'Farrell 135+
(Richard Woollacott) *t.k.h: trckd ldrs: mstkes 10th and 14th: stl gng wl after 4 out: shkn up to chal whn nt fluent 2 out: led after last: nt qckn and hdd nr fin* **9/2**[2]
/04- **3** *4* **Cnoc Seoda (IRE)**[29] 2754 8-10-4 **118**.............................(t) TomO'Brien 120
(Paul Henderson) *in tch towards rr: rdn after 4 out: sme prog but hanging after 3 out: kpt on to take 3rd after last* **25/1**
021- **4** *3* **Bally Legend**[21] 2925 8-11-11 **139**.. IanPopham 141+
(Caroline Keevil) *lw: jinked s: mde most: hrd pressed after 4 out: hdd 2 out: 3rd and btn whn blnd last: wknd* **5/1**[3]
F23- **5** *3 ¼* **Polisky (FR)**[29] 2754 6-10-13 **127**...................................(tp) NickScholfield 123
(Paul Nicholls) *hld up in last pair: tried to creep into the r after 4 out: shkn up and no rspnse after 3 out* **12/1**
014- **6** *12* **Forest Walker (IRE)**[51] 2293 6-11-0 **128**........................... HarrySkelton 119
(Dan Skelton) *lw: wl in tch: mstke 12th: prog to press ldr 4 out: upsides 3 out: wknd qckly bef next* **9/2**[2]
150- **P** **American Spin**[20] 2953 9-10-12 **126**.....................................(v) JamieMoore
(Luke Dace) *racd wd: pressed ldng pair: wknd rapidly u.str.p after 9th: t.o whn p.u bef 12th* **14/1**
004- **P** **On Trend (IRE)**[17] 3006 7-10-13 **127**.........................(p) AndrewThornton
(Nick Gifford) *lw: mostly pressed ldr tl wknd qckly and mstke 4 out: bhd whn p.u bef next* **7/1**
302- **F** **Merrion Square (IRE)**[21] 2931 7-11-5 **133**.........................(t) DarylJacob
(Paul Nicholls) *hld up in last pair: nt fluent 9th: stl there but in tch and pushed along whn fell 4 out: winded* **4/1**[1]

6m 25.9s (10.50) **Going Correction** +0.625s/f (Soft) **9** Ran SP% **117.1**
Speed ratings (Par 109): **107,106,105,104,103 99,** , ,
toteswingers 1&2 £6.00, 1&3 £19.90, 2&3 £24.10 CSF £37.13 CT £692.55 TOTE £6.80: £2.10, £1.70, £6.40; EX 35.20 Trifecta £1255.90 Pool: £1,815.95 - 1.08 winning units..
Owner Simon Munir **Bred** Serge Dubois **Trained** Upper Lambourn, Berks

FOCUS
Good prize money produced a decent handicap chase and in turn a close finish. The winner seems a better chaser than hurdler, while the second has been rated as running a pb in defeat and would probably have won without the jumping errors.

3322 WILLIAM HILL - IN THE APP STORE H'CAP HURDLE (8 hdls) 2m
3:40 (3:40) (Class 3) (0-135,132) 3-Y-0+ **£12,996** (£3,816; £1,908; £954)

Form RPR
131- **1** **Three Kingdoms (IRE)**[22] 2893 4-11-8 **131**.................... JackQuinlan(3) 144+
(John Ferguson) *prom: lft in 2nd pl 5th: led bef 2 out: rdn and hdd sn after last: rallied wl to ld post* **7/2**[2]
252- **2** *shd* **Vibrato Valtat (FR)**[20] 2947 4-11-1 **121**..............................(t) DarylJacob 134+
(Paul Nicholls) *lw: hld up in rr: stdy prog gng wl fr 3 out: trckd wnr after 2 out: produced to ld sn after last: styd on but hdd post* **7/2**[2]
155- **3** *18* **Tidal Way (IRE)**[34] 2668 4-11-1 **124**.........................(p) KielanWoods(3) 120
(Charlie Longsdon) *trckd ldrs: mstke 2nd: rdn in 4th bef 2 out: sn lft bhd by ldrs: tk modest 3rd after last* **20/1**
0/2- **4** *2 ¼* **Bohemian Rhapsody (IRE)**[29] 2755 4-10-11 **117**.......... ConorO'Farrell 110
(Seamus Durack) *hld up in detached last: mstke 1st and smetimes j.lft: sme prog 3 out but nvr gng wl enough: wl btn 5th after 2 out* **11/4**[1]
0/4- **5** *nk* **Right Step**[71] 1943 6-10-10 **116**...(t) JamieMoore 113+
(Pat Phelan) *wl in tch: clsd on ldrs 3 out: rdn to chal 2 out: 6 l down in 3rd and btn whn blnd last: wknd* **33/1**
/11- **6** *12* **Fergall (IRE)**[15] 3031 6-11-9 **132**.............................. WayneKavanagh(3) 112
(Seamus Mullins) *hld up towards rr: blnd 2nd: sltly hmpd 5th: rdn and wknd wl bef 2 out* **14/1**
020- **7** *1* **Specialagent Alfie**[20] 2951 7-11-7 **127**..............................(t) TomCannon 108
(Nick Gifford) *trckd ldrs: hmpd 5th: rdn after 3 out: wknd bef 2 out* **12/1**
/20- **8** *13* **Seventh Sky (GER)**[20] 2951 6-11-6 **126**............................(tp) MarkGrant 92
(Charlie Mann) *chsd clr ldr: lft in ld and sltly hmpd 5th: appeared to be gng wl after 3 out: hdd & wknd rapidly bef 2 out* **14/1**
024/ **P** **Somemothersdohavem**[244] 5573 4-11-6 **126**...................... AidanColeman
(Venetia Williams) *in tch: sltly hmpd 5th: wknd sn after 3 out: wl bhd whn p.u bef 2 out* **14/1**
230- **F** **Milord (GER)**[20] 2951 4-10-13 **124**...................................(p) EdCookson(5)
(Kim Bailey) *led after nthing else wanted to and sn clr: 6 l up and coming bk to field whn fell 5th* **8/1**[3]

4m 4.4s (6.30) **Going Correction** +0.625s/f (Soft)
WFA 4 from 5yo+ 5lb **10** Ran SP% **117.6**
Speed ratings (Par 107): **109,108,99,98,98 92,92,85,** ,
toteswingers 1&2 £3.80, 1&3 £14.10, 2&3 £22.90 CSF £16.77 CT £214.42 TOTE £4.10: £1.90, £1.50, £6.00; EX 14.70 Trifecta £212.30 Pool: £3,684.14 - 13.00 winning units..
Owner Bloomfields **Bred** Darley **Trained** Cowlinge, Suffolk

FOCUS
A competitive handicap hurdle and a really close finish. They went no pace until Milord, in first-time cheekpieces, went on and that gelding was clear when coming down at the fifth. The first two are on the upgrade and powered clear.
T/Jkpt: £10,847.50 to a £1 stake. Pool: £99,308.10 - 6.50 winning units T/Plt: £127.70 to a £1 stake. Pool: £143,617.43 - 820.90 winning units T/Qpdt: £87.10 to a £1 stake. Pool: £7,112.06 - 60.38 winning units JN

3023 LEICESTER (R-H)
Friday, December 27

OFFICIAL GOING: Hurdle course - soft (heavy in places; good to soft in places on the back straight); chase course - good to soft (good in places; soft on flat course crossings) (hdl 7.3; chs 7.8)
Wind: Blustery Weather: Sunny spells

3323 TOTEPLACEPOT RACING'S FAVOURITE BET H'CAP CHASE (12 fncs) 2m
12:35 (12:35) (Class 3) (0-125,125)
4-Y-0+ **£6,498** (£1,908; £954; £477)

Form RPR
334- **1** **Baile Anrai (IRE)**[13] 3091 9-11-9 **122**..................................(b) RyanMahon 127
(Dan Skelton) *chsd ldr tl led after 2nd: hdd 8th: rdn and outpcd bef next: rallied appr last: styd on u.p to ld fnl 50yds* **15/8**[1]
101- **2** *1* **Christopher Wren (USA)**[26] 2845 6-11-12 **125**...............(p) TomCannon 129
(Nick Gifford) *a.p: chsd wnr 3rd: led 3 out: rdn flat: hdd and unable qck fnl 50yds* **4/1**[3]
26/- **3** *3* **Prince Of Dreams**[264] 5198 6-11-7 **123**......................... JoshuaMoore(3) 123
(Ed de Giles) *a.p: led 8th: hdd 3 out: ev ch next: rdn appr last: styd on same pce flat* **10/3**[2]
P05- **4** *44* **Jack The Gent (IRE)**[28] 2785 9-11-11 **124**.................... RichieMcLernon 95
(George Moore) *led: blnd 2nd: sn hdd and lost pl: tk clsr order 7th: wknd 4 out: mstke next* **12/1**
604- **5** *1 ¼* **Le Bacardy (FR)**[26] 2845 7-11-7 **120**...................................(p) LeeEdwards 80
(Tony Carroll) *hld up: mstke 3rd (water): sn lost tch* **6/1**
/06- **P** **Wessex King (IRE)**[28] 2797 9-11-3 **119**........................ JakeGreenall(3)
(Henry Daly) *prom: hmpd 2nd: chsd wnr next tl hit 5th: sn wknd: bhd whn p.u bef 7th* **7/1**

4m 5.5s (-2.70) **Going Correction** -0.15s/f (Good) **6** Ran SP% **112.3**
Speed ratings (Par 107): **100,99,98,76,75**
toteswingers 1&2 £2.80, 1&3 £1.40, 2&3 £3.10 CSF £10.03 TOTE £3.50: £1.60, £1.80; EX 8.60 Trifecta £29.80 Pool: £581.00 - 14.60 winning units..
Owner Massive **Bred** Fred Williams **Trained** Alcester, Warwicks

FOCUS
A modest handicap, run at a good gallop. The winner is probably better over further but the race panned out for him. The second has been rated to his recent C&D win.

3324 TOTEPOOL HOME OF KING SIZE POOLS (S) HURDLE (10 hdls) 2m 4f 110y
1:10 (1:10) (Class 5) 4-Y-0+ **£1,949** (£572; £286; £143)

Form RPR
0P2- **1** **Stow**[22] 2894 8-10-11 117...(p) JoshWall(7) 125+
(Michael Blake) *mde all: clr fr 3 out: blnd last* **11/4**[1]
/5P- **2** *15* **Going Wrong**[20] 2956 10-10-12 120...(t) RyanMahon 98
(Dan Skelton) *prom: rdn after 7th: wknd 3 out: sn hung rt and wnt mod 2nd bef next: blnd last* **3/1**[2]
24P- **3** *14* **Woody Waller**[36] 2618 8-10-12 0...(tp) PaulMoloney 85
(Sophie Leech) *hld up: pushed along 5th: hdwy to go 3rd 3 out: sn wknd* **14/1**
003- **4** *39* **Tisfreetdream (IRE)**[24] 2877 12-11-4 93.................................(p) JackDoyle 49
(Peter Pritchard) *chsd ldrs: rdn after 7th: wknd bef next* **20/1**
P46- **5** *9* **Sublime Talent (IRE)**[19] 2977 7-10-5 0............................(tp) ConorRing(7) 34
(Evan Williams) *hld up: hdwy 4th: chsd wnr appr 3 out: rdn and wknd bef next* **5/1**
000- **6** *1* **Thinger Licht (FR)**[17] 3012 4-11-8 108.................................... LeeEdwards 43
(Tony Carroll) *chsd ldrs: lost pl 4th: bhd fr next* **33/1**
144- **P** **Persian Herald**[10] 3149 5-11-5 105.............................(bt) TrevorWhelan(3)
(Neil King) *chsd wnr tl rdn and wknd after 7th: bhd whn p.u 2 out* **9/1**
415- **F** **Belle De Fontenay (FR)**[12] 3117 8-11-0 115..........(p) ConorShoemark(5)
(Conor Dore) *hld up: fell 3rd* **4/1**[3]

5m 22.1s (-2.60) **Going Correction** -0.15s/f (Good) **8** Ran SP% **112.7**
Speed ratings (Par 103): **98,92,86,72,68 68,** ,
toteswingers 1&2 £2.00, 1&3 £4.10, 2&3 £13.00 CSF £11.18 TOTE £3.00: £1.10, £1.30, £4.70; EX 14.00 Trifecta £124.90 Pool: £822.57 - 4.93 winning units..There was no bid for the winner.
Owner Mrs J M Haines **Bred** Plantation Stud **Trained** Trowbridge, Wilts

FOCUS
An ordinary seller that turned into a procession. The second has been rated in line with the best of his recent runs.

3325 TOTEQUADPOT FOUR PLACES IN FOUR RACES H'CAP CHASE (FOR THE LEICESTERSHIRE SILVER FOX) (11 fncs 4 omitted) 2m 4f 110y
1:40 (1:46) (Class 3) (0-125,124) 4-Y-0+ **£7,596** (£2,244; £1,122; £561; £280)

521/ **1** **Good Order**[247] 5496 8-11-11 **123**...(t) AlainCawley 129+
(Tom George) *a.p: jnd ldr 3 out: sn pushed along: led last: styd on u.p* **8/1**
/F0- **2** *1* **Majorica King (FR)**[28] 2797 7-10-12 **115**..................... ThomasGarner(5) 121+
(Oliver Sherwood) *hld up: hdwy 7th: led 4 out: blnd 2 out: hdd last: unable qck towards fin* **8/1**
004- **3** *16* **The Chazer (IRE)**[20] 2945 8-11-11 **123**................................ PaulMoloney 113
(Richard Lee) *hld up: hdwy after 7th: rdn and wknd appr last* **5/1**[3]
66P- **4** *10* **Lough Coi (IRE)**[27] 2804 7-9-9 **98** oh1...........................(tp) JamesBanks(5) 79
(Anthony Middleton) *chsd ldrs: drvn along after 7th: wknd 2 out* **10/1**
21P/ **5** *15* **Glens Boy (IRE)**[650] 4918 9-11-4 **116**................................. RichieMcLernon 83
(Jonjo O'Neill) *led to 2nd: chsd ldrs: wknd appr 2 out* **4/1**[2]
/P5- **6** *1 ½* **Tafika**[26] 2847 9-10-12 **110**...(p) DominicElsworth 76
(Paul Webber) *led 2nd to 4 out: rdn and wknd after next* **7/2**[1]
1F0- **P** **Midnight Macarena**[24] 2874 8-10-4 **107**..........................(p) MattCrawley(5)
(Lucy Wadham) *prom tl wknd 7th: bhd whn p.u bef 2 out* **16/1**
/35- **P** **Chestertern**[27] 2803 6-11-6 **118**... SeanQuinlan
(Jennie Candlish) *prom: mstke 1st: lost pl after next: bhd and rdn 5th: j. slowly next: sn p.u* **4/1**[2]

5m 12.2s (-6.70) **Going Correction** -0.15s/f (Good) course record **8** Ran SP% **116.1**
Speed ratings (Par 107): **106,105,99,95,90 89,** ,
toteswingers 1&2 £14.90, 1&3 £3.60, 2&3 £9.40 CSF £68.62 CT £354.86 TOTE £6.00: £2.20, £2.80, £1.30; EX 73.10 Trifecta £291.70 Pool: £909.31 - 2.33 winning units..
Owner Sharon C Nelson & Dermot O'Donohoe **Bred** P C Nelson **Trained** Slad, Gloucs

FOCUS
A competive handicap chase in which the first two dominated up the straight. The winner is on the upgrade and there should be more to come from him, while the second has been rated to his chase mark.

3326 YOUR FAVOURITE POOL BETS AT TOTEPOOL.COM NOVICES' HURDLE (10 hdls) 2m 4f 110y

2:10 (2:11) (Class 4) 4-Y-0+ **£3,249** (£954; £477; £238)

Form RPR

1- **1** **Mosspark (IRE)**[44] 2457 5-11-5 0 NoelFehily 131+
(Emma Lavelle) *a.p: chsd ldr 7th: pushed along bef next: rdn to ld appr 2 out: sn clr: mstke last: styd on* **1/3**[1]

/62- **2** *11* **Bhakti (IRE)**[20] 2954 6-10-12 0 RichieMcLernon 114
(Mark Rimell) *led: rdn appr 3 out: hdd bef next: wknd appr last* **4/1**[2]

500- **3** *2 1/4* **Cadeau George**[13] 3092 4-10-12 0 AndrewTinkler 110
(Ben Pauling) *hld up: hdwy 5th: rdn and wknd 2 out* **50/1**

/04- **4** *25* **Seas Of Green**[17] 3005 6-10-5 0 AdamWedge 78
(Paul Cowley) *hld up: hdwy 3 out: rdn and wknd bef next* **12/1**[3]

0- **5** *85* **Sand Artist (IRE)**[32] 2720 5-10-7 0 CallumWhillans(5)
(Venetia Williams) *prom: mstke 1st: lost pl 5th: sn bhd* **25/1**

6- **6** *1* **High Aspirations (IRE)**[41] 2509 5-10-5 0 JoshWall(7)
(Michael Blake) *hld up: rdn and wknd after 7th* **33/1**

/0P- **P** **Special Vintage**[8] 3177 7-10-12 0 WayneHutchinson
(Graeme McPherson) *chsd ldr and nt fluent 1st: sn given reminders: rdn after 4th: lost 2nd 7th: sn wknd: bhd whn p.u bef next* **100/1**

5m 23.3s (-1.40) **Going Correction** -0.15s/f (Good)
WFA 4 from 5yo+ 6lb **7** Ran SP% **112.4**
Speed ratings (Par 105): **96,91,90,81,49 48,**
toteswingers 1&2 £1.02, 1&3 £2.80, 2&3 £9.50 CSF £1.98 TOTE £1.20: £1.10, £1.50; EX 2.00 Trifecta £12.30 Pool: £983.23 - 59.67 winning units..

Owner N Mustoe & Tim Syder **Bred** Mrs Anthea Smyth **Trained** Hatherden, Hants

FOCUS
A novice hurdle lacking in depth. The first two have been rated pretty close to their marks, with seeminhgly a big step up from the third.

3327 CHELTENHAM ANTE POST BETTING AT TOTEPOOL.COM NOVICES' CHASE (18 fncs) 2m 7f 110y

2:45 (2:45) (Class 3) 4-Y-0+ **£6,486** (£2,026; £1,091)

Form RPR

/10- **1** **Ely Brown (IRE)**[34] 2672 8-11-0 0 (p) NoelFehily 141+
(Charlie Longsdon) *chsd ldrs: led 8th: hit 14th: rdn appr last: styd on wl* **13/8**[1]

123- **2** *16* **Beeves (IRE)**[19] 2969 6-11-7 138 WayneHutchinson 138
(Donald McCain) *led to 2nd: pushed along at various stages: drvn along after 8th: styd on same pce fr 3 out: mstke next: wnt 2nd appr last* **9/2**[3]

F02- **3** *11* **Sixty Something (FR)**[17] 3011 7-10-11 132 JakeGreenall(3) 121
(Paul Webber) *led 2nd to 8th: chsd wnr: pushed along after 13th: rdn and wknd appr last* **7/4**[2]

/02- **F** **Cloudy Spirit**[32] 2719 8-10-7 0 PaulMoloney
(Andrew Hollinshead) *hld up: mstke 6th: fell 10th* **5/1**

5m 55.7s (-8.30) **Going Correction** -0.15s/f (Good) **4** Ran SP% **109.3**
Speed ratings (Par 107): **107,101,98,**
CSF £8.54 TOTE £3.00; EX 7.70 Trifecta £8.10 Pool: £558.48 - 51.51 winning units..

Owner Countrywide Vehicle Rentals Taxi Hire **Bred** James Meagher **Trained** Over Norton, Oxon

FOCUS
Only four runners, but a competitive novice chase.

3328 BET TOTETRIFECTA ON ALL RACES H'CAP HURDLE (FOR THE LEICESTERSHIRE BRONZE FOX) (8 hdls) 2m

3:15 (3:15) (Class 3) (0-125,132) 3-Y-0+ **£6,498** (£1,908; £954; £477)

Form RPR

301- **1** **Act Of Kalanisi (IRE)**[11] 3132 7-11-12 **132** 7ex...(bt) ChristopherWard(7) 143+
(Dr Richard Newland) *mde all: clr appr 2 out: blnd last: styd on wl* **7/4**[1]

/33- **2** *8* **Headly's Bridge (IRE)**[8] 3169 7-11-2 **115** GerardTumelty 118
(Simon Earle) *hld up: hdwy 5th: chsd wnr appr 2 out: sn rdn: styng on same pce whn mstke last* **5/1**[3]

532- **3** *nk* **Hartside (GER)**[6] 3201 4-10-10 **116** MrRWinks(7) 118
(Peter Winks) *chsd ldrs: lost pl 4th: outpcd after next: rallied appr last: styd on* **9/2**[2]

/13- **4** *1 1/2* **Wily Fox**[36] 2625 6-10-12 **118** KieronEdgar(7) 119
(James Eustace) *trckd ldrs: t.k.h: rdn after 3 out: styd on same pce appr last* **15/2**

151/ **5** *6* **Veloce (IRE)**[263] 5220 5-11-9 **122** (t) AdrianLane 117
(Donald McCain) *chsd wnr to 3rd: remained handy: rdn after 3 out: wknd appr last* **10/1**

401- **6** *hd* **Lost In Newyork (IRE)**[22] 2898 6-9-8 **100** oh15 ow1.. CharlieDeutsch(7) 94
(Nick Kent) *hld up: hdwy appr 3 out: rdn and wknd after next* **16/1**

000- **7** *16* **Heurtevent (FR)**[26] 2848 4-10-4 **103** LeeEdwards 81
(Tony Carroll) *prom: chsd wnr 3rd to 5th: rdn and wknd after 3 out* **33/1**

060- **8** *29* **Touch Back (IRE)**[27] 2828 7-11-8 **121** RichieMcLernon 70
(Jonjo O'Neill) *hld up: pushed along and wknd after 5th* **8/1**

3m 54.9s (-6.10) **Going Correction** -0.15s/f (Good)
WFA 4 from 5yo+ 5lb **8** Ran SP% **112.0**
Speed ratings (Par 107): **109,105,104,104,101 101,93,78**
toteswingers 1&2 £2.00, 1&3 £3.90, 2&3 £6.00 CSF £10.79 CT £32.27 TOTE £3.00: £1.20, £2.10, £2.00; EX 13.50 Trifecta £36.00 Pool: £698.95 - 14.55 winning units..

Owner C E Stedman,Dr R D P And Mrs L J Newland **Bred** Mrs Joan Keaney **Trained** Claines, Worcs

FOCUS
Not the strongest of handicaps for the grade. The winner was well in on his recent win but this looks another step up from him under his claiming rider, backed up by a good time. The third and fourth have been rated close to their marks.

T/Plt: £19.30 to a £1 stake. Pool: £71,045.18 - 2,681.69 winning units T/Qpdt: £12.40 to a £1 stake. Pool: £4,323.90 - 256.10 winning units CR

3283 WETHERBY (L-H)

Friday, December 27

OFFICIAL GOING: Soft
Wind: Very strong; half behind Weather: Very windy; showers

3329 WILLIAM HILL - DOWNLOAD THE APP MARES' NOVICES' HURDLE (11 hdls) 2m 4f

12:15 (12:16) (Class 4) 4-Y-0+ **£3,249** (£954; £477; £238)

Form RPR

212- **1** **Run Ructions Run (IRE)**[23] 2883 4-11-5 112 (p) DougieCostello 116+
(Tim Easterby) *trckd ldrs: upsides 6th: led 8th: 5 l ahd whn hit last: easily* **8/11**[1]

2 *5* **Poncho**[23] 4-10-12 0 TomScudamore 97
(Mark Rimell) *hld up: hdwy to trck ldrs bef 3rd: chsd wnr appr 3 out: kpt on: no imp* **16/1**

/15- **3** *27* **Falcon's Present**[23] 2885 5-10-12 0 RichieMcGrath 72
(John Weymes) *j.rt: set slow pce tl after 5th: j. slowly next 2: hdd 8th: wknd bef next* **10/1**

600- **4** *1* **Definitely Better (IRE)**[8] 3168 5-10-12 0 PaddyBrennan 69
(Tom George) *chsd ldrs: drvn 8th: sn wknd: bhd whn j.rt last 3* **7/1**[3]

000/ **5** *20* **Minden March**[886] 1203 8-10-12 0 TomSiddall 49
(Peter Maddison) *in rr: hmpd 3rd: bhd fr 6th: t.o 8th* **66/1**

03- **B** **Gold Show**[23] 2883 4-10-7 0 TonyKelly(5)
(Edwin Tuer) *trckd ldrs: b.d 3rd* **9/4**[2]

P **Classical Chloe**[94] 5-10-12 0 BrianHughes
(Tim Fitzgerald) *chsd ldrs: drvn 8th: sn wknd: t.o whn p.u bef next* **66/1**

350- **F** **Lacocodanza**[30] 2752 4-10-12 0 BarryKeniry
(George Moore) *trckd ldrs: fell 3rd* **20/1**

5m 36.7s (37.20) **Going Correction** +0.90s/f (Soft) **8** Ran SP% **123.9**
Speed ratings (Par 105): **61,59,48,47,39 , ,**
toteswingers 1&2 £6.10, 1&3 £2.90, 2&3 £24.50 CSF £16.62 TOTE £2.00: £1.10, £3.80, £3.00; EX 19.90 Trifecta £94.40 Pool: £2,085.44 - 16.56 winning units..

Owner Tom Ford **Bred** Minch Bloodstock & AV Bloodstock **Trained** Great Habton, N Yorks

FOCUS
Away bend put back to split chase and hurdles tracks. With the defection of Flementime this mares' novices' hurdle turned into a fairly modest contest, weakened even further when the only threat to the winner on paper, Gold Show, was brought down at an early stage. It turned out to be a straightforward assignment for the odds-on favourite.

3330 WILLIAM HILL - IN THE APP STORE NOVICES' HURDLE (9 hdls) 2m 110y

12:45 (12:46) (Class 4) 4-Y-0+ **£3,422** (£997; £499)

Form RPR

152- **1** **Secrete Stream (IRE)**[30] 2748 4-10-12 0 BrianHughes 128+
(Malcolm Jefferson) *hld up in mid-div: hdwy to trck ldrs 4th: clr 2nd appr 3 out: shkn up to ld between last 2: j.lft: wnt clr: eased towards fin* **9/4**[1]

65/- **2** *11* **Allied Answer**[58] 3080 5-10-12 0 JamesReveley 116+
(Steve Gollings) *led 2nd to 6th: led again bef next: hdd between last 2: no ch w wnr* **16/1**

630- **3** *18* **Rocky Stone (IRE)**[14] 3061 5-10-12 0 JasonMaguire 94
(Donald McCain) *chsd ldrs: drvn 5th: outpcd appr 3 out: kpt on to take modest 3rd last* **33/1**

4 *3 1/2* **Retrieve (AUS)**[412] 6-10-12 0 DenisO'Regan 92
(John Ferguson) *hld up in rr: hdwy 6th: 3rd and pushed along next: wknd last* **5/2**[2]

/16- **5** *nk* **Clan William (IRE)**[30] 2748 5-11-5 0 RyanMania 97
(Sue Smith) *nt fluent: led: j.lft 1st: hdd 2nd: led 6th: hdd bef next: wknd appr last* **9/1**

40- **6** *6* **Utopian**[42] 2499 4-10-12 0 RichieMcGrath 84
(Rose Dobbin) *stdd s: hld up in rr: hdwy 5th: outpcd appr 3 out: nvr a threat* **80/1**

03- **7** *1 1/2* **Choisan (IRE)**[26] 2840 4-10-12 0 DougieCostello 83
(Tim Easterby) *prom: nt fluent 4th: lost pl 6th* **20/1**

8 *4 1/2* **Sleepy Eye (IRE)**[82] 4-10-12 0 BrianHarding 78
(Jedd O'Keeffe) *chsd ldrs: lost pl after 6th* **20/1**

0- **9** *2 1/4* **Ever Fortune (USA)**[15] 3034 4-10-12 0 TomScudamore 76
(Brian Ellison) *hld up in rr: hdwy 5th: lost pl after next: sn bhd* **16/1**

P **Swiftly Done (IRE)**[48] 6-10-12 0 PaddyBrennan
(Declan Carroll) *stdd s: hld up in rr: nt fluent 4th: eased and bhd after 6th: p.u bef next* **12/1**

363- **P** **Pulpitarian (USA)**[19] 2968 5-10-12 119 PeterBuchanan
(Lucinda Russell) *chsd ldrs: lost pl 6th: sn bhd: t.o whn p.u bef next* **6/1**[3]

0- **P** **Baile Atha Cliath (IRE)**[32] 2507 4-10-12 0 BarryKeniry
(Declan Carroll) *hld up in mid-div: t.k.h: lost pl after 6th: t.o whn p.u bef next* **100/1**

450- **P** **Oorayvic (IRE)**[180] 847 6-10-7 0 JonathanEngland(5)
(Sue Smith) *t.k.h: sn trcking ldrs: lost pl and blnd 6th: sn bhd: t.o whn p.u between last 2* **66/1**

4m 8.8s (13.00) **Going Correction** +0.90s/f (Soft)
WFA 4 from 5yo+ 5lb **13** Ran SP% **119.3**
Speed ratings (Par 105): **105,99,91,89,89 86,86,83,82, , ,**
toteswingers 1&2 £8.40, 1&3 £12.90, 2&3 £62.30 CSF £35.95 TOTE £3.00: £1.50, £4.70, £4.70; EX 48.50 Trifecta £735.70 Pool: £2,202.03 - 2.24 winning units..

Owner Mrs M E Dixon **Bred** Michael Bolger **Trained** Norton, N Yorks

FOCUS
An interesting novices hurdle, run at a fair pace, with the front pair pulling well clear of the remainder and both look horses to keep onside.

3331 WILLIAM HILL - EXCLUSIVE MOBILE OFFERS NOVICES' CHASE (16 fncs) 2m 4f 110y

1:15 (1:15) (Class 3) 4-Y-0+ **£6,498** (£1,908; £954)

Form RPR

/12- **1** **Many Clouds (IRE)**[35] 2658 6-11-5 140 LeightonAspell 157+
(Oliver Sherwood) *trckd ldng pair: cl 2nd 10th: led next: pushed clr bef 2 out: 12 l ahd last: eased run-in* **8/15**[1]

/11- **2** *16* **Indian Castle (IRE)**[30] 2747 5-11-5 137 JasonMaguire 140
(Donald McCain) *t.k.h: led to 3rd: w ldr: led 6th: hdd 11th: drvn next: rdn bef 4 out: one pce fr 3 out: eased clsng stages* **2/1**[2]

/44- **3** *5* **Pinerolo**[15] 3037 7-10-13 112 RyanMania 126
(Sue Smith) *w ldr: led 3rd: hdd and hit 6th: lost pl 13th: sn bhd: 12 l down in 3rd last: kpt on: flattered* **14/1**[3]

5m 30.4s (22.60) **Going Correction** +1.35s/f (Heav) **3** Ran SP% **105.2**
Speed ratings (Par 107): **110,103,102**
CSF £1.92 TOTE £1.40; EX 2.00 Trifecta £2.90 Pool: £2,560.93 - 659.18 winning units..

Owner Trevor Hemmings **Bred** Aidan Aherne **Trained** Upper Lambourn, Berks

FOCUS
Only three runners, but an intriguing contest.

3332 WILLIAM HILL - BET ON THE MOVE INTRODUCTORY JUVENILE HURDLE (9 hdls) 2m 110y
1:45 (1:53) (Class 4) 3-Y-0 **£3,249** (£954; £477; £238)

Form RPR

1- **1** **Handiwork**[22] 2899 3-11-5 0 .... JasonMaguire 119
(Steve Gollings) *trckd ldrs: cl 2nd after 6th: styd on u.p to land upsides last: led run-in: kpt on wl clsng stages* **3/1**[2]

2 *1* **Royal Skies (IRE)**[90] 3-11-0 0 .... DenisO'Regan 114+
(John Ferguson) *trckd ldr: led after 6th: pushed along next: jnd last: sn hdd and no ex: eased nr fin* **10/11**[1]

3 *21* **Pearl Castle (IRE)**[93] 3-11-0 0 .... BrianHughes 95
(John Quinn) *trckd ldrs: t.k.h: clr 3rd and drvn after 6th: grad wknd* **4/1**[3]

4 *15* **Kolonel Kirkup**[98] 3-11-0 0 .... BarryKeniry 77
(Michael Dods) *t.k.h: trckd ldrs: lost pl bef 3 out* **25/1**

0- **5** *17* **Amour Collonges (FR)**[20] 2960 3-11-0 0 .... PaddyBrennan 60
(Chris Grant) *j.rt: set v stdy pce to 3rd: hdd after 6th: sn lost pl and bhd* **25/1**

6 *17* **Khelac**[71] 3-10-9 0 .... JoeColliver(5) 43
(Micky Hammond) *hld up in rr: bhd fr 6th* **25/1**

0- **7** *9* **Bold And Free**[22] 2899 3-10-9 0 .... TonyKelly(5) 34
(David Thompson) *t.k.h in rr: lost pl 6th: sn wl bhd* **50/1**

P **Janaab (IRE)**[76] 3-11-0 0 .... JamesReveley
(Tim Easterby) *hld up in rr: nt fluent 4th: sme hdwy 6th: sn wknd: t.o whn p.u bef last* **12/1**

4m 21.3s (25.50) **Going Correction** +1.35s/f (Heav) **8** Ran SP% **118.6**
Speed ratings (Par 104): **94,93,83,76,68 60,56,**
toteswingers 1&2 £1.20, 1&3 £2.10, 2&3 £1.50 CSF £6.42 TOTE £4.80: £1.30, £1.10, £1.60; EX 7.30 Trifecta £15.60 Pool: £3,786.49 - 180.94 winning units..
Owner C Johnstone **Bred** The Queen **Trained** Scamblesby, Lincs

FOCUS
Just a steady early pace for this interesting juvenile hurdle, which featured some fair Flat performers making their respective debuts in this discipline. The front pair certainly look useful recruits in this sphere.

3333 WILLIAM HILL CASTLEFORD H'CAP CHASE (13 fncs) 2m
2:15 (2:21) (Class 2) (0-150,150) 4-Y-0+ **£14,427** (£5,247)

Form RPR

/04- **1** **Pepite Rose (FR)**[222] 392 6-11-2 **140** .... LiamTreadwell 154+
(Venetia Williams) *j. v big 1st and rdr briefly lost iron: hld up: handy 3rd 6th: led appr 4 out: clr 2 out: 12 l ahd sn after last: tired and drvn rt out* **4/1**[3]

/11- **2** *11* **King Of The Wolds (IRE)**[38] 2574 6-10-8 **132** .... BrianHughes 133
(Malcolm Jefferson) *w ldr: pckd landing 6th: led next: hdd and outpcd appr 4 out: lft 5 l 2nd 3 out* **13/8**[1]

5/6- **P** **Wilde Pastures (IRE)**[48] 2359 8-9-13 **130** .... (p) DaleIrving(7)
(James Ewart) *chsd ldrs: drvn 7th: sn lost pl: wknd 9th: t.o whn p.u bef next* **10/1**

/00- **F** **His Excellency (IRE)**[20] 2952 5-11-7 **145** .... (b) TomScudamore
(David Pipe) *hld up in rr: outpcd 8th: poor 4th after next: keeping on whn fell 4 out* **15/2**

1/2- **F** **Majala (FR)**[62] 2081 7-11-12 **150** .... (t) PaddyBrennan
(Tom George) *led: blnd 1st: hdd 7th: rallied and chsd wnr appr 4 out: 4 l down whn fell 3 out* **9/4**[2]

4m 12.7s (16.90) **Going Correction** +1.35s/f (Heav) **5** Ran SP% **109.7**
Speed ratings (Par 109): **111,105, , ,**
CSF £11.28 TOTE £4.70: £1.90, £1.20; EX 12.00 Trifecta £13.90 Pool: £3,567.61 - 191.90 winning units..
Owner Falcon's Line Ltd **Bred** Pegasus Breeding Ltd **Trained** Kings Caple, H'fords

FOCUS
Only a small field for the feature on the card, where only two managed to complete after a decent early pace in the conditions began to show in the home straight.

3334 WILLIAM HILL - NO. 1 DOWNLOADED BETTING APP H'CAP HURDLE (DIV I) (13 hdls) 3m 1f
2:50 (2:52) (Class 5) (0-95,95) 4-Y-0+ **£1,949** (£572; £286; £143)

Form RPR

550- **1** **Millers Reef (IRE)**[82] 1785 7-11-7 **90** .... RichieMcGrath 99+
(Keith Dalgleish) *hld up in rr: smooth hdwy to trck ldrs 10th: led on bit appr next: shkn up and 3 l clr last: comf* **7/1**

202- **2** *4 ½* **Definite Lady (IRE)**[19] 2980 7-11-12 **95** .... (b) TomScudamore 98
(Mark Rimell) *chsd ldr: drvn 10th: upsides next: kpt on same pce appr last* **5/1**[3]

0B4- **3** *11* **Optical High**[24] 2877 4-10-4 **78** .... JonathanEngland(5) 69
(Sue Smith) *led: increased pce 8th: hdd appr 3 out: wknd between last 2* **7/2**[2]

033- **4** *11* **Blue Cove**[8] 3179 8-10-9 **78** .... TomSiddall 58
(Lynn Siddall) *hld up in rr: hdwy to trck ldrs 7th: pushed along 9th: outpcd after next: distant 4th appr 3 out* **7/2**[2]

400- **5** *26* **Makellys Blackpool**[29] 2767 4-9-12 **72** .... HarryChalloner(5) 26
(Richard Ford) *hit 2nd: chsd ldrs 7th: drvn 9th: lost pl next: sn bhd: t.o 3 out* **14/1**

/03- **6** *33* **Crushed Ice**[34] 2680 7-10-13 **82** .... BrianHughes 3
(Malcolm Jefferson) *chsd ldng pair: drvn 10th: sn wknd: blnd next: sn t.o in last* **9/4**[1]

7m 0.5s (44.00) **Going Correction** +1.80s/f (Heav)
WFA 4 from 6yo+ 7lb **6** Ran SP% **111.0**
Speed ratings (Par 103): **101,99,96,92,84 73**
toteswingers 1&2 £7.20, 1&3 £4.10, 2&3 £3.40 CSF £39.26 CT £137.70 TOTE £6.40: £3.30, £2.20; EX 46.60 Trifecta £102.00 Pool: £3,701.65 - 27.21 winning units..
Owner M C MacKenzie **Bred** Pat And Oliver McCarthy **Trained** Carluke, S Lanarks

FOCUS
A low-grade staying handicap hurdle that looked the stronger of the two divisions, despite the non-runners leaving only the six.

3335 WILLIAM HILL - NO. 1 DOWNLOADED BETTING APP H'CAP HURDLE (DIV II) (13 hdls) 3m 1f
3:25 (3:26) (Class 5) (0-95,95) 4-Y-0+ **£1,949** (£572; £286; £143)

Form RPR

65P- **1** **Adili (IRE)**[12] 3119 4-10-0 **79** .... GLavery(10) 86
(Brian Ellison) *in rr: hdwy 8th: chsng ldrs and drvn after 10th: styd on to ld last: drvn rt out* **11/1**[3]

5/3- **2** *1 ¼* **Stickleback**[37] 2596 4-11-3 **86** .... JasonMaguire 92
(Micky Hammond) *hld up in rr: hdwy to chse ldrs 8th: cl 2nd last: styd on same pce* **4/1**[2]

/PF- **3** *8* **Gorey Lane (IRE)**[27] 2818 7-11-5 **95** .... (v) StephenMulqueen(7) 95
(John Norton) *chsd ldrs: led after 10th: hdd last: one pce* **28/1**

4/6- **4** *1 ¾* **Waywood Princess**[36] 2620 8-10-4 **78** .... HarryChalloner(5) 74
(John Bryan Groucott) *w ldrs: led 9th: hdd next: drvn 3 out: one pce appr last* **4/1**[2]

P50- **5** *3 ½* **Delightfully (FR)**[42] 2497 9-11-2 **92** .... (vt) GrantCockburn(7) 86
(Lucinda Russell) *mid-div: hdwy to chse ldrs 8th: drvn and outpcd 10th: modest 5th 3 out: kpt on: nvr a threat* **4/1**[2]

0P4- **6** *6* **Burnthill (IRE)**[27] 2827 8-9-12 **74** .... (tp) GeraldQuinn(7) 63
(Claire Dyson) *w ldrs: led briefly 10th: wl outpcd bef next: no threat after* **7/2**[1]

01P/ **7** *7* **Desert Tommy**[216] 12-10-8 **84** .... (p) NathanMoscrop(7) 64
(Lucinda Egerton) *led: drvn 8th: hdd next: lost pl sn after 10th: sn bhd* **20/1**

10P- **8** *13* **Almond Court (IRE)**[82] 1789 10-10-12 **81** .... KennyJohnson 48
(Robert Johnson) *trckd ldrs: upsides 8th: drvn 10th: lost pl bef next: sn bhd* **20/1**

/50- **9** *17* **Desert Nova (IRE)**[28] 2787 11-10-4 **73** .... BrianHughes 23
(Mark Campion) *mid-div: chsd ldrs 8th: lost pl sn after 10th: sn bhd: t.o 2 out* **20/1**

0/0- **P** **Irish By Name (IRE)**[58] 2156 7-11-0 **90** .... JohnDawson(7)
(John Wade) *in rr: wl bhd 10th: t.o whn p.u bef next* **16/1**

34P- **P** **Reckless Romeo (IRE)**[26] 2842 4-10-8 **77** .... RichieMcGrath
(Richard Ford) *in rr: last and drvn 8th: wl bhd 10th: t.o whn p.u bef next* **16/1**

7m 6.6s (50.10) **Going Correction** +1.80s/f (Heav)
WFA 4 from 7yo+ 7lb **11** Ran SP% **120.1**
Speed ratings (Par 103): **91,90,88,87,86 84,82,78,72,**
toteswingers 1&2 £8.00, 1&3 £77.80, 2&3 £77.80 CSF £53.73 CT £1230.36 TOTE £11.90: £2.90, £1.90, £8.50; EX 76.60 Trifecta £1333.90 Pool: £3,027.76 - 1.70 winning units..
Owner Brian Ellison & Chris Lowther **Bred** His Highness The Aga Khan's Studs S C **Trained** Norton, N Yorks

FOCUS
More competitive than the first division regarding runners and any one of four could have won the race jumping the last, but a weak staying handicap hurdle nonetheless.
T/Plt: £28.60 to a £1 stake. Pool: £53,710.88 - 1,367.10 winning units T/Qpdt: £9.00 to a £1 stake. Pool: £3,185.53 - 260.52 winning units WG

3336 - 3337a (Foreign Racing) - See Raceform Interactive

3303
LEOPARDSTOWN (L-H)
Friday, December 27

OFFICIAL GOING: Soft (yielding to soft in places on chase course)

3338a PADDY POWER DIAL-A-BET CHASE (GRADE 1) (11 fncs) 2m 1f
1:20 (1:20) 5-Y-0+ **£52,845** (£15,447; £7,317; £2,439)

RPR

1 **Benefficient (IRE)**[55] 2229 7-11-12 157 .... BryanCooper 166+
(A J Martin, Ire) *chsd ldrs in 4th: tk clsr order in 3rd bef 4 out: clsd on outer into st to ld narrowly last: drifted lft u.p run-in: all out towards fin: kpt on wl* **9/1**

2 *¾* **Hidden Cyclone (IRE)**[41] 2503 8-11-12 153 .... (p) AndrewJMcNamara 165+
(John Joseph Hanlon, Ire) *chsd ldr: mod 2nd bef 1/2-way: tk clsr order 3 out: almost on terms next where pckd sltly: led narrowly into st tl hdd last: short of room between horses run-in and swtchd in 3rd: kpt on wl cl home: hld* **8/1**

3 *½* **Arvika Ligeonniere (FR)**[19] 2991 8-11-12 161 .... RWalsh 165+
(W P Mullins, Ire) *hld up towards rr: j.rt 2nd and next: clsr in 5th after 1/2-way: wnt 4th bef 2 out and sn clsd to chal into st: ev ch far side fr last: no ex u.p in 3rd cl home* **7/4**[1]

4 *15* **Sizing Europe (IRE)**[55] 2234 11-11-12 167 .... AELynch 152
(Henry De Bromhead, Ire) *led: over 6 l clr bef 1/2-way: slow 5th and reduced advantage: j. sltly rt 5 out and reminder: almost jnd bef 2 out and hdd into st: dropped to 4th bef last: no ex* **11/4**[2]

5 *14* **Baily Green (IRE)**[83] 1776 7-11-12 157 .... (t) DJCasey 138
(M F Morris, Ire) *chsd ldrs: 3rd 1/2-way: pushed along in 4th bef 3 out and sn no ex u.p: wknd* **10/1**

6 *17* **Rubi Light (FR)**[19] 2991 8-11-12 152 .... (t) DavyRussell 123
(Robert Alan Hennessy, Ire) *chsd ldrs in 5th: dropped towards rr bef 3 out: pushed along in mod 6th fr next: wknd* **20/1**

7 *13* **Kid Cassidy (IRE)**[40] 2532 7-11-12 156 .... APMcCoy 110
(Nicky Henderson) *w.w in rr: mstkes 4 out and next: no imp after: bad mstke last: t.o* **9/2**[3]

4m 8.5s (-13.50) **Going Correction** -0.425s/f (Good) **7** Ran SP% **116.2**
Speed ratings: **114,113,113,106,99 91,85**
CSF £74.91 TOTE £12.30: £4.30, £3.00; DF 96.00 Trifecta £436.70.
Owner A Shiels & Niall Reilly **Bred** Peter Tomany **Trained** Summerhill, Co. Meath

FOCUS
Three second-season chasers finished clear, with the fourth well below last year's form.

3339a PADDY POWER FUTURE CHAMPIONS NOVICE HURDLE (GRADE 1) (8 hdls) 2m
1:50 (1:54) 4-Y-0+ **£42,276** (£12,357; £5,853; £1,951)

RPR

1 **The Tullow Tank (IRE)**[26] 2852 5-11-10 140 .... DannyMullins 147+
(Philip Fenton, Ire) *chsd ldrs: pushed along fr 2 out and wnt 3rd between last 2: swtchd rt and qcknd on outer to ld bef last: drew clr run-in* **9/4**[2]

2 *8* **King Of The Picts (IRE)**[47] 2407 4-11-7 133 .... PCarberry 136
(John Patrick Shanahan, Ire) *led: slt mstke 4 out and hdd: regained advantage fr next: rdn into st and hdd bef last: no imp on wnr run-in: kpt on same pce* **33/1**

3 *2 ¾* **Moyle Park (IRE)**[33] 2704 5-11-10 .... RWalsh 137
(W P Mullins, Ire) *chsd ldrs: clsr in 2nd bef 1/2-way: dropped to 3rd 4 out where slt mstke: impr into 2nd gng wl into st: sn pushed along and dropped to 3rd bef last where mstke: no ex run-in* **6/5**[1]

4 *6* **Arctic Fire (GER)**[26] 2852 4-11-7 138 .... PaulTownend 127
(W P Mullins, Ire) *chsd ldrs in 4th: t.k.h: clsr in 2nd at 4th and led next: hdd fr 3 out: no ex u.p in 4th bef last: kpt on one pce* **5/1**[3]

5 *16* **Art Of Payroll (GER)**[48] 2377 4-11-7 127 .... BryanCooper 111
(D T Hughes, Ire) *hld up in tch: rdn and no imp in 6th after 2 out: kpt on one pce* **33/1**

The Form Book Jumps, Raceform Ltd, Compton, RG20 6NL.

6 35 **The Game Changer (IRE)**19 2989 4-11-7 128.................. DavyRussell 76
(C F Swan, Ire) *hld up in tch: rdn in cl 5th fr 2 out and sn no ex u.p: wknd between last 2: t.o* **8/1**

P **Gambling Girl (IRE)**26 2852 4-11-0 132.........................1 RobbiePower
(Mrs John Harrington, Ire) *in rr: sme mstkes: pushed along after 3 out and no ex: t.o whn p.u bef last* **16/1**

4m 5.8s (-1.70) **Going Correction** +0.30s/f (Yiel)
WFA 4 from 5yo 5lb 7 Ran SP% **115.8**
Speed ratings: **116,112,110,107,99 82,**
CSF £55.01 TOTE £2.70: £2.10, £6.60; DF 48.50 Trifecta £456.80.
Owner Barry Connell **Bred** Aidan Aherne **Trained** Carrick-On-Suir, Co Tipperary

FOCUS
Some high-class performers have won the Royal Bond Novice Hurdle and this event in the same year and The Tullow Tank emulated Istabraq, Hurricane Fly and Jezki by completing the Grade 1 double. The runner-up set a good pace and helps set the level.

3340 - 3349a (Foreign Racing) - See Raceform Interactive

3141
CATTERICK (L-H)
Saturday, December 28

OFFICIAL GOING: Soft (6.9)
Wind: 1/2 against Weather: Cloudy

3350 WATCH ON 3 DEVICES RACINGUK.COM/ANYWHERE MAIDEN HURDLE (DIV I) (8 hdls) 2m
12:25 (12:27) (Class 4) 3-Y-0+ **£3,249** (£954; £477; £238)

Form RPR

/54- 1 **Yorkist (IRE)**55 2241 5-10-13 102.............................. NathanMoscrop(7) 123+
(Brian Ellison) *prom: led 4th: jnd 2 out: sn rdn: asserted appr last: kpt on run-in* **7/2**3

310/ 2 4 1/2 **Fair Loch**29 5179 5-11-6 0.. HarryHaynes 120+
(K R Burke) *trckd ldrs: upsides 2 out: sn rdn: one pce and hld in 2nd fr appr last* **9/2**

\- 3 4 1/2 **Benzanno (IRE)**77 4-11-6 0.. JasonMaguire 116+
(Donald McCain) *in tch: slow 4th and briefly lost pl: pushed along to chse ldng pair appr 2 out: rdn after 2 out: one pce* **9/4**2

4 11 **Rainbow Peak (IRE)**420 7-11-6 0...................................... DenisO'Regan 108+
(John Ferguson) *hld up in midfield: hdwy and in tch appr 2 out: pushed along and sn hld in 4th after 2 out* **2/1**1

5 12 **Time Of My Life (IRE)**142 4-11-1 0..............................(t) JoeColliver(5) 91
(Patrick Holmes) *trckd ldrs: grad wknd appr 2 out* **33/1**

P/ 6 29 **Persian Peril**71 2216 9-11-6 0... HarrySkelton 62
(Alan Swinbank) *midfield: pushed along after 3 out: wknd appr 2 out* **25/1**

000- 7 17 **Torrington Deal**24 2883 5-10-13 0...................................... BarryKeniry 38
(Malcolm Jefferson) *led: hdd 4th: wknd after 3 out* **100/1**

00- 8 15 **Auto Mac**11 3144 5-11-6 0.. BrianHarding 30
(Mike Sowersby) *hld up: mstke 3rd: a bhd* **100/1**

0- 9 13 **Escape To The West**32 2738 5-11-1 0..................... SamanthaDrake(5) 17
(Joanne Foster) *hld up in rr: a bhd* **100/1**

3P/ P **Pelican Rock (IRE)**14 2846 4-11-1 0.................................. AdamNicol(5)
(David Thompson) *midfield: hit 2nd: wknd after 5th: t.o whn p.u bef 2 out* **200/1**

3m 54.5s (2.00) **Going Correction** +0.30s/f (Yiel)
WFA 3 from 4yo 13lb 4 from 5yo+ 5lb 10 Ran SP% **114.8**
Speed ratings (Par 105): **107,104,102,97,91 76,68,60,54,**
CSF £18.75 TOTE £4.60: £1.10, £1.60, £1.40; EX 20.90 Trifecta £25.80 Pool: £485.12 - 14.05 winning units..
Owner Mike And Eileen Newbould **Bred** Con O'Keeffe **Trained** Norton, N Yorks

FOCUS
The first division of this maiden hurdle was run at a steady pace and the four market leaders finished clear of the rest. Jockeys who rode in the opener described the ground as "soft" and "loose".

3351 WATCH ON 3 DEVICES RACINGUK.COM/ANYWHERE MAIDEN HURDLE (DIV II) (8 hdls) 2m
12:55 (12:55) (Class 4) 3-Y-0+ **£3,249** (£954; £477; £238)

Form RPR

?- 1 **Aalim**23 2899 3-10-7 0... DenisO'Regan 113+
(John Ferguson) *hld up in tch: smooth hdwy after 3 out to trck ldr appr next: led on bit between last 2: nudged clr run-in: comf* **11/8**1

52- 2 6 **Dark Dune (IRE)**13 3106 5-11-6 0...................................... JamesReveley 113
(Tim Easterby) *led: rdn appr 2 out: hdd between last 2: kpt on but no ch w wnr run-in* **7/1**

/22- 3 2 1/2 **Spin Cast**33 2718 5-10-13 110.. MissHBethell(7) 111
(Brian Ellison) *trckd ldrs: rdn and ev ch 2 out: nt fluent last: no ex* **5/1**3

4 3 1/4 **Zip Wire (IRE)**66 4-11-6 0.. JasonMaguire 109+
(Donald McCain) *nt fluent: in tch on inner: swtchd towards outer appr 3 out: rdn and hdwy to chse ldr appr 2 out: mstke 2 out: sn hld in 4th* **9/4**2

5 12 **Mohawk Ridge**60 7-11-1 0.. JonathanEngland(5) 95
(James Moffatt) *prom: slow 4th: wknd appr 2 out* **20/1**

4/5- 6 21 **Dissidancer (IRE)**29 2792 5-10-13 0............................. JohnDawson(7) 74
(John Wade) *trckd ldrs: wknd after 3 out* **50/1**

7 2 1/4 **Young Jay**82 3-10-4 0.. JohnKington(3) 59
(Andrew Crook) *midfield: wknd after 3 out* **50/1**

6/0- P **Bellingo**11 3147 6-10-13 0...(p) KennyJohnson
(Robert Johnson) *racd keenly: hld up: lost tch after 4th: t.o whn hit 3 out: p.u bef next* **200/1**

5- F **Spring Back**32 2738 5-10-8 0.. TonyKelly(5)
(Edwin Tuer) *hld up in rr: slow 2nd: pushed along whn fell 5th* **100/1**

3m 56.5s (4.00) **Going Correction** +0.30s/f (Yiel)
WFA 3 from 4yo+ 13lb 9 Ran SP% **112.2**
Speed ratings (Par 105): **102,99,97,96,90 79,78, ,**
toteswingers: 1&2 £1.90, 1&3 £1.80, 2&3 £7.50. CSF £11.05 TOTE £2.40: £1.20, £2.70, £2.40; EX 9.30 Trifecta £33.40 Pool: £365.60 - 8.19 winning units..
Owner Bloomfields **Bred** Darley **Trained** Cowlinge, Suffolk

FOCUS
As with the first leg, the second division of this maiden hurdle lacked depth, but the winner did it nicely.

3352 JULIE CALDERBANK "MY SOULMATE" MEMORIAL H'CAP CHASE (15 fncs) 2m 3f
1:25 (1:28) (Class 5) (0-100,93) 4-Y-0+ **£3,249** (£954; £477; £238)

Form RPR

P13- 1 **Pistol Basc (FR)**25 2870 9-11-0 86...................................... TonyKelly(5) 96
(Rebecca Menzies) *in tch: led 3 out: sn rdn: drvn out run-in: jst hld on* **11/2**3

P/5- 2 hd **Moonlight Maggie**28 2825 6-10-2 74..................... AodhaganConlon(5) 85+
(Tom George) *hld up: hdwy to trck ldrs after 4 out: wnt 2nd 3 out: nt fluent 2 out: sn rdn: kpt on run-in: clsng at fin* **6/1**

320- 3 8 **Pindar (GER)**16 3038 9-10-12 84..............................(p) SamanthaDrake(5) 87
(Joanne Foster) *trckd ldrs: lost pl after 10th: rallied appr 2 out: wnt 3rd fnl 75yds: no threat to ldng pair* **16/1**

F51- 4 1 1/2 **River Purple**18 3015 6-11-9 90...(t) BrianHarding 93+
(John Mackie) *trckd ldr: led 9th: faltered appr 3 out and sn dropped to 4th: plugged on* **10/3**2

546- 5 3 **Dorlesh Way (IRE)**24 2880 6-9-9 67 oh6.................... HarryChalloner(5) 66
(Patrick Holmes) *led: hdd nt fluent 8th: hdd 9th: remained cl up tl wknd 2 out* **7/1**

031- 6 38 **Milan Royale**24 2880 8-11-12 93.. HarryHaynes 52
(Kevin Hunter) *hld up: pushed along bef 8th: sn struggling* **15/8**1

24/- 7 1 **Chicago Alley**555 774 12-11-7 88...................................... LeeEdwards 46
(Dave Roberts) *in tch: nt fluent 8th: rdn after 4 out: sn wknd* **18/1**

4m 58.2s (9.40) **Going Correction** +0.30s/f (Yiel) 7 Ran SP% **111.2**
Speed ratings (Par 103): **92,91,88,87,86 70,70**
CSF £35.26 TOTE £8.00: £4.30, £3.60; EX 40.90 Trifecta £465.60 Part won. Pool: £620.90 - 0.91 winning units..
Owner Panther Racing Ltd **Bred** Sebastien & Alain Dufrancatel **Trained** Stearsby, N Yorks

FOCUS
Not a strong race for the grade with the top-weight rated 93, but the pace was sound.

3353 YORKSHIRE-OUTDOORS.CO.UK (S) H'CAP HURDLE (8 hdls) 2m
1:55 (1:58) (Class 5) (0-95,94) 3-Y-0+ **£2,737** (£798; £399)

Form RPR

6F0- 1 **Newdane Dancer (IRE)**51 2306 6-10-2 75..........(b) ColmMcCormack(5) 84
(Dianne Sayer) *midfield: rdn and stl only 8th 3 out: hdwy into 3rd appr 2 out: styd on to ld fnl 100yds* **10/1**

003- 2 2 3/4 **Qasser (IRE)**12 3140 4-10-11 86.. RyanHatch(7) 92
(Harry Whittington) *hld up: smooth hdwy 5th: sn trckd ldr: led on bit bef 2 out: rdn appr last: hdd 100yds out: no ex* **3/1**1

044- 3 4 1/2 **Johnnys Legacy (IRE)**2 3264 6-11-9 94...................(p) PeterCarberry(3) 96
(Conor Dore) *prom: led 4th: rdn whn hdd appr last: one pce: lost 2nd between last 2* **9/2**3

354- 4 9 **Highland River**8 3192 7-10-3 71.......................................(b1) LeeEdwards 65
(Dave Roberts) *chsd ldrs: wnt in snatches: rdn 3 out: sn outpacd by ldrs: wnt poor 4th nr fin* **7/1**

003- 5 nk **Ghaabesh (IRE)**2 3264 6-10-11 79.......................................(t) LiamHeard 71
(Barry Leavy) *trckd ldrs: rdn after 3 out: wknd after 2 out: lost 4th nr fin* **7/2**2

PFP- 6 1 3/4 **Two Oscars (IRE)**50 2333 7-10-3 74..............................(p) JohnKington(3) 64
(Andrew Crook) *hld up: sme hdwy 3 out: wknd bef 2 out* **33/1**

420- 7 15 **Queen Of Epirus**11 3141 5-11-10 92.................................... HarryHaynes 67
(Brian Rothwell) *prom: rdn appr 3 out: sn wknd* **16/1**

000/ P **Ptolomeos**143 5163 10-10-5 78..1 AdamNicol(5)
(Sean Regan) *led: hdd 4th: sn wknd: p.u bef 2 out* **25/1**

00P- P **Breeze With Ease (IRE)**28 2818 9-10-4 79..........(tp) GrahamWatters(7)
(Barry Murtagh) *hld up: a bhd: t.o whn p.u bef last* **28/1**

300/ P **So Bazaar (IRE)**461 1616 6-10-12 80.................................. BrianHarding
(Andrew Wilson) *hld up: a bhd: p.u bef 2 out* **33/1**

6P0- P **D'Argent Cloud**11 3141 5-10-6 81..............................(t) CraigGallagher(7)
(Brian Ellison) *prom: lost pl 5th: sn struggling: p.u bef 2 out* **10/1**

3m 57.3s (4.80) **Going Correction** +0.30s/f (Yiel)
WFA 4 from 5yo+ 5lb 11 Ran SP% **115.1**
Speed ratings (Par 103): **100,98,96,91,91 90,83, , ,**
CSF £38.76 CT £154.75 TOTE £12.80: £3.00, £1.50, £1.90; EX 52.80 Trifecta £316.70 Part won. Pool: £422.39 - 0.15 winning units..There was no bid for the winner. Qasser was claimed by Alan Swinbank for £5,000.
Owner E G Tunstall **Bred** Spratstown Stud A T **Trained** Hackthorpe, Cumbria

FOCUS
A typically moderate selling handicap.

3354 COME RACING NEW YEAR'S DAY NOVICES' LIMITED H'CAP CHASE (12 fncs) 2m
2:25 (2:26) (Class 3) (0-125,124) 4-Y-0+ **£9,514** (£2,902; £1,516; £823)

Form RPR

1P5- 1 **Croco Bay (IRE)**24 2882 6-11-0 124........................ HarryChalloner(5) 135+
(Peter Atkinson) *w ldr: lft in front 7th: c clr on bit after 3 out: hit last: easily* **9/1**

224- 2 10 **Phase Shift**42 2515 5-11-1 120......................................(t) JasonMaguire 116
(Brian Ellison) *hld up: hdwy after 4 out: wnt 2nd bef 2 out: nt fluent 2 out: plugged on and no threat wnr* **10/1**

022- 3 1/2 **Big Water (IRE)**11 3142 5-11-4 123.................................. JamesReveley 119
(Alan Swinbank) *trckd ldng pair: lft 2nd 7th: rdn and sn outpcd by wnr 3 out: lost 2nd bef 2 out: plugged on* **15/8**1

155- 4 2 3/4 **Dartford Warbler (IRE)**21 2955 6-10-12 122......... JonathanEngland(5) 114
(Sue Smith) *hld up in tch: nt fluent 4 out: sn rdn: hld in 4th fr 3 out* **4/1**2

211- F **Suprise Vendor (IRE)**28 2804 7-10-8 120.................. DaraghBourke(7)
(Stuart Coltherd) *hld up in tch: fell 5th* **9/2**3

23- F **Sir Valentino (FR)**25 2876 4-10-12 122................................. AlainCawley
(Tom George) *led: fell 7th* **9/2**3

4m 2.1s (2.00) **Going Correction** +0.30s/f (Yiel)
WFA 4 from 5yo+ 5lb 6 Ran SP% **110.2**
Speed ratings (Par 107): **107,102,101,100,**
CSF £76.89 TOTE £8.40: £3.50, £2.80; EX 50.70 Trifecta £171.80 Pool: £345.12 - 1.50 winning units..
Owner P G Atkinson **Bred** D Caverley **Trained** Yafforth, N Yorks

FOCUS
An open-looking handicap chase, but the winner could be called some way from home.

3355 BUY YOUR 2014 ANNUAL BADGE TODAY H'CAP CHASE (19 fncs) 3m 1f 110y
3:00 (3:00) (Class 4) (0-110,108) 4-Y-0+ **£4,548** (£1,335; £667; £333)

Form RPR
/05- **1** **The Panama Kid (IRE)**[211] 566 9-11-11 **107**.................... HarrySkelton 121+
(Malcolm Jefferson) *trckd ldr: rdn and upsides bef 3 out: drvn 2 out: led run-in: styd on* **7/2**[2]
452- **2** 2 ½ **Twice Lucky**[28] 2818 9-9-10 **83**.................................. JonathanEngland(5) 93
(Sue Smith) *hld up: wnt prom 7th: led 11th: jnd bef 3 out: sn rdn: hdd run-in: no ex* **5/4**[1]
/26- **3** 33 **Allanard (IRE)**[31] 2749 9-11-7 **108**............................(p) HarryChalloner(5) 85
(Martin Todhunter) *w ldr: led 9th tl 11th: outpcd by ldng pair after 13th: hit 5 out: sn wl btn in 3rd* **6/1**[3]
P60- **4** 2 **Trouble In Paris (IRE)**[47] 2416 6-9-13 **86**............................ TonyKelly(5) 61
(Barry Murtagh) *nt a fluent: hld up: struggling fr 13th* **7/2**[2]
44P- **P** **Sycho Fred (IRE)**[25] 2872 12-10-0 **82** oh13......................(t) BrianHarding
(Mike Sowersby) *led narrowly: hdd 9th: blnd 10th and dropped to rr: hit 13th: p.u sn after* **16/1**

6m 49.6s (7.60) **Going Correction** +0.30s/f (Yiel) **5** Ran SP% **109.1**
Speed ratings (Par 105): **100,99,89,88,**
CSF £8.56 TOTE £3.70: £2.50, £1.10; EX 10.30 Trifecta £29.00 Pool: £453.52 - 11.69 winning units..
Owner Mrs D W Davenport **Bred** J M And Mrs Davenport **Trained** Norton, N Yorks
■ Stewards' Enquiry : Harry Skelton two-day ban; used whip above permitted level (11th-12th Jan)

FOCUS
The first two pulled well clear in this ordinary handicap chase.

3356 GOODBYE 2013 HELLO 2014 CONDITIONAL JOCKEYS' H'CAP HURDLE (12 hdls) 3m 1f 110y
3:35 (3:35) (Class 4) (0-105,101) 4-Y-0+ **£3,249** (£954; £477; £238)

Form RPR
533- **1** **Pudsey House**[11] 3145 6-11-6 **101**..............................(b) JohnDawson(6) 116+
(John Wade) *trckd ldrs: led bef 6th: rdn clr after 2 out: eased towards fin* **3/1**[2]
5P0- **2** 19 **Acordingtoscript (IRE)**[16] 3040 7-10-10 **85**.................. HarryChalloner 80
(Martin Todhunter) *hld up: smooth hdwy after 8th: only 2 l down whn lft 2nd 2 out: sn rdn: wknd last* **10/1**
465- **3** 1 ¾ **Carmela Maria**[11] 3145 8-11-3 **92**.......................................(b) AdamNicol 82
(Mike Sowersby) *hld up: rdn 8th: lft poor 3rd 2 out: plugged on: nvr threatened* **15/2**
P44- **4** 38 **Oh Right (IRE)**[25] 2870 9-9-11 **75** oh3..........................(p) EmmaSayer(3) 27
(Dianne Sayer) *hld up: nt fluent 4th: a bhd* **11/1**
P0P- **5** 30 **Ballyreesode (IRE)**[27] 2842 8-11-1 **93**...............................(p) RyanHatch(3) 15
(Susan Corbett) *chsd ldrs: hit 8th: stl 2nd 3 out: wknd bef 2 out* **33/1**
600- **6** 29 **Danceintothelight**[11] 3145 6-11-4 **96**................................. JoeColliver(3)
(Micky Hammond) *trckd ldrs: led 5th: hdd bef 6th: lost pl after 7th: sn bhd: t.o* **12/1**
4/6- **7** 16 **Alf The Audacious**[17] 3021 7-11-6 **101**......................... CallumBewley(6)
(Sue Smith) *trckd ldrs: blnd 7th and lost pl: sn bhd: t.o* **11/4**[1]
342- **F** **Auberge (IRE)**[29] 2789 9-11-9 **98**................................ ColmMcCormack 88
(Evelyn Slack) *led: hdd 5th: trckd ldrs: rdn to chse wnr after 3 out: abt to be chal for 2nd whn fell 2 out* **4/1**[3]

6m 41.2s (13.60) **Going Correction** +0.30s/f (Yiel) **8** Ran SP% **111.5**
Speed ratings (Par 105): **91,85,84,72,63 54,49,**
toteswingers: 1&2 £6.60, 1&3 £8.10, 2&3 £6.40. CSF £30.35 CT £198.54 TOTE £4.60: £1.10, £2.20, £3.30; EX 33.80 Trifecta £286.80 Pool: £425.46 - 1.11 winning units..
Owner John Wade **Bred** East Burrow Farm **Trained** Mordon, Co Durham

FOCUS
Very few got competitive in this moderate handicap hurdle and they finished well strung out.
T/Plt: £152.40 to a £1 stake. Pool: £61,148.54 - 292.86 winning units T/Qpdt: £44.60 to a £1 stake. Pool: £4,040.00 - 67.00 winning units AS

2940 CHEPSTOW (L-H)
Saturday, December 28
OFFICIAL GOING: Heavy (chs 4.8, hdl 5.2)
Wind: medium to fresh, half against Weather: showers, brighter spells

3357 DOWNLOAD THE CORAL MOBILE APP MAIDEN HURDLE (11 hdls) 2m 4f
12:30 (12:31) (Class 4) 4-Y-0+ **£3,119** (£915; £457; £228)

Form RPR
/22- **1** **Deputy Dan (IRE)**[20] 2978 5-11-0 122............................ LeightonAspell 137+
(Oliver Sherwood) *hld up in tch in midfield: hdwy after 4th: chsd ldr 6th: led 8th: drew wl clr fr 2 out: styd on strly: readily* **10/11**[1]
1/0- **2** 19 **Ceasar Milan (IRE)**[63] 2079 5-11-0 0.................................. DarylJacob 115
(Paul Nicholls) *hld up in tch towards rr: hdwy 7th: chsd ldrs next: chsd wnr 3 out: rdn and btn sn after next: plugged on to hold 2nd* **5/2**[2]
53- **3** 2 ¼ **Minella On Line (IRE)**[35] 2667 4-11-0 0......................... JamieMoore 114
(Rebecca Curtis) *chsd ldrs: rdn on long run after 7th: blnd 8th: 3rd and btn whn mstke next: no ch w wnr but plugged on fr next* **14/1**
14- **4** 6 **Tullyesker Hill (IRE)**[20] 2978 4-11-0 0.......................... TomScudamore 107
(David Pipe) *wl in tch in midfield: rdn and struggling bef 8th: no ch w ldrs 3 out: plugged on to go modest 4th next* **8/1**[3]
/04- **5** 2 ½ **Dan's Wee Man**[22] 2924 4-10-9 0................................ JamesBanks(5) 105
(Andy Turnell) *hld up in tch towards rr: mstke 1st and 2nd: rdn and lost tch w ldrs on long run after 7th: no ch whn blnd 3 out: plugged on past btn horses fr next* **50/1**
06- **6** ½ **Bajan Blu**[37] 2614 5-11-0 0.. DonalDevereux 104
(David Brace) *hld up in tch in rr: mstke 2nd: hdwy 6th: rdn and lost tch w ldrs on long run to next: n.d after but plugged on steadily fr 3 out* **66/1**
432- **7** 8 **Little Jon**[25] 2875 5-11-0 0................................... SamTwiston-Davies 99
(Nigel Twiston-Davies) *t.k.h: led after 1st tl 8th: 4th and btn whn mstke next: sn fdd: t.o* **12/1**
/56- **8** 17 **Kayf Moss**[13] 3116 5-11-0 0... RhysFlint 79
(John Flint) *chsd ldr after 1st tl 6th: lost pl sn after next: t.o 8th* **100/1**
0/0- **9** 6 **Mortlestown (IRE)**[97] 1632 5-11-0 0.................................. TomSiddall 73
(Martin Keighley) *j.big 1st: in tch in midfield: hdwy to chse ldrs 6th: drvn and btn bef next: fdd bef 3 out: t.o 2 out* **20/1**
5/0- **10** 7 **Exmoor Mist**[21] 2940 5-11-0 0.. JackDoyle 66
(Victor Dartnall) *in tch in midfield: hdwy to chse ldrs 6th tl rdn and btn bef 8th: sn dropped out: t.o bef 2 out* **50/1**
5- **11** 6 **Ampleforth**[20] 2978 5-11-0 0......................................(p) WillKennedy 60
(Ian Williams) *wl in tch in midfield: rdn and btn bef 8th: sn bhd: t.o bef 3 out* **50/1**
0- **12** 3 **Solid Concrete (IRE)**[14] 3092 7-10-0 0.......................... MrLKilgarriff(7) 50
(Neil Mulholland) *mstkes: in tch in midfield: j. slowly 4th: lost pl and rdn after next: t.o sn after 7th* **150/1**
4/6- **13** 7 **Electric Mayhem**[236] 146 6-11-0 0............................ WayneHutchinson 50
(Nick Mitchell) *in tch in midfield: rdn and dropped out on long run after 7th: t.o next* **100/1**
60- **14** 7 **Twopoundsofbutter (IRE)**[21] 2940 6-10-11 0............. MichaelByrne(3) 43
(Tim Vaughan) *a in rr: lost tch 6th: t.o after next* **100/1**
/00- **15** 63 **Nash Point (IRE)**[44] 2471 4-11-0 0................................. RichardJohnson
(Tim Vaughan) *nt fluent: led tl after 1st: chsd ldrs tl lost pl and mstke 5th: bhd next and sn lost tch: wl t.o bef 8th* **100/1**

4m 56.6s (-5.20) **Going Correction** +0.05s/f (Yiel)
WFA 4 from 5yo+ 6lb **15** Ran SP% **123.2**
Speed ratings (Par 105): **112,104,103,101,100 99,96,89,87,84 82,81,78,75,50**
CSF £3.16 TOTE £2.10: £1.10, £1.30, £3.40; EX 4.50 Trifecta £28.40 Pool: £1544.86 - 40.70 winning units..
Owner Tim Syder **Bred** Conna Stud **Trained** Upper Lambourn, Berks

FOCUS
Some talented horses have won this race down the years, including Our Father in 2011 and What A Friend in 2007, so this winner should be worth following.

3358 CORAL.CO.UK BEST PRICE GUARANTEED ON HORSE RACING NOVICES' LIMITED H'CAP CHASE (18 fncs) 3m
1:00 (1:00) (Class 3) (0-125,125) 4-Y-0+ **£6,498** (£1,908; £954; £477)

Form RPR
232- **1** **Hansupfordetroit (IRE)**[36] 2651 8-11-0 **125**.............. RobertWilliams(5) 134+
(Bernard Llewellyn) *j.rt: mde all: j.big 1st: hung rt briefly bnd after 7th: travelling best and drew clr 15th: 4 l clr 2 out: rdn last: kpt on and a holding on* **7/2**[2]
243- **2** 1 ½ **Seven Woods (IRE)**[46] 2438 7-11-5 **125**.........................(t) PaddyBrennan 130
(Tom George) *chsd wnr thrght: upsides wnr 13th: rdn and outpcd after next: 4 l down and hit 2 out: rallied gamely u.p and kpt on flat* **3/1**[1]
/F3- **3** 26 **Billy Dutton**[45] 2460 7-11-0 **120**.. JamesDavies 98
(Chris Down) *in tch in midfield: chsd ldng pair 8th: rdn and struggling after 15th: wknd next: wl hld but plugged on to hold 3rd flat* **9/2**[3]
223- **4** 2 **Bertie Boru (IRE)**[22] 2925 6-11-3 **123**.................................... TomO'Brien 101
(Philip Hobbs) *hld up in tch in rr: mstke and pckd 11th: mstke 13th: rdn and struggling next: btn whn mstke 3 out: no ch after: plugged on* **9/2**[3]
0/5- **5** 1 **Cheat The Cheater (IRE)**[45] 2451 6-9-12 **111** oh4......(p) GeraldQuinn(7) 86
(Claire Dyson) *chsd ldrs: pushed along and lost pl bef 8th: rallied to chse ldrs 12th: wknd u.p after 14th: wl btn 3 out: plugged on* **10/1**
/40- **P** **Xaarcet (IRE)**[22] 2928 6-10-9 **115**.. JoeTizzard
(Colin Tizzard) *in tch: j.big 1st: mstke and reminders 4th: dropped to last and rapidly lost tch after 13th: eased and p.u bef next* **5/1**

6m 23.15s (1.15) **Going Correction** +0.125s/f (Yiel) **6** Ran SP% **109.3**
Speed ratings (Par 107): **103,102,93,93,92**
CSF £13.92 CT £41.70 TOTE £3.90: £2.20, £1.80; EX 12.70 Trifecta £45.30 Pool: £1112.53 - 18.38 winning units..
Owner Alex James **Bred** Stephen Weston **Trained** Fochriw, Caerphilly

FOCUS
A modest-looking handicap but a taking winner.

3359 CORAL SPIN CASINO FOR IPAD H'CAP HURDLE (12 hdls) 3m
1:30 (1:30) (Class 2) (0-145,132) 4-Y-0+ **£9,747** (£2,862; £1,431; £715)

Form RPR
223- **1** **Awaywiththegreys (IRE)**[15] 3060 6-11-10 **130**................... JamieMoore 135
(Peter Bowen) *chsd ldrs: j. slowly and rdn briefly 6th: chsd ldr bef 8th: rdn 3 out: str chal between last 2: outj. last: sn drvn to ld: styd on gamely: all out* **12/1**
4/6- **2** nk **Ugly Bug**[21] 2944 7-10-7 **120**.. KevinJones(7) 125
(Seamus Mullins) *led: rdn 2 out: jnd between last 2: bold jump last: sn hdd: battled on gamely u.p tl no ex and btn cl home* **8/1**
PU2- **3** 7 **Brackloon High (IRE)**[21] 2944 8-10-9 **120**..................... JamesBanks(5) 118
(Brendan Powell) *chsd ldrs: rdn 7th: no ex u.p 2 out: kpt on same pce after* **11/1**
453- **4** 6 **Pure Science (IRE)**[27] 2850 5-11-3 **123**................. SamTwiston-Davies 116
(Nigel Twiston-Davies) *hld up in tch in last trio: mstke 2nd and 7th: effrt to chse ldng trio bef 3 out: no prog and mstke 2 out: plugged on* **7/1**[3]
/41- **5** 15 **Moorlands Mist**[21] 2944 6-11-2 **132**...................... ThomasCheesman(10) 111
(Philip Hobbs) *wl in tch in midfield: sltly hmpd 6th: rdn and effrt bef 9th: btn 3 out: wknd next* **9/4**[1]
/40- **6** 1 ½ **Seventh Sign**[29] 2798 4-11-10 **130**...........................(b) WayneHutchinson 106
(Alan King) *wl in tch in midfield: mstke 7th: rdn and struggling jst bef 9th: wknd after 3 out* **25/1**
133/ **7** 5 **Lamps**[367] 3256 6-11-5 **125**...(b) TomCannon 96
(Michael Blake) *hld up in tch in rr: stl travelling wl after 8th: rdn and btn jst bef next: sn wknd and bhd: t.o* **10/1**
124- **8** 2 ½ **Lookout Mountain (IRE)**[21] 2944 5-10-13 **124**.....(vt) MauriceLinehan(5) 92
(Jonjo O'Neill) *in tch in midfield: j. slowly and reminder 6th: hdwy to chse ldrs next: rdn and struggling whn j. slowly 9th: wknd bef next: t.o* **13/2**[2]
043- **9** 67 **Makethe Mostofnow (IRE)**[12] 3130 8-11-4 **124**.............. PaulMoloney 25
(Evan Williams) *hld up in tch in last trio: rdn on long run after 8th: sn lost tch and wl t.o 9th* **14/1**
230- **P** **Abruzzi**[15] 3069 5-10-9 **120**.. BenPoste(5)
(Tom Symonds) *nt fluent 1st: chsd ldr tl lost pl rapidly after 7th: last next and sn lost tch: wl t.o 9th tl p.u last* **8/1**

6m 13.3s (11.10) **Going Correction** +0.05s/f (Yiel) **10** Ran SP% **114.5**
Speed ratings (Par 109): **83,82,80,78,73 73,71,70,48,**
CSF £102.11 CT £1089.28 TOTE £15.70: £3.60, £2.80, £3.40; EX 170.50 Trifecta £1160.70 Part won. Pool: £1547.66 - 0.71 winning units..
Owner Karen Bowen, Saith O Ni & The Hedonists **Bred** Domenico Fonzo **Trained** Little Newcastle, Pembrokes

FOCUS
Plenty had some sort of chance leaving the back straight, but the field steadily started to thin out.

3360 CORAL.CO.UK FUTURE CHAMPIONS FINALE JUVENILE HURDLE (GRADE 1) (8 hdls) 2m 110y
2:00 (2:03) (Class 1) 3-Y-0 **£19,932** (£7,479; £3,745; £1,865; £938)

Form RPR
110- **1** **Le Rocher (FR)**[55] 2262 3-11-0 0.................................. RichardJohnson 139+
(Nick Williams) *chsd ldr tl 2nd: styd chsng ldrs: led and blnd 3 out: mstke next: drvn between last 2: styd on strly and asserted flat: drvn out* **11/2**

The Form Book Jumps, Raceform Ltd, Compton, RG20 6NL.

12- **2** 2½ **Kentucky Hyden (IRE)**[14] 3078 3-11-0 135 DavidBass 133
(Nicky Henderson) *led tl 3rd: styd pressing ldr tl led again bef 5th: hdd 3 out: outpcd u.p and swtchd lft between last 2: rallied u.p last: no ex and btn fnl 100yds* **2/1**[2]

11- **3** 16 **Violet Dancer**[22] 2927 3-11-0 134 JamieMoore 121
(Gary Moore) *t.k.h: hld up wl in tch: mstke 4th: trckd ldrs on long run bef next: mstke 5th: rdn next: wknd u.p between last 2* **11/4**[3]

4 18 **Solar Impulse (FR)**[191] 3-11-0 DarylJacob 101
(Paul Nicholls) *chsd ldrs: wnt 2nd at 2nd: led and hit next: mstke 4th: hdd bef next: rdn and btn 5th: sn wknd: t.o between last 2* **15/8**[1]

0- **5** 50 **Arty Campbell (IRE)**[12] 3127 3-11-0 0 PaulMoloney 49
(Bernard Llewellyn) *mstkes: hld up in rr: blnd 1st: lost tch 3rd: t.o after next* **33/1**

4m 6.5s (-4.10) **Going Correction** +0.05s/f (Yiel) **5** Ran SP% **113.1**
Speed ratings (Par 116): **111,109,102,93,70**
CSF £17.64 TOTE £6.20: £2.20, £1.30; EX 14.00 Trifecta £33.50 Pool: £3376.80 - 75.51 winning units..
Owner John White & Anne Underhill **Bred** Mme Sylvie Ringler And Roger Frieh **Trained** George Nympton, Devon

FOCUS
This didn't seem an overly strong field for a Grade 1 considering the previous form of these, but the pace appeared fair for the conditions.

3361 CORAL WELSH GRAND NATIONAL (A H'CAP CHASE) (GRADE 3) (22 fncs) 3m 5f 110y
2:35 (2:41) (Class 1) 4-Y-0+
£56,950 (£21,370; £10,700; £5,330; £2,680; £1,340)

Form RPR

/33- **1** **Mountainous (IRE)**[21] 2943 8-10-0 **137** oh5 PaulMoloney 147
(Richard Lee) *in tch in midfield: clsd and chsd ldrs after 17th: pressed ldr 2 out: ev ch last: drvn to ld flat: all out and hld on gamely cl home* **20/1**

P/4- **2** hd **Hawkes Point**[21] 2943 8-10-0 **137** RyanMahon 146
(Paul Nicholls) *chsd ldrs: jnd ldrs travelling strly 18th: led 3 out: rdn between last 2: hdd flat: drvn and rallied gamely towards fin: jst hld* **14/1**

/15- **3** ½ **Tidal Bay (IRE)**[35] 2673 12-11-12 **163** DarylJacob 172
(Paul Nicholls) *hld up in rr: stdy prog fr 15th: chsd ldng pair last: drvn and swtchd rt flat: kpt on wl towards fin: nvr quite getting to ldng pair* **10/1**

F3P- **4** 7 **One In A Milan (IRE)**[24] 2889 8-9-7 **137** oh11 ConorRing[(7)] 139
(Evan Williams) *in tch in midfield: pushed along briefly bef 12th: hdwy on inner bef 18th: 4th and drvn between last 2: no imp* **50/1**

/25- **5** 3¾ **Merry King (IRE)**[28] 2815 6-10-3 **140** RichieMcLernon 139
(Jonjo O'Neill) *hld up in tch in midfield: pushed along and hdwy after 17th: chsd ldrs 19th: rdn and btn 2 out: wknd bef last* **9/1**[3]

/12- **6** 2¼ **Vintage Star (IRE)**[28] 2822 7-10-2 **139** ow2 RyanMania 137
(Sue Smith) *in tch in midfield: hdwy to chse ldrs 11th: wnt 2nd 13th tl led 18th: hdd 3 out: btn after 2 out: wknd last* **10/1**

/00- **7** 4½ **Amigo (FR)**[29] 2798 6-10-0 **137** oh2 (bt[1]) ConorO'Farrell 128
(David Pipe) *in tch in midfield: rdn and outpcd bef 3 out: no threat to ldrs and plugged on same pce after* **20/1**

1/5- **8** 1¼ **Goonyella (IRE)**[34] 2708 6-10-1 **138** AELynch 128
(J T R Dreaper, Ire) *hld up in tch towards rr: rdn and effrt after 15th: no prog 19th: outpcd and wl hld 3 out: plugged on* **8/1**[2]

203/ **9** 8 **Teaforthree (IRE)**[266] 5177 9-10-11 **153** PatrickCorbett[(5)] 137+
(Rebecca Curtis) *chsd ldr tl after 6th: chsd ldrs after: j.rt 14th: rdn bef 18th: wknd bef 3 out* **14/1**

/41- **P** **Hey Big Spender (IRE)**[28] 2822 10-10-7 **144** 4ex (t) JoeTizzard
(Colin Tizzard) *hld up in tch towards rr: mstke 11th: rdn and struggling 16th lost tch next: t.o whn p.u 18th* **20/1**

/03- **P** **Well Refreshed**[21] 2953 9-10-1 **141** ow2 JoshuaMoore[(3)]
(Gary Moore) *hld up in tch in rr: sme prog whn blnd bdly 13th: sn rdn and nt rcvr: wl bhd whn p.u 17th* **10/1**

/16- **P** **Harouet (FR)**[27] 2841 8-10-0 **137** oh7 (p) JamieMoore
(Peter Bowen) *a in rr: mstke 4th: lost tch 13th: t.o whn p.u 16th* **100/1**

/00- **P** **Chartreux (FR)**[21] 2937 8-10-0 **137** oh3 PaddyBrennan
(Tom George) *in tch in midfield: mstke 12th: rdn and btn after 17th: bhd whn p.u 3 out* **66/1**

/03- **P** **Ace High**[35] 2670 9-9-7 **137** oh5 KieronEdgar[(7)]
(David Pipe) *chsd ldrs tl 6th: steadily lost pl and bhd whn rdn after 11th: lost tch 14th: t.o whn p.u 16th* **14/1**

/00- **P** **Wyck Hill (IRE)**[21] 2937 9-10-3 **140** TomO'Brien
(David Bridgwater) *in tch in midfield: rdn after 11th: struggling and lost tch 15th: tailing off whn p.u next* **22/1**

201- **P** **Knock A Hand (IRE)**[13] 3109 8-10-0 **137** 4ex (b) RichardJohnson
(Richard Lee) *chsd ldrs: wnt after 6th tl led 8th: hdd 18th: sn rdn: wknd bef 3 out: wl btn and wkng whn p.u 2 out* **16/1**

4/2- **P** **Red Rocco (IRE)**[35] 2670 6-10-0 **137** oh7 AdamWedge
(Nigel Twiston-Davies) *in tch in midfield: mstke 11th: rdn and struggling 13th: sn dropped out: wl bhd whn p.u 17th* **25/1**

/24- **P** **Highland Lodge (IRE)**[28] 2815 7-10-6 **143** LeightonAspell
(Emma Lavelle) *led tl 7th: chsd ldr tl 13th: styd chsng ldrs tl wknd qckly 3 out: j.rt next: bhd whn p.u last* **13/2**[1]

/26- **P** **Tour Des Champs (FR)**[42] 2502 6-10-0 **137** oh5 SamTwiston-Davies
(Nigel Twiston-Davies) *in tch in midfield: blnd 8th: rdn after 11th: struggling 14th: sn bhd: t.o whn p.u 18th* **14/1**

2/0- **P** **Goulanes (IRE)**[42] 2502 7-10-6 **143** (b[1]) TomScudamore
(David Pipe) *in tch in midfield: mstke 11th: rdn and struggling bef 18th: bhd whn p.u 3 out* **20/1**

7m 54.9s (-0.10) **Going Correction** +0.125s/f (Yiel) **20** Ran SP% **126.0**
Speed ratings (Par 113): **105,104,104,102,101 101,100,99,97, , , , , , , ,**
CSF £252.69 CT £2983.79 TOTE £21.90: £4.70, £4.20, £2.60, £14.30; EX 276.80 Trifecta £3151.20 Pool: £56628.48 - 13.47 winning units..
Owner Walters Plant Hire & James & Jean Potter **Bred** Lady Melissa Brooke **Trained** Byton, H'fords

■ Stewards' Enquiry : Daryl Jacob two-day ban; used whip above permitted level (11th-12th Jan)
Paul Moloney four-day ban; used whip above permitted level (11th-14th Jan)

FOCUS
Always usually a dour test, this year's renewal had a slightly lopsided look to it considering the presence of the classy topweight. His presence meant nearly half of the field were running from out of the weights.

3362 CORAL.CO.UK MONEY BACK IF YOUR HORSE FALLS H'CAP CHASE (16 fncs) 2m 3f 110y
3:10 (3:15) (Class 2) 4-Y-0+ **£14,620** (£4,293; £2,146; £1,073)

Form RPR

001- **1** **Renard (FR)**[21] 2945 8-11-7 **135** LiamTreadwell 148+
(Venetia Williams) *racd in midfield: wnt 3rd 10th: chsd clr ldr after 12th: clsd to press ldr 3 out: led bef 2 out: clr and in command last: styd on wl: comf* **7/1**[3]

/50- **2** 12 **Tranquil Sea (IRE)**[150] 1168 11-11-8 **139** GavinSheehan[(3)] 142+
(Warren Greatrex) *hld up in last pair: stdy prog 11th: chsd ldng pair bef 13th: rdn 3 out: no threat to wnr fr 2 out: plugged on to go 2nd flat* **17/2**

3/4- **3** 6 **Mail De Bievre (FR)**[48] 2415 8-11-12 **140** PaddyBrennan 139+
(Tom George) *j.rt: racd keenly: chsd ldr tl led and mstke 2nd: 6 l clr after 11th: rdn and hdd after 3 out: drvn and btn between last 2: lost 2nd and wknd flat* **9/2**[1]

/40- **4** 15 **Poole Master**[21] 2939 8-11-2 **130** (b[1]) TomScudamore 110
(David Pipe) *led tl 2nd: chsd ldr tl 12th: 4th and btn bef 3 out: sn wknd* **10/1**

/11- **5** 8 **Get It On (IRE)**[60] 2149 8-10-9 **130** ConorRing[(7)] 102
(Evan Williams) *hld up off the pce in midfield: clsd and in tch after 5th: rdn and struggling after 11th: wl btn next: t.o 3 out* **7/1**[3]

P/5- **P** **Green Belt Elite (FR)**[214] 520 9-10-6 **125** CallumWhillans[(5)]
(Venetia Williams) *hld up in midfield: clsd and in tch after 5th: rdn and struggling 11th: sn wknd and t.o whn p.u next* **25/1**

/23- **P** **Simply Wings (IRE)**[36] 2645 9-11-5 **133** JamieMoore
(Richard Lee) *j.rt: racd in midfield: clsd and in tch after 5th: wnt 4th and j.rt 11th: rdn and btn bef next: t.o whn p.u 2 out* **8/1**

/6P- **P** **Frontier Spirit (IRE)**[21] 2939 9-11-4 **132** SamTwiston-Davies
(Nigel Twiston-Davies) *racd in midfield: clsd and in tch after 5th: j. slowly and rdn after 8th: mstke next: lost tch after 11th: t.o and p.u next* **16/1**

211- **P** **Coverholder (IRE)**[20] 2969 6-11-12 **140** RyanMania
(Sue Smith) *a towards rr: j.rt 3rd: rdn after 7th: nvr travelling wl after: lost tch after 11th: t.o whn p.u next* **8/1**

P22- **P** **Un Bon P'Tit Gars (FR)**[28] 2811 5-10-11 **125** RichardJohnson
(Nick Williams) *chsd ldrs: blnd 1st: stl 3rd whn blnd and lost pl 10th: in rr whn hit next: sn eased and p.u* **5/1**[2]

0P0- **P** **Vif Argent (FR)**[15] 3065 4-10-0 **120** ConorO'Farrell
(David Pipe) *hld up in rr: a wl bhd: t.o 9th tl p.u 2 out* **20/1**

5m 8.6s (-2.70) **Going Correction** +0.125s/f (Yiel)
WFA 4 from 5yo+ 5lb **11** Ran SP% **116.2**
Speed ratings (Par 109): **110,105,102,96,93 , , , ,**
CSF £64.53 CT £298.76 TOTE £7.20: £2.40, £3.10, £2.30; EX 70.40 Trifecta £515.30 Pool: £3590.34 - 5.22 winning units..
Owner Roa Arkle Partnership **Bred** Guillaume Moinon & Pierre Julienne **Trained** Kings Caple, H'fords

FOCUS
This was run at a terrific gallop and, as a result, not many got into contention.

3363 CORAL BACKING "MACMILLAN CANCER SUPPORT" STANDARD OPEN NATIONAL HUNT FLAT RACE 2m 110y
3:45 (3:45) (Class 5) 4-6-Y-0 **£1,949** (£572; £286; £143)

Form RPR

4- **1** **Justanother Muddle**[230] 246 4-11-0 0 MarcGoldstein 117+
(Sheena West) *chsd ldrs: sltly hmpd and lft upsides ldr after 2f: mde rest: drew clr 4f out: 8 l clr and hanging lft over 1f out: pushed along and a holding runner-up fnl f* **25/1**

2 1¼ **Ashford Wood (IRE)**[208] 624 5-11-0 0 RichardJohnson 114+
(Tim Vaughan) *in tch: rdn and outpacved 7f out: 6th and looked wl btn over 4f out: styd on past btn horses to go 2nd over 2f out: 8 l down over 1f out: styd on wl but nvr getting to wnr* **10/3**[2]

3 13 **Keep Presenting (IRE)** 4-11-0 0 TomScudamore 101
(Rebecca Curtis) *chsd ldrs tl led after 2f: sn hdd and chsd wnr tl 1/2-way: rdn and outpcd 4f out: chsd clr wnr over 3f out: no imp: 3rd and wl hld fnl 2f* **8/1**

2/ **4** 1¼ **Bar A Mine (FR)**[266] 5187 4-11-0 0 DarylJacob 100
(Paul Nicholls) *hld up in tch towards rr: hdwy 7f out: rdn over 3f out: modest 3rd and no imp u.p over 3f out: 4th and wl hld fnl 2f* **13/8**[1]

5 12 **Castletown (IRE)**[244] 5-11-0 0 (t) RhysFlint 88
(Laura Young) *chsd ldrs: pushed rt bnd after 2f: in tch in midfield after: rdn and outpcd 6f out: no ch but plugged on past btn horses fnl 2f* **40/1**

42/ **6** 12 **Shadow Cruise (IRE)**[312] 4299 4-10-9 0 RobertWilliams[(5)] 76
(Bernard Llewellyn) *chsd ldr tl pushed rt bnd after 2f: in tch in midfield tl chsd wnr 1/2-way: rdn and outpcd over 4f out: 4th and btn 3f out: sn fdd: t.o* **16/1**

12- **7** 3½ **Capilla (IRE)**[36] 2654 5-11-7 0 AdamWedge 80
(Evan Williams) *in tch in midfield: trckd ldrs 5f out: rdn and btn 4f out: wknd 3f out: t.o and eased ins fnl f* **5/1**[3]

8 9 **Rocket Scientist** 4-11-0 0 JoeTizzard 64
(Colin Tizzard) *in tch in midfield: wknd 6f out: t.o fnl 4f* **10/1**

00- **9** 41 **Proper Job**[23] 2912 5-10-7 0 MrJoshuaNewman[(7)] 23
(Polly Gundry) *t.k.h: wl in tch in midfield: pushed rt bnd after 2f out: lost tch 6f out: wl t.o fnl 5f* **40/1**

10 5 **Hot Pepper** 5-11-0 0 JamesDavies 18
(Chris Down) *in tch towards rr: rdn and struggling 7f out: lost tch and wl t.o fnl 5f* **50/1**

6- **11** 35 **Caldey**[12] 3133 4-10-7 0 JamieMoore
(Keith Goldsworthy) *led tl hung rt bnd and hdd after 2f: dropped to rr and u.p 10f out: lost tch and wl t.o fnl 5f: eased fnl 3f* **66/1**

4m 4.6s (-0.40) **Going Correction** +0.05s/f (Yiel)
WFA 4 from 5yo 5lb **11** Ran SP% **116.1**
Speed ratings: **102,101,95,94,89 83,81,77,58,55 39**
CSF £103.63 TOTE £45.20: £6.50, £1.40, £2.90; EX 183.90 Trifecta £1211.00 Pool: £3398.59 - 2.10 winning units..
Owner Saloop **Bred** Saloop Ltd **Trained** Falmer, E Sussex

FOCUS
Probably just a modest event.
T/Jkpt: Not won. T/Plt: £498.50 to a £1 stake. Pool: £211032.08 - 309.00 winning tickets T/Qpdt: £218.30 to a £1 stake. Pool: £13218.46 - 44.80 winning tickets SP

3161 **NEWBURY** (L-H)
Saturday, December 28

OFFICIAL GOING: Chase course - soft (heavy in places); hurdle course - heavy (soft in places)
Wind: Virtually nil Weather: Sunny

3364 BETFRED FUN AND FRIENDLY JUVENILE HURDLE (8 hdls) 2m 110y
12:15 (12:15) (Class 3) 3-Y-O **£6,498** (£1,908; £954; £477)

Form RPR
6- **1** **Baradari (IRE)**[29] 2796 3-10-12 0 AidanColeman 119+
(Venetia Williams) *in rr but wl in tch: chal 3 out: led gng wl after 2 out: pushed out run-in: readily* **11/4**[2]
25- **2** 5 **Cadoudoff (FR)**[14] 3078 3-11-8 124 NoelFehily 121
(Charlie Longsdon) *led 2nd to next: styd upsides and stl chalng 2 out: chsd wnr bef last: kpt run-in on but a readily hld* **9/4**[1]
312- **3** 5 **Sleepy Haven (IRE)**[22] 2927 3-11-4 123 SeanQuinlan 111
(Jennie Candlish) *chsd ldrs: rdn 3 out: hung lft and outpcd after 2 out: stl hanging whn kpt on to re-take 3rd appr last: no ch w ldng duo* **5/1**[3]
4 3 ¼ **Ronaldinho (IRE)**[75] 3-10-12 0 RobertThornton 103+
(Alan King) *led to 2nd: led again next: hrd pressed but kpt slt advantage tl after 2 out: wknd appr last* **9/4**[1]
0- **5** 15 **Candyman Can (IRE)**[10] 3161 3-10-12 0 MarkGrant 90
(Dominic Ffrench Davis) *in rr but in tch: j. slowly 4th: rdn after 4 out: no ch fr next* **20/1**
4m 13.91s (3.91) **Going Correction** +0.30s/f (Yiel) 5 Ran SP% **109.6**
Speed ratings (Par 106): **102,99,97,95,88**
CSF £9.43 TOTE £3.60: £1.50, £2.00; EX 10.70 Trifecta £20.10 Pool: £668.98 - 24.86 winning units..
Owner A Brooks **Bred** His Highness The Aga Khan's Studs S C **Trained** Kings Caple, H'fords

FOCUS
Rail moved out on hurdles track. Considering the field size they went a sound enough gallop in this 4-y-o event and the form looks solid enough, rated around the penalised runner-up.

3365 BETFRED MOBILE LOTTO NOVICES' LIMITED H'CAP CHASE (17 fncs) 2m 6f 110y
12:45 (12:45) (Class 3) (0-125,123) 4-Y-O+ **£6,498** (£1,908; £954; £477)

Form RPR
/52- **1** **Saroque (IRE)**[12] 3129 6-10-8 **112** AidanColeman 129+
(Venetia Williams) *led: hit 5th: blnd 4 out: narrowly hdd next: sn led again: nt fluent 2 out: drvn clr run-in: comf* **5/2**[1]
311- **2** 4 **Glen Countess (IRE)**[15] 3058 6-10-11 **115** (t) BrendanPowell 122
(Brendan Powell) *chsd wnr fr 11th: slt ld and rdn 3 out: sn hdd: nt qckn appr last: styd on clsng stages* **8/1**
0/4- **3** ¾ **Ultimatum Du Roy (FR)**[24] 2887 5-10-1 **110** KillianMoore(5) 118+
(Alex Hales) *in rr but in tch: j. slowly 8th: trckd ldrs fr 12th: one pce u.p fr 3 out: blnd next and last: kpt on again to press for 2nd clsng stages but no ch w wnr* **7/1**
323- **4** 1 ½ **Ballylifen (IRE)**[35] 2662 6-11-0 **118** (tp) APMcCoy 124
(Jonjo O'Neill) *in rr but in tch: nt fluent 6th: reminders after next: sltly hmpd 10th: chsd ldrs 12th: rdn 4 out: sn outpcd: styd on again u.p clsng stages* **3/1**[2]
/31- **P** **Castle Conflict (IRE)**[28] 2805 8-11-2 **123** JakeGreenall(3)
(Henry Daly) *bmpd 1st: chsd ldrs: wnt 2nd 7th tl hit 11th: rdn and wknd 13th: no ch whn blnd 2 out and p.u* **7/2**[3]
/24- **U** **De Blacksmith (IRE)**[46] 2438 5-11-4 **122** ColinBolger
(Gary Moore) *wnt rt 1st: chsd ldrs tl mstke and uns rdr 10th* **10/1**
5m 54.88s (7.88) **Going Correction** +0.525s/f (Soft) 6 Ran SP% **108.5**
Speed ratings (Par 107): **107,105,105,104,**
toteswingers 1&2 £2.80, 1&3 £25.40, 2&3 £13.90 CSF £19.57 TOTE £3.40: £2.50, £2.80; EX 21.50 Trifecta £78.00 Pool: £853.12 - 8.20 winning units..
Owner A Brooks **Bred** Miss Mary Condon **Trained** Kings Caple, H'fords

FOCUS
A modest novice handicap, run at a fair gallop. The winner is on the upgrade.

3366 BETFRED MANDARIN H'CAP CHASE (21 fncs) 3m 2f 110y
1:15 (1:15) (Class 3) (0-130,130) 4-Y-O+ **£9,097** (£2,671; £1,335; £667)

Form RPR
1F3- **1** **Financial Climate (IRE)**[18] 3006 6-10-9 **118** ThomasGarner(5) 130+
(Oliver Sherwood) *in tch: hdwy to cl on ldrs 17th: mstke 4 out: chsd ldr 2 out: styd on u.p run-in to ld fnl 100yds: hld on wl* **4/1**[2]
16P- **2** ¾ **Faultless Feelings (IRE)**[24] 2889 7-11-7 **125** (p) IanPopham 134
(Martin Keighley) *j.w: led: rdn 2 out: styd on wl and kpt on run-in: hdd and nt qckn fnl 100yds* **13/2**
1/2- **3** 9 **Denali Highway (IRE)**[42] 2517 6-11-11 **129** AndrewThornton 130
(Caroline Bailey) *hit 2nd: chsd ldrs: wnt 2nd 14th: rdn and hit 4 out: lost 2nd 2 out: outpcd after last* **4/1**[2]
/P2- **4** 11 **Howard's Legacy (IRE)**[46] 2438 7-11-12 **130** AidanColeman 123
(Venetia Williams) *hld up in rr but wl in tch: hit 10th: trckd ldrs fr 17th: hit 4 out: wknd bef last* **6/1**[3]
B50- **5** 12 **Jaunty Journey**[35] 2670 10-10-5 **109** BrianHughes 90
(Nigel Twiston-Davies) *chsd ldrs: rdn 13th: hit 15th: sn bhd* **13/2**
P/P- **F** **Shaking Hands (IRE)**[12] 3131 9-10-13 **124** (bt) TomBellamy(7)
(David Pipe) *chsng ldr whn fell 6th* **12/1**
/00- **U** **Restless Harry**[35] 2672 9-11-4 **122** CharliePoste
(Robin Dickin) *trcking ldrs whn mstke: hmpd and uns rdr 6th* **7/2**[1]
6m 55.97s (9.97) **Going Correction** +0.525s/f (Soft) 7 Ran SP% **110.9**
Speed ratings (Par 107): **106,105,103,99,96** ,
toteswingers 1&2 £11.20, 1&3 £1.10, 2&3 £26.70 CSF £27.45 TOTE £4.30: £1.30, £4.10; EX 34.40 Trifecta £232.00 Pool: £1965.84 - 6.35 winning units..
Owner Mrs Sara Fillery **Bred** Mrs E M Motherway **Trained** Upper Lambourn, Berks

FOCUS
A fair staying handicap which looked wide open and it saw changing fortunes on the run-in. There's a case for rating the form a few pounds higher.

3367 BETFRED GOALS GALORE CHALLOW NOVICES' HURDLE (GRADE 1) (10 hdls) 2m 5f
1:45 (1:49) (Class 1) 4-Y-O+ **£20,026** (£7,573; £3,838; £1,959; £1,031)

Form RPR
/11- **1** **Captain Cutter (IRE)**[23] 2900 6-11-7 130 APMcCoy 150+
(Nicky Henderson) *hld up in rr but in tch: hdwy appr 3 out whn nt fluent: chal 2 out: sn drvn to ld: styd on strly run-in* **8/1**
112- **2** 4 ½ **Timesremembered (IRE)**[42] 2505 5-11-7 144 AidanColeman 146
(Emma Lavelle) *in tch: hdwy 4 out: chal 3 out: slt ld appr 2 out: hdd sn after: kpt on same pce run-in* **11/4**[2]
/12- **3** 4 ½ **Oscar Rock (IRE)**[28] 2819 5-11-7 140 BrianHughes 141
(Malcolm Jefferson) *chsd ldrs: rdn and ev ch 3 out: hit next and outpcd: styd on again u.p run-in* **2/1**[1]
/11- **4** 6 **Shantou Magic (IRE)**[48] 2393 6-11-7 0 NoelFehily 134
(Charlie Longsdon) *led tl hdd appr 2 out: sn btn* **7/1**
211- **5** 3 ¼ **Kaki De La Pree (FR)**[13] 3108 6-11-7 140 FelixDeGiles 132
(Tom Symonds) *chsd ldrs: rdn after 4 out: wknd next: no ch whn hit last* **8/1**
121- **U** **Creepy (IRE)**[42] 2505 5-11-7 138 IanPopham
(Martin Keighley) *chsd ldrs and t.k.h early: disputing cl 2nd whn mstke and uns rdr 4 out* **5/1**[3]
5m 18.3s (-0.70) **Going Correction** +0.30s/f (Yiel) 6 Ran SP% **111.4**
Speed ratings (Par 117): **113,111,109,107,106**
CSF £30.07 TOTE £5.50: £2.70, £1.70; EX 17.50 Trifecta £40.40 Pool: £3315.66 - 61.44 winning units..
Owner John P McManus **Bred** Mrs S Brennan **Trained** Upper Lambourn, Berks

FOCUS
This Grade 1 event has a rich history. It was an open line-up this year and proved a proper test, with the first pair pulling clear from the penultimate flight. The second and third set the level in a solid renewal.

3368 BETFRED "RACING'S BIGGEST SUPPORTER" NOVICES' CHASE (FOR THE HALLOWE'EN TROPHY) (15 fncs) 2m 2f 110y
2:15 (2:19) (Class 3) 4-Y-O+ **£7,797** (£2,289; £1,144; £572)

Form RPR
2- **1** **Vukovar (FR)**[20] 2976 4-10-8 0 (t) NoelFehily 148+
(Harry Fry) *mde all: clr fr 11th: blnd 3 out: v easily* **4/6**[1]
0/1- **2** 21 **Open Hearted**[15] 3057 6-11-7 145 AndrewTinkler 135
(Nicky Henderson) *chsd ldrs: shkn up 8th: blnd 9th: chsd wnr fr next: nvr any ch but wl clr of 3rd* **15/8**[2]
P- **3** 34 **Festive Affair (IRE)**[15] 3057 5-11-0 0 APMcCoy 108
(Jonjo O'Neill) *nt fluent early: chsd wnr to 10th: wknd into 3rd after 11th: wl bhd whn hit 3 out* **10/1**[3]
103- **4** 30 **Kentford Legend**[33] 2712 6-11-0 96 AndrewThornton 62
(Seamus Mullins) *hit 1st: j. slowly 6th: sn t.o* **40/1**
4m 43.7s (13.70) **Going Correction** +0.525s/f (Soft)
WFA 4 from 5yo+ 5lb 4 Ran SP% **106.3**
Speed ratings (Par 107): **92,83,68,56**
CSF £2.27 TOTE £1.50; EX 2.10 Trifecta £2.60 Pool: £1996.62 - 555.27 winning units..
Owner Gdm Partnership **Bred** Thierry Cypres **Trained** Seaborough, Dorset

FOCUS
An impressive win for ex-French 4-y-o Vukovar.

3369 BETFRED RACING FOLLOW US ON FACEBOOK H'CAP HURDLE (10 hdls) 2m 5f
2:50 (2:50) (Class 2) 4-Y-O+ **£11,573** (£3,418; £1,709; £854; £427)

Form RPR
/33- **1** **Whisper (FR)**[21] 2949 5-11-8 **140** AndrewTinkler 150+
(Nicky Henderson) *trckd ldr: drvn to chal 2 out: sn led: hit last: rdn and styd on strly run-in* **13/8**[1]
532- **2** 7 **Pateese (FR)**[29] 2798 8-11-0 **139** (p) ChrisDavies(7) 141
(Philip Hobbs) *chsd ldrs in 3rd: drvn 3 out: chsd wnr after 2 out: no imp u.p whn mstke last* **9/2**[3]
1/1- **3** ¾ **Stopped Out**[45] 2454 8-11-12 **144** (p) RichieMcGrath 144
(Philip Kirby) *led: rdn 3 out: jnd 2 out and sn hdd: outpcd bef last: styd on again to cl on 2nd nr fin but no ch w wnr* **8/1**
F- **4** 3 **Black River (FR)**[28] 2811 4-10-11 **134** HarryDerham(5) 131
(Paul Nicholls) *hld up in rr: hdwy 3 out: sn shkn up and outpcd: in last pl fnl flight: styd on again run-in: gng on clsng stages* **7/4**[2]
003/ **5** 9 **Kazlian (FR)**[21] 4665 5-11-4 **136** BrendanPowell 126
(Johnny Farrelly) *in rr: hdwy to cl on ldrs 3 out: wknd bef next* **16/1**
5m 34.08s (15.08) **Going Correction** +0.30s/f (Yiel)
WFA 4 from 5yo+ 6lb 5 Ran SP% **109.6**
Speed ratings (Par 109): **83,80,80,78,75**
CSF £9.09 TOTE £2.30: £1.50, £1.80; EX 6.20 Trifecta £25.60 Pool: £744.52 - 21.78 winning units..
Owner Walters Plant Hire Ltd **Bred** Hubert & Sandra Hosselet **Trained** Upper Lambourn, Berks
■ Stewards' Enquiry : Richie McGrath two-day ban; careless riding (11th-12th Jan).

FOCUS
A fair little handicap. There was just a steady gallop on early doors and those held up were at a disadvantage. The winner can probably rate a bit higher.

3370 BETFRED CALL US ON 0800 221221 INTRODUCTORY HURDLE (8 hdls) 2m 110y
3:25 (3:25) (Class 4) 4-Y-O+ **£3,532** (£1,328)

Form RPR
1- **1** **Stand To Reason (IRE)**[23] 2906 5-11-5 0 APMcCoy 133+
(Nicky Henderson) *t.k.h: trckd ldr wh blnd 3 out: sn rcvrd and travelling wl: drvn to chal and styng on whn lft wl clr last* **11/8**[2]
06- **2** 16 **Midnight Thunder (IRE)**[21] 2940 4-11-0 0 BrendanPowell 107
(Colin Tizzard) *in tch: j. slowly 2nd: hdwy to chse ldrs 3 out: wknd and hit 2 out: lft mod 2nd last* **7/1**[3]
3- **U** **Benbecula**[34] 2695 4-11-0 0 NoelFehily
(Richard Mitchell) *t.k.h: led: racd wd 2nd to 4 out and hrd pressed tl hdd wl bef 3 out whn wknd, blnd and uns rdr* **16/1**
0- **U** **Balady (IRE)**[66] 2027 4-10-7 0 MarkGrant
(Dominic Ffrench Davis) *in rr but in tch tl wknd and mstke 3 out: no ch whn blnd and uns rdr 2 out* **66/1**
/11- **F** **Wilde Blue Yonder (IRE)**[29] 2802 4-11-5 0 RobertThornton 133+
(Alan King) *w ldr 2nd tl led wl bef 3 out: rdn and mstke 2 out: jnd and u.p but stl finding whn fell last* **11/10**[1]
4m 13.74s (3.74) **Going Correction** +0.30s/f (Yiel) 5 Ran SP% **109.6**
Speed ratings (Par 105): **103,95, , ,**
CSF £10.59 TOTE £2.00: £1.50, £3.20; EX 10.10 Trifecta £12.30 Pool: £1360.13 - 82.36 winning units..
Owner Seasons Holidays **Bred** Coleman Bloodstock Limited **Trained** Upper Lambourn, Berks

FOCUS
A dramatic little event. The winner and faller are well above average but have some way to go to be considered as candidates for top novice races.
T/Plt: £78.00 to a £1 stake. Pool: £79817.92 - 746.49 winning tickets T/Qpdt: £15.30 to a £1 stake. Pool: £6256.45 - 301.25 winning tickets ST

The Form Book Jumps, Raceform Ltd, Compton, RG20 6NL.

3371 - 3373a (Foreign Racing) - See Raceform Interactive

3336 LEOPARDSTOWN (L-H)

Saturday, December 28

OFFICIAL GOING: Chase course - yielding to soft; hurdle course - soft (soft to heavy in places)

3374a WOODIESDIY.COM CHRISTMAS HURDLE (GRADE 1) (12 hdls) 3m
1:50 (1:50) 4-Y-0+ **£42,276** (£12,357; £5,853; £1,951)

RPR

1 **Zaidpour (FR)**[27] 2855 7-11-10 155 .... RWalsh 159+
(W P Mullins, Ire) *w.w in rr of quartet: tk clsr order bef 8th where mstke: pushed along in cl 3rd between last 2: swtchd rt to chal last: kpt on wl u.p to ld fnl 100yds* **5/4**[1]

2 4 ¼ **Rule The World**[27] 2855 6-11-10 150 .... DavyRussell 155+
(M F Morris, Ire) *trckd ldr: nt fluent 1st: led briefly fr 8th: in front again 4 out: nt fluent and jnd 2 out: narrow advantage u.p fr last: strly pressed and hdd fnl 100yds: no ex and eased cl home* **10/3**[3]

3 3 ½ **Mala Beach (IRE)**[48] 2408 5-11-10 148 .... RobbieColgan 152
(Gordon Elliott, Ire) *chsd ldrs in 3rd for most tl got on terms 2 out: rdn and disp into st: hung lft fr last where nt fluent and sn no ex u.p in 3rd: kpt on same pce* **7/4**[2]

4 33 **Whatuthink (IRE)**[13] 3123 11-11-10 142 .... (vt) PatrickMangan 119
(Oliver McKiernan, Ire) *led tl hdd briefly fr 8th: cl 2nd 4 out: pushed along fr 3 out and wknd u.p bef next* **16/1**

6m 22.8s (2.80) **Going Correction** -0.30s/f (Good) 4 Ran SP% **109.8**
Speed ratings: **83,81,80,69**
CSF £5.80 TOTE £1.90; DF 3.80 Trifecta £4.00.
Owner Mrs S Ricci **Bred** H H The Aga Khan's Studs Sc **Trained** Muine Beag, Co Carlow

FOCUS
In contrast to the general trend of the season most of the best races at this meeting have been well supported and suitably competitive. Solwhit was a non-runner due to being lame. The runner-up helps set the level, with a pb from the third on this step up in trip.

3376a LEXUS CHASE (GRADE 1) (17 fncs) 3m
2:55 (2:57) 5-Y-0+ **£75,609** (£23,170; £10,975; £3,658; £1,219)

RPR

1 **Bobs Worth (IRE)**[35] 2673 8-11-10 .... BarryGeraghty 165+
(Nicky Henderson) *trckd ldrs: 3rd 1/2-way: nt fluent 11th: slt mstke 3 out and niggled along bhd ldrs in 4th: rdn in 3rd bef last and styd on wl u.p run-in to ld ins fnl 100yds* **11/4**[1]

2 1 ½ **First Lieutenant (IRE)**[56] 2234 8-11-10 167 .... (p) DJCasey 163+
(M F Morris, Ire) *trckd ldr: cl 2nd 1/2-way: led briefly fr 11th: cl 2nd bef 3 out and disp next: led fr last and rdn: sn strly pressed and hdd ins fnl 100yds: no ex* **7/1**[3]

3 1 **Rubi Ball (FR)**[30] 2778 8-11-10 .... RWalsh 162
(W P Mullins, Ire) *led: over 1 l clr 1/2-way: slt mstke 11th and hdd briefly: slow next: narrow advantage bef 3 out and jnd next: hdd fr last where pckd sltly: sn no ex u.p in 3rd: kpt on same pce* **8/1**

4 3 ¾ **Sir Des Champs (FR)**[20] 2991 7-11-10 173 .... DavyRussell 158+
(W P Mullins, Ire) *trckd ldrs: cl 4th bef 3 out: rdn into st and no imp on ldrs after slt mstke last: kpt on same pce* **11/4**[1]

5 2 **Lyreen Legend (IRE)**[249] 5489 6-11-10 152 .... BryanCooper 156
(D T Hughes, Ire) *hld up in tch: clsr in 5th appr st: no imp on ldrs u.p bef last: kpt on same pce* **14/1**

6 2 ½ **Foildubh (IRE)**[20] 2985 9-11-10 151 .... PCarberry 154
(John Patrick Ryan, Ire) *w.w towards rr: clsr in 6th bef 3 out: rdn fr next and no imp on ldrs into st: kpt on same pce fr last* **33/1**

7 nk **Lord Windermere (IRE)**[28] 2815 7-11-10 154 .... DougieCostello 153
(J H Culloty, Ire) *w.w in rr: slt mstke 7th: hdwy on outer 2 out: rdn in 6th into st and sn no imp on ldrs: kpt on same pce* **7/1**[3]

8 nse **Unioniste (FR)**[21] 2938 5-11-9 .... NickScholfield 152
(Paul Nicholls) *on toes befhand: chsd ldrs: 4th 1/2-way: niggled along in 5th bef 3 out and no ex u.p in 7th fr after next: kpt on same pce run-in* **9/2**[2]

9 28 **Prince De Beauchene (FR)**[28] 2815 10-11-10 154 .... PaulTownend 125
(W P Mullins, Ire) *hld up in tch: nt fluent in rr 5 out: mstke 3 out and no imp on ldrs fr next: wknd* **20/1**

6m 17.1s (-13.90) **Going Correction** -0.45s/f (Good) 9 Ran SP% **122.0**
Speed ratings: **105,104,104,102,102 101,101,101,91**
CSF £24.40 TOTE £3.40: £1.80, £2.00, £1.40; DF 28.00 Trifecta £194.70.
Owner The Not Afraid Partnership **Bred** Mrs L Eadie **Trained** Upper Lambourn, Berks

FOCUS
The race of the Irish season so far. They raced in a tight group the whole way, and the fifth and sixth help set the standard.

3375 - 3379a (Foreign Racing) - See Raceform Interactive

3343 LIMERICK (R-H)

Saturday, December 28

OFFICIAL GOING: Heavy

3380a LIBERTY INSURANCE NOVICE HURDLE (GRADE 3) (14 hdls) 3m
1:35 (1:36) 4-Y-0+ **£15,060** (£4,402; £2,085; £695)

RPR

1 **Faugheen (IRE)**[21] 2963 5-11-3 .... EmmetMullins 149+
(W P Mullins, Ire) *mde all: far fr fluent at times but extended advantage bef 2 out and sn in command: stdd at last: easily* **8/13**[1]

2 5 **The Job Is Right**[20] 2983 5-11-6 126 .... (b) APHeskin 139
(Michael Hourigan, Ire) *chsd ldr in 3rd tl pushed along into 2nd after 3 out: no imp on wnr appr next: kpt on same pce* **12/1**

3 31 **Azorian (IRE)**[13] 3122 5-11-0 139 .... MPFogarty 108
(Eoin Griffin, Ire) *chsd ldrs in 4th tl prog into 2nd 4 out: pushed along after 3 out and sn no ex: jst dropped to 4th whn lft modest 3rd last* **11/4**[2]

4 1 ¾ **Royal Moll (IRE)**[39] 2586 6-10-7 .... AlanCrowe 93
(W P Mullins, Ire) *w.w: no threat bef 3 out: lft modest 4th 2 out* **16/1**

P **Kilbarry Beauty (IRE)**[21] 2963 6-10-7 121 .... NiallPMadden
(John E Kiely, Ire) *hld up towards rr: dropped to rr w a circ to r and sn detached: p.u* **33/1**

P **Lots Of Memories (IRE)**[20] 2983 6-11-6 129 .... ShaneButler
(P G Fahey, Ire) *trckd ldr in 2nd tl pushed along after 4 out: wknd qckly: p.u bef 2 out* **10/1**[3]

U **The Housekeeper (IRE)**[38] 2608 6-10-7 .... KevinSexton 103+
(David Harry Kelly, Ire) *t.k.h in rr tl prog 4 out: clsd to dispute 3rd whn mstke: uns rdr 2 out* **25/1**

6m 15.6s (375.60) 7 Ran SP% **118.0**
CSF £10.62 TOTE £1.40: £1.02, £3.40; DF 8.80 Trifecta £12.00.
Owner Mrs S Ricci **Bred** Dr John Waldron **Trained** Muine Beag, Co Carlow

FOCUS
The winner did not need to be at his best but coasted home. The progressive runner-up has been rated to a fair pb.

3381 - 3384a (Foreign Racing) - See Raceform Interactive

3085 DONCASTER (L-H)

Sunday, December 29

OFFICIAL GOING: Good to soft (chs 7.0; hdl 7.8)
Wind: light 1/2 against Weather: fine and sunny, cold

3385 THOROUGHBRED BREEDERS' ASSOCIATION FILLIES' JUVENILE MAIDEN HURDLE (THE SUNDAY £5K BONUS RACE) (8 hdls) 2m 110y
12:10 (12:10) (Class 5) 3-Y-0 **£2,599** (£763; £381; £190)

Form RPR

1 **Red Four**[60] 3-10-12 0 .... AndrewTinkler 98
(George Baker) *chsd ldrs: j.lft 3rd: reminders after 5th: 3rd 2 out: j.lft last: 2nd last 150yds: styd on to ld nr fin* **12/1**

3- 2 nk **Haatefina**[21] 2975 3-10-12 0 .... DaveCrosse 101+
(Mark Usher) *led: qcknd pce after 5th: 4 l clr next: 7 l ahd whn blnd bdly last: hdd nr fin* **20/1**

2- 3 5 **Morning With Ivan (IRE)**[25] 2881 3-10-12 0 .... DenisO'Regan 93
(Martin Todhunter) *hld up in rr: hdwy 4th: chsd ldrs appr 3 out: kpt on same pce fr 2 out* **9/4**[1]

34- 4 4 ½ **Maypole Lass**[22] 2934 3-10-12 112 .... (t) PaddyBrennan 89
(Renee Robeson) *chsd ldrs: one pce fr 3 out* **4/1**[2]

5 1 ½ **Colleen Bawn (FR)**[91] 3-10-12 0 .... HarrySkelton 87
(Dan Skelton) *hld up: hdwy appr 3 out: sn drvn: one pce* **9/2**[3]

5- 6 11 **Aminah**[22] 2934 3-10-12 0 .... LiamTreadwell 76
(Venetia Williams) *t.k.h: sn trcking ldrs: lost pl bef 3 out* **15/2**

7 7 **Pixie Cut (IRE)**[23] 3-10-12 0 .... JamieMoore 69
(Alistair Whillans) *t.k.h: trckd ldrs: lost pl after 5th* **7/1**

036- 8 9 **Multilicious**[39] 2592 3-10-9 0 .... JakeGreenall(3) 60
(Tim Walford) *in rr: pckd 2nd: bhd and pushed along 4th: bhd whn blnd next: t.o 3 out* **50/1**

5- 9 37 **Super Cookie**[32] 2750 3-10-9 0 .... JackQuinlan(3) 23
(Noel Quinlan) *hld up in rr: drvn after 5th: lost pl bef 3 out: sn bhd: t.o* **16/1**

4m 3.5s (-1.20) **Going Correction** -0.425s/f (Good) 9 Ran SP% **113.5**
Speed ratings (Par 99): **85,84,82,80,79 74,71,66,49**
toteswingers 1&2 £15.10, 1&3 £5.50, 2&3 £5.90 CSF £201.76 TOTE £14.10: £4.30, £5.20, £1.10; EX 298.30 Trifecta £1018.80 Pool: £2090.78 - 1.53 winning units..
Owner Lady Cobham **Bred** Lady Cobham **Trained** Manton, Wilts

FOCUS
This was just an ordinary race of its type. It was steadily run and has been given a token rating through the third.

3386 QUICKSILVERSLOTS PLAY £500 ROULETTE NOVICES' LIMITED H'CAP CHASE (12 fncs) 2m 110y
12:40 (12:40) (Class 3) (0-140,145) 4-Y-0+
£6,256 (£1,848; £924; £462; £231; £116)

Form RPR

11U- 1 **Next Sensation (IRE)**[29] 2816 6-10-12 133 .... (t) TomScudamore 150+
(Michael Scudamore) *led 1st: mde rest: styd on wl fr 3 out: 7 l ahd whn eased last 50yds* **4/1**[2]

U10- 2 6 **God's Own (IRE)**[44] 2490 5-11-2 137 .... PaddyBrennan 145+
(Tom George) *chsd ldrs: 2nd 5th: hit 8th: kpt on same pce fr 3 out* **8/1**

222- 3 4 ½ **Turn Over Sivola (FR)**[34] 2716 6-10-11 132 .... RobertThornton 132
(Alan King) *hld up: hdwy to chse ldrs 5th: 3rd 7th: one pce fr 3 out* **5/1**[3]

/24- 4 1 **Royal Guardsman (IRE)**[23] 2928 6-10-5 126 oh2 .... NoelFehily 125
(Ali Brewer) *in rr: hdwy 8th: sn chsng ldrs: one pce fr 3 out* **7/2**[1]

/56- 5 ½ **Sound Investment (IRE)**[22] 2935 5-10-5 126 oh2 .... (t) DarylJacob 124
(Paul Nicholls) *in rr: hdwy to chse ldrs whn hit 5th: outpcd 8th: kpt on fr 3 out* **7/1**

113- 6 9 **Robbie**[15] 3088 9-10-12 133 .... JamesReveley 123
(Keith Reveley) *chsd ldrs: mstke 4th: drvn and lost pl bef 4 out* **9/1**

/41- 7 33 **Doynosaur**[17] 3037 6-10-6 127 .... DenisO'Regan 83
(K R Burke) *hld up in rr: sme hdwy 6th: lost pl appr 4 out: sn bhd and eased: t.o* **14/1**

121- U **Mwaleshi**[8] 3202 8-11-5 145 .... JonathanEngland(5)
(Sue Smith) *led to 1st: chsd ldrs: blnd and uns rdr 4th* **7/1**

3m 56.8s (-8.20) **Going Correction** -0.425s/f (Good) 8 Ran SP% **111.7**
Speed ratings (Par 107): **102,99,97,96,96 92,76,**
toteswingers 1&2 £7.50, 1&3 £5.80, 2&3 £10.80 CSF £33.39 CT £158.39 TOTE £4.80: £1.50, £3.20, £2.20; EX 40.00 Trifecta £272.70 Pool: £2526.36 - 6.94 winning units..
Owner Mark Blandford **Bred** Mrs Regina McAuliffe **Trained** Bromsash, H'fords

FOCUS
Eight runners started this competitive-looking chase, but only one counted from some way out. The winner's time was pretty good. He took another step up and has developed into a smart novice.

3387 QUICKSILVERSLOTS PLAY £500 RAINBOW RICHES H'CAP HURDLE (11 hdls) 3m 110y
1:15 (1:15) (Class 3) (0-140,140) 4-Y-0+ **£5,848** (£1,717; £858; £429)

Form RPR

205- 1 **Mister Dillon**[16] 3069 6-10-11 130 .... NicodeBoinville(5) 137+
(Nicky Henderson) *chsd ldrs: led bef 2 out: drvn rt out* **8/1**

1/P- 2 1 ½ **Western Jo (IRE)**[29] 2807 5-10-9 123 .... RichardJohnson 128
(Philip Hobbs) *nt fluent in rr: hdwy appr 3 out: chsng wnr between last 2: j.lft last: styd on same pce last 100yds* **14/1**

302- 3 3 ½ **Corkage (IRE)**[15] 3085 10-10-9 123 .... (v) JamesReveley 126
(Keith Reveley) *led to 5th: led appr 3 out: hdd and hit 2 out: kpt on same pce* **12/1**

426- 4 1 ½ **Drum Valley**[22] 2949 5-11-4 132 .... LeightonAspell 132
(Oliver Sherwood) *chsd ldrs: one pce fr 2 out* **6/1**[2]

UF4- 5 4 ½ **Midnight Oscar (IRE)**[15] 3085 6-10-6 120 .... (v[1]) NickScholfield 116
(Kim Bailey) *chsd ldrs: dropped bk 8th: hdwy next: one pce fr 2 out* **7/1**[3]

213- **6** 3½ **Don't Be Late (IRE)**[29] 2813 5-11-3 **131**......................(p) RichieMcLernon 123
(Jonjo O'Neill) *in rr: hdwy 8th: sn chsng ldrs: drvn next: wknd run-in* **9/1**

1/1- **7** 1¾ **Cowards Close (IRE)**[236] 163 6-10-11 **125**......................(t) DarylJacob 115
(Paul Nicholls) *chsd ldrs: drvn 8th: one pce fr next* **3/1**[1]

2/2- **8** 1¾ **Henryville**[41] 2569 5-10-4 **118**.. RyanMahon 106
(Harry Fry) *detached in last: hdwy appr 3 out: one pce* **9/1**

113- **9** *hd* **Sivola De Sivola (FR)**[57] 2220 7-11-4 **132**........................ PaddyBrennan 120
(Tom George) *racd wd: chsd ldr: led 5th: drvn 7th: hdd appr 3 out: fdd 2 out* **16/1**

102- **10** 3¾ **Al Co (FR)**[38] 2624 8-11-7 **135**.. DonalDevereux 119
(Peter Bowen) *in rr: hdwy to chse ldrs 5th: drvn and lost pl 3 out* **16/1**

/PF- **11** *42* **Opening Batsman (IRE)**[29] 2815 7-11-12 **140**....................(t) NoelFehily 82
(Harry Fry) *racd v wd: chsd ldrs: lost pl after 8th: sn bhd: t.o 2 out: virtually p.u* **16/1**

5m 50.4s (-8.60) **Going Correction** -0.425s/f (Good) **11** Ran SP% **114.9**
Speed ratings (Par 107): **96,95,94,93,92 91,90,90,90,88 75**
toteswingers 1&2 £30.00, 1&3 £10.40, 2&3 £29.00 CSF £109.17 CT £1332.03 TOTE £8.30: £2.30, £4.20, £3.00; EX 121.80 Trifecta £1326.20 Pool: £3499.60 - 1.97 winning units..
Owner Elite Racing Club **Bred** Elite Racing Club **Trained** Upper Lambourn, Berks

FOCUS
The early pace was steady in this decent contest and one got the impression that it developed into a sprint. Improvement from the winner with a bigger step up from the second.

3388 QUICKSILVERSLOTS GET UP TO £200 FREEPLAYS "NATIONAL HUNT" NOVICES' HURDLE (10 hdls) 2m 3f 110y
1:45 (1:46) (Class 4) 4-Y-0+ **£3,249** (£954; £477; £238)

Form RPR

1/2- **1** **Oscar Hoof (IRE)**[37] 2657 5-10-12 0................................ AndrewTinkler 129+
(Nicky Henderson) *w ldrs: led 3rd to 5th: led 7th: hit last: drvn clr* **11/10**[1]

4/3- **2** 4½ **Elmore Back (IRE)**[31] 2761 4-10-12 0.................................... MarkGrant 121
(Charlie Mann) *chsd ldrs: cl 2nd 3 out: kpt on same pce run-in* **20/1**

31- **3** *nse* **Powerstown Dreams (IRE)**[30] 2788 4-10-12 0..... SamTwiston-Davies 121
(Steve Gollings) *mid-div: chsd ldrs 3rd: drvn after 6th: 3rd 2 out: styd on run-in* **18/1**

31- **4** 3½ **Swallowshide**[38] 2631 4-11-5 0.. AidanColeman 124
(Emma Lavelle) *in rr: hdwy 6th: drvn appr 3 out: lft 4th 2 out: kpt on same pce* **4/1**[2]

505- **5** *8* **Land Of Vic**[24] 2907 5-10-5 0... DonalDevereux 102
(Peter Bowen) *led to 3rd: chsd ldrs: outpcd appr 3 out: kpt on between last 2* **66/1**

0/4- **6** 3¼ **Mr Bridger**[45] 2479 4-10-12 0.. DarylJacob 107
(Paul Nicholls) *hld up: hdwy 4th: chsng ldrs 6th: wkng whn mstke 2 out* **25/1**

452/ **7** 2¼ **No Substitute (IRE)**[715] 3722 8-10-12 0......................... RobertThornton 104
(Alan King) *in rr: hdwy 7th: one pce fr next* **20/1**

/5P- **8** *hd* **Operatic Heights (IRE)**[56] 2252 4-10-12 0.................. RichardJohnson 103
(Tim Vaughan) *mid-div: sme hdwy 7th: fdd next* **100/1**

0/ **9** *8* **Pure Oxygen (IRE)**[297] 4621 5-10-12 0.................................... NoelFehily 102+
(Harry Fry) *chsng ldrs 3rd: wknd 2 out: 6th whn mstke last* **16/1**

/04- **10** *6* **Favourable Fellow (IRE)**[26] 2871 4-10-12 0.............. RichieMcGrath 89
(Geoffrey Harker) *t.k.h in rr: kpt on fr 3 out: nvr a factor* **100/1**

/06- **11** *5* **The Kvilleken**[45] 2476 5-10-12 0.. IanPopham 84
(Martin Keighley) *in rr: hdwy 6th: hung rt and lost pl bef 3 out* **100/1**

50- **12** 4½ **Whichwaytobougie**[12] 3144 4-10-12 0.................................. JamesReveley 80
(Keith Reveley) *chsd ldrs: lost pl 6th* **80/1**

0/5- **13** 1¼ **Steel Summit (IRE)**[231] 246 4-10-12 0.......................... WayneHutchinson 79
(David Dennis) *hdwy to chse ldrs 3rd: drvn 5th: lost pl after 7th* **100/1**

162- **14** 2½ **Lemony Bay**[30] 2783 4-10-12 0.. LeightonAspell 76
(Oliver Sherwood) *w ldrs: led 5th: hdd 7th: wkng whn mstke next* **5/1**[3]

036- **15** *21* **All Riled Up**[120] 1472 5-10-5 0.. JamieMoore 48
(Harry Chisman) *in rr: bhd fr 6th: t.o 3 out* **150/1**

46- **16** 2¾ **Crazy Chester (IRE)**[7] 3225 4-10-9 0.............................. JakeGreenall(3) 52
(Michael Easterby) *in rr: bhd fr 6th: t.o 2 out* **100/1**

4P/ **17** *13* **Serious Mixture**[245] 19 6-10-12 0.. JackDoyle 39
(Hilary Parrott) *mid-div: hdwy to chse ldrs 4th: lost pl 7th: bhd whn blnd next: t.o* **125/1**

0F0- **18** 3½ **Presentings Return (IRE)**[11] 3163 4-10-12 0............. RichieMcLernon 36
(Jonjo O'Neill) *mid-div: chsng ldrs 6th: lost pl after next: sn bhd: t.o 2 out* **100/1**

/40- **F** **Bodega**[21] 2978 5-10-12 0.. WillKennedy 117
(Ian Williams) *hld up in rr: hdwy 6th: 4th and keeping on whn fell 2 out* **33/1**

P **Tire Larigot (FR)**[253] 6-10-12 0.. PaddyBrennan
(Tom George) *mid-div: lost pl 7th: bhd whn p.u bef next* **100/1**

00- **U** **Sir Harry Hotspur**[22] 2954 5-10-12 0.................................... HarryHaynes
(John Mackie) *in tch: blnd and uns rdr 2nd* **150/1**

4m 40.3s (-11.00) **Going Correction** -0.425s/f (Good) **21** Ran SP% **123.5**
Speed ratings (Par 105): **105,103,103,101,98 97,96,96,93,90 88,86,86,85,77 75,70,69, ,**
toteswingers 1&2 £4.40, 1&3 £5.40, 2&3 £52.80 CSF £29.40 TOTE £2.20: £1.30, £4.40, £4.10; EX 25.90 Trifecta £240.10 Pool: £2651.28 - 8.28 winning units..
Owner The Hoof Partnership **Bred** John Bergin **Trained** Upper Lambourn, Berks

FOCUS
Lots of runners but not many were of serious interest. Four pulled clear. The cosy winner set a decent standard and is rated to his mark.

3389 QUICKSILVERSLOTS £1 TO WIN £500 H'CAP CHASE (17 fncs 1 omitted) 3m
2:20 (2:22) (Class 3) (0-135,132) 4-Y-0+ **£6,498** (£1,908; £954; £477)

Form RPR

163- **1** **Mart Lane (IRE)**[15] 3091 8-11-12 **132**......................(b) WayneHutchinson 146+
(Dr Richard Newland) *chsd ldr: led 7th: drvn clr 4 out: styd on wl* **9/2**[2]

533- **2** *7* **Categorical**[25] 2884 10-10-8 **114**.. JamesReveley 118
(Keith Reveley) *chsd ldrs: outpcd 6 out: hdwy appr 3 out: 4th whn hit last: styd on to take 2nd fnl strides* **9/1**

/05- **3** ½ **Mr Syntax (IRE)**[17] 3036 9-11-0 **120**..............................(t) DenisO'Regan 123
(Tim Fitzgerald) *last whn j. slowly 1st: nt fluent in rr: hdwy 6 out: 3rd 3 out: kpt on run-in* **16/1**

023/ **4** *2* **Real Milan (IRE)**[249] 5496 8-11-12 **132**..................................(t) NoelFehily 125+
(Donald McCain) *chsd ldrs: bmpd 1st: 2nd whn blnd 4 out: wknd and lost two pls clsng stages* **7/2**[1]

132- **5** *19* **Susquehanna River (IRE)**[31] 2754 6-10-9 **115**...... SamTwiston-Davies 103
(Nigel Twiston-Davies) *in rr: outpcd 7 out: sme hdwy 5 out: 5th and wkng whn mstke 3 out* **9/2**[2]

4P6- **6** *42* **Savant Bleu (FR)**[23] 2931 7-11-5 **125**.. SamThomas 64
(Kim Bailey) *j.lft 1st: chsd ldrs: lost pl after 9th: mstke 7 out: bhd 5 out: t.o* **18/1**

0FP- **P** **Havingotascoobydo (IRE)**[22] 2943 8-10-12 **118**................. TomSiddall
(Martin Keighley) *led to 7th: lost pl bef 3 out: poor 6th whn p.u bef 2 out* **10/1**

5/6- **P** **Yellow Ball (FR)**[15] 3097 5-11-4 **124**.. LiamTreadwell
(Venetia Williams) *rr-div: lost pl 9th: sn bhd: t.o whn p.u bef 6 out* **10/1**

/34- **P** **Regal Presence (IRE)**[54] 2283 6-10-6 **112**..................(p) AidanColeman
(Victor Dartnall) *chsd ldrs: rem inders after 9th: lost pl 5 out: sn bhd: t.o whn p.u bef 2 out* **11/2**[3]

5m 55.9s (-16.10) **Going Correction** -0.425s/f (Good) **9** Ran SP% **113.3**
Speed ratings (Par 107): **109,106,106,105,99 85, , ,**
CSF £42.90 CT £588.33 TOTE £4.60: £1.50, £2.10, £4.50; EX 38.00 Trifecta £658.20 Pool: £2759.06 - 3.14 winning units..
Owner Jim Stewart **Bred** Ronnie O'Neill **Trained** Claines, Worcs

FOCUS
Another race where it paid to race handily. A big step up from the easy winner who should be competitive in higher grade.

3390 CROWNHOTEL-BAWTRY.COM NOVICES' H'CAP HURDLE (8 hdls) 2m 110y
2:55 (2:56) (Class 4) (0-115,115) 3-Y-0+ **£3,249** (£954; £477; £238)

Form RPR

34- **1** **Nesterenko (GER)**[27] 2858 4-11-11 **114**............................ AndrewTinkler 126+
(Nicky Henderson) *chsd ldrs: drvn 5th: styd on to chal next: led appr last: drvn clr last 75yds* **15/2**

/52- **2** *9* **Figaro**[24] 2900 5-11-9 **112**..(t) RichardJohnson 117+
(Tim Vaughan) *chsd ldr: led and hit 3 out: nt fluent next: hdd appr last: kpt on same pce last 100yds* **4/1**[1]

33- **3** *11* **Dewala**[31] 2767 4-11-2 **105**.. RyanMahon 97
(Michael Appleby) *chsd ldrs: cl 3rd 3 out: one pce fr next* **11/2**[3]

430- **4** 2¼ **Even If**[15] 3094 5-11-5 **108**.. RichieMcLernon 98
(Jonjo O'Neill) *mid-div: hdwy appr 3 out: one pce fr 2 out* **14/1**

0/6- **5** *6* **Pinotage**[24] 2904 5-10-13 **102**.. DenisO'Regan 86
(Peter Niven) *in rr: sme hdwy after 5th: blnd 2 out: nvr a factor* **28/1**

045- **6** 1¼ **Join The Clan (IRE)**[27] 2858 4-11-5 **113**.................(p) MauriceLinehan(5) 96
(Jonjo O'Neill) *chsd ldrs: wknd appr 2 out* **11/1**

504- **7** *9* **Ballyhooley Boy (IRE)**[16] 3070 6-11-11 **114**...................... CharliePoste 88
(Robin Dickin) *in rr: hdwy on outside 7th: rdn and lost pl appr next* **14/1**

006- **8** *5* **Ghost Of A Smile (IRE)**[16] 3070 5-10-13 **107**............ RobertMcCarth(5) 76
(Ian Williams) *prom: drvn and lost pl after 5th* **12/1**

210- **9** 1¾ **Little Pop**[44] 2492 5-11-12 **115**................................... SamTwiston-Davies 82
(Nigel Twiston-Davies) *led: hdd appr 3 out: sn wknd: blnd 2 out: sn eased* **5/1**[2]

304- **10** *12* **Rock A Doodle Doo (IRE)**[57] 2225 6-11-12 **115**......... AndrewThornton 70
(Sally Hall) *mid-div: drvn 5th: lost pl and bhd 3 out* **9/1**

F05- **11** *10* **Sleeping City (FR)**[24] 2910 6-11-4 **107**.. JackDoyle 52
(Victor Dartnall) *in rr: sme hdwy 5th: lost pl bef next* **11/1**

334- **F** **Seaside Rock (IRE)**[13] 3127 3-10-0 **102**.............................. RichieMcGrath 70
(Keith Dalgleish) *in rr: modest 8th whn fell 2 out* **28/1**

3m 54.3s (-10.40) **Going Correction** -0.425s/f (Good)
WFA 3 from 4yo 13lb 4 from 5yo+ 5lb **12** Ran SP% **118.4**
Speed ratings (Par 105): **107,102,97,96,93 93,88,86,85,80 75,**
CSF £38.21 CT £179.35 TOTE £7.50: £2.70, £1.90, £2.10; EX 30.60 Trifecta £84.10 Pool: £2039.72 - 18.18 winning units..
Owner Juergen Meyer **Bred** A Pereira **Trained** Upper Lambourn, Berks

FOCUS
A modest but competitive contest, run at an ordinary gallop. A big step up from the impressive winner.

3391 PARK HILL HOSPITAL MARES' H'CAP HURDLE (10 hdls) 2m 3f 110y
3:25 (3:26) (Class 4) (0-120,111) 3-Y-0+ **£3,249** (£954; £477; £238)

Form RPR

/56- **1** **Iron Butterfly**[19] 3012 4-11-7 **106**.. PaulMoloney 112+
(James Eustace) *hld up towards rr: hdwy to chse ldrs 3 out: outpcd next: 4th last: styd on wl to ld last 50yds* **7/1**

035- **2** 1¼ **Queen Spud**[25] 2891 4-10-5 **90**....................................(p) RichardJohnson 95
(Henry Daly) *w ldr: led 3rd tl after 7th: led appr 3 out: j.lft and hit last: hdd and no ex last 50yds* **13/2**

120- **3** 3½ **In By Midnight**[22] 2948 5-11-9 **108**.............................. PaddyBrennan 108
(Tom George) *trckd ldrs: upsides 3 out: kpt on same pce appr last: tk 3rd nr fin* **11/2**[3]

/21- **4** ¾ **Favorite Girl (GER)**[28] 2848 5-11-7 **106**................................ RyanMahon 105
(Michael Appleby) *trckd ldrs: chal 3 out: edgd rt and fdd last 100yds* **11/4**[1]

001- **5** *9* **Sparkling Hand**[8] 3212 7-11-4 **103**....................................(p) HarryHaynes 93
(Peter Atkinson) *led to 3rd: led briefly after 7th: 4th and one pce whn hit 2 out: sn fdd* **11/1**

/32- **6** *7* **Entertain Me**[14] 3113 9-10-13 **108**............................ JosephPalmowski(10) 91
(Robin Dickin) *in rr: pushed along 5th: chsd ldrs next: reminders 7th: wknd appr 2 out* **11/1**

603- **7** *19* **Tara Muck**[29] 2824 6-11-5 **104**.................................. SamTwiston-Davies 68
(Nigel Twiston-Davies) *chsd ldrs: lost pl after 7th: sn bhd* **5/1**[2]

0/6- **8** 3¼ **September Blaze**[45] 2477 6-11-12 **111**.................................. DenisO'Regan 72
(Paul Webber) *chsd ldrs: edgd rt and lost pl after 3 out: bhd whn eased run-in* **16/1**

/55- **9** *hd* **Kathleen Frances**[19] 3010 6-11-9 **108**..................................(t) JackDoyle 69
(Ali Brewer) *in rr: sme hdwy 6th: lost pl bef 3 out: sn eased* **14/1**

4m 42.5s (-8.80) **Going Correction** -0.425s/f (Good)
WFA 4 from 5yo+ 5lb **9** Ran SP% **113.8**
Speed ratings (Par 105): **100,99,98,97,94 91,83,82,82**
CSF £51.10 CT £268.06 TOTE £7.80: £2.20, £2.20, £1.80; EX 56.90 Trifecta £278.30 Pool: £2206.66 - 5.94 winning units..
Owner Harold Nass **Bred** Rockville Pike Partnership **Trained** Newmarket, Suffolk

■ Stewards' Enquiry : Paul Moloney two-day ban; used whip above permitted level (15th-16th Jan).

FOCUS
The early fractions weren't particularly quick and this isn't strong form. It's rated around the third and fourth.

T/Jkpt: Not won. T/Plt: £107.30. Pool: £105,626.01 - 718.24 winning units. T/Qpdt: £27.70. Pool: £10,123.23 - 270.05 winning units. WG

The Form Book Jumps, Raceform Ltd, Compton, RG20 6NL.

[2968]KELSO (L-H)

Sunday, December 29

OFFICIAL GOING: Soft (5.8)

Wind: Fresh, half against Weather: Overcast

3392 MATT BOOKIE CONGRATULATES KELSO GROUND STAFF "NATIONAL HUNT" MAIDEN HURDLE (11 hdls) 2m 6f 110y

12:00 (12:02) (Class 5) 4-Y-0+ **£2,599** (£763; £381; £190)

Form RPR

3- **1** **Masterleaderman (IRE)**[51] 2342 5-11-0 0 RyanMania 102+
(Michael Smith) *prom: hdwy to ld 2 out: shkn up and hung edgd lft appr last: drvn out run-in* **11/4**[2]

/62- **2** *3 1/4* **Hellorboston (IRE)**[18] 3018 5-11-0 0 (p) JasonMaguire 100+
(Donald McCain) *led: rdn 4 out: nt fluent next: hdd 2 out: kpt on same pce fr last* **8/13**[1]

054/ **3** *3 1/2* **Blueside Boy (IRE)**[365] 3341 5-10-7 0 GrahamWatters(7) 93
(Lucinda Russell) *prom: hdwy to chal 4th: effrt and pushed along 2 out: one pce fr last* **10/1**[3]

046/ **4** *shd* **Lord Usher (IRE)**[261] 5279 6-11-0 0 BrianHarding 94
(George Charlton) *hld up: smooth hdwy to trck ldrs 3 out: shkn up whn nt fluent next: outpcd bef last* **12/1**

/06- **5** *3* **Thorlak (FR)**[17] 3036 6-11-0 0 BrianHughes 91
(James Ewart) *prom: effrt and shkn up 2 out: nt fluent last: sn wknd* **14/1**

P4- **6** *6* **Allforthelove**[18] 3018 5-10-7 0 MrKitAlexander(7) 85
(N W Alexander) *disp ld tl rdn and wknd fr 2 out* **50/1**

5- **7** *28* **Prairie Lad**[28] 2838 5-10-7 0 CallumBewley(7) 56
(Sandy Thomson) *towards rr: outpcd and drvn 1/2-way: n.d after* **16/1**

000- **8** *1 1/4* **Marlee Massie (IRE)**[51] 2337 4-11-0 0 PeterBuchanan 55
(N W Alexander) *hld up bhd ldng gp: mstke 5 out: wknd fr next: t.o* **100/1**

P/0- **9** *27* **Mr Mansson (IRE)**[17] 3038 6-11-0 68 AdrianLane 28
(Lucy Normile) *in tch: struggling 5 out: lost tch fr next: t.o* **100/1**

P- **10** *32* **Ruberslaw**[18] 3018 7-11-0 0 BarryKeniry
(Simon Shirley-Beavan) *hld up: outpcd whn blnd 5 out: sn lost tch: t.o* **50/1**

5m 53.3s (12.30) **Going Correction** +0.075s/f (Yiel) **10** Ran SP% **123.8**
Speed ratings (Par 103): **81,79,78,78,77 75,65,65,55,44**
toteswingers 1&2 £1.10, 1&3 £4.90, 2&3 £4.30 CSF £5.30 TOTE £3.00: £1.20, £1.10, £3.00; EX 5.30 Trifecta £33.40 Pool: £1957.91 - 43.89 winning units..
Owner East-West Partnership **Bred** J Costello **Trained** Kirkheaton, Northumberland

FOCUS
Fresh ground on all bends, inner line used and distances reduced by about 15yds per circuit. A modest staying novice hurdle which was slowly run. The cosy winner is rated to his mark with the second a stone+ off.

3393 BLACK SWAN LEES HOTEL KELSO MARES' NOVICES' HURDLE (8 hdls) 2m 110y

12:30 (12:32) (Class 4) 4-Y-0+ **£3,898** (£1,144; £572; £286)

Form RPR

235- **1** **Retrieve The Stick**[25] 2883 4-10-12 0 BrianHughes 98+
(Malcolm Jefferson) *trckd ldr: led 3 out: pushed along and clr whn edgd lft after 2 out: kpt on strly* **9/4**[2]

03/ **2** *19* **High Fair**[365] 3344 7-10-5 0 StephenMulqueen(7) 77
(Sandy Forster) *t.k.h: prom: effrt bef 2 out: chsng (clr) wnr whn mstke last: no imp* **40/1**

232- **3** *2* **Texas Rose (IRE)**[44] 2495 6-10-7 103 TonyKelly(5) 75
(Rebecca Menzies) *t.k.h: led at stdy pce to 3 out: sn rdn: outpcd appr next: btn whn lost 2nd last* **8/11**[1]

004- **4** *15* **Innocent Girl (IRE)**[20] 2998 4-10-12 0 PeterBuchanan 63
(Lucinda Russell) *in tch: stdy hdwy bef 3 out: rdn and wknd bef next* **5/1**[3]

4m 2.0s (0.20) **Going Correction** +0.075s/f (Yiel) **4** Ran SP% **107.8**
Speed ratings (Par 105): **102,93,92,85**
CSF £28.13 TOTE £2.20; EX 39.10 Trifecta £67.10 Pool: £588.25 - 6.57 winning units..
Owner Newstead Racing Partnership **Bred** Mrs M Barker **Trained** Norton, N Yorks

FOCUS
An ordinary mares' novice. The winner is probably the best guide.

3394 FLOORS CASTLE HORSE TRIALS H'CAP CHASE (17 fncs) 2m 7f 110y

1:05 (1:05) (Class 4) (0-120,112) 4-Y-0+ **£3,768** (£1,106; £553; £276)

Form RPR

5/5- **1** **Or De Grugy (FR)**[79] 1852 11-11-6 106 PeterBuchanan 116
(N W Alexander) *mde all: rdn 2 out: styd on strly fr last* **7/2**[3]

6F3- **2** *4 1/2* **Polarbrook (IRE)**[29] 2805 6-11-12 112 (b) JasonMaguire 120+
(Donald McCain) *mstkes in rr: outpcd 11th: rallied 3 out: effrt and chsd (clr) wnr between last 2: hit last: kpt on same pce* **7/2**[3]

432- **3** *1 3/4* **Farm Pixie (IRE)**[26] 2870 7-10-2 95 GrahamWatters(7) 97
(Ann Hamilton) *in tch: rdn and outpcd 12th: rallied 4 out: plugged on fr 2 out: nt pce to chal* **9/4**[1]

6/0- **4** *2 1/2* **Fog Patches (IRE)**[18] 3019 7-10-9 102 (p) GrantCockburn(7) 104
(Lucinda Russell) *prom: rdn bef 4 out: hung lft and outpcd fr 2 out* **3/1**[2]

314- **5** *1 1/4* **More Equity**[21] 2971 11-11-11 111 RyanMania 110
(Dianne Sayer) *chsd wnr tl rdn and wknd between last 2* **10/1**

6m 9.0s (1.00) **Going Correction** 0.0s/f (Good) **5** Ran SP% **109.3**
Speed ratings (Par 105): **98,96,95,95,94**
CSF £15.48 TOTE £4.90: £2.00, £2.50; EX 17.40 Trifecta £40.50 Pool: £434.79 - 8.04 winning units..
Owner Lord Cochrane And Partners **Bred** Earl La Grugerie **Trained** Kinneston, Perth & Kinross

FOCUS
A moderate handicap. The winner is rated in line with the best of last season's figures.

3395 MONTEITH MEMORIAL H'CAP CHASE (BETFAIR SCOTTISH CHASE SERIES QUALIFIER) (11 fncs 1 omitted) 2m 1f

1:35 (1:38) (Class 4) (0-120,120) 4-Y-0+ **£5,848** (£1,717; £858; £429)

Form RPR

5U4- **1** **Ballycool (IRE)**[50] 2361 6-9-9 94 oh1 (t) DerekFox(5) 110+
(Lucinda Russell) *hld up in tch: smooth hdwy to chse ldr bef 2 out (usual 3 out): led and edgd lft bef last: sn clr* **10/3**[2]

2F4- **2** *19* **Rocking Blues (FR)**[17] 3039 8-11-2 110 JasonMaguire 109
(Rose Dobbin) *chsd ldrs: outpcd 7th: rallied 3 out (usual 4 out): sn rdn: styd on fr last to take 2nd towards fin: nt pce of wnr* **11/4**[1]

025- **3** *2* **Endeavor**[20] 2996 8-10-13 107 RyanMania 103
(Dianne Sayer) *in tch: hdwy to chse ldr 7th: led 3 out (usual 4 out) to bef last: sn outpcd* **10/1**

3/6- **4** *7* **Prosecco (IRE)**[57] 2222 11-11-12 120 PeterBuchanan 108
(Lucinda Russell) *led to 3 out (usual 4 out): rdn and outpcd after next* **9/1**[3]

220- **5** *24* **Prince Tam**[17] 3039 9-9-7 94 oh2 CallumBewley(7) 58
(Harriet Graham) *chsd ldrs: lft 2nd 3rd: rdn and wknd fr 3 out (usual 4 out)* **18/1**

313- **U** **Cloverhill Lad (IRE)**[8] 3213 9-10-7 101 BrianHarding
(Stuart Coltherd) *in tch whn bdly hmpd and uns rdr 3rd* **9/1**[3]

/22- **F** **Little Glenshee (IRE)**[21] 2969 7-11-5 120 MrKitAlexander(7)
(N W Alexander) *chsng ldr whn fell heavily 3rd* **11/4**[1]

4m 18.6s (0.60) **Going Correction** 0.0s/f (Good) **7** Ran SP% **110.8**
Speed ratings (Par 105): **98,89,88,84,73 ,**
toteswingers 1&2 £3.50, 1&3 £9.00, 2&3 £18.10 CSF £12.55 TOTE £4.50: £2.40, £2.10; EX 16.50 Trifecta £116.60 Pool: £1077.93 - 6.92 winning units..
Owner Mr And Mrs T P Winnell **Bred** Edward McKinley **Trained** Arlary, Perth & Kinross

FOCUS
The first fence in the home straight was bypassed on the final circuit. A modest handicap. Seemingly a big step up from the easy winner.

3396 PETER & GILLIAN ALLAN CATERERS H'CAP HURDLE (5 hdls 6 omitted) 2m 6f 110y

2:10 (2:10) (Class 4) (0-115,113) 4-Y-0+ **£3,898** (£1,144; £572; £286)

Form RPR

21- **1** **Mr Utah**[26] 2866 6-11-7 113 TonyKelly(5) 113
(Rebecca Menzies) *in tch: stdy hdwy 2 out (usual 4 out): cl 3rd whn blnd next: rallied and led bef omitted 2 out: styd on gamely u.p* **13/2**

/04- **2** *3/4* **Quel Elite (FR)**[19] 3013 9-11-4 105 BrianHughes 105
(James Moffatt) *hld up: stdy hdwy and lft 4th last (usual 3 out): chsd wnr bef omitted 2 out: kpt on wl u.p: hld nr fin* **9/2**[2]

/P0- **3** *13* **Caerlaverock (IRE)**[22] 2956 8-10-6 100 ShaunDobbin(7) 86
(Rose Dobbin) *hld up towards rr: outpcd whn n.m.r on bnd sing fnl circ: hdwy whn hmpd last (usual 3 out): sn rdn and outpcd: rallied and swtchd lft after omitted last: kpt on: nt rch first two* **16/1**

010- **4** *2* **Amethyst Rose (IRE)**[21] 2974 6-10-8 95 RyanMania 80
(Stuart Coltherd) *hld up: hdwy 2 out (usual 4 out): lft 2nd next: sn rdn: one pce bypassing omitted 2 out* **5/1**[3]

501- **5** *3/4* **Jack Albert (IRE)**[20] 2997 6-10-0 87 oh2 (b) BrianHarding 71
(Dianne Sayer) *cl up: led 1st to 2 out (usual 4 out): lft in ld next: hdd bef omitted 2 out: sn one pce* **8/1**

26P- **6** *10* **Bescot Springs (IRE)**[21] 2971 8-11-8 109 PeterBuchanan 83
(Lucinda Russell) *hld up: struggling 2 out (usual 4 out): nvr on terms* **8/1**

0/3- **7** *11* **Nodda High Kid**[56] 2245 7-10-3 95 CallumWhillans(5) 58
(Donald Whillans) *led to 1st: cl up tl rdn and wknd 2 out (usual 4 out)* **12/1**

F12- **F** **Dickie Henderhoop (IRE)**[28] 2844 8-10-10 104 (b) MrRWilson(7)
(Lucy Normile) *in tch: hdwy to ld 2 out (usual 4 out): jst in front and shkn up whn fell heavily next* **10/1**

423- **B** **Romany Ryme**[18] 3018 7-11-2 110 JonathonBewley(7)
(George Bewley) *trckd ldrs: cl 3rd and gng wl whn b.d last (usual 3 out)* **4/1**[1]

5m 41.2s (0.20) **Going Correction** +0.075s/f (Yiel) **9** Ran SP% **113.1**
Speed ratings (Par 105): **102,101,97,96,96 92,88, ,**
toteswingers 1&2 £5.20, 1&3 £40.00, 2&3 £20.30 CSF £35.56 CT £445.40 TOTE £8.20: £1.90, £2.40, £4.80; EX 49.30 Trifecta £1181.90 Part won..
Owner Premier Racing Partnerships **Bred** Dr B Mayoh **Trained** Stearsby, N Yorks
■ Stewards' Enquiry : Shaun Dobbin two-day ban; used whip with excessive force (12th-13th Jan).

FOCUS
Both hurdles in the home straight were omitted on each circuit because of the low sun. A dramatic handicap chase. The first two are rated pretty much to their marks.

3397 CHILDREN'S IMMUNOLOGY TRUST NOVICES' LIMITED H'CAP CHASE (12 fncs 5 omitted) 2m 7f 110y

2:45 (2:45) (Class 3) (0-125,120) 4-Y-0+ **£6,498** (£1,908; £954)

Form RPR

113- **1** **Settledoutofcourt (IRE)**[22] 2959 7-10-9 110 PeterBuchanan 117
(Lucinda Russell) *mde all: rdn whn hrd pressed bef omitted 2 out: styd on gamely last 200yds* **6/5**[1]

/P2- **2** *3 1/2* **Abbey Storm (IRE)**[63] 2099 7-11-5 120 JasonMaguire 125
(Donald McCain) *mstkes: chsd ldrs: hdwy to press wnr 9th: ev ch and rdn bef omitted 2 out: hung lft and outpcd passing omitted last* **13/8**[2]

134- **3** *19* **Indigo Rock (IRE)**[44] 2494 7-11-5 120 RyanMania 111
(Michael Smith) *chsd wnr to 9th: hit 2 out (usual 4 out): rdn and wknd appr omitted 2 out* **10/3**[3]

6m 4.3s (-3.70) **Going Correction** 0.0s/f (Good) **3** Ran SP% **106.6**
Speed ratings (Par 107): **106,104,98**
CSF £3.42 TOTE £2.20; EX 5.30 Trifecta £6.00 Pool: £1744.51 - 214.89 winning units..
Owner Andrew McAllister **Bred** Sean Naughton **Trained** Arlary, Perth & Kinross

FOCUS
Both fences in the straight were bypassed, variously on account of damage and low sun. The first two were pretty much to their marks in this ordinary handicap.

3398 ISLE OF SKYE BLENDED SCOTCH WHISKY H'CAP HURDLE (THE SUNDAY £5K BONUS RACE) (6 hdls 4 omitted) 2m 2f

3:15 (3:15) (Class 4) (0-120,120) 4-Y-0+ **£4,548** (£1,335; £667; £333)

Form RPR

52P- **1** **Ubaltique (FR)**[57] 2221 5-11-12 120 (b1) JasonMaguire 130+
(Donald McCain) *bhd and sn pushed along briefly: smooth hdwy after 2 out (usual 4 out): led gng wl appr omitted last: rdn and r.o wl* **8/1**

4P3- **2** *3* **Another Mattie (IRE)**[32] 2748 6-11-4 112 (t) PeterBuchanan 117
(N W Alexander) *hld up: mstke 2 out (usual 4 out): effrt bef omitted 2 out: wnt 2nd passing omitted last: nt rch wnr* **8/1**

325- **3** *1 3/4* **Trust Thomas**[26] 2868 5-10-2 103 GrahamWatters(7) 107
(Ann Hamilton) *hld up in midfield: stdy hdwy 2 out (usual 4 out): led bef omitted 2 out: hdd appr omitted last: one pce* **4/1**[1]

010/ **4** *4* **Dante's Frolic**[270] 5121 5-10-11 105 RyanMania 104
(Michael Smith) *hld up: hdwy and prom after last (usual 3 out): rdn and one pce passing omitted 2 out* **14/1**

F20- **5** *4 1/2* **Captain Brown**[36] 2668 5-11-4 117 TonyKelly(5) 112
(James Moffatt) *led tl rdn and hdd bef omitted 2 out: sn btn* **9/1**

/56- **6** *1 1/2* **Plus Jamais (FR)**[22] 2936 6-10-8 102 BrianHarding 95
(Jim Goldie) *hld up: rdn and outpcd 2 out (usual 4 out): rallied passing omitted 2 out: nvr rchd ldrs* **5/1**[2]

245- **7** *1 3/4* **Funky Munky**[15] 2879 8-10-5 102 (p) EwanWhillans(3) 94
(Alistair Whillans) *chsd ldrs tl rdn and wknd bef omitted 2 out* **10/1**

460- **8** 2¾ **Cool Baranca (GER)**^{8} 3212 7-11-1 **116**........................ CallumBewley$^{(7)}$ 105
(Dianne Sayer) *in tch: hdwy and cl up 2 out (usual 4 out): rdn and wknd passing omitted 2 out* **25/1**

/45- **9** 2½ **Sacre Toi (FR)**^{18} 3021 7-11-2 **110**..................................(b^{1}) BrianHughes 96
(James Ewart) *cl up tl rdn and wknd passing omitted 2 out* **6/1**^{3}

551- **10** 13 **Granaruid (IRE)**^{28} 2844 10-11-0 **113**..............(p) ConorShoemark$^{(5)}$ 86
(Alison Hamilton) *prom: drvn along 1/2-way: struggling bef last (usual 3 out)* **12/1**

346- **11** 11 **Rhymers Ha**^{32} 2751 6-11-3 **118**..................................(p) CraigNichol$^{(7)}$ 80
(Lucinda Russell) *prom tl rdn and wknd after 2 out (usual 4 out)* **10/1**

4m 25.3s (-1.70) **Going Correction** +0.075s/f (Yiel) **11** Ran SP% **119.6**
Speed ratings (Par 105): **106,104,103,102,100 99,98,97,96,90 85**
toteswingers 1&2 £46.30, 1&3 £13.70, 2&3 £7.10 CSF £71.88 CT £298.74 TOTE £8.60: £1.90, £2.20, £1.70; EX 84.80 Trifecta £1138.30 Part won..
Owner T G Leslie **Bred** Arnaud Chaille-Chaille **Trained** Cholmondeley, Cheshire

FOCUS
Both hurdles in the home straight were omitted due to the low sun. An open handicap, run at a fair gallop. The winner was well in on the best of last year's form and is rated back to that level.
T/Plt: £168.10. Pool: £55,094.73 - 239.25 winning units. T/Qpdt: £53.20. Pool: £3309.60 - 46.00 winning units. RY

3399 - 3401a (Foreign Racing) - See Raceform Interactive

3371 LEOPARDSTOWN (L-H)
Sunday, December 29

OFFICIAL GOING: Hurdle course - soft; chase course - yielding to soft

3402a RYANAIR HURDLE (GRADE 1) (8 hdls) 2m
2:00 (2:00) 4-Y-0+ **£48,780** (£15,447; £7,317; £2,439; £1,626)

RPR

1 **Hurricane Fly (IRE)**^{42} 2552 9-11-10 175.................................... RWalsh 170+
(W P Mullins, Ire) *hld up at mod early pce: in rr of quintet at 1/2-way: clsr in 4th bef 2 out and sn clsd on outer travelling best to ld narrowly at last: rdn clr run-in and kpt on wl* **11/10**^{1}

2 2½ **Jezki (IRE)**^{28} 2855 5-11-10 161.. APMcCoy 167+
(Mrs John Harrington, Ire) *hld up at mod early pce: nt fluent 2nd: mod 3rd 1/2-way: wnt 2nd 4 out: clsd on ldr into st: sn short of room between horses and swtchd in 4th bef last where nt fluent: rdn into 2nd fnl 100yds: nt trble wnr* **15/8**^{2}

3 3¼ **Our Conor (IRE)**^{70} 4767 4-11-7 161.................................. DannyMullins 161+
(D T Hughes, Ire) *chsd ldr in 2nd at mod early pce: t.k.h: mod 4th 1/2-way: clsd in 3rd fr 2 out: got on terms between last 2 and sn strly pressed: hdd narrowly last and sn no imp on wnr: dropped to 3rd fnl 100yds* **3/1**^{3}

4 3¾ **Captain Cee Bee (IRE)**^{29} 2835 12-11-10 149.................... MarkWalsh 160
(Edward P Harty, Ire) *hld up at mod early pce tl qcknd tempo to ld after 1st: sn clr: nt fluent 2nd: reduced advantage whn mstke 2 out: strly pressed into st and hdd bef last: no ex in 4th run-in* **66/1**

5 4 **Thousand Stars (FR)**^{203} 685 9-11-10 164.................. PaulTownend 156
(W P Mullins, Ire) *led at mod early pce tl hdd after 1st: mod 2nd 1/2-way: lost pl 4 out and dropped to 4th bef next: no imp on principals fr 2 out: kpt on same pce fr last* **25/1**

3m 59.8s (-7.70) **Going Correction** -0.05s/f (Good)
WFA 4 from 5yo+ 5lb **5** Ran SP% **112.7**
Speed ratings: **117,115,114,112,110**
CSF £3.75 TOTE £1.80: £1.02, £1.50; DF 3.30 Trifecta £3.80.
Owner George Creighton & Mrs Rose Boyd **Bred** Agricola Del Parco **Trained** Muine Beag, Co Carlow

FOCUS
A vintage renewal and a three-way tussle that we have been waiting for since last March. Tactics were always going to be paramount and, after expected pacesetter Thousand Stars took them down to the first at little more than a crawl, Mark Walsh swiftly moved to send Captain Cee Bee on and he found himself 15 lengths clear by the third hurdle. He was reeled in after the second last and that left the way clear for the principals to fight it out. The fourth, who was clear for much of the race, helps set the level, with the runner-up also close to his best. The ratce rates on a par with recent renewals.

3403a IFG EUROPEAN BREEDERS FUND MARES HURDLE (GRADE 3) (10 hdls) 2m 4f
2:35 (2:35) 4-Y-0+ **£18,495** (£5,406; £2,560; £853)

RPR

1 **Theatre Bird (IRE)**^{24} 2913 5-10-13 .... BryanCooper 137+
(Sean Thomas Doyle, Ire) *mde all: 2 l clr 1/2-way: extended advantage bef 4 out: pressed bef 2 out: styd on wl u.p fr bef last* **14/1**

2 4½ **Caoimhe's Delight (IRE)**^{21} 2986 7-10-13 113...................... JohnAllen 132
(Sean O'Brien, Ire) *trckd ldr: 2nd 1/2-way: slt mstke 4 out: pushed along in 3rd fr next and no imp on wnr after 2 out: kpt on same pce run-in into 2nd fnl 50yds* **33/1**

3 1½ **Jennies Jewel (IRE)**^{14} 3123 6-11-2 139.......................... IanMcCarthy 134
(Jarlath P Fahey, Ire) *chsd ldrs: mstke 1st and nt fluent next: 4th 1/2-way: pushed along fr 3 out and sn no imp on wnr: mod 5th between last 2: kpt on fr last into nvr threatening 3rd cl home* **3/1**^{3}

4 ½ **Upsie (FR)**^{42} 2542 5-11-5 147.. APMcCoy 136+
(W P Mullins, Ire) *chsd ldrs: 3rd 1/2-way: tk clsr order in 2nd bef 2 out: rdn between last 2 and no imp on wnr fr last: no ex u.p run-in and wknd qckly nr fin* **10/11**^{1}

5 11 **Urticaire (FR)**^{22} 2962 5-10-13 .... DavyRussell 119
(W P Mullins, Ire) *hld up in tch: 5th 1/2-way: hdwy on outer fr 3 out: slt mstke in 4th next: no imp on wnr bef last where mstke and dropped to 5th: one pce run-in* **11/4**^{2}

6 8 **Ellaway Rose (IRE)**^{62} 2134 5-10-13 99........................... AELynch 111
(J P Kenny, Ire) *w.w in rr: last 1/2-way: niggled along in mod 6th bef 2 out: kpt on one pce* **66/1**

P **Fantastic Gold**^{28} 2854 7-10-13 99...........................(tp) DannyMullins
(M O Cullinane, Ire) *hld up in tch: 6th 1/2-way: dropped to rr after 3 out: wknd and trailing whn p.u bef last* **66/1**

5m 12.9s (6.50) **Going Correction** -0.05s/f (Good) **7** Ran SP% **116.6**
Speed ratings: **85,83,82,82,78 74,**
CSF £236.17 TOTE £14.70: £2.90, £4.90; DF 313.80 Trifecta £2039.80.
Owner T Merrigan **Bred** Robert Merrigan **Trained** Ballindaggin, Co Wexford

FOCUS
This race provided the Mullins family with a magic moment last year when Zuzka gave Patrick his record-breaking win but there was no luck for the Closutton clan this time as the hot favourite faltered. The winner made all and coped well with the tacky underfoot conditions. The second and sixth help set the standard, with the progressive, front-running winner to a pb.

3404a TOPAZ NOVICE CHASE (GRADE 1) (17 fncs) 3m
3:05 (3:05) 4-Y-0+ **£39,634** (£11,585; £5,487; £1,829)

RPR

1 **Carlingford Lough (IRE)**^{28} 2853 7-11-10 150.................... APMcCoy 154+
(John E Kiely, Ire) *w.w in rr: nt fluent 8th: tk clsr order fr 10th: clsd to trck ldrs in 4th into st: chal in 2nd bef last where nt fluent: styd on wl u.p to ld ins fnl 100yds* **5/1**^{3}

2 1½ **Morning Assembly (IRE)**^{42} 2551 6-11-10 .... RWalsh 152
(P A Fahy, Ire) *prom early: settled bhd ldrs: 3rd 1/2-way: tk clsr order appr st and led gng wl bef last: rdn and strly pressed run-in: hdd ins fnl 100yds and no ex* **11/8**^{1}

3 7½ **Foxrock (IRE)**^{29} 2834 5-11-9 .... DannyMullins 144
(T M Walsh, Ire) *chsd ldrs: nt fluent 2nd: 4th 1/2-way: slt mstke 3 out: niggled along in 6th whn mstke next: kpt on u.p between last 2 into 3rd fr last: nt trble principals* **7/1**

4 7 **My Murphy (IRE)**^{15} 3104 7-11-10 130.............................. RobbiePower 138
(W J Burke, Ire) *led fr 1st tl hdd bef next: clsr in 2nd fr 9th: regained advantage after 10th and led and disp after: mstke 5 out: disp 2 out: sn pushed along and dropped to 5th at last: kpt on one pce* **25/1**

5 hd **Bright New Dawn (IRE)**^{21} 2993 6-11-10 .... DavyRussell 137
(D T Hughes, Ire) *trckd ldrs tl led bef 2nd: clr whn j.rt 8th: reduced advantage whn j.rt again next: hdd after 10th and led and disp after: rdn on terms into st and no ex in 3rd bef last: one pce run-in* **7/2**^{2}

6 2¼ **Mad Brian (IRE)**^{35} 2708 7-11-10 141.............................. KeithDonoghue 135
(Mrs Gillian Callaghan, Ire) *chsd ldrs: 5th 1/2-way: rdn bef st and sn no imp on ldrs: kpt on one pce* **9/1**

P **Sizing Rio (IRE)**^{28} 2853 5-11-9 142.. AELynch
(Henry De Bromhead, Ire) *hld up: 6th 1/2-way: wknd qckly after 3 out and p.u injured bef next* **10/1**

6m 17.5s (-13.50) **Going Correction** -0.275s/f (Good) **7** Ran SP% **116.4**
Speed ratings: **111,110,108,105,105 104,**
CSF £13.43 TOTE £4.70: £2.20, £1.10; DF 10.80 Trifecta £70.50.
Owner John P McManus **Bred** Kenilworth House Stud **Trained** Dungarvan, Co Waterford

FOCUS
There was no Ballycasey and no Don Cossack, which was disappointing, but this was still an up-to-scratch renewal. The winner is rated 150 and was at the top of his game. This was a true test and stamina came into play in the final half-mile. It is form that can be trusted. The second, fourth and fifth help set the standard.

3201 HAYDOCK (L-H)
Monday, December 30

OFFICIAL GOING: Soft (heavy in places on chase course; chs 5.6; hdl 5.5) changing to heavy after race 3 (1.20)
The first fence in the back straight was omitted on each circuit of each chase.
Wind: Strong, against Weather: Wet early

3413 APOLLOBET ONLINE GAMES AND CASINO CONDITIONAL JOCKEYS' H'CAP HURDLE 3m
12:20 (12:20) (Class 4) (0-115,112)
4-Y-0+ **£3,898** (£1,144; £572; £286)

Form RPR

/06- **1** **Moscow Presents (IRE)**^{29} 2844 5-11-9 **112**..................(p) AdamNicol$^{(3)}$ 118+
(Philip Kirby) *a.p: led after 4 out: asserted appr last: abt 4 l clr run-in: all out towards fin: hld on grimly* **16/1**

054- **2** ½ **American Life (FR)**^{10} 3191 6-10-8 **102**.........................(bt) MarkMarris$^{(8)}$ 105
(Anthony Middleton) *hld up in rr: mstke 4th: hdwy 4 out: chsd ldrs bef 3 out: no imp tl tk 2nd run-in: styd on to cl on wnr towards fin* **13/2**

/54- **3** 1¾ **Cloudingstar (IRE)**^{32} 2771 6-11-2 **105**..................(t) MauriceLinehan$^{(3)}$ 106
(Jonjo O'Neill) *trckd ldrs: upsides wnr fr bef 3 out: rdn abt 3 l down last: lost 2nd run-in: kpt on u.p but hld after* **4/1**^{2}

P25/ **4** 7 **Nodebateaboutit**^{295} 4687 8-11-7 **107**..........................(t) GavinSheehan 101
(Tom George) *hld up in tch: pushed along appr 8th: hdwy 4 out: outpcd bef 3 out: kpt on one pce and no imp after* **7/1**

324- **5** 1½ **Nicene Creed**^{29} 2842 8-11-1 **101**...................................(tp) HarryDerham 95
(Sophie Leech) *hld up: pushed along and outpcd appr 3 out: plugged on but no imp* **9/2**^{3}

413- **6** 2 **Amore Mio (GER)**^{29} 2843 8-10-13 **105**..........................(tp) CraigNichol$^{(6)}$ 96
(Lucinda Russell) *led: hdd 4th: regained ld 6th: pushed along and hdd after 4 out: wknd after 3 out* **11/4**^{1}

/10- **7** 12 **Upbeat Cobbler (FR)**^{37} 2663 5-11-4 **107**.......................... JakeGreenall$^{(3)}$ 89
(Henry Daly) *in tch: lost pl 8th: blnd 4 out: bhd after* **8/1**

062/ **8** 4 **Sphinx (FR)**^{408} 2481 15-11-6 **106**..(b) TonyKelly 81
(Edwin Tuer) *hld up: pushed along after 8th: outpcd after 4 out: n.d* **33/1**

/0P- **9** 45 **Outlaw Tom (IRE)**^{19} 3019 9-11-1 **107**.....................(v) GrantCockburn$^{(6)}$ 37
(Lucinda Russell) *prom: led 4th: hdd 6th: mstke 8th: rdn and wknd 4 out: t.o* **40/1**

6m 1.4s (1.40) **Going Correction** +0.025s/f (Yiel) **9** Ran SP% **113.1**
Speed ratings (Par 105): **98,97,97,94,94 93,89,88,73**
toteswingers 1&2 £20.30, 1&3 £12.90, 2&3 £6.90 CSF £113.38 CT £500.69 TOTE £19.30: £4.80, £2.30, £1.60; EX 161.20 Trifecta £1558.30 Pool: £2459.03 - 1.18 winning units..
Owner Boretech & Tony Sadler **Bred** J Duggan **Trained** Middleham, N Yorks

FOCUS
Course at standard configuration with shared bends. Bend out of back straight moved out 8yds and bend at winning post out 3yds, adding 34yds per circuit to advertised distances. They went a sound gallop in this 3m conditional jockeys' handicap and the first three pulled clear. Straightforward form.

3414 APOLLOBET IN-PLAY BETTING VETERANS' H'CAP CHASE 2m 5f
12:50 (12:50) (Class 2) (0-145,145)
10-Y-0+ **£13,814** (£4,116; £2,083; £1,067; £559)

Form RPR

/00- **1** **Kilcrea Asla (IRE)**^{30} 2812 12-9-10 **120**.......................... KillianMoore$^{(5)}$ 125
(Graeme McPherson) *hld up: rdn in 4th pl appr 12th: wnt 3rd for press bef 4 out: clsd to take 2nd fnl 110yds: styd on gamely to ld towards fin* **16/1**

The Form Book Jumps, Raceform Ltd, Compton, RG20 6NL.

/54- **2** *1 ½* **Gansey (IRE)**[23] 2939 11-10-11 **130** .... RyanMania 136+
(Sue Smith) *trckd ldrs: wnt 2nd after 8th: mstke 10th: led 11th: hdd briefly appr 4 out: edgd rt bef next: abt 2 l up last: all out run-in: hdd and no ex towards fin* **9/4**[1]

/23- **3** *1 ½* **Charingworth (IRE)**[26] 2889 10-10-11 **130** .... JasonMaguire 134
(Kim Bailey) *a.p: wnt 2nd appr 12th: sn pushed along: led briefly bef 4 out: rdn bef 2 out: abt 2 l down whn nt fluent last: lost 2nd fnl 110yds: kpt on same pce u.p* **7/1**[2]

3/2- **4** *33* **Baby Run (FR)**[23] 2937 13-11-8 **141** .... SamTwiston-Davies 123
(Nigel Twiston-Davies) *led: rdn appr 9th: hdd 11th: wknd 4 out: eased whn wl btn after 3 out* **9/4**[1]

260- **5** *47* **Gauvain (GER)**[16] 3082 11-11-5 **145** .... (t) MrCSmith(7) 67
(Philip Hobbs) *in rr: mstke 1st: sn detached and nvr travelling wl: t.o bef 9th: nvr on terms* **8/1**[3]

PP4- **P** **The Knoxs (IRE)**[4] 3273 10-10-12 **134** .... JonathanEngland(3)
(Sue Smith) *j.lft in rr: slithered on landing 4th: nt rcvr and sn p.u* **9/1**

U65/ **P** **Lucky Sunny (IRE)**[354] 3592 10-10-0 **119** oh7 .... AidanColeman
(Venetia Williams) *t.k.h: prom: wknd 11th: bhd whn p.u bef 4 out* **12/1**

5m 32.8s (7.30) **Going Correction** +0.025s/f (Yiel) 7 Ran SP% **108.7**
Speed ratings: **87,86,85,73,55 ,**
toteswingers 1&2 £10.00, 1&3 £9.00, 2&3 £4.50 CSF £48.97 TOTE £15.70: £6.90, £1.60; EX 66.40 Trifecta £385.40 Pool: £2507.62 - 4.87 winning units..
Owner Mrs Laura Day **Bred** J Day **Trained** Upper Oddington, Gloucs

FOCUS
The first fence in the back straight was omitted. In very testing conditions this veterans' chase became a war of attrition. The winner is rated back to the level of his Chepstow win.

3415 EBF STALLIONS APOLLOBET FREE DOWNLOAD APP "NATIONAL HUNT" NOVICES' HURDLE (QUALIFIER) 2m
1:20 (1:21) (Class 4) 4-6-Y-O **£3,898** (£1,144; £572; £286)

Form RPR

/32- **1** **Goohar (IRE)**[17] 3061 4-10-9 118 .... JakeGreenall(3) 117+
(Henry Daly) *trckd ldrs: upsides bef 3 out: led jst bef 2 out: hdd run-in: plld off rail fnl 200yds: rallied to regain ld narrowly fnl 110yds: all out* **2/1**[2]

12- **2** *hd* **Desoto County**[17] 3063 4-10-12 0 .... JasonMaguire 116+
(Donald McCain) *hld up: nt travel smoothly after 3rd but in tch: trckd ldrs appr 3 out: 3rd bef 2 out: wnt 2nd last: styd on to ld run-in: sn edgd lft: hdd narrowly fnl 110yds: rallied for press fnl strides* **8/11**[1]

60- **3** *3 ½* **Highpower (IRE)**[17] 3061 4-10-12 0 .... APMcCoy 111
(Jonjo O'Neill) *disp ld: def advantage after 4 out: hdd jst bef 2 out: stl ch run-in: no ex fnl 75yds* **13/2**[3]

000- **4** *29* **Echo Foxtrot**[8] 3226 4-10-5 0 .... GeraldQuinn(7) 82
(Claire Dyson) *trckd ldrs: pushed along appr 3 out: one pce 2 out: wl btn whn hit last* **66/1**

5/0- **5** *26* **Wheelavim**[35] 2720 5-10-12 0 .... TommyPhelan 56
(Claire Dyson) *hld up: detcached after 4th: nt fluent whn toiling 4 out: nvr on terms* **100/1**

550- **6** *21* **Clues And Arrows (IRE)**[13] 3144 5-10-12 0 .... RichieMcLernon 35
(Jonjo O'Neill) *disp ld tl rdn after 4 out: sn hmpd: wknd bef 3 out: t.o* **20/1**

0/0- **7** *28* **Lord Westhead (IRE)**[22] 2981 4-10-12 0 .... AdrianLane
(Danielle McCormick) *bhd: detached after 4th: t.o* **100/1**

0/ **F** **Dibdabs (IRE)**[225] 402 5-10-5 0 .... (t) StephenMulqueen(7)
(Maurice Barnes) *t.k.h: in tch: hit 3rd: fell 4th* **7/1**

4m 0.1s (-4.10) **Going Correction** +0.025s/f (Yiel) 8 Ran SP% **125.3**
Speed ratings: **111,110,109,94,81 71,57,**
toteswingers 1&2 £1.10, 1&3 £2.60, 2&3 £2.20 CSF £4.42 TOTE £3.40: £1.40, £1.10, £1.30; EX 4.80 Trifecta £14.80 Pool: £3419.72 - 172.91 winning units..
Owner Rod Brereton & Kate Maxwell **Bred** Darley **Trained** Stanton Lacy, Shropshire

FOCUS
Any price bar four in this interesting novice hurdle. The winner is rated in line with his good Bangor run.

3416 THE LAST FLING CHASE (HANDICAP SPONSORED BY CLASSIC LODGES LTD) 3m 4f
1:55 (1:55) (Class 2) (0-145,143) 4-Y-O+ **£14,295** (£4,197; £2,098; £1,049)

Form RPR

/50- **1** **Across The Bay (IRE)**[23] 2937 9-11-12 **143** .... (bt) JasonMaguire 152
(Donald McCain) *hld up: hdwy 14th: rdn whn chsng ldrs appr last (usual 2 out): styd on run ins fnl 200yds: led cl home* **8/1**

/46- **2** *½* **Wellforth (IRE)**[30] 2807 9-10-10 **127** .... (p) DavidEngland 135
(Barry Brennan) *a cl up: led 16th: mstke and hdd 2 out (usual 4 out): over 2 l down last: rallied run-in: chal cl home: jst hld* **40/1**

FP1- **3** *¾* **Pete The Feat (IRE)**[20] 3006 9-11-8 **139** .... NoelFehily 146
(Charlie Longsdon) *in tch: led appr 10th: hdd 16th: regained ld 2 out (usual 4 out): rdn bef last where over 2 l up (usual 2 out): hdd cl home* **17/2**

U02- **4** *3 ¾* **Sir Du Bearn (FR)**[14] 3131 7-10-13 **130** .... DonalDevereux 134
(Peter Bowen) *hld up: hdwy 14th: pushed along after 16th: outpcd bef 2 out (usual 4 out): rallied but no imp whn mstke last (usual 2 out): styd on: nt rch ldrs* **10/1**

136- **5** *nk* **Hunters Lodge (IRE)**[23] 2953 7-10-10 **127** .... (p) SamTwiston-Davies 130
(Nigel Twiston-Davies) *in rr: pushed along appr 13th: hdwy and hung lft appr last (usual 2 out): styd on run-in: nt rch ldrs* **17/2**

512- **6** *27* **Herdsman (IRE)**[29] 2841 8-10-12 **129** .... RyanMania 105
(Sue Smith) *prom: mstke 12th: pushed along whn mstke 14th: wknd bef 2 out (usual 4 out)* **13/2**[2]

252- **7** *½* **Bob Ford (IRE)**[30] 2803 6-10-11 **128** .... APMcCoy 103
(Rebecca Curtis) *t.k.h: led: hdd appr 10th: remained handy: rdn after 16th: wknd after 2 out (usual 4 out)* **3/1**[1]

2/5- **8** *38* **Ballyoliver**[51] 2373 9-10-12 **129** .... AidanColeman 66
(Venetia Williams) *midfield: lost pl 14th: rallied 2 out but no real imp on ldrs (usual 4 out): wknd bef last (usual 2 out)* **7/1**[3]

P/0- **P** **Monsieur Cadou (FR)**[57] 2246 8-10-5 **122** .... PaddyBrennan
(Tom George) *hld up: blnd 12th and wnt wrong: sn p.u: fatally injured* **7/1**[3]

F13/ **P** **Beamazed**[413] 2379 9-10-9 **126** .... BrianHughes
(Malcolm Jefferson) *prom tl wnt wrong and p.u bef 10th: fatally injured* **16/1**

7m 30.5s (14.50) **Going Correction** +0.025s/f (Yiel) 10 Ran SP% **112.9**
Speed ratings (Par 109): **80,79,79,78,78 70,70,59, ,**
toteswingers 1&2 £49.60, 1&3 £9.10, 2&3 £51.60 CSF £217.73 CT £2747.30 TOTE £9.30: £2.60, £7.20, £2.10; EX 415.10 Trifecta £2594.90 Part won..
Owner Scotch Piper Syndicate **Bred** Noel McLoughlin **Trained** Cholmondeley, Cheshire

FOCUS
The going was changed to heavy all round ahead of this competitive 3m 4f handicap chase. Because of stricken horses only the normal four out and two out were jumped on the final circuit. The winner had slipped to a very good mark and should still be competitive when reassessed.

3417 APOLLOBET BEST ODDS GUARANTEED "FIXED BRUSH" NOVICES' HURDLE 2m 4f
2:30 (2:30) (Class 4) 4-7-Y-O **£3,898** (£1,144; £572; £286)

Form RPR

12- **1** **Urban Hymn (FR)**[38] 2659 5-10-12 0 .... BrianHughes 141+
(Malcolm Jefferson) *mde all: effrtlessly drew clr 3 out: easily* **8/11**[1]

321- **2** *20* **Algernon Pazham (IRE)**[19] 3023 4-10-12 129 .... SamTwiston-Davies 121
(Nigel Twiston-Davies) *hld up: hdwy to trck ldrs 6th: rdn and outpcd bef 3 out: tk poor 2nd last: no ch w wnr* **4/1**[3]

3- **3** *60* **El Indio (IRE)**[50] 2386 6-10-5 0 .... GeraldQuinn(7) 61
(Claire Dyson) *hld up: rdn appr 4 out: sn lost tch: lft poor 3rd last* **33/1**

4 *46* **Saint Brieuc (FR)**[457] 4-10-7 0 .... JoeColliver(5) 15
(Simon West) *t.k.h: chsd wnr: mstke 4th and rdr lost iron briefly: lost 2nd bef next: bhd whn mstke 6th: t.o: lft poor 4th last* **50/1**

0/1- **F** **Howaboutnow (IRE)**[39] 2621 6-11-5 0 .... JasonMaguire 124
(Donald McCain) *prom: wnt 2nd bef 5th: rdn and outpcd by wnr bef 3 out: sn no ch: wl btn and losing 2nd whn fell last* **10/3**[2]

4m 50.9s (-2.10) **Going Correction** +0.025s/f (Yiel)
WFA 4 from 5yo+ 6lb 5 Ran SP% **105.9**
Speed ratings: **105,97,73,54,**
CSF £3.74 TOTE £1.70: £1.40, £1.50; EX 4.10 Trifecta £14.00 Pool: £3756.25 - 200.25 winning units..
Owner Mr & Mrs G Calder **Bred** Jean-Jacques Augier **Trained** Norton, N Yorks

FOCUS
A one-sided fixed brush novice hurdle. The impressive winner took a bug step forward and looks a tremendous prospect.

3418 NICK CARTER 30TH BIRTHDAY NOVICES' LIMITED H'CAP CHASE 2m 4f
3:05 (3:05) (Class 3) (0-125,125) 4-Y-O+ **£6,498** (£1,908; £954; £477)

Form RPR

/13- **1** **Bobcatbilly (IRE)**[12] 3155 7-10-8 **114** .... APMcCoy 123+
(Ian Williams) *chsd ldrs: wnt 2nd 4 out: chal fr 2 out: rdn to ld after last: sn edgd lft: kpt on wl towards fin* **6/4**[1]

/33- **2** *2 ¾* **Supreme Asset (IRE)**[18] 3037 5-11-5 **125** .... JasonMaguire 129
(Donald McCain) *hld up: hdwy 4 out: led 2 out: hdd after last: sn rdn: kpt on u.p but hld towards fin* **4/1**[2]

/5P- **3** *2* **No Duffer**[40] 2599 6-10-5 **111** oh2 .... AndrewTinkler 115+
(Henry Daly) *chsd ldrs: wnt 2nd 7th: lost 2nd 4 out: rdn appr 2 out whn stl chsng ldrs: styd on same pce run-in* **6/1**

200- **4** *¾* **Presence Felt (IRE)**[16] 3085 5-10-9 **115** .... (b[1]) RichieMcLernon 118
(Jonjo O'Neill) *led: abt 3 l clr whn blnd 3 out: sn rdn: hdd 2 out: u.p and nt qckn bef last: kpt on u.p run-in* **14/1**

5/0- **5** *18* **Saints And Sinners (IRE)**[19] 3028 5-10-11 **120** .... JakeGreenall(3) 111
(Michael Easterby) *chsd ldr to 7th: wknd bef 4 out* **7/1**

3F4- **6** *5* **Sands Cove (IRE)**[18] 3045 6-11-3 **123** .... (t) NoelFehily 105
(Charlie Mann) *in rr: outpcd after 4 out: nvr a threat* **5/1**[3]

5m 6.7s (-3.30) **Going Correction** +0.025s/f (Yiel) 6 Ran SP% **110.1**
Speed ratings (Par 107): **107,105,105,104,97 95**
toteswingers 1&2 £1.90, 1&3 £2.80, 2&3 £4.60 CSF £7.83 TOTE £2.10: £1.40, £1.60; EX 4.30 Trifecta £24.80 Pool: £3300.88 - 99.70 winning units..
Owner P J Vogt **Bred** Con Troy **Trained** Portway, Worcs

FOCUS
Quite an interesting novice handicap, and there were four almost in a line at the penultimate fence. There's probably more to come from the winner.

3419 APOLLOBET FREE £50 BETS "FIXED BRUSH" H'CAP HURDLE (JOCKEY CLUB G'ROOTS JUMPS SERIES QUALIFIER 2m 4f
3:35 (3:35) (Class 4) (0-120,120) 4-Y-O+ **£3,898** (£1,144; £572; £286)

Form RPR

01/- **1** **No No Bingo (IRE)**[251] 5481 7-11-0 **108** .... (p) NoelFehily 113
(Charlie Longsdon) *prom: lost pl 5th: impr to trck ldrs 3 out: rdn appr last: styd on to ld fnl 150yds: edgd lft: kpt on gamely* **5/1**[3]

P55- **2** *½* **The Jugopolist (IRE)**[25] 2894 6-10-6 **110** .... (v[1]) PaulO'Brien(10) 113
(Rebecca Curtis) *handy: chal 3 out: led 2 out: rdn appr last: hdd fnl 150yds: styd on u.p* **7/1**

/P5- **3** *nk* **Basford Bob (IRE)**[23] 2956 8-10-11 **105** .... SeanQuinlan 109
(Jennie Candlish) *hld up: hdwy appr 3 out: rdn bef last: styd on towards fin* **10/1**

/52- **4** *½* **Teochew (IRE)**[23] 2948 5-11-6 **117** .... GavinSheehan(3) 120
(Warren Greatrex) *led: hdd 5th: remained handy: pushed along 3 out: rdn and nt qckn 2 out: styd on fnl 110yds* **11/4**[1]

100/ **5** *3 ½* **Sole Survivor (FR)**[733] 3394 6-10-3 **100** .... (t) JakeGreenall(3) 100
(Paul Webber) *prom: led 5th: hdd 2 out: rdn and stl ev ch last: no ex fnl 110yds* **25/1**

352- **6** *3 ¼* **Dundee**[23] 2936 5-11-3 **111** .... RobertThornton 110
(Alan King) *hld up: hdwy 6th: effrt to chse ldrs whn stmbld 2 out: one pce run-in* **3/1**[2]

000- **7** *3 ½* **Hold Court (IRE)**[23] 2944 6-11-12 **120** .... PaulMoloney 112
(Evan Williams) *hld up: hdwy on outer after 4 out: sn prom: wknd 2 out* **5/1**[3]

5m 4.0s (11.00) **Going Correction** +0.025s/f (Yiel) 7 Ran SP% **110.4**
Speed ratings (Par 105): **79,78,78,78,77 75,74**
toteswingers 1&2 £3.50, 1&3 £7.90, 2&3 £7.60 CSF £35.71 TOTE £5.20: £2.60, £3.10; EX 22.10 Trifecta £695.40 Pool: £2422.84 - 2.61 winning units..
Owner R Jenner & J Green **Bred** D Hickey **Trained** Over Norton, Oxon

FOCUS
They went a very steady gallop and as a result five of the seven runners were still in with a chance at the last. Sound recent form was very thin on the ground. The winner was well in on his chase form.

T/Plt: £68.50. Pool: £92,584.84 - 985.31 winning units. T/Qpdt: £5.80. Pool: £7525.83 - 956.20 winning units. DO

[3043]TAUNTON (R-H)

Monday, December 30

OFFICIAL GOING: Heavy (4.4)

Wind: mild breeze across Weather: sunny periods

3420 TOTEJACKPOT CONDITIONAL JOCKEYS' H'CAP HURDLE (10 hdls) 2m 3f 110y

12:40 (12:40) (Class 4) (0-110,107) 4-Y-0+ **£4,106** (£1,197; £598)

Form				RPR
603-	1		**The Happy Warrior**[24] 2920 5-9-9 **81** oh3 .... GaryDerwin(5) (Bob Buckler) *a.p: led 6th: rdn whn 6 l clr 2 out: narrowly hdd run-in: rallied gamely to regain ld fnl stride* **10/1**[3]	95
323-	2	*nse*	**Superciliary**[20] 3007 4-10-9 **98** .... LouisMuspratt(8) (Chris Gordon) *hld up towards rr: gd prog after 3 out to chse wnr next: sn rdn: tk slt advantage run-in: hdd fnl stride* **20/1**	112
0/0-	3	*28*	**Waldorf Salad**[58] 2210 5-11-3 **101** .... HarryChalloner(3) (Venetia Williams) *trckd ldrs: rdn after 3 out: one pce fr next: wnt modest 3rd towards fin* **12/1**	87
030/	4	*nk*	**Extremely So**[270] 5148 7-11-6 **101** .... GilesHawkins (Chris Down) *mid-div on outer: rdn appr 3 out: wnt 3rd but no ch w front pair 2 out: lost modest 3rd towards fin* **16/1**	88
200-	5	*3/4*	**Kilrye (IRE)**[4] 3288 6-9-13 **86** ....(bt[1]) KieronEdgar(6) (David Pipe) *hld up towards rr: rdn after 3 out: no imp tl styd on appr last: wnt 5th run-in* **12/1**	71
/24-	6	*3 3/4*	**Yes Daddy (IRE)**[179] 879 5-11-6 **104** .... MichaelByrne(3) (Tim Vaughan) *trckd ldrs: mstke 5th: rdn after 3 out: wkng in 4th whn mstke last* **11/1**	85
/02-	7	*1/2*	**Lights Of Broadway (IRE)**[25] 2896 7 11 5 **103** .... RobertWilliams(3) (Bernard Llewellyn) *mid-div: rdn after 3 out: nvr threatened ldrs* **5/1**[1]	84
463-	8	*1/2*	**Amuse Me**[50] 2397 7-10-13 **104** .... PatrickCowley(10) (Jonjo O'Neill) *hld up towards rr: pushed along bef 4th: rdn after 7th: nvr any imp* **8/1**[2]	84
F00-	9	*1/2*	**Kartanian (IRE)**[25] 2908 7-11-7 **105** ....(b[1]) JamesBest(3) (Philip Hobbs) *mid-div: trckd ldrs 3rd: rdn to chse wnr after 3 out tl wknd bef next* **8/1**[2]	85
006-	10	*3 3/4*	**Veratan (FR)**[12] 3157 6-10-4 **88** .... CallumWhillans(3) (Venetia Williams) *trckd ldrs early: pushed along fr 3rd: towards rr 5th: nvr any danger after* **5/1**[1]	64
050-	11	*12*	**Nether Stream (IRE)**[40] 2598 9-11-4 **104** .... JakeHodson(5) (David Dennis) *mid-div tl wknd 3 out* **50/1**	68
401/	12	*2 3/4*	**Cridda Boy**[359] 3523 7-11-12 **107** ....(t) AdamWedge (Richard Woollacott) *mid-div: trckd ldrs 4th: rdn after 3 out: sn wknd* **20/1**	68
/50-	13	*72*	**Cantabilly (IRE)**[18] 3047 10-10-9 **90** ....(v[1]) MattGriffiths (Ron Hodges) *led tl 6th: sn rdn: wknd after next: t.o* **40/1**
650-	P		**Mount Odell**[36] 2696 5-11-4 **102** .... JoshuaMoore(3) (Gary Moore) *hld up towards rr: rdn bef 3 out: sn wknd: t.o whn p.u bef next* **11/1**

4m 59.7s (13.70) **Going Correction** +0.80s/f (Soft)

WFA 4 from 5yo+ 5lb 14 Ran SP% **116.5**

Speed ratings (Par 105): **104,103,92,92,92 90,90,90,90,88 83,82,54,**

toteswingers 1&2 £39.40, 1&3 £39.40, 2&3 £39.40 CSF £191.73 CT £2411.53 TOTE £14.80: £5.10, £5.00, £7.00; EX 267.20 TRIFECTA Not won..

Owner Nick Elliott **Bred** H G Llewellyn **Trained** Henley, Somerset

FOCUS

Both bends split. A competitive, if only modest opener and not a race for the faint hearted following 19mm of overnight rainfall, which had prompted course officials to change the official going description from soft, heavy in places to heavy all round. The deteriorating conditions meant they went steadier than is often the case in this type of contest and it developed into something of a sprint with two of them pulling well clear of the remainder. The first two are on the upgrade.

3421 TOTEPOOL MOBILE NOVICES' H'CAP CHASE (6 fncs 11 omitted) 2m 7f 110y

1:10 (1:12) (Class 4) (0-110,110) 4-Y-0+ **£4,106** (£1,197; £598)

Form				RPR
P11-	1		**Milosam (IRE)**[32] 2765 6-10-1 **85** ....(b) TomO'Brien (Philip Hobbs) *mde all: clr ldr bypassing 4 out: idling and hanging lft sn after bypassing omitted last: drvn out* **6/4**[1]	97+
4FP-	2	*1 1/4*	**Possibly Flora**[20] 3015 8-10-7 **91** ....(t) RhysFlint (Richard Woollacott) *mid-div: hdwy in bk st fnl time: rdn to chse wnr after bypassing omitted 4 out: styd on bypassing last: hld towards fin* **33/1**	96
323/	3	*46*	**Now Listen To Me**[712] 3794 10-10-13 **104** ....(t) KevinJones(7) (Charles Whittaker) *disp ld tl rdn bypassing omitted 13th: sn wknd into modest 3rd: t.o* **11/1**	63
/P6-	P		**Shades Of Autumn (IRE)**[32] 2766 8-10-0 **84** ....(v) ConorO'Farrell (Linda Blackford) *trckd ldrs tl rdn ent bk st fnl time: sn wknd: t.o whn p.u bypassing omitted 4 out* **14/1**
/20-	P		**Moorland Sunset**[47] 2462 6-11-12 **110** .... IanPopham (Caroline Keevil) *trckd ldrs tl rdn bypassing omitted 12th: sn wknd: t.o whn p.u after bypassing omitted 4 out* **8/1**[3]
/P0-	P		**Decimus (IRE)**[45] 2490 6-11-12 **110** .... NickScholfield (Jeremy Scott) *a bhd: reminders after 4th: wknd in bk st fnl time: t.o whn p.u bef 2 out (usual 3 out)* **3/1**[2]
05P-	P		**Phone Home (IRE)**[20] 3004 6-11-12 **110** .... DarylJacob (Nick Mitchell) *hld up: reminders after 4th: disp 3rd on long run bef ent bk st fnl time: drvn bypassing omitted 13th: sn wknd: t.o whn awkward 2 out: p.u bef last* **8/1**[3]
32P-	P		**Pod**[30] 2825 5-10-0 **87** oh11 ow3 .... JamesBest(3) (Caroline Keevil) *a bhd: struggling after 4th: sn t.o and p.u* **9/1**

6m 9.5s (-6.50) **Going Correction** -0.15s/f (Good) 8 Ran SP% **115.2**

Speed ratings (Par 105): **104,103,88, , ,**

toteswingers 1&2 £16.80, 1&3 £2.40, 2&3 £46.90 CSF £40.50 CT £416.94 TOTE £2.50: £1.10, £8.20, £2.90; EX 51.10 Trifecta £449.40 Pool: £2015.01 - 3.36 winning units..

Owner Rob Croker **Bred** James Canty **Trained** Withycombe, Somerset

FOCUS

The combination of low sunlight and unsafe ground meant only six fences were jumped in this near 3m chase, so as a result the form amounts to very little. However, the long run between the fences ensured they went quick enough in the testing conditions and that set up a thrilling finish. The idling winner was value for further.

3422 TOTEQUADPOT FOUR PLACES IN FOUR RACES NOVICES' HURDLE (10 hdls) 2m 3f 110y

1:45 (1:45) (Class 4) 4-Y-0+ **£4,106** (£1,197; £598)

Form				RPR
122-	1		**Horizontal Speed (IRE)**[30] 2808 5-11-4 128 .... RichardJohnson (Philip Hobbs) *led 2nd: mde rest: stmbld bdly 5th: pushed along and in command whn nt fluent last: styd on wl* **11/10**[1]	129+
1/3-	2	*4 1/2*	**Foggy's Wall (IRE)**[24] 2924 5-10-12 0 .... DarylJacob (Paul Nicholls) *mid-div: hdwy after 5th: rdn after 3 out: chsd wnr next: styd on but a being hld* **11/4**[2]	116+
/63-	3	*6*	**Dream Deal**[39] 2614 5-10-12 0 .... NickScholfield (Jeremy Scott) *led tl 2nd: trckd wnr tl 7th: rdn after 3 out: styd on same pce fr next: regained 3rd towards fin* **4/1**[3]	109
00/-	4	*1 1/4*	**Daveron (IRE)**[630] 5343 5-10-9 0 .... MattGriffiths(3) (Jeremy Scott) *trckd ldrs: chal briefly 3 out: sn rdn: styd on same pce fr next: lost 3rd towards fin* **100/1**	108
50-	5	*16*	**Powerful Action (IRE)**[22] 2978 5-10-9 0 .... JamesBest(3) (Philip Hobbs) *trckd ldrs: rdn after 3 out: wknd bef next* **25/1**	92
0-	6	*1 1/4*	**Pure Poteen (IRE)**[33] 2745 5-10-12 0 ....(t) DougieCostello (Neil Mulholland) *trckd ldrs: pushed along after 6th: wknd after 3 out* **50/1**	90
6/0-	7	*2*	**Billy My Boy**[237] 160 4-10-9 0 .... GilesHawkins(3) (Chris Down) *mid-div: hdwy appr 3 out: sn rdn: wknd bef 2 out* **50/1**	88
016-	8	*23*	**Larks Rising**[22] 2981 5-10-12 0 .... TomO'Brien (Caroline Keevil) *mid-div: rdn after 3 out: sn wknd: t.o* **33/1**	65
00-	9	*19*	**More Tricks**[11] 3168 5-9-12 0 .... MrFTett(7) (James Frost) *a bhd: t.o* **200/1**	39
432-	10	*22*	**Another Brandy (IRE)**[42] 2570 5-10-9 0 .... MichaelByrne(3) (Neil Mulholland) *mid-div tl wknd 7th: t.o* **10/1**	24
0-	11	*8*	**Gladstone (IRE)**[16] 3092 5-10-12 0 .... AndrewThornton (Polly Gundry) *a towards rr: wknd 7th: t.o* **100/1**	16
P		**Saint Helena (IRE)**[78] 5-10-5 0 .... MattieBatchelor (Jim Best) *hld up towards rr: rdn after 6th: sn wknd: t.o whn p.u bef 2 out* **33/1**
P		**Alfie Joe**[239] 4-10-7 0 .... CharlieWallis(5) (Ron Hodges) *t.k.h: trckd ldrs tl dropped to rr 4th: rdn after next: sn lost tch: p.u bef 7th* **100/1**
40-	P		**Kilfinichen Bay (IRE)**[44] 2513 5-10-12 0 .... WillKennedy (Violet M Jordan) *mid-div tl wknd after 7th: t.o whn p.u bef 2 out* **66/1**

5m 3.4s (17.40) **Going Correction** +0.80s/f (Soft)

WFA 4 from 5yo 5lb 14 Ran SP% **122.0**

Speed ratings (Par 105): **97,95,92,92,85 85,84,75,67,59 55, , ,**

toteswingers 1&2 £1.20, 1&3 £1.40, 2&3 £2.70 CSF £4.15 TOTE £1.70: £1.10, £1.40, £1.90; EX 5.20 Trifecta £13.50 Pool: £3761.39 - 208.44 winning units..

Owner Favourites Racing **Bred** Dick White **Trained** Withycombe, Somerset

FOCUS

An informative novices' hurdle and a likeable performance from the winner.

3423 SEASON'S GREETINGS FROM TOTEPOOL MARES' NOVICES' HURDLE (LISTED RACE) (9 hdls) 2m 1f

2:20 (2:20) (Class 1) 3-Y-0+ **£11,546** (£4,334; £2,170; £1,082; £542)

Form				RPR
111-	1		**Down Ace (IRE)**[34] 2725 6-11-2 122 .... DougieCostello (Fergal O'Brien) *trckd ldrs: chal 2 out: disp ld bef last: wandered u.p run-in: kpt on wl to edge ahd nring fin* **7/2**[2]	127+
F31-	2	*nk*	**Blue Buttons (IRE)**[11] 3168 5-11-2 125 ....(t) RyanMahon (Harry Fry) *trckd ldrs: rdn to chal gng to 2 out: disp ld bef last: kpt on gamely u.p: narrowly hdd nring fin* **7/2**[2]	126
312-	3	*11*	**As I Am (IRE)**[9] 3203 5-11-7 139 .... ConorShoemark (Don Cantillon) *j.lft thrght: led: rdn appr 2 out: hdd bef last where hmpd: no ex flat* **1/1**[1]	125+
04-	4	*5*	**Dolores Delightful (FR)**[211] 615 3-10-3 0 .... RichardJohnson (Nick Williams) *hld up: nt fluent 4th: hdwy 5th: chal sn after 3 out tl rdn bef next: styng on at same pce in hld 4th whn nt fluent last* **10/1**[3]	99
0/0-	5	*2 3/4*	**Miner Distraction**[11] 3168 5-11-2 0 .... NickScholfield (Jeremy Scott) *hld up: tk clsr order 5th: rdn after 3 out: outpcd bef next* **66/1**	107
010-	6	*17*	**Neston Grace**[24] 2932 5-11-2 115 .... JamesDavies (Simon Hodgson) *trckd ldrs: rdn after 6th: wknd after 3 out: t.o* **33/1**	90
25-	7	*19*	**Roja Dove (IRE)**[20] 3005 4-11-5 124 .... TrevorWhelan (Neil King) *trckd ldrs: rdn after 5th: wknd after 3 out: t.o* **25/1**	74

4m 17.5s (9.50) **Going Correction** +0.80s/f (Soft)

WFA 3 from 4yo 13lb 4 from 5yo+ 5lb 7 Ran SP% **111.8**

Speed ratings (Par 111): **109,108,103,101,100 92,83**

toteswingers 1&2 £1.10, 1&3 £1.30, 2&3 £1.90 CSF £15.44 TOTE £4.10: £2.10, £2.10; EX 15.40 Trifecta £22.90 Pool: £4498.94 - 146.86 winning units..

Owner Paul Sullivan **Bred** Mrs C J Berry **Trained** Coln St. Dennis, Gloucs

FOCUS

A good turn out for this mares' Listed race and it produced a stirring finish. Big steps up from the first two, but the form looks believable.

3424 STEVE LOGAN MEMORIAL (COUNTY CONTRACTORS) H'CAP CHASE (14 fncs 3 omitted) 2m 7f 110y

2:55 (2:55) (Class 3) (0-130,130) 4-Y-0+ **£6,498** (£1,908; £954; £477)

Form				RPR
30U-	1		**Theatrical Star**[31] 2800 7-11-12 **130** .... JoeTizzard (Colin Tizzard) *disp ld: clr ldr after 9th: pushed along whn jnd appr 2 out: clr again appr last: styd on wl: pushed out* **7/2**[2]	140+
4/0-	2	*7*	**Mic's Delight (IRE)**[54] 2288 9-11-2 **120** .... JackDoyle (Victor Dartnall) *trckd ldrs: pckd 10th: chal gng wl after 3 out (usual 4 out): ev ch whn pckd 2 out: sn rdn and hld: styd on same pce* **9/1**[3]	124+
/04-	3	*9*	**Talkonthestreet (IRE)**[26] 2889 6-11-0 **118** ....(p) RichardJohnson (Philip Hobbs) *trckd ldrs: chalng whn wnt lft and awkward 3 out (usual 4 out): sn rdn: wknd next* **2/1**[1]	111
600-	4	*18*	**Firebird Flyer (IRE)**[19] 3028 6-11-4 **122** .... AdamWedge (Evan Williams) *hld up bhd ldrs: wnt 4th gng to 3 out (usual 4 out): sn rdn: wknd bef next: t.o* **10/1**	105
P/4-	5	*56*	**No Secrets (IRE)**[30] 2812 9-11-11 **129** ....(t) ConorO'Farrell (David Pipe) *disp ld tl after 9th: pushed along after next: rdn after 11th: wknd after 3 out (usual 4 out) t.o whn virtually p.u run-in* **2/1**[1]	48

The Form Book Jumps, Raceform Ltd, Compton, RG20 6NL.

3/3- P Speedy Bruere (FR)[19] 3023 7-10-12 123 JakeHodson(7)
(David Bridgwater) *trckd ldrs: rdn after 9th: wknd 3 out (usual 4 out) t.o whn p.u bef last* **16/1**

6m 12.3s (-3.70) **Going Correction** -0.15s/f (Good) **6** Ran SP% **113.9**
Speed ratings (Par 107): **100,97,94,88,70**
toteswingers 1&2 £6.40, 1&3 £1.20, 2&3 £5.10 CSF £31.39 TOTE £5.30: £2.90, £4.20; EX 41.90 Trifecta £149.00 Pool: £3960.43 - 19.92 winning units..
Owner Brocade Racing **Bred** R D Chugg And C M A Aston **Trained** Milborne Port, Dorset

FOCUS
Only seven of the usual 14 fences were jumped in this decent handicap chase and, as a result, is probably worth treating the form with a degree of caution. The winner is rated back to form.

3425 TOTEPOOL.COM H'CAP HURDLE (12 hdls) 3m 110y
3:25 (3:25) (Class 5) (0-95,95) 4-Y-O+ **£2,737** (£798; £399)

Form RPR
S05- **1** **Residence And Spa (IRE)**[24] 2920 5-10-3 **75** MarkQuinlan(3) 82
(Helen Rees) *hld up towards rr: rdn and stdy prog fr after 9th: 5th appr 2 out: 6 l 3rd at the last: str run fnl 120yds: led nring fin* **20/1**

035- **2** *nk* **Matako (FR)**[22] 2980 10-11-10 **93** IanPopham 102+
(Caroline Keevil) *travelled wl in mid-div: hdwy 8th: led 2 out: 4 l clr last: rdn and idling flat: hdd towards fin* **7/1[3]**

640- **3** *5* **Midnight Mustang**[36] 2690 6-10-4 **80** CharlieDeutsch(7) 82
(Andrew J Martin) *trckd ldrs: rdn after 3 out: ev ch bef next tl bef last: no ex whn lost 2nd run-in* **6/1[2]**

06P- **4** *18* **Dont Call Me Oscar (IRE)**[26] 2887 6-10-11 **80** (bt) TomO'Brien 64
(Mark Gillard) *trckd ldrs: j.rt at times: led 9th: rdn and hdd 2 out where stmbld: wknd* **25/1**

/00- **5** *3* **Thedeboftheyear**[55] 2284 9-11-5 **95** KieronEdgar(7) 76
(Chris Down) *led tl 2nd: trckd ldr: rdn after 3 out: wknd next* **10/3[1]**

/5P- **6** *10* **Acosta**[15] 3114 9-10-0 **72** (b) WayneKavanagh(3) 43
(Dr Jeremy Naylor) *trckd ldr: led 8th tl 9th: sn rdn: wknd bef 2 out: t.o* **25/1**

12F/ **7** *6* **Dushy Valley (IRE)**[365] 3378 6-10-12 **81** NickSchofield 46
(Paul Henderson) *mid-div: rdn after 8th: wknd after 3 out: t.o* **10/1**

0/6- **8** *8* **Lady From Geneva**[241] 99 6-11-4 **92** ConorShoemark(5) 49
(Brendan Powell) *mid-div: rdn after 9th: sn wknd: t.o* **7/1[3]**

000- **9** *21* **Ask The Boss**[36] 2689 8-10-13 **89** MikeyEnnis(7) 25
(Tim Dennis) *mid-div: rdn after 9th: wknd after 3 out: t.o* **25/1**

/00- **P** **Miss Tinks**[18] 3047 7-10-7 **76** (t[1]) DarylJacob
(Richard Woollacott) *hld up towards rr: hdwy 9th: sn rdn and wknd sn after next: t.o whn p.u bef 2 out* **14/1**

2/P- **P** **Sudden Light (IRE)**[14] 3138 7-10-2 **71** (bt[1]) MattieBatchelor
(Jim Best) *led 2nd tl 8th: sn rdn: wknd after next: t.o whn p.u bef 2 out* **22/1**

P/0- **P** **Just Watch Ollie (IRE)**[24] 2920 7-9-7 **69** oh2 LouisMuspratt(7)
(John Coombe) *struggling 8th: a towards rr: t.o whn p.u bef 2 out* **50/1**

230- **P** **Theoystercatcher (IRE)**[131] 1339 7-11-7 **90** RichardJohnson
(Tim Vaughan) *a towards rr: t.o whn p.u after 3 out* **6/1[2]**

504- **P** **Hurricane Ivan (IRE)**[27] 2875 5-11-12 **95** (t) AlainCawley
(Fergal O'Brien) *towards rr: nvr travelling: detached 5th: losing tch whn p.u after 7th* **14/1**

6m 26.1s (22.10) **Going Correction** +0.80s/f (Soft) **14** Ran SP% **121.7**
Speed ratings (Par 103): **96,95,94,88,87 84,82,79,73,**
toteswingers 1&2 £34.90, 1&3 £22.80, 2&3 £7.90 CSF £146.20 CT £965.46 TOTE £29.50: £8.90, £2.40, £2.50; EX 273.00 Trifecta £1360.80 Part won..
Owner Mrs H E Rees **Bred** Bigwigs Bloodstock **Trained** Chalmington, Dorset

FOCUS
Recent winning form was extremely hard to come by in this handicap hurdle. The winner was well in on his best form.

3426 COLLECT TOTEPOOL WINNINGS AT BETFRED SHOPS H'CAP HURDLE (9 hdls) 2m 1f
3:55 (3:55) (Class 5) (0-95,95) 3-Y-O+ **£2,737** (£798; £399)

Form RPR
/41- **1** **Sarenice (FR)**[168] 1000 7-11-9 **92** HaddenFrost 100+
(James Frost) *racd wd: trckd ldr: led after 3 out: r.o wl fr last: rdn out* **10/1**

012- **2** *1 ½* **Dalrymple (IRE)**[32] 2766 7-11-2 **90** (t) CharlieWallis(5) 97+
(Nick Ayliffe) *mid-div: rdn after 6th: chsd ldrs after 3 out: styng on at same pce in 3rd whn untidy last: wnt 2nd towards fin* **9/2[2]**

100- **3** *1* **Whispering Harry**[27] 2877 4-11-1 **84** RichardJohnson 88
(Henry Oliver) *led tl 2nd: disp fr 4th: rdn and hdd whn kpt to inner appr 2 out: styd on but no ex whn lost 2nd towards fin* **8/1**

/26- **4** *6* **Wise Hawk**[47] 2460 8-10-10 **82** JamesBest(3) 81
(Jackie Du Plessis) *mid-div: hdwy 5th: rdn in cl 4th after 3 out: fdd fnl 120yds* **7/1[3]**

604- **5** *9* **Going Nowhere Fast (IRE)**[17] 3062 8-11-1 **89** (p) RobertWilliams(5) 78
(Bernard Llewellyn) *hld up towards rr: hdwy after 6th: rdn after 3 out: nvr threatened ldrs* **7/1[3]**

533- **6** *3 ¾* **Pennant Dancer**[26] 2886 6-10-8 **82** (vt) AodhaganConlon(5) 67
(Debra Hamer) *trckd ldrs: disp ld 5th tl rdn after 3 out: wknd bef next* **20/1**

030- **7** *8* **Miles Of Sunshine**[9] 3195 8-11-9 **92** ConorO'Farrell 69
(Ron Hodges) *mid-div: rdn after 3 out: sn wknd* **25/1**

005- **8** *4* **Drummond**[25] 2898 4-10-9 **81** (tp) MarkQuinlan(3) 54
(Bernard Llewellyn) *a towards rr: nvr a factor* **25/1**

544- **9** *hd* **Cruise In Style (IRE)**[39] 2629 7-11-2 **95** (bt) JonPark(10) 68
(Kevin Bishop) *hld up towards rr: midfield whn nt fluent 3 out: sn rdn: wkng whn wnt lft and hit 2 out* **12/1**

004- **10** *13* **Light The World (FR)**[18] 3047 5-11-1 **91** (p) JakeHodson(7) 51
(Kevin Frost) *trckd ldrs: rdn after 5th: wknd 3 out* **12/1**

2/0- **11** *17* **Supernoverre (IRE)**[97] 1643 7-11-5 **88** (p) TomO'Brien 31
(Alan Jones) *a towards rr: t.o fr after 3 out* **20/1**

010- **12** *22* **Sylvan Legend**[24] 2920 5-10-12 **81** IanPopham
(Caroline Keevil) *a towards rr: wknd 3 out: t.o* **3/1[1]**

/0P- **P** **Jambobo**[180] 635 4-10-11 **80** (tp) JamesDavies
(Chris Down) *t.k.h: led 2nd: jnd 4th: rdn after 6th: sn wknd: t.o whn p.u bef 2 out* **50/1**

4m 23.3s (15.30) **Going Correction** +0.80s/f (Soft)
WFA 4 from 5yo+ 5lb **13** Ran SP% **122.9**
Speed ratings (Par 103): **96,95,94,92,87 86,82,80,80,74 66,55,**
toteswingers 1&2 £2.60, 1&3 £19.10, 2&3 £10.40 CSF £53.34 CT £391.73 TOTE £8.60: £2.60, £2.30, £3.10; EX 26.20 Trifecta £265.40 Pool: £3490.44 - 9.86 winning units..
Owner Mrs J F Bury **Bred** G Roy & Mme G Roy **Trained** Scorriton, Devon

FOCUS
A trappy finale. The winner is still on the upgrade and there may be more to come.
T/Jkpt: Not won. T/Plt: £553.40. Pool: £100,257.43 - 132.25 winning units. T/Qpdt: £36.10. Pool: £13,489.03 - 276.50 winning units. TM

3188 UTTOXETER (L-H)
Tuesday, December 31

OFFICIAL GOING: Heavy (some standing water in chute)
Wind: Moderate, across Weather: Overcast

3427 32RED CASINO MAIDEN HURDLE (7 hdls 2 omitted) 2m
12:40 (12:40) (Class 5) 4-Y-O+ **£2,859** (£839; £419; £209)

Form RPR
120/ **1** **Cheltenian (FR)**[294] 4719 7-11-0 0 RichardJohnson 129+
(Philip Hobbs) *t.k.h and a travelling strly: sn prom: wnt 2nd at 3rd: led 4th: effrtlessly drew clr fr last: v easily* **2/7[1]**

3/3- **2** *7* **Fergal Mael Duin**[61] 2178 5-11-0 113 SeanQuinlan 117+
(David Bridgwater) *led: hdd 4th: chsd wnr after: stl ev ch 3 out but a fighting losing battle: no ch w wnr and wl outpcd fr last* **9/2[2]**

0U0- **3** *34* **Camptown Lady**[17] 3092 4-10-7 0 DougieCostello 73
(Laura Young) *hld up in rr: hmpd 3 out: kpt on fr bef last: nvr a threat* **100/1**

46- **4** *1 ¼* **Sukiyaki (IRE)**[5] 3258 4-11-0 0 NoelFehily 84
(Charlie Longsdon) *hld up: j.lft fnl 3: blnd 3 out: sn outpcd: kpt on run-in wout troubling ldrs* **10/1[3]**

/05- **5** *6* **Ergo Sum**[26] 2893 6-10-11 0 RobertDunne(3) 73
(Robin Mathew) *hld up: hdwy to chse ldrs after 3rd: unable to go w front two after 3 out: no imp after: wl btn bef last* **50/1**

6 *17* **Early Bonnet (IRE)**[234] 5-10-2 0 ConorShoemark(5) 49
(Kim Bailey) *chsd ldr to 3rd: remained handy tl rdn appr 3 out: sn wknd* **33/1**

0/6- **7** *44* **Whileaway (USA)**[43] 2563 4-10-9 0 (t) JamesBanks(5) 12
(Andy Turnell) *chsd ldrs: rdn and wknd after 4th: struggling whn blnd 3 out: t.o* **33/1**

4m 14.5s (22.50) **Going Correction** +1.775s/f (Heav) **7** Ran SP% **113.9**
Speed ratings (Par 103): **114,110,93,92,89 81,59**
toteswingers 1&2 £1.10, 1&3 £11.20, 2&3 £13.50 CSF £2.06 TOTE £1.20: £1.10, £1.80; EX 2.40 Trifecta £46.60.
Owner R S Brookhouse **Bred** Jean-Charles Haimet & J-Pascal Liberge **Trained** Withycombe, Somerset

FOCUS
Common bends and hurdles course at longest. After further morning rain the ground was changed to heavy. The first hurdle in the back straight had to be omitted. The form makes plenty of sense.

3428 32RED.COM H'CAP HURDLE (7 hdls 2 omitted) 2m
1:10 (1:10) (Class 5) (0-100,100) 3-Y-O+ **£2,729** (£801; £400; £200)

Form RPR
5/3- **1** **Come On Annie**[21] 3012 7-11-1 **96** MrsAlexDunn(7) 107+
(Alexandra Dunn) *hld up and confidently rdn: hdwy travelling wl bef 3 out: cl up appr 2 out: rdn to ld run-in: drew away towards fin* **2/1[1]**

040- **2** *2 ¼* **Lean Burn (USA)**[18] 3062 7-10-0 **79** HarryChalloner(5) 84
(Barry Leavy) *hld up: niggled along after 4th: hdwy 3 out: led last: rdn and hdd run-in: styd on same pce towards fin* **4/1[2]**

323- **3** *3 ½* **Detour Ahead**[18] 3058 5-11-4 **99** (p) ConorRing(7) 102
(Jennie Candlish) *a.p: led appr 3 out: rdn and hdd jst bef last: one pce fnl 100yds* **6/1[3]**

000- **4** *15* **Catching On (IRE)**[15] 3128 5-11-8 **96** RichieMcLernon 83
(Jonjo O'Neill) *led: hdd appr 3 out: u.p whn mstke 2 out: wknd after* **8/1**

0F0- **5** *16* **Maxdelas (FR)**[19] 3047 7-10-0 **81** (t) RyanHatch(7) 52
(Roy Brotherton) *hld up in midfield: hdwy appr 4th: ev ch 3 out: sn rdn and wknd* **7/1**

PFP/ **6** *10* **Lucky Prince**[312] 4372 6-11-3 **98** GaryDerwin(7) 59
(Brian Eckley) *chsd ldrs: lost pl 4th: rdn after: wknd 3 out* **25/1**

S0U- **7** *½* **Prickles**[19] 3048 8-11-6 **94** (p) DarylJacob 54
(Richard Woollacott) *prom tl rdn and wknd bef 3 out* **12/1**

8 *16* **Milans Cross (IRE)**[165] 1033 5-11-12 **100** SeanQuinlan 44
(Jennie Candlish) *hld up in tch: lost pl bef 4th: sn u.p: bhd and n.d whn mstke 2 out* **16/1**

045- **P** **Cloudy Deal (IRE)**[10] 3210 6-11-5 **93** (t) JasonMaguire
(Martin Todhunter) *in tch: rdn and wknd bef 3 out: wl bhd whn p.u bef last* **16/1**

4m 18.8s (26.80) **Going Correction** +1.775s/f (Heav)
WFA 4 from 5yo+ 5lb **9** Ran SP% **114.5**
Speed ratings (Par 103): **104,102,101,93,85 80,80,72,**
toteswingers 1&2 £2.40, 1&3 £2.50, 2&3 £7.50 CSF £10.72 CT £39.77 TOTE £2.70: £1.10, £1.90, £2.30; EX 12.30 Trifecta £24.60.
Owner Mrs Ann Trotman **Bred** Mickley Stud **Trained** Wellington, Somerset

FOCUS
A modest 2m handicap hurdle run at a sensible pace in the testing conditions. Three in a line at the last, but ultimately a comfortable and confidently ridden winner. She built on a good recent run in a stronger race.

3429 32RED NOVICES' H'CAP CHASE (LIMITED HANDICAP) (12 fncs) 2m
1:40 (1:40) (Class 3) (0-125,129) 4-Y-O+ **£6,388** (£1,928; £993; £526)

Form RPR
41/- **1** **Tresor De Bontee (FR)**[290] 4794 6-10-11 112 RichardJohnson 123+
(Richard Lee) *in tch: clsd to take 2nd appr 3 out: sn pressed ldr: rdn bef last: led narrowly run-in: styd on wl fnl strides* **9/4[1]**

431- **2** *½* **Lord Of House (GER)**[5] 3294 5-11-11 129 7ex (t) GavinSheehan(3) 138
(Charlie Mann) *led: shkn up appr 2 out: rdn whn pressed bef last: hdd narrowly run-in: kpt on wl* **5/2[2]**

530- **3** *21* **Munsaab (IRE)**[24] 2935 7-11-7 122 (tp) NoelFehily 110
(Charlie Longsdon) *chsd ldrs: wnt 2nd appr 6th: lost 2nd bef 3 out: rdn and outpcd bef next and dropped to last: n.d to front pair after but kpt on to take 3rd cl home* **5/1[3]**

/4F- **4** *nse* **Regal One (IRE)**[30] 2845 5-10-13 114 SeanQuinlan 102
(David Bridgwater) *hld up: hdwy to chse ldrs 8th: wnt 3rd appr 2 out: no imp on front pair: lost 3rd cl home* **8/1**

31U- **P** **Batu Ferringhi (FR)**[23] 2977 7-11-2 117 (p) AndrewTinkler
(Jamie Snowden) *chsd ldr tl appr 6th: rdn bef next: wknd 8th: t.o whn p.u bef 4 out* **15/2**

0/P- **P** **Ironic (FR)**[30] 2845 5-10-9 110 (t) PaddyBrennan
(Tom George) *nt a fluent: hld up: lft bhd bef 4 out: p.u bef 3 out* **11/1**

4m 15.5s (20.50) **Going Correction** +1.475s/f (Heav) **6** Ran SP% **107.2**
Speed ratings (Par 107): **107,106,96,96,**
toteswingers 1&2 £1.10, 1&3 £3.60, 2&3 £4.40 CSF £7.80 TOTE £2.80: £1.60, £1.70; EX 7.00 Trifecta £20.80.
Owner Glass Half Full **Bred** F Martineau **Trained** Byton, H'fords

FOCUS
Two unexposed chasers finished well clear. The form makes sense on time.

3430 £32 BONUS AT 32RED.COM H'CAP HURDLE (8 hdls 2 omitted) 2m 4f 110y
2:10 (2:10) (Class 3) (0-130,130) 3-Y-0 **£5,697** (£1,683; £841; £421; £210)

Form RPR
21- **1** **Madness Light (FR)**[17] 3092 4-11-3 **124**....................(t) GavinSheehan[(3)] 130+
(Warren Greatrex) *trckd ldrs: rdn to ld after 3 out: styd on run-in* **4/1**[2]

115- **2** *2 ¼* **Flicka Williams (IRE)**[17] 3081 6-11-12 **130**.................... DougieCostello 133
(Tony Coyle) *hld up: hdwy after 5th: chsng ldrs whn mstke 3 out: wnt 2nd 2 out: big effrt run-in: styd on same pce fnl 100yds* **13/2**

/00- **3** *17* **Notus De La Tour (FR)**[31] 2813 7-11-8 **126**....................(p) ConorO'Farrell 111
(David Pipe) *chsd ldr: led approachng 5th: hdd after 5th: rdn and stl ev ch 3 out: btn bef 2 out: plugged on but n.d after* **11/2**

1/0- **4** *21* **Quick Decisson (IRE)**[38] 2668 5-10-12 **116**................ RichardJohnson 80
(Philip Hobbs) *trckd ldrs: wnt 2nd appr 5th: led after flight: hdd after 3 out: wknd bef last* **7/2**[1]

021- **5** *2* **Di Kaprio (FR)**[21] 3013 7-11-4 **122**.. LiamHeard 84
(Barry Leavy) *led: hdd appr 5th: sn wknd* **14/1**

045- **6** *42* **Bob's World**[10] 3201 4-10-12 **116**..............................(p) SeanQuinlan 36
(Jennie Candlish) *hld up in rr: struggling 5th: nvr able to trble ldrs: t.o* **7/1**

51/- **P** **Oscatara (IRE)**[382] 3039 6-11-7 **125**................................ JasonMaguire
(Donald McCain) *hld up: sme hdwy after 5th: no imp on ldrs: rdn and stopped qckly sn after: bhd whn p.u bef 3 out* **5/1**[3]

3/0- **P** **Woodpole Academy (IRE)**[24] 2935 6-11-7 **130**............... AdamNicol[(5)]
(Philip Kirby) *midfield: hdwy appr 5th: rdn and wknd bef 3 out: wl bhd bef 2 out* **20/1**

5m 31.6s (32.60) **Going Correction** +1.775s/f (Heav)
WFA 4 from 5yo+ 6lb **8 Ran SP% 111.5**
Speed ratings (Par 107): **108,107,100,92,91 75, ,**
toteswingers 1&2 £6.30, 1&3 £5.80, 2&3 £16.40 CSF £28.47 CT £138.46 TOTE £4.30: £1.70, £1.90, £2.10; EX 22.50 Trifecta £267.40.
Owner Mrs T Brown **Bred** Alexa Leherissier & Laurent Baudry **Trained** Upper Lambourn, Berks

FOCUS
An open looking handicap hurdle, run at a sound pace. Just the first four home were seriously involved in the home straight. The first two are on the upgrade but nothing else really got home.

3431 ST14 CONSTRUCTION H'CAP CHASE (12 fncs) 2m
2:40 (2:40) (Class 4) (0-115,115) 4-Y-0 **£4,431** (£1,309; £654; £327; £163)

Form RPR
564- **1** **George Nympton (IRE)**[23] 2977 7-11-11 **114**............(t) RichardJohnson 125
(Brian Barr) *in tch: trckd ldrs after 8th: wnt 2nd 2 out: styd on to ld fnl 75yds: in control cl home* **11/1**

412- **2** *¾* **Massena (IRE)**[32] 2797 6-11-4 **107**.................................... LiamTreadwell 121+
(Venetia Williams) *prom: j. slowly 5th: led appr 3 out: j. awkwardly 2 out: rdr lost irons and nvr able to regain them: hdd fnl 75yds: kpt on but hld cl home* **11/10**[1]

0PP- **3** *10* **The Sneezer (IRE)**[10] 3197 10-11-0 **110**.......................... KieronEdgar[(7)] 110
(Alexandra Dunn) *prom: led 3rd: rdn and hdd appr 3 out: sn one pce* **25/1**

003- **4** *4 ½* **Fintan**[13] 3164 10-10-6 **95**.. DougieCostello 91
(Laura Young) *hld up: mstke 6th: no imp fr 3 out* **4/1**[2]

/5P- **5** *3 ½* **Morgan's Bay**[26] 2895 8-11-7 **110**...................................... PaddyBrennan 102
(Tom George) *hld up: effrt to chse ldrs appr 4 out: disp 2nd briefly 2 out: sn wknd* **9/2**[3]

32P- **6** *9* **Marky Bob (IRE)**[17] 3093 8-11-5 **115**.............................. MikeyEnnis[(7)] 98
(Hugo Froud) *led: hdd 3rd: remained handy: rdn and wknd 4 out* **16/1**

6/6- **P** **Superman De La Rue (FR)**[21] 3004 7-11-9 **112**............... AdamWedge
(David Rees) *in tch: rdn and wknd bef 4 out: bhd whn p.u bef 3 out* **8/1**

4m 17.6s (22.60) **Going Correction** +1.475s/f (Heav) **7 Ran SP% 115.0**
Speed ratings (Par 105): **102,101,96,94,92 88,**
toteswingers 1&2 £4.60, 1&3 £24.50, 2&3 £18.30 CSF £25.29 TOTE £8.00: £3.50, £1.60; EX 25.30 Trifecta £291.40.
Owner Miss Daisy Hitchins **Bred** Huw G Davies **Trained** Longburton, Dorset

FOCUS
The favourite's blunder at the second-last fence proved crucial. The winner had slipped to a good mark.

3432 ST14 CONSTRUCTION H'CAP HURDLE (10 hdls 2 omitted) 3m
3:10 (3:10) (Class 5) (0-100,105) 4-Y-0+ **£2,729** (£801; £400; £200)

Form RPR
404- **1** **Over My Head**[21] 3014 5-9-13 **78**................................... GeraldQuinn[(7)] 89
(Claire Dyson) *mde all: pushed along and gng clr whn hit 3 out: styd on wl* **5/1**[3]

30P- **2** *19* **Earcomesthedream (IRE)**[12] 3179 10-11-11 **97**...............(b) JackDoyle 93
(Peter Pritchard) *prom: reminder after 3rd: lft 2nd 3 out: no imp on wnr after* **16/1**

001- **3** *39* **Crookstown (IRE)**[5] 3265 6-12-5 **105** 7ex............................. DarylJacob 57
(Ben Case) *hld up: hdwy 5th: trckd ldrs after 6th: gng wl 7th: wnt 2nd: shkn up and over 6 l down bef 3 out where blnd and lost 2nd: sn btn* **2/1**[1]

/0P- **4** *16* **Bravo Riquet (FR)**[38] 2680 7-11-9 **95**........................(vt) LeeEdwards 31
(Robin Mathew) *hld up: pushed along after 6th: struggling 7th: nvr a threat* **7/1**

000- **P** **Gilded Age**[28] 2877 7-11-2 **88**..(tp) TomMessenger
(Mandy Rowland) *hld up: u.p bef 7th: lost tch sn after: t.o whn p.u bef 2 out* **25/1**

0/0- **P** **Midnight Return (IRE)**[43] 2563 7-9-9 **72** oh2.............. HarryChalloner[(5)]
(Richard Ford) *midfield: lost pl bef 7th: toiling after: t.o whn p.u bef 3 out* **25/1**

066- **P** **Terntheothercheek**[18] 3062 4-9-7 **72** oh1.......................(p) ConorRing[(7)]
(Jennie Candlish) *trckd ldrs: hit 4th: blnd and lost pl 6th: sn bhd: t.o whn p.u bef 7th* **8/1**

/36- **P** **Goodacres Garden (IRE)**[22] 2999 6-11-1 **87**..................... JasonMaguire
(Donald McCain) *trckd ldrs: rdn and lost pl 5th: bhd and struggling 6th: sme hdwy bef 7th: toiling sn after: t.o whn p.u bef 3 out* **3/1**[2]

6m 42.8s (52.80) **Going Correction** +1.775s/f (Heav)
WFA 4 from 5yo+ 7lb **8 Ran SP% 112.2**
Speed ratings (Par 103): **83,76,63,58, , ,**
toteswingers 1&2 £8.20, 1&3 £2.70, 2&3 £7.40 CSF £70.83 CT £207.90 TOTE £5.20: £1.50, £3.60, £1.40; EX 82.20 Trifecta £283.30.
Owner Ms Ingrid Heritage **Bred** Mrs Jane Smith **Trained** Cleeve Prior, Worcs

FOCUS
This turned in to a severe stamina test with the eventual one-two taking each other on until four out. Weak form.

3433 SIGNS 2000 MAIDEN OPEN NATIONAL HUNT FLAT RACE 2m
3:40 (3:40) (Class 6) 4-6-Y-0 **£1,949** (£572; £286; £143)

Form RPR
1 **Definitly Red (IRE)**[66] 4-11-2 0... DarylJacob 118+
(Steve Gollings) *trckd ldrs: led over 2f out: drew clr fnl f: styd on wl* **13/8**[1]

2 *9* **Final Nudge (IRE)**[317] 4-11-2 0.. NoelFehily 109
(David Dennis) *hld up in rr: hdwy over 4f out: effrt whn chsng ldrs 3f out: rdn to take 2nd 2f out: unable to go w wnr fr 1f out: one pce* **8/1**

2- **3** *9* **Binge Drinker (IRE)**[69] 2026 4-11-2 0................................ JamieMoore 100
(Rebecca Curtis) *chsd ldr tl rdn 3f out: no ex u.p over 1f out* **15/8**[2]

5- **4** *18* **Bostin (IRE)**[26] 2912 5-11-2 0... PaddyBrennan 82
(Brian Barr) *led: rdn and hdd over 2f out: wknd wl over 1f out* **25/1**

5 *28* **Laird Of Monksford (IRE)** 4-11-2 0................................ JasonMaguire 54
(Donald McCain) *hld up: hdwy 6f out: rdn over 4f out: sn wl btn* **9/2**[3]

0- **6** *65* **Monart Diamond**[47] 2472 4-11-2 0.................................. RichardJohnson
(Tim Vaughan) *hld up: pushed along over 6f out: t.o fnl 4f* **16/1**

0- **7** *166* **Sunsational Girl**[31] 2809 4-10-2 0...................................... GaryDerwin[(7)]
(Brian Eckley) *prom: pushed along and wknd 1/2-way: t.o: virtually p.u* **66/1**

4m 12.1s (25.70) **Going Correction** +1.775s/f (Heav) **7 Ran SP% 113.4**
Speed ratings: **106,101,97,88,74 41,**
toteswingers 1&2 £3.00, 1&3 £1.40, 2&3 £2.80 CSF £15.21 TOTE £2.80: £1.80, £3.00; EX 16.20 Trifecta £56.00.
Owner P J Martin **Bred** James Keegan **Trained** Scamblesby, Lincs

FOCUS
A fair bumper run at a sound pace in the conditions and almost certainly an above-average winner.
T/Plt: £7.20. Pool: £116,585.79 - 11,812.98 winning units. T/Qpdt: £7.40. Pool: £7085.22 - 699.16 winning units. DO

2975 WARWICK (L-H)
Tuesday, December 31

OFFICIAL GOING: Soft (heavy in places; chs 5.5; hdl 4.8)
Wind: Fresh behind Weather: Overcast

3434 32RED CASINO NOVICES' H'CAP HURDLE (9 hdls) 2m 3f
12:50 (12:50) (Class 5) (0-100,100) 3-Y-0+ **£1,949** (£572; £286; £143)

Form RPR
22/ **1** **Mudita Moment (IRE)**[577] 548 8-11-4 **92**........................ AidanColeman 108+
(Venetia Williams) *hld up: hdwy 5th: chsd ldr next: hit 3 out: led appr 2 out: clr whn j.rt last: easily* **2/1**[1]

33P/ **2** *6* **Landenstown Pearl (IRE)**[919] 950 7-10-3 **80**............... JackQuinlan[(3)] 85+
(Sarah Humphrey) *led: rdn and hdd appr 2 out: styd on same pce* **20/1**

000- **3** *12* **Young Lou**[11] 3188 4-10-6 **80**.. CharliePoste 72
(Robin Dickin) *chsd ldrs: j. slowly 1st: lost pl after 4th: in rr and drvn along 6th: styd on to go poor 3rd flat* **25/1**

006- **4** *1* **Lightentertainment (IRE)**[36] 2711 5-11-12 **100**............ MarcGoldstein 91
(Chris Gordon) *hld up: hdwy 5th: rdn and wknd after 3 out* **20/1**

5F0- **5** *6* **June French (FR)**[54] 2312 5-10-0 **74** oh5....................(t) DavidEngland 59
(Giles Smyly) *prom: chsd ldr after 4th tl 6th: sn pushed along: wknd after 3 out* **8/1**[2]

340- **6** *1 ¼* **Mighty Mambo**[29] 2862 6-10-13 **87**....................................(tp) DavidBass 71
(Lawney Hill) *hld up: hdwy 5th: rdn and wknd after 3 out* **12/1**[3]

050- **7** *6* **Powertakeoff (IRE)**[26] 2898 5-10-3 **82**..................... ChristopherWard[(5)] 60
(Henry Oliver) *prom tl rdn and wknd after 3 out* **25/1**

/00- **8** *33* **Downtown Manhattan (IRE)**[17] 3094 6-11-4 **97**....... MauriceLinehan[(5)] 42
(Jonjo O'Neill) *in rr: pushed along after 3rd: bhd fr 5th* **14/1**

0PP- **P** **Haling Park (UAE)**[16] 3119 7-9-11 **74** oh10...............(b[1]) TrevorWhelan[(3)]
(Clarissa Caroe) *hld up: a in rr: bhd fr 5th: p.u bef 2 out* **100/1**

6/0- **P** **Landerbee (IRE)**[44] 2536 6-10-5 **86**................................. KevinJones[(7)]
(Seamus Mullins) *hld up: plld hrd: hdwy 5th: wknd next: bhd whn p.u bef 2 out* **20/1**

/30- **P** **Stage King**[23] 2978 7-11-10 **98**...(t) APMcCoy
(Warren Greatrex) *hld up in tch: wknd after 3 out: p.u bef next* **2/1**[1]

000- **P** **Forrardon Xmoor**[15] 3136 4-11-2 **90**................................. WillKennedy
(Miss Jessica Westwood) *t.k.h: trckd ldr tl after 4th: rdn and wknd next: bhd whn p.u bef 2 out* **33/1**

4m 39.1s (-3.60) **Going Correction** -0.125s/f (Good)
WFA 4 from 5yo+ 5lb **12 Ran SP% 118.0**
Speed ratings (Par 103): **102,99,94,94,91 90,88,74, , ,**
toteswingers 1&2 £9.10, 1&3 £14.10, 2&3 £26.10 CSF £45.27 CT £793.72 TOTE £3.00: £1.10, £3.80, £3.90; EX 39.70 Trifecta £457.60.
Owner John Moorhouse & John Nicholls (Trading) **Bred** John J Cleary **Trained** Kings Caple, H'fords

FOCUS
The going was testing after further rain leading up to the meeting. The jockeys reported it was "a mixture of heavy and soft, but not too bad." A moderate novices' handicap hurdle, but the first two defied long absences. The winner should rate higher and the form is best rated around the third and fourth.

3435 32RED ON THE APP STORE CONDITIONAL JOCKEYS' H'CAP HURDLE (12 hdls) 3m 1f
1:20 (1:20) (Class 4) (0-120,118) 4-Y-0+ **£3,119** (£915; £457; £228)

Form RPR
361/ **1** **Gunna Be A Devil (IRE)**[791] 2262 9-11-3 **112**................ MattGriffiths[(3)] 120
(Jeremy Scott) *led to 6th: led 7th: rdn appr 2 out: styd on gamely u.p* **16/1**

551- **2** *nk* **Kilrush (IRE)**[34] 2744 7-11-4 **110**.. MichaelByrne 119+
(Neil Mulholland) *hld up: mstkes: hdwy 9th: pushed along to chse wnr appr 2 out: ev ch whn hit last: styd on u.p* **10/1**

RP0- **3** *22* **Sarando**[24] 2944 8-11-8 **114**...(tp) KillianMoore 100
(Alex Hales) *chsd ldrs: rdn after 3 out: wknd bef next* **20/1**

000- **4** *½* **Mission Complete (IRE)**[21] 3013 7-11-4 **118**............ JamesHuxham[(8)] 104
(Jonjo O'Neill) *hld up: drvn along 8th: nvr nrr* **8/1**

265- **5** *4 ½* **Knockraheen (IRE)**[24] 2936 5-11-2 **116**.................. TommieMO'Brien[(8)] 97
(Jonjo O'Neill) *hld up: nt fluent 2nd: hdwy 7th: hit next: rdn and wknd after 3 out: mstke next* **7/2**[1]

U4P- **6** *25* **Hot Whiskey (IRE)**[30] 2847 5-11-4 **110**.............................. JoshuaMoore 66
(Brendan Powell) *chsd ldrs tl rdn and wknd after 3 out* **12/1**

The Form Book Jumps, Raceform Ltd, Compton, RG20 6NL.

0/0- 7 1 ½ **Nutin Fancy (IRE)**[37] 2691 7-11-1 **110**..........................(b[1]) JamesBest(3) 65
(Philip Hobbs) *prom: rdn 8th: sn wknd* **7/1[3]**

552- 8 3 ¾ **Alberobello (IRE)**[36] 2715 5-11-2 **116**..........................(t) ChrisMeehan(8) 67
(Jeremy Scott) *hld up: hdwy 4th: chsd wnr next: led 6th to 7th: ev ch 3 out: rdn and wknd bef next* **7/2[1]**

1PF- P **Dom Lukka (FR)**[34] 2744 5-11-1 **110**..........................(p) KielanWoods(3)
(Charlie Longsdon) *prom: lost pl after 7th: rdn and wknd after 9th: bhd whn hit 2 out: sn p.u* **4/1[2]**

6m 20.1s (5.10) **Going Correction** -0.125s/f (Good) 9 Ran SP% **115.5**
Speed ratings (Par 105): **86,85,78,78,77 69,68,67,**
toteswingers 1&2 £6.70, 1&3 £25.90, 2&3 £21.00 CSF £160.78 CT £3194.14 TOTE £12.60: £4.00, £2.30, £4.40; EX 117.20 Trifecta £276.30.
Owner R J Lock **Bred** Terry Cassidy **Trained** Brompton Regis, Somerset
■ Stewards' Enquiry : Matt Griffiths seven-day ban; used whip above permitted level (14th-20th Jan).

FOCUS
A competitive conditionals' staying handicap and another winner to defy a long absence. The winner may still be capable of a bit better than this.

3436 WHITSON BLOODSTOCK NOVICES' CHASE (17 fncs) 2m 4f 110y
1:50 (1:50) (Class 4) 4-Y-0+ **£4,873** (£1,431; £715)

Form RPR

/43- 1 **Barrakilla (IRE)**[27] 2882 6-11-0 130.................................... PaulMoloney 137+
(Evan Williams) *mde virtually all: rdn out* **5/6[1]**

/35- 2 2 ½ **Persian Snow (IRE)**[36] 2714 7-11-0 130..........................(t) TomO'Brien 133
(Philip Hobbs) *trckd wnr: pushed along appr 2 out: rdn flat: styd on same pce* **13/8[2]**

324- 3 54 **Rio Milan (IRE)**[11] 3189 7-11-0 0..........................(t) AlainCawley 79
(Fergal O'Brien) *hld up: nt fluent: bhd fr 11th* **7/1[3]**

5m 13.1s (-7.90) **Going Correction** -0.125s/f (Good) 3 Ran SP% **105.2**
Speed ratings (Par 105): **110,109,88**
CSF £2.48 TOTE £1.80; EX 2.50 Trifecta £2.90.
Owner Mr & Mrs William Rucker **Bred** Brian Griffin **Trained** Llancarfan, Vale Of Glamorgan

FOCUS
A decent novices' chase, despite the small field. The form is rated around the second.

3437 32RED H'CAP CHASE (JOCKEY CLUB GRASSROOTS JUMPS SERIES QUALIFIER) (18 fncs) 3m 110y
2:20 (2:20) (Class 4) (0-120,109) 4-Y-0+ **£4,093** (£1,202; £601; £300)

Form RPR

/00- 1 **Wood Yer (IRE)**[25] 2931 7-11-12 **109**..................(tp) SamTwiston-Davies 118
(Nigel Twiston-Davies) *w ldr tl led 8th: reminders appr 12th: styd on u.p* **9/2**

132- 2 3 **Roseneath (IRE)**[26] 2902 9-11-0 **97**..........................(tp) APMcCoy 103
(Alex Hales) *a.p: pushed along to chse wnr appr 2 out: rdn flat: styd on same pce* **2/1[1]**

/32- 3 3 **Samurai Way**[9] 3223 11-11-10 **107**.................................... AidanColeman 112
(Venetia Williams) *led to 8th: remained handy: jnd wnr 11th tl rdn 15th: lost 2nd whn hit 2 out: no ex last* **9/4[2]**

P24- 4 13 **Elite Beneficial (IRE)**[23] 2979 8-10-4 **92**..........................(p) BenPoste(5) 85
(Rosemary Gasson) *chsd ldrs tl rdn and wknd 2 out* **11/4[3]**

6m 30.8s (3.80) **Going Correction** -0.125s/f (Good) 4 Ran SP% **109.0**
Speed ratings (Par 105): **88,87,86,81**
CSF £13.68 TOTE £6.40; EX 14.80 Trifecta £20.80.
Owner Miss Katharine J Holland **Bred** J Harold-Barry **Trained** Naunton, Gloucs

FOCUS
Another small field for this handicap chase with the top weight 11lb below the race ceiling and a steady gallop early on. The second and third set the level.

3438 EBF STALLIONS/32RED.COM MARES' "NATIONAL HUNT" NOVICES' HURDLE (11 hdls) 2m 5f
2:50 (2:50) (Class 4) 4-Y-0+ **£2,227** (£2,227; £505; £252)

Form RPR

2/4- 1 **Tickity Bleue**[33] 2767 5-10-12 0.................................... RobertThornton 111+
(Alan King) *hld up: nt fluent 6th: hdwy sn after: led appr 2 out: shkn up bef last: rdn and hung rt flat: r.o: jnd on line* **11/4[2]**

/00- 1 dht **Molly's A Diva**[12] 3168 6-10-12 0.................................... NickScholfield 111+
(Kim Bailey) *hld up: hdwy appr 3 out: wnt 2nd last: rdn and edgd rt flat: r.o to join rival on line* **9/2[3]**

553- 3 13 **Mrs Jordan (IRE)**[12] 3168 5-10-12 110.......................... AidanColeman 101
(Venetia Williams) *led 2nd: rdn and hdd appr 2 out: wknd flat* **5/6[1]**

02- 4 13 **Leith Hill Legasi**[29] 2864 4-10-9 0.......................... KielanWoods(3) 85
(Charlie Longsdon) *chsd ldrs: pushed along appr 7th: wknd after next* **16/1**

/P3- 5 ½ **Fine Moment**[23] 2981 5-10-12 0..........................(t) BrianHughes 85
(Kevin Frost) *prom: chsd ldr 6th tl rdn and wknd appr 2 out* **25/1**

/00- 6 1 ¾ **Ereyna**[13] 3159 4-10-9 0.................................... JoshuaMoore(3) 83
(Renee Robeson) *led to 2nd: chsd ldr to 6th: rdn and wknd appr 3 out* **40/1**

5m 23.2s (8.20) **Going Correction** -0.125s/f (Good)
WFA 4 from 5yo+ 6lb 6 Ran SP% **111.6**
Speed ratings (Par 105): **79,79,74,69,68 68**
WIN: Tickity Bleue £1.80, Molly's A Diva £2.30; PL: Tickity Bleue £2.20, Molly's A Diva £1.80; EX: TB/MAD £5.40, MAD/TB £5.20; CSF: TB/MAD £7.59, MAD/TB £8.65; Trifecta: TB/MAD/MJ £9.00, MAD/TB/MJ £17.40.
Owner J Perriss **Bred** J F Perriss **Trained** Andoversford, Gloucs
Owner Let's Live Racing **Bred** Wood Farm Stud **Trained** Barbury Castle, Wilts

FOCUS
An ordinary mares' novices' hurdle that produced a terrific finish and a dead-heat. The form is rated around the third.

3439 32REDBINGO.COM H'CAP CHASE (17 fncs) 2m 4f 110y
3:20 (3:21) (Class 4) (0-105,105) 4-Y-0+ **£3,768** (£1,106; £553; £276)

Form RPR

453- 1 **Free World (FR)**[13] 3156 9-11-0 100.......................... MissLBrooke(7) 110+
(Lady Susan Brooke) *a.p: chsd ldr 7th: led 9th: rdn flat: styd on wl* **14/1**

/03- 2 3 **Todareistodo**[40] 2618 7-11-6 99.................................... MarkGrant 106
(Jim Old) *hld up: hdwy 10th: chsd wnr appr 2 out: sn rdn: styd on same pce flat* **4/1[2]**

131- 3 ½ **Midnight Charmer**[21] 3008 7-10-9 93.......................... JamesBanks(5) 99
(Emma Baker) *hld up: hdwy appr 11th: rdn after 3 out: styd on* **4/1[2]**

606- 4 1 ½ **Minellaforlunch (IRE)**[26] 2897 6-11-7 100..................(p) DenisO'Regan 104
(Henry Oliver) *led to 9th: chsd wnr tl pushed along after 3 out: styd on same pce fr next* **3/1[1]**

232- 5 6 **Fitandproperjob**[20] 3027 7-10-5 84..........................(vt) PaulMoloney 82
(Anthony Middleton) *hld up: hdwy 11th: rdn after 3 out: wknd next* **8/1[3]**

5/0- 6 1 ½ **Craiglands (IRE)**[23] 2980 11-10-2 86..........................(v) RobertMcCarth(5) 83
(Ian Williams) *mid-div: hdwy after 10th: rdn 14th: wknd 3 out* **8/1[3]**

356- 7 18 **Topaze Collonges (FR)**[17] 3093 6-11-9 105..............(b) KielanWoods(3) 84
(Charlie Longsdon) *chsd ldrs: pushed along 6th: wknd 9th* **17/2**

066- P **Arrayan**[17] 3094 8-11-12 105.................................... NickScholfield
(Alexandra Dunn) *prom: lost pl 6th: bhd fr 10th: p.u bef 13th* **25/1**

31P- P **Shalamiyr (FR)**[40] 2615 8-11-6 99.................................... WillKennedy
(Sarah-Jayne Davies) *chsd ldr to 7th: rdn and wknd after 10th: bhd whn p.u bef 14th* **12/1**

5m 18.1s (-2.90) **Going Correction** -0.125s/f (Good) 9 Ran SP% **116.0**
Speed ratings (Par 105): **100,98,98,98,95 95,88, ,**
CSF £71.21 CT £271.90 TOTE £13.90: £3.10, £1.90, £1.80; EX 60.20 Trifecta £383.60.
Owner Lady Susan Brooke **Bred** Jean-Christian Raymond **Trained** Dolau, Powys

FOCUS
A moderate but competitive handicap chase and a surprise winner. The form is rated around the second to fourth.

3440 CONNOLLY'S RED MILLS BUMPER CHALLENGE STANDARD OPEN NATIONAL HUNT FLAT RACE 2m
3:50 (3:50) (Class 6) 4-6-Y-0 **£1,559** (£457; £228; £114)

Form RPR

1 **Call Me Vic (IRE)**[604] 6-10-9 0.......................... AodhaganConlon(5) 119+
(Tom George) *mde all: shkn up and clr fr over 1f out: styd on wl* **16/1**

3- 2 9 **Monbeg Theatre (IRE)**[47] 2472 4-11-0 0.......................... SamTwiston-Davies 110
(Jamie Snowden) *hld up in tch: rdn to chse wnr over 1f out: styd on same pce* **7/2[2]**

1- 3 1 ¼ **Bandit Country (IRE)**[26] 2905 4-11-7 0.................................... APMcCoy 116
(Jonjo O'Neill) *hld up: hdwy 1/2-way: rdn to chse wnr over 2f out tl over 1f out: styd on same pce* **4/7[1]**

2- 4 7 **Trapper Peak (IRE)**[37] 2703 4-11-0 0.......................... AndrewThornton 102
(Caroline Bailey) *mid-div: hdwy 1/2-way: chsd wnr over 5f out tl rdn and wknd over 2f out* **20/1**

5 6 **Templebraden (IRE)** 6-11-0 0.................................... LeightonAspell 96
(Henry Oliver) *prom tl rdn and wknd 3f out* **33/1**

6 1 ¼ **Too Much Too Soon (IRE)** 4-11-0 0.......................... DenisO'Regan 95
(Paul Webber) *hld up: hdwy over 3f out: wknd over 2f out* **14/1**

7 3 ¼ **Rascal (IRE)** 4-11-0 0.................................... HarrySkelton 91
(Dan Skelton) *trckd ldrs: wnt 2nd 10f out tl pushed along over 5f out: wknd 4f out* **10/1[3]**

8 2 ¾ **A Keen Sense (GER)**[290] 4-11-0 0..........................(t) AidanColeman 89
(David Dennis) *hld up: rdn and wknd over 5f out* **50/1**

26- 9 1 **Driving Well (IRE)**[37] 2703 5-11-0 0.......................... NickScholfield 88
(Arthur Whiting) *chsd ldr 6f: rdn and wknd 5f out* **50/1**

- 10 4 ½ **Call Me Emma (IRE)**[290] 5-10-7 0.......................... WayneHutchinson 76
(Richard Phillips) *hld up: hdwy 7f out: wknd 4f out* **20/1**

5- 11 19 **Tanner Hill (IRE)**[28] 2878 5-10-11 0.......................... MarkQuinlan(3) 64
(James Evans) *trckd ldrs: plld hrd: wknd over 5f out* **66/1**

3m 49.5s (-1.40) **Going Correction** -0.125s/f (Good) 11 Ran SP% **125.4**
Speed ratings: **98,93,92,89,86 85,84,82,82,80 70**
toteswingers 1&2 £5.90, 1&3 £6.50, 2&3 £1.10 CSF £72.11 TOTE £20.50: £4.50, £1.10, £1.10; EX 94.00 Trifecta £168.10.
Owner C B Compton **Bred** R P Walshe **Trained** Slad, Gloucs

FOCUS
This bumper was won by Swing Bowler when last run in 2011 and produced another potentially useful sort. The form is rated around the second and third.
T/Plt: £872.20. Pool: £60,681.31 - 50.78 winning units. T/Qpdt: £54.20. Pool: £5473.71 - 74.71 winning units. CR

3441 - 3447a (Foreign Racing) - See Raceform Interactive

3350 CATTERICK (L-H)
Wednesday, January 1

OFFICIAL GOING: Soft (heavy in places; chs 6.5, hdl 6.3)
Wind: fresh 1/2 behind Weather: wet and windy

3448 HAPPY NEW YEAR NOVICES' HURDLE (10 hdls) 2m 3f
12:30 (12:30) (Class 4) 4-Y-0+ **£4,873** (£1,431; £715; £357)

Form RPR

30- 1 **Emral Silk**[51] 2426 6-11-6 0.................................... ShaneByrne 118+
(Sue Smith) *trckd ldrs: hit 4th: mstke 6th: chsd ldr next: led appr 2 out: wnt clr between last 2: hit last: v easily* **16/1**

5- 2 13 **The Backup Plan (IRE)**[41] 2627 5-11-6 0.......................... JasonMaguire 99
(Donald McCain) *led: j.rt: mstke 3rd: drvn and hdd appr 2 out: no ch w wnr* **7/1[3]**

4/0- 3 2 ½ **Admiral Hawke (IRE)**[26] 2932 8-10-13 112..............(t) NathanMoscrop(7) 96
(Brian Ellison) *trckd ldrs: 3rd after 3 out: rdn appr next: one pce* **15/8[1]**

2U1- 4 33 **Most Honourable**[28] 2881 4-10-6 116.......................... DaraghBourke(7) 56
(Michael Smith) *chsd ldr to 7th: drvn 3 out: lost pl appr next: sn bhd* **15/8[1]**

/15- 5 8 **King Rolfe (IRE)**[40] 2657 6-11-9 0.......................... MichaelByrne(3) 61
(Tim Vaughan) *chsd ldrs: drvn 3 out: lost pl appr next: sn bhd* **4/1[2]**

6 80 **Cottam Maybel**[152] 5-10-10 0.................................... JakeGreenall(3)
(Michael Easterby) *trckd ldrs: lost pl after 5th: sn bhd: t.o 3 out: eventually completed* **50/1**

4m 55.7s (19.60) **Going Correction** +1.175s/f (Heav)
WFA 4 from 5yo+ 11lb 6 Ran SP% **109.9**
Speed ratings (Par 105): **105,99,98,84,81 47**
CSF £107.45 TOTE £15.80: £4.60, £1.90; EX 169.00 Trifecta £158.00.
Owner Mrs A Ellis **Bred** Mrs P A Broad **Trained** High Eldwick, W Yorks

FOCUS
A moderate novices' hurdle. A big step up from the easy winner.

3449 YORKSHIRE-OUTDOORS.CO.UK ADVENTURE ACTIVITIES H'CAP CHASE (12 fncs) 2m
1:05 (1:07) (Class 5) (0-100,99) 5-Y-0+ **£3,422** (£997; £499)

Form RPR

U40- 1 **Cara Court (IRE)**[20] 3040 8-10-8 **86**..........................(p) SamanthaDrake(5) 89
(Joanne Foster) *mde all: drvn appr 3 out: kpt on run-in* **4/1[3]**

32U- 2 2 **Bocamix (FR)**[20] 3039 8-11-9 **99**.......................... JohnKington(3) 102
(Andrew Crook) *hmpd by loose horse 2nd: trckd wnr: upsides after 4 out: rdn between last 2: kpt on same pce* **7/2[2]**

332- 3 10 **Forestside (IRE)**[15] 3143 9-10-6 **84**.......................... TonyKelly(5) 77
(Barry Murtagh) *nt fluent: outpcd and lost pl 5th: sme hdwy appr 3 out: one pce fr 2 out* **2/1[1]**

554- **U** **Decent Lord (IRE)**[21] 3020 10-10-5 **78**............................(p) SeanQuinlan
(Jennie Candlish) *chsng wnr whn blnd and uns rdr 1st* **2/1**[1]

4m 11.9s (11.80) **Going Correction** +0.80s/f (Soft) **4** Ran SP% **108.9**
Speed ratings: **102,101,96,**
CSF £16.46 TOTE £4.90; EX 13.20 Trifecta £232.20 Part won..
Owner Miss J E Foster **Bred** L W Doran **Trained** Menston, W Yorks

FOCUS
Modest handicap form, rated around the second.

3450 DINE AND VIEW AT CATTERICK RACES BEGINNERS' CHASE (19 fncs) 3m 1f 110y

1:40 (1:41) (Class 4) 5-Y-0+ **£7,147** (£2,098; £1,049)

Form				RPR
110/	**1**		**Dungeel (IRE)**[327] 4102 8-11-0 0.. JasonMaguire (Donald McCain) *mde all: drvn after 4 out: styd on: unchal* **10/11**[1]	129+
/P4-	**2**	*1 ½*	**Son Of Flicka**[28] 2882 10-11-0 124.................................. DougieCostello (Tony Coyle) *chsd wnr: clr 2nd 12th: hit 3 out: j.lft last 2: kpt on same pce* **11/2**[3]	124
4-	**3**	*41*	**Colonel Iain**[22] 3011 8-11-0 0... AndrewTinkler (John Ferguson) *trckd ldr: mstke 6th and 10th: blnd and lost pl 12th: hdwy and in tch 14th: outpcd and hit 4 out: sn bhd: t.o* **13/8**[2]	99

7m 2.3s (20.30) **Going Correction** +0.95s/f (Soft) **3** Ran SP% **105.9**
Speed ratings: **106,105,92**
CSF £4.82 TOTE £1.90; EX 3.90 Trifecta £2.50.
Owner Martin Kemp **Bred** Mccracken Family **Trained** Cholmondeley, Cheshire

FOCUS
Only three runners. The first two should go on to rate higher.

3451 60/53 NEW YEAR CELEBRATION H'CAP HURDLE (10 hdls) 2m 3f

2:15 (2:15) (Class 4) (0-115,111) 4-Y-0+ **£5,198** (£1,526; £763; £381)

Form				RPR
1/6-	**1**		**Grate Fella (IRE)**[31] 2848 6-11-8 **107**.................................... ShaneByrne (Sue Smith) *hld up in rr: hdwy to trck ldrs 7th: led appr 2 out: drvn clr run-in* **9/2**[2]	113+
2-	**2**	*2 ¼*	**Summerlea (IRE)**[15] 3141 8-10-10 **95**.............................. JasonMaguire (Micky Hammond) *hld up in rr: hdwy 6th: chsng ldrs appr 2 out: kpt on and upsides last: styd on same pce* **6/1**[3]	98
536-	**3**	*6*	**Logical Approach (IRE)**[15] 3149 7-10-6 **96**...................(b[1]) TonyKelly(5) (David Thompson) *chsd ldr: lft in ld 5th: hdd after 3 out: rallied between last 2: one pce* **10/1**	94
320-	**4**	*11*	**Kodicil (IRE)**[25] 2956 6-11-12 **111**.................................. DougieCostello (Tim Walford) *in rr: hdwy 7th: sn drvn: one pce* **9/1**	97
031-	**5**	*1 ¼*	**Kayfrou**[19] 3062 9-9-9 **90**..(t) GLavery(10) (Brian Ellison) *in rr: hdwy 6th: chsng ldrs after 3 out: hung lft and one pce* **7/4**[1]	75
P/2-	**6**	*16*	**Prime Contender**[222] 456 12-11-6 **105**...........................(v) SeanQuinlan (Jennie Candlish) *w ldrs: led after 3 out: hdd appr next: wknd between last 2* **16/1**	74
3/0-	**7**	*44*	**Short Takes (USA)**[27] 2904 6-10-13 **105**...................... JamesCowley(7) (Donald McCain) *mid-div: lost pl after 7th: sn bhd: t.o 2 out* **20/1**	30
110-	**8**	*28*	**Amir Pasha (UAE)**[28] 2879 9-11-0 **104**...........................(p) JoeColliver(5) (Micky Hammond) *chsd ldrs: lost pl after 6th: t.o 3 out* **20/1**	
4F-	**P**		**Force Of Habit**[28] 2880 8-10-11 **101**.........................(p) SamanthaDrake(5) (Joanne Foster) *chsd ldrs: wknd after 3 out: sn bhd: t.o whn p.u bef 2 out* **50/1**	
U0P-	**F**		**Jukebox Melody (IRE)**[21] 3019 8-11-2 **108**................(b) JohnDawson(7) (John Wade) *led: fell 5th* **20/1**	
/46-	**P**		**Latest Fashion (IRE)**[15] 3144 8-9-10 **88**................ StephenMulqueen(7) (Christopher Wilson) *chsd ldrs: lost pl after 3 out: sn bhd: t.o whn p.u bef last* **14/1**	

5m 3.6s (27.50) **Going Correction** +1.325s/f (Heav) **11** Ran SP% **116.7**
Speed ratings (Par 105): **95,94,91,86,86 79,61,49, ,**
CSF £29.90 CT £257.82 TOTE £7.80: £2.80, £3.30, £3.20; EX 41.40 Trifecta £194.10 Part won..
Owner Mrs M Ashby **Bred** L K I Bloodstock Ltd **Trained** High Eldwick, W Yorks

FOCUS
An open-looking handicap run in miserable conditions. The winner was back to the level of his Sedgefield win.

3452 WATCH ON 3 DEVICES RACINGUK.COM/ANYWHERE H'CAP CHASE (15 fncs) 2m 3f

2:50 (2:51) (Class 4) (0-120,119) 5-Y-0+ **£7,322** (£2,273; £1,224)

Form				RPR
25F-	**1**		**Alderbrook Lad (IRE)**[15] 3143 8-10-5 **103**........................ JoeColliver(5) (Micky Hammond) *mde all: shkn up and wnt clr appr last: easily* **7/2**[3]	121+
013-	**2**	*8*	**Billy Cuckoo (IRE)**[11] 3211 8-11-10 **117**......................(v) DougieCostello (Tony Coyle) *chsd wnr: drvn approaching 3 out: one pce* **2/1**[2]	120
126-	**3**	*10*	**Claragh Native (IRE)**[18] 3000 9-11-7 **110**.................(p) HarryChalloner(5) (Martin Todhunter) *hld up in rr: hdwy 8th: trcking ldrs 10th: drvn appr 3 out: wknd appr last* **9/2**	107
153-	**P**		**Ballybriggan (IRE)**[20] 3039 10-11-11 **118**........................ JasonMaguire (Donald McCain) *hld up in rr: sme hdwy 8th: nt fluent and lost pl 11th: bhd and drvn next: sn t.o: p.u bef 2 out* **15/8**[1]	

5m 7.0s (18.20) **Going Correction** +1.10s/f (Heav) **4** Ran SP% **108.5**
Speed ratings: **105,101,93,**
CSF £10.77 TOTE £4.40; EX 9.90 Trifecta £46.30.
Owner Masters Of The Hall **Bred** A Malone **Trained** Middleham Moor, N Yorks

FOCUS
Not form to go overboard about or to be too confident over.

3453 RACING AGAIN ON 9TH JANUARY NOVICES' HURDLE (12 hdls) 3m 1f 110y

3:25 (3:27) (Class 4) 5-Y-0+ **£4,873** (£1,431; £715; £357)

Form				RPR
23-	**1**		**I Need Gold (IRE)**[25] 2954 6-10-12 0........................... JasonMaguire (Donald McCain) *led at v stdy pce: increased gallop 9th: drvn appr 2 out: clr between last 2: eased towards fin* **13/8**[2]	115+
14-	**2**	*3 ¼*	**Five In A Row (IRE)**[32] 2819 6-10-12 0........................ DougieCostello (Brian Ellison) *chsd wnr: drvn 9th: styd on same pce appr 2 out: tk 2nd nr fin* **10/11**[1]	108
0/	**3**	*½*	**Ballythomas**[395] 7-10-7 0.. TonyKelly(5) (David Thompson) *hld up in rr: hdwy 3 out: chsng wnr appr next: kpt on same pce* **50/1**	107
1-	**4**	*14*	**Dream Flyer (IRE)**[25] 2954 7-10-12 0........................... DaraghBourke(7) (Michael Smith) *trckd ldrs: drvn appr 2 out: sn wknd* **5/1**[3]	102
P-	**P**		**Frosty Dawn**[17] 3116 6-10-0 0.. JoeColliver(5) (Mike Sowersby) *j.rt: chsd ldrs: mstke 8th and sn lost pl: t.o 3 out: p.u bef next* **150/1**	

7m 16.4s (48.80) **Going Correction** +1.475s/f (Heav) **5** Ran SP% **109.8**
Speed ratings: **83,82,81,77,**
CSF £3.58 TOTE £1.50: £1.10, £1.10; EX 3.90 Trifecta £15.20.
Owner Deva Racing Golden Partnership **Bred** George Blackburn **Trained** Cholmondeley, Cheshire

FOCUS
A potentially informative little novices' hurdle in which Jason Maguire seized the initiative at the start where no one wanted to make the running. Not form to take too literally.
T/Plt: £2,105.50 to a £1 stake. Pool: £41,390.05 - 14.35 winning tickets. T/Qpdt: £39.70 to a £1 stake. Pool: £3,037.80 - 56.60 winning tickets. WG

3078 CHELTENHAM (L-H)

Wednesday, January 1

OFFICIAL GOING: Soft (heavy in places; 6.5)
The 5th, 6th, 8th, 14th and 15th fences were omitted due to standing water.
Wind: Very strong across Weather: Rain

3454 NEPTUNE INVESTMENT MANAGEMENT NOVICES' HURDLE (10 hdls) 2m 4f 110y

12:10 (12:11) (Class 3) 4-Y-0+
£6,256 (£1,848; £924; £462; £231; £116)

Form				RPR
01-	**1**		**Aubusson (FR)**[25] 2940 5-11-1 0.................................... MissEKelly(7) (Nick Williams) *chsd ldrs: chal 4 out: slt ld next: hrd pressed and drvn last: styd on strly run-in* **9/1**	137+
624-	**2**	*2 ¼*	**Regal Diamond (IRE)**[25] 2933 6-11-2 0............................ TomO'Brien (Peter Bowen) *led to 4th: styd pressing ldr: chal 3 out: stl upsides next and chal last: styd on run-in to hold 2nd but no imp on wnr* **22/1**	129
1-	**3**	*nk*	**Racing Pulse (IRE)**[20] 3036 5-11-8 0............................ JamesReveley (John Quinn) *chsd ldrs: led 4th to 4 out: styd front rnk: rdn appr last: kpt on to cl on 2nd run-in but no imp on wnr* **15/8**[1]	135+
111-	**4**	*6*	**Ballyalton (IRE)**[19] 3070 7-11-12 140.................................... APMcCoy (Ian Williams) *in rr but in tch: hdwy to trck ldrs 2 out: rdn last: wknd fnl 120yds* **3/1**[2]	132
/11-	**5**	*3 ¼*	**Royal Regatta (IRE)**[31] 2850 6-11-12 133.................... RichardJohnson (Philip Hobbs) *in rr but in tch: hdwy to chse ldrs 2 out: rdn last: sn wknd* **3/1**[2]	129
2-	**6**	*2 ¾*	**Vivaldi Collonges (FR)**[61] 2197 5-11-2 0............................ DarylJacob (Paul Nicholls) *chsd ldrs: hit 3 out: rdn next: wknd bef last* **7/1**[3]	117

5m 29.97s (28.97) **Going Correction** +1.325s/f (Heav) **6** Ran SP% **111.6**
Speed ratings (Par 107): **97,96,96,93,92 91**
CSF £128.10 TOTE £11.00: £4.50, £4.10; EX 232.40 Trifecta £1111.60 Part won..
Owner Mrs Jane Williams **Bred** Serge Dubois **Trained** George Nympton, Devon

FOCUS
Heavy rain led to some very testing ground, with standing water in places, and the runners had to contest with a strong wind too. Jockeys in the first confirmed the ground to be heavy. Bobs Worth won this event three years ago before taking the Albert Bartlett at the festival. This looked a hot novice hurdle, with some smart prospects on show, but the conditions led to a very steady pace and the merit of the form is questionable. Big steps forward from the first two.

3455 FOUNDATION DEVELOPMENTS LTD H'CAP CHASE (13 fncs 9 omitted) 3m 2f 110y

12:45 (12:46) (Class 2) (0-145,139)
5-Y-0+
£12,512 (£3,696; £1,848; £924; £462; £232)

Form				RPR
/11-	**1**		**Mendip Express (IRE)**[32] 2803 8-11-7 **139**...................(t) MrWBiddick(5) (Harry Fry) *in rr: mstke 11th: hdwy to trck ldrs at omitted 4 out: led at omitted 3rd last: styd on wl* **7/1**[3]	156+
024-	**2**	*5*	**Alfie Spinner (IRE)**[25] 2953 9-11-1 **128**.................................... APMcCoy (Nick Williams) *sn led: hdd at omitted 3rd last: styd on same pce run-in* **7/1**[3]	136
U4P-	**3**	*1 ½*	**Ballypatrick (IRE)**[26] 2923 8-10-10 **123**....................... DominicElsworth (Mick Channon) *pressed ldrs: rdn omitted 3rd last: styd on run-in but no ch w wnr* **20/1**	130
/05-	**4**	*2 ¼*	**Our Island (IRE)**[39] 2670 9-10-6 **119**.............................(p) AidanColeman (Tim Vaughan) *pressed ldr: rdn omitted 3rd last: styd on same pce fr omitted 2nd last* **8/1**	123
/P0-	**5**	*24*	**Quinz (FR)**[33] 2800 10-11-10 **137**.................................... RichardJohnson (Philip Hobbs) *in tch to 1/2-way* **25/1**	117
/01-	**6**	*3 ¼*	**De La Bech**[25] 2943 7-11-1 **128**... TomO'Brien (Philip Hobbs) *chsd ldrs: wknd bef omitted 4th last* **5/1**[1]	105
41P-	**7**	*3*	**Handy Andy (IRE)**[32] 2812 8-11-4 **131**................................(t) JoeTizzard (Colin Tizzard) *in rr: hit 8th: wknd bef omitted 4th last* **16/1**	105
253-	**P**		**Pigeon Island**[19] 3067 11-11-5 **132**........................(vt) SamTwiston-Davies (Nigel Twiston-Davies) *a in rr: t.o whn p.u bef omitted 4th last* **16/1**	
2F1-	**P**		**Bendant**[40] 2650 9-10-4 **117**...(v) IanPopham (Debra Hamer) *chsd ldrs: wknd after bypassed 4th last: t.o whn p.u bef omitted 2 out* **25/1**	
/51-	**P**		**Alvarado (IRE)**[46] 2502 9-11-12 **139**....................................... PaulMoloney (Fergal O'Brien) *in rr: blnd 10th: t.o whn p.u sn after* **12/1**	
530-	**P**		**Bradley**[25] 2953 10-11-5 **132**...(b[1]) PaddyBrennan (Fergal O'Brien) *chsd ldrs: wknd omitted 4th last: t.o whn p.u bef last* **8/1**	
00U-	**U**		**Restless Harry**[4] 3366 10-10-9 **122**.. CharliePoste (Robin Dickin) *in tch tl blnd and uns rdr 9th* **11/2**[2]	
F/2-	**P**		**Allthekingshorses (IRE)**[27] 2909 8-10-6 **122**...............(tp) JamesBest(3) (Philip Hobbs) *blnd and rdr lost irons 2nd: t.o whn p.u bef omitted 4th last* **12/1**	

7m 22.16s (28.36) **Going Correction** +1.325s/f (Heav) **13** Ran SP% **118.9**
Speed ratings: **110,108,108,107,100 99,98, , , ,**
CSF £54.43 CT £933.86 TOTE £6.60: £2.70, £2.40, £7.10; EX 41.70 Trifecta £2176.40.
Owner The Mendip Syndicate **Bred** Miss E Hamilton **Trained** Seaborough, Dorset

The Form Book Jumps, Raceform Ltd, Compton, RG20 6NL.

FOCUS
Nine fences were omitted in this good handicap chase, with a particularly long jumping-free run between what is normally the fifth-last and the final fence. It turned into a real slog and only a handful gave their running. The winner is a high-class novice and there is more to come.

3456 CHELTENHAM PONY CLUB RACEDAY NOVICES' CHASE (REGISTERED THE DIPPER NOVICES' STEEPLE CHASE) GRADE 2
(11 fncs 6 omitted) **2m 5f**
1:20 (1:20) (Class 1) 5-Y-0+ **£18,224** (£6,838; £3,424; £1,705)

/21- **1** **Oscar Whisky (IRE)**[19] 3064 9-11-7 0 BarryGeraghty 154+
(Nicky Henderson) *trckd ldr: chal fr 7th: upsides fr omitted 4 out tl slt ld omitted 2 out: rdn last: drvn out run-in and a doing enough* **5/6**[1]

113- **2** ¾ **Taquin Du Seuil (FR)**[25] 2950 7-11-7 147 APMcCoy 154+
(Jonjo O'Neill) *trckd ldrs in 3rd: qckncd to chal omitted 2 out: drvn and stmbld on landing last: tried to rally and kpt on but a jst hld* **6/4**[2]

/0F- **3** 14 **Close House**[19] 3064 7-11-0 0 (t) PaddyBrennan 133+
(David Pipe) *nvr jumping w much fluency in cl 4th: hdwy to cl on ldng duo omitted 2nd last: sn rdn: nt fluent again and wknd last* **10/1**[3]

342- **4** 1½ **Timesawastin (IRE)**[25] 2945 8-11-0 128 PaulMoloney 132
(Evan Williams) *sn led: rdn and jnd omitted 2nd last: wknd bef last* **25/1**

5m 44.2s (24.80) **Going Correction** +1.45s/f (Heav) 4 Ran SP% **107.5**
Speed ratings: **110,109,104,103**
CSF £2.51 TOTE £1.80; EX 2.30 Trifecta £3.00.
Owner Walters Plant Hire Ltd **Bred** Stephanie Hanly **Trained** Upper Lambourn, Berks

FOCUS
A good running of this Grade 2 event, which was won by subsequent Arkle winner My Way De Solzen in 2007 and by Champion Court when it was last run in 2012. It wasn't exactly a dawdle, but the lack of obstacles contributed to all four runners being more or less in line passing the omitted second-last, before the big guns sprinted away. The first two are obvious Jewcon material but still 7-10lb shy of what is likely to be required to win.

3457 REWARDS4RACING H'CAP HURDLE (12 hdls) 3m
1:55 (1:55) (Class 2) 4-Y-0+ **£12,558** (£3,742; £1,894; £970; £508)

Form RPR

/12- **1** **Return Spring (IRE)**[19] 3069 7-10-13 **134** RichardJohnson 142+
(Philip Hobbs) *chsd ldrs: wnt 2nd 4 out: led wl bef last: drvn and styd on wl run-in* **7/2**[1]

/5P- **2** 3¼ **Quartz De Thaix (FR)**[25] 2943 10-11-7 **142** (b[1]) LiamTreadwell 145
(Venetia Williams) *t.k.h: chal fr 5th tl led 7th: rdn 2 out: hdd wl bef last: swtchd lft and sn ev ch: kpt on u.p run-in: no imp on wnr but wl clr of 3rd* **16/1**

0/3- **3** 28 **Florafern**[39] 2663 9-9-11 **123** ThomasGarner(5) 98
(Oliver Sherwood) *in rr: hdwy fr 2 out: tk wl: hld 3rd run-in* **15/2**

11/ **4** 7 **Whispering Gallery**[316] 4304 8-11-9 **144** BarryGeraghty 114
(John Ferguson) *sn stdd towards rr but in tch: hdwy and racd wd after 4 out: trckd ldrs 2 out: wknd bef last and dropped to wl hld 4th run-in* **11/2**[3]

/0U- **5** 11 **The Giant Bolster**[25] 2938 9-11-3 **145** JakeHodson(7) 102
(David Bridgwater) *led tl hdd and hit 7th: sn drvn: wknd bef 2 out* **7/1**

500- **P** **Burton Port (IRE)**[19] 3067 10-11-0 **135** APMcCoy
(Jonjo O'Neill) *chsd ldrs: pushed along and hit 7th: blnd 8th: in tch again 3 out: wknd next and p.u bef last* **12/1**

/44- **P** **Poungach (FR)**[14] 3165 8-11-12 **147** (p) DarylJacob
(Paul Nicholls) *in rr: hit 6th: t.o whn p.u bef last* **12/1**

113/ **P** **Grand Vision (IRE)**[656] 4883 8-11-6 **141** JoeTizzard
(Colin Tizzard) *t.k.h: sn chsng ldrs: hit 4 out: wknd 3 out: t.o whn p.u bef last* **4/1**[2]

5/ **P** **Astigos (FR)**[45] 7-10-0 **121** oh1 AidanColeman
(Venetia Williams) *in rr: hit 8th: hdwy 3 out: chsd ldrs sn after: hit 2 out and wknd: t.o whn p.u bef last* **8/1**

6m 28.69s (27.69) **Going Correction** +1.45s/f (Heav) 9 Ran SP% **114.2**
Speed ratings (Par 109): **111,109,100,98,94 , , ,**
CSF £54.19 CT £394.35 TOTE £4.10: £1.70, £5.30, £2.60; EX 69.30 Trifecta £735.50.
Owner D J Jones **Bred** A V Bloodstock **Trained** Withycombe, Somerset

FOCUS
Big Buck's took this race five years ago before embarking on an 18-race winning streak. This was a decent handicap, but the deteriorating conditions took their toll. The first two finished clear and there's a case for rating the form a lot higher.

3458 FAIRLAWNE H'CAP CHASE (GRADE 3) (11 fncs 6 omitted) 2m 5f
2:30 (2:30) (Class 1) 5-Y-0+ **£28,977** (£11,187; £5,852; £3,167)

Form RPR

321- **1** **Double Ross (IRE)**[18] 3082 8-11-5 **140** SamTwiston-Davies 146+
(Nigel Twiston-Davies) *blnd 1st: hit 4th and sn chsng ldrs: led appr omitted 3rd last: rdn run-in and kpt on wl* **11/8**[1]

/02- **2** 4½ **Cedre Bleu (FR)**[11] 3199 7-11-6 **141** (bt) DarylJacob 143
(Paul Nicholls) *in rr but in tch: blnd 9th: stdy hdwy to trck ldrs omitted 3rd last: wnt 2nd appr last: sn rdn: fnd no ex and one pce run-in* **9/2**[2]

040- **3** 11 **Kumbeshwar**[46] 2503 7-11-10 **145** (b) WayneHutchinson 134
(Alan King) *pressed ldr: pushed along fr 8th: stl ev ch u.p omitted 2nd last: wknd run-in* **12/1**

/01- **4** 11¾ **Pickamus (FR)**[28] 2889 11-11-1 **136** RobertThornton 113
(Henry Daly) *led but hrd pressed tl hdd appr omitted 3rd last: wknd appr last* **14/1**

/00- **P** **Carrickboy (IRE)**[46] 2503 10-11-7 **142** LiamTreadwell
(Venetia Williams) *chsd ldrs: wknd omitted 4th last: t.o whn p.u bef last* **11/2**[3]

130- **P** **Drumshambo (USA)**[18] 3080 8-11-12 **147** AidanColeman
(Venetia Williams) *in tch tl wknd 9th: t.o whn p.u bef last* **10/1**

/26- **P** **Ackertac (IRE)**[33] 2800 9-11-10 **145** (b) RichardJohnson
(Tim Vaughan) *in tch fr 4th: hit 8th: blnd and bhd 10th: t.o whn p.u bef last* **6/1**

5m 47.37s (27.97) **Going Correction** +1.575s/f (Heav) 7 Ran SP% **113.4**
Speed ratings: **109,107,103,98, ,**
CSF £8.26 CT £50.00 TOTE £2.40: £1.80, £2.50; EX 8.10 Trifecta £64.90.
Owner Options O Syndicate **Bred** T McIlhagga **Trained** Naunton, Gloucs

■ Stewards' Enquiry : Wayne Hutchinson seven-day ban; used whip above permitted level (15th-21st Jan)

FOCUS
The weights rose 10lb at the overnight stage in this decent handicap chase. The winner is rated in line with his C&D win.

3459 DORNAN ENGINEERING HURDLE (10 hdls) 2m 4f 110y
3:05 (3:05) (Class 2) 4-Y-0+ **£15,640** (£4,620; £2,310)

Form RPR

1/1- **1** **Annie Power (IRE)**[39] 2665 6-11-5 159 RWalsh 164+
(W P Mullins, Ire) *trckd ldr: chal 2 out and sn led: nt fluent last: shkn up and c readily clr: easily* **2/5**[1]

/22- **2** 8 **Zarkandar (IRE)**[18] 3083 7-11-12 166 DarylJacob 161
(Paul Nicholls) *racd in 3rd tl hdwy to go 2nd sn after 2 out: pushed along to chal and nt fluent last: sn no ex and easily outpcd by wnr* **2/1**[2]

F/0- **3** 37 **Empire Levant (USA)**[18] 3088 7-11-4 132 NickScholfield 121
(Paul Nicholls) *led tl hit 2 out and hdd: sn wl bhd* **33/1**[3]

5m 25.46s (24.46) **Going Correction** +1.575s/f (Heav) 3 Ran SP% **107.7**
Speed ratings (Par 109): **116,112,98**
CSF £1.61 TOTE £1.40; EX 1.20 Trifecta £1.10.
Owner Mrs S Ricci **Bred** Eamon Cleary **Trained** Muine Beag, Co Carlow

FOCUS
A fascinating event despite the small field, with a very impressive winner.

3460 EBF "HIGH SHERIFF OF GLOUCESTERSHIRE'S" "JUNIOR" STANDARD OPEN NATIONAL HUNT FLAT RACE (LISTED RACE) 1m 6f 110y
3:40 (3:40) (Class 1) 4-Y-0 **£11,888** (£4,452; £2,224; £1,110)

Form RPR

1- **1** **Modus**[71] 2015 4-10-12 0 TomO'Brien 123+
(Robert Stephens) *in tch: hdwy 3f out: led wl over 1f out: pushed clr: easily* **5/1**[3]

1- **2** 13 **Adeupas D'Ycy (FR)**[26] 2926 4-10-12 0 BarryGeraghty 108
(Nicky Henderson) *in tch: hdwy 3f out: chsd wnr wl over 1f out and kpt on but nvr any ch* **7/2**[2]

3 ¾ **Solstice Star** 4-10-12 0 AidanColeman 107+
(Anthony Honeyball) *in rr: hdwy 3f out: styd on to take 3rd wl over 1f out: clsd on 2nd nr fin but nvr any ch w wnr* **22/1**

4 7 **City Supreme (IRE)** 4-10-9 0 RachaelGreen(3) 98
(Anthony Honeyball) *in rr: hdwy over 3f out: styd on fnl 2f: nvr a threat* **16/1**

3- **5** 2 **Looks Like Power (IRE)**[71] 2015 4-10-12 0 RobertThornton 96
(Debra Hamer) *chsd ldr: led over 3f out: hdd wl over 1f out: sn btn* **33/1**

6 10 **Colin's Brother** 4-10-12 0 SamTwiston-Davies 84
(Nigel Twiston-Davies) *in rr: styd on fnl 2f: nvr a threat* **12/1**

1- **7** ½ **Lady Buttons**[25] 2960 4-10-0 0 AdamNicol(5) 76
(Philip Kirby) *chsd ldrs: wknd 3f out* **6/1**

11- **8** ½ **Coyaba**[32] 2830 4-10-12 0 IanPopham 83
(Martin Keighley) *chsd ldrs: rdn over 3f out: sn wknd* **9/4**[1]

9 4 **Sandy Beach** 4-10-12 0 JoeTizzard 78
(Colin Tizzard) *chsd ldrs tl wknd over 3f out* **16/1**

21- **10** 18 **Puzzle Time**[42] 2604 4-10-5 0 PaddyBrennan 49
(Giles Bravery) *led tl hdd over 3f out: sn wknd* **16/1**

3m 43.22s (223.22) 10 Ran SP% **116.6**
CSF £22.85 TOTE £6.20: £2.10, £1.70, £6.70; EX 22.60 Trifecta £727.20.
Owner D J Deer **Bred** D J And Mrs Deer **Trained** Penhow, Newport

FOCUS
One of the best races of its type, this was won by The New One when it was last held two years ago. The hurdles were left in place due to the ground and the runners had to weave their way past them. Given the atrocious conditions it's understandable that a lot of these inexperienced youngsters didn't give their running. The winner looks a good prospect.
T/Jkpt: £4,612.10 to a £1 stake. Pool: £74,704.28 - 11.50 winning units T/Plt: £1,147.10 to a £1 stake. Pool: £148,329.64 - 94.39 winning units T/Qpdt: £6.40 to a £1 stake. Pool: £16,104.51 - 1,846.30 winning units ST

[3168]EXETER (R-H)
Wednesday, January 1
3461 Meeting Abandoned - waterlogged

[3148]FAKENHAM (L-H)
Wednesday, January 1
OFFICIAL GOING: Soft (5.2) changing to heavy after race 4 (2.05)
Wind: Strong; against Weather: Rain

3468 BET TOTEJACKPOT (S) HURDLE (11 hdls) 2m 4f
12:20 (12:20) (Class 5) 4-Y-0+ **£2,053** (£598; £299)

Form RPR

P21- **1** **Stow**[5] 3324 9-11-2 117 (p) JoshWall(7) 113+
(Michael Blake) *in tch: nt fluent 2nd: trckd ldrs 7th: wnt 2nd bef 3 out: led bef 2 out and sn clr: eased flat: v easily* **1/3**[1]

230- **2** 23 **County Zen (FR)**[15] 3149 11-11-2 97 MissBAndrews(7) 87
(Caroline Fryer) *led: reminders after 7th: drvn bef 3 out: hdd bef 2 out and immediately btn: tired flat but plugged to hold 2nd* **20/1**

420- **3** 7 **Monroe Park (IRE)**[27] 2894 9-10-13 77 (p) JosephAkehurst(7) 77
(Alan Blackmore) *chsd ldr: rdn bef 8th: 3rd and btn 3 out: wknd wl bef next* **50/1**

44P- **4** 7 **Persian Herald**[5] 3324 6-11-9 105 (bt) TrevorWhelan(3) 78
(Neil King) *in tch: reminders after 3rd: drvn and dropped to last pair bef 5th: nvr gng after: lost tch u.p sn after 3 out* **9/2**[2]

4P6- **P** **Safe Investment (USA)**[68] 2067 10-10-13 0 (vt) CharlieDeutsch(7)
(Lawney Hill) *chsd ldrs tl rdn and lost pl after 7th: lost tch bef 3 out: t.o whn blnd 2 out: p.u last* **12/1**[3]

P **Good As New**[12] 4-9-11 0 JackQuinlan(3)
(Denis Quinn) *a in rr: rdn and qckly lost tch 7th: t.o and blnd next: immediately p.u* **66/1**

5m 34.6s (22.00) **Going Correction** +1.225s/f (Heav)
WFA 4 from 5yo+ 12lb 6 Ran SP% **109.1**
Speed ratings (Par 103): **105,95,93,90,**
CSF £8.00 TOTE £1.30: £1.10, £4.70; EX 7.20 Trifecta £86.90.No bid for the winner. Persian Herald was claimed by Mrs J B Pye for £4,000.
Owner Mrs J M Haines **Bred** Plantation Stud **Trained** Trowbridge, Wilts

FOCUS
A weak seller.

3469 FAKENHAM RACECOURSE ANNUAL MEMBERS MAIDEN HURDLE (9 hdls) 2m
12:55 (12:55) (Class 5) 4-Y-0+ **£2,053** (£598; £299)

Form RPR

- **1** **Fennell Bay (IRE)**[77] 5-11-2 0 .... JackQuinlan(3) 115+
(John Ferguson) *chsd ldrs: 3rd and rdn after 3 out: led between last 2: sn clr and styd on strly: rdn out* **11/8**[1]

6/0- **2** *14* **Cappielow Park**[15] 3149 5-10-12 85 .... (p) MikeyEnnis(7) 99
(Fleur Hawes) *chsd ldrs: wnt 2nd sn after 5th: led bef 3 out: rdn and hdd between last 2: sn brushed aside by wnr: mstke last: tired flat but hld on gamely for 2nd* **66/1**

3 *nk* **Polstar (FR)**[108] 5-11-5 0 .... JamesDavies 98
(Harry Whittington) *in tch in midfield: chsd ldrs after 5th: rdn and ev ch after 3 out: no ex u.p and btn between last 2: plugged on flat* **7/1**

50- **4** *26* **Focail Maith**[6] 3269 6-11-2 117 .... (p) TrevorWhelan(3) 72
(Neil King) *in tch in midfield: hdwy 6th: 4th and cl enough 3 out: rdn and btn bef next: wknd between last 2: t.o* **7/2**[2]

5 *6* **Ossie's Dancer**[47] 5-11-5 0 .... LeightonAspell 66
(Martin Smith) *nt a fluent: in tch in rr: rdn and btn 3 out: wl bhd and blnd next: t.o* **50/1**

6 *48* **Impertinent**[71] 4-10-0 0 .... ConorO'Farrell
(Noel Quinlan) *chsd ldr tl led 4th: hdd bef 3 out and sn dropped out: t.o bef 2 out* **20/1**

P **Rockweiller**[70] 7-11-5 0 .... JamieMoore
(Steve Gollings) *in tch in midfield: 5th and drvn bef 3 out: sn struggling: lost tch bef 2 out: t.o whn p.u between last 2* **9/1**

P2/ **P** **Intent (IRE)**[309] 4434 5-10-12 0 .... TomMessenger
(Chris Bealby) *hld up in tch in rr: mstke 6th: sn lost tch and p.u next* **13/2**[3]

P **Wrecking Ball (IRE)**[48] 4-10-4 0 .... JoshuaMoore(3)
(Amy Weaver) *led tl 4th: lost pl qckly sn after next: tailing off whn eased and p.u 6th* **25/1**

00/ **P** **Izza Diva**[249] 5572 6-10-7 0 .... BenPoste(5)
(John Holt) *in tch in last trio: rdn and lost tch 5th: t.o whn p.u after 6th* **100/1**

0P0- **P** **Secret Island**[10] 3226 5-10-12 0 .... MarcGoldstein
(Anthony Day) *in tch in midfield on outer: lost pl and struggling u.p after 5th: t.o whn p.u after 6th* **100/1**

4m 27.95s (22.55) **Going Correction** +1.475s/f (Heav)
WFA 4 from 5yo+ 11lb 11 Ran SP% **114.2**
Speed ratings (Par 103): **102,95,94,81,78 54,,,,**
CSF £127.81 TOTE £3.00: £1.30, £13.70, £3.10; EX 81.30 Trifecta £185.40 Part won..
Owner Bloomfields **Bred** J R Wills **Trained** Cowlinge, Suffolk

FOCUS
An intriguing maiden hurdle. The winner is entitled to rate a lot higher on his Flat form.

3470 FAKENHAM AMATEUR RIDERS' H'CAP CHASE (16 fncs) 2m 5f 110y
1:30 (1:33) (Class 5) (0-100,100) 5-Y-0+ **£3,520** (£1,152; £620)

Form RPR

2U3- **1** **Full Ov Beans**[16] 3139 10-10-8 87 .... MissAEStirling(5) 99+
(Michael Gates) *chsd ldr tl lft in ld: hmpd 2nd and almost carried out bnd sn after: mde rest: mstke 4th and 10th: drew clr fr 11th: in n.d fr next: rdn out* **7/2**[3]

4U4- **2** *57* **Minella Ranger (IRE)**[43] 2575 8-10-9 90 .... MrGBranton(7) 45
(Paul Henderson) *sn bhd and nvr gng wl: lft 3rd 2nd: niggled along fr 5th: lost tch 9th: t.o after 11th: wnt poor 2nd sn after 2 out* **5/2**[2]

061- **3** *16* **Zhukov (IRE)**[6] 3248 12-11-4 99 7ex .... (b) MrGGorman(7) 38
(Kevin Tork) *j.lft 1st: lft chsng wnr and hmpd 2nd: mstke 6th and 10th: rdn and struggling after next: wl btn and slowing fr 13th: t.o next: lost 2nd sn after 2 out* **12/1**

405- **U** **King Ozzy (IRE)**[15] 3151 10-11-5 100 .... (tp) MrJoeHill(7)
(Lawney Hill) *led: j. bdly lft: sddle slipped and uns rdr 2nd* **6/1**

452- **R** **Upton Mead (IRE)**[6] 3246 7-11-5 100 .... (b) MrMJPKendrick(7)
(Kevin Tork) *sltly hmpd and ref 1st* **7/4**[1]

6m 8.0s (26.20) **Going Correction** +1.25s/f (Heav) 5 Ran SP% **109.1**
Speed ratings: **102,81,75,,**
CSF £12.56 TOTE £3.90: £1.80, £1.30; EX 11.50 Trifecta £103.80.
Owner Michael Gates **Bred** Miss A Thompson **Trained** Clifford Chambers, Warwicks
■ Amaury De Lusignan (8-1) was withdrawn. Rule 4 applies to board prices prior to withdrawal. Deduction - 10p in the pound. New market formed.

FOCUS
A weak handicap chase but no shortage of drama. The winner is rated back to his best.

3471 POW GRANDSTAND FOR PRIVATE FUNCTIONS H'CAP HURDLE (11 hdls) 2m 4f
2:05 (2:05) (Class 3) (0-125,125) 4-Y-0+ **£6,173** (£1,812; £906; £453)

Form RPR

600- **1** **Maller Tree**[25] 2944 7-11-5 125 .... (v) KieronEdgar(3) 135+
(David Dennis) *w ldr and travelled strly thrght: hit 6th: led sn after 3 out and readily wnt clr: in n.d whn hit last: easily* **12/1**

122- **2** *22* **Brass Monkey (IRE)**[6] 3249 7-10-0 102 .... TrevorWhelan(3) 89
(Neil King) *chsd ldrs: 3rd and rdn bef 3 out: no ch w wnr but wnt 2nd wl bef last: no imp* **7/2**[2]

006- **3** *2 ¼* **Daliance (IRE)**[11] 3195 5-9-12 102 .... (p) MattCrawley(5) 86
(Lucy Wadham) *in tch in midfield: rdn bef 8th: wnt modest 4th 3 out: no ch w wnr but plugged on to go 3rd between last 2: mstke last* **5/1**

/40- **4** *6* **Vasco D'Ycy (FR)**[39] 2671 5-11-3 119 .... JackQuinlan(3) 98
(Sarah Humphrey) *led: mstke 3 out: sn hdd and drvn: sn brushed aside by wnr and wl btn next: lost 2 pls between last 2* **4/1**[3]

313- **5** *1 ½* **Wither Yenot (IRE)**[15] 3151 7-10-3 109 .... MrMJPKendrick(7) 86
(Ben Case) *nvr really jumping fluently: in tch in last pair: rdn 5th: struggling 8th: lost tch after 3 out: no ch whn nt clr run flat* **5/1**

144/ **P** **Bantry Bere (IRE)**[1025] 4750 10-10-6 112 .... MikeyEnnis(7)
(Fleur Hawes) *in tch in rr: mstke 3rd: rdn after next: sn struggling: losing tch whn p.u 6th* **33/1**

50F- **P** **Occasionally Yours (IRE)**[43] 2574 10-10-12 111 .... MarcGoldstein
(Alan Blackmore) *in tch in midfield: rdn and lost pl 5th: rallied u.p after next: lost pl again and bhd after 7th: t.o whn p.u 3 out* **20/1**

403- **P** **Scots Gaelic (IRE)**[23] 3000 7-11-10 123 .... JamieMoore
(John Quinn) *chsd ldrs: rdn and wknd after 8th: dropped to last 3 out and lost tch: t.o whn p.u 2 out* **10/3**[1]

5m 43.6s (31.00) **Going Correction** +1.725s/f (Heav) 8 Ran SP% **114.0**
Speed ratings (Par 107): **107,98,97,94,94 ,,**
CSF £54.35 CT £241.25 TOTE £15.80: £3.40, £1.90, £2.10; EX 79.00 TRIFECTA Not won..
Owner Favourites Racing **Bred** Phil Toft **Trained** Hanley Swan, Worcestershire

FOCUS
A fair handicap hurdle. There's a case for rating the form up to 10lb higher.

3472 PHYLLIS AND WILFRED TARRANT MEMORIAL NOVICES' H'CAP CHASE (16 fncs) 2m 5f 110y
2:40 (2:40) (Class 5) (0-100,98) 5-Y-0+ **£2,937** (£997)

Form RPR

5P2- **1** **Tony Dinozzo (FR)**[21] 3026 7-11-12 98 .... (p) JamieMoore 110
(Peter Bowen) *chsd ldr: led 3rd tl 4th: chsd ldr after tl led bef 13th: drew clr fr 3 out: in command whn lft wl clr last: eased flat* **2/1**[1]

454- **2** *57* **Bit Of A Clown (IRE)**[16] 3139 8-11-7 93 .... TomCannon 48
(Nick Gifford) *racd wd: in tch: mstke 6th and rdn: nvr travelling after but rallied to chse ldrs 8th: wknd12th: lft poor 3rd 3 out: t.o whn lft 2nd last* **5/2**[2]

34P- **F** **Killegney**[13] 3179 10-10-11 90 .... (v[1]) MissAEStirling(7) 87
(Michael Gates) *led tl 3rd: led again next: hdd bef 13th: rdn and wknd bef 2 out: 12 l down whn fell last* **10/1**

FP3- **F** **Shannon Spirit (IRE)**[15] 3152 9-11-9 95 .... LeightonAspell
(Paul Henderson) *chsd ldrs: 3rd and outpcd by ldng pair after 11th: effrt to dispute 4 l 2nd whn fell 3 out* **6/1**

P2F- **R** **Jim Job Jones**[41] 2619 10-9-7 72 oh1 .... (tp) ConorRing(7)
(Neil Mulholland) *in tch: rdn 8th: j. slowly next: struggling and j. slowly 11th: lost tch next: lft poor 3rd and ref 3 out* **4/1**[3]

U4U- **P** **Ninfea (IRE)**[15] 3152 6-11-6 95 .... (p) TrevorWhelan(3)
(Neil King) *in tch in rr: mstke 2nd: j. slowly next: mstke 6th: sn rdn and struggling: lost tch 11th: t.o whn p.u 13th* **14/1**

6m 10.5s (28.70) **Going Correction** +1.25s/f (Heav) 6 Ran SP% **111.9**
Speed ratings: **97,76,,,**
CSF £7.71 TOTE £2.20: £1.10, £1.80; EX 7.40 Trifecta £4.20.
Owner John Andrews **Bred** P D Jones, S Jones, T Jones **Trained** Little Newcastle, Pembrokes

FOCUS
A modest handicap chase in which only two completed. This was possibly a step up from the winner.

3473 FAKENHAM GOLF CLUB 125 YEAR ANNIVERSARY H'CAP HURDLE (13 hdls) 2m 7f 110y
3:15 (3:15) (Class 4) (0-110,108) 4-Y-0+ **£3,249** (£954; £477; £238)

Form RPR

21F- **1** **The Young Master**[19] 2690 5-11-2 103 .... (p) ConorShoemark(5) 114+
(Neil Mulholland) *taken down early: chsd ldr 3rd: led sn after 3 out and readily drew clr: mstke last: r.o strly* **11/4**[1]

351- **2** *34* **Mistral Reine**[15] 3151 5-11-9 105 .... LeightonAspell 82
(Lucy Wadham) *racd wd: in tch: hdwy to chse ldrs 8th: rdn bef 3 out: 3rd and no ch w wnr between last 2: wnt poor 2nd last* **4/1**[2]

/05- **3** *2 ¼* **Torrential Raine**[31] 2842 6-10-13 102 .... JoshWall(7) 77
(Michael Blake) *in tch in rr: rdn and effrt bef 3 out: chsd clr wnr after 3 out: no imp and wl btn between last 2: lost 2nd last* **11/4**[1]

422- **4** *34* **Larteta (FR)**[20] 3029 5-11-5 108 .... MikeyEnnis(7) 49
(Sarah Humphrey) *led tl rdn and hdd after 3 out: sn wknd: 4th and t.o next* **7/1**[3]

234- **5** *¾* **Riddlestown (IRE)**[15] 3151 7-11-3 102 .... TrevorWhelan(3) 42
(Caroline Fryer) *in tch: rdn after next: drvn and struggling next: last and fading whn blnd 3 out: t.o bef next* **15/2**

5/3- **P** **Peterbrown (IRE)**[239] 163 6-11-11 107 .... TomCannon
(Nick Gifford) *chsd ldr tl 3rd: chsd ldrs after: rdn bef 8th: dropped to last and mstke 9th: sn lost tch: t.o whn p.u 3 out* **8/1**

6m 57.3s (50.90) **Going Correction** +1.975s/f (Heav) 6 Ran SP% **108.7**
Speed ratings (Par 105): **94,82,81,70,70**
CSF £13.22 TOTE £2.90: £1.80, £2.20; EX 13.10 Trifecta £74.70.
Owner Dajam Ltd **Bred** Brendan Boyle **Trained** Limpley Stoke, Wilts

FOCUS
A trappy handicap hurdle. The easy winner is rated in line with the level of his recent Flat win.
T/Plt: £33.10 to a £1 stake. Pool: £50,433.51 - 1,110.52 winning tickets. T/Qpdt: £16.70 to a £1 stake. Pool: £3,803.10 - 168.30 winning tickets. SP

2996 MUSSELBURGH (R-H)
Wednesday, January 1

OFFICIAL GOING: Soft (good to soft in places; 6.3)
Wind: Slight, behind Weather: Overcast, dry

3474 TOTEPLACEPOT FIRST FOOT JUVENILE HURDLE (9 hdls) 2m
12:25 (12:25) (Class 3) 4-Y-0 **£7,797** (£2,289; £1,144; £572)

Form RPR

11- **1** **Rutherglen**[10] 3224 4-11-8 0 .... BrianHughes 127+
(John Quinn) *t.k.h: led to 3rd: w ldr: led after 4 out: rdn and edgd rt 2 out: edgd lft after last: drvn clr* **4/5**[1]

2- **2** *6* **Thorpe (IRE)**[33] 2790 4-10-7 0 .... DerekFox(5) 108
(Lucinda Russell) *t.k.h: nt fluent on occasions: cl up: led 3rd: j.lft 4 out: sn hdd: effrt and rdn next: one pce fr last* **9/2**[3]

3 *7* **Bushel (USA)**[144] 4-10-12 0 .... DenisO'Regan 103+
(John Ferguson) *novicey on occasions: hld up in tch: stdy hdwy to chse ldrs after 4 out: shkn up and edgd rt after next: sn outpcd* **7/2**[2]

4 *10* **Love Marmalade (IRE)**[88] 4-10-9 0 .... EwanWhillans(3) 91
(Alistair Whillans) *t.k.h: hld up in tch: stdy hdwy after 4 out: shkn up and wknd after next* **25/1**

41- **5** *35* **Magic Skyline (IRE)**[36] 2733 4-10-4 110 .... (t) CraigGallagher(7) 70
(Brian Ellison) *plld hrd early: cl up: overj. 1st: pushed along after 4 out: wknd fr next* **12/1**

3m 43.7s (-4.70) **Going Correction** -0.40s/f (Good) 5 Ran SP% **107.5**
Speed ratings: **95,92,88,83,66**
CSF £4.60 TOTE £1.40: £1.10, £1.90; EX 5.30 Trifecta £7.90.
Owner The Beer Swigging Strangers **Bred** Frank Brady **Trained** Settrington, N Yorks

FOCUS
Bends and hurdles moved to fresh ground. A useful performance from the winner, who's a potential 130+ hurdler.

3475 TOTEQUADPOT FOUR PLACES IN FOUR RACES H'CAP HURDLE (12 hdls) 2m 4f
1:00 (1:00) (Class 4) (0-120,120) 4-Y-0+ **£6,498** (£1,908; £954; £477)

Form RPR

136- **1** **Call Box (IRE)**[19] 3072 9-11-3 118 .... (p) CraigNichol(7) 130+
(S R B Crawford, Ire) *trckd ldrs: led after 4 out: qcknd clr next: comf* **3/1**[1]

444- 2 8 **Los Nadis (GER)**[23] 2996 10-11-8 **116** RyanMania 115
(Jim Goldie) *led to 3rd: w ldr to 8th: drvn and outpcd after 4 out: rallied to chse (clr) wnr appr 2 out: kpt on: no imp* **5/1**[2]

/P5- 3 4 ½ **Divers (FR)**[23] 3000 10-11-12 **120** (b) TimmyMurphy 117+
(Donald McCain) *hld up: hit 4 out: effrt and pushed along next: edgd rt whn nt fluent 2 out: sn no ex* **5/1**[2]

/10- 4 1 ½ **Unex Canaletto**[25] 2936 5-10-12 **106** BrianHughes 99
(James Ewart) *prom: effrt and pushed along bef 3 out: outpcd fr next* **7/1**[3]

524- 5 9 **Biggar (IRE)**[33] 2792 6-10-6 **107** GrahamWatters(7) 94
(Lucinda Russell) *in tch: pushed along and outpcd 1/2-way: rallied 2 out: no imp whn blnd last* **5/1**[2]

/24- 6 10 **Merchant Of Dubai**[23] 3000 9-11-4 **112** DenisO'Regan 88
(Jim Goldie) *hld up: hit 3rd: rdn after 4 out: wknd next: btn whn hit last* **5/1**[2]

16P- 7 15 **Damascus Steel (IRE)**[24] 2970 6-11-4 **112** BrianHarding 81
(Alison Hamilton) *t.k.h: w ldr: led 3rd to after 4 out: rdn next: styd chsng wnr tl wknd appr 2 out* **12/1**

4m 47.5s (-4.00) **Going Correction** -0.40s/f (Good) **7 Ran SP% 111.9**
Speed ratings (Par 105): **92,88,87,86,82 78,72**
CSF £17.58 TOTE £4.10: £2.00, £3.20; EX 17.50 Trifecta £120.00.
Owner Pircan Partnership **Bred** David Fenton **Trained** Larne, Co Antrim

FOCUS
A pretty uncompetitive handicap as it turned out, the winner having matters under control a long way out.

3476 TOTEPOOL.COM SCOTTISH PREMIER CHASE (H'CAP) (16 fncs) 2m 4f
1:35 (1:35) (Class 3) (0-140,139) 5-Y-0+ **£16,245** (£4,770; £2,385; £1,192)

Form RPR

503- 1 **Mr Moonshine (IRE)**[25] 2937 10-11-9 **136** RyanMania 146+
(Sue Smith) *trckd ldr: led 5 out: rdn whn pressed 2 out: styd on gamely fr last* **4/1**[2]

366- 2 2 ¼ **Viva Colonia (IRE)**[25] 2952 9-11-12 **139** TimmyMurphy 147
(Brian Ellison) *t.k.h: hld up: smooth hdwy bef 4 out: chsd wnr next: effrt after 2 out: swtchd lft run-in: kpt on: hld nr fin* **4/1**[2]

323- 3 7 **Bar De Ligne (FR)**[33] 2782 8-10-11 **124** (p) PeterBuchanan 126
(Steve Gollings) *prom: rdn and outpcd 4 out: rallied 2 out: chsd clr ldng pair last: no imp* **9/2**[3]

/34- 4 nk **Upsilon Bleu (FR)**[33] 2800 6-11-10 **137** DenisO'Regan 141
(Pauline Robson) *t.k.h early: trckd ldrs: nt fluent 10th: wnt 2nd bef 4 out to next: sn outpcd: lost 3rd last: no imp* **11/4**[1]

4F0- 5 8 **Sleep In First (FR)**[24] 2970 8-11-0 **127** BrianHughes 122
(James Ewart) *in tch: hmpd and mstke 3rd: effrt and rdn 4 out: wknd fr next* **25/1**

330- 6 8 **Full Jack (FR)**[33] 2800 7-11-4 **131** BrianHarding 118
(Pauline Robson) *prom: j.rt and blkd 3rd: sn dropped to last pl and pushed along: struggling fr 10th: n.d after* **12/1**

013- 7 11 **Quito Du Tresor (FR)**[33] 2793 10-10-5 **125** (p) CraigNichol(7) 99
(Lucinda Russell) *prom: nt fluent and rdn 5 out: sn drvn and outpcd: struggling fr next: no ch whn hit last* **10/1**

651- P **Kealigolane (IRE)**[23] 3001 10-11-0 **127** RichieMcLernon
(Barry Murtagh) *led to 5 out: rdn and wknd qckly next: no ch whn p.u bef 2 out* **10/1**

5m 0.7s (-0.50) **Going Correction** +0.225s/f (Yiel) **8 Ran SP% 114.6**
Speed ratings: **110,109,106,106,102 99,95,**
CSF £20.97 CT £73.86 TOTE £5.40: £1.70, £2.70, £2.00; EX 25.10 Trifecta £159.40.
Owner DG Pryde,J Beaumont,DP Van Der Hoeven 1 **Bred** T McIlhagga **Trained** High Eldwick, W Yorks

FOCUS
A useful contest which was run at a sound pace. Solid form, the winner's best figure for over a year.

3477 TOTEPOOL MOBILE HOGMANEIGH HURDLE H'CAP (9 hdls) 2m
2:10 (2:10) (Class 2) 4-Y-0+ **£25,992** (£7,632; £3,816; £1,908)

Form RPR

221- 1 **Strongpoint (IRE)**[23] 3000 10-11-2 **130** [1] PeterBuchanan 137+
(S R B Crawford, Ire) *led to 2nd: cl up: led bef 2 out: drvn out fr last* **9/1**

301- 2 4 **Ifandbutwhynot (IRE)**[34] 2758 8-11-11 **139** TimmyMurphy 142
(David O'Meara) *hld up: smooth hdwy bef 3 out: drifted rt bef last: effrt and chsd wnr last: kpt on same pce fnl 150yds* **13/2**[2]

/30- 3 2 ¼ **Local Hero (GER)**[165] 1046 7-11-5 **140** (p) PaulBohan(7) 140
(Steve Gollings) *prom: effrt and chsd wnr bef 2 out to last: kpt on same pce u.p* **14/1**

630- 4 1 ½ **Runswick Royal (IRE)**[18] 3088 5-11-5 **140** GrahamWatters(7) 140
(Ann Hamilton) *midfield: effrt and hdwy bef 3 out: nt fluent 2 out: kpt on same pce bef last* **17/2**[3]

3/4- 5 ¾ **Streets Of Newyork**[24] 2970 7-10-0 **114** oh5 BarryKeniry 113+
(Brian Ellison) *bhd: pushed along whn nt fluent 5th: rallied 3 out: styd on wl fr last: nt pce to chal* **12/1**

/32- 6 9 **Titus Bolt (IRE)**[24] 2970 5-9-7 **114** oh1 (v) GrantCockburn(7) 104
(Jim Goldie) *t.k.h early: cl up: led 2nd: mstke 4 out: hdd and edgd lft bef 2 out: sn wknd* **20/1**

214- 7 5 **Ultimate**[32] 2822 8-10-7 **128** CraigGallagher(7) 112
(Brian Ellison) *cl up: ev ch and rdn bef 3 out: wknd fr next* **10/1**

221- 8 10 **New Year's Eve**[83] 1839 6-10-9 **123** DenisO'Regan 103
(John Ferguson) *t.k.h early: hld up: shkn up bef 3 out: sn wknd: no ch whn mstke last* **7/2**[1]

230- 9 ½ **Bygones Of Brid (IRE)**[25] 2935 11-10-5 **126** (p) CraigNichol(7) 100
(Karen McLintock) *prom tl rdn and wknd bef 3 out* **25/1**

U03/ 10 shd **Wyse Hill Teabags**[256] 5405 9-11-2 **130** RyanMania 103
(Jim Goldie) *hld up: pushed along 1/2-way: nvr on terms* **20/1**

564- 11 2 ¾ **Deepsand (IRE)**[25] 2958 5-11-0 **128** (tp) BrianHarding 99
(Tim Easterby) *midfield: rdn after 4 out: wknd bef next* **16/1**

/4U- 12 2 ½ **Rumble Of Thunder (IRE)**[178] 901 8-10-13 **127** RichieMcGrath 95
(Philip Kirby) *hld up: struggling after 4 out: sn btn* **33/1**

110/ 13 17 **Hidden Justice (IRE)**[230] 4767 5-11-10 **138** BrianHughes 89
(John Quinn) *hld up in midfield: struggling 4 out: sn btn* **11/1**

/11- U **Zaplamation (IRE)**[25] 2958 9-10-4 **125** DeanPratt(7)
(John Quinn) *t.k.h in midfield: mstke and uns rdr 1st* **11/1**

3m 37.9s (-10.50) **Going Correction** -0.40s/f (Good) **14 Ran SP% 118.4**
Speed ratings (Par 109): **110,108,106,106,105 101,98,93,93,93 92,90,82,**
CSF £62.60 CT £823.97 TOTE £12.10: £4.20, £1.90, £5.20; EX 87.70 Trifecta £786.70.
Owner S McAlister **Bred** Seamus Murphy **Trained** Larne, Co Antrim

FOCUS
A useful and competitive handicap. It was run at a good pace, though not that many ever threatened to land a serious blow. The winner built on his recent course victory.

3478 HAPPY NEW YEAR FROM TOTEPOOL H'CAP CHASE (18 fncs) 3m
2:45 (2:45) (Class 4) (0-115,112) 5-Y-0+ **£6,498** (£1,908; £954; £477)

Form RPR

314- 1 **Swing Hard (IRE)**[11] 3211 6-11-12 **112** RyanMania 123+
(Sue Smith) *trckd ldrs: led 11th: mde rest: rdn bef 2 out: styd on gamely fr last* **5/1**[3]

/21- 2 2 ¼ **Presented (IRE)**[32] 2818 7-11-3 **103** TimmyMurphy 112
(Brian Ellison) *prom: outpcd after 10th: rallied and cl up next: rdn bef 4 out: kpt on same pce fr last* **12/5**[1]

023- 3 3 **The Magic Bishop**[41] 2623 9-11-8 **108** BrianHughes 115
(Malcolm Jefferson) *hld up: smooth hdwy to trck ldrs 4 out: effrt and swtchd between horses 2 out: sn rdn: one pce whn mstke last* **7/2**[2]

006- 4 3 ½ **Riguez Dancer**[32] 2820 10-11-12 **112** (b) AdrianLane 115
(Donald McCain) *in tch: effrt and rdn appr 4 out: outpcd next: no imp fr 2 out* **9/1**

/P5- 5 9 **Everaard (USA)**[28] 2884 8-11-7 **107** (tp) RichieMcGrath 102
(Philip Kirby) *mostly j.lft: led to 2nd: cl up: niggled fr 1/2-way: outpcd 12th: struggling after 5 out: n.d after* **5/1**[3]

313- 6 3 ¼ **Lord Of Drums (IRE)**[15] 3143 8-11-8 **108** PeterBuchanan 99
(Lucinda Russell) *t.k.h: led 2nd: hdd 11th: rallied: rdn and wknd bef 4 out* **15/2**

/64- P **Daasij (IRE)**[11] 3213 9-11-0 **100** BrianHarding
(N W Alexander) *bhd: outpcd fr 1/2-way: struggling whn mstke 6 out: sn btn: t.o whn p.u 4 out* **16/1**

6m 14.0s (10.60) **Going Correction** +0.225s/f (Yiel) **7 Ran SP% 112.6**
Speed ratings: **91,90,89,88,85 84,**
CSF £17.53 TOTE £5.40: £3.00, £1.70; EX 21.70 Trifecta £61.60.
Owner DP van der Hoeven, DG Pryde & J Beaumont **Bred** Paddy Kinsella **Trained** High Eldwick, W Yorks

FOCUS
A fair handicap, and the finish was fought out by a couple of unexposed and progressive sorts. The winner was back to the level of his Newcastle win.

3479 COLLECT TOTEPOOL WINNINGS AT BETFRED SHOPS H'CAP HURDLE (14 hdls) 3m 110y
3:20 (3:20) (Class 3) (0-140,128) 4-Y-0+ **£12,996** (£3,816; £1,908; £954)

Form RPR

323- 1 **Any Given Moment (IRE)**[18] 3085 8-10-7 **109** RyanMania 112
(Sandy Thomson) *chsd ldr: led 9th: qcknd clr bef 3 out: gd jump last: rdn and styd on strly* **11/4**[1]

21- 2 1 ¾ **Tantamount**[25] 2936 5-10-7 **116** CraigNichol(7) 117+
(Lucinda Russell) *t.k.h: hld up in tch: smooth hdwy to chse wnr bef 2 out: rdn and ch run-in: hung rt: hld towards fin* **11/4**[1]

120- 3 3 ½ **Capellanus (IRE)**[25] 2935 8-11-5 **128** CraigGallagher(7) 127
(Brian Ellison) *t.k.h: hld up in tch: nt fluent and outpcd 4 out: rallied after next: kpt on wl fr last: nt pce of first two* **9/2**[3]

/61- 4 8 **Arctic Court (IRE)**[54] 2345 10-11-7 **123** DenisO'Regan 115
(Jim Goldie) *led at stdy pce: hdd 9th: drvn and outpcd after 3 out: btn bef last* **4/1**[2]

2/1- 5 11 **Alderley Rover (IRE)**[32] 2807 10-11-9 **125** TimmyMurphy 109
(Donald McCain) *chsd ldrs: hit 6th: stdy hdwy after 4 out: rdn and wknd bef 2 out* **4/1**[2]

6m 0.1s (3.40) **Going Correction** -0.40s/f (Good) **5 Ran SP% 111.5**
Speed ratings (Par 107): **78,77,76,73,70**
CSF £10.92 TOTE £3.10: £2.10, £2.50; EX 5.50 Trifecta £47.80.
Owner Mr & Mrs A M Thomson **Bred** W Lazy T Ranch **Trained** Lambden, Berwicks

FOCUS
A bit of a disappointing turnout for the money, with the top-weight rated 12lb below the ceiling. The pace was steady until the winner pressed on after the fourth-last. Not form to be too confident in.
T/Plt: £78.70 to a £1 stake. Pool: £73,635.62 - 682.72 winning tickets. T/Qpdt: £22.00 to a £1 stake. Pool: £5,290.00 - 177.35 winning tickets. RY

3480 - 3493a (Foreign Racing) - See Raceform Interactive

2217 AYR (L-H)
Thursday, January 2

OFFICIAL GOING: Heavy (chs 7.5, hdl 7.8)
Wind: Fresh, half against Weather: Overcast, dry

3494 EBF "NATIONAL HUNT" NOVICES' HURDLE (QUALIFIER) (9 hdls) 2m
12:20 (12:22) (Class 4) 4-7-Y-0 **£3,898** (£1,144; £572; £286)

Form RPR

3/2- 1 **Fine Rightly (IRE)**[18] 3126 6-10-13 0 MrSCrawford(3) 111+
(S R B Crawford, Ire) *j.lft thrght: t.k.h: trckd ldrs: stmbld 4 out: smooth hdwy to press ldr next: pushed along bef 2 out: led bef last: styd on strly* **1/10**[1]

3- 2 2 **The Orange Rogue (IRE)**[18] 3112 7-11-2 0 BrianHarding 101
(N W Alexander) *j.w: led: rdn after 2 out: hdd whn nt fluent last: kpt on same pce* **10/1**[2]

5- 3 9 **Sudski Star (IRE)**[24] 2998 6-11-2 0 (t) BrianHughes 92
(Patrick Griffin, Ire) *trckd ldr to bef 3 out: sn rdn and outpcd: no imp fr next* **50/1**

300- 4 7 **You'resomedreamer (IRE)**[43] 2593 6-11-2 0 PeterBuchanan 85
(Lucinda Russell) *in tch: effrt bef 3 out: wknd bef next: btn whn nt fluent last* **28/1**[3]

4m 4.9s (1.80) **Going Correction** +0.325s/f (Yiel) **4 Ran SP% 105.4**
Speed ratings: **108,107,102,99**
CSF £1.67 TOTE £1.10; EX 1.60 Trifecta £6.40.
Owner Miss Patricia Duffin **Bred** Miss Patricia Duffin **Trained** Larne, Co Antrim

FOCUS
Divided bends. A planned 7.30am inspection was cancelled after just 3.5mm of rain fell in the preceding 24 hours, though steady rain had set in by the time of this opener. This was as one-sided a betting heat as you'll find in novice hurdles all season. The winner can rate a lot higher.

3495 BETVICTOR NON-RUNNER FREE BET CHELTENHAM 2014 MAIDEN HURDLE (11 hdls) 2m 4f
12:50 (12:50) (Class 5) 5-Y-0+ **£2,274** (£667; £333; £166)

Form RPR

P/4- 1 **Rinnagree Rosie**[12] 3208 8-10-7 0 AdrianLane 98
(Lucy Normile) *hld up in tch: pushed along and outpcd bef 4 out: rallied next: wnt 2nd last: styd on wl to ld cl home* **20/1**

U32- **2** *nk* **Frankie's Promise (IRE)**[32] 2838 6-11-0 109 BrianHarding 108+
(N W Alexander) *nt jump wl: led: rdn bef 2 out: styd on wl fr last: hdd cl home* **5/4**[1]

3/ **3** *4 1/2* **Little Boy Boru (IRE)**[7] 3300 6-10-11 0 EwanWhillans(3) 100
(S R B Crawford, Ire) *hld up: rdn along and hdwy after 4 out: styd on fr 2 out: no imp fr last* **28/1**

2/ **4** *6* **Mclovin (IRE)**[43] 2606 8-10-11 0 MrSCrawford(3) 97
(S R B Crawford, Ire) *hld up: nt fluent 2nd: smooth hdwy to chse ldr bef 2 out: rdn and tired whn lost 2nd last: sn btn* **7/2**[2]

0/6- **5** *3/4* **Finaghy Ayr (IRE)**[61] 2217 6-10-7 0 GrahamWatters(7) 93
(Ian Duncan) *pressed ldr: drvn after 4 out: outpcd fr 2 out* **33/1**

23- **6** *13* **Vasco Pierji (FR)**[30] 2871 5-11-0 0 JasonMaguire 89
(Donald McCain) *chsd ldrs: drvn and outpcd after 7th: no ch after* **11/2**

7 *9* **Happy River (IRE)**[606] 7-11-0 0 PeterBuchanan 71
(Lucinda Russell) *hld up bhd ldng gp: stdy hdwy and prom 1/2-way: rdn and outpcd after 4 out: btn fr next* **9/2**[3]

5/0- **8** *18* **Marlee Mourinho (IRE)**[25] 2968 8-11-0 0 JamesReveley 53
(N W Alexander) *prom tl lost pl bef 6th: struggling fr next: t.o* **66/1**

5m 16.2s (4.20) **Going Correction** +0.325s/f (Yiel) **8** Ran SP% **112.9**
Speed ratings: **104,103,102,99,99 94,90,83**
CSF £45.78 TOTE £15.90: £2.60, £1.10, £6.40; EX 31.60 Trifecta £946.00.
Owner The Silver Tops **Bred** Mrs M Morrison (camp Farm Racing) **Trained** Duncrievie, Perth & Kinross

FOCUS
Not an especially strong-looking maiden event, with the favourite entering the contest off a rating of 109. The pace increased at about halfway.

3496 CHELTENHAM 2014 NRFB AT BETVICTOR.COM NOVICES' CHASE (15 fncs 4 omitted) 3m 1f
1:20 (1:20) (Class 4) 5-Y-0+ **£4,758** (£1,636)

Form RPR

/31- **1** **Swatow Typhoon (IRE)**[12] 3209 7-11-7 128 (p) JasonMaguire 135+
(Donald McCain) *racd lazily: nt fluent on occasions: led tl nt fluent and hdd 6th: drvn to regain ld after 8th: jnd whn lft wl clr fr 4 out (usual 5 out): ears pricked and rdn whn blnd next: idled and kpt up to work: drvn out* **4/6**[1]

P0/ **2** *126* **Cherry's Bay**[228] 8-10-7 0 (p) AdrianLane
(Sandy Forster) *disp ld tl lost pl 9th: lft poor 2nd 4 out (usual 5 out) and rdr looked to pull up: continued: t.o* **40/1**[3]

01- **F** **Milborough (IRE)**[23] 3011 8-11-7 133 DougieCostello
(Tim Vaughan) *t.k.h: trckd ldrs: pckd 1st: hdwy to ld 6th: hdd after 8th: styd upsides: ev ch whn fell 4 out (usual 5 out)* **5/4**[2]

7m 12.3s (22.40) **Going Correction** +0.65s/f (Soft) **3** Ran SP% **106.9**
Speed ratings: **90, ,**
CSF £7.48 TOTE £2.40; EX 2.40 Trifecta £3.00.
Owner G E Fitzpatrick **Bred** Glenn Turley **Trained** Cholmondeley, Cheshire

FOCUS
The last fence down the back and the second in the home straight were omitted from all chases. Impossible form to rate accurately.

3497 BACK OF THE NET AT BETVICTOR.COM H'CAP CHASE (15 fncs 4 omitted) 3m 1f
1:50 (1:50) (Class 5) (0-100,94) 5-Y-0+ **£2,599** (£763; £381; £190)

Form RPR

5/3- **1** **Arc Warrior (FR)**[22] 3022 10-10-7 75 (t) BrianHarding 89
(William Amos) *t.k.h: hld up: smooth hdwy 9th: nt fluent 3 out (usual 4 out): wnt 2nd gng wl bef next: rdn to ld last: kpt on strly* **14/1**

54U- **2** *1 1/4* **Lord Fox (IRE)**[7] 3283 7-10-6 79 BenPoste(5) 92
(Shaun Harris) *trckd ldrs on outside: led 10th: rdn and hung lft after 2 out: hdd whn hit last: kpt on: hld towards fin* **9/2**[2]

046/ **3** *21* **Too Cool To Fool (IRE)**[251] 5549 11-11-3 85 JamesReveley 76
(Jim Goldie) *prom: nt fluent 11th: wnt 2nd after 4 out (usual 5 out): rdn and wknd appr 2 out* **6/1**

444- **4** *4 1/2* **Alexander Oats**[33] 2818 11-10-9 82 (b[1]) HarryChalloner(5) 69
(Robert Goldie) *hld up: stdy hdwy 10th: drvn and outpcd after 4 out (usual 5 out): no imp fr next* **9/1**

560- **5** *1 3/4* **Boris The Blade**[22] 3022 12-11-4 91 (b) SamanthaDrake(5) 76
(Tina Jackson) *chsd ldrs: mstke 4th: hdwy to ld 9th: hdd next: cl up tl wknd after 4 out (usual 5 out)* **10/1**

635- **6** *3 1/4* **Cilliseal (IRE)**[43] 2594 9-11-1 88 (bt) DerekFox(5) 70
(Noel C Kelly, Ire) *hld up bhd ldng gp: outpcd and detached after 8th: n.d fr next* **10/1**

522- **7** *41* **Fozy Moss**[22] 3022 8-10-6 81 DaraghBourke(7) 53
(Stuart Coltherd) *t.k.h: pressed ldr to 8th: prom whn mstke next: outpcd whn nt fluent 4 out (usual 5 out): wknd bef next: no ch whn mstke last* **5/1**[3]

113- **F** **Snuker**[25] 2974 7-11-12 94 BrianHughes
(James Ewart) *led: hit 7th: hdd 9th: chsng ldrs whn fell next* **5/2**[1]

7m 4.6s (14.70) **Going Correction** +0.65s/f (Soft) **8** Ran SP% **112.6**
Speed ratings: **102,101,94,93,92 91,78,**
CSF £74.21 CT £422.69 TOTE £12.80: £3.40, £3.10, £3.30; EX 126.20 Trifecta £1729.30 Part won..
Owner J John Paterson **Bred** Mme Katherine Aalen And Ian Hanamy **Trained** Rochester, Northumberland

FOCUS
This was hard work in the conditions and a finish fought out between the two lowest in the weights. The winner has the potential to rate a lot higher on old hurdles form.

3498 DOWNLOAD THE BETVICTOR APP NOW H'CAP CHASE (14 fncs 3 omitted) 2m 4f
2:20 (2:21) (Class 4) (0-120,120) 5-Y-0+ **£4,548** (£1,335; £667; £333)

Form RPR

P36- **1** **Wicklow Lad**[12] 3205 10-10-11 112 (v) MrKitAlexander(7) 132+
(N W Alexander) *mde virtually all: rdn after 3 out (usual 4 out): styd on gamely whn pressed after last* **7/2**[2]

P/P- **2** *2 1/4* **And The Man**[13] 3190 8-11-4 112 BrianHarding 126
(Nicky Richards) *hld up: drvn and outpcd 9th: plenty to do whn nt fluent 3 out (usual 4 out): gd hdwy to chse wnr between last 2: edgd lft: kpt on fr last: hld nr fin* **14/1**

55P- **3** *12* **Oil Burner**[22] 3019 9-9-13 96 TonyKelly(3) 101
(William Amos) *t.k.h: in tch: nt fluent and stmbld 6th: rdn fr 8th: rallied bef 2 out: no imp bef last* **5/1**

/25- **4** *1/2* **Ros Castle (IRE)**[25] 2971 8-11-5 120 ShaunDobbin(7) 121
(Rose Dobbin) *hld up in tch: blnd 4 out (usual 5 out): sn pushed along: rallied after next: no imp fr 2 out* **5/1**

4U5- **5** *hd* **Ultra Du Chatelet (FR)**[36] 2749 6-10-13 107 (t) PeterBuchanan 107
(Lucinda Russell) *hld up on ins: stdy hdwy after 4 out (usual 5 out): sn rdn: no imp fr 2 out* **11/4**[1]

/SP- **6** *9* **Alfred Oats**[33] 2820 10-10-1 95 BrianHughes 87
(Robert Goldie) *w wnr to 3 out (usual 4 out): rdn and wknd after next* **16/1**

/25- **7** *nk* **Stormin Exit (IRE)**[26] 2939 11-11-12 120 JamesReveley 114
(Jim Goldie) *chsd ldrs: led briefly 6th: mstke 8th: rdn and wknd bef 3 out* **9/2**[3]

5m 32.8s (9.90) **Going Correction** +0.65s/f (Soft) **7** Ran SP% **113.0**
Speed ratings: **106,105,100,100,100 96,96**
CSF £43.17 CT £241.92 TOTE £4.10: £2.00, £4.70; EX 52.20 Trifecta £587.70.
Owner Clan Gathering **Bred** Mrs R E Hambro **Trained** Kinneston, Perth & Kinross

FOCUS
Few got involved behind the winner, who made virtually all. He was value for further and is rated in line with his best Irish form.

3499 NON-RUNNER FREE BET CHELTENHAM 2014 AT BETVICTOR.COM H'CAP HURDLE (12 hdls) 2m 5f 110y
2:50 (2:51) (Class 3) (0-140,127) 4-Y-0 **£6,330** (£1,870; £935; £468; £234)

Form RPR

103- **1** **Trucking Along (IRE)**[12] 3201 8-11-7 125 [1] MrSCrawford(3) 134+
(S R B Crawford, Ire) *t.k.h: hld up in last pl: hit 8th: smooth hdwy to ld 2 out: j.lft last: rdn and styd on strly* **5/2**[2]

P14- **2** *3* **Makhzoon (USA)**[32] 2844 10-10-8 116 (v) DiarmuidO'Regan(7) 119
(N W Alexander) *led: rdn and hdd 2 out: rallied last: kpt on same pce last 100yds* **8/1**

/13- **3** *9* **Tikkandemickey (IRE)**[22] 3017 8-10-11 119 CallumBewley(7) 113
(Raymond Shiels) *t.k.h early: in tch: rdn bef 3 out: edgd lft and sn outpcd: plugged on to take 3rd pl run-in: no ch w first two* **11/2**[3]

214- **4** *1 1/4* **Talkin Sence (IRE)**[25] 2969 9-11-5 127 DaraghBourke(7) 120
(Stuart Coltherd) *chsd ldr tl rdn and outpcd after 3 out: no imp whn lost 3rd pl run-in* **6/1**

1/6- **5** *17* **Golden Sparkle (IRE)**[55] 2345 8-10-12 120 GrahamWatters(7) 100
(Ian Duncan) *hld up in tch: stdy hdwy to chse ldrs after 4 out: rdn whn mstke next: sn btn* **14/1**

031- **P** **West Brit (IRE)**[115] 1535 6-11-7 122 (t) PeterBuchanan
(R Mike Smith) *mstkes: hld up in tch: struggling fr 7th: t.o whn p.u after 4 out* **28/1**

342- **P** **One For Harry (IRE)**[13] 3191 6-11-3 118 (p) BrianHarding
(Nicky Richards) *trckd ldrs: stdy hdwy whn mstke 4 out: rdn and wknd bef next: p.u after 3 out* **9/4**[1]

5m 47.8s (7.50) **Going Correction** +0.325s/f (Yiel) **7** Ran SP% **110.2**
Speed ratings (Par 107): **99,97,94,94,88 ,**
CSF £20.48 TOTE £3.30: £1.70, £3.50; EX 26.10 Trifecta £104.40.
Owner Mrs Denise Bailey **Bred** Michael Doyle **Trained** Larne, Co Antrim

FOCUS
Only the topweight was rated within a stone of the ceiling, so this didn't look a conspicuously strong 0-140, though the runner-up did at least ensure a fair tempo in the conditions. A personal best from the cosy winner.

3500 VICTOR'S LIVE CASINO NOW OPEN STANDARD OPEN NATIONAL HUNT FLAT RACE 2m
3:20 (3:20) (Class 6) 4-6-Y-0 **£1,711** (£498; £249)

Form RPR

- **1** **Uppertown Cave (IRE)**[81] 5-11-5 0 JasonMaguire 114+
(Donald McCain) *t.k.h: hld up in tch: stdy hdwy on outside and cl up after 5f: wnt 2nd 1/2-way: shkn up to ld over 1f out: sn drvn clr* **12/5**[1]

42- **2** *6* **Gilnockie**[21] 3042 6-11-5 0 BrianHughes 105
(James Ewart) *led: rdn over 2f out: hdd over 1f out: kpt on same pce fnl f* **4/1**[3]

3 *4* **Turtle Cask (IRE)** 5-11-2 0 EwanWhillans(3) 101
(Alistair Whillans) *t.k.h: chsd ldr to 1/2-way: cl up tl pushed along and outpcd fnl 2f* **14/1**

4 *24* **Touch Of Steel (IRE)** 5-10-12 0 DaleIrving(7) 77
(James Ewart) *hld up in tch: drvn and outpcd over 6f out: plugged on fnl 2f: no ch w first three* **12/1**

5 *3/4* **Throthethatch (IRE)**[66] 5-10-12 0 GrahamWatters(7) 76
(Lucinda Russell) *hld up in tch: stdy hdwy 1/2-way: drvn and outpcd over 5f out: btn fnl 3f* **5/2**[2]

3- **6** *40* **The Squinty Bridge**[61] 2223 6-10-12 0 CraigNichol(7) 36
(Lucinda Russell) *t.k.h: cl up tl outpcd over 6f out: lost tch fr 4f out* **4/1**[3]

0P/ **7** *91* **Jackofhearts**[462] 1657 6-11-5 0 JamesReveley
(Jean McGregor) *cl up to 1/2-way: sn struggling: t.o fnl 4f* **50/1**

3m 59.5s (2.00) **Going Correction** +0.325s/f (Yiel)
WFA 5 from 6yo 3lb **7** Ran SP% **114.3**
Speed ratings: **108,105,103,91,90 70,25**
CSF £12.45 TOTE £3.20: £2.00, £1.50; EX 15.60 Trifecta £72.40.
Owner Paul & Clare Rooney **Bred** Declan McCann **Trained** Cholmondeley, Cheshire

FOCUS
One or two fairly nicely-bred types opposed in a bumper, run at an ordinary gallop. The second sets the level.
T/Plt: £256.90. Pool: £46,425.79 - 131.88 winning units. T/Qpdt: £72.60. Pool: £4122.30 - 42.00 winning units. RY

3029 HUNTINGDON (R-H)
Thursday, January 2

OFFICIAL GOING: Heavy
Wind: medium, across Weather: dry and bright

3501 32RED CASINO NOVICES' HURDLE (8 hdls) 2m 110y
12:10 (12:10) (Class 4) 4-Y-0+ **£3,119** (£915; £457; £228)

Form RPR

1/2- **1** **Steel City**[27] 2924 6-11-5 0 AndrewThornton 120+
(Seamus Mullins) *chsd ldrs: clsd 5th: led bef next: gng clr and wandered lft 2 out: in command and wnt lft flat: comf* **16/1**[3]

3/ **2** *24* **Arthur's Oak**[249] 4 6-11-5 0 AidanColeman 99
(Venetia Williams) *chsd clr ldng pair: clsd and cl enough 3 out: rdn and btn bef next: wl hld whn lft 2nd and hmpd last* **16/1**[3]

3/0- **3** *19* **Jolly Valentine**[21] 3034 6-11-2 0 TrevorWhelan(3) 80
(Neil King) *racd off the pce in midfield: 4th and no threat to ldrs 3 out: lft 3rd and swvd lft last: t.o* **100/1**

4 *35* **Star Date (IRE)**[64] 5-11-5 0 LeightonAspell 41
(Oliver Sherwood) *t.k.h: hld up off the pce in last trio: nvr on terms w ldrs: t.o 3 out: mstke 2 out: lft 4th last* **50/1**

1- **F** **Mijhaar**[34] 2783 6-11-12 0 DenisO'Regan 107
(John Ferguson) *led: t.k.h after 1st: drew wl clr after 3rd: hdd bef 3 out: pushed along and btn bef 2 out: stl 2nd but wkng and tired whn fell last* **1/2**[1]

13- **P** **Gunner Fifteen (IRE)**[26] 2940 6-11-5 0 NoelFehily
(Fergal O'Brien) *a bhd and nvr on terms w ldrs: nt fluent 1st: mstke 2nd and 3rd: hmpd after 4th: t.o 3 out: p.u next* **9/4**[2]

4m 10.2s (15.30) **Going Correction** +1.05s/f (Soft) 6 Ran SP% **112.2**
Speed ratings (Par 105): **106,94,85,69,**
CSF £185.66 TOTE £11.90: £3.20, £4.20; EX 93.90 Trifecta £945.80.

Owner J T Brown **Bred** J T Brown **Trained** Wilsford-Cum-Lake, Wilts

FOCUS
This eight-race card survived an early morning inspection and the going was reported by the jockeys as "very heavy, horrible ground." There was a fresh breeze against the runners in the straight. Quite an interesting novices' hurdle and, although the betting suggested it was a match, it did not turn out that way. The winner threatened this sort of figure when winning a bumper.

3502 32RED H'CAP CHASE (17 fncs 2 omitted) 3m
12:40 (12:40) (Class 5) (0-100,100) 5-Y-0+ **£2,144** (£629; £314; £157)

Form RPR

223- **1** **Flemi Two Toes (IRE)**[21] 3033 8-11-6 **97** (p) JackQuinlan(3) 110+
(Sarah Humphrey) *nt a fluent: in tch in midfield: chsd ldrs 12th: rdn on long run to 2 out: 5 l down and looked hld last: chsd wnr flat: styd on dourly u.p to ld cl home* **7/2**[2]

PU4- **2** *nk* **Tarraco (FR)**[44] 2578 7-10-12 **86** AidanColeman 97
(Venetia Williams) *led tl 13th: w ldr tl led again on long run to 2 out: drvn and forged clr 2 out: 3 l clr last: kpt on u.p tl hdd and no ex cl home* **3/1**[1]

U65- **3** *2 ¼* **Bally Sands (IRE)**[13] 3193 10-11-7 **98** (v[1]) RobertDunne(3) 106
(Robin Mathew) *pressed ldr tl led 13th: hdd on long run to 2 out: drvn and sltly outpcd 2 out: swtchd lft between last 2: 3 l down last: styd on same pce and lost 2nd flat* **11/2**

42F- **4** *25* **Tinelyra (IRE)**[7] 3277 8-11-1 **89** (t) PaddyBrennan 77
(Fergal O'Brien) *hld up in rr: stdy prog 10th: clr in ldng quartet and travelling wl 14th: rdn bef 2 out: no rspnse and sn btn: wknd flat* **9/2**[3]

55U- **5** *32* **Genny Wren**[38] 2722 8-11-9 **97** SamJones 48
(Renee Robeson) *in tch in last trio: mstke 11th: rdn bef next: 5th and lost tch 15th: t.o next* **8/1**

54P- **6** *4* **Epee Celeste (FR)**[7] 3267 8-11-12 **100** DaveCrosse 47
(Michael Chapman) *chsd ldrs: rdn after 9th: lost pl and last whn j. slowly 12th: t.o 15th* **22/1**

444- **7** *½* **Noble Witness (IRE)**[13] 3193 11-11-11 **99** (p) AdamPogson 46
(Charles Pogson) *in tch in midfield: j.lft 1st: mstke and pckd 2nd: chsd ldrs after 7th: rdn and lost tch 15th: t.o* **12/1**

/56- **P** **Dunkelly Castle (IRE)**[36] 2744 10-11-7 **100** (t) ThomasGarner(5)
(Brendan Powell) *j.lft: in tch in last trio: rdn 12th: struggling next: losing tch whn p.u 15th* **10/1**

6m 27.3s (17.00) **Going Correction** +0.775s/f (Soft) 8 Ran SP% **113.0**
Speed ratings: **102,101,101,92,82 80,80,**
CSF £14.64 CT £54.72 TOTE £4.10: £1.30, £1.40, £2.20; EX 16.60 Trifecta £71.10.

Owner A Whyte, J Custerson, D Nott **Bred** C Kenneally **Trained** West Wratting, Cambs

FOCUS
The last fence in the back straight was omitted in all chases due to false ground. This moderate handicap chase proved an attritional test, although those that raced up with the pace stayed there. The winner was a 120 hurdle at best and may match that over fences.

3503 32RED CASINO H'CAP HURDLE (10 hdls) 2m 4f 110y
1:10 (1:12) (Class 5) (0-100,100) 4-Y-0+ **£1,949** (£572; £286; £143)

Form RPR

003- **1** **Boomtown**[13] 3192 9-10-11 **92** (t) GeraldQuinn(7) 98+
(Claire Dyson) *planted himself briefly s: sn rcvrd and led: mde rest and racd wdr than rivals: pushed clr bef 2 out: styd on: rdn out* **9/4**[1]

0/0- **2** *7* **Fidelor (FR)**[88] 1797 8-11-7 **95** WillKennedy 94
(Alex Hales) *led early: sn hdd and chsd wnr after: mstke 2nd: mstke 3 out: rdn and btn bef 2 out: plugged on* **7/2**[3]

F/2- **3** *9* **Just Benny (IRE)**[243] 122 9-11-12 **100** RichardJohnson 89
(Richard Phillips) *t.k.h: chsd clr ldng pair: rdn 3 out: no hdwy and wl hld in 4th next: hung lft flat but plugged on to go 3rd again nr fin* **10/3**[2]

PP6- **4** *1 ½* **Chapel House**[7] 3261 11-9-10 **75** ow1 JamesBanks(5) 63
(Richard Harper) *hld up in rr: rdn and effrt bef 3 out: wnt 3rd but no imp bef 2 out: lost 3rd nr fin* **13/2**

605- **P** **Was My Valentine**[19] 3094 7-10-12 **96** (p) JackSavage(10)
(Jo Davis) *hld up in last pair: rdn after 7th: mstke next and sn wknd: wl bhd whn p.u last* **4/1**

5m 20.0s (21.00) **Going Correction** +1.05s/f (Soft) 5 Ran SP% **109.4**
Speed ratings (Par 103): **102,99,95,95,**
CSF £10.29 TOTE £3.40: £1.60, £2.10; EX 11.10 Trifecta £33.00.

Owner FSF Racing **Bred** Gainsborough Stud Management Ltd **Trained** Cleeve Prior, Worcs

FOCUS
A low-grade handicap hurdle that turned into a procession. The form is rated around the second.

3504 32RED.COM H'CAP CHASE (14 fncs 2 omitted) 2m 4f 110y
1:40 (1:40) (Class 4) (0-120,117) 5-Y-0+ **£4,045** (£1,383)

Form RPR

563- **1** **Ringa Bay**[47] 2512 9-11-5 **117** (p) JakeHodson(7) 121+
(David Bridgwater) *mde all: rdn bnd bef 2 out: lft 5 l clr 2 out: idling and wandered last: doing little and edging lft flat: a holding rival: rdn out* **5/2**[3]

/P4- **2** *¾* **Mentalist (FR)**[19] 3093 6-11-10 **115** AidanColeman 118
(Venetia Williams) *wl in tch in 3rd: mstke 9th: drvn and little rspnse on long run to 2 out: lft 5 l 2nd and mstke 2 out: steadily clsd on idling wnr flat* **6/4**[1]

341- **U** **Strawberry Hill (IRE)**[36] 2741 8-11-5 **110** IanPopham 114+
(Caroline Keevil) *pressed wnr: shkn up and ev ch whn mstke: slipped on landing and uns rdr 2 out* **13/8**[2]

5m 27.55s (22.25) **Going Correction** +0.775s/f (Soft) 3 Ran SP% **106.7**
Speed ratings: **88,87,**
CSF £6.23 TOTE £3.30; EX 7.70 Trifecta £4.90.

Owner D G Bridgwater **Bred** Helshaw Grange Stud Ltd **Trained** Icomb, Gloucs

■ Stewards' Enquiry : Aidan Coleman two-day ban: use of whip (16-17 Jan)

FOCUS
Only three lined up for this modest chase, but it produced an exciting finish. The winner was well in on the best of his form from last season.

3505 32RED H'CAP HURDLE (12 hdls) 3m 2f
2:10 (2:10) (Class 3) (0-135,126) 4-Y-0+ **£5,815** (£1,707; £853; £426)

Form RPR

/12- **1** **Beauboreen (IRE)**[33] 2807 7-11-6 **120** SeanQuinlan 128+
(Jennie Candlish) *hld up in tch in rr: blnd 7th: hdwy to trck ldrs after 7th: led and blnd 2 out: clr last: styd on wl: rdn out* **11/4**[1]

/20- **2** *7* **Dawn Twister (GER)**[34] 2798 7-11-3 **122** MattCrawley(5) 122
(Lucy Wadham) *in tch in midfield: mstke 7th: mstke and rdn 9th: chsd ldng pair 2 out: no threat to wnr but kpt on to go 2nd flat* **11/2**

225- **3** *1 ¼* **Neptune Equester**[18] 3108 11-11-5 **119** APMcCoy 116
(Brian Ellison) *pressed ldr: rdn bef 9th: drvn and btn bef 2 out: swtchd rt and plugged on flat* **4/1**[2]

/32- **4** *2 ¼* **Arkose (IRE)**[40] 2678 10-11-12 **126** (v) LeightonAspell 123
(Oliver Sherwood) *led: rdn and mstke 3 out: hdd and blnd next: 2nd and btn last: hung lft: wknd and lost 2 pls flat* **4/1**[2]

/05- **5** *74* **Promised Wings (GER)**[36] 2742 7-11-6 **120** (b) TomCannon 41
(Chris Gordon) *pressed ldr tl j. slowly 5th: immediately drvn and off the bridle after: dropped to last but stl in tch 7th: wknd 3 out: eased next: t.o* **9/1**

002- **F** **Phare Isle (IRE)**[28] 2903 9-11-1 **115** (tp) DarylJacob 109
(Ben Case) *chsd ldrs: 3rd and rdn bef 2 out: no imp and btn between last 2: 5th whn fell last* **9/2**[3]

6m 48.2s (25.30) **Going Correction** +1.05s/f (Soft) 6 Ran SP% **110.2**
Speed ratings (Par 107): **103,100,100,99,77**
CSF £17.07 TOTE £3.60: £2.40, £3.70; EX 19.90 Trifecta £116.50.

Owner Mrs Hall & Exors of the Late Hall **Bred** Richard Hall **Trained** Basford Green, Staffs

FOCUS
Just a fair staying handicap hurdle with the top weight rated 9lb below the race ceiling. The winner is on the upgrade and the second ran pretty much to his mark.

3506 32REDPOKER.COM MAIDEN HURDLE (10 hdls) 2m 5f 110y
2:40 (2:40) (Class 5) 4-Y-0+ **£1,949** (£572; £286; £143)

Form RPR

2F2- **1** **Carole's Destrier**[26] 2940 6-11-3 119 MichaelByrne(3) 132+
(Neil Mulholland) *hld up in tch: hdwy to trck ldrs after 5th: j. into ld next: gng best after 3 out: readily c clr between last 2: comf* **11/8**[2]

022- **2** *16* **Cloud Creeper (IRE)**[36] 2740 7-11-6 120 RichardJohnson 123+
(Philip Hobbs) *hld up in tch: hdwy to chse ldrs 6th: hit next: sn clr in ldng trio: blnd 3 out: rdn and chsd wnr bef 2 out: btn between last 2: eased flat* **6/5**[1]

0/3- **3** *20* **Westerly Breeze (IRE)**[38] 2720 6-11-6 0 IanPopham 101
(Martin Keighley) *pressed ldrs: drew clr in ldng trio after 7th: rdn and btn in 3rd bef 2 out: wknd between last 2* **9/1**

5/ **4** *57* **Arfur Didit (IRE)**[304] 4572 6-11-3 0 JackQuinlan(3) 39
(Sarah Humphrey) *chsd ldrs: rdn and struggling after 6th: bhd next: t.o 3 out* **40/1**

/F0- **5** *50* **Anshantor (IRE)**[25] 2978 8-11-3 0 JakeGreenall(3)
(Henry Daly) *t.k.h: chsd ldrs: hdwy to ld 3rd: hdd bef 6th: wknd 7th: 4th and t.o 3 out: lost action and eased to a walk towards fin: dismntd immediately after fin* **20/1**

P- **6** *½* **Zaffaran Rain (IRE)**[44] 2579 5-10-13 0 DaveCrosse
(K F Clutterbuck) *led tl 3rd: styd w ldrs tl led again bef 6th: outj. and hdd 6th: wknd next: wl t.o 3 out* **66/1**

P **Shubaat**[516] 7-11-6 0 DenisO'Regan
(John Ferguson) *wl in tch in midfield: mstke 5th: rdn bef 7th: 4th and wknd wl bef 3 out: t.o whn p.u next* **7/1**[3]

105- **P** **Amazing Scenes (IRE)**[17] 3136 5-11-6 0 BrendanPowell
(Brendan Powell) *in tch in rr: rdn after 5th: lost tch bef 7th: wl t.o and p.u 3 out* **33/1**

5m 27.0s (16.40) **Going Correction** +1.05s/f (Soft) 8 Ran SP% **121.7**
Speed ratings (Par 103): **112,106,98,78,60 59, ,**
CSF £3.73 TOTE £3.90: £1.20, £1.10, £2.40; EX 4.40 Trifecta £11.90.

Owner Mrs C Skipworth **Bred** Larkinglass Ltd **Trained** Limpley Stoke, Wilts

■ Stewards' Enquiry : Jake Greenall 10-day ban: failed to dismount horse when it appeared to have gone lame (16-25 Jan)

FOCUS
A fair maiden hurdle and the pair who set the standard on official ratings had it between themselves from the third-last. The winner can rate higher.

3507 HUNTINGDON RACECOURSE/HBLB MARES' STANDARD OPEN NATIONAL HUNT FLAT RACE (LISTED RACE) 2m 110y
3:10 (3:10) (Class 1) 5-6-Y-0
£9,966 (£3,739; £1,872; £932; £469; £234)

Form RPR

1- **1** **Bitofapuzzle**[33] 2809 6-11-0 0 (t) NoelFehily 116+
(Harry Fry) *mde all: gng best over 2f out: clr whn m green over 1f out: styd on wl fnl f: readily* **5/2**[2]

1- **2** *4* **Tara Mist**[29] 2892 5-11-0 0 RichardJohnson 112+
(Henry Daly) *hld up wl in tch in last pair: hdwy to chse ldr 4f out: rdn and effrt 2f out: styd on same pce after* **9/4**[1]

1/3- **3** *11* **Delta Forty**[30] 2878 6-11-0 0 AndrewThornton 101
(Keith Reveley) *chsd ldrs: rdn 3f out: 3rd and btn over 1f out: edgd lft and wknd fnl f* **11/1**

1- **4** *3 ¾* **Cloudante (IRE)**[11] 3228 6-10-7 0 JamesCowley(7) 97
(Donald McCain) *chsd ldrs: rdn and outpcd 3f out: no threat to wnr but plugged on fnl f* **10/1**

2- **5** *¾* **Chantara Rose**[11] 3228 5-11-0 0 AidanColeman 97
(Anthony Honeyball) *wl in tch in midfield: rdn and outpcd over 2f out: btn 2f out: plugged on fnl f* **14/1**

/12- **6** *4* **Rouquine Sauvage**[36] 2745 6-11-0 0 (t) APMcCoy 96
(Anthony Honeyball) *t.k.h: hld up wl in tch in rr: effrt to go 4th jst over 2f out: sn btn: wknd over 1f out* **4/1**[3]

/3- **7** *11* **Rose Of The World (IRE)**[71] 2026 6-11-0 0 (t) SamJones 82
(Jo Davis) *wl in tch in midfield: rdn and dropped to rr 4f out: bhd fnl 2f* **20/1**

2- **8** *17* **Notnowivorheadache**[97] 1671 5-10-11 0 JamesBest(3) 65
(Paul Webber) *chsd ldr: rdn over 4f out: lost pl over 2f out: sn wknd: bhd fnl f* **25/1**

4m 4.0s (14.90) **Going Correction** +1.05s/f (Soft) 8 Ran SP% **112.0**
Speed ratings: **106,104,98,97,96 94,89,81**
CSF £8.16 TOTE £3.00: £1.10, £1.10, £2.70; EX 7.30 Trifecta £42.60.

Owner Richard Barber **Bred** R J & S A Carter **Trained** Seaborough, Dorset

FOCUS
A Listed mares' bumper featuring five previous winners, which had originally been scheduled to take place at the abandoned Boxing Day meeting here. The winner looks a decent prospect.

3508 32RED STANDARD OPEN NATIONAL HUNT FLAT RACE 2m 110y
3:40 (3:40) (Class 6) 4-6-Y-O £1,559 (£457; £228; £114)

Form RPR

/3- **1** **River Deep (IRE)**54 2375 5-11-5 0 RichardJohnson 111+
(Philip Hobbs) *led for 2f: chsd ldr tl led again 7f out: rdn: rn green and edgd lft over 1f out: kpt on and a holding runner-up ins fnl f* **4/5**1

0/ **2** ½ **Zeroeshadesofgrey (IRE)**266 5263 5-11-2 0 TrevorWhelan(3) 110
(Neil King) *chsd ldrs: rdn and ev ch 2f out: carried lft over 1f out: kpt on u.p but hld fnl 100yds* **13/2**2

- **3** 14 **I'm A Joker** 5-11-2 0 JackQuinlan(3) 96
(Sarah Humphrey) *wl in tch in last trio: hdwy to chse ldrs 3f out: wknd u.p over 1f out* **8/1**3

5- **4** 10 **Double U Dot Ede'S**45 2570 5-10-9 0 PaddyBradley(10) 86
(Pat Phelan) *wl in tch in midfield: rdn and outpcd over 2f out: wl hld fnl 2f* **16/1**

5 1½ **Blacksmiths Arms** 4-10-4 0 JakeGreenall(3) 73
(Michael Easterby) *t.k.h: chsd ldr tl led after 2f: hdd 7f out: pressed wnr after tl wknd 2f out* **16/1**

6 12 **Broughtons Warrior** 6-11-5 0 LeightonAspell 73
(Willie Musson) *hld up wl in tch in rr: hdwy and cl enough in 5th 3f out: wknd 2f out* **13/2**2

0/ **7** 74 **Linden Rose**259 5364 5-10-12 0 JamieMoore
(Steph Hollinshead) *chsd ldrs: rdn and lost pl qckly 3f out: sn t.o* **33/1**

8 9 **Chandler Bing** 5-11-5 0 BrendanPowell
(Eugene Stanford) *wl in tch in last trio: rdn and lost tch rapidly 4f out: sn t.o* **20/1**

4m 5.6s (16.50) **Going Correction** +1.05s/f (Soft)
WFA 4 from 5yo+ 11lb **8** Ran SP% **112.8**
Speed ratings: **103,102,96,91,90 85,50,46**
CSF £6.21 TOTE £1.70: £1.10, £2.10, £2.00; EX 6.00 Trifecta £31.10.
Owner Bradley Partnership **Bred** Miss Elizabeth Kennedy **Trained** Withycombe, Somerset

FOCUS
This bumper was full of inexperienced sorts, but the time was only 1.6sec slower than the preceding Listed race. Steps up from the first two.
T/Plt: £406.20. Pool: £46,463.80 - 83.50 winning units. T/Qpdt: £21.00. Pool: £7073.00 - 249.10 winning units. SP

3229 LINGFIELD (L-H)
Friday, January 3
3509 Meeting Abandoned - waterlogged

3474 MUSSELBURGH (R-H)
Friday, January 3
OFFICIAL GOING: Soft (good to soft in places) changing to soft after race 1 (12.40)
Wind: Fairly strong, across Weather: Overcast, showers

3516 LAUDERDALE PONY CLUB MAIDEN HURDLE (9 hdls) 2m
12:40 (12:40) (Class 5) 4-Y-0+ £3,249 (£954; £477; £238)

Form RPR

1 **Rockabilly Riot (IRE)**177 4-10-7 0 DenisO'Regan 102+
(Martin Todhunter) *hld up on ins: smooth hdwy appr 3 out: led after last: sn pushed along and edgd lft: kpt on wl* **33/1**

544- **2** 1½ **Final Assault (IRE)**34 2823 5-11-5 110 PeterBuchanan 112+
(Lucinda Russell) *hld up in midfield: stdy hdwy bef 2 out: effrt and chsd wnr run-in: n.m.r and swtchd rt last 150yds: kpt on* **10/3**2

3- **3** 3¼ **Katachenko (IRE)**25 3002 5-11-5 0 JasonMaguire 107
(Donald McCain) *trckd ldr: led and hit 3 out: rdn next: hdd after last: kpt on same pce* **5/1**3

/52- **4** shd **King Of Strings (IRE)**26 2968 5-11-5 0 DougieCostello 107
(Tim Walford) *t.k.h: prom: hdwy and ev ch 2 out: kpt on same pce fr last* **9/4**1

5 2¼ **Empresario (IRE)**27 2961 5-11-5 0 (tp) DGHogan 106
(Denis Gerard Hogan, Ire) *t.k.h: led: hdd 3 out: rallied: hung rt and outpcd fr last* **7/1**

3- **6** 7 **Yourholidayisover (IRE)**35 2792 7-11-0 0 JoeColliver(5) 98
(Patrick Holmes) *prom: rdn and outpcd 3 out: sn hung rt: n.d after* **25/1**

540- **7** 1¾ **Shine A Diamond (IRE)**37 2748 6-10-12 0 GrahamWatters(7) 96
(Lucinda Russell) *hld up: stdy hdwy bef 3 out: pushed along and no imp bef next* **66/1**

53- **8** 14 **Sudski Star (IRE)**1 3494 6-11-5 0 JamesReveley 82
(Patrick Griffin, Ire) *cl up: struggling after 4 out: btn next* **33/1**

45- **9** 2 **Landecker (IRE)**34 2823 6-11-5 0 BrianHarding 80
(N W Alexander) *nt fluent on occasions: bhd: stdy hdwy 1/2-way: rdn and wknd 3 out* **12/1**

366- **10** hd **Bellorophon (IRE)**18 3128 5-10-12 0 CraigNichol(7) 80
(Keith Dalgleish) *nt fluent on occasions: hld up: struggling 4 out: sn btn* **12/1**

0- **11** 23 **Bassett Road (IRE)**26 2968 6-11-2 0 EwanWhillans(3) 57
(Keith Dalgleish) *prom tl lost pl 1/2-way: struggling whn mstke 3 out: t.o* **66/1**

0/0- **P** **Red Mystique (IRE)**73 306 5-10-12 69 (t) StephenMulqueen(7)
(Maurice Barnes) *a bhd: struggling 1/2-way: t.o whn p.u after 3 out* **250/1**

3m 50.5s (2.10) **Going Correction** +0.175s/f (Yiel)
WFA 4 from 5yo+ 11lb **12** Ran SP% **111.5**
Speed ratings (Par 103): **101,100,98,98,97 93,93,86,85,84 73,**
CSF £133.18 TOTE £32.00: £7.00, £1.60, £1.50; EX 196.90 Trifecta £1358.60 Part won..
Owner James-Douglas Gordon **Bred** John Cullinan **Trained** Orton, Cumbria

FOCUS
Rails on bends moved 2yds. Ground conditions were fairly testing and runners had to contend with a strong, gusting wind, especially down the back. The opener was run in a time 15.5sec slower than standard. This was probably an ordinary maiden hurdle but the winner can rate higher on his Flat form.

3517 32RED.COM H'CAP CHASE (12 fncs) 2m
1:10 (1:10) (Class 5) (0-100,100) 5-Y-0+ £3,249 (£954; £477; £238)

Form RPR

114- **1** **Civil Unrest (IRE)**30 2879 8-11-5 100 (b) DaleIrving(7) 109+
(James Ewart) *mde all: clr 4 out: hrd pressed appr last: drvn out run-in* **7/2**2

/41- **2** 1¾ **Coax**17 3143 6-11-12 100 RichieMcGrath 109+
(Patrick Holmes) *hld up: stdy hdwy 4 out: chsd wnr next: effrt and jst over 1 l down whn mstke last: one pce run-in* **11/2**3

U41- **3** 9 **Ballycool (IRE)**5 3395 7-11-7 100 7ex (t) DerekFox(5) 99
(Lucinda Russell) *nt fluent on occasions: in tch: drvn and outpcd bef 4 out: rallied 2 out: kpt on: no ch w first two* **5/4**1

125- **4** 4½ **Jim Tango (FR)**17 3143 10-10-13 87 (p) RichardJohnson 82
(Karen McLintock) *hld up in tch: stdy hdwy 5 out: rdn and outpcd 3 out: hld whn blnd next* **11/1**

323- **5** 20 **Forestside (IRE)**2 3449 9-10-10 84 (p) JamesReveley 57
(Barry Murtagh) *chsd clr ldng pair: stdy hdwy after 5 out: rdn and wknd bef next* **8/1**

/64- **6** 19 **Overlaw**38 2737 12-10-5 86 DaraghBourke(7) 40
(Stuart Coltherd) *w wnr to bef 4 out: wknd next: t.o* **16/1**

4m 5.5s (13.10) **Going Correction** +0.675s/f (Soft) **6** Ran SP% **107.4**
Speed ratings: **94,93,88,86,76 66**
CSF £20.22 TOTE £4.60: £2.40, £3.00; EX 19.20 Trifecta £20.80.
Owner The Ancrum Pointer 1 **Bred** D And Mrs Noonan **Trained** Langholm, Dumfries & G'way

FOCUS
A modest handicap chase. The winner is rated in line with the best of this season's hurdle form.

3518 32RED CASINO H'CAP HURDLE (9 hdls) 2m
1:40 (1:40) (Class 4) (0-105,103) 4-Y-0+ £3,249 (£954; £477; £238)

Form RPR

1 **Benalex Park**29 2915 5-10-13 90 (bt1) DGHogan 101+
(Denis Gerard Hogan, Ire) *t.k.h: hld up in tch: smooth hdwy bef 3 out: chalng whn hit last: led run-in: drvn out* **14/1**

/12- **2** 1¾ **Pass Muster**28 2921 7-11-6 102 AdamNicol(5) 109+
(Philip Kirby) *chsd ldrs: wnt 2nd 1/2-way: led after 4 out: rdn 2 out: edgd rt and hdd run-in: kpt on same pce towards fin* **11/4**2

565- **3** 7 **Knockturnal (IRE)**31 2865 6-10-6 83 (b1) BrianHughes 83
(Malcolm Jefferson) *t.k.h: cl up: rdn and outpcd 2 out: plugged on fr last: no ch w first two* **14/1**

3/3- **4** 3 **Shan Valley (IRE)**57 2306 8-9-12 82 ow1 DaraghBourke(7) 80
(Stuart Coltherd) *t.k.h: cl up: led after 3rd to after 4 out: rdn bef next: one pce and hung rt after 2 out: 3rd and hld whn j.rt and mstke last* **5/1**3

022- **5** 2¼ **Cadore (IRE)**35 2794 6-11-2 100 (p) GrantCockburn(7) 95
(Lucy Normile) *hld up: rdn after 4 out: sme hdwy 2 out: nvr able to chal* **5/2**1

0P5- **6** 1 **Flogarose (FR)**13 3212 5-10-9 86 DougieCostello 82
(Lucy Normile) *hld up in midfield: stdy hdwy after 4 out: rdn and outpcd fr 2 out* **15/2**

006- **7** 8 **Inniscastle Boy**35 2792 5-11-0 91 (v) GaryBartley 77
(Jim Goldie) *hld up in tch: lost pl 1/2-way: sn rdn: n.d after* **25/1**

P50- **8** 1½ **Bow Fiddle (IRE)**165 1072 8-10-3 85 JoeColliver(5) 69
(Patrick Holmes) *t.k.h: hld up: sme hdwy after 4 out: wknd after next* **40/1**

330/ **9** 7 **The Starboard Bow**652 5011 7-11-12 103 (p) PeterBuchanan 80
(Lucinda Russell) *led to 3rd: cl up tl rdn and wknd after 4 out* **8/1**

3m 53.1s (4.70) **Going Correction** +0.175s/f (Yiel) **9** Ran SP% **114.4**
Speed ratings (Par 105): **95,94,90,89,88 87,83,82,79**
CSF £53.34 CT £561.88 TOTE £9.70: £4.10, £1.40, £2.40; EX 69.60 Trifecta £1799.20 Part won..
Owner Winonesoon Syndicate **Bred** D E And Mrs J Cash **Trained** Cloughjordan, Co Tipperary

FOCUS
Modest handicap form. The time was 2.6sec slower than the opening maiden hurdle. A big step up from the winner but it's believable on his Flat form.

3519 32RED NOVICES' CHASE (12 fncs) 2m
2:10 (2:11) (Class 4) 5-Y-0+ £3,898 (£1,144; £572; £286)

Form RPR

3/P- **1** **Witness In Court (IRE)**76 1976 7-11-0 129 JasonMaguire 135+
(Donald McCain) *j.w: mde all: clr after 4 out: kpt on strly: unchal* **7/4**2

U23- **2** 8 **Jet Master (IRE)**19 3109 8-11-0 127 (t) BrianHughes 126
(N W Alexander) *hld up in tch: stdy hdwy whn nt fluent 7th: 3 l down and chsng wnr whn nt fluent 4 out: mstke next: sn no imp: hld whn mstke last* **6/4**1

/P1- **3** 17 **Reaping The Reward (IRE)**183 884 10-11-0 130 PeterBuchanan 111
(Lucinda Russell) *chsd wnr to bef 4 out: sn rdn and wknd* **5/2**3

066- **4** 56 **Lillioftheballet (IRE)**35 2794 7-10-2 81 HarryChalloner(5) 43
(Jim Goldie) *j.lft: in tch: outpcd whn blnd 7th: sn lost tch: t.o* **33/1**

3m 59.8s (7.40) **Going Correction** +0.675s/f (Soft) **4** Ran SP% **107.9**
Speed ratings: **108,104,95,67**
CSF £4.89 TOTE £3.10; EX 5.30 Trifecta £8.30.
Owner T G Leslie **Bred** Michael Ronayne **Trained** Cholmondeley, Cheshire

FOCUS
A fair novice chase. There's probably more to come from the winner.

3520 MACKIE MOTORS BRECHIN H'CAP HURDLE (14 hdls) 3m 110y
2:40 (2:40) (Class 4) (0-105,102) 4-Y-0+ £3,249 (£954; £477; £238)

Form RPR

122- **1** **Hartforth**33 2842 6-10-9 90 CallumWhillans(5) 102+
(Donald Whillans) *hld up: stmbld and nrly uns rdr bnd bef 2nd: rdn and hdwy to chse ldr after 4 out: led 2 out: drew clr* **9/2**3

6/3- **2** 12 **Solidago (IRE)**25 2997 7-11-10 100 (v1) RichardJohnson 100
(S R B Crawford, Ire) *t.k.h: hld up on outside: hdwy and cl up 1/2-way: led 9th: rdn and hdd 2 out: sn one pce* **3/1**1

635- **3** 13 **Ryton Runner (IRE)**156 1164 6-11-5 102 (p) CraigNichol(7) 91
(Lucinda Russell) *prom: drvn and outpcd 4 out: plugged on fr 2 out: no ch w first two* **15/2**

0/P- **4** 5 **Highlander Ted**44 2596 6-11-0 90 (p) PeterBuchanan 75
(Tim Walford) *hld up in midfield: stdy hdwy after 4 out: drvn and no imp fr next* **8/1**

/00- **5** 16 **Yourlookinathim (IRE)**223 471 8-10-4 80 GaryBartley 46
(Jim Goldie) *led tl nt fluent and hdd 9th: wknd bef 3 out* **28/1**

The Form Book Jumps, Raceform Ltd, Compton, RG20 6NL.

220- **P** **Burns Night**[35] 2789 8-11-0 **95**..(p) AdamNicol(5)
(Philip Kirby) *prom: mstke and lost pl 8th: struggling fr next: t.o whn p.u bef 3 out* **12/1**

643- **P** **Vallani (IRE)**[25] 2999 9-9-9 **78**.. GrantCockburn(7)
(Lucinda Russell) *bhd and sn niggled along: struggling 1/2-way: t.o whn p.u bef 3 out* **4/1**[2]

/04- **P** **Blackmore**[25] 2997 7-11-7 **102**.. JoeColliver(5)
(N W Alexander) *hld up: rdn whn nt fluent 9th: sn btn: t.o whn p.u bef 2 out* **20/1**

P15- **P** **Stitched In Time (IRE)**[25] 2999 7-11-0 **97**.................... ShaunDobbin(7)
(Rose Dobbin) *t.k.h: cl up tl wknd after 4 out: tailedd off whn p.u bef 2 out* **17/2**

5m 58.3s (1.60) **Going Correction** +0.175s/f (Yiel) **9** Ran SP% **112.5**
Speed ratings (Par 105): **104,100,96,94,89** , , ,
CSF £18.25 CT £96.56 TOTE £4.90: £1.70, £1.60, £2.30; EX 16.20 Trifecta £176.20.
Owner The Brave Lads Partnership **Bred** Bishop Wilton Stud **Trained** Hawick, Borders

FOCUS
The wind had eased by now but this still turned into a slog, with only the first two still seriously in contention from the home turn. Not form to be confindent about.

3521 KILMANY CUP (HANDICAP CHASE) (18 fncs) 3m
3:10 (3:10) (Class 3) (0-135,133) 5-Y-0+ **£7,797** (£2,289; £1,144; £572)

Form RPR

2/0- **1** **Isla Pearl Fisher**[33] 2841 11-11-1 **122**.............................. PeterBuchanan 130
(N W Alexander) *nt fluent on occasions: in tch: hdwy to chse wnr 5 out: led 3 out: styd on strly fr next* **11/2**[3]

331- **2** *3* **Kris Cross (IRE)**[41] 2662 7-10-9 **123**..........................(t) GrantCockburn(7) 129
(Lucinda Russell) *pressed ldr: blkd 1st: led 11th: mstke next: rdn whn nt fluent 4 out: hdd whn hit next: rallied: nt fluent last: kpt on* **11/8**[1]

116- **3** *3 1/2* **Rossini's Dancer**[26] 2972 9-11-5 **133**......................(p) MrKitAlexander(7) 133
(N W Alexander) *led to 11th: rdn and outpcd 5 out: rallied 3 out: no imp fr next* **11/1**

206- **4** *13* **Lively Baron (IRE)**[41] 2670 9-11-2 **123**...........................(bt) JasonMaguire 114
(Donald McCain) *nt fluent: chsd ldrs: outpcd 12th: struggling fr next: n.d after* **6/4**[2]

6m 24.0s (20.60) **Going Correction** +0.675s/f (Soft) **4** Ran SP% **105.8**
Speed ratings: **92,91,89,85**
CSF £13.26 TOTE £5.80; EX 16.70 Trifecta £52.20.
Owner Mrs J E B Gammell **Bred** Mrs D Marshall **Trained** Kinneston, Perth & Kinross

FOCUS
They went a reasonable pace in this fair handicap chase. The winner is rated back to his very best.

3522 READ AIDAN COLEMAN EVERY FRIDAY RACINGUK.COM INTERMEDIATE OPEN NATIONAL HUNT FLAT RACE 2m
3:40 (3:40) (Class 6) 4-6-Y-0 **£1,949** (£572; £286; £143)

Form RPR

5- **1** **Coozan George**[56] 2347 5-11-5 0.. BrianHughes 104+
(Malcolm Jefferson) *t.k.h: prom: smooth hdwy to ld wl over 1f out: rdn and r.o strly fnl f* **11/4**[3]

332- **2** *5* **Cousin Guillaume (FR)**[31] 2871 5-11-5 0.................... RichardJohnson 97
(Karen McLintock) *t.k.h: led at slow pce: rdn over 2f out: hdd wl over 1f out: kpt on same pce fnl f* **6/4**[1]

3 *7* **Always Tipsy** 5-10-12 0.. MrKitAlexander(7) 90+
(N W Alexander) *t.k.h: hld up in tch: rdn and outpcd over 4f out: styd on wl fr 2f out: no ch w first two* **16/1**

3/5- **4** *1 1/4* **Il Testone (FR)**[229] 389 5-10-12 0.......................... DiarmuidO'Regan(7) 89
(Chris Grant) *chsd ldrs: drvn and outpcd over 2f out: n.d after* **16/1**

5 *1 1/2* **Elfego Baca (IRE)**[89] 5-10-12 0.. CraigNichol(7) 87
(Lucinda Russell) *plld hrd early: cl up: ev ch over 3f out: rn green and outpcd fr 2f out* **9/4**[2]

6- **6** *23* **Lachlan Mor**[38] 2738 5-10-12 0.. DaraghBourke(7) 64
(Stuart Coltherd) *hld up in tch: struggling 5f out: sn lost tch: t.o* **40/1**

3m 51.8s (9.00) **Going Correction** +0.175s/f (Yiel) **6** Ran SP% **111.6**
Speed ratings: **84,81,78,77,76 65**
CSF £7.21 TOTE £3.70: £1.30, £1.50; EX 7.60 Trifecta £54.60.
Owner A N Barrett **Bred** A N Barrett **Trained** Norton, N Yorks

FOCUS
A modest, steadily run bumper. The second and fourth set the level.
T/Plt: £564.70. Pool: £99,228.06 - 126.26 winning units. T/Qpdt: £95.40. Pool: £8230.87 - 63.80 winning units. RY

3208 NEWCASTLE (L-H)
Saturday, January 4

OFFICIAL GOING: Heavy (soft in places; 5.0)
Wind: Almost nil Weather: Overcast, dry

3523 CATHERINE DORNAN 90TH BIRTHDAY/EBF MARES' NOVICES' HURDLE (11 hdls) 2m 4f
12:00 (12:02) (Class 4) 4-Y-0+ **£3,898** (£1,144; £572; £286)

Form RPR

351- **1** **Retrieve The Stick**[6] 3393 5-11-8 0..................................(p) BrianHughes 104+
(Malcolm Jefferson) *t.k.h early: chsd ldrs: effrt and rdn bef 3 out: hdwy to ld appr next: sn hrd pressed: hung lft fr last: drvn out* **11/8**[1]

2 *nk* **Nosey Box (IRE)**[9] 3299 8-10-11 0..................................(t) DerekFox(5) 97
(Noel C Kelly, Ire) *led to 4 out: rallied and ev ch fr next: bmpd run-in: kpt on u.p: hld nr fin* **7/4**[2]

P54- **3** *3 1/4* **The Flaming Matron (IRE)**[14] 3212 8-11-1 105...(t) DiarmuidO'Regan(7) 102
(N W Alexander) *w ldr: led 4 out: jst hdd whn nt fluent 2 out: rdn and kpt on same pce fr last* **5/2**[3]

540- **4** *dist* **Beyondtemptation**[32] 2869 6-10-13 74.......................... JohnKington(3)
(Jonathan Haynes) *chsd ldrs: mstke and outpcd 6th: lost tch 4 out: t.o* **100/1**

5m 21.4s (0.30) **Going Correction** +0.10s/f (Yiel) **4** Ran SP% **108.0**
Speed ratings (Par 105): **103,102,101,**
CSF £4.22 TOTE £2.00; EX 3.60 Trifecta £4.60.
Owner Newstead Racing Partnership **Bred** Mrs M Barker **Trained** Norton, N Yorks

FOCUS
Fresh ground on bend into straight. They went an ordinary pace in this pretty modest event for mares. Probably a step up from the winner.

3524 STRAIGHTLINE CONSTRUCTION H'CAP CHASE (13 fncs) 2m 110y
12:35 (12:35) (Class 4) (0-120,111) 5-Y-0+ **£5,198** (£1,526; £763; £381)

Form RPR

13U- **1** **Cloverhill Lad (IRE)**[6] 3395 10-10-9 **101**..................... DaraghBourke(7) 111+
(Stuart Coltherd) *pressed ldr: led 3rd to next: cl up: led 5 out: clr 2 out: kpt on wl run-in* **5/1**

3/6- **2** *2 1/4* **Dancing Art (IRE)**[49] 2512 8-11-11 **110**.......................... JamesReveley 120+
(Keith Reveley) *prom: outpcd and pushed along 5 out: rallied whn nt fluent next: rdn whn pckd 3 out: chsd wnr bef last: kpt on* **15/8**[1]

5/3- **3** *9* **Dotties Dilema (IRE)**[45] 2595 6-11-9 **108**...................... PeterBuchanan 106
(Lucinda Russell) *led to 3rd: cl up: rdn and pressed wnr bef 4 out: sn rdn: lost 2nd bef last: wknd run-in* **2/1**[2]

/55- **4** *16* **Rupert Bear**[23] 3039 8-11-7 **111**.. MissCWalton(5) 95
(James Walton) *j. deliberately on occasions: t.k.h: hld up in tch: hdwy to ld 4th: hdd 5 out: nt fluent and wknd next* **7/2**[3]

4m 23.2s (2.10) **Going Correction** +0.175s/f (Yiel) **4** Ran SP% **107.0**
Speed ratings: **102,100,96,89**
CSF £14.37 TOTE £5.60; EX 8.10 Trifecta £21.70.
Owner Coltherd Turnbull **Bred** D Lynam **Trained** Selkirk, Borders

FOCUS
Not a strong handicap for the grade. A chase personal best from the winner.

3525 S V RUTTER H'CAP HURDLE (13 hdls) 2m 6f
1:05 (1:05) (Class 4) (0-105,105) 4-Y-0+ **£3,249** (£954; £477; £238)

Form RPR

F02- **1** **Total Assets**[26] 2999 6-11-7 **100**.. RyanMania 103+
(Simon Waugh) *prom: hdwy to ld bef 3 out: sn rdn: hrd pressed fr last: hld on gamely* **16/1**

F05- **2** *1/2* **Madam Lilibet (IRE)**[15] 3192 5-10-9 **95**................. JosephPalmowski(7) 95
(Sharon Watt) *hld up: stdy hdwy 1/2-way: rdn and outpcd bef 4 out: rallied and lft 4 l 3rd 3 out: wnt 2nd last: styd on u.p: hld nr fin* **8/1**[3]

/PP- **3** *hd* **Wayne Manor (IRE)**[100] 1664 5-10-12 **98**..................(t) GrantCockburn(7) 102+
(Lucinda Russell) *hld up: hmpd 2nd: stdy hdwy and in tch 8th: effrt and wnt 2nd 3 out: hmpd next: clsd on wnr last: kpt on: hld towards fin* **40/1**

PPP- **4** *17* **Notonebuttwo (IRE)**[24] 3022 7-10-8 **87**...................(vt[1]) RichieMcGrath 70
(Chris Grant) *prom: nt fluent and outpcd 9th: rallied bef 3 out: lft mod 4th next: no imp* **16/1**

66- **5** *6* **Milan Flyer (IRE)**[57] 2337 8-10-5 **89**.. DerekFox(5) 70
(Noel C Kelly, Ire) *hmpd 2nd: hld up: nt fluent 7th: stdy hdwy after next: outpcd after next: sme late hdwy: nvr on terms* **12/1**

0P5- **6** *28* **Ballyreesode (IRE)**[7] 3356 9-10-6 **85**..............................(p) BrianHarding 34
(Susan Corbett) *cl up: hmpd and lft in ld briefly 2nd: cl up: led 8th to after next: ev ch tl wknd after 3 out* **28/1**

PP4- **7** *1 1/4* **Shooting Times**[50] 2497 9-10-13 **92**..............................(b) PeterBuchanan 40
(Lucinda Russell) *cl up: led after 2nd: hdd 8th: cl up tl rdn and wknd after 4 out* **12/1**

036- **8** *14* **Crushed Ice**[8] 3334 8-10-3 **82**.. BrianHughes 16
(Malcolm Jefferson) *t.k.h: cl up: led after 9th: hit next: hdd bef 3 out: outpcd whn blnd 3 out: sn btn* **9/1**

2P6- **B** **Bollin Fiona**[54] 2416 10-10-11 **95**.. CallumWhillans(5)
(Donald Whillans) *hld up: b.d 2nd* **25/1**

566- **F** **Northern Acres**[23] 3040 8-10-4 **90**.. DiarmuidO'Regan(7) 88
(N W Alexander) *hld up bhd ldng gp: stdy hdwy and prom 4 out: 3 l down and disputing 2nd pl whn fell 2 out* **3/1**[1]

13/- **F** **Grey Area (IRE)**[255] 5495 9-11-5 **105**.. MrTDavidson(7)
(Tristan Davidson) *led tl fell heavily 2nd* **4/1**[2]

5/5- **P** **Hotgrove Boy**[23] 3040 7-9-9 **79** oh3.. HarryChalloner(5)
(Stuart Coltherd) *bhd: rdn and struggling bef 4 out: t.o whn p.u bef 2 out* **17/2**

6P1- **U** **Cumbrian Farmer**[18] 3141 7-10-5 **91**..............................(p) JonathonBewley(7)
(George Bewley) *in tch tl blnd and uns rdr 4th* **20/1**

5m 54.4s (18.40) **Going Correction** +0.30s/f (Yiel) **13** Ran SP% **118.3**
Speed ratings (Par 105): **78,77,77,71,69 59,58,53,** , , ,
CSF £131.75 CT £4979.00 TOTE £12.50: £3.90, £2.70, £13.50; EX 185.20 Trifecta £800.00 Part won. Pool of £1066.69 - 0.30 winning units..
Owner Northumberland Racing Club **Bred** H L Kirpalani & Shade Oak Stud **Trained** Mitford, Northumberland

FOCUS
Just a modest handicap hurdle, but there was an abundance of incident and a three-way finish, the trio finishing well clear. The winner is rated in line with her recent run, and the third was unlucky.

3526 MARRIOTT INTERACTIVE H'CAP CHASE (19 fncs) 3m
1:40 (1:42) (Class 3) (0-125,125) 5-Y-£6,963 (£2,057; £1,028; £514; £257)

Form RPR

0/5- **1** **Knockgraffon King (IRE)**[24] 3019 9-10-13 **112**.............. JasonMaguire 129+
(Donald McCain) *nt fluent on occasions: prom: hdwy to ld 12th: ears pricked and rdn whn nt fluent 4 out: styd on wl fr last* **7/2**[1]

053- **2** *2 1/2* **Rolecarr (IRE)**[27] 2972 11-11-5 **125**.......................... GrahamWatters(7) 135
(Ann Hamilton) *prom: hdwy to chse wnr after 5 out: effrt and clsd next: rdn after 3 out: one pce fr last* **7/2**[1]

432- **3** *10* **War On (IRE)**[14] 3209 7-10-11 **110**.. BrianHughes 111
(Chris Grant) *led to 9th: cl up: chal 12th to next: outpcd after 5 out: rallied to chse clr ldng pair 3 out: no imp* **4/1**[2]

F23- **4** *4 1/2* **Gwladys Street (IRE)**[13] 3223 7-10-7 **106**........................(p) RyanMahon 105
(William Kinsey) *nt fluent: hld up in tch: struggling fr 10th: sn detached: rallied 3 out: styd on: n.d* **4/1**[2]

253- **5** *24* **Bertie Milan (IRE)**[26] 3001 9-10-2 **101**..............................(p) BrianHarding 86
(N W Alexander) *cl up: led 9th to 12th: drvn and outpcd after 5 out: wknd 3 out* **9/2**[3]

331- **P** **Etxalar (FR)**[20] 3107 11-10-9 **108**..............................(t) PeterBuchanan
(Lucinda Russell) *chsd ldrs: outpcd whn mstke and stmbld 13th: sn struggling: t.o whn p.u bef 4 out* **8/1**

6m 22.0s (-0.50) **Going Correction** +0.175s/f (Yiel) **6** Ran SP% **113.7**
Speed ratings: **107,106,102,101,93**
CSF £16.62 TOTE £4.00: £2.50, £2.70; EX 16.40 Trifecta £58.20.
Owner Hollyville Partnership **Bred** Patrick Boyle **Trained** Cholmondeley, Cheshire

FOCUS
A fair handicap chase. The winner is rated better than the bare result.

3527 ST. JAMES PLACE H'CAP HURDLE (9 hdls) 2m
2:15 (2:16) (Class 4) (0-115,115) 4-Y-0+ **£3,898** (£1,144; £572; £286)

Form RPR
202- **1** **Sam Lord**[9] 3274 10-11-2 **105** DominicElsworth 107
(James Moffatt) *chsd clr ldr: hdwy and ev ch bef 3 out: rdn to ld run-in: styd on wl* **11/2**[3]

611- **2** *1 1/4* **Circus Star (USA)**[9] 3288 6-11-5 **115** MrJDixon(7) 118+
(John Dixon) *t.k.h: led and clr: blnd 4th: hit next: jnd by rivals bef 3 out: qcknd after 3 out: rdn next: edgd lft and hdd run-in: rallied: hld towards fin* **4/1**[2]

003- **3** *1* **Spanish Fleet**[20] 3106 6-10-2 **98** JohnDawson(7) 98
(John Wade) *prom: reminders after 3rd: outpcd 5th: rallied after 3 out: styd on wl fr last: hld towards fin* **11/1**

352- **4** *15* **Lysino (GER)**[14] 3210 5-10-13 **102** BrianHarding 89
(Chris Grant) *hld up: hdwy and in tch after 4 out: nt fluent next: wknd 2 out* **5/2**[1]

/06- **5** *17* **Pertemps Networks**[14] 3201 10-11-4 **110** (t) JakeGreenall(3) 78
(Michael Easterby) *hld up in tch: stdy hdwy and prom bef 3 out: rdn and wknd appr next* **12/1**

432- **6** *1 3/4* **Nautical Twilight**[14] 3212 4-10-8 **109** (p) BrianHughes 66
(Malcolm Jefferson) *chsd ldrs: blnd 3rd: effrt and ch bef 3 out: wknd appr next* **7/1**

400- **7** *13* **Call Of Duty (IRE)**[9] 3274 9-10-6 **100** ColmMcCormack(5) 53
(Dianne Sayer) *bhd: shortlived effrt bef 4 out: btn bef next* **40/1**

064- **8** *2 1/2* **Badea**[20] 3106 5-10-8 **97** DenisO'Regan 48
(Martin Todhunter) *hld up: struggling 1/2-way: nvr on terms* **6/1**

P30- **P** **Leroy Parker (IRE)**[23] 3041 6-10-9 **98** (b) RichieMcGrath
(Barry Murtagh) *prom: drvn along 4th: rallied: wknd 4 out: t.o whn p.u bef 2 out* **28/1**

4m 12.7s (2.70) **Going Correction** +0.30s/f (Yiel)
WFA 4 from 5yo+ 11lb **9** Ran SP% **112.7**
Speed ratings (Par 105): **105,104,103,96,87 87,80,79,**
CSF £27.47 CT £230.79 TOTE £6.00: £2.40, £1.30, £4.00; EX 23.20 Trifecta £217.70.
Owner Bowes Lodge Stables **Bred** Wickfield Farm Partnership **Trained** Cartmel, Cumbria

FOCUS
An ordinary handicap hurdle. The winner ran to his mark.

3528 BARBOUR H'CAP CHASE (16 fncs) 2m 4f
2:50 (2:50) (Class 5) (0-100,100) 5-Y-0+ **£2,599** (£763; £381; £190)

Form RPR
4/F- **1** **Dingo Bay**[50] 2498 8-10-8 **82** BrianHughes 97+
(John Wade) *j.w: cl up: chal 6 out: led 4 out: qcknd clr bef 2 out: styd on wl* **9/4**[1]

50P- **2** *7* **Samson Collonges (FR)**[24] 3022 8-9-11 **74** oh15 TonyKelly(3) 82
(Rebecca Menzies) *cl up: effrt and chsd wnr 4 out: sn rdn: kpt on same pce fr 2 out* **20/1**

160- **3** *8* **Monbeg (IRE)**[9] 3275 7-11-0 **88** (p) DenisO'Regan 90
(Martin Todhunter) *hld up: nt fluent and outpcd 7th: drvn along whn nt fluent 5 out: styd on fr 2 out: no imp* **12/1**

522- **4** *6* **Indian Voyage (IRE)**[20] 3107 6-10-13 **94** (t) StephenMulqueen(7) 93+
(Maurice Barnes) *mstkes: hld up in tch: hdwy 1/2-way: effrt whn blnd 4 out: kpt on same pce fr next* **9/2**[2]

665- **5** *11* **Vardas Supreme (IRE)**[16] 3180 11-10-0 **77** (tp) JonathanEngland(3) 68
(Richard Drake) *nt fluent on occasions: led: reminders after 6th: jnd 6 out: hdd whn hit 4 out: sn btn* **16/1**

2U4- **6** *3/4* **Ben Akram (IRE)**[23] 3041 6-11-12 **100** PeterBuchanan 85
(Lucinda Russell) *nt fluent on occasions: hld up in tch: rdn and wknd bef 4 out* **13/2**[3]

1F3- **7** *1* **Tresor De L'Isle (FR)**[20] 3107 7-11-0 **95** (p) DaleIrving(7) 78
(James Ewart) *in tch: mstke 7th: outpcd whn hit 10th: struggling fr 5 out* **8/1**

123/ **P** **Mr Chippy (IRE)**[736] 3441 10-11-6 **94** JasonMaguire
(Donald McCain) *prom on outside: mstke and outpcd 9th: nt fluent and wknd 5 out: t.o whn p.u after next* **9/2**[2]

5m 32.1s (4.90) **Going Correction** +0.175s/f (Yiel) **8** Ran SP% **109.9**
Speed ratings: **97,94,91,88,84 83,83,**
CSF £37.44 CT £408.07 TOTE £2.20: £2.00, £4.70, £3.80; EX 46.90 Trifecta £550.60.
Owner Miss Maria D Myco **Bred** G J White **Trained** Mordon, Co Durham

FOCUS
A modest handicap chase. The winner is rated to his best.

3529 EBF STALLIONS MARES' STANDARD OPEN NATIONAL HUNT FLAT RACE 2m
3:25 (3:25) (Class 6) 4-7-Y-0 **£1,949** (£572; £286; £143)

Form RPR
\- **1** **Oleohneh (IRE)** 6-11-3 0 BrianHughes 104+
(Malcolm Jefferson) *hld up in tch: smooth hdwy to ld over 2f out: shkn up over 1f out: qcknd clr: readily* **5/4**[1]

30- **2** *8* **Conjola**[23] 3042 7-11-3 0 RichieMcGrath 91
(Geoffrey Harker) *led 6f: pressed ldr: effrt and ev ch over 3f out to over 1f out: kpt on same pce fnl f* **5/1**[2]

0/0- **3** *8* **Kastela Stari**[57] 2347 7-11-3 0 BrianHarding 83
(Tim Fitzgerald) *hld up: stdy hdwy over 4f out: rdn 3f out: chsd clr ldng pair 1f out: no imp* **10/1**

00- **4** *1 3/4* **Silver Storm**[23] 3042 6-11-0 0 EwanWhillans(3) 81
(Tristan Davidson) *cl up: led after 6f to over 2f out: sn rdn: wknd appr fnl f* **7/1**

5 *1 3/4* **Presidential Lady (IRE)** 5-11-3 0 PeterBuchanan 80
(Chris Grant) *in tch: rn green after 4f: effrt u.p over 4f out: hung lft and wknd over 2f out* **6/1**[3]

0- **6** *42* **Camden Vine**[39] 2738 6-10-10 0 MrJDixon(7) 38
(Victor Thompson) *prom: drvn along 1/2-way: rdn and wknd over 5f out: t.o* **66/1**

5- **7** *79* **Madame Flirt**[32] 2871 5-10-12 0 HarryChalloner(5)
(Dianne Sayer) *prom: drvn 1/2-way: struggling fr 6f out: t.o* **20/1**

8 *5* **Polly's Rose** 5-11-3 0 RyanMania
(Ian Semple) *hld up: stdy hdwy and in tch over 6f out: rdn and wknd 4f out: t.o* **10/1**

4m 14.8s (10.40) **Going Correction** +0.30s/f (Yiel) **8** Ran SP% **112.3**
Speed ratings: **86,82,78,77,76 55,15,13**
CSF £7.34 TOTE £2.10: £1.20, £1.10, £4.40; EX 7.60 Trifecta £71.90.
Owner T A Stephenson & Mrs S Jefferson **Bred** Miss Mary O'Sullivan **Trained** Norton, N Yorks

FOCUS
Hard to think that this was anything other than a pretty weak bumper.

T/Plt: £1,043.10 to a £1 stake. Pool of £141115.43 - 98.75 winning tickets. T/Qpdt: £103.00 to a £1 stake. Pool of £16243.76 - 116.70 winning tickets. RY

2947 SANDOWN (R-H)
Saturday, January 4
3531 Meeting Abandoned - waterlogged

3289 WINCANTON (R-H)
Saturday, January 4
3536 Meeting Abandoned - waterlogged

3543 - 3549a (Foreign Racing) - See Raceform Interactive

3134 PLUMPTON (L-H)
Sunday, January 5

OFFICIAL GOING: Heavy (chs 3.7, hdl 3.8)
Wind: medium, against Weather: showers

3550 ATTHERACES.COM EXCLUSIVE BARRY GERAGHTY BLOG NOVICES' HURDLE (9 hdls) 2m
12:50 (12:50) (Class 4) 4-Y-0+ **£3,249** (£954; £477; £238)

Form RPR
1- **1** **Dubawi Island (FR)**[14] 3226 5-11-12 0 AidanColeman 126+
(Venetia Williams) *hld up in tch in midfield: clsd to trck ldrs 3 out: led and gng best bnd bef next: hrd pressed and rdn between last 2: fnd ex and sn asserted flat: wl in command and eased towards fin* **8/13**[1]

\- **2** *2 3/4* **Civil War (IRE)**[82] 5-11-5 0 JamieMoore 112
(Gary Moore) *hld up in last trio: mstke 5th: clsd to chse ldrs 3 out: rdn and effrt bef 2 out: drvn and str chal between last 2: no ex and one pce flat* **9/2**[3]

6F- **3** *6* **Warrant Officer**[20] 3134 4-10-7 0 MarcGoldstein 94
(Sheena West) *chsd ldrs: cl 6th and nt clr run after 3 out: rdn and effrt bnd bef next: 3rd and styd on same pce between last 2* **14/1**

03- **4** *2 1/2* **Torero**[20] 3134 5-11-2 0 JoshuaMoore(3) 104
(Diana Grissell) *nt a fluent: led: j. slowly and mstke 1st: sn hdd: chsd ldr tl after 6th: mstke 3 out: rdn and outpcd bnd bef next: kpt on same pce fr 2 out* **4/1**[2]

646- **5** *10* **Kaki Island (IRE)**[17] 3175 6-11-5 0 TomCannon 95
(Chris Gordon) *t.k.h: chsd ldrs: hmpd and j. into 1st: sn led and clr next: rdn and hdd bnd bef 2 out: btn whn j.lft 2 out: sn wknd* **16/1**

00- **6** *2 1/2* **Moratab (IRE)**[18] 3163 5-11-5 0 NickScholfield 91
(Keiran Burke) *chsd ldrs: wnt 2nd after 3 out: rdn and ev ch wl bef 3 out: lost pl and struggling bef 2 out: wknd 2 out* **33/1**

7 *32* **See More Power (IRE)**[231] 9-11-5 0 TomO'Brien 59
(Paul Henderson) *hld up in last pair: lost tch qckly after 6th: t.o 2 out* **50/1**

P- **P** **Saint Helena (IRE)**[6] 3422 6-10-12 0 MattieBatchelor
(Jim Best) *t.k.h: hld up in rr: sme hdwy after 4th: blnd and dropped to last again 6th: sn eased and t.o: p.u last* **50/1**

005- **F** **Sportsreport (IRE)**[168] 1053 6-11-5 0 AndrewThornton
(Seamus Mullins) *midfield whn j.big: cannoned into rival and fell 1st* **50/1**

4m 21.8s (21.00) **Going Correction** +1.325s/f (Heav)
WFA 4 from 5yo+ 11lb **9** Ran SP% **121.5**
Speed ratings (Par 105): **100,98,95,94,89 88,72, ,**
CSF £4.24 TOTE £1.80: £1.10, £1.40, £3.40; EX 4.50 Trifecta £31.80.
Owner Andrew Brooks & Julian Taylor **Bred** Darley Stud Management Co Ltd **Trained** Kings Caple, H'fords

FOCUS
Rails moved to outer winter line on back straight, all bends on fresh ground and inner strip opened down the hill on chase course. The going was heavy after a dry night which enabled the meeting to pass an inspection. The jockeys reported it was riding "very heavy". There were several non-runners in this novice hurdle and it turned into a two-horse race in the straight. The cosy winner was value for further.

3551 FOLLOW @ATTHERACES ON TWITTER NOVICES' CHASE (10 fncs 2 omitted) 2m 1f
1:20 (1:20) (Class 3) 5-Y-0+ **£7,147** (£2,098; £1,049; £524)

Form RPR
234/ **1** **Brick Red**[275] 5157 7-10-12 0 AidanColeman 120+
(Venetia Williams) *trckd ldrs: mstke 7th: led on bit bef bypassed 2 out: clr last: v easily: nt extended* **4/6**[1]

3/1- **2** *6* **King Spirit (IRE)**[246] 118 6-11-4 130 BrendanPowell 106
(Brendan Powell) *w ldr tl led bef 8th: rdn and hdd after 3 out (actual 2 out): stl ev ch tl brushed aside by wnr bypassing 2 out: mstke last: plugged on flat* **5/2**[2]

5F3- **3** *1 1/4* **Head Spin (IRE)**[21] 3119 6-10-12 0 AndrewThornton 99
(Seamus Mullins) *hld up in tch in last pair: effrt and ev ch 3 out (actual 2 out): rdn to ld on long run to last: hdd bef bypassed 2 out: sn brushed aside by wnr: 3rd and styd on same pce flat* **25/1**

500- **4** *31* **Tchang Goon (FR)**[20] 3139 10-10-12 62 (p) DaveCrosse 68
(Zoe Davison) *led: mstke 2nd: reminders after 6th: hdd bef 8th: dropped to last 3 out (actual 2 out): sn lost tch u.p: t.o* **100/1**

626- **U** **Marcus Antonius**[16] 3183 7-10-12 116 LeightonAspell
(Jim Boyle) *t.k.h: j.rt: hld up in last pair: blnd and uns rdr 4th* **6/1**[3]

4m 40.0s (17.00) **Going Correction** +1.025s/f (Soft) **5** Ran SP% **107.7**
Speed ratings: **101,98,97,83,**
CSF £2.68 TOTE £1.40: £1.40, £1.10; EX 2.70 Trifecta £12.10.
Owner Julian Taylor & Andrew Brooks **Bred** Raimon Bloodstock **Trained** Kings Caple, H'fords

FOCUS
Due to the ground the first fence in the straight was omitted in all races. An interesting novice chase. The easy winner was a 144 hurdler at best and can probably match that over fences.

3552 AT THE RACES SKY 415 & EBF STALLIONS "NATIONAL HUNT" NOVICES' HURDLE (QUALIFIER) (12 hdls) 2m 5f
1:50 (1:50) (Class 3) 4-7-Y-0 **£5,718** (£1,679; £839; £419)

Form RPR
2- **1** **Marcilhac (FR)**[20] 3136 5-11-2 131 AidanColeman 130+
(Venetia Williams) *j.rt at times: w ldr thrght: rdn and led bef 2 out: drvn to ld and j.rt 2 out: 4 l clr last: drvn out: a holding 2nd* **5/4**[1]

2/3- **2** *1* **Brave Vic (IRE)**[22] 3092 6-10-13 0 JoshuaMoore(3) 123
(Gary Moore) *chsd ldng pair: clsd to ld bef 3 out: wnt clr w wnr wl bef 2 out: rdn and hdd bef 2 out: 4 l down and looked wl hld last: rallied gamely and kpt on flat* **7/2**[3]

11- **3** *33* **Spirit Oscar (IRE)**[10] 3247 6-11-5 123 LeightonAspell 105
(Oliver Sherwood) *led: rdn and hdd bef 3 out: 3rd and wknd wl bef 2 out: j.lft last: eased flat* **6/4**[2]

00- **4** *51* **Wunfurlez**[20] 3136 6-11-2 0 SamThomas 38
(Diana Grissell) *hld up in last pair: clsd and trckd ldrs after 8th: wknd after next: j. slowly and mstke 3 out: sn t.o: eased flat* **100/1**

0- **5** *26* **Underwood (FR)**[20] 3136 6-11-2 0 TomSiddall 12
(Michael Roberts) *a in rr: rdn and struggling after 8th: t.o after next: blnd 3 out* **100/1**

5m 39.4s (22.40) **Going Correction** +1.325s/f (Heav) 5 Ran SP% **108.6**
Speed ratings: **110,109,97,77,67**
CSF £6.01 TOTE £3.10: £1.70, £1.70; EX 4.80 Trifecta £7.00.
Owner A Brooks **Bred** S C E A Du Haras Des Sablonnets Et Al **Trained** Kings Caple, H'fords

FOCUS
Despite the small field plenty of interest in this novice hurdle but it proved a severe test in the conditions. The idling winner was value for further.

3553 AT THE RACES VIRGIN 534 H'CAP HURDLE (12 hdls) 2m 5f
2:20 (2:20) (Class 5) (0-100,99) 4-Y-0+ **£2,395** (£698; £349)

Form RPR

2/1- **1** **Mudita Moment (IRE)**[5] 3434 9-12-2 99 7ex AidanColeman 117+
(Venetia Williams) *hld up in tch: trckd ldng trio 9th: jnd ldr on bit after 3 out: j. bdly rt and mstke 2 out: rdn to ld between last 2: mstke last: drvn flat: asserted fnl 100yds: styd on* **4/6**[1]

0U5- **2** *3/4* **Sweet Boy Vic (IRE)**[20] 3138 6-10-5 74 (t) MarcGoldstein 87
(Chris Gordon) *wl in tch in midfield: hdwy to join ldrs 6th: rdn to ld after 3 out: clr w wnr next: hdd between last 2: stl ev ch and mstke last: no ex fnl 100yds* **7/1**[2]

/00- **3** *33* **Marmalade Man**[31] 2908 8-11-9 92 AndrewThornton 72
(Seamus Mullins) *j.rt: w ldr: reminder after 5th: rdn to ld after 8th: hdd after 3 out: wknd bef next* **8/1**

0/5- **4** *5* **Strange Bird (IRE)**[39] 2744 9-10-11 80 LeightonAspell 55
(Richard Rowe) *mde most tl 7th: stl cl 4th and mstke 3 out: wknd bef next* **14/1**

005- **R** **Romney Marsh**[31] 2896 13-11-0 90 MrFTett(7)
(Roger Curtis) *wl in tch in midfield: chsd ldrs 7th: rdn and wknd 9th: wl t.o whn rn out last* **25/1**

5PP- **P** **Zelos Diktator**[21] 3119 8-10-5 84 MikeyHamill(10)
(Sean Curran) *w ldrs: led 7th: rdn and hdd after next: losing tch whn mstke next: t.o whn p.u bef 2 out* **25/1**

004- **P** **Brians Well (IRE)**[24] 3029 7-11-12 95 (t) BrendanPowell
(Brendan Powell) *hld up in tch in rr: nt fluent 1st: rdn and lost tch bef 3 out: t.o whn p.u bef 2 out* **15/2**[3]

5m 43.4s (26.40) **Going Correction** +1.325s/f (Heav) 7 Ran SP% **109.7**
Speed ratings (Par 103): **102,101,89,87,** ,
CSF £5.63 CT £17.36 TOTE £1.50: £1.10, £3.40; EX 5.50 Trifecta £23.80.
Owner John Moorhouse & John Nicholls (Trading) **Bred** John J Cleary **Trained** Kings Caple, H'fords

FOCUS
A very moderate handicap hurdle. The winner is rated in line with his recent win.

3554 AT THE RACES SUSSEX NATIONAL (A H'CAP CHASE) (16 fncs 4 omitted) 3m 5f
2:50 (2:50) (Class 3) (0-130,129) 5-Y-0+ **£15,856** (£4,836; £2,526; £1,371)

Form RPR

/61- **1** **Reblis (FR)**[20] 3137 9-10-13 119 JoshuaMoore(3) 132+
(Gary Moore) *in tch in midfield: chsd ldng pair and rdn 13th: hit next: led on long run to last: sn clr and idling bnd ent st: drvn out flat* **5/1**[2]

0/6- **2** *4 1/2* **Smoking Aces (IRE)**[29] 2945 10-11-5 122 (b) APMcCoy 129+
(Jonjo O'Neill) *j.lft and mstkes: in tch in rr: rdn after 6th: hdwy u.p after 12th: lft 4th and pckd next: drvn and styd on to chse wnr bypassing 2 out: kpt on but nvr a threat* **7/2**[1]

/04- **3** *8* **Monkerty Tunkerty**[30] 2931 11-11-12 129 WillKennedy 125
(Miss Jessica Westwood) *chsd ldr tl 8th: stydd prom: wnt 2nd again after 11th: led 3 out: rdn and hdd on long run to last: 3rd and btn bypassing 2 out: wknd last* **8/1**

4/4- **4** *15* **Mortimers Cross**[14] 3223 13-10-13 116 (t) RichardJohnson 105
(John Needham) *chsd ldrs: wnt 2nd 8th: mstke 10th: led 11th: hdd and mstke 3 out: wknd bnd ent st* **8/1**

252- **P** **According To Them (IRE)**[10] 3250 10-9-11 105 oh32 ow2(t) ConorShoemark(5)
(Daniel Steele) *hld up in tch in rr: sme hdwy after 10th: mstke 11th: rdn and lost tch qckly after next: t.o whn p.u 14th* **80/1**

251- **F** **Leg Iron (IRE)**[28] 2979 9-10-10 113 MarcGoldstein
(Sheena West) *chsd ldrs: 4th and wl in tch whn fell 13th* **6/1**[3]

PP3- **P** **Halley (FR)**[16] 3191 7-11-9 126 PaddyBrennan
(Tom George) *led: pckd 10th: hdd next: sn lost pl and bhd 12th: t.o after 13th tl p.u 3 out (actual 2 out)* **6/1**[3]

204- **P** **Ballybough Gorta (IRE)**[29] 2937 7-11-12 129 (v) JamieMoore
(Peter Bowen) *in tch in rr: nt fluent 7th: sn rdn and nvr travelling wl after: losing tch whn p.u 12th* **5/1**[2]

122- **P** **Adrenalin Flight (IRE)**[49] 2537 8-10-11 114 AndrewThornton
(Seamus Mullins) *chsd ldrs: rdn and lost pl after 8th: stl in tch but struggling whn p.u qckly 12th* **7/1**

8m 1.5s (23.50) **Going Correction** +1.025s/f (Soft) 9 Ran SP% **120.1**
Speed ratings: **108,106,104,100,** , , ,
CSF £24.65 CT £141.43 TOTE £6.10: £2.20, £2.00, £2.70; EX 23.90 Trifecta £255.80.
Owner Kingsley, Avery, Farr, Glover, Humphreys **Bred** Robert Adenot **Trained** Lower Beeding, W Sussex

FOCUS
The feature race and a gruelling test of stamina, with eventually just four completing. The winner looks to have more to offer.

3555 AT THE RACES ON FACEBOOK H'CAP CHASE (11 fncs 3 omitted) 2m 4f
3:20 (3:20) (Class 4) (0-105,105) 5-Y-0+ **£3,898** (£1,144; £572; £286)

Form RPR

52R- **1** **Upton Mead (IRE)**[4] 3470 7-11-7 100 (b) RichardJohnson 110+
(Kevin Tork) *chsd ldr tl led 2nd: mde rest: rdn and forged 3 l clr whn lft wl clr bnd ent st: eased flat* **9/4**[1]

322- **2** *29* **Overnight Fame (IRE)**[23] 3058 10-11-7 105 (p) AodhaganConlon(5) 80
(Tom George) *led tl 2nd: chsd ldr after: ev ch whn stmbld on landing 8th: rdn and trying to rally whn mstke next: wknd after 3 out (actual 2 out): lft modest 2nd bnd ent st* **9/4**[1]

/64- **3** *15* **Badb Catha (IRE)**[35] 2849 8-9-7 79 oh17 MrFTett(7) 39
(Roger Curtis) *a in rr: pushed along after 6th: lost tch w ldrs after 7th: wnt modest 4th and mstke 8th: wl btn whn lft 3rd bnd ent st: t.o* **25/1**

0/5- **4** *9* **Abbey Dore (IRE)**[47] 2578 11-10-0 79 oh1 (v[1]) MarkGrant 30
(Jonathan Geake) *chsd ldrs: rdn after 6th: drvn and struggling after next: lost tch 9th: lft 4th bnd ent st: t.o* **5/1**[3]

0/0- **S** **Browns Brook (IRE)**[26] 3015 8-10-2 81 AidanColeman 79
(Venetia Williams) *chsd ldrs: rdn after 7th: ev ch whn lft 2nd next: drvn after 3 out (actual 2 out): 3 l down and looked btn whn stmbld and slipped up bnd ent st* **5/2**[2]

5m 35.8s (28.50) **Going Correction** +1.025s/f (Soft) 5 Ran SP% **110.6**
Speed ratings: **84,72,66,62,**
CSF £8.01 TOTE £2.60: £1.30, £1.40; EX 5.70 Trifecta £32.60.
Owner Tork Racing **Bred** Francis Small **Trained** Leigh, Surrey

FOCUS
A small field in this moderate handicap chase and another success for a course specialist. It's difficult to know what he achieved.

3556 COMPARE THE ODDS ON ATTHERACES.COM H'CAP HURDLE (9 hdls) 2m
3:50 (3:50) (Class 4) (0-110,105) 4-Y-0+ **£3,249** (£954; £477; £238)

Form RPR

/51- **1** **Beau Lake (IRE)**[22] 3094 10-11-3 99 GavinSheehan(3) 109+
(Suzy Smith) *mde all: qcknd after 3 out: j.rt 2 out and last: r.o wl* **7/4**[2]

P55- **2** *4 1/2* **Hold The Bucks (USA)**[10] 3249 8-10-1 85 ow5 ConorShoemark(5) 86
(Daniel Steele) *chsd wnr thrght: hit 3 out: rdn and pressed wnr bef next: sltly outpcd 2 out: swtchd lft and rallied between last 2: styd on same pce flat* **8/1**[3]

/30- **3** *6* **Edmaaj (IRE)**[51] 2492 6-11-12 105 APMcCoy 104
(Jonjo O'Neill) *t.k.h: hld up in tch in rr: clsd after 6th: rdn and effrt after 3 out: no imp: btn whn nt fluent last* **5/6**[1]

024/ **4** *23* **Kingsfold Flare**[550] 866 7-11-2 95 JamieMoore 76
(Gary Moore) *t.k.h: hld up in 3rd and clsd to chse ldrs 3 out: wknd next: mstke last* **16/1**

4m 26.6s (25.80) **Going Correction** +1.325s/f (Heav) 4 Ran SP% **107.9**
Speed ratings (Par 105): **88,85,82,71**
CSF £12.44 TOTE £2.80; EX 14.10 Trifecta £19.10.
Owner Sergio Gordon-Watson & Graham Willetts **Bred** Larry Murphy **Trained** Lewes, E Sussex

FOCUS
A moderate handicap hurdle with the field reduced by withdrawals to just four, but a third course specialist to score on the day. The form is rated around the second and third.
T/Plt: £3.90 to a £1 stake. Pool: £106,662.14 - 19,612.99 winning tickets. T/Qpdt: £4.00 to a £1 stake. Pool: £6,105.03 - 1,103.70 winning tickets. SP

3557 - 3558a (Foreign Racing) - See Raceform Interactive

2376 NAAS (L-H)
Sunday, January 5

OFFICIAL GOING: Soft (soft to heavy in places)

3559a SLANEY NOVICE HURDLE (GRADE 2) (11 hdls) 2m 4f
1:30 (1:30) 5-Y-0+ **£20,312** (£5,937; £2,812)

RPR

1 **Briar Hill (IRE)**[21] 3122 6-11-10 RWalsh 150+
(W P Mullins, Ire) *trckd ldr in 2nd: niggled along 3 out and sn clsd on outer to get on terms bef next: led narrowly between last 2: nt fluent last and kpt on wl u.p run-in* **1/3**[1]

2 *2 1/4* **Apache Jack (IRE)**[28] 2990 6-11-3 BryanCooper 141
(D T Hughes, Ire) *led: nt fluent 2nd: slt mstke 7th: jnd bef 2 out and hdd narrowly u.p between last 2: kpt on wl fr last wout matching wnr* **10/1**[3]

3 *3/4* **Very Wood (FR)**[35] 2852 5-11-0 135 PCarberry 139
(Noel Meade, Ire) *w.w in rr of trio: slt mstke 5th: nt fluent 4 out and mstke next: rdn bef 2 out and no imp on ldrs: kpt on wl towards fin wout threatening principals* **10/3**[2]

5m 4.0s (3.10) 3 Ran SP% **107.2**
CSF £3.51 TOTE £1.40; DF 3.40 Trifecta £3.20.
Owner Andrea & Graham Wylie **Bred** Victor Connolly **Trained** Muine Beag, Co Carlow

FOCUS
It was visually unimpressive by Briar Hill but it might just have been one of those races.

3560 - 3563a (Foreign Racing) - See Raceform Interactive

3113 SOUTHWELL (L-H)
Monday, January 6

OFFICIAL GOING: Heavy (soft in places; 5.7)
The inside two-thirds of fences were on un-raced fresh ground and bends moved where possible.
Wind: strong across Weather: fine and sunny but windy Rails: Both bends moved to fresh ground

3564 BET TOTEPLACEPOT WITH TOTEPOOL H'CAP CHASE (13 fncs) 2m
12:25 (12:25) (Class 5) (0-100,93) 5-Y-0+ **£2,599** (£763; £381; £190)

Form RPR

PPP- **1** **The Informant**[21] 3139 8-10-7 74 (p) AndrewThornton 87+
(Seamus Mullins) *j.rt: led to 2nd: chsd ldr: led 9th: hdd appr 3 out: hit 2 out: styd on to ld last 100yds: drvn rt out* **7/1**

54U- **2** *3/4* **Decent Lord (IRE)**[5] 3449 10-10-11 78 SeanQuinlan 88
(Jennie Candlish) *chsd ldrs: pushed along 8th: upsides 100yds out: no ex clsng stages* **7/4**[1]

00- **3** *1 1/2* **Cooldine Run (IRE)**[15] 3227 10-11-5 93 (t) MrJJarrett(7) 103
(John Needham) *hld up: hdwy to chse ldrs 7th: led appr 3 out: hit 2 out: hdd and no ex last 100yds* **5/1**[3]

222- **4** *11* **Morestead (IRE)**[11] 3248 9-11-9 90 (v) APMcCoy 88
(Brendan Powell) *hmpd 1st: swtchd ins and led 2nd: clr 6th: hdd 9th: sn hrd drvn: wknd appr 3 out* **5/2**[2]

000- **5** *19* **Strathaird (IRE)**[41] 2737 10-9-12 68 oh20 ow1 (p) JohnKington(3) 47
(Andrew Crook) *in rr: hit 1st: sme hdwy 7th: bhd fr 4 out* **33/1**

P05- **U** **Teenage Dream (IRE)**[29] 2976 6-11-10 **91**....................(vt[1]) CharliePoste
(Derek Shaw) *in rr: reminders 7th: 5th and styng on whn blnd and uns rdr 4 out* **5/1**[3]

4m 28.7s (26.70) **Going Correction** +1.525s/f (Heav) **6** Ran SP% **113.7**
Speed ratings: **94,93,92,87,77**
CSF £20.96 TOTE £11.40: £3.60, £1.60; EX 23.20 Trifecta £122.90.

Owner Dr & Mrs John Millar **Bred** Mrs J D Richards, Mrs C L Shaw & Mrs V Gilmou **Trained** Wilsford-Cum-Lake, Wilts

FOCUS
The inside two-thirds of fences were on unraced fresh ground and bends moved where possible. A run-of-the-mill handicap, with the winner rated to his hurdles mark.

3565 WIN BIG WITH THE TOTEJACKPOT NOVICES' H'CAP CHASE (19 fncs) 3m 110y

12:55 (12:55) (Class 4) (0-110,110) 5-Y-0+ **£3,994** (£1,240; £667)

Form RPR

356- **1** **High Ron**[43] 2700 9-11-4 **102**... AndrewThornton 108
(Caroline Bailey) *led: reminders 7th: narrowly hdd 11th: led 4 out: sn drvn: narrowly hdd 2 out: n.m.r and edgd rt run-in: led nr fin: all out* **8/1**

022- **2** *shd* **Shouldavboughtgold (IRE)**[11] 3283 7-11-11 **109**...(tp) RichardJohnson 116+
(William Kinsey) *trckd ldr: narrow ld 11th: blnd and hdd 4 out: narrow ld 2 out: edgd lft run-in: hdd and carried rt nr fin* **6/4**[1]

1FU- **3** *42* **What A Good Night (IRE)**[17] 3193 6-11-1 **99**........ SamTwiston-Davies 75
(Nigel Twiston-Davies) *chsd ldrs: wknd 4 out: sn bhd: t.o* **6/1**

/U6- **P** **Old Way (IRE)**[55] 2430 8-11-0 **98**... AidanColeman
(Venetia Williams) *in rr: drvn 9th: lost pl and reminders bef next: sn bhd: p.u bef 15th* **4/1**[3]

4/3- **P** **Off The Wall (IRE)**[21] 3129 7-11-12 **110**....................(bt) TomScudamore
(David Pipe) *chsd ldrs 10th: 4th and wkng whn blnd 4 out: sn eased and wl bhd: t.o whn p.u bef next* **3/1**[2]

6m 58.5s (35.50) **Going Correction** +1.525s/f (Heav) **5** Ran SP% **110.4**
Speed ratings: **104,103,90, ,**
CSF £21.32 TOTE £7.10: £2.50, £1.30; EX 22.10 Trifecta £90.40.

Owner Mrs Gillian Burke **Bred** Gillian & Micheal Burke **Trained** Holdenby, Northants

FOCUS
A novice handicap which probably took little winning. The winner is rated back to the best of last year's form.

3566 ROULETTE AND BLACKJACK AT TOTEPOOL.COM CASINO MARES' H'CAP HURDLE (13 hdls) 3m 110y

1:25 (1:26) (Class 4) (0-120,116) 4-Y-0+ **£3,249** (£954; £477; £238)

Form RPR

/11- **1** **Hopatina (IRE)**[46] 2620 8-11-1 **108**................................. MichaelByrne(3) 115+
(Neil Mulholland) *hld up wl in tch: jnd ldrs 9th: led 3 out: drvn clr between last 2* **3/1**[2]

2/P- **2** *6* **Fortuna Rose**[218] 606 8-10-12 **102**.. MarkGrant 103
(Julian Smith) *hld up but wl in tch: jnd ldrs 8th: chsd wnr fr 3 out: kpt on same pce* **6/1**[3]

241- **3** *21* **Fountains Mary**[25] 3044 6-11-1 **105**...............................(b) AidanColeman 85
(Anthony Honeyball) *nt fluent: chsd ldrs: reminders 3 out: lost pl bef next: tk poor 3rd appr last* **5/2**[1]

060- **4** *23* **Lady Fingers**[27] 3010 6-10-8 **98**................................ SamTwiston-Davies 55
(Nigel Twiston-Davies) *mde most: hdd 3 out: lost pl bef next: lost poor 3rd and mstke last: sn eased* **5/2**[1]

011- **P** **Gulf Punch**[20] 3145 7-11-12 **116**.......................................(p) JasonMaguire
(Donald McCain) *w ldr: reminders 10th: sn lost pl and bhd: t.o whn p.u bef 2 out* **6/1**[3]

6m 58.7s (43.70) **Going Correction** +1.40s/f (Heav) **5** Ran SP% **110.7**
Speed ratings (Par 105): **86,84,77,70,**
CSF £19.39 TOTE £3.60: £1.70, £3.70; EX 23.20 Trifecta £62.80.

Owner J R Baigent **Bred** Avon Thoroughbreds **Trained** Limpley Stoke, Wilts

FOCUS
A moderate mares' handicap which saw another step forward from the winner.

3567 YOUR FAVOURITE POOL BETS AT TOTEPOOL.COM NOVICES' HURDLE (11 hdls) 2m 4f 110y

1:55 (1:55) (Class 4) 4-Y-0+ **£3,249** (£954; £477; £238)

Form RPR

234- **1** **No No Mac (IRE)**[31] 2932 5-11-6 123.. NoelFehily 121+
(Charlie Longsdon) *trckd ldrs: led 8th: drvn clr between last 2: kpt rt up to work* **8/11**[1]

50- **2** *1 3/4* **Ampleforth**[9] 3357 6-11-1 0... RobertMcCarth(5) 116+
(Ian Williams) *hld up towards rr: hdwy 7th: chsd wnr after 3 out: styd on same pce between last 2: keeping on at fin* **16/1**

/00- **3** *22* **Lecale Lad (IRE)**[22] 3115 7-11-6 0................................ RichardJohnson 94
(Tim Vaughan) *hld up in rr: hdwy 7th: modest 4th 3 out: poor 3rd next* **33/1**

4/4- **4** *5* **The Clock Leary (IRE)**[23] 3092 6-11-6 0.......................... AidanColeman 92
(Venetia Williams) *j.rt: led to 8th: sn drvn: wknd appr 2 out: poor 4th whn hit last* **9/4**[2]

5 *2* **Silent Knight (IRE)**[71] 5-11-6 0.. JasonMaguire 87
(Warren Greatrex) *chsd ldrs: drvn 6th: outpcd and lost pl 3 out* **5/1**[3]

554- **6** *2* **Cusheen Bridge (IRE)**[22] 3115 6-11-6 0.......................... AdamPogson 85
(Charles Pogson) *chsd ldrs: 3rd and wkng whn mstke 2 out* **16/1**

66- **P** **High Aspirations (IRE)**[10] 3326 6-11-6 0............................ NickScholfield
(Michael Blake) *t.k.h: sn trcking ldrs: lost pl 7th: sn bhd: t.o whn p.u after 3 out* **50/1**

0- **P** **He's A Gentleman**[20] 3147 7-11-3 0.................................... JakeGreenall(3)
(Michael Easterby) *mid-div: hit 3rd: drvn and lost pl 7th: sn bhd: p.u after next* **50/1**

P- **P** **Carrigeen Aspen (IRE)**[18] 3177 7-10-8 0.................. ThomasGarner(5)
(Oliver Sherwood) *in rr: bhd and drvn 7th: sn bhd: t.o whn p.u bef 2 out* **50/1**

5m 37.1s (24.10) **Going Correction** +1.40s/f (Heav) **9** Ran SP% **125.9**
Speed ratings (Par 105): **110,109,100,99,98 97, , ,**
CSF £17.00 TOTE £1.80: £1.10, £4.20, £7.90; EX 20.20 Trifecta £211.00.

Owner R Jenner & J Green **Bred** Mrs Kathleen McKeever **Trained** Over Norton, Oxon

FOCUS
No real depth to this novice and the leading pair came well clear. Arguably a step up from the winner.

3568 DOWNLOAD THE TOTEPOOL MOBILE APP NOVICES' HURDLE (9 hdls) 2m

2:30 (2:30) (Class 4) 4-Y-0+ **£3,119** (£915; £457; £228)

Form RPR

101- **1** **Wadswick Court (IRE)**[25] 3034 6-11-12 0............................. NoelFehily 133+
(Charlie Longsdon) *mde all: drvn and styd on strly fr 2 out* **5/4**[1]

2 *6* **Earth Amber**[86] 5-10-12 0.. DavidBass 114+
(Nicky Henderson) *trckd ldrs: handy 2nd 3 out: rdn next: sn btn* **7/4**[2]

000- **3** *38* **Tashkaldou (FR)**[18] 3175 5-11-5 0...................................(t) HarrySkelton 82
(Dan Skelton) *chsd ldrs: handy 3rd 6th: drvn and one pce next* **20/1**

20- **4** *6* **Bally Braes (IRE)**[29] 2978 6-11-5 0...................... SamTwiston-Davies 76
(Nigel Twiston-Davies) *in rr: drvn along 3rd: sme hdwy 5th: sn struggling: tk poor 4th last* **3/1**[3]

50- **5** *3 1/2* **Epic Storm (IRE)**[21] 1152 6-11-5 0.. TomSiddall 73
(Martin Keighley) *trckd ldrs: outpcd 5th: modest 4th sn after 3 out: j.rt and wknd last* **33/1**

0- **6** *45* **Spirit Minded**[53] 2479 6-10-12 0.. DavidEngland 21
(Giles Smyly) *t.k.h: trckd ldrs: lost pl 5th: sn bhd: t.o 3 out* **100/1**

P- **7** *9* **Dustland Fairytale (IRE)**[18] 3175 6-10-12 0................. RobertThornton 12
(Ian Williams) *t.k.h: trckd ldrs 5th: wknd qckly 3 out: sn bhd: t.o next* **100/1**

4m 21.2s (24.20) **Going Correction** +1.40s/f (Heav) **7** Ran SP% **115.5**
Speed ratings (Par 105): **95,92,73,70,68 45,41**
CSF £3.94 TOTE £2.50: £1.20, £1.60; EX 5.00 Trifecta £30.80.

Owner The Chosen Few **Bred** L W Doran **Trained** Over Norton, Oxon

FOCUS
A novice which predictably developed into a match between the two market leaders. Form worth being fairly positive about.

3569 CHELTENHAM ANTE POST BETTING AT TOTEPOOL.COM H'CAP HURDLE (11 hdls) 2m 4f 110y

3:00 (3:00) (Class 5) (0-100,100) 4-Y-0+ **£2,241** (£658; £329; £164)

Form RPR

552- **1** **Bold Tara**[22] 3119 7-9-13 **80**..(tp) OllieGarner(7) 96
(Martin Keighley) *chsd ldrs: drvn 7th: upsides 3 out and last: led last 75yds: kpt rt up to work* **8/1**

031- **2** *2* **The Happy Warrior**[7] 3420 6-9-11 **78**............................... GaryDerwin(7) 93
(Bob Buckler) *w ldr: led 8th: jnd last: hdd and no ex* **7/4**[1]

232- **3** *21* **Superciliary**[7] 3420 5-11-0 **98**.................................... LouisMuspratt(10) 96
(Chris Gordon) *in rr: drvn and hdwy 7th: 3rd 3 out: wknd next: blnd last* **9/2**[2]

030- **4** *3 1/2* **Taradrewe**[181] 932 7-11-8 **96**.. AidanColeman 87
(Anthony Honeyball) *in rr: drvn 5th: mstke 3 out: sme hdwy and poor 4th appr next* **5/1**[3]

460- **5** *2 1/2* **Cleve Cottage**[38] 2786 6-11-7 **100**...................................... AdamNicol(5) 87
(Philip Kirby) *chsd ldrs: wknd appr 3 out* **8/1**

636- **6** *16* **Snowed In (IRE)**[11] 3288 5-11-7 **95**.................................(p) SeanQuinlan 66
(Jennie Candlish) *in rr-div: lost pl 7th: poor 6th after 3 out* **14/1**

341- **7** *7* **Peqeno Diablo (IRE)**[11] 3251 9-9-7 **74**.......................(tp) GeraldQuinn(7) 38
(Claire Dyson) *led to 8th: wknd next: sn bhd* **10/1**

FU5- **P** **Song Of Pride (GER)**[22] 3119 10-10-0 **74** oh1...........(b) TomMessenger
(Mandy Rowland) *chsd ldrs: wknd 6th: t.o whn p.u bef next* **50/1**

060- **P** **Agesilas (FR)**[30] 2954 6-11-3 **94**.. JohnKington(3)
(Andrew Crook) *chsd ldrs: lost pl 7th: sn bhd: t.o whn p.u bef 2 out* **14/1**

606- **P** **Gilanto (IRE)**[36] 2840 7-11-12 **100**.. NickScholfield
(Michael Blake) *in rr: drvn 4th: sme hdwy 7th: sn lost pl and bhd: t.o whn p.u bef 2 out* **20/1**

5m 40.9s (27.90) **Going Correction** +1.40s/f (Heav) **10** Ran SP% **122.6**
Speed ratings (Par 103): **102,101,93,91,90 84,82, , ,**
CSF £24.28 CT £75.83 TOTE £6.30: £2.00, £1.30, £1.80; EX 29.50 Trifecta £93.50.

Owner Mrs Anne Lee-Warner **Bred** Mrs Anne Lee-Warner **Trained** Condicote, Gloucs

FOCUS
Probably form to view quite positively for the level, the winner seeing off a well-treated rival, with the pair well clear of the rest. The winner is rated back to the level of his 2012 best.

3570 COLLECT TOTEPOOL WINNINGS AT BETFRED SHOPS MARES' "NATIONAL HUNT" MAIDEN HURDLE (9 hdls) 2m

3:30 (3:30) (Class 5) 4-Y-0+ **£1,997** (£620; £333)

Form RPR

0P6- **1** **A Shade Of Bay**[11] 3289 6-11-5 0.. JasonMaguire 110
(Kim Bailey) *in rr: hdwy: reminders and modest 3rd sn after 3 out: chsng ldrs appr next: led appr last: drvn rt out* **20/1**

123- **2** *2 1/2* **Lily Waugh (IRE)**[27] 3005 7-11-5 0................................. RobertThornton 107
(Anthony Honeyball) *chsd ldrs: 2nd 6th: drvn to ld narrowly 2 out: hdd and hit last: no ex* **8/13**[1]

224- **3** *6* **Born To Benefit (IRE)**[18] 3171 8-11-5 106....................(t) PaddyBrennan 102
(Fergal O'Brien) *chsd ldr: led 5th: hdd 2 out: edgd rt and one pce* **5/1**[2]

0/P- **P** **Graylyn Amber**[37] 2825 9-11-5 81.. CharliePoste
(Robin Dickin) *led: drvn and hdd 5th: wknd appr 3 out: sn t.o: 5th whn p.u bef 2 out* **50/1**

222- **U** **Playhara (IRE)**[23] 3098 5-11-5 0.. AndrewTinkler
(Nicky Henderson) *chsd ldrs: nt fluent 3rd: blnd and uns rdr next* **5/1**[2]

0- **P** **Frangipani Lady**[233] 372 5-11-5 0.. NoelFehily
(Nick Williams) *chsd ldrs: wknd appr 3 out: tired and distant 4th whn p.u bef next: b.b.v* **8/1**[3]

4m 24.0s (27.00) **Going Correction** +1.40s/f (Heav) **6** Ran SP% **113.1**
Speed ratings (Par 103): **88,86,83, ,**
CSF £35.43 TOTE £17.90: £4.90, £1.10; EX 41.50 Trifecta £119.40.

Owner The Real Partnership **Bred** Mrs S Steer-Fowler **Trained** Andoversford, Gloucs

FOCUS
Fair form in this mares' maiden. It has been rated through the second.
T/Plt: £22.50 to a £1 stake. Pool: £82900.70 - 2683.01 winning tickets T/Qpdt: £4.20 to a £1 stake. Pool: £8108.76 - 1421.4 winning tickets WG

3420 TAUNTON (R-H)

Monday, January 6

3571 Meeting Abandoned - waterlogged

The Form Book Jumps, Raceform Ltd, Compton, RG20 6NL.

3357 CHEPSTOW (L-H)
Tuesday, January 7
3585 Meeting Abandoned - waterlogged

3323 LEICESTER (R-H)
Tuesday, January 7
OFFICIAL GOING: Hurdle course - heavy (6.3); chase course - soft (heavy in places; 5.4)
Wind: Light behind Weather: Fine

3592 NOMAD NOVICES' HURDLE (4 hdls 4 omitted) 2m
12:45 (12:45) (Class 4) 4-Y-0+ **£4,548** (£1,335; £667; £333)

Form RPR
03- 1 **Hint Of Mint**[33] 2906 5-11-5 0 .... WayneHutchinson 126+
(Nick Williams) *chsd ldrs: rdn to ld after bypassed 2 out: styd on wl* **10/1**
120- 2 *6* **Uhlan Bute (FR)**[25] 3066 6-11-12 127 .... AidanColeman 127
(Venetia Williams) *chsd ldrs: rdn and ev ch last (usual 3 out): styd on same pce fnl f* **15/8**[2]
0/1- 3 *nk* **Milo Man (IRE)**[57] 2420 6-11-12 0 .... PaulMoloney 127
(Evan Williams) *led: rdn and hdd after bypassed 2 out: no ex fnl f* **11/10**[1]
FF4- 4 *11* **Cantony**[28] 3010 5-10-9 0 .... JakeGreenall(3) 104
(Henry Daly) *hld up: hdwy 2 out: mstke last (usual 3 out): sn wknd* **20/1**
216- 5 *22* **Ashes House (IRE)**[19] 3177 8-11-12 125 ....(p) APMcCoy 101
(Rebecca Curtis) *chsd ldr tl rdn and wknd after last (usual 3 out)* **4/1**[3]
400- 6 *6* **Benefitofhindsight**[12] 3278 5-11-2 0 .... KielanWoods(3) 81
(Ben Pauling) *hld up: effrt and mstke 2 out (usual 5th): sn wknd* **100/1**
46- 7 *20* **Last Chance Ranch**[33] 2899 4-10-0 0 .... OllieGarner(7) 49
(Derek Shaw) *sn pushed along in rr: wknd appr 2 out (usual 5th)* **100/1**
46- 8 *15* **Ravens Nest**[28] 1920 4-10-7 0 .... DavidBass 34
(Ben Pauling) *hld up: wknd 2 out (usual 5th)* **50/1**
000- 9 *26* **Alwayslookback (IRE)**[35] 2876 5-11-0 0 .... BenPoste(5) 20
(Rosemary Gasson) *hld up: a in rr: wknd 2 out (usual 5th)* **100/1**
00- P **Hollywood All Star (IRE)**[22] 3128 5-11-5 0 .... FelixDeGiles
(Graeme McPherson) *hld up: j.rt 2nd: sn p.u* **100/1**

3m 56.9s (-4.10) **Going Correction** +0.05s/f (Yiel)
WFA 4 from 5yo+ 11lb 10 Ran SP% **122.2**
Speed ratings (Par 105): **112,109,108,103,92 89,79,71,58,**
CSF £31.21 TOTE £12.00: £2.00, £1.10, £1.10; EX 47.70 Trifecta £87.40.
Owner Sandie & David Newton **Bred** Mrs J S Newton **Trained** George Nympton, Devon

FOCUS
After the first, Wayne Hutchinson confirmed conditions were tough, describing the ground as "hard work", while Jake Greenall described it as "proper heavy". They only jumped four in this fair novice hurdle and the market was dominated by those who had already won a race and were therefore competing under a penalty. However, they were upset by a horse they were attempting to give 7lb. The second and third set the level.

3593 DOVE (S) HURDLE (6 hdls 4 omitted) 2m 4f 110y
1:15 (1:15) (Class 5) 4-Y-0+ **£2,599** (£763; £381; £190)

Form RPR
552- 1 **The Jugopolist (IRE)**[8] 3419 7-10-10 110 ....(v) PaulO'Brien(10) 114
(Rebecca Curtis) *chsd ldrs: led last (usual 3 out): rdn bypassed 2 out: styd on wl* **11/4**[2]
211- 2 *3 3/4* **Stow**[6] 3468 9-11-5 125 ....(p) JoshWall(7) 116
(Michael Blake) *chsd ldr to appr 3rd: sn lost pl: hdwy 2 out (usual 7th): rdn after last (usual 3 out: chsd wnr fnl f: no ex fnl 50yds* **5/4**[1]
00F/ 3 *10* **Zanir (FR)**[668] 4779 10-11-6 0 .... WayneHutchinson 100
(Graeme McPherson) *prom: rdn after last (usual 3 out): wknd fnl 100yds* **8/1**
5P2- 4 *2 1/4* **Going Wrong**[11] 3324 11-11-6 115 ....(t) HarrySkelton 98
(Dan Skelton) *led to last (usual 3 out): sn rdn: wknd after bypassed 2 out* **7/1**
15F- 5 *5* **Belle De Fontenay (FR)**[11] 3324 9-11-0 115.........(p) ConorShoemark(5) 92
(Conor Dore) *hld up: hdwy appr last (usual 3 out): sn rdn and wknd* **5/1**[3]
544- 6 *4 1/2* **Highland River**[10] 3353 8-11-6 71 ....(b) LeeEdwards 88
(Dave Roberts) *hld up: hdwy to chse ldr appr 3rd: rdn and wknd bef last (usual 3 out)* **66/1**

5m 34.6s (9.90) **Going Correction** +0.05s/f (Yiel) 6 Ran SP% **112.9**
Speed ratings (Par 103): **83,81,77,76,75 73**
CSF £6.95 TOTE £3.60: £2.10, £1.20; EX 8.10 Trifecta £36.60.The winner was bought by John Cornwall for 7,200gns.
Owner C R Trembath **Bred** Thomas Horgan **Trained** Newport, Dyfed

FOCUS
A fair race of its type. The front three in the market were reopposing after all running in a C&D seller a month earlier. The winner is rated similar to that form.

3594 LEICESTER ANNUAL MEMBERS NOVICES' LIMITED H'CAP CHASE (18 fncs) 2m 7f 110y
1:50 (1:50) (Class 3) (0-140,137) 5-Y-0+ **£6,498** (£1,908; £954; £477)

Form RPR
3/0- 1 **Edmund Kean (IRE)**[52] 2504 7-11-2 132 .... TomScudamore 138+
(David Pipe) *trckd ldrs: led 7th to next: led 13th: rdn out* **3/1**[2]
/25- 2 *2 1/2* **Whats Happening (IRE)**[20] 3162 7-11-7 137 ....(t) PaddyBrennan 141
(Tom George) *led to 3rd: remained handy: nt fluent 2 out: sn rdn to chse wnr: styd on same pce flat* **9/1**
/11- 3 *2* **Muldoon's Picnic (IRE)**[84] 1918 8-11-6 136 .... JasonMaguire 137
(Kim Bailey) *hld up: mstke 3 out: rdn appr last: styd on same pce u.p flat* **4/1**[3]
1U3- 4 *nse* **Le Reve (IRE)**[24] 3079 6-11-2 132 .... LeightonAspell 133
(Lucy Wadham) *trckd ldrs: lft in ld 6th: hdd next: led 8th to 13th: ev ch 3 out: sn rdn: styd on same pce flat* **4/1**[3]
/14- U **Renard D'Irlande (FR)**[40] 2757 9-10-11 127 .... AidanColeman
(Venetia Williams) *trckd ldr tl led 3rd: blnd and uns rdr 6th* **5/2**[1]
401- U **San Telm (IRE)**[21] 3150 9-10-9 128 .... JoshuaMoore(3)
(Renee Robeson) *hld up: mstke and uns rdr 6th* **10/1**

6m 5.8s (1.80) **Going Correction** +0.325s/f (Yiel) 6 Ran SP% **112.7**
Speed ratings: **110,109,108,108,**
CSF £26.94 TOTE £3.70: £1.90, £5.30; EX 27.70 Trifecta £119.30.
Owner Walters Plant Hire & James & Jean Potter **Bred** Mervyn Chamney **Trained** Nicholashayne, Devon

FOCUS
A good, tight-knit handicap where 10lb covered all six runners and all could have been given a chance coming into the race. The winner could be a decent novice.

3595 HOSE THORNS H'CAP CHASE (15 fncs) 2m 4f 110y
2:25 (2:25) (Class 5) (0-100,98) 5-Y-0+ **£3,249** (£954; £477; £238)

Form RPR
342- 1 **Carli King (IRE)**[19] 3180 8-11-12 98 .... TomMessenger 110+
(Caroline Bailey) *w ldr tl rdn to ld 2 out: styd on wl* **5/2**[1]
P/6- 2 *10* **Thedreamstillalive (IRE)**[55] 2462 14-10-6 78 ....(t) MarkGrant 80
(Jim Old) *led: rdn and hdd 2 out: wknd flat* **20/1**
3U1- 3 *3 3/4* **Crescent Beach (IRE)**[37] 2849 7-11-4 90 .... DenisO'Regan 88
(Henry Oliver) *hld up: hdwy 11th: sn rdn: styd on same pce fr 3 out: wnt 3rd last* **11/2**
/23- 4 *4 1/2* **Lord Landen (IRE)**[38] 2825 9-11-8 94 ....(t) PaddyBrennan 88
(Fergal O'Brien) *hld up: mstke 2nd: nt fluent next: hdwy 9th: rdn after 4 out: wknd 2 out* **7/2**[3]
243- P **Meirig's Dream (IRE)**[28] 3015 8-10-5 77 .... JamesDavies
(Philip Hobbs) *prom: j.rt 9th: rdn and wkng whn mstke 2 out: p.u bef last* **3/1**[2]
531- P **Phoenix Des Mottes (FR)**[23] 3114 11-9-9 72 oh2.......... JoeCornwall(5)
(John Cornwall) *prom: pushed along 6th: wknd 11th: bhd whn p.u bef 4 out* **16/1**
/42- P **Bringewood Belle**[16] 3222 11-10-0 72 oh12..............(bt[1]) TommyPhelan
(John Needham) *chsd ldrs: mstke 3rd: lost pl next: wknd 7th: bhd whn p.u bef 4 out* **20/1**
/4P- U **Thorncliffer**[33] 2902 10-9-10 75 .... OllieGarner(7)
(Derek Shaw) *mstke and uns rdr 1st* **10/1**
FU6- P **Kevin Fancy (IRE)**[37] 2849 8-9-12 73 oh32 ow1.......... GavinSheehan(3)
(John Upson) *a in rr: bhd fr 5th: p.u bef 4 out* **100/1**

5m 27.9s (9.00) **Going Correction** +0.325s/f (Yiel) 9 Ran SP% **116.7**
Speed ratings: **95,91,89,88, , , ,**
CSF £47.32 CT £257.45 TOTE £4.10: £1.10, £4.60, £2.10; EX 63.10 Trifecta £296.90.
Owner Varley, Lloyd & Bailey **Bred** Eamon Fitzgerald **Trained** Holdenby, Northants

FOCUS
With the topweight rated 98, this was undoubtedly a weak race. The second and thirs set the level.

3596 GROBY NOVICES' H'CAP CHASE (12 fncs) 2m
2:55 (2:55) (Class 4) (0-110,109) 5-Y-0+ **£5,198** (£1,526; £763; £381)

Form RPR
122- 1 **Massena (IRE)**[7] 3431 7-11-10 107 .... AidanColeman 122+
(Venetia Williams) *w ldr: j. slowly 3rd: led 5th to next: led appr 4 out: hdd 2 out: led again last: sn hdd: styd on u.p to ld fnl 50yds* **1/1**[1]
613- 2 *3/4* **Un Anjou (FR)**[27] 3027 6-11-12 109 ....(p) NoelFehily 121
(David Dennis) *hld up: hdwy 5th: chsd wnr 4 out: led 2 out: sn rdn: hdd last: rallied to ld flat: sn hung rt: hdd and no ex fnl 50yds* **4/1**[2]
363- 3 *18* **Bin End**[11] 3318 8-11-5 102 ....(p) FelixDeGiles 96
(Barry Brennan) *hld up: hdwy 4th: rdn whn mstke 4 out: wknd next: wnt 3rd last* **14/1**
23F- 4 *6* **Moorlands Jack**[35] 2873 9-11-5 102 ....(p) NickScholfield 90
(Jeremy Scott) *prom: rdn appr 4 out: wknd bef next* **8/1**[3]
030- 5 *1 1/4* **Brassbound (USA)**[45] 2677 6-11-11 108 .... AndrewThornton 95
(Caroline Bailey) *prom: lost pl 4th: n.d after* **16/1**
655/ 6 *2* **Egypt Mill Spirit (IRE)**[666] 4829 8-11-3 100 .... PaddyBrennan 85
(Tom George) *led to 5th: led 6th tl appr 4 out: wknd after next* **10/1**
/02- 7 *28* **Rasheed**[33] 2904 6-11-11 108 ....(b) LeightonAspell 83
(Lucy Wadham) *hld up: hdwy and mstke 4 out: wknd bef next* **20/1**
/03- 8 *40* **Islandmagee (IRE)**[47] 2617 7-11-8 105 .... PaulMoloney 22
(Evan Williams) *hld up: plld hrd: nt fluent 7th: bhd fr next* **10/1**

4m 10.2s (2.00) **Going Correction** +0.325s/f (Yiel) 8 Ran SP% **116.6**
Speed ratings: **108,107,98,95,95 94,80,60**
CSF £6.07 CT £34.24 TOTE £1.70: £1.10, £1.20, £4.10; EX 6.00 Trifecta £51.70.
Owner Miss V M Williams **Bred** Frank Dunne **Trained** Kings Caple, H'fords

FOCUS
Not the strongest of races and it revolved around the well backed favourite. The winner is rated in line with his unlucky recent second.

3597 CHIEFTAIN H'CAP HURDLE (4 hdls 4 omitted) 2m
3:30 (3:30) (Class 4) (0-110,108) 4-Y-0+ **£5,198** (£1,526; £763; £381)

Form RPR
F3P/ 1 **Scotsbrook Legend**[377] 3254 6-10-0 85 .... PeterCarberry(3) 104+
(Shaun Lycett) *hld up: hdwy 2 out (usual 5th): led last (usual 3 out): rdn clr whn hung lft bypassed 2 out and again bypassed last* **25/1**
/02- 2 *19* **Santo Thomas (FR)**[22] 3132 8-11-11 107 .... AidanColeman 106
(Venetia Williams) *sn prom: ev ch last (usual 3 out): sn rdn: wknd bypassed 2 out* **13/8**[1]
/23- 3 *1 1/4* **Toowoomba (IRE)**[43] 2718 6-11-9 105 .... RichardJohnson 103
(Philip Hobbs) *prom: ev ch last (usual 3 out): sn rdn and wknd* **2/1**[2]
202- 4 *5* **Kayfton Pete**[21] 3149 8-11-9 105 .... AdamPogson 99
(Charles Pogson) *w ldr tl led appr 2 out (usual 5th): hdd last (usual 3 out): sn rdn and wknd* **10/1**
00- 5 *21* **Vedani (IRE)**[53] 2492 5-11-12 108 ....(t) LeeEdwards 80
(Tony Carroll) *hld up: bhd and pushed along 2nd: hdwy appr last (usual 3 out): sn wknd* **11/2**[3]
005- 6 *5* **Dealing River**[37] 2846 7-11-4 100 .... AndrewThornton 67
(Caroline Bailey) *prom: racd keenly: mot fluent 1st: rdn after 2 out (usual 5th): wknd bef last (usual 3 out)* **14/1**
3P1- 7 *27* **Kilflora**[12] 3269 11-11-4 107 ....(p) GeraldQuinn(7) 47
(Claire Dyson) *racd keenly: led tl rdn: hdd and mstke 2 out (usual 5th): wknd bef last (usual 3 out)* **12/1**

3m 59.9s (-1.10) **Going Correction** +0.05s/f (Yiel) 7 Ran SP% **114.1**
Speed ratings (Par 105): **104,94,93,91,80 78,64**
CSF £67.98 TOTE £32.60: £12.50, £2.20; EX 72.30 Trifecta £415.30.
Owner A E Price **Bred** A E And P E Price **Trained** Clapton-on-the-Hill, Gloucs

FOCUS
The closing race looked to be between the front two in the market but it was turned into a procession by the outsider of the field. He produced a massive step up.
T/Plt: £29.70 to a £1 stake. Pool: £108,723.35 - 2,666.59 winning ticket. T/Qpdt: £33.60 to a £1 stake. Pool: £7,292.12 - 160.20 winning ticket. CR

[3385]DONCASTER (L-H)

Wednesday, January 8

OFFICIAL GOING: Good to soft (soft in places; chs 6.8; hdl 7.0)
All hurdles re-sited.
Wind: light 1/2 against Weather: fine

3598 1STSECURITYSOLUTIONS.CO.UK MAIDEN HURDLE (DIV I) (10 hdls) 2m 3f 110y
12:10 (12:10) (Class 5) 4-Y-0+ **£2,599** (£763; £381; £190)

Form RPR

020/ **1** **Softsong (FR)**[131] 5013 6-11-6 125 LiamTreadwell 132+
(James Evans) *trckd ldrs: upsides 3 out: led next: drvn clr appr last: styd on strly* **5/1**[3]

23- **2** *10* **Minella Friend (IRE)**[56] 2457 5-11-6 124 PaulMoloney 123
(Evan Williams) *trckd ldrs: cl 3rd 3 out: sn outpcd: styd on between last 2: tk modest 2nd last 75yds* **85/40**[1]

3- **3** *5* **Nordic Quest (IRE)**[27] 3034 5-11-6 0 DavidBass 121
(Nicky Henderson) *trckd ldrs: t.k.h: led narrowly appr 3 out: hdd next: wknd run-in* **7/2**[2]

2/3- **4** *20* **Thomas Junior (FR)**[47] 2654 5-11-6 0 TomScudamore 104
(David Pipe) *mstkes: chsd ldrs 6th: 4th 3 out: wknd between last 2* **8/1**

2/6- **5** *27* **Easter Dancer**[253] 41 7-10-13 0 AidanColeman 69
(Emma Lavelle) *in rr: bhd and drvn 7th: t.o: b.b.v* **12/1**

55- **6** *4 ½* **Attimo (GER)**[46] 2661 5-11-6 0 NoelFehily 72
(Charlie Mann) *t.k.h in rr: bhd fr 7th: t.o* **16/1**

40P- **7** *17* **Kilfinichen Bay (IRE)**[9] 3422 6-10-13 0 CharlieDeutsch(7) 57
(Violet M Jordan) *mid-div: drvn 7th: sn lost pl: bhd fr next: t.o* **200/1**

FP/ **8** *1 ¼* **Perfect Shot (IRE)**[288] 2888 8-11-6 0 WillKennedy 56
(Sarah-Jayne Davies) *mid-div: drvn 7th: sn lost pl and bhd: t.o* **150/1**

00U- **9** *36* **Sir Harry Hotspur**[10] 3388 6-11-6 0 DonalDevereux 23
(John Mackie) *led to 3rd: lost pl bef 3 out: sn heavily eased: hopelessly t.o: virtually p.u* **250/1**

0- **P** **Namibian (IRE)**[27] 3034 6-11-6 0 DenisO'Regan
(John Ferguson) *racd wd: chsd ldrs: lost pl 6th: sn bhd: t.o next: p.u bef 3 out* **6/1**

4- **F** **Save The Bees**[22] 3144 6-11-6 0 DougieCostello
(Declan Carroll) *w ldr: mstke and led 3rd: hdd appr 3 out: sn wknd: distant 7th whn fell last* **50/1**

4m 44.6s (-6.70) **Going Correction** -0.175s/f (Good) **11** Ran SP% **113.4**
Speed ratings (Par 103): **106,102,100,92,81 79,72,72,57,**
CSF £15.97 TOTE £7.50: £1.80, £1.40, £1.60; EX 19.40 Trifecta £45.20.
Owner Andrew Cohen & Alan Kaplan **Bred** Wertheimer & Frere **Trained** Broadwas, Worcs

FOCUS
All hurdles re-sited. An ordinary maiden hurdle, won in dominant fashion by the form horse. There may be more to come from the winner.

3599 PEGLER YORKSHIRE H'CAP HURDLE (8 hdls) 2m 110y
12:40 (12:40) (Class 4) (0-120,121) 4-Y-0+ **£3,119** (£915; £457; £228)

Form RPR

1U2- **1** **Forced Family Fun**[23] 3127 4-10-7 **113** BrianHughes 109+
(John Quinn) *trckd ldrs: led between last 2: hrd drvn last 100yds: hld on* **5/1**[3]

406- **2** *½* **Mojolika**[30] 3000 6-11-8 **116** APMcCoy 124+
(Tim Easterby) *hld up in rr: hdwy appr 3 out: swtchd lft and 2nd last: kpt on: no ex clsng stages* **15/2**

/24- **3** *5* **Bohemian Rhapsody (IRE)**[12] 3322 5-11-9 **117** ConorO'Farrell 122
(Seamus Durack) *hld up towards rr: chsng ldrs 3 out: one pce between last 2* **4/1**[2]

341- **4** *2 ¾* **Nesterenko (GER)**[10] 3390 5-11-6 **121** 7ex MrFMitchell(7) 122
(Nicky Henderson) *in rr and sn pushed along: hdwy bef 5th: w ldrs 3 out: nt clr run and swtchd lft between last 2: kpt on to take 4th last 100yds* **9/4**[1]

22- **5** *1 ½* **Stephen Hero (IRE)**[12] 3317 4-11-0 **120** HarrySkelton 108
(Dan Skelton) *hld up: hdwy 3rd: chsng ldrs 5th: led narrowly 3 out: hdd between last 2: wknd last 100yds* **12/1**

/P2- **6** *7* **Great Value (IRE)**[38] 2848 9-11-12 **120** (t) WayneHutchinson 114
(Graeme McPherson) *in rr: hdwy 5th: chsng ldrs next: nt clr run and swtchd lft between last 2: wknd run-in* **28/1**

323- **7** *6* **Hartside (GER)**[12] 3328 5-11-4 **119** MrRWinks(7) 107
(Peter Winks) *in rr: reminders 4th: bhd next: kpt on fr 2 out: nvr on terms* **22/1**

254- **8** *4* **Groomed (IRE)**[178] 967 6-10-13 **107** RyanMania 91
(Sue Smith) *chsd ldrs: wknd between last 2* **20/1**

004- **9** *18* **Dark And Dangerous (IRE)**[43] 2729 6-11-4 **112** (v) BrendanPowell 80
(Brendan Powell) *led: hdd appr 3 out: sn lost pl and bhd* **20/1**

1/2- **10** *15* **Boston Blue**[48] 2617 7-11-5 **118** JoshHamer(5) 73
(Tony Carroll) *trckd ldrs: hit 3rd: led briefly appr 3 out: lost pl bef 2 out: bhd whn eased run-in* **40/1**

436/ **11** *2 ½* **Minsky Mine (IRE)**[370] 2930 7-10-8 **105** JonathanEngland(3) 57
(Michael Appleby) *chsd ldrs: lost pl 5th: sn bhd* **33/1**

/23- **F** **Phantom Prince (IRE)**[25] 3094 5-11-2 **115** ConorShoemark(5)
(Brendan Powell) *chsd ldrs: drvn 5th: 9th and outpcd whn fell next* **25/1**

3m 58.8s (-5.90) **Going Correction** -0.175s/f (Good)
WFA 4 from 5yo+ 11lb **12** Ran SP% **113.4**
Speed ratings (Par 105): **106,105,103,102,101 98,95,93,84,77 76,**
CSF £35.62 CT £162.93 TOTE £3.80: £1.90, £2.90, £2.10; EX 36.40 Trifecta £134.40.
Owner The Top Silk Syndicate **Bred** M B Hawtin **Trained** Settrington, N Yorks
■ Stewards' Enquiry : Harry Skelton two-day ban: careless riding (Jan 22-23)

FOCUS
The front pair drew away late on and the form looks fair for the level. The first three are on the upgrade.

3600 1STSECURITYSOLUTIONS.CO.UK MAIDEN HURDLE (DIV II) (10 hdls) 2m 3f 110y
1:10 (1:10) (Class 5) 4-Y-0+ **£2,599** (£763; £381; £190)

Form RPR

3/2- **1** **Act Alone**[238] 309 5-11-1 0 NicodeBoinville(5) 130+
(Nicky Henderson) *trckd ldrs: t.k.h: cl 2nd 3 out: led between last 2: drvn wl clr* **7/2**[2]

5/4- **2** *14* **Sir Pitt**[23] 3128 7-11-6 125 DonalDevereux 115
(Peter Bowen) *led: hdd between last 2: fdd last 100yds* **7/4**[1]

3 *shd* **Benenden (IRE)**[45] 6-11-6 0 LiamTreadwell 115
(Michael Scudamore) *nt fluent 1st: in rr: hdwy on outside 5th: chsng ldrs next: cl 3rd 3 out: outpcd whn nt fluent next: styd on wl fnl 150yds* **10/1**

205- **4** *5* **Mister Newby (IRE)**[32] 2954 8-11-6 115 (t) RichardJohnson 109
(Richard Phillips) *hld up: hdwy 7th: handy 4th next: one pce* **5/1**[3]

43- **5** *3 ¼* **Smiles For Miles (IRE)**[24] 3116 6-11-6 0 TomScudamore 106
(David Pipe) *in rr: hdwy 7th: outpcd appr next: kpt on between last 2* **10/1**

00/- **6** *16* **Ginger Fizz**[106] 5394 7-10-10 0 KielanWoods(3) 88
(Ben Case) *t.k.h: j.rt 2nd: trckd ldrs next: wknd 3 out* **40/1**

500- **7** *25* **Whichwaytobougie**[10] 3388 5-11-6 0 JamesReveley 70
(Keith Reveley) *chsd ldrs: lost pl and blnd 6th: sn bhd: t.o 3 out* **100/1**

6P- **8** *2 ¾* **My Destination (IRE)**[18] 3208 5-11-6 0 DougieCostello 67
(Declan Carroll) *prom: hit 5th: lost pl next: sme hdwy appr 3 out: sn wknd: t.o* **50/1**

40- **9** *4 ½* **Rozener (IRE)**[42] 2748 8-11-6 0 RichieMcGrath 63
(Henry Hogarth) *chsd ldrs: drvn 7th: sn lost pl and bhd: t.o* **100/1**

10/- **F** **Abigail Lynch (IRE)**[278] 5163 6-10-13 0 (t) AndrewTinkler
(George Baker) *in rr: hdwy 7th: lost pl and poor 8th whn fell 3 out* **8/1**

0P- **P** **Donapollo**[19] 3182 6-11-6 0 (t) RobertThornton
(Ian Williams) *in rr: blnd 1st: sme hdwy 7th: lost pl and bhd whn p.u bef next* **100/1**

4m 44.7s (-6.60) **Going Correction** -0.175s/f (Good) **11** Ran SP% **111.9**
Speed ratings (Par 103): **106,100,100,98,97 90,80,79,77,**
CSF £9.71 TOTE £3.20: £1.90, £1.10, £3.60; EX 10.40 Trifecta £33.60.
Owner S W Group Logistics Limited **Bred** Stratford Place Stud **Trained** Upper Lambourn, Berks

FOCUS
Less depth than division one, but an authoritative winner who looks a fair prospect.

3601 CHECK OUT THE ALL NEW FREEBETS.CO.UK NOVICES' CHASE (15 fncs) 2m 3f
1:40 (1:40) (Class 3) 5-Y-0+ **£6,498** (£1,908; £954; £477)

Form RPR

/26- **1** **Western Warhorse (IRE)**[40] 2798 6-10-12 129 TomScudamore 143+
(David Pipe) *led and sn clr: j. boldly: jnd briefly 9th: hit 3 out: styd on wl: edgd rt run-in: hld on towards fin* **2/1**[2]

121/ **2** *nk* **Victor Hewgo**[282] 5071 9-10-12 0 JamesReveley 143+
(Keith Reveley) *trckd ldrs after 8th: chsd wnr 4 out: effrt between last 2: 3 l down last: styd on last 75yds: no ex towards fin* **14/1**

151- **3** *16* **Karinga Dancer**[25] 3087 8-11-4 0 (t) NoelFehily 141
(Harry Fry) *j.lft: hdwy 9th: chsng ldrs whn nt fluent 11th: effrt and disp 2nd 2 out: wknd last* **8/11**[1]

/43- **4** *22* **Walkabout Creek (IRE)**[48] 2622 7-10-12 128 JasonMaguire 113
(Steve Gollings) *chsd wnr: drvn 10th: 3rd and one pce whn hit 4 out: lost pl after next* **12/1**[3]

3- **5** *71* **My Dads Horse**[47] 2643 8-10-12 0 PaulMoloney 45
(Evan Williams) *mstkes in last: blnd 7th: bhd fr 9th: t.o 4 out: eased and eventually completed* **20/1**

4m 44.4s (-4.60) **Going Correction** -0.125s/f (Good) **5** Ran SP% **110.4**
Speed ratings: **104,103,97,87,57**
CSF £22.11 TOTE £2.00: £1.30, £1.80; EX 20.80 Trifecta £40.10.
Owner R S Brookhouse **Bred** Harry Kavanagh **Trained** Nicholashayne, Devon

FOCUS
This looked quite a decent novice chase and it saw a thoroughly likeable effort from the winner. The frst two are rated in line with their best hurdles form.

3602 DOWNLOAD THE ALL NEW FREEBETS.CO.UK "NATIONAL HUNT" NOVICES' HURDLE (8 hdls) 2m 110y
2:10 (2:10) (Class 4) 4-Y-0+ **£3,119** (£915; £457; £228)

Form RPR

/13- **1** **Diamond King (IRE)**[26] 3061 6-11-12 0 JasonMaguire 136+
(Donald McCain) *mde all: styd on wl fr 3 out: j.lft next: reminders and clr between last 2: eased towards fin* **2/5**[1]

423- **2** *3 ¾* **Uppingham**[26] 3063 5-11-5 0 BrianHughes 120
(Malcolm Jefferson) *hld up in tch: chsd wnr 2 out: no imp* **9/1**[3]

6- **3** *5* **Themanfrom Minella (IRE)**[19] 3187 5-11-5 0 (t) DarylJacob 116
(Ben Case) *chsd wnr: one pce fr 2 out* **4/1**[2]

26- **4** *12* **I Got Power**[22] 3147 5-11-5 0 JamesReveley 105+
(Keith Reveley) *stdd s: hld up in rr: hdwy 5th: modest 4th next: one pce whn hit 2 out* **25/1**

050- **5** *3 ½* **Trillerin Minella (IRE)**[20] 3175 6-11-5 0 WayneHutchinson 100
(Graeme McPherson) *in tch: drvn appr 3 out: sn outpcd: one pce fr 2 out* **33/1**

40- **6** *1* **Vermouth Bleu (FR)**[20] 3175 5-11-5 0 APMcCoy 100
(Jonjo O'Neill) *t.k.h: trckd ldrs: drvn appr 3 out: hit 2 out: hung lft and sn fdd* **14/1**

000- **7** *4 ½* **Grand Gigolo (FR)**[26] 3061 5-11-0 0 RobertMcCarth(5) 94
(Ian Williams) *in rr: sme hdwy after 5th: hung lft: lost pl and hit next* **200/1**

0/P- **8** *5* **Ifits A Fiddle**[65] 2266 5-10-12 0 (t) RichardJohnson 82
(Richard Phillips) *in rr-div: effrt and modest 5th 3 out: wknd next* **33/1**

560- **9** *1 ¾* **Viacometti (FR)**[21] 3163 5-11-5 0 PaddyBrennan 87
(Tom George) *mid-div: hdwy to chse ldrs 5th: sn drvn: lost pl appr next* **50/1**

5/ **10** *61* **First Lad**[235] 7-11-5 0 ConorO'Farrell 26
(Nicholas Pomfret) *nt fluent in rr: lost pl 5th: sn bhd: t.o next* **200/1**

/0- **11** *2* **Daylan (IRE)**[27] 3042 6-11-5 0 DougieCostello 24
(Tony Coyle) *stdd s: in rr: sme hdwy after 5th: sn wknd and bhd: t.o 3 out: eventually completed* **25/1**

4m 2.4s (-2.30) **Going Correction** -0.175s/f (Good) **11** Ran SP% **124.6**
Speed ratings (Par 105): **98,96,93,88,86 86,84,81,80,52 51**
CSF £5.60 TOTE £1.40: £1.10, £1.40, £1.40; EX 6.20 Trifecta £14.30.
Owner Mrs Diana L Whateley **Bred** Cleaboy Stud **Trained** Cholmondeley, Cheshire

FOCUS
Little depth to this novice hurdle. The easy winner was value for further.

3603 BIG CASINO BONUS.CO.UK H'CAP CHASE (18 fncs) 3m
2:45 (2:45) (Class 4) (0-120,120) 5-Y-0+ **£3,768** (£1,106; £553; £276)

Form RPR

/41- **1** **Ifyousayso (IRE)**[34] 2897 7-11-7 **115** (t) PaddyBrennan 125+
(Tom George) *chsd ldrs: 2nd 4th: led narrowly 3 out: 3 l ahd whn hit last: hrd drvn and styd on fr next* **11/2**[2]

5/6- **2** *1 ¼* **Triangular (USA)**[221] 587 9-11-12 **120** (tp) NoelFehily 126
(Harry Fry) *chsd ldrs 4th: 3rd 11th: styd on to chse wnr last 75yds: no ex* **4/1**[1]

/U6- **3** *3 ¾* **Honest John**[28] 3019 10-11-4 **112** JasonMaguire 117
(Steve Gollings) *led: hdd 3 out: one pce fr next* **14/1**

245- **4** *9* **My Flora**[26] 3058 10-11-9 **117**................................ HarrySkelton 113
(Dan Skelton) *in rr: hdwy 11th: modest 4th appr 4 out: one pce* **25/1**

332- **5** *3 ½* **Categorical**[10] 3389 11-11-6 **114**........................ JamesReveley 107
(Keith Reveley) *chsd ldrs: drvn 11th: outpcd 13th: one pce and modest 5th 2 out* **9/1**

P/5- **6** *20* **Glens Boy (IRE)**[12] 3325 10-11-7 **115**........................ APMcCoy 89
(Jonjo O'Neill) *prom: chsd ldrs 11th: outpcd appr 4 out: lost pl appr 3 out* **8/1**

532- **7** *¾* **Tickatack (IRE)**[40] 2784 9-10-9 **103**........................ WayneHutchinson 76
(Graeme McPherson) *in rr-div: hdwy to chse ldrs 11th: outpcd appr 4 out: wknd 3 out* **9/1**

/3P- **8** *5* **Mr Supreme (IRE)**[13] 3283 9-10-9 **103**........................ RichieMcGrath 72
(Keith Reveley) *hld up in rr: mstke 7th: bhd fr 13th* **28/1**

151/ **9** *6* **Bruslini (FR)**[543] 5115 9-11-4 **112**........................ MrGBarfoot-Saunt 75
(Tracey Barfoot-Saunt) *chsd ldrs: lost pl 9th: bhd fr 12th* **150/1**

463- **10** *26* **Sail And Return**[85] 1916 10-11-9 **117**..................(t) SamTwiston-Davies 57
(Phil Middleton) *in rr: bhd fr 14th: t.o 2 out* **11/1**

1F5- **11** *¾* **Danandy (IRE)**[29] 3004 7-11-10 **118**........................ TomO'Brien 57
(Philip Hobbs) *nt fluent: prom: lost pl 9th: bhd fr 12th: t.o 3 out* **10/1**

/3P- **P** **Global Warming (IRE)**[50] 2578 10-10-2 **96**..................(p) AidanColeman
(Emma Lavelle) *chsd ldrs: hit 2nd: lost pl and reminders 11th: bhd fr next: t.o whn p.u bef 2 out* **13/2**[3]

6m 5.0s (-7.00) **Going Correction** -0.125s/f (Good) **12** Ran SP% **111.9**
Speed ratings: **106,105,104,101,100 93,93,91,89,80 80,**
CSF £26.52 CT £286.24 TOTE £5.20: £1.60, £2.70, £3.60; EX 33.80 Trifecta £231.90.
Owner The Joaly Partnership **Bred** S Delaney **Trained** Slad, Gloucs

FOCUS
The right horses dominated and the form looks sound. The winner is on the upgrade and there's probably more to come.

3604 SUPER BINGO BONUSES BONUS.CO.UK MARES' H'CAP HURDLE (10 hdls) 2m 3f 110y
3:20 (3:21) (Class 4) (0-120,116) 4-Y-0+ **£3,119** (£915; £457; £228)

Form RPR

23- **1** **Chasse En Mer (FR)**[18] 3212 4-10-11 **114**........................ RobertThornton 107+
(Caroline Bailey) *trckd ldrs: upsides 2 out and last: kpt on to ld last 75yds* **5/1**[3]

352- **2** *1 ¼* **Queen Spud**[10] 3391 5-10-0 **90**..................(p) RichardJohnson 95+
(Henry Daly) *w ldrs: led narrowly 7th: j.lft 2 out: hdd and no ex last 75yds* **11/8**[1]

541- **3** *13* **Dardanella**[45] 2697 7-11-8 **112**........................ JamieMoore 106
(Richard Lee) *trckd ldrs: upsides 3 out: 3rd and wl hld whn mstke last: sn fdd* **7/2**[2]

0/3- **4** *¾* **My Legal Lady**[247] 144 9-11-6 **110**..................(v[1]) TomScudamore 102
(Stuart Howe) *chsd ldrs: led narrowly 6th: hdd next: drvn appr 3 out: wknd appr 2 out* **12/1**

002- **5** *18* **Kimora (IRE)**[13] 3264 8-10-2 **92**..................(p) AidanColeman 70
(Marc Barber) *led to 6th: sn drvn and outpcd: rallied appr 3 out: wknd bef 2 out* **14/1**

20/- **6** *18* **Tharaya**[946] 784 9-10-5 **102**........................ GeraldQuinn[(7)] 61
(Claire Dyson) *chsd ldrs: outpcd and pushed along 5th: bhd fr 3 out: t.o next* **25/1**

4m 46.2s (-5.10) **Going Correction** -0.175s/f (Good)
WFA 4 from 5yo+ 11lb **6** Ran SP% **99.2**
Speed ratings (Par 105): **103,102,97,97,89 82**
CSF £9.89 TOTE £3.70: £1.40, £1.20; EX 10.40 Trifecta £23.10.
Owner Mrs Susan Carsberg **Bred** N Madamet & Mme B Gabeur **Trained** Holdenby, Northants
■ Rule 4 of 10p in the pound applies to all bets; Withdrawn: Kykate

FOCUS
A modest mares' hurdle. Kykate had to be withdrawn after receiving a kick at the start. The winner is on the upgrade.

3605 BINGO BONUS CODES @ BINGOBONUSCODES.CO.UK H'CAP HURDLE (11 hdls) 3m 110y
3:50 (3:50) (Class 5) (0-100,100) 4-Y-0+ **£2,599** (£763; £381; £190)

Form RPR

204- **1** **Top Billing**[27] 3040 5-11-1 **89**..................(p) DenisO'Regan 102+
(Nicky Richards) *hld up in rr: stdy hdwy 7th: cl 2nd 2 out: led last: wnt clr: easily* **4/1**[1]

P46- **2** *4 ½* **Burnthill (IRE)**[12] 3335 9-9-7 **74**..................(tp) GeraldQuinn[(7)] 79
(Claire Dyson) *w ldr: drvn to ld appr 3 out: hdd and hit last: kpt on same pce* **9/2**[2]

604- **3** *15* **Blue Sea Of Ibrox (IRE)**[13] 3265 6-10-0 **74** oh2..........(b) DavidEngland 63
(Alan Brown) *hld up: hdwy to trck ldrs 4th: drvn 3 out: one pce and modest 3rd last* **12/1**

/03- **4** *12* **Another Dimension (IRE)**[35] 2879 8-11-0 **95**.............. ShaunDobbin[(7)] 78
(Rose Dobbin) *trckd ldrs 4th: cl 2nd 3 out: 3rd whn mstke 2 out: wknd last* **7/1**[3]

056- **5** *17* **Milan Of Hope (IRE)**[25] 3086 7-11-9 **97**........................ AdamPogson 60
(Charles Pogson) *prom: lost pl 5th: reminders next: t.o 8th: poor 10th appr 3 out: kpt on* **25/1**

0/5- **6** *¾* **Minden March**[12] 3329 9-9-7 **74** oh10........................ DanielHiskett[(7)] 37
(Peter Maddison) *chsd ldrs: drvn 8th: wknd appr next* **40/1**

65P- **7** *9* **Balinderry (IRE)**[13] 3283 7-10-9 **90**..................(p) PaulBohan[(7)] 45
(Steve Gollings) *chsd ldrs: drvn 7th: lost pl appr 2 out* **7/1**[3]

6F4- **8** *26* **Wheelavher**[58] 2423 8-10-0 **74** oh4..................(t) TommyPhelan 5
(Claire Dyson) *chsd ldrs: lost pl after 7th: sn bhd: t.o* **20/1**

04P- **9** *3 ½* **Oak Wood (IRE)**[39] 2827 6-10-12 **89**........................ GavinSheehan[(3)] 17
(John Upson) *t.k.h: led: hdd appr 3 out: sn lost pl and bhd: t.o* **25/1**

44P/ **10** *18* **Ravens Secret**[757] 3110 9-11-12 **100**........................ MrGBarfoot-Saunt 12
(Tracey Barfoot-Saunt) *in rr: bhd fr 5th: t.o after 7th* **100/1**

00P/ **11** *5* **Polo Springs**[560] 839 7-9-9 **74** oh3..................(t) KillianMoore[(5)]
(Graeme McPherson) *in rr: hdwy to chse ldrs whn blnd 7th: lost pl after next: sn bhd: t.o* **12/1**

/05- **P** **Thurnham**[36] 2875 8-11-7 **95**........................ JamesReveley
(Keith Reveley) *prom: mstke and lost pl 3rd: reluctant and bhd after next: hopelessly t.o 7th: p.u bef 3 out* **16/1**

/00- **P** **Lucas Pitt**[48] 2614 7-10-4 **78**........................ TomScudamore
(Michael Scudamore) *in rr: bhd fr 8th: t.o whn p.u bef 3 out* **14/1**

P/0- **P** **Mumbles Bay (IRE)**[138] 1364 8-10-0 **74** oh5..............(v[1]) DonalDevereux
(Peter Bowen) *prom: lost pl 6th: reminders next: sn bhd: t.o whn p.u bef 3 out* **8/1**

6m 6.6s (7.60) **Going Correction** -0.175s/f (Good) **14** Ran SP% **118.1**
Speed ratings (Par 103): **80,78,73,69,64 64,61,53,51,46 44,,,**
CSF £20.70 CT £200.82 TOTE £4.80: £3.40, £1.90, £3.00; EX 16.40 Trifecta £128.30.
Owner Jimmy Dudgeon & Partners **Bred** Newsells Park Stud **Trained** Greystoke, Cumbria

FOCUS
A pretty poor handicap that provided a decent test of stamina. A big step up from the easy winner who will probably win again.
T/Jkpt: £4733.30. Pool: £10,000.00 - 1.5 winning units. T/Plt: £19.20. Pool: £118,724.91 - 4501.44 wining units. T/Qpdt: £9.30. Pool: £8728.58 - 689.67 winning units. WG

3154 LUDLOW (R-H)
Wednesday, January 8
3606 Meeting Abandoned - waterlogged

3448 CATTERICK (L-H)
Thursday, January 9
OFFICIAL GOING: Heavy (soft in places; chs 6.0, hdl 6.1)
Wind: Breezy, half against Weather: Cloudy

3613 RACINGUK.COM FILLIES' JUVENILE HURDLE (7 hdls 1 omitted) 2m
12:35 (12:35) (Class 4) 4-Y-0 **£3,898** (£1,144; £572; £286)

Form RPR

415- **1** **Magic Skyline (IRE)**[8] 3474 4-11-3 110..................(t) APMcCoy 110+
(Brian Ellison) *led to 3rd: cl up: regained ld next: shkn up and clr whn mstke 2 out: styd on wl* **15/8**[2]

0- **2** *14* **Pixie Cut (IRE)**[11] 3385 4-10-7 0........................ EwanWhillans[(3)] 84
(Alistair Whillans) *cl up: led 3rd to next: chsd wnr: outpcd bef 2 out: no imp bef last* **10/1**

5- **3** *25* **Colleen Bawn (FR)**[11] 3385 4-10-10 0........................ HarrySkelton 59
(Dan Skelton) *cl up: effrt and pushed along after 3 out: wknd bef next* **7/4**[1]

246- **4** *7* **Lebanna**[33] 2960 4-10-10 0........................ DougieCostello 52
(Tim Easterby) *nt fluent: hld up in tch: pushed along 4 out: struggling after next* **13/2**[3]

5 *20* **Terpsichore**[96] 4-10-10 0..................(t) DaveCrosse 32
(Barry Brennan) *prom: outpcd after 4 out: lost tch fr next* **100/1**

P **Flawless Filly (IRE)**[88] 4-10-10 0........................ RichieMcGrath
(Rose Dobbin) *t.k.h: hld up in tch: hit 2nd: struggling after 3 out: btn whn nt fluent next: sn p.u* **13/2**[3]

4m 4.6s (12.10) **Going Correction** +0.75s/f (Soft) **6** Ran SP% **107.9**
Speed ratings: **99,92,79,76,66**
CSF £17.65 TOTE £1.90: £1.10, £3.30; EX 11.40 Trifecta £30.00.
Owner Mike And Eileen Newbould **Bred** Rabbah Bloodstock Limited **Trained** Norton, N Yorks

FOCUS
After 19mm of rain overnight and more showers in the morning, conditions were very testing. All bends and hurdles moved to fresh ground. The first hurdle and first fence in the back straight had to be omitted. A very modest juvenile fillies' hurdle run at a surprisingly good pace in the conditions and they came home well strung out. The winner is rated in line with her Flat form.

3614 GO RACING AT WETHERBY THIS SATURDAY NOVICES' HURDLE (8 hdls 2 omitted) 2m 3f
1:05 (1:05) (Class 4) 4-Y-0+ **£3,249** (£954; £477; £238)

Form RPR

032- **1** **Getabuzz**[14] 3284 6-11-6 108..................(b[1]) APMcCoy 124+
(Tim Easterby) *hld up in tch: smooth hdwy 3 out: led gng wl appr next: pushed clr fr last* **5/2**[2]

03B- **2** *9* **Gold Show**[13] 3329 5-10-10 0........................ TonyKelly[(3)] 106
(Edwin Tuer) *t.k.h: in tch: effrt whn hit 2 out: sn chsng wnr: kpt on same pce fr last* **7/1**

5- **3** *5* **Mohawk Ridge**[12] 3351 8-11-6 0........................ BrianHughes 108
(James Moffatt) *t.k.h: chsd ldr: led after 3 out: hdd whn hit next: outpcd bef last* **25/1**

/52- **4** *6* **Sealous Scout (IRE)**[25] 3110 6-11-6 0........................ JasonMaguire 101
(Donald McCain) *led: rdn and hdd after 3 out: outpcd fr next* **11/4**[3]

626- **5** *74* **Johnny Og**[50] 2593 5-11-6 0........................ IanPopham 27
(Martin Keighley) *cl up: hit and outpcd 4 out: lost tch fr next: virtually p.u fr last* **15/8**[1]

040- **P** **Favourable Fellow (IRE)**[11] 3388 5-11-6 0.................. RichieMcGrath
(Geoffrey Harker) *bhd: outpcd 4 out: lost tch next: t.o whn p.u bef 2 out* **50/1**

4m 53.5s (17.40) **Going Correction** +0.75s/f (Soft) **6** Ran SP% **108.3**
Speed ratings (Par 105): **93,89,87,84,53**
CSF £17.91 TOTE £3.60: £1.70, £4.10; EX 15.80 Trifecta £72.40.
Owner Langham Hall Stud Three **Bred** Peter Botham **Trained** Great Habton, N Yorks

FOCUS
Again the pace was sound considering the testing underfoot conditions. A big step up from the winner in headgear.

3615 W.L. AND HECTOR CHRISTIE MEMORIAL TROPHY (NOVICES' LIMITED H'CAP CHASE) (11 fncs 1 omitted) 2m
1:35 (1:35) (Class 3) (0-125,120) 5-Y-0+ **£7,797** (£2,289; £1,144; £572)

Form RPR

5F1- **1** **Alderbrook Lad (IRE)**[8] 3452 8-10-6 **110** 7ex.................. JoeColliver[(5)] 121+
(Micky Hammond) *mde all: hrd pressed after 4 out: shkn up after 2 out: clr last: eased run-in: shkn up and kpt on wl towards fin* **7/2**[3]

314- **2** *1* **Smadynium (FR)**[19] 3201 6-11-4 **117**........................ JasonMaguire 123
(Donald McCain) *prom on outside: outpcd 5th: sn struggling: rallied bef 3 out: j.lft next: chsd (eased-down) wnr run-in: kpt on fin* **9/2**

554- **3** *4 ½* **Dartford Warbler (IRE)**[12] 3354 7-11-6 **119**.................. RyanMania 119
(Sue Smith) *chsd wnr: rdn and ev ch after 4 out: one pce after 2 out: lost 2nd run-in* **8/1**

252- **4** *½* **Desgrey**[14] 3288 6-11-1 **114**........................ BrianHughes 116
(Peter Niven) *hld up in tch: stdy hdwy 5th: chsng ldrs and effrt whn nt fluent 3 out: outpcd whn hit next: sn no imp* **10/1**

11F- **5** *28* **Suprise Vendor (IRE)**[12] 3354 8-11-7 **120**.................. APMcCoy 104
(Stuart Coltherd) *chsd ldrs: mstke 2nd: drvn and outpcd after 7th: btn fnl 3* **11/4**[2]

/50- **F** **Veauce De Sivola (FR)**[75] 2087 5-10-11 **114**.................. JamesReveley
(Nick Williams) *hld up in tch: cl 4th and gng wl whn fell 6th* **9/4**[1]

4m 5.9s (5.80) **Going Correction** +0.525s/f (Soft)
WFA 5 from 6yo+ 3lb **6** Ran SP% **118.0**
Speed ratings: **106,105,103,103,89**
CSF £20.44 TOTE £4.30: £2.50, £2.40; EX 22.00 Trifecta £115.10.
Owner Masters Of The Hall **Bred** A Malone **Trained** Middleham Moor, N Yorks

FOCUS
A tight-looking novices' handicap chase, but a decisive all-the-way winner who was again better than the bare result.

3616 WATCH ON 3 DEVICES RACINGUK.COM/ANYWHERE NOVICES' HURDLE (7 hdls 1 omitted) 2m
2:05 (2:05) (Class 4) 4-Y-O+ **£3,249** (£954; £477; £238)

Form RPR
541- **1** **Yorkist (IRE)**[12] 3350 6-11-5 108 NathanMoscrop(7) 125+
(Brian Ellison) *t.k.h: trckd ldrs: led gng wl bef 2 out: pushed along 1 l in front whn lft 12 l clr last* **5/2**[2]
1- **2** *12* **Askamore Darsi (IRE)**[30] 3016 5-11-5 0 JasonMaguire 105
(Donald McCain) *led to 2nd: cl up: rdn and outpcd after 3 out: rallied next: one pce whn lft 12 l 2nd last* **7/2**[3]
0- **3** *19* **Nexius (IRE)**[23] 3144 5-10-12 0 CraigNichol(7) 86
(Keith Dalgleish) *nt fluent on occasions in rr: rdn and outpcd bef 3 out: no imp bef next: lft mod 3rd after last* **16/1**
6- **4** *2 ¼* **Khelac**[13] 3332 4-10-2 0 JoeCollier(5) 74
(Micky Hammond) *trckd ldrs: rdn after 3 out: wknd bef next* **25/1**
50- **5** *7* **Danby's Legend**[49] 2621 7-11-5 0 BrianHughes 77
(Malcolm Jefferson) *hld up in tch: drvn and outpcd after 3 out: btn next* **16/1**
522- **U** **Dark Dune (IRE)**[12] 3351 6-11-5 113 JamesReveley 103
(Tim Easterby) *cl up: led 2nd: rdn and hdd bef 2 out: 15 l 3rd and hld whn bdly hmpd and uns rdr after next* **15/8**[1]
P- **P** **Janaab (IRE)**[13] 3332 4-10-7 0 (t) RichieMcGrath
(Tim Easterby) *t.k.h: nt fluent in rr: outpcd bef 4 out: sn struggling: t.o whn p.u after 2 out* **50/1**
F **El Massivo (IRE)**[94] 4-10-7 0 DougieCostello 105+
(Brian Ellison) *hld up in tch: smooth hdwy 3 out: effrt and 1 l down whn fell last* **8/1**
0/5- **P** **Pennine Josie**[23] 3147 5-10-12 0 [1] BrianHarding
(James Moffatt) *bhd: struggling fnl circ: t.o whn p.u after 2 out* **100/1**

4m 1.5s (9.00) **Going Correction** +0.75s/f (Soft)
WFA 4 from 5yo+ 11lb 9 Ran SP% **115.2**
Speed ratings (Par 105): **107,101,91,90,86** , , ,
CSF £11.89 TOTE £3.30: £1.20, £1.80, £4.10; EX 11.10 Trifecta £135.90.
Owner Mike And Eileen Newbould **Bred** Con O'Keeffe **Trained** Norton, N Yorks

FOCUS
The outcome changed with a dramatic incident at the final flight. The winner is on the upgrade.

3617 NORTH YORKSHIRE GRAND NATIONAL H'CAP CHASE (FOR THE DENYS SMITH CHALLENGE TROPHY) (21 fncs 2 omitted) 3m 6f
2:35 (2:35) (Class 3) (0-135,135) 5-Y-O+**£12,685** (£3,869; £2,021; £1,097)

Form RPR
F31- **1** **Sun Cloud (IRE)**[29] 3019 7-11-0 123 BrianHughes 140+
(Malcolm Jefferson) *hld up towards rr: stdy hdwy and cl up after 14th: led gng wl 3 out: lft 4 l clr next: kpt on strly* **4/1**[2]
211- **2** *11* **Merlin's Wish**[14] 3267 9-11-2 125 IanPopham 132+
(Martin Keighley) *mstkes: cl up: pushed along whn blnd and outpcd 5 out: rallied to chse (clr) wnr last: plugged on: no imp* **9/4**[1]
32F- **3** *½* **The Thirsty Bricky (IRE)**[23] 3150 12-10-0 112 TonyKelly(3) 116
(David Thompson) *hld up: stdy hdwy 15th: rdn bef 3 out: lft 6 l 3rd and hmpd next: no imp* **22/1**
462- **4** *2 ½* **Wellforth (IRE)**[10] 3416 10-11-4 127 (p) DavidEngland 130+
(Barry Brennan) *cl up: led fr 6th tl rdn and hdd 3 out: lft 4 l 2nd next: wknd last* **12/1**
434- **F** **Diamond Harry**[55] 2491 11-11-12 135 JamesReveley 136
(Nick Williams) *hld up on outside: stdy hdwy and prom 14th: pushed along and jst over 2 l down whn fell heavily 2 out* **8/1**
/2P- **P** **Mister Marker (IRE)**[40] 2822 10-11-12 135 BrianHarding
(Nicky Richards) *hld up in tch: outpcd after 14th: t.o whn p.u bef 5 out* **12/1**
5P/ **P** **Carrigeen Lechuga (IRE)**[39] 2856 9-11-2 130 MissEALalor(5)
(R H Lalor, Ire) *nt fluent in rr: stdy hdwy and in tch 14th: wknd next: t.o whn p.u 4 out* **22/1**
/FP- **P** **Chac Du Cadran (FR)**[47] 2670 8-10-9 118 (p) TomMessenger
(Chris Bealby) *led to 6th: cl up tl lost pl 14th: t.o whn p.u bef 17th* **9/2**[3]
5P2- **P** **Green Wizard (IRE)**[40] 2817 8-11-3 126 RyanMania
(Sue Smith) *chsd ldrs: struggling after 14th: t.o whn p.u bef 17th* **7/1**

8m 5.4s (12.40) **Going Correction** +0.525s/f (Soft) 9 Ran SP% **116.6**
Speed ratings: **104,101,100,100,** , , ,
CSF £14.21 CT £168.22 TOTE £4.90: £1.50, £1.20, £5.40; EX 14.90 Trifecta £294.60.
Owner Boundary Garage (Bury) Limited **Bred** Mrs Rose & Miss Lucy Barry **Trained** Norton, N Yorks

FOCUS
An unrelenting gallop and a true test of stamina in the underfoot conditions. There were just five still in with a shout four out and just four completed. The winner is on the upgrade and is developing into a decent staying handicapper. Solid form.

3618 YORKSHIRE-OUTDOORS.CO.UK ADVENTURE ACTIVITIES H'CAP HURDLE (8 hdls 2 omitted) 2m 3f
3:05 (3:05) (Class 4) (0-115,113) 4-Y-O+ **£4,223** (£1,240; £620; £310)

Form RPR
323- **1** **Hit The Top (IRE)**[14] 3271 7-11-12 113 RyanMania 122+
(Sue Smith) *chsd ldrs: led and hit 4 out: rdn bef 2 out: edgd lft and styd on strly fr last* **7/1**[3]
22- **2** *2 ¾* **Summerlea (IRE)**[8] 3451 8-10-1 95 CraigNichol(7) 98
(Micky Hammond) *hld up in tch: effrt and edgd lft bef 2 out: chsd wnr last: kpt on: nt pce to chal* **5/2**[2]
600- **3** *1 ½* **Jokers And Rogues (IRE)**[23] 3144 6-10-6 100 JohnDawson(7) 104+
(John Wade) *t.k.h: hld up in tch: stdy hdwy and chsng wnr whn mstkes 2 out and last: kpt on same pce* **14/1**
F35- **4** *8* **Knight Valliant**[23] 3141 11-10-5 92 SeanQuinlan 86
(Barbara Butterworth) *hld up in tch: stdy hdwy 3 out: pushed along and outpcd next: sn no imp* **15/2**
415- **5** *shd* **Redpender (IRE)**[32] 2970 8-11-6 107 BrianHughes 100
(James Moffatt) *t.k.h: trckd ldrs: wnt 2nd 4 out: rdn bef 2 out: sn outpcd* **2/1**[1]
/10- **6** *7* **Welsh Bard (IRE)**[246] 168 5-11-12 113 JasonMaguire 99
(Donald McCain) *cl up: led after 2nd to 4th: nt fluent and outpcd 4 out: struggling after next* **10/1**
020/ **7** *½* **Patavium (IRE)**[160] 5074 11-10-8 98 TonyKelly(3) 84
(Edwin Tuer) *t.k.h: prom on outside: struggling 3 out: btn next* **25/1**
/60- **8** *11* **Pierrers Bounty (IRE)**[20] 3189 7-11-12 113 RichieMcGrath 88
(Henry Hogarth) *led to after 2nd: regained ld 4th to 4 out: rdn and sn struggling: btn after next* **20/1**

4m 59.3s (23.20) **Going Correction** +0.75s/f (Soft) 8 Ran SP% **110.5**
Speed ratings (Par 105): **81,79,79,75,75 72,72,68**
CSF £23.82 CT £224.87 TOTE £6.50: £2.60, £1.40, £4.60; EX 15.00 Trifecta £236.90.
Owner Mrs S Smith **Bred** S G And W R Deacon **Trained** High Eldwick, W Yorks

FOCUS
There were five still in with a shout turning for home. A big step up from the winner with the second too his mark.

3619 TUNSTALL STANDARD NATIONAL HUNT FLAT RACE (CONDITIONAL JOCKEYS' AND AMATEUR RIDERS') 2m
3:35 (3:35) (Class 5) 4-6-Y-O **£2,053** (£598; £299)

Form RPR
32- **1** **Gone Forever**[40] 2830 4-10-0 0 CraigGallagher(7) 99+
(Brian Ellison) *t.k.h: cl up: led over 2f out: hung lft: pushed out fnl f* **5/2**[2]
2- **2** *2* **Rons Dream**[24] 3133 4-9-7 0 MrSPBowen(7) 90+
(Peter Bowen) *in tch: effrt and swtchd rt 5f out: drvn over 3f out: rallied to chse wnr over 1f out: styd on: hld nr fin* **15/8**[1]
3 *6* **Landmarque** 5-11-2 0 JackQuinlan(3) 103
(Tony Coyle) *hld up: stdy hdwy 5f out: shkn up and outpcd 2f out: kpt on fnl f: no ch w first two* **11/1**
54- **4** *hd* **Ride The Range (IRE)**[28] 3042 5-10-12 0 LHall(7) 103
(Chris Grant) *cl up: chal over 3f out to over 2f out: outpcd wl over 1f out* **14/1**
5 *4 ½* **Sir Safir** 4-10-2 0 AdamNicol(5) 86
(Peter Niven) *hld up in tch: stdy hdwy on outside 1/2-way: effrt over 2f out: edgd lft and wknd appr fnl f* **6/1**[3]
0- **6** *12* **Be A Dreamer**[23] 3147 6-10-9 0 Zachery-JamesGaughan(10) 86
(Sue Smith) *led at ordinary gallop: rdn and hdd over 2f out: sn wknd* **50/1**
7 *18* **Guns At Midnight** 6-11-2 0 JakeGreenall(3) 68
(Tim Walford) *in tch tl rdn and wknd over 3f out* **12/1**
8 *2* **Wabanaki Legend** 5-10-5 0 MrJTeal(7) 59
(Malcolm Jefferson) *in tch: pushed along 1/2-way: struggling fnl 5f* **16/1**
0- **9** *2 ¼* **Clarence Beeks (IRE)**[33] 2960 4-9-11 0 GLavery(10) 52
(Brian Ellison) *hld up: stdy hdwy on outside 1/2-way: rdn and wknd wl over 2f out* **25/1**

4m 3.7s (16.80) **Going Correction** +0.75s/f (Soft)
WFA 4 from 5yo+ 11lb 9 Ran SP% **112.0**
Speed ratings: **88,87,84,83,81 75,66,65,64**
CSF £7.21 TOTE £2.50: £1.20, £1.50, £3.30; EX 7.40 Trifecta £70.50.
Owner P J Martin **Bred** Juddmonte Farms Ltd **Trained** Norton, N Yorks

FOCUS
All but one was still in with a chance turning for home and four were still in with a shot over a furlong out. Ordinary bumper form.
T/Plt: £36.80 to a £1 stake. Pool of £90984.43 - 1801.85 winning tickets. T/Qpdt: £10.10 to a £1 stake. Pool of £8360.29 - 606.55 winning tickets. RY

3245 FONTWELL (L-H)
Thursday, January 9
3620 Meeting Abandoned - Waterlogged

3501 HUNTINGDON (R-H)
Friday, January 10
3627 Meeting Abandoned - Waterlogged

3270 SEDGEFIELD (L-H)
Friday, January 10

OFFICIAL GOING: Heavy (soft in places; 4.6)
Final fence omitted on all circuits; ground. Hurdles moved in off outer rail, common bends and fresher ground provided where possible.
Wind: fresh across Weather: Cloudy

3634 BETFRED NOVICES' HURDLE (BETFRED HURDLE SERIES QUALIFIER) (10 hdls) 2m 4f
12:45 (12:45) (Class 4) 4-Y-O+ **£3,508** (£1,030; £515; £257)

Form RPR
322- **1** **Sir Mangan (IRE)**[29] 3036 6-11-6 115 JasonMaguire 125+
(Donald McCain) *mde all: rdn clr after 2 out* **10/11**[1]
5/5- **2** *19* **Dare To Endeavour**[21] 3189 7-11-6 116 PaddyBrennan 110
(Tom George) *in tch: hdwy to trck ldr bef 3 out: rdn appr 2 out: sn hld in 2nd* **11/4**[2]
165- **3** *23* **Riskier**[33] 2972 9-11-6 0 BrianHughes 90
(John Wade) *trckd ldr: nt fluent 7th: rdn appr 3 out: sn struggling: lft poor 3rd appr 2 out* **17/2**
/P6- **4** *34* **Native Optimist (IRE)**[40] 2838 7-11-1 0 MissCWalton(5) 49
(Sheena Walton) *hld up in rr: a bhd* **80/1**
/66- **5** *14* **Cadgers Hole**[31] 3016 7-11-6 0 TomSiddall 35
(Lynn Siddall) *hld up: a bhd: t.o after 7th* **250/1**
3- **P** **Carrybridge (IRE)**[45] 2738 7-10-13 0 TimmyMurphy
(S R B Crawford, Ire) *trckd ldr: pushed along in 3rd whn wnt wrong and p.u appr 2 out* **4/1**[3]

5m 7.3s (14.60) **Going Correction** +0.85s/f (Soft) 6 Ran SP% **111.2**
Speed ratings (Par 105): **104,96,87,73,68**
CSF £3.76 TOTE £2.40: £1.10, £2.70; EX 4.10 Trifecta £11.50.
Owner Frank McAleavy **Bred** Patrick F Doyle **Trained** Cholmondeley, Cheshire

The Form Book Jumps, Raceform Ltd, Compton, RG20 6NL.

FOCUS
Hurdles moved in off outer rail, common bends and fresher ground provided where possible. This modest novice hurdle was run at a routine gallop and the taxing underfoot conditions played a big part. The winner was the form pick but is progressive and should win more races.

3635 NO DEPOSIT FREE BETS WITH BOOKMAKERS.CO.UK H'CAP CHASE (14 fncs 3 omitted) 2m 6f

1:15 (1:15) (Class 5) (0-100,100) 5-Y-0+ **£2,989** (£877; £438; £219)

Form RPR

P34- **1** **Baltic Pathfinder (IRE)**[15] 3275 10-11-9 **97**........................ ShaneByrne 113+
(Sue Smith) *trckd ldrs: led 8th: hit 11th: clr bef 2 out: easily* **6/1**[3]

2FR- **2** *20* **Jim Job Jones**[9] 3472 10-9-9 **74** oh3....................(tp) ConorShoemark(5) 61
(Neil Mulholland) *led narrowly: hdd 8th: rdn 11th: no ch w wnr fr bef 2 out* **13/2**

3 *1 ¼* **Debt To Society (IRE)**[90] 1883 7-11-6 **99**................(t) HarryChalloner(5) 84
(Richard Ford) *midfield: trckd ldr 9th: outpcd 10th: hld in 3rd fr bef 2 out* **13/2**

6P4- **4** *14* **Lough Coi (IRE)**[14] 3325 8-11-2 **95**..............................(tp) JamesBanks(5) 66
(Anthony Middleton) *sn pushed along in rr: a bhd* **9/2**[2]

203- **F** **Pindar (GER)**[13] 3352 10-10-5 **84**...........................(p) SamanthaDrake(5)
(Joanne Foster) *in tch: fell 9th* **7/1**

/54- **P** **Mannered**[70] 2201 9-11-5 **100**.. JohnDawson(7)
(John Wade) *w ldr: wknd after 9th: t.o whn p.u after 2 out* **17/2**

60P- **U** **My Friend Riquet (FR)**[26] 7-10-0 **74** oh6........................... LeeEdwards
(Dave Roberts) *hld up: uns rdr 10th* **10/1**

454- **U** **Yukon Delta (IRE)**[20] 3209 7-9-10 **77**...................(p) StephenMulqueen(7)
(Robert Johnson) *hld up: uns rdr 2nd* **4/1**[1]

5m 54.0s (21.00) **Going Correction** +1.025s/f (Soft) **8** Ran SP% **111.3**
Speed ratings: **102,98,97,92,** , ,
CSF £41.74 CT £252.62 TOTE £7.60: £2.20, £2.30, £1.20; EX 46.80 Trifecta £111.30.
Owner John Regan & John Conroy **Bred** Christopher Maye **Trained** High Eldwick, W Yorks

FOCUS
Again the sapping surface had a huge bearing on this weak handicap and the majority were in trouble before the turn for home. The easy winner was value for further.

3636 COMPARE BOOKIES FREE BETS WITH BOOKMAKERS.CO.UK NOVICES' H'CAP HURDLE (8 hdls) 2m 1f

1:45 (1:45) (Class 5) (0-100,92) 4-Y-0+ **£2,339** (£686; £343; £171)

Form RPR

020- **1** **Next Hight (IRE)**[29] 3040 7-11-6 **89**........................... JonathanEngland(3) 105+
(Sue Smith) *trckd ldr: rdn to ld appr 2 out: kpt on to go clr* **15/8**[1]

050- **2** *16* **Rose Red**[42] 2787 7-11-3 **86**.. JamesBest(3) 86
(Rob Summers) *midfield: nt fluent 3 out: sn rdn: styd on fr appr 2 out: wnt 2nd bef last: no threat wnr* **13/2**[3]

/F0- **3** *1 ½* **W Six Times**[20] 3210 8-9-11 **68**...................................... CallumWhillans(5) 65
(Alistair Whillans) *hld up: rdn after 3 out: styd on after 2 out: wnt 3rd towards fin: nvr threatened* **7/1**

053- **4** *1* **Kathlatino**[15] 3284 7-10-12 **83**... JoeColliver(5) 79
(Micky Hammond) *in tch: rdn 3 out: one pce* **4/1**[2]

3- **5** *6* **Arkansas Dave (IRE)**[15] 3301 7-11-5 **92**...........................(tp) MrSFox(7) 86
(Mark Michael McNiff, Ire) *led: rdn whn hdd appr 2 out: lost 2nd bef last: wknd* **14/1**

064- **6** *2 ½* **Jebulani**[45] 2733 4-11-0 **92**... BrianHarding 67
(Barry Murtagh) *hld up: smooth hdwy to trck ldr after 3 out: rdn appr 2 out: sn wknd* **11/1**

335- **7** *10* **Mrs Grass**[26] 3110 7-10-9 **78**.. JohnKington(3) 55
(Jonathan Haynes) *trckd ldrs: wknd appr 2 out* **20/1**

54P- **8** *11* **Exit To Freedom**[15] 3265 8-11-0 **80**................................(p) DenisO'Regan 46
(John Wainwright) *trckd ldrs: wknd appr 2 out* **9/1**

/P0- **9** *11* **Needwood Park**[15] 3274 6-11-12 **92**...............................(p) KennyJohnson 47
(Ray Craggs) *hld up: hit 3rd: bhd fr 5th* **50/1**

4m 20.1s (13.20) **Going Correction** +0.85s/f (Soft)
WFA 4 from 6yo+ 11lb **9** Ran SP% **112.3**
Speed ratings (Par 103): **102,94,93,93,90 89,84,79,74**
CSF £14.34 CT £68.07 TOTE £2.60: £1.20, £2.10, £2.90; EX 15.40 Trifecta £89.40.
Owner Mrs S Smith **Bred** Gestut Wittekindshof **Trained** High Eldwick, W Yorks
■ Stewards' Enquiry : Mr S Fox two-day ban: used whip above permitted level (Jan 29-30)

FOCUS
A very weak novice handicap, run at an average gallop. A big step forward from the winner.

3637 COMPARE BOOKMAKER ODDS AT BOOKMAKERS.CO.UK H'CAP CHASE (11 fncs 2 omitted) 2m 110y

2:15 (2:15) (Class 5) (0-100,100) 5-Y-0+ **£2,989** (£877; £438; £219)

Form RPR

232- **1** **Pamak D'Airy (FR)**[30] 3020 11-11-9 **100**..........................(p) TonyKelly(3) 108
(Henry Hogarth) *chsd ldng pair: moved upsides after 7th: led last (normal 2 out): rdn clr extended run-in* **3/1**[3]

/44- **2** *7* **Mia's Vio (IRE)**[12] 3399 9-11-7 **100**.................................(t) DerekFox(5) 101
(Noel C Kelly, Ire) *hld up: hdwy into 3rd after 2 out: styd on: wnt 2nd ins fnl f: no threat wnr* **9/4**[1]

036- **3** *8* **Panthers Run**[26] 3107 14-9-11 **74** oh5...........................(t) JohnKington(3) 66
(Jonathan Haynes) *w ldr: outpcd in 3rd after 9th: dropped to 4th after 2 out: plugged on: regained 3rd towards fin* **16/1**

P04- **4** *2 ¼* **Fred Bojangals (IRE)**[26] 3107 12-11-12 **100**...................... SeanQuinlan 92
(Barbara Butterworth) *led narrowly: rdn whn hdd last: lost 2nd ins fnl f: tied up and lost 3rd towards fin* **13/2**

4/0- **5** *35* **Chicago Alley**[13] 3352 13-10-11 **85**.. LeeEdwards 40
(Dave Roberts) *hld up: hit 8th: a bhd* **16/1**

401- **F** **Cara Court (IRE)**[9] 3449 8-11-0 **93** 7ex...................(p) SamanthaDrake(5)
(Joanne Foster) *in tch: blnd and fell 6th* **5/2**[2]

4m 26.4s (17.80) **Going Correction** +1.025s/f (Soft) **6** Ran SP% **109.4**
Speed ratings: **99,95,91,90,74**
CSF £10.02 TOTE £3.40: £1.50, £1.40; EX 10.00 Trifecta £85.60.
Owner Hogarth Racing **Bred** Claude Yves Pelsy **Trained** Stillington, N Yorks

FOCUS
A moderate little handicap. It was run at a sound gallop considering the ground. The winner is rated to his mark.

3638 HORSE RACING FREE BETS AT BOOKMAKERS.CO.UK H'CAP HURDLE (13 hdls) 3m 3f 110y

2:45 (2:47) (Class 4) (0-120,115) 4-Y-0+ **£3,898** (£1,144; £572; £286)

Form RPR

1F1- **1** **The Young Master**[9] 3473 5-11-2 **110** 7ex.............(p) ConorShoemark(5) 119+
(Neil Mulholland) *trckd ldng pair: led narrowly after 3 out: stl on bit appr last: rdn and kpt on run-in* **15/8**[1]

542- **2** *1 ½* **American Life (FR)**[11] 3413 7-10-8 **102**.......................(vt) JamesBanks(5) 110
(Anthony Middleton) *hld up: rdn and hdwy to chse ldr after 2 out: kpt on: wnt 2nd post* **4/1**[2]

061- **3** *hd* **Moscow Presents (IRE)**[11] 3413 6-11-4 **112**.................(p) AdamNicol(5) 120
(Philip Kirby) *trckd ldr: upsides after 3 out: rdn and ev ch last: one pce run-in: lost 2nd post* **9/2**[3]

042- **4** *¾* **Quel Elite (FR)**[12] 3396 10-11-2 **105**.................................(p) BrianHughes 112
(James Moffatt) *hld up: rdn and hdwy to chse ldr after 2 out: one pce run-in* **8/1**

15P- **5** *14* **Big Sound**[40] 2843 7-10-11 **100**.....................................(p) PeterBuchanan 93
(Tim Walford) *in tch: nt fluent 3 out and dropped to rr: rdn appr 2 out: sn btn* **11/1**

/P4- **6** *¾* **Mister Philson (IRE)**[30] 3019 9-11-4 **107**......................(p) TimmyMurphy 99
(S R B Crawford, Ire) *led at stdy pce: slow 4th and 9th: hdd after 3 out: wknd 2 out* **9/2**[3]

7m 30.6s (38.60) **Going Correction** +0.85s/f (Soft) **6** Ran SP% **110.6**
Speed ratings (Par 105): **78,77,77,77,73 73**
CSF £9.62 TOTE £2.40: £1.20, £2.40; EX 7.10 Trifecta £21.40.
Owner Dajam Ltd **Bred** Brendan Boyle **Trained** Limpley Stoke, Wilts

FOCUS
This modest marathon handicap did not present quite the stamina sapping test one could have expected due to the steady gallop and there was a tight finish from the last. The form is given a token rating.

3639 COMPARE BOOKMAKERS AT BOOKMAKERS.CO.UK H'CAP HURDLE (10 hdls) 2m 4f

3:15 (3:15) (Class 5) (0-100,100) 4-Y-0+ **£2,339** (£686; £343; £171)

Form RPR

/P5- **1** **Markem (IRE)**[68] 2245 7-11-3 **98**...................................(t) ShaunDobbin(7) 102+
(Rose Dobbin) *midfield: smooth hdwy after 3 out: rdn to ld bef 2 out: kpt on wl* **12/1**

465- **2** *4 ½* **Caught By Witness (IRE)**[15] 3264 9-10-0 **79**..............(t) JamesBanks(5) 78
(Anthony Middleton) *hld up: stl only 8th appr 2 out: styd on: wnt 2nd post* **10/1**

540- **3** *shd* **Willie Hall**[29] 3040 10-10-8 **82**...(p) BrianHarding 82
(William Amos) *led: rdn whn hdd bef 2 out: one pce: lost 2nd post* **4/1**[1]

056- **4** *nk* **Bollin Julie**[29] 3038 7-9-9 **74**.. CallumWhillans(5) 74
(Donald Whillans) *hld up in tch: hdwy after 3 out: chsd ldng pair bef 2 out: kpt on same pce* **5/1**[3]

S45- **5** *2 ¼* **Indigo Island (IRE)**[26] 3106 5-10-7 **88**........................ CallumBewley(7) 84
(Robert Bewley) *racd keenly: trckd ldr: rdn after 3 out: wknd run-in* **25/1**

0/0- **6** *½* **One In A Row (IRE)**[15] 3270 7-10-4 **78**........................... PaddyBrennan 74
(Alan Swinbank) *midfield: rdn after 3 out: nt fluent 2 out: one pce and nvr threatened* **15/2**

7 *20* **Ivanka (IRE)**[233] 438 6-11-7 **100**...(t) DerekFox(5) 76
(Noel C Kelly, Ire) *hld up in rr: nvr threatened* **7/1**

121/ **8** *½* **Orlittlebylittle**[601] 342 8-11-12 **100**..................................... JasonMaguire 75
(Donald McCain) *in tch: rdn after 3 out: sn wknd* **9/2**[2]

P/0- **9** *½* **Desert Tommy**[14] 3335 13-10-7 **84**.................................(p) JakeGreenall(3) 59
(Lucinda Egerton) *trckd ldr: lost pl 5th: reminders after 6th: sn struggling in rr* **66/1**

0/P- **10** *6* **Politelysed**[29] 3040 8-9-7 **74**.. StephenMulqueen(7) 43
(Robert Johnson) *hld up: nvr threatened* **16/1**

PU4- **F** **King's Chorister**[32] 2999 8-10-4 **85**..............................(t) CraigNichol(7) 84
(Barry Murtagh) *midfield: rdn after 3 out: wknd after 2 out: 7th whn fell last* **9/1**

5m 12.2s (19.50) **Going Correction** +0.85s/f (Soft) **11** Ran SP% **117.1**
Speed ratings (Par 103): **95,93,93,93,92 91,83,83,83,81**
CSF £124.83 CT £570.99 TOTE £17.80: £4.30, £4.10, £1.50; EX 127.60 Trifecta £2619.60 Part won..
Owner Mr & Mrs Duncan Davidson **Bred** Eamonn Garrett **Trained** South Hazelrigg, Northumbria

FOCUS
An ordinary handicap. They went a fair gallop but it paid to race handily. The second, fourth and fifth set the level.

3640 BOOKMAKER FREE BETS AT BOOKMAKERS.CO.UK MAIDEN OPEN NATIONAL HUNT FLAT RACE 2m 1f

3:45 (3:45) (Class 6) 4-6-Y-0 **£1,559** (£457; £228; £114)

Form RPR

2- **1** **Master Dee (IRE)**[24] 3147 5-11-6 0................................... JasonMaguire 104+
(Donald McCain) *mde all: rdn over 2f out: kpt on wl* **4/7**[1]

2 *4* **Duncomplaining (IRE)** 5-11-6 0.................................... DougieCostello 100
(William Kinsey) *trckd ldrs: rdn over 2f out: kpt on: wnt 2nd ins fnl f* **11/2**[3]

3 *3 ¼* **Astaroland (FR)** 4-10-8 0... SeanQuinlan 85
(Jennie Candlish) *midfield: pushed along 4f out: hdwy to chse wnr over 1f out: no ex and lost 2nd ins fnl f* **9/1**

\- **4** *3 ½* **Maxed Out King (IRE)**[244] 6-11-6 0..................................... ShaneByrne 93
(Sue Smith) *racd keenly: hld up in tch: wnt prom 1/2-way: rdn over 2f out: sn one pce in 4th* **14/1**

5- **5** *6* **Donna's Diamond (IRE)**[32] 3002 5-11-6 0......................... DenisO'Regan 87
(Chris Grant) *trckd ldr: rdn 4f out: wknd fnl 2f* **5/1**[2]

0- **6** *3* **Wildest Dreams (IRE)**[56] 2499 5-10-13 0....................... AlistairFindlay(7) 84
(Jane Walton) *hld up: pushed along 3f out: minor late hdwy: nvr threatened* **40/1**

7 *57* **Diamond Native (IRE)** 6-11-6 0....................................... RichieMcGrath 27
(Brian Storey) *trckd ldrs: rdn and lost pl 1/2-way: sn bhd* **33/1**

60- **8** *3 ½* **Rossington**[42] 2788 5-10-13 0..[1] GLavery(7) 24
(John Wainwright) *hld up: a bhd: t.o* **125/1**

4m 13.8s (12.50) **Going Correction** +0.85s/f (Soft)
WFA 4 from 5yo+ 11lb **8** Ran SP% **118.5**
Speed ratings: **104,102,100,98,96 94,67,66**
CSF £4.53 TOTE £1.50: £1.10, £1.90, £3.00; EX 6.40 Trifecta £28.60.
Owner Paul & Clare Rooney **Bred** B Kavanagh **Trained** Cholmondeley, Cheshire

FOCUS
The first four each held every chance in what was probably a fair bumper. The winner built on his Catterick run.

T/Plt: £33.40 to a £1 stake. Pool: £110874.41 - 2418.70 winning tickets T/Qpdt: £11.50 to a £1 stake. Pool: £8020.59 - 515.10 winning tickets AS

3317 KEMPTON (R-H)

Saturday, January 11

OFFICIAL GOING: Soft (heavy in places on hurdle course)

All rail moved out 2yds on to fresh ground and all distances as advertised.

Wind: Virtually nil Weather: Sunny

3641 WILLIAM HILL - IN THE APP STORE JUVENILE HURDLE (8 hdls) 2m

11:55 (11:55) (Class 4) 4-Y-O £3,898 (£1,144; £572; £286)

Form RPR

1 **Goodwood Mirage (IRE)**99 4-10-12 0 APMcCoy 113+
(Jonjo O'Neill) *t.k.h: bmpd 2nd: trckd ldrs: wnt 2nd after 3 out: chal: bmpd and mstke 2 out: rallied to chal again and blnd last: styd on u.p to ld last stride* **6/4**1

0- 2 *shd* **The Green Ogre**24 3161 4-10-12 0 TomCannon 107
(Gary Moore) *in rr: stdy hdwy fr 3 out to ld and bmpd 2 out: styd on wl appr last: kpt on run-in: hdd last stride* **33/1**

3 *7* **Grey Blue (IRE)**95 4-10-12 0 BarryGeraghty 100
(Nicky Henderson) *in tch: chsd ldrs fr 3 out and rt there next: sn rdn: outpcd run-in* **9/2**3

62- 4 *8* **Sun Wild Life (FR)**32 3003 4-10-12 120 DougieCostello 92
(Robert Walford) *led: jnd 3rd: and again next: hdd 3 out and sn rdn: wknd fr 2 out* **5/2**2

5- 5 *11* **After Eight Sivola (FR)**91 1862 4-10-12 0 RichardJohnson 87+
(Nick Williams) *blnd 1st: chsd ldr: chal and mstke 3rd: upsides and j. slowly 4 out: slt ld and hit 3 out: hdd appr next: sn wknd* **9/2**3

6 *8* **Fruity Bun**437 4-10-0 0 (t) JamesBanks(5) 66
(Keiran Burke) *rdn 4 out: a in rr* **100/1**

7 *½* **Hidden Link**106 4-10-12 0 FelixDeGiles 72
(Tom Symonds) *bmpd 2nd: in tch to 3 out: wknd sn after and mstke 2 out* **33/1**

05- 8 *hd* **Classic Art**15 3317 4-10-12 0 ColinBolger 72
(Roger Teal) *chsd ldrs: rdn after 4th: btn next* **100/1**

4m 9.17s (11.07) **Going Correction** +0.30s/f (Yiel) 8 Ran SP% **112.8**
Speed ratings: **84,83,80,76,70 66,66,66**
CSF £42.97 TOTE £2.10: £1.10, £5.30, £1.50; EX 40.50 Trifecta £118.80.
Owner Lady Bamford & Alice Bamford **Bred** Mrs Chris Harrington **Trained** Cheltenham, Gloucs

FOCUS

All rail moved out 2yds on to fresh ground and all distances as advertised. The jockeys reported the ground to be riding as described, with some adding that it was "tiring". Last year's winner of this juvenile event, L'Unique, went on to take the Grade 1 Anniversary Hurdle at Aintree, while 2012 scorer Sadler's Risk was sixth in that year's Triumph Hurdle. This edition lacked strength in depth, however, and the time was slow. Not an easy race to put a figure on.

3642 WILLIAM HILL - DOWNLOAD THE APP H'CAP CHASE (16 fncs) 2m 4f 110y

12:25 (12:25) (Class 3) (0-135,135) 5-Y-O+

£6,256 (£1,848; £924; £462; £231; £116)

Form RPR

530- 1 **King Edmund**21 3197 11-11-12 **135** TomCannon 144
(Chris Gordon) *hld up in rr: stdy hdwy fr 10th: trckd ldrs next: led after 3 out: rdn appr last: hld on all out* **25/1**

211/ 2 *½* **Ice 'N' Easy (IRE)**270 5331 8-10-11 **120** (t) NoelFehily 129
(Charlie Longsdon) *towards rr but in tch: hdwy 12th: chsd ldrs 4 out: rdn bef next: rallied to chse wnr sn after 2 out: kpt on wl u.p run-in: clsng fin: nt quite get up* **5/1**3

/3P- 3 *12* **Shangani (USA)**35 2939 8-11-12 **135** LiamTreadwell 133
(Venetia Williams) *chsd ldrs: hit 8th: rdn next: sn chsng ldrs again: chal 4 out: rdn next and styd disputing 2nd tl no ex after 2 out* **8/1**

11F- 4 *8* **Toby Lerone (IRE)**35 2939 7-11-1 **124** HarrySkelton 114
(Dan Skelton) *led to 2nd: chsd ldr: chal 5th and 7th: led 11th: narrowly hdd 12th: chal 4 out: sn led u.p: hdd after 3 out: btn next* **11/2**

343- 5 *9* **Barlow (IRE)**48 2693 7-10-12 **121** (p) APMcCoy 105
(Warren Greatrex) *led 2nd: hdd and hit 11th and hdd: led next: jnd 4 out: sn hdd: wknd after 3 out* **4/1**2

S13- 6 *10* **Sergeant Dick (IRE)**44 2757 9-11-3 **126** (t) FelixDeGiles 99
(Barry Brennan) *pressed ldrs: chal 12th: stl upsides 4 out: wknd sn after* **10/1**

/03- 7 *10* **Aegean Dawn**21 3207 9-11-11 **134** DougieCostello 44
(Robert Walford) *blnd 1st: in rr: pushed along 11th: no rspnse and no ch after* **7/2**1

PP4- 8 *16* **Arthur's Pass**28 3090 10-11-6 **129** RhysFlint 73
(Tom George) *t.k.h: chsd ldrs to 4 out: sn wknd* **16/1**

/56- P **Mister Snowball (FR)**63 2370 7-10-3 **112** TomScudamore
(Chris Down) *hit 4th: in rr tl p.u bef 10th* **10/1**

5m 18.0s (1.40) **Going Correction** +0.30s/f (Yiel) 9 Ran SP% **113.3**
Speed ratings: **109,108,104,101,97 93,90,84,**
CSF £144.53 CT £1105.75 TOTE £34.60: £5.00, £1.60, £2.40; EX 192.40 Trifecta £846.20.
Owner Anthony Ward-Thomas **Bred** Simon Tindall **Trained** Morestead, Hants

FOCUS

A fair handicap chase run at a reasonable gallop. The winner is rated back to his best.

3643 WILLIAMHILL.COM NOVICES' HURDLE (12 hdls) 3m 110y

1:00 (1:00) (Class 3) 4-Y-O+ £5,848 (£1,717; £858; £429)

Form RPR

/23- 1 **Closing Ceremony (IRE)**50 2649 5-11-2 125 RichardJohnson 126+
(Emma Lavelle) *led 3rd: in command whn rdn after 2 out: c clr last: readily* **10/11**1

533- 2 *14* **Minella On Line (IRE)**14 3357 5-11-2 0 APMcCoy 116+
(Rebecca Curtis) *chsd ldrs: hit 8th: chsd wnr after 3 out and sn rdn: no imp 2 out: styd on same pce sn after* **9/4**2

3/3- 3 *7* **Harry's Farewell**55 2536 7-11-2 0 AndrewThornton 105
(Polly Gundry) *chsd ldrs: outpcd 8th and sn rdn: styd on to take 3rd after 3 out: wknd bef 2 out* **7/1**3

6- 4 *2¼* **Garde Fou (FR)**28 3092 8-11-2 0 RhysFlint 102
(Paul Henderson) *in rr: pushed along 3 out: styd on appr last whn nt fluent: styd on to cl on 3rd nr fin but nvr a threat* **50/1**

/42- 5 *20* **Spencer Lea**20 3225 6-10-13 109 RobertDunne(3) 92
(Andrew Price) *led: hdd and hit 5th styd chsng wnr to 3 out: sn wknd* **9/1**

25- 6 *39* **Back In June**36 2929 6-11-2 0 NickScholfield 43
(Paul Henderson) *blnd 1st and 7th: a in rr: t.o fr 4 out* **33/1**

6m 30.0s (14.00) **Going Correction** +0.30s/f (Yiel) 6 Ran SP% **110.6**
Speed ratings (Par 107): **89,84,82,81,75 62**
CSF £3.17 TOTE £2.30: £1.10, £1.80; EX 3.20 Trifecta £5.10.
Owner The High Altitude Partnership **Bred** Ms Margaret Treacy **Trained** Hatherden, Hants

FOCUS

They went a steady pace in this ordinary novice hurdle. Straightforward form.

3644 WILLIAMHILL.COM LEVY BOARD TOLWORTH HURDLE NOVICES' HURDLE (GRADE 1) (8 hdls) 2m

1:35 (1:38) (Class 1) 4-Y-O+

£18,224 (£6,838; £3,424; £1,705; £857; £428)

Form RPR

/31- 1 **Royal Boy (FR)**22 3182 7-11-7 138 APMcCoy 150+
(Nicky Henderson) *trckd ldrs: wnt 2nd after 3 out: slt ld sn after: jnd and narrowly hdd 2 out but styd upsides: stl chalng last u.p: styd on wl to ld cl home* **9/1**

11- 2 *½* **Josses Hill (IRE)**24 3163 6-11-7 0 BarryGeraghty 150+
(Nicky Henderson) *in tch: nt fluent 4th and 4 out: chal after 3 out and slt ld next put remained hrd pressed at last: kpt on u.p: hdd cl home* **5/1**3

- 3 *11* **Upazo (FR)**28 3100 6-11-7 0 RWalsh 140
(W P Mullins, Ire) *hld up in rr: hdwy after 3 out: nt fluent u.p 2 out: kpt on to take 3rd wl bef last but no imp on ldng duo* **3/1**2

112- 4 *4½* **Garde La Victoire (FR)**29 3070 5-11-7 138 RichardJohnson 136
(Philip Hobbs) *t.k.h: hit 2nd: chsd ldr 3rd: rdn after 3 out: mstke 2 out: btn sn after* **7/1**

/11- 5 *4½* **The Liquidator**55 2530 6-11-7 0 TomScudamore 131
(David Pipe) *led: rdn appr 3 out: hdd sn after: wknd 2 out* **11/8**1

51F- 6 *1¼* **Prince Siegfried (FR)**22 3184 8-11-7 138 DenisO'Regan 129
(John Ferguson) *hld up in rr: nt fluent 3rd: drvn and hdwy after 3 out: nvr rchd ldrs: btn bef next* **20/1**

3m 58.29s (0.19) **Going Correction** +0.30s/f (Yiel) 6 Ran SP% **111.0**
Speed ratings: **111,110,105,103,100 100**
CSF £50.02 TOTE £9.90: £4.70, £2.80; EX 26.90 Trifecta £144.40.
Owner Michael Buckley **Bred** Earl Haras Du Luy **Trained** Upper Lambourn, Berks

FOCUS

A race with an illustrious role of honour, with Noland in 2006 the last winner to go on to Cheltenham festival victory. Originally scheduled for Sandown last Saturday, the race was reopened when that fixture was washed out. Irving was the most notable absentee from the line-up. Nicky Henderson won two of the three previous runnings with Minella Class and Captain Conan, and the stable enjoyed a 1-2 here. The first two are on the upgrade and the form looks solid enough.

3645 WILLIAMHILL.COM CHASE (LISTED RACE) (16 fncs) 2m 4f 110y

2:10 (2:10) (Class 1) 5-Y-O+ £17,386 (£6,712; £3,511; £1,900)

Form RPR

4/3- 1 **Captain Chris (IRE)**30 3032 10-11-10 165 (t) RichardJohnson 175+
(Philip Hobbs) *in tch: trckd ldr 12th: led 4 out: c clr appr next: styd on strly* **15/8**1

02U- 2 *23* **Champion Court (IRE)**16 3262 9-11-6 157 APMcCoy 148
(Martin Keighley) *led: wnt wd bnd after 7th: rdn and hdd 4 out: no ch w wnr after but kpt on to hold clr 2nd fr 3 out* **11/4**2

/11- 3 *9* **Twinlight (FR)**34 2985 7-11-10 162 RWalsh 147
(W P Mullins, Ire) *trckd ldr: hit 3rd: blnd 10th: rdn and btn 4 out: mstke last: tk wl hld 3rd run-in* **11/4**2

041- 4 *1½* **Pepite Rose (FR)**15 3333 7-10-11 148 LiamTreadwell 129
(Venetia Williams) *hit 1st: in rr: hit 7th: hdwy 12th: tk 3rd 4 out: sn rdn: no ch w ldng duo next: lost wl hld 3rd run-in* **7/1**3

504- P **Tataniano (FR)**15 3320 10-11-0 143 NoelFehily
(Richard Rowe) *a in rr: pushed along 10th: t.o whn p.u bef 12th* **50/1**

P/6- P **Ghizao (GER)**30 3032 10-11-6 153 NickScholfield
(Paul Nicholls) *chsd ldrs: blnd 3rd: nt fluent 8th: sn reminders to chse ldr: wknd fr 11th: t.o whn p.u bef 3 out* **14/1**

5m 14.85s (-1.75) **Going Correction** +0.30s/f (Yiel) 6 Ran SP% **109.2**
Speed ratings: **115,106,102,102,**
CSF £7.23 TOTE £2.60: £1.70, £1.70; EX 7.10 Trifecta £18.20.
Owner Mrs Diana L Whateley **Bred** Mrs Noreen Walsh **Trained** Withycombe, Somerset

FOCUS

The first running of this Listed event. Captain Chris is rated back to his best and there's a case for rating the form higher still, but not on time.

3646 WILLIAM HILL LANZAROTE HURDLE (H'CAP) (LISTED RACE) (10 hdls) 2m 5f

2:40 (2:42) (Class 1) 4-Y-O+

£25,627 (£9,616; £4,815; £2,398; £1,206; £603)

Form RPR

541- 1 **Saphir Du Rheu (FR)**35 2949 5-11-7 **145** HarryDerham(5) 158+
(Paul Nicholls) *in tch: hdwy 5th: blnd 4 out: led appr 2 out: drvn clr bef last: readily* **6/1**3

3/1- 2 *6* **If In Doubt (IRE)**42 2828 6-10-13 **132** APMcCoy 139+
(Philip Hobbs) *in rr: nt fluent 1st: hdwy 3 out and sn chsng ldrs: ev ch 2 out: chsd wnr u.p appr last: no imp but hld on wl for 2nd* **5/1**2

/21- 3 *1* **Like Minded**35 2935 10-11-2 **135** (t) HarrySkelton 140
(Dan Skelton) *in tch: hdwy to chse ldrs 4 out: styd on fr 2 out to press for 2nd run-in but no ch w wnr and no ex into 3rd in clsng stages* **16/1**

121- 4 *5* **Spirit Of Shankly**50 2659 6-11-3 **136** (t) NoelFehily 136
(Charlie Longsdon) *in rr: sme hdwy 4 out: rdn next and outpcd: styd on again fr 2 out: nt rch ldrs* **8/1**

3F6- 5 *7* **Kaylif Aramis**21 3200 7-10-7 **133** (t) RyanHatch(7) 127
(Nigel Twiston-Davies) *chsd ldrs: hit 3rd: wnt 2nd 6th: slt ld after 3 out: hdd appr 2 out: wknd bef last* **7/1**

3F1- 6 *5* **Foxcub (IRE)**31 3028 6-11-4 **137** FelixDeGiles 124
(Tom Symonds) *chsd ldrs: wnt 2nd 4 out: led appr 3 out: hdd sn after: wknd after next* **33/1**

142- 7 *73* **Home Run (GER)**35 2949 6-10-4 **130** (b) TomBellamy(7) 102
(David Pipe) *in tch: rdn and wknd 3 out* **12/1**

/02- P **Art Professor (IRE)**21 3206 10-10-12 **131** LiamTreadwell
(Venetia Williams) *chsd ldr to 4 out: wknd next: t.o whn p.u bef 2 out* **16/1**

013- P **Gores Island (IRE)**45 2742 8-10-2 **121** TomCannon
(Gary Moore) *chsd ldrs to 4 out: t.o whn p.u bef 2 out* **33/1**

0/3- P **River Maigue (IRE)**35 2951 7-11-9 **142** BarryGeraghty
(Nicky Henderson) *in rr: hdwy to trck ldrs 4 out: travelling wl 3 out: rdn sn after and wknd qckly: p.u bef last* **6/1**3

001- P **Maller Tree**10 3471 7-11-5 **138** (v) TomScudamore
(David Dennis) *led: hdd 4 out: wknd next: t.o whn p.u bef 2 out* **33/1**

026- P **Party Rock (IRE)**16 3292 7-11-5 **145** ConorRing(7)
(Jennie Candlish) *sn behnd: blnd 5th: t.o whn p.u bef 2 out* **25/1**

The Form Book Jumps, Raceform Ltd, Compton, RG20 6NL.

311- **F** **Junction Fourteen (IRE)**[16] 3263 5-11-4 **137**.............. RichardJohnson 131
(Emma Lavelle) *in rr: hdwy 4 out: chsd ldrs 3 out: ev ch and rdn 2 out: wkng in 4th whn fell last* **9/2**[1]

5m 25.3s (7.80) **Going Correction** +0.30s/f (Yiel) **13** Ran SP% **119.2**
Speed ratings (Par 111): **97,94,94,92,89 87,60,, ,**
CSF £35.22 CT £452.67 TOTE £7.40: £2.60, £1.90, £4.10; EX 37.80 Trifecta £502.50.
Owner The Stewart Family **Bred** Claude Duval **Trained** Ditcheat, Somerset

FOCUS
A very competitive renewal of this Listed handicap, which has been run over 2m5f since 2007. The pace was good and the form looks solid. A number came here on the back of easy wins last time. Another big step forward from the impressive winner, who is verging on top class.

3647 WILLIAM HILL - BET ON THE MOVE H'CAP CHASE (18 fncs) 3m
3:15 (3:15) (Class 2) (0-145,144) 5-Y-0+
£11,573 (£3,418; £1,709; £854; £427; £214)

Form RPR

0P/- **1** **Planet Of Sound**[280] 5176 12-11-12 **144**....................(t) RichardJohnson 152+
(Philip Hobbs) *chsd ldrs: led 9th: drvn and styd on fr 3 out: mstke last: sn rcvrd and kpt on wl run-in* **10/1**

134- **2** *2* **Jump City (FR)**[36] 2925 8-11-0 **132**...................................... DarylJacob 136
(Paul Nicholls) *in rr: hdwy 9th: chsd wnr fr 4 out: kpt on u.p fr 3 out: no imp fr 2 out* **8/1**[3]

040- **3** *6* **Native Gallery (IRE)**[42] 2813 9-11-1 **133**.............................. NoelFehily 131
(Ben De Haan) *in rr: hdwy 4 out: tk 3rd u.p 3 out: kpt on same pce and no imp on ldng duo: hld on for 3rd in clsng stages* **5/1**[2]

04P- **4** *nk* **On Trend (IRE)**[15] 3321 8-10-6 **124**.................................(p) TomCannon 124
(Nick Gifford) *chsd ldrs: blnd 9th: rdn 11th: styd in tch: and kpt on u.p fr 3 out to press for 2nd in clsng stages* **12/1**

/P1- **5** *17* **Relax (FR)**[26] 3131 9-11-0 **132**... LiamTreadwell 116
(Venetia Williams) *led 3rd: hit 6th and sn hdd: hit 12th: chsd wnr 13th: wknd after 14th* **4/1**[1]

F20- **6** *4* **Buddy Bolero (IRE)**[35] 2953 8-11-12 **144**..................(p) TomScudamore 123
(David Pipe) *led to 3rd: led after 6th: hdd and nt fluent 9th: wknd 13th* **4/1**[1]

/03- **7** *26* **Nadiya De La Vega (FR)**[28] 3090 8-11-6 **138**........................ APMcCoy 104
(Nicky Henderson) *in rr: hdwy fr 12th and styng on whn blnd 14th and nt rcvr* **5/1**[2]

1/1- **P** **Good Order**[15] 3325 9-10-11 **129**.......................................(t) AlainCawley
(Tom George) *nvr jumping w much fluency in rr: t.o whn p.u bef 3 out* **8/1**[3]

6m 18.86s (3.46) **Going Correction** +0.30s/f (Yiel) **8** Ran SP% **112.3**
Speed ratings: **106,105,103,103,97 96,87,**
CSF £81.07 CT £447.00 TOTE £13.00: £4.10, £2.20, £1.80; EX 122.20 Trifecta £513.30.
Owner C G M Lloyd-Baker **Bred** C G M Lloyd-Baker **Trained** Withycombe, Somerset

FOCUS
A fair handicap, but there were doubts over a few of these going into the race. The winner's best figure for nearly two years.

3648 WILLIAM HILL - DOWNLOAD THE APP H'CAP HURDLE (8 hdls) 2m
3:50 (3:50) (Class 3) (0-140,140) 4-Y-0+ **£5,848** (£1,717; £858; £429)

Form RPR

/42- **1** **Lyvius**[29] 3066 6-11-4 **132**... BarryGeraghty 140+
(Nicky Henderson) *in rr tl hdwy after 3 out: chal and bmpd 2 out: slt ld sn after: hrd pressed and u.p run-in: asserted last strides* **5/2**[1]

221- **2** *hd* **Deep Trouble (IRE)**[35] 2951 7-11-5 **133**.............................. DarylJacob 141+
(Ben Case) *hld up in rr: stdy hdwy fr 2 out to press wnr fr last: styd upsides u.p tl no ex last strides* **10/3**[2]

B/0- **3** *8* **Lexi's Boy (IRE)**[35] 2958 6-11-6 **134**..................................... NoelFehily 133
(Donald McCain) *chsd ldrs: slt ld appr 2 out: sn bmpd and hdd sn after: wknd and j. slowly last* **8/1**

530/ **4** *1¼* **Kudu Country (IRE)**[280] 5178 8-10-11 **125**.................... DougieCostello 123
(Tom Tate) *led tl hdd appr 2 out but styd chalng tl wknd bef last* **33/1**

/45- **5** *5* **Right Step**[15] 3322 7-9-6 **116**..(t) PaddyBradley[(10)] 110
(Pat Phelan) *chsd ldrs: wnt 2nd and rdn 3 out: wknd 2 out* **10/1**

/F0- **6** *1¾* **Urcalin (FR)**[42] 2828 6-10-3 **117**.. TomCannon 108
(David Arbuthnot) *chsd ldrs: dropped to rr 4 out: sme hdwy again after 3 out: no prog appr next* **14/1**

0/F- **7** *14* **Swnymor (IRE)**[63] 1866 5-10-13 **137**............................. PaulO'Brien[(10)] 114
(Rebecca Curtis) *towards rr: hdwy 4th: chsd ldrs 3 out: wknd bef next* **7/1**[3]

P/P- **8** *1* **First Avenue**[126] 1520 9-11-2 **140**.................................. NathanAdams[(10)] 116
(Laura Mongan) *a in rr* **28/1**

U10- **9** *6* **Honour System (IRE)**[49] 2668 7-10-8 **122**........................ DenisO'Regan 92
(John Ferguson) *chsd ldr to 4 out: wknd next* **22/1**

0/1- **10** *5* **Moujik Borget (FR)**[49] 2668 6-10-13 **127**.......................... LiamTreadwell 92
(Venetia Williams) *chsd ldrs tl wknd after 3 out* **7/1**[3]

4m 4.54s (6.44) **Going Correction** +0.30s/f (Yiel) **10** Ran SP% **114.3**
Speed ratings (Par 107): **95,94,90,90,87 86,79,79,76,73**
CSF £11.02 CT £56.08 TOTE £3.40: £1.50, £1.60, £2.50; EX 10.60 Trifecta £47.90.
Owner Trevor Hemmings **Bred** Gestut Hof Ittlingen **Trained** Upper Lambourn, Berks

FOCUS
A decent handicap hurdle which was run at a fairly steady tempo. It's worth being fairly positive about the first two.
T/Jkpt: Not won. £56,530.47 carried forward to Wolverhampton, 20th January. T/Plt: £131.70 to a £1 stake. Pool of £142,632.84 - 790.36 winning units T/Qpdt: £26.60 to a £1 stake. Pool of £11,114.43 - 309.15 winning units ST

3434 WARWICK (L-H)
Saturday, January 11

OFFICIAL GOING: Heavy (soft in places) changing to soft on chase course after race 4 (1.55)
Wind: Fresh half-behind Weather: Cloudy with sunny spells

3649 LEVY BOARD WARWICK MARES' HURDLE (LISTED RACE) (F&M) (9 hdls) 2m 3f
12:10 (12:10) (Class 1) 4-Y-0+
£11,390 (£4,274; £2,140; £1,066; £536; £268)

Form RPR

1/3- **1** **Glens Melody (IRE)**[28] 3084 6-11-8 0.. DJCasey 139+
(W P Mullins, Ire) *hld up: hdwy appr 5th: led 2 out: rdn and edgd rt flat: styd on* **7/4**[1]

/46- **2** *¾* **Mischievous Milly (IRE)**[42] 2813 6-11-8 137.................. LeightonAspell 138+
(Oliver Sherwood) *hld up: hdwy 6th: rdn and ev ch fr 2 out: nt clr run and swtchd lft flat: styd on* **4/1**[2]

/11- **3** *nk* **Hidden Identity (IRE)**[60] 2433 8-11-0 138....................... AidanColeman 129
(Tim Vaughan) *hld up: hdwy 3 out: sn rdn: r.o* **4/1**[2]

0/2- **4** *2½* **Prima Porta**[70] 2226 8-11-0 136.. PaulMoloney 126
(Evan Williams) *hld up: hdwy 6th: outpcd after 3 out: r.o flat* **4/1**[2]

6/2- **5** *2¾* **Flementime (IRE)**[32] 3010 6-11-0 0.. IanPopham 125
(Martin Keighley) *trckd ldr: mstke 4th: led 6th: rdn and hdd whn mstke 2 out: no ex and hung rt flat* **12/1**[3]

524- **6** *3¼* **Teochew (IRE)**[12] 3419 6-11-0 117..(p) DarylJacob 120
(Warren Greatrex) *led to 6th: rdn and wkng whn mstke 2 out* **28/1**

1P5/ **U** **Queens Grove**[268] 5358 8-11-0 129.. JamesBest
(Kevin Bishop) *chsd ldrs: pushed along 6th: lost pl whn blnd and uns rdr 3 out* **66/1**

4m 40.9s (-1.80) **Going Correction** -0.075s/f (Good) **7** Ran SP% **109.0**
Speed ratings (Par 111): **100,99,99,98,97 95,**
CSF £8.25 TOTE £2.60: £1.30, £2.90; EX 11.10 Trifecta £29.70.
Owner Ms Fiona McStay **Bred** Mrs Fiona McStay **Trained** Muine Beag, Co Carlow

FOCUS
Both David Casey and Aidan Coleman described the ground as "tacky". A race that had been saved from Sandown's abandoned meeting a week earlier, they went a fairly steady gallop and the class act in the line-up prevailed. It was steadily run and the first four were all below their best.

3650 BETFRED GOALS GALORE NOVICES' H'CAP HURDLE (8 hdls) 2m
12:45 (12:45) (Class 4) (0-110,108)
4-Y-0+ **£3,249** (£954; £477; £238)

Form RPR

0/3- **1** **Dungeness**[32] 3014 6-10-13 **95**.. AidanColeman 104+
(Venetia Williams) *led: hdd appr 2 out: rallied to ld last: styd on wl* **6/1**[3]

360- **2** *4* **Bold Cuffs**[44] 2755 5-11-6 **102**...(t) JoeTizzard 106+
(Colin Tizzard) *mid-div: hdwy 3rd: chsd ldr 3 out: led bef next: hdd whn mstke last: no ex u.p flat* **7/1**

/35- **3** *1½* **Tracking Time**[181] 966 7-11-3 **104**................................... KillianMoore[(5)] 105
(Andrew J Martin) *chsd ldr to 3 out: sn rdn: styd on same pce fr next* **20/1**

1F4- **4** *1* **The Game Is A Foot (IRE)**[44] 2766 7-11-3 **106**........ JosephAkehurst[(7)] 106
(Gary Moore) *prom: rdn after 3 out: styd on same pce fr next* **5/1**[2]

016- **5** *8* **Lost In Newyork (IRE)**[15] 3328 7-9-11 **86**.................. CharlieDeutsch[(7)] 78
(Nick Kent) *hld up: hdwy appr 3 out: rdn and wknd bef next* **6/1**[3]

F40- **6** *1¼* **Who's Jeff (IRE)**[41] 2848 6-11-5 **104**.................................. JamesBest[(3)] 95
(Philip Hobbs) *hld up: hmpd 4th: hdwy next: rdn and wknd appr 2 out* **12/1**

40/- **7** *¾* **Cropley (IRE)**[147] 3340 5-11-0 **96**.................................. RichieMcLernon 88
(Jonjo O'Neill) *hld up: rdn and wknd after 3 out* **20/1**

02P- **8** *14* **Dude Alert (IRE)**[36] 2927 4-10-4 **98**.. AdamWedge 62
(Anna Newton-Smith) *prom: nt fluent 1st: pushed along 4th: wknd next* **50/1**

535- **9** *¾* **Tempuran**[7] 2628 5-11-9 **105**... SeanQuinlan 80
(David Bridgwater) *hld up: rdn 5th: wknd bef next* **20/1**

600- **10** *12* **Frozen Over**[24] 3163 6-11-6 **102**.. JamesDavies 65
(Chris Down) *hld up: hdwy 4th: rdn and wknd after 3 out* **20/1**

/13- **P** **Windpfeil (IRE)**[202] 810 8-10-2 **91**................................(p) MissCBoxall[(7)]
(Dominic Ffrench Davis) *mid-div: lost pl after 3rd: wknd appr 3 out: bhd whn p.u bef last* **25/1**

/24- **U** **Don Pooleoni (IRE)**[52] 2598 9-11-2 **108**.................. MartinMcIntyre[(10)]
(Harry Fry) *trckd ldrs tl blnd and uns rdr 4th* **11/4**[1]

3m 53.4s (-3.10) **Going Correction** -0.075s/f (Good)
WFA 4 from 5yo+ 11lb **12** Ran SP% **117.0**
Speed ratings (Par 105): **104,102,101,100,96 95,95,88,88,82 ,**
CSF £41.26 CT £793.21 TOTE £7.60: £1.90, £2.90, £6.50; EX 56.70 Trifecta £755.30 Part won. Pool of £1007.07 - 0.29 winning units..
Owner The Bellamy Partnership **Bred** Design & Planning & Mickley Stud **Trained** Kings Caple, H'fords

FOCUS
Modest form, with the favourite departing down the back. The winner is on the upgrade.

3651 BETFRED GOALS GALORE EXTRA NOVICES' CHASE (18 fncs) 3m 110y
1:20 (1:20) (Class 2) 5-Y-0+ **£11,573** (£3,418; £1,709; £854)

Form RPR

/11- **1** **Corrin Wood (IRE)**[25] 3146 7-11-8 144.............................. JasonMaguire 159+
(Donald McCain) *mde all: j.rt at times: rdn appr 2 out: styd on wl* **2/1**[2]

111- **2** *2½* **Black Thunder (FR)**[28] 3095 7-11-8 153................................. DarylJacob 157
(Paul Nicholls) *a.p: chsd wnr 6th: rdn appr 2 out: styd on same pce flat* **10/11**[1]

13/ **3** *34* **Court Victory (IRE)**[728] 3728 9-11-0 0............................. AidanColeman 115
(Emma Lavelle) *chsd wnr to 6th: remained handy tl wknd after 14th* **11/1**

F11- **4** *1½* **Via Sundown (FR)**[28] 3097 6-11-8 134.............................. JoshuaMoore 123
(Gary Moore) *hld up: hdwy 12th: pushed along 14th: mstke next: sn wknd* **6/1**[3]

6m 13.1s (-13.90) **Going Correction** -0.375s/f (Good) **4** Ran SP% **108.3**
Speed ratings: **107,106,95,94**
CSF £4.42 TOTE £3.00; EX 4.90 Trifecta £19.20.
Owner Dermot Hanafin **Bred** Margaret Nevin **Trained** Cholmondeley, Cheshire

FOCUS
Just the four runners, but all three to have run this season had created a fine impression and it was certainly a true test at the distance. The first two are smart novices.

3652 BETFRED MOBILE H'CAP CHASE (FOR THE EDWARD COURAGE CUP) (12 fncs) 2m
1:55 (1:55) (Class 3) (0-135,135) 5-Y-0+ **£6,498** (£1,908; £954; £477)

Form RPR

/02- **1** **Dare Me (IRE)**[231] 474 10-11-4 **127**................................. AidanColeman 147+
(Venetia Williams) *sn prom: led after 8th: wnt clr appr 2 out: easily* **7/1**

354- **2** *14* **Al Alfa**[29] 3065 7-10-3 **115**.. JamesBest[(3)] 120
(Philip Hobbs) *a.p: chsd wnr after 8th: rdn 3 out: sn outpcd* **9/2**[2]

221- **3** *6* **Dolatulo (FR)**[28] 3096 7-11-12 **135**..........................(p) SamTwiston-Davies 135
(Warren Greatrex) *chsd ldr tl led 5th: hdd bef next: mstke 7th: rdn after 3 out: styd on same pce* **7/2**[1]

PP5- **4** *7* **Nozic (FR)**[28] 3093 13-10-3 **112**... DaveCrosse 104
(Zoe Davison) *prom tl rdn and wknd 9th* **16/1**

4/P- **5** *8* **Dunowen Point (IRE)**[35] 2939 8-11-12 **135**...................... JasonMaguire 119
(Donald McCain) *hld up: pushed along appr 6th: a in rr* **6/1**

324- **6** *5* **Sew On Target (IRE)**[28] 3082 9-11-7 **130**............................. JoeTizzard 109
(Colin Tizzard) *led to 5th: led again bef next: hdd after 8th: rdn and wknd after 3 out* **5/1**[3]

351- 7 9 **Granville Island (IRE)**[21] 3204 7-10-13 **122**........................ SeanQuinlan 97
(Jennie Candlish) *hld up: sme hdwy 6th: wknd after next* **8/1**
641- P **George Nympton (IRE)**[11] 3431 8-10-13 **122**.............(t) RobertThornton
(Brian Barr) *hld up: a in rr: bhd whn p.u bef 7th* **11/1**
6/3- U **Prince Of Dreams**[15] 3323 7-10-11 **123**........................ JoshuaMoore(3)
(Ed de Giles) *hld up: hdwy 6th: cl up whn blnd and uns rdr next* **12/1**
3m 55.9s (-9.70) **Going Correction** -0.375s/f (Good) **9** Ran SP% **116.9**
Speed ratings: **109,102,99,95,91 89,84, ,**
CSF £39.82 CT £130.35 TOTE £7.10: £2.20, £2.20, £1.50; EX 47.20 Trifecta £348.10.
Owner Shire Birds **Bred** Aaron Metcalfe **Trained** Kings Caple, H'fords
FOCUS
No hanging around here, in what was a good, competitive handicap, and it produced a clear-cut winner. This rates a personal best from him.

3653 PERTEMPS NETWORK H'CAP HURDLE (SERIES QUALIFIER) (12 hdls) 3m 1f
2:25 (2:25) (Class 2) 5-Y-0+
£11,573 (£3,418; £1,709; £854; £427; £214)

Form RPR
234- 1 **Uncle Jimmy (IRE)**[57] 2490 7-10-1 **133**.............. ThomasCheesman(10) 142+
(Philip Hobbs) *hld up: hdwy 7th: shkn up to ld and hit 2 out: rdn out* **15/2**[2]
3/P- 2 2 ¾ **Grand Vision (IRE)**[10] 3457 8-10-11 **140**............................ MrMLegg(7) 143
(Colin Tizzard) *hld up in tch: racd keenly early: rdn after 3 out: chsd wnr last: styd on same pce flat* **12/1**
162- 3 2 ¼ **Drop Out Joe**[28] 3086 6-10-4 **129**.................................... KielanWoods(3) 131
(Charlie Longsdon) *a.p: rdn after 3 out: styd on same pce appr last* **20/1**
021- 4 nk **Bygones Sovereign (IRE)**[22] 3186 8-9-7 **122** oh4......(p) KieronEdgar(7) 123
(David Pipe) *led: hdd appr 2 out: styd on same pce* **10/1**
114- 5 13 **Ballyculla (IRE)**[21] 3207 7-10-11 **133**................................ JasonMaguire 124
(Warren Greatrex) *hld up: nt fluent 8th: pushed along after 3 out: mstke last: nt trble ldrs* **10/1**
114- 6 11 **Oscar Fortune (IRE)**[36] 2929 6-10-9 **131**...................... RichieMcLernon 112
(Jonjo O'Neill) *hld up: hdwy 7th: rdn and wknd after 3 out* **10/1**
63F- 7 1 ¾ **Who Owns Me (IRE)**[23] 3178 8-9-7 **122** oh1............ MrHAABannister(7) 97
(Charlie Mann) *prom: lost pl after 6th: sn bhd* **22/1**
355- 8 1 ¼ **Billy Twyford (IRE)**[16] 3263 7-10-3 **125**............................(t) DavidBass 99
(Lawney Hill) *hld up: hdwy 7th: rdn and wknd after 3 out* **10/1**
11P- 9 3 ½ **Cyrien Star**[22] 3191 7-10-5 **130**.. JakeGreenall(3) 100
(Henry Daly) *w ldr to 7th: lost 2nd 9th: wknd after 3 out* **17/2**
32P- P **Seymour Eric**[26] 3131 9-11-2 **138**..(p) IanPopham
(Martin Keighley) *chsd ldrs: reminder after 2nd: pushed along 5th: nt fluent and lost pl 7th: sn bhd: p.u bef 2 out* **25/1**
224/ F **Tidal Dance (IRE)**[312] 4577 7-10-0 **122** oh1.............. AidanColeman
(Venetia Williams) *hld up: fell 3rd* **5/2**[1]
/4F- P **African Gold (IRE)**[32] 3011 6-11-12 **148**..............(t) SamTwiston-Davies
(Nigel Twiston-Davies) *hld up: rdn and wknd appr 8th: bhd whn p.u bef 3 out* **8/1**[3]
6m 21.3s (6.30) **Going Correction** -0.075s/f (Good) **12** Ran SP% **119.0**
Speed ratings: **86,85,84,84,80 76,76,75,74, ,**
CSF £90.48 CT £1734.74 TOTE £7.20: £2.60, £4.20, £5.30; EX 117.60 Trifecta £1608.80 Part won. Pool of £2145.11 - 0.11 winning units..
Owner Andy Ash **Bred** Michael M Byrne **Trained** Withycombe, Somerset
FOCUS
A typically open qualifier for the final of the series at the festival in March, especially after the well-backed favourite Tidal Dance came down at the third. A step up from the progressive winner. The first eight home qualify for the final.

3654 NEPTUNE INVESTMENT MANAGEMENT NOVICES' HURDLE (REGISTERED AS LEAMINGTON NOVICES' HURDLE) (GRADE 2) (11 hdls) 2m 5f
3:00 (3:01) (Class 1) 5-Y-0+ **£15,734** (£5,950; £3,016; £1,539; £810)

Form RPR
221- 1 **Deputy Dan (IRE)**[14] 3357 6-11-4 132............................ LeightonAspell 147+
(Oliver Sherwood) *hld up: hdwy appr 7th: led 3 out: clr bef next: rdn whn mstke last: styd on* **5/2**[2]
1P2- 2 9 **Masters Hill (IRE)**[28] 3081 8-11-4 135.................................. JoeTizzard 136
(Colin Tizzard) *trckd ldr to 4th: remained handy: wnt 2nd again 7th: led next: hdd 3 out: sn rdn: styd on same pce fr next* **9/1**
413- 3 7 **Splash Of Ginge**[22] 3184 6-11-4 135................ SamTwiston-Davies 131
(Nigel Twiston-Davies) *hld up: hdwy 7th: rdn to chse wnr appr 2 out tl wknd bef last* **16/1**
213- 4 7 **Potters Cross**[28] 3081 7-11-4 134..................................(t) PatrickCorbett 122
(Rebecca Curtis) *trckd ldrs: wnt 2nd 4th tl 7th: rdn and wknd after 3 out* **25/1**
21U- 5 26 **Creepy (IRE)**[14] 3367 6-11-7 137... IanPopham 105
(Martin Keighley) *led: nt fluent 3rd: hdd 8th: rdn and wknd after 3 out* **8/1**
431- P **Garrahalish (IRE)**[16] 3278 6-11-4 129................................ CharliePoste
(Robin Dickin) *trckd ldrs: pushed along after 6th: wknd bef next: bhd whn p.u bef 2 out* **50/1**
101- P **Killala Quay**[36] 2929 7-11-7 142.. JasonMaguire
(Charlie Longsdon) *prom tl rdn and wknd appr 7th: bhd whn p.u bef 2 out* **9/2**[3]
F **Rathvinden (IRE)**[34] 2982 6-11-7 0... DJCasey
(W P Mullins, Ire) *hld up: hdwy and pckd 8th: disputing cl 2nd whn fell 3 out* **2/1**[1]
5m 9.5s (-5.50) **Going Correction** -0.075s/f (Good) **8** Ran SP% **112.9**
Speed ratings: **107,103,100,98,88 , ,**
CSF £24.22 TOTE £3.00: £1.40, £2.20, £3.00; EX 27.80 Trifecta £345.60.
Owner Tim Syder **Bred** Conna Stud **Trained** Upper Lambourn, Berks
FOCUS
A race won by the subsequent Neptune winner twice since 2005, No Refuge and just last year The New One, but it looks fairly safe to assume that Deputy Dan, a good winner though he was, won't be going on to success in the same race. He still produced a biggish step up on his previous form.

3655 BETFRED CLASSIC CHASE (H'CAP) (GRADE 3) (22 fncs) 3m 5f
3:35 (3:35) (Class 1) 5-Y-0+
£34,170 (£12,822; £6,420; £3,198; £1,608; £804)

Form RPR
132- 1 **Shotgun Paddy (IRE)**[28] 3095 7-11-7 **145**...................... LeightonAspell 158+
(Emma Lavelle) *hld up in tch: chsd ldr 17th: led appr 2 out: hit last: rdn out* **9/1**[3]
01P/ 2 6 **Carruthers**[301] 4797 11-11-7 **150**........................(t) NicodeBoinville(5) 157
(Mark Bradstock) *chsd ldrs: led 8th: hdd appr 2 out: styd on same pce last* **28/1**
001- 3 6 **Royale Knight**[34] 2971 8-10-0 **124** oh3............................. BrendanPowell 124
(Dr Richard Newland) *hld up: hdwy 15th: rdn after 3 out: styd on same pce* **9/1**[3]
202- 4 2 ½ **Loch Ba (IRE)**[21] 3205 8-10-8 **132**................................ DominicElsworth 135+
(Mick Channon) *hld up: blnd 14th: hdwy appr 16th: sn outpcd: styd on fr 2 out* **8/1**[2]
532- 5 nse **Any Currency (IRE)**[29] 3068 11-10-8 **132**.........................(p) IanPopham 129
(Martin Keighley) *chsd ldrs: pushed along after 10th: rdn 17th: wknd appr 2 out* **20/1**
/3P- 6 4 ½ **Safran De Cotte (FR)**[21] 3205 8-9-13 **126**...................... JakeGreenall(3) 119
(Henry Daly) *chsd ldrs: drvn along 18th: wknd appr 2 out* **12/1**
/6P- 7 2 ¾ **Emperor's Choice (IRE)**[21] 3205 7-10-4 **128**.................. AidanColeman 118
(Venetia Williams) *hld up: hdwy 13th: rdn appr 16th: wknd 4 out* **8/1**[2]
0P1- P **Noble Legend**[16] 3287 7-10-11 **135**.................................... AndrewThornton
(Caroline Bailey) *led to 2nd: remained handy: led appr 6th: hdd 8th: chsd ldr to 17th: sn lost pl and p.u bef next* **10/1**
P1P/ P **Master Overseer (IRE)**[301] 4797 11-11-8 **146**............(bt[1]) ConorO'Farrell
(David Pipe) *prom: pushed along and lost pl 7th: bhd fr 9th: p.u bef 13th* **22/1**
F01- P **Major Malarkey (IRE)**[36] 2923 11-10-2 **126**...................(v) AdamWedge
(Nigel Twiston-Davies) *hld up: a in rr: rdn after 15th: bhd whn p.u bef 18th* **33/1**
41P- P **Hey Big Spender (IRE)**[14] 3361 11-11-8 **146**......................(t) JoeTizzard
(Colin Tizzard) *a in rr and nvr gng wl: bhd whn p.u bef 7th* **16/1**
P/2- P **Victors Serenade (IRE)**[62] 2388 9-10-13 **137**............... RobertThornton
(Anthony Honeyball) *hld up: mstke 10th: rdn and wknd appr 16th: bhd whn p.u bef 18th* **16/1**
2/F- U **Vesper Bell (IRE)**[35] 2937 8-11-4 **142**.. DJCasey
(W P Mullins, Ire) *hld up: hdwy whn blnd and uns rdr 14th* **8/1**[2]
/00- P **Same Difference (IRE)**[42] 2815 8-11-6 **144**.........(v) SamTwiston-Davies
(Nigel Twiston-Davies) *hld up: a in rr: nt fluent 12th: mstke 15th: sn drvn along: wknd bef next: bhd whn p.u bef 2 out* **12/1**
331- P **Boyfromnowhere (IRE)**[55] 2537 7-10-0 **129**.............(p) PatrickCorbett(5)
(Rebecca Curtis) *led 2nd tl appr 6th: chsd ldrs: drvn along 16th: wknd after next: bhd whn p.u bef 3 out* **7/1**[1]
7m 30.1s (-10.90) **Going Correction** -0.375s/f (Good) **15** Ran SP% **117.6**
Speed ratings: **100,98,96,96,95 94,93, , , , , , , ,**
CSF £236.63 CT £2324.15 TOTE £9.50: £3.00, £9.80, £3.70; EX 360.80 Trifecta £4429.90.
Owner Axom (XXXVI) **Bred** Mrs Richella Rohan **Trained** Hatherden, Hants
FOCUS
This was always going to be a thorough test, even with the ground on the chase course seemingly not riding as deep as advertised, and the race was fought out by a pair of grinders. A big step forward from the winner.

3656 BETFRED TV "NEWCOMERS" STANDARD OPEN NATIONAL HUNT FLAT RACE 2m
4:05 (4:06) (Class 6) 4-6-Y-0 **£1,559** (£457; £228; £114)

Form RPR
1 **Millicent Silver** 5-10-12 0.. SamTwiston-Davies 96+
(Nigel Twiston-Davies) *hdwy after 3f: rdn over 4f out: sn outpcd: rallied u.p over 1f out: styd on to ld nr fin* **11/2**
2 hd **Meetmeatthemoon (IRE)** 5-10-9 0................................. JamesBest(3) 96
(Philip Hobbs) *hld up: hdwy 1/2-way: chsd ldr 4f out: led 2f out: sn rdn: hdd nr fin* **7/2**[2]
3 3 ¼ **Superior Fire (IRE)** 4-10-4 0.. KielanWoods(3) 88
(Charlie Longsdon) *racd keenly: trckd ldr: rdn over 2f out: styd on same pce ins fnl f* **10/3**[1]
4 1 **Dawson City** 5-11-5 0.. AndrewThornton 99+
(Polly Gundry) *trckd ldrs: rdn and outpcd over 3f out: rallied over 1f out: styd on* **8/1**
- 5 3 **Wolftrap (IRE)** 5-11-5 0... RhysFlint 97
(Laura Young) *hld up: hdwy 1/2-way: led 4f out: rdn and hdd 2f out: edgd lft: wknd ins fnl f* **16/1**
6 1 ½ **Midnight Memories** 4-9-13 0 ow2................................ RobertDunne(3) 77
(Steph Hollinshead) *hld up: hdwy 1/2-way: rdn over 3f out: wknd over 1f out* **14/1**
7 1 ¼ **Izzy Piccolina (IRE)** 6-10-7 0.. JamesBanks(5) 86
(Geoffrey Deacon) *led: plld hrd: hdd 4f out: rdn over 2f out: wknd over 1f out* **28/1**
8 22 **Jeans Lady** 5-10-5 0... OllieGarner(7) 64
(Martin Keighley) *hld up: bhd fnl 6f* **12/1**
9 33 **Vagner (FR)** 5-11-0 0.. AodhaganConlon(5) 38
(Tom George) *prom tl rdn and wknd over 5f out* **4/1**[3]
3m 58.3s (7.40) **Going Correction** -0.075s/f (Good)
WFA 4 from 5yo+ 11lb **9** Ran SP% **115.5**
Speed ratings: **78,77,76,75,74 73,72,61,45**
CSF £25.09 TOTE £6.90: £2.20, £2.30, £1.40; EX 18.20 Trifecta £38.70.
Owner John Goodman **Bred** Owen Brennan / John Goodman **Trained** Naunton, Gloucs
FOCUS
A steadily run newcomers' bumper, run in a slow time.
T/Plt: £579.50 to a £1 stake. Pool of £108073.22 - 136.14 winning tickets. T/Qpdt: £73.10 to a £1 stake. Pool of £8890.61 - 89.88 winning tickets. CR

3329 WETHERBY (L-H)
Saturday, January 11
OFFICIAL GOING: Soft (heavy in places; chs 5.0, hdl 4.8)
Wind: fresh 1/2 behind Weather: fine but cold

3657 EBF STALLIONS "NATIONAL HUNT" NOVICES' HURDLE QUALIFIER (11 hdls) 2m 4f
12:35 (12:35) (Class 4) 4-7-Y-0 **£3,768** (£1,106; £553; £276)

Form RPR
/11- 1 **Red Sherlock**[27] 3115 5-11-8 0... TimmyMurphy 129+
(David Pipe) *mde all: qcknd pce 6th: j. bdly lft last 2: v easily* **1/6**[1]
312- 2 3 ¾ **Bonnet's Vino**[25] 3151 6-10-10 108.............................. MissGAndrews(5) 106
(Pam Sly) *hld up in rr: hdwy 7th: chsd wnr fr 3 out: no imp* **9/1**[3]
3 2 ¼ **The Ramblin Kid**[95] 1812 6-11-2 0............................ WayneHutchinson 106
(Micky Hammond) *chsd ldrs: one pce whn mstke 2 out* **25/1**
024- 4 15 **Herecomestrouble**[25] 3147 7-11-2 0.................................... BrianHughes 95
(Malcolm Jefferson) *trckd ldrs: t.k.h: wknd 2 out* **20/1**
1- 5 51 **Ocean Waves (IRE)**[92] 1854 5-11-2 0.................................. BrianHarding 39
(Jedd O'Keeffe) *j.lft 1st: chsd ldrs: lost pl 7th: t.o and reminders next: eventually completed* **15/2**[2]

The Form Book Jumps, Raceform Ltd, Compton, RG20 6NL.

P **Apache Pilot**[237] 6-10-9 0........................(t) StephenMulqueen(7)
(Maurice Barnes) *t.k.h: chsd ldrs: pushed along 5th: lost pl and nt fluent next: t.o whn p.u after 8th* **150/1**

5m 26.8s (27.30) **Going Correction** +1.125s/f (Heav) **6** Ran SP% **116.7**
Speed ratings: **90,88,87,81,61**
CSF £3.00 TOTE £1.10: £1.02, £2.40; EX 2.50 Trifecta £15.00.
Owner The Johnson Family **Bred** David Johnson **Trained** Nicholashayne, Devon

FOCUS
An easy success for the odds-on favourite. The facile winner can rate higher, while the third and fourth have been rated to their bumper marks.

3658 STAR SPORTS CHELTENHAM PREVIEW NIGHT NOVICES' CHASE (16 fncs) 2m 4f 110y
1:10 (1:10) (Class 4) 5-Y-0+ **£3,768** (£1,106; £553; £276)

Form RPR
413- **1** **Yesyoucan (IRE)**[41] 2839 9-11-7 139........................ WayneHutchinson 119+
(Brian Ellison) *mde virtually all: stdy on fr 3 out: rdn rt out* **5/6**[1]

613- **2** 4 **My Idea**[33] 2996 8-11-0 105........................(t) StephenMulqueen(7) 112
(Maurice Barnes) *trckd ldrs: 2nd 3 out: kpt on same pce* **22/1**

/43- **3** 7 **Pistol (IRE)**[36] 2922 5-10-9 130........................(b) TomO'Brien 96
(Philip Hobbs) *chsd ldrs: drvn 11th: 4th whn hit next: hit 4 out: 3rd and one pce whn hit 2 out* **9/4**[2]

2/0- **4** 14 **Mitchell's Way**[56] 2519 7-11-0 122........................ PaddyBrennan 87
(Alan Swinbank) *trckd ldrs: drvn 4 out: 4th whn hit next: sn wknd* **15/2**[3]

/60- **P** **Alf The Audacious**[14] 3356 8-11-0 0........................ RyanMania
(Sue Smith) *w wnr: hit 7th and reminders: blnd 9th: lost pl and j.lft next: t.o 12th: p.u bef next* **12/1**

5m 29.5s (21.70) **Going Correction** +0.675s/f (Soft)
WFA 5 from 7yo+ 4lb **5** Ran SP% **109.1**
Speed ratings: **85,83,80,75,**
CSF £14.45 TOTE £1.60: £1.10, £3.50; EX 10.10 Trifecta £24.40.
Owner Prism Bloodstock **Bred** Thomas Steele **Trained** Norton, N Yorks

FOCUS
They went an even gallop in this ordinary event. The second has been rated back to his best.

3659 WATCH ON 3 DEVICES RACINGUK.COM/ANYWHERE H'CAP HURDLE (9 hdls) 2m 110y
1:45 (1:45) (Class 4) (0-110,110) 4-Y-0+ **£3,119** (£915; £457; £228)

Form RPR
5/2- **1** **Allied Answer**[15] 3330 6-11-11 109........................ WayneHutchinson 116+
(Steve Gollings) *trckd ldrs: led narrowly 2 out: edgd lft between last 2: hdd last: styd on to ld post* **9/4**[1]

253- **2** shd **Trust Thomas**[13] 3398 6-10-12 103........................ GrahamWatters(7) 110+
(Ann Hamilton) *hld up towards rr: mstke 2nd: hdwy appr 3 out: upsides 2 out: carried lft between last 2: led narrowly last: hdd fnl stride* **9/2**[2]

0/3- **3** ¾ **Forward Flight (IRE)**[16] 3270 8-11-2 100........................ RyanMania 105+
(Sue Smith) *trckd ldrs: led appr 3 out: hdd 2 out: swtchd lft appr last: styng on at fin* **5/1**[3]

263- **4** 10 **Pertuis (IRE)**[16] 3288 8-11-2 105........................(p) JoeCollliver(5) 100
(Micky Hammond) *mid-div: drvn 6th: sn chsng ldrs: upsides next: wknd between last 2* **8/1**

6/0- **5** 2 **Right To Rule (IRE)**[16] 3288 5-11-7 105........................ AdrianLane 98
(Donald McCain) *hld up in rr: hdwy 6th: upsides next: one pce fr 2 out* **25/1**

F43- **6** 2¼ **Memory Cloth**[16] 3274 7-11-5 110........................ NathanMoscrop(7) 102
(Brian Ellison) *mid-div: hdwy appr 3 out: drvn and wandered appr 2 out: one pce* **15/2**

060- **7** 3 **Crooked Arrow (IRE)**[87] 1924 6-10-3 90........................ KyleJames(3) 78
(Marjorie Fife) *stdd s: hld up in rr: effrt 6th: sme hdwy appr next: nvr a factor* **11/1**

6/0- **8** 10 **Three White Socks (IRE)**[16] 3271 7-11-10 108........................ JamieMoore 86
(Brian Ellison) *drvn to chse ldrs 3rd: lost pl 6th: sn bhd* **33/1**

/00- **9** 2¼ **Bonnie Burnett (IRE)**[39] 2868 7-10-13 97........................ TomO'Brien 73
(Brian Rothwell) *stdd s: hld up in rr: sme hdwy appr 3 out: sn wknd* **25/1**

006- **10** 11 **Hi Dancer**[39] 2868 11-10-9 103........................ RyanDClark(10) 68
(Ben Haslam) *chsd ldrs: led appr 5th: hdd appr next: lost pl bef 3 out* **22/1**

0PF- **11** nse **Jukebox Melody (IRE)**[10] 3451 8-11-3 108........................(b) JohnDawson(7) 81
(John Wade) *w ldrs: j.lft 4th: mstke next: led appr 6th: hdd appr 3 out: lost pl bef 2 out: bhd whn eased run-in* **66/1**

101/ **P** **Wordy's Boy**[682] 4589 9-11-11 109........................ AdamPogson
(Charles Pogson) *led: hdd appr 5th: lost pl next: t.o whn p.u bef 3 out* **25/1**

4m 12.9s (17.10) **Going Correction** +1.125s/f (Heav) **12** Ran SP% **117.1**
Speed ratings (Par 105): **104,103,103,98,97 96,95,90,89,84 84,**
CSF £11.52 CT £46.03 TOTE £3.30: £1.50, £1.90, £1.70; EX 12.20 Trifecta £117.30.
Owner P J Martin **Bred** D D And Mrs Jean P Clee **Trained** Scamblesby, Lincs

FOCUS
A moderate event run at a respectable pace. The second has been rated as running a small personal best and the third as improving to his bumper mark.

3660 DOWNLOAD THE NEW RACING UK IPAD APP H'CAP CHASE (13 fncs) 2m
2:15 (2:15) (Class 2) (0-145,145) 5-Y-0+ **£11,710** (£3,459; £1,729; £865; £432)

Form RPR
/P1- **1** **Desert Cry (IRE)**[23] 3170 8-11-6 139........................ TimmyMurphy 156+
(Donald McCain) *hld up in rr: hdwy 5th: 2nd appr 4 out: j.lft and led next: j.lft last: drvn clr* **8/1**[3]

/33- **2** 7 **Grey Gold (IRE)**[21] 3197 9-11-5 138........................ JamieMoore 146
(Richard Lee) *chsd ldr: led appr 4 out: hdd and hit 3 out: kpt on same pce appr last* **4/1**[1]

554- **3** 1½ **Elenika (FR)**[21] 3197 6-10-0 124........................ HarryChalloner(5) 129
(Venetia Williams) *chsd ldrs: outpcd 9th: rallied to chse ldrs next: kpt on to take modest 3rd run-in* **4/1**[1]

/41- **4** 1 **Filbert (IRE)**[42] 2816 8-11-2 135........................ TomO'Brien 140
(Philip Hobbs) *hdwy 4th: sn chsng ldrs: outpcd 9th: 3rd 3 out: blnd next: one pce* **6/1**[2]

5/F- **5** 2½ **Doeslessthanme (IRE)**[244] 249 10-11-12 145........................(t) RichieMcGrath 147
(Richard Ford) *chsd ldrs: one pce fr 3 out* **66/1**

00F- **6** 3 **His Excellency (IRE)**[15] 3333 6-11-5 145........................(b) MikeyEnnis(7) 145
(David Pipe) *chsd ldrs: hit 7th and lost pl: hdwy 9th: rdn 3 out: one pce* **14/1**

612- **7** 18 **De Boitron (FR)**[28] 3091 10-11-12 145........................ RyanMania 126
(Sue Smith) *in rr: bhd 9th: sme hdwy next: sn lost pl and bhd* **8/1**[3]

411- **8** 5 **Oscar Hill (IRE)**[38] 2890 8-11-4 144........................ JakeHodson(7) 130+
(David Bridgwater) *led: clr 5th: j. bdly rt 7th: j. bdly rt and blnd next: hdd appr 4 out: wknd 3 out* **8/1**[3]

P/4- **P** **Rody (FR)**[42] 2816 9-11-11 144........................(t) PaddyBrennan
(Tom George) *mid-div: drvn 6th: lost pl 9th: sn bhd: t.o whn p.u bef 2 out* **6/1**[2]

4m 2.2s (6.40) **Going Correction** +0.675s/f (Soft) **9** Ran SP% **110.1**
Speed ratings: **111,107,106,106,105 103,94,92,**
CSF £38.11 CT £137.65 TOTE £10.00: £3.10, £1.80, £1.80; EX 45.00 Trifecta £163.90.
Owner N.Y.P.D Racing **Bred** Fin A Co S R L **Trained** Cholmondeley, Cheshire

FOCUS
The pace was always going to be decent in this, with confirmed front-runner Oscar Hill, who was chasing a hat-trick on his third outing for David Bridgewater, taking part. The cosy winner is on the upgrade and there's a case for rating the race higher through the second and third.

3661 WETHERBYRACING.CO.UK H'CAP HURDLE (11 hdls) 2m 4f
2:50 (2:50) (Class 3) (0-135,129) 4-Y-0+ **£5,393** (£1,583; £791; £395)

Form RPR
/3F- **1** **Embsay Crag**[16] 3286 8-10-3 106........................ RichieMcGrath 111
(Philip Kirby) *hld up in rr: hdwy to trck ldrs 4th: upsides 3 out: edgd rt and led narrowly 2 out: all out* **7/1**

/31- **2** hd **Shimla Dawn (IRE)**[37] 2903 6-11-8 125........................ PeterBuchanan 130
(Tim Walford) *hld up in rr: hdwy to trck ldrs 5th: hit 8th: narrow ld next: hdd 2 out: swtchd lft between last 2: styd on last 50yds: jst hld* **7/1**

4/5- **3** 10 **Mcmurrough (IRE)**[49] 2671 10-11-12 129........................(b) BrianHughes 125
(Malcolm Jefferson) *chsd ldr: upsides 3 out: kpt on one pce fr next* **4/1**[2]

003- **4** 1 **Notus De La Tour (FR)**[11] 3430 8-11-1 125........................(b[1]) MikeyEnnis(7) 119
(David Pipe) *led: hdd 3 out: one pce fr next* **9/2**[3]

0/1- **5** 6 **Lord Protector (IRE)**[36] 2932 7-11-4 121........................ TomO'Brien 110
(Philip Hobbs) *chsd ldrs: outpcd 3 out: no threat after* **3/1**[1]

110/ **6** 13 **Chavoy (FR)**[262] 5512 9-11-0 120........................ TonyKelly(3) 95
(Rebecca Menzies) *in rr: drvn 7th: sme hdwy next: lost pl appr 3 out* **9/1**

6/5- **7** 6 **Allow Me**[16] 3273 9-10-11 119........................ ColmMcCormack(5) 88
(Dianne Sayer) *in rr: pushed along 5th: mstke 7th: sme hdwy next: lost pl appr 3 out* **20/1**

P/1- **8** 29 **Society Shares (IRE)**[26] 3130 9-11-0 117........................ WayneHutchinson 57
(Graeme McPherson) *chsd ldrs: drvn and lost pl 8th: sn bhd: t.o next* **9/1**

5m 22.2s (22.70) **Going Correction** +1.125s/f (Heav) **8** Ran SP% **112.9**
Speed ratings (Par 107): **99,98,94,94,92 86,84,72**
CSF £52.87 CT £221.42 TOTE £7.00: £2.00, £2.80, £1.80; EX 61.90 Trifecta £122.80.
Owner Grange Park Racing IV & Partner **Bred** Mrs Glenda Swinglehurst **Trained** Middleham, N Yorks

■ Stewards' Enquiry : Richie McGrath caution: careless riding.

FOCUS
Being held up proved to be a positive in this contest. The first two are on the upgrade and have the potential to rate higher.

3662 TOTEPOOL MEDIEVAL DAY - SATURDAY 1ST FEBRUARY H'CAP CHASE (16 fncs) 2m 4f 110y
3:25 (3:25) (Class 4) (0-120,118) 5-Y-0+ **£3,768** (£1,106; £553; £276)

Form RPR
541- **1** **Chicklemix**[23] 3176 8-10-11 108........................ MissGAndrews(5) 114
(Pam Sly) *chsd ldrs: hit 12th: chsd ldr next: kpt on to ld last 100yds* **7/1**[3]

531- **2** 2½ **Free World (FR)**[11] 3439 10-10-6 105........................ MissLBrooke(7) 109
(Lady Susan Brooke) *t.k.h: w ldrs: led 2nd: stdd after next: 1 l ahd whn hit last: sn hdd and no ex* **8/1**

353- **3** 7 **Cocacobana (IRE)**[26] 3131 9-11-10 116........................ WayneHutchinson 114
(Graeme McPherson) *in tch: drvn 9th: sn outpcd: j.rt last 4: modest 3rd 3 out: one pce whn hit next* **15/2**

/4F- **4** 23 **Whats Up Woody (IRE)**[21] 3211 9-11-9 115........................ BrianHughes 87
(John Wade) *w ldrs: drvn 4 out: wknd next* **8/1**

026/ **5** 20 **Requin (FR)**[262] 5496 9-11-12 118........................(p) JackDoyle 70
(Victor Dartnall) *chsd ldrs: reminders 5th: rdn and lost pl appr 4 out: sn bhd* **5/1**[2]

/P0- **6** 3½ **Dusky Bob (IRE)**[49] 2670 9-11-8 114........................(t) TimmyMurphy 63
(Brian Ellison) *towards rr: nt fluent 8th: bhd fr 11th* **9/1**

/41- **P** **Ravens Brook (IRE)**[20] 3222 8-11-1 107........................(p) JamieMoore
(Richard Lee) *led to 2nd: chsd ldrs: pushed along 7th: lost pl 9th: sn bhd: t.o whn p.u bef 4 out* **13/8**[1]

5m 35.9s (28.10) **Going Correction** +0.675s/f (Soft) **7** Ran SP% **111.2**
Speed ratings: **73,72,69,60,53 51,**
CSF £54.52 TOTE £10.60: £4.60, £4.10; EX 35.70 Trifecta £230.10.
Owner Michael H Sly Dr T Davies Mrs Pam Sly **Bred** Mrs P Sly **Trained** Thorney, Cambs

FOCUS
Ordinary form at a moderate level. The first three have been rated pretty close to their pre-race marks.

3663 RACING UK ANYWHERE AVAILABLE NOW FILLIES' "JUNIOR" STANDARD OPEN NATIONAL HUNT FLAT RACE 1m 5f
3:55 (3:56) (Class 6) 4-Y-0 **£1,642** (£478; £239)

Form RPR
1 **Molly Cat** 4-10-10 0........................ PaddyBrennan 105+
(Alan Swinbank) *hld up towards rr: racd wd: stdy hdwy 6f out: led on bit over 2f out: rdn clr over 1f out: eased towards fin* **9/4**[1]

32- **2** 10 **May Hay**[24] 3167 4-10-10 0........................ AndrewTinkler 89
(Anthony Carson) *led: drvn 3f out: sn hdd: kpt on one pce* **9/4**[1]

03- **3** 1½ **Bulas Belle**[21] 3214 4-10-3 0........................ CraigNichol(7) 87
(Edwin Tuer) *trckd ldrs: drvn over 4f out: one pce fnl 2f* **9/2**[2]

4 4 **Georgian Firebird** 4-10-7 0........................ JohnKington(3) 82
(Alan Swinbank) *mid-div: hdwy 6f out: drvn over 3f out: one pce* **14/1**

4- **5** 6 **Montjen (IRE)**[24] 3167 4-10-3 0........................ GemmaTutty(7) 74
(Karen Tutty) *stdd s: hld up in rr: hdwy 6f out: sn outpcd: rallied 3f out: wknd over 1f out* **7/1**[3]

0- **6** 9 **Lola**[35] 2960 4-10-10 0........................ BarryKeniry 62
(Michael Dods) *chsd ldrs: drvn over 4f out: wknd 3f out* **25/1**

7 2¾ **Hopefull** 4-10-10 0........................ PeterBuchanan 59
(R Mike Smith) *in rr: drvn 6f out: sn lost pl and bhd* **25/1**

8 41 **Claraty** 4-10-5 0........................ HarryChalloner(5) 5
(James Unett) *mid-div: sme hdwy 6f out: sn lost pl and bhd: t.o 3f out: eventually completed* **40/1**

3m 25.4s (205.40) **8** Ran SP% **109.0**
CSF £6.33 TOTE £2.50: £1.20, £1.10, £2.30; EX 6.40 Trifecta £23.50.
Owner Elm Row Racing Syndicate **Bred** Meon Valley Stud **Trained** Melsonby, N Yorks

FOCUS
Not a bad race of its type, and it saw a particularly impressive performance by a newcomer. The second, third and fifth set the level.

T/Plt: £27.80 to a £1 stake. Pool: £68811.15 - 1800.83 winning tickets T/Qpdt: £18.50 to a £1 stake. Pool: £5262.42 - 210.30 winning tickets WG

3664 - 3666a (Foreign Racing) - See Raceform Interactive

3441 PUNCHESTOWN (R-H)

Saturday, January 11

OFFICIAL GOING: Soft to heavy (soft in places)

3667a MOSCOW FLYER NOVICE HURDLE (GRADE 2) (9 hdls) 2m

2:20 (2:23) 5-Y-0+ **£20,312** (£5,937; £2,812; £937)

RPR

1 **Vautour (FR)**[35] 2961 5-11-0 .... PaulTownend 145+
(W P Mullins, Ire) *chsd ldrs: 3rd 1/2-way: wnt 2nd after 2 out and led bef last: sn strly pressed and hdd narrowly run-in: rallied wl to regain advantage cl home* **1/4**[1]

2 ¾ **Western Boy (IRE)**[16] 3304 5-11-0 .... DavyRussell 144+
(P A Fahy, Ire) *hld up in tch: 5th 1/2-way: tk clsr order bhd ldrs gng wl bef 2 out where nt fluent: rdn into 2nd bef last and sn clsd u.p to ld narrowly run-in: hdd cl home* **7/1**[2]

3 11 **Mr Fiftyone (IRE)**[41] 2852 5-11-0 132 .... RobbiePower 133
(Mrs John Harrington, Ire) *chsd ldrs: clsr in 2nd bef 3rd: nt fluent 2 out and sn pushed along in 3rd: rdn in 4th between last 2 and no imp on ldrs: kpt on u.p fr last into mod 3rd run-in* **8/1**[3]

4 3 **Chicago (IRE)**[13] 3406 5-11-0 127 .... PatrickMangan 130
(John Patrick Shanahan, Ire) *led: mstke 2nd and nt fluent next: pressed into st and hdd bef last: sn no ex u.p in 3rd: dropped to mod 4th run-in* **11/1**

5 3¾ **Captainofthefleet (IRE)**[14] 3379 7-11-2 119 .... KeithDonoghue 128
(Eamonn O'Connell, Ire) *hld up in rr: mstke 4 out: rdn in 5th after 2 out and no imp on ldrs bef st: one pce after* **33/1**

6 51 **Easter Hunt (IRE)**[13] 3406 5-11-0 .... (t) BryanCooper 75
(M F Morris, Ire) *chsd ldrs: 4th 1/2-way: slt mstke 5th and pushed along: nt fluent next: no imp on ldrs bef 3 out: wknd: completely t.o* **25/1**

3m 56.4s (-8.60) **6** Ran SP% **118.7**
CSF £3.42 TOTE £1.20: £1.02, £1.10; DF 3.20 Trifecta £4.70.
Owner Mrs S Ricci **Bred** Haras De Saint Voir & Patrick Joubert **Trained** Muine Beag, Co Carlow
■ Stewards' Enquiry : Davy Russell one-day ban: used whip down shoulder in the forehand (tbn)

FOCUS
A narrow success for a well-touted horse. The third and fourth help set the standard.

3668 - 3670a (Foreign Racing) - See Raceform Interactive

3392 KELSO (L-H)

Sunday, January 12

3671 Meeting Abandoned - Frost

3550 PLUMPTON (L-H)

Monday, January 13

OFFICIAL GOING: Heavy (hdl 3.6; chs 4.0)
Wind: half against, modest Weather: showers

3686 RACE PASSES AT TIMEFORM.COM NOVICES' HURDLE (9 hdls) 2m

1:00 (1:01) (Class 4) 4-Y-0+ **£3,249** (£954; £477; £238)

Form RPR

202- 1 **Uhlan Bute (FR)**[6] 3592 6-11-11 127 .... AidanColeman 125
(Venetia Williams) *chsd ldrs: nt fluent 2nd: chsd ldr bef 3 out: led and travelling wl bef 2 out: rdn and jnd bef last: drvn and kpt on gamely flat* **8/11**[1]

1F3- 2 nk **Raven's Tower (USA)**[17] 3317 4-10-13 119 .... DavidBass 113
(Ben Pauling) *t.k.h: hld up towards rr: hdwy to chse ldrs 4th: rdn and effrt after 3 out: lft 2nd 2 out: str chal bef last: kpt on gamely flat: a jst hld* **11/4**[2]

0/4- 3 8 **Daveron (IRE)**[14] 3422 6-11-5 0 .... NickScholfield 112
(Jeremy Scott) *nt a fluent: t.k.h early: chsd ldrs tl 6th and outpcd bef 3 out: rallied and lft 3rd whn hmpd 2 out: kpt on but no imp after* **12/1**

50- 4 17 **Hermosa Vaquera (IRE)**[34] 3003 4-10-0 0 .... AdamWedge 75
(Anna Newton-Smith) *hld up in midfield: j.rt and bmpd rival 3rd: clr in ldng quintet bef 3 out: drvn and wknd bef 2 out* **66/1**

6- 5 1 **Freddy Q (IRE)**[52] 2644 5-11-5 0 .... (t) RichieMcLernon 93
(Roger Teal) *led: rdn and hdd bef 2 out: btn whn lft 4th and hmpd 2 out: wknd bef last* **20/1**

00- 6 13 **Spartilla**[28] 3134 5-10-12 0 .... MrJPearce(7) 80
(Daniel O'Brien) *hld up off the pce in rr: lost tch bef 6th and t.o bef 3 out: kpt on past btn horses bef 2 out: n.d* **66/1**

300- 7 20 **On The Move**[189] 920 6-10-9 0 .... RachaelGreen(3) 57
(Anthony Honeyball) *hld up in midfield: mstke 4th: lost pl next: lost tch bef 3 out: t.o bef 2 out* **66/1**

6/ 8 11 **Harlequins Gleams**[277] 5247 6-11-5 0 .... AndrewThornton 49
(Anna Newton-Smith) *j.lft: in tch in midfield: bmpd 3rd: lost tch bef 3 out: t.o bef 2 out* **100/1**

PP- 9 12 **Saint Helena (IRE)**[8] 3550 6-10-12 0 .... MattieBatchelor 30
(Jim Best) *hld up off the pce in last pair: clsd after 4th: wknd wl bef 3 out: t.o bef 2 out* **100/1**

2- U **Minority Interest**[28] 3134 5-11-5 0 .... TomCannon 108
(Daniel O'Brien) *chsd ldr tl bef 3 out: sn drvn: chsd wnr bef 2 out: hrd drvn but keeping on whn blnd and uns rdr 2 out* **6/1**[3]

4m 25.6s (24.80) **Going Correction** +1.55s/f (Heav)
WFA 4 from 5yo+ 11lb **10** Ran SP% **117.8**
Speed ratings (Par 105): **100,99,95,87,86 80,70,64,58,**
CSF £2.98 TOTE £1.40: £1.10, £1.10, £3.40; EX 3.50 Trifecta £16.40.
Owner R Elliott & N Coe **Bred** Herve D'Armaille **Trained** Kings Caple, H'fords
■ Stewards' Enquiry : Mr J Pearce ten-day ban: failed to take all reasonable and permissable measures to obtain best possible placing (Jan 29-30,Feb 1-2,4-7,11-12)

FOCUS
Effectively a match and so it played out. The form is rated around the first two.

3687 TIMEFORM JURY H'CAP CHASE (8 fncs 4 omitted) 2m 1f

1:30 (1:30) (Class 5) (0-100,94) 5-Y-0+ **£2,599** (£763; £381; £190)

Form RPR

/36- 1 **Brandon Thomas (IRE)**[18] 3283 8-10-13 81 .... TomCannon 90
(Nick Gifford) *hld up in last pair: hdwy 4th: 5th and drvn after next: rallied and 5 l 3rd 3 out (actual 2 out): styd on u.p to chal last: led flat: forged clr* **11/4**[2]

P1U- 2 4½ **Sablazo (FR)**[18] 3248 8-10-10 78 .... NickScholfield 82
(Andy Turnell) *led tl 2nd: chsd ldrs tl led again bef 6th: drvn on long run to last: hdd flat: no ex* **20/1**

/05- 3 ½ **Enchanting Smile (FR)**[48] 2726 7-11-6 88 .... (t) TommyPhelan 92
(Mark Gillard) *t.k.h: hld up in rr: hdwy and mstke 3rd: jnd ldr and wnt clr bef 6th: rdn bypassing 2 out: stl ev ch last: no ex flat* **50/1**

F33- 4 23 **Head Spin (IRE)**[8] 3551 6-10-12 80 .... AndrewThornton 61
(Seamus Mullins) *in tch in midfield: lost tch after 5th: no ch after: plugged on into poor 4th last* **7/4**[1]

/2P- 5 21 **Goring Two (IRE)**[28] 3139 9-11-4 86 .... (b) AdamWedge 46
(Anna Newton-Smith) *chsd ldrs: wnt 2nd 3rd tl led on long run after 5th: hdd bef next and struggling in 3rd whn blnd 6th: mstke next: wknd on long run to last: t.o* **12/1**

0/P- P **Autumn Day (IRE)**[48] 2727 9-11-1 83 .... LeightonAspell
(Luke Dace) *hld up in rr: rdn and no rspnse after 4th: tailing off whn p.u after next* **25/1**

/P3- P **Zen Factor**[48] 2727 9-11-4 86 .... JamieMoore
(Jonathan Portman) *chsd ldrs tl mstke and lost pl 3rd: dropped to last and drvn after 4th: sn lost tch: t.o whn p.u bef last* **10/1**

U3F- P **Join The Navy**[23] 3196 9-11-12 94 .... (tp) LiamTreadwell
(Kate Buckett) *t.k.h: hld up in tch in midfield: blnd 2nd: rdn and lost tch after 5th: t.o whn p.u bef last* **8/1**[3]

044- F **Go Annie**[66] 2348 6-10-7 75 .... (bt) SamJones
(Jo Davis) *racd on outer: in tch in midfield: rdn and lost tch after 5th: t.o whn fell 3 out (actual 2 out)* **33/1**

442- P **Further More (IRE)**[32] 3048 7-11-5 87 .... (b[1]) AidanColeman
(Emma Lavelle) *chsd ldr tl led 2nd: hdd on long run after 5th: sn btn: losing tch whn p.u 3 out* **8/1**[3]

4m 41.6s (18.60) **Going Correction** +1.125s/f (Heav) **10** Ran SP% **115.5**
Speed ratings: **101,98,98,87,77 , , , ,**
CSF £54.48 CT £2228.45 TOTE £3.50: £1.10, £4.60, £12.60; EX 60.90 Trifecta £2169.40 Part won..
Owner S Hubbard Rodwell **Bred** R J Whitford **Trained** Findon, W Sussex

FOCUS
The first fence in the back straight and home straight was omitted in all chase races. The finish of this weaj handicap was more reminiscent of a staying chase with the field being strung out some way from home. The winner had slipped to a good mark in race run to suit.

3688 RACING WELFARE CHARITY RACEDAY 31ST MARCH H'CAP CHASE (12 fncs 6 omitted) 3m 2f

2:00 (2:00) (Class 5) (0-100,100) 5-Y-0+ **£2,662** (£826; £445)

Form RPR

3F3- 1 **Royaume Bleu (FR)**[18] 3277 9-10-12 91 .... KillianMoore(5) 106+
(Alex Hales) *t.k.h: w ldr tl led 6th: mde rest: rdn and drew clr bypassing 2 out: eased flat* **8/1**

6F2- 2 16 **Flugzeug**[46] 2765 6-9-10 77 oh2 ow3 .... KevinJones(7) 73
(Seamus Mullins) *racd wd: chsd ldrs: wnt 2nd after 9th: lft clr w wnr next: rdn and 2 l down after 3 (actual 2 out): btn bypassing 2 out: wknd but hung on to 2nd flat* **15/2**

312- 3 shd **Glenwood Prince (IRE)**[28] 3137 8-11-12 100 .... (t) NickScholfield 96
(Jeremy Scott) *racd in last pair: nvr really travelling: reminders after 7th: sme hdwy 9th: wknd on long run to next: lft modest 3rd 10th: plugged on and almost snatched 2nd* **6/4**[1]

1/4- F **Tarabela**[18] 3281 11-11-12 100 .... (t) BrendanPowell
(Johnny Farrelly) *patiently rdn: hld up in rr: stdy hdwy 8th: trckd ldng pair on long run after next: 3 l 3rd and stl gng wl whn sltly hmpd and fell 10th* **7/1**[3]

5/2- P **Beware Chalk Pit (IRE)**[42] 2863 10-11-5 93 .... MarkGrant
(Jonathan Geake) *chsd ldrs: rdn after 6th: drvn and lost tch after 9th: t.o whn p.u 10th* **8/1**

F/0- P **Dushy Valley (IRE)**[14] 3425 7-10-8 82 .... TomO'Brien
(Paul Henderson) *led tl 6th: styd w wnr tl rdn and dropped to 4th on long run after 9th: struggling whn lost action and p.u qckly 10th: dismntd* **3/1**[2]

7m 31.25s (40.55) **Going Correction** +1.125s/f (Heav) **6** Ran SP% **111.5**
Speed ratings: **82,77,77, ,**
CSF £58.46 TOTE £9.20: £3.00, £3.40; EX 60.50 Trifecta £352.70.
Owner The Royaume Bleu Racing Partnership **Bred** F Besnouin, D Besnouin & I Besnouin **Trained** Edgcote, Northants

FOCUS
They appeared to go a fair gallop, considering the conditions, and it proved a severe test. The form is rated around the first two.

3689 EBF STALLIONS MARES' "NATIONAL HUNT" NOVICES' HURDLE (12 hdls) 2m 5f

2:30 (2:31) (Class 4) 4-Y-0+ **£3,443** (£1,011; £505; £252)

Form RPR

104- 1 **Toubeera**[45] 2801 8-11-12 125 .... AidanColeman 136+
(Venetia Williams) *mde most tl after 9th: pushed along bef next: led after 3 out: drvn ahd and in command 2 out: kpt on* **1/2**[1]

11F- 2 9 **Massannie (IRE)**[177] 1045 6-11-12 132 .... TomScudamore 127
(David Pipe) *planted s and slowly away: t.k.h: sn rcvrd and jnd ldr 2nd: led after 9th: hdd after next: rdn and btn bef 2 out: plugged on* **2/1**[2]

3 61 **Cove (IRE)**[316] 7-11-2 0 .... TomCannon 56
(Nick Gifford) *in tch in last pair: mstke 6th: rdn and chsd clr ldng pair after 8th: lost tch bef 3 out: no ch whn hung rt and rel to r bnd bef 2 out: continued t.o* **12/1**[3]

05- 4 21 **Present Trend (IRE)**[25] 3181 5-11-2 0 .... NoelFehily 35
(Charlie Longsdon) *chsd clr ldng pair: mstke 5th: rdn and dropped to 4th after 8th: t.o next* **20/1**

5P0/ P **Whatagoa (IRE)**[323] 4406 7-11-2 0 .... LeightonAspell
(Richard Rowe) *a in rr: rdn and lost tch 8th: t.o whn p.u 3 out* **100/1**

5m 49.95s (32.95) **Going Correction** +1.55s/f (Heav) **5** Ran SP% **113.4**
Speed ratings (Par 105): **99,95,72,64,**
CSF £1.99 TOTE £1.20: £1.10, £1.30; EX 1.90 Trifecta £4.80.
Owner Richard Britten-Long **Bred** Mrs H I S Calzini **Trained** Kings Caple, H'fords

The Form Book Jumps, Raceform Ltd, Compton, RG20 6NL.

FOCUS
An uncompetitive mares' event and not one to be confident about.

3690 SIS LIVE NOVICES' LIMITED H'CAP CHASE (9 fncs 5 omitted) 2m 4f
3:00 (3:00) (Class 3) (0-125,124) 5-Y-0+ **£8,122** (£2,385; £1,192; £596)

Form RPR

223- **1** **No Buts**[34] [3004] 6-10-12 **115**.. TomScudamore 135+
(David Bridgwater) *chsd ldr tl led on long run after 6th: readily drew clr on long run to last: easily* **11/4**[2]

24U- **2** *14* **De Blacksmith (IRE)**[16] [3365] 6-11-5 **122**........................... JamieMoore 127
(Gary Moore) *chsd ldrs: rdn and effrt in 3rd bef 7th: chsd clr wnr bypassing 2 out: plugged on but no imp* **5/1**[3]

521- **3** *4* **Saroque (IRE)**[16] [3365] 7-11-3 **120**.................................... AidanColeman 124
(Venetia Williams) *led tl hdd on long run after 6th: rdn and mstke next: 3rd and btn bypassing 2 out: plugged on* **7/4**[1]

413- **4** *11* **Itoldyou (IRE)**[28] [3137] 8-10-2 **110** oh7........................ ConorShoemark(5) 100
(Linda Jewell) *hld up in tch in rr: rdn and effrt after 6th: sn struggling and wknd bef next: wnt poor 4th last* **8/1**

/14- **5** *12* **Lord Of The Dunes**[230] [521] 6-10-7 **110** oh8...............(t) BrendanPowell 95
(Colin Tizzard) *chsd ldrs: 4th and rdn on long run after 6th: wknd 3 out (actual 2 out): t.o* **12/1**

26U- **P** **Marcus Antonius**[8] [3551] 7-10-13 **116**.............................. LeightonAspell
(Jim Boyle) *in tch in last trio: rdn and struggling on long run after 6th: lost tch and j. slowly next: t.o whn p.u last* **25/1**

102- **P** **Avoca Promise (IRE)**[29] [3109] 9-11-7 **124**......................(b[1]) FelixDeGiles
(Tom Symonds) *racd wd: in tch in last trio: j.rt 6th: sn rdn and reluctant: sn lost tch and wl bhd whn p.u next* **8/1**

5m 29.3s (22.00) **Going Correction** +1.125s/f (Heav) **7** Ran SP% **113.5**
Speed ratings: **101,95,93,89,84** ,
CSF £16.77 TOTE £3.10: £1.70, £2.50; EX 17.80 Trifecta £41.70.
Owner Wontcostalot Partnership **Bred** Wontcostalot Partnership **Trained** Icomb, Gloucs

FOCUS
Few landed a blow behind the progressive winner, who produced a big step up. The second is rated to the level of his October C&D run.

3691 FOLLOW @TIMEFORM1948 ON TWITTER H'CAP HURDLE (14 hdls) 3m 1f 110y
3:30 (3:30) (Class 4) (0-115,115) 4-Y-0+ **£3,249** (£954; £477; £238)

Form RPR

000- **1** **Virginia Ash (IRE)**[37] [2944] 6-11-2 105..........................(p) BrendanPowell 112
(Colin Tizzard) *midfield: hdwy 9th: drvn and chsd ldrs bef 3 out: led bef 2 out: battled on v gamely to assert fnl 100yds: all out* **11/4**[1]

211- **2** *¾* **Night Of Passion (IRE)**[22] [3227] 6-10-11 100..............(p) NickScholfield 106
(Jeremy Scott) *racd wd: bhd and nt go early pce: hdwy into midfield 9th: chsd ldrs 11th: drvn and ev ch bef 2 out: hit last: battled on gamely tl no ex and btn fnl 100yds* **3/1**[2]

P03- **3** *20* **Sarando**[13] [3435] 9-11-9 112...(tp) WillKennedy 103
(Alex Hales) *chsd ldr tl 3rd: chsd ldr again 7th: led 9th tl drvn and hdd bef 2 out: wknd between last 2* **16/1**

1F5- **4** *25* **Royal Native (IRE)**[37] [2944] 6-11-9 115.......................(t) RachaelGreen(3) 76
(Anthony Honeyball) *in tch in midfield: rdn and struggling after 10th: wl btn 3 out: lft poor 4th next: t.o* **8/1**

5/P- **P** **The Red Laird**[24] [3191] 11-11-1 107................................ TrevorWhelan(3)
(Neil King) *chsd ldrs: rdn after 5th: drvn and struggling after 10th: wknd after next and wl btn whn p.u 3 out* **28/1**

1/4- **P** **Bangkok Pete (IRE)**[56] [2565] 9-11-6 112................... WayneKavanagh(3)
(Jamie Poulton) *chsd ldrs: wnt 2nd 3rd tl 7th: rdn and lost pl bef 10th: lost tch 11th: t.o whn p.u 2 out* **25/1**

105- **P** **Kind Of Easy (IRE)**[30] [3092] 8-11-11 114........................(b[1]) NoelFehily
(Emma Lavelle) *racd wd: t.k.h: chsd ldrs: reminder after 7th: wknd qckly bef 3 out: t.o whn p.u 2 out* **8/1**

663- **P** **Rocky Bender (IRE)**[24] [3193] 9-11-2 105........................ AidanColeman
(Venetia Williams) *in tch in midfield: rdn and struggling after 10th: lost tch bef 3 out: t.o whn p.u 2 out* **13/2**[3]

231- **P** **Flemi Two Toes (IRE)**[11] [3502] 8-10-13 105................(p) JackQuinlan(3)
(Sarah Humphrey) *in tch towards rr: rdn after 7th: lost tch after 10th: t.o whn p.u 3 out* **8/1**

U5U- **P** **Curtain Razer (IRE)**[34] [3006] 8-11-12 115.......................... TomCannon
(Chris Gordon) *led tl 9th: styd pressing ldr tl rdn and btn after 3 out: 4th and wkng whn eased and p.u 2 out* **33/1**

1/0- **P** **Milans Well (IRE)**[162] [1205] 8-10-12 101.......................... AndrewTinkler
(Brendan Powell) *sn detached in last: lost tch after 5th: t.o whn p.u 7th* **16/1**

003- **P** **Cadeau George**[17] [3326] 5-11-10 113.................................... DavidBass
(Ben Pauling) *in tch towards rr: rdn after 6th: struggling 8th: t.o 11th tl p.u 2 out* **33/1**

7m 10.5s (45.50) **Going Correction** +1.55s/f (Heav) **12** Ran SP% **123.3**
Speed ratings (Par 105): **92,91,85,77,** , , , , ,
CSF £11.76 CT £113.23 TOTE £4.00: £1.50, £1.40, £5.00; EX 13.70 Trifecta £337.20.
Owner J P Romans **Bred** Peter O'Reilly **Trained** Milborne Port, Dorset
■ Stewards' Enquiry : Nick Scholfield two-day ban: used whip above permitted level (Jan 27-28)

FOCUS
They got racing a long way out and it made for a slow-motion finish. No less than two thirds of the field were pulled up. The winner is rated back to the level of last season's win in this race.

3692 FOLLOW @PLUMPTONRACEDAY ON TWITTER H'CAP HURDLE (7 hdls 2 omitted) 2m
4:00 (4:01) (Class 5) (0-100,106) 4-Y-0+ **£2,395** (£698; £349)

Form RPR

P02- **1** **Clonusker (IRE)**[28] [3140] 6-10-1 74................................(t) GerardTumelty 90+
(Linda Jewell) *chsd ldrs: mstke 5th: wnt 2nd bypassing next: led wl bef 2 out: j.lft 2 out: in command and wandered between last 2: comf* **8/1**

/00- **2** *11* **Goochypoochyprader**[39] [2896] 7-11-11 98...............(t) RichardJohnson 100
(Nick Lampard) *chsd ldr tl after 5th: styd chsng ldrs: rdn after 3 out: chsd clr wnr next: no imp but plugged on to hold 2nd flat* **9/2**[2]

420- **3** *4½* **Jaja De Jau**[189] [924] 5-11-1 91...............................(t) RachaelGreen(3) 88
(Anthony Honeyball) *hld up in tch towards rr: nt clr run after 5th: gd hdwy bef 3 out: rdn and chsd ldrs bef 2 out: no ex and plugged on same pce between last 2* **9/1**

/02- **4** *2½* **Fidelor (FR)**[11] [3503] 8-11-8 95.. WillKennedy 89
(Alex Hales) *in tch in midfield: rdn and hdwy to chse ldrs 3 out: chsd wnr after 3 out tl 2 out: wknd flat* **12/1**

2/4- **5** *1¼* **Little Roxy (IRE)**[55] [2581] 9-10-6 79................................. AdamWedge 73
(Anna Newton-Smith) *in tch in midfield: rdn to chse ldrs bef 3 out: keeping on same pce whn mstke 2 out: plugged on* **7/1**

/60- **6** *2½* **Maccabees**[34] [3009] 5-10-12 85.. HaddenFrost 75
(Roger Curtis) *racd wd: hld up off the pce in last pair: hung rt bnd after 5th: hdwy past btn horse bef 2 out: styd on flat: n.d* **20/1**

/0P- **7** *½* **Landerbee (IRE)**[13] [3434] 7-10-0 80................................. KevinJones(7) 70
(Seamus Mullins) *t.k.h: hld up in detached last: sme hdwy bypassing 6th: rdn after 3 out: kpt on past btn horses fr 2 out: n.d* **20/1**

305- **8** *13* **Lady Bridget**[32] [3043] 6-10-2 82....................................(bt) JakeHodson(7) 59
(Mark Gillard) *chsd ldrs: drvn bypassing 6th: wknd after 3 out* **6/1**[3]

0UP/ **9** *2¼* **Quinola Des Obeaux (FR)**[338] 10-11-5 95....................... JamesBest(3) 70
(Rob Summers) *led tl sn after 3 out: wknd bef last: fdd between last 2* **50/1**

65P- **10** *16* **Rosoff (IRE)**[28] [3139] 12-10-2 75.......................................(b) TomCannon 34
(Laura Mongan) *in tch in midfield: effrt u.p bef 3 out: btn 3 out and wknd bef next: t.o and mstke last* **20/1**

005- **11** *½* **Sporting Club Girl**[18] [3245] 4-10-0 85 oh5......................... MattieBatchelor 31
(Jim Best) *in tch in midfield: rdn and effrt bypassing 6th: sn struggling: wknd next: t.o* **33/1**

/1P- **P** **Bathwick Junior**[55] [2581] 7-11-4 91................................... NickScholfield
(Michael Blake) *in tch in midfield: rdn and btn bef 3 out: wl bhd whn p.u 2 out* **4/1**[1]

0/0- **P** **Strictly Cissbury**[255] [95] 5-10-9 82.................................. BrendanPowell
(Brendan Powell) *a towards rr: rdn and struggling after 4th: lost tch bef 3 out: t.o whn p.u 2 out* **28/1**

4m 26.6s (25.80) **Going Correction** +1.55s/f (Heav)
WFA 4 from 5yo+ 11lb **13** Ran SP% **116.4**
Speed ratings (Par 103): **97,91,89,88,87 86,85,79,78,70 70,** ,
CSF £39.19 CT £334.65 TOTE £8.70: £3.10, £2.20, £5.10; EX 54.00 Trifecta £178.80.
Owner Valence Racing **Bred** J P Jones **Trained** Sutton Valence, Kent

FOCUS
A moderate handicap. The easy winner built on his improved recent C&D run, and there's a case for rating the form a few pounds higher.
T/Plt: £142.90. Pool: £110,175.12 - 562.69 winning units. T/Qpdt: £45.30. Pool: £7126.97 - 116.30 winning units. SP

3168 EXETER (R-H)
Tuesday, January 14

OFFICIAL GOING: Soft (heavy in places; chs 5.8, hdl 5.7)
The middle hurdle in the home straight and the hurdle on the bend after the winning post was omitted on all circuits of all hurdle races due to the ground.
Wind: virtually nil Weather: cloudy with sunny periods

3693 32RED CASINO H'CAP CHASE (12 fncs) 2m 1f 110y
12:55 (12:55) (Class 4) (0-120,117) 5-Y-0+ **£3,898** (£1,144; £572; £286)

Form RPR

415- **1** **Umberto D'Olivate (FR)**[26] [3172] 6-11-12 **117**..................... FelixDeGiles 135+
(Robert Walford) *in tch: tk clsr order 6th: rdn to chse ldr appr 4 out: led 3 out: rdn clr between last 2: styd on wl* **8/1**

605- **2** *5* **Kingcora (FR)**[27] [3155] 6-11-4 **109**................................... AidanColeman 121+
(Venetia Williams) *in tch: rdn and stdy prog into 3rd 4 out: styd on to go 2nd at the last but nvr threatening to rch wnr* **3/1**[2]

122- **3** *19* **Ray Diamond**[26] [3172] 9-10-6 **100**.. JamesBest(3) 97
(Jackie Du Plessis) *trckd ldr: rdn to ld appr 4 out: hdd 3 out: hld in 2nd whn stmbld 2 out: wknd last* **5/2**[1]

65F- **4** *7* **Milarrow (IRE)**[39] [2931] 7-11-4 **109**..............................(b[1]) BrendanPowell 95
(Colin Tizzard) *trckd ldr tl nt fluent 7th: rdn after next: sn lost pl: plugged on fr 4 out: wnt 4th at the last* **9/1**

324- **5** *6* **Royal Riviera**[29] [3129] 8-10-12 **103**...........................(t) SamTwiston-Davies 83
(Nigel Twiston-Davies) *hld up but in tch: rdn after 8th: nvr threatened: wknd 3 out* **9/1**

PP3- **6** *6* **The Sneezer (IRE)**[14] [3431] 11-10-12 **110**.......................... KieronEdgar(7) 84
(Alexandra Dunn) *racd freely: led tl rdn appr 4 out: wknd 3 out* **20/1**

/26- **7** *5* **Ballincurrig (IRE)**[39] [2928] 8-11-1 **113**.......................(t) MissBAndrews(7) 82
(Dan Skelton) *trckd ldr: rdn appr 4 out: sn wknd* **5/1**[3]

UU5- **8** *32* **Swincombe Stone**[35] [3007] 7-11-0 **105**............................ RobertThornton 42
(Anthony Honeyball) *nt a fluent: hld up but in tch: rdn after 8th: wknd next: t.o* **25/1**

5PP- **P** **Humbel Ben (IRE)**[26] [3172] 11-10-8 **99**..............................(p) TomO'Brien
(Alan Jones) *hld up: struggling 6th: lost tch 8th: p.u bef next* **100/1**

4m 27.5s (8.50) **Going Correction** +0.90s/f (Soft) **9** Ran SP% **110.9**
Speed ratings: **106,103,95,92,89 86,84,70,**
CSF £31.33 CT £74.33 TOTE £10.50: £2.50, £1.70, £1.20; EX 49.60 Trifecta £91.70.
Owner Mrs S De Wilde **Bred** J P Rivoire **Trained** Child Okeford, Dorset
■ This meeting was arranged at short notice.

FOCUS
The opening time was 25.5sec slower than standard, suggesting that the ground for this swiftly arranged fixture was pretty testing. Felix De Giles called it "soft and hard work" and Sam Twiston-Davies said it was "dead and holding". They finished well strung out in this modest handicap chase. The form makes sense, with the winner producing a big step up.

3694 32RED ON THE APP STORE "NATIONAL HUNT" NOVICES' HURDLE (DIV I) (8 hdls 2 omitted) 2m 3f
1:25 (1:25) (Class 4) 5-Y-0+ **£3,249** (£954; £477; £238)

Form RPR

262- **1** **Strollawaynow (IRE)**[31] [3092] 7-10-12 118......................... TomCannon 123+
(David Arbuthnot) *trckd ldrs: rdn after 6th: led 2 out: styd on strly fr last: drvn out* **11/10**[1]

144- **2** *3¾* **Tullyesker Hill (IRE)**[17] [3357] 5-10-12 0......................... ConorO'Farrell 120
(David Pipe) *trckd ldrs: rdn and ev ch 2 out: styd on but no ex fr last* **5/1**[3]

/21- **3** *18* **Steel City**[12] [3501] 6-11-5 0... AndrewThornton 112
(Seamus Mullins) *w ldr: blnd 2nd: led 4th: rdn and hdd bef 2 out (usual 3 out): sn hld: fdd fr last* **5/2**[2]

435- **4** *5* **Smiles For Miles (IRE)**[6] [3600] 6-10-12 0.................(t) TomScudamore 97+
(David Pipe) *hld up towards rr: stdy prog fr 3rd: rdn after 6th: nvr threatened: styd on same pce fr 2 out (usual 3 out)* **8/1**

605- **5** *7* **Here's Herbie**[58] [2536] 6-10-7 0.................................. MissLucyGardner(5) 90
(Sue Gardner) *hld up towards rr: styd on steadily fr bef 2 out: nvr threatened ldrs* **125/1**

505- **6** *1½* **Powerful Action (IRE)**[15] [3422] 6-10-12 0......................... RichardJohnson 88
(Philip Hobbs) *trckd ldrs: rdn after 6th: sn hld: wknd bef last* **12/1**

06- **7** *12* **Pure Poteen (IRE)**[15] [3422] 6-10-12 0...........................(t) DougieCostello 82+
(Neil Mulholland) *led: mstke and hdd 4th: w ldr: led briefly after 6th: sn rdn: wknd next* **50/1**

54- **8** *14* **Bostin (IRE)**[14] 3433 6-10-5 0 MikeyHamill(7) 62
(Brian Barr) *bdly hmpd 1st: a towards rr: t.o* **100/1**

0P/- **9** *12* **Folly Farm (IRE)**[314] 4593 6-10-12 0 (t) TomO'Brien 50
(Richard Woollacott) *mid-div: rdn after 6th: wknd bef next: t.o* **200/1**

300- **U** **Bandol (IRE)**[47] 2761 6-10-9 0 RobertDunne(3)
(Laura Young) *hld up towards rr: blnd and uns rdr 6th* **200/1**

F **Ziggerson Hill** 7-10-2 0 JamesBest(3)
(Jackie Du Plessis) *hld up towards rr: fell 3rd* **100/1**

2- **U** **Springhill Lad**[230] 544 7-10-12 0 MarkGrant
(Geoffrey Deacon) *stmbld bdly and uns rdr 1st* **33/1**

4m 55.1s (12.40) **Going Correction** +0.775s/f (Soft) **12** Ran SP% **120.3**
Speed ratings: **104,102,94,92,89 89,84,78,73,** ,
CSF £7.63 TOTE £2.50: £1.20, £1.70, £1.40; EX 9.10 Trifecta £21.10.
Owner A T A Wates **Bred** Mrs E M Codd **Trained** Beare Green, Surrey

FOCUS
A reasonable novice hurdle which should produce a few winners. The first two sat just off the pace before drawing well clear. Another step up from the winner, who was the form pick.

3695 32RED ON THE APP STORE "NATIONAL HUNT" NOVICES' HURDLE (DIV II) (10 hdls) 2m 3f
2:00 (2:00) (Class 4) 5-Y-0+ **£3,249** (£954; £477; £238)

Form RPR

2F- **1** **Knight Of Noir (IRE)**[54] 2631 5-10-12 0 APMcCoy 122+
(David Pipe) *hld up towards rr: nt fluent 2nd: stdy prog fr after 5th: pushed along to chse ldrs 2 out: chal last: sn led: r.o wl to assert towards fin: pushed out* **7/1**[3]

U44- **2** *1 ¼* **Cool George**[26] 3169 6-10-9 117 JamesBest(3) 118
(Jackie Du Plessis) *disp tl clr ldr 4th: rdn between last 2: kpt on gamely but no ex whn hdd run-in* **3/1**[2]

161- **3** *4 ½* **Prideofthecastle (IRE)**[39] 2924 7-11-5 0 TomScudamore 120
(David Pipe) *disp ld tl 4th: trckd ldrs: rdn after 2 out: styd on but nt gng pce to chal* **3/1**[2]

/23- **4** *3* **Sky Watch (IRE)**[29] 3136 7-10-12 122 (t) NoelFehily 111
(Warren Greatrex) *prom: rdn and ev ch appr 2 out: no ex appr last* **6/4**[1]

0- **5** *8* **Silvergrove**[26] 3173 6-10-12 0 (t) DarylJacob 103
(Richard Woollacott) *mid-div: hdwy 6th: rdn bef 2 out: sn one pce* **100/1**

4/5- **6** *3 ¼* **Know More Oats (IRE)**[38] 2946 6-10-9 0 GilesHawkins(3) 100
(Victor Dartnall) *trckd ldrs: nt fluent 5th: effrt after next: one pce fr 2 out* **25/1**

000- **7** *25* **Bonds Conquest**[29] 3136 5-10-12 0 AndrewThornton 74
(Seamus Mullins) *nt fluent 4th: a towards rr: nvr any danger to ldrs* **100/1**

40- **8** *½* **Tribulation (IRE)**[38] 2940 6-10-12 0 DougieCostello 80
(Robert Walford) *cl up: mstke 2nd: rdn appr 2 out where blnd: wknd: t.o* **14/1**

000- **9** *5* **More Tricks**[15] 3422 6-9-12 0 MrFTett(7) 61
(James Frost) *a towards rr: wknd after 6th: t.o* **200/1**

0/0- **10** *40* **Beat The Bounds**[66] 2375 5-10-12 0 BrendanPowell 28
(Martin Hill) *midfield early: towards rr 3rd: wknd after 6th: mstke 2 out: t.o* **100/1**

320- **11** *13* **Another Brandy (IRE)**[15] 3422 6-10-9 0 MichaelByrne(3) 15
(Neil Mulholland) *trckd ldrs tl after 4th: mstke next: sn bhd: t.o* **25/1**

5/6- **12** *8* **Brogeen Boy (IRE)**[32] 3063 6-10-12 0 TomO'Brien
(Alan Jones) *mainly towards rr: t.o after 6th* **100/1**

50- **P** **Canarbino Girl**[35] 3005 7-9-12 0 MrLDrowne(7)
(Caroline Keevil) *mid-div tl wknd 5th: t.o whn p.u bef 2 out* **200/1**

4m 55.7s (13.00) **Going Correction** +0.775s/f (Soft) **13** Ran SP% **121.8**
Speed ratings: **103,102,100,99,95 94,84,83,81,64 59,56,**
CSF £29.20 TOTE £6.60: £3.10, £1.70, £1.40; EX 28.70 Trifecta £94.90.
Owner Wayne Clifford **Bred** C Berry **Trained** Nicholashayne, Devon

FOCUS
This was run in a slightly slower time than the first division. A step forward from the cosy winner.

3696 32RED H'CAP CHASE (18 fncs) 3m
2:35 (2:35) (Class 4) (0-105,105) 5-Y-0+ **£3,898** (£1,144; £572; £286)

Form RPR

55P- **1** **Barton Gift**[19] 3277 7-9-12 **82** (b[1]) NicodeBoinville(5) 107+
(John Spearing) *mid-div: trckd ldrs 4th: disp 14th: clr ldr appr 4 out: styd on strly to draw wl clr after 3 out: v easily* **3/1**[2]

P/5- **2** *32* **Tuskar Rock (FR)**[123] 1579 11-11-7 **105** CallumWhillans(5) 100+
(Venetia Williams) *disp ld tl rdn appr 4 out: sn hld by wnr but clr of remainder: wknd last* **11/1**

/5P- **3** *7* **Ballyegan (IRE)**[54] 2619 9-10-7 **86** (t) GerardTumelty 70
(Bob Buckler) *nt a fluent: trckd ldrs tl awkward and rdr lost iron and pl 14th: sn rdn: no ch fr next: plugged on past wkng horses fr 2 out: wnt 3rd at the last* **9/1**

253- **4** *2 ¼* **Cornish Ice**[26] 3176 10-11-11 **104** (b) CharliePoste 85
(Robin Dickin) *prom: nt fluent 8th (water): rdn along fr 12th: outpcd after 14th: rallied bk into disp 3rd: no ch w ldng pair next: blnd 3 out: wknd last* **7/1**

322- **5** *3 ¾* **Roseneath (IRE)**[14] 3437 10-11-4 **97** (tp) APMcCoy 74
(Alex Hales) *mid-div: trckd ldrs 7th: reminder 11th: rdn in disp 3rd bef 4 out: sn wl hld: wknd after 2 out* **2/1**[1]

/55- **6** *15* **Cheat The Cheater (IRE)**[17] 3358 7-10-13 **99** (p) GeraldQuinn(7) 59
(Claire Dyson) *disp ld: pushed along fr 11th: hdd 14th: wknd bef next: t.o* **9/2**[3]

450/ **7** *8* **Ball Hopper (IRE)**[447] 1984 10-11-4 **97** AndrewThornton 49
(Richenda Ford) *a towards rr: lost tch fr 14th: t.o* **16/1**

4P6- **P** **Mallusk (IRE)**[19] 3281 9-11-2 **95** (t) DominicElsworth
(Shaun Lycett) *hld up: blnd 7th: reminder: sn hdwy 12th: wknd after 14th: t.o whn p.u bef 4 out* **16/1**

/FU- **P** **Keltic Crisis (IRE)**[19] 3279 10-11-8 **104** JamesBest(3)
(Sophie Leech) *hld up: hdwy 11th: wknd after 13th: t.o whn p.u bef 4 out* **40/1**

0F6- **P** **Vintage Tea**[26] 3176 7-11-12 **105** (t) DarylJacob
(Richard Woollacott) *mid-div tl dropped to last pair 10th: wknd 14th: t.o whn p.u bef 4 out* **20/1**

6m 29.9s (20.60) **Going Correction** +0.90s/f (Soft) **10** Ran SP% **126.3**
Speed ratings: **104,93,91,90,89 84,81,** , ,
CSF £38.88 CT £283.07 TOTE £4.70: £1.40, £2.50, £4.00; EX 38.40 Trifecta £319.70.
Owner Mercy Rimell & Kate Ive **Bred** Mrs Mercy Rimell **Trained** Kinnersley, Worcs

FOCUS
A modest handicap chase. The winner was well in on his old form but arguably exceeded that here.

3697 32RED.COM MAIDEN HURDLE (9 hdls 2 omitted) 2m 5f 110y
3:05 (3:06) (Class 5) 5-Y-0+ **£2,111** (£620; £310; £155)

Form RPR

1 **Royal Player**[247] 5-11-0 0 RichardJohnson 119+
(Philip Hobbs) *mde all: hit 2nd: 7 l clr last: looked to be idling whn drvn run-in: a holding on* **5/1**[2]

554- **2** *3* **Tinker Time (IRE)**[52] 2661 6-11-0 112 LiamHeard 114
(Bob Buckler) *trckd wnr after 6th: rdn appr 2 out: lost 2nd between last 2: styd on again after last: regained 2nd and edgd lft fnl 100yds* **14/1**

/22- **3** *nk* **Major Milborne**[26] 3175 6-11-0 118 BrendanPowell 112
(Jamie Snowden) *trckd ldrs: rdn appr 2 out: chsd wnr between last 2 tl no ex fnl 100yds* **11/2**[3]

4 *2 ¾* **Kudu Shine**[253] 8-11-0 0 ConorO'Farrell 109
(Richard Woollacott) *trckd ldrs: rdn appr 2 out: styd on same pce* **20/1**

406/ **5** *20* **Romany Quest**[541] 1031 7-10-7 0 MrCSmith(7) 91
(Linda Blackford) *mid-div: hdwy after 6th: rdn after next: wknd appr 2 out* **100/1**

/00- **6** *35* **Rafafie**[38] 2940 6-10-9 0 MissLucyGardner(5) 54
(Sue Gardner) *hld up towards rr: nvr any danger: t.o fr after 6th* **66/1**

0- **7** *15* **Genson**[29] 3133 5-11-0 0 DarylJacob 39
(Richard Woollacott) *mid-div: rdn after 6th: sn wknd: t.o* **100/1**

/35- **8** *16* **Just Fee**[26] 3168 7-10-7 0 DaveCrosse 16
(Nick Mitchell) *mid-div: struggling bef 4th: wkng whn mstke 7th: t.o* **33/1**

636/ **9** *10* **Letmespeak (IRE)**[226] 9-11-0 0 (p) JackDoyle 13
(Victor Dartnall) *trckd wnr most of way tl after 5th: wknd sn after 7th: t.o* **40/1**

0- **10** *3* **Moorlands George**[105] 1712 6-11-0 0 NickScholfield 10
(Jeremy Scott) *a towards rr: t.o fr 5th* **40/1**

0FP/ **11** *26* **Clovers Boy**[744] 3502 9-11-0 0 WillKennedy
(Sue Gardner) *mid-div: rdn after 5th: sn wknd: t.o* **150/1**

0- **12** *9* **Landulph Lass**[26] 3168 7-10-4 0 JamesBest(3)
(Jackie Du Plessis) *a in rr: t.o fr 6th* **150/1**

/0F- **13** *6* **Pullmen**[53] 2644 6-11-0 0 TomO'Brien
(Paul Henderson) *mid-div tl after 6th: t.o* **100/1**

P/0- **P** **Crowcombe Park**[83] 2027 6-10-7 0 JamesDavies
(Kevin Bishop) *struggling after 3rd: a in rr: tailing off whn p.u bef 5th* **100/1**

/22- **P** **Allow Dallow (IRE)**[25] 3189 7-11-0 123 APMcCoy
(Jonjo O'Neill) *mid-div: nudged along 4th: rdn after 5th: nvr any imp: wkng whn p.u after 7th: b.b.v* **4/7**[1]

5m 55.2s (22.20) **Going Correction** +0.775s/f (Soft) **15** Ran SP% **121.7**
Speed ratings: **90,88,88,87,80 67,62,56,52,51 42,39,36,** ,
CSF £64.95 TOTE £6.40: £1.70, £2.80, £1.50; EX 58.70 Trifecta £187.20.
Owner Mrs Diana L Whateley **Bred** Mrs R M Wilson **Trained** Withycombe, Somerset

FOCUS
There wasn't much strength in depth to this and only half a dozen or so were ever in it. The principals showed fair form.

3698 32REDPOKER.COM VETERANS' H'CAP CHASE (18 fncs) 3m
3:40 (3:41) (Class 2) (0-150,148)
10-Y-0+

£11,573 (£3,418; £1,709; £854; £427; £214)

Form RPR

F20- **1** **Pineau De Re (FR)**[24] 3207 11-10-11 **133** SamTwiston-Davies 151+
(Dr Richard Newland) *travelled wl bhd ldng bunch: hit 7th: hdwy 13th: lost pl whn nt clr run on bnd after 14th: cruised up to ld 4 out: wl in command after: hit last: v easily* **11/4**[1]

/32- **2** *5* **Tullamore Dew (IRE)**[19] 3285 12-10-4 **126** TomCannon 132
(Nick Gifford) *in tch: pushed along after 11th: rdn appr 4 out: styd on to go 2nd run-in: no ch w v easy wnr* **7/2**[2]

5P4- **3** *1 ¼* **Junior**[19] 3285 11-11-12 **148** (b) ConorO'Farrell 154
(David Pipe) *prom: nt fluent 2nd: rdn to disp ld after 14th tl next: styd on same pce fr 3 out* **20/1**

FR4- **4** *10* **Triggerman**[51] 2693 12-9-6 **122** oh3 ow2 (b) ThomasCheesman(10) 123
(Philip Hobbs) *racd keenly: trckd ldrs: rdn after 4 out: styd on same pce* **13/2**[3]

044- **5** *2 ½* **Alderluck (IRE)**[39] 2923 11-9-7 **122** (b) MikeyEnnis(7) 116
(David Pipe) *trckd ldrs: jnd ldrs 11th: rdn and ev ch appr 4 out: grad fdd fr after 3 out* **7/1**

/50- **6** *5* **Ballyoliver**[15] 3416 10-10-4 **126** AidanColeman 115
(Venetia Williams) *trckd ldrs tl after 10th: in last pair but wl in tch: rdn appr 4 out: grad fdd fr 3 out* **13/2**[3]

410/ **P** **Richard's Sundance (IRE)**[306] 4751 12-10-11 **133** (p[1]) JackDoyle
(Victor Dartnall) *pressed ldrs tl wknd rapidly and p.u appr 4 out* **13/2**[3]

/PF- **P** **Shaking Hands (IRE)**[17] 3366 10-10-2 **124** (bt) TomScudamore
(David Pipe) *led: reminders appr 8th: rdn and hdd after 11th: bk pressing ldrs 14th: wkng whn hmpd and p.u jst bef 4 out* **16/1**

6m 26.2s (16.90) **Going Correction** +0.90s/f (Soft) **8** Ran SP% **112.0**
Speed ratings: **107,105,104,101,100 99,** ,
CSF £12.74 CT £152.12 TOTE £3.20: £1.10, £1.80, £4.70; EX 14.10 Trifecta £104.90.
Owner J A Provan **Bred** Michel Hardy **Trained** Claines, Worcs

FOCUS
Quite a valuable prize for this veterans' handicap, in which all eight were still in with a chance on the home turn. The time was 3.7sec quicker than the earlier 0-105 handicap. The easy winner is rated to the level of his best Irish form.

3699 32REDBET.COM H'CAP HURDLE (9 hdls 2 omitted) 2m 5f 110y
4:10 (4:13) (Class 5) (0-100,102) 4-Y-0+ **£2,111** (£620; £310; £155)

Form RPR

2/P- **1** **Admiral Blake**[69] 2291 7-10-1 **75** DougieCostello 86+
(Laura Young) *hld up towards rr: stdy prog whn mstke 7th: rdn and stdy hdwy appr 2 out: 8 l 5th jumping last: str run to ld fnl 50yds: rdn out* **11/2**[2]

041- **2** *2 ¼* **Cash Injection**[26] 3174 5-11-0 **95** (t) TomBellamy(7) 102
(Richard Woollacott) *chsd ldrs: rdn into clr ld appr 2 out: 7 l clr last: no ex whn hdd fnl 50yds* **6/1**[3]

051- **3** *3* **Residence And Spa (IRE)**[15] 3425 6-10-3 **80** MarkQuinlan(3) 84
(Helen Rees) *hld up towards rr: rdn and hdwy after 7th: styd on fr next: wnt 3rd run-in: nt rch ldrs* **7/1**

6/1- **4** *2 ¾* **Catcher Star (IRE)**[19] 3284 6-11-2 **90** (p) TomCannon 91
(Nick Gifford) *mid-div: pushed along after 5th: rdn after 7th: disp hld 3rd 2 out: kpt on same pce fr last* **5/2**[1]

565- **5** *9* **Free Falling**[35] 3009 8-10-5 **79**..........(v) WillKennedy 73
(Alastair Lidderdale) *led: rdn and hdd appr 2 out: kpt chsng wnr tl no ex and lost 3 pls run-in* **16/1**

0P6- **6** *7* **Comical Red**[26] 3174 6-9-7 **74** oh5.......... ThomasCheesman(7) 59
(Mark Gillard) *mid-div: hdwy to chse ldrs 3rd: rdn after 7th: wknd between last 2* **20/1**

303- **7** *3/4* **General Girling**[35] 3009 7-10-4 **78**.......... IanPopham 62
(Caroline Keevil) *chsd ldrs: rdn and wknd 2 out* **10/1**

5/0- **8** *29* **Count Vettori (IRE)**[62] 2458 8-11-2 **100**.......... JonPark(10) 55
(Kevin Bishop) *mid-div: pushed along and hdwy 6th: chsd ldrs next: rdn and wkng whn mstke 2 out: t.o* **20/1**

245- **9** *1* **Nicene Creed**[15] 3413 9-11-12 **100**..........(tp) RichieMcLernon 54
(Sophie Leech) *mid-div: rdn after 6th: wknd after next: t.o* **8/1**

306- **10** *3 1/4* **Brunette'Sonly (IRE)**[29] 3138 9-10-11 **85**.......... AndrewThornton 35
(Seamus Mullins) *racd wd: trckd ldr: rdn after 4th: lost pl after next: t.o* **16/1**

00P- **11** *6* **Miss Tinks**[15] 3425 8-10-0 **74** oh1..........(t) ConorO'Farrell 18
(Richard Woollacott) *a towards rr: t.o fr 6th* **50/1**

/00- **P** **Forgotten Promise**[47] 2766 7-9-7 **74** oh2..........[1] CiaranMckee(7)
(Brian Barr) *a towards rr: struggling 6th: t.o whn p.u bef 2 out* **100/1**

005- **P** **Kilrye (IRE)**[15] 3420 7-10-10 **84**..........(bt) TomScudamore
(David Pipe) *mid-div: hdwy after 6th: jst gone 3rd whn wknd rapidly and p.u bef 2 out* **12/1**

6m 6.2s (33.20) **Going Correction** +0.775s/f (Soft) **13** Ran SP% **122.9**
Speed ratings (Par 103): **70,69,68,67,63 61,61,50,50,48 46, ,**
CSF £38.80 CT £241.30 TOTE £6.70: £2.10, £2.10, £2.40; EX 50.60 Trifecta £347.60.
Owner Mrs Laura Young **Bred** Mrs Laura Young **Trained** Broomfield, Somerset
■ Duke's Affair was withdrawn. Price at time of withdrawal 16/1. Rule 4 does not apply.

FOCUS
A fair handicap hurdle, and the form seems sound. A step up from the winner.
T/Jkpt: Not won. T/Plt: £67.80 to a £1 stake. Pool of £120719.66, 1299.49 winning tickets
T/Qpdt: £28.40 to a £1 stake. Pool of £10196.42 - 265.40 winning tickets. TM

3127 FFOS LAS (L-H)
Tuesday, January 14
3700 Meeting Abandoned - Waterlogged

3229 LINGFIELD (L-H)
Tuesday, January 14
3707 Meeting Abandoned - Waterlogged

3364 NEWBURY (L-H)
Wednesday, January 15

OFFICIAL GOING: Soft (chs 6.2, hdl 6.0)
Wind: Moderate across Weather: Overcast, damp

3714 BETFRED TV JUVENILE HURDLE (8 hdls) 2m 110y
12:50 (12:50) (Class 4) 4-Y-O **£3,249** (£954; £477; £238)

Form RPR

41- **1** **Dawalan (FR)**[28] 3161 4-11-5 131.......... BarryGeraghty 128+
(Nicky Henderson) *mde all at modest pce tl qcknd appr 3 out: shkn up and edgd lft bef last: rdn run-in and sn hanging lft: drvn out clsng stages* **4/9**[1]

2 *1 1/2* **Carry On Sydney**[86] 4-10-12 0.......... LeightonAspell 115+
(Oliver Sherwood) *in tch: outpcd whn pce qcknd appr 3 out: styd on to chse ldrs fr 2 out: wnt 2nd after last and kpt on wl clsng stages but no imp on wnr* **20/1**

3 *2 3/4* **Prince Khurram**[118] 4-10-12 0.......... JasonMaguire 114+
(Donald McCain) *chsd ldrs in 3rd: drvn to chse wnr after 2 out: nt fluent last and sn dropped to 3rd: kpt on same pce* **4/1**[2]

4 *15* **Astrum**[130] 4-10-9 0.......... TrevorWhelan(3) 98
(Neil King) *trckd wnr and t.k.h off modest pce: drvn to chal 2 out: sn wknd* **40/1**

41- **5** *2 3/4* **Ivanhoe**[30] 3127 4-11-5 109.......... NickScholfield 102
(Michael Blanshard) *in tch early: towards rr whn nt fluent 4th: no ch w ldrs fr 3 out* **16/1**

6 *5* **Interior Minister**[153] 4-10-12 0.......... APMcCoy 91
(Jonjo O'Neill) *in tch: chsd ldrs appr 3 out: sn rdn and wknd* **12/1**[3]

7 *32* **Hurricane John (IRE)**[88] 4-10-12 0.......... AidanColeman 57
(Venetia Williams) *reminders after 4 out: sn rdn: a bhd: t.o fr 3 out* **33/1**

4m 21.9s (11.90) **Going Correction** +0.275s/f (Yiel) **7** Ran SP% **113.0**
Speed ratings: **83,82,81,73,72 70,55**
CSF £12.23 TOTE £1.30: £1.20, £4.90; EX 13.00 Trifecta £42.80.
Owner Simon Munir & Isaac Souede **Bred** H H The Aga Khan's Studs Sc **Trained** Upper Lambourn, Berks

FOCUS
All rails moved in on both courses. This was always likely to be a tactical affair and so it proved as the gallop only began to warm up exiting the back straight. They looked to get through the ground well enough over the final three flights. The winner looked to have a bity in hand and the fourth helps with the level.

3715 BETFRED GOALS GALORE NOVICES' CHASE (13 fncs) 2m 1f
1:20 (1:20) (Class 3) 5-Y-O+ **£6,498** (£1,908; £954; £477)

Form RPR

P3- **1** **Festive Affair (IRE)**[18] 3368 6-10-13 0.......... APMcCoy 130+
(Jonjo O'Neill) *mde all: jnd fr 2 out and drvn along: stl hrd pressed last: edgd lft whn rdn run-in: styd on willingly clsng stages* **10/1**[3]

/1F- **2** *nk* **Dark Lover (GER)**[71] 2282 9-11-9 143.......... DarylJacob 141+
(Paul Nicholls) *trckd wnr fr 4th: blnd 7th but hld 2nd: mstke 4 out and lost 2nd: rallied to chal fr 2 out and stl upside last: pressed wnr clsng stages tl no ex clsng stages* **5/6**[1]

4/1- **3** *2 1/2* **Brick Red**[10] 3551 7-11-5 0.......... AidanColeman 133
(Venetia Williams) *trckd wnr to 4th: styd cl 3rd tl wnt 2nd briefly 3 out: drvn to chal 2 out and stl upsides last: outpcd by ldng duo fnl 120yds* **11/8**[2]

034- **4** *24* **Merchant Of Milan**[20] 3280 6-10-13 0.......... BrendanPowell 107
(Brendan Powell) *in rr but in tch: hdwy 8th: drvn next: blnd and wknd 4 out* **66/1**

004- **5** *59* **Tchang Goon (FR)**[10] 3551 10-10-13 62..........(p) DaveCrosse 44
(Zoe Davison) *a in rr: losing tch whn j. slowly 8th: hit next and t.o* **100/1**

4m 12.73s (4.73) **Going Correction** +0.275s/f (Yiel) **5** Ran SP% **108.2**
Speed ratings: **99,98,97,86,58**
CSF £19.47 TOTE £6.90: £2.50, £1.10; EX 14.80 Trifecta £23.30.
Owner John P McManus **Bred** Noel O'Brien **Trained** Cheltenham, Gloucs

FOCUS
This was the weakest running of this traditionally strong novice chase for some years, but it was run at a fair gallop and served up a cracking finish between three useful performers. The form looks believable.

3716 BETFRED "DOUBLE DELIGHT" NOVICES' HURDLE (10 hdls) 2m 3f
1:50 (1:50) (Class 4) 5-Y-O+ **£3,573** (£1,049; £524; £262)

Form RPR

141- **1** **Cole Harden (IRE)**[59] 2536 5-11-5 120..........(t) JasonMaguire 138+
(Warren Greatrex) *mde all: drvn clr fr 2 out: unchal* **4/1**[3]

1- **2** *8* **Full Shift (FR)**[46] 2823 5-11-5 0.......... APMcCoy 130+
(Nicky Henderson) *chsd ldrs: rdn to go 2nd after 2 out: styd on to hold that position run-in but nvr any ch w wnr* **5/2**[2]

051- **3** *1 1/4* **Brother Brian (IRE)**[28] 3166 6-11-5 0.......... TomO'Brien 129+
(Hughie Morrison) *chsd wnr: hit 3 out: sn rdn and no ch w wnr: lost 2nd after 2 out: kpt on same pce run-in* **11/8**[1]

0/4- **4** *40* **The Ould Lad (IRE)**[28] 3166 6-10-12 0.......... AlainCawley 81
(Tom George) *in rr: hit 4 out: hdwy appr 3 out but nvr any ch w ldng trio: t.o* **9/1**

0- **5** *2 3/4* **Herons Heir (IRE)**[26] 3187 6-10-12 0.......... HarrySkelton 78+
(Dan Skelton) *t.k.h: pckd 1st: chsd ldrs fr 3rd: nt fluent 6th: wnt 3rd after 4 out but sn no ch w ldng trio: wknd 2 out: lost poor 4th run-in: t.o* **8/1**

2/0- **6** *8* **Master Cynk**[26] 3189 7-10-7 0.......... AodhaganConlon(5) 70
(Tom George) *j. slowly 4th and 5th: towards rr most of way: t.o fr 3 out* **66/1**

6/3- **7** *13* **Bay Fortuna**[228] 588 5-10-12 0.......... DarylJacob 57
(Mark Usher) *t.k.h: a in rr: t.o whn blnd 3 out* **50/1**

05- **8** *hd* **Sand Artist (IRE)**[19] 3326 6-10-12 0.......... AidanColeman 57
(Venetia Williams) *a in rr: t.o bef 3 out* **100/1**

05- **9** *42* **Venez Horace (FR)**[52] 2703 5-10-12 0.......... DavidEngland 15
(Giles Smyly) *hit 3rd: bhd fr 5th: t.o* **100/1**

45- **10** *34* **Church Bray**[31] 3116 6-10-12 0.......... SamTwiston-Davies
(Nigel Twiston-Davies) *in rr: hit 2nd: j. slowly 4th: hit 5th: sn bhd: t.o whn rdn 7th* **66/1**

4m 46.82s (-1.18) **Going Correction** +0.275s/f (Yiel) **10** Ran SP% **118.7**
Speed ratings: **113,109,109,92,91 87,82,82,64,50**
CSF £15.15 TOTE £5.90: £1.80, £1.60, £1.10; EX 13.90 Trifecta £20.80.
Owner Mrs Jill Eynon & Robin Eynon **Bred** Mrs J O'Callaghan **Trained** Upper Lambourn, Berks

FOCUS
A fair novice hurdle that proved a demanding test and the principals came a long way clear in the home straight. A big step up from the winner.

3717 BETFRED "HAT TRICK HEAVEN" H'CAP CHASE (FOR THE HARWELL TROPHY) (18 fncs) 3m
2:25 (2:25) (Class 3) (0-130,129) 5-Y-O+ **£6,498** (£1,908; £954; £477)

Form RPR

OUU- **1** **Restless Harry**[14] 3455 10-11-5 **122**.......... CharliePoste 150+
(Robin Dickin) *in tch fr 8th: chsd ldrs 12th: chalng whn bmpd 4 out and sn led: sn clr after next: v easily* **5/1**[2]

F1P- **2** *17* **Bendant**[14] 3455 9-10-13 **116**.......... TomO'Brien 122
(Debra Hamer) *hit 6th: dropped to rr fr 8th: blnd 13th: hdwy next: chsd wnr after 2 out but nvr any ch: mstke last: hld on for wl hld 2nd* **20/1**

F31- **3** *3 1/2* **Financial Climate (IRE)**[18] 3366 7-11-4 **126**.......... ThomasGarner(5) 131+
(Oliver Sherwood) *in rr: hdwy fr 12th: wnt 3rd 3 out but nvr nr wnr: blnd and dropped to 3rd 2 out: styd on again run-in to cl on wl hld 2nd* **9/2**[1]

631- **4** *shd* **Ringa Bay**[13] 3504 9-10-10 **120**..........(p) JakeHodson(7) 124
(David Bridgwater) *chsd ldrs: hit 14th and 4 out: sn rdn and outpcd: styd on again last and kpt on run-in to cl on wl hld 3rd* **10/1**

6P6- **5** *1/2* **Golden Call (IRE)**[47] 2785 10-11-8 **125**.......... RichardJohnson 131+
(Jennie Candlish) *led 3rd: hrd pressed fr 8th to 14th: stl slt ld whn blnd bdly 4 out and sn hdd: outpcd 3 out: styd on again clsng stages to press for wl hld 4th* **20/1**

/2P- **6** *2* **Winds And Waves (IRE)**[63] 2451 8-11-3 **123**.......... JakeGreenall(3) 123
(Henry Daly) *in rr and rdn 7th: wl bhd fr 4 out: styd on fr 2 out to cl on wl hld 5th clsng stages* **7/1**[3]

522- **7** *26* **Dunlough Bay (IRE)**[20] 3279 8-11-8 **125**..........(p) DenisO'Regan 105
(Paul Webber) *in rr: hit 5th: hit 13th: hdwy and mstke 14th: blnd 4 out and sn wknd* **14/1**

042- **8** *3 1/4* **Tullyraine (IRE)**[63] 2451 10-11-7 **124**.......... SamTwiston-Davies 95
(Nigel Twiston-Davies) *led to 3rd: rdn and wknd after 13th* **9/2**[1]

3/1- **P** **Railway Dillon (IRE)**[33] 3059 9-11-9 **126**..........(bt) JasonMaguire
(Donald McCain) *pressed ldr 8th to 14th: wknd 4 out: t.o whn p.u bef 2 out* **7/1**[3]

1P0- **P** **Handy Andy (IRE)**[14] 3455 8-11-12 **129**..........(t) JoeTizzard
(Colin Tizzard) *hit 1st: in tch 8th: wknd 13th: t.o whn p.u bef 4 out* **8/1**

P1P- **P** **Duke Of Monmouth (IRE)**[41] 2901 7-11-0 **117**.......... DominicElsworth
(Charlie Mann) *in tch 8th: rdn and bhd 12th: t.o whn p.u bef 4 out* **16/1**

6m 7.21s (1.21) **Going Correction** +0.275s/f (Yiel) **11** Ran SP% **120.3**
Speed ratings: **108,102,101,101,100 100,91,90, ,**
CSF £95.33 CT £482.17 TOTE £5.90: £2.50, £5.20, £2.50; EX 153.20 Trifecta £747.20.
Owner R G Whitehead **Bred** R J Francome **Trained** Alcester, Warwicks

FOCUS
A staying handicap that looked very competitive on paper and it was run at a true gallop. Solid form, the easy winner rated back to the level of his chase best.

3718 EUROPEAN BREEDERS' FUND/THOROUGHBRED BREEDERS' ASSOCIATION MARES' NOVICES' CHASE (16 fncs) 2m 4f
3:00 (3:00) (Class 4) 5-Y-O+ **£3,573** (£1,049; £524)

Form RPR

221- **1** **Baby Shine (IRE)**[20] 3279 8-11-4 132.......... LeightonAspell 139+
(Lucy Wadham) *trckd ldr: chal 7th: led next but jnd tl asserted 3 out: sn wl clr: v easily* **4/5**[1]

1/1- **2** *24* **Definite Memories (IRE)**[48] 2769 7-11-4 128.......... DenisO'Regan 119+
(David Bridgwater) *led: jnd 7th: narrowly hdd next: styd chalng tl rdn and mstke 3 out: sn no ch w easy wnr but wl clr of 3rd: eased clsng stages* **11/4**[2]

650/ 3 *13* **Miss Milborne**^{309} 4723 8-10-12 0 .... BrendanPowell 90
(Jamie Snowden) *a in 3rd: outpcd 8th and tendency to jump rt and no ch after but kpt on as wl hld 2nd eased clsng stages* **3/1**^{3}

5m 13.48s (10.48) **Going Correction** +0.275s/f (Yiel) **3** Ran SP% **107.2**
Speed ratings: **90,80,75**
CSF £3.19 TOTE £1.80; EX 2.40 Trifecta £3.00.
Owner P A Philipps,T S Redman & Mrs L Redman **Bred** Kevin Francis O'Donnell **Trained** Newmarket, Suffolk

FOCUS
This select mares' novice chase looked a tight affair beforehand. The form is rated around the first two.

3719 BETFRED MOBILE "JUNIOR" STANDARD OPEN NATIONAL HUNT FLAT RACE 1m 4f 110y
3:35 (3:35) (Class 5) 4-Y-O **£2,053** (£598; £299)

Form RPR

1- **1** **Pitter Patter**^{69} 2318 4-10-7 0 .... ConorShoemark$^{(5)}$ 112+
(Fergal O'Brien) *sn led: drvn along over 2f out: hld on all out u.p fnl f* **4/1**^{3}

2- **2** *1 ½* **Diaktoros (IRE)**^{39} 2960 4-10-12 0 .... APMcCoy 108+
(Ben Haslam) *trckd ldrs: chsd wnr ins fnl 4f: styd on u.p fnl f but a hld* **6/4**^{1}

3 *5* **Palermo Don** 4-10-12 0 .... JasonMaguire 101+
(Donald McCain) *in tch: chsd ldrs in 3rd fr 3f out: no imp u.p fnl 2f* **11/4**^{2}

0- **4** *7* **Flute Bowl**^{28} 3167 4-10-5 0 .... JamieMoore 83
(Gary Moore) *in rr: rdn fr over 3f out: mod prog fnl 2f* **20/1**

3- **5** *3 ¼* **Morello Royale (IRE)**^{28} 3167 4-10-5 0 .... BrendanPowell 78
(Colin Tizzard) *pressed ldrs: rdn over 3f out: sn no ch but kpt on again clsng stages* **5/1**

6 *nse* **Manhattan Mead** 4-10-12 0 .... MarcGoldstein 85
(Michael Madgwick) *in tch: rdn to chse ldrs 5f out: no ch fnl 3f but kpt on clsng stages* **100/1**

0- **7** *¾* **Dan's Quest**^{46} 2830 4-10-12 0 .... CharliePoste 84
(Robin Dickin) *in rr: hdwy to chse ldrs 1/2-way: rdn and no ch over 3f out but kpt on again clsng stages* **33/1**

8 *22* **Onefortheboyz** 4-10-2 0 .... MikeyHamill$^{(10)}$ 51
(Sean Curran) *a in rr: t.o fnl 3f* **66/1**

9 *1* **Bel Ami Rich** 4-10-12 0 .... FelixDeGiles 49
(Barry Brennan) *chsd ldrs: wknd qckly over 3f out: t.o* **33/1**

10 *23* **Iskrabob** 4-10-12 0 .... ColinBolger 15
(Philip Hide) *a in rr: t.o* **40/1**

3m 4.8s (-1.00) **10** Ran SP% **118.9**
CSF £10.21 TOTE £3.70: £1.70, £1.30, £1.50; EX 11.20 Trifecta £44.20.
Owner Nicholas Jones **Bred** Coln Valley Stud **Trained** Coln St. Dennis, Gloucs

FOCUS
An interesting junior bumper. The winner looks a fair prospect.

3720 BETFRED "RACING'S BIGGEST SUPPORTER" OPEN HUNTERS' CHASE (17 fncs) 2m 6f 110y
4:10 (4:10) (Class 6) 6-Y-O+ **£987** (£303; £151)

Form RPR

32F- **1** **Foundry Square (IRE)**^{88} 1976 8-11-5 135 ....(p) MrWTelfer$^{(7)}$ 120+
(S Flook) *in tch: chsd ldrs fr 12th: wnt 2nd next: chal 2 out: sn led: drvn out run-in* **3/1**^{2}

2/0- **2** *7* **Seigneur Des Bois (FR)**^{10} 8-11-11 110 ....(p) MrTEllis$^{(5)}$ 116
(D Buckett) *chsd ldrs: rdn 13th: styng on whn mstke 3 out: kpt on again fr 2 out: styd on to take 2nd fnl 120yds but no ch w wnr* **33/1**

41P/ **3** *4 ½* **Offshore Account (IRE)**^{19} 14-11-13 119.........(bt^{1}) MrDominicSutton$^{(7)}$ 117
(Tracey L Bailey) *chsd ldrs: hit 2nd: chsd ldr 12th: led 13th: jnd 2 out: sn hdd wknd run-in and dropped to 3rd fnl 120yds* **12/1**

1P2/ **4** *8* **Minella Theatre (IRE)**^{266} 5500 11-11-5 108...................(tp) MrJoeHill$^{(7)}$ 101
(Alan Hill) *rdn 13th: a bhd* **12/1**

04P/ **F** **Ninetieth Minute (IRE)**^{19} 11-11-13 0 .... MrPGerety$^{(7)}$
(J J O'Shea) *in rr: hdwy 12th: clsng on ldrs and gng ok whn fell 13th* **5/1**^{3}

/1P- **P** **Charles Bruce (IRE)**^{45} 11-11-11 103 .... MrFTett$^{(5)}$
(A Campbell) *led: hit 3rd: hdd and hit next: styd chsng ldrs: hit 10th: wknd 12th: t.o whn p.u bef 4 out* **25/1**

11F/ **P** **Bold Addition (FR)**^{286} 5138 9-12-6 136 .... MrWBiddick
(Mrs F J Browne) *in rr: drvn and sme hdwy to cl on ldrs after 13th: nvr on terms and sn wknd: p.u bef 2 out* **5/6**^{1}

100- **P** **Himalayan Express**^{17} 10-11-13 117 .... MissPFuller$^{(7)}$
(Mrs David Plunkett) *led 4th: hdd13th: sn wknd: t.o whn p.u bef 2 out* **50/1**

6m 5.83s (18.83) **Going Correction** +0.275s/f (Yiel) **8** Ran SP% **120.4**
Speed ratings: **78,75,74,71, , ,**
CSF £79.42 TOTE £3.20: £1.10, £3.40, £2.60; EX 92.60 Trifecta £297.60.
Owner B J Mould **Bred** W H Neville **Trained** Leominster, Herefordshire

FOCUS
The opening hunter chase of the season. It was run at a searching early gallop. The second sets the level and the winner is decent in this company.
T/Plt: £6.80 to a £1 stake. Pool: £81823.80 - 8660.70 winning tickets T/Qpdt: £3.60 to a £1 stake. Pool: £5166.57 - 1045.76 winning tickets ST

3523 NEWCASTLE (L-H)
Wednesday, January 15

OFFICIAL GOING: Heavy (4.6)
Wind: Light, half behind Weather: Overcast, showers

3721 STP CONSTRUCTION "NATIONAL HUNT" NOVICES' HURDLE (8 hdls 1 omitted) 2m
12:40 (12:40) (Class 4) 4-Y-O+ **£3,249** (£954; £477; £238)

Form RPR

1- **1** **Stellar Notion (IRE)**^{33} 3063 6-11-5 0 .... PaddyBrennan 131+
(Tom George) *t.k.h: led after 2nd: maintained stdy pce: shkn up whn hrd pressed run-in: kpt on strly* **10/11**^{1}

P32- **2** *3 ½* **Another Mattie (IRE)**^{17} 3398 7-11-5 114...................(t) PeterBuchanan 117+
(N W Alexander) *hld up in tch: stdy hdwy 1/2-way: chsd wnr after 4 out: effrt bef 2 out: ev ch run-in: drifted lft: one pce* **6/4**^{2}

45- **3** *22* **River Bollin**^{39} 2960 4-10-7 0 .... DougieCostello 83
(Tim Easterby) *nt fluent on occasions: in tch: effrt 3 out: outpcd by first two fr next* **20/1**

34/- **4** *1* **Ortolan (GER)**^{1404} 4583 9-11-5 0 .... HenryBrooke 94
(Donald McCain) *t.k.h: cl up: led 1st to after next: pressed wnr to after 4 out: rdn and wknd fr next* **10/1**^{3}

P46- **5** *20* **Allforthelove**^{17} 3392 6-11-5 0 .... BrianHarding 74
(N W Alexander) *led to 1st: cl up: rdn and outpcd 4 out: struggling bef next: t.o* **50/1**

4m 21.5s (11.50) **Going Correction** +0.65s/f (Soft)
WFA 4 from 6yo+ 11lb **5** Ran SP% **108.2**
Speed ratings (Par 105): **97,95,84,83,73**
CSF £2.53 TOTE £1.40: £1.60, £1.10; EX 2.60 Trifecta £9.90.
Owner R S Brookhouse **Bred** Meadhill Stables **Trained** Slad, Gloucs

FOCUS
All bends and hurdles moved to fresh ground. Clearly not much depth to this novice, but still hard not be taken with the performance of the winner. He was value for further and looks a decent prospect.

3722 COMPLETE BUILDING SERVICES H'CAP CHASE (13 fncs) 2m 110y
1:10 (1:10) (Class 5) (0-100,98) 5-Y-O+ **£2,599** (£763; £381; £190)

Form RPR

4U2- **1** **Decent Lord (IRE)**^{9} 3564 10-10-6 78...................(v^{1}) SeanQuinlan 96+
(Jennie Candlish) *cl up: led 7th: mde rest: gng clr whn nt fluent 4 out: nt fluent 2 out: kpt on wl* **4/1**^{3}

502- **2** *12* **Mumgos Debut (IRE)**^{25} 3213 6-11-2 88 .... PeterBuchanan 92
(Lucinda Russell) *led to 7th: chsd wnr: effrt 4 out: outpcd between last 2* **9/4**^{2}

664- **3** *4 ½* **Turf Trivia**^{29} 3143 7-11-5 91...................(b) BarryKeniry 91
(George Moore) *prom: drvn and outpcd 4 out: no imp fr next* **11/1**

005- **4** *4 ½* **Strathaird (IRE)**^{9} 3564 10-9-11 72 oh25...................(p) JohnKington$^{(3)}$ 67
(Andrew Crook) *bhd and detached: outpcd 1/2-way: hdwy after 4 out: styd on fr next: nvr able to chal* **100/1**

205- **5** *25* **Prince Tam**^{17} 3395 10-11-0 89 .... JonathanEngland$^{(3)}$ 72
(Harriet Graham) *prom: hit 1st: drvn and outpcd after 5 out: btn whn hit 2 out* **7/1**

/51- **F** **Edmund (IRE)**^{25} 3213 7-11-12 98...................(t) BrianHughes
(Ann Hamilton) *in tch: mstke 4th: disputing ld and gng wl whn fell 7th* **7/4**^{1}

4m 29.1s (8.00) **Going Correction** +0.65s/f (Soft) **6** Ran SP% **109.0**
Speed ratings: **107,101,99,97,85**
CSF £13.07 TOTE £5.30: £3.00, £1.40; EX 14.40 Trifecta £60.10.
Owner Mrs Judith Ratcliff **Bred** Lar O'Toole **Trained** Basford Green, Staffs

FOCUS
A modest handicap. The winner improved to the level of his best hurdle form.

3723 PIN POINT RECRUITMENT H'CAP HURDLE (8 hdls 1 omitted) 2m
1:40 (1:40) (Class 5) (0-100,100) 4-Y-O+ **£2,599** (£763; £381; £190)

Form RPR

122- **1** **Blake Dean**^{26} 3188 6-10-7 88 .... CallumBewley$^{(7)}$ 98+
(Sue Smith) *pressed ldr: led whn hit 3 out: rdn whn pricked ears and idled bef last: hdd briefly towards fin: battled on gamely* **10/11**^{1}

205/ **2** *nse* **Scimon Templar (FR)**^{282} 5217 6-11-2 90 .... BrianHarding 97+
(Pauline Robson) *hld up in tch: stdy hdwy 4 out: chsng wnr whn hit 2 out: sn drvn: rallied last: led briefly towards fin: jst hld* **10/3**^{2}

065- **3** *7* **Rosquero (FR)**^{20} 3270 9-10-5 79...................(p) KennyJohnson 80
(Robert Johnson) *led: rdn and hdd bef 3 out: kpt on same pce after next* **22/1**

005/ **4** *34* **Jasper Massini (IRE)**^{316} 4582 9-11-12 100 .... RichieMcGrath 65
(Philip Kirby) *bhd: hdwy u.p after 4 out: no ch w first three fr next* **10/1**

0/6- **5** *9* **Copt Hill**^{246} 283 6-10-5 79 .... ^{1} DougieCostello 35
(Tracy Waggott) *cl up: pckd 2nd: rdn and wknd bef 3 out* **9/1**^{3}

235/ **6** *1 ½* **Carters Rest**^{228} 11-11-5 93...................(tp) AdrianLane 48
(Iain Jardine) *prom: rdn 4 out: wknd bef next* **25/1**

3/2- **7** *15* **High Fair**^{17} 3393 8-10-9 90 .... StephenMulqueen$^{(7)}$ 30
(Sandy Forster) *hld up: struggling bef 4 out: sn btn* **25/1**

000- **8** *¾* **Call Of Duty (IRE)**^{11} 3527 9-11-2 95 .... ColmMcCormack$^{(5)}$ 34
(Dianne Sayer) *nt fluent in rr: struggling 4 out: sn btn* **25/1**

0- **9** *13* **Milans Cross (IRE)**^{15} 3428 6-11-7 95 .... SeanQuinlan 21
(Jennie Candlish) *towards rr: struggling bef 4 out: sn btn* **20/1**

4m 17.2s (7.20) **Going Correction** +0.65s/f (Soft) **9** Ran SP% **115.2**
Speed ratings (Par 103): **108,107,104,87,82 82,74,74,67**
CSF £3.97 CT £33.04 TOTE £2.10: £1.40, £1.30, £6.70; EX 5.30 Trifecta £61.00.
Owner Widdop Wanderers **Bred** Lordship Stud **Trained** High Eldwick, W Yorks

FOCUS
A modest handicap which was run at a sound pace under the conditions. The idling winner was value for further and is rated back to his best.

3724 KETHOSE NAGI, MISS GALAXY NE H'CAP HURDLE (9 hdls 2 omitted) 2m 4f
2:10 (2:11) (Class 4) (0-120,120) 4-Y-O+ **£3,249** (£954; £477; £238)

Form RPR

U05- **1** **Big Society (IRE)**^{25} 3207 8-11-9 117 .... PaddyBrennan 129+
(Tom George) *nt fluent: cl up on outside: led 6th: drew clr fr 3 out: easily* **7/2**^{1}

P00- **2** *8* **Rock Relief (IRE)**^{31} 3108 8-11-12 120 .... RyanMania 118+
(Chris Grant) *prom: nt fluent and outpcd 4 out: rallied next: wnt 2nd and plugged on fr last: no ch w easy wnr* **8/1**

/26- **3** *½* **Walser (IRE)**^{20} 3273 7-11-6 114...................(b) BrianHughes 108
(John Wade) *chsd ldrs: drvn after 4 out: one pce bef 2 out* **14/1**

133- **4** *20* **Tikkandemickey (IRE)**^{13} 3499 8-11-4 119 .... CallumBewley$^{(7)}$ 93
(Raymond Shiels) *t.k.h: in tch: hdwy to chal 6th: rdn and outpcd after next: sn n.d* **11/1**

5F3- **5** *1 ½* **Just Cameron**^{31} 3110 7-11-5 113 .... RichieMcGrath 89
(Philip Kirby) *t.k.h: prom: hdwy to chse wnr 4 out: rdn bef next: outpcd fr 2 out: lost 2nd whn hit last* **13/2**^{3}

P53- **6** *32* **Basford Bob (IRE)**^{16} 3419 9-10-12 106 .... SeanQuinlan 47
(Jennie Candlish) *hld up: smooth hdwy on outside 6th: rdn and wknd bef 3 out: t.o* **5/1**^{2}

13P- **P** **Mrs Eff**^{29} 3145 8-10-13 110...................(t) KyleJames$^{(3)}$
(Philip Kirby) *nt fluent in rr: struggling bef 4 out: t.o whn p.u next* **22/1**

015- **P** **Sparkling Hand**^{17} 3391 8-10-7 101...................(p) HenryBrooke
(Peter Atkinson) *cl up to 4 out: sn rdn and wknd: t.o whn p.u next* **17/2**

553/ **P** **Baileys Concerto (IRE)**^{278} 5266 8-10-11 110....... ColmMcCormack$^{(5)}$
(Dianne Sayer) *hld up: struggling bef 4 out: t.o whn p.u next* **25/1**

0P4- **P** **Northern Oscar (IRE)**^{20} 3269 6-10-11 105 .... PeterBuchanan
(Tim Walford) *hld up in midfield: struggling 6th: t.o whn p.u 3 out* **7/1**

1/P- **P** **Picks Milan (IRE)**^{230} 556 8-10-13 112 .... JoeColliver$^{(5)}$
(Philip Kirby) *led to 6th: rdn and wknd after next: t.o whn p.u 3 out* **20/1**

5m 33.0s (11.90) **Going Correction** +0.65s/f (Soft) **11** Ran SP% **114.3**
Speed ratings (Par 105): **102,98,98,90,90 77, , , ,**
CSF £29.85 CT £346.25 TOTE £5.00: £2.00, £3.60, £2.50; EX 38.60 Trifecta £387.20.
Owner Simon Clarke & David Thorpe **Bred** Mrs Mary O'Connor **Trained** Slad, Gloucs

FOCUS
Quite a few patently failed to cope with conditions here, the field well strung out a long way from home. Arguably a personal best from the winner.

3725 CARRAWAY FINANCE H'CAP CHASE (19 fncs) 3m
2:45 (2:49) (Class 3) (0-140,132) 5-Y-O+ **£6,498** (£1,908; £954; £477)

Form RPR
- 111- **1** **Tutchec (FR)**[45] 2841 7-11-3 **123** BrianHarding 135+
  (Nicky Richards) *cl up: mstke 10th: chsd ldr gng wl bef 4 out: nt fluent next: lft in ld 2 out: gng clr whn nt fluent and stmbld bdly last: rcvrd and stydon wl* **4/1**[3]
- 2/P- **2** *5* **Fentara**[46] 2805 9-11-3 **123** (tp) PeterBuchanan 130+
  (Tim Walford) *cl up: led after 6 out: nt fluent 3 out: mstke and hdd next: one pce fr last* **5/1**
- 233- **3** *17* **Imperial Vic (IRE)**[38] 2971 9-11-12 **132** RyanMania 118
  (Michael Smith) *nt fluent on occasions: mde most to after 6 out: outpcd by first two fr 4 out* **11/10**[1]
- 532- **4** *12* **Rolecarr (IRE)**[11] 3526 11-10-12 **125** GrahamWatters[(7)] 99
  (Ann Hamilton) *chsd ldrs tl rdn and wknd bef 4 out* **3/1**[2]

6m 32.9s (10.40) **Going Correction** +0.65s/f (Soft) **4** Ran SP% **109.3**
Speed ratings: **108,106,100,96**
CSF £19.94 TOTE £2.90; EX 17.10 Trifecta £21.30.
Owner Club 4 Racing **Bred** William Ewart **Trained** Greystoke, Cumbria

FOCUS
A dramatic conclusion to this staying handicap. Another step forward from the winner.

3726 NORTH SEA LOGISTICS H'CAP HURDLE (11 hdls 2 omitted) 3m
3:20 (3:20) (Class 4) (0-115,115) 4-Y-O+ **£3,249** (£954; £477; £238)

Form RPR
- 505- **1** **Wolf Shield (IRE)**[32] 3085 7-11-7 **110** BarryKeniry 116
  (George Moore) *disp ld: wnt on 4 out: jnd next: hdd 2 out: rallied and regained ld last 75yds: styd on wl* **3/1**[2]
- 23B- **2** *1 ¼* **Romany Ryme**[17] 3396 8-11-0 **110** JonathonBewley[(7)] 116
  (George Bewley) *in tch: outpcd bef 4 out: rallied bef next: led and hit 2 out: sn rdn: hdd last 75yds: one pce* **4/1**[3]
- F46- **3** *16* **Micro Mission (IRE)**[67] 2357 8-11-5 **115** DiarmuidO'Regan[(7)] 105
  (Chris Grant) *chsd ldrs: drvn and outpcd 4 out: rallied bef 2 out: kpt on: no ch w first two* **10/1**
- 251- **4** *4 ½* **Simarthur**[35] 3018 7-11-12 **115** (v) PeterBuchanan 104
  (Lucinda Russell) *hld up in tch: stdy hdwy 1/2-way: effrt and ch 3 out: wknd fr next* **5/2**[1]
- 523- **5** *14* **Magic Present**[25] 3208 7-11-7 **110** (b) BrianHughes 85
  (Malcolm Jefferson) *t.k.h: nt fluent on occasions: slt ld to 4 out: wknd appr next* **8/1**
- 4/1- **6** *32* **Snapping Turtle (IRE)**[34] 3040 9-10-4 **98** CallumWhillans[(5)] 37
  (Donald Whillans) *hld up: stdy hdwy 1/2-way: struggling after 4 out: t.o* **5/1**
- 2/0- **P** **Sphinx (FR)**[16] 3413 16-10-13 **105** (b) TonyKelly[(3)]
  (Edwin Tuer) *t.k.h: chsd ldrs: lost pl 4th: pushed along after next: rallied: wknd after 4 out: t.o whn p.u bef last* **33/1**

6m 31.4s (17.40) **Going Correction** +0.65s/f (Soft) **7** Ran SP% **113.4**
Speed ratings (Par 105): **97,96,91,89,85 74,**
CSF £15.37 CT £103.40 TOTE £4.00: £2.20, £2.30; EX 18.40 Trifecta £107.30.
Owner Mrs J M Gray **Bred** Terence Conroy **Trained** Middleham Moor, N Yorks

FOCUS
The leading pair came a long way clear in another race where plenty failed to cope with conditions. The winner is rated back to form.

3727 SWARLANDFENCE.CO.UK MARES' MAIDEN OPEN NATIONAL HUNT FLAT RACE 2m
3:55 (3:55) (Class 6) 4-6-Y-O **£1,559** (£457; £228; £114)

Form RPR
- **1** **Just For Pleasure (IRE)** 4-9-13 0 GrantCockburn[(7)] 91+
  (Lucinda Russell) *hld up: stdy hdwy 1/2-way: drvn and outpcd 4f out: rallied 2f out: led ins fnl f: styd on wl* **11/2**[3]
- 6- **2** *1 ¾* **Nearly May**[195] 885 6-10-8 0 RyanNichol[(10)] 98
  (Donald Whillans) *pressed ldr: rdn over 3f out: rallied to ld over 2f out: hdd ins fnl f: kpt on same pce towards fin* **50/1**
- 4- **3** *1 ¼* **Lilly's Legend**[25] 3214 4-10-6 0 DougieCostello 85
  (Tim Walford) *trckd ldrs: rdn over 3f out: rallied 2f out: edgd lft: kpt on same pce ins fnl f* **3/1**[2]
- 54- **4** *1 ¼* **Sheilas Lady**[31] 3112 6-11-1 0 JohnKington[(3)] 96
  (Andrew Crook) *led: rdn and hdd over 2f out: kpt on same pce over 1f out* **20/1**
- **5** *11* **Lochnell (IRE)** 5-10-11 0 NathanMoscrop[(7)] 85
  (Brian Ellison) *hld up: hdwy to chse ldrs over 6f out: rdn and wknd fr 2f out* **16/1**
- 5- **6** *5* **Presidential Lady (IRE)**[11] 3529 5-11-4 0 PeterBuchanan 80
  (Chris Grant) *in tch: drvn and outpcd over 3f out: n.d after* **20/1**
- 0- **7** *15* **Ceilidh (IRE)**[54] 2660 6-11-4 0 BrianHarding 70
  (N W Alexander) *t.k.h: hld up: pushed along over 3f out: wknd over 2f out* **50/1**
- 2- **8** *12* **Shanendou (IRE)**[49] 2752 5-11-4 0 PaddyBrennan 62
  (Tom George) *racd wd: hld up: smooth hdwy and cl up over 3f out: rdn and wknd qckly over 1f out: eased* **5/6**[1]
- **9** *3 ¾* **Thatlldoforus** 6-11-4 0 BrianHughes 49
  (Alistair Whillans) *hld up in tch: drvn and outpcd 1/2-way: sn struggling: nvr on terms* **28/1**

4m 25.4s (21.00) **Going Correction** +0.65s/f (Soft)
WFA 4 from 5yo 11lb 5 from 6yo 3lb **9** Ran SP% **117.7**
Speed ratings: **73,72,71,70,65 62,55,49,47**
CSF £242.17 TOTE £8.50: £1.40, £7.90, £1.50; EX 253.50 Trifecta £2320.50 Part won..
Owner Let's Live Racing **Bred** R Bryan **Trained** Arlary, Perth & Kinross

FOCUS
Probably not a strong bumper, particularly with the favourite well below form. The third, fourth and sixth set the level.
T/Plt: £108.90 to a £1 stake. Pool: £68794.35 - 460.75 winning tickets T/Qpdt: £54.10 to a £1 stake. Pool: £5575.16 - 76.20 winning tickets RY

[3154] LUDLOW (R-H)
Thursday, January 16

OFFICIAL GOING: Heavy (soft in places; 6.1)
Wind: light across Weather: cloudy

3728 LUDLOW FOR FUNCTIONS NOVICES' HURDLE (8 hdls 1 omitted) 2m
1:10 (1:10) (Class 4) 4-Y-O+ **£3,898** (£1,144; £572; £286)

Form RPR
- 1- **1** **Mountain King**[39] 2981 5-11-4 0 RichardJohnson 130+
  (Philip Hobbs) *a.p: chsd ldr appr 5th: led and edgd rt bef 3 out: clr next: comf* **11/8**[1]
- 305- **2** *12* **Muckle Roe (IRE)**[44] 2876 5-10-11 0 RyanHatch[(7)] 114
  (Nigel Twiston-Davies) *hld up: hdwy appr 3 out: sn rdn: wnt 2nd flat: no ch w wnr* **12/1**
- 52- **3** *3 ¼* **Red Seventy**[42] 2906 5-10-11 0 (p) TomBellamy[(7)] 113
  (David Pipe) *plld hrd: led 2nd: rdn and hdd whn mstke 3 out: styd on same pce fr next* **7/2**[2]
- 644- **4** *17* **Gallic Warrior (FR)**[53] 2695 7-11-4 113 AlainCawley 95
  (Fergal O'Brien) *led and nt fluent 1st: hdd next: chsd ldr to appr 5th: rdn and wknd 3 out* **9/1**
- **5** *1* **Huff And Puff**[470] 7-11-4 0 SamThomas 93
  (Venetia Williams) *mid-div: hdwy 5th: wknd 3 out* **8/1**
- /50- **6** *1 ¾* **Steel Summit (IRE)**[18] 3388 5-10-13 0 AnthonyFreeman[(5)] 91
  (David Dennis) *prom: rdn after 5th: wknd appr 3 out* **80/1**
- /00- **7** *12* **Secure Investment**[39] 2978 6-11-4 0 LeightonAspell 79
  (Oliver Sherwood) *hld up: nvr nrr* **100/1**
- **8** *10* **King's Warrior (FR)**[82] 7-11-4 0 PaddyBrennan 72
  (Tom George) *hld up: hdwy appr 3 out: sn rdn and wknd* **7/1**[3]
- 4- **9** *4* **Home For Tea**[29] 3160 5-11-4 0 FelixDeGiles 65
  (Tom Symonds) *prom tl rdn and wknd after 5th: in rr whn blnd 2 out* **33/1**
- 465- **10** *1 ½* **Iouascore (IRE)**[34] 3063 7-10-11 0 MissLBrooke[(7)] 64
  (Lady Susan Brooke) *mid-div: mstke 2nd: nt fluent 4th: bhd fr next* **200/1**
- 6- **11** *6* **Early Bonnet (IRE)**[16] 3427 6-10-6 0 ConorShoemark[(5)] 51
  (Kim Bailey) *hld up: hdwy after 5th: sn wknd* **66/1**
- P/0- **12** *7* **Perfect Shot (IRE)**[8] 3598 8-10-11 0 MrJMahot[(7)] 51
  (Sarah-Jayne Davies) *hld up: a in rr: bhd fr 5th* **150/1**
- 0/0- **13** *4* **Femme D'Espere**[44] 2876 8-10-8 0 RobertDunne[(3)] 40
  (Trevor Wall) *a in rr: bhd fr 5th* **150/1**

3m 56.2s (6.70) **Going Correction** +0.70s/f (Soft) **13** Ran SP% **114.1**
Speed ratings (Par 105): **111,105,103,94,94 93,87,82,80,79 76,73,71**
CSF £19.33 TOTE £2.10: £1.20, £3.30, £1.90; EX 17.60 Trifecta £103.70.
Owner Mrs Diana L Whateley **Bred** R D Chugg And J R H Fowler **Trained** Withycombe, Somerset

FOCUS
All bends and hurdles moved to fresh ground. False wings removed from fences leaving 6yds of fresh ground. Hurdle course on inside line throughout. The ground was pretty testing and they were soon strung out in the opener. The winner looks a fair recruit.

3729 SIDNEY PHILLIPS NOVICES' H'CAP CHASE (16 fncs 1 omitted) 2m 4f
1:40 (1:40) (Class 4) (0-110,110) 5-Y-O+ **£4,548** (£1,335; £667; £333)

Form RPR
- /50- **1** **Buywise (IRE)**[31] 3128 7-11-4 **102** AdamWedge 135+
  (Evan Williams) *mid-div: hdwy 5th: led and blnd 4 out: clr fr 2 out: comf* **11/2**[2]
- /04- **2** *7* **Take The Mick**[43] 2891 7-10-6 **95** CallumWhillans[(5)] 116
  (Venetia Williams) *chsd ldrs: rdn and ev ch appr 4 out: styd on same pce fr 2 out* **7/1**[3]
- P14- **3** *17* **Bincombe**[28] 3172 6-11-5 **103** RichardJohnson 114
  (Philip Hobbs) *chsd ldrs: led appr 9th: j.lft next and 12th: rdn and hdd 4 out: wkng whn mstke 2 out* **2/1**[1]
- 103- **4** *26* **Carhue Princess (IRE)**[42] 2896 8-10-6 **90** FelixDeGiles 67
  (Tom Symonds) *led to 2nd: chsd ldr tl pushed along appr 9th: wknd 12th* **18/1**
- 000- **5** *shd* **Dropzone (USA)**[143] 1391 5-10-12 **100** CharliePoste 73
  (Richard Lee) *a in rr: drvn along after 8th: lost tch fr 12th* **16/1**
- 1/5- **6** *11* **Supreme Bob (IRE)**[57] 2598 8-11-12 **110** DaveCrosse 79
  (Lucy Jones) *mid-div: hdwy appr 9th: wknd after 12th* **11/1**
- /33- **P** **Marju King (IRE)**[102] 1783 8-11-2 **103** (p) JoshuaMoore[(3)]
  (Phil Middleton) *hld up: drvn along 8th: bhd fr next: p.u bef 12th* **9/1**
- 512- **P** **Red Rock (FR)**[50] 2741 9-11-5 **103** (p) LeightonAspell
  (Emma Lavelle) *led 2nd: blnd 6th: hdd appr 9th: wkng whn blnd next: sn p.u* **8/1**
- /03- **F** **Crystal Swing**[49] 2771 7-11-3 **108** DanielHiskett[(7)]
  (Richard Phillips) *fell 1st* **25/1**
- /P0- **P** **Flora Lea**[49] 2770 7-10-1 **88** RobertDunne[(3)]
  (Andrew Price) *mstke 1st: a in rr: bhd whn p.u bef 9th* **66/1**
- /3P- **P** **Still Believing (IRE)**[31] 3129 6-11-5 **110** ConorRing[(7)]
  (Evan Williams) *a in rr: pushed along 9th: wknd 12th: bhd whn mstke 4 out: j. slowly next: sn p.u* **14/1**

5m 16.4s (12.00) **Going Correction** +0.70s/f (Soft)
WFA 5 from 6yo+ 4lb **11** Ran SP% **113.8**
Speed ratings: **104,101,94,84,83 79, , , ,**
CSF £42.88 CT £101.83 TOTE £6.00: £3.00, £2.60, £1.90; EX 59.60 Trifecta £367.10.
Owner T Hywel Jones **Bred** Mrs A Stack **Trained** Llancarfan, Vale Of Glamorgan

FOCUS
This novice handicap was run at a fair lick and the first three had it between them a good way from the finish. The easy winner should win more races over fences.

3730 HIS ROYAL HIGHNESS THE PRINCE OF WALES CHALLENGE TROPHY (AN AMATEUR RIDERS' H'CAP CHASE) (17 fncs 2 omitted) 3m
2:10 (2:11) (Class 3) (0-125,122) 5-Y-**£9**,**105** (£2,844; £1,422; £711; £355)

Form RPR
- 44P- **1** **Rhum (FR)**[41] 2923 9-11-0 **115** (vt) MrHAABannister[(5)] 123+
  (Nigel Twiston-Davies) *prom: lost pl 4th: hdwy 12th: rdn appr 4 out: styd on to ld nr fin* **10/1**[3]
- UF5- **2** *½* **Shalimar Fromentro (FR)**[34] 3068 8-11-7 **122** (p) MissEKelly[(5)] 131+
  (Nick Williams) *prom: rdn appr 4 out: led flat: hung lft, idled and hdd towards fin* **7/2**[1]
- 224- **3** *1* **Rydalis (FR)**[21] 3293 9-11-5 **118** MrJHamilton[(3)] 126+
  (Venetia Williams) *led to appr 2nd: led 4th: hdd after 9th: led again 12th: clr whn blnd 2 out: sn rdn and wnt lft: hdd flat* **7/2**[1]
- P41- **4** *2* **Le Grand Chene (FR)**[21] 3281 8-9-11 **96** (t) MrFMitchell[(3)] 98
  (Sophie Leech) *hld up: hdwy 5th: rdn appr 4 out: styd on* **20/1**

/00- **5** 3/4 **Cool Bob (IRE)**[27] 3188 11-9-7 **96** oh5....................(t) MrStanSheppard(7) 97
(Matt Sheppard) *hld up: hdwy appr 4 out: kpt on* **50/1**

/24- **6** 5 **Taffy Thomas**[68] 2370 10-10-1 **104**....................(t) MrSPBowen(7) 101
(Peter Bowen) *hld up: hdwy 12th: rdn appr 4 out: styd on same pce fr next* **10/1**[3]

2R1- **7** 5 **Upton Mead (IRE)**[11] 3555 7-10-4 **107** 7ex....................(b) MrPJohn(7) 99
(Kevin Tork) *chsd ldr: led appr 2nd: hdd 4th: led again after 9th: hdd 12th: rdn and wknd 4 out* **14/1**

003- **8** 6 **Mauricetheathlete (IRE)**[44] 2867 11-10-9 **112** ow2.......... MrJSKnox(7) 97
(Martin Keighley) *mid-div: reminders 3rd: wknd 4 out* **25/1**

31P- **9** 6 **Lava Lamp (GER)**[63] 2468 7-11-4 **119**.................................... MrFTett(5) 98
(Evan Williams) *hld up: pushed along 10th: n.d* **20/1**

12P/ **10** 25 **Victory Gunner (IRE)**[268] 5474 16-10-13 **114**................ MissLBrooke(5) 68
(Richard Lee) *a in rr: pushed along 8th: bhd fr 11th* **25/1**

4P6- **P** **Epee Celeste (FR)**[14] 3502 8-9-9 **96** oh1..................(b) MissAliceMills(5)
(Michael Chapman) *chsd ldrs: lost pl appr 6th: mstke 8th: sn wknd: bhd whn p.u bef 12th* **25/1**

P62- **U** **Five Star Wilsham (IRE)**[90] 1959 10-11-0 **117**............... MissVWade(7)
(Jeremy Scott) *hld up: hdwy 5th: ev ch whn blnd and uns rdr 4 out* **10/1**[3]

/FP- **P** **Big News**[29] 3158 8-11-6 **116**..(t) MrWBiddick
(Richard Lee) *prom: pushed along 9th: wknd 12th: sn p.u* **5/1**[2]

6m 32.6s (24.30) **Going Correction** +0.70s/f (Soft) **13** Ran SP% **118.1**
Speed ratings: **87,86,86,85,85 83,82,80,78,69 , ,**
CSF £41.60 CT £151.00 TOTE £12.60: £3.50, £2.10, £2.00; EX 64.10 Trifecta £761.50.
Owner N A Twiston-Davies **Bred** Thierry Cypres & Jean-Francois Naudin **Trained** Naunton, Gloucs
■ Stewards' Enquiry : Mr J S Knox two-day ban: weighed-in 2lb heavy (Jan 30,Feb 2)

FOCUS
A competitive amateurs' handicap run at a solid pace. It was a race with a bizarre finish and the form is of limited value. The fortunate winner is on a decent mark.

3731 LUDLOW RACECOURSE BOOKMAKERS MARES' H'CAP HURDLE (10 hdls 2 omitted) 3m
2:40 (2:40) (Class 3) (0-125,122) 4-Y-0+ **£6,498** (£1,908; £954; £477)

Form RPR

326- **1** **Top Totti**[40] 2948 6-11-4 **114**.. RichardJohnson 133+
(Henry Daly) *a.p: chsd ldr after 6th: led appr 3 out: clr fr next: easily* **9/4**[1]

113- **2** 19 **Midnight Belle**[32] 3117 7-11-9 **119**....................................... FelixDeGiles 119
(Tom Symonds) *hld up: hdwy 7th: chsd wnr appr 3 out: styng on same pce whn mstke next* **3/1**[2]

234/ **3** 11 **Animation (IRE)**[302] 4876 10-9-11 **100**..............(v) MissJodieHughes(7) 84
(Lucy Jones) *led: racd keenly: rdn: hdd & wknd appr 3 out: bhd whn mstke last* **16/1**

511/ **4** 2 1/2 **Too Generous**[367] 3660 6-11-5 **122**.................................... MikeyEnnis(7) 104
(David Pipe) *chsd ldr tl after 6th: rdn and wknd appr 3 out* **11/2**[3]

F11- **5** 24 **Mini Muck**[39] 2980 8-11-0 **117**... RyanHatch(7) 75
(Nigel Twiston-Davies) *trckd ldrs: rdn after 7th: wknd bef next: bhd whn hit last* **3/1**[2]

463- **P** **Russie With Love**[63] 2477 8-10-12 **108**.................................... JamesDavies
(Chris Down) *hld up: pushed along 6th: stmbld and wknd next: bhd whn p.u bef 3 out* **12/1**

6m 14.0s (21.70) **Going Correction** +0.70s/f (Soft) **6** Ran SP% **109.7**
Speed ratings (Par 107): **91,84,81,80,72**
CSF £9.17 TOTE £2.30: £1.10, £2.20; EX 11.60 Trifecta £89.60.
Owner Hamer, Hawkes & Hellin **Bred** E R Hanbury **Trained** Stanton Lacy, Shropshire

FOCUS
A fair handicap for mares run at a steady pace. The form could prove at least 5lb out either way.

3732 CLIVE PAVILION NOVICES' LIMITED H'CAP CHASE (12 fncs 1 omitted) 2m
3:10 (3:10) (Class 3) (0-140,135) 5-Y-0+ **£7,876** (£2,524; £1,402)

Form RPR

312- **1** **Lord Of House (GER)**[16] 3429 6-11-7 **135**...........................(t) MarkGrant 140
(Charlie Mann) *trckd ldr: mstkes 4th and 7th: led 2 out: hung lft flat: styd on u.p* **7/2**[3]

23F- **2** nk **Sir Valentino (FR)**[19] 3354 5-10-7 **124** oh2....................... PaddyBrennan 126+
(Tom George) *trckd ldrs: ev ch fr 2 out: hmpd flat: kpt on* **11/2**

012- **3** 15 **Rio De Sivola (FR)**[27] 3183 5-10-8 **125**............................ RichardJohnson 111
(Nick Williams) *led: pushed along appr 4 out: hdd 2 out: sn wknd* **6/4**[1]

0/4- **R** **Duaiseoir (IRE)**[52] 2719 8-10-8 **122**.................................... SamThomas
(Venetia Williams) *hld up: pushed along after 4th: bhd fr 6th: j. slowly 2 out: ref last* **11/1**

314- **F** **Zarzal (IRE)**[31] 3132 6-11-2 **130**... AdamWedge
(Evan Williams) *hld up: hdwy 8th: 2 1/2 l 4th and rdn whn fell 3 out* **3/1**[2]

4m 15.3s (16.80) **Going Correction** +0.70s/f (Soft)
WFA 5 from 6yo+ 3lb **5** Ran SP% **110.9**
Speed ratings: **86,85,78, ,**
CSF £20.98 TOTE £3.30: £1.40, £2.30; EX 20.00 Trifecta £39.10.
Owner Good Lord Partnership **Bred** R Venn Bloodstock Ltd **Trained** Upper Lambourn, Berks
■ Stewards' Enquiry : Mark Grant one-day ban: careless riding (Jan 30)

FOCUS
A fair race of its type, run at a good gallop. A small pb from the winner and the second should win over fences.

3733 LUDLOW MARES' MAIDEN HURDLE (10 hdls 1 omitted) 2m 5f
3:40 (3:40) (Class 4) 4-Y-0+ **£3,898** (£1,144; £572; £286)

Form RPR

055- **1** **Land Of Vic**[18] 3388 6-11-4 0.. DonalDevereux 117+
(Peter Bowen) *chsd ldr: led appr 3 out: mstke last: rdn out* **7/2**[2]

523- **2** 4 1/2 **Princess Caetani (IRE)**[37] 3010 5-11-4 112.................. RichardJohnson 113
(David Dennis) *hld up: hdwy 5th: chsd wnr appr 3 out: ev ch fr next tl hit last: no ex flat* **7/4**[1]

3 44 **Abundantly**[88] 5-11-4 0.. SamThomas 73+
(Venetia Williams) *prom: led appr 6th: rdn after next: hdd & wknd appr 3 out: nt fluent last* **8/1**

4 17 **Painted Gold**[243] 8-10-11 0.. MrJMahot(7) 50
(Sarah-Jayne Davies) *prom: drvn along 6th: wknd after next* **50/1**

00P- **5** hd **Amber Flush**[32] 3115 5-11-4 96...................................... FelixDeGiles 50
(Tom Symonds) *hld up: a in rr: bhd fr 7th* **100/1**

/3- **6** 6 **Bilidn**[42] 2907 6-11-4 0... MarkGrant 44
(Ben De Haan) *hld up: racd keenly: hdwy 6th: wknd bef 3 out* **7/2**[2]

0/0- **7** 22 **Goldie Horn**[58] 715 6-10-11 0....................................(t) RyanHatch(7) 22
(Nigel Twiston-Davies) *hld up: hdwy 7th: rdn and wknd bef next* **50/1**

00- **8** 95 **Materiana (IRE)**[52] 2724 6-11-1 0.................................. RobertDunne(3)
(Andrew Hollinshead) *mstke 1st: a in rr: pushed along after 5th: sn lost tch* **200/1**

U00- **P** **Party Girls (FR)**[28] 3168 6-10-11 0..................................(t) MikeyEnnis(7)
(David Pipe) *plld hrd and prom: lost pl 5th: sn bhd: p.u bef next* **100/1**

202- **P** **Forgivienne**[29] 3159 7-11-4 108... AdamWedge
(Evan Williams) *led: hdd & wknd appr 6th: bhd p.u bef next* **5/1**[3]

0/6- **P** **Aroseforoscar**[28] 3168 5-11-4 0... JamesDavies
(Chris Down) *chsd ldrs: pushed along and lost pl 5th: hdwy next: wknd after 7th: p.u bef 3 out* **50/1**

5m 30.1s (15.30) **Going Correction** +0.70s/f (Soft) **11** Ran SP% **116.9**
Speed ratings (Par 105): **98,96,79,73,72 70,62,26, ,**
CSF £10.31 TOTE £4.00: £1.60, £1.50, £3.40; EX 18.20 Trifecta £81.00.
Owner W Hill **Bred** Stewart Pike **Trained** Little Newcastle, Pembrokes

FOCUS
An ordinary event for mares in which the first two came a long way clear. The form is rated around the second to her mark.

3734 LUDLOW INTERMEDIATE NATIONAL HUNT FLAT RACE (CONDITIONAL JOCKEYS' AND AMATEUR RIDERS' RACE) 2m
4:10 (4:10) (Class 5) 4-6-Y-O **£2,599** (£763; £381; £190)

Form RPR

4- **1** **Buckhorn Timothy**[212] 760 5-10-11 0.................................. MrMLegg(7) 112+
(Colin Tizzard) *mainly trckd ldr tl led over 3f out: styd on wl: drew clr fnl f* **9/1**

3- **2** 7 **Onenightinvienna (IRE)**[37] 3016 5-11-1 0........................ JamesBest(3) 105
(Philip Hobbs) *in tch: clsd 6f out: drvn to chse wnr 2f out: sn no imp* **5/2**[2]

13- **3** 6 **Henllan Harri (IRE)**[40] 2946 6-11-4 0............................... MrSPBowen(7) 106
(Peter Bowen) *in tch: rdn over 4f out: styd on same pce fnl 3f* **9/4**[1]

4 7 **Laraghcon Boy (IRE)**[53] 5-10-11 0.................................... RyanHatch(7) 92
(Tony Carroll) *chsd ldrs: rdn 5f out: one pce fnl 3f* **16/1**

0- **5** 1/2 **Foxtail Hill (IRE)**[48] 2788 5-10-13 0............................ PatrickCorbett(5) 92
(Rebecca Curtis) *led tl hung rt and hdd over 3f out: rdn and grad wknd* **16/1**

6 33 **Primo Milano** 5-10-11 0.. ConorRing(7) 59
(Evan Williams) *in tch in rr: n.m.r bnd after 4f: sn pushed along: lost tch 7f out: t.o* **8/1**

7 1 **Chain Of Beacons** 5-10-11 0.. CharlieDeutsch(7) 58
(Charlie Longsdon) *chsd ldrs tl wknd 4f out: t.o* **13/2**[3]

2- **8** 1 1/4 **Thatchers Gold (IRE)**[224] 647 6-10-11 0................. MrAlexEdwards(7) 56
(Dave Roberts) *mid-div: pushed along after 6f: sn lost tch: t.o* **16/1**

0/ **9** 32 **Sammy Blade**[642] 5415 6-10-11 0..................................... MissAEStirling(7) 24
(Alan Phillips) *mid-div tl outpcd by ldrs 6f out: nudged along after and sn lost tch: t.o* **100/1**

10 88 **Randall** 6-10-13 0... NicodeBoinville(5)
(Martin Bosley) *in tch towards rr: rdn after 7f: sn lost tch: wl t.o* **25/1**

3m 53.9s (10.00) **Going Correction** +0.70s/f (Soft)
WFA 5 from 6yo 3lb **10** Ran SP% **116.3**
Speed ratings: **103,99,96,93,92 76,75,75,59,15**
CSF £31.67 TOTE £10.20: £2.20, £1.60, £1.10; EX 31.00 Trifecta £78.40.
Owner The Buckhorn Racing Team **Bred** M M Hooker **Trained** Milborne Port, Dorset

FOCUS
A pretty weak bumper, and not form to treat very positively. A step up from the winner.
T/Plt: £29.00 to a £1 stake. Pool of £71,773.75 - 1805.40 winning units. T/Qpdt: £17.40 to a £1 stake. Pool of £4,031.07 - 170.90 winning units. CR

3264 MARKET RASEN (R-H)
Thursday, January 16

OFFICIAL GOING: Heavy (soft in places; 5.2)
Wind: light, half behind Weather: dry and bright

3735 CALVERTS CARPETS YORK NOVICES' HURDLE (10 hdls) 2m 3f
1:30 (1:30) (Class 4) 4-Y-0+ **£3,249** (£954; £477; £238)

Form RPR

214/ **1** **Enchanted Garden**[206] 4547 6-11-5 0................................ BrianHughes 121+
(Malcolm Jefferson) *hld up in tch: hdwy after 3rd: clr in ldng quintet 6th: chsd clr ldng pair sn after 3 out: steadily clsd: lft 3 l 2nd and hmpd next: pressing ldr whn j.rt and mstke last: sn led: styd on: rdn out* **8/1**

/32- **2** 4 1/2 **Fergal Mael Duin**[16] 3427 6-11-5 113............................. SeanQuinlan 117
(David Bridgwater) *w ldr: clr fr after 5th: rdn to ld whn lft 3 l clr 2 out: sn drvn and 1 l ahd whn mstke last: sn hdd: swtchd lft flat: no ex and wknd towards fin* **9/4**[1]

3 19 **Lyric Street (IRE)**[100] 6-11-5 0.. JasonMaguire 100
(Donald McCain) *chsd ldng pair: rdn and btn sn after 3 out: wl hld whn lft 3rd next* **9/1**

3/2- **4** 15 **Arthur's Oak**[14] 3501 6-11-5 0.. AidanColeman 83
(Venetia Williams) *chsd ldrs: clr in ldng quintet 6th: wknd after 3 out: wl btn whn lft 4th next: t.o* **8/1**

54- **5** 9 **Spookydooky (IRE)**[78] 2156 6-11-5 0...................................(t) APMcCoy 74
(Jonjo O'Neill) *in tch in midfield on outer: lost tch after 6th: t.o but plugged on past btn horses after 3 out: blnd last* **9/2**[3]

040- **6** 1/2 **Agent Louise**[186] 970 6-10-7 0.. AdamNicol(5) 66
(Mike Sowersby) *hld up in last pair: rdn and lost tch after 5th: t.o bef 3 out: plugged on past btn horses fr 2 out* **150/1**

040- **7** dist **Not Another Monday (IRE)**[48] 2783 6-11-5 0.................. BarryKeniry 23
(George Moore) *in tch in midfield: outpcd whn mstke 6th: lost tch next: t.o sn after 3 out* **100/1**

PP- **8** nk **Frosty Dawn**[15] 3453 6-10-7 0.. JoeColliver(5) 16
(Mike Sowersby) *hld up in rr: mstke 4th: lost tch after next: t.o bef 3 out* **200/1**

50- **9** 20 **Shinooki (IRE)**[46] 2850 7-11-5 0.. DougieCostello 3
(Alex Hales) *in tch in midfield: 6th and outpcd 6th: t.o sn after 3 out: fdd bef next* **80/1**

0/0- **U** **Mackeson**[57] 2602 5-11-5 0.. TomMessenger
(Chris Bealby) *in tch in midfield whn blnd and uns rdr 2nd* **200/1**

16/ **F** **Ready Token (IRE)**[275] 5334 6-11-5 0................................ NoelFehily 114
(Charlie Longsdon) *led: clr w rival fr 5th: jst hdd whn fell 2 out* **5/2**[2]

4m 57.3s (17.90) **Going Correction** +1.125s/f (Heav) **11** Ran SP% **113.6**
Speed ratings (Par 105): **107,105,97,90,87 86,65,65,57, ,**
CSF £26.62 TOTE £8.50: £2.40, £1.10, £2.60; EX 28.80 Trifecta £134.50.
Owner Mrs D W Davenport **Bred** Mrs S Camacho **Trained** Norton, N Yorks

FOCUS
The going was heavy, soft in places. After riding in the opener Jason Maguire reported it as heavy ground and Dougie Costello's assessment was 'very holding'. A fair novices' hurdle run at an honest pace. The winner is rated in line with his Flat form.

3736 CALVERTS CARPETS AND FLOORING YORK H'CAP HURDLE (8 hdls) 2m 1f
2:00 (2:00) (Class 4) (0-120,118) 4-Y-0+ **£3,249** (£954; £477; £238)

Form RPR

411- **1** **Yorkist (IRE)**[7] 3616 6-11-2 **115** 7ex............................ NathanMoscrop(7) 132+
(Brian Ellison) *t.k.h: hld up in midfield: smooth hdwy to ld bef 2 out: sn in command: untidy jump last: easily* **11/8**[1]

/02- **2** *10* **Cappielow Park**[15] 3469 5-10-1 **100**..............................(p) KieronEdgar(7) 99
(Fleur Hawes) *led: mstke 4th: rdn and hdd bef 2 out: sn brushed aside by wnr: plugged on for clr 2nd* **20/1**

214- **3** *4 ½* **Favorite Girl (GER)**[18] 3391 6-10-11 **106**................ JonathanEngland(3) 99
(Michael Appleby) *t.k.h: chsd ldr tl after 3rd: rdn and btn after 3 out: plugged on to go modest 3rd between last 2* **3/1**[2]

464- **4** *8* **Chalk It Down (IRE)**[35] 3034 5-11-9 **115**.......................... APMcCoy 100
(Warren Greatrex) *mounted on crse: t.k.h: chsd ldrs after 1st: wnt 2nd after 3rd tl after 3 out: rdn and wknd bef next* **10/3**[3]

24U- **5** *27* **Mulligan's Man (IRE)**[21] 3272 7-11-11 **117**...................... JasonMaguire 75
(Donald McCain) *hld up off the pce in 5th: pushed along and no rspnse sn after 3 out: wl btn next: t.o* **8/1**

6/ **P** **Crouching Harry (IRE)**[74] 2260 5-11-12 **118**................ TomMessenger
(Anabel K Murphy) *hld up off the pce in last: struggling 5th: rdn and lost tch next: t.o whn p.u last* **25/1**

4m 26.15s (19.45) **Going Correction** +1.125s/f (Heav) **6** Ran SP% **109.9**
Speed ratings (Par 105): **99,94,92,88,75**
CSF £22.58 TOTE £2.40: £2.20, £3.60; EX 32.60 Trifecta £144.80.
Owner Mike And Eileen Newbould **Bred** Con O'Keeffe **Trained** Norton, N Yorks

FOCUS
They went a steady pace for this uncompetitive handicap. The easy winner was well in on his recent win but there's probably still more to come.

3737 CALVERTS CARPETS YORK H'CAP HURDLE (10 hdls) 2m 5f
2:30 (2:31) (Class 3) (0-140,138) 4-Y-0+ **£5,523** (£1,621; £810; £405)

Form RPR

3/0- **1** **Lamps**[19] 3359 7-10-6 **125**...(b) JoshWall(7) 127
(Michael Blake) *reluctant to line up: chsd ldr tl after 5th: cl 3rd and rdn bef 2 out: ev ch last: drvn and edgd lft flat: led fnl 100yds: styd on: rdn out* **4/1**[3]

/11- **2** *1 ¼* **Joanne One (IRE)**[64] 2463 6-10-8 **120**................................(t) APMcCoy 122
(Jamie Snowden) *chsd ldrs tl wnt 2nd after 5th: j. into ld 7th: mstke and hdd next: led again 2 out: hit last: drvn flat: hdd and no ex fnl 100yds* **7/4**[1]

5/P- **3** *1* **Astigos (FR)**[15] 3457 7-10-3 **115**....................................... AidanColeman 115
(Venetia Williams) *led tl out j. and hdd 6th: led again next: rdn and hdd 2 out: stl ev ch last: one pce and swtchd rt flat* **2/1**[2]

010- **4** *11* **Beyeh (IRE)**[21] 3263 6-10-10 **125**.............................. JonathanEngland(3) 115
(Michael Appleby) *in tch in midfield: mstke 4th: lost pl 6th: rdn and no imp after 3 out* **10/1**

521- **5** *11* **The Jugopolist (IRE)**[9] 3593 7-10-1 **118** 7ex...............(v) JoeCornwall(5) 99
(John Cornwall) *in tch in last pair: rdn bef 3 out: no imp and wknd bef 2 out* **22/1**

/24- **6** *32* **Superior Quality (IRE)**[74] 2249 9-11-12 **138**.....................(t[1]) NoelFehily 109
(Charlie Longsdon) *in tch in last pair: hdwy to chse ldng trio 6th: cl 4th after 3 out: wknd qckly bef next: t.o and eased flat* **12/1**

5m 43.4s (34.60) **Going Correction** +1.125s/f (Heav) **6** Ran SP% **110.8**
Speed ratings (Par 107): **79,78,78,73,69 57**
CSF £11.50 TOTE £6.50: £2.40, £1.20; EX 14.30 Trifecta £45.10.
Owner The Moonlighters **Bred** Kilboy Estate **Trained** Trowbridge, Wilts

FOCUS
They went a messy gallop for this handicap with the front three fighting out a thrilling finish. The winner is rated 5lb off his best with the third setting the level.

3738 CALVERTS CARPETS YORK H'CAP CHASE (12 fncs) 2m 2f
3:00 (3:01) (Class 3) (0-135,129) 5-Y-0+ **£6,498** (£1,908; £954; £477)

Form RPR

/21- **1** **Firth Of The Clyde**[50] 2751 9-11-10 **127**............................ BrianHughes 139+
(Malcolm Jefferson) *hld up wl in tch in last pair: mstke 7th: hdwy to trck ldrs bef 3 out: chal gng best 2 out: led bef last: r.o wl: pushed out: comf* **11/4**[2]

/43- **2** *3 ½* **Flaming Gorge (IRE)**[30] 3150 9-11-3 **127**.................... KieronEdgar(7) 132
(Fleur Hawes) *led tl 6th: styd upsides ldr: ev ch and rdn bef 2 out: hung rt and unable qck last: styd on same pce flat* **6/1**

3 *15* **Upepito (FR)**[496] 6-11-12 **129**.. AidanColeman 122
(Venetia Williams) *w ldr tl led 6th: rdn bef 2 out: hdd between last 2: 3rd and btn whn blnd last: wknd flat* **6/4**[1]

303- **4** *2 ¼* **Munsaab (IRE)**[16] 3429 8-11-0 **120**.................................(p) KielanWoods(3) 108
(Charlie Longsdon) *wl in tch in midfield: rdn after 9th: 4th and unable qck whn mstke and pckd 3 out: btn next: plugged on flat* **11/2**[3]

/3P- **5** *12* **Speedy Bruere (FR)**[17] 3424 8-11-4 **121**.......................(v[1]) SeanQuinlan 100
(David Bridgwater) *chsd ldrs: rdn and lost pl after 8th: btn 3 out: wl btn whn j.rt next: wknd* **16/1**

054- **6** *19* **Jack The Gent (IRE)**[20] 3323 10-11-3 **120**...................... BarryKeniry 82
(George Moore) *chsd ldrs: hit 5th: mstke 7th: rdn after next: wknd bef 3 out: t.o whn hit last* **22/1**

363- **P** **Great Oak (IRE)**[30] 3153 8-11-6 **123**................................ DougieCostello
(Tim Vaughan) *hld up wl in tch in last pair: hdwy and mstke 7th: lost pl after next: t.o whn p.u 3 out* **25/1**

4m 48.95s (13.95) **Going Correction** +0.975s/f (Soft) **7** Ran SP% **110.4**
Speed ratings: **108,106,99,98,93 85,**
CSF £18.07 TOTE £2.50: £2.70, £2.70; EX 14.90 Trifecta £41.10.
Owner Robert H Goldie **Bred** Robert H Goldie **Trained** Norton, N Yorks
■ Stewards' Enquiry : Kieron Edgar three-day ban: used whip without giving gelding time to respond (Jan 31-Feb 2)

FOCUS
A decent contest run at a steady pace.

3739 CALVERTS CARPETS AND FLOORING YORK H'CAP CHASE (14 fncs) 2m 6f 110y
3:30 (3:30) (Class 4) (0-115,113) 5-Y-0+ **£3,898** (£1,144; £572; £286)

Form RPR

/43- **1** **Ultimatum Du Roy (FR)**[19] 3365 6-11-8 **109**.......................... APMcCoy 119+
(Alex Hales) *in tch: lft 3rd 2nd: mstke 8th: wnt 2nd sn after 11th: led next: readily wnt between last 2: in command and nt pushed flat: easily* **11/10**[1]

004- **2** *1 ¼* **Around A Pound (IRE)**[21] 3268 9-10-13 **100**................... JasonMaguire 100
(Nick Kent) *hld up in rr: lft 4th 2nd: clsd to trck ldng pair sn after 11th: chal next: outpcd and j.lft last: kpt on flat but flattered by proximity to wnr* **6/1**

253- **3** *53* **Plum Pudding (FR)**[42] 2911 11-10-9 **103**.....................(p) JakeHodson(7) 50
(David Bridgwater) *led tl hdd after 11th: sn lost pl and bhd: blnd 2 out: t.o but plugged on to go poor 3rd flat* **11/2**[3]

004- **4** *1 ¾* **Presence Felt (IRE)**[17] 3418 6-11-12 **113**................(v[1]) RichieMcLernon 58
(Jonjo O'Neill) *w ldr: mstke 2nd: led after 11th: hdd and mstke next: sn outpcd and btn whn j. slowly 2 out: fdd and tired whn j. slowly last: lost 3rd flat: t.o* **3/1**[2]

3/1- **U** **Legendary Hop**[67] 2396 8-11-1 **102**................................ TomMessenger
(Chris Bealby) *chsd ldng pair tl blnd and uns rdr 2nd* **10/1**

6m 16.9s (30.90) **Going Correction** +0.975s/f (Soft) **5** Ran SP% **111.4**
Speed ratings: **85,84,66,65,**
CSF £8.08 TOTE £2.00: £1.10, £4.80; EX 7.40 Trifecta £26.60.
Owner D Allen **Bred** E A R L Detouillon **Trained** Edgcote, Northants

FOCUS
The pace was fair for this modest handicap. The easy winner stood out on recent form.

3740 CALVERTS CARPETS AND FLOORING CONDITIONAL JOCKEYS' H'CAP HURDLE (10 hdls) 2m 3f
4:00 (4:00) (Class 4) (0-110,110) 4-Y-0+ **£3,119** (£915; £457; £228)

Form RPR

204- **1** **Kodicil (IRE)**[15] 3451 6-11-11 **109**.......................................(b[1]) TonyKelly 116+
(Tim Walford) *mde all: clr w runner-up after 3 out: hit 2 out: styd on gamely flat: drvn out* **12/1**

056- **2** *4* **Murtys Delight (IRE)**[34] 3061 7-11-2 **106**...............(t) ChristopherWard(6) 108
(Dr Richard Newland) *wl in tch in midfield: wnt 2nd and drew clr w wnr after 3 out: j.rt and sltly hmpd last: rdn and fnd little flat: one pce* **7/4**[1]

065- **3** *13* **In The Gate (IRE)**[32] 3115 6-11-2 **103**............................(t) KielanWoods(3) 92
(Charlie Longsdon) *hld up in tch in last trio: hdwy 7th: rdn and chsd clr ldng pair after 3 out: no imp and wl hld whn j.rt and mstke next: j.rt and mstke last 2* **7/2**[3]

01P- **4** *3 ½* **King Zeal (IRE)**[37] 3012 10-11-2 **105**..........................(t) NathanAdams(5) 91
(Barry Leavy) *wl in tch in midfield: rdn and outpcd by ldng pair after 3 out: 4th and wl hld whn j.rt next* **20/1**

500- **5** *7* **Expanding Universe (IRE)**[21] 3249 7-11-9 **110**.............. JoshHamer(3) 91
(Tony Carroll) *chsd wnr tl after 3 out: sn rdn and struggling: wknd and wl hld in 5th between last 2* **11/1**

3/3- **6** *22* **Trozulon (FR)**[21] 3280 7-11-4 **105**................................ HarryChalloner(3) 62
(Venetia Williams) *chsd ldrs tl lost pl and rdn 7th: lost tch after next: t.o 2 out* **3/1**[2]

5/P- **7** *1 ¼* **Reelwill (FR)**[32] 3113 9-9-9 **84** oh17.................................. OllieGarner(5) 39
(Derek Shaw) *in tch in last pair: rdn after 7th: lost tch 3 out: t.o next* **66/1**

023- **8** *7* **Bold Raider (IRE)**[48] 2786 7-11-4 **110**...................... TommieMO'Brien(8) 58
(Jonjo O'Neill) *in tch in last trio: mstke 2nd: rdn 7th: sn struggling and lost tch after next: t.o 2 out* **14/1**

5m 3.6s (24.20) **Going Correction** +1.125s/f (Heav) **8** Ran SP% **112.5**
Speed ratings (Par 105): **94,92,86,85,82 73,72,69**
CSF £33.44 CT £91.18 TOTE £9.30: £3.70, £1.10, £2.30; EX 44.50 Trifecta £177.20.
Owner D & S Woodall **Bred** Tally-Ho Stud **Trained** Sheriff Hutton, N Yorks

FOCUS
This handicap, confined to conditional riders, was run at a decent gallop. The winner improved to the level of his Flat form.
T/Plt: £25.50 to a £1 stake. Pool of £58,308.56 -1667.17 winning units. T/Qpdt: £8.70 to a £1 stake. Pool of £3,596.00 - 303.75 winning units. SP

3289 WINCANTON (R-H)
Thursday, January 16

OFFICIAL GOING: Heavy (soft in places; chs 5.4, hdl 5.3)
Wind: quite strong half across Weather: overcast with heavy rain showers from 3.45

3741 HIGOS INSURANCE SERVICES GLASTONBURY H'CAP HURDLE (JOCKEY CLUB GRASSROOTS JUMPS SERIES QUALIFIER) (10 hdls 1 omitted) 2m 6f
1:20 (1:20) (Class 3) (0-125,125) 4-Y-0+ **£5,393** (£1,583; £791; £395; £15)

663- **1** **Bob Tucker (IRE)**[26] 3195 7-10-6 **110**............................ JamesBanks(5) 115
(Brendan Powell) *mid-div: hdwy after 7th: rdn to chse ldrs 2 out: led sn after last: kpt on wl: rdn out* **8/1**[3]

053- **2** *¾* **Kilmurvy (IRE)**[27] 3186 6-11-9 **122**................................(tp) NickScholfield 126
(Jeremy Scott) *in tch: rdn and dropped in rr after 3 out: hdwy between last 2: styd on strly fr last: wnt 2nd fnl stride* **5/1**[2]

04P- **3** *shd* **Bravo Bravo**[85] 2020 7-10-11 **110**..(b) TomO'Brien 115
(Mark Gillard) *led: rdn appr 2 out: kpt on v gamely even whn hdd sn after last: lost 2nd fnl stride* **00/1**

1/6- **4** *½* **Minellahalfcentury (IRE)**[71] 2288 6-11-5 **118**...................(t) DarylJacob 121
(Paul Nicholls) *mid-div: hdwy after 3 out: rdn to chse ldrs after next: cl 4th last: styd on same pce* **3/1**[1]

1/0- **5** *2* **Barton Stacey (IRE)**[52] 2715 9-10-8 **114**..........................(p) MrMHeard(7) 116
(David Pipe) *racd keenly on outer: mid-div: hdwy after 7th: rdn and ev ch 2 out: hld in 3rd whn awkward last: no ex* **33/1**

205- **6** *¾* **Westaway (IRE)**[26] 3195 7-11-0 **113**................................... TomCannon 115
(David Arbuthnot) *mid-div: rdn appr 2 out: no imp tl styd on fr last: nvr rchd ldrs* **10/1**

512- **7** *4 ½* **Kilrush (IRE)**[16] 3435 8-11-1 **117**.................................. MichaelByrne(3) 115
(Neil Mulholland) *hld up towards rr: nt fluent 2nd: pushed aong after 6th: rdn after 3 out: sme late prog: nvr a danger* **12/1**

000- **8** *5* **Whisky Yankee (IRE)**[27] 3186 7-11-7 **125**................ MauriceLinehan(5) 116
(Jonjo O'Neill) *tk keen old: trckd ldrs: rdn appr 2 out: wknd bef last* **12/1**

0P2- **9** *½* **Old Tricks (IRE)**[21] 3292 7-11-7 **120**............................(p) BrendanPowell 111
(Colin Tizzard) *mid-div tl dropped towards rr: 6th: rdn after 3 out: nt a danger after* **9/1**

012- **10** *8* **Weather Babe**[52] 2713 6-11-9 **122**.................................. TomScudamore 105
(David Pipe) *trckd ldrs: rdn after 3 out: wknd between last 2: eased run-in* **14/1**

/03- **11** *1 ½* **Tolkeins Tango (IRE)**[37] 3013 6-11-0 **113**........................... JackDoyle 94
(Victor Dartnall) *a towards rr* **20/1**

133- **12** *2* **Golanova**[51] 2729 6-10-13 **112**.. JamieMoore 91
(Gary Moore) *mid-div: rdn after 3 out: sn btn* **12/1**

40P- **13** *11* **Xaarcet (IRE)**[19] 3358 7-11-1 **114**.. JoeTizzard 82
(Colin Tizzard) *trckd ldr: chal 6th tl rdn appr 2 out: sn wknd* **16/1**

466- **P** **Halifax (IRE)**[35] 3031 6-11-3 **116**....................(p) AndrewTinkler
(Tony Newcombe) *struggling after 5th: a in rr: t.o 7th: p.u bef 2 out* **25/1**
5m 49.1s (22.60) **Going Correction** +0.775s/f (Soft) **14** Ran SP% **122.0**
Speed ratings (Par 107): **89,88,88,88,87 87,85,84,83,80 80,79,75,**
CSF £47.07 CT £1269.06 TOTE £13.20: £3.70, £2.90, £4.20; EX 71.50 Trifecta £1189.00 Part won..
Owner Nigel M Davies **Bred** Mrs Mary Mangan **Trained** Upper Lambourn, Berks

FOCUS
All hurdles and fences moved out 4yds on to fresh ground. A modest, but competitive handicap. They finished in a bit of a heap off a steady pace.

3742 HIGOS INSURANCE SERVICES PLATINUM H'CAP CHASE (JOCKEY CLUB GRASSROOTS JUMPS SERIES QUALIFIER) (17 fncs) 2m 5f
1:50 (1:51) (Class 3) (0-130,130) 5-Y-0+
£7,820 (£2,310; £1,155; £577; £288; £145)

Form RPR
/60- **1** **Bennys Mist (IRE)**[40] 2937 8-11-9 **127**.................... LiamTreadwell 143+
(Venetia Williams) *nt fluent 1st: trckd ldr: pressed ldr 10th tl led after 13th: wnt lft and hit 3 out: hit next: in command last: styd on strly* **11/4**[1]
146- **2** *7* **Forest Walker (IRE)**[20] 3321 7-11-8 **126**....................(t) HarrySkelton 131
(Dan Skelton) *in tch: hdwy 4 out: sn rdn: wnt 2nd 2 out: styd on but a being hld by wnr* **9/2**[3]
/02- **3** *7* **Mic's Delight (IRE)**[17] 3424 10-11-2 **120**.................... JackDoyle 120
(Victor Dartnall) *trckd ldrs: jnd ldr 13th: rdn to chse wnr appr 3 out tl 2 out: styd on same pce* **9/2**[3]
0P3- **4** *12* **Paddy The Stout (IRE)**[21] 3294 9-10-5 **109**....................(t) TomO'Brien 97
(Paul Henderson) *hld up: hdwy 4 out: rdn in disp 3rd next: wknd after 2 out* **12/1**
F/P- **5** *15* **Marie Des Anges (FR)**[76] 2194 6-10-9 **113**.................... RobertThornton 84
(Anthony Honeyball) *hld up: effrt after 4 out: wknd bef next* **10/1**
/23- **6** *1 ¼* **Denali Highway (IRE)**[19] 3366 7-11-10 **128**.................... AndrewThornton 98
(Caroline Bailey) *trckd ldrs: nt fluent 4th: rdn after 13th: wknd after 4 out* **7/2**[2]
P54- **P** **Falcon Island**[21] 3294 9-11-6 **124**....................(p) JoeTizzard
(Colin Tizzard) *hld up in tch: dropped to last and reminders after 8th: t.o 11th: p.u 4 out* **22/1**
6PP- **P** **Frontier Spirit (IRE)**[19] 3362 10-11-12 **130**.................... SamTwiston-Davies
(Nigel Twiston-Davies) *led tl after 13th: losing pl whn stmbld 4 out: sn wknd: p.u bef next* **12/1**
5m 38.4s (13.20) **Going Correction** +0.775s/f (Soft) **8** Ran SP% **114.1**
Speed ratings: **105,102,99,95,89 88, ,**
CSF £15.92 CT £52.74 TOTE £6.40: £2.10, £1.70, £2.20; EX 20.20 Trifecta £114.60.
Owner Mezzone Family **Bred** Flan O'Neill **Trained** Kings Caple, H'fords

FOCUS
Fair form. The winner is rated to a similar level to last season's Newbury win.

3743 HIGOS INSURANCE SERVICES SOMERSET NATIONAL H'CAP CHASE (22 fncs) 3m 3f 110y
2:20 (2:22) (Class 3) (0-130,129) 5-Y-0+
£12,512 (£3,696; £1,848; £924; £462; £232)

Form RPR
1/0- **1** **Flying Award (IRE)**[60] 2537 10-10-13 **121**.................... MissLucyGardner(5) 130+
(Sue Gardner) *hld up: tk clsr order 13th: wnt 4th 18th: rdn to chse ldng pair appr 3 out: chalng whn nt fluent last: styd on wl to ld fnl 75yds* **14/1**
414- **2** *nk* **Samstown**[26] 3205 7-10-7 **113**.................... EwanWhillans(3) 120
(Alistair Whillans) *j.lft thrght: mid-div: hdwy 12th: led 18th: rdn whn hrd pressed after 4 out: styd on gamely whn hdd fnl 75yds* **5/2**[1]
/6P- **3** *2 ¼* **Yellow Ball (FR)**[18] 3389 6-11-4 **121**.................... LiamTreadwell 126
(Venetia Williams) *in tch: trckd ldrs 11th: hmpd 14th: pressed ldr 18th tl rdn bef next: kpt on w ev ch last: no ex run-in* **14/1**
5/4- **4** *36* **Nodebateaboutit**[17] 3413 9-10-8 **111**....................(t) AndrewThornton 80
(Tom George) *hld up: struggling 16th: sn no ch: wnt t.o 4th towards fin* **9/2**[2]
012- **5** *½* **Musical Wedge**[21] 3267 10-10-5 **115**.................... GeraldQuinn(7) 83
(Claire Dyson) *chsd ldr: nt fluent 12th or 14th (water): rdn after next: kpt chsng ldrs tl grad fdd fr after 4 out: t.o* **12/1**
0P0- **6** *23* **Whispering Jack**[40] 2945 9-10-11 **114**....................(p) NickScholfield 59
(Keiran Burke) *j.lft most of way: trckd ldr: led 5th tl 18th: sn rdn: wknd after next: t.o* **25/1**
043- **P** **Monkerty Tunkerty**[11] 3554 11-11-12 **129**.................... WillKennedy
(Miss Jessica Westwood) *chsd ldrs: blnd bdly 7th: dropped to last 15th: sn u.p: wknd 18th: tailing off whn p.u bef 3 out* **5/1**[3]
043- **P** **Cnoc Seoda (IRE)**[20] 3321 9-11-1 **118**....................(t) TomO'Brien
(Paul Henderson) *hld up: mstke 16th: p.u bef next* **12/1**
/2P- **P** **Red Rocco (IRE)**[19] 3361 7-11-12 **129**.................... SamTwiston-Davies
(Nigel Twiston-Davies) *led tl 5th: chsd ldrs: rdn after 17th: wknd after next: p.u bef 3 out* **9/2**[2]
7m 30.8s (22.60) **Going Correction** +0.775s/f (Soft) **9** Ran SP% **114.2**
Speed ratings: **98,97,97,86,86 80, , ,**
CSF £50.56 CT £511.69 TOTE £15.80: £5.50, £1.20, £4.30; EX 83.10 Trifecta £1100.50.
Owner Mr & Mrs P George & Mrs B Russell **Bred** James V Neville **Trained** Longdown, Devon

FOCUS
A modest marathon handicap. The winner is rated back to the level of his Perth win.

3744 HIGOS INSURANCE SERVICES LANGPORT H'CAP HURDLE (7 hdls 1 omitted) 2m
2:50 (2:54) (Class 3) (0-130,130) 4-Y-0+ **£6,498** (£1,908; £954; £477)

Form RPR
/04- **1** **Quick Decisson (IRE)**[16] 3430 6-10-12 **116**.................... TomO'Brien 124+
(Philip Hobbs) *chsd ldrs: led appr 2 out: sn rdn: styd on wl* **5/1**[2]
/00- **2** *3 ¼* **Alaivan (IRE)**[26] 3200 8-11-7 **130**.................... MauriceLinehan(5) 135
(Jonjo O'Neill) *mid-div: hdwy 4th: chal after 3 out: rdn and ev ch next: hld appr last: kpt on* **10/1**
/01- **3** *1 ¼* **Ut Majeur Aulmes (FR)**[37] 3012 6-11-2 **120**.................... JackDoyle 123
(Victor Dartnall) *mid-div: hdwy 3 out to trck ldrs: rdn to chse wnr between last 2: kpt on same pce fr last where sn lost 2nd* **7/2**[1]
3/0- **4** *12* **Chesil Beach Boy**[21] 3292 11-11-6 **129**....................(t) MrsMRoberts(5) 120+
(John Coombe) *hld up towards rr: stdy hdwy after 3 out: 5th whn wnt rt next: styd on to go wl hld 4th fnl strides* **14/1**
415- **5** *nk* **Brinestine (USA)**[55] 2647 5-11-6 **124**.................... DarylJacob 115
(Paul Nicholls) *hld up towards rr of mid-div: smooth hdwy after 3 out: rdn into 4th between last 2: nvr threatened ldrs: fdd run-in* **13/2**
6/0- **6** *8* **Poet**[52] 2717 9-11-6 **124**.................... DominicElsworth 109
(Clive Cox) *prom: led after 3 out tl rdn bef next: wknd between last 2* **6/1**[3]

40P- **7** *¾* **Union Saint (FR)**[31] 3130 6-11-8 **126**.................... HaddenFrost 108
(James Frost) *mid-div: pushed along and lost pl after 3 out: nt a danger after but sme late prog* **33/1**
223- **8** *½* **Canadian Diamond (IRE)**[34] 3066 7-11-4 **127**.................... JamesBanks(5) 108
(Brendan Powell) *mid-div: rdn after 3 out: nvr any imp* **14/1**
230- **9** *2 ¼* **Quite By Chance**[62] 2492 5-10-13 **117**.................... JoeTizzard 96
(Colin Tizzard) *trckd ldrs: rdn after 3 out: wknd bef next* **12/1**
020- **10** *11* **Quaddick Lake (IRE)**[21] 3263 11-11-10 **128**.................... NickScholfield 101
(Jeremy Scott) *a towards rr* **14/1**
/00- **11** *11* **Look For Love**[28] 3169 6-10-7 **116**.................... MissLucyGardner(5) 73
(Sue Gardner) *a in rr: wnt bdly rt 2 out: t.o* **33/1**
066- **12** *1 ¾* **Advisor (FR)**[35] 3043 8-10-0 **104** oh3.................... TommyPhelan 59
(Mark Gillard) *led tl 2nd: prom: rdn along fr 3rd: wknd after 3 out: t.o* **100/1**
035- **13** *3 ¼* **Decoy (FR)**[28] 3169 8-10-9 **123**....................(p) AnthonyFox(10) 75
(David Pipe) *led 2nd: pushed along after 3rd: hdd after 3 out: sn wknd: t.o* **16/1**
0/0- **14** *6* **Grams And Ounces**[35] 3031 7-10-11 **115**....................(t) JamieMoore 61
(John Flint) *mid-div tl mstke 3 out: sn wknd: t.o* **20/1**
P00- **P** **Kim Tian Road (IRE)**[35] 3043 8-10-10 **114**.................... BrendanPowell
(Martin Hill) *a towards rr: wknd appr 2 out: p.u bef last* **33/1**
3m 57.8s (8.90) **Going Correction** +0.775s/f (Soft) **15** Ran SP% **123.7**
Speed ratings (Par 107): **108,106,105,99,99 95,95,94,93,88 82,81,80,77,**
CSF £53.01 CT £203.35 TOTE £6.00: £2.70, £2.30, £1.70; EX 86.30 Trifecta £906.50.
Owner Owners For Owners: Quick Decisson **Bred** Oak Hill Stud **Trained** Withycombe, Somerset

FOCUS
A fair handicap and sound form. A step up from the winner.

3745 HIGOS INSURANCE SERVICES STREET NOVICES' LIMITED H'CAP CHASE (17 fncs) 2m 5f
3:20 (3:21) (Class 3) (0-140,134) 5-Y-0+ **£8,935** (£3,360)

Form RPR
234- **1** **Bertie Boru (IRE)**[19] 3358 7-10-7 **122**.................... TomO'Brien 129
(Philip Hobbs) *racd in 4th: j.lft at times: rdn after 13th: lft 3rd but sn chsng ldr after 4 out: led between last 2: drifted rt run-in: kpt on wl* **10/1**
321- **2** *2 ¼* **Hansupfordetroit (IRE)**[19] 3358 9-10-12 **132**.................... RobertWilliams(5) 138
(Bernard Llewellyn) *w ldr: nt fluent 1st: led 8th: lft 6 l clr 4 out: rdn after 3 out: hdd bef last: kpt on but a being hld run-in* **3/1**[3]
/05- **P** **Bathwick Brave (IRE)**[21] 3279 7-10-12 **127**....................(t) NickScholfield
(Johnny Farrelly) *nt a fluent: hld up 5th: slow jump 10th: sn lost tch: p.u bef 4 out* **8/1**
F13- **F** **Flaming Charmer (IRE)**[47] 2811 6-10-9 **124**....................(t) BrendanPowell 95
(Colin Tizzard) *trckd ldng pair: rdn after 13th: lft 2nd briefly after 4 out: wknd bef next: fell last* **9/5**[1]
/UP- **F** **Wilton Milan (IRE)**[40] 2941 6-11-5 **134**.................... DarylJacob
(Paul Nicholls) *led tl nt fluent 8th: w ldr: gng wl enough whn knuckled on landing and fell 4 out* **2/1**[2]
5m 42.4s (17.20) **Going Correction** +0.775s/f (Soft) **5** Ran SP% **114.2**
Speed ratings: **98,97, , ,**
CSF £40.21 TOTE £9.70: £3.80, £1.90; EX 12.10 Trifecta £24.90.
Owner Unity Farm Holiday Centre Ltd **Bred** John Leahy **Trained** Withycombe, Somerset

FOCUS
Not a bad little handicap. The finishers are rated to their marks.

3746 HIGOS INSURANCE SERVICES LTD CREWKERNE "NATIONAL HUNT" NOVICES' HURDLE (DIV I) (7 hdls 1 omitted) 2m
3:50 (3:50) (Class 4) 4-Y-0+ **£3,898** (£1,144; £572; £286)

Form RPR
4/3- **1** **Baltimore Rock (IRE)**[31] 3128 5-11-4 0.................... TomScudamore 113+
(David Pipe) *in tch: hdwy into 2nd at the 3rd: clsd on clr ldr 3 out: led between last 2: kpt on: rdn out* **4/6**[1]
062- **2** *2* **Midnight Thunder (IRE)**[19] 3370 5-11-4 0.................... JoeTizzard 112+
(Colin Tizzard) *led: clr 3rd: hit 3 out: blnd 2 out: sn rdn and hdd: rallied briefly last: hld again sn after but wl clr of remainder* **6/4**[2]
/00- **3** *26* **Billy My Boy**[17] 3422 5-11-1 0.................... GilesHawkins(3) 85
(Chris Down) *trckd ldrs: rdn after 3 out: wl clr of remainder in 3rd but no ch w ldng duo sn after* **12/1**
/50- **4** *11* **Rosa Fleet (IRE)**[37] 3010 6-10-11 0.................... LiamTreadwell 67
(Venetia Williams) *racd keenly: in tch: no ch w ldrs fr after 4th: wnt modest 4th 2 out* **10/1**[3]
400- **5** *14* **Barton Heather**[27] 3189 5-10-8 0....................(t) MichaelByrne(3) 53
(Neil Mulholland) *chsd ldrs tl 3rd: lost tch w front 3 after next: chal for modest 4th 2 out: wknd bef last* **16/1**
00- **6** *7* **Carpies Boy**[52] 2724 5-10-8 0....................(t) WilliamFeatherstone(10) 53
(Warren Greatrex) *slowly away: bhd: no ch fr after 4th: t.o* **50/1**
/05- **7** *10* **Wheelavim**[17] 3415 6-11-4 0.................... TommyPhelan 43
(Claire Dyson) *chsd ldrs tl lost tch after 4th: remained in modest 4th tl wknd 2 out: t.o* **100/1**
P **Wansbeck**[249] 6-11-4 0.................... HaddenFrost
(James Frost) *lost tch 4th: t.o whn p.u bef 2 out* **50/1**
4m 3.4s (14.50) **Going Correction** +0.775s/f (Soft) **8** Ran SP% **127.6**
Speed ratings (Par 105): **94,93,80,74,67 64,59,**
CSF £2.40 TOTE £1.50: £1.10, £1.10, £3.50; EX 2.60 Trifecta £7.60.
Owner R S Brookhouse **Bred** Lynn Lodge Stud And Foxtale Farm **Trained** Nicholashayne, Devon

FOCUS
A race that concerned only two on paper and the pair had it between them from a long way out. The winner is rated similar to his recent run.

3747 HIGOS INSURANCE SERVICES LTD CREWKERNE "NATIONAL HUNT" NOVICES' HURDLE (DIV II) (7 hdls 1 omitted) 2m
4:20 (4:20) (Class 4) 4-Y-0+ **£3,898** (£1,144; £572; £286)

Form RPR
110/ **1** **Vieux Lion Rouge (FR)**[309] 4738 5-11-4 0.................... TomScudamore 130+
(David Pipe) *trckd clr ldr: hit 4th: clsd on ldr after 3 out: led between last 2: sn in command: readily* **4/9**[1]
553- **2** *4* **Revaader**[21] 3289 6-10-11 95.................... TommyPhelan 113+
(Mark Gillard) *led: sn clr: rdn appr 2 out: hdd bef last: sn hld by wnr: edgd lft but fin wl clr of remainder* **6/1**[2]
/65- **3** *22* **Winged Crusader (IRE)**[28] 3177 6-11-4 0.................... SamTwiston-Davies 96
(Nigel Twiston-Davies) *hld up in tch: no ch fr 3 out: wnt modest 3rd sn after last* **10/1**
500- **4** *nk* **Barton Rose**[27] 3189 5-10-8 0.................... MichaelByrne(3) 89
(Neil Mulholland) *hld up: no ch fr 3 out: chal for modest 3rd sn after last: nvr any danger to ldrs* **40/1**

The Form Book Jumps, Raceform Ltd, Compton, RG20 6NL.

106- **5** *7* **Lemons Ground**[31] 3134 5-11-4 0.................................... BrendanPowell 93
(Jamie Snowden) *trckd ldrs: rdn but no ch fr 3 out: remained modest 3rd tl blnd last* **7/1**[3]
160- **6** *21* **Larks Rising**[17] 3422 6-11-4 0.................................... TomO'Brien 68
(Caroline Keevil) *trckd ldrs: rdn after 3 out: sn wknd: t.o* **33/1**
/60- **7** *4* **Un Bleu A L'Aam (FR)**[29] 3163 6-11-4 0.................................... JackDoyle 64
(Victor Dartnall) *hld up in tch: struggling 4th: wknd 3 out: t.o* **12/1**
40- **F** **Beatrix Kiddo (IRE)**[29] 3159 5-10-11 0.................................... HarrySkelton
(Dan Skelton) *hld up: wknd after 3 out: t.o whn fell last* **25/1**

3m 58.8s (9.90) **Going Correction** +0.775s/f (Soft) **8** Ran SP% **122.0**
Speed ratings (Par 105): **106,104,93,92,89 78,76,**
CSF £4.30 TOTE £1.30: £1.10, £1.40, £1.90; EX 4.30 Trifecta £14.20.
Owner Prof Caroline Tisdall & John Gent **Bred** F M Cottin **Trained** Nicholashayne, Devon

FOCUS

The second division of the novice hurdle and another where few landed a blow.
T/Jkpt: Not won. T/Plt: £76.80 to a £1 stake. Pool of £87928.51 - 835.30 winning tickets. T/Qpdt: £13.50 to a £1 stake. Pool of £5616.77 - 306.14 winning tickets TM

3578 THURLES (R-H)

Thursday, January 16

OFFICIAL GOING: Soft (yielding in places on chase course)

3750a FAME AND GLORY & SANS FRONTIERES COOLMORE NATIONAL HUNT SIRES EBF MARES NOVICE CHASE (GRADE 2) (14 fncs) 2m 4f

2:15 (2:15) 5-Y-0+ **£28,437** (£8,312; £3,937; £1,312)

RPR

1 **Byerley Babe (IRE)**[18] 3410 7-11-0.................................... PhillipEnright 138+
(Robert Tyner, Ire) *w.w: nt fluent 1st: sltly hmpd between horses 3rd: 8th 1/2-way: tk clsr order bhd ldrs after 5 out: clsd gng wl bef 2 out where slt mstke: rdn to chal last and led narrowly run-in: all out: jst* **3/1**[2]
2 *nse* **Une Artiste (FR)**[35] 3030 6-11-0 140.................................... BarryGeraghty 137
(Nicky Henderson) *hld up in tch: 5th 1/2-way: tk clsr order bef 8th: nt fluent disputing 3rd 5 out: prog fr 2 out to ld between last 2: sn strly pressed and jnd last: hdd narrowly run-in: kpt on wl towards fin: jst hld* **6/5**[1]
3 *1 1/2* **Caoimhe's Delight (IRE)**[18] 3403 8-11-0 123................(p) PaulTownend 136
(Sean O'Brien, Ire) *trckd ldr: 2nd 1/2-way: pushed along 3 out: rdn fr next to chal between last 2: no imp on ldrs in 3rd fr last: kpt on wl* **12/1**
4 *6 1/2* **Kates Benefit (IRE)**[39] 2986 8-11-0 132.................................... DannyMullins 130
(David Kenneth Budds, Ire) *led: j.lft at times: narrow advantage whn nt fluent 2 out: rdn and hdd between last 2: no ex u.p in 4th at last: kpt on same pce* **7/1**[3]
5 *18* **Carrigeen Lonicera (IRE)**[11] 3561 8-11-0 113.................. MissEALalor 111
(R H Lalor, Ire) *chsd ldrs early: slt mstke in 9th at 6th: rdn and no imp on ldrs after 5 out: kpt on fr 2 out* **50/1**
6 *1 3/4* **Backinthere (IRE)**[39] 2986 9-11-0 123.................................... APHeskin 110
(Eamonn Francis Gallagher, Ire) *chsd ldrs: 3rd 1/2-way: niggled along in 4th bef 8th: reminders fr next: rdn in 6th after 3 out and no imp bef next: kpt on one pce* **12/1**
7 *16* **Pur Style (FR)**[46] 2854 6-11-0 104.................................... BryanCooper 93
(E J O'Grady, Ire) *chsd ldrs: 4th 1/2-way: clsr in 2nd on outer 5 out: slt mstke in 5th 3 out and no imp on ldrs after: wknd and slt mstke in mod 8th 2 out* **50/1**
8 *3 1/4* **Miss Palm (IRE)**[25] 3232 10-11-0 101.................................... AELynch 92
(D Deacon, Ire) *towards rr: bad mstke 8th: rdn and no imp fr 5th: mod 9th bef 2 out: one pce* **33/1**
9 *14* **Mini Vic (IRE)**[15] 3490 10-11-0 109................................(t) MPFogarty 76
(Miss Elizabeth Doyle, Ire) *hld up in tch: j.rt 3rd: 6th 1/2-way: mstke 8th: rdn in 8th and no imp on ldrs bef 3 out: wknd and eased fr next: t.o* **66/1**
P **Aibrean (IRE)**[11] 3561 10-11-0 127.................................... PCarberry 110+
(S R B Crawford, Ire) *hld up: mstke 4th: 7th 1/2-way: slt mstke in 8th 5 out: no imp on ldrs in 5th whn mstke 2 out and wnt bdly lft: p.u between last 2* **7/1**[3]
P **Chiltern Hills (IRE)**[11] 3561 7-11-0..(p) RWalsh
(W P Mullins, Ire) *towards rr: rdn and no imp fr 5 out: trailing whn p.u bef 2 out* **16/1**

5m 8.1s (-20.10) **11** Ran SP% **125.1**
CSF £7.79 TOTE £8.00: £1.20, £1.50, £2.50; DF 8.40 Trifecta £71.80.
Owner John P McManus **Bred** Rachel Ryan **Trained** Kinsale, Co Cork

FOCUS

The progressive winner rates a personal bestr, the second, fourth and fifth helping with the standard.

3751a KINLOCH BRAE CHASE (GRADE 2) (14 fncs) 2m 4f

2:45 (2:45) 6-Y-0+ **£20,312** (£5,937; £2,812; £937)

RPR

1 **Texas Jack (IRE)**[63] 2483 8-11-8 150.................................... PCarberry 159+
(Noel Meade, Ire) *w.w: clsr in 5th 1/2-way: hdwy in 4th 3 out: clsd gng best between last 2 to chal last: rdn to ld run-in and styd on wl towards fin* **4/1**[2]
2 *3/4* **Baily Green (IRE)**[20] 3338 8-11-8 156................................(t) DJCasey 157
(M F Morris, Ire) *chsd ldrs: 4th 1/2-way: clsr in 2nd fr 8th: disp 4 out and led narrowly 2 out: hdd bef last where mstke: kpt on wl in 3rd fr last into 2nd cl home wout troubling wnr* **5/1**[3]
3 *1/2* **Last Instalment (IRE)**[704] 4278 9-11-10 150.................... BryanCooper 159
(Philip Fenton, Ire) *chsd ldrs: tk clsr order at 5th: cl 2nd 1/2-way: almost on terms fr 5 out: disp 3 out tl hdd narrowly fr next: sn clsd u.p to chal between horses at last: no ex nr fin and dropped to 3rd* **9/4**[1]
4 *9* **Prince De Beauchene (FR)**[19] 3376 11-11-8 151.................. RWalsh 149
(W P Mullins, Ire) *led and disp: 1 l clr 1/2-way: almost jnd fr 5 out: hdd 3 out where mstke: rdn in 4th 2 out and sn no imp on ldrs: kpt on one pce* **8/1**
5 *8* **Realt Dubh (IRE)**[39] 2985 10-11-3 150..............................(t) BarryGeraghty 135
(Noel Meade, Ire) *w.w towards rr: mstke 2nd: 6th 1/2-way: rdn in 5th bef 2 out where slt mstke and no imp on ldrs: kpt on one pce* **10/1**
6 *1 1/4* **Argocat (IRE)**[75] 2235 6-11-8 151.................................... PaulTownend 139
(T J Taaffe, Ire) *hld up: last 1/2-way: rdn and no imp on ldrs in 6th bef 2 out: kpt on one pce* **5/1**[3]
7 *33* **Quito De La Roque (FR)**[70] 2320 10-11-8 155..............(p) DavyRussell 107
(C A Murphy, Ire) *led and disp: 3rd 1/2-way: niggled along in 6th after 5 out: no imp fr next where slt mstke and dropped to rr after 3 out: wknd* **7/1**

5m 11.4s (-16.80) **7** Ran SP% **116.8**
CSF £25.06 TOTE £2.80: £1.70, £5.10; DF 17.00 Trifecta £47.80.
Owner Robert Watson **Bred** Fergal O'Donnell **Trained** Castletown, Co Meath

FOCUS

Most of the column inches won't be about the winner but it was a victory that portrayed Texas Jack as the classy horse he is and realistically as a very solid Grade 2 horse with the ability to run well in the highest company. He probably just had to run up to his mark.

3516 MUSSELBURGH (R-H)

Friday, January 17

OFFICIAL GOING: Good to soft (6.7)

Wind: Light, half against Weather: Overcast

3755 IMA CONDITIONAL JOCKEYS' H'CAP CHASE (BETFAIR SCOTTISH CHASE SERIES QUALIFIER) (18 fncs) 3m

1:15 (1:15) (Class 5) (0-100,95) 5-Y-0+ **£3,249** (£954; £477; £238)

Form RPR

444- **1** **Oh Right (IRE)**[20] 3356 10-10-3 72..........................(b) ColmMcCormack 85+
(Dianne Sayer) *in tch on ins: hdwy to ld 6 out: rdn clr bef 4 out: styd on strly fr next* **14/1**
P6- **2** *4 1/2* **Gibbstown (IRE)**[11] 3580 8-10-4 73.......................................(p) DerekFox 82
(Paul Stafford, Ire) *t.k.h: in tch: hdwy to ld 9th: hdd 6 out: rdn whn nt fluent 3 out: kpt on same pce fr next* **7/1**[3]
F/5- **3** *4* **Tears From Heaven (USA)**[49] 2789 8-10-2 79...(p) DiarmuidO'Regan[(8)] 86
(Chris Grant) *prom: pushed along and edgd rt after 5 out: effrt next: outpcd bef 3 out: 3rd and hld whn mstke last* **9/2**[2]
522- **4** *15* **Twice Lucky**[20] 3355 10-10-11 83.......................... JonathanEngland[(3)] 75
(Sue Smith) *cl up: led bef 3rd to 9th: cl up tl rdn and outpcd after 5 out: no imp fr next* **7/4**[1]
/0P- **5** *6* **The Shrimp (IRE)**[70] 2339 7-10-0 69 oh3...................(p) CallumWhillans 55
(Sandy Thomson) *nt fluent on occasions: led to bef 3rd: cl up tl lost pl 6 out: struggling after next: sn n.d* **17/2**
650- **6** *20* **Quinder Spring (FR)**[48] 2818 10-11-6 95...............(p) GrantCockburn[(6)] 63
(Lucinda Russell) *hld up: rdn and outpcd 6 out: struggling fr next: nvr on terms* **16/1**
/2P- **7** *1 1/4* **Silver Steel (FR)**[220] 707 11-11-6 89..........................(t) HarryChalloner 56
(Richard Ford) *hld up: mstke 12th: hdwy to chse ldrs after 5 out: rdn and wknd next* **20/1**
205- **8** *25* **Call Me Mulligan (IRE)**[52] 2735 10-11-5 94..............(b) JohnDawson[(6)] 39
(John Wade) *chsd ldrs: drvn and outpcd 7th: lost tch fnl circ: t.o* **9/2**[2]

6m 6.8s (3.40) **Going Correction** -0.05s/f (Good) **8** Ran SP% **113.1**
Speed ratings: **92,90,89,84,82 75,75,66**
CSF £103.03 CT £514.79 TOTE £13.70: £2.80, £2.30, £1.40; EX 77.40 Trifecta £248.60.
Owner Andrew Sayer **Bred** Martin Keating **Trained** Hackthorpe, Cumbria

FOCUS

Bottom bend shared and at innermost position. Hurdles re-sited on fresh ground. A weak handicap but solid enough form.

3756 BLUEBIRD CARE (S) HURDLE (9 hdls) 2m

1:45 (1:45) (Class 5) 4-Y-0+ **£2,599** (£763; £381; £190)

Form RPR

250- **1** **Stormin Exit (IRE)**[15] 3498 11-11-4 0.................................... JamesReveley 111+
(Jim Goldie) *cl up: lft in ld 1st: hmpd by loose horse 5th: rdn 3 out: styd on strly fr next* **8/1**
231- **2** *7* **Lac Sacre (FR)**[8] 3118 5-10-13 112..............................(tp) JoshHamer[(5)] 105
(Tony Carroll) *in tch: stdy hdwy 1/2-way: effrt and chsd wnr 2 out: edgd rt: kpt on same pce fr last* **5/2**[3]
223- **3** *12* **Spin Cast**[20] 3351 6-10-11 110.................................... MissHBethell[(7)] 98
(Brian Ellison) *t.k.h: chsd ldrs: lft 2nd 1st: mstke 5th: effrt 3 out: outpcd next: btn run-in* **9/4**[2]
/00- **4** *8* **Moheebb (IRE)**[47] 2840 10-11-4 99..............................(p) KennyJohnson 88
(Robert Johnson) *t.k.h: chsd ldrs: outpcd 4 out: struggling whn nt fluent next: no ch whn mstke last* **100/1**
230- **R** **That'll Do Nicely (IRE)**[197] 879 11-10-11 87........... MissJRRichards[(7)]
(Nicky Richards) *ref to r* **28/1**
521- **F** **Western Approaches**[36] 3043 7-10-11 109......................(t) WillKennedy
(Ian Williams) *led: fell 1st* **2/1**[1]

3m 50.4s (2.00) **Going Correction** -0.05s/f (Good) **6** Ran SP% **108.2**
Speed ratings (Par 103): **93,89,83,79,**
CSF £26.72 TOTE £9.20: £3.80, £1.50; EX 47.20 Trifecta £92.30.There was no bid for the winner.
Owner Thomson Fyffe Racing **Bred** Jamie Davidson **Trained** Uplawmoor, E Renfrews

FOCUS

Not a bad seller. The winner and fourth look the best guides.

3757 COSMIC CASE MARES' NOVICES' HURDLE (9 hdls) 2m

2:15 (2:15) (Class 4) 4-Y-0+ **£3,249** (£954; £477; £238)

Form RPR

14- **1** **Cloudante (IRE)**[15] 3507 6-11-0 0.................................... JasonMaguire 119+
(Donald McCain) *mostly j.w: mde all: rdn and qcknd bef 3 out: clr whn nt fluent last: unchal* **10/1**
23- **2** *4 1/2* **Morning With Ivan (IRE)**[19] 3385 4-9-12 109............ HarryChalloner[(5)] 101
(Martin Todhunter) *t.k.h: chsd wnr: effrt whn nt fluent 2 out: kpt on same pce* **8/1**[3]
3/6- **3** *6* **Maison De Ville (GER)**[44] 2883 6-11-0 0.................................... APMcCoy 108
(David O'Meara) *hld up in tch: rdn after 4 out: rallied next: no imp fr 2 out* **8/1**[3]
/15- **4** *8* **Brijomi Queen (IRE)**[48] 2810 7-11-6 0.................................... DenisO'Regan 108
(Nicky Richards) *chsd ldrs: drvn and outpcd bef 3 out: no imp fr next* **5/2**[2]
226- **5** *1 3/4* **Rathvawn Belle (IRE)**[40] 2973 7-11-0 110...................... WilsonRenwick 98
(Lucinda Russell) *t.k.h: hld up: rdn and hung rt 3 out: no imp fr next* **10/1**
4- **6** *10* **Stephanie Frances (IRE)**[45] 2876 6-11-0 0.................................... HarrySkelton 91
(Dan Skelton) *nt fluent on occasions: prom: hit 2nd: stdy hdwy after 4 out: hung rt and wknd bef 2 out* **11/8**[1]
7 *1 1/4* **Pink Mischief**[78] 4-10-0 0.................................... JohnKington[(3)] 78
(Andrew Crook) *t.k.h: hld up on ins: nt fluent 3rd: struggling fr 4 out: sn btn* **100/1**
6- **8** *50* **Cottam Maybel**[16] 3448 5-10-7 0.................................... MrHAABannister[(7)] 43
(Michael Easterby) *nt fluent in rr: mstke 1st: lost tch fr 4 out: t.o* **200/1**

3m 51.1s (2.70) **Going Correction** -0.05s/f (Good)
WFA 4 from 5yo+ 11lb **8** Ran SP% **112.6**
Speed ratings (Par 105): **91,88,85,81,80 75,75,50**
CSF £82.01 TOTE £6.20: £2.40, £2.00, £3.00; EX 56.50 Trifecta £327.50.
Owner Thomson Fyffe Racing **Bred** Martin Allen **Trained** Cholmondeley, Cheshire

FOCUS
A modest mares' novice but the winner looks a fair recruit.

3758 FORTH ONE BOOGIE IN MORNING H'CAP HURDLE (9 hdls) 2m
2:45 (2:45) (Class 3) (0-130,129) 4-Y-0+ **£6,498** (£1,908; £954; £477)

Form RPR
122- 1 **Clever Cookie**[48] 2823 6-10-12 **115**.......... WilsonRenwick 124+
(Peter Niven) *t.k.h: hld up in tch: smooth hdwy to chse ldrs after 4 out: cl up whn mstke 2 out: sn rdn: led last 100yds: drvn out* 11/2[3]
326- 2 *nk* **Titus Bolt (IRE)**[16] 3477 5-10-9 **112**.......... HenryBrooke 119
(Jim Goldie) *led: rdn bef 2 out: hit last: kpt on: hdd last 100yds: rallied: jst hld* 9/1
12U- 3 *6* **Smart Ruler (IRE)**[70] 2344 8-11-0 **117**.......... BrianHughes 118
(James Moffatt) *trckd ldrs: effrt and rdn bef 2 out: outpcd fr last* 9/1
303- 4 *½* **Sud Pacifique (IRE)**[40] 2970 6-11-1 **118**..........(b) JasonMaguire 119
(Donald McCain) *prom: hit 5th: effrt and drvn bef 2 out: edgd lft: outpcd bef last* 5/1[2]
121- 5 *7* **Sky Khan**[143] 1418 5-11-8 **125**..........(b[1]) DenisO'Regan 122
(Richard Guest) *t.k.h: hld up in tch: effrt and shkn up bef 2 out: sn outpcd* 8/1
220- 6 *3 ¼* **Discovery Bay**[56] 2647 6-11-11 **128**.......... APMcCoy 123
(Brian Ellison) *t.k.h: in tch: effrt after 4 out: rdn and wknd bef 2 out* 2/1[1]
540- 7 *19* **Groomed (IRE)**[9] 3599 6-10-1 **107**.......... JonathanEngland(3) 82
(Sue Smith) *chsd ldrs to 4 out: sn struggling: btn next* 14/1
610- 8 *4 ½* **Stormy Weather (FR)**[48] 2821 8-11-5 **129**..........(p) NathanMoscrop(7) 100
(Brian Ellison) *hld up: rdn after 4 out: btn next* 10/1
253- 9 *1 ¾* **Endeavor**[19] 3395 9-9-12 **106**..........(p) EmmaSayer(5) 75
(Dianne Sayer) *prom: lost pl 2nd: struggling fr 1/2-way: nvr on terms* 33/1
3m 44.1s (-4.30) **Going Correction** -0.05s/f (Good) **9** Ran SP% **115.2**
Speed ratings (Par 107): **108,107,104,104,101 99,89,87,86**
CSF £53.07 CT £438.32 TOTE £6.40: £2.40, £3.00, £2.90; EX 38.60 Trifecta £658.00.
Owner Francis Green Racing Ltd **Bred** Mrs J A Niven **Trained** Barton-le-Street, N Yorks

FOCUS
A decent handicap and the form should prove sound. The time was much the quickest of the three C&D races and there's probably more to come from the winner.

3759 BUY YOUR 2014 ANNUAL MEMBERS BADGE TODAY H'CAP CHASE (16 fncs) 2m 4f
3:20 (3:20) (Class 3) (0-140,136) 5-Y-0+ **£7,797** (£2,289; £1,144; £572)

Form RPR
233- 1 **Bar De Ligne (FR)**[16] 3476 8-10-12 **122**..........(p) APMcCoy 138+
(Steve Gollings) *cl up: led after 5 out: kpt on strly to go clr fr 2 out: eased towards fin* 11/4[1]
531- 2 *7* **Drumlang (IRE)**[43] 2895 8-10-5 **115**..........(p) WillKennedy 121
(Ian Williams) *trckd ldrs: effrt and chsd wnr 3 out: one pce whn pckd last* 10/1
0U0/ 3 *1 ¾* **Mister First (FR)**[16] 3484 8-10-12 **122**.......... TomO'Brien 127
(Robert Alan Hennessy, Ire) *hld up: stdy hdwy after 5 out: effrt 3 out: rdn and one pce fr last* 20/1
P4P- 4 *9* **The Knoxs (IRE)**[18] 3414 11-11-10 **134**.......... RyanMania 130
(Sue Smith) *nt fluent on occasions: in tch: effrt 4 out: outpcd fr next* 28/1
032- 5 *3 ¼* **Palos Conti (FR)**[48] 2820 11-10-0 **110**.......... DougieCostello 105
(Brian Ellison) *led: rdn and hdd after 5 out: mstke and lost 2nd 3 out: sn btn* 15/2[3]
F36- 6 *5* **Aneyeforaneye (IRE)**[22] 3287 8-11-1 **125**.......... BrianHughes 114
(Malcolm Jefferson) *hld up in tch: effrt bef 4 out: wknd fr next* 8/1
412- 7 *½* **Maggio (FR)**[69] 2358 9-11-7 **136**..........(t[1]) DerekFox(5) 123
(Patrick Griffin, Ire) *bhd: pushed along 1/2-way: nvr on terms* 16/1
02P- 8 *51* **Balinroab (IRE)**[27] 3205 7-10-5 **115** ow1.......... DenisO'Regan 56
(Richard Guest) *hld up: struggling 6 out: t.o* 8/1
/62- F **Storming Gale (IRE)**[39] 3001 8-10-13 **123**..........(t) JasonMaguire
(Donald McCain) *midfield: fell 1st* 11/1
F14- P **Rudemeister (IRE)**[93] 1923 8-10-13 **123**..........(t) WilsonRenwick
(Lucinda Russell) *bhd: hmpd 1st: nt fluent next: struggling 6 out: t.o whn p.u bef 4 out* 11/2[2]
1F6- P **Dorset Naga**[54] 2693 8-10-9 **119**..........(t) RobertThornton
(Anthony Honeyball) *midfield: lost pl whn nt fluent 10th: sn struggling: t.o whn p.u bef 4 out* 14/1
4m 55.4s (-5.80) **Going Correction** -0.05s/f (Good) **11** Ran SP% **114.2**
Speed ratings: **109,106,105,101,100 98,98,78, ,**
CSF £29.78 CT £455.37 TOTE £3.70: £1.90, £2.50, £5.70; EX 20.70 Trifecta £920.00.
Owner P J Martin **Bred** Neustrian Associates **Trained** Scamblesby, Lincs

FOCUS
A fair handicap. The easy winner improved in line with the best of his hurdle form.

3760 RACING UK - YOUR HOME FROM HOME STANDARD OPEN NATIONAL HUNT FLAT RACE 2m
3:55 (3:55) (Class 5) 4-6-Y-0 **£1,949** (£572; £286; £143)

Form RPR
1 **El Namoose** 5-11-4 0.......... DenisO'Regan 115+
(John Ferguson) *hld up in tch: smooth hdwy 3f out: shkn up to ld appr fnl f: kpt on strly: readily* 11/4[1]
2 *4* **Racing Europe (IRE)**[54] 5-11-4 0.......... APMcCoy 108+
(Brian Ellison) *trckd ldr: lft in ld briefly after 6f: led again over 4f out: rdn over 2f out: hdd appr fnl f: edgd lft and one pce ins fnl f* 3/1[2]
2- 3 *4* **Lawsons Thorns (IRE)**[111] 1690 5-11-4 0.......... HarrySkelton 103
(Dan Skelton) *t.k.h: in tch: effrt over 2f out: kpt on same pce fr over 1f out* 7/1
2- 4 *shd* **Warriors Tale**[76] 2223 5-11-4 0.......... BrianHarding 103
(Nicky Richards) *t.k.h: prom: smooth hdwy and ev ch over 2f out: rdn and outpcd over 1f out* 3/1[2]
5- 5 *7* **Amazing Eight**[33] 3112 5-10-11 0.......... MrHAABannister(7) 97
(Michael Easterby) *cl up: led after 6f: hdd over 4f out: rdn and wknd wl over 1f out* 33/1
6 *6* **Sonny Thyne** 5-11-4 0.......... PeterBuchanan 92
(Lucinda Russell) *bhd: pushed along and outpcd 5f out: n.d after* 40/1
0- 7 *8* **Revanna**[70] 2347 5-10-11 0.......... WilsonRenwick 77
(Peter Niven) *hld up: rdn over 3f out: sn btn* 20/1
/42- U **Gurkha Brave (IRE)**[39] 3002 6-11-4 0.......... BrianHughes
(Karen McLintock) *led tl jinked lft and uns rdr after 6f* 5/1[3]
3m 46.3s (3.50) **Going Correction** -0.05s/f (Good) **8** Ran SP% **116.0**
Speed ratings: **89,87,85,84,81 78,74,**
CSF £11.27 TOTE £3.40: £1.20, £1.50, £2.40; EX 12.20 Trifecta £90.80.
Owner Bloomfields **Bred** Darley **Trained** Cowlinge, Suffolk

FOCUS
Probably a fair bumper and the winner could prove decent.

T/Jkpt: Not won. T/Plt: £731.60 to a £1 stake. Pool: £116342.36 - 116.08 winning tickets T/Qpdt: £72.80 to a £1 stake. Pool: £12086.17 - 122.80 winning tickets RY

3357 CHEPSTOW (L-H)
Friday, January 17
3761 Meeting Abandoned - waterlogged

3195 ASCOT (R-H)
Saturday, January 18
OFFICIAL GOING: Heavy (chs 5.5; hdl 5.4)
Wind: Moderate, across Weather: Overcast

3768 ASCOT BADGEHOLDERS JUVENILE HURDLE (9 hdls) 2m
12:40 (12:41) (Class 3) 4-Y-0
£5,630 (£1,663; £831; £415; £207; £104)

Form RPR
4- 1 **Astre De La Cour (FR)**[22] 3317 4-10-12 0.......... LeightonAspell 115+
(Robert Walford) *t.k.h: trckd ldng pair: wnt 2nd 6th and pressed ldr: led 2 out: shkn up and in command last: rdn out* 2/1[2]
11- 2 *4* **Handiwork**[22] 3332 4-11-8 128.......... SamTwiston-Davies 119
(Steve Gollings) *t.k.h: trckd ldr: led 4th: upped the pce after next: rdn and hdd 2 out: one pce* 11/8[1]
31- 3 *3 ½* **Vandross (IRE)**[23] 3245 4-11-1 116.......... TrevorWhelan(3) 112
(Neil King) *reluctant ldr at sedate pce: hdd 4th: blnd 6th and dropped to 5th: rallied to go 3rd 2 out: styd on but unable to threaten* 9/1
462- 4 *15* **Mandy's Boy (IRE)**[41] 2975 4-10-12 120.......... WillKennedy 91
(Ian Williams) *hld up in last pair: chsd ldng pair after 3 out to 2 out: wknd* 8/1
5 *22* **Masquerading (IRE)**[115] 4-10-12 0.......... NoelFehily 81
(Jonjo O'Neill) *in tch: chsd ldng pair 3 out where nt fluent: sn pushed along and wknd* 5/1[3]
0- 6 *34* **Green Special (ITY)**[94] 1920 4-10-12 0.......... LeeEdwards 35
(Dave Roberts) *hld up in last: mstke 4th: wknd 3 out: wl t.o* 66/1
4m 15.1s (27.70) **Going Correction** +1.30s/f (Heav) **6** Ran SP% **114.7**
Speed ratings: **82,80,78,70,59 42**
CSF £5.55 TOTE £3.20: £1.80, £1.60; EX 4.90 Trifecta £22.20.
Owner The Front Runners Partnership **Bred** J Delepine **Trained** Child Okeford, Dorset

FOCUS
It was no surprise they went steady in this opener, considering the ground, which Leighton Aspell described as "very soft". A fair juvenile hurdle that was dominated by the pair at the head of the market. More to come from the winner, with the second and third close to their marks.

3769 ROSLING KING LLP NOVICES' H'CAP CHASE (16 fncs) 2m 3f
1:15 (1:15) (Class 3) (0-125,125) 5-Y-£9,495 (£2,805; £1,402; £702; £351)

Form RPR
421- 1 **Ballinvarrig (IRE)**[30] 3172 7-11-9 **122**.......... PaddyBrennan 133+
(Tom George) *trckd ldrs: mstke 7th: lost pl next: mstke 12th but sn cl up: rdn bef 2 out: clsd to ld after last: drvn and all out* 7/2[2]
/32- 2 *1 ¼* **Benefit Cut (IRE)**[86] 2050 8-11-7 **120**..........(t) SamTwiston-Davies 129
(Renee Robeson) *j.w: led: hdd and stmbld 2 out: styd on to chal after last: one pce* 10/1
313- 3 *1 ¼* **Cloudy Bob (IRE)**[38] 3028 7-11-12 **125**.......... ColinBolger 131
(Pat Murphy) *mostly chsd ldr to 4 out: outpcd and sn dropped to 5th: rallied 2 out: kpt on fr last to take 3rd fnl stride* 16/1
052- 4 *shd* **Kingcora (FR)**[4] 3693 6-10-10 **109**.......... LiamTreadwell 119+
(Venetia Williams) *w.w: mstke 10th: prog to press ldr whn blnd 4 out and rdr nrly off: led and mstke 2 out: sn 2 l clr: tired and hdd after last* 15/8[1]
632- 5 *18* **Fair Bramble**[30] 3171 8-10-4 **103**..........(v) LeightonAspell 94
(Oliver Sherwood) *mstke 1st: prom: mstke 12th and dropped to last: sn btn: j.rt 2 out* 12/1
131- 6 *19* **Bobcatbilly (IRE)**[19] 3418 8-11-5 **118**.......... NoelFehily 85
(Ian Williams) *hld up in last: prog and cl up fr 11th: wknd rapidly after 3 out: t.o* 7/2[2]
332- F **Pearls Legend**[31] 3156 7-11-5 **118**.......... JamieMoore
(John Spearing) *wl in tch tl fell 7th* 8/1[3]
4m 59.6s (13.20) **Going Correction** +0.65s/f (Soft) **7** Ran SP% **113.0**
Speed ratings: **98,97,96,96,89 81,**
CSF £34.28 CT £487.79 TOTE £4.60: £2.20, £4.80; EX 38.60 Trifecta £185.40.
Owner Lady Hilda Clarke & S W Clarke **Bred** James Browne **Trained** Slad, Gloucs

FOCUS
No hanging around here in a race littered with jumping errors. The winner is the type to rate higher.

3770 OLBG.COM MARES' HURDLE (REGISTERED AS THE WARFIELD MARES' HURDLE RACE) (GRADE 2) (13 hdls) 3m
1:50 (1:50) (Class 1) 4-Y-0+
£22,780 (£8,548; £4,280; £2,132; £1,072; £536)

Form RPR
/11- 1 **Highland Retreat**[54] 2713 7-11-5 133.......... NoelFehily 147+
(Harry Fry) *j.w: pressed ldr: led 7th: gng best 3 out: rdn 2 out: jnd last: edgd rt flat but styd on gamely* 5/1[3]
111- 2 *2* **Carole's Spirit**[28] 3203 6-11-5 137.......... LeightonAspell 146+
(Robert Walford) *in tch: pushed along to chse ldng pair 10th: clsd to take 2nd 2 out: sn chalng: upsides whn j.rt last: no ex fnl 100yds: eased nr fin* 3/1[2]
511- 3 *3* **Mickie**[22] 3319 6-11-0 145.......... RichardJohnson 137
(Henry Daly) *cl up: pressed wnr fr 9th: outj. next 2 and drvn: lost 2nd 2 out: one pce after* 11/8[1]
/24- 4 *3 ¾* **Prima Porta**[7] 3649 8-11-0 136.......... AdamWedge 133
(Evan Williams) *hld up: pushed along to chse ldng pair 10th: tried to cl bef 2 out: fdd bef last* 12/1
254- 5 *23* **Utopie Des Bordes (FR)**[22] 3319 6-11-5 140.......... DavidBass 120
(Nicky Henderson) *led at modest pce to 7th: pushed along fr next: dropped to 5th and struggling 10th: wl btn after* 5/1[3]
413- 6 *12* **Tweedledrum**[28] 3198 7-11-5 125..........(p) BenPoste 106
(Tom Symonds) *pressed ldrs: lost pl once pce lifted fr 8th: nt fluent next and sn last: t.o* 50/1
6m 20.5s (24.50) **Going Correction** +1.30s/f (Heav) **6** Ran SP% **110.1**
Speed ratings (Par 115): **111,110,109,108,100 96**
CSF £19.72 TOTE £6.00: £2.30, £2.10; EX 17.40 Trifecta £30.00.
Owner Richard Barber **Bred** Richard Bridges **Trained** Seaborough, Dorset

The Form Book Jumps, Raceform Ltd, Compton, RG20 6NL.

FOCUS
A good mares' hurdle in which they got racing from quite a way out. A big step up from the winner with a smaller one from the second.

3771 KELTBRAY HOLLOWAY'S HURDLE (A LIMITED H'CAP) (GRADE 2) (11 hdls) 2m 3f 110y
2:25 (2:25) (Class 1) 4-Y-0+

£22,780 (£8,548; £4,280; £2,132; £1,072; £536)

Form RPR
/F0- **1** **Irish Saint (FR)**[28] 3200 5-11-5 **140** .... NoelFehily 152+
(Paul Nicholls) *j.w: pressed ldr: led 3 out: drew rt away bef next: pushed along bef last: impressive* **6/1**[3]
0/0- **2** *11* **Imperial Leader (IRE)**[49] 2813 6-10-7 **128** .... (t) SamTwiston-Davies 128
(Nigel Twiston-Davies) *nt a fluent: trckd ldng pair: rdn after 3 out: kpt on to take 2nd 2 out: no ch w wnr* **8/1**
303- **3** *2* **Bourne**[23] 3286 8-10-4 **125** .... (b) HenryBrooke 123
(Donald McCain) *trckd ldrs: rdn and bdly outpcd once pce lifted 1/2-way: 7th and struggling 3 out: styd on to take 3rd bef last* **5/1**[2]
110- **4** *11* **Thomas Crapper**[36] 3069 7-10-13 **134** .... CharliePoste 122
(Robin Dickin) *t.k.h: trckd ldrs: rdn and nt pce to cl fr 3 out: wl btn after* **9/2**[1]
111- **5** *5* **The Skyfarmer**[36] 3066 6-11-5 **140** .... RichardJohnson 123
(Philip Hobbs) *led: set mod pce to 1/2-way: hdd 3 out: sn no ch w wnr: lost 2nd and wknd 2 out* **5/1**[2]
1/U- **6** *6* **Get Back In Line (IRE)**[51] 2758 6-10-1 **127** .... MauriceLinehan[(5)] 103
(Jonjo O'Neill) *plld hrd in last trio: prog to chse ldrs after 7th: lost pl 3 out: jst pushed along and no ch after: mstke 2 out* **7/1**
/12- **7** *11* **Knight Of Pleasure**[35] 3096 5-10-10 **131** .... JamieMoore 95
(Gary Moore) *taken down early: hld up in tch: outpcd and rdn after 7th: mstke 3 out: wl btn after* **12/1**
112/ **8** *6* **Minella Forfitness (IRE)**[266] 5574 7-11-10 **145** .... DavidBass 103
(Nicky Henderson) *mostly in last: mstke 4th: blnd 7th and lost tch: wl btn fr next* **10/1**
/01- **9** *8* **Citizenship**[30] 3169 8-11-0 **135** .... LiamTreadwell 85
(Venetia Williams) *a in rr: struggling in last pair after 7th: no ch after next* **8/1**

5m 5.2s (20.50) **Going Correction** +1.30s/f (Heav) **9** Ran SP% **117.3**
Speed ratings (Par 115): **111,106,105,101,99 97,92,90,87**
CSF £53.50 CT £259.84 TOTE £7.20: £2.60, £2.90, £1.80; EX 55.60 Trifecta £263.10.
Owner Mrs Johnny de la Hey **Bred** S C E A Haras Du Ma **Trained** Ditcheat, Somerset

FOCUS
What had looked a competitive handicap was blown apart by Irish Sain, who produced a big step up. The second was close to his mark.

3772 SODEXO H'CAP CHASE (17 fncs) 2m 5f 110y
3:00 (3:00) (Class 2) 5-Y-0+

£31,280 (£9,240; £4,620; £2,310; £1,155; £580)

Form RPR
/1R- **1** **Bury Parade (IRE)**[30] 3170 8-11-6 **143** ....[1] NoelFehily 157+
(Paul Nicholls) *trckd ldrs: clsd to ld bef 2 out gng strly: drew clr bef last: easily* **11/2**[3]
/3P- **2** *5* **Grandioso (IRE)**[35] 3082 7-11-5 **147** .... (t) HarryDerham[(5)] 155
(Paul Nicholls) *trckd ldrs: moved up to chal after 3 out gng easily: upsides 2 out: styd on but no match for wnr after* **4/1**[1]
0U1- **3** *6* **Theatrical Star**[19] 3424 8-11-0 **137** .... JoeTizzard 140
(Colin Tizzard) *mde most: rdn and hdd bef 2 out where nt fluent: easily outpcd: kpt on fr last* **9/2**[2]
011- **4** *4 ½* **Renard (FR)**[21] 3362 9-11-7 **144** .... LiamTreadwell 142
(Venetia Williams) *mostly pressed ldr: pushed along after 11th: lost 2nd after 3 out: sn wl outpcd* **4/1**[1]
403- **5** *16* **What A Warrior (IRE)**[28] 3199 7-10-9 **132** .... SamTwiston-Davies 118
(Nigel Twiston-Davies) *pressed ldrs: pushed along fr 12th: wknd fr 4 out* **7/1**
/00- **6** *12* **Big Fella Thanks**[42] 2937 12-11-7 **149** .... (t) AodhaganConlon[(5)] 119
(Tom George) *hld up in last but wl in tch: pushed along fr 12th: j.lft 4 out and wknd: fin tired* **7/1**
002- **7** *4 ½* **Gus Macrae (IRE)**[28] 3197 10-9-13 **127** .... (tp) PatrickCorbett[(5)] 92
(Rebecca Curtis) *hld up in tch: sing to be outpcd whn nt fluent 13th: sn btn* **17/2**

5m 31.6s (5.60) **Going Correction** +0.65s/f (Soft) **7** Ran SP% **109.1**
Speed ratings: **115,113,111,109,103 99,97**
CSF £25.45 CT £95.84 TOTE £5.70: £2.30, £2.30; EX 24.00 Trifecta £138.00.
Owner HighclereThoroughbredRacing- Bury Parade **Bred** J R Weston **Trained** Ditcheat, Somerset

FOCUS
A decent handicap chase, run at a fair gallop, and it was dominated by the two Nicholls' runners. A step up from the winner with the second improving for a claimer.

3773 SODEXO CLARENCE HOUSE CHASE (GRADE 1) (13 fncs) 2m 1f
3:35 (3:36) (Class 1) 5-Y-0+

£59,199 (£22,375; £11,256; £5,680; £2,908; £1,512)

Form RPR
211- **1** **Sire De Grugy (FR)**[22] 3320 8-11-7 169 .... JamieMoore 174+
(Gary Moore) *tended to jump lft: hld up: prog to trck ldng pair 9th: clsd to ld bef 2 out: sn bounded clr: fine jump last: impressive* **5/4**[1]
132- **2** *11* **Hidden Cyclone (IRE)**[22] 3338 9-11-7 155 .... (p) AndrewJMcNamara 165
(John Joseph Hanlon, Ire) *led to after 1st: pressed ldr after: trying to chal whn mstke 8th: upsides bef 2 out: sn lft bhd by wnr* **4/1**[3]
/55- **3** *15* **Kauto Stone (FR)**[42] 2952 8-11-7 153 .... (b) SamTwiston-Davies 145
(Paul Nicholls) *led after 1st and set str pce: hdd & wknd bef 2 out* **16/1**
/23- **4** *3 ¼* **Days Hotel (IRE)**[41] 2985 9-11-7 159 .... RichardJohnson 142
(Henry De Bromhead, Ire) *chsd ldng pair: rdn 8th: lost 3rd next: wknd* **10/1**
442- **5** *7* **Oiseau De Nuit (FR)**[22] 3320 12-11-7 154 .... (t) JoeTizzard 137
(Colin Tizzard) *in tch: outpcd and struggling fr 8th: wl btn fr next* **28/1**
421- **6** *25* **Lancetto (FR)**[28] 3197 9-11-7 141 .... (p) AdamWedge 122
(Evan Williams) *chsd ldrs to 7th: sn wknd: t.o* **50/1**
/12- **U** **Somersby (IRE)**[42] 2952 10-11-7 164 .... DominicElsworth
(Mick Channon) *taken down early: hld up: mstke and uns rdr 5th* **11/4**[2]

4m 19.1s (4.50) **Going Correction** +0.65s/f (Soft) **7** Ran SP% **111.5**
Speed ratings: **115,109,102,101,97 86,**
CSF £6.58 TOTE £1.90: £1.10, £2.10; EX 6.00 Trifecta £52.80.
Owner The Preston Family & Friends Ltd **Bred** La Grugerie **Trained** Lower Beeding, W Sussex
■ New sponsors for this event, which was formerly the Victor Chandler Chase.

FOCUS
Not a strong edition of the race, with Sprinter Sacre on the shelf for the time being, and the combination of 2012 winner Somersby departing early and runner-up Hidden Cyclone making numerous jumping errors left Sire De Grugy with a fairly straightforward task. He rates a personal best, in a good time for the grade.

3774 EBF STALLIONS "NATIONAL HUNT" NOVICES' HURDLE (QUALIFIER) (12 hdls) 2m 6f
4:05 (4:06) (Class 3) 4-7-Y-0

£5,630 (£1,663; £831; £415; £207; £104)

Form RPR
211- **1** **Champagne West (IRE)**[23] 3292 6-11-12 132 .... RichardJohnson 143+
(Philip Hobbs) *hld up in last: prog and mstke 7th: hdwy to ld next: rdn to gain upper hand 2 out: clr last: kpt on wl* **11/8**[1]
/31- **2** *4* **Knock House (IRE)**[33] 3136 5-11-8 131 .... DominicElsworth 131
(Mick Channon) *led: nt fluent 2nd and 6th: hdd 8th: w wnr tl jst bef 2 out: kpt on same pce after* **7/2**[2]
/02- **3** *14* **Ceasar Milan (IRE)**[21] 3357 6-11-2 0 .... SamTwiston-Davies 111+
(Paul Nicholls) *chsd ldr to 7th: outpcd by ldng pair fr 3 out: no ch after: clung on for 3rd nr fin* **7/2**[2]
131- **4** *½* **Call The Cops (IRE)**[30] 3175 5-11-8 0 .... AndrewTinkler 118
(Nicky Henderson) *wl in tch: mstke 7th: rdn and outpcd fr next: n.d after: kpt on fr last* **11/1**
/21- **5** *1 ¾* **Delgany Demon**[23] 3282 6-10-13 0 .... TrevorWhelan[(3)] 110
(Neil King) *cl up: mstke 7th: rdn and struggling bdly next: no ch after: kpt on after 2 out* **33/1**
314- **6** *1* **Swallowshide**[20] 3388 5-11-8 130 .... LeightonAspell 114
(Emma Lavelle) *chsd ldr to 7th: shkn up and lost tch bef 3 out: wl bhd whn mstke 2 out: kpt on fr last* **8/1**[3]
43- **7** *27* **By The Boardwalk (IRE)**[56] 2661 6-11-2 120 .... SamThomas 91
(Kim Bailey) *in tch: j.rt 2nd: mstke 7th: wknd next: wl t.o* **20/1**

5m 51.9s (25.90) **Going Correction** +1.30s/f (Heav) **7** Ran SP% **113.7**
Speed ratings: **104,102,97,97,96 96,86**
CSF £6.50 TOTE £2.20: £1.20, £2.30; EX 7.30 Trifecta £20.60.
Owner R S Brookhouse **Bred** Peter Byrne **Trained** Withycombe, Somerset

FOCUS
Another likeable effort from the progressive Champagne West, who rates a decent novice.
T/Plt: £150.10. Pool: £154,424.94 - 750.66 winning units. T/Qpdt: £37.90. Pool: £10,177.50 - 198.35 winning units. JN

3413 HAYDOCK (L-H)
Saturday, January 18

OFFICIAL GOING: Heavy (chs 5.5, hdl 5.7)
Wind: Moderate, half behind Weather: Cloudy

3775 TATE CONTRACTS H'CAP HURDLE 3m
12:20 (12:20) (Class 3) (0-135,128) 4-Y-0+

£6,498 (£1,908; £954; £477)

Form RPR
033/ **1** **Extreme Impact**[619] 154 8-10-6 **115** .... ConorRing[(7)] 120
(Evan Williams) *prom: pushed along appr 9th: rdn to ld last: styd on gamely whn pressed run-in: a doing enough cl home* **22/1**
424- **2** *nk* **Quel Elite (FR)**[8] 3638 10-10-7 **109** .... (p) BrianHughes 114
(James Moffatt) *hld up: hdwy 7th: chalng gng wl whn mstke 2 out: sn rdn: duelled w wnr run-in: kpt on: hld cl home* **12/1**
/62- **3** *10* **Ugly Bug**[21] 3359 8-11-2 **125** .... KevinJones[(7)] 123
(Seamus Mullins) *led: pushed along appr 3 out: rdn bef 2 out: hdd last: sn unable to go w front pair: wknd fnl 100yds* **7/2**[1]
606- **4** *¾* **Hada Men (USA)**[28] 3207 9-11-11 **127** .... AidanColeman 121
(Venetia Williams) *hld up: niggled along bef 7th: struggling 9th: sme hdwy appr 2 out: kpt on run-in but nvr able to trble ldrs* **15/2**
051- **5** *9* **Saphir River (FR)**[23] 3286 8-11-5 **128** .... (tp) CraigNichol[(7)] 113
(Lucinda Russell) *hld up in rr: hdwy appr 8th: pushed along in tch after next: effrt appr 3 out: no imp fr next: wknd bef last* **7/1**
/P2- **6** *hd* **Western Jo (IRE)**[20] 3387 6-11-10 **126** .... TomO'Brien 113
(Philip Hobbs) *midfield: hdwy appr 9th: chsd ldrs 3 out: mstke 2 out: wknd bef last* **9/2**[3]
110- **7** *22* **Brave Buck**[28] 3195 6-10-2 **104** .... TomScudamore 76
(Henry Daly) *prom: mstke 6th: pushed along and lost pl appr 9th: sn bhd and struggling* **4/1**[2]
23- **8** *40* **Champagne Rian (IRE)**[42] 2942 6-11-8 **124** .... APMcCoy 47
(Rebecca Curtis) *in tch: rdn after 7th: sn lost pl: bhd and struggling 9th: hit 3 out: t.o* **13/2**

5m 58.1s (-1.90) **Going Correction** -0.30s/f (Good) **8** Ran SP% **110.0**
Speed ratings (Par 107): **91,90,87,87,84 84,76,63**
CSF £226.06 CT £1087.06 TOTE £30.00: £4.10, £2.90, £1.40; EX 282.20 Trifecta £918.30.
Owner Gareth Morse,Iwan Thomas,Charles Footman **Bred** Juddmonte Farms Ltd **Trained** Llancarfan, Vale Of Glamorgan

FOCUS
All chases run around Flat Course bend out of the back straight returning to Chase course in home straight adding about 110yds per circuit. Official distances amended pre-race and as shown. The first pair drew clear late on in this fair staying handicap. The winner was well treated on old form and the second is rated back to his best.

3776 G4S EVENTS GRADUATION CHASE 2m 5f
12:55 (12:55) (Class 2) 5-Y-0+ **£12,660** (£3,740; £1,870; £936; £468)

Form RPR
/F1- **1** **Benvolio (IRE)**[31] 3162 7-11-4 142 .... DarylJacob 145+
(Paul Nicholls) *mde virtually all: pressed fr 4 out: styd on run-in: drvn out* **11/8**[1]
120- **2** *1* **Maggio (FR)**[1] 3759 9-11-0 135 .... (t) BrianHughes 139
(Patrick Griffin, Ire) *racd w zest: a.p: led briefly 4 out: continued to chal wnr: rdn bef last: kpt on: hld fnl 75yds* **33/1**
403- **3** *5* **Trustan Times (IRE)**[34] 3108 8-11-0 137 .... JamesReveley 137+
(Tim Easterby) *hld up: nt fluent 3rd: mstke 4th: clsd appr 4 out: chsd ldrs bef next: rdn and hung lft appr 2 out: one pce fnl 100yds: eased whn btn towards fin* **13/8**[2]
255/ **4** *8* **Fill The Power (IRE)**[273] 5404 8-11-0 129 .... RyanMania 128
(Sue Smith) *prom: pushed along appr 10th: rdn after 4 out: wknd after next* **8/1**

1FP/ **5** *8* **Rival D'Estruval (FR)**^{273} 5404 9-11-7 143.................... WilsonRenwick 127
(Pauline Robson) *j.lft at times: hld up in rr: shkn up 3 out: btn bef next* **7/1**^{3}

5m 19.7s (-5.80) **Going Correction** -0.025s/f (Good) **5** Ran SP% **106.8**
Speed ratings: **110,109,107,104,101**
CSF £23.65 TOTE £2.20: £1.70, £5.40; EX 19.00 Trifecta £39.50.
Owner Dobson, Sutton & Woodhouse **Bred** Mrs Mary And Paul Motherway **Trained** Ditcheat, Somerset

FOCUS
A good-quality graduation chase. There was a routine gallop on and the field got sorted out from the third-last. The winner didn't need to improve to land a steadily run race.

3777 RACING POST CELEBRATES 200,000 SOCIAL FOLLOWERS NOVICES' CHASE (GRADE 2) 2m 5f
1:30 (1:30) (Class 1) 5-Y-0+ **£17,911** (£7,059; £3,805)

Form RPR
132- **1** **Taquin Du Seuil (FR)**^{17} 3456 7-11-7 147.............................. APMcCoy 157+
(Jonjo O'Neill) *hld up: nt fluent 5th: led 10th: travelling strly and effrtlessly gng clr whn mstke 2 out: v easily* **8/11**^{1}

11P- **2** *17* **Coverholder (IRE)**^{21} 3362 7-11-4 137........................ JonathanEngland 130
(Sue Smith) *w ldr: stl trying to chal but pushed along and fighting losing battle whn nt fluent 3 out: sn no ch w wnr and wl btn* **16/1**

01P- **3** *23* **Knock A Hand (IRE)**^{21} 3361 9-11-4 138..................(b) TomScudamore 106
(Richard Lee) *led: hdd 10th: sn pushed along and dropped to rr: wknd bef 4 out: sn lost tch* **8/1**^{3}

4/2- **P** **O'Faolains Boy (IRE)**^{28} 3196 7-11-0 0........................... BarryGeraghty
(Rebecca Curtis) *hld up: shkn up and sn struggling in rr appr 8th: bhd and losing tch whn p.u bef 10th* **9/4**^{2}

5m 16.4s (-9.10) **Going Correction** -0.025s/f (Good) **4** Ran SP% **105.7**
Speed ratings: **116,109,100,**
CSF £8.76 TOTE £1.50; EX 9.50 Trifecta £14.50.
Owner Martin Broughton & Friends 1 **Bred** Marc Boudot **Trained** Cheltenham, Gloucs

FOCUS
This Grade 2 novice chase rather fell apart. The easy winner was a class above these but probably ran a personal best.

3778 SKY BET SUPREME TRIAL NOVICES' HURDLE (REGISTERED AS THE ROSSINGTON MAIN NOVICES' HURDLE) (GRADE 2) 2m
2:05 (2:05) (Class 1) 4-Y-0+
£15,661 (£5,876; £2,942; £1,465; £737; £368)

Form RPR
/11- **1** **Zamdy Man**^{57} 2657 5-11-11 136.. AidanColeman 150+
(Venetia Williams) *led: hdd 4th: remained prom: regained ld 6th: pushed along appr 3 out: rdn whn pressed 2 out: extended advantage last: styd on* **7/2**^{2}

3- **2** *1 ¾* **Un Temps Pour Tout (IRE)**^{69} 2414 5-11-11 147........ TomScudamore 147+
(David Pipe) *a.p: wnt 2nd 6th: ev ch 2 out: nt qckn appr last: kpt on run-in but a hld* **11/8**^{1}

1/1- **3** *22* **Meadowcroft Boy**^{48} 2840 5-11-8 0............................ EwanWhillans 122
(Alistair Whillans) *t.k.h: prom: led 4th: hdd 6th: wknd appr 3 out* **9/2**^{3}

11- **4** *3 ¼* **Stand To Reason (IRE)**^{21} 3370 6-11-8 0....................... BarryGeraghty 120
(Nicky Henderson) *nt a fluent: hld up bhd: nvr nr ldrs* **7/2**^{2}

253- **5** *6* **Abracadabra Sivola (FR)**^{43} 2927 4-10-7 115.................... DarylJacob 98
(Nick Williams) *hld up: nt fluent 6th: struggling and bhd after* **20/1**

4- **6** *30* **River Clare (IRE)**^{36} 3063 6-11-4 0.................................. CiaranMckee 83
(John O'Shea) *hld up: struggling and bhd after 6th: t.o* **100/1**

3m 54.8s (-9.40) **Going Correction** -0.30s/f (Good)
WFA 4 from 5yo+ 11lb **6** Ran SP% **110.5**
Speed ratings (Par 115): **111,110,99,97,94 79**
CSF £8.77 TOTE £3.10: £1.90, £1.30; EX 9.80 Trifecta £27.50.
Owner Muhammad Nadeem Khan **Bred** The Kathryn Stud **Trained** Kings Caple, H'fords

FOCUS
A fascinating affair. There was a solid gallop on, which found out all bar the first pair, who came well clear and look smart novices. The time was good compared with the next.

3779 STANJAMES.COM CHAMPION HURDLE TRIAL (GRADE 2) 2m
2:40 (2:40) (Class 1) 4-Y-0+ **£42,913** (£16,228; £8,226; £4,198; £2,211)

Form RPR
/15- **1** **Melodic Rendezvous**^{49} 2821 8-11-8 152........................ NickScholfield 157+
(Jeremy Scott) *chsd ldrs: lft prom 6th: hit 2 out: led run-in 1f out: styd on wl* **7/4**^{2}

212- **2** *4 ½* **Ptit Zig (FR)**^{28} 3200 5-11-12 159.. DarylJacob 155
(Paul Nicholls) *chsd ldr: wanted to lug lft whn hit and lft in ld 6th: nt fluent 3 out: rdn appr last: hdd run-in 1f out: no ex fnl 75yds* **1/1**^{1}

613- **3** *11* **Jumps Road**^{35} 3083 7-11-4 135.................................. BrendanPowell 135
(Colin Tizzard) *in tch: lft prom 6th: effrt appr 3 out: one pce last: sn lft bhd by front two* **28/1**

253- **4** *nse* **Morning Royalty (IRE)**^{28} 3206 7-11-4 130....................... BrianHughes 136
(James Moffatt) *hld up: rdn after 3 out: in tch whn hit 2 out: sn n.d to ldrs: kpt on u.p run-in* **50/1**

012- **5** *2* **Ifandbutwhynot (IRE)**^{17} 3477 8-11-8 141....................... TimmyMurphy 139
(David O'Meara) *hld up: hdwy to chse ldrs 3 out: pushed along after 2 out: rdn and btn after last* **16/1**

011- **U** **Act Of Kalanisi (IRE)**^{22} 3328 8-11-4 143..........................(bt) APMcCoy
(Dr Richard Newland) *nt a fluent: led: hit 5th: blnd and uns rdr 6th* **15/2**^{3}

3m 56.4s (-7.80) **Going Correction** -0.30s/f (Good) **6** Ran SP% **109.4**
Speed ratings (Par 115): **107,104,99,99,98**
CSF £3.78 TOTE £2.50: £1.20, £1.80; EX 4.40 Trifecta £28.40.
Owner Cash For Honours **Bred** Mrs N A Ward **Trained** Brompton Regis, Somerset

FOCUS
A Grade 2 that essentially looked a match and it played out so as the two market leaders fought it out from the penultimate flight. The winner is rated in line with his Wincanton win and is potential 160+ horse.

3780 PETER MARSH CHASE (A LIMITED H'CAP) (GRADE 2) 3m 1f
3:15 (3:15) (Class 1) 5-Y-0+
£28,475 (£10,685; £5,350; £2,665; £1,340; £670)

Form RPR
2F1- **1** **Wychwoods Brook**^{35} 3093 8-9-11 137 oh7...................... ConorRing$^{(7)}$ 149+
(Evan Williams) *a.p: mstke 8th: led and nt fluent 3 out: mstke and hdd 2 out: stl chalng whn mstke last: rallied to regain ld fnl 75yds: styd on* **16/1**

126- **2** *1 ½* **Vintage Star (IRE)**^{21} 3361 8-10-8 141................................. RyanMania 147
(Sue Smith) *midfield: hdwy 10th: rdn bef 4 out: led 2 out: hung lft fr bef last: hdd fnl 75yds: no ex* **6/1**

255- **3** *nk* **Merry King (IRE)**^{21} 3361 7-10-4 137 oh1.................(v^{1}) RichieMcLernon 144
(Jonjo O'Neill) *prom: rdn and outpcd appr 3 out: styd on u.p run-in: clsd at fin* **9/2**^{2}

/F4- **4** *½* **Katenko (FR)**^{42} 2938 8-11-8 155.. AidanColeman 163+
(Venetia Williams) *prom: dropped to midfield 4th: hit 9th: rdn and outpcd bef 4 out: rallied and in contention 2 out: kpt on u.p towards fin* **3/1**^{1}

/1P- **5** *6* **Sydney Paget (IRE)**^{23} 3285 7-10-9 142.......................... JasonMaguire 144
(Donald McCain) *led: dived at 4th: rdn and hdd 3 out: wknd bef last* **11/2**^{3}

/52- **6** *21* **Valoroso**^{22} 3321 9-10-4 137 oh8.....................................(t) ConorO'Farrell 115
(Richard Woollacott) *hld up in rr: u.p after 12th: nvr a threat* **25/1**

0/1- **P** **Chance Du Roy (FR)**^{42} 2937 10-10-10 143........................ TomO'Brien
(Philip Hobbs) *midfield: dropped to rr 4th: rdn after 6th: bhd whn hit 9th: p.u bef 12th* **11/1**

UF1- **P** **Vino Griego (FR)**^{43} 2930 9-11-7 157..........................(v) JoshuaMoore$^{(3)}$
(Gary Moore) *hld up: pushed along after 12th: bhd whn p.u bef last* **16/1**

1F1- **P** **Night Alliance (IRE)**^{28} 3205 9-10-4 137 oh3............(b) TomScudamore
(Dr Richard Newland) *midfield: wnt prom 4th: mstke 5th: rdn and wknd after 12th: bhd whn p.u bef 3 out* **8/1**

11F/ **F** **The Minack (IRE)**^{700} 4375 10-11-5 152.............................. DarylJacob
(Paul Nicholls) *hld up in tch: fell 1st* **12/1**

6m 21.7s (-8.80) **Going Correction** -0.025s/f (Good) **10** Ran SP% **115.6**
Speed ratings: **113,112,112,112,110 103,,,,**
CSF £109.11 CT £511.81 TOTE £17.90: £4.60, £2.60, £1.70; EX 132.40 Trifecta £785.60.
Owner Kevin & Anne Glastonbury **Bred** D T And A T Goldsworthy **Trained** Llancarfan, Vale Of Glamorgan

■ Stewards' Enquiry : Richie McLernon four-day ban: used whip above permitted level (Jan 2-5)

FOCUS
A very competitive edition of this well established handicap and it served up a real test.

3781 NRC CHELTENHAM PREVIEW HERE MARCH 5TH "FIXED BRUSH" NOVICES' HURDLE 2m 4f
3:50 (3:50) (Class 4) 4-7-Y-0 **£3,898** (£1,144; £572; £286)

Form RPR
21- **1** **Wuff (IRE)**^{29} 3189 6-11-11 0...(t) PaddyBrennan 130+
(Tom George) *in tch: wnt cl 2nd appr 3 out: chal fr 2 out: over 2 l down run-in abt 1f out: rallied and styd on gamely to ld fnl stride* **7/4**^{1}

443- **2** *shd* **Straidnahanna (IRE)**^{37} 3036 5-11-5 117.............................. RyanMania 122
(Sue Smith) *led: hdd appr 2nd: remained prom: regained ld 6th: nt fluent whn pressed 2 out and last: sn edgd lft: over 2 l clr run-in 1f out: all out towards fin: hdd fnl stride* **7/4**^{1}

/22- **3** *16* **Greensalt (IRE)**^{28} 3208 6-11-5 115................................... JasonMaguire 108
(Donald McCain) *midfield: hdwy 7th: chsd ldrs appr 3 out: wknd bef last* **4/1**^{2}

504- **4** *2* **Garde Ville (FR)**^{23} 3245 4-10-7 117..........................(bt) TomScudamore 93
(David Pipe) *hld up: shkn up bef 2 out: kpt on for press run-in: nvr trbld ldrs* **12/1**^{3}

0- **5** *3 ¼* **Voyage A New York (FR)**^{86} 2037 5-11-5 0................. WilsonRenwick 102
(Lucinda Russell) *t.k.h: prom: led appr 2nd: hdd 6th: pushed along and wknd appr 3 out* **40/1**

4- **6** *8* **Love Marmalade (IRE)**^{17} 3474 4-10-4 0.................... EwanWhillans$^{(3)}$ 81
(Alistair Whillans) *hld up: struggling appr 3 out: nvr a threat* **33/1**

165- **7** *8* **Clan William (IRE)**^{22} 3330 6-11-8 110................... JonathanEngland$^{(3)}$ 91
(Sue Smith) *chsd ldrs tl rdn and wknd bef 3 out* **20/1**

236- **8** *hd* **Vasco Pierji (FR)**^{16} 3495 5-11-5 0...................................... AdrianLane 84
(Donald McCain) *hld up: hit 6th: struggling bef 3 out: nvr a threat* **33/1**

4m 55.6s (2.60) **Going Correction** -0.30s/f (Good)
WFA 4 from 5yo+ 12lb **8** Ran SP% **113.5**
Speed ratings: **82,81,75,74,73 70,67,66**
CSF £4.75 TOTE £2.30: £1.10, £1.40, £1.20; EX 5.70 Trifecta £11.50.
Owner R S Brookhouse **Bred** Mrs Miriam Tarrant **Trained** Slad, Gloucs

FOCUS
The two market principals dominated the finish of this modest novice hurdle. There's a case for rating the form higher through the third and fourth.
T/Jkpt: Not won. T/Plt: £34.20. Pool: £107,821.14 - 2295.31 winning units. T/Qpdt: £6.30. Pool: £7350.84 - 859.58 winning units. DO

3420 TAUNTON (R-H)
Saturday, January 18

OFFICIAL GOING: Heavy (4.5)
Wind: very strong across Weather: heavy rain

3782 EBF STALLIONS "NATIONAL HUNT" NOVICES' HURDLE (QUALIFIER) (10 hdls) 2m 3f 110y
12:30 (12:31) (Class 4) 4-7-Y-0 **£4,223** (£1,240; £620; £310)

Form RPR
221- **1** **Horizontal Speed (IRE)**^{19} 3422 6-11-5 128.................. ChrisDavies$^{(7)}$ 138+
(Philip Hobbs) *mde all: drew wl clr after 3 out: rdn briefly after last: unchal* **4/6**^{1}

121- **2** *41* **Kayfleur**^{31} 3159 5-11-1 120... RobertThornton 89
(Henry Daly) *in tch: trckd wnr fr after 5th: pushed along after 3 out: sn no ch w wnr: fin tired jst hld on for 2nd* **5/2**^{2}

00- **3** *nk* **Spending Time**^{70} 2375 5-10-9 0.................................... MrMLegg$^{(7)}$ 87
(Colin Tizzard) *mid-div: struggling after 6th: no ch fr 3 out: plugged on fr 2 out: nrly snatched 2nd* **8/1**^{3}

00- **4** *7* **Brave Encounter (IRE)**^{30} 3173 6-10-13 0........................ JamesBest$^{(3)}$ 80
(Sue Gardner) *towards rr: struggling in last after 5th: plugged on appr 2 out: wnt modest 4th towards fin* **100/1**

060- **5** *½* **The Kvilleken**^{20} 3388 6-11-2 0.. IanPopham 80
(Martin Keighley) *trckd ldrs: rdn after 3 out: sn no ch: tired whn lost 2 pls run-in* **14/1**

63- **6** *3* **Y A Bon (IRE)**^{243} 412 6-11-2 0.................................... HaddenFrost 77
(Martin Hill) *mid-div: wnt 4th after 6th: rdn after 3 out: sn no ch: tired run-in* **25/1**

3/4- **7** *21* **Power Of God (IRE)**^{37} 3046 6-10-13 0......................... MichaelByrne$^{(3)}$ 56
(Tim Vaughan) *in tch: rdn after 7th: sn wknd: t.o* **14/1**

0- **8** *2 ½* **Castarnie**^{66} 2457 6-11-2 0... FelixDeGiles 53
(Robert Walford) *rdn after 6th: a towards rr: t.o* **66/1**

000- **9** *38* **Proper Job**^{21} 3363 6-11-2 0.......................................(p) AndrewThornton 15
(Polly Gundry) *mid-div: rdn after 6th: sn wknd: t.o* **66/1**

0/0- **P** **Starship Trouper**^{70} 2375 6-11-2 0............................... DougieCostello
(Neil Mulholland) *nt fluent: trckd wnr tl after 5th: sn bhd: t.o whn p.u bef 7th* **66/1**

5m 10.5s (24.50) **Going Correction** +1.40s/f (Heav) **10** Ran SP% **122.3**
Speed ratings: **107,90,90,87,87 86,77,76,61,**
CSF £2.76 TOTE £1.40: £1.10, £1.10, £2.90; EX 2.50 Trifecta £12.40.

The Form Book Jumps, Raceform Ltd, Compton, RG20 6NL.

Owner Favourites Racing **Bred** Dick White **Trained** Withycombe, Somerset

FOCUS

Hurdles moved out by two sections and all bends moved out by 3-4yds. Second and third fences in back straight omitted. Taunton's first ever meeting on a Saturday got under way in worsening conditions with a fair novices' hurdle on heavy ground. It was much the fastest of the hurdles races and looks a step up from the winner.

3783 BATHWICK TYRES TAUNTON NOVICES' HURDLE (9 hdls) 2m 1f

1:05 (1:06) (Class 4) 4-Y-0+ **£4,223** (£1,240; £620; £310)

Form RPR

40- **1** **All But Grey**[31] 3163 8-11-1 0 MichealNolan(3) 105+
(Carroll Gray) *trckd ldr: led after 3 out: nt fluent next: styd on wl: pushed out* **11/1**

/30- **2** 3 **Rugged Jack (FR)**[30] 3173 7-11-4 0 JackDoyle 98
(Victor Dartnall) *trckd ldrs: rdn after 3 out: chsd wnr bef next: jnd for hld 2nd at the last: styd on fnl 120yds* **7/2**[2]

500- **3** 1 1/4 **Devil's Dyke (USA)**[36] 3061 6-11-4 0 PaulMoloney 97
(Evan Williams) *racd wdst: mid-div: hdwy after 3 out: sn rdn into 3rd: chal for hld 2nd at the last: no ex fnl 120yds* **4/1**[3]

00U- **4** 16 **Bandol (IRE)**[4] 3694 6-11-1 0 RobertDunne(3) 81
(Laura Young) *hld up: sme prog 3 out but no ch w ldrs: plugged on into modest 4th run-in* **100/1**

/00- **5** 5 **Be Bop Boru (IRE)**[42] 2940 7-11-1 0 MichaelByrne(3) 76
(Tim Vaughan) *in tch tl rdn after 3 out: no threat after* **13/2**

425- **6** 1 **Newforge House (IRE)**[23] 3278 6-10-13 0 JamesBanks(5) 75
(Brendan Powell) *led tl after 3 out: sn rdn: wkng whn mstke next* **6/1**

00- **7** 9 **Baksheesh**[51] 2761 5-11-1 0 JamesBest(3) 66
(Sue Gardner) *wknd 3 out: a towards rr: t.o* **100/1**

646- **8** 21 **Georgea (IRE)**[49] 2824 5-10-11 0 DougieCostello 38
(Gary Moore) *t.k.h: hld up: hdwy 4th: wknd after 3 out: mstke last: t.o* **20/1**

00P- **9** 11 **Arcas (IRE)**[30] 3173 5-10-13 0 CharlieWallis(5) 34
(Alan Jones) *mid-div: rdn after 6th: sn wknd: t.o* **200/1**

P **Vauban Du Seuil (FR)**[223] 5-11-4 0 RyanMahon
(Harry Fry) *mid-div: nt fluent 2nd: wknd after 3 out: bhd whn p.u bef next* **9/4**[1]

4m 41.3s (33.30) **Going Correction** +1.50s/f (Heavy) **10** Ran SP% **116.2**

Speed ratings (Par 105): **81,79,79,71,69 68,64,54,49,**

CSF £49.71 TOTE £14.50: £3.60, £1.10, £1.60; EX 53.40 Trifecta £160.00.

Owner R J Napper and N P Searle **Bred** R Napper & N P Searle **Trained** Moorland, Somerset

FOCUS

A modest novice hurdle. A step forward from the winner, with the form rated around the third.

3784 BATHWICK TYRES BRIDGWATER H'CAP HURDLE (12 hdls) 3m 110y

1:40 (1:43) (Class 3) (0-130,128) 4-Y-0+ **£5,848** (£1,717; £858; £429)

Form RPR

/34- **1** **Lienosus (IRE)**[36] 3060 8-11-12 **128** PaulMoloney 140+
(Evan Williams) *racd wd: a.p: led after 9th tl after 3 out: led again bef last: shkn up to assert after last: eased towards fin* **9/1**

422- **2** 3 3/4 **American Life (FR)**[8] 3638 7-10-0 **105** (vt) KielanWoods(3) 110
(Anthony Middleton) *racd wd: trckd ldrs: rdn after 3 out: chsd wnr next: styd on same pce fr last* **11/2**

053- **3** 17 **Buckhorn Tom**[55] 2691 6-10-5 **114** (p) MrMLegg(7) 101
(Colin Tizzard) *prom in centre/inner: dropped to 6th and btn whn rdn after 3 out: modest 5th whn nt fluent last: plugged on to snatch 3rd past wkng horses fnl strides* **4/1**[2]

U23- **4** nk **Brackloon High (IRE)**[21] 3359 9-10-13 **120** JamesBanks(5) 106
(Brendan Powell) *kpt to inner: trckd ldrs tl 3rd: last but wl in tch: nudged along after 7th: rdn to ld after 3 out tl bef next: wknd last* **13/2**

051- **5** shd **Woodford County**[29] 3191 7-10-10 **119** MrCGethings(7) 106
(Philip Hobbs) *racd centre: prom: rdn to chse ldrs after 3 out: wknd last* **7/2**[1]

0F5- **6** 74 **Robin Will (FR)**[29] 3191 9-10-5 **110** (p[1]) MichealNolan(3) 22
(Richard Woollacott) *hld up bhd ldrs: kpt wd: wknd 3 out: t.o* **10/1**

2/4- **P** **Awesome Freddie**[23] 3286 9-10-13 **115** HarrySkelton
(Dan Skelton) *kpt to inner: trckd ldrs: rdn after 9th: sn btn: t.o whn p.u bef 2 out* **5/1**[3]

56P- **P** **Mister Snowball (FR)**[7] 3642 7-10-13 **115** (p) RobertThornton
(Chris Down) *racd wd: prom: led 3rd tl after 9th: sn rdn: wknd qckly after next: t.o whn p.u bef 2 out* **28/1**

644/ **P** **Tenby Jewel (IRE)**[388] 3202 9-10-9 **111** TommyPhelan
(Mark Gillard) *racd centre: led tl 3rd: trckd ldrs: rdn after 9th: sn wknd: t.o whn p.u bef 2 out* **66/1**

6m 47.2s (43.20) **Going Correction** +1.60s/f (Heavy) **9** Ran SP% **111.6**

Speed ratings (Par 107): **94,92,87,87,87 63,,,**

CSF £55.54 CT £226.23 TOTE £8.50: £2.60, £1.80, £1.60; EX 59.30 Trifecta £437.40.

Owner Mr & Mrs William Rucker **Bred** Fergus Jones **Trained** Llancarfan, Vale Of Glamorgan

FOCUS

A fairly decent staying handicap hurdle in which they went a respectable, even gallop given the very testing underfoot conditions. The cosy winner belatedly fulfilled the promise of last season's form.

3785 BATHWICK TYRES BATH NOVICES' H'CAP CHASE (13 fncs 4 omitted) 2m 7f 110y

2:15 (2:15) (Class 4) (0-110,110) 5-Y-0+ **£4,659** (£1,446; £779)

Form RPR

501- **1** **Buywise (IRE)**[2] 3729 7-11-11 **109** 7ex PaulMoloney 130+
(Evan Williams) *mid-div: hdwy to trck ldrs after 8th: chalng whn nt fluent 3 out: led after 2 out: sn clr: easily* **5/4**[1]

/34- **2** 9 **Water Wagtail**[55] 2691 7-11-11 **109** RobertThornton 116+
(Emma Lavelle) *sn upsides ldr: led 4 out: jnd next: rdn and hdd after 2 out: styd on same pce* **15/2**[3]

FP2- **3** 10 **Possibly Flora**[19] 3421 9-10-7 **91** (t) DougieCostello 86
(Richard Woollacott) *hld up: hdwy appr 9th: wnt cl 3rd 4 out: sn rdn: hld fr next: styd on same pce* **10/1**

/56- **P** **Saint Peray (FR)**[37] 3044 8-10-1 **85** SamJones
(Bob Buckler) *trckd ldrs tl rdn after 9th: wknd 4 out: poor 4th whn p.u bef 2 out* **7/1**[2]

313- **P** **Russe Blanc (FR)**[29] 3190 7-11-1 **102** (p) MichealNolan(3)
(Richard Lee) *trckd ldrs: pushed along after 8th: rdn after 9th: wknd 4 out: tailing off whn p.u bef 3 out* **7/1**[2]

4F1- **P** **Midnight Lira**[30] 3171 7-11-4 **105** JamesBest(3)
(Caroline Keevil) *led tl 9th: sn rdn: sn wknd: tailing off whn p.u bef 4 out* **11/1**

2/0- **P** **Whenindoubtdoit (IRE)**[254] 185 7-11-12 **110** (b[1]) TomCannon
(David Arbuthnot) *trckd ldrs: hit 3rd: nt fluent 7th: sn pushed along: rdn and dropped to rr: wknd bef 4 out: t.o whn p.u bef 3 out* **33/1**

005- **P** **Ashcott Boy**[38] 2568 6-10-4 **91** MichaelByrne(3)
(Neil Mulholland) *mid-div: hdwy to join ldrs 8th: led 9th tl 4 out: wknd qckly: p.u bef next* **50/1**

/62- **P** **Guanciale**[23] 3281 7-10-11 **100** (t) JamesBanks(5)
(Brendan Powell) *a in rr: t.o whn p.u bef 4 out* **10/1**

6m 34.9s (18.90) **Going Correction** +0.90s/f (Soft) **9** Ran SP% **112.6**

Speed ratings: **104,101,97,, , , ,**

CSF £11.29 CT £63.79 TOTE £2.20: £1.20, £2.60, £2.20; EX 13.40 Trifecta £113.80.

Owner T Hywel Jones **Bred** Mrs A Stack **Trained** Llancarfan, Vale Of Glamorgan

FOCUS

A modest staying novices' handicap chase run at a decent tempo which took its toll in the conditions with only three finishers. The easy winner confirmed the merit of his recent easy win and is probably capable of better.

3786 BATHWICK TYRES YEOVIL H'CAP HURDLE (10 hdls) 2m 3f 110y

2:50 (2:50) (Class 3) (0-135,130) 4-Y-0+ **£5,848** (£1,717; £858; £429)

Form RPR

/03- **1** **Virak (FR)**[59] 2601 5-11-5 **130** JackSherwood(7) 142+
(Paul Nicholls) *disp ld: mstke 3 out: sn pushed into a commanding advantage: rdn briefly after last: pushed out* **5/1**

214/ **2** 42 **Sustainability (IRE)**[274] 5375 9-10-11 **120** HarryChalloner(5) 89
(Venetia Williams) *disp ld tl rdn after 3 out: qckly btn: fin tired but a holding on for 2nd* **7/2**[3]

134- **3** 2 1/4 **Wily Fox**[22] 3328 7-10-7 **118** KieronEdgar(7) 85
(James Eustace) *trckd ldrs: mstke 2nd: nvr really travelling after: nt fluent next: rdn after 6th: lft btn 3rd next: clsd on tiring runner-up fr 2 out but nvr any threat* **7/4**[1]

000/ **4** 98 **Tiger O'Toole (IRE)**[317] 4616 9-11-7 **125** PaulMoloney
(Evan Williams) *racd wd: hld up: 5th: losing tch whn mstke 6th: continued t.o fr next* **10/1**

3/4- **P** **Roudoudou Ville (FR)**[42] 2940 9-11-2 **120** JackDoyle
(Victor Dartnall) *racd wd: trckd ldrs: rdn in 3rd after 6th: appeared to lose action and p.u bef next* **11/4**[2]

5m 15.9s (29.90) **Going Correction** +1.70s/f (Heavy) **5** Ran SP% **111.0**

Speed ratings (Par 107): **108,91,90,51,**

CSF £22.18 TOTE £10.80: £2.60, £1.60; EX 20.60 Trifecta £112.00.

Owner Hills Of Ledbury (Aga) **Bred** B Thierry, S Thierry & E Labataille **Trained** Ditcheat, Somerset

FOCUS

A decent small-field handicap hurdle in which they went a sedate gallop until the tempo increased down the back straight. Not form to be confident about.

3787 BATHWICK TYRES NOVICES' LIMITED H'CAP CHASE (9 fncs 3 omitted) 2m 110y

3:25 (3:26) (Class 3) (0-125,123) 5-Y-0+ **£7,147** (£2,098; £1,049; £524)

Form RPR

4F5- **1** **Tornado In Milan (IRE)**[28] 3204 8-10-13 **115** PaulMoloney 126+
(Evan Williams) *t.k.h: kpt wd: disp ld: hit 4th: outrt ldr after 3 out: rdn after last: enough in hand to repel late surge of runner-up* **3/1**[2]

565- **2** 3/4 **Sound Investment (IRE)**[20] 3386 6-11-7 **123** (t) RyanMahon 131+
(Paul Nicholls) *trckd ldrs: hmpd 1st: jnd wnr 4 out: rdn and ev ch next: looked hld after 2 out: str run fnl 120yds: nvr quite reeling in wnr* **7/4**[1]

044- **3** 6 **Noche De Reyes (FR)**[28] 3202 5-11-0 **119** AlainCawley 117
(Tom George) *hld up bhd ldrs: trckd ldrs 4 out: sn rdn: kpt on same pce fr 3 out* **4/1**[3]

F46- **4** 35 **Sands Cove (IRE)**[19] 3418 7-11-6 **122** (t) MarkGrant 88
(Charlie Mann) *trckd ldrs: jnd ldrs 4th: rdn next: sn wknd: t.o* **8/1**

5 1 1/4 **Itsuptoyou (IRE)**[259] 128 10-10-9 **111** RobertThornton 76
(Arthur Whiting) *hld up bhd ldrs: hdwy 4 out: sn rdn: wknd next: t.o* **25/1**

/13- **P** **Workbench (FR)**[37] 3045 6-11-7 **123** (t) HarrySkelton
(Dan Skelton) *diputed ld tl rdn after 4th: wknd 4 out: t.o whn p.u bef 3 out* **11/2**

4m 27.8s (13.80) **Going Correction** +1.00s/f (Soft)

WFA 5 from 6yo+ 3lb **6** Ran SP% **111.7**

Speed ratings: **107,106,103,87,86**

CSF £9.01 TOTE £4.20: £2.30, £1.40; EX 11.20 Trifecta £49.70.

Owner Mr & Mrs William Rucker **Bred** Garry Hadden **Trained** Llancarfan, Vale Of Glamorgan

FOCUS

A fair novice handicap chase. The winner is capable of better still.

3788 BATHWICK TYRES MIDSOMER NORTON H'CAP HURDLE (9 hdls) 2m 1f

4:00 (4:02) (Class 5) (0-100,100) 4-Y-0+ **£2,737** (£798; £399)

Form RPR

U00- **1** **Withy Mills**[37] 3047 9-10-3 **80** (bt) JamesBest(3) 88
(Kevin Bishop) *mid-div: hdwy 3 out: sn rdn: styng on in disp 2nd whn hit last: str run to ld fnl 175yds: drvn out* **14/1**

003- **2** 3 **Whispering Harry**[19] 3426 5-11-0 **88** RobertThornton 92
(Henry Oliver) *trckd ldrs: hit 3 out: led next: sn rdn: no ex whn hdd fnl 175yds* **11/4**[1]

3/P- **3** 1 1/4 **Just Spot**[87] 2029 7-10-13 **97** JonPark(10) 100
(Kevin Bishop) *mid-div: rdn and hdwy after 3 out: styd on to dispute cl 2nd briefly last: no ex fnl 120yds* **16/1**

/03- **4** 7 **Juicy Legend**[23] 3251 7-10-5 **79** TomCannon 75
(Chris Gordon) *trckd ldrs: chalng but short of room after 3 out: sn rdn: styd on same pce fr next* **12/1**

P00- **5** 3 1/2 **Moneymix**[42] 2954 7-10-1 **75** (b[1]) WillKennedy 67
(Ali Brewer) *towards rr: reminders after 4th: hdwy into midfield next: drvn after 3 out: styd on but nvr gng pce to get involved* **8/1**[3]

FU4- **6** 1 **Pagham Belle**[33] 3140 6-10-6 **83** (t) MarkQuinlan(3) 77
(Nigel Hawke) *led tl 2nd: prom: led after 3 out: rdn and hdd whn mstke 2 out: no ex fr last* **13/2**[2]

/6F- **7** 4 1/2 **Chance Encounter (IRE)**[23] 3290 8-11-2 **97** MrCSmith(7) 84
(Linda Blackford) *awkward 1st: led next: rdn and hdd after 3 out: fdd fr next* **8/1**[3]

440- **8** 7 **Karl Marx (IRE)**[43] 2920 4-10-4 **89** TommyPhelan 58
(Mark Gillard) *nvr bttr than mid-div* **25/1**

300- **9** 1 3/4 **Miles Of Sunshine**[19] 3426 9-10-11 **85** IanPopham 63
(Ron Hodges) *t.k.h: trckd ldrs: rdn after 3 out: sn wknd* **20/1**

500- **10** nk **Nether Stream (IRE)**[19] 3420 10-11-5 **100** JakeHodson(7) 78
(David Dennis) *chsd ldrs tl wknd after 3 out* **33/1**

0P/- **11** 58 **Businessmoney Judi**[429] 2441 8-11-11 **99** (t) PaulMoloney 19
(Keiran Burke) *a towards rr: wknd bef 2 out: t.o* **28/1**

04/- **12** 3 3/4 **Zouti (FR)**[313] 4702 6-10-10 **91** MrGGorman(7) 7
(Gary Moore) *mid-div tl after 5th: sn bhd: t.o* **25/1**

006- **13** *10* **Moratab (IRE)**[13] 3550 5-11-12 **100**....................................(t) FelixDeGiles 6
(Keiran Burke) *mid-div tl wknd after 3 out: t.o* **14/1**
0PP- **P** **Jambobo**[19] 3426 5-10-1 **75**..(b) JamesDavies
(Chris Down) *a towards rr: bhd whn p.u jst bef 2 out* **66/1**
420/ **P** **Whichever**[649] 5325 8-11-12 **100**.. SeanQuinlan
(Richard Phillips) *a towards rr: t.o whn p.u bef 2 out* **25/1**
U03- **P** **Camptown Lady**[18] 3427 5-10-13 **87**............................ DougieCostello
(Laura Young) *a towards rr: t.o whn p.u bef 2 out* **17/2**

4m 40.2s (32.20) **Going Correction** +1.80s/f (Heav)
WFA 4 from 5yo+ 11lb **16** Ran SP% **123.8**
Speed ratings (Par 103): **96,94,94,90,89 88,86,83,82,82 54,53,48, ,**
CSF £50.21 CT £659.39 TOTE £15.40: £3.50, £1.40, £4.70, £2.70; EX 68.70 Trifecta £404.20.
Owner Slabs And Lucan **Bred** K Bishop **Trained** Spaxton, Somerset

FOCUS
A low-grade handicap, and fairly sound form.
T/Plt: £60.20. Pool: £77,642.05 - 941.44 winning units. T/Qpdt: £17.30. Pool: £4850.90 - 206.50 winning units. TM

3789 - (Foreign Racing) - See Raceform Interactive

3557 NAAS (L-H)
Saturday, January 18

OFFICIAL GOING: Soft to heavy

3790a LIMESTONE LAD HURDLE (GRADE 3) (10 hdls) 2m 3f
1:00 (1:01) 5-Y-0+ **£16,250** (£4,750; £2,250; £750)

RPR
1 **Rule The World**[21] 3374 7-11-8 150.................................... BryanCooper 163+
(M F Morris, Ire) *mde all: 2 l clr 1/2-way: stl gng wl into st: reduced advantage 2 out: rdn and in command whn stepped at last: styd on wl* **5/4**[1]
2 *7 ½* **Jennies Jewel (IRE)**[20] 3403 7-10-10 139........................ DannyMullins 143
(Jarlath P Fahey, Ire) *trckd ldr: mstke in 2nd at 5th: tk clsr order bhd ldr 2 out: sn rdn and no ex u.p bef last where j.big: kpt on same pce* **6/1**[3]
3 *9* **Dunguib (IRE)**[1040] 4791 11-10-13 148........................... BrianO'Connell 138
(Philip Fenton, Ire) *hld up in rr: t.k.h: slt mstke 3rd and nt fluent at times after: 5th 1/2-way: tk clsr order in 4th fr 3 out: pushed along and no imp on ldrs between last 2: kpt on fr last into mod 3rd run-in* **13/2**
4 *4 ½* **Upsie (FR)**[20] 3403 6-10-13 145... RWalsh 133
(W P Mullins, Ire) *chsd ldrs: 4th 1/2-way: slt mstke in 3rd at 3 out: rdn fr next and no imp on wnr bef last: wknd run-in and dropped to mod 4th* **11/4**[2]
5 *17* **Rathlin**[172] 1157 9-10-13 140..(t) DavyRussell 118
(M F Morris, Ire) *chsd ldrs: 3rd 1/2-way: dropped to 5th after 3 out and no imp bef next: one pce after* **7/1**
6 *19* **Mourad (IRE)**[18] 3443 9-11-8 154....................................... PaulTownend 106
(W P Mullins, Ire) *hld up towards rr: reminders in 5th after 2nd: nt fluent 4th: dropped to rr bef next where reminders again after: detached fr 6th and no imp after 3 out: one pce* **16/1**

4m 52.5s (0.90) **6** Ran SP% **117.1**
CSF £10.07 TOTE £2.20: £1.20, £2.20; DF 10.10 Trifecta £133.80.
Owner Gigginstown House Stud **Bred** Mrs P G Wilkins And R J McAlpine **Trained** Fethard, Co Tipperary

FOCUS
A really good performance from Rule the World as he gave the biggest indicator yet of being back to something like his best.

3791a WOODLANDS PARK 100 CLUB NOVICE CHASE (GRADE 2) (16 fncs) 3m
1:35 (1:35) 5-Y-0+ **£21,666** (£6,333; £3,000; £1,000)

RPR
1 **Foxrock (IRE)**[20] 3404 6-11-5 142...................................... DannyMullins 146+
(T M Walsh, Ire) *chsd ldrs: nt fluent 5th: disp 2nd 1/2-way: slt mstke 10th: wnt cl 2nd bef 12th and on terms next: led narrowly after 3 out: kpt on wl fr last and extended advantage run-in* **11/8**[1]
2 *7* **Sizing Gold (IRE)**[34] 3124 7-11-5 .... AELynch 139+
(Henry De Bromhead, Ire) *chsd ldrs: disp 2nd 1/2-way: hdwy on inner to dispute after 3 out: rdn in 2nd after 2 out and no imp on wnr u.p fr last: tired nr fin and jst hld on for 2nd* **7/4**[2]
3 *shd* **Clar Na Mionn (IRE)**[23] 3314 7-11-5 131........................... PhillipEnright 139
(V T O'Brien, Ire) *w.w: detached in 4th 1/2-way: tk clsr order bhd ldrs bef 12th: rdn in 4th into st and wnt mod 3rd 2 out: kpt on wl fr last and jst failed for 2nd: nt trble wnr* **20/1**
4 *49* **Rogue Angel (IRE)**[18] 3441 6-11-5 131...........................(b) BryanCooper 90
(M F Morris, Ire) *led: nt fluent 3rd: jnd 4 out: rdn fr next and hdd: sn wknd and dropped to mod 4th 2 out: eased: t.o* **6/1**[3]
5 *30* **Ipsos Du Berlais (FR)**[22] 3341 8-11-5 137.........................(p) PCarberry 60
(Noel Meade, Ire) *w.w: in rr whn j. sltly rt 6th: detached bef 1/2-way: completely t.o* **6/1**[3]

6m 55.4s (7.30) **5** Ran SP% **111.8**
CSF £4.45 TOTE £2.80: £1.70, £1.10; DF 2.10 Trifecta £42.90.
Owner Barry Connell **Bred** Geoffrey Thompson **Trained** Kill, Co Kildare

FOCUS
Despite some erratic jumping at times, there's little doubt that Foxrock stays and has an engine. He's rated to the best view of his previous form.

3277 TOWCESTER (R-H)
Sunday, January 19

OFFICIAL GOING: Heavy
Wind: Light; across Weather: Fine

3796 HAYGAIN HAY STEAMERS CLEAN HEALTHY FORAGE MAIDEN HURDLE (7 hdls 1 omitted) 2m
1:10 (1:10) (Class 4) 4-Y-0+ **£3,898** (£1,144; £572; £286)

Form RPR
004- **1** **Pink Gin**[31] 3175 6-11-4 0...(t) MarkGrant 112+
(Jim Old) *led tl rdn and hdd 2 out: 2 l down whn lft in ld last: all out* **12/1**[3]
502- **2** *6* **Ampleforth**[13] 3567 6-11-4 111..(p) WillKennedy 106
(Ian Williams) *a.p: rdn appr 2 out: wkng whn lft 2nd and mstke last* **6/1**[2]
30- **3** *2 ¾* **Grey Earl**[30] 3194 7-11-4 0... JamieMoore 102
(Richard Lee) *hld up: hdwy 5th: rdn and wkng whn lft 3rd last* **66/1**
24- **4** *15* **Alanjou (FR)**[107] 1743 4-10-7 114..................................... BrendanPowell 79
(Jamie Snowden) *w wnr tl rdn and wknd appr 2 out* **6/1**[2]
3- **5** *3 ¾* **Polstar (FR)**[18] 3469 5-11-4 0.. JamesDavies 84
(Harry Whittington) *chsd ldrs: ev ch appr 2 out: sn rdn: wknd bef last* **14/1**
5P- **6** *hd* **Collingbourneducis (IRE)**[34] 3134 4-10-0 0............. MissAEStirling[(7)] 72
(Michael Gates) *hld up: racing keenly: bhd fr 4th* **150/1**
030/ **7** *5* **Thom Thumb (IRE)**[645] 5415 8-11-1 0............................. JamesBest[(3)] 78
(Paul Webber) *chsd ldrs tl rdn and wknd appr 2 out* **66/1**
5- **8** *8* **Silent Knight (IRE)**[13] 3567 5-11-4 0..................................... NoelFehily 70
(Warren Greatrex) *hld up: bhd fr 4th* **16/1**
00- **9** *2* **There You Are**[45] 2893 5-11-4 0..................................... RichieMcLernon 68
(Jonjo O'Neill) *hld up: bhd fr 5th* **100/1**
30F- **F** **Milord (GER)**[23] 3322 5-11-4 124.................................... JasonMaguire 114+
(Kim Bailey) *hld up: pushed along 4th: hdwy after next: led 2 out: sn rdn: 2 l up whn fell last* **8/15**[1]
06- **P** **Spirit Minded**[13] 3568 6-10-11 0.......................................(t) DavidEngland
(Giles Smyly) *hld up: bhd fr 4th: p.u bef 2 out* **200/1**

4m 14.4s (6.50) **Going Correction** +0.575s/f (Soft)
WFA 4 from 5yo+ 11lb **11** Ran SP% **119.2**
Speed ratings (Par 105): **106,103,101,94,92 92,89,85,84,**
CSF £83.11 TOTE £17.20: £2.70, £1.60, £6.70; EX 62.50 Trifecta £1711.80 Part won..
Owner Mrs J Fowler & C Jenkins **Bred** Peter Guntrip **Trained** Barbury Castle, Wilts

FOCUS
The third-last was omitted in all hurdle races and it was stamina-sapping ground at this, the stiffest of British tracks. There's a case for rating the form higher.

3797 TRY GG.COM ON YOUR MOBILE H'CAP CHASE (18 fncs) 3m 110y
1:40 (1:40) (Class 5) (0-100,99) 5-Y-0+ **£3,249** (£954; £477; £238)

Form RPR
232- **1** **Smart Exit (IRE)**[31] 3178 7-11-9 **99**...........................(p) JoshuaMoore[(3)] 110+
(Renee Robeson) *chsd ldrs: led 4th to 10th: led next: rdn appr last: all out* **7/2**[2]
0P2- **2** *nk* **Samson Collonges (FR)**[15] 3528 8-9-11 **73** oh1.............. TonyKelly[(3)] 82
(Rebecca Menzies) *led tl after 1st: remained handy: ev ch 3 out: sn rdn: styd on u.p* **14/1**
/31- **3** *½* **Mansonien L'As (FR)**[24] 3277 8-11-8 **95**.......................(p) JasonMaguire 107+
(Donald McCain) *prom: lost pl 2nd: reminders after 6th: hdwy 15th: rdn appr 2 out: styd on u.p* **11/8**[1]
/13- **4** *¾* **Somerby (IRE)**[68] 2441 11-11-0 **87**..............................(t) AndrewThornton 96
(Richenda Ford) *led after 1st: hdd 4th: chsd ldrs: nt clr run and j. slowly 9th: drvn along and outpcd 15th: swtchd rt after 2 out: rallied flat: styd on* **22/1**
004- **5** *1* **Top Benefit (IRE)**[31] 3180 12-10-1 **79**................................ JamesBanks[(5)] 85
(Richard Harper) *hld up: hdwy 7th: rdn after 15th: outpcd next: rallied last: styd on* **33/1**
/30- **6** *1* **Black Is Beautiful (FR)**[30] 3193 6-11-6 **93**........................ JamieMoore 98
(Richard Lee) *hld up in tch: rdn after 6th: led 10th to next: drvn along 13th: styd on u.p* **11/2**[3]
B22- **F** **Kilvergan Boy (IRE)**[24] 3277 10-10-1 **74**..............(p) SamTwiston-Davies
(Nigel Twiston-Davies) *hld up: mstke 11th: fell next* **12/1**
333- **P** **Miss Saffron**[56] 2700 11-11-2 **94**................................ MissLucyGardner[(5)]
(Sue Gardner) *hld up: hdwy 11th: pushed along 13th: wknd 2 out: p.u bef last* **14/1**
PP0- **P** **Bishophill Jack (IRE)**[30] 3193 8-11-12 **99**.....................(p) NickScholfield
(Kim Bailey) *chsd ldrs: lost pl 9th: bhd fr 12th: p.u bef 2 out* **28/1**
360- **F** **Artic Night (FR)**[28] 3227 8-10-12 **85**...............................(bt) DavidEngland
(Nigel Twiston-Davies) *hld up: fell 2nd* **66/1**

6m 49.5s (12.60) **Going Correction** +0.575s/f (Soft) **10** Ran SP% **113.0**
Speed ratings: **102,101,101,101,101 100, , , ,**
CSF £43.98 CT £95.83 TOTE £4.10: £1.30, £4.10, £1.10; EX 46.30 Trifecta £161.10.
Owner The Ravenstone Partnership **Bred** G T Morrow **Trained** Tyringham, Bucks

FOCUS
There was a tight finish to this moderate staying handicap. The first fouer ran pretty much to their marks.

3798 FREE TIPS EVERY DAY AT GG.COM H'CAP HURDLE (9 hdls 2 omitted) 2m 5f
2:10 (2:12) (Class 3) (0-130,130) 4-Y-0+ **£6,498** (£1,908; £954; £477)

Form RPR
404- **1** **Oscar Prairie (IRE)**[24] 3292 9-10-8 **122**..........(b) WilliamFeatherstone[(10)] 126+
(Warren Greatrex) *hld up: hdwy appr 2 out: led last: pushed out* **7/1**[3]
266/ **2** *2* **Sunny Ledgend**[290] 5140 9-11-0 **125**.................................. MrJMartin[(7)] 127
(Andrew J Martin) *led to 2 out: ev ch last: sn rdn: styd on same pce flat* **14/1**
02F- **3** *4 ½* **Phare Isle (IRE)**[17] 3505 9-10-3 **114**.........................(tp) MrMJPKendrick[(7)] 113
(Ben Case) *a.p: chsd ldr 7th: led 2 out tl last: no ex flat* **8/1**
/P3- **4** *7* **Astigos (FR)**[3] 3737 7-10-11 **115**.. AidanColeman 106
(Venetia Williams) *hld up: hdwy 7th: rdn appr 2 out: wknd bef last* **15/8**[1]
534- **5** *9* **Pure Science (IRE)**[22] 3359 6-11-4 **122**.................. SamTwiston-Davies 104
(Nigel Twiston-Davies) *sn prom: chsd ldr after 2nd tl rdn and wknd appr 2 out* **5/2**[2]
0P5/ **6** *46* **Spirit River (FR)**[35] 9-11-12 **130**.. LeeEdwards 66
(Dave Roberts) *chsd ldr tl after 2nd: remained handy tl rdn and wknd wl bef 2 out* **33/1**
PF0/ **P** **Round The Horn (IRE)**[379] 3502 14-10-3 **107**.........................(t) MarkGrant
(Jim Old) *hld up: rdn and wknd bef 2 out: p.u bef last* **22/1**
031/ **P** **Sweeps Hill (NZ)**[820] 2114 10-11-12 **130**...................... RichieMcLernon
(Jonjo O'Neill) *hld up: hdwy appr 2 out: wknd qckly and p.u bef last* **16/1**
51/- **P** **Fishing Bridge (IRE)**[297] 4977 9-11-7 **125**.........................(p) PaulMoloney
(David Rees) *chsd ldrs: hit 5th: pushed along next: lost pl whn mstke 7th: sn wknd: bhd whn p.u bef 2 out* **16/1**

5m 49.3s (22.10) **Going Correction** +0.575s/f (Soft) **9** Ran SP% **112.7**
Speed ratings (Par 107): **80,79,77,74,71 53, , ,**
CSF £92.22 CT £794.27 TOTE £9.20: £2.40, £2.30, £2.60; EX 115.30 Trifecta £673.70.
Owner Warren Greatrex **Bred** Noel O'Connor **Trained** Upper Lambourn, Berks

FOCUS
A modest handicap. They went a routine gallop and the principals came clear after the last. Probably not a race to get carried away with.

3799 DON'T MISS OUT WITH GG.COM ALERTS H'CAP CHASE (12 fncs) 2m 110y
2:40 (2:40) (Class 5) (0-100,99) 5-Y-0+ **£3,249** (£954; £477; £238)

Form RPR
35U- **1** **Freckle Face**[31] 3180 7-11-12 **99**.. TommyPhelan 118+
(Bill Turner) *hld up: nt fluent 6th: hdwy 9th: led appr 2 out: sn lft clr* **10/3**[2]
446- **2** *19* **Highland River**[12] 3593 8-10-8 **81**......................................(b) LeeEdwards 80
(Dave Roberts) *led tl after 3rd: chsd ldr tl pushed along 5th: drvn along 8th: styd on same pce fr 3 out: wnt 2nd last* **7/1**[3]

363- **3** *7* **Panthers Run**[9] 3637 14-9-11 **73** oh4..............................(t) JohnKington[(3)] 65
(Jonathan Haynes) *chsd ldr tl after 3rd: rdn and hdd after 3 out: lft 2nd and j.rt next: sn wknd* **11/1**

455/ **4** *½* **Beauchamp Viking**[478] 1659 10-10-8 **81**..............................(t) ColinBolger 72
(Hugo Froud) *prom: rdn after 3 out: wnt 2nd briefly after 2 out: sn wknd* **16/1**

034- **F** **Fintan**[19] 3431 11-11-6 **93**.............................. DougieCostello 102
(Laura Young) *chsd ldrs: wnt 2nd after 5th: led after 3 out: sn rdn and hdd: cl 2nd whn fell next* **10/3**[2]

/32- **U** **Hector's House**[59] 2615 8-10-0 **76** oh2 ow3.................... RobertDunne[(3)] 65
(Nikki Evans) *hld up: rdn after 9th: in rr whn nt clr run: j. slowly and uns rdr 2 out* **11/4**[1]

U/5- **P** **Mezarat (ITY)**[210] 807 9-9-8 **74** ow1..............................(p) MissAEStirling[(7)]
(Michael Gates) *hld up: hdwy whn slipped bdly on landing and lost pl 6th: hdwy 8th: wknd after 3 out: p.u bef next* **9/1**

4m 25.5s (9.40) **Going Correction** +0.575s/f (Soft) 7 Ran SP% **109.5**
Speed ratings: **100,91,87,87,** ,
CSF £23.81 TOTE £3.90: £2.00, £3.90; EX 25.90 Trifecta £215.00.
Owner Mrs Christine Goldsmith **Bred** B J Goldsmith **Trained** Sigwells, Somerset

FOCUS
A weak handicap in which only two mattered off the home turn. This rates a step up from the winner.

3800 VISIT THE FORUM ON GG.COM NOVICES' HURDLE (10 hdls 2 omitted) 3m
3:10 (3:10) (Class 4) 5-Y-O+ **£3,898** (£1,144; £572; £286)

Form RPR

4/F- **1** **Tidal Dance (IRE)**[8] 3653 7-10-12 121.............................. AidanColeman 130+
(Venetia Williams) *hld up: hdwy bef 2 out: led appr and mstke last: styd on wl* **5/6**[1]

12- **2** *7* **Knockanrawley (IRE)**[31] 3177 6-11-4 131.............................. JasonMaguire 126
(Kim Bailey) *trckd ldrs: led 6th to next: led 8th: rdn and hdd appr last: styd on same pce* **5/2**[2]

3- **3** *2¾* **Ivy Gate (IRE)**[31] 3173 6-10-7 0.............................. MauriceLinehan[(5)] 117
(Jonjo O'Neill) *led tl after 1st: remained handy: led again 7th: hdd next: ev ch 2 out: sn rdn: no ex whn nt fluent last* **16/1**

/62- **4** *6* **Sybarite (FR)**[29] 3195 8-10-12 116.............................. SamTwiston-Davies 113
(Nigel Twiston-Davies) *hld up: hdwy to join ldrs 6th: rdn appr 2 out: wknd bef last* **9/2**[3]

5- **5** *4½* **Kaikias (IRE)**[43] 2942 7-10-12 0..............................(b[1]) RichieMcLernon 108
(Jonjo O'Neill) *nt fluent 1st: chsd ldrs tl rdn and wknd appr 2 out* **40/1**

3- **6** *81* **Spike Mac (IRE)**[101] 1838 9-10-12 0.............................. AndrewThornton 26
(Richard Harper) *led after 1st: hdd 6th: sn wknd* **150/1**

6m 44.5s (29.50) **Going Correction** +0.575s/f (Soft) 6 Ran SP% **110.3**
Speed ratings: **73,70,69,67,66 39**
CSF £3.16 TOTE £2.30: £1.30, £1.60; EX 3.20 Trifecta £16.40.
Owner Pinks Gym & Leisure Wear Ltd **Bred** Mrs C Ross **Trained** Kings Caple, H'fords

FOCUS
They went steadily in this fair little staying novice and the form is rated around the consistent runner-up.

3801 CGA FOXHUNTER TRIAL HUNTERS' CHASE (14 fncs 4 omitted) 3m 110y
3:40 (3:42) (Class 6) 5-Y-O+ **£1,247** (£387; £193; £96)

Form RPR

446/ **1** **Pearlysteps**[287] 5199 11-11-9 128.............................. MissJCWilliams[(5)] 140+
(Henry Daly) *hld up: hdwy 5th: mstke 11th: led last (normal 3 out): sn clr* **6/4**[1]

2- **2** *34* **Gunmoney (IRE)**[246] 9-11-7 0.............................. MrJRussell[(7)] 103
(G T H Bailey) *led: nt fluent 4th: hdd after 7th: led again 12th: hdd last (normal 3 out): sn rdn and wknd* **2/1**[2]

/ **3** *nk* **Viking Splash (IRE)**[246] 11-11-11 115..............................(p) MrDKemp[(3)] 103
(David Kemp) *prom: rdn after 13th: wknd last (normal 3 out)* **14/1**

2- **4** *½* **Alskamatic**[14] 8-11-7 0.............................. MissEEMacMahon[(7)] 102
(Richard J Bandey) *hld up: bhd 9th and pushed along 9th: n.d* **14/1**

U40/ **5** *33* **Nalim (IRE)**[322] 8-11-11 0.............................. MissHBethell[(3)] 69
(W A Bethell) *hld up: bhd fr 11th* **20/1**

1PP- **6** *32* **Charles Bruce (IRE)**[4] 3720 11-11-13 103.............................. MrFTett[(5)] 41
(A Campbell) *chsd ldr tl led after 7th: clr after 9th tl hdd 12th: rdn and wknd bef last (normal 3 out)* **33/1**

1U1/ **7** *dist* **Lorikarad (FR)**[668] 5019 10-12-3 116..............................(p) MrLRPayter[(5)]
(Miss C C Jones) *hld up: mstke 9th: sme hdwy bef next: sn wknd* **5/1**[3]

3/- **P** **Roskeen Boy (IRE)**[21] 9-11-9 0.............................. MrJSole[(5)]
(Miss Louise Allan) *prom: mstke and lost pl 7th: bhd fr 9th: p.u bef last (normal 3 out)* **100/1**

400/ **U** **Horatio Caine (FR)**[316] 7-11-7 0.............................. MissCChugg[(7)]
(Mrs Julie Mansell) *mstke and uns rdr 2nd* **33/1**

6m 42.4s (5.50) **Going Correction** +0.575s/f (Soft) 9 Ran SP% **115.0**
Speed ratings: **114,103,103,102,92 82,** , ,
CSF £4.79 TOTE £2.60: £1.40, £1.40, £3.00, EX 5.40 Trifecta £26.60.
Owner The Glazeley Partnership **Bred** W P Jenks **Trained** Stanton Lacy, Shropshire

FOCUS
The final two fences in this hunter chase were omitted due to low sun, ensuring an extremely long run-in. The winner cn probably win more of these.

3802 BEST RACING BLOGS ON GG.COM H'CAP HURDLE (7 hdls 1 omitted) 2m
4:10 (4:10) (Class 4) (0-120,120) 4-Y-O+ **£3,898** (£1,144; £572; £286)

Form RPR

354- **1** **Twoways (IRE)**[24] 3288 8-10-10 **104**.............................. ConorO'Farrell 110
(Mark Rimell) *hld up: hdwy appr 2 out: led flat: edgd lft: drvn out* **16/1**

331- **2** *¾* **It's A Doddle (IRE)**[34] 3128 6-11-5 **113**.............................. RichieMcLernon 118
(Jonjo O'Neill) *mid-div: hdwy 4th: rdn appr last: ev ch flat: styd on* **11/4**[1]

22- **3** *2¾* **Smart Money (IRE)**[36] 3094 7-11-5 **113**.............................. AidanColeman 115
(Venetia Williams) *trckd ldrs: plld hrd: lft 2nd after 3rd: lft in ld bef next: rdn appr last: hdd and no ex flat* **11/4**[1]

332- **4** *3¾* **Headly's Bridge (IRE)**[23] 3328 8-11-3 **118**.............................. RyanHatch[(7)] 117
(Simon Earle) *hld up: hdwy 4th: rdn appr 2 out: no ex last* **3/1**[2]

PP5/ **5** *15* **Dashing George (IRE)**[273] 5433 12-11-5 **120**.............................. MrRWinks[(7)] 107
(Peter Winks) *prom: lft 2nd briefly and hmpd 3rd: lft 2nd again next: rdn and ev ch appr 2 out: wknd bef last* **25/1**

0- **6** *1½* **Kilavalley (IRE)**[36] 3094 7-10-10 **111**..............................(p) MikeyEnnis[(7)] 93
(Hugo Froud) *hld up: a in rr* **66/1**

2P0- **7** *34* **Rosslyn Castle**[32] 3163 5-11-4 **112**.............................. JamieMoore 60
(Jonjo O'Neill) *mid-div: hmpd 3rd: hdwy next: rdn and wknd after 5th* **20/1**

/10- **8** *24* **Cawdor House Bert**[34] 3130 7-11-5 **113**.............................. PaulMoloney 37
(David Rees) *hld up: hdwy 5th: rdn and wknd bef next* **40/1**

034- **F** **The Weatherman (IRE)**[77] 2245 7-10-8 **102**.............................. HenryBrooke
(Donald McCain) *led tl after 2nd: chsng ldr whn fell next* **9/1**[3]

255- **U** **Sirop De Menthe (FR)**[34] 3134 4-10-10 **115**..............................(v[1]) WillKennedy
(Miss Jessica Westwood) *plld hrd: trckd ldr tl led after 2nd: sn hung lft and clr: hung bdly lft: hit rails and uns rdr bef 4th* **14/1**

4m 15.1s (7.20) **Going Correction** +0.575s/f (Soft)
WFA 4 from 5yo+ 11lb 10 Ran SP% **113.4**
Speed ratings (Par 105): **105,104,103,101,93 93,76,64,** ,
CSF £57.92 CT £161.55 TOTE £13.50: £3.20, £1.40, £1.30; EX 66.00 Trifecta £658.60.
Owner Mark Rimell **Bred** M And Mrs J Cummins **Trained** Leafield, Oxon

FOCUS
There was a fair gallop on in this modest handicap and the form should work out. A step up from the winner.
T/Plt: £125.00 to a £1 stake. Pool: £144,686.84 - 844.43 winning units T/Qpdt: £20.70 to a £1 stake. Pool: £12,016.09 - 429.08 winning units CR

3803 - (Foreign Racing) - See Raceform Interactive

3480 FAIRYHOUSE (R-H)
Sunday, January 19

OFFICIAL GOING: Soft (soft to heavy in places)

3804a SOLERINA MARES NOVICE HURDLE (GRADE 3) (10 hdls) 2m 2f
1:20 (1:20) 4-Y-O+ **£16,250** (£4,750; £2,250; £750)

RPR

1 **Gitane Du Berlais (FR)**[43] 2934 4-10-4 131.............................. PaulTownend 130+
(W P Mullins, Ire) *trckd ldr in 2nd: nt fluent 2nd and next: led bef 5th and extended advantage bef 4 out: stl travelling wl appr st: pressed between last 2: j.big last and kpt on wl u.p towards fin* **1/1**[1]

2 *5* **Vicky De L'Oasis (FR)**[50] 2810 5-11-1 131.............................. RWalsh 136
(W P Mullins, Ire) *hld up: slt mstke in 5th at 4th: nt fluent 4 out: sn clsd and wnt 2nd appr st: rdn fr 2 out and no imp on wnr fr last: kpt on wl: nt rch wnr* **10/3**[2]

3 *22* **Romantic Fashion (IRE)**[21] 3407 7-10-13.............................. MPFogarty 112
(Mrs Prunella Dobbs, Ire) *chsd ldrs: slt mstke in 4th at 3rd: hdwy into 3rd bef 4 out: pushed along bef next and sn no imp on ldrs: kpt on one pce* **12/1**

4 *5½* **Dantes Firth (IRE)**[8] 3668 7-10-13.............................. RogerLoughran 108
(Thomas Foley, Ire) *chsd ldrs: 3rd 1/2-way: wnt 2nd fr 5th: rdn in 3rd into st and no imp on ldrs: wknd* **12/1**

5 *82* **Fair Funny (IRE)**[13] 3581 6-10-13 102.............................. JohnCullen 25
(Edward U Hales, Ire) *hld up: 6th 1/2-way: no imp in mod 6th bef 3 out: wknd and eased: completely t.o* **50/1**

6 *31* **Honey Bach (IRE)**[24] 3313 7-10-13 111..............................(t) PCarberry
(B R Hamilton, Ire) *w.w: 7th 1/2-way: no imp in mod 5th bef 3 out: wknd and eased: completely t.o* **14/1**

P **Akatara (IRE)**[7] 3680 7-11-3 104.............................. JodyMcGarvey
(Michael J Bowe, Ire) *in rr: detached bef 4th: t.o whn p.u bef 3 out* **66/1**

P **Theatre Bird (IRE)**[21] 3403 6-11-6 130.............................. BryanCooper
(Sean Thomas Doyle, Ire) *led: nt fluent 2nd: hdd bef 5th where mstke and dropped to 3rd: pushed along and wknd bef 4 out: p.u bef next* **9/2**[3]

4m 45.7s (-3.70)
WFA 4 from 5yo+ 11lb 8 Ran SP% **116.8**
CSF £4.80 TOTE £2.50: £1.02, £1.50, £2.10; DF 5.70 Trifecta £30.60.
Owner Simon Munir & Isaac Souede **Bred** J M Lucas, L Collet & C Collet **Trained** Muine Beag, Co Carlow

FOCUS
The allowance she got was significant but it was a pretty impressive performance from the winner, who is rated to her mark.

3806a UNDERWRITING EXCHANGE DAN MOORE MEMORIAL H'CAP CHASE (GRADE A) (13 fncs) 2m 1f
2:20 (2:20) 4-Y-O+
£50,000 (£15,833; £7,500; £2,500; £1,666; £833)

RPR

1 **Turban (FR)**[15] 3543 7-11-2 **140**.............................. RWalsh 155+
(W P Mullins, Ire) *w.w in rr of mid-div: 9th 1/2-way: prog to chse ldrs bef 4 out: clsr in 3rd next: led gng wl between last 2 and wnt clr bef last: styd on wl* **11/2**[2]

2 *6* **Competitive Edge (IRE)**[23] 3341 7-10-12 **136**.............................. APMcCoy 144
(Conor O'Dwyer, Ire) *hld up in tch: 7th 1/2-way: tk clsr order 4 out: cl 2nd bef next where slt mstke: effrt fr 2 out: rdn in 2nd between last 2 and no imp on wnr bef last: kpt on same pce* **7/2**[1]

3 *4* **Lastoftheleaders (IRE)**[23] 3340 11-11-4 **142**.............................. DavyRussell 146
(A J Martin, Ire) *hld up towards rr: 12th 1/2-way: hdwy fr 4 out to chse ldrs in 4th after next: rdn and no imp on ldrs in 3rd between last 2: mstke last: kpt on one pce* **8/1**

4 *4¼* **Torphichen**[18] 3491 9-11-7 **145**.............................. MarkWalsh 145
(E J O'Grady, Ire) *racd in mid-div: 8th 1/2-way: tk clsr order fr 3 out and wnt 5th appr st: no ex u.p fr 2 out: kpt on one pce in 4th* **12/1**

5 *2¼* **Il Fenomeno (ITY)**[22] 3382 8-9-10 **127** oh4..............................(b) JJBurke[(7)] 125
(Noel Meade, Ire) *towards rr: 10th 1/2-way: hdwy in 8th fr 3 out: rdn into mod 6th after next and kpt on u.p into 5th fr last* **18/1**

6 *5* **Harpsy Cord (IRE)**[23] 3347 8-10-6 **130**.............................. AELynch 123
(Henry De Bromhead, Ire) *led briefly fr 1st: sn settled bhd ldrs: 3rd 1/2-way: clsr in 2nd fr 6th: almost on terms bef 4 out and gained narrow advantage bef 3 out: hdd after next and no ex: wknd* **12/1**

7 *6½* **Perfect Smile (IRE)**[24] 3307 9-10-8 **132**.............................. PCarberry 118
(Noel Meade, Ire) *w.w towards rr: 11th 1/2-way: mstke 5th: pushed along in 10th after 3 out and no imp u.p in 7th between last 2: kpt on one pce* **6/1**[3]

8 *8* **Fosters Cross (IRE)**[36] 3100 12-10-11 **135**.............................. MPFogarty 113
(Thomas Mullins, Ire) *chsd ldrs tl led bef 1/2-way: jnd bef 4 out and no imp in 6th fr next: one pce after* **20/1**

9 *19* **Savello (IRE)**[24] 3307 8-11-8 **146**.............................. BryanCooper 105
(A J Martin, Ire) *chsd ldrs: 5th 1/2-way: pushed along after 3 out whn short of room briefly: no imp bef 2 out: wknd* **8/1**

P **Cadspeed (FR)**[29] 3219 11-10-3 **127** oh6.............................. PaulTownend
(W P Mullins, Ire) *prom: settled bhd ldrs fr 1st: 4th 1/2-way: rdn and wknd 4 out: dropped to rr 2 out where mstke: p.u bef last* **12/1**

P **Beneficial Spirit (IRE)**[24] 3306 11-9-10 **127** oh6.............................. AndrewRing[(7)]
(P J Rothwell, Ire) *in rr: mstke 2nd and slt mstke next: last 1/2-way: trailing whn p.u bef 4 out* **25/1**

P **Shrapnel (IRE)**[24] 3314 8-10-11 **135**..............................(tp) RobbieColgan
(Gordon Elliott, Ire) *reminders after s: hld up in mid-div: 6th 1/2-way: dropped to rr 4 out and p.u after next* **14/1**

P **Majala (FR)**[23] 3333 8-11-10 **148**......................................(t) PaddyBrennan
(Tom George) *trckd ldrs tl led after 1st: hdd bef 1/2-way: mstke 6th and dropped to 3rd: remained prom tl mstke 8th and lost pl: dropped towards rr whn nt fluent 2 out: p.u bef last* **9/1**

4m 23.1s (-7.90) **13** Ran SP% **127.7**
CSF £27.81 CT £163.27 TOTE £5.50: £2.20, £1.70, £2.10; DF 34.70 Trifecta £153.30.
Owner Edward O'Connell **Bred** B Provot **Trained** Muine Beag, Co Carlow

FOCUS
A very taking display here from Turban who jumped superbly and looked totally uncomplicated. Personal bests from the first two.

3807 - 3809a (Foreign Racing) - See Raceform Interactive

[3222]BANGOR-ON-DEE (L-H)
Monday, January 20

3810 Meeting Abandoned - waterlogged

[3592]LEICESTER (R-H)
Tuesday, January 21

OFFICIAL GOING: Hurdle course - heavy (soft in places; 6.7); chase course - soft (good to soft in places; heavy on flat course crossings; 7.3)
Wind: Light; across Weather: Fine

3816 CROXTON PARK NOVICES' HURDLE (10 hdls) 2m 4f 110y
1:10 (1:10) (Class 4) 4-Y-0+ **£3,898** (£1,144; £572; £286)

Form RPR

163- **1** **Cogry**[32] 3189 5-11-5 0.................................. SamTwiston-Davies 122
(Nigel Twiston-Davies) *trckd ldrs: wnt 2nd after 6th: led appr 2 out: drvn out: hung rt nr fin* **6/4**[2]

/62- **2** 1 1/2 **Saffron Wells (IRE)**[35] 3148 6-11-2 0........................... TrevorWhelan(3) 121
(Neil King) *hld up: hdwy 7th: ev ch 2 out: sn rdn: styng on whn hmpd nr fin* **12/1**[3]

322- **3** nk **Come On Laurie (IRE)**[26] 3278 6-11-5 **126**..................... AidanColeman 121
(Lawney Hill) *hld up: hdwy after 7th: ev ch 2 out: sn rdn: nt fluent last: styd on same pce flat* **1/1**[1]

4 23 **De Kerry Man (IRE)**[309] 6-11-5 0... SamJones 97
(Fiona Kehoe) *got loose prior to the s: led: rdn: hdd & wknd appr 2 out* **100/1**

4/U- **5** 8 **Whiskey Chaser (IRE)**[26] 3282 6-11-5 0.......................... HenryBrooke 90
(Donald McCain) *trckd ldrs: racd keenly: ev ch 3 out: sn rdn and wknd* **33/1**

/36- **P** **Tiller Belle**[237] 544 6-10-12 0... AndrewTinkler
(Nicky Henderson) *prom: racd keenly: mstke 4th: rdn and wknd after 7th: bhd whn p.u bef 2 out* **16/1**

60- **P** **Ll Cool Horse**[66] 2507 5-11-5 0.. FelixDeGiles
(Tom Gretton) *racd keenly: trckd ldr tl after 6th: wknd next: bhd whn p.u bef last* **100/1**

5m 26.9s (2.20) **Going Correction** +0.125s/f (Yiel) **7** Ran SP% **108.5**
Speed ratings (Par 105): **100,99,99,90,87** ,
CSF £16.04 TOTE £2.10: £1.60, £3.50; EX 12.20 Trifecta £23.30.
Owner Graham And Alison Jelley **Bred** R D And Mrs J S Chugg **Trained** Naunton, Gloucs
■ Stewards' Enquiry : Sam Twiston-Davies one-day ban: careless riding (Feb 4)

FOCUS
They got sorted out from the third-last in this opening novice hurdle and the principals fought out a tough finish. A step up from the winner, with the second improving in line with his bumper form.

3817 BROOK "HANDS AND HEELS" H'CAP CHASE (CONDITIONALS & AMATEURS) (RACING EXCELLENCE INITIATIVE) (15 fncs) 2m 4f 110y
1:40 (1:40) (Class 5) (0-100,98) 5-Y-0+ **£3,249** (£954; £477; £238)

Form RPR

325- **1** **Fitandproperjob**[21] 3439 8-10-12 **84**.............................(vt) CharlieDeutsch 95+
(Anthony Middleton) *hld up: hdwy 9th: blnd 3 out: led on bit appr last: pushed clr* **9/2**[2]

/62- **2** 10 **Thedreamstillalive (IRE)**[14] 3595 14-10-5 **77**...........(t) MrHAABannister 80
(Jim Old) *chsd ldrs: led 4th tl appr 6th: led again bef 4 out: shkn up after 2 out: hdd whn blnd last: no ex flat* **9/2**[2]

34P- **3** 5 **Double Chocolate**[46] 2923 11-11-12 **98**.......................(v[1]) CiaranMckee 95
(John O'Shea) *led tl j. slowly: 3rd: led again appr 6th: hdd bef 4 out: wknd next* **7/1**

P64- **4** 3 3/4 **Chapel House**[19] 3503 11-9-13 **74**.................................. MrJBargary(3) 66
(Richard Harper) *sn prom: ev ch 2 out: sn pushed along: wknd last* **6/1**[3]

613- **5** 8 **Zhukov (IRE)**[20] 3470 12-11-2 **93**....................................(b) MrFPenford(5) 77
(Kevin Tork) *prom tl pushed along and wknd appr 4 out* **25/1**

4PF- **P** **Killegney**[20] 3472 10-11-2 **88**...(v) MissAEStirling
(Michael Gates) *hld up: bhd fr 5th: p.u bef 9th* **16/1**

4PU- **P** **Thorncliffer**[14] 3595 10-10-3 **75**...(t) OllieGarner
(Derek Shaw) *chsd ldr: j.rt 2nd: led next: hdd 4th: mstke and lost pl 7th: hit next: sn wknd: bhd whn p.u bef 4 out* **8/1**

2F4- **P** **Tinelyra (IRE)**[19] 3502 8-10-11 **88**...[1] MrRHogg(5)
(Fergal O'Brien) *hld up: a in rr: pushed along 8th: bhd fr 10th: p.u bef 4 out* **5/2**[1]

PPP- **P** **Dramatic Victory (IRE)**[62] 2603 7-10-0 **72** oh36.................... ConorRing
(John Upson) *chsd ldrs: pushed along 9th: wkng whn mstke 11th: bhd whn p.u bef next* **100/1**

5m 23.5s (4.60) **Going Correction** +0.125s/f (Yiel) **9** Ran SP% **113.6**
Speed ratings: **96,92,90,88,85** ,,,
CSF £25.24 CT £138.10 TOTE £5.80: £1.90, £2.10, £1.70; EX 16.30 Trifecta £100.90.
Owner S E D Racing Partnership **Bred** John Allen **Trained** Granborough, Bucks

FOCUS
A trappy handicap of its type. It was run at a fair gallop and the runner-up sets the level.

3818 EBF STALLIONS MARES' "NATIONAL HUNT" NOVICES' HURDLE (8 hdls) 2m
2:15 (2:15) (Class 3) 4-Y-0+ **£6,498** (£1,908; £954; £477)

Form RPR

/31- **1** **Legacy Gold (IRE)**[42] 3010 6-11-8 0................................. TomScudamore 126+
(David Pipe) *mde all: mstke 4th: shkn up flat: comf* **1/6**[1]

121- **2** 3 3/4 **Run Ructions Run (IRE)**[25] 3329 5-11-12 114...........(p) DougieCostello 122+
(Tim Easterby) *trckd ldrs: wnt 2nd 3rd: rdn appr 2 out: styd on same pce last: eased whn hld nr fin* **4/1**[2]

P35- **3** 18 **Fine Moment**[21] 3438 6-11-2 0.......................................(t) RobertThornton 93
(Kevin Frost) *chsd ldrs: rdn appr 2 out: wkng whn blnd last* **20/1**[3]

\- **4** 35 **Crazy Jane (IRE)** 5-11-2 0.. FelixDeGiles 58
(Tom Gretton) *hld up: hdwy 5th: rdn and wknd bef next* **100/1**

0- **5** 28 **Ruby Mac (IRE)**[44] 2981 6-10-11 0...................................... JoshHamer(5) 30
(Tony Carroll) *chsd wnr: wandered into 3rd: mstke next: blnd and wknd 5th* **100/1**

4m 4.8s (3.80) **Going Correction** +0.125s/f (Yiel) **5** Ran SP% **112.4**
Speed ratings (Par 107): **95,93,84,66,52**
CSF £1.43 TOTE £1.10: £1.10, £1.20; EX 1.40 Trifecta £2.00.
Owner R S Brookhouse **Bred** C K Johnson **Trained** Nicholashayne, Devon

FOCUS
The cosy winner is rated below her best in beating her only serious rival.

3819 DICK CHRISTIAN NOVICES' CHASE (12 fncs) 2m
2:50 (2:50) (Class 3) 5-Y-0+ **£6,498** (£1,908; £954; £477)

Form RPR

F23- **1** **Ahyaknowyerself (IRE)**[31] 3202 8-11-0 140.......(b) SamTwiston-Davies 114+
(Dr Richard Newland) *trckd ldr after 2nd: nt fluent 4th: led 6th: rdn appr last: styd on wl* **1/2**[1]

633- **2** 7 **Bin End**[14] 3596 8-11-0 102...(p) FelixDeGiles 104
(Barry Brennan) *led to 6th: sn pushed along: rdn and ev ch fr 3 out tl styd on same pce appr last* **14/1**[3]

1/5- **3** 5 **Veloce (IRE)**[25] 3328 6-11-0 0...(t) HenryBrooke 100
(Donald McCain) *trckd ldr tl after 2nd: remained handy: pushed along bef 4 out: rdn and ev ch fr 3 out tl no ex appr last* **9/4**[2]

045- **4** 24 **Tchang Goon (FR)**[6] 3715 10-10-7 62.............................(p) MrHGMiller(7) 75
(Zoe Davison) *hld up: rdn and wknd appr 4 out* **100/1**

4m 11.2s (3.00) **Going Correction** +0.125s/f (Yiel) **4** Ran SP% **105.1**
Speed ratings: **97,93,91,79**
CSF £6.24 TOTE £1.50; EX 4.60 Trifecta £8.60.
Owner G Carstairs & R Marker **Bred** Tim Hegarty **Trained** Claines, Worcs

FOCUS
The winner was well below his mark but there's a case for rating the form up to 6lb higher.

3820 SIS+ H'CAP CHASE (18 fncs) 2m 7f 110y
3:25 (3:25) (Class 4) (0-115,115) 5-Y-0+ **£4,548** (£1,335; £667; £333)

Form RPR

001- **1** **Wood Yer (IRE)**[21] 3437 8-11-11 **114**..................(tp) SamTwiston-Davies 123+
(Nigel Twiston-Davies) *disputed ld tl led 12th: rdn appr last: styd on wl* **10/1**

P42- **2** 3 **Mentalist (FR)**[19] 3504 6-11-12 **115**.................................. AidanColeman 122
(Venetia Williams) *hld up: hit 13th: hdwy appr 4 out: rdn to chse wnr 2 out: styd on same pce flat* **5/1**[3]

13P- **3** 1 1/2 **Young Hurricane (IRE)**[26] 3293 8-11-11 **114**.....................(t) DarylJacob 119
(Dr Richard Newland) *hld up in tch: chsd wnr 4 out tl rdn 2 out: no ex flat* **6/1**

421- **4** 20 **Carli King (IRE)**[14] 3595 8-11-2 **105**................................ TomMessenger 96
(Caroline Bailey) *disp ld tl mstke 12th: rdn appr 3 out: wkng whn mstke 2 out* **2/1**[2]

25F/ **5** 53 **Grey Wulff (IRE)**[743] 3664 9-11-7 **110**....................................... NoelFehily 42
(Emma Lavelle) *hld up in tch: chsd wnr 13th tl appr 4 out: wknd bef next* **7/4**[1]

6m 3.5s (-0.50) **Going Correction** +0.125s/f (Yiel) **5** Ran SP% **109.7**
Speed ratings: **105,104,103,96,79**
CSF £52.55 TOTE £9.10: £2.60, £1.90; EX 27.20 Trifecta £63.00.
Owner Miss Katharine J Holland **Bred** J Harold-Barry **Trained** Naunton, Gloucs

FOCUS
There was a sound enough gallop on in this modest staying handicap, but all five held a chance at the top of the home straight and it produced a tight finish. Solid-looking form.

3821 HUMBERSTONE H'CAP HURDLE (10 hdls) 2m 4f 110y
3:55 (3:55) (Class 4) (0-110,108) 4-Y-0+ **£4,548** (£1,335; £667; £333)

Form RPR

560- **1** **Kayf Moss**[24] 3357 6-11-0 **96**...(b[1]) RhysFlint 112+
(John Flint) *mde virtually all: racd keenly: mstke 3rd: clr 2 out: sn rdn: edgd lft flat: styd on* **6/1**[3]

606- **2** 5 **Midnight Request**[32] 3188 5-10-6 **88**..................................... FelixDeGiles 100
(Tom Symonds) *a.p: chsd wnr and mstke 3 out: sn rdn: edgd rt flat: kpt on* **10/3**[1]

652- **3** 19 **Caught By Witness (IRE)**[11] 3639 9-9-9 **82** oh3.........(t) JamesBanks(5) 74
(Anthony Middleton) *hld up: hdwy 3 out: rdn and wknd next* **8/1**

002- **4** 7 **Goochypoochyprader**[8] 3692 7-10-11 **98**..............(t) ConorShoemark(5) 84
(Nick Lampard) *w wnr: nt fluent 5th: rdn appr 3 out: wknd bef next* **8/1**

/00- **5** 10 **Market Option (IRE)**[42] 3013 8-11-12 **108**........................ AidanColeman 83
(Venetia Williams) *trckd ldrs: pushed along bef 5th: rdn and wknd after 3 out* **7/2**[2]

222- **6** 8 **Brass Monkey (IRE)**[20] 3471 7-11-3 **102**.......................... TrevorWhelan(3) 69
(Neil King) *chsd ldrs tl rdn and wknd 3 out* **7/1**

505- **7** 25 **Epic Storm (IRE)**[15] 3568 6-11-1 **97**....................................... TomSiddall 39
(Martin Keighley) *hld up: racd keenly: rdn and wknd appr 3 out* **25/1**

233- **8** 17 **Detour Ahead**[21] 3428 6-11-3 **99**..(p) NoelFehily 24
(Jennie Candlish) *prom: j.rt 4th: nt fluent 7th: sn rdn and wknd* **6/1**[3]

5m 24.9s (0.20) **Going Correction** +0.125s/f (Yiel) **8** Ran SP% **112.4**
Speed ratings (Par 105): **104,102,94,92,88 85,75,69**
CSF £25.92 CT £159.04 TOTE £5.90: £1.80, £1.40, £2.90; EX 32.70 Trifecta £152.80.
Owner L H & Mrs T Evans **Bred** Mrs Vashti Hasdell **Trained** Kenfig Hill, Bridgend

FOCUS
This looked an open handicap and they went a fair gallop, but they finished well strung out as underfoot conditions played a big part. The first two should still be competitive when reassessed.

T/Plt: £41.00 to a £1 stake. Pool: £74,035.52 - 1,316.37 winning units T/Qpdt: £11.20 to a £1 stake. Pool: £4,845.48 - 317.47 winning units CR

[3657]WETHERBY (L-H)

Tuesday, January 21

OFFICIAL GOING: Soft (heavy in places; chs 4.8, hdl 4.6)

Wind: Light; against Weather: Cloudy and cold

3822 WATCH ON 3 DEVICES RACINGUK.COM/ANYWHERE JUVENILE MAIDEN HURDLE (9 hdls) 2m 110y

12:20 (12:21) (Class 5) 4-Y-O £2,053 (£598; £299)

Form				RPR
3-	1		**Certification (IRE)**[34] 3161 4-10-12 0 .... DenisO'Regan (John Ferguson) *led at stdy pce: hdd after 3rd: led again 4th: mde rest: jnd by runner-up 3 out: pushed out and asserted fnl 75yds* **5/4**[1]	107+
302-	2	2 1/4	**Rayak (IRE)**[34] 3161 4-10-12 121 .... APMcCoy (Jonjo O'Neill) *hld up: hdwy bef 3 out: upsides sn after: chsd along appr last: outpcd by wnr fnl 75yds* **13/8**[2]	104+
24-	3	4 1/2	**Chebsey Beau**[45] 2960 4-10-12 0 .... BrianHughes (John Quinn) *a.p: rdn appr 2 out: styd on same pce fr bef last and unable to go w front two* **7/1**	98
	4	3 1/4	**Investment Expert (IRE)**[25] 4-10-12 0 .... (t) RichardJohnson (Brian Ellison) *in tch: effrt to chse ldrs 2 out: sn hung lft and no imp* **6/1**[3]	95
0-	5	13	**Young Jay**[24] 3351 4-10-9 0 .... (t) JohnKington(3) (Andrew Crook) *hld up: hdwy appr 3 out: sn chsd ldrs: effrt sn after: wknd after 2 out* **66/1**	81
64-	6	1/2	**Khelac**[12] 3616 4-10-7 0 .... JoeColliver(5) (Micky Hammond) *prom: led after 3rd: hdd next: lost pl bef 3 out: wknd 2 out* **33/1**	80
6-	7	2 1/2	**Spencers Lad**[14] 3214 4-10-12 0 .... WilsonRenwick (Michael Easterby) *plld hrd: hld up: pushed along 2 out: sn lft bhd* **40/1**	78
	P		**Poetic Star**[449] 4-10-12 0 .... BarryKeniry (Ben Haslam) *plld hrd: chsd ldrs: rdn and wknd after 6th: t.o whn p.u bef last* **100/1**	

4m 26.8s (31.00) **Going Correction** +1.40s/f (Heav) 8 Ran SP% **117.2**

Speed ratings: **83,81,79,78,72 71,70,**

CSF £3.77 TOTE £2.30: £1.10, £1.10, £1.50; EX 4.30 Trifecta £15.00.

Owner Bloomfields **Bred** Darley **Trained** Cowlinge, Suffolk

■ Stewards' Enquiry : Joe Colliver Fine: £140, failed to report reason for poor performance at scales.

FOCUS

The opening contest was an ordinary juvenile maiden hurdle in which noone wanted to make the running on ground officially described as soft, heavy in places, resulting in a particularly steady gallop until the tempo increased down the back straight. The cosy winenr can rate higher but the form is suspect.

3823 TOTEPOOL MEDIEVAL DAY - SATURDAY 1ST FEBRUARY H'CAP CHASE (16 fncs) 2m 4f 110y

12:50 (12:51) (Class 4) (0-120,120) 5-Y-O+ £3,969 (£1,157; £578)

Form				RPR
6/1-	1		**Sharney Sike**[40] 3041 8-10-1 102 ow2 .... DaraghBourke(7) (Stuart Coltherd) *hld up: nt fluent 6th and 8th: effrt appr 4 out: lft in ld 3 out: pressed tl styd on and fnd ex towards fin* **5/2**[1]	112+
350-	2	3/4	**Be My Deputy (IRE)**[53] 2785 9-11-7 115 .... (b) PeterBuchanan (Lucinda Russell) *racd keenly: prom: pushed along appr 4 out: lft chalng after 3 out: edgd lft run-in whn ev ch: kpt on but hld towards fin* **7/1**	122
010/	3	3 1/2	**Harris Hawk**[348] 4077 9-11-3 111 .... BrianHughes (John Wade) *prom: nt travel wl after 7th: lost pl 8th: rallied and tried to chal fr bef 2 out tl one pce fnl 75yds* **5/1**[3]	115
20P-	4	36	**Purcell's Bridge (FR)**[45] 2955 7-11-10 118 .... WilsonRenwick (Rose Dobbin) *racd keenly: in tch: dropped to rr and mstke 12th: pushed along last but stl in tch whn hmpd 3 out: wl bhd after* **7/1**	97
F34-	U		**Kykate**[26] 3287 8-11-11 119 .... (t) RyanMahon (William Kinsey) *hld up in tch: hdwy 8th: cl up and pushed along whn bdly hmpd and uns rdr 3 out* **5/1**[3]	
22F-	F		**Little Glenshee (IRE)**[23] 3395 8-11-12 120 .... BrianHarding (N W Alexander) *led: stl abt 2 l up and pushed along sltly whn fell 3 out* **4/1**[2]	
0-	U		**Sir Lynx (IRE)**[62] 2599 7-10-8 102 .... (t) TomMessenger (Chris Bealby) *hld up tl blnd and uns rdr 3rd* **25/1**	

5m 35.3s (27.50) **Going Correction** +1.475s/f (Heav) 7 Ran SP% **110.8**

Speed ratings: **106,105,104,90, ,**

CSF £18.65 CT £75.82 TOTE £4.30: £2.70, £4.40; EX 21.30 Trifecta £153.30.

Owner John Hogg **Bred** John Hogg **Trained** Selkirk, Borders

■ Stewards' Enquiry : Peter Buchanan one-day ban: careless riding (Feb 4)

FOCUS

A fair handicap chase in which the whole complexion of the contest changed three out. The form is rated around the second and third.

3824 WETHERBYRACING.CO.UK H'CAP HURDLE (13 hdls) 3m 1f

1:20 (1:20) (Class 5) (0-100,98) 4-Y-O+ £1,949 (£572; £286; £143)

Form				RPR
303-	1		**Rocky Stone (IRE)**[25] 3330 6-11-9 95 .... JasonMaguire (Donald McCain) *in tch: effrt to chse ldrs appr 3 out: led jst after last: drvn out and kpt on* **11/2**[2]	99+
5P5-	2	1/2	**Big Sound**[11] 3638 7-11-5 98 .... (p) GrantCockburn(7) (Tim Walford) *in tch: chsd ldr appr 3 out: led narrowly jst bef last: hdd jst after last: styd on u.p: jst hld* **9/1**	102+
041-	3	4 1/2	**Over My Head**[21] 3432 6-10-8 87 .... (t) GeraldQuinn(7) (Claire Dyson) *led: mstke 4 out: j.lft 3 out: rdn whn hit next: hdd jst bef last: no ex fnl 75yds* **9/2**[1]	87
P64-	4	13	**Native Optimist (IRE)**[11] 3634 7-10-9 86 .... MissCWalton(5) (Sheena Walton) *hld up: j. slowly 2nd: blnd 4th: nt fluent 6th: hdwy appr 3 out: kpt on to take 4th bef last: no imp on ldrs* **50/1**	75
0P4-	5	3/4	**Bravo Riquet (FR)**[21] 3432 8-10-13 92 .... (t) JakeHodson(7) (Robin Mathew) *in tch: pushed along appr 9th: rdn to chse ldrs appr 3 out: one pce and no imp fr 2 out* **20/1**	77
PP4-	6	8	**Notonebuttwo (IRE)**[17] 3525 7-10-13 85 .... (vt) RichieMcGrath (Chris Grant) *prom: rdn appr 3 out: wknd 2 out* **20/1**	62
5P1-	7	17	**Adili (IRE)**[25] 3335 5-10-5 87 .... GLavery(10) (Brian Ellison) *hld up: struggling 8th: nvr on terms w ldrs* **8/1**	47
505/	8	1 1/4	**Roseville Cottage (IRE)**[305] 4911 7-11-4 90 .... BrianHughes (John Wade) *prom tl rdn and wknd after 4 out* **10/1**	49
PF3-	9	1/2	**Gorey Lane (IRE)**[25] 3335 8-11-2 95 .... (v) StephenMulqueen(7) (John Norton) *hld up: hdwy into midfield 5th: chsd ldrs after 4 out: sn rdn: wknd 2 out* **16/1**	53
/06-	10	1	**One In A Row (IRE)**[11] 3639 7-10-4 76 .... RichardJohnson (Alan Swinbank) *hld up: midfield bef 5th: struggling 10th* **7/1**[3]	33
0/0-	11	14	**Mini The Minx (IRE)**[51] 2843 8-10-0 77 .... (b[1]) CallumWhillans(5) (Donald Whillans) *in tch: u.p and lost pl after 7th: wknd bef 9th* **16/1**	20
653-	P		**Carmela Maria**[24] 3356 9-10-13 90 .... (p) JoeColliver(5) (Mike Sowersby) *in rr: bhd and struggling bef 5th: t.o whn p.u after 7th* **25/1**	
0/5-	P		**Filbert Fox (IRE)**[41] 3022 8-10-3 78 .... (p) EwanWhillans(3) (Alistair Whillans) *hld up in midfield: mstke 2nd: struggling after 7th: bhd after: t.o whn p.u bef 3 out* **16/1**	
04P-	P		**Blackmore**[18] 3520 7-11-9 95 .... BrianHarding (N W Alexander) *chsd ldrs: lost pl after 4th: struggling and bhd 8th: t.o whn p.u bef 3 out* **50/1**	
/64-	P		**Waywood Princess**[25] 3335 9-10-0 77 .... HarryChalloner(5) (John Bryan Groucott) *chsd ldrs tl wknd 8th: t.o whn p.u bef 2 out* **14/1**	

6m 50.1s (33.60) **Going Correction** +1.40s/f (Heav) 15 Ran SP% **117.9**

Speed ratings (Par 103): **102,101,100,96,96 93,88,87,87,87 82, , , ,**

CSF £49.45 CT £241.94 TOTE £5.80: £1.90, £3.30, £2.70; EX 57.20 Trifecta £142.30.

Owner Penketh And Sankey Jech Racing Club **Bred** James Cregan **Trained** Cholmondeley, Cheshire

FOCUS

A modest staying handicap in which they went an even gallop. A step up from the winner over this longer trip.

3825 STAR SPORTS CHELTENHAM PREVIEW - 3RD MARCH INTERACTIVE H'CAP CHASE (18 fncs) 3m 1f

1:55 (1:55) (Class 3) (0-135,132) 5-Y-O+ £6,388 (£1,928; £993; £526)

Form				RPR
P/0-	1		**Rose Of The Moon (IRE)**[45] 2937 9-11-12 132 .... APMcCoy (David O'Meara) *hld up: hit 3rd: hdwy appr 10th: mstke 12th: led 13th: styd on wl fr 2 out: pushed along bef last: drew clr run-in* **3/1**[2]	142+
3/4-	2	9	**Real Milan (IRE)**[23] 3389 9-11-11 131 .... (tp) JasonMaguire (Donald McCain) *hld up in tch: prom after 9th: chalng whn nt fluent 4 out: 3 out and whn rdn 2 out: one pce appr last: wl btn run-in* **11/4**[1]	131
361-	3	6	**Wicklow Lad**[19] 3498 10-10-8 121 .... (v) MrKitAlexander(7) (N W Alexander) *prom: blnd 5th: outpcd bef 4 out: no imp after* **6/1**	115
P01/	4	19	**Aachen**[596] 585 10-11-8 128 .... LiamTreadwell (Venetia Williams) *hld up: handy 6th: blnd 10th: wknd bef 4 out* **6/1**	105
121/	P		**Tartan Snow**[292] 5138 14-10-9 122 .... MrJHamilton(7) (Stuart Coltherd) *hld up: mstke 6th: struggling 11th: t.o whn p.u bef 4 out* **25/1**	
/2P-	P		**Beau Dandy (IRE)**[62] 2594 9-10-0 106 oh7 .... RichieMcGrath (Chris Grant) *prom: reminders at times fr bef 6th: wknd bef 10th: struggling after: t.o whn p.u bef 3 out* **9/1**	
P2P-	P		**Green Wizard (IRE)**[12] 3617 8-11-2 122 .... RyanMania (Sue Smith) *led: hdd 13th: wknd after 14th: t.o whn p.u bef 3 out: b.b.v* **9/2**[3]	

6m 45.9s (36.50) **Going Correction** +1.475s/f (Heav) 7 Ran SP% **112.3**

Speed ratings: **100,97,95,89, ,**

CSF £11.69 TOTE £3.80: £2.20, £2.00; EX 8.50 Trifecta £59.80.

Owner Middleham Park Racing XXXIII & Partners **Bred** Mrs Teresa Mulcahy **Trained** Nawton, N Yorks

FOCUS

A fairly decent staying handicap chase, and the feature race on the card. The winner was back to the level of his early novice form.

3826 DOWNLOAD NEW RACING UK IPAD APP "NATIONAL HUNT" NOVICES' HURDLE (9 hdls) 2m 110y

2:30 (2:31) (Class 4) 4-Y-O+ £3,119 (£915; £457; £228)

Form				RPR
/33-	1		**Tiqris**[34] 3163 6-11-4 130 .... (t) RichardJohnson (Philip Hobbs) *in tch: gng wl to ld 3 out: r.o to draw clr run-in* **5/4**[1]	125+
521-	2	4	**Secrete Stream (IRE)**[25] 3330 5-11-11 125 .... BrianHughes (Malcolm Jefferson) *midfield: hdwy after 6th: nt fluent 3 out: effrt to take 2nd and try to chal whn nt fluent 2 out: rdn bef last: nt fluent last: styd on same pce run-in and unable to go w wnr* **9/4**[2]	128+
11-	3	6	**Stonebrook (IRE)**[37] 3112 6-11-4 0 .... APMcCoy (Donald McCain) *hld up: stdy hdwy appr 3 out: pushed along bef 2 out: styd on to take 3rd towards fin: nt trble front two* **11/4**[3]	114+
/01-	4	1 1/2	**Tough Trade**[44] 2968 5-11-11 0 .... DenisO'Regan (Chris Grant) *hld up in midfield: hdwy appr 3 out: cl up whn swtchd lft between last 2: shkn up whn hit last: kpt on same pce* **25/1**	120
300/	5	17	**Ballyvoque (IRE)**[458] 1932 8-11-4 0 .... RyanMania (George Charlton) *prom: nt fluent 6th: led sn after: hdd 3 out: rdn and wknd bef last* **66/1**	97
/00	6	1 1/2	**Daylan (IRE)**[13] 3602 6-11-1 0 .... JackQuinlan(3) (Tony Coyle) *midfield: rdn and hdwy to chse ldrs appr 3 out: sn no imp: wknd bef last* **100/1**	93
50P-	7	5	**Oorayvic (IRE)**[25] 3330 7-11-1 0 .... JonathanEngland(3) (Sue Smith) *midfield: hdwy 5th: one pce fr 2 out* **100/1**	88
464-	8	4	**Lebanna**[12] 3613 4-10-0 0 .... BrianHarding (Tim Easterby) *in rr: pushed along bef 4th: kpt on fr 3 out: nvr trbld ldrs* **66/1**	66
	9	1/2	**Island Heights (IRE)**[100] 5-11-4 0 .... WilsonRenwick (Lucinda Russell) *hld up: rdn and hdwy on outer after 6th: no imp on ldrs: wknd 3 out* **25/1**	84
000-	10	nse	**Runswick Days (IRE)**[52] 2823 7-10-11 0 .... JohnDawson(7) (John Wade) *prom tl rdn and wknd bef 3 out* **100/1**	83
0/F-	11	2 3/4	**Dibdabs (IRE)**[22] 3415 6-10-11 0 .... (t) StephenMulqueen(7) (Maurice Barnes) *led: nt fluent 2nd: blnd 5th: hdd after 6th: wknd 2 out* **50/1**	81
0P-	12	19	**Well Related**[89] 2049 7-11-4 0 .... RichieMcGrath (Henry Hogarth) *a bhd: struggling after 6th: nvr on terms* **100/1**	62
	13	25	**Devil At Midnight (IRE)**[9] 6-10-13 0 .... (t) SamanthaDrake(5) (Richard Drake) *prom tl wknd 6th: bhd whn hit 3 out: t.o* **100/1**	37
	14	4	**Minden Dawn** 8-10-4 0 .... DanielHiskett(7) (Peter Maddison) *midfield tl rdn and wknd 6th: t.o* **100/1**	26

4m 15.6s (19.80) **Going Correction** +1.40s/f (Heav)

WFA 4 from 5yo+ 11lb 14 Ran SP% **120.5**

Speed ratings (Par 105): **109,107,104,103,95 94,92,90,90,90 89,80,68,66**

CSF £4.24 TOTE £2.40: £1.10, £1.20, £1.80; EX 4.10 Trifecta £9.10.

Owner R S Brookhouse **Bred** Pitchall Stud **Trained** Withycombe, Somerset

FOCUS
A decent novices' hurdle in which the correct horses came to the fore off an even gallop. The first two are rated below their best.

3827 NEW RACING UK ANYWHERE AVAILABLE NOW H'CAP CHASE (18 fncs) 3m 1f
3:05 (3:05) (Class 4) (0-110,110) 5-Y-0+ **£3,969** (£1,157; £578)

Form RPR
/31- **1** **Arc Warrior (FR)**[19] 3497 10-10-0 **84**..............................(t) BrianHarding 99+
(William Amos) *hld up: hdwy 14th: led 2 out: drvn clr and styd on wl run-in* **12/1**
31P- **2** *11* **Basford Ben**[26] 3283 6-10-11 **95**......................................(p) SeanQuinlan 100
(Jennie Candlish) *hld up: hdwy appr 10th: led bef 4 out: blnd and hdd 3 out: one pce run-in* **9/1**
41P- **3** *4* **Royal Chatelier (FR)**[44] 2979 9-11-5 **110**............................. JoshWall(7) 110
(Michael Blake) *j.rt a few times: prom: led 6th: hdd appr 10th: led again 12th: hdd after 14th: stl ev ch 3 out: rdn bef 2 out: one pce appr last* **16/1**
5/2- **4** *6* **Mighty Mobb (IRE)**[33] 3176 7-11-11 **109**.............................. RichardJohnson 105
(Philip Hobbs) *in tch: nt fluent 4th: led after 14th: hdd appr 4 out: regained ld and mstke 3 out: hdd 2 out: tired bef last* **9/4**[1]
P/P- **5** *5* **Dermatologiste**[63] 2578 11-11-1 **99**..............................(p) AndrewThornton 90
(Caroline Bailey) *prom: reminders fr bef 7th: led appr 10th: hdd 12th: pckd 14th: pushed along bef 4 out: wknd bef next* **16/1**
444- **6** *3 ½* **Camden George (IRE)**[41] 3022 13-10-8 **92**.......................... RyanMania 77
(Sue Smith) *hld up: pushed along bef 4 out: nvr able to trble ldrs* **8/1**
234- **7** *15* **Gwladys Street (IRE)**[17] 3526 7-11-5 **103**........................ RyanMahon 73
(William Kinsey) *disp ld: hdd 6th: lost pl 10th: blnd 11th: wknd 13th* **7/1**[3]
233- **P** **The Magic Bishop**[20] 3478 9-11-10 **108**.............................. BrianHughes
(Malcolm Jefferson) *hld up: hdwy 10th to trck ldrs: bmpd 14th: wknd qckly: t.o whn p.u bef 4 out* **7/2**[2]
02/ **P** **Carrigeen Kariega (IRE)**[15] 3580 9-11-5 **110**.................... MrJRLalor(7)
(R H Lalor, Ire) *disp ld tl after 5th: lost pl bef 10th: sn bhd: t.o whn p.u bef 4 out* **10/1**

6m 48.9s (39.50) **Going Correction** +1.475s/f (Heav) **9** Ran SP% **115.2**
Speed ratings: **95,91,90,88,86 85,80, ,**
CSF £111.31 CT £1731.65 TOTE £9.10: £3.10, £2.70, £2.50; EX 141.00 Trifecta £1276.50.
Owner J John Paterson **Bred** Mme Katherine Aalen And Ian Hanamy **Trained** Rochester, Northumberland

FOCUS
A modest staying handicap chase. The easy winner improved to the level of his old hurdle form.

3828 BRAMHAM HALL FOR CONFERENCES & EVENTS H'CAP HURDLE (10 hdls 1 omitted) 2m 4f
3:35 (3:35) (Class 5) (0-100,100) 4-Y-0+ **£2,053** (£598; £299)

Form RPR
004- **1** **Catching On (IRE)**[21] 3428 6-11-7 **95**.......................... RichieMcLernon 106+
(Jonjo O'Neill) *led: hdd 2nd: remained prom: led after 8th: gng clr whn mstke last: drvn out and styd on* **11/2**[3]
031- **2** *9* **Boomtown**[19] 3503 9-11-5 **100**..(t) GeraldQuinn(7) 100
(Claire Dyson) *w ldr: led 2nd: hdd after 8th: stl ev ch next: kpt on same pce u.p fr bef last: n.d to wnr after* **14/1**
4- **3** *3* **Abolitionist (IRE)**[5] 3749 6-11-8 **96**.. APMcCoy 94
(John Joseph Hanlon, Ire) *hld up in midfield: hdwy after 8th: sn chsd ldrs: rdn bef last: one pce* **6/4**[1]
1P6- **4** *13* **Hi Candy (IRE)**[31] 3212 4-10-4 **100**................................ RyanDClark(10) 72
(Ben Haslam) *trckd ldrs tl rdn and wknd after 8th* **33/1**
U3U- **5** *2 ½* **Doyenthedecenthing**[26] 3284 6-10-4 **78**..............................(t[1]) BrianHughes 60
(John Davies) *racd keenly: prom: rdn bef 9th: sn btn* **7/2**[2]
50/- **6** *16* **The Boozy Bishop (IRE)**[608] 401 9-9-10 **77** oh4 ow3. JohnDawson(7) 43
(Sheena Walton) *in tch tl rdn and wknd 9th* **80/1**
/00- **7** *11* **Armedandbeautiful**[42] 3010 6-11-7 **100**....................... NicodeBoinville(5) 55
(Tom Gretton) *hld up: struggling bef 6th: t.o* **8/1**
114/ **8** *3* **Mootabar (IRE)**[274] 5451 7-10-8 **85**.......................... JonathanEngland(3) 37
(Chris Fairhurst) *hld up: hdwy to chse ldrs briefly after 8th: sn wknd: t.o* **12/1**
0/6- **P** **Tharaya**[13] 3604 9-11-11 **99**...(t) NickScholfield
(Claire Dyson) *midfield early: hld up: wnt wrong and p.u bef 4th: dismntd* **66/1**
400- **P** **Rozener (IRE)**[13] 3600 8-11-10 **98**.................................... RichieMcGrath
(Henry Hogarth) *mstkes: hld up: struggling bef 6th: t.o whn p.u bef last* **25/1**

5m 28.6s (29.10) **Going Correction** +1.40s/f (Heav)
WFA 4 from 6yo+ 12lb **10** Ran SP% **112.6**
Speed ratings (Par 103): **97,93,92,87,86 79,75,74, ,**
CSF £69.29 CT £169.16 TOTE £6.40: £1.80, £2.90, £1.10; EX 86.60 Trifecta £278.70.
Owner Mrs Gay Smith **Bred** Gareth Adair **Trained** Cheltenham, Gloucs

FOCUS
A modest handicap hurdle. The winner rates back to form.
T/Jkpt: £7,100.00 to a £1 stake. Pool: £10,000.00 - 1.00 winning unit T/Plt: £55.90 to a £1 stake. Pool: £76,168.25 - 994.10 winning units T/Qpdt: £29.90 to a £1 stake. Pool: £5,543.87 - 137.00 winning units DO

3613 CATTERICK (L-H)
Wednesday, January 22

OFFICIAL GOING: Soft (hdl 6.1; chs 5.7)
Wind: light behind Weather: overcast

3829 BHEST RACING TO SCHOOL NOVICES' HURDLE (11 hdls 1 omitted) 3m 1f 110y
1:10 (1:11) (Class 4) 5-Y-0+ **£3,249** (£954; £477; £238)

Form RPR
211- **1** **The Last Samuri (IRE)**[53] 2808 6-11-12 131.................. JasonMaguire 132+
(Donald McCain) *hld up in tch: clsr order 6th: chsd ldr after 3 out: rdn to ld jst bef last: kpt on* **4/9**[1]
2 *11* **Rare Legend (IRE)**[374] 3653 7-10-12 0.................................. APMcCoy 111+
(John Joseph Hanlon, Ire) *trckd ldr: led 5th: rdn appr 2 out: hdd jst bef last: sn hld in 2nd: eased fnl 100yds* **2/1**[2]
/65- **3** *6* **Finaghy Ayr (IRE)**[20] 3495 6-10-5 0.......................... GrahamWatters(7) 99
(Ian Duncan) *midfield: wnt 3rd appr 2 out: sn no match ldng pair: hit last* **22/1**[3]
0F- **4** *6* **Generous Chief (IRE)**[42] 3018 6-10-12 0.............................. BrianHughes 92
(Chris Grant) *hld up in tch: rdn after 3 out: hit 2 out: wknd* **100/1**
6- **5** *70* **Native Spa (IRE)**[41] 3042 6-10-12 0....................................... RyanMania 22
(Michael Smith) *prom: led between 4th and 5th: rdn after 3 out: sn btn: eased after 2 out* **25/1**
0UP- **P** **Tropical Sky (IRE)**[36] 3148 6-10-5 0....................................(t) GLavery(7)
(Michael Chapman) *hld up: a bhd: t.o whn p.u after 7th* **250/1**
P0- **P** **Ruberslaw**[24] 3392 8-10-12 0.. BarryKeniry
(Iain Jardine) *led: hit 1st: hdd 4th: hit 6th: sn struggling: t.o whn p.u after 7th* **250/1**

6m 57.0s (29.40) **Going Correction** +0.625s/f (Soft) **7** Ran SP% **112.6**
Speed ratings: **79,75,73,71,50 ,**
CSF £1.62 TOTE £1.70: £1.10, £1.20; EX 2.00 Trifecta £5.10.
Owner Paul & Clare Rooney **Bred** Edmond Coleman **Trained** Cholmondeley, Cheshire

FOCUS
This essentially looked a match and the two clear market leaders dominated from two out. It looked hard work in the ground off the home bend, but Tony McCoy labelled it "just soft". The pace was steady and the first two are rated 10lb+ off their marks.

3830 YORKSHIRE-OUTDOORS.CO.UK H'CAP HURDLE (7 hdls 1 omitted) 2m
1:40 (1:41) (Class 5) (0-100,100) 4-Y-0+ **£2,737** (£798; £399)

Form RPR
0/3- **1** **Seven Summits (IRE)**[225] 708 7-11-7 **95**......................... PaulMoloney 107+
(Sophie Leech) *in tch: trckd ldr gng wl after 2 out (normal 3 out): led last: edgd rt: drvn out* **9/4**[1]
/65- **2** *1 ½* **Copt Hill**[7] 3723 6-10-5 **79**.. BrianHughes 87
(Tracy Waggott) *led: rdn after 2 out (normal 3 out): hdd last: one pce run-in* **9/1**
F01- **3** *1* **Newdane Dancer (IRE)**[25] 3353 7-10-4 **83**..........(b) ColmMcCormack(5) 93+
(Dianne Sayer) *in tch: hit 5th: sn rdn: chsd ldng pair on extended run to last: nt fluent last: one pce run-in* **4/1**[3]
/65- **4** *40* **Pinotage**[24] 3390 6-11-12 **100**.. DenisO'Regan 67
(Peter Niven) *trckd ldrs: wknd on extended run to last* **12/1**
005- **5** *11* **Stanley Bridge**[41] 3038 7-11-2 **97**................................... CraigNichol(7) 53
(Barry Murtagh) *in tch: lost pl 5th: sn btn* **10/1**
0- **P** **Monthly Medal**[71] 2449 11-10-12 **93**..........................(t) MissSMDoolan(7)
(Wilf Storey) *a bhd: p.u bef last* **100/1**
363- **F** **Logical Approach (IRE)**[21] 3451 7-11-4 **95**....................(b) TonyKelly(3)
(David Thompson) *prom: upsides whn fell 2 out (normal 3 out)* **3/1**[2]
34F- **P** **Seaside Rock (IRE)**[24] 3390 4-10-12 **97**........................(p) WilsonRenwick
(Keith Dalgleish) *hld up in tch: nt fluent 4th: sn reminders and struggling: already btn whn hmpd by faller 2 out (normal 3 out): t.o whn p.u bef last* **12/1**

4m 1.4s (8.90) **Going Correction** +0.625s/f (Soft)
WFA 4 from 5yo+ 11lb **8** Ran SP% **111.2**
Speed ratings (Par 103): **102,101,100,80,75 , ,**
CSF £21.28 CT £72.94 TOTE £1.90: £1.10, £2.80, £2.00; EX 28.90 Trifecta £203.40.
Owner C J Leech **Bred** Barronstown Stud **Trained** Elton, Gloucs
■ Stewards' Enquiry : Colm McCormack seven-day ban: used whip above permitted level (Feb 5-11)

FOCUS
They went a sound gallop in this moderate handicap and the principals came well clear. The penultimate flight was bypassed due to damage in the preceding novice. The first three all deserve credit.

3831 RICHMOND BEGINNERS' CHASE (15 fncs) 2m 3f
2:10 (2:10) (Class 4) 5-Y-0+ **£4,659** (£1,446; £779)

Form RPR
32U- **1** **Holywell (IRE)**[27] 3291 7-11-0 0...(p) APMcCoy 143+
(Jonjo O'Neill) *hld up: hdwy after 4 out to chse ldr 3 out: j. to front 2 out: pushed clr run-in* **10/11**[1]
220- **2** *4 ½* **Shotavodka (IRE)**[32] 3200 8-11-0 0................................. TomScudamore 140+
(David Pipe) *led: nt fluent 4th and hdd: chsd clr ldr in 2nd: led again appr 3 out: hdd 2 out: sn rdn: stl ev ch last: no ex and sn hld run-in* **11/10**[2]
242- **3** *17* **Phase Shift**[25] 3354 6-10-7 120...................................(t) DenisO'Regan 113
(Brian Ellison) *hld up: rdn after 4 out: lft modest 3rd 3 out: nvr threatened ldng pair* **12/1**[3]
/5P- **F** **Hotgrove Boy**[18] 3525 7-10-7 0.. DaraghBourke(7) 103+
(Stuart Coltherd) *prom: led 4th: clr 5th tl 4 out: hdd appr 3 out: 4 l down and hld in 3rd whn stmbld and fell 3 out* **125/1**
P **March Seventeenth (IRE)**[24] 6-11-0 0..........................(b[1]) ConorO'Farrell
(John Joseph Hanlon, Ire) *prom: lost pl after 5th: hit 8th: sn t.o: p.u bef last* **100/1**

5m 2.9s (14.10) **Going Correction** +0.525s/f (Soft) **5** Ran SP% **109.5**
Speed ratings: **91,89,81, ,**
CSF £2.33 TOTE £2.20: £1.10, £1.60; EX 3.10 Trifecta £5.10.
Owner Mrs Gay Smith **Bred** Patrick Doyle **Trained** Cheltenham, Gloucs

FOCUS
Another event that was essentially a match. A step up from the winner on his previous chase form.

3832 RACINGUK.COM H'CAP HURDLE (10 hdls) 2m 3f
2:40 (2:41) (Class 3) (0-135,129) 4-Y-0+ **£6,498** (£1,908; £954; £477)

Form RPR
2P1- **1** **Ubaltique (FR)**[24] 3398 6-11-12 **129**..............................(b) JasonMaguire 137+
(Donald McCain) *hld up: nt fluent 6th and 3 out: smooth hdwy to trck ldr appr 2 out: led jst bef last: drvn out run-in* **4/1**[2]
231- **2** *1 ½* **Hit The Top (IRE)**[13] 3618 7-11-4 **121**................................... RyanMania 125+
(Sue Smith) *led: nt fluent 2 out: sn rdn: edgd lft between last 2: hdd jst bef last: kpt on but a hld run-in* **10/3**[1]
361- **3** *7* **Maybe I Wont**[27] 3271 9-11-3 **120**..................................... BrianHughes 117
(James Moffatt) *trckd ldrs: nt fluent 6th and 7th: rdn bef 2 out: sn one pce in 4th: wnt 3rd run-in* **9/1**
300- **4** *4* **Bygones Of Brid (IRE)**[21] 3477 11-11-6 **123**..................(v[1]) DarylJacob 117
(Karen McLintock) *prom: rdn 2 out: wknd and lost 3rd run-in* **5/1**
4U0- **5** *9* **Rumble Of Thunder (IRE)**[21] 3477 8-11-8 **125**........... RichieMcGrath 108
(Philip Kirby) *hld up: nvr threatened* **18/1**
P/3- **6** *3 ½* **Shanen (IRE)**[95] 1980 8-10-10 **113**..................................(t) DenisO'Regan 95
(Pauline Robson) *in tch: rdn after 3 out: wknd after 2 out* **9/2**[3]
005- **7** *26* **Ubaldo Des Menhies (FR)**[37] 3132 6-11-4 **121**..................... APMcCoy 75
(Jonjo O'Neill) *hld up: rdn after 3 out: sn btn* **5/1**

5m 0.2s (24.10) **Going Correction** +0.625s/f (Soft) **7** Ran SP% **109.9**
Speed ratings (Par 107): **74,73,70,68,64 63,52**
CSF £16.58 CT £101.63 TOTE £3.20: £2.20, £3.00; EX 10.10 Trifecta £40.60.
Owner T G Leslie **Bred** Arnaud Chaille-Chaille **Trained** Cholmondeley, Cheshire

FOCUS
This was run at a fair gallop and the form looks solid for the class, with the first pair clear at the business end. The winner is on the upgrade.

3833 CHELTENHAM PREVIEW EVENING 28TH FEBRUARY H'CAP CHASE (12 fncs) 2m
3:15 (3:16) (Class 3) (0-125,123) 5-Y-0+ £7,797 (£2,289; £1,144; £572)

Form RPR
211- 1 **Cloudy Joker (IRE)**35 3155 6-11-9 120 JasonMaguire 132+
(Donald McCain) *in tch: smooth hdwy to trck ldr 2 out: led last: rdn clr run-in* 5/2[1]

/3U- 2 6 **Prince Of Dreams**11 3652 7-11-12 123 FelixDeGiles 131
(Ed de Giles) *in tch: nt fluent 4 out: hdwy 3 out: rdn to ld 2 out: nt fluent and hdd last: no ex* 10/3[2]

5/P- 3 4 **Lucky Sunny (IRE)**23 3414 11-11-1 112 LiamTreadwell 116
(Venetia Williams) *chsd ldr: upsides 7th: led 4 out: hit 2 out and hdd: hld in 3rd whn nt fluent last* 6/1

2U2- 4 18 **Bocamix (FR)**21 3449 8-9-13 99 JohnKington(3) 89
(Andrew Crook) *hld up: blnd 4 out: sn rdn and btn* 11/2

/60- P **Saddle Pack (IRE)**63 2597 11-9-12 100 MissCWalton(5)
(James Walton) *hld up: hit 1st: a bhd: p.u bef 3 out* 17/2

511- U **Arkaim**60 2677 6-11-0 114 KielanWoods(3) 118
(Pam Sly) *led: jnd 7th: hdd 4 out: 2 l down disputing 3rd whn uns rdr 2 out* 4/1[3]

4m 5.6s (5.50) **Going Correction** +0.525s/f (Soft) 6 Ran SP% **111.8**
Speed ratings: **107,104,102,93,**
CSF £11.42 TOTE £3.00: £1.60, £3.30; EX 7.40 Trifecta £31.90.
Owner D McCain Jnr **Bred** Miss Penny Downes **Trained** Cholmondeley, Cheshire

FOCUS
A competitive handicap, run at a solid gallop. Another step forward from the winner with the second to his mark.

3834 RACING AGAIN 31ST JANUARY H'CAP CHASE (19 fncs) 3m 1f 110y
3:45 (3:45) (Class 5) (0-100,96) 5-Y-0+ £3,249 (£954; £477; £238)

Form RPR
PP0- 1 **Over And Above (IRE)**57 2735 8-10-0 70 oh7 (bt) RichieMcGrath 79
(Henry Hogarth) *in tch: nt fluent 13th: rdn and outpcd in 4th after 4 out: styd on after 2 out: led jst after last* 17/2

522- 2 4 **Bennys Well (IRE)**33 3193 8-10-12 82 RyanMania 88
(Sue Smith) *prom: led after 8th: hdd 14th: rdn to ld again 3 out: hit 2 out: reduced advantage whn nt fluent last: sn hdd and no ex* 2/1[1]

54P- 3 2 ½ **Mannered**12 3635 9-11-3 94 JohnDawson(7) 95
(John Wade) *t.k.h early: prom: led 14th: rdn whn hdd 3 out: hld in 3rd after 2 out* 8/1

P41- 4 19 **Esme Rides A Gaine**42 3022 12-10-2 79 StephenMulqueen(7) 61
(Christopher Wilson) *sn pushed along towards rr: nvr threatened* 12/1

01F- 5 nk **Cara Court (IRE)**12 3637 8-11-0 89 (p) SamanthaDrake(5) 71
(Joanne Foster) *led: hdd after 8th: pushed along and lost pl after 11th: hit 5 out: sn btn* 11/2[3]

155- 6 48 **Salut Honore (FR)**27 3281 8-11-7 96 KillianMoore(5) 69
(Alex Hales) *in tch: hit 11th: rdn after 4 out: wknd after 2 out: eased run-in* 4/1[2]

P/P- P **Barnevelder (IRE)**53 2818 9-10-10 80 (bt) AdrianLane
(Sandy Forster) *hld up: nt a fluent: rdn and bhd after 11th: p.u bef 12th* 6/1

7m 3.8s (21.80) **Going Correction** +0.525s/f (Soft) 7 Ran SP% **112.3**
Speed ratings: **87,85,85,79,79 64,**
CSF £26.07 TOTE £10.90: £3.30, £1.70; EX 35.60 Trifecta £306.70.
Owner Hogarth Racing **Bred** Leslie Tucker **Trained** Stillington, N Yorks

FOCUS
A moderate staying handicap that saw changing fortunes in the home straight. The winner is rated back to the best of last season's form.

3835 LEYBURN STANDARD NATIONAL HUNT FLAT RACE (CONDITIONALS & AMATEURS) 2m
4:15 (4:15) (Class 5) 4-6-Y-0 £2,053 (£598; £299)

Form RPR
0/2- 1 **Zeroeshadesofgrey (IRE)**20 3508 5-11-1 0 TrevorWhelan(3) 118+
(Neil King) *prom: led 4f out: pushed clr over 1f out: comf* 9/4[1]

2 6 **Big Mike (IRE)**277 6-11-1 0 JackQuinlan(3) 109
(Sarah Humphrey) *in tch: rdn 3f out: styd on to go 2nd ins fnl f: no ch w wnr* 8/1

3 3 **Philosofy** 4-10-0 0 AdamWedge 88
(David O'Meara) *in tch: rdn to chse wnr over 2f out: no ex and lost 2nd ins fnl f* 11/2[3]

4 8 **Take The Cash (IRE)**73 5-10-11 0 NickSlatter(7) 98
(Donald McCain) *trckd ldrs on outer: rdn over 2f out: sn btn in 4th* 11/4[2]

00- 5 15 **Zuileka**75 2347 5-10-4 0 MissAlexandraWilson(7) 76
(James Moffatt) *led: hdd 4f out: wknd* 100/1

- 6 4 ½ **Halkirk (IRE)** 5-10-13 0 ConorShoemark(5) 79
(Alan Swinbank) *t.k.h early: hld up in tch: rdn 3f out: sn wknd* 6/1

7 20 **On Vacation (IRE)**59 6-11-1 0 (t) MichealNolan(3) 59
(John Joseph Hanlon, Ire) *hld up: a bhd* 28/1

8 4 **Belanna** 5-10-8 0 JoshuaMoore(3) 48
(Tim Easterby) *trckd ldrs: wknd over 4f out* 12/1

9 8 **Vortex Star** 5-10-13 0 JoeCornwall(5) 47
(Michael Chapman) *hld up: bhd fr 1/2-way* 100/1

4m 1.6s (14.70) **Going Correction** +0.625s/f (Soft)
WFA 4 from 5yo 11lb 5 from 6yo 3lb 9 Ran SP% **111.3**
Speed ratings: **88,85,83,79,72 69,59,57,53**
CSF £19.79 TOTE £3.20: £1.10, £2.90, £2.80; EX 21.40 Trifecta £86.60.
Owner Mrs J K Buckle **Bred** Joe Fogarty **Trained** Newmarket, Suffolk

FOCUS
The first six had a chance turning for home in this modest bumper, but the majority got found out as soon as the winner turned the taps on. Arguably another step forward from the winner.
T/Plt: £8.00. Pool: £67,402.08 - 6109.37 winning units. T/Qpdt: £3.80. Pool: £3253.01 - 628.35 winning units. AS

3564 SOUTHWELL (L-H)
Wednesday, January 22

OFFICIAL GOING: Heavy (5.7)
Wind: Almost nil Weather: Fine

3836 32RED CASINO H'CAP CHASE (21 fncs) 3m 2f
12:50 (12:50) (Class 4) (0-110,110) 5-Y-0+ £3,898 (£1,144; £572; £286)

Form RPR
561- 1 **High Ron**16 3565 9-11-7 105 AndrewThornton 118+
(Caroline Bailey) *chsd ldr: led 2nd: mde rest: lft abt 8 l clr 17th: reduced advantage bef 3 out: rdn and over 2 l clr last: styd on wl* 9/2[3]

/U4- 2 3 ½ **Badgers Cove (IRE)**59 2700 10-11-8 106 (p) CharliePoste 114
(Robin Dickin) *hld up in rr: hdwy to trck ldrs 11th: nt fluent 12th: rdn after: nt fluent 14th: lft abt 8 l 2nd 17th: clsd on wnr bef 3 out: over 2 l down last: no further imp run-in* 3/1[1]

/10- 3 28 **Jump Up**59 2691 8-11-2 100 TomO'Brien 78
(Peter Bowen) *chsd ldrs: pushed along and lost pl 15th: lost tch w ldrs 4 out* 9/2[3]

41U- 4 3 ½ **Faith Keeper (IRE)**34 3176 9-11-12 110 PaddyBrennan 85
(Fergal O'Brien) *hld up: a in rr: nt fluent 13th: struggling 4 out and lost tch w ldrs: nvr a threat* 8/1

505- 5 13 **Jat Punjabi**33 3190 10-11-11 109 (p) MarkGrant 71
(Jo Hughes) *hld up in tch: pckd 1st: nt fluent 14th: u.p appr 15th: mstke next: outpcd after: lost tch w ldrs 4 out* 12/1

505- U **Jaunty Journey**25 3366 11-11-5 103 (p) SamTwiston-Davies
(Nigel Twiston-Davies) *led to 2nd: racd in 2nd after: abt 1 l down whn blnd and uns rdr 17th* 4/1[2]

P/2- P **Emma Soda**38 3111 9-11-0 101 PeterCarberry(3)
(Paul Davies) *chsd ldrs: u.p fr bef 12th: bhd 16th: p.u bef 17th* 6/1

7m 30.3s (44.30) **Going Correction** +1.55s/f (Heav) 7 Ran SP% **114.5**
Speed ratings: **93,91,83,82,78 ,**
CSF £18.98 CT £63.37 TOTE £5.10: £2.50, £2.50; EX 21.40 Trifecta £75.20.
Owner Mrs Gillian Burke **Bred** Gillian & Micheal Burke **Trained** Holdenby, Northants

FOCUS
Both bends moved to fresh ground where possible. Modest form, but a progressive winner.

3837 32RED ON THE APP STORE H'CAP CHASE (13 fncs) 2m
1:20 (1:50) (Class 4) (0-110,110) 5-Y-0+ £3,898 (£1,144; £572; £286)

Form RPR
003- 1 **Cooldine Run (IRE)**16 3564 10-10-2 93 (t) MrJarrett(7) 103+
(John Needham) *hld up in rr: impr on bit to go 2nd bef 3 out: led gng wl 2 out: asserted run-in: sn clr* 3/1[3]

1/4- 2 13 **Stormhoek (IRE)**33 3190 9-11-12 110 (vt) SamTwiston-Davies 115+
(Nigel Twiston-Davies) *sweating: chsd ldr to 6th: shkn up appr 9th: wnt 2nd 4 out: led bef 3 out: rdn whn hdd 2 out: a fighting losing battle: eased qckly whn btn after last* 7/4[1]

U21- 3 35 **Decent Lord (IRE)**7 3722 10-10-2 86 7ex (v) SeanQuinlan 48
(Jennie Candlish) *chsd ldrs: wnt 2nd 6th: mstke and lost 2nd 4 out: sn u.p: lft bhd by ldrs bef 3 out: j. sltly rt fnl three whn wl btn* 2/1[2]

212- 4 3 ¾ **Hopeand**27 3268 9-11-9 107 (t) AdamPogson 65
(Charles Pogson) *led: rdn and hdd bef 3 out: sn wknd* 6/1

4m 24.9s (22.90) **Going Correction** +1.55s/f (Heav) 4 Ran SP% **109.0**
Speed ratings: **104,97,80,78**
CSF £8.76 TOTE £6.20; EX 11.80 Trifecta £31.00.
Owner J L Needham **Bred** John P A Kenny **Trained** Ludlow, Shropshire

FOCUS
Just the four runners, but it was run at an honest gallop and the front pair drew clear. The cosy winner was nicely in but thuis arguably rates a step up.

3838 32RED.COM NOVICES' HURDLE (9 hdls) 2m
1:50 (2:20) (Class 4) 5-Y-0+ £3,249 (£954; £477; £238)

Form RPR
1UP- 1 **Anay Turge (FR)**49 2890 9-10-12 125 (tp) KieronEdgar(7) 127+
(Nigel Hawke) *settled chsng ldrs: wnt 2nd gng wl bef 2 out: sn upsides: led on bit last: drvn clr run-in* 3/1[2]

11F- 2 3 **Long Lunch**33 3184 5-11-5 0 (t) NoelFehily 122
(Charlie Longsdon) *t.k.h: trckd ldr: upsides fr 5th: led bef 2 out: sn pressed: pushed along and hdd last: one pce fnl 75yds and wl hld by wnr* 4/6[1]

5- 3 6 **Ossie's Dancer**21 3469 5-10-12 0 LeightonAspell 109
(Martin Smith) *t.k.h: hld up: hdwy bef 2 out: sn chsd ldng two: one pce and no further imp fr last* 100/1

0- 4 22 **Parting Way (IRE)**33 3187 6-10-12 0 RichardJohnson 87
(Tim Vaughan) *hld up in rr: niggled along appr 3 out: sn outpcd: plugged on fr 2 out: nvr a threat* 33/1

0/5- 5 ½ **Flemensmix**67 2507 6-10-12 0 NickScholfield 87
(Kim Bailey) *midfield: pushed along after 3 out: hdwy to chse ldrs bef 2 out: sn no imp and btn* 8/1[3]

3/P- 6 31 **Bishops Gate (IRE)**32 3208 8-10-12 0 BrianHarding 56
(Nicky Richards) *led: pushed along and hdd bef 2 out: sn wknd* 8/1[3]

50- 7 2 ¾ **Veyranno (FR)**35 3166 5-10-12 0 (t) PaddyBrennan 53
(Tom George) *hld up: mstke 5th: struggling 3 out: nvr a threat* 66/1

050/ 8 13 **Hydrant**93 2491 8-10-12 0 RobertThornton 40
(Richard Guest) *t.k.h: hld up: struggling after 3 out: sn wl btn: t.o* 14/1

9 14 **Absolute Return**270 5-10-7 0 (t) AodhaganConlon(5) 26
(Tom George) *chsd ldrs: pushed along whn mstke 3 out: sn wknd: t.o* 50/1

4m 22.7s (25.70) **Going Correction** +1.65s/f (Heav) 9 Ran SP% **121.3**
Speed ratings: **101,99,96,85,85 69,68,61,54**
CSF £5.86 TOTE £4.20: £1.40, £1.10, £11.70; EX 7.20 Trifecta £192.80.
Owner Mrs K Wetherall **Bred** Mme Annick Penouilh **Trained** Stoodleigh, Devon

FOCUS
This was dominated by the front pair in the betting, although the favourite was turned over. The winner's best hurdles run but he's still over a stone off his best chase rating.

3839 32RED H'CAP HURDLE (9 hdls) 2m
2:20 (2:50) (Class 4) (0-110,108) 4-Y-0+ £3,249 (£954; £477; £238)

Form RPR
4P4- 1 **Persian Herald**21 3468 6-11-5 104 JonathanEngland(3) 110
(Sue Smith) *led: hdd 3rd: remained w ldr: pushed along and regained ld after 3 out: drew clr appr last: drvn out and styd on wl* 8/1

022- **2** *6* **Santo Thomas (FR)**[15] 3597 8-11-11 **107**........................ AidanColeman 107
(Venetia Williams) *in tch: clsd to take 2nd 2 out: rdn and no imp on wnr appr last: kpt on same pce* **7/4**[1]

/04- **3** *7* **Tokyo Javilex (FR)**[47] 2920 7-10-8 **93**..........................(t) MarkQuinlan(3) 87
(Nigel Hawke) *hld up: hdwy appr 5th: rdn appr 2 out where mstke whn stl in contention: one pce sn after* **6/1**[3]

4 *14* **Alizari (IRE)**[19] 818 5-11-2 **105**.. MikeyHamill(7) 86
(Barry Brennan) *prom: led 3rd: hdd after 3 out: stl handy whn hit 2 out: sn rdn and wknd* **50/1**

24U- **5** *4* **Don Pooleoni (IRE)**[11] 3650 9-11-12 **108**........................... NoelFehily 83
(Harry Fry) *hld up: hdwy to trck ldrs bef 5th: rdn after 2 out: sn btn* **2/1**[2]

/26- **6** *4* **Prime Contender**[21] 3451 12-11-7 **103**..............................(v) SeanQuinlan 76
(Jennie Candlish) *prom: nt fluent 4th: blnd 6th: sn lost pl: wknd after 3 out* **16/1**

1/P- **7** *26* **Wordy's Boy**[11] 3659 9-11-9 **105**.. AdamPogson 50
(Charles Pogson) *hld up: struggling and lost tch 3 out: t.o* **14/1**

6/0- **8** *hd* **Minsky Mine (IRE)**[14] 3599 7-11-1 **102**.......................... CharlieWallis(5) 47
(Michael Appleby) *in tch: j. carefully and lost pl 4th: sn rdn and bhd: struggling and lost tch 3 out: t.o* **16/1**

4m 21.5s (24.50) **Going Correction** +1.65s/f (Heav) **8 Ran SP% 115.5**
Speed ratings (Par 105): **104,101,97,90,88 86,73,73**
CSF £23.43 CT £92.19 TOTE £6.10: £1.40, £1.20, £1.30; EX 17.50 Trifecta £219.90.
Owner The Cartmel Syndicate **Bred** J W P Clark **Trained** High Eldwick, W Yorks

FOCUS
Moderst form, but a strongly run race and a personal best from the winner.

3840 32REDPOKER.COM MARES' MAIDEN HURDLE (13 hdls) 3m 110y
2:55 (3:21) (Class 5) 5-Y-O+ £1,949 (£572; £286; £143)

Form RPR

200- **1** **Truckers Darling (IRE)**[27] 3278 7-10-12 100.................. LeightonAspell 110+
(Don Cantillon) *hld up in rr: hdwy appr 9th: led 3 out: over 2 l ahd last: styd on wl run-in* **6/1**

/22- **2** *3 1/4* **Floral Spinner**[97] 1946 7-10-5 107.. RyanWhile(7) 107
(Bill Turner) *hld up: hdwy appr 3 out: chsd wnr bef 2 out: rdn jst over 2 l down last: one pce run-in* **5/2**[2]

522- **3** *55* **Comedinewithme**[27] 3247 6-10-12 107............................ BrendanPowell 82
(Jamie Snowden) *trckd ldrs: chsd wnr briefly bef 2 out: sn btn and tired* **5/4**[1]

043- **4** *22* **Blue Sea Of Ibrox (IRE)**[14] 3605 6-10-12 72................(b) DavidEngland 30
(Alan Brown) *trckd ldrs: led appr 9th: rdn and hdd 3 out: wknd qckly* **20/1**

P- **P** **Classical Chloe**[26] 3329 6-10-12 0.................................(t) GerardTumelty
(Sara Ender) *plld hrd early: hld up: bhd 3rd: struggling whn nt fluent 5th: t.o whn p.u bef 7th* **100/1**

P6- **P** **Zaffaran Rain (IRE)**[20] 3506 5-10-12 0...............................(t) DaveCrosse
(K F Clutterbuck) *w ldr tl rdn appr 9th: wknd 4 out: t.o whn p.u after 3 out* **33/1**

P **Russett Star**[241] 6-10-12 0... NoelFehily
(Charlie Longsdon) *led: hdd appr 9th where mstke: rdn and wknd 4 out: t.o whn p.u bef 2 out* **16/1**

546- **P** **Grape Tree Flame**[33] 3189 6-10-12 0................................... TomO'Brien
(Peter Bowen) *midfield: hdwy to chse ldrs appr 4 out: wknd qckly after 3 out: t.o whn p.u bef 2 out* **9/2**[3]

7m 0.3s (45.30) **Going Correction** +1.65s/f (Heav) **8 Ran SP% 120.1**
Speed ratings: **93,91,74,67, , ,**
CSF £22.82 TOTE £11.20: £2.50, £1.50, £1.10; EX 29.60 Trifecta £78.30.
Owner Mrs Catherine Reed **Bred** B Kavanagh **Trained** Newmarket, Suffolk

FOCUS
The front pair drew a long way clear of the favourite. A big step up from the winner.

3841 32REDBET.COM "NATIONAL HUNT" MAIDEN HURDLE (11 hdls) 2m 4f 110y
3:25 (3:52) (Class 5) 5-Y-O+ £2,111 (£620; £310; £155)

Form RPR

5- **1** **Templebraden (IRE)**[22] 3440 7-11-0 0........................... LeightonAspell 122+
(Henry Oliver) *racd wd and w zest: trckd ldrs: wnt 2nd at 2nd: led 5th: nt fluent 7th: shkn up appr last: sn clr: eased run-in* **20/1**

434- **2** *15* **Glowinginthedark (IRE)**[53] 2826 6-11-0 119.......................... NoelFehily 104
(Charlie Longsdon) *racd in 2nd pl tl j. slowly 2nd: remained prom: effrt bef 2 out: rdn and no imp on wnr between last 2: sn no ch* **4/5**[1]

2- **3** *3 1/2* **Paradise Valley (IRE)**[41] 3035 5-11-0 0...................... DominicElsworth 102
(Mick Channon) *led: hdd 5th: remained prom: rdn appr 2 out: btn between last 2* **7/4**[2]

5P0- **4** *36* **Operatic Heights (IRE)**[24] 3388 5-11-0 0.................... RichardJohnson 76
(Tim Vaughan) *hld up in rr: pushed along after 3 out: sn lft bhd* **8/1**[3]

5m 48.5s (35.50) **Going Correction** +1.65s/f (Heav) **4 Ran SP% 107.8**
Speed ratings: **98,92,90,77**
CSF £38.15 TOTE £20.10; EX 31.40 Trifecta £35.40.
Owner Jack McGrath **Bred** Maurice Harrington **Trained** Broomhall, Worcs

FOCUS
Something of a turn up here, with neither of the front pair in the market looking happy on the ground. Not an easy race to rate but the winner could be a fair sort.

3842 32REDBINGO.COM H'CAP HURDLE (13 hdls) 3m 110y
3:55 (4:20) (Class 5) (0-100,97) 4-Y-O+ £1,949 (£572; £286; £143)

Form RPR

/P1- **1** **Admiral Blake**[8] 3699 7-10-11 **82** 7ex................................ DougieCostello 90+
(Laura Young) *hld up: hdwy 3 out: led appr 2 out: rdn bef last: styd on to draw clr run-in: eased cl home* **2/1**[1]

600- **2** *2 1/2* **Gonalston Cloud (IRE)**[56] 2748 7-11-3 **95**................ CharlieDeutsch(7) 98
(Nick Kent) *hld up: hdwy 9th: rdn whn chalng fr 2 out: unable to go w wnr run-in: styd on same pce* **12/1**

334- **3** *10* **Blue Cove**[26] 3334 9-10-7 **78**.. TomSiddall 73
(Lynn Siddall) *led: hdd appr 2 out: rdn and stl cl up bef last: no ex run-in* **6/1**

521- **4** *27* **Bold Tara**[16] 3569 7-10-12 **90**...(tp) OllieGarner(7) 55
(Martin Keighley) *rel to r: s.s: in rr: hdwy to go prom 3rd: stl ev ch after 3 out: rdn and wknd appr 2 out* **4/1**[3]

450- **P** **Photogenique (FR)**[33] 3188 11-10-0 **74** oh7 ow3............. JamesBest(3)
(Rob Summers) *in tch: lost pl 7th: struggling and bhd 8th: t.o whn p.u after 3 out* **50/1**

501- **S** **Millers Reef (IRE)**[26] 3334 8-11-12 **97**........................... WilsonRenwick 103+
(Keith Dalgleish) *trckd ldrs: nt fluent 8th: stl gng wl abt 2 l down whn n.m.r and slipped up on bnd after 3 out* **5/2**[2]

565- **P** **Milan Of Hope (IRE)**[14] 3605 7-11-8 **93**...........................(p) AdamPogson
(Charles Pogson) *prom: mstke 7th: wknd 9th: sn rdn: bhd and struggling whn blnd 4 out: p.u bef next* **12/1**

7m 6.4s (51.40) **Going Correction** +1.65s/f (Heav) **7 Ran SP% 113.5**
Speed ratings (Par 103): **83,82,79,70, ,**
CSF £24.19 CT £123.12 TOTE £3.80: £1.90, £4.00; EX 25.00 Trifecta £180.50.
Owner Mrs Laura Young **Bred** Mrs Laura Young **Trained** Broomfield, Somerset
■ Stewards' Enquiry : Charlie Deutsch five-day ban: careless riding (Feb 5-9)

FOCUS
Low-grade handicap form. The winner built on his recent victory.
T/Plt: £4820.20. Pool: £69002.00 - 10.45 winning units. T/Qpdt: £1202.80. Pool: £6339.34 - 3.90 winning units. DO

3843 - 3849a (Foreign Racing) - See Raceform Interactive

3468 FAKENHAM (L-H)
Thursday, January 23

OFFICIAL GOING: Soft (heavy in places) changing to heavy after race 2 (1.30)
Wind: almost nil Weather: brightening after heavy morning rain; 5 degrees

3850 HOE NOVICES' HURDLE (13 hdls) 2m 7f 110y
1:00 (1:00) (Class 4) 5-Y-O+ £3,119 (£915; £457; £228)

Form RPR

/54- **1** **Moss On The Mill**[35] 3173 6-10-12 0.................................... DarylJacob 112+
(Ben Case) *settled trcking ldrs: wnt 2nd gng wl after 3 out: led sn after next: in command bef last: styd on wl* **9/4**[2]

02- **2** *4 1/2* **Canuspotit**[39] 3115 7-10-7 0.. MattCrawley(5) 109
(Lucy Wadham) *settled trcking ldrs: nt fluent 10th: mstke next: wnt 2nd after 2 out: hrd drvn and wl hld bef last* **1/1**[1]

035/ **3** *14* **Social Overdrive (IRE)**[324] 4577 8-10-7 90.................. JamesBanks(5) 93
(Emma Baker) *chsd ldr: drew level and hit 10th: drvn after next: sn btn: styd on: lft poor 3rd at last* **16/1**

2P- **4** *8* **Speckled Door**[54] 2826 6-10-12 0................................... AndrewThornton 85
(Caroline Bailey) *towards rr: rdn and outpcd bef 2 out: styd on into poor 4th nr fin* **10/1**

0/3- **5** *nk* **Ballythomas**[22] 3453 7-10-9 0.. TonyKelly(3) 87
(David Thompson) *bhd: blnd 7th: 8 l last whn hit 9th: rdn and struggling bef 2 out* **9/2**[3]

5/4- **6** *1/2* **Arfur Didit (IRE)**[21] 3506 6-10-9 0................................. JackQuinlan(3) 85
(Sarah Humphrey) *settled in 3rd: hit 5th and 6th: nt fluent 9th: rdn and wknd bef 2 out* **33/1**

7 *nse* **Carn Rock** 6-10-5 0.. MissAEStirling(7) 84
(Michael Gates) *in rr: hit 10th: lost tch bef next* **100/1**

P/0- **F** **Steepleofcopper (IRE)**[67] 2536 8-10-5 0................. JosephAkehurst(7) 101
(Alan Jessop) *led but wavering and rdn into hurdles: abt 6 l clr tl 9th: jnd whn hit 3 out: rdn and hdd sn after next: 6 l 3rd whn fell heavily last* **150/1**

6m 46.8s (40.40) **Going Correction** +1.40s/f (Heav) **8 Ran SP% 118.5**
Speed ratings: **88,86,81,79,79 78,78,**
CSF £5.29 TOTE £1.70: £1.10, £1.10, £4.40; EX 5.50 Trifecta £49.80.
Owner Steve Hemstock **Bred** S D Hemstock **Trained** Edgcote, Northants

FOCUS
Fresh ground all way round on Hurdle course. The official going was changed from soft to soft, heavy in places following steady rainfall prior to racing. A very ordinary race but a step up from the winner.

3851 HORNINGTOFT NOVICES' H'CAP HURDLE (11 hdls) 2m 4f
1:30 (1:30) (Class 4) (0-120,120) 4-Y-O+ £3,119 (£915; £457; £228)

Form RPR

432- **1** **Akdam (IRE)**[28] 3245 4-11-1 **120**......................................(p) JoshHamer(5) 119+
(Tony Carroll) *modest hurdling technique thrght: settled cl 4th: hrd drvn to go 2nd after 3 out: led next: sn 5 l clr: idling bdly after: hopped over last: plugged on* **10/1**

202- **2** *5* **Make Me A Fortune (IRE)**[28] 3270 6-11-8 **110**.................(p) DarylJacob 111
(Steve Gollings) *settled in 3rd: relegated 4th and nt fluent 8th: rdn and outpcd next: drvn and rallied to go 5 l 2nd bef last: no further imp* **9/4**[2]

041- **3** *7* **Kodicil (IRE)**[7] 3740 6-11-4 **109**.......................................(b) TonyKelly(3) 104
(Tim Walford) *led: hrd drvn after 3 out: hdd and hit next: tired whn losing wl-btn 2nd bef last* **11/10**[1]

P/2- **4** *2 1/4* **Calaf**[42] 3043 6-11-7 **114**.. MauriceLinehan(5) 106
(Jonjo O'Neill) *t.k.h in 2nd: chal ldr 8th: drvn and wknd after next: fin slowly* **6/1**[3]

020- **P** **The Master Remover (IRE)**[35] 3175 5-10-12 **100**............. TomCannon
(Chris Gordon) *a last: rdn after 3rd and nvr travelling: lost tch u.p 7th: t.o after next: p.u 2 out* **16/1**

5m 37.6s (25.00) **Going Correction** +1.40s/f (Heav)
WFA 4 from 5yo+ 12lb **5 Ran SP% 107.6**
Speed ratings (Par 105): **106,104,101,100,**
CSF £31.43 TOTE £7.60: £3.10, £1.40; EX 20.40 Trifecta £17.90.
Owner Stephen Louch **Bred** His Highness The Aga Khan's Studs S C **Trained** Cropthorne, Worcs

FOCUS
This was hard work for these novices and it saw something of an upset. The winner is rated in line with his Fontwell second.

3852 LONGHAM CONDITIONAL JOCKEYS' H'CAP HURDLE (11 hdls) 2m 4f
2:00 (2:00) (Class 5) (0-100,100) 4-Y-O+ £1,949 (£572; £286; £143)

Form RPR

P6/- **1** **Campbonnais (FR)**[226] 722 9-11-12 **100**.......................(p) AdamWedge 112+
(Ali Brewer) *settled in rr: wnt 3rd at 7th: wnt 2nd gng wl 3 out: mstke next: rdn to ld between last two: sn asserted* **12/1**

412- **2** *8* **Cash Injection**[9] 3699 5-11-7 **95**.................................(t) MattGriffiths 100
(Richard Woollacott) *cl up: wnt 2nd and nt fluent 7th: led next: drvn and hdd between last two: 4 l 2nd and btn whn hit last* **5/4**[1]

352- **3** *12* **Torran Sound**[106] 1824 7-11-12 **100**................................(p) JoshuaMoore 90
(Lawney Hill) *hld up towards rr: effrt 7th: cl 3rd bef 3 out: sn drvn and fdd: wl btn in 8 l 3rd next* **13/2**[3]

P6P- **4** *15* **Epee Celeste (FR)**[7] 3730 8-11-2 **90**.................................(b) JoeCornwall 65
(Michael Chapman) *led after 1st but sn urged along: hdd 6th and dropped out qckly u.p: styd on into remote 4th after 2 out* **33/1**

P/2- **5** *26* **Landenstown Pearl (IRE)**[23] 3434 8-10-12 **86**.................. JackQuinlan 35
(Sarah Humphrey) *chsd ldrs tl drvn 7th: sn struggling: hopelessly t.o* **7/2**[2]

203- **6** *5* **Monroe Park (IRE)**[22] 3468 9-10-4 **78** ow1........................(p) JoshHamer 22
(Alan Blackmore) *led tl after 1st: pressed ldr tl led 6th: hdd 8th: drvn and fading whn j. slowly 3 out: hopelessly t.o* **10/1**

302- P County Zen (FR)[22] 3468 11-11-4 95 KieronEdgar(3)
(Caroline Fryer) *chsd ldrs tl drvn 5th: nvr travelling after: last after 6th: t.o and p.u after 8th* 10/1
5m 39.0s (26.40) **Going Correction** +1.40s/f (Heavy) 7 Ran SP% **108.8**
Speed ratings (Par 103): **103,99,95,89,78 76,**
CSF £25.88 CT £97.36 TOTE £19.50: £7.40, £1.30; EX 38.90 Trifecta £204.70.
Owner Miss Ali Brewer **Bred** Patrick Lemarie & Patrick Le Gougouec **Trained** Eastbury, Berks

FOCUS
A gruelling test in which the winner posted his best figure since 2012.

3853 WENDLING H'CAP CHASE (18 fncs) 3m 110y
2:30 (2:30) (Class 3) (0-130,127) 5-Y-0+ £9,701 (£2,480; £1,335)

Form RPR
212- 1 Presented (IRE)[22] 3478 7-10-5 106 (p) DarylJacob 114
(Brian Ellison) *nt fluent and occasionally j.rt in 3rd or 4th: mstke 7th: rdn 11th: blnd 12th: bdly outpcd in 12 l 4th at 15th: rallied u.p bef last where jst over 3 l 3rd: lft in ld: idling and all out* 10/3[2]
045- 2 1 1/4 Galway Jack (IRE)[33] 3211 9-11-12 127 AndrewThornton 133
(Caroline Bailey) *j. soundly and racd enthusiastically in ld: pressed fr 15th: rdn and hdd 2 out: 3 l 2nd and nt qckn whn lft 2nd and impeded by faller at last: kpt on same pce after* 4/1[3]
134- 3 2 Goring One (IRE)[49] 2909 9-10-13 114 AdamWedge 118
(Anna Newton-Smith) *chsd ldrs: 7 l 3rd and rdn and outpcd 15th: 15 l 4th at next: tried to rally bef last: lft 3rd but nt able to get in a blow* 7/1
4P2- P That's The Deal (IRE)[37] 3150 10-9-10 102 JoeCornwall(5)
(John Cornwall) *a last: rdn 6th: struggling 9th: t.o and p.u14th* 9/1
P10- P Colebrooke[40] 3097 6-11-9 127 (p) JoshuaMoore(3)
(Renee Robeson) *nt fluent 2nd: v slow next: wl in tch tl 12th: dropping out rapidly whn j. bdly rt 14th and p.u* 12/1
P21- F Tony Dinozzo (FR)[22] 3472 7-10-2 103 TomO'Brien 110+
(Peter Bowen) *2nd tl led 2 out: sn rdn: 3 l clr whn j. awkwardly last and fell* 15/8[1]
6m 54.5s (18.80) **Going Correction** +0.95s/f (Soft) 6 Ran SP% **108.1**
Speed ratings: **107,106,105, ,**
CSF £15.72 TOTE £3.20: £2.30, £1.90; EX 14.10 Trifecta £52.00.
Owner Miss C A Carr **Bred** Miss Catherine M Walsh **Trained** Norton, N Yorks

FOCUS
A soundly run feature. The first three and the faller are rated pretty close to their marks.

3854 BEETLEY MARES' MAIDEN HURDLE (9 hdls) 2m
3:00 (3:00) (Class 5) 4-Y-0+ £1,949 (£572; £286; £143)

Form RPR
3- 1 Slipper Satin (IRE)[34] 2577 4-10-4 0 JackQuinlan(3) 105+
(Noel Quinlan) *settled cl up: led 2 out: sn urged clr: 15 l ahd whn nt fluent last: eased flat* 14/1[3]
2- 2 16 Earth Amber[17] 3568 5-11-4 0 DavidBass 97
(Nicky Henderson) *nvr really looked happy: midfield: mstkes 3rd and 6th: hrd drvn bef 3 out: wnt 2nd after next but wnr sn clr: styd on* 2/5[1]
3 15 Wasabi (IRE)[244] 5-11-4 0 WillKennedy 82
(John Berry) *prom: nt fluent 5th: led 6th tl rdn and hdd and hit 3 out: fdd qckly next: fin tired* 28/1
550- 4 24 Kathleen Frances[25] 3391 7-11-4 104 (t) JackDoyle 57
(Ali Brewer) *nt fluent 4th: towards rr of cl bunch tl 3 out: stopped rapidly bef next: hopelessly t.o* 5/1[2]
F Miss Fortywinks[232] 5-11-4 0 AndrewThornton 76
(Seamus Mullins) *hld up: hdwy to 2nd after 6th: led next: rdn and hdd 2 out: 20 l 4th and tired whn crashing fall last: winded but rcvrd* 20/1
044- P Seas Of Green[27] 3326 7-11-4 95 SamThomas
(Paul Cowley) *prom tl 6th: fading qckly whn j.rt and mstke 3 out: t.o and p.u next* 16/1
00- P Scolt Head Island[61] 2675 8-11-4 0 DavidEngland
(Caroline Bailey) *j.rt 2nd: nt fluent 3rd: led tl 6th: slowed to almost nil and continued hopelessly t.o tl p.u 2 out* 150/1
4m 33.1s (27.70) **Going Correction** +1.40s/f (Heavy)
WFA 4 from 5yo+ 11lb 7 Ran SP% **109.5**
Speed ratings (Par 103): **86,78,70,58, ,**
CSF £19.64 TOTE £13.10: £5.40, £1.10; EX 24.40 Trifecta £253.10.
Owner Yallop Racing & Gee Geez.Co.Uk **Bred** J Murphy **Trained** Newmarket, Suffolk

FOCUS
A moderate mares' hurdle. The winner is rated in line with her best Flat form.

3855 EAST BILNEY H'CAP CHASE (16 fncs) 2m 5f 110y
3:30 (3:30) (Class 5) (0-100,100) 5-Y-0+ £2,088 (£617; £308; £154; £77)

Form RPR
U31- 1 Full Ov Beans[22] 3470 10-10-13 94 MissAEStirling(7) 105+
(Michael Gates) *led tl 2nd: t.k.h in 2nd tl lft in ld 6th: continued to set sn gallop: hrd pressed fr 3 out: stl on bit bef last where mstke whn gng 2 l ahd: lft w big advantage* 11/2[3]
/P6- 2 29 Got Attitude (IRE)[36] 3164 11-11-12 100 LeeEdwards 86
(Tony Carroll) *cl up: hit 3rd: hmpd 6th: blnd 7th: nt fluent 11th: mstke 13th: rdn and lost tch w ldng pair next: lft poor 2nd at last: pulling himself up flat but jst hld the rest* 16/1
31P- 3 2 1/4 Phoenix Des Mottes (FR)[16] 3595 11-9-9 74 oh4 JoeCornwall(5) 53
(John Cornwall) *cl 2nd or 3rd tl 11th: sn rdn: 10 l 4th and outpcd 3 out: poor 5th between last two: hrd drvn flat: snatched poor 3rd* 33/1
613- 4 nse Bill The Lad (IRE)[28] 3281 7-11-0 88 SamThomas 69
(Paul Cowley) *last mostly: nt fluent 5th: 7 l last at 11th: nt fluent next and lost tch: poor 4th 2 out: lft remote 3rd at last tl fnl strides* 3/1[2]
U01- 5 shd Cruising Bye[38] 3129 8-11-9 97 TomO'Brien 79
(Peter Bowen) *blnd 5th: drvn 9th: blnd next: outpcd whn mstke 13th: remote last 2 out: kpt on u.p after last* 11/4[1]
2P5- F Goring Two (IRE)[10] 3687 9-10-12 86 (v[1]) AndrewThornton
(Anna Newton-Smith) *led at fast pce fr 2nd tl fell 6th* 12/1
313- F Midnight Charmer[23] 3439 8-11-0 93 JamesBanks(5) 101
(Emma Baker) *settled towards rr: effrt 11th: drvn and sustained effrt fr 3 out tl jst outpcd nring last: 2 l down whn crumpled on landing and fell last* 3/1[2]
6m 2.5s (20.70) **Going Correction** +0.95s/f (Soft) 7 Ran SP% **108.6**
Speed ratings: **100,89,88,88,88 ,**
CSF £66.40 TOTE £6.30: £2.40, £7.00; EX 101.60 Trifecta £834.20.
Owner Michael Gates **Bred** Miss A Thompson **Trained** Clifford Chambers, Warwicks

FOCUS
A fair race for the grade. The winner's recent C&D win could be rated at least this high.

3856 GATELEY H'CAP HURDLE (9 hdls) 2m
4:00 (4:00) (Class 5) (0-100,96) 4-Y-0+ £1,949 (£572; £286; £143)

Form RPR
005- 1 Straits Of Messina (IRE)[76] 2351 5-11-9 93 FelixDeGiles 102+
(Tom Symonds) *hld up: effrt 5th: wnt 2nd after next and sn clr w one rival: led gng best after 3 out: 3 l clr last: idled and drifted rt: all out* 15/8[1]
5/3- 2 1 3/4 Grand Article (IRE)[106] 1824 10-10-0 70 oh5 AdamWedge 75
(Paul Cowley) *led after 1st: mstke 5th: rdn and hdd after 3 out: tried to rally flat: a hld* 9/1
506- 3 19 Clues And Arrows (IRE)[24] 3415 6-11-3 87 RichieMcLernon 73
(Jonjo O'Neill) *cl up tl 6th: rdn and bdly outpcd bef 3 out: styd on* 4/1[3]
001- 4 3/4 Walter De La Mare (IRE)[28] 3264 7-11-12 96 TomMessenger 82
(Anabel K Murphy) *hld up last tl 1/2-way: effrt 6th: wnt 10 l 3rd but outpcd 3 out: no ch after* 8/1
305/ 5 50 Tayarat (IRE)[279] 5386 9-11-0 89 JoeCornwall(5) 25
(Michael Chapman) *led tl after 1st: drvn and lost tch 5th: sn hopelessly t.o* 20/1
065- P Lilac Belle[37] 3149 8-10-8 83 (tp) KillianMoore(5)
(Alex Hales) *pushed along 4th: sn labouring: last and drvn 5th: t.o and p.u 2 out* 9/4[2]
4m 33.7s (28.30) **Going Correction** +1.40s/f (Heavy) 6 Ran SP% **111.4**
Speed ratings (Par 103): **85,84,74,74,49**
CSF £17.55 TOTE £3.10: £1.20, £3.40; EX 20.00 Trifecta £124.10.
Owner Lost In Space **Bred** Pat O'Rourke **Trained** Harewood End, H'fords

FOCUS
The market can often be the best guide in races of this nature and that certainly proved the case here. Low-grade form.
T/Plt: £60.60. Pool: £64,404.13 - 774.87 winning units. T/Qpdt: £22.20. Pool: £4573.28 - 151.79 winning units. IM

3649 WARWICK (L-H)
Thursday, January 23

OFFICIAL GOING: Soft (heavy in places on hurdle course; chs 6.4; hdl 5.3)
Wind: Moderate behind Weather: Sunny spells

3857 RACINGUK.COM JUVENILE HURDLE (8 hdls) 2m
1:20 (1:21) (Class 4) 4-Y-0 £3,249 (£954; £477; £238)

Form RPR
12- 1 Hawk High (IRE)[58] 2733 4-11-5 123 (p) APMcCoy 117+
(Tim Easterby) *hld up in tch: hdwy after 3 out: chal 2 out: slt ld last and sn 2 l clr: idled clsng stages and drvn out* 6/4[2]
32- 2 nk Haatefina[25] 3385 4-10-5 0 DaveCrosse 101
(Mark Usher) *led: rdn after 3 out: jnd and hit 2 out: narrowly hdd and nt fluent last: sn 2 l down but rallied as wnr idled clsng stages* 7/1[3]
1- 3 9 Red Four[25] 3385 4-10-12 0 (p) AndrewTinkler 99
(George Baker) *chsd ldr: nt fluent 4 out: rdn after 3 out: wknd bef next* 12/1
4 4 1/2 Stiff Upper Lip (IRE)[73] 4-10-12 0 LeightonAspell 95
(Oliver Sherwood) *chsd ldrs: hit 4 out: wknd after next* 20/1
5 23 Strong Conviction[116] 4-10-12 0 NickScholfield 71
(Simon Hodgson) *in tch tl wknd 4 out* 25/1
6 48 Rock Diamond (IRE)[24] 4-10-5 0 BrendanPowell 16
(Brendan Powell) *in rr: nt fluent 4th: wknd 4 out* 100/1
F Dido 4-10-12 0 HaddenFrost
(Alexandra Dunn) *nt fluent in rr: wl bhd whn fell 4th* 66/1
1- P Mahican (IRE)[46] 2975 4-11-5 0 DenisO'Regan
(John Ferguson) *disputed 2nd: hit 3 out: sn rdn and btn: t.o whn p.u bef last* 5/4[1]
(3.50) **Going Correction** +0.40s/f (Soft) 8 Ran SP% **115.7**
Speed ratings: **107,106,102,100,88 64, ,**
CSF £12.04 TOTE £2.00: £1.10, £2.70, £3.70; EX 14.70 Trifecta £24.20.
Owner Trevor Hemmings **Bred** Gleadhill House Stud Ltd **Trained** Great Habton, N Yorks

FOCUS
Tony McCoy called the ground "soft and tacky", with Nick Scholfield saying it was "hard work as it is drying out". Just fair juvenile form, particularly with the favourite misfiring, but the winner can rate higher.

3858 REWARDS4RACING.COM H'CAP CHASE (18 fncs 2 omitted) 3m 2f
1:50 (1:50) (Class 4) (0-120,119) 5-Y-0+ £3,898 (£1,144; £572; £286)

Form RPR
3/P- 1 Union Jack D'Ycy (FR)[50] 2889 6-11-9 116 AidanColeman 127+
(Venetia Williams) *chsd ldrs: hit 14th: chsd ldr 4 out: led appr 2 out and nt fluent: styd on wl u.p* 7/1[3]
653- 2 2 1/2 Bally Sands (IRE)[21] 3502 10-10-2 98 (v) RobertDunne(3) 103
(Robin Mathew) *chsd ldrs: chal 8th: led next: rdn and hdd appr 2 out: styd on u.p run-in but no imp on wnr* 4/1[2]
/02- 3 1 Present To You (IRE)[60] 2700 9-10-11 111 JakeHodson(7) 115
(David Bridgwater) *mde most tl hdd 9th: styd chalng 12th to next: dropped to 3rd and rdn 4 out: rallied u.p fr 2 out: kpt on run-in to press for 2nd but no imp on wnr* 8/1
130- 4 12 Franklin Roosevelt (IRE)[47] 2953 8-11-12 119 (b) TomScudamore 111
(David Pipe) *in rr and reminder after 4th: hdwy 12th: styd on u.p fr 4 out to take wl-hld 4th run-in* 7/1[3]
346- 5 4 Incentivise (IRE)[48] 2923 11-11-4 114 MichealNolan(3) 103
(Richard Lee) *in tch: hit 6th: in rr 9th: lost pl 12th and sn rdn: hit 14th and no ch after* 12/1
6/2- 6 23 My Boy Paddy (IRE)[85] 2157 10-11-10 117 (p) SamTwiston-Davies 93
(Nigel Twiston-Davies) *hit 3rd: chsd ldrs 11th: wknd 4 out* 8/1
2/5- P Only Witness (IRE)[42] 3044 9-11-8 115 (p) BrendanPowell
(Brendan Powell) *prom early: in rr 6th: t.o whn p.u bef 12th* 40/1
521- P Dark Glacier (IRE)[34] 3193 9-11-11 118 (v) JamieMoore
(Peter Bowen) *pressed ldrs early: wknd 11th: t.o whn p.u bef next* 7/1[3]
6/4- F Master Neo (FR)[40] 3097 8-11-4 114 (tp) MarkQuinlan(3)
(Nigel Hawke) *chsd ldrs early: hit 3rd: wknd 11th: bhd whn fell next* 3/1[1]
6m 53.34s (0.64) **Going Correction** +0.175s/f (Yiel) 9 Ran SP% **114.9**
Speed ratings: **106,105,104,101,100 92, , ,**
CSF £35.87 CT £229.85 TOTE £6.10: £4.70, £1.70, £3.40; EX 54.70 Trifecta £386.90.
Owner Ian Josephs **Bred** Mme Anne Vallee & Claude Gouin **Trained** Kings Caple, H'fords
■ Stewards' Enquiry : Robert Dunne four-day ban: used whip above permitted level (Feb 6-9)

FOCUS
The early pace was relatively brisk and, predictably, this turned into a slog. The form is rated around the second.

3859 TURFTV H'CAP CHASE (JOCKEY CLUB GRASSROOTS JUMPS SERIES QUALIFIER) (16 fncs 1 omitted) 2m 4f 110y

2:20 (2:22) (Class 4) (0-120,120) 5-Y-0+ **£3,898** (£1,144; £572; £286)

Form RPR

4/3- **1** **Time To Think**[40] 3093 9-11-5 **113** APMcCoy 125+
(Seamus Mullins) *in rr: nt fluent 7th: rdn along appr 10th: drvn fr 13th: styd on after 3 out: disp 2nd u.p 2 out: chsd ldr and hit last: styd on wl to ld last strides: all out* **2/1**[1]

300- **2** *nk* **Have You Seen Me (IRE)**[41] 3065 11-11-12 **120** SamTwiston-Davies 129
(Nigel Twiston-Davies) *chsd ldr: led after 5th: rdn after 3 out: styd on u.p fr last: hdd last strides* **7/2**[2]

12P- **3** *3* **Brody Bleu (FR)**[224] 728 7-11-9 **117** WayneHutchinson 124
(Robert Walford) *in tch: hdwy to chse ldrs fr 12th: rdn 3 out: styng on u.p whn hit last: kpt on again clsng stages* **13/2**

121/ **4** *8* **Gentle Bob (IRE)**[686] 4727 9-11-6 **114** PaddyBrennan 113
(Tom George) *slt ld: hit 3rd: hdd after 5th: styd pressing ldr: chal and hit 3 out: stl ev ch next: wknd bef last* **5/1**[3]

/24- **5** *½* **Mr Muddle**[36] 3164 7-11-9 **117** MarcGoldstein 118
(Sheena West) *chsd ldrs: hit 5th: rdn 10th: hit 14th: wknd bef 2 out: no ch w ldrs whn blnd last* **9/1**

/05- **6** *hd* **Saints And Sinners (IRE)**[24] 3418 6-11-9 **117** WilsonRenwick 114
(Michael Easterby) *in rr but in tch: pushed along 4 out: styd on same pce fr 2 out* **11/2**

5m 23.37s (2.37) **Going Correction** +0.175s/f (Yiel) **6** Ran SP% **110.9**
Speed ratings: **102,101,100,97,97 97**
CSF £9.44 TOTE £2.60: £1.50, £2.00; EX 6.90 Trifecta £40.40.
Owner Mrs Fay Hewett **Bred** M E R Allsopp **Trained** Wilsford-Cum-Lake, Wilts

FOCUS
Just a fair handicap chase, but solid-looking form.

3860 JOHN MALONE GODFATHER OF MORTGAGES RETIREMENT H'CAP HURDLE (12 hdls) 3m 1f

2:50 (2:51) (Class 3) (0-130,128) 4-Y-0+ **£6,498** (£1,908; £954; £477)

Form RPR

/22- **1** **Kris Spin (IRE)**[47] 2942 6-11-12 **125** RichardJohnson 129+
(Richard Lee) *trckd ldrs off mod pce: qcknd to ld 3 out: drvn 2 out: nt fluent last: styd on wl u.p run-in* **7/1**[3]

/F1- **2** *¾* **Tidal Dance (IRE)**[4] 3800 7-12-1 **128** 7ex AidanColeman 130
(Venetia Williams) *chsd ldrs off mod pce: chsd wnr 3 out: drvn and swtchd lft 2 out: nt fluent last: kpt on u.p but a hld* **5/4**[1]

051- **3** *16* **Big Society (IRE)**[8] 3724 8-11-11 **124** 7ex PaddyBrennan 115+
(Tom George) *led and hit 1st: sn hdd: sn pressing ldr off mod pce: drvn: hit 4 out and sn dropped to 3rd: u.p whn hit 3 out and next: no ch w ldng duo whn mstke last* **5/2**[2]

512- **4** *13* **Mistral Reine**[22] 3473 5-10-6 **105** LeightonAspell 78
(Lucy Wadham) *trckd ldrs off mod pce: rdn whn pce qcknd after 4 out: btn next* **9/1**

/2F- **5** *13* **Dreams Of Milan (IRE)**[28] 3266 6-11-10 **123** JasonMaguire 83
(Donald McCain) *led 2nd at mod pce: sn jnd but kpt slt ld tl hdd and nt fluent 3 out: sn rdn and btn* **7/1**[3]

6m 53.66s (38.66) **Going Correction** +0.40s/f (Soft) **5** Ran SP% **108.0**
Speed ratings (Par 107): **54,53,48,44,40**
CSF £16.22 TOTE £7.40: £3.40, £1.20; EX 17.80 Trifecta £44.80.
Owner Six To Five Against **Bred** Neill Patrick Francis Doran **Trained** Byton, H'fords

FOCUS
They went a very sedate pace for two-thirds of the trip and the form may not prove that solid. It's been given a token rating through the second.

3861 CALL STAR SPORTS ON 08000 521 321 NOVICES' CHASE (16 fncs 1 omitted) 2m 4f 110y

3:20 (3:22) (Class 3) 5-Y-0+ **£6,498** (£1,908; £954; £477)

Form RPR

352- **1** **Persian Snow (IRE)**[23] 3436 8-11-0 130 (t) RichardJohnson 136+
(Philip Hobbs) *trckd ldr: hit 5th: j. slowly 4 out: chal 2 out: slt ld sn after: drvn last: styd on strly run-in* **8/13**[1]

231- **2** *8* **No Buts**[10] 3690 6-11-7 117 TomScudamore 137
(David Bridgwater) *led: rdn after 3 out: jnd next: sn hdd: wl there last: btn u.p fnl 150yds: eased cl home* **6/4**[2]

200- **3** *dist* **Another Brandy (IRE)**[9] 3695 6-10-11 0 MichaelByrne[(3)] 86
(Neil Mulholland) *a in 3rd: in tch 9th: btn next: t.o fr 11th* **33/1**[3]

060- **4** *1 ½* **Pure Poteen (IRE)**[9] 3694 6-11-0 0 (t) DougieCostello 85
(Neil Mulholland) *a in 4th: in tch 9th: btn next: t.o fr 11th* **50/1**

5m 24.46s (3.46) **Going Correction** +0.175s/f (Yiel) **4** Ran SP% **106.8**
Speed ratings: **100,96,81,81**
CSF £1.91 TOTE £1.60; EX 1.80 Trifecta £3.10.
Owner D R Peppiatt **Bred** Garryhankard House Stud **Trained** Withycombe, Somerset

FOCUS
No depth to this novice chase. The first two are rated to their marks.

3862 CGA FOXHUNTER TRIAL OPEN HUNTERS' CHASE (16 fncs 2 omitted) 3m 110y

3:50 (3:53) (Class 6) 5-Y-0+ **£987** (£303; £151)

Form RPR

1/1- **1** **Little Legend**[261] 165 10-11-13 108 (p) MissCHaydon[(7)] 120+
(Miss C M E Haydon) *mde all: pushed along 2 out: drvn clr fr last: comf* **11/10**[1]

424- **2** *5* **Loose Preformer (IRE)**[178] 1134 8-11-11 0 MrBGibbs[(5)] 107
(Michael Hawker) *hit 2nd: j. slowly 5th: in rr 7th: hdwy 10th: chsd wnr and rdn 2 out: styd on same pce appr last* **12/1**

P23/ **3** *2 ¼* **Ben's Folly (IRE)**[11] 9-11-7 0 (p) MissLBrooke[(5)] 100
(R A Owen) *chsd ldrs: styd on to take 3rd appr last: nvr rchd wnr and styd on one pce* **4/1**[2]

/0P- **4** *2 ½* **Schindler's Prince (IRE)**[18] 9-11-7 0 MrJMRidley[(5)] 98
(Mrs H S M Ridley) *disp 2nd: rdn along 10th: drvn to cl on wnr 3 out: no prog u.p next: wknd last* **6/1**

4F/ **P** **Carronhills (IRE)**[1063] 4333 12-11-5 0 MissLeandaTickle[(7)]
(P J Tolman) *chsd ldrs 7th: wknd 11th: t.o whn p.u bef 3 out* **5/1**[3]

/ **P** **Rockers Field (IRE)**[27] 12-11-5 0 (b) MrBFurnival[(7)]
(B A Furnival) *chsd ldrs: hit 8th: rdn after 9th: t.o whn p.u bef 12th* **40/1**

6m 38.92s (11.92) **Going Correction** +0.175s/f (Yiel) **6** Ran SP% **108.7**
Speed ratings: **87,85,84,83,**
CSF £13.07 TOTE £1.90: £1.70, £1.90; EX 11.70 Trifecta £22.00.
Owner Michael Haydon **Bred** D F Evans **Trained** Aylesbury, Bucks

FOCUS
A fairly ordinary hunter chase. The winner and fourth are rated in line with last year's hunter chase marks.

3863 CONNOLLY'S RED MILLS BUMPER CHALLENGE INTERMEDIATE OPEN NATIONAL HUNT FLAT RACE 2m

4:20 (4:22) (Class 6) 5-6-Y-0 **£1,559** (£457; £228; £114)

Form RPR

3- **1** **Battle Born**[62] 2660 5-10-12 0 NoelFehily 112+
(Charlie Longsdon) *mde virtually all: drvn over 2f out: styd on strly u.p fr over 1f out* **6/4**[1]

2 *2 ½* **King's Odyssey (IRE)** 5-10-12 0 DenisO'Regan 110+
(Denis Coakley) *hld up towards rr: gd hdwy 4f out: trckd ldrs 3f out: drvn and styd on to chse wnr over 1f out: kpt on but no imp* **20/1**

3 *4* **Otago Trail (IRE)**[88] 6-10-12 0 AidanColeman 107+
(Venetia Williams) *pressed wnr tl drvn over 3f out: no imp over 2f out: dropped to 3rd over 1f out and styd on same pce* **10/1**

- **4** *6* **Point Guard (IRE)** 6-10-12 0 RobertThornton 100+
(Don Cantillon) *hld up in rr: drvn 4f out: styd on but green fr over 2f out: styd on to take 4th over 1f out: nvr a threat* **8/1**

3- **5** *5* **Surging Seas (IRE)**[69] 2499 5-10-12 0 DougieCostello 95
(Tony Coyle) *chsd ldrs: rdn 3f out: wknd 2f out* **6/1**[3]

6 *3 ½* **Vesuvhill (FR)** 5-10-9 0 KielanWoods[(3)] 91
(Ben Case) *chsd ldrs: rdn over 3f out: wknd wl over 2f out* **50/1**

7 *1 ¼* **Royalraise (IRE)**[116] 5-10-12 0 LeightonAspell 90
(Oliver Sherwood) *t.k.h towards rr: hdwy 6f out: rdn 3f out: sn btn* **16/1**

5- **8** *5* **Saddlers Encore (IRE)**[61] 2667 5-10-12 0 RichardJohnson 85
(Philip Hobbs) *chsd ldrs tl over 3f out* **5/1**[2]

9 *12* **Latelo** 6-10-12 0 MarkGrant 73
(Charlie Mann) *chsd ldrs: rdn along 4f out: wknd over 3f out* **10/1**

265/ **10** *27* **Turoyal (FR)**[298] 5041 6-10-12 0 PaulMoloney 46
(Laura Hurley) *a in rr: t.o* **80/1**

11 *6* **Flobury** 6-10-5 0 LiamHeard 33
(Barry Leavy) *in tch to 1/2-way: t.o* **100/1**

12 *nk* **So Sudden** 5-10-5 0 TomScudamore 32
(Mark Rimell) *chsd ldrs to 1/2-way: t.o* **33/1**

- **13** *11* **Just Like Beth** 6-9-12 0 KevinJones[(7)] 21
(Giuseppe Fierro) *prom early: sn bhd* **66/1**

3m 57.37s (6.47) **Going Correction** +0.40s/f (Soft) **13** Ran SP% **119.5**
Speed ratings: **99,97,95,92,90 88,87,85,79,65 62,62,57**
CSF £40.60 TOTE £2.80: £1.40, £7.90, £2.30; EX 46.40 Trifecta £708.50.
Owner Alan Halsall **Bred** Mrs S C Welch **Trained** Over Norton, Oxon

FOCUS
A decent bumper which was run at a very steady initial pace. It's a race that should produce winners.
T/Plt: £53.70. Pool: £59,500.21 - 807.41 winning units. T/Qpdt: £6.50. Pool: £3494.80 - 396.10 winning units. ST

3864 - 3865a (Foreign Racing) - See Raceform Interactive

2682 GOWRAN PARK (R-H)

Thursday, January 23

OFFICIAL GOING: Soft (soft to heavy in places)

3866a JOHN MULHERN GALMOY HURDLE (GRADE 2) (13 hdls) 3m

2:15 (2:15) 5-Y-0+ **£21,666** (£6,333; £3,000; £1,000)

RPR

1 **Mala Beach (IRE)**[26] 3374 6-11-8 148 RobbieColgan 156+
(Gordon Elliott, Ire) *chsd ldr in 2nd: nt fluent 10th and next: pushed along fr 3 out and sn clsd to chal fr next: led between last 2 and wnt clr last: styd on wl* **10/3**[2]

2 *8* **Un Beau Matin (IRE)**[12] 3670 6-11-3 134 BryanCooper 142
(Gordon Elliott, Ire) *attempted to make all: extended ld bef 6th: reduced advantage after 3 out and jnd fr next: hdd between last 2 and sn no ex: kpt on same pce run-in* **7/1**[3]

3 *11* **Jetson (IRE)**[26] 3372 9-11-3 139 BarryGeraghty 131
(Mrs John Harrington, Ire) *chsd ldrs: slt mstke in 5th at 6th: mstke 3 out and rdn: no imp on ldrs and wnt mod 3rd next: kpt on one pce* **14/1**

4 *9* **Bishopsfurze (IRE)**[12] 3670 9-11-3 133 PaulTownend 122
(W P Mullins, Ire) *sn chsd ldrs: 4th 1/2-way: slt mstke on outer in 6th 4 out: no imp on ldrs u.p fr next: kpt on one pce* **20/1**

5 *5 ½* **Aughnacurraveel (IRE)**[56] 2778 10-11-3 130 PCarberry 117
(Thomas P Cummins, Ire) *hld up in tch: t.k.h early: clsr in 5th after 3 out: rdn and no imp on ldrs bef next: kpt on one pce* **20/1**

6 *14* **Zaidpour (FR)**[26] 3374 8-11-10 158 RWalsh 110
(W P Mullins, Ire) *chsd ldrs: slt mstke in 4th at 6th: niggled along in 3rd bef 9th where slt mstke: reminders after: no imp on ldrs in 3rd 3 out: n.d u.p next where nt fluent: wknd* **1/2**[1]

7 *8 ½* **Mazuri Cowboy (IRE)**[12] 3670 9-11-3 129 MartinFerris 94
(Eoin Doyle, Ire) *w.w: tk clsr order bef 4 out: rdn in mod 7th next and n.d into st: mstke 2 out: wknd* **33/1**

P **Its Who You Are (IRE)**[17] 3584 5-10-6 PaddyKennedy
(Jeffrey Ian Mulhern, Ire) *hld up in rr: nt fluent 10th: sn pushed along and no imp: trailing bef 4 out and p.u bef next* **150/1**

6m 19.8s (-9.10) **8** Ran SP% **122.0**
CSF £26.11 TOTE £4.30: £1.30, £1.40, £2.00; DF 25.30 Trifecta £132.90.
Owner C Jones **Bred** R Guiry **Trained** Trim, Co Meath

FOCUS
The front-running runner-up helps to set the standard.

3868a GOFFS THYESTES H'CAP CHASE (GRADE A) (17 fncs) 3m 1f

3:15 (3:15) 5-Y-0+

£50,000 (£15,833; £7,500; £2,500; £1,666; £833)

RPR

1 **On His Own (IRE)**[47] 2937 10-11-6 **142** PaulTownend 159+
(W P Mullins, Ire) *sn led: slow 6th and jnd briefly: over 1 l clr 1/2-way: mstke 4 out and hdd: regained advantage bef next: edgd lft bef 2 out where j.rt: wandered bef last and j.rt again: styd on wl u.p* **12/1**

2 *6* **Los Amigos (IRE)**[32] 3235 7-10-4 **126** AELynch 137
(J T R Dreaper, Ire) *chsd ldrs: 5th 1/2-way: clsr in 3rd into st: rdn 3 out and no imp on wnr bef last: rdn into mod 2nd run-in: kpt on same pce* **5/1**[1]

3 1 3/4 **Oscars Business (IRE)**[39] 3125 10-9-12 **120**..................(t) PhillipEnright 129
(Robert Tyner, Ire) *chsd ldrs: 6th 1/2-way: cl 4th bef 4 out: clsd u.p fr next: sltly hmpd 2 out: no imp on ldrs in 4th bef last: kpt on u.p run-in into 3rd fnl stride* **12/1**

4 shd **Balnaslow (IRE)**[28] 3314 7-10-11 **133**................................ BryanCooper 142
(W P Mullins, Ire) *hld up: hdwy to chse ldrs in 6th after 4 out: clsd to chal in 2nd fr next: no imp on wnr u.p bef last where mstke: wknd run-in and denied 3rd fnl stride* **8/1**[2]

5 6 **Cootamundra (IRE)**[60] 2708 11-10-13 **135**........................ RobbieMoran 140
(J A Berry, Ire) *w.w towards rr: slt mstke 5th: tk clsr order in mid-div 1/2-way: clsr in 7th after 4 out: slt mstke in cl 6th 3 out: rdn and no imp on wnr in 5th at last: kpt on one pce* **16/1**

6 nk **Sole Witness (IRE)**[11] 3684 10-10-0 **125**............................ BenDalton(3) 128
(C A McBratney, Ire) *chsd ldr: disp briefly 6th: 2nd 1/2-way on terms again fr 13th and led narrowly fr 4 out: hdd bef next and rdn into st: mstke 3 out and sn no ex in 5th: kpt on one pce* **22/1**

7 13 **Panther Claw (IRE)**[27] 3341 8-10-6 **128**.....................(b[1]) BarryGeraghty 118
(Paul Nolan, Ire) *chsd ldrs: 3rd 1/2-way: rdn fr 12th and no imp on ldrs fr 4 out: mod 7th whn slt mstke last: one pce run-in* **8/1**[2]

8 1/2 **Ipsos Du Berlais (FR)**[5] 3791 8-10-8 **137**............................(p) GerFox(7) 126
(Noel Meade, Ire) *hld up: slt mstke in rr at 5th: sme hdwy u.p bef 4 out: no imp on ldrs in mod 8th whn mstke next: kpt on one pce* **16/1**

9 10 **Vesper Bell (IRE)**[12] 3655 8-11-7 **143**... RWalsh 124
(W P Mullins, Ire) *hld up in tch: niggled along in 12th after 13th and no imp bef next: one pce after* **8/1**[2]

10 13 **Playing (FR)**[19] 3548 11-10-7 **134**...................................(p) KevinSexton(5) 101
(Thomas Foley, Ire) *racd in mid-div: 9th 1/2-way: rdn and no imp on ldrs in mod 9th after 4 out: kpt on one pce fr next* **14/1**

11 48 **Hunting Party (IRE)**[27] 3341 8-10-6 **128**................................ PCarberry 46
(D T Hughes, Ire) *hld up in rr of mid-div: pushed along and no imp bef 4 out: wknd and eased into st: completely t.o* **10/1**

12 14 **Lookoutnow (IRE)**[27] 3347 9-10-8 **133**......................... MichaelButler(3) 37
(Eoin Doyle, Ire) *prom early: settled bhd ldr in 2nd fr first: 4th 1/2-way: rdn and wknd fr 13th: completely t.o* **9/1**[3]

P **Uncle Junior (IRE)**[69] 2491 13-10-12 **134**..................................(p) DJCasey
(W P Mullins, Ire) *w.w in rr: j.rt 4th and several times after: slt mstke 11th: t.o whn p.u bef 3 out* **25/1**

P **Tarquinius (FR)**[12] 3669 11-10-4 **126**...............................(tp) MartinFerris
(Gordon Elliott, Ire) *chsd ldrs: 7th 1/2-way: reminders after 12th: no imp on ldrs in mod 8th whn p.u bef 3 out* **25/1**

P **Caduceus (IRE)**[53] 2856 10-9-12 **120**..................................... APHeskin
(P Hughes, Ire) *towards rr: pushed along fr 11th and no imp: trailing whn p.u bef 3 out* **25/1**

P **Groody Hill (IRE)**[22] 3484 8-10-7 **129**..................................[1] AlanCrowe
(C Roche, Ire) *racd in mid-div: 8th 1/2-way: dropped towards rr bef 4 out and p.u bef next* **11/1**

P **Rich Revival (IRE)**[27] 3341 10-10-11 **133**........................... BrianO'Connell
(Miss Elizabeth Doyle, Ire) *towards rr: bmpd in air by rival at 4th: reminders after 9th: no imp bef 4 out: trailing whn p.u bef next* **14/1**

P **Archie Meade (IRE)**[23] 3441 9-9-13 **121**................................(t) DJHoward
(Daniel John Howard, Ire) *in rr of mid-div: slt mstke 4th and rdr lost iron briefly: no imp whn mstke 13th: trailing whn p.u bef 3 out* **20/1**

6m 36.7s (396.70) **18** Ran SP% **138.6**
CSF £76.06 CT £773.77 TOTE £17.70: £4.60, £1.90, £2.10, £2.00; DF 103.80.
Owner Andrea & Graham Wylie **Bred** Ms Margaret Treacy **Trained** Muine Beag, Co Carlow

FOCUS
A renewal in keeping with recent years. Competitive, lacking the presence of a real star off top weight and plenty in with a chance turning for home. The tempo increased quickly heading on to the final circuit and there were plenty left toiling when it did. The winner was at his very best.

3867 - 3870a (Foreign Racing) - See Raceform Interactive

3598 DONCASTER (L-H)

Friday, January 24

OFFICIAL GOING: Good to soft (soft in places; chs 6.8, hdl 7.0)
Wind: fresh against Weather: Cloudy

3871 SKY BET "BEST ODDS GUARANTEED" NOVICES' H'CAP HURDLE (8 hdls) 2m 110y

1:10 (1:11) (Class 5) (0-100,100) 4-Y-0+ **£1,949** (£572; £286; £143)

Form RPR

0/0- 1 **Easydoesit (IRE)**[11] 812 6-11-10 **98**...................................... NoelFehily 104+
(Tony Carroll) *prom: rdn to ld between last 2: kpt on wl* **12/1**

055- 2 5 **Ergo Sum**[24] 3427 7-11-3 **94**... RobertDunne(3) 96
(Robin Mathew) *racd keenly: led: rdn whn hdd between last 2: one pce and no ch w wnr run-in* **12/1**

033- 3 1 1/4 **Spanish Fleet**[20] 3527 6-11-5 **100**................................... JohnDawson(7) 100
(John Wade) *in tch: hdwy to chse ldr appr 3 out: rdn bef 2 out: one pce in 3rd fr appr last* **15/2**

063- 4 1 1/2 **Daliance (IRE)**[23] 3471 5-11-7 **100**..............................(p) MattCrawley(5) 99+
(Lucy Wadham) *hld up in midfield: wnt a little in snatches: rdn bef 3 out: stl bhd 2 out: styd on fr bef last: nrst fin* **10/3**[1]

004- 5 3 1/2 **Dalstontosiloth (IRE)**[40] 3110 6-10-13 **94**................... CallumBewley(7) 91
(Barry Murtagh) *midfield: hdwy to chse ldrs bef 3 out: rdn 2 out: hit last: no ex* **33/1**

035- 6 5 **Finmerello**[62] 2679 8-11-2 **90**...(p) JasonMaguire 81
(Kim Bailey) *hld up: pushed along and sme hdwy whn sltly hmpd by faller 2 out: no further imp* **7/1**[3]

004- 7 1 **Echo Foxtrot**[25] 3415 5-10-9 **90**.................................... GeraldQuinn(7) 82
(Claire Dyson) *hld up: rdn 3 out: nvr threatened ldrs* **25/1**

0/P- 8 25 **So Bazaar (IRE)**[27] 3353 7-10-1 **75**....................................(t) BrianHarding 43
(Andrew Wilson) *hld up: nvr threatened* **80/1**

524- 9 2 1/4 **Monita Bonita**[29] 3270 5-11-9 **97**.................................... DougieCostello 62
(Tim Easterby) *chsd ldrs: already wkng whn sltly hmpd by faller 2 out* **11/2**[2]

505- 10 2 1/4 **Danby's Legend**[15] 3616 7-11-1 **99**.................................[1] JakeHolliday(10) 62
(Malcolm Jefferson) *midfield on outer: wknd 3 out* **10/1**

00P/ 11 6 **I'm So Special (IRE)**[325] 4573 8-10-9 **83**........................(t) RichardJohnson 41
(Susan Johnson) *prom: wknd after 3 out* **20/1**

P/0- 12 62 **Arte Del Calcio**[14] 2292 5-11-4 **92**...................................... LeeEdwards
(Tony Carroll) *racd keenly in midfield: hit 4th: wknd bef 3 out* **50/1**

653- F **Knockturnal (IRE)**[21] 3518 6-10-9 **83**..............................(b) BrianHughes 82
(Malcolm Jefferson) *midfield on inner: swtchd to outer bef 3 out: sn hdwy: 2 l down and stl gng wl whn fell 2 out: fatally injured* **7/1**[3]

4m 2.9s (-1.80) **Going Correction** -0.05s/f (Good) **13** Ran SP% **114.4**
Speed ratings (Par 103): **102,99,99,98,96 94,93,82,81,80 77,48,**
CSF £131.86 CT £1153.98 TOTE £13.00: £4.40, £5.20, £2.60; EX 181.60 Trifecta £1187.90 Part won..
Owner T R Pearson **Bred** Tinnakill Bloodstock & Alan Byrne **Trained** Cropthorne, Worcs
■ Noel Fehily's 100th winner of the season, his first century.
■ Stewards' Enquiry : Brian Hughes caution: careless riding.

FOCUS
Hurdle dividing rail moved to provided fresh ground where possible. After riding the winner of the first, Noel Fehily said the ground was "a bit dead and a bit tacky." An ordinary race. The winner is entitled to rate higher on Flat form.

3872 SKY VEGAS APP NOVICES' HURDLE (8 hdls) 2m 110y

1:40 (1:42) (Class 4) 4-Y-0+ **£3,119** (£915; £457; £228)

Form RPR

3- 1 **Pearl Castle (IRE)**[28] 3332 4-10-7 0.................................. BrianHughes 124+
(John Quinn) *in tch: smooth hdwy to trck ldrs 3 out: led appr last: qcknd clr: impressive* **17/2**

264- 2 16 **I Got Power**[16] 3602 5-11-4 0... JamesReveley 117
(Keith Reveley) *hld up in rr: hdwy into midfield after 4th: pushed along after 3 out: hit 2 out: kpt on fr appr last: wnt 2nd towards fin* **33/1**

1P- 3 1 **Dubai Prince (IRE)**[29] 3258 6-11-11 0................................ DenisO'Regan 123
(John Ferguson) *in tch: hdwy to ld 3 out: hdd appr last: sn outpcd by wnr: rdn and no ex run-in: lost 2nd towards fin* **7/2**[3]

2/5- 4 2 1/4 **Spring Steel (IRE)**[244] 483 5-11-4 0.................................. DavidBass 113
(Ben Pauling) *led: hdd 3 out: sn rdn and one pce* **50/1**

/25- 5 2 3/4 **Varom (FR)**[63] 2659 5-11-4 0... DarylJacob 112
(Paul Nicholls) *prom: rdn 3 out: one pce* **2/1**[1]

6 3 **Area Fifty One**[104] 6-11-4 0... BarryGeraghty 107
(Nicky Henderson) *in tch: hdwy to trck ldrs 3 out: rdn after 2 out: wknd run-in* **9/4**[2]

5- 7 6 **Time Of My Life (IRE)**[27] 3350 5-10-13 0.......................... JoeColliver(5) 101
(Patrick Holmes) *hld up: hdwy into midfield after 5th: nvr threatened ldrs* **100/1**

/03- 8 7 **Jolly Valentine**[22] 3501 6-11-1 0.................................. TrevorWhelan(3) 94
(Neil King) *hld up: nvr threatened* **150/1**

9 1 **Triple Eight (IRE)**[29] 6-10-13 0....................................... AdamNicol(5) 93
(Philip Kirby) *in tch: wknd after 3 out* **100/1**

145- 10 12 **Mister Jones**[38] 3144 6-11-4 0... RyanMania 81
(Sue Smith) *midfield: reminder after 4th: nvr threatened* **20/1**

/06- 11 7 **Master Cynk**[9] 3716 7-11-4 0.. PaddyBrennan 74
(Tom George) *midfield: wknd bef 3 out* **100/1**

6/0- 12 1 3/4 **Fly By Knight**[110] 1793 5-11-4 0.................................... PeterBuchanan 72
(Tim Walford) *hld up: nvr threatened* **150/1**

03- 13 3/4 **Nexius (IRE)**[15] 3616 5-11-4 0....................................... WilsonRenwick 72
(Keith Dalgleish) *hld up in midfield: nvr threatened* **100/1**

5- 14 2 3/4 **Princeofthedesert**[50] 2900 8-11-4 0.................................. AdamPogson 69
(Garry Woodward) *prom: wknd 3 out* **150/1**

0- 15 16 **Langarve Lass (IRE)**[260] 187 5-10-11 0.............................. NoelFehily 46
(Neil Mulholland) *a towards rr* **150/1**

3/0- 16 1 1/2 **Miss Lucky Penny**[35] 3189 8-10-6 0............................ RobertMcCarth(5) 44
(Ian Williams) *hld up: a towards rr* **40/1**

17 1 **Vaillant Creek (FR)**[89] 5-11-4 0.................................... DougieCostello 50
(Alex Hales) *hld up: nvr threatened* **50/1**

U **Great Demeanor (USA)**[256] 4-10-2 0........................ ColmMcCormack(5)
(Dianne Sayer) *hld up: t.o whn uns rdr 3 out* **150/1**

3m 59.4s (-5.30) **Going Correction** -0.05s/f (Good)
WFA 4 from 5yo+ 11lb **18** Ran SP% **118.2**
Speed ratings (Par 105): **110,102,102,100,99 98,95,92,91,86 82,81,81,80,72 72,71,**
CSF £232.14 TOTE £11.00: £3.00, £6.50, £1.50; EX 181.40 Trifecta £1264.90.
Owner Mr & Mrs Paul Gaffney **Bred** Mogeely Stud **Trained** Settrington, N Yorks

FOCUS
This looked a fair novice on paper and it was won in terrific style. There should be more to come from the winner.

3873 SKY BET "FREE BET CLUB" NOVICES' CHASE (18 fncs) 3m

2:10 (2:10) (Class 4) 5-Y-0+ **£3,768** (£1,106; £553; £276)

Form RPR

1/2- 1 **Victor Hewgo**[16] 3601 9-11-0 0...................................... JamesReveley 135+
(Keith Reveley) *trckd ldrs: led after 3 out: sn in command: rdn clr after last: comfortaby* **6/4**[2]

4/3- 2 8 **Dreamy George (IRE)**[41] 3087 8-11-0 0............................ DenisO'Regan 125+
(John Ferguson) *hld up in tch: hdwy to chse ldrs 4 out: rdn 3 out: kpt on to go 2nd last: nt threat wnr* **25/1**

232- 3 1 1/4 **Beeves (IRE)**[28] 3327 7-11-7 135.................................(b[1]) JasonMaguire 131
(Donald McCain) *w ldr: hit 5 out: sn rdn: nt fluent 3 out: sn outpcd in 4th: plugged on after last: wnt 3rd fnl 100yds* **5/1**[3]

4/2- 4 nk **Perfect Candidate (IRE)**[104] 1863 7-11-0 119................ PaddyBrennan 123
(Fergal O'Brien) *j. slowly in rr: bhd tl kpt on after 2 out* **33/1**

224- 5 3 1/2 **Up To Something (FR)**[35] 3185 6-11-7 140.....................(tp) NoelFehily 126
(Charlie Longsdon) *led narrowly: hdd after 3 out: lost 2nd last: wknd and lost 2 more pls fnl 100yds* **11/8**[1]

3- 6 33 **Danners (IRE)**[29] 3279 8-10-9 0.......................................(p) MrMWall(5) 98
(Giles Smyly) *trckd ldrs: wnt prom 9th: mstke 4 out: wknd after 3 out* **20/1**

00F/ 7 43 **Newton Thistle**[446] 2218 7-11-0 0...................................... DavidBass 42
(Ben Pauling) *hld up: t.o after 12th* **250/1**

6m 9.9s (-2.10) **Going Correction** -0.05s/f (Good) **7** Ran SP% **110.7**
Speed ratings: **101,98,97,97,96 85,71**
CSF £29.53 TOTE £2.00: £1.90, £6.80; EX 19.00 Trifecta £82.60.
Owner Sir Ian Good **Bred** J Good, C Anderson And K G Reveley **Trained** Lingdale, Redcar & Cleveland

FOCUS
An interesting novice chase. The winner can rate higher.

3874 SKY BET "HOME OF PRICE BOOST" H'CAP CHASE (18 fncs) 3m

2:45 (2:46) (Class 4) (0-120,119) 5-Y-0+ **£3,768** (£1,106; £553; £276)

Form RPR

051- 1 **The Panama Kid (IRE)**[27] 3355 10-11-5 **112**..................(b) BrianHughes 129+
(Malcolm Jefferson) *trckd ldr: led bef 3 out: rdn clr after 2 out: eased towards fin: comf* **7/1**

3P0- 2 8 **Mr Supreme (IRE)**[16] 3603 9-10-6 **99**............................ RichieMcGrath 104+
(Keith Reveley) *hld up: hdwy 11th: chsd ldrs 4 out: outpcd by wnr after 3 out: plugged on run-in: wnt 2nd post* **7/1**

151- **3** *shd* **Badger Foot (IRE)**[34] 3211 9-10-13 **111**.....(t) DerekFox(5) 118
(Lucinda Russell) *hld up in tch: hit 10th: hdwy and cl up 4 out: outpcd by ldr 3 out: wnt 2nd last: one pce: lost 2nd post* **9/1**

424- **4** *hd* **Be Definite (IRE)**[54] 2847 10-11-5 **112**.....(p) PaddyBrennan 117
(Tom George) *trckd ldrs: rdn in 2nd 3 out: sn outpcd by wnr: hit last and lost 2nd: one pce* **16/1**

145- **5** *27* **More Equity**[26] 3394 12-11-3 **110**..... RyanMania 90
(Dianne Sayer) *in tch: wknd after 5 out* **33/1**

U63- **6** *30* **Honest John**[16] 3603 10-11-5 **112**..... JasonMaguire 65
(Steve Gollings) *led: hdd bef 3 out: wknd* **2/1**[1]

FF5- **7** *29* **Minella Definitely (IRE)**[48] 2941 7-11-12 **119**.....(tp) NoelFehily 45
(Neil Mulholland) *mstkes in rr: bhd fr12th* **7/2**[2]

3/5- **P** **Milo Milan (IRE)**[85] 2179 9-11-7 **117**.....(bt[1]) MichealNolan(3)
(Richard Lee) *mstkes: midfield: dropped to rr 9th: bhd after 12th: t.o whn p.u bef 2 out* **11/2**[3]

6m 6.7s (-5.30) **Going Correction** -0.05s/f (Good) **8** Ran SP% **114.8**
Speed ratings: **106,103,103,103,94 84,74,**
CSF £54.17 CT £445.27 TOTE £7.90: £1.90, £2.10, £2.40; EX 69.50 Trifecta £734.00.
Owner Mrs D W Davenport **Bred** J M And Mrs Davenport **Trained** Norton, N Yorks

FOCUS
Fair form. The easy winner built on his recent victory.

3875 SKY BET BEST ODDS GUARANTEED H'CAP HURDLE (11 hdls) 3m 110y
3:15 (3:16) (Class 3) (0-140,135) 4-Y-0+ **£5,525** (£1,715; £923)

Form RPR

/46- **1** **Kaysersberg (FR)**[64] 2624 7-11-0 **123**..... RichardJohnson 128+
(Neil King) *trckd ldr: nt fluent 4th: led jst after 4 out: rdn clr 2 out: kpt on wl* **85/40**[2]

204- **2** *10* **Wakanda (IRE)**[41] 3086 5-10-10 **119**..... RyanMania 117
(Sue Smith) *hld up in tch: tk clsr order 4 out: rdn and 2 l down whn hit 3 out: sn outpcd by wnr: hit last* **15/2**

1/0- **3** *32* **Atlantic Roller (IRE)**[70] 2490 7-11-6 **129**..... DarylJacob 108
(Paul Nicholls) *racd keenly: trckd ldr: upsides 6th: pushed along and dropped to 3rd after 4 out: btn whn hit 3 out: eased* **13/8**[1]

/14- **P** **Tornado Bob (IRE)**[188] 1042 9-11-12 **135**.....(b) JasonMaguire
(Donald McCain) *led: hit 4 out and sn hdd: wknd qckly: p.u bef 3 out* **3/1**[3]

5m 58.0s (-1.00) **Going Correction** -0.05s/f (Good) **4** Ran SP% **106.9**
Speed ratings (Par 107): **99,95,85,**
CSF £13.99 TOTE £4.30; EX 14.70 Trifecta £30.00.
Owner Mrs Julien Turner & Andrew Merriam **Bred** Mme Marquerite De Tarragon **Trained** Newmarket, Suffolk

FOCUS
Just the four runners, and with Tornado Bob disappointing this may not have taken much winning. The race is given a token rating through the second.

3876 SKY BINGO APP NOVICES' H'CAP CHASE (15 fncs) 2m 3f
3:50 (3:50) (Class 5) (0-100,100) 5-Y-0+ **£2,144** (£629; £314; £157)

Form RPR

441- **1** **Oh Right (IRE)**[7] 3755 10-9-9 **74** oh2.....(b) HarryChalloner(5) 90+
(Dianne Sayer) *led: rdn whn hdd bef 4 out: led again 3 out: blnd 2 out: hld on towards fin* **7/1**[3]

042- **2** *1 ½* **Take The Mick**[8] 3729 7-11-7 **95**..... LiamTreadwell 110+
(Venetia Williams) *midfield: in tch whn mstke 5 out: rdn and styd on after 3 out: wnt 2nd jst after last: clsng at fin but a hld* **13/8**[1]

443- **3** *10* **Johnnys Legacy (IRE)**[27] 3353 7-11-3 **94**..... PeterCarberry(3) 100
(Conor Dore) *prom: led bef 4 out: hdd 3 out: nt fluent last: no ex run-in* **20/1**

/P2- **4** *¾* **Malibu Sun**[45] 3008 7-11-7 **95**..... DavidBass 100
(Ben Pauling) *prom: upsides whn blnd 3 out: lost 2nd after last: wknd run-in: lost 3rd nr fin* **12/1**

0/0- **5** *19* **Tallulah Mai**[151] 1391 7-11-12 **100**..... WillKennedy 86
(Alastair Lidderdale) *hld up in midfield: wknd after 2 out* **50/1**

U13- **6** *14* **Crescent Beach (IRE)**[17] 3595 7-11-0 **88**..... RobertThornton 67
(Henry Oliver) *trckd ldrs: lost pl 9th: wknd after 5 out* **14/1**

400- **7** *12* **Shine A Diamond (IRE)**[21] 3516 6-11-9 **97**..... PeterBuchanan 60
(Lucinda Russell) *hld up: nvr threatened* **16/1**

244- **P** **Foot The Bill**[70] 2498 9-11-11 **99**..... BrianHarding
(Patrick Holmes) *hld up: nt fluent 6th: bhd whn hit 8th: t.o whn p.u bef 3 out* **25/1**

0/5- **P** **Sole Survivor (FR)**[25] 3419 7-11-12 **100**.....(t) DenisO'Regan
(Paul Webber) *hld up: hit 1st: tk clsr order 6th: nt fluent 8th: wknd 5 out: t.o whn p.u bef 3 out* **15/2**

/5P- **P** **Shady Sadie (IRE)**[43] 3040 7-10-9 **83**.....(t) WilsonRenwick
(Rose Dobbin) *hld up: a towards rr: p.u bef 3 out* **50/1**

006- **F** **Khazium (IRE)**[47] 2980 5-10-2 **87**.....(tp) GeraldQuinn(7)
(Claire Dyson) *midfield: wkng whn fell 6 out* **50/1**

0/0- **P** **On The Case**[263] 140 6-10-8 **82**..... PaddyBrennan
(Tom George) *hld up: hdwy 6 out: in tch whn blnd 5 out: struggling whn hit next: p.u after 3 out* **9/2**[2]

4m 54.9s (5.90) **Going Correction** -0.05s/f (Good)
WFA 5 from 6yo+ 3lb **12** Ran SP% **115.3**
Speed ratings: **85,84,80,79,71 65,60,, ,**
CSF £18.22 CT £214.67 TOTE £9.10: £2.50, £1.90, £2.30; EX 27.80 Trifecta £584.30.
Owner Andrew Sayer **Bred** Martin Keating **Trained** Hackthorpe, Cumbria

FOCUS
A moderate handicap but the form makes sense.

3877 SKY BET MOBILE MAIDEN HURDLE (10 hdls) 2m 3f 110y
4:20 (4:28) (Class 5) 4-Y-0+ **£2,053** (£598; £299)

Form RPR

4- **1** **Rainbow Peak (IRE)**[27] 3350 8-11-5 0..... DenisO'Regan 135+
(John Ferguson) *racd keenly: trckd ldr: led gng wl between last 2: pushed out run-in: shade cosily* **12/1**

1- **2** *1 ¾* **Call Me Vic (IRE)**[24] 3440 7-11-5 0..... PaddyBrennan 129+
(Tom George) *led: rdn whn hdd between last 2: nt fluent last: kpt on but a hld* **9/4**[1]

232- **3** *16* **Uppingham**[16] 3602 5-11-5 0..... BrianHughes 116
(Malcolm Jefferson) *trckd ldrs: mstke 5th: rdn 3 out: sn outpcd by ldng pair and already hld in 3rd whn hit 2 out* **13/2**[3]

53- **4** *5* **Broadway Symphony (IRE)**[36] 3177 7-11-5 0..... MarkGrant 110
(Tracey L Bailey) *in tch: rdn 3 out: one pce in 4th fr 2 out* **25/1**

2- **5** *3 ¼* **Jimmy The Jetplane (IRE)**[237] 584 6-11-5 0..... JasonMaguire 107
(Kim Bailey) *midfield: rdn and outpcd appr 3 out: plugged on after 2 out: nvr threatened* **33/1**

/32- **6** *13* **Dakar Run**[90] 2089 5-11-5 **127**..... RichieMcLernon 99
(Jonjo O'Neill) *hld up in midfield: hdwy 7th: in tch 3 out: wknd after 2 out* **8/1**

36- **7** *10* **Yourholidayisover (IRE)**[21] 3516 7-11-0 0..... JoeColliver(5) 89
(Patrick Holmes) *hld up in midfield: hdwy and in tch appr 3 out: wknd after 2 out* **100/1**

660- **8** *15* **Bellorophon (IRE)**[21] 3516 5-11-5 0..... WilsonRenwick 72
(Keith Dalgleish) *hld up: nvr threatened* **150/1**

1/- **9** *1 ½* **Sergeant Thunder**[288] 5254 5-11-5 0..... DarylJacob 76
(Paul Nicholls) *midfield: nt fluent 3 out: wnt lft and mstke 2 out: wknd* **3/1**[2]

40F- **10** *11* **Bodega**[26] 3388 6-11-5 0..... WillKennedy 61
(Ian Williams) *midfield: wknd bef 3 out* **8/1**

0P- **11** *40* **The Perfect Crime (IRE)**[36] 3175 5-11-0 0..... RobertMcCarth(5) 25
(Ian Williams) *hld up: a bhd* **150/1**

0/3- **12** *3* **Accordingtojodie (IRE)**[251] 367 8-11-5 0..... BarryGeraghty 22
(Nicky Henderson) *trckd ldrs: nt fluent 6th: wknd qckly appr 3 out: eased* **11/1**

/06- **13** *10* **Bayley's Dream**[71] 2471 5-11-5 0..... PaulMoloney 13
(Paul Webber) *midfield: wknd after 7th* **100/1**

6P0- **14** *2 ¼* **My Destination (IRE)**[16] 3600 5-11-5 0..... DominicElsworth 11
(Declan Carroll) *hld up in rr: a bhd* **150/1**

/U5- **15** *9* **Princess Bella (IRE)**[33] 3228 5-10-12 0..... NoelFehily
(Fergal O'Brien) *j. slowly in rr: a bhd* **100/1**

006- **16** *10* **Benefitofhindsight**[17] 3592 5-11-5 0..... DavidBass
(Ben Pauling) *hld up: t.o bef 3 out* **150/1**

4F- **17** *24* **Save The Bees**[16] 3598 6-11-5 0..... DougieCostello
(Declan Carroll) *t.k.h: hld up: mstke 6th: t.o bef 3 out* **80/1**

4m 46.5s (-4.80) **Going Correction** -0.05s/f (Good) **17** Ran SP% **121.0**
Speed ratings (Par 103): **107,106,99,97,96 91,87,81,80,76 60,59,55,54,50 46,37**
CSF £39.30 TOTE £14.10: £4.00, £1.90, £2.60; EX 64.40 Trifecta £547.30.
Owner Bloomfields **Bred** P D Savill **Trained** Cowlinge, Suffolk
■ Farmer's Friend was withdrawn. Price at time of withdrawal 150-1. Rule 4 does not apply.

FOCUS
A number of interesting sorts in this maiden hurdle, and form to be positive about. The winner can rate higher yet on his Flat form.
T/Jkpt: Not won. T/Plt: £732.10 to a £1 stake. Pool: £127244.52 - 126.86 winning tickets T/Qpdt: £55.90 to a £1 stake. Pool: £8566.46 - 113.39 winning tickets AS

3501 HUNTINGDON (R-H)
Friday, January 24

OFFICIAL GOING: Heavy (soft in places on hurdle course; chs 5.1, hdl 5.3)
First fence in the back straight omitted on all circuits of the chase course.
Wind: almost nil Weather: quite bright; 6 degrees

3878 32RED ON APP STORE "NATIONAL HUNT" NOVICES' H'CAP HURDLE (10 hdls) 2m 4f 110y
12:50 (12:50) (Class 4) (0-105,105) 4-Y-0+ **£3,249** (£954; £477; £238)

Form RPR

/03- **1** **Waldorf Salad**[25] 3420 6-11-7 **100**..... AidanColeman 117+
(Venetia Williams) *mde all: rdn 7 l clr bef 2 out: kpt on gamely and in n.d after* **7/1**

U52- **2** *11* **Sweet Boy Vic (IRE)**[19] 3553 6-10-2 **81**..... MarcGoldstein 86
(Chris Gordon) *prom: pushed along bef 7th: rdn to chse wnr who was already clr bef 2 out: no imp: wnt rt last* **11/4**[1]

/34- **3** *9* **Dougalstar (FR)**[68] 2536 5-10-8 **97**..... MikeyHamill(10) 93
(Sean Curran) *chsd ldrs: rdn bef 6th: mstke next: brief effrt in 4th 3 out: nt qckn after: blnd next: jst won duel for poor 3rd* **28/1**

060- **4** *nse* **Ghost Of A Smile (IRE)**[26] 3390 6-11-10 **103**..... WillKennedy 98
(Ian Williams) *t.k.h: hld up: hit 3rd: effrt and last of five w ch 3 out: nt qckn after: duelling for poor 3rd whn mstke last* **12/1**

336- **5** *7* **Vinnieslittle Lamb (IRE)**[45] 3010 6-11-12 **105**..... AlainCawley 92
(David Bridgwater) *midfield: pushed along after 5th: nvr looked to be gng wl enough after: struggling fr 3 out* **12/1**

066- **6** *2 ¼* **Bajan Blu**[27] 3357 6-11-11 **104**..... DonalDevereux 89
(David Brace) *clsd to chse wnr fr 3rd tl rdn and dropped out qckly bef 2 out* **5/1**[3]

000- **7** *nk* **Downtown Manhattan (IRE)**[24] 3434 7-10-13 **92**..... APMcCoy 76
(Jonjo O'Neill) *nvr bttr than midfield: rdn 3 out: sn lost tch: hit next* **8/1**

050- **8** *6* **Shipton**[37] 3166 5-11-2 **100**..... JamesBanks(5) 78
(Brendan Powell) *last pair: struggling bdly after 7th: plugged on flat* **50/1**

/P0- **P** **Reelwill (FR)**[8] 3740 9-9-7 **79** oh12.....(v[1]) OllieGarner(7)
(Derek Shaw) *midfield tl mstke 6th: struggling after: t.o and p.u 2 out* **150/1**

603- **F** **Snapchat (IRE)**[38] 3149 7-11-11 **104**..... ConorO'Farrell
(Seamus Durack) *hld up in last pair tl 6th: prog to midfield whn fell 8th* **7/2**[2]

5m 14.8s (15.80) **Going Correction** +0.85s/f (Soft) **10** Ran SP% **110.6**
Speed ratings (Par 105): **103,98,95,95,92 91,91,89, ,**
CSF £25.49 CT £479.51 TOTE £8.40: £2.50, £1.40, £3.60; EX 31.10 Trifecta £595.10.
Owner Alan Parker **Bred** A Parker **Trained** Kings Caple, H'fords

FOCUS
Shared bend turning in to back straight. A moderate novice handicap and the form looks believable despite a big step up from the winner.

3879 32RED H'CAP CHASE (17 fncs 2 omitted) 3m
1:20 (1:21) (Class 4) (0-110,109) 5-Y-0+ **£3,898** (£1,144; £572; £286)

Form RPR

/2F- **1** **Trojan Sun**[40] 3113 8-11-12 **109**.....(t) FelixDeGiles 115
(Tom Symonds) *settled in 3rd or 4th: wnt 2nd 3 out: rdn and upsides 2 out tl last: all out to edge clr fnl 100yds* **10/3**[2]

/06- **2** *1 ¾* **Craiglands (IRE)**[24] 3439 12-10-0 **83** oh1.....(v) WillKennedy 87
(Ian Williams) *led tl 2nd: j. rather tentatively tl 1/2-way: led narrowly 8th tl jnd u.p 2 out: ev ch tl v one pce fnl 100yds* **12/1**

1F0/ **3** *nk* **Chapolimoss (FR)**[572] 845 10-11-12 **109**.....(t) AidanColeman 113+
(Lawney Hill) *settled in last mostly: nt fluent 13th: effrt after next: hrd rdn 4th whn j.lft 2 out and last: no imp tl styd on into 3rd cl home* **8/1**

143- **4** *1 ¾* **Hollow Blue Sky (FR)**[36] 3172 7-11-12 **109**..... SamTwiston-Davies 110
(Nigel Twiston-Davies) *trckd ldrs: wnt 3rd jst after 3 out: sn u.p: 4 l 3rd 2 out: ev ch but no imp after: lost 3rd nr fin* **11/8**[1]

243- **5** *24* **Chasers Chance (IRE)**[29] 3293 11-10-11 **94**.....(p) TomO'Brien 71
(Paul Henderson) *in last pair mostly and nt a fluent: hit 11th: sn lost tch: t.o after 3 out* **6/1**[3]

/22- **P** **Ya Hafed**[43] 3033 6-11-10 **107**............ LeightonAspell
(Sheena West) *slt advantage 2nd tl 8th: cl 2nd tl hrd drvn and lost 3rd and fading whn blnd 3 out: remote 5th whn p.u last* **9/1**

6m 44.1s (33.80) **Going Correction** +1.375s/f (Heav) **6** Ran SP% **108.3**
Speed ratings: **98,97,97,96,88**
CSF £33.12 TOTE £3.90: £1.60, £5.10; EX 46.00 Trifecta £190.00.
Owner I A Low **Bred** Ian Low **Trained** Harewood End, H'fords

FOCUS
This produced a bunched finish but they came home in slow motion. Probably not strong form.

3880 32RED.COM NOVICES' HURDLE (8 hdls) 2m 110y
1:50 (1:51) (Class 4) 4-Y-0+ **£3,249** (£954; £477; £238)

Form RPR

210- **1** **New Year's Eve**[23] 3477 6-11-8 123............[1] JackQuinlan(3) 128+
(John Ferguson) *t.k.h: mstke 5th: nrly a 2nd tl led on bit bef 2 out: qcknd and 4 l clr last: hrd hld* **6/4**[1]

2 *8* **Anton Chigurh**[90] 5-10-13 0............ JamesBanks(5) 108+
(Brendan Powell) *racd keenly: led tl rdn and hdd bef 2 out: no ch w v easy wnr but a clr of rest* **11/2**[2]

/55- **3** *3 ¼* **Generous Ransom (IRE)**[37] 3166 6-11-4 0............ WayneHutchinson 104
(Nick Gifford) *chsd ldrs: 3 l 3rd and rdn 3 out: sn outpcd by ldng pair: 6 l 3rd and wl hld next* **6/4**[1]

6/P- **4** *16* **Scuderia (IRE)**[78] 2316 7-11-4 0............ BrendanPowell 87
(Jamie Snowden) *towards rr: rdn and outpcd 3 out: sn wl btn: kpt on after last to go poor 4th cl home* **66/1**

0/6- **5** *6* **Ultra Klass (FR)**[29] 3278 6-11-4 0............ AndrewTinkler 83
(Jamie Snowden) *chsd ldrs: pushed along after 5th: wknd after next: poor 4th whn tired jumps 2 out and last* **20/1**

6 *1 ¼* **Trafords Hero**[256] 273 6-11-4 0............ MarkGrant 80
(Geoffrey Deacon) *a towards rr: rdn and struggling fr 3 out* **50/1**

204- **7** *8* **Bally Braes (IRE)**[18] 3568 6-11-4 0............ SamTwiston-Davies 72
(Nigel Twiston-Davies) *last and rdn bef 4th: hanging to outside and nvr travelling after: t.o bef 2 out* **8/1**[3]

0/P- **8** *12* **Kingscombe (USA)**[52] 2876 5-11-4 0............ AndrewThornton 60
(Linda Jewell) *j. modly and racd wd: chsd ldr after 3rd tl next: wknd qckly and blnd 5th: t.o bef 2 out: eased* **150/1**

4m 8.0s (13.10) **Going Correction** +0.85s/f (Soft) **8** Ran SP% **115.4**
Speed ratings (Par 105): **103,99,97,90,87 86,83,77**
CSF £10.84 TOTE £1.80: £1.10, £2.20, £1.10; EX 7.70 Trifecta £21.00.
Owner Bloomfields **Bred** Newsells Park Stud **Trained** Cowlinge, Suffolk

FOCUS
Not much strength in depth, but a quality performance from a talented if quirky winner. He may still be capable of better given his bumper form.

3881 32RED NOVICES' CHASE (17 fncs 2 omitted) 3m
2:20 (2:20) (Class 3) 5-Y-0+ **£6,657** (£2,067; £1,113)

Form RPR

321- **1** **Loose Chips**[29] 3259 8-11-4 138............(b) AidanColeman 144+
(Charlie Longsdon) *mde all and j. much bttr than only serious rival: hrd drvn to go clr after 3 out: pressed again 2 out tl last but rdr nvr taking any chs and sn urged clr flat* **5/4**[1]

131- **2** *8* **Yesyoucan (IRE)**[13] 3658 9-11-8 139............ APMcCoy 142
(Brian Ellison) *plentiful mstkes in 2nd: hunging bdly lft whn j.lft 14th and violently so next where on his nose: sn 8 l down: rallied u.p 2 out and cl up at last and nt fluent: edgd rt and fnd nil flat: eased fnl 100yds* **9/4**[2]

2PU- **3** *dist* **Flichity (IRE)**[29] 3266 9-10-7 65............ JoeCornwall(5)
(John Cornwall) *j.lft: last and rdn 4th: t.o fr 7th: clambered over 3 out: stl coming to last as wnr fin* **125/1**[3]

/04- **U** **Fourovakind**[29] 3279 9-10-7 130............ JamesBanks(5)
(Harry Whittington) *chsd ldng pair fr 4th: mstke 12th (water): 7 l 3rd and struggling whn landed bdly and uns rdr next* **9/4**[2]

6m 37.0s (26.70) **Going Correction** +1.375s/f (Heav) **4** Ran SP% **106.8**
Speed ratings: **110,107, ,**
CSF £4.42 TOTE £2.40; EX 4.80 Trifecta £20.20.
Owner Barrels Of Courage **Bred** Peter Lamyman **Trained** Over Norton, Oxon

FOCUS
A fair novice chase. The first two are rated to their marks.

3882 PERTEMPS NETWORK H'CAP HURDLE (SERIES QUALIFIER) (12 hdls) 3m 2f
2:55 (2:55) (Class 2) 5-Y-0+
£11,573 (£3,418; £1,709; £854; £427; £214)

Form RPR

131- **1** **Josies Orders (IRE)**[34] 3195 6-10-8 **122**............(b) MauriceLinehan(5) 131+
(Jonjo O'Neill) *trckd ldrs gng wl: led 2 out: pushed 3 l clr last: comf* **4/1**[3]

202 **2** *7* **Dawn Twister (GER)**[22] 3505 7-10-13 **122**............(p) LeightonAspell 121
(Lucy Wadham) *chsd ldrs: nt fluent 5th: rdn and effrt whn hit 3 out: 4 l 4th next: plugged on into 2nd flat but no ch w wnr* **8/1**

01U- **3** *¾* **San Telm (IRE)**[17] 3594 9-10-12 **124**............ JoshuaMoore(3) 122
(Renee Robeson) *a 2nd or 3rd: drvn and ev ch 2 out: chsd wnr vainly after tl lost 2nd cl home* **16/1**

122- **4** *¾* **Cannon Fodder**[28] 3319 7-11-7 **130**............ MarcGoldstein 128
(Sheena West) *led: drvn after 3 out: hdd and mstke next: kpt on gamely at one pce after* **9/1**

114- **5** *13* **Milan Bound (IRE)**[41] 3081 6-11-9 **132**............ APMcCoy 116
(Jonjo O'Neill) *bhd: 8th whn mstke 7th: btn after 3 out* **11/4**[1]

300- **6** *3 ¾* **Monetary Fund (USA)**[62] 2672 8-11-6 **129**............ AidanColeman 109
(Venetia Williams) *racd on ins and trying to keep away fr others: prom tl 9th: rdn and wknd next: wnt rt last* **7/2**[2]

2PP- **7** *1* **Seymour Eric**[13] 3653 9-11-5 **135**............ OllieGarner(7) 114
(Martin Keighley) *j.rt: rn in snatches: drvn bef 7th: brief effrt to press ldrs next: struggling after 3 out* **25/1**

432- **8** *19* **Seven Woods (IRE)**[27] 3358 8-11-2 **125**............(t) AlainCawley 85
(Tom George) *prom tl mstke 3rd: lost pl whn drvn 8th: t.o after 3 out: sn eased* **9/1**

/0F- **9** *20* **Mahogany Blaze (FR)**[63] 2646 12-11-6 **129**............(t) SamTwiston-Davies 69
(Nigel Twiston-Davies) *bhd: rdn and struggling on wd outside 9th: t.o after next: sn eased* **50/1**

6m 52.8s (29.90) **Going Correction** +0.85s/f (Soft) **9** Ran SP% **111.7**
Speed ratings: **88,85,85,85,81 80,79,74,67**
CSF £34.12 CT £448.56 TOTE £5.40: £1.80, £2.10, £4.70; EX 46.10 Trifecta £554.60.
Owner John P McManus **Bred** Mrs E Moore **Trained** Cheltenham, Gloucs

FOCUS
A fair staying handicap, in which the first eight home qualify for the final of the series at Cheltenham in March. The form is rated around the second.

3883 32RED CASINO H'CAP CHASE (13 fncs 3 omitted) 2m 4f 110y
3:25 (3:25) (Class 5) (0-100,100) 5-Y-0+ **£2,274** (£667; £333; £166)

Form RPR

/0S- **1** **Browns Brook (IRE)**[19] 3555 8-10-7 **81**............ AidanColeman 108+
(Venetia Williams) *cl 2nd tl led 10th: clr w one rival after 3 out: rdn and looked to be gng best whn lft clr 2 out: 12 l advantage last: styd on stoutly* **5/2**[2]

P4P- **2** *21* **Regal Park (IRE)**[29] 3250 7-10-6 **83**............(v[1]) JoshuaMoore(3) 85
(Gary Moore) *settled in 3rd: j. slowly 6th and 7th: wnt 2nd at 10th: drew clr w wnr fr 3 out: 3 l down and rdn whn blnd next: wl hld after: nt fluent last* **15/2**

361- **3** *11* **Brandon Thomas (IRE)**[11] 3687 8-11-0 **88** 7ex............ TomCannon 77
(Nick Gifford) *j. slowly 1st: nt fluent 8th (water): chsd ldrs tl drvn 8th: racd v idly fr 3 out and remote 3rd next* **9/4**[1]

200- **4** *7* **Amaury De Lusignan (IRE)**[36] 3174 8-11-4 **92**............ TomO'Brien 72
(Paul Henderson) *led at decent pce tl j. hesitantly and hdd 10th: sn rdn: lost tch tamely 3 out* **11/1**

05U- **5** *4 ½* **King Ozzy (IRE)**[23] 3470 10-11-5 **100**............(tp) MrJoeHill(7) 81
(Lawney Hill) *chsd ldrs: reminder 10th: becoming outpcd whn hmpd 3 out: wl bhd after* **28/1**

P6P- **6** *29* **Mallusk (IRE)**[10] 3696 9-11-7 **95**............(bt[1]) SamTwiston-Davies 42
(Shaun Lycett) *a last: j. slowly 1st: mstke 5th and reminder: nvr travelling: t.o fr 9th* **16/1**

/52- **F** **Moonlight Maggie**[27] 3352 7-10-1 **80**............ AodhaganConlon(5)
(Tom George) *mstke 3rd: hld up in last pair: hdwy 10th: disputing cl 3rd and gng wl whn fell 3 out* **4/1**[3]

5m 35.2s (29.90) **Going Correction** +1.375s/f (Heav) **7** Ran SP% **108.8**
Speed ratings: **98,90,85,83,81 70,**
CSF £18.88 TOTE £3.00: £1.40, £4.10; EX 23.20 Trifecta £58.50.
Owner Mrs Vida Bingham **Bred** Stephen Lanigan-O'Keeffe **Trained** Kings Caple, H'fords

FOCUS
A weak handicap. The winner should go in again.

3884 32RED.COM H'CAP HURDLE (THE JOCKEY CLUB GRASSROOTS JUMPS SERIES QUALIFIER) (10 hdls) 2m 5f 110y
4:00 (4:01) (Class 4) (0-120,120) 4-Y-0+ **£3,249** (£954; £477; £238)

Form RPR

600- **1** **Touch Back (IRE)**[28] 3328 8-11-10 **118**............(p) APMcCoy 125
(Jonjo O'Neill) *tended to jump indifferently: settled in rr tl effrt 7th: 4th at next: 3 l 3rd and hrd rdn 2 out: stl 2 l down at last: only clsd grad but galvanised to get up on line despite edging lft fnl strides: brilliant ride* **7/2**[2]

313- **2** *nse* **Theatrebar**[33] 3225 6-11-6 **114**............ FelixDeGiles 121
(Tom Symonds) *led: hrd drvn after 3 out: 2 l clr last: kpt on but pipped on post* **7/2**[2]

0/4- **3** *2* **Secret Edge**[53] 182 6-11-4 **119**............ StephenO'Donovan(7) 125
(Alan King) *cl up: wnt 2nd at 6th: drvn and ev ch fr 2 out tl hit last whn looking hld: sn lost 2nd: no ex fnl 100yds* **25/1**

312- **4** *20* **Chase The Spud**[69] 2507 6-11-7 **120**............ ConorShoemark(5) 105
(Fergal O'Brien) *plld hrd: chsd ldrs: rdn and wknd 3 out* **7/1**[3]

1/1- **5** *12* **No No Bingo (IRE)**[25] 3419 8-11-0 **111**............(p) KielanWoods(3) 89
(Charlie Longsdon) *chsd ldrs: rdn 7th: wknd next: eased last* **8/1**

621/ **6** *28* **Miss Tique (FR)**[673] 5014 6-11-11 **119**............ AidanColeman 64
(Venetia Williams) *settled in rr: stl in tch 3 out: sn fdd: t.o whn flattened last* **16/1**

562- **P** **Murtys Delight (IRE)**[8] 3740 7-10-12 **106**............(t) SamTwiston-Davies
(Dr Richard Newland) *t.k.h: nt fluent 2nd: pressed ldr tl nt fluent 6th and rdn: sn hanging and racing awkwardly: nt run on: t.o and p.u 2 out* **2/1**[1]

5m 31.7s (21.10) **Going Correction** +0.85s/f (Soft) **7** Ran SP% **111.1**
Speed ratings (Par 105): **95,94,94,86,82 72,**
CSF £15.47 CT £246.61 TOTE £4.60: £2.30, £2.00; EX 29.70 Trifecta £264.00.
Owner John P McManus **Bred** John O'Connor **Trained** Cheltenham, Gloucs
■ Stewards' Enquiry : A P McCoy caution: careless riding.

FOCUS
A modest handicap. The winner and third were both well in on the best of their old form.
T/Plt: £313.90 to a £1 stake. Pool: £68365.81 - 158.95 winning tickets T/Qpdt: £37.10 to a £1 stake. Pool: £4648.45 - 92.70 winning tickets IM

3454 CHELTENHAM (L-H)
Saturday, January 25

OFFICIAL GOING: Heavy (soft in places; 6.3)
Wind: Moderate across Weather: Sunny spells

3885 JCB TRIUMPH HURDLE TRIAL (A JUVENILE HURDLE) (REGISTERED AS THE FINESSE JUVENILE HURDLE) (GRADE 2) (8 hdls) 2m 1f
12:40 (12:40) (Class 1) 4-Y-0
£17,085 (£6,411; £3,210; £1,599; £804; £402)

Form RPR

101- **1** **Le Rocher (FR)**[28] 3360 4-11-7 141............ RichardJohnson 149+
(Nick Williams) *str: lw: trckd ldr: hit 2nd: nt fluent 3rd: chal 3 out: led wl bef last: drvn clr run-in: readily* **2/1**[2]

122- **2** *10* **Kentucky Hyden (IRE)**[28] 3360 4-11-7 138............ BarryGeraghty 138
(Nicky Henderson) *mstke 2nd: sn chsng ldrs: chal 2 out: rdn wl bef last and styd on to take 2nd u.p run-in but no ch w wnr* **15/2**[3]

41- **3** *5* **Vicenzo Mio (FR)**[29] 3317 4-11-7 143............ DarylJacob 134
(Paul Nicholls) *lw: led: jnd 2 out: rdn and hdd wl bef last: no ex u.p and dropped to 3rd run-in* **11/10**[1]

331- **4** *7* **Ballyglasheen (IRE)**[42] 3078 4-11-7 135............ PaulMoloney 127
(Evan Williams) *in tch: hit 4th and sn drvn along towards rr: no ch after but styd on same pce to take 4th run-in* **25/1**

4- **5** *2 ¼* **Ronaldinho (IRE)**[28] 3364 4-11-0 0............ WayneHutchinson 119
(Alan King) *lw: in tch: hdwy to chse ldrs 4th: wknd 2 out* **33/1**

1- **6** *37* **Goodwood Mirage (IRE)**[14] 3641 4-11-4 0............ APMcCoy 101
(Jonjo O'Neill) *plld hrd in rr: sme hdwy to cl on ldrs whn mstke 2 out: nvr any threat and sn wl bhd* **9/1**

4m 25.09s (13.79) **Going Correction** +1.25s/f (Heav) **6** Ran SP% **109.5**
Speed ratings: **117,112,109,106,105 88**
CSF £15.71 TOTE £3.10: £2.00, £2.70; EX 13.20 Trifecta £19.90.

Owner John White & Anne Underhill **Bred** Mme Sylvie Ringler And Roger Frieh **Trained** George Nympton, Devon

FOCUS

The track endured 12mm of overnight rain which changed the going to heavy, soft in places and stamina was at a premium over all distances on both courses. The tricky downhill third-last fence was left out due to waterlogged ground on the landing side, a significant omission in all chases. This Grade 2 juvenile event often has a significant bearing on the Triumph Hurdle. Katchit was the most recent winner to back up at the Festival (2007), but Franchoek placed the following season and Walkon finished runner-up in 2009, that trio trained by Alan King. King also saddled Grumeti to place in 2012 and Rolling Star was sent off favourite in the Triumph last year prior to running below par. It was a select field this season, with four last-time-out winners, including the 1-2 from the Grade 1 Finale at Chepstow last month and it was that form which came to the fore. Le Rocher now heads the juvenile ratings and is within a few pounds of a typical Triumph winner.

3886 TIMEFORM NOVICES' H'CAP CHASE (16 fncs 1 omitted) 2m 5f

1:15 (1:15) (Class 2) 5-Y-0+

£15,640 (£4,620; £2,310; £1,155; £577; £290)

Form — RPR

112- **1** **Indian Castle (IRE)**[29] 3331 6-11-3 **135**.............................. JasonMaguire 146+
(Donald McCain) *trckd ldrs: wnt 2nd after 13th: rdn bef 2 out: slt ld last: in command sn after but idled clsng stages and sn drvn out* **14/1**

621- **2** *1 3/4* **Annacotty (IRE)**[30] 3260 6-11-12 **144**..................................(b) IanPopham 151+
(Martin Keighley) *lw: w ldr tl led 4th: pckd 3 out: pushed along omitted original 3rd last: narrowly hdd last: rallied as wnr idled clsng stages and sn no imp* **8/1**

14U- **3** *2 1/4* **Renard D'Irlande (FR)**[18] 3594 9-10-9 **127**...................... AidanColeman 131
(Venetia Williams) *chsd ldrs: disp 2nd and omitted 3rd last: tl appr 2 out: styd on same pce u.p run-in* **6/1**[3]

342- **4** *4* **Ohio Gold (IRE)**[30] 3259 8-11-0 **132**....................................(t) JoeTizzard 132
(Colin Tizzard) *chsd ldrs: disp 2nd at omitted 3rd last: sn rdn: btn after 2 out* **9/2**[2]

311- **5** *13* **Samingarry (FR)**[49] 2941 7-10-8 **126**.. APMcCoy 115
(Nigel Hawke) *hit 2nd: in rr: hit 7th and 11th: sn pushed along: no prog whn sltly hmpd 3 out* **6/1**[3]

1F2- **6** *12* **Dark Lover (GER)**[10] 3715 9-11-10 **142**............................... DarylJacob 121
(Paul Nicholls) *lw: in tch: chsd ldrs fr 8th: btn whn hmpd 3 out* **8/1**

013- **7** *2* **Tempest River (IRE)**[44] 3030 8-10-12 **130**................ WayneHutchinson 103
(Ben Case) *hit 3rd and 3 out: a towards rr* **25/1**

8 *15* **Shanpallas (IRE)**[30] 3307 6-11-2 **137**..................................... RJJones(3) 98
(C Byrnes, Ire) *hmpd 4th: nvr jumping w any real fluency and a bhd* **28/1**

P1P- **9** *11* **Super Villan**[48] 2979 9-10-0 **118** oh3...................................(b) JamieMoore 65
(Mark Bradstock) *narrow ld tl hdd 4th: chsd ldr tl lost 2nd and wknd fr 13th* **14/1**

424- **F** **Timesawastin (IRE)**[24] 3456 8-10-11 **129**........................... PaulMoloney
(Evan Williams) *in tch whn fell 4th* **12/1**

221- **P** **The Italian Yob (IRE)**[50] 2928 6-11-0 **132**..................... RichardJohnson
(Nick Williams) *hit 1st: in rr: hit 6th: in tch next: j. slowly 11th: wknd qckly: t.o whn p.u bef 13th: b.b.v* **4/1**[1]

5m 34.7s (15.30) **Going Correction** +1.025s/f (Soft) 11 Ran SP% **117.3**
Speed ratings: **111,110,109,107,103 98,97,91,87,**
CSF £121.25 CT £753.77 TOTE £14.10: £3.50, £3.00, £2.20; EX 167.70 Trifecta £2015.70 Part won..

Owner Askew Dick Hernon Reynard **Bred** Robert McCarthy **Trained** Cholmondeley, Cheshire

FOCUS

There looked to be plenty of pace in the race, and with Super Villan duelling with Annacotty early on, that's how it turned out, the race developing into a real stamina test. A good effort from the winner, backed up by the time.

3887 FREEBETS.COM TROPHY CHASE (A H'CAP) (GRADE 3) (16 fncs 1 omitted) 2m 5f

1:50 (1:50) (Class 1) 5-Y-0+

£28,475 (£10,685; £5,350; £2,665; £1,340; £670)

Form — RPR

662- **1** **Wishfull Thinking**[49] 2938 11-11-12 **156**...................(t) RichardJohnson 162+
(Philip Hobbs) *hld up towards rr but in tch: hdwy 12th: slt ld 2 out and drvn: hrd pressed fnl 150yds: styd on strly fnl 75yds* **9/1**

211- **2** *1 3/4* **Double Ross (IRE)**[24] 3458 8-11-4 **148**.................. SamTwiston-Davies 152+
(Nigel Twiston-Davies) *hit 1st: led 2nd: hdd 4th: styd cl 2nd tl chal fr 10th tl led sn after omitted 3rd last: travelling wl whn narrowly hdd 2 out and again last: rdn to chal fnl 150yds: no ex and one pce fnl 75yds* **3/1**[1]

200- **3** *5* **Tap Night (USA)**[42] 3082 7-10-12 **142**.. APMcCoy 141
(Lucinda Russell) *lw: in rr: nt fluent 10th: hdwy fr omitted 3rd last: styd on to chse ldng duo last but no imp run-in* **9/2**[2]

246- **4** *12* **Sew On Target (IRE)**[14] 3652 9-10-0 **130** oh2................. BrendanPowell 117
(Colin Tizzard) *chsd ldrs: lost position 13th: gd prog to trck ldrs after omitted 3rd last: wknd bef last* **14/1**

3P3- **5** *1 1/4* **Shangani (USA)**[14] 3642 8-10-4 **134**................................. AidanColeman 122
(Venetia Williams) *hit 4th: in tch: chsd ldrs fr 6th: rdn after omitted 3rd last: wknd sn after 2 out: hit last* **11/2**[3]

022- **6** *8* **Cedre Bleu (FR)**[24] 3458 7-10-13 **143**..................................(bt) DarylJacob 123
(Paul Nicholls) *chsd ldrs: nt fluent 7th: shkn up 2 out and sn btn* **8/1**

114- **7** *1/2* **Renard (FR)**[7] 3772 9-10-13 **143**...................................... SamThomas 122
(Venetia Williams) *lw: led to 2nd: styd chsng ldrs tl wknd omitted 3rd last* **16/1**

005- **8** *12* **Ulck Du Lin (FR)**[35] 3197 6-10-7 **137**................................ BarryGeraghty 103
(Paul Nicholls) *a towards rr* **11/1**

403- **9** *11* **Kumbeshwar**[24] 3458 7-10-13 **143**..............................(b) WayneHutchinson 106
(Alan King) *led 4th: hrd pressed fr 10th tl hdd after omitted 3rd last: sn btn* **16/1**

/P3- **P** **Our Mick**[49] 2938 8-10-10 **140**..(b[1]) JasonMaguire
(Donald McCain) *lw: pressed ldrs early: hit 2nd: bhd whn hit 7th: blnd 8th: t.o whn p.u bef 10th* **8/1**

5m 35.56s (16.16) **Going Correction** +1.025s/f (Soft) 10 Ran SP% **117.6**
Speed ratings: **110,109,107,102,102 99,99,94,90,**
CSF £37.85 CT £141.29 TOTE £8.00: £2.50, £1.70, £2.20; EX 27.50 Trifecta £547.20.

Owner Mrs Diana L Whateley **Bred** Cobhall Court Stud **Trained** Withycombe, Somerset

FOCUS

This very competitive handicap was run at a sound enough gallop and it began to hot up bypassing the usual third-last. Decent form, the winner trated to the best of last season's form.

3888 ARGENTO CHASE (REGISTERED AS THE COTSWOLD STEEPLE CHASE) (GRADE 2) (19 fncs 2 omitted) 3m 1f 110y

2:25 (2:25) (Class 1) 5-Y-0+

£56,950 (£21,370; £10,700; £5,330; £2,680; £1,340)

Form — RPR

0U5- **1** **The Giant Bolster**[24] 3457 9-11-0 157.......................(v[1]) TomScudamore 165+
(David Bridgwater) *prom whn j. slowly 4th and 5th: styd wl in tch tl j. slowly 3 out: rdn and styd on strly to chal 2 out: slt ld sn after tl forged clr fnl 150yds* **6/1**[3]

3/2- **2** *7* **Rocky Creek (IRE)**[56] 2815 8-11-5 157................................ DarylJacob 162
(Paul Nicholls) *lw: trckd ldrs: qcknd to chal 2 out and stl upsides last: no ex and btn fnl 150yds: jst hld on for 2nd clsng stages* **6/4**[1]

/13- **3** *hd* **Harry Topper**[50] 2930 7-11-10 153.................................(p) JasonMaguire 170
(Kim Bailey) *in tch: j. slowly 3rd and 6th: dropped towards rr 10th: hdwy 13th: j. slowly 16th: drvn omitted 3rd last: outpcd next: styd on again to cl on 2nd nr fin: no ch w wnr* **6/1**[3]

161- **4** *4 1/2* **Houblon Des Obeaux (FR)**[35] 3199 7-11-6 159............ AidanColeman 160
(Venetia Williams) *w ldr: led 5th: narrowly hdd 15th: styd chalng tl drvn to ld bef 2 out: hdd sn after: wknd run-in* **7/2**[2]

UU1- **5** *7* **Restless Harry**[10] 3717 10-11-6 141.................................... CharliePoste 152
(Robin Dickin) *pressed ldrs: rdn omitted 3rd last: wknd bef next* **14/1**

2U2- **6** *3 1/2* **Champion Court (IRE)**[14] 3645 9-11-6 157........................ IanPopham 149
(Martin Keighley) *led to 5th: styd chalng tl led again 15th: drvn and hdd appr 2 out: wknd sn after* **9/1**

53P- **7** *31* **Pigeon Island**[24] 3455 11-11-4 129.......................(vt) SamTwiston-Davies 126
(Nigel Twiston-Davies) *j. slowly 3rd: hit 6th: a in rr* **66/1**

7m 7.9s (29.70) **Going Correction** +1.025s/f (Soft) 7 Ran SP% **109.0**
Speed ratings: **95,92,92,91,89 88,78**
CSF £14.71 TOTE £6.50: £2.90, £1.80; EX 16.30 Trifecta £138.80.

Owner Simon Hunt & Gary Lambton **Bred** Gestut Fahrhof **Trained** Icomb, Gloucs

FOCUS

Not much of a Gold Cup trial in recent years and it's unlikely that trend will be changing soon judged by this result. They went a steady pace, which contributed to five jumping the second-last together and the race only being decided from there. The Giant Bolster was still 10lb off last year's Gold Cup mark, with Rocky Creek well below his Hennessy run.

3889 NEPTUNE INVESTMENT MANAGEMENT NOVICES' HURDLE (REG' AS THE CLASSIC NOVICES' HURDLE RACE) (GRADE 2) (10 hdls) 2m 4f 110y

3:00 (3:00) (Class 1) 4-Y-0+ **£17,165** (£6,491; £3,290; £1,679; £884)

Form — RPR

111- **1** **Red Sherlock**[14] 3657 5-11-9 0....................................... TomScudamore 148+
(David Pipe) *lw: trckd ldrs: chal 2 out: sn led: flashed tail bef last: drvn and kpt finding run-in: styd on strly clsng stages* **9/4**[2]

F- **2** *2 1/2* **Rathvinden (IRE)**[14] 3654 6-11-12 0................................. BarryGeraghty 148+
(W P Mullins, Ire) *str: hld up in rr but in tch: j. slowly 3 out: stdy hdwy appr 2 out: chsd wnr sn after: styd on u.p run-in for clr 2nd but no imp on wnr* **6/4**[1]

011- **3** *29* **Aubusson (FR)**[24] 3454 5-11-12 140....................................... MissEKelly 121
(Nick Williams) *lw: sn chsng ldrs: led after 3 out: hdd after 2 out: sn lft bhd by ldng duo but styd on for wl-btn 3rd* **7/1**[3]

242- **4** *42* **Regal Diamond (IRE)**[24] 3454 6-11-5 130.......................(p) JamieMoore 70
(Peter Bowen) *chsd ldrs: hit 4th: j. slowly 5th: drvn to ld 3 out: hdd sn after: wknd fr 2 out* **16/1**

1U5- **5** *26* **Creepy (IRE)**[14] 3654 6-11-12 137...................................... IanPopham 51
(Martin Keighley) *w ldr tl slt ld 5th: hdd 4 out: wknd after 3 out* **14/1**

211- **P** **Madness Light (FR)**[25] 3430 5-11-12 135..............................(t) APMcCoy
(Warren Greatrex) *slt ld but hrd pressed tl hdd 5th: styd upsides and led 4 out: hdd next: sn wknd: t.o whn p.u bef 2 out* **7/1**[3]

5m 20.15s (19.15) **Going Correction** +1.25s/f (Heav) 6 Ran SP% **108.3**
Speed ratings (Par 115): **113,112,101,85,75**
CSF £5.77 TOTE £2.80: £1.90, £1.60; EX 5.70 Trifecta £21.90.

Owner The Johnson Family **Bred** David Johnson **Trained** Nicholashayne, Devon

FOCUS

A Grade 2 novice that has produced three winners who went on to land the Albert Bartlett at the Festival, most recently At Fishers Cross last season. It was a fascinating affair this time around. There was a tactical gallop set and all of the runners took a keen early hold, but the form looks outstanding with the two clear market leaders dominating from the penultimate hurdle. The first two are both Festival material.

3890 GALLIARDHOMES.COM CLEEVE HURDLE (GRADE 2) (12 hdls) 3m

3:35 (3:38) (Class 1) 5-Y-0+

£34,170 (£12,822; £6,420; £3,198; £1,608; £804)

Form — RPR

125- **1** **Knockara Beau (IRE)**[43] 3067 11-11-0 145......................... JanFaltejsek 154
(George Charlton) *slt ld tl after 4th: led again 5th: hdd after 6th: lost position and dropped to last pl after 3 out: styd on again fr 2 out to dispute 2nd and hit last: styd on gamely u.p to ld fnl 150yds: all out* **66/1**

/4U- **2** *shd* **At Fishers Cross (IRE)**[35] 3198 7-11-4 160...........................(p) APMcCoy 159
(Rebecca Curtis) *in rr: j. slowly 5th: hit 8th: hdwy fr 2 out: chsd ldrs and clsng last: styd on gamely u.p fnl 150yds: clsng on wnr last strides: jst failed* **5/1**

111/ **3** *3/4* **Big Buck's (FR)**[420] 2774 11-11-8 174..................... SamTwiston-Davies 160
(Paul Nicholls) *lw: trckd ldrs in 3rd: wnt 2nd 4 out: led 3 out: rdn wl bef last: hdd fnl 150yds: no ex fnl 50yds but kpt on gamely* **6/5**[1]

131- **4** *7* **Reve De Sivola (FR)**[35] 3198 9-11-8 162.......................... RichardJohnson 153
(Nick Williams) *in rr: nt fluent 3rd: hdwy fr 8th: chsd ldrs after 2 out and rdn wl bef last: wknd run-in* **11/4**[2]

5P2- **5** *2 3/4* **Quartz De Thaix (FR)**[24] 3457 10-11-0 147...................(b) AidanColeman 142
(Venetia Williams) *w wnr: led after 4th: hdd 5th: led after 6th: hdd 3 out: rdn 2 out: wknd wl bef last* **33/1**

1FF/ **6** *39* **Boston Bob (IRE)**[25] 3443 9-11-4 150................................ BarryGeraghty 137
(W P Mullins, Ire) *in rr: stdy hdwy to trck ldrs 2 out: rdn sn after: wknd qckly wl bef last* **9/2**[3]

6m 25.81s (24.81) **Going Correction** +1.25s/f (Heav) 6 Ran SP% **111.4**
Speed ratings: **108,107,107,105,104 91**
CSF £344.14 TOTE £57.40: £8.30, £2.10; EX 311.20 Trifecta £397.90.

Owner J I A Charlton **Bred** George Durrheim & Mrs Maria Mulcahy Durr **Trained** Stocksfield, Northumberland

The Form Book Jumps, Raceform Ltd, Compton, RG20 6NL.

FOCUS
This year's Cleeve was the undoubted highlight of the meeting as it signalled the hugely anticipated comeback of four-time World Hurdle winner Big Buck's, but there was a right turn-up. Knockara Beau is rated in line with his best course form of the last couple of years, At Fishers Cross arguably produced a personal best and Big Buck's is rated a stone+ off his best.

3891 STEEL PLATE AND SECTIONS H'CAP HURDLE (8 hdls) 2m 1f
4:10 (4:13) (Class 2) 4-Y-0+ **£16,245** (£4,770; £2,385; £1,192)

Form RPR

/14- **1** **Lac Fontana (FR)**[69] 2530 5-10-12 **127** DarylJacob 143+
(Paul Nicholls) *hld up in rr stdy hdwy fr 2 out to chal last: led sn after: pushed clr* **4/1**[1]

5/P- **2** *5* **Totalize**[35] 3200 5-11-0 **129** JamieMoore 137
(Brian Ellison) *in rr: hit 3rd: n.m.r on inner and pushed along after 3 out: hdwy fr 2 out to chal last: sn outpcd by wnr but kpt on wl for 2nd* **8/1**[2]

411- **3** *6* **Amore Alato**[30] 3258 5-11-6 **135** APMcCoy 137
(Nick Williams) *lw: chsd ldrs: slt ld 2 out: jnd last: hdd u.p sn after: styd on same pce* **4/1**[1]

414- **4** *8* **Nesterenko (GER)**[17] 3599 5-10-11 **126** BarryGeraghty 120
(Nicky Henderson) *towards rr: hdwy fr 4 out to trck ldrs after next: trckd ldrs 2 out: rdn and wknd bef last* **8/1**[2]

/04- **5** *½* **Ruacana**[49] 2951 5-11-9 **141** JackQuinlan(3) 135
(John Ferguson) *trckd ldrs: rdn after 2 out: sn outpcd* **14/1**

041- **6** *1 ¼* **Quick Decisson (IRE)**[9] 3744 6-10-12 **127** RichardJohnson 119
(Philip Hobbs) *lw: slt ld to 2 out but stl upsides: wknd u.p bef last* **4/1**[1]

150- **7** *10* **Waterunder (IRE)**[35] 3200 7-11-7 **136** (t) TomScudamore 118
(David Pipe) *chsd ldrs: ev ch 2 out: wknd sn after* **16/1**

/03- **8** *3 ½* **Lexi's Boy (IRE)**[14] 3648 6-11-5 **134** JasonMaguire 113
(Donald McCain) *pressed ldrs: chal 2 out: wknd qckly u.p wl bef last* **11/1**[3]

010- **9** *8* **Citizenship**[7] 3771 8-11-6 **135** AidanColeman 106
(Venetia Williams) *hld up towards rr: effrt to cl 2 out: sn wknd* **12/1**

230- **10** *1 ¾* **Hartside (GER)**[17] 3599 5-9-10 **118** MrRWinks(7) 87
(Peter Winks) *chsd ldrs to 3 out: wknd bef next* **33/1**

4m 27.92s (16.62) **Going Correction** +1.25s/f (Heav) **10** Ran SP% **113.7**
Speed ratings (Par 109): **110,107,104,101,100 100,95,93,90,89**
CSF £35.20 CT £134.66 TOTE £5.60: £2.00, £3.00, £1.80; EX 38.80 Trifecta £144.10.
Owner Potensis Limited **Bred** S C A La Perrigne **Trained** Ditcheat, Somerset

FOCUS
This looked a reasonably competitive race. A big step forward from the easy winner.
T/Jkpt: Not won. T/Plt: £727.90. Pool: £261,034.02 - 261.77 winning units. T/Qpdt: £71.10. Pool: £16,896.31 - 175.73 winning units. ST

3871 DONCASTER (L-H)
Saturday, January 25

OFFICIAL GOING: Good to soft (soft in places) changing to soft after race 4 (2.05)
Wind: fresh against Weather: Cloudy, storm between 4th and 5th

3892 SKY BET BEST ODDS GUARANTEED H'CAP HURDLE (10 hdls) 2m 3f 110y
12:25 (12:25) (Class 3) (0-140,133) 4-Y-0+ **£5,393** (£1,583; £791; £395)

Form RPR

3/0- **1** **Master Of The Game (IRE)**[56] 2813 8-11-3 **124** (t[1]) AndrewTinkler 138+
(Nicky Henderson) *mde all: clr after 3 out: rdn after 2 out: kpt on wl* **16/1**

/26- **2** *15* **McIlhatton (IRE)**[30] 3263 6-11-4 **125** NickScholfield 125
(Paul Nicholls) *hld up: smooth hdwy appr 3 out: wnt 2nd jst after 3 out: rdn 2 out: sn no imp on wnr* **15/2**[3]

062- **3** *¾* **Mojolika**[17] 3599 6-11-1 **122** DougieCostello 121
(Tim Easterby) *hld up: short of room and stl plenty to do appr 3 out: styd on after 3 out: wnt 3rd fnl 100yds* **15/2**[3]

/12- **4** *1* **Centasia**[37] 3168 7-11-4 **125** (t) TomScudamore 123
(David Pipe) *in tch: rdn appr 3 out: one pce and sn no ch w wnr: lost 3rd fnl 100yds* **3/1**[1]

112- **5** *12* **Taigan (FR)**[189] 1042 7-11-6 **127** DavidEngland 114
(Giles Smyly) *hld up: rdn 3 out: nvr threatened ldrs* **33/1**

P23- **6** *2 ¼* **Pas Trop Tard (FR)**[30] 3273 7-11-5 **133** (t) StephenMulqueen(7) 118
(Maurice Barnes) *prom: rdn appr 3 out: sn wknd* **25/1**

4/P- **7** *2 ¼* **Somemothersdohavem**[29] 3322 5-11-2 **123** LiamTreadwell 108
(Venetia Williams) *in tch: briefly chsd wnr appr 3 out: wknd 2 out* **9/1**

136- **8** *14* **Robbie**[27] 3386 10-11-11 **132** JamesReveley 103
(Keith Reveley) *hld up in rr: pushed along appr 3 out: nvr threatened ldrs* **16/1**

/04- **9** *14* **Jetnova (IRE)**[65] 2630 9-11-2 **123** RobertThornton 81
(Alan King) *midfield: rdn after 7th: sn btn* **16/1**

0/0- **10** *½* **Hidden Justice (IRE)**[24] 3477 5-11-5 **133** DeanPratt(7) 91
(John Quinn) *midfield: rdn 3 out: sn wknd* **8/1**

534- **11** *10* **Kayaan**[45] 3028 7-10-13 **123** KielanWoods(3) 72
(Pam Sly) *hld up: nvr threatened* **20/1**

/32- **P** **Elmore Back (IRE)**[27] 3388 5-11-3 **124** NoelFehily
(Charlie Mann) *in tch: lost pl after 7th: wknd 3 out: p.u bef last* **5/1**[2]

4m 47.84s (-3.46) **Going Correction** +0.175s/f (Yiel) **12** Ran SP% **115.5**
Speed ratings (Par 107): **113,107,106,106,101 100,99,94,88,88 84,**
CSF £125.43 CT £983.42 TOTE £19.00: £3.20, £2.80, £2.40; EX 111.60 Trifecta £878.20 Part won..
Owner Mr & Mrs R Kelvin-Hughes **Bred** R Sexton **Trained** Upper Lambourn, Berks

FOCUS
Hurdle dividing rail moved to provided fresh ground where possible. This had the look of a fair contest before the off, as it contained a couple of interesting types making their handicap debuts, but the winner made all and never looked like being pegged back. A big step up from the winner.

3893 RACING POST LIGHTNING NOVICES' CHASE (GRADE 2) (12 fncs) 2m 110y
12:55 (12:55) (Class 1) 5-Y-0+ **£17,369** (£6,517; £3,263; £1,625; £817)

Form RPR

/11- **1** **Valdez**[56] 2811 7-11-4 152 RobertThornton 154
(Alan King) *hld up in tch: nt fluent 1st: chsd ldr after 5 out: rdn 3 out: led jst after last: kpt on* **15/8**[1]

050/ **2** *3 ¼* **Arnaud (IRE)**[43] 3072 6-11-4 142 DenisO'Regan 152+
(C Byrnes, Ire) *led: stl gng wl whn hit 2 out: reduced advantage whn nt fluent last: hdd sn after: no ex* **14/1**

221- **3** *1* **Fox Appeal (IRE)**[36] 3185 7-11-7 152 LeightonAspell 155
(Emma Lavelle) *trckd ldr: mstke 1st: hit 5 out: rdn and outpcd in 3rd whn mstke 3 out: styd on after 2 out* **2/1**[2]

102- **4** *10* **God's Own (IRE)**[27] 3386 6-11-0 137 PaddyBrennan 138
(Tom George) *in tch on outside: nt fluent 6th and 7th: rdn after 4 out: sn btn: j.rt last 3* **17/2**

/21- **5** *1* **Caid Du Berlais (FR)**[50] 2922 5-11-4 0 NickScholfield 139
(Paul Nicholls) *hld up in tch: rdn after 5 out: sn btn* **10/3**[3]

4m 7.0s (2.00) **Going Correction** +0.425s/f (Soft)
WFA 5 from 6yo+ 3lb **5** Ran SP% **108.4**
Speed ratings: **112,110,110,105,104**
CSF £20.43 TOTE £2.60: £1.30, £2.60; EX 11.90 Trifecta £35.60.
Owner Riverdee Stable **Bred** David & Julie Andrews **Trained** Barbury Castle, Wilts

FOCUS
All of the declared runners had shown more than enough since going chasing to suggest they could develop in to very useful performers at the very least, as between them they had run 11 times over fences, winning seven and finishing no worse than third in the other four, but the contest was dealt a blow when likely favourite Rock On Ruby was taken out due to the ground. Decent novice form and the winner is worth his place in the Arkle.

3894 TRM-EXCELLENCE IN EQUINE NUTRITION H'CAP CHASE (12 fncs) 2m 110y
1:30 (1:30) (Class 2) 5-Y-0+
£14,076 (£4,158; £2,079; £1,039; £519; £261)

Form RPR

122- **1** **Simply Ned (IRE)**[44] 3037 7-10-11 **138** BrianHarding 150+
(Nicky Richards) *hld up in tch: smooth hdwy 5 out: trckd ldr gng wl fr 4 out: pushed along to ld appr last: idled run-in: drvn out* **6/1**

344- **2** *1 ½* **Upsilon Bleu (FR)**[24] 3476 6-10-8 **135** WilsonRenwick 145+
(Pauline Robson) *in tch: hdwy 4 out: led narrowly 3 out: sn rdn: hdd appr last: kpt on but a hld by wnr* **4/1**[3]

512- **3** *12* **Last Shot (FR)**[30] 3294 7-10-3 **130** LiamTreadwell 131
(Venetia Williams) *w ldr: led 5 out: jnd 4 out: hdd 3 out: nt fluent 2 out: wknd* **8/1**

112- **4** *11* **King Of The Wolds (IRE)**[29] 3333 7-10-5 **132** BrianHughes 121
(Malcolm Jefferson) *in tch: lost pl after 6th: rdn 5 out: sn btn* **3/1**[1]

100- **5** *11* **Conquisto**[44] 3032 9-11-12 **153** NoelFehily 132
(Steve Gollings) *hld up: mstke 6th: sn struggling* **9/1**

01- **6** *8* **Bellenos (FR)**[36] 3183 6-10-7 **134** HarrySkelton 106
(Dan Skelton) *hld up in tch: rdn appr 4 out: sn wknd* **7/2**[2]

6/0- **P** **Shooters Wood (IRE)**[42] 3080 10-10-10 **137** (t) NickScholfield
(Paul Nicholls) *trckd ldng pair: lost pl 5th and sn dropped to rr: p.u bef 6th* **16/1**

/4P- **P** **Rody (FR)**[14] 3660 9-11-3 **144** (bt[1]) PaddyBrennan
(Tom George) *led narrowly: hit 5 out and hdd: sn wknd: p.u bef 2 out* **16/1**

4m 6.3s (1.30) **Going Correction** +0.425s/f (Soft) **8** Ran SP% **114.4**
Speed ratings: **113,112,106,101,96 92,,**
CSF £30.88 CT £192.90 TOTE £8.50: £2.10, £1.60, £1.80; EX 41.30 Trifecta £194.80.
Owner David & Nicky Robinson **Bred** Miss Irene Hatton **Trained** Greystoke, Cumbria

FOCUS
Plenty of these had something to prove for one reason or another and quite a few proved to be disappointing, so this may not be strong form despite the winning time being quicker than the Grade 2 novice chase that preceded it. The winner rates a decent northern novice.

3895 OLBG.COM MARES' HURDLE (REGISTERED AS THE DONCASTER MARES' HURDLE) (GRADE 2) (8 hdls) 2m 110y
2:05 (2:05) (Class 1) 4-Y-0+ **£21,031** (£8,044; £4,150; £2,190)

Form RPR

/11- **1** **Annie Power (IRE)**[24] 3459 6-11-5 165 RWalsh 162+
(W P Mullins, Ire) *mde all: clr on bit after 2 out: nt fluent last: easily* **1/6**[1]

/52- **2** *15* **Doyly Carte**[63] 2669 6-11-5 140 HenryBrooke 140
(Donald McCain) *trckd ldr: rdn 2 out: one pce and sn no ch w wnr* **16/1**[3]

315- **3** *7* **Alasi**[44] 3032 10-11-0 138 DominicElsworth 129
(Paul Webber) *in tch: rdn appr 3 out: sn struggling: lft 3rd and sltly hmpd by faller 2 out* **20/1**

321- **4** *½* **Pass The Time**[3] 2763 5-11-0 123 (p) NoelFehily 128
(Neil Mulholland) *hld up: j.lft 3rd and 3 out: nvr threatened* **80/1**

/12- **F** **Cockney Sparrow**[56] 2821 5-11-5 147 DougieCostello 140
(John Quinn) *trckd ldr: pushed along and 2 l down in dispute of 2nd whn fell 2 out* **4/1**[2]

4m 4.3s (-0.40) **Going Correction** +0.425s/f (Soft) **5** Ran SP% **117.6**
Speed ratings (Par 115): **117,109,106,106,**
CSF £5.61 TOTE £1.10: £1.02, £5.00; EX 5.30 Trifecta £28.10.
Owner Mrs S Ricci **Bred** Eamon Cleary **Trained** Muine Beag, Co Carlow

FOCUS
Annie Power was value for much more than the official margin and will be a major player at the Festival regardless of her target.

3896 ALBERT BARTLETT NOVICES' HURDLE (REGISTERED AS THE RIVER DON NOVICES' HURDLE) (GRADE 2) (11 hdls) 3m 110y
2:40 (2:41) (Class 1) 4-Y-0+
£15,661 (£5,876; £2,942; £1,465; £737; £368)

Form RPR

121- **1** **Urban Hymn (FR)**[26] 3417 6-11-10 0 BrianHughes 141+
(Malcolm Jefferson) *led: nt a fluent: mstke 2 out: sn rdn: strly pressed whn hit last: hdd narrowly run-in: rallied to ld again post* **9/4**[1]

131- **2** *shd* **Blakemount (IRE)**[35] 3208 6-11-10 136 RyanMania 140+
(Sue Smith) *trckd ldr: rdn to chal 2 out: upsides last: led narrowly run-in: kpt on: hdd post* **7/1**[3]

101- **3** *12* **Warden Hill (IRE)**[42] 3086 6-11-10 124 DominicElsworth 129
(Mick Channon) *in tch: rdn and outpcd by ldng pair 3 out: dropped to 5th 2 out: plugged on after last: wnt 3rd fnl 100yds* **10/1**

51- **4** *1* **Walk On Al (IRE)**[41] 3116 6-11-10 0 HarrySkelton 126
(Dan Skelton) *hld up: rdn and hdwy into 3rd 3 out: wknd run-in: lost 3rd fnl 100yds* **33/1**

311- **5** *3 ¼* **Sausalito Sunrise (IRE)**[35] 3207 6-11-12 140 TomO'Brien 126
(Philip Hobbs) *hld up: rdn after 4 out: nvr threatened* **3/1**[2]

122- **6** *20* **Timesremembered (IRE)**[28] 3367 6-11-12 143 LeightonAspell 117
(Emma Lavelle) *in tch: pushed along bef 3 out: sn wknd* **3/1**[2]

/01- **7** *16* **Aerial (FR)**[44] 3046 8-11-10 139 NickScholfield 87
(Paul Nicholls) *trckd ldr: rdn bef 3 out: sn wknd* **16/1**

6m 19.1s (20.10) **Going Correction** +0.80s/f (Soft) **7** Ran SP% **111.2**
Speed ratings (Par 115): **99,98,95,94,93 87,82**
CSF £17.44 TOTE £2.80: £2.10, £2.80; EX 20.00 Trifecta £122.30.
Owner Mr & Mrs G Calder **Bred** Jean-Jacques Augier **Trained** Norton, N Yorks

FOCUS
Some nice prospects lined up for this staying event, and it developed into a proper slog in what was testing conditions. The early gallop wasn't quick The winner is rated to his mark in a fair renewal.

3897 SKY BET CHASE (A H'CAP) (FORMERLY THE GREAT YORKSHIRE CHASE) (LISTED RACE) (18 fncs) 3m
3:15 (3:17) (Class 1) (0-155,153) 5-Y-0+

£42,712 (£16,027; £8,025; £3,997; £2,010; £1,005)

Form RPR

/26- 1 **The Rainbow Hunter**[63] 2674 10-10-9 136 NickScholfield 148
(Kim Bailey) *midfield: hdwy 12th: nt fluent 5 out: chsd ldr 4 out: rdn to ld appr 2 out: styd on* 25/1

341- 2 1 1/2 **Baile Anrai (IRE)**[29] 3323 10-10-0 127 (b) HarrySkelton 138
(Dan Skelton) *hld up: hdwy 12th: chsd ldrs bef 4 out: rdn 3 out: wnt 2nd last: styd on run-in but a hld* 25/1

310- 3 8 **Unioniste (FR)**[28] 3376 6-11-7 153 HarryDerham(5) 155
(Paul Nicholls) *midfield: hit 5 out: sn rdn: styd on after 2 out: wnt 3rd towards fin* 11/4[1]

465- 4 2 3/4 **Solix (FR)**[35] 3205 8-10-4 131 (v[1]) WillKennedy 130
(Ian Williams) *led: rdn 4 out: hdd appr 2 out: slow last and lost 2nd: wknd: lost 3rd towards fin* 33/1

/15- 5 2 1/4 **Niceonefrankie**[57] 2800 8-10-13 140 LiamTreadwell 139
(Venetia Williams) *midfield: nt fluent 5 out: sn rdn: plugged on* 14/1

/40- 6 3/4 **Roberto Goldback (IRE)**[49] 2937 12-11-4 150 NicodeBoinville(5) 145
(Nicky Henderson) *hld up: rdn 5 out: plugged on after 3 out: nvr threatened* 25/1

411- 7 nk **Kruzhlinin (GER)**[48] 2972 7-11-3 144 HenryBrooke 139
(Donald McCain) *hld up: nt a fluent: rdn after 5 out: plugged on after 3 out: nvr threatened* 14/1

4/4- 8 12 **Time For Rupert (IRE)**[35] 3198 10-11-2 143 DenisO'Regan 126
(Paul Webber) *midfield: wknd after 5 out* 9/1

P/5- 9 34 **Auroras Encore (IRE)**[30] 3285 12-11-5 146 RyanMania 95
(Sue Smith) *trckd ldrs: wknd after 5 out* 50/1

403- P **Native Gallery (IRE)**[14] 3647 9-10-4 131 (t) LeightonAspell
(Ben De Haan) *midfield: wknd qckly after 6 out: p.u bef 4 out* 9/1

301- P **Night In Milan (IRE)**[42] 3091 8-10-11 138 (b) JamesReveley
(Keith Reveley) *prom: wknd 4 out: p.u bef 2 out* 12/1

153- P **Gullinbursti (IRE)**[38] 3165 8-11-3 144 (t) NoelFehily
(Emma Lavelle) *hld up: rdn after 10th: p.u bef 11th* 11/2[2]

631- P **Mart Lane (IRE)**[27] 3389 9-11-1 142 (b) TomO'Brien
(Dr Richard Newland) *trckd ldrs: hit 1st: lost pl after 8th: sn struggling: t.o whn p.u bef 11th* 16/1

33F- P **According To Trev (IRE)**[38] 3162 8-9-13 133 (vt) RyanHatch(7)
(Nigel Twiston-Davies) *in tch: lost pl after 7th: sn bhd: p.u after 9th* 20/1

4F2- P **The Druids Nephew (IRE)**[49] 2943 7-10-3 135 (p) JamesBanks(5)
(Andy Turnell) *midfield: mstke 6th: wknd 5 out: t.o whn p.u bef 2 out* 13/2[3]

6m 23.3s (11.30) **Going Correction** +0.80s/f (Soft) 15 Ran SP% 123.5
Speed ratings: **113,112,109,108,108 107,107,103,92, , , , ,**
CSF £509.80 CT £2279.67 TOTE £40.60: £8.50, £4.80, £1.80; EX 1257.90 Trifecta £7188.60.
Owner May We Never Be Found Out Partnership **Bred** M Massarella **Trained** Andoversford, Gloucs
■ Stewards' Enquiry : Harry Skelton two-day ban: used whip above permitted level (Feb 8-9)

FOCUS
A really competitive handicap but not many of these got seriously involved. The Rainbow Hunter belatedly built on the form of last year's Ascot win.

3898 EBF STALLIONS PARK HILL HOSPITAL MARES' STANDARD OPEN NATIONAL HUNT FLAT RACE 2m 110y
3:50 (3:50) (Class 6) 4-7-Y-0 £1,624 (£477; £238; £119)

Form RPR

3- 1 **Side Step**[52] 2892 5-11-0 0 AndrewTinkler 109
(Nicky Henderson) *midfield: rdn and hdwy over 4f out: wnt 2nd 2f out: styd on to ld post* 7/2[1]

313- 2 nk **Balmusette**[80] 2298 5-11-7 0 JamesReveley 116
(Keith Reveley) *led: 5 l up and stl gng wl 2f out: rdn over 1f out: wandered and reduced advantage ins fnl f: hdd post* 9/2[2]

32- 3 11 **Ebony Empress (IRE)**[49] 2946 5-10-11 0 MichaelByrne(3) 99
(Neil Mulholland) *trckd ldrs: rdn over 4f out: one pce in 3rd fnl 2f* 9/1

5- 4 3 1/2 **Ellin's Tower**[252] 372 5-10-9 0 (t) EdCookson(5) 94
(Kim Bailey) *trckd ldr: rdn over 4f out: one pce in 4th fnl 2f* 11/1

5 9 **Well Connected** 5-11-0 0 NoelFehily 85
(Emma Lavelle) *hld up: pushed along over 6f out: plugged on: nvr threatened* 7/1

6 2 1/2 **Lily Little Legs (IRE)**[48] 5-11-0 0 WillKennedy 83
(Ian Williams) *trckd ldr: rdn over 5f out: wknd over 3f out* 8/1

7 29 **Royal Roo** 5-11-0 0 ConorO'Farrell 54
(Mark Rimell) *midfield: wknd over 4f out* 20/1

8 18 **Star Of Salford** 5-11-0 0 HaddenFrost 36
(David Pipe) *midfield: pushed along over 6f out: sn btn* 5/1[3]

6- 9 23 **Eternal Vine**[52] 2885 5-11-0 0 BrianHughes 13
(Malcolm Jefferson) *trckd ldrs: lost pl 1/2-way: t.o fnl 6f* 50/1

10 3 3/4 **Elegant Stride (IRE)** 4-10-3 0 LeightonAspell
(Don Cantillon) *hld up: pushed along over 6f out: sn btn: t.o* 8/1

4m 11.2s (12.10) **Going Correction** +0.80s/f (Soft)
WFA 4 from 5yo 11lb 10 Ran SP% 116.8
Speed ratings: **103,102,97,96,91 90,76,68,57,55**
CSF £19.02 TOTE £3.30: £2.30, £1.60, £2.00; EX 26.10 Trifecta £88.60.
Owner The Queen **Bred** The Queen **Trained** Upper Lambourn, Berks

FOCUS
This didn't look a bad contest of its type, but two of the experienced runners came miles clear. They looks above-average mares.
T/Plt: £85.20. Pool: £158,176.44 - 1354.46 winning units. T/Qpdt: £12.60. Pool £13,489.76 - 787.65 winning units. AS

3427 UTTOXETER (L-H)
Saturday, January 25

3899 Meeting Abandoned - waterlogged

3906 - 3907a (Foreign Racing) - See Raceform Interactive

3399 LEOPARDSTOWN (L-H)
Saturday, January 25

OFFICIAL GOING: Soft (yielding last 2f on hurdle course)

3908a BOYLESPORTS.COM KILLINEY NOVICE CHASE (GRADE 2) (14 fncs) 2m 5f
2:15 (2:16) 5-Y-0+ £21,666 (£6,333; £3,000; £1,000)

RPR

1 **Djakadam (FR)**[28] 3375 5-10-8 PaulTownend 146+
(W P Mullins, Ire) *sn trckd ldr in 2nd tl led 5th: hdd 6 out: bk on terms 3 out: slt mstke 2 out: led last: styd on wl to draw clr clsng stages* 6/4[1]

2 4 **Bright New Dawn (IRE)**[27] 3404 7-11-5 135[1] BryanCooper 152
(D T Hughes, Ire) *led tl hdd 5th: led again 6 out tl hdd last: no ex w wnr run-in: kpt on same pce* 2/1[2]

3 17 **Mullaghanoe River (IRE)**[14] 3664 6-11-5 136 PCarberry 139
(Noel Meade, Ire) *trckd ldr in 2nd whn slow at 2nd and dropped to 3rd: nt qckn w principals 3 out: reduced deficit bef last but nvr on terms and wknd run-in* 10/3[3]

4 38 **Road To Riches (IRE)**[30] 3308 7-11-5 147 RobbieColgan 103
(Noel Meade, Ire) *a in rr of quartet: no imp whn mstke 3 out: sn adrift* 6/1

5m 26.0s (-10.00) **Going Correction** -0.10s/f (Good)
WFA 5 from 6yo+ 4lb 4 Ran SP% 110.7
Speed ratings: **115,113,107,92**
CSF £5.10 TOTE £2.00; DF 4.50 Trifecta £7.50.
Owner Mrs S Ricci **Bred** Richard Corveller **Trained** Muine Beag, Co Carlow

FOCUS
This is usually a good race, and the winner could be very useful. He's rated in line with his hurdles form.

3910a BOYLESPORTS.COM HURDLE (EXTENDED H'CAP HURDLE) (GRADE B) (8 hdls) 2m
3:25 (3:25) (0-150,142) 4-Y-0+

£50,000 (£15,833; £7,500; £2,500; £1,666; £833)

RPR

1 **Gilgamboa (IRE)**[25] 3445 6-10-9 128 MarkWalsh 142+
(E Bolger, Ire) *racd towards mid-div tl tk clsr order in 5th 1/2-way: travelled wl into cl 3rd bef 2 out: disp appr last: kpt on strly to assert clsng stages* 10/1

2 1 1/4 **Flaxen Flare (IRE)**[35] 3200 5-11-0 142 (b) MrDJO'Leary(7) 152
(Gordon Elliott, Ire) *trckd ldrs in 3rd tl prog into 2nd after 3 out: disp appr last: kpt on wl tl hdd and no ex w wnr clsng stages* 16/1

3 2 1/4 **Quick Jack (IRE)**[71] 2492 5-9-12 119 PCarberry 129+
(A J Martin, Ire) *w.w towards rr tl prog on outer 2 out in 10th: gd hdwy to chse ldrs in 3rd bef last: nvr quite on terms: kpt on same pce* 7/4[1]

4 11 **Sea Light (IRE)**[27] 3400 6-9-12 117 DJCasey 116
(C Byrnes, Ire) *chsd ldrs: pushed along after 2 out and no imp in 6th bef last: kpt on same pce into 4th clsng strides* 4/1[2]

5 hd **Blacklough (IRE)**[41] 3121 6-10-7 126 AndrewLeigh 125
(W J Austin, Ire) *racd in mid-div tl clsd to chse ldrs 1/2-way: prog into 4th after 2 out: sn rdn and nt qckn w principals: kpt on same pce: dropped to 5th clsng strides* 16/1

6 1 **Snake Eyes (IRE)**[86] 2178 6-10-4 123 RobbiePower 121
(Nicky Henderson) *towards rr whn mstke 3rd: prog into mid-div on inner 1/2-way: plenty to do 2 out: prog into 7th appr last: kpt on same pce* 12/1

7 2 1/2 **Maxim Gorky (IRE)**[29] 3340 7-10-1 127 JJBurke(7) 122
(Noel Meade, Ire) *hld up towards rr: prog after 2 out: kpt on fr bef last: nvr on terms* 33/1

8 3/4 **Massini's Trap (IRE)**[36] 3184 5-10-8 134 JodyMcGarvey(5) 127
(J A Nash, Ire) *w.w tl tk clsr order appr 2 out: kpt on wl on outer fr bef last: nvr nrr* 50/1

9 1 **Ballyadam Brook (IRE)**[36] 2488 10-10-6 125 APHeskin 119
(Terence O'Brien, Ire) *led and sn clr: advantage reduced 3 out and sn hdd: no ex bef last* 40/1

10 hd **Blood Cotil (FR)**[21] 3547 5-11-6 141 PaulTownend 132
(W P Mullins, Ire) *racd in mid-div tl prog towards outer 2 out: bit short of room home turn: sn one pce* 9/1[3]

11 1 1/2 **Leah Claire (IRE)**[28] 3373 8-10-5 127 BenDalton(3) 119
(W McCreery, Ire) *chsd ldrs: prog into 5th 2 out: sn pushed along and no ex* 12/1

12 3/4 **Sailors Warn (IRE)**[385] 3524 7-11-2 138 SJHassett(3) 129
(E J O'Grady, Ire) *racd towards rr: nvr a threat: kpt on one pce fr 2 out* 50/1

13 hd **Big Generator**[30] 3306 8-9-10 115 (t) MarkEnright 106
(Paul Nolan, Ire) *trckd ldr in 2nd tl led after 3 out: hdd bef last: sn no ex and wknd bdly run-in* 33/1

14 1 3/4 **Il Fenomeno (ITY)**[6] 3806 8-10-7 133 (b) GerFox(7) 122
(Noel Meade, Ire) *chsd ldrs in 4th tl wknd after 2 out* 33/1

15 6 1/2 **Dysios (IRE)**[28] 3373 6-10-6 125 AELynch 108
(Denis W Cullen, Ire) *nvr bttr than mid-div: no threat bef 2 out* 16/1

16 3 1/2 **Fosters Cross (IRE)**[6] 3806 12-10-9 128 DGHogan 107
(Thomas Mullins, Ire) *w.w: no imp 3 out* 33/1

17 nse **The Game Changer (IRE)**[29] 3339 5-10-6 127 BryanCooper 104
(C F Swan, Ire) *nvr bttr than mid-div: no threat after 3 out* 16/1

18 6 1/2 **Diplomat (USA)**[127] 1614 5-10-6 132 KevinSexton(5) 103
(D K Weld, Ire) *chsd ldrs tl no ex after 3 out: sn wknd* 33/1

19 15 **Sullane Chief (IRE)**[48] 2992 6-10-3 129 ConorWalsh(7) 87
(P C O'Connor, Ire) *slowly away and racd in rr: hdwy whn hmpd 2 out: sn no ex* 14/1

20 9 **Princeton Plains (IRE)**[42] 3100 8-10-10 129 AndrewJMcNamara 78
(Edward P Harty, Ire) *w.w: no threat 3 out* 33/1

21 12 **Primroseandblue (IRE)**[42] 3100 10-10-7 126 (t) DannyMullins 63
(W P Mullins, Ire) *nvr bttr than mid-div: no threat 3 out* 66/1

22 shd **Rocky Wednesday (IRE)**[7] 3793 7-10-11 130 (p) RobbieColgan 67
(Gordon Elliott, Ire) *a towards rr: nvr a factor* 25/1

F **Reizovic (IRE)**[760] 3375 9-9-13 118 DavidSplaine
(John E Kiely, Ire) *hld up towards rr: prog to chse ldrs towards outer whn fell 2 out* 25/1

P **Way Up In The Air (IRE)**[48] 2986 7-10-5 **124**.................... PhillipEnright
(Robert Tyner, Ire) *nvr bttr than mid-div: no threat 3 out: p.u bef last* **20/1**

3m 48.6s (-18.90) **Going Correction** -0.90s/f (Hard) **24** Ran SP% **159.0**
Speed ratings: **111,110,109,103,103 103,101,101,101,100 100,99,99,98,95 93,93,90,83,78 72,72, ,**
CSF £179.47 CT £438.15 TOTE £13.80: £3.80, £4.30, £1.90, £1.90; DF 233.20 Trifecta £958.70.
Owner John P McManus **Bred** K McManus **Trained** Bruree, Co Limerick

FOCUS
A really strong race, as one would expect for the money on offer. The winner ansd third are probably capable of better.

3909 - 3912a (Foreign Racing) - See Raceform Interactive

3245 FONTWELL (L-H)
Sunday, January 26

3913 Meeting Abandoned - waterlogged

3634 SEDGEFIELD (L-H)
Sunday, January 26

OFFICIAL GOING: Heavy (soft in places; 4.6) changing to heavy after race 1 (1.10)
Wind: fresh across Weather: wet initially, dry and sunny after second

3920 BETFRED NOVICES' HURDLE (QUALIFIER) (BETFRED HURDLE SERIES QUALIFIER) (8 hdls 2 omitted) 2m 4f
1:10 (1:10) (Class 4) 4-Y-0+ **£3,798** (£1,122; £561; £280; £140)

Form RPR
321- 1 **Getabuzz**[17] 3614 6-11-11 117...(b) DougieCostello 124+
(Tim Easterby) *hld up in tch: smooth hdwy after 2 out (normal 3 out): led last (normal 2 out): rdn and sn in command extended run-in: eased nr fin* **4/1**[3]

4- 2 2 1/4 **Maxed Out King (IRE)**[16] 3640 6-11-5 0............................ ShaneByrne 113+
(Sue Smith) *hld up: pushed along and hdwy after 2 out (normal 3 out): hit last (normal 2 out): styd on extended run-in: wnt 2nd ins fnl f* **12/1**

231- 3 10 **Masquerade (IRE)**[44] 3061 5-11-11 0.................................. NoelFehily 109
(Warren Greatrex) *led: rdn whn hdd last (normal 2 out): wknd and lost 2nd ins fnl f* **5/2**[2]

F46- 4 3/4 **Fairweather Friend**[39] 3159 5-10-12 0............................... SeanQuinlan 95
(Jennie Candlish) *in tch: nt fluent last (normal 2 out): one pce extended run-in* **16/1**

2- 5 11 **Great Choice (IRE)**[37] 3194 5-11-5 0............................ TomScudamore 95+
(David Pipe) *trckd ldr: rdn appr last (normal 2 out): wknd extended run-in* **5/4**[1]

516- 6 50 **Our Boy Ben**[46] 3017 5-11-11 0... BrianHughes 47
(Malcolm Jefferson) *hld up: hit 6th: hung lft: btn next: t.o* **10/1**

60- 7 47 **Cottam Maybel**[9] 3757 5-10-12 0.. BrianHarding
(Michael Easterby) *in tch: bhd after 6th: t.o* **100/1**

460- 8 11 **Crazy Chester (IRE)**[28] 3388 5-11-2 0.............................. JakeGreenall[(3)]
(Michael Easterby) *in tch: slow 1st: struggling fr 1/2-way: t.o after 6th* **66/1**

5m 22.4s (29.70) **Going Correction** +1.35s/f (Heav) **8** Ran SP% **118.2**
Speed ratings (Par 105): **94,93,89,88,84 64,45,41**
CSF £49.74 TOTE £4.80: £1.60, £2.70, £1.30; EX 48.50 Trifecta £106.20.
Owner Langham Hall Stud Three **Bred** Peter Botham **Trained** Great Habton, N Yorks

FOCUS
Common bends, hurdles sited on outer, chase course dolled off inner. Quite an interesting race, run in testing conditions. What should have been the last hurdle in the home straight was missed out all day. The winner is a potential 130+ horse on Flat form.

3921 FREE BETS ON YOUR MOBILE AT BOOKMAKERS.CO.UK NOVICES' CHASE (18 fncs 3 omitted) 3m 3f
1:40 (1:40) (Class 4) 5-Y-0+ **£4,288** (£1,259; £629; £314)

Form RPR
/4P- 1 **Alpha Victor (IRE)**[42] 3108 9-11-3 130............................... PeterBuchanan 118+
(William Kinsey) *trckd ldr: led jst after last (normal 2 out): styd on to go clr* **7/2**[2]

- 2 13 **Mondo Cane (IRE)**[637] 7-11-3 0... AdamPogson 106
(Charles Pogson) *hld up: wnt prom 12th: led 15th: rdn whn hdd jst after last (normal 2 out): sn no ch w wnr* **33/1**

F/ 3 6 **Isaacstown Lad (IRE)**[323] 4648 7-11-3 0............................ BrianHarding 99
(William Amos) *hld up: tk clsr order 12th: outpcd and briefly dropped bk to 5th after 15th: upsides again 2 out (normal 3 out): no ex and hld in 3rd extended run-in* **9/2**[3]

311- 4 19 **Swatow Typhoon (IRE)**[24] 3496 7-11-13 126................... JasonMaguire 97
(Donald McCain) *led: j. slowly and wnt in snatches: rdn after 12th: hdd 15th: hit 2 out (normal 3 out): wknd* **4/7**[1]

40F- 5 34 **Harrys Whim**[36] 3209 9-10-3 62..............................(t) StephenMulqueen[(7)] 53
(Maurice Barnes) *in tch: briefly prom 12th: stl in tch 2 out (normal 3 out): wknd* **25/1**

7m 41.5s (52.50) **Going Correction** +1.125s/f (Heav) **5** Ran SP% **110.8**
Speed ratings: **67,63,61,55,45**
CSF £51.25 TOTE £4.20: £1.90, £6.90; EX 78.20 Trifecta £99.60.
Owner Denton,Kinsey,Osborne Hse,Wesley-Yates **Bred** Miss Penny Downes **Trained** Ashton, Cheshire

FOCUS
The final fence was omitted on all circuits throughout the day in all chases. The winner is rated in line with the best of this season's hurdles form.

3922 JEAN DAWSON MEMORIAL H'CAP HURDLE (8 hdls 2 omitted) 2m 4f
2:10 (2:10) (Class 4) (0-120,116) 4-Y-0+ **£3,898** (£1,144; £572; £286)

Form RPR
P51- 1 **Markem (IRE)**[16] 3639 7-10-6 **103**..................................(t) ShaunDobbin[(7)] 111+
(Rose Dobbin) *in tch: trckd ldrs 1/2-way: rdn to ld appr last (normal 2 out): hit last: styd on* **3/1**[2]

/33- 2 3/4 **Comeback Colin**[77] 2393 6-11-6 **110**.................................... RyanMania 116
(Sue Smith) *trckd ldr: led after 5th: hit 6th: rdn whn hdd appr last (normal 2 out): nt fluent last: kpt on but a jst hld* **3/1**[2]

50F- 3 3 1/4 **Forty Crown (IRE)**[50] 2959 8-11-6 **110**......................... WilsonRenwick 112
(John Wade) *hld up in tch: reminders 1/2-way: rdn and outpcd after 6th: wnt 3rd appr last (normal 2 out): styd on extended run-in: nrst fin* **7/1**[3]

106- 4 2 1/2 **Welsh Bard (IRE)**[17] 3618 5-11-6 **110**............................ JasonMaguire 109
(Donald McCain) *sn pushed along in rr: bhd tl styd on fr appr last (normal 2 out)* **16/1**

600- 5 28 **Pierrers Bounty (IRE)**[17] 3618 7-11-4 **108**..................(p) RichieMcGrath 79
(Henry Hogarth) *led: hdd after 5th: rdn and btn after 6th* **12/1**

/22- 6 6 **Mixologist**[38] 3169 7-11-12 **116**..(t) NoelFehily 81
(Warren Greatrex) *trckd ldrs on inner: nt fluent 6th: upsides whn mstke 2 out (normal 3 out): wknd qckly appr last (normal 2 out)* **5/2**[1]

021- 7 dist **Sam Lord**[22] 3527 10-11-6 **110**....................................... DominicElsworth
(James Moffatt) *trckd ldrs: wknd after 6th: sn t.o* **7/1**[3]

5m 17.03s (24.33) **Going Correction** +1.35s/f (Heav) **7** Ran SP% **117.1**
Speed ratings (Par 105): **105,104,103,102,91 88,**
CSF £13.31 TOTE £4.40: £2.00, £2.60; EX 13.80 Trifecta £98.80.
Owner Mr & Mrs Duncan Davidson **Bred** Eamonn Garrett **Trained** South Hazelrigg, Northumbria

FOCUS
A competitive handicap run at a fair gallop. The first two are on the upgrade.

3923 FRAZER HINES & JOHN O'LOAN H'CAP CHASE (FOR THE GLENUGIE/INGHAM CUP) (14 fncs 2 omitted) 2m 4f
2:45 (2:45) (Class 3) (0-140,139) 5-Y-0+ **£6,256** (£1,848; £924; £462)

Form RPR
222- 1 **Tahiti Pearl (IRE)**[31] 3287 10-11-2 **129**.................................. RyanMania 140+
(Sue Smith) *mde all: pushed clr extended run-in: easily* **4/1**

066- 2 10 **Consigliere (FR)**[36] 3197 11-11-2 **136**............................(b) KieronEdgar[(7)] 135
(David Pipe) *trckd ldr: rdn after 2 out (normal 3 out): one pce and sn no ch w wnr* **9/4**[1]

502- 3 19 **Tranquil Sea (IRE)**[29] 3362 12-11-12 **139**.............................. NoelFehily 119
(Warren Greatrex) *trckd ldr: rdn after 2 out (normal 3 out): sn wknd* **5/2**[2]

/P5- 4 7 **Dunowen Point (IRE)**[15] 3652 8-11-6 **133**....................... JasonMaguire 106
(Donald McCain) *hld up: nvr threatened* **11/4**[3]

5m 20.2s (17.20) **Going Correction** +1.125s/f (Heav) **4** Ran SP% **106.0**
Speed ratings: **110,106,98,95**
CSF £12.56 TOTE £2.50; EX 12.60 Trifecta £26.20.
Owner M B Scholey & R H Scholey **Bred** Thomas Webb **Trained** High Eldwick, W Yorks

FOCUS
This was quite an easy race to sum up. There's a case for rating the form a few pounds higher.

3924 HORSE RACING FREE BETS AT BOOKMAKERS.CO.UK H'CAP HURDLE (7 hdls 2 omitted) 2m 2f 110y
3:20 (3:20) (Class 5) (0-100,95) 4-Y-0+ **£2,599** (£763; £381; £190)

Form RPR
403- 1 **Willie Hall**[16] 3639 10-10-13 **82**...(p) BrianHarding 88+
(William Amos) *w ldr: led 3rd: mde rest: hit 5th: rdn and 5 l up last (normal 2 out): idled extended run-in: fnd more whn jnd 100yds out* **6/4**[1]

455- 2 1 **Indigo Island (IRE)**[16] 3639 5-10-11 **87**......................... CallumBewley[(7)] 89
(Robert Bewley) *in tch: cl up after 5th: 5 l down last (normal 2 out): kpt on: upsides 100yds out: hld nr fin* **9/2**[3]

0/5- 3 1 1/4 **Grand Vintage (IRE)**[31] 3271 8-11-7 **95**.................. ColmMcCormack[(5)] 96
(Evelyn Slack) *hld up in tch: rdn and outpcd after 5th: 13 l down in 4th last (normal 2 out): styd on wl* **10/1**

002- 4 27 **Douchkirk (FR)**[47] 3009 7-11-10 **93**....................................(b) WillKennedy 71
(John Berry) *trckd ldrs: rdn and outpcd in 3rd after 2 out (normal 3 out): wknd extended run-in* **3/1**[2]

044- 5 6 **Fred Bojangals (IRE)**[16] 3637 12-10-9 **85**...........(p) MissEButterworth[(7)] 52
(Barbara Butterworth) *led narrowly: hdd 3rd: lost pl 4th: btn after 5th* **10/1**

/56- 6 1 1/4 **Minden March**[18] 3605 9-9-7 **69** oh5.............................. DanielHiskett[(7)] 35
(Peter Maddison) *hld up in rr: a bhd* **25/1**

000- P **Bonnie Burnett (IRE)**[15] 3659 7-11-10 **93**............................. TomO'Brien
(Brian Rothwell) *hld up: rdn 4th: t.o after 5th: p.u bef last* **7/1**

4m 54.4s (25.70) **Going Correction** +1.35s/f (Heav) **7** Ran SP% **117.7**
Speed ratings (Par 103): **99,98,98,86,84 83,**
CSF £9.53 TOTE £2.80: £1.70, £4.70; EX 12.10 Trifecta £100.00.
Owner R H Hall **Bred** G E Leech **Trained** Rochester, Northumberland

FOCUS
A moderate contest. The winner is probably still capable of a bit better than this.

3925 NO DEPOSIT FREE BETS WITH BOOKMAKERS.CO.UK H'CAP CHASE (14 fncs 2 omitted) 2m 4f
3:50 (3:50) (Class 5) (0-100,95) 5-Y-0+ **£3,249** (£954; £477; £238)

Form RPR
041- 1 **Prince Blackthorn (IRE)**[54] 2870 8-10-9 **78**.................... BrianHarding 90+
(William Amos) *in tch: rdn to chse ldr whn hit last (normal 2 out): led over 1f out: kpt on* **11/4**[2]

336- 2 2 3/4 **Cloudy Dawn**[61] 2735 9-9-11 **69**............................ JonathanEngland[(3)] 77
(Sue Smith) *led: rdn after 2 out (normal 3 out): hit last (normal 2 out): hdd over 1f out: plugged on but a hld* **2/1**[1]

605- 3 4 **Wave Breaker (IRE)**[79] 2336 7-10-7 **76**.......................(p) DougieCostello 81
(Robert Johnson) *prom: rdn after 12th: hit last (normal 2 out): hld in 3rd fr over 1f out* **8/1**

603- 4 3 1/2 **Monbeg (IRE)**[22] 3528 7-11-4 **87**.....................................(p) DenisO'Regan 87
(Martin Todhunter) *hld up: slow 11th: rdn 12th: no imp on ldrs* **5/1**

/04- 5 1 1/4 **Samtheman**[47] 3015 9-11-7 **95**................................... JoeColliver[(5)] 93
(Micky Hammond) *hld up: hit 10th: nvr threatened* **10/1**

/0P- 6 8 **Runswick Relax**[79] 2339 8-10-13 **82**.............................. WilsonRenwick 74
(John Wade) *trckd ldrs: hit 12th: wknd next* **9/2**[3]

5m 33.3s (30.30) **Going Correction** +1.125s/f (Heav) **6** Ran SP% **115.1**
Speed ratings: **84,82,81,79,79 76**
CSF £9.41 CT £37.21 TOTE £2.90: £1.30, £1.50; EX 7.60 Trifecta £21.50.
Owner J M Stenhouse **Bred** Miss Carmel McGinn **Trained** Rochester, Northumberland

FOCUS
A weak event run at a sound tempo. The three that went to the last with every chance all made a mistake. The second and third are rated pretty much to their marks.

3926 BOOKMAKERS.CO.UK STANDARD OPEN NATIONAL HUNT FLAT RACE 2m 1f
4:20 (4:20) (Class 6) 4-6-Y-0 **£1,559** (£457; £228; £114)

Form RPR
1 **Royal Supreme (IRE)** 4-10-7 0... WilsonRenwick 100+
(Keith Dalgleish) *in tch: trckd ldr gng wl over 3f out: led on bit over 1f out: pushed clr* **10/1**

2 7 **Silver Gent (IRE)**[70] 6-11-4 0... JasonMaguire 104+
(Donald McCain) *led narrowly: drvn whn hdd over 1f out: one pce* **4/5**[1]

5- 3 6 **Con Forza (IRE)**[43] 3098 5-11-4 0.. NoelFehily 97
(Warren Greatrex) *trckd ldrs: outpcd in 5th over 2f out: plugged on: wnt 3rd ins fnl f* **7/2**[2]

4 3 1/2 **Apterix (FR)**[122] 4-10-7 0 .... CraigGallagher(7) 90
(Brian Ellison) *in tch: rdn to chse ldr over 3f out: wknd and lost 3rd ins fnl f* **5/1**[3]

2/0- 5 8 **Allbarnone**[254] 359 6-11-4 0 .... DougieCostello 86
(William Kinsey) *hld up: rdn over 3f out: wknd over 1f out* **14/1**

5- 6 42 **Blacksmiths Arms**[24] 3508 4-10-4 0 .... JakeGreenall(3) 33
(Michael Easterby) *w ldr: wknd qckly 5f out: t.o* **20/1**

4m 26.8s (25.50) **Going Correction** +1.35s/f (Heav)
WFA 4 from 5yo+ 11lb 6 Ran SP% **115.0**
Speed ratings: **94,90,87,86,82 62**
CSF £19.36 TOTE £14.10: £6.50, £1.10; EX 33.00 Trifecta £104.50.
Owner Equus Syndicate **Bred** Stephanie Hanly **Trained** Carluke, S Lanarks

FOCUS
Interestingly, four went wide in this while two remained closer to the inside rail in the back and home straights. The latter route proved to be most beneficial considering the result. Hard to put a figure on the form.
T/Plt: £228.40. Pool: £119,891.45 - 383.04 winning units. T/Qpdt: £12.90. Pool: £8720.52 - 499.70 winning units. AS

3906 LEOPARDSTOWN (L-H)
Sunday, January 26

OFFICIAL GOING: Chase course - heavy (soft in places); hurdle course - soft to heavy (soft last 2f)

3928a FRANK WARD SOLICITORS ARKLE NOVICE CHASE (GRADE 1) (11 fncs) 2m 1f
1:30 (1:30) 5-Y-0+ **£43,333** (£12,666; £6,000; £2,000)

RPR

1 **Trifolium (FR)**[31] 3308 7-11-12 145 .... BryanCooper 158+
(C Byrnes, Ire) *chsd ldr in 2nd tl led narrowly fr 3 out: extended advantage fr next and in command into st: clr whn edgd lft bef jumping last: rdn and styd on wl run-in* **7/1**

2 9 **Felix Yonger (IRE)**[31] 3314 8-11-12 154 .... RWalsh 151+
(W P Mullins, Ire) *chsd ldrs: 3rd 1/2-way: mstke 4 out and niggled along in 5th next: slt mstke whn lft 4th 2 out and hmpd sltly: rdn bef st and clsd u.p into mod 2nd fr last: kpt on same pce* **5/2**[2]

3 3 3/4 **Mozoltov**[43] 3103 8-11-12 .... PaulTownend 145
(W P Mullins, Ire) *chsd ldrs: 4th 1/2-way: tk clsr order in 3rd bef 2 out where slt mstke: rdn into 2nd bef st: no imp on wnr fr last and sn dropped to 3rd: kpt on one pce* **7/2**[3]

4 18 **Ted Veale (IRE)**[31] 3308 7-11-12 .... PCarberry 131+
(A J Martin, Ire) *w.w: mod 6th bef 4 out: no imp on ldrs bef 2 out where lft mod 5th: rdn into mod 4th bef last: kpt on one pce* **25/1**

5 17 **Defy Logic (IRE)**[31] 3308 7-11-12 150 .... APMcCoy 118+
(Paul Nolan, Ire) *attempted to make all: slt mstke 4th: 2 l clr 1/2-way: bad mstke 3 out and hdd narrowly: rdn and wknd qckly fr next: eased bef last: b.b.v* **11/8**[1]

6 35 **Irish Thistle (IRE)**[14] 3683 7-11-12 130 .... DavyRussell 75+
(H Rogers, Ire) *hld up towards rr: j.rt 3rd and several times after: detached next: lft remote 6th 2 out: nvr a factor* **66/1**

F **Mallowney (IRE)**[21] 3558 8-11-12 136 .... AndrewJMcNamara
(Timothy Doyle, Ire) *chsd ldrs: nt fluent 2nd: tk clsr order bhd ldrs after 3 out: cl up disputing 3rd whn fell next* **20/1**

4m 15.6s (-6.40) **Going Correction** 0.0s/f (Good) 7 Ran SP% **115.5**
Speed ratings: **115,110,109,100,92 76,**
CSF £25.62 TOTE £8.50: £2.50, £1.70; DF 27.70 Trifecta £124.20.
Owner Gigginstown House Stud **Bred** Haras De La Rousseliere Scea & J Poirier **Trained** Ballingarry, Co Limerick
■ Stewards' Enquiry : Bryan Cooper severe caution: continued hitting gelding when race was clearly won.

FOCUS
No Champagne Fever, but otherwise this was the best Ireland had to offer in the 2m novice chasing division. As expected, the gallop was generous from the outset and there were plenty struggling leaving the back straight. The result caused a massive shake-up in the Racing Post Arkle market at the Cheltenham Festival and, if anything, it made the picture even hazier than it was beforehand. The winner is progressive.

3930a BHP INSURANCE IRISH CHAMPION HURDLE (GRADE 1) (8 hdls) 2m
2:35 (2:35) 4-Y-0+ **£59,583** (£17,416; £8,250; £2,750)

RPR

1 **Hurricane Fly (IRE)**[28] 3402 10-11-10 175 .... RWalsh 163+
(W P Mullins, Ire) *settled bhd ldr in 2nd: got in cl 2nd: clsd into st and led narrowly bef last where slt mstke and hdd briefly: rallied wl run-in to regain advantage far side and styd on wl to extend advantage towards fin* **4/7**[1]

2 1 1/2 **Our Conor (IRE)**[28] 3402 5-11-8 161 .... DannyMullins 159+
(D T Hughes, Ire) *hld up in 3rd: hdwy gng wl fr 2 out to chal: led briefly fr last: sn hdd u.p and kpt on wl towards fin wout matching wnr* **5/1**[3]

3 1 1/4 **Captain Cee Bee (IRE)**[28] 3402 13-11-10 149 .... MarkWalsh 160
(Edward P Harty, Ire) *led: reduced advantage bef 4th: rdn and strly pressed between last 2: hdd narrowly bef last: no imp on ldrs in 3rd run-in: kpt on wl towards fin to hold 3rd* **50/1**

4 1/2 **Jezki (IRE)**[28] 3402 6-11-10 166 .... APMcCoy 160+
(Mrs John Harrington, Ire) *settled in rr of quartet: t.k.h: nt fluent 5th: tk clsr order bhd ldrs fr 2 out where pushed along: clsd on outer and rdn bef last: no imp on ldrs run-in: kpt on same pce* **3/1**[2]

3m 53.0s (-14.50) **Going Correction** -0.725s/f (Firm) 4 Ran SP% **107.3**
Speed ratings: **107,106,105,105**
CSF £3.84 TOTE £1.50; DF 3.00 Trifecta £18.70.
Owner George Creighton & Mrs Rose Boyd **Bred** Agricola Del Parco **Trained** Muine Beag, Co Carlow

FOCUS
Hurricane Fly proved the quickest in a 2f sprint and is rated some way below his best.

3931a SYNERGY SECURITY SOLUTIONS NOVICE HURDLE (GRADE 2) (10 hdls) 2m 4f
3:10 (3:12) 5-Y-0+ **£21,395** (£6,254; £2,962; £987)

RPR

1 **Sure Reef (IRE)**[29] 3371 5-11-0 .... RWalsh 139+
(W P Mullins, Ire) *trckd ldrs in 3rd at mod early pce: tk clsr order in 2nd and tk keen bef 6th: lost pl 3 out and dropped to rr bef next: lost tch into st: rallied into 3rd bef last and styd on wl run-in to ld ins fnl 50yd* **9/4**[1]

2 3/4 **Moonshine Lad (IRE)**[31] 3311 6-11-3 130 .... PCarberry 140
(Gordon Elliott, Ire) *w.w at mod early pce: tk clsr order fr 3 out: cl 3rd bef next and rdn to ld bef last: sn strly pressed u.p and hdd ins fnl 50yds: no ex* **4/1**[2]

3 2 1/2 **Gilt Shadow (IRE)**[56] 2852 6-11-3 140 .... MrSCrawford 138
(S R B Crawford, Ire) *hld up at mod early pce: tk clsr order bhd ldrs bef 4 out and wnt 2nd bef next where nt fluent: rdn into st and no imp on ldrs in 4th fr last: kpt on wl into 3rd nr fin: nt trble principals* **9/4**[1]

4 1/2 **Wounded Warrior (IRE)**[14] 3681 5-11-0 .... BryanCooper 134
(Noel Meade, Ire) *trckd ldr in 2nd at mod early pce: lost pl bef 6th: pushed along in 4th bef 2 out: no imp on ldrs in 5th bef last where slt mstke: kpt on into nvr threatening 4th cl home* **9/2**[3]

5 1/2 **Gallant Tipp (IRE)**[66] 2638 6-11-3 128 .... APMcCoy 137
(E J O'Grady, Ire) *led at mod early pce: nt fluent 3rd: strly pressed fr 2 out and hdd bef last where nt fluent: sn no ex u.p in 3rd: wknd nr fin* **10/1**

6 5 1/2 **Mr Fiftyone (IRE)**[15] 3667 5-11-0 131 .... RobbiePower 128
(Mrs John Harrington, Ire) *chsd ldrs in 4th at mod early pce: mstke 3 out: rdn into st in 4th and sn no imp on ldrs: wknd bef last* **16/1**

4m 59.8s (-6.60) **Going Correction** -0.725s/f (Firm) 6 Ran SP% **114.7**
Speed ratings: **84,83,82,82,82 80**
CSF £12.13 TOTE £2.80: £1.60, £2.30; DF 13.10 Trifecta £38.20.
Owner Andrea & Graham Wylie **Bred** Michael Woodlock & Seamus Kennedy **Trained** Muine Beag, Co Carlow

FOCUS
A deeply unsatisfactory race. It's hard to imagine that any of these were particularly suited by the complete lack of any sort of gallop. The standard is set around the third, fourth and fifth.

3494 AYR (L-H)
Monday, January 27

OFFICIAL GOING: Heavy (chs 7.0; hdl 7.1)
Second fence in home st and last fence in back st omitted all chases. Divided bends and both tracks 6m from innermost line.
Wind: Light, half against Weather: Overcast

3934 BETVICTOR MERSEYSIDE DERBY RED CARD REFUND MARES' NOVICES' HURDLE (12 hdls) 2m 5f 110y
12:45 (12:45) (Class 4) 4-Y-0+ **£3,313** (£973; £486; £243)

Form RPR

1 **Layla Joan (IRE)**[26] 3481 6-11-6 0 .... JasonMaguire 123+
(Gordon Elliott, Ire) *hld up in last pl: smooth hdwy after 4 out: led gng wl 2 out: shkn up briefly and qcknd run-in: readily* **4/11**[1]

2- 2 3 1/4 **Nosey Box (IRE)**[23] 3523 8-10-9 102 .... (tp) DerekFox(5) 102
(Noel C Kelly, Ire) *in tch: effrt and pushed along 3 out: ev ch 2 out to last: kpt on: nt pce of ready wnr* **17/2**[2]

/41- 3 23 **Rinnagree Rosie**[25] 3495 8-11-6 103 .... AdrianLane 85
(Lucy Normile) *chsd ldrs: hdwy and ev ch 8th: drvn and outpcd after 3 out: sn n.d* **18/1**

4 6 **Midnight Streaker**[27] 3447 5-11-0 0 .... APMcCoy 76
(B Arthey, Ire) *cl up: led 7th to 2 out: sn pushed along: wkng whn j.lft last* **17/2**[2]

404- 5 33 **Beyondtemptation**[23] 3523 6-10-11 70 .... [1] JohnKington(3) 40
(Jonathan Haynes) *nt fluent: prom: effrt 4 out: hung lft and wknd next: hld whn mstke 2 out* **250/1**

02- P **Pixie Cut (IRE)**[18] 3613 4-9-11 0 .... CallumWhillans(5)
(Alistair Whillans) *t.k.h: led at stdy pce: hdd 7th: struggling after next: lost tch and p.u after 4 out* **16/1**[3]

5m 55.7s (15.40) **Going Correction** +0.60s/f (Soft)
WFA 4 from 5yo+ 12lb 6 Ran SP% **105.9**
Speed ratings (Par 105): **96,94,86,84,72**
CSF £3.54 TOTE £1.30: £1.02, £3.40; EX 4.00 Trifecta £15.10.
Owner W T Murphy **Bred** N Elliott **Trained** Trim, Co Meath

FOCUS
Divided bends and both tracks 6m from innermost line. An ordinary mares' event. It was steadily run and the winner is value for further.

3935 BETVICTOR NON-RUNNER FREE BET CHELTENHAM 2014 "NATIONAL HUNT" MAIDEN HURDLE (9 hdls) 2m
1:15 (1:16) (Class 5) 4-Y-0+ **£1,949** (£572; £286; £143)

Form RPR

442- 1 **Final Assault (IRE)**[24] 3516 5-11-4 110 .... PeterBuchanan 113+
(Lucinda Russell) *hld up in tch: stdy hdwy 1/2-way: chsd ldr 3 out: chalng whn lft 5 l clr last: kpt on strly* **7/4**[2]

2/4- 2 10 **Mclovin (IRE)**[15] 3679 8-11-1 0 .... MrSCrawford(3) 105
(S R B Crawford, Ire) *chsd ldrs: drvn 3 out: sn one pce: lft 5 l 2nd last: no imp* **6/4**[1]

/U5- 3 12 **Marrakech Trader (NZ)**[77] 2422 7-11-4 0 .... WilsonRenwick 87
(Rose Dobbin) *blnd 1st: hld up bhd ldng gp: rdn and outpcd 3 out: no imp fr next: lft 3rd last* **33/1**

4 15 **Haughtons Bridge (IRE)**[32] 3300 6-11-4 0 .... APMcCoy 72
(J J Lambe, Ire) *chsd clr ldr: clsd 1/2-way: ev ch 4 out: nt fluent and wknd next* **14/1**

/00- 5 32 **Marlee Mourinho (IRE)**[25] 3495 8-11-4 0 .... BrianHarding 40
(N W Alexander) *in tch: pushed along 1/2-way: lost tch fr 4 out: t.o* **150/1**

32- F **The Orange Rogue (IRE)**[25] 3494 7-11-4 0 .... LucyAlexander 110
(N W Alexander) *led and clr to 1/2-way: rdn and qcknd bef 3 out: rdn and jnd whn fell last* **7/2**[3]

4m 13.2s (10.10) **Going Correction** +0.60s/f (Soft) 6 Ran SP% **108.9**
Speed ratings (Par 103): **98,93,87,79,63**
CSF £4.61 TOTE £2.20: £1.50, £1.40; EX 4.60 Trifecta £39.50.
Owner Mrs S Russell & A M Russell **Bred** Gerard Mullins **Trained** Arlary, Perth & Kinross

FOCUS
Modest novice form. The cosy winner is on the upgrade.

3936 NON-RUNNER NO BET CHAMPIONSHIP RACES AT CHELTENHAM H'CAP CHASE (15 fncs 4 omitted) 3m 1f
1:45 (1:45) (Class 5) (0-100,100) 5-Y-0+ **£2,274** (£667; £333; £166)

Form RPR

5P3- 1 **Oil Burner**[25] 3498 9-11-7 95 .... BrianHarding 114+
(William Amos) *hld up: stdy hdwy 9th: pressed ldr 4 out (usual 6 out): led 2 out: styd on strly to draw clr fr last* **11/1**

6/3- 2 10 **Too Cool To Fool (IRE)**[25] 3497 11-10-7 81 .... JamesReveley 92
(Jim Goldie) *hld up in midfield: stdy hdwy to ld 11th: rdn and hdd 2 out: kpt on same pce fr last* **5/1**[2]

0P5- **3** *26* **The Shrimp (IRE)**[10] 3755 7-9-9 **74** oh16..................(p) HarryChalloner(5) 58
(Sandy Thomson) *chsd ldrs: mstke and outpcd 9th: sn struggling: sme late hdwy: no ch w first two* **66/1**

P/P- **4** *2 1/2* **Sam Patch**[264] 172 11-9-9 **74** oh1.............................. CallumWhillans(5) 55
(Donald Whillans) *hld up in midfield: stdy hdwy to chse ldrs 1/2-way: drvn and outpcd after 4 out (usual 6 out): btn fnl 2* **66/1**

4U2- **5** *shd* **Lord Fox (IRE)**[25] 3497 7-10-7 **86**.. BenPoste(5) 68
(Shaun Harris) *prom: hit 4 out (usual 6 out): rdn and wknd fr next* **11/4**[1]

4PF- **P** **Cottiers Den (IRE)**[32] 3283 7-10-11 **85**........................... WilsonRenwick
(Martin Todhunter) *nt fluent: sn towards rr and drvn along: lost tch and p.u bef 10th* **15/2**

444- **P** **Alexander Oats**[25] 3497 11-10-0 **74**................................(b) BrianHughes
(Robert Goldie) *led to 11th: rdn and outpcd next: wkng whn mstke 3 out (usual 4 out): p.u next* **11/1**

P **Paudi The Punter (IRE)**[32] 3297 8-11-6 **94**.................(tp) JasonMaguire
(Gordon Elliott, Ire) *hld up in midfield: hit and reminders 4th: struggling fr 6th: lost tch and p.u after 8th* **7/1**[3]

P22- **P** **Samson Collonges (FR)**[8] 3797 8-9-11 **74** oh2................. TonyKelly(3)
(Rebecca Menzies) *cl up: nt fluent 7th: mstke and outpcd 10th: wknd after 4 out (usual 6 out): t.o whn p.u bef 2 out* **7/1**[3]

/04- **P** **Fog Patches (IRE)**[29] 3394 8-11-5 **100**....................(p) GrantCockburn(7)
(Lucinda Russell) *bhd: struggling whn p.u and dismntd bef 5th* **12/1**

0/2- **P** **Cherry's Bay**[25] 3496 8-10-0 **74** oh25................................(b) AdrianLane
(Sandy Forster) *chsd ldrs tl lost pl qckly after 8th: t.o whn p.u bef next* **150/1**

220- **P** **Fozy Moss**[25] 3497 8-10-0 **81**.. DaraghBourke(7)
(Stuart Coltherd) *towards rr: drvn and outpcd bef 9th: losing tch whn p.u bef 11th* **22/1**

7m 7.2s (17.30) **Going Correction** +0.70s/f (Soft) **12** Ran SP% **112.5**
Speed ratings: **100,96,88,87,87** , , , , ,
CSF £62.29 CT £3422.44 TOTE £10.90: £3.10, £2.00, £13.80; EX 68.80 Trifecta £2941.90 Part won..
Owner J W Clark **Bred** J M Castle **Trained** Rochester, Northumberland

FOCUS
No less than seven of the 12 runners pulled up with the winner the only one to pass the stamina test.

3937 CHELTENHAM 2014 NRFB AT BETVICTOR.COM H'CAP HURDLE (9 hdls) 2m
2:15 (2:18) (Class 4) (0-120,117) 4-Y-0+ **£3,313** (£973; £486; £243)

Form RPR

566- **1** **Plus Jamais (FR)**[29] 3398 7-10-8 **99**.................................. BrianHughes 111+
(Jim Goldie) *pressed ldr: led 2 out: rdn clr fr last* **9/4**[1]

3P1- **2** *7* **Rhymers Stone**[37] 3210 6-10-7 **105**...............................(p) CraigNichol(7) 110
(Lucinda Russell) *led: rdn and jst hdd whn hit 2 out: one pce fr last* **3/1**[3]

530- **3** *8* **Endeavor**[10] 3758 9-10-13 **104**..(p) RyanMania 99
(Dianne Sayer) *chsd ldrs: rdn and outpcd appr 2 out: sn no imp w ldng pair* **20/1**

4P4/ **4** *2 1/2* **Shanroe Society (IRE)**[27] 3446 8-11-0 **105**........................... APMcCoy 99
(J J Lambe, Ire) *hld up in tch: pushed along after 4 out: effrt u.p next: edgd lft and sn no imp* **5/2**[2]

2- **5** *4* **Glenconkeyne (IRE)**[11] 3753 7-11-7 **117**..........................(t) DerekFox(5) 107
(Noel C Kelly, Ire) *nt fluent on occasions: hld up in tch: outpcd after 4 out: sn n.d* **10/1**

0- **6** *4 1/2* **Gunner Lindley (IRE)**[50] 2970 7-10-4 **102**.................. DaraghBourke(7) 89
(Stuart Coltherd) *hld up in tch: effrt after 4 out: outpcd whn hit next: sn btn* **8/1**

4m 12.2s (9.10) **Going Correction** +0.60s/f (Soft) **6** Ran SP% **109.3**
Speed ratings (Par 105): **101,97,93,92,90 88**
CSF £9.09 CT £89.28 TOTE £3.30: £1.50, £1.60; EX 9.10 Trifecta £87.30.
Owner Alba-Eire Syndicate **Bred** Ecurie Passing **Trained** Uplawmoor, E Renfrews

FOCUS
An uncompetitive handicap and a progressive winner who can probably win another.

3938 DOWNLOAD THE BETVICTOR APP NOW H'CAP HURDLE (12 hdls) 3m 110y
2:50 (2:50) (Class 4) (0-120,118) 4-Y-0+ **£3,313** (£973; £486; £243)

Form RPR

0/6- **1** **Chavoy (FR)**[16] 3661 9-11-9 **118**......................................(t) TonyKelly(3) 127+
(Rebecca Menzies) *confidently rdn in rr: smooth hdwy to ld bef 2 out: pushed along and edgd rt run-in: r.o strly* **16/1**

622- **2** *5* **Hellorboston (IRE)**[29] 3392 6-11-6 **112**.......................(b[1]) JasonMaguire 116+
(Donald McCain) *cl up: rdn and ev ch bef 2 out: kpt on same pce fr last* **7/2**[2]

136- **3** *11* **Amore Mio (GER)**[28] 3413 9-10-13 **105**......................(tp) PeterBuchanan 97
(Lucinda Russell) *chsd ldr: rdn bef 3 out: ev ch bef 2 out: sn outpcd by first two* **5/1**[3]

6P6- **4** *7* **Bescot Springs (IRE)**[29] 3396 9-10-8 **107**.....................(v) CraigNichol(7) 91
(Lucinda Russell) *prom: effrt and rdn after 3 out: wknd between last 2* **0/1**

3/3- **5** *15* **Little Boy Boru (IRE)**[25] 3495 6-10-10 **105**..................[1] MrSCrawford(3) 74
(S R B Crawford, Ire) *hld up: hdwy into midfield 1/2-way: rdn and wknd 4 out: sn btn* **5/1**[3]

3/F- **6** *21* **Grey Area (IRE)**[23] 3525 9-10-6 **105**.............................. DaraghBourke(7) 53
(Tristan Davidson) *nt fluent on occasions: led tl rdn and hdd bef 2 out: sn wknd: eased run-in* **5/2**[1]

210- **P** **Solis (GER)**[188] 867 11-10-13 **105**.....................................(p) RyanMania
(Dianne Sayer) *hld up in midfield: lost pl bef 7th: struggling fr next: t.o whn p.u bef 2 out* **33/1**

0P3/ **P** **City Of Doral**[51] 2964 12-10-12 **104**.. APMcCoy
(J J Lambe, Ire) *hld up: stdy hdwy bef 4 out: rdn bef next: hung lft and sn wknd: p.u bef 2 out* **12/1**

6m 42.5s (10.70) **Going Correction** +0.60s/f (Soft) **8** Ran SP% **110.6**
Speed ratings (Par 105): **106,104,100,98,93 87**, ,
CSF £67.94 CT £312.24 TOTE £16.80: £3.50, £1.40, £1.80; EX 67.00 Trifecta £347.70.
Owner Masoud Khadem **Bred** Jean-Luc Couetil Et Al **Trained** Stearsby, N Yorks

FOCUS
A moderate handicap and a step up from the impressive winner.

3939 BACK OF THE NET AT BETVICTOR.COM H'CAP CHASE (13 fncs 4 omitted) 2m 4f
3:20 (3:21) (Class 4) (0-115,115) 5-Y-0+ **£4,327** (£1,343; £723)

Form RPR

/P2- **1** **And The Man**[25] 3498 8-11-12 **115**.................................. BrianHarding 126+
(Nicky Richards) *hld up in tch: smooth hdwy to chse ldr after 3 out (usual 4 out): rdn to ld last: edgd lft run-in: styd on strly* **7/2**[3]

0/ **2** *3 1/4* **See Double You (IRE)**[21] 3580 11-10-5 **101**............. MrRMPMcNally(7) 109
(Ronan M P McNally, Ire) *t.k.h: chsd ldrs: led 4 out (usual 6 out): rdn whn pckd 2 out: hdd last: kpt on same pce run-in* **11/2**

263- **3** *30* **Allanard (IRE)**[30] 3355 10-11-1 **104**..............................(v) WilsonRenwick 82
(Martin Todhunter) *hld up in tch: drvn and outpcd 4 out (usual 6 out): wnt mod 3rd 2 out: no ch w first two* **12/1**

0/ **F** **Jim Bowie (IRE)**[22] 3562 9-10-10 **99**.. APMcCoy
(J J Lambe, Ire) *in tch: fell 6th* **9/4**[1]

/50- **P** **Lord Redsgirth (IRE)**[207] 883 9-11-7 **110**..................... DougieCostello
(Lucy Normile) *w ldr: led 3rd to 4 out (usual 6 out): rdn and wknd appr 3 out: t.o whn p.u bef last* **14/1**

131- **P** **Settledoutofcourt (IRE)**[29] 3397 8-11-11 **114**................ PeterBuchanan
(Lucinda Russell) *led to 3rd: w ldr: ev ch after 4 out (usual 6 out): rdn and wknd bef 2 out: p.u bef last* **5/2**[2]

5m 34.01s (11.11) **Going Correction** +0.70s/f (Soft) **6** Ran SP% **111.3**
Speed ratings: **105,103,91**, ,
CSF £21.73 TOTE £4.20: £1.80, £2.80; EX 26.10 Trifecta £176.10.
Owner Little Green Syndicate **Bred** A Buller **Trained** Greystoke, Cumbria

FOCUS
A modest handicap. The winner has the potential to rate higher.

3940 COME PLAY AT VICTOR'S LIVE CASINO H'CAP HURDLE (11 hdls) 2m 4f
3:50 (3:51) (Class 5) (0-100,98) 4-Y-0+ **£2,053** (£598; £299)

Form RPR

040- **1** **Ancient Times (USA)**[46] 3040 7-10-5 **80**........................(p) KyleJames(3) 90+
(Philip Kirby) *mde all: rdn and hrd pressed fr 3 out: drifted lft u.p run-in: styd on gamely* **10/3**[2]

F03- **2** *1/2* **W Six Times**[17] 3636 8-9-9 **72** oh5.............................. CallumWhillans(5) 81+
(Alistair Whillans) *t.k.h: prom: stdy hdwy to chal 2 out: carried lft u.p run-in: kpt on: hld towards fin* **3/1**[1]

2/4- **3** *7* **See The Legend**[57] 2843 9-10-13 **85**..................................... AdrianLane 85
(Sandy Forster) *chsd ldrs: effrt and ev ch 3 out: rdn whn nt fluent next: outpcd by first two fr last* **16/1**

354- **4** *1/2* **Knight Valliant**[18] 3618 11-10-12 **91**........................ MissEButterworth(7) 91
(Barbara Butterworth) *hld up: stdy hdwy bef 3 out: kpt on fr last: nvr able to chal* **14/1**

0/0- **5** *8* **The Starboard Bow**[24] 3518 7-11-12 **98**.......................(p) PeterBuchanan 90
(Lucinda Russell) *t.k.h in midfield: pushed along after 4 out: rallied bef next: wknd after 2 out* **22/1**

66F- **6** *20* **Northern Acres**[23] 3525 8-11-6 **92**.................................. LucyAlexander 64
(N W Alexander) *t.k.h: hld up: hit 4 out: effrt bef next: sn wknd* **9/2**[3]

P02- **7** *36* **Acordingtoscript (IRE)**[30] 3356 8-10-13 **85**................... WilsonRenwick 21
(Martin Todhunter) *hld up: hdwy and in tch bef 4 out: rdn and wknd fr next* **6/1**

104- **8** *6* **Amethyst Rose (IRE)**[29] 3396 7-11-0 **93**..................... DaraghBourke(7) 23
(Stuart Coltherd) *hld up: rdn and outpcd after 4 out: btn next* **5/1**

350- **P** **Mrs Grass**[17] 3636 7-9-11 **72**.. JohnKington(3)
(Jonathan Haynes) *cl up tl wknd after 4 out: t.o whn p.u bef next* **66/1**

5m 27.7s (15.70) **Going Correction** +0.60s/f (Soft) **9** Ran SP% **115.6**
Speed ratings (Par 103): **92,91,89,88,85 77,63,60**,
CSF £14.18 CT £137.70 TOTE £4.50: £1.40, £2.20, £2.80; EX 17.60 Trifecta £256.40.
Owner L & D Racing **Bred** Ocala Horses, Llc **Trained** Middleham, N Yorks
■ Stewards' Enquiry : Kyle James three-day ban: careless riding (Feb 10-12); two-day ban: used whip above permitted level (Feb 13-14)

FOCUS
A weak affair with a tight finish. The winner was well treated on last year's C&D win.
T/Plt: £43.80 to a £1 stake. Pool: £99,691.48 - 1660.55 winning units. T/Qpdt: £31.40 to a £1 stake. Pool: £7740.52 - 181.90 winning units. RY

3686 PLUMPTON (L-H)
Monday, January 27
3941 Meeting Abandoned - Waterlogged

3229 LINGFIELD (L-H)
Tuesday, January 28
3948 Meeting Abandoned - waterlogged

3782 TAUNTON (R-H)
Tuesday, January 28

OFFICIAL GOING: Heavy (4.2)
The two middle fences in the back straight were omitted in all chases due to ground. All bends moved out 2-4 yds.
Wind: quite strong across Weather: showers

3955 BHEST RACING TO SCHOOL CONDITIONAL JOCKEYS' H'CAP HURDLE (12 hdls) 3m 110y
1:40 (1:40) (Class 5) (0-100,107) 4-Y-0+ **£2,737** (£798; £399)

Form RPR

031- **1** **Waldorf Salad**[4] 3878 6-12-2 **107** 7ex......................... HarryChalloner(3) 128+
(Venetia Williams) *mde all: clr 9th: nt fluent 2 out: styd on dourly: pushed out* **5/4**[1]

P66- **2** *3 1/2* **Comical Red**[14] 3699 6-9-9 **74** oh5....................(b[1]) ThomasCheesman(5) 87+
(Mark Gillard) *trckd ldrs: rdn to chse wnr appr 3 out: drew wl clr of remainder: keeping on whn nodded last but a being hld* **28/1**

42P- **3** *19* **Blazing Bouncer**[40] 3179 9-11-7 **95**...............................(tp) MichealNolan 89
(Richard Woollacott) *hld up: hdwy after 7th: rdn into 3rd 3 out: sn wknd: t.o* **20/1**

030- **4** *17* **General Girling**[14] 3699 7-10-4 **78**... JamesBest 55
(Caroline Keevil) *trckd wnr tl rdn after 8th: wknd bef 3 out: t.o* **20/1**

35U- **5** *1/2* **Kalamill (IRE)**[47] 3044 7-11-12 **100**...............................(t) PeterCarberry 77
(Shaun Lycett) *hld up towards rr: stdy prog fr after 7th: rdn into btn 4th after 3 out: sn wknd: t.o* **12/1**

443- **6** *75* **Bob Keown (IRE)**[37] 3227 6-11-2 **98**..................................... PaulO'Brien(8)
(Rebecca Curtis) *trckd ldrs: pushed along after 3rd: in rr 7th: t.o fr next: continued* **3/1**[2]

/00- **P** **Count Vettori (IRE)**[14] 3699 8-10-13 **95** JonPark(8)
(Kevin Bishop) *struggling 7th: a in rr: tailing off whn p.u bef 9th* **25/1**
F05- **P** **June French (FR)**[28] 3434 6-10-0 **74** oh5 (t) ConorShoemark
(Giles Smyly) *trckd ldrs tl drvn after 7th: qckly lost tch: p.u bef next* **33/1**
/43- **P** **Uncle Pettit (IRE)**[43] 3138 6-10-10 **84** HarryDerham
(Jonathan Portman) *mid-div tl wknd: t.o whn p.u bef 3 out* **17/2**[3]
43P- **P** **Redlynch Rock (IRE)**[93] 2110 6-11-2 **95** (t) GaryDerwin(5)
(Bob Buckler) *prom tl rdn after 8th: sn bhd: t.o whn p.u bef 3 out* **50/1**
P05- **P** **Langarve Lady (IRE)**[33] 3289 6-10-10 **84** (p) MichaelByrne
(Neil Mulholland) *trckd ldrs: awkward on landing 1st: nudged along after 4th: losing pl whn rdn after 7th: tailing off whn p.u bef 9th* **14/1**

6m 43.5s (39.50) **Going Correction** +1.825s/f (Heav) **11** Ran SP% **116.0**
Speed ratings (Par 103): **109,107,101,96,96 72,,,,**
CSF £44.69 CT £495.78 TOTE £2.40: £1.20, £7.90, £3.70; EX 40.90 Trifecta £706.10.
Owner Alan Parker **Bred** A Parker **Trained** Kings Caple, H'fords

FOCUS
All bends moved out 2-4 yds. The course passed a morning inspection and, for the second meeting running, the going was very hard work. This weak handicap for conditional riders rather fell apart as the majority struggled to handle such taxing ground. Arguably another step forward from the winner.

3956 EPDS RACING WELFARE BTO SERIES 2014 NOVICES' HURDLE (9 hdls) 2m 1f
2:10 (2:11) (Class 4) 4-Y-0+ **£3,935** (£1,147; £573)

Form RPR
/13- **1** **Milo Man (IRE)**[21] 3592 6-11-11 127 PaulMoloney 133+
(Evan Williams) *nt a fluent: led: hdd after 3 out: led again bef next: styd on strly to draw clr bef last: comf* **4/6**[1]
2 *11* **Liberty One (IRE)**[65] 8-11-4 0 DarylJacob 109+
(Richard Woollacott) *mid-div: wnt 16 l 4th 2 out: styd on wl fr last: wnt 2nd towards fin but no ch w wnr* **20/1**
/34- **3** *3/4* **Thomas Junior (FR)**[20] 3598 5-11-4 0 TomScudamore 107
(David Pipe) *trckd wnr: chal 3 out: sn led: rdn and hdd bef next: sn hld: no ex whn lost 2nd towards fin* **4/1**[2]
4 *9* **John Louis**[535] 6-11-4 0 AidanColeman 100
(Venetia Williams) *trckd ldrs: rdn into 3rd after 3 out: wknd last* **7/1**[3]
060- **5** *3 1/4* **Henwood (IRE)**[80] 2369 6-11-4 0 JoeTizzard 95
(Colin Tizzard) *t.k.h early: hdwy into midfield 3rd: no ch w ldrs fr 3 out: plugged on* **50/1**
401- **6** *1* **All But Grey**[10] 3783 8-11-8 108 MichealNolan(3) 102
(Carroll Gray) *in tch: trckd ldrs 4th: chalng whn mstke 3 out: sn rdn and wknd* **14/1**
0P- **7** *25* **Passing Fiesta**[231] 715 5-10-11 0 WillKennedy 62
(Sarah-Jayne Davies) *mid-div tl wknd 3 out: t.o* **150/1**
0/P- **8** *1 1/2* **Le Pergolese (FR)**[43] 3134 8-11-1 0 [1] MarkQuinlan(3) 68
(Nigel Hawke) *nt a fluent: a towards rr: t.o fr after 5th* **200/1**
/00- **9** *4 1/2* **Exmoor Mist**[31] 3357 6-11-4 0 JackDoyle 63
(Victor Dartnall) *mid-div tl wknd after 6th: t.o* **20/1**
004/ **10** *11* **Calusa Star**[302] 5065 5-11-4 0 RichardJohnson 52
(Philip Hobbs) *trckd ldrs tl lost pl after 4th: wknd after 6th: t.o* **14/1**
0/ **11** *2 1/4* **Indiana Oscar**[263] 211 6-10-11 0 MrRobertHawker(7) 50
(Carroll Gray) *mid-div tl after 5th: sn t.o* **100/1**
P **Medal Of Valour (JPN)**[824] 6-11-4 0 TommyPhelan
(Mark Gillard) *trckd ldrs tl 5th: sn bhd: t.o whn p.u bef 3 out* **125/1**
0/ **P** **Artists Boy**[292] 5262 7-11-4 0 JamesDavies
(Chris Down) *nt fluent 2nd: a towards rr: t.o after 5th: p.u after next* **200/1**
003- **F** **Billy My Boy**[12] 3746 5-11-1 0 GilesHawkins(3)
(Chris Down) *a towards rr: tailing off whn fell 3 out* **66/1**

4m 38.3s (30.30) **Going Correction** +1.825s/f (Heav) **14** Ran SP% **122.2**
Speed ratings (Par 105): **101,95,95,91,89 89,77,76,74,69 68,,,**
CSF £21.21 TOTE £2.00: £1.30, £5.00, £1.10; EX 24.00 Trifecta £101.10.
Owner Mr & Mrs William Rucker **Bred** S G Deacon **Trained** Llancarfan, Vale Of Glamorgan

FOCUS
Little strength in depth to this novice hurdle and the form is straightforward enough. The winner is rated in line with his bumper win.

3957 BATHWICK TYRES H'CAP HURDLE (9 hdls) 2m 1f
2:40 (2:40) (Class 3) (0-135,132) 4-Y-0+ **£5,848** (£1,717; £858; £429)

Form RPR
3/4- **1** **Helium (FR)**[263] 202 9-10-1 **114** MrsAlexDunn(7) 116+
(Alexandra Dunn) *t.k.h: trckd ldrs: led narrowly 3rd: disp after 3 out: hdd briefly run-in: edgd lft: hld on* **17/2**
/04- **2** *hd* **Chesil Beach Boy**[12] 3744 11-11-4 **129** (t) MrsMRoberts(5) 131+
(John Coombe) *hld up bhd ldrs: trckd ldrs 4th: chal 6th: j.rt last 2: rdn into narrow advantage briefly run-in: kpt on: jst hld* **5/1**[3]
/10- **3** *15* **Moujik Borget (FR)**[17] 3648 6-11-7 **127** AidanColeman 114
(Venetia Williams) *trckd ldrs: kpt to inner in home st: chal briefly after 3 out: sn rdn: hld in 3rd fr next: fdd run-in* **3/1**[1]
016- **4** *3 1/2* **Shammick Boy (IRE)**[40] 3169 9-11-12 **132** JackDoyle 117
(Victor Dartnall) *trckd ldrs: rdn along fr after 4th: styd chsng ldrs but nt pce to mount chal fr after 3 out: fading in 4th whn mstke last* **6/1**
115- **5** *2 1/2* **Get It On (IRE)**[31] 3362 9-10-10 **123** ConorRing(7) 104
(Evan Williams) *trckd ldrs: rdn after 3 out: wknd next* **7/2**[2]
350- **6** *7* **Decoy (FR)**[12] 3744 8-10-5 **118** (p) MikeyEnnis(7) 92
(David Pipe) *led tl 3rd: w wnr tl rdn after 5th: hld fr 3 out: wknd 2 out* **3/1**[1]

4m 35.1s (27.10) **Going Correction** +1.825s/f (Heav) **6** Ran SP% **113.7**
Speed ratings (Par 107): **109,108,101,100,99 95**
CSF £49.22 TOTE £10.00: £4.00, £2.70; EX 50.70 Trifecta £230.90.
Owner Dunn Racing **Bred** Adrian Von Gunten **Trained** Wellington, Somerset
■ Stewards' Enquiry : Mrs Alex Dunn caution: careless riding

FOCUS
A tight-looking handicap, run at a routine gallop, and the first pair had it to themselves from the top of the home straight. The winner was well in on his course win last year.

3958 IRIS SHARP MEMORIAL H'CAP CHASE (13 fncs 4 omitted) 2m 7f 110y
3:10 (3:10) (Class 4) (0-115,115) 5-Y-0+ **£4,327** (£1,343; £723)

Form RPR
1P3- **1** **Royal Chatelier (FR)**[7] 3827 9-11-4 **110** MichealNolan(3) 115
(Michael Blake) *trckd ldrs: rdn on long run after 9th: wnt 8 l 2nd after 4 out: 3 l down last: str run fnl 75yds: led nr fin* **8/1**
111- **2** *nk* **Milosam (IRE)**[29] 3421 7-10-0 **89** (b) TomO'Brien 97+
(Philip Hobbs) *trckd ldr: disp most of way fr 4th: outrt ldr after 9th: 8 l clr after 4 out: sn rdn: 3 l up last: no ex whn hdd towards fin* **2/1**[1]
622- **3** *31* **Tin Pot Man (IRE)**[68] 2619 8-10-6 **95** (t) PaulMoloney 80
(Evan Williams) *in tch: rdn bef 4 out: wnt 3rd bef 3 out: nvr rchd ldrs: wknd and eased last* **5/1**[3]
F03- **P** **Donnas Palm (IRE)**[33] 3246 10-11-11 **114** (vt) JamieMoore
(Gary Moore) *nt a fluent: led: rchd for 2nd: jnd 4th: rdn and hdd on long run after 9th: wknd bef 4 out where lft 4th: pckd bdly 2 out: sn p.u* **9/1**
0- **P** **Friendly Society (IRE)**[46] 3065 9-11-5 **113** (b) ThomasGarner(5)
(Noel Williams) *missed s: last: awkward and nrly uns rdr 3rd: mstke next: reminders: rdn after 8th: losing tch whn hit next: t.o whn p.u bef 4 out* **13/2**
422- **U** **Mentalist (FR)**[7] 3820 6-11-12 **115** AidanColeman
(Venetia Williams) *disp 4th most of way: rdn on long run after 9th: wkng whn uns rdr 4 out* **11/4**[2]

6m 35.8s (19.80) **Going Correction** +0.925s/f (Soft) **6** Ran SP% **111.1**
Speed ratings: **104,103,93,,,**
CSF £24.77 TOTE £9.70: £3.60, £1.40; EX 30.90 Trifecta £114.90.
Owner The Moonlighters **Bred** Marc Trinquet And Olivier Trinquet **Trained** Trowbridge, Wilts
■ Stewards' Enquiry : Micheal Nolan seven-day ban: use of whip (12-17 Feb)

FOCUS
There was no hanging around in this modest staying handicap.

3959 AID TRAINING H'CAP HURDLE (10 hdls) 2m 3f 110y
3:40 (3:40) (Class 4) (0-110,108) 4-Y-0+ **£3,935** (£1,147; £573)

Form RPR
/31- **1** **Come On Annie**[28] 3428 8-10-12 **101** MrsAlexDunn(7) 118+
(Alexandra Dunn) *hld up bhd: smooth prog after 6th: wnt sltly lft 3 out: wnt 2nd after 3 out: led sn after last: eased ahd: readily* **11/2**[3]
062- **2** *3* **Midnight Request**[7] 3821 5-10-6 **88** FelixDeGiles 98+
(Tom Symonds) *led: pushed clr after 3 out: rdn and jnd whn nt fluent last: sn hdd and hld: kpt on same pce* **7/4**[1]
0/4- **3** *36* **Extremely So**[29] 3420 8-11-4 **100** JamesDavies 74
(Chris Down) *trckd ldr: rdn 3 out: lost 2nd bef next: wknd between last 2: jst hld on for modest 3rd* **14/1**
FP4- **4** *shd* **Should I Stay (FR)**[33] 3249 6-11-6 **105** (p) JoshuaMoore(3) 79
(Gary Moore) *in tch: trckd ldrs 4th: rdn after 3 out: sn no ch: plugged on: jst failed to snatch modest 3rd fnl stride* **20/1**
001- **5** *17* **Withy Mills**[10] 3788 9-10-2 **87** (bt) JamesBest(3) 44
(Kevin Bishop) *trckd ldrs: hit 2nd: rdn after 7th: wknd after 3 out: t.o* **16/1**
050- **6** *5* **Lady Bridget**[15] 3692 6-9-7 **82** oh1 (bt) ThomasCheesman(7) 34
(Mark Gillard) *trckd ldrs: rdn after 7th: sn wknd: t.o* **25/1**
032- **7** *7* **Bedouin Bay**[40] 3174 7-11-2 **105** MrRobertHawker(7) 50
(Johnny Farrelly) *hld up towards rr: hdwy 6th: rdn 3 out: wknd qckly: t.o* **12/1**
05F- **8** *dist* **Sedgemoor Top Bid (IRE)**[40] 3176 6-11-0 **99** MarkQuinlan(3)
(Nigel Hawke) *trckd ldrs: rdn along after 3rd: wknd after 6th: continued wl-t.o* **100/1**
055- **P** **River Dancing (IRE)**[33] 3290 7-10-12 **94** NickScholfield
(Andy Turnell) *mid-div tl wknd appr 3 out: t.o whn p.u bef 2 out* **25/1**
566- **P** **Hassadin**[107] 1890 8-10-6 **95** JoshWall(7)
(Michael Blake) *mid-div: struggling to hold pl after 6th: wknd bef 3 out: t.o whn p.u bef 2 out* **4/1**[2]
54F- **P** **Delphi Mountain (IRE)**[65] 2696 9-11-4 **103** MichealNolan(3)
(Richard Woollacott) *mid-div: blnd 1st: wknd after 7th: t.o whn p.u after 3 out* **33/1**
000- **P** **Kartanian (IRE)**[29] 3420 8-11-5 **101** (b) RichardJohnson
(Philip Hobbs) *mid-div on outer: lost pl after 5th: sme prog u.p 7th: wknd sn after 3 out: p.u bef next* **7/1**
P0/- **P** **Green Hackle (IRE)**[283] 5410 9-11-12 **108** SamJones
(Oliver Sherwood) *in tch on outer: rdn after 5th: wknd after next: t.o whn p.u after 3 out* **50/1**

5m 20.9s (34.90) **Going Correction** +1.825s/f (Heav) **13** Ran SP% **122.8**
Speed ratings (Par 105): **103,101,87,87,80 78,75,59,,,,,**
CSF £15.39 CT £135.68 TOTE £6.40: £2.10, £1.40, £4.30; EX 19.30 Trifecta £152.40.
Owner Mrs Ann Trotman **Bred** Mickley Stud **Trained** Wellington, Somerset

FOCUS
A moderate handicap, run at a sound gallop considering underfoot conditions. Another big step forward from the winner and the second should still be competitive off his new mark.

3960 ATLAS PACKAGING H'CAP CHASE (8 fncs 4 omitted) 2m 110y
4:10 (4:10) (Class 4) (0-120,115) 5-Y-0+ **£4,223** (£1,240; £620; £310)

Form RPR
542- **1** **Al Alfa**[17] 3652 7-11-12 **115** RichardJohnson 126+
(Philip Hobbs) *mde all: nt fluent 3 out and 2 out: kpt on wl: rdn out* **5/4**[1]
145- **2** *3 1/2* **Lord Of The Dunes**[15] 3690 6-10-13 **102** (t) JoeTizzard 107
(Colin Tizzard) *disp 4th: wnt 3rd gng to 4 out: rdn to chse wnr 3 out: kpt on but a being hld fr next* **7/2**[2]
/F5- **3** *12* **Coolbeg (IRE)**[54] 2895 8-10-13 **102** FelixDeGiles 95
(Heather Main) *disp 4th: rdn after 4 out: wnt 3rd after next: kpt on same pce* **12/1**
532- **4** *1* **Benny The Swinger (IRE)**[68] 2629 9-10-5 **94** TomCannon 87
(Chris Gordon) *trckd ldrs: hit 2nd: chal 4 out: sn rdn: hld bef next: sn lost 2nd: kpt on same pce* **6/1**[3]
3/3- **5** *15* **Mon Chevalier (IRE)**[68] 2629 11-11-4 **110** MichealNolan(3) 94
(Carroll Gray) *hld up but in tch: rdn bef 4 out: nt pce to get involved: wknd bef last* **10/1**
P36- **P** **The Sneezer (IRE)**[14] 3693 11-11-4 **107** NickScholfield
(Alexandra Dunn) *trckd ldr: shkn up after 3rd: drvn after next: wknd bef 4 out: t.o whn p.u bef 3 out* **10/1**
/6P- **P** **Cranky Corner**[45] 3093 10-10-8 **104** ChrisDavies(7)
(Helen Nelmes) *hld up: sme hdwy on long run after 4th: nvr threatened ldrs: wknd 4 out: tailing off whn p.u bef next* **40/1**

4m 27.2s (13.20) **Going Correction** +0.925s/f (Soft) **7** Ran SP% **109.3**
Speed ratings: **105,103,97,97,90**
CSF £5.76 CT £28.27 TOTE £2.10: £1.20, £2.00; EX 5.90 Trifecta £43.70.
Owner James Drummond **Bred** Countess Goess-Saurau **Trained** Withycombe, Somerset

FOCUS
Not a bad handicap for the grade and it was run at a solid gallop. There was a long run to the first, as what would normally have been the opening fence was omitted. Arguably a personal best from the winner.

3961 EBF STALLIONS MARES' STANDARD OPEN NATIONAL HUNT FLAT RACE 2m 1f
4:40 (4:40) (Class 5) 4-7-Y-0 **£2,737** (£798; £399)

Form RPR
1 **Rhythm Star** 4-10-5 0 BrendanPowell 97+
(Jamie Snowden) *mid-div: hdwy 1/2-way: disp 2nd 4f out: rdn over 2f out: led over 1f out: styd on wl* **14/1**
2/ **2** *2 3/4* **Western Diva (IRE)**[274] 35 5-11-2 0 TomScudamore 104
(David Pipe) *led: rdn 2f out: sn hdd: kpt on same pce* **11/4**[2]

The Form Book Jumps, Raceform Ltd, Compton, RG20 6NL.

50- **3** 1 **Buckboru (IRE)**[71] 2570 6-11-2 0 DougieCostello 103
(Laura Young) *hld up towards rr: hdwy fr 4f out: rdn in 4th over 2f out: styd on wl but nvr quite rching ldrs* **100/1**

2- **4** 15 **Ivor's Queen (IRE)**[75] 2479 5-11-2 0 JoeTizzard 88
(Colin Tizzard) *trckd ldrs: rdn over 2f out: wknd over 1f out* **9/4**[1]

20- **5** 16 **Makadamia**[62] 2752 5-10-11 0 MrSWaley-Cohen(5) 72
(David Pipe) *mid-div tl wknd over 3f out: t.o* **7/2**[3]

6 1 ¾ **Catcharose (IRE)** 4-10-5 0 FelixDeGiles 59
(Jennifer Mason) *hld up towards rr: sme prog 4f out: sn rdn: wknd over 2f out: t.o* **50/1**

63- **7** 11 **Dream Destiny**[33] 3295 5-11-2 0 (t) TommyPhelan 59
(Mark Gillard) *trckd ldr tl rdn 4f out: wknd 3f out: t.o* **33/1**

0- **8** 8 **Bow Quest**[244] 544 7-10-13 0 JoshuaMoore(3) 51
(Gary Moore) *hld up towards rr: midfield 6f out: rdn over 4f out: wknd 3f out: t.o* **33/1**

5- **9** 2 ½ **Kentford Myth**[41] 3167 4-9-12 0 KevinJones(7) 38
(Seamus Mullins) *mid-div: struggling 1/2-way: sn bhd: t.o* **13/2**

10 1 ¼ **Over The Air** 6-11-2 0 JamieMoore 48
(John Spearing) *trckd ldrs: rdn over 4f out: sn wknd: t.o* **25/1**

0- **11** 14 **Mrs Winchester (IRE)**[47] 3049 5-11-2 0 IanPopham 34
(Caroline Keevil) *mid-div tl wknd 5f out: t.o* **66/1**

12 dist **Festival Folklore (IRE)** 6-11-2 0 LeightonAspell
(Henry Oliver) *chsd ldrs tl 6f out: sn wl bhd: t.o* **33/1**

13 47 **Mini Island (IRE)** 5-10-9 0 MrRobertHawker(7)
(Richard Hawker) *a in rr: t.o fnl 5f* **80/1**

4m 40.2s (37.80) **Going Correction** +1.825s/f (Heav)
WFA 4 from 5yo 11lb 5 from 6yo+ 3lb **13 Ran SP% 118.0**
Speed ratings: **84,82,82,75,67 66,61,57,56,56 49,28,6**
CSF £49.71 TOTE £20.90: £4.30, £1.40, £8.60; EX 77.80 Trifecta £4327.50 Part won..
Owner ValueRacingClub.co.uk **Bred** Mrs J A Thomas **Trained** Lambourn, Berks

FOCUS
A fair mares' bumper, run at an ordinary gallop, and the form is rated around the runner-up and the fourth.
T/Jkpt: Not won. T/Plt: £22.60 to a £1 stake. Pool: £146,647.51 - 4731.97 winning units. T/Qpdt: £19.40 to a £1 stake. Pool: £10,156.98 - 386.45 winning units. TM

3816 LEICESTER (R-H)
Wednesday, January 29
3962 Meeting Abandoned - Waterlogged.

3728 LUDLOW (R-H)
Wednesday, January 29
3968 Meeting Abandoned - Waterlogged

3721 NEWCASTLE (L-H)
Wednesday, January 29
3975 Meeting Abandoned - Waterlogged.

3796 TOWCESTER (R-H)
Thursday, January 30
3982 Meeting Abandoned - waterlogged

3741 WINCANTON (R-H)
Thursday, January 30

OFFICIAL GOING: Heavy (soft in places)
Hurdle on stable bend omitted on all circuits of all hurdle races. Start of 2m5f chase moved to road crossing.
Wind: mild across Weather: overcast

3988 FITANDFURNISH.CO.UK NOVICES' HURDLE (7 hdls 1 omitted) 2m
1:40 (1:45) (Class 3) 4-Y-0+ **£5,523** (£1,621; £810; £405)

Form RPR
0/1- **1** **Vieux Lion Rouge (FR)**[14] 3747 5-11-8 0 TomScudamore 118+
(David Pipe) *mde all: in command whn lft clr 2 out: unchal* **1/4**[1]

506- **2** 6 **Steel Summit (IRE)**[14] 3728 5-10-11 0 AnthonyFreeman(5) 100
(David Dennis) *mid-div: hdwy after 3 out: rdn whn lft 2nd and hmpd 2 out: styd on but no ch w wnr* **33/1**

05P- **3** 10 **Amazing Scenes (IRE)**[28] 3506 5-11-2 0 (t) BrendanPowell 89
(Brendan Powell) *w wnr tl rdn after 3 out: lft 3rd next: styd on same pce* **20/1**

0- **4** 1 ½ **King's Warrior (FR)**[14] 3728 7-11-2 0 PaddyBrennan 88
(Tom George) *hld up towards rr: hdwy into midfield 3 out: styd on steadily fr next: lft 4th 2 out: nvr threatened ldrs* **8/1**[3]

000- **5** 3 ½ **Ma'Ire Rua (IRE)**[56] 2906 7-11-2 0 JackDoyle 84
(Alan Jones) *t.k.h early: mid-div: rdn after 3 out: styd on same pce fr next* **100/1**

0- **6** 1 **A Keen Sense (GER)**[30] 3440 5-11-2 0 AidanColeman 83
(David Dennis) *mid-div: rdn after 3 out: styd on same pce fr next: nvr a threat* **50/1**

/5F- **7** 4 ½ **Upham Running (IRE)**[47] 3092 6-11-2 0 LiamTreadwell 79
(Kate Buckett) *hld up towards rr: nt fluent 3rd: hdwy after 3 out: rdn bef next: no further imp* **100/1**

8 ½ **Dream Lucky** 9-10-13 0 MattGriffiths(3) 78
(Richard Woollacott) *mid-div tl lost pl 4th: sme late prog but nvr any danger after* **66/1**

540- **9** nk **Bostin (IRE)**[16] 3694 6-10-11 0 HarryDerham(5) 78
(Brian Barr) *mid-div tl wknd after 3 out* **50/1**

60- **10** 2 **Early Bonnet (IRE)**[14] 3728 6-10-4 0 EdCookson(5) 69
(Kim Bailey) *mid-div tl wknd after 3 out* **50/1**

2U- **11** 28 **Springhill Lad**[16] 3694 7-11-2 0 MarkGrant 48
(Geoffrey Deacon) *a towards rr: t.o after 3 out* **25/1**

0U0- **12** 18 **No No Cardinal (IRE)**[128] 1643 5-11-2 81 (t1) TommyPhelan 30
(Mark Gillard) *trckd ldrs tl wknd after 3 out: t.o* **100/1**

/51- **F** **Lady Charisma**[61] 2824 5-11-1 0 RichardJohnson 100
(Philip Hobbs) *trckd ldrs: wnt 2nd after 3 out: pushed along and 2 l down whn fell next* **7/2**[2]

3m 56.8s (7.90) **Going Correction** +0.475s/f (Soft) **13 Ran SP% 135.2**
Speed ratings (Par 107): **99,96,91,90,88 88,85,85,85,84 70,61,**
CSF £24.74 TOTE £1.60: £1.02, £6.40, £4.40; EX 17.90 Trifecta £199.00.
Owner Prof Caroline Tisdall & John Gent **Bred** F M Cottin **Trained** Nicholashayne, Devon

FOCUS
Start of 2m5f chase moved to road crossing. The ground was riding as advertised, but was quite holding. There was little depth to this novice hurdle. The easy winner was value for further and is sure to rate higher.

3989 NEW RACING UK ANYWHERE AVAILABLE NOW H'CAP HURDLE (9 hdls 1 omitted) 2m 4f
2:10 (2:15) (Class 3) (0-140,138) 4-Y-0+
£12,512 (£3,696; £1,848; £924; £462; £232)

Form RPR
40P- **1** **Alder Mairi (IRE)**[34] 3319 7-10-8 **120** AndrewThornton 128+
(Seamus Mullins) *trckd ldrs: led appr 2 out: styd on wl: rdn out* **18/1**

42- **2** 2 **Silsol (GER)**[22] 3023 5-10-9 **121** (t) DarylJacob 126
(Paul Nicholls) *mid-div: pckd 5th: hdwy 3 out: rdn to chse ldrs bef 2 out: styd on but a being hld by wnr fr last* **7/1**[3]

214- **3** 1 ¾ **Bygones Sovereign (IRE)**[19] 3653 8-10-3 **122** (p) TomBellamy(7) 125
(David Pipe) *led: clr 3rd tl 5th: sn pushed along: rdn and hdd appr 2 out: kpt on gamely to regain 3rd at the last: styd on* **6/1**[2]

114- **4** 10 **Shantou Magic (IRE)**[33] 3367 7-11-12 **138** NoelFehily 134
(Charlie Longsdon) *mid-div: hdwy appr 6th: rdn to dispute 2nd but hanging rt fr 2 out: hld in 3rd whn nt fluent last: wknd* **10/3**[1]

50F- **5** 5 **Veauce De Sivola (FR)**[21] 3615 5-10-2 **114** RichardJohnson 102
(Nick Williams) *hld up bhd: hdwy fr 6th: rdn in 7th after 3 out: nvr threatened ldrs: wknd bef last* **10/1**

P20- **6** ¾ **Old Tricks (IRE)**[14] 3741 7-10-1 **120** (t) MrMLegg(7) 108
(Colin Tizzard) *mid-div early: pushed along towards rr 3rd: styd on again appr 2 out but nvr any danger* **9/1**

021- **7** 10 **Uhlan Bute (FR)**[17] 3686 6-11-1 **127** AidanColeman 107
(Venetia Williams) *chsd ldr tl rdn appr 2 out: wknd* **7/1**[3]

0P0- **8** 3 ¾ **Union Saint (FR)**[14] 3744 6-10-13 **125** HaddenFrost 99
(James Frost) *a towards rr* **33/1**

200- **9** 2 **Quaddick Lake (IRE)**[14] 3744 11-10-13 **125** BrendanPowell 97
(Jeremy Scott) *mid-div: rdn after 3 out: wknd next* **16/1**

114/ **10** 11 **Minella Special (IRE)**[289] 5340 8-9-13 **118** MrGBranton(7) 79
(Paul Henderson) *a bhd: t.o* **33/1**

5F- **11** 4 ½ **Ainsi Fideles (FR)**[65] 2733 4-10-2 **126** (tp) TomScudamore 83+
(David Pipe) *trckd ldrs: led briefly appr 2 out: sn rdn: fnd nil: eased whn btn between last 2* **15/2**

210/ **12** 51 **Martial Law (IRE)**[474] 770 8-10-1 **113** (p) ConorO'Farrell 18
(David Pipe) *bhd fr 6th: t.o* **25/1**

4P3- **P** **Bravo Bravo**[14] 3741 7-10-1 **113** (b) PaddyBrennan
(Mark Gillard) *chsd ldrs tl wknd 6th: t.o whn p.u bef 2 out* **20/1**

5m 4.2s (7.40) **Going Correction** +0.625s/f (Soft)
WFA 4 from 5yo+ 12lb **13 Ran SP% 118.9**
Speed ratings (Par 107): **110,109,108,104,102 102,98,96,95,91 89,69,**
CSF £133.50 CT £856.95 TOTE £26.10: £5.20, £2.50, £2.10; EX 211.80 Trifecta £1192.20 Part won. Pool of £1589.69 - 0.01..
Owner F G Matthews **Bred** Alan Inglis **Trained** Wilsford-Cum-Lake, Wilts

FOCUS
The pace was generous in this decent handicap hurdle and the form looks sound. The winner is rated back to her best novice form.

3990 DICK HUNT H'CAP CHASE (FOR THE DICK HUNT TROPHY) (17 fncs) 2m 5f
2:40 (2:45) (Class 3) (0-140,140) 5-Y-0+
£15,640 (£4,620; £2,310; £1,155; £577; £290)

Form RPR
601- **1** **Bennys Mist (IRE)**[14] 3742 8-11-5 **133** AidanColeman 143+
(Venetia Williams) *pressed ldr most of way tl led 13th: rdn appr 3 out: hdd 2 out: rallied to take narrow advantage last: styd on wl to assert run-in: rdn out* **9/4**[1]

P23- **2** 3 **Rouge Et Blanc (FR)**[54] 2957 9-10-8 **127** ThomasGarner(5) 134+
(Oliver Sherwood) *hld up: hmpd 7th: hdwy 11th: wnt 2nd 3 out: led and nt fluent 2 out: sn rdn: hdd last: no ex* **11/1**

00P- **3** 8 **Carrickboy (IRE)**[29] 3458 10-11-12 **140** LiamTreadwell 136
(Venetia Williams) *hld up: hdwy to trck ldrs 13th: rdn appr 3 out: styd on same pce* **16/1**

04- **4** 2 ¾ **Coolking**[51] 3004 7-10-1 **118** ow1 JoshuaMoore(3) 111
(Lawney Hill) *led tl 13th: rdn and ev ch appr 3 out: hld fr bef 2 out: styd on same pce* **16/1**

423- **5** 4 ½ **Ultragold (FR)**[47] 3097 6-10-7 **121** (t) JoeTizzard 113
(Colin Tizzard) *in tch: wnt 3rd 10th: hit 4 out: sn rdn: one pce fr next* **9/4**[1]

6/5- **6** 22 **Requin (FR)**[19] 3662 9-10-0 **117** ow2 (p) GilesHawkins(3) 89
(Victor Dartnall) *trckd ldrs tl dropped last 11th: remained in tch tl wknd bef 3 out: t.o* **14/1**

3FP/ **7** 30 **Webberys Dream**[294] 5258 11-10-1 **115** IanPopham 52
(Jeremy Scott) *chsd ldrs tl 10th: sn struggling but in tch: hmpd 13th: wknd next: t.o* **20/1**

/U0- **F** **Forgotten Gold (IRE)**[54] 2939 8-11-7 **135** PaddyBrennan
(Tom George) *in tch whn fell 7th* **8/1**[2]

341- **F** **Bertie Boru (IRE)**[14] 3745 7-10-11 **125** TomO'Brien
(Philip Hobbs) *mstke 1st: in last pair: sltly hmpd 7th: fell 13th* **9/1**[3]

5m 36.1s (10.90) **Going Correction** +0.775s/f (Soft) **9 Ran SP% 114.2**
Speed ratings: **110,108,105,104,103 94,83, ,**
CSF £26.55 CT £318.11 TOTE £3.60: £1.60, £3.00, £4.90; EX 32.40 Trifecta £250.10.
Owner Mezzone Family **Bred** Flan O'Neill **Trained** Kings Caple, H'fords

FOCUS
Quite a valuable handicap chase. There's probably still more to come from the winner.

3991 CARLING EUROPEAN BREEDERS' FUND MARES' "NATIONAL HUNT" NOVICES' HURDLE (10 hdls 1 omitted) 2m 6f
3:10 (3:15) (Class 4) 4-Y-0+ **£3,898** (£1,144; £572; £286)

Form RPR
31- **1** **Tagrita (IRE)**[42] 3173 6-11-6 125 DarylJacob 124+
(Paul Nicholls) *mde all: in command between last 2: comf* **1/3**[1]
/30- **2** 3 1/2 **Brantingham Breeze**[51] 3005 6-10-4 0 RichardO'Dea(10) 107+
(Emma Lavelle) *hld up bhd ldng trio: hdwy into 2nd 2 out: sn rdn: kpt on but no ch w easy wnr* **10/1**[3]
/05- **3** 8 **Miner Distraction**[31] 3423 6-11-0 0 NickScholfield 100
(Jeremy Scott) *racd keenly: trckd wnr tl rdn appr 2: sn outpcd* **7/2**[2]
/6P- **4** 13 **Aroseforoscar**[14] 3733 5-11-0 0 JamesDavies 86
(Chris Down) *trckd wnr: rdn appr 2 out: sn btn* **33/1**
00P- **F** **Party Girls (FR)**[14] 3733 6-11-0 0 (bt[1]) ConorO'Farrell
(David Pipe) *racd keenly early: hld up last but in tch: wnt 5th at the 6th where mstke: fell 3 out* **50/1**
0/0- **P** **Kris Magic (IRE)**[255] 412 7-11-0 0 LiamHeard
(Colin Heard) *hld up bhd ldng trio: wknd 7th: t.o whn p.u bef 2 out* **100/1**

5m 49.5s (23.00) **Going Correction** +0.775s/f (Soft) 6 Ran SP% **112.2**
Speed ratings (Par 105): **89,87,84,80,**
CSF £4.81 TOTE £1.30: £1.10, £3.40; EX 3.70 Trifecta £8.00.
Owner Axom XLVIII **Bred** John Kidd **Trained** Ditcheat, Somerset

FOCUS
An uncompetitive event which proved easy pickings for the winner. She was value for further and is rated close to her mark in a steadily run race.

3992 RED AND YELLA MICKEY BOLEY MEMORIAL NOVICES' LIMITED H'CAP CHASE (13 fncs) 2m
3:40 (3:45) (Class 3) (0-140,138) 5-Y-0+ **£9,495** (£2,805; £1,402; £702)

Form RPR
/13- **1** **Brick Red**[15] 3715 7-11-5 **135** AidanColeman 144+
(Venetia Williams) *trckd ldr: chal after 2 out: narrow ld sn after last: nudged clr: readily* **9/4**[2]
103- **2** 1 **Notarfbad (IRE)**[67] 2694 8-10-11 **127** NickScholfield 132
(Jeremy Scott) *led: rdn after 3 out: hdd sn after last: kpt on but a being readily hld* **5/1**
1/1- **3** 9 **Tresor De Bontee (FR)**[30] 3429 7-10-6 **122** RichardJohnson 118
(Richard Lee) *trckd ldng pair: effrt appr 3 out: nvr quite got on terms: kpt on same pce* **15/8**[1]
0F3- **4** 3 1/2 **Close House**[29] 3456 7-11-8 **138** (t) TomScudamore 131
(David Pipe) *racd last of 4 but wl in tch: j. sltly rt at times: outpcd after 4 out: nvr threatened* **3/1**[3]

4m 12.1s (12.20) **Going Correction** +0.925s/f (Soft) 4 Ran SP% **107.2**
Speed ratings: **106,105,101,99**
CSF £11.75 TOTE £3.20; EX 11.00 Trifecta £19.50.
Owner Julian Taylor & Andrew Brooks **Bred** Raimon Bloodstock **Trained** Kings Caple, H'fords

FOCUS
A fair event run at a decent gallop. The cosy winner improved to his hurdles mark.

3993 CGA FOXHUNTER TRIAL OPEN HUNTERS' CHASE (FOR THE STEWART TORY MEMORIAL CHALLENGE TROPHY) (21 fncs) 3m 1f 110y
4:10 (4:15) (Class 6) 5-Y-0+ **£935** (£290; £145; £72)

Form RPR
4/ **1** **Shy John**[32] 8-11-5 0 MrPMason(7) 130+
(P W Mason) *travelled strly most of way: hld up bhd ldrs: smooth prog to join ldr after 4 out: led 2 out: rdn out run-in* **13/2**[3]
0/P- **2** 1 1/4 **Richard's Sundance (IRE)**[16] 3698 12-11-13 127(p) MrMatthewHampton(7) 135
(Victor Dartnall) *led tl 11th: prom: led 14th: rdn after 3 out: 1 l down whn untidy last: swtchd lft: styd on fnl 120yds but nvr quite getting there* **4/1**[2]
/4P- **3** 27 **Coombe Hill**[25] 13-12-3 117 MrDEdwards(3) 109
(Mrs C Fear) *trckd ldrs: jnd ldr 17th: rdn after next: wkng whn lft 3rd 3 out: t.o* **6/4**[1]
2/4- **4** 1 1/4 **Minella Theatre (IRE)**[15] 3720 11-11-5 104 (tp) MrJoeHill(7) 97
(Alan Hill) *hld up bhd ldrs: trckd ldrs 8th: rdn appr 4 out: sn btn: lft 4th 3 out: t.o* **12/1**
5 36 **Gosser Time**[11] 11-11-5 0 (b) MrJAPonting(7) 65
(P Ponting) *hld up: jnd ldr 8th: led 11th tl 14th: blnd next: sn rdn: wknd after 17th: t.o* **66/1**
313/ **F** **Martys Mission (IRE)**[32] 12-11-11 109 MrADoyle(5)
(Miss Becky Furber) *trcking ldrs whn fell 8th* **4/1**[2]
/02- **F** **Seigneur Des Bois (FR)**[15] 3720 8-11-11 110 (p) MrTEllis(5) 113
(D Buckett) *trckd ldrs: nt fluent 2nd: rdn to chse ldng pair after 4 out: styng on at same pce whn fell next* **8/1**

7m 18.1s (38.60) **Going Correction** +1.075s/f (Soft) 7 Ran SP% **113.6**
Speed ratings: **83,82,74,73,62** ,
CSF £32.44 TOTE £6.90: £3.30, £2.20; EX 25.80 Trifecta £75.10.
Owner Shy John Partnership **Bred** A J Mason **Trained** Bibury, Gloucs

FOCUS
An ordinary hunter chase. The winner should take more of these.

3994 CONNOLLY'S RED MILLS BUMPER CHALLENGE STANDARD OPEN NATIONAL HUNT FLAT RACE 2m
4:40 (4:42) (Class 6) 4-6-Y-0 **£1,624** (£477; £238; £119)

Form RPR
42/ **1** **Jolly's Cracked It (FR)**[294] 5247 5-11-4 0 NoelFehily 112+
(Harry Fry) *trckd ldrs: wnt 2nd over 2f out: shkn up to ld over 1f out: styd on strly fnl f: rdn out* **7/2**[1]
2 3 1/4 **Davy Doubt (IRE)**[304] 5-11-4 0 TomScudamore 108+
(David Pipe) *disp ld tl clr ldr 4f out: rdn over 2f out: hdd over 1f out: styd on but nt gng pce of wnr* **7/2**[1]
3 8 **Fight Commander (IRE)**[96] 5-11-4 0 LeightonAspell 100
(Oliver Sherwood) *mid-div: hdwy to chse ldrs 3f out: sn rdn: styd on to go 3rd over 1f out but nt gng pce of front pair* **14/1**
3- **4** 1 3/4 **Dashaway (IRE)**[45] 3133 5-11-4 0 NickScholfield 98
(Jeremy Scott) *trckd ldrs: rdn over 2f out: styd on same pce* **6/1**[3]
1- **5** shd **Brother Tedd**[49] 3035 5-11-11 0 RichardJohnson 105
(Philip Hobbs) *racd keenly: hld up towards rr of midfield: hdwy on outer fr 4f out: effrt over 2f out: sn one pce* **4/1**[2]
- **6** 2 1/2 **Ugolin De Beaumont (FR)** 6-11-4 0 SamJones 96
(Bob Buckler) *trckd ldrs: rdn wl over 2f out: sn wknd* **50/1**
7 nk **Millanisi Boy** 5-11-4 0 ConorO'Farrell 95
(Richard Woollacott) *mid-div: lost pl 1/2-way and nudged along: rdn in last trio 3f out: styd on fnl 2f but n.d* **50/1**
3- **8** nk **Thats Yer Man (IRE)**[56] 2912 6-10-11 0 MrCSmith(7) 95
(Linda Blackford) *disp ld tl rdn 4f out: one pce fnl 2f* **28/1**
9 2 **Gold Carrot** 6-11-1 0 JoshuaMoore(3) 93
(Gary Moore) *hld up towards rr of midfield: hdwy to chse ldrs but nt best of runs wl over 2f out: sn rdn: wknd over 1f out* **8/1**
5- **10** 13 **Wolftrap (IRE)**[19] 3656 5-11-4 0 DougieCostello 80
(Laura Young) *a towards rr* **12/1**
5- **11** 1/2 **Knight ofthe Realm**[49] 3049 5-10-11 0 MrLDrowne(7) 80
(Caroline Keevil) *a towards rr* **50/1**
12 7 **Are We There** 5-10-11 0 MrRobertHawker(7) 73
(Carroll Gray) *a towards rr* **100/1**
13 3 1/4 **Capel Le Ferne (IRE)** 6-11-4 0 DarylJacob 69
(Robert Walford) *mid-div tl wknd over 2f out* **25/1**

3m 57.7s (14.40) **Going Correction** +0.925s/f (Soft) 13 Ran SP% **118.4**
Speed ratings: **101,99,95,94,94 93,93,92,91,85 85,81,80**
CSF £14.65 TOTE £4.10: £1.80, £1.70, £3.80; EX 23.40 Trifecta £184.50.
Owner Gdm Partnership **Bred** Henrietta Charlet & Daniel Charlesworth **Trained** Seaborough, Dorset

FOCUS
This appeared to be a decent bumper and the first two, who pulled clear, look well above average. There's a case for rating the form up to 7lb higher.
T/Plt: £38.30 to a £1 stake. Pool of £84571.20 - 1610.38 winning tickets. T/Qpdt: £14.30 to a £1 stake. Pool of £4605.09 - 237.79 winning tickets. TM

3995 - 4001a (Foreign Racing) - See Raceform Interactive

3829 CATTERICK (L-H)
Friday, January 31

OFFICIAL GOING: Soft (heavy in places) changing to heavy after race 3 (2.10)
First fence in back straight omitted for all chases. Bends moved out and all hurdle positions moved to provided fresh ground.
Wind: Fresh, half behind Weather: Overcast, raining

4002 YEAR OF THE HORSE CONDITIONAL JOCKEYS' (S) HURDLE (10 hdls) 2m 3f
1:10 (1:10) (Class 5) 4-Y-0+ **£2,737** (£798; £399)

Form RPR
142- **1** **Makhzoon (USA)**[29] 3499 10-11-4 119 (v) DiarmuidO'Regan(5) 117+
(N W Alexander) *chsd ldr: rdn and outpcd after 3 out: rallied to ld next: styd on strly fr last* **4/6**[1]
65F- **2** 2 3/4 **Hunters Belt (IRE)**[45] 3142 10-11-2 122 (vt) GrahamWatters(3) 108
(Barry Murtagh) *trckd ldrs: smooth hdwy to ld briefly bef 2 out: rdn and kpt on same pce appr last* **11/4**[2]
5F5- **3** 31 **Belle De Fontenay (FR)**[24] 3593 9-11-6 114 (p) ConorShoemark 78
(Conor Dore) *led: qcknd whn nt fluent 6th: rdn and hdd bef 2 out: sn btn: no ch whn nt fluent last* **4/1**[3]

4m 59.1s (23.00) **Going Correction** +1.15s/f (Heav) 3 Ran SP% **106.7**
Speed ratings (Par 103): **97,95,82**
CSF £2.73 TOTE £1.50; EX 2.60 Trifecta £3.10.
Owner The Ladies Who **Bred** Vision Bloodstock Et Al **Trained** Kinneston, Perth & Kinross

FOCUS
Bends moved out and all hurdle positions moved to provide fresh ground. A weak contest. The winner is rated to the level of his recent runs.

4003 BHEST RACING TO SCHOOL JUVENILE HURDLE (8 hdls) 2m
1:40 (1:42) (Class 4) 4-Y-0 **£3,249** (£954; £477; £238)

Form RPR
21- **1** **Aalim**[34] 3351 4-11-5 126 DenisO'Regan 112+
(John Ferguson) *hld up last but in tch: hit 2nd: j.big next: stdy hdwy gng wl bef 2 out: led on bit last: shkn up briefly nr fin: readily* **1/9**[1]
4- **2** 1 1/4 **Kolonel Kirkup**[35] 3332 4-10-12 0 BarryKeniry 93
(Michael Dods) *t.k.h early: prom: wnt 2nd 3rd: led gng wl bef 2 out: hdd last: kpt on: no ch w wnr* **8/1**[2]
50- **3** nk **Marlborough House**[65] 2750 4-10-12 0 HenryBrooke 93
(Chris Grant) *in tch: rdn and outpcd after 3 out: rallied u.p and chsd ldrs last: kpt on run-in* **9/1**[3]
60- **4** 20 **Spencers Lad**[10] 3822 4-10-9 0 JakeGreenall(3) 78
(Michael Easterby) *chsd ldrs: rdn along whn blnd 2 out: sn wknd* **33/1**
U- **5** 21 **Great Demeanor (USA)**[7] 3872 4-10-12 0 RyanMania 52
(Dianne Sayer) *led: mstke 3 out: hdd bef next: sn lost tch: t.o* **33/1**

4m 12.4s (19.90) **Going Correction** +1.15s/f (Heav) 5 Ran SP% **117.0**
Speed ratings: **96,95,95,85,74**
CSF £2.48 TOTE £1.10: £1.10, £2.90; EX 2.50 Trifecta £5.10.
Owner Bloomfields **Bred** Darley **Trained** Cowlinge, Suffolk

FOCUS
An uncompetitive juvenile event, with the easy winner standing out.

4004 FREE RACEDAYS WITH THE RACEGOERS CLUB NOVICES' H'CAP CHASE (11 fncs 1 omitted) 2m
2:10 (2:11) (Class 4) (0-110,110) 5-Y-0+ **£4,548** (£1,335; £667; £333)

Form RPR
110- **1** **Proud Times (USA)**[56] 2932 8-11-7 **105** (p) JackDoyle 120
(Ali Brewer) *pressed ldr: chal 4th: led and drvn 2 out: styd on wl fr last* **9/2**
5PF- **2** 3 **Hotgrove Boy**[9] 3831 7-10-0 **84** oh8 BrianHarding 96
(Stuart Coltherd) *led: jnd 4th: rdn and hdd 2 out: rallied: kpt on same pce last 100yds* **3/1**[2]
044- **3** 12 **Blackwater King (IRE)**[62] 2804 6-11-12 **110** HenryBrooke 110
(Donald McCain) *t.k.h: chsd clr ldng pair: rdn after 4 out: sn no imp* **7/2**[3]
251- **4** 12 **Fitandproperjob**[10] 3817 8-10-3 **84** ow3 (vt) PaulMoloney 75
(Anthony Middleton) *hld up in tch: outpcd 4 out: struggling fr next* **5/2**[1]
/01- **P** **Easydoesit (IRE)**[7] 3871 6-10-9 **98** ColmMcCormack(5)
(Tony Carroll) *nt fluent on occasions: in tch: struggling fr 4th: t.o whn p.u bef 2 out* **13/2**

4m 6.9s (6.80) **Going Correction** +0.525s/f (Soft) 5 Ran SP% **107.3**
Speed ratings: **104,102,96,90,**
CSF £17.21 TOTE £6.10: £1.40, £1.20; EX 26.70 Trifecta £66.40.
Owner Crowcombe Racing & Miss Ali Brewer **Bred** Timothy Thornton & Meg & Mike Buckley **Trained** Eastbury, Berks

FOCUS
Only two mattered in the home straight. Much the fastest race on the card and the winner is rated in line with his Flat/hurdles mark.

4005 EUROPEAN BREEDERS' FUND "NATIONAL HUNT" NOVICES' HURDLE (QUALIFIER) (10 hdls) 2m 3f
2:45 (2:45) (Class 4) 4-7-Y-0 **£3,898** (£1,144; £572; £286)

Form RPR

131- **1** **Classic Move (IRE)**^{40} 3225 5-11-8 **122** HenryBrooke 129+
(Donald McCain) *mde all: rdn bef 2 out: kpt on strly to go clr: unchal* **5/4**^{2}

453- **2** *23* **River Bollin**^{16} 3721 4-10-4 0 DougieCostello 88
(Tim Easterby) *nt fluent on occasions: hld up: rdn and hdwy after 3 out: chsd (clr) wnr whn nt fluent last: no imp* **12/1**

450- **3** *1 1/4* **Mister Jones**^{7} 3872 6-11-2 0 RyanMania 98
(Sue Smith) *hld up in tch: stdy hdwy after 3 out: rdn and kpt on same pce fr next* **6/1**^{3}

/11- **4** *1/2* **Vice Et Vertu (FR)**^{47} 3106 5-11-12 **130** RichardJohnson 110
(Henry Daly) *t.k.h: chsd ldrs: wnt 2nd 5th: hit 3 out: outpcd fr 2 out: lost 2nd last* **6/5**^{1}

0P0- **5** *23* **Oorayvic (IRE)**^{10} 3826 7-10-13 0 JonathanEngland$^{(3)}$ 75
(Sue Smith) *midfield: drvn and outpcd 4 out: n.d after* **16/1**

00P- **6** *5* **Thatildee (IRE)**^{50} 3036 6-11-2 0 DenisO'Regan 70
(Chris Grant) *bhd: struggling fnl circ: nvr on terms* **66/1**

0- **7** *69* **Devil At Midnight (IRE)**^{10} 3826 6-10-11 0 SamanthaDrake$^{(5)}$ 1
(Richard Drake) *chsd wnr to 5th: struggling bef next: t.o* **80/1**

0P0- **P** **Well Related**^{10} 3826 7-11-2 0 RichieMcGrath
(Henry Hogarth) *bhd: lost tch fr 5th: t.o whn p.u bef 2 out* **100/1**

5m 4.6s (28.50) **Going Correction** +1.15s/f (Heav)
WFA 4 from 5yo+ 11lb **8** Ran SP% **121.5**
Speed ratings: **86,76,75,75,65 63,34,**
CSF £17.73 TOTE £2.80: £1.10, £1.90, £1.80; EX 12.80 Trifecta £72.50.
Owner T G Leslie **Bred** Jim Mernagh **Trained** Cholmondeley, Cheshire

FOCUS
This was one-way traffic for the winner, who was left with little to beat with the favourite underperforming.

4006 WATT FENCES H'CAP HURDLE (10 hdls 2 omitted) 3m 1f 110y
3:20 (3:20) (Class 3) (0-125,125) 4-Y-0+ **£6,498** (£1,908; £954; £477)

Form RPR

221- **1** **Hartforth**^{28} 3520 6-9-12 **102** CallumWhillans$^{(5)}$ 111+
(Donald Whillans) *prom: hdwy to press ldr 2 out (usual 3 out): led whn lft 7 l clr last: drew further clr* **10/1**

222- **2** *23* **American Life (FR)**^{13} 3784 7-10-11 **110** (vt) PaulMoloney 107+
(Anthony Middleton) *hld up: stdy hdwy on outside and prom 7th: effrt bef omitted 2 out: one pce whn lft 7 l 2nd last: sn btn* **8/1**^{3}

613- **3** *23* **Moscow Presents (IRE)**^{21} 3638 6-11-1 **119** (p) AdamNicol$^{(5)}$ 82
(Philip Kirby) *cl up tl rdn and wknd bef omitted 2 out: hld whn lft modest 3rd last* **11/1**

6/1- **4** *7* **Campbonnais (FR)**^{8} 3852 9-10-1 **100** (p) AdamWedge 56
(Ali Brewer) *in tch: stdy hdwy 7th: wknd after 2 out (usual 3 out)* **9/4**^{2}

P52- **5** *5* **Big Sound**^{10} 3824 7-9-7 **99** oh1 (p) GrantCockburn$^{(7)}$ 50
(Tim Walford) *hld up in tch: drvn and outpcd fr 6th: lost tch fr 2 out (usual 3 out)* **2/1**^{1}

1PP- **6** *44* **Duke Of Monmouth (IRE)**^{16} 3717 7-11-5 **118** (b^{1}) MarkGrant 25
(Charlie Mann) *led tl rdn and hdd 2 out (usual 3 out): sn struggling* **20/1**

/15- **7** *dist* **Alderley Rover (IRE)**^{30} 3479 10-11-12 **125** HenryBrooke
(Donald McCain) *bhd: lost tch fr 6th: continued* **20/1**

331- **F** **Pudsey House**^{34} 3356 7-10-9 **115** (b) JohnDawson$^{(7)}$ 118
(John Wade) *cl up: led 2 out (usual 3 out): hdd and 4 l down whn fell last* **16/1**

3B2- **F** **Romany Ryme**^{16} 3726 8-10-12 **118** JonathonBewley$^{(7)}$
(George Bewley) *hld up in tch: fell 3rd* **16/1**

6m 52.8s (25.20) **Going Correction** +1.15s/f (Heav) **9** Ran SP% **113.9**
Speed ratings (Par 107): **107,99,92,90,89 75, , ,**
CSF £85.01 CT £891.35 TOTE £12.00: £2.50, £2.30, £2.90; EX 46.70 Trifecta £383.00.
Owner The Brave Lads Partnership **Bred** Bishop Wilton Stud **Trained** Hawick, Borders
■ Big Sound was Tim Walford's final runner. The licence now passes to his son Mark Walford.

FOCUS
The ground played its part in this moderate handicap. Another step up from the progressive winner.

4007 NEW RACING UK ANYWHERE AVAILABLE NOW H'CAP CHASE (14 fncs 1 omitted) 2m 3f
3:55 (3:55) (Class 3) (0-125,122) 5-Y-0+ **£7,797** (£2,289; £1,144; £572)

Form RPR

510- **1** **Granville Island (IRE)**^{30} 3032 7-11-12 **122** SeanQuinlan 120
(Jennie Candlish) *t.k.h: hld up in tch: hdwy and ev ch bef 3 out: rdn next: drifted to stands' rail after last: edgd lft and styd on to ld towards fin* **13/2**

32F- **2** *1 1/4* **Pearls Legend**^{13} 3769 7-11-8 **118** JamieMoore 124
(John Spearing) *cl up: led after 4 out: rdn and 2 l clr last: hdd and no ex towards fin* **3/1**^{1}

132- **3** *4 1/2* **Billy Cuckoo (IRE)**^{30} 3452 8-11-4 **117** (b) JakeGreenall$^{(3)}$ 120
(Tony Coyle) *cl up: rdn and outpcd after 4 out: rallied next: nt fluent 2 out: sn no imp* **9/2**^{3}

244- **4** *1 3/4* **Qoubilai (FR)**^{94} 2149 10-11-6 **116** ^{1} DougieCostello 117
(Tony Coyle) *nt fluent on occasions: hld up in tch: stdy hdwy 8th: hit 4 out: rdn and no imp fr next* **16/1**

34U- **5** *6* **Kykate**^{10} 3823 8-11-9 **119** (t) RyanMahon 114
(William Kinsey) *prom: hdwy 8th: rdn and outpcd whn nt fluent 2 out: btn last* **7/1**

504- **6** *61* **Arctic Ben (IRE)**^{41} 3204 10-11-10 **120** RichardJohnson 53
(Henry Daly) *nt fluent on occasions: mde most to after 4 out: rdn and wknd qckly next* **5/1**

411- **P** **Chicklemix**^{20} 3662 8-10-13 **114** MissGAndrews$^{(5)}$
(Pam Sly) *nt fluent in rr: rdn and outpcd 7th: struggling fr next: t.o whn p.u 3 out* **4/1**^{2}

5m 11.7s (22.90) **Going Correction** +0.525s/f (Soft) **7** Ran SP% **111.6**
Speed ratings: **72,71,69,68,66 40,**
CSF £25.68 TOTE £9.70: £4.10, £1.60; EX 31.80 Trifecta £97.60.
Owner P and Mrs G A Clarke **Bred** Gareth Metcalfe **Trained** Basford Green, Staffs

FOCUS
This saw changing fortunes after the last. Ordinary handicap form.

4008 YORKSHIRE-OUTDOORS.CO.UK MARES' STANDARD OPEN NATIONAL HUNT FLAT RACE 2m
4:25 (4:25) (Class 6) 4-6-Y-0 **£2,053** (£598; £299)

Form RPR

3- **1** **Philosofy**^{9} 3835 4-10-6 0 RichardJohnson 95
(David O'Meara) *t.k.h: cl up: effrt and ev ch over 1f out: led ins fnl f: hld on wl u.p* **4/1**^{2}

033- **2** *shd* **Bulas Belle**^{20} 3663 4-9-13 0 CraigNichol$^{(7)}$ 95
(Edwin Tuer) *t.k.h: cl up: led 1/2-way: rdn and hrd pressed over 1f out: hdd ins fnl f: rallied: jst hld* **8/1**^{3}

1- **3** *19* **Oleohneh (IRE)**^{27} 3529 6-11-10 0 BrianHughes 94
(Malcolm Jefferson) *t.k.h: in tch: stdy hdwy 1/2-way: rdn over 2f out: edgd rt and wknd over 1f out* **8/15**^{1}

4 *hd* **Money Maid (IRE)**^{280} 6-11-3 0 GerardTumelty 87
(Simon Earle) *led at stdy pce to 1/2-way: cl up tl shkn up and wknd 2f out* **9/1**

P **Who's Emma** 4-10-6 0 BarryKeniry
(Chris Fairhurst) *rn green in tch: outpcd 1/2-way: broke down over 6f out: fatally injured* **33/1**

4m 17.7s (30.80) **Going Correction** +1.15s/f (Heav)
WFA 4 from 5yo 11lb 5 from 6yo 3lb **5** Ran SP% **109.3**
Speed ratings: **69,68,59,59,**
CSF £31.15 TOTE £3.60: £2.00, £2.80; EX 19.10 Trifecta £26.50.
Owner Direct Racing Partnership **Bred** Fittocks Stud Ltd **Trained** Nawton, N Yorks

FOCUS
The first pair came right away in this ordinary mares' bumper, with the third seemingly well below the level of his recent win.
T/Plt: £170.40 to a £1 stake. Pool: £63594.01 - 272.39 winning tickets T/Qpdt: £87.60 to a £1 stake. Pool: £3815.40 - 32.20 winning tickets RY

3357 CHEPSTOW (L-H)
Friday, January 31
4009 Meeting Abandoned - waterlogged

KEMPTON (A.W) (R-H)
Friday, January 31

OFFICIAL GOING: Standard to slow
Weather: Overcast; rain gradually increasing until heavy after race 6.

4016 DINE IN THE PANORAMIC STANDARD OPEN NATIONAL HUNT FLAT RACE (DIV I) 2m (P)
1:50 (1:50) (Class 4) 4-6-Y-0 **£3,249** (£954; £477; £238)

Form RPR

1 **One For The Guv'Nr (IRE)** 5-11-4 0 DavidBass 111
(Nicky Henderson) *prom: led 2f out: rdn and battted on gamely through fnl f* **13/2**^{3}

2 *nk* **Shout It Aloud** 5-11-1 0 MichaelByrne$^{(3)}$ 110
(Tim Vaughan) *v tall: trckd ldrs and t.k.h on inner: effrt and swtchd to outer over 2f out: ev ch 1f out: kpt on wl cl home but jst hld* **33/1**

3 *1* **There Is No Point (IRE)** 5-10-11 0 APMcCoy 102
(Jonjo O'Neill) *trckd ldrs on ins: effrt 4f out: w wnr 2f out tl drvn and ev ch wl ins fnl f: nt qckn after* **3/1**^{1}

4/ **4** *3/4* **Graffiti Art**^{316} 4885 5-10-11 0 BrendanPowell 101
(Brendan Powell) *mounted outside paddock: towards rr: rdn and hdwy over 1f out: kpt on nicely ins fnl f* **20/1**

2- **5** *3 1/4* **Go Odee Go (IRE)**^{50} 3049 6-11-4 0 HarrySkelton 105
(Dan Skelton) *mounted outside paddock: prom: disp ld 2f out tl drvn over 1f out: fading ins fnl f* **9/2**^{2}

6 *hd* **Cochinillo (IRE)** 5-11-4 0 DarylJacob 105
(Ben Case) *bhd: hdwy over 1f out: styng on steadily ins fnl f* **33/1**

/25- **7** *hd* **Southfield Vic (IRE)**^{75} 2534 5-11-4 0 JackSherwood$^{(7)}$ 112
(Paul Nicholls) *led: rdn and hdd 2f out: lost pl tamely and hanging lft after* **3/1**^{1}

8 *1 1/2* **The Cider Maker** 4-10-7 0 JoeTizzard 92
(Colin Tizzard) *midfield: rdn 3f out: one pce after* **16/1**

9 *5* **Kincora Fort (IRE)** 5-11-4 0 WayneHutchinson 98
(Noel Williams) *mounted outside paddock: nvr bttr than midfield: btn over 2f out: rn green* **33/1**

10 *13* **The Dodgy Dealer** 5-11-4 0 TomScudamore 85
(Nigel Hawke) *a bhd: lost tch 3f out: t.o* **25/1**

11 *1 1/4* **Italian Symphony (IRE)** 4-10-0 0 (t) AndrewTinkler 66
(Brendan Powell) *cl up tl pushed along and lost pl 4f out: t.o* **20/1**

4- **12** *5* **Supari**^{36} 3295 5-11-4 0 WillKennedy 79
(Sarah-Jayne Davies) *towards rr and drvn 6f out: t.o* **66/1**

13 *1 1/2* **Webbswood (IRE)** 5-10-8 0 MikeyHamill$^{(10)}$ 78
(Sean Curran) *last early: rdn and struggling over 3f out: t.o* **50/1**

14 *4 1/2* **Be My Witness (IRE)** 5-10-1 0 JosephPalmowski$^{(10)}$ 66
(Robin Dickin) *trckd ldrs on outside tl 1/2-way: t.o over 3f out* **50/1**

2- **15** *15* **Sirrah Star (IRE)**^{71} 2634 6-10-11 0 NoelFehily 51
(Neil Mulholland) *midfield: rdn and wknd over 3f out: t.o* **8/1**

3m 44.66s (14.56) **Going Correction** +0.45s/f (Slow)
WFA 4 from 5yo+ 11lb **15** Ran SP% **126.1**
Speed ratings: **81,80,80,79,78 78,78,77,74,68 67,65,64,62,54**
CSF £216.74 TOTE £10.30: £3.00, £7.70, £2.60; EX 244.60 Trifecta £2384.80.
Owner Bradley Partnership **Bred** Chris Kinane **Trained** Upper Lambourn, Berks

FOCUS
A hastily arranged bumpers card due to the current wet weather throughout the country. The track was super harrowed about 90mm, double the amount for a usual Flat meeting. The opener was a conventional bumper. It was steadily run and it paid to race handily.

4017 DINE IN THE PANORAMIC STANDARD OPEN NATIONAL HUNT FLAT RACE (DIV II) 2m (P)
2:20 (2:20) (Class 4) 4-6-Y-0 **£3,249** (£954; £477; £238)

Form RPR

1 **Clondaw Banker (IRE)**^{90} 5-10-13 0 NicodeBoinville$^{(5)}$ 110+
(Nicky Henderson) *trckd ldr: shkn up to ld jst over 1f out: kpt on wl: pushed out* **13/8**^{1}

1- **2** *2* **Molly Cat**[20] 3663 4-10-7 0 PaddyBrennan 97
(Alan Swinbank) *mid-div: hdwy 4f out: chsd ldrs over 2f out: rdn over 1f out: kpt on to go 2nd ins fnl f: a being hld by wnr* **11/4**[2]

052- **3** *1* **Mr Shantu (IRE)**[58] 2885 5-11-4 0 APMcCoy 107
(Jonjo O'Neill) *trckd ldrs: rdn over 2f out: styd on ins fnl f: wnt 3rd fnl 75yds* **7/1**[3]

/33- **4** *1* **Black Cow (IRE)**[63] 2788 6-11-4 0 DarylJacob 106
(Paul Nicholls) *sn prom: led 1/2-way: rdn over 2f out: hdd jst over 1f out: kpt on but no ex fnl 120yds* **9/1**

5 *1 ¼* **Henrybrowneyes (IRE)** 5-10-13 0 RobertMcCarth(5) 105
(Ian Williams) *hld up towards rr: pushed along and hdwy over 2f out: swtchd lft over 1f out: fin strly: improve* **33/1**

204- **6** *1* **Royal Ripple (IRE)**[63] 2788 6-11-4 0 TomO'Brien 104
(Paul Henderson) *mid-div: hdwy to chse ldrs over 2f out: sn rdn: kpt on same pce* **33/1**

3- **7** *¾* **Rough Fighter (USA)**[67] 2724 5-10-13 0 JamesBanks(5) 103
(Andy Turnell) *trckd ldrs: rdn over 2f out: fdd ins fnl f* **16/1**

46- **8** *1 ¾* **The Snappy Poet**[55] 2946 5-11-4 0 [1] NickScholfield 101
(Jeremy Scott) *led tl 1/2-way: kpt pressing ldr: rdn over 2f out: sn one pce* **40/1**

6- **9** *5* **Greybougg**[76] 2513 5-11-1 0 [1] MarkQuinlan(3) 96
(Nigel Hawke) *hld up towards rr: hdwy into midfield 4f out: rdn whn hung lft over 2f out: wknd over 1f out* **66/1**

0- **10** *1 ¾* **Elegant Stride (IRE)**[6] 3898 4-9-11 0 PeterCarberry(3) 77
(Don Cantillon) *hld up towards rr: sme prog whn hmpd over 2f out: sn rdn: wknd over 1f out* **33/1**

4- **11** *1* **Knight's Reward**[50] 3049 4-10-4 0 MichaelByrne(3) 83
(Tim Vaughan) *t.k.h in midfield: outpcd over 2f out: wknd over 1f out* **25/1**

0- **12** *13* **Rocket Scientist**[34] 3363 5-11-4 0 JoeTizzard 81
(Colin Tizzard) *mid-div: hdwy 6f out: rdn over 4f out: sn wknd* **50/1**

0- **13** *¾* **Wild Legend (IRE)**[247] 544 5-10-11 0 LeightonAspell 73
(Richard Rowe) *a towards rr* **100/1**

14 *3 ¼* **Terra Firma** 4-10-7 0 BrendanPowell 66
(Brendan Powell) *mid-div: hdwy 4f out: rdn 3f out: sn wknd* **20/1**

15 *2* **Crazy Train** 5-10-11 0 (t[1]) SamTwiston-Davies 68
(Keiran Burke) *a towards rr* **33/1**

- **16** *40* **Littleton Lad (IRE)** 6-10-11 0 [1] MrHGMiller(7) 35
(Zoe Davison) *t.k.h early: hld up towards rr: struggling 1/2-way: sn detached: t.o* **100/1**

3m 40.9s (10.80) **Going Correction** +0.45s/f (Slow)
WFA 4 from 5yo+ 11lb **16** Ran SP% **121.4**
Speed ratings: **91,90,89,89,88 87,87,86,84,83 82,76,75,74,73 53**
CSF £5.01 TOTE £2.80: £1.50, £1.30, £2.00; EX 8.90 Trifecta £49.90.
Owner A D Spence **Bred** William Flood **Trained** Upper Lambourn, Berks

FOCUS
They began to wind up the gallop 4f out in this second division of the standard open bumper, and the form ought to work out. It's rated around the first three.

4018 MIX BUSINESS WITH PLEASURE AT KEMPTON "JUMPERS' BUMPER" NATIONAL HUNT FLAT RACE (DIV I) 2m (P)

2:55 (2:55) (Class 4) 4-Y-0+ **£3,249** (£954; £477; £238)

Form RPR

2/3- **1** **Ellnando Queen**[99] 2043 6-10-8 0 GavinSheehan(3) 114
(Warren Greatrex) *mde all: set brisk pce: 7 l clr after 6f: given breather 6f out: plld out ex over 1f out and wl in command after: galloped on strly* **8/1**[3]

04P- **2** *5* **Ourmanmassini (IRE)**[36] 3263 6-11-4 0 (t) PaddyBrennan 116
(Suzy Smith) *towards rr on inner: hdwy 3f out: urged into 2nd 1f out but no ch w easy wnr* **25/1**

324- **3** *1 ½* **Aldopicgros (FR)**[52] 3003 4-10-7 0 DarylJacob 104
(Paul Nicholls) *trckd ldrs: wnt 2nd over 2f out: sn rdn: one pce and btn over 1f out: lost 2nd 1f out* **9/2**[2]

214- **4** *2 ¾* **Spirit Of Shankly**[20] 3646 6-11-4 0 (t) NoelFehily 112
(Charlie Longsdon) *trckd ldrs on inner: effrt 3f out: sn rdn w v limited rspnse: btn wl over 1f out* **8/15**[1]

153- **5** *4* **Jack By The Hedge**[88] 2266 5-11-4 0 IanPopham 108
(Caroline Keevil) *prom: wnt 2nd 4f out: sn rdn: grad wknd fnl 2f* **33/1**

614- **6** *2 ¾* **Buxom (IRE)**[58] 2888 7-10-11 0 (p) BrendanPowell 98
(Jamie Snowden) *nvr bttr than midfield: rdn and struggling 3f out: plugged on* **20/1**

523- **7** *1 ¼* **Saffron Prince**[60] 2858 6-11-4 0 TomScudamore 104
(David Bridgwater) *chsd ldr tl rdn and lost pl tamely 5f out* **25/1**

145- **8** *1 ½* **Factor Fifty (IRE)**[96] 2104 5-11-1 0 KyleJames(3) 102
(Philip Kirby) *a midfield: rdn and btn 3f out* **14/1**

05/ **9** *6* **Sleepy (FR)**[707] 4493 8-11-4 0 RichieMcLernon 96
(Sophie Leech) *bhd: fdd rapidly wl over 2f out: t.o* **66/1**

/56- **10** *5* **Cut'N'Shut**[50] 3035 7-10-11 0 MrHGMiller(7) 91
(Zoe Davison) *stmbld bdly after 3f: in last trio: drvn 6f out: no rspnse: t.o fnl 2f* **100/1**

/30- **11** *11* **Keppel Isle (IRE)**[118] 1764 5-11-4 0 TomCannon 80
(Laura Mongan) *t.k.h: prom: wnt 2nd 5f out tl 4f out: fdd bdly wl over 2f out: t.o* **50/1**

500/ **12** *19* **Lagan Katie**[1186] 2142 8-10-4 0 RyanWhile(7) 54
(Bill Turner) *last trio: plld hrd early: bdly t.o fnl 3f* **66/1**

13 *14* **Miss Morn (IRE)** 8-10-1 0 JosephPalmowski(10) 40
(Robin Dickin) *drvn 6f out: bdly t.o fnl 3f* **66/1**

3m 35.0s (4.90) **Going Correction** +0.45s/f (Slow)
WFA 4 from 5yo 11lb 5 from 6yo+ 3lb **13** Ran SP% **124.0**
Speed ratings (Par 105): **105,102,101,100,98 97,96,95,92,90 84,75,68**
CSF £188.97 TOTE £16.30: £2.30, £2.90, £1.50; EX 159.40 Trifecta £1407.40.
Owner Mrs R Vaughan **Bred** Mrs R I Vaughan **Trained** Upper Lambourn, Berks

FOCUS
This was confined to horses eligible for NH novices' hurdles. The winner made all in style, in one of the better times on the card..

4019 MIX BUSINESS WITH PLEASURE AT KEMPTON "JUMPERS' BUMPER" NATIONAL HUNT FLAT RACE (DIV II) 2m (P)

3:30 (3:30) (Class 4) 4-Y-0+ **£3,249** (£954; £477; £238)

Form RPR

414- **1** **Sign Of A Victory (IRE)**[63] 2802 5-11-4 0 AndrewTinkler 118+
(Nicky Henderson) *trckd ldrs: led 2f out: qcknd up wl: in command fnl f: pushed out: readily* **13/8**[1]

0/P- **2** *2 ¼* **Supreme Present**[77] 2495 6-10-11 0 (t) JasonMaguire 106+
(Kim Bailey) *hld up: hdwy over 2f out: rdn over 1f out: r.o wl to go 2nd ins fnl f: a being readily hld by wnr* **16/1**

13F- **3** *1 ¼* **Saint Roque (FR)**[48] 3081 8-11-4 0 (t) DarylJacob 112
(Paul Nicholls) *trckd ldrs: chal travelling wl 2f out: sn rdn: nt pce of wnr: lost 2nd ins fnl f* **2/1**[2]

464- **4** *3* **Sukiyaki (IRE)**[31] 3427 5-11-4 0 NoelFehily 109
(Charlie Longsdon) *in tch: rdn to chse ldrs 2f out: kpt on same pce* **10/1**

350- **5** *3 ¾* **Berkeley Avenue**[46] 3134 5-11-4 0 (tp) APMcCoy 105
(Warren Greatrex) *led: rdn and hdd 2f out: sn one pce* **10/1**

252- **6** *3* **Simply A Legend**[50] 3034 5-11-4 0 RobertThornton 102
(Alan King) *hld up: hdwy over 2f out to chse ldrs: sn rdn: wknd ent fnl f* **8/1**[3]

0- **7** *¾* **Highfields Dancer**[213] 862 6-11-1 0 JoshuaMoore(3) 102
(Gary Moore) *mid-div: travelling strly over 3f out: effrt over 2f out: wknd jst over 1f out* **50/1**

4- **8** *10* **Castle Cheetah (IRE)**[43] 3177 6-11-4 0 IanPopham 92
(Martin Keighley) *sn disputing ld: rdn over 3f out: sn hdd: wknd 2f out* **20/1**

50P- **9** *13* **Canarbino Girl**[17] 3695 7-10-4 0 MrLDrowne(7) 72
(Caroline Keevil) *in tch on outer: rdn 4f out: sn wknd* **100/1**

005- **10** *½* **Mac's Grey (IRE)**[73] 2573 7-10-11 0 MrHGMiller(7) 78
(Zoe Davison) *in tch: rdn over 4f out: sn btn* **100/1**

F- **11** *5* **Dido**[8] 3857 4-10-2 0 ChristopherWard(5) 62
(Alexandra Dunn) *tk str hold: in tch on outer: rdn over 3f out: sn wknd* **66/1**

3m 38.8s (8.70) **Going Correction** +0.45s/f (Slow)
WFA 4 from 5yo+ 11lb **11** Ran SP% **116.8**
Speed ratings (Par 105): **96,94,94,92,90 89,89,84,77,77 74**
CSF £28.73 TOTE £2.50: £1.20, £2.80, £1.10; EX 47.40 Trifecta £99.70.
Owner Matt & Lauren Morgan **Bred** John Hore **Trained** Upper Lambourn, Berks

FOCUS
This was confined to horses eligible for NH novices' hurdles. A fair contest and a promising winner. The third and fourth help set the level.

4020 KEMPTON FOR WEDDINGS "JUMPERS" BUMPER' NATIONAL HUNT FLAT RACE 2m (P)

4:05 (4:09) (Class 4) 5-Y-0+ **£3,249** (£954; £477; £238)

Form RPR

/52- **1** **Domtaline (FR)**[56] 2925 7-11-0 0 DarylJacob 123
(Paul Nicholls) *settled trcking ldrs: shkn up and clsd to ld gng wl over 2f out: clr 1f out: rdn and styd on gamely* **4/1**[2]

/22- **2** *1* **Daymar Bay (IRE)**[61] 2845 8-11-0 0 AidanColeman 122
(Emma Lavelle) *mounted outside paddock: racd keenly in rr: hdwy over 2f out: wnt 2nd ins fnl f: drvn and kpt on stoutly but wnr a in control* **10/1**

5U0- **3** *3 ½* **Hazy Tom (IRE)**[48] 3090 8-11-0 0 NoelFehily 118
(Charlie Longsdon) *hld up in rr: hdwy and chsd ldrs 5f out: sn rdn: one pce and no imp fnl 2f but snatched 3rd* **6/1**[3]

020- **4** *shd* **Rasheed**[24] 3596 6-10-9 0 (b) MattCrawley(5) 118
(Lucy Wadham) *towards rr: effrt 4f out: ev ch 3f out: sn racing awkwardly u.p: no ex over 1f out: lost 3rd nr fin* **16/1**

/03- **5** *5* **Empire Levant (USA)**[30] 3459 7-11-0 0 NickScholfield 113
(Paul Nicholls) *trckd ldrs: led 5f out: 3 l clr briefly home turn: drvn and hdd over 2f out: fdd over 1f out* **10/1**

/46- **6** *3 ¾* **Star In Flight**[58] 2882 7-11-0 0 JasonMaguire 110
(Donald McCain) *led for 6f: prom tl 5f out: fdd tamely over 2f out* **25/1**

33P- **7** *3 ½* **Marju King (IRE)**[15] 3729 8-10-11 0 (t) KielanWoods(3) 106
(Phil Middleton) *settled towards rr: pushed along and prog 6f out: 2nd briefly home turn: drvn and lost pl tamely* **66/1**

2/2- **8** *½* **Lidar (FR)**[43] 3170 9-11-0 0 (b) WayneHutchinson 106
(Alan King) *midfield: btn 3f out* **6/1**[3]

53P- **9** *2 ¼* **Bally Lagan (IRE)**[43] 3180 6-11-0 0 (t) CharliePoste 103
(Robin Dickin) *sn pushed along in detached last: nvr on terms: t.o* **100/1**

/22- **10** *1 ½* **French Opera**[48] 3080 11-11-0 0 AndrewTinkler 107
(Nicky Henderson) *prom on outer: shkn up 5f out: lost pl 3f out: t.o and eased fnl f* **3/1**[1]

435- **11** *26* **Barlow (IRE)**[20] 3642 7-10-11 0 GavinSheehan(3) 76
(Warren Greatrex) *prom tl drvn 5f out: qckly lost pl: t.o and eased over 1f out* **11/1**

1/U- **12** *9* **Kuilsriver (IRE)**[48] 3096 7-10-9 0 (v[1]) ThomasGarner(5) 67
(Nick Gifford) *dropped to rr and struggling 1/2-way: t.o fnl 4f* **14/1**

200- **13** *5* **Escort'men (FR)**[83] 2366 8-11-0 0 WillKennedy 62
(Ian Williams) *t.k.h: led after 6f: hdd 5f out and lost grnd v qckly: t.o over 3f out* **25/1**

3m 32.6s (2.50) **Going Correction** +0.45s/f (Slow) **13** Ran SP% **122.8**
Speed ratings: **111,110,108,108,106 104,102,102,101,100 87,82,80**
CSF £44.14 TOTE £4.60: £1.80, £3.40, £2.10; EX 43.10 Trifecta £355.50.
Owner Sparkes & Gibson **Bred** Mme Marinette Avril & Mlle Marie Avril **Trained** Ditcheat, Somerset
■ Stewards' Enquiry : Matt Crawley one-day ban; careless riding (14th Feb).

FOCUS
Runners must have taken part in at least one chase, but could not have won a class 1 or 2 chase. An interesting contest and the fastest race on the card.

4021 BOOK NOW FOR SILVER CUPS DAY 15.03.14 "JUMPERS' BUMPER" NATIONAL HUNT FLAT RACE 2m (P)

4:40 (4:40) (Class 4) 4-Y-0+ **£3,249** (£954; £477; £238)

Form RPR

/41- **1** **Caulfields Venture (IRE)**[118] 1765 8-11-4 0 AidanColeman 119
(Emma Lavelle) *trckd ldrs: led jst over 2f out: kpt on wl: rdn out* **16/1**

214- **2** *2* **Bally Legend**[35] 3321 9-11-4 0 TomO'Brien 117
(Caroline Keevil) *mid-div: hdwy whn nt nt clr run over 2f out: rdn and r.o strly to chse wnr over 1f out: kpt on but a being hld fnl f* **9/2**[2]

UP2- **3** *hd* **Heronry (IRE)**[49] 3060 6-11-1 0 JeremiahMcGrath(3) 117
(Nicky Henderson) *mid-div: nt clr run over 2f out: sn rdn: hdwy to chse wnr briefly over 1f out: kpt on same pce fnl f* **6/1**[3]

21P- **4** *3* **Dawn Commander (GER)**[98] 2065 7-11-4 0 BrendanPowell 114
(Renee Robeson) *hld up towards rr: c wd ent st: hdwy over 2f out: sn rdn: styd on to take 4th ins fnl f* **20/1**

343- **5** *nk* **Southfield Theatre (IRE)**[36] 3292 6-11-4 0 DarylJacob 114
(Paul Nicholls) *mid-div: rdn 3f out: chsd ldrs over 2f out: styd on but nvr gng pce to mount chal* **5/6**[1]

220/ **6** *nk* **Shakalakaboomboom (IRE)**[657] 5406 10-11-1 0 PeterCarberry(3) 113
(Nicky Henderson) *mid-div: hdwy over 2f out: sn rdn: 4th over 1f out: no ex fnl 120yds* **12/1**

/0P- **7** *1 ¾* **Ballybach (IRE)**[64] 2764 10-11-4 0 TomCannon 112
(Nick Gifford) *hld up towards rr: rdn and sme hdwy over 2f out: kpt on fnl f: nvr trbld ldrs* **66/1**

U2P/ **8** *1 ½* **Picaroon**[397] 10-10-11 0 MrsAlexDunn(7) 110
(Alexandra Dunn) *racd keenly: led tl rdn jst over 2f out: wknd fnl f* **33/1**

F0P- **9** ½ **Midnight Macarena**[35] 3325 9-10-1 0..........................(p) LukeIngram(10) 103
(Lucy Wadham) *hld up towards rr: c wd into st: styd on fr over 1f out but nvr threatening to get involved* **66/1**

P06- **10** *18* **Whispering Jack**[15] 3743 9-11-4 0......................(p) SamTwiston-Davies 92
(Keiran Burke) *trckd ldr: rdn 3f out: sn wknd: t.o* **66/1**

/22- **11** *nse* **Georgian King**[36] 3263 11-11-4 0.. IanPopham 92
(Martin Keighley) *mid-div: rdn 3f out: sn wknd: t.o* **25/1**

00P/ **12** *3 ½* **Kapricorne (FR)**[626] 276 7-10-13 0..................... CharlieWallis(5) 88
(Sophie Leech) *a towards rr: t.o* **100/1**

60P/ **13** *7* **Estates Recovery (IRE)**[439] 2502 9-11-4 0..................... LeightonAspell 81
(Luke Dace) *trckd ldrs tl pushed along over 5f out: sn bhd: t.o* **50/1**

12P- **14** *1 ¼* **Moscow Mule**[243] 600 11-10-13 0............................... EdCookson(5) 80
(Laura Hurley) *in tch: rdn 3f out: sn wknd* **100/1**

3m 33.6s (3.50) **Going Correction** +0.45s/f (Slow) **14** Ran SP% **120.6**
Speed ratings (Par 105): **109,108,107,106,106 106,105,104,104,95 95,93,89,89**
CSF £82.49 TOTE £16.50: £4.50, £1.40, £1.70; EX 118.80 Trifecta £685.50.
Owner C F Colquhoun **Bred** Michael Crean **Trained** Hatherden, Hants

FOCUS
For horses which had never run on the Flat, had run at least once over 2m7f+ since 2011, and had not won any class 1 or 2 race. This didn't look all that competitive, but there was something of a turn-up. The winner will be well handicapped if he can transfer this level back to jumping.

4022 KEMPTON.CO.UK "JUMPERS' BUMPER" NATIONAL HUNT FLAT RACE 2m (P)
5:10 (5:10) (Class 3) 4-Y-0+ **£6,330** (£1,870; £935; £468; £234)

Form RPR

313- **1** **Sgt Reckless**[36] 3258 7-11-4 0............................. DominicElsworth 129
(Mick Channon) *settled midfield: smooth prog 4f out: rdn to ld over 1f out: kpt on strly: impressive* **15/8**[1]

/16- **2** *1 ½* **Ranjaan (FR)**[48] 3088 6-11-4 0.................................(t) DarylJacob 127
(Paul Nicholls) *prom chsng clr ldng pair: clsd 4f out: drvn to ld over 2f out: hdd over 1f out: nt qckn* **7/2**[2]

303- **3** *nk* **Edmaaj (IRE)**[26] 3556 6-11-4 0.. APMcCoy 127
(Jonjo O'Neill) *settled chsng ldrs: rdn and outpcd over 2f out: styd on u.p after: unable to chal* **12/1**

122- **4** *1 ¼* **Benbane Head (USA)**[105] 1956 10-11-4 0.........................(t) IanPopham 125
(Martin Keighley) *disp ld at gd pce and clr w one rival: drvn and hdd 2f out: styd on steadily ins fnl f* **16/1**

012- **5** *hd* **Christopher Wren (USA)**[35] 3323 7-11-4 0...................... TomCannon 125
(Nick Gifford) *midfield: drvn and racing awkwardly 3f out: sn bdly outpcd: decided to run on late and fin strly: gave himself too much to do* **33/1**

141- **6** *10* **Staigue Fort**[113] 1828 6-11-4 0... AidanColeman 115
(Emma Lavelle) *mounted outside paddock: disp ld: rdn and hdd over 2f out: drvn and btn over 1f out* **20/1**

/14- **7** ½ **Tuscan Gold**[40] 237 7-11-4 0.. LeightonAspell 115
(Laura Mongan) *bhd: n.d fnl 3f* **66/1**

6/6- **8** *1* **Adiynara (IRE)**[47] 3117 6-11-3 0...................................(p) NoelFehily 113
(Neil Mulholland) *a abt same pl: btn 3f out* **50/1**

3- **9** *9* **Benzanno (IRE)**[34] 3350 5-11-4 0... JasonMaguire 105
(Donald McCain) *plld hrd in rr: rdn and btn 3f out: t.o* **8/1**[3]

0/ **10** *1* **Troopingthecolour**[44] 5131 8-11-4 0...................(t) SamTwiston-Davies 104
(Steve Gollings) *bhd: struggling 4f out: t.o* **7/2**[2]

110/ **11** *hd* **Sonoran Sands (IRE)**[643] 5649 6-11-4 0...................... BrendanPowell 104
(Brendan Powell) *t.k.h in last: struggling 4f out: t.o* **66/1**

6F3- **12** *6* **Warrant Officer**[26] 3550 4-10-7 0..................................... MarcGoldstein 87
(Sheena West) *chsd clr ldng pair: 8 l 3rd at 1/2-way: lost pl rapidly 5f out: t.o* **66/1**

0FF- **P** **Milord (GER)**[12] 3796 5-11-4 0... NickScholfield
(Kim Bailey) *prom in chsng gp 10f: t.o and eased over 1f out: p.u clsng stages* **16/1**

3m 33.5s (3.40) **Going Correction** +0.45s/f (Slow)
WFA 4 from 5yo 11lb 5 from 6yo+ 3lb **13** Ran SP% **123.9**
Speed ratings (Par 107): **109,108,108,107,107 102,102,101,97,96 96,93,**
CSF £8.19 TOTE £3.10: £1.80, £1.60, £4.20; EX 11.40 Trifecta £112.00.
Owner Mrs T P Radford **Bred** Miss Bridget Coyle **Trained** West Ilsley, Berks

FOCUS
For horses that had run at least once over hurdles but have not won any class 1 or 2 race. Probably the best race on the card. The winner is a useful novice.

4023 KEMPTON PARK CHASE DAY 22.02.14 "JUMPERS' BUMPER" NATIONAL HUNT FLAT RACE 2m (P)
5:40 (5:40) (Class 4) 4-Y-0+ **£3,249** (£954; £477; £238)

Form RPR

122- **1** **Pass Muster**[28] 3518 7-11-1 0.. KyleJames(3) 113
(Philip Kirby) *trckd ldrs: led over 2f out: sn rdn 3 l clr: jst hld on: all out* **16/1**

411- **2** *nse* **Dawalan (FR)**[16] 3714 4-10-7 0... DavidBass 101
(Nicky Henderson) *mid-div: pushed along and hdwy fr 3f out: rdn to chse ldrs over 2f out: wnt 2nd over 1f out: str run whn chal fnl 120yds: jst failed* **10/11**[1]

43- **3** ½ **Cool Sky**[45] 3144 5-11-4 0.. JasonMaguire 112
(Donald McCain) *towards rr of mid-div: nt clr run and swtchd lft over 2f out: sn rdn and hdwy: str run to chal runner-up ins fnl f: no ex nring fin* **8/1**[3]

316- **4** *5* **Tealissio**[36] 3249 8-10-13 0..................................(t) MattCrawley(5) 107
(Lucy Wadham) *mid-div: rdn over 2f out: styd on ent fnl f: wnt 4th fnl 50yds* **50/1**

116- **5** *1 ½* **Kettlewell**[19] 1913 5-11-4 0..(t) APMcCoy 105
(Warren Greatrex) *disp ld: clr ldr whn qcknd pce over 4f out: rdn and hdd over 2f out: sn hld: no ex ins fnl f* **4/1**[2]

353- **6** *2 ¾* **Spoil Me (IRE)**[58] 2887 7-11-10 0................................ RichieMcLernon 109
(Jonjo O'Neill) *in tch: rdn into 3rd over 3f out: one pce fnl 2f* **33/1**

104- **7** ½ **Invicta Lake (IRE)**[42] 3186 7-11-4 0............................(p) PaddyBrennan 102
(Suzy Smith) *hld up towards rr: sme late prog: nvr trbld ldrs* **20/1**

300- **8** *hd* **Kyles Faith (IRE)**[50] 3029 6-10-11 0.............................. OllieGarner(7) 102
(Martin Keighley) *hld up towards rr: sme late prog: nvr a danger* **100/1**

250/ **9** *nk* **Spanish Treasure (GER)**[329] 4645 8-11-4 0.................. NickScholfield 102
(Andy Turnell) *nvr bttr than mid-div* **33/1**

553- **10** *1* **Tidal Way (IRE)**[35] 3322 5-10-11 0.....................(tp) CharlieDeutsch(7) 101
(Charlie Longsdon) *in tch: rdn over 3f out: wknd over 1f out* **14/1**

000- **11** *1* **Pyleigh Lass**[79] 2458 8-10-11 0... IanPopham 93
(Martin Keighley) *chsd ldrs: rdn over 3f out: sn wknd* **50/1**

233- **12** ¾ **Houseparty**[45] 3148 6-10-11 0... MrHGMiller(7) 99
(Zoe Davison) *hld up towards rr: sme prog u.p over 2f out: nvr a threat: wknd over 1f out* **100/1**

10/- **13** ½ **Dont Do Mondays (IRE)**[287] 5376 7-11-4 0.................. TomScudamore 98
(David Bridgwater) *disp ld tl over 4f out: rdn over 3f out: wknd over 2f out* **66/1**

4- **14** *1 ¾* **Stay In My Heart (IRE)**[52] 3007 5-10-11 0..................... LeightonAspell 90
(Laura Mongan) *mid-div: rdn over 3f out: sn wknd* **66/1**

215- **15** *1 ¼* **Aazif (IRE)**[167] 1290 5-11-4 0.. WillKennedy 95
(Ian Williams) *a towards rr* **10/1**

3/P- **16** *11* **Cinematique (IRE)**[250] 486 6-11-4 0................................. TomCannon 84
(Laura Mongan) *a towards rr* **100/1**

3m 36.1s (6.00) **Going Correction** +0.45s/f (Slow)
WFA 4 from 5yo 11lb 5 from 6yo+ 3lb **16** Ran SP% **125.7**
Speed ratings (Par 105): **103,102,102,100,99 98,97,97,97,97 96,96,95,95,94 88**
CSF £30.69 TOTE £16.60: £3.40, £1.20, £2.40; EX 48.80 Trifecta £556.70.
Owner C B Construction (Cleveland) Limited **Bred** Darley **Trained** Middleham, N Yorks

FOCUS
For horses that had run at least once over hurdles but have not won any class 1, 2 or 3 race. This was run at an uneven gallop and the principals finished well clear. The winn, third and fourth set the level.
T/Jkpt: Not won. T/Plt: £197.00 to a £1 stake. Pool: £79366.69 - 293.96 winning tickets T/Qpdt: £30.10 to a £1 stake. Pool: £5595.83 - 137.50 winning tickets TM

3127 FFOS LAS (L-H)
Saturday, February 1

OFFICIAL GOING: Heavy (5.7)
Hurdles sited on fresh ground tight to Chase course. Fences sited towards outer of Chase course.
Wind: Strong; against Weather: Blustery showers and bright spells

4024 BURNS HEALTHY PET NOVICES' HURDLE (7 hdls 1 omitted) 2m
1:30 (1:31) (Class 4) 4-Y-0+ **£3,898** (£1,144; £572; £286)

Form RPR

053/ **1** **Horatio Hornblower (IRE)**[420] 2914 6-11-3 0............. TomScudamore 118+
(Nick Williams) *t.k.h: chsd ldrs: pressed ldrs fr 4th: ev ch and looked to be travelling best bypassing 3 out: led last: drvn and hdd fnl 100yds: kpt on gamely to ld again on post* **7/2**[3]

042- **2** *nse* **Filatore (IRE)**[47] 3128 5-11-3 112...................................(p) PaulMoloney 118+
(Bernard Llewellyn) *t.k.h: chsd ldrs: drew clr in ldng trio bypassing 3 out: ev ch next: mstke last: drvn to ld fnl 100yds: kpt on u.p: hdd on post* **3/1**[2]

345- **3** *2 ½* **Pure Science (IRE)**[13] 3798 6-11-3 120.................. SamTwiston-Davies 115
(Nigel Twiston-Davies) *chsd ldrs tl led after 2nd: rdn 2 out: hdd last: no ex and one pce flat* **11/4**[1]

244- **4** *26* **Gate Please (IRE)**[47] 3130 9-10-12 121.....................(t) PatrickCorbett(5) 89
(Rebecca Curtis) *led tl after 2nd: styd pressing ldrs: rdn on long run after 5th: wknd u.p bypassing 3 out* **6/1**

2/4- **5** *21* **Bar A Mine (FR)**[35] 3363 5-11-3 0.................................... NickScholfield 68
(Paul Nicholls) *wl in tch in midfield: mstke 4th: rdn sn after next: wknd on long run to next: t.o whn mstke 2 out* **6/1**

/06- **6** *15* **Comte D'Anjou**[56] 2947 5-11-3 0.................................... BrendanPowell 53
(Nick Williams) *hld up in tch in last trio: 6th and rdn sn after 5th: sn btn and t.o bef next* **10/1**

05- **7** *6* **Wicklewood**[51] 3047 8-11-3 75..(t) TommyPhelan 47
(Mark Gillard) *chsd ldrs tl 2nd: shuffled bk into last trio next: wknd bef 5th: t.o on long run to 2 out* **100/1**

8 *50* **Kagouillot (FR)**[559] 5-10-10 0.. MrPJohn(7)
(Reginald Brown) *wl in tch in midfield: mstke 1st: rdn and struggling after 4th: lost tch on long run after next: t.o bef 2 out* **50/1**

FP/ **P** **Shays River (IRE)**[279] 8 9-11-3 0.............................(bt[1]) AdamWedge
(Evan Williams) *hld up in rr: lost tch 4th: t.o on long run after next: p.u last* **50/1**

4m 8.0s (19.50) **Going Correction** +1.375s/f (Heav) **9** Ran SP% **116.5**
Speed ratings (Par 105): **106,105,104,91,81 73,70,45,**
CSF £14.93 TOTE £5.50: £2.40, £1.10, £1.40; EX 16.40 Trifecta £46.90.
Owner Huw & Richard Davies **Bred** H Davies & R Davies **Trained** George Nympton, Devon

FOCUS
Hurdles sited on fresh ground tight to chase course. Fences sited towards outer of chase course. The course survived a 7.30am inspection. After riding in the first Tom Scudamore said it's heavy but sloppy and wet and they are getting through it. The first hurdle in the home straight was omitted. A fair novices´ hurdle run at an honest pace. There should be more to come from the winner.

4025 BURNS PET NUTRITION WELSH CHAMPION HURDLE (LIMITED H'CAP) (8 hdls 2 omitted) 2m 4f
2:05 (2:05) (Class 2) 4-Y-0+
£31,280 (£9,240; £4,620; £2,310; £1,155; £580)

Form RPR

411- **1** **Saphir Du Rheu (FR)**[21] 3646 5-11-5 **158**.................... HarryDerham(5) 162+
(Paul Nicholls) *mde all: wnt clr w runner-up 2 out: hdd bef last: outj. rival and led again last: r.o wl u.p and a holding rival flat* **2/1**[2]

331- **2** *hd* **Whisper (FR)**[35] 3369 6-10-13 **147**................................. AndrewTinkler 152+
(Nicky Henderson) *t.k.h: chsd ldrs: chsd wnr after bypassed 3 out: clr w wnr fr next: rdn to ld bef last: hit last and hdd: r.o wl u.p but a jst hld flat* **6/4**[1]

/P2- **3** *19* **Grand Vision (IRE)**[21] 3653 8-10-8 **142**........................ BrendanPowell 127
(Colin Tizzard) *wl in tch in midfield: rdn on long run after 6th: 4th and btn 2 out: wnt 3rd but no threat to ldrs between last 2: plugged on* **5/1**[3]

231- **4** *1 ¾* **Awaywiththegreys (IRE)**[35] 3359 7-10-4 **136**............(p) DonalDevereux 121
(Peter Bowen) *racd wdst: chsd wnr tl nt fluent and lost ch 5th: rdn and btn bef 2 out: wknd between last 2* **8/1**

420- **5** *2 ¼* **Home Run (GER)**[21] 3646 6-9-11 **130**............................(b) KieronEdgar(7) 119
(David Pipe) *hld up wl in tch in last pair: rdn and struggling bypassing 3 out: wknd next* **11/1**

/F0- **6** *1* **Swnymor (IRE)**[21] 3648 5-9-13 **132**.........................(t) PatrickCorbett(5) 118
(Rebecca Curtis) *hld up wl in tch in last pair: effrt to chse ldng pair bef 2 out: sn rdn and no imp: wknd between last 2* **16/1**

5m 31.55s (40.65) **Going Correction** +1.65s/f (Heav) **6** Ran SP% **115.3**
Speed ratings (Par 109): **84,83,76,75,74 74**
CSF £5.86 TOTE £2.40: £1.50, £1.10; EX 5.40 Trifecta £10.20.
Owner The Stewart Family **Bred** Claude Duval **Trained** Ditcheat, Somerset
■ Stewards' Enquiry : Andrew Tinkler four-day ban: use of whip (16-19 Feb)

FOCUS
A race which Medinas won in 2013 prior to landing the Coral Cup, it was short on numbers but not on quality. It was run at a steady pace with the first two home fighting out a thrilling finish. Another step forward from the progreesive winner, but not a proper test at the trip.

4026 BURNS PET NUTRITION WEST WALES NATIONAL (HANDICAP CHASE) (17 fncs 5 omitted) 3m 4f
2:40 (2:40) (Class 2) 5-Y-0+ **£18,990** (£5,610; £2,805; £1,404; £702)

Form RPR

6P0- **1** **Emperor's Choice (IRE)**[21] 3655 7-10-5 **126** .... LiamTreadwell 140+
(Venetia Williams) *in tch in midfield: rdn after 10th: pressed ldrs and bk on bridle after 14th: chsng ldr and j.lft 2 out: drvn to ld and gng clr whn j. awkwardly last: styd on wl flat* **9/2**[1]

004- **2** *8* **Firebird Flyer (IRE)**[33] 3424 7-10-0 **121** oh1 .... AdamWedge 127
(Evan Williams) *in tch in midfield: clsd to trck ldrs 11th: chsd ldr sn after 14th: led next: rdn and hdd between last 2: btn last: wknd flat but hld on for 2nd cl home* **14/1**

/62- **3** *½* **Smoking Aces (IRE)**[27] 3554 10-10-1 **122** ....(b) RichieMcLernon 131+
(Jonjo O'Neill) *in tch in midfield: clsd on ldrs 10th: cl 5th after 14th: mstke 15th: rdn and outpcd bypassing next: wnt 3rd between last 2: no threat to wnr but styd on u.p flat* **6/1**[2]

P43- **4** *6* **Junior**[18] 3698 11-11-12 **147** ....(b) ConorO'Farrell 149
(David Pipe) *chsd ldrs: wnt 2nd 10th tl led after 13th: rdn and hdd 15th: drvn bypassing next: 3rd and btn 2 out: wknd bef last* **20/1**

331- **5** *26* **Mountainous (IRE)**[35] 3361 9-11-9 **144** .... PaulMoloney 131
(Richard Lee) *chsd ldrs: cl 4th after 14th: rdn and struggling after next: wknd 2 out: heavily eased fnl 100yds: t.o* **8/1**

242- **P** **Alfie Spinner (IRE)**[31] 3455 9-10-7 **128** .... TomScudamore
(Nick Williams) *chsd ldr tl 10th: styd chsng ldrs tl lost pl rapidly after 13th: t.o whn p.u 15th* **7/1**

/01- **P** **Flying Award (IRE)**[16] 3743 10-10-0 **126** .... MissLucyGardner[(5)]
(Sue Gardner) *a bhd: rdn along briefly after 7th: rdn again and no hdwy after 10th: tailing off whn p.u next* **16/1**

314- **P** **Ringa Bay**[17] 3717 9-9-10 **124** oh1 ow3........(p) JakeHodson[(7)]
(David Bridgwater) *in tch in midfield: mstke and lost pl 4th: bhd and nvr gng wl after: lost tch 10th: t.o whn p.u next* **16/1**

024- **P** **Sir Du Bearn (FR)**[33] 3416 8-10-9 **130** .... DonalDevereux
(Peter Bowen) *a towards rr: in tch but struggling u.p after 10th: lost tch 12th: t.o whn p.u 14th* **12/1**

365- **P** **Hunters Lodge (IRE)**[33] 3416 8-10-6 **127** ....(p) SamTwiston-Davies
(Nigel Twiston-Davies) *a towards rr: j. slowly 10th: sn rdn and no rspnse: tailing off whn p.u next* **12/1**

016- **P** **De La Bech**[31] 3455 7-10-7 **128** .... TomO'Brien
(Philip Hobbs) *chsd ldrs: rdn and lost pl after mstke 12th: lost tch after next: t.o whn p.u 15th* **13/2**[3]

520- **P** **Bob Ford (IRE)**[33] 3416 7-10-0 **126** .... PatrickCorbett[(5)]
(Rebecca Curtis) *led: clr 2nd tl after 7th: hdd after 13th: sn dropped out and bhd: t.o whn p.u 15th* **7/1**

7m 58.7s (38.40) **Going Correction** +1.65s/f (Heav) **12** Ran SP% **120.5**
Speed ratings: **111,108,108,106,99** , , , , ,
CSF £65.92 CT £388.61 TOTE £4.40: £1.90, £5.00, £1.90; EX 83.00 Trifecta £455.50.
Owner The Bellamy Partnership **Bred** Pat Browne **Trained** Kings Caple, H'fords

FOCUS
The first fence in the back straight and second fence (open ditch) in the home straight were omitted. A fiercely competitive staying handicap which took some getting in these gruelling conditions, especially after Bob Ford set such a strong early pace. The winner had slipped to a good mark and is rated back to form.

4027 BURNS HEALTHY PET H'CAP CHASE (11 fncs 4 omitted) 2m 3f 110y
3:10 (3:13) (Class 3) (0-130,128) 5-Y-0+ **£6,498** (£1,908; £954; £477)

Form RPR

404- **1** **Poole Master**[35] 3362 9-11-12 **128** ....(b) TomScudamore 145+
(David Pipe) *clr w runner-up thrght: led tl 5th: styd w ldr tl led again and travelling strly bef 9th: sn wl clr: easily* **4/1**[3]

PPP- **2** *39* **Frontier Spirit (IRE)**[16] 3742 10-11-9 **125** ....(v[1]) SamTwiston-Davies 98
(Nigel Twiston-Davies) *w ldr and clr of field thrght: led 5th tl rdn and hdd bef 9th: sn btn: j. slowly 2 out: j. slowly again and lost 2nd last: battled bk to go 2nd again towards fin* **8/1**

043- **3** *1 ½* **The Chazer (IRE)**[36] 3325 9-11-4 **120** .... IanPopham 91
(Richard Lee) *hld up in rr: hdwy to go 7 l 3rd 8th: rdn and wknd next: plugged on to go modest 2nd last: plugged on but lost 2nd towards fin* **7/1**

45P- **4** *9* **Triptico (FR)**[42] 3205 8-11-8 **124** .... PaulMoloney 86
(Evan Williams) *in tch in midfield: pushed along and struggling 6th: rdn and wknd 9th: 4th and wl hld bypassing 3 out: t.o* **9/4**[1]

/5P- **P** **Green Belt Elite (FR)**[35] 3362 10-11-7 **123** .... LiamTreadwell
(Venetia Williams) *j.rt and mstkes: in tch in midfield: wknd 8th: t.o sn after next tl p.u 9th* **8/1**

01P- **P** **Maller Tree**[21] 3646 7-10-13 **115** ....(v) DougieCostello
(David Dennis) *chsd ldrs tl rdn and dropped to last after 6th: t.o 8th: p.u next* **11/4**[2]

5m 29.0s (27.90) **Going Correction** +1.65s/f (Heav) **6** Ran SP% **112.2**
Speed ratings: **110,94,93,90,**
CSF £32.15 TOTE £4.90: £2.10, £3.60; EX 41.50 Trifecta £200.80.
Owner G Thompson **Bred** Wood Farm Stud **Trained** Nicholashayne, Devon

FOCUS
An interesting contest with a number of well handicapped runners in the field. It was run at a fair pace and the easy winner is rated back to his best.

4028 PROFESSIONAL SECURITY MANAGEMENT H'CAP HURDLE (8 hdls 2 omitted) 2m 4f
3:45 (3:46) (Class 3) (0-130,128) 4-Y-0+ **£6,498** (£1,908; £954; £477)

Form RPR

601- **1** **Kayf Moss**[11] 3821 6-10-8 **110** ....(b) TomO'Brien 133+
(John Flint) *mde virtually all: drew wl clr after 6th: in n.d whn hit 2 out: eased flat* **6/4**[1]

533- **2** *27* **Buckhorn Tom**[14] 3784 6-10-11 **113** ....(p) BrendanPowell 104
(Colin Tizzard) *chsd wnr tl after 3rd: mstke and lost pl 5th: 4th and wl btn u.p after 6th: plugged on to go modest 2nd towards fin* **7/1**

430- **3** *2 ¼* **Makethe Mostofnow (IRE)**[35] 3359 9-11-0 **123** .... ConorRing[(7)] 112
(Evan Williams) *wl in tch in midfield: chsd clr wnr on losng run after 6th: wl btn bef 2 out: lost 2nd towards fin* **8/1**

P0P- **4** *19* **Oscar Magic (IRE)**[37] 3259 7-11-12 **128** ....(t) SamTwiston-Davies 98
(Nigel Twiston-Davies) *chsd ldrs: wnt 2nd after 3rd: upsides wnr 5th tl after next: sn btn: 4th and wkng 2 out: t.o* **9/2**[2]

1/P- **5** *10* **Fishing Bridge (IRE)**[13] 3798 9-11-4 **120** .... AdamWedge 80
(David Rees) *in tch in midfield: rdn and btn sn after 6th: wknd bef next: t.o 2 out* **20/1**

022- **6** *34* **Scales (IRE)**[45] 3157 8-10-5 **110** .... MichealNolan[(3)] 36
(Richard Lee) *in tch in midfield: hdwy to chse ldrs 5th: rdn and btn after next: sn wknd and t.o 2 out* **8/1**

000- **7** *5* **Whisky Yankee (IRE)**[16] 3741 7-11-6 **122** .... RichieMcLernon 43
(Jonjo O'Neill) *a in last pair: lost tch 6th: t.o on long run to next* **6/1**[3]

100- **8** *40* **Radmores Revenge**[42] 3201 11-11-8 **124** .... PaulMoloney
(Sophie Leech) *a in rr: lost tch 6th: t.o on long run to next* **20/1**

5m 22.7s (31.80) **Going Correction** +1.80s/f (Heav) **8** Ran SP% **116.7**
Speed ratings (Par 107): **108,97,96,88,84 71,69,53**
CSF £13.22 CT £61.46 TOTE £2.90: £1.10, £2.30, £2.90; EX 8.90 Trifecta £53.90.
Owner L H & Mrs T Evans **Bred** Mrs Vashti Hasdell **Trained** Kenfig Hill, Bridgend

FOCUS
They went a sound gallop for this handicap with the field finishing well strung out. There's a case for rating the form a lot higher through the beaten horses.

4029 IWEC ELECTRICAL MAIDEN HURDLE (9 hdls 3 omitted) 3m
4:20 (4:21) (Class 4) 5-Y-0+ **£3,898** (£1,144; £572; £286)

Form RPR

404- **1** **Copper Birch (IRE)**[45] 3155 6-11-0 116 .... PaulMoloney 126+
(Evan Williams) *chsd ldrs: wnt 2nd and travelling best after 7th: led bypassing 3 out and sn clr: eased flat* **9/4**[1]

243- **2** *21* **Red Devil Lads (IRE)**[45] 3166 5-11-0 0 .... TomO'Brien 101
(Rebecca Curtis) *mstkes: led tl rdn and hdd bypassing 3 out: sn btn but plugged on for clr 2nd* **4/1**[3]

42- **3** *20* **Gorsky Island**[48] 3116 6-11-0 0 .... PaddyBrennan 80
(Tom George) *chsd ldrs: wnt 2nd bypassing 6th: rdn and btn 3rd on long run bef 2 out: t.o whn j.rt 2 out* **5/2**[2]

5- **4** *8* **Castletown (IRE)**[35] 3363 6-11-0 0 ....(t) DougieCostello 72
(Laura Young) *racd in last quartet: pushed along and clsd after 5th: 4th and cl enough 7th: wknd wl bef 2 out: t.o whn j.rt 2 out* **10/1**

55- **5** *20* **Kaikias (IRE)**[13] 3800 7-11-0 0 ....(b) RichieMcLernon 52
(Jonjo O'Neill) *nt a fluent: chsd ldrs: rdn and struggling sn after 7th: sn bhd: t.o bef 2 out* **14/1**

004- **6** *120* **Brave Encounter (IRE)**[14] 3782 6-10-9 0 .... MissLucyGardner[(5)]
(Sue Gardner) *a bhd: rdn and lost tch after 5th: wl t.o fr 7th* **50/1**

P/0- **P** **Clovers Boy**[18] 3697 9-11-0 0 .... WillKennedy
(Sue Gardner) *sn bhd: t.o whn p.u after 5th* **100/1**

003- **P** **Spending Time**[14] 3782 5-11-0 0 .... BrendanPowell
(Colin Tizzard) *wl in tch in midfield: lost tch qckly 7th: sn eased and p.u wl bef 2 out* **7/1**

\- **P** **Mountain Cliche (IRE)**[258] 7-11-0 0 .... TomScudamore
(Jo Hughes) *chsd ldr tl bypassing 6th: rdn and lost pl next: t.o whn p.u bef 2 out* **16/1**

260- **P** **Driving Well (IRE)**[32] 3440 6-11-0 0 .... NickScholfield
(Arthur Whiting) *in tch towards rr: clsd after 5th: rdn and btn 7th: sn lost tch and t.o: p.u 2 out* **50/1**

6m 37.3s (48.30) **Going Correction** +1.80s/f (Heav) **10** Ran SP% **118.4**
Speed ratings: **91,84,77,74,68** , , , ,
CSF £12.10 TOTE £3.40: £1.40, £1.90, £1.10; EX 14.20 Trifecta £33.10.
Owner Mrs Janet Davies **Bred** Jarlath O'Dwyer **Trained** Llancarfan, Vale Of Glamorgan

FOCUS
This maiden hurdle was run at a sound pace, proving a brutal test in the conditions. The easy winner is rated back to his best.

4030 WALTERS UK STANDARD OPEN NATIONAL HUNT FLAT RACE 2m
4:50 (4:52) (Class 6) 4-6-Y-0 **£1,949** (£572; £286; £143)

Form RPR

2- **1** **Foryourinformation**[80] 2456 5-10-13 0 ....(t) PatrickCorbett[(5)] 120+
(Rebecca Curtis) *in tch in midfield: clsd to ldrs and gng wl 4f out: led over 2f out: 4 l clr over 1f out: drvn ins fnl f: kpt on and a holding on* **4/1**[3]

2 *½* **Obistar (FR)** 4-10-8 0 .... TomScudamore 110+
(David Pipe) *chsd ldrs: rdn and outpcd in 6th 4f out: rallied and hdwy 3f out: chsd clr wnr over 1f out: styd on wl fnl f: nvr quite getting to wnr* **11/4**[2]

2- **3** *13* **Ashford Wood (IRE)**[35] 3363 6-11-4 0 .... DougieCostello 107
(Tim Vaughan) *chsd ldrs: 4th and outpcd u.p over 3f out: no imp whn hung lft u.p over 1f out: wnt 3rd ins fnl f: no threat to ldng pair* **2/1**[1]

4 *1 ½* **Southsea Island (IRE)**[304] 5132 6-10-8 0 .... PaulO'Brien[(10)] 105
(Rebecca Curtis) *t.k.h: led tl rdn and hdd over 2f out: 3rd and wknd over 1f out: lost 4th ins fnl f* **20/1**

5 *16* **Rock On Rocky** 6-11-4 0 .... CharliePoste 89
(Matt Sheppard) *t.k.h: chsd ldr tl 4f out: 5th and btn 3f out: wknd 2f out* **50/1**

4- **6** *17* **Picodean**[47] 3133 6-11-4 0 .... TomO'Brien 72
(Robert Stephens) *in tch towards rr: rdn and wknd 5f out: t.o fnl 3f* **16/1**

120- **7** *31* **Capilla (IRE)**[35] 3363 6-11-4 0 .... ConorRing[(7)] 48
(Evan Williams) *in tch in midfield: clsd to trck ldrs 6f out: 3rd and rdn 3f out: sn btn: fdd bdly 2f out: t.o and eased ins fnl f* **9/2**

00- **8** *24* **Castanum (IRE)**[77] 2513 5-11-1 0 .... RobertDunne[(3)] 17
(Laura Young) *in tch in rr tl lost tch over 5f out: sn t.o* **100/1**

9 *47* **Magnum Too (IRE)** 5-10-11 0 .... MrMatthewBarber[(7)]
(Beth Roberts) *hld up in tch in rr: hdwy into midfield 12f out: lost pl and bhd 6f out: sn t.o* **66/1**

2/6- **S** **Shadow Cruise (IRE)**[35] 3363 5-11-4 0 .... DonalDevereux
(Bernard Llewellyn) *in tch in midfield: rdn and struggling 5f out: wkng whn stmbld and fell over 4f out: fatally injured* **25/1**

P **Bobtail** 4-10-8 0 .... TommyPhelan
(Mark Gillard) *in tch towards rr: lost tch qckly 6f out: t.o whn rdr p.u to catch stricken rival 4f out* **50/1**

4m 7.6s (24.70) **Going Correction** +1.80s/f (Heav)
WFA 4 from 5yo 9lb 5 from 6yo 1lb **11** Ran SP% **119.1**
Speed ratings: **110,109,103,102,94 86,70,58,35,**
CSF £14.92 TOTE £4.60: £1.50, £2.10, £1.10; EX 18.50 Trifecta £37.40.
Owner Carl Hinchy **Bred** Whitley Stud **Trained** Newport, Dyfed

FOCUS
A fair bumper run at a sound gallop with the front two looking nice types. The field were called back after a false start which thankfully did not adversely affect any runners. A step up from the winner.
T/Plt: £36.40 to a £1 stake. Pool: £130,721.51 - 2,621.2 winning units T/Qpdt: £25.30 to a £1 stake. Pool: £6,660.00 - 194.70 winning units SP

2947 SANDOWN (R-H)

Saturday, February 1

OFFICIAL GOING: Heavy (soft in places back straight; 4.5)

An all-chase card after the scheduled hurdle races, inlcuding the Contenders Hurdle, were abandoned due to waterlogging.

Wind: Brisk; ahead Weather: Sunny spells early

4031 BETFRED "DOUBLE DELIGHT" NOVICES' LIMITED H'CAP CHASE (17 fncs) 2m 4f 110y

1:15 (1:15) (Class 3) (0-125,124) 5-Y-0+

£9,384 (£2,772; £1,386; £693; £346; £174)

Form RPR

213- **1** **Saroque (IRE)**[19] 3690 7-11-4 119 AidanColeman 130+
(Venetia Williams) *mde all: mstke 12th: styd on wl u.p fr 2 out* **3/1**[1]

1F4- **2** 2 1/4 **Toby Lerone (IRE)**[21] 3642 7-11-8 123 HarrySkelton 131
(Dan Skelton) *chsd wnr thrght: rdn and styd on fr 3 out: ev ch u.p last: styd on same pce run-in* **9/2**[2]

341- **3** 28 **Spanish Arch (IRE)**[37] 3266 7-11-1 119 (bt[1]) KielanWoods[(3)] 99
(Charlie Longsdon) *in tch: chsd ldrs fr 7th: rdn 4 out: wknd sn after 3 out* **3/1**[1]

415- **4** 2 3/4 **Gandalfe (FR)**[65] 2762 9-10-11 112 (b) AndrewThornton 90
(David Arbuthnot) *hit 4th: chsd ldrs fr 6th: blnd 10th: j. slowly next: rdn and hit 4 out: mstke and wknd 3 out* **14/1**

433- **5** 14 **Pistol (IRE)**[21] 3658 5-11-6 124 (b) RichardJohnson 84
(Philip Hobbs) *hdwy to chse ldrs 6th: pushed along appr 7th: rdn next: hit 9th: blnd and bhd 10th: mod prog u.p after 4 out: nvr any ch and sn wknd* **6/1**[3]

52P- **6** 16 **According To Them (IRE)**[27] 3554 10-10-3 101 oh30(t) MattieBatchelor 51
(Daniel Steele) *j. slowly and bhd fr 3rd: lost tch fr 9th* **100/1**

31P- **P** **Castle Conflict (IRE)**[35] 3365 9-11-5 123 JakeGreenall[(3)]
(Henry Daly) *chsd ldrs early: bhd and j. slowly 7th: wknd and p.u bef 9th* **8/1**

4F4- **P** **Regal One (IRE)**[32] 3429 6-10-11 112 RobertThornton
(David Bridgwater) *in rr fr 6th: blnd 8th: hit 13th: t.o whn p.u bef 2 out* **8/1**

5m 36.31s (17.91) **Going Correction** +1.05s/f (Soft)
WFA 5 from 6yo+ 2lb **8 Ran SP% 112.3**
Speed ratings: **107,106,95,94,89 83,,**
CSF £16.72 CT £42.12 TOTE £3.80: £1.30, £1.50, £1.40; EX 14.40 Trifecta £36.10.

Owner A Brooks **Bred** Miss Mary Condon **Trained** Kings Caple, H'fords

FOCUS
Aidan Coleman described the ground as "very hard work and quite holding." Little got into this and the first two were clear. Arguably a small personal best from the winner.

4032 BETFRED "GOALS GALORE" H'CAP CHASE (13 fncs) 2m

1:50 (1:50) (Class 2) (0-150,148) 5-Y-0+

£15,640 (£4,620; £2,310; £1,155; £577; £290)

Form RPR

332- **1** **Grey Gold (IRE)**[21] 3660 9-11-2 **138** JamieMoore 149+
(Richard Lee) *trckd ldrs: wnt 2nd 9th: drvn to take slt ld appr 3 out: styd on gamely u.p run-in* **4/1**[1]

P11- **2** 3/4 **Desert Cry (IRE)**[21] 3660 8-11-11 **147** JasonMaguire 158+
(Donald McCain) *hld up in rr: stdy hdwy after 4 out to trck ldrs next: wnt 2nd travelling wl fr 2 out: stl gng wl whn j. slowly last: sn drvn and swtchd rt: ev ch fnl 150yds: fnd no ex clsng stages* **9/2**[2]

541- **3** 18 **Rebel Rebellion (IRE)**[56] 2939 9-11-10 **146** (tp) RyanMahon 140
(Paul Nicholls) *chsd ldr: led 8th: drvn to chal 3 out: wknd bef last* **8/1**

131- **4** 7 **Eastlake (IRE)**[49] 3080 8-11-2 **148** TommieMO'Brien[(10)] 134
(Jonjo O'Neill) *hld up towards rr: in tch 6th: stdy hdwy fr 4 out to chal 3 out: wknd next* **8/1**

414- **5** 3 1/4 **Filbert (IRE)**[21] 3660 8-10-13 **135** RichardJohnson 117
(Philip Hobbs) *in rr tl hdwy after 4 out: chsd ldrs appr next: wknd sn after* **7/1**

110- **6** hd **Oscar Hill (IRE)**[21] 3660 8-11-8 **144** RobertThornton 126
(David Bridgwater) *led: sn clr: j. slowly 4 out: hdd appr 3 out and sn btn* **10/1**

030- **7** 3 1/2 **Kumbeshwar**[7] 3887 7-11-4 **140** (b) WayneHutchinson 118
(Alan King) *chsd ldrs: wknd 9th* **5/1**[3]

414- **8** 8 **Pepite Rose (FR)**[21] 3645 7-11-11 **147** AidanColeman 117
(Venetia Williams) *in tch: hdwy after 4 out: wknd sn after next* **7/1**

4m 13.63s (11.83) **Going Correction** +1.05s/f (Soft) **8 Ran SP% 111.2**
Speed ratings: **112,111,102,99,97 97,95,91**
CSF £21.48 CT £130.23 TOTE £4.20: £1.20, £1.60, £3.00; EX 14.70 Trifecta £74.60.

Owner Mrs M A Boden **Bred** James Keegan And Jeff Hamilton **Trained** Byton, H'fords

■ Stewards' Enquiry : Jamie Moore two-day ban: use of whip (16-17 Feb)

FOCUS
Having been well strung out early, the field bunched right up coming to the Pond Fence and it was a pair of old rivals who fought out the finish. The winner was well in on his best form.

4033 BETFRED TV SCILLY ISLES NOVICES' CHASE (GRADE 1) (17 fncs) 2m 4f 110y

2:25 (2:25) (Class 1) 5-Y-0+ **£22,780** (£8,548; £4,280)

Form RPR

211- **1** **Oscar Whisky (IRE)**[31] 3456 9-11-4 156 BarryGeraghty 154+
(Nicky Henderson) *trckd ldrs in 3rd: nt flunt 7th: 8th and 4 out: wnt 2nd 3 out: rdn after 2 out: styd on to take slt ld whn nt fluent last: styd on strly* **1/6**[1]

/16- **2** 9 **Manyriverstocross (IRE)**[56] 2950 9-11-4 138 RobertThornton 143+
(Alan King) *t.k.h: trckd ldr: chal 8th: sn led: pushed along after 3 out: narrowly hdd last: sn no ch w wnr* **16/1**[3]

F11- **3** 33 **Benvolio (IRE)**[14] 3776 7-11-4 142 DarylJacob 122
(Paul Nicholls) *led: jnd 8th: sn hdd: drvn along fr 12th: lost 2nd 3 out and sn btn: no ch whn blnd last* **5/1**[2]

5m 33.74s (15.34) **Going Correction** +1.05s/f (Soft) **3 Ran SP% 108.2**
Speed ratings: **112,108,96**
CSF £3.10 TOTE £1.30; EX 2.80 Trifecta £3.00.

Owner Walters Plant Hire Ltd **Bred** Stephanie Hanly **Trained** Upper Lambourn, Berks

FOCUS
A disappointing turnout for this Grade 1 prize, and the red-hot favourite made hard enough work of winning. There's a case to rate the form a few pounds higher.

4034 BETFRED MOBILE VETERANS' H'CAP CHASE (17 fncs) 2m 4f 110y

3:00 (3:01) (Class 2) (0-150,143)
10-Y-0+ **£15,640** (£4,620; £2,310; £1,155; £577)

Form RPR

1/4- **1** **Aachen**[11] 3825 10-10-8 123 AidanColeman 127+
(Venetia Williams) *trckd ldrs: pckd 2nd: nt fluent 11th (water): chsd ldr after 3 out: led last: drvn out* **6/4**[1]

0/1- **2** 1 **Tatenen (FR)**[63] 2812 10-11-11 140 AndrewThornton 141
(Richard Rowe) *trckd ldr: chal 10th: hit 12th: styd upsides tl led after 4 out: rdn fr 3 out: hdd last: one pce u.p* **10/3**[3]

301- **3** 12 **King Edmund**[21] 3642 11-11-12 141 TomCannon 130
(Chris Gordon) *chsd ldrs in 4th: cl up 7th: rdn 3 out: wknd bef last* **4/1**

454- **4** 67 **Tchang Goon (FR)**[11] 3819 10-9-7 115 oh53 (p) MrHGMiller[(7)] 37
(Zoe Davison) *a last: wl bhd fr 9th: t.o* **100/1**

111- **5** 23 **Fine Parchment (IRE)**[57] 2931 11-10-13 135 (tp) MrHAABannister[(7)] 34
(Charlie Mann) *led: jnd fr 10th tl hdd after 4 out: wknd rapidly bef 2 out: v tired whn t.o and j.v.slowly last: virtually p.u run-in* **3/1**[2]

5m 43.56s (25.16) **Going Correction** +1.15s/f (Heav) **5 Ran SP% 109.1**
Speed ratings: **98,97,93,67,58**
CSF £6.89 TOTE £2.30: £1.20, £1.50; EX 5.80 Trifecta £27.70.

Owner Tony Bloom **Bred** Darley **Trained** Kings Caple, H'fords

FOCUS
This looked fairly competitive, despite the small field, and it went to the least exposed member of the field. The form is rated around the second.

4035 BETFRED MASTERS H'CAP CHASE (22 fncs) 3m 110y

3:35 (3:35) (Class 2) 5-Y-0+

£31,280 (£9,240; £4,620; £2,310; £1,155; £580)

Form RPR

P15- **1** **Relax (FR)**[21] 3647 9-11-1 **132** AidanColeman 144
(Venetia Williams) *led but hrd pressed tl hdd 8th: styd chalng but u.p after 4 out: kpt on gamely to ld sn after last: kpt on wl* **9/1**

231- **2** 3 **Ardkilly Witness (IRE)**[37] 3291 8-11-2 **133** LeightonAspell 141
(Dr Richard Newland) *in tch: chsd ldrs fr 12th: hit 18th: led u.p appr 2 out: kpt slt ld tl hdd sn after last: styd on same pce* **9/2**[1]

U13- **3** 3 **Theatrical Star**[14] 3772 8-11-4 **135** JoeTizzard 140
(Colin Tizzard) *chsd ldrs tl dropped to rr 12th: sn wl bhd: styd on again appr 3 out: r.o wl after 2 out to take 3rd run-in: styd on wl clsng stages but nt rch ldng duo* **10/1**

0/5- **4** 11 **Soll**[56] 2953 9-11-7 **138** MarkGrant 133
(Jo Hughes) *chsd ldrs: hmpd 16th: sn rdn: wknd u.p after 3 out* **11/2**[2]

/65- **5** 1/2 **Fruity O'Rooney**[98] 2070 11-11-6 **137** (v) JamieMoore 134
(Gary Moore) *in tch: chsd ldrs fr 10th: chalng whn lft in ld 16th: hit 4 out: jnd 3 out: hdd appr next: wknd bef last* **20/1**

342- **6** 6 **Jump City (FR)**[21] 3647 8-11-1 **132** DarylJacob 122
(Paul Nicholls) *in rr: hdwy 18th: wknd u.p fr 3 out* **8/1**

4P4- **7** 5 **On Trend (IRE)**[21] 3647 8-10-5 **122** TomCannon 105
(Nick Gifford) *rdn along fr 11th: a towards rr* **9/2**[1]

P13- **P** **Pete The Feat (IRE)**[33] 3416 10-11-9 **143** KielanWoods[(3)]
(Charlie Longsdon) *chsd ldrs: wknd 14th: t.o whn p.u bef 17th* **10/1**

512/ **P** **Roalco De Farges (FR)**[644] 5652 9-11-0 **131** RichardJohnson
(Philip Hobbs) *in rr: hdwy 11th: chsd ldrs fr 16th: nt fluent 4 out: wknd sn after: t.o whn p.u bef 2 out* **6/1**[3]

212- **U** **Hansupfordetroit (IRE)**[16] 3745 9-10-12 **132** MarkQuinlan[(3)]
(Bernard Llewellyn) *w ldr tl narrow ld fr 8th tl blnd and uns rdr 16th (water)* **16/1**

6m 49.26s (21.46) **Going Correction** +1.15s/f (Heav) **10 Ran SP% 116.0**
Speed ratings: **111,110,109,105,105 103,101,,,**
CSF £50.20 CT £417.80 TOTE £10.50: £3.00, £2.20, £3.60; EX 56.00 Trifecta £670.60.

Owner The Bellamy Partnership **Bred** Marc Trinquet & Mlle Marie Trinquet **Trained** Kings Caple, H'fords

FOCUS
Plenty of potential front-runners in opposition here and it proved a thorough test of stamina, with the runners finishing very tired. The form amongst the principals is sound.

4036 BETFRED "STILL TREBLE ODDS ON LUCKY 15S" H'CAP CHASE (13 fncs) 2m

4:10 (4:10) (Class 3) (0-130,130) 5-Y-0+

£9,384 (£2,772; £1,386; £693; £346; £174)

Form RPR

464- **1** **Sew On Target (IRE)**[7] 3887 9-11-10 128 JoeTizzard 136
(Colin Tizzard) *chsd ldrs: chal fr 5th: hit 6th: styd upsides tl led 2 out: drvn out run-in* **11/4**[2]

3P5- **2** 6 **Speedy Bruere (FR)**[16] 3738 8-10-13 117 RobertThornton 119
(David Bridgwater) *chsd ldrs: nt fluent 4 out: styd on u.p to take 2nd after last but no imp on wnr* **10/1**

526- **3** 3 **Roger Beantown (IRE)**[37] 3259 9-11-9 127 (p) DaveCrosse 126
(Zoe Davison) *chsd ldrs: rdn after 4 out: styng on same pce whn mstke 2 out: tk one pce 3rd run-in* **16/1**

123- **4** 1 3/4 **Last Shot (FR)**[7] 3894 7-11-12 130 AidanColeman 129
(Venetia Williams) *narrow ldr but a hrd pressed: rdn after 4 out: hdd 2 out: wknd last* **3/1**[3]

132- **5** 23 **Un Anjou (FR)**[25] 3596 6-10-11 115 (p) RichardJohnson 93
(David Dennis) *mstkes in rr: hdwy 7th: wknd 4 out* **2/1**[1]

/40- **6** 24 **Regal D'Estruval (FR)**[263] 282 9-10-13 117 DarylJacob 66
(Dr Richard Newland) *pressed ldr to 6th: wknd 7th: mstke 4 out: t.o* **8/1**

4m 21.64s (19.84) **Going Correction** +1.15s/f (Heav) **6 Ran SP% 111.1**
Speed ratings: **96,93,91,90,79 67**
CSF £25.98 TOTE £2.90: £1.70, £3.20; EX 19.70 Trifecta £223.50.

Owner A Selway **Bred** Gerry Canavan **Trained** Milborne Port, Dorset

FOCUS
The drop in grade helped the winner in what was an ordinary race.

T/Plt: £60.90 to a £1 stake. Pool: £145,891.62 - 1,747.38 winning units T/Qpdt: £33.10 to a £1 stake. Pool: £5,521.74 - 123.40 winning units ST

[3822]WETHERBY (L-H)

Saturday, February 1

OFFICIAL GOING: Heavy

Wind: Fairly strong; half against Weather: Overcast

4037 WILMOT-SMITH MEMORIAL MARES' NOVICES' HURDLE (9 hdls) 2m 110y

1:00 (1:00) (Class 4) 4-Y-0+ **£3,285** (£957; £479)

Form RPR

1 **Aurore D'Estruval (FR)**[58] 4-10-4 0 BrianHughes 111+
(John Quinn) *j.w: trckd ldrs: led gng wl 3 out: qcknd clr on bit after next: v easily* **8/15**[1]

/UP- 2 13 **Clara Peggotty**[63] 2824 7-11-0 0 FelixDeGiles 96
(Tom Gretton) *chsd ldr: led briefly appr 3 out: outpcd by wnr fr next: hld whn nt fluent last* **50/1**

640- 3 5 **Lebanna**[11] 3826 4-10-4 0 BrianHarding 82
(Tim Easterby) *nt fluent on occasions: in tch: stdy hdwy bef 3 out: shkn up next: outpcd fr last* **16/1**[3]

0- 4 60 **Pink Mischief**[15] 3757 4-10-1 0 JohnKington(3) 20
(Andrew Crook) *led tl hdd appr 3 out: sn struggling: t.o* **80/1**

31- U **Slipper Satin (IRE)**[9] 3854 4-10-7 0 JackQuinlan(3)
(Noel Quinlan) *cl up: stmbld bdly and uns rdr 1st* **2/1**[2]

4m 30.2s (34.40) **Going Correction** +2.225s/f (Heav)
WFA 4 from 6yo+ 9lb 5 Ran SP% **107.6**
Speed ratings (Par 105): **108,101,99,71,**
CSF £18.06 TOTE £1.70: £1.10, £14.10; EX 19.40 Trifecta £59.00.
Owner Carl Hinchy **Bred** Marie-Francoise Le Gentil **Trained** Settrington, N Yorks

FOCUS
A straightforward task for the winner, who was left with little to beat.

4038 PLAY THE £1MILLION SCOOP6 TODAY NOVICES' HURDLE (12 hdls) 2m 6f

1:35 (1:36) (Class 4) 5-Y-0+ **£3,249** (£954; £477; £238)

Form RPR

12- 1 **Flemenson (IRE)**[88] 2279 5-11-5 130 APMcCoy 132+
(Jonjo O'Neill) *j.rt to 1/2-way: pressed ldr: drvn and outpcd after 4 out: rallied next: led 2 out: rdn clr fr last* **4/5**[1]

221- 2 3¾ **Sir Mangan (IRE)**[22] 3634 6-11-5 125 HenryBrooke 127
(Donald McCain) *led: rdn along 4 out: hdd 2 out: rallied and ev ch last: one pce run-in* **6/4**[2]

021- 3 25 **Total Assets**[28] 3525 6-10-12 106 RyanMania 102+
(Simon Waugh) *chsd clr ldrs: hdwy and cl up 1/2-way: ev ch tl rdn and wknd after 3 out* **10/1**[3]

000- 4 61 **Marlee Massie (IRE)**[34] 3392 5-10-12 0 LucyAlexander 34
(N W Alexander) *nt fluent in rr: lost tch 1/2-way: t.o* **125/1**

0P/ 5 4½ **Henry Jenkins**[364] 3997 7-10-12 0 BrianHughes 30
(Malcolm Jefferson) *bhd: struggling fr 1/2-way: t.o* **50/1**

0- P **Miss Twiggy**[82] 2422 6-9-11 0 ow2 GLavery(10)
(Brian Ellison) *a bhd: lost tch 1/2-way: t.o whn p.u bef 3 out* **66/1**

600- P **Crazy Chester (IRE)**[6] 3920 5-10-12 0 WilsonRenwick
(Michael Easterby) *hld up: struggling 1/2-way: t.o whn p.u bef 3 out* **100/1**

6m 15.3s (48.50) **Going Correction** +2.225s/f (Heav) 7 Ran SP% **109.9**
Speed ratings: **100,98,89,67,65** ,
CSF £2.14 TOTE £1.60: £1.10, £1.10; EX 1.80 Trifecta £3.50.
Owner Mrs Gay Smith **Bred** Grange Stud **Trained** Cheltenham, Gloucs

FOCUS
This served up a real test. The first two are rated to their marks.

4039 BET TOTEQUADPOT WITH TOTEPOOL H'CAP CHASE (14 fncs 2 omitted) 2m 4f 110y

2:10 (2:12) (Class 2) (0-150,143) 5-Y-0+**£11,734** (£3,579; £1,869; £1,015)

Form RPR

123- 1 **No Planning**[42] 3205 7-11-1 132 RyanMania 146+
(Sue Smith) *cl up: led 5th: mde rest: styng on strly whn lft 10 l clr 3 out: kpt on* **6/4**[1]

/F5- 2 15 **Doeslessthanme (IRE)**[21] 3660 10-11-12 143 (tp) RichieMcGrath 139
(Richard Ford) *hld up: stdy hdwy bef 4 out: effrt and lft 10 l 2nd next: no ch w wnr* **16/1**

163- 3 7 **Rossini's Dancer**[29] 3521 9-10-8 132 (p) MrKitAlexander(7) 119
(N W Alexander) *in tch: outpcd 8th: rallied 3 out: no ch w first two* **25/1**

1/2- 4 19 **Ice 'N' Easy (IRE)**[21] 3642 8-10-8 125 (tp) NoelFehily 100
(Charlie Longsdon) *t.k.h: prom tl rdn and wknd bef 4 out* **85/40**[2]

140- R **Ultimate**[31] 3477 8-11-11 142 APMcCoy
(Brian Ellison) *led to 5th: chsd wnr: lost 2nd whn blnd bdly 4 out: lft mod 3rd next: last and no ch whn j.v.slowly: bec lodged on fence and rdr dismntd last* **6/1**[3]

/53- U **Mcmurrough (IRE)**[21] 3661 10-11-8 139 (b) BrianHughes
(Malcolm Jefferson) *chsd ldrs: wnt 2nd bef 4 out: sn rdn: jst over 3 l down and one pce whn blnd and uns rdr 3 out* **13/2**

5m 48.7s (40.90) **Going Correction** +2.225s/f (Heav) 6 Ran SP% **109.3**
Speed ratings: **111,105,102,95,**
CSF £20.19 TOTE £2.60: £1.40, £5.70; EX 21.00 Trifecta £215.00.
Owner Mrs Jacqueline Conroy **Bred** Mrs S Johnson **Trained** High Eldwick, W Yorks

FOCUS
A fair handicap, run a a sound enough gallop. There's a case for rating the form a few pounds higher.

4040 DOWNLOAD THE TOTEPOOL MOBILE APP H'CAP HURDLE (13 hdls) 3m 1f

2:45 (2:48) (Class 3) (0-135,132) 4-Y-0+ **£5,393** (£1,583; £791; £395)

Form RPR

3F0- 1 **Who Owns Me (IRE)**[21] 3653 8-11-0 120 (b[1]) NoelFehily 133+
(Charlie Mann) *in tch: drvn and outpcd 8th: gd hdwy to ld 3 out: clr between last 2: kpt on wl* **17/2**

215- 2 5 **Kilbree Chief (IRE)**[63] 2819 6-11-0 120 PeterBuchanan 126
(Lucinda Russell) *chsd ldrs: drvn and outpcd 4 out: rallied next: chsd wnr bef 2 out: kpt on same pce appr last* **11/2**[3]

30U- 3 18 **Milano Magic (IRE)**[51] 3041 8-10-3 109 (p) LucyAlexander 96
(N W Alexander) *led to 6th: cl up: drvn and outpcd bef 4 out: rallied 2 out: kpt on fr last: no ch w first two* **10/1**

121- 4 5 **Beauboreen (IRE)**[30] 3505 7-11-8 128 SeanQuinlan 112
(Jennie Candlish) *hld up: niggled along 9th: hdwy and cl up bef 3 out: wknd next* **4/1**[2]

FOP- 5 10 **Master Of The Hall (IRE)**[37] 3285 10-11-7 132 JoeColliver(5) 104
(Micky Hammond) *cl up: led 6th: clr w one other after 4 out: rdn and hdd next: wknd 2 out* **28/1**

512- 6 1 **Rattlin**[37] 3286 6-10-5 118 CallumBewley(7) 89
(Sue Smith) *cl up: ev ch and clr w ldr after 4 out: rdn and wknd bef next* **11/8**[1]

136- F **Tweedledrum**[14] 3770 7-11-0 125 (p) BenPoste(5)
(Tom Symonds) *hld up in tch: fell 2nd* **15/2**

7m 10.31s (53.81) **Going Correction** +2.225s/f (Heav) 7 Ran SP% **112.3**
Speed ratings (Par 107): **102,100,94,93,89 89,**
CSF £51.50 CT £472.72 TOTE £8.90: £3.80, £3.40; EX 55.00 Trifecta £340.60.
Owner Fromthestables.com Racing **Bred** Mrs Claire Berry **Trained** Upper Lambourn, Berks

FOCUS
Not the strongest event for the class. The race was set up for the closers leaving the back straight and only two mattered from the second-last. The form is rated around the second.

4041 TOTEPOOL TOWTON NOVICES' CHASE (GRADE 2) (16 fncs 2 omitted) 3m 1f

3:20 (3:22) (Class 1) 5-Y-0+ **£18,184** (£7,332; £4,077)

Form RPR

101- 1 **Ely Brown (IRE)**[36] 3327 9-11-4 140 (p) NoelFehily 148+
(Charlie Longsdon) *t.k.h: w ldr: led 8th: jnd 10th: asserting whn nt fluent 2 out: kpt on strly* **2/1**[2]

01F- 2 9 **Milborough (IRE)**[30] 3496 8-11-0 133 MichaelByrne 136
(Tim Vaughan) *in tch: lft 2nd bnd bef 9th: ev ch fr next tl hit and outpcd 3 out: kpt on same pce fr next* **11/1**

3 98 **Strike Fast (IRE)**[1001] 9-11-0 0 HarryChalloner 36
(William Kinsey) *in tch: outpcd whn lft 3rd bnd bef 9th: lost tch fr next: t.o* **40/1**

112- U **Green Flag (IRE)**[37] 3260 7-11-4 143 PeterBuchanan
(Lucinda Russell) *trckd ldrs: clipped heels stmbld and uns rdr bnd bef 9th* **1/1**[1]

1P2- P **Coverholder (IRE)**[14] 3777 7-11-4 133 JonathanEngland
(Sue Smith) *slt ld to 8th: cl 2nd whn broke down bdly bnd bef 9th: fatally injured* **6/1**[3]

7m 17.6s (68.20) **Going Correction** +2.225s/f (Heav) 5 Ran SP% **108.4**
Speed ratings: **79,76,44,** ,
CSF £18.71 TOTE £2.20: £1.10, £4.00; EX 16.30 Trifecta £150.00.
Owner Countrywide Vehicle Rentals Taxi Hire **Bred** James Meagher **Trained** Over Norton, Oxon

FOCUS
A dramatic Grade 2 novice chase. The winner is on the upgrade and rates a decent novice.

4042 CGA FOXHUNTER TRIAL OPEN HUNTER CHASE (16 fncs 2 omitted) 3m 1f

3:55 (3:55) (Class 6) 6-Y-0+ **£987** (£303; £151)

Form RPR

1/2- 1 **Palypso De Creek (FR)**[250] 11-11-7 118 MissCVHart(7) 125
(Mrs J Dawson) *prom: effrt 3 out: led last: rdn and r.o wl* **6/4**[1]

4/1- 2 2 **Doctor Kingsley**[20] 12-11-11 117 MrPMann(7) 127
(Mrs Pauline Harkin) *chsd ldrs: rdn and outpcd bef 4 out: rallied bef 2 out: chsd wnr run-in: kpt on: no imp* **3/1**[2]

P/P- 3 nk **Always Right (IRE)**[269] 170 12-12-1 140 MrCDawson(3) 129+
(John Wade) *t.k.h: prom: hdwy to ld 3 out: hit and hdd last: kpt on same pce run-in* **3/1**[2]

/44- 4 14 **Captain Americo (IRE)**[13] 12-11-3 110 MrRLindsay(7) 108
(Mrs B Ewart) *cl up: led 8th: rdn bef 4 out: hdd whn mstke next: sn outpcd* **8/1**[3]

P/0- 5 34 **Croan Rock (IRE)**[20] 9-11-7 103 (tp) MrGCrow(3) 71
(R A Owen) *hld up bhd ldng gp: hit 2nd: struggling 4 out: sn btn* **25/1**

0/6- 6 14 **Newyearsresolution (IRE)**[13] 10-11-3 78 MissAWaugh(7) 57
(Simon Waugh) *t.k.h: bhd: struggling fnl circ: nvr on terms* **33/1**

3P5/ 7 24 **Viking Rebel (IRE)**[48] 12-11-3 81 MrWHRReed(7) 33
(W T Reed) *hld up: outpcd 9th: lost tch after 5 out: t.o* **100/1**

2/P- P **Melua Maid (IRE)**[13] 12-11-0 86 (p) MrJDixon(7)
(Mrs B Ewart) *cl up: blnd and rdr lost both irons 2nd: p.u bef next* **50/1**

0/2- P **Killary Bay (IRE)**[247] 557 10-11-11 103 MissHBethell(3)
(Mrs T Corrigan) *led to 8th: cl up tl rdn and wknd bef 4 out: p.u next* **25/1**

3/3- P **Playing The Field (IRE)**[263] 288 9-12-0 88 MissCWalton
(Mrs Alison Christmas) *nt fluent in rr: struggling fnl circ: t.o whn p.u bef 4 out* **33/1**

7m 32.5s (83.10) **Going Correction** +2.225s/f (Heav) 10 Ran SP% **117.6**
Speed ratings: **56,55,55,50,39 35,27,** , ,
CSF £6.16 TOTE £2.60: £2.00, £1.30, £2.20; EX 8.70 Trifecta £26.00.
Owner M N Dawson **Bred** Suc Yves Chopin & Mme Francoise Roux **Trained** Grainthorpe, Lincs

FOCUS
This is always a decent hunter chase. The first two are rated to their marks with the third a stone+ off.

4043 WETHERBYRACING.CO.UK STANDARD OPEN NATIONAL HUNT FLAT RACE 2m 110y

4:30 (4:30) (Class 6) 4-6-Y-0 **£1,642** (£478; £239)

Form RPR

1 **Relic Rock (IRE)**[524] 1373 6-11-4 0 APMcCoy 113+
(Steve Gollings) *trckd ldrs: smooth hdwy to ld 2f out: drvn and kpt on wl fnl f* **2/1**[1]

2 1 **Bryden Boy (IRE)** 4-10-8 0 SeanQuinlan 102+
(Jennie Candlish) *hld up: stdy hdwy and prom 3f out: effrt and chsd wnr over 1f out: drifted lft ins fnl f: kpt on: hld nr fin* **40/1**

3 2½ **Pithivier (FR)** 4-10-8 0 WilsonRenwick 99
(Peter Niven) *t.k.h: chsd ldr: led over 3f out to 2f out: rdn and one pce fnl f* **11/4**[2]

4 2¼ **Bobs Lord Tara** 4-10-8 0 DominicElsworth 97
(Alan Swinbank) *hld up in midfield: effrt and pushed along 3f out: kpt on same pce fr 2f out* **10/1**

2- 5 hd **Rock On Bollinski**[42] 3214 4-10-8 0 BrianHughes 97
(Tim Fitzgerald) *hld up in midfield: stdy hdwy over 3f out: rdn over 2f out: one pce over 1f out* **8/1**

6 10 **Itstimeforapint (IRE)**[111] 6-10-11 0 CraigNichol(7) 97
(Lucinda Russell) *led to 3f out: sn rdn and outpcd: n.d after* **20/1**

7 2¼ **Farragon (IRE)** 4-10-1 0 GrahamWatters(7) 85
(Lucinda Russell) *hld up: pushed along over 3f out: nvr able to chal* **22/1**

8 2¾ **Backforce** 6-10-11 0 NathanMoscrop(7) 92
(Noel Wilson) *t.k.h in midfield: effrt and edgd lft over 2f out: sn btn* **100/1**

9 hd **Kings Folly (IRE)** 6-10-11 0 MrSFox(7) 92
(Lucinda Russell) *bhd: pushed along over 3f out: sn btn* **50/1**

10 *10* **Verdasco (FR)** 5-11-4 0 AdrianLane 82
(Donald McCain) *hld up towards rr: outpcd over 5f out: btn fnl 3f* **8/1**

11 *2 ¼* **Manor Brook (IRE)** 6-10-11 0 NoelFehily 73
(Charlie Longsdon) *t.k.h: prom: stdy hdwy over 4f out: rdn and wknd over 2f out* **15/2[3]**

4m 30.8s (40.60) **Going Correction** +2.225s/f (Heavy)
WFA 4 from 5yo+ 9lb **11** Ran SP% **117.6**
Speed ratings: **93,92,91,90,90 85,84,83,83,78 77**
CSF £102.77 TOTE £2.90: £1.10, £12.50, £1.80; EX 55.80 Trifecta £624.80.
Owner P J Martin **Bred** Sean O'Loughlin **Trained** Scamblesby, Lincs

FOCUS
This bumper ought to produce its share of future winners. The winner looks well above average.
T/Plt: £107.70 to a £1 stake. Pool: £81,555.44 - 552.45 winning units T/Qpdt: £76.10 to a £1 stake. Pool: £4,317.24 - 41.96 winning units RY

4044 - 4050a (Foreign Racing) - See Raceform Interactive

[3755]MUSSELBURGH (R-H)

Sunday, February 2

OFFICIAL GOING: Soft (good to soft in places; 6.0)
All fences, hurdles and rails moved to provide fresh ground.
Wind: Fresh, half against Weather: Bright

4051 PERTEMPS NETWORK H'CAP HURDLE (SERIES QUALIFIER) (14 hdls) 3m 110y
1:00 (1:00) (Class 2) 5-Y-0+
£12,512 (£3,696; £1,848; £924; £462; £232)

Form RPR

3/0- 1 **Wyse Hill Teabags**[32] 3477 9-10-9 **130** RyanMania 133+
(Jim Goldie) *mde all: rdn bef 2 out: gd jump last: kpt on strly run-in* **10/1**

051- 2 *2* **Mister Dillon**[35] 3387 7-11-2 **137** BarryGeraghty 137
(Nicky Henderson) *trckd ldrs: effrt and wnt 2nd bef 2 out: sn rdn: edgd rt and kpt on run-in: hld towards fin* **7/1[3]**

/16- 3 *1 ¾* **Crowning Jewel**[71] 2672 8-11-2 **137** JamesReveley 135
(Keith Reveley) *chsd wnr: rdn bef 2 out: sn lost 2nd: kpt on same pce between last 2* **10/1**

231- 4 *2 ¼* **Any Given Moment (IRE)**[32] 3479 8-9-7 **121** oh7 GrantCockburn(7) 117
(Sandy Thomson) *hld up in midfield: stdy hdwy after 4 out: effrt and rdn next: kpt on same pce fr 2 out* **18/1**

240- 5 *2 ¼* **Attaglance**[50] 3082 8-11-12 **147** (t) BrianHughes 141
(Malcolm Jefferson) *in tch: stdy hdwy and cl up bef 3 out: rdn and outpcd next: no imp bef last* **25/1**

3/5- 6 *23* **Pay The King (IRE)**[77] 2529 7-9-9 **121** oh5 HarryDerham(5) 92
(Paul Nicholls) *hld up: stdy hdwy bef 4 out: pushed along bef next: sn n.d* **5/2[1]**

203- 7 *5* **Capellanus (IRE)**[32] 3479 8-10-7 **128** DenisO'Regan 94
(Brian Ellison) *hld up: hmpd 4 out: sn rdn along and no imp* **28/1**

8 *10* **Golden Plan (IRE)**[10] 3867 8-9-9 **121** oh1 KillianMoore(5) 77
(Mark Fahey, Ire) *midfield: hit 3rd: rdn fr 1/2-way: outpcd whn hmpd 4 out: btn next* **22/1**

0P0- 9 *¾* **Malt Master (IRE)**[57] 2949 7-10-9 **130** APMcCoy 85
(Nicky Henderson) *nt fluent on occasions: hld up on outside: drvn along fr 1/2-way: struggling fr 4 out* **7/1[3]**

006- F **Monetary Fund (USA)**[9] 3882 8-10-6 **127** AidanColeman
(Venetia Williams) *trckd ldrs on ins: stl gng wl whn fell 4 out* **7/2[2]**

614- P **Arctic Court (IRE)**[32] 3479 10-10-2 **123** WilsonRenwick
(Jim Goldie) *hld up: bdly hmpd 4 out: sn btn: t.o whn p.u next* **25/1**

5m 38.2s (-18.50) **Going Correction** -0.45s/f (Good) **11** Ran SP% **114.7**
Speed ratings: **111,110,109,109,108 101,99,96,95,**
CSF £72.40 CT £721.37 TOTE £11.30: £3.40, £2.20, £2.40; EX 84.00 Trifecta £937.10.
Owner Mr & Mrs Philip C Smith **Bred** Gail And Stuart Smales **Trained** Uplawmoor, E Renfrews

FOCUS
All fences, hurdles and rails moved to provide fresh ground. This qualifier was run at an uneven gallop and the principals dominated from two out as those held up struggled to make an impact. The first eight home became eligible for a run in the final come March and the form looks believable.

4052 ALBERT BARTLETT SCOTTISH TRIAL (NOVICES' HURDLE) (14 hdls) 3m 110y
1:30 (1:30) (Class 2) 5-Y-0+ **£12,996** (£3,816; £1,908; £954)

Form RPR

1- 1 **Seeyouatmidnight**[53] 3017 6-11-1 0 RyanMania 146+
(Sandy Thomson) *led to 4th: pressed ldr: led bef 9th: rdn bef 3 out: nt fluent next: styd on strly* **22/1**

13- 2 *9* **Racing Pulse (IRE)**[32] 3454 5-11-1 144 APMcCoy 137
(John Quinn) *nt fluent on occasions: t.k.h: prom: wnt 2nd 9th: rdn along bef 3 out: effrt whn nt fluent next: kpt on same pce last* **4/11[1]**

4- 3 *16* **Medieval Chapel (FR)**[44] 3182 6-10-12 0 BarryGeraghty 119
(Nicky Henderson) *in tch: hdwy and cl up 4 out: effrt and rdn bef next: wknd bef 2 out* **5/1[2]**

313- 4 *41* **Powerstown Dreams (IRE)**[35] 3388 5-10-12 0 SamTwiston-Davies 76
(Steve Gollings) *hld up in tch: pushed along fr 1/2-way: struggling 4 out: btn bef next* **12/1**

2P1- P **Clondaw Hero (IRE)**[86] 2342 6-11-1 0 JasonMaguire
(Donald McCain) *cl up: led 4th: reminders 8th: hdd bef next: struggling fr 4 out: t.o whn p.u bef 2 out* **9/1[3]**

5m 36.2s (-20.50) **Going Correction** -0.45s/f (Good) **5** Ran SP% **112.0**
Speed ratings: **114,111,106,92,**
CSF £33.69 TOTE £12.20: £5.00, £1.10; EX 40.10 Trifecta £133.60.
Owner Mrs A M Thomson **Bred** Miss F A Evans **Trained** Lambden, Berwicks

FOCUS
The winner rates a smart novice and the second was again below his Newcastle level.

4053 JOHN SMITH'S SCOTTISH CHAMPION CHASE (H'CAP) (FOR THE BOWES-LYON TROPHY) (12 fncs) 2m
2:00 (2:00) (Class 3) (0-140,140) 5-Y-0+ **£12,996** (£3,816; £1,908; £954)

Form RPR

41P- 1 **Swift Arrow (IRE)**[65] 2793 8-11-4 **132** HenryBrooke 138
(Donald McCain) *hld up in tch: nt fluent 5th: rdn after 5 out: rallied next: led and hit 3 out: hld on wl fr last* **22/1**

0F6- 2 *½* **His Excellency (IRE)**[22] 3660 6-11-12 **140** (b) TomScudamore 146
(David Pipe) *cl up: nt fluent 5th: rdn along after 5 out: rallied 3 out: chsd wnr next: nt fluent last: kpt on: hld nr fin* **4/1[2]**

1/0- 3 *2 ¼* **Kie (IRE)**[71] 2666 6-11-6 **134** JasonMaguire 136
(Donald McCain) *led: rdn and hdd 2 out: rallied: kpt on same pce between last 2* **9/2[3]**

501- 4 *nse* **Stormin Exit (IRE)**[16] 3756 11-10-5 **119** JamesReveley 124+
(Jim Goldie) *in tch: hit and outpcd 5 out: rallied 2 out: styd on run-in: nvr able to chal* **10/1**

130- 5 *2 ¼* **Quito Du Tresor (FR)**[32] 3476 10-10-2 **123** (p) CraigNichol(7) 123
(Lucinda Russell) *prom: effrt bef 4 out: drvn and outpcd bef 2 out* **14/1**

3- 6 *14* **Upepito (FR)**[17] 3738 6-11-0 **128** AidanColeman 119
(Venetia Williams) *nt fluent on occasions: cl up tl rdn and wknd 3 out: btn whn mstke next* **5/4[1]**

263- 7 *8* **Claragh Native (IRE)**[32] 3452 9-10-3 **117** LucyAlexander 95
(Martin Todhunter) *mstkes: sn bhd: struggling fr 1/2-way: nvr on terms* **14/1**

3m 55.9s (3.50) **Going Correction** +0.25s/f (Yiel) **7** Ran SP% **109.4**
Speed ratings: **101,100,99,99,98 91,87**
CSF £98.93 TOTE £16.20: £5.80, £2.20; EX 93.20 Trifecta £272.50.
Owner Mrs C Strang Steel **Bred** Paul Stacey **Trained** Cholmondeley, Cheshire

FOCUS
A fair handicap, run at a decent gallop. A small personal best from the winner.

4054 JOHN SMITH'S SCOTTISH TRIUMPH HURDLE TRIAL (JUVENILE HURDLE) (LISTED RACE) (9 hdls) 2m
2:30 (2:30) (Class 1) 4-Y-0
£11,390 (£4,274; £2,140; £1,066; £536; £268)

Form RPR

2- 1 **Broughton (GER)**[50] 3089 4-11-0 0 DenisO'Regan 129+
(John Ferguson) *trckd ldrs: wnt 2nd 1/2-way: led on bit bef 2 out: shkn up and qcknd clr run-in: readily* **5/6[1]**

32- 2 *5* **Clarcam (FR)**[38] 3305 4-11-5 133 (t) JasonMaguire 124
(Gordon Elliott, Ire) *poached 5 l at s: led: rdn and nt fluent 3 out: hdd bef next: kpt on same pce* **7/1**

22- 3 *3 ¾* **Thorpe (IRE)**[32] 3474 4-11-0 111 PeterBuchanan 114
(Lucinda Russell) *hld up on ins: pushed along and effrt bef 3 out: styd on fr last: nvr able to chal* **20/1**

4 *¾* **Space Ship**[37] 3336 4-11-0 0 SamTwiston-Davies 114
(Robert Alan Hennessy, Ire) *t.k.h: chsd ldr to 1/2-way: rdn and effrt bef 2 out: outpcd fr last* **6/1[3]**

5 *14* **Hawker**[81] 4-11-0 0 JackQuinlan 101
(John Ferguson) *hld up: pushed along and hdwy after 4 out: no imp fr next* **25/1**

U14- 6 *½* **Most Honourable**[32] 3448 4-11-5 116 RyanMania 104
(Michael Smith) *hld up: struggling after 4 out: btn next* **20/1**

4- 7 *61* **Investment Expert (IRE)**[12] 3822 4-11-0 0 (t) TomScudamore 38
(Brian Ellison) *t.k.h: in tch: lost pl 1/2-way: lost tch fr 4 out* **33/1**

12- P **Adeupas D'Ycy (FR)**[32] 3460 4-11-0 0 BarryGeraghty
(Nicky Henderson) *plld hrd early: in tch: hdwy 1/2-way: sixth and outpcd whn p.u qckly appr 3 out: fatally injured* **4/1[2]**

3m 43.6s (-4.80) **Going Correction** -0.45s/f (Good) **8** Ran SP% **117.7**
Speed ratings: **94,91,89,89,82 82,51,**
CSF £7.23 TOTE £1.90: £1.10, £1.60, £2.90; EX 7.50 Trifecta £43.70.
Owner Bloomfields **Bred** Gestut Westerberg **Trained** Cowlinge, Suffolk

FOCUS
The field stood still for around 15secs as the tape went up, but once Clarcam set off there was a fair enough gallop on and this looks sound form. The easy winner was value for further.

4055 JOHN SMITH'S SCOTTISH FUTURE CHAMPIONS NOVICES' CHASE (16 fncs) 2m 4f
3:00 (3:00) (Class 3) 5-Y-0+ **£7,797** (£2,289; £1,144; £572)

Form RPR

/25- 1 **Ericht (IRE)**[38] 3259 8-10-12 135 BarryGeraghty 146+
(Nicky Henderson) *a gng wl: prom: wnt 2nd 6th: led bef 3 out: clr bef next: easily* **2/1[1]**

331- 2 *9* **Bar De Ligne (FR)**[16] 3759 8-11-6 132 (p) APMcCoy 138
(Steve Gollings) *chsd ldr to 6th: cl up: drvn after 5 out: rallied to chse (clr) wnr bef 2 out: no imp* **7/2[2]**

211- 3 *6* **Funny Star (FR)**[52] 3045 6-11-6 141 (tp) DarylJacob 133
(Paul Nicholls) *prom: nt fluent: pushed along fr 10th: drvn bef 4 out: no imp fr next* **4/1[3]**

/P1- 4 *5* **Witness In Court (IRE)**[30] 3519 7-11-3 135 JasonMaguire 126
(Donald McCain) *led: mstke 5 out: sn drvn: hdd bef 3 out: sn wknd* **4/1[3]**

132- 5 *16* **My Idea**[22] 3658 8-10-10 112 (t) StephenMulqueen(7) 108
(Maurice Barnes) *nt fluent: bhd: struggling fr 1/2-way: nvr on terms* **100/1**

P13- P **Reaping The Reward (IRE)**[30] 3519 10-10-12 130 PeterBuchanan
(Lucinda Russell) *hld up: mstke 3rd: outpcd after 9th: struggling and p.u after next* **22/1**

5/1- U **Top Of The Range (IRE)**[72] 2643 7-11-3 138 AndrewTinkler
(Nicky Henderson) *hld up in tch: overj. and uns rdr 1st* **7/1**

5m 1.6s (0.40) **Going Correction** +0.25s/f (Yiel) **7** Ran SP% **113.4**
Speed ratings: **109,105,103,101,94 ,**
CSF £9.53 TOTE £3.10: £1.60, £2.20; EX 10.80 Trifecta £26.60.
Owner Mrs Christopher Hanbury **Bred** Mrs M McDonagh **Trained** Upper Lambourn, Berks

FOCUS
This was one-way traffic for Ericht, and this rates a step up.

4056 JOHN SMITH'S SCOTTISH COUNTY HURDLE (H'CAP) (9 hdls) 2m
3:30 (3:30) (Class 2) 4-Y-0+
£15,640 (£4,620; £2,310; £1,155; £577; £290)

Form RPR

221- 1 **Clever Cookie**[16] 3758 6-10-0 **124** oh2 WilsonRenwick 139+
(Peter Niven) *hld up: smooth hdwy 4 out: poised to chal whn nt fluent 2 out: led last: rdn clr: readily* **5/1[2]**

303- 2 *8* **Local Hero (GER)**[32] 3477 7-10-9 **140** (p) PaulBohan(7) 143
(Steve Gollings) *cl up: rdn and led 2 out: hdd last: kpt on same pce run-in* **7/1**

236- 3 *1 ¾* **Pas Trop Tard (FR)**[8] 3892 7-9-13 **130** (t) StephenMulqueen(7) 132
(Maurice Barnes) *led: rdn and hdd 2 out: kpt on same pce bef last* **28/1**

421- 4 *1 ½* **Lyvius**[22] 3648 6-11-2 **140** BarryGeraghty 140
(Nicky Henderson) *hld up: rdn along 4 out: hdwy u.p next: styd on fr 2 out: nt pce to chal* **13/2**

123- 5 *1 ½* **Sametegal (FR)**[38] 3261 5-11-7 **150** HarryDerham(5) 148
(Paul Nicholls) *prom: effrt and rdn bef 3 out: outpcd fr next* **11/4[1]**

111- 6 *nse* **Yorkist (IRE)**[17] 3736 6-10-8 **132** APMcCoy 130
(Brian Ellison) *in tch on ins: rdn and effrt 3 out: outpcd after next* **7/1**

300- 7 14 **Dumbarton (IRE)**[38] 3273 6-10-1 **125** BrianHughes 109
(James Moffatt) *t.k.h: hld up: hdwy and in tch 4 out: rdn and wknd next* **28/1**

/04- 8 6 **Orsippus (USA)**[98] 2100 8-10-8 **132** RyanMania 110
(Michael Smith) *chsd ldrs: outpcd whn hit 4 out: sn struggling: btn next* **20/1**

130- F **Franciscan**[50] 3088 6-10-4 **128** (p) HenryBrooke
(Donald McCain) *cl up: hdwy and ev ch 4 out: rdn and disputing 2nd whn fell next* **14/1**

304- F **Runswick Royal (IRE)**[32] 3477 5-10-8 **139** GrahamWatters(7)
(Ann Hamilton) *midfield on outside: lost pl whn fell 4th* **6/1**[3]

3m 37.7s (-10.70) **Going Correction** -0.45s/f (Good) **10** Ran SP% **114.3**
Speed ratings (Par 109): **108,104,103,102,101 101,94,91,** ,
CSF £38.02 CT £873.26 TOTE £7.50: £2.30, £2.30, £5.20; EX 51.60 Trifecta £524.20.

Owner Francis Green Racing Ltd **Bred** Mrs J A Niven **Trained** Barton-le-Street, N Yorks

FOCUS
A traditionally strong handicap. Despite the the field being tightly bunched there was a fair pace set and the form ought to work out. The winner should still be competitive when reassessed.

4057 CGA SCOTTISH FOXHUNTER CHASE (OPEN HUNTERS' CHASE) 3m 3f
4:00 (4:01) (Class 3) 5-Y-0+ **£6,239** (£1,935; £967; £484)

Form RPR

/11- 1 **That's Rhythm (FR)**[240] 657 14-11-11 126 MissPFuller(7) 132
(Miss Sally Duckett) *chsd ldrs: lft 2nd 12th: effrt and led 3 out (usual 4 out): hld on gamely fr last* **11/1**

2 ½ **Walden (IRE)**[37] 3348 7-11-5 0 (p) MrWThompson(7) 126
(I R Ferguson, Ire) *hld up and bhd: gd hdwy bef 3 out (usual 4 out): chsd wnr bef last: kpt on u.p run-in: jst hld* **13/2**

122- 3 6 **Brassick**[124] 1709 7-12-1 128 (t) MrTWeston 124
(Mrs A Rucker) *hld up: stdy hdwy and in tch 13th: effrt and chsng ldrs whn n.m.r 2 out (usual 3 out): one pce fr last* **7/2**[1]

1/1- 4 2 **Penmore Mill (IRE)**[21] 9-11-13 119 MrTEllis(5) 123
(F A Hutsby) *prom: lft 3rd 12th: effrt and led briefly bef 3 out: outpcd fr last* **13/2**

015- 5 6 **General Hardi**[232] 747 13-11-9 112 MrCDawson(3) 113
(John Wade) *hld up in midfield: stdy hdwy after 4 out (usual 5 out): effrt next: wknd after 2 out (usual 3 out)* **66/1**

2U1- 6 ½ **Special Portrait (IRE)**[21] 10-11-11 109 (t) MrPGerety(7) 117
(Mark Hughes) *midfield: drvn and outpcd 14th: sme late hdwy: nvr rchd ldrs* **20/1**

412/ 7 4 **Marufo (IRE)**[28] 12-11-11 129 (p) MrDominicSutton(7) 113
(Tracey L Bailey) *t.k.h: cl up: led 9th to bef 3 out (usual 4 out): wknd fr next* **25/1**

/13- P **Back On The Road (IRE)**[14] 12-11-11 109 MrJamieAlexander(7)
(N W Alexander) *bhd: blnd 11th: struggling fnl circ: t.o whn p.u bef 3 out (usual 4 out)* **50/1**

5/0- P **Ballycolin**[270] 170 11-11-7 113 MrSFox(5)
(Ian Duncan) *mstkes in rr: struggling fnl circ: t.o whn p.u bef 4 out (usual 5 out)* **14/1**

22/- U **King Fontaine (IRE)**[21] 11-11-5 116 MissETodd(7)
(J J O'Shea) *in tch: hit: stmbld and uns rdr 11th* **12/1**

154- F **Themilanhorse (IRE)**[197] 1040 8-11-11 127 MrJamesFerguson(7)
(John Ferguson) *t.k.h: cl up: led 4th to 9th: upsides whn fell heavily 12th* **5/1**[2]

P/0- U **Pentiffic (NZ)**[266] 238 11-12-1 122 MrJHamilton(3)
(Venetia Williams) *led to 4th: prom: lost pl whn hit 13th: sn struggling: no ch whn mstke: stmbld and uns rdr 4 out (usual 5 out)* **6/1**[3]

6m 56.4s (7.60) **Going Correction** +0.25s/f (Yiel) **12** Ran SP% **114.6**
Speed ratings: **98,97,96,95,93 93,92,** , ,
CSF £76.26 TOTE £10.30: £3.60, £3.20, £1.70; EX 86.70 Trifecta £352.20.

Owner Mr and Mrs R H F Fuller **Bred** Scea Du Haras Des Sablonets **Trained** Moreton-In-Marsh, Gloucs

■ Stewards' Enquiry : Mr W Thompson four-day ban: use of whip (TBA)

FOCUS
This well-contested hunter chase was run over a further distance this season and provided a proper test. It served up a cracking finish and the final fence was bypassed. Decent hunter chase form.

4058 CONDITIONAL JOCKEYS' FESTIVAL TRIAL H'CAP HURDLE (12 hdls) 2m 4f
4:30 (4:30) (Class 3) (0-135,128) 4-Y-0+ **£6,498** (£1,908; £954; £477)

Form RPR

U05- 1 **Rumble Of Thunder (IRE)**[11] 3832 8-11-3 **122** AdamNicol(3) 128+
(Philip Kirby) *pressed ldr: led 3 out: rdn next: kpt on strly fr last* **6/1**

034- 2 2 **Sud Pacifique (IRE)**[16] 3758 6-10-10 **118** (b) NickSlatter(6) 122
(Donald McCain) *t.k.h: hld up in tch: stdy hdwy bef 3 out: effrt and chsd wnr last: kpt on same pce run-in* **3/1**[3]

03P- 3 1 ¾ **Scots Gaelic (IRE)**[32] 3471 7-10-12 **120** DeanPratt(6) 123
(John Quinn) *t.k.h: prom: sltly outpcd 3 out: rallied next: hit last: edgd rt run-in: styd on: nrst fin* **2/1**[1]

/65- 4 3 **Golden Sparkle (IRE)**[31] 3499 8-10-11 **116** GrahamWatters(3) 115
(Ian Duncan) *cl up: effrt and ev ch 2 out: rdn and outpcd fr last* **12/1**

442- 5 3 ¼ **Los Nadis (GER)**[32] 3475 10-11-0 **116** TonyKelly 112
(Jim Goldie) *led: rdn and hdd 3 out: rallied: wknd after next* **11/4**[2]

160- 6 29 **Tom Wade (IRE)**[185] 1173 7-11-0 **116** BenPoste 92
(Shaun Harris) *t.k.h: hld up in tch: stdy hdwy bef 3 out: wknd next* **20/1**

4m 50.6s (-0.90) **Going Correction** -0.45s/f (Good) **6** Ran SP% **111.7**
Speed ratings (Par 107): **83,82,81,80,79 67**
CSF £24.23 TOTE £7.50: £2.90, £1.50; EX 30.20 Trifecta £106.20.

Owner The Well Oiled Partnership **Bred** Rathasker Stud **Trained** Middleham, N Yorks

FOCUS
A modest handicap. The third and fourth help set the level.

T/Plt: £350.00 to a £1 stake. Pool: £115093.01 - 240.00 winning tickets T/Qpdt: £33.40 to a £1 stake. Pool: £9130.20 - 201.70 winning tickets RY

3664 PUNCHESTOWN (R-H)
Sunday, February 2

OFFICIAL GOING: Heavy (soft in places)

4062a BOYLESPORTS FREE WIFI COMING TO OUR SHOPS TIED COTTAGE CHASE (GRADE 2) (11 fncs) 2m
3:10 (3:11) 5-Y-0+ **£21,666** (£6,333; £3,000; £1,000)

RPR

1 **Arvika Ligeonniere (FR)**[37] 3338 9-11-12 157 RWalsh 166+
(W P Mullins, Ire) *trckd ldr in 2nd: travelled wl to ld 3 out and drew clr after next: in command appr last: easily* **2/7**[1]

2 14 **Toner D'Oudairies (FR)**[27] 3579 7-11-7 150 (tp) BryanCooper 147+
(Gordon Elliott, Ire) *hld up in rr tl prog into 3rd after 3 out: chsd wnr in 2nd after next: sn no imp: kpt on same pce* **6/1**[2]

3 14 **Rathlin**[15] 3790 9-11-10 157 (t) MarkEnright 136
(M F Morris, Ire) *racd in 3rd tl pushed along and dropped to 4th after 3 out: sn no ex: kpt on one pce into 3rd at last* **10/1**[3]

4 shd **Special Tiara**[77] 2532 7-11-12 153 DavyRussell 138
(Henry De Bromhead, Ire) *led tl hdd 3 out: sn no ex and dropped to 4th at last* **10/1**[3]

4m 7.7s (-10.90) **4** Ran SP% **110.2**
CSF £2.77 TOTE £1.30; DF 2.60 Trifecta £5.00.
Owner Mrs S Ricci **Bred** Yves Lepage **Trained** Muine Beag, Co Carlow

FOCUS
Best to rate the winner to his mark, as the fourth is better on quicker ground and third has no recent form.

3836 SOUTHWELL (L-H)
Monday, February 3

OFFICIAL GOING: Heavy (5.9)
The first hurdle and fence in the back straight were omitted.
Wind: quite strong against in home straight Weather: overcast; 5 degrees

4066 BET TOTEPLACEPOT AT TOTEPOOL.COM H'CAP CHASE (17 fncs 2 omitted) 3m 110y
12:45 (12:46) (Class 5) (0-100,98) 5-Y-0+ **£2,371** (£696; £348; £174)

Form RPR

/06- 1 **The Last Bridge**[43] 3227 7-10-8 **80** RichardJohnson 98+
(Susan Johnson) *off pce in last trio: drvn 9th: wnt 3rd bef 12th: nt fluent next: urged and jst after 14th: 4 l clr whn landed v awkwardly 2 out: galloped on stoutly flat* **5/2**[1]

134- 2 8 **Somerby (IRE)**[15] 3797 11-11-1 **87** (t) AdamWedge 94
(Richenda Ford) *off pce in last trio: effrt 11th: disp 2nd and rdn home turn: one pce after: 3rd at last: wnt 2nd but no ch w wnr flat* **5/1**[3]

F31- 3 ¾ **Royaume Bleu (FR)**[21] 3688 9-11-7 **98** KillianMoore(5) 106
(Alex Hales) *t.k.h in 3rd bhd clr ldrs: rdn and effrt whn hit 12th: chsd wnr vainly fr 3 out tl after last* **6/1**

440- 4 24 **Noble Witness (IRE)**[32] 3502 11-11-7 **93** (p) AdamPogson 79
(Charles Pogson) *led: sn clr w one rival: hdd bef 6th: led briefly 14th: drvn and fdd bef next* **10/1**

6P4- 5 10 **Epee Celeste (FR)**[11] 3852 8-10-10 **87** (b) JoeCornwall(5) 59
(Michael Chapman) *pressed ldr and sn 12 l clr of rest: led bef 6th: hdd 14th and immediately lost tch: t.o* **33/1**

/P5- R **Dermatologiste**[13] 3827 11-11-7 **93** (b[1]) AndrewThornton
(Caroline Bailey) *caused false s and then lft at s* **9/2**[2]

64P- F **Waywood Princess**[13] 3824 9-9-7 **72** NickSlatter(7)
(John Bryan Groucott) *in rr tl fell 3rd* **14/1**

P01- P **Over And Above (IRE)**[12] 3834 8-10-6 **78** (bt) RichieMcGrath
(Henry Hogarth) *settled in 4th bhd clr ldng pair: hit 10th: drvn and lost tch after next: t.o and p.u 14th* **8/1**

FU3- P **What A Good Night (IRE)**[28] 3565 6-11-10 **96** SamTwiston-Davies
(Nigel Twiston-Davies) *in rr and nt a fluent: effrt and in tch 11th: wknd 13th: t.o and p.u after next* **8/1**

6m 37.9s (14.90) **Going Correction** +0.65s/f (Soft) **9** Ran SP% **118.6**
Speed ratings: **102,99,99,91,88** , , ,
CSF £16.51 CT £69.02 TOTE £2.90: £1.90, £2.20, £1.20; EX 17.20 Trifecta £40.20.
Owner I K Johnson **Bred** I K Johnson **Trained** Madley, H'fords
■ Stewards' Enquiry : Adam Wedge one-day ban: careless riding (Feb 17)

FOCUS
Both straights, Golf Club bend and bend into home straight moved inside for fresh ground. A dramatic start. Moderate form. The second and third are rated to their marks in a good time for the grade.

4067 BET AT TOTEPOOL.COM ON YOUR MOBILE NOVICES' H'CAP CHASE (14 fncs 2 omitted) 2m 4f 110y
1:15 (1:15) (Class 4) (0-110,105) 5-Y-0+ **£3,898** (£1,144; £572; £286)

Form RPR

/2F- 1 **Farbreaga (IRE)**[46] 3176 8-11-9 **105** JeremiahMcGrath(3) 116+
(Jamie Poulton) *mstke 1st: w ldrs: nt fluent 10th: rdn to ld bef 3 out: hrd pressed whn untidy last but outj. rival at last and in command after* **9/2**[3]

245- 2 3 ¼ **Royal Riviera**[20] 3693 8-11-8 **101** (t) SamTwiston-Davies 111
(Nigel Twiston-Davies) *hld up trcking ldrs: effrt 9th: chsd wnr 3 out: chal and nt fluent 2 out: stl on terms whn mstke last: nt rcvr* **7/1**

0/0- 3 8 **Ball Hopper (IRE)**[20] 3696 10-11-1 **94** (t) AndrewThornton 97
(Richenda Ford) *in rr whn hmpd 5th: effrt 11th: 4th home turn: rdn and outpcd whn mstke 3 out: sn 3rd: 8 l 3rd at last: eased whn btn* **8/1**

62P- 4 13 **Guanciale**[16] 3785 7-11-7 **100** (t) BrendanPowell 86
(Brendan Powell) *prom: led after 5th tl rdn and hdd bef 3 out: dropped out tamely* **6/1**

PU3- 5 1 ¾ **Flichity (IRE)**[10] 3881 9-9-9 **79** oh17 JoeCornwall(5) 63
(John Cornwall) *t.k.h: mde most tl after 5th: rdn next: in tch tl struggling bef 11th* **50/1**

/0P- 6 4 ½ **Fashion Faux Pas (IRE)**[53] 3033 7-11-7 **100** NickScholfield 80
(Paul Henderson) *nt fluent 2nd: nrly a last: hit 8th: rdn and lost tch next* **16/1**

/36- P **Trozulon (FR)**[18] 3740 7-11-10 **103** AidanColeman
(Venetia Williams) *pressed ldrs on outer: cl 3rd but shkn up whn blnd 11th: nt rcvr: p.u next* **7/2**[2]

The Form Book Jumps, Raceform Ltd, Compton, RG20 6NL.

05F- **F** **Stagecoach Jasper**[65] 2818 8-10-7 **93**........................ CallumBewley[(7)]
(Sue Smith) *w ldrs tl fell 5th* **5/2**[1]
5m 38.0s (21.00) **Going Correction** +0.65s/f (Soft) **8** Ran SP% **114.7**
Speed ratings: **86,84,81,76,76 74,** , ,
CSF £35.55 CT £243.89 TOTE £5.10: £2.30, £1.90, £2.20; EX 29.50 Trifecta £261.40.
Owner Miss V Markowiak **Bred** Daniel O'Mahony **Trained** Telscombe, E Sussex

FOCUS
An ordinary handicap. A big step up from the winner but he threatened this sort of figure over hurdles.

4068 TEXT YOUR BETS TO TOTEPOOL ON 60021 NOVICES' HURDLE (9 hdls 2 omitted) 2m 4f 110y
1:45 (1:45) (Class 4) 4-Y-0+ **£3,119** (£915; £457; £228)

Form RPR
25- **1** **Flementine (IRE)**[23] 3649 6-10-11 0.................................... IanPopham 120+
(Martin Keighley) *racd keenly in 2nd or 3rd tl led 6th: 5 l clr last: pushed along and styd on wl* **4/6**[1]
2 *2 ¼* **Spyder**[465] 6-11-4 0.. LeightonAspell 122
(Lucy Wadham) *trckd ldrs: mstke 5th: wnt 2nd 3 out: rdn and drew clr of rest next: wl hld by wnr after* **14/1**[3]
/32- **3** *2 ½* **Brave Vic (IRE)**[29] 3552 6-11-1 123.............................. JoshuaMoore[(3)] 120
(Gary Moore) *prom: drvn and outpcd bef 2 out: 10 l 3rd at last: rallied and kpt on stoutly flat* **6/4**[2]
33- **4** *22* **El Indio (IRE)**[35] 3417 7-10-11 0...................................... GeraldQuinn[(7)] 97
(Claire Dyson) *led at slow pce tl 2nd: rdn and lost tch qckly sn after 3 out* **16/1**
024- **5** *11* **Leith Hill Legasi**[34] 3438 5-10-8 0.................................. KielanWoods[(3)] 79
(Charlie Longsdon) *midfield: rdn bef 6th: struggling 3 out* **16/1**
05F- **6** *12* **Sportsreport (IRE)**[29] 3550 6-11-4 0.............................. AndrewThornton 74
(Seamus Mullins) *t.k.h: sn pressing ldrs: 3rd and looked to be gng wl at 6th: rdn and fdd tamely after next: t.o* **50/1**
/40- **7** *16* **Power Of God (IRE)**[16] 3782 6-11-4 0............................. RichardJohnson 58
(Tim Vaughan) *bhd: rdn 3rd: nvr travelling after: t.o bef 3 out* **20/1**
450- **8** *½* **Church Bray**[19] 3716 6-11-4 0................................... SamTwiston-Davies 58
(Nigel Twiston-Davies) *bhd: mstke 4th: t.o after 3 out* **25/1**
50- **9** *68* **Princeofthedesert**[10] 3872 8-11-4 0.................................. AdamPogson
(Garry Woodward) *led 2nd: set mod pce tl hdd 6th: lost pl v rapidly and sn hopelessly t.o* **50/1**
5m 30.3s (17.30) **Going Correction** +1.05s/f (Soft) **9** Ran SP% **130.9**
Speed ratings (Par 105): **109,108,107,98,94 90,83,83,57**
CSF £14.57 TOTE £1.60: £1.10, £3.50, £1.10; EX 24.20 Trifecta £47.90.
Owner Figjam II **Bred** R McCarthy **Trained** Condicote, Gloucs

FOCUS
An uncompetitive novice hurdle. The winner was the form pick and is rated 10lb off best.

4069 DOWNLOAD THE TOTEPOOL MOBILE APP "NATIONAL HUNT" NOVICES' HURDLE (8 hdls 1 omitted) 2m
2:15 (2:15) (Class 4) 4-Y-0+ **£3,249** (£954; £477; £238)

Form RPR
UP1- **1** **Anay Turge (FR)**[12] 3838 9-11-10 128..........................(tp) KieronEdgar[(7)] 125+
(Nigel Hawke) *pressed ldr: led gng wl 2 out: racd rather idly but a in command after: 3 l clr last: pushed out* **1/1**[1]
1P- **2** *2 ¼* **Vivaccio (FR)**[54] 3023 5-11-10 122.................................... AidanColeman 116+
(Venetia Williams) *settled in 3rd: pushed along and chsd wnr after 2 out: no imp after* **5/2**[2]
3P0- **3** *7* **Mission To Mars (IRE)**[66] 2802 5-11-3 0.............. SamTwiston-Davies 103
(Nigel Twiston-Davies) *led at v stdy pce: rdn and hdd 2 out: sn btn: plugged on in 3rd pl* **14/1**
26- **4** *1* **Rendezvous Peak**[66] 2788 5-10-12 0.............................. MattCrawley[(5)] 102
(Lucy Wadham) *taken down early: settled in last pl on outside tl effrt bef 2 out: sn cajoled along and fnd nil: mstke last* **33/1**
001- **5** *26* **Vikekhal (FR)**[49] 3134 5-11-10 0... JamieMoore 82
(Gary Moore) *a abt same pl: rdn and struggling after 3 out: t.o* **9/2**[3]
60- **6** *hd* **High Holloa**[237] 715 5-10-10 0...................................... AndrewThornton 68
(Caroline Bailey) *towards rr: mstke 5th and reminders: sn struggling: nt fluent next: t.o bef 2 out* **66/1**
F00- **7** *5* **Presentings Return (IRE)**[36] 3388 5-11-3 0........................... APMcCoy 70
(Jonjo O'Neill) *chsd ldrs: mstke 5th: sn drvn and no rspnse: struggling bdly bef 2 out: t.o* **10/1**
4m 17.3s (20.30) **Going Correction** +1.05s/f (Soft) **7** Ran SP% **116.9**
Speed ratings (Par 105): **91,89,86,85,72 72,70**
CSF £4.06 TOTE £2.40: £1.30, £2.90; EX 5.70 Trifecta £33.70.
Owner Mrs K Wetherall **Bred** Mme Annick Penouilh **Trained** Stoodleigh, Devon

FOCUS
A modest affair. The winner is rated to the level of his recent C&D run.

4070 WE'LL DOUBLE YOUR DEPOSIT AT TOTEPOOL CASINO H'CAP HURDLE (11 hdls 2 omitted) 3m 110y
2:50 (2:50) (Class 4) (0-115,115) 4-Y-0+ **£3,119** (£915; £457; £228)

Form RPR
/00- **1** **Heavenstown (IRE)**[67] 2771 8-10-12 **106**..............(b[1]) NicodeBoinville[(5)] 113+
(John Spearing) *t.k.h: led 3rd: 6 l clr and rdn bef 2 out: kpt finding plenty after: 3 l ahd last: rdn out* **16/1**
/05- **2** *2* **Barton Stacey (IRE)**[18] 3741 9-11-11 **114**.................(b) TomScudamore 117
(David Pipe) *settled towards rr: pushed along and stdy prog bef 8th: 3rd and rdn home turn: nt qckn after: wnt wl hld 2nd after last* **8/1**
5/2- **3** *¾* **Silver Wren**[94] 2193 7-11-5 **108**.. SamJones 111
(Renee Robeson) *hmpd after 1st: trckd ldrs: j. slowly 4th: wnt 3rd at 8th and 2nd bef 2 out: sn rdn and one pce: lost 2nd after last* **16/1**
111- **4** *3 ½* **Hopatina (IRE)**[28] 3566 8-11-9 **115**............................... MichaelByrne[(3)] 114
(Neil Mulholland) *impeded 1st: bhd: pushed along after 7th: drvn to pass fading rivals after 3 out: 5th home turn: plugged on but nvr able to chal* **4/1**[2]
002- **5** *¾* **Gonalston Cloud (IRE)**[12] 3842 7-9-13 **95**................ CharlieDeutsch[(7)] 94
(Nick Kent) *trckd ldrs: rdn to go 2nd bef 8th: hit next: lost 2nd after 3 out: 4th and struggling home turn: plodded on* **3/1**[1]
655- **6** *22* **Knockraheen (IRE)**[34] 3435 6-11-12 **115**.. APMcCoy 93
(Jonjo O'Neill) *bmpd rival at 1st: rdr lost iron briefly: lost gd pl and nt fluent 3rd: chsd ldrs: brief effrt 8th: sn rdn and struggling: t.o bef 2 out* **4/1**[2]
442- **7** *27* **Golden Calf (IRE)**[43] 3227 7-10-13 **102**...........................(p) JamieMoore 51
(Peter Bowen) *chsd wnr 3rd tl 7th: rdn and dropped out qckly bef 3 out: t.o and eased* **8/1**
05U- **U** **Jaunty Journey**[12] 3836 11-11-0 **103**.....................(p) SamTwiston-Davies
(Nigel Twiston-Davies) *led tl j. awkwardly: bmpd rival and uns rdr 1st* **10/1**
502- **P** **Yazdi (IRE)**[39] 3265 5-10-11 **100**.. DenisO'Regan
(Henry Oliver) *midfield: rdn and wknd 8th: t.o and p.u after 3 out* **14/1**
0- **P** **See More Power (IRE)**[29] 3550 9-10-5 **94**......................... NickScholfield
(Paul Henderson) *a last: rdn and struggling after 7th: t.o and p.u 3 out* **50/1**
215- **P** **The Jugopolist (IRE)**[18] 3737 7-11-7 **115**..................(v) JoeCornwall[(5)]
(John Cornwall) *bhd: pushed along 4th: nvr gng wl: rdn and struggling 7th: t.o and p.u after 3 out* **50/1**
220- **P** **Ifyouthinkso**[65] 2827 7-11-1 **104**..............................(p) WillKennedy
(Lucy Jones) *lft in ld after schemozzle 1st: hdd 3rd: pushed along 6th: lost 2nd bef 8th: sn t.o: p.u after 3 out* **6/1**[3]
6m 38.0s (23.00) **Going Correction** +1.05s/f (Soft) **12** Ran SP% **133.0**
Speed ratings (Par 105): **105,104,104,103,102 95,87,** , ,
CSF £154.73 CT £2136.95 TOTE £21.70: £6.70, £4.10, £3.60; EX 180.10 Trifecta £2954.30.
Owner Malcolm Page **Bred** Thistletown Stud **Trained** Kinnersley, Worcs

FOCUS
A moderate handicap, but solid enough form for the class.

4071 FOLLOW @TOTEPOOL ON TWITTER H'CAP HURDLE (9 hdls 2 omitted) 2m 4f 110y
3:20 (3:20) (Class 5) (0-100,96) 4-Y-0+ **£2,274** (£667; £333; £166)

Form RPR
/32- **1** **Alaccordion**[253] 490 9-10-7 77.. CharliePoste 86+
(Violet M Jordan) *trckd ldrs: wnt 3rd after 5th and 2nd after 3 out: sn led but drvn and wanting to hang rt after: 4 l clr 2 out: plugged on after: all out* **12/1**
060- **2** *1 ¾* **Veratan (FR)**[35] 3420 7-11-4 88...................................... AidanColeman 94
(Venetia Williams) *nt fluent in rr and rdn fr 2nd: nvr looked to be travelling wl: hit 3rd and reminders: 6th after 3 out: laboured prog under driving after: wnt 2nd bef last where 3 l down and mstke: nt rcvr* **3/1**[1]
655- **3** *4 ½* **Free Falling**[20] 3699 8-10-6 76.....................................(v) FelixDeGiles 76
(Alastair Lidderdale) *rdn to ld after 1st: hdd bef 6th: sn drvn: chsd wnr vainly after 3 out tl bef last: lost two pl clsng stages* **6/1**[3]
003- **4** *½* **Marmalade Man**[29] 3553 8-11-3 87.................................. AndrewThornton 88
(Seamus Mullins) *j. modly: reminders 3rd: j. slowly 6th: chsd ldrs: 3rd briefly after 3 out: hrd drvn after but v one pce* **7/1**
330- **5** *11* **Detour Ahead**[13] 3821 6-11-5 96..................................(tp) ConorRing[(7)] 85
(Jennie Candlish) *chsd ldrs: rdn after 5th: struggling fr 3 out* **8/1**
362- **P** **Cloudy Dawn**[8] 3925 9-9-4 70 oh1.............. Zachery-JamesGaughan[(10)]
(Sue Smith) *dropped bk last and rdn 5th: t.o and p.u next* **9/2**[2]
355- **P** **Landenstown Star (IRE)**[43] 3227 9-10-7 77...............(tp) TommyPhelan
(Mark Gillard) *rdn to begin: in rr and nt travelling: rdn and labouring 5th: t.o and p.u 2 out* **6/1**[3]
024- **P** **Fidelor (FR)**[21] 3692 8-11-11 95.. WillKennedy
(Alex Hales) *led tl after 1st: pressed ldr tl led again bef 6th: hdd after 3 out and dropped out v rapidly: t.o and p.u next* **10/1**
000- **P** **Home Girl (IRE)**[61] 2886 6-10-1 71.................................. DougieCostello
(Susan Johnson) *nvr bttr than midfield: rdn after 5th: mstke next and struggling: t.o and p.u 2 out* **20/1**
5m 33.8s (20.80) **Going Correction** +1.05s/f (Soft) **9** Ran SP% **116.9**
Speed ratings (Par 103): **102,101,99,99,95** , , ,
CSF £49.75 CT £244.75 TOTE £4.80: £3.50, £2.80, £2.90; EX 54.70 Trifecta £366.70.
Owner Farmers & Cricketers Partnership **Bred** F K Jennings **Trained** Moreton Morrell, Warwicks

FOCUS
This weak event proved hard work. The first two are on the upgrade.

4072 LIKE TOTEPOOL ON FACEBOOK H'CAP HURDLE (8 hdls 1 omitted) 2m
3:50 (3:50) (Class 5) (0-100,100) 4-Y-0+ **£2,274** (£667; £333; £166)

Form RPR
032- **1** **Whispering Harry**[16] 3788 5-11-4 **92**.............................. RichardJohnson 101+
(Henry Oliver) *hit 1st: chsd ldrs: cl to chal 3 out: sn rdn to ld and gng best: clr between last two: readily* **9/4**[1]
U46- **2** *7* **Pagham Belle**[16] 3788 6-10-9 **83**.................................(t) TomScudamore 84
(Nigel Hawke) *cl up: led briefly after 3 out: sn drvn: tired between last two: 7 l 2nd whn hopped over last* **3/1**[2]
03P- **3** *10* **Camptown Lady**[16] 3788 5-10-8 **82**.............................. DougieCostello 71
(Laura Young) *towards rr: drvn and bdly outpcd in 6th after 3 out: rallied bef last: fin wl to snatch modest 3rd* **6/1**[3]
334- **4** *1 ¼* **Chankillo**[54] 3025 5-11-4 **92**.. WillKennedy 80
(Sarah-Jayne Davies) *chsd ldrs tl mstke 5th: poor 4th and struggling after next: plugged on* **10/1**
022- **5** *nk* **Cappielow Park**[18] 3736 5-11-5 **100**........................(p) MikeyEnnis[(7)] 87
(Fleur Hawes) *t.k.h: 2nd tl led 4th: mde most after tl drvn and hdd after 3 out: fdd to mod 3rd 2 out: lost two pls clsng stages* **7/1**
02P- **6** *3 ¼* **Lodgician (IRE)**[55] 3015 12-11-2 **97**........................(vt) RyanHatch[(7)] 81
(Nigel Twiston-Davies) *chsd ldrs: rdn 3 out: no rspnse: sn struggling* **14/1**
363/ **7** *22* **Marleno (GER)**[368] 3957 8-11-12 **100**................................(t) PaulMoloney 62
(Anthony Middleton) *last pair: nt fluent 4th and lost tch: t.o 3 out* **7/1**
P/0- **8** *17* **Quinola Des Obeaux (FR)**[21] 3692 10-10-13 **90**.............. JamesBest[(3)] 35
(Rob Summers) *t.k.h early: led tl 4th and again bef next: sn hdd and dropped rt out: t.o bef 2 out* **20/1**
4m 14.3s (17.30) **Going Correction** +1.05s/f (Soft) **8** Ran SP% **115.6**
Speed ratings (Par 103): **98,94,89,88,88 87,76,67**
CSF £9.91 CT £34.55 TOTE £2.80: £1.70, £1.20, £2.00; EX 12.10 Trifecta £78.20.
Owner R G Whitehead **Bred** S A Brookshaw **Trained** Broomhall, Worcs

FOCUS
A moderate handicap that took a lot of getting. A step up from the winner with the second to his mark.
T/Jkpt: Not won. T/Plt: £56.90 to a £1 stake. Pool: £94471.08 - 1210.56 winning tickets T/Qpdt: £12.80 to a £1 stake. Pool: £8276.45 - 475.94 winning tickets IM

3735 MARKET RASEN (R-H)
Tuesday, February 4

OFFICIAL GOING: Soft (heavy in places on chase course)
Wind: Light across Weather: Fine

4073 WATCH RACING UK ON SKY CHANNEL 432 JUVENILE MAIDEN HURDLE (8 hdls) 2m 1f
1:20 (1:20) (Class 4) 4-Y-0 **£3,119** (£915; £457; £228)

Form RPR
2- **1** **Carry On Sydney**[20] 3714 4-10-12 0.................................. LeightonAspell 122+
(Oliver Sherwood) *mde all: shkn up flat: r.o wl: eased towards fin* **8/15**[1]

4- **2** *8* **Astrum**[20] 3714 4-10-9 0 TrevorWhelan(3) 109
(Neil King) *hld up: hdwy 4th: chsd wnr appr 2 out: sn rdn: styd on same pce last* **10/1**
243- **3** *11* **Chebsey Beau**[14] 3822 4-10-12 0 BrianHughes 98
(John Quinn) *prom: chsd wnr 4th tl rdn appr 2 out: wknd bef last* **5/1**[2]
044- **4** *12* **Garde Ville (FR)**[17] 3781 4-10-12 113 TomScudamore 88
(Lisa Williamson) *hld up: mstke 3rd: sn given reminder: bhd fr 6th* **14/1**
6- **5** *7* **Interior Minister**[20] 3714 4-10-12 0 APMcCoy 79
(Jonjo O'Neill) *chsd wnr to 4th: mstke 6th: sn wknd: bhd whn j.lft last* **9/1**[3]
0- **6** *6* **Hurricane John (IRE)**[20] 3714 4-10-12 0 AidanColeman 73
(Venetia Williams) *prom: lost pl 4th: sn pushed along: wknd 6th* **66/1**

4m 14.6s (7.90) **Going Correction** +0.575s/f (Soft) **6** Ran SP% **109.1**
Speed ratings: **104,100,95,89,86 83**
CSF £6.38 TOTE £1.70: £1.10, £3.90; EX 7.30 Trifecta £16.80.
Owner The Sydney Arms Partnership **Bred** Mrs James Wigan **Trained** Upper Lambourn, Berks

FOCUS
Rail moved in 8m to provide fresh ground on hurdles track and on common bend. The easy winner is on the upgrade along with the second.

4074 EBF STALLIONS MARES' "NATIONAL HUNT" MAIDEN HURDLE (8 hdls) 2m 1f
1:50 (1:50) (Class 4) 4-Y-0+ **£3,768** (£1,106; £553; £276)

Form RPR
504- **1** **Rosa Fleet (IRE)**[19] 3746 6-11-3 0 AidanColeman 117+
(Venetia Williams) *hld up in tch: tk clsr order 5th: led and mstke last: r.o wl: eased nr fin* **7/1**
353- **2** *8* **Fine Moment**[14] 3818 6-11-3 0 (t) BrianHughes 104
(Kevin Frost) *chsd ldrs: wnt 2nd after 3rd: rdn to ld 2 out: hdd last: no ex flat* **4/1**[3]
423- **3** *2 ¼* **Rising Teal**[40] 3247 5-11-3 105 LeightonAspell 103
(Lucy Wadham) *chsd ldrs: led after 3rd: drvn along after 3 out: hdd and mstke next: hit last: wknd flat* **13/8**[1]
0/3- **4** *3* **Be My Present**[280] 46 7-11-3 0 [1] WilsonRenwick 99
(Rose Dobbin) *prom: rdn appr 2 out: styd on same pce* **7/1**
0/0- **5** *28* **Dream Mistress**[75] 2621 5-11-3 0 TomMessenger 71
(Chris Bealby) *hld up: nt fluent 2nd and next: wknd 5th* **100/1**
4- **6** *15* **Crazy Jane (IRE)**[14] 3818 5-11-3 0 FelixDeGiles 56
(Tom Gretton) *hld up: wknd 5th* **66/1**
55- **7** *nk* **All For Lily**[157] 1472 5-11-3 0 AdamPogson 56
(Charles Pogson) *hld up: racd keenly: wknd after 5th* **40/1**
000- **8** *7* **Miss Dimples (IRE)**[48] 3159 5-11-3 0 WillKennedy 49
(Sarah-Jayne Davies) *led: hmpd 1st: hdd after 3rd: rdn and wknd bef next* **100/1**
43- **9** *3 ¾* **Lilly's Legend**[20] 3727 4-10-7 0 DougieCostello 35
(Mark Walford) *hld up: rdn and wknd bef 4th* **10/3**[2]
P/P- **P** **Silk Sky**[51] 3116 8-11-0 0 (v[1]) JackQuinlan(3)
(Phil McEntee) *chsd ldr: j.rt 1st: rdn and wknd after 3rd: bhd fr next: p.u bef 2 out* **200/1**

4m 14.1s (7.40) **Going Correction** +0.575s/f (Soft)
WFA 4 from 5yo+ 9lb **10** Ran SP% **112.6**
Speed ratings (Par 105): **105,101,100,98,85 78,78,75,73,**
toteswingers 1&2 £4.00, 2&3 £1.90, 1&3 £4.80 CSF £34.11 TOTE £8.70: £2.40, £1.40, £1.20; EX 48.80 Trifecta £106.40.
Owner Mezzone Family **Bred** J F C Maxwell **Trained** Kings Caple, H'fords

FOCUS
A moderate mares' maiden. It was run at a sound gallop and only four mattered off the home turn. A massive step up from the wasy winner but she can win again.

4075 EBF STALLIONS "NATIONAL HUNT" NOVICES' HURDLE QUALIFIER (10 hdls) 2m 5f
2:20 (2:20) (Class 3) 4-7-Y-0 **£5,718** (£1,679; £839; £419)

Form RPR
3/3- **1** **Panama Petrus (IRE)**[89] 2316 6-11-2 0 AidanColeman 126+
(Venetia Williams) *a.p: led 2 out: nt fluent last: drvn out* **11/4**[2]
312- **2** *½* **Shimla Dawn (IRE)**[24] 3661 6-11-8 131 DougieCostello 130+
(Mark Walford) *a.p: chsd ldr 3rd: led 3 out: rdn and hdd next: ev ch last: styd on gamely* **4/5**[1]
353- **3** *19* **Tracking Time**[24] 3650 7-10-9 105 MrJMartin(7) 106
(Andrew J Martin) *led to 1st: chsd ldr to 3rd: remained handy: rdn appr 2 out: wknd bef last* **16/1**
545- **4** *5* **Spookydooky (IRE)**[19] 3735 6-11-2 0 (t) APMcCoy 103+
(Jonjo O'Neill) *hld up: mstke and outpcd 7th: n.d* **12/1**
03F- **5** *7* **Owen Na View (IRE)**[55] 3023 6-11-2 121 PaddyBrennan 93
(Fergal O'Brien) *trckd ldrs tl rdn and wknd appr 2 out* **16/1**
42- **6** *1 ½* **Maxed Out King (IRE)**[9] 3920 6-11-2 0 ShaneByrne 92
(Sue Smith) *plld hrd: trckd ldr tl led 1st: hdd 3 out: rdn and wknd bef next* **6/1**[3]
406- **7** *17* **Agent Louise**[19] 3735 6-10-4 0 AdamNicol(5) 68
(Mike Sowersby) *hld up: wknd 6th* **100/1**
/0U- **P** **Mackeson**[19] 3735 5-11-2 0 TomMessenger
(Chris Bealby) *hld up: nt fluent 2nd: drvn along after 5th: bhd fr next: p.u bef 3 out* **200/1**

5m 20.4s (11.60) **Going Correction** +0.575s/f (Soft) **8** Ran SP% **117.5**
Speed ratings: **100,99,92,90,88 87,80,**
CSF £5.67 TOTE £3.70: £1.10, £1.10, £2.00; EX 7.50 Trifecta £45.50.
Owner Andrew Brooks & Julian Taylor **Bred** J F C Maxwell **Trained** Kings Caple, H'fords

FOCUS
The two market principals dominated this novice hurdle from two out and it's straightforward form. The first two are decent.

4076 WHISTLE AND FLUTE BARNETBY H'CAP HURDLE (10 hdls) 2m 5f
2:50 (2:50) (Class 4) (0-120,120) 4-Y-0+ **£3,119** (£915; £457; £228)

Form RPR
622- **1** **Saffron Wells (IRE)**[14] 3816 6-11-3 **114** TrevorWhelan(3) 127+
(Neil King) *hld up: hdwy 7th: led appr 2 out: styd on wl* **4/1**[2]
1/4- **2** *11* **Too Generous**[19] 3731 6-11-5 **120** MikeyEnnis(7) 119
(David Pipe) *chsd ldr tl appr 7th: rdn after 3 out: styd on same pce fr next* **5/1**[3]
/61- **3** *¾* **Grate Fella (IRE)**[34] 3451 6-11-6 **114** RyanMania 113
(Sue Smith) *prom: led after 7th: rdn and hdd 2 out: nt fluent last: wknd flat* **2/1**[1]
520- **4** *8* **Venceremos**[73] 2663 7-10-7 **104** (p) KielanWoods(3) 95
(Charlie Longsdon) *mid-div: pckd and lost pl 6th: hdwy after next: rdn and wknd 2 out* **10/1**
5P0- **5** *3* **Balinderry (IRE)**[27] 3605 7-9-7 **94** oh7 (p) PaulBohan(7) 82
(Steve Gollings) *led: hdd after 7th: rdn and wknd appr 2 out* **14/1**
2F3- **U** **Phare Isle (IRE)**[16] 3798 9-10-13 **114** (tp) MrMJPKendrick(7) 118
(Ben Case) *hld up: hdwy 7th: ev ch whn blnd 2 out: uns rdr sn after* **11/2**
PF0- **P** **Jukebox Melody (IRE)**[24] 3659 8-10-4 **105** (b) JohnDawson(7)
(John Wade) *chsd ldrs tl rdn and wknd after 3 out: bhd whn p.u bef last* **40/1**
- **P** **Cyprusormilan**[212] 914 7-11-6 **114** RichardJohnson
(Nikki Evans) *hld up: rdn and wknd appr 3 out: bhd whn p.u bef next* **16/1**

5m 17.4s (8.60) **Going Correction** +0.575s/f (Soft) **8** Ran SP% **109.5**
Speed ratings (Par 105): **106,101,101,98,97 , ,**
CSF £22.36 CT £45.66 TOTE £4.50: £1.10, £1.80, £1.50; EX 20.00 Trifecta £34.00.
Owner Mark Harrod & Peter Beadles **Bred** Denis And Mrs Teresa Bergin **Trained** Newmarket, Suffolk

FOCUS
This looks to be sound form for the class. The easy winner was well in on his recent run but this rates a step up.

4077 LADIES DAY IS SATURDAY 19TH JULY NOVICES' LIMITED H'CAP CHASE (14 fncs) 2m 4f
3:20 (3:20) (Class 3) (0-125,125) 5-Y-0+ **£6,498** (£1,908; £954; £477)

Form RPR
322- **1** **Benefit Cut (IRE)**[17] 3769 8-11-4 **122** (t) SamTwiston-Davies 142+
(Renee Robeson) *mde all: clr fr 3 out: easily* **6/4**[1]
056- **2** *9* **Saints And Sinners (IRE)**[12] 3859 6-10-8 **115** JakeGreenall(3) 115
(Michael Easterby) *prom: outpcd 8th: rallied to go 3rd appr 3 out: styd on same pce: wnt 2nd flat* **7/2**[2]
543- **3** *nk* **Dartford Warbler (IRE)**[26] 3615 7-11-1 **119** RyanMania 119
(Sue Smith) *chsd wnr to 8th: pushed along 10th: rdn to go 2nd again appr 3 out: styd on same pce: lost 2nd flat* **7/1**[3]
F02- **4** *40* **Majorica King (FR)**[39] 3325 8-10-11 **120** ThomasGarner(5) 90
(Oliver Sherwood) *blnd 1st: hld up: hdwy 8th: hit next: sn rdn and wknd: bhd whn j.rt 3 out* **8/1**
532- **5** *3 ¼* **Mystifiable**[56] 3012 6-10-11 **115** (t) PaddyBrennan 72
(Fergal O'Brien) *prom: blnd 4th: chsd wnr 8th: hit 10th: rdn and wknd appr 3 out* **7/2**[2]
4- **P** **Benevolent (IRE)**[75] 2622 7-11-7 **125** TomMessenger
(Chris Bealby) *in tch tl rdn and wknd appr 9th: bhd whn p.u bef next* **33/1**

5m 20.6s (14.90) **Going Correction** +0.925s/f (Soft) **6** Ran SP% **111.0**
Speed ratings: **107,103,103,87,85**
CSF £7.28 TOTE £2.70: £1.70, £3.60; EX 8.40 Trifecta £39.00.
Owner Howard Cooke & Terence Jenner **Bred** B Kendellen **Trained** Tyringham, Bucks

FOCUS
It was evident from an early stage this was a novice handicap as there was some errant jumping. The winner was well in on his Ascot run but this rates a step up.

4078 ERIC AND LUCY PAPWORTH H'CAP CHASE (14 fncs) 2m 6f 110y
3:50 (3:50) (Class 4) (0-115,110) 5-Y-0+ **£4,183** (£1,521)

Form RPR
/22- **1** **Divine Intavention (IRE)**[264] 329 10-11-6 **109** MrMWall(5) 118+
(Martin Keighley) *chsd ldrs: blnd 10th: drvn along appr 3 out: lft 2nd next: lft clr whn hmpd by loose horse bef last: all out* **11/8**[1]
/36- **2** *23* **Doubletoilntrouble (IRE)**[68] 2754 8-10-12 **96** (tp) PaddyBrennan 75
(Fergal O'Brien) *prom: lost pl 4th: bhd fr 7th: lft remote 2nd last* **16/1**
636- **P** **Honest John**[11] 3874 10-11-12 **110** APMcCoy
(Steve Gollings) *led to 5th: mstke 7th: wknd after 9th: bhd whn p.u bef 11th* **11/4**[2]
43F- **P** **Lukey Luke**[51] 3107 11-10-12 **96** PeterBuchanan 100
(James Turner) *hld up: hdwy 10th: 2 l down and rdn whn lft in ld 2 out: wnt lame and p.u bef last* **14/1**
246- **U** **Taffy Thomas**[19] 3730 10-11-3 **101** (t) TomO'Brien 110+
(Peter Bowen) *chsd ldrs: led 6th: rdn and 2 l ahd whn blnd and uns rdr 2 out* **9/2**[3]
/1U- **P** **Legendary Hop**[19] 3739 8-11-4 **102** TomMessenger
(Chris Bealby) *w ldr tl led 5th: hdd next: rdn and wknd after 9th: bhd whn p.u bef 11th* **11/1**

6m 13.1s (27.10) **Going Correction** +0.925s/f (Soft) **6** Ran SP% **107.8**
Speed ratings: **89,81, , ,**
CSF £18.24 TOTE £2.00: £1.50, £3.50; EX 21.20 Trifecta £20.10.
Owner H Wilson **Bred** James Nolan **Trained** Condicote, Gloucs

FOCUS
This moderate staying handicap was an incident-packed affair thanks to high drama in the home straight. The winner was thrown in on his best hunter form and is rated a stone off his best.

4079 CGA FOXHUNTER TRIAL OPEN HUNTERS' CHASE (17 fncs) 3m 1f
4:20 (4:20) (Class 6) 5-Y-0+ **£960** (£314; £169)

Form RPR
265- **1** **Qualviro (FR)**[204] 998 10-11-7 115 (v) MrBGibbs(5) 122+
(Tim Vaughan) *chsd ldrs: lost pl 8th: tk clsr order and mstke 11th: led after 14th: clr fr 3 out: easily* **5/1**[3]
3/1- **2** *42* **Nowurhurlin (IRE)**[37] 7-11-9 111 (p) MissETodd(7) 84
(Mrs S J Stilgoe) *prom: chsd wnr after 14th: wknd next* **14/1**
505/ **3** *30* **Classinaglass**[23] 7-11-11 115 MrHAABannister(5) 54
(Mrs Stephanie Easterby) *hld up: nt fluent 1st: pushed along 11th: hdwy next: rdn and wknd bef 3 out* **11/8**[1]
PPP/ **U** **Galant Nuit (FR)**[23] 10-11-5 118 MrTRFStrawson(7)
(Mrs R Burt) *prom: racd keenly: lost pl 8th: mstke 10th: wknd 12th: bhd whn blnd: hmpd and uns rdr 4 out* **2/1**[2]
066- **F** **Oranger (FR)**[2] 12-12-1 87 (b) MrJMartin(5)
(Andrew J Martin) *chsd ldr to 11th: rdn 13th: wkng whn fell next* **50/1**
6/P- **P** **Copper's Gold (IRE)**[23] 10-11-5 79 (p) MrJLyttle(7)
(R A Owen) *mde most tl 12th: rdn and wknd after 14th: p.u bef next* **66/1**
242- **P** **Loose Preformer (IRE)**[12] 3862 8-12-2 112 MrMWall
(Michael Hawker) *hld up: blnd 3rd: nt fluent 5th: hdwy 7th: chsd ldr 10th tl led 12th: hdd after 14th: sn rdn and wknd: bhd whn p.u bef next* **9/1**

6m 58.5s (27.20) **Going Correction** +0.925s/f (Soft) **7** Ran SP% **112.2**
Speed ratings: **93,79,69, , ,**
CSF £59.16 TOTE £5.30: £3.00, £3.30; EX 44.00 Trifecta £154.20.
Owner Double Trouble Partnership **Bred** E A R L Detouillon Raphael & Frederiqu **Trained** Aberthin, Vale of Glamorgan

FOCUS
A hunter chase that served up a proper test and only three got home. The winner is rated to his mark.

T/Plt: £5.30 to a £1 stake. Pool of £86951.96 - 11762.40 winning tickets. T/Qpdt: £2.90 to a £1 stake. Pool of £5249.80 - 1332.05 winning tickets. CR

3106 CARLISLE (R-H)

Wednesday, February 5

OFFICIAL GOING: Heavy (5.4)

Wind: Fairly strong, half against Weather: Overcast, showers

4080 32RED CASINO INTERACTIVE PLANNING H'CAP CHASE (11 fncs 1 omitted) 2m

1:20 (1:21) (Class 4) (0-115,110) 5-Y-0+ **£3,768** (£1,106; £553; £276)

Form RPR

224- **1** **Indian Voyage (IRE)**[32] 3528 6-10-2 93..............(t) StephenMulqueen(7) 112+
(Maurice Barnes) *chsd clr ldr: clsd 1/2-way: gd jump to ld 3 out: clr bef last: kpt on strly* **7/4**[1]

51F- **2** *9* **Edmund (IRE)**[21] 3722 7-11-0 98.................................(t) BrianHughes 108
(Ann Hamilton) *cl up chsng gp: hit 5th and next: sn rcvrd and cl up bef 4 out: chsd wnr 2 out: no imp bef last* **7/2**[2]

F42- **3** *1 ½* **Rocking Blues (FR)**[38] 3395 9-11-12 110...................... WilsonRenwick 116
(Rose Dobbin) *hld up chsng gp: hdwy and prom 5 out: effrt 3 out: outpcd fr next* **11/2**[3]

031- **4** *9* **Cooldine Run (IRE)**[14] 3837 10-10-12 103 ow1.............(t) MrJJarrett(7) 100
(John Needham) *t.k.h: hld up: effrt bef 3 out: outpcd bef last* **6/1**

532- **5** *2* **Peachey Moment (USA)**[41] 3272 9-11-4 109.......(p) MissJRRichards(7) 104
(Nicky Richards) *led and clr: rdn and hdd 3 out: wknd fr next* **7/1**

321- **6** *8* **Pamak D'Airy (FR)**[26] 3637 11-11-4 105.........................(p) TonyKelly(3) 94
(Henry Hogarth) *prom: drvn along after 4 out: wknd bef 2 out* **14/1**

60P- **7** *8* **Saddle Pack (IRE)**[14] 3833 11-10-8 97.......................... MissCWalton(5) 78
(James Walton) *hld up: nt fluent 6th: struggling after 5 out: nvr on terms* **28/1**

4m 16.9s (0.80) **Going Correction** +0.15s/f (Yiel) **7 Ran SP% 110.9**
Speed ratings: **104,99,98,94,93 89,85**
CSF £8.11 TOTE £2.50: £1.10, £3.00; EX 11.10 Trifecta £60.10.
Owner D Carr & M Carlyle **Bred** Victor Stud Bloodstock Ltd **Trained** Farlam, Cumbria

FOCUS
Hurdles on new hurdles course with all hurdles on outside, chase bends on inside line. Horrible conditions and the ground certainly appeared more testing on the hurdles course. A modest race for the grade with the second and third setting the level.

4081 32RED NOVICES' HURDLE (8 hdls) 2m 1f

1:50 (1:50) (Class 4) 4-Y-0+ **£3,249** (£954; £477; £238)

Form RPR

53- **1** **Mohawk Ridge**[27] 3614 8-11-3 0.. BrianHughes 118
(James Moffatt) *mde virtually all: hrd pressed fr 3 out: mstke and rdn next: styd on gamely to forge clr last 100yds* **5/1**

123- **2** *10* **Sleepy Haven (IRE)**[39] 3364 4-11-0 123............................. SeanQuinlan 107
(Jennie Candlish) *t.k.h: prom: hit 2nd: effrt and disp ld between last 2: wknd last 100yds* **6/4**[1]

360- **3** *9* **Vasco Pierji (FR)**[18] 3781 5-11-3 0...................................... AdrianLane 98
(Donald McCain) *hld up: pushed along after 3 out: plugged on to take modest 3rd between last 2: no ch w first two* **20/1**

024- **4** *6* **Lord Brendy**[56] 3017 6-11-3 0... KennyJohnson 92
(Robert Johnson) *taken early to post: chsd ldrs: hit 4 out: nt fluent and outpcd next: no imp bef 2 out* **11/4**[2]

5 *39* **I'm A Rocker (IRE)**[59] 5-11-3 0..................................... JasonMaguire 53
(Donald McCain) *pressed wnr: ev ch 3 out tl rdn and swvd lft bnd bef next: sn wknd* **9/2**[3]

FU- **6** *32* **Shirls Son Sam**[29] 2420 6-11-3 0.. BarryKeniry 21
(Chris Fairhurst) *t.k.h: hld up in tch: struggling bef 3 out: sn btn: t.o* **200/1**

/F0- **P** **Dibdabs (IRE)**[15] 3826 6-10-10 0.........................(t[1]) StephenMulqueen(7)
(Maurice Barnes) *hld up: blnd 3rd: struggling 3 out: lost tch bef next: t.o whn p.u bef last* **33/1**

4m 43.5s (14.30) **Going Correction** +1.125s/f (Heav)
WFA 4 from 5yo+ 9lb **7 Ran SP% 109.7**
Speed ratings (Par 105): **111,106,102,99,80 65,**
CSF £12.29 TOTE £4.80: £2.30, £1.10; EX 9.60 Trifecta £136.60.
Owner K Bowron **Bred** Old Mill Stud Ltd And Oomswell Ltd **Trained** Cartmel, Cumbria

FOCUS
Average form. A step up from the winner with the second rated 8lb off.

4082 32RED.COM NOVICES' H'CAP CHASE (16 fncs 2 omitted) 3m 110y

2:20 (2:20) (Class 4) (0-110,103) 5-Y-0+ **£3,898** (£1,144; £572; £286)

Form RPR

20P- **1** **Fozy Moss**[9] 3936 8-10-4 81..(t) BrianHarding 88
(Stuart Coltherd) *t.k.h early: w ldr: hit 9th: led next: rdn whn hrd pressed between last 2: edgd lft run-in: styd on gamely* **12/1**

323- **2** *hd* **Farm Pixie (IRE)**[38] 3394 8-10-11 95......................... GrahamWatters(7) 103
(Ann Hamilton) *in tch: nt fluent and outpcd 11th: rallied 4 out: effrt and chal between last 2: kpt on fr last: hld nr fin* **13/2**

1P2- **3** *21* **Basford Ben**[15] 3827 6-11-4 95......................................(p) SeanQuinlan 86
(Jennie Candlish) *hld up: hit 6th: rdn after 8th: outpcd 10th: plugged on fr 3 out: no ch w first two* **5/1**[3]

PFP- **4** *7* **Cottiers Den (IRE)**[9] 3936 7-10-8 85........................... WilsonRenwick 63
(Martin Todhunter) *nt fluent: prom: drvn and outpcd 1/2-way: no imp fr 4 out* **9/2**[2]

0P0/ **5** *8* **Rojo Vivo**[364] 4063 8-11-7 98.. RichieMcGrath 68
(Henry Hogarth) *chsd ldrs: drvn and outpcd 10th: n.d after* **20/1**

4/3- **6** *9* **Blueside Boy (IRE)**[38] 3392 6-11-11 102......................... PeterBuchanan 63
(Lucinda Russell) *cl up: chal bef 5 out to bef 3 out: wknd qckly fr next* **7/1**

400- **7** *2 ¼* **Uppercut De L'Orne (FR)**[41] 3278 6-11-12 103............. JasonMaguire 62
(Donald McCain) *hld up: stdy hdwy and prom whn nt fluent 5 out: nt fluent and pckd next: sn btn* **5/1**[3]

FP5- **P** **Whiskey Ridge (IRE)**[41] 3283 8-11-2 93.............................. RyanMania
(Sue Smith) *led tl nt fluent and hdd 10th: struggling 5 out: p.u bef next* **7/2**[1]

6m 49.6s (7.00) **Going Correction** +0.15s/f (Yiel) **8 Ran SP% 112.0**
Speed ratings: **94,93,87,84,82 79,78,**
CSF £82.64 CT £441.85 TOTE £12.60: £2.50, £2.30, £1.40; EX 95.10 Trifecta £195.10.
Owner John Hogg **Bred** John Hogg **Trained** Selkirk, Borders
■ Stewards' Enquiry : Brian Harding caution: careless riding.

FOCUS
The front pair drew clear, but a couple of the key contenders failed to produce. A personal best from the winner with the second to his mark.

4083 32RED EBF MARES' "NATIONAL HUNT" NOVICES' HURDLE (10 hdls) 2m 3f 110y

2:55 (2:55) (Class 4) 4-Y-0+ **£4,223** (£1,240; £620; £310)

Form RPR

001- **1** **Truckers Darling (IRE)**[14] 3840 7-10-13 110................... KieronEdgar(7) 113+
(Don Cantillon) *t.k.h: prom: smooth hdwy 3 out: led and rdn clr after next: 5 l up last: hld on wl towards fin* **11/10**[1]

154- **2** *nk* **Brijomi Queen (IRE)**[19] 3757 7-11-6 113......................... DenisO'Regan 113
(Nicky Richards) *hld up in tch: hdwy to chse wnr bef 2 out: 5 l down whn mstke last: kpt on wl last 100yds: jst hld* **11/8**[2]

034- **3** *35* **Spring Over (IRE)**[59] 2973 8-10-7 102..................... GrahamWatters(7) 72
(Ian Duncan) *led: hit 4 out: rdn and hdd bef 2 out: sn wknd* **11/1**[3]

302- **4** *29* **Conjola**[32] 3529 7-11-0 0.. RichieMcGrath 43
(Geoffrey Harker) *mstkes: w ldr to 3 out: rdn and wknd bef next* **16/1**

50F- **5** *dist* **Lacocodanza**[40] 3329 5-11-0 0.. BarryKeniry
(George Moore) *prom: nt fluent 2nd: rdn and lost tch fr 3 out: t.o* **20/1**

5m 36.6s (27.80) **Going Correction** +1.125s/f (Heav) **5 Ran SP% 108.7**
Speed ratings (Par 105): **89,88,74,63,**
CSF £2.93 TOTE £2.40: £1.10, £1.10; EX 3.60 Trifecta £9.90.
Owner Mrs Catherine Reed **Bred** B Kavanagh **Trained** Newmarket, Suffolk
■ Stewards' Enquiry : Denis O'Regan two-day ban: used whip above permitted level (Nov 19-20)

FOCUS
Run in the driving rain, this was a race that concerned only two and the pair duly drew clear. The winner didn't need to improve to win, and is rated to her mark.

4084 32RED NOVICES' LIMITED H'CAP CHASE (11 fncs 1 omitted) 2m

3:30 (3:30) (Class 3) (0-125,125) 5-Y-0+ **£6,498** (£1,908; £954; £477)

Form RPR

332- **1** **Supreme Asset (IRE)**[37] 3418 6-11-7 125....................... JasonMaguire 131+
(Donald McCain) *in tch: lft cl 2nd 5 out: gng wl whn hit 2 out: rdn to ld run-in: styd on wl* **6/5**[1]

F11- **2** *3* **Alderbrook Lad (IRE)**[27] 3615 8-10-9 118....................... JoeColliver(5) 121
(Micky Hammond) *chsd clr ldr: blnd 6th: 5 l down whn lft in ld next: rdn whn hit last: hdd and no ex run-in* **11/4**[2]

/50- **3** *12* **Allow Me**[25] 3661 9-10-12 116... JamesReveley 108
(Dianne Sayer) *in tch: outpcd whn lft 3rd 5 out: rallied next: wkng whn hit 2 out* **8/1**

554- **4** *26* **Rupert Bear**[32] 3524 8-10-2 111 oh4................................ MissCWalton(5) 73
(James Walton) *j. deliberately in rr: lost tch fr 3rd: nvr on terms* **11/2**[3]

1F5- **U** **Suprise Vendor (IRE)**[27] 3615 8-10-7 118.................. DaraghBourke(7)
(Stuart Coltherd) *led and sn clr: 5 l in front whn blnd and uns rdr 5 out* **10/1**

4m 20.7s (4.60) **Going Correction** +0.15s/f (Yiel) **5 Ran SP% 107.7**
Speed ratings: **94,92,86,73,**
CSF £4.84 TOTE £2.30: £1.10, £1.60; EX 3.20 Trifecta £15.00.
Owner Lucky Bin Racing **Bred** Catherine Armitage **Trained** Cholmondeley, Cheshire

FOCUS
The field were soon quite well strung out. The winner has improved with each race over fences, and the second ran to his mark.

4085 32RED CASINO H'CAP HURDLE (8 hdls) 2m 1f

4:00 (4:00) (Class 4) (0-120,115) 4-Y-0+ **£3,573** (£1,049; £524; £262)

Form RPR

541- **1** **Twoways (IRE)**[17] 3802 8-11-7 110.................................. ConorO'Farrell 121+
(Mark Rimell) *hld up in tch: stdy hdwy 3 out: led after next: sn rdn: styd on wl fr last* **9/2**[3]

40P- **2** *2 ¼* **Hallmark Star**[41] 3284 5-10-7 103.................................. CraigNichol(7) 109
(Lucinda Russell) *cl up: jnd ldr 1/2-way: led bef 2 out to after 2 out: sn rdn and rallied: edgd rt after last: kpt on: hld towards fin* **15/2**

210- **3** *41* **Sam Lord**[10] 3922 10-11-7 110.......................................(b[1]) BrianHughes 75
(James Moffatt) *cl up: led 1/2-way to bef 2 out: sn rdn and wknd* **12/1**

456- **4** *4* **Bob's World**[36] 3430 5-11-12 115...................................(p) SeanQuinlan 76
(Jennie Candlish) *hld up in tch: hit and rdn 3 out: wknd bef next* **10/3**[2]

34F- **5** *25* **The Weatherman (IRE)**[17] 3802 7-10-13 102................. JasonMaguire 38
(Donald McCain) *led to 4th: cl up tl rdn and wknd 3 out* **6/1**

201- **P** **Next Hight (IRE)**[26] 3636 7-10-8 100......................... JonathanEngland(3)
(Sue Smith) *nt fluent: chsd ldrs: drvn and outpcd 3 out: wknd bef next: t.o whn p.u after last* **7/4**[1]

4m 46.1s (16.90) **Going Correction** +1.125s/f (Heav) **6 Ran SP% 111.4**
Speed ratings (Par 105): **105,103,84,82,71**
CSF £34.34 TOTE £3.20: £1.80, £3.80; EX 54.70 Trifecta £474.60.
Owner Mark Rimell **Bred** M And Mrs J Cummins **Trained** Leafield, Oxon

FOCUS
With the two at the head of the market disappointing, Twoways wasn't left with much to beat. He's on the upgrade though.

4086 32RED.COM H'CAP CHASE (10 fncs 1 omitted) 2m 5f

4:30 (4:30) (Class 4) (0-115,115) 5-Y-0+ **£3,898** (£1,144; £572; £286)

Form RPR

31P- **1** **Etxalar (FR)**[32] 3526 11-11-5 108.................................(t) PeterBuchanan 119+
(Lucinda Russell) *j.w: mde all: pushed clr bef 3 out: idled run-in: kpt on wl* **5/1**

341- **2** *1 ¼* **Baltic Pathfinder (IRE)**[26] 3635 10-10-13 102................... ShaneByrne 110
(Sue Smith) *prom: hdwy bef 5 out: rdn and outpcd next: rallied to chse wnr run-in: kpt on: hld nr fin* **7/2**[2]

42P- **3** *2 ¼* **Hawaii Klass**[189] 1162 9-11-7 115.............................. CallumWhillans(5) 120
(Donald Whillans) *t.k.h: prom: hdwy to chse (clr) wnr bef 3 out to run-in: one pce* **8/1**

4P4- **4** *12* **Royal Sam (IRE)**[41] 3283 9-11-3 106............................. WilsonRenwick 99
(Martin Todhunter) *in tch: rdn and outpcd after 5 out: no imp fr 3 out* **7/1**

/44- **5** *¾* **Mortimers Cross**[31] 3554 13-11-4 114.............................(t) MrJJarrett(7) 106
(John Needham) *chsd wnr: drvn and lost 2nd bef 3 out: btn next* **9/2**[3]

535- **6** *shd* **Bertie Milan (IRE)**[32] 3526 9-10-9 98............................(v[1]) LucyAlexander 93
(N W Alexander) *nt fluent on occasions: chsd ldrs on outside: rdn after 9th: struggling after 5 out: sn no ch* **9/4**[1]

5m 52.5s (7.40) **Going Correction** +0.15s/f (Yiel) **6 Ran SP% 111.5**
Speed ratings: **91,90,89,85,84 84**
CSF £22.50 TOTE £4.10: £2.30, £2.30; EX 19.20 Trifecta £99.00.
Owner Dig In Racing **Bred** Elie Lellouche And Bertrand Clin **Trained** Arlary, Perth & Kinross

FOCUS
Moderate form. The winner is rated in line with his upgraded course win.
T/Plt: £28.30 to a £1 stake. Pool: £71097.24 - 1831.87 winning tickets T/Qpdt: £6.70 to a £1 stake. Pool: £3145.67 - 345.64 winning tickets RY

3728 LUDLOW (R-H)

Wednesday, February 5

OFFICIAL GOING: Heavy

Wind: very breezy Weather: raining

4087 WEDDING RECEPTIONS AT LUDLOW CLAIMING HURDLE (8 hdls 1 omitted) 2m

1:40 (1:40) (Class 4) 4-Y-0+ **£3,898** (£1,144; £572; £286)

Form RPR

66P- 1 **Arrayan**[36] 3439 9-11-3 105 (b[1]) NickScholfield 120+
(Alexandra Dunn) *racd keenly: cl up tl led gng best bef 3 out: sn clr: unchal* 7/2[2]

030- 2 18 **Islandmagee (IRE)**[29] 3596 7-10-10 103 (vt[1]) ConorRing(7) 101
(Evan Williams) *led: rdn and hdd bef 3 out: hit 3 out and sn lost tch w wnr: struggled on to retain 2nd* 4/1[3]

P51- 3 1 3/4 **Edlomond (IRE)**[73] 2698 8-11-0 120 (t) RyanWhile(7) 103
(Bill Turner) *trckd ldrs: rdn and outpcd after 5th: tried to rally 3 out: disp poor 2nd at last: fin tired* 7/4[1]

5/6- 4 6 **Spirit River (FR)**[17] 3798 9-11-12 125 LeeEdwards 103
(Dave Roberts) *cl up: nt fluent 5th: sn rdn: struggling in 3rd bef 3 out* 8/1

465- 5 46 **Sublime Talent (IRE)**[40] 3324 8-11-3 108 (vt[1]) AdamWedge 47
(Evan Williams) *a in last: t.o wl bef 3 out* 4/1[3]

4m 9.0s (19.50) **Going Correction** +1.40s/f (Heav) 5 Ran SP% **109.7**

Speed ratings (Par 105): **107,98,97,94,71**

CSF £16.98 TOTE £4.60: £2.10, £3.20; EX 18.00 Trifecta £88.60.

Owner Dunn Racing **Bred** West Stow Stud Ltd **Trained** Wellington, Somerset

FOCUS

It was touch and go whether the meeting went ahead on near-waterlogged ground. All bends moved to provide best ground available, hurdles moved to extreme outside. The extreme conditions must be borne in mind when assessing the worth of the form. They took things understandably steady in this ordinary claimer. The winner is rated back to form.

4088 DOWNTON NOVICES' CHASE (17 fncs 2 omitted) 3m

2:10 (2:10) (Class 4) 5-Y-0+ **£5,198** (£1,526; £763)

Form RPR

/01- 1 **Edmund Kean (IRE)**[29] 3594 7-11-7 137 TomScudamore 144+
(David Pipe) *tended to jump lft: mde all: 4 l clr and rdn last: tired and edgd rt flat: hung on gamely* 4/6[1]

233- 2 1/2 **The Romford Pele (IRE)**[68] 2799 7-11-0 134 APMcCoy 138+
(Rebecca Curtis) *tended to lack fluency: chsd wnr: drvn bef 14th: outj. at fnl four fences: 4 l down at last: kpt on u.p and nrly got up* 6/5[2]

P/P- 3 53 **Shays River (IRE)**[4] 4024 9-11-0 0 (t) AdamWedge 82
(Evan Williams) *a in last: lost tch after 9th: bdly t.o fr 12th: hacked on* 33/1[3]

6m 42.7s (34.40) **Going Correction** +1.70s/f (Heav) 3 Ran SP% **108.4**

Speed ratings: **110,109,92**

CSF £1.90 TOTE £2.00; EX 1.90 Trifecta £1.70.

Owner Walters Plant Hire & James & Jean Potter **Bred** Mervyn Chamney **Trained** Nicholashayne, Devon

FOCUS

Effectively a match, but still a decent little event with the first two useful novices. The form makes sense.

4089 ATTWOOD MEMORIAL TROPHY H'CAP CHASE (16 fncs 1 omitted) 2m 4f

2:40 (2:40) (Class 3) (0-135,133) 5-Y-**£12,660** (£3,740; £1,870; £936; £468)

Form RPR

011- 1 **Buywise (IRE)**[18] 3785 7-10-13 **120** PaulMoloney 139+
(Evan Williams) *dropped out towards rr: prog gng wl fr 13th: led next: sn in command: 5 l clr last: galloped on strly* 15/8[1]

543- 2 9 **Elenika (FR)**[25] 3660 6-11-2 **123** AidanColeman 130+
(Venetia Williams) *settled trcking ldrs: effrt on inner to go 2nd at 14th: sn rdn: chsd wnr vainly after* 7/2[3]

323- 3 33 **Cootehill (IRE)**[49] 3158 10-11-8 **129** SamTwiston-Davies 101
(Nigel Twiston-Davies) *towards rr: drvn bef 13th: sn struggling: t.o 2 out: fin tired* 16/1

312- 4 6 **Free World (FR)**[25] 3662 10-9-9 **109** MissLBrooke(7) 75
(Lady Susan Brooke) *t.k.h: led 2nd tl outj. 10th: wknd after 12th: t.o 3 out* 20/1

21F- 5 10 **Tony Dinozzo (FR)**[13] 3853 7-10-0 **107** (p) JamieMoore 63
(Peter Bowen) *presed ldr: led 9th: drvn and hdd 13th: dropped out rapidly: t.o and tired whn blnd last* 7/1

514- P **Gallox Bridge**[75] 2645 9-11-12 **133** (t) RichardJohnson
(Tim Vaughan) *led tl 2nd: prom tl poor jump 9th: dropped out rapidly and sn t.o: p.u 13th* 10/1

462- P **Forest Walker (IRE)**[20] 3742 7-11-3 **124** (t) HarrySkelton
(Dan Skelton) *mostly last: pushed along bef 9th: nt gng wl enough after: drvn and lost tch bef 13th: t.o and p.u 2 out* 3/1[2]

5m 36.1s (31.70) **Going Correction** +1.80s/f (Heav) 7 Ran SP% **114.2**

Speed ratings: **108,104,91,88,84** ,

CSF £9.27 TOTE £2.70: £1.20, £2.60; EX 9.40 Trifecta £76.80.

Owner T Hywel Jones **Bred** Mrs A Stack **Trained** Llancarfan, Vale Of Glamorgan

FOCUS

This fair handicap was won in 2010 by Sunnyhillboy, who was runner-up in the Byrne Group Plate next time out, while last year's winner Grandioso followed up in a Grade 2 novice chase.

4090 MICHAEL LUMSDEN MEMORIAL MARES' H'CAP HURDLE (FOR THE HENLEY HALL GOLD CUP) (10 hdls 1 omitted) 2m 5f

3:15 (3:15) (Class 3) (0-135,130) 4-Y-**£7,912** (£2,337; £1,168; £585; £292)

Form RPR

551- 1 **Land Of Vic**[20] 3733 6-10-11 **115** DonalDevereux 127+
(Peter Bowen) *led at v slow pce tl after 2nd: prom chsng clr ldr tl clsd to ld bef 3 out where wnt lft: sn clr: styd on dourly flat* 7/1

261- 2 7 **Top Totti**[20] 3731 6-11-12 **130** RichardJohnson 134
(Henry Daly) *settled chsng ldrs: effrt in 4 l 4th home turn: drvn to go 2nd between last two: 3 l down at last: no further imp and fin tired* 9/1

3PP- 3 3 **Still Believing (IRE)**[20] 3729 6-9-13 **110** ConorRing(7) 111
(Evan Williams) *settled in rr: in last whn nt fluent 6th: effrt and looked gng wl after next: outpcd by ldng pair after 2 out: rdn and kpt on same steadily although hld after* 33/1

222- 4 3 3/4 **Floral Spinner**[14] 3840 7-9-8 **105** RyanWhile(7) 102
(Bill Turner) *midfield: rdn after 7th: plugged on same pce fr next* 10/1

241- 5 1 1/2 **Benefique Royale**[60] 2948 6-10-5 **109** DarylJacob 106
(Nick Williams) *racd keenly: led after 2nd and sn 10 l clr: rdn and hdd bef 3 out: wknd grad* 11/4[2]

533- 6 30 **Mrs Jordan (IRE)**[36] 3438 6-10-6 **110** AidanColeman 84
(Venetia Williams) *prom in chsng gp tl rdn and dropped out qckly after 7th: sn t.o* 6/1[3]

02F- 7 35 **Cloudy Spirit**[40] 3327 9-11-11 **129** PaulMoloney 60
(Andrew Hollinshead) *prom in chsng gp tl lost pl 7th: t.o whn j.lft 2 out: virtually p.u after* 20/1

311- 8 9 **Come On Annie**[8] 3959 8-9-11 **108** 7ex MrsAlexDunn(7) 78
(Alexandra Dunn) *t.k.h in last: effrt after 7th and wnt 2nd briefly: 3 l 3rd home turn: rdn and floundering 3 out: t.o and virtually p.u flat* 7/4[1]

5m 53.7s (38.90) **Going Correction** +1.60s/f (Heav) 8 Ran SP% **116.6**

Speed ratings (Par 107): **89,86,85,83,83 71,58,55**

CSF £66.86 CT £1942.51 TOTE £10.40: £2.70, £2.00, £6.00; EX 63.60 Trifecta £1154.80.

Owner W Hill **Bred** Stewart Pike **Trained** Little Newcastle, Pembrokes

FOCUS

Quite a competitive mares' handicap. The first two home both won at the most recent Ludlow meeting. The winner is on the upgrade and the next two are rated close to their marks.

4091 BROMFIELD "NATIONAL HUNT" MAIDEN HURDLE (8 hdls 1 omitted) 2m

3:50 (3:50) (Class 4) 4-Y-0+ **£3,898** (£1,144; £572; £286)

Form RPR

5- 1 **Minella Reception (IRE)**[51] 3128 8-11-3 115 (t) APMcCoy 113+
(Rebecca Curtis) *mde all: set stdy pce: taken wd fr wl bef 3 out: hrd drvn whn hit last: hung on gamely: all out* 8/15[1]

/43- 2 hd **Daveron (IRE)**[23] 3686 6-11-3 110 NickScholfield 112+
(Jeremy Scott) *prom in 3rd: shkn up home turn: drvn and chsd wnr hrd fr 2 out: 1 l down bef last: kpt battling on but jst hld fnl strides* 4/1[2]

6/0- 3 14 **When Ben When (IRE)**[83] 2472 5-10-10 0 (t) MrSamPainting(7) 98
(Colin Tizzard) *racd keenly in 2nd tl drvn 2 out: sn hanging bdly lft and fading: eased after last* 12/1[3]

40/ 4 9 **Liars Poker (IRE)**[81] 7-11-3 0 LeightonAspell 89
(Oliver Sherwood) *settled midfield: effrt bef 3 out to trck ldrs briefly: sn rdn and btn* 14/1

0F0- 5 3/4 **Etania**[49] 3163 6-10-10 0 WillKennedy 81
(Ian Williams) *midfield: effrt in 4th home turn: sn rdn and no ch w ldng trio: hit last* 25/1

00/- 6 6 **Florida Quays (IRE)**[299] 5264 6-11-3 0 NoelFehily 82
(David Dennis) *chsd ldrs tl rdn and wknd bef 3 out* 12/1[3]

056/ 7 35 **The Mobb (IRE)**[288] 5468 6-11-3 0 LeeEdwards 47
(Dave Roberts) *s.s: rcvrd to chse ldrs bef 4th: rdn and wknd qckly bef 3 out: tired whn mstke next: t.o* 100/1

40- 8 3 **Home For Tea**[20] 3728 5-11-3 0 FelixDeGiles 44
(Tom Symonds) *midfield: rdn and struggling bef 3 out: t.o* 50/1

P- 9 79 **Sarahs Doll**[51] 3128 6-10-7 0 RobertDunne(3)
(Dai Burchell) *last pair: hopelessly t.o after 5th* 100/1

0/ 10 3 1/2 **Tedney Express (IRE)**[480] 1838 7-11-3 0 (t) AdamWedge
(Evan Williams) *stdd s: plld v hrd in last pair: hopelessly t.o after 5th* 25/1

4m 17.6s (28.10) **Going Correction** +1.90s/f (Heav) 10 Ran SP% **118.9**

Speed ratings (Par 105): **105,104,97,93,93 90,72,71,31,29**

CSF £2.97 TOTE £1.90: £1.10, £1.40, £2.60; EX 3.10 Trifecta £15.50.

Owner Options O Syndicate **Bred** Elms Stud Co Ltd **Trained** Newport, Dyfed

FOCUS

Few got into this very ordinary maiden hurdle, in which the first two came clear off a steady pace. Both are probably capable of better.

4092 CGA FOXHUNTER TRIAL HUNTERS' CHASE (FOR THE LUDLOW GOLD CUP) (17 fncs 2 omitted) 3m

4:20 (4:20) (Class 5) 6-Y-0+ **£2,560** (£838; £451)

Form RPR

6/1- 1 **Pearlysteps**[17] 3801 11-12-0 128 MrOGreenall 130+
(Henry Daly) *j. soundly: led at slow pce tl 6th: led again 8th: styd on wl flat: readily* 1/2[1]

F22/ 2 2 3/4 **Made In Time (IRE)**[530] 1349 9-11-11 0 (t) MissLeandaTickle(7) 131
(Rebecca Curtis) *racd keenly in 2nd tl led 6th tl 8th: pressed wnr rest of way: hit 11th: drvn and stl on terms nring last: kpt on but alway hld flat* 9/1[3]

3/P- 3 99 **The General Lee (IRE)**[241] 12-11-9 112 MissLBrooke(5) 28
(Lady Susan Brooke) *settled 4th: t.o bef 10th: two fences bhd fr bef 14th: lft 3rd 2 out* 25/1

P/2- P **Pathian Prince**[265] 335 11-11-3 100 MrWMaskill(7)
(E R Clough) *nt jump wl in last pair: rdn and struggling 7th: t.o bef 10th: two fences bhd whn eventually p.u last* 33/1

2F1- P **Foundry Square (IRE)**[21] 3720 8-11-7 135 (p) MrWTelfer(7)
(S Flook) *hit several fences: settled in 3rd: floundering bdly bef 14th: 3rd but a fence bhd whn p.u 2 out* 3/1[2]

6m 50.7s (42.40) **Going Correction** +1.90s/f (Heav) 5 Ran SP% **108.5**

Speed ratings: **105,104,71,** ,

CSF £5.46 TOTE £1.50: £1.20, £1.90; EX 5.20 Trifecta £25.50.

Owner The Glazeley Partnership **Bred** W P Jenks **Trained** Stanton Lacy, Shropshire

FOCUS

The first two showed useful hunter chase form. The winner, who was 10lb off his Towcester form, will be tough to beat in this grade.

4093 ONIBURY MAIDEN HURDLE (10 hdls 1 omitted) 2m 5f

4:50 (4:50) (Class 4) 4-Y-0+ **£3,898** (£1,144; £572; £286)

Form RPR

022- 1 **Ampleforth**[17] 3796 6-11-4 113 (v) WillKennedy 116+
(Ian Williams) *settled towards rr of bunch: wnt 3rd after 7th: pressed ldr fr home turn but outj. at fnl three: nrly upsides at last: led flat: sed to get upper hand 75yds out but v tired and hanging lft and inconveniencing rival after* 11/4[2]

315- 2 2 3/4 **Tara Road**[47] 3182 6-11-4 0 APMcCoy 112+
(Rebecca Curtis) *racd wd: cl up: led 6th tl after 7th: led again bef 3 out: drvn and slt advantage after: hdd after last: btn whn bdly squeezed for room fnl 75yds* 11/10[1]

0/P- 3 4 1/2 **Island Cruise (IRE)**[48] 3177 6-11-4 0 (t) ColinBolger 107+
(Pat Murphy) *cl up: rdn and lost tch bef 3 out: 20 l 3rd at last: styng on wl fnl 100yds* 66/1

6- 4 39 **Eastern Witness (IRE)**[48] 3173 7-11-4 0 AidanColeman 77
(Venetia Williams) *led at mod pce tl 6th: led again bef next: rdn and hdd bef 3 out: dropped out steadily: lost poor 3rd at last: fin v tired* 3/1[3]

436- 5 43 **Oscar's Pet (IRE)**[68] 2801 6-10-11 0 FelixDeGiles 18
(Tom Symonds) *last pair: hit 5th: lost tch bef next: hopelessly t.o bef 3 out* 8/1

The Form Book Jumps, Raceform Ltd, Compton, RG20 6NL.

060- **6** *31* **Modeligo (IRE)**[54] 3070 5-11-4 0 CharliePoste
(Matt Sheppard) *hit 4th: chsd ldrs tl rdn and wknd 7th: hopelessly t.o and hacked on fr next* **100/1**

5m 59.3s (44.50) **Going Correction** +2.20s/f (Heav) 6 Ran SP% **112.9**
Speed ratings (Par 105): **103,101,100,85,69 57**
CSF £6.51 TOTE £4.80: £2.00, £1.20; EX 5.90 Trifecta £60.00.
Owner Macable Partnership **Bred** Plantation Stud **Trained** Portway, Worcs
■ Stewards' Enquiry : Will Kennedy caution: careless riding.

FOCUS
A weak maiden hurdle run in the worst of the ground and in descending darkness. The first two came close together after the last and the time was very slow. The winner is rated in line with his Southwell run.
T/Plt: £114.40 to a £1 stake. Pool: £67415.75 - 429.85 winning tickets T/Qpdt: £11.70 to a £1 stake. Pool: £5019.97 - 316.61 winning tickets IM

3892 DONCASTER (L-H)
Thursday, February 6

OFFICIAL GOING: Good to soft (good in places on hurdle course; hdl 7.0, chs 6.5)
Wind: fresh against Weather: cloudy, rain after 5th

4101 EVENTMASTERS CORPORATE HOSPITALITY NOVICES' CHASE (12 fncs) 2m 110y
1:20 (1:25) (Class 3) 5-Y-0+ **£6,498** (£1,908)

Form RPR
/21- **1** **Rock On Ruby (IRE)**[52] 3135 9-11-7 0 (t) NoelFehily 152+
(Harry Fry) *mde all: nt fluent 3 out (j.w in main): pckd sltly on landing last: rdn clr: comf* **2/7**[1]

213- **2** *10* **Mr Mole (IRE)**[48] 3185 6-11-7 147 (t) APMcCoy 142
(Paul Nicholls) *trckd wnr: nt fluent 5 out: l down whn mstke 3 out: sn rdn: hit last: sn btn: eased fnl 75yds* **3/1**[2]

4m 7.9s (2.90) **Going Correction** +0.15s/f (Yiel) 2 Ran SP% **102.8**
Speed ratings: **99,94**
TOTE £1.20.
Owner The Festival Goers **Bred** John O'Dwyer **Trained** Seaborough, Dorset

FOCUS
All hurdles moved to fresh take-offs and landings. This match totally revolved around 2012 Champion Hurdle winner Rock On Ruby. He jumped well enough and is a leading Arkle contender.

4102 EVENTMASTERS LTD EBF "NATIONAL HUNT" NOVICES' HURDLE (QUALIFIER) (10 hdls) 2m 3f 110y
1:50 (1:55) (Class 4) 4-7-Y-0 **£3,573** (£1,049; £524; £262)

Form RPR
14- **1** **Vaniteux (FR)**[42] 3258 5-11-12 132 BarryGeraghty 143+
(Nicky Henderson) *midfield: smooth hdwy 3 out: led jst after 2 out: qcknd clr after last: impressive* **8/11**[1]

111- **2** *12* **Portway Flyer (IRE)**[62] 2921 6-11-7 120 RobertMcCarth(5) 128
(Ian Williams) *hld up in tch: nt fluent 5th: smooth hdwy 3 out: chsd wnr between last 2: one pce and no ch w wnr after last* **5/1**[3]

112- **3** *3 ¾* **Gone Too Far**[78] 2602 6-11-12 125 APMcCoy 124
(Alan King) *t.k.h in tch: hit 5th: nt fluent 3 out: chsd ldrs whn hit 2 out: sn outpcd: wnt 3rd jst after last* **11/4**[2]

054- **4** *1 ¼* **Vinstar (FR)**[69] 2783 5-11-2 117 (t) JasonMaguire 110
(Donald McCain) *trckd ldr: led 3 out: sn rdn: hdd jst after 2 out: no ex after last* **20/1**

5 *½* **Benzel (IRE)**[67] 6-11-2 0 DougieCostello 110
(Jonjo O'Neill) *led: hdd 3 out: sn one pce* **33/1**

30- **6** *12* **Ronnie Lawson (IRE)**[78] 2602 5-11-2 0 DenisO'Regan 98
(John Ferguson) *trckd ldrs: hit 2 out: sn rdn: hung lft between last 2: wknd* **33/1**

7 *14* **The Purchaser (IRE)**[270] 6-11-2 0 TomMessenger 84
(Chris Bealby) *hld up: nt fluent 4th: btn bef 3 out* **100/1**

8 *3 ¾* **Garton Star (IRE)**[263] 5-11-2 0 RyanMahon 80
(Harry Fry) *hld up: struggling after 4 out* **66/1**

0/1- **9** *36* **Fair Dreamer**[63] 2912 6-11-2 0 NoelFehily 44
(Harry Fry) *in tch: wknd qckly appr 3 out* **14/1**

0/P- **10** *70* **Izza Diva**[36] 3469 6-10-9 0 PaulMoloney
(John Holt) *prom tl after 3rd: lost tch bef 4 out: t.o* **100/1**

4m 56.6s (5.30) **Going Correction** +0.50s/f (Soft) 10 Ran SP% **122.0**
Speed ratings: **109,104,102,102,102 97,91,90,75,47**
CSF £5.24 TOTE £1.50: £1.02, £1.80, £1.40; EX 6.30 Trifecta £12.90.
Owner Mr & Mrs R Kelvin-Hughes **Bred** Jacques Cypres **Trained** Upper Lambourn, Berks

FOCUS
An interesting novices' hurdle, but they went a very steady pace and things didn't quicken up until approaching three out. The winner stepped up and looks a decent novice, with the next three pretty much to their marks.

4103 EVENTMASTERS.CO.UK NOVICES' HURDLE (8 hdls) 2m 110y
2:25 (2:30) (Class 4) 5-Y-0+ **£3,119** (£915; £457; £228)

Form RPR
1 **First Mohican**[117] 6-10-12 0 RobertThornton 123+
(Alan King) *midfield: smooth hdwy to trck ldr 3 out: led jst after 2 out: rdn bef last: drvn and rdr dropped rein run-in: rcvrd and hld on towards fin* **7/2**[2]

5- **2** *¾* **Huff And Puff**[21] 3728 7-10-12 0 LiamTreadwell 122+
(Venetia Williams) *trckd ldrs: rdn and outpcd in 5th whn hit 2 out: styd on fr appr last: wnt 2nd 125yds out* **20/1**

0/2- **3** *4* **Fair Loch**[40] 3350 6-10-12 0 BrianHughes 120+
(K R Burke) *t.k.h: trckd ldrs: chal on bit 2 out: rdn appr last: lost 2nd 125yds out: wknd* **13/2**[3]

4/ **4** *2 ¾* **Attwaal (IRE)**[142] 3141 5-10-9 0 TrevorWhelan(3) 115
(Neil King) *hld up: hit 4th: rdn after 2 out: kpt on: wnt 4th post* **66/1**

2- **5** *nk* **Civil War (IRE)**[32] 3550 5-10-12 0 JamieMoore 115
(Gary Moore) *midfield on inner: hdwy to chse ldrs 3 out: rdn bef 2 out: 3 l down in 3rd last: wknd and lost 2 pls run-in* **18/1**

4- **6** *10* **Retrieve (AUS)**[41] 3330 7-10-12 0 DenisO'Regan 107
(John Ferguson) *hld up: hdwy appr 2 out: rdn 2 out: sn wknd* **7/2**[2]

/21- **7** *1 ½* **Allied Answer**[26] 3659 6-11-5 116 APMcCoy 112
(Steve Gollings) *led narrowly: jst hdd whn hit 2 out: wknd* **8/1**

3- **8** *2 ½* **Lyric Street (IRE)**[21] 3735 6-10-12 0 JasonMaguire 103
(Donald McCain) *trckd ldrs: pushed along appr 3 out: wknd bef 2 out* **28/1**

P/1- **9** *7* **Electrolyser (IRE)**[66] 2858 9-11-5 0 BarryGeraghty 103
(Nicky Henderson) *hld up in midfield: rdn appr 3 out: sn btn* **5/2**[1]

35- **10** *½* **Polstar (FR)**[18] 3796 5-10-12 0 JamesDavies 96
(Harry Whittington) *hld up in midfield: wknd appr 3 out* **100/1**

006- **11** *21* **Daylan (IRE)**[16] 3826 6-10-12 0 DougieCostello 77
(Tony Coyle) *w ldr: wknd appr 3 out* **100/1**

0- **12** *10* **Triple Eight (IRE)**[13] 3872 6-10-7 0 AdamNicol(5) 68
(Philip Kirby) *hld up in midfield: wknd appr 3 out* **100/1**

00- **13** *36* **Devil At Midnight (IRE)**[6] 4005 6-10-7 0 SamanthaDrake(5) 35
(Richard Drake) *hld up in rr: a bhd* **200/1**

000- **14** *7* **Brasingaman Espee**[51] 3144 5-10-12 0 (t) BarryKeniry 29
(George Moore) *hld up in midfield: hit 5th: wknd appr 3 out* **200/1**

4m 7.8s (3.10) **Going Correction** +0.50s/f (Soft) 14 Ran SP% **116.4**
Speed ratings: **112,111,109,108,108 103,102,101,98,98 88,83,66,63**
CSF £68.39 TOTE £3.40: £2.10, £5.40, £2.60; EX 90.40 Trifecta £518.00.
Owner W H Ponsonby **Bred** Bottisham Heath Stud **Trained** Barbury Castle, Wilts

FOCUS
Another interesting novices' hurdle, featuring a few decent ex-Flat performers. The race should produce winners and the first pair are well above average.

4104 LARKSHILL ENGINEERING H'CAP CHASE (18 fncs) 3m
3:00 (3:05) (Class 3) (0-135,133) 5-Y-0+ **£6,498** (£1,908; £954; £477)

Form RPR
P65- **1** **Golden Call (IRE)**[22] 3717 10-11-3 124 DougieCostello 139+
(Jennie Candlish) *mde all: rdn 4 out: strly pressed 3 out tl last: styd on wl and sn in command run-in* **11/2**[2]

/P2- **2** *4* **Fentara**[22] 3725 9-10-13 123 (t) JakeGreenall(3) 133
(Mark Walford) *in tch: hdwy and upsides 3 out: sn rdn: stl ev ch last: no ex run-in* **4/1**[1]

P/0- **3** *2 ¾* **Harry The Viking**[54] 3091 9-11-8 129 (b[1]) NickScholfield 139
(Paul Nicholls) *prom: rdn and ev ch 2 out: no ex run-in* **6/1**[3]

5/4- **4** *3 ½* **Fill The Power (IRE)**[19] 3776 8-11-6 127 RyanMania 132
(Sue Smith) *trckd ldr: nt fluent 7th: pushed along fr 8th: dropped to rr 11th: styd on again after 2 out: wnt modest 4th after last* **4/1**[1]

3F6- **5** *5* **Storm Survivor (IRE)**[47] 3199 8-11-11 132 (v) APMcCoy 134
(Jonjo O'Neill) *hld up: rdn after 5 out: sn no imp on ldrs* **7/1**

/60- **6** *22* **Mr Gardner (IRE)**[68] 2812 11-11-0 121 BarryGeraghty 108
(Polly Gundry) *trckd ldrs: wknd after 6 out* **15/2**

P40- **P** **Arthur's Pass**[26] 3642 10-11-6 127 AlainCawley
(Tom George) *hld up: mstke 12th: p.u bef 5 out* **28/1**

P24- **P** **Howard's Legacy (IRE)**[40] 3366 8-11-9 130 LiamTreadwell
(Venetia Williams) *hld up in tch: hdwy to trck ldrs 11th: nt fluent 4 out: wknd 3 out: p.u bef last* **6/1**[3]

6m 9.9s (-2.10) **Going Correction** +0.15s/f (Yiel) 8 Ran SP% **111.7**
Speed ratings: **109,107,106,105,103 96, ,**
CSF £27.03 CT £132.76 TOTE £3.70: £1.10, £1.70, £2.70; EX 30.00 Trifecta £224.70.
Owner M M Allen **Bred** George Halford **Trained** Basford Green, Staffs

FOCUS
A decent staying handicap chase and there were three in a line jumping two out. Plenty of these were well in on old form and the second is probably the best guide.

4105 SOCIALMEDIABUZ.COM H'CAP HURDLE (11 hdls) 3m 110y
3:35 (3:40) (Class 3) (0-130,128) 4-Y-0+ **£5,393** (£1,583; £791; £395)

Form RPR
P55- **1** **Everaard (USA)**[36] 3478 8-10-2 104 (tp) RichieMcGrath 115+
(Philip Kirby) *prom: outpcd and briefly dropped to 5th after 4 out: rallied 3 out: hit 2 out but sn led: sn clr: idled towards fin* **16/1**

/60- **2** *5* **Viva Steve (IRE)**[58] 3004 6-11-6 122 DominicElsworth 124
(Mick Channon) *led: nt fluent 4 out: hdd jst after 2 out: sn rdn and no ch w wnr* **20/1**

156- **3** *5* **Abnaki (IRE)**[55] 3060 9-11-7 128 (b) MauriceLinehan(5) 126
(Jonjo O'Neill) *in tch: rdn bef 4 out: one pce in 3rd after 2 out* **33/1**

10P- **4** *9* **Colebrooke**[14] 3853 6-11-4 120 (b) JamieMoore 109
(Renee Robeson) *trckd ldrs: wnt prom after 7th: rdn 3 out: wknd after 2 out* **33/1**

53P- **5** *11* **Keltic Rhythm (IRE)**[48] 3186 7-10-5 110 (t) TrevorWhelan(3) 89
(Neil King) *in tch: rdn appr 3 out: wknd 2 out* **7/1**[3]

1FF- **6** *8* **Streams Of Whiskey (IRE)**[68] 2817 7-11-3 119 BrianHarding 91
(Nicky Richards) *trckd ldrs: rdn 3 out: wknd* **9/1**

041- **7** *33* **Top Billing**[29] 3605 5-10-4 106 ow1 (p) DenisO'Regan 48
(Nicky Richards) *hld up: rdn bef 3 out: sn btn* **9/2**[2]

30P- **8** *42* **Abruzzi**[40] 3359 6-11-2 118 (p) FelixDeGiles 22
(Tom Symonds) *hld up: pushed along fr 4th: t.o fr 4 out* **7/1**[3]

/50- **P** **Union Du Chenet (FR)**[70] 2755 6-10-11 113 (p) DavidBass
(Nicky Henderson) *midfield: nt fluent 5th and 6th: struggling 4 out: p.u bef 3 out* **16/1**

6/F- **P** **One Conemara (IRE)**[83] 2490 6-11-7 123 BarryGeraghty
(Nicky Henderson) *hld up in tch: wknd after 4 out: p.u bef 3 out* **13/8**[1]

6m 9.9s (10.90) **Going Correction** +0.50s/f (Soft) 10 Ran SP% **113.7**
Speed ratings (Par 107): **102,100,98,95,92 89,79,65, ,**
CSF £266.79 CT £9900.49 TOTE £20.00: £4.70, £4.80, £5.00; EX 211.50 Trifecta £3297.60 Not won..
Owner Tennant, Sharpe & Boston **Bred** F & F Investments **Trained** Middleham, N Yorks

FOCUS
A useful staying handicap hurdle, but not that many got into it. The winner is rated back to the level of last season's best and was value for a bit further.

4106 BOOK FESTIVAL HOSPITALITY WITH EVENTMASTERS H'CAP CHASE (15 fncs) 2m 3f
4:10 (4:15) (Class 3) (0-130,130) 5-Y-0+ **£6,498** (£1,908; £954; £477)

Form RPR
323- **1** **Billy Cuckoo (IRE)**[6] 4007 8-10-13 117 (b) DougieCostello 125+
(Tony Coyle) *prom: led 3 out: sn rdn: bit slow last: kpt on wl* **11/2**[3]

215- **2** *2 ¼* **Di Kaprio (FR)**[37] 3430 8-11-10 128 LiamHeard 132
(Barry Leavy) *led: hdd 3 out: sn rdn: kpt on but a hld by wnr* **11/1**

/31- **3** *2 ¾* **Clondaw Knight (IRE)**[89] 2356 6-11-4 122 WilsonRenwick 125
(Lucinda Russell) *in tch: rdn after 3 out: disp 2nd last: no ex fnl 100yds* **13/8**[1]

534- **4** *nk* **Thunderstorm (IRE)**[42] 3259 9-11-6 124 APMcCoy 126
(Philip Hobbs) *hld up: reminder after 8th: rdn 5 out: hdwy 4 out to chse ldr 3 out: no ex fnl 100yds* **11/4**[2]

5/5- **5** *10* **Dashing George (IRE)**[18] 3802 12-10-12 123 MrRWinks(7) 114
(Peter Winks) *trckd ldr: rdn after 3 out: wknd appr last* **33/1**

00F- **6** *14* **Shadows Lengthen**[42] 3287 8-11-7 128 JakeGreenall(3) 109
(Michael Easterby) *hld up: hit 4th and 8th: btn whn anther mstke 3 out* **11/1**

504- **7** *29* **Oh Crick (FR)**[74] 2694 11-11-6 **124**..............................(b) RobertThornton 77
(Alan King) *in tch: trckd ldr whn nt fluent 5 out: hit 3 out: wknd* **8/1**
4m 57.2s (8.20) **Going Correction** +0.15s/f (Yiel) **7** Ran SP% **110.9**
Speed ratings: **88,87,85,85,81 75,63**
CSF £53.78 CT £134.40 TOTE £8.10: £3.00, £5.30; EX 49.70 Trifecta £143.40.
Owner Gary Dewhurst & Tony Coyle **Bred** James Robinson **Trained** Norton, N Yorks
FOCUS
A good handicap chase, but another race where it paid to be handy as the front pair were up there throughout. Straightforward form.

4107 EVENTMASTERS CATERING SERVICES CONDITIONAL JOCKEYS' H'CAP HURDLE (8 hdls) 2m 110y

4:40 (4:45) (Class 5) (0-100,100) 4-Y-0+ **£2,053** (£598; £299)

Form RPR
402- **1** **Lean Burn (USA)**[37] 3428 8-10-2 **79**.................................. ConorRing(3) 82
(Barry Leavy) *hld up: smooth hdwy 3 out: chsd ldrs 2 out: sn rdn: kpt on to ld towards fin* **5/2**[1]
344- **2** *½* **Baraboy (IRE)**[47] 3210 4-10-4 **91**.............................. GrahamWatters(3) 83
(Barry Murtagh) *hld up: smooth hdwy 3 out: led 2 out: rdn appr last: one pce fnl 100yds: hdd towards fin* **20/1**
014- **3** *2 ¾* **Walter De La Mare (IRE)**[14] 3856 7-11-7 **95**................. MichealNolan 95
(Anabel K Murphy) *hld up in tch: hdwy 3 out: chsd ldrs 2 out: kpt on* **20/1**
640- **4** *5* **Inside Knowledge (USA)**[36] 2787 8-11-2 **90**...............(p) TrevorWhelan 86
(Garry Woodward) *prom: rdn and outpcd 2 out: plugged on after last* **9/1**
050- **5** *3* **Wheelavim**[21] 3746 6-10-8 **88**.. GeraldQuinn(6) 82
(Claire Dyson) *led: jst hdd whn hit 2 out: grad wknd* **100/1**
523- **6** *1* **Caught By Witness (IRE)**[16] 3821 9-10-5 **79**.................(t) JakeGreenall 71
(Anthony Middleton) *midfield: rdn 3 out: sn one pce and no imp on ldrs* **6/1**
004- **7** *12* **Torgamah Lad (IRE)**[46] 3226 6-11-7 **98**.................... HarryChalloner(3) 83+
(Venetia Williams) *in tch: collided w rail and dropped to rr after 4 out: wknd after 3 out* **4/1**[3]
500- **8** *29* **Bow Fiddle (IRE)**[34] 3518 8-10-4 **81**................................ NickSlatter(3) 36
(Patrick Holmes) *trckd ldrs: rdn 3 out: wknd after 2 out* **25/1**
4FP- **9** *24* **Force Of Habit**[36] 3451 8-11-4 **95**...............................(p) JohnDawson(3) 28
(Joanne Foster) *midfield: wknd bef 3 out* **50/1**
051- **F** **Straits Of Messina (IRE)**[14] 3856 5-11-9 **100**.................... BenPoste(3)
(Tom Symonds) *in tch: fell 4th* **10/3**[2]
4m 16.2s (11.50) **Going Correction** +0.50s/f (Soft)
WFA 4 from 5yo+ 9lb **10** Ran SP% **112.3**
Speed ratings (Par 103): **92,91,90,88,86 86,80,66,55,**
CSF £51.09 CT £806.55 TOTE £3.30: £1.60, £2.90, £4.30; EX 36.60 Trifecta £328.40.
Owner N Heath **Bred** George Ruggiero Jr **Trained** Forsbrook, Staffs
FOCUS
A modest conditional jockeys' handicap hurdle and they went no pace early. The first three ran pretty much to their marks.
T/Jkpt: £10667.40 to a £1 stake. Pool: £112,684.17 - 7.50 winning units. T/Plt: £973.80 to a £1 stake. Pool: £10,6833.42 - 80.08 winning units. T/Qpdt: £588.70 to a £1 stake. Pool: £9148.76 - 11.50 winning units. AS

3878 HUNTINGDON (R-H)

Thursday, February 6

OFFICIAL GOING: Hurdle course - soft (heavy in places); chase course - heavy (soft in places) (chs 5.3, hdl 5.9)
The first fence in the back straight and last fence in the home straight were omitted.
Wind: medium, against Weather: rain

4108 32RED.COM H'CAP HURDLE (12 hdls) 3m 2f

1:10 (1:10) (Class 4) (0-110,110) 4-Y-0+ **£3,249** (£954; £477; £238)

Form RPR
/11- **1** **Mudita Moment (IRE)**[32] 3553 9-11-12 **110**.................... AidanColeman 117+
(Venetia Williams) *chsd ldr: rdn and effrt between last 2: led last: styd on wl flat: rdn out* **7/4**[1]
602- **2** *1 ¾* **Bebinn (IRE)**[42] 3280 7-11-2 **100**.......................................(p) CharliePoste 103
(Ben Case) *led and set stdy gallop: rdn after 3 out: drvn and hdd last: kpt on u.p but a hld flat* **13/2**
543- **3** *3 ¼* **Cloudingstar (IRE)**[38] 3413 7-11-7 **105**.......................(t) RichieMcLernon 105
(Jonjo O'Neill) *hld up in tch: trckd ldng trio 3 out: rdn and effrt between last 2: stl cl enough last: outpcd fnl 150yds* **5/2**[2]
4P0- **4** *8* **Feast Of Fire (IRE)**[186] 1205 7-11-2 **103**.................... GavinSheehan(3) 97
(Mike Sowersby) *t.k.h: hld up in tch: hdwy 8th: rdn and btn bef 2 out: pushed into modest 4th flat: eased fnl 75yds* **33/1**
/04- **5** *2 ¾* **Genstone Trail**[46] 3227 8-11-0 **98**.............................. WayneHutchinson 90
(Alan King) *t.k.h: hdwy to chse ldrs 3rd: c wdst and ev ch whn mstke 2 out: 4th and btn whn hit last: wknd flat: eased fnl 75yds* **10/3**[3]
53P- **6** *20* **Carmela Maria**[16] 3824 9-10-1 **90**...................................(b) JoeColliver(5) 59
(Mike Sowersby) *chsd ldrs: pushed along and lost pl after 7th: rdn and btn 9th: lost tch next* **28/1**
7m 8.3s (45.40) **Going Correction** +1.575s/f (Heav) **6** Ran SP% **107.7**
Speed ratings (Par 105): **93,92,91,89,88 82**
CSF £12.09 TOTE £2.30: £1.20, £2.80; EX 13.20 Trifecta £22.70.
Owner John Moorhouse & John Nicholls (Trading) **Bred** John J Cleary **Trained** Kings Caple, H'fords
FOCUS
The track received only 5mm of the forecast overnight rain, so it passed a morning inspection, and though conditions were testing jockeys reported it was not as bad as feared. The first circuit was taken very steadily, and the field were still bunched going to the back straight for the final time. The cosy winner probably still has more to offer.

4109 32RED CASINO H'CAP CHASE (12 fncs 4 omitted) 2m 4f 110y

1:40 (1:41) (Class 4) (0-110,108) 5-Y-0+ **£3,898** (£1,144; £572; £286)

Form RPR
0S1- **1** **Browns Brook (IRE)**[13] 3883 8-10-13 **95**....................... AidanColeman 120+
(Venetia Williams) *in tch in midfield: trckd ldrs 8th: led after 3 out and sn wnt clr: in command whn j.lft 2 out: eased flat: easily* **6/4**[1]
P44- **2** *23* **Lough Coi (IRE)**[27] 3635 8-10-3 **90**..............................(vt) JamesBanks(5) 85
(Anthony Middleton) *chsd ldrs: reminder after 3rd: rdn and after next: hdwy to join ldr on long run after 6th: 3rd and rdn whn mstke 3 out: sn wl btn: plugged on to go 2nd flat* **13/2**
326- **3** *6* **Moleskin (IRE)**[49] 3172 11-11-5 **108**...............(bt) MrMatthewHampton(7) 99
(Victor Dartnall) *mde most tl rdn and hdd after 3 out: sn brushed aside and wl btn: lost 2nd flat* **5/1**[2]
5F4- **4** *26* **Milarrow (IRE)**[23] 3693 7-11-11 **107**..............................(b) BrendanPowell 73
(Colin Tizzard) *chsd ldr: upsides ldr on long run after 6th: rdn and struggling whn j. slowly next: lost pl and bhd 8th: t.o after 3 out* **6/1**[3]
352- **P** **Ring Bo Ree (IRE)**[63] 2911 11-11-6 **102**.......................(p) PaddyBrennan
(Tom George) *wl in tch in midfield: cl 4th and rdn after 7th: wkng whn mstke next: sn lost tch: t.o whn p.u 2 out* **9/1**
P5F- **P** **Goring Two (IRE)**[14] 3855 9-10-3 **85**...............................(p) AdamWedge
(Anna Newton-Smith) *in tch in last pair: rdn on long run after 6th: losing tch and j. slowly 8th: p.u next* **20/1**
345- **P** **Riddlestown (IRE)**[36] 3473 7-11-7 **103**.............................. HarrySkelton
(Caroline Fryer) *in tch in last pair: pushed along on long run after 6th: rdn and struggling in 6th after 8th: blnd bdly next: sn eased and p.u next* **8/1**
5m 35.8s (30.50) **Going Correction** +1.575s/f (Heav) **7** Ran SP% **110.2**
Speed ratings: **104,95,92,83, ,**
CSF £10.96 TOTE £2.50: £1.20, £2.10; EX 11.40 Trifecta £57.40.
Owner Mrs Vida Bingham **Bred** Stephen Lanigan-O'Keeffe **Trained** Kings Caple, H'fords
FOCUS
The last fence in the home straight and first in the back straight were omitted in all chases. The water jump, which would have been the first in this, was omitted first time round. This was gruelling stuff, especially with three horses taking each other on mid-race. As a result the winner only had to bide his time to pick up the pieces. The winner was well in on his recent win but this looks another step forward.

4110 32RED NOVICES' LIMITED H'CAP CHASE (JOCKEY CLUB GRASSROOTS JUMPS SERIES QUALIFIER) (15 fncs 4 omitted) 3m

2:15 (2:15) (Class 3) (0-125,125) 5-Y-0+ **£6,498** (£1,908; £954; £477)

Form RPR
/52- **1** **Dare To Endeavour**[27] 3634 7-10-11 **115**.......................... PaddyBrennan 130+
(Tom George) *mostly chsd ldr tl led after 3 out and travelling best bef next: 2 l clr last: sn readily asserted: easily* **7/1**
121- **2** *10* **Beforeall (IRE)**[42] 3246 6-11-7 **125**............................... LeightonAspell 129
(Oliver Sherwood) *chsd ldrs: 4th and rdn after 3 out: no ex u.p and hld in 3rd next: no ch w wnr but plugged on to snatch 2nd towards fin* **11/4**[2]
431- **3** *½* **Ultimatum Du Roy (FR)**[21] 3739 6-10-12 **116**.................... DarylJacob 122+
(Alex Hales) *hld up in tch: cl 4th 11th: rdn and effrt to press wnr bef 2 out: 2 l down and btn whn mstke last: wknd flat and lost 2nd towards fin* **9/4**[1]
515- **4** *30* **Woodford County**[19] 3784 7-11-1 **119**........................... RichardJohnson 92
(Philip Hobbs) *mstkes: in tch in last pair: rdn and struggling whn hit 11th: wknd next: t.o after 3 out: plugged on to go poor 4th flat* **10/3**[3]
/PP- **5** *1 ¾* **My Silver Lilly**[58] 3014 7-10-4 **111** oh37............................ JackQuinlan(3) 82
(Clive Drew) *in tch in last pair: rdn after 10th: sn struggling and lost tch after next: t.o after 3 out: plugged on flat* **250/1**
/32- **6** *7* **Henry King (IRE)**[54] 3093 10-11-2 **120**.................................(t) JackDoyle 91
(Victor Dartnall) *j.lft: led tl after 3 out: sn rdn: wknd rapidly bnd bef 2 out: 4th and wl btn 2 out: lost 2 pls and eased flat: t.o* **6/1**
6m 48.2s (37.90) **Going Correction** +1.575s/f (Heav) **6** Ran SP% **107.7**
Speed ratings: **99,95,95,85,84 82**
CSF £24.87 TOTE £5.60: £2.80, £1.60; EX 26.70 Trifecta £83.00.
Owner Nationwide Acquisitions PLC **Bred** Direct Sales (uk) Ltd **Trained** Slad, Gloucs
FOCUS
There was some fair previous chase form on offer here, though the winner was one of the least-exposed types. He stepped up massively on his hurdles form.

4111 32RED JUVENILE HURDLE (FOR THE CHATTERIS FEN TROPHY) (8 hdls) 2m 110y

2:50 (2:53) (Class 2) 4-Y-0

£9,384 (£2,772; £1,386; £693; £346; £174)

Form RPR
133- **1** **Harristown**[63] 2899 4-10-12 122...................................(p) KielanWoods 122
(Charlie Longsdon) *chsd ldr: upsides bef 3 out: rdn bef 2 out: bttr jump than rival last and sn led: kpt on wl: rdn out* **20/1**
61- **2** *1* **Baradari (IRE)**[40] 3364 4-11-2 0.................................... AidanColeman 126+
(Venetia Williams) *walked through s and reluctant ldr: broke into gallop after 150yds and set fair pce after: jnd bef 3 out: u.p 2 out: dived: blnd and unbalanced last: sn hdd: hung rt flat and one pce fnl 100yds* **3/1**[1]
2- **3** *8* **Royal Skies (IRE)**[41] 3332 4-10-12 0................................. JackQuinlan 114
(John Ferguson) *wl in tch in midfield: rdn and effrt to chse ldng pair bef 2 out: no imp between last 2* **3/1**[1]
113- **4** *6* **Violet Dancer**[40] 3360 4-11-6 132...................................... JoshuaMoore 119+
(Gary Moore) *hld up in tch in midfield: effrt to chse ldrs sn after 3 out: drvn and btn between last 2: blnd bdly and rdr lost iron last* **5/1**[3]
55- **5** *1* **After Eight Sivola (FR)**[26] 3641 4-10-12 0.................. RichardJohnson 106
(Nick Williams) *t.k.h: hld up in tch in rr: clsd after 5th: rdn and btn bnd bef 2 out: wknd between last 2* **50/1**
4- **6** *6* **Alco Sivola (FR)**[50] 3161 4-10-12 0................................... DarylJacob 100
(Nick Williams) *t.k.h: hld up in tch in midfield: clsd after 5th: wknd bnd bef 2 out* **8/1**
1- **7** *23* **Muhtaris (IRE)**[58] 3003 4-10-12 0............................ SamTwiston-Davies 85
(John Ferguson) *chsd ldrs: j.big 2nd: rdn bef 3 out: wknd bef 2 out: bhd whn mstke 2 out: t.o* **10/3**[2]
P- **8** *12* **Memberof (FR)**[102] 2098 4-11-2 0............................... WayneHutchinson 69
(Alan King) *hld up in tch in last pair: clsd 4th: rdn and wknd sn after 3 out: bhd next: t.o* **11/1**
4m 36.1s (41.20) **Going Correction** +1.575s/f (Heav) **8** Ran SP% **115.9**
Speed ratings: **66,65,61,58,58 55,44,39**
CSF £82.14 TOTE £33.50: £4.40, £1.60, £2.10; EX 138.70 Trifecta £445.70.
Owner Kyuna Memories **Bred** Juddmonte Farms Ltd **Trained** Over Norton, Oxon
FOCUS
Some decent juveniles have taken this prize in the past, such as Chris Pea Green, Songe and Afsoun, and this looked a fair renewal. However, no one wanted to lead and the field stood still for around 45 seconds before eventually setting off at a sedate pace. This played into the hands of the leaders. The first two are on the upgrade.

4112 32RED H'CAP HURDLE (10 hdls) 2m 4f 110y

3:25 (3:25) (Class 2) 4-Y-0+ **£12,021** (£3,529; £1,764; £882)

Form RPR
613- **1** **Prideofthecastle (IRE)**[23] 3695 7-10-7 **124**.................. TomScudamore 132+
(David Pipe) *mde all: drew clr and mstke 2 out: rdn and edgd lft between last 2: wnt rt and mstke last: rdn out* **9/2**[3]
02P- **2** *4* **Art Professor (IRE)**[26] 3646 10-11-0 **131**........................ AidanColeman 132
(Venetia Williams) *chsd ldrs: 3rd and outpcd u.p bef 2 out: chsd clr wnr 2 out: 5 l down last: kpt on* **7/2**[2]
313- **3** *4 ½* **Vandross (IRE)**[19] 3768 4-9-12 **129** oh8 ow1...................... JackQuinlan(3) 114
(Neil King) *chsd ldrs: cl 4th and rdn bef 3 out: outpcd bef 2 out: wnt 3rd last: kpt on same pce flat* **16/1**

F4- **4** *10* **Black River (FR)**[40] 3369 5-11-1 **132** .... DarylJacob 118
(Paul Nicholls) *chsd ldr: rdn and no ex bef 2 out: 3rd and btn 2 out: lost 3rd last: wknd flat* **6/4**[1]

022- **5** *1 ½* **Dawn Twister (GER)**[13] 3882 7-10-5 **122** ....(p) LeightonAspell 108
(Lucy Wadham) *racd wdst: in tch: hdwy to chse ldrs 6th: lost pl next: rdn and struggling bef 3 out: wknd bef 2 out* **11/2**

26P- **6** *16* **Party Rock (IRE)**[26] 3646 7-11-12 **143** .... SeanQuinlan 111
(Jennie Candlish) *hld up in tch in rr: mstke and pushed along 6th: rdn and mstke next: wknd 3 out* **11/1**

5m 26.2s (27.20) **Going Correction** +1.575s/f (Heav)
WFA 4 from 5yo+ 10lb **6** Ran SP% **110.0**
Speed ratings (Par 109): **111,109,107,103,103 97**
CSF £19.74 TOTE £4.10: £1.50, £2.50; EX 23.20 Trifecta £122.60.
Owner Bryan Drew **Bred** Patrick Cronin **Trained** Nicholashayne, Devon

FOCUS
A competitive handicap, in which the winner dictated matters and produced a big step up on his previous form.

4113 CGA FOXHUNTER TRIAL HUNTERS' CHASE (15 fncs 4 omitted) 3m
4:00 (4:00) (Class 6) 5-Y-0+ **£987** (£303)

Form RPR

/1P- **1** **Brunswick Gold (IRE)**[39] 9-11-13 127 .... MrStuartRobinson[(7)] 130
(Miss Rose Grissell) *led 2nd: travelled and j. bttr than rival tl rdn and hdd after 2 out: 2 l down and looked btn last: tired and gng v slowly flat: lft in ld towards fin* **8/15**[1]

22- **2** *3 ½* **Gunmoney (IRE)**[18] 3801 9-11-5 107 ....(p) MrJRussell[(7)] 122
(G T H Bailey) *led tl 2nd: rdn and upsides wnr 11th: led after 2 out: 2 l clr last: gng lft under rt-hand drive flat: racd nr stands' rail and slowed bdly fnl 100yds: hdd towards fin* **13/8**[2]

7m 1.9s (51.60) **Going Correction** +1.575s/f (Heav) **2** Ran SP% **103.3**
Speed ratings: **77,75**
TOTE £1.30.
Owner Dr C Hargreaves & S C Robinson **Bred** J P Murphy **Trained** Robertsbridge, East Sussex

FOCUS
There was not much between these two for most of the way, but it developed into a farce after the last. The pair are rated pretty much to their marks.

4114 EBF STALLIONS MARES' STANDARD OPEN NATIONAL HUNT FLAT RACE 2m 110y
4:30 (4:30) (Class 6) 4-7-Y-0 **£1,819** (£534; £267; £133)

Form RPR

4- **1** **Avispa**[92] 2298 5-11-2 0 .... WayneHutchinson 109+
(Alan King) *hld up in tch in last pair: cl 3rd 5f out: rdn and led 2f out: forged clr 1f out: styd on wl: rdn out* **6/4**[2]

2 *6* **Promanco**[311] 5-11-2 0 .... NoelFehily 102+
(Charlie Longsdon) *chsd ldrs: wnt 2nd 7f out tl led 3f out: sn wnt clr w wnr: rdn and hdd 2f out: no ex and btn 1f out: plugged on* **5/4**[1]

25/ **3** *27* **Molly Maid (IRE)**[288] 5511 6-11-2 0 .... MarkGrant 75
(Dominic Ffrench Davis) *chsd ldrs: cl 4th 5f out: rdn and outpcd 3f out: sn wl btn: wnt modest 3rd 2f out* **12/1**

4 *7* **Our Cat (IRE)**[102] 6-11-2 0 .... PaddyBrennan 68
(Fergal O'Brien) *led tl rdn and hdd 3f out: sn btn: 4th and wknd 2f out: t.o* **8/1**[3]

0- **5** *47* **Just Like Beth**[14] 3863 6-10-9 0 .... KevinJones[(7)] 21
(Giuseppe Fierro) *chsd ldr tl 7f out: sn rdn and dropped to rr: t.o fnl 4f* **66/1**

6 *32* **Western Dolly** 5-10-13 0 .... JackQuinlan[(3)]
(Caroline Fryer) *in tch: rdn and lost tch rapidly 4f out: sn t.o* **18/1**

4m 13.05s (23.95) **Going Correction** +1.575s/f (Heav) **6** Ran SP% **110.0**
Speed ratings: **106,103,90,87,65 50**
CSF £3.53 TOTE £2.60: £1.20, £1.40; EX 3.70 Trifecta £12.30.
Owner The Wasp Partnership **Bred** R D And Mrs J S Chugg **Trained** Barbury Castle, Wilts

FOCUS
Not a strong contest, but the market leaders pulled clear and look decent. There's a case for rating the form a lot higher through the third.
T/Plt: £20.00 to a £1 stake. Pool: £65,996.34 - 2397.53 winning units. T/Qpdt: £10.80 to a £1 stake. Pool: £5594.13 - 382.69 winning units. SP

3955 TAUNTON (R-H)
Thursday, February 6
4115 Meeting Abandoned - Waterlogged

3222 BANGOR-ON-DEE (L-H)
Friday, February 7
4122 Meeting Abandoned - Waterlogged

3641 KEMPTON (R-H)
Friday, February 7

OFFICIAL GOING: Heavy (soft in places on chase course; chs 3.7; hdl 3.2)
Wind: Fresh, across (away from stands) Weather: Fine but cloudy

4129 BETDAQ THE SPORTS BETTING EXCHANGE CONDITIONAL JOCKEYS' H'CAP HURDLE (8 hdls) 2m
1:30 (1:30) (Class 4) (0-115,112) 4-Y-0+ **£3,119** (£915; £457; £228)

Form RPR

502- **1** **Loyaute (FR)**[54] 3117 7-11-10 **110** .... GilesHawkins 122+
(Chris Down) *trckd ldr: mstke 3rd: led sn after 3 out and sent 5 l clr: shkn up after 2 out: styd on wl: readily* **7/1**[3]

/31- **2** *3 ¾* **Baltimore Rock (IRE)**[22] 3746 5-11-6 **112** .... KieronEdgar[(6)] 121+
(David Pipe) *t.k.h: hld up in last trio: nt fluent 3rd: prog 3 out: chsd wnr and nt fluent 2 out: sn rdn: nt fluent last: styd on but no imp* **8/11**[1]

222- **3** *11* **Santo Thomas (FR)**[16] 3839 8-11-4 **107** .... HarryChalloner[(3)] 105
(Venetia Williams) *trckd ldng pair: rdn to chse wnr on long run after 3 out: no imp and dropped to 3rd sn after 2 out: wknd last* **5/1**[2]

0P0- **4** *4 ½* **Xaarcet (IRE)**[22] 3741 7-11-2 **112** .... LewisGordon[(10)] 106
(Colin Tizzard) *in tch: nt fluent 3 out: pushed along and no imp on long run to 2 out: one pce after* **25/1**

12/- **5** *¾* **Pilgreen (FR)**[1049] 5013 9-11-8 **108** .... HarryDerham 99
(Robert Walford) *hld up in last trio: in tch 3 out: pushed along and no prog bef 2 out: drvn and kpt on one pce bef last* **12/1**

060- **6** *10* **Drussell (IRE)**[53] 3132 8-11-3 **103** .... NicodeBoinville 84
(Martin Bosley) *wl in tch: shkn up and no prog bef 2 out: sn wknd* **20/1**

040- **7** *2 ¼* **Dark And Dangerous (IRE)**[30] 3599 6-11-9 **109** ....(v) JoshuaMoore 88
(Brendan Powell) *led at gd pce: hdd sn after 3 out and rdn: wknd wl bef 2 out* **16/1**

/00- **8** *25* **Dalmo**[257] 505 5-10-11 **103** .... ChristopherWard[(6)] 57
(Dr Richard Newland) *a in last trio: rdn and lost tch after 5th: t.o* **16/1**

4m 8.8s (10.70) **Going Correction** +0.80s/f (Soft) **8** Ran SP% **115.1**
Speed ratings (Par 105): **105,103,97,95,95 90,88,76**
CSF £13.11 CT £28.72 TOTE £12.40: £2.70, £1.10, £1.10; EX 18.70 Trifecta £61.20.
Owner Upton Racing 2 **Bred** Haras De Mezeray **Trained** Mutterton, Devon

FOCUS
All rails moved out 3yds on to fresh ground, all distances as advertised. After 15mm of rain overnight the ground has eased slightly to Heavy on the hurdles course and Heavy, soft in places on the chase course. They went a sensible pace in this opening conditional jockeys' event and the winning time being 26.8sec outside standard demonstrates how testing conditions were.

4130 BETDAQ £25 NO LOSE MOBILE BET NOVICES' HURDLE (10 hdls) 2m 5f
2:00 (2:00) (Class 4) 4-Y-0+ **£3,249** (£954; £477; £238)

Form RPR

/51- **1** **Boogie In The Barn (IRE)**[67] 2864 6-11-4 0 .... NickScholfield 128+
(Jeremy Scott) *pressed ldr: led after 6th: gng best and in command after 3 out: slowed into 2 out and jnd sn after it: pushed along to assert again bef last* **8/1**

1- **2** *3 ½* **Hot Whiskey N Ice (IRE)**[71] 2773 5-11-4 0 .... WayneHutchinson 119
(Noel Williams) *mostly chsd ldng trio: rdn after 7th: outpcd 3 out: kpt on bef 2 out: tk 2nd nr fin* **9/2**[3]

621- **3** *½* **Strollawaynow (IRE)**[24] 3694 7-11-11 122 .... TomCannon 126
(David Arbuthnot) *mde most to after 6th: pressed wnr and clr w him fr 3 out: sn rdn: hld whn lft nrly upsides after 2 out: one pce bef last: lost 2nd nr fin* **2/1**[1]

5/0- **4** *12* **Fourth Act (IRE)**[119] 1861 5-11-4 0 .... JoeTizzard 106
(Colin Tizzard) *in tch: chsd ldrs 7th: rdn and lft bhd 3 out: no imp after* **25/1**

5 *19* **Albert Bridge**[118] 6-11-4 0 .... RichardJohnson 87
(Emma Lavelle) *nt a fluent: hld up: chsd ldrs 6th tl wknd 3 out: t.o* **9/4**[2]

10/ **6** *2 ½* **Call Carlo**[290] 5475 7-11-4 0 .... AidanColeman 87
(Venetia Williams) *sloppy rnd of jumping: a in rr: rdn 7th: no ch 3 out: blnd next* **20/1**

2/0- **P** **No Substitute (IRE)**[40] 3388 9-11-4 125 .... RobertThornton
(Alan King) *a in rr: rdn 7th: wknd bef 3 out: t.o whn p.u bef 2 out* **7/1**

5m 37.2s (19.70) **Going Correction** +0.80s/f (Soft) **7** Ran SP% **114.5**
Speed ratings (Par 105): **94,92,92,87,80 79,**
CSF £43.62 TOTE £10.00: £2.60, £3.00; EX 45.60 Trifecta £125.90.
Owner Bradley Partnership **Bred** Patrick Gardiner **Trained** Brompton Regis, Somerset

FOCUS
They went a very steady pace in this novice hurdle which suited those ridden prominently.

4131 BETDAQ £500 IN FREE BETS H'CAP CHASE (12 fncs) 2m
2:30 (2:30) (Class 3) (0-135,127) 5-Y-0 **£6,279** (£1,871; £947; £485; £254)

Form RPR

P34- **1** **Paddy The Stout (IRE)**[22] 3742 9-10-4 **105** ....(t) TomO'Brien 111+
(Paul Henderson) *sn off the pce: struggling whn blnd 7th: rdn and styd on to take 2nd after 4 out: lft in ld next: mstke last: all out to hang on* **10/1**

/P5- **2** *nk* **Overclear**[56] 3065 12-11-2 **117** .... JackDoyle 121
(Victor Dartnall) *sn off the pce: nt fluent 4th and mstke next: rdn and no prog 8th: kpt on after 4 out: lft cl 2nd next and wobbled: given ch after wnr's mstke last: grad clsd: jst failed* **12/1**

032- **3** *10* **Notarfbad (IRE)**[8] 3992 8-11-12 **127** .... NickScholfield 119
(Jeremy Scott) *disp ld at str pce and mostly clr of rest: hdd 7th: wknd 4 out: lft in 3rd pl next: tired and no imp* **7/2**[3]

P54- **4** *12* **Nozic (FR)**[27] 3652 13-10-9 **110** ....(b) DaveCrosse 91
(Zoe Davison) *chsd clr ldng pair: clsng whn nt fluent 6th: lost grnd fr next: wknd after 4 out* **13/2**

/65- **5** *20* **Ted Dolly (IRE)**[103] 2116 10-11-7 **122** .... FelixDeGiles 82
(Tom Symonds) *sn wl off the pce in last: brief prog to chse clr ldng trio 6th: wknd 8th: t.o* **33/1**

/P3- **F** **Lucky Sunny (IRE)**[16] 3833 11-10-9 **110** .... AidanColeman 116
(Venetia Williams) *tended to jump lft: disp ld at str pce and clr of rest: led 7th: drawing clr whn mstke 4 out: 6 l up but u.p whn fell 3 out* **3/1**[2]

235- **P** **Ultragold (FR)**[8] 3990 6-11-6 **121** ....(t) JoeTizzard
(Colin Tizzard) *nt fluent 3rd: chsd clr ldng pair to 4th: lost pl rapidly after next: t.o whn p.u bef 7th* **9/4**[1]

4m 14.0s (13.70) **Going Correction** +0.875s/f (Soft) **7** Ran SP% **111.0**
Speed ratings: **100,99,94,88,78 ,**
CSF £100.60 TOTE £10.00: £3.80, £0.00; EX 110.70 Trifecta £617.20.
Owner The Pearly Kings Partnership **Bred** Sean Hourigan **Trained** Whitsbury, Hants

FOCUS
A couple of these took each other on from the off in this decent handicap chase and the first two home picked up the pieces.

4132 BETDAQ NO PREMIUM CHARGE NOVICES' H'CAP HURDLE (10 hdls) 2m 5f
3:05 (3:05) (Class 4) (0-110,109) 4-Y-0+ **£3,249** (£954; £477; £238)

Form RPR

/33- **1** **Harry's Farewell**[27] 3643 7-11-9 **106** .... NickScholfield 121+
(Polly Gundry) *hld up in rr: stdy prog after 6th: trckd ldrs 3 out: led bef 2 out gng strly: sn clr: 9 l ahd last: eased flat* **7/1**[3]

354- **2** *7* **Smiles For Miles (IRE)**[24] 3694 6-11-12 **109** ....(t) TomScudamore 114+
(David Pipe) *hld up in rr: short of room on bnd after 2nd: stdy prog fr 6th to trck ldrs next: led 3 out: rdn and hdd bef 2 out: kpt on but no ch w wnr* **5/1**[2]

424- **3** *2 ½* **Coup De Grace (IRE)**[15] 3195 5-11-2 **102** .... JoshuaMoore[(3)] 103
(Pat Phelan) *nt fluent: chsd ldrs: wl in tch 3 out: sn rdn: kpt on but nvr able to chal: mstke last* **9/2**[1]

4 *1* **Minella Gathering (IRE)**[57] 3052 5-10-12 **95** .... TomO'Brien 95
(Paul Henderson) *nt fluent in rr: shoved along after 4th: prog on wd outside 7th: chsd ldrs and in tch 3 out: rdn and outpcd sn after: kpt on fr 2 out* **40/1**

533- **5** *7* **Tracking Time**[3] 4075 7-11-1 **105** .... MrJMartin[(7)] 99
(Andrew J Martin) *hld up towards rr: prog to trck ldng pair after 6th: rdn and lost grnd qckly after 3 out: plugged on again fr next* **8/1**

121- **6** *36* **Easy Beesy**[50] 3179 6-11-5 **102**................................ SamTwiston-Davies 58
(Charles Egerton) *prom: w ldr 7th to 3 out: wknd rapidly jst bef 2 out: t.o*
5/1[2]

540- **P** **Micquus (IRE)**[82] 2536 5-10-11 **94**..(v) MarkGrant
(Jonathan Geake) *hld up in last pair: short of room bnd after 7th: struggling 5th: sn wknd: t.o bef 3 out: p.u bef 2 out* **100/1**

060- **P** **Master Cynk**[14] 3872 7-11-5 **102**.. PaddyBrennan
(Tom George) *hld up in rr: stl towards rr after 6th but gng bttr than many: jst in tch whn mstke 3 out and reminder: pushed along and wknd: p.u bef 2 out* **14/1**

510- **P** **Boss In Boots (IRE)**[48] 3195 6-11-8 **105**..................... AndrewThornton
(Seamus Mullins) *in tch: reminders after 4th: nt gng wl after: wknd after 7th: t.o whn p.u bef 2 out* **8/1**

4P6- **P** **Hot Whiskey (IRE)**[38] 3435 6-11-8 **105**..........................(p) AndrewTinkler
(Brendan Powell) *mde most to 6th: wknd rapidly: t.o after next: p.u bef 3 out* **25/1**

/2P- **P** **Foxes Bridge**[85] 2474 6-11-7 **104**...................................... BrendanPowell
(Colin Tizzard) *prom: drvn and nt look keen after 7th: wknd rapidly 3 out: t.o whn p.u bef 2 out* **33/1**

0P5- **P** **Amber Flush**[22] 3733 5-10-10 **93**... FelixDeGiles
(Tom Symonds) *a in rr: short of room bnd after 2nd: wknd after 4th: t.o whn p.u after 6th* **33/1**

653- **P** **In The Gate (IRE)**[22] 3740 6-11-4 **101**...................................(t) NoelFehily
(Charlie Longsdon) *pressed ldr: led 6th: hdd & wknd rapidly 3 out: t.o whn p.u bef next* **9/1**

/24- **P** **Upton Wood**[57] 3044 8-11-9 **106**.. JamesDavies
(Chris Down) *chsd ldrs: n.m.r bnd after 4th: sn drvn and struggling: wknd rapidly 6th: t.o whn p.u bef next* **16/1**

5m 43.6s (26.10) **Going Correction** +0.80s/f (Soft) **14** Ran SP% **121.9**
Speed ratings (Par 105): **82,79,78,78,75 61,,,, ,,,**
CSF £41.51 CT £180.15 TOTE £9.10: £2.60, £1.90, £2.60; EX 54.00 Trifecta £219.10.
Owner J P Selby **Bred** J Selby **Trained** Ottery St Mary, Devon

FOCUS
The pace didn't look that strong in this novices' handicap hurdle and the field remained tightly bunched for a long way, but the conditions eventually took their toll.

4133 BETDAQ £25 NO LOSE MOBILE BET GRADUATION CHASE (16 fncs) 2m 4f 110y
3:35 (3:35) (Class 2) 5-Y-0+ **£12,512** (£3,696; £1,848; £924)

Form RPR
212- **1** **Une Artiste (FR)**[22] 3750 6-10-3 140.. DavidBass 132+
(Nicky Henderson) *trckd ldr: led 4 out: gng best next: pressed and drvn whn gd jump last: edgd lft but styd on wl* **4/9**[1]

P35- **2** *3* **Shangani (USA)**[13] 3887 8-11-7 132................................. AidanColeman 144
(Venetia Williams) *led at mod pce: awkward 3rd: rdn and hdd whn mstke 4 out: kpt on wl fr next and tried to chal last: one pce flat* **6/1**[3]

43P- **3** *27* **Cnoc Seoda (IRE)**[22] 3743 9-10-11 117...........................(t) TomO'Brien 106
(Paul Henderson) *nt a fluent: in tch: pushed along and steadily lost tch fr 10th: t.o* **50/1**

1/0- **4** *6* **Batonnier (FR)**[69] 2813 8-10-10 0..................................... RobertThornton 123+
(Alan King) *t.k.h: hld up: hit 8th: cl up 4 out: disputing 2 l 2nd whn hit 3 out and slithered on landing: nt rcvr and eased: dismntd after fin* **4/1**[2]

5m 28.1s (11.50) **Going Correction** +0.875s/f (Soft) **4** Ran SP% **105.5**
Speed ratings: **113,111,101,99**
CSF £3.36 TOTE £1.60; EX 3.20 Trifecta £12.10.
Owner Simon Munir **Bred** E Clayeux & D Clayeux **Trained** Upper Lambourn, Berks

FOCUS
This revolved about the favourite.

4134 BETDAQ 3% COMMISSION H'CAP CHASE (18 fncs) 3m
4:10 (4:10) (Class 3) (0-140,139) 5-Y-0+
£6,256 (£1,848; £924; £462; £231; £116)

Form RPR
/62- **1** **Triangular (USA)**[30] 3603 9-10-11 **124**................................(tp) NoelFehily 131
(Harry Fry) *hld up in rr: stdy prog fr 13th: chsd ldrs bef 3 out where lft cl 2nd: led 2 out: jnd last: hld on nr fin* **4/1**[2]

010- **2** *¾* **Midnight Appeal**[62] 2939 9-11-12 **139**....................(b) WayneHutchinson 146
(Alan King) *hld up in tch: prog to trck ldrs 11th: wnt 2nd whn lft in ld and hmpd 3 out: hdd next: rallied and upsides last: nt qckn nr fin* **7/1**

22P- **3** *2½* **Adrenalin Flight (IRE)**[33] 3554 8-10-1 **114**........................ RyanMahon 119
(Seamus Mullins) *mde most tl j. slowly and hdd 10th: sn lost pl and shoved along: struggling 4 out: rallied fr next: styd on and clsd on ldng pair fr last* **10/1**

/P3- **4** *nk* **Summery Justice (IRE)**[56] 3059 10-11-1 **128**............... AidanColeman 133
(Venetia Williams) *in tch: nt fluent 6th: nt fluent 11th and reminder: struggling fr 13th: styd on again fr 3 out: clsng on ldng pair fr last but jst lost out in battle for 3rd* **4/1**[2]

525- **5** *12* **Shuil Royale (IRE)**[43] 3293 9-10-4 **117**............................ TomCannon 110
(David Arbuthnot) *pressed ldr fr 4th tl led 10th: hdd next: w ldr to 14th: wknd 3 out* **6/1**[3]

5/P- **6** *10* **Arbeo (IRE)**[105] 2065 8-10-10 **123**.. SamThomas 109
(Diana Grissell) *chsd ldrs: lost grnd qckly after 13th and wl bhd 4 out: tried to rally bef next: sn wknd* **12/1**

00P- **F** **Chartreux (FR)**[41] 3361 9-11-1 **128**...............................(t) PaddyBrennan 135
(Tom George) *pressed ldr to 4th: remained w ldrs: led 11th: gd jumps 14th and next: 3 l up and rdn but gng strly whn fell 3 out* **10/1**

3/3- **P** **Court Victory (IRE)**[27] 3651 9-10-12 **128**...................... GavinSheehan(3)
(Emma Lavelle) *nt fluent 1st: hld up and sn last: nt fluent 8th: no real prog whn pushed along fr 12th: wl bhd 3 out: j.lft 2 out and p.u* **3/1**[1]

6m 29.9s (14.50) **Going Correction** +0.875s/f (Soft) **8** Ran SP% **117.7**
Speed ratings: **110,109,108,108,104 101,,**
CSF £32.65 CT £264.06 TOTE £4.60: £1.60, £2.10, £3.00; EX 23.40 Trifecta £281.30.
Owner Gdm Partnership **Bred** Flaxman Holdings Ltd **Trained** Seaborough, Dorset
■ Stewards' Enquiry : Wayne Hutchinson two-day ban: use of whip (21 - 22 Feb)

FOCUS
A good staying handicap chase.

4135 BETDAQ VALUE YOU CAN BET ON MAIDEN OPEN NATIONAL HUNT FLAT RACE 2m
4:40 (4:40) (Class 5) 4-6-Y-0 **£1,949** (£572; £286; £143)

Form RPR
3/2- **1** **Third Act (IRE)**[125] 1771 5-11-4 0... JoeTizzard 112+
(Colin Tizzard) *t.k.h: hld up in tch: prog to ld over 3f out: pushed along and in command 2f out: eased nr fin* **13/8**[1]

2 *6* **Etheridge Annie** 5-10-4 0.. MikeyEnnis(7) 94
(Hugo Froud) *t.k.h: cl up: rdn wl over 3f out and looked to be struggling to stay on terms: rallied over 2f out: wnt 2nd over 1f out: styd on but no ch w wnr* **40/1**

3 *4* **Goneinaglance** 5-10-4 0.. MrJMartin(7) 90
(Andrew J Martin) *t.k.h: w ldrs: rdn over 3f out: outpcd over 2f out: kpt on again fnl f to snatch 3rd last stride* **66/1**

4 *nse* **Summer Sounds (IRE)** 5-11-4 0.. FelixDeGiles 97
(Tom Symonds) *cl up: w ldrs fr 1/2-way: upsides over 3f out: styd chsng ldrs but steadily outpcd fnl 2f* **10/1**

5 *nk* **Less Time (IRE)** 5-11-4 0.. APMcCoy 97
(Jonjo O'Neill) *hld up in rr: prog on outer 4f out to trck wnr 3f out: shkn up and no imp over 2f out: lost 2nd over 1f out: fdd* **15/8**[2]

6 *14* **Rattleandrun (IRE)**[257] 6-11-4 0...................................... BrendanPowell 83
(Brendan Powell) *t.k.h: w ldrs: hmpd bnd after 4f: rdn and steadily wknd over 3f out* **33/1**

0- **7** *3½* **Littleton Lad (IRE)**[7] 4017 6-10-11 0................................ MrHGMiller(7) 79
(Zoe Davison) *t.k.h: led at mod pce: veered lft bnd after 4f: hdd over 3f out: sn btn* **150/1**

8 *shd* **Darloa (IRE)** 5-11-4 0.. JackDoyle 85+
(Victor Dartnall) *in tch: pushed along at rr of main gp 4f out: wl hld in 6th whn stmbld v bdly over 1f out: wknd* **10/1**

0- **9** *14* **Top Show**[96] 2254 5-11-4 0... PaulMoloney 65
(Dean Ivory) *in tch tl rdn and wknd 4f out: sn bhd* **66/1**

05/ **10** *1¼* **Bridgetown**[681] 5130 6-11-4 0.. JamesDavies 64
(Simon Hodgson) *in tch in rr: urged along sn after 1/2-way: wknd 4f out: sn bhd* **100/1**

11 *16* **Brean Play Percy** 4-10-8 0.. RichardJohnson 38
(Philip Hobbs) *t.k.h: hld up in rr: shkn up and no prog over 4f out: wl btn 3f out: eased whn no ch* **7/1**[3]

4m 12.5s (20.00) **Going Correction** +0.80s/f (Soft)
WFA 4 from 5yo+ 9lb **11** Ran SP% **113.6**
Speed ratings: **82,79,77,76,76 69,68,68,61,60 52**
CSF £77.90 TOTE £2.50: £1.30, £11.50, £11.00; EX 68.40 Trifecta £2298.50.
Owner Mrs Jean R Bishop **Bred** Liam Brady **Trained** Milborne Port, Dorset

FOCUS
An interesting bumper, though as is so often the case with races like this there was no pace on at all until well past halfway.
T/Jkpt: Not won. £7958.60 carried forward to Newbury on Saturday the 8th of February. T/Plt: £285.60 to a £1 stake. Pool: £147,350.52 - 376.63 winning units. T/Qpdt: £81.20 to a £1 stake. Pool: £12,094.05 - 110.20 winning units. JN

3721 NEWCASTLE (L-H)
Friday, February 7
4136 Meeting Abandoned - Waterlogged

3714 NEWBURY (L-H)
Saturday, February 8
OFFICIAL GOING: Heavy (hdl 5.3, chs 5.4)
The first two fences in the home straight were omitted.
Wind: Strong across Weather: Changeable

4143 CASH OUT YOUR SATURDAY MULTIPLES WITH BETFAIR NOVICES' HURDLE (8 hdls) 2m 110y
1:20 (1:20) (Class 3) 4-Y-0+ **£6,498** (£1,908; £954; £477)

Form RPR
1- **1** **Calipto (FR)**[71] 2796 4-11-2 0... DarylJacob 137+
(Paul Nicholls) *trckd ldrs in 3rd chal travelling wl 2 out and sn led: drvn out run-in* **4/6**[1]

320- **2** *5* **Little Jon**[42] 3357 6-10-9 0.. RyanHatch(7) 129
(Nigel Twiston-Davies) *led: jnd 2 out: sn hdd and dropped to cl 3rd: rallied to chse wnr last and kpt on wl but nvr any ch* **16/1**

102- **3** *5* **Seedling**[71] 2802 5-11-2 0.. APMcCoy 125
(Charles Egerton) *trckd ldr: chal 2 out and wnt 2nd briefly sn after: dropped to 3rd last and sn no ch w ldng duo* **11/4**[2]

4 *30* **Justification**[79] 2637 6-11-2 0.. JamieMoore 100
(Gary Moore) *nt fluent in rr: hdwy to cl on ldrs 3 out: styd in tch tl wknd fr 2 out* **6/1**[3]

/06- **5** *43* **No No Charlie (IRE)**[89] 2426 7-11-2 0................................ NoelFehily 51
(Charlie Longsdon) *towards rr: lost tch fr 3 out: t.o* **33/1**

4m 8.37s (-1.63) **Going Correction** +0.175s/f (Yiel) **5** Ran SP% **109.8**
Speed ratings (Par 107): **110,107,105,91,70**
CSF £11.27 TOTE £1.50: £1.10, £4.40; EX 11.70 Trifecta £33.10.
Owner Ian Fogg & Chris Giles **Bred** Andre Priolet **Trained** Ditcheat, Somerset

FOCUS
All rails moved in on both courses. The ground was given as heavy (GoingStick: Hurdle 5.3, Chase 5.4) and the winning time of this opening novice hurdle was 20.37sec outside the standard. There was a strong wind, roughly against them, in the home straight. This didn't look a particularly strong race for the track. The winner was the form pick but this still rates a step up.

4144 READ NICHOLLS AND MCCAIN EXCLUSIVELY ON BETFAIR H'CAP HURDLE (12 hdls) 3m 110y
1:50 (1:50) (Class 2) (0-145,139) 4-Y-0+
£12,512 (£3,696; £1,848; £924; £462; £232)

Form RPR
64F- **1** **Upswing (IRE)**[44] 3292 6-11-1 **128**.. APMcCoy 133
(Jonjo O'Neill) *hld up in rr: nt fluent 5th: stdy hdwy 3 out: trckd ldr after 2 out: styd on wl u.p after last to ld fnl 140yds: gamely* **11/4**[1]

F/1- **2** *½* **Rydon Pynes**[95] 2279 6-10-12 **125**..................................... HaddenFrost 129
(Martin Hill) *in tch: trckd ldrs after 4 out: led after 3 out: 3 l clr and drvn appr last: hdd fnl 140yds: kpt on but no ex clsng stages* **9/1**

234- **3** *3* **Brackloon High (IRE)**[21] 3784 9-10-6 **119**..................... RichardJohnson 121
(Brendan Powell) *chsd ldrs: rdn 3 out: hit 2 out: rallied styd styd on for 3rd run-in but no imp on ldng duo* **16/1**

532- **4** *nk* **Kilmurvy (IRE)**[23] 3741 6-10-12 **125**...............................(tp) NickScholfield 126
(Jeremy Scott) *led and blnd 2: styd pressing ldrs and led 6th: hdd next: styd chalng and led after 4 out: jnd 3 out: hdd sn after: nt fluent last: styd on same pce u.p run-in* **7/1**[3]

001- **5** *23* **Virginia Ash (IRE)**[26] 3691 6-10-2 **115**.......................(p) BrendanPowell 93
(Colin Tizzard) *led to 2nd: styd pressing ldrs: led 5th: hdd next: led again 7th: hdd after 4 out: rdn bef next: sn wknd* **9/1**

136- **6** *1 ¼* **Scholastica**[43] 3319 7-10-12 **125**.......................... FelixDeGiles 101
(Tom Symonds) *chsd ldrs: lost position 7th: sme prog u.p bef 3 out: wknd sn after* **16/1**

415- **7** *3 ¼* **Moorlands Mist**[42] 3359 7-10-12 **132**..................... ThomasCheesman[(7)] 105
(Philip Hobbs) *in tch: drvn along after 5th: wknd bef 3 out* **8/1**

322- **8** *10* **Pateese (FR)**[42] 3369 9-11-5 **139**.......................(p) ChrisDavies[(7)] 102
(Philip Hobbs) *in tch: hdwy appr 3 out: sn wknd* **12/1**

152- **P** **Flicka Williams (IRE)**[39] 3430 7-11-11 **138**.................... DougieCostello
(Tony Coyle) *in rr: pushed along after 4 out: wknd and p.u bef next* **16/1**

142- **F** **Andy Kelly (IRE)**[50] 3186 5-11-0 **130**............................ GavinSheehan[(3)] 121
(Emma Lavelle) *led after 2f: sn hrd pressed: narrowly hdd 5th: styd chalng to 3 out: wknd next: 5th and no ch whn fell last* **4/1**[2]

6m 22.5s (14.20) **Going Correction** +0.175s/f (Yiel) **10** Ran SP% **115.6**
Speed ratings (Par 109): **84,83,82,82,75 75,73,70, ,**
CSF £27.74 CT £334.51 TOTE £3.60: £1.50, £3.10, £3.40; EX 34.70 Trifecta £311.70.
Owner John P McManus **Bred** Darren Quaid **Trained** Cheltenham, Gloucs

FOCUS
A decent handicap hurdle, if not a strong race for the class, and it was understandably run at a steady pace. The first two stuck to the inside in the long home straight. The third and fourth set the level.

4145 BETFAIR DENMAN CHASE (GRADE 2) (14 fncs 4 omitted) 3m
2:25 (2:25) (Class 1) 5-Y-0+ **£28,810** (£11,020; £5,685; £3,000)

Form RPR

133- **1** **Harry Topper**[14] 3888 7-11-10 156.................................(p) JasonMaguire 170+
(Kim Bailey) *trckd ldr to 5th: reminders after 6th: wnt 2nd again 9th: led bef omitted 4th last: clr fr omitted 3rd last: styd on strly* **7/2**[3]

/13- **2** *25* **Al Ferof (FR)**[44] 3262 9-11-10 168.. DarylJacob 145
(Paul Nicholls) *chsd ldrs: drvn to chse wnr bef omitted 4th last but no imp: no ch fr omitted 3rd last* **5/4**[1]

F44- **3** *24* **Katenko (FR)**[21] 3780 8-11-6 156...................................... AidanColeman 117
(Venetia Williams) *led tl hdd bef omitted 4th last: wknd qckly* **9/4**[2]

2/U- **4** *37* **Walkon (FR)**[105] 2071 9-11-0 151..................................(p) RobertThornton 74
(Alan King) *trckd ldr 5th to 9th: hit 12th: wknd wl bef omitted 4th last: t.o whn mstke 2 out* **10/1**

F1P- **P** **Vino Griego (FR)**[21] 3780 9-11-10 154.............................(v) JamieMoore
(Gary Moore) *a in last pl: rdn and lost pl 11th: sn t.o: p.u bef 2 out* **20/1**

6m 6.56s (0.56) **Going Correction** +0.45s/f (Soft) **5** Ran SP% **111.3**
Speed ratings: **117,108,100,88,**
CSF £8.84 TOTE £3.40: £2.30, £1.20; EX 8.60 Trifecta £21.40.
Owner D J Keyte **Bred** The Round Oak Partnership **Trained** Andoversford, Gloucs

FOCUS
This has to rate a step up from Harry Topper, and there's a case for rating the form a lot higher.

4146 BETFAIR CASH OUT CHASE (REGISTERED AS THE GAME SPIRIT CHASE) (GRADE 2) (11 fncs 2 omitted) 2m 1f
3:00 (3:01) (Class 1) 5-Y-0+ **£28,475** (£10,685; £5,350; £2,665)

Form RPR

/24- **1** **Module (FR)**[58] 3032 7-11-2 157....................................... PaddyBrennan 158
(Tom George) *led tl narrowly hdd 9th: sn led again: rdn 2 out: narrowly hdd last: rallied u.p to ld again fnl 75yds: styd on wl* **11/8**[1]

111- **2** *nk* **Dodging Bullets**[43] 3318 6-11-5 155...................................... DarylJacob 161
(Paul Nicholls) *trckd wnr to 5th: pushed along to gor 2nd again 2 out: slt ld last and sn rdn: hdd and no ex fnl 75yds* **2/1**[2]

122- **3** *2 ½* **Raya Star (IRE)**[50] 3185 8-11-0 149................................. RobertThornton 154
(Alan King) *trckd ldrs: wnt 2nd 5th: led and hit 9th: hdd sn after: rdn 2 out and sn dropped to 3rd: rallied run-in and kpt on clsng stages: nt trble ldng duo* **13/2**

112- **4** *29* **Desert Cry (IRE)**[7] 4032 8-11-6 152.................................. JasonMaguire 140
(Donald McCain) *nt fluent 1st: hit: rdn after 8th: no ch fr 9th: tired whn veered bdly lft 2 out* **4/1**[3]

4m 21.55s (13.55) **Going Correction** +0.45s/f (Soft) **4** Ran SP% **108.8**
Speed ratings: **86,85,84,71**
CSF £4.62 TOTE £2.20; EX 3.70 Trifecta £6.00.
Owner Simon W Clarke **Bred** David Lumet & Jean-Marie Baradeau **Trained** Slad, Gloucs

FOCUS
With no natural front-runner in the line-up this predictably turned into a messy, tactical affair. Module was favoured by the weights and is rated back to the level of his Exeter run.

4147 BETFAIR HURDLE H'CAP (GRADE 3) (8 hdls) 2m 110y
3:35 (3:36) (Class 1) 4-Y-0+
£86,848 (£32,589; £16,317; £8,128; £4,087; £2,043)

Form RPR

133- **1** **Splash Of Ginge**[28] 3654 6-10-3 **134**................................. RyanHatch[(7)] 143
(Nigel Twiston-Davies) *led to 4th: chal 3 out: sn led: styd on wl u.p run in* **33/1**

1U- **2** *1 ¾* **Dell' Arca (IRE)**[49] 3200 5-10-12 **136**........................... TomScudamore 144
(David Pipe) *chsd ldrs: sltly hmpd 3 out: sn rdn: styd on wl u.p to take 2nd last strides: no imp on wnr* **15/2**[2]

F01- **3** *nk* **Irish Saint (FR)**[21] 3771 5-11-7 **145** 5ex...........................(t) NoelFehily 152
(Paul Nicholls) *in tch: chsd ldrs after 4 out: chsd wnr fr 2 out: kpt on u.p but no imp run-in: dropped to 3rd last strides* **6/1**[1]

0/1- **4** *2* **Cheltenian (FR)**[39] 3427 8-10-10 **134**.......................... RichardJohnson 140
(Philip Hobbs) *in tch: hdwy 3 out: chsd ldrs sn after: disp 2nd 2 out: one pce u.p run-in* **8/1**[3]

30/- **5** *nse* **Swing Bowler**[333] 4723 7-10-12 **136**............................ ConorO'Farrell 143+
(David Pipe) *chsd ldrs: bmpd 3 out: rdn and one pce next: styd on again u.p run-in: gng on cl home* **20/1**

002- **6** *1 ½* **Alaivan (IRE)**[23] 3744 8-10-1 **130**............................ MauriceLinehan[(5)] 133
(Jonjo O'Neill) *in tch: fr 4th: drvn and hdwy fr 2 out: kpt on run-in: styd on clsng stages* **10/1**

234- **7** *1 ¼* **Chris Pea Green**[49] 3200 5-11-1 **142**........................... JoshuaMoore[(3)] 144
(Gary Moore) *in rr: hdwy after 3 out: styd on u.p appr last: kpt on run-in* **16/1**

/01- **8** *¾* **Vendor (FR)**[70] 2813 6-11-0 **138**..................................... JackDoyle 139
(Alan King) *slowly away and bhd: stl in rr 3 out: hdwy fr 2 out: kpt on wl run-in but nt rch ldrs* **16/1**

9 *3 ½* **Smashing (FR)**[44] 3312 5-11-5 **143**................................... AELynch 144+
(W P Mullins, Ire) *in rr: gd hdwy appr 3 out and sn n.m.r: rdn 2 out: styd on same pce* **10/1**

133- **10** *5* **Jumps Road**[21] 3779 7-10-11 **135**............................. BrendanPowell 128
(Colin Tizzard) *in rr: rdn after 3 out: styd on same pce fr next* **33/1**

/P2- **11** *12* **Totalize**[14] 3891 5-10-5 **129**... AidanColeman 110
(Brian Ellison) *in rr: rdn 3 out: nvr nr ldrs* **12/1**

/06- **12** *1 ¼* **Poet**[23] 3744 9-9-9 **124**.. JamesBanks[(5)] 104
(Clive Cox) *chsd ldrs: rdn 3 out: sn btn* **20/1**

212- **13** *1 ½* **Deep Trouble (IRE)**[28] 3648 7-11-2 **140**............................ DarylJacob 118
(Ben Case) *in rr: sme hdwy 3 out: wknd next* **25/1**

/50- **14** *1 ¼* **Gibb River (IRE)**[70] 2813 8-11-4 **142**................................. APMcCoy 119
(Nicky Henderson) *bhd most of way* **20/1**

/0F- **15** *3 ½* **Recession Proof (FR)**[49] 3200 8-10-7 **134**.................... JakeGreenall[(3)] 107
(John Quinn) *chsd ldrs tl wknd appr 3 out* **20/1**

114/ **16** *10* **Montbazon (FR)**[697] 4833 7-11-2 **140**............................ RobertThornton 103
(Alan King) *in rr: sme hdwy after 4 out: wknd after next* **20/1**

/10- **17** *4 ½* **Rolling Star (FR)**[49] 3200 5-11-12 **150**............................. BarryGeraghty 109
(Nicky Henderson) *chsd ldrs to 3 out* **14/1**

11U- **18** *25* **Act Of Kalanisi (IRE)**[21] 3779 8-11-0 **143**...........(bt) ChristopherWard[(5)] 77
(Dr Richard Newland) *chsd ldr: led 4th: wnt rt 3 out and sn hdd: wknd qckly* **33/1**

323- **P** **Prompter**[58] 3031 7-10-3 **127**.. DominicElsworth
(Jonjo O'Neill) *in rr: t.o whn p.u bef last* **50/1**

/24- **F** **Far West (FR)**[77] 2669 5-11-3 **146**................................. HarryDerham[(5)] 153
(Paul Nicholls) *chsd ldrs: sltly hmpd 3 out: sn rdn: styng on u.p to dispute 4 l 5th whn fell last* **10/1**

4m 7.44s (-2.56) **Going Correction** +0.175s/f (Yiel) **20** Ran SP% **129.0**
Speed ratings (Par 113): **113,112,112,111,111 110,109,109,107,105 99,99,98,97,96 91,89,77, ,**
CSF £246.95 CT £1736.30 TOTE £43.70: £8.10, £2.20, £1.80, £3.20; EX 592.50 Trifecta £5765.70.
Owner J D Neild **Bred** Stewart Pike **Trained** Naunton, Gloucs

FOCUS
Perhaps not a vintage edition of Britain's richest handicap hurdle, but it was typically competitive and the form looks rock solid. The weights went up 2lb following the defection of original topweight Melodic Rendezvous, with Irving another notable absentee. Novices had won three of the previous four runnings and the winner, second and fourth here all come into this category. Six-year-olds have now won four of the last six runnings (were the first three home in 2013), with the winner one of just two runners of that age this year. The pace appeared sound, shared between Act Of Kalanisi and the winner.

4148 IJF 50TH ANNIVERSARY NOVICES' CHASE (14 fncs 4 omitted) 3m
4:10 (4:10) (Class 3) 5-Y-0+ **£7,797** (£2,289; £1,144; £572)

Form RPR

/U1- **1** **Smad Place (FR)**[87] 2459 7-11-5 148.............................. RobertThornton 154+
(Alan King) *trckd ldr: hit 3rd: chal 8th: led next: jnd fr 12th: shkn up whn pressed omitted 3rd last: jnd last: narrowly hdd sn after: rallied and qcknd to ld again fnl 150yds: kpt on wl* **9/4**[2]

/31- **2** *2* **Sam Winner (FR)**[56] 3079 7-11-8 147..................................... DarylJacob 153
(Paul Nicholls) *led: j.big 3rd: jnd 8thm hdd 9th: styd pressing wnr and upsides fr 12th: pushed along omitted 3rd last: chal last: sn slt ld: hdd and no ex fnl 150yds* **5/2**[3]

111- **3** *31* **Mendip Express (IRE)**[38] 3455 8-11-5 147...................(t) MrWBiddick[(3)] 131
(Harry Fry) *chsd ldrs in 3rd: hit 11th: rdn pushed along omitted 4th: last: btn omitted 3rd last* **11/10**[1]

36- **4** *dist* **Danners (IRE)**[15] 3873 8-10-9 0... MrMWall[(5)] 64
(Giles Smyly) *a in last: lost tch fr 10th: t.o* **66/1**

6m 24.36s (18.36) **Going Correction** +0.45s/f (Soft) **4** Ran SP% **108.5**
Speed ratings: **87,86,76,59**
CSF £8.08 TOTE £3.10; EX 6.90 Trifecta £8.10.
Owner Mrs Peter Andrews **Bred** Eric Aubree & Mme Maryse Aubree **Trained** Barbury Castle, Wilts

FOCUS
A key trial for Cheltenham. It was steadily run with relatively fast finishing fractions compared with the earlier race over the trip. Smad Place was rated 161 over hurdles at his best and can probably match that over fences.

4149 BETFAIR COMMITS £40 MILLION TO BRITISH RACING (A STANDARD OPEN NATIONAL HUNT FLAT RACE) (LISTED) 2m 110y
4:40 (4:40) (Class 1) 4-6-Y-0
£11,390 (£4,274; £2,140; £1,066; £536; £268)

Form RPR

1- **1** **Definitly Red (IRE)**[39] 3433 5-11-3 0............................... JasonMaguire 124+
(Steve Gollings) *chsd ldrs: rdn to ld ins fnl 2f and hung rt: styd on wl fnl f* **6/1**[3]

1/ **2** *3 ¼* **Tea For Two**[303] 5262 5-10-10 0.. MissEKelly[(7)] 121+
(Nick Williams) *chsd ldrs: rdn and green whn n.m.r ins fnl 2f: tk 2nd fnl 150yds: no imp on wnr* **14/1**

/21- **3** *5* **Mountain Of Mourne (IRE)**[44] 3295 5-10-10 0.................. MrCSmith[(7)] 117
(Linda Blackford) *disp ld 3f: styd chsng ldr: chal 6f out: led 5f out: rdn 3f out: hdd ins fnl 2f: one pce and dropped to 3rd fnl 150yds* **25/1**

41- **4** *15* **Justanother Muddle**[42] 3363 5-11-3 0............................ MarcGoldstein 101
(Sheena West) *disp ld tl led after 3f: jnd 6f out: hdd 5f out: wknd 2f out* **20/1**

1/1- **5** *8* **Seven Nation Army (IRE)**[50] 3187 5-11-7 0.................. TomScudamore 97
(David Pipe) *chsd ldrs: rdn and btn 4f out* **11/4**[2]

41- **6** *13* **Buckhorn Timothy**[23] 3734 5-11-3 0...................................... JoeTizzard 80
(Colin Tizzard) *chsd ldrs: wknd u.p 3f out* **16/1**

1- **7** *44* **Imagine The Chat**[54] 3133 5-11-3 0... APMcCoy 36
(Rebecca Curtis) *in rr: rdn and btn 5f out* **9/1**

41- **8** *dist* **Thomas Brown**[72] 2759 5-11-3 0.. NoelFehily
(Harry Fry) *in rr: reminders 10f out: wknd 7 out: virtually p.u 6f out* **5/4**[1]

4m 7.9s (3.60) **Going Correction** +0.175s/f (Yiel)
WFA 4 from 5yo 9lb **8** Ran SP% **116.6**
Speed ratings: **98,96,94,87,83 77,56,40**
CSF £84.89 TOTE £7.50: £2.00, £2.50, £3.50; EX 44.50 Trifecta £1143.50.
Owner P J Martin **Bred** James Keegan **Trained** Scamblesby, Lincs
■ Stewards' Enquiry : Miss E Kelly four-day ban: use of whip (22-25 Feb)

FOCUS
An interesting Listed bumper run in bad ground, and a couple of the main players failed to give their running. Al Ferof won this event in 2010, when the race held Grade 2 status. The winner built on his Uttoxeter win.

T/Jkpt: Part won. £21,998.90 to a £1 stake. Pool: £30,984.70 - 0.50 winning tickets. T/Plt: £48.10 to a £1 stake. Pool: £200,572.31 - 3041.56 winning tickets T/Qpdt: £27.30 to a £1 stake. Pool: 11,156.13 - 301.95 winning tickets ST

3427 UTTOXETER (L-H)

Saturday, February 8

4150 Meeting Abandoned - Waterlogged

3857 WARWICK (L-H)

Saturday, February 8

OFFICIAL GOING: Heavy (soft in places) changing to soft (heavy in places) after race 4 (3.15)

The last fence before the hill and the last flight in the back straight were omitted.
Wind: Strong behind Weather: Overcast turning showery after race 4

4157 STARSPORTSBET.CO.UK H'CAP HURDLE (7 hdls 1 omitted) 2m

1:35 (1:35) (Class 4) (0-120,120) 4-Y-0+ **£4,873** (£1,431; £715; £357)

Form RPR

132- **1** **Keel Haul (IRE)**[44] 3269 6-10-13 **107**................................ DenisO'Regan 117+
(Henry Oliver) *a.p: chsd ldr appr 2 out: led last: shkn up flat: styd on wl* **3/1**[1]

1P4- **2** 3 ¼ **King Zeal (IRE)**[23] 3740 10-10-9 **103**.................................(t) LiamHeard 106
(Barry Leavy) *led: clr fr 5th tl rdn appr 2 out: hdd last: styd on same pce flat* **16/1**

243- **3** 1 ¾ **Bohemian Rhapsody (IRE)**[31] 3599 5-11-10 **118**.......... ConorO'Farrell 120
(Seamus Durack) *hld up: hdwy appr 2 out: styd on same pce flat* **3/1**[1]

644- **4** 7 **Chalk It Down (IRE)**[23] 3736 5-11-5 **113**................................ DJCasey 107
(Warren Greatrex) *plld hrd: trckd ldr to 3rd: remained handy tl rdn and wknd appr 2 out* **16/1**

030- **5** 1 **Dormouse**[44] 3269 9-11-5 **116**.......................................(p) MichealNolan(3) 110
(Anabel K Murphy) *hld up: wknd appr 2 out* **6/1**[3]

/P0- **6** 1 ¼ **Somemothersdohavem**[14] 3892 5-11-12 **120**................ LiamTreadwell 112
(Venetia Williams) *hld up: nt fluent 5th: wknd appr 2 out* **7/2**[2]

/60- **7** 10 **The Pier (IRE)**[59] 3028 8-11-7 **115**..................................(t) AndrewTinkler 97
(Anna Brooks) *prom: chsd ldr 5th tl rdn and wknd appr 2 out* **40/1**

4/3- **8** 12 **Switched Off**[257] 512 9-11-11 **119**...[1] AdrianLane 89
(Kevin Frost) *hld up: hdwy 5th: rdn and wknd bef 2 out* **25/1**

23P/ **P** **Valrene**[314] 5037 8-11-2 **110**.. CharliePoste
(Robin Dickin) *hld up: rdn and wknd after 4th: bhd whn p.u bef 2 out* **25/1**

P/ **P** **Ten Bob (IRE)**[654] 5591 8-11-10 **118**.................................... RichieMcLernon
(Jonjo O'Neill) *hld up: plld hrd: hdwy to trck ldr 3rd tl wknd qckly 5th: bhd whn p.u bef 2 out* **14/1**

3m 51.5s (-5.00) **Going Correction** -0.15s/f (Good) **10** Ran SP% **115.1**
Speed ratings (Par 105): **106,104,103,100,99 98,93,87, ,**
CSF £46.09 CT £155.69 TOTE £3.50: £1.20, £9.40, £1.50; EX 64.80 Trifecta £770.30.
Owner R G Whitehead **Bred** Aaron Stronge **Trained** Broomhall, Worcs

FOCUS
A dry day with a strong wind (behind the runners in the home straight) but, given the track had soaked up 20mm of rain since Thursday evening and had survived a morning inspection, conditions were testing. The last fence before the hill and the last hurdle in the back straight were omitted in all races. Mainly exposed performers in a fair handicap. The gallop was reasonable but very few figured and the first three pulled clear. The cosy winner is on the upgrade.

4158 OLBG.COM MARES' HURDLE (LISTED RACE) (9 hdls 2 omitted) 2m 5f

2:05 (2:05) (Class 1) 4-Y-0+ **£12,529** (£4,701; £2,354; £1,172)

Form RPR

/31- **1** **Glens Melody (IRE)**[28] 3649 6-11-5 141.................................. DJCasey 143+
(W P Mullins, Ire) *led at stdy pce tl qcknd after 3 out: hdd and blnd next: rallied u.p to ld flat: all out* **1/1**[1]

462- **2** ½ **Mischievous Milly (IRE)**[28] 3649 6-11-5 138.................. LeightonAspell 140
(Oliver Sherwood) *trckd wnr: wnt upsides 4th: rdn to ld 2 out: sn edgd lft: hdd flat: styd on* **5/2**[2]

/60- **3** 15 **L'Unique (FR)**[83] 2533 5-11-5 138............................... WayneHutchinson 125
(Alan King) *chsd ldrs tl rdn and wknd appr 2 out* **5/1**[3]

113- **4** 50 **Hidden Identity (IRE)**[28] 3649 8-11-0 137........................ MichaelByrne 70
(Tim Vaughan) *hld up: hdwy appr 6th: nt fluent 3 out: rdn and wknd bef next* **7/1**

5m 15.2s (0.20) **Going Correction** +0.10s/f (Yiel) **4** Ran SP% **107.7**
Speed ratings (Par 111): **103,102,97,78**
CSF £3.81 TOTE £2.00; EX 3.10 Trifecta £6.40.
Owner Ms Fiona McStay **Bred** Mrs Fiona McStay **Trained** Muine Beag, Co Carlow

FOCUS
The inaugural running of a Listed mares-only event featuring the trio who filled the first three placings in the same grade over 2m3f at this course last month. A modest gallop only picked up after the third-last hurdle and the first two pulled clear in the straight. The first two are rated a bit better than the bare result.

4159 STAR SPORTS KINGMAKER NOVICES' CHASE (GRADE 2) (10 fncs 2 omitted) 2m

2:40 (2:40) (Class 1) 5-Y-0+ **£22,780** (£8,548; £4,280; £2,132; £1,072)

Form RPR

F15- **1** **Balder Succes (FR)**[63] 2950 6-11-7 145.................. WayneHutchinson 157+
(Alan King) *j.w: disp ld tl wnt on 5th: shkn up appr 2 out: rdn out* **6/5**[1]

131- **2** 3 ½ **Brick Red**[9] 3992 7-11-4 141.. LiamTreadwell 149
(Venetia Williams) *hld up in tch: chsd wnr 6th: rdn appr 2 out: styd on same pce flat* **5/2**[2]

112- **3** 34 **Valco De Touzaine (FR)**[49] 3202 5-11-2 144.......(t) SamTwiston-Davies 115
(Paul Nicholls) *chsd ldrs tl rdn and wknd after 3 out* **3/1**[3]

121- **4** 2 ¼ **Lord Of House (GER)**[23] 3732 6-11-4 138..............................(t) MarkGrant 113
(Charlie Mann) *disp ld to 5th: wknd 8th* **9/1**

544- **5** 32 **Tchang Goon (FR)**[7] 4034 10-11-0 62...............................(p) MrHGMiller 77
(Zoe Davison) *hld up: a in rr: bhd fr 5th* **200/1**

4m 3.1s (-2.50) **Going Correction** +0.10s/f (Yiel)
WFA 5 from 6yo+ 1lb **5** Ran SP% **109.5**
Speed ratings: **110,108,91,90,74**
CSF £4.72 TOTE £1.70: £1.10, £2.40; EX 5.90 Trifecta £13.00.
Owner Masterson Holdings Limited **Bred** Damien Bellanger Et Al **Trained** Barbury Castle, Wilts

FOCUS
A race won in 2009 by the high-class Gauvain and the following year by subsequent Cheltenham Gold Cup and dual King George winner Long Run. This renewal looked to lack a potential superstar but the winner confirmed himself to be bordering on smart. The gallop was an ordinary one and the first two pulled clear from the fourth-last fence. Balder Succes is rated back form but nearly 10lb shy of the typical Arkle winner.

4160 CALL STAR SPORTS ON 08000 521 321 H'CAP CHASE (15 fncs 2 omitted) 2m 4f 110y

3:15 (3:15) (Class 2) 5-Y-0+

£18,768 (£5,544; £2,772; £1,386; £693; £348)

Form RPR

031- **1** **Mr Moonshine (IRE)**[38] 3476 10-11-4 **143**.............................. RyanMania 156+
(Sue Smith) *mde all: shkn up appr last: rdn clr flat* **13/2**

521- **2** 4 **Persian Snow (IRE)**[16] 3861 8-10-5 **130**.........................(t) TomO'Brien 139
(Philip Hobbs) *a.p: hmpd 1st: trckd wnr 3rd: wnt upsides 11th: rdn and ev ch last: no ex fnl 110yds* **5/2**[1]

312- **3** 5 **No Buts**[16] 3861 6-10-5 **130**... SeanQuinlan 135
(David Bridgwater) *chsd wnr 2nd to 3rd: remained handy: rdn appr 2 out: styd on same pce* **7/2**[2]

232- **4** 6 **Rouge Et Blanc (FR)**[9] 3990 9-10-0 **130**..................... ThomasGarner(5) 128
(Oliver Sherwood) *hld up: rdn and wknd appr 2 out* **5/1**[3]

2FP- **5** 4 ½ **Majala (FR)**[20] 3806 8-11-8 **147**...(t) DenisO'Regan 142
(Tom George) *hld up: hdwy 8th: rdn and wknd appr 2 out* **6/1**

30P- **6** 16 **Drumshambo (USA)**[38] 3458 8-11-6 **145**........................ LiamTreadwell 123
(Venetia Williams) *chsd ldrs: pushed along 9th: wknd 11th* **7/1**

3/0- **P** **Mr Cracker (IRE)**[192] 1168 9-10-12 **140**........................ MichaelByrne(3)
(Tim Vaughan) *w wnr whn slipped on landing 1st and sn lost pl: nt fluent next and 3rd: wknd appr 10th: p.u bef next* **25/1**

5m 22.4s (1.40) **Going Correction** +0.35s/f (Yiel) **7** Ran SP% **111.4**
Speed ratings: **111,109,107,105,103 97,**
CSF £22.71 CT £63.88 TOTE £4.80: £3.50, £1.30; EX 19.20 Trifecta £60.00.
Owner DG Pryde,J Beaumont,DP Van Der Hoeven 1 **Bred** T McIlhagga **Trained** High Eldwick, W Yorks

FOCUS
A decent handicap in which the ordinary gallop suited those right up with the pace. The two horses who won their previous start pulled clear on the approach to the home turn. The winner is rated in line with the best of his novice form.

4161 D.A.D H'CAP HURDLE (10 hdls 2 omitted) 3m 1f

3:50 (3:50) (Class 4) (0-120,120) 4-Y-0+ **£4,873** (£1,431; £715; £357)

Form RPR

442- **1** **Tullyesker Hill (IRE)**[25] 3694 5-11-3 **118**.......................(p) TomBellamy(7) 128+
(David Pipe) *a.p: led 2 out: rdn clr flat* **5/2**[1]

03P- **2** 5 **Cadeau George**[26] 3691 5-10-11 **105**...................................... DavidBass 110+
(Ben Pauling) *led tl appr 2nd: chsd ldr tl led again appr 2 out: hdd 2 out: rdn and blnd last: no ex flat* **50/1**

6P3- **3** 18 **Yellow Ball (FR)**[23] 3743 6-11-12 **120**.............................. LiamTreadwell 106
(Venetia Williams) *led appr 2nd: rdn and hdd befiore 2 out: sn wknd* **12/1**

145- **4** 3 ¼ **Premier Portrait (IRE)**[60] 3013 7-11-1 **114**...................... EdCookson(5) 96
(Kim Bailey) *hld up: hdwy appr 7th: rdn and wknd bef 2 out* **16/1**

055- **5** 25 **Promised Wings (GER)**[37] 3505 7-11-9 **117**..................(v) TomCannon 74
(Chris Gordon) *chsd ldrs: pushed along 3rd: rdn and lost pl next: bhd fr 6th* **33/1**

/33- **6** nk **Westerly Breeze (IRE)**[37] 3506 6-10-11 **105**........................ IanPopham 61
(Martin Keighley) *chsd ldrs: nt fluent 6th: rdn and wknd after 3 out* **14/1**

64- **7** 30 **Garde Fou (FR)**[28] 3643 8-10-10 **104**.................................... TomO'Brien 30
(Paul Henderson) *hld up: a in rr: bhd fr 7th* **14/1**

5/F- **P** **Mac Steamy (IRE)**[283] 68 8-11-2 **110**.....................................(t) RyanMahon
(William Kinsey) *hld up: rdn and wknd appr 7th: bhd whn p.u bef 3 out* **50/1**

120- **P** **Kilrush (IRE)**[23] 3741 8-11-6 **117**.................................... MichaelByrne(3)
(Neil Mulholland) *hld up: hdwy appr 7th: wknd bef next: bhd whn p.u bef 2 out* **14/1**

231- **P** **He's The Daddy**[44] 3280 7-11-1 **109**.......................(t) SamTwiston-Davies
(Nigel Twiston-Davies) *hld up in tch: rdn and wknd bef 3 out: bhd whn p.u bef next* **11/2**[3]

312- **F** **It's A Doddle (IRE)**[20] 3802 6-11-9 **117**......................... RichieMcLernon 94
(Jonjo O'Neill) *hld up: hdwy after 3 out: 5th and wkng whn fell next* **4/1**[2]

112- **P** **Night Of Passion (IRE)**[26] 3691 6-11-1 **109**.......................(p) NickScholfield
(Jeremy Scott) *hld up: rdn after 6th: wknd bef next: bhd whn p.u bef 2 out* **8/1**

6m 24.5s (9.50) **Going Correction** +0.35s/f (Yiel) **12** Ran SP% **115.5**
Speed ratings (Par 105): **98,96,90,89,81 81,71, , ,**
CSF £122.18 CT £1263.57 TOTE £3.70: £1.20, £11.90, £5.00; EX 136.60 Trifecta £706.70.
Owner Bryan Drew **Bred** Miss Patricia McGlynn **Trained** Nicholashayne, Devon

FOCUS
A fair handicap in which a decent gallop saw the field finish at lengthy intervals. The first two pulled clear in the home straight, with a step up from the winner.

4162 STARSPORTSBET.CO.UK NOVICES' CHASE (18 fncs 2 omitted) 3m 2f

4:25 (4:27) (Class 3) 5-Y-0+ **£9,615** (£3,003; £1,617)

Form RPR

1U2- **1** **Midnight Prayer**[52] 3162 9-11-7 135......................... WayneHutchinson 146+
(Alan King) *trckd ldr: led 14th: clr after 3 out: easily* **8/13**[1]

/U1- **2** 53 **Count Guido Deiro (IRE)**[44] 3293 7-11-7 128........ SamTwiston-Davies 111
(Nigel Twiston-Davies) *led: pushed along 12th: hdd 14th: wknd after 3 out* **2/1**[2]

36- **3** 93 **Spike Mac (IRE)**[20] 3800 9-11-0 0.................................... AndrewThornton
(Richard Harper) *bhd fr 3rd* **100/1**

4P1- **R** **Alpha Victor (IRE)**[13] 3921 9-11-7 130........................... PeterBuchanan
(William Kinsey) *ref 1st* **7/1**[3]

7m 11.3s (18.60) **Going Correction** +0.60s/f (Soft) **4** Ran SP% **108.7**
Speed ratings: **95,78,50,**
CSF £2.33 TOTE £1.40; EX 2.50 Trifecta £15.80.
Owner The Legends Partnership **Bred** J P L Reynolds **Trained** Barbury Castle, Wilts

The Form Book Jumps, Raceform Ltd, Compton, RG20 6NL.

FOCUS
A race won last year but subsequent Scottish National winner Godsmejudge and, although this year's renewal wasn't a strong one for the money on offer, it threw up a very useful performance from the wide-margin winner. It's impossible to put an accurate figure on this performance.

4163 FOLLOW US ON TWITTER @STARSPORTS_BET NOVICES' HURDLE (9 hdls 2 omitted) 2m 5f
4:55 (4:55) (Class 3) 4-Y-0+ £6,498 (£1,908; £954; £477)

Form RPR
1- **1** **Royal Player**[25] 3697 5-11-11 0 TomO'Brien 131+
(Philip Hobbs) *mde all: shkn up and 4 l ahd whn lft wl clr 2 out* 11/4[3]
212- **2** 10 **Algernon Pazham (IRE)**[40] 3417 5-11-4 125 SamTwiston-Davies 114
(Nigel Twiston-Davies) *hld up: hdwy 3 out: rdn and wkng whn lft 2nd and hmpd next* 2/1[2]
26- **3** 16 **Vivaldi Collonges (FR)**[38] 3454 5-11-4 0 NickScholfield 99
(Paul Nicholls) *chsd ldrs: nt fluent 6th: rdn and wkng whn lft 3rd 2 out* 15/8[1]
/56- **4** 61 **Know More Oats (IRE)**[25] 3695 6-11-1 0 GilesHawkins[(3)] 34
(Victor Dartnall) *chsd wnr to 6th: wknd next* 25/1
6/F- **F** **Ready Token (IRE)**[23] 3735 6-11-1 0 KielanWoods[(3)] 117
(Charlie Longsdon) *prom: chsd wnr 6th: 4 l down and rdn whn fell 2 out* 8/1

5m 22.4s (7.40) **Going Correction** +0.60s/f (Soft) 5 Ran SP% **109.7**
Speed ratings (Par 107): **109,105,99,75,**
CSF £8.81 TOTE £2.60: £1.70, £1.30; EX 7.30 Trifecta £9.70.
Owner Mrs Diana L Whateley **Bred** Mrs R M Wilson **Trained** Withycombe, Somerset

FOCUS
Only a handful of runners but a useful novice hurdle in which a modest gallop picked up turning for home. The winner is the type to rate higher and win again.
T/Plt: £23.90 to a £1 stake. Pool: £106,047.71 - 3235.60 winning units. T/Qpdt: £11.80 to a £1 stake. Pool: £4851.60 - 301.80 winning units. CR

4164 - 4170a (Foreign Racing) - See Raceform Interactive

3693 EXETER (R-H)
Sunday, February 9

OFFICIAL GOING: Heavy
Scheduled chases abandoned. Middle flight in home straight omitted, flight after winning post moved to back straight.
Wind: quite strong breeze behind Weather: sunny periods with snow/rain showers

4171 BATHWICK TYRES "NATIONAL HUNT" NOVICES' HURDLE (8 hdls 2 omitted) 2m 3f
1:25 (1:25) (Class 4) 4-Y-0+ £4,548 (£1,335; £667; £333)

Form RPR
/24- **1** **Arthur's Oak**[24] 3735 6-11-4 0 AidanColeman 120+
(Venetia Williams) *mde all: styd on dourly fr 2 out: rdn out* 9/2[3]
54- **2** 7 **Castletown (IRE)**[8] 4029 6-11-4 0 (t) DougieCostello 111+
(Laura Young) *mid-div: rdn and hdwy appr 2 out: styd on wl fr last: wnt 2nd towards fin* 20/1
/33- **3** 3 ¾ **Unowhatimeanharry**[74] 2740 6-11-4 115 PaulMoloney 107
(Helen Nelmes) *t.k.h: trckd wnr: rdn appr 2 out: hld by wnr whn lost 2nd briefly between last 2: regained 2nd at the last tl no ex nring fin* 9/4[2]
4 5 **Dormello Mo (FR)**[109] 4-11-0 123 DarylJacob 99
(Paul Nicholls) *hld up towards rr: hdwy fr 3rd: trckd ldrs 6th: rdn bef 2 out: chsd wnr briefly between last 2: no ex fr last* 13/8[1]
05- **5** 11 **Silvergrove**[26] 3695 6-11-4 0 (t) ConorO'Farrell 97
(Richard Woollacott) *mid-div: hdwy 6th: sn rdn: styd on but nvr any real imp on ldrs* 12/1
636- **6** 14 **Y A Bon (IRE)**[22] 3782 6-11-4 0 HaddenFrost 77
(Martin Hill) *mid-div: rdn after 6th: sn btn* 33/1
7 8 **Wilde And Willing (IRE)** 6-11-4 0 AndrewThornton 69
(Seamus Mullins) *a towards rr* 25/1
0- **8** nk **Tresor De La Vie (FR)**[105] 2106 7-11-4 0 (tp) JackDoyle 69
(Victor Dartnall) *t.k.h: trckd wnr tl rdn appr 2 out: wknd bef last* 20/1
003- **9** 3 ¾ **Another Brandy (IRE)**[17] 3861 6-11-1 0 MichaelByrne[(3)] 65
(Neil Mulholland) *hld up towards rr of midfield: hdwy 6th: sn rdn: wknd bef next* 40/1
- **10** 26 **Master Max** 7-11-4 0 NickScholfield 39
(Jeremy Scott) *untidy 1st: a bhd: t.o fr after 6th* 25/1
0- **11** 1 **Hot Pepper**[43] 3363 6-11-4 0 JamesDavies 38
(Chris Down) *mid-div tl wknd after 6th: t.o* 100/1
P **Saint Breiz (FR)**[665] 8-10-11 0 MrRobertHawker[(7)]
(Carroll Gray) *trckd ldrs: sddle slipped after 2nd: nt rcvr and p.u bef next* 33/1
00- **U** **Back By Midnight**[87] 2472 5-10-13 0 JamesBanks[(5)]
(Emma Baker) *t.k.h: trckd ldrs: rdn after 6th: fading in 7th whn blnd and uns rdr 2 out* 100/1
0- **U** **Catch The Katt**[83] 2570 7-10-11 0 (b[1]) DaveCrosse
(Richard Mitchell) *mid-div tl 3rd: in rr whn stmbld bdly and uns rdr after 6th* 250/1

5m 3.3s (20.60) **Going Correction** +1.05s/f (Soft)
WFA 4 from 5yo+ 9lb 14 Ran SP% **122.7**
Speed ratings (Par 105): **98,95,93,91,86 80,77,77,75,64 64, , ,**
CSF £86.92 TOTE £5.00: £1.70, £4.80, £1.70; EX 28.80 Trifecta £192.20.
Owner Mrs J K Burt **Bred** J L Burt **Trained** Kings Caple, H'fords

FOCUS
Hurdle course out wide, tight to chase course on mostly fresh ground. A modest novice hurdle but the time compared favourably to the following handicap. A big step up from the winner.

4172 BATHWICK TYRES TAUNTON CONDITIONAL JOCKEYS' TRAINING SERIES H'CAP HURDLE (8 hdls 2 omitted) 2m 3f
1:55 (1:55) (Class 4) (0-110,110) 4-Y-0 £4,431 (£1,309; £654; £327; £163)

Form RPR
312- **1** **The Happy Warrior**[34] 3569 6-10-0 89 GaryDerwin[(5)] 96+
(Bob Buckler) *disp tl after 2nd: trckd ldr: rdn into ld whn blnd 2 out and rdr lost iron: rcvrd bef last: styd on: rdn out* 5/2[2]
06- **2** 2 ½ **Kilavalley (IRE)**[21] 3802 7-11-6 107 (p) ConorRing[(3)] 108
(Hugo Froud) *hld up bhd ldrs: hdwy into 3rd after 6th: rdn bef next: wnt 2nd between last 2: styd on but a being hld fr last* 25/1
/P3- **3** 2 ½ **Just Spot**[22] 3788 7-10-8 100 JonPark[(8)] 98
(Kevin Bishop) *hld up bhd ldrs: rdn into 4th appr 2 out: wnt 3rd bef last: styd on* 10/1
/56- **4** 6 **Supreme Bob (IRE)**[24] 3729 8-11-6 109 AlanJohns[(5)] 101
(Lucy Jones) *hld up bhd ldrs: rdn after 6th: sn hld: wnt 4th run-in* 9/1

P14/ **5** 1 ½ **Mystic Appeal (IRE)**[294] 5440 8-11-1 107 (p) ChrisMeehan[(8)] 98
(Jeremy Scott) *t.k.h: disp tl after 2nd: trckd ldrs: rdn bef 2 out: sn btn* 10/1
/31- **6** 3 ¼ **Dungeness**[29] 3650 6-11-2 103 TomBellamy[(3)] 96+
(Venetia Williams) *disp tl clr ldr after 2nd: drvn along w stirrup leather broke on home turn: hdd bef next: lost 2 pls between last 2: wknd run-in* 2/1[1]
5F0- **7** 97 **Sedgemoor Top Bid (IRE)**[12] 3959 6-10-6 95 ThomasCheesman[(5)]
(Nigel Hawke) *hld up bhd ldrs: rdn after 3rd: wknd after 6th: t.o* 66/1
212- **P** **The Rattler Obrien (IRE)**[59] 3044 8-11-4 102 (p) ConorShoemark
(Martin Hill) *trckd ldrs: pushed along after 2nd: drvn after next: sn dropped to rr: tailing off whn p.u bef 6th* 5/1[3]

5m 9.0s (26.30) **Going Correction** +1.05s/f (Soft) 8 Ran SP% **112.1**
Speed ratings (Par 105): **86,84,83,81,80 79,38,**
CSF £51.80 CT £529.16 TOTE £3.70: £1.20, £4.40, £3.60; EX 48.60 Trifecta £219.40.
Owner Nick Elliott **Bred** H G Llewellyn **Trained** Henley, Somerset

FOCUS
Plenty of drama in this modest handicap hurdle, and a slow-motion finish. The time was 5.7sec slower than the previous novice hurdle. This rates a small step up from the winner.

4173 BATHWICK TYRES PLYMOUTH NOVICES' HURDLE (LISTED RACE) (7 hdls 1 omitted) 2m 1f
2:25 (2:25) (Class 1) 4-Y-0+ £11,390 (£4,274; £2,140; £1,066; £536)

Form RPR
522- **1** **Vibrato Valtat (FR)**[44] 3322 5-11-3 129 (t) DarylJacob 140+
(Paul Nicholls) *hld up 5th: wnt 4th after 3rd: travelling strly whn upsides ldr run-in: qcknd ahd fnl 75yds: readily* 7/5[1]
331- **2** 3 ¼ **Tiqris**[19] 3826 6-11-9 130 (t) RichardJohnson 131
(Philip Hobbs) *chsd clr ldr: clsd on ldr appr 2 out: slt ld last: sn rdn: outpcd by wnr fnl 75yds* 7/2[3]
532- **3** 6 **Revaader**[24] 3747 6-10-10 103 TommyPhelan 113
(Mark Gillard) *j.lft most of way: led: sn clr: j. quite bdly lft 2 out: rdn and hung lft after 2 out: hdd whn nt fluent last: sn hld* 33/1
031- **4** 27 **Hint Of Mint**[33] 3592 5-11-9 127 WayneHutchinson 98
(Nick Williams) *hld up 4th: struggling bef 5th: sn detached: wnt modest 4th bef last: t.o* 10/1
3- **5** 33 **Chocala (IRE)**[72] 2796 4-10-7 0 RobertThornton 68
(Alan King) *chsd ldrs: nudged along after 4th: rdn after next: wknd next: t.o* 2/1[2]

4m 30.3s (14.80) **Going Correction** +1.05s/f (Soft)
WFA 4 from 5yo+ 9lb 5 Ran SP% **109.3**
Speed ratings (Par 111): **107,105,102,89,74**
CSF £6.68 TOTE £2.40: £1.50, £2.10; EX 6.20 Trifecta £33.20.
Owner Axom XLIII **Bred** Mme C Duperret & Mlle A-M Duperret **Trained** Ditcheat, Somerset

FOCUS
There are some star names on this Listed event's roll of honour, Melodic Rendezvous taking the race 12 months ago. It was run at a solid gallop. The easy winner was value for lot further and comfirmed the merit of his good Sandown run, while the next two ran to their best.

4174 PERTEMPS NETWORK H'CAP HURDLE (SERIES QUALIFIER) (10 hdls 2 omitted) 2m 7f 110y
2:55 (2:56) (Class 2) 5-Y-0+
£12,512 (£3,696; £1,848; £924; £462; £232)

Form RPR
120/ **1** **Fingal Bay (IRE)**[429] 2893 8-11-7 **142** RichardJohnson 152+
(Philip Hobbs) *trckd ldrs: led 5th: wnt sltly rt whn 1 1/2 l up last: sn rdn: a holding on* 9/2[2]
/12- **2** ½ **If In Doubt (IRE)**[29] 3646 6-11-0 **135** TomO'Brien 143
(Philip Hobbs) *hld up towards rr: smooth hdwy fr after 6th: rdn to chse wnr after 2 out: 1 1/2 l down last: styd on wl fnl 75yds: nvr quite getting there* 6/1
/02- **3** 10 **Imperial Leader (IRE)**[22] 3771 6-10-8 **129** (t) SamTwiston-Davies 129
(Nigel Twiston-Davies) *in tch: wnt 4th after 8th: rdn bef 2 out: wnt 3rd bef last: styd on same pce* 13/2
P25- **4** 3 ½ **Quartz De Thaix (FR)**[15] 3890 10-11-12 **147** (b) AidanColeman 142
(Venetia Williams) *led tl 4th: prom: rdn after 7th: kpt in tch: styd on same pce fr 2 out: lft 4th at last* 20/1
/44- **5** 14 **Broadway Buffalo (IRE)**[89] 2433 6-11-4 **139** (t) ConorO'Farrell 121
(David Pipe) *hld up towards rr: hdwy after 7th: rdn to chse ldrs appr 2 out: wknd between last 2* 12/1
206- **6** 1 ¼ **Old Tricks (IRE)**[10] 3989 7-10-0 **121** oh4 (p) BrendanPowell 101
(Colin Tizzard) *prom: led 4th tl next: pressed wnr tl rdn appr 2 out: wknd between last 2* 25/1
F21- **7** 33 **Carole's Destrier**[38] 3506 6-10-6 **130** MichaelByrne[(3)] 76
(Neil Mulholland) *in tch: rdn appr 8th: sn wknd: t.o* 11/2[3]
36F- **8** 6 **Tweedledrum**[8] 4040 7-9-13 **125** (p) BenPoste[(5)] 65
(Tom Symonds) *a struggling in rr: t.o* 40/1
/24- **9** nk **Berkeley Barron (IRE)**[106] 2079 6-10-6 **130** (t) MichealNolan[(3)] 70
(Philip Hobbs) *mid-div: struggling bef 5th: wknd 8th: t.o* 16/1
121- **10** 2 ¾ **Return Spring (IRE)**[39] 3457 7-11-5 **143** JamesBest[(3)] 80
(Philip Hobbs) *trckd ldrs: rdn after 7th: wknd after next: t.o* 14/1
05P- **P** **Bathwick Brave (IRE)**[24] 3745 7-10-7 **128** (t) DougieCostello
(Johnny Farrelly) *mid-div: rdn after 6th: losing pl whn p.u bef 8th* 50/1
1/0- **F** **Top Gamble (IRE)**[86] 2490 6-10-12 **133** (t) TomScudamore 130
(David Pipe) *mid-div: hdwy fr 6th: rdn to chse wnr appr 2 out: styng on at same pce in hld 4th whn fell last* 3/1[1]

6m 17.4s (18.40) **Going Correction** +1.05s/f (Soft) 12 Ran SP% **119.4**
Speed ratings: **111,110,107,106,101 101,90,88,88,87 ,**
CSF £31.07 CT £178.13 TOTE £4.60: £1.50, £2.10, £3.20; EX 22.90 Trifecta £205.40.
Owner Mrs R J Skan **Bred** James Kinsella **Trained** Withycombe, Somerset

FOCUS
The first running of this Exeter qualifier for the Pertemps Final, and a competitive, well contested event. The first eight home qualify for the final. The pace was sound and the form should pay to follow.

4175 BATHWICK TYRES BRIDGWATER NOVICES' HURDLE (9 hdls 2 omitted) 2m 5f 110y
3:25 (3:25) (Class 4) 5-Y-0+ £4,431 (£1,309; £654; £327; £163)

Form RPR
041- **1** **Toubeera**[27] 3689 8-11-12 130 AidanColeman 136+
(Venetia Williams) *trckd ldrs: led appr 2 out: sn rdn: styd on wl fr last: rdn out* 10/3[3]
/03- **2** 4 ½ **Howlongisafoot (IRE)**[57] 3086 5-10-12 0 DarylJacob 119+
(Paul Nicholls) *in tch: wnt 2nd appr 2 out: sn rdn and edgd lft: ev ch last tl hung towards paddock entrnce run-in: hld after* 3/1[2]

234- **3** *9* **Sky Watch (IRE)**[26] 3695 7-10-9 120 (t) GavinSheehan(3) 111
(Warren Greatrex) *racd wd: hld up towards rr: hdwy after 5th: rdn to chse ldng pair whn wnt rt and nt fluent 2 out: styd on same pce* **4/1**

4 *31* **Paddy The Oscar (IRE)**[434] 11-10-5 0 ConorRing(7) 77
(Grace Harris) *disp ld: outrt ldr after 7th tl rdn bef next: wknd between last 2* **16/1**

5- **5** *15* **Farasi Kubwa**[49] 3225 6-10-12 0 LiamTreadwell 62
(Venetia Williams) *trckd ldrs: pushed along whn nt fluent 6th: rdn after next: wknd bef 2 out: t.o* **16/1**

0- **6** *7* **Dream Lucky**[10] 3988 9-10-9 0 MattGriffiths(3) 55
(Richard Woollacott) *mid-div tl after 3rd: towards rr: wknd after 7th: t.o* **50/1**

000- **7** *1 1/2* **Baksheesh**[22] 3783 5-10-12 0 WillKennedy 54
(Sue Gardner) *a towards rr: t.o* **200/1**

8 *nk* **Exmoor Challenge** 5-10-12 0 LiamHeard 53
(Jeremy Scott) *a towards rr: t.o* **66/1**

4- **9** *1 1/4* **Kudu Shine**[26] 3697 8-10-12 0 ConorO'Farrell 52
(Richard Woollacott) *disp ld tl after 7th: sn rdn: wknd next: t.o* **11/4**[1]

00- **10** *18* **Moorlands George**[26] 3697 6-10-12 0 NickScholfield 34
(Jeremy Scott) *mid-div tl wknd after 7th: t.o* **50/1**

604- **11** *dist* **Pure Poteen (IRE)**[17] 3861 6-10-12 0 (t) DougieCostello
(Neil Mulholland) *mid-div tl 4th: hit next: sn bhd: t.o* **50/1**

6m 2.2s (29.20) **Going Correction** +1.05s/f (Soft) 11 Ran SP% **114.4**
Speed ratings: **88,86,83,71,66 63,63,63,62,56 39**
CSF £13.56 TOTE £4.30: £1.60, £1.30, £1.40; EX 12.30 Trifecta £29.00.

Owner Richard Britten-Long **Bred** Mrs H I S Calzini **Trained** Kings Caple, H'fords

FOCUS
Not much depth to this novice hurdle. The winner was rated to her Plumpton form.

4176 BATHWICK TYRES BARNSTAPLE H'CAP HURDLE (10 hdls 2 omitted) 2m 7f 110y
4:00 (4:01) (Class 4) (0-125,105) 4-Y-O **£4,431** (£1,309; £654; £327; £163)

Form RPR

/4F- **1** **Tarabela**[27] 3688 11-11-10 103 (t) BrendanPowell 115+
(Johnny Farrelly) *hld up in chsng gp: hdwy appr 5th: chsd clr ldr 7th: clsd on ldr after next: led bef 2 out: sn clr and wl in command: hit last: eased nr fin* **5/1**[2]

63P- **2** *19* **Rocky Bender (IRE)**[27] 3691 9-11-9 102 (b[1]) AidanColeman 91
(Venetia Williams) *j.rt: led: clr 3rd: rdn after 8th: hdd bef 2 out: sn wknd but wl clr of remainder* **5/2**[1]

005- **3** *17* **Thedeboftheyear**[41] 3425 10-10-6 92 KieronEdgar(7) 58
(Chris Down) *trckd ldrs in chsng gp: chsd clr ldr 5th tl 7th: wknd after next: t.o* **5/2**[1]

P/0- **4** *18* **Kapricorne (FR)**[9] 4021 7-10-4 83 PaulMoloney 31
(Sophie Leech) *hld up: wnt poor 4th after 8th: nvr any danger: t.o* **12/1**

5P3- **5** *8* **Ballyegan (IRE)**[26] 3696 9-10-0 79 (t) GerardTumelty 19
(Bob Buckler) *chsd clr ldr tl rdn after 6th: sn no ch: t.o* **8/1**

/4P- **6** *33* **Tara Tavey (IRE)**[45] 3250 9-10-5 94 JonPark(10)
(Kevin Bishop) *trckd ldrs in chsng gp: reminders after 3rd: wknd after 5th: t.o fr 7th* **20/1**

00- **7** *5* **Solid Concrete (IRE)**[43] 3357 8-10-4 90 MrLKilgarriff(7)
(Neil Mulholland) *trckd ldr in chsng gp: rdn after 4th: sn lost pl: t.o fr 7th* **12/1**

012- **P** **Clouds Of Mist**[252] 595 9-11-2 100 MissLucyGardner(5)
(Sue Gardner) *hld up in chsng gp: hdwy 5th: wknd 7th: t.o whn p.u after 8th* **15/2**[3]

6m 35.6s (36.60) **Going Correction** +1.05s/f (Soft) 8 Ran SP% **116.8**
Speed ratings (Par 105): **81,74,69,63,60 49,47,**
CSF £18.87 CT £38.61 TOTE £3.90: £1.40, £1.30, £1.80; EX 21.40 Trifecta £79.80.

Owner G2 Recruitment Solutions Ltd **Bred** Mrs S M Reeks **Trained** Bridgwater, Somerset

FOCUS
A weak staying handicap. They came home at wide intervals and the time was 18secs slower than the earlier Pertemps Qualifier. The form is rated around the first two.

4177 BATHWICK TYRES INTERMEDIATE OPEN NATIONAL HUNT FLAT RACE 2m 1f
4:30 (4:30) (Class 6) 4-6-Y-O **£1,624** (£477; £238; £119)

Form RPR

0- **1** **Trickaway (IRE)**[113] 1974 6-11-4 0 RichardJohnson 105+
(Philip Hobbs) *mde all: hung lft fr 2f out: rdn ent fnl f: swishing tail but on top fnl 75yds: rdn out* **11/10**[1]

2 *3* **Dancing Shadow (IRE)** 5-11-4 0 JackDoyle 100+
(Victor Dartnall) *in tch: prom 7f out: rdn to chal whn hung lft fr over 2f out: kpt pressing wnr but hanging lft: hld fnl 75yds* **15/2**

3 *30* **Essteepee** 5-11-1 0 MichaelByrne(3) 70
(Tim Vaughan) *hld up last but in tch: wnt prom 7f out tl 6f out: rdn to chse ldng pair 3f out: wknd over 1f out* **7/1**[3]

4 *46* **Harry Partridge** 5-11-4 0 WillKennedy 24
(Sue Gardner) *in tch: upsides ldr after 6f tl 6f out: wknd 4f out: t.o* **14/1**

0- **5** *1 3/4* **Wolfe Mountain (IRE)**[55] 3133 5-11-4 0 IanPopham 22
(Linda Blackford) *t.k.h: trckd ldrs: jnd wnr after 4f tl 5f out: rdn 4f out: wknd 3f out: t.o* **16/1**

6 *25* **Flinstone (IRE)**[112] 5-11-4 0 RichieMcLernon
(Jonjo O'Neill) *trckd ldrs: nudged along 5f out: wknd 3f out: t.o* **3/1**[2]

P **Mr Toy Boy** 4-10-8 0 PaulMoloney
(Helen Nelmes) *racd wd: in tch: prom 7f out tl 6f out: sn wknd: t.o whn p.u 4f out* **20/1**

4m 37.6s (28.80) **Going Correction** +1.05s/f (Soft)
WFA 4 from 5yo+ 9lb 7 Ran SP% **114.2**
Speed ratings: **74,72,58,36,36 24,**
CSF £10.31 TOTE £2.80: £1.50, £2.60; EX 6.80 Trifecta £56.80.

Owner The Mount Fawcus Partnership **Bred** Oliver Carter **Trained** Withycombe, Somerset

FOCUS
Fingal Bay took this bumper in 2011 and the two divisions last year were won by a useful pair from the David Pipe stable, but this didn't look a strong race. The first two finished well clear but it's difficult to assess the worth of the form.

T/Plt: £30.00 to a £1 stake. Pool: £120,943.45 - 2937.35 winning units. T/Qpdt: £3.90 to a £1 stake. Pool: £9160.07 - 1734.25 winning units. TM

3927 LEOPARDSTOWN (L-H)
Sunday, February 9
OFFICIAL GOING: Soft to heavy

4178a GALA RETAIL SPRING JUVENILE HURDLE (GRADE 1) (8 hdls) 2m
1:15 (1:15) 4-Y-O **£40,666** (£11,916; £5,666; £1,916)

RPR

1 **Guitar Pete (IRE)**[45] 3305 4-11-0 132 (v) BarryGeraghty 138
(D T Hughes, Ire) *chsd ldrs: wnt mod 2nd bef 3rd: clsd steadily on ldr fr 4 out and almost on terms 2 out: led gng best into st and sn clr: kpt on wl run-in* **9/2**[3]

2 *2 1/4* **Tiger Roll (IRE)**[91] 2392 4-11-0 BryanCooper 136+
(Gordon Elliott, Ire) *hld up: pushed along in 4th after 3 out: clsd u.p into 2nd bef last where mstke: no imp on wnr run-in where rdr lost whip: kpt on same pce* **16/1**

3 *3 3/4* **Plinth (IRE)**[44] 3336 4-11-0 APMcCoy 133+
(A P O'Brien, Ire) *chsd ldrs: slt mstke in 5th 4 out: mstke next: sn niggled along in 5th: rdn after 2 out and wnt mod 3rd bef last where slow: no imp on wnr: kpt on same pce run-in* **9/4**[2]

4 *1 1/2* **Ivan Grozny (FR)**[22] 3789 4-11-0 135 RWalsh 131
(W P Mullins, Ire) *settled bhd ldr in 2nd: dropped to mod 3rd bef 3rd: nt fluent next: slt mstke in 3rd 2 out: rdn between last 2 and nt qckn: kpt on same pce in 4th run-in* **9/10**[1]

5 *5 1/2* **Henry Higgins (IRE)**[45] 3305 4-11-0 MarkWalsh 125
(Charles O'Brien, Ire) *w.w in rr: nt fluent 2 out: wnt mod 5th bef last: kpt on one pce* **50/1**

6 *9 1/2* **Orgilgo Bay (IRE)**[49] 3224 4-11-0 126 MarkBolger 116
(John C McConnell, Ire) *led and clr: reduced advantage 4 out: pushed along and pressed bef 2 out: hdd u.p bef st and wknd* **20/1**

3m 50.4s (-17.10) **Going Correction** -0.75s/f (Firm) 6 Ran SP% **114.2**
Speed ratings: **112,110,109,108,105 100**
CSF £58.39 TOTE £4.10: £1.90, £2.60; DF 39.70 Trifecta £256.10.

Owner Mrs P Sloan **Bred** P J Burke **Trained** The Curragh, Co Kildare

FOCUS
The jockeys were unanimous with their description of the ground – dead and hard work. Despite the small field, there was no shortage of early pace and the generous gallop found out quite a few in the jumping department. The time was good, the winner is progressing but perhaps the Irish team for the Triumph Hurdle isn't as strong as it looked before this. The form fits in with the race averages.

4180a DELOITTE NOVICE HURDLE (GRADE 1) (9 hdls) 2m 2f
2:15 (2:18) 5-Y-O+ **£43,333** (£12,666; £6,000; £2,000)

RPR

1 **Vautour (FR)**[29] 3667 5-11-9 143 RWalsh 150+
(W P Mullins, Ire) *mde all: 1 l clr 1/2-way: stl gng wl into st: pushed out bef last and in command: styd on wl run-in: comf* **7/4**[2]

2 *3* **The Tullow Tank (IRE)**[44] 3339 6-11-10 150 DannyMullins 148+
(Philip Fenton, Ire) *chsd ldrs: 3rd 1/2-way: nt fluent 4 out: slt mstke 2 out: rdn into 2nd bef last and sn no imp on wnr: kpt on wl run-in: nvr on terms* **9/10**[1]

3 *12* **King Of The Picts (IRE)**[44] 3339 5-11-9 141 PCarberry 135
(John Patrick Shanahan, Ire) *chsd ldrs: nt fluent in 4th at 1st: slt mstkes 3rd and next: rdn in 4th between last 2 and no imp on ldrs bef last where slt mstke: kpt on one pce into mod 3rd* **33/1**

4 *1 1/4* **Quickpick Vic (IRE)**[14] 3927 7-11-10 141 DavyRussell 135
(A J Martin, Ire) *trckd ldr in 2nd: stl gng wl whn nt fluent 2 out: sn pushed along and no ex into st: dropped to 3rd u.p bef last: one pce run-in and dropped to 4th* **6/1**[3]

5 *14* **Draycott Place (IRE)**[18] 3844 5-11-9 AELynch 120
(John Patrick Ryan, Ire) *w.w: last 1/2-way: clsr in 5th fr 3 out: rdn fr next and no imp on ldrs into st: one pce after* **200/1**

6 *58* **Azorian (IRE)**[43] 3380 6-11-10 136 BryanCooper 63
(Eoin Griffin, Ire) *t.k.h on way to s: hld up: 5th 1/2-way: rdn in rr 3 out and no ex u.p next: wknd into st and eased: completely t.o* **16/1**

4m 22.5s (-18.30) **Going Correction** -0.75s/f (Firm) 6 Ran SP% **112.6**
Speed ratings: **110,108,103,102,96 70**
CSF £3.85 TOTE £2.50: £1.90, £1.02; DF 3.70 Trifecta £31.10.

Owner Mrs S Ricci **Bred** Haras De Saint Voir & Patrick Joubert **Trained** Muine Beag, Co Carlow

FOCUS
Any letdown that might have been felt at the manner of his victory at Punchestown the previous month were firmly put in reverse by the impressive Vautour who established himself as the leading contender for Supreme Novices' Hurdle glory with this performance. The form is rated around the second and third.

4181a DR. P.J. MORIARTY NOVICE CHASE (GRADE 1) (14 fncs) 2m 5f
2:45 (2:47) 5-Y-O+ **£43,437** (£14,687)

RPR

1 **Ballycasey (IRE)**[77] 2707 7-11-10 148 RWalsh 156+
(W P Mullins, Ire) *mde all: nt fluent 4 out: narrow advantage whn slt mstke 2 out: strly pressed appr last: kpt on wl u.p run-in* **2/1**[2]

2 *4* **Don Cossack (GER)**[70] 2853 7-11-10 152 BryanCooper 153
(Gordon Elliott, Ire) *trckd ldr in 2nd: almost on terms bef 2 out: rdn into st and ev ch whn edgd lft bef last where nt fluent: sn no imp on wnr: kpt on same pce* **1/1**[1]

U **Carlingford Lough (IRE)**[42] 3404 8-11-10 151 APMcCoy 152+
(John E Kiely, Ire) *w.w in rr of trio: nt fluent 8th: rdn into st and clsd far side to chal bef last where squeezed for room: pckd sltly and uns rdr* **11/4**[3]

5m 34.9s (-1.10) **Going Correction** +0.25s/f (Yiel) 3 Ran SP% **110.0**
Speed ratings: **112,110,**
CSF £4.51 TOTE £2.30; DF 4.30 Trifecta £4.20.

Owner Mrs S Ricci **Bred** R Tanner **Trained** Muine Beag, Co Carlow

■ Stewards' Enquiry : Bryan Cooper six-day ban, reduced on appeal to five; careless riding (Feb 27,Mar 1,2,5,6)

The Form Book Jumps, Raceform Ltd, Compton, RG20 6NL.

FOCUS
Only three runners and two finishers, but a thoroughly absorbing contest nonetheless. The progressive winner improved past the solid runner-up.

4183a HENNESSY GOLD CUP CHASE (GRADE 1) (17 fncs) 3m
3:50 (3:50) 5-Y-0+
£76,666 (£25,333; £12,000; £4,000; £2,666; £666)

RPR
1 **Last Instalment (IRE)**[24] 3751 9-11-10 154 BrianO'Connell 168+
(Philip Fenton, Ire) *chsd ldrs: tk clsr order in 2nd fr 1st tl led fr next: slt mstke 3rd: pushed along fr 2 out and sn clr: styd on wl run-in* **8/1**
2 8 1/2 **Tidal Bay (IRE)**[43] 3361 13-11-10 168 RWalsh 160+
(Paul Nicholls) *w.w: tk clsr order bef 7th: wnt cl 2nd bef 10th where nt fluent: dropped to rr 3 out: no imp in mod 6th between last 2: rallied and kpt on wl in 5th fr last into nvr threatening 2nd* **5/2**[2]
3 1/2 **First Lieutenant (IRE)**[43] 3376 9-11-10 167 (p) BryanCooper 159
(M F Morris, Ire) *chsd ldrs: niggled along in 5th after 4 out: rdn after 2 out and wnt 2nd into st: no imp on wnr fr last and dropped to 3rd cl home* **7/4**[1]
4 1/2 **Texas Jack (IRE)**[24] 3751 8-11-10 154 PCarberry 159
(Noel Meade, Ire) *w.w in rr: tk clsr order fr 4 out: rdn in 3rd bef last where slt mstke: no ex run-in and dropped to 4th nr fin* **14/1**
5 4 **Lyreen Legend (IRE)**[43] 3376 7-11-10 154 BarryGeraghty 155
(D T Hughes, Ire) *chsd ldrs: clsr in 3rd on outer bef 12th: rdn in 2nd after 2 out and no imp on wnr into st: dropped to 4th bef last: one pce run-in* **13/2**
6 12 **Lord Windermere (IRE)**[43] 3376 8-11-10 153 DavyRussell 143
(J H Culloty, Ire) *chsd ldrs: tk clsr order after 4 out and disp 2nd next: sn pushed along and no imp in 5th between last 2: kpt on one pce* **6/1**[3]
7 47 **Roi Du Mee (FR)**[39] 3491 9-11-10 159 (t) DavyCondon 104
(Gordon Elliott, Ire) *led tl hdd fr 2nd: nt fluent 7th: dropped to 3rd briefly bef 10th: remained prom in 2nd tl rdn and wknd bef 2 out: eased: t.o* **14/1**

6m 26.7s (-4.30) **Going Correction** +0.25s/f (Yiel) 7 Ran SP% **117.0**
Speed ratings: **117,114,114,113,112 108,92**
CSF £29.43 TOTE £10.20: £3.50, £2.10; DF 38.80 Trifecta £84.50.
Owner Gigginstown House Stud **Bred** John O'Mahony **Trained** Carrick-On-Suir, Co Tipperary

FOCUS
A terrific performance by Last Intalment on only his second run since his comeback, and two years after he had confirmed his credentials as a top-class novice on the corresponding day. The fourth and fifth help with the standard.

4184 - 4185a (Foreign Racing) - See Raceform Interactive

4002 CATTERICK (L-H)
Monday, February 10

OFFICIAL GOING: Heavy (soft in places; 5.8)
The first fence in the back straight was omitted on all circuits of all chases.
Wind: Almost nil Weather: Sunny

4186 RACINGUK.COM NOVICES' HURDLE (12 hdls) 3m 1f 110y
1:50 (1:50) (Class 4) 5-Y-0+ **£3,764** (£1,097; £548)

Form RPR
1 **Capote (IRE)**[64] 6-10-12 0 APMcCoy 132+
(Jonjo O'Neill) *mostly chsd wnr: nt fluent 6th: taken wd in bk st on both circs: hdwy to ld 2 out: drvn along and styd on strly fr last* **4/1**[2]
231- 2 1 3/4 **I Need Gold (IRE)**[40] 3453 6-11-5 130 JasonMaguire 136+
(Donald McCain) *led at ordinary gallop: rdn and hdd 2 out: rallied u.p and ev ch last: kpt on run-in: hld towards fin* **2/9**[1]
0F4- 3 dist **Generous Chief (IRE)**[19] 3829 6-10-12 0 BrianHughes 89
(Chris Grant) *in tch: stdy hdwy 4 out: rdn and wknd bef 2 out: distant 3rd whn nt fluent last* **66/1**[3]
54U- 4 9 **Yukon Delta (IRE)**[31] 3635 7-10-12 85 KennyJohnson 80
(Robert Johnson) *chsd ldrs: wnt 2nd briefly after 7th: nt fluent and outpcd 9th: lost tch bef 2 out: t.o* **100/1**

6m 46.9s (19.30) **Going Correction** +0.825s/f (Soft) 4 Ran SP% **104.3**
Speed ratings: **103,102,90,87**
CSF £5.30 TOTE £4.60; EX 6.10 Trifecta £6.80.
Owner Trevor Hemmings **Bred** Michael Long **Trained** Cheltenham, Gloucs

FOCUS
Two useful novices dominated. The form is rated around the third.

4187 CHELTENHAM PREVIEW EVENING FEBRUARY 28TH H'CAP HURDLE (8 hdls) 2m
2:20 (2:20) (Class 4) (0-115,115) 4-Y-0+ **£3,764** (£1,097; £548)

Form RPR
430- 1 **Hawaii Five Nil (IRE)**[59] 3070 6-11-8 111 APMcCoy 118+
(Jonjo O'Neill) *trckd ldrs: smooth hdwy 3 out: led and rdn next: edgd lft fr last: drvn out* **11/4**[1]
/00- 2 1 1/4 **Short Takes (USA)**[40] 3451 6-10-13 102 JasonMaguire 106
(Donald McCain) *chsd ldrs: hdwy and ev ch after 3 out: rdn and sltly outpcd next: rallied to press wnr last: sn ev ch: kpt on: hld nr fin* **28/1**
300- 3 1 1/2 **Hartside (GER)**[16] 3891 5-11-5 115 MrRWinks(7) 118
(Peter Winks) *prom: outpcd after 3 out: sn rdn: rallied and cl up in last: kpt on same pce last 50yds* **8/1**
P41- 4 6 **Persian Herald**[19] 3839 6-11-4 110 JonathanEngland(3) 108
(Sue Smith) *led: rdn whn hit and hdd 2 out: rallied: wknd fr last* **3/1**[2]
000- 5 2 3/4 **Vodka Red (IRE)**[51] 3210 6-9-7 89 oh8 StephenMulqueen(7) 82
(Robert Johnson) *hld up: rdn after 3 out: hdwy bef next: hung lft and no imp between last 2* **11/1**
524- 6 14 **Lysino (GER)**[37] 3527 5-10-13 102 WilsonRenwick 86
(Chris Grant) *j.lft 1st: hld up: hdwy to chal after 3rd: rdn and wknd bef 2 out: no ch whn blnd bdly last* **4/1**[3]
3B2- 7 11 **Gold Show**[32] 3614 5-11-0 106 TonyKelly(3) 74
(Edwin Tuer) *hld up in tch: struggling bef 3 out: btn next* **5/1**
5/6- 8 29 **Carters Rest**[26] 3723 11-9-11 93 (tp) DaleIrving(7) 32
(Iain Jardine) *hld up in tch: struggling bef 3 out: lost tch bef next: t.o* **33/1**

4m 3.4s (10.90) **Going Correction** +0.825s/f (Soft) 8 Ran SP% **114.2**
Speed ratings (Par 105): **105,104,103,100,99 92,86,72**
CSF £63.13 CT £551.16 TOTE £3.10: £1.10, £4.70, £2.30; EX 62.00 Trifecta £162.00.
Owner Regulatory Finance Solutions Limited **Bred** John Supple **Trained** Cheltenham, Gloucs

FOCUS
Not bad form for the class. The winner is rated in line with his bumper form.

4188 WEATHERBYS HAMILTON INSURANCE NOVICES' LIMITED H'CAP CHASE (17 fncs 2 omitted) 3m 1f 110y
2:50 (2:50) (Class 3) (0-125,125) 5-Y-0+ **£6,498** (£1,908; £954; £477)

Form RPR
443- 1 **Pinerolo**[45] 3331 8-10-8 112 RyanMania 136+
(Sue Smith) *pressed ldr: led after 4 out: drew clr fr next: easily* **13/8**[1]
PP1- 2 22 **Harris (IRE)**[55] 3145 7-10-8 112 JamesReveley 109
(William Kinsey) *nt fluent on occasions: chsd ldrs: drvn and outpcd 13th: rallied 2 out: kpt on to take 2nd nr fin: no ch w wnr* **5/1**[3]
112- 3 nk **Alderbrook Lad (IRE)**[5] 4084 8-10-9 118 JoeColliver(5) 113
(Micky Hammond) *led: hit 10th: hit 4 out: sn rdn and hdd: kpt on same pce fr next: lost 2nd nr fin* **11/2**
/04- 4 50 **Mitchell's Way**[30] 3658 7-11-2 120 APMcCoy 64
(Alan Swinbank) *in tch: hdwy and cl up 11th: hit 13th: rdn and wknd 3 out: t.o* **6/1**
5/1- P **Diocles (IRE)**[55] 3142 8-11-7 125 JasonMaguire
(Donald McCain) *nt fluent in last pl: outpcd 13th: no ch whn p.u after 3 out* **9/4**[2]

6m 51.4s (9.40) **Going Correction** +0.55s/f (Soft) 5 Ran SP% **115.2**
Speed ratings: **107,100,100,84,**
CSF £10.38 TOTE £2.50: £1.30, £2.50; EX 11.30 Trifecta £45.90.
Owner McGoldrick Racing Syndicates (2) **Bred** W Goldie **Trained** High Eldwick, W Yorks

FOCUS
This handicap fell apart. A step up from the winner with the second 5lb off his recent win.

4189 YORKSHIRE-OUTDOORS.CO.UK H'CAP HURDLE (10 hdls) 2m 3f
3:20 (3:20) (Class 4) (0-115,110) 4-Y-0+ **£3,898** (£1,144; £572; £286)

Form RPR
/44- 1 **The Clock Leary (IRE)**[35] 3567 6-11-12 110 AidanColeman 118
(Venetia Williams) *t.k.h: in tch: stdy hdwy 4 out: rdn and ev ch 2 out: styd on gamely run-in to ld towards fin* **10/3**[2]
221- 2 1/2 **Blake Dean**[26] 3723 6-10-9 93 RyanMania 100
(Sue Smith) *led: hrd pressed and rdn 2 out: kpt on fr last: hdd and no ex towards fin* **3/1**[1]
122- 3 19 **Bonnet's Vino**[30] 3657 6-11-7 108 KielanWoods(3) 103
(Pam Sly) *chsd ldrs: wnt 2nd 1/2-way: effrt and ch after 3 out: rdn and wknd fr next* **6/1**
0/0- 4 22 **Patavium (IRE)**[32] 3618 11-10-8 95 TonyKelly(3) 61
(Edwin Tuer) *hld up in tch: drvn and outpcd 4 out: n.d after* **33/1**
003- 5 22 **Jokers And Rogues (IRE)**[32] 3618 6-10-11 102 JohnDawson(7) 46
(John Wade) *hld up in tch: stdy hdwy after 5th: drvn and outpcd 7th: lost tch bef 2 out* **7/1**
534- 6 28 **Kathlatino**[31] 3636 7-9-9 84 oh1 JoeColliver(5)
(Micky Hammond) *in tch: nt fluent 3rd: drvn and outpcd 6th: lost tch after next: t.o* **22/1**
4/ P **De Chissler (IRE)**[41] 3446 7-11-2 100 WilsonRenwick
(Martin Todhunter) *mstkes: chsd ldr: outpcd whn hit 6th: sn struggling: t.o whn p.u bef 2 out* **11/2**[3]
/05- P **Right To Rule (IRE)**[30] 3659 5-11-5 103 (p) JasonMaguire
(Donald McCain) *hld up: nt fluent 2nd: struggling 6th: t.o whn p.u bef 2 out* **7/1**

4m 57.0s (20.90) **Going Correction** +0.825s/f (Soft) 8 Ran SP% **110.0**
Speed ratings (Par 105): **89,88,80,71,62 50, ,**
CSF £13.01 CT £51.20 TOTE £4.00: £1.30, £1.60, £2.00; EX 13.90 Trifecta £38.80.
Owner Brooks, Vanderson, Pummell & Martin **Bred** Francis Small **Trained** Kings Caple, H'fords

FOCUS
This principals had this to themselves from four out. A step up from the winner but the form is believable.

4190 WEATHERBYS PRIVATE BANKING H'CAP CHASE (19 fncs) 3m 1f 110y
3:50 (3:50) (Class 3) (0-140,129) 5-Y-0+ **£7,988** (£2,480; £1,335)

Form RPR
126- 1 **Herdsman (IRE)**[42] 3416 9-11-10 127 RyanMania 138+
(Sue Smith) *chsd ldr: nt fluent 3rd: blnd 8th: led and pckd 11th: pushed clr 3 out: kpt on wl fr last* **11/2**[3]
551- 2 2 1/4 **Everaard (USA)**[4] 4105 8-10-0 103 oh1 (tp) RichieMcGrath 109
(Philip Kirby) *in tch: pushed along fnl circ: rallied to chse wnr appr 3 out: kpt on run-in: nt gng pce to chal* **2/1**[2]
R44- 3 65 **Triggerman**[27] 3698 12-11-2 119 (b) RichardJohnson 84
(Philip Hobbs) *chsd ldrs: wnt 2nd after 11th: rdn and outpcd appr 3 out: sn lost tch* **9/1**
/P1- U **Union Jack D'Ycy (FR)**[18] 3858 6-11-6 123 AidanColeman
(Venetia Williams) *nt fluent on occasions: hld up in tch: hit and uns rdr 9th* **7/4**[1]
434- P **Mr Watson (IRE)**[64] 2976 7-11-10 127 (b) APMcCoy
(Jonjo O'Neill) *t.k.h: led: hit 3rd: hdd 11th: sn lost pl and struggling: p.u bef 4 out* **13/2**

6m 53.4s (11.40) **Going Correction** +0.55s/f (Soft) 5 Ran SP% **108.4**
Speed ratings: **104,103,83, ,**
CSF £16.76 TOTE £4.60: £1.30, £1.70; EX 19.10 Trifecta £116.00.
Owner Trevor Hemmings **Bred** Eddie Flavin **Trained** High Eldwick, W Yorks

FOCUS
What was already a below-par handicap for a 0-140 was further weakened by the late withdrawal of Real Milan. The form is rated around the first two.

4191 RACING AGAIN ON 25TH FEBRUARY MARES' STANDARD OPEN NATIONAL HUNT FLAT RACE 2m
4:20 (4:20) (Class 5) 4-6-Y-0 **£2,053** (£598; £299)

Form RPR
4- 1 **Georgian Firebird**[30] 3663 4-10-5 PaddyBrennan 98+
(Alan Swinbank) *in tch: swtchd lft and gd hdwy to ld over 1f out: clr whn edgd rt ins fnl f: pushed out* **6/1**[3]
503- 2 9 **Buckboru (IRE)**[13] 3961 6-11-1 DougieCostello 99
(Laura Young) *t.k.h: hld up in tch: hdwy and cl up over 3f out: rdn and sltly outpcd 2f out: rallied to chse (clr) wnr ins fnl f: no imp* **7/4**[2]
1- 3 1 **Star Lily (IRE)**[75] 2752 5-11-8 JamesReveley 105
(Keith Reveley) *cl up: chal 1/2-way: led over 3f out to over 1f out: no ex and lost 2nd ins fnl f* **5/4**[1]
4 2 **Lady Busanda** 4-10-0 JoeColliver(5) 86
(George Moore) *chsd ldrs: hdwy to chal 1/2-way: outpcd over 3f out: rallied over 1f out: nvr rchd ldrs* **33/1**

5 ¾ **Preacher's Belle** 5-10-10 .... AdamNicol(5) 95
(Philip Kirby) *in tch: hdwy and ev ch 3f out to over 1f out: outpcd fnl f* **14/1**

0- 6 13 **Belanna**[19] 3835 5-11-1 .... (b[1]) BrianHarding 82
(Tim Easterby) *led: jnd 1/2-way: rdn and hdd over 3f out: wknd over 2f out* **28/1**

4m 7.7s (20.80) **Going Correction** +0.825s/f (Soft)
WFA 4 from 5yo+ 9lb 6 Ran SP% **108.1**
Speed ratings: **81,76,76,75,74 68**
CSF £15.73 TOTE £5.10: £2.10, £1.60; EX 15.30 Trifecta £25.70.
Owner Mrs Lizzy Wilson **Bred** Brown Moss Stud **Trained** Melsonby, N Yorks

FOCUS
Ordinary form, but an impressive winner. The form is rated around the second and third.
T/Plt: £267.20 to a £1 stake. Pool of £91271.23 - 249.27 winning tickets. T/Qpdt: £25.80 to a £1 stake. Pool of £8060.94 - 231.0 winning tickets. RY

3686 PLUMPTON (L-H)
Monday, February 10
4192 Meeting Abandoned - Waterlogged

3934 AYR (L-H)
Tuesday, February 11

OFFICIAL GOING: Heavy (soft in places; chs 7.6; hdl 7.8)
Both tracks 7m from innermost line with divided bends.
Wind: Fresh, half against Weather: Overcast Rails: Both tracks 7m from the innermost line; divided bends

4199 BETVICTOR NON-RUNNER FREE BET CHELTENHAM 2014 MAIDEN HURDLE (9 hdls) 2m
1:50 (1:50) (Class 5) 4-Y-0+ **£2,079** (£610; £305; £152)

Form RPR

113- 1 **Stonebrook (IRE)**[21] 3826 6-11-3 0 .... APMcCoy 127+
(Donald McCain) *a gng wl: prom: hdwy to chal after 4 out: led last: shkn up and asserted run-in: cosily* **8/11**[1]

05- 2 2 **Voyage A New York (FR)**[24] 3781 5-11-3 0 .... WilsonRenwick 118
(Lucinda Russell) *chsd ldrs: wnt 2nd 4th: led after 4 out: sn hrd pressed: hdd last: kpt on: nt pce of wnr* **25/1**

262- 3 10 **Titus Bolt (IRE)**[25] 3758 5-11-3 117 .... RyanMania 111
(Jim Goldie) *led and clr to 1/2-way: nt fluent and stmbld 4 out: sn hdd: rallied u.p and ev ch bef next: outpcd fr 2 out* **11/4**[2]

/60- 4 10 **Bobs Lady Tamure**[76] 2748 7-10-3 0 .... (t) StephenMulqueen(7) 91
(Maurice Barnes) *hld up: stdy hdwy to chse ldrs 4 out: rdn and wknd after next* **100/1**

32F- 5 dist **The Orange Rogue (IRE)**[15] 3935 7-11-3 0 .... LucyAlexander
(N W Alexander) *j.lft: chsd clr ldr to 4th: drvn and struggling fr next: continued: t.o* **12/1**

5- 6 46 **The Village (IRE)**[110] 2061 5-11-3 0 .... PeterBuchanan
(Lucinda Russell) *bhd: struggling fr 1/2-way: continued: t.o* **80/1**

7 5 **Alkali (IRE)**[119] 4-10-0 0 .... AELynch
(S R B Crawford, Ire) *bhd: struggling fr 1/2-way: continued: t.o* **33/1**

46- P **Love Marmalade (IRE)**[24] 3781 4-10-4 0 .... EwanWhillans(3)
(Alistair Whillans) *bhd: lost tch fnl circ: t.o whn p.u bef 4 out* **66/1**

P **Moss Street**[10] 4045 4-10-7 0 .... JasonMaguire
(Gordon Elliott, Ire) *hld up: lost tch and p.u bef 4 out* **8/1**[3]

0/P- P **Knockcairn (IRE)**[101] 2217 7-10-3 0 .... GrahamWatters(7)
(Ian Duncan) *in tch: struggling 1/2-way: t.o whn p.u after 4 out* **150/1**

4m 11.2s (8.10) **Going Correction** +0.70s/f (Soft)
WFA 4 from 5yo+ 9lb 10 Ran SP% **114.5**
Speed ratings (Par 103): **107,106,101,96,** , , , ,
CSF £23.79 TOTE £1.60: £1.10, £5.90, £1.40; EX 26.50 Trifecta £48.20.
Owner John P McManus **Bred** George Ward **Trained** Cholmondeley, Cheshire

FOCUS
Both tracks 7m from innermost line with divided bends. A moderate maiden hurdle but it was run at a stern pace on the testing surface. The winner built on his hurdles debut run and should rate higher.

4200 BETVICTOR.COM "NATIONAL HUNT" NOVICES' HURDLE (12 hdls) 2m 5f 110y
2:20 (2:20) (Class 4) 4-Y-0+ **£3,573** (£1,049; £524; £262)

Form RPR

1- 1 **Layla Joan (IRE)**[15] 3934 6-11-11 125 .... (t) APMcCoy 140+
(Gordon Elliott, Ire) *hld up in tch: smooth hdwy to chse wnr 4 out: led on bit 2 out: shkn up briefly after last: sn clr: readily* **5/4**[1]

/21- 2 6 **Fine Rightly (IRE)**[40] 3494 6-11-8 0 .... MrSCrawford(3) 130+
(S R B Crawford, Ire) *nt fluent on occasions: led 2nd: rdn and hdd 2 out: rallied: no ch w wnr fr last* **7/5**[2]

224- 3 19 **Mysteree (IRE)**[66] 2954 6-11-11 125 .... PeterBuchanan 109
(Lucinda Russell) *prom: pushed along after 4 out: hung lft and wknd bef 2 out* **8/1**[3]

4 43 **Doubledisdoubledat (IRE)**[394] 7-10-11 0 .... DaraghBourke(7) 59
(Stuart Coltherd) *led to 2nd: chsd ldr to 4 out: sn rdn and lost tch: t.o* **50/1**

P0P- P **Ruberslaw**[20] 3829 8-11-4 0 .... AdrianLane
(Iain Jardine) *mstkes: sn in rr: struggling fr 4th: t.o whn p.u bef 7th* **150/1**

12- P **Askamore Darsi (IRE)**[33] 3616 5-11-4 0 .... JasonMaguire
(Donald McCain) *chsd ldrs: reminders 4th: outpcd after next: rallied and cl up 7th: wknd bef 4 out: t.o whn p.u bef next* **10/1**

5m 55.7s (15.40) **Going Correction** +0.70s/f (Soft) 6 Ran SP% **108.9**
Speed ratings (Par 105): **100,97,90,75,**
CSF £3.19 TOTE £2.00: £1.20, £1.40; EX 3.40 Trifecta £11.50.
Owner W T Murphy **Bred** N Elliott **Trained** Trim, Co Meath

FOCUS
A fair race for the grade, dominated as the market suggested by the two Irish raiders. The winner built on her recent easy win and can go in again.

4201 CHELTENHAM 2014 NRFB AT BETVICTOR.COM CONDITIONAL JOCKEYS' H'CAP HURDLE (11 hdls) 2m 4f
2:55 (2:55) (Class 5) (0-100,100) 4-Y-0+ **£2,144** (£629; £314; £157)

Form RPR

032- 1 **W Six Times**[15] 3940 8-10-5 79 .... CallumWhillans 91+
(Alistair Whillans) *trckd ldrs: led gng wl 4 out: drew clr fr next: rdn out fr 2 out* **8/1**

401- 2 7 **Ancient Times (USA)**[15] 3940 7-10-11 88 .... (p) AdamNicol(3) 93
(Philip Kirby) *led to 6th: drvn to regain ld bef next: hdd 4 out: drvn and chsd (clr) wnr bef 2 out: kpt on: no imp* **6/1**[3]

052- 3 19 **Madam Lilibet (IRE)**[38] 3525 5-11-4 97 .... JosephPalmowski(5) 83
(Sharon Watt) *bhd: drvn along 1/2-way: hdwy u.p after 4 out: no imp bef 2 out* **10/1**

5/2- 4 ¾ **Scimon Templar (FR)**[27] 3723 6-11-6 94 .... TonyKelly 79
(Pauline Robson) *prom: drvn and effrt bef 3 out: wknd fr next* **5/1**[2]

50P- 5 28 **Mrs Grass**[15] 3940 7-10-0 74 oh5 .... JoeColliver 31
(Jonathan Haynes) *midfield: drvn along 7th: wknd fr next: t.o* **100/1**

PP3- 6 2 ¼ **Wayne Manor (IRE)**[38] 3525 5-11-6 100 .... (t) GrantCockburn(6) 55
(Lucinda Russell) *hld up: outpcd whn nt fluent 4 out: sn struggling: t.o* **8/1**

/43- 7 22 **See The Legend**[15] 3940 9-10-8 85 .... StephenMulqueen(3) 18
(Sandy Forster) *prom: hdwy and ev ch after 4 out: wknd bef 2 out: virtually p.u run-in: t.o* **10/1**

01S- 8 4 **Millers Reef (IRE)**[20] 3842 8-11-6 97 .... CraigNichol(3) 26
(Keith Dalgleish) *hld up in midfield: stdy hdwy to chse ldrs after 4 out: rdn and wknd next: t.o* **7/2**[1]

065- P **Thorlak (FR)**[44] 3392 7-11-3 99 .... DaleIrving(8)
(James Ewart) *bhd: drvn along and struggling fr 6th: no ch whn p.u bef last* **8/1**

040- P **Amethyst Rose (IRE)**[15] 3940 7-10-9 91 .... DaraghBourke(8)
(Stuart Coltherd) *w ldr: led 6th to bef next: sn struggling: t.o whn p.u bef 3 out* **20/1**

5m 24.6s (12.60) **Going Correction** +0.70s/f (Soft) 10 Ran SP% **110.4**
Speed ratings (Par 103): **102,99,91,91,80 79,70,68,** ,
CSF £52.31 CT £459.38 TOTE £6.10: £2.60, £1.80, £2.30; EX 21.10 Trifecta £203.80.
Owner Mrs L M Whillans **Bred** East Burrow Farm **Trained** Newmill-On-Slitrig, Borders

FOCUS
This conditional riders' handicap was turned into a procession. The winner was up 10lb on her recent C&D run behind the second.

4202 BACK OF THE NET AT BETVICTOR.COM NOVICES' CHASE (18 fncs) 2m 5f
3:25 (3:29) (Class 4) 5-Y-0+ **£4,327** (£1,343; £723)

Form RPR

452- 1 **Tiny Dancer (IRE)**[72] 2843 6-11-0 103 .... BrianHughes 116+
(Alan Swinbank) *chsd ldrs: lft cl 2nd 10th: nt fluent 13th: led bef 4 out: drawing clr whn hit next: kpt on strly: unchal* **12/1**

5- 2 24 **Vasco Du Mee (FR)**[10] 4048 5-10-11 0 .... APMcCoy 92
(Gordon Elliott, Ire) *nt fluent: hld up: niggled along after 9th: rallied whn lft cl 3rd next: mstke 5 out: effrt and chsd (clr) wnr 3 out: no imp* **10/1**[3]

323- 3 28 **Ballyben (IRE)**[52] 3209 6-10-7 106 .... CraigNichol(7) 61
(Lucinda Russell) *cl up: lft cl 2nd 4th: lft in ld 10th: rdn and hdd bef 4 out: wknd and lost 2nd next* **5/2**[2]

0F5- U **Harrys Whim**[16] 3921 9-10-0 62 .... (t) StephenMulqueen(7)
(Maurice Barnes) *led: hit: stmbld bdly and uns rdr 4th* **80/1**

/24- F **She Ranks Me (IRE)**[52] 3206 7-10-7 0 .... (p) JasonMaguire
(Donald McCain) *t.k.h early: cl up: lft in ld 4th: 2 l up whn fell 10th* **4/6**[1]

6m 4.4s (22.40) **Going Correction** +1.025s/f (Soft)
WFA 5 from 6yo+ 2lb 5 Ran SP% **106.6**
Speed ratings: **98,88,78,** ,
CSF £88.28 TOTE £10.70: £3.50, £2.80; EX 71.60 Trifecta £68.10.
Owner Ms A Findlay **Bred** John Blake **Trained** Melsonby, N Yorks

FOCUS
No shortage of drama in this novice chase. The winner was left with little to beat but is clearly a better chaser than hurdler.

4203 DOWNLOAD THE BETVICTOR APP NOW H'CAP CHASE (12 fncs) 2m
4:00 (4:00) (Class 5) (0-100,88) 5-Y-0+ **£2,599** (£763; £381; £190)

Form RPR

/32- 1 **Too Cool To Fool (IRE)**[15] 3936 11-11-5 81 .... JamesReveley 104+
(Jim Goldie) *hld up bhd ldng gp: gd hdwy to chse ldr after 5 out: led next: pushed clr fr 3 out* **2/1**[1]

/55- 2 17 **Soul Angel**[58] 3107 10-10-11 73 .... (v) AdrianLane 77
(Sandy Forster) *prom: hdwy to ld 5 out: rdn and hdd next: outpcd by wnr fr 3 out: hld whn j.lft last* **16/1**

235- 3 5 **Forestside (IRE)**[39] 3517 9-11-4 80 .... APMcCoy 81
(Barry Murtagh) *nt fluent: hld up in tch: hit 3rd: hdwy to chse ldrs whn hit 4 out: sn rdn: outpcd fr next: hld whn j.lft last* **7/1**

633- 4 17 **Panthers Run**[23] 3799 14-10-4 69 .... (t) JohnKington(3) 50
(Jonathan Haynes) *prom: rdn and outpcd after 7th: sn struggling: n.d after* **33/1**

054- 5 26 **Strathaird (IRE)**[27] 3722 10-9-9 62 oh9 .... (p) JoeColliver(5) 17
(Andrew Crook) *bhd and detached: struggling fr 1/2-way: nvr on terms* **20/1**

PF2- P **Hotgrove Boy**[11] 4004 7-11-4 87 .... DaraghBourke(7)
(Stuart Coltherd) *cl up: hit and pckd 3rd: mstke 7th: rdn and wknd bef 4 out: t.o whn p.u bef last* **5/2**[2]

022- P **Mumgos Debut (IRE)**[27] 3722 6-11-12 88 .... PeterBuchanan
(Lucinda Russell) *t.k.h: led to 5 out: rdn and wknd fr next: t.o whn p.u bef last* **9/2**[3]

4m 26.7s (16.00) **Going Correction** +1.025s/f (Soft) 7 Ran SP% **106.2**
Speed ratings: **101,92,90,81,68** ,
CSF £25.33 TOTE £2.80: £1.10, £7.50; EX 28.90 Trifecta £101.00.
Owner Johnnie Delta Racing **Bred** Simon Young **Trained** Uplawmoor, E Renfrews

FOCUS
The easy winner improved to his hurdles mark.

4204 BETVICTOR'S LIVE CASINO H'CAP CHASE (17 fncs) 2m 4f
4:30 (4:30) (Class 3) (0-140,130) 5-Y-O+ £7,797 (£2,289; £1,144; £572)

Form RPR
P21- 1 **And The Man**[15] 3939 8-11-1 **119**.. BrianHarding 130+
(Nicky Richards) *prom: pushed along 6 out: effrt 4 out: sn chsng ldr: rdn to ld appr last: kpt on wl: eased nr fin* **11/4**[1]
613- 2 *1 1/4* **Wicklow Lad**[21] 3825 10-11-1 **119**................................(v) LucyAlexander 127
(N W Alexander) *chsd ldrs: chal 9th: led bef 4 out: sn rdn: hdd last: kpt on towards fin: nt rch wnr* **11/2**
3/ 3 *22* **Barneys Honour (IRE)**[16] 3929 10-11-4 **122**......................... APMcCoy 111
(Gordon Elliott, Ire) *hld up: mstke 6th: hdwy to chse ldrs 4 out: rdn and wknd 2 out* **4/1**[3]
0/3- 4 *10* **Mister First (FR)**[25] 3759 8-11-3 **121**... AELynch 98
(Robert Alan Hennessy, Ire) *hld up: hit and outpcd 5 out: pushed along and no imp next: sn btn* **7/1**
542- 5 *16* **Gansey (IRE)**[43] 3414 12-11-12 **130**....................................... RyanMania 89
(Sue Smith) *cl up: chal 3rd: led 10th to bef 4 out: wknd fr next* **7/2**[2]
/64- P **Prosecco (IRE)**[44] 3395 12-10-13 **117**.............................. PeterBuchanan
(Lucinda Russell) *hld up in tch: struggling bef 12th: btn bef 4 out: t.o whn p.u bef 2 out* **18/1**
/1P- P **Railway Dillon (IRE)**[27] 3717 9-11-8 **126**.....................(bt) JasonMaguire
(Donald McCain) *mde most to 10th: cl up to 4 out: 5th and wkng whn blnd next: p.u bef 2 out* **8/1**

5m 43.8s (20.90) **Going Correction** +1.025s/f (Soft) **7** Ran SP% **113.1**
Speed ratings: **99,98,89,85,79** ,
CSF £17.86 CT £58.52 TOTE £3.10: £1.80, £3.90; EX 19.20 Trifecta £64.20.
Owner Little Green Syndicate **Bred** A Buller **Trained** Greystoke, Cumbria

FOCUS
This hotly contested feature was run at a decent gallop. The first two were the only ones to pass the stamina test in the ground, and the winner is progressive.

4205 GOOD LUCK STEVE KNIGHT STANDARD OPEN NATIONAL HUNT FLAT RACE 2m
5:00 (5:02) (Class 6) 4-6-Y-O £1,711 (£498; £249)

Form RPR
1 **Heritage Way** 5-11-0 0.. MrSCrawford[(3)] 116+
(S R B Crawford, Ire) *t.k.h early: hld up: smooth hdwy 3f out: led gng wl over 1f out: pushed out fnl f: comf* **5/1**
2 *1 3/4* **The Unsub (IRE)** 6-11-3 0.. APMcCoy 111
(Gordon Elliott, Ire) *prom: effrt and hdwy over 3f out: ev ch and rdn over 1f out: chsd wnr ins fnl f: r.o* **4/1**[3]
3 *2* **Gold Opera (IRE)**[108] 5-11-3 0... LucyAlexander 109
(N W Alexander) *led at slow pce 4f: cl up: regained ld 1/2-way: rdn and hung lft over 2f out: hdd over 1f out: kpt on same pce ins fnl f* **14/1**
1- 4 *7* **Uppertown Cave (IRE)**[40] 3500 5-11-10 0........................ JasonMaguire 109
(Donald McCain) *hld up: hdwy and prom over 3f out: rdn and hung lft over 2f out: sn no imp* **7/4**[1]
2- 5 *nk* **Hail The Brave (IRE)**[58] 3112 5-10-12 0............................ AdamNicol[(5)] 102
(Philip Kirby) *t.k.h: prom: rdn and outpcd over 3f out: rallied over 1f out: nvr able to chal* **3/1**[2]
0- 6 *16* **Hopefull**[31] 3663 4-10-0 0.. PeterBuchanan 69
(R Mike Smith) *t.k.h: in tch: hdwy over 5f out: rdn and outpcd over 3f out: sn n.d* **66/1**
7 *15* **Thatsmylot (IRE)** 5-10-10 0... DaraghBourke[(7)] 71
(Stuart Coltherd) *hld up in tch: stdy hdwy over 4f out: rdn and wknd 3f out* **50/1**
- 8 *10* **Sir Tommy** 5-10-10 0..(t) StephenMulqueen[(7)] 61
(Maurice Barnes) *t.k.h: cl up: led and maintained slow pce after 4f: hdd 1/2-way: rdn and wknd over 3f out* **25/1**
0- 9 *10* **Diamond Native (IRE)**[32] 3640 6-10-10 0........................ MrJHamilton[(7)] 51
(Brian Storey) *plld hrd: hld up: struggling 1/2-way: sn lost tch* **100/1**

4m 26.0s (28.50) **Going Correction** +0.70s/f (Soft)
WFA 4 from 5yo+ 9lb **9** Ran SP% **113.0**
Speed ratings: **56,55,54,50,50 42,34,29,24**
CSF £24.24 TOTE £7.40: £1.90, £1.60, £3.60; EX 29.70 Trifecta £194.90.
Owner S R B Crawford **Bred** A W Buller **Trained** Larne, Co Antrim

FOCUS
An intriguing finale, but with this developing into nothing more than a mad 3f dash, there has to be a big question mark over the form moving forward. However, it could have been a good bumper for the track.
T/Plt: £143.50 to a £1 stake. Pool: £104,741.10 - 532.78 winning units. T/Qpdt: £84.90 to a £1 stake. Pool: £5570.61 - 48.50 winning units. RY

3229 LINGFIELD (L-H)
Tuesday, February 11
4206 Meeting Abandoned - waterlogged

3357 CHEPSTOW (L-H)
Wednesday, February 12
4213 Meeting Abandoned - Waterlogged

4051 MUSSELBURGH (R-H)
Wednesday, February 12

OFFICIAL GOING: Good (good to soft in places) changing to good to soft after race 1 (1:40), changing to soft after race 4 (3:15)
Bottom bend moved out 2m.
Wind: Fresh, half behind Weather: Overcast, showers

4220 RURAL INSURANCE AMATEUR RIDERS' H'CAP CHASE 3m 3f
1:40 (1:45) (Class 5) (0-100,100) 5-Y-O+ £3,119 (£967; £483; £242)

Form RPR
/53- 1 **Tears From Heaven (USA)**[26] 3755 8-9-12 **79**...............(p) MrRSmith[(7)] 90+
(Chris Grant) *hld up in tch: hdwy after 5 out: rdn to ld next: styd on strly fr 2 out* **4/1**[1]
P53- 2 *1 1/4* **The Shrimp (IRE)**[16] 3936 7-9-11 **74** oh16...................(p) MrJHamilton[(3)] 82
(Sandy Thomson) *stdd in tch: drvn and outpcd 8th: rallied and prom after 5 out: drvn and no imp bef next: styd on strly fr last: tk 2nd cl home* **11/1**
552- 3 *nk* **Soul Angel**[1] 4203 10-9-7 **74** oh1.....................................(p) MrTHamilton[(7)] 82
(Sandy Forster) *chsd ldrs: rdn whn j.lft 3 out: effrt and chsng wnr whn mstke last: kpt on: lost 2nd cl home* **11/2**[2]
5/3- 4 *2 1/4* **Get Ready To Go (IRE)**[281] 162 10-9-8 **75**...........(p) MrTGreenwood[(7)] 82
(Richard Ford) *chsd ldrs: disp ld fr 14th: led 15th to 4 out: sn rdn and rallied: one pce fr last* **6/1**[3]
032- 5 *43* **Miss Sunflower**[204] 1089 12-9-9 **74** oh4.............(p) MissJoannaMason[(5)] 41
(Tina Jackson) *mstkes in rr: struggling fnl circ: nvr on terms: t.o* **25/1**
2PP- 6 *2* **Ballyvoneen (IRE)**[48] 3267 9-10-1 **82**..............................(b) MrBenJay[(7)] 47
(Neil King) *t.k.h: cl up: led 3rd: nt fluent 8th: blnd and hdd 15th: rdn and wknd bef 4 out: t.o* **4/1**[1]
0P1- 7 *6* **Fozy Moss**[7] 4082 8-10-11 **85** 7ex...(t) MissCWalton 45
(Stuart Coltherd) *sn bhd and pushed along: struggling fnl circ: nvr on terms: t.o* **13/2**
04P- P **Fog Patches (IRE)**[16] 3936 8-11-7 **100**.................................(p) MrSFox[(5)]
(Lucinda Russell) *led to 3rd: prom: outpcd 6th: struggling and p.u after 12th* **12/1**
3- P **Debt To Society (IRE)**[33] 3635 7-10-13 **94**.....................(tp) MrRDDay[(7)]
(Richard Ford) *nt jump wl in rr: lost tch and p.u after 7th* **10/1**

7m 0.6s (11.80) **Going Correction** +0.50s/f (Soft) **9** Ran SP% **112.0**
Speed ratings: **102,101,101,100,88 87,85,** ,
CSF £43.89 CT £238.86 TOTE £4.60: £2.40, £4.20, £3.10; EX 54.40 Trifecta £378.30.
Owner Mrs S Sunter **Bred** Bock, McMillin, Sion, Culbertson Et Al **Trained** Newton Bewley, Co Durham

FOCUS
Bottom bend moved out 2m. With it starting to rain quite heavily prior to racing, the ground certainly looked more testing than had been advertised, and it was changed to good to soft (from predominantly good) after this opening contest. The winner is rated back to his best.\n\x\x The field were soon well strung out in what was a weak staying handicap chase, run in wet and very windy conditions.

4221 BET & WATCH WITH RACINGUK'S APP NOVICES' HURDLE (12 hdls) 2m 4f
2:10 (2:18) (Class 4) 4-Y-O+ £3,249 (£954; £477; £238)

Form RPR
1- 1 **Fennell Bay (IRE)**[42] 3469 5-11-11 0.................................. DenisO'Regan 126+
(John Ferguson) *trckd ldrs gng wl: led bef 3 out: j. sltly rt 3 out and last: qcknd clr on bridle run-in: readily* **8/11**[1]
32- 2 *5* **Ollie G**[75] 2795 6-11-4 0... BrianHughes 107
(Chris Grant) *t.k.h: prom: hdwy to chse wnr bef 3 out: rdn and ev ch next: kpt on same pce fr last* **16/1**[3]
1/1- 3 *1* **Plan Again (IRE)**[116] 1975 7-11-11 0................................. JasonMaguire 113
(Donald McCain) *nt fluent on occasions: t.k.h: hld up in tch: hdwy to chse ldrs after 3 out: effrt next: j.lft last: one pce* **7/4**[2]
5- 4 *10* **Elfego Baca (IRE)**[40] 3522 5-11-4 0.............................. PeterBuchanan 96
(Lucinda Russell) *hld up: shkn up and hdwy bef 3 out: no imp bef next* **40/1**
/40- 5 *14* **Politeness (FR)**[93] 2420 5-11-4 0.. BrianHarding 82
(Rose Dobbin) *hld up in tch: hit 8th: effrt bef 3 out: wknd after next* **66/1**
- 6 *40* **Martin Chuzzlewit (IRE)**[124] 5-11-4 0.......................... WilsonRenwick 42
(Martin Todhunter) *t.k.h: cl up: led bef 4th: hdd bef 3 out: sn wknd: t.o* **20/1**
P- P **Apache Pilot**[32] 3657 6-10-11 0...............................(t) StephenMulqueen[(7)]
(Maurice Barnes) *led at slow pce to bef 4th: cl up tl rdn and wknd after 4 out: t.o whn p.u next* **200/1**

5m 5.6s (14.10) **Going Correction** -0.15s/f (Good) **7** Ran SP% **109.3**
Speed ratings (Par 105): **65,63,62,58,53 37,**
CSF £11.05 TOTE £1.80: £1.10, £3.90; EX 11.70 Trifecta £22.20.
Owner Bloomfields **Bred** J R Wills **Trained** Cowlinge, Suffolk

FOCUS
There was little depth to this novice hurdle, which was run at a steady pace early. There'a probably more to come from the winner.

4222 EDINBURGH EVENING NEWS H'CAP CHASE (BETFAIR SCOTTISH CHASE SERIES QUALIFIER) (16 fncs) 2m 4f
2:40 (2:45) (Class 4) (0-110,109) 5-Y-O+ £5,198 (£1,526; £763; £381)

Form RPR
325- 1 **Alpha One (IRE)**[48] 3275 8-11-12 **109**................................ DenisO'Regan 109
(Chris Grant) *hld up in tch: effrt after 4 out: rdn and outpcd next: rallied whn lft 2 l 2nd last: styd on wl to ld towards fin* **8/1**
141- 2 *1* **Civil Unrest (IRE)**[40] 3517 8-11-1 **105**................................(b) DaleIrving[(7)] 104
(James Ewart) *chsd ldrs: effrt and chsng (clr) wnr whn blnd 3 out: sn one pce: 18 l down whn lft 2 l in front last: kpt on: hdd towards fin* **11/2**[3]
136- 3 *7* **Lord Of Drums (IRE)**[42] 3478 8-11-11 **108**..................... PeterBuchanan 102
(Lucinda Russell) *chsd ldrs: blnd and outpcd 5 out: lft modest 4th last: plugged on towards fin* **15/2**
303- 4 *3/4* **Endeavor**[16] 3937 9-11-9 **106**... RyanMania 98
(Dianne Sayer) *prom: mstke 8th: effrt and chsd wnr bef 4 out to next: sn outpcd: btn whn lft 10 l 3rd last* **18/1**
131- P **Pistol Basc (FR)**[46] 3352 10-10-7 **93**.................................... TonyKelly[(3)]
(Rebecca Menzies) *hld up: struggling fnl circ: t.o whn p.u 4 out* **15/2**
21P/ P **New Shuil (IRE)**[1125] 3552 10-10-9 **99**.............................. JohnDawson[(7)]
(John Wade) *mstkes in rr: lost tch and p.u bef 11th* **22/1**
50P- P **Lord Redsgirth (IRE)**[16] 3939 9-11-8 **105**........................ DougieCostello
(Lucy Normile) *bhd: pushed along 1/2-way: struggling 6 out: t.o whn p.u bef last* **10/1**

032- **F** **Brieryhill Boy**[48] 3275 7-11-0 **97** .... BrianHarding 116+
(William Amos) *led: rdn and drew clr fr 4 out: 18 l in front whn fell last* **3/1**[1]

642- **P** **Radio Nowhere (IRE)**[62] 3041 6-11-5 **102** ....(b) JasonMaguire
(Donald McCain) *prom: pushed along 1/2-way: rdn along and struggling 11th: t.o whn p.u 4 out* **9/2**[2]

5m 18.2s (17.00) **Going Correction** +0.50s/f (Soft) **9** Ran SP% **111.9**
Speed ratings: **86,85,82,82, , , ,**
CSF £49.98 CT £340.58 TOTE £10.00: £2.30, £1.80, £2.40; EX 39.40 Trifecta £341.70.
Owner John Wade **Bred** Miss Elizabeth Behan & Teresa Behan **Trained** Newton Bewley, Co Durham

FOCUS
Late drama here, with Brieryhill Boy clear and in complete control when taking off too far out and coming down at the last. There's a case for rating the form up to 5lb higher.

4223 DOWNLOAD THE FREE RACING APP H'CAP HURDLE (12 hdls) 2m 4f
3:15 (3:20) (Class 4) (0-105,104) 4-Y-0+ **£3,249** (£954; £477; £238)

Form RPR

/04- **1** **Blue Kascade (IRE)**[111] 2035 7-10-12 **90** .... RyanMania 98+
(Sandy Thomson) *in tch: hdwy 6th: led 8th: mde rest: clr whn nt fluent last: styd on strly* **5/1**[1]

015- **2** *10* **Jack Albert (IRE)**[45] 3396 7-10-4 **87** ow2........(b) ColmMcCormack[(5)] 85
(Dianne Sayer) *midfield: stdy hdwy 7th: rdn and 5th whn blnd 3 out: rallied whn hit last: sn chsng (clr) wnr: no imp* **8/1**

000- **3** *3 ½* **Runswick Days (IRE)**[22] 3826 7-10-8 **93** .... JohnDawson[(7)] 88
(John Wade) *hld up in midfield: pushed along after 4 out: styd on fr 2 out: nvr able to chal* **40/1**

/45- **4** *2 ¼* **Ellistrin Belle**[101] 2243 6-10-7 **90** .... CallumWhillans[(5)] 82
(Donald Whillans) *hld up: hdwy to chse ldrs after 4 out: rdn and chsd wnr 2 out to run-in: sn outpcd* **16/1**

036- **5** *1 ¼* **Iktiview**[23] 3264 6-10-10 **93** ....(bt) AdamNicol[(5)] 84
(Philip Kirby) *in tch: rdn and lost pl 5th: no imp tl styd on fr 2 out: nt pce to chal* **28/1**

P40- **6** *10* **Shooting Times**[39] 3525 9-11-0 **92** ....(b) PeterBuchanan 74
(Lucinda Russell) *midfield: lost pl 7th: sn struggling: rallied 2 out: nvr rchd ldrs* **28/1**

031- **7** *½* **Willie Hall**[17] 3924 10-10-11 **89** ....(p) BrianHarding 72
(William Amos) *cl up: led 6th to 8th: rdn and effrt 3 out: wkng whn j.lft last* **6/1**[3]

464- **8** *¾* **Tweedo Paradiso (NZ)**[57] 3141 7-10-12 **90** .... WilsonRenwick 71
(Rose Dobbin) *hld up on ins: hdwy to chse ldrs 1/2-way: rdn and wknd fr 2 out* **9/1**

9 *3* **Pairc Na Leasa (IRE)**[37] 3582 8-10-13 **96** .... HarryChalloner[(5)] 74
(Martin Todhunter) *bhd: struggling fnl circ: sme hdwy whn mstke last: nvr on terms* **11/2**[2]

10 *26* **Seancill Oir (IRE)**[42] 3481 9-11-7 **104** .... NicodeBoinville[(5)] 59
(S Donohoe, Ire) *chsd ldrs tl rdn and wknd bef 2 out* **8/1**

446- **11** *shd* **Mister D (IRE)**[101] 2245 8-10-10 **95** .... JonathonBewley[(7)] 50
(George Bewley) *led to 6th: cl up tl wknd after 4 out: btn whn hit 2 out* **40/1**

530- **12** *22* **Sudski Star (IRE)**[40] 3516 6-11-3 **95** ....(t) JamesReveley 30
(Patrick Griffin, Ire) *hld up: struggling fr 1/2-way: t.o* **12/1**

/32- **P** **Some Lad (IRE)**[262] 493 9-10-10 **88** .... DenisO'Regan
(Alison Hamilton) *hld up: nt fluent 8th: sn pushed along: struggling after next: t.o whn p.u bef 2 out* **14/1**

3U6- **P** **Karingo**[139] 1664 7-11-6 **98** .... DougieCostello
(Lucy Normile) *hld up: pushed along 8th: sn btn: t.o whn p.u bef 4 out* **20/1**

/0P- **P** **Darlington County (IRE)**[96] 2334 6-11-8 **100** ....(b[1]) JasonMaguire
(Donald McCain) *chsd ldrs: reminders 4th: lost pl bef 6th: struggling next: t.o whn p.u bef 3 out* **16/1**

4m 58.0s (6.50) **Going Correction** -0.15s/f (Good) **15** Ran SP% **121.2**
Speed ratings (Par 105): **81,77,75,74,74 70,70,69,68,58 58,49, , ,**
CSF £42.26 CT £1448.87 TOTE £6.90: £2.70, £3.50, £15.00; EX 54.30 Trifecta £2744.30.
Owner Mrs A M Thomson **Bred** Peter Greene & Joe Fallon **Trained** Lambden, Berwicks
■ Stewards' Enquiry : Colm McCormack three-day ban: weighed in 2lb heavy (Feb 26-28)

FOCUS
Ordinary handicap form. The easy winner is rated back to the best of his 2012 form.

4224 WATER TIGHT GREEN COMPLIANCE H'CAP HURDLE (9 hdls) 2m
3:50 (3:55) (Class 3) (0-135,132) 4-Y-0+
£6,256 (£1,848; £924; £462; £231; £116)

Form RPR

522- **1** **Figaro**[45] 3390 6-10-9 **115** ....(t) RichardJohnson 125+
(Tim Vaughan) *trckd ldrs: hdwy to dispute ld appr 2 out: led last: drvn out* **5/1**[3]

33F- **2** *½* **Roman Flight (IRE)**[11] 2910 6-11-0 **127** ....(v) KieronEdgar[(7)] 135+
(David Dennis) *t.k.h: hld up: smooth hdwy to ld appr 2 out: hdd and rdn last: kpt on: hld nr fin* **4/1**[2]

363- **3** *11* **Pas Trop Tard (FR)**[10] 4056 7-11-3 **130** ....(t) StephenMulqueen[(7)] 127
(Maurice Barnes) *led: rdn whn hit 3 out: hdd appr next: outpcd by first two fr last* **7/1**

532- **4** *1 ¼* **Trust Thomas**[32] 3659 6-10-3 **109** .... WilsonRenwick 104
(Ann Hamilton) *hld up: hdwy on outside and cl up bef 3 out: rdn and hung rt after next: outpcd bef last* **15/2**

U21- **5** *1 ¼* **Forced Family Fun**[35] 3599 4-10-5 **121** .... BrianHughes 105
(John Quinn) *t.k.h in midfield: hdwy bef 3 out: effrt and rdn next: wknd appr last* **5/2**[1]

100- **6** *hd* **Honour System (IRE)**[32] 3648 7-10-13 **119** .... DenisO'Regan 113
(John Ferguson) *hld up: n.m.r bnd after 4 out: effrt and hdwy bef next: no imp fr 2 out* **16/1**

F05- **7** *8* **Sleep In First (FR)**[42] 3476 8-10-4 **110** .... RyanMania 96
(James Ewart) *chsd ldrs: mstke 1st: rdn and outpcd bef 3 out: btn whn mstke next* **25/1**

/42- **8** *2* **Sir Pitt**[35] 3600 7-10-9 **120** .... HarryChalloner[(5)] 104
(John Bryan Groucott) *cl up: ev ch 4 out: rdn and wknd fr next* **18/1**

516- **9** *1 ½* **Kitchapoly (FR)**[103] 2200 4-10-12 **128** .... JasonMaguire 100
(Donald McCain) *nt fluent in rr: hdwy after 4 out: effrt whn stmbld next: sn btn* **18/1**

23/ **10** *37* **Fisher**[413] 3269 5-11-5 **132** .... DeanPratt[(7)] 77
(John Quinn) *in tch: rdn and outpcd after 4 out: lost tch fr next: t.o* **28/1**

321- **11** *16* **Town Mouse**[101] 2248 4-10-8 **127** .... TrevorWhelan[(3)] 46
(Neil King) *plld hrd: cl up tl rdn and wknd after 4 out: lost tch fr next: t.o* **22/1**

3m 42.5s (-5.90) **Going Correction** -0.15s/f (Good)
WFA 4 from 5yo+ 9lb **11** Ran SP% **117.6**
Speed ratings (Par 107): **108,107,102,101,101 100,96,95,95,76 68**
CSF £25.18 CT £141.66 TOTE £6.60: £1.90, £2.60, £2.70; EX 34.30 Trifecta £235.50.
Owner Pearn's Pharmacies Ltd **Bred** Cheveley Park Stud Ltd **Trained** Aberthin, Vale of Glamorgan

FOCUS
Only fair form for the level. The first two were well in on thir best Flat form and both posted biggish hurdling bests.

4225 CGA HUNTERS' CHASE (16 fncs) 2m 4f
4:25 (4:25) (Class 6) 5-Y-0+ **£1,247** (£387; £193; £96)

Form RPR

P/1- **1** **Habbie Simpson**[258] 557 9-11-9 126 .... MrTHamilton[(7)] 116+
(Miss J M Furness) *nt fluent on occasions: chsd clr ldng trio: rdn and hdwy to chse ldr 4 out: nrly 3 l down and styng on wl whn lft in ld 2 out: styd on strly: eased nr fin* **5/2**[2]

5/4- **2** *1 ¼* **Pena Dorada (IRE)**[17] 7-11-9 107 .... MissRMcDonald[(7)] 110
(Alan J Brown) *hld up: hdwy after 5 out: effrt and lft 4 l 2nd 2 out: kpt on fr last: nt rch eased-down wnr* **10/1**

13P- **3** *22* **Back On The Road (IRE)**[10] 4057 12-11-13 109.. MrJamieAlexander[(7)] 92
(N W Alexander) *bhd: strugging fr 1/2-way: hdwy bef 4 out: lft 4th 2 out: styd on fr last: no ch w first two* **33/1**

465/ **4** *10* **Oaklands Bobby**[256] 12-11-5 90 .... MissETodd[(7)] 76
(R G Russ) *led at str gallop and clr w one other to 1/2-way: mde most to 5 out: rdn and outpcd fr next: btn whn lft 15 l 3rd 2 out* **33/1**

/P2- **5** *26* **Beggar's Velvet (IRE)**[59] 8-11-13 129 .... MrDHolmes[(7)] 56
(D Holmes) *mstkes in rr: struggling fnl circ: nvr on terms* **8/1**[3]

1- **6** *24* **Molten Brown**[17] 9-11-9 0 .... MissJWalton[(7)] 28
(Miss C Marshall) *nt fluent in rr: struggling fr 1/2-way: t.o* **40/1**

033/ **U** **Golan Way**[431] 2925 10-11-7 0 .... MrBGibbs[(5)]
(Tim Vaughan) *hld up in tch: stmbld and uns rdr 2nd* **1/1**[1]

/P4- **F** **Glen Lord**[17] 11-11-9 69 ....(t) MrGCrow[(3)] 90
(Mrs N C Neill) *chsd clr ldng pair: hdwy 1/2-way: led 5 out: sn clr: nrly 3 l up whn fell 2 out* **66/1**

0/ **P** **Big Whitfield**[59] 8-11-5 0 .... MrNOrpwood[(7)]
(David Thompson) *t.k.h: disp ld and clr of rest to 1/2-way: outpcd whn blnd 11th: sn btn: t.o whn p.u bef 4 out* **66/1**

6FP/ **P** **Quix**[263] 8-11-7 0 .... MrSFox[(5)]
(Miss G E J Anderson) *mstkes in rr: no ch fnl circ: t.o whn p.u bef 4 out* **66/1**

144/ **U** **Silent Snow (IRE)**[374] 9-11-9 0 .... MrWHRReed[(7)]
(W T Reed) *hld up: mstke 1st: plenty to do whn uns rdr 9th* **50/1**

5m 19.3s (18.10) **Going Correction** +0.50s/f (Soft) **11** Ran SP% **113.5**
Speed ratings: **83,82,73,69,59 49, , , ,**
CSF £24.10 TOTE £3.40: £2.00, £3.70, £5.20; EX 21.90 Trifecta £127.00.
Owner Sandy Love **Bred** Moniabrock Farming **Trained** Lauder, Borders

FOCUS
Run at a searching gallop, there was no great depth to this hunters' chase, with it looking a match on paper. The cosy winner was a 135+ horse at best and should win more of these.

4226 SUZANNE & NIGEL 10 YEARS TOGETHER STANDARD OPEN NATIONAL HUNT FLAT RACE 2m
4:55 (4:55) (Class 6) 4-6-Y-0 **£1,949** (£572; £286; £143)

Form RPR

55- **1** **Donna's Diamond (IRE)**[33] 3640 5-10-10 0 .... DiarmuidO'Regan[(7)] 112+
(Chris Grant) *mde all: rdn along 2f out: sn hrd pressed: styd on gamely ins fnl f* **16/1**

1- **2** *1 ½* **Hurricane Hollow**[105] 2160 4-11-0 0 .... WilsonRenwick 107+
(Keith Dalgleish) *t.k.h: hld up in tch: stdy hdwy over 3f out: rdn and chal over 1f out to ins fnl f: hld last 50yds* **3/1**[1]

51- **3** *9* **Coozan George**[40] 3522 5-11-10 0 .... BrianHughes 108
(Malcolm Jefferson) *trckd ldrs: effrt and rdn over 2f out: outpcd by first two fr over 1f out* **7/2**[2]

0- **4** *¾* **Nathans Pride (IRE)**[54] 3187 6-11-3 .... AlanJohns[(10)] 111
(Tim Vaughan) *hld up in tch: effrt and rdn over 2f out: hung rt and outpcd over 1f out* **5/1**[3]

3/ **5** *1 ½* **Apachee Prince (IRE)**[298] 5407 5-11-0 0 .... EwanWhillans[(3)] 99
(Alistair Whillans) *hld up: shkn up and hdwy on outside over 2f out: no imp fr over 1f out* **7/2**[2]

0- **6** *1* **Lord Fendale (IRE)**[65] 3002 5-10-12 0 .... NicodeBoinville[(5)] 98
(S Donohoe, Ire) *cl up: rdn over 3f out: wknd over 1f out* **50/1**

3- **7** *8* **Always Tipsy**[40] 3522 5-10-10 0 .... MrKitAlexander[(7)] 90
(N W Alexander) *t.k.h: hld up on outside: rdn over 3f out: sn btn* **20/1**

5- **8** *15* **Albatros Tresor (FR)**[105] 2160 4-10-0 0 .... GrantCockburn[(7)] 65
(Lucinda Russell) *hld up: pushed along over 3f out: wknd over 2f out* **20/1**

0- **9** *11* **Drive The Bus (IRE)**[66] 2995 5-11-3 0 .... DGHogan 64
(Denis Gerard Hogan, Ire) *chsd ldrs: lost pl 4f out: sn struggling* **12/1**

5- **10** *3 ¼* **General Tiberius**[48] 3276 5-11-3 0 .... JasonMaguire 61
(K R Burke) *hld up: reminders after 6f: rallied: wknd 4f out* **28/1**

0- **P** **Castle Eden (IRE)**[53] 3214 4-10-7 0 .... AdrianLane
(Colin Teague) *in tch: struggling and lost pl after 6f: lost tch and p.u ent st* **200/1**

3m 40.4s (-2.40) **Going Correction** -0.15s/f (Good)
WFA 4 from 5yo+ 9lb **11** Ran SP% **115.1**
Speed ratings: **100,99,94,94,93 93,89,81,76,74**
CSF £59.61 TOTE £22.00: £4.70, £1.10, £1.60; EX 85.50 Trifecta £264.40.
Owner D&D Armstrong Ltd **Bred** C Kenneally **Trained** Newton Bewley, Co Durham

FOCUS
An above average bumper for the track, which should still produce winners.
T/Plt: £371.50 to a £1 stake. Pool: £109,060.45 - 214.28 winning tickets T/Qpdt: £70.20 to a £1 stake. Pool: £9077.44 - 95.64 winning tickets RY

3245 FONTWELL (L-H)
Thursday, February 13
4227 Meeting Abandoned - waterlogged

The Form Book Jumps, Raceform Ltd, Compton, RG20 6NL.

[3392]KELSO (L-H)

Thursday, February 13

OFFICIAL GOING: Good to soft (soft in places; 6.2)

Fresh ground on all bends and all distances as advertised.

Wind: Fresh, half against Weather: Cloudy

4234 DAVID MERRY FARRIER NOVICES' HURDLE (8 hdls) 2m 110y

1:55 (1:55) (Class 4) 4-Y-O+ £3,249 (£954; £477; £238)

Form RPR

450- 1 **Landecker (IRE)**[41] 3516 6-11-3 0 LucyAlexander 121+
(N W Alexander) *hld up bhd ldng gp: hdwy to chse ldrs whn nt fluent 3 out: nrly 4 l down whn lft 2nd last: styd on wl to ld cl home* **50/1**

41- 2 *nse* **Rainbow Peak (IRE)**[20] 3877 8-11-10 0 DenisO'Regan 127
(John Ferguson) *cl up gng wl: led on bit 2 out: lft nrly 4 l clr last: sn rdn: kpt on: hdd cl home* **4/11**[1]

6/4- 3 *20* **Lord Usher (IRE)**[46] 3392 7-11-3 0 JanFaltejsek 104
(George Charlton) *chsd ldrs: pushed along and outpcd bef 2 out: no imp whn lft 3rd last: one pce* **14/1**[3]

0- 4 *8* **Island Heights (IRE)**[23] 3826 5-11-3 0 WilsonRenwick 96
(Lucinda Russell) *in tch: hdwy to chal 4 out to appr next: outpcd bef 2 out: hld whn lft 4th last* **33/1**

0/3- 5 *2 3/4* **Spitz (FR)**[117] 1975 6-11-3 0[1] BrianHarding 92
(Rose Dobbin) *hld up on ins: rdn after 3 out: no imp whn blnd next: sn btn* **20/1**

4- 6 *8* **Apterix (FR)**[18] 3926 4-10-7 0 JamesReveley 75
(Brian Ellison) *hld up: stdy hdwy after 3 out: shkn up bef next: no imp and eased bef last* **16/1**

/5P- 7 *3 1/4* **Pennine Josie**[35] 3616 5-10-7 0 TonyKelly[(3)] 75
(James Moffatt) *bhd: struggling 1/2-way: sme late hdwy: nvr on terms* **100/1**

05- 8 *1/2* **Westend Theatre (IRE)**[85] 2593 5-10-10 0 AlistairFindlay[(7)] 82
(Jane Walton) *prom tl rdn and wknd appr 3 out* **66/1**

10- 9 *2* **Roc De Prince**[67] 2968 5-11-10 0 (t) BrianHughes 87
(James Ewart) *in tch: pushed along bef 3 out: rdn and wknd bef next* **20/1**

005- 10 *42* **Zuileka**[22] 3835 5-10-7 0 JonathanEngland[(3)] 35
(James Moffatt) *midfield on outside: struggling fr 4th: t.o* **100/1**

U5- 11 *10* **Great Demeanor (USA)**[13] 4003 4-10-7 0 RyanMania 23
(Dianne Sayer) *led: mstke and hdd 4 out: wknd fr next: t.o* **66/1**

/2F- F **Master Red (IRE)**[75] 2806 5-11-3 0 JasonMaguire 121
(Donald McCain) *cl up: nt fluent 4th: led next: blnd and hdd 2 out: styd upsides: ev ch whn fell and down for sme time last* **3/1**[2]

4m 10.6s (8.80) **Going Correction** +0.55s/f (Soft)
WFA 4 from 5yo+ 9lb 12 Ran SP% **130.3**
Speed ratings (Par 105): **101,100,91,87,86 82,81,80,80,60 55,**
CSF £78.14 TOTE £61.20: £14.20, £1.10, £3.70; EX 232.30 Trifecta £711.70.
Owner Mrs N Hodge **Bred** Mrs Patricia Furlong **Trained** Kinneston, Perth & Kinross

FOCUS

Fresh ground on all bends and all distances as advertised. Brian Hughes reported the ground to be dead and hard work. There was little pace on early, with nobody wanting to go on, and the race produced a shock result. The runner-up is rated a stone+ off.

4235 KELSO ANNUAL MEMBERS NOVICES' LIMITED H'CAP CHASE (12 fncs) 2m 1f

2:25 (2:25) (Class 3) (0-140,135) 5-Y-O+ £6,498 (£1,908; £954; £477)

Form RPR

F5U- 1 **Suprise Vendor (IRE)**[8] 4084 8-10-0 120 ow2 DaraghBourke[(7)] 124
(Stuart Coltherd) *pressed ldr: sltly outpcd 3 out: rallied and ev ch bef last: kpt on wl to ld post* **8/1**

P51- 2 *shd* **Croco Bay (IRE)**[47] 3354 7-11-8 135 RichieMcGrath 138
(Peter Atkinson) *t.k.h early: led: qcknd 3 out: hrd pressed bef last: kpt on run-in: hdd post* **4/1**[2]

211- 3 *1/2* **Firth Of The Clyde**[28] 3738 9-11-8 135 BrianHughes 139+
(Malcolm Jefferson) *hld up in tch: rdn and outpcd after 5 out: rallied between last 2: kpt on wl u.p fr last* **2/1**[1]

P4/- 4 *1 1/2* **Cayman Islands**[307] 5272 6-10-10 123 DenisO'Regan 124
(John Ferguson) *prom: effrt 3 out: sn rdn: kpt on same pce fr last* **10/1**

644- 5 *8* **Tour D'Argent (FR)**[68] 2957 7-10-12 125 JasonMaguire 123
(Donald McCain) *prom: nt fluent 1st: blnd 4 out: rdn next: no imp whn hit 2 out* **5/1**[3]

460- 6 *50* **Rhymers Ha'**[46] 3398 7-10-3 116 oh2 (p) PeterBuchanan 65
(Lucinda Russell) *bhd: lost tch 1/2-way: t.o* **11/1**

/15- F **Rockawango (FR)**[54] 3202 8-11-3 130 (tp) NickScholfield
(James Ewart) *hld up: fell 2nd* **8/1**

4m 27.4s (9.40) **Going Correction** +0.35s/f (Yiel) 7 Ran SP% **109.6**
Speed ratings: **91,90,90,90,86 62,**
CSF £36.97 TOTE £9.90: £4.50, £2.40; EX 65.90 Trifecta £141.10.
Owner Aidan Gunning **Bred** P Travers **Trained** Selkirk, Borders

FOCUS

A fair handicap chase that produced a tight finish. Small steps up from the fist two with the third rated similar to his recent win.

4236 AMATEUR JOCKEYS' ASSOCIATION AMATEUR RIDERS' H'CAP CHASE (17 fncs) 2m 7f 110y

2:55 (2:55) (Class 3) (0-135,132) 5-Y-O+ £6,862 (£2,128; £1,063; £532)

Form RPR

2PP- 1 **Mister Marker (IRE)**[35] 3617 10-11-7 132 MissJRRichards[(5)] 143
(Nicky Richards) *w ldrs: led 1/2-way: hdd 3 out: rdn and sltly outpcd next: rallied to regain ld last 100yds: hld on gamely* **8/1**

/51- 2 *shd* **Or De Grugy (FR)**[46] 3394 12-10-0 111 MrKitAlexander[(5)] 122
(N W Alexander) *cl up: led 3 out: rdn next: hdd last 100yds: rallied: jst hld* **8/1**

513- 3 *17* **Badger Foot (IRE)**[20] 3874 9-9-12 111 (t) MissRMcDonald[(7)] 109
(Lucinda Russell) *hld up in tch: nt fluent 4 out: effrt to chse clr ldrs bef 2 out: sn no imp* **8/1**

254- 4 *12* **Ros Castle (IRE)**[42] 3498 8-10-9 118 MrJHamilton[(3)] 105
(Rose Dobbin) *hld up bhd ldng gp: blnd 8th: rdn bef 4 out: no imp fr next* **5/1**[3]

455- 5 *6* **More Equity**[20] 3874 12-10-2 108 MissCWalton 88
(Dianne Sayer) *bhd: outpcd bef 12th: no imp whn mstke 2 out* **50/1**

511- 6 *3/4* **The Panama Kid (IRE)**[20] 3874 10-10-12 125 (b) MrJTeal[(7)] 104
(Malcolm Jefferson) *prom: rdn and outpcd 4 out: btn fnl 2* **3/1**[1]

354- 7 *6* **Fiddlers Reel**[60] 3111 11-10-1 114 MrTHamilton[(7)] 90
(Jane Clark) *in tch: mstkes 7th and next: sn lost pl: struggling fr 11th* **9/2**[2]

P22- 8 *14* **Abbey Storm (IRE)**[46] 3397 8-11-0 120 MrDerekO'Connor 81
(Donald McCain) *nt fluent: slt ld to 1/2-way: cl up tl rdn and wknd after 3 out* **9/2**[2]

6m 10.8s (2.80) **Going Correction** +0.35s/f (Yiel) 8 Ran SP% **113.3**
Speed ratings: **109,108,103,99,97 97,95,90**
CSF £66.51 CT £527.47 TOTE £9.80: £1.70, £2.10, £3.10; EX 84.40 Trifecta £543.20.
Owner Jimmy Dudgeon **Bred** Mrs M M Kelly **Trained** Greystoke, Cumbria

FOCUS

The front pair drew right away in this staying handicap. The winner is rated back to his best.

4237 TIMEFORM MOREBATTLE HURDLE (10 hdls) 2m 2f

3:25 (3:25) (Class 2) 4-Y-O+ £12,996 (£3,816; £1,908; £954)

Form RPR

04F- 1 **Runswick Royal (IRE)**[11] 4056 5-11-3 139 BrianHughes 144
(Ann Hamilton) *trckd ldrs: stdy hdwy bef 2 out: rdn and led between last 2: edgd lft after last: hld on wl cl home* **9/2**[3]

442- 2 *1/2* **Upsilon Bleu (FR)**[19] 3894 6-11-3 144 WilsonRenwick 144
(Pauline Robson) *chsd ldr: nt fluent 3rd: led and pushed along bef 2 out: hdd between last 2: rallied and ev ch whn n.m.r briefly last: kpt on: hld nr fin* **14/1**

431- 3 *8* **Special Catch (IRE)**[54] 3206 7-11-3 134 JamesReveley 137
(Keith Reveley) *hld up: stdy hdwy whn hit 2 out: sn outpcd by ldng pair* **10/3**[2]

522- 4 *5* **Doyly Carte**[19] 3895 6-11-0 140 JasonMaguire 129
(Donald McCain) *chsd ldrs: drvn along bef 2 out: wknd between last 2* **10/3**[2]

004- 5 *8* **Bygones Of Brid (IRE)**[22] 3832 11-11-3 120 (v) RyanMania 126
(Karen McLintock) *led: rdn and hdd bef 2 out: sn wknd* **33/1**

/64- F **Duke Of Navan (IRE)**[49] 3261 6-11-7 145 BrianHarding 136
(Nicky Richards) *t.k.h: hld up in tch: pushed along and outpcd after 3 out: no imp next: 5th and btn whn fell last* **2/1**[1]

4m 37.9s (10.90) **Going Correction** +0.90s/f (Soft) 6 Ran SP% **107.3**
Speed ratings (Par 109): **111,110,107,105,101**
CSF £48.60 TOTE £5.70: £2.20, £2.60; EX 65.20 Trifecta £151.50.
Owner Ian Hamilton **Bred** Chesters Stud Ltd **Trained** Great Bavington, Northumbland

FOCUS

Although run at a good gallop, this isn't form to take seriously, with neither of the two market leaders giving their running. The winner is rated back to his best.

4238 IVAN STRAKER MEMORIAL CHASE (19 fncs) 3m 2f

3:55 (3:56) (Class 2) 5-Y-O+ £12,512 (£3,696; £1,848; £924)

Form RPR

54U- 1 **Long Run (FR)**[49] 3262 9-10-12 163 (p) MrSWaley-Cohen 128+
(Nicky Henderson) *t.k.h: pressed ldr: nt fluent 6th: chal 1/2-way: led gng wl 3 out: rdn clr fr last* **2/5**[1]

251- 2 *6* **Knockara Beau (IRE)**[19] 3890 11-10-12 146 JanFaltejsek 122+
(George Charlton) *led at stdy pce: slipped after 14th: sn rcvrd: hdd 3 out: sn rdn: rallied and ev ch last: outpcd run-in* **9/4**[2]

/01- 3 *16* **Isla Pearl Fisher**[41] 3521 11-10-12 127 LucyAlexander 106
(N W Alexander) *in tch: wnt 3rd 14th: outpcd by first two 4 out: sn no imp* **25/1**[3]

326- 4 *8* **Heez A Steel (IRE)**[64] 3022 13-10-12 93 AlistairFindlay 98
(Jane Walton) *chsd ldrs: outpcd and lost 3rd pl 14th: n.d after* **300/1**

7m 12.5s (25.30) **Going Correction** +0.70s/f (Soft) 4 Ran SP% **106.4**
Speed ratings: **89,87,82,79**
CSF £1.66 TOTE £1.30; EX 1.80 Trifecta £2.10.
Owner Robert Waley-Cohen **Bred** Mrs Marie-Christine Gabeur **Trained** Upper Lambourn, Berks

FOCUS

An intriguing match that played out pretty much as expected. Not form to take seriously with the first two rated stones off in a slowly run race.

4239 CGA FOXHUNTER TRIAL OPEN HUNTERS' CHASE (15 fncs 2 omitted) 2m 7f 110y

4:25 (4:27) (Class 6) 5-Y-O+ £1,871 (£580; £290; £145)

Form RPR

1/P- 1 **Tartan Snow**[23] 3825 14-12-2 122 MrJHamilton[(3)] 120+
(Stuart Coltherd) *hld up in tch: stdy hdwy fnl circ: led 3 out (usual 4 out): drew clr bef omitted 2 out: kpt on strly: unchal* **13/2**[2]

1/- 2 *20* **Moscow Menace (IRE)**[18] 7-11-8 87 MrTHamilton[(7)] 96
(Miss K Scott) *t.k.h early: chsd ldrs: outpcd 4 out (usual 5 out): rallied bef omitted 2 out: chsd (clr) wnr run-in: no imp* **10/1**

45P/ 3 *3* **Douglas Julian**[18] 12-12-5 123 MrDerekO'Connor 98
(Miss K Scott) *cl up: led 5th: blnd and rdr dropped whip 4 out (usual 5 out): hdd next: chsd wnr: outpcd bef omitted 2 out: lost 2nd run-in* **14/1**

242/ 4 *3 1/2* **Noir Et Vert (FR)**[18] 13-11-6 91 ow2 MrJamieAlexander[(7)] 88
(N W Alexander) *hld up in tch: stdy hdwy 1/2-way: effrt bef 3 out (usual 4 out): no imp bef omitted 2 out* **20/1**

21S/ 5 *15* **Sacred Mountain**[25] 13-12-1 109 MissCWalton 82
(James Walton) *chsd ldrs: chal 3rd to 5th: cl up tl lost pl after 10th: outpcd 4 out (usual 5 out): btn bef omitted 2 out* **12/1**

0/4- P **Charming Knight (IRE)**[285] 114 13-11-4 59 MissJWalton[(7)]
(Jane Walton) *bhd: lost tch fnl circ: t.o whn p.u bef 2 out (usual 3 out)* **100/1**

POP/ R **Sammy Spiderman**[18] 11-11-8 65 MissEDunkley[(7)]
(Miss K Scott) *bhd: hmpd 1st: outpcd after 10th: sme hdwy after 4 out (usual 5 out): sn n.d: no ch whn ref last* **66/1**

444- F **Captain Americo (IRE)**[12] 4042 12-11-8 108 (p) MrTDavidson[(3)] 80
(Mrs B Ewart) *led to 5th: cl up: effrt and ev ch bef 3 out (usual 4 out): outpcd bef omitted 2 out: sixth and btn whn fell heavily last* **8/1**[3]

/33- F **Barachois Silver**[25] 10-10-13 79 MrSFox[(5)]
(Mrs J M Hollands) *cl up: j.rt and fell heavily 1st* **20/1**

11- U **Harbour Court**[251] 658 8-12-5 120 MrJETudor
(Alan Hill) *hld up: bdly hmpd and uns rdr 1st* **8/13**[1]

6m 21.0s (13.00) **Going Correction** +0.70s/f (Soft) 10 Ran SP% **121.8**
Speed ratings: **106,99,98,97,92 , , , ,**
CSF £66.38 TOTE £6.80: £2.30, £2.40, £3.60; EX 73.30 Trifecta £1575.70.
Owner R V Westwood **Bred** R V Westwood **Trained** Selkirk, Borders

FOCUS
Much of the interest in this hunters' chase was lost when red-hot favourite Harbour Court was out of the race at the first. Tartan Snow is rated 6lb off last season's Aintree win.

4240 EBF STALLIONS MARES' STANDARD OPEN NATIONAL HUNT FLAT RACE 2m 110y

4:55 (4:55) (Class 6) 4-7-Y-0 £1,949 (£572; £286; £143)

Form RPR

1 **Knocklayde Express (IRE)** 5-10-13 0 MrSCrawford(3) 104
(S R B Crawford, Ire) *t.k.h: hld up: smooth hdwy over 3f out: effrt and ev ch 2f out: drifted lft over 1f out: styd on wl fnl f to ld nr fin* **3/1**[1]

- 2 *hd* **Tara Mac** 5-11-2 0 WilsonRenwick 104
(Keith Dalgleish) *prom: hdwy to ld 2f out: kpt on fnl f: hdd nr fin* **5/1**[3]

3 *7* **Bespoke Lady (IRE)**[26] 5-11-2 0 JasonMaguire 98
(Donald McCain) *led: reminders 1/2-way: rallied: drvn and hdd 2f out: sn outpcd by first two* **7/2**[2]

5- 4 *9* **Lady Of Provence**[258] 567 5-10-13 0 JeremiahMcGrath(3) 90
(Nicky Henderson) *in tch: smooth hdwy and ev ch over 2f out: rdn and wknd over 1f out* **11/2**

5- 5 *1 ¾* **Lochnell (IRE)**[29] 3727 5-10-9 0 NathanMoscrop(7) 88
(Brian Ellison) *in tch: pushed along 3f out: outpcd fr 2f out* **18/1**

6 *8* **Blue Bellini** 6-11-2 0 DenisO'Regan 81
(Chris Grant) *hld up: rdn over 6f out: plugged on fr over 1f out: nvr able to chal* **16/1**

7 *4* **Just Annie** 6-11-2 0 RyanMania 77
(Lucy Normile) *hld up: hdwy to chse ldrs over 5f out: rdn and wknd over 2f out* **22/1**

8 *3 ¼* **Bossy Beccy** 5-10-11 0 MissCWalton(5) 74
(James Walton) *hld up: struggling over 5f out: n.d after* **100/1**

9 *14* **Tara Springs** 5-11-2 0 BrianHarding 62
(Barry Murtagh) *in tch: drvn and outpcd 4f out: btn over 2f out* **50/1**

10 *15* **Queens Regatta (IRE)** 5-11-2 0 LucyAlexander 48
(Bruce Mactaggart) *cl up tl rdn and wknd over 3f out* **33/1**

62- 11 *1 ½* **Nearly May**[29] 3727 6-10-11 0 CallumWhillans(5) 47
(Donald Whillans) *cl up: rdn over 3f out: wknd qckly 2f out* **8/1**

12 *56* **Classy Chassis (IRE)** 6-11-2 0 AdrianLane
(Iain Jardine) *hld up in tch: struggling 1/2-way: sn lost tch: t.o* **40/1**

4m 11.8s (15.60) **Going Correction** +0.90s/f (Soft) **12** Ran SP% **114.2**
Speed ratings: **99,98,95,91,90 86,84,83,76,69 69,42**
CSF £16.53 TOTE £3.60: £2.10, £2.20, £1.30; EX 19.50 Trifecta £117.80.
Owner Colm McHenry **Bred** Colm McHenry **Trained** Larne, Co Antrim
■ Stewards' Enquiry : Mr S Crawford four-day ban: used whip above permitted level (Feb 27,Mar 1,3,5)

FOCUS
The market leaders dominated this ordinary mares' bumper. The fifth sets the level.
T/Plt: £811.10 to a £1 stake. Pool of £80480.82 - 72.43 winning tickets. T/Qpdt: £104.70 to a £1 stake. Pool of £6064.91 - 42.86 winning tickets. RY

3816 LEICESTER (R-H)

Thursday, February 13

OFFICIAL GOING: Soft (heavy in places; 5.8)
The 2nd fence in the home straight was omitted on all circuits of all chases; false ground.
Wind: Fresh behind Weather: Cloudy with sunny spells

4241 WREN H'CAP CHASE (11 fncs 1 omitted) 2m

2:10 (2:10) (Class 4) (0-115,115) 5-Y-0+ £4,548 (£1,335; £667; £333)

Form RPR

221- 1 **Massena (IRE)**[37] 3596 7-11-12 115 AidanColeman 141+
(Venetia Williams) *trckd ldr: led appr 3 out: sn clr: eased flat* **1/1**[1]

11U- 2 *22* **Arkaim**[22] 3833 6-11-8 114 KielanWoods(3) 113
(Pam Sly) *hld up: led appr 3 out: rdn and wknd bef next* **10/1**

/42- 3 *4 ½* **Stormhoek (IRE)**[22] 3837 9-11-7 110 (vt) SamTwiston-Davies 104
(Nigel Twiston-Davies) *chsd ldrs: pushed along 7th: rdn and wknd appr 3 out: lft poor 3rd last* **5/1**[3]

215- 4 *32* **Engai (GER)**[166] 1478 8-11-12 115 TomScudamore 77
(David Bridgwater) *hld up: hdwy 7th: wknd 3 out* **16/1**

103- P **Molko Jack (FR)**[49] 3272 10-9-11 91[1] JamesBanks(5)
(Michael Mullineaux) *a in rr: nt fluent 2nd: bhd and pushed along next: p.u bef last* **20/1**

2/4- F **Little Jimmy**[79] 2727 7-10-0 89 FelixDeGiles 88
(Tom Gretton) *hld up: hdwy 5th: rdn and wknd after 3 out: poor 3rd whn fell last* **3/1**[2]

4m 13.8s (5.60) **Going Correction** +0.50s/f (Soft) **6** Ran SP% **111.4**
Speed ratings: **106,95,92,76,**
CSF £10.95 CT £33.62 TOTE £1.50: £1.10, £4.00; EX 11.60 Trifecta £27.30.
Owner Miss V M Williams **Bred** Frank Dunne **Trained** Kings Caple, H'fords

FOCUS
An all-chase card. Aidan Coleman said of the ground: "It's more soft than heavy", while Tom Scudamore described it as "very holding." This interesting handicap was run at a decent gallop. A seemingly big step up from the easy winner and there's a case for rating the form higher.

4242 WEATHERBYS HAMILTON INSURANCE NOVICES' H'CAP CHASE (10 fncs 2 omitted) 2m

2:40 (2:40) (Class 4) (0-110,110) 5-Y-0+ £4,548 (£1,335; £667; £333)

Form RPR

F50- 1 **Lord Navits (IRE)**[245] 730 6-10-5 89 (vt[1]) AlainCawley 113+
(David Bridgwater) *hld up: racd keenly: hdwy to ld 4th: clr next: easily* **8/1**[3]

043- 2 *10* **Tokyo Javilex (FR)**[22] 3839 7-10-8 92 (t) SamTwiston-Davies 105
(Nigel Hawke) *hld up: hdwy and nt fluent 8th: rdn to chse wnr appr last: styd on same pce* **7/2**[1]

0/0- 3 *3 ¼* **Dont Do Mondays (IRE)**[13] 4023 7-11-12 110 TomScudamore 120
(David Bridgwater) *lft in ld 1st: hdd 4th: chsd wnr tl rdn appr last: no ex flat* **4/1**[2]

005- 4 *8* **Dropzone (USA)**[28] 3729 5-10-9 98 (p) RobertDunne(3) 97
(Richard Lee) *prom: pushed along 7th: rdn and wknd 3 out* **10/1**

43P- 5 *2 ¼* **Kastani Beach (IRE)**[59] 3137 8-10-10 101 KevinJones(7) 99
(Seamus Mullins) *chsd ldr 1st to 4th: rdn and wknd appr 3 out* **10/1**

/65- 6 *30* **Ultra Klass (FR)**[20] 3880 6-11-5 103 (p) AndrewTinkler 71
(Jamie Snowden) *prom: lost pl 6th: wknd 3 out* **16/1**

/60- 7 *13* **September Blaze**[46] 3391 7-11-10 108 DominicElsworth 63
(Paul Webber) *hld up: a in rr: wknd appr 3 out* **33/1**

332- B **Bin End**[23] 3819 8-11-4 102 (p) FelixDeGiles
(Barry Brennan) *b.d 1st* **4/1**[2]

PFP- F **Killegney**[23] 3817 10-9-9 86 ow1[1] MissAEStirling(7)
(Michael Gates) *led and fell 1st* **50/1**

/00- P **Star Presenter (IRE)**[74] 2848 6-10-13 97 PaulMoloney
(Paul Webber) *hld up: a in rr: wkng whn j.rt 3 out: bhd whn p.u bef last* **8/1**[3]

4m 12.1s (3.90) **Going Correction** +0.50s/f (Soft)
WFA 5 from 6yo+ 1lb **10** Ran SP% **113.4**
Speed ratings: **110,105,103,99,98 83,76,, ,**
CSF £36.31 CT £128.92 TOTE £8.80: £2.30, £1.50, £2.00; EX 47.00 Trifecta £358.80.
Owner Jobarry Partnership **Bred** Miss Mary O'Sullivan **Trained** Icomb, Gloucs

FOCUS
Modest novice handicap form. Killegney and Bin End came down at the first and that fence, which would have been the second-last, was bypassed on the final circuit. The easy winner was up 10lb on his best hurdles form.

4243 ROA OWNERS JACKPOT H'CAP CHASE (16 fncs 2 omitted) 2m 7f 110y

3:10 (3:10) (Class 5) (0-100,102) 5-Y-0+ £3,249 (£954; £477; £238)

Form RPR

034- 1 **Kentford Legend**[47] 3368 7-11-12 96 AndrewThornton 111
(Seamus Mullins) *a.p: j.rt 5th: led 7th: hdd and nt fluent 3 out: sn rdn: styd on u.p to ld fnl 50yds* **8/1**

136- 2 *2 ¾* **Crescent Beach (IRE)**[20] 3876 7-11-2 86 PaddyBrennan 99
(Henry Oliver) *hld up: racd keenly: hdwy 13th: led 3 out: rdn appr last: hdd and no ex fnl 50yds* **16/1**

S11- 3 *4 ½* **Browns Brook (IRE)**[7] 4109 8-12-4 102 7ex AidanColeman 112
(Venetia Williams) *chsd ldrs: rdn appr last: styd on same pce* **6/4**[1]

061- 4 *2 ½* **The Last Bridge**[10] 4066 7-11-3 87 7ex RichardJohnson 94
(Susan Johnson) *chsd ldrs: lost pl 5th: sn pushed along: hdwy 10th: rdn and outpcd appr 3 out: styd 2 on flat* **7/2**[2]

210/ 5 *¾* **Killfinnan Castle (IRE)**[694] 4994 11-10-6 76 WillKennedy 80
(Violet M Jordan) *hld up: hdwy 13th: rdn appr 2 out: wknd bef last* **66/1**

U25- 6 *10* **Lord Fox (IRE)**[17] 3936 7-10-11 86 BenPoste(5) 80
(Shaun Harris) *led 2nd to 4th: led 5th to next: chsd ldrs: rdn appr 3 out: wknd bef next* **7/1**[3]

404- 7 *13* **Noble Witness (IRE)**[10] 4066 11-11-9 93 (p) AdamPogson 74
(Charles Pogson) *led to 2nd: led 4th to next: led 6th to 7th: remained handy tl rdn and wknd 3 out* **28/1**

462- 8 *60* **Highland River**[25] 3799 8-10-9 79 (b) LeeEdwards
(Dave Roberts) *in rr whn mstke 4th: sn rdn: bhd fr 7th* **33/1**

045- P **Top Benefit (IRE)**[25] 3797 12-10-3 78 JamesBanks(5)
(Richard Harper) *hld up: hdwy 5th: wknd 9th: bhd whn p.u bef last* **25/1**

P5R- P **Dermatologiste**[10] 4066 11-11-9 93 (p) PaulMoloney
(Caroline Bailey) *prom: reminders 3rd: lost pl next: bhd fr 8th: p.u after 13th* **16/1**

/5P- P **Mezarat (ITY)**[25] 3799 9-9-10 73 (p) MissAEStirling(7)
(Michael Gates) *nt fluent in rr: bhd fr 8th: mstke next: sn p.u* **50/1**

F/0- F **Newton Thistle**[20] 3873 7-9-9 70 oh5 NicodeBoinville(5)
(Ben Pauling) *chsd ldrs: disputing cl 3rd whn fell 10th* **12/1**

6m 16.1s (12.10) **Going Correction** +0.50s/f (Soft) **12** Ran SP% **119.0**
Speed ratings: **99,98,96,95,95 92,87,67,, ,**
CSF £112.50 CT £296.98 TOTE £10.50: £3.10, £1.70, £1.80; EX 96.00 Trifecta £338.50.
Owner D I Bare **Bred** D I Bare **Trained** Wilsford-Cum-Lake, Wilts

FOCUS
A low-grade handicap chase. A big step up from the winner with a smaller one from the second.

4244 CAVALRY H'CAP CHASE (13 fncs 2 omitted) 2m 4f 110y

3:40 (3:40) (Class 3) (0-140,135) 5-Y-0+ £6,498 (£1,908; £954; £477)

Form RPR

243- 1 **Rydalis (FR)**[28] 3730 9-10-10 119 AidanColeman 127+
(Venetia Williams) *hld up in tch: led 2 out: rdn flat: idled towards fin: jst hld on* **6/1**

P1P- 2 *¾* **Noble Legend**[33] 3655 7-11-12 135 AndrewThornton 139
(Caroline Bailey) *chsd ldrs: wnt 2nd 9th tl led appr 3 out: rdn and hdd next: rallied u.p flat* **11/2**[3]

133- 3 *7* **Cloudy Bob (IRE)**[26] 3769 7-11-2 125 ColinBolger 122
(Pat Murphy) *led: mstke 2nd: sn hdd: chsd ldr to 4th: remained handy: rdn after 3 out: styd on same pce appr last* **15/8**[1]

002- 4 *15* **Have You Seen Me (IRE)**[21] 3859 11-10-7 123 RyanHatch(7) 105
(Nigel Twiston-Davies) *plld hrd: w ldr tl led after 2nd: hdd bef 3 out: rdn and wknd appr last* **12/1**

231- P **Billy Cuckoo (IRE)**[7] 4106 8-11-1 124 7ex (b) DougieCostello
(Tony Coyle) *hld up: bhd fr 5th: p.u bef 3 out* **16/1**

221- P **Benefit Cut (IRE)**[9] 4077 8-11-6 129 7ex (t) SamTwiston-Davies
(Renee Robeson) *prom: chsd ldr 4th tl mstke 9th: rdn and wknd appr 3 out: bhd whn p.u bef last* **2/1**[2]

5m 26.8s (7.90) **Going Correction** +0.50s/f (Soft) **6** Ran SP% **111.4**
Speed ratings: **104,103,101,95,**
CSF £36.16 TOTE £6.30: £2.10, £2.30; EX 39.40 Trifecta £85.90.
Owner Mrs Vida Bingham **Bred** Jean-Luc Couetil & Marie-Celine Couetil **Trained** Kings Caple, H'fords

FOCUS
A fair handicap chase run at a sound gallop. The winner is rated to her best, with the second to his mark.

4245 FERNIE NOVICES' LIMITED H'CAP CHASE (16 fncs 2 omitted) 2m 7f 110y

4:10 (4:10) (Class 3) (0-140,133) 5-Y-0 £6,330 (£1,870; £935; £468; £234)

Form RPR

1P3- 1 **Knock A Hand (IRE)**[26] 3777 9-11-8 133 (b) RichardJohnson 143
(Richard Lee) *a.p: chsd ldr 3rd tl led 12th: rdn appr 2 out: styd on u.p* **9/2**[3]

/24- 2 *7* **Titchwood (IRE)**[59] 3131 6-11-2 127 APMcCoy 131
(Jonjo O'Neill) *trckd ldrs: racd keenly: chal 3 out: rdn appr last: no ex flat: eased whn hld towards fin* **9/4**[2]

4U3- 3 *7* **Renard D'Irlande (FR)**[19] 3886 9-11-2 127 AidanColeman 122
(Venetia Williams) *hld up in tch: rdn after 3 out: wknd appr last* **7/4**[1]

/12- 4 *3* **Definite Memories (IRE)**[29] 3718 7-11-3 128 AlainCawley 120
(David Bridgwater) *hld up: hdwy appr 3 out: rdn bef next: wknd last* **16/1**

420- 5 *32* **Tullyraine (IRE)**[29] 3717 10-10-12 123 SamTwiston-Davies 83
(Nigel Twiston-Davies) *led: hit 11th: hdd next: rdn and wknd appr 3 out* **9/2**[3]

6m 10.5s (6.50) **Going Correction** +0.50s/f (Soft) **5** Ran SP% **109.4**
Speed ratings: **109,106,104,103,92**
CSF £15.06 TOTE £6.20: £2.30, £2.80; EX 16.80 Trifecta £37.60.
Owner Alan Halsall **Bred** Patrick Monahan **Trained** Byton, H'fords

FOCUS
An interesting event run in a time 5.6sec quicker than the previous handicap over the trip. The winenr is rated back to his Carlisle mark, with the second to form.

4246 CGA FOXHUNTER TRIAL NOVICES' HUNTERS' CHASE (FOR THE DICK SAUNDERS TROPHY) (13 fncs 2 omitted) 2m 4f 110y
4:40 (4:40) (Class 6) 6-Y-0+ **£1,559** (£483; £241; £121)

Form RPR
4/1- **1** **Shy John**[14] 3993 8-11-11 124 .... MrPMason(7) 115+
(P W Mason) *hld up: hdwy appr 3 out: led next: drvn out* **4/6**[1]
2 ½ **Spotthestripe**[690] 9-11-0 0 ....[1] MrRGSpencer(7) 101
(G J Tarry) *a.p: chsd ldr 5th: led 7th to next: led 9th: hdd after 10th: ev ch 2 out: sn rdn: styd on u.p* **50/1**
2/4- **3** 5 **Swallows Delight (IRE)**[288] 57 9-12-0 100 .... MrDMansell 104
(Mrs Julie Mansell) *led to 7th: led again next: hdd 9th: led after 10th: rdn and hdd 2 out: styd on same pce last* **8/1**[3]
3/- **4** 2 **Kiestown Chief (IRE)**[32] 11-11-7 0 .... MrDerekSmith(7) 101
(R C Garton) *prom: rdn bef 3 out: styd on same pce appr last* **25/1**
P/3- **5** 5 **Chief Heckler (IRE)**[11] 8-11-9 0 .... MrAlexEdwards(5) 97
(Philip Rowley) *hld up: racd keenly: hdwy 8th: rdn after 3 out: styd on same pce fr next* **8/1**[3]
6/0- **6** 38 **Dunraven Prince (IRE)**[11] 7-11-9 84 ....(p) MrBGibbs(5) 72
(David Brace) *hld up: hdwy appr 3 out: rdn and wkng whn mstke next* **14/1**
7 30 **Comealong Cornwall**[19] 12-11-7 0 ....(t) MrMWall 21
(M J Wall) *chsd ldrs: rdn appr 3 out: wknd bef next* **20/1**
0PP/ **8** 11 **If And When**[32] 6-12-0 0 .... MrGBarfoot-Saunt 17
(Mrs V J Morse) *hld up: hdwy 4th: lost pl whn mstke 7th: bhd fr 9th* **150/1**
50P/ **9** 4 **Send For Tim (IRE)**[250] 11-11-7 0 .... MrJJInsole(7) 13
(Mrs Gaye Williams) *mid-div: lost pl 8th: bhd fr next* **150/1**
324/ **F** **Mister Teddy**[32] 9-11-9 111 .... MrTEllis(5)
(F A Hutsby) *chsd ldrs: disputing cl 4th whn fell 3 out* **9/2**[2]
5m 36.6s (17.70) **Going Correction** +0.50s/f (Soft) **10** Ran SP% **119.0**
Speed ratings: **86,85,83,83,81 66,55,51,49,**
CSF £52.79 TOTE £2.40: £1.10, £4.80, £1.60; EX 37.10 Trifecta £158.70.
Owner Shy John Partnership **Bred** A J Mason **Trained** Bibury, Gloucs
■ Stewards' Enquiry : Mr R G Spencer four-day ban: used whip above permitted level (Feb 27,Mar 1,3,5)
FOCUS
A modest hunter chase. The winner is rated a stone off his recent win.
T/Plt: £65.40 to a £1 stake. Pool of £99687.50 - 1111.16 winning units. T/Qpdt: £21.40 to a £1 stake. Pool of £7904.54 - 273.15 winning units. CR

3850 FAKENHAM (L-H)
Friday, February 14

OFFICIAL GOING: Heavy (5.8)
Fresh 8ft strip of ground all way round on Chase course.
Wind: strong gusting winds Weather: very overcast; 6 degrees

4247 TOTEPOOL VALENTINE'S DAY (S) H'CAP HURDLE (8 hdls 1 omitted) 2m
1:15 (1:15) (Class 5) (0-100,100) 4-Y-0+ **£2,053** (£598; £299)

Form RPR
500- **1** **Powertakeoff (IRE)**[45] 3434 6-10-4 78 .... PaddyBrennan 85+
(Henry Oliver) *dropped out last early: smooth prog in 2nd bef 3 out: led next: sn 4 l clr and in command: eased fnl 100yds* **2/1**[1]
060- **2** 3½ **Slaney Star (IRE)**[79] 2740 6-11-11 99 .... APMcCoy 102
(Jim Best) *chsd ldrs: reminder 3rd: nvr really gng wl after: hrd rdn 3rd fr bef 3 out tl wnt 2nd bef last: no ch w wnr* **2/1**[1]
225- **3** 2½ **Cappielow Park**[11] 4072 5-11-5 100 ....(p) MikeyEnnis(7) 100
(Fleur Hawes) *settled in rr: pushed along after 5th: effrt whn hit 2 out: sn hrd rdn and no further imp: tk 3rd bef last* **4/1**[2]
5P6- **4** 15 **Collingbourneducis (IRE)**[26] 3796 4-10-6 97 .... MissAEStirling(7) 72
(Michael Gates) *a abt same pl: rdn and struggling after 3 out* **12/1**
02P- **5** 4½ **County Zen (FR)**[22] 3852 11-11-4 92 ....(b) HarrySkelton 75
(Caroline Fryer) *led at fast pce tl bef 2nd: led again 5th: u.p 3 out: hdd next: sn btn: fin tired* **8/1**[3]
445- **P** **Mad Professor (IRE)**[75] 2849 11-9-9 74 oh12 ....(b) JoeCornwall(5)
(John Cornwall) *chsd ldrs: lost pl 5th: sn drvn: t.o after 3 out: p.u last* **66/1**
00P- **P** **Scolt Head Island**[22] 3854 8-10-0 74 ....(b[1]) DavidEngland
(Caroline Bailey) *tk str hold early: led bef 2nd tl hdd u.p 5th: reluctant and sn t.o: eventually p.u last* **25/1**
4m 21.1s (15.70) **Going Correction** +1.00s/f (Soft)
WFA 4 from 5yo+ 9lb **7** Ran SP% **110.8**
Speed ratings (Par 103): **100,98,97,89,87** ,
CSF £6.20 CT £12.14 TOTE £5.40: £3.50, £1.10; EX 7.20 Trifecta £28.30.There was no bid for the winner. Cappielow Park was claimed by Miss Ali Brewer for £6,000.
Owner Mrs Heather Oliver **Bred** Niall Kelly **Trained** Broomhall, Worcs
FOCUS
Fresh 8ft strip of ground all way round on chase course. Wet and windy conditions. The going description was changed to heavy all round following the opener, a weak selling handicap. The winner is rated in line with the best of his Irish form.

4248 ANDY DON MEMORIAL BEGINNERS' CHASE (18 fncs) 3m 110y
1:45 (1:45) (Class 4) 5-Y-0+ **£4,659** (£1,446; £779)

Form RPR
/00- **1** **Destroyer Deployed**[63] 3069 8-11-0 124 .... RichardJohnson 131+
(Tim Vaughan) *pressed ldr fr 3rd: j. slowly 9th: led bef 15th: forged rt away fr 2 out: 10 l ahd last: v easily* **7/4**[2]
113- **2** 17 **Spirit Oscar (IRE)**[40] 3552 6-10-7 121 .... LeightonAspell 112+
(Oliver Sherwood) *led at stdy pce tl bef 15th: landed awkwardly next and rdn: stl ev ch 2 out: sn labouring in grnd and wl btn* **4/5**[1]
U35- **3** 46 **Flichity (IRE)**[11] 4067 9-10-9 62 .... JoeCornwall(5) 68
(John Cornwall) *mstke 2nd: last after and nt jump wl: j. slowly 5th and rdn: struggling 7th: t.o fr 10th* **100/1**
363- **U** **Spike Mac (IRE)**[6] 4162 9-11-0 0 .... AndrewThornton
(Richard Harper) *last whn mstke and uns rdr 2nd* **100/1**
2- **U** **Mondo Cane (IRE)**[19] 3921 7-11-0 0 .... AdamPogson
(Charles Pogson) *blnd bdly 3rd and rdr lost iron: chsd ldng pair after tl mstke 12th, sprawled on landing and uns rdr* **7/1**[3]
6m 56.0s (20.30) **Going Correction** +1.00s/f (Soft) **5** Ran SP% **106.4**
Speed ratings: **107,101,86,** ,
CSF £3.43 TOTE £2.50: £1.10, £1.10; EX 4.00 Trifecta £18.70.
Owner The Craftsmen **Bred** A W Buller **Trained** Aberthin, Vale of Glamorgan

FOCUS
Little depth to this beginners' chase. The first two matched strides until the third-last. The winner looks like proving a better chaser than hurdler.

4249 TOTEPOOL NOVICES' H'CAP HURDLE (13 hdls) 2m 7f 110y
2:15 (2:15) (Class 4) (0-115,112) 4-Y-0+ **£3,573** (£1,049; £524; £262)

Form RPR
124- **1** **Mistral Reine**[22] 3860 5-11-4 104 .... LeightonAspell 108+
(Lucy Wadham) *settled in 3rd: wnt 2nd 3 out: sn led gng much the best: drew rt away fr 2 out: canter* **6/4**[1]
5UP- **2** 18 **Curtain Razer (IRE)**[32] 3691 8-11-12 112 .... TomCannon 96
(Chris Gordon) *led at sedate pce: hdd sn after 3 out: rdn and qckly lost tch w wnr: plugged on* **8/1**
260- **3** 6 **Zafaraban (IRE)**[19] 3195 7-11-0 100 .... LeeEdwards 79
(Aytach Sadik) *pressed ldr: off bridle at rdn at several stages: drvn upsides bef 10th tl 3 out: sn floundering in 3rd: eased flat* **20/1**
013- **4** 65 **Crookstown (IRE)**[45] 3432 7-11-3 103 .... DarylJacob 16
(Ben Case) *a 4th: hit 9th: lost tch rapidly bef 3 out: sn t.o: hopped over last* **7/4**[2]
134- **U** **Itoldyou (IRE)**[32] 3690 8-11-3 103 ....(t) AndrewThornton
(Linda Jewell) *last tl slithered on landing and uns rdr 7th* **4/1**[3]
6m 42.3s (35.90) **Going Correction** +1.175s/f (Heav) **5** Ran SP% **112.2**
Speed ratings (Par 105): **87,81,79,57,**
CSF £12.88 TOTE £2.80: £1.10, £3.70; EX 15.20 Trifecta £84.80.
Owner Sara Dennis And Dominic And Sarah Reilly **Bred** Elms Stud Co Ltd & Miss J Winter **Trained** Newmarket, Suffolk
FOCUS
A modest novice handicap. The first two are rated in line with the best of this season's form.

4250 TIM BARCLAY MEMORIAL H'CAP CHASE (16 fncs) 2m 5f 110y
2:45 (2:45) (Class 3) (0-125,123) 5-Y-0+ **£6,822** (£2,003; £1,001; £500)

Form RPR
/55- **1** **Dashing George (IRE)**[8] 4106 12-11-5 123 .... MrRWinks(7) 129+
(Peter Winks) *rdr lurchd and lost iron briefly 1st: led next and plenty of gd jumps after: hit 12th: drew clr 3 out: 6 l ahd next: pushed out flat* **12/1**
0U- **2** 11 **Sir Lynx (IRE)**[24] 3823 7-10-5 102 ....(t) TomMessenger 97
(Chris Bealby) *settled in 3rd: mstke 13th: lft 6 l 2nd but rdn and floundering after mstke next: all out to hold poor 2nd fr last* **25/1**
46U- **3** 1¾ **Taffy Thomas**[10] 4078 10-10-4 101 ....(t) TomO'Brien 97+
(Peter Bowen) *hld up last: sprawled bdly 6th: 4th whn mstke and reminder 13th: mstke next: plugged on same pce after: ev ch of mod 2nd at last* **7/2**[3]
432- **4** 4½ **Elenika (FR)**[9] 4089 6-11-12 123 .... AidanColeman 117+
(Venetia Williams) *trcking ldrs and in tch tl pckd bdly 12th and relegated last: lost plenty of momentum: no imp after mstke next: plugged home* **11/10**[1]
311- **U** **Full Ov Beans**[22] 3855 10-9-9 99 ow1 .... MissAEStirling(7)
(Michael Gates) *led tl 2nd: pressed ldr: mstke 8th: 3 l 2nd and stl gng wl enough whn sprawled bdly and uns rdr 3 out* **3/1**[2]
6m 3.4s (21.60) **Going Correction** +1.175s/f (Heav) **5** Ran SP% **106.4**
Speed ratings: **107,103,102,100,**
CSF £132.39 TOTE £11.10: £4.30, £8.60; EX 93.00 Trifecta £252.70.
Owner P Winks **Bred** Miss Irene Hatton **Trained** Little Houghton, S Yorks
FOCUS
They went a fair pace in this ordinary handicap chase, which was littered with jumping errors. The winner is rated in line with the best of his 2013 form.

4251 EBF STALLIONS "NATIONAL HUNT" NOVICES' HURDLE (QUALIFIER) (11 hdls) 2m 4f
3:20 (3:20) (Class 3) 4-7-Y-0 **£5,848** (£1,717; £858; £429)

Form RPR
115- **1** **Doctor Harper (IRE)**[63] 3070 6-11-12 137 .... TomScudamore 137+
(David Pipe) *mde all: set leisurely pce: shkn up after 3 out: drew rt away on bridle between last two* **1/1**[1]
236- **2** 12 **Robbers Roost (IRE)**[50] 3271 6-11-2 0 .... RichardJohnson 112
(Tim Vaughan) *chsd wnr fr 3rd: nrly 3 l down and rdn whn mstke 2 out: kpt on steadily but wnr wl clr after* **33/1**
221- **3** 1 **Saffron Wells (IRE)**[10] 4076 6-11-5 114 .... TrevorWhelan(3) 118
(Neil King) *trckd ldrs: hit 6th and 7th: 3rd fr next: rdn after 3 out: plugged on same pce* **7/4**[2]
4- **4** 34 **De Kerry Man (IRE)**[24] 3816 6-11-2 0 .... SamJones 76
(Fiona Kehoe) *last tl wnt 4th after 8th where tiring rapidly: continued t.o* **40/1**
/11- **P** **Bobble Boru (IRE)**[50] 3289 6-11-1 0 .... AidanColeman
(Venetia Williams) *racd keenly: pressed wnr tl 3rd: 4th and struggling bdly after mstke 8th: continued t.o tl p.u last* **4/1**[3]
5m 45.9s (33.30) **Going Correction** +1.35s/f (Heav) **5** Ran SP% **111.7**
Speed ratings: **87,82,81,68,**
CSF £22.53 TOTE £2.10: £1.10, £5.60; EX 15.90 Trifecta £50.00.
Owner The Johnson Family **Bred** Stephen O'Flynn **Trained** Nicholashayne, Devon
FOCUS
An ordinary novice event which saw a pillar-to-post win from the favourite. He was the form pick here and remains capable of better.

4252 WILLIAM BULWER-LONG MEMORIAL NOVICES' FOX HUNTERS' CHASE (16 fncs) 2m 5f 110y
3:55 (3:56) (Class 6) 5-Y-0+ **£1,280** (£419; £225)

Form RPR
3P/ **1** **Jack Bene (IRE)**[235] 826 8-11-5 115 .... MrJSole(5) 114
(Miss Louise Allan) *settled in 3rd: wnt 2nd bef 12th: rdn bef 2 out: led last: sn began to assert then floundered under driving fnl 100yds and jst hung on* **1/1**[1]
330/ **2** hd **Mister Chancer (IRE)**[20] 9-11-3 0 .... MissCVHart(7) 114
(Richard J Bandey) *2nd tl led bef 7th: drvn fr 2 out: jnd and nt fluent last: over 1 l down 100yds out: rallied bravely and jst failed* **7/2**[3]
2/3- **3** 48 **Earl Grez (FR)**[33] 9-11-4 94 ow1 ....(tp) MrJoeHill(7) 67
(Alan Hill) *set v slow pce tl hdd bef 7th: rdn and lost 2nd bef 12th: fnd nil after: 8 l 3rd and labouring whn mstke 2 out: continued t.o* **3/1**[2]
640/ **R** **Lang Shining (IRE)**[33] 10-11-10 0 .... MrMWall
(Lady Blandford) *reluctant to s: wnt v unwillingly to 1st and ref* **12/1**
4/ **R** **Mr Maybe (IRE)**[19] 9-11-3 0 ....(t) MrMJPKendrick(7)
(John Whyte) *v reluctant to go down: threw rdr leaving paddock: mulish at s and ref to r* **14/1**
6m 25.1s (43.30) **Going Correction** +1.35s/f (Heav) **5** Ran SP% **111.6**
Speed ratings: **75,74,57,** ,
CSF £5.17 TOTE £1.90: £1.30, £2.00; EX 5.20 Trifecta £9.80.
Owner Robert Clifton-Brown **Bred** Mrs Margaret Lucey **Trained** Exning, Suffolk

FOCUS
A weak novice hunter chase run at a very slow pace in driving rain and strong wind. Not form to take seriously, the first two rated close to their old marks.

4253 EBF STALLIONS MARES' INTERMEDIATE OPEN NATIONAL HUNT FLAT RACE 2m
4:30 (4:30) (Class 5) 4-7-Y-0 **£2,309** (£673; £336)

Form RPR
22- **1** **Rons Dream**[36] 3619 4-10-7 0 DonalDevereux 95+
(Peter Bowen) *mde all: set v slow pce: sauntered rt away fnl 2f* **1/4**[1]
2 22 **Inca Dove** 5-11-3 0 BrendanPowell 78
(Renee Robeson) *3rd tl wnt 2nd 6f out: rdn and lost tch w v easy wnr over 2f out* **4/1**[2]
0- **3** 2 ¼ **Ella's Promise**[57] 3181 5-11-3 0 RichardJohnson 74
(Barry Brennan) *4th and shkn up 1/2-way: wnt 3rd 5f out: plugged on steadily but no ch after* **20/1**
6- **4** 77 **Western Dolly**[8] 4114 5-11-0 0 JackQuinlan(3)
(Caroline Fryer) *2nd tl rdn 6f out: hopelessly t.o over 4f out* **33/1**
P- **5** 52 **Ricardo's Girl (IRE)**[259] 567 5-10-10 0 (p) PaulBohan(7)
(Steve Gollings) *sn last: drvn 1/2-way: continued v reluctantly and sn hopelessly t.o: fin eventually* **8/1**[3]
4m 40.8s (41.00) **Going Correction** +1.525s/f (Heav)
WFA 4 from 5yo 9lb **5** Ran SP% **118.8**
Speed ratings: **58,47,45,7,**
CSF £2.09 TOTE £1.20: £1.10, £1.90; EX 2.20 Trifecta £8.90.
Owner Mrs Tania Stepney **Bred** Peter E Clinton **Trained** Little Newcastle, Pembrokes

FOCUS
An uncompetitive mares' bumper run in badly poached ground. Arguably a step forward from the easy winner.
T/Plt: £387.30 to a £1 stake. Pool: £88212.03 - 166.26 winning tickets T/Qpdt: £188.20 to a £1 stake. Pool: £7617.22 - 29.94 winning tickets IM

4031 SANDOWN (R-H)
Friday, February 14
4254 Meeting Abandoned - waterlogged

3768 ASCOT (R-H)
Saturday, February 15
OFFICIAL GOING: Heavy changing to soft (heavy in places) after race 1 (1.30)
Wind: Fresh, half against Weather: Changeable with showers

4261 NEPTUNE INVESTMENT MANAGEMENT NOVICES' HURDLE (11 hdls) 2m 3f 110y
1:30 (1:33) (Class 2) 5-Y-0+ **£15,640** (£4,620; £2,310; £1,155)

Form RPR
32- **1** **Un Temps Pour Tout (IRE)**[28] 3778 5-11-8 147 TomScudamore 149+
(David Pipe) *trckd ldr: led sn after 3 out: sn drew clr: eased after last* **40/85**[1]
411- **2** 16 **Cole Harden (IRE)**[31] 3716 5-11-8 132 (t) GavinSheehan 129+
(Warren Greatrex) *racd wd and tended to jump lft: led to after 3 out: one pce and sn no ch w wnr* **11/4**[2]
0/2- **3** 28 **Our Pollyanna (IRE)**[87] 2600 7-10-7 0 RobertThornton 86
(Alan King) *hld up in last: chsd ldng pair and mstke 7th: wknd 3 out: v tired whn mstke last* **20/1**
111- **4** 29 **Irish Cavalier (IRE)**[94] 2453 5-11-8 0 BarryGeraghty 72
(Rebecca Curtis) *chsd ldng pair to 7th: wknd and mstke next: mstke 3 out: sn t.o* **8/1**[3]
5m 3.6s (18.90) **Going Correction** +1.05s/f (Soft) **4** Ran SP% **110.5**
Speed ratings: **104,97,86,74**
CSF £2.27 TOTE £1.50; EX 2.00 Trifecta £8.60.
Owner Professor Caroline Tisdall & Bryan Drew **Bred** Felix Talbot **Trained** Nicholashayne, Devon

FOCUS
The ground was changed to soft, heavy in places following this contest. Only four runners took part in the opener and it had the look of an interesting contest prior to the off. A step up from the easy winner and there's a case for rating the form up to 6lb higher.

4262 RSA TRIAL NOVICES' CHASE (REGISTERED AS REYNOLDSTOWN NOVICES' CHASE) (GRADE 2) (£8K FIELDSIZE BONUS) (20 fncs) 3m
2:05 (2:05) (Class 1) 5-Y-0+ **£18,091** (£6,869; £3,480; £1,781; £936)

Form RPR
/2P- **1** **O'Faolains Boy (IRE)**[28] 3777 7-11-0 0 BarryGeraghty 150+
(Rebecca Curtis) *cl up: trckd ldng pair 15th: rdn 3 out: clsd to ld after 2 out: drvn and kpt on wl fr last* **8/1**
121- **2** 2 ½ **Many Clouds (IRE)**[50] 3331 7-11-4 145 LeightonAspell 151+
(Oliver Sherwood) *cl up: trckd ldr 9th: upsides fr 12th: led 3 out: hdd and outpcd by wnr sn after 2 out: kpt on again nr fin* **2/1**[2]
323- **3** 4 ½ **Third Intention (IRE)**[51] 3260 7-11-7 143 (t) JoeTizzard 149
(Colin Tizzard) *t.k.h: cl up: tended to jump lft fr 1/2-way: chsd ldng pair 11th to 15th: rdn 3 out: wnt 3rd again after 2 out: threatened to cl on runner-up flat: wknd fnl 100yds* **20/1**
211- **4** 32 **Baby Shine (IRE)**[31] 3718 8-10-7 137 RichardJohnson 112
(Lucy Wadham) *hld up: hmpd 4th: mstke 13th: hdwy after 15th: wknd fr 3 out* **11/2**[3]
011- **5** 25 **Ely Brown (IRE)**[14] 4041 9-11-7 143 (p) NoelFehily 92
(Charlie Longsdon) *led to 5th: lost pl and mstke 11th: last fr 13th: wknd 15th: t.o* **10/1**
6/1- **P** **Gevrey Chambertin (FR)**[84] 2672 6-11-0 0 (p) TomScudamore
(David Pipe) *racd freely: w ldr: led 5th: jnd 12th: hdd 3 out: stl upsides bef 2 out: stopped to nil sn after: poor 5th whn p.u bef last* **13/8**[1]
6m 21.5s (18.00) **Going Correction** +0.575s/f (Soft) **6** Ran SP% **111.8**
Speed ratings: **93,92,90,80,71**
CSF £25.07 TOTE £8.80: £3.30, £1.70; EX 24.40 Trifecta £335.30.
Owner Trembath, Hyde, Outhart & Hill **Bred** Tom And P Phelan **Trained** Newport, Dyfed

FOCUS
A race with a good recent history in producing RSA Chase winners, with Albertas Run (2008) and Bobs Worth, who was actually runner-up in this in 2012, both going on to victory, plus Burton Port, successful here in 2010, going on to finish second a month later. There was a bit of a turn up in this year's edition, with a step up from O'Faolains Boy.

4263 WEATHERBYS HAMILTON INSURANCE CHASE (LIMITED H'CAP) (LISTED RACE) (20 fncs) 3m
2:40 (2:40) (Class 1) 5-Y-0+
£22,780 (£8,548; £4,280; £2,132; £1,072; £536)

Form RPR
U15- **1** **Restless Harry**[21] 3888 10-10-7 **141** CharliePoste 150
(Robin Dickin) *cl up: pushed along 15th: led 16th to next: rallied to chal 2 out: w ldr after tl drvn to take narrow ld last 100yds* **4/1**[2]
3/0- **2** nk **Teaforthree (IRE)**[49] 3361 10-11-1 **149** NoelFehily 158
(Rebecca Curtis) *awkward jump 1st: cl up: gd jump to ld 12th: hdd and mstke 16th: dropped to 3rd next: rallied to ld 2 out: sn jnd: tremendous battle after: jst hdd and hld last 100yds* **5/1**
614- **3** 3 **Houblon Des Obeaux (FR)**[21] 3888 7-11-10 **158** LiamTreadwell 166+
(Venetia Williams) *sloppy rnd of jumping in rr: pushed along fr 11th: lost tch fr 16th: poor 6th after 3 out: styd on relentlessly after: tk 3rd flat and clsd on ldng pair fin* **9/2**[3]
/1P- **4** 5 **Chance Du Roy (FR)**[28] 3780 10-10-9 **143** (p) TomO'Brien 146
(Philip Hobbs) *t.k.h early: hld up: blnd 14th: prog next: led 4 out: hdd 2 out: wknd last* **12/1**
322- **5** 6 **Tullamore Dew (IRE)**[32] 3698 12-10-1 **138** oh12 GavinSheehan(3) 135
(Nick Gifford) *led 3rd to 9th: losing pl whn mstke 15th and dropped to last: nvr on terms after: plugged on* **12/1**
24P- **6** 53 **Highland Lodge (IRE)**[49] 3361 8-10-5 **139** LeightonAspell 115
(Emma Lavelle) *racd freely: led to 3rd: led 9th to 12th: nt fluent 15th: wknd 4 out: eased and t.o* **9/4**[1]
2/6- **F** **Wetak (FR)**[235] 838 7-10-9 **143** (t) TomScudamore
(David Pipe) *w.w in rr: in tch 15th: shkn up and lost tch fr next: 6th whn fell 3 out* **8/1**
6m 18.3s (14.80) **Going Correction** +0.575s/f (Soft) **7** Ran SP% **112.1**
Speed ratings: **98,97,96,95,93 75,**
CSF £23.24 CT £91.21 TOTE £4.40: £2.20, £2.10; EX 17.10 Trifecta £65.10.
Owner R G Whitehead **Bred** R J Francome **Trained** Alcester, Warwicks
■ Stewards' Enquiry : Charlie Poste two-day ban; used whip above permitted level (1st-2nd Mar)
Noel Fehily two-day ban; used whip above permitted level (1st-2nd Mar)

FOCUS
A good-quality handicap chase that provided a thorough test at the distance. Solid form, the winner to the level of his last two runs.

4264 GREAT BRITISH DRAMA H'CAP HURDLE (11 hdls) 2m 3f 110y
3:15 (3:15) (Class 2) 4-Y-0+
£24,760 (£7,352; £3,676; £1,832; £920; £464)

Form RPR
F65- **1** **Kaylif Aramis**[35] 3646 7-10-7 **131** (t) RyanHatch(7) 138+
(Nigel Twiston-Davies) *hld up towards rr: prog after 7th: wnt 2nd bef 2 out gng strly: clsd to ld between last 2: rdn clr* **11/2**[2]
2P2- **2** 5 **Art Professor (IRE)**[9] 4112 10-11-1 **132** LiamTreadwell 134
(Venetia Williams) *hld up towards rr: prog 7th: rdn to chse ldr after 3 out tl bef next: kpt on to take 2nd again last: no threat to wnr* **16/1**
3/6- **3** 7 **Leo Luna**[119] 1970 5-11-4 **135** JamieMoore 133
(Gary Moore) *mstkes: hld up in midfield: prog 8th: rdn 3 out: kpt on one pce fr 2 out to take 3rd nr fin* **25/1**
211- **4** nk **Heath Hunter (IRE)**[51] 3270 7-10-8 **125** (p) TomScudamore 121
(David Pipe) *prom: chsd ldr 5th: led 8th: 3 l clr after 3 out and gng wl: hdd & wknd between last 2* **5/1**[1]
143- **5** 7 **Bygones Sovereign (IRE)**[16] 3989 8-10-0 **124** (p) KieronEdgar(7) 113
(David Pipe) *won fierce battle for early ld and set gd pce: rdn fr 5th: hdd 8th: lost 2nd after 3 out: steadily fdd* **8/1**
PP0- **6** 2 ½ **Seymour Eric**[22] 3882 9-10-13 **130** (b[1]) IanPopham 115
(Martin Keighley) *prom in chsng gp: rdn after 7th: struggling next: no ch after 3 out: plugged on* **33/1**
213- **7** 10 **Like Minded**[35] 3646 10-11-6 **137** (t) HarrySkelton 112
(Dan Skelton) *hld up wl in rr: prog after 7th: gng wl enough 3 out: sn rdn and no imp on ldrs: wknd 2 out* **15/2**
F16- **8** nse **Foxcub (IRE)**[35] 3646 6-11-1 **137** BenPoste(5) 112
(Tom Symonds) *hld up towards rr: mstke 6th: rdn and no prog 3 out: wl bhd whn mstke last* **50/1**
113- **9** ½ **Changing The Guard**[198] 1178 8-10-13 **135** (t) ChristopherWard(5) 110
(Dr Richard Newland) *t.k.h: hld up in last pair: sltly hmpd 1st: prog after 7th: chsd ldrs next: rdn and no hdwy after 3 out: wknd 2 out* **33/1**
033- **10** 1 ¼ **Bourne**[28] 3771 8-10-8 **125** (b) AdrianLane 103
(Donald McCain) *hld up: prog to chse ldrs whn blnd 5th: nvr rcvrd: wl bhd after 3 out* **7/1**[3]
/13- **P** **Stopped Out**[49] 3369 9-11-12 **143** (p) RichieMcGrath
(Philip Kirby) *unable to ld: mostly chsd ldr to 5th: prom tl wknd qckly 3 out: t.o whn p.u bef last* **25/1**
460- **P** **Dan Breen (IRE)**[56] 3200 9-10-8 **132** (bt) TomBellamy(7)
(David Pipe) *unable to ld: prom in chsng gp: wknd qckly after 6th: t.o whn p.u bef 8th* **25/1**
/U0- **P** **Kuilsriver (IRE)**[15] 4020 7-10-4 **126** ThomasGarner(5)
(Nick Gifford) *unable to ld: prom tl wknd rapidly after 4th: t.o whn p.u bef 7th* **25/1**
P **Lough Kent**[112] 5-11-5 **136** BarryGeraghty
(Nicky Henderson) *hld up in last pair: hmpd 1st: no prog 6th: wknd next: t.o whn p.u bef 8th* **15/2**
0/0- **F** **Two Rockers (IRE)**[84] 2672 7-11-11 **142** RobertThornton
(Alan King) *hld up: fell 1st* **11/2**[2]
4m 59.8s (15.10) **Going Correction** +1.05s/f (Soft) **15** Ran SP% **123.7**
Speed ratings (Par 109): **111,109,106,106,103 102,98,98,98,97 , , , ,**
CSF £82.57 CT £2061.93 TOTE £6.70: £2.90, £4.70, £5.90; EX 89.60 Trifecta £3089.80 Part won..
Owner The Grangers **Bred** Mrs Isobel Phipps Coltman **Trained** Naunton, Gloucs

The Form Book Jumps, Raceform Ltd, Compton, RG20 6NL.

FOCUS
Plenty of these looked of interest for one reason or another, so this is likely to be strong handicap form. The early leader set a good gallop.

4265 **BETFAIR ASCOT CHASE (GRADE 1)** (17 fncs) **2m 5f 110y**
3:50 (3:53) (Class 1) 5-Y-O+
£84,655 (£32,050; £16,165; £8,200; £4,240; £2,245)

Form RPR
/31- **1** **Captain Chris (IRE)**[35] 3645 10-11-7 169..................(t) RichardJohnson 176+
(Philip Hobbs) *hld up: prog 8th: awkward next: trckd ldng pair after 11th: swept into ld after 3 out: stormed clr: impressive* **8/11**[1]
101- **2** *19* **Cloudy Too (IRE)**[51] 3285 8-11-7 157.......................... JonathanEngland 156
(Sue Smith) *trckd ldr to 2nd and fr 8th: chal and upsides fr 13th tl wnr swept past after 3 out: kpt on but no ch* **7/1**[3]
413/ **3** *12* **Hunt Ball (IRE)**[119] 9-11-7 161.. AndrewTinkler 146
(Nicky Henderson) *hld up: mstke 8th: prog to chse ldng trio 12th: lost tch 3 out: plugged on to take remote 3rd last* **20/1**
234/ **4** *4* **Medermit (FR)**[674] 5376 10-11-7 159.............................. RobertThornton 139
(Alan King) *hld up in rr: lost tch fr 12th: wl bhd 3 out: tk remote 4th nr fin* **12/1**
553- **5** *1 ½* **Kauto Stone (FR)**[28] 3773 8-11-7 152..................................(b) PCarberry 140
(Paul Nicholls) *led at str pce: jnd 13th: hdd & wknd after 3 out* **16/1**
/1U- **6** *19* **Riverside Theatre**[51] 3262 10-11-7 163........................(b) BarryGeraghty 119
(Nicky Henderson) *nt fluent: racd wd: in tch: pushed along 8th: sn struggling: wknd 12th: t.o* **11/2**[2]
6/2- **P** **Sunny Ledgend**[27] 3798 9-11-7 127....................................... MrJMartin
(Andrew J Martin) *chsd ldr 2nd to 8th: wknd 11th: poor 6th whn blnd 4 out: t.o whn p.u bef last* **100/1**
/12- **P** **Rolling Aces (IRE)**[71] 2930 8-11-7 152...............................(p) NoelFehily
(Paul Nicholls) *wl in tch: disp 2nd pl 9th to 11th: wknd qckly 4 out: t.o whn p.u bef 2 out* **15/2**
5m 28.8s (2.80) **Going Correction** +0.575s/f (Soft) **8** Ran SP% **116.9**
Speed ratings: **117,110,105,104,103 96, ,**
CSF £7.10 TOTE £1.60: £1.10, £2.10, £4.20; EX 6.60 Trifecta £69.90.
Owner Mrs Diana L Whateley **Bred** Mrs Noreen Walsh **Trained** Withycombe, Somerset

FOCUS
There was no great depth to this Grade 1, but there's little doubt it was won by a truly high-class performer. Capyain Chris is rated in line with his Kempton romp, and the form looks solid.

4266 **ASCOT SPONSORS' CLUB "NATIONAL HUNT" NOVICES' HURDLE (£5K FIELD SIZE BONUS)** (9 hdls) **2m**
4:20 (4:24) (Class 2) 4-Y-O+ **£9,470** (£2,858; £1,472; £779)

Form RPR
11- **1** **Mountain King**[30] 3728 5-11-7 0.................................... RichardJohnson 130
(Philip Hobbs) *t.k.h: cl up: mstke 6th: prog to join ldr next: rdn and upsides 2 out: sn outpcd: wl hld whn lft 2nd at last: kpt on u.p to ld fnl 100yds* **11/10**[1]
011- **2** *nk* **Wadswick Court (IRE)**[40] 3568 6-11-10 133.......................... NoelFehily 135+
(Charlie Longsdon) *t.k.h: led at modest pce to 3rd: led again 6th: rdn and hdd 2 out: hld whn lft 5 l clr and sltly hmpd last: hung lft and idled bdly: hdd 100yds out: kpt on nr fin* **9/1**
0- **3** *nk* **Art Mauresque (FR)**[91] 2500 4-11-1 0.............................. BarryGeraghty 122
(Paul Nicholls) *t.k.h: hld up in tch: shkn up and nt qckn bef 2 out: wl hld after: lft 2nd at last: clsd to chal w wnr flat: no ex nr fin* **4/1**[3]
31P- **4** *5* **Garrahalish (IRE)**[35] 3654 6-11-7 128.................................. CharliePoste 124
(Robin Dickin) *plld hrd: led 3rd to 6th: lft bhd fr 3 out: n.d after but lost little further grnd: sltly hmpd last* **20/1**
11F- **F** **Wilde Blue Yonder (IRE)**[49] 3370 5-11-10 0............... RobertThornton 145+
(Alan King) *hld up in last: prog after 3 out: led 2 out: rdn 4 l clr and wl in command whn fell last* **5/2**[2]
4m 9.3s (21.90) **Going Correction** +1.05s/f (Soft)
WFA 4 from 5yo+ 9lb **5** Ran SP% **111.0**
Speed ratings (Par 109): **87,86,86,84,**
CSF £11.14 TOTE £2.00: £1.30, £2.60; EX 10.50 Trifecta £18.00.
Owner Mrs Diana L Whateley **Bred** R D Chugg And J R H Fowler **Trained** Withycombe, Somerset

FOCUS
This contest has produced some quality horses down the years. Sprinter Sacre won on the bridle in 2011, while juvenile hurdlers Balder Succes (2012) and Far West (2013) took the last two renewals. There was late drama when Wilde Blue Yonder, who was heading for a big personal best, came down. The finishers are all rated within a few pounds of their marks.

4267 **MILLGATE STANDARD OPEN NATIONAL HUNT FLAT RACE** **2m**
4:50 (4:51) (Class 4) 4-6-Y-O **£3,249** (£954; £477; £238)

Form RPR
1- **1** **A Vos Gardes (FR)**[94] 2456 4-10-4 0.......................... CharlieDeutsch(7) 118+
(Charlie Longsdon) *hld up in tch: prog to join ldrs 6f out: rdn to go 2nd over 2f out: led over 1f out: wandered and green in front: kpt on* **7/2**[2]
2 *1* **Ondorun (IRE)**[132] 5-10-13 0.. GavinSheehan(3) 119
(Emma Lavelle) *cl up: trckd ldr over 5f out tl rdn and nt qckn over 2f out: styd on again to take 2nd last 100yds: clsng at fin* **14/1**
3 *2 ¼* **No Dice (IRE)** 5-11-2 0.. TomScudamore 117
(David Pipe) *racd quite keenly: led: set mod pce early: shkn up over 2f out: hdd over 1f out: no ex* **9/4**[1]
4 *1* **Royal Vacation (IRE)** 4-10-7 0.. JoeTizzard 107+
(Colin Tizzard) *hld up in rr: dropped to last and rdn 1/2-way: sn bhd: styd on fr over 3f out: tk 4th fnl f and gaining at fin* **4/1**[3]
5 *3 ¼* **The Wexfordian (IRE)**[83] 5-11-2 0.. IanPopham 113
(Martin Keighley) *t.k.h: hld up in last pair: prog to join ldrs 6f out: last of four w a ch 3f out: rdn and steadily fdd fnl 2f* **12/1**
6 *32* **Golden Milan (IRE)**[259] 6-11-2 0..................................... BarryGeraghty 81
(Rebecca Curtis) *hld up in tch: prog to join ldrs 6f out: wknd qckly over 4f out: t.o* **5/1**
11/ **7** *2 ½* **Devenish Island**[321] 5041 5-11-4 0............................ CallumWhillans(5) 85
(Karen McLintock) *t.k.h: trckd ldr to 1/2-way: sn pushed along: wknd qckly 5f out: t.o* **12/1**
8 *12* **Medburn Cutler** 4-10-7 0.. AndrewTinkler 57
(George Baker) *t.k.h: hld up in rr: lost tch 7f out: t.o* **33/1**
06- **9** *6* **Be A Dreamer**[37] 3619 6-10-13 0................................. JonathanEngland(3) 60
(Sue Smith) *trckd ldng pair: wnt 2nd 1/2-way tl wknd rapidly over 5f out: t.o* **50/1**
(19.20) **Going Correction** +1.05s/f (Soft)
WFA 4 from 5yo+ 9lb **9** Ran SP% **116.6**
Speed ratings: **94,93,92,91,90 74,73,67,64**
CSF £51.62 TOTE £4.00: £1.70, £4.10, £1.20; EX 60.90 Trifecta £270.40.
Owner The Rollright Stones **Bred** U J And B Lenouvel De Vulpian **Trained** Over Norton, Oxon

FOCUS
Some nice types have taken this race down the years, so the winner is well worth following. Not an easy race to put a figure on.
T/Plt: £129.30 to a £1 stake. Pool: £166908.31 - 942.07 winning tickets T/Qpdt: £30.40 to a £1 stake. Pool: £10806.67 - 262.85 winning tickets JN

3775 HAYDOCK (L-H)
Saturday, February 15

OFFICIAL GOING: Heavy (chs 4.4, hdl 4.2)
Wind: strong 1/2 against Weather: rain until after race 2

4268 **BETFRED "GOALS GALORE" VICTOR LUDORUM JUVENILE HURDLE** **2m**
1:45 (1:45) (Class 2) 4-Y-O **£9,747** (£2,862; £1,431; £715)

Form RPR
535- **1** **Abracadabra Sivola (FR)**[28] 3778 4-10-12 115..... SamTwiston-Davies 130+
(Nick Williams) *mde all: nt fluent 4th: jnd 2 out: fnd ex run-in: hld on wl towards fin* **9/1**
1- **2** *½* **Aurore D'Estruval (FR)**[14] 4037 4-10-10 0............................ BrianHughes 127+
(John Quinn) *trckd ldrs: 2nd after 6th: upsides 2 out: drvn and kpt on same pce last 50yds* **6/4**[1]
02- **3** *17* **The Green Ogre**[35] 3641 4-10-12 0.................................... JoshuaMoore 114
(Gary Moore) *hld up in rr: shkn up 6th: outpcd next: styd on and slty hmpd 2 out: kpt on to take modest 3rd nr fin* **20/1**
112- **4** *1* **Handiwork**[28] 3768 4-11-6 130.. APMcCoy 119
(Steve Gollings) *chsd ldrs: drvn 3 out: modest 3rd and j.rt next: one pce* **7/2**[2]
25- **5** *5* **Cafe Au Lait (GER)**[63] 3089 4-10-12 0.............................. PaulMoloney 106
(C Von Der Recke, Germany) *chsd ldrs: 2nd 4th: drvn 3 out: wknd clsng stages* **12/1**
121- **6** *11* **Hawk High (IRE)**[23] 3857 4-11-6 135...........................(p) DougieCostello 106
(Tim Easterby) *t.k.h in rr: shkn up 6th: drvn next: wknd between last 2* **7/1**
P **Sea Claria (FR)**[94] 4-10-5 0.. AidanColeman
(Venetia Williams) *chsng ldr whn j. slowly: wnt rt-handed 1st and lost pl: detached last whn reminders 4th: t.o whn p.u after next* **6/1**[3]
4m 13.3s (9.10) **Going Correction** +0.875s/f (Soft) **7** Ran SP% **111.5**
Speed ratings: **112,111,103,102,100 94,**
CSF £22.59 TOTE £10.10: £3.80, £1.70; EX 25.60 Trifecta £678.30.
Owner The Arthur White Partnership **Bred** G Trapenard **Trained** George Nympton, Devon

FOCUS
Chasers utilised Flat course bend out of the back Straight. Stable bend and bend out of back straight both out from innermost configuration and changes combined added 34yds per circuit to advertised distances on both courses. Rain continued to come down and the ground was very testing. Although this isn't the race it once was, 2012 winner Une Artiste went on to win the Fred Winter at the festival. The pace the winner set here was just steady and the first two finished well clear, showing useful juvenile form. A big step up from the winner.

4269 **BETFRED MOBILE HURDLE (REGISTERED AS THE RENDLESHAM HURDLE) (GRADE 2)** **3m**
2:20 (2:20) (Class 1) 4-Y-O+
£20,786 (£7,800; £3,905; £1,945; £978; £489)

Form RPR
11- **1** **Seeyouatmidnight**[13] 4052 6-11-6 142.................................. RyanMania 154+
(Sandy Thomson) *mde all: styd on gamely fr 3 out: hld on wl clsng stages* **6/1**[3]
113- **2** *1 ¼* **Mickie**[28] 3770 6-10-11 144... JakeGreenall 144
(Henry Daly) *hld up: hdwy to trck ldrs 3rd: cl 2nd appr 3 out: styd on same pce last 100yds* **5/1**[2]
161- **3** *13* **Celestial Halo (IRE)**[77] 2814 10-11-12 165.........(bt) SamTwiston-Davies 147
(Paul Nicholls) *sn chsng ldrs: 3rd 3 out: sn drvn and hung lft: wknd appr next* **6/5**[1]
040- **4** *7* **Cross Kennon (IRE)**[56] 3207 10-11-4 140...................(b[1]) SeanQuinlan 132
(Jennie Candlish) *chsd ldrs: drvn 8th: outpcd and lost pl appr 3 out* **10/1**
/UF- **5** *35* **Quincy Des Pictons (FR)**[70] 2939 10-11-4 135.................... JamesBest 95
(Alan Jones) *chsd ldrs: drvn and lost pl 9th: sn bhd: t.o* **100/1**
254- **6** *7* **Quartz De Thaix (FR)**[6] 4174 10-11-4 147..................(b) AidanColeman 88
(Venetia Williams) *in rr: detached 2nd: drvn 4th: remainder 6th: sn bhd: t.o 9th* **8/1**
341- **7** *2 ¾* **Lienosus (IRE)**[28] 3784 8-11-4 140.. PaulMoloney 85
(Evan Williams) *chsd ldrs: drvn 7th: lost pl 9th: sn bhd: t.o* **17/2**
6m 11.6s (11.60) **Going Correction** +0.875s/f (Soft) **7** Ran SP% **108.1**
Speed ratings (Par 115): **115,114,110,107,96 93,93**
CSF £31.80 TOTE £5.70: £2.40, £1.80; EX 23.80 Trifecta £53.90.
Owner Mrs A M Thomson **Bred** Miss F A Evans **Trained** Lambden, Berwicks

FOCUS
Not the strongest of Grade 2s, but another step forward from the progressive winner who is entitled to be rated top of the novice hurdle pile on this run. The time was relatively good.

4270 **BETFRED GRAND NATIONAL TRIAL (HANDICAP CHASE) (GRADE 3)** **3m 5f**
2:55 (2:56) (Class 1) 5-Y-O+
£42,712 (£16,027; £8,025; £3,997; £2,010; £1,005)

Form RPR
2PP/ **1** **Rigadin De Beauchene (FR)**[301] 5404 9-10-5 **131**...... RobertDunne(3) 150+
(Venetia Williams) *w ldrs: led 14th: drew clr 2 out: lft wl clr last: heavily eased last 100yds* **16/1**
P01- **2** *10* **Emperor's Choice (IRE)**[14] 4026 7-10-8 **131** 5ex........... AidanColeman 128
(Venetia Williams) *mid-div: hdwy 8th: drvn 16th: outpcd bef next: kpt on and modest 3rd 3 out: lft 20 l 2nd last* **11/2**[3]
024- **3** *30* **Loch Ba (IRE)**[35] 3655 8-10-7 **130**.............................. DominicElsworth 98
(Mick Channon) *in tch: reminders and lost pl 4th: bhd whn hit 13th: t.o 4 out: styd on fr 2 out: tk distant 3rd last 50yds* **15/2**
/1P- **4** *1 ¼* **Nuts N Bolts**[51] 3285 8-11-1 **138**.................................(t) PeterBuchanan 102
(Lucinda Russell) *mid-div: lost pl 15th: in rr whn mstke 4 out: kpt on fr 2 out: tk distant 4th clsng stages* **14/1**
4/0- **5** *2* **Our Father (IRE)**[77] 2815 8-11-8 **145**................................(t) ConorO'Farrell 107
(David Pipe) *in rr: shkn up 3rd and next: hdwy 8th: chsng ldrs 13th: drvn 16th: 3rd next: wknd next* **5/1**[2]
/42- **6** *2 ¼* **Hawkes Point**[49] 3361 9-11-6 **143**.. RyanMahon 103
(Paul Nicholls) *in rr: hit 6th: hdwy to chse ldrs 12th: lost pl and hit 14th: sn bhd: kpt on fr 2 out* **10/1**
/54- **7** *1 ¼* **Soll**[14] 4035 9-11-1 **138**...(p) MarkGrant 96
(Jo Hughes) *chsd ldrs: lost pl after 15th: bhd fr 4 out* **25/1**

501- U **Across The Bay (IRE)**[47] 3416 10-11-12 149..............(bt) JasonMaguire
(Donald McCain) *in rr: drvn along 5th: bhd fr 13th: blnd and uns rdr 16th* **18/1**

624- F **Wellforth (IRE)**[37] 3617 10-10-9 132..............(p) FelixDeGiles
(Barry Brennan) *w ldrs: fell 8th* **66/1**

03P- P **Well Refreshed**[49] 3361 10-11-1 141.............. JoshuaMoore(3)
(Gary Moore) *in rr: hit 8th: lost pl and hmpdc 15th: sn bhd: t.o whn p.u bef 4 out* **22/1**

2PP- U **Red Rocco (IRE)**[30] 3743 7-10-4 127..............(v[1]) SamTwiston-Davies 124
(Nigel Twiston-Davies) *mde most to 14th: cl 2nd whn mstke 4 out: wknd 2 out: 14 l 2nd whn blnd and uns rdr last* **16/1**

553- P **Merry King (IRE)**[28] 3780 7-11-2 139..............(v) APMcCoy
(Jonjo O'Neill) *in rr: hmpd 8th: outpcd and reminder 13th: sn bhd: t.o whn p.u after 15th: b.b.v* **9/2**[1]

F11- F **Wychwoods Brook**[28] 3780 8-10-12 142.............. ConorRing(7)
(Evan Williams) *chsd ldrs: upsides 12th: wknd appr 4 out: in rr whn fell heavily 3 out* **11/1**

U34- P **Le Reve (IRE)**[39] 3594 6-10-8 131..............(p) DougieCostello
(Lucy Wadham) *mid-div: chsd ldrs 12th: lost pl 16th: t.o whn p.u bef 3 out* **18/1**

8m 9.3s (37.70) **Going Correction** +0.875s/f (Soft) 14 Ran SP% **118.1**
Speed ratings: **83,80,71,71,71 70,70,,,**
CSF £100.32 CT £729.43 TOTE £20.60: £6.00, £2.40, £3.10; EX 109.00 Trifecta £1069.20.
Owner Andrew Wiles **Bred** Raymond Bellanger **Trained** Kings Caple, H'fords
■ Stewards' Enquiry : Conor Ring ten-day ban; continued riding on a clearly tired horse (1st-10th Mar)

FOCUS
Billed as the Grand National Trial since 2011, no winner of this event has ever gone on to Aintree success but Neptune Collonges, the 2012 Grand National winner, had been narrowly beaten here, while Teaforthree, only tenth last year, went on to be third at Aintree. Leading ante-post fancy Monbeg Dude was an absentee. This time, the six Grand National entries were well well beaten in what proved a real slog in the conditions. A terrific training performance by Venetia Williams. A biggish personal best from Rigadin De Beauchene, with the runner-up 12lb off and the rest well below par.

4271 PERTEMPS NETWORK H'CAP HURDLE (SERIES QUALIFIER) 3m
3:30 (3:34) (Class 2) 5-Y-0+ **£12,021** (£3,529; £1,764; £882)

Form RPR

322/ 1 **Top Wood (FR)**[388] 3789 7-11-7 130..............(t) ConorO'Farrell 138+
(David Pipe) *mde all: jnd whn j.rt 2 out: drvn 3 l ahd run-in: all out* **25/1**

P34- 2 1 ½ **Astigos (FR)**[27] 3798 7-10-8 117.............. AidanColeman 120
(Venetia Williams) *hld up in mid-div: hdwy to teracks ldrs 4th: 2nd 8th: upsides whn bmpd 2 out: kpt on same pce last 100yds* **11/2**[3]

051- 3 31 **Wolf Shield (IRE)**[31] 3726 7-10-11 120.............. BarryKeniry 92
(George Moore) *chsd ldrs: drvn 8th: sn outpcd: kpt on fr 3 out: tk distant 3rd run-in* **20/1**

242- 4 ¾ **Quel Elite (FR)**[28] 3775 10-10-5 114..............(p) BrianHughes 85
(James Moffatt) *in rr: hdwy 7th: modestr 4th 3 out: one pce* **12/1**

1/2- 5 1 ¼ **Open Day (IRE)**[126] 1867 8-11-12 135.............. APMcCoy 105
(Jonjo O'Neill) *hld up in rr: gd hdwy 8th: wnt modest 3rd after next: j.rt last: sn wknd* **10/1**

1U3- 6 8 **San Telm (IRE)**[22] 3882 9-10-12 124.............. JoshuaMoore(3) 86
(Renee Robeson) *mid-div: sme hdwy 9th: nvr a factor* **17/2**

/61- 7 shd **Chavoy (FR)**[19] 3938 9-11-4 130..............(t) TonyKelly(3) 92
(Rebecca Menzies) *in rr: blnd 5th: sn bhd: t.o 7th: nvr on terms* **14/1**

3/1- 8 24 **Extreme Impact**[28] 3775 8-10-5 121.............. ConorRing(7) 59
(Evan Williams) *prom: drvn and lost pl 6th: sn t.o* **11/1**

4P4- P **The Knoxs (IRE)**[29] 3759 11-11-4 127.............. RyanMania
(Sue Smith) *in rr: t.o 7th: p.u bef 9th* **25/1**

0U6- P **Viking Blond (FR)**[70] 2943 9-11-2 125..............(v) SamTwiston-Davies
(Nigel Twiston-Davies) *chsd ldrs: reminders 3rd: lost pl next: t.o whn p.u after 6th* **20/1**

222- P **American Life (FR)**[15] 4006 7-10-1 110..............(vt) PaulMoloney
(Anthony Middleton) *in rr: bhd fr 7th: t.o 9th: p.u bef last* **16/1**

3/1- P **Horatio Hornblower (IRE)**[14] 4024 6-10-8 117.............. JasonMaguire
(Nick Williams) *nt fluent 1st 2: chsd ldrs: wknd after 9th: eased and bhd next: t.o whn p.u bef 2 out* **5/1**[2]

121- P **Flemenson (IRE)**[14] 4038 5-11-2 130..............(p) MauriceLinehan(5)
(Jonjo O'Neill) *prom: drvn and lost pl after 6th: bhd whn hit 8th: t.o next: p.u bef 2 out* **4/1**[1]

6m 17.3s (17.30) **Going Correction** +0.875s/f (Soft) 13 Ran SP% **117.5**
Speed ratings: **106,105,95,94,94 91,91,83,,**
CSF £150.40 CT £2812.57 TOTE £24.60: £7.10, £2.60, £6.40; EX 243.30 Trifecta £1618.80 Part won..
Owner Lady Clarke **Bred** Francois Couvreur **Trained** Nicholashayne, Devon

FOCUS
The eight finishers all qualify for the series final at Cheltenham. It proved a rigorous test of stamina in the condition and the first two came a long way clear. A personal best from the winner with the second stepping up on the best of his British runs.

4272 ALBERT BARTLETT NOVICES' HURDLE (REGISTERED AS THE PRESTIGE NOVICES' HURDLE) (GRADE 2) 3m
4:05 (4:06) (Class 1) 4-Y-0+
£15,661 (£5,876; £2,942; £1,465; £737; £368)

Form RPR

411- 1 **Toubeera**[6] 4175 8-11-1 130.............. AidanColeman 136
(Venetia Williams) *hld up in rr: hdwy to trck ldrs 5th: led 2 out: styd on strly* **5/1**[2]

115- 2 12 **Kaki De La Pree (FR)**[49] 3367 7-11-11 138.............. FelixDeGiles 135
(Tom Symonds) *chsd ldrs: drvn 8th: led 3 out: hdd next: kpt on same pce* **11/1**[3]

123- 3 25 **Oscar Rock (IRE)**[49] 3367 6-11-8 139.............. BrianHughes 106
(Malcolm Jefferson) *chsd ldrs: drvn 8th: reminders and sn lost pl: distant 6th 3 out: poor 4th last: tk 3rd clsng stages* **11/8**[1]

B1- 4 3 ¼ **Sego Success (IRE)**[74] 2874 6-11-8 0.............. APMcCoy 105
(Alan King) *trckd ldrs 5th: drvn 3 out: modest 3rd whn hit 2 out: wknd and lost distant 3rd clsng stages* **14/1**

3/0- 5 12 **Caledonia**[77] 2819 7-11-4 0.............. JamesReveley 88
(Jim Goldie) *led: hdd 8th: led briefly appr 3 out: wknd bef 2 out* **20/1**

211- 6 13 **Wuff (IRE)**[28] 3781 6-11-8 129..............(t) PaddyBrennan 78
(Tom George) *chsd ldrs: drvn 8th: sn bhd* **5/1**[2]

041- P **Copper Birch (IRE)**[14] 4029 6-11-8 125.............. PaulMoloney
(Evan Williams) *chsd ldrs: lost pl 3rd: sn bhd: t.o whn p.u bef 7th* **16/1**

432- P **Straidnahanna (IRE)**[28] 3781 5-11-4 121.............. RyanMania
(Sue Smith) *w ldr: hit 7th: led next: hdd appr 3 out: sn lost pl: bhd whn p.u bef 2 out* **11/1**[3]

122- P **Knockanrawley (IRE)**[27] 3800 6-11-8 131.............. JasonMaguire
(Kim Bailey) *in rr: reminders 3rd: sme hdwy 6th: sn reminders and lost pl: t.o 9th: p.u bef next* **25/1**

6m 19.6s (19.60) **Going Correction** +0.875s/f (Soft) 9 Ran SP% **113.3**
Speed ratings (Par 115): **102,98,89,88,84 80,,**
CSF £55.87 TOTE £5.20: £2.00, £2.80, £1.30; EX 61.20 Trifecta £151.60.
Owner Richard Britten-Long **Bred** Mrs H I S Calzini **Trained** Kings Caple, H'fords

FOCUS
A race that has been won by some smart novices. Brindisi Breeze beat Harry Topper in it two years ago before winning the Albert Bartlett Novices' Hurdle at Cheltenham. It proved a gruelling test and only two really saw it out.

4273 BETFRED SUPPORTS JACK BERRY HOUSE NOVICES' LIMITED H'CAP CHASE 2m 5f
4:35 (4:36) (Class 3) (0-140,132) 5-Y-0+ **£8,321** (£2,583; £1,391)

Form RPR

316- 1 **Bobcatbilly (IRE)**[28] 3769 8-10-8 118.............. APMcCoy 130+
(Ian Williams) *chsd ldrs: led 10th: clr 3 out: 15 l ahd whn eased last 100yds* **3/1**[1]

023- 2 13 **Sixty Something (FR)**[50] 3327 8-11-5 132.............. JakeGreenall(3) 130
(Paul Webber) *chsd ldrs: blnd and reminders 7th: sn lost pl: kpt on to take modest 2nd 3 out* **9/2**[3]

136- 3 56 **Sergeant Dick (IRE)**[35] 3642 9-11-1 125..............(t) SamTwiston-Davies 91
(Barry Brennan) *chsd ldrs: led 6th: hdd 9th: wknd 3 out: sn bhd: t.o whn eased run-in* **8/1**

0/1- P **Dungeel (IRE)**[45] 3450 8-11-6 130.............. JasonMaguire
(Donald McCain) *reminders 3rd: sn bhd: t.o whn p.u bef 7th* **11/2**

20P- P **Bob Ford (IRE)**[14] 4026 7-10-11 126.............. PatrickCorbett(5)
(Rebecca Curtis) *led: j.lft 1st: hdd 6th: lost pl 8th: sn bhd: t.o whn p.u bef 10th* **4/1**[2]

P **Gardefort (FR)**[97] 5-11-6 132.............. AidanColeman
(Venetia Williams) *hld up: jnd ldrs 8th: led next: hdd 10th: wknd qckly after 4 out: t.o 4th whn p.u bef 2 out* **3/1**[1]

5m 39.0s (13.50) **Going Correction** +0.875s/f (Soft) 6 Ran SP% **114.7**
Speed ratings: **109,104,82,,**
CSF £17.21 TOTE £4.50: £2.10, £3.10; EX 22.20 Trifecta £111.90.
Owner P J Vogt **Bred** Con Troy **Trained** Portway, Worcs

FOCUS
A decent novice handicap chase but one where the conditions played a big part. A step up from the winner, and there's a case for rating the form higher.

4274 CGA FOXHUNTER TRIAL WALRUS OPEN HUNTERS' CHASE 3m 1f
5:05 (5:05) (Class 3) 5-Y-0+ **£6,239** (£1,935; £967; £484)

Form RPR

130/ 1 **Ockey De Neulliac (FR)**[20] 12-11-12 115.............. MissCWalton 125
(N Mechie) *mde all: pckd 3 out: tired run-in: all out to hold on nr fin* **8/1**

12P/ 2 1 **Current Exchange (IRE)**[27] 9-11-8 117.............. MrPGerety(7) 126
(Mrs Sheila Crow) *hld up in rr: hdwy 6th: 2nd 12th: rallied to take 6 l 2nd sn after last: kpt on: jst hld* **7/1**[2]

00/ 3 15 **Onetwobeat**[34] 9-11-0 0.............. MrSFox(5) 100
(Mrs T R Kinsey) *chsd ldrs: lost pl and hit 5th: mstke 9th and 11th: hdwy and modest 5th 3 out: kpt on to take 3rd nr fin* **66/1**

1/5- 4 ½ **Chiquilline (FR)**[34] 8-11-12 115.............. MrSDrinkwater(3) 110
(T Lacey) *hld up in rr: hdwy 9th: 3rd 4 out: kpt on one pce to take modest 4th nr fin* **20/1**

/10- 5 nk **What A Laugh**[34] 9-12-4 122.............. MrWBiddick 112
(G D Hanmer) *hld up in rr: hdwy 10th: 2nd 3 out: wknd sn after last* **15/2**[3]

/0U- 6 21 **Pentiffic (NZ)**[13] 4057 11-12-1 116.............. MrJHamilton(3) 91
(Venetia Williams) *chsd ldrs: drvn 4th: lost pl 12th: sn bhd: t.o* **10/1**

F/P- P **Carronhills (IRE)**[23] 3862 12-11-5 104.............. MissLeandaTickle(7)
(P J Tolman) *in rr: t.o 9th: p.u bef 11th* **50/1**

/P3- P **Always Right (IRE)**[14] 4042 12-12-1 132.............. MrCDawson(3)
(John Wade) *in rr: nt fluent 2nd: hdwy and in tch 5th: j. slowly and lost pl 10th: bhd 12th: t.o whn p.u bef 3 out* **2/1**[1]

P/F- P **Ninetieth Minute (IRE)**[20] 11-12-1 131.............. MrGCrow(3)
(J J O'Shea) *j. slowly: prom: lost pl 3rd: bhd and reminders 6th: t.o 12th: p.u bef 2 out* **16/1**

P/P- P **Radetsky March (IRE)**[265] 11-11-11 108..............(p) MissPFuller(7)
(Miss Sally Duckett) *chsd ldrs: outpcd 10th: rallied whn hit 4 out: sn lost pl: bhd whn p.u bef next* **12/1**

3/3- P **Ben's Folly (IRE)**[23] 3862 9-11-7 106..............(p) MissLBrooke(5)
(R A Owen) *chsd ldrs: lost pl 12th: sn bhd: t.o whn p.u bef 3 out* **28/1**

341/ P **Bobs Law (IRE)**[13] 10-11-8 116.............. MrSPBowen(7)
(Mickey Bowen) *chsd ldrs: drvn along 3rd: lost pl 9th: bhd whn p.u bef 12th* **7/1**[2]

P **Flan The Man (IRE)**[27] 8-11-5 0.............. MrWTelfer(7)
(Miss S Randell) *chsd ldrs: wknd after 12th: t.o whn p.u bef 2 out* **33/1**

6m 57.1s (26.60) **Going Correction** +0.875s/f (Soft) 13 Ran SP% **118.5**
Speed ratings: **92,91,86,86,86 79,,,,**
CSF £59.95 TOTE £11.00: £3.30, £2.40, £7.70; EX 58.40 Trifecta £1797.00.
Owner N Mechie **Bred** Michel J Collin **Trained** Thirsk, North Yorks

FOCUS
A relatively valuable hunter chase and a suitably competitive field, but probably not a strong event of its type. The first two are rated pretty much to their best.
T/Jkpt: Not won. T/Plt: £1,448.60 to a £1 stake. Pool: £164550.19 - 82.92 winning tickets T/Qpdt: £99.90 to a £1 stake. Pool: £10447.69 - 77.35 winning tickets WG

3988 WINCANTON (R-H)
Saturday, February 15

OFFICIAL GOING: Heavy (chs 5.7, hdl 6.2)
Wind: strong across Weather: heavy showers

4275 BATHWICK TYRES SALISBURY H'CAP HURDLE (10 hdls 1 omitted) 2m 6f
1:20 (1:21) (Class 4) (0-105,110) 4-Y-0+ **£3,249** (£954; £477; £238)

Form RPR

4F1- 1 **Tarabela**[6] 4176 11-11-11 110 7ex..............(t) MrRobertHawker(7) 115
(Johnny Farrelly) *hld up towards rr: stdy prog fr 6th: rdn to chse ldng pair appr 2 out: chalng strly whn hit last: styd on gamely to ld on nod fnl stride* **5/1**[2]

522- 2 nse **Sweet Boy Vic (IRE)**[22] 3878 6-10-4 82.............. TomCannon 87
(Chris Gordon) *disp ld: rdn and hdd appr 2 out: rallied to regain ld bef last: strly pressed but kpt on gamely fr last: lost on nod* **3/1**[1]

The Form Book Jumps, Raceform Ltd, Compton, RG20 6NL.

506- **3** *10* **The Wealerdealer (IRE)**[79] 2761 7-11-2 **101**................(b[1]) MrMHeard[(7)] 97
(David Pipe) *trckd ldrs: gng wl whn nt fluent 3 out: sn rdn* **7/1**[3]

304- **4** *8* **General Girling**[18] 3955 7-10-0 **78** oh1............................(p) AdamWedge 65
(Caroline Keevil) *mid-div: rdn and stdy prog after 3 out: wnt 4th next: styd on but nvr threatened to get on terms w front 3* **25/1**

0/4- **5** *7* **Mic Aubin (FR)**[262] 542 11-11-2 **94**.. DavidBass 77
(Jennifer Mason) *prom: rdn after 3 out: wknd appr 2 out: blnd last* **20/1**

0/0- **6** *¾* **Cropley (IRE)**[35] 3650 5-11-1 **93**................................... RichieMcLernon 72
(Jonjo O'Neill) *hld up towards rr: stdy prog fr 6th: rdn after 3 out: nvr threatened ldrs* **12/1**

660- **7** *6* **Advisor (FR)**[30] 3744 8-11-8 **100**.. TommyPhelan 73
(Mark Gillard) *hld up towards rr: reminder after 3rd: sme late prog u.p: nvr any danger* **100/1**

605- **8** *1* **Henwood (IRE)**[18] 3956 6-11-1 **100**...................................... MrMLegg[(7)] 72
(Colin Tizzard) *trckd ldrs: pushed along after 6th: rdn after 3 out: wknd bef next* **8/1**

PU/- **9** *nk* **Pimbury (IRE)**[279] 12-9-9 **78** oh1.................................. HarryDerham[(5)] 50
(Fiona Shaw) *a towards rr* **100/1**

000- **10** *7* **Master Cardor Visa (IRE)**[83] 2690 9-10-6 **89**............... JamesBanks[(5)] 54
(Emma Baker) *a towards rr* **16/1**

/60- **11** *3½* **Russian Song (IRE)**[250] 690 10-11-8 **100**.......................(p) DarylJacob 61
(Fiona Shaw) *trckd ldrs: rdn after 6th: wknd after next* **33/1**

050- **12** *1½* **Warsaw Pact (IRE)**[138] 1700 11-9-7 **78** oh2.................... MrLKilgarriff[(7)] 38
(Steven Dixon) *dwlt: bhd: hdwy into midfield 3rd: rdn after 7th: wknd after 3 out* **33/1**

UP5- **13** *35* **Ballyhilty Bridge**[58] 3174 8-10-12 **90**................................ NickScholfield 15
(Paul Henderson) *mid-div tl appr 6th: sn bhd: t.o* **16/1**

0P- **14** *27* **See More Power (IRE)**[12] 4070 9-10-5 **90**...................... MrGBranton[(7)]
(Paul Henderson) *disp ld tl rdn after 7th: sn wknd: t.o* **100/1**

/23- **P** **Just Benny (IRE)**[44] 3503 9-11-5 **97**.......................... WayneHutchinson
(Richard Phillips) *mid-div tl wknd 3 out: tailing off whn p.u bef next* **14/1**

004- **P** **Duke's Affair**[51] 3290 6-11-2 **97**....................................... MattGriffiths[(3)]
(Jeremy Scott) *hld up towards rr: rdn and wknd 3 out: p.u bef next* **20/1**

03F- **P** **Snapchat (IRE)**[22] 3878 7-11-12 **104**................................ BrendanPowell
(Seamus Durack) *mid-div: trckd ldrs 3 out: sn rdn: wknd qckly and p.u bef next* **9/1**

5m 54.5s (28.00) **Going Correction** +1.075s/f (Soft) **17** Ran SP% **123.6**
Speed ratings (Par 105): **92,91,88,85,82 82,80,80,79,77 76,75,62,53,** ,
CSF £19.27 CT £108.90 TOTE £6.00: £1.70, £1.50, £2.10, £5.20; EX 23.30 Trifecta £66.30.
Owner G2 Recruitment Solutions Ltd **Bred** Mrs S M Reeks **Trained** Bridgwater, Somerset

FOCUS
The pace was not overly strong in this staying handicap hurdle but they finished strung out, with the first two well clear. They are rated in line with their good recent runs.

4276 COUNTRY GENTLEMEN'S ASSOCIATION JANE SEYMOUR MARES' NOVICES' HURDLE (LISTED RACE) (9 hdls 1 omitted) 2m 4f

1:55 (1:55) (Class 1) 4-Y-0+ **£11,443** (£4,327; £2,193; £1,119; £589)

Form RPR

311- **1** **Tagrita (IRE)**[16] 3991 6-11-2 125.. DarylJacob 135+
(Paul Nicholls) *a.p: led after 2 out: drifted lft bef last: styd on wl: rdn out* **11/4**[1]

224- **2** *4½* **Cannon Fodder**[22] 3882 7-11-2 129................................ MarcGoldstein 128
(Sheena West) *led: rdn whn nt fluent 2 out: hdd bef last: kpt on gamely but sn hld* **15/2**

001- **3** *37* **Molly's A Diva**[46] 3438 7-11-2 115..................................... NickScholfield 90
(Kim Bailey) *hld up bhd ldrs: struggling to hold pl after 5th: styd chsng ldng 4 tl outpcd appr 2 out: plugged on into go modest 3rd run-in* **5/1**[3]

122- **4** *½* **The Pirate's Queen (IRE)**[77] 2810 5-11-2 0............. WayneHutchinson 90
(Alan King) *hld up bhd ldrs: disputing cl 3rd 3 out: rdn and outpcd bef next: wknd last* **3/1**[2]

/14- **5** *19* **Woodland Walk**[58] 3168 6-11-2 115................................. RichieMcLernon 71
(Emma Lavelle) *trckd ldrs: rdn appr 2 out: sn wknd: t.o* **25/1**

UP2- **P** **Clara Peggotty**[14] 4037 7-11-2 0... DavidBass
(Tom Gretton) *trckd ldrs tl 6th: sn struggling and detached: p.u bef 3 out* **100/1**

312- **F** **Blue Buttons (IRE)**[47] 3423 6-11-2 126........................(t) BrendanPowell
(Harry Fry) *trcking ldrs whn fell heavily 4th* **3/1**[2]

5m 17.6s (20.80) **Going Correction** +1.075s/f (Soft) **7** Ran SP% **109.9**
Speed ratings (Par 111): **101,99,84,84,76** ,
CSF £21.51 TOTE £2.90: £2.10, £3.20; EX 18.70 Trifecta £104.30.
Owner Axom XLVIII **Bred** John Kidd **Trained** Ditcheat, Somerset

FOCUS
Only two mattered in this Listed novice once in the straight and the winner looks a good prospect. The form could be rated a lot higher.

4277 BATHWICK TYRES YEOVIL H'CAP HURDLE (THE JOCKEY CLUB GRASSROOTS JUMPS SERIES QUALIFIER) (10 hdls 1 omitted) 2m 6f

2:30 (2:32) (Class 3) (0-135,131) 4-Y-**£7,596** (£2,244; £1,122; £561; £280)

Form RPR

/64- **1** **Minellahalfcentury (IRE)**[30] 3741 6-11-1 **120**..................(tp) DarylJacob 126+
(Paul Nicholls) *mde all: rdn between last 2: styd on wl run-in: drvn out* **9/4**[1]

631- **2** *2* **Bob Tucker (IRE)**[30] 3741 7-10-4 **114**.............................. JamesBanks[(5)] 119
(Brendan Powell) *trckd ldrs: rdn to chse wnr bef 2 out: ev ch whn nt fluent last: styd on but a being hld after* **9/2**[2]

041- **3** *8* **Oscar Prairie (IRE)**[27] 3798 9-10-13 **128**........(b) WilliamFeatherstone[(10)] 125
(Warren Greatrex) *racd wdst: hld up but in tch: rdn and hdwy into 4th after 3 out: wnt 3rd between last 2: styd on but no further imp on ldng pair* **12/1**

/15- **4** *21* **Seebright**[51] 3292 7-11-12 **131**... JackDoyle 106
(Victor Dartnall) *hld up bhd ldrs: tk clsr order 5th: rdn to chse wnr after 3 out tl bef next: wknd between last 2* **11/1**

/01- **5** *2¾* **Lamps**[30] 3737 7-11-4 **130**..(b) JoshWall[(7)] 104
(Michael Blake) *reluctant to line up: slowly away: in last pair in tch: drvn along bef 6th: nvr threatened: wknd after 3 out* **6/1**[3]

542- **6** *19* **Tinker Time (IRE)**[32] 3697 6-10-12 **117**................................ LiamHeard 70
(Bob Buckler) *trckd ldrs: rdn after 3 out: wknd bef next: t.o* **8/1**

404- **7** *7* **Experimentalist**[24] 3263 6-10-9 **117**........................(t) MichaelByrne[(3)] 63
(Tim Vaughan) *trckd ldrs: rdn after 3 out: wknd bef next: t.o* **20/1**

126- **8** *32* **Angles Hill (IRE)**[64] 3069 7-11-6 **125**............................... NickScholfield 39
(Richard Woollacott) *trckd ldrs tl after 3rd: in last trio: rdn along after 7th: wknd after 3 out: t.o* **8/1**

145- **P** **Milan Bound (IRE)**[22] 3882 6-11-11 **130**......................... RichieMcLernon
(Jonjo O'Neill) *trckd ldrs: lost pl 6th: sn nudged along: rdn after 3 out: wknd qckly: t.o whn p.u bef next* **8/1**

5m 52.0s (25.50) **Going Correction** +1.075s/f (Soft) **9** Ran SP% **117.4**
Speed ratings (Par 107): **96,95,92,84,83 76,74,62,**
CSF £13.51 CT £99.91 TOTE £2.80: £1.20, £1.60, £3.50; EX 12.20 Trifecta £101.40.
Owner Jeffrey Hordle & Peter Hart **Bred** J Mangan **Trained** Ditcheat, Somerset

FOCUS
Not many got into it, despite the steady pace, and they finished strung out. The winner is on a good mark and is rated back to his best.

4278 BATHWICK TYRES BRIDGWATER H'CAP HURDLE (7 hdls 1 omitted) 2m

3:05 (3:05) (Class 3) (0-130,125) 4-Y-0 **£6,330** (£1,870; £935; £468; £234)

Form RPR

243- **1** **Aldopicgros (FR)**[15] 4018 4-10-7 **120**........................... HarryDerham[(5)] 116+
(Paul Nicholls) *mid-div: hdwy appr 3 out: rdn bef 2 out: led between last 2: strly pressed fnl 120yds: hld on: all out* **5/1**[3]

324- **2** *hd* **Headly's Bridge (IRE)**[27] 3802 8-11-3 **116**................. AndrewThornton 121+
(Simon Earle) *trckd ldrs: rdn appr 2 out: chsd wnr between last 2: styd on strly fnl 120yds: jst hld* **8/1**

200- **3** *3* **Seventh Sky (GER)**[50] 3322 7-11-11 **124**..........................(t) DarylJacob 125
(Charlie Mann) *mid-div: hdwy 3 out: sn rdn: styng on in 3rd whn swtchd rt after 2 out: disputing 2nd at the last: no ex fnl 120yds* **10/1**

304- **4** *5* **Dragon's Den (IRE)**[94] 2461 7-10-12 **111**.................. WayneHutchinson 107
(Chris Down) *hld up bhd: hdwy after 3 out: sn rdn: styd on same pce fr next* **20/1**

122- **5** *6* **Dalrymple (IRE)**[47] 3426 8-9-7 **99** oh4...............................(t) OllieGarner[(7)] 89
(Nick Ayliffe) *hld up towards rr: struggling 4th: styd on fr 2 out: styd on wout ever threatening to rch ldrs* **20/1**

214- **6** *2* **Zafranagar (IRE)**[64] 3066 9-10-7 **111**......................... RobertMcCarth[(5)] 99
(Ian Williams) *hld up towards rr: rdn appr 2 out: styd on wout ever threatening to get involved* **9/1**

P04- **7** *7* **Xaarcet (IRE)**[8] 4129 7-10-10 **109**................................... BrendanPowell 90
(Colin Tizzard) *led tl 2nd: lft in ld 4th: rdn and hdd after 2 out: grad fdd* **16/1**

416- **8** *nk* **Quick Decisson (IRE)**[21] 3891 6-11-5 **125**.................. MrCGethings[(7)] 106
(Philip Hobbs) *mid-div: tk clsr order 4th: rdn after 3 out: grad fdd* **11/4**[1]

013- **9** *26* **Ut Majeur Aulmes (FR)**[30] 3744 6-11-10 **123**........................ JackDoyle 78
(Victor Dartnall) *mid-div: hdwy 4th: rdn appr 2 out: wknd bef last: eased run-in* **9/2**[2]

000- **U** **Quaddick Lake (IRE)**[16] 3989 11-11-6 **122**.................... MattGriffiths[(3)]
(Jeremy Scott) *racd keenly: led 2nd tl blnd and uns rdr 4th* **20/1**

41P- **P** **George Nympton (IRE)**[35] 3652 8-11-0 **120**................(t) MikeyHamill[(7)]
(Brian Barr) *trckd ldrs: sltly hmpd 3rd: rdn after next: wknd 3 out: t.o whn p.u bef 2 out* **66/1**

050- **P** **Ubaldo Des Menhies (FR)**[24] 3832 6-11-4 **117**.......... RichieMcLernon
(Jonjo O'Neill) *lost tch 3rd: t.o whn p.u bef 2 out* **25/1**

4m 3.0s (14.10) **Going Correction** +1.075s/f (Soft)
WFA 4 from 6yo+ 9lb **12** Ran SP% **117.2**
Speed ratings (Par 107): **107,106,105,102,99 98,95,95,82,** ,
CSF £40.43 CT £388.20 TOTE £6.20: £2.30, £2.20, £3.50; EX 47.60 Trifecta £299.10.
Owner Million In Mind Partnership **Bred** S C I De Cercy & Maurice Goin **Trained** Ditcheat, Somerset

FOCUS
The pace was consistent and several were still travelling well on the turn into the straight. A step up from the winner under a claimer.

4279 BATHWICK TYRES KINGWELL HURDLE (GRADE 2) (7 hdls 1 omitted) 2m

3:35 (3:36) (Class 1) 4-Y-0+
£34,170 (£12,822; £6,420; £3,198; £1,608; £804)

Form RPR

151- **1** **Melodic Rendezvous**[28] 3779 8-11-10 156....................... NickScholfield 157+
(Jeremy Scott) *trckd ldr tl nudged along in 4th after 3 out: rdn bef next: styd on between last 2: squeezed through on nrside rail to ld run-in: on top at fin* **1/1**[1]

222- **2** *½* **Zarkandar (IRE)**[45] 3459 7-11-10 165.................................(b) DarylJacob 156
(Paul Nicholls) *trckd ldrs: mstke 4th: wnt 2nd 3 out: led appr 2 out: sn rdn: bmpd sltly whn chal fnl 170yds: sn hdd: hld nring fin* **11/10**[2]

/35- **3** *6* **Grumeti**[51] 3261 6-11-2 151.. WayneHutchinson 142
(Alan King) *hld up bhd ldrs: hdwy 3 out: rdn to chse wnr next tl appr last: kpt on same pce* **7/1**[3]

323- **4** *20* **Notarfbad (IRE)**[8] 4131 8-11-2 124...................................... MattGriffiths 124
(Jeremy Scott) *led at only a reasonable pce: rdn and hdd appr 2 out: sn outpcd* **100/1**

331/ **5** *3* **Golden Chieftain (IRE)**[340] 4721 9-11-2 148.............(tp) BrendanPowell 119
(Colin Tizzard) *trckd ldr tl after 4th: outpcd after 3 out* **33/1**

534- **6** *44* **Red Riverman**[50] 3318 6-11-2 120..................................(v[1]) DaveCrosse 75
(Nigel Twiston-Davies) *hld up bhd ldrs: rdn bef 3 out: wknd sn after: t.o* **100/1**

4m 8.4s (19.50) **Going Correction** +1.075s/f (Soft) **6** Ran SP% **115.0**
Speed ratings (Par 115): **94,93,90,80,79 57**
CSF £2.64 TOTE £2.10: £1.30, £1.10; EX 2.50 Trifecta £1.80.
Owner Cash For Honours **Bred** Mrs N A Ward **Trained** Brompton Regis, Somerset

FOCUS
As is often the case, another small field lined up for this Champion Hurdle trial, but it was an interesting contest and a close finish between two smart types. Melodic Rendezvous can rate higher and Zarkandar is rated close to the level of his win in this race last year. The result stood after a stewards' enquiry.

4280 BATHWICK TYRES EBF STALLIONS "NATIONAL HUNT" NOVICES' HURDLE (QUALIFIER) (9 hdls 1 omitted) 2m 4f

4:15 (4:15) (Class 3) 4-7-Y-0 **£6,498** (£1,908; £954; £477)

Form RPR

2F1- **1** **Knight Of Noir (IRE)**[32] 3695 5-11-8 0..........................(t) NickScholfield 135+
(David Pipe) *hld up bhd: racd wd: nt fluent 6th: nudged along: hdwy after 3 out: w.w trcking ldrs: led last: pushed clr: readily* **3/1**[2]

2 *6* **Brother Du Berlais (FR)**[170] 5-11-7 126......................... HarryDerham[(5)] 130
(Paul Nicholls) *trckd ldr: led appr 2 out: rdn and hdd last: sn readily hld by wnr* **4/1**[3]

F12- **3** *2* **Tidal Dance (IRE)**[23] 3860 7-11-3 133........................ HarryChalloner[(5)] 124
(Venetia Williams) *led: hmpd 2nd: rdn and hdd appr 2 out: rallied appr last: no ex run-in* **15/8**[1]

4 18 **Boondooma (IRE)**42 3545 7-11-2 118 .... DarylJacob 100
(Dr Richard Newland) *racd keenly: in tch: trckd ldrs 3 out: effrt bef next: wknd bef last* **9/2**

22P- 5 8 **Allow Dallow (IRE)**32 3697 7-11-2 124 .... (t) RichieMcLernon 92
(Jonjo O'Neill) *hld up: sme minor prog after 3 out: nvr threatened ldrs: wknd between last 2* **14/1**

00- 6 25 **Castarnie**28 3782 6-11-2 0 .... WayneHutchinson 67
(Robert Walford) *trckd ldr: j.rt 2nd: rdn after 3 out: sn wknd: t.o* **100/1**

444/ P **Hell's Spirit (IRE)**413 3354 6-10-11 0 .... AnthonyFreeman(5)
(David Dennis) *trckd ldrs: hit 6th: rdn after 3 out: sn wknd: t.o whn p.u bef 2 out* **20/1**

50- P **Saddlers Encore (IRE)**23 3863 5-10-9 0 .... MrCSmith(7)
(Philip Hobbs) *trckd ldrs tl pushed along after 4th: in tch: rdn after next: wknd after 3 out: t.o whn p.u bef 2 out* **50/1**

00- P **Genson**32 3697 5-11-2 0 .... DaveCrosse
(Richard Woollacott) *a towards rr: lost tch 3 out: p.u bef 2 out* **100/1**

5m 28.1s (31.30) **Going Correction** +1.075s/f (Soft) **9** Ran SP% **113.3**
Speed ratings: **80,77,76,69,66 56,, ,**
CSF £15.05 TOTE £4.40: £1.80, £2.10, £1.10; EX 14.70 Trifecta £45.40.
Owner Wayne Clifford **Bred** C Berry **Trained** Nicholashayne, Devon
FOCUS
This looked a fair novice event, with the winner proving much the best. The first two are on the upgrade.

4281 BATHWICK TYRES SALISBURY NOVICES' HURDLE (7 hdls 1 omitted) 2m
4:45 (4:46) (Class 4) 4-Y-0+ **£3,898** (£1,144; £572; £286)

Form RPR

P- 1 **Saint Breiz (FR)**6 4171 8-10-9 0 .... JonPark(7) 111
(Carroll Gray) *hld up towards rr: hdwy u.p after 3 out: led sn after last: styd on: rdn out* **66/1**

21- 2 2 **Carry On Sydney**11 4073 4-11-0 125 .... LeightonAspell 109
(Oliver Sherwood) *towards rr of midfield: hdwy appr 3 out: rdn to chse ldrs appr 2 out: styd on fr last: wnt 2nd nring fin* **9/4**2

/0F- 3 nk **Somerset Lias (IRE)**86 2631 6-11-2 0 .... SamJones 109
(Bob Buckler) *trckd ldr: rdn after 3 out: sltly hmpd 2 out: styd on fr last: wnt 3rd nring fin* **18/1**

/55- 4 ½ **Flemensmix**24 3838 6-10-11 0 .... EdCookson(5) 109
(Kim Bailey) *mid-div: hdwy 3 out: rdn to chse ldrs bef next: styd on same pce: wnt 4th nring fin* **25/1**

3U- 5 nk **Benbecula**14 3370 5-11-2 0 .... DaveCrosse 108
(Richard Mitchell) *led: j.lft 1st: clr 3rd tl rdn appr 2 out: hdd sn after last: no ex whn lost 3 pls nring fin* **20/1**

/60- 6 9 **Electric Mayhem**49 3357 7-11-2 0 .... WayneHutchinson 99
(Nick Mitchell) *mid-div: rdn after 4th: hdwy to chse ldrs next: styd on same pce fr 2 out* **66/1**

2- 7 11 **Anton Chigurh**22 3880 5-10-11 0 .... JamesBanks(5) 91
(Brendan Powell) *trckd ldr: bmpd 1st: rdn whn bdly hmpd 2 out: no ch after: wknd last* **8/1**3

5- 8 6 **Strong Conviction**23 3857 4-10-7 0 .... JamesDavies 73
(Simon Hodgson) *in tch: rdn after 3 out: wknd next* **66/1**

0/0- 9 31 **Indiana Oscar**18 3956 6-10-9 0 .... MrRobertHawker(7) 51
(Carroll Gray) *a towards rr: t.o fr 4th* **100/1**

60/ 10 5 **Fuse Wire**521 1555 7-10-11 0 .... CharlieWallis(5) 46
(Dai Burchell) *taken to s early: mid-div: rdn after 3 out: sn wknd: t.o* **100/1**

4/0- 11 1¾ **Calusa Star**18 3956 5-10-9 0 .... ChrisDavies(7) 44
(Philip Hobbs) *mid-div: rdn bef 3 out: sn wknd: t.o* **50/1**

5/4- 12 17 **Miller's Maverick**277 298 6-11-2 0 .... NickScholfield 27
(Grant Cann) *a bhd: t.o fr after 3rd* **40/1**

/52- F **Fascino Rustico**51 3258 6-11-2 0 .... (t) DarylJacob 121+
(Paul Nicholls) *hld up towards rr: hdwy whn short of room 3 out: travelling wl and abt to mount chal whn stmbld and fell 2 out* **4/5**1

U00- P **No No Cardinal (IRE)**16 3988 5-11-2 75 .... (t) TommyPhelan
(Mark Gillard) *trckd ldrs tl wknd after 3 out: t.o whn p.u bef 2 out* **100/1**

000- P **Castanum (IRE)**14 4030 5-11-2 0 .... TomCannon
(Laura Young) *a bhd: t.o 3rd: p.u bef 2 out* **100/1**

4m 12.4s (23.50) **Going Correction** +1.075s/f (Soft)
WFA 4 from 5yo+ 9lb **15** Ran SP% **124.1**
Speed ratings (Par 105): **84,83,82,82,82 77,72,69,53,51 50,42,, ,**
CSF £219.43 TOTE £74.70: £16.20, £1.30, £4.90; EX 451.10 Trifecta £1479.40 Part won..
Owner Riverdance Consortium 2 **Bred** Scea Des Prairies & Mme M Le Moigne **Trained** Moorland, Somerset
■ Stewards' Enquiry : Dave Crosse four-day; used whip above permitted level (1st-4th March).
FOCUS
A big-field maiden with little depth. The complexion of the race changed at the second-last when Fascino Rustico, who had barely broken sweat and looked set for a comfortable victory, seemed to stumble on landing, and his jockey had no chance of keeping the partnership intact. The time was slow and this is ordinary form.
T/Plt: £12.40 to a £1 stake. Pool: £85434.47 - 5021.82 winning tickets T/Qpdt: £4.90 to a £1 stake. Pool: £4051.06 - 611.00 winning tickets TM

4282 - (Foreign Racing) - See Raceform Interactive

3864 GOWRAN PARK (R-H)
Saturday, February 15

OFFICIAL GOING: Heavy

4283a RED MILLS CHASE (GRADE 2) (14 fncs) 2m 4f
2:25 (2:25) 5-Y-0+ **£21,666** (£6,333)

RPR

1 **Argocat (IRE)**30 3751 6-11-8 150 .... BrianO'Connell 157
(T J Taaffe, Ire) *chsd ldrs in 3rd for most: niggled along and dropped to rr briefly at 5th: nt fluent 5 out: clsr in 2nd after 4 out and disp next: rdn to ld bef 2 out: mstke last and strly pressed: kpt on wl: all out* **10/1**

2 ¾ **Turban (FR)**27 3806 7-11-3 151 .... RWalsh 152+
(W P Mullins, Ire) *w.w: tk clsr order in rr of quartet 4 out: cl up whn pckd sltly next: clsd into 2nd bef 2 out: rdn bef last and kpt on wl u.p run-in wout rching wnr* **5/4**1

F **Aupcharlie (IRE)**294 5578 8-11-3 147 .... AELynch
(Henry De Bromhead, Ire) *chsd ldr in 2nd for most: slt mstke 5 out: dropped to 3rd bef 3 out: sn rdn and stl in tch u.p whn fell 2 out* **4/1**3

U **Bog Warrior (IRE)**338 4749 10-11-3 150 .... BryanCooper
(A J Martin, Ire) *led: 3 l clr 1/2-way: reduced advantage bef 4 out: jnd next: sn pushed along and dropped to cl 3rd u.p whn blnd and uns rdr 2 out* **13/8**2

5m 19.4s (8.10) **4** Ran SP% **111.6**
CSF £24.02 TOTE £8.30; DF 30.30 Trifecta £14.40.
Owner Mrs Fitri Hay **Bred** B Bellaud & Caragh Bloodstock **Trained** Straffan, Co Kildare
■ Stewards' Enquiry : Brian O'Connell three-day ban: used whip above shoulder height (tbn)
FOCUS
The winner is rated in line with his penultimate run. The runner-up was just off his handicap form off a slower pace.

4285a RED MILLS TRIAL HURDLE (GRADE 2) (9 hdls) 2m
3:35 (3:41) 4-Y-0+ **£21,666** (£6,333; £3,000; £1,000)

RPR

1 **Un De Sceaux (FR)**34 3680 6-11-7 156 .... RWalsh 164+
(W P Mullins, Ire) *mde all: rn sltly off bnd after 3rd: a in command: v easily* **1/14**1

2 16 **Midnight Game**90 2552 7-11-4 140 .... BryanCooper 144
(W P Mullins, Ire) *chsd ldr thrght: rdn in mod 2nd and no imp on easy wnr 2 out: kpt on one pce* **10/1**2

3 12 **Chicago (IRE)**35 3667 5-11-3 127 .... PatrickMangan 130
(John Patrick Shanahan, Ire) *w.w in rr of quartet tl wnt mod 3rd at 4th: rdn and no ex bef 2 out: kpt on one pce* **20/1**3

4 67 **The Four Elms (IRE)**42 3543 6-11-4 116 .... (t) PhillipEnright 69
(John J Walsh, Ire) *chsd ldrs in 3rd tl dropped to rr at 4th where slow: no imp 4 out: wknd: completely t.o* **66/1**

4m 10.5s (9.60) **4** Ran SP% **108.7**
CSF £1.74 TOTE £1.10; DF 1.40 Trifecta £1.70.
Owner Edward O'Connell **Bred** Haras De La Rousseliere Et Al **Trained** Muine Beag, Co Carlow
FOCUS
The winner made all in great style. The race has been rated around the balance of the first three.

4286 - 4288a (Foreign Racing) - See Raceform Interactive

4024 FFOS LAS (L-H)
Sunday, February 16
4289 Meeting Abandoned - waterlogged

4016 KEMPTON (A.W) (R-H)
Sunday, February 16

OFFICIAL GOING: Standard to slow
Wind: mild breeze across Weather: sunny periods

4296 DINE IN THE PANORAMIC STANDARD OPEN NATIONAL HUNT FLAT RACE 2m (P)
1:30 (1:30) (Class 4) 4-6-Y-0 **£3,249** (£954; £477; £238)

Form RPR

4/ 1 **Bringithomeminty**308 5310 5-11-2 0 .... BarryGeraghty 118+
(Nicky Henderson) *hld up in midfield: nt clr run over 3f out: swtchd lft jst over 2f out: str run and qckng to ld over 1f out: r.o strly: impressive* **2/1**1

2 8 **Alibi De Sivola (FR)** 4-10-7 0 .... DarylJacob 102+
(Paul Nicholls) *hld up in midfield: nt clr run on inner over 2f out: swtchd rt and hdwy 2f out: 3rd whn swtchd lft and rn green ins fnl f: wnt 2nd and styd on wl fnl 150yds: no ch w wnr* **8/1**

22- 3 6 **Flamenco Lad**72 2926 4-10-7 0 .... BrendanPowell 96
(Martin Hill) *sn led: clr and rdn over 2f out: hdd and immediately outpcd by wnr over 1f out: lost 2nd and one pce fnl f* **5/1**2

4 2½ **Little Louie** 5-10-13 0 .... JoshuaMoore(3) 102
(Gary Moore) *hld up in rr: rdn over 3f out: no hdwy and plenty to do over 2f out: prog over 1f out: styd on strly ins fnl f: nvr trbld ldrs* **40/1**

5 1 **Rainy City (IRE)** 4-10-2 0 .... HarryDerham(5) 92
(Paul Nicholls) *chsd ldrs: rdn into 2nd briefly over 2f out: 3rd and outpcd over 1f out: kpt on same pce after* **8/1**

3- 6 1½ **Swincombe Star**87 2634 5-11-2 0 .... TomSiddall 99
(Robert Walford) *chsd ldr: pushed along 1/2-way: rdn over 2f out: rn green and btn ent fnl f: kpt on same pce* **10/1**

7 1½ **Pearly Legend** 6-10-6 0 .... MichaelByrne(3) 91
(Neil Mulholland) *in tch in midfield: rdn and outpcd over 2f out: wl hld and one pce fnl f* **100/1**

8 ½ **The Bailiff (IRE)** 5-11-2 0 .... TomScudamore 97
(David Pipe) *chsd ldr: rdn and outpcd over 2f out: wknd sn after* **6/1**3

9 ½ **Twojayslad** 5-11-2 0 .... WillKennedy 97
(Ian Williams) *hld up in last quartet: rdn over 3f out: sme hdwy ent fnl 2f: no further imp fr over 1f out* **33/1**

2/4- 10 2¼ **Malibu Rock**76 2864 6-11-2 0 .... PaddyBrennan 94
(Suzy Smith) *chsd ldrs: rdn and unable qck over 2f out: sn lost pl: wknd 2f out* **14/1**

4- 11 1 **Sea Tiger**72 2926 4-10-7 0 .... WayneHutchinson 84
(Alan King) *in tch in midfield: clsd to chse ldrs and stl travelling wl over 3f out: rdn over 2f out: sn wknd* **8/1**

40- 12 5 **Ronnie Rockcake**78 2830 4-10-7 0 .... DavidBass 79
(Ben Pauling) *chsd ldrs: losing pl whn n.m.r wl over 2f out: sn wknd* **100/1**

003- 13 4 **Lymm Grey**56 3228 5-10-9 0 .... SamJones 77
(Jo Davis) *in tch in midfield on outer: rdn and lost pl over 3f out: lost tch and bhd fnl 2f* **150/1**

14 9 **Boldwood** 5-11-2 0 .... LiamTreadwell 75
(James Evans) *in tch towards rr: lost pl 5f out: sn lost tch: t.o 3f out* **200/1**

15 6 **Tarantelle** 5-10-9 0 .... JamieMoore 62
(John Spearing) *in tch in last trio: rdn and struggling over 3f out: lost tch over 2f out: t.o* **25/1**

P **Gaiety Star** 5-10-9 0 .... AndrewThornton
(John O'Neill) *hld up in tch in rr: eased and p.u over 6f out: dismntd* **100/1**

3m 33.6s (3.50) **Going Correction** +0.35s/f (Slow)
WFA 4 from 5yo+ 9lb **16** Ran SP% **126.7**
Speed ratings: **105,101,98,96,96 95,94,94,94,93 92,90,88,83,80**
CSF £19.13 TOTE £3.80: £1.90, £3.20, £1.40; EX 24.10 Trifecta £70.80.
Owner Walters Plant Hire Ltd **Bred** G W Turner And Miss S J Turner **Trained** Upper Lambourn, Berks

FOCUS
The only standard bumper on the card, the pace wasn't bad at all and they finished quite well spread out. A big step up from the impressive winner.

4297 MIX BUSINESS WITH PLEASURE AT KEMPTON "JUMPERS' BUMPER" NATIONAL HUNT FLAT RACE (DIV I) 2m (P)

2:00 (2:00) (Class 4) 4-Y-O+ **£3,249** (£954; £477; £238)

Form RPR

142- **1** **Five In A Row (IRE)**[46] 3453 6-11-2 0 APMcCoy 110
(Brian Ellison) *in tch: swtchd lft and hdwy to ld 2f out: kpt on wl whn strly chal ent fnl f: asserted fnl 100yds: drvn out* **9/2**[3]

/P2- **2** *1* **Supreme Present**[16] 4019 6-10-9 0 (t) JasonMaguire 102
(Kim Bailey) *mid-div: smooth hdwy 3f out: nt clr run tl 2f out: sn shkn up: str chal ent fnl f: ev ch tl no ex fnl 100yds* **7/2**[2]

1- **3** *10* **Bennachie (IRE)**[208] 1094 5-11-2 0 RichardJohnson 99
(Tim Vaughan) *in tch: rdn wl over 2f out: styd on fr over 1f out: wnt 3rd ins fnl f: no ch w ldng pair* **8/1**

2- **4** *1 ½* **Lily Mars (IRE)**[52] 3295 7-10-6 0 MichaelByrne(3) 91
(Neil Mulholland) *trckd ldrs: rdn wl over 2f out: styd on same pce* **20/1**

252- **5** *1 ¼* **A Tail Of Intrigue (IRE)**[56] 3226 6-11-2 0 WillKennedy 96
(Ian Williams) *led: jnd after 6f: rdn and hdd jst over 2f out: sn hld: fdd wl ins fnl f* **10/1**

0- **6** *nk* **Gold Carrot**[17] 3994 6-10-13 0 JoshuaMoore(3) 96
(Gary Moore) *hld up towards rr: rdn and stdy prog fr over 2f out: styd on wout ever threatening to rch ldrs* **8/1**

7 *shd* **Tsar Alexandre (FR)**[308] 7-10-13 0 GavinSheehan(3) 96
(Warren Greatrex) *trckd ldrs: rdn over 2f out: sn one pce* **14/1**

/30- **8** *2* **Bay Fortuna**[32] 3716 5-11-2 0 WayneHutchinson 94
(Mark Usher) *hld up towards rr: rdn 3f out: sme late prog: nvr a danger* **25/1**

/32- **9** *1* **Foggy's Wall (IRE)**[48] 3422 6-10-11 0 HarryDerham(5) 93
(Paul Nicholls) *trckd ldr: disp after 6f tl rdn over 2f out: sn one pce: fdd fnl f* **11/4**[1]

0- **10** *7* **Mr Lennygreengrass (IRE)**[86] 2660 7-11-2 0 PaddyBrennan 86
(Fergal O'Brien) *hld up towards rr: hdwy wl over 2f out: sn rdn: wknd over 1f out* **100/1**

400- **11** *½* **Bostin (IRE)**[17] 3988 6-10-9 0 MikeyHamill(7) 85
(Brian Barr) *mid-div: rdn over 4f out: wknd over 1f out* **100/1**

0P0- **12** *6* **Canarbino Girl**[16] 4019 7-10-2 0 MrLDrowne(7) 72
(Caroline Keevil) *mid-div tl wknd over 3f out* **200/1**

00- **13** *12* **Top Show**[9] 4135 5-11-2 0 PaulMoloney 67
(Dean Ivory) *mid-div tl rdn over 4f out: sn in rr* **100/1**

/ **14** *3 ¾* **San Siro (IRE)**[315] 8-10-9 0 MrFMitchell(7) 64
(Philip Mitchell) *a in rr* **66/1**

3m 35.4s (5.30) **Going Correction** +0.35s/f (Slow)
WFA 5 from 6yo+ 1lb **14** Ran SP% **118.6**
Speed ratings (Par 105): **100,99,94,93,93 92,92,91,91,87 87,84,78,76**
CSF £19.65 TOTE £3.60: £1.50, £1.50, £3.40; EX 19.30 Trifecta £112.90.
Owner P J Martin **Bred** Ms M Maher **Trained** Norton, N Yorks

■ Stewards' Enquiry : Michael Byrne two-day ban; careless riding (2nd-3rd Mar)

FOCUS
For horses currently eligible for NH novice hurdles. The pace was steady but the front pair were still able to draw well clear. The fourth and sixth help set the level.

4298 MIX BUSINESS WITH PLEASURE AT KEMPTON "JUMPERS' BUMPER" NATIONAL HUNT FLAT RACE (DIV II) 2m (P)

2:30 (2:30) (Class 4) 4-Y-O+ **£3,249** (£954; £477; £238)

Form RPR

/21- **1** **Zulu Oscar**[99] 2375 5-11-2 0 RyanMahon 119+
(Harry Fry) *racd keenly trcking ldrs: led 2f out: qcknd up wl whn rdn to draw clr: wl in command fnl f: readily* **11/4**[1]

4P2- **2** *2 ¼* **Ourmanmassini (IRE)**[16] 4018 6-11-2 0 (t) AidanColeman 117
(Suzy Smith) *mid-div: rdn and hdwy over 2f out: r.o wl to chse wnr ent fnl f but a being hld* **10/1**[3]

106- **3** *¾* **Neston Grace**[48] 3423 6-10-9 0 JamesDavies 109
(Simon Hodgson) *mid-div: rdn wl over 2f out: no imp tl r.o ent fnl f: wnt 3rd sn after: nt rch ldrs* **33/1**

- **4** *3* **As De Mee (FR)**[125] 4-10-2 0 HarryDerham(5) 104
(Paul Nicholls) *mid-div: hdwy over 2f out: rdn to chse wnr over 1f out tl ent fnl f: sn no ex* **11/4**[1]

204- **5** *1 ¾* **Chase The Wind (IRE)**[62] 3134 5-10-13 0 (t) GavinSheehan(3) 112
(Warren Greatrex) *prom: led 4f out: rdn and hdd 2f out: sn one pce* **8/1**[2]

112- **6** *9* **Joanne One (IRE)**[31] 3737 6-10-9 0 (t) BrendanPowell 96
(Jamie Snowden) *trckd ldrs: struggling to hold pce 4f out: wknd 3f out* **11/4**[1]

/53- **7** *1 ¾* **Crackerjack**[66] 3047 7-10-11 0 JamesBanks(5) 101
(Emma Baker) *mid-div: rdn wl over 2f out: wknd wl over 1f out* **66/1**

8 *1 ¾* **Smart Story**[286] 7-11-2 0 PaddyBrennan 99
(Fergal O'Brien) *hld up towards rr: sme hdwy over 2f out: sn rdn: wknd over 1f out* **33/1**

4- **9** *2 ¼* **Captain Ocana (IRE)**[65] 3064 9-11-2 0 TomO'Brien 97
(Paul Henderson) *a towards rr* **66/1**

425- **10** *8* **Sonofagun (FR)**[60] 3164 8-11-2 0 WillKennedy 89
(Ian Williams) *led tl 4f out: sn rdn: wknd over 2f out* **25/1**

11 *35* **Thomastown (IRE)**[475] 7-11-2 0 TomScudamore 54
(Kevin Frost) *trckd ldrs on outer tl 6f out: wknd 4f out* **66/1**

PPP/ **12** *7* **Redinga**[303] 5374 8-10-9 0 (t) AndrewThornton 40
(Linda Jewell) *trckd ldrs tl lost pl rapidly after 7f: sn wl bhd* **200/1**

/PP- **13** *¾* **Niceboy (IRE)**[52] 3251 10-10-9 0 MrFMitchell(7) 46
(Daniel Steele) *in last pair: rn wd on stable bnd: t.o after 6f* **200/1**

14 *99* **Chunck** 7-11-2 0 RichardJohnson
(Edward Creighton) *a bhd: t.o 1/2-way* **50/1**

3m 35.1s (5.00) **Going Correction** +0.35s/f (Slow)
WFA 4 from 5yo 9lb 5 from 6yo+ 1lb **14** Ran SP% **117.4**
Speed ratings (Par 105): **101,99,99,98,97 92,91,90,89,85 68,64,64,14**
CSF £32.42 TOTE £4.40: £1.80, £1.70, £8.90; EX 24.90 Trifecta £522.20.
Owner Caroline Fry & Susie Dilhorne **Bred** R Robinson **Trained** Seaborough, Dorset

FOCUS
For horses currently eligible for NH novice hurdles. A couple of the key contenders failed to meet expectations and it's likely the form of the first division is stronger. The winenr and fifth were rated pretty much to their marks.

4299 BOOK NOW FOR SILVER CUPS DAY 15.03.14 "JUMPERS' BUMPER" NATIONAL HUNT FLAT RACE 2m 2f

3:00 (3:01) (Class 4) 4-Y-O+ **£3,249** (£954; £477; £238)

Form RPR

1P4- **1** **Dawn Commander (GER)**[16] 4021 7-11-2 0 BrendanPowell 119
(Renee Robeson) *mid-div: hdwy on inner 3f out: rdn over 2f out: sn swtchd lft: styd on strly to ld fnl 75yds: wl on top at fin* **9/2**[3]

235- **2** *1 ¼* **Polisky (FR)**[51] 3321 7-11-2 0 (t) DarylJacob 118
(Paul Nicholls) *pushed along ealry: midfield: hdwy to trck ldrs after 2f: upsides ldr 2f out: drvn jst over 1f out: ev ch fnl f tl fnl 75yds: wnt 2nd nring fin* **4/1**[2]

/20- **3** *nk* **Henryville**[49] 3387 6-11-2 0 RyanMahon 117
(Harry Fry) *mid-div on outer: hdwy over 5f out: rdn to ld 2f out: strly pressed and hld on to narrow advantage fr over 1f out tl hdd and no ex fnl 75yds* **4/1**[2]

224- **4** *1 ¾* **Benbane Head (USA)**[16] 4022 10-11-2 0 (t) IanPopham 116
(Martin Keighley) *trckd ldr: pressed ldr w a circ to go tl led over 5f out: led 5f out: rdn and hdd 2f out: kpt on same pce* **9/4**[1]

/60- **5** *2* **Lady From Geneva**[48] 3425 7-10-6 0 JoshuaMoore(3) 107
(Brendan Powell) *chsd ldrs tl outpcd 4f out: in rr w plenty to do 3f out: styd on wl fr over 1f out but no threat to ldrs* **66/1**

536- **6** *2 ¼* **Spoil Me (IRE)**[16] 4023 7-11-8 0 RichieMcLernon 117
(Jonjo O'Neill) *hld up towards rr: hdwy on outer fr 4f out: rdn 3f out: styd on same pce fnl 2f* **16/1**

P6P- **7** *½* **Hot Whiskey (IRE)**[9] 4132 6-11-2 0 (t) LeightonAspell 111
(Brendan Powell) *hld up towards rr: hdwy into midfield over 3f out: sn rdn: styd on same pce* **25/1**

225/ **8** *2 ¼* **High Kite (IRE)**[424] 3142 8-10-13 0 GavinSheehan(3) 109
(Warren Greatrex) *in tch: rdn over 2f out: nt pce to get on terms: fdd fnl f* **14/1**

F1P- **9** *9* **Midnight Lira**[29] 3785 7-10-6 0 JamesBest(3) 93
(Caroline Keevil) *in tch: rdn over 3f out: wknd over 1f out* **16/1**

103- **10** *11* **Halucha (IRE)**[66] 3044 9-11-2 0 (p) LiamTreadwell 89
(Paul Webber) *led tl 5f out: sn rdn: wknd over 2f out* **25/1**

004- **11** *1 ¾* **Amaury De Lusignan (IRE)**[23] 3883 8-10-9 0 MrGBranton(7) 87
(Paul Henderson) *mid-div tl dropped to rr over 8f out: sn struggling: bhd fnl 4f* **66/1**

4m 0.6s (4.20) **Going Correction** +0.35s/f (Slow) **11** Ran SP% **118.1**
Speed ratings (Par 105): **104,103,103,102,101 100,100,99,95,90 89**
CSF £22.34 TOTE £7.30: £2.60, £2.80, £1.02; EX 23.90 Trifecta £124.10.
Owner Nick Brown Racing **Bred** W Lohmann Jr **Trained** Tyringham, Bucks

■ Stewards' Enquiry : Mr G Branton five-day ban; used whip when out of contention (tba)

FOCUS
For horses that have not run on the Flat, have run at least once over 2m7f+ and who have not won a Class 1 or 2 race. They appeared to go a reasonable gallop. The third and seventh set the level.

4300 KEMPTON PARK CHASE DAY 22.02.14 "JUMPERS' BUMPER" NATIONAL HUNT FLAT RACE (DIV I) 2m 2f

3:35 (3:35) (Class 4) 4-Y-O+ **£3,249** (£954; £477; £238)

Form RPR

420/ **1** **Presenting Arms (IRE)**[348] 4574 7-10-9 0 (t) GaryDerwin(7) 130
(Harry Fry) *mid-div: hdwy over 3f out: rdn to ld jst over 1f out: r.o wl* **40/1**

422- **2** *1 ¼* **Silsol (GER)**[17] 3989 5-10-11 0 (t) HarryDerham(5) 129
(Paul Nicholls) *prom: led after 9f: drvn wl over 1f out: hdd jst over 1f out: kpt on but hld fnl f* **5/2**[1]

150- **3** *4* **Aazif (IRE)**[16] 4023 5-11-2 0 WillKennedy 125
(Ian Williams) *mid-div: hdwy over 2f out: sn rdn: styd on fnl f: snatched 3rd fnl stride* **20/1**

3- **4** *shd* **Grey Blue (IRE)**[36] 3641 4-10-7 0 BarryGeraghty 116
(Nicky Henderson) *hld up towards rr: gd hdwy fr 3f out: mounting chal whn squeezed out wl over 1f out: swtchd lft: rdn and r.o to go 3rd sn after but nt pce to rch ldrs: lost 3rd fnl stride* **5/1**[3]

226- **5** *3 ½* **Mixologist**[21] 3922 7-10-13 0 (t) GavinSheehan(3) 121
(Warren Greatrex) *hld up towards rr of midfield: sme prog 3f out: sn rdn: styd on steadily wout ever threatening to get on terms* **10/1**

4- **6** *1 ¼* **Zip Wire (IRE)**[50] 3351 5-11-2 0 JasonMaguire 120
(Donald McCain) *trckd ldrs: rdn over 3f out: kpt on tl no ex fnl f* **11/2**

416- **7** *1 ¼* **Staigue Fort**[16] 4022 6-11-2 0 AidanColeman 119
(Emma Lavelle) *hld up towards rr: sme hdwy on outer ent st: styd on wout ever threatening to get involved* **14/1**

/21- **8** *1 ¾* **Koolala (IRE)**[80] 2767 6-10-9 0 APMcCoy 110
(Paul Webber) *led tl 9f out: prom: rdn and ev ch briefly over 2f out: sn hld: wknd ent fnl f* **3/1**[2]

305- **9** *1 ¼* **Dormouse**[8] 4157 9-10-11 0 (p) JoshHamer(5) 116
(Anabel K Murphy) *mid-div tl outpcd 3f out* **66/1**

040- **9** *dht* **Invicta Lake (IRE)**[16] 4023 7-11-2 0 (p) DarylJacob 116
(Suzy Smith) *prom for 6f: trckd ldrs: rdn wl over 2f out: sn outpcd* **20/1**

135- **11** *6* **Castlemorris King**[210] 1054 6-10-9 0 MikeyHamill(7) 110
(Brian Barr) *hld up towards rr: rdn wl over 2f out: nvr any imp* **50/1**

/40- **12** *3* **Couldhavehaditall (IRE)**[83] 2718 6-11-2 0 LiamTreadwell 107
(Paul Webber) *mid-div on outer: hdwy to trck ldrs over 9f out: rdn 4f out: wknd over 2f out* **25/1**

14U- **13** *2* **Gud Day (IRE)**[74] 2890 6-11-2 0 (t) PaddyBrennan 105
(Fergal O'Brien) *a towards rr* **40/1**

0P6- **14** *2 ½* **Darkestbeforedawn (IRE)**[78] 2828 7-11-2 0 TomO'Brien 102
(Caroline Keevil) *prom tl rdn 4f out: sn wknd* **66/1**

40- **15** *3* **Castle Cheetah (IRE)**[16] 4019 6-11-2 0 IanPopham 99
(Martin Keighley) *mid-div tl wknd 3f out* **66/1**

4m 0.5s (4.10) **Going Correction** +0.35s/f (Slow)
WFA 4 from 5yo 9lb 5 from 6yo+ 1lb **15** Ran SP% **126.1**
Speed ratings (Par 105): **104,103,101,101,100 99,98,98,97,97 94,93,92,91,90**
CSF £136.79 TOTE £53.20: £14.80, £1.40, £4.30; EX 428.80 Trifecta £2765.40 Part won..
Owner J M Dare **Bred** Ms Iona Maguire **Trained** Seaborough, Dorset

FOCUS
For horses which have run at least once over hurdles and have not won at Class 1, 2 or 3 level. A massive step up from the surprise winner but the form has a fairly solid look.

4301 KEMPTON PARK CHASE DAY 22.02.14 "JUMPERS' BUMPER" NATIONAL HUNT FLAT RACE (DIV II) 2m 2f

4:05 (4:08) (Class 4) 4-Y-0+ £3,249 (£954; £477; £238)

Form RPR

225- 1 **Knightly Escapade**[77] 2840 6-11-2 0 APMcCoy 105
(Brian Ellison) *mid-div: hdwy over 2f out: sn nt clr tl swtchd rt jst over 1f out: qcknd up wl to ld jst ins fnl f: r.o: rdn out* **9/1**

0F2- 2 ¾ **Watt Broderick (IRE)**[89] 2573 5-10-11 0 RobertMcCarth(5) 104
(Ian Williams) *hld up towards rr: gd hdwy on outer ent st: led wl over 1f out: sn rdn: hdd jst ins fnl f: kpt on* **40/1**

25- 3 3 **Civil War (IRE)**[10] 4103 5-11-2 0 JamieMoore 101
(Gary Moore) *mid-div: hdwy over 3f out: rdn and ev ch 2f out: kpt on same pce fnl f* **2/1**[1]

/31- 4 nk **Ellnando Queen**[16] 4018 6-10-12 0 GavinSheehan(3) 100
(Warren Greatrex) *trckd ldr: led after 9f: rdn whn strly pressed over 2f out: sn hdd: kpt on same pce: regained 4th nring fin* **7/2**[2]

155- 5 ¾ **Brinestine (USA)**[31] 3744 5-10-9 0 AndriasGuerin(7) 100
(Paul Nicholls) *mid-div: hdwy over 3f out: led briefly 2f out: sn rdn: ev ch ent fnl f: no ex fnl 100yds* **5/1**[3]

553- 6 ½ **Generous Ransom (IRE)**[23] 3880 6-11-2 0 DarylJacob 100
(Nick Gifford) *trckd ldrs: chal 3f out: rdn whn outpcd 2f out: hld after* **9/1**

234- 7 ¾ **Lord Landen (IRE)**[40] 3595 9-11-2 0 (t) PaddyBrennan 99
(Fergal O'Brien) *in tch: rdn over 2f out: sn outpcd* **50/1**

312- 8 2¼ **Drumlang (IRE)**[30] 3759 8-11-2 0 WillKennedy 97
(Ian Williams) *trckd ldrs: rdn and ev ch 2f out: wknd over 1f out* **12/1**

060- 9 1¼ **Bayley's Dream**[23] 3877 5-11-2 0 (t) PaulMoloney 96
(Paul Webber) *hld up towards rr: rdn 3f out: nvr finding pce to get involved* **40/1**

353- 10 10 **Chemistry Master**[62] 3132 6-10-6 0 (t) MartinMcIntyre(10) 86
(Harry Fry) *towards rr of mid-div on outer: stdy prog fr over 6f out: rdn over 3f out: wknd over 2f out* **8/1**

P/0- 11 16 **Businessmoney Judi**[29] 3788 8-10-9 0 (tp) NickScholfield 63
(Keiran Burke) *led for 9f: chsd ldr: rdn over 3f out: wknd over 2f out* **50/1**

01P- 12 10 **Big John Cannon (IRE)**[51] 3317 4-10-7 0 AidanColeman 51
(Sarah-Jayne Davies) *a towards rr* **66/1**

4m 4.8s (8.40) **Going Correction** +0.35s/f (Slow)
WFA 4 from 5yo 9lb 5 from 6yo+ 1lb 12 Ran SP% **121.3**
Speed ratings (Par 105): **95,94,93,93,92 92,92,91,90,86 79,74**
CSF £308.83 TOTE £8.60: £2.20, £7.20, £1.60; EX 257.70 Trifecta £1969.60.
Owner Mrs J A Martin **Bred** M Meacock & The Late I Stewart-Brown **Trained** Norton, N Yorks
■ Rule 4 of 5p in the pound applies to all bets; Withdrawn: Juno The Muffinman

FOCUS
For horses which have run at least once over hurdles and have not won at Class 1, 2 or 3 level. It was the slowest race over the trip and the form looks ordinary.

4302 KEMPTON.CO.UK "JUMPERS' BUMPER" NATIONAL HUNT FLAT RACE 2m (P)

4:40 (4:40) (Class 3) 4-Y-0+ £6,330 (£1,870; £935; £468; £234)

Form RPR

/11- 1 **My Tent Or Yours (IRE)**[52] 3261 7-11-2 0 APMcCoy 143+
(Nicky Henderson) *travelled strly in mid-div: hdwy on bridle 4f out: wnt 2nd wl over 3f out: led on bit over 2f out: nudged along ent fnl f: easily* **1/5**[1]

162- 2 4½ **Ranjaan (FR)**[16] 4022 6-10-11 0 (t) HarryDerham(5) 135
(Paul Nicholls) *hld up towards rr: hdwy over 4f out: wnt 2nd over 2f out: sn rdn: nvr finding pce to get on terms and no ch w wnr but kpt on wl* **5/1**[2]

030- 3 4½ **Capellanus (IRE)**[14] 4051 8-11-8 0 RichardJohnson 137
(Brian Ellison) *hld up towards rr: hdwy fr 4f out: rdn to chse ldng pair over 2f out: kpt on but nvr any ch* **20/1**

453- 4 11 **Ballygrooby Bertie (IRE)**[90] 2563 6-11-2 0 (t) PaddyBrennan 120
(Fergal O'Brien) *hld up towards rr: hdwy u.p over 2f out: styd on wout ever threatening to rch ldrs* **66/1**

200- 5 7 **Valid Reason**[24] 3186 7-11-2 0 (t) PaulMoloney 113
(Dean Ivory) *hld up towards rr: styd on fnl 2f: nvr any danger* **33/1**

214- 6 4 **Dispour (IRE)**[64] 3089 4-10-7 0 JasonMaguire 101
(Donald McCain) *disp for 4f: trckd clr ldr tl 3f out: sn rdn: wknd over 1f out* **12/1**[3]

510/ 7 2½ **Gifted Leader (USA)**[862] 5201 9-11-2 0 WillKennedy 106
(Ian Williams) *hld up towards rr: sme minor late prog: nvr any danger* **100/1**

23P- 8 2 **Prompter**[8] 4147 7-11-2 0 RichieMcLernon 104
(Jonjo O'Neill) *disp ld tl clr ldr after 4f out: sn clr: shkn up 4f out: hdd over 2f out: sn wknd* **20/1**

03P- 9 8 **Donnas Palm (IRE)**[19] 3958 10-11-2 0 (v) JamieMoore 96
(Gary Moore) *mid-div tl wknd over 3f out* **50/1**

606- 10 1¼ **Tom Wade (IRE)**[14] 4058 7-10-11 0 BenPoste(5) 95
(Shaun Harris) *mid-div: rdn over 3f out: wknd over 2f out* **66/1**

352- 11 2 **O'Callaghan Strand (AUS)**[74] 2884 8-10-6 0 PatrickCowley(10) 93
(Jonjo O'Neill) *in tch: pushed along over 5f out: wknd over 3f out* **50/1**

505- 12 7 **Berkeley Avenue**[16] 4019 5-10-6 0 (tp) WilliamFeatherstone(10) 86
(Warren Greatrex) *a towards rr* **50/1**

5PP- 13 13 **Green Belt Elite (FR)**[15] 4027 10-11-2 0 AidanColeman 73
(Venetia Williams) *chsd ldrs: rdn over 4f out: sn btn* **33/1**

3m 25.7s (-4.40) **Going Correction** +0.35s/f (Slow)
WFA 4 from 5yo 9lb 5 from 6yo+ 1lb 13 Ran SP% **133.0**
Speed ratings (Par 107): **125,122,120,115,111 109,108,107,103,102 101,98,91**
CSF £1.90 TOTE £1.30: £1.02, £1.20, £4.90; EX 3.10 Trifecta £14.40.
Owner John P McManus **Bred** F Dunne **Trained** Upper Lambourn, Berks

FOCUS
For horses which have run at least once over hurdles or fences. The easy winner stood out and this was much the fastest time on the card. The runner-up is rated to his best.

4303 KEMPTON FOR WEDDINGS "JUMPERS' BUMPER" NATIONAL HUNT FLAT RACE 2m (P)

5:10 (5:10) (Class 4) 5-Y-0+ £3,249 (£954; £477; £238)

Form RPR

/P6- 1 **Tanks For That (IRE)**[64] 3080 11-11-0 0 BarryGeraghty 125
(Nicky Henderson) *mid-div: hdwy 3f out: rdn to chse ldr 2f out: led jst over 1f out: kpt on u.str.p whn jnd fnl 100yds: jst hld on* **9/2**[3]

11F- 2 nse **Tzora**[211] 1046 9-11-0 0 HaddenFrost 125
(Martin Hill) *hld up towards rr: hdwy on outer fr 3f out: pushed along and clsng on ldrs over 1f out: str chal fnl 100yds: kpt on: jst hld* **12/1**

222- 3 2¾ **Daymar Bay (IRE)**[16] 4020 8-11-0 0 AidanColeman 122
(Emma Lavelle) *racd keenly: trckd ldr: led over 7f out: rdn over 2f out: hdd jst over 1f out: kpt on same pce* **11/4**[1]

221- 4 1¾ **Divine Intavention (IRE)**[12] 4078 10-10-9 0 MrMWall(5) 120
(Martin Keighley) *trckd ldrs: rdn over 2f out: kpt on same pce* **25/1**

521- 5 hd **Domtaline (FR)**[16] 4020 7-10-10 0 AlexChadwick(10) 126
(Paul Nicholls) *cl up: rdn to chse ldr briefly over 2f out: kpt on same pce tl no ex fnl 75yds* **3/1**[2]

132- 6 nse **The Nephew (IRE)**[109] 2155 6-11-0 0 RichieMcLernon 120
(Jonjo O'Neill) *hld up bhd: hdwy over 2f out: pushed along to chse ldrs over 1f out: kpt on but nvr finding pce to chal* **20/1**

624- 7 ¾ **All That Remains (IRE)**[78] 2828 9-11-0 0 (t) APMcCoy 119
(Brian Ellison) *trckd ldrs: rdn over 2f out: no ex ent fnl f* **6/1**

/05- 8 hd **Tallulah Mai**[23] 3876 7-10-2 0 JamesBanks(5) 112
(Alastair Lidderdale) *mid-div: rdn over 3f out: kpt on fnl f but nvr any real imp on ldrs* **100/1**

PP0- 9 shd **Golden Gael**[71] 2948 8-10-7 0 NickScholfield 112
(Jeremy Scott) *hld up towards rr: hdwy over 3f out: sn rdn: chsd ldrs over 1f out: no ex ins fnl f* **50/1**

/06- 10 1¼ **First Fandango**[112] 2100 7-11-0 0 (t) RichardJohnson 118
(Tim Vaughan) *mid-div: rdn 4f out: kpt on fnl 2f but no imp on ldrs* **12/1**

560- 11 1¾ **Fredo (IRE)**[70] 2979 10-10-9 0 RobertMcCarth(5) 116
(Ian Williams) *hld up towards rr: rdn wl over 2f out: kpt on but nvr gng pce to get on terms* **33/1**

536- 12 13 **Marley Roca (IRE)**[65] 3065 10-11-0 0 LiamTreadwell 103
(Paul Webber) *mid-div tl wknd wl over 2f out* **66/1**

312- 13 29 **Osmosia (FR)**[60] 3164 9-10-7 0 (p) TomCannon 67
(Chris Gordon) *led tl over 7f out: chsd ldr: pushed along 5f out: wknd over 2f out: t.o* **66/1**

3m 34.0s (3.90) **Going Correction** +0.35s/f (Slow) 13 Ran SP% **117.0**
Speed ratings: **104,103,102,101,101 101,101,101,101,100 99,93,78**
CSF £52.60 TOTE £7.10: £1.70, £2.70, £2.00; EX 46.60 Trifecta £301.80.
Owner Mrs Christopher Hanbury **Bred** B O'Connell **Trained** Upper Lambourn, Berks

FOCUS
For horses which have run in at least once chase since 2011 and have not won a Class 1 or 2 chase. The third sets the level.
T/Plt: £71.10 to a £1 stake. Pool: £98,942.49 - 1,015.79 winning ticket. T/Qpdt: £26.20 to a £1 stake. Pool: £6,729.76 - 189.40 winning units. TM

4073 MARKET RASEN (R-H)

Sunday, February 16

OFFICIAL GOING: Soft (good to soft in places; 6.8)
Wind: moderate 1/2 against Weather: fine but cold

4304 WATCH RACING UK ON SKY 432 NOVICES' HURDLE (10 hdls) 2m 5f

1:50 (1:50) (Class 4) 4-Y-0+ £3,249 (£954; £477; £238)

Form RPR

/63- 1 **Maison De Ville (GER)**[30] 3757 6-10-10 0 JamesReveley 115+
(Brian Ellison) *led: hit 3rd: hdd 5th: styd on to ld appr 2 out: drew clr between last 2: eased towards fin* **4/1**[2]

2- 2 8 **At Reception (IRE)**[107] 2195 7-10-12 0 MauriceLinehan(5) 111
(Jonjo O'Neill) *trckd ldrs: drvn 3 out: kpt on to take 2nd run-in: no imp* **4/1**[2]

3 1¼ **Yasir (USA)**[5] 6-11-0 0 PeterCarberry(3) 110
(Conor Dore) *hld up in rr: hdwy to chse wnr appr 2 out: kpt on same pce* **14/1**

2/1- 4 2¾ **Deadly Sting (IRE)**[112] 2104 5-11-3 0 DougieCostello 107
(Jonjo O'Neill) *in rr: shkn up after 3rd: drvn along after 5th: hdwy to chse ldrs 3 out: outpcd appr next: kpt on run-in* **6/4**[1]

5 11 **Withoutdefavourite (IRE)**[105] 6-11-3 0 DenisO'Regan 100
(Henry Oliver) *trckd ldrs: upsides 5th: drvn to ld 3 out: sddle slipped and hdd appr next: eased and sn bhd* **13/2**[3]

6 hd **Always Archie**[274] 7-10-7 0 AlanJohns(10) 97
(Tim Vaughan) *w ldr: led 5th: hdd 3 out: wknd appr next* **11/1**

5m 16.1s (7.30) **Going Correction** +0.20s/f (Yiel) 6 Ran SP% **108.3**
Speed ratings (Par 105): **94,90,90,89,85 85**
CSF £18.73 TOTE £3.30: £1.30, £2.10; EX 17.00 Trifecta £170.60.
Owner Mrs J A Martin & Mrs C L Ellison **Bred** Gestut Etzean **Trained** Norton, N Yorks

FOCUS
This looks just ordinary form, but a few of these will improve with time. A step up from the winner.

4305 RASEN ROCKS IN AUGUST H'CAP HURDLE (THE JOCKEY CLUB GRASSROOTS JUMPS SERIES QUALIFIER) (8 hdls) 2m 1f

2:20 (2:20) (Class 4) (0-115,118) 4-Y-0+ £3,249 (£954; £477; £238)

Form RPR

212- 1 **Run Ructions Run (IRE)**[26] 3818 5-11-8 **118** (p) CraigNichol(7) 125+
(Tim Easterby) *trckd ldrs: hdwy on ins to ld sn after 2 out: drvn clr run-in: styd on strly* **6/4**[1]

51F- 2 6 **Straits Of Messina (IRE)**[10] 4107 5-10-11 **100** FelixDeGiles 100
(Tom Symonds) *chsd ldrs 4th: upsides 2 out: lft 3 l 2nd last: kpt on same pce* **5/1**[3]

F53- 3 26 **Belle De Fontenay (FR)**[16] 4002 9-11-3 **111** (p) ConorShoemark(5) 85
(Conor Dore) *chsd ldrs: drvn 3 out: outpcd appr next: lft poor 3rd last* **25/1**

P00- 4 6 **Rosslyn Castle**[28] 3802 5-11-7 **110** DominicElsworth 78
(Jonjo O'Neill) *in rr: drvn 4th: j. bdly lft 3 out: sme hdwy appr next: lost pl and j.lft: lft poor 4th last* **9/1**

5/5- 5 3¾ **Tayarat (IRE)**[24] 3856 9-9-9 **89** oh5 JoeCornwall(5) 53
(Michael Chapman) *led: hdd 4th: sn drvn: lost pl 3 out: sn bhd: j. bdly lft last* **40/1**

151- 6 1¼ **Magic Skyline (IRE)**[38] 3613 4-11-3 **115** (t) JamesReveley 69
(Brian Ellison) *j.lft: in rr: sme hdwy after 3 out: lost pl and bhd appr next* **6/1**

P42- F **King Zeal (IRE)**[8] 4157 10-11-2 **105** (t) LiamHeard 106
(Barry Leavy) *w ldr: led 4th: hdd sn after 2 out: 1 ld down and looking hld whn fell last* **7/2**[2]

4m 11.5s (4.80) **Going Correction** +0.20s/f (Yiel)
WFA 4 from 5yo+ 9lb 7 Ran SP% **109.5**
Speed ratings (Par 105): **96,93,80,78,76 75,**
CSF £8.79 CT £111.39 TOTE £2.40: £1.10, £2.80; EX 12.50 Trifecta £98.80.
Owner Tom Ford **Bred** Minch Bloodstock & AV Bloodstock **Trained** Great Habton, N Yorks

FOCUS
A modest handicap run at a sound pace. The winner is on the upgrade and there is probably more to come.

4306 1ST SECURITY SOLUTIONS H'CAP HURDLE (10 hdls) 2m 3f
2:50 (2:51) (Class 3) (0-135,135) 4-Y-0+ £5,523 (£1,621; £810; £405)

Form RPR
101- 1 **New Year's Eve**[23] 3880 6-10-11 123 JackQuinlan(3) 130+
(John Ferguson) *trckd ldrs: led sn after 3 out: drvn clr last 150yds: won gng away* 13/8[1]
051- 2 3 ½ **Rumble Of Thunder (IRE)**[14] 4058 8-11-3 126 RichieMcGrath 127
(Philip Kirby) *trckd ldrs: cl 2nd sn after 3 out: upsides last: styd on same pce* 11/2[3]
340- 3 6 **Kayaan**[22] 3892 7-10-9 121 KielanWoods(3) 117
(Pam Sly) *hld up in rr: t.k.h: hdwy 7th: chsng ldng pair after 3 out: 3 l down and wl hld whn mstke last* 7/1
343- 4 5 **Wily Fox**[29] 3786 7-10-2 118 KieronEdgar(7) 109
(James Eustace) *hld up: hdwy to chse ldrs 4th: drvn 3 out: one pce* 4/1[2]
413- 5 2 ¾ **Kodicil (IRE)**[24] 3851 6-10-7 116 (b) DougieCostello 103
(Mark Walford) *led to 3rd: led 6th tl sn after 3 out: one pce* 8/1
530- 6 18 **Tidal Way (IRE)**[16] 4023 5-10-13 122 (tp) NoelFehily 91
(Charlie Longsdon) *in rr: outpcd 7th: sn bhd* 8/1
316/ 7 15 **Mubrook (USA)**[238] 5574 9-10-4 120 (b) CraigGallagher(7) 74
(Brian Ellison) *w ldr: led 3rd: hdd 6th: sn drvn and lost pl: wl bhd fr 3 out* 25/1

4m 38.6s (-0.80) **Going Correction** +0.20s/f (Yiel) 7 Ran SP% **112.0**
Speed ratings (Par 107): **109,107,105,102,101 94,87**
CSF £10.76 CT £47.09 TOTE £2.50: £1.20, £2.70; EX 11.50 Trifecta £48.30.
Owner Bloomfields **Bred** Newsells Park Stud **Trained** Cowlinge, Suffolk

FOCUS
A fair handicap. The winner built on his recent victory but has the potential to do better yet.

4307 LATE GREAT TED MUNNELLY BIRTHDAY MEMORIAL NOVICES' HURDLE (8 hdls) 2m 1f
3:20 (3:20) (Class 3) 4-Y-0+ £5,697 (£1,683; £841; £421; £210)

Form RPR
21- 1 **Kilcooley (IRE)**[87] 2627 5-11-2 0 NoelFehily 131+
(Charlie Longsdon) *trckd ldrs: upsides 3rd: led next: styd on strly to forge clr between last 2: eased clsng stages* 7/4[1]
31- 2 13 **Certification (IRE)**[26] 3822 4-10-13 124 DenisO'Regan 110
(John Ferguson) *chsd ldrs: 2nd after 3 out: drvn: hung rt and carried hd awkwardly next: no imp* 2/1[2]
3 1 ¾ **Lord Of Scotland (FR)**[136] 5-11-12 0 RobertThornton 121
(Alan King) *in rr: hdwy to chse ldrs 5th: 3rd appr 2 out: keeping on one pce whn mstke last* 4/1[3]
31U- 4 12 **Slipper Satin (IRE)**[15] 4037 4-10-3 129 JackQuinlan(3) 92
(Noel Quinlan) *chsd ldrs: cl 2nd 3 out: wknd between last 2* 5/1
5 4 **Markttag**[124] 4-10-2 0 MauriceLinehan(5) 86
(Jonjo O'Neill) *in tch: drvn 4th: chsng ldrs 3 out: lost pl bef next* 25/1
5- 6 6 **Boruma (IRE)**[57] 3214 4-10-7 0 JamesReveley 80
(Dianne Sayer) *in rr: bhd fr 3 out* 50/1
0- 7 8 **Hidden Link**[36] 3641 4-10-7 0 FelixDeGiles 72
(Tom Symonds) *in rr: reminders 5th: bhd fr next* 80/1
U50- 8 44 **Great Demeanor (USA)**[3] 4234 4-10-7 0 RyanMania 28
(Dianne Sayer) *towards rr: nt fluent 4th: bhd fr 3 out: t.o* 100/1
P- 9 8 **Benidorm**[63] 3106 6-10-9 0 MrJHamilton(7) 29
(John Wainwright) *sn drvn clr: jnd 3rd: hdd next: wknd 3 out: sn bhd: t.o* 125/1

4m 12.1s (5.40) **Going Correction** +0.20s/f (Yiel)
WFA 4 from 5yo+ 9lb 9 Ran SP% **115.2**
Speed ratings (Par 107): **95,88,88,82,80 77,73,53,49**
CSF £5.66 TOTE £2.20: £1.10, £1.10, £2.00; EX 6.10 Trifecta £21.00.
Owner J H & S M Wall **Bred** Fergal O'Mahoney **Trained** Over Norton, Oxon

FOCUS
Punters only wanted to know about four of these, and that bunch dominated the outcome. The winner impressed but the time was nothing special.

4308 1ST SECURITY SOLUTIONS H'CAP HURDLE (12 hdls) 3m
3:55 (3:55) (Class 4) (0-120,120) 4-Y-0+ £4,223 (£1,240; £620; £310)

Form RPR
456- 1 **Join The Clan (IRE)**[49] 3390 5-10-13 112 MauriceLinehan(5) 124+
(Jonjo O'Neill) *trckd ldrs: led appr 2 out: drew clr run-in* 11/4[2]
F3U- 2 6 **Phare Isle (IRE)**[12] 4076 9-11-0 115 (tp) MrMJPKendrick(7) 117
(Ben Case) *chsd ldrs 3rd: outpcd 8th: rallied to chse ldrs 3 out: 3rd next: kpt on to take 2nd last 150yds* 7/2[3]
F30- 3 1 ½ **Gorey Lane (IRE)**[26] 3824 8-10-0 94 oh1 (v) AdrianLane 96
(John Norton) *chsd ldrs: mstke 9th: outpcd 2 out: kpt on run-in: tk 3rd post* 14/1
132- 4 shd **Theatrebar**[23] 3884 6-11-12 120 FelixDeGiles 121
(Tom Symonds) *led: qcknd pce 7th: drvn next: hdd appr 2 out: fdd and lost 2 pls last 100yds* 5/2[1]
045- 5 13 **Genstone Trail**[10] 4108 8-10-3 97 GerardTumelty 84
(Alan King) *in rr: hdwy to chse ldrs 7th: outpcd next: sme hdwy 3 out: lost pl bef next* 6/1
42F- 6 15 **Auberge (IRE)**[50] 3356 10-9-13 98 EmmaSayer(5) 70
(Evelyn Slack) *in rr: hdwy to chse ldrs 7th: outpcd and lost pl next: bhd fr 3 out* 13/2

5m 59.9s (9.40) **Going Correction** +0.20s/f (Yiel) 6 Ran SP% **111.7**
Speed ratings (Par 105): **92,90,89,89,85 80**
CSF £12.79 CT £107.64 TOTE £4.50: £3.10, £2.20; EX 10.80 Trifecta £97.40.
Owner John P McManus **Bred** Felix Talbot **Trained** Cheltenham, Gloucs

FOCUS
An already modest contest was weakened by three non-runners, who had all run the previous day. A big step up from the easy winner.

4309 RASEN ROOF H'CAP HURDLE (10 hdls) 2m 3f
4:30 (4:30) (Class 5) (0-100,100) 4-Y-0+ £2,339 (£686; £343; £171)

Form RPR
P45- 1 **Epee Celeste (FR)**[13] 4066 8-10-1 80 (b) JoeCornwall(5) 85
(Michael Chapman) *w ldr: styd on to ld last: hung lft and drew clr* 20/1
/00- 2 6 **Swing State**[58] 3192 9-10-4 78 LeeEdwards 78
(Tom Gretton) *chsd ldrs: drvn 6th: outpcd 3 out: 4th whn mstke next: sltly hmpd and lft 3rd last: kpt on to take 2nd last 75yds* 16/1
445- 3 5 **Ivans Back (IRE)**[52] 3265 9-10-1 82 CharlieDeutsch(7) 76
(Nick Kent) *stdd s: t.k.h: hdwy to trck ldrs 3 out: upsides next: sltly hmpd and lft cl 2nd last: wknd fnl 75yds* 6/1[3]
02P- 4 10 **Yazdi (IRE)**[13] 4070 5-11-12 100 (v[1]) DenisO'Regan 82
(Henry Oliver) *prom 3rd: outpcd 3 out: no ch after* 4/1[2]
/25- 5 shd **Landenstown Pearl (IRE)**[24] 3852 8-10-9 86 JackQuinlan(3) 68
(Sarah Humphrey) *chsd ldrs: drvn 6th: lost pl bef 3 out* 15/2
360- 6 6 **Multilicious**[49] 3385 4-10-6 90 DougieCostello 56
(Mark Walford) *in tch: outpcd and lost pl 6th* 33/1
622- 7 55 **Midnight Request**[19] 3959 5-11-9 97 FelixDeGiles 18
(Tom Symonds) *chsd ldrs: drvn 6th: lost pl next: sn bhd: eased between last 2: virtually p.u: t.o* 11/10[1]
606- F **Drumgooland (IRE)**[77] 2846 7-11-0 95 ow1 MrJMahot(7) 97+
(Sarah-Jayne Davies) *mde most: nt fluent 4th: j.lft 2 out: hdd whn fell last* 14/1

4m 46.0s (6.60) **Going Correction** +0.20s/f (Yiel)
WFA 4 from 5yo+ 9lb 8 Ran SP% **113.9**
Speed ratings (Par 103): **94,91,89,85,85 82,59,**
CSF £267.96 CT £2150.04 TOTE £22.20: £4.00, £3.00, £1.90; EX 334.90 Trifecta £1461.80.
Owner Mrs S M Richards **Bred** E A R L Haras De Trefontaine **Trained** Market Rasen, Lincs

FOCUS
A weak handicap. The winner is rated in line with the best of his British hurdles runs.

4310 CONNOLLY'S RED MILLS BUMPER CHALLENGE STANDARD OPEN NATIONAL HUNT FLAT RACE 2m 1f
5:00 (5:00) (Class 6) 4-6-Y-0 £1,559 (£457; £228; £114)

Form RPR
32- 1 **Monbeg Theatre (IRE)**[47] 3440 5-11-4 0 SamTwiston-Davies 106+
(Jamie Snowden) *trckd ldrs: led 4f out: drvn clr over 1f out: kpt on* 2/1[1]
321- 2 1 **Gone Forever**[38] 3619 4-10-9 0 CraigGallagher(7) 102+
(Brian Ellison) *chsd ldrs: outpcd 6f out: hdwy over 3f out: chsd wnr over 1f out: styd on* 9/2[3]
3 4 **Arden Denis (IRE)**[91] 5-11-4 0 FelixDeGiles 100
(Tom Symonds) *led 6f: chsd ldrs: drvn 6f out: kpt on same pce to take 3rd nr fin* 20/1
4 ¾ **Orby's Man (IRE)**[98] 5-11-4 0 [1] NoelFehily 99
(Charlie Longsdon) *hld up in rr: hdwy to trck ldrs after 5f: chsd wnr over 3f out: one pce* 5/2[2]
3- 5 7 **Astaroland (FR)**[37] 3640 4-10-9 0 SeanQuinlan 83
(Jennie Candlish) *in rr: hdwy 6f out: sn chsng ldrs: wknd over 1f out* 8/1
6 5 **Periquest** 5-11-4 0 DougieCostello 87
(Alex Hales) *in rr: drvn 7f out: sn outpcd and lost pl: kpt on fnl 3f* 25/1
5- 7 11 **Sir Safir**[38] 3619 4-10-9 0 WilsonRenwick 67
(Peter Niven) *mid-div: outpcd over 4f out: sn lost pl* 10/1
6- 8 7 **Midnight Memories**[36] 3656 4-10-2 0 ow3 RobertDunne(3) 56
(Steph Hollinshead) *chsd ldrs: lost pl 4f out* 33/1
9 3 ½ **Singapore Story (FR)** 5-11-1 0 TrevorWhelan(3) 66
(Neil King) *in rr: drvn 8f out: sme hdwy 5f out: lost pl over 3f out* 50/1
0- 10 4 ½ **Flobury**[24] 3863 6-10-11 0 RyanMania 54
(Barry Leavy) *w ldr: led after 6f: hdd 4f out: sn lost pl* 150/1

4m 12.6s (11.50) **Going Correction** +0.20s/f (Yiel)
WFA 4 from 5yo+ 9lb 10 Ran SP% **114.5**
Speed ratings: **80,79,77,77,74 71,66,63,61,59**
CSF £10.50 TOTE £3.40: £1.30, £1.90, £5.00; EX 9.00 Trifecta £106.60.
Owner Tim Dykes & Lynda Lovell **Bred** John Deegan & James L O'Toole **Trained** Lambourn, Berks

FOCUS
An open-looking bumper. The first two and the fifth set an ordinary level.
T/Jkpt: £16,996.90 to a £1 stake. Pool: £23,939.38 - 1.00 winning ticket. T/Plt: £254.20 to a £1 stake. Pool: £114,015.13 - 327.31 winning ticket. T/Qpdt: £64.70 to a £1 stake. Pool: £8,003.64 - 91.54 winning ticket. WG

4311 - (Foreign Racing) - See Raceform Interactive

3679 NAVAN (L-H)
Sunday, February 16

OFFICIAL GOING: Heavy

4312a LADBROKES BOYNE HURDLE (GRADE 2) (12 hdls) 2m 5f
2:10 (2:10) 5-Y-0+ £21,666 (£6,333; £3,000; £1,000)

RPR
1 **Dunguib (IRE)**[29] 3790 11-11-3 148 BrianO'Connell 156+
(Philip Fenton, Ire) *chsd ldrs in 3rd: nt fluent 3rd: wnt 2nd fr 5th and led narrowly bef 5 out: gng best bef 3 out and wnt clr bef next: eased run-in: easily* 11/4[2]
2 6 **Zaidpour (FR)**[24] 3866 8-11-10 158 (p) RWalsh 152
(W P Mullins, Ire) *settled bhd ldrs after 1st: slt mstke 4th and niggled along after: reminder after next: nt fluent 6th: rdn fr 4 out and wnt 3rd briefly next: no imp 2 out: kpt on u.p into mod 2nd run-in* 5/4[1]
3 3 ¼ **Un Beau Matin (IRE)**[24] 3866 6-11-3 136 BryanCooper 142
(Gordon Elliott, Ire) *attempted to make all: j. sltly rt 2nd and at times after: reduced advantage bef 6th and hdd bef 5 out: rdn and no imp on wnr bef 2 out: slow last and dropped to mod 3rd run-in: kpt on one pce* 7/2[3]
4 22 **Jennies Jewel (IRE)**[29] 3790 7-10-10 139 IanMcCarthy 113
(Jarlath P Fahey, Ire) *chsd ldr in 2nd: lost pl fr 5th: pushed along after 4 out and dropped to rr briefly bef next: no imp on wnr in 3rd bef 2 out: dropped to rr whn mstke last* 5/1

5m 26.8s (10.80) 4 Ran SP% **110.0**
CSF £6.89 TOTE £3.70; DF 7.40 Trifecta £13.00.
Owner Daniel Harnett/Mrs E A Lawlor **Bred** Liam Meade **Trained** Carrick-On-Suir, Co Tipperary

FOCUS
The winner was best in on old figures and won easily. It's been rated around the front-running third.

4314a FLYINGBOLT NOVICE CHASE (GRADE 2) (12 fncs) 2m 1f
3:10 (3:10) 5-Y-0+ £20,312 (£5,937; £2,812)

RPR
1 **Bright New Dawn (IRE)**[22] 3908 7-11-4 142 BryanCooper 152+
(D T Hughes, Ire) *led and disp tl settled bhd ldr in 2nd fr 4th: slt mstke 7th: got on terms after 4 out and led narrowly bef next: disp 2 out: sn led again u.p and extended advantage run-in: kpt on wl* 5/4[1]
2 7 **Mallowney (IRE)**[21] 3928 8-11-4 139 AndrewJMcNamara 145
(Timothy Doyle, Ire) *led and disp tl wnt 1 l clr fr 4th: racd keenly: jnd after 4 out and hdd narrowly bef next: disp 2 out: sn rdn in cl 2nd and no imp on wnr fr last: kpt on same pce* 13/8[2]
3 53 **Shrapnel (IRE)**[15] 4047 8-11-7 134 (tp) DavyCondon 95
(Gordon Elliott, Ire) *hld up in rr: reminders after 4th and again after next: slow 7th and detached: no imp on ldrs appr st: lft remote 3rd 3 out: j.rt at times: one pce* 16/1

F **Irish Thistle (IRE)**[21] 3928 7-11-4 130..............................(p) DavyRussell
(H Rogers, Ire) *settled bhd ldrs in 3rd: slt mstke 5th: pushed along and u.p bef 3 out where fell* **16/1**

U **Some Tikket (IRE)**[24] 3869 7-11-4 130.. RWalsh
(D T Hughes, Ire) *w.w towards rr: slt mstke in 4th at 4th: pushed along and u.p bef 3 out where hmpd by faller and uns rdr* **9/2**[3]

4m 36.7s (3.40) 5 Ran SP% **112.5**
CSF £3.96 TOTE £1.80: £1.02, £2.00; DF 4.30 Trifecta £19.20.
Owner Gigginstown House Stud **Bred** Mrs Marilyn Syme **Trained** The Curragh, Co Kildare

FOCUS
The winner kept on best after the last. The first two have been rated close to their marks.

4315a TEN UP NOVICE CHASE (GRADE 2) (17 fncs) 3m
3:45 (3:45) 5-Y-0+ **£20,312** (£5,937; £2,812; £937)

RPR

1 **Foxrock (IRE)**[29] 3791 6-11-8 142.. DannyMullins 146+
(T M Walsh, Ire) *led and disp tl slt mstke 4 out and dropped to 3rd: regained narrow advantage fr next: nt fluent last and hdd: rallied run-in and styd on wl to ld again cl home* **4/6**[1]

2 ½ **My Murphy (IRE)**[49] 3404 8-11-3 135.. RobbiePower 140+
(W J Burke, Ire) *hld up: racd keenly: slt mstke in rr at 9th: tk clsr order 4 out: nt fluent 2 out: no imp in 4th between last 2: rdn into 3rd at last and clsd u.p run-in into nvr nrr 2nd: nt trble wnr* **7/2**[2]

3 nk **Clar Na Mionn (IRE)**[29] 3791 7-11-3 131............................ PhillipEnright 139
(V T O'Brien, Ire) *led and disp: t.k.h: slow 3rd: cl 2nd fr 4 out: rdn to ld narrowly fr last: no ex u.p nr fin and hdd: dropped to 3rd fnl strides* **6/1**[3]

4 14 **Cootamundra (IRE)**[24] 3868 11-11-3 135............................ RobbieMoran 125
(J A Berry, Ire) *hld up bhd ldrs: tk clsr order bef 3 out where nt fluent: clsd into 3rd between last 2: slt mstke last and no ex u.p in 4th: wknd* **8/1**

5 16 **Civena (IRE)**[46] 3482 8-10-10 123.. AFO'Neill 102
(J A Berry, Ire) *led and disp: led narrowly fr 4 out tl hdd fr next: pushed along disputing 3rd whn mstke 2 out and dropped to rr: no ex: wknd* **20/1**

6m 48.3s (19.00) 5 Ran SP% **112.4**
CSF £3.73 TOTE £1.40: £1.20, £1.50; DF 3.70 Trifecta £11.00.
Owner Barry Connell **Bred** Geoffrey Thompson **Trained** Kill, Co Kildare

FOCUS
Not a great deal of depth to this Grade 2. The race was pretty unremarkable until it finally developed after the second-last. The first three have all been rated close to their marks.

4316 - 4317a (Foreign Racing) - See Raceform Interactive

4080 CARLISLE (R-H)
Monday, February 17
4318 Meeting Abandoned - Waterlogged

4066 SOUTHWELL (L-H)
Monday, February 17

OFFICIAL GOING: Standard
Wind: fresh 1/2 against Weather: overcast, breezy and cold, light showers

4324 TOTEPLACEPOT RACING'S FAVOURITE BET "JUMPERS' BUMPER" NATIONAL HUNT FLAT RACE 2m (F)
2:00 (2:00) (Class 4) 4-Y-0+ **£3,165** (£935; £467; £234; £117)

Form RPR

/PP- 1 **Direct Approach (IRE)**[69] 3014 10-11-2 0........................... TomSiddall 105+
(Lynn Siddall) *hld up: hdwy to trck ldrs after 6f: upsides on outer over 2f out: led jst ins fnl f: styd on strly: readily* **50/1**

155- 2 2 ¾ **King Rolfe (IRE)**[47] 3448 6-11-2 0...............................(t) RichardJohnson 102
(Tim Vaughan) *t.k.h: trckd ldrs: shkn up over 5f out: led over 2f out: hdd jst ins fnl f: no ex* **7/4**[1]

PP- 3 2 **Classical Chloe**[26] 3840 6-10-2 0.......................(t) MrJoshuaNewman(7) 93
(Sara Ender) *sn chsng ldrs on outer: drvn over 4f out: one pce fnl 2f* **50/1**

146- 4 2 ¼ **Buxom (IRE)**[17] 4018 7-10-9 0......................................(v) BrendanPowell 91
(Jamie Snowden) *led 4f: chsd ldrs: outpcd over 4f out: hdwy over 2f out: one pce* **3/1**[3]

433- 5 1 ½ **Johnnys Legacy (IRE)**[24] 3876 7-10-13 0................(p) PeterCarberry(3) 96
(Conor Dore) *trckd ldr: led after 4f: set modest pce: increased gallop after 7f: hdd over 4f out: lost pl over 2f out* **6/1**

330- 6 1 **Houseparty**[17] 4023 6-10-9 0... MrHGMiller(7) 95
(Zoe Davison) *hld up in rr: drvn over 4f out: sn outpcd: nvr a factor* **16/1**

031- 7 2 ¾ **Exemplary**[14] 3290 7-10-9 0.. MrsAlexDunn(7) 92
(Alexandra Dunn) *t.k.h: w ldr: led over 4f out: hdd over 2f out: wknd over 1f out* **5/2**[2]

4m 3.6s (18.10) **Going Correction** +0.45s/f (Slow)
WFA 5 from 6yo+ 1lb 7 Ran SP% **114.0**
Speed ratings (Par 105): **72,70,69,68,67 67,65**
CSF £136.91 TOTE £38.00: £7.90, £1.70; EX 318.20 Trifecta £1863.00.
Owner G Kennington **Bred** Michael McInerney **Trained** Colton, N Yorks

FOCUS
For horses which have run at least twice over hurdles and are currently eligible for novice hurdles. They went an ordinary gallop in this modest affair and the entire field still had a chance of sorts 4f out. Very suspect form.

4325 TOTEJACKPOT WIN BIG FOR SMALL STAKE "JUMPERS' BUMPER" NATIONAL HUNT FLAT RACE 2m (F)
2:30 (2:30) (Class 4) 5-Y-0+ **£3,165** (£935; £467; £234; £117)

Form RPR

/12- 1 **Any Given Day (IRE)**[248] 736 9-11-0 0............................ JasonMaguire 140+
(Donald McCain) *led 2f: w ldr: led over 4f out: pushed clr over 2f out: easily* **7/2**[2]

213- 2 15 **Dolatulo (FR)**[37] 3652 7-11-3 0...............................(t) GavinSheehan(3) 129+
(Warren Greatrex) *w ldr: led after 2f: drvn and hdd over 4f out: hung rt 2f out: no ch w wnr* **8/13**[1]

22P- 3 4 ½ **Ski Sunday**[114] 2078 9-11-0 0...............................(t) RichardJohnson 115
(Tim Vaughan) *chsd ldng trio: drvn 9f out: outpcd over 4f out: kpt on to take modest 3rd over 1f out* **6/1**[3]

546- 4 4 **Jack The Gent (IRE)**[32] 3738 10-11-0 0............................ BarryKeniry 111
(George Moore) *w ldrs on outer: drvn over 4f out: wknd over 1f out* **12/1**

0PU- 5 14 **My Friend Riquet (FR)**[38] 3635 7-10-7 0............(t) MrAlexEdwards(7) 97
(Dave Roberts) *drvn and outpcd over 8f out: bhd fnl 5f* **50/1**

620- 6 9 **Highland River**[4] 4243 8-11-0 0.. LeeEdwards 88
(Dave Roberts) *in rr: outpcd over 8f out: bhd fnl 5f* **33/1**

3m 50.5s (5.00) **Going Correction** +0.45s/f (Slow) 6 Ran SP% **111.0**
Speed ratings: **105,97,95,93,86 81**
CSF £5.89 TOTE £4.10: £2.20, £1.10; EX 6.60 Trifecta £11.60.
Owner T G Leslie **Bred** Ralph And Helen O'Brien **Trained** Cholmondeley, Cheshire

FOCUS
For horses which have run in at least one chase in 2011 and have not won a Class 1 or 2 chase. There was a solid gallop set here. An easy win for class act Any Given Day, who is a stone+ better hurdler than the runner-up.

4326 TOTEQUADPOT FOUR PLACES IN FOUR RACES "JUMPERS' BUMPER" NATIONAL HUNT FLAT RACE 2m 2f
3:00 (3:00) (Class 4) 4-Y-0+ **£3,165** (£935; £467; £234; £117)

Form RPR

044- 1 **Mitchell's Way**[7] 4188 7-11-2 0.. PaddyBrennan 110+
(Alan Swinbank) *trckd ldrs gng wl: upsides over 2f out: rdn to ld appr fnl f: styd on* **4/1**[2]

/2P- 2 2 ¼ **Sin Bin (IRE)**[95] 2475 8-11-2 0......................................(t) DarylJacob 106
(Paul Nicholls) *w ldrs on inner: led over 4f out: hdd appr fnl f: styd on same pce* **11/10**[1]

P/0- 3 2 ¾ **Picaroon**[17] 4021 10-10-9 0.. MrsAlexDunn(7) 103
(Alexandra Dunn) *t.k.h: trckd ldrs after 5f: hung rt over 2f out: kpt on same pce* **6/1**[3]

13P- 4 2 **Silver Dragon**[53] 3265 6-11-2 0.. DougieCostello 101
(Tony Coyle) *hld up: hdwy on outer over 7f out: sn chsng ldrs: upsides over 3f out: one pce fnl 2f* **6/1**[3]

030- 5 9 **Mauricetheathlete (IRE)**[32] 3730 11-10-9 0..................... NickSlatter(7) 92
(Martin Keighley) *mde most: hdd over 4f out: lost pl 3f out* **16/1**

2P4- 6 5 **Guanciale**[14] 4067 7-11-2 0..(t) BrendanPowell 87
(Brendan Powell) *w ldrs: chal 4f out: rdn over 2f out: wknd over 1f out* **10/1**

4P0- 7 39 **Oak Wood (IRE)**[40] 3605 6-10-9 0...................................... ConorRing(7) 48
(John Upson) *w ldrs: drvn over 8f out: lost pl over 5f out: sn bhd: t.o 2f out* **50/1**

P/0- 8 17 **Ravens Secret**[40] 3605 9-11-2 0.............................. MrGBarfoot-Saunt 31
(Tracey Barfoot-Saunt) *chsd ldrs: drvn over 8f out: sn lost pl and bhd: t.o 3f out* **50/1**

6/0- 9 15 **The Mobb (IRE)**[12] 4091 6-11-2 0.. LeeEdwards 16
(Dave Roberts) *in rr: drvn 8f out: sn bhd: t.o 4f out* **50/1**

4m 18.8s (5.10) **Going Correction** +0.45s/f (Slow) 9 Ran SP% **117.0**
Speed ratings (Par 105): **106,105,103,102,98 96,79,71,65**
CSF £8.85 TOTE £3.60: £1.50, £1.10, £2.10; EX 10.00 Trifecta £33.20.
Owner Ontoawinner 2 **Bred** Mrs P M Grainger **Trained** Melsonby, N Yorks

FOCUS
A modest affair. The first pair dominated from the 2f marker. The cosy winner is a 120 hurdler.

4327 TOTEEXACTA "JUMPERS' BUMPER" NATIONAL HUNT FLAT RACE 2m 2f
3:30 (3:30) (Class 4) 4-Y-0+ **£3,165** (£935; £467; £234; £117)

Form RPR

31/ 1 **Gogeo (IRE)**[18] 2750 7-11-2 0.. PaddyBrennan 131+
(Alan Swinbank) *hld up in rr: hdwy 7f out: sn trcking ldrs: led over 2f out: edgd lft and pushed clr: v comf* **5/4**[1]

444- 2 6 **Qoubilai (FR)**[17] 4007 10-11-2 0...................................... DougieCostello 121
(Tony Coyle) *hld up in rr: hdwy on outer over 8f out: sn trcking ldrs: led over 4f out: hdd over 2f out: no ch w wnr* **10/1**

564- 3 4 **Bob's World**[12] 4085 5-11-2 0......................................(t) SeanQuinlan 117
(Jennie Candlish) *sn in rr: hdwy over 7f out: sn chsng ldrs: drvn over 4f out: modest 3rd over 1f out: one pce* **8/1**

P04- 4 8 **Operatic Heights (IRE)**[26] 3841 5-10-13 0...............(v[1]) JakeGreenall(3) 109
(Alan McCabe) *w ldrs: led 10f out: hdd over 4f out: wknd over 1f out* **25/1**

0/0- 5 25 **Hollow Tree**[282] 215 6-11-2 0.. JasonMaguire 84
(Donald McCain) *chsd ldrs: drvn and lost pl after 5f: sn plld wd and bhd: kpt on fnl 2f* **3/1**[2]

464- 6 4 ½ **Moaning Butcher**[16] 3224 4-10-7 0...................................(v) LeeEdwards 71
(Dave Roberts) *reminders after s: sn chsng ldrs: rdn and outpcd over 5f out: sn lost pl* **50/1**

102/ 7 11 **Zakatal**[422] 2738 8-11-2 0.. AndrewThornton 69
(Simon Earle) *hld up: hdwy after 4f: sn chsng ldrs: lost pl over 4f out: bhd whn eased clsng stages* **6/1**[3]

0PP- 8 7 **Rose Of Marron (IRE)**[78] 2850 7-10-9 0............................ ConorRing(7) 62
(John Upson) *mde most tl 10f out: lost pl over 4f out* **100/1**

350- 9 28 **Galley Slave (IRE)**[125] 1917 9-10-11 0............................ JoeCornwall(5) 34
(Michael Chapman) *in rr: bhd after 6f: sn t.o* **50/1**

3/0- 10 31 **Eseej (USA)**[118] 2013 9-11-2 0.. MarkGrant 3
(Geoffrey Deacon) *chsd ldrs: drvn over 7f out: lost pl 6f out: sn bhd: hopelessly t.o* **10/1**

/00- 11 66 **Perfect Shot (IRE)**[32] 3728 8-10-9 0................................ MrRJarrett(7)
(Sarah-Jayne Davies) *chsd ldrs: lost pl over 9f out: bhd and hung rt over 6f out: sn t.o: virtually p.u: eventually completed* **50/1**

4m 14.2s (0.50) **Going Correction** +0.45s/f (Slow)
WFA 4 from 5yo+ 9lb 11 Ran SP% **123.7**
Speed ratings (Par 105): **116,113,111,108,96 94,90,86,74,60 31**
CSF £16.51 TOTE £2.60: £1.30, £2.90, £2.70; EX 16.90 Trifecta £80.60.
Owner Mrs J Porter **Bred** Peter Nolan **Trained** Melsonby, N Yorks

FOCUS
For horses which have run at least once over hurdles and, since 2011, have not won a Class 1, 2 or 3 race. Straightforward enough form. The easy winner was entitled to this sort of rating on Flat form.

4328 TOTEPOOL.COM "JUMPERS' BUMPER" NATIONAL HUNT FLAT RACE 2m (F)
4:00 (4:00) (Class 3) 4-Y-0+ **£6,330** (£1,870; £935; £468; £234)

Form RPR

U03- 1 **Hazy Tom (IRE)**[17] 4020 8-10-9 0............................ CharlieDeutsch(7) 135+
(Charlie Longsdon) *trckd ldrs: cl 2nd 6f out: drvn over 4f out: led 3f out: hung rt and kpt on fnl 2f* **3/1**[2]

1/3- 2 3 ½ **Masterful Act (USA)**[18] 1443 7-11-8 0............................ JasonMaguire 138
(Alan McCabe) *led: rdn and hdd 3f out: swtchd rt 2f out: kpt on same pce* **2/7**[1]

PPP- 3 18 **Dreambrook Lady (IRE)**[59] 3186 8-10-6 0.................. GavinSheehan(3) 113+
(Warren Greatrex) *chsd ldr: outpcd and lft bhd over 4f out: eased whn no ch fnl 2f* **16/1**[3]

440- 4 5 **Hellesbelles (IRE)**[53] 3274 6-10-9 0............................ RichardJohnson 102
(Tim Vaughan) *trckd ldrs: outpcd and lost pl after 6f: bhd fnl 6f* **25/1**

1/0- **5** *9* **Bruslini (FR)**[40] 3603 9-11-2 0 .... MrGBarfoot-Saunt 100
(Tracey Barfoot-Saunt) *s.i.s: in last thrght: sn pushed along: lost tch 8f out* **50/1**

0/3- **U** **Tantalized**[266] 506 5-10-9 0 .... LeeEdwards
(Dave Roberts) *jinxed and uns rdr s* **50/1**

3m 50.6s (5.10) **Going Correction** +0.45s/f (Slow)
WFA 5 from 6yo+ 1lb **6** Ran SP% **116.4**
Speed ratings (Par 107): **105,103,94,91,87**
CSF £4.42 TOTE £3.50: £1.10, £1.10; EX 6.20 Trifecta £27.00.
Owner Alan Halsall **Bred** Messrs T & J Hayes **Trained** Over Norton, Oxon

FOCUS
Runners must have contested at least one chase or hurdle but, after 2011, must not have won a Class 1 race. The two market leaders dominated and the winner is rated in line with his hurdles form.

4329 TOTETRIFECTA AVAILABLE ON ALL RACES MAIDEN OPEN NATIONAL HUNT FLAT RACE 2m (F)
4:30 (4:30) (Class 4) 4-6-Y-O **£3,165** (£935; £467; £234; £117)

Form RPR

1 **Great Try (IRE)** 5-11-2 0 .... DarylJacob 110+
(Paul Nicholls) *hld up in mid-div: smooth hdwy to trck ldrs 5f out: led 2f out: sn wnt clr: easily* **3/1**[2]

2 *9* **Its A Sting (IRE)**[154] 1593 5-11-2 0 ....[1] DougieCostello 94
(Tony Coyle) *hld up in rr: hdwy 6f out: chsng ldrs and swtchd rt over 2f out: 2nd 1f out: no ch w wnr* **8/1**[3]

4- **3** *1 ¾* **Laraghcon Boy (IRE)**[32] 3734 5-11-2 0 .... LeeEdwards 92
(Tony Carroll) *w ldr: led 6f out: hdd 2f out: kpt on same pce* **8/1**[3]

40- **4** *12* **Supari**[17] 4016 5-11-2 0 .... WillKennedy 80
(Sarah-Jayne Davies) *chsd ldrs: drvn 6f out: outpcd over 4f out: wknd fnl f* **33/1**

\- **5** *2 ½* **Ruaraidh Hugh (IRE)** 5-11-2 0 .... TomMessenger 78
(Chris Bealby) *in rr: drvn 9f out: hdwy jst over 7f out: outpcd and lost pl over 4f out* **25/1**

6 *2 ¼* **At First Light** 5-10-4 0 .... NicodeBoinville[(5)] 68
(Jonathan Geake) *chsd ldrs: drvn 6f out: outpcd over 4f out* **12/1**

4- **7** *hd* **Bobs Lord Tara**[16] 4043 4-10-7 0 .... PaddyBrennan 66
(Alan Swinbank) *hld up in rr: effrt 6f out: drvn and outpcd 5f out: nvr a factor* **6/4**[1]

0- **8** *10* **Jeans Lady**[37] 3656 5-10-9 0 .... IanPopham 58
(Martin Keighley) *chsd ldrs: drvn over 7f out: lost pl over 5f out* **20/1**

9 *4* **Bold Prince Rupert (IRE)** 4-10-7 0 .... GerardTumelty 52
(Sara Ender) *in rr: lost pl 6f out: sn bhd* **25/1**

50- **10** *9* **Todoistodare**[61] 3167 4-10-0 0 .... BrendanPowell 36
(Brendan Powell) *led: hdd 6f out: lost pl 4f out: bhd and eased 2f out* **16/1**

0- **11** *12* **Vortex Star**[26] 3835 5-10-11 0 .... JoeCornwall[(5)] 40
(Michael Chapman) *chsd ldrs: drvn 7f out: sn lost pl and bhd: t.o 3f out* **50/1**

3m 55.3s (9.80) **Going Correction** +0.45s/f (Slow)
WFA 4 from 5yo 9lb **11** Ran SP% **118.2**
Speed ratings: **93,88,87,81,80 79,79,74,72,67 61**
CSF £25.35 TOTE £3.70: £1.70, £1.60, £2.10; EX 28.80 Trifecta £91.90.
Owner Trevor Hemmings **Bred** Gleadhill House Stud Ltd **Trained** Ditcheat, Somerset

FOCUS
A taking debut winner emerged from this modest contest. The third and fourth set the level.
T/Plt: £17.00 to a £1 stake. Pool: £73400.02 - 3142.31 winning tickets T/Qpdt: £4.40 to a £1 stake. Pool: £6590.65 - 1101.87 winning tickets WG

3955 TAUNTON (R-H)
Tuesday, February 18

OFFICIAL GOING: Heavy (3.6)
An all-hurdles card, with the scheduled chases abandoned. Middle flight in back straight omitted.
Wind: Virtually nil Weather: Overcast with sunny periods

4330 ASPEN WAITE R & D TAX SPECIALISTS H'CAP HURDLE (10 hdls 2 omitted) 3m 110y
2:05 (2:05) (Class 5) (0-100,100) 4-Y-0+ **£2,395** (£698; £349)

Form RPR

662- **1** **Comical Red**[21] 3955 6-9-8 **75** ....(b) ThomasCheesman[(7)] 97+
(Mark Gillard) *trckd ldrs: rdn along briefly after 7th: bk gng wl in front after 3 out: sn drew clr: rdn briefly after last: eased fnl 100yds* **9/4**[2]

413- **2** *20* **Over My Head**[28] 3824 6-10-6 **87** ....(t) GeraldQuinn[(7)] 87
(Claire Dyson) *led: j. sltly lft and bmpd 1st: rdn and hdd after 3 out: a holding on for 2nd but no ch w wnr fr next* **15/8**[1]

302- **3** *4* **Brantingham Breeze**[19] 3991 6-11-2 **100** .... RichardO'Dea[(10)] 96
(Emma Lavelle) *hld up last but wl in tch: hdwy into 4th whn mstke 3 out: sn rdn into 3rd: styd on same pce* **5/1**[3]

000- **4** *19* **More Tricks**[35] 3695 6-9-10 **77** .... MrFTett[(7)] 54
(James Frost) *trckd ldrs: rdn after 7th: btn 3 out: wnt modest 4th run-in* **16/1**

500- **5** *3 ¾* **Clear Mix**[104] 2291 6-10-1 **75** ....(t) WillKennedy 48
(Sue Gardner) *nvr fluent: trckd ldrs: rdn to chse ldng pair 3 out: wknd bef 2 out: blnd last: sn lost modest 4th* **16/1**

55P- **6** *18* **Landenstown Star (IRE)**[15] 4071 9-9-9 **76** oh1 ow2 ....(b[1]) JPKiely[(7)] 31
(Mark Gillard) *nt a fluent: trckd ldr tl rdn after 7th: wknd next: t.o* **6/1**

050- **7** *14* **Sporting Club Girl**[36] 3692 4-10-0 **85** oh5 .... MattieBatchelor 15
(Jim Best) *hld up in last pair wl in tch: struggling after 6th: wknd bef 3 out: t.o* **66/1**

6m 52.6s (48.60) **Going Correction** +1.25s/f (Heav)
WFA 4 from 6yo+ 11lb **7** Ran SP% **109.8**
Speed ratings (Par 103): **72,65,64,58,57 51,46**
CSF £6.51 CT £15.30 TOTE £3.40: £2.30, £1.30; EX 3.40 Trifecta £21.10.
Owner N J McMullan **Bred** Roseland Thoroughbreds Ltd **Trained** Holwell, Dorset

FOCUS
Weak handicap form and, despite going a steady pace for much of the way, they finished strung out. Arguably a step forward from the winner.

4331 EBF STALLIONS MARES' "NATIONAL HUNT" NOVICES' HURDLE (8 hdls 2 omitted) 2m 3f 110y
2:35 (2:36) (Class 4) 4-Y-0+ **£3,627** (£1,057; £528)

Form RPR

/02- **1** **Fairytale Theatre (IRE)**[75] 2907 7-10-12 0 ....(t) DarylJacob 111+
(Paul Nicholls) *mde all: hit 3 out: sn drew clr and in command after: pushed out run-in* **30/100**[1]

2 *14* **Young Cheddar (IRE)**[31] 7-10-7 0 .... ConorShoemark[(5)] 91
(Polly Gundry) *chsd clr ldrs: clsd on ldrs after 5th: rdn after 3 out: wnt 2nd bef next: styd on but a being readily hld by wnr* **16/1**

20- **3** *23* **Shanendou (IRE)**[34] 3727 5-10-12 0 .... PaddyBrennan 76
(Tom George) *trckd wnr: rdn after 3 out: wknd bef next: t.o* **5/1**[2]

450/ **P** **Applause For Amy (IRE)**[30] 7-10-5 0 .... MrJBargary[(7)]
(Mary Sanderson) *chsd clr ldrs: rdn appr 3 out: sn wknd: t.o whn p.u bef last* **25/1**

4- **P** **Money Maid (IRE)**[18] 4008 6-10-12 0 .... GerardTumelty
(Simon Earle) *hld up: struggling 4th: tailing off whn p.u bef next* **14/1**[3]

0/5- **F** **Dervla (IRE)**[275] 391 6-10-5 0 .... KevinJones[(7)]
(Seamus Mullins) *racd keenly: hld up: rdn after 5th: sn wknd: t.o whn fell heavily 2 out* **40/1**

5m 15.9s (29.90) **Going Correction** +1.25s/f (Heav) **6** Ran SP% **112.4**
Speed ratings (Par 105): **90,84,75, ,**
CSF £6.94 TOTE £1.20: £1.10, £7.40; EX 9.00 Trifecta £38.00.
Owner R J H Geffen **Bred** J J & Dan Melody **Trained** Ditcheat, Somerset

FOCUS
No depth to this mares' hurdle and it was won easily by the red-hot favourite. She's been given a token rating to her mark.

4332 BATHWICK TYRES TAUNTON NOVICES' H'CAP HURDLE (8 hdls 2 omitted) 2m 3f 110y
3:10 (3:10) (Class 3) (0-125,120) 4-Y-0 **£6,330** (£1,870; £935; £468; £234)

Form RPR

023- **1** **Ceasar Milan (IRE)**[31] 3774 6-11-7 **117** ....(t) HarryDerham[(5)] 132+
(Paul Nicholls) *trckd ldr: disp ld after 5th: clr ldr after 3 out: drew steadily clr: comf* **11/10**[1]

3/6- **2** *23* **King Of Glory**[137] 1749 6-11-7 **112** .... AidanColeman 107+
(Venetia Williams) *trckd ldrs: prom 5th: sn disputing ld w wnr: rdn after 3 out: sn hld: wkng whn nt fluent last* **4/1**[3]

05P- **3** *56* **Was My Valentine**[47] 3503 7-10-4 **95** ....(vt[1]) SamJones 31
(Jo Davis) *led tl rdn after 5th: wknd 3 out: t.o* **25/1**

422- **4** *1 ½* **Filatore (IRE)**[17] 4024 5-11-6 **116** ....(p) RobertWilliams[(5)] 51
(Bernard Llewellyn) *nvr that fluent: trckd ldrs: wnt prom 5th: sn rdn: btn bef next: wnt poor 4th run-in: t.o* **10/3**[2]

234- **5** *41* **Auld Sthock (IRE)**[64] 3136 6-11-10 **115** .... JamieMoore 9
(Gary Moore) *hld up: rdn after 5th: wnt 4th bef next: wknd after 3 out: lost poor 4th run-in: virtually p.u* **10/1**

126- **P** **Wooly Bully**[70] 3003 4-11-5 **120** .... WayneHutchinson
(Alan King) *nvr travelling fr 4th: sn lost tch: t.o whn p.u bef 3 out* **12/1**

5m 9.9s (23.90) **Going Correction** +1.25s/f (Heav)
WFA 4 from 5yo+ 9lb **6** Ran SP% **111.3**
Speed ratings (Par 107): **102,92,70,69,53**
CSF £6.06 TOTE £2.70: £2.00, £1.50; EX 7.00 Trifecta £87.00.
Owner The Stewart & Wylie Families **Bred** Pat O'Donovan **Trained** Ditcheat, Somerset

FOCUS
The two who appealed as being potential improvers now switching to handicaps came clear. The winner improved in line with the best of his bumper form.

4333 BATHWICK TYRES H'CAP HURDLE (7 hdls 2 omitted) 2m 1f
3:45 (3:45) (Class 2) 4-Y-0+ **£11,818** (£3,567; £1,837; £974)

Form RPR

031- **1** **Virak (FR)**[31] 3786 5-11-5 **140** .... JackSherwood[(7)] 149+
(Paul Nicholls) *trckd ldrs: led appr 3 out: clr bef 2 out: rdn out* **5/2**[2]

F51- **2** *8* **Tornado In Milan (IRE)**[31] 3787 8-10-6 **120** .... PaulMoloney 125+
(Evan Williams) *led tl after 3rd: prom tl tried to duck out and hit rails by stable entrnce after 4th: dropped to 7 l 4th: rdn after 3 out: lft 12 l 2nd 2 out: styd on same pce* **11/2**[3]

/41- **3** *7* **Helium (FR)**[21] 3957 9-9-11 **118** .... MrsAlexDunn[(7)] 111
(Alexandra Dunn) *trckd ldrs tl lost pl appr 3 out: no ch sn after but styd on to regain 3rd run-in* **11/2**[3]

042- **4** *1 ¼* **Chesil Beach Boy**[21] 3957 11-10-13 **132** ....(vt) MrsMRoberts[(5)] 124
(John Coombe) *racd keenly early: trckd ldrs 3rd: wnt 2nd sn after 3 out: c wd and lost 2nd bef 2 out: hld after: lft 3rd 2 out: lost 3rd run-in* **7/1**

P41- **F** **Leviathan**[59] 0201 7-10-11 **125** .... AidanColeman 118
(Venetia Williams) *trckd ldr: led after 3rd: hdd bef 3 out: rdn sn after: hld in 11 l 2nd whn fell 2 out* **15/8**[1]

000- **P** **Look For Love**[33] 3744 6-10-0 **114** oh2 .... WillKennedy
(Sue Gardner) *hld up: nt fluent 3rd: rdn after 4th: sn wknd: tailing off whn p.u bef next* **20/1**

4m 24.8s (16.80) **Going Correction** +1.25s/f (Heav) **6** Ran SP% **111.4**
Speed ratings (Par 109): **110,106,102,102,**
CSF £15.98 TOTE £3.60: £2.20, £1.70; EX 13.90 Trifecta £38.50.
Owner Hills Of Ledbury (Aga) **Bred** B Thierry, S Thierry & E Labataille **Trained** Ditcheat, Somerset

FOCUS
Not a strong race for the grade and yet another wide-margin winner on the afternoon. He's rated close to latest course form.

4334 BATHWICK TYRES BRIDGWATER H'CAP HURDLE (8 hdls 2 omitted) 2m 3f 110y
4:15 (4:15) (Class 5) (0-100,99) 4-Y-0+ **£2,395** (£698; £349)

Form RPR

3FP- **1** **Join The Navy**[36] 3687 9-10-12 **92** .... KieronEdgar[(7)] 99
(Kate Buckett) *hld up bhd: smooth prog fr after 5th: pushed into ld appr 2 out: sn rdn: styd on: drvn rt out* **50/1**

055- **2** *½* **Here's Herbie**[35] 3694 6-11-7 **99** ....(t) MissLucyGardner[(5)] 106
(Sue Gardner) *hld up towards rr: hdwy appr 5th: rdn to chse ldrs appr 2 out: styd on wl fr last: clsng on wnr at fin* **20/1**

121- **3** *4 ½* **The Happy Warrior**[9] 4172 6-10-9 **89** .... GaryDerwin[(7)] 92
(Bob Buckler) *chsd ldrs: rdn whn lost pl after 5th: in tch: styd on again after 2 out: wnt 3rd towards fin* **15/8**[1]

005- **4** *3/4* **Moneymix**[31] 3788 7-10-1 **74**......(b) WillKennedy 75
(Ali Brewer) *prom: led 3rd: rdn and hdd appr 2 out: styd chsng wnr tl drifted lft after last: no ex fnl 120yds* **12/1**

040- **5** *6* **Torgamah Lad (IRE)**[12] 4107 6-11-11 **98**...... AidanColeman 95+
(Venetia Williams) *mid-div: hdwy after 5th: rdn to chse ldng pair 2 out tl fdd run-in* **15/2**

0U4- **6** *23* **Bandol (IRE)**[31] 3783 6-10-12 **85**...... DougieCostello 57
(Laura Young) *hld up towards rr: sme prog into midfield after 5th: rdn after 3 out: wknd bef next: t.o* **16/1**

/40- **7** *24* **Leeroar (IRE)**[82] 2766 6-11-5 **92**......(p) SamJones 40
(Jo Davis) *mid-div: pushed along after 4th: wknd bef 3 out: sn t.o* **33/1**

43- **8** *28* **Railway Vic (IRE)**[61] 3174 7-11-0 **87**...... HaddenFrost
(James Frost) *a towards rr: wknd 3 out: t.o* **14/1**

300- **P** **Sun Quest**[141] 1699 10-10-13 **93**...... MrLKilgarriff(7)
(Steven Dixon) *chsd ldrs tl 5th: sn bhd: t.o whn p.u bef 3 out* **66/1**

66P- **P** **Hassadin**[21] 3959 8-10-12 **92**......(p) JoshWall(7)
(Michael Blake) *towards rr: pushed along after 3rd: t.o whn p.u after 3 out* **7/1**[3]

225- **P** **Prince Freddie**[60] 3188 6-10-3 **76**......(p) JamieMoore
(Roy Brotherton) *mid-div: hdwy to sit promly 3rd tl rdn after next: wknd after 5th: t.o whn p.u bef 2 out* **14/1**

015- **P** **Withy Mills**[21] 3959 9-10-11 **87**......(bt) JamesBest(3)
(Kevin Bishop) *chsd ldrs tl after 5th: t.o 3 out: sn p.u* **22/1**

00P- **P** **Hunky Dorey**[64] 3128 8-10-1 **74**...... PaddyBrennan
(Alexandra Dunn) *kpt wd: led tl 3rd: prom: j.lft next: rdn after 5th: wknd bef 3 out: t.o whn p.u bef 2 out* **9/2**[2]

5m 14.1s (28.10) **Going Correction** +1.25s/f (Heav) **13** Ran SP% **119.6**
Speed ratings (Par 103): **93,92,91,90,88 79,69,58,, ,,**
CSF £781.45 CT £2826.91 TOTE £38.30: £9.40, £6.40, £1.30; EX 532.90 Trifecta £2192.40 Part won. Pool: £2,923.22 - 0.38 winning units..
Owner Mrs D Buckett **Bred** Mrs F Wilson **Trained** Upham, Hants

FOCUS
A number of these were struggling from quite a way out and a pair of outsiders came to the fore. The winner is rated in line with the best of his chase form.

4335 FOLLOW YOUR DREAMS STANDARD NATIONAL HUNT FLAT RACE (CONDITIONALS & AMATEURS) 2m 1f
4:50 (4:50) (Class 5) 4-6-Y-O **£2,053** (£598; £299)

Form RPR

32- **1** **Onenightinvienna (IRE)**[33] 3734 5-11-1 0...... JamesBest(3) 115
(Philip Hobbs) *pressed ldr tl pushed along after 8f: sn rdn in 3rd: kpt chsng ldrs: regained 2nd over 2f out: chal ent fnl f: styd on to ld fnl 100yds: all out* **4/1**[3]

2 *3/4* **Pressies Girl (IRE)**[323] 5093 6-10-6 0...... HarryDerham(5) 107
(Paul Nicholls) *trckd ldrs: stmbld a couple of times after 5f: trckd ldr after 8f: led over 2f out: sn rdn: edgd lft ent fnl f: hdd fnl 100yds: no ex* **5/2**[2]

0- **3** *27* **Millanisi Boy**[19] 3994 5-11-4 0...... AdamWedge 87
(Richard Woollacott) *hld up in tch: rdn to dispute 3rd 4f out: wl hld over 2f out: wnt modest 3rd ins fnl f: t.o* **14/1**

2- **4** *9* **Davy Doubt (IRE)**[19] 3994 5-10-11 0...... KieronEdgar(7) 78
(David Pipe) *led: rdn and hdd over 2f out: sn wknd: t.o* **1/1**[1]

0- **5** *18* **Are We There**[19] 3994 5-10-11 0...... MrRobertHawker(7) 60
(Carroll Gray) *last but wl in tch: rdn along after 7f: sn lost tch: t.o* **66/1**

0- **6** *18* **Thymeandthymeagain**[61] 3181 5-10-8 0...... MichaelByrne(3) 35
(Hugo Froud) *hld up in tch: rdn and wknd 5f out: t.o* **33/1**

4m 23.3s (20.90) **Going Correction** +1.25s/f (Heav) **6** Ran SP% **109.7**
Speed ratings: **100,99,86,82,74 65**
CSF £13.70 TOTE £5.30: £2.50, £2.10; EX 11.60 Trifecta £55.40.
Owner Peter Luff **Bred** Colm Griffin **Trained** Withycombe, Somerset

FOCUS
The front pair drew well clear of the disappointing favourite in what was an ordinary bumper. It has been rated around the first three.
T/Plt: £31.70 to a £1 stake. Pool: £84,824.17 - 1,951.76 winning units T/Qpdt: £16.70 to a £1 stake. Pool: £5,714.85 - 252.05 winning units TM

4037 WETHERBY (L-H)
Tuesday, February 18

OFFICIAL GOING: Heavy (soft in places)
The first fence in the back straight was omitted.
Wind: Fresh; half behind Weather: Fine; breezy

4336 NEW RACING UK ANYWHERE AVAILABLE NOW CONDITIONAL JOCKEYS' H'CAP HURDLE (9 hdls) 2m 110y
1:45 (1:45) (Class 5) (0-100,95) 4-Y-0+ **£2,053** (£598; £299)

Form RPR

021- **1** **Lean Burn (USA)**[12] 4107 8-10-13 **85**...... ConorRing(3) 90+
(Barry Leavy) *chsd ldrs: upsides 3 out: 3rd last: styd on wl to ld last 50yds* **10/3**[1]

/34- **2** *2 1/4* **Shan Valley (IRE)**[46] 3518 8-10-6 **81**...... DaraghBourke(6) 84+
(Stuart Coltherd) *hld up in rr: stdy hdwy 6th: w ldrs next: led 2 out: nt fluent last: hung lft and hdd last 50yds* **4/1**[2]

045- **3** *1 1/4* **Beyondtemptation**[22] 3934 6-10-1 **70**...... JoeColliver 71
(Jonathan Haynes) *led to 2 out: kpt on same pce run-in* **66/1**

442- **4** *2 1/4* **Baraboy (IRE)**[12] 4107 4-11-0 **95**...... GrahamWatters(3) 84
(Barry Murtagh) *hld up in mid-div: hdwy 3 out: kpt on same pce appr last* **7/1**

/P0- **5** *1* **Politelysed**[39] 3639 8-10-2 **74**...... StephenMulqueen(3) 71
(Robert Johnson) *hld up in rr: stdy hdwy appr 3 out: chsng ldrs between last 2: one pce* **20/1**

040- **6** *3* **Tom Sang (FR)**[64] 3140 7-10-7 **76**......(t) ThomasGarner 70
(Jamie Snowden) *mid-div: hdwy to chse ldrs 3 out: wknd between last 2* **5/1**[3]

00P- **7** *7* **Rayadour (IRE)**[102] 2336 5-10-10 **82**......(t) CraigNichol(3) 71
(Micky Hammond) *chsd ldrs: nt fluent 5th: lost pl appr 3 out* **33/1**

P05- **8** *6* **Oorayvic (IRE)**[18] 4005 7-11-6 **92**...... JonathanEngland(3) 76
(Sue Smith) *chsd ldrs: upsides 4th: wknd after 2 out* **6/1**

420- **9** *12* **Chapelle du Roi (USA)**[77] 2877 5-11-7 **90**......(p) MichealNolan 59
(Robert Stephens) *j.lft: chsd ldrs: mstke 2nd: drvn 6th: sn lost pl and bhd* **9/1**

060- **10** *19* **Hi Dancer**[38] 3659 11-11-2 **95**...... RyanDClark(10) 45
(Ben Haslam) *in rr: rdn 6th: sn bhd* **12/1**

4m 8.0s (12.20) **Going Correction** +0.45s/f (Soft)
WFA 4 from 5yo+ 9lb **10** Ran SP% **113.4**
Speed ratings (Par 103): **89,87,87,86,85 84,81,78,72,63**
CSF £16.59 CT £715.36 TOTE £3.60: £1.40, £1.70, £10.10; EX 17.00 Trifecta £317.80.
Owner N Heath **Bred** George Ruggiero Jr **Trained** Forsbrook, Staffs

FOCUS
A moderate handicap, confined to conditional riders. The winner is closing in on the best of last season's form.

4337 EBF/TBA MARES' NOVICES' H'CAP CHASE (16 fncs 2 omitted) 2m 6f 110y
2:15 (2:15) (Class 4) (0-110,109) 5-Y-0+ **£4,093** (£1,202; £601; £300)

Form RPR

1UP- **1** **Legendary Hop**[14] 4078 8-11-2 **99**...... TomMessenger 103
(Chris Bealby) *w ldr: led 8th: hdd 3 out: lft 2nd next: styd on run-in: led nr fin* **8/1**

3PP- **2** *nk* **Mrs Eff**[34] 3724 8-11-7 **107**......(t) KyleJames(3) 114+
(Philip Kirby) *in rr: drvn 8th: hdwy 4 out: led and j. bdly lft 2 out: 4 l ahd last: wandered and hung rt: tired and hdd nr fin* **12/1**

325- **3** *1 1/4* **Fair Bramble**[31] 3769 8-11-3 **100**......(p) LeightonAspell 101
(Oliver Sherwood) *chsd ldrs: j.rt 7th and 11th: outpcd and lost pl 4 out: lft modest 4th 2 out: 10 l 3rd last: styd on wl last 75yds* **7/2**[2]

210- **4** *3/4* **Tea Caddy**[67] 3058 8-11-7 **107**......(t) GavinSheehan(3) 109
(Jamie Snowden) *hld up: hmpd 7th: hdwy 12th: sn chsng ldrs: outpcd and lost pl 4 out: lft modest 3rd 2 out: 12 l 4th last: styd on wl last 75yds* **13/2**

/2P- **P** **Cherry's Bay**[22] 3936 8-10-0 **83** oh34......(p) AdrianLane
(Sandy Forster) *in rr: nt fluent 6th: outpcd and reminders 8th: sn bhd: t.o whn p.u bef next* **100/1**

034- **F** **Lady Of Verona (IRE)**[72] 2974 7-10-1 **91**...... CraigNichol(7) 93
(Lucinda Russell) *chsd ldrs: fell 2nd* **11/4**[1]

543- **P** **The Flaming Matron (IRE)**[45] 3523 8-11-8 **105**......(t) LucyAlexander
(N W Alexander) *led: hdd 8th: wkng whn hit 4 out: sn bhd: p.u bef last* **13/2**

1/3- **U** **Hidden Horizons (IRE)**[19] 3996 8-11-12 **109**......(p) PeterBuchanan 110
(S R B Crawford, Ire) *chsd ldrs: cl 2nd 4 out: 2 l 2nd whn blnd and uns rdr 2 out* **11/2**[3]

6m 6.9s (29.90) **Going Correction** +1.025s/f (Soft) **8** Ran SP% **110.7**
Speed ratings: **89,88,88,88, ,,**
CSF £85.47 CT £379.54 TOTE £11.40: £2.70, £2.50, £1.50; EX 116.60 Trifecta £895.40 Part won. Pool: £1,193.94 - 0.31 winning units..
Owner Messrs Duke,Umpleby,Holmes & Bealby **Bred** B G Duke **Trained** Barrowby, Lincs

FOCUS
A modest mares' novice handicap in which they finished in a heap. Very suspect form.

4338 DOWNLOAD THE NEW RACINGUK IPAD APP H'CAP HURDLE (12 hdls) 2m 6f
2:50 (2:50) (Class 4) (0-115,113) 4-Y-0+ **£3,285** (£957; £479)

Form RPR

/55- **1** **Captain Clayton (IRE)**[71] 2997 7-10-7 **101**...... RyanDClark(7) 109
(Simon West) *hld up in rr: hmpd 5th: hdwy 9th: chsng ldr appr next: upsides 2 out: led last: drvn out* **33/1**

001- **2** *2* **Heavenstown (IRE)**[15] 4070 8-11-4 **110**......(b) NicodeBoinville(5) 116
(John Spearing) *chsd ldr 3rd: led 5th: hdd last: no ex* **6/1**[3]

0F3- **3** *12* **Forty Crown (IRE)**[23] 3922 8-11-10 **111**...... WilsonRenwick 108
(John Wade) *prom: chsd ldrs 7th: modest 3rd appr 3 out: kpt on same pce* **5/1**[2]

100- **4** *nk* **Brave Buck**[31] 3775 6-10-12 **102**...... JakeGreenall(3) 97
(Henry Daly) *chsd ldrs: drvn 7th: lost pl 9th: hdwy appr next: disputing modest 3rd 2 out: kpt on one pce* **6/1**[3]

463- **5** *1* **Micro Mission (IRE)**[34] 3726 8-11-5 **113**...... DiarmuidO'Regan(7) 106
(Chris Grant) *chsd ldrs: drvn 9th: one pce* **9/1**

505- **6** *15* **Delightfully (FR)**[53] 3335 10-9-10 **90**......(bt) GrantCockburn(7) 68
(Lucinda Russell) *in rr: reminders after 9th: nvr a factor* **10/1**

3/P- **7** *16* **Baileys Concerto (IRE)**[34] 3724 8-11-4 **105**...... BrianHughes 67
(Dianne Sayer) *hld up in rr: hdwy 7th: lost pl bef 3 out* **66/1**

/32- **8** *nk* **Stickleback**[53] 3335 5-9-12 **90**......(p) JoeColliver(5) 51
(Micky Hammond) *in rr: bdly hmpd 5th: sn drvn: bhd fr 9th* **9/2**[1]

/F6- **9** *5* **Grey Area (IRE)**[22] 3938 9-10-9 **103**...... DaraghBourke(7) 59
(Tristan Davidson) *led to 5th: lost pl bef 3 out* **12/1**

511- **10** *7* **Markem (IRE)**[23] 3922 7-11-1 **109**......(t) CraigNichol(7) 58
(Rose Dobbin) *chsd ldrs: drvn 9th: fdd appr next: modest 6th whn hit 2 out: sn lost pl and fin v tired* **5/1**[2]

1/5- **U** **You Know Yourself (IRE)**[286] 170 11-11-10 **111**...... ShaneByrne
(Sue Smith) *mid-div: blnd and uns rdr 5th* **25/1**

5m 33.7s (6.90) **Going Correction** +0.45s/f (Soft) **11** Ran SP% **115.1**
Speed ratings (Par 105): **105,104,99,99,99 93,88,88,86,83**
CSF £216.35 CT £1177.69 TOTE £27.30: £7.80, £2.40, £2.30; EX 313.80 Trifecta £1655.30.
Owner Wild West Racing **Bred** Nicholas O'Neill **Trained** Middleham Moor, N Yorks
■ Jockey Ryan D Clark's first winner under rules.

FOCUS
A wide-open handicap. A personal best from the winner with the second back to his best.

4339 GOODBYE AND GOOD LUCK BEN ATKINSON H'CAP CHASE (16 fncs 2 omitted) 3m 1f
3:25 (3:25) (Class 3) (0-140,126) 5-Y-0+ **£6,498** (£1,908; £954; £477)

Form RPR

/44- **1** **Fill The Power (IRE)**[12] 4104 8-11-12 **126**...... RyanMania 144+
(Sue Smith) *mde all: drvn 4 out: styd on strly: drew clr appr 2 out: 12 l ahd last: eased clsng stages* **2/1**[1]

0/3- **2** *18* **Harris Hawk**[28] 3823 9-10-11 **111**......(p) BrianHughes 107
(John Wade) *chsd ldng pair: drvn 12th: chsd wnr next: regained modest 2nd sn after last* **3/1**[3]

/PP- **3** *3 3/4* **Camden (IRE)**[67] 3059 8-11-5 **119**......(p) LeightonAspell 111
(Oliver Sherwood) *w wnr: drvn 11th: modest 2nd 3 out: wknd last* **7/2**

011- **4** *12* **Wood Yer (IRE)**[28] 3820 8-11-4 **118**......(tp) SamTwiston-Davies 102
(Nigel Twiston-Davies) *in rr: drvn 10th: hit 12th: sn given reminders and lost pl* **5/2**[2]

6m 32.0s (22.60) **Going Correction** +1.025s/f (Soft) **4** Ran SP% **109.1**
Speed ratings: **104,98,97,93**
CSF £8.10 TOTE £2.90; EX 7.70 Trifecta £18.90.
Owner McGoldrick Racing Syndicates **Bred** Patrick Condon **Trained** High Eldwick, W Yorks

FOCUS
A fair little handicap and sound form. The winner built on his promising recent run.

4340 WATCH ON 3 DEVICES RACINGUK.COM/ANYWHERE NOVICES' HURDLE (11 hdls) 2m 4f
3:55 (3:56) (Class 4) 4-Y-0+ £3,119 (£915; £457; £228)

Form RPR
212- 1 **Fine Rightly (IRE)**[7] 4200 6-11-6 0 MrSCrawford(3) 135+
(S R B Crawford, Ire) *mde all: j.lft 1st: wnt clr between last 2: v easily* 8/11[1]
51- 2 7 **Templebraden (IRE)**[27] 3841 7-11-9 0 LeightonAspell 120
(Henry Oliver) *trckd wnr: t.k.h: nt fluent 3rd: upsides 6th: drvn appr 3 out: no ch w wnr* 13/8[2]
/35- 3 13 **Ballythomas**[26] 3850 7-11-0 0 TonyKelly(3) 105
(David Thompson) *wnt modest 3rd 7th: drvn next: one pce* 25/1
000- 4 31 **Secure Investment**[33] 3728 6-10-12 0 ThomasGarner(5) 69
(Oliver Sherwood) *hld up: outpcd and lost tch after 7th: t.o 3 out* 40/1
3- 5 3 3/4 **Mistariva (IRE)**[54] 3282 7-11-3 0 LiamTreadwell 65
(Venetia Williams) *nt fluent: hit 3rd: 3rd 5th: reminders next: reminders and lost pl 7th: sn bhd: t.o 3 out* 9/1[3]

5m 14.4s (14.90) **Going Correction** +0.45s/f (Soft) **5** Ran SP% **112.3**
Speed ratings (Par 105): **88,85,80,67,66**
CSF £2.36 TOTE £1.70: £1.30, £1.10; EX 2.60 Trifecta £10.60.
Owner Miss Patricia Duffin **Bred** Miss Patricia Duffin **Trained** Larne, Co Antrim

FOCUS
An uncompetitive novice hurdle. Arguably a step up from the winner with the next two pretty much to their marks.

4341 WETHERBY RACECOURSE & CONFERENCE CENTRE H'CAP CHASE (12 fncs 1 omitted) 2m
4:30 (4:30) (Class 4) (0-120,122) 5-Y-0+ £3,768 (£1,106; £553; £276)

Form RPR
211- 1 **Massena (IRE)**[5] 4241 7-11-12 **122** 7ex CallumWhillans(5) 143+
(Venetia Williams) *led: nt fluent and hdd 5th: led after 8th: clr whn shkn up between last 2: pushed out* 4/7[1]
3U1- 2 13 **Cloverhill Lad (IRE)**[45] 3524 10-10-8 **106** DaraghBourke(7) 111
(Stuart Coltherd) *trckd ldrs: led 5th: hdd next: chsd wnr 4 out: no imp* 4/1[2]
216- 3 3 3/4 **Pamak D'Airy (FR)**[13] 4080 11-10-10 **104** (p) TonyKelly(3) 105
(Henry Hogarth) *hit 1st: jnd ldrs next: led 6th: hdd after 8th: one pce fr 3 out* 12/1
3/6- 4 10 **Mister Wall Street (FR)**[71] 2996 9-10-12 **103** BrianHughes 94
(Rebecca Menzies) *w ldrs: nudged along 8th: wknd bef next* 8/1[3]
0P- 5 11 **Champagne Agent (IRE)**[69] 3017 8-11-12 **117** (p) PeterBuchanan 103
(Lucinda Russell) *last fr 2nd: drvn 8th: sn bhd* 16/1

4m 9.3s (13.50) **Going Correction** +1.025s/f (Soft) **5** Ran SP% **108.3**
Speed ratings: **107,100,98,93,88**
CSF £3.34 TOTE £1.30: £1.10, £1.80; EX 3.00 Trifecta £5.80.
Owner Miss V M Williams **Bred** Frank Dunne **Trained** Kings Caple, H'fords

FOCUS
An easy win for the in-form Massena, who is rated to a similar level as his recent win.

4342 RACINGUK.COM/ANYWHERE: 3 DEVICES, 1 PRICE MARES' STANDARD OPEN NATIONAL HUNT FLAT RACE 2m 110y
5:00 (5:00) (Class 6) 4-6-Y-0 £1,642 (£478; £239)

Form RPR
10- 1 **Lady Buttons**[48] 3460 4-10-7 0 AdamNicol(5) 109+
(Philip Kirby) *trckd ldrs: upsides over 5f out: led on bit over 2f out: wnt clr appr fnl f: v easily* 10/11[1]
1- 2 8 **Millicent Silver**[38] 3656 5-11-0 0 RyanHatch(7) 103
(Nigel Twiston-Davies) *trckd ldr: upsides over 5f out: shkn up over 3f out: rdn over 2f out: no ch w wnr* 5/4[2]
56- 3 11 **Presidential Lady (IRE)**[34] 3727 5-10-7 0 DiarmuidO'Regan(7) 85
(Chris Grant) *led: pushed along 6f out: rdn over 3f out: hdd over 2f out: one pce* 10/1[3]

4m 7.8s (17.60) **Going Correction** +0.45s/f (Soft)
WFA 4 from 5yo 9lb **3** Ran SP% **105.9**
Speed ratings: **76,72,67**
CSF £2.31 TOTE £1.60; EX 1.90 Trifecta £2.30.
Owner Mrs Jayne Sivills **Bred** Keith Sivills **Trained** Middleham, N Yorks

FOCUS
A cakewalk for the promising winner, who is rated back to form.
T/Plt: £38.50 to a £1 stake. Pool: £82,389.07 - 1,561.31 winning units T/Qpdt: £8.20 to a £1 stake. Pool: £5,224.47 - 467.75 winning units WG

4101 DONCASTER (L-H)
Wednesday, February 19

OFFICIAL GOING: Good to soft (soft in places; chs 6.9, hdl 7.2)
Wind: moderate 1/2 against Weather: fine

4343 BETDAQ 3% COMMISSION BRITISH STALLION STUDS EBF "NATIONAL HUNT" NOVICES' HURDLE (QUALIFIER) (8 hdls) 2m 110y
1:45 (1:45) (Class 4) 4-7-Y-0 £3,898 (£1,144; £572; £286)

Form RPR
130/ 1 **Un Ace (FR)**[319] 5179 6-11-2 0 NickScholfield 128+
(Kim Bailey) *hld up in rr: hdwy 5th: 4th and chsng ldrs whn stmbld 3 out: 4th last: styd on strly to ld last 125yds: wnt clr* 7/1[2]
11- 2 8 **Stellar Notion (IRE)**[35] 3721 6-11-8 0 PaddyBrennan 125+
(Tom George) *sn trcking ldrs: effrt 3 out: styd on to ld 1f out: sn hdd and no ex* 5/6[1]
21- 3 1 1/4 **Master Dee (IRE)**[40] 3640 5-11-2 0 JasonMaguire 116
(Donald McCain) *chsd ldrs: narrow ld 2 out: hdd and no ex run-in* 8/1[3]
/24- 4 shd **Rhapando**[74] 2947 5-11-2 0 DenisO'Regan 115
(Paul Webber) *chsd ldr: reminders 3rd: led after 5th: jnd next: hdd narrowly 2 out: kpt on one pce appr last* 11/1
333- 5 15 **In The Rough (IRE)**[62] 3175 5-11-2 0 APMcCoy 102
(Jonjo O'Neill) *in rr: bhd and reminders 5th: nvr on terms* 7/1[2]
/55- 6 nk **Morning Reggie**[74] 2947 5-11-2 0 LeightonAspell 101
(Oliver Sherwood) *chsd ldrs: lost pl 3 out* 10/1
00U- 7 7 **Back By Midnight**[10] 4171 5-10-11 0 JamesBanks(5) 95
(Emma Baker) *t.k.h towards rr: sme hdwy 5th: lost pl bef next* 200/1
220/ 8 43 **Master Malt**[319] 5179 6-11-2 0 RichieMcLernon 56
(Jonjo O'Neill) *chsd ldrs: drvn 5th: sn lost pl and bhd: t.o* 20/1
0- 9 35 **Master Wickham (IRE)**[86] 2724 5-11-2 0 CharliePoste 25
(Paul Webber) *chsd ldrs: lost pl after 4th: sn bhd t.o* 100/1
3- P **Spiculas (IRE)**[100] 2426 5-11-2 0 JamesReveley
(Keith Reveley) *in rr: bhd whn p.u bef 5th* 33/1
000- U **Devil At Midnight (IRE)**[13] 4103 6-10-11 0 SamanthaDrake(5)
(Richard Drake) *led: hdd after 5th: lost pl and bhd whn mstke and uns rdr next* 200/1

4m 5.0s (0.30) **Going Correction** +0.40s/f (Soft) **11** Ran SP% **117.8**
Speed ratings: **115,111,110,110,103 103,100,79,63,**
CSF £13.57 TOTE £8.60: £2.70, £1.20, £2.70; EX 19.70 Trifecta £78.70.
Owner Ace In The Pack Partnership **Bred** Jacques Lauriot **Trained** Andoversford, Gloucs

FOCUS
It was a drying day with a light wind across the track. The ground was riding "a bit dead" according to Nick Scholfield after the first. This interesting novice event was run at a fair gallop and the first four came clear from the second-last. Sound form, and the winner should rate higher.

4344 BETDAQ NO PREMIUM CHARGE NOVICES' CHASE (18 fncs) 3m
2:20 (2:20) (Class 4) 5-Y-0+ £3,768 (£1,106; £553; £276)

Form RPR
2U1- 1 **Holywell (IRE)**[28] 3831 7-11-7 0 (p) APMcCoy 140+
(Jonjo O'Neill) *nt fluent: reminders after 7th: chsd ldrs next: drvn after 14th: kpt on and upsides last: styd on to ld last 150yds* 10/11[1]
/21- 2 3/4 **Victor Hewgo**[26] 3873 9-11-7 132 JamesReveley 138
(Keith Reveley) *trckd ldrs: pushed along appr 4 out: styd on to ld narrowly last: hdd and no ex run-in* 5/2[2]
142- 3 3 **Firm Order (IRE)**[71] 3006 9-11-7 127 (p) DenisO'Regan 135
(Paul Webber) *led: j.rt 1st: j. boldly: hdd narrowly last: kpt on same pce* 14/1
/1U- 4 24 **Top Of The Range (IRE)**[17] 4055 7-11-7 138 BarryGeraghty 118
(Nicky Henderson) *t.k.h: trckd ldrs 7th: pushed along 13th: lost pl 3 out* 4/1[3]
5/3- P **Social Overdrive (IRE)**[27] 3850 8-10-9 0 JamesBanks(5)
(Emma Baker) *chsd ldrs: nt fluent 2nd: lost pl 7th: sn drvn: bhd fr 11th: t.o whn p.u bef 4 out* 100/1

6m 6.3s (-5.70) **Going Correction** +0.025s/f (Yiel) **5** Ran SP% **108.6**
Speed ratings: **110,109,108,100,**
CSF £3.60 TOTE £2.00: £1.10, £1.50; EX 4.40 Trifecta £10.30.
Owner Mrs Gay Smith **Bred** Patrick Doyle **Trained** Cheltenham, Gloucs

FOCUS
There was a superb finish to this good-quality staying novice chase. The winner is rated in line with his chase form to date.

4345 BETDAQ FREE PREMIER LEAGUE GAME SATURDAY JUVENILE HURDLE (8 hdls) 2m 110y
2:50 (2:51) (Class 4) 4-Y-0 £3,119 (£915; £457; £228)

Form RPR
31- 1 **Pearl Castle (IRE)**[26] 3872 4-11-5 0 BrianHughes 129+
(John Quinn) *trckd ldrs: upsides whn stmbld on landing 3 out: swtchd lft between last 2: led narrowly last: drvn clr last 75yds* 4/6[1]
33- 2 2 1/4 **Zamoyski**[63] 2392 4-10-12 0 RichardJohnson 116
(Steve Gollings) *led at v stdy pce: increased gallop 4th: jnd 3 out: hdd narrowly last: styd on same pce last 100yds* 8/1[3]
45- 3 4 **Ronaldinho (IRE)**[25] 3885 4-10-12 0 WayneHutchinson 113
(Alan King) *trckd ldrs: cl-up 3 out: styd on same pce appr last* 7/2[2]
4 2 1/4 **She's Late**[135] 4-10-12 0 APMcCoy 110
(Jonjo O'Neill) *trckd ldrs: upsides 2 out: fdd appr last* 10/1
1P- 5 13 **Mahican (IRE)**[27] 3857 4-11-5 0 (b[1]) DenisO'Regan 109+
(John Ferguson) *chsd ldrs: fading whn hmpd between last 2* 12/1
2- 6 8 **Mr Vendman (IRE)**[59] 3224 4-10-7 0 RobertMcCarth(5) 92
(Ian Williams) *t.k.h in rr: bhd fr 5th: j. bdly lft and blnd 2 out* 33/1
624- 7 34 **Mandy's Boy (IRE)**[32] 3768 4-10-12 120 (p) JasonMaguire 55
(Ian Williams) *in rr: nt fluent 4th: bhd fr next: t.o whn j.lft last* 16/1
05- 8 6 **Young Jay**[29] 3822 4-10-9 0 (t) JohnKington(3) 49
(Andrew Crook) *in rr: nt fluent 4th: bhd 5th: j.lft 3 out: sn t.o* 100/1

4m 7.9s (3.20) **Going Correction** +0.40s/f (Soft) **8** Ran SP% **119.9**
Speed ratings: **108,106,105,104,97 94,78,75**
CSF £7.89 TOTE £2.40: £1.10, £1.70, £1.60; EX 8.70 Trifecta £32.30.
Owner Mr & Mrs Paul Gaffney **Bred** Mogeely Stud **Trained** Settrington, N Yorks
■ Stewards' Enquiry : Brian Hughes two-day ban: careless riding (Mar 5-6)

FOCUS
This was steadily run and it isn't form to ber confident about, but it might work out.

4346 BETDAQ £25 NO LOSE MOBILE BET DONCASTER VETERANS' H'CAP CHASE (18 fncs) 3m
3:25 (3:26) (Class 2) (0-150,146) 10-Y-0+ £12,021 (£3,529; £1,764; £882)

Form RPR
023- 1 **Tranquil Sea (IRE)**[24] 3923 12-10-12 **135** GavinSheehan(3) 146+
(Warren Greatrex) *hld up in rr: stdy hdwy 14th: 2nd 3 out: led appr next: pushed out* 12/1
/40- 2 2 **Time For Rupert (IRE)**[25] 3897 10-11-4 **138** (p) DenisO'Regan 143
(Paul Webber) *led to 4th: w ldr: led 14th: hdd appr 2 out: kpt on same pce* 11/4[1]
53U- 3 hd **Mcmurrough (IRE)**[18] 4039 10-11-5 **139** (b) BrianHughes 144
(Malcolm Jefferson) *chsd ldrs: hit 6th and reminders: rdn and outpcd 14th: rallied 2 out: 4th last: styd on wl fnl 100yds* 12/1
P42- 4 1 **Son Of Flicka**[49] 3450 10-10-4 **124** DougieCostello 128
(Tony Coyle) *chsd ldrs: drvn 11th: sn lost pl and bhd: hdwy 3 out: 5th last: kpt on to take 4th last 100yds* 10/1
006- 5 4 1/2 **Big Fella Thanks**[32] 3772 12-11-10 **144** (tp) PaddyBrennan 143
(Tom George) *racd wd: hld up in rr: hdwy 8th: trcking ldrs 11th: 3rd 3 out: wknd and lost 2 pls fnl 150yds* 10/1
/41- 6 1 1/4 **Aachen**[18] 4034 10-10-6 **126** LiamTreadwell 125
(Venetia Williams) *chsd ldrs: hit 10th: drvn 4 out: wknd last* 4/1[2]
655- 7 2 3/4 **Fruity O'Rooney**[18] 4035 11-11-1 **135** (p) JamieMoore 130
(Gary Moore) *prom: drvn and outpcd 14th: kpt on one pce fr 3 out* 7/1[3]
00P- 8 3/4 **Burton Port (IRE)**[49] 3457 10-11-11 **145** DavyRussell 143+
(Jonjo O'Neill) *in rr: drvn 9th: bhd 11th: kpt on fr 2 out* 8/1
325- 9 9 **Categorical**[42] 3603 11-9-9 **120** oh7 HarryChalloner(5) 109
(Keith Reveley) *mid-div: lost pl 11th: no ch after* 25/1
1P1/ 10 55 **Massini's Maguire (IRE)**[732] 4375 13-11-12 **146** RichardJohnson 108
(Tim Vaughan) *w ldr: led 4th to 14th: lost pl 3 out: t.o whn eased run-in: virtually p.u* 10/1

6m 6.0s (-6.00) **Going Correction** +0.025s/f (Yiel) **10** Ran SP% **116.8**
Speed ratings: **111,110,110,109,108 108,107,106,103,85**
CSF £46.93 CT £417.18 TOTE £12.00: £3.50, £1.60, £3.50; EX 70.50 Trifecta £1415.00.
Owner No Dramas Partnership 1 **Bred** Edward Curtin **Trained** Upper Lambourn, Berks

FOCUS
A decent contest of its type, run at a solid gallop. The winner is rated close to his best form of last year.

4347 BETDAQ £500 IN FREE BETS H'CAP HURDLE (11 hdls) 3m 110y
3:55 (3:56) (Class 3) (0-130,130) 4-Y-0+ **£5,393** (£1,583; £791; £395)

Form RPR
406- **1** **Seventh Sign**[53] 3359 5-11-9 **127**..(b) NoelFehily 138+
(Alan King) *trckd ldrs: led between last 2: drvn out* **22/1**
/02- **2** *5* **Matthew Riley (IRE)**[60] 3207 7-11-8 **126**........................ RichieMcGrath 131
(Philip Kirby) *in rr: effrt 7th: drvn to chse ldrs 3 out: 4th 2 out: styd on to chse wnr sn after last: no real imp* **3/1**[1]
461- **3** *3 ½* **Kaysersberg (FR)**[26] 3875 7-11-12 **130**........................ RichardJohnson 132
(Neil King) *t.k.h: trckd ldrs: led appr 3 out: hdd between last 2: kpt on same pce* **7/1**[3]
526- **4** *6* **Dundee**[51] 3419 6-10-7 **111**.. WayneHutchinson 108
(Alan King) *hld up: hdwy to trck ldrs 7th: one pce fr 2 out* **8/1**
240- **5** *12* **Lookout Mountain (IRE)**[53] 3359 6-11-5 **123**........................(vt) APMcCoy 110
(Jonjo O'Neill) *in rr: hdwy 7th: sn chsng ldrs: drvn 3 out: wknd between last 2* **17/2**
31F- **6** *8* **Pudsey House**[19] 4006 7-10-7 **118**..............................(b) JohnDawson[(7)] 95
(John Wade) *led: hit 1st: hdd next: w ldrs: wknd 2 out* **33/1**
/52- **7** *23* **Rev It Up (IRE)**[78] 2867 8-11-9 **127**..............................(v) DougieCostello 84
(Tim Vaughan) *w ldr: led 2nd to 7th: led after 8th: hdd & wknd bef next* **25/1**
211- **8** *1 ½* **Mr Utah**[52] 3396 7-11-1 **122**.. TonyKelly[(3)] 77
(Henry Hogarth) *prom: lost pl 4th: in rr and reminders 7th: bhd next* **33/1**
022- **9** *9* **Make Me A Fortune (IRE)**[27] 3851 6-10-8 **112**................(p) DarylJacob 59
(Steve Gollings) *in rr: hdwy 6th: outpcd appr 3 out: sn lost pl* **9/1**
022- **10** *27* **Canuspotit**[27] 3850 7-10-11 **115**.. LeightonAspell 38
(Lucy Wadham) *t.k.h: sn trcking ldrs: led 7th: hdd after next: sn wknd: bhd whn eased last: t.o* **18/1**
0/6- **P** **Shakalakaboomboom (IRE)**[19] 4021 10-11-12 **130**...... BarryGeraghty
(Nicky Henderson) *mid-div: lost pl 5th: bhd and drvn after 7th: t.o whn p.u bef 3 out* **12/1**
134- **P** **Potters Cross**[39] 3654 7-11-7 **130**..............................(t) PatrickCorbett[(5)]
(Rebecca Curtis) *chsd ldrs: hit 8th: sn lost pl: eased and bhd whn p.u bef next* **9/2**[2]
35P- **P** **Chestertern**[54] 3325 7-10-11 **115**.. JasonMaguire
(Jennie Candlish) *chsd ldrs: reminders and lost pl 4th: bhd whn blnd 6th: t.o whn p.u after next* **14/1**

6m 3.6s (4.60) **Going Correction** +0.40s/f (Soft) 13 Ran SP% **121.0**
Speed ratings (Par 107): **108,106,105,103,99 96,89,89,86,77 , ,**
CSF £87.53 CT £531.62 TOTE £18.70: £4.20, £1.70, £2.60; EX 131.00 Trifecta £1035.50.
Owner Masterson Holdings Limited **Bred** Newsells Park Stud **Trained** Barbury Castle, Wilts

FOCUS
They got sorted out from the top of the home straight in this fair staying handicap. A step up from the winner.

4348 CGA FOXHUNTER TRIAL OPEN HUNTERS' CHASE (19 fncs) 3m 2f
4:25 (4:26) (Class 6) 5-Y-0+ **£1,247** (£387; £193; £96)

Form RPR
/21- **1** **Palypso De Creek (FR)**[18] 4042 11-11-11 120............... MissCVHart[(7)] 126+
(Mrs J Dawson) *chsd ldrs: drvn to ld appr 4 out: styd on wl* **6/4**[1]
F1P- **2** *3 ½* **Foundry Square (IRE)**[14] 4092 8-11-7 127....................(p) MrWTelfer[(7)] 115
(S Flook) *hld up: hdwy 7th: reminders 9th: chsng ldrs 12th: outpcd appr 4 out: chsd wnr between last 2: no real imp* **4/1**[2]
0P4- **3** *1* **Schindler's Prince (IRE)**[27] 3862 9-11-5 96.............. MrJMRidley[(5)] 109
(Mrs H S M Ridley) *in rr: hdwy appr 4 out: styd on and 4th last: tk 3rd last 50yds* **33/1**
/05- **4** *3* **Croan Rock (IRE)**[18] 4042 9-11-3 94.............................. MrJLyttle[(7)] 107
(R A Owen) *w ldrs: led 5th to 13th: 2nd 2 out: wknd fnl 75yds* **50/1**
2/U- **5** *10* **King Fontaine (IRE)**[17] 4057 11-11-7 116......................... MrGCrow[(3)] 97
(J J O'Shea) *in rr: heawady 12th: sn chsng ldrs: outpcd 4 out: wknd appr 2 out* **7/1**
PP6- **6** *30* **Charles Bruce (IRE)**[31] 3801 11-11-7 95......................... MrJBargary[(7)] 74
(A Campbell) *led to 5th: drvn 12th: outpcd 14th: wknd appr 4 out: sn bhd: t.o* **33/1**
2/0- **7** *4 ½* **Marufo (IRE)**[17] 4057 12-11-11 120........................(tp) MrDominicSutton[(7)] 74
(Tracey L Bailey) *t.k.h: trckd ldrs 4th: led 13th: hdd appr out: wknd bef 2 out: bhd whn eased last: t.o* **8/1**
530- **P** **Keenan's Future (IRE)**[54] 13-11-7 100....................(tp) MissAEStirling[(3)]
(S Rea) *in rr: outpcd whn hit 13th: t.o 15th: p.u bef 3 out* **18/1**
P/2- **U** **Beneficial Reform (IRE)**[45] 9-12-0 127.......................... MrTWeston
(Mrs A Rucker) *t.k.h: trckd ldrs: nt fluent 6th: handy 4th whn blnd and uns rdr 14th* **5/1**[3]

6m 54.9s (11.90) **Going Correction** +0.025s/f (Yiel) 9 Ran SP% **113.4**
Speed ratings: **82,80,80,79,76 67,66, ,**
CSF £7.66 TOTE £2.30: £1.10, £2.00, £5.90; EX 7.60 Trifecta £143.20.
Owner M N Dawson **Bred** Suc Yves Chopin & Mme Francoise Roux **Trained** Grainthorpe, Lincs

FOCUS
This fair hunter chase was run at a sound gallop. The idling winner is rated value for further and to his mark.

4349 SIS LIVE STANDARD OPEN NATIONAL HUNT FLAT RACE 2m 110y
4:55 (4:57) (Class 6) 4-6-Y-0 **£1,559** (£457; £228; £114)

Form RPR
/21- **1** **Zeroeshadesofgrey (IRE)**[28] 3835 5-11-6 0................ TrevorWhelan[(3)] 115+
(Neil King) *chsd ldrs: led over 3f out: styd on wl last 150yds* **9/2**[3]
1- **2** *2* **Relic Rock (IRE)**[18] 4043 6-11-9 0.................................... JasonMaguire 113
(Steve Gollings) *chsd ldrs: rdn 3f out: sn outpcd: styd on wl fnl f: tk 2nd nr fin* **9/1**
3 *nk* **Some Buckle (IRE)**[115] 5-11-2 0.................................... PaddyBrennan 106
(Tom George) *trckd ldrs: hdwy on inner to trck ldrs over 4f out: upsides over 3f out: fdd clsng stages* **7/2**[1]
2- **4** *hd* **Racing Europe (IRE)**[33] 3760 5-11-2 0.......................... RichardJohnson 106
(Brian Ellison) *chsd ldrs: rdn 3f out: sn outpcd: styd on wl last 150yds* **4/1**[2]
3- **5** *4 ½* **Keep Presenting (IRE)**[53] 3363 5-11-2 0......................... BarryGeraghty 101
(Rebecca Curtis) *led: hdd over 3f out: one pce whn swtchd lft over 1f out* **7/1**
5- **6** *2* **Smart Motive**[99] 2436 4-10-7 0...................................... WayneHutchinson 90
(Alan King) *hld up in rr: hdwy to chse ldrs over 3f out: edgd rt 2f out: wknd fnl f* **16/1**
1- **7** *6* **Mont Royale**[136] 1792 6-11-9 0... APMcCoy 100
(Jonjo O'Neill) *chsd ldr: drvn over 3f out: sn lost pl* **5/1**

8 *3 ½* **Road To Freedom** 5-11-2 0... LeightonAspell 90
(Lucy Wadham) *in rr: hdwy 6f out: sn wl in tch: lost pl over 3f out* **66/1**
9 *4* **Teescomponents Max** 5-11-2 0...................................... JamesReveley 86
(Keith Reveley) *hld up in rr: hdwy 6f out: sn chsng ldrs: lost pl over 3f out* **25/1**
10 *78* **Gentlemans Token** 6-11-2 0.. AndrewThornton 8
(Clive Mulhall) *in rr-div: reminders over 8f out: sn lost pl and bhd: t.o 4f out: eventually completed* **100/1**

4m 12.2s (13.10) **Going Correction** +0.40s/f (Soft)
WFA 4 from 5yo 9lb 5 from 6yo 1lb 10 Ran SP% **111.8**
Speed ratings: **85,84,83,83,81 80,77,76,74,37**
CSF £42.00 TOTE £6.60: £1.90, £2.60, £1.90; EX 46.00 Trifecta £302.50.
Owner Mrs J K Buckle **Bred** Joe Fogarty **Trained** Newmarket, Suffolk

FOCUS
An above-average bumper. It developed into something of a sprint off the home turn, but the first four were nicely clear at the finish. The form makes sense.
T/Plt: £15.50 to a £1 stake. Pool: £99,045.33 - 4660.83 winning units. T/Qpdt: £9.30 to a £1 stake. Pool: £6418.99 - 12.50 winning units. WG

4087 LUDLOW (R-H)
Wednesday, February 19

OFFICIAL GOING: Heavy (soft in places; 6.3)
Wind: Light against Weather: Cloudy with sunny spells

4350 ONNY MAIDEN HURDLE (8 hdls 1 omitted) 2m
2:10 (2:10) (Class 4) 4-Y-0+ **£3,898** (£1,144; £572; £286)

Form RPR
0F0- **1** **Bodega**[26] 3877 6-11-2 120.. WillKennedy 113
(Ian Williams) *w ldr tl led 5th: drvn out* **11/4**[1]
406- **2** *2 ½* **Vermouth Bleu (FR)**[42] 3602 5-10-6 0.................... TommieMO'Brien[(10)] 111
(Jonjo O'Neill) *a.p: chsd wnr 3 out: hit next: rdn flat: styd on* **17/2**
3 *7* **Lochnagar (GER)**[210] 5-11-2 0.. AidanColeman 105+
(Venetia Williams) *chsd ldrs: nt fluent: hit 3 out and next: sn rdn: no ex flat* **7/2**[3]
230- **4** *4 ½* **Saffron Prince**[19] 4018 6-11-2 115...................................... TomScudamore 99
(David Bridgwater) *chsd ldrs: ev ch appr 3 out: sn rdn: wkng whn mstke last* **3/1**[2]
5/0- **5** *1 ½* **Scribe (IRE)**[12] 2718 6-11-2 0..(vt) SeanQuinlan 97
(David Evans) *hld up: hdwy appr and mstke 3 out: rdn and wknd bef last* **33/1**
46- **6** *4 ½* **River Clare (IRE)**[32] 3778 6-10-9 0................................. CiaranMckee[(7)] 93
(John O'Shea) *mid-div: hdwy 5th: rdn appr 3 out: sn wknd* **12/1**
0P0- **7** *23* **Passing Fiesta**[22] 3956 5-10-4 0.. BenPoste[(5)] 62
(Sarah-Jayne Davies) *hld up: hdwy appr 3 out: sn rdn and wknd* **100/1**
8 *3 ¼* **Alberto's Dream** 5-11-2 0.. FelixDeGiles 66
(Tom Symonds) *hld up: hmpd 1st: j. slowly 5th: sn wknd* **33/1**
0- **9** *1 ¼* **Kagouillot (FR)**[18] 4024 5-10-9 0... PaulJohn[(7)] 65
(Reginald Brown) *led to 5th: rdn and wknd bef next* **100/1**
0/ **10** *18* **Nowweareseven**[400] 3670 7-10-9 0......................... SamTwiston-Davies 40
(Nigel Twiston-Davies) *hld up: sme hdwy after 5th: wknd bef next: bhd whn blnd last* **10/1**
5/0- **11** *25* **Sleepy (FR)**[19] 4018 8-11-2 0.. PaulMoloney 22
(Sophie Leech) *hld up: bhd fr 4th* **50/1**
P0- **12** *99* **Sarahs Doll**[14] 4091 6-10-6 0... RobertDunne[(3)]
(Dai Burchell) *j.rt: sn bhd* **250/1**
/P3- **P** **Shays River (IRE)**[19] 4088 9-11-2 0......................................(bt) AdamWedge
(Evan Williams) *mid-div: lost pl 4th: bhd fr next: p.u bef last* **25/1**

4m 1.6s (12.10) **Going Correction** +0.85s/f (Soft) 13 Ran SP% **115.3**
Speed ratings (Par 105): **103,101,98,96,95 93,81,79,79,70 57,8,**
CSF £24.89 TOTE £4.90: £2.10, £2.90, £1.10; EX 29.30 Trifecta £197.10.
Owner Paul Williams **Bred** Mrs Claire Massey **Trained** Portway, Worcs

FOCUS
The water jump and the hurdle by the golf clubhouse (first one past the stands) had to be omitted due to the state of the ground. The going was officially heavy with soft places. Will Kennedy called it "testing" and Aidan Coleman described it as "gluey and soft." The size of this field masked its lack of competitiveness and this looks to be just modest form. The winner is rated 5lb off his best.

4351 SHUKERS LAND ROVER H'CAP HURDLE (10 hdls 1 omitted) 2m 5f
2:40 (2:42) (Class 4) (0-115,115) 4-Y-0+ **£5,198** (£1,526; £763; £381)

Form RPR
PP3- **1** **Still Believing (IRE)**[14] 4090 6-11-0 **110**............................ ConorRing[(7)] 113+
(Evan Williams) *a.p: jnd ldr 2 out: rdn to ld flat: r.o* **8/1**
534- **2** *1 ½* **Broadway Symphony (IRE)**[26] 3877 7-11-12 **115**.............. MarkGrant 116
(Tracey L Bailey) *hld up in tch: racd keenly: hit 3 out: led next: rdn: hung lft and hdd flat: styd on same pce* **9/1**
332- **3** *12* **Buckhorn Tom**[18] 4028 6-11-9 **112**..................................(p) BrendanPowell 104
(Colin Tizzard) *led tl after 5th: led again appr and hit 3 out: hdd and hit next: blnd and wknd last* **6/1**
62P- **4** *10* **Murtys Delight (IRE)**[26] 3884 7-11-6 **109**.............(t) SamTwiston-Davies 88
(Dr Richard Newland) *chsd ldrs tl rdn and wknd appr 3 out* **15/2**
005- **5** *½* **Market Option (IRE)**[29] 3821 8-11-3 **106**.......................... AidanColeman 85
(Venetia Williams) *chsd ldrs: drvn along after 6th: wknd appr 3 out* **7/2**[1]
406- **6** *30* **Who's Jeff (IRE)**[39] 3650 6-10-12 **101**.................................. TomO'Brien 60
(Philip Hobbs) *hld up: plld hrd: hdwy 4th: led after next: hdd & wknd appr 3 out* **11/2**[3]
443/ **7** *32* **Annaluna (IRE)**[24] 4270 5-10-13 **102**.............................. DominicElsworth 19
(David Evans) *hld up: effrt after 7th: wknd bef next* **33/1**
214- **8** *9* **Kings Apollo**[62] 3174 5-10-6 **95**.. FelixDeGiles 3
(Tom Symonds) *hld up: a in rr: drvn along after 7th: sn wknd* **5/1**[2]
542- **P** **Captain Cardington (IRE)**[70] 3025 5-10-9 **105**..........(v) CiaranMckee[(7)]
(John O'Shea) *chsd ldrs: rdn after 5th: sn wknd: bhd fr next: p.u bef 3 out* **16/1**
F2- **R** **Juno The Muffinman (IRE)**[66] 3118 5-11-6 **112**.......... MichaelByrne[(3)]
(Tim Vaughan) *ref to r* **20/1**

5m 32.6s (17.80) **Going Correction** +0.85s/f (Soft) 10 Ran SP% **115.0**
Speed ratings (Par 105): **100,99,94,91,90 79,67,63, ,**
CSF £76.16 CT £463.82 TOTE £13.00: £2.70, £4.00, £1.30; EX 85.80 Trifecta £332.00.
Owner R E R Williams **Bred** Declan Moran **Trained** Llancarfan, Vale Of Glamorgan

The Form Book Jumps, Raceform Ltd, Compton, RG20 6NL.

FOCUS
An ordinary handicap hurdle which was wide open. The first two are on the upgrade.

4352 WEATHERBYS HAMILTON INSURANCE H'CAP CHASE (12 fncs 1 omitted) 2m
3:15 (3:15) (Class 4) (0-110,110) 5-Y-0+ £4,279 (£2,150; £1,075; £538; £269)

Form RPR
124- 1 **Riddleofthesands (IRE)**[63] 3156 10-11-2 100.....(t) SamTwiston-Davies 107
(Nigel Twiston-Davies) *chsd clr ldr to 4th: remained handy: rdn appr 4 out: hung lft bef last: styd on u.p to ld nr fin* 13/2
P3F- 2 ½ **Lucky Sunny (IRE)**[12] 4131 11-11-12 110........................ AidanColeman 118+
(Venetia Williams) *led and sn clr tl appr 4 out: blnd next: rdn bef last: hdd nr fin* 9/4[1]
P03- 3 1½ **Moulin De La Croix**[55] 3248 10-10-9 100..................(t) JackSherwood(7) 104
(Oliver Sherwood) *prom: chsd ldr appr 4 out: rdn and hung lft appr last: n.m.r and unable qck towards fin* 8/1
124- 4 9 **Free World (FR)**[14] 4089 10-11-2 107.............................. MissLBrooke(7) 105
(Lady Susan Brooke) *chsd ldrs: wnt 2nd 4th: rdn appr 4 out: wknd flat* 8/1
22F- 5 10 **Think Its All Over (USA)**[59] 3222 7-10-11 95.................. AdamWedge 82
(Evan Williams) *hld up: effrt appr 4 out: wknd appr 2 out* 10/3[2]
314- 6 18 **Cooldine Run (IRE)**[14] 4080 10-10-11 102......................(t) MrJarrett(7) 77
(John Needham) *hld up: 5th whn blnd and rdr lost iron 7th: sn bhd* 11/2[3]
PPP- P **Humbel Ben (IRE)**[36] 3693 11-10-12 96.............................(tp) TomO'Brien
(Alan Jones) *sn pushed along and bhd: p.u bef 4 out* 25/1

4m 16.4s (17.90) **Going Correction** +1.125s/f (Heav) 7 Ran SP% **108.6**
Speed ratings: **100,99,99,94,89 80,**
CSF £20.16 TOTE £4.90: £2.30, £1.70; EX 14.30 Trifecta £105.50.
Owner N A Twiston-Davies **Bred** Terence Kelly **Trained** Naunton, Gloucs
■ Stewards' Enquiry : Aidan Coleman four-day ban: used whip above permitted level (Mar 5-8)

FOCUS
Question marks over a few of these coming into the contest and it turned into a messy sort of race with a close finish. The winner is rated to his mark.

4353 WEATHERBYS CHELTENHAM FESTIVAL BETTING GUIDE H'CAP HURDLE (8 hdls 1 omitted) 2m
3:45 (3:46) (Class 3) (0-125,125) 4-Y-0+ £9,495 (£2,805; £1,402; £702; £351)

Form RPR
312- 1 **Baltimore Rock (IRE)**[12] 4129 5-11-3 116..................... TomScudamore 129+
(David Pipe) *hld up: hdwy appr 3 out: led last: rdn out* 6/4[1]
230- 2 3¾ **Canadian Diamond (IRE)**[34] 3744 7-11-5 125................ MikeyHamill(7) 130
(Brendan Powell) *a.p: chsd ldr appr 4th: led next: hdd 3 out: ev ch last: rdn and hung lft flat: styd on same pce* 7/1
321- 3 ½ **Whispering Harry**[16] 4072 5-10-5 104.............................. DominicElsworth 108
(Henry Oliver) *led: hit 4th: hdd next: led again 3 out: rdn and hdd last: no ex flat* 13/2[3]
000- 4 24 **Hold Court (IRE)**[51] 3419 7-11-5 118.................................(p) PaulMoloney 105
(Evan Williams) *chsd ldrs tl rdn and wknd after 2 out* 9/4[2]
006- 5 12 **Thinger Licht (FR)**[54] 3324 5-10-6 105.................................. LeeEdwards 73
(Tony Carroll) *prom tl wknd appr 3 out* 33/1
/00- 6 2 **Grams And Ounces**[34] 3744 7-10-11 110..............................(t) RhysFlint 76
(John Flint) *hld up: wkng whn mstke 3 out* 16/1
1/6- 7 23 **Miss Tique (FR)**[26] 3884 6-11-4 117.................................. AidanColeman 60
(Venetia Williams) *chsd ldr to appr 4th: rdn and wknd bef 3 out* 12/1

4m 0.3s (10.80) **Going Correction** +0.85s/f (Soft) 7 Ran SP% **113.1**
Speed ratings (Par 107): **107,105,104,92,86 85,74**
CSF £12.32 CT £51.95 TOTE £2.40: £1.10, £3.20; EX 14.60 Trifecta £64.50.
Owner R S Brookhouse **Bred** Lynn Lodge Stud And Foxtale Farm **Trained** Nicholashayne, Devon

FOCUS
A fair race and a decent performance from the winner, who's on the upgrade.

4354 TEME CONDITIONAL JOCKEYS' H'CAP CHASE (17 fncs 2 omitted) 3m
4:15 (4:19) (Class 4) (0-105,105) 5-Y-0+ £6,173 (£1,812; £906; £453)

Form RPR
422- 1 **Take The Mick**[26] 3876 7-11-5 101.............................. CallumWhillans(3) 125+
(Venetia Williams) *mde all: clr fr 3 out: easily* 9/4[1]
442- 2 21 **Lough Coi (IRE)**[13] 4109 8-10-4 88..........................(vt) CharlieDeutsch(5) 87
(Anthony Middleton) *hld up: hdwy 9th: chsd wnr 11th: rdn and wknd 3 out* 8/1
062- 3 shd **Craiglands (IRE)**[26] 3879 12-10-4 83...............................(v) KielanWoods 83
(Ian Williams) *prom: pushed along 9th: rdn and wknd 3 out* 10/1
31P- 4 22 **Flemi Two Toes (IRE)**[37] 3691 8-11-9 102........................(p) JackQuinlan 79
(Sarah Humphrey) *hld up: hdwy appr 10th: wknd bef 4 out* 12/1
103- 5 5 **Jump Up**[28] 3836 8-11-3 96...(v[1]) MichaelByrne 68
(Peter Bowen) *prom: rdn after 13th: wknd bef next* 25/1
0P0- 6 nk **Midnight Macarena**[19] 4021 9-11-12 105.......................(p) MichealNolan 77
(Lucy Wadham) *prom: chsd wnr 8th: j.rt next: lost 2nd 11th: wknd 4 out* 33/1
414- 7 39 **Le Grand Chene (FR)**[34] 3730 8-11-0 96........................(t) KieronEdgar(3) 29
(Sophie Leech) *hld up: j.rt 6th: hdwy 11th: wknd 13th* 16/1
443/ P **Night Safe (IRE)**[328] 4980 13-11-3 102............................(p) RyanHatch(6)
(Nigel Twiston-Davies) *chsd ldrs: stmbld 10th: sn lost pl: bhd fr 12th: p.u bef 4 out* 12/1
000- P **Gran Torino (IRE)**[71] 3007 9-11-6 102................................ AdamWedge(3)
(Evan Williams) *hld up: wknd 11th: bhd whn p.u bef 4 out* 12/1
5U5- P **Genny Wren**[48] 3502 8-10-10 89...(t) JoshuaMoore
(Renee Robeson) *hld up: bhd fr 9th: p.u bef next* 15/2[3]
112- P **Milosam (IRE)**[22] 3958 7-10-11 93...................................(b) JamesBest(3)
(Philip Hobbs) *chsd wnr tl pushed along 8th: rdn appr 10th: wknd 13th: bhd whn p.u bef 3 out* 4/1[2]

6m 33.3s (25.00) **Going Correction** +1.125s/f (Heav) 11 Ran SP% **118.5**
Speed ratings: **103,96,95,88,86 86,73,,,**
CSF £21.52 CT £153.92 TOTE £3.00: £1.30, £4.00, £2.70; EX 28.10 Trifecta £314.30.
Owner Sir Geoffrey & Lady Vos **Bred** G C And Mrs V M Vos **Trained** Kings Caple, H'fords

FOCUS
Back-to-back wins in this race for Venetia Williams. A step up from the winner and there's a case for rating the form a few pounds higher.

4355 CGA FOXHUNTER TRIAL HUNTERS' CHASE (FOR THE MAGNUS-ALLCROFT MEMORIAL TROPHY) (15 fncs 2 omitted) 2m 4f
4:45 (4:49) (Class 5) 5-Y-0+ £2,495 (£774; £386; £193)

Form RPR
2/2- 1 **Made In Time (IRE)**[14] 4092 9-11-13 129............(t) MissLeandaTickle(7) 128+
(Rebecca Curtis) *a.p: chsd ldr 9th: led 11th: hdd bef 4 out: led appr last: styd on wl* 5/4[1]
3/F- 2 6 **Martys Mission (IRE)**[20] 3993 12-11-13 109............ MrDavidPrichard(3) 116
(Miss Becky Furber) *hld up: hdwy 11th: rdn appr 4 out: styd on to go 2nd towards fin: no ch w wnr* 12/1
/03- 3 1 **Fresh Air And Fun (IRE)**[54] 11-11-11 112....................... MrLRPayter(5) 116
(Alastair Ralph) *mid-div: hdwy 12th: rdn appr 4 out: styd on to go 3rd nr fin* 28/1
222- 4 ¾ **Rob Conti (FR)**[123] 1969 9-12-1 131.................................. MrDMaxwell(5) 119
(Philip Hobbs) *mid-div: hdwy 8th: led appr 4 out: mstke 2 out: hdd appr last: no ex flat* 7/2[2]
32F/ 5 16 **Bermuda Boy (FR)**[38] 9-11-9 114..............................(tp) MrJHamilton(3) 98
(S Flook) *hld up: hdwy 9th: rdn after 12th: wknd 2 out* 20/1
2/5- 6 44 **Cool Friend (IRE)**[294] 63 11-11-13 114.............................. MrOGreenall 71
(Oliver Greenall) *hld up: drvn along 11th: wknd 4 out* 8/1[3]
500/ P **Safari Adventures (IRE)**[436] 2974 12-11-5 0.......(t) MrRichardPatrick(7)
(Richard A Thomas) *a in rr: bhd fr 6th: p.u bef 9th* 66/1
/P3- P **The General Lee (IRE)**[14] 4092 12-11-11 108.............. MissLBrooke(5)
(Lady Susan Brooke) *hld up: bhd fr 8th: p.u bef next* 22/1
P50/ P **Tara Royal**[24] 9-12-6 0...(t) MrPYork
(P York) *led: hdd 2nd: chsd ldr tl led again 8th: hdd 11th: rdn and wknd after next: bhd whn p.u bef 4 out* 11/1
P **Walter Wallace (IRE)**[38] 9-11-7 0.......................... MrMatthewBarber(5)
(S Flook) *chsd ldrs to 11th: bhd whn p.u bef 4 out* 40/1
/1P- P **Rebel Alliance (IRE)**[257] 655 9-11-9 0......................(t) MrWHickman(7)
(Richard A Thomas) *led 2nd to 8th: rdn and wknd appr 4 out: blnd next: sn p.u* 33/1
22/ P **Sawago (FR)**[357] 4455 8-11-5 94...................................(tp) MrWMaskill(7)
(Miss E Rodney) *hld up: a in rr: bhd fr 10th: p.u bef 4 out* 40/1
P/ P **Wiston Dreamer**[268] 8-11-5 0...(p) MrEDavid(7)
(R E Luke) *prom: t.k.h: wknd appr 4 out: blnd next: sn p.u* 80/1

5m 33.1s (28.70) **Going Correction** +1.125s/f (Heav) 13 Ran SP% **116.9**
Speed ratings: **87,84,84,83,77 59,,,,,,,**
CSF £15.45 TOTE £2.50: £1.10, £3.60, £4.20; EX 13.80 Trifecta £404.80.
Owner John P McManus **Bred** J And J Lawler **Trained** Newport, Dyfed

FOCUS
An above-average renewal of this hunter chase. The cosy winner was close to his recent level.

4356 ANNUAL MEMBERS CHELTENHAM PREVIEW ON 27TH FEBRUARY MAIDEN HURDLE (10 hdls 2 omitted) 3m
5:15 (5:15) (Class 4) 4-Y-0+ £3,898 (£1,144; £572; £286)

Form RPR
624- 1 **Sybarite (FR)**[31] 3800 8-11-4 116............................ SamTwiston-Davies 117+
(Nigel Twiston-Davies) *hld up: hdwy 6th: chsd ldr appr 3 out: sn rdn: led last: styd on wl* 7/2[2]
/P3- 2 7 **Island Cruise (IRE)**[14] 4093 6-11-4 0..................................(t) ColinBolger 110
(Pat Murphy) *trckd ldr: led 2nd to 5th: led again after 7th: rdn and hdd last: no ex flat* 20/1
363- 3 27 **Master Butcher (IRE)**[81] 2808 7-10-8 0.......................... PaulO'Brien(10) 83
(Rebecca Curtis) *plld hrd: hld up in tch: rdn and wknd 3 out* 11/2[3]
224- 4 20 **Floral Spinner**[14] 4090 7-10-11 105................................. BrendanPowell 56
(Bill Turner) *chsd ldrs: outpcd 6th: rallied appr 3 out: sn wknd* 13/2
424- P **Regal Diamond (IRE)**[25] 3889 6-11-4 130...................... DonalDevereux
(Peter Bowen) *led to 2nd: led again 5th: j.big 7th: sn hdd: wknd appr 3 out: p.u bef next* 5/6[1]

6m 19.8s (27.50) **Going Correction** +0.85s/f (Soft) 5 Ran SP% **110.3**
Speed ratings (Par 105): **88,85,76,70,**
CSF £44.12 TOTE £3.10: £2.30, £5.20; EX 42.20 Trifecta £152.10.
Owner H R Mould **Bred** Mme Andre Vagne And Bruno Vagne **Trained** Naunton, Gloucs

FOCUS
A good test on churned up ground for these maiden hurdlers. The winner was close to the best of his recent runs.
T/Plt: £30.10 to a £1 stake. Pool: £69,638.71 - 1683.64 winning units. T/Qpdt: £9.00 to a £1 stake. Pool: 4478.66 - 366.34 winning units. CR

4357 - 4363a (Foreign Racing) - See Raceform Interactive

4199 AYR (L-H)
Thursday, February 20

OFFICIAL GOING: Heavy (soft in places; chs - 7.3, hdl 7.5)
Penultimate fence in back straight omitted all chases.
Wind: Fairly strong, across Weather: Overcast, showers

4364 KERR & SMITH AYR DAF MAIDEN HURDLE (9 hdls) 2m
2:20 (2:21) (Class 5) 4-Y-0+ £2,395 (£698; £349)

Form RPR
623- 1 **Titus Bolt (IRE)**[9] 4199 5-11-2 119.................................. JamesReveley 112+
(Jim Goldie) *led to 2nd: w ldr: led bef 3 out: rdn next: hld on wl run-in* 4/6[1]
02P- 2 ¾ **Pixie Cut (IRE)**[24] 3934 4-9-9 0.................................... HarryChalloner(5) 95+
(Alistair Whillans) *t.k.h: cl up: led 2nd to bef 3 out: rdn bef next: styd on fr last: hld towards fin* 20/1
6- 3 12 **Itstimeforapint (IRE)**[19] 4043 6-11-2 0............................ PeterBuchanan 99
(Lucinda Russell) *hld up: outpcd after 4 out: styd on fr 2 out: no ch w first two* 50/1
604- 4 2 **Bobs Lady Tamure**[9] 4199 7-10-2 0....................(t) StephenMulqueen(7) 91
(Maurice Barnes) *t.k.h: in tch: hdwy and cl up bef 3 out: rdn and wknd next* 20/1
4/5- 5 21 **Scorpions Sting (IRE)**[110] 2217 5-11-2 0......................... NickScholfield 76
(James Ewart) *t.k.h: chsd ldrs tl rdn and wknd bef 3 out* 14/1[3]
P **King Vahe (IRE)**[72] 5-11-2 0.. KennyJohnson
(Robert Johnson) *mstkes in rr: struggling 4 out: t.o whn p.u bef next* 250/1
322- U **Frankie's Promise (IRE)**[49] 3495 6-11-2 109................. LucyAlexander
(N W Alexander) *cl up: nt fluent and uns rdr 1st* 15/8[2]
U53- F **Marrakech Trader (NZ)**[24] 3935 7-11-2 0........................ WilsonRenwick 89
(Rose Dobbin) *t.k.h early: prom: effrt and rdn bef 3 out: wknd next: 4th and btn whn fell last* 40/1

4m 20.7s (17.60) **Going Correction** +1.25s/f (Heav)
WFA 4 from 5yo+ 9lb 8 Ran SP% **115.8**
Speed ratings (Par 103): **106,105,99,98,88 ,,**
CSF £17.56 TOTE £1.40: £1.02, £3.90, £6.10; EX 19.20 Trifecta £244.60.
Owner Ian G M Dalgleish **Bred** Patrick Brady **Trained** Uplawmoor, E Renfrews

FOCUS
Both tracks 10m from innermost line, divided bends. An ordinary maiden. The winner and fourth are rated in line with recent C&D form.

4365 3B CONSTRUCTION LTD H'CAP HURDLE (12 hdls) 2m 5f 110y
2:50 (2:52) (Class 4) (0-120,120) 4-Y-O+ **£3,573** (£1,049; £524; £262)

Form RPR
321- **1** **Too Cool To Fool (IRE)**[9] 4203 11-10-4 **98** JamesReveley 97
(Jim Goldie) *pressed ldr: led 4 out to after next: sn rdn: rallied: styd on to hd idling ldr last 50yds: drvn out* **2/1**[1]
421- **2** *nk* **Makhzoon (USA)**[20] 4002 10-11-4 **119** (v) DiarmuidO'Regan[(7)] 119
(N W Alexander) *led to 4 out: rdn and regained ld after next: hung rt and idled on run-in: hdd last 50yds: kpt on towards fin* **11/2**[3]
/35- **3** *¾* **Little Boy Boru (IRE)**[24] 3938 6-10-4 **105** GerFox[(7)] 103
(S R B Crawford, Ire) *in tch: stdy hdwy bef 3 out: rdn and outpcd bef next: rallied appr last: kpt on run-in: hld last 50yds* **8/1**
3- **4** *shd* **Romantic Fashion (IRE)**[32] 3804 7-11-6 **114** PaulMoloney 112
(Mrs Prunella Dobbs, Ire) *chsd ldrs: drvn and outpcd bef 2 out: rallied appr last: kpt on run-in* **5/2**[2]
11P- **5** *1 ¾* **Vinny Gambini (IRE)**[56] 3286 7-11-10 **118** WilsonRenwick 114
(Rose Dobbin) *hld up in tch: stdy hdwy bef 3 out: rdn and outpcd bef next: rallied last: kpt on same pce run-in* **8/1**
12F- **F** **Dickie Henderhoop (IRE)**[53] 3396 9-10-3 **104** (b) MikeyEnnis[(7)]
(Lucy Normile) *in tch on outside: fell 3rd* **9/1**

6m 16.5s (36.20) **Going Correction** +1.25s/f (Heavy) **6** Ran SP% **109.5**
Speed ratings (Par 105): **84,83,83,83,82**
CSF £12.55 TOTE £3.40: £2.90, £3.10; EX 13.40 Trifecta £56.00.
Owner Johnnie Delta Racing **Bred** Simon Young **Trained** Uplawmoor, E Renfrews

FOCUS
A modest handicap and a bunched finish. The winner is rated below the best of his 2013 hurdle form.

4366 Q8OILS H'CAP HURDLE (9 hdls) 2m
3:20 (3:22) (Class 5) (0-100,100) 4-Y-O+ **£2,274** (£667; £333; £166)

Form RPR
653- **1** **Rosquero (FR)**[36] 3723 9-10-5 **79** (v[1]) KennyJohnson 86+
(Robert Johnson) *mde all: rdn 3 out: kpt on strly fr last* **17/2**
/24- **2** *4* **Scimon Templar (FR)**[9] 4201 6-11-3 **94** TonyKelly[(3)] 97
(Pauline Robson) *prom: nt fluent 4th: effrt and chsd wnr 3 out: drvn next: nt fluent last: kpt on same pce* **11/4**[2]
020- **3** *25* **Acordingtoscript (IRE)**[24] 3940 8-10-8 **82** WilsonRenwick 60
(Martin Todhunter) *pressed wnr and sn clr of rest: rdn whn hit and lost 2nd 3 out: wknd bef next* **16/1**
225- **4** *2 ¾* **Cadore (IRE)**[48] 3518 6-11-3 **98** (p) MikeyEnnis[(7)] 73
(Lucy Normile) *hld up bhd ldng gp: shortlived effrt after 4 out: hung lft and no imp fr next* **13/2**[3]
640- **5** *16* **Badea**[47] 3527 5-11-1 **94** HarryChalloner[(5)] 53
(Martin Todhunter) *hld up: struggling 1/2-way: nvr on terms* **33/1**
U4F- **6** *1 ½* **King's Chorister**[41] 3639 8-10-8 **82** (t) LucyAlexander 40
(Barry Murtagh) *hld up: struggling after 5th: btn after next* **10/1**
/05- **7** *14* **The Starboard Bow**[24] 3940 7-11-9 **97** (p) PeterBuchanan 41
(Lucinda Russell) *prom: drvn and outpcd 1/2-way: sn btn* **12/1**
543/ **P** **Double Whammy**[763] 3805 8-11-12 **100** JasonMaguire
(Iain Jardine) *bhd: pushed along after 3rd: struggling fr 1/2-way: t.o whn p.u bef 3 out* **14/1**
000- **P** **Heurtevent (FR)**[55] 3328 5-11-7 **95** LeeEdwards
(Tony Carroll) *chsd ldrs: drvn and outpcd whn hit 4 out: sn struggling: t.o whn p.u next* **9/4**[1]

4m 20.5s (17.40) **Going Correction** +1.25s/f (Heavy) **9** Ran SP% **113.6**
Speed ratings (Par 103): **106,104,91,90,82 81,74, ,**
CSF £32.40 CT £369.06 TOTE £8.50: £2.40, £1.30, £6.40; EX 32.10 Trifecta £235.90.
Owner Alan Kidd Dave Bamlet Racing R Johnson **Bred** Denis Fontaine **Trained** Newburn, Tyne & Wear
■ The first winner since March 2012 for veteran jockey Kenny Johnson.

FOCUS
A weak handicap. The winner is rated back to his best.

4367 KERR & SMITH CUMNOCK VAUXHALL NOVICES' CHASE (11 fncs 1 omitted) 2m
3:50 (3:51) (Class 4) 5-Y-O+ **£3,898** (£1,144; £572; £286)

Form RPR
2FF- **1** **Little Glenshee (IRE)**[30] 3823 8-10-5 120 LucyAlexander 111
(N W Alexander) *cl up: wnt 2nd 1/2-way to 4 out: regained 2nd 2 out: effrt and led run-in: hld on gamely* **5/2**[2]
/44- **2** *shd* **Up And Go (FR)**[69] 3057 6-10-12 137 JasonMaguire 118
(Donald McCain) *cl up: led 4th: rdn appr last: hdd run-in: rallied: jst hld* **5/4**[1]
004- **3** *9* **You'resomedreamer (IRE)**[49] 3494 6-10-12 93 PeterBuchanan 110
(Lucinda Russell) *hld up bhd ldng gp: effrt and rdn bef 4 out: one pce fr last* **33/1**
241- **4** *8* **Indian Voyage (IRE)**[15] 4080 6-10-12 103 (t) StephenMulqueen[(7)] 110
(Maurice Barnes) *in tch: hdwy to chse ldr 4 out: nt fluent and stmbld next: sn rdn: wknd after 2 out* **8/1**
300- **5** *22* **Sudski Star (IRE)**[8] 4223 6-10-12 95 JamesReveley 86
(Patrick Griffin, Ire) *led to 4th: cl up: outpcd 4 out: hld whn blnd next: sn btn* **66/1**
15F- **P** **Rockawango (FR)**[7] 4235 8-11-5 130 (tp) NickScholfield
(James Ewart) *chsd ldrs: outpcd 1/2-way: struggling bef 4 out: t.o whn p.u bef 2 out* **9/2**[3]

4m 31.4s (20.70) **Going Correction** +1.525s/f (Heavy) **6** Ran SP% **106.7**
Speed ratings: **109,108,104,100,89**
CSF £5.69 TOTE £1.80: £1.10, £3.00; EX 8.50 Trifecta £70.80.
Owner Turcan Barber Douglas Miller Dunning 1 **Bred** Alexander Family **Trained** Kinneston, Perth & Kinross

FOCUS
A fairly decent novice chase. The form could be rated higher through the winner and second's hurdles form.

4368 IMPERIAL FLYER H'CAP CHASE (17 fncs 2 omitted) 3m 1f
4:20 (4:20) (Class 4) (0-120,118) 5-Y-O+ **£4,548** (£1,335; £667; £333)

Form RPR
313- **1** **The Friary (IRE)**[67] 3111 7-11-3 **114** (tp) DerekFox[(5)] 122
(Lucinda Russell) *in tch: hit 12th: hdwy to ld bef 2 out: hrd pressed fr last: edgd rt and styd on gamely u.p* **5/1**[3]
P46- **2** *hd* **Mister Philson (IRE)**[15] 4094 9-10-8 **107** (p) GerFox[(7)] 115
(S R B Crawford, Ire) *cl up: led 6th: jnd 9th: rdn and hdd bef 2 out: rallied bef last: ev ch whn blkd: kpt on: hld nr fin* **5/1**[3]
P31- **3** *20* **Oil Burner**[24] 3936 9-10-13 **105** JamesReveley 97
(William Amos) *sn chsng ldrs: chal after 9th to bef 2 out: sn rdn and wknd* **6/4**[1]
0P0- **4** *34* **Outlaw Tom (IRE)**[52] 3413 10-11-1 **107** (p) PeterBuchanan 74
(Lucinda Russell) *led to 6th: pckd 9th: pushed along 5 out: rdn and wknd after next* **18/1**
/51- **P** **Knockgraffon King (IRE)**[47] 3526 9-11-12 **118** (b[1]) JasonMaguire
(Donald McCain) *chsd ldrs: hit and lost pl 2nd: struggling fr 1/2-way: t.o whn p.u bef 4 out* **5/2**[2]

7m 26.1s (36.20) **Going Correction** +1.525s/f (Heavy) **5** Ran SP% **107.2**
Speed ratings: **103,102,96,85,**
CSF £26.01 TOTE £5.90: £3.70, £1.90; EX 16.60 Trifecta £41.20.
Owner Mrs S Russell & A M Russell **Bred** Michael And Fiona O'Connor **Trained** Arlary, Perth & Kinross
■ Stewards' Enquiry : Ger Fox four-day ban: used whip above permitted level (Mar 6-9)

FOCUS
A fair staying handicap. The first two are rated to their marks.

4369 IAIN WATT HAULAGE H'CAP HURDLE (9 hdls) 2m
4:50 (4:53) (Class 3) (0-135,135) 4-Y-O+ **£6,498** (£1,908; £954; £477)

Form RPR
51- **1** **Great Link**[48] 2886 5-9-12 **112** (t) JoshHamer[(5)] 112+
(Tony Carroll) *prom: hdwy to ld 3 out: drvn out fr last* **7/1**[3]
031- **2** *1 ¼* **Trucking Along (IRE)**[33] 3793 8-11-9 **135** MrSCrawford[(3)] 134
(S R B Crawford, Ire) *hld up in tch: stdy hdwy 3 out: effrt and pushed along after next: chsd wnr run-in: kpt on* **3/1**[2]
322- **3** *nse* **Another Mattie (IRE)**[36] 3721 7-10-5 **114** (t) LucyAlexander 112
(N W Alexander) *chsd ldrs: lost pl 3rd: rallied 4 out: rdn and outpcd bef 2 out: hung lft and rallied bef last: kpt on run-in: no imp* **9/4**[1]
014- **4** *2 ¼* **Stormin Exit (IRE)**[18] 4053 11-10-11 **120** JamesReveley 117
(Jim Goldie) *led to bef 3 out: sn rdn along: kpt on same pce fr last* **10/1**
421- **5** *¾* **Final Assault (IRE)**[24] 3935 5-10-3 **112** PeterBuchanan 107
(Lucinda Russell) *pressed ldr: led briefly bef 3 out: rdn and kpt on same pce between last 2* **9/4**[1]

4m 19.5s (16.40) **Going Correction** +1.25s/f (Heavy)
WFA 4 from 5yo+ 9lb **5** Ran SP% **108.1**
Speed ratings (Par 107): **109,108,108,107,106**
CSF £26.65 TOTE £10.70: £4.30, £2.10; EX 31.40 Trifecta £95.40.
Owner Carl Hodgson **Bred** Granham Farm And P Hearson Bloodstock **Trained** Cropthorne, Worcs

FOCUS
A modest little handicap. A step up from the winner but there's probably more to come.

4370 KERR & SMITH GLASGOW IVECO STANDARD NATIONAL HUNT FLAT RACE (CONDITIONAL JOCKEYS/AMATEUR RIDERS) 2m
5:20 (5:22) (Class 6) 4-6-Y-O **£1,711** (£498; £249)

Form RPR
1 **Clan Chief** 5-10-11 0 MrKitAlexander[(7)] 106+
(N W Alexander) *trckd ldrs: rdn and outpcd over 3f out: rallied to ld over 1f out: pushed clr ins fnl f* **25/1**
221- **2** *6* **Flying Eagle (IRE)**[90] 2654 6-11-4 0 MrSPBowen[(7)] 107
(Peter Bowen) *t.k.h: led at slow pce: rdn over 2f out: hdd over 1f out: kpt on same pce* **4/5**[1]
3 *3 ¾* **Cottenwood (IRE)** 6-10-11 0 MrCJMiller[(7)] 96
(Nicky Richards) *plld hrd: in tch: hdwy and ev ch 3f out: rdn and outpcd wl over 1f out* **9/1**[3]
4 *2 ¼* **John Mor** 5-11-1 0 MrSCrawford[(3)] 94
(S R B Crawford, Ire) *t.k.h: hld up in last: stdy hdwy over 3f out: sn outpcd: rallied 2f out: sn no imp* **15/8**[2]
6- **5** *5* **Sonny Thyne**[34] 3760 5-10-11 0 GrahamWatters[(7)] 89
(Lucinda Russell) *chsd ldr: rdn and outpcd over 3f out: btn fnl 2f* **20/1**

4m 32.4s (34.90) **Going Correction** +1.25s/f (Heavy)
WFA 4 from 5yo 9lb 5 from 6yo 1lb **5** Ran SP% **108.9**
Speed ratings: **62,59,57,56,53**
CSF £45.99 TOTE £10.60: £4.10, £1.10; EX 45.30 Trifecta £77.50.
Owner Clan Gathering **Bred** Alexander Family **Trained** Kinneston, Perth & Kinross

FOCUS
An ordinary bumper which turned into something of a sprint up the home straight off a slow gallop. Very suspect form.
T/Plt: £248.90 to a £1 stake. Pool: £59,608.00 - 174.76 winning units. T/Qpdt: £57.90 to a £1 stake. Pool: 4629.20 - 59.10 winning units. RY

4108 HUNTINGDON (R-H)
Thursday, February 20

OFFICIAL GOING: Chase course - soft (heavy in places on stable bend); hurdle course - soft (good to soft in places; heavy in places on stable bend; chs 5.9, hdl 6.7)
The last fence in the home straight and the first fence in the back straight were omitted.
Wind: light to medium, across Weather: showers clearing, bright spells

4371 GET FREE BETS @STANJAMES ON TWITTER NOVICES' H'CAP HURDLE (8 hdls) 2m 110y
2:10 (2:10) (Class 4) (0-105,105) 4-Y-O+ **£3,249** (£954; £477; £238)

Form RPR
653- **1** **Winged Crusader (IRE)**[35] 3747 6-11-8 **101** SamTwiston-Davies 110+
(Nigel Twiston-Davies) *in tch in midfield: wnt 2nd and travelling strly after 3 out: led between last 2: stmbld sltly last: rdn and styd on wl flat: rdn out* **9/2**[2]
032- **2** *5* **Qasser (IRE)**[54] 3353 5-10-6 **90** JamesBanks[(5)] 92
(Harry Whittington) *t.k.h: hld up in tch towards rr: clsd to trck ldrs after 3 out: wnt 2nd between last 2: 1 l down last: sn drvn and btn: outpcd fnl 150yds* **7/2**[1]
335- **3** *1 ½* **Tracking Time**[13] 4132 7-11-5 **105** MrJMartin[(7)] 105
(Andrew J Martin) *chsd ldrs: hdwy after 3rd: drvn bef 3 out: cl 3rd 2 out: no ex and outpcd in 3rd whn mstke last: one pce flat* **7/2**[1]
0/0- **4** *3 ¾* **Allusive Power (IRE)**[72] 3012 5-10-11 **90** CharliePoste 86
(Anna Brooks) *chsd ldr: mstke 4th: led 3 out: drvn and hrd pressed bef next: hdd between last 2: 4th and btn last: wknd flat* **25/1**

/55- **5** *shd* **Bold Adventure**[21] 3284 10-11-4 **97** .... LeightonAspell 94
(Willie Musson) *hld up in tch in last pair: rdn and outpcd after 5th: 5th and styng on whn j.lft last: n.d but plugged on flat* **13/2**[3]

050- **6** *8* **Epic Storm (IRE)**[30] 3821 6-10-11 **90** .... TomSiddall 79
(Martin Keighley) *in tch in midfield: rdn and struggling whn mstke 3 out: wl hld whn mstke next: wknd between last 2* **11/1**

000- **7** *1 ½* **Mr Fickle (IRE)**[70] 3034 5-11-9 **105** .... JoshuaMoore(3) 94
(Gary Moore) *a towards rr: in tch: mstke 5th: sn rdn and no hdwy: n.d fr next* **10/1**

36P- **8** *20* **Goodacres Garden (IRE)**[51] 3432 7-10-5 **87** .... PeterCarberry(3) 54
(Shaun Lycett) *chsd ldrs: rdn and lost pl after 4th: bhd 5th: wknd next: t.o flat* **9/1**

5F6- **9** *23* **Sportsreport (IRE)**[17] 4068 6-11-0 **93** .... AndrewThornton 37
(Seamus Mullins) *led: mstke 1st: hdd 3 out: fdd rapidly bef next: t.o flat* **14/1**

4m 13.55s (18.65) **Going Correction** +1.175s/f (Heav) **9** Ran SP% **113.9**
Speed ratings (Par 105): **103,100,99,98,98 94,93,84,73**
CSF £20.79 CT £60.38 TOTE £4.00: £1.10, £2.80, £1.90; EX 21.50 Trifecta £47.40.
Owner Imperial Racing Partnership No 6 **Bred** Mrs Hugh Baird **Trained** Naunton, Gloucs

FOCUS
The consensus amongst the jockeys after the opener was that the ground was "very holding". None of the nine runners in this modest novice handicap had been successful over hurdles before. A big step up from the winner.

4372 STANJAMES.COM WHO ARE YOU WITH H'CAP CHASE (FOR THE JOHN BIGG OXO MEMORIAL TROPHY) (12 fncs 4 omitted) 2m 4f 110y

2:40 (2:40) (Class 4) (0-115,114) 5-Y-0+ **£3,898** (£1,144; £572; £286)

Form RPR

434- **1** **Hollow Blue Sky (FR)**[27] 3879 7-11-7 **109** .... SamTwiston-Davies 121+
(Nigel Twiston-Davies) *in tch: hdwy to chse ldrs 9th: wnt 2nd and gng best after 3 out: led between last 2: 2 l ld and mstke last: sn in command: idling and drvn fnl 100yds: eased towards fin* **11/4**[1]

1/4- **2** *12* **Gentle Bob (IRE)**[28] 3859 9-11-12 **114** .... PaddyBrennan 116
(Tom George) *led: mstke 4th: jnd and u.p whn mstke 2 out: sn hdd: 2 l down and hld whn mstke last: wknd flat: eased towards fin* **11/2**[3]

032- **3** *13* **Todareistodo**[51] 3439 8-11-0 **102** .... MarkGrant 88
(Jim Old) *in tch in last pair: hdwy to chse ldrs 7th: wnt 2nd 3 out: 3rd and wknd u.p bef next* **6/1**

2/0- **4** *12* **Petit Ecuyer (FR)**[293] 98 8-10-11 **102** .... JoshuaMoore(3) 76
(Barry Brennan) *hld up in tch in rr: effrt to chse ldng trio sn after 3 out: drvn and wknd bef next: wl btn and j.lft 2 out* **50/1**

305- **5** *33* **Brassbound (USA)**[44] 3596 6-11-3 **105** .... AndrewThornton 46
(Caroline Bailey) *chsd ldr and j.big 2nd: lost 2nd 8th and sn dropped out: t.o bef 2 out* **14/1**

03F- **P** **Crystal Swing**[35] 3729 7-11-6 **108** .... WayneHutchinson
(Richard Phillips) *mstke 1st: chsd ldr tl 2nd: styd prom tl lost pl and rdn after 7th: lost tch 3 out: t.o 2 out* **9/1**

2F1- **P** **Trojan Sun**[27] 3879 8-11-10 **112** ....(t) FelixDeGiles
(Tom Symonds) *in tch in midfield: dropped to rr but stl in tch whn mstke 8th: mstke and lost tch next: t.o whn p.u after 3 out* **9/2**[2]

452- **P** **Lord Of The Dunes**[23] 3960 6-11-2 **104** ....(t) JoeTizzard
(Colin Tizzard) *chsd ldrs: rdn and fdd rapidly after 3 out: t.o whn p.u bef next* **9/2**[2]

5m 36.1s (30.80) **Going Correction** +1.60s/f (Heav) **8** Ran SP% **111.3**
Speed ratings: **105,100,95,90,78 , ,**
CSF £17.55 CT £79.28 TOTE £2.90: £1.10, £3.10, £1.90; EX 21.60 Trifecta £85.70.
Owner The Hollow Partnership **Bred** E A R L Elevage Des Loges **Trained** Naunton, Gloucs

FOCUS
The last fence in the home straight and first fence in the back straight were omitted in all chases, while the water jump was omitted on the first circuit in this race. Despite the early pace looking modest and the field remaining closely packed in the first half of the contest, they eventually finished very tired. The winner rates a personal best.

4373 STANJAMES.COM ON TWITTER AND FACEBOOK NOVICES' CHASE (10 fncs 2 omitted) 2m 110y

3:10 (3:10) (Class 3) 5-Y-0+ **£6,657** (£2,067; £1,113)

Form RPR

202- **1** **Shotavodka (IRE)**[29] 3831 8-11-0 0 .... APMcCoy 137+
(David Pipe) *j.lft: mde virtually all: rdn and asserted flat: styd on wl* **4/11**[1]

016- **2** *7* **Bellenos (FR)**[26] 3894 6-11-7 134 ....(t) HarrySkelton 134
(Dan Skelton) *t.k.h: trckd ldrs: wnt 2nd 2 out: rdn and effrt last: no ex and outpcd flat: btn whn rdr looked down and eased towards fin* **4/1**[2]

13F- **3** *4* **Flaming Charmer (IRE)**[35] 3745 6-11-7 122 .... JoeTizzard 128
(Colin Tizzard) *t.k.h: chsd ldrs: jnd wnr after 4th tl after 3 out: 3rd and btn next: wknd between last 2* **8/1**[3]

50- **F** **Wicklewood**[19] 4024 8-10-7 0 ....(t) RyanHatch(7)
(Mark Gillard) *in tch in last tl fell 4th* **150/1**

/4R- **R** **Duaiseoir (IRE)**[35] 3732 8-10-7 119 .... MrJHamilton(7)
(Venetia Williams) *chsd ldrs: 4th and pushed along after 4th: struggling and j.lft fr 6th: lost tch after 3 out: t.o whn ref last* **20/1**

4m 41.3s (31.10) **Going Correction** +1.60s/f (Heav) **5** Ran SP% **109.8**
Speed ratings: **90,86,84, ,**
CSF £2.42 TOTE £1.20: £1.10, £1.80; EX 2.20 Trifecta £4.10.
Owner Mrs Jane Gerard-Pearse **Bred** Alastair Pim **Trained** Nicholashayne, Devon

FOCUS
The water jump was omitted on the first circuit. An uncompetitive novice chase in which they went an ordinary pace, possibly being mindful of the conditions. The winner scored with a bit in hand and the next two ran to their marks.

4374 STANJAMES.COM SIDNEY BANKS MEMORIAL NOVICES' HURDLE (LISTED RACE) (10 hdls) 2m 4f 110y

3:40 (3:40) (Class 1) 4-Y-0+ **£11,888** (£4,452; £2,224; £1,110)

Form RPR

11- **1** **Mosspark (IRE)**[55] 3326 6-11-3 135 .... AidanColeman 141+
(Emma Lavelle) *w ldr tl led 3 out: drew clr and in command 2 out: styd on wl: rdn out* **9/2**[3]

144- **2** *5* **Spirit Of Shankly**[20] 4018 6-11-7 136 ....(t) NoelFehily 138
(Charlie Longsdon) *hld up wl in tch: rdn and effrt 3 out: chsd clr wnr next: kpt on but no imp* **7/2**[2]

12- **3** *1* **Carraig Mor (IRE)**[89] 2661 6-11-3 0 .... RobertThornton 134
(Alan King) *t.k.h: hld up in tch in last pair: hdwy to chse ldrs after 5th: led 7th tl next: rdn and btn bef 2 out: 3rd and hld whn mstke 2 out: plugged on same pce after* **4/6**[1]

124- **4** *22* **Chase The Spud**[27] 3884 6-11-3 120 .... PaddyBrennan 121
(Fergal O'Brien) *led: mstke 6th: hdd next: sn dropped to 4th and drvn: wknd after 3 out* **33/1**

231- **5** *51* **Chasse En Mer (FR)**[43] 3604 4-10-4 121 .... RichardJohnson 47
(Caroline Bailey) *t.k.h: chsd ldrs: hdwy to join ldrs 6th tl mstke 7th: sn dropped to last and lost tch: t.o* **25/1**

5m 16.6s (17.60) **Going Correction** +1.175s/f (Heav)
WFA 4 from 6yo 10lb **5** Ran SP% **107.2**
Speed ratings (Par 111): **113,111,110,102,82**
CSF £18.88 TOTE £5.20: £1.60, £1.50; EX 12.10 Trifecta £21.80.
Owner N Mustoe & Tim Syder **Bred** Mrs Anthea Smyth **Trained** Hatherden, Hants

FOCUS
Some very decent novices have taken this Listed hurdle over the years, including French Holly, Refinement and Time For Rupert since 1998. They didn't go a great pace and there wasn't much separating the quintet for well over a circuit, but again they finished tired. The winner is on the upgrade with the second and fourth setting the level.

4375 "LIKE" STANJAMESBET ON FACEBOOK MARES' NOVICES' HURDLE (10 hdls) 2m 5f 110y

4:10 (4:10) (Class 4) 4-Y-0+ **£3,249** (£954; £477; £238)

Form RPR

/05- **1** **Carolina Wren**[64] 3159 5-10-12 0 .... SamJones 113+
(Renee Robeson) *chsd ldrs tl hdwy to ld after 6th: mde rest: rdn between last 2: styd on wl: rdn out* **10/1**[3]

/4P- **2** *6* **Cabaret Girl**[61] 3203 7-10-12 0 .... AndrewThornton 107
(John O'Neill) *hld up wl in tch in last pair: trckd ldng pair 7th: c towards stands' rail and outpcd 2 out: j.rt last: edgd lft but kpt on u.p flat to go 2nd cl home* **11/4**[2]

232- **3** *½* **Princess Caetani (IRE)**[35] 3733 5-10-12 112 .... RichardJohnson 107
(David Dennis) *hld up wl in tch in rr: hdwy to chse wnr 7th: rdn and unable qck 2 out: edgd lft u.p between last 2: plugged on same pce flat and lost 2nd cl home* **4/9**[1]

245- **4** *66* **Leith Hill Legasi**[17] 4068 5-10-12 0 .... NoelFehily 41
(Charlie Longsdon) *w ldr tl after 6th: 4th and struggling u.p after 7th: wknd next: t.o bef 2 out* **16/1**

4- **5** *24* **Painted Gold**[35] 3733 8-10-12 0 .... WillKennedy 17
(Sarah-Jayne Davies) *mde most tl after 6th: sn rdn: dropped to last next: sn lost tch and t.o after 3 out* **66/1**

5m 40.55s (29.95) **Going Correction** +1.175s/f (Heav) **5** Ran SP% **112.4**
Speed ratings (Par 105): **92,89,89,65,56**
CSF £37.64 TOTE £9.30: £2.20, £2.10; EX 32.30 Trifecta £47.30.
Owner Mrs P Robeson **Bred** Mrs Peter Robeson **Trained** Tyringham, Bucks

FOCUS
A weak mares' novices hurdle, but a bit of a turn up. The time was slow and the winner stepped up.

4376 CGA FOXHUNTER TRIAL OPEN HUNTERS' CHASE (15 fncs 4 omitted) 3m

4:40 (4:40) (Class 6) 5-Y-0+ **£987** (£303; £151)

Form RPR

1 **Certain Flight (IRE)**[18] 9-11-12 0 .... MrWBiddick 120+
(K J Cumings) *a travelling wl: in tch tl hdwy to chse ldr 9th: led next: cruised clr 3 out: v easily* **10/11**[1]

245/ **2** *15* **Dead Or Alive (IRE)**[12] 11-11-5 113 .... MrGWheeler(7) 99
(Miss Rose Grissell) *j.lft: led tl mstke and hdd 10th: no ch w wnr whn j.lft 2 out: plugged on* **12/1**[3]

651- **3** *24* **Qualviro (FR)**[16] 4079 10-11-11 120 ....(v) MrBGibbs(5) 78
(Tim Vaughan) *bmpd 1st: in tch in rr: hdwy to chse ldrs 11th: 3rd and no imp after 3 out: wl btn whn j.lft 2 out: mstke last: wknd flat* **6/4**[2]

1/P- **4** *3 ½* **Ide No Idea (IRE)**[39] 10-11-5 84 ....(p) MrRStearn(7) 71
(Caroline Fryer) *bmpd 1st: chsd ldr tl 9th: sn rdn and struggling next: lost tch after 3 out: t.o* **40/1**

B34/ **P** **Bluegun (IRE)**[25] 12-11-12 0 .... MissGAndrews
(S R Andrews) *hld up in tch: mstke 4th: hdwy to chse ldrs 7th: struggling and mstke 12th: lost tch after next: t.o whn p.u last* **16/1**

7m 3.65s (53.35) **Going Correction** +1.60s/f (Heav) **5** Ran SP% **108.4**
Speed ratings: **75,70,62,60,**
CSF £10.53 TOTE £2.40: £1.10, £2.80; EX 9.40 Trifecta £17.30.
Owner R Dunsford **Bred** Joe Magee **Trained** South Molton, Devon

FOCUS
This uncompetitive hunter chase was run in unpleasant conditions and it turned into a one-horse race. The easy winner can rate higher.

4377 STANJAMES.COM ON THE ROAD TO CHELTENHAM H'CAP HURDLE (10 hdls) 2m 4f 110y

5:10 (5:10) (Class 4) (0-110,110) 4-Y-0+ **£3,249** (£954; £477; £238)

Form RPR

P44 **1** **Should I Stay (FR)**[23] 3959 6-11-1 **102** ....(p) JoshuaMoore(3) 107+
(Gary Moore) *mde all: rdn and j.lft 2 out: kpt on wl u.p flat: rdn out* **15/2**

130- **2** *5* **Hail Tiberius**[2] 3264 7-10-8 **92** ....(t) TomSiddall 92
(Martin Keighley) *t.k.h: hld up in rr: clsd and in tch after 5th: wnt 2nd 2 out: rdn: no ex and edgd lft flat* **2/1**[1]

320/ **3** *6* **Ussee (FR)**[354] 4538 6-11-8 **106** .... DarylJacob 99
(Ben Case) *chsd ldrs: clsd and wl in tch after 5th: rdn and effrt after 3 out: styd on same pce between last 2* **4/1**[2]

4/P- **4** *15* **Tenby Jewel (IRE)**[33] 3784 9-11-5 **110** .... RyanHatch(7) 88
(Mark Gillard) *w ldr tl after 6th: sn rdn: cl 4th 3 out: wknd u.p bef next: plugged on* **12/1**

666- **5** *2 ¾* **Bajan Blu**[27] 3878 6-11-5 **103** ....(t) JamieMoore 78
(David Brace) *t.k.h: hld up in last pair: clsd and wl in tch after 5th: rdn and effrt after 3 out: 4th and btn next: wknd between last 2* **4/1**[2]

0/2- **6** *3 ¼* **Val D'Allier (FR)**[134] 1820 5-11-12 **110** ....(t) MarkGrant 82
(Jim Old) *hld up off the pce in midfield: clsd and chsd ldrs after 5th: rdn and btn after 3 out: wknd bef next* **9/2**[3]

5m 31.7s (32.70) **Going Correction** +1.175s/f (Heav) **6** Ran SP% **111.0**
Speed ratings (Par 105): **84,82,79,74,73 71**
CSF £22.97 TOTE £7.20: £4.90, £1.60; EX 23.10 Trifecta £100.50.
Owner M L Bloodstock Ltd **Bred** M L Bloodstock Limited **Trained** Lower Beeding, W Sussex

FOCUS
A modest handicap hurdle, rated around the first two.

T/Plt: £37.20 to a £1 stake. Pool: £63,265.17 - 1238.51 winning units. T/Qpdt: £15.40 to a £1 stake. Pool: £3092.57 - 148.32 winning units. SP

[3920]SEDGEFIELD (L-H)

Thursday, February 20

OFFICIAL GOING: Heavy (soft in places; 4.7)

Wind: fresh across Weather: mixture of sunshine and cloud

4378 COMPARE BOOKMAKERS AT BOOKMAKERS.CO.UK CONDITIONAL JOCKEYS' H'CAP HURDLE (8 hdls) 2m 1f

2:00 (2:00) (Class 4) (0-110,108) 4-Y-0+ **£3,378** (£992; £496; £248)

Form RPR

002- **1** **Short Takes (USA)**[10] 4187 6-11-0 **102**.........................(b) NickSlatter(6) 116+
(Donald McCain) *trckd ldr: upsides 3 out: led 2 out: rdn clr: hit last: easily* **2/1**[2]

030- **2** *24* **Choisan (IRE)**[55] 3330 5-11-6 **105**.................................... CraigNichol(3) 95
(Tim Easterby) *trckd ldr: hit 3 out but led narrowly: hdd 2 out: drvn and sn no ch w wnr: mstke last* **9/4**[3]

414- **3** *3 1/4* **Persian Herald**[10] 4187 6-11-9 **108**.......................... JonathanEngland(3) 95
(Sue Smith) *hld up in tch: reminders and outpcd after 5th: no threat after* **15/8**[1]

100- **4** *33* **Amir Pasha (UAE)**[50] 3451 9-11-3 **102**..........................(p) JoeColliver(3) 64
(Micky Hammond) *led: hdd 3 out: sn wknd* **10/1**

4m 28.3s (21.40) **Going Correction** +1.375s/f (Heav) **4** Ran SP% **108.0**

Speed ratings (Par 105): **104,92,91,75**

CSF £6.81 TOTE £2.30; EX 6.60 Trifecta £9.80.

Owner T P McMahon and D McMahon **Bred** Rosa Colasanti **Trained** Cholmondeley, Cheshire

FOCUS

Divided bends, hurdles on the outer rail. An uncompetitive handicap hurdle won by a wide margin. A personal best from the winner.

4379 BETFRED NOVICES' HURDLE (BETFRED HURDLE SERIES QUALIFIER) (8 hdls) 2m 1f

2:30 (2:30) (Class 4) 4-Y-0+ **£3,378** (£992; £496; £248)

Form RPR

/11- **1** **Vieux Lion Rouge (FR)**[21] 3988 5-12-0 132................. TomScudamore 141+
(David Pipe) *mde all: rdn after 2 out: kpt on wl: eased towards fin* **4/7**[1]

3- **2** *12* **Prince Khurram**[36] 3714 4-10-7 0....................................(t) BrianHarding 106
(Donald McCain) *trckd ldr: nt fluent 5th: rdn 2 out: sn one pce and no ch w wnr: nt fluent last* **7/4**[2]

244- **3** *9* **Lord Brendy**[15] 4081 6-11-2 108.................................... DougieCostello 105
(Robert Johnson) *in tch: rdn and outpcd by ldng pair after 3 out: hit last: wnt modest 3rd towards fin* **16/1**[3]

3/P- **4** *1/2* **Classic Rally (IRE)**[70] 3036 8-11-2 0.......................... BrianHughes 103
(Malcolm Jefferson) *trckd ldr: rdn and outpcd by ldng pair after 3 out: lost 3rd nr fin* **25/1**

/00- **5** *78* **Femme D'Espere**[35] 3728 8-10-2 0.. JoshWall(7) 18
(Trevor Wall) *hld up: lost tch after 5th: t.o* **100/1**

05- **6** *28* **Dermo's Dilemma**[92] 2592 4-10-0 0.................................... JohnDawson(7)
(Chris Grant) *hld up: lost tch 1/2-way: t.o* **100/1**

4m 28.1s (21.20) **Going Correction** +1.375s/f (Heav)

WFA 4 from 5yo+ 9lb **6** Ran SP% **111.7**

Speed ratings (Par 105): **105,99,95,94,58 45**

CSF £1.90 TOTE £1.40; £1.10, £1.40; EX 1.80 Trifecta £4.70.

Owner Prof Caroline Tisdall & John Gent **Bred** F M Cottin **Trained** Nicholashayne, Devon

FOCUS

What had looked a match ultimately proved a one-sided affair. The easy winner is on the upgrade.

4380 FREE BETS ON YOUR MOBILE AT BOOKMAKERS.CO.UK H'CAP CHASE (14 fncs 2 omitted) 2m 4f

3:00 (3:00) (Class 5) (0-100,93) 5-Y-0+ **£2,599** (£763; £381; £190)

Form RPR

P5P- **1** **Whiskey Ridge (IRE)**[15] 4082 8-11-8 **89**........................... RyanMania 102+
(Sue Smith) *mde all: pressed by runner-up fr 3 out (normal 4 out): rdn next: hld on wl extended run-in* **4/1**[1]

/P4- **2** *2 1/4* **Sam Patch**[24] 3936 11-9-11 **69**................................... CallumWhillans(5) 80
(Donald Whillans) *in tch: pressed wnr fr 3 out (normal 4 out): kpt on but a jst hld* **5/1**[3]

44P- **3** *11* **Alexander Oats**[24] 3936 11-10-2 **69**................................(b) BrianHughes 69
(Robert Goldie) *prom: rdn and outpcd by ldng pair after 3 out (normal 4 out): no threat after* **5/1**[3]

053- **4** *2 1/4* **Wave Breaker (IRE)**[25] 3925 7-10-9 **76**.....................(tp) DougieCostello 75
(Robert Johnson) *prom on outer: mstke 9th: rdn and lost pl after 10th: plugged on again extended run-in* **9/2**[2]

5FF- **5** *7* **Stagecoach Jasper**[17] 4067 8-11-12 **93**........................... ShaneByrne 85
(Sue Smith) *hld up: hit 9th: rdn after 11th: sn no imp: hit last (normal 2 out)* **5/1**[3]

045- **6** *3/4* **Samtheman**[25] 3925 9-11-6 **92**.. JoeColliver(5) 82
(Micky Hammond) *trckd ldrs: mstke 10th: sn btn* **8/1**

4P3- **U** **Mannered**[29] 3834 9-11-4 **92**.. JohnDawson(7)
(John Wade) *hld up: uns at 4th* **11/2**

5m 20.6s (17.60) **Going Correction** +0.925s/f (Soft) **7** Ran SP% **114.7**

Speed ratings: **101,100,95,94,92 91,**

CSF £24.34 CT £101.06 TOTE £4.30: £2.00, £3.80; EX 22.80 Trifecta £124.40.

Owner Widdop Wanderers **Bred** Tankardstown Stud **Trained** High Eldwick, W Yorks

FOCUS

The final fence had to be omitted because of ground conditions, resulting in a run-in of around 4f. The first two are rated back to last year's marks in this weak handicap. Only the first two were seriously involved from four out.

4381 WEATHERBYS CHELTENHAM FESTIVAL BETTING GUIDE MARES' H'CAP HURDLE (10 hdls) 2m 4f

3:30 (3:30) (Class 4) (0-120,116) 4-Y-0+ **£3,378** (£992; £496; £248)

Form RPR

40/- **1** **Lua De Itapoan**[827] 2557 9-10-3 **93**.................................... BrianHughes 110+
(Malcolm Jefferson) *trckd ldr: led bef 3 out: rdn 2 out: styd on wl and sn clr: hit last* **6/1**[3]

11P- **2** *28* **Gulf Punch**[45] 3566 7-11-5 **116**..................................(p) JamesCowley(7) 105
(Donald McCain) *hld up: reminders and lost tch after 5th: wl bhd tl styd on after last: wnt 2nd post* **8/1**

011- **3** *1/2* **Truckers Darling (IRE)**[15] 4083 7-11-3 **114**..................... KieronEdgar(7) 105
(Don Cantillon) *hld up: hdwy after 7th: cl up whn nt fluent 3 out: rdn appr 2 out: sn outpcd by wnr: tied up run-in and lost 2nd post* **1/1**[1]

464- **4** *3/4* **Fairweather Friend**[25] 3920 5-10-12 **102**............................ SeanQuinlan 90
(Jennie Candlish) *led: hdd bef 3 out: sn btn* **2/1**[2]

5m 22.4s (29.70) **Going Correction** +1.375s/f (Heav) **4** Ran SP% **108.7**

Speed ratings (Par 105): **95,83,83,83**

CSF £36.88 TOTE £11.20; EX 39.60 Trifecta £40.80.

Owner T Pearcy **Bred** D L Pearcy **Trained** Norton, N Yorks

FOCUS

A weak mares' handicap hurdle but a fine training feat by Malcolm Jefferson. Seemingly a big step up from the winner.

4382 SEDGEFIELDERS CAN'T WAIT UNTIL OCTOBER H'CAP CHASE (19 fncs 2 omitted) 3m 3f

4:00 (4:00) (Class 4) (0-120,120) 5-Y-0+ **£4,028** (£1,182; £591; £295)

Form RPR

222- **1** **Bennys Well (IRE)**[29] 3834 8-9-11 **94** oh12.............. JonathanEngland(3) 111+
(Sue Smith) *mde all: clr bef 3 out (normal 4 out): styd on wl: eased towards fin* **8/1**[3]

340- **2** *16* **Gwladys Street (IRE)**[30] 3827 7-10-5 **99**....................(v[1]) RyanMahon 100+
(William Kinsey) *in tch: hit 4th: lost pl and dropped to rr after 13th: styd on again after 2 out (normal 3 out): wnt 2nd 1f out: no threat to wnr* **7/2**[2]

13F- **3** *7* **Snuker**[49] 3497 7-10-0 **94**... BrianHughes 87
(James Ewart) *trckd ldr: hit 15th: rdn after next: sn outpcd by wnr: wknd extended run-in: lost 2nd 1f out* **7/2**[2]

/5P- **4** *2* **Rapidolyte De Ladalka (FR)**[69] 3059 9-11-12 **120**............ BarryKeniry 108
(Simon Shirley-Beavan) *hld up reminders after 12th: sn struggling in rr: plugged on extended run-in: nvr threatened* **8/1**[3]

313- **5** *99* **Mansonien L'As (FR)**[32] 3797 8-10-2 **96**..........................(b) AdrianLane
(Donald McCain) *trckd ldr: wknd after 3 out (normal 4 out): t.o* **10/3**[1]

311- **P** **Arc Warrior (FR)**[30] 3827 10-10-3 **97**...............................(t) BrianHarding
(William Amos) *hld up: tk clsr order 11th: rdn after 15th: sn wknd: p.u bef last (normal 2 out)* **10/3**[1]

7m 20.2s (31.20) **Going Correction** +0.925s/f (Soft) **6** Ran SP% **112.8**

Speed ratings: **90,85,83,82,53**

CSF £36.21 TOTE £7.30: £4.20, £3.00; EX 29.20 Trifecta £131.20.

Owner Mrs A Ellis **Bred** J Costello **Trained** High Eldwick, W Yorks

FOCUS

A severe test of stamina in the conditions but an all-the-way winner. The form could be at least 5lb out either way.

4383 HORSE RACING FREE BETS AT BOOKMAKERS.CO.UK H'CAP CHASE (11 fncs 2 omitted) 2m 110y

4:30 (4:30) (Class 5) (0-100,98) 5-Y-0+ **£2,662** (£826; £445)

Form RPR

643- **1** **Turf Trivia**[36] 3722 7-11-3 **89**...(b) BarryKeniry 101+
(George Moore) *trckd ldng pair: led gng wl extended run-in: pushed clr ins fnl f* **5/1**

1F5- **2** *2 3/4* **Cara Court (IRE)**[29] 3834 8-10-11 **88**....................(p) SamanthaDrake(5) 92
(Joanne Foster) *j.rt: led 2nd: hdd bef 5th: led again 8th: rdn 3 out (normal 4 out): hdd extended run-in: no ex* **4/1**[2]

213- **3** *29* **Decent Lord (IRE)**[29] 3837 10-11-2 **88**..........................(b[1]) SeanQuinlan 72
(Jennie Candlish) *led tl 2nd: trckd ldr: led again bef 5th: hdd 8th: sn rdn: wknd extended run-in* **9/2**[3]

62P- **P** **Cloudy Dawn**[17] 4071 9-9-11 **72** oh2.......................... JonathanEngland(3)
(Sue Smith) *in tch: pushed along and lost pl after 4th: bhd after 6th: hit 8th: p.u bef 2 out (normal 3 out)* **6/4**[1]

0P/- **P** **Celts Espere**[344] 4741 11-9-9 **74** oh22 ow2.........................(p) JoshWall(7)
(Trevor Wall) *sn wl bhd: p.u bef 7th* **33/1**

1/0- **P** **Orlittlebylittle**[41] 3639 8-11-12 **98**.. AdrianLane
(Donald McCain) *in tch: reminder after 6th: sn struggling in rr: p.u bef 3 out (normal 4 out)* **6/1**

4m 31.4s (22.80) **Going Correction** +0.925s/f (Soft) **6** Ran SP% **112.1**

Speed ratings: **83,81,68,,,**

CSF £24.86 TOTE £7.10: £3.60, £3.50; EX 16.70 Trifecta £45.50.

Owner Mrs Mary Hatfield & Mrs Susan Kramer **Bred** London Thoroughbred Services Ltd **Trained** Middleham Moor, N Yorks

FOCUS

A weak handicap chase run in a heavy shower. The early pace was strong and it only concerned the first two from at the top of the final hill. The winner is rated back to form.

4384 COMPARE BOOKIES FREE BETS WITH BOOKMAKERS.CO.UK STANDARD OPEN NATIONAL HUNT FLAT RACE 2m 1f

5:00 (5:00) (Class 6) 4-6-Y-0 **£1,559** (£457; £228; £114)

Form RPR

1 **Tom Lamb** 4-10-4 0.. AdamNicol(5) 106+
(Sally Hall) *trckd ldng pair: led over 1f out: pushed clr: comf* **7/1**

35- **2** *7* **Surging Seas (IRE)**[28] 3863 5-11-4 0.......................... DougieCostello 105
(Tony Coyle) *led narrowly: hdd over 5f out: remained prom: rdn to ld again over 2f out: hdd over 1f out: one pce and sn no ch w wnr* **3/1**[2]

3 *11* **Silver Vogue** 6-11-4 0.. RyanMania 95
(Sue Smith) *w ldr: led over 5f out: hdd over 2f out: grad wknd* **10/1**

1- **4** *1 1/4* **Starplex**[61] 3214 4-10-9 0.. GrantCockburn(7) 91
(Lucinda Russell) *hld up in tch: rdn over 3f out: sn no imp on ldrs* **11/2**[3]

5- **5** *6* **Laird Of Monksford (IRE)**[51] 3433 5-11-4 0...................... AdrianLane 87
(Donald McCain) *trckd ldng pair: rdn 4f out: sn wknd* **8/1**

6 *2 1/2* **Rough King (IRE)**[95] 5-11-4 0... SeanQuinlan 86
(Jennie Candlish) *hld up in tch: rdn over 3f out: sn btn* **11/8**[1]

4m 30.5s (29.20) **Going Correction** +1.375s/f (Heav)

WFA 4 from 5yo 9lb 5 from 6yo 1lb **6** Ran SP% **115.2**

Speed ratings: **86,82,77,76,74 72**

CSF £29.02 TOTE £13.40: £9.80, £3.20; EX 35.50 Trifecta £173.80.

Owner Miss S E Hall **Bred** Miss S E Hall **Trained** Middleham Moor, N Yorks

FOCUS

A bumper run at a sound pace and they came home well strung out. The form is given a token rating through the second.

T/Plt: £983.40 to a £1 stake. Pool: £63,113.84 - 46.85 winning units. T/Qpdt: £211.20 to a £1 stake. Pool: £3528.87 - 12.36 winning units. AS

2913 CLONMEL (R-H)

Thursday, February 20

OFFICIAL GOING: Heavy

4386a SUREHAUL MERCEDES-BENZ NOVICE HURDLE (GRADE 3) (14 hdls) 3m

2:45 (2:44) 4-Y-0+ **£17,062** (£4,987; £2,362; £787)

RPR

1 **Don Poli (IRE)**21 3998 5-10-13 .... BryanCooper 145+
(W P Mullins, Ire) *chsd ldrs: prog 3 out into 3rd: led bef next and sn pushed clr: styd on wl* **9/2**3

2 3 1/4 **Goonyella (IRE)**54 3361 7-11-2 .... AELynch 145
(J T R Dreaper, Ire) *sn trckd ldrs: pushed along in 3rd appr 2 out and sn chsd ldr in 2nd: hung lft after last: kpt on wl* **16/1**

3 8 1/2 **Seskinane (IRE)**39 3683 8-11-2 132.. DavyRussell 136
(Brian M McMahon, Ire) *racd in mid-div: nt fluent 4th: tk clsr order to chse ldrs bef 2 out in 4th: no imp in 3rd appr last: kpt on same pce* **20/1**

4 13 **Captainofthefleet (IRE)**40 3667 7-11-2 123........................ KeithDonoghue 125
(Eamonn O'Connell, Ire) *led tl strly pressed after 3 out and hdd bef next: sn no ex: lft modest 4th at last* **12/1**

5 25 **Shantou Ed (IRE)**19 4045 5-10-13 .... MarkWalsh 95
(P A Fahy, Ire) *hld up in rr: nt fluent at times: sme prog after 3 out: no imp after next* **8/1**

6 50 **The Winkler (IRE)**28 3865 5-10-13 .... MichaelButler 45
(Eoin Doyle, Ire) *hld up towards rr: dropped to rr bef 4 out and sn adrift: t.o* **14/1**

P **The Job Is Right**54 3380 6-11-8 130..............................(b) BarryGeraghty
(Michael Hourigan, Ire) *chsd ldrs in 3rd tl prog into 2nd at 4th: dropped to 3rd 4 out and sn pushed along: wknd qckly and p.u bef 2 out* **13/2**

P **Railway Zira (IRE)**40 3668 6-10-9 .... SeanFlanagan
(David Harry Kelly, Ire) *hld up towards rr: sme prog on outer w a circ to r: no imp after 3 out: sn dropped to rr and p.u* **20/1**

P **Moonshine Lad (IRE)**25 3931 6-11-2 137.. PCarberry
(Gordon Elliott, Ire) *hld up towards rr: pushed along w a circ to r and sn adrift: p.u after 5 out* **5/2**1

F **Double Irish (IRE)**55 3337 6-11-2 .... DannyMullins 130+
(Gordon Elliott, Ire) *chsd ldrs: t.k.h: prog into 3rd w a circ to r: wnt 2nd 4 out and on terms after next: hdd bef 2 out and sn one pce: wl hld in 4th whn fell last* **4/1**2

6m 32.0s (392.00) **10** Ran SP% **121.0**
CSF £73.62 TOTE £5.80: £1.60, £5.10, £3.70; DF 75.00.
Owner Gigginstown House Stud **Bred** Brian J Griffiths And John Nicholson **Trained** Muine Beag, Co Carlow

FOCUS
The runner-up ran in line with his chase best. The winner was less exposed and ran to a personal best.

4171 EXETER (R-H)

Friday, February 21

OFFICIAL GOING: Soft (heavy in places; chs 5.5, hdl 5.8)
Penultimate flight omitted on all circuits of the hurdle course; unsuitable ground.
Wind: quite strong behind Weather: showers with sunny periods

4391 BATHWICK TYRES "NATIONAL HUNT" NOVICES' HURDLE (8 hdls 2 omitted) 2m 3f

2:20 (2:20) (Class 4) 4-Y-0+ **£3,249** (£954; £477; £238)

Form RPR

2- 1 **Liberty One (IRE)**24 3956 8-11-3 0.. DarylJacob 124
(Richard Woollacott) *trckd ldrs: rdn appr 2 out: wnt 2nd between last 2: chal last: sn led: styd on: drvn out* **7/1**3

624- 2 1 1/2 **Sun Wild Life (FR)**41 3641 4-10-7 118.. FelixDeGiles 112
(Robert Walford) *trckd ldrs: rdn after 6th: styd on fr 2 out: wnt 2nd run-in: kpt on* **10/1**

442- 3 4 **Cool George**38 3695 6-11-0 118.. JamesBest(3) 119
(Jackie Du Plessis) *prom: led appr 2 out where nt fluent: sn rdn: hdd sn after last: no ex* **2/1**2

13- 4 31 **Pleasant Company (IRE)**63 3182 6-11-3 0.................. TomScudamore 92
(David Pipe) *racd keenly: led: rdn and hdd appr 2 out: lost 2nd between last 2: wkng in 5th whn lft 4th at the last* **10/11**1

006- 5 2 1/4 **Rafafie**38 3697 6-10-12 0.. MissLucyGardner(5) 88
(Sue Gardner) *trckd ldrs: nt fluent 3rd: rdn appr 2 out: sn hld: wknd bef last* **40/1**

0- 6 33 **Exmoor Challenge**12 4175 5-11-0 0.. MattGriffiths(3) 52
(Jeremy Scott) *mid-div tl wknd after 6th: t.o* **66/1**

00- 7 22 **Hot Pepper**12 4171 6-11-3 0.. JamesDavies 30
(Chris Down) *hld up: struggling 3rd: grad lost tch: t.o* **100/1**

564- U **Know More Oats (IRE)**13 4163 6-11-0 0........................ GilesHawkins(3) 100
(Victor Dartnall) *mid-div: rdn appr 2 out: wnt hld 4th and hung lft between last 2: v awkward whn unseating rdr last* **25/1**

050- U **Sand Artist (IRE)**37 3716 6-11-3 0.. AidanColeman
(Venetia Williams) *hld up: pushed along whn nt fluent and uns rdr 4th* **33/1**

5m 11.9s (29.20) **Going Correction** +1.55s/f (Heav)
WFA 4 from 5yo+ 9lb **9** Ran SP% **119.0**
Speed ratings (Par 105): **100,99,97,84,83 69,60, ,**
CSF £64.83 TOTE £10.30: £1.90, £2.70, £1.10; EX 33.90 Trifecta £102.40.
Owner D G Staddon **Bred** John O'Doherty **Trained** South Molton, Devon

FOCUS
Hurdle course on same line as 9th February which increased distances by about 90yds per circuit. There were heavy showers pre-racing on top of ground already very testing so conditions were extremely demanding. The middle flight in the home straight was omitted from all hurdles races. A big step up from the winner with the second back to form.

4392 CALL STAR SPORTS 08000521321 MARES' H'CAP HURDLE (8 hdls 2 omitted) 2m 3f

2:50 (2:50) (Class 3) (0-130,125) 4-Y-0+ **£6,498** (£1,908; £954; £477)

Form RPR

132- 1 **Midnight Belle**36 3731 7-11-6 119.. FelixDeGiles 121
(Tom Symonds) *trckd ldrs: rdn to dispute 6 l 2nd after 6th: 3 l down last: styd on to ld fnl 75yds: drvn out* **15/2**

251- 2 2 1/4 **Flementime (IRE)**18 4068 6-11-12 125.. IanPopham 125
(Martin Keighley) *led: drew 6 l clr after 6th: rdn after 2 out: 3 l up but tiring jumping last: no ex whn hdd fnl 75yds* **11/4**1

053- 3 11 **Miner Distraction**22 3991 6-10-8 107.. NickScholfield 98
(Jeremy Scott) *trckd ldrs: rdn after 6th: styd on into 3rd between last 2: hit last: no ex* **11/1**

021- 4 1 1/4 **Loyaute (FR)**14 4129 7-11-7 120.. JamesDavies 108
(Chris Down) *prom: rdn in 6 l 2nd after 6th: one pce and hld bef next* **4/1**3

P61- 5 9 **A Shade Of Bay**46 3570 6-11-2 115.. JasonMaguire 98
(Kim Bailey) *hld up in tch: nudged along bef 3rd: rdn after 6th: btn bef next: wknd between last 2* **15/2**

/P5- P **Marie Des Anges (FR)**36 3742 6-10-8 107..................(t) AidanColeman
(Anthony Honeyball) *trckd ldrs tl hit 3rd: sn pushed along: plenty to do 6th: styng on and on heels on 3rd/4th 2 out: tired qckly and p.u bef last* **8/1**

415- P **Benefique Royale**16 4090 6-10-10 109.. BrendanPowell
(Nick Williams) *hld up last but in tch: rdn after 4th: qckly btn: t.o whn p.u after 6th* **7/2**2

5m 15.9s (33.20) **Going Correction** +1.55s/f (Heav) **7** Ran SP% **111.9**
Speed ratings (Par 107): **92,91,86,85,82 ,**
CSF £27.73 TOTE £7.80: £5.40, £1.10; EX 20.40 Trifecta £202.50.
Owner Mrs Patricia Holtorp **Bred** Mrs Patricia Ellen Holtorp **Trained** Harewood End, H'fords

FOCUS
A modest event. The first two were close to their marks in a slow-motion finish.

4393 EQUINE INVESTMENTS UK LEADING TIPSTER H'CAP HURDLE (9 hdls 3 omitted) 2m 7f 110y

3:20 (3:20) (Class 4) (0-120,117) 4-Y-0+ **£3,898** (£1,144; £572; £286)

Form RPR

/36- 1 **Storm Alert**91 2655 7-11-0 110.. MissLucyGardner(5) 116
(Sue Gardner) *hld up: trckd ldrs: 4th: rdn bef 2 out: wnt 2nd between last 2: styd on dourly to ld fnl 100yds: rdn out* **11/2**2

5P/- 2 1 1/2 **Lundy Sky**311 5328 9-11-10 115.. JamieMoore 118
(Tony Newcombe) *led tl 4th: prom: rdn bef 2 out: led bef last: kpt on but no ex whn hdd fnl 100yds* **12/1**

066- 3 11 **Old Tricks (IRE)**12 4174 7-11-12 117..............................(p) BrendanPowell 110
(Colin Tizzard) *trckd ldrs: rdn after 8th: styd on same pce fr 2 out: wnt 3rd run-in* **8/1**

4- 4 1 1/4 **Paddy The Oscar (IRE)**12 4175 11-10-7 105.................. ConorRing(7) 96
(Grace Harris) *w ldr: led 4th: rdn appr 2 out: hdd bef last: fdd* **20/1**

000- 5 7 **Pyleigh Lass**21 4023 8-11-6 111..(t) IanPopham 95
(Martin Keighley) *trckd ldrs: rdn after 8th: wknd next* **20/1**

342- 6 22 **Astigos (FR)**6 4271 7-11-12 117.. AidanColeman 79
(Venetia Williams) *hld up wl in tch: trckd ldrs 4th tl 6th: rdn after 8th: btn bef next: t.o* **6/5**1

015- 7 2 **Virginia Ash (IRE)**13 4144 6-11-7 112..............................(p) JoeTizzard 72
(Colin Tizzard) *cl up: rn in snatches: rdn after 5th: wknd after 8th: t.o* **13/2**3

POP- 8 1 3/4 **Decimus (IRE)**53 3421 7-11-10 115.. NickScholfield 73
(Jeremy Scott) *racd wd: bhd: slow 1st: hdwy 6th: nt fluent next and dropped to rr: rdn after 8th: sn wknd: t.o* **9/1**

6m 35.2s (36.20) **Going Correction** +1.55s/f (Heav) **8** Ran SP% **112.5**
Speed ratings (Par 105): **101,100,96,96,94 86,86,85**
CSF £62.87 CT £519.81 TOTE £8.00: £1.10, £4.40, £3.00; EX 43.00 Trifecta £823.10 Part won..
Owner D V Gardner **Bred** S Raymond **Trained** Longdown, Devon

FOCUS
The overall gallop was fairly steady but the principals kept those positions throughout most of the final circuit. A personal best from the winner.

4394 EQUINE INVESTMENTS 11TH YEAR STILL GOING STRONG MARES' NOVICES' HURDLE (7 hdls 1 omitted) 2m 1f

3:50 (3:50) (Class 4) 4-Y-0+ **£4,328** (£1,574)

Form RPR

311- 1 **Legacy Gold (IRE)**31 3818 6-11-12 133.. TomScudamore 136+
(David Pipe) *trckd ldr: pushed into ld between last 2: in command run-in: nudged out* **1/6**1

323- 2 1 3/4 **Revaader**12 4173 6-10-12 103.. TommyPhelan 113
(Mark Gillard) *led: rdn: hanging lft and hdd bef last: sn hld by wnr but kpt on* **9/2**2

F- F **Miss Fortywinks**29 3854 5-10-5 0.. KevinJones(7)
(Seamus Mullins) *chsd clr ldrs: rdn and lost tch after 5th: t.o whn fell last* **33/1**3

P **Moniques Gift** 6-10-12 0.. JamesDavies
(Chris Down) *veered bdly lft s: last and detached: rcvrd sltly after 1st but t.o rapidly bef next: p.u after 5th* **100/1**

4m 37.9s (22.40) **Going Correction** +1.55s/f (Heav) **4** Ran SP% **107.8**
Speed ratings (Par 105): **109,108, ,**
CSF £1.43 TOTE £1.10; EX 1.30 Trifecta £1.70.
Owner R S Brookhouse **Bred** C K Johnson **Trained** Nicholashayne, Devon

FOCUS
An easy win for the form choice, who was value for further and is a decent mare.

4395 STAR SPORTS FESTIVAL PREVIEW EVENING NOVICES' LIMITED H'CAP CHASE (18 fncs) 3m

4:20 (4:20) (Class 3) (0-140,134) 5-Y-0+ **£9,495** (£2,805; £1,402; £702; £351)

Form RPR

521- 1 **Dare To Endeavour**15 4110 7-11-1 127.. PaddyBrennan 137+
(Tom George) *trckd ldrs: rdn and j.rt fr 4 out: led 2 out: styd on wl: rdn out* **9/2**3

131- 2 2 3/4 **Saroque (IRE)**20 4031 7-11-0 126.. AidanColeman 130
(Venetia Williams) *led: rdn bef 4 out: j. sltly rt: hdd 2 out: styd on same pce: a jst holding on for 2nd run-in* **3/1**1

41F- 3 nk **Bertie Boru (IRE)**[22] 3990 7-10-13 **125** TomO'Brien 130
(Philip Hobbs) *rn in snatches: trckd ldrs tl 8th: rdn after 10th: bit to do 12th: on heels of ldrs after 14th: mstke 3 out: disp 2nd fr next: hld in 3rd but kpt on fr last* **9/1**

21P- 4 17 **Dark Glacier (IRE)**[29] 3858 9-10-4 **116** (v) JamieMoore 108
(Peter Bowen) *trckd ldrs: hrd rdn after 14th: nt pce to get on terms: wknd after 2 out* **15/2**

UPF- 5 18 **Wilton Milan (IRE)**[36] 3745 6-11-8 **134** (t) DarylJacob 111
(Paul Nicholls) *trckd ldrs: chal after 14th tl rdn bef next: grad fdd: wnt rt 2 out: t.o* **9/2**[3]

21P- P **The Italian Yob (IRE)**[27] 3886 6-11-6 **132** NoelFehily
(Nick Williams) *hld up in tch: trckd ldrs 7th: rdn after 14th: wknd qckly and p.u bef 4 out* **7/2**[2]

222/ P **Master Todd (IRE)**[327] 5039 9-10-8 **120** NickScholfield
(Grant Cann) *hld up last: j.rt: nt fluent 8th (water): wknd 12th: t.o whn p.u bef 4 out* **16/1**

6m 32.9s (23.60) **Going Correction** +1.225s/f (Heav) **7** Ran SP% **111.2**
Speed ratings: **109,108,107,102,96** ,
CSF £17.89 TOTE £5.30: £3.20, £1.40; EX 15.00 Trifecta £143.60.
Owner J B Property Developments (Midlands) Ltd **Bred** Direct Sales (uk) Ltd **Trained** Slad, Gloucs

FOCUS
An open-looking handicap, but probably not the the strongest for the grade with the top weight rated 6lb below the ceiling for the grade. However, the form seems solid enough.

4396 BATHWICK TYRES PLYMOUTH H'CAP CHASE (18 fncs) 3m
4:50 (4:50) (Class 4) (0-120,119) 5-Y-0+ **£5,198** (£1,526; £763; £381)

Form RPR

1/3- 1 **Thomas Wild**[283] 294 9-11-3 **113** MichealNolan(3) 116
(Philip Hobbs) *hld up but in tch: wnt 4th after 14th: rdn in 3rd bef 4 out: wnt 2nd between last 2 but hld by ldr: lft in ld whn ldr bdly hmpd by paddock entrnce: lucky* **13/2**

/44- 2 1 ¼ **Nodebateaboutit**[36] 3743 9-10-11 **104** (tp) PaddyBrennan 118+
(Tom George) *hld up in tch: hdwy 14th: chal sn after: rdn to ld 3 out: clr next: comf in command whn broadsided by loose horse by paddock entrnce run-in: brought to a stand stl: hdd sn after: nt time to rcvr: v unlucky* **4/1**[2]

P/0- 3 4 ½ **Victory Gunner (IRE)**[36] 3730 16-10-13 **109** JakeGreenall(3) 106
(Richard Lee) *w ldr: led briefly 6th: led 9th: jnd 11th: rdn appr 4 out: hdd 3 out: lost 2nd between last 2: styd on same pce* **33/1**

564- 4 25 **Supreme Bob (IRE)**[12] 4172 8-11-1 **108** WillKennedy 80
(Lucy Jones) *awkward s and nrly uns rdr: last: hit 7th: rdn after 14th: wnt 4th 4 out: wknd 2 out: t.o whn hmpd by loose rider run-in* **14/1**

/52- 5 43 **Tuskar Rock (FR)**[38] 3696 11-10-5 **103** CallumWhillans(5) 32
(Venetia Williams) *trckd ldrs: jnd ldrs 12th: rdn after 14th: wknd after next: t.o* **6/1**[3]

F33- 6 1 ¼ **Billy Dutton**[55] 3358 8-11-6 **113** JamesDavies 41
(Chris Down) *mid-div: rdn after 14th: sn wknd: t.o* **11/4**[1]

P31- 7 10 **Royal Chatelier (FR)**[24] 3958 9-11-1 **115** JoshWall(7) 33
(Michael Blake) *mid-div: struggling and bhd fr 9th: slow next: sn drvn: lost tch fr 12th: t.o* **12/1**

PFP- 8 18 **Shaking Hands (IRE)**[38] 3698 10-11-12 **119** (bt) TomScudamore 19
(David Pipe) *led: hdd briefly 6th: reminders after next: hdd 9th: upsides whn nt fluent 11th: slow whn lost pl rapidly 13th: t.o after next* **9/1**

P/0- P **Webberys Dream**[22] 3990 11-10-13 **109** (p) MattGriffiths(3)
(Jeremy Scott) *trckd ldrs: rdn after 10th: wknd after 12th: t.o whn p.u bef 4 out* **22/1**

14P- U **Ringa Bay**[20] 4026 9-11-5 **119** (p) JakeHodson(7)
(David Bridgwater) *blnd and uns rdr 2nd* **8/1**

6m 38.6s (29.30) **Going Correction** +1.225s/f (Heav) **10** Ran SP% **117.0**
Speed ratings: **100,99,98,89,75 75,71,65**, ,
CSF £33.81 CT £805.38 TOTE £7.70: £2.20, £2.60, £10.40; EX 32.00 Trifecta £445.60.
Owner C L T **Bred** Miss S J Turner **Trained** Withycombe, Somerset

FOCUS
Absolute carnage here thanks to loose horse Ringa Bay who, having made a nuisance of himself throughout, veered violently across the track towards the stands' rail after the last fence, cutting right across Nodebateaboutit, who was brought to a complete standstill having had the race in the bag. The lucky winner is rated below his best, with the second rated as an 11-length winner.
T/Plt: £159.90 to a £1 stake. Pool: £69267.48 - 316.06 winning tickets T/Qpdt: £37.70 to a £1 stake. Pool: £4930.85 - 96.7 winning tickets TM

4157 WARWICK (L-H)
Friday, February 21

OFFICIAL GOING: Soft (good to soft in places on chase course; chs 6.7, hdl 6.3)
Fifth fence omitted on all circuits of the chase course.
Wind: Brisk behind Weather: Overcast

4397 EBF STALLIONS "NATIONAL HUNT" NOVICES' HURDLE (QUALIFIER) (9 hdls) 2m 3f
2:10 (2:10) (Class 4) 4-7-Y-0 **£3,898** (£1,144; £572; £286)

Form RPR

631- 1 **Cogry**[31] 3816 5-11-8 126 SamTwiston-Davies 113+
(Nigel Twiston-Davies) *trckd ldrs: nt fluent 2nd: trckd ldr fr 5th: j. slowly 4 out: drvn next: styd on to ld appr 2 out: sn clr: readily* **4/6**[1]

041- 2 6 **Pink Gin**[33] 3796 6-11-8 121 (t) MarkGrant 106+
(Jim Old) *led tl after 1st: led again bef next: hrd pressed fr 4 out tl rdn: hdd and blnd 2 out: mstke last: styd on to hold 2nd but no ch w wnr* **5/1**[2]

3 ½ **Super Lunar (IRE)**[320] 5-11-2 0 RobertThornton 96
(Alan King) *hld up towards rr but in tch: stdy hdwy 3 out to trck ldrs: rdn 2 out: styd on to dispute 2nd bef last but no ch w wnr: one pce into 3rd run-in* **11/2**[3]

5- 4 6 **I'm A Rocker (IRE)**[16] 4081 5-11-2 0 AdrianLane 90
(Donald McCain) *in rr: sme hdwy bef 2 out: sn shkn up: hung bdly lft and hd to one side bef last and run-in: nt keen* **25/1**

06- 5 1 **A Keen Sense (GER)**[22] 3988 5-11-2 0 LeightonAspell 89
(David Dennis) *chsd ldrs: rdn 3 out: wknd next* **40/1**

P- 6 56 **Georgie Lad (IRE)**[113] 2181 6-11-2 0 RichardJohnson 33
(Philip Hobbs) *j. slowly 3rd: chsd ldrs: nt fluent 4 out: drvn to chal next: wknd qckly wl bef 2 out* **7/1**

2/5- U **Vineman**[63] 3194 7-11-2 0 SeanQuinlan
(David Bridgwater) *t.k.h: led after first: veered off crse, hit rails and uns rdr bnd bef next* **50/1**

4m 41.97s (-0.73) **Going Correction** +0.15s/f (Yiel) **7** Ran SP% **112.8**
Speed ratings: **107,104,104,101,101 77**,
CSF £4.39 TOTE £1.60: £1.10, £3.30; EX 4.90 Trifecta £11.10.
Owner Graham And Alison Jelley **Bred** R D And Mrs J S Chugg **Trained** Naunton, Gloucs

FOCUS
Not a bad novice hurdle, but it was steadily run and the first two are rated below their best.

4398 WARWICK "HANDS AND HEELS" H'CAP HURDLE (FOR CONDITIONAL JOCKEYS AND AMATEUR RIDERS) (8 hdls) 2m
2:40 (2:42) (Class 5) (0-100,100) 4-Y-0+ **£1,949** (£572; £286; £143)

Form RPR

0/0- 1 **Dorry K (IRE)**[65] 3163 5-10-6 **80** JackSherwood 88+
(Jim Best) *trckd ldrs: led wl bef 2 out: shkn up whn hrd pressed after 2 out: nt fluent last: kpt on wl run-in* **16/1**

165- 2 1 ¾ **Lost In Newyork (IRE)**[41] 3650 7-10-10 **84** CharlieDeutsch 89
(Nick Kent) *in rr: hdwy 4th: chsd wnr appr 2 out: chal sn after and ev ch last: kpt on same pce* **11/4**[1]

143- 3 3 ¼ **Walter De La Mare (IRE)**[15] 4107 7-11-8 **96** MissJoannaMason 97
(Anabel K Murphy) *j. slowly 2nd: in rr: hdwy fr 3 out: chsd ldng duo fr 2 out but no imp* **12/1**

000- 4 2 ¾ **Kyles Faith (IRE)**[21] 4023 6-11-7 **100** MrHRLCornock(5) 98
(Martin Keighley) *in tch: chsd ldrs fr 3 out: sn drvn: styd on same pce* **5/1**[2]

325- 5 1 ½ **Tribal Dance (IRE)**[94] 2571 8-11-12 **100** CiaranMckee 97
(John O'Shea) *chsd ldrs: drvn 3 out: one pce fr 2 out* **25/1**

462- 6 6 **Pagham Belle**[18] 4072 6-10-10 **84** (t) KieronEdgar 78
(Nigel Hawke) *in rr: j. slowly 2nd: drvn 4 out: mod prog fr 2 out* **6/1**[3]

00- 7 10 **Spunky**[107] 2291 5-10-6 **85** (tp) MrRichardPatrick(5) 66
(Marc Barber) *chsd ldr after 3rd: led 3 out: sn drvn: hdd wl bef 2 out and mstke: no ch whn blnd last* **66/1**

350- 8 nk **Tempuran**[22] 3650 5-11-12 **100** RyanHatch 80
(David Bridgwater) *in tch 4th: rdn 3 out: sn wknd* **9/1**

003- 9 ¾ **Young Lou**[52] 3434 5-9-13 **78** (b[1]) MrTWWheeler(5) 58
(Robin Dickin) *chsd ldrs: bdly hmpd and lost pl 3rd: rallied to chse ldrs bef next: wknd 3 out* **9/1**

05/- 10 27 **Queenswood Bay**[575] 1086 8-10-3 **80** PaulJohn(3) 33
(David Dennis) *in tch 4th: wknd 3 out: no ch whn hmpd 2 out* **20/1**

50P- 11 5 **Photogenique (FR)**[30] 3842 11-9-9 **74** oh10.. MissGeorgiaHenderson(5) 22
(Rob Summers) *sn bhd* **66/1**

123/ F **Philharmonic Hall**[749] 3715 6-11-12 **100** MrMatthewBarber
(Marc Barber) *led and veered rt 3rd: hdd 3 out: sn wknd: no ch whn fell 2 out* **33/1**

060- U **Benefitofhindsight**[28] 3877 5-10-9 **88** MrHBeswick(5)
(Ben Pauling) *led tl bdly bmpd and uns rdr 3rd* **8/1**

3m 58.03s (1.53) **Going Correction** +0.15s/f (Yiel) **13** Ran SP% **116.8**
Speed ratings (Par 103): **102,101,99,98,97 94,89,89,88,75 72**, ,
CSF £57.47 CT £563.36 TOTE £15.80: £4.30, £1.40, £3.70; EX 44.00 Trifecta £420.70.
Owner The K Team **Bred** Twinacre Nurseries Ltd **Trained** Lewes, E Sussex

FOCUS
A moderate handicap. The winner is entitled to rate 100+ on her Flat form, with the next four all close to their marks.

4399 GAMBLE FAMILY DAY AT WARWICK RACES NOVICES' H'CAP CHASE (17 fncs 1 omitted) 3m 110y
3:10 (3:10) (Class 4) (0-110,110) 5-Y-0+ **£3,898** (£1,144; £572; £286)

Form RPR

5P3- 1 **No Duffer**[53] 3418 7-11-11 **109** AndrewTinkler 122+
(Henry Daly) *chsd ldrs: hit 3rd: drvn and outpcd appr 10th: styd on wl u.p fr 3 out: nt fluent and disputing 2nd 2 out: slt ld appr last: hrd pressed run-in: hld on all out* **11/2**[3]

/24- 2 nk **Mighty Mobb (IRE)**[31] 3827 7-11-10 **108** (p) RichardJohnson 121+
(Philip Hobbs) *blnd 1st: in rr: hdwy 7th: chsd ldr 3 out: hit 2 out and sn chalng: upsides and u.p fr last: no ex last strides* **8/1**

P23- 3 8 **Basford Ben**[16] 4082 6-10-11 **95** (p) SeanQuinlan 100
(Jennie Candlish) *in tch: chsd ldrs 8th: lost pl and rdn bef 4 out: kpt on fr 2 out to take 3rd after last but no imp on ldng duo* **14/1**

U42- 4 7 **Badgers Cove (IRE)**[30] 3836 10-11-8 **106** (p) CharliePoste 103
(Robin Dickin) *towards rr and rdn 7th: dropped away 9th: styd on again fr 2 out to take modest 4th fnl 120yds* **8/1**

54P- 5 18 **Comeonginger (IRE)**[57] 3293 7-11-11 **109** TomCannon 93
(Chris Gordon) *led: jnd and u.p 2 out: hdd appr last: wknd rapidly run-in* **20/1**

342- 6 10 **Water Wagtail**[34] 3785 7-11-8 **106** RobertThornton 74
(Emma Lavelle) *chsd ldr to 4 out: wknd 3 out: no ch whn hit last* **11/4**[1]

556- 7 24 **Cheat The Cheater (IRE)**[38] 3696 7-9-12 **89** (tp) GeraldQuinn(7) 33
(Claire Dyson) *hit 6th and 7th: a in rr* **15/2**

/FP- P **Mac Steamy (IRE)**[13] 4161 8-11-9 **107** (t) RyanMahon
(William Kinsey) *chsd ldrs early: tailed off whn p.u bef 12th* **40/1**

0/P- P **Getting Ready (IRE)**[63] 3183 7-11-12 **110** SamTwiston-Davies
(Nigel Twiston-Davies) *in rr: j. slowly 8th: p.u bef next* **16/1**

5P1- U **Barton Gift**[38] 3696 7-10-12 **101** (b) NicodeBoinville(5) +
(John Spearing) *trckd ldrs: cl 2nd and travelling wl whn mstke and uns rdr 12th* **9/2**[2]

6m 24.74s (-2.26) **Going Correction** -0.05s/f (Good) **10** Ran SP% **114.0**
Speed ratings: **101,100,98,96,90 87,79**, , ,
CSF £47.85 CT £581.22 TOTE £7.30: £2.20, £2.10, £4.00; EX 47.80 Trifecta £464.10.
Owner David Robey **Bred** Mrs R Crank **Trained** Stanton Lacy, Shropshire
■ Stewards' Enquiry : Andrew Tinkler two-day ban: used whip in incorrect place (Mar 7-8)

FOCUS
A fair novice handicap chase and quite a test in the conditions. The winner belatedly fulfilled the promise of his best bumper form.

4400 STAR SPORTS BUDBROOKE CHASE (A H'CAP) (16 fncs 1 omitted) 2m 4f 110y
3:40 (3:40) (Class 2) (0-150,150) 5-Y-0+
£18,768 (£5,544; £2,772; £1,386; £693; £348)

Form RPR

212- 1 **Persian Snow (IRE)**[13] 4160 8-10-8 **132** (t) RichardJohnson 142+
(Philip Hobbs) *chsd ldrs: blnd 10th: chsd ldr next: nt fluent 3 out: led 2 out: drvn clr fr last* **7/2**[2]

630- 2 8 **Greywell Boy**[69] 3080 7-10-0 **124** oh2 PaulMoloney 125
(Nick Williams) *chsd ldrs: lost position after 9th: rcvrd next: styd on under pressur fr 3 out to take 2nd after last but no ch w wnr* **9/1**

The Form Book Jumps, Raceform Ltd, Compton, RG20 6NL.

011- 3 4 **Bennys Mist (IRE)**22 3990 8-11-2 **140** LiamTreadwell 140+
(Venetia Williams) *led: rdn after 3 out: hdd next: no ch w wnr whn blnd last and lost 2nd: kpt on again clsng stages* **8/1**3

231- 4 4 1/2 **No Planning**20 4039 7-11-2 **140** RyanMania 135
(Sue Smith) *chsd ldr: chal 6th to 7th: dropped to 3rd 12th: rdn 3 out: no ch w ldrs whn hit 2 out* **5/2**1

/11- 5 2 1/4 **Uxizandre (FR)**95 2565 6-11-12 **150** APMcCoy 143
(Alan King) *a in rr: mstke 2nd: hit 6th and 10th: j. slowly 12th and outpcd: no prog whn hit 2 out: modest hdwy run-in* **5/2**1

035- 6 nk **What A Warrior (IRE)**34 3772 7-10-6 **130** SamTwiston-Davies 120
(Nigel Twiston-Davies) *j. slowly and in rr: mstke 2nd: hit 6th and 10th: j. slowly 12th and outpcd: wl bhd fr 3 out: kpt on wl run-in but nvr a threat* **8/1**3

5m 12.83s (-8.17) **Going Correction** -0.05s/f (Good) **6** Ran SP% **111.6**
Speed ratings: **113,109,108,106,105 105**
CSF £30.43 TOTE £4.10: £1.60, £4.00; EX 42.90 Trifecta £255.00.
Owner D R Peppiatt **Bred** Garryhankard House Stud **Trained** Withycombe, Somerset

FOCUS
A decent handicap chase and they looked to go a solid pace. Another step up from the winner.

4401 WHITSON BLOODSTOCK JUVENILE HURDLE (8 hdls) 2m
4:10 (4:10) (Class 4) 4-Y-O **£3,898** (£1,144; £572; £286)

Form RPR

F32- 1 **Raven's Tower (USA)**39 3686 4-11-5 124 DavidBass 115
(Ben Pauling) *in tiuch: chsd ldrs 4th: wnt 2nd bef 2 out: styd on u.p fr last to ld fnl 75yds* **5/2**1

322- 2 1/2 **Haatefina**29 3857 4-10-5 117 DaveCrosse 101
(Mark Usher) *led: hdd after 3rd: led again 4th: rdn bef 2 out: nt fluent last: hdd fnl 75yds: no ex u.p* **7/2**2

20- 3 6 **Ninepointsixthree**42 3245 4-10-5 0 CiaranMckee(3) 101
(John O'Shea) *chsd ldr: led after 3rd: hdd next: rdn and outpcd 3 out: kpt on u.p fr 2 out to take 3rd fnl 75yds* **66/1**

4 1 3/4 **Amoruccio (FR)** 4-10-12 0 SamTwiston-Davies 99
(Paul Webber) *chsd ldrs: rdn after 3 out: styd on same pce fr 2 out: mstke and no ex last* **16/1**

10- 5 nk **Muhtaris (IRE)**15 4111 4-11-5 0 (p) DenisO'Regan 107
(John Ferguson) *trckd ldrs: hit 3 out: styd wl there: pushed along appr 2 out: styd on same pce* **4/1**3

26- 6 6 **Mr Vendman (IRE)**2 4345 4-10-7 0 RobertMcCarth(5) 95
(Ian Williams) *blnd 1st: in rr: pushed along 4 out: mod prog fr 2 out* **33/1**

555- 7 15 **After Eight Sivola (FR)**15 4111 4-10-12 117 RichardJohnson 96
(Nick Williams) *chsd ldrs: rdn and hit 3 out: wknd sn after: blnd 2 out* **9/2**

65- 8 4 1/2 **Interior Minister**17 4073 4-10-12 0 APMcCoy 73
(Jonjo O'Neill) *bhd fr 1/2-way* **11/1**

9 12 **Bahumbug** 4-10-12 0 AndrewThornton 61
(Seamus Mullins) *a in rr* **100/1**

06- 10 1 3/4 **Hurricane John (IRE)**17 4073 4-10-12 0 LiamTreadwell 60
(Venetia Williams) *hit 2nd: bhd fr 1/2-way* **33/1**

F **London Skolar**77 4-10-9 0 JackQuinlan(3)
(James Eustace) *bhd fr 1/2-way: t.o whn fell 2 out* **20/1**

3m 57.18s (0.68) **Going Correction** +0.15s/f (Yiel) **11** Ran SP% **116.3**
Speed ratings: **104,103,100,99,99 96,89,86,80,80**
CSF £10.87 TOTE £3.20: £1.50, £1.30, £11.80; EX 11.30 Trifecta £320.70.
Owner Faithful Friends **Bred** Darley **Trained** Bourton-On-The-Water, Gloucs

FOCUS
An ordinary juvenile contest. The first three were all fairly close to their marks.

4402 IRISH RACEDAY HERE ON 9TH MARCH H'CAP CHASE (20 fncs 2 omitted) 3m 5f
4:40 (4:40) (Class 3) (0-130,123) 5-Y-O+ **£6,498** (£1,908; £954; £477)

Form RPR

326- 1 **Loughalder (IRE)**75 2979 8-10-2 **99** (tp) CharliePoste 117+
(Matt Sheppard) *trckd ldr fr 5th: drvn to ld appr last: sn clr: readily* **13/2**

532- 2 7 **Bally Sands (IRE)**29 3858 10-10-0 **100** ow1 (v) RobertDunne(3) 108
(Robin Mathew) *mde most tl hdd appr last: sn no ch w wnr but hld on wl for 2nd clsng stages* **5/2**1

P1U- 3 2 1/4 **Union Jack D'Ycy (FR)**11 4190 6-11-12 **123** LiamTreadwell 127
(Venetia Williams) *pressed ldr to 3rd: dropped to 3rd 5th: styd prom: pressed ldrs 4 out: to next: sn outpcd: kpt on again to cl on 2nd nr fin but no ch w wnr* **7/2**2

445- 4 hd **Alderluck (IRE)**38 3698 11-11-1 **119** (b) MikeyEnnis(7) 123
(David Pipe) *in rr: hdwy 12th: styd on and pckd 4 out: kpt on u.p fr 2 out to dispute 3rd and cl on 2nd nr fin but no ch w wnr* **5/1**3

600- 5 17 **Fredo (IRE)**5 4303 10-11-2 **118** (p) RobertMcCarth(5) 108
(Ian Williams) *chsd ldrs: blnd 15th: no ch after* **8/1**

/44- 6 16 **Counting House (IRE)**76 2941 11-11-12 **123** MarkGrant 94
(Jim Old) *in rr: lost tch fr 15th: no ch whn blnd 2 out* **14/1**

125- 7 6 **Musical Wedge**36 3743 10-10-9 **113** GeraldQuinn(7) 78
(Claire Dyson) *chsd ldrs: wknd qckly 4 out* **16/1**

304/ P **Trigger The Light**348 4687 13-11-12 **123** RobertThornton
(Alan King) *in tch: hit 12th: wknd 4 out: t.o whn p.u bef last* **10/1**

P/0- P **Estates Recovery (IRE)**21 4021 9-11-3 **114** LeightonAspell
(Luke Dace) *in rr whn hit 9th: blnd 11th: t.o whn p.u bef 14th* **33/1**

7m 40.58s (-0.42) **Going Correction** -0.05s/f (Good) **9** Ran SP% **116.5**
Speed ratings: **98,96,95,95,90 86,84, ,**
CSF £24.32 CT £66.96 TOTE £7.20: £2.10, £1.10, £2.40; EX 26.20 Trifecta £114.40.
Owner Simon Gegg & Tony Scrivin **Bred** Tom Burns **Trained** Eastnor, H'fords

FOCUS
A decent marathon handicap chase, but they went a sensible pace in the conditions and all bar one were still closely packed a mile from home. Those that raced close to the pace were at an advantage, however. A big step up from the winner with the second rated in line with his recent course win.

4403 EBF STALLIONS MARES' STANDARD OPEN NATIONAL HUNT FLAT RACE 2m
5:10 (5:10) (Class 6) 4-7-Y-O **£1,819** (£534; £267; £133)

Form RPR

0- 1 **Midnight Jazz**65 3167 4-10-2 0 KielanWoods(3) 95
(Ben Case) *in tch: hdwy to chse ldr over 5f out: led 4f out: drvn and styd on wl fnl 2f* **16/1**

3- 2 2 1/4 **Jennys Surprise (IRE)**64 3181 6-10-9 0 ConorShoemark(5) 102
(Fergal O'Brien) *chsd ldr to 5f out: chsd wnr fr over 3f out: kpt on u.p but a hld* **9/1**

3 9 **Bel Esprit (IRE)** 5-11-0 0 RhysFlint 93
(Robert Stephens) *chsd ldrs: rdn 5f out: outpcd 4f out: styd on again u.p to take 3rd fnl 120yds but no ch w ldng duo* **50/1**

2- 4 1 **Meetmeatthemoon (IRE)**41 3656 5-11-0 0 RichardJohnson 92
(Philip Hobbs) *in rr: hdwy 6f out: rdn over 4f out: sn one pce: styd on again clsng stages* **9/4**1

5 1 **Beautiful Gem (FR)** 4-10-5 0 HarrySkelton 82
(Dan Skelton) *in rr: hdwy over 4f out: chsd ldrs 3 out: sn outpcd* **14/1**

6 6 **Hinton Magic** 5-11-0 0 APMcCoy 85
(Jonjo O'Neill) *hld up in rr: rdn and sme hdwy to cl on ldrs over 3f out: sn btn* **17/2**3

35- 7 3 **Morello Royale (IRE)**37 3719 4-9-12 0 MrMLegg(7) 73
(Colin Tizzard) *in tch: hdwy to chse ldrs 1/2-way: wknd 4f out* **14/1**

3- 8 8 **Goneinaglance**14 4135 5-10-7 0 MrJMartin(7) 74
(Andrew J Martin) *chsd ldrs 10f* **25/1**

9 44 **Native Princess** 4-10-5 0 SamTwiston-Davies 21
(Renee Robeson) *in rr: sme hdwy 1/2-way: wknd 6f out* **9/1**

2/2- S **Western Diva (IRE)**24 3961 5-11-0 0 HaddenFrost
(David Pipe) *led: hdd 4f out: wkng whn slipped up on bnd and fell over 3f out* **5/2**2

3m 49.71s (-1.19) **Going Correction** +0.15s/f (Yiel)
WFA 4 from 5yo+ 9lb **10** Ran SP% **114.9**
Speed ratings: **108,106,102,101,101 98,96,92,70,**
CSF £149.85 TOTE £28.20: £7.00, £2.60, £11.20; EX 222.90 Trifecta £1908.70 Part won..
Owner D Allen **Bred** David Allen **Trained** Edgcote, Northants

FOCUS
A modest mares' bumper. The second and fourth help set the level.
T/Jkpt: Not won. T/Plt: £95.00 to a £1 stake. Pool: £90809.72 - 697.62 winning tickets T/Qpdt: £44.70 to a £1 stake. Pool: £5500.03 - 90.95 winning tickets ST

3357 CHEPSTOW (L-H)
Saturday, February 22

OFFICIAL GOING: Heavy (ch 3.6, hdl 4.8)
Wind: Brisk across Weather: Sunny spells

4411 32RED MAIDEN HURDLE (7 hdls 4 omitted) 2m 4f
1:20 (1:21) (Class 4) 4-Y-0+ **£3,119** (£915; £457; £228)

Form RPR

010/ 1 **Monkey Kingdom**322 5179 6-10-12 0 (t) PatrickCorbett(5) 118+
(Rebecca Curtis) *mde virtually all: 2 l clr on 2f run-in: sn drvn: wkng clsng stages: jst lasted* **4/5**1

6- 2 shd **Queen's Star**74 3005 5-10-10 0 TomO'Brien 110
(Andrew Balding) *chsd wnr fr 4th: 2 l 2nd last: styd on wl u.p on 2f run-in: edgd lft fnl 50yds: jst failed* **14/1**

5PP- 3 nk **Phone Home (IRE)**54 3421 7-11-3 110 DominicElsworth 117
(Nick Mitchell) *in rr: hdwy after 5th: drvn and plenty to do in 4th at last: styd on wl on 2f run-in: fin strly: nt quite get up* **6/1**2

53- 4 6 **Ossie's Dancer**31 3838 5-11-3 0 ColinBolger 112
(Martin Smith) *in tch: hdwy after 5th: styng on one pce in 3rd whn hit last: styd on same pce 2f run-in* **16/1**

- 5 23 **Almost Gemini (IRE)**120 5-11-3 0 MarkGrant 88
(Charlie Mann) *in rr: hit 4th: hdwy after 5th: wknd fr 2 out* **12/1**

303- 6 2 **Grey Earl**34 3796 7-11-3 0 JamieMoore 86
(Richard Lee) *in rr whn hit 3rd and 4th: hdwy after 5th: wknd fr 2 out* **8/1**3

7 1 1/2 **The Bogman's Ball**301 8-10-10 0 ConorRing(7) 85
(Grace Harris) *chsd ldrs: wknd after 2 out* **50/1**

6/5- 8 60 **Romany Quest**39 3697 7-10-10 0 MrCSmith(7) 25
(Linda Blackford) *pressed wnr 2nd: rdn after 3rd: wknd 4th: t.o* **33/1**

9 30 **Cloudy Smith** 5-10-3 0 GaryDerwin(7)
(Brian Eckley) *a in rr* **100/1**

60P- 10 25 **Driving Well (IRE)**21 4029 6-10-10 0 [1] RyanHatch(7)
(Arthur Whiting) *t.o fr 3rd* **66/1**

64- P **Eastern Witness (IRE)**17 4093 7-11-3 0 LiamTreadwell
(Venetia Williams) *nt fluent and in rr 3rd: wknd and p.u bef next* **14/1**

0/0- P **Morebutwhen**77 2946 7-10-10 0 TomCannon
(Richard King) *chsd ldrs: hit 4th: sn wknd: t.o whn p.u bef 2 out* **80/1**

5m 6.51s (4.71) **Going Correction** +0.325s/f (Yiel) **12** Ran SP% **116.5**
Speed ratings (Par 105): **103,102,102,100,91 90,89,65,53,43 ,**
CSF £13.37 TOTE £1.90: £1.10, £3.10, £2.10; EX 13.20 Trifecta £59.90.
Owner Carl Hinchy **Bred** R Aston **Trained** Newport, Dyfed

FOCUS
An ordinary maiden hurdle run at a steady pace. The winner is entitled to rate higher on bumper form.

4412 32RED NOVICES' LIMITED H'CAP CHASE (14 fncs 4 omitted) 3m
1:55 (1:57) (Class 3) (0-125,124) 5-Y-O+ **£6,498** (£1,908; £954; £477)

Form RPR

154- 1 **Woodford County**16 4110 7-10-13 **116** (p) TomO'Brien 128+
(Philip Hobbs) *led: hdd 3 out: rallied to chal next: slt ld last: asserted at omitted fnl fence: drvn out* **11/2**

513- 2 1 **Big Society (IRE)**30 3860 8-11-3 **120** RhysFlint 129
(Tom George) *chsd wnr fr 3rd: chal 4 out: led next: jnd 2 out: narrowly hdd last: no imp fr omitted fnl fence* **11/2**

04U- 3 8 **Fourovakind**29 3881 9-11-4 **124** (b1) JeremiahMcGrath(3) 125
(Harry Whittington) *in tch: hdwy 10th: chsd ldrs fr 4 out: styd on same pce fr omitted fnl fence* **5/1**3

234- 4 7 **Ballylifen (IRE)**56 3365 7-10-4 **117** JamesHuxham(10) 113
(Jonjo O'Neill) *chsd ldrs: blnd 7th: sn rcvrd: chsd ldrs 4 out: wknd fr 2 out* **7/2**2

030- 5 16 **Tolkeins Tango (IRE)**37 3741 6-10-9 **112** JackDoyle 93
(Victor Dartnall) *in rr: j. slowly 4th: hdwy appr 4 out: sn wknd* **9/1**

P3P- P **Bravo Bravo**23 3989 7-10-3 **113** (b) RyanHatch(7)
(Mark Gillard) *chsd wnr to 3rd: sn bhd: t.o whn p.u bef 12th* **20/1**

221- P **Goodtoknow**62 3223 6-11-5 **122** JamieMoore
(Richard Lee) *j.big 1st: hit 5th: hdwy sn after: hit 9th: j. slowly 10th: wknd 4 out: p.u next* **11/4**1

6m 35.95s (13.95) **Going Correction** +0.325s/f (Yiel) **7** Ran SP% **111.1**
Speed ratings: **76,75,73,70,65 ,**
CSF £33.08 CT £153.99 TOTE £6.00: £2.70, £2.70; EX 26.10 Trifecta £105.20.
Owner E & A England and A & A Heywood **Bred** Wendy Robinson **Trained** Withycombe, Somerset

FOCUS
Owing to the recent rainfall, the last fence in the back straight and the last in the home straight were omitted for this comptitive limited handicap chase, and they jumped nine fences per circuit rather than 11. The run-in was over 2f and it was a factor in the outcome of a protracted battle. The first three were all entitled to be this good on hurdles form.

4413 32RED.COM H'CAP HURDLE (6 hdls 2 omitted) 2m 110y
2:30 (2:30) (Class 3) (0-135,129) 4-Y-0+ £6,498 (£1,908; £954; £477)

Form RPR
/15- 1 **Lord Protector (IRE)**42 3661 7-11-2 **119** TomO'Brien 127+
(Philip Hobbs) *chsd ldrs: chal 2 out (omitted 4th last): upsides last: sn led on 2f run-in: drvn out* **13/5**1
P06- 2 1 3/4 **Somemothersdohavem**14 4157 5-11-1 **118** LiamTreadwell 123
(Venetia Williams) *chsd ldrs: chal 2 out: (omitted 4th last) led sn after: jnd last: hdd on 2f run-in: kpt on same pce u.p* **7/2**2
42P- 3 5 **Captain Cardington (IRE)**3 4351 5-9-9 **105** (b1) CiaranMckee(7) 105
(John O'Shea) *led tl after 1st: rdn and ev ch 2 out (omitted 4th last): styd on same pce 2f run-in* **12/1**
0P1- 4 1/2 **Alder Mairi (IRE)**23 3989 7-11-10 **127** AndrewThornton 128
(Seamus Mullins) *led after 1st: jnd 2 out (omitted 4th last): one pce last: edgd lft u.p and no ex 2f run-in* **7/2**2
F06- 5 1 **Swnymor (IRE)**21 4025 5-11-2 **129** (t) PaulO'Brien(10) 128
(Rebecca Curtis) *chsd ldrs: ev ch 2 out (omitted 4th last): sn one pce: kpt on u.p 2f run-in* **4/1**3
1P0- 6 44 **Lava Lamp (GER)**37 3730 7-11-2 **119** AdamWedge 74
(Evan Williams) *a in rr: t.o fr 1/2-way* **20/1**
0/4- 7 20 **Tiger O'Toole (IRE)**35 3786 9-11-4 **121** PaulMoloney 56
(Evan Williams) *a in rr: t.o fr 1/2-way* **16/1**
4m 12.59s (1.99) **Going Correction** +0.325s/f (Yiel) 7 Ran SP% **110.6**
Speed ratings (Par 107): **108,107,104,104,104 83,74**
CSF £11.54 TOTE £2.80: £1.20, £2.50; EX 12.50 Trifecta £129.70.
Owner Louisville Syndicate **Bred** Joan And John Ronayne **Trained** Withycombe, Somerset

FOCUS
Mainly exposed performers in a fair handicap. They went no great pace and plenty held chances two out, yet the form has a solid feel. A step up from the winner with the third to fifth setting the level.

4414 RIFLES H'CAP CHASE SUPPORTING CARE FOR CASUALTIES (FOR THE BOMBAY HUNT CUP) (10 fncs 2 omitted) 2m 110y
3:05 (3:05) (Class 2) 5-Y-0+ £15,825 (£4,675; £2,337; £1,170; £585)

Form RPR
041- 1 **Poole Master**21 4027 9-10-8 **139** (b) TomBellamy(7) 147
(David Pipe) *trckd ldrs: shkn up and outpcd 4 out: sn bk chsng ldr: chal 2 out to last: rdn and one pce omitted fnl fence: rallied to ld last strides* **9/2**2
321- 2 nk **Grey Gold (IRE)**21 4032 9-11-7 **145** JamieMoore 153
(Richard Lee) *in rr: hdwy 5th: chsd ldrs 4 out: rdn fr next: chal 2 out to last: led u.p omitted fnl fence: hdd last strides* **3/1**1
421- 3 3 **Al Alfa**25 3960 7-9-11 **124** oh2 JamesBest(3) 129
(Philip Hobbs) *chsd ldrs: led after 5th: drvn and jnd fr 3 out tl hdd omitted fnl fence: no ex* **5/1**3
615- 4 18 **Fago (FR)**57 3320 6-11-12 **150** 1 RyanMahon 137
(Paul Nicholls) *in rr: hdwy after 5th: clsd on ldrs and nt fluent 4 out: effrt 3 out: wl hld in 4th fr 2 out* **9/2**2
225- 5 7 **Saved By John (IRE)**70 3080 9-10-6 **133** (t) MichaelByrne(3) 115
(Tim Vaughan) *led: hdd after 5th: wknd and hit 3 out* **8/1**
155- 6 4 **Get It On (IRE)**25 3957 9-10-4 **128** PaulMoloney 104
(Evan Williams) *bhd most of way* **22/1**
234- 7 2 **Last Shot (FR)**21 4036 7-10-4 **128** LiamTreadwell 104
(Venetia Williams) *pressed ldrs to 5th: wknd after 4 out* **10/1**
4PP- 8 14 **Rody (FR)**28 3894 9-10-11 **140** (tp) AodhaganConlon(5) 100
(Tom George) *in tch: rdn 4 out: wknd and mstke next* **22/1**
020- P **Gus Macrae (IRE)**35 3772 10-9-12 **127** (tp) PatrickCorbett(5)
(Rebecca Curtis) *blnd and bhd fr 1st: t.o whn p.u bef 5th* **10/1**
4m 11.39s (-5.71) **Going Correction** 0.0s/f (Good) 9 Ran SP% **116.0**
Speed ratings: **113,112,111,102,99 97,96,90,**
CSF £19.23 CT £67.93 TOTE £4.50: £2.00, £1.10, £1.80; EX 15.50 Trifecta £34.40.
Owner G Thompson **Bred** Wood Farm Stud **Trained** Nicholashayne, Devon

FOCUS
They went relatively hard up front in a race where plenty liked to set the pace. The last fence was bypassed owing to the ground and the long run-in proved a factor in the outcome. Strong handicap form with the first two on the upgrade.

4415 PERTEMPS NETWORK H'CAP HURDLE (SERIES QUALIFIER) (8 hdls 4 omitted) 3m
3:40 (3:41) (Class 2) 5-Y-0+
£12,512 (£3,696; £1,848; £924; £462; £232)

Form RPR
206- 1 **Buddy Bolero (IRE)**42 3647 8-11-7 **135** (p) KieronEdgar(5) 148+
(David Pipe) *chsd ldrs: pushed along and outpcd 6th: sn rcvrd: pressed ldrs 2 out: chal last: sn led on 2f run-in and c readily clr* **12/1**
221- 2 10 **Kris Spin (IRE)**30 3860 6-11-6 **132** MichealNolan(3) 134
(Richard Lee) *in tch chsd ldrs 6th: led appr 2 out: jnd last: sn hdd on 2f run-in and no ch w wnr but kpt on for 2nd* **10/1**
314- 3 5 **Awaywiththegreys (IRE)**21 4025 7-11-12 **135** JamieMoore 132
(Peter Bowen) *in tch pushed along to chse ldrs fr 5th: chal 2 out: no ex last and styd on same pce 2f run-in* **12/1**
602- 4 23 **Viva Steve (IRE)**16 4105 6-10-13 **122** DominicElsworth 96
(Mick Channon) *led tl appr 4th: styd chsng ldrs to 2 out: wknd wl bef last* **8/1**
123- 5 6 **Tidal Dance (IRE)**7 4280 7-11-10 **133** LiamTreadwell 101
(Venetia Williams) *pressed ldrs: rdn along fr 5th: wknd bef 2 out* **5/1**2
3P4- 6 9 **One In A Milan (IRE)**56 3361 9-10-13 **122** PaulMoloney 81
(Evan Williams) *chsd ldrs tl rdn and bhd fr 5th* **8/1**
1P0- 7 49 **Cyrien Star**42 3653 7-11-4 **127** TomO'Brien 37
(Henry Daly) *chsd ldrs to 5th: sn wknd* **12/1**
421- 8 56 **Tullyesker Hill (IRE)**14 4161 5-10-12 **128** (p) TomBellamy(7)
(David Pipe) *in rr whn rdn and hit 5th: no ch after* **9/4**1
623- P **Ugly Bug**35 3775 8-10-8 **124** KevinJones(7)
(Seamus Mullins) *led appr 4th: hdd appr 2 out and mstke: sn btn: p.u bef last* **7/1**3
6m 15.2s (13.00) **Going Correction** +0.325s/f (Yiel) 9 Ran SP% **114.3**
Speed ratings: **91,87,86,78,76 73,57,38,**
CSF £120.91 CT £1469.61 TOTE £15.60: £4.10, £2.80, £2.40; EX 103.50 Trifecta £648.30 Part won..
Owner Malcolm C Denmark **Bred** Mary Fanning McCormack **Trained** Nicholashayne, Devon

FOCUS
A fairly competitive handicap run at a fair pace. They finished well strung out. A big hurdles best from the winner.

4416 32RED FREE £10 BONUS H'CAP CHASE (10 fncs 2 omitted) 2m 110y
4:10 (4:12) (Class 5) (0-100,94) 5-Y-0+ £2,144 (£629; £314; £157)

Form RPR
023- 1 **Jeanry (FR)**108 2289 11-11-5 **94** JoshWall(7) 107+
(Arthur Whitehead) *in tch: hdwy appr 4 out: trckd ldr 2 out: led after last and forged clr wl bef omitted fnl fence: eased considerably clsng stages* **20/1**
1U2- 2 7 **Sablazo (FR)**40 3687 8-10-11 **79** LiamTreadwell 81
(Andy Turnell) *chsd ldrs: chal fr 4 out tl slt ld 3 out: rdn and hdd after last: no ch w wnr fr wl bef omitted fnl fence: jst hld on for 2nd last strides* **8/1**
12P- 3 nk **Mister Wiseman**68 3139 12-10-13 **88** (vt) ThomasCheesman(7) 89
(Nigel Hawke) *led to 2nd: styd pressing ldrs: slt ld appr 4 out to 3 out: outpcd 2 out: rallied fr omitted fnl fence to cl on 2nd last stride but nvr any ch w wnr* **14/1**
05P- 4 hd **Ashcott Boy**35 3785 6-11-3 **88** MichaelByrne(3) 91
(Neil Mulholland) *in rr: hit 5th and 4 out: blnd 3 out and plenty to do: styd on fr 2 out: kpt on fr omitted fnl fence to cl on 2nd but nvr any ch w wnr* **10/1**
PP1- 5 27 **The Informant**47 3564 8-10-12 **80** (p) AndrewThornton 54
(Seamus Mullins) *chsd ldrs: drvn along fr 5th: pressed ldrs u.p fr 4 out: wkng whn stmbld after 3 out* **6/1**2
5/4- 6 10 **Beauchamp Viking**34 3799 10-10-11 **79** (t) ColinBolger 43
(Hugo Froud) *bhd most of way* **25/1**
P3P- 7 6 **Zen Factor**40 3687 9-11-3 **85** (b1) PaulMoloney 43
(Jonathan Portman) *led 2nd: kpt slt advantage tl appr 4 out: sn wknd* **11/1**
50U- 8 3 **Ilewin Kim**74 3015 8-10-7 **75** JamieMoore 30
(Gary Brown) *a in rr* **17/2**
32U- U **Hector's House**34 3799 8-9-9 **70** OllieGarner(7)
(Nikki Evans) *pressed ldrs to 1st: bmpd: rdn and lost poition 2nd: sme hdwy u.p after 5th: wknd out: no ch w ldrs whn blnd and uns rdr next* **13/2**3
053- U **Enchanting Smile (FR)**40 3687 7-11-6 **88** (t1) TommyPhelan
(Mark Gillard) *blnd and uns rdr 2nd* **6/1**2
613- P **Brandon Thomas (IRE)**29 3883 8-11-6 **88** (p) TomCannon
(Nick Gifford) *chsd ldrs tl wknd bef 4 out: t.o whn p.u bef last* **7/2**1
4m 25.72s (8.62) **Going Correction** +0.325s/f (Yiel) 11 Ran SP% **118.5**
Speed ratings: **79,75,75,75,62 58,55,53, ,**
CSF £172.71 CT £2330.11 TOTE £29.10: £5.90, £2.60, £4.00; EX 213.00 Trifecta £508.70.
Owner A J Whitehead **Bred** Jean Biraben And Henri Soler **Trained** Aston on Clun, Shropshire

FOCUS
They went a fair gallop in this poor handicap chase. The easy winner is rated back to his best.

4417 32RED NEW AVALON II SLOT MAIDEN NATIONAL HUNT FLAT RACE (CONDITIONALS & AMATEURS) 2m 110y
4:45 (4:45) (Class 6) 4-6-Y-O £1,559 (£457; £228; £114)

Form RPR
23- 1 **Binge Drinker (IRE)**53 3433 5-10-9 0 PaulO'Brien(10) 111+
(Rebecca Curtis) *disp ld tl led after 3f: rdn over 2f out: styd on wl fnl f* **8/11**1
2 7 **Theunnamedsoldier** 6-10-12 0 MrRobertHawker(7) 102
(Nigel Hawke) *in rr: hdwy 6f out: drvn to chse wnr 3f out: kpt on u.p fnl 2f but no imp* **20/1**
3 6 **Doctor Look Here (IRE)** 4-10-5 0 MissLucyGardner(5) 86
(Sue Gardner) *sn bhd: pushed along and green fr 1/2-way: hdwy fr 3f out: styd on wl to take 3rd over 1f out but no ch w ldng duo* **8/1**2
5- 4 1 1/4 **Rock On Rocky**21 4030 6-11-0 0 BenPoste(5) 94
(Matt Sheppard) *in tch: rdn and one pce 3f out: kpt on again fr over 1f out: nvr a threat* **14/1**
5 4 1/2 **Orchard Mist** 5-10-7 0 RobertWilliams(5) 83
(Bernard Llewellyn) *chsd ldrs: lost position 5f out: styd on again fnl 2f but nvr any threat* **10/1**3
6 1 1/2 **Johns Luck (IRE)** 5-11-0 0 ConorShoemark(5) 88
(Neil Mulholland) *in rr: hdwy 6f out: chsd wnr 4f out to 3f out: wknd 2f out* **8/1**2
5/0- 7 26 **Jaunty Inflight**286 250 5-10-12 0 GaryDerwin(7) 62
(Brian Eckley) *chsd ldrs: rdn 4f out: sn btn* **25/1**
8 65 **Thyne River (IRE)** 4-9-10 0 MrSPBowen(7)
(Bernard Llewellyn) *a in rr* **16/1**
30- 9 4 1/2 **Thats Yer Man (IRE)**23 3994 6-10-12 0 MrCSmith(7)
(Linda Blackford) *pressed wnr to 1/2-way: wknd 6f out* **14/1**
P **Cashback Dreamer (IRE)** 6-10-12 0 ConorRing(7)
(Grace Harris) *t.o 1/2-way: sn p.u* **50/1**
4m 15.28s (10.28) **Going Correction** +0.325s/f (Yiel)
WFA 4 from 5yo+ 9lb 10 Ran SP% **119.0**
Speed ratings: **88,84,81,81,79 78,66,35,33,**
CSF £22.10 TOTE £1.70: £1.02, £3.30, £4.10; EX 17.20 Trifecta £116.60.
Owner Miss Rebecca Curtis **Bred** Cyril O'Hara **Trained** Newport, Dyfed

FOCUS
An ordinary bumper run at a sound pace for the conditions. The form is rated around the fourth.
T/Plt: £136.20 to a £1 stake. Pool: £90,482.17 - 484.90 winning units. T/Qpdt: £36.90 to a £1 stake. Pool: £6959.50 - 139.50 winning units. ST

4129 KEMPTON (R-H)
Saturday, February 22

OFFICIAL GOING: Soft (heavy on lakeside bend; chs 4.8, hdl 4.2)
Wind: Moderate, across Weather: Fine, mild

4418 REWARDS4RACING H'CAP CHASE (THE JOCKEY CLUB GRASSROOTS JUMPS SERIES QUALIFIER) (16 fncs) 2m 4f 110y
1:30 (1:30) (Class 3) (0-130,130) 5-Y-0+ £6,498 (£1,908; £954; £477)

Form RPR
212- 1 **Present View**71 3059 6-11-8 **126** BrendanPowell 145+
(Jamie Snowden) *w ldr: led 9th: mde rest: clr 3 out: readily* **5/2**1
211- 2 10 **Ballinvarrig (IRE)**35 3769 7-11-9 **127** PaddyBrennan 134
(Tom George) *trckd ldrs: nt fluent 4th: mstke 9th: chsd wnr 11th to 12th: wnt 2nd again and mstke 3 out: j.rt next: no imp* **11/4**2
023- 3 3 **Mic's Delight (IRE)**37 3742 10-11-0 **118** (b1) DenisO'Regan 123
(Victor Dartnall) *hld up in rr: stdy prog fr 8th: trckd wnr 12th tl mstke 3 out: hld whn mstke 2 out: one pce* **10/1**

2P3- **4** *4* **Brody Bleu (FR)**[30] 3859 7-10-13 **117** .... FelixDeGiles 116
(Robert Walford) *trckd ldrs: in tch whn blnd 12th: rdn and btn after next* **11/1**

2F2- **5** *6* **Pearls Legend**[22] 4007 7-11-2 **120** .... RobertThornton 116
(John Spearing) *trckd ldrs: mstke 9th: wl on terms 13th: shkn up and wknd bef 3 out* **10/1**

164- **6** *7* **Lost Legend (IRE)**[89] 2714 7-11-9 **127** ....(p) APMcCoy 112
(Jonjo O'Neill) *hld up: last 1/2-way: lost tch w ldrs 12th: nudged along after next: no prog* **16/1**

31P/ **7** *8* **Jackies Solitaire**[321] 5198 6-11-10 **128** .... AidanColeman 105
(Anthony Honeyball) *hld up in rr: nt fluent 4th: lost tch 12th: drvn and no prog after next* **25/1**

432- **8** *24* **Flaming Gorge (IRE)**[37] 3738 9-11-11 **129** .... LeightonAspell 82
(Fleur Hawes) *led to 9th: wknd 11th: t.o* **16/1**

/2P- **F** **Sunny Ledgend**[7] 4265 9-11-2 **127** ....(p) MrJMartin(7)
(Andrew J Martin) *trckd ldrs: blnd 7th: mstkes after and steadily lost pl: struggling in 7th whn fell 12th* **7/1**[3]

411/ **P** **Tiptoeaway (IRE)**[493] 1884 9-11-12 **130** .... BarryGeraghty
(Tim Easterby) *racd wd: in tch to 7th: wknd next: wl t.o whn p.u after 4 out* **16/1**

5m 18.0s (1.40) **Going Correction** +0.15s/f (Yiel) **10** Ran SP% **115.7**
Speed ratings: **103,99,98,96,94 91,88,79,,**
CSF £10.20 CT £56.84 TOTE £3.20: £1.60, £2.10, £2.40; EX 10.50 Trifecta £53.60.

Owner Sir Chips Keswick **Bred** Richard Mathias **Trained** Lambourn, Berks

FOCUS
All rail moved back to inside configuration and distances as advertised. Following a dry night, the going was given as soft, heavy on the bend adjacent to the lake before racing started. Jockeys were spilt on the ground following the first. Paddy Brennan said it was "really hard work", while Brendan Powell was more upbeat, and said it was soft but his horse carried him round on it like was good ground. A fair handicap started the meeting off, which was run at a respectable gallop considering conditions. The easy winner was on a good mark but this rates a step up.

4419 BETBRIGHT.COM ADONIS JUVENILE HURDLE (GRADE 2) (8 hdls) 2m
2:05 (2:06) (Class 1) 4-Y-O
£15,661 (£5,876; £2,942; £1,465; £737; £368)

Form RPR

2- **1** **Activial (FR)**[85] 2796 4-10-12 0 .... NoelFehily 128+
(Harry Fry) *trckd ldng pair: cl up 3 out: led sn after 2 out: rdn and r.o wl fr last* **9/4**[1]

3- **2** *3 1/2* **Commissioned (IRE)**[70] 3078 4-10-12 0 ....(b[1]) DenisO'Regan 121
(John Ferguson) *trckd ldrs: clsd bef 2 out: swtchd lft and chsd wnr last: styd on but hung lft flat and no imp* **4/1**[3]

4- **3** *3 1/4* **Solar Impulse (FR)**[56] 3360 4-11-5 131 ....(t) DavidCottin 125
(Paul Nicholls) *mde most: hit 2nd: rdn bef 2 out: hdd sn after it: readily outpcd* **9/2**

4 *1 1/2* **Alcala (FR)**[151] 4-10-12 0 .... DarylJacob 117+
(Paul Nicholls) *hld up in midfield: gng wl on long run after 3 out: shkn up after 2 out: styd on but nt pce to be involved* **7/2**[2]

16- **5** *1* **Goodwood Mirage (IRE)**[28] 3885 4-11-2 0 ....[1] APMcCoy 122+
(Jonjo O'Neill) *t.k.h: j.lft: hld up in last: prog after 3 out: rdn 2 out: kpt on one pce and nvr able to threaten* **8/1**

1- **6** *5* **Fitzwilly**[125] 1044 4-11-2 0 .... WillKennedy 114
(Mick Channon) *t.k.h: w ldr: led briefly 5th: wknd 2 out* **33/1**

7 *8* **Agreement (IRE)**[204] 4-10-12 0 .... BarryGeraghty 103
(Rebecca Curtis) *trckd ldrs: blnd 3 out: sn rdn: wknd jst bef 2 out* **16/1**

410- **8** *27* **Duroble Man**[76] 2975 4-11-5 0 .... RobertThornton 82
(Alan King) *hld up in last pair: rdn and wknd on long run after 3 out: t.o* **25/1**

3m 59.6s (1.50) **Going Correction** +0.35s/f (Yiel) **8** Ran SP% **115.0**
Speed ratings: **110,108,106,105,105 102,98,85**
CSF £11.80 TOTE £3.30: £1.10, £2.00, £2.00; EX 10.00 Trifecta £70.00.

Owner Potensis Limited **Bred** Francis Maze **Trained** Seaborough, Dorset

FOCUS
This has proved to be a really good race for future hurdling stars in recent times, with the likes of Zarkandar (2011 Triumph Hurdle winner), Binocular and Punjabi (both subsequent Champion Hurdle winners) among some well-known names to land this Grade 2. The pace looked sound from the off for this renewal, but there wasn't much to separate the whole field heading off the final bend. Activial built on his recent run but this is still a long way shy of Grade 1 form. The next two were close to their marks.

4420 BETBRIGHT MOBILE PENDIL NOVICES' CHASE (GRADE 2) (16 fncs) 2m 4f 110y
2:40 (2:40) (Class 1) 5-Y-O+ **£17,451** (£6,599; £3,345; £1,707; £899)

Form RPR

151- **1** **Balder Succes (FR)**[14] 4159 6-11-7 151 .... WayneHutchinson 158+
(Alan King) *trckd ldng pair: pushed along to go 2nd after 3 out: upsides next: narrow ld last: rdn and styd on wl: won quite decisively* **9/4**[2]

024- **2** *1 1/4* **God's Own (IRE)**[28] 3893 6-11-0 137 .... PaddyBrennan 149
(Tom George) *nt a fluent: trckd ldrs: sltly outpcd 3 out: wnt 3rd next and clsd on ldng pair: swtchd lft bef last: styd on to take 2nd post* **6/1**[3]

213- **3** *nse* **Fox Appeal (IRE)**[28] 3893 7-11-7 152 .... AidanColeman 155
(Emma Lavelle) *pressed ldr: led 3 out: sn pressed and drvn: jnd 2 out: narrowly hdd last: styd on but lost 2nd post* **5/4**[1]

F26- **4** *18* **Dark Lover (GER)**[28] 3886 9-11-7 140 ....(p) DarylJacob 140
(Paul Nicholls) *nt a fluent: wl in tch: rdn after 13th: wknd bef next (3 out)* **10/1**

211- **5** *1* **Loose Chips**[29] 3881 8-11-4 139 ....(b) NoelFehily 133
(Charlie Longsdon) *led: rdn and hdd 3 out: sn wknd* **7/1**

445- **P** **Tchang Goon (FR)**[14] 4159 10-11-0 62 ....(p) MrHGMiller
(Zoe Davison) *j.lft: a last: lost tch 9th: t.o whn p.u bef 3 out* **250/1**

5m 11.1s (-5.50) **Going Correction** +0.15s/f (Yiel) **6** Ran SP% **111.5**
Speed ratings: **116,115,115,108,108**
CSF £15.43 TOTE £3.20: £1.60, £2.80; EX 16.40 Trifecta £40.20.

Owner Masterson Holdings Limited **Bred** Damien Bellanger Et Al **Trained** Barbury Castle, Wilts

FOCUS
Only five of the six made any appeal on what they'd done over fences, but three came right away. The time was almost seven seconds quicker than the 0-130 handicap chase over the same trip earlier on the card. Balder Succes is closing in on the level of a Grade 1-winning novice chaser, and the form looks solid.

4421 SKY BET DOVECOTE NOVICES' HURDLE (GRADE 2) (8 hdls) 2m
3:15 (3:15) (Class 1) 4-Y-O+
£15,661 (£5,876; £2,942; £1,465; £737; £368)

Form RPR

111- **1** **Irving**[64] 3184 6-11-9 143 .... NickScholfield 149+
(Paul Nicholls) *nt a fluent: wl in tch: trckd ldr 5th: clsng whn hit 2 out: sn led: guessed at last: easily* **4/6**[1]

113- **2** *5* **Amore Alato**[28] 3891 5-11-9 135 .... RichardJohnson 139
(Nick Williams) *fast away: led and clr: tried to kick on bef 2 out: hdd sn after 2 out: styd on but no ch w wnr* **8/1**[3]

4/2- **3** *5* **Cup Final (IRE)**[100] 2476 5-11-2 0 .... APMcCoy 125
(Nicky Henderson) *hld up in 5th: pushed along bef 2 out and sn outpcd: styd on steadily after to take 3rd flat: do bttr* **8/1**[3]

1- **4** *3* **First Mohican**[16] 4103 6-11-6 0 .... RobertThornton 128+
(Alan King) *t.k.h: wl in tch: mstke 3 out: chsd ldng pair 2 out: wl hld whn blnd last: fdd* **5/1**[2]

32- **5** *3/4* **Germany Calling (IRE)**[127] 1958 5-11-2 0 ....(t) NoelFehily 121
(Charlie Longsdon) *t.k.h: trckd ldr to 5th: steadily lost pl bef 2 out: nt knocked abt* **28/1**

6 *9* **Vaihau (FR)**[145] 5-11-2 0 .... RichieMcLernon 113
(Jonjo O'Neill) *hld up in last pair: no prog bef 2 out: steadily wknd* **50/1**

1P3- **7** *37* **Dubai Prince (IRE)**[29] 3872 6-11-6 0 ....[1] DenisO'Regan 92
(John Ferguson) *hld up in last pair: wknd bef 2 out: t.o and eased* **16/1**

3m 57.9s (-0.20) **Going Correction** +0.35s/f (Yiel) **7** Ran SP% **110.2**
Speed ratings (Par 115): **114,111,109,107,107 102,84**
CSF £6.29 TOTE £1.50: £1.10, £3.70; EX 5.40 Trifecta £16.20.

Owner Axom XLIX **Bred** Gestut Schlenderhan **Trained** Ditcheat, Somerset

FOCUS
This had looked a competitive heat but Irving bolted up after being given an uncomplicated ride. He was value for further and looks a strong Supreme Novices' contender. The second is rated to his best.

4422 BETBRIGHT CHASE (H'CAP) (GRADE 3) (18 fncs) 3m
3:50 (3:50) (Class 1) 5-Y-O+
£56,950 (£21,370; £10,700; £5,330; £2,680; £1,340)

Form RPR

142- **1** **Bally Legend**[22] 4021 9-10-12 **138** .... IanPopham 146
(Caroline Keevil) *wl in tch: rdn to chse ldng trio after 15th: clsd fr 3 out: drvn to ld last: styd on wl* **28/1**

1R1- **2** *1 1/4* **Bury Parade (IRE)**[35] 3772 8-11-12 **152** .... NoelFehily 160+
(Paul Nicholls) *hld up in rr: rn wd bnd after 9th: prog fr 4 out: clsng on ldrs whn nt clr run and swtchd lft bef last: r.o to take 2nd flat: unable to chal* **15/2**[3]

26P- **3** *1* **Tour Des Champs (FR)**[56] 3361 7-10-1 **127** ......(v[1]) SamTwiston-Davies 133
(Nigel Twiston-Davies) *led at gd pce: mstke 5th: hdd and mstke 3 out: kpt on fr next but a hld* **9/2**[1]

102- **4** *nk* **Midnight Appeal**[15] 4134 9-10-13 **139** ....(b) RobertThornton 144
(Alan King) *towards rr whn blnd 4th: prog fr 7th: prom next: chsd ldr 13th: led 3 out: hdd & wknd last* **14/1**

312- **5** *1 1/2* **Ardkilly Witness (IRE)**[21] 4035 8-10-10 **136** .... LeightonAspell 141
(Dr Richard Newland) *hld up in rr: mstke 11th: trying to make prog after 4 out whn squeezed out: rallied after next: j.rt 2 out and last: nrst fin* **7/1**[2]

155- **6** *1 1/2* **Niceonefrankie**[28] 3897 8-10-11 **137** .... AidanColeman 139
(Venetia Williams) *towards rr of main gp: 9th after 4 out and rdn: styd on fr next: nrst fin* **8/1**

P/1- **7** *12* **Planet Of Sound**[42] 3647 12-11-8 **148** ....(t) RichardJohnson 137
(Philip Hobbs) *wl in tch: rdn to chse ldng trio after 15th: no imp bef next: wknd* **10/1**

110- **8** *2* **Standing Ovation (IRE)**[99] 2487 7-10-7 **133** ....(tp) ConorO'Farrell 122
(David Pipe) *chsd ldr to 13th: styd prom tl wknd bef 3 out* **10/1**

426- **9** *4* **Jump City (FR)**[21] 4035 8-10-3 **132** .... HarryDerham(3) 115
(Paul Nicholls) *towards rr whn mstkes 4th and 6th: no real prog fr 12th: wl btn after* **16/1**

3P2- **10** *10* **Grandioso (IRE)**[35] 3772 7-11-7 **147** ....(t) DarylJacob 125
(Paul Nicholls) *wl in tch: chsd ldrs in 6th after 15th: wknd fr next (3 out)* **7/1**[2]

412- **11** *4* **Baile Anrai (IRE)**[28] 3897 10-10-6 **132** ....(b) HarrySkelton 101
(Dan Skelton) *a in last pair: j. slowly 5th: bhd fr 12th: t.o* **12/1**

252- **12** *3/4* **Whats Happening (IRE)**[46] 3594 7-10-12 **138** ....(tp) PaddyBrennan 106
(Tom George) *chsd ldng pair to 12th: wkng whn blnd next: sn wl in rr* **16/1**

/64- **P** **Bless The Wings (IRE)**[63] 3199 9-11-3 **143** .... WayneHutchinson
(Alan King) *a in rr: dropped to last pair and mstke 12th: sn bhd: t.o whn p.u bef 3 out* **16/1**

6m 11.0s (-4.40) **Going Correction** +0.15s/f (Yiel) **13** Ran SP% **119.7**
Speed ratings: **113,112,112,111 111,107,106,105,101 100,100,**
CSF £228.92 CT £1143.67 TOTE £30.70: £6.40, £2.10, £2.00; EX 230.90 Trifecta £4258.20.

Owner Brian Derrick **Bred** V Thorne, B Derrick And P R Rodford **Trained** Motcombe, Dorset
■ Another new sponsor for this event, previously backed by the Racing Post and Racing Plus.

FOCUS
This is traditionally a strong handicap with some depth. For instance, last year's sixth, Same Difference, went on to land the Kim Muir on his next start. Small personal bests from the first two in a solid renewal.

4423 JOCKEY CLUB H'CAP HURDLE (THE JOCKEY CLUB GRASSROOTS JUMPS SERIES QUALIFIER) (10 hdls) 2m 5f
4:25 (4:25) (Class 3) (0-135,130) 4-Y-O+ **£5,848** (£1,717; £858; £429)

Form RPR

12- **1** **Full Shift (FR)**[38] 3716 5-11-6 **124** .... APMcCoy 139+
(Nicky Henderson) *wl in tch: trckd ldng pair after 6th: wnt 2nd 3 out: led on long run bef next: sn jnd: shkn up to assert last: styd on wl* **5/2**[2]

10/- **2** *3 1/4* **Songsmith**[665] 5649 6-10-13 **117** .... LeightonAspell 127
(Lucy Wadham) *hld up in rr: mstke 5th: gd prog fr 7th to trck ldrs 3 out: jnd wnr bef next: shkn up and looked hld whn mstke last: one pce* **12/1**

332- **3** *11* **Minella On Line (IRE)**[42] 3643 5-10-10 **114** .... BarryGeraghty 114
(Rebecca Curtis) *chsd ldng pair tl after 6th: styd in tch: cl up after 3 out: sn rdn: outpcd fr next: mstke last* **5/2**[2]

11- 4 10 **Royal Player**[14] 4163 5-11-12 **130** RichardJohnson 118
(Philip Hobbs) *pressed ldr: led 4th: nvr allowed untrbld ld: hdd & wknd on long run to 2 out* **9/4**[1]
4/0- 5 1 3/4 **Minella Special (IRE)**[23] 3989 8-10-12 **116** PaddyBrennan 102
(Paul Henderson) *hld up in last: wl off the pce 6th: sme prog fr next: threatened to cl on long gp after 3 out: shkn up and wknd 2 out* **20/1**
0P4- 6 1 3/4 **Colebrooke**[16] 4105 6-10-13 **117** (b) BrendanPowell 104
(Renee Robeson) *led to 4th: mstke 5th but pressed ldr to 3 out: wknd bef next* **12/1**[3]
/00- 7 44 **Hidden Justice (IRE)**[28] 3892 5-11-11 **129** DenisO'Regan 70
(John Quinn) *hld up in rr: struggling fr 7th: wknd after 3 out: wl t.o* **16/1**
005- P **Valid Reason**[6] 4302 7-11-7 **125** (t[1]) RobertThornton
(Dean Ivory) *in tch: blnd bdly 2nd: wknd 6th: wl bhd whn p.u bef next* **16/1**

5m 20.2s (2.70) **Going Correction** +0.35s/f (Yiel) **8** Ran SP% **114.6**
Speed ratings (Par 107): **108,106,102,98,98 97,80,**
CSF £73.54 CT £274.75 TOTE £2.20: £1.10, £7.20, £1.50; EX 88.20 Trifecta £207.10.
Owner John P McManus **Bred** Mme Catherine Niederhauser Dietrich **Trained** Upper Lambourn, Berks

FOCUS
A fair handicap, in which two quickened away from their rivals. A big step forward from the winner.

4424 RACINGUK.COM STANDARD OPEN NATIONAL HUNT FLAT RACE 2m
4:55 (4:55) (Class 5) 4-6-Y-O **£1,949** (£572; £286; £143)

Form RPR
1- 1 **Aqalim**[72] 3049 4-11-0 0 DenisO'Regan 104+
(John Ferguson) *fractious to post: hld up in tch: trckd ldng pair over 2f out: rdn and swtchd rt 1f out: r.o between rivals to ld post* **2/1**[2]
6- 2 *nse* **Colin's Brother**[52] 3460 4-10-7 0 SamTwiston-Davies 97
(Nigel Twiston-Davies) *t.k.h: trckd ldr after 5f to 6f out: wnt 2nd again 3f out and sn upsides: rdn to ld narrowly fnl f: hdd post* **11/1**[3]
1- 3 *nk* **Clondaw Banker (IRE)**[22] 4017 5-11-4 0 NicodeBoinville[(5)] 113
(Nicky Henderson) *trckd ldr 5f and again 6f out: led 3f out: jnd over 2f out: narrowly hdd ins fnl f: styd on but lost 2nd last strides* **1/1**[1]
4 5 **Hurricane Vic** 4-10-7 0 RobertThornton 92
(Alan King) *hld up in tch: rdn to chse ldrs 3f out: outpcd fr 2f out* **12/1**
5 1 1/4 **Champagne Chaser** 4-10-7 0 RichardJohnson 91
(Tim Vaughan) *t.k.h early: hld up in tch: pushed along and rn green 3f out: outpcd fr 2f out* **16/1**
6 1 **Murrayana (IRE)** 4-10-7 0 JoeTizzard 90
(Colin Tizzard) *trckd ldrs: rdn and outpcd fr over 2f out* **14/1**
000- 7 11 **Top Show**[6] 4297 5-11-2 0 [1] PaddyBrennan 88
(Dean Ivory) *led at mod pce: reminder 1/2-way: rdn 4f out: hdd & wknd 3f out* **100/1**

4m 3.5s (11.00) **Going Correction** +0.35s/f (Yiel)
WFA 4 from 5yo 9lb **7** Ran SP% **112.9**
Speed ratings: **86,85,85,83,82 82,76**
CSF £23.14 TOTE £2.40: £1.10, £4.10; EX 19.20 Trifecta £45.10.
Owner Bloomfields **Bred** Darley **Trained** Cowlinge, Suffolk

FOCUS
Three experienced horses came clear after this developed into a sprint, meaning it wasn't a proper test. Not a strong bumper for the track.
T/Jkpt: £7551.30 to a £1 stake. Pool: £53,178.64 - 5.00 winning units. T/Plt: £19.50 to a £1 stake. Pool: £173,826.56 - 6505.47 winning units. T/Qpdt: £13.70 to a £1 stake. Pool : £8446.45 - 453.25 winning units. JN

3721 NEWCASTLE (L-H)
Saturday, February 22

OFFICIAL GOING: Heavy (soft in places in home straight; 4.3)
Wind: Fresh, half against Weather: Cloudy, bright

4425 BETFRED RACING FOLLOW US ON FACEBOOK NOVICES' CHASE (17 fncs 2 omitted) 3m
1:50 (1:50) (Class 2) 5-Y-O+ **£11,573** (£3,418; £1,709; £854)

Form RPR
431- 1 **Pinerolo**[12] 4188 8-11-4 127 RyanMania 136
(Sue Smith) *led to 11th: sn rdn and styd cl up: nt fluent 5 out: effrt and rdn bef 3 out: led next: styd on gamely u.p run-in* **9/4**[2]
/41- 2 1/2 **Bucking The Trend**[74] 3004 6-11-4 132 DougieCostello 135
(Tim Vaughan) *cl up: led 11th: hit 4 out and next: sn rdn: hdd 2 out: rallied and ev ch last: kpt on run-in: hld towards fin* **7/2**[3]
011- 3 32 **Edmund Kean (IRE)**[17] 4088 7-11-7 139 TomScudamore 118
(David Pipe) *nt fluent on occasions: trckd ldrs: hdwy and ev ch 12th: shkn up and outpcd 4 out: 4 l 3rd and one pce whn blnd 2 out: wknd* **10/11**[1]
3- 4 89 **Strike Fast (IRE)**[21] 4041 9-10-13 0 PeterBuchanan 7
(William Kinsey) *in tch: outpcd 9th: lost tch fr next: t.o* **66/1**

6m 28.6s (6.10) **Going Correction** +0.40s/f (Soft) **4** Ran SP% **106.9**
Speed ratings: **105,104,94,64**
CSF £9.57 TOTE £3.30; EX 11.70 Trifecta £20.00.
Owner McGoldrick Racing Syndicates (2) **Bred** W Goldie **Trained** High Eldwick, W Yorks

FOCUS
Rails after Winning Post brought out and narrowed to provide fresh ground to beyond the road crossing. Rail realigned at 3m start bend to provide best ground possible. Dividing rail after 2nd hurdle in back straight to keep horses off worst of ground. After six dry days the ground was very holding. The third fence in the back straight was omitted because of bad ground. A good-class novices' chase run at a sound pace in the testing conditions. The first two were pretty much to their marks, with the third well below his previous level.

4426 BETFRED WIN GOLD CUP TICKETS ON FACEBOOK H'CAP HURDLE (8 hdls 1 omitted) 2m
2:20 (2:20) (Class 2) (0-145,137) 4-Y-**£9,495** (£2,805; £1,402; £702; £351)

Form RPR
116- 1 **Yorkist (IRE)**[20] 4056 6-10-12 **130** NathanMoscrop[(7)] 136+
(Brian Ellison) *t.k.h: in tch: hdwy to ld 4 out: qcknd after next: hrd pressed and rdn bef last: styd on gamely run-in* **6/1**[2]
623- 2 1 3/4 **Mojolika**[28] 3892 6-10-11 **122** BrianHarding 124
(Tim Easterby) *hld up: hdwy and prom 4 out: rdn to chse wnr bef 2 out: effrt and ev ch bef last: kpt on same pce last 75yds* **7/1**[3]
P11- 3 15 **Ubaltique (FR)**[31] 3832 6-11-12 **137** (b) JasonMaguire 126
(Donald McCain) *hld up: smooth hdwy to chse ldrs 2 out: sn rdn and outpcd by first two* **7/1**[3]
130/ 4 2 1/4 **Angelot Du Berlais (FR)**[12] 4737 5-10-11 **125** JoshuaMoore[(3)] 110
(Dr Richard Newland) *t.k.h: cl up tl rdn and wknd bef 2 out* **10/1**
613- 5 3/4 **Grate Fella (IRE)**[18] 4076 6-10-3 **114** BrianHughes 98
(Sue Smith) *cl up: ev ch 4 out: sn pushed along and outpcd bef next: n.d after* **9/2**[1]
0/4- 6 1 3/4 **Kudu Country (IRE)**[42] 3648 8-10-13 **124** DougieCostello 106
(Tom Tate) *led: nt fluent 4th: hdd 4 out: rallied: wknd qckly after 2 out* **6/1**[2]
640- 7 28 **Deepsand (IRE)**[52] 3477 5-11-3 **128** (t) JamesReveley 82
(Tim Easterby) *hld up: hdwy u.p bef 3 out: wkng whn blnd next* **7/1**[3]
221- P **Figaro**[10] 4224 6-10-11 **122** (t) TomScudamore
(Tim Vaughan) *cl up tl rdn and wknd after 4 out: t.o whn p.u bef next* **9/2**[1]

4m 16.9s (6.90) **Going Correction** +0.70s/f (Soft) **8** Ran SP% **111.5**
Speed ratings (Par 109): **110,109,101,100,100 99,85,**
CSF £44.45 CT £292.73 TOTE £6.60: £2.10, £2.40, £2.50; EX 47.50 Trifecta £255.80.
Owner Mike And Eileen Newbould **Bred** Con O'Keeffe **Trained** Norton, N Yorks

FOCUS
The first hurdle in the back straight had to be omitted. An open-looking handicap but in the end the first two pulled clear. The winner is back on the upgrade.

4427 BETFRED EIDER (HANDICAP CHASE) (23 fncs 2 omitted) 4m 1f
2:55 (2:55) (Class 2) (0-150,145) 5-Y-O+
£37,140 (£11,028; £5,514; £2,748; £1,380; £696)

Form RPR
00P- 1 **Wyck Hill (IRE)**[56] 3361 10-11-0 **133** (t) TomScudamore 148+
(David Bridgwater) *a gng wl: prom: led 17th: rdn whn nt fluent last: styd on wl run-in* **9/1**[3]
623- 2 3/4 **Smoking Aces (IRE)**[21] 4026 10-9-12 **122** (b) MauriceLinehan[(5)] 136+
(Jonjo O'Neill) *rn in snatches: towards rr: reminders 5th: hdwy and in tch 6 out: rdn and outpcd after next: rallied to chse wnr 2 out: kpt on u.p run-in* **6/1**[1]
4P3- 3 2 **Ballypatrick (IRE)**[52] 3455 8-10-0 **122** GavinSheehan[(3)] 132
(Mick Channon) *in tch: hdwy and ev ch 6 out: rdn after next: rallied: kpt on same pce between last 2* **10/1**
3P6- 4 6 **Safran De Cotte (FR)**[42] 3655 8-10-0 **122** JakeGreenall[(3)] 127
(Henry Daly) *cl up: ev ch 6 out: rdn 4 out: outpcd between last 2* **7/1**[2]
320- 5 1/2 **Seven Woods (IRE)**[29] 3882 8-10-9 **128** (t) AlainCawley 132
(Tom George) *midfield on outside: stdy hdwy 16th: rdn and outpcd after 5 out: rallied bef 2 out: no imp bef last* **16/1**
121- 6 3 1/2 **Presented (IRE)**[30] 3853 7-9-9 **119** oh8 (p) HarryChalloner[(5)] 119
(Brian Ellison) *hld up in tch: hdwy and ev ch 6 out: hit and rdn next: wknd after 2 out* **20/1**
013- 7 18 **Royale Knight**[42] 3655 8-10-0 **122** JoshuaMoore[(3)] 104
(Dr Richard Newland) *hld up bhd ldng gp: rdn after 17th: struggling fr 5 out* **9/1**[3]
434- 8 2 **Junior**[21] 4026 11-11-5 **145** (b) MikeyEnnis[(7)] 125
(David Pipe) *in tch: rdn 15th: wknd fr 17th* **16/1**
054- 9 1/2 **Our Island (IRE)**[52] 3455 9-10-0 **119** oh2 (p) DougieCostello 99
(Tim Vaughan) *in tch: drvn and outpcd bef 11th: no ch fr 6 out* **9/1**[3]
610- P **Chavoy (FR)**[7] 4271 9-10-8 **130** (t) TonyKelly[(3)]
(Rebecca Menzies) *bhd: pushed along whn hmpd 15th: sn struggling: t.o whn p.u 6 out* **33/1**
/0P- P **Tarquinius (FR)**[30] 3868 11-10-1 **120** (tp) WilsonRenwick
(Gordon Elliott, Ire) *mstkes in rr: outpcd whn blnd 15th: struggling bef 6 out: t.o whn p.u bef 4 out* **25/1**
151- P **Relax (FR)**[21] 4035 9-11-1 **139** CallumWhillans[(5)]
(Venetia Williams) *disp ld to 17th: hit 11th: struggling after next: t.o whn p.u after 5 out* **10/1**
313- P **Financial Climate (IRE)**[38] 3717 7-10-2 **126** ThomasGarner[(5)]
(Oliver Sherwood) *nt fluent on occasions in rr: struggling bef 16th: t.o whn p.u 6 out* **11/1**
311- F **Sun Cloud (IRE)**[44] 3617 7-11-2 **135** BrianHughes
(Malcolm Jefferson) *hld up: stdy hdwy 12th: fell 15th* **11/1**
114- P **Swatow Typhoon (IRE)**[27] 3921 7-10-5 **124** (b[1]) BrianHarding
(Donald McCain) *nt fluent on occasions: mde most to 17th: wknd qckly next: t.o whn p.u bef 5 out* **14/1**
323- P **War On (IRE)**[49] 3526 7-9-7 **119** oh12 DiarmuidO'Regan[(7)]
(Chris Grant) *midfield: lost pl bef 6th: lost tch and p.u after 14th* **25/1**

9m 11.4s (3.60) **Going Correction** +0.40s/f (Soft) **16** Ran SP% **125.5**
Speed ratings: **111,110,110,108,108 107,103,103,102, , , , ,**
CSF £62.35 CT £569.96 TOTE £10.10: £2.30, £2.40, £3.40, £3.00; EX 60.50 Trifecta £1560.30.
Owner John P McManus **Bred** T Simmons **Trained** Icomb, Gloucs

FOCUS
Only the Grand National itself and the Midlands version at Uttoxeter are run over further than this 4m1f trip. Surprisingly the last eight runnings have been won by horses carrying 11st or more. Just half a dozen were still in with a chance on the home turn and only about half the field finished the course. The winner had slipped to a good mark and is rated back to his best in a solid renewal.

4428 BETFRED GOALS GALORE NOVICES' HURDLE (11 hdls 2 omitted) 2m 6f
3:25 (3:25) (Class 3) 5-Y-O+ **£5,907** (£1,893; £1,052)

Form RPR
3- 1 **The Ramblin Kid**[42] 3657 6-10-12 0 JasonMaguire 125+
(Micky Hammond) *cl up: led 5th: mde rest: rdn 2 out: clr last: styd on strly* **14/1**
33- 2 7 **Ivy Gate (IRE)**[34] 3800 6-10-7 122 MauriceLinehan[(5)] 117
(Jonjo O'Neill) *prom: hdwy to chal 1/2-way: hit 4 out: rdn and outpcd bef 2 out: rallied to chse (clr) wnr run-in: no imp* **4/1**[3]
/31- 3 10 **Panama Petrus (IRE)**[18] 4075 6-11-3 126 CallumWhillans[(5)] 122
(Venetia Williams) *chsd ldrs: hit 7th: hdwy and ev ch 3 out: sn chsng wnr: wknd and lost 2nd run-in* **7/4**[1]
0P0- P **Almond Court (IRE)**[57] 3335 11-10-5 76 KennyJohnson
(Robert Johnson) *led to 5th: lost pl bef next: sn struggling: t.o whn p.u 4 out* **200/1**
211- F **Getabuzz**[27] 3920 6-11-1 125 (b) CraigNichol[(7)]
(Tim Easterby) *in tch: pushed along after 4 out: 4 l 4th and outpcd whn fell heavily next* **3/1**[2]
B2F- F **Romany Ryme**[22] 4006 8-10-5 118 (p) JonathonBewley[(7)] 105
(George Bewley) *hld up in tch: outpcd after 4 out: rallied after next: 6 l 4th and styng on whn fell next* **4/1**[3]
04P- P **Lucky Cody (IRE)**[77] 2954 5-10-5 0 NathanMoscrop[(7)]
(Brian Ellison) *bhd and sn detached: t.o whn p.u bef 6th* **28/1**
P **Salmonliv** 7-10-5 0 RyanDClark[(7)]
(Noel Wilson) *cl up: lost pl after 5th: lost tch after next: t.o whn p.u 4 out* **100/1**

6m 5.5s (29.50) **Going Correction** +0.70s/f (Soft) **8** Ran SP% **113.0**
Speed ratings: **74,71,67, , ,**
CSF £67.59 TOTE £13.20: £2.60, £1.50, £1.30; EX 69.20 Trifecta £450.30.
Owner Joe Buzzeo **Bred** Goldford Stud **Trained** Middleham Moor, N Yorks

The Form Book Jumps, Raceform Ltd, Compton, RG20 6NL.

FOCUS
This proved a severe test in the conditions and in the end only the first three completed. The second sets the level.

4429 BETFRED RACING'S BIGGEST SUPPORTER NOVICES' HURDLE (8 hdls 1 omitted) 2m
3:55 (3:58) (Class 4) 4-Y-O+ £3,328 (£1,033; £556)

Form RPR
22U- 1 **Dark Dune (IRE)**44 3616 6-11-2 113 JamesReveley 121+
(Tim Easterby) *prom: taken wd fr 3rd: led on bit 3 out: stl gng wl whn lft nrly 4 l clr last: rdn and r.o wl* 11/8[1]

04- 2 6 **Island Heights (IRE)**9 4234 5-11-2 0 WilsonRenwick 111
(Lucinda Russell) *chsd ldrs: mstke 4th: rdn and outpcd after 3 out: rallied and lft nrly 4 l 2nd last: kpt on same pce* 8/1

544- 3 24 **Ride The Range (IRE)**44 3619 5-11-2 0 BrianHughes 86
(Chris Grant) *in tch: hdwy after 4 out: rdn and wknd next: lft modest 3rd last* 7/2[3]

30- F **Lyric Street (IRE)**16 4103 6-11-2 0 JasonMaguire 112
(Donald McCain) *led and clr to 1/2-way: rdn and hdd 3 out: rallied: 2 l down and keeping on whn fell heavily last* 9/4[2]

004- P **Silver Storm**49 3529 6-10-6 0 EwanWhillans(3)
(Tristan Davidson) *nt fluent in rr: struggling fr 3rd: t.o whn p.u 4 out* 33/1

005- P **Lordenshaws (IRE)**102 2443 7-11-2 0 KennyJohnson
(Robert Johnson) *hld up: nt fluent 2nd: taken wd bef 3rd: struggling fr next: t.o whn p.u 4 out* 100/1

4m 21.4s (11.40) **Going Correction** +0.70s/f (Soft) 6 Ran SP% **110.1**
Speed ratings (Par 105): **99,96,84, ,**
CSF £12.48 TOTE £2.50: £1.50, £3.00; EX 12.70 Trifecta £37.00.
Owner Habton Farms **Bred** P Turley **Trained** Great Habton, N Yorks

FOCUS
Moderate novice hurdle form. The cosy winner stood out and is rated close to form.

4430 BETFRED TV H'CAP CHASE (15 fncs 1 omitted) 2m 4f
4:30 (4:31) (Class 3) (0-135,134) 5-Y-O+
£6,256 (£1,848; £924; £462; £231; £116)

Form RPR
132- 1 **Wicklow Lad**11 4204 10-10-8 **123** (v) MrKitAlexander(7) 132+
(N W Alexander) *hld up in tch: hdwy to chse ldr 4 out: led last: rdn and styd on wl* 4/1[2]

662- 2 2¾ **Consigliere (FR)**27 3923 11-11-12 **134** (p) TomScudamore 139
(David Pipe) *cl up: led 6 out: rdn bef 2 out: hdd last: kpt on same pce run-in* 5/1

P22- 3 2¾ **Fentara**16 4104 9-11-0 **125** (t) JakeGreenall(3) 128
(Mark Walford) *in tch: pushed along 6 out: rdn 4 out: effrt after 2 out: kpt on same pce fr last* 11/4[1]

/11- 4 23 **Sharney Sike**32 3823 8-10-0 **108** oh2 BrianHarding 88
(Stuart Coltherd) *nt fluent on occasions: hld up: hdwy and in tch 9th: effrt and rdn 4 out: wknd fr next* 15/2

425- 5 9 **Gansey (IRE)**11 4204 12-11-8 **130** RyanMania 101
(Sue Smith) *led 2nd to 6 out: cl up: rdn bef 4 out: wknd fr next* 8/1

4/2- 6 21 **Sustainability (IRE)**35 3786 9-10-13 **124** RobertDunne(3) 74
(Venetia Williams) *led to 2nd: j.lft next: cl up tl rdn and wknd bef 4 out* 9/2[3]

502- P **Be My Deputy (IRE)**32 3823 9-10-9 **117** (b) PeterBuchanan
(Lucinda Russell) *in tch: outpcd after 8th: struggling after next: t.o whn p.u bef 4 out* 12/1

5m 30.2s (3.00) **Going Correction** +0.40s/f (Soft) 7 Ran SP% **112.1**
Speed ratings: **110,108,107,98,95 86,**
CSF £23.23 CT £62.18 TOTE £4.70: £2.60, £3.00; EX 20.40 Trifecta £102.40.
Owner Clan Gathering **Bred** Mrs R E Hambro **Trained** Kinneston, Perth & Kinross

FOCUS
Just three in serious contention over the final three fences. Fair form, with the winner rated to his best.

4431 BETFRED GOALS GALORE EXTRA STANDARD OPEN NATIONAL HUNT FLAT RACE 2m
5:00 (5:00) (Class 6) 4-6-Y-O £1,624 (£477; £238; £119)

Form RPR
1 **Grove Silver (IRE)**55 5-11-3 0 SeanQuinlan 115+
(Jennie Candlish) *hld up: smooth hdwy 5f out: led gng wl over 2f out: sn qcknd clr: readily* 12/1

2 5 **One For Arthur (IRE)**90 5-11-3 0 PeterBuchanan 110
(Lucinda Russell) *hld up in tch: hdwy over 4f out: chsd wnr over 2f out: kpt on same pce fnl f* 13/2

3- 3 11 **Pithivier (FR)**21 4043 4-10-8 0 WilsonRenwick 90
(Peter Niven) *t.k.h: prom: hdwy and ev ch over 3f out: outpcd by first two fnl 2f* 3/1[2]

3- 4 1 **Redkalani (IRE)**72 3042 6-11-3 0 JamesReveley 98
(Keith Reveley) *cl up on outside: led over 3f out to over 2f out: outpcd whn rdr dropped whip over 1f out* 15/2

3- 5 8 **Howaboutnever (IRE)**101 2456 6-11-3 0 JasonMaguire 90
(Donald McCain) *cl up: drvn and outpcd over 6f out: sme late hdwy: nvr rchd ldrs* 5/2[1]

6- 6 ½ **Purple Harry**69 3112 6-10-12 0 SamanthaDrake(5) 90
(Tina Jackson) *led to over 3f out: rdn and wknd over 2f out* 20/1

13- 7 29 **Oleohneh (IRE)**22 4008 6-11-3 0 BrianHughes 61
(Malcolm Jefferson) *hld up in tch: struggling over 3f out: sn btn* 9/2[3]

0- 8 6 **Backforce**21 4043 6-10-10 0 NathanMoscrop(7) 55
(Noel Wilson) *in tch: struggling over 5f out: sn btn* 40/1

9 59 **Messina Straights**307 6-10-10 0 JonathonBewley(7)
(George Bewley) *hld up: struggling 1/2-way: t.o* 66/1

4m 16.0s (11.60) **Going Correction** +0.70s/f (Soft)
WFA 4 from 5yo 9lb 5 from 6yo 1lb 9 Ran SP% **113.2**
Speed ratings: **99,96,91,90,86 86,71,68,39**
CSF £84.06 TOTE £15.00: £3.50, £1.70, £2.10; EX 82.30 Trifecta £330.10.
Owner Alan Baxter Anthony Bloor Dave Cheetham **Bred** Gerald McStay **Trained** Basford Green, Staffs

FOCUS
Probably just an ordinary bumper and again they came home well strung out. The fourth sets the level.
T/Plt: £215.10 to a £1 stake. Pool: £101,917.61 - 344.85 winning units. T/Qpdt: £13.00 to a £1 stake. Pool: £8704.22 - 492.85 winning units. RY

4044 FAIRYHOUSE (R-H)
Saturday, February 22

OFFICIAL GOING: Soft to heavy

4432a WINNING FAIR JUVENILE HURDLE (GRADE 2) (10 hdls) 2m
1:25 (1:25) 4-Y-O £20,312 (£5,937; £2,812; £937)

RPR
1 **Abbyssial (IRE)**30 3864 4-11-0 134 PaulTownend 134+
(W P Mullins, Ire) *mde all: nt fluent 1st: pressed bef 2 out where nt fluent: gng best and in command between last 2: rdn fr last and swished tail: reduced advantage u.p towards fin* 11/4[2]

2 ½ **Adriana Des Mottes (FR)**53 3444 4-10-7 RWalsh 126+
(W P Mullins, Ire) *chsd ldrs in 3rd tl wnt 2nd fr 5th: pushed along bef 2 out: sn rdn and no imp on wnr bef last: rallied nr fin and kpt on wl wout rching wnr* 8/11[1]

3 2½ **Gerdago (IRE)**83 2851 4-11-0 118 (t) EddieO'Connell 131
(K J Condon, Ire) *hld up in tch: 7th 1/2-way: tk clsr order bhd ldrs appr st: rdn into 3rd between last 2: no imp on ldrs u.p bef last: kpt on same pce* 25/1

4 23 **Blue Hell (FR)**131 4-11-0 DannyMullins 110
(Anthony Mullins, Ire) *chsd ldrs: 5th 1/2-way: tk clsr order in 3rd bef 2 out: pushed along and no ex in 4th between last 2: nt fluent last: one pce run-in* 12/1

5 9 **Henry Higgins (IRE)**13 4178 4-11-0 MarkWalsh 101
(Charles O'Brien, Ire) *towards rr: tk clsr order in 5th after 4th: clsr in 3rd after 3 out: rdn next and sn no ex u.p in 5th: wknd* 12/1

6 1¾ **Bertimont (FR)**112 2239 4-11-0 132 LiamMcKenna 97
(J J Lambe, Ire) *w.w in rr: nt fluent 1st and 3rd: tk clsr order in 8th fr 5th: rdn in mod 6th bef 2 out: one pce* 33/1

7 20 **All Pepper (GER)**104 4-11-0 DJCasey 77
(W P Mullins, Ire) *chsd ldrs: 4th 1/2-way: pushed along bef 3 out and sn no ex u.p: wknd: slt mstke in remote 7th at last* 8/1[3]

8 38 **Achtung**14 4164 4-11-0 (t) ChrisTimmons 39
(Luke Comer, Ire) *chsd ldr in 2nd: slt mstke 2nd and nt fluent next: lost pl 5th: sn pushed along and wknd bef next: completely t.o* 100/1

9 17 **Elishpour (IRE)**57 3336 4-11-0 RobbieColgan 22
(A J Martin, Ire) *hld up in tch: 6th bef 1/2-way: sn lost pl and dropped to rr after 4th: no imp after and sn wknd: completely t.o* 33/1

4m 6.0s (-6.00) **Going Correction** -0.10s/f (Good) 9 Ran SP% **121.8**
Speed ratings: **111,110,109,98,93 92,82,63,55**
CSF £5.52 TOTE £4.20: £1.70, £1.02, £3.50; DF 9.90 Trifecta £22.70.
Owner Mrs Violet O'Leary **Bred** J J Murphy & G Adare **Trained** Muine Beag, Co Carlow

FOCUS
The winner ran to a small personal best depsite flashing his tail late on.

4435a AT THE RACES BOBBYJO CHASE (GRADE 2) (20 fncs) 3m 1f
3:10 (3:09) 5-Y-O+ £21,666 (£6,333; £3,000; £1,000)

RPR
1 **On His Own (IRE)**30 3868 10-11-3 153 RWalsh 161+
(W P Mullins, Ire) *trckd ldrs tl led and disp fr 2nd: narrow advantage fr 5th and extended advantage fr 11th: nt fluent 3 out and slt mstke next where pressed: rdn and sn in command again: styd on wl* 11/8[1]

2 12 **Mount Benbulben (IRE)**58 3262 9-11-10 160 DannyMullins 160
(Gordon Elliott, Ire) *hld up in tch: mstke 2nd and rdr lost iron briefly: slt mstke 7th: clsr in 3rd fr 12th: cl 2nd fr 3 out: rdn and no imp on wnr fr after next: kpt on one pce* 13/8[2]

3 4¾ **Buckers Bridge (IRE)**28 3909 8-11-8 145 AELynch 152
(Henry De Bromhead, Ire) *hld up towards rr: tk clsr order in 3rd fr 5 out: rdn in 3rd after 3 out and no imp on ldrs bef next: kpt on one pce* 20/1

4 33 **Lion Na Bearnai (IRE)**21 4047 12-11-8 140 (p) DavyRussell 116
(Thomas Gibney, Ire) *led fr 1st tl jnd next: settled bhd ldrs: in 4th bef 3rd: clsr in 2nd bef 11th: sn niggled along and dropped to 4th bef 4 out: sn no imp and trailing: one pce* 16/1

P **Quito De La Roque (FR)**20 4064 10-11-8 150 (p) BrianO'Connell
(C A Murphy, Ire) *chsd ldrs: slt mstke 7th: pushed along in 4th fr 12th: mstke next: mstke in 5th 5 out: j.lft next and trailing whn p.u bef 2 out* 14/1

P **Roi Du Mee (FR)**13 4183 9-11-10 155 (t) BryanCooper
(Gordon Elliott, Ire) *trckd ldrs tl led and disp fr after 2nd: mstke 5th and hdd: mstke 8th and dropped to rr: reminders after: detached u.p fr 10th and p.u bef 13th* 8/1[3]

P **Make A Track (IRE)**28 3909 8-11-3 147 DJCasey
(C F Swan, Ire) *chsd ldrs: disp 3rd at 10th: sn wknd to rr: no imp on ldrs whn mstke 12th: sn rdn and no ex u.p: trailing whn p.u bef 3 out* 14/1

6m 54.0s (-8.00) **Going Correction** +0.075s/f (Yiel) 7 Ran SP% **115.3**
Speed ratings: **115,111,109,99, ,**
CSF £1.25 TOTE £2.30: £1.20, £1.90; DF 5.40 Trifecta £71.00.
Owner Andrea & Graham Wylie **Bred** Ms Margaret Treacy **Trained** Muine Beag, Co Carlow

FOCUS
The winner skipped along at his own pace. He's rated close to the race average.

3245 FONTWELL (L-H)
Sunday, February 23

OFFICIAL GOING: Heavy (5.7)
Wind: strong, behind Weather: overcast, dry

4439 BET PLACEPOT WITH TOTEPOOL JOSH GIFFORD MEMORIAL NOVICES' CHASE (FOR THE JOSH GIFFORD CUP) (11 fncs 5 omitted) 2m 6f
2:10 (2:10) (Class 2) 5-Y-O+ £12,972 (£4,052; £2,182)

Form RPR
114- 1 **Via Sundown (FR)**43 3651 6-11-6 134 JoshuaMoore 144
(Gary Moore) *chsd ldr 2nd tl j. into narrow ld last downhill fence (actual 3 out): hdd bypassing 2 out: led again last: battled on wl u.p flat: rdn out* 7/2[3]

113- 2 ½ **Benvolio (IRE)**22 4033 7-11-6 140 (p) DarylJacob 145+
(Paul Nicholls) *led: j. slowly 2nd and 6th (open ditch): reminder after 6th: rdn and anther reminder on long run after 7th: outj. and hdd last downhill fence (actual 3 out): led again bypassing 2 out: hdd last: kpt on* 10/11[1]

052- **3** *3 1/2* **Lamb Or Cod (IRE)**[59] 3291 7-10-12 130....................(t) RichardJohnson 132
(Philip Hobbs) *chsd ldr tl hmpd and dropped to 3rd 2nd: chsd ldrs after: ev ch last downhill fence (actual 3 out): outpcd next (actual 2 out): plugged on same pce after* **2/1**[2]

PP0- **P** **Niceboy (IRE)**[7] 4298 10-10-12 61.. CharlieWallis
(Daniel Steele) *sn lost tch: t.o 3rd tl p.u 8th* **150/1**

5m 51.9s (8.90) **Going Correction** +0.675s/f (Soft) 4 Ran SP% **108.6**
Speed ratings: **110,109,108,**
CSF £7.47 TOTE £4.60; EX 7.30 Trifecta £7.40.
Owner The Old Brokers **Bred** Elevage Avicole Lozach Le Yan Et Al **Trained** Lower Beeding, W Sussex

FOCUS
Overcast and breezy after a dry night, with a strong wind behind them up the straight. The second-last fence and the first fence down the back straight were omitted owing to the heavy ground. Fresh ground on bends not used since October. Hurdles sited middle down back straight and inner on home straight. A good little novice chase, rated around the first two.

4440 TOTEPOOL HOME OF POOL BETTING H'CAP CHASE (FOR THE CERTAIN JUSTICE CHALLENGE TROPHY) (11 fncs 5 omitted) 2m 6f

2:40 (2:40) (Class 4) (0-115,111) 5-Y-0+ **£4,808** (£1,411; £705; £352)

Form RPR

34U- **1** **Itoldyou (IRE)**[9] 4249 8-11-4 **103**..(t) TomCannon 119
(Linda Jewell) *bhd: sme hdwy and lft 3rd 7th: wnt 10 l 2nd 8th (4 out): rdn and steadily clsd after next: led last: plugged on to go clr: rdn out* **8/1**[3]

5/U- **2** *8* **West Cork Flash (IRE)**[283] 325 10-11-2 **101**...........(p) RichardJohnson 112+
(Paul Henderson) *led: wnt clr after 6th: 10 l ahd after last downhill fence (actual 3 out): rdn bypassing 2 out: hdd last: no ex and wknd flat* **12/1**

560- **3** *25* **Topaze Collonges (FR)**[54] 3439 7-11-5 **104**.......................(b) NoelFehily 87
(Charlie Longsdon) *chsd ldrs: lost pl and reminders after 4th: nvr travelling after: lft 4th and hmpd 7th: no ch after: wnt poor 3rd after last downhill fence* **17/2**

4P3- **4** *1 1/4* **Double Chocolate**[33] 3817 11-10-11 **96**.....................(v) RobertThornton 78
(John O'Shea) *w ldr tl rdn and after 6th: nvr travelling after: dropped to 3rd and btn 8th (4 out): 4th and wl bhd after next* **8/1**[3]

P32- **5** *54* **Venetian Lad**[97] 2567 9-11-8 **107**.. MarcGoldstein 35
(Lydia Richards) *a towards rr: 5th and lost tch after 7th: t.o fr last downhill fence (actual 3 out)* **5/1**[2]

524- **U** **Kingcora (FR)**[36] 3769 6-11-12 **111**.................................... LiamTreadwell
(Venetia Williams) *chsd ldrs tl blnd bdly: sprawled on landing and uns rdr 7th* **10/11**[1]

5m 56.25s (13.25) **Going Correction** +0.675s/f (Soft) 6 Ran SP% **109.5**
Speed ratings: **102,99,90,89,69**
CSF £75.97 TOTE £8.20: £4.40, £4.20; EX 100.80 Trifecta £323.60.
Owner Valence Racing Too **Bred** James O'Leary **Trained** Sutton Valence, Kent

FOCUS
This was a proper test of the distance. The winner rates a personal bdset and the form could be rated a few pounds higher.

4441 TOTEPOOL NATIONAL SPIRIT HURDLE (GRADE 2) (10 hdls) 2m 4f

3:10 (3:10) (Class 1) 4-Y-0+
£28,475 (£10,685; £5,350; £2,665; £1,340; £670)

Form RPR

011- **1** **Kayf Moss**[22] 4028 6-11-3 130...(b) RhysFlint 144
(John Flint) *mde all: rdn and forged clr after 2 out: wnt lft last: drvn flat: battled on gamely fnl 100yds: jst lasted home* **16/1**

3/P- **2** *hd* **Meister Eckhart (IRE)**[106] 2374 8-11-3 150.................. RobertThornton 144
(Alan King) *hld up in midfield: clsd to trck ldrs 5th: rdn bef 2 out: styd on u.p flat: clsng whn short of room: swtchd rt and bmpd rival fnl 100yds: styd on wl towards fin: jst hld* **9/2**[2]

340- **3** *1 1/2* **Chris Pea Green**[15] 4147 5-11-5 142................................... JoshuaMoore 145
(Gary Moore) *hld up in midfield: clsd to trck ldrs 5th: rdn and effrt bef 2 out: chsd wnr flat: styd on u.p and pressing ldr whn bmpd and pushed rt fnl 100yds: no ex and one pce after* **6/1**[3]

111- **4** *6* **Saphir Du Rheu (FR)**[22] 4025 5-11-7 165............................ DarylJacob 142
(Paul Nicholls) *chsd wnr 2nd: clsd to trck ldr 5th: shkn up to chal 2 out: drvn and unable qck between last 2: lost 2nd and wknd flat* **2/5**[1]

333- **5** *54* **Unowhatimeanharry**[14] 4171 6-11-3 113............................ PaulMoloney 82
(Helen Nelmes) *hld up in rr: wnt 5th 5th but nvr on terms w ldrs: t.o after 3 out* **100/1**

154- **6** *7* **Princely Hero (IRE)**[4] 3250 10-11-3 97.............................. TomCannon 75
(Chris Gordon) *chsd wnr tl 2nd: steadily lost pl: last 5th: lost tch and t.o after next* **150/1**

5m 10.3s (10.90) **Going Correction** +0.925s/f (Soft) 6 Ran SP% **111.4**
Speed ratings (Par 115): **115,114,114,111,90 87**
CSF £81.93 TOTE £11.40: £3.30, £2.00; EX 57.80 Trifecta £135.50.
Owner L H & Mrs T Evans **Bred** Mrs Vashti Hasdell **Trained** Kenfig Hill, Bridgend

■ Stewards' Enquiry : Robert Thornton one-day ban: careless riding (Mar 9)
Joshua Moore two-day ban: used whip above permitted level (Mar 9-10)
Rhys Flint seven-day ban: used whip above the permitted level (Mar 9-15): Fine: £500.

FOCUS
Owing to a patch of unraceable ground, a balloon-shaped railing after the last promised to make the run-in something of a slalom. Fortunately, the small field for a below-par renewal of this Grade 2 prize coped with it well. They went a fair pace and the outcome was a surprising one. The form looks solid enough although Saphir Du Rheu was a stone+ off.

4442 TOTEPOOL.COM SUPPORTS THE RACEHORSE SANCTUARY NOVICES' HURDLE (11 hdls) 2m 6f 110y

3:45 (3:45) (Class 4) 5-Y-0+ **£4,158** (£1,221; £610; £305)

Form RPR

12- **1** **Hot Whiskey N Ice (IRE)**[16] 4130 5-10-12 0............ WayneHutchinson 122+
(Noel Williams) *chsd ldr: rdn to ld bef 2 out: j.rt 2 out: drvn flat: pressed and edgd lft fnl 100yds: fnd ex and styd on: drvn out* **3/1**[3]

032- **2** *3/4* **Howlongisafoot (IRE)**[14] 4175 5-10-12 120......................... DarylJacob 119
(Paul Nicholls) *hld up wl in tch: mstke 3rd: trckd ldrs and nt fluent 5th: mstke 7th: rdn and effrt bef 2 out: 3rd and looked hld between last 2: rallied u.p flat: wnt 2nd towards fin: kpt on* **3/1**[3]

323- **3** *1 1/2* **Brave Vic (IRE)**[20] 4068 6-10-9 123.................................... JoshuaMoore(3) 117
(Gary Moore) *led tl rdn and hdd bef 2 out: rallied u.p flat: pressing wnr whn short of room on inner fnl 100yds: no ex and wknd towards fin* **5/2**[2]

231- **4** *40* **Closing Ceremony (IRE)**[43] 3643 5-11-5 125............. RichardJohnson 104
(Emma Lavelle) *chsd ldrs: 4th and rdn after 3 out: wknd bef next: t.o whn eased flat* **9/4**[1]

3P4/ **P** **Heathyards Flyer**[318] 5242 11-10-12 0............................. GerardTumelty
(Nick Lampard) *a detached last and nvr travelling wl: lost tch 4th: t.o and p.u 8th* **100/1**

05- **P** **Underwood (FR)**[49] 3552 6-10-12 0....................................... TomCannon
(Michael Roberts) *chsd ldrs tl lost pl qckly u.p after 7th: t.o whn j. slowly next: p.u bef 2 out* **200/1**

6m 1.1s (18.60) **Going Correction** +0.925s/f (Soft) 6 Ran SP% **110.8**
Speed ratings: **104,103,103,89,**
CSF £12.28 TOTE £4.10: £2.00, £2.20; EX 13.90 Trifecta £46.00.
Owner Whitehorsemen **Bred** G Durrheim & Mrs Maria Mulcahy Durrheim **Trained** Blewbury, Oxon

FOCUS
Not a bad novice hurdle. The idling winner is on the upgrade, with the next two to their marks.

4443 DOWNLOAD TOTEPOOL LIVE INFO APP FOXHUNTER TRIAL (AN OPEN HUNTERS' CHASE) (WHITELAW CHALLENGE CUP) (13 fncs 6 omitted) 3m 2f 110y

4:20 (4:21) (Class 6) 5-Y-0+ **£1,559** (£483; £241; £121)

Form RPR

/P2- **1** **Richard's Sundance (IRE)**[24] 3993 12-11-13 127(p)
MrMatthewHampton(7) 130+
(Victor Dartnall) *mde virtually all: 3 l clr 3 out (actual 2 out): drvn and kpt on bypassing 2 out: in command last: styd on: rdn out* **5/4**[1]

10- **2** *9* **Adept Approach (IRE)**[21] 8-11-13 0.................................... MrPGHall(3) 120
(P G Hall) *chsd ldrs: wnt 2nd 10th (4 out): 3 l down 3 out (actual 2 out): drvn and no ex bypassing 2 out: hld whn j.lft last: eased towards fin* **11/4**[2]

P/P- **3** *dist* **Man From Moscow**[7] 11-11-5 79................................(v) MrWHickman(7) 63
(Mrs H Norman) *w wnr tl 9th: sn u.p: dropped to 3rd and struggling next (actual 4 out): t.o bef 3 out (actual 2 out)* **14/1**

/PP- **4** *18* **Radetsky March (IRE)**[8] 4274 11-12-6 108.......................(p) MrTWeston 53
(Miss Sally Duckett) *hld up in tch: 4th and mstke 10th: struggling and j.lft next (actual 3 out): t.o bef next* **7/2**[3]

222/ **F** **Behind The Scenes (IRE)**[385] 12-11-9 85................................ MrPBull(3)
(A Coveney) *a towards rr: mstke 7th: lost tch after 9th: t.o whn fell last downhill fence (actual 3 out)* **14/1**

0/ **P** **Arkendale (IRE)**[15] 12-11-5 107......................................(t) MrJBargary(7)
(Miss K L Mellor) *a in rr: lost tch 10th (4 out): t.o next tl p.u last* **33/1**

7m 24.2s (23.10) **Going Correction** +1.05s/f (Soft) 6 Ran SP% **109.6**
Speed ratings: **107,104,89,84,**
CSF £4.99 TOTE £2.20: £1.40, £1.90; EX 5.70 Trifecta £30.00.
Owner Mrs Lucy Barlow & Mrs Sara Vernon **Bred** Miss Lillian Barry **Trained** Brayford, Devon

FOCUS
A reasonable hunter chase and only four finished. The winner stood out in this grade.

4444 TOTEEXACTA PICK THE FIRST AND SECOND H'CAP HURDLE (9 hdls) 2m 2f 110y

4:50 (4:50) (Class 4) (0-115,114) 4-Y-0+ **£3,119** (£915; £457; £228)

Form RPR

021- **1** **Clonusker (IRE)**[41] 3692 6-10-0 **88** oh1..........................(t) GerardTumelty 98+
(Linda Jewell) *t.k.h: chsd ldrs until j. ahd 2nd: mde rest: drew clr and travelling best after 3 out: 5 l clr and mstke last: drvn and faltered flat: tired but hld on gamely fnl 100yds: all out* **10/1**

300- **2** *1 1/2* **Quite By Chance**[38] 3744 5-11-12 **114**.................................. JoeTizzard 117
(Colin Tizzard) *hld up in tch in last trio: hdwy and clr in ldng quartet after 5th: chsd clr wnr bef 2 out: plugged on and pressing wnr flat: no ex and hld towards fin* **6/1**

F44- **3** *2 1/4* **The Game Is A Foot (IRE)**[43] 3650 7-10-11 **106**...... JosephAkehurst(7) 107
(Gary Moore) *in tch towards rr: 5th and rdn after 5th: styd jst in tch tl looked btn bef 2 out: rallied u.p flat: wnt 3rd and styng on wl fnl 100yds: nt rch ldrs* **5/2**[1]

101- **4** *2 1/2* **Proud Times (USA)**[23] 4004 8-11-10 **112**..............................(p) JackDoyle 111
(Ali Brewer) *chsd ldrs: rdn and chsd wnr after 3 out tl bef next: styd on same pce u.p flat* **4/1**[2]

465- **5** *2 1/2* **Kaki Island (IRE)**[49] 3550 6-11-0 **102**................................... TomCannon 100
(Chris Gordon) *led tl 2nd: chsd wnr tl after 3 out: btn between last 2: wknd flat* **12/1**

2P0- **6** *86* **Dude Alert (IRE)**[43] 3650 4-10-0 **98** oh4.................................. AdamWedge
(Anna Newton-Smith) *in tch in rr: rdn and j.lft 5th: lost tch and t.o after next* **33/1**

324- **P** **Just Cloudy**[94] 2620 10-10-12 **100**..(t) DarylJacob
(Robert Walford) *wl in tch in midfield tl rdn and dropped out qckly after 5th: t.o whn p.u next* **11/2**[3]

024- **P** **Goochypoochyprader**[33] 3821 7-10-5 **98**..............(t) ConorShoemark(5)
(Nick Lampard) *dropped to rr and rdn after 1st: mstke 2nd and nvr travelling after: lost tch 4th: mstke next: t.o whn p.u bef 6th* **6/1**

4m 58.0s (23.70) **Going Correction** +1.30s/f (Heav)
WFA 4 from 5yo+ 9lb 8 Ran SP% **112.3**
Speed ratings (Par 105): **102,101,100,99,98 62, ,**
CSF £65.61 CT £195.98 TOTE £8.10: £3.10, £2.90, £1.60; EX 77.20 Trifecta £310.90.
Owner Valence Racing **Bred** J P Jones **Trained** Sutton Valence, Kent

FOCUS
A moderate handicap.

4445 CHELTENHAM ANTE POST BETTING AT TOTEPOOL.COM STANDARD OPEN NATIONAL HUNT FLAT RACE 2m 2f 110y

5:20 (5:20) (Class 6) 4-6-Y-O **£1,559** (£457; £228; £114)

Form RPR

3- **1** **Otago Trail (IRE)**[31] 3863 6-11-3 0.................................... LiamTreadwell 120+
(Venetia Williams) *mde all: drew wl clr fr 7f out: heavily eased ins fnl f* **5/4**[1]

2 *69* **Beaufort Boy (IRE)** 5-11-3 0... JamieMoore 45
(Gary Moore) *hld up in tch: hdwy 1/2-way: chsd clr wnr 4f out: no imp and sn wl btn: t.o over 2f out: tired but plugged on to hold 2nd* **6/1**[3]

3 *2* **Face To Face** 5-11-3 0... TomScudamore 43
(David Pipe) *chsd ldr tl 4f out: 3rd and t.o 3 out: plugged on and battling for poor 2nd fnl f* **9/4**[2]

4 *44* **Toohighforme (IRE)** 5-11-3 0.. TomCannon
(Nick Gifford) *chsd ldrs tl rdn and dropped to 4th 1/2-way: lost tch 6f out: sn wl t.o* **8/1**

5 *35* **Ollisu Lad (IRE)** 5-11-3 0... RichardJohnson
(Tim Vaughan) *a bhd: lost tch 7f out: sn wl t.o* **8/1**

4m 50.8s (22.10) **Going Correction** +1.30s/f (Heav) 5 Ran SP% **111.7**
Speed ratings: **105,75,75,56,41**
CSF £9.36 TOTE £2.80: £2.20, £2.20; EX 7.70 Trifecta £17.20.
Owner Mrs Marie Shone **Bred** Dan O'Brien **Trained** Kings Caple, H'fords

FOCUS
A moderate bumper but the pace was not bad considering the small field. The winner could be decent but the form is pretty much unrateable.
T/Plt: £669.30 to a £1 stake. Pool: £96,758.76 - 105.53 winning units. T/Qpdt: £38.10 to a £1 stake. Pool: £7808.40 - 151.62 winning units. SP

[3796]TOWCESTER (R-H)

Sunday, February 23

OFFICIAL GOING: Heavy (6.4)

Wind: strong against Weather: overcast with some light rain; 11 degrees

4446 HAYGAIN HAY STEAMERS CLEAN HEALTHY FORAGE H'CAP HURDLE (12 hdls) 3m

2:00 (2:00) (Class 5) (0-100,99) 4-Y-O+ **£2,599** (£763; £381; £190)

Form RPR

/0F- **1** **Newton Thistle**[10] 4243 7-9-9 **73** oh3 NicodeBoinville[(5)] 91+
(Ben Pauling) *prom: led 9th: drew rt away after next: hit 2 out: v tired and str reminders after last but nvr in any danger* **7/1**[3]

1S0- **2** *19* **Millers Reef (IRE)**[12] 4201 8-11-10 **97** WilsonRenwick 96
(Keith Dalgleish) *settled in rr: effrt gng wl 8th: chsd wnr fr 3 out but immediately outpcd: no ch fr next: fin tired* **9/2**[2]

0P2- **3** *10* **Earcomesthedream (IRE)**[54] 3432 11-11-10 **97** (b) RyanMahon 86
(Peter Pritchard) *led: clr tl 3rd: rdn and hdd 9th: fdd steadily fr 3 out: remote 3rd next* **10/1**

343- **4** *9* **Blue Cove**[32] 3842 9-10-4 **77** TomSiddall 57
(Lynn Siddall) *hld up: effrt 7th: rdn 9th: struggled on w no ch fr next: 35 l 4th 2 out* **9/4**[1]

462- **5** *1 1/4* **Miss Mayfair (IRE)**[59] 3251 7-11-2 **89** AidanColeman 68
(Lawney Hill) *midfield: rdn 3 out: sn lost tch: 36 l 5th 2 out* **9/2**[2]

451- **6** *5* **Volio Vincente (FR)**[88] 2743 7-9-11 **73** oh2 JamesBest[(3)] 47
(Carroll Gray) *midfield: rdn and lost tch 3 out: t.o and v tired bef next* **10/1**

P00- **7** *21* **Oak Wood (IRE)**[6] 4326 6-10-5 **85** ConorRing[(7)] 38
(John Upson) *prom: j. slowly 4th and 9th: dropped out qckly: t.o and v tired after next* **33/1**

0/0- **P** **Captain P K (IRE)**[127] 1982 7-10-2 **80** (t) DerekFox[(5)]
(Noel C Kelly, Ire) *j.lft in detached last: struggling 8th: t.o and p.u 2 out* **14/1**

6- **P** **Trafords Hero**[30] 3880 6-11-12 **99** MarkGrant
(Geoffrey Deacon) *towards rr: hit 6th: rdn and struggling next: t.o after 9th: p.u wl bef 2 out* **33/1**

6m 57.5s (42.50) **Going Correction** +1.075s/f (Soft) **9** Ran SP% **110.4**
Speed ratings (Par 103): **72,65,62,59,58 57,50, ,**
CSF £36.40 CT £296.17 TOTE £9.60: £2.90, £1.50, £2.60; EX 40.30 Trifecta £604.10.
Owner J H And N J Foxon **Bred** J H And N J Foxon **Trained** Bourton-On-The-Water, Gloucs

FOCUS
This was a moderate handicap to open proceedings. It was run at a fair enough gallop and all bar the first pair were in trouble from the third-last. The surface certainly looked hard work. The winner is rated in line with his best bumper form.

4447 HAYGAIN HAY STEAMERS CLEAN HEALTHY FORAGE (S) H'CAP HURDLE (8 hdls) 2m

2:30 (2:31) (Class 5) (0-100,99) 4-Y-O+ **£1,949** (£572; £286; £143)

Form RPR

006- **1** **Drombeg West**[75] 3014 7-10-0 **73** oh4 AndrewTinkler 81+
(Anna Brooks) *trckd ldrs gng wl: led 3 out: in command bef next: tired and drvn fr last but hung on gamely* **8/1**

602- **2** *1 3/4* **Slaney Star (IRE)**[9] 4247 6-11-12 **99** (v[1]) TomScudamore 105+
(Jim Best) *pushed along much of way: mde nrly all tl 3 out: sn outpcd by wnr: hit 2 out: 5 l down whn sprawled at last: clsd u.p but a hld* **3/1**[1]

635/ **3** *17* **Converti**[6] 962 10-10-0 **76** JamesBest[(3)] 63
(Carroll Gray) *in rr and rdn after 3rd: virtually t.o 3 out: remote 7th whn crossed by puller up at next: pluged on u.p: tk poor 3rd nr fin* **14/1**

P54- **4** *1 1/2* **Captain Sharpe**[80] 2898 6-10-12 **90** (t) RobertWilliams[(5)] 78
(Bernard Llewellyn) *pressed ldrs: 4th and rdn and jst getting outpcd whn pckd bdly 3 out: 12 l 3rd and wl btn next: lost a pl nr fin* **10/1**

24P- **5** *hd* **Fidelor (FR)**[20] 4071 8-11-5 **92** (b[1]) WillKennedy 77
(Alex Hales) *prom: nt fluent 4th: sn drvn and nt travelling: wl btn 3 out* **8/1**

404- **6** *hd* **Inside Knowledge (USA)**[17] 4107 8-11-2 **89** (p) AdamPogson 74
(Garry Woodward) *prom: led briefly 4th: drvn and fdd 3 out* **9/1**

050- **7** *13* **Drummond**[6] 3426 5-10-2 **78** (bt) MarkQuinlan[(3)] 50
(Bernard Llewellyn) *nvr bttr than midfield: rdn whn mstke 5th: no ch after* **50/1**

FPF- **8** *5* **Killegney**[10] 4242 10-11-3 **90** (v) BrendanPowell 57
(Michael Gates) *bhd: drvn after 3rd: no rspnse: t.o fr next* **50/1**

410- **9** *17* **Peqeno Diablo (IRE)**[48] 3569 9-9-8 **74** (tp) GeraldQuinn[(7)] 24
(Claire Dyson) *racd wd: nvr bttr than midfield: t.o 3 out* **6/1**[3]

034- **P** **Tisfreetdream (IRE)**[58] 3324 13-11-3 **95** (bt) NicodeBoinville[(5)]
(Peter Pritchard) *prom tl 3rd and drvn 3 out: sn btn: midfield but v tired whn p.u next* **20/1**

035- **P** **Ghaabesh (IRE)**[57] 3353 7-10-3 **81** (t) HarryChalloner[(5)]
(Barry Leavy) *wl bhd: drvn after 3rd: t.o next: p.u 2 out* **5/1**[2]

660- **P** **Echoes Of Joy**[75] 3014 5-11-0 **87** SeanQuinlan
(David Evans) *wore a nosenet: veered lft s: last whn mstke 2nd: prog to midfield after 4th: pckd bdly next: rdn and fdd 3 out: t.o and p.u last* **50/1**

4m 24.2s (16.30) **Going Correction** +1.075s/f (Soft) **12** Ran SP% **114.6**
Speed ratings (Par 103): **102,101,92,91,91 91,85,82,74, ,**
CSF £30.98 CT £329.22 TOTE £11.40: £3.20, £1.50, £5.00; EX 48.70 Trifecta £1015.50.There was no bid for the winner.
Owner Mrs J M Owen **Bred** Steve Hadley **Trained** Alderton, Northants

FOCUS
An ordinary handicap, run at a sound tempo and again the ground played a big part. The winner was potentially well in on a Worcester run.

4448 TRY GG.COM ON YOUR MOBILE H'CAP CHASE (14 fncs) 2m 3f 110y

3:00 (3:01) (Class 4) (0-120,117) 5-Y-O+ **£3,898** (£1,144; £572; £286)

Form RPR

5U1- **1** **Freckle Face**[35] 3799 7-11-5 **110** TommyPhelan 128+
(Bill Turner) *hld up: wnt 2nd bef 10th: led gng wl 2 out: easily drew clr: revelled in conditions* **8/1**

P54- **2** *17* **Pensnett Bay**[70] 3113 9-11-7 **112** (b) MarkGrant 108
(Jo Hughes) *led: blnd 2nd: hrd pressed 3 out: drvn and hdd next: immediately outpcd: fin tired* **9/1**

22U- **3** *7* **Mentalist (FR)**[26] 3958 6-11-10 **115** AidanColeman 104
(Venetia Williams) *settled handy: effrt 10th: wnt 3 l 3rd and rdn 3 out: sn rdn and btn: 8 l 3rd next: fin tired* **7/2**[3]

611- **4** *22* **High Ron**[32] 3836 9-11-7 **112** AndrewThornton 79
(Caroline Bailey) *taken wd: prom tl pushed along after 4th: nvr gng wl after: t.o fr 10th* **10/3**[2]

P52- **P** **Speedy Bruere (FR)**[22] 4036 8-11-5 **117** JakeHodson[(7)]
(David Bridgwater) *pressed ldr tl mstke 6th and rdr lost iron: lost 2nd bef 10th: slowed alarmingly after 3 out: t.o and p.u next* **5/2**[1]

F32- **P** **Polarbrook (IRE)**[56] 3394 7-11-9 **114** (b) JasonMaguire
(Donald McCain) *nt travelling in last: pushed along after 4th: reminders and fnd nil bef 7th: hit 8th: t.o and p.u 2 out* **6/1**

5m 26.6s (8.40) **Going Correction** +0.575s/f (Soft) **6** Ran SP% **109.3**
Speed ratings: **106,99,96,87, ,**
CSF £63.39 TOTE £5.80: £3.30, £3.90; EX 58.50 Trifecta £117.50.
Owner Mrs Christine Goldsmith **Bred** B J Goldsmith **Trained** Sigwells, Somerset

FOCUS
Not a bad little handicap. Another step up from the easy winner, and there's a case for rating the form up to 10lb higher.

4449 HARRY HARRIS MEMORIAL H'CAP HURDLE (12 hdls) 3m

3:35 (3:35) (Class 3) (0-140,124) 4-Y-O+ **£7,876** (£2,524; £1,402)

Form RPR

3P2- **1** **Cadeau George**[15] 4161 5-10-12 **110** (p) DavidBass 116
(Ben Pauling) *disp ld tl nt fluent 6th: led bef 8th tl next: hrd drvn 3rd and briefly outpcd home turn: rallied 2 out: led last: styd on dourly* **6/1**[3]

31F- **2** *3 1/2* **Wayward Glance**[63] 3223 6-11-10 **122** (p) WilsonRenwick 124
(Keith Dalgleish) *settled cl up: chal 3 out: rdn to ld bef next where 2 l clr: hdd and clipped last: no ex flat* **6/1**[3]

030- **3** *67* **Halucha (IRE)**[7] 4299 9-10-6 **107** (p) JakeGreenall[(3)] 42
(Paul Webber) *disp ld: led 6th tl bef 8th: rdn and dropped out qckly after next: t.o 3 out: lft v remote 3rd bef last* **16/1**

324- **P** **Arkose (IRE)**[52] 3505 10-11-12 **124** (v) LeightonAspell
(Oliver Sherwood) *cl up tl mstke 7th: last and rdn and labouring next: lost tch after 9th: sn t.o: p.u last* **5/1**[2]

561- **P** **Join The Clan (IRE)**[7] 4308 5-11-2 **119** 7ex MauriceLinehan[(5)]
(Jonjo O'Neill) *trckd ldrs: wnt 2nd at 8th: led narrowly next: hrd rdn and hdd bef 2 out: sn btn: poor 3rd whn p.u bef last: dismntd* **4/5**[1]

6m 43.5s (28.50) **Going Correction** +1.375s/f (Heav) **5** Ran SP% **106.7**
Speed ratings (Par 107): **107,105,83, ,**
CSF £34.65 TOTE £9.10: £3.40, £1.50; EX 24.10 Trifecta £78.80.
Owner Genesis Racing Partnership **Bred** Exors Of The Late Brian William Gillbard **Trained** Bourton-On-The-Water, Gloucs

FOCUS
This modest staying handicap served up a severe test. A step up from the winner with the second to his mark, in a relatively good time.

4450 DON'T MISS OUT WITH GG.COM ALERTS NOVICES' HURDLE (8 hdls) 2m

4:10 (4:10) (Class 4) 4-Y-O+ **£3,898** (£1,144; £572; £286)

Form RPR

531- **1** **Son Of Suzie**[65] 3194 6-11-2 0 PaddyBrennan 109+
(Fergal O'Brien) *j.rt 1st: cl up: led gng best bef 2 out: narrow advantage after tl pushed clr after last* **11/8**[1]

6- **2** *3/4* **Neighbourhood (USA)**[72] 2280 6-10-13 0 MarkQuinlan[(3)] 108+
(James Evans) *settled in rr: effrt after 3 out: rdn and wnt cl 2nd and hit next: stl upsides but hld whn hit last: kpt on steadily* **8/1**

55/ **3** *16* **Mister Frosty (IRE)**[19] 2396 8-10-13 0 JackQuinlan[(3)] 93
(Michael Squance) *hld up: effrt to go cl up at 5th: mstke next: sn rdn: 8 l 3rd and tiring 2 out: plugged on* **20/1**

523- **4** *10* **Mr Shantu (IRE)**[23] 4017 5-11-2 0 RichieMcLernon 84
(Jonjo O'Neill) *prom: wnt 2nd at 5th: rdn next: floundering bef 2 out* **5/1**[3]

0- **5** *3* **Luckster**[4] 3161 4-10-7 0 SeanQuinlan 69
(David Evans) *towards rr: lost tch tamely 3 out* **33/1**

\- **6** *1 3/4* **Paddocks Lounge (IRE)**[294] 7-11-2 0 MattieBatchelor 76
(Jim Best) *plld hrd: cl up tl dropped bk last and rdn 5th: struggling after next* **14/1**

4- **7** *6* **John Louis**[26] 3956 6-11-2 0 AidanColeman 77
(Venetia Williams) *plld hrd: led after 2nd: blnd next: drvn and hdd bef 2 out: fdd tamely: lost modest 4th sn after 2 out and eased* **5/2**[2]

8 *35* **Offherocker**[38] 7-10-2 0 GeraldQuinn[(7)] 28
(Claire Dyson) *led tl after 2nd: lost pl 5th: struggling whn mstke next: sn t.o* **100/1**

4m 27.5s (19.60) **Going Correction** +1.375s/f (Heav)
WFA 4 from 5yo+ 9lb **8** Ran SP% **113.8**
Speed ratings (Par 105): **106,105,97,92,91 90,87,69**
CSF £13.11 TOTE £2.00: £1.10, £2.30, £3.90; EX 13.40 Trifecta £73.50.
Owner Mrs R Mackness **Bred** Caroline Mackness **Trained** Coln St. Dennis, Gloucs

FOCUS
The first pair locked horns from the penultimate flight in this modest novice hurdle. The winner can rate higher.

4451 BEST RACING BLOGS ON GG.COM NOVICES' H'CAP CHASE (16 fncs) 2m 6f

4:40 (4:40) (Class 4) (0-110,105) 5-Y-O+ **£3,898** (£1,144; £572; £286)

Form RPR

3U4- **1** **Nail 'M (IRE)**[66] 3176 6-11-10 **103** (p) SamTwiston-Davies 118
(Nigel Hawke) *settled cl up: 4th and rdn at 13th: drvn into 2nd wl bef 2 out: led bef last: grad edgd clr: idling flat and kpt rt up to work* **8/1**

221- **2** *3* **Take The Mick**[4] 4354 7-11-8 **101** AidanColeman 115
(Venetia Williams) *led narrowly: jnd 12th: drvn wl bef 2 out: hdd appr last: kpt on same pce and a hld flat* **8/13**[1]

050- **3** *17* **I Know The Code (IRE)**[65] 3191 9-10-10 **89** TomSiddall 84
(Lynn Siddall) *hit 4th: bhd: lft last at 8th: t.o 12th: plugged on into remote 3rd after last* **25/1**

321- **4** *3 1/2* **Smart Exit (IRE)**[35] 3797 7-11-11 **104** (p) TomO'Brien 98
(Renee Robeson) *trckd ldrs: hit 11th: 3 l 3rd and rdn 13th: wknd bef 2 out: lost poor 3rd flat* **5/1**[2]

433- **5** *26* **Cloudingstar (IRE)**[17] 4108 7-11-12 **105** (t) RichieMcLernon 70
(Jonjo O'Neill) *w ldr tl 3 out: rdn and fdd qckly up hill bef next: lost poor 4th at last and eased: t.o* **15/2**[3]

/03- **P** **Ball Hopper (IRE)**[20] 4067 10-10-13 **92** (t) AndrewThornton
(Richenda Ford) *immediately detached in last: awkward jump 7th: t.o and p.u next* **20/1**

/U4- **P** **Roparta Avenue**[96] 2582 7-10-7 **86** LeightonAspell
(Diana Grissell) *towards rr: pushed along after 6th: p.u 9th: stirrup leather broke* **40/1**

6m 3.7s (10.70) **Going Correction** +0.575s/f (Soft) **7** Ran SP% **112.5**
Speed ratings: **103,101,95,94,85 ,**
CSF £13.89 CT £119.53 TOTE £8.80: £4.30, £1.50; EX 17.90 Trifecta £113.70.
Owner David Mitchell & D R Mead **Bred** Peter & Des Dundon **Trained** Stoodleigh, Devon

FOCUS
A moderate novice handicap. They went a fair gallop and it saw a slow-motion finish. A step up from the winner with the second below his best.

4452 FOLLOW GG.COM ON FACEBOOK AND TWITTER "NEWCOMERS" STANDARD OPEN NATIONAL HUNT FLAT RACE 2m
5:10 (5:10) (Class 5) 4-5-Y-0 **£1,949** (£572; £286; £143)

Form RPR
1 **Big Jim** 5-11-4 0 WillKennedy 96+
(Alex Hales) *v big: pressed ldr in v slow r: rdn and running green whn carried lft home turn: led over 2f out: sn urged clr* **6/1**3
2 9 **Eaton Rock (IRE)** 5-11-4 0 FelixDeGiles 86
(Tom Symonds) *v tall: led at v slow pce and hanging lft thrght: rdn whn rn wd home turn and hdd: sn outpcd* **9/4**1
3 22 **Graasp The Nettle** 4-10-9 0 AidanColeman 55
(Harry Whittington) *4th and struggling 1/2-way: plodded into remote 3rd 1f out* **11/4**2
4 15 **Time And Again (FR)** 4-10-6 0 MichaelByrne(3) 40
(Tim Vaughan) *cl up: drvn wl over 2f out: fdd bdly after: hopelessly t.o* **9/4**1
P **Ilewinbrittania** 5-10-11 0 JackSavage(7)
(Gary Brown) *lost tch after 6f: sn hopelessly t.o and plld himself up bef 1/2-way* **10/1**

4m 24.4s (22.10) **Going Correction** +1.375s/f (Heav)
WFA 4 from 5yo 9lb 5 Ran SP% **111.6**
Speed ratings: **99,94,83,76,**
CSF £20.02 TOTE £5.90: £2.30, £2.00; EX 25.40 Trifecta £68.60.
Owner Gumbrills Racing Partnership **Bred** John S C And Mrs K A Fry **Trained** Edgcote, Northants
FOCUS
No previous form to go on here and they raced steadily early on. The hurdles were not removed as is usually the case due to the heavy ground.
T/Jkpt: Not won. T/Plt: £394.00 to a £1 stake. Pool: £123,662.78 - 229.08 winning units. T/Qpdt: £67.50 to a £1 stake. Pool: £8182.14 - 89.65 winning units. IM

4453 - 4454a (Foreign Racing) - See Raceform Interactive

4164 NAAS (L-H)
Sunday, February 23
OFFICIAL GOING: Soft to heavy

4455a WOODLANDS PARK 100 CLUB NAS NA RIOGH NOVICE CHASE (GRADE 2) (13 fncs) 2m 4f
2:50 (2:50) 5-Y-0+ **£21,666** (£6,333; £3,000)

RPR
1 **Mozoltov**28 3928 8-11-5 150 BryanCooper 154+
(W P Mullins, Ire) *mde all: clr whn bad mstke and almost uns rdr 1st where rdr lost irons briefly: j. sltly lft at times: extended clr advantage into st: j.lft and mstke last: easily* **2/13**1
2 35 **Folsom Blue (IRE)**21 4064 7-11-5 134 BenDalton 120+
(Conor O'Dwyer, Ire) *hld up wl bhd ldr: remote 2nd 1/2-way: slow 5 out and dropped to rr: regained remote 2nd after 3 out: no imp on easy wnr thrght: disp 2nd whn slow last: kpt on one pce to hold 2nd* **9/2**2
3 nk **Summer Star (IRE)**49 3561 6-10-12 MsKWalsh 110
(T M Walsh, Ire) *hld up wl bhd ldr: remote 3rd 1/2-way: wnt remote 2nd 5 out tl dropped to rr of trio again after 3 out: no imp on wnr thrght: swtchd fr next and disp 2nd at last: kpt on same pce run-in: jst hld for 2nd* **33/1**3

5m 48.3s (19.30) 3 Ran SP% **107.8**
CSF £1.41 TOTE £1.10; DF 1.40 Trifecta £1.20.
Owner Gigginstown House Stud **Bred** Mrs C A Brown **Trained** Muine Beag, Co Carlow
FOCUS
Basically a non-event, and there would have been precious little to say about this rewarding schooling-session for the long odds-on winner.

4456a PADDY POWER SHOPS BETTER VALUE NOVICE HURDLE (GRADE 2) (8 hdls) 2m
3:25 (3:26) 4-Y-0+ **£22,750** (£6,650; £3,150; £1,050)

RPR
1 **Real Steel (IRE)**21 4060 6-11-4 128 BrianO'Connell 142+
(Philip Fenton, Ire) *mde all: 2 l clr whn slt mstke 4th: extended advantage 3 out tl jnd bef next: sn rdn w narrow ld: styd on wl u.p run-in* **7/1**
2 3 1/4 **Vicky De L'Oasis (FR)**35 3804 5-10-10 130 RWalsh 131
(W P Mullins, Ire) *chsd ldrs: j.rt 1st: 4th 1/2-way: tk clsr order in 3rd bef 2 out: rdn and wnt 2nd u.p fr after last: no imp on wnr run-in: kpt on same pce* **13/8**1
3 1/2 **Minella Foru (IRE)**84 2852 5-11-6 133 MarkWalsh 141+
(Edward P Harty, Ire) *w.w towards rr: j.big 1st: niggled along fr 4 out: tk clsr order bhd ldrs in rr bef 2 out: rdn into 4th bef last: n.m.r run-in and kpt on between horses into nvr threatening 3rd cl home* **12/1**
4 nk **Empire Of Dirt (IRE)**29 3911 7-11-4 130 BryanCooper 138
(C A Murphy, Ire) *trckd ldr in 2nd for most tl got on terms bef 2 out: sn rdn in 2nd and no imp on wnr u.p in 3rd fr last: dropped to 4th cl home* **5/1**3
5 9 **Kylestyle (IRE)**38 3748 5-11-3 130 AndrewJMcNamara 129
(F Flood, Ire) *chsd ldrs: 3rd 1/2-way: rdn bef 2 out and sn no imp on wnr in 5th: kpt on one pce* **9/1**
6 10 **City Slicker (IRE)**43 3670 6-11-7 140 1 APMcCoy 124
(W P Mullins, Ire) *on toes befhand: w.w in rr: nt fluent 1st and 3rd: t.k.h: sme hdwy bhd ldrs fr 4 out: pushed along in 4th after next and no ex u.p fr 2 out: dropped to rr bef last: eased* **9/4**2

3m 56.5s (-7.00) 6 Ran SP% **115.7**
CSF £20.22 TOTE £9.70: £3.70, £1.02; DF 31.30 Trifecta £197.30.
Owner Gigginstown House Stud **Bred** T Hendy **Trained** Carrick-On-Suir, Co Tipperary
FOCUS
A minor upset here.

4457a PADDY POWER YOUR LOCAL BETTING SHOP CHASE (GRADE 2) (10 fncs) 2m
4:00 (4:00) 5-Y-0+ **£24,375** (£7,125; £3,375)

RPR
1 **Days Hotel (IRE)**36 3773 9-11-10 152 AELynch 157
(Henry De Bromhead, Ire) *led and disp tl in front bef 1/2-way: mstke 3 out and jnd briefly: gng wl 2 out and brought to nrside: rdn and styd on wl run-in to extend advantage nr fin* **4/1**2
2 5 1/2 **Toner D'Oudaires (FR)**21 4062 7-11-7 152 (tp) BryanCooper 150+
(Gordon Elliott, Ire) *trckd ldrs: niggled along fr 5th: tk clsr order bhd ldr fr 4 out: j.lft in 2nd 2 out and sn rdn: no imp on wnr fr after last: kpt on same pce* **5/1**3
3 47 **Twinlight (FR)**43 3645 7-11-10 157 RWalsh 117+
(W P Mullins, Ire) *led and disp out wd: j. sltly rt at times: 2nd bef 1/2-way: almost on terms whn nt fluent 5 out: mstke next and dropped to 3rd briefly: pushed along in 2nd into st and sn no ex: wknd and eased* **4/11**1

4m 18.6s (-4.70) 3 Ran SP% **110.0**
CSF £15.56 TOTE £4.00; DF 9.40 Trifecta £11.40.
Owner James Treacy **Bred** James Treacy **Trained** Knockeen, Co Waterford
FOCUS
A poor turn-out, and not a very satisfactory race with the short-priced favourite failing to do himself justice. The winner is rated back to his best.

4458 - 4459a (Foreign Racing) - See Raceform Interactive

4220 MUSSELBURGH (R-H)
Monday, February 24
OFFICIAL GOING: Soft (heavy in places)
Wind: Light, half behind Weather: Overcast, dull

4460 NEW RACING UK ANYWHERE AVAILABLE NOW MAIDEN HURDLE (12 hdls) 2m 4f
1:50 (1:50) (Class 5) 4-Y-0+ **£2,599** (£763; £381; £190)

Form RPR
33- 1 **Katachenko (IRE)**52 3516 5-11-3 0 JasonMaguire 121+
(Donald McCain) *mde all: j.lft fr 1/2-way: qcknd clr 3 out: styd on strly: easily* **7/4**1
42U- 2 12 **Gurkha Brave (IRE)**38 3760 6-11-3 0 JamesReveley 104
(Karen McLintock) *chsd wnr: effrt and rdn whn nt fluent 3 out: outpcd fr next* **13/2**
/32- 3 1 3/4 **Solidago (IRE)**52 3520 7-11-3 100 (v) TomO'Brien 103
(S R B Crawford, Ire) *in tch: effrt and pushed along after 4 out: no imp whn nt fluent 2 out: hld whn mstke last* **5/2**2
503- 4 3 **Marlborough House**24 4003 4-10-7 107 BrianHughes 88
(Chris Grant) *chsd ldrs: drvn and outpcd 4 out: no imp fr next* **11/1**
F/3- 5 49 **Isaacstown Lad (IRE)**29 3921 7-11-3 0 BrianHarding 49
(William Amos) *bhd: rdn and outpcd fr 3rd: struggling fnl circ: t.o* **4/1**3

4m 50.1s (-1.40) **Going Correction** -0.075s/f (Good)
WFA 4 from 5yo+ 10lb 5 Ran SP% **106.6**
Speed ratings (Par 103): **99,94,93,92,72**
CSF £11.92 TOTE £2.50: £1.60, £1.90; EX 10.00 Trifecta £21.60.
Owner Trevor Hemmings **Bred** Charles Harte **Trained** Cholmondeley, Cheshire
FOCUS
All hurdles moved and the bottom bend moved in. Hurdle and Chase used same bend. A seven-race card which lost some of its lustre when 15mm of overnight rain resulted in 22 non-runners. An ordinary maiden hurdle in which they went a sensible gallop. The winner should go on to rate higher.

4461 WATCH CHELTENHAM WITH RACING UK ANYWHERE H'CAP HURDLE (14 hdls) 3m 110y
2:20 (2:20) (Class 5) (0-100,100) 4-Y-0+ **£3,422** (£997; £499)

Form RPR
353- 1 **Ryton Runner (IRE)**52 3520 6-11-5 100 (p) CraigNichol(7) 103
(Lucinda Russell) *midfield on ins: drvn and outpcd 4 out: rallied and cl up next: led run-in: styd on wl u.p* **9/1**
/P4- 2 hd **Highlander Ted**52 3520 6-10-13 87 (p) PeterBuchanan 90
(Mark Walford) *led to 2nd: led 4th: j.rt next: rdn bef 2 out: hung lft between last 2: hdd run-in: rallied: hld nr fin* **10/1**
F43- 3 1 1/2 **Generous Chief (IRE)**14 4186 6-11-0 95 DiarmuidO'Regan(7) 98
(Chris Grant) *hld up in midfield: blnd and pushed along 8th: rallied bef 3 out: effrt and cl up whn carried lft briefly between last 2: kpt on fr last: hld fnl 50yds* **25/1**
4U4- 4 1 3/4 **Yukon Delta (IRE)**14 4186 7-10-11 85 KennyJohnson 85
(Robert Johnson) *s.i.s: hld up: hdwy and prom 6th: drvn along 3 out: rallied: kpt on same pce fr last* **80/1**
344- 5 5 **Merrydown Vintage (IRE)**69 3145 7-11-6 94 (p) TomO'Brien 89
(S R B Crawford, Ire) *cl up: led 2nd to 4th: w ldr: ev ch tl rdn and outpcd 2 out: no imp fr last* **15/2**3
003- 6 4 1/2 **Runswick Days (IRE)**12 4223 7-10-11 92 JohnDawson(7) 82
(John Wade) *chsd ldrs: drvn along bef 3 out: outpcd fr next* **14/1**
644- 7 2 **Native Optimist (IRE)**34 3824 7-10-6 85 MissCWalton(5) 73
(Sheena Walton) *hld up: hdwy and in tch after 4 out: rdn and wknd after next* **16/1**
031- 8 3 3/4 **Rocky Stone (IRE)**34 3824 6-11-12 100 JasonMaguire 87
(Donald McCain) *prom: hdwy and cl up bef 3 out: sn pushed along: wknd fr next* **9/4**1
3P4- 9 7 **Silver Dragon**7 4326 6-11-9 97 DougieCostello 78
(Tony Coyle) *nt fluent in rr: hit and outpcd 9th: nvr on terms* **5/1**2
555- 10 1 1/4 **More Equity**11 4236 12-11-7 100 EmmaSayer(5) 76
(Dianne Sayer) *bhd: outpcd fr 8th: nvr on terms* **25/1**
43P- 11 24 **Vallani (IRE)**52 3520 9-9-9 76 GrantCockburn(7) 28
(Lucinda Russell) *bhd and sn pushed along: struggling fnl circ: nvr on terms* **15/2**3

5m 53.1s (-3.60) **Going Correction** -0.075s/f (Good) 11 Ran SP% **111.5**
Speed ratings (Par 103): **102,101,101,100,99 97,97,96,93,93 85**
CSF £88.03 CT £2110.98 TOTE £10.20: £2.90, £3.30, £4.70; EX 88.30 Trifecta £1545.30.
Owner County Set Four **Bred** Premier Bloodstock **Trained** Arlary, Perth & Kinross
FOCUS
A modest staying handicap hurdle in which they went an honest gallop. The first two ran to their marks.

4462 HENRY REILLY MEMORIAL H'CAP CHASE (BETFAIR SCOTTISH CHASE SERIES QUALIFIER) (16 fncs) 2m 4f
2:50 (2:50) (Class 5) (0-100,99) 5-Y-0+ **£3,898** (£1,144; £572; £286)

Form RPR
U46- 1 **Ben Akram (IRE)**51 3528 6-11-12 99 PeterBuchanan 107+
(Lucinda Russell) *in tch: hdwy on outside 9th: drvn to ld bef 2 out: hrd pressed last: styd on wl towards fin* **15/2**
/F1- 2 3/4 **Dingo Bay**51 3528 8-11-5 92 BrianHughes 97
(John Wade) *cl up: rdn and outpcd bef 4 out: rallied bef next: drvn and ev ch last: hung rt run-in: kpt on: hld cl home* **15/8**1

The Form Book Jumps, Raceform Ltd, Compton, RG20 6NL.

411- **3** *3 ¼* **Oh Right (IRE)**[31] 3876 10-10-5 **83**........................(b) ColmMcCormack(5) 86
(Dianne Sayer) *led: rdn and qcknd whn nt fluent 4 out: nt fluent next: hdd bef 2 out: rallied: one pce fr last* **5/1**

523- **4** *15* **Soul Angel**[12] 4220 10-10-1 **74**...(v) AdrianLane 61
(Sandy Forster) *cl up tl drvn and outpcd after 5 out: no imp fr next* **9/2**[3]

52F- **5** *15* **Moonlight Maggie**[31] 3883 7-10-2 **80**....................... AodhaganConlon(5) 60
(Tom George) *prom: mstkes 4th and 10th: rdn and outpcd bef 4 out: wknd next* **11/4**[2]

5m 8.9s (7.70) **Going Correction** +0.40s/f (Soft) **5** Ran SP% **108.1**
Speed ratings: **100,99,98,92,86**
CSF £21.69 TOTE £8.30: £3.20, £1.60; EX 22.60 Trifecta £55.40.
Owner Mrs Michelle Gleeson **Bred** William Scallan **Trained** Arlary, Perth & Kinross

FOCUS
A modest handicap chase. The first three were all fairly close to their pre-race marks.

4463 RACINGUK.COM/ANYWHERE: 3 DEVICES, 1 PRICE H'CAP HURDLE (9 hdls) 2m
3:20 (3:20) (Class 4) (0-120,115) 4-Y-0+ **£3,898** (£1,144; £572; £286)

Form RPR

433- **1** **Cool Sky**[24] 4023 5-11-8 **111**.. JasonMaguire 114+
(Donald McCain) *hld up in tch: stdy hdwy 3 out: effrt and ev ch last: led run-in: rdn and r.o wl* **6/4**[1]

432- **2** *¾* **Bellgrove (IRE)**[87] 2792 6-11-9 **112**................................. DougieCostello 114+
(Ian Semple) *t.k.h early: led: hdd whn nt fluent 5th: led next: rdn bef 3 out: hrd pressed last: hdd run-in: kpt on: hld nr fin* **9/2**[3]

U3F- **3** *6* **Lone Foot Laddie (IRE)**[78] 2970 5-11-0 **110**............ GrahamWatters(7) 105
(Lucinda Russell) *hld up in tch: hdwy bef 2 out: effrt and cl 3rd whn nt fluent 2 out: outpcd run-in* **11/1**

600- **4** *21* **Cool Baranca (GER)**[57] 3398 8-11-5 **113**........................ EmmaSayer(5) 86
(Dianne Sayer) *w ldr: led 5th to next: drvn and wknd bef 3 out* **12/1**

060- **5** *3 ¾* **Tom Wade (IRE)**[8] 4302 7-11-7 **115**...................................... BenPoste(5) 84
(Shaun Harris) *prom: hdwy and cl up 4 out: sn pushed along: hung rt and wknd after next* **11/1**

0/4- **U** **Dante's Frolic**[57] 3398 6-11-1 **104**.. RyanMania 95
(Michael Smith) *t.k.h: trckd ldrs: effrt and ev ch 3 out: sn rdn: 3 l 3rd and one pce whn mstke and uns rdr last* **11/4**[2]

3m 50.7s (2.30) **Going Correction** -0.075s/f (Good) **6** Ran SP% **109.2**
Speed ratings (Par 105): **91,90,87,77,75**
CSF £8.30 CT £45.29 TOTE £2.20: £1.10, £2.00; EX 7.00 Trifecta £48.90.
Owner Norte Sur Partnership **Bred** Miss K J Keir **Trained** Cholmondeley, Cheshire

FOCUS
A fair contest which produced an exciting, close-fought finish between the two handicap debutants.

4464 MUSSELBURGH INTERACTIVE NOVICES' LIMITED H'CAP CHASE (18 fncs) 3m
3:50 (3:50) (Class 3) (0-125,125) 5-Y-0+ **£6,797** (£2,337)

Form RPR

312- **1** **Kris Cross (IRE)**[52] 3521 7-10-12 122......................(tp) GrantCockburn(7) 131+
(Lucinda Russell) *mostly j.lft: mde all: clr after 5 out: rdn and styd on wl fr 3 out: unchal* **15/8**[2]

/31- **2** *12* **King's Grace**[60] 3275 8-10-12 115...................................... JasonMaguire 118
(Donald McCain) *nt fluent at any stage: chsd wnr: hit and outpcd 5 out: sn drvn: rallied next: outpcd fr 2 out* **1/1**[1]

2P3- **U** **Hawaii Klass**[19] 4086 9-10-7 115............................... CallumWhillans(5)
(Donald Whillans) *nt fluent: chsd ldrs: drvn and outpcd after 5 out: 4 l 3rd and styng on whn blnd bdly and uns rdr next* **4/1**[3]

6m 8.6s (5.20) **Going Correction** +0.40s/f (Soft) **3** Ran SP% **104.8**
Speed ratings: **107,103,**
CSF £4.05 TOTE £2.50; EX 3.90 Trifecta £3.00.
Owner Ms Deborah Thomson **Bred** Richard Healy **Trained** Arlary, Perth & Kinross

FOCUS
The feature race was a fair staying handicap chase, but the initial field of ten was decimated by seven morning non-runners on account of the testing ground after an unexpected bout of heavy overnight rain. A small personal best from the winner.

4465 WATCH ON 3 DEVICES RACINGUK.COM/ANYWHERE H'CAP HURDLE (12 hdls) 2m 4f
4:20 (4:20) (Class 5) (0-100,100) 4-Y-0+ **£3,249** (£954; £477; £238)

Form RPR

013- **1** **Newdane Dancer (IRE)**[33] 3830 7-10-7 **86**..........(p) ColmMcCormack(5) 92
(Dianne Sayer) *cl up: led 1/2-way: hrd pressed fr 2 out: drvn and styd on wl fr last* **7/1**[3]

342- **2** *1 ¾* **Shan Valley (IRE)**[6] 4336 8-10-0 **81**................................ DaleIrving(7) 84
(Stuart Coltherd) *t.k.h: nt fluent on occasions in rr: hdwy and prom 5th: effrt and ev ch 2 out to run-in: kpt on: hld towards fin* **3/1**[2]

041- **3** *5* **Blue Kascade (IRE)**[12] 4223 7-11-12 **100**............................ RyanMania 99
(Sandy Thomson) *led to 1/2-way: pressed wnr to bef 3 out: rdn and outpcd fr next* **11/8**[1]

333- **4** *6* **Spanish Fleet**[31] 3871 6-11-5 **100**.................................. JohnDawson(7) 92
(John Wade) *hld up: stdy hdwy 1/2-way: drvn and outpcd 4 out: rallied next: styd on fr 2 out: nt pce to chal* **17/2**

00P/ **5** *32* **Patriot (IRE)**[477] 2212 10-10-10 **91**...........................(p) GrahamWatters(7) 51
(Barry Murtagh) *chsd ldrs: rdn after 4 out: wknd bef next* **66/1**

0P5- **6** *6* **Mrs Grass**[13] 4201 7-9-11 **74** oh5...................................... JohnKington(3) 28
(Jonathan Haynes) *midfield: struggling fr 1/2-way: btn fr 4 out* **20/1**

0- **7** *½* **Pairc Na Leasa (IRE)**[12] 4223 8-11-2 **95**..................... HarryChalloner(5) 49
(Martin Todhunter) *bhd: struggling fnl circ: nvr on terms* **9/1**

0/6- **8** *1* **The Boozy Bishop (IRE)**[34] 3828 9-9-11 **74** oh5 ow2.. MissCWalton(5) 29
(Sheena Walton) *hld up: stdy hdwy 7th: rdn and wknd after 4 out* **50/1**

P4P/ **P** **Reland (FR)**[441] 2977 9-10-2 **83**................................. GrantCockburn(7)
(Mrs Jackie Stephen) *towards rr: struggling fr 1/2-way: t.o whn p.u bef 3 out* **25/1**

4m 50.8s (-0.70) **Going Correction** -0.075s/f (Good) **9** Ran SP% **112.2**
Speed ratings (Par 103): **98,97,95,92,80 77,77,77,**
CSF £27.12 CT £44.96 TOTE £7.50: £1.70, £1.20, £1.60; EX 32.50 Trifecta £71.00.
Owner E G Tunstall **Bred** Spratstown Stud A T **Trained** Hackthorpe, Cumbria

■ Stewards' Enquiry : Miss C Walton three-day ban: careless riding (Mar 10,16,17)

FOCUS
An ordinary handicap hurdle. The first three are all rated similar to their recent runs.

4466 DOWNLOAD NEW RACING RACING UK ANYWHERE TODAY MARES' NOVICES' HURDLE (9 hdls) 2m
4:50 (4:50) (Class 4) 4-Y-0+ **£3,249** (£954; £477; £238)

Form RPR

232- **1** **Morning With Ivan (IRE)**[38] 3757 4-10-7 113................ WilsonRenwick 102+
(Martin Todhunter) *t.k.h: trckd ldrs: smooth hdwy to ld 2 out: rdn and edgd lft after last: r.o wl* **1/1**[1]

516- **2** *2 ¾* **Magic Skyline (IRE)**[8] 4305 4-10-12 115.................(t) NathanMoscrop(7) 110
(Brian Ellison) *t.k.h: led: nt fluent and pushed along 3 out: hdd next: rallied: one pce run-in* **11/4**[2]

/34- **3** *3* **Be My Present**[20] 4074 7-10-9 0.. CraigNichol(7) 103
(Rose Dobbin) *pressed ldr: rdn and ev ch 3 out: one pce between last 2* **11/4**[2]

/0P- **4** *28* **Teaatreids (IRE)**[60] 3270 6-11-2 0.. WillKennedy 75
(Brian Ellison) *in tch: hit 3rd: struggling after next: t.o* **50/1**[3]

3m 57.0s (8.60) **Going Correction** -0.075s/f (Good)
WFA 4 from 6yo+ 9lb **4** Ran SP% **105.3**
Speed ratings (Par 105): **75,73,72,58**
CSF £3.90 TOTE £1.90; EX 3.70 Trifecta £4.20.
Owner Island Intermodal Services **Bred** J S Bolger **Trained** Orton, Cumbria

FOCUS
A modest small-field mares' novices' hurdle which was steadily run. The first three are all rated close to their marks.
T/Jkpt: Not won. T/Plt: £137.70 to a £1 stake. Pool: £91518.30 - 484.96 winning tickets T/Qpdt: £11.20 to a £1 stake. Pool: £7536.75 - 495.00 winning tickets RY

3686 PLUMPTON (L-H)
Monday, February 24

OFFICIAL GOING: Soft (heavy in places; hdl 4.2, chs 4.6)
Wind: light to medium, half against Weather: dry and bright

4467 ATTHERACES.COM EXCLUSIVE BARRY GERAGHTY BLOG MAIDEN HURDLE (9 hdls) 2m
2:05 (2:05) (Class 5) 4-Y-0+ **£2,190** (£638; £319)

Form RPR

5- **1** **Albert Bridge**[17] 4130 6-11-2 0.. AidanColeman 128+
(Emma Lavelle) *led tl 2nd: chsd ldr tl led again 6th: rdn bef 2 out: styd on strly and drew wl clr flat: readily* **7/2**[2]

253- **2** *10* **Civil War (IRE)**[8] 4301 5-11-2 0.. JamieMoore 117+
(Gary Moore) *hld up in tch in midfield: clsd on ldrs bef 3 out: rdn to chse wnr bef 2 out: no ex between last 2: readily outpcd flat* **13/8**[1]

00- **3** *16* **Bow Quest**[27] 3961 7-10-6 0.. JoshuaMoore(3) 92
(Gary Moore) *hld up towards rr: modest 9th and sme hdwy bef 3 out: styd on steadily past btn horses after: wnt 3rd and j.lft last: no ch w ldng pair* **66/1**

65- **4** *8* **Freddy Q (IRE)**[42] 3686 5-11-2 0..................................(t) RichieMcLernon 92
(Roger Teal) *t.k.h: chsd ldrs tl led 2nd: hdd 6th: stl cl 2nd whn mstke next: rdn and wknd bef 2 out: lost 3rd last* **20/1**

4F- **5** *8* **Bawden Rocks**[278] 434 5-11-2 0..................................... TomScudamore 83
(David Bridgwater) *chsd ldrs: j.big 2nd: cl 4th after 3 out: sn rdn and btn: wknd qckly bef next: t.o* **20/1**

00- **6** *7* **Langarve Lass (IRE)**[31] 3872 5-10-9 0..................................... NoelFehily 69
(Neil Mulholland) *in tch in midfield: outpcd after 6th: n.d after: 6th and no ch whn j.lft 2 out: t.o* **100/1**

2U- **7** *20* **Minority Interest**[42] 3686 5-11-2 0... TomCannon 61
(Daniel O'Brien) *chsd ldr tl 2nd: chsd ldrs tl 5th and struggling u.p bef 3 out: wknd wl bef 2 out: t.o* **4/1**[3]

006- **8** *2 ½* **Spartilla**[42] 3686 5-10-9 0... MrJPearce(7) 54
(Daniel O'Brien) *hld up in tch in rr: struggling and outpcd 6th: sn lost tch: t.o after next* **66/1**

3- **9** *31* **Wasabi (IRE)**[32] 3854 5-10-9 0.. DaveCrosse 16
(John Berry) *hld up in last pair: struggling whn mstke 6th: sn lost tch and t.o next* **25/1**

PP0- **P** **Saint Helena (IRE)**[42] 3686 6-10-9 0............................... MattieBatchelor
(Jim Best) *in tch in midfield tl wknd 6th: sn lost tch and t.o next tl p.u 2 out* **100/1**

0/P- **P** **Whatagoa (IRE)**[42] 3689 7-10-9 0.................................... LeightonAspell
(Richard Rowe) *in tch in midfield: rdn and struggling 6th: sn lost tch and wl bhd: t.o whn p.u 2 out* **100/1**

126- **P** **Rouquine Sauvage**[53] 3507 6-10-9 0.. APMcCoy
(Anthony Honeyball) *t.k.h: nt fluent: hld up in last quartet: sme hdwy bef 6th: 6th and no imp whn j.big 3 out: sn wknd and wl bhd whn p.u next* **5/1**

6/0- **P** **Harlequins Gleams**[42] 3686 6-11-2 0.......................... AndrewThornton
(Anna Newton-Smith) *wl in tch in midfield tl wknd 6th: t.o next tl p.u 2 out* **100/1**

400- **P** **Home For Tea**[19] 4091 5-11-2 0.. FelixDeGiles
(Tom Symonds) *a bhd: nt fluent 1st: rdn and lost tch after 5th: t.o after next tl p.u last* **66/1**

4m 14.2s (13.40) **Going Correction** +1.00s/f (Soft) **14** Ran SP% **118.8**
Speed ratings (Par 103): **106,101,93,89,85 81,71,70,54, , , ,**
CSF £9.15 TOTE £3.50: £1.40, £1.10, £13.20; EX 10.90 Trifecta £1331.30.
Owner The Cheyne Walkers **Bred** Miss K Rausing **Trained** Hatherden, Hants

FOCUS
It was a drying day but the ground was still demanding and that was advertised in the opening novice hurdle as two came well clear. A massive step up from the winner on his Kempton run.

4468 ATTHERACES.COM & EBF STALLIONS/TBA MARES' NOVICES' CHASE (14 fncs) 2m 4f
2:35 (2:35) (Class 4) 5-Y-0+ **£4,288** (£1,259)

Form RPR

24F- **1** **She Ranks Me (IRE)**[13] 4202 7-10-12 0...............................(p) APMcCoy 126+
(Donald McCain) *w ldr whn bmpd 1st and 2nd: reminder after 9th and off the bridle: rallied u.p and upsides rival 11th tl after next: styd on and pressing ldr again last: drvn to ld flat: sn in command* **Evs**[2]

114- 2 2 3/4 **Baby Shine (IRE)**[9] 4262 8-11-10 134.............................. LeightonAspell 138+
(Lucy Wadham) *mde most: j.rt at times: bmpd rival 1st and 2nd: mstke 10th: 2 l clr and rdn bef 2 out: hit 2 out: drvn between last 2: mstke last: sn hdd and btn: eased towards fin* **5/6**[1]

5m 28.3s (21.00) **Going Correction** +1.20s/f (Heav) 2 Ran SP% **104.6**
Speed ratings: **106,104**
TOTE £1.60.
Owner Roger O'Byrne **Bred** Patrick O'Keeffe **Trained** Cholmondeley, Cheshire

FOCUS
This mares' contest is usually a stepping stone to the mares' final of this series, switched this season to Cheltenham's April meeting. It was a match race but threatened to end at the very first fence as two runners collided, and then did so again at the next. It was a tactical affair from there on. The winner was a 138 hurdler at best but may struggle to match that over fences.

4469 AT THE RACES SKY 415 H'CAP HURDLE (9 hdls) 2m
3:10 (3:10) (Class 4) (0-115,113) 4-Y-0+ **£3,249** (£954; £477; £238)

Form RPR

552- 1 **Hold The Bucks (USA)**[50] 3556 8-9-11 **87** oh2............ GavinSheehan(3) 93
(Daniel Steele) *chsd ldr tl 6th: 4th and outpcd u.p bef next: rallied to chse ldng pair bef 2 out: wnt 2nd and pressing ldr 2 out: led last: edgd lft u.p flat: drvn out* **15/2**

316- 2 1 3/4 **Dungeness**[15] 4172 6-11-2 **103**.. AidanColeman 107
(Venetia Williams) *led: rdn along bef 3 out: 3 l clr and drvn bef 2 out: hdd last: kpt on same pce flat: eased cl home* **5/4**[1]

/45- 3 13 **Little Roxy (IRE)**[42] 3692 9-10-0 **87** oh10........................... AdamWedge 78
(Anna Newton-Smith) *wl in tch in midfield: 5th and rdn bef 6th: outpcd 3 out: plugged on but n.d after* **25/1**

164- 4 1 1/2 **Tealissio**[24] 4023 8-11-9 **110**..(t) LeightonAspell 103
(Lucy Wadham) *hld up in tch in last pair: hdwy to chse ldrs after 5th: wnt 2nd next: rdn and no ex bef 2 out: 3rd and mstke 2 out: wknd between last 2* **11/4**[2]

F4P- 5 19 **Regal One (IRE)**[23] 4031 6-11-7 **108**.........................(t[1]) TomScudamore 86
(David Bridgwater) *chsd ldrs: 3rd and rdn 3 out: sn btn and wknd bef next* **5/1**[3]

550/ 6 60 **Osgood**[24] 7-10-8 **95**.. JamieMoore 6
(Gary Moore) *t.k.h: hld up in rr: clsd after 5th: effrt bef 3 out: stl cl enough 3 out: sn wknd and t.o next* **20/1**

F30- U **Warrant Officer**[24] 4022 4-11-3 **113**.................................. MarcGoldstein
(Sheena West) *wl in tch in midfield tl blnd bdly and uns rdr 5th* **14/1**

4m 18.0s (17.20) **Going Correction** +1.20s/f (Heav)
WFA 4 from 6yo+ 9lb 7 Ran SP% **114.8**
Speed ratings (Par 105): **105,104,97,96,87 57,**
CSF £18.17 CT £227.67 TOTE £9.70: £3.80, £1.30; EX 20.40 Trifecta £180.80.
Owner D Steele **Bred** David E Hager II **Trained** Henfield, W Sussex
■ A first training success for Daniel Steele, who completed a double later on the card.

FOCUS
The gallop increased markedly on the far side in this moderate handicap and most got caught out at that stage. Ordinary handicap form.

4470 WINDSOR AMATEUR RIDERS' H'CAP CHASE (FOR THE GAY KINDERSLEY MEMORIAL SALVER) (18 fncs) 3m 2f
3:40 (3:41) (Class 4) (0-115,111) 5-Y-0+ **£3,840** (£1,257; £677)

Form RPR

2P6- 1 **According To Them (IRE)**[23] 4031 10-9-11 **85** oh14...(t) MrFMitchell(3) 98+
(Daniel Steele) *trckd ldrs: effrt to chal 2 out: sn rdn to ld and asserted bef last: r.o: rdn out* **10/1**

023- 2 14 **Present To You (IRE)**[32] 3858 9-11-9 **111**.................. MrSDrinkwater(3) 110
(David Bridgwater) *led: rdn and hdd sn after 2 out: sn btn: wknd flat and jst hld 2nd* **8/11**[1]

PP6- 3 shd **Ballyvoneen (IRE)**[12] 4220 9-9-8 **86** oh3 ow1..................(p) MrBenJay(7) 89
(Neil King) *nt a fluent: trckd ldrs on outer: mstke 14th: rdn and outpcd bef 2 out: wl hld in 3rd whn j.big last: plugged on* **5/2**[2]

/P5- P **Thats Ben (IRE)**[98] 2560 9-10-2 **94**................................(p) MrSPBowen(7)
(Tom Gretton) *w ldr: rdn bef 3 out: dropped to last and qckly btn bef 2 out: t.o whn p.u last* **15/2**[3]

7m 26.6s (35.90) **Going Correction** +1.40s/f (Heav) 4 Ran SP% **107.3**
Speed ratings: **100,95,95,**
CSF £18.70 TOTE £7.60; EX 17.00 Trifecta £35.40.
Owner D Steele **Bred** Imelda Grogan **Trained** Henfield, W Sussex

FOCUS
A well established amateur riders' handicap. The routine gallop meant the field were tightly grouped until around four out. Suspect form, with the winner rated back to his best Irish form.

4471 AT THE RACES VIRGIN 534 H'CAP HURDLE (14 hdls) 3m 1f 110y
4:10 (4:10) (Class 5) (0-100,100) 4-Y-0+ **£2,190** (£638; £319)

Form RPR

/54- 1 **Strange Bird (IRE)**[50] 3553 9-10-0 **74** oh1....................... AidanColeman 98+
(Richard Rowe) *w ldr tl led 10th: clr and travelling best next: mstke 3 out: drew wl clr after: rdn between last 2: wnt rt after last: eased flat* **9/2**[2]

600- 2 32 **Twopoundsofbutter (IRE)**[58] 3357 7-11-12 **100**.......(t) RichardJohnson 89
(Tim Vaughan) *hld up in tch: hdwy to chse ldrs 9th: wnt 2nd after 10th: no imp on wnr bef 3 out: tired but plugged on to hold 2nd flat* **11/2**

523- 3 4 1/2 **Torran Sound**[32] 3852 7-11-8 **99**...................................(p) JoshuaMoore(3) 85
(Lawney Hill) *several positions: drvn and outpcd after 10th: 4th and no ch 3 out: wnt poor 3rd between last 2* **5/1**[3]

606- 4 18 **Maccabees**[21] 3692 5-10-1 **82**... MrFTett(7) 49
(Roger Curtis) *t.k.h: hld up in tch in last trio: hdwy to chse ldrs after 9th: 3rd and wl btn bef 3 out: lost 3rd between last 2: t.o* **20/1**

603- 5 23 **Zafaraban (IRE)**[10] 4249 7-11-7 **95**...................................(b[1]) LeeEdwards 39
(Aytach Sadik) *chsd ldrs: rdn 9th: wknd after next: t.o bef 3 out* **12/1**

313- U **Royaume Bleu (FR)**[21] 4066 9-10-9 **88**........................... KillianMoore(5)
(Alex Hales) *chsd ldrs tl blnd and uns rdr 9th* **3/1**[1]

/0P- P **Dushy Valley (IRE)**[42] 3688 7-9-11 **74**.............................. JamesBest(3)
(Paul Henderson) *hmpd and dropped to rr 2nd: off the bridle after but jst abt in tch tl 8th: t.o whn p.u after 11th* **7/1**

0P0- P **Landerbee (IRE)**[42] 3692 7-9-13 **80** ow3........................... KevinJones(7)
(Seamus Mullins) *hld up in last pair: blnd bdly and rdr lost irons 1st: dashed up to ldrs and plld out next: rdr unable to stop and eventually uns 1 1/2 circs later* **15/2**

0PP- P **Alfie Alexander (IRE)**[70] 3138 6-9-9 **74** oh5................(b) JamesBanks(5)
(Mark Hoad) *reminder sn after s: mde most tl 10th: sn drvn and dropped out: t.o whn p.u after next* **33/1**

7m 14.25s (49.25) **Going Correction** +1.40s/f (Heav) 9 Ran SP% **114.9**
Speed ratings (Par 103): **80,70,68,63,56 , , ,**
CSF £29.60 CT £127.75 TOTE £5.30: £2.60, £2.20, £2.30; EX 40.00 Trifecta £339.10.
Owner Richard Rowe Racing Partnership **Bred** M O'Sullivan **Trained** Sullington, W Sussex
■ Stewards' Enquiry : Killian Moore caution: careless riding.

FOCUS
A weak handicap, run at a routine gallop. The winner is rated up 10lb on the best of last season's form.

4472 COMPARE PRICES AT ATTHERACES.COM/ODDS MARES' H'CAP HURDLE (12 hdls) 2m 5f
4:40 (4:40) (Class 4) (0-105,105) 4-Y-0+ **£3,249** (£954; £477; £238)

Form RPR

004- 1 **Barton Rose**[39] 3747 5-10-11 **93**...................................... MichaelByrne(3) 108+
(Neil Mulholland) *v confidently rdn: hld up in tch in rr: stdy hdwy 8th: trckd ldrs after next: led 2 out and readily asserted bef last: v easily* **11/4**[1]

022- 2 6 **Bebinn (IRE)**[18] 4108 7-11-9 **102**..................................(p) CharliePoste 103
(Ben Case) *chsd ldr tl led 8th: mstke next: clr in ldng trio and rdn after 3 out: hdd next: no ch w wnr but kpt on for clr 2nd* **7/2**[2]

055- 3 20 **La Madonnina (IRE)**[225] 969 6-10-9 **88**............................... IanPopham 69
(Caroline Keevil) *chsd ldrs on inner: mstke and pckd 6th: ev ch 9th tl rdn and btn after 3 out: mstke 2 out: wknd between last 2* **16/1**

054- 4 6 **Niki Royal (FR)**[73] 3058 9-11-1 **94**................................(t) AndrewTinkler 67
(Jamie Snowden) *reluctant to line up and led into s: nvr gng wl a rdn along in rr: in tch tl after 9th: no ch but plugged on past btn horses fr bef 2 out: snatched 4th cl home* **8/1**

553- 5 hd **Free Falling**[21] 4071 8-10-0 **79** oh3....................................(v) AidanColeman 52
(Alastair Lidderdale) *led tl hdd 10th: sn rdn: styd preeing ldrs tl wknd bef 3 out: lost tch bef 2 out* **4/1**[3]

063- 6 23 **Marie Deja La (FR)**[91] 2715 8-11-3 **96**..............................(b) TomCannon 46
(Chris Gordon) *in tch in midfield: hdwy to chse ldrs 8th: clr in ldng quartet 3 out: sn wknd u.p: t.o between last 2* **10/1**

365- 7 16 **Oscar's Pet (IRE)**[19] 4093 6-11-3 **96**.................................(p) FelixDeGiles 30
(Tom Symonds) *hld up in tch towards rr: rdn bef 9th: 5th and struggling whn mstke 3 out: sn wknd and wl bhd: t.o* **14/1**

00P- 8 13 **Be Kind**[124] 2023 8-9-8 **80** oh13 ow1.. JPKiely(7)
(Tim Vaughan) *mstkes: chsd ldrs: rdn and lost pl after 7th: rallied after 9th: 6th and struggling whn mstke next: sn wknd and bhd: t.o and eased flat* **20/1**

233- P **Rising Teal**[20] 4074 5-11-12 **105**... LeightonAspell
(Lucy Wadham) *hld up in tch towards rr: hdwy to chse ldrs 8th: wknd bef 3 out: t.o whn p.u next* **9/1**

5m 55.1s (38.10) **Going Correction** +1.60s/f (Heav) 9 Ran SP% **116.4**
Speed ratings (Par 105): **91,88,81,78,78 69,63,58,**
CSF £13.33 CT £128.22 TOTE £5.20: £2.00, £1.20, £4.60; EX 11.60 Trifecta £200.40.
Owner Lady Clarke **Bred** Lady H J Clarke **Trained** Limpley Stoke, Wilts

FOCUS
An ordinary mares' handicap in which only the principals mattered from three out. A massive step up from the facile winner with the second to her mark.

4473 AT THE RACES ON FACEBOOK INTERMEDIATE OPEN NATIONAL HUNT FLAT RACE 2m 2f
5:10 (5:11) (Class 6) 4-6-Y-0 **£1,916** (£558; £279)

Form RPR

1 **Virtuel D'Oudon (FR)**[71] 5-11-4 0................................... TomScudamore 107+
(David Pipe) *mde all: rdn and forged ahd 2f out: clr and hanging lft ins fnl f: styd on* **7/4**[1]

0- 2 4 **Mercers Court (IRE)**[66] 3194 6-11-1 0........................... TrevorWhelan(3) 103
(Neil King) *t.k.h: hld up wl in tch in rr: effrt 5f out: chsd ldng pair wl over 3f out: swtchd rt over 1f out: kpt on u.p to chse wnr ins fnl f: no imp* **7/1**

/- 3 2 1/2 **Exitas (IRE)** 6-11-4 0.. LeightonAspell 102
(Oliver Sherwood) *t.k.h: hld up in tch in last trio: hdwy into midfield on outer after 3f: wnt 2nd 6f out: rdn and no ex ent fnl 2f: lost 3rd and one pce ins fnl f* **7/1**

6- 4 21 **Vesuvhill (FR)**[32] 3863 5-11-4 0... DarylJacob 86
(Ben Case) *t.k.h: chsd ldrs: rdn and outpcd 4f out: wknd 3f out* **7/2**[2]

5 13 **Tara Bridge** 6-11-4 0.. TomCannon 67
(Chris Gordon) *chsd ldrs: wnt 2nd 8f out tl 6f out: drvn and lost pl over 4f out: sn wknd: t.o* **25/1**

6 17 **Killshannon (IRE)**[113] 5-10-11 0...................................... JakeHodson(7) 50
(David Bridgwater) *chsd ldr tl 8f out: styd chsng ldrs tl rdn and lost pl qckly over 4f out: sn bhd: t.o* **12/1**

4- 7 99 **Little Louie**[8] 4296 5-11-1 0.. JoshuaMoore(3)
(Gary Moore) *t.k.h: hld up in tch in last pair: rdn 5f out: sn lost tch: wl t.o and virtually p.u fnl f* **4/1**[3]

5m 0.3s (35.00) **Going Correction** +1.80s/f (Heav)
WFA 5 from 6yo 1lb 7 Ran SP% **115.1**
Speed ratings: **94,92,91,81,76 68,24**
CSF £15.09 TOTE £2.40: £1.70, £4.40; EX 15.90 Trifecta £104.50.
Owner Stephen Quinlan **Bred** Mme F Marionneau & Mlle V Dasque **Trained** Nicholashayne, Devon

FOCUS
An ordinary bumper.
T/Plt: £221.20 to a £1 stake. Pool: £86144.91 - 284.18 winning tickets T/Qpdt: £95.40 to a £1 stake. Pool: £6179.35 - 47.90 winning tickets SP

4186 CATTERICK (L-H)
Tuesday, February 25

OFFICIAL GOING: Good to soft (soft in places; chs 7.0, hdl 7.3)
Wind: strong 1/2 behind Weather: fine but becoming overcast, showers race 3, cold and windy

4474 CHELTENHAM PREVIEW EVENING 28TH FEBRUARY NOVICES' CHASE (19 fncs) 3m 1f 110y
2:20 (2:20) (Class 4) 5-Y-0+ **£5,198** (£1,526)

Form RPR

/21- 1 **Bit Of A Jig (IRE)**[84] 2867 7-11-7 129.............................. JasonMaguire 138+
(Donald McCain) *mde all: reminders bef 4th: 6th and 11th: drvn 12th: hld on wl fr 2 out* **11/8**[2]

UU2- 2 2 **Dursey Sound (IRE)**[70] 3146 6-11-7 137...................(b) RichieMcLernon 135
(Jonjo O'Neill) *hit 3rd: effrt appr 3 out: rdn between last 2: 2 l down last: kpt on same pce* **8/13**[1]

7m 3.5s (21.50) **Going Correction** +0.15s/f (Yiel) 2 Ran SP% **104.0**
Speed ratings: **72,71**
TOTE £2.00.
Owner Let's Live Racing **Bred** W Henry **Trained** Cholmondeley, Cheshire

FOCUS
Only two runners for this staying event, but both are useful.

4475 DOWNLOAD NEW RACING UK IPAD APP LADY AMATEUR RIDERS' H'CAP HURDLE (10 hdls) 2m 3f

2:50 (2:51) (Class 5) (0-100,100) 4-Y-0+ **£2,634** (£810; £405)

Form RPR

222- **1** **Summerlea (IRE)**[8] 3618 8-11-11 **99** MissCWalton 106+
(Micky Hammond) *hld up in rr: gd hdwy to trck ldrs 3 out: 2nd appr next: led appr last: drvn clr* **13/2**[3]

004- **2** *5* **Kyles Faith (IRE)**[4] 4398 6-11-7 **100** MissCVHart[(5)] 101
(Martin Keighley) *w ldr: led appr 6th: hdd appr last: kpt on same pce* **2/1**[1]

434- **3** *4 ½* **Blue Sea Of Ibrox (IRE)**[34] 3840 6-10-0 **74** oh2 (b) MissHBethell 70
(Alan Brown) *hld up in rr: hdwy 4th: chsd ldr 3 out: one pce between last 2* **14/1**

P1U- **4** *nk* **Cumbrian Farmer**[52] 3525 7-10-12 **91** (p) MissJWalton[(5)] 87
(George Bewley) *mid-div: hdwy 3 out: outpcd appr next: kpt on between last 2* **7/1**

552- **5** *8* **Indigo Island (IRE)**[30] 3924 5-11-0 **91** MissSMDoolan[(3)] 80
(Robert Bewley) *chsd ldrs: hit 6th: outpcd after 3 out: wknd next* **17/2**

/0P- **6** *6* **Orlittlebylittle**[5] 4383 8-11-3 **98** (b) MissKYoung[(7)] 81
(Donald McCain) *mid-div: effrt 3 out: wknd after next* **16/1**

/53- **7** *2 ¾* **Grand Vintage (IRE)**[30] 3924 8-11-9 **97** MissHannahWatson 78
(Evelyn Slack) *chsd ldrs: lost pl and 7th whn blnd 2 out* **17/2**

620- **P** **Rare Coincidence**[185] 1374 13-10-2 **79** (p) MissJRRichards[(3)]
(Alan Berry) *led tl hdd and lost pl appr 6th: bhd 7th: t.o whn p.u bef 2 out* **50/1**

/00- **U** **Canadian Dreamer (IRE)**[67] 3191 7-11-5 **100** MrsVSollitt[(7)]
(Graeme McPherson) *detached last whn swvd and uns rdr appr s* **9/2**[2]

4m 55.7s (19.60) **Going Correction** +0.65s/f (Soft) **9 Ran SP% 112.9**
Speed ratings (Par 103): **84,81,80,79,76 73,72, ,**
CSF £19.99 CT £174.54 TOTE £6.50: £2.10, £1.60, £5.00; EX 21.40 Trifecta £165.80.
Owner Straightline Construction Ltd **Bred** Mrs Clodagh McStay **Trained** Middleham Moor, N Yorks

FOCUS
This was run at just an ordinary pace. A step up from the winner with the next two to their marks.

4476 YORKSHIRE-OUTDOORS.CO.UK ADVENTURE ACTIVITIES MAIDEN HURDLE (8 hdls) 2m

3:20 (3:20) (Class 5) 4-Y-0+ **£2,737** (£798; £399)

Form RPR

30- **1** **Benzanno (IRE)**[25] 4022 5-11-2 0 JasonMaguire 123+
(Donald McCain) *mde all: j.lft 3 out: rdn clr and j.lft last* **5/4**[1]

42- **2** *18* **Kolonel Kirkup**[25] 4003 4-10-7 107 BarryKeniry 96
(Michael Dods) *trckd ldrs: 2nd 3 out: kpt on same pce fr next* **9/2**[3]

040- **3** *1 ¼* **Rock A Doodle Doo (IRE)**[58] 3390 7-10-11 113 AdamNicol[(5)] 105
(Sally Hall) *chsd wnr: 3rd and drvn whn hit 2 out: kpt on one pce* **13/8**[2]

04- **4** *33* **Pink Mischief**[24] 4037 4-9-11 0 JohnKington[(3)] 55
(Andrew Crook) *in rr: hdwy to chse ldrs 4th: outpcd and j.lft next: wknd bef 2 out* **50/1**

646- **5** *7* **Khelac**[35] 3822 4-10-2 0 JoeColliver[(5)] 55
(Micky Hammond) *in tch: chsd ldrs 4th: wknd next* **12/1**

00- **6** *23* **Escape To The West**[59] 3350 6-10-11 0 SamanthaDrake[(5)] 41
(Joanne Foster) *chsd ldrs: lost pl after 4th: sn bhd: t.o 2 out* **100/1**

0F5- **7** *11* **Lacocodanza**[20] 4083 5-10-9 0 BrianHarding 23
(George Moore) *in rr: bhd fr 3rd: t.o* **40/1**

4/6- **8** *9* **Hope For Glory**[91] 2104 5-11-2 0 DougieCostello 21
(Jason Ward) *in rr: bhd fr 5th: t.o* **33/1**

P0P- **9** *22* **Well Related**[25] 4005 7-11-2 0 RichieMcGrath
(Henry Hogarth) *mid-div: drvn and outpcd 3rd: mstke next: sn bhd: t.o 2 out: eventually completed* **100/1**

10 *15* **Olynard (IRE)**[8] 8-10-13 0 KielanWoods[(3)]
(Michael Mullineaux) *in rr: bhd and drvn 4th: sn t.o: eventually completed* **100/1**

3m 58.1s (5.60) **Going Correction** +0.65s/f (Soft)
WFA 4 from 5yo+ 9lb **10 Ran SP% 118.7**
Speed ratings (Par 103): **112,103,102,85,82 70,65,60,49,42**
CSF £7.72 TOTE £2.20: £1.10, £1.80, £1.10; EX 7.20 Trifecta £13.20.
Owner T G Leslie **Bred** Nanallac Stud **Trained** Cholmondeley, Cheshire

FOCUS
They went a decent pace for this modest maiden hurdle, where only three could be seriously considered on paper. The winer has the potential to rate higher on Flat form.

4477 EA3DY ADDEY II'CAP CHASE (1? fnoo) 2m

3:50 (3:51) (Class 4) (0-110,110) 5-Y-0+ **£6,657** (£2,067; £1,113)

Form RPR

214- **1** **Divine Intavention (IRE)**[9] 4303 10-11-6 **109** MrMWall[(5)] 134+
(Martin Keighley) *chsd ldr: lft in ld 3rd: clr fr 5th: j.rt last: styd on strly* **12/5**[2]

4F- **2** *49* **Little Jimmy**[12] 4241 7-10-4 **88** (p) FelixDeGiles 79
(Tom Gretton) *in rr: hdwy 4th: chsng ldrs next: modest 2nd 8th: no ch w wnr* **7/2**[3]

5/P- **3** *47* **Mister Stickler (IRE)**[115] 2222 10-11-12 **110** BrianHughes 49
(Chris Grant) *chsd ldrs: dropped to rr 6th: sn bhd: t.o whn lft distant 3rd 2 out* **16/1**

445- **F** **Fred Bojangals (IRE)**[30] 3924 12-10-13 **97** (tp) SeanQuinlan 88
(Barbara Butterworth) *chsd ldrs: one pce fr 4 out: modest 3rd whn fell 2 out* **50/1**

U12- **F** **Cloverhill Lad (IRE)**[7] 4341 10-11-1 **106** DaraghBourke[(7)] 92
(Stuart Coltherd) *in rr: bhd whn hit 5th: modest 4th whn fell 2 out* **11/1**

431- **F** **Turf Trivia**[5] 4383 7-10-12 **96** 7ex (b) BarryKeniry
(George Moore) *chsd ldrs: outpcd 7th: in rr whn fell next* **9/1**

3F2- **U** **Lucky Sunny (IRE)**[6] 4352 11-11-12 **110** AidanColeman
(Venetia Williams) *led: blnd and uns rdr 3rd* **9/4**[1]

4m 0.6s (0.50) **Going Correction** +0.15s/f (Yiel) **7 Ran SP% 108.6**
Speed ratings: **104,79,56, , ,**
CSF £10.38 CT £90.60 TOTE £3.90: £2.20, £1.50; EX 12.90 Trifecta £151.70.
Owner H Wilson **Bred** James Nolan **Trained** Condicote, Gloucs

FOCUS
The race basically fell apart in what had looked a competitive heat on paper, with only three of the seven runners completing. The easy winner is rated back to his best.

4478 EPDS RACING WELFARE BTO SERIES 2014 H'CAP HURDLE (12 hdls) 3m 1f 110y

4:20 (4:21) (Class 4) (0-110,109) 4-Y-0+ **£3,573** (£1,049; £524; £262)

Form RPR

261- **1** **Brae On (IRE)**[79] 2974 6-10-5 **95** JonathonBewley[(7)] 98
(George Bewley) *hld up in rr: hdwy 7th: sn chsng ldrs: led briefly appr 2 out: led last: drvn out* **3/1**[1]

4/0- **2** *1 ¾* **Mootabar (IRE)**[35] 3828 7-9-11 **83** JonathanEngland[(3)] 85
(Chris Fairhurst) *hld up towards rr: hdwy 6th: sn chsng ldrs: led 2 out: hdd last: no ex* **14/1**

P04- **3** *2* **Feast Of Fire (IRE)**[19] 4108 7-11-0 **100** GavinSheehan[(3)] 99
(Mike Sowersby) *in rr: hdwy 6th: sn chsng ldrs: outpcd appr 2 out: styd on to take 3rd appr last* **9/1**

523- **4** *2 ¾* **Madam Lilibet (IRE)**[14] 4201 5-10-5 **95** (p) JosephPalmowski[(7)] 92
(Sharon Watt) *chsd ldrs: drvn 7th: outpcd appr 2 out: kpt on to take 4th appr last* **4/1**[2]

442- **5** *8* **Qoubilai (FR)**[8] 4327 10-11-11 **108** DougieCostello 98
(Tony Coyle) *chsd ldrs: wknd between last 2* **7/1**

/26- **6** *¾* **Spiekeroog**[83] 2879 8-11-6 **103** DavidEngland 92
(Alan Brown) *chsd ldrs: lost pl 6th: rallied and hit 8th: outpcd after 3 out: styd on and swtchd lft between last 2: sn wknd* **33/1**

005- **7** *4 ½* **Pierrers Bounty (IRE)**[30] 3922 7-11-6 **103** (p) RichieMcGrath 88
(Henry Hogarth) *led: drvn 9th: hdd appr 2 out: wknd between last 2* **13/2**[3]

3P6- **8** *20* **Carmela Maria**[19] 4108 9-10-0 **88** (b) AdamNicol[(5)] 55
(Mike Sowersby) *w ldrs: drvn 7th: lost pl next: sn bhd: t.o 9th* **8/1**

064- **9** *24* **Welsh Bard (IRE)**[30] 3922 5-11-12 **109** (b) JasonMaguire 54
(Donald McCain) *in rr: reminders and lost pl 7th: rallied briefly next: sn bhd: hit 9th: sn t.o: blnd 2 out* **7/1**

6m 44.0s (16.40) **Going Correction** +0.65s/f (Soft) **9 Ran SP% 114.1**
Speed ratings (Par 105): **100,99,98,98,95 95,93,87,80**
CSF £42.22 CT £337.99 TOTE £3.30: £1.20, £3.20, £2.90; EX 48.50 Trifecta £1327.10.
Owner West Coast Racing Partnership **Bred** Pat Moore **Trained** Bonchester Bridge, Borders

FOCUS
A dour staying performance from the winner, who's on the upgrade.

4479 WATCH ON 3 DEVICES RACINGUK.COM/ANYWHERE MARES' NOVICES' HURDLE (10 hdls) 2m 3f

4:50 (4:50) (Class 4) 4-Y-0+ **£3,573** (£1,049; £524; £262)

Form RPR

141- **1** **Cloudante (IRE)**[39] 3757 6-11-6 0 JasonMaguire 103+
(Donald McCain) *mde all: j.lft 3rd: increased pce 3 out: wnt clr between last 2: eased clsng stages* **1/7**[1]

2 *6* **Miss Mohawk (IRE)**[49] 5-11-0 0 DavidEngland 81
(Alan Brown) *chsd ldrs: 2nd appr 2 out: kpt on same pce: no ch w wnr* **16/1**

/05- **3** *1 ¼* **Dream Mistress**[21] 4074 5-11-0 0 AdamWedge 80
(Chris Bealby) *mid-div: hdwy to chse ldrs 6th: 3rd and one pce 2 out* **8/1**[2]

060- **4** *2 ¼* **Agent Louise**[21] 4075 6-10-9 0 AdamNicol[(5)] 78
(Mike Sowersby) *chsd wnr: outpcd after 3 out: styd on between last 2 to take modest 4th* **14/1**

000- **5** *13* **Bow Fiddle (IRE)**[19] 4107 8-11-0 74 (t) RichieMcGrath 65
(Patrick Holmes) *hld up in rr: hdwy to chse ldrs 6th: wknd between last 2* **12/1**[3]

6 *8* **Simmply Sam** 7-10-11 0 KyleJames[(3)] 57
(Marjorie Fife) *chsd ldrs: 2nd 6th: upsides 3 out: lost pl sn after 2 out* **16/1**

PP0- **7** *16* **Frosty Dawn**[40] 3735 6-10-11 0 GavinSheehan[(3)] 41
(Mike Sowersby) *in rr: hdwy to chse ldrs 6th: lost pl 3 out: sn bhd* **100/1**

46- **8** *98* **Crazy Jane (IRE)**[21] 4074 5-11-0 0 FelixDeGiles
(Tom Gretton) *in rr: hdwy to chse ldrs 6th: reminders and lost pl next: sn bhd: t.o 2 out: eventually completed* **20/1**

0P- **P** **Manyshadesofblack (IRE)**[72] 3110 6-11-0 0 BrianHarding
(Tina Jackson) *mid-div: lost pl after 4th: sn bhd: t.o 6th: p.u bef next* **100/1**

5m 1.1s (25.00) **Going Correction** +0.65s/f (Soft) **9 Ran SP% 131.5**
Speed ratings (Par 105): **73,70,69,69,63 60,53,12,**
CSF £7.11 TOTE £1.20: £1.02, £2.90, £2.00; EX 7.10 Trifecta £54.20.
Owner Thomson Fyffe Racing **Bred** Martin Allen **Trained** Cholmondeley, Cheshire
■ Stewards' Enquiry : Gavin Sheehan Fine: £140, failed to report mare was unsuited by the good to soft ground.

FOCUS
This mares' novice hurdle centred around the long odds-on favourite, who was value for further. The time was poor.

4480 WE RACE AGAIN ON MARCH 5TH MAIDEN NATIONAL HUNT FLAT RACE (CONDITIONALS & AMATEURS) 2m

5:20 (5:20) (Class 5) 4-6-Y-O **£2,053** (£598; £299)

Form RPR

3- **1** **Landmarque**[47] 3619 5-11-2 0 JakeGreenall[(3)] 105
(Tony Coyle) *chsd ldrs: outpcd 6f out: hdwy over 3f out: 3rd over 1f out: styd on wl to ld towards fin* **3/1**[1]

/26- **2** *½* **Serenity Now (IRE)**[102] 2499 6-10-12 0 NathanMoscrop[(7)] 105
(Brian Ellison) *led: hdd narrowly 2f out: regained narrow ld last 75yds: hdd nr fin* **4/1**[2]

3 *hd* **Palm Grey (IRE)** 6-11-2 0 JonathanEngland[(3)] 105
(Sue Smith) *in rr: hdwy after 6f: sn chsng ldrs: 2nd 4f out: led narrowly 2f out: hdd and no ex ins fnl f* **20/1**

65- **4** *10* **Shantou Tiger (IRE)**[92] 2724 5-10-12 0 NickSlatter[(7)] 96
(Donald McCain) *chsd ldrs: hung rt bnd after 5f: drvn over 5f out: sn lost pl* **12/1**[3]

5 *8* **Tommy O'Dwyer (IRE)** 5-11-2 0 JackQuinlan[(3)] 89
(John Ferguson) *gave problems and uns rdr gng to s: in rr: sn drvn along: detached last after 6f: t.o over 3f out: kpt on over 1f out: nvr a factor* **4/1**[2]

2- **6** *5* **Big Mike (IRE)**[34] 3835 6-10-12 0 MrWDegnan[(7)] 84
(Sarah Humphrey) *chsd ldrs: drvn 4f out: wknd over 1f out* **3/1**[1]

0- **7** *49* **Trooper Royal**[66] 3214 4-10-3 0 DaraghBourke[(7)] 31
(Sue Smith) *hld up in mid-div: hdwy after 6f: drvn 6f out: sn lost pl: t.o 3f out* **12/1**[3]

8 14 **True Gold** 4-10-0 0 .... KielanWoods(3) 11
(Michael Mullineaux) *in rr: hdwy after 6f: drvn 6f out: sn lost pl and bhd: t.o 3f out* **66/1**

3m 55.4s (8.50) **Going Correction** +0.65s/f (Soft)
WFA 4 from 5yo+ 9lb **8** Ran SP% **111.6**
Speed ratings: **104,103,103,98,94 92,67,60**
CSF £14.41 TOTE £3.10: £1.20, £2.20, £4.80; EX 14.30 Trifecta £137.40.
Owner C E Whiteley **Bred** C E Whiteley **Trained** Norton, N Yorks

FOCUS
An interesting bumper with a fair level of form on offer. The form is rated around the winner, second and fifth.
T/Plt: £29.90 to a £1 stake. Pool: £70,652.30 - 1723.51 winning units. T/Qpdt: £8.00 to a £1 stake. Pool: £5435.65 - 500.80 winning units. WG

[4241] LEICESTER (R-H)
Tuesday, February 25

OFFICIAL GOING: Good to soft (soft in places; 6.1)
Wind: Light behind Weather: Fine turning showery after race 3

4481 SQUIRE OSBALDESTON H'CAP CHASE (18 fncs) 2m 7f 110y
2:10 (2:10) (Class 4) (0-105,105) 5-Y-0+ **£5,198** (£1,526; £763; £381)

Form RPR
214- 1 **Carli King (IRE)**[35] 3820 8-11-12 **105** .... (p) TomMessenger 116
(Caroline Bailey) *led to 3rd: chsd ldrs: led again appr 4 out: rdn after 2 out: styd on u.p* **9/2**[2]
422- 2 nk **Lough Coi (IRE)**[6] 4354 8-10-2 **88** .... (vt) CharlieDeutsch(7) 99
(Anthony Middleton) *hld up: hdwy 8th: jnd wnr 4 out: rdn and rdr bec unbalanced flat: styd on* **4/1**[1]
451- 3 23 **Epee Celeste (FR)**[9] 4309 8-9-10 **80** .... (b) JoeCornwall(5) 72
(Michael Chapman) *chsd ldrs: led 3rd tl j.lft and hdd 7th: drvn along 12th: wknd 2 out* **11/2**[3]
044- 4 2 **Handsome Buddy (IRE)**[125] 2023 7-10-13 **92** .... (v) BrendanPowell 82
(Michael Gates) *prom: rdn after 4 out: wknd 2 out* **25/1**
435- 5 1 ½ **Chasers Chance (IRE)**[32] 3879 11-10-8 **87** .... (p) RichardJohnson 74
(Paul Henderson) *hld up: hdwy 11th: rdn and wknd appr 4 out* **7/1**
1U4- 6 10 **Faith Keeper (IRE)**[34] 3836 9-11-10 **103** .... PaddyBrennan 83
(Fergal O'Brien) *chsd ldrs: j. slowly 5th: led 7th: rdn and hdd appr 4 out: wknd bef next* **7/1**
PP5- 7 28 **My Silver Lilly**[19] 4110 7-9-11 **79** .... TrevorWhelan(3) 32
(Clive Drew) *hld up: a in rr: wknd 13th* **12/1**
/05- 8 2 ¼ **Bruslini (FR)**[8] 4328 9-11-10 **103** .... MrGBarfoot-Saunt 54
(Tracey Barfoot-Saunt) *prom: lost pl 4th: bhd fr 9th* **66/1**
1/F- P **Oscar The Myth (IRE)**[72] 3114 8-10-9 **88** .... (tp) NickScholfield
(Jeremy Scott) *prom: j. slowly and lost pl 5th: reminders after next: bhd whn p.u bef 10th* **9/2**[2]

6m 4.8s (0.80) **Going Correction** +0.125s/f (Yiel) **9** Ran SP% **109.8**
Speed ratings: **103,102,95,94,94 90,81,80,**
CSF £21.64 CT £91.58 TOTE £5.20: £2.00, £1.70, £2.00; EX 19.90 Trifecta £71.60.
Owner Varley, Lloyd & Bailey **Bred** Eamon Fitzgerald **Trained** Holdenby, Northants

FOCUS
The pace was honest for this modest handicap, with the front two pulling a long way clear. A big step up from the winner.

4482 PROSTATE AWARENESS NOVICES' H'CAP CHASE (15 fncs) 2m 4f 110y
2:40 (2:40) (Class 5) (0-100,100) 5-Y-0+ **£3,249** (£954; £477; £238)

Form RPR
256- 1 **Lord Fox (IRE)**[12] 4243 7-10-5 **84** .... BenPoste(5) 93
(Shaun Harris) *mde all: rdn 3 out: drvn flat: jst hld on* **9/2**[1]
246- 2 nk **Me And Ben (IRE)**[66] 3203 7-11-9 **97** .... (t) PaddyBrennan 106
(Fergal O'Brien) *hld up: hdwy 10th: chsd wnr 2 out: styd on u.p* **6/1**[2]
P23- 3 12 **Possibly Flora**[38] 3785 9-11-3 **91** .... (t) DarylJacob 88
(Richard Woollacott) *chsd ldrs: rdn and nt fluent 3 out: wknd flat* **6/1**[2]
P05/ 4 27 **No Through Road**[312] 5383 7-10-0 **74** .... (t) LiamTreadwell 47
(Michael Scudamore) *hld up: bhd fr 8th* **15/2**[3]
01U- 5 6 **Smart Catch (IRE)**[82] 2897 8-11-8 **96** .... LeeEdwards 63
(Tony Carroll) *chsd wnr: j.lft 1st: chal 4 out: sn rdn: wknd after next* **20/1**
0U2- 6 8 **Sir Lynx (IRE)**[11] 4250 7-11-12 **100** .... (t) TomMessenger 60
(Chris Bealby) *hld up: nt fluent 3rd: drvn along 11th: sn wknd* **12/1**
45P- 7 nse **Riddlestown (IRE)**[19] 4109 7-11-11 **99** .... HarrySkelton 59
(Caroline Fryer) *hld up: hdwy 8th: rdn and wknd appr 4 out* **16/1**
335- 8 ¾ **Johnnys Legacy (IRE)**[8] 4324 7-11-3 **94** .... PeterCarberry(3) 53
(Conor Dore) *chsd ldrs: hmpd 1st: rdn and wknd 11th* **16/1**
050- F **Tallulah Mai**[9] 4303 7-11-6 **99** .... JamesBanks(5)
(Alastair Lidderdale) *hld up: hdwy 9th: wknd after 11th: disputing poor 5th whn fell 4 out* **33/1**
P3F- P **Shannon Spirit (IRE)**[55] 3472 9-11-2 **90** .... TomO'Brien
(Paul Henderson) *chsd ldrs tl wknd 6th: bhd whn p.u bef 4 out* **16/1**
4- P **Toe To Toe (IRE)**[187] 1341 6-11-7 **95** .... NickScholfield
(Lucy Jones) *sn bhd and nt jump wl: p.u after 5th* **25/1**
604- P **Wah Wah Taysee (IRE)**[82] 2893 7-11-12 **100** .... TomScudamore
(David Bridgwater) *hld up: hdwy 5th: wknd appr 4 out: sn p.u* **9/2**[1]

5m 27.3s (8.40) **Going Correction** +0.25s/f (Yiel) **12** Ran SP% **113.6**
Speed ratings: **94,93,89,79,76 73,73,73, , ,**
CSF £30.08 CT £161.57 TOTE £5.80: £1.90, £2.40, £2.50; EX 34.10 Trifecta £167.90.
Owner Miss H Ward **Bred** Miss Violet Sweeney **Trained** Carburton, Notts

FOCUS
An ordinary novice handicap where two came clear. The winner is rated back to his Ayr level.

4483 CAPTAIN MACHELL H'CAP CHASE (12 fncs) 2m
3:10 (3:10) (Class 4) (0-120,120) 5-Y-0+ **£6,498** (£1,908; £954; £477)

Form RPR
5P5- 1 **Morgan's Bay**[56] 3431 9-10-13 **107** .... PaddyBrennan 113+
(Tom George) *trckd ldr: upsides and nt fluent 4 out: led next: shkn up flat: styd on wl* **13/8**[1]
P61- 2 5 **Barenger (IRE)**[61] 3268 7-11-5 **113** .... (p) JackDoyle 113
(Ali Brewer) *chsd ldrs: chal 3 out tl rdn appr last: styd on same pce flat* **2/1**[2]
0P0- 3 19 **Ballybach (IRE)**[25] 4021 10-11-6 **114** .... TomCannon 96
(Nick Gifford) *led to 3 out: wknd next* **5/1**
423- 4 4 **Phase Shift**[34] 3831 6-11-12 **120** .... (t) DenisO'Regan 98
(Brian Ellison) *hld up: pushed along after 8th: wknd 4 out* **9/2**[3]

4m 17.3s (9.10) **Going Correction** +0.375s/f (Yiel) **4** Ran SP% **106.3**
Speed ratings: **92,89,80,78**
CSF £5.17 TOTE £2.60; EX 6.00 Trifecta £17.50.
Owner Simon W Clarke **Bred** Richard Mathias **Trained** Slad, Gloucs

FOCUS
This handicap was run at a sound pace. The winner was back to the best of last season's form, with the second to his mark.

4484 RUTLAND WATER NOVICES' CHASE (18 fncs) 2m 7f 110y
3:40 (3:40) (Class 3) 5-Y-0+ **£7,797** (£2,289; £1,144; £572)

Form RPR
3P5- 1 **Keltic Rhythm (IRE)**[19] 4105 7-10-11 0 .... TrevorWhelan(3) 113+
(Neil King) *mde all: clr fr 4 out: easily* **6/1**[3]
0/3- 2 13 **Miss Milborne**[41] 3718 8-10-7 125 .... BrendanPowell 91
(Jamie Snowden) *chsd ldrs: pushed along at various stages: hmpd 6th: wnt 2nd 13th: outpcd fr 4 out* **9/4**[2]
403- 3 12 **Midnight Mustang**[57] 3425 7-10-7 0 .... MrJMartin(7) 87
(Andrew J Martin) *mid-div: pushed along and nt fluent 13th: wknd after next* **16/1**
055/ 4 2 **Cosway Spirit (IRE)**[735] 4431 7-11-0 0 .... DavidBass 85
(Ben Pauling) *hld up: a towards rr: wknd after 14th* **20/1**
353- 5 25 **Flichity (IRE)**[11] 4248 9-10-9 62 .... JoeCornwall(5) 63
(John Cornwall) *chsd wnr to 13th: wknd after next* **33/1**
/00- 6 32 **Ravens Secret**[8] 4326 9-11-0 0 .... MrGBarfoot-Saunt 34
(Tracey Barfoot-Saunt) *a in rr: bhd fr 8th* **50/1**
001- U **Destroyer Deployed**[11] 4248 8-11-7 129 .... RichardJohnson
(Tim Vaughan) *chsd ldrs: cl 3rd whn blnd and uns rdr 6th* **8/11**[1]
5/0- P **First Lad**[48] 3602 7-11-0 0 .... JackDoyle
(Nicholas Pomfret) *hld up: a in rr: hmpd 6th: bhd whn hit 10th: p.u bef 4 out* **100/1**

6m 11.8s (7.80) **Going Correction** +0.50s/f (Soft) **8** Ran SP% **119.5**
Speed ratings: **107,102,98,98,89 79, ,**
CSF £21.10 TOTE £5.90: £1.80, £1.10, £3.10; EX 22.70 Trifecta £126.40.
Owner Stephen Lower Insurance Services Ltd **Bred** Michael Fennessy **Trained** Newmarket, Suffolk

FOCUS
An uncompetitive novice chase. Modest form, but it makes sense.

4485 CGA FOXHUNTER MAIDEN HUNTERS' CHASE (18 fncs) 2m 7f 110y
4:10 (4:10) (Class 6) 6-Y-0+ **£1,559** (£483; £241; £121)

Form RPR
222- 1 **Gunmoney (IRE)**[19] 4113 9-11-10 113 .... (p) MrJRussell(7) 114+
(G T H Bailey) *led to 3rd: chsd ldrto 8th: led again 14th: blnd 2 out: drvn along and edgd lft flat: styd on* **3/1**[1]
2 2 ¼ **All Great N Theory (IRE)**[16] 8-11-10 0 .... MrDRenney(7) 107
(Mrs Julie Marles) *chsd ldrs: led 8th to 14th: outpcd after 4 out: rallied last: r.o to go 2nd nr fin* **13/2**[3]
2/- 3 1 ¾ **Blazing Whale**[9] 9-12-0 0 .... MrRGHenderson(3) 105
(E Walker) *hld up: hdwy 11th: chsd wnr 4 out: rdn appr last: styd on same pce flat: lost 2nd nr fin* **7/1**
4 9 **Illicit Illusion (IRE)**[37] 6-12-0 0 .... MrSDrinkwater(3) 97
(T Lacey) *chsd ldrs: lost pl after 8th: hdwy 4 out: rdn and wknd after next* **8/1**
4/F- 5 3 ¼ **Mister Teddy**[12] 4246 9-11-12 111 .... MrTEllis(5) 94
(F A Hutsby) *prom: rdn after 14th: wknd appr 3 out* **10/1**
U00- 6 ½ **Patricktom Boru (IRE)**[23] 7-11-10 0 .... MrEDavid(7) 95
(R W J Willcox) *mid-div: hdwy 7th: rdn and wknd after 3 out* **50/1**
UP0/ 7 14 **Panama Canal (IRE)**[16] 9-11-10 0 .... MrTRFStrawson(7) 81
(S Robinson) *prom: rdn 13th: wknd appr 4 out* **33/1**
3/4- 8 1 ½ **Kiestown Chief (IRE)**[12] 4246 11-11-10 100 .... MrDerekSmith(7) 80
(R C Garton) *chsd ldr: led 3rd to 8th: rdn appr 4 out: wknd bef next* **14/1**
P/0- P **Send For Tim (IRE)**[12] 4246 11-11-10 48 .... MrJJInsole(7)
(Mrs Gaye Williams) *hld up: bhd fr 10th: p.u bef 13th* **200/1**
4- P **Glidewell**[282] 12-11-10 0 .... MissADalton(7)
(A N Dalton) *prom: nt fluent and lost pl 4th: bhd fr 9th: p.u bef 4 out* **22/1**
P **Quantum Theory (IRE)**[268] 10-12-3 0 .... MrWBiddick
(G D Hanmer) *hld up: hdwy 13th: rdn and wknd bef 4 out: bhd whn p.u bef next* **7/2**[2]
00/ P **Timarello (IRE)**[16] 11-11-10 0 .... MrTWeston
(G J Tarry) *hld up: hdwy appr 9th: wknd 12th: bhd whn p.u bef 4 out* **28/1**
P **Sitting Back (IRE)**[30] 10-11-10 0 .... MissTWorsley(7)
(Ms G Howell) *hld up: bhd fr 9th: bhd whn p.u bef 13th* **100/1**
4/ P **Neighbours Lady**[60] 7-11-7 0 .... MrJarrett(3)
(Patrick J Hanly) *mid-div: blnd and lost pl 6th: bhd fr 13th: p.u bef 3 out* **33/1**

6m 17.2s (13.20) **Going Correction** +0.625s/f (Soft) **14** Ran SP% **117.1**
Speed ratings: **103,102,101,98,97 97,92,92, , , ,**
CSF £21.21 TOTE £5.30: £1.30, £2.80, £2.90; EX 30.00 Trifecta £224.50.
Owner R G Russell **Bred** D McMahon **Trained** Holdenby, Northants

FOCUS
Plenty of pace on for this ordinary hunter chase. It paid to race handy. The idling winner was below his best.

4486 DANIEL LAMBERT H'CAP CHASE (15 fncs) 2m 4f 110y
4:40 (4:40) (Class 4) (0-105,104) 5-Y-0+ **£4,548** (£1,335; £667; £333)

Form RPR
340- 1 **Lord Landen (IRE)**[9] 4301 9-10-7 **90** .... (t) ConorShoemark(5) 109+
(Fergal O'Brien) *a.p: chsd ldr 5th tl led 7th: clr fr 3 out: easily* **13/2**
/34- 2 12 **Carpincho (FR)**[87] 2805 10-11-12 **104** .... RichardJohnson 105
(Sarah Humphrey) *led to 7th: chsd wnr to 11th: rdn to go 2nd 3 out: styd on same pce fr next* **10/3**[1]
5/6- 3 7 **Egypt Mill Spirit (IRE)**[49] 3596 8-11-6 **98** .... PaddyBrennan 96+
(Tom George) *hld up: hdwy 10th: rdn whn mstke 2 out: sn wknd* **7/1**
34F- 4 9 **Fintan**[37] 3799 11-10-12 **93** .... RobertDunne(3) 84
(Laura Young) *hld up: hdwy 8th: chsd wnr 11th: blnd next: wknd 3 out* **8/1**
/03- 5 14 **Witch's Hat (IRE)**[68] 3180 11-10-5 **83** .... (t) MarkGrant 57
(Jim Old) *chsd ldr to 5th: remained handy tl rdn and wknd 2 out* **16/1**
P62- 6 4 ½ **Got Attitude (IRE)**[33] 3855 11-11-3 **95** .... (tp) LeeEdwards 65
(Tony Carroll) *prom tl wknd 4 out* **20/1**
514- 7 2 ¾ **Fitandproperjob**[25] 4004 8-10-8 **91** .... (vt) JamesBanks(5) 59
(Anthony Middleton) *hld up: a in rr: wknd appr 4 out* **10/1**
452- 8 11 **Royal Riviera**[22] 4067 8-11-9 **101** .... (t) SamTwiston-Davies 59
(Nigel Twiston-Davies) *hld up: a in rr: pushed along after 5th: rdn and wknd appr 4 out* **5/1**[2]
0/5- 9 1 ¾ **Killfinnan Castle (IRE)**[12] 4243 11-10-0 **78** oh2 .... WillKennedy 34
(Violet M Jordan) *hld up: a in rr: wknd appr 4 out* **28/1**
1P3- P **Phoenix Des Mottes (FR)**[33] 3855 11-9-9 **78** oh8 .... JoeCornwall(5)
(John Cornwall) *prom: mstke and lost pl 2nd: bhd whn p.u after 5th* **66/1**

11U- P **Full Ov Beans**[11] 4250 10-11-6 98 JamieMoore
(Michael Gates) *prom to 8th: bhd fr 13th: p.u bef 4 out* 11/2[3]

5m 33.4s (14.50) **Going Correction** +0.75s/f (Soft) 11 Ran SP% **116.8**
Speed ratings: **102,97,94,91,86 84,83,79,78,**
CSF £28.70 CT £158.40 TOTE £6.60: £2.70, £1.10, £3.40; EX 33.20 Trifecta £342.60.
Owner The B Lucky Partnership **Bred** Richard And Marie Hennessy **Trained** Coln St. Dennis, Gloucs

FOCUS
A modest handicap, run at a solid gallop. The winner improved to the level of his old hurdle form.
T/Jkpt: Not won. T/Plt: £121.40 to a £1 stake. Pool: £127,694.73 - 767.41 winning units. T/Qpdt: £46.30 to a £1 stake. Pool: £6844.81 - 109.35 winning units. CR

3222 BANGOR-ON-DEE (L-H)
Wednesday, February 26

OFFICIAL GOING: Heavy (chs 4.1, hdl 5.0)
The fence on the paddock bend was omitted in all chases.
Wind: Half against, moderate Weather: Cloudy with bright intervals

4487 CLWYD SPECIAL RIDING CENTRE MARES' "NATIONAL HUNT" NOVICES' HURDLE (9 hdls) 2m 1f
2:30 (2:30) (Class 4) 4-Y-0+ **£3,119** (£915; £457; £228)

Form RPR
- 1 **Churchtown Love (IRE)**[388] 6-10-12 0 BarryGeraghty 113+
(Rebecca Curtis) *chsd ldr: led 3rd: mde rest and racd enthusiastically: shkn up appr last: kpt finding more: styd on wl to draw clr run-in* **10/3**[2]

041- 2 3 ½ **Rosa Fleet (IRE)**[22] 4074 6-11-5 119 AidanColeman 117+
(Venetia Williams) *led: hdd 3rd: remained prom: swtchd rt appr 2 out: sn ev ch and nt fluent 2 out: rdn bef last: one pce run-in* **4/5**[1]

31- 3 11 **Shuil Gealach (IRE)**[260] 715 6-10-12 0 PaulMoloney 99
(Paul Webber) *hld up in tch: mstke 5th: disp 2nd briefly after 3 out: pushed along and outpcd fr 2 out: n.d after* **9/2**[3]

050- 4 18 **Zuileka**[13] 4234 5-10-12 0 BrianHughes 79
(James Moffatt) *hld up: hdwy to go prom after 4th: wnt 2nd briefly appr 3 out: wknd bef 2 out* **125/1**

0/5- 5 3 ¾ **Taffy Dare (IRE)**[95] 2675 5-10-12 0 WayneHutchinson 75
(Alan King) *hld up: rdn after 3 out: sn btn* **12/1**

606- 6 20 **High Holloa**[23] 4069 5-10-12 0 DavidEngland 55
(Caroline Bailey) *chsd ldrs: rdn and lost pl 4 out: sn wknd* **100/1**

P **Teeton Blackvelvet** 5-10-12 0 TomMessenger
(Caroline Bailey) *racd keenly on outer: handy: stmbld 2nd: lost pl and dropped to rr after 4th: struggling and bhd whn mstke 5th: t.o whn p.u bef 4 out* **66/1**

4m 30.8s (19.90) **Going Correction** +1.375s/f (Heav) 7 Ran SP% **107.8**
Speed ratings (Par 105): **108,106,101,92,90 81,**
CSF £5.87 TOTE £4.20: £1.90, £1.30; EX 8.20 Trifecta £17.60.
Owner A J Rhead **Bred** The Red Marble Syndicate **Trained** Newport, Dyfed

FOCUS
A modest mares' novice hurdle to open the card, but one run at a fair gallop and the form is straightforward. The second sets the level.

4488 EXCEL SIGNS NOVICES' H'CAP CHASE (11 fncs 1 omitted) 2m 1f 110y
3:00 (3:01) (Class 4) (0-110,103) 5-Y-0+ **£3,768** (£1,106; £553; £276)

Form RPR
501- 1 **Lord Navits (IRE)**[13] 4242 6-11-10 101 (vt) AlainCawley 124+
(David Bridgwater) *mde all: steadily drew clr fr 3 out: eased run-in* **7/4**[1]

231- 2 14 **Jeanry (FR)**[4] 4416 11-11-3 101 7ex JoshWall(7) 106
(Arthur Whitehead) *in tch: chsd wnr fr 7th: u.p after 3 out: no imp: no ch bef last* **11/4**[2]

65P- 3 11 **Kayalar (IRE)**[19] 3119 6-11-2 93 PaulMoloney 93
(Evan Williams) *chsd ldrs: racd in 2nd pl fr 4th to 7th: outpcd after 4 out: wnt mod 3rd appr 2 out: no real imp* **16/1**

36P- 4 9 **Trozulon (FR)**[23] 4067 7-11-12 103 AidanColeman 91
(Venetia Williams) *hld up in rr: wnt 3rd whn pckd 7th: rdn whn chsd ldrs appr 3 out: no imp: dropped to last and btn bef 2 out* **5/1**

4/4- P **Ortolan (GER)**[42] 3721 9-11-4 95 JasonMaguire
(Donald McCain) *chsd wnr to 4th and reminders: dived at 5th: in rr and j. slowly 6th: wl bhd whn p.u bef 4 out* **3/1**[3]

5m 0.8s (38.70) **Going Correction** +2.225s/f (Heav) 5 Ran SP% **110.6**
Speed ratings: **103,96,91,87,**
CSF £7.19 TOTE £2.80: £2.50, £1.10; EX 6.70 Trifecta £21.60.
Owner Jobarry Partnership **Bred** Miss Mary O'Sullivan **Trained** Icomb, Gloucs

FOCUS
This ordinary novices' handicap was run at a sound gallop and it saw another winner from the front. The runner-up sets the level. Another big step forward from the easy winner.

4489 WEATHERBYS HAMILTON INSURANCE H'CAP HURDLE (12 hdls) 3m
3:30 (3:31) (Class 3) (0-130,130) 4-Y-0+ **£6,498** (£1,908; £954; £477)

Form RPR
P1R- 1 **Alpha Victor (IRE)**[18] 4162 9-11-7 130 HarryChalloner(5) 144+
(William Kinsey) *trckd ldrs: pushed along whn lost pl and outpcd after 7th: rallied 4 out: led 3 out: drew clr appr last: styd on wl* **25/1**

5UU- 2 11 **Jaunty Journey**[23] 4070 11-10-0 104 oh1 (v[1]) SamTwiston-Davies 108
(Nigel Twiston-Davies) *led: hdd 2nd: ramained w ldr: regained ld 8th: hdd 3 out: rdn bef next: one pce appr last: no ch w wnr sn after* **9/2**[3]

424- 3 4 **Quel Elite (FR)**[11] 4271 10-10-9 113 (v[1]) BrianHughes 111
(James Moffatt) *trckd ldrs: pushed along and sltly outpcd bef 4 out: rallied 3 out: one pce and no imp fr 2 out* **9/2**[3]

212- 4 6 **Sir Mangan (IRE)**[25] 4038 6-11-7 125 JasonMaguire 117
(Donald McCain) *prom: led 2nd: mstke and hdd 8th: remained w ldr tl u.p after 3 out: wknd bef next* **5/2**[1]

06F- 5 ¾ **Monetary Fund (USA)**[24] 4051 8-11-9 127 AidanColeman 118
(Venetia Williams) *hld up in rr: hdwy appr 8th: chsd ldrs tl rdn and wknd after 3 out* **3/1**[2]

/10- 6 24 **Extreme Impact**[11] 4271 8-10-9 120 (p) ConorRing(7) 87
(Evan Williams) *rdn thrght: prom tl lost pl after 6th: lost tch 7th: t.o* **13/2**

6m 20.9s (29.90) **Going Correction** +1.375s/f (Heav) 6 Ran SP% **107.1**
Speed ratings (Par 107): **105,101,100,98,97 89**
CSF £117.67 TOTE £18.90: £8.80, £3.30; EX 174.60 Trifecta £512.10.
Owner Denton,Kinsey,Osborne Hse,Wesley-Yates **Bred** Miss Penny Downes **Trained** Ashton, Cheshire

FOCUS
Not a strong staying handicap for the class. A personal best from the winner.

4490 HAMPTON VETERINARY GROUP H'CAP CHASE (16 fncs 2 omitted) 3m 110y
4:00 (4:02) (Class 4) (0-120,119) 5-Y-0+ **£3,861** (£1,198; £645)

Form RPR
303- 1 **Makethe Mostofnow (IRE)**[25] 4028 9-11-12 119 PaulMoloney 130+
(Evan Williams) *j.lft: prom: hmpd and lost pl briefly 11th: rallied to ld 12th: pressed appr 2 out: styd on to drew away run-in* **8/1**

465- 2 2 ½ **Incentivise (IRE)**[34] 3858 11-10-13 109 MichealNolan(3) 116
(Richard Lee) *prom: outpcd bef 3 out: sn rallied to take 2nd: ev ch appr 2 out: kpt on u.p run-in: no imp fnl 100yds* **5/1**[2]

044- 3 ¾ **Presence Felt (IRE)**[41] 3739 6-11-0 112 (v) MauriceLinehan(5) 118
(Jonjo O'Neill) *hld up: effrt to chse ldrs 3 out: kpt on u.p appr last: no imp on wnr fnl 100yds: one pce cl home* **7/1**[3]

423- P **Stormhoek (IRE)**[13] 4241 9-11-1 108 (vt) SamTwiston-Davies
(Nigel Twiston-Davies) *racd on and off the bridle: in rr but in tch: effrt whn j. awkwardly and bmpd 11th: sn lost pl: bhd whn p.u bef 4 out* **7/1**[3]

212- P **Take The Mick**[3] 4451 7-10-8 101 AidanColeman
(Venetia Williams) *led: hdd 12th: rdn appr 3 out: wknd sn after: bhd whn p.u bef 2 out* **5/6**[1]

7m 14.6s (54.80) **Going Correction** +2.225s/f (Heav) 5 Ran SP% **107.3**
Speed ratings: **101,100,99, ,**
CSF £40.78 TOTE £9.30: £3.00, £1.70; EX 31.00 Trifecta £79.30.
Owner Mrs Janet Davies **Bred** Thomas Hanley **Trained** Llancarfan, Vale Of Glamorgan

FOCUS
This was run at a routine gallop and the form is best rated around the first two.

4491 BANGORBET H'CAP HURDLE (11 hdls) 2m 4f
4:30 (4:30) (Class 4) (0-115,115) 4-Y-0+ **£3,195** (£992; £534)

Form RPR
222- 1 **Hellorboston (IRE)**[30] 3938 6-11-12 115 (b) JasonMaguire 120+
(Donald McCain) *led: hdd 4th: racd u.p fr after 5th: abt 2 l down 2 out: drew level last: sn led: drvn out* **9/4**[2]

111- 2 ½ **Mudita Moment (IRE)**[20] 4108 9-11-12 115 AidanColeman 121+
(Venetia Williams) *j.rt most of way: led 4th: rdn appr 2 out where abt 2 l down: jnd last: sn hdd: kpt on u.p run-in* **10/11**[1]

554- 3 59 **Flemensmix**[11] 4281 6-11-5 113 EdCookson(5) 72
(Kim Bailey) *chsd ldrs: pushed along and outpcd after 6th: no imp after: wl btn* **5/1**[3]

02P- P **Forgivienne**[41] 3733 7-11-5 108 AdamWedge
(Evan Williams) *in rr: mstke 1st: struggling bef 6th: t.o whn sn p.u: b.b.v* **16/1**

5m 24.2s (32.20) **Going Correction** +1.375s/f (Heav) 4 Ran SP% **105.7**
Speed ratings (Par 105): **90,89,66,**
CSF £4.68 TOTE £3.20; EX 4.60 Trifecta £6.70.
Owner Thomson Fyffe Racing **Bred** Miss Yvonne Prendiville **Trained** Cholmondeley, Cheshire

FOCUS
An uncompetitive handicap dominated by the first pair. The winner is closing in on his best bumper mark.

4492 RACING UK STANDARD OPEN NATIONAL HUNT FLAT RACE 2m 1f
5:00 (5:01) (Class 6) 4-6-Y-O **£1,642** (£478; £239)

Form RPR
31- 1 **Battle Born**[34] 3863 5-11-3 0 CharlieDeutsch(7) 125+
(Charlie Longsdon) *racd in cl 2nd pl: led gng wl over 3f out: effrtlessly drew clr wl over 1f out: v easily* **4/5**[1]

2 31 **Fearless Tunes (IRE)**[291] 6-11-3 0 JasonMaguire 83
(Donald McCain) *racd keenly: led: hdd over 3f out: sn rdn: no ch fr 2f out: wl btn* **3/1**[2]

3 1 ½ **Creative Boru (IRE)**[271] 6-11-3 0 BarryGeraghty 81
(Rebecca Curtis) *chsd ldrs: niggled along to try and cl over 4f out: rdn over 2f out whn no imp: plugged on after but no ch* **7/2**[3]

4 55 **Buckontupence (IRE)**[276] 6-11-3 0 DougieCostello 26
(James Evans) *in rr: outpcd over 6f out: lft bhd 5f out: t.o* **20/1**

4m 22.9s (17.60) **Going Correction** +1.375s/f (Heav)
WFA 5 from 6yo 1lb 4 Ran SP% **107.5**
Speed ratings: **113,98,97,71**
CSF £3.44 TOTE £1.80; EX 5.10 Trifecta £6.20.
Owner Alan Halsall **Bred** Mrs S C Welch **Trained** Over Norton, Oxon

FOCUS
What looked an interesting bumper was completely taken apart by the winner, who looks a smart prospect.
T/Plt: £223.40 to a £1 stake. Pool of £55315.63 - 180.70 winning tickets. T/Qpdt: £98.30 to a £1 stake. Pool of £3003.60 - 22.60 winning tickets. DO

3229 LINGFIELD (L-H)
Wednesday, February 26

OFFICIAL GOING: Standard
This AW bumper card replaced a scheduled turf fixture which was cancelled due to waterlogging.
Wind: medium, half behind Weather: bright spells, light showers

4493 GO BANANAS FOR FAIRTRADE "JUMPERS' BUMPER" NATIONAL HUNT FLAT RACE 1m 7f 169y
2:10 (2:10) (Class 4) 4-Y-0+ **£3,898** (£1,144; £572; £286)

Form RPR
050- 1 **Very Noble (FR)**[90] 2761 5-11-2 0 (t) NickScholfield 96
(Paul Nicholls) *hld up in midfield: travelling wl but stuck bhd horses 2f out: clsd to trck ldrs and nt clr run over 1f out: gap opened and qcknd ins fnl f to ld fnl 75yds: r.o wl* **6/1**[3]

0/6- 2 ¾ **Ginger Fizz**[49] 3600 7-10-6 0 (t) KielanWoods(3) 88
(Ben Case) *t.k.h: led for 1f: chsd ldr after: rdn and ev ch 2f out: led ins fnl f: kpt on tl hdd and one pce fnl 75yds* **7/1**

613- 3 nk **Shaddaii (FR)**[238] 876 8-11-2 0 (t) IanPopham 95
(Caroline Keevil) *hld up in tch midfield: effrt u.p to chse ldrs over 1f out: ev ch ins fnl f: styd on same pce fnl 75yds* **16/1**

433/ 4 ¾ **Theredballoon**[701] 5117 8-11-2 0 [1] AndrewTinkler 94
(David Elsworth) *chsd ldrs: rdn over 1f out: n.m.r ins fnl f: kpt on towards fin* **10/1**

326- 5 nk **The Nephew (IRE)**[10] 4303 6-11-2 0 RichieMcLernon 94
(Jonjo O'Neill) *hld up in last trio: hdwy on outer over 2f out: wdst bnd 2f out: kpt on ins fnl f* **6/4**[1]

130- **6** *hd* **The Stig (FR)**[72] 3134 6-11-2 0 .... APMcCoy 94
(Nick Littmoden) *chsd ldr tl led after 1f: drvn wl over 1f out: hdd ins fnl f: no ex and wknd towards fin* **4/1**[2]

506- **7** *2 ½* **Mariet**[14] 3140 5-10-9 0 .... PaddyBrennan 84
(Suzy Smith) *hld up in last trio: sme hdwy 1/2-way: rdn and struggling over 2f out: styd on same pce and no imp over 1f out* **20/1**

PP1- **8** *¾* **Direct Approach (IRE)**[9] 4324 10-11-8 0 .... TomSiddall 97
(Lynn Siddall) *chsd ldrs: rdn and unable qck wl over 1f out: wknd ins fnl f* **25/1**

300- **9** *¾* **Keppel Isle (IRE)**[26] 4018 5-11-2 0 .... TomCannon 90
(Laura Mongan) *hld up in rr: rdn and struggling over 2f out: kpt on same pce 2f* **33/1**

3m 32.0s (-6.00) **Going Correction** -0.475s/f (Stan)
WFA 5 from 6yo+ 1lb **9** Ran SP% **113.3**
Speed ratings (Par 105): **96,95,95,95,94 94,93,93,92**
CSF £45.02 TOTE £10.10: £1.90, £2.20, £4.20; EX 49.40 Trifecta £909.80.
Owner Paul K Barber & Ian J Fogg **Bred** Mlle M Drion **Trained** Ditcheat, Somerset

FOCUS
For horses that have have run at least once over hurdles but have not won on the Flat or won any Class 1, 2 or 3 race. They finished in a heap off a slow pace. The form is given a token rating through the third.

4494 FAIRTRADE MARK 20TH CELEBRATION "JUMPERS' BUMPER" NATIONAL HUNT FLAT RACE 1m 7f 169y
2:40 (2:40) (Class 4) 5-Y-0+ **£3,898** (£1,144; £572; £286)

Form RPR

142- **1** **One Lucky Lady**[238] 877 6-10-2 0 .... NicodeBoinville(5) 92
(Nicky Henderson) *t.k.h: pressed ldr tl rdn to ld over 1f out: kpt on and a doing enough ins fnl f: rdn out* **4/6**[1]

450- **2** *¾* **Noble Friend (IRE)**[96] 2642 6-11-0 0 .... TomCannon 98
(Chris Gordon) *chsd ldrs: nt clr run 2f out: swtchd rt and effrt u.p over 1f out: pressed ldr ins fnl f: r.o but a hld* **33/1**

335- **3** *¾* **Harry Hunt**[90] 2757 7-11-0 0 .... NoelFehily 97
(Graeme McPherson) *hld up wl in tch in last pair: rdn and effrt jst over 2f out: 3rd and styd on same pce u.p ins fnl f* **9/4**[2]

22P- **4** *2* **Ya Hafed**[33] 3879 6-11-0 0 .... LeightonAspell 95
(Sheena West) *led and set stdy gallop: qcknd over 2f out: rdn and hdd over 1f out: 4th and styd on same pce ins fnl f* **8/1**[3]

0/0- **5** *8* **Asker (IRE)**[71] 3151 6-10-7 0 .... (p) MrHGMiller(7) 87
(Zoe Davison) *hld up wl in tch in last pair: rdn over 3f out: outpcd and btn over 2f out* **20/1**

3m 34.5s (-3.50) **Going Correction** -0.475s/f (Stan) **5** Ran SP% **109.6**
Speed ratings: **89,88,88,87,83**
CSF £22.32 TOTE £1.40: £1.20, £3.50; EX 19.10 Trifecta £35.30.
Owner S W Group Logistics Limited **Bred** Ken Knox **Trained** Upper Lambourn, Berks

FOCUS
For horses which, since 2011, have run at least once over 2m6f or further, and have not won a Class 1 or 2 race. A race run at an early dawdle, given a token rating through the second.

4495 "BET AND WATCH" AT 888SPORT.COM "JUMPERS' BUMPER" NATIONAL HUNT FLAT RACE 1m 7f 169y
3:10 (3:10) (Class 4) 4-Y-0+ **£3,898** (£1,144; £572; £286)

Form RPR

P22- **1** **Supreme Present**[10] 4297 6-10-9 0 .... (t) APMcCoy 107
(Kim Bailey) *chsd ldng pair: swtchd rt and effrt over 1f out: r.o wl u.p to ld fnl 100yds: rdn out* **5/4**[1]

1- **2** *1 ¾* **One For The Guv'Nr (IRE)**[26] 4016 5-11-2 0 .... DavidBass 112
(Nicky Henderson) *t.k.h: chsd ldr: upsides and stl travelling wl 2f out: rdn and edgd lft over 1f out: led 1f out: hdd and one pce fnl 100yds* **7/4**[2]

/0P- **3** *2* **Shooters Wood (IRE)**[32] 3894 10-11-2 0 .... (t) NickScholfield 110
(Paul Nicholls) *led: rdn and jnd 2f out: hdd over 1f out: styd on same pce ins fnl f* **6/1**[3]

434- **4** *10* **Fred Le Macon (FR)**[62] 3282 5-11-2 0 .... RobertThornton 100
(Alan King) *hld up in tch: 4th and rdn over 3f out: sn outpcd and wl hld over 2f out* **7/1**

300/ **5** *19* **Generous June (IRE)**[309] 5483 6-10-6 0 .... KielanWoods(3) 74
(Paddy Butler) *in tch in rr: rdn 9f out: lost tch wl over 2f out* **66/1**

560- **6** *42* **Cut'N'Shut**[26] 4018 7-10-9 0 .... MrHGMiller(7) 39
(Zoe Davison) *in tch in midfield on outer: dropped to last and struggling 5f out: t.o fnl 3f: fin lame* **66/1**

3m 21.9s (-16.10) **Going Correction** -0.475s/f (Stan) **6** Ran SP% **110.6**
Speed ratings (Par 105): **121,120,119,114,104 83**
CSF £3.54 TOTE £2.20: £1.30, £1.60; EX 4.60 Trifecta £12.70.
Owner Lucky Bin Racing & Little Lodge Farm **Bred** R D And Mrs J S Chugg **Trained** Andoversford, Gloucs

FOCUS
For horses currently eligible for NH Novice hurdles. One of the more interesting races on the card, and it was run in the quickest time.

4496 "CASH IN" EARLY AT 888SPORT.COM "JUMPERS' BUMPER" NATIONAL HUNT FLAT RACE 1m 7f 169y
3:40 (3:40) (Class 4) 4-Y-0+ **£3,898** (£1,144; £572; £286)

Form RPR

444- **1** **Chalk It Down (IRE)**[18] 4157 5-11-2 0 .... APMcCoy 84+
(Warren Greatrex) *hld up wl in tch in midfield: stuck bhd ldng trio fr 2f out: swtchd rt ins fnl f: qcknd wl u.p fnl 100yds to ld cl home* **11/10**[1]

P22- **2** *nk* **Ourmanmassini (IRE)**[10] 4298 6-11-2 0 .... (t) PaddyBrennan 82
(Suzy Smith) *hld up wl in tch in midfield: hdwy u.p to ld 1f out: edgd lft but r.o ins fnl f: hdd cl home* **7/4**[2]

366- **3** *2 ½* **Spoil Me (IRE)**[10] 4299 7-11-8 0 .... RichieMcLernon 86
(Jonjo O'Neill) *t.k.h: w ldr tl led 4f out: hdd and rdn wl over 1f out: outpcd fnl 100yds* **9/2**[3]

0/F- **4** *¾* **Rosa Imperialis**[62] 3289 5-10-9 0 .... FelixDeGiles 72
(Robert Walford) *chsd ldrs: hdwy to join ldr over 2f out: drvn to ld wl over 1f out: hdd 1f out: outpacd ins fnl f* **33/1**

00P- **5** *1 ¼* **First Of Never (IRE)**[62] 3265 8-11-2 0 .... TomSiddall 78
(Lynn Siddall) *hld up wl in tch in last pair: rdn and effrt over 1f out: kpt on same pce and no imp* **66/1**

006/ **6** *10* **Sparrow Hills (IRE)**[318] 5321 10-10-9 0 .... MrLKilgarriff(7) 68
(Steven Dixon) *led and set stdy gallop: hdd 4f out: sn u.p: lost pl over 2f out: wknd over 1f out: fin lame* **33/1**

3m 30.0s (-8.00) **Going Correction** -0.475s/f (Stan)
WFA 5 from 6yo+ 1lb **6** Ran SP% **109.5**
Speed ratings (Par 105): **101,100,99,99,98 93**
CSF £3.06 TOTE £1.70: £1.10, £1.80; EX 3.40 Trifecta £7.00.
Owner John P McManus **Bred** Michael Ryan **Trained** Upper Lambourn, Berks

FOCUS
Runners must have contested, since 2011, at least one hurdle, but must not have run on the Flat or won a Class 1 or 2 race. A moderate race but it served up a thrilling finish. Another slow time.

4497 £88 IN FREE BETS AT 888SPORT.COM "JUMPERS' BUMPER" NATIONAL HUNT FLAT RACE 1m 7f 169y
4:10 (4:10) (Class 4) 5-Y-0+ **£3,898** (£1,144; £572; £286)

Form RPR

/34- **1** **Earls Quarter (IRE)**[88] 2811 8-11-0 0 .... (t) APMcCoy 124+
(Ian Williams) *chsd ldng pair: wnt 2nd 4f out: led over 1f out and sn rdn clr: r.o wl: rdn out* **7/2**[3]

035- **2** *2 ½* **Empire Levant (USA)**[26] 4020 7-11-0 0 .... NickScholfield 121+
(Paul Nicholls) *hld up in tch in last pair: effrt to chse ldng pair over 1f out: styd on to go 2nd wl ins fnl f: no threat to wnr* **5/4**[1]

/51- **3** *2 ½* **Alfraamsey**[157] 1627 6-11-0 0 .... MarcGoldstein 119
(Sheena West) *led: rdn 2f out: hdd over 1f out and sn brushed aside by wnr: one pce and lost 2nd wl ins fnl f* **5/2**[2]

100- **4** *2 ¾* **Stormy Weather (FR)**[40] 3758 8-11-0 0 .... (p) JamieMoore 116
(Brian Ellison) *hld up in tch in rr: rdn over 2f out: no real imp: no ch w wnr but kpt on ins fnl f to go 4th cl home* **10/1**

U5U- **5** *½* **Akula (IRE)**[89] 2782 7-11-0 0 .... ColinBolger 115
(Mark H Tompkins) *chsd ldr tl 4f out: rdn and unable qck over 2f out: outpcd and wl hld 1f out* **12/1**

3m 29.5s (-8.50) **Going Correction** -0.475s/f (Stan) **5** Ran SP% **112.0**
Speed ratings: **102,100,99,98,97**
CSF £8.54 TOTE £5.70: £2.50, £1.40; EX 7.60 Trifecta £23.60.
Owner Patrick Kelly **Bred** Victor Connolly **Trained** Portway, Worcs

FOCUS
For 5yo+ which have run at least once over fences and have not won at Class 1 or 2 level. A warm race, despite the small field. The form is rated around the first three.

4498 HALF LENGTH REFUNDS AT 888SPORT.COM STANDARD OPEN NATIONAL HUNT FLAT RACE 1m 7f 169y
4:40 (4:40) (Class 4) 4-6-Y-0 **£3,898** (£1,144; £572; £286)

Form RPR

/64- **1** **Vodka 'n Tonic (IRE)**[106] 2439 5-11-2 0 .... AndrewTinkler 107+
(Nicky Henderson) *mde all: sn clr: 3 l clr over 2f out: rdn and fnd ex 2f out: in command and styd on wl after: eased towards fin* **7/1**[3]

2- **2** *4* **Inner Drive (IRE)**[109] 2375 6-11-2 0 .... RobertThornton 102
(Alan King) *t.k.h: hld up off the pce in midfield: wnt 3rd 1/2-way: chsd clr wnr over 4f out: clsd 3f out: rdn and no imp jst over 2f out: styd on same pce fnl 2f* **4/5**[1]

3 *4 ½* **Agha Des Mottes (FR)**[87] 4-11-0 0 .... APMcCoy 96
(Ian Williams) *hld up off the pce in last pair: hdwy into midfield 7f out: wnt 3rd over 4f out: clsd on wnr 3f out: rdn and outpcd over 2f out: wl hld and one pce* **11/4**[2]

4 *¾* **Family Motto** 5-11-2 0 .... TomCannon 97
(Chris Gordon) *chsd clr wnr tl over 4f out: 4th and kpt on same pce fnl 2f* **50/1**

0- **5** *25* **Capel Le Ferne (IRE)**[27] 3994 6-11-2 0 .... [1] FelixDeGiles 72
(Robert Walford) *taken down early: t.k.h: hld up off the pce in last pair: rdn and struggling 5f out: sn lost tch: t.o fnl 3f* **33/1**

6 *8* **Misirlou (FR)** 4-10-7 0 .... NoelFehily 55
(Tim Vaughan) *led main gp tl 8f out: rdn and lost pl 5f out: t.o fnl 3f* **8/1**

7 *43* **Gartan Boy** 6-10-13 0 .... JeremiahMcGrath(3) 21
(Anabel K Murphy) *racd off the pce in midfield: rdn and struggling 5f out: sn lost tch: t.o over 3f out* **66/1**

3m 23.7s (-14.30) **Going Correction** -0.475s/f (Stan)
WFA 4 from 5yo+ 9lb **7** Ran SP% **112.2**
Speed ratings: **116,114,111,111,98 94,73**
CSF £12.69 TOTE £8.40: £3.50, £1.10; EX 16.20 Trifecta £32.90.
Owner Bradley Partnership **Bred** Ms C Corrigan & Tom Conway **Trained** Upper Lambourn, Berks

FOCUS
A conventional bumper. A step forward from the winner with the second below his Wincanton form.

4499 DORMANSLAND FAIRTRADE VILLAGE MARES' INTERMEDIATE OPEN NATIONAL HUNT FLAT RACE 1m 7f 169y
5:10 (5:10) (Class 6) 4-6-Y-0 **£1,711** (£498; £249)

Form RPR

4- **1** **Double Dealites**[66] 3229 4-10-2 0 .... JeremiahMcGrath(3) 81
(Jamie Poulton) *hld up wl in tch in last pair: hdwy to chse ldrs wl over 1f out: rdn to chse ldr 1f out: styd on to ld fnl 50yds: rdn out* **8/1**

54- **2** *¾* **Ellin's Tower**[32] 3898 5-11-0 0 .... (t) NickScholfield 89
(Kim Bailey) *led and set stdy gallop: rdn and qcknd 3 l clr 2f: drvn ins fnl f: hdd and no ex wl ins fnl f* **7/2**[2]

3 *2 ¾* **Prettyasapicture** 5-11-0 0 .... RobertThornton 87
(Alan King) *hld up wl in tch towards rr: hdwy to chse ldrs over 2f out: styd on same pce fr over 1f out: wnt 3rd ins fnl f* **11/4**[1]

4 *¾* **Bus Named Desire** 6-11-0 0 .... SeanQuinlan 86
(David Bridgwater) *t.k.h: hld up wl in tch in midfield: chsd ldrs 1/2-way: rdn to chse clr ldr 2f out: 3rd and btn 1f out: styd on same pce and lost 3rd ins fnl f* **16/1**

5 *½* **Minx Of The Lamp** 5-11-0 0 .... [1] GerardTumelty 85
(Alan King) *hld up in tch in rr: rdn and effrt ent fnl 2f: no threat to ldrs but kpt on fnl f* **7/1**

4/ **6** *1 ¼* **Hortense Mancini**[303] 36 5-10-9 0 .... [1] MattCrawley(5) 84
(Lucy Wadham) *hld up wl in tch in midfield: rdn over 2f out: outpcd and btn whn hung lft over 1f out: styd on same pce after* **6/1**

3- **7** *½* **Seas The Moment (IRE)**[66] 3230 5-11-0 0 .... TomCannon 84
(Chris Gordon) *chsd ldrs: rdn and outpcd wl over 1f out: wknd ent fnl f* **5/1**[3]

0- **8** *6* **Crazy Train**[26] 4017 5-10-9 0 .... (t) JamesBanks(5) 78
(Keiran Burke) *t.k.h: w ldr tl rdn and outpcd ent fnl 2f: wknd over 1f out* **33/1**

9 *7* **Pomegranate** 6-10-9 0 .... KieronEdgar(5) 71
(Tracey Barfoot-Saunt) *t.k.h: chsd ldrs tl rdn and lost pl jst over 2f out: wknd over 1f out: bhd fnl f* **33/1**

3m 33.9s (-4.10) **Going Correction** -0.475s/f (Stan)
WFA 4 from 5yo+ 9lb **9** Ran SP% **115.2**
Speed ratings: **91,90,89,88,88 88,87,84,81**
CSF £36.08 TOTE £9.40: £3.30, £1.60, £1.10; EX 36.20 Trifecta £123.90.
Owner Miss V Markowiak **Bred** R C Moules **Trained** Telscombe, E Sussex

FOCUS
A conventional mares' bumper. Another very slowly run race. The second and sixth set the level.

T/Plt: £27.70 to a £1 stake. Pool of £64497.04 - 1694.87 winning tickets. T/Qpdt: £2.30 to a £1 stake. Pool of £5946.99 - 1884.66 winning tickets. SP

4275 WINCANTON (R-H)

Wednesday, February 26

OFFICIAL GOING: Heavy (soft in places; 5.4)

The flight on the stable bend was omitted in all hurdle races due to the state of ground.

Wind: mild across Weather: sunny with light showers

4500 HIGOS FOR ALL YOUR COMMERCIAL NEEDS MARES' NOVICES' HURDLE (10 hdls 1 omitted) 2m 6f

2:20 (2:20) (Class 4) 5-Y-0+ **£3,249** (£954; £477; £238)

Form RPR

021- **1** **Fairytale Theatre (IRE)**[8] 4331 7-11-3 0 ....(t) DarylJacob 118+
(Paul Nicholls) *mounted on trck: mde all: racd keenly: nt a fluent: pushed clr after 2 out: readily* **2/9**[1]

2- **2** *14* **Young Cheddar (IRE)**[8] 4331 7-10-5 0 .... ConorShoemark[(5)] 91
(Polly Gundry) *nt a fluent: trckd ldrs: awkward 5th: wnt 2nd after next: rdn appr 2 out: sn outpcd by wnr* **5/1**[2]

005- **3** *8* **Barton Heather**[41] 3746 5-10-7 92 ....(t) MichaelByrne[(3)] 81
(Neil Mulholland) *trckd wnr tl after 6th: rdn and outpcd after 3 out: styd on again after 2 out: sn wnt 3rd run-in* **10/1**[3]

000- **4** *¾* **Two Mile Bridge (IRE)**[62] 3290 8-10-10 89 .... TomO'Brien 80
(Paul Henderson) *hld up bhd ldrs: wnt 3rd after 3 out: sn rdn: outpcd bef next: no ex whn lost 3rd run-in* **33/1**

6P4- **5** *25* **Aroseforoscar**[27] 3991 5-10-10 95 .... JamesDavies 65
(Chris Down) *hld up bhd ldrs: struggling after 6th: wknd after 3 out: t.o* **14/1**

5m 49.5s (23.00) **Going Correction** +0.825s/f (Soft) **5** Ran SP% **117.2**
Speed ratings: **91,85,83,82,73**
CSF £2.37 TOTE £1.20: £1.10, £1.90; EX 2.00 Trifecta £7.20.
Owner R J H Geffen **Bred** J J & Dan Melody **Trained** Ditcheat, Somerset

FOCUS
Hurdles moved out on to fresh ground. Starts of 2m5f and 2m6f moved road crossing. There was no depth to this mares' hurdle and the result was an exact repeat of the previous week's Taunton race. The winner is on the upgrade.

4501 HIGOS MOTOR DEAL H'CAP HURDLE (10 hdls 1 omitted) 2m 6f

2:50 (2:50) (Class 4) (0-110,105) 4-Y-0+ **£3,249** (£954; £477; £238)

Form RPR

053- **1** **Thedeboftheyear**[17] 4176 10-10-8 87 ....(p) JamesDavies 89
(Chris Down) *mde all: rdn after 3 out: drifted rt run-in: kpt on gamely: a holding on* **6/1**

P/P- **2** *1¼* **Mobaasher (USA)**[24] 11-11-5 103 .... MissLucyGardner[(5)] 104
(Patricia Shaw) *trckd wnr tl rdn after 3 out: wnt lft next: sn chsng wnr: styd on fr last but nvr quite getting there* **20/1**

4- **3** *1½* **Minella Gathering (IRE)**[19] 4132 5-11-2 95 .... TomO'Brien 95
(Paul Henderson) *trckd ldrs tl dropped to 6th at the 7th: sn u.p 3 out: stdy hdwy between last 2: wnt 3rd run-in: styd on* **7/2**[3]

4/5- **4** *1½* **Mystic Appeal (IRE)**[17] 4172 8-11-9 105 ....(p) MattGriffiths[(3)] 103
(Jeremy Scott) *in tch: nudged along at times: trckd ldrs after 5th: drvn after 3 out: styd on same pce tl no ex run-in* **3/1**[2]

463- **5** *19* **West End Classic (IRE)**[224] 1019 7-11-2 100 .... BenPoste[(5)] 83
(Tracey Watkins) *hld up in last pair: hdwy 3 out: rdn to chse wnr bef 2 out tl wknd bef last: collapsed after fin* **10/1**

50F- **P** **Prasina Russata (IRE)**[70] 3163 7-11-9 102 ....[1] TomScudamore
(David Pipe) *hld up last: looked to hang lft most of way: pushed along on stable bnd: hdwy 7th: rdn after 3 out: qckly btn: p.u bef next* **9/4**[1]

0/0- **P** **Ctappers**[7] 2510 5-11-12 105 .... RichardJohnson
(Michael Madgwick) *trckd ldrs tl wknd after 7th: t.o whn p.u bef next* **14/1**

5m 56.0s (29.50) **Going Correction** +0.825s/f (Soft) **7** Ran SP% **112.8**
Speed ratings (Par 105): **79,78,78,77,70** ,
CSF £92.27 TOTE £6.10: £2.40, £9.00; EX 89.40 Trifecta £396.40.
Owner Culm Valley Racing **Bred** Wood Farm Stud **Trained** Mutterton, Devon

FOCUS
Ordinarty form, with a couple of the key contenders failing to give their running. The winner was still a stone off last season's best.

4502 HIGOS INSURANCE SERVICES H'CAP CHASE (17 fncs) 2m 5f

3:20 (3:20) (Class 3) (0-130,124) 5-Y-0+ **£6,498** (£1,908; £954; £477)

Form RPR

P0P- **1** **Vif Argent (FR)**[60] 3362 5-11-3 117 ....(b[1]) TomScudamore 129+
(David Pipe) *cl up in 4th: chal 13th: led after 4 out: rdn whn jnd next: asserted after 2 out: kpt on wl* **9/4**[2]

/31- **2** *7* **Time To Think**[34] 3859 9-11-5 117 .... AndrewThornton 122
(Seamus Mullins) *led tl 5th: led after 8th: rdn appr 4 out: hdd sn after: rallied and ev ch 3 out tl no ex appr last* **8/1**

/3F- **3** *1* **Opera Og (IRE)**[88] 2812 8-11-5 117 .... LiamTreadwell 127+
(Venetia Williams) *trckd ldrs: cl 3rd whn slipped on landing 4 out: rcvring but u.p whn hit 3 out: styd on same pce fr next* **2/1**[1]

331/ **4** *26* **Roll The Dice (IRE)**[318] 5319 8-11-0 112 .... RichardJohnson 89
(Philip Hobbs) *j.lft at times: prom: led 5th tl after 8th: pushed along on stable bnd: prom 10th: rdn and lost pl bef 4 out: fdd fr 3 out: t.o* **3/1**[3]

315- **5** *3½* **Miss Tenacious**[62] 3294 7-11-12 124 .... JackDoyle 98
(Ron Hodges) *cl up in 5th: effrt after 4 out: fdd fr next: t.o* **10/1**

5m 43.8s (18.60) **Going Correction** +1.075s/f (Soft) **5** Ran SP% **109.3**
WFA 5 from 7yo+ 2lb
Speed ratings: **107,104,103,94,92**
CSF £17.40 TOTE £3.70: £2.30, £3.60; EX 20.70 Trifecta £51.70.
Owner Stef Stefanou **Bred** Francois Rimaud **Trained** Nicholashayne, Devon

FOCUS
A fair event. The winner was back to the level of her French form.

4503 HIGOS INSURANCE SERVICES PLATINUM NOVICES' H'CAP HURDLE (7 hdls 1 omitted) 2m

3:50 (3:50) (Class 3) (0-130,126) 4-Y-0+ **£5,523** (£1,621; £810; £405)

Form RPR

321- **1** **Keel Haul (IRE)**[18] 4157 6-11-1 115 .... DenisO'Regan 125+
(Henry Oliver) *trckd ldrs: wnt 2nd bef 3 out: rdn to cl on clr ldr bef 2 out: travelling best whn ldng between last 2: kpt on: drvn out run-in* **11/4**[3]

411- **2** *1¾* **Twoways (IRE)**[21] 4085 8-11-6 120 .... ConorO'Farrell 124
(Mark Rimell) *hld up in last: plenty to do whn nt fluent 3 out: making prog u.p but 13 l down 2 out: 3 l down last: kpt on but nvr quite rching wnr* **14/1**

622- **3** *7* **Midnight Thunder (IRE)**[41] 3746 5-10-10 110 ....(t) BrendanPowell 108+
(Colin Tizzard) *led: clr after 3 out: wnt rt 2 out: sn rdn and hdd: lost 3rd and no ex sn after last* **6/4**[1]

412- **4** *6* **Easily Pleased (IRE)**[138] 1857 8-11-1 115 .... HaddenFrost 105
(Martin Hill) *hld up: hdwy u.p after 3 out: wnt hld 3rd bef next: nvr threatened principals: kpt on same pce* **20/1**

52F- **5** *14* **Fascino Rustico**[11] 4281 6-11-12 126 ....(t) DarylJacob 102
(Paul Nicholls) *hld up: hdwy fr 4th: disp 2nd after 3 out: sn rdn: wknd tamely bef next: t.o* **9/4**[2]

3U5- **6** *7* **Benbecula**[11] 4281 5-10-13 113 .... DaveCrosse 86
(Richard Mitchell) *j.rt at times: trckd ldr tl bef 3 out: wknd bef next: t.o* **25/1**

3m 59.2s (10.30) **Going Correction** +0.825s/f (Soft) **6** Ran SP% **112.7**
Speed ratings (Par 107): **107,106,102,99,92 89**
CSF £34.09 TOTE £3.50: £1.70, £4.40; EX 25.50 Trifecta £51.70.
Owner R G Whitehead **Bred** Aaron Stronge **Trained** Broomhall, Worcs

FOCUS
Run at a decent gallop, the runners were soon quite well strung out. The winner is still on the upgrade.

4504 HIGOS FOR YOUR HOME INSURANCE H'CAP HURDLE (8 hdls) 2m

4:20 (4:22) (Class 5) (0-100,100) 4-Y-0+ **£1,949** (£572; £286; £143)

Form RPR

005- **1** **Be Bop Boru (IRE)**[39] 3783 7-10-10 84 .... RichardJohnson 101+
(Tim Vaughan) *hld up towards rr: hdwy after 4th: tk narrow advantage gng to 2 out: 2 l clr last: pushed out* **3/1**[2]

/01- **2** *4½* **Dorry K (IRE)**[5] 4398 5-10-6 80 .... TomScudamore 88
(Jim Best) *trckd ldrs: chal 3 out: rdn and ev ch 2 out: hld whn wnt lft last: kpt on same pce* **2/1**[1]

/00- **3** *2* **Businessmoney Judi**[10] 4301 8-11-4 99 ....(tp) MrMatthewHampton[(7)] 104
(Keiran Burke) *led: hit 4th: rdn and hdd appr 2 out: styd on same pce* **66/1**

400- **4** *1* **Karl Marx (IRE)**[39] 3788 4-9-10 86 ....(b[1]) ThomasCheesman[(7)] 81
(Mark Gillard) *trckd ldrs: rdn after 3 out: styd on same pce fr next* **33/1**

P33- **5** *4½* **Just Spot**[17] 4172 7-11-2 100 .... JonPark[(10)] 100
(Kevin Bishop) *hld up: rdn after 3 out: no imp tl styd on appr last: nvr trbld ldrs* **12/1**

600- **6** *1* **Un Bleu A L'Aam (FR)**[41] 3747 6-11-8 96 .... JackDoyle 95
(Victor Dartnall) *mid-div: hdwy after 4th: rdn after 3 out: styd on same pce fr next* **7/1**

440- **7** *2¾* **Take The Crown**[184] 1400 5-10-5 79 .... DenisO'Regan 76
(Henry Oliver) *trckd ldrs: hit 4th: rdn after 3 out: fdd between last 2* **7/1**

66F- **8** *14* **Gizzit (IRE)**[76] 3048 8-11-4 92 ....(p) AndrewThornton 78
(Karen George) *hld up bhd: hit 4th: rdn after 3 out: wknd next* **25/1**

644- **9** *21* **Flashy Star**[114] 2271 5-11-0 88 .... TomO'Brien 49
(Paul Henderson) *hmpd 2 out: a towards rr: t.o* **20/1**

264- **F** **Wise Hawk**[58] 3426 9-10-5 82 .... JamesBest[(3)]
(Jackie Du Plessis) *racd keenly: trckd ldrs: rdn after 3 out: wkng whn fell heavily next* **6/1**[3]

3P0/ **P** **Generous Bob**[793] 3324 7-10-12 89 .... WayneKavanagh[(3)]
(Seamus Mullins) *mid-div tl 3rd: sn struggling towards rr: wknd after 3 out: hmpd next: p.u bef last* **66/1**

4m 5.6s (16.70) **Going Correction** +0.825s/f (Soft)
WFA 4 from 5yo+ 9lb **11** Ran SP% **119.8**
Speed ratings (Par 103): **91,88,87,87,85 84,83,76,65,**
CSF £9.46 CT £321.30 TOTE £3.50: £1.10, £2.00, £10.10; EX 13.60 Trifecta £441.30.
Owner The Oak Syndicate **Bred** Robert McCarthy **Trained** Aberthin, Vale of Glamorgan

FOCUS
The two at the head of the market both appealed as well handicapped and duly dominated the closing stages. The winner should still be well in when reassessed.

4505 DICK AND SUE WOODHOUSE MEMORIAL OPEN HUNTERS' CHASE (FOR THE DICK WOODHOUSE TROPHY) (17 fncs) 2m 5f

4:50 (4:51) (Class 6) 5-Y-0+ **£935** (£290; £145; £72)

Form RPR

4/0- **1** **Double Bank (IRE)**[24] 11-11-7 0 .... MrMWoodward[(7)] 105+
(Ms Emma Oliver) *nt fluent: led 2nd tl 6th: led 12th: in command fr after 3 out: styd on wl* **6/4**[1]

/03- **2** *6* **Picaroon**[9] 4326 10-11-11 125 .... MrsAlexDunn[(3)] 102+
(Alexandra Dunn) *racd keenly: trckd ldrs: led appr 6th where mstke: stmbld 11th: sn hdd: chsd wnr: mstke 4 out: styd on same pce fr next* **9/4**[2]

044- **3** *2¾* **Latest Trend (IRE)**[32] 8-11-9 105 .... MissBAndrews[(5)] 96
(S Penny) *hld up bhd ldrs: disp 4th fr 8th: rdn after 4 out: wnt 3rd 2 out: styd on same pce* **3/1**[3]

4/P- **4** *5* **Restezen D'Armor (FR)**[45] 9-11-7 115 ....(p) MrRobertHawker[(7)] 93
(Mrs O C Jackson) *led tl 2nd: chsd ldrs: rdn after 4 out: 3rd and hld whn mstke 3 out: lost 3rd next: one pce after* **14/1**

006/ **5** *36* **Checkerboard (IRE)**[87] 11-12-0 113 ....(p) MrJoshuaGuerriero 66
(Mrs Kayley Woollacott) *trckd ldrs: reminders after 10th: rdn bef 4 out: nvr threatened: wknd 3 out: t.o* **12/1**

5m 53.8s (28.60) **Going Correction** +1.075s/f (Soft) **5** Ran SP% **110.1**
Speed ratings: **88,85,84,82,69**
CSF £5.46 TOTE £2.30: £1.60, £1.40; EX 5.90 Trifecta £11.90.
Owner J D Cole **Bred** Sean Hourigan **Trained** Lower Ashton, Devon

FOCUS
A steadily run hunters' chase and the field bunched up rounding for home. The winner is rated to the level of his old hurdle form but this is not a race to be confident about.

T/Plt: £160.20 to a £1 stake. Pool of £62520.97 - 284.75 winning tickets. T/Qpdt: £19.70 to a £1 stake. Pool of £4865.91 - 182.49 winning tickets. TM

4350 LUDLOW (R-H)

Thursday, February 27

OFFICIAL GOING: Soft (6.4)

Hurdle behind golf clubhouse omitted all races.

Wind: moderate across Weather: sunny spells

4506 BET LIVE AT CORBETTSPORTS.COM "NATIONAL HUNT" NOVICES' HURDLE (8 hdls 1 omitted) 2m

2:00 (2:00) (Class 4) 4-Y-0+ **£3,898** (£1,144; £572; £286)

Form RPR

4/4- **1** **Kings Bandit (IRE)**69 3194 6-11-2 0 JasonMaguire 123+
(Donald McCain) *t.k.h: mde all: pushed along 3 out: rdn after next: drawing clr whn hit last: r.o wl* **3/1**2

526- **2** *8* **Simply A Legend**27 4019 5-11-2 119 RobertThornton 111
(Alan King) *t.k.h: trckd ldrs: hdwy to chse wnr 4th: rdn appr 3 out: j. sltly rt 2 out: sn one pce: hld whn j.rt last* **11/10**1

0/4- **3** *½* **Troyan (IRE)**81 2981 7-11-2 0 CharliePoste 111
(Robin Dickin) *trckd wnr to 3rd: styd prom: chsng ldng pair whn rdn appr 3 out: kpt on same pce* **17/2**

/04- **4** *27* **Wing Mira (IRE)**89 2806 6-11-2 0 LiamTreadwell 87
(Venetia Williams) *towards rr: hdwy 5th: sn outpcd and no ch w 1st 3 but kpt on steadily* **16/1**

40/ **5** *12* **Herecomesthehollow (IRE)**765 3897 8-11-2 0 SamTwiston-Davies 72
(Nigel Twiston-Davies) *prom: trckd wnr 3rd to 4th: rdn next: sn wknd* **5/1**3

400- **6** *2* **Ronnie Rockcake**11 4296 4-10-7 0 DavidBass 61
(Ben Pauling) *a towards rr: lost tch after 5th* **66/1**

50- **7** *29* **Silent Knight (IRE)**39 3796 5-11-2 0 NoelFehily 41
(Warren Greatrex) *in tch: niggled along after slow jump 4th: wknd after next: t.o* **14/1**

006- **8** *7* **Carpies Boy**42 3746 5-10-6 0 (t) WilliamFeatherstone(10) 34
(Warren Greatrex) *a towards rr: lost tch after 5th: t.o* **150/1**

P0/ **P** **Bit Of A Scruff (IRE)**736 4450 7-11-2 0 JackDoyle
(Hilary Parrott) *t.k.h early: hld up in rr: hdwy 5th: sn wknd: t.o whn p.u bef 3 out* **150/1**

4m 2.2s (12.70) **Going Correction** +0.825s/f (Soft)
WFA 4 from 5yo+ 9lb **9** Ran SP% **115.2**
Speed ratings (Par 105): **101,97,96,83,77 76,61,58,**
CSF £6.92 TOTE £3.00: £2.10, £1.10, £1.60; EX 7.70 Trifecta £33.60.
Owner Mrs Diana L Whateley **Bred** Rathbarry Stud **Trained** Cholmondeley, Cheshire

FOCUS
Hurdles moved to outside of track for fresh ground. A modest novice hurdle but the easy winner could be decent. The form is rated through the second.

4507 BET ON YOUR MOBILE AT CORBETTSPORTS.COM NOVICES' LIMITED H'CAP CHASE (17 fncs) 2m 4f

2:30 (2:30) (Class 3) (0-140,130) 5-Y-0+ **£7,985** (£2,410; £1,241; £658)

Form RPR

6/2- **1** **Benbens (IRE)**71 3155 9-10-12 120 SamTwiston-Davies 137+
(Nigel Twiston-Davies) *mde all: reluctant briefly paddock bnd after 9th: rdn appr 4 out: styd on strly to draw clr fr next where nt fluent: in command whn hit last: eased flat* **5/6**1

111- **2** *9* **Cloudy Joker (IRE)**36 3833 6-11-6 128 JasonMaguire 132
(Donald McCain) *racd in 3rd tl trckd wnr 9th: 3 l down and niggled along whn blnd 4 out: hld by wnr fr next* **3/1**2

14F- **3** *34* **Zarzal (IRE)**42 3732 6-11-8 130 AdamWedge 104
(Evan Williams) *hld up in rr: blnd bdly 3rd: struggling 12th: wnt mod 3rd next: t.o* **6/1**3

02P- **4** *54* **Avoca Promise (IRE)**45 3690 9-11-0 122 FelixDeGiles 36
(Tom Symonds) *trckd ldr to 9th: carried lft bnd sn after: drvn along fr 10th: relegated to last 13th: virtually p.u flat: t.o* **7/1**

P35- **U** **Midnight Choice**91 2766 9-9-12 111 oh37 BenPoste(5)
(James Evans) *last whn stmbld and uns rdr 1st* **66/1**

5m 21.1s (16.70) **Going Correction** +0.925s/f (Soft) **5** Ran SP% **107.8**
Speed ratings: **103,99,85,64,**
CSF £3.73 TOTE £1.70: £1.10, £1.60; EX 3.10 Trifecta £16.00.
Owner Mrs S Such **Bred** Patrick Collins **Trained** Naunton, Gloucs

FOCUS
A fair novice handicap run at an honest pace, with the market leaders in control a long way from home. A step up from the winner with a personal best from the runner-up in defeat.

4508 FOLLOW @CORBETTSPORTS ON TWITTER MARES' H'CAP HURDLE (10 hdls 2 omitted) 3m

3:00 (3:00) (Class 3) (0-125,117) 4-Y-0+ **£5,848** (£1,717; £858; £429)

Form RPR

153- **1** **Midnight Cataria**71 3159 5-11-10 113 WayneHutchinson 117+
(Alan King) *hld up in tch: clsd 7th: chal 3 out: led next: drvn clr flat* **20/1**

413- **2** *5* **Dardanella**50 3604 7-11-8 111 JamieMoore 110
(Richard Lee) *in tch: wnt 2nd after 7th: chal 2 out: ev ch whn hit last: no ex flat* **20/1**

4/3- **3** *nk* **Annimation (IRE)**42 3731 10-10-4 100 (v) MissJodieHughes(7) 100
(Lucy Jones) *disp ld tl def advantage 7th: drvn appr 3 out: hdd and nt fluent 2 out: kpt on flat* **33/1**

115- **4** *1 ½* **Mini Muck**42 3731 8-11-12 115 SamTwiston-Davies 113
(Nigel Twiston-Davies) *towards rr: hdwy 7th: chsng ldrs whn n.m.r appr 3 out: rdn next: kpt on same pce* **14/1**

013- **5** *15* **Molly's A Diva**12 4276 7-11-12 115 (p) JasonMaguire 97
(Kim Bailey) *in rr: hdwy 7th: sn rdn along: hung lft and wknd 3 out* **11/2**2

100- **6** *2* **Upbeat Cobbler (FR)**59 3413 6-11-2 105 RichardJohnson 85
(Henry Daly) *chsd ldrs tl rdn and wknd appr 3 out* **6/1**3

P31- **7** *10* **Still Believing (IRE)**8 4351 6-11-7 117 7ex ConorRing(7) 87
(Evan Williams) *hld up towards rr: hdwy 6th: struggling next: lost tch 3 out: t.o* **7/1**

P/P- **P** **Valrene**19 4157 8-11-4 107 CharliePoste
(Robin Dickin) *in rr: hit 4th and 5th: wknd 7th: t.o whn p.u bef 3 out* **25/1**

/23- **P** **Silver Wren**24 4070 7-11-6 109 SamJones
(Renee Robeson) *disp ld to 7th: sn rdn and wknd: bhd whn p.u bef 3 out: fatally injured* **15/2**

114/ **P** **Dancingtilmidnight**432 3183 7-11-11 114 (t) NoelFehily
(Harry Fry) *chsd ldrs: rdn after 7th: wknd qckly: p.u bef 3 out* **13/8**1

6m 14.3s (22.00) **Going Correction** +0.825s/f (Soft) **10** Ran SP% **115.0**
Speed ratings (Par 107): **96,94,94,93,88 88,84, , ,**
CSF £318.00 CT £12348.30 TOTE £19.40: £5.20, £6.10, £10.90; EX 176.40 Trifecta £1026.60 Part won..
Owner Mrs K Holmes **Bred** Pitchall Stud **Trained** Barbury Castle, Wilts

FOCUS
An ordinary mares' handicap, rated around the third and fourth.

4509 FORBRA GOLD CUP (HANDICAP CHASE) (19 fncs) 3m

3:30 (3:32) (Class 3) (0-140,135) 5-Y-0+ **£12,660** (£3,740; £1,870; £936; £468)

Form RPR

042- **1** **Firebird Flyer (IRE)**26 4026 7-10-12 121 AdamWedge 134
(Evan Williams) *in tch: hdwy 11th: mstke next: chal 2 out: sn led: styd on wl* **7/2**2

U0F- **2** *2 ¼* **Forgotten Gold (IRE)**28 3990 8-11-12 135 PaddyBrennan 145
(Tom George) *cl up: led narrowly 9th: rdn 2 out: sn hdd: one pce* **8/1**

2/P- **3** *2 ¼* **Roalco De Farges (FR)**26 4035 9-11-5 128 RichardJohnson 135
(Philip Hobbs) *in tch: clsd 11th: wnt 2nd 4 out: rdn 2 out: kpt on same pce* **10/3**1

123/ **4** *27* **Brass Tax (IRE)**412 3597 8-11-12 135 APMcCoy 117
(Ben Case) *led: mstke 5th: hdd 9th: styd cl up: rdn appr 4 out: wknd 3 out* **5/1**3

506- **5** *6* **Ballyoliver**44 3698 10-11-1 124 LiamTreadwell 98
(Venetia Williams) *chsd ldrs: reminder 10th: rdn along fr next: wknd 15th: t.o* **13/2**

324- **6** *1 ¼* **Rouge Et Blanc (FR)**19 4160 9-11-0 128 ThomasGarner(5) 101
(Oliver Sherwood) *hld up towards rr: hdwy 12th: rdn and wknd appr 4 out: t.o* **10/1**

233- **P** **Cootehill (IRE)**22 4089 10-11-5 128 SamTwiston-Davies
(Nigel Twiston-Davies) *towards rr: wkng whn hit 15th: t.o whn p.u bef 2 out: collapsed fatally* **16/1**

220- **P** **Lamboro Lad (IRE)**110 2373 9-10-13 122 (tp) JamieMoore
(Peter Bowen) *chsd ldrs: losing pl whn mstke 13th: wknd 15th: t.o whn p.u bef 2 out* **8/1**

6m 24.7s (16.40) **Going Correction** +0.925s/f (Soft) **8** Ran SP% **112.5**
Speed ratings: **109,108,107,98,96 96, ,**
CSF £29.89 CT £99.07 TOTE £3.10: £1.10, £4.40, £2.30; EX 27.40 Trifecta £237.20.
Owner R E R Williams **Bred** Paul McWilliams **Trained** Llancarfan, Vale Of Glamorgan

FOCUS
A fair staying handicap. A small step up from the in-form winner with the second rated back to his best.

4510 £25 FREE BET AT CORBETTSPORTS.COM "NATIONAL HUNT" NOVICES' H'CAP HURDLE (10 hdls 1 omitted) 2m 5f

4:00 (4:00) (Class 3) (0-130,128) 4-Y-0+ **£6,498** (£1,908; £954; £477)

Form RPR

425- **1** **Spencer Lea**47 3643 6-10-7 109 RichardJohnson 119+
(Andrew Price) *hld up in rr: hdwy 6th: chal 2 out: sn led: hit last: styd on wl to draw clr flat* **7/2**2

103- **2** *11* **Big Casino**63 3263 8-11-9 125 SamTwiston-Davies 125
(Nigel Twiston-Davies) *led: nt fluent 4th: jnd 2 out: sn hdd: no ex flat* **5/2**1

524- **3** *10* **Sealous Scout (IRE)**49 3614 6-10-8 110 JasonMaguire 101
(Donald McCain) *prom tl drvn and lost pl after 7th: sn no ch w ldrs: pushed along to pass two tired rivals flat* **15/2**

622- **4** *2 ¾* **Bhakti (IRE)**62 3326 7-11-2 118 ConorO'Farrell 103
(Mark Rimell) *chsd ldrs: hit 7th: sn wnt 2nd: rdn and wknd 3 out: lost modest 3rd flat* **11/2**3

005- **5** *3* **Expanding Universe (IRE)**42 3740 7-10-1 108 ow2 JoshHamer(5) 91
(Tony Carroll) *cl up: mstke 6th: rdn and wknd after next: lost poor 4th flat* **15/2**

1P4- **6** *67* **Garrahalish (IRE)**12 4266 6-11-12 128 CharliePoste 43
(Robin Dickin) *in tch tl rdn and wknd 7th: t.o* **9/1**

534- **P** **Ballygrooby Bertie (IRE)**11 4302 6-10-12 114 (t) PaddyBrennan
(Fergal O'Brien) *a in rr: wknd 7th: t.o whn p.u bef 3 out* **8/1**

5m 30.5s (15.70) **Going Correction** +0.825s/f (Soft) **7** Ran SP% **110.8**
Speed ratings (Par 107): **103,98,95,93,92 67,**
CSF £12.20 TOTE £4.10: £2.20, £1.70; EX 13.60 Trifecta £67.70.
Owner Mrs Carol Davis **Bred** Mrs C Davis **Trained** Leominster, H'fords

FOCUS
A modest novice handicap. This rates a step up from the winner.

4511 CGA FOXHUNTER (AN OPEN HUNTERS' CHASE) (FOR THE CHASE MEREDITH MEMORIAL TROPHY) (19 fncs) 3m

4:30 (4:30) (Class 5) 6-Y-0+ **£2,560** (£838; £451)

Form RPR

0/5- **1** **Qrackers (FR)**60 10-11-7 99 (t) MissHannahWatson(3) 130+
(Miss V Collins) *j.w: prom: trckd ldr 5th tl led 13th: drew wl clr fr 15th: brushed through last: v easily* **9/2**3

545/ **2** *34* **Island Life (IRE)**25 11-11-11 123 (p) MrWTelfer(7) 98
(S Flook) *trckd ldr to 5th: styd prom tl wknd 15th: plugged on to take remote 2nd flat* **11/2**

/35- **3** *5* **Chief Heckler (IRE)**14 4246 8-11-10 93 MrMWall 87
(Philip Rowley) *t.k.h: led to 13th: nt fluent 15th: sn no ch w wnr: tired whn mstke last: lost remote 2nd flat* **3/1**2

4/0- **P** **Noble Ben (IRE)**33 12-11-5 101 MrJMRidley(5)
(Mrs H S M Ridley) *hld up in rr: clsd 10th: chsd ldng pair 14th: rdn and wknd appr 4 out: lost poor 3rd whn mstke 2 out: sn p.u* **9/1**

/ **P** **Lord Bellamy (IRE)**33 12-11-3 0 MrMWilesmith(7)
(Martin Wilesmith) *in tch tl steadily lost pl fr 7th: wl bhd whn p.u bef 12th* **66/1**

1/0- **P** **Lorikarad (FR)**11 10-11-13 116 (p) MrLRPayter(5)
(Miss C C Jones) *nt fluent: a bhd: lost tch 11th: t.o whn p.u after 15th* **5/2**1

615- **P** **Bay To Go (IRE)**33 8-11-7 110 MrSDavies-Thomas(7)
(Mrs H M Kemp) *in tch: mstke 12th: wknd 14th: wl bhd whn p.u bef 4 out* **8/1**

6m 29.3s (21.00) **Going Correction** +0.925s/f (Soft) **7** Ran SP% **109.7**
Speed ratings: **102,90,89, , ,**
CSF £26.66 TOTE £7.40: £2.70, £3.60; EX 19.30 Trifecta £134.60.
Owner Miss Sarah A Dawson **Bred** Eric Becq **Trained** Basingstoke, Hants

The Form Book Jumps, Raceform Ltd, Compton, RG20 6NL.

FOCUS
They went a sound gallop for this weak hunters' chase. The impressive winner is rated back to his best.

4512 FOLLOW @BETTINGBARON AT CORBETT SPORTS CONDITIONAL JOCKEYS' H'CAP HURDLE (9 hdls) 2m
5:00 (5:00) (Class 4) (0-120,116) 4-Y-0+ **£3,898** (£1,144; £572; £286)

Form RPR
453- **1** **Pure Science (IRE)**[26] 4024 6-11-6 116 RyanHatch(6) 127
(Nigel Twiston-Davies) *cl up: drvn to ld appr 3 out: sn jnd by rival: asserted u.p and edgd lft flat* **1/1**[1]
312- **2** 2 **Lac Sacre (FR)**[27] 3756 5-11-5 112 (tp) JoshHamer(3) 121
(Tony Carroll) *hld up last but wl in tch: clsd after 5th: chal gng wl 3 out: rdn flat: nt qckn* **7/1**
600- **3** 13 **The Pier (IRE)**[19] 4157 8-11-9 113 (t) NicodeBoinville 109
(Anna Brooks) *t.k.h: trckd ldrs: relegated to last 4th but stl wl in tch: chsd ldng pair appr 3 out: wknd after 2 out* **6/1**[3]
223- **4** 1 1/4 **Santo Thomas (FR)**[20] 4129 8-10-12 105 CallumWhillans(3) 101
(Venetia Williams) *in tch: rdn after 5th: wknd 3 out: hit 2 out and last* **10/3**[2]
3/0- **5** 14 **Dovils Date**[88] 2848 5-11-9 116 MichaelByrne(3) 99
(Tim Vaughan) *led tl hdd appr 3 out: sn wknd* **12/1**

4m 0.7s (11.20) **Going Correction** +0.825s/f (Soft) **5** Ran SP% **107.6**
Speed ratings (Par 105): **105,104,97,96,89**
CSF £7.72 TOTE £1.70: £1.30, £2.20; EX 8.30 Trifecta £26.20.
Owner H R Mould **Bred** Castlemartin Stud And Skymarc Farm **Trained** Naunton, Gloucs

FOCUS
This handicap, confined to conditional riders, was run at a steady pace. The form is rated around the second.
T/Plt: £151.90 to a £1 stake. Pool: £67,915.29 - 326.36 winning units. T/Qpdt: £90.30 to a £1 stake. Pool: £3327.45 - 27.26 winning units. RL

4330 TAUNTON (R-H)
Thursday, February 27

OFFICIAL GOING: Heavy
The middle hurdle and middle two fences in the back straight were omitted due to the state of the ground.
Wind: strong across Weather: heavy showers

4513 RURAL LIVING SHOW 12TH APRIL (S) HURDLE (8 hdls 2 omitted) 2m 3f 110y
2:10 (2:10) (Class 5) 4-Y-0+ **£2,737** (£798; £399)

Form RPR
112- **1** **Stow**[51] 3593 9-11-5 125 (p) JoshWall(7) 118
(Michael Blake) *mde all: clr 5th tl 3 out: pushed clr again bef next: kpt on wl: rdn out* **1/1**[1]
6P1- **2** 3 1/4 **Arrayan**[22] 4087 9-11-12 123 (b) NickScholfield 114
(Alexandra Dunn) *w wnr most of way: rdn appr 2 out and sn hld: kpt on same pce* **7/4**[2]
6- **3** 13 **Fruity Bun**[15] 3641 4-9-9 0 (t) JamesBanks(5) 75
(Keiran Burke) *hld up 4th: wnt 3rd after 5th: rdn in 6 l 3rd after 3 out: wl hld whn nt fluent next* **66/1**
F00- **4** 1 1/4 **Sedgemoor Top Bid (IRE)**[18] 4172 6-11-3 90 (p) TomScudamore 91
(Nigel Hawke) *trckd ldrs: rdn after 3 out: sn btn* **25/1**
F22- **P** **Sir Dylan**[60] 1525 5-10-10 100 ChrisDavies(7)
(Ronald Harris) *hld up in last pair: rdn after 4th: sn t.o: p.u bef 3 out* **10/1**[3]
/5U- **P** **Vineman**[6] 4397 7-11-3 0 SeanQuinlan
(David Bridgwater) *detached in last: nudged along fr 4th: sme prog after 5th: wknd bef 3 out: t.o whn p.u sn after* **14/1**

5m 15.9s (29.90) **Going Correction** +1.375s/f (Heavy)
WFA 4 from 5yo+ 9lb **6** Ran SP% **107.5**
Speed ratings (Par 103): **95,93,88,88,**
CSF £2.76 TOTE £2.00: £1.60, £1.10; EX 3.60 Trifecta £28.00.There was no bid for the winner.
Owner Mrs J M Haines **Bred** Plantation Stud **Trained** Trowbridge, Wilts

FOCUS
Essentially a match and straightforward form. The first two are rated 10lb off.

4514 ELIZABETH WATERS BIRTHDAY NOVICES' HURDLE (8 hdls 2 omitted) 2m 3f 110y
2:40 (2:40) (Class 4) 4-Y-0+ **£3,593** (£1,047; £523)

Form RPR
2- **1** **Fayette County (IRE)**[126] 2030 7-11-3 0 DougieCostello 124+
(Tim Vaughan) *t.k.h: trckd ldrs: wnt 2nd after 5th: led appr 2 out: kpt on wl to assert fr last: rdn out* **11/8**[1]
4- **2** 2 3/4 **Vicente (FR)**[123] 2109 5-11-3 0 [1] DarylJacob 118+
(Paul Nicholls) *in tch: tk clsr order 3 out: chal gng to 2 out: ev ch whn rdn between last 2: hld sn after last: kpt on* **2/1**[2]
25- **3** 10 **Great Choice (IRE)**[32] 3920 5-11-3 0 (t) TomScudamore 110
(David Pipe) *hld up: hdwy after 5th: trckd ldng pair appr 2 out: sn rdn: kpt on same pce* **4/1**[3]
00- **4** 27 **Tresor De La Vie (FR)**[18] 4171 7-11-0 0 (p) GilesHawkins(3) 81
(Victor Dartnall) *led at stdy pce: rdn and hdd appr 2 out: sn wknd: t.o* **25/1**
06- **5** 3 **Dream Lucky**[18] 4175 9-11-0 0 MattGriffiths(3) 78
(Richard Woollacott) *trckd ldrs tl after 5th: rdn and wknd after 3 out: t.o* **66/1**
055- **6** 2 **Silvergrove**[18] 4171 6-11-3 0 (t) PaulMoloney 76
(Richard Woollacott) *trckd ldrs: rdn after 3 out: sn wknd: t.o* **10/1**
/P0- **7** 15 **Le Pergolese (FR)**[30] 3956 8-10-10 0 (t[1]) MrRobertHawker(7) 61
(Nigel Hawke) *a towards rr: t.o after 3 out* **100/1**
366- **8** 15 **Y A Bon (IRE)**[18] 4171 6-11-3 0 HaddenFrost 46
(Martin Hill) *losing tch whn nt fluent 4th: a bhd: t.o* **33/1**
/60- **9** 4 **Brogeen Boy (IRE)**[44] 3695 6-11-3 0 (p) TomO'Brien 42
(Alan Jones) *a towards rr: t.o after 3 out* **100/1**
\- **F** **Billeragh Milan (IRE)**[297] 7-11-3 0 SeanQuinlan
(David Bridgwater) *in tch whn fell 3rd* **33/1**

5m 16.9s (30.90) **Going Correction** +1.375s/f (Heavy) **10** Ran SP% **117.7**
Speed ratings (Par 105): **93,91,87,77,75 75,69,63,61,**
CSF £4.37 TOTE £2.60: £1.30, £1.10, £1.30; EX 7.20 Trifecta £8.80.
Owner John P McManus **Bred** T G Mooney **Trained** Aberthin, Vale of Glamorgan

FOCUS
This went to script. The winner built on his Carlisle run.

4515 ROYAL BATH & WEST NOVICES' LIMITED H'CAP CHASE (9 fncs 3 omitted) 2m 110y
3:10 (3:11) (Class 3) (0-140,138) 5-Y-0+ **£6,498** (£1,908; £954; £477)

Form RPR
652- **1** **Sound Investment (IRE)**[40] 3787 6-10-9 125 (t) DarylJacob 145+
(Paul Nicholls) *j.w: trckd ldr: led after 1st tl bef 4th: chal 4 out: led 3 out: sn clr: easily* **11/8**[1]
111- **2** 23 **Massena (IRE)**[9] 4341 7-11-4 134 7ex AidanColeman 134+
(Venetia Williams) *led: slow 1st and hdd: prom: led bef 4th: jnd 4 out: sn rdn: nt fluent and hdd next: wknd 2 out* **11/4**[2]
214- **3** 15 **Lord Of House (GER)**[19] 4159 6-11-5 138 (t) GavinSheehan(3) 118
(Charlie Mann) *chsd ldrs: wnt 3rd after 4th: rdn bef next: dropped to 4th and no ch after 4 out: regained modest 3rd after 2 out* **11/2**
5- **4** 2 **Itsuptoyou (IRE)**[40] 3787 10-9-12 119 oh12 KieronEdgar(5) 97
(Arthur Whiting) *hld up bhd ldrs: wnt 4th after 4th: rdn into 3rd after 4 out but sn no ch w ldng pair: lost modest 3rd after 2 out* **33/1**
512- **P** **Tornado In Milan (IRE)**[9] 4333 8-10-6 122 PaulMoloney
(Evan Williams) *chsd ldr: hit 3rd and 4th: sn struggling: losing tch whn p.u bef 4 out* **3/1**[3]

4m 23.1s (9.10) **Going Correction** +0.80s/f (Soft) **5** Ran SP% **112.1**
Speed ratings: **110,99,92,91,**
CSF £5.91 TOTE £2.50: £1.30, £2.20; EX 5.10 Trifecta £16.30.
Owner Andrea & Graham Wylie **Bred** Mrs Jacinta McGeough **Trained** Ditcheat, Somerset

FOCUS
Not a bad little novice handicap and a big step up from the impressive winner.

4516 MICRON BIO-SYSTEMS NOVICES' H'CAP HURDLE (10 hdls 2 omitted) 3m 110y
3:40 (3:40) (Class 4) (0-115,115) 4-Y-0+ **£3,593** (£1,047; £523)

Form RPR
0F5- **1** **Veauce De Sivola (FR)**[28] 3989 5-11-8 111 (t) DarylJacob 125+
(Nick Williams) *travelled wl in last: tk clsr order after 7th: short of room whn mounting chal on bnd bef 2 out: sn upsides: led last: rdn clr run-in* **11/4**[3]
621- **2** 3 1/4 **Comical Red**[9] 4330 6-9-7 89 7ex (b) ThomasCheesman(7) 97
(Mark Gillard) *trckd ldrs: led appr 3 out: rdn whn hrd pressed bef next: kpt on gamely: hdd last: sn no ex* **15/8**[1]
542- **3** 12 **Smiles For Miles (IRE)**[20] 4132 6-11-8 111 (t) TomScudamore 108
(David Pipe) *trckd ldrs: chal after 3 out: rdn appr 2 out: sn hld* **9/4**[2]
/0F- **4** 9 **Upham Atom**[84] 2909 11-11-7 115 (p) KieronEdgar(5) 102
(Kate Buckett) *led tl rdn appr 3 out: btn bef 2 out* **14/1**
12P- **5** 2 **Clouds Of Mist**[18] 4176 9-10-6 100 MissLucyGardner(5) 85
(Sue Gardner) *trckd ldr: pressed ldr fr 4th tl rdn after 3 out: wknd next* **12/1**

6m 49.2s (45.20) **Going Correction** +1.375s/f (Heavy) **5** Ran SP% **106.6**
Speed ratings (Par 105): **82,80,77,74,73**
CSF £7.97 TOTE £3.90: £2.10, £1.10; EX 6.30 Trifecta £21.20.
Owner Paul Duffy **Bred** Gilles Trapenard **Trained** George Nympton, Devon

FOCUS
Fair form for the class. A big step up from the winner but he can probably go on to rate higher.

4517 BATHWICK TYRES H'CAP HURDLE (8 hdls 2 omitted) 2m 3f 110y
4:10 (4:10) (Class 3) (0-140,136) 4-Y-0+ **£5,523** (£1,621; £810; £405)

Form RPR
231- **1** **Ceasar Milan (IRE)**[9] 4332 6-10-11 124 7ex (t) HarryDerham(3) 131+
(Paul Nicholls) *trckd ldrs: chal after 3 out: surrendered narrow advantage whn nt fluent 2 out: sn drvn: led fnl 120yds: hld on: all out* **4/6**[1]
062- **2** nk **Somemothersdohavem**[5] 4413 5-10-8 118 AidanColeman 123+
(Venetia Williams) *trckd ldrs: led 3 out: briefly hdd 2 out: sn drvn in narrow advantage: hdd fnl 120yds: remained w ev ch but leaning on wnr: hld nring fin* **11/4**[2]
015- **3** 24 **Lamps**[12] 4277 7-11-6 130 (v[1]) PaulMoloney 115
(Michael Blake) *reluctant to line up: little slowly away: sn pressing ldr: pushed along and kpt wd appr 3 out: rdn sn after: outpcd bef next: wknd bef last* **20/1**
1PP- **4** 36 **Maller Tree**[26] 4027 7-11-7 136 (v) KieronEdgar(5) 81
(David Dennis) *j.lft: led: mstke 2nd: pushed along after 5th: rdn and hdd 3 out: sn wknd: t.o* **28/1**
0F0- **P** **Recession Proof (FR)**[19] 4147 8-11-3 130 (b) JakeGreenall(3)
(John Quinn) *hld up bhd ldrs: nt fluent 5th: sn nudged along: rdn after 3 out: wknd qckly: t.o whn p.u bef last* **7/1**[3]

5m 8.7s (22.70) **Going Correction** +0.80s/f (Soft) **5** Ran SP% **107.4**
Speed ratings (Par 107): **109,108,99,84,**
CSF £2.83 TOTE £1.80: £1.10, £1.30; EX 3.80 Trifecta £10.40.
Owner The Stewart & Wylie Families **Bred** Pat O'Donovan **Trained** Ditcheat, Somerset
■ Stewards' Enquiry : Aidan Coleman one-day ban: careless riding (15 Mar)

FOCUS
The two market leaders dominated off the home turn. The winner built on his recent facile win and probably took another step up to beat a well-in and in-form rival.

4518 CGA FOXHUNTER (HUNTERS' CHASE) (FOR THE RICHARD WILLIAMS MEMORIAL TROPHY) (13 fncs 4 omitted) 2m 7f 110y
4:40 (4:40) (Class 6) 6-Y-0+ **£1,975** (£607; £303)

Form RPR
/F2- **1** **Martys Mission (IRE)**[8] 4355 12-12-1 109 MrDavidPrichard(3) 108+
(Miss Becky Furber) *j.w: cl up: rdn to ld appr 3 out: idled fnl 120yds: drvn out* **11/8**[1]
263/ **2** 1 1/2 **Swansbrook (IRE)**[25] 11-11-9 112 MrMLegg(5) 98
(Mrs Sue Popham) *hld up: trckd ldrs 5th: rdn afer 4 out: sn chsng wnr: kpt on whn wnr idled fnl 120yds: a being hld* **7/2**[3]
3 3/4 **Meilyr**[627] 11-11-9 0 MrMatthewHampton(5) 96
(Mrs C Lawrence) *hld up but in tch: nt fluent 8th: rdn after 4 out: styd on into 3rd 2 out: kpt on run-in* **33/1**
P06/ **4** hd **Coup Royale (FR)**[312] 5433 10-12-0 113 (t) MrWBiddick 97
(Mrs Claire Hitch) *nt fluent 1st: sn led: hit 3rd: hdd whn restrained bk to last pair after next: plenty to do after 4 out: styd on fr after 3 out: jst failed to snatch 3rd* **8/1**
02F- **5** 4 **Seigneur Des Bois (FR)**[28] 3993 8-11-13 110 (p) MrTEllis(5) 98+
(D Buckett) *trckd ldrs: prom 8th tl rdn after 4 out: styd on same pce fr next tl fdd last* **3/1**[2]

2/0- **P** **My Fella (IRE)**[39] 11-11-7 82 MrGBall(7)
(Andrew Quick) *trckd ldrs: j.lft whn ldng 4 out: sn rdn and hdd: wknd after next: p.u run-in* **33/1**

054/ **P** **Quil Est Beau (FR)**[39] 10-11-7 73 MissVWade(7)
(Mrs Jo Sleep) *cl up tl rdn after 9th: wknd bef 4 out: t.o whn p.u bef 3 out* **33/1**

4P/- **P** **Mrs Peacock (IRE)**[46] 9-11-2 0 (t) MissEKelly(5)
(N J Edwards) *trckd ldrs: led after 4th tl rdn 4 out: wknd bef next: bhd whn p.u 2 out* **14/1**

6m 55.5s (39.50) **Going Correction** +0.80s/f (Soft) **8** Ran SP% **115.9**
Speed ratings: **66,65,65,65,63** , ,
CSF £6.83 TOTE £2.50: £1.10, £1.70, £9.40; EX 6.20 Trifecta £169.20.
Owner Miss Becky Furber **Bred** Miss Sabrina Boyle **Trained** Shepton Mallet, Somerset
■ Becky Furber's first winner under rules.

FOCUS
The fair winner rates value for further in this modest hunter chase. The form is rated around the first two.

4519 SOMERSET MILITARY TATTOO 6TH SEPTEMBER H'CAP HURDLE (8 hdls 2 omitted) 2m 3f 110y
5:10 (5:10) (Class 5) (0-100,99) 4-Y-0+ **£2,737** (£798; £399)

Form RPR

2/2- **1** **The Darling Boy**[76] 3062 9-11-12 97 (tp) TomScudamore 100
(David Pipe) *kpt to inner: mde virtually all: rdn whn hrd pressed after 2 out: kpt on strly: hld on wl* **3/1**[2]

FP1- **2** *hd* **Join The Navy**[9] 4334 9-11-9 99 7ex KieronEdgar(5) 102
(Kate Buckett) *racd wd: detached in last: pushed along after 4th: smooth hdwy into 4th 3 out: rdn for str chal between last 2: kpt on strly w ev ch run-in: jst hld* **7/2**[3]

530- **3** *2 1/2* **Crackerjack**[11] 4298 7-10-13 89 JamesBanks(5) 90
(Emma Baker) *kpt to inner: t.k.h: trckd wnr: rdn and ev ch briefly appr 2 out: kpt on heels of ldng pair tl no ex fnl 75yds* **5/1**

054- **4** *18* **Moneymix**[9] 4334 7-10-3 74 (b) WillKennedy 59
(Ali Brewer) *kpt wd in bk st: prom: nt fluent 2nd: hit 5th: rdn after 3 out: wknd bef next* **11/4**[1]

160- **5** *52* **Award Winner**[116] 2253 11-11-10 95 (p) BrendanPowell 25
(Brendan Powell) *racd wd: led tl 2nd: prom: rdn after 5th: wknd next: t.o* **20/1**

225- **6** *26* **Dalrymple (IRE)**[12] 4278 8-11-5 95 (t) CharlieWallis(5)
(Nick Ayliffe) *racd wd: in tch: hit 4th: rdn bef next: wknd sn after 3 out: t.o* **11/2**

/00- **P** **Supernoverre (IRE)**[59] 3426 8-10-13 84 (p) TomO'Brien
(Alan Jones) *kpt on inner: in tch tl wknd rapidly 5th: sn t.o and p.u* **28/1**

5m 17.5s (31.50) **Going Correction** +1.375s/f (Heav) **7** Ran SP% **114.2**
Speed ratings (Par 103): **92,91,90,83,62 52,**
CSF £14.17 CT £49.45 TOTE £3.50: £2.90, £1.70; EX 8.10 Trifecta £36.70.
Owner Mrs Doone Hulse **Bred** G Russell **Trained** Nicholashayne, Devon

FOCUS
A moderate handicap hurdle. The first three are rated pretty much to their marks.
T/Plt: £3.30 to a £1 stake. Pool: £70,184.63 - 15,217.55 winning units. T/Qpdt: £2.40 to a £1 stake. Pool: £3939.49 - 1175.42 winning units. TM

4520 - 4522a (Foreign Racing) - See Raceform Interactive

4404 THURLES (R-H)
Thursday, February 27

OFFICIAL GOING: Heavy

4523a BOYLESPORTS MICHAEL PURCELL MEMORIAL NOVICE HURDLE (GRADE 2) (12 hdls) 2m 4f
4:05 (4:05) 5-Y-0+ **£21,666** (£6,333; £3,000; £1,000)

RPR

1 **Giantofaman (IRE)**[42] 3752 6-11-3 (b) PCarberry 140+
(D T Hughes, Ire) *led: over 1 l clr 1/2-way: nt fluent 6th and hdd: remained prom tl regained narrow advantage between last 2: rdn clr bef last and extended advantage run-in: comf* **7/1**[3]

2 *8* **Gallant Tipp (IRE)**[32] 3931 6-11-3 132 MarkWalsh 131
(E J O'Grady, Ire) *hld up towards rr: slt mstke 1st: 6th 1/2-way: tk clsr order bhd ldrs bef st: rdn into mod 2nd bef last where nt fluent: kpt on same pce: nt trble wnr* **4/1**[2]

3 *2 3/4* **Draycott Place (IRE)**[18] 4180 5-11-1 DavyRussell 126
(John Patrick Ryan, Ire) *chsd ldrs: 4th 1/2-way: pushed along in 6th bef 2 out: no imp on ldrs between last 2: kpt on fr last into mod 3rd run-in* **33/1**

4 *1 1/2* **The Pounds (IRE)**[26] 4044 8-11-3 123 (t) RogerLoughran 127
(Thomas Foley, Ire) *chsd ldrs: 2nd 1/2-way: disp 4 out: rdn in cl 3rd between last 2 and sn no ex u.p: dropped to 4th run-in* **8/1**

5 *1/2* **Horendus Hulabaloo (IRE)**[42] 3752 5-11-1 120 AELynch 124
(M F Morris, Ire) *chsd ldrs: 3rd 1/2-way: tk clsr order fr 6th and on terms next: rdn in cl 2nd between last 2 and sn no imp on wnr: wknd bef last* **16/1**

6 *1/2* **Urano (FR)**[52] 3581 6-11-3 RWalsh 126
(W P Mullins, Ire) *hld up in rr: last 1/2-way: mstke 4 out and next: tk clsr order bhd ldrs bef st: rdn to chal between horses bef last: sn no ex in 4th: wknd* **5/6**[1]

7 *42* **Band Of Blood (IRE)**[33] 3911 6-11-3 128 BrianO'Connell 84
(Philip Fenton, Ire) *hld up: 5th 1/2-way: pushed along in 6th bef 4 out and sn dropped to rr: nt fluent and detached 2 out: wknd and eased: t.o* **7/1**[3]

5m 13.1s (313.10) **7** Ran SP% **119.5**
CSF £37.20 TOTE £8.90: £1.40, £2.70; DF 35.70 Trifecta £197.80.
Owner Mrs A N Durkan **Bred** Ronnie O'Neill **Trained** The Curragh, Co Kildare

FOCUS
The runer-up set the standard but the progressive winner improved past him.

4524 - 4526a (Foreign Racing) - See Raceform Interactive

4343 DONCASTER (L-H)
Friday, February 28

OFFICIAL GOING: Good (chs 7.7, hdl 8.1)
Wind: almost nil Weather: fine

4527 BETDAQ £25 NO LOSE MOBILE BET NOVICES' H'CAP HURDLE (8 hdls) 2m 110y
2:10 (2:14) (Class 4) (0-105,105) 4-Y-0+ **£3,249** (£954; £477; £238)

Form RPR

350- **1** **Polstar (FR)**[22] 4103 5-10-12 98 RyanHatch(7) 105+
(Harry Whittington) *chsd ldrs: outpcd 5th: hdwy to ld 3 out: drvn clr appr last* **9/2**[1]

453- **2** *6* **Ivans Back (IRE)**[12] 4309 9-9-10 82 CharlieDeutsch(7) 83
(Nick Kent) *hld up in rr: hdwy to trck ldrs wnt 2nd 2 out: kpt on same pce* **5/1**[2]

050- **3** *6* **Danby's Legend**[35] 3871 7-11-2 95 BrianHughes 92
(Malcolm Jefferson) *prom: outpcd and j.rt 3 out: styd on to take modest 3rd last 100yds* **12/1**

60U- **4** *7* **Benefitofhindsight**[7] 4398 5-10-9 88 JamesDavies 78
(Ben Pauling) *w ldr: led 4th: hdd 3 out: wknd last 150yds* **16/1**

01P- **5** *1 1/4* **Easydoesit (IRE)**[28] 4004 6-11-12 105 NoelFehily 93
(Tony Carroll) *hld up in rr: hdwyappr 3 out: nvr on terms* **7/1**[3]

505- **6** *5* **Wheelavim**[22] 4107 6-9-13 85 GeraldQuinn(7) 69
(Claire Dyson) *led to 4th: w ldrs tl wknd 3 out* **25/1**

35- **7** *45* **Arkansas Dave (IRE)**[49] 3636 7-10-4 90 (t) MrSFox(7) 33
(Mark Michael McNiff, Ire) *j.lft in rr: drvn 4th: bhd whn j. bdly lft 3 out: t.o* **50/1**

440/ **8** *18* **Generous Spender**[418] 3537 8-11-7 100 LiamTreadwell 27
(Heather Cobb) *hld up in rr: reminders after 2nd: sn bhd: t.o 3 out* **100/1**

005- **B** **Vodka Red (IRE)**[18] 4187 6-9-9 81 (b[1]) StephenMulqueen(7)
(Robert Johnson) *hld up in rr: b.d 1st* **7/1**[3]

245- **F** **Biggar (IRE)**[58] 3475 6-11-5 105 (p) GrahamWatters(7)
(Lucinda Russell) *chsd ldrs: fell 1st* **12/1**

552- **B** **Ergo Sum**[35] 3871 7-10-13 95 RobertDunne(3)
(Robin Mathew) *mid-div: b.d 1st* **9/2**[1]

3m 59.5s (-5.20) **Going Correction** -0.475s/f (Good) **11** Ran SP% **106.1**
Speed ratings (Par 105): **93,90,87,84,83 81,59,51**, ,
CSF £22.43 CT £182.85 TOTE £5.20: £2.10, £1.80, £3.60; EX 27.30 Trifecta £386.90.
Owner Dixon,Ellis,Lynds,Travers,Watkins **Bred** Comte Jean-Jacques De La Rochette **Trained** Sparsholt, Oxforshire
■ Rule 4 of 10p in the pound applies to all bets; Withdrawn: Lysino

FOCUS
Hurdle dividing rail moved on to fresh ground where possible. A modest novices' handicap at best, in which they finished strung out. The time wasn't bad for the grade and the winner stepped up.

4528 BETDAQ NO PREMIUM CHARGE EBF STALLIONS MARES' "NATIONAL HUNT" NOVICES' HURDLE (10 hdls) 2m 3f 110y
2:40 (2:41) (Class 4) 4-Y-0+ **£3,573** (£1,049; £524; £262)

Form RPR

/02- **1** **Bull And Bush (IRE)**[80] 3005 5-10-12 0 WayneHutchinson 116+
(Alan King) *hld up: hdwy to trck ldrs 6th: led narrowly 2 out: drvn out* **5/4**[2]

/16- **2** *3 3/4* **Free Thinking**[90] 2810 6-11-2 0 MrSWaley-Cohen(3) 120+
(Nicky Henderson) *t.k.h: trckd ldrs: led and mstke 3 out: hdd next: styd on same pce run-in* **4/5**[1]

100- **3** *20* **Wyfield Rose**[80] 3005 5-10-12 0 BrendanPowell 91
(Jamie Snowden) *trckd ldrs 3rd: 4th and outpcd 3 out: kpt on to take poor 3rd last* **16/1**[3]

003- **4** *2 3/4* **Cinnomhor**[87] 2865 6-10-5 97 DiarmuidO'Regan(7) 89
(Chris Grant) *w ldr 3rd: nt flent 7th: led briefly appr 3 out: modest 3rd whn mstke 2 out: wknd last* **33/1**

/P0- **5** *52* **Izza Diva**[22] 4102 6-10-12 0 (t) CharliePoste 36
(John Holt) *j.lft: mde most tl hdd appr 3 out: sn lost pl and bhd: t.o 2 out* **125/1**

550- **6** *3/4* **All For Lily**[24] 4074 5-10-12 0 AdamPogson 35
(Charles Pogson) *t.k.h: trckd ldrs: j.lft 1st: outpcd and lost pl 5th: rallied appr 7th: lot plce bef 7th: sn bhd: t.o next* **100/1**

4m 44.4s (-6.90) **Going Correction** -0.475s/f (Good) **6** Ran SP% **110.6**
Speed ratings (Par 105): **94,92,84,83,62 62**
CSF £2.59 TOTE £2.20: £1.40, £1.10; EX 3.00 Trifecta £7.70.
Owner W A Harrison-Allan **Bred** M Conaghan **Trained** Barbury Castle, Wilts

FOCUS
The betting suggested this mares' novice hurdle was a two-horse race and the market principals duly pulled well clear. The fourth sets the level.

4529 BETDAQ £500 IN FREE BETS CONDITIONAL JOCKEYS' NOVICES' HURDLE (8 hdls) 2m 110y
3:10 (3:10) (Class 4) 4-Y-0+ **£3,249** (£954; £477; £238)

Form RPR

141- **1** **Sign Of A Victory (IRE)**[28] 4019 5-10-13 0 JeremiahMcGrath(3) 130+
(Nicky Henderson) *trckd ldng pair: led 3 out: wnt clr bef last: v easily* **1/4**[1]

433- **2** *10* **Chebsey Beau**[24] 4073 4-10-1 0 DeanPratt(6) 101
(John Quinn) *w ldr: led briefly appr 3 out: hit 2 out: eased whn no ch w wnr clsng stages* **4/1**[2]

0P0- **3** *11* **The Perfect Crime (IRE)**[35] 3877 5-11-2 0 KielanWoods 94
(Ian Williams) *in tch: hdwy and cl 3rd 3 out: one pce: j.lft last* **100/1**

4 *2* **Verano (GER)**[130] 5-11-2 0 (t) GavinSheehan 94+
(Charlie Mann) *hld up in rr: nt fluent 3rd: hdwy 5th: 4th and chsng ldrs whn mstke next: one pce* **14/1**

5 *1 1/2* **Mr Maynard**[302] 5-11-2 0 JoshuaMoore 92
(Renee Robeson) *in tch: chsd ldrs 3 out: lost pl appr next* **10/1**[3]

50- **6** *8* **Time Of My Life (IRE)**[35] 3872 5-11-2 0 JoeColliver 83
(Patrick Holmes) *in tch: hdwy to chse ldrs 3 out: lost pl appr next* **16/1**

00- **7** *4* **Triple Eight (IRE)**[22] 4103 6-10-13 0 AdamNicol(3) 79
(Philip Kirby) *led: nt fluent 3rd: hdd appr 3 out: sn wknd* **20/1**

0U0/ **8** *12* **Midnight Sequel**[25] 5470 5-10-9 0 MichaelByrne 60
(Neil Mulholland) *in rr: shkn up 3rd: bhd and drvn next: sn bhd* **33/1**

3m 59.8s (-4.90) **Going Correction** -0.475s/f (Good)
WFA 4 from 5yo+ 9lb **8** Ran SP% **130.3**
Speed ratings (Par 105): **92,87,82,81,80 76,74,69**
CSF £2.48 TOTE £1.30: £1.02, £1.30, £18.30; EX 2.70 Trifecta £67.30.
Owner Matt & Lauren Morgan **Bred** John Hore **Trained** Upper Lambourn, Berks

FOCUS
There was little strength in depth to this novices' hurdle, in which the favourite could not have won any easier.

4530 BETDAQ FREE PREMIER LEAGUE GAME SATURDAYS NOVICES' CHASE (15 fncs) 2m 3f
3:45 (3:45) (Class 3) 5-Y-0+ **£6,498** (£1,908; £954; £477)

Form RPR
512- **1** **Croco Bay (IRE)**[15] 4235 7-11-7 137 RichieMcGrath 119+
(Peter Atkinson) *t.k.h: set modest pce: hdd 7th: led 4 out: pushed clr run-in: eased towards fin* **1/1**[1]
1/P- **2** *10* **Oscatara (IRE)**[59] 3430 7-11-0 0 JasonMaguire 104+
(Donald McCain) *t.k.h: trckd wnr: led 7th: outj. and hdd 4 out: hit next: 3 l down whn hung lft between last 2: hld whn j.lft last: eased fnl 50yds* **13/8**[2]
060- **3** *9* **One In A Row (IRE)**[38] 3824 7-10-11 0 JohnKington(3) 90
(Andrew Crook) *trckd ldng pair: j.rt 6th and next: pushed along 10th: one pce and rdn 4 out* **100/1**
514- **4** *34* **Simarthur**[44] 3726 7-11-0 115 (p) PeterBuchanan 66
(Lucinda Russell) *chsd ldrs: mstke 4th: drvn: outpcd and reminders 8th: sn bhd: t.o 4 out: virtually p.u run-in* **9/2**[3]

4m 46.5s (-2.50) **Going Correction** -0.20s/f (Good) **4** Ran SP% **107.3**
Speed ratings: **97,92,89,74**
CSF £3.06 TOTE £1.70; EX 4.10 Trifecta £13.60.
Owner P G Atkinson **Bred** D Caverley **Trained** Yafforth, N Yorks

FOCUS
Predictably the two market leaders dominated in this novices' chase. The winner is rated a stone+ off his best with the second again well below his best hurdles form.

4531 BETDAQ 3% COMMISSION MARES' H'CAP HURDLE (8 hdls) 2m 110y
4:20 (4:20) (Class 3) (0-125,123) 4-Y-0+ **£5,393** (£1,583; £791; £395)

Form RPR
214- **1** **Pass The Time**[34] 3895 5-11-12 123 (p) NoelFehily 128+
(Neil Mulholland) *hld up in mid-div: stdy hdwy 5th: w ldrs next: j.lft 2 out: led narrowly last: drvn rt out* **6/1**[2]
210- **2** *1* **Koolala (IRE)**[12] 4300 6-11-2 113 DominicElsworth 115
(Paul Webber) *lost pl 1st and sn detached in last: hdwy after 5th: lft clr 3rd last: styd on to take 2nd post* **7/2**[1]
104- **3** *hd* **Beyeh (IRE)**[43] 3737 6-11-9 123 JonathanEngland(3) 126
(Michael Appleby) *w ldrs: led 2nd: hit 5th: hdd last: styd on same pce last 50yds* **15/2**
542- **4** *5* **Brijomi Queen (IRE)**[23] 4083 7-11-1 112 DenisO'Regan 110
(Nicky Richards) *mid-div: hdwy to chse ldrs appr 3 out: lft modest 4th and hmpd last: kpt on one pce* **7/2**[1]
15P- **5** *2 1/4* **Sparkling Hand**[44] 3724 8-10-3 100 (p) HenryBrooke 95
(Peter Atkinson) *in rr: shkn up and hdwy 4th: outpcd next: kpt on and hung lft between last 2: lft modest 5th and sltly hmpd last* **10/1**
B20- **6** *12* **Gold Show**[18] 4187 5-10-6 106 TonyKelly(3) 90
(Edwin Tuer) *chsd ldrs: drvn 5th: outpcd and lost pl appr next* **18/1**
344- **7** *2* **Maypole Lass**[61] 3385 4-10-1 107 (t) BrendanPowell 83
(Renee Robeson) *chsd ldrs: reminders 3rd: drvn 5th: outpcd whn nt fluent 3 out: wknd between last 2* **9/1**
326- **8** *15* **Nautical Twilight**[55] 3527 4-10-1 107 BrianHughes 67
(Malcolm Jefferson) *chsd ldrs 4th: lost pl appr 3 out: sn bhd* **20/1**
250- **F** **Roja Dove (IRE)**[60] 3423 5-11-7 121 TrevorWhelan(3) 122
(Neil King) *led to 2nd: w ldrs: disputing cl 3rd and keeping on same pce whn fell last* **13/2**[3]

3m 58.1s (-6.60) **Going Correction** -0.475s/f (Good)
WFA 4 from 5yo+ 9lb **9** Ran SP% **112.9**
Speed ratings (Par 107): **96,95,95,93,92 86,85,78,**
CSF £27.22 CT £158.20 TOTE £7.80: £2.40, £1.80, £1.30; EX 31.60 Trifecta £182.50.
Owner Dajam Ltd **Bred** M Burbidge **Trained** Limpley Stoke, Wilts

FOCUS
A fair mares' handicap hurdle, in which several were in contention at the third-last. Straightforward form.

4532 BETDAQ VALUE YOU CAN BET ON H'CAP CHASE (15 fncs) 2m 3f
4:55 (4:55) (Class 3) (0-135,132) 5-Y-0+ **£6,498** (£1,908; £954; £477)

Form RPR
0F6- **1** **Shadows Lengthen**[22] 4106 8-11-1 124 JakeGreenall(3) 132+
(Michael Easterby) *hld up: hdwy and 3rd 4 out: hit next: 2nd 2 out: led appr last: styd on wl* **7/1**
464- **2** *5* **Jack The Gent (IRE)**[11] 4325 10-10-9 115 BarryKeniry 119
(George Moore) *led: j. boldly: hdd and no ex appr last* **9/2**[3]
360- **3** *3 1/2* **Robbie**[34] 3892 10-11-12 132 JamesReveley 134
(Keith Reveley) *chsng ldr whn mstke 1st: dropped to rr 8th: outpcd and lost pl 10th: kpt on fr 3 out: styd on run-in: tk 3rd nr fin* **4/1**[2]
124- **4** *1* **King Of The Wolds (IRE)**[31] 3894 7-11-9 129 BrianHughes 130
(Malcolm Jefferson) *chsd ldr 3rd: drvn after 4 out: kpt on one pce fr 2 out: j.lft last* **6/4**[1]
101- **5** *23* **Granville Island (IRE)**[28] 4007 7-11-7 127 SeanQuinlan 115
(Jennie Candlish) *t.k.h in rr: wnt 3rd 9th: blnd 11th: wknd next: bhd whn eased run-in* **4/1**[2]

4m 40.6s (-8.40) **Going Correction** -0.20s/f (Good) **5** Ran SP% **110.7**
Speed ratings: **109,106,105,105,95**
CSF £35.44 TOTE £9.30: £3.00, £1.80; EX 42.60 Trifecta £162.20.
Owner T A F Frost **Bred** London Thoroughbred Services Ltd **Trained** Sheriff Hutton, N Yorks

FOCUS
A competitive-looking handicap chase, which was run at a good pace. The winner is rated back to the level of last season's form.

4533 EXPERT GUIDE TO DONCASTER AT DONCASTERRACECOURSETIPS.CO.UK H'CAP HURDLE (10 hdls) 2m 3f 110y
5:25 (5:25) (Class 4) (0-110,110) 4-Y-0+ **£3,119** (£915; £457; £228)

Form RPR
400- **1** **Groomed (IRE)**[42] 3758 6-11-4 105 JonathanEngland(3) 111
(Sue Smith) *chsd ldrs: drvn and lost pl 5th: rallied appr 3 out: cl 3rd next: 2nd last: led last 100yds: drvn out* **10/1**
021- **2** *1 1/2* **Short Takes (USA)**[8] 4378 6-11-6 104 (b) JasonMaguire 108
(Donald McCain) *trckd ldrs: drvn and lost pl 7th: hdwy to join ldrs next: led 2 out: edgd rt: edgd lft and hdd run-in: no ex last 75yds* **10/3**[1]
000- **3** *3 1/4* **Grand Gigolo (FR)**[51] 3602 5-10-8 97 RobertMcCarth(5) 98
(Ian Williams) *nt fluent 1st: sn mid-div: chsng ldrs 3 out: sn outpcd: 5th last: styd on wl to take 3rd line* **4/1**[3]
000- **4** *shd* **Armedandbeautiful**[38] 3828 6-10-12 96 JamesReveley 97
(Tom Gretton) *in rr: drvn 7th: outpcd appr next: 6th last: styd on wl to take 4th line* **20/1**
P4P- **5** *hd* **Northern Oscar (IRE)**[44] 3724 6-11-7 105 PeterBuchanan 106
(Mark Walford) *trckd ldrs: narrow ld 3 out: hdd next: wl hld whn eased sltly and lost 2 pls fnl strides* **9/1**
66P- **6** *5* **Halifax (IRE)**[43] 3741 6-11-12 110 AndrewTinkler 106
(Tony Newcombe) *trckd ldrs: upsides 3 out: nt fluent next: hung lft between last 2: wknd last* **7/2**[2]
0PP/ **7** *30* **Barnack**[726] 4657 8-10-2 89 (t) KielanWoods(3) 58
(Pam Sly) *prom: cl up 7th: led briefly appr next: wknd appr 2 out* **50/1**
030- **8** *13* **Jolly Valentine**[35] 3872 6-11-7 105 DominicElsworth 63
(Neil King) *in rr: hdwy to chse ldrs 6th: lost pl 2 out* **11/1**
P10- **9** *3/4* **Kilflora**[52] 3597 11-11-2 107 (p) GeraldQuinn(7) 64
(Claire Dyson) *led: hdd appr 3 out: lost pl bef 2 out: sn bhd* **33/1**
266- **10** *27* **Prime Contender**[37] 3839 12-11-2 100 (v) SeanQuinlan 33
(Jennie Candlish) *w ldr: wknd appr 3 out: sn bhd: t.o* **16/1**
100/ **11** *7* **Parc Des Princes (USA)**[306] 12 8-11-7 105 DenisO'Regan 31
(Nicky Richards) *nt fluent in rr: bhd and reminders 6th: t.o 3 out* **16/1**

4m 39.6s (-11.70) **Going Correction** -0.475s/f (Good) **11** Ran SP% **114.2**
Speed ratings (Par 105): **104,103,102,102,101 99,87,82,82,71 68**
CSF £42.22 CT £157.46 TOTE £11.80: £3.50, £1.60, £2.10; EX 49.50 Trifecta £492.90.
Owner Mrs S Smith **Bred** Rathbarry Stud **Trained** High Eldwick, W Yorks
■ Stewards' Enquiry : Jonathan England two-day ban: use of whip (15-16 Mar)

FOCUS
Only a modest handicap hurdle. The winner is rated back to something like his best.
T/Jkpt: £1,523.70 to a £1 stake. Pool: £22534.43 - 10.50 winning tickets T/Plt: £37.00 to a £1 stake. Pool: £110270.97 - 2172.77 winning tickets T/Qpdt: £24.00 to a £1 stake. Pool: £6328.46 - 195.08 winning tickets WG

4143 NEWBURY (L-H)
Friday, February 28

OFFICIAL GOING: Heavy (hdl 4.8, chs 5.5)
The open ditch in the home straight was omitted.
Wind: Moderate across Weather: Overcast/rain

4534 FLOOR V DAVIS HL1979 JUVENILE HURDLE (8 hdls) 2m 110y
1:45 (1:45) (Class 4) 4-Y-0 **£3,249** (£954; £477; £238)

Form RPR
4- **1** **Stiff Upper Lip (IRE)**[36] 3857 4-10-12 0 LeightonAspell 103+
(Oliver Sherwood) *trckd ldr: chal fr 4th tl led gng wl appr 2 out: sn clr: eased fnl 100yds* **15/8**[2]
50- **2** *20* **Strong Conviction**[13] 4281 4-10-12 0 NickScholfield 75
(Simon Hodgson) *chsd ldrs and lft 3rd 4 out: sn no ch but kpt on appr last to take mod 2nd fnl 150yds* **14/1**
3 *8* **Theionlady (IRE)** 4-10-5 0 ConorO'Farrell 60
(Richard Woollacott) *in rr: mod prog fr 2 out: edgd lft run-in and kpt on to take mod 3rd fnl 110yds* **14/1**
203- **4** *7* **Ninepointsixthree**[7] 4401 4-10-12 0 APMcCoy 63
(John O'Shea) *led and nt fluent 1st: jnd fr 4th tl rdn and hdd appr 2 out sn lft bhd by wnr: wknd bdly bef last: dropped two plcd fnl 150yds* **11/10**[1]
500- **5** *52* **Todoistodare**[11] 4329 4-10-5 0 RichieMcLernon 1
(Brendan Powell) *a wl bhd: t.o after 4 out* **66/1**
F **Cherry Tiger**[122] 4-10-12 0 PaulMoloney
(Graeme McPherson) *t.k.h early: chsng ldrs in 3rd whn fell 4 out* **8/1**[3]
P- **U** **Bobtail**[27] 4030 4-10-5 0 ThomasCheesman(7)
(Mark Gillard) *in r tl bdly hmpd and uns rdr 4 out* **100/1**

4m 21.06s (11.06) **Going Correction** +0.50s/f (Soft) **7** Ran SP% **109.3**
Speed ratings: **93,83,79,76,52 ,**
CSF £23.61 TOTE £2.50: £1.70, £4.10; EX 18.50 Trifecta £88.50.
Owner Richard Hitchcock Alan King **Bred** B Kennedy **Trained** Upper Lambourn, Berks

FOCUS
Rails moved out since last meeting on both courses. A very weak juvenile event by course standards and they went for home a long way out. The second is probably the best guide to the level.

4535 PHYSICOOL "NATIONAL HUNT" NOVICES' HURDLE (IN AID OF WEST BERKSHIRE MENCAP) (10 hdls) 2m 5f
2:20 (2:21) (Class 4) 5-Y-0+ **£3,249** (£954; £477; £238)

Form RPR
2- **1** **Big Hands Harry**[70] 3182 5-10-12 0 BarryGeraghty 131+
(Nicky Henderson) *trckd ldrs: chal 2 out: sn led travelling wl: edgd lft and green bef last: clr run-in: easily* **8/11**[1]
2 *10* **Ziga Boy (FR)**[133] 5-10-12 0 JackDoyle 111
(Alan King) *in tch: hdwy to trck ldrs after 4 out: chal travelling wl 2 out: drvn and kpt on last but no ch w wnr* **14/1**[3]
033- **3** *11* **Flintham**[92] 2768 5-10-7 90 NicodeBoinville(5) 100
(Mark Bradstock) *narrow ldr but hrd pressed tl narrowly hdd 6th: led again 4 out: drvn 3 out: jnd next and sn hdd and no ch w ldng duo but kpt on wl for clr 3rd* **80/1**
/20- **4** *8* **Fine Words**[72] 3166 6-10-12 0 RobertThornton 92
(Alan King) *in rr: hdwy 4 out: trckd ldrs appr next: wknd 3 out* **16/1**
05- **5** *26* **Foxtail Hill (IRE)**[43] 3734 5-10-12 0 JamieMoore 66
(Rebecca Curtis) *chsd ldrs tl wknd u.p 3 out* **66/1**
412- **6** *14* **Pink Gin**[7] 4397 6-11-4 121 (t) MarkGrant 58
(Jim Old) *mstke 1st: chsd ldrs: rdn 4 out: wkng whn blnd 3 out: t.o* **16/1**
511- **7** *14* **Boogie In The Barn (IRE)**[21] 4130 6-11-4 0 NickScholfield 44
(Jeremy Scott) *w ldr tl led and propped 6th: hdd 4 out: wknd after 4 out: t.o* **11/4**[2]
5- **8** *23* **Withoutdefavourite (IRE)**[12] 4304 6-10-12 0 RichardJohnson 15
(Henry Oliver) *in rr: lost tch after 4 out: t.o* **33/1**
6/ **9** *11* **Lightning Moley (IRE)**[1381] 409 11-10-7 0 (t) BenPoste(5) 4
(Tracey Watkins) *in rr: lost tch after 4 out: t.o* **100/1**
P **Abbey Court (IRE)**[467] 6-10-12 0 DavidBass
(Nicky Henderson) *chsd ldrs: j. slowly 4th: wknd after 4 out: t.o whn p.u bef 2 out* **20/1**
5F0- **P** **Upham Running (IRE)**[29] 3988 6-10-7 0 KieronEdgar(5)
(Kate Buckett) *hmpd and in rr 1st: sn wl bhd: t.o whn p.u bef 3 out* **100/1**
0- **P** **Smart Story**[12] 4298 7-10-12 0 PaddyBrennan
(Fergal O'Brien) *blnd bdly 1st: p.u bef next* **100/1**
00- **P** **Matripajo (IRE)**[72] 3163 5-10-12 0 APMcCoy
(Jonjo O'Neill) *in rr: sme hdwy 6th: sn wknd: t.o whn p.u bef 3 out* **33/1**

5m 24.38s (5.38) **Going Correction** +0.50s/f (Soft) **13** Ran SP% **119.3**
Speed ratings: **109,105,101,97,88 82,77,68,64, , ,**
CSF £13.04 TOTE £1.60: £1.10, £2.40, £10.30; EX 13.60 Trifecta £192.50.

Owner A D Spence **Bred** R J Spencer And Mickley Stud **Trained** Upper Lambourn, Berks

FOCUS

An impressive winner who was value for further and is rated in line with his hurdling debut.

4536 BERRY BROS & RUDD H'CAP CHASE (FOR THE GEOFFREY GILBEY TROPHY) (12 fncs 1 omitted) 2m 1f

2:50 (2:50) (Class 3) (0-130,126) 5-Y-0+ **£6,975** (£2,385)

Form RPR

151- **1** **Umberto D'Olivate (FR)**[45] 3693 6-11-11 **125**.................... FelixDeGiles 135+
(Robert Walford) *led: drvn fr 9th: hdd u.p appr omitted 3rd last: rallied to take slt ld last: styd on strly* **4/6**[1]

/33- **2** *5* **Stone Light (FR)**[71] 3171 6-11-1 **115**.................................. AidanColeman 120
(Venetia Williams) *racd in cl 3rd: trckd ldrs 9th: led gng wl appr omitted 3rd last but sn hrd pressed whn lft 2 l ahd 2 out: narrowly hdd last: no ex and btn run-in* **9/2**[3]

3F2- **F** **Sir Valentino (FR)**[43] 3732 5-11-10 **125**............................ PaddyBrennan 129
(Tom George) *trckd ldr: chalng and travelling wl whn fell 2 out* **11/4**[2]

4m 23.19s (15.19) **Going Correction** +0.80s/f (Soft)
WFA 5 from 6yo+ 1lb **3** Ran SP% **104.8**
Speed ratings: **96,93,**
CSF £3.45 TOTE £1.60; EX 3.10 Trifecta £4.80.

Owner Mrs S De Wilde **Bred** J P Rivoire **Trained** Child Okeford, Dorset

FOCUS

A tight little handicap, run at a routine gallop, and the trio of chasers were almost upsides two from home. The form makes sense with the winner close to his mark.

4537 AGETUR UK NOVICES' LIMITED H'CAP CHASE (15 fncs 2 omitted) 2m 6f 110y

3:25 (3:25) (Class 3) (0-125,122) 5-Y-0+ **£6,498** (£1,908; £954; £477)

Form RPR

2F1- **1** **Farbreaga (IRE)**[25] 4067 8-10-10 **111**................................... TomO'Brien 125+
(Jamie Poulton) *tendency to jump lft: trckd ldr: slt ld 3 out: drvn ommitted 3rd last: styd on wl fr 2 out to go clr last: comf* **4/1**[3]

220- **2** *15* **Dunlough Bay (IRE)**[44] 3717 8-11-7 **122**..................(p) RichieMcLernon 122
(Paul Webber) *in tch: hdwy 12th: trckd ldrs 3 out: pressed wnr omitted 3rd last: rdn and mstke 2 out: sn no ch but kpt on wl for 2nd run-in* **10/1**

313- **3** *2 ¾* **Ultimatum Du Roy (FR)**[22] 4110 6-11-1 **116**.......................... APMcCoy 113
(Alex Hales) *in rr: nt fluent 1st: j. slowly 8th: hdwy 12th: chal and hit 3 out: rdn omitted 3rd last: styd on same pce fr 2 out* **9/4**[1]

/24- **4** *4* **Perfect Candidate (IRE)**[35] 3873 7-11-4 **119**................. PaddyBrennan 110
(Fergal O'Brien) *chsd ldrs: pushed along 6th: dropped to rr 9th: hit 12th: styd on same pce fr omitted 3rd last* **3/1**[2]

3P3- **5** *27* **Young Hurricane (IRE)**[38] 3820 8-10-12 **113**.....(bt) SamTwiston-Davies 86
(Dr Richard Newland) *led and blnd 1st: rdn: mstke and hdd 3 out: wknd omitted 3rd last: no ch whn wnt lft and blnd last* **5/1**

335- **6** *48* **Pistol (IRE)**[27] 4031 5-11-1 **119**.. RichardJohnson 31
(Philip Hobbs) *chsd ldrs: chal 9th to 10th: rdn and hit 12th: sn wknd: mstke 3 out: t.o* **8/1**

6m 1.36s (14.36) **Going Correction** +0.80s/f (Soft)
WFA 5 from 6yo+ 2lb **6** Ran SP% **112.6**
Speed ratings: **107,101,100,99,90 73**
CSF £37.47 TOTE £5.40: £2.30, £6.10; EX 45.40 Trifecta £159.00.

Owner Miss V Markowiak **Bred** Daniel O'Mahony **Trained** Telscombe, E Sussex

FOCUS

This modest novice handicap was run at a good gallop and provided a decent test. The winner is on the upgrade and there's a case for rating the form up to 4lb higher.

4538 RR ELITE NOVICES' H'CAP HURDLE (IN AID OF WEST BERKSHIRE MENCAP) (8 hdls) 2m 110y

4:00 (4:00) (Class 4) (0-120,119) 4-Y-0+ **£3,898** (£1,144; £572; £286)

Form RPR

213- **1** **Whispering Harry**[9] 4353 5-10-13 **104**.......................... RichardJohnson 110+
(Henry Oliver) *nt fluent 1st: trckd ldr: rdn to chal 2 out and sn led: blnd last: hung rt u.p run-in: hld on all out* **2/1**[1]

040- **2** *½* **Fond Memory (IRE)**[77] 3070 6-11-5 **110**................ SamTwiston-Davies 115+
(Nigel Twiston-Davies) *in rr: j. slowly 3rd: hit 4 out: rdn and styd on fr 3 out to take 3rd 2 out: c to stands' side and styd on u.p to chse wnr last: kpt on wl clsng stages but a jst hld* **13/2**

51- **3** *6* **Minella Reception (IRE)**[23] 4091 8-11-9 **114**......................(t) APMcCoy 112
(Rebecca Curtis) *led: rdn and jnd 2 out: sn hdd: no imp on wnr and lost 2nd whn mstke last: one pce* **2/1**[1]

432- **4** *7* **Daveron (IRE)**[23] 4091 6-11-7 **112**.. NickScholfield 102
(Jeremy Scott) *in tch: nt fluent 4 out: rdn and sme hdwy appr 3 out: wknd next* **5/1**[2]

31F- **5** *9* **Rior (IRE)**[70] 3186 7-11-1 **106**... TomO'Brien 87
(Paul Henderson) *chsd ldrs in 3rd: rdn and effrt 3 out: wknd sn after* **6/1**[3]

4m 21.95s (11.95) **Going Correction** +0.80s/f (Soft) **5** Ran SP% **111.0**
Speed ratings (Par 105): **103,102,99,96,92**
CSF £14.22 TOTE £3.10: £1.70, £2.60; EX 14.40 Trifecta £41.60.

Owner R G Whitehead **Bred** S A Brookshaw **Trained** Broomhall, Worcs

FOCUS

A modest little novice handicap, weakened by the non-runners There was no hanging about and it served up a tight finish. The first two are on the upgrade.

4539 FREDK SAGE CO LTD H'CAP CHASE (IN AID OF WEST BERKSHIRE MENCAP) (14 fncs 2 omitted) 2m 4f

4:35 (4:35) (Class 4) (0-120,115) 5-Y-0+ **£3,898** (£1,144; £572)

Form RPR

143- **1** **Bincombe**[43] 3729 6-11-0 **103**.. RichardJohnson 121+
(Philip Hobbs) *mde all: c easily clr fr omitted 3rd last: unchal* **5/6**[1]

244- **2** *19* **Be Definite (IRE)**[35] 3874 10-11-8 **111**........................(p) PaddyBrennan 114
(Tom George) *disp 2nd tl j. slowly 5th (water): hit 10th and dropped on ldng duo: styd on to chse wnr 3 out but no ch fr omitted 3rd last* **15/8**[2]

245- **3** *27* **Mr Muddle**[36] 3859 7-11-12 **115**.. MarcGoldstein 87
(Sheena West) *hit 3rd: disp 2nd tl chsd wnr 7th: nt fluent 8th and 9th: wknd into 3rd whn blnd 3 out and wl bhd fr omitted 3rd last: no ch whn hit 2 out: t.o* **9/2**[3]

5m 23.42s (20.42) **Going Correction** +1.10s/f (Heav) **3** Ran SP% **107.5**
Speed ratings: **103,95,84**
CSF £2.75 TOTE £1.50; EX 2.00 Trifecta £2.10.

Owner Martin Short **Bred** R D And Mrs J S Chugg **Trained** Withycombe, Somerset

FOCUS

With his two rivals failing to really fire this ordinary handicap provided a straightforward opportunity for the winner. The form is rated around the first two.

4540 RICKETY BRIDGE MARES' STANDARD OPEN NATIONAL HUNT FLAT (IN AID OF WEST BERKSHIRE MENCAP) 2m 110y

5:10 (5:10) (Class 6) 4-6-Y-0 **£1,624** (£477; £238; £119)

Form RPR

3/2- **1** **No Pushover**[71] 3181 5-11-2 0.. BarryGeraghty 97+
(Nicky Henderson) *led at mod pce tl hdd 10f out: styd trcking ldr: chal over 3f out tl drvn to take narrow ld fr 2f out: hld on all out* **2/5**[1]

2- **2** *nk* **Etheridge Annie**[21] 4135 5-10-9 0.. MikeyEnnis(7) 96
(Hugo Froud) *t.k.h off mod pce and chsd ldrs: drvn and outpcd 3f out: styd on stands' rail and kpt on fr over 1f out: str run clsng stages to take 2nd: nt quite get up* **4/1**[2]

3 *2* **Tyre Hill Lady** 5-11-2 0.. AidanColeman 94
(David Dennis) *in rr off mod pce: hdwy over 3f out: pushed along to press wnr fr over 2f out: sn rdn: chal over 1f out: no ex and dropped to 3rd clsng stages* **8/1**[3]

0- **4** *6* **Izzy Piccolina (IRE)**[48] 3656 6-10-9 0........................ MissRachelKing(7) 88
(Geoffrey Deacon) *t.k.h off mod pce: led 10f out: rdn and jnd over 3f out: hdd 2f out: wknd into 4th fnl f* **25/1**

5 *12* **Cloudbusting** 6-10-9 0.. MrHGMiller(7) 76
(Zoe Davison) *chsd ldrs off mod pce: rdn 4f out: sn btn* **33/1**

00- **6** *34* **Mrs Winchester (IRE)**[31] 3961 5-11-2 0...................................... IanPopham 42
(Caroline Keevil) *chsd ldrs of mod pce and t.k.h: wknd ins fnl 3f* **50/1**

4m 34.95s (30.65) **Going Correction** +1.10s/f (Heav) **6** Ran SP% **111.3**
Speed ratings: **71,70,69,67,61 45**
CSF £2.23 TOTE £1.40: £1.10, £2.40; EX 2.80 Trifecta £4.80.

Owner The Perfect Day Partnership **Bred** R F And S D Knipe **Trained** Upper Lambourn, Berks

FOCUS

The market leaders dominated in this modest bumper for the track.

T/Plt: £210.90 to a £1 stake. Pool: £74303.86 - 257.10 winning tickets T/Qpdt: £61.80 to a £1 stake. Pool: £4876.21 - 58.30 winning tickets ST

4527 DONCASTER (L-H)

Saturday, March 1

OFFICIAL GOING: Good (chs 7.7 hdl 8.6)

Wind: almost nil Weather: fine

4541 PARK HILL HOSPITAL NOVICES' CHASE (18 fncs) 3m

1:45 (1:45) (Class 4) 5-Y-0+ **£3,898** (£1,144; £572)

Form RPR

212- **1** **Victor Hewgo**[10] 4344 9-11-7 132.. JamesReveley 143+
(Keith Reveley) *led tl appr 2nd: trckd ldr: led 3 out: styd on strly: eased clsng stages: v readily* **4/5**[1]

/10- **2** *11* **Cowards Close (IRE)**[62] 3387 7-11-0 125..........................(t) DarylJacob 129+
(Paul Nicholls) *chsd ldr: mstke 1st: led appr next: increased pce 12th: drvn 4 out: hdd and blnd next: no ch w wnr* **5/4**[2]

35- **3** *56* **My Dads Horse**[52] 3601 8-11-0 0.. PaulMoloney 101
(Evan Williams) *nt fluent: sn detached in last: hit 7th: j.rt 10th: sme hdwy 12th: lost tch and bhd 4 out: t.o* **14/1**[3]

6m 0.8s (-11.20) **Going Correction** -0.425s/f (Good) **3** Ran SP% **106.7**
Speed ratings: **101,97,78**
CSF £2.18 TOTE £1.70; EX 1.70 Trifecta £1.80.

Owner Sir Ian Good **Bred** J Good, C Anderson And K G Reveley **Trained** Lingdale, Redcar & Cleveland

FOCUS

Hurdle dividing rail moved on to fresh ground where possible. This was nothing more than a straight match and it played out as the market anticipated. The winner stepped up on recent course form.

4542 WILLIAM HILL - BET ON THE MOVE MARES' NOVICES' HURDLE (LISTED RACE) (11 hdls) 3m 110y

2:20 (2:20) (Class 1) 4-Y-0+ **£11,546** (£4,334; £2,170; £1,082; £542)

Form RPR

/51- **1** **Mayfair Music (IRE)**[86] 2907 5-11-2 0.............................. BarryGeraghty 136+
(Nicky Henderson) *hld up: smooth hdwy to join ldr 3 out: led appr next: pushed clr run-in: eased towards fin: readily* **15/8**[1]

242- **2** *4 ½* **Cannon Fodder**[14] 4276 7-11-2 129.................................... MarcGoldstein 128
(Sheena West) *chsd ldrs: hrd drvn bef 3 out: styd on to take 2nd between last 2: no ch w wnr* **10/1**

111- **3** *1 ½* **Toubeera**[14] 4272 8-11-7 144.. AidanColeman 132
(Venetia Williams) *mde most: hdd appr 2 out: kpt on same pce* **11/4**[3]

123- **4** *7* **Luci Di Mezzanotte**[98] 2675 6-11-2 115.........................(p) LeightonAspell 120
(Oliver Sherwood) *racd in last: hrd drvn 7th: outpcd next: kpt on to take modest 4th 2 out: nvr a factor* **33/1**

511- **5** *13* **Land Of Vic**[24] 4090 6-11-2 125.. DonalDevereux 109
(Peter Bowen) *w ldr: drvn 3 out: lost pl appr next* **14/1**

11- **U** **Layla Joan (IRE)**[18] 4200 6-11-2 145.......................................(t) PCarberry
(Gordon Elliott, Ire) *hld up in 5th: stmbld bdly landing and uns rdr 1st* **9/4**[2]

5m 53.4s (-5.60) **Going Correction** -0.425s/f (Good) **6** Ran SP% **110.9**
Speed ratings (Par 111): **91,89,89,86,82**
CSF £19.33 TOTE £2.70: £1.30, £2.10; EX 16.10 Trifecta £49.90.

Owner Mrs E Roberts **Bred** Mrs Marilyn Syme **Trained** Upper Lambourn, Berks

FOCUS

Some likeable mares on show in this Listed contest. A big step up from the cosy winner with the second to her mark.

4543 WILLIAM HILL - IN THE APP STORE H'CAP CHASE (12 fncs) 2m 110y

2:55 (2:55) (Class 2) (0-145,145) 5-Y-0+ **£12,996** (£3,816; £1,908; £954)

Form RPR

F52- **1** **Doeslessthanme (IRE)**[28] 4039 10-11-1 **139**..........(tp) HarryChalloner(5) 148
(Richard Ford) *led: narrowly hdd 2 out: slt ld last: hld on gamely* **11/2**[3]

223- **2** *½* **Turn Over Sivola (FR)**[62] 3386 7-10-11 **130**................. RobertThornton 139
(Alan King) *trckd ldrs 2nd: cl 2nd 7th: narrow ld 2 out: hdd last: no ex towards fin* **3/1**[1]

221- **3** *½* **Simply Ned (IRE)**[35] 3894 7-11-12 **145**............................... BrianHarding 154
(Nicky Richards) *hld up in rr: hdwy 6th: trcking ldrs 4 out: cl 3rd next: kpt on towards fin* **9/2**[2]

335- **4** *17* **Kings Grey (IRE)**[77] 3090 10-11-4 **137**................................ JamesReveley 130
(Keith Reveley) *chsd ldrs: wknd between last 2* **16/1**

The Form Book Jumps, Raceform Ltd, Compton, RG20 6NL.

/32- **5** *13* **Shadrack (IRE)**[79] 3039 10-10-0 **119** ..... RichieMcGrath 101
(Keith Reveley) *chsd ldrs: lost pl 8th* **13/2**
1P1- **6** *1 ¾* **Swift Arrow (IRE)**[27] 4053 8-11-3 **136** ..... HenryBrooke 116
(Donald McCain) *hld up in rr: hdwy 6th: chsng ldrs whn hit 12th: sn outpcd: lost pl after next* **20/1**
231- **7** *2 ¾* **Lucky Landing (IRE)**[136] 1921 8-11-3 **136** ..... DougieCostello 114
(Tony Coyle) *hld up in rr: hit 2nd: hdwy to trck ldrs 6th: lost pl bef 4 out* **12/1**
3U2- **8** *9* **Prince Of Dreams**[38] 3833 7-10-4 **123** ..... JoshuaMoore 92
(Ed de Giles) *t.k.h: trckd ldrs: lost pl appr 4 out* **9/1**
/20- **9** *10* **Lidar (FR)**[29] 4020 9-11-7 **140** ..... (b) BarryGeraghty 107
(Alan King) *t.k.h: sn trcking ldrs: hit 3rd: reminders 7th: hit 8th: sn rdn and lost pl: bhd fr 4 out* **7/1**

3m 54.6s (-10.40) **Going Correction** -0.425s/f (Good) 9 Ran SP% **112.7**
Speed ratings: **107,106,106,98,92 91,90,86,81**
CSF £22.58 CT £79.23 TOTE £6.40: £1.50, £1.60, £2.00; EX 30.40 Trifecta £157.40.
Owner R J Hewitt **Bred** Mrs Karin Osthus **Trained** Garstang, Lancs

FOCUS
This hotly-contested handicap chase was run at a searching gallop and served up a thrilling finish as a trio of runners pulled clear. Good handicap form.

4544 WILLIAM HILL GRIMTHORPE CHASE (H'CAP) (19 fncs) 3m 2f
3:30 (3:30) (Class 2) 5-Y-0+ **£32,490** (£9,540; £4,770; £2,385)

Form RPR
01P- **1** **Night In Milan (IRE)**[35] 3897 8-10-12 **136** ..... (b) JamesReveley 149+
(Keith Reveley) *j. soundly: w ldr: led 2nd to 8th: led 4 out: styd on wl and 5 l ahd last: drvn out* **14/1**
F65- **2** *5* **Storm Survivor (IRE)**[23] 4104 8-10-5 **129** ..... (v) RichieMcLernon 136
(Jonjo O'Neill) *in rr: hit 6th: hdwy next: chsng ldrs 12th: 3rd 4 out: 2nd 2 out: kpt on same pce* **12/1**
140- **3** *shd* **Renard (FR)**[35] 3887 9-11-3 **141** ..... AidanColeman 148
(Venetia Williams) *in tch: chsd ldrs 7th: drvn 4 out: kpt on to take 3rd last: styd on towards fin* **16/1**
651- **4** *14* **Golden Call (IRE)**[23] 4104 10-10-8 **132** ..... (t) DougieCostello 130
(Jennie Candlish) *led to 2nd: w ldr: led 12th: hdd 4 out: 2nd whn hit next: hung lft and wknd last* **8/1**[3]
341- **5** *7* **Monbeg Dude (IRE)**[78] 3067 9-11-8 **146** ..... PCarberry 136
(Michael Scudamore) *hld up in rr: blnd and last 3rd: sme hdwy and poor 6th 5 out: sn rdn: kpt on: nvr on terms* **5/1**[1]
332- **6** *30* **Court By Surprise (IRE)**[84] 2953 9-10-10 **134** ..... BarryGeraghty 94
(Emma Lavelle) *in tch: chsd ldrs 7th: wknd 3 out: t.o* **11/2**[2]
52P- **7** *12* **Wayward Prince**[84] 2938 10-11-12 **150** ..... (t) JackDoyle 99
(Hilary Parrott) *in rr: reminders 4th: bhd next: t.o and reminders 11th* **25/1**
4/P- **8** *9* **Mon Parrain (FR)**[120] 2199 8-11-6 **144** ..... (t) DarylJacob 85
(Paul Nicholls) *in rr: pushed along 5th: bhd fr 14th: t.o* **9/1**
31P- **9** *8* **Mart Lane (IRE)**[35] 3897 9-11-3 **141** ..... (b) LeightonAspell 75
(Dr Richard Newland) *chsd ldrs 3rd: outpcd and hit 13th: lost pl next: sn bhd: t.o 2 out* **20/1**
/03- **P** **Harry The Viking**[23] 4104 9-10-5 **129** ..... (b) NickScholfield
(Paul Nicholls) *prom: lost pl 4th: bhd fr 12th: t.o whn p.u bef 3 out* **5/1**[1]
/5P- **P** **Godsmejudge (IRE)**[84] 2953 8-11-10 **148** ..... RobertThornton
(Alan King) *chsd ldrs: drvn 11th: lost pl next: sn bhd: t.o whn p.u bef 4 out* **11/1**
/42- **P** **Real Milan (IRE)**[39] 3825 9-10-5 **129** ..... (tp) BrianHarding
(Donald McCain) *in tch 7th: lost pl 12th: bhd 4 out: sn t.o: p.u bef last* **8/1**[3]

6m 22.9s (-20.10) **Going Correction** -0.425s/f (Good) 12 Ran SP% **118.1**
Speed ratings: **113,111,111,107,104 95,92,89,86, ,**
CSF £168.08 CT £2711.22 TOTE £17.70: £4.90, £3.30, £6.80; EX 176.90 Trifecta £3928.30.
Owner Richard Collins **Bred** Commandant Brendan Healy **Trained** Lingdale, Redcar & Cleveland

FOCUS
A fiercely competitive renewal of this valuable staying handicap which featured both the Scottish and Welsh National winners. Improvement from Night In Milan in a solid-looking renewal.

4545 SAINT GOBAIN WEBER H'CAP HURDLE (11 hdls) 3m 110y
4:05 (4:06) (Class 2) (0-145,134) 4-Y-0+ **£12,996** (£3,816; £1,908; £954)

Form RPR
P41- **1** **Dawn Commander (GER)**[13] 4299 7-11-7 **129** ..... JoshuaMoore 133+
(Renee Robeson) *trckd ldrs: t.k.h: upsides 3 out: led next: drvn out* **9/2**[3]
623- **2** *3 ¾* **Drop Out Joe**[49] 3653 6-11-4 **129** ..... KielanWoods(3) 131
(Charlie Longsdon) *set stdy pce: increased gallop 7th: jnd 3 out: hdd next: hung lft between last 2: kpt on same pce* **9/4**[1]
143- **3** *14* **Awaywiththegreys (IRE)**[7] 4415 7-11-12 **134** ..... (p) BarryGeraghty 124
(Peter Bowen) *chsd ldr: upsides 3 out: kpt on one pce appr next* **3/1**[2]
211- **4** *3* **Hartforth**[29] 4006 6-10-2 **115** ..... CallumWhillans(5) 101
(Donald Whillans) *chsd ldrs: drvn 7th: outpcd appr 3 out: kpt on to take poor 4th last* **6/1**
221- **5** *½* **Ampleforth**[24] 4093 6-10-5 **113** ..... (v) WillKennedy 98
(Ian Williams) *chsd ldrs: drvn appr 3 out: sn btn* **6/1**
P40- **P** **Low Gales (IRE)**[79] 3044 8-10-0 **108** oh2 ..... (p) MarkGrant
(Charlie Mann) *hld up wl in tch: hdwy to trck ldrs 8th: wknd next: t.o last whn p.u bef last* **9/1**

6m 0.5s (1.50) **Going Correction** -0.425s/f (Good) 6 Ran SP% **112.5**
Speed ratings (Par 109): **80,78,74,73,73**
CSF £15.49 TOTE £4.90: £2.40, £1.60; EX 17.60 Trifecta £61.60.
Owner Nick Brown Racing **Bred** W Lohmann Jr **Trained** Tyringham, Bucks

FOCUS
Some in-form runners in this handicap hurdle. The winner is rated back to his bset, with the second to his mark.

4546 REGISTER NOW FOR WEARAHATDAY NOVICES' HURDLE (4 hdls 6 omitted) 2m 3f 110y
4:40 (4:45) (Class 4) 4-Y-0+ **£3,573** (£1,049; £524; £262)

Form RPR
/12- **1** **Tistory (FR)**[73] 3166 7-11-9 131 ..... BarryGeraghty 130+
(Nicky Henderson) *trckd ldrs: upsides on bridle normal 3 out: led sn after normal 2 out: c clr easily* **8/11**[1]
0- **2** *6* **Tsar Alexandre (FR)**[13] 4297 7-10-13 0 ..... (t) GavinSheehan(3) 112
(Warren Greatrex) *led: drvn last (normal 4 out): hdd normal 2 out: kpt on same pce: no ch w wnr* **25/1**
3/0- **3** *4* **Go West Young Man (IRE)**[79] 3034 6-10-13 0 ..... JakeGreenall(3) 108
(Henry Daly) *hld up: hdwy to trck ldrs 3rd (normal 6th) effrt appr normal 2 out: kpt on one pce* **14/1**
642- **4** *6* **I Got Power**[36] 3872 5-11-2 115 ..... JamesReveley 102
(Keith Reveley) *hld up in rr: hdwy to trck ldrs appr last (normal 4 out): wknd between normal last 2* **6/1**[3]

232- **5** *16* **Minella Friend (IRE)**[52] 3598 5-11-2 124 ..... PaulMoloney 90
(Evan Williams) *chsd ldrs: drvn last (normal 4 out): wknd normal 2 out* **11/4**[2]
320/ **6** *15* **Monksgold (IRE)**[372] 4370 6-11-2 0 ..... RobertThornton 71
(Alan King) *in rr: sme hdwy after last (normal 4 out): carried hd awkwardly: lost pl bef normal 2 out* **12/1**
P- **7** *½* **March Seventeenth (IRE)**[38] 3831 6-11-2 0 ..... BarryKeniry 71
(Brian Ellison) *chsd ldrs: lost pl 3rd (normal 6th): bhd normal 3 out* **50/1**
F60- **8** *32* **Ziggie (IRE)**[88] 2874 7-11-2 0 ..... HenryBrooke 39
(Donald McCain) *mid-div: lost pl 3rd (normal 6th): bhd next: t.o* **33/1**
6/5- **9** *17* **Lapworth (IRE)**[86] 2905 7-11-2 0 ..... CharliePoste 22
(Michael Appleby) *chsd ldrs: blnd 2nd (normal 5th): lost pl bef last (normal 4 out): sn bhd: t.o next (normal 3 out)* **66/1**

4m 33.3s (-18.00) **Going Correction** -0.675s/f (Firm) 9 Ran SP% **123.5**
Speed ratings (Par 105): **109,106,105,102,96 90,90,77,70**
CSF £26.86 TOTE £1.80: £1.10, £4.50, £2.90; EX 21.90 Trifecta £326.70.
Owner Mrs Judy Wilson **Bred** Gerard Ferte **Trained** Upper Lambourn, Berks

FOCUS
With the three hurdles in the home straight omitted on both circuits on account of the low sunlight, this novices' hurdle was more like a Flat race and the form has to be treated with caution. The easy stood out and is rated to his mark.

4547 WILLIAM HILL DOWNLOAD THE APP STANDARD NATIONAL HUNT FLAT RACE (CONDITIONALS & AMATEURS) 2m 110y
5:15 (5:15) (Class 6) 4-6-Y-0 **£1,949** (£572; £286; £143)

Form RPR
52/ **1** **Aiaam Al Namoos**[381] 4192 5-10-9 0 ..... JohnDawson(7) 106+
(John Wade) *mid-div: hdwy 6f out: chsd ldr 2f out: rdn and styd on to ld last 100yds* **16/1**
4- **2** *1 ¼* **The Grey Taylor (IRE)**[65] 3276 5-10-9 0 ..... PaulBohan(7) 105
(Steve Gollings) *led: drvn 3f out: hdd and no ex ins fnl f* **11/2**[3]
- **3** *4* **Vinnie Red (IRE)** 5-11-2 0 ..... AdamWedge 101
(Evan Williams) *hld up: hdwy to chse ldrs 6f out: drvn and hung lft in 3rd over 1f out: kpt on one pce* **14/1**
4- **4** *1 ¾* **Chicoria (IRE)**[97] 2703 5-10-13 0 ..... JakeGreenall(3) 99
(Henry Daly) *t.k.h: sn trcking ldr: kpt on one pce fnl 2f* **12/1**
5 *½* **Head Of The Class (IRE)**[62] 5-10-9 0 ..... MrJohnWilley(7) 99
(Brian Ellison) *stdd s: t.k.h in rr: hdwy 6f out: sn chsng ldrs: outpcd over 3f out: kpt on one pce fnl 2f* **50/1**
4/5- **6** *1* **Arthur Mc Bride (IRE)**[93] 2759 5-10-11 0 ..... ConorShoemark(5) 98
(Fergal O'Brien) *in rr: hdwy 6f out: outpcd over 2f out: kpt on fnl f* **11/2**[3]
- **7** *¾* **Bedale Lane (IRE)** 5-10-4 0 ..... AdamNicol(5) 90
(Philip Kirby) *mid-div: hdwy 10f out: one pce fnl 3f* **14/1**
8 *hd* **Acertain Circus** 4-10-5 0 ..... KielanWoods(3) 89
(Pam Sly) *chsd ldrs: wknd fnl f* **25/1**
2- **9** *39* **Shout It Aloud**[29] 4016 5-10-13 0 ..... MichaelByrne(3) 62
(Tim Vaughan) *t.k.h: sn trcking ldrs: lost pl 3f out: sn bhd: t.o* **7/2**[2]
10 *3 ¼* **Tinos Tank (IRE)** 5-10-9 0 ..... MrFMitchell(7) 59
(Hilary Parrott) *unruly and rel to r: detached in last: sme hdwy 6f out: hung lft and lost pl over 2f out: sn bhd: t.o* **11/1**
1- **11** *6* **Mike McCann (IRE)**[132] 2001 6-11-4 0 ..... MrNMcParlan(5) 61
(Michael O'Hare, Ire) *prom: drvn and lost pl over 4f out: sn bhd: t.o whn eased 2f out: virtually p.u* **3/1**[1]

3m 52.0s (-7.10) **Going Correction** -0.425s/f (Good)
WFA 4 from 5yo+ 7lb 11 Ran SP% **119.0**
Speed ratings: **99,98,96,95,95 95,94,94,76,74 71**
CSF £102.94 TOTE £13.80: £4.60, £1.80, £3.10; EX 95.40 Trifecta £771.40 Part won..
Owner John Wade **Bred** Rabbah Bloodstock Limited **Trained** Mordon, Co Durham
■ Stewards' Enquiry : John Dawson two-day ban: use of whip (15, 26 Mar)

FOCUS
This was run at a strong gallop throughout.
T/Plt: £170.10 to a £1 stake. Pool: £145,318.36 - 623.58 winning tickets. T/Qpdt: £77.50 to a £1 stake. Pool: £10,864.78 - 103.62 winning tickets. WG

4234 KELSO (L-H)
Saturday, March 1

OFFICIAL GOING: Good to soft (soft in places; 6.4)
Wind: Light, half behind Weather: Cloudy, bright

4548 TERRY FRAME JOINERS NOVICES' HURDLE (8 hdls) 2m 110y
1:55 (1:55) (Class 4) 4-Y-0+ **£3,249** (£954; £477; £238)

Form RPR
122- **1** **Desoto County**[61] 3415 5-11-1 0 ..... JasonMaguire 114+
(Donald McCain) *trckd ldrs: smooth hdwy to ld bef last: rdn and r.o strly run-in* **8/13**[1]
531- **2** *3 ½* **Mohawk Ridge**[24] 4081 8-11-8 120 ..... BrianHughes 113
(James Moffatt) *led: rdn bef 2 out: hdd bef last: kpt on: nt pce of wnr* **4/1**[2]
40- **3** *1 ¾* **The Chief Villain**[13] 4313 6-10-9 0 ow1 ..... AnthonyFox(7) 105
(S R B Crawford, Ire) *hld up: stdy hdwy 3 out: rdn next: styd on fr last: nvr able to chal* **66/1**
406- **4** *1 ¾* **Utopian**[64] 3330 5-10-10 0 ..... CraigNichol(5) 102
(Rose Dobbin) *in tch: effrt and drvn bef 2 out: one pce bef last* **20/1**
1- **5** *5* **Rockabilly Riot (IRE)**[57] 3516 4-11-0 0 ..... DenisO'Regan 96
(Martin Todhunter) *prom: smooth hdwy appr 2 out: shkn up briefly and outpcd whn nt fluent last: sn btn: nt knocked abt* **5/1**[3]
/35- **6** *nk* **Spitz (FR)**[16] 4234 6-11-1 0 ..... WilsonRenwick 97
(Rose Dobbin) *hld up in midfield: effrt and rdn after 3 out: no outpcd fr next* **10/1**
/06- **7** *1* **Neville Woods**[82] 3002 7-10-8 0 ..... AlistairFindlay(7) 96
(J L Gledson) *t.k.h: sn chsng ldr: rdn and ev ch after 3 out: wknd after next* **66/1**
0- **8** *15* **Alkali (IRE)**[18] 4199 4-9-9 0 ..... GrantCockburn(5) 66
(S R B Crawford, Ire) *nt fluent: in rr on outside: struggling bef 3 out: sn btn* **28/1**
56- **9** *30* **The Village (IRE)**[18] 4199 5-11-1 0 ..... PeterBuchanan 51
(Lucinda Russell) *towards rr: struggling bef 3 out: lost tch bef next: t.o* **33/1**
0- **P** **Thatsmylot (IRE)**[18] 4205 5-10-8 0 ..... DaraghBourke(7)
(Stuart Coltherd) *nt fluent in rr: struggling bef 3 out: sn btn and p.u* **66/1**

4m 8.0s (6.20) **Going Correction** +0.30s/f (Yiel)
WFA 4 from 5yo+ 7lb 10 Ran SP% **123.3**
Speed ratings (Par 105): **97,95,94,93,91 91,90,83,69,**
CSF £3.63 TOTE £1.70: £1.10, £1.20, £11.60; EX 4.30 Trifecta £82.10.
Owner Paul & Clare Rooney **Bred** Miss K Rausing **Trained** Cholmondeley, Cheshire

FOCUS
All bends moved out on to better ground increasing hurdles by 10yds per circuit. This proved straightforward for the odds-on favourite. It was steadily run and the first two are rated below their best.

4549 CYRIL ALEXANDER MEMORIAL NOVICES' LIMITED H'CAP CHASE (12 fncs) 2m 1f
2:30 (2:30) (Class 3) (0-125,125) 4-Y-0+ **£6,498** (£1,908; £954; £477)

Form RPR
232- **1** **Jet Master (IRE)**[57] 3519 8-11-7 **125**..............................(t) LucyAlexander 136+
(N W Alexander) *confidently rdn in rr: stdy hdwy to chse ldrs 3 out: 2nd whn nt fluent next: led on bit bef last: readily drew clr run-in* **9/2**[2]
142- **2** *11* **Smadynium (FR)**[51] 3615 6-11-4 **122**..............................(b) JasonMaguire 123+
(Donald McCain) *nt fluent: prom on outside: outpcd 7th: rallied whn nt fluent 4 out: sn drvn: rallied bef 2 out: chsd (clr) wnr run-in: no imp* **6/1**
/34- **3** *5* **Inoogoo (IRE)**[92] 2793 9-10-2 **113** oh7 ow2................ GrahamWatters(7) 106
(Brian Ellison) *mde most tl rdn and hdd bef last: sn outpcd: lost 2nd run-in* **11/2**[3]
524- **4** *2 ½* **Desgrey**[51] 3615 6-10-10 **114**..............................(p) WilsonRenwick 105
(Peter Niven) *in tch: reminders after 4th: effrt and rdn after 3 out: no imp fr next* **7/1**
120/ **5** *1* **Makbullet**[304] 5178 7-11-2 **120**.............................. BrianHughes 110
(Michael Smith) *prom: wnt 2nd 4 out to bef 2 out: wknd appr last* **20/1**
413- **6** *9* **Ballycool (IRE)**[57] 3517 7-10-2 **111** oh6..............................(t) DerekFox(5) 92
(Lucinda Russell) *bhd: outpcd fr 4th: sme late hdwy: nvr on terms* **8/1**
433- **7** *2* **Dartford Warbler (IRE)**[25] 4077 7-11-1 **119**.............................. RyanMania 98
(Sue Smith) *nt fluent on occasions: w ldrs tl outpcd 4 out: btn bef 2 out* **3/1**[1]
5U1- **8** *17* **Suprise Vendor (IRE)**[16] 4235 8-10-12 **123**................ DaraghBourke(7) 96
(Stuart Coltherd) *w ldrs: rdn whn nt fluent 4 out: lost pl whn mstke next: sn btn* **8/1**

4m 20.1s (2.10) **Going Correction** +0.30s/f (Yiel) **8** Ran SP% **112.3**
Speed ratings (Par 107): **107,101,99,98,97 93,92,84**
CSF £30.44 CT £149.05 TOTE £4.80: £1.90, £2.10, £2.10; EX 23.70 Trifecta £389.00.
Owner H W Turcan & Sir Simon Dunning **Bred** Roger G English **Trained** Kinneston, Perth & Kinross
■ Stewards' Enquiry : Graham Watters three-day ban: weighed in 2lb heavy (15-17 Mar)

FOCUS
With the leaders taking each other on and going a good gallop, this was set up for the patiently ridden winner. This rates a step up and he can win more chases.

4550 £1.25 MILLION SCOOP6 PREMIER KELSO HURDLE (NOVICES' HURDLE) (GRADE 2) (10 hdls) 2m 2f
3:05 (3:05) (Class 1) 4-Y-0+
£19,932 (£7,479; £3,745; £1,865; £938; £469)

Form RPR
211- **1** **Clever Cookie**[27] 4056 6-11-8 136.............................. WilsonRenwick 145+
(Peter Niven) *t.k.h early: hld up: smooth hdwy after 4 out: led gng wl between last 2: sn shkn up: edgd lft and kpt on strly to draw clr run-in* **13/8**[1]
116- **2** *8* **Fergall (IRE)**[64] 3322 7-11-8 130.............................. WayneKavanagh 136
(Seamus Mullins) *led at decent gallop: rdn whn hit 2 out: hdd between last 2: kpt on: no ch w wnr* **12/1**
312- **3** *6* **Hit The Top (IRE)**[38] 3832 7-11-5 127.............................. RyanMania 126
(Sue Smith) *chsd ldr: nt fluent 3 out: rdn bef next: kpt on same pce* **9/1**
212- **4** *2 ¾* **Secrete Stream (IRE)**[39] 3826 5-11-5 127.............................. BrianHughes 126
(Malcolm Jefferson) *midfield: effrt and hdwy after 3 out: rdn and no imp fr next* **10/3**[2]
1/6- **5** *6* **Mister Nibbles (IRE)**[35] 3907 6-11-8 0.............................. MrBGCrawford 123
(S R B Crawford, Ire) *hld up in tch: stdy hdwy bef 3 out: pushed along and outpcd bef next: n.d after* **7/1**[3]
014- **6** *3 ¾* **Tough Trade**[39] 3826 5-11-5 120.............................. DenisO'Regan 115
(Chris Grant) *hld up: rdn and outpcd 4 out: rallied bef 2 out: nvr on terms* **50/1**
501- **7** *11* **Landecker (IRE)**[16] 4234 6-11-5 128.............................. LucyAlexander 105
(N W Alexander) *blnd 1st and a bhd: struggling whn mstke 6th: nvr on terms* **16/1**
/43- **8** *9* **Lord Usher (IRE)**[16] 4234 7-11-1 107.............................. PeterBuchanan 93
(George Charlton) *chsd ldrs tl rdn and wknd fr 4 out* **100/1**
613- **9** *2 ¾* **Maybe I Wont**[38] 3832 9-11-5 120.............................. TonyKelly 97
(James Moffatt) *hld up: mstke 4th: outpcd whn mstke 4 out: sn btn* **80/1**
30F- **10** *22* **Franciscan**[27] 4056 6-11-5 128..............................(p) JasonMaguire 75
(Donald McCain) *hld up in tch: outpcd after 6th: btn 3 out: t.o* **8/1**

4m 28.4s (1.40) **Going Correction** +0.30s/f (Yiel) **10** Ran SP% **112.5**
Speed ratings (Par 115): **108,104,101,100,97 96,91,87,86,76**
CSF £22.08 TOTE £2.50: £1.10, £3.10, £2.90; EX 21.80 Trifecta £139.50.
Owner Francis Green Racing Ltd **Bred** Mrs J A Niven **Trained** Barton-le-Street, N Yorks

FOCUS
Decent prize-money for this Grade 2 event. Another step up from Clever Cookie and there's probably more to come.

4551 PREMIER TRAFFIC MANAGEMENT H'CAP CHASE (HAMILTON MEMORIAL TROPHY) (BETFAIR SCOTTISH CHASE SERIES) (14 fncs 2 omitted) 2m 5f 110y
3:40 (3:41) (Class 4) (0-110,110) 5-Y-0+ **£3,898** (£1,144; £572; £286)

423- **1** **Rocking Blues (FR)**[24] 4080 9-11-11 **109**.............................. WilsonRenwick 116+
(Rose Dobbin) *in tch on outside: hdwy to chse ldr 5th: effrt and rdn after 2 out (usual 3 out): led appr last: hld on gamely u.p run-in* **7/1**
540- **2** *nk* **Fiddlers Reel**[16] 4236 11-11-12 **110**.............................. RyanMania 116
(Jane Clark) *cl up: led 4th: rdn 2 out (usual 3 out): hdd appr last: rallied run-in: kpt on: hld nr fin* **8/1**
34F- **3** *3* **Lady Of Verona (IRE)**[11] 4337 7-10-2 **91**.............................. CraigNichol(5) 94
(Lucinda Russell) *hld up bhd ldng gp: hdwy to chse ldrs 3 out (usual 4 out): kpt on u.p fr last: nt rch first two* **11/1**
114- **4** *4 ½* **Sharney Sike**[7] 4430 8-11-1 **106**.............................. DaraghBourke(7) 105
(Stuart Coltherd) *hld up: stdy hdwy 1/2-way: nt fluent and rdn 3 out (usual 4 out): no imp after next* **5/1**[2]
325- **5** *25* **Peachey Moment (USA)**[24] 4080 9-11-9 **107**................ DenisO'Regan 83
(Nicky Richards) *bhd: rdn along and outpcd 1/2-way: n.d after* **13/2**[3]
/36- **6** *10* **Blueside Boy (IRE)**[24] 4082 6-10-13 **97**.............................. PeterBuchanan 64
(Lucinda Russell) *chsd ldrs tl rdn and wknd after 4 out (usual 5 out)* **5/2**[1]
03P/ **7** *4* **Collyns Avenue**[439] 3116 11-11-0 **105**..............................(p) NathanMoscrop(7) 69
(Tristan Davidson) *t.k.h: prom: nt fluent and pushed along 10th: rdn and wknd bef 2 out (usual 3 out)* **28/1**
/PP- **P** **Accordion To Paddy (IRE)**[78] 3076 10-10-1 **85**..............(t) IanPopham
(Michael O'Hare, Ire) *in tch tl outpcd fr 10th: t.o whn p.u bef last* **25/1**
0U3- **P** **Milano Magic (IRE)**[28] 4040 8-11-9 **107**..............................(p) LucyAlexander
(N W Alexander) *led to 4th: lost pl next: t.o fnl circ: p.u bef 3 out (usual 4 out)* **7/1**

5m 46.0s (16.80) **9** Ran SP% **110.3**
CSF £56.84 CT £573.96 TOTE £8.00: £2.50, £3.50, £3.30; EX 26.70 Trifecta £517.80.
Owner J Filmer-Wilson & Mrs D Davidson **Bred** Mme Genevieve Mongin **Trained** South Hazelrigg, Northumbria

FOCUS
Due to the low sun the second-last was omitted on both circuits for what was just a modest handicap. The third sets the level.

4552 BEST ODDS GUARANTEED AT TOTEPOOL.COM PREMIER CHASE (LISTED RACE) (17 fncs) 2m 7f 110y
4:15 (4:15) (Class 1) 5-Y-0+ **£15,661** (£5,876; £2,942; £1,465; £737)

Form RPR
202- **1** **Maggio (FR)**[42] 3776 9-10-12 135..............................(t) BrianHughes 144+
(Patrick Griffin, Ire) *trckd ldrs: wnt 2nd 11th: led 4 out: rdn clr after 2 out: styd on wl run-in* **8/1**
311- **2** *4 ½* **Mr Moonshine (IRE)**[21] 4160 10-11-2 149.............................. RyanMania 144
(Sue Smith) *cl up: led 10th: nt fluent and hdd 4 out: rdn after next: no imp bef 2 out tl rallied last: kpt on: nt rch wnr* **5/4**[1]
110- **3** *11* **Kruzhlinin (GER)**[35] 3897 7-11-2 143.............................. JasonMaguire 139
(Donald McCain) *prom: outpcd after 12th: rallied to chse ldrs whn blnd 4 out: sn rdn: no imp whn j.lft last* **2/1**[2]
332- **4** *17* **Scotswell**[83] 2971 8-10-12 121.............................. LucyAlexander 117
(Harriet Graham) *led to 10th: cl up tl rdn and wknd after 4 out* **22/1**
PF0- **5** *39* **Opening Batsman (IRE)**[62] 3387 8-11-4 145.............................. IanPopham 97
(Harry Fry) *in tch: struggling fr 10th: no ch whn hit 4 out: t.o* **5/1**[3]

6m 5.7s (-2.30) **Going Correction** +0.30s/f (Yiel) **5** Ran SP% **109.9**
Speed ratings: **115,113,109,104,91**
CSF £19.33 TOTE £10.00: £3.10, £1.30; EX 16.70 Trifecta £45.00.
Owner M Deren **Bred** Haras Du Reuilly **Trained** Oldtown, Co Dublin

FOCUS
As usual, a small field for this Listed chase, but an interesting race nonetheless. A minor step up from the winner but there's a case for rating the form up to 10lb higher.

4553 ANDERSON AWARD WINNING BUTCHER - NORTH BERWICK H'CAP HURDLE (11 hdls) 2m 6f 110y
4:50 (4:51) (Class 4) (0-110,108) 4-Y-0+ **£3,249** (£954; £477; £238)

Form RPR
213- **1** **Total Assets**[28] 4038 6-11-10 **106**.............................. PeterBuchanan 115
(Simon Waugh) *in tch: hdwy and cl up 3 out: led after next: j.lft last: drvn out* **14/1**
303- **2** *1 ¾* **Gorey Lane (IRE)**[13] 4308 8-10-4 **93**..............................(v) DaraghBourke(7) 100
(John Norton) *prom: smooth hdwy to ld briefly 2 out: sn rdn: ev ch last: kpt on run-in: hld nr fin* **11/1**
155- **3** *8* **Redpender (IRE)**[51] 3618 8-11-5 **106**.............................. CraigNichol(5) 106
(James Moffatt) *hld up: smooth hdwy and in tch 4 out: effrt and rdn bef 2 out: sn outpcd by first two* **7/1**
2F6- **4** *1 ¾* **Auberge (IRE)**[13] 4308 10-10-11 **98**.............................. EmmaSayer(5) 96
(Evelyn Slack) *hld up: pushed along 4 out: hdwy 2 out: kpt on fr last: nvr able to chal* **33/1**
P46- **5** *2 ½* **Notonebuttwo (IRE)**[39] 3824 7-9-7 **82** oh1..........(vt) DiarmuidO'Regan(7) 79
(Chris Grant) *prom on ins: rdn and outpcd bef 2 out: hld whn mstke last* **5/1**[2]
450- **6** *1 ¾* **Funky Munky**[12] 3398 9-11-0 **99**.............................. EwanWhillans(3) 94
(Alistair Whillans) *hld up: rdn after 4 out: hdwy 2 out: no imp bef last* **16/1**
463- **7** *¾* **Master Murphy (IRE)**[70] 3210 9-10-4 **93**.............................. AlistairFindlay(7) 87
(Jane Walton) *midfield: rdn and outpcd 3 out: sme late hdwy: nvr rchd ldrs* **11/1**
430- **8** *5* **See The Legend**[18] 4201 9-10-3 **85**.............................. AdrianLane 74
(Sandy Forster) *midfield: nt fluent and pushed along 4 out: effrt bef next: wknd fr 2 out* **25/1**
10P- **9** *2 ½* **Solis (GER)**[33] 3938 11-11-2 **103**.............................. ColmMcCormack(5) 90
(Dianne Sayer) *midfield: nt fluent and outpcd 7th: n.d after* **33/1**
3/P- **10** *nk* **Bow School (IRE)**[289] 341 13-11-11 **107**.............................. DenisO'Regan 94
(Alison Hamilton) *cl up: led 1/2-way: rdn and hdd 2 out: wknd between last 2* **33/1**
3/P- **11** *¾* **Double Whammy**[9] 4366 8-10-13 **95**..............................(p) JasonMaguire 81
(Iain Jardine) *hld up: pushed along bef 3 out: btn bef next* **16/1**
235- **12** *1 ½* **Magic Present**[45] 3726 7-11-12 **108**..............................(b) BrianHughes 93
(Malcolm Jefferson) *prom: drvn and outpcd after 3 out: btn next* **12/1**
503- **13** *54* **Mister Jones**[29] 4005 6-11-4 **100**.............................. RyanMania 36
(Sue Smith) *prom: hit 5th: lost pl 4 out: sn struggling: t.o* **4/1**[1]
260- **14** *4 ½* **Azerodegree (IRE)**[92] 2792 5-11-1 **104**.............................. MrSFox(7) 36
(Harriet Graham) *nt fluent: bhd on outside: struggling fnl circ: t.o* **33/1**
15 *75* **Mooney's Cottage (IRE)**[8] 4406 9-10-8 **90**..............................(t) IanPopham
(Michael O'Hare, Ire) *led to 1/2-way: rdn whn blnd 3 out: sn btn: t.o* **33/1**
1PP/ **P** **Caught In The Act (IRE)**[427] 3343 7-10-3 **85**.............................. LucyAlexander
(N W Alexander) *hld up: nt fluent 7th: effrt bef 3 out: sn btn: no ch whn p.u bef last* **6/1**[3]

5m 56.1s (15.10) **Going Correction** +0.30s/f (Yiel) **16** Ran SP% **124.8**
Speed ratings (Par 105): **85,84,81,81,80 79,79,77,76,76 76,75,56,55,29**
CSF £152.15 CT £1169.36 TOTE £12.70: £2.50, £3.00, £1.60, £4.20; EX 203.40 Trifecta £814.70 Part won..
Owner Northumberland Racing Club **Bred** H L Kirpalani & Shade Oak Stud **Trained** Mitford, Northumberland

FOCUS
An ordinary handicap in which the second and third set the level.

4554 CGA FOXHUNTER (AN OPEN HUNTERS' CHASE) (17 fncs) 2m 7f 110y
5:25 (5:26) (Class 6) 5-Y-0+ **£1,247** (£387; £193; £96)

Form RPR
/42- **1** **Pena Dorada (IRE)**[17] 4225 7-11-6 107.................... MissRMcDonald(7) 113
(Alan J Brown) *prom chsng gp: hdwy to ld appr 2 out: styd on strly fr last* **8/1**
1/2- **2** *4 ½* **Moscow Menace (IRE)**[16] 4239 7-11-6 98.................... MrTHamilton(7) 108
(Miss K Scott) *in tch chsng gp: blnd 12th: rdn 4 out: rallied 2 out: chsd wnr bef last: kpt on: no imp* **7/1**[2]
/P1- **3** *½* **Tartan Snow**[16] 4239 14-11-13 122.................... MrJHamilton(3) 110
(Stuart Coltherd) *hld up: stdy hdwy 1/2-way: chsd ldrs 4 out: rdn after next: one pce appr last* **11/10**[1]

The Form Book Jumps, Raceforml Ltd, Compton, RG20 6NL.

2/2- **4** 1/2 **Buckstruther (IRE)**[279] 496 12-11-6 99........................ MrNOrpwood(7) 107
(Alastair Bell) *hld up: stdy hdwy 12th: rdn and outpcd after 4 out: styd on fr 2 out: nrst fin* **28/1**

/0P- **5** 22 **Ballycolin**[27] 4057 11-11-5 108........................ MrSFox(5) 84
(Ian Duncan) *hld up: stdy hdwy and in tch 7th: rdn and outpcd 12th: rallied 4 out: wknd fr 2 out* **16/1**

3P3- **6** 3/4 **Back On The Road (IRE)**[17] 4225 12-11-9 108.... MrJamieAlexander(7) 90
(N W Alexander) *hld up: rdn and outpcd 12th: sme hdwy bef 2 out: nvr able to chal* **33/1**

4P5/ **7** 5 **Tommysteel (IRE)**[20] 9-11-13 103........................ MrTDavidson(3) 85
(Victor Thompson) *hld up in midfield: lost pl 9th: struggling hit 12th: n.d after* **50/1**

/10- **8** 1 **Moon Over Miami (GER)**[267] 655 13-11-6 114............ MrDHolmes(7) 81
(D Holmes) *nt fluent on occasions: t.k.h: led and clr to 11th: hdd 5 out: wknd bef 3 out* **28/1**

054/ **9** 10 **Ashtonmore**[20] 11-11-3 0........................ MrBCampbell(7) 69
(Miss V Renwick) *bhd: struggling fnl circ: no ch whn mstke 3 out* **100/1**

324- **10** 2 1/2 **Gin Cobbler**[76] 8-11-6 103........................ MrTSpeke(7) 70
(Victor Thompson) *cl up: chsd clr ldr 9th: led 5 out to appr 2 out: sn wknd* **80/1**

010/ **P** **Sotovik (IRE)**[20] 13-11-9 117........................ MissATaylor(7)
(Miss D V Carter) *sn chsng clr ldr: blnd 6th: struggling fr 10th: t.o whn p.u bef 2 out* **66/1**

4PP/ **P** **Supreme Builder**[41] 13-11-10 95........................ MissCWalton
(Miss G E J Anderson) *prom: lost pl 4th: t.o whn p.u after 10th* **100/1**

U16- **P** **Special Portrait (IRE)**[27] 4057 10-11-13 109....................(t) MrGCrow(3)
(Mark Hughes) *hld up in midfield: stdy hdwy 1/2-way: struggling bef 4 out: btn whn p.u bef 2 out* **10/1**

P/3- **P** **Douglas Julian**[16] 4239 12-11-11 117........................ MrKitAlexander(5)
(Miss K Scott) *prom: outpcd whn hit 11th: sn struggling: t.o whn p.u bef 3 out* **15/2**[3]

16- **P** **Molten Brown**[17] 4225 9-11-6 0........................ MissJWalton(7)
(Miss C Marshall) *bhd: struggling fnl circ: t.o whn p.u bef 2 out* **100/1**

6m 17.0s (9.00) **Going Correction** +0.30s/f (Yiel) **15** Ran SP% **115.5**
Speed ratings: **97,95,95,95,87 87,85,85,82,81** , , , ,
CSF £57.26 TOTE £11.00: £2.90, £2.40, £1.10; EX 50.10 Trifecta £83.90.
Owner Alan J Brown **Bred** J P Dwan **Trained** Hawick, Borders

FOCUS
This looked less competitive than the field size suggested.
T/Plt: £41.00 to a £1 stake. Pool: £87,248.13 - 1,550.56 winning tickets. T/Qpdt: £17.40 to a £1 stake. Pool: £4,601.50 - 194.70 winning tickets. RY

4534 NEWBURY (L-H)
Saturday, March 1

OFFICIAL GOING: Heavy (hdl 5.6, chs 5.6)
The open ditch was omitted.
Wind: Virtually nil Weather: Some sunny spells

4555 MOORE OF DEVIZES LTD SUPPORTING GREATWOOD H'CAP HURDLE (10 hdls) 2m 5f
1:30 (1:31) (Class 4) (0-120,117) 4-Y-0+ **£3,898** (£1,144; £572; £286)

Form RPR

056- **1** **Westaway (IRE)**[44] 3741 7-11-8 113........................ TomCannon 122+
(David Arbuthnot) *bmpd 1st: trckd ldr after 3rd: led appr 2 out: drvn clr fr last: comf* **3/1**[1]

2/5- **2** 13 **Pilgreen (FR)**[22] 4129 9-11-0 105........................ FelixDeGiles 102
(Robert Walford) *chsd ldrs: hit 2nd: rdn 3 out: outpcd 2 out: rallied tl press run-in to take 2nd last strides but no ch w wnr* **12/1**

14/- **3** hd **Kings Bayonet**[646] 423 7-11-12 117........................ WayneHutchinson 113
(Alan King) *t.k.h: hld up in rr: stdy hdwy appr 3 out: trckd ldrs travelling wl 2 out: rdn and no imp bef last and no ch w wnr: no ex run-in and dropped to 3rd last strides* **16/1**

432- **4** nk **Red Devil Lads (IRE)**[28] 4029 5-11-8 113........................ APMcCoy 112+
(Rebecca Curtis) *led: drvn and hit 3 out: hdd appr next and mstke: nt fluent last and no ch w wnr: kpt on again u.p clsng stages to press for wl-hld 2nd* **7/2**[2]

454- **5** 4 **Premier Portrait (IRE)**[21] 4161 7-11-3 113........................ EdCookson(5) 105
(Kim Bailey) *chsd ldrs: rdn and lost pl 3 out: kpt on again run-in but nvr any ch* **11/2**[3]

F50- **6** hd **Minella Definitely (IRE)**[36] 3874 7-11-12 117....................(tp) NoelFehily 108
(Neil Mulholland) *chsd ldrs: pushed along 5th: styd in tch tl rdn 3 out and lost position next: styd on again run-in* **12/1**

/4P- **7** 13 **Bangkok Pete (IRE)**[47] 3691 9-11-2 110................ JeremiahMcGrath(3) 88
(Jamie Poulton) *in rr: hdwy 6th: chsd ldrs after 4 out: wknd 3 out* **8/1**

PUU- **8** 37 **What An Oscar (IRE)**[76] 3113 9-11-12 117............ SamTwiston-Davies 58
(Nigel Twiston-Davies) *wnt lft 1st: chsd ldr to 3rd: wknd btn: t.o* **25/1**

542- **9** 1 1/2 **Castletown (IRE)**[20] 4171 6-11-12 117........................(t) RichardJohnson 57
(Laura Young) *in rr: hdwy 5th: chsd ldrs next: wknd after 4 out* **7/1**

034- **P** **Torero**[55] 3550 5-11-6 111........................ AndrewThornton
(Diana Grissell) *in rr: mstke 6th: pushed along bef 3 out: p.u 2 out whn struggling* **28/1**

5m 17.06s (-1.94) **Going Correction** +0.075s/f (Yiel) **10** Ran SP% **114.8**
Speed ratings (Par 105): **106,101,100,100,99 99,94,80,79,**
CSF £37.87 CT £493.58 TOTE £3.80: £1.50, £5.00, £3.30; EX 47.60 Trifecta £1100.70.
Owner P M Claydon **Bred** Seamus Kennedy & Jan Kennedy **Trained** Beare Green, Surrey

FOCUS
Rails moved in from yesterday (Friday) for fresh ground. Wayne Hutchinson described the going as "very, very holding and hard work". This rates a step forward from the winner, with the next three close to their marks.

4556 BETFAIR SUPPORTING GREATWOOD H'CAP HURDLE (12 hdls) 3m 110y
2:05 (2:05) (Class 3) (0-130,130) 4-Y-0+ **£7,797** (£2,289; £1,144; £572)

Form RPR

550- **1** **Billy Twyford (IRE)**[49] 3653 7-11-5 123........................(t) APMcCoy 127
(Lawney Hill) *t.k.h early: hld up in rr but in tch: hdwy appr 3 out: slt ld 2 out: sn hdd: styd on u.p to ld again fnl 120yds: drvn out* **9/4**[1]

F01- **2** 1 **Who Owns Me (IRE)**[28] 4040 8-11-12 130........................(b) NoelFehily 133
(Charlie Mann) *led: hdd appr 3 out: sn drvn: outpcd 2 out: styd on again u.p run-in to chse wnr fnl 75yds: kpt on but a hld* **7/2**[3]

343- **3** 3 1/2 **Brackloon High (IRE)**[21] 4144 9-11-1 119................(p) RichardJohnson 122+
(Brendan Powell) *trckd ldr tl jnd for 2nd fr 6th to 4 out: styd cl up: led after 3 out: hdd next: led again last: hdd fnl 120yds: wknd into 3rd fnl 75yds* **11/4**[2]

555- **4** 9 **Promised Wings (GER)**[21] 4161 7-10-11 115................(v) TomCannon 106
(Chris Gordon) *chsd ldrs: rdn after 5th and disp 2nd fr next tl led appr 3 out: hdd: btn after 2 out* **15/2**

/00- **5** 4 1/2 **Frizzo (FR)**[80] 3028 7-11-2 120........................(b) WayneHutchinson 106
(Alan King) *in rr: hdwy to chse ldrs 3 out: wknd after 2 out* **5/1**

6m 21.57s (13.27) **Going Correction** +0.35s/f (Yiel) **5** Ran SP% **108.1**
Speed ratings (Par 107): **92,91,90,87,86**
CSF £10.02 TOTE £3.00: £1.50, £2.00; EX 10.30 Trifecta £19.60.
Owner Andy Weller **Bred** Jeff Hamilton **Trained** Aston Rowant, Oxon

FOCUS
They went fairly steady early on and the form looks modest for the level. The winner is rated close to his mark.

4557 BARBURY INTERNATIONAL SUPPORTING GREATWOOD VETERANS' H'CAP CHASE (19 fncs 2 omitted) 3m 2f 110y
2:40 (2:40) (Class 2) (0-150,150) 10-Y-0+

£12,512 (£3,696; £1,848; £924; £462; £232)

Form RPR

P34- **1** **Summery Justice (IRE)**[22] 4134 10-10-4 128................ LiamTreadwell 137+
(Venetia Williams) *in rr: hdwy and blnd 14th: wnt 2nd after 16th: styd on u.p fr 2 out: edgd rt and led bef last whn nt fluent: drvn out* **9/2**[2]

0P0- **2** 7 **Burton Port (IRE)**[10] 4346 10-11-3 141........................(p) APMcCoy 143+
(Jonjo O'Neill) *led 2nd: jnd fr 7th to 10th: sn asserted: blnd 14th: rdn 3 out: bmpd and hdd appr last: no ex after last: wknd clsng stages* **6/1**[3]

3P0- **3** 21 **Pigeon Island**[35] 3888 11-10-4 128........................(vt) SamTwiston-Davies 106
(Nigel Twiston-Davies) *in rr: hit 12th and 13th: stl plenty to do after 16th but styd on fr 2 out: kpt on to take wl hld 3rd run-in* **9/1**

225- **4** 7 **Tullamore Dew (IRE)**[14] 4263 12-10-4 128........................ TomCannon 99
(Nick Gifford) *in rr but in tch: hdwy 16th: styd on to take wl-hld 3rd 2 out: wknd into 4th run-in* **7/1**

P/P- **5** 10 **Master Overseer (IRE)**[49] 3655 11-11-5 143............(tp) TomScudamore 104
(David Pipe) *led to 2nd: rdn 13th: wl bhd fr next: mod prog u.p after 2 out* **10/1**

P/2- **6** 38 **Carruthers**[49] 3655 11-11-7 150........................(t) NicodeBoinville(5) 73
(Mark Bradstock) *chsd ldr 4th: chal 7th to 10th: lost 2nd after 16th: wknd qckly wl bef 2 out* **9/4**[1]

13P- **U** **Pete The Feat (IRE)**[28] 4035 10-11-3 141........................ NoelFehily
(Charlie Longsdon) *trckd ldrs: 5 l 3rd whn mstke and uns rdr 12th* **6/1**[3]

6m 46.18s (0.18) **Going Correction** +0.35s/f (Yiel) **7** Ran SP% **109.1**
Speed ratings: **113,110,104,102,99 88,**
CSF £28.06 TOTE £5.30: £2.50, £3.10; EX 30.60 Trifecta £231.20.
Owner Mrs H Brown **Bred** Michael Long **Trained** Kings Caple, H'fords

FOCUS
The second fence up the straight was bypassed in all chases. With three horses who like to make the running in the field this was always likely to be run at a good gallop. The winner is rated back to the best of his 2012 form, and the second may still be capable of 150+ figures.

4558 LADBROKES SUPPORTING GREATWOOD H'CAP HURDLE (8 hdls) 2m 110y
3:15 (3:15) (Class 3) (0-140,132) 4-Y-0+ **£7,830** (£2,541; £1,432)

Form RPR

330- **1** **Jumps Road**[21] 4147 7-11-11 131........................ BrendanPowell 128+
(Colin Tizzard) *chsd ldrs: hit 4th: rdn 3 out: one pce and u.p in 5th whn lft 3rd 2 out: rallied u.p to chal last: led sn after: hld on all out* **13/2**

661/ **2** nk **Kuda Huraa (IRE)**[280] 5064 6-11-3 123................ WayneHutchinson 120
(Alan King) *hld up in rr: stdy hdwy 3 out: trcking ldrs whn lft cl 2nd 2 out: sn led: drvn: stmbld and lost momentum whn pressed last and sn hdd: rallied u.p clsng stages: jst failed* **16/1**

F01- **3** 9 **Bodega**[10] 4350 6-11-3 123........................(p) APMcCoy 112
(Ian Williams) *led to 2nd: chsd ldrs: chal and hit 3 out: 2 l 3rd and rdn whn lft in slt ld 2 out: sn hdd & wknd bef last* **6/1**[3]

003- **F** **Seventh Sky (GER)**[14] 4278 7-11-5 125................(t) NoelFehily 122
(Charlie Mann) *led 2nd: jnd 3 out: 1 l in front and travelling ok whn fell 2 out* **7/2**[2]

3F2- **U** **Roman Flight (IRE)**[17] 4224 6-11-7 132................(v) KieronEdgar(5) 108
(David Dennis) *in rr: j. slowly 3rd: blnd 4 out: no ch whn nt fluent 3 out: wl bhd whn bdly hmpd and uns rdr 2 out* **8/1**

312- **B** **Tiqris**[20] 4173 6-11-9 129........................(t) RichardJohnson 131+
(Philip Hobbs) *trckd ldrs: 1 l 2nd and travelling wl whn bdly hmpd and b.d 2 out* **11/8**[1]

4m 16.73s (6.73) **Going Correction** +0.625s/f (Soft) **6** Ran SP% **108.9**
Speed ratings (Par 107): **109,108,104, ,**
CSF £76.23 TOTE £8.60: £3.50, £4.30; EX 68.50 Trifecta £423.00.
Owner Chasing Gold Racing Club **Bred** T H Chadney **Trained** Milborne Port, Dorset

FOCUS
An ordinary contest for the grade and the complexion of the race changed two out when Seventh Sky fell and brought down the favourite. The winner was again well below his best.

4559 STANJAMES.COM SUPPORTING GREATWOOD GOLD CUP H'CAP CHASE (GRADE 3) (14 fncs 2 omitted) 2m 4f
3:50 (3:55) (Class 1) 5-Y-0+

£28,475 (£10,685; £5,350; £2,665; £1,340; £670)

Form RPR

352- **1** **Shangani (USA)**[22] 4133 8-10-12 132........................ TomScudamore 142+
(Venetia Williams) *towards rr but in tch: hdwy 9th: led 11th: jnd and rdn 2 out: narrowly hdd last: pushed bdly lft run-in: c rt and rallied to keep on crse and ld fnl 100yds: kpt on strly clsng satges* **3/1**[1]

413- **2** 1 3/4 **Rebel Rebellion (IRE)**[28] 4032 9-11-12 146................(bt[1]) RyanMahon 153
(Paul Nicholls) *hit 2nd: chsd ldrs: chal 2 out: slt ld last and edgd lft but gng off crse run-in: pushed rt and hdd fnl 100yds: no ex* **7/1**

324- **3** 6 **Elenika (FR)**[15] 4250 6-10-3 123........................ LiamTreadwell 124
(Venetia Williams) *in tch tl lost pl 3rd: hdwy to chse ldrs after 10th: drvn along and one pce fr 2 out* **9/2**[3]

206- **4** 1 3/4 **Tara Rose**[85] 2925 9-10-5 125........................(t) SamTwiston-Davies 124
(Nigel Twiston-Davies) *in rr: nt fluent 8th and next: styd on same pce fr 4 out and no imp on ldrs* **8/1**

050- **5** 13 **Ulck Du Lin (FR)**[35] 3887 6-10-13 133........................(t) NoelFehily 118
(Paul Nicholls) *in tch: hdwy to chse ldrs 9th: wknd after 11th* **7/2**[2]

551- **6** 1 3/4 **Dashing George (IRE)**[15] 4250 12-10-2 129........................ MrRWinks(7) 115
(Peter Winks) *led tl hit 4th and hdd: chal 6th tl led 8th: hdd 11th: wknd wl bef 2 out* **10/1**

FP5- **7** 1 ¼ **Majala (FR)**[21] 4160 8-11-8 **142**..(t) PaddyBrennan 127
(Tom George) *chsd ldr: led 4th: pressed fr 6th tl hdd 8th: hit 9th: wknd and blnd 3 out* **6/1**

5m 10.67s (7.67) **Going Correction** +0.625s/f (Soft) **7** Ran SP% **112.4**
Speed ratings: **109,108,105,105,100 99,98**
CSF £22.76 CT £91.17 TOTE £3.40: £2.20, £3.00; EX 21.30 Trifecta £78.10.
Owner The Bellamy Partnership **Bred** Aleyrion Bloodstock Ltd **Trained** Kings Caple, H'fords
■ Stewards' Enquiry : Tom Scudamore four-day ban: use of whip (15-18 Mar)

FOCUS
Not the strongest edition of this race, with nearly all the runners having one thing or another to prove on recent form, but it served up a cracking duel from a fair way out, with Shangani coming out on top of Rebel Rebellion, but only after the pair had to dive back onto the correct course, with Ryan Mahon, who rode the runner-up, unaware in the moment that he was heading the wrong side of the railing on the run-in. The winner is rated close to his best.

4560 GREATWOOD NOVICES' LIMITED H'CAP CHASE (FOR THE JACKY UPTON TROPHY) (13 fncs 2 omitted) 2m 2f 110y
4:25 (4:26) (Class 3) (0-125,123) 5-Y-O+ **£7,147** (£2,098; £1,049; £524)

Form RPR
242- **1** **Headly's Bridge (IRE)**[14] 4278 8-11-2 **120**.................. AndrewThornton 134+
(Simon Earle) *in tch: pressed ldrs fr 8th: led after 3 out: travelling wl but pressed whn lft clr 2 out: in n.d after and sn c clr* **14/1**
223- **2** *19* **Smart Money (IRE)**[41] 3802 7-10-10 **114**......................... LiamTreadwell 110+
(Venetia Williams) *led to 7th: styd pressing ldrs: hit 9th: led after 10th: sn hdd: no ch whn lft mod 2nd 2 out: no ch whn mstke last* **9/2**[2]
341- **3** *9* **Paddy The Stout (IRE)**[22] 4131 9-10-6 **110**.......................(t) TomO'Brien 96
(Paul Henderson) *in rr: nt fluent: styd on fr 2 out to take mod 3rd after last* **14/1**
/44- **4** *3* **The Ould Lad (IRE)**[45] 3716 6-10-8 **112**........................... PaddyBrennan 94
(Tom George) *pressed ldrs: led 7th: chal 4th: stl upsides 8th: wknd fr 10th* **9/4**[1]
22P- **5** 1 ¾ **Un Bon P'Tit Gars (FR)**[63] 3362 6-11-5 **123**........... SamTwiston-Davies 103
(Nick Williams) *chsd ldrs: rdn appr 10th: no ch fr 3 out* **9/2**[2]
363- **6** *37* **Sergeant Dick (IRE)**[14] 4273 9-11-4 **122**.............................(t) APMcCoy 64
(Barry Brennan) *j. slowly 3rd: chsd ldrs: led and hit 7th: hdd after 10th: sn wknd* **10/1**
3/3- **F** **Cody Wyoming**[109] 2437 8-10-0 **109** oh4.................... NicodeBoinville[(5)] 110
(Heather Main) *tk keen old early: chsd ldrs: hit 9th: chalng and gng ok whn wnt lft and fell 2 out* **9/1**
/13- **P** **Tresor De Bontee (FR)**[30] 3992 7-11-4 **122**................. RichardJohnson
(Richard Lee) *bhd fr 6th: t.o whn p.u bef 3 out* **13/2**[3]

4m 42.88s (12.88) **Going Correction** +0.90s/f (Soft) **8** Ran SP% **112.9**
Speed ratings: **108,100,96,94,94 78, ,**
CSF £74.64 CT £904.77 TOTE £14.50: £3.50, £1.90, £3.60; EX 77.60 Trifecta £433.20.
Owner Mrs P L Bridel **Bred** Islanmore Stud **Trained** Tytherington, Wilts

FOCUS
No hanging around in what had looked an open handicap. The impressive winner was up 12lb on the best of his hurdle figures.

4561 WEST BERKSHIRE RACING CLUB "JUNIOR" BUMPER (A JUNIOR STANDARD OPEN NATIONAL HUNT FLAT RACE) 1m 4f 110y
5:00 (5:00) (Class 6) 4-Y-O **£1,711** (£498; £249)

Form RPR
1 **Puisque Tu Pars (FR)** 4-10-12 0.. JamieMoore 108+
(Gary Moore) *lost position 6f out: rdn in rr and green over 4f out: styd on u.p but stl green over 2f out: led wl over 1f out: styd on wl u.p* **5/1**[2]
2 3 ½ **McCabe Creek (IRE)** 4-10-12 0................................ WayneHutchinson 103+
(Alan King) *in rr: gd hdwy over 3f out: trckd ldr travelling wl appr fnl 2f: drvn to chal wnr fr wl over 1f out: no ex fnl 110yds* **8/1**
322- **3** *3* **May Hay**[49] 3663 4-10-5 0.. RyanMahon 91
(Anthony Carson) *led: rdn over 2f out: hdd wl over 1f out: one pce fnl f* **8/1**
4 *7* **L'Amiral David (FR)** 4-10-12 0... GerardTumelty 88
(Alan King) *in rr: hdwy to cl on ldrs fr 3f out: wknd ins fnl 2f* **8/1**
5 *1* **Glamorous Sister (IRE)** 4-10-5 0... TomO'Brien 79
(Robert Stephens) *in rr: hdwy over 2f out: sn drvn and one pce* **20/1**
12- **6** 3 ¼ **Hurricane Hollow**[17] 4226 4-11-5 0.. APMcCoy 89
(Keith Dalgleish) *in tch: chsd ldrs 4f out: rdn 3f out: wknd ins fnl 2f* **5/4**[1]
7 *10* **Radmores Jewel** 4-9-12 0... CiaranMckee[(7)] 59
(John O'Shea) *sn chsng ldr: wknd fr 3f out* **50/1**
0- **8** 4 ½ **Medburn Cutler**[14] 4267 4-10-12 0.................................... AndrewTinkler 59
(George Baker) *chsd ldrs: rdn and btn 3f out* **50/1**
9 *9* **Act Of Supremacy (IRE)** 4-10-12 0.......................... SamTwiston-Davies 46
(Charles Egerton) *chsd ldrs: wknd ins fnl 3f* **7/1**[3]
10 *11* **Ticinese** 4-10-12 0.. FelixDeGiles 29
(Heather Main) *bhd most of way* **40/1**

3m 3.65s (-2.15) **10** Ran SP% **118.1**
CSF £43.48 TOTE £6.80: £2.30, £3.00, £2.70; EX 50.20 Trifecta £91.40.
Owner Dedman Properties **Bred** Mlle Isabelle Mauger **Trained** Lower Beeding, W Sussex

FOCUS
An average junior bumper, but both the front pair showed plenty. The third is probably the best guide.
T/Jkpt: Not won. T/Plt: £949.60 to a £1 stake. Pool: £151,244.27 - 116.26 winning tickets.
T/Qpdt: £91.40 to a £1 stake. Pool: £10,234.55 - 116.26 winning tickets. ST

4562 - 4568a (Foreign Racing) - See Raceform Interactive

[4371] HUNTINGDON (R-H)
Sunday, March 2

OFFICIAL GOING: Soft (heavy in places; chs 5.4, hdl 5.0)
The 1st fence in the back straight was omitted all circuits. In the 2nd race the water jump was omitted on the 1st circuit.
Wind: Fresh across Weather: Overcast

4569 32RED FREE £10 BONUS MAIDEN HURDLE (8 hdls) 2m 110y
2:00 (2:02) (Class 4) 4-Y-O+ **£3,249** (£954; £477; £238)

Form RPR
4/4- **1** **Attwaal (IRE)**[24] 4103 5-11-1 0... JamieMoore 104+
(Neil King) *hld up: t.k.h: hdwy 5th: led last: rdn out* **6/4**[1]
/00- **2** 3 ¾ **Goldie Horn**[45] 3733 6-10-8 0...................................(t) SamTwiston-Davies 90
(Nigel Twiston-Davies) *trckd ldrs: led appr 4th: hdd last: styd on same pce flat* **40/1**
6- **3** 2 ¾ **Broughtons Warrior**[59] 3508 6-11-1 0.. DarylJacob 94
(Willie Musson) *hld up in tch: chsd wnr 3 out: ev ch next: no ex flat* **25/1**
04- **4** *7* **King's Warrior (FR)**[31] 3988 7-11-1 0................................ PaddyBrennan 88
(Tom George) *hld up: plld hrd: blnd 4th: hdwy after next: ev ch 2 out: wknd flat* **9/4**[2]
5 2 ¼ **Saint John Henry (FR)** 4-10-7 0..................................... TomScudamore 79
(David Pipe) *hld up: hdwy after 5th: mstke 2 out: wkng whn blnd last* **5/1**[3]
0/0- **6** 1 ¾ **Fuse Wire**[15] 4281 7-10-12 0...................................... RobertDunne[(3)] 83
(Dai Burchell) *prom: rdn after 3 out: wknd appr last* **150/1**
6- **7** 1 ½ **Paddocks Lounge (IRE)**[7] 4450 7-11-1 0.......................... MattieBatchelor 82
(Jim Best) *hld up: pushed along after 5th: outpcd after 3 out* **20/1**
05- **8** *nk* **Luckster**[7] 4450 4-10-7 0... DominicElsworth 73
(David Evans) *chsd ldrs: rdn after 3 out: wknd appr last* **14/1**
0- **9** *20* **Offherocker**[7] 4450 7-10-1 0.................................... JWStevenson[(7)] 54
(Claire Dyson) *plld hrd: disp ld tl appr 4th: rdn and wknd after 3 out* **250/1**
10 *27* **Mexican Mick**[470] 5-10-12 0... KielanWoods[(3)] 34
(Charlie Longsdon) *disp ld tl appr 4th: wknd bef 3 out* **18/1**
0/6- **11** *6* **Cool Chief**[291] 309 5-10-8 0...................................... JosephAkehurst[(7)] 28
(Alan Blackmore) *hld up: t.k.h: mstke 3rd: wknd 5th* **250/1**

4m 20.4s (25.50) **Going Correction** +1.40s/f (Heav)
WFA 4 from 5yo+ 7lb **11** Ran SP% **111.9**
Speed ratings (Par 105): **96,94,92,89,88 87,87,86,77,64 61**
CSF £71.00 TOTE £2.40: £1.20, £4.80, £4.70; EX 35.30 Trifecta £543.60.
Owner Dr & Mrs Clive Layton **Bred** Darley **Trained** Newmarket, Suffolk

FOCUS
Jamie Moore described the ground as "sticky" while Paddy Brennan thought it was "very testing". No depth to this maiden hurdle, which was run at a steady pace, and the form is weak. The winner didn't need to run to his Doncaster mark.

4570 HOG ROAST CATERING COMPANY H'CAP CHASE (13 fncs 3 omitted) 2m 4f 110y
2:30 (2:31) (Class 4) (0-105,102) 5-Y-O+ **£3,898** (£1,144; £572; £286)

Form RPR
312- **1** **Ratify**[72] 3190 10-11-9 **102**... RobertDunne[(3)] 109+
(Dai Burchell) *mde all: set stdy pce: nt fluent 9th: qckng appr 2 out: j.rt last: pushed out* **11/10**[1]
4F2- **2** *7* **Little Jimmy**[5] 4477 7-10-12 **88**..(p) FelixDeGiles 88
(Tom Gretton) *trckd wnr to 4th: remained handy: shkn up to go 2nd again 2 out: styd on same pce flat* **7/4**[2]
2P0- **3** *24* **Silver Steel (FR)**[44] 3755 11-10-8 **87**.........................(t) HarryChalloner[(3)] 70
(Richard Ford) *t.k.h: trckd wnr 4th tl rdn appr 2 out: wkng whn hit last* **15/2**[3]
644- **4** *57* **Chapel House**[40] 3817 11-9-7 **76** oh7.......................... MrMJPKendrick[(7)]
(Richard Harper) *s.s: hld up: pushed along 7th: nt fluent 9th: wknd 3 out* **8/1**

5m 28.7s (23.40) **Going Correction** +1.10s/f (Heav) **4** Ran SP% **106.9**
Speed ratings: **99,96,87,65**
CSF £3.44 TOTE £2.00; EX 3.60 Trifecta £5.60.
Owner J J King **Bred** Mrs R Lyon **Trained** Briery Hill, Blaenau Gwent

FOCUS
The first fence in the back straight was omitted in all chase races. The winner was rated 7lb off his best in this weak race and should still be competitive when reassessed.

4571 ON THE MOVE WITH ATACANTER HORSEBOXES H'CAP HURDLE (JOCKEY CLUB GRASSROOTS SERIES QUALIFIER) (10 hdls) 2m 5f 110y
3:00 (3:00) (Class 4) (0-115,115) 4-Y-O+ **£3,249** (£954; £477; £238)

Form RPR
604- **1** **Ghost Of A Smile (IRE)**[37] 3878 6-10-6 **100**............... RobertMcCarth[(5)] 106+
(Ian Williams) *hld up: plld hrd: hdwy 7th: led 2 out: shkn up flat: styd on wl* **9/4**[1]
343- **2** *6* **Thomas Junior (FR)**[33] 3956 5-11-6 **109**......................... TomScudamore 114+
(David Pipe) *trckd ldrs: chal 7th: slipped on landing 3 out: sn rdn: stl ev ch 2 out: no ex whn hit last* **5/2**[2]
334- **3** 1 ¾ **El Indio (IRE)**[27] 4068 7-10-8 **104**.................................... GeraldQuinn[(7)] 102
(Claire Dyson) *w ldr tl led 3rd: hdd 5th: led again 7th: rdn and hdd 2 out: no ex last* **16/1**
3/0- **4** *18* **Annaluna (IRE)**[11] 4351 5-10-9 **98**..............................(v) DominicElsworth 78
(David Evans) *hld up: hdwy appr 6th: rdn and wknd after 3 out* **33/1**
3F1- **5** *1* **Embsay Crag**[50] 3661 8-11-10 **113**.................................... RichieMcGrath 92
(Philip Kirby) *hld up: a in rr: pushed along 6th: wknd 3 out* **4/1**[3]
2/0- **6** 4 ½ **Zakatal**[13] 4327 8-11-12 **115**... AndrewThornton 90
(Simon Earle) *prom: pushed along 7th: wknd next* **16/1**
033- **P** **Sarando**[48] 3691 9-11-7 **110**..(tp) WillKennedy
(Alex Hales) *led to 3rd: led 5th to 7th: sn rdn: wknd bef next: bhd whn p.u bef last* **11/2**

5m 38.2s (27.60) **Going Correction** +1.40s/f (Heav) **7** Ran SP% **109.4**
Speed ratings (Par 105): **105,102,102,95,95 93,**
CSF £7.78 TOTE £3.10: £1.60, £1.60; EX 10.00 Trifecta £111.50.
Owner S J Cox **Bred** Kevin Talbot **Trained** Portway, Worcs

FOCUS
The market leaders came to the fore in this modest handicap hurdle. A step up from the winner with the second arguably unlucky.

4572 32RED H'CAP CHASE (THE JOCKEY CLUB GRASSROOTS JUMPS SERIES QUALIFIER) (17 fncs 2 omitted) 3m
3:30 (3:30) (Class 3) (0-125,125) 5-Y-O+ **£7,797** (£2,289; £1,144; £572)

Form RPR
0/3- **1** **Chapolimoss (FR)**[37] 3879 10-10-10 **109**........................(t) NickScholfield 125+
(Lawney Hill) *hld up: hdwy 14th: led last: r.o strly* **11/4**[1]
064- **2** *15* **Lively Baron (IRE)**[58] 3521 9-11-6 **119**.......................(tp) HenryBrooke 120
(Donald McCain) *trckd ldrs: pushed along 11th: drvn to chse ldr 3 out: ev ch next: wknd last* **7/1**
431- **3** *4* **Rydalis (FR)**[17] 4244 9-11-12 **125**...................................... AidanColeman 120
(Venetia Williams) *trckd ldr: led 12th: hit 14th: hdd last: wknd flat* **3/1**[2]
FF6- **4** *11* **Streams Of Whiskey (IRE)**[24] 4105 7-11-11 **124**............. BrianHarding 109
(Nicky Richards) *prom: rdn after 3 out: wknd bef next* **3/1**[2]
PP2- **P** **Frontier Spirit (IRE)**[29] 4027 10-11-12 **125**..........(v) SamTwiston-Davies
(Nigel Twiston-Davies) *led: nt fluent 6th: hdd 12th: rdn and wknd after 3 out: bhd whn p.u bef next* **9/2**[3]

6m 32.5s (22.20) **Going Correction** +1.10s/f (Heav) **5** Ran SP% **107.3**
Speed ratings: **107,102,100,97,**
CSF £18.49 TOTE £3.20: £1.20, £3.80; EX 18.20 Trifecta £46.40.
Owner A Barr,J Basquill,A Hill,H Mullineux **Bred** Mme Micheline Boucheron **Trained** Aston Rowant, Oxon

FOCUS
A good test in the ground. The easy winner threatened this sort of rating on better ground in 2011.

4573 32RED.COM H'CAP HURDLE (8 hdls) 2m 110y
4:00 (4:04) (Class 4) (0-115,117) 4-Y-0+ **£3,249** (£954; £477; £238)

Form RPR

P/1- **1** **Scotsbrook Legend**[54] 3597 6-10-4 **96**........................ PeterCarberry(3) 110+
(Shaun Lycett) *hld up: hdwy 3 out: led after next: sn clr: easily* **9/4**[1]

003- **2** *15* **Hartside (GER)**[20] 4187 5-11-7 **117**.................................... MrRWinks(7) 114
(Peter Winks) *prom: outpcd 5th: rallied after 3 out: styd on same pce fr next* **9/2**[2]

P03- **3** *nk* **Mission To Mars (IRE)**[27] 4069 5-11-5 **108**........... SamTwiston-Davies 105
(Nigel Twiston-Davies) *led after 1st: hdd 3 out: rallied to ld next: sn hdd and btn* **8/1**

/40- **4** *11* **Thundering Home**[87] 2910 7-10-13 **105**........................ GavinSheehan(3) 91
(Richard Mitchell) *prom: mstke 3rd: lost pl next: n.d after: bhd whn hmpd 2 out* **7/1**[3]

504- **5** *14* **Focail Maith**[60] 3469 6-11-9 **112**.................................... DominicElsworth 84
(Neil King) *prom: mstke 2nd: rdn and wkng whn hmpd 2 out* **10/1**

533- **6** *13* **Belle De Fontenay (FR)**[14] 4305 9-11-0 **108**.........(p) ConorShoemark(5) 67
(Conor Dore) *led tl after 1st: chsd ldr: mstke 4th: lost 2nd next: wknd appr 3 out: bhd whn hmpd next* **9/1**

306- **7** *11* **Houseparty**[13] 4324 6-10-8 **104**.. MrHGMiller(7) 52
(Zoe Davison) *hld up: bhd fr 5th* **50/1**

/24- **F** **Broughtons Bandit**[243] 856 7-11-4 **107**.......................... LeightonAspell 70
(Willie Musson) *hld up: hdwy 5th: rdn and wknd after 3 out: poor 6th whn fell next* **11/1**

065- **F** **No No Charlie (IRE)**[22] 4143 7-11-4 **110**......................(t) KielanWoods(3) 101
(Charlie Longsdon) *trckd ldrs: wnt 2nd 5th: led and hit 3 out: rdn and hdd whn fell next* **7/1**[3]

4m 16.0s (21.10) **Going Correction** +1.40s/f (Heavy) **9** Ran SP% **114.4**
Speed ratings (Par 105): **106,98,98,93,87 80,75, ,**
CSF £13.08 CT £67.30 TOTE £3.10: £1.50, £1.70, £2.10; EX 12.40 Trifecta £57.60.
Owner A E Price **Bred** A E And P E Price **Trained** Clapton-on-the-Hill, Gloucs

FOCUS
They got racing from quite a way out. The winner took another step forward and the form is rated around the next two home.

4574 32RED CASINO MAIDEN HURDLE (10 hdls) 2m 4f 110y
4:30 (4:30) (Class 4) 4-Y-0+ **£3,249** (£954; £477; £238)

Form RPR

63- **1** **Themanfrom Minella (IRE)**[53] 3602 5-11-2 0..................(t) DarylJacob 124+
(Ben Case) *trckd ldrs: a gng wl: led 2 out: rdn flat: r.o wl: eased nr fin* **11/4**[1]

342- **2** *3 ½* **Glowinginthedark (IRE)**[39] 3841 6-11-2 117..............(b[1]) AidanColeman 117
(Charlie Longsdon) *led: hit 5th: reminders bef next: drvn along and hdd 7th: led again 3 out: hdd next: styd on same pce flat* **3/1**[2]

5- **3** *7* **Benzel (IRE)**[24] 4102 6-11-2 0.. RichieMcLernon 112+
(Jonjo O'Neill) *hld up: hdwy 7th: mstke 2 out: sn rdn: hit last: no ex flat* **7/2**[3]

4 *8* **Pirates Cay**[666] 7-11-2 0... RobertThornton 103
(Alan King) *hld up: plld hrd: hdwy 7th: rdn and wknd after 2 out* **10/1**

2- **5** *2 ½* **Silver Gent (IRE)**[35] 3926 6-11-2 0.................................... HenryBrooke 101
(Donald McCain) *trckd ldr: plld hrd: led 7th: hdd next: sn rdn and wknd* **7/1**

6/2- **6** *53* **Rossoneri (IRE)**[112] 2393 7-11-2 0......................... SamTwiston-Davies 47
(Nigel Twiston-Davies) *hld up: rdn and wknd after 7th* **13/2**

5m 24.4s (25.40) **Going Correction** +1.40s/f (Heavy) **6** Ran SP% **108.8**
Speed ratings (Par 105): **107,105,103,99,99 78**
CSF £10.75 TOTE £4.80: £2.50, £1.40; EX 14.50 Trifecta £62.30.
Owner Mrs Carolyn Kendrick **Bred** G Durrheim And Maria Mulcahy Durrheim **Trained** Edgcote, Northants

FOCUS
Ordinary novice form. The cosy winner is on the upgrade.

4575 32RED IMMORTAL ROMANCE SLOT STANDARD OPEN NATIONAL HUNT FLAT RACE 2m 110y
5:00 (5:00) (Class 6) 4-6-Y-0 **£1,559** (£457; £228; £114)

Form RPR

1 **Ordo Ab Chao (IRE)**[127] 5-11-4 0................................ RobertThornton 122+
(Alan King) *hld up: hdwy 1/2-way: led over 1f out: shkn up and r.o wl* **6/1**

21- **2** *6* **No No Romeo (IRE)**[114] 2354 5-11-4 0........................ CharlieDeutsch(7) 119+
(Charlie Longsdon) *a.p: led over 3f out: rdn and hdd over 1f out: styd on same pce fnl f* **5/2**[2]

6- **3** *6* **Too Much Too Soon (IRE)**[61] 3440 5-11-4 0................. DenisO'Regan 107+
(Paul Webber) *hld up: nt clr run over 3f out: hdwy over 2f out: rdn over 1f out: wknd fnl f* **14/1**

6- **4** *21* **Nimbus Gale (IRE)**[100] 2660 5-11-4 0............................ LeightonAspell 84
(Oliver Sherwood) *trckd ldrs: led 6f out: rdn and hdd 3f out: wknd wl over 1f out* **5/1**[3]

5 *1 ¼* **Mister Chairman (IRE)** 6-10-11 0................................ MrFMitchell(7) 83
(Nicky Henderson) *sn pushed along in rr: hdwy over 4f out: rdn and wknd 2f out* **8/1**

- **6** *1* **Piccadilly Circus** 5-11-4 0.. TomScudamore 82
(David Pipe) *trckd ldrs: pushed along over 5f out: rdn and wknd over 2f out* **2/1**[1]

00- **7** *94* **Littleton Lad (IRE)**[23] 4135 6-10-11 0..........................(p) MrHGMiller(7)
(Zoe Davison) *led: hung lft 12f out: hdd 6f out: sn wknd* **200/1**

0/ **8** *39* **Winneys Boy**[648] 409 6-11-1 0...................................... PeterCarberry(3)
(Shaun Lycett) *chsd ldrs: lost pl 10f out: bhd fr 1/2-way* **100/1**

4m 10.7s (21.60) **Going Correction** +1.40s/f (Heavy) **8** Ran SP% **112.1**
Speed ratings: **105,102,99,89,88 88,44,25**
CSF £20.54 TOTE £10.40: £3.00, £1.10, £2.80; EX 22.90 Trifecta £214.30.
Owner A R W Marsh **Bred** Miss Pauline Kavanagh **Trained** Barbury Castle, Wilts

FOCUS
The winner looks decent and should win more races. The second set a decent standard.

T/Plt: £25.80 to a £1 stake. Pool: £86,275.54 - 2436.65 winning units. T/Qpdt: £7.70 to a £1 stake. Pool: £6189.32 - 590.47 winning units. CR

[4378] SEDGEFIELD (L-H)
Sunday, March 2

OFFICIAL GOING: Soft (6.1)
Final fence in the home straight omitted all chases due to false ground.
Wind: Light, half against, changing to fresh, half against after race 4 Weather: Overcast

4576 BETFRED NOVICES' HURDLE (QUALIFIER) (10 hdls) 2m 4f
2:10 (2:10) (Class 4) 4-Y-0+ **£3,544** (£1,047; £523; £262; £131)

Form RPR

4- **1** **Take The Cash (IRE)**[39] 3835 5-11-2 0........................... JasonMaguire 132+
(Donald McCain) *mde all: rdn and drew clr between last 2: styd on strly* **4/1**[2]

4/1- **2** *13* **Enchanted Garden**[45] 3735 6-11-9 0................................. BrianHughes 124
(Malcolm Jefferson) *chsd ldrs: stdy hdwy 3 out: rdn bef next: rallied to chse (clr) wnr whn nt fluent last: styd on: no imp* **8/13**[1]

1U4- **3** *7* **Slipper Satin (IRE)**[14] 4307 4-10-4 122........................ JackQuinlan(3) 103
(Noel Quinlan) *pressed wnr: ev ch and rdn 3 out: outpcd by wnr after next: no ex whn lost 2nd last* **4/1**[2]

0P6- **4** *27* **Thatildee (IRE)**[30] 4005 6-11-2 0...................................... RyanMania 83
(Chris Grant) *t.k.h: in tch tl rdn and wknd bef 3 out* **25/1**[3]

450/ **5** *48* **Squealy Keely**[308] 15 6-10-9 0.................................... PeterBuchanan 28
(James Turner) *hld up in tch: struggling fr 1/2-way: t.o* **80/1**

056- **6** *60* **Dermo's Dilemma**[10] 4379 4-10-0 0........................ DiarmuidO'Regan(7)
(Chris Grant) *hld up in tch: outpcd 4 out: sn lost tch: t.o* **80/1**

5m 12.0s (19.30) **Going Correction** +0.925s/f (Soft)
WFA 4 from 5yo+ 8lb **6** Ran SP% **108.2**
Speed ratings (Par 105): **98,92,90,79,60 36**
CSF £6.71 TOTE £3.50: £1.60, £1.10; EX 9.20 Trifecta £17.20.
Owner Trevor Hemmings **Bred** Miss Joanne Mulcahy **Trained** Cholmondeley, Cheshire

FOCUS
Hurdles on outer, divided bends and chasers dolled of inner rail. A modest novice hurdle but the winner looks decent. The form makes sense.

4577 COLLINS SEAFOODS H'CAP HURDLE (13 hdls) 3m 3f 110y
2:40 (2:40) (Class 4) (0-110,110) 4-Y-0 **£3,544** (£1,047; £523; £262; £131)

Form RPR

605- **1** **Boris The Blade**[59] 3497 12-9-10 **85**........................(b) SamanthaDrake(5) 95+
(Tina Jackson) *led: rdn and hdd 2 out: sn hung lft: rallied to ld last: styd on gamely* **25/1**

P03- **2** *2* **Caerlaverock (IRE)**[63] 3396 9-10-9 **98**........................(b) CraigNichol(5) 105
(Rose Dobbin) *hld up: smooth hdwy to press wnr bef 3 out: led and rdn next: hdd last: kpt on same pce run-in* **10/1**

525- **3** *15* **Big Sound**[30] 4006 7-10-13 **102**................................(tp) GrantCockburn(5) 94
(Mark Walford) *hld up: rdn and hdwy bef 3 out: wnt 3rd and effrt bef next: wknd fr last* **5/1**[3]

264- **4** *9* **Heez A Steel (IRE)**[17] 4238 13-10-2 **93**........................ AlistairFindlay(7) 76
(Jane Walton) *prom: pushed along and outpcd 3 out: lost 3rd and struggling bef next: n.d after* **16/1**

363- **5** *29* **Amore Mio (GER)**[34] 3938 9-11-5 **103**..........................(tp) PeterBuchanan 57
(Lucinda Russell) *prom: rdn whn blnd 9th: struggling fr next: t.o* **15/2**

551- **6** *8* **Captain Clayton (IRE)**[12] 4338 7-11-5 **110**........................ RyanDClark(7) 56
(Simon West) *hld up: rdn and outpcd bef 4 out: sn btn: t.o: lame* **9/2**[2]

P3U- **7** *15* **Mannered**[10] 4380 9-10-1 **92**... JohnDawson(7) 23
(John Wade) *chsd wnr to bef 3 out: sn rdn and wknd: t.o* **22/1**

/5P- **P** **Filbert Fox (IRE)**[40] 3824 8-9-9 **84** oh11.................(v[1]) CallumWhillans(5)
(Alistair Whillans) *prom: reminders 4th: drvn and lost pl bef 9th: t.o whn p.u bef 3 out* **50/1**

234- **P** **Madam Lilibet (IRE)**[5] 4478 5-10-4 **95**...............(p) JosephPalmowski(7)
(Sharon Watt) *hld up: stdy hdwy bef 6th: rdn and struggling fr next: t.o whn p.u bef 3 out* **5/1**[3]

611- **P** **Brae On (IRE)**[5] 4478 6-10-13 **102** 7ex...................... JonathonBewley(5)
(George Bewley) *hld up: stdy hdwy whn hit 4 out: sn rdn and struggling: t.o whn p.u bef next* **10/3**[1]

7m 14.5s (22.50) **Going Correction** +0.925s/f (Soft) **10** Ran SP% **111.5**
Speed ratings (Par 105): **104,103,99,96,88 86,81, , ,**
CSF £237.39 CT £1435.89 TOTE £20.70: £5.30, £2.90, £2.50; EX 243.60 Trifecta £2197.20.
Owner Simon Bodsworth & Howard Thompson **Bred** R Robinson **Trained** Liverton, Cleveland

FOCUS
This marathon handicap was run at a proper gallop. The form has been rated fairly positively.

4578 WRAGGS SEAFOODS LTD H'CAP CHASE (14 fncs 2 omitted) 2m 4f
3:10 (3:10) (Class 4) (0-115,113) 5-Y-0+
£6,256 (£1,848; £924; £462; £231; £116)

Form RPR

441- **1** **Mitchell's Way**[13] 4326 7-11-12 **113**................................. PaulMoloney 126+
(Alan Swinbank) *hld up in tch: stdy hdwy 9th: led bef 2 out (usual 3 out): rdn bef omitted last: r.o wl* **9/2**[2]

4F4- **2** *4* **Whats Up Woody (IRE)**[50] 3662 9-11-11 **112**.................. BrianHughes 120
(John Wade) *chsd ldrs: effrt and lft jst over 2 l 2nd last (usual 2 out): sn rdn: kpt on same pce passing omitted last* **6/1**

5P1- **3** *8* **Whiskey Ridge (IRE)**[10] 4380 8-10-10 **97**......................... RyanMania 98
(Sue Smith) *disp ld to 2 out (usual 3 out): rdn and outpcd whn lft 3rd last: sn no imp on ldrs* **9/2**[2]

501/ **4** *½* **Work Boy**[858] 2146 13-11-3 **109**................................. SamanthaDrake(5) 109
(Richard Drake) *bhd: rdn and outpcd 1/2-way: rallied after 2 out (usual 3 out): kpt on: no imp passing omitted last* **66/1**

2P3- **5** *27* **Mister Wiseman**[8] 4416 12-9-8 **88**......................(vt) ThomasCheesman(7) 61
(Nigel Hawke) *slt ld tl nt fluent and hdd 3 out (usual 4 out): sn drvn along: rallied: wknd appr last (usual 2 out)* **7/1**

320- **6** *40* **Ballymoat**[79] 3065 7-11-9 **110**...................................(t) RichardJohnson 43
(Tim Vaughan) *hld up: drvn and outpcd bef 8th: rallied to ld 3 out (usual 4 out): hdd bef next: outpcd whn hmpd last (usual 2 out): sn btn* **11/2**[3]

412- **P** **Baltic Pathfinder (IRE)**[25] 4086 10-11-3 **104**..................... ShaneByrne
(Sue Smith) *prom: outpcd whn j. slowly 9th: struggling next: p.u bef 4 out (usual 5 out)* **6/1**

304- **F** **See What Happens (IRE)**[92] 2820 8-11-11 **112**.......... WilsonRenwick 120
(Martin Todhunter) *hld up in tch: mstke 10th: hdwy on outside after 2 out (usual 3 out): 2 l 2nd and styng on whn fell last (usual 2 out)* **4/1**[1]

5m 12.0s (9.00) **Going Correction** +0.575s/f (Soft) **8** Ran SP% **114.3**
Speed ratings: **105,103,100,100,89 73, ,**
CSF £31.54 CT £127.44 TOTE £6.70: £2.90, £2.20, £2.20; EX 44.70 Trifecta £281.00.
Owner Ontoawinner 2 **Bred** Mrs P M Grainger **Trained** Melsonby, N Yorks

FOCUS
A competitive handicap in which all but one could be given a real chance. Straightforward form.

4579 JOHNNY RIDLEY BOOKMAKERS H'CAP HURDLE (10 hdls) 2m 4f
3:40 (3:40) (Class 4) (0-120,118) 4-Y-O **£3,418** (£1,009; £504; £252; £126)

Form RPR
/33- **1** **Forward Flight (IRE)**[50] 3659 8-10-13 **105** RyanMania 118+
(Sue Smith) *trckd ldr: led after 3 out: pushed clr fr next: eased towards fin* **5/4**[1]
P2P/ **2** 15 **Safari Journey (USA)**[694] 5279 10-11-2 **115** NathanMoscrop(7) 110
(Lucinda Egerton) *hld up in tch: smooth hdwy and cl up bef 3 out: effrt and pushed along bef next: chsd (clr) wnr bef last: no imp* **33/1**
404- **3** 4 1/2 **Vasco D'Ycy (FR)**[60] 3471 5-11-6 **115** JackQuinlan(3) 106
(Sarah Humphrey) *led: rdn and hdd after 3 out: one pce fr next* **3/1**[2]
5/0- **4** 1 3/4 **Fiddleesticks (IRE)**[136] 1935 6-10-7 **99** (t) DougieCostello 90
(William Kinsey) *hld up in tch: hdwy after 4 out: rdn after next: rallied and chsd wnr bef 2 out: outpcd and lost two pls whn mstke last* **6/1**
/P0- **5** 1/2 **Baileys Concerto (IRE)**[12] 4338 8-10-8 **100** BrianHughes 89
(Dianne Sayer) *hld up in tch: rdn and struggling bef 3 out: rallied between last 2: nvr able to chal* **12/1**
311/ **6** 27 **Keeneland (IRE)**[644] 451 7-11-12 **118** JasonMaguire 80
(Donald McCain) *chsd ldrs: lost pl appr 6th: struggling after next: t.o* **11/2**[3]

5m 17.6s (24.90) **Going Correction** +1.40s/f (Heav) **6** Ran SP% **109.7**
Speed ratings (Par 105): **106,100,98,97,97 86**
CSF £28.18 TOTE £2.00: £1.50, £6.40; EX 22.70 Trifecta £95.30.
Owner John P McManus **Bred** Limestone And Tara Studs **Trained** High Eldwick, W Yorks
FOCUS
The progressive winner took this apart from two out. Probably not the strongest form and the time was comparatively slow.

4580 WILLS PROPERTY SERVICES LTD H'CAP CHASE (19 fncs 2 omitted) 3m 3f
4:10 (4:10) (Class 4) (0-120,115) 5-Y-O+ **£4,471** (£1,349; £695; £368)

Form RPR
U41- **1** **Nail 'M (IRE)**[7] 4451 6-11-7 **110** 7ex (p) JasonMaguire 119+
(Nigel Hawke) *nt fluent: chsd ldrs: hit and outpcd 4 out (usual 5 out): rallied bef last: led passing omitted last: styd on u.p* **6/4**[1]
221- **2** 1 **Bennys Well (IRE)**[10] 4382 8-11-0 **106** JonathanEngland(3) 111
(Sue Smith) *led: rdn 2 out (usual 3 out): hdd passing omitted last: rallied: hld towards fin* **9/2**[3]
2PP- **3** 6 **Beau Dandy (IRE)**[40] 3825 9-10-3 **99** (b) DiarmuidO'Regan(7) 99
(Chris Grant) *cl up: wnt 2nd after 11th to 14th: rdn and outpcd after 3 out (usual 4 out): rallied bef omitted last: styd on: no imp* **3/1**[2]
0P4- **4** 4 **Purcell's Bridge (FR)**[40] 3823 7-11-12 **115** WilsonRenwick 112
(Rose Dobbin) *in tch: smooth hdwy to chse ldr 14th: effrt and pushed along bef last (usual 2 out): hung lft and wknd bef omitted last* **12/1**
P61- **U** **Acrai Rua (IRE)**[87] 2902 11-11-4 **110** (tp) TonyKelly(3)
(Tim Fitzgerald) *chsd ldr to after 11th: outpcd fr 14th: 5th and wl btn whn blnd bdly and uns rdr last (usual 2 out)* **16/1**
33P- **P** **The Magic Bishop**[40] 3827 9-11-5 **108** BrianHughes
(Malcolm Jefferson) *hld up in tch: rdn and outpcd: sn n.d: t.o whn p.u bef last (usual 2 out)* **6/1**

7m 18.2s (29.20) **Going Correction** +0.975s/f (Soft) **6** Ran SP% **111.0**
Speed ratings: **95,94,92,91,**
CSF £8.68 TOTE £2.80: £1.90, £1.10; EX 7.90 Trifecta £36.40.
Owner David Mitchell & D R Mead **Bred** Peter & Des Dundon **Trained** Stoodleigh, Devon
FOCUS
A moderate marathon handicap. The winner is rated similar to his recent win.

4581 COMPARE BOOKMAKERS ODDS AT BOOKMAKERS.CO.UK H'CAP CHASE (11 fncs 2 omitted) 2m 110y
4:40 (4:40) (Class 5) (0-100,96) 5-Y-O+ **£2,599** (£763; £381; £190)

Form RPR
432- **1** **Tokyo Javilex (FR)**[17] 4242 7-11-8 **92** (t) JasonMaguire 108+
(Nigel Hawke) *j. deliberately in rr early: hdwy 4 out (usual 5 out): wnt 2nd after next: pushed along to ld bef omitted last: drvn clr* **10/11**[1]
1F5- **2** 4 1/2 **Sendiym (FR)**[113] 2361 7-11-7 **91** (b) BrianHughes 96
(Dianne Sayer) *cl up: led 3 out (usual 4 out): rdn after last: hdd bef omitted last: kpt on same pce fnl 150yds* **5/1**[3]
U24- **3** 20 **Bocamix (FR)**[39] 3833 8-11-9 **96** JohnKington(3) 83
(Andrew Crook) *prom: mstke 7th: rallied 4 out (usual 5 out): ev ch after 2 out: wknd after last* **6/1**
334- **4** 5 **Panthers Run**[19] 4203 14-9-9 **70** oh7 (t) JoeColliver(5) 50
(Jonathan Haynes) *cl up: hit 6th: led next to 3 out (usual 4 out): lost tch fr 2 out* **25/1**
F52- **U** **Cara Court (IRE)**[10] 4383 8-10-13 **88** (p) SamanthaDrake(5)
(Joanne Foster) *led: j.rt 5th: hdd 7th: rallied and ev ch whn mstke and uns rdr 3 out (usual 4 out)* **7/2**[2]

4m 24.6s (16.00) **Going Correction** +0.975s/f (Soft) **5** Ran SP% **109.4**
Speed ratings: **101,98,89,87,**
CSF £5.90 TOTE £1.90: £1.70, £2.10; EX 6.00 Trifecta £14.40.
Owner D R Mead **Bred** Scea Ecurie Jc Laisis **Trained** Stoodleigh, Devon
FOCUS
A weak handicap. The cosy winner builto on his recent chase debut.

4582 BOOKMAKERS ON YOUR MOBILE AT BOOKMAKERS.CO.UK STANDARD OPEN NATIONAL HUNT FLAT RACE 2m 1f
5:10 (5:10) (Class 6) 4-6-Y-O **£1,559** (£457; £228; £114)

Form RPR
22- **1** **Degooch (IRE)**[87] 2905 5-11-4 0 JasonMaguire 115
(Donald McCain) *in tch: smooth hdwy to ld over 2f out: rdn and edgd lft over 1f out: drvn and styd on wl fnl f* **11/4**[2]
2- **2** 1 1/2 **Bryden Boy (IRE)**[29] 4043 4-10-10 0 SeanQuinlan 105
(Jennie Candlish) *t.k.h: hld up bhd ldng gp: smooth hdwy 1/2-way: chal gng wl 2f out: sn rdn: kpt on fnl f: hld towards fin* **5/2**[1]
2- **3** 1 3/4 **Tara Mac**[17] 4240 5-10-11 0 WilsonRenwick 104
(Keith Dalgleish) *hld up: hdwy to chse ldrs 4f out: rdn over 2f out: kpt on ins fnl f* **5/2**[1]
4 10 **Transient Bay (IRE)** 4-10-7 0 KyleJames(3) 93
(Philip Kirby) *t.k.h: mde most to over 2f out: sn rdn: wknd over 1f out* **14/1**
5 18 **Buzzard Flight** 5-11-4 0 RyanMania 83
(Sue Smith) *cl up: ev ch fr 5f out to over 2f out: wknd over 1f out* **14/1**
6 8 **Aregra (FR)** 4-10-10 0 BrianHughes 67
(Peter Niven) *prom: drvn and outpcd over 4f out: sn btn* **8/1**[3]

0/ **7** 1 3/4 **Hi Bob**[376] 4306 6-10-11 0 NathanMoscrop(7) 74
(Lucinda Egerton) *t.k.h early: chsd ldrs tl rdn and wknd over 3f out* **50/1**
8 69 **Europe (IRE)** 5-10-11 0 MrMJohnson(7) 5
(Sara Ender) *bhd: struggling fr 1/2-way: t.o* **66/1**
9 1/2 **Annie's Act** 5-10-6 0 SamanthaDrake(5)
(Joanne Foster) *hld up in tch: outpcd 1/2-way: struggling fnl 6f: t.o* **40/1**

4m 25.0s (23.70) **Going Correction** +1.40s/f (Heav)
WFA 4 from 5yo+ 7lb **9** Ran SP% **114.1**
Speed ratings: **100,99,98,93,85 81,80,48,48**
CSF £9.85 TOTE £3.50: £1.10, £1.40, £1.10; EX 9.90 Trifecta £17.30.
Owner Paul & Clare Rooney **Bred** David Harvey **Trained** Cholmondeley, Cheshire
FOCUS
Not a bad bumper. It was dominated by the form horses.
T/Jkpt: £8034.90 to a £1 stake. Pool: £33,950.67 - 3.0 winning units. T/Plt: £25.60 to a £1 stake. Pool: £11,4674.82 - 3257.44 winning units. T/Qpdt: £7.10 to a £1 stake. Pool: £7422.90 - 764.66 winning units. RY

4583 - 4591a (Foreign Racing) - See Raceform Interactive

4324 SOUTHWELL (L-H)
Monday, March 3

OFFICIAL GOING: Soft (heavy in places; 5.5)
The first fence and hurdle in the back straight were omitted in all races.
Wind: almost nil Weather: fine, sunny, mild

4592 BEST ODDS GUARANTEED AT TOTEPOOL.COM NOVICES' LIMITED H'CAP CHASE (12 fncs 1 omitted) 2m
2:00 (2:00) (Class 3) (0-125,122) 5-Y-O+ **£6,498** (£1,908; £954; £477)

Form RPR
011- **1** **Lord Navits (IRE)**[5] 4488 6-10-7 **108** 7ex (vt) AlainCawley 117+
(David Bridgwater) *mde all: hit 3 out: shkn up and wnt clr between last 2: eased towards fin* **4/11**[1]
3UP- **2** 9 **Elsafeer (IRE)**[67] 3272 9-11-0 **115** RichardJohnson 112
(Tim Vaughan) *hld up in last: hdwy 4 out: chsd wnr appr next: one pce between last 2* **5/1**[2]
13P- **3** 33 **Workbench (FR)**[44] 3787 6-11-7 **122** (t) HarrySkelton 86
(Dan Skelton) *j.rt: chsd wnr: drvn 4 out: wknd qckly next* **5/1**[2]
445- **4** 6 **Radsoc De Sivola (FR)**[67] 3268 9-10-2 **108** oh58 JoeCornwall(5) 66
(John Cornwall) *chsd ldng pair: drvn 4th: outpcd appr 3 out: sn bhd* **100/1**[3]

4m 13.6s (11.60) **Going Correction** +0.55s/f (Soft) **4** Ran SP% **107.6**
Speed ratings: **93,88,72,69**
CSF £2.72 TOTE £1.20; EX 2.40 Trifecta £3.60.
Owner Jobarry Partnership **Bred** Miss Mary O'Sullivan **Trained** Icomb, Gloucs
FOCUS
An uncompetitive handicap chase in which the easy winner stood out on recent form. There's a case for rating the race a little higher.

4593 TOTEPOOL.COM BEST ODDS ON IRISH LOTTO H'CAP CHASE (14 fncs 2 omitted) 2m 4f 110y
2:30 (2:30) (Class 3) (0-135,129) 5-Y-O+ **£6,657** (£2,067; £1,113)

Form RPR
452- **1** **Galway Jack (IRE)**[39] 3853 9-11-10 **127** AndrewThornton 133
(Caroline Bailey) *j. soundly: led: drvn appr 3 out: hdd between last 2: lft in ld last: kpt on gamely* **7/4**[1]
2/3- **2** 1 3/4 **Balzaccio (FR)**[102] 2630 9-11-3 **120** PaddyBrennan 126+
(Fergal O'Brien) *hld up wl in tch: nt fluent 10th: effrt 3 out: lft 1 l 2nd last: kpt on same pce* **11/4**[2]
31P- **3** 11 **Billy Cuckoo (IRE)**[18] 4244 8-11-6 **123** (v) DougieCostello 117
(Tony Coyle) *chsd wnr: drvn 7th: wknd sn after 2 out: lft modest 3rd last* **10/1**
516- **P** **Dashing George (IRE)**[2] 4559 12-11-5 **129** MrRWinks(7)
(Peter Winks) *in last: drvn 3rd: wknd 8th: p.u bef next* **7/1**
40P- **P** **Arthur's Pass**[25] 4104 10-11-8 **125** (p) RhysFlint
(Tom George) *chsd ldrs: drvn 8th: lost pl and hit next: bhd 4 out: t.o whn p.u bef next* **12/1**
2PP- **F** **Green Wizard (IRE)**[41] 3825 8-11-5 **122** RyanMania 128
(Sue Smith) *chsd ldrs: drvn on ins to chse wnr 3 out: narrow ld between last 2: slt advantage whn fell last* **4/1**[3]

5m 24.1s (7.10) **Going Correction** +0.55s/f (Soft) **6** Ran SP% **112.3**
Speed ratings: **108,107,103, ,**
CSF £7.31 TOTE £2.80: £2.20, £1.80; EX 8.50 Trifecta £28.20.
Owner Mrs M E Moody **Bred** John O'Mahony **Trained** Holdenby, Northants
FOCUS
This six-runner event looked competitive beforehand and there were four in contention in the straight. The winner and faller are rated pretty much to their marks.

4594 WE'LL DOUBLE YOUR DEPOSIT AT TOTEPOOL CASINO "NATIONAL HUNT" NOVICES' HURDLE (9 hdls 2 omitted) 2m 4f 110y
3:00 (3:00) (Class 4) 4-Y-O+ **£3,119** (£915; £457; £228)

Form RPR
222- **1** **Cloud Creeper (IRE)**[60] 3506 7-11-2 123 RichardJohnson 121+
(Philip Hobbs) *hld up wl in tch: hdwy to chse ldrs 6th: led appr 2 out: forged clr between last 2: pushed out* **1/1**[1]
2U- **2** 10 **Mondo Cane (IRE)**[17] 4248 7-11-2 0 AdamPogson 106
(Charles Pogson) *w ldr: led 2nd to 4th: led after 3 out: hdd appr next: clr 2nd last: one pce* **20/1**
/00- **3** nk **Mortlestown (IRE)**[65] 3357 6-11-2 0 IanPopham 106
(Martin Keighley) *t.k.h: hdwy to trck ldrs 6th: outpcd 3 out: styd on to take modest 3rd between last 2* **12/1**
65- **4** 1 **Max Ward (IRE)**[145] 1819 5-10-9 0 MrSDrinkwater(7) 105
(Charlie Brooks) *t.k.h: dropped in rr 2nd: stdy hdwy appr 2 out: sn rdn: one pce* **50/1**
512- **5** 2 **Templebraden (IRE)**[13] 4340 7-11-9 125 LeightonAspell 111
(Henry Oliver) *led to 2nd: w ldrs: led 4th tl after 3 out: sn lost pl: kpt on between last 2* **11/4**[2]
3- **6** 1/2 **Benenden (IRE)**[54] 3600 6-11-2 0 TomScudamore 104
(Michael Scudamore) *hld up wl in tch: hdwy to chse ldrs 2nd: nt fluent 6th: one pce appr 2 out* **7/2**[3]
U50- **7** 38 **Princess Bella (IRE)**[38] 3877 5-10-9 0 PaddyBrennan 58
(Fergal O'Brien) *chsd ldrs: drvn 5th: lost pl bef 3 out: sn bhd: t.o whn eased between last 2* **66/1**

5m 21.9s (8.90) **Going Correction** +0.65s/f (Soft) **7** Ran SP% **114.8**
Speed ratings (Par 105): **109,105,105,104,103 103,89**
CSF £20.26 TOTE £2.00: £1.10, £6.20; EX 25.20 Trifecta £214.00.
Owner Mick Fitzgerald Racing Club **Bred** J And P Bannon **Trained** Withycombe, Somerset

FOCUS
This was a decent novice hurdle that came down to three according to the betting. It didn't quite work out that way with the favourite winning without having the deal with much of a threat in the straight. The cosy winner was close to his mark, with his main form rivals well below form.

4595 PLAY BLACKJACK AND ROULETTE AT TOTEPOOL.COM NOVICES' H'CAP HURDLE (11 hdls) 2m 4f 110y

3:35 (3:35) (Class 5) (0-100,100) 4-Y-0+ **£1,949** (£572; £286; £143)

Form RPR

041- **1** **Barton Rose**[7] 4472 5-12-2 **100** 7ex.. NoelFehily 110+
(Neil Mulholland) *hld up in rr: stdy hdwy 3 out: jnd ldr appr next: led sn after 2 out: pushed out: readily* **4/5**[1]

321- **2** *2 ½* **Alaccordion**[28] 4071 9-10-13 **83**.. CharliePoste 86
(Violet M Jordan) *chsd ldrs: 4th and outpcd 2 out: styd on to dispute 2nd last: no real imp* **5/1**[2]

P/0- **3** *¾* **I'm So Special (IRE)**[38] 3871 8-10-9 **79**.......................(t) RichardJohnson 82
(Susan Johnson) *hld up in rr: hdwy 3 out: 3rd appr next: disputing 2nd whn hit last: kpt on same pce* **20/1**

605- **4** *5* **Lady From Geneva**[15] 4299 7-11-6 **90**.............................. BrendanPowell 89
(Brendan Powell) *trckd ldrs: led sn after 3 out: hdd sn after 2 out: wknd last* **10/1**

05P- **5** *18* **Langarve Lady (IRE)**[34] 3955 6-11-0 **84**..........................(p) DarylJacob 67
(Neil Mulholland) *in rr: hit 6th and next: sme hdwy bef 2 out: sn wknd* **25/1**

600- **6** *9* **Bellorophon (IRE)**[38] 3877 5-11-12 **96**.......................... WilsonRenwick 66
(Keith Dalgleish) *trckd ldrs: lost pl bef 2 out* **8/1**[3]

343- **7** *3 ½* **Dougalstar (FR)**[38] 3878 5-11-1 **95**................................ MikeyHamill[(10)] 62
(Sean Curran) *mid-div: pushed along 2nd: reminders 4th: lost pl next* **10/1**

P64- **8** *2 ¾* **Hi Candy (IRE)**[41] 3828 4-10-8 **97**.................................... RyanDClark[(10)] 52
(Ben Haslam) *mid-div: pushed along 3rd: lost pl 6th* **25/1**

040- **9** *1 ¼* **Echo Foxtrot**[38] 3871 5-11-3 **87**.. JamieMoore 50
(Claire Dyson) *chsd ldrs: lost pl bef 2 out* **20/1**

255- **10** *2 ¼* **Landenstown Pearl (IRE)**[15] 4309 8-10-10 **83**.............. JackQuinlan[(3)] 44
(Sarah Humphrey) *led to 2nd: lost pl 3 out* **20/1**

0/U- **P** **Mysula**[289] 369 7-10-0 **77**...(t) GeraldQuinn[(7)]
(Claire Dyson) *led 2nd: hdd sn after 3 out: sn wknd: t.o whn p.u bef last* **50/1**

5/0- **P** **Queenswood Bay**[10] 4398 8-10-5 **75**.............................. TommyPhelan
(David Dennis) *in rr: nt fluent 4th: hdwy to chse ldrs 6th: lost pl and blnd 2 out: t.o whn p.u bef last* **28/1**

5m 25.1s (12.10) **Going Correction** +0.65s/f (Soft)
WFA 4 from 5yo+ 8lb **12** Ran SP% **128.9**
Speed ratings (Par 103): **102,101,100,98,92 88,87,86,85,84 ,**
CSF £5.51 CT £56.74 TOTE £2.00: £1.10, £2.20, £5.00; EX 9.10 Trifecta £122.10.
Owner Lady Clarke **Bred** Lady H J Clarke **Trained** Limpley Stoke, Wilts

FOCUS
This handicap hurdle revolved around the favourite, who confirmed the merit of her recent easy win.

4596 20 NEW CASINO GAMES AT TOTEPOOL.COM H'CAP HURDLE (11 hdls) 2m 4f 110y

4:05 (4:05) (Class 4) (0-120,120) 4-Y-0+ **£3,119** (£915; £457; £228)

Form RPR

21P- **1** **My Oh Mount Brown (IRE)**[67] 3286 7-11-12 **120**................. NoelFehily 125+
(Alan McCabe) *t.k.h: jnd ldr 3rd: led sn after 2 out: drvn and hung lft: styd on strly: readily* **4/1**[3]

343- **2** *3 ½* **Sky Watch (IRE)**[22] 4175 7-11-7 **118**...........................(t) GavinSheehan[(3)] 116
(Warren Greatrex) *hld up: hdwy 5th: chsd wnr between last 2: no imp* **3/1**[2]

/50- **3** *1 ¾* **Kent Street (IRE)**[107] 2516 9-10-5 **102**..................... JonathanEngland[(3)] 97
(Sue Smith) *w ldrs: drvn and outpcd and reminder 3 out: kpt on appr next: 4th last: styd on same pce* **2/1**[1]

243- **4** *3 ¼* **Rio Milan (IRE)**[62] 3436 8-11-9 **117**................................(t) PaddyBrennan 109
(Fergal O'Brien) *mde most: hdd sn after 2 out: wknd last* **5/1**

406- **5** *1* **Pembroke House**[85] 2978 7-10-13 **107**.............................. WillKennedy 98
(Sarah-Jayne Davies) *trckd ldrs 2nd: effrt appr 2 out: one pce* **12/1**

135- **6** *16* **Kodicil (IRE)**[15] 4306 6-11-6 **114**....................................(b) DougieCostello 89
(Mark Walford) *t.k.h: w ldrs: drvn 3 out: lost pl bef next: sn bhd and eased: blnd last* **8/1**

5m 27.9s (14.90) **Going Correction** +0.65s/f (Soft) **6** Ran SP% **113.8**
Speed ratings (Par 105): **97,95,95,93,93 87**
CSF £16.94 CT £29.90 TOTE £4.40: £2.30, £1.90; EX 12.60 Trifecta £35.80.
Owner Craig and Maureen Buckingham **Bred** James Dillon **Trained** Averham Park, Notts

FOCUS
There were five non-runners but this still looked a wide-open affair beforehand. The pace was ordinary. The easy winner threatened this sort of rating when bolting up at Uttoxeter.

4597 DOWNLOAD THE TOTEPOOL LIVE INFO APP H'CAP HURDLE (8 hdls 1 omitted) 2m

4:35 (4:35) (Class 5) (0-100,100) 4-Y-0+ **£1,949** (£572; £286; £143)

Form RPR

/P0- **1** **Wordy's Boy**[40] 3839 9-11-12 **100**.. AdamPogson 111+
(Charles Pogson) *mde all: clr tl appr 5th: styd on wl to forge clr bef last: drvn out* **12/1**

433- **2** *9* **Walter De La Mare (IRE)**[10] 4398 7-11-8 **96**......................... APMcCoy 98
(Anabel K Murphy) *hld up in rr: shkn up 3 out: kpt on to chse wnr between last 2: no imp* **5/2**[2]

001- **3** *3* **Powertakeoff (IRE)**[17] 4247 6-10-10 **84**.......................... PaddyBrennan 84
(Henry Oliver) *trckd wnr: stmbld on landing 3rd: drvn appr 2 out: 3rd and one pce whn hit last* **5/4**[1]

606- **4** *1* **Drussell (IRE)**[24] 4129 8-11-5 **100**...................................... RyanHatch[(7)] 98
(Martin Bosley) *chsd ldrs: drvn 3 out: one pce next* **9/2**[3]

250- **5** *2 ¼* **Poetic Power (IRE)**[76] 3149 5-10-11 **92**........................ GeraldQuinn[(7)] 88
(Claire Dyson) *chsd ldrs: hit 3rd: effrt 3 out: one pce* **6/1**

4m 13.8s (16.80) **Going Correction** +0.65s/f (Soft) **5** Ran SP% **113.2**
Speed ratings (Par 103): **84,79,78,77,76**
CSF £42.74 TOTE £15.60: £4.70, £1.30; EX 42.00 Trifecta £130.10.
Owner Wordingham Plant Hire **Bred** L Wordingham **Trained** Farnsfield, Notts

FOCUS
Modest handicap form. The winner is rated to the level of his 2012 C&D win.

4598 £5 FREE IRISH LOTTO BET AT TOTEPOOL.COM INTERMEDIATE NATIONAL HUNT FLAT RACE (CONDITIONALS/AMATEURS) 2m

5:05 (5:05) (Class 6) 4-6-Y-0 **£1,559** (£457; £228; £114)

Form RPR

3/ **1** **Celtic Agent**[509] 1792 6-10-13 0.. AdamNicol[(5)] 110+
(Philip Kirby) *trckd ldrs: led on bit 4f out: clr over 1f out: v easily* **7/2**[3]

2 *12* **Gwendoliner (IRE)** 5-10-6 0.. BenPoste[(5)] 88
(Tom Symonds) *t.k.h: in tch: jnd ldrs 5f out: w wnr 3f out: one pce and hung lft over 1f out* **16/1**

3 *10* **Heston** 5-11-1 0.. MichealNolan[(3)] 85
(Robert Stephens) *trckd ldrs: led briefly 5f out: one pce fnl 3f* **12/1**

5- **4** *28* **Less Time (IRE)**[24] 4135 5-10-13 0........................ MauriceLinehan[(5)] 57
(Jonjo O'Neill) *t.k.h: sn trcking ldrs: drvn 5f out: wknd over 3f out: bhd whn eased ins fnl f* **2/1**[1]

24- **5** *10* **Trapper Peak (IRE)**[62] 3440 5-11-4 0.............................. JoshuaMoore 47
(Caroline Bailey) *led at modest pce: increased gallop 7f out: hdd 5f out: lost pl over 3f out* **3/1**[2]

6 *10* **Primitive Sam** 6-11-4 0.. AdamWedge 37
(Chris Bealby) *hld up in rr: drvn over 5f out: sn lost pl and bhd* **50/1**

7 *17* **Always Summat** 4-10-3 0.. MrHAABannister[(7)] 12
(Michael Easterby) *chsd ldrs: drvn 7f out: sn lost pl: bhd fnl 4f: t.o whn eased over 1f out* **5/1**

4m 10.8s (19.40) **Going Correction** +0.65s/f (Soft)
WFA 4 from 5yo+ 7lb **7** Ran SP% **112.8**
Speed ratings: **77,71,66,52,47 42,33**
CSF £52.33 TOTE £3.50: £2.00, £6.60; EX 58.60 Trifecta £282.70.
Owner Mrs Susan Johnson **Bred** Mrs S Johnson **Trained** Middleham, N Yorks

FOCUS
This was a below-average bumper run at a steady pace. Seemingly big step up from the impressive winner, but not an easy race to put a figure on.
T/Plt: £14.80 to a £1 stake. Pool: £70813.70 - 3491.18 winning tickets T/Qpdt: £7.90 to a £1 stake. Pool: £5346.44 - 495.80 winning tickets WG

4391 EXETER (R-H)

Tuesday, March 4

OFFICIAL GOING: Heavy (soft in places; chs 6.4, hdl 6.5)
Wind: Mild; across Weather: Overcast

4599 CALL STAR SPORTS ON 08000 521 321 H'CAP HURDLE (10 hdls) 2m 3f

2:00 (2:00) (Class 4) (0-115,112) 4-Y-0+ **£3,898** (£1,144; £572; £286)

Form RPR

552- **1** **Here's Herbie**[14] 4334 6-10-13 **104**............................(t) MissLucyGardner[(5)] 118+
(Sue Gardner) *hld up towards rr: hdwy appr 4th: rdn after 7th: 8 l down chsng ldr next: mstke last: styd on strly to ld run-in: pushed out* **10/3**[1]

444- **2** *10* **Gallic Warrior (FR)**[47] 3728 7-11-10 **110**......................... PaddyBrennan 117+
(Fergal O'Brien) *racd freely: led: hit 5th: 8 l clr appr 3 out: rdn and hdd after last: eased whn btn towards fin* **11/2**[3]

P60- **3** *26* **Darkestbeforedawn (IRE)**[16] 4300 7-11-12 **112**.............. TomO'Brien 88
(Caroline Keevil) *trckd ldr: rdn appr 3 out in clr 3rd: wknd 2 out* **6/1**

PP0- **4** *3 ¼* **Green Belt Elite (FR)**[16] 4302 10-11-12 **112**.................... AidanColeman 85
(Venetia Williams) *trckd ldrs whn hit 1st: hit 3rd: in last pair and struggling bef 4th: bhd 6th: styd on steadily fr 3 out: wnt modest 4th at the last* **14/1**

/34- **5** *3* **My Legal Lady**[55] 3604 9-11-8 **108**..............................(v) TomScudamore 78
(Stuart Howe) *trckd ldrs: hit 6th and stmbld: rdn in 3rd after 7th: wknd and j.lft fr next: lost modest 4th at the last* **10/1**

000- **6** *7* **Exmoor Mist**[35] 3956 6-10-13 **99**.. JackDoyle 62
(Victor Dartnall) *mid-div tl wknd after 7th: t.o* **9/2**[2]

410- **7** *39* **Monderon (FR)**[86] 2980 7-10-11 **104**........................ MrRobertHawker[(7)] 28
(Richard Hawker) *untidy 1st: hld up towards rr: rdn in midfield after 6th: wknd after next: t.o* **10/1**

323- **8** *4 ½* **Superciliary**[33] 3569 5-11-5 **105**.. TomCannon 24
(Chris Gordon) *hld up towards rr: rdn in midfield 5th: wknd after 7th: t.o* **14/1**

/32- **P** **Royal Opera**[256] 784 6-11-3 **110**.. JPKiely[(7)]
(Stephen Hughes) *mstke 7th: a towards rr: t.o whn p.u bef 3 out* **28/1**

016- **P** **All But Grey**[35] 3956 8-11-5 **108**...................................... MichealNolan[(3)]
(Carroll Gray) *mid-div tl wknd after 7th: t.o whn p.u bef next* **9/1**

4m 53.9s (11.20) **Going Correction** +0.725s/f (Soft) **10** Ran SP% **115.9**
Speed ratings (Par 105): **105,100,89,88,87 84,67,65, ,**
CSF £22.29 CT £105.47 TOTE £4.00: £1.60, £1.90, £2.10; EX 20.20 Trifecta £114.60.
Owner D V Gardner **Bred** D V Gardner Woodhayes Stud **Trained** Longdown, Devon

FOCUS
The hurdle course had been moved in and they were racing on ground that hadn't been used since December, but it was still hard work, with Paddy Brennan describing it as "soft/heavy and horrible". Although only a modest race, the front pair pulled clear and look worth keeping on side at a similar level. The winner built on his recent run.

4600 EBF STALLIONS MARES' "NATIONAL HUNT" NOVICES' HURDLE (10 hdls) 2m 3f

2:30 (2:30) (Class 4) 4-Y-0+ **£3,573** (£1,049; £524; £262)

Form RPR

11P- **1** **Bobble Boru (IRE)**[18] 4251 6-11-6 0.............................. AidanColeman 110
(Venetia Williams) *trckd ldr: led 3rd tl appr 3 out: led bef 2 out: sn clr: enough in hand and a holding on fr last: rdn out* **2/1**[2]

1F2- **2** *1 ¼* **Massannie (IRE)**[50] 3689 6-12-4 130.............................. TomScudamore 121+
(David Pipe) *reluctant to line up: sn led: reluctant and hdd 3rd: bk on an even keel bef 4th trcking ldr: led appr 3 out: hdd bef 2 out: sn looked wl hld 2nd: r.o again fr last* **11/10**[1]

5/3- **3** *23* **Molly Maid (IRE)**[26] 4114 6-11-0 0.. MarkGrant 80
(Dominic Ffrench Davis) *racd keenly: trckd ldrs: hit 1st: rdn appr 3 out: disputing hld 2nd 2 out: wknd* **20/1**

04- **4** *41* **Delineate (IRE)**[75] 3181 5-11-0 0...................................... GerardTumelty 39
(G C Maundrell) *in tch: stmbld bdly after mstke 2nd: struggling in last 4th: wknd after 7th: wnt modest 4th next: t.o* **18/1**

0PF- **P** **Party Girls (FR)**[33] 3991 6-10-7 0......................................(bt) MrMHeard[(7)]
(David Pipe) *racd keenly: plld way through to dispute 3rd after 3rd: rdn after 7th: wknd qckly: p.u bef 3 out* **25/1**

032- **U** **Buckboru (IRE)**[22] 4191 6-11-0 0.. DougieCostello
(Laura Young) *trcking ldrs whn tried to duck out and uns rdr 4th* **11/2**[3]

5m 11.7s (29.00) **Going Correction** +0.725s/f (Soft) **6** Ran SP% **110.2**
Speed ratings (Par 105): **67,66,56,39,**
CSF £4.56 TOTE £2.60: £1.10, £1.70; EX 4.60 Trifecta £19.20.

Owner Mrs B Grainger **Bred** Jimmy Coffey **Trained** Kings Caple, H'fords

FOCUS

A race that ultimately took little winning, with favourite Massannie putting in a bit of a moody display and third favourite Buckboru swerving and unseating. It was slowly run and isn't form to dwell on.

4601 HIGOS INSURANCE SERVICES DEVON NATIONAL H'CAP CHASE (£5K FIELD SIZE BONUS) (21 fncs) 3m 6f 110y

3:00 (3:00) (Class 3) (0-125,125) 5-Y£01,077 (£3,272; £1,636; £819; £409)

Form RPR

01P- **1** **Flying Award (IRE)**[31] [4026] 10-11-7 **125**................ MissLucyGardner(5) 137+
(Sue Gardner) *hld up bhd ldrs: tk clsr order 10th: led bef 4 out: styd on gamely: rdn out* **9/2**[2]

044- **2** *3* **Coolking**[33] [3990] 7-11-3 **116**.. AidanColeman 122
(Lawney Hill) *led: hit 12th: rdn and hdd bef 4 out: rallied briefly after 2 out: styd on but a being hld fr last* **9/2**[2]

454- **3** *4* **Alderluck (IRE)**[11] [4402] 11-10-12 **118**............................(b) MikeyEnnis(7) 123
(David Pipe) *prom: chsng ldrs whn nt fluent 16th: rdn to dispute 2nd bef 4 out tl no ex fr 2 out* **3/1**[1]

/23- **4** *11* **Armedanddangerous (IRE)**[75] [3178] 9-10-3 **102**.......(p) DougieCostello 93
(Tom Gretton) *trckd ldrs: nudged along after 9th: j.lft and bmpd 13th: lost pl u.p bef next: plugged on fr 4 out but nvr a danger to ldrs* **3/1**[1]

250- **5** *32* **Musical Wedge**[11] [4402] 10-10-12 **111**.................................... JamieMoore 82
(Claire Dyson) *hld up bhd ldrs: pushed along after 10th: rdn in cl 3rd after 15th: wknd appr 4 out: t.o* **16/1**

342- **P** **Somerby (IRE)**[29] [4066] 11-10-0 **99** oh12............................(t) AdamWedge
(Richenda Ford) *hld up last but in tch: wknd after 15th: t.o whn p.u bef 4 out* **10/1**

62U- **U** **Five Star Wilsham (IRE)**[47] [3730] 10-10-11 **117**............. MissVWade(7)
(Jeremy Scott) *trcking ldrs whn bdly hmpd and uns rdr 13th* **7/1**[3]

8m 16.8s (28.20) **Going Correction** +1.05s/f (Soft) **7** Ran SP% **113.8**

Speed ratings: **105,104,103,100,92** ,

CSF £24.87 CT £69.18 TOTE £4.70: £2.60, £3.00; EX 23.80 Trifecta £52.00.

Owner Mr & Mrs P George & Mrs B Russell **Bred** James V Neville **Trained** Longdown, Devon

FOCUS

Not a strong contest for the level, but the class horse of the race prevailed. The idling winner was value for a bit further.

4602 WEATHERBYS CHELTENHAM FESTIVAL BETTING GUIDE NOVICES' LIMITED H'CAP CHASE (18 fncs) 3m

3:30 (3:30) (Class 3) (0-125,125) 5-Y-0+ **£6,498** (£1,908; £954; £477)

Form RPR

0/2- **1** **Farmer Matt (IRE)**[88] [2922] 8-10-10 **114**..........................(t) PaddyBrennan 124+
(Fergal O'Brien) *trckd ldrs: nt fluent 4th and 10th: led after 2 out: styd on wl: pushed out* **3/1**[3]

212- **2** *1 ¼* **Beforeall (IRE)**[26] [4110] 6-11-7 **125**................................... LeightonAspell 132
(Oliver Sherwood) *led: nt fluent whn jnd 12th: rdn and briefly hdd appr 4 out: hdd after 2 out: styd on gamely fr last: hld nring fin* **11/4**[2]

556- **3** *16* **Knockraheen (IRE)**[29] [4070] 6-10-8 **112**...................(b[1]) RichieMcLernon 105
(Jonjo O'Neill) *trckd ldrs: hit 9th: rdn and ch briefly appr 4 out: sn btn: hit 2 out: regained modest 3rd at the last* **10/1**

1P0- **4** *8* **Super Villan**[38] [3886] 9-10-11 **115**......................................(b) JamieMoore 99
(Mark Bradstock) *trckd ldr: jnd ldr 12th: led briefly appr 4 out: sn rdn and ev ch tl 2 out: wknd into 4th at the last* **9/2**

230- **5** *6* **Ballytober**[73] [3205] 8-11-7 **125**.....................................(t) RichardJohnson 104
(Philip Hobbs) *racd in cl 5th: effrt appr 4 out where nt fluent: nvr fnd pce to chal: wknd 2 out* **9/4**[1]

6m 30.3s (21.00) **Going Correction** +1.05s/f (Soft) **5** Ran SP% **109.7**

Speed ratings: **107,106,101,98,96**

CSF £11.64 TOTE £4.50: £2.50, £1.60; EX 11.20 Trifecta £38.70.

Owner Steve Hemstock **Bred** Vincent And Jimmy Lawler **Trained** Coln St. Dennis, Gloucs

FOCUS

A competitive handicap, despite the small field, and the form looks solid. There's probably more to come from the winner.

4603 RACING UK NOVICES' HURDLE (12 hdls) 2m 7f 110y

4:00 (4:00) (Class 4) 4-Y-0+ **£3,487** (£1,192)

Form RPR

1- **1** **Capote (IRE)**[22] [4186] 6-11-4 0.................................... MauriceLinehan(5) 137+
(Jonjo O'Neill) *trckd ldr: led appr 3 out: sn wl in command: easily* **Evs**[1]

P1- **2** *24* **Saint Breiz (FR)**[17] [4281] 8-11-2 117.......................... MrRobertHawker(7) 102
(Carroll Gray) *led: rdn and hdd appr 3 out: sn wl hld by wnr: wknd last* **16/1**[2]

P **Chinatown Boy (IRE)**[311] 6-11-3 0....................................... DarylJacob
(Paul Nicholls) *j. sltly lft at times: trckd ldr: hit 4th: nudged along bef 6th: reminder after 7th: rdn after 9th: sn wknd: p.u bef next* **Evs**[1]

6m 31.1s (32.10) **Going Correction** +0.725s/f (Soft) **3** Ran SP% **105.9**

Speed ratings (Par 105): **75,67,**

CSF £8.03 TOTE £2.40; EX 4.20 Trifecta £4.20.

Owner Trevor Hemmings **Bred** Michael Long **Trained** Cheltenham, Gloucs

FOCUS

With Chinatown Boy never looking happy, Capote was left with only the outsider to beat and he did so with ease. The winner is a decent novice.

4604 RACING EXCELLENCE CONDITIONAL JOCKEYS' TRAINING SERIES H'CAP HURDLE (8 hdls) 2m 1f

4:30 (4:30) (Class 4) (0-105,105) 4-Y-0+ **£3,249** (£954; £477; £238)

Form RPR

302- **1** **Rugged Jack (FR)**[45] [3783] 7-11-6 **99**.............................. ConorShoemark 103+
(Victor Dartnall) *trckd ldrs: rdn and lost pl after 4th: stdy prog fr 3 out: led sn after last: drvn out* **11/4**[2]

506- **2** *2* **Lady Bridget**[35] [3959] 6-9-11 **79**..........................(bt) ThomasCheesman(3) 80
(Mark Gillard) *trckd ldrs: hit 1st: rdn after 5th: looking hld in 3rd whn lft 2nd 3 out: led sn after 2 out: mstke last: sn hdd: no ex* **9/1**

/54- **3** *8* **Milor De La Borie (FR)**[289] [390] 5-11-2 **95**.........................(p) RyanHatch 87
(David Pipe) *trckd ldr: rdn whn lft in ld 3 out: hdd sn after 2 out: wknd run-in* **6/1**[3]

0/6- **4** *16* **Florida Quays (IRE)**[27] [4091] 6-11-2 **95**.................. ChristopherWard 70
(David Dennis) *hld up: struggling and detached 5th: sme prog after 3 out: wknd bef last* **8/1**

PPP/ **P** **Francly Flora**[1605] [1716] 13-9-10 **80**.. ChrisMeehan(5)
(James Payne) *hld up bhd ldrs: v awkward and nrly uns rdr 2nd and next: nt rcvr and sn t.o: p.u bef 5th* **66/1**

232- **F** **Revaader**[11] [4394] 6-11-9 **105**.. JakeHodson(3) 113+
(Mark Gillard) *led: hit 4th: looked in command whn fell 3 out* **11/10**[1]

4m 35.4s (19.90) **Going Correction** +0.725s/f (Soft) **6** Ran SP% **111.2**

Speed ratings (Par 105): **82,81,77,69,**

CSF £24.63 TOTE £3.00: £2.40, £6.20; EX 25.60 Trifecta £64.00.

Owner G D Hake **Bred** Breeding & Racing Enterprise Ltd **Trained** Brayford, Devon

■ Stewards' Enquiry : Conor Shoemark seven-day ban: used whip contrary to race conditions (Mar 21-23,25,28-30)

FOCUS

Weak form, especially when considering top weight Revaader was clear and with the race at her mercy when falling at the first in the straight. The winner was fortunate and the next two ran close to their marks.

T/Plt: £32.90 to a £1 stake. Pool: £74,377.01 - 1,648.82 winning units T/Qpdt: £14.10 to a £1 stake. Pool: £3,628.34 - 190.00 winning units TM

4425 NEWCASTLE (L-H)

Tuesday, March 4

OFFICIAL GOING: Soft (good to soft in places in the home straight; 5.9)

First hurdle in the back straight and middle fence in the back straight omitted

Wind: Fresh; half against Weather: Cloudy

4605 CBBF "RUN FOREST RUN" "NATIONAL HUNT" NOVICES' HURDLE (8 hdls 1 omitted) 2m

2:20 (2:20) (Class 4) 4-Y-0+ **£3,119** (£915; £457; £228)

Form RPR

131- **1** **Stonebrook (IRE)**[21] [4199] 6-11-7 0.. APMcCoy 120+
(Donald McCain) *mde all: wandered appr 3rd and 3 out: 3 l clr last: shkn up briefly run-in: readily* **2/9**[1]

/33- **2** *2 ¼* **Delta Forty**[61] [3507] 6-10-8 0.. JamesReveley 97+
(Keith Reveley) *nt fluent on occasions: pressed wnr: racd wd fr 3rd to 4 out: effrt and shkn up appr last: edgd rt and kpt on run-in: no ch w wnr* **4/1**[2]

/54- **3** *17* **Il Testone (FR)**[60] [3522] 5-11-1 0.. HenryBrooke 83
(Chris Grant) *prom: rdn and outpcd after 3 out: plugged on fr last: no ch w first two* **33/1**

3- **4** *1* **Silver Vogue**[12] [4384] 6-11-1 0.. RyanMania 82
(Sue Smith) *t.k.h: chsd ldrs to 3 out: sn pushed along and outpcd: btn after next* **12/1**[3]

05P- **5** *2 ½* **Lordenshaws (IRE)**[10] [4429] 7-11-1 0.......................... KennyJohnson 80
(Robert Johnson) *hld up in tch: nt fluent 4 out: outpcd and j.lft 3 out: btn whn j.lft next* **100/1**

0- **6** *34* **Tara Springs**[19] [4240] 5-10-8 0.. BrianHarding 38
(Barry Murtagh) *hld up in tch: nt fluent 4th: struggling after next: t.o* **100/1**

4m 18.3s (8.30) **Going Correction** +0.125s/f (Yiel) **6** Ran SP% **114.4**

Speed ratings (Par 105): **84,82,74,73,72 55**

CSF £1.77 TOTE £1.30: £1.10, £1.40; EX 1.80 Trifecta £6.00.

Owner John P McManus **Bred** George Ward **Trained** Cholmondeley, Cheshire

FOCUS

Rail after Winning Post moved out 3m, bend into home straight and at 3m moved back inside. The going was soft, good to soft in places in the home straight. The fourth flight was omitted for all hurdle races. An uncompetitive novice hurdle, run at a steady pace. The easy winner stood out.

4606 CBBF HP, LEASING AND REFINANCE H'CAP CHASE (17 fncs 2 omitted) 3m

2:50 (2:50) (Class 4) (0-120,119) 5-Y-0+ **£3,768** (£1,106; £553; £276)

Form RPR

24P- **1** **Frank The Slink**[68] [3287] 8-10-10 **103**................................ JasonMaguire 116+
(Micky Hammond) *mde all: rdn 4 out: styd on wl fr next: rdn out* **4/1**[3]

053- **2** *6* **Mr Syntax (IRE)**[65] [3389] 10-11-12 **119**...............................(t) BrianHughes 126
(Tim Fitzgerald) *t.k.h: chsd wnr to 3rd: cl up: regained 2nd 10th: effrt and pushed along 4 out: one pce fr 2 out* **11/4**[2]

P02- **3** *10* **Mr Supreme (IRE)**[39] [3874] 9-10-5 **98**............................... RichieMcGrath 98
(Keith Reveley) *t.k.h: in tch: stdy hdwy whn nt fluent and outpcd 12th: shortlived effrt bef 4 out: hld whn hit 2 out* **11/8**[1]

232- **4** *19* **Farm Pixie (IRE)**[27] [4082] 8-10-7 **100**.............................. WilsonRenwick 82
(Ann Hamilton) *t.k.h: chsd wnr fr 3rd to 10th: drvn and outpcd 12th: rallied u.p after 5 out: outpcd whn nt fluent next: sn btn* **4/1**[3]

6m 20.8s (-1.70) **Going Correction** -0.325s/f (Good) **4** Ran SP% **108.8**

Speed ratings: **89,87,83,77**

CSF £14.45 TOTE £5.10; EX 14.70 Trifecta £42.00.

Owner M H O G **Bred** G A Greaves **Trained** Middleham Moor, N Yorks

FOCUS

The seventh fence was omitted for all chases. There wasn't much pace on for this handicap. The winner probably ran to a similar level as his C&D second in November.

4607 CLOSE BROTHERS BUSINESS FINANCE CONDITIONAL JOCKEYS' H'CAP HURDLE (10 hdls 1 omitted) 2m 4f

3:20 (3:20) (Class 5) (0-100,100) 4-Y-0+ **£1,949** (£572; £286; £143)

Form RPR

051- **1** **Be Bop Boru (IRE)**[6] [4504] 7-11-0 **91** 7ex......................... MichaelByrne(3) 106+
(Tim Vaughan) *hld up: stdy hdwy and cl up 6th: led 3 out: shkn up and qcknd clr bef last: readily* **10/11**[1]

24U- **2** *8* **Solway Dornal**[149] [1789] 9-9-11 **74** oh2.....................(p) GrantCockburn(3) 76
(Lisa Harrison) *led: rdn and hdd 3 out: kpt on fr next: no ch w wnr* **33/1**

005- **3** *2 ¼* **Marlee Mourinho (IRE)**[36] [3935] 8-10-2 **81**............ DiarmuidO'Regan(5) 81
(N W Alexander) *prom: drvn and outpcd bef 3 out: rallied after next: styd on fr last: nt rch first two* **14/1**

564- **4** *shd* **Bollin Julie**[53] [3639] 7-10-0 **74**.. CallumWhillans 74
(Donald Whillans) *cl up: rdn bef 3 out: kpt on same pce fr next* **7/1**[3]

422- **5** *1 ¼* **Shan Valley (IRE)**[8] [4465] 8-10-5 **85**................................ DaraghBourke(6) 84
(Stuart Coltherd) *hld up: stdy hdwy to chse ldrs bef 3 out: rdn next: wknd after last* **5/1**[2]

065- **6** *17* **Thinger Licht (FR)**[13] [4353] 5-11-9 **100**............................ JoshHamer(3) 81
(Tony Carroll) *hld up in tch: outpcd after 6th: rallied next: struggling bef 3 out: sn btn* **15/2**

P56- **7** *12* **Ballyreesode (IRE)**[59] [3525] 9-9-10 **80**........................ JamesCorbett(10) 49
(Susan Corbett) *t.k.h: pressed ldr to 4 out: sn struggling: t.o* **20/1**

346- **8** *shd* **Kathlatino**[22] [4189] 7-10-4 **81**.. JoeColliver(3) 50
(Micky Hammond) *hld up: pushed along and outpcd bef 4 out: btn next: t.o* **20/1**

5/0- **P** **Solway Legend**[293] 316 7-10-6 **80** TonyKelly
(Lisa Harrison) *prom tl outpcd after 6th: lost tch next: t.o whn p.u bef 3 out* **50/1**

5m 22.5s (1.40) **Going Correction** +0.125s/f (Yiel) **9** Ran SP% **114.4**
Speed ratings (Par 103): **102,98,97,97,97 90,85,85,**
CSF £36.91 CT £272.41 TOTE £1.90: £1.10, £3.30, £3.80; EX 23.20 Trifecta £230.20.
Owner The Oak Syndicate **Bred** Robert McCarthy **Trained** Aberthin, Vale of Glamorgan

FOCUS
A weak handicap, run at a steady pace. The well-in winner should at least go on to match his 111 bumper best.

4608 CLOSE BROTHERS BUSINESS FINANCE H'CAP HURDLE (8 hdls 1 omitted) 2m

3:50 (3:50) (Class 4) (0-110,110) 4-Y-0+ **£3,119** (£915; £457; £228)

Form RPR
P12- **1** **Rhymers Stone**[36] 3937 6-11-2 **105** (p) CraigNichol(5) 110+
(Lucinda Russell) *cl up: hmpd 3rd: nt fluent next: rdn bef 3 out: rallied: led run-in: styd on wl* **15/8**[1]

143- **2** ¾ **Persian Herald**[12] 4378 6-11-3 **108** DaraghBourke(7) 111
(Sue Smith) *led: rdn 3 out: hdd run-in: kpt on: hld towards fin* **4/1**[3]

121- **3** 1¾ **Light The City (IRE)**[18] 3274 7-11-9 **110** JakeGreenall(3) 111
(Ruth Carr) *chsd ldrs: hdwy and cl up 3rd: rdn and outpcd 3 out: rallied and disp 2nd pl bef last: one pce run-in* **11/4**[2]

/02- **4** 46 **Broctune Papa Gio**[112] 2449 7-11-5 **103** JamesReveley 58
(Keith Reveley) *prom: taken wd bef 3rd: struggling after next: lost tch after 4 out: t.o* **11/4**[2]

4m 11.5s (1.50) **Going Correction** +0.125s/f (Yiel) **4** Ran SP% **108.1**
Speed ratings (Par 105): **101,100,99,76**
CSF £8.94 TOTE £2.80; EX 8.70 Trifecta £19.00.
Owner G Adam **Bred** Miss Carrie Key-Forestal **Trained** Arlary, Perth & Kinross

FOCUS
An open affair despite the small field size. The form makes sense.

4609 CLOSE BROTHERS BUSINESS FINANCE NOVICES' HURDLE (10 hdls 1 omitted) 2m 4f

4:20 (4:23) (Class 4) 4-Y-0+ **£3,119** (£915; £457; £228)

Form RPR
22U- **1** **Frankie's Promise (IRE)**[12] 4364 6-11-2 109 (p) LucyAlexander 114+
(N W Alexander) *nt fluent on occasions: t.k.h: chsd ldrs: hdwy to ld bef 2 out: clr last: styd on strly: eased towards fin* **15/8**[2]

1/3- **2** 4 **Wild Card**[139] 1924 7-11-9 118 JasonMaguire 110
(Donald McCain) *t.k.h: chsd ldrs: hdwy to ld 3 out: hdd bef next: kpt on same pce fr last* **4/7**[1]

65- **3** nk **Native Spa (IRE)**[41] 3829 6-10-11 0 AdamNicol(5) 103
(Michael Smith) *led at ordinary gallop: rdn and hdd 3 out: sn rdn: kpt on fr last: no imp* **16/1**[3]

6- **4** 66 **Blue Bellini**[19] 4240 6-10-9 0 DenisO'Regan 30
(Chris Grant) *in tch tl outpcd after 6th: lost tch next: t.o* **25/1**

5m 26.6s (5.50) **Going Correction** +0.125s/f (Yiel) **4** Ran SP% **108.2**
Speed ratings (Par 105): **94,92,92,65**
CSF £3.47 TOTE £3.00; EX 3.30 Trifecta £5.90.
Owner Brian Castle **Bred** Sean And Batt Leahy **Trained** Kinneston, Perth & Kinross

FOCUS
The pace was steady for this novices' hurdle. The winner was better than the bare result and is rated to his mark.

4610 CLOSE BROTHERS BUSINESS FINANCE H'CAP CHASE (15 fncs 1 omitted) 2m 4f

4:50 (4:50) (Class 3) (0-130,123) 5-Y-0+ **£6,498** (£1,908; £954; £477)

Form RPR
250- **1** **Categorical**[13] 4346 11-11-2 **113** JamesReveley 123+
(Keith Reveley) *mde all: blnd and rdr lost iron briefly 9th: sn rcvrd: pushed along 4 out: styd on strly to draw clr fr 2 out* **3/1**[3]

411- **2** 11 **Clondaw Flicka (IRE)**[68] 3283 6-11-7 **118** (p) PeterBuchanan 118
(Lucinda Russell) *nt fluent on occasions: chsd ldrs: chal 9th: ev ch and rdn 4 out: outpcd fr 2 out* **11/10**[1]

300- **3** 10 **Sergeant Pink (IRE)**[18] 2939 8-11-9 **120** HenryBrooke 109
(Dianne Sayer) *chsd ldrs: drvn along bef 5 out: wknd fr next* **11/1**

62F- **4** 45 **Storming Gale (IRE)**[46] 3759 8-11-12 **123** (t) JasonMaguire 65
(Donald McCain) *nt fluent: in tch: hit and rdn 6 out: lost tch fr next: t.o* **5/2**[2]

5m 17.1s (-10.10) **Going Correction** -0.325s/f (Good) **4** Ran SP% **109.5**
Speed ratings: **107,102,98,80**
CSF £7.07 TOTE £3.60; EX 9.90 Trifecta £29.90.
Owner Rug, Grub & Pub Partnership **Bred** Darley **Trained** Lingdale, Redcar & Cleveland

FOCUS
The gallop was honest for this fair handicap chase. The winner is rated back to last season's best.

4611 TOO "CLOSE" TO CALL "NEWCOMERS" STANDARD OPEN NATIONAL HUNT FLAT RACE 2m

5:20 (5:20) (Class 6) 4-5-Y-0 **£1,559** (£457; £228; £114)

Form RPR
1 **Ustica (IRE)** 4-10-10 0 RichieMcGrath 95+
(Philip Kirby) *prom: hdwy to ld over 3f out: pushed along 2f out: styd on wl fnl f* **20/1**

2 1¾ **Whadaurmeddlewimei** 4-10-7 0 EwanWhillans(3) 93
(Alistair Whillans) *hld up in midfield: stdy hdwy whn n.m.r over 4f out: swtchd lft effrt wl over 1f out: sn chsng wnr: kpt on fnl f* **20/1**

3 7 **Corsair Prince** 4-10-10 0 JamesReveley 86
(Keith Reveley) *hld up: stdy hdwy and in tch 1/2-way: poised to chal gng wl 3f out: effrt 2f out: outpcd fnl f* **9/2**[3]

4 5 **Imperial Prince (IRE)** 5-11-4 0 RyanMania 89
(Michael Smith) *pressed ldr: drvn and outpcd 4f out: rallied fnl f: kpt on: nt rch first three* **14/1**

5 nk **Chiron (IRE)** 5-11-4 0 WilsonRenwick 89
(Keith Dalgleish) *cl up: hdwy to chal over 3f out to over 2f out: sn outpcd: btn fnl f* **12/1**

6 nk **Ardenlee Lad (IRE)** 4-10-5 0 AdamNicol(5) 81
(Philip Kirby) *hld up: pushed along and rn green over 5f out: hdwy over 3f out: kpt on same pce fnl 2f* **8/1**

7 9 **Teddy Tee (IRE)** 5-11-4 0 BrianHarding 80
(Nicky Richards) *hld up: effrt and drvn over 4f out: wknd over 2f out* **8/1**

8 1¾ **The Last Leg (IRE)** 5-11-4 0 JasonMaguire 78
(Karen McLintock) *led and green: rdn and hdd over 3f out: sn wknd* **4/1**[2]

9 nk **Wicked Spice (IRE)** 5-11-4 0 DenisO'Regan 78
(Nicky Richards) *hld up in midfield: lost pl 6f out: pushed along over 3f out: nvr able to chal* **7/2**[1]

10 ¾ **Alizee De Janeiro (FR)** 4-9-12 0 GrantCockburn(5) 62
(Lucinda Russell) *hld up: rdn along 4f out: nvr on terms* **12/1**

11 11 **Silver Crossing** 5-10-11 0 JohnDawson(7) 66
(John Wade) *midfield: drvn along over 4f out: wknd 3f out* **50/1**

12 4½ **Master Spider (IRE)** 5-10-8 0 JamesCorbett(10) 61
(Susan Corbett) *t.k.h in rr: struggling 5f out: nvr on terms* **80/1**

13 4 **Valnamixe Du Mee (FR)** 5-11-4 0 KennyJohnson 57
(Robert Johnson) *plld hrd in rr: struggling over 4f out: sn btn* **66/1**

14 ¾ **Mighty Cliche (IRE)** 5-10-13 0 ColmMcCormack(5) 57
(Dianne Sayer) *hld up: rdn over 5f out: btn fnl 3f* **40/1**

4m 8.0s (3.60) **Going Correction** +0.125s/f (Yiel)
WFA 4 from 5yo 7lb **14** Ran SP% **121.3**
Speed ratings: **96,95,91,89,88 88,84,83,83,82 77,75,73,72**
CSF £354.65 TOTE £23.50: £8.30, £7.30, £2.00; EX 242.20 Trifecta £2863.20 Pool: £3,817.66 - 0.08 winning units..
Owner Mrs N J McGrath **Bred** Desmond Devereux **Trained** Middleham, N Yorks

FOCUS
This "newcomers" bumper was run at a decent pace.
T/Plt: £358.50 to a £1 stake. Pool: £71,699.53 - 145.99 winning units T/Qpdt: £56.20 to a £1 stake. Pool: £5,228.56 - 68.80 winning units RY

4474 CATTERICK (L-H)

Wednesday, March 5

OFFICIAL GOING: Good to soft (soft in places; chs 6.8, hdl 7.4)
Wind: fresh 1/2 behind Weather: overcast, cool and very breezy

4612 YORKSHIRE-OUTDOORS.CO.UK ADVENTURE ACTIVITIES (S) HURDLE (8 hdls) 2m

2:15 (2:15) (Class 5) 4-Y-0+ **£2,737** (£798; £399)

Form RPR
51P- **1** **Waltz Darling (IRE)**[96] 2786 6-11-6 117 JamesReveley 108+
(Keith Reveley) *w ldr: led 2nd: drvn clr run-in* **7/2**[3]

122- **2** 5 **Lac Sacre (FR)**[6] 4512 5-11-4 112 (tp) JoshHamer(5) 105
(Tony Carroll) *hld up towards rr: hdwy 3 out: chsd wnr appr next: hrd drvn between last 2: no imp* **13/8**[1]

3/3- **3** 7 **Barneys Honour (IRE)**[10] 4454 10-11-9 125 (tp) JasonMaguire 97
(Gordon Elliott, Ire) *chsd ldrs: 2nd appr 4th: drvn after 3 out: outpcd appr next: kpt on to take modest 3rd last* **11/4**[2]

01P- **4** 3¼ **Next Hight (IRE)**[28] 4085 7-11-6 100 RyanMania 95
(Sue Smith) *strated v slowly: drvn and hdwy 4th: chsd wnr briefly bef 2 out: 3rd whn mstke 2 out: wknd last* **5/1**

/60- **5** 8 **The Boozy Bishop (IRE)**[9] 4465 9-10-10 69 (p) MissCWalton(5) 78
(Sheena Walton) *led to 2nd: chsd wnr: lost pl bef 2 out* **150/1**

P- **6** 22 **King Vahe (IRE)**[13] 4364 5-10-8 0 MrTSpeke(7) 56
(Robert Johnson) *t.k.h: trckd ldrs: wknd 3 out: sn bhd* **125/1**

004- **7** 23 **Moheebb (IRE)**[47] 3756 10-11-1 95 (b) KennyJohnson 33
(Robert Johnson) *s.s: nt fluent in rr: bhd fr 5th: t.o 3 out* **33/1**

604- **8** 44 **Spencers Lad**[33] 4003 4-10-4 0 JakeGreenall(3)
(Michael Easterby) *trckd ldrs: t.k.h: nt fluent 3rd: drvn 5th: sn lost pl and bhd: t.o whn blnd 2 out* **20/1**

3m 57.7s (5.20) **Going Correction** +0.50s/f (Soft)
WFA 4 from 5yo+ 7lb **8** Ran SP% **112.8**
Speed ratings (Par 103): **107,104,101,99,95 84,72,50**
CSF £9.64 TOTE £4.20: £1.40, £2.00, £1.02; EX 12.60 Trifecta £21.10.There was no bid for the winner. Lac Sacre was claimed by J. L. Flint for £5000.
Owner Mrs M B Thwaites & M E Foxton **Bred** Ms Natalie Cleary **Trained** Lingdale, Redcar & Cleveland

FOCUS
A fair selling hurdle in which they went an honest gallop. A tricky one to assess which could be rated up to 10lb higher.

4613 DINE AND VIEW AT CATTERICK RACES NOVICES' H'CAP CHASE (19 fncs) 3m 1f 110y

2:45 (2:45) (Class 4) (0-110,108) 5-Y-0+ **£5,198** (£1,526; £763; £381)

Form RPR
P12- **1** **Harris (IRE)**[23] 4188 7-11-11 **107** (p) JamesReveley 115+
(William Kinsey) *trckd ldng pair: 2nd 9th: led 14th: reminders 4 out: drvn and lft clr 2 out: pushed out* **6/4**[1]

521- **2** 21 **Tiny Dancer (IRE)**[22] 4202 6-11-12 **108** PaddyBrennan 110
(Alan Swinbank) *hld up in rr: handy 3rd 13th: mstke 15th: chsd wnr appr 3 out: almost 3 l down whn blnd next: rdn and wl hld whn j.rt last: heavily eased last 50yds* **15/8**[2]

42P- **3** 22 **Radio Nowhere (IRE)**[21] 4222 6-11-6 **102** (b) JasonMaguire 70
(Donald McCain) *led: drvn and hdd 14th: upsides 4 out: wknd next* **8/1**

01P- **4** 6 **Over And Above (IRE)**[30] 4066 8-10-0 **82** oh4 (bt) RichieMcGrath 48
(Henry Hogarth) *t.k.h: trckd ldr: 3rd whn hit 10th: j. slowly and lost pl next: hmpd 13th: sn bhd: t.o 4 out* **16/1**

32/- **F** **Swingbridge (IRE)**[318] 5422 6-11-10 **106** HenryBrooke
(Chris Grant) *in rr: mstke 5th: hdwy to chse ldrs12th: 4th whn fell next* **6/1**[3]

6m 45.6s (3.60) **Going Correction** +0.25s/f (Yiel) **5** Ran SP% **106.1**
Speed ratings: **104,97,90,88,**
CSF £4.51 TOTE £2.80: £2.20, £1.10; EX 4.50 Trifecta £11.60.
Owner Harris Syndicate **Bred** James G Kehoe **Trained** Ashton, Cheshire

FOCUS
A modest small-field staying novice handicap chase. The form is rated around the first two.

4614 FOLLOW US ON TWITTER @CATTERICKRACES MARES' NOVICES' HURDLE (8 hdls) 2m

3:15 (3:16) (Class 4) 4-Y-0+ **£3,249** (£954; £477; £238)

Form RPR
321- **1** **Morning With Ivan (IRE)**[9] 4466 4-10-11 113 WilsonRenwick 106+
(Martin Todhunter) *mde all: qcknd pce 3rd: drvn clr between last 2: styd on wl* **2/5**[1]

2- **2** 10 **Gold Chain (IRE)**[118] 2307 4-10-4 0 LucyAlexander 89+
(Dianne Sayer) *t.k.h: trckd ldrs: outpcd 5th: drvn next: styd on appr 2 out: chsd wnr between last 2: wl hld whn hit last* **3/1**[2]

P- **3** 11 **Flawless Filly (IRE)**[55] 3613 4-10-4 0 RichieMcGrath 78
(Rose Dobbin) *trckd wnr: nt fluent and 3rd 5th: chsd wnr bef 2 out: 3rd and wl btn whn j.lft last* **10/1**[3]

0- 4 *nse* **Just Chilly**[98] 2752 5-10-12 0 PeterBuchanan 86
(Lucinda Russell) *trckd ldrs: 2nd 5th: wknd between last 2* **40/1**

P **Don't Tell**[138] 4-10-4 0 BarryKeniry
(George Moore) *t.k.h: lost pl 5th: bhd whn blnd next: sn t.o: p.u between last 2* **100/1**

4m 3.6s (11.10) **Going Correction** +0.50s/f (Soft)
WFA 4 from 5yo+ 7lb **5** Ran SP% **108.9**
Speed ratings (Par 105): **92,87,81,81,**
CSF £1.96 TOTE £1.50: £1.10, £1.50; EX 1.90 Trifecta £3.30.
Owner Island Intermodal Services **Bred** J S Bolger **Trained** Orton, Cumbria

FOCUS
A modest mares' novice hurdle. The winner has the potential to rate a lot higher on Flat form.

4615 GO RACING IN YORKSHIRE H'CAP HURDLE (10 hdls) 2m 3f
3:45 (3:45) (Class 5) (0-100,100) 4-Y-0+ **£2,737** (£798; £399)

Form RPR

/04- 1 **Patavium (IRE)**[23] 4189 11-11-0 **91** TonyKelly(3) 96
(Edwin Tuer) *prom: effrt and handy 3rd appr 2 out: led appr last: kpt on wl* **14/1**

131- 2 *3 ¾* **Newdane Dancer (IRE)**[9] 4465 7-11-0 **93** 7ex (p) ColmMcCormack(5) 96
(Dianne Sayer) *prom: drvn and outpcd 6th: rallied 3 out: chsng ldrs between last 2: kpt on to take 2nd run-in* **4/1**[1]

050- 3 *1 ½* **Oorayvic (IRE)**[15] 4336 7-10-13 **90** JonathanEngland(3) 92+
(Sue Smith) *in tch: chsng ldrs and hit 7th: led appr 2 out: hit 2 out: hdd and hit last: kpt on same pce* **9/2**[2]

P05- 4 *13* **Politelysed**[15] 4336 8-9-11 **74** oh1 HarryChalloner(3) 63
(Robert Johnson) *hld up in rr: hdwy 6th: chsng ldrs next: one pce appr 2 out* **6/1**[3]

024- 5 *5* **Douchkirk (FR)**[38] 3924 7-11-5 **93** (b) WillKennedy 77
(John Berry) *chsd ldr: led 6th: hdd appr 2 out: wknd between last 2* **10/1**

4/P- 6 *9* **De Chissler (IRE)**[23] 4189 7-11-9 **97** WilsonRenwick 73
(Martin Todhunter) *led: hdd 6th: reminders next: wknd appr 2 out* **12/1**

4F6- 7 *2 ½* **King's Chorister**[13] 4366 8-10-5 **79** (t) LucyAlexander 53
(Barry Murtagh) *in rr: drvn 5th: sme hdwy 3 out: nvr on terms* **10/1**

00P- 8 *3 ¼* **Bonnie Burnett (IRE)**[38] 3924 7-11-1 **89** DougieCostello 60
(Brian Rothwell) *hld up in rr: hdwy 6th: fdd bef 2 out* **25/1**

004- 9 *1* **Amir Pasha (UAE)**[13] 4378 9-11-7 **100** (p) JoeColliver(5) 70
(Micky Hammond) *mid-div: sme hdwy 3 out: sn wknd* **16/1**

/FR- 10 *1* **Dun To Perfection**[277] 579 7-10-0 **84** JamesCorbett(10) 53
(Susan Corbett) *in tch: hdwy 6th: sn drvn: lost pl 3 out* **40/1**

006/ 11 *3 ¼* **Gunpoint (IRE)**[899] 1670 10-9-9 **74** oh6 SamanthaDrake(5) 40
(Richard Drake) *in rr: bhd and drvn 6th: t.o after next: kpt on fr 2 out* **66/1**

453- 12 *1* **Beyondtemptation**[15] 4336 6-9-11 **74** oh2 JohnKington(3) 39
(Jonathan Haynes) *chsd ldrs: lost pl after 7th* **20/1**

405- 13 *23* **Politeness (FR)**[21] 4221 5-11-7 **100** CraigNichol(5) 44
(Rose Dobbin) *chsd ldrs: drvn 3 out: sn lost pl: t.o* **14/1**

000- P **Lisdonagh House (IRE)**[75] 3192 12-10-3 **77** TomSiddall
(Lynn Siddall) *reluctant in last: t.o after 3rd: p.u bef 2 out* **11/1**

4F5- P **The Weatherman (IRE)**[28] 4085 7-11-9 **97** JasonMaguire
(Donald McCain) *prom: nt fluent 1st: lost pl and hit next: bhd and reminders 4th: t.o 7th: p.u bef 2 out* **8/1**

46P- P **Latest Fashion (IRE)**[63] 3451 8-10-11 **85** PeterBuchanan
(Christopher Wilson) *in rr: blnd 4th: lost pl 7th: t.o next: p.u bef 2 out* **66/1**

4m 49.2s (13.10) **Going Correction** +0.50s/f (Soft) **16** Ran SP% **131.0**
Speed ratings (Par 103): **92,90,89,84,82 78,77,76,75,75 73,73,63, ,**
CSF £72.93 CT £310.32 TOTE £21.40: £4.00, £1.60, £1.40, £1.50; EX 95.00 Trifecta £564.60.
Owner J A Nixon **Bred** M Channon **Trained** Birkby, N Yorks

FOCUS
A moderate big-field handicap hurdle in which they went a proper gallop. The winner is rated in line with last year's C&D run, with the second to his mark.

4616 CATTERICKBRIDGE.CO.UK NOVICES' H'CAP CHASE (12 fncs) 2m
4:15 (4:15) (Class 4) (0-110,105) 5-Y-0+ **£5,198** (£1,526; £763; £381)

Form RPR

400- 1 **Dark And Dangerous (IRE)**[26] 4129 6-11-12 **105** (v) BrendanPowell 110+
(Brendan Powell) *led: hdd 9th: led appr next: hld on wl in clsng stages* **9/4**[1]

FP0- 2 *1 ¼* **Force Of Habit**[27] 4107 8-10-1 **85** (p) JohnDawson(5) 87
(Joanne Foster) *hld up: hdwy to trck ldrs appr 3 out: j.rt 2 out: chsd wnr 3 l down last: kpt on same pce last 50yds* **14/1**

525- 3 *11* **Indigo Island (IRE)**[8] 4475 5-10-12 **91** HenryBrooke 84
(Robert Bewley) *chsd wnr: led 9th: hdd appr next: disputing 2nd whn hit last: sn wknd* **5/1**[3]

034- 4 *3 ½* **Endeavor**[21] 4222 9-11-11 **104** RyanMania 95
(Dianne Sayer) *chsd ldrs: nt fluent 2nd: outpcd 8th: wknd after 2 out* **9/4**[1]

000- 5 *6* **Shine A Diamond (IRE)**[40] 3876 6-11-2 **95** PeterBuchanan 82
(Lucinda Russell) *trckd ldrs: hit 4th: n.m.r and hit 9th: 2 l 2nd whn hit 2 out: sn wknd* **7/2**[2]

4m 9.2s (9.10) **Going Correction** +0.25s/f (Yiel) **5** Ran SP% **107.1**
Speed ratings: **87,86,80,79,76**
CSF £23.16 TOTE £2.90: £1.40, £5.30; EX 34.50 Trifecta £102.30.
Owner North South Alliance **Bred** Roundhill Stud And A Stroud **Trained** Upper Lambourn, Berks

FOCUS
A modest novice handicap chase. The winner didn't need to improve on previous chase runs.

4617 JOHN WADE SKIP HIRE NOVICES' HUNTERS' CHASE (19 fncs) 3m 1f 110y
4:45 (4:45) (Class 6) 5-Y-0+ **£1,559** (£483; £241; £121)

Form RPR

1 **Rosie Du Berlais (IRE)**[332] 8-10-12 0 MrPDennis(7) 95+
(Philip Kirby) *t.k.h: trckd ldrs: led 12th: styd on wl fr 2 out: 5 l ahd whn hit last: drvn out* **11/4**[1]

30U/ 2 *7* **Scrum V**[297] 10-11-5 79 MrJLyttle(7) 93
(Mrs N Naughton) *j.rt: t.k.h: trckd ldrs: outpcd and hit 15th: rallied and chsd wnr appr 3 out: kpt on one pce* **9/2**[3]

PPP/ 3 *18* **Silk And Roses**[38] 11-10-12 67 (tp) MrTHamilton(7) 70
(Mrs Wendy Hamilton) *in tch: pushed along 8th: reminders and lost pl after 11th: kpt on appr 3 out: tk modest 3rd appr last* **4/1**[2]

440/ 4 *17* **Another Dark Rum**[24] 10-11-5 82 MrNOrpwood(7) 63
(S J Leadbetter) *in tch: chsd ldrs sn after 4 out: 3rd whn j. slowly 2 out: wknd appr last* **16/1**

/66- 5 *1 ¾* **Newyearsresolution (IRE)**[32] 4042 10-11-5 78 MissAWaugh(7) 60
(Simon Waugh) *in tch: mstke 12th: outpcd 14th: bhd fr 4 out* **10/1**

5/4- 6 *1 ¼* **Oaklands Bobby**[21] 4225 12-11-9 90 MrCDawson(3) 59
(R G Russ) *t.k.h: led: hdd appr 12th: lost pl 2 out* **4/1**[2]

P0P/ F **French Seventyfive**[17] 7-11-5 84 MissETodd(7)
(Miss Gill Boanas) *w ldrs: mstke 1st: led briefly appr 12th: cl 3rd whn fell next* **8/1**

6m 56.5s (14.50) **Going Correction** +0.25s/f (Yiel) **7** Ran SP% **110.9**
Speed ratings: **87,84,79,74,73 73,**
CSF £14.70 TOTE £2.30: £2.10, £2.40; EX 13.20 Trifecta £36.80.
Owner Mrs S Frank **Bred** Neilus Madigan **Trained** Middleham, N Yorks

FOCUS
A moderate hunters' chase run in a relatively slow time.

4618 FLAT SEASON NEXT MARES' STANDARD NATIONAL HUNT FLAT RACE (CONDITIONALS AND AMATEURS) 2m
5:15 (5:15) (Class 5) 4-6-Y-0 **£2,053** (£598; £299)

Form RPR

1 **Degenerous (IRE)**[42] 3849 6-10-11 0 PeterCarberry(3) 100
(Sarah Dawson, Ire) *mde all: qcknd pce 7f out: 6 l clr over 4f out and 1f out: kpt on: unchal* **16/1**

41- 2 *1 ½* **Georgian Firebird**[23] 4191 4-10-10 0 JakeGreenall(3) 98
(Alan Swinbank) *trckd ldrs: 3rd 4f out: chsd wnr over 2f out: styd on: unable to chal* **9/4**[1]

34- 3 *1 ¼* **Donna's Pride**[91] 2885 5-10-9 0 ColmMcCormack(5) 98
(Keith Reveley) *hld up: hdwy 6f out: 4th 4f out: 3rd 2f out: styd on same pce* **7/2**[3]

4 *3* **Toola Boola** 4-9-13 0 MrPDennis(7) 87
(Philip Kirby) *hld up: hdwy 6f out: drvn and lost pl over 4f out: kpt on fnl 2f: tk 4th ins fnl f: gng on at fin* **11/4**[2]

0- 5 *4 ½* **Bossy Beccy**[20] 4240 5-10-9 0 MissCWalton(5) 91
(James Walton) *w ldrs: lost pl after 6f: kpt on over 2f out: modest 4th over 1f out* **100/1**

110/ 6 *13* **Diligent**[691] 5394 6-11-3 0 NickSlatter(7) 93+
(Donald McCain) *hld up: hdwy to trck ldrs after 3f: clr 2nd over 4f out: wknd fnl 2f* **13/2**

4- 7 *19* **Lady Busanda**[23] 4191 4-10-1 0 JoeColliver(5) 54
(George Moore) *chsd wnr: lost pl over 4f out: sn bhd* **20/1**

8 *hd* **One Act** 5-10-7 0 MrHAABannister(7) 62
(Michael Easterby) *in rr: sn pushed along: reminders after 6f: bhd fnl 7f* **14/1**

3m 55.7s (8.80) **Going Correction** +0.50s/f (Soft)
WFA 4 from 5yo+ 7lb **8** Ran SP% **111.3**
Speed ratings: **98,97,96,95,92 86,76,76**
CSF £49.55 TOTE £20.30: £5.30, £1.10, £1.10; EX 77.30 Trifecta £317.50.
Owner Dr J F Dawson **Bred** Mrs Patricia Doran **Trained** Banbridge, Co Down
■ Sarah Dawson's first winner in Britain.

FOCUS
An ordinary bumper in which they went an even gallop. The form is rated aound the second and third.
T/Plt: £9.70 to a £1 stake. Pool of £89749.88- 6701.27 winning tickets T/Qpdt: £9.00 to a £1 stake. Pool of £4996.39 - 410.0 winning tickets. WG

4439 FONTWELL (L-H)
Wednesday, March 5
4619 Meeting Abandoned - Waterlogged

4080 CARLISLE (R-H)
Thursday, March 6

OFFICIAL GOING: Heavy (soft in places) changing to soft after race 3 (3.15)
First fence after the winning post omitted all chases
Wind: Breezy, half against Weather: Overcast

4625 APOLLOBET FREE £50 BETS "HANDS AND HEELS" H'CAP HURDLE (CONDITIONALS & AMATEURS) (10 hdls) 2m 3f 110y
2:10 (2:12) (Class 4) (0-120,116) 4-Y-0+ **£3,119** (£915; £457; £228)

Form RPR

510- 1 **Granaruid (IRE)**[67] 3398 11-11-5 **112** (p) MrTHamilton(3) 114+
(Alison Hamilton) *pressed ldr: led gng wl 2 out: pushed clr fr last* **11/4**[2]

1P2- 2 *4 ½* **Gulf Punch**[14] 4381 7-11-7 **116** (p) MrHStock(5) 112
(Donald McCain) *prom: effrt and rdn 2 out: chsd wnr last: kpt on same pce* **5/1**

353- 3 *11* **Little Boy Boru (IRE)**[14] 4365 6-10-10 **105** (p) AnthonyFox(5) 92
(S R B Crawford, Ire) *led at ordinary gallop: qcknd 3 out: rdn and hdd next: rallied: lost 2nd and wknd last* **11/8**[1]

5F2- 4 *4 ½* **Hunters Belt (IRE)**[34] 4002 10-11-12 **116** (vt) DiarmuidO'Regan 96
(Barry Murtagh) *cl up tl rdn and wknd fr 2 out* **4/1**[3]

5m 15.7s (6.90) **Going Correction** +0.375s/f (Yiel) **4** Ran SP% **105.4**
Speed ratings (Par 105): **101,99,94,93**
CSF £13.70 TOTE £4.20; EX 12.00 Trifecta £23.70.
Owner J P G Hamilton **Bred** S Donohoe And R Donohoe **Trained** Denholm, Borders

FOCUS
Hurdles on New Hurdles course and hurdles moved to inside line. Inside of chase course dolled out 3yds. The winning jockey in the first said the ground was "not too bad, a bit tacky". They went a reasonable gallop in this very ordinary handicap. The winner is a 120 horse at best and may still be capable of a bit better than this.

4626 DW CONSTRUCTION & JOINERY LTD NOVICES' H'CAP CHASE (16 fncs 1 omitted) 2m 5f
2:40 (2:40) (Class 4) (0-110,110) 5-Y-0+ **£3,898** (£1,144; £572; £286)

Form RPR

3F3- 1 **Snuker**[14] 4382 7-10-8 **92** (p) BrianHughes 102+
(James Ewart) *led or disp ld to 3 out: sn rdn: mstke and outpcd next: rallied last: styd on wl to ld nr fin* **11/4**[1]

13P- 2 *½* **Russe Blanc (FR)**[47] 3785 7-11-4 **102** (p) CharliePoste 109
(Richard Lee) *led or disp ld to 3 out: rallied and ev ch next: regained ld last: styd on: hdd nr fin* **5/1**

/3U- 3 *2 ¾* **Hidden Horizons (IRE)**[16] 4337 8-11-5 **110** (p) MrBGCrawford(7) 113
(S R B Crawford, Ire) *nt fluent on occasions: hld up: outpcd 9th: rallied whn nt fluent 2 out: styd on wl fr last* **5/1**

034- 4 *nk* **Monbeg (IRE)**[39] 3925 7-10-2 **86** (v[1]) WilsonRenwick 89
(Martin Todhunter) *prom: hdwy and ev ch whn hit 4 out: sn rdn and outpcd next: styd on fr last: no imp* **9/1**

/33- 5 3 1/4 **Dotties Dilema (IRE)**[61] 3524 6-11-7 **105** PeterBuchanan 106
(Lucinda Russell) *t.k.h: cl up: hdwy to ld 3 out: rdn and hdd last: wknd and lost two pls last 125yds* **9/2**[3]

FF5- 6 6 **Stagecoach Jasper**[14] 4380 8-9-12 **89** DaraghBourke(7) 87
(Sue Smith) *trckd ldrs: hit 4th: mstke and outpcd 5 out: no imp fr next* **7/2**[2]

5m 38.7s (-6.40) **Going Correction** -0.20s/f (Good) 6 Ran SP% **110.4**
Speed ratings: **104,103,102,102,101 99**
CSF £16.00 TOTE £2.50: £1.20, £2.10; EX 19.70 Trifecta £71.10.
Owner Mrs Percy, Mr Down & Mr Boyd **Bred** Mr And Mrs N M L Ewart **Trained** Langholm, Dumfries & G'way
■ Stewards' Enquiry : Charlie Poste caution: careless riding.

FOCUS
A modest novice handicap chase. The form has a fairly solid look to it, with the second to fifth pretty much to their marks.

4627 APOLLOBET IN-PLAY BETTING "NATIONAL HUNT" NOVICES' HURDLE (10 hdls) 2m 3f 110y
3:15 (3:15) (Class 4) 4-Y-0+ **£3,195** (£992; £534)

Form RPR
1 **Volcanic (FR)**[179] 5-11-2 0 JasonMaguire 125+
(Donald McCain) *j.lft: t.k.h: in tch: a gng wl: led on bit 2 out: drifted to stands' rail and qcknd clr fr last: canter* **2/5**[1]

653- 2 21 **Riskier**[55] 3634 9-11-2 115 BrianHughes 90
(John Wade) *led to 1st: cl up: led 5th: drvn and hdd 2 out: sn outpcd by easy wnr* **11/4**[2]

56- 3 78 **Boruma (IRE)**[18] 4307 4-10-7 0 JamesReveley 3
(Dianne Sayer) *cl up: led 1st to bef 4th: wknd fr 6th: t.o* **16/1**[3]

P **Beau Ballistic (IRE)**[70] 3300 6-10-13 0 PeterCarberry(3)
(Sarah Dawson, Ire) *plld hrd: chsd ldrs: led bef 4th to next: wknd after 4 out: t.o whn p.u bef 2 out* **28/1**

5m 15.3s (6.50) **Going Correction** +0.375s/f (Yiel)
WFA 4 from 5yo+ 7lb 4 Ran SP% **107.4**
Speed ratings (Par 105): **102,93,62,**
CSF £1.86 TOTE £1.20; EX 1.90 Trifecta £3.50.
Owner Elite Racing Club **Bred** Guy Cherel And Emmanuel Cherel **Trained** Cholmondeley, Cheshire

FOCUS
A decidedly uncompetitive event. The facile winner was value for further and may be a lot better than this.

4628 APOLLOBET BEST ODDS H'CAP CHASE (11 fncs 1 omitted) 2m
3:45 (3:45) (Class 4) (0-120,115) 5-Y-0+ **£4,548** (£1,335; £667; £333)

Form RPR
64P- 1 **Prosecco (IRE)**[23] 4204 12-11-9 **112** PeterBuchanan 118
(Lucinda Russell) *chsd ldrs: hdwy to ld 4 out: hdd 2 out: rallied to ld last 100yds: gamely* **10/1**

12F- 2 1/2 **Cloverhill Lad (IRE)**[9] 4477 10-10-10 **106** DaraghBourke(7) 111
(Stuart Coltherd) *cl up: j.lft 5 out: led 2 out: hdd last 100yds: kpt on: hld nr fin* **6/1**[3]

005- 3 1 1/2 **Sudski Star (IRE)**[14] 4367 6-10-3 **92** BrianHughes 96
(Patrick Griffin, Ire) *trckd ldrs: outpcd after 5 out: rallied to chse ldrs after 3 out: edgd rt and kpt on u.p fr last* **9/1**

1F2- 4 1 1/2 **Edmund (IRE)**[29] 4080 7-10-9 **98** (t) WilsonRenwick 100
(Ann Hamilton) *in tch: pushed along and outpcd 5 out: rallied bef 2 out: kpt on run-in: nt pce to chal* **5/4**[1]

503- 5 10 **Allow Me**[29] 4084 9-11-12 **115** JamesReveley 109
(Dianne Sayer) *led: hit 5th: hdd and rdn 4 out: wknd after next* **11/4**[2]

P/P- P **Gold Cygnet (IRE)**[133] 2031 9-10-13 **109** MrSFox(7)
(Theresa Gibson) *j.lft in rr: outpcd whn mstke 6th: sn struggling: no ch whn hit 2 out: sn p.u* **25/1**

4m 18.6s (2.50) **Going Correction** -0.20s/f (Good) 6 Ran SP% **108.3**
Speed ratings: **85,84,84,83,78**
CSF £59.39 TOTE £7.60: £2.90, £2.10; EX 35.70 Trifecta £141.60.
Owner Tay Valley Chasers Racing Club **Bred** W Sheldon **Trained** Arlary, Perth & Kinross

FOCUS
Ordinary handicap chase form. The winner is rated back to form with the second to his mark.

4629 APOLLOBET FREE DOWNLOAD APP NOVICES' H'CAP HURDLE (8 hdls) 2m 1f
4:15 (4:15) (Class 4) (0-120,116) 4-Y-0+ **£3,119** (£915; £457; £228)

Form RPR
F35- 1 **Just Cameron**[50] 3724 7-11-9 **113** RichieMcGrath 118+
(Philip Kirby) *t.k.h early: pressed ldr: led 4 out: rdn and clr between last 2: drvn out run-in* **9/4**[1]

0P2- 2 3 1/2 **Hallmark Star**[29] 4085 5-10-13 **108** (p) CraigNichol(5) 107
(Lucinda Russell) *prom: stdy hdwy 3 out: drvn and outpcd bef next: rallied to chse (clr) wnr run-in: kpt on: nt pce to chal* **5/1**[3]

210- 3 8 **Allied Answer**[28] 4103 6-11-12 **116** APMcCoy 107
(Steve Gollings) *trckd ldrs: smooth hdwy to press wnr bef 2 out: sn rdn: outpcd bef last: lost 2nd run-in: wknd* **5/2**[2]

444- 4 2 **Garde Ville (FR)**[30] 4073 4-10-5 **108** ThomasGarner(5) 89
(Lisa Williamson) *hld up in tch: stdy hdwy 3 out: sn rdn: no imp fr next* **33/1**

212- 5 11 **Blake Dean**[24] 4189 6-10-10 **100** RyanMania 80
(Sue Smith) *led to 4 out: sn drvn along: wknd bef 2 out* **5/2**[2]

4m 33.3s (4.10) **Going Correction** +0.375s/f (Yiel)
WFA 4 from 5yo+ 7lb 5 Ran SP% **107.5**
Speed ratings (Par 105): **105,103,99,98,93**
CSF £12.54 TOTE £2.80: £1.70, £2.60; EX 22.20 Trifecta £39.70.
Owner Mr and Mrs Paul Chapman **Bred** Mrs A E And Miss S J Dixon **Trained** Middleham, N Yorks

FOCUS
Just a fair handicap hurdle. A step forward from the winner and the form could be rated a few pounds higher.

4630 APOLLOBET ONLINE GAMES AND CASINO H'CAP CHASE (17 fncs 2 omitted) 3m 2f
4:45 (4:45) (Class 4) (0-110,109) 5-Y-0+ **£4,223** (£1,240; £620; £310)

Form RPR
/2P- 1 **Emma Soda**[43] 3836 9-10-9 **95** (b[1]) PeterCarberry(3) 107+
(Paul Davies) *mde all: clr bef 4 out: rdn and styd on strly fr 2 out* **13/2**

233- 2 3 **Basford Ben**[13] 4399 6-10-12 **95** (p) SeanQuinlan 100
(Jennie Candlish) *cl up: effrt and chsd (clr) wnr bef 4 out: kpt on fr 2 out: nt rch wnr* **7/2**[2]

FP4- 3 3/4 **Cottiers Den (IRE)**[29] 4082 7-10-0 **83** oh6 (e[1]) WilsonRenwick 88
(Martin Todhunter) *prom: n.m.r and lost pl bnd after 1st: drvn and outpcd 10th: rallied bef 4 out: styd on fr 2 out: kpt on run-in: nrst fin* **5/1**

532- 4 80 **The Shrimp (IRE)**[22] 4220 7-9-9 **83** oh9 (p) GrantCockburn(5) 7
(Sandy Thomson) *in tch: bmpd 4th: rdn and outpcd after 10th: lost tch fr 5 out: t.o* **4/1**[3]

FPP- P **Big News**[49] 3730 8-11-12 **109** (t) JamieMoore
(Richard Lee) *t.k.h: in tch: j.lft 4th and next: wnt 2nd 12th to bef 4 out: wknd next: no ch whn p.u appr last* **3/1**[1]

P10- P **Fozy Moss**[22] 4220 8-10-4 **87** (t) BrianHarding
(Stuart Coltherd) *w ldr: hit 2nd: outpcd 10th: rallied next: wknd bef 4 out: p.u next* **6/1**

7m 15.8s (8.60) **Going Correction** -0.20s/f (Good) 6 Ran SP% **111.5**
Speed ratings: **78,77,76,52,**
CSF £28.97 TOTE £5.40: £3.70, £1.20; EX 33.00 Trifecta £117.60.
Owner P S Davies **Bred** Richard Mathias **Trained** Bromyard, H'fords

FOCUS
There were doubts over all these before this modest handicap chase. The first three all ran to their marks.

4631 CONNOLLY'S RED MILLS BUMPER CHALLENGE INTERMEDIATE OPEN NATIONAL HUNT FLAT RACE 2m 1f
5:15 (5:15) (Class 6) 4-6-Y-0 **£1,559** (£457; £228; £114)

Form RPR
40- 1 **Bobs Lord Tara**[17] 4329 4-10-10 0 APMcCoy 97+
(Alan Swinbank) *hld up in tch: smooth hdwy 4f out: led gng wl over 1f out: pushed along and sn clr* **6/5**[1]

4/ 2 9 **Garth (IRE)**[730] 4695 6-10-13 0 DerekFox(5) 93
(Lucinda Russell) *hld up in tch: outpcd 1/2-way: rallied to chse wnr over 1f out: sn one pce* **12/1**

3 22 **Cliff Lane (IRE)**[116] 5-10-13 0 (t) CraigNichol(5) 71
(Lucinda Russell) *led: rdn over 3f out: hdd over 1f out: sn btn: fin tired* **13/8**[2]

/33- 4 27 **Proud Jack**[284] 497 6-11-4 0 BrianHughes 44
(Ann Hamilton) *trckd ldrs: wnt 2nd over 5f out to over 3f out: wknd over 2f out* **14/1**

0- 5 41 **Queens Regatta (IRE)**[21] 4240 5-10-11 0 LucyAlexander
(Bruce Mactaggart) *bhd: struggling fnl circ: t.o* **100/1**

4- 6 18 **Calton Entry (IRE)**[97] 2795 5-11-4 0 DougieCostello
(Ian Semple) *pressed ldr: struggling over 6f out: eased whn no ch fnl 2f* **8/1**[3]

4m 36.5s (12.30) **Going Correction** +0.375s/f (Yiel)
WFA 4 from 5yo+ 7lb 6 Ran SP% **110.0**
Speed ratings: **86,81,71,58,39 30**
CSF £15.71 TOTE £1.90: £1.10, £3.00; EX 20.60 Trifecta £46.80.
Owner John Wills **Bred** J R Wills **Trained** Melsonby, N Yorks

FOCUS
They went just a modest pace in this ordinary bumper. The winner is rated to his mark.
T/Plt: £300.50 to a £1 stake. Pool: £50,373.13 - 122.36 winning units. T/Qpdt: £36.10 to a £1 stake. Pool: £3973.85 - 81.30 winning units. RY

4500 WINCANTON (R-H)
Thursday, March 6

OFFICIAL GOING: Soft (heavy in places; chs 5.7, hdl 5.4)
Hurdle on stable bend omitted due to state of ground.
Wind: mild across Weather: overcast

4632 BATHWICK TYRES POOLE MAIDEN HURDLE (7 hdls 1 omitted) 2m
2:30 (2:30) (Class 4) 4-Y-0+ **£3,249** (£954; £477; £238)

Form RPR
/05- 1 **Gentleman Jon**[113] 2457 6-11-1 0 JoeTizzard 114+
(Colin Tizzard) *trckd ldr: led appr 2 out: j. sltly lft last 2: rdn bef last: kpt on wl run-in: asserted fnl 100yds* **7/1**

023- 2 2 **The Green Ogre**[19] 4268 4-10-7 127 JoshuaMoore 102
(Gary Moore) *in tch: trckd ldrs 3 out: rdn to chal between last 2: ev ch run-in untl no ex fnl 100yds* **5/2**[1]

20- 3 3/4 **Anton Chigurh**[19] 4281 5-10-10 0 JamesBanks(5) 108
(Brendan Powell) *in tch: disp cl 4th after 3 out: rdn after 2 out: kpt on same pce fr last* **20/1**

3- 4 nk **Lochnagar (GER)**[15] 4350 5-11-1 0 LiamTreadwell 109
(Venetia Williams) *j.rt: trckd ldrs: chalng whn j.rt 2 out: sn rdn: kpt on same pce fr last* **5/1**[3]

/45- 5 2 **Volt Face (FR)**[77] 3175 5-11-1 0[1] TomScudamore 106
(David Pipe) *hld up towards rr: stdy prog after 3rd: rdn to chse ldrs between last 2: kpt on but nt pce to chal* **3/1**[2]

0- 6 hd **Norfolk Sky**[50] 2265 5-10-8 0 DaveCrosse 100
(Brian Barr) *mid div: smooth hdwy after 3 out on outer: trcking ldrs next: sn rdn: kpt on but nt pce to chal* **25/1**

60- 7 18 **Paddocks Lounge (IRE)**[4] 4569 7-11-1 0 MattieBatchelor 88
(Jim Best) *hld up towards rr: sme prog into midfield after 3 out: no further imp fr next: wl btn* **150/1**

8 1 **King's Ciel**[83] 5-10-5 0[1] MikeyHamill(10) 87
(Sean Curran) *hld up towards rr: nudged along after 4th: nvr a danger: wknd bef 2 out: wl btn* **200/1**

9 3 3/4 **Warrior Conquest**[711] 9-11-1 0 BrendanPowell 83
(Jamie Snowden) *led: rdn and hdd appr 2 out: grad fdd: t.o* **33/1**

2- 10 13 **Obistar (FR)**[33] 4030 4-10-7 0 ConorO'Farrell 62
(David Pipe) *t.k.h in midfield: rdn after 3 out: sn btn: t.o* **7/1**

630- 11 6 **Dream Destiny**[37] 3961 5-10-8 0 (t) TomO'Brien 57
(Mark Gillard) *trckd ldrs: rdn after 3 out: sn wknd: stmbld next: mstke last: t.o* **200/1**

550- 12 3 **Western Movie**[83] 3061 6-11-1 0 RichardJohnson 61
(Philip Hobbs) *mid-div: hit 3rd: sme prog after 3 out: wknd next: t.o* **33/1**

60/- 13 11 **My Space**[298] 8-10-8 0 (t[1]) IanPopham 43
(Fiona Shaw) *hld up towards rr: pckd 1st: sme prog 3 out: wknd bef next: t.o* **250/1**

P3P- 14 6 **Shays River (IRE)**[15] 4350 9-11-1 0 (t) AdamWedge 44
(Evan Williams) *in tch tl 4th: wknd after 3 out: t.o* **200/1**

F- 15 11 **Cherry Tiger**[6] 4534 4-10-7 0 PaulMoloney 25
(Graeme McPherson) *mid-div: rdn after 3 out: wknd next: t.o* **33/1**

0- 16 4 **Tomorrow Night**[84] 3049 4-10-2 0 ow2 TomCannon 16
(Jennifer Mason) *mid-div tl wknd appr 3 out: t.o* **100/1**

/40- 17 6 **Miller's Maverick**[19] 4281 6-11-1 0 NickScholfield 23
(Grant Cann) *a towards rr: lost tch after 4th: t.o* **250/1**

P **Margh Arhansek (IRE)** 7-11-1 0 AndrewTinkler
(Tony Newcombe) *a towards rr: t.o whn p.u bef last* **200/1**

4m 0.4s (11.50) **Going Correction** +0.75s/f (Soft)
WFA 4 from 5yo+ 7lb 18 Ran SP% **117.1**
Speed ratings (Par 105): **101,100,99,99,98 98,89,88,87,80 77,76,70,67,62 60,57,**
CSF £22.96 TOTE £8.70: £2.50, £1.50, £5.00; EX 29.90 Trifecta £360.70.
Owner J P Romans **Bred** R Kent & Mrs N O'Neil **Trained** Milborne Port, Dorset

FOCUS
Starts of 2m5f and 2m6f moved to Road crossing. Andrew Tinkler described the ground as "heavy, sticky and hard work". Ordinary form, with them going a steady gallop and several holding a chance at the top of the straight. They finished in a heap. The cosy winner can rate higher.

4633 BATHWICK TYRES TERRY BIDDLECOMBE FIRST AND LAST H'CAP CHASE (13 fncs) 2m
3:00 (3:00) (Class 4) (0-105,105) 5-Y-0+ **£3,898** (£1,144; £572; £286)

Form RPR
1 **Martin Cash (IRE)**[70] 3297 8-10-7 **93** MrGTreacy(7) 99+
(Paul Henderson) *hld up last but wl in tch: smooth hdwy to ld gng wl appr 3 out: in command after: readily* **11/2**

5U5- 2 4 ½ **King Ozzy (IRE)**[41] 3883 10-11-1 **94** (tp) NickScholfield 92
(Lawney Hill) *trckd ldng trio: rdn into 3rd 3 out: kpt on fr last to go 2nd towards fin: nt pce to threaten wnr* **7/2**[3]

302- 3 *hd* **Islandmagee (IRE)**[29] 4087 7-11-9 **102** (t) AdamWedge 100
(Evan Williams) *trckd ldrs: chal 9th tl next: ev ch briefly appr 3 out: rdn bef 2 out: a being readily hld by wnr: no ex whn lost 2nd towards fin* **3/1**[2]

53U- 4 3 **Enchanting Smile (FR)**[12] 4416 7-10-9 **88** (t) TommyPhelan 87
(Mark Gillard) *nvr fluent: trckd ldr: led 2nd: bked rt off 5th (water): hdd next: rdn after 4 out: one pce fr next* **11/4**[1]

530- 5 25 **Wait No More (IRE)**[165] 1626 9-11-5 **101** (p) MichaelByrne(3) 86
(Neil Mulholland) *led tl 2nd: trckd ldr: hmpd 5th: led next: rdn and hdd whn blnd 3 out: qckly btn* **9/2**

4m 21.8s (21.90) **Going Correction** +0.825s/f (Soft) 5 Ran SP% **107.5**
Speed ratings: **78,75,75,74,61**
CSF £22.96 TOTE £6.50: £2.60, £1.70; EX 29.80 Trifecta £99.30.
Owner Mrs J L Chappell **Bred** Michael Heskin **Trained** Whitsbury, Hants

FOCUS
A really messy race, with them dawdling around, and plenty of credit goes to winning rider Gordon Treacy. Weak form, but it makes sense.

4634 BATHWICK TYRES SALISBURY H'CAP HURDLE (7 hdls 1 omitted) 2m
3:35 (3:35) (Class 3) (0-130,130) 4-Y-0 **£6,330** (£1,870; £935; £468; £234)

Form RPR
523- 1 **Red Seventy**[49] 3728 5-10-13 **117** (p) TomScudamore 121+
(David Pipe) *t.k.h: disp ld tl clr ldr after 2nd: jnd after 3 out: 1 l up last: kpt on wl: rdn out* **7/2**[1]

044- 2 2 **Dragon's Den (IRE)**[19] 4278 7-10-6 **110** LeightonAspell 113
(Chris Down) *hld up bhd ldrs: jnd wnr sn after 3 out: short of room on stands' side rails appr 2 out tl swtchd rt bef last where nt fluent: sn rdn: kpt on but a being hld* **7/2**[1]

413- 3 9 **Helium (FR)**[16] 4333 9-10-5 **116** MrsAlexDunn(7) 108
(Alexandra Dunn) *trckd ldrs: rdn after 3 out: kpt on same pce fr next* **6/1**

424- 4 4 ½ **Chesil Beach Boy**[16] 4333 11-11-12 **130** DominicElsworth 118
(John Coombe) *cl up: rdn after 3 out: kpt on but nvr gng pce to threaten* **9/2**[3]

00U- 5 3 ¼ **Quaddick Lake (IRE)**[19] 4278 11-10-8 **122** ChrisMeehan(10) 107
(Jeremy Scott) *t.k.h: disp ld tl after 2nd: trckd wnr tl sn after 3 out: sn rdn: kpt on same pce fr next* **5/1**

103- 6 18 **Moujik Borget (FR)**[37] 3957 6-11-8 **126** LiamTreadwell 92
(Venetia Williams) *trckd ldrs: pushed along after 3rd: rdn after next: btn sn after 3 out: t.o* **4/1**[2]

3m 57.4s (8.50) **Going Correction** +0.75s/f (Soft) 6 Ran SP% **113.6**
Speed ratings (Par 107): **108,107,102,100,98 89**
CSF £16.53 TOTE £3.30: £1.80, £1.90; EX 12.00 Trifecta £33.70.
Owner Terry Neill **Bred** Sir Eric Parker **Trained** Nicholashayne, Devon

FOCUS
Ordinary form, with a few of these failing to give their running. Arguably a step up from the winner.

4635 BATHWICK TYRES BRIDGWATER H'CAP CHASE (21 fncs) 3m 1f 110y
4:05 (4:05) (Class 3) (0-125,127) 5-Y-0+ **£6,330** (£1,870; £935)

Form RPR
/21- 1 **Benbens (IRE)**[7] 4507 9-12-4 **127** 7ex SamTwiston-Davies 136+
(Nigel Twiston-Davies) *trckd ldr: nt fluent 12th: mstkes 15th: 16th and next: rdn to chal after 3 out: led on landing 2 out: mstke last: styd on: rdn out* **8/11**[1]

/31- 2 2 ¼ **Thomas Wild**[13] 4396 9-11-2 **114** MichealNolan(3) 119
(Philip Hobbs) *trckd ldr: stmbld 12th: pushed along after 17th: rdn to ld bef 3 out: nt fluent and hdd 2 out: styd on same pce* **4/1**[3]

P33- 3 13 **Yellow Ball (FR)**[26] 4161 6-11-12 **121** LiamTreadwell 117
(Venetia Williams) *led: stmbld 7th: mstke 16th: rdn whn hit 4 out: hdd bef next: sn hld* **5/2**[2]

6m 55.6s (16.10) **Going Correction** +0.825s/f (Soft) 3 Ran SP% **106.5**
Speed ratings: **108,107,103**
CSF £3.54 TOTE £1.70; EX 2.90 Trifecta £3.30.
Owner Mrs S Such **Bred** Patrick Collins **Trained** Naunton, Gloucs

FOCUS
A shambles of a race, with the jumping of each of the three runners falling to pieces on the final circuit. The first two are rated similar to their recent wins.

4636 BATHWICK TYRES DORCHESTER H'CAP HURDLE (9 hdls 1 omitted) 2m 4f
4:35 (4:36) (Class 5) (0-100,100) 4-Y-0+ **£1,949** (£572; £286; £143)

Form RPR
500- 1 **Warsaw Pact (IRE)**[19] 4275 11-9-7 **74** oh5 MrLKilgarriff(7) 82
(Steven Dixon) *towards rr of mid-div: pushed along and stdy prog fr 5th: drvn after 3 out: str chal bef next: led appr last: styd on wl* **33/1**

P0P- 2 5 **Landerbee (IRE)**[10] 4471 7-9-10 **77** KevinJones(7) 82+
(Seamus Mullins) *hld up bhd: smooth hdwy fr 5th: led bef 2 out: sn rdn whn strly pressed: hdd between last 2: looked hld whn mstke last: jst hld on for 2nd* **14/1**

122- 3 *hd* **Cash Injection**[42] 3852 5-11-9 **100** (t) MichealNolan(3) 103
(Richard Woollacott) *mid-div: trckd ldrs 3 out: sn rdn: styd on same pce fr next: jst failed to snatch 2nd fnl strides* **5/1**[3]

044- 4 6 **General Girling**[19] 4275 7-10-3 **77** (p) IanPopham 74
(Caroline Keevil) *led tl 2nd: pressed ldr: rdn to ld after 3 out tl bef next: one pce after: lost 3rd nr post* **17/2**

/04- 5 2 ¾ **Kapricorne (FR)**[25] 4176 7-10-2 **76** RichieMcLernon 72+
(Sophie Leech) *hld up towards rr: stdy prog fr 6th: nvr threatened: styd on same pce fr 2 out* **33/1**

2UU- 6 18 **Hector's House**[12] 4416 8-10-1 **78** RobertDunne(3) 54
(Nikki Evans) *hld up towards rr: hdwy after 4th: rdn after next: wknd after 3 out: t.o* **20/1**

00U- 7 9 **Canadian Dreamer (IRE)**[9] 4475 7-11-12 **100** WayneHutchinson 67
(Graeme McPherson) *mid-div: rdn appr 3 out: wknd sn after: t.o* **5/1**[3]

022- 8 4 ½ **Slaney Star (IRE)**[11] 4447 6-11-11 **99** (b[1]) TomScudamore 62
(Jim Best) *led 2nd: rdn appr 5th: hdd after 3 out: wknd bef next: t.o* **5/1**[3]

06P/ P **Giant Sequoia (USA)**[456] 2856 10-10-13 **87** PaulMoloney
(Sophie Leech) *mid-div on outer: dropped to rr rapidly 5th: p.u bef next* **3/1**[1]

12- P **Boomtown**[44] 3828 9-11-5 **100** (t) GeraldQuinn(7)
(Claire Dyson) *trckd ldr: rdn after 3 out: sn wknd: tailing off whn p.u bef next* **10/1**

405- P **Torgamah Lad (IRE)**[16] 4334 6-11-9 **97** LiamTreadwell
(Venetia Williams) *mid-div: hdwy to trck ldrs after 4th: wknd after next: tailing off whn p.u bef 3 out* **9/2**[2]

/0P- P **Strictly Cissbury**[52] 3692 5-10-3 **77** (p) BrendanPowell
(Brendan Powell) *chsd ldrs: rdn after 4th: blnd next: qckly dropped to rr: tailing off whn p.u bef 6th* **66/1**

5m 19.9s (23.10) **Going Correction** +0.75s/f (Soft) 12 Ran SP% **131.6**
Speed ratings (Par 103): **83,81,80,78,77 70,66,64,,**
CSF £452.53 CT £2733.29 TOTE £46.80: £12.20, £5.30, £2.50; EX 747.60 Trifecta £4828.50 Part won..
Owner S Dixon **Bred** Saad Bin Mishrif **Trained** Winterslow, Wilts
■ A belated first winner under rules for Luke Kilgarriff.
■ Stewards' Enquiry : Mr L Kilgarriff 15-day ban: used whip above permitted level (Mar 20,21,26-28,30,Apr 1-5,7,10,12-13)

FOCUS
A few of the fancied runners failed to give their running and the form looks moderate. The winner was thrown in on old form.

4637 BATHWICK TYRES H'CAP CHASE (17 fncs) 2m 5f
5:05 (5:05) (Class 4) (0-110,109) 5-Y-0+ **£3,898** (£1,144; £572; £286)

Form RPR
305- 1 **Tolkeins Tango (IRE)**[12] 4412 6-11-9 **106** JackDoyle 116+
(Victor Dartnall) *trckd ldrs: hit 2nd: led 4 out: rdn and idling whn hdd after 3 out: led again bef last: kpt on fr last: drvn out* **5/2**[2]

/45- 2 ¾ **Mic Aubin (FR)**[19] 4275 11-10-9 **92** FelixDeGiles 100
(Jennifer Mason) *trckd ldr: v awkward 11th: sn pushed along: chal briefly 4 out: rdn bk upsides next: led sn after: hdd bef last: kpt on: hld towards fin* **9/2**[3]

/0P- 3 18 **Webberys Dream**[13] 4396 11-11-2 **102** (p) MattGriffiths(3) 91
(Jeremy Scott) *led: rdn after 13th: narrowly hdd next: wknd after 3 out* **7/1**

/35- 4 6 **Mon Chevalier (IRE)**[37] 3960 11-11-7 **107** (p) MichealNolan(3) 89
(Carroll Gray) *hld up last of 5: hdwy 13th: rdn bef next: hld sn after: wknd after 3 out* **8/1**

214- 5 27 **Rossa Parks (IRE)**[84] 3033 8-11-12 **109** NoelFehily 64
(Neil Mulholland) *trckd ldng trio: pckd 1st: effrt after 13th: wknd after next: t.o* **6/4**[1]

5m 44.1s (18.90) **Going Correction** +0.825s/f (Soft) 5 Ran SP% **110.4**
Speed ratings: **97,96,89,87,77**
CSF £13.54 TOTE £4.50: £2.00, £2.00; EX 12.50 Trifecta £72.30.
Owner Mrs Sonia M Hall **Bred** Michael C Walsh **Trained** Brayford, Devon

FOCUS
The front pair drew clear in a race that took little winning. The winner improved to his hurdles mark.

4638 BATHWICK TYRES MAIDEN OPEN NATIONAL HUNT FLAT RACE 2m
5:40 (5:40) (Class 6) 4-6-Y-0 **£1,624** (£477; £238; £119)

Form RPR
1 **Earthmoves (FR)** 4-10-10 0 DarylJacob 95+
(Paul Nicholls) *trckd ldrs: jnd ldr over 2f out running green: led over 1f out: sn rdn: jst hld on: all out* **11/4**[2]

0- 2 *shd* **The Cider Maker**[34] 4016 4-10-10 0 JoeTizzard 95
(Colin Tizzard) *t.k.h: trckd ldrs: rdn over 2f out where sltly outpcd: kpt on wl fnl f: clsng wl fnl 75yds: jst failed* **6/1**

3 3 ¼ **Kublai (FR)** 4-10-10 0 RichardJohnson 92
(Philip Hobbs) *hld up bhd ldrs: hdwy 5f out: effrt 3f out: sn sltly outpcd: kpt on ins fnl f: wnt 3rd towards fin* **7/2**[3]

4 *nk* **Our Chief (IRE)** 5-11-4 0 TomScudamore 99
(David Pipe) *led at stdy pce: qcknd pce 7f out: rdn over 2f out: hdd over 1f out: kpt on same pce: lost 3rd towards fin* **6/4**[1]

5 1 ¾ **Somerset Jem** 5-11-1 0 JamesBest(3) 98
(Kevin Bishop) *hld up: effrt over 3f out: kpt on but nt pce to chal fnl 2f* **25/1**

6 4 ½ **Krackatoa King** 6-10-13 0 JamesBanks(5) 93
(Noel Williams) *trckd ldr: nudged along after 3f: rdn over 5f out: outpcd 3f out: kpt on fnl f* **14/1**

7 31 **Grand Lad (IRE)**[306] 6-11-4 0 NickScholfield 62
(Grant Cann) *kpt wd away fr bunch: in tch tl wknd 3f out: t.o* **66/1**

4m 16.2s (32.90) **Going Correction** +0.75s/f (Soft)
WFA 4 from 5yo+ 7lb 7 Ran SP% **115.2**
Speed ratings: **47,46,45,45,44 42,26**
CSF £19.81 TOTE £4.10: £1.70, £3.00; EX 14.10 Trifecta £47.50.
Owner R M Penny **Bred** Jean-Francois Vermand **Trained** Ditcheat, Somerset

FOCUS
This looked a reasonable bumper on paper but it was slowly run and they finished in a heap. It's been given a token rating through the second.
T/Plt: £1047.20 to a £1 stake. Pool: £74,755.10 - 52.11 winning units. T/Qpdt: £116.80 to a £1 stake. Pool: 4429.50 - 28.06 winning units. TM

4639 - 4645a (Foreign Racing) - See Raceform Interactive

4364 AYR (L-H)

Friday, March 7

OFFICIAL GOING: Heavy (chs 7.3, hdl 7.5)

First hurdle in the home straight and penultimate fence in the back straight omitted all races

Wind: Fairly strong, half against, changing to light, half against before race 5

Weather: Cloudy, bright

4646 TOTEPOOL.COM BEST ODDS ON IRISH LOTTO NOVICES' CHASE (11 fncs 1 omitted) 2m

1:50 (1:50) (Class 4) 5-Y-O+ **£4,548** (£1,335)

Form				RPR
/21-	1		**Eduard (IRE)**[96] 2839 6-11-7 140 BrianHarding (Nicky Richards) *chsd ldr: nt fluent 5 out: clsng whn blnd next: sn rcvrd: shkn up briefly and led between last 2: j. sltly lft last: drvn clr* **30/100**[1]	142+
/26-	2	11	**Imjoeking (IRE)**[90] 2957 7-11-0 128 PeterBuchanan (Lucinda Russell) *led at modest gallop: pushed along whn nt fluent 2 out: hdd between last 2: j. sltly lft last: sn outpcd* **11/4**[2]	123

4m 32.9s (22.20) **Going Correction** +1.45s/f (Heav) 2 Ran SP% **103.6**
Speed ratings: **102,96**
TOTE £1.30.

Owner Kingdom Taverns Ltd **Bred** Cecil And Martin McCracken **Trained** Greystoke, Cumbria

FOCUS
Divided bends and both tracks 12m from innermost lines. Divided bends and both tracks 12m from innermost lines. A disappointing turnout. The duo took things pretty steadily in ground described as "very hard work" and "very deep" and the time was 50sec slower than standard. The winner is a decent novice but it's hard to say this represents a step up.

4647 WE'LL DOUBLE YOUR DEPOSIT AT TOTEPOOL CASINO NOVICES' HURDLE (8 hdls 1 omitted) 2m

2:20 (2:20) (Class 4) 4-Y-O+ **£3,898** (£1,144; £572; £286)

Form				RPR
0/4-	1		**Avidity**[112] 2493 5-11-1 0 BrianHughes (James Ewart) *trckd ldr gng wl: led on bit 2 out: clr bef last: readily* **7/2**[2]	116+
231-	2	8	**Titus Bolt (IRE)**[15] 4364 5-11-8 119 JamesReveley (Jim Goldie) *led: rdn and hdd 2 out: kpt on fr last: nt pce of wnr* **5/6**[1]	112
46P-	3	5	**Love Marmalade (IRE)**[24] 4199 4-10-4 0 EwanWhillans(3) (Alistair Whillans) *t.k.h: in tch: effrt and hdwy bef 2 out: 3rd and one pce whn mstke last* **20/1**	94
0-	4	¾	**Got The Nac (IRE)**[112] 2499 5-11-1 0 WilsonRenwick (S R B Crawford, Ire) *prom: hdwy and ev ch bef 2 out: sn rdn and edgd lft: outpcd between last 2* **20/1**	99
63-	5	6	**Itstimeforapint (IRE)**[15] 4364 6-11-1 0 PeterBuchanan (Lucinda Russell) *hld up: nt fluent 3rd: hdwy and prom 3 out (usual 4 out): rdn and outpcd bef next: hld whn mstke 2 out* **6/1**[3]	95+
	6	57	**Golan Sun (IRE)**[16] 4357 6-10-8 0 MrSFox(7) (Paul Stafford, Ire) *hld up: stdy hdwy 4th: nt fluent next: sn rdn and wknd bef omitted 3 out: t.o* **66/1**	36
	7	49	**Ebony Roc (IRE)**[6] 4562 4-10-7 0 DavyCondon (Gordon Elliott, Ire) *hld up: outpcd whn nt fluent 3 out (usual 4 out): sn rdn and wknd: t.o* **11/1**	
00-	P		**Alkali (IRE)**[6] 4548 4-9-9 0 GrantCockburn(5) (S R B Crawford, Ire) *mstkes towards rr: struggling fr 1/2-way: t.o whn p.u bef 2 out* **66/1**	
55-	P		**Lochnell (IRE)**[22] 4240 5-10-1 0 NathanMoscrop(7) (Brian Ellison) *hld up in midfield: outpcd whn mstke 3 out (usual 4 out): lost tch and p.u bef 2 out* **25/1**	

4m 20.8s (17.70) **Going Correction** +1.25s/f (Heav)
WFA 4 from 5yo+ 7lb 9 Ran SP% **115.8**
Speed ratings (Par 105): **105,101,98,98,95 66,42, ,**
CSF £6.73 TOTE £3.50: £1.10, £1.10, £3.90; EX 7.20 Trifecta £50.20.

Owner Leeds Plywood And Doors Ltd **Bred** Mrs Glenda Swinglehurst **Trained** Langholm, Dumfries & G'way

FOCUS
A modest novice hurdle but a big step up from the easy winner.

4648 BEST ODDS GUARANTEED AT TOTEPOOL.COM H'CAP HURDLE (FOR THE JAMES BARCLAY CHALLENGE TROPHY) (9 hdls 2 omitted) 2m 4f

2:50 (2:50) (Class 4) (0-115,115) 4-Y-O+ **£4,882** (£1,669)

Form				RPR
042-	1		**Island Heights (IRE)**[13] 4429 5-11-4 107 WilsonRenwick (Lucinda Russell) *chsd ldrs: nt fluent 6th: smooth hdwy to ld bef 2 out: sn clr: v easily* **11/8**[2]	115+
103-	2	24	**Sam Lord**[30] 4085 10-11-6 109 (v[1]) BrianHughes (James Moffatt) *led at stdy pce: rdn and hdd 3 out: rallied and regained ld briefly bef next: no ch w easy wnr* **6/1**[3]	92
034-	P		**The Tracey Shuffle**[91] 8-11-5 115 [1] NathanMoscrop(7) (Brian Ellison) *t.k.h: cl up: chal 6th: led next: hdd bnd bef omitted 3 out: nt keen and sn lost tch: p.u bef 2 out* **1/1**[1]	

5m 44.1s (32.10) **Going Correction** +1.25s/f (Heav) 3 Ran SP% **106.4**
Speed ratings (Par 105): **85,75,**
CSF £6.82 TOTE £2.40; EX 4.70 Trifecta £5.20.

Owner Straightline Construction Ltd **Bred** Fiona And Michael O'Connor **Trained** Arlary, Perth & Kinross

FOCUS
A modest handicap, and with the favourite not running his race it didn't take much winning. It's difficult to know what the winner achieved.

4649 PLAY BLACKJACK AND ROULETTE AT TOTEPOOL.COM H'CAP HURDLE (10 hdls 2 omitted) 3m 110y

3:25 (3:25) (Class 4) (0-105,105) 4-Y-O+ **£3,898** (£1,144; £572; £286)

Form				RPR
653-	1		**Finaghy Ayr (IRE)**[44] 3829 6-11-0 100 GrahamWatters(7) (Ian Duncan) *in tch: hdwy to ld whn hit 3 out (usual 4 out): rdn whn nt fluent next: hrd pressed fr last: styd on gamely towards fin* **13/2**	101+
P64-	2	shd	**Bescot Springs (IRE)**[39] 3938 9-11-7 105 (v) CraigNichol(5) (Lucinda Russell) *hld up in tch: hdwy and prom 3 out (usual 4 out): effrt and chsd wnr bef next: ev ch and drvn last: kpt on wl: jst hld* **9/2**[3]	105
P6B-	3	8	**Bollin Fiona**[62] 3525 10-10-11 95 CallumWhillans(5) (Donald Whillans) *chsd ldrs: drvn after 3 out (usual 4 out): rallied whn hit next: outpcd appr last* **14/1**	88
635-	4	7	**Amore Mio (GER)**[5] 4577 9-11-10 103 (tp) PeterBuchanan (Lucinda Russell) *led to 3 out (usual 4 out): rallied and sn ev ch: hung lft and outpcd next: 4th and hld whn hit last* **11/4**[1]	90
665-	5	3 ¼	**Milan Flyer (IRE)**[62] 3525 8-10-5 89 DerekFox(5) (Noel C Kelly, Ire) *bhd: pushed along and outpcd 1/2-way: sme hdwy appr 2 out: nvr rchd ldrs* **4/1**[2]	71
413-	6	8	**Rinnagree Rosie**[39] 3934 8-11-10 103 AdrianLane (Lucy Normile) *in tch: hdwy and cl up 1/2-way: ev ch and rdn 3 out: wknd bef next* **8/1**	77
465-	P		**Allforthelove**[51] 3721 6-10-10 89 LucyAlexander (N W Alexander) *cl up tl lost pl bef 6th: struggling fr next: t.o whn p.u bef 2 out* **6/1**	

7m 2.3s (30.50) **Going Correction** +1.25s/f (Heav) 7 Ran SP% **110.2**
Speed ratings (Par 105): **101,100,98,96,95 92,**
CSF £33.09 TOTE £5.10: £3.30, £2.40; EX 31.90 Trifecta £180.20.

Owner Ronald Lilley **Bred** A Steele **Trained** Coylton, Ayrshire

FOCUS
A very ordinary handicap hurdle. A small step up from the winner.

4650 20 NEW CASINO GAMES AT TOTEPOOL.COM H'CAP HURDLE (10 hdls 2 omitted) 3m 110y

4:00 (4:00) (Class 3) (0-135,120) 4-Y-O+ **£6,657** (£2,067; £1,113)

Form				RPR
243-	1		**Mysteree (IRE)**[24] 4200 6-11-12 120 PeterBuchanan (Lucinda Russell) *chsd ldrs: chal 6th: led and hung lft bef 2 out: continued to hang lft but drew clr between last 2* **13/8**[1]	124+
635-	2	14	**Micro Mission (IRE)**[17] 4338 8-11-2 110 BrianHughes (Chris Grant) *chsd ldr: led and jnd 6th: hdd and carried lft bef 2 out: sn rdn and swtchd rt: outpcd by wnr after 2 out* **2/1**[2]	99
353-	3	71	**Ballythomas**[17] 4340 7-10-13 110 TonyKelly(3) (David Thompson) *prom: hdwy 6th: rdn and outpcd after 3 out (usual 4 out): lost tch bef omitted 3 out: t.o* **15/2**	28
425-	P		**Los Nadis (GER)**[33] 4058 10-11-8 116 HenryBrooke (Jim Goldie) *led to 6th: drvn and struggling fr next: 4th and no ch whn blnd 2 out: sn p.u* **7/2**[3]	

6m 59.0s (27.20) **Going Correction** +1.25s/f (Heav) 4 Ran SP% **105.4**
Speed ratings (Par 107): **106,101,78,**
CSF £5.05 TOTE £2.70; EX 6.90 Trifecta £13.70.

Owner Mrs Lynne Maclennan **Bred** Lar & Fiona Cloke **Trained** Arlary, Perth & Kinross

FOCUS
A weak race for the Class, run in a time 3.7sec quicker than the previous 0-105 handicap. The easy winner is rated back to his best.

4651 DOWNLOAD THE TOTEPOOL LIVE INFO APP H'CAP CHASE (15 fncs 2 omitted) 2m 4f

4:35 (4:35) (Class 3) (0-140,139) 5-Y-O+ **£7,797** (£2,289; £1,144; £572)

Form				RPR
/13-	1		**Jimmy The Hat (IRE)**[65] 3483 8-10-2 115 (bt[1]) DavyCondon (Gordon Elliott, Ire) *hld up in tch: stdy hdwy whn hit 5 out: smooth hdwy to ld next: qcknd clr on bridle after 3 out: eased down last 100yds* **9/1**	132+
PP1-	2	5	**Mister Marker (IRE)**[22] 4236 10-11-1 135 MissJRRichards(7) (Nicky Richards) *cl up: led 8th to 10th: chsng ldr and pushed along whn stmbld bnd bef 4 out: rallied and ev ch 4 out: hit next: wnt 2nd after 2 out: kpt on: flattered by proximity to eased-down wnr* **4/1**[3]	136
144-	3	5	**Stormin Exit (IRE)**[15] 4369 11-10-6 119 JamesReveley (Jim Goldie) *led to 8th: regained ld 10th: rdn and hdd 4 out: outpcd after 2 out* **10/3**[2]	116
321-	4	43	**Wicklow Lad**[13] 4430 10-10-8 128 (v) MrKitAlexander(7) (N W Alexander) *chsd ldrs: hdwy to chal 8th to bef 10th: outpcd after 5 out: lost tch fr next: t.o* **6/4**[1]	80
651/	F		**Lackamon**[317] 5503 9-11-12 139 RyanMania (Sue Smith) *in tch: fell 4th* **7/1**	

5m 46.9s (24.00) **Going Correction** +1.45s/f (Heav) 5 Ran SP% **105.6**
Speed ratings: **110,108,106,88,**
CSF £38.70 TOTE £9.20: £3.90, £1.70; EX 49.60 Trifecta £192.60.

Owner Ms Annie Flora Joan Bowles **Bred** J F C Maxwell **Trained** Trim, Co Meath

FOCUS
A fair handicap chase in which they went a reasonable gallop. A big step up in form from the easy winner.

4652 £5 FREE IRISH LOTTO BET AT TOTEPOOL.COM CONDITIONAL JOCKEYS' H'CAP CHASE (17 fncs 2 omitted) 3m 1f

5:10 (5:10) (Class 5) (0-100,90) 5-Y-O+ **£2,662** (£826; £445)

Form				RPR
P62-	1		**Gibbstown (IRE)**[49] 3755 8-11-1 79 (p) DerekFox (Paul Stafford, Ire) *hld up in tch: hit 10th: smooth hdwy to chse ldr 4 out: led 2 out: sn rdn clr* **7/2**[2]	91+
234-	2	16	**Soul Angel**[11] 4462 10-10-7 74 (v) CraigNichol(3) (Sandy Forster) *w ldr: led 10th: rdn and hdd 2 out: sn no ch w wnr* **5/1**[3]	70
531-	3	52	**Tears From Heaven (USA)**[23] 4220 8-10-11 83 (p) DiarmuidO'Regan(8) (Chris Grant) *prom: hit 3rd: sn pushed along: hdwy u.p 11th: struggling 4 out: losing tch whn hit next: t.o* **3/1**[1]	27
1/P-	P		**Shadow Boxer**[86] 3022 9-11-12 90 CallumWhillans (Donald Whillans) *led to 10th: sn drvn along: outpcd next: lost tch 5 out: t.o whn p.u bef next* **5/1**[3]	
22P-	U		**Samson Collonges (FR)**[39] 3936 8-10-8 75 TonyKelly(3) (Rebecca Menzies) *prom: blnd and uns rdr 6th* **5/1**[3]	
/PP-	P		**Heart O Annandale (IRE)**[257] 798 7-11-4 85 DaraghBourke(3) (Alistair Whillans) *mstkes: prom: wnt 2nd 11th to 4 out: wknd bef next: 3rd and btn whn blnd 2 out: sn p.u* **15/2**	

7m 32.4s (42.50) **Going Correction** +1.45s/f (Heav) 6 Ran SP% **109.0**
Speed ratings: **90,84,68, ,**
CSF £19.51 TOTE £5.60: £2.10, £2.40; EX 20.80 Trifecta £44.00.

Owner Mrs L Skelly **Bred** John And Ann Goold **Trained** Oldtown, Co. Dublin

FOCUS
A very moderate handicap chase. There's a case for rating the form a bit higher through the second.

T/Plt: £120.70 to a £1 stake. Pool: £52155.82 - 315.24 winning tickets T/Qpdt: £114.90 to a £1 stake. Pool: £3183.31 - 20.50 winning tickets RY

[4481]LEICESTER (R-H)

Friday, March 7

OFFICIAL GOING: Soft (heavy in places; 5.6)

Wind: Light behind Weather: Cloudy

4653 QUEENS ROYAL LANCERS H'CAP CHASE (12 fncs) 2m

2:10 (2:10) (Class 4) (0-115,114) 5-Y-O+ **£4,659** (£1,446; £779)

Form RPR

1U2- **1** **Arkaim**[22] 4241 6-11-9 **114**........ KielanWoods(3) 125+
(Pam Sly) *chsd ldr tl led after 2nd: clr fr 4th to 7th: wnt clr again 4 out: rdn appr last: eased flat* **5/1**[3]

P51- **2** *27* **Morgan's Bay**[10] 4483 9-11-12 **114** 7ex........ PaddyBrennan 95
(Tom George) *prom: chsd wnr 4th: pushed along appr 4 out: wknd next* **11/8**[1]

055- **3** *2 ¾* **Brassbound (USA)**[15] 4372 6-11-0 **102**........(p) AndrewThornton 69
(Caroline Bailey) *prom to 5th* **5/1**[3]

32B- **P** **Bin End**[22] 4242 8-11-0 **102**........(p) SamTwiston-Davies
(Barry Brennan) *hld up: pushed along 3rd: rdn appr 5th: sn wl bhd: p.u bef 3 out* **11/4**[2]

3F6/ **P** **Playing With Fire (IRE)**[787] 3671 10-11-2 **104**........[1] CharliePoste
(Robin Dickin) *led: blnd 2nd: sn hdd: chsesd wnr to 4th: wknd after next: bhd whn p.u bef 3 out* **12/1**

4m 21.9s (13.70) **Going Correction** +0.70s/f (Soft) 5 Ran SP% **109.8**
Speed ratings: **93,79,78,** ,
CSF £12.82 TOTE £4.90: £1.90, £1.90; EX 15.90 Trifecta £30.30.
Owner G A Libson D L Bayliss G Taylor P M Sly **Bred** Harton Limited **Trained** Thorney, Cambs

FOCUS
There was no hanging about in this moderate handicap and only two mattered from a long way out. The ground was no doubt heavy. An easy winner but form to be confident about.

4654 LEICESTER INTERACTIVE NOVICES' H'CAP CHASE (18 fncs) 2m 7f 110y

2:40 (2:40) (Class 5) (0-100,97) 5-Y-O+ **£2,380** (£865)

Form RPR

400- **1** **Leeroar (IRE)**[17] 4334 6-11-9 87........ SamJones 91
(Jo Davis) *hmpd 1st: led sn after: hdd 11th: chsd ldr: rdn appr 4 out: led last: styd on u.p* **9/1**[3]

643- **2** *1 ¼* **Badb Catha (IRE)**[61] 3555 8-9-7 64 oh2........ MrFTett(7) 67
(Roger Curtis) *chsd ldr after 1st tl led 11th: rdn and nt fluent 4 out: hdd last: unable qck towards fin* **14/1**

P4/- **F** **No More Whispers (IRE)**[278] 9-10-6 70........(p) DaveCrosse
(Marc Barber) *w ldr whn hmpd and lft in ld 1st: sn hdd: chsd ldrs: pushed along after 10th: 4 l 3rd whn fell 12th* **11/4**[2]

401- **U** **Lord Landen (IRE)**[10] 4486 9-12-0 97 7ex........(t) ConorShoemark(5)
(Fergal O'Brien) *led: j.lft and uns rdr 1st* **8/15**[1]

6m 31.8s (27.80) **Going Correction** +0.70s/f (Soft) 4 Ran SP% **108.6**
Speed ratings: **81,80,** ,
CSF £65.71 TOTE £11.50; EX 28.30 Trifecta £34.50.
Owner The Hard Hat Gang **Bred** Henry Morgan **Trained** East Garston, Berks
■ Stewards' Enquiry : Mr F Tett seven-day ban: used whip above permitted level (Mar 21,26-28,30,Apr 1-2)
Sam Jones seven-day ban: used whip above permitted level (Mar 21-27)

FOCUS
A poor handicap run in a slow time, given a token rating through the second.

4655 MALLARD PAWNBROKERS HUNTERS' CHASE (18 fncs) 2m 7f 110y

3:15 (3:15) (Class 3) 6-Y-O+ **£9,193** (£2,932; £1,510; £799)

Form RPR

P/2- **1** **Current Exchange (IRE)**[20] 4274 9-11-7 117........ MrPGerety(7) 124
(Mrs Sheila Crow) *a.p: pckd 1st: chsd ldr 12th: led 3 out: rdn bef next: hdd last: rallied to ld nr fin* **5/2**[1]

2F3/ **2** *nk* **Court Red Handed (IRE)**[26] 9-11-3 120........(t) MrMJPKendrick(7) 120
(Mrs S Case) *hld up: hdwy after 4th: mstke 12th: rdn and outpcd after 4 out: rallied appr last: styd on wl* **6/1**

1/3- **3** *½* **Benedictus (IRE)**[68] 9-11-13 129........ MrJBarber(5) 127+
(Jack Barber) *prom: nt fluent and lost pl 4th: hdwy 12th: led and wnt lft last: rdn and edgd rt flat: hdd nr fin* **7/1**[2]

/11- **4** *6* **Little Legend**[43] 3862 10-11-13 119........(p) MissCHaydon(5) 122
(Miss C M E Haydon) *led to 3 out: sn pushed along: no ex last* **4/1**[3]

34P- **P** **Lady Myfanwy**[197] 1344 13-11-0 90........ MissHLewis(7)
(Mrs Myfanwy Miles) *chsd ldr 2nd to 4th: remained handy tl lost pl after 8th: bhd fr 10th: p.u bef 14th* **33/1**

5/2- **P** **Island Life (IRE)**[8] 4511 11-11-11 123........(b) MrWTelfer(7)
(S Flook) *prom: chsd ldr 4th tl hit 12th: wknd 14th: bhd whn p.u bef next* **25/1**

105- **P** **What A Laugh**[20] 4274 9-12-4 114........ MrWBiddick
(G D Hanmer) *hld up: hdwy 10th: rdn and wknd after 2 out: p.u bef last* **4/1**[3]

6m 19.3s (15.30) **Going Correction** +0.70s/f (Soft) 7 Ran SP% **114.6**
Speed ratings: **102,101,101,99,** ,
CSF £18.03 TOTE £3.10: £1.50, £3.80; EX 24.10 Trifecta £86.60.
Owner Alastair Crow **Bred** R Guiry **Trained** Shrewsbury, Shropshire
■ Stewards' Enquiry : Mr P Gerety two-day ban: used whip above permitted level (Mar 21,26)

FOCUS
This was a fair hunter chase and it provided a war of attrition from the third-last fence. The winner is rated to the level of his recent Haydock run.

4656 LEICESTERSHIRE AND DERBYSHIRE YEOMANRY H'CAP CHASE (AMATEUR RIDERS) (15 fncs) 2m 4f 110y

3:50 (3:50) (Class 5) (0-100,99) 5-Y-O+ **£3,119** (£967; £483; £242)

Form RPR

622- **1** **Thedreamstillalive (IRE)**[45] 3817 14-9-11 **75**.......(t) MrHAABannister(5) 81
(Jim Old) *mde all: set stdy pce tl qcknd appr 4 out: rdn bef last: all out* **2/1**[2]

005- **2** *nse* **Cool Bob (IRE)**[50] 3730 11-11-0 **94**........(t) MrStanSheppard(7) 100
(Matt Sheppard) *hld up: outpcd bef 4 out: rallied appr last: styd on wl* **9/1**

3P0- **3** *8* **Bally Lagan (IRE)**[35] 4020 6-9-13 **79**........(tp) MrTWWheeler(7) 77
(Robin Dickin) *chsd wnr: chal 4 out tl rdn appr last: no ex flat* **4/1**[3]

6U3- **4** *17* **Taffy Thomas**[21] 4250 10-11-5 **99**........(t) MrSPBowen(7) 88
(Peter Bowen) *chsd ldrs: ev ch whn hit 4 out: mstke next: sn rdn: wknd after 2 out* **5/4**[1]

5m 50.8s (31.90) **Going Correction** +0.70s/f (Soft) 4 Ran SP% **107.8**
Speed ratings: **67,66,63,57**
CSF £14.53 TOTE £5.10; EX 5.60 Trifecta £16.00.
Owner J A B Old **Bred** Frank O'Malley **Trained** Barbury Castle, Wilts

FOCUS
With the ground at its most demanding there was predictably a slow-motion finish to this weak handicap. The first two are rated pretty much to their marks.

4657 SHERWOOD RANGERS YEOMANRY H'CAP CHASE (18 fncs) 2m 7f 110y

4:25 (4:25) (Class 4) (0-110,108) 5-Y-O+ **£4,548** (£1,335; £667; £333)

Form RPR

341- **1** **Kentford Legend**[22] 4243 7-11-9 **105**........ AndrewThornton 124+
(Seamus Mullins) *mde all: clr to 13th: c clr again fr 3 out: styd on wl* **6/4**[2]

222- **2** *11* **Lough Coi (IRE)**[10] 4481 8-9-13 **88**........(vt) CharlieDeutsch(7) 95
(Anthony Middleton) *hld up: tk clsr order 13th: shkn up appr 4 out: wnt 2nd 2 out: styd on same pce* **5/4**[1]

225- **3** *19* **Roseneath (IRE)**[52] 3696 10-10-10 **97**........(tp) KillianMoore(5) 85
(Alex Hales) *chsd wnr: mstke 11th: rdn tk clsr order 13th: rdn 4 out: wknd 2 out* **9/1**

1F5- **4** *40* **Tony Dinozzo (FR)**[30] 4089 7-11-11 **107**........(p) JamieMoore 55
(Peter Bowen) *hld up: tk clsr order 13th: rdn and wknd after next* **7/1**[3]

6m 18.4s (14.40) **Going Correction** +0.70s/f (Soft) 4 Ran SP% **106.9**
Speed ratings: **104,100,94,80**
CSF £3.84 TOTE £2.60; EX 5.40 Trifecta £10.40.
Owner D I Bare **Bred** D I Bare **Trained** Wilsford-Cum-Lake, Wilts

FOCUS
A moderate staying handicap. It was run at a solid gallop. The form makes sense.

4658 THRUSTERS HUNTERS' CHASE (12 fncs) 2m

5:00 (5:00) (Class 6) 5-Y-O+ **£1,559** (£483; £241; £121)

Form RPR

6- **1** **Siro Demur (FR)**[70] 8-11-7 95........ MrAlexEdwards(5) 115+
(Philip Rowley) *a.p: led 3 out: pushed out* **5/1**[3]

423- **2** *3 ½* **Delta Borget (FR)**[12] 9-11-5 103........ MissLeandaTickle(7) 108
(L Jefford) *hld up: hdwy 8th: rdn to go 2nd last: styd on: nt rch wnr* **10/1**

/43- **3** *3 ¼* **Swallows Delight (IRE)**[22] 4246 9-11-12 100........ MrDMansell 105
(Mrs Julie Mansell) *mid-div: hdwy 8th: drvn along and mstke 4 out: styd on u.p: nt trble ldrs* **7/2**[2]

5P0/ **4** *6* **Areuwitmenow (IRE)**[19] 9-11-9 89........ MissAEStirling(3) 102
(S Rea) *trckd ldrs: rdn appr 2 out: hmpd last: wknd flat* **33/1**

360/ **5** *10* **I'm So Lucky**[40] 12-11-7 139........(t) MrTEllis(5) 94
(Mrs S E Busby) *led to 7th: led again 4 out: hdd next: sn rdn: blnd and wknd last* **15/8**[1]

6 *12* **Blackstown Flyer (IRE)**[40] 7-11-5 0........ MrTAMcclorey(7) 81
(G T H Bailey) *trckd ldrs: led 7th: hdd 4 out: mstke next: sn rdn: wknd 2 out* **6/1**

00P- **7** *1* **Himalayan Express**[51] 3720 10-12-1 115........ MrJMartin(5) 85
(Mrs David Plunkett) *hld up: hdwy after 7th: rdn and wknd bef 4 out* **25/1**

/04- **8** *12* **Petit Ecuyer (FR)**[15] 4372 8-11-11 99........ MissAliceMills(5) 68
(Barry Brennan) *hld up: a in rr* **20/1**

P **Fairymount (IRE)**[278] 9-11-12 0........(t) MrWBiddick
(G D Hanmer) *hld up: wknd appr 4 out: p.u bef next* **8/1**

P **Ooson (IRE)**[27] 7-11-5 0........(v[1]) MrRobertHawker(7)
(Mrs O C Jackson) *trckd ldr to 4th: pushed along 6th: rdn and wknd after 8th: p.u bef next* **100/1**

4m 20.3s (12.10) **Going Correction** +0.70s/f (Soft) 10 Ran SP% **120.7**
Speed ratings: **97,95,93,90,85 79,79,73,** ,
CSF £51.24 TOTE £9.90: £2.60, £4.10, £1.90; EX 61.50 Trifecta £205.90.
Owner Philip Rowley **Bred** Serge Hamon **Trained** Bridgnorth, Shropshire

FOCUS
A rare hunter chase over the minimum trip and the ground played a big part in proceedings. The form looks solid enough.
T/Plt: £1,653.50 to a £1 stake. Pool: £66118.19 - 29.19 winning tickets T/Qpdt: £42.20 to a £1 stake. Pool: £6109.61 - 107.02 winning tickets CR

[4031]SANDOWN (R-H)

Friday, March 7

OFFICIAL GOING: Soft (good to soft in the back straight on chase course; heavy in places on hurdle course; chs 5.8, hdl 5.2)

Wind: Moderate, half against Weather: Fine, mild

4659 ANNINGTON AMATEUR RIDERS' H'CAP HURDLE (FOR MILITARY AMATEUR RIDERS) (8 hdls) 2m 110y

2:00 (2:00) (Class 4) (0-115,115) 4-Y-O+ **£3,119** (£967; £483; £242)

Form RPR

U6P- **1** **Old Way (IRE)**[42] 3565 8-10-9 **97**........(b) MrJSole(5) 103+
(Venetia Williams) *prom: trckd ldr 3rd: led bef 2 out and sn clr: slow into last and briefly looked vulnerable: rdn and kpt on wl* **4/1**[2]

3P5- **2** *2 ¾* **Kastani Beach (IRE)**[22] 4242 8-10-10 **100**........ LtColEricaBridge(7) 101
(Seamus Mullins) *hld up in last and wl off the pce: no prog tl after 3 out: styd on to take 2nd last: no imp on wnr flat* **7/1**

441- **3** *11* **Should I Stay (FR)**[15] 4377 6-11-4 **108**........(p) MajorFelixWheeler(7) 100
(Gary Moore) *pressed ldr: led after 2nd: hit 5th: rdn and hdd bef 2 out: hung lft after: lost 2nd last: fdd* **4/1**[2]

2P3- **4** *3 ¼* **Captain Cardington (IRE)**[13] 4413 5-11-3 **105**....(v) MissSallyRandell(5) 92
(John O'Shea) *led to after 2nd: lost pl next: rdn 3 out: outpcd bef 2 out* **6/1**[3]

1- **5** *11* **Great Link**[15] 4369 5-12-3 **114**........(t) MissLucyGardner 90
(Tony Carroll) *hld up off the pce in 5th: clsd steadily on ldrs fr 3 out: wl in tch bef 2 out: wknd rapidly sn after 2 out* **11/4**[1]

244- **6** *4* **Alanjou (FR)**[47] 3796 4-10-13 **109**........(p) MajorAlexMichael(5) 73
(Jamie Snowden) *trckd ldng pair: wl on terms 3 out: wknd qckly bef 2 out* **15/2**

/20- **P** **Boston Blue**[16] 3599 7-11-11 **115**........ CaptMaxChenery(7)
(Tony Carroll) *hld up in 6th and off the pce: no prog 3 out: t.o whn p.u bef last* **16/1**

4m 11.9s (4.70) **Going Correction** +0.45s/f (Soft)
WFA 4 from 5yo+ 7lb 7 Ran SP% **111.1**
Speed ratings (Par 105): **106,104,99,98,92 90,**
CSF £29.23 TOTE £5.10: £2.60, £3.20; EX 32.50 Trifecta £172.30.
Owner B C Dice **Bred** Wertheimer Et Frere **Trained** Kings Caple, H'fords

FOCUS
A modest handicap. The winner is rated in line with his best form from the last couple of years.

4660 CHARLES STANLEY H'CAP CHASE (13 fncs) 2m
2:30 (2:30) (Class 3) (0-125,125) 5-Y-0+ £7,797 (£2,289; £1,144; £572)

Form RPR
302- 1 **Greywell Boy**[14] 4400 7-11-9 **122** RichardJohnson 129
(Nick Williams) *trckd ldr fr 5th: rdn 4 out: led next: hrd pressed fr last: hld on wl* **5/4**[1]
643- 2 ¾ **Bullet Street (IRE)**[99] 2762 6-11-1 **114** PaulMoloney 120
(Evan Williams) *hld up in last: prog 3 out and cl up: trckd wnr after next and stl gng wl: rdn after last: fnd little and a jst hld* **3/1**[2]
464- 3 1½ **Sands Cove (IRE)**[48] 3787 7-11-7 **120** (t) NoelFehily 125
(Charlie Mann) *sweating: patiently rdn in rr: asked for effrt and in tch after 3 out: nt fluent next and rdn: kpt on same pce fr last* **7/1**[3]
F53- 4 4½ **Coolbeg (IRE)**[38] 3960 8-10-3 **102** ow1 FelixDeGiles 103
(Heather Main) *trckd ldr: dived at 4th: dropped to 3rd next: mstke 8th: lost pl after 3 out but stl gng wl enough: rdn after 2 out: fdd flat* **8/1**
442- 5 13 **Wings Of Smoke (IRE)**[76] 3204 9-11-9 **125** (vt) MichaelByrne(3) 116
(Tim Vaughan) *hld up: nt fluent 1st: mstke 5th: cl up whn nt fluent 9th: wnt 2nd after 3 out tl after next: wknd v rapidly flat* **8/1**
F0P- 6 43 **Train Of Thought (IRE)**[114] 2461 6-11-2 **115** (p) AdamWedge 59
(Evan Williams) *led to 3 out: wknd rapidly: t.o* **16/1**
4m 8.8s (7.00) **Going Correction** +0.625s/f (Soft) 6 Ran SP% **110.0**
Speed ratings: **107,106,105,103,97 75**
CSF £5.44 TOTE £2.20: £1.50, £1.50; EX 5.30 Trifecta £16.90.
Owner Chasing Gold Racing Club **Bred** Shade Oak Stud **Trained** George Nympton, Devon

FOCUS
The winner was on a fair mark and is rated 3lb off last season's best.

4661 GRAND MILITARY GOLD CUP (CHASE FOR MILITARY AMATEUR RIDERS) (SPONSORED BY THE MILITARY MUTUAL) (22 fncs) 3m 110y
3:05 (3:05) (Class 3) 6-Y-0+ £6,239 (£1,935; £967; £484)

Form RPR
30P- 1 **Bradley**[65] 3455 10-11-9 128 MissSallyRandell(5) 139
(Fergal O'Brien) *j.rt: trckd ldr fr 5th: led 10th: mde rest: shkn up and styd on strly fr last* **10/3**[3]
34P- 2 2¾ **Le Reve (IRE)**[20] 4270 6-11-9 129 (p) MajorAlexMichael(5) 135
(Lucy Wadham) *wl plcd: trckd ldng pair 15th: cl enough fr 3 out: rdn to take 2nd last: styd on but no imp on wnr* **3/1**[2]
654- 3 5 **Solix (FR)**[41] 3897 8-11-7 129 (v) CaptHarryWallace(7) 132
(Ian Williams) *tended to jump lft: led to 10th: chsd wnr after: cl enough 2 out: lost 2nd and fdd last* **5/2**[1]
352- 4 17 **Polisky (FR)**[19] 4299 7-11-9 126 (t) MrJSole(5) 114
(Paul Nicholls) *j. slowly 3rd: hld up in rr: prog to trck ldrs 12th: cl 4th after 4 out: rdn and fnd nil next: wknd* **5/1**
360- 5 1½ **Marley Roca (IRE)**[19] 4303 10-11-7 122 CaptMaxChenery(7) 113
(Paul Webber) *wl in rr: rchd 5th 4 out: no imp on ldrs bef next: fdd* **20/1**
253- 6 21 **Neptune Equester**[64] 3505 11-11-7 123 MajorFelixWheeler(7) 94
(Sandy Thomson) *appeared nt to jump fluently: a in rr: pushed along 1/2-way: bhd fr 17th: t.o* **14/1**
P/1- 7 3¾ **Jack Bene (IRE)**[21] 4252 8-12-0 115 MissLucyGardner 90
(Miss Louise Allan) *prom: j. v slow 3rd and slow again next: wknd rapidly fr 4 out: t.o* **12/1**
P14/ P **Qualypso D'Allier (FR)**[530] 1607 10-11-10 96 ow3. MrRobertSkinner(7)
(Richard Woollacott) *a in rr: lost tch 15th: t.o whn p.u bef last* **50/1**
/0P- F **Estates Recovery (IRE)**[14] 4402 9-11-7 109 LtColEricaBridge(7)
(Luke Dace) *chsd ldr to 5th: mstke next: sn lost pl: last whn fell 12th* **100/1**
6m 40.8s (13.00) **Going Correction** +0.625s/f (Soft) 9 Ran SP% **115.4**
Speed ratings: **104,103,101,96,95 88,87, ,**
CSF £14.14 TOTE £4.60: £1.50, £1.70, £1.10; EX 15.20 Trifecta £59.10.
Owner J C Collett **Bred** P A Broad **Trained** Coln St. Dennis, Gloucs

FOCUS
A straightforward renewal of this historic race.

4662 CHARLES STANLEY H'CAP HURDLE (11 hdls) 2m 6f
3:40 (3:40) (Class 3) (0-135,128) 4-Y-0+ £7,797 (£2,289; £1,144; £572)

Form RPR
240- 1 **Berkeley Barron (IRE)**[26] 4174 6-11-12 **128** RichardJohnson 135+
(Philip Hobbs) *hld up in last trio: mstke 7th: rdn next: wl off the pce in 7th 3 out: styd on bef 2 out as ldrs tired: clsd qckly to ld bef last: drvn clr* **10/1**
PP3- 2 7 **Phone Home (IRE)**[13] 4411 7-11-2 **118** DominicElsworth 117
(Nick Mitchell) *in tch: rdn after 8th and struggling to make hdwy: kpt on as ldrs tired but mstke 2 out: lft in 2nd pl last: v tired and no imp on wnr* **14/1**
U36- 3 2¾ **San Telm (IRE)**[20] 4271 9-11-7 **123** JoshuaMoore 119
(Renee Robeson) *trckd ldng pair: cl up and clr of rest 3 out: sn rdn: tried to chal 2 out: tired and hld bef last where lft in 3rd pl* **12/1**
311- 4 ½ **Waldorf Salad**[38] 3955 6-11-9 **125** LiamTreadwell 123
(Venetia Williams) *led to 3rd: w ldr and gd pce fr next: drvn 3 out: upsides next: wknd last* **7/2**[3]
561- 5 2½ **Westaway (IRE)**[6] 4555 7-11-4 **120** 7ex TomCannon 113
(David Arbuthnot) *w ldr: led 3rd: set gd pce after: drvn wl bef 2 out: hdd & wknd bef last* **11/4**[2]
251- 6 1¼ **Spencer Lea**[8] 4510 6-11-0 **116** 7ex NoelFehily 108
(Andrew Price) *hld up in last trio: sme prog 8th but nt on terms: rdn and no imp on ldrs on long run to 2 out* **5/2**[1]
030- 7 55 **Nataani (IRE)**[146] 1868 11-10-11 **123** (vt) JackSavage(10) 60
(Jo Davis) *chsd ldrs: rdn after 5th: struggling to stay in tch fr next: wknd 3 out: t.o* **40/1**
2P- F **American Life (FR)**[20] 4271 7-10-2 **109** (bt) JamesBanks(5) 109
(Anthony Middleton) *hld up in last trio: rdn after 8th: kpt on as ldrs tired bef 2 out: tried to chal between last 2: more than 2 l down and hld whn fell last* **20/1**
05P- P **Valid Reason**[13] 4423 7-11-9 **125** (t) PaulMoloney
(Dean Ivory) *lost tch 5th: sn wl t.o: p.u bef 3 out* **16/1**
5m 35.4s (5.40) **Going Correction** +0.45s/f (Soft) 9 Ran SP% **114.0**
Speed ratings (Par 107): **108,105,104,104,103 102,82, ,**
CSF £131.10 CT £1688.08 TOTE £8.30: £2.90, £3.20, £2.10; EX 122.50 Trifecta £926.00.
Owner Mrs Peter Prowting **Bred** Fred Williams **Trained** Withycombe, Somerset

FOCUS
The top weight was rated 7lb below the ceiling. The complexion of this race changed dramatically early in the straight, as the leaders began to paddle. The second and the faller set the level.

4663 QUEEN ELIZABETH THE QUEEN MOTHER MEMORIAL H'CAP CHASE (FOR MILITARY AMATEUR RIDERS) (17 fncs) 2m 4f 110y
4:15 (4:15) (Class 4) (0-115,112) 5-Y-0+ £4,367 (£1,354; £676; £338)

Form RPR
005- 1 **Fredo (IRE)**[14] 4402 10-11-11 **112** (v[1]) CaptHarryWallace(7) 128+
(Ian Williams) *trckd ldng pair: nt fluent 11th: wnt 2nd after 4 out: upsides whn outj. 3 out and next: urged along and fnlly led after last: styd on* **3/1**[2]
P56- 2 5 **Tafika**[70] 3325 10-11-6 **107** (p) CaptMaxChenery(7) 117
(Paul Webber) *led 4th: mde most after: mstkes 5th and 10th: battled on wl whn jnd 3 out: hdd and tired after last* **2/1**[1]
623- 3 13 **Craiglands (IRE)**[16] 4354 12-10-7 **87** oh4 (v) MissLucyGardner 84
(Ian Williams) *led to 4th tl hdd: led briefly 8th: rdn 11th: lost 2nd after 4 out: steadily fdd* **3/1**[2]
255- 4 22 **Tribal Dance (IRE)**[14] 4398 8-11-1 **100** MrJSole(5) 74
(John O'Shea) *in tch in rr to 7th: sn bhd: t.o fr 10th: won sprint for 4th fr last* **6/1**[3]
656- 5 1½ **Ultra Klass (FR)**[22] 4242 6-10-13 **98** (t) MajorAlexMichael(5) 71
(Jamie Snowden) *in tch to 7th: bhd whn blnd 10th: t.o and mstke 12th* **8/1**
5m 31.1s (12.70) **Going Correction** +0.625s/f (Soft) 5 Ran SP% **108.7**
Speed ratings: **100,98,93,84,84**
CSF £9.46 TOTE £4.90: £2.40, £1.10; EX 10.10 Trifecta £22.00.
Owner Mrs Jacky Allen **Bred** Gestut Hof Ittlingen **Trained** Portway, Worcs

FOCUS
In these conditions this was quite a test. Ordinary hunter chase form.

4664 SSAFA FORCES AND FAMILIES "NATIONAL HUNT" NOVICES' HURDLE (8 hdls) 2m 110y
4:50 (4:51) (Class 4) 4-Y-0+ £3,898 (£1,144; £572; £286)

Form RPR
460- 1 **In Fairness (IRE)**[79] 3166 5-11-1 0 DavidBass 105+
(Nicky Henderson) *hld up in tch: prog to ld 2 out and kicked on: rdn and edgd lft flat: styd on wl* **7/1**
111- 2 3 **Mountain King**[20] 4266 5-12-1 135 RichardJohnson 116
(Philip Hobbs) *hld up in tch: prog 2 out: sn rdn: chsd wnr last: styd on but nt pce to chal* **2/1**[2]
3- 3 3½ **Fight Commander (IRE)**[36] 3994 5-11-1 0 LeightonAspell 98
(Oliver Sherwood) *trckd ldrs: shkn up to chal 2 out: lost 2nd and outpcd fr last: kpt on* **11/2**[3]
066- 4 10 **Comte D'Anjou**[34] 4024 5-11-1 0 (p) NickScholfield 89
(Nick Williams) *trckd ldr: cl enough bef 2 out: wknd bef last* **12/1**
04- 5 1 **Parting Way (IRE)**[44] 3838 6-10-12 0 MichaelByrne(3) 87
(Tim Vaughan) *mstke 1st and nt a fluent: hld up in last: prog into 5th 2 out: nudged along and lft bhd by ldrs bef last* **50/1**
/04- 6 4 **Willpower (IRE)**[86] 3023 5-10-12 0 PeterCarberry(3) 83
(Nicky Henderson) *trckd ldrs: lost pl 3 out: sn rdn: stl jst in tch whn mstke 2 out: wknd* **25/1**
6- 7 7 **Rattleandrun (IRE)**[28] 4135 6-11-1 0 BrendanPowell 76
(Brendan Powell) *wl in tch: rdn and sing to struggle whn mstke 2 out: wknd* **100/1**
525- P **A Tail Of Intrigue (IRE)**[19] 4297 6-10-10 124 RobertMcCarth(5)
(Ian Williams) *mstkes: led at mod pce: hdd and mstke 2 out: immediately btn and eased: p.u bef last: b.b.v* **11/8**[1]
4m 14.0s (6.80) **Going Correction** +0.45s/f (Soft) 8 Ran SP% **117.8**
Speed ratings (Par 105): **102,100,98,94,93 91,88,**
CSF £22.65 TOTE £10.90: £1.80, £1.20, £1.80; EX 30.40 Trifecta £83.00.
Owner Simon Munir & Isaac Souede **Bred** Kevin Talbot **Trained** Upper Lambourn, Berks

FOCUS
With the runner-up, who is rated 135, giving a stone away to the rest, it probably didn't need a great performance from the winner. He's rated as improving to the level of his bumper form in a steadily run race.
T/Jkpt: £28,634.90 to a £1 stake. Pool: £262150.53 - 6.50 winning tickets T/Plt: £165.50 to a £1 stake. Pool: £106422.26 - 469.21 winning tickets T/Qpdt: £31.90 to a £1 stake. Pool: £10383.67 - 240.75 winning tickets JN

4646 AYR (L-H)
Saturday, March 8

OFFICIAL GOING: Heavy (7.7)
First hurdle in home straight and penultimate fence in back straight omitted all races.
Wind: Strong, across Weather: Overcast

4665 TOTEJACKPOT WIN BIG FOR A SMALL STAKE NOVICES' HURDLE (10 hdls 2 omitted) 3m 110y
1:55 (1:56) (Class 4) 4-Y-0+ £3,994 (£1,240; £667)

Form RPR
312- 1 **I Need Gold (IRE)**[26] 4186 6-11-10 130 HenryBrooke 138+
(Donald McCain) *mde virtually all: hrd pressed and rdn bef 2 out: styd on gamely fr last* **85/40**[2]
2P- 2 ½ **Moonshine Lad (IRE)**[16] 4386 6-11-10 138 DavyCondon 138+
(Gordon Elliott, Ire) *prom on outside: hdwy to chse wnr 6th: chal gng wl whn stmbld bef 2 out: styd on u.p fr last: hld towards fin* **8/11**[1]
306- 3 85 **Full Jack (FR)**[66] 3476 7-11-3 117 WilsonRenwick 46
(Pauline Robson) *chsd ldrs: nt fluent 6th: outpcd after next: lost tch w first two fr 3 out (usual 4 out)* **13/2**[3]
4- P **Doubledisdoubledat (IRE)**[25] 4200 7-10-10 0 DaraghBourke(7)
(Stuart Coltherd) *t.k.h early: chsd wnr to 6th: outpcd whn nt fluent next: lost tch 3 out (usual 4 out): t.o whn p.u bef next* **33/1**
P **Firth Of Bavard** 7-11-3 0 BrianHughes
(Robert Goldie) *nt fluent: hld up in tch: struggling 1/2-way: t.o whn p.u bef 7th* **100/1**
6m 51.0s (19.20) **Going Correction** +0.90s/f (Soft) 5 Ran SP% **107.2**
Speed ratings (Par 105): **105,104,77, ,**
CSF £3.97 TOTE £2.90: £1.10, £2.10; EX 3.40 Trifecta £5.70.
Owner Deva Racing Golden Partnership **Bred** George Blackburn **Trained** Cholmondeley, Cheshire
■ Stewards' Enquiry : Davy Condon two-day ban: used whip above permitted level (Mar 22-23)

FOCUS
Divided bends moved overnight and rails moved out from previous day, 13m from innermost lines. Conditions remained very testing, not helped by a strong, very gusty cross wind. The first hurdle in the home straight was again omitted. A severe test of stamina in the conditions. The winner is a bit better than his current mark.

4666 TOTESCOOP6 SATURDAY'S BIG TV BET H'CAP CHASE (15 fncs 2 omitted) 2m 4f
2:30 (2:30) (Class 4) (0-110,110) 5-Y-O+ **£4,548** (£1,335; £667)

Form RPR
0/2- **1** **See Double You (IRE)**[13] 4458 11-11-4 **109**............. MrRMPMcNally(7) 123+
(Ronan M P McNally, Ire) *cl up: led 5th to 9th: chal 5 out: regained ld whn hit next: kpt on strly fr 2 out* **11/8**[1]
133- **2** 2 ¾ **Badger Foot (IRE)**[23] 4236 9-11-5 **110**......................(t) GrahamWatters(7) 118
(Lucinda Russell) *trckd ldrs: smooth hdwy to chse wnr 3 out: effrt and ch next: sn rdn and edgd lft: one pce fr last* **7/2**[3]
211- **3** 9 **Too Cool To Fool (IRE)**[16] 4365 11-10-12 **96**................ JamesReveley 98
(Jim Goldie) *led to 5th: regained ld 9th: hdd appr 4 out: outpcd after next* **6/4**[2]
5m 57.5s (34.60) **Going Correction** +0.90s/f (Soft) 3 Ran SP% **104.3**
Speed ratings: **66,64,61**
CSF £5.31 TOTE £2.30; EX 4.90 Trifecta £4.80.
Owner Red Neds Racing Club **Bred** Michael And Mrs B C Lenihan **Trained** Ireland
FOCUS
The penultimate fence in the back straight was omitted and the pace was very steady, with the lead repeatedly changing hands until the turn for home. The form is rated around the second.

4667 CHELTENHAM ANTE POST AT TOTEPOOL.COM H'CAP HURDLE (8 hdls 1 omitted) 2m
3:05 (3:06) (Class 4) (0-120,111) 4-Y-O+ **£3,898** (£1,144; £572; £286)

Form RPR
661- **1** **Plus Jamais (FR)**[40] 3937 7-11-7 **106**................................. BrianHughes 111+
(Jim Goldie) *w ldr: chal 3rd: led next: drvn along whn nt fluent last: edgd rt and styd on wl run-in* **1/1**[1]
215- **2** 1 ¼ **Final Assault (IRE)**[16] 4369 5-11-7 **111**................................ DerekFox(5) 113
(Lucinda Russell) *in tch: stdy hdwy after 3 out (usual 4 out): wnt 2nd and effrt bef next: sn edgd lft: styd on fr last: hld nr fin* **5/2**[2]
242- **3** 11 **Scimon Templar (FR)**[16] 4366 6-11-1 **100**................... WilsonRenwick 91
(Pauline Robson) *t.k.h early: led: hdd whn hit 4th: styd upsides: ev ch tl outpcd and lost 2nd bef 2 out: n.d after* **7/2**[3]
54P- **4** 64 **Indepub**[135] 2034 5-11-4 **103**... LucyAlexander 30
(Martin Todhunter) *nt fluent on occasions: chsd ldrs to 3rd: outpcd next: lost tch fr 3 out (usual 4 out): t.o* **16/1**
4m 21.1s (18.00) **Going Correction** +0.90s/f (Soft) 4 Ran SP% **106.7**
Speed ratings (Par 105): **91,90,84,52**
CSF £3.84 TOTE £1.90; EX 5.20 Trifecta £7.10.
Owner Alba-Eire Syndicate **Bred** Ecurie Passing **Trained** Uplawmoor, E Renfrews
FOCUS
They went a steady gallop in the testing conditions and the first two had it to themselves. They are both rated to their marks.

4668 TOTEPOOL HOME OF POOL BETTING MARES' H'CAP HURDLE (10 hdls 2 omitted) 2m 5f 110y
3:40 (3:42) (Class 3) (0-130,120) 4-Y-O+ **£6,498** (£1,908; £954; £477)

Form RPR
34- **1** **Romantic Fashion (IRE)**[16] 4365 7-11-6 **114**....................... MPFogarty 117+
(Mrs Prunella Dobbs, Ire) *nt fluent on occasions: mde virtually all: rdn bef 2 out: hit last: styd on gamely* **11/4**[1]
654- **2** 2 ¼ **Golden Sparkle (IRE)**[34] 4058 8-10-13 **114**.............. GrahamWatters(7) 114
(Ian Duncan) *in tch: stdy hdwy after 3 out (usual 4 out): effrt and chsd wnr bef last: kpt on same pce run-in* **5/1**[3]
FF1- **3** 3 **Little Glenshee (IRE)**[16] 4367 8-11-12 **120**.................... LucyAlexander 118
(N W Alexander) *cl up: drvn and outpcd bef omitted 3 out: rallied bef last: styd on to take 3rd towards fin: nt rch first two* **4/1**[2]
4U5- **4** 1 ¼ **Kykate**[36] 4007 8-11-1 **112**...............................(t) HarryChalloner(3) 108
(William Kinsey) *prom: smooth hdwy to chse wnr bef 2 out: sn rdn: lost 2nd and one pce whn hit last: sn outpcd* **9/1**
126- **5** 58 **Rattlin**[35] 4040 6-11-7 **118**.............................. JonathanEngland(3) 56
(Sue Smith) *cl up tl rdn and wknd after 3 out (usual 4 out)* **11/4**[1]
343- **6** 13 **Spring Over (IRE)**[31] 4083 8-10-6 **100**................................ BrianHughes 25
(Ian Duncan) *in tch: outpcd 7th: lost tch fr next: t.o* **12/1**
6m 3.5s (23.20) **Going Correction** +0.90s/f (Soft) 6 Ran SP% **107.7**
Speed ratings (Par 107): **93,92,91,90,69 64**
CSF £15.18 TOTE £2.80: £1.80, £2.60; EX 15.70 Trifecta £57.80.
Owner Ms K Tottenham **Bred** Robert Quinn And David Duane **Trained** Dunganstown, Co Wicklow
FOCUS
They went a sound gallop in this mares' handicap hurdle. The form is rated around the second and third.

4669 BEST ODDS GUARANTEED AT TOTEPOOL.COM H'CAP CHASE (FOR THE HUGH BARCLAY CHALLENGE TROPHY) (17 fncs 2 omitted) 3m 1f
4:15 (4:16) (Class 3) (0-130,127) 5-Y-O+ **£7,988** (£2,480; £1,335)

Form RPR
462- **1** **Mister Philson (IRE)**[16] 4368 9-10-1 **107**......................(p) CraigNichol(5) 116
(S R B Crawford, Ire) *in tch: drvn and outpcd 12th: hdwy after 5 out: no imp tl styd on bef last: led run-in: drvn out* **7/2**[2]
142- **2** ¾ **Samstown**[51] 3743 7-10-12 **116**...................................... EwanWhillans(3) 124
(Alistair Whillans) *in tch: hdwy whn nt fluent 5th: ev ch fr 4 out: sn rdn: led briefly after last: kpt on: hld towards fin* **11/8**[1]
1P1- **3** 3 ¼ **Etxalar (FR)**[31] 4086 11-10-12 **113**...............................(t) PeterBuchanan 119
(Lucinda Russell) *cl up: hdwy to ld 5 out: mstke next: sn rdn: nt fluent last: sn hdd and one pce* **7/1**[3]
51P- **P** **Kealigolane (IRE)**[66] 3476 10-11-12 **127**......................... JamesReveley
(Barry Murtagh) *led: blnd 7th: nt fluent next: hit and hdd 10th: sn struggling: lost tch and p.u bef 12th* **22/1**
1PP- **P** **Railway Dillon (IRE)**[25] 4204 9-11-3 **125**....................(tp) NickSlatter(7)
(Donald McCain) *cl up: led 10th: hdd 5 out: cl up whn mstke and outpcd 4 out: struggling fr next: t.o whn p.u after 2 out* **10/1**
223- **P** **Fentara**[14] 4430 9-11-9 **124**.......................................(bt[1]) DougieCostello
(Mark Walford) *hld up in tch: nt fluent 12th: rdn and outpcd next: rallied bef 4 out: rdn and wknd 2 out: p.u appr last* **7/2**[2]
7m 7.0s (17.10) **Going Correction** +0.90s/f (Soft) 6 Ran SP% **112.5**
Speed ratings: **108,107,106, ,**
CSF £9.26 TOTE £4.60: £1.90, £3.00; EX 10.50 Trifecta £35.20.
Owner Leonard Phillips **Bred** Brittas House Stud & Grenane House **Trained** Larne, Co Antrim

FOCUS
This proved a severe test of stamina and the complexion of the race changed dramatically at the final fence. Ordinary form, rated around the first three.

4670 TOTEEXACTA PICK FIRST AND SECOND H'CAP HURDLE (FOR THE AYRSHIRE YEOMANRY CUP) (9 hdls 2 omitted) 2m 4f
4:50 (4:52) (Class 3) (0-140,132) 4-Y-O+ **£6,498** (£1,908; £954; £477)

Form RPR
331- **1** **Forward Flight (IRE)**[6] 4579 8-10-6 **112** 7ex......................... RyanMania 116+
(Sue Smith) *nt fluent on occasions: in tch: hit 3rd: hdwy to chal bef 2 out: rdn and led between last 2: styd on wl run-in* **13/8**[2]
2 nk **Man With Van (IRE)**[35] 4044 8-11-9 **132**...................... MrSCrawford(3) 136+
(S R B Crawford, Ire) *hld up in tch: stdy hdwy bef 2 out: sn pushed along and hdwy to chse wnr whn nt fluent last: kpt on: hld nr fin* **6/5**[1]
152- **3** 2 ½ **Kilbree Chief (IRE)**[35] 4040 6-11-5 **125**......................... PeterBuchanan 126
(Lucinda Russell) *led: rdn and edgd lft bef 2 out: hdd between last 2: rallied: kpt on run-in* **8/1**[3]
0P5- **4** 20 **Master Of The Hall (IRE)**[35] 4040 10-11-2 **127**............(p) JoeColliver(5) 108
(Micky Hammond) *cl up tl rdn and wknd fr 2 out* **22/1**
002- **5** 2 ½ **Rock Relief (IRE)**[52] 3724 8-11-0 **120**.............................. HenryBrooke 99
(Chris Grant) *chsd ldrs: drvn and outpcd 6th: lost tch bef omitted 3 out* **12/1**
5m 35.7s (23.70) **Going Correction** +0.90s/f (Soft) 5 Ran SP% **106.7**
Speed ratings (Par 107): **88,87,86,78,77**
CSF £3.81 TOTE £3.00: £2.80, £1.10; EX 4.70 Trifecta £11.70.
Owner John P McManus **Bred** Limestone And Tara Studs **Trained** High Eldwick, W Yorks
FOCUS
Again they went a decent pace and the bottom weight had to withstand the challenge of the topweight. The first two looked well in and are rated close to form.

4671 DOWNLOAD THE TOTEPOOL LIVE INFO APP STANDARD OPEN NATIONAL HUNT FLAT RACE 2m
5:25 (5:28) (Class 6) 4-6-Y-O **£1,624** (£477; £238; £119)

Form RPR
2- **1** **The Unsub (IRE)**[25] 4205 6-11-2 0...................................... DavyCondon 111+
(Gordon Elliott, Ire) *prom: shkn up to ld over 2f out: clr whn flashed tail over 1f out: drvn out* **1/1**[1]
2 7 **Waddingstown (IRE)**[49] 5-10-11 0...................................... DerekFox(5) 104
(Lucinda Russell) *led to over 2f out: rallied: kpt on same pce fr over 1f out* **9/1**[3]
1- **3** 3 ¼ **Seldom Inn**[86] 3042 6-11-9 0.. RyanMania 109
(Sandy Thomson) *chsd ldrs: drvn along 3f out: kpt on same pce fr 2f out* **4/1**[2]
4 nk **Kingswell Theatre** 5-10-11 0.. CraigNichol(5) 101
(Lucinda Russell) *in tch: drvn and outpcd over 3f out: rallied 2f out: styd on strly fnl f: nvr able to chal* **4/1**[2]
5 15 **Major Ridge (IRE)** 5-11-2 0.. HenryBrooke 86
(Robert Bewley) *hld up in tch: rdn and outpcd whn edgd lft over 2f out: sn btn* **20/1**
6 12 **Bengairn** 6-11-2 0... JamesReveley 74
(Jim Goldie) *hld up: struggling 3f out: sn btn* **16/1**
7 33 **Belfastdarknstormy (IRE)**[48] 3809 6-10-13 0............(t) MrSCrawford(3) 41
(B Arthey, Ire) *cl up tl rdn and wknd over 3f out: t.o* **66/1**
4m 21.1s (23.60) **Going Correction** +0.90s/f (Soft)
WFA 4 from 5yo+ 7lb 7 Ran SP% **112.1**
Speed ratings: **77,73,71,71,64 58,41**
CSF £10.83 TOTE £2.00: £1.40, £5.00; EX 12.30 Trifecta £35.80.
Owner John Earls **Bred** J Earls **Trained** Trim, Co Meath
FOCUS
Almost certainly an ordinary bumper, run at a very steady pace until in line for home. The winner and third set the level.
T/Plt: £22.00 to a £1 stake. Pool: £65,079.70 - 2153.78 winning units. T/Qpdt: £10.30 to a £1 stake. Pool: £2756.98 - 196.90 winning units. RY

4411 CHEPSTOW (L-H)
Saturday, March 8
OFFICIAL GOING: Heavy changing to soft after race 1 (2.10)
Wind: Moderate across Weather: Sunny

4672 FOLLOW @BETVICTORRACING TODAY "NATIONAL HUNT" MAIDEN HURDLE (10 hdls 2 omitted) 3m
2:10 (2:11) (Class 4) 4-Y-O+ **£3,119** (£915; £457; £228)

Form RPR
362- **1** **Robbers Roost (IRE)**[22] 4251 6-11-0 0........................ MichaelByrne(3) 112
(Tim Vaughan) *in rr but in tch: hdwy and nt fluent 7th: wnt 2nd appr 3 out: slt ld next: hrd pressed last: pushed along 2f run-in: styd on strly thrght fnl f* **3/1**[3]
6- **2** 6 **Always Archie**[20] 4304 7-10-7 0.................................. AlanJohns(10) 107
(Tim Vaughan) *led: narrowly hdd 2 out: stl chalng last: no ex and one pce 2f run-in* **8/1**
2/P- **3** 9 **Master Todd (IRE)**[15] 4395 9-11-3 0.............................. NickScholfield 98
(Grant Cann) *chsd ldrs: wl hld in 3rd whn lft in 3rd 2 out* **5/2**[2]
0- **4** 8 **The Bogman's Ball**[14] 4411 8-11-3 0................................ PaulMoloney 89
(Grace Harris) *chsd ldr tl wknd appr 3 out* **18/1**
2P5- **F** **Allow Dallow (IRE)**[21] 4280 7-11-3 122......................(t) RichieMcLernon 112+
(Jonjo O'Neill) *hld up in rr but in tch: stdy hdwy 3 out: 3 l 3rd and travelling wl whn fell 2 out* **6/4**[1]
/00- **P** **Jaunty Inflight**[14] 4417 5-10-10 0................................ GaryDerwin(7)
(Brian Eckley) *a in rr: j. slowly 6th: rdn and lost tch 7th: t.o whn p.u after 2 out* **100/1**
6m 25.73s (23.53) **Going Correction** +0.30s/f (Yiel) 6 Ran SP% **110.9**
Speed ratings (Par 105): **72,70,67,64, ,**
CSF £24.46 TOTE £3.60: £1.80, £3.70; EX 18.50 Trifecta £56.70.
Owner The Oxymorons **Bred** Alex Heskin **Trained** Aberthin, Vale of Glamorgan

The Form Book Jumps, Raceform Ltd, Compton, RG20 6NL.

FOCUS
The last obstacle was omitted in all hurdle races, due to the ground conditions. With not much solid form under rules to go on, this has to be modest form at best. The pace wasn't particularly quick early. The form is rated around the first four.

4673 BETVICTOR NON-RUNNER NO BET AT CHELTENHAM NOVICES' CHASE (18 fncs) 3m
2:45 (2:47) (Class 4) 5-Y-0+ **£4,045** (£1,383)

Form				RPR
0PP-	1		**Bob Ford (IRE)**[21] 4273 7-10-9 123.............................(t) PatrickCorbett(5) (Rebecca Curtis) *mde virtually all: nt fluent and jnd fr 9th: hit 12th: asserted fr 4 out: hit next: sn wl clr: comf* 8/15[1]	131+
364-	2	43	**Danners (IRE)**[28] 4148 8-11-0 0.. CharliePoste (Giles Smyly) *chsd ldrs in 3rd: hit 5th: pushed along after 7th: chsd wnr 8th: chal fr 9th: nt fluent 11th: hit 4 out and wknd next* 9/4[2]	106
34-	P		**Strike Fast (IRE)**[14] 4425 9-11-0 0.................................(p) RyanMahon (William Kinsey) *chsd wnr tl after 7th: wknd 11th: t.o whn p.u bef 4 out* 9/1[3]	

6m 29.16s (7.16) **Going Correction** +0.30s/f (Yiel) **3** Ran SP% **106.0**
Speed ratings: **100,85,**
CSF £2.07 TOTE £1.10; EX 1.80 Trifecta £1.60.
Owner The Bob Ford Partnership **Bred** Lorcan Allen **Trained** Newport, Dyfed

FOCUS
Two of the four declared had stood out on chasing form under rules, but one of those runners, Alpha Victor, didn't run due to unsuitable ground, which appeared to leave the way clear for the winner. Bob Ford is rated to his Bangor mark.

4674 DOWNLOAD THE BETVICTOR APP NOW NOVICES' H'CAP HURDLE (6 hdls 2 omitted) 2m 110y
3:20 (3:23) (Class 4) (0-120,120) 4-Y-0+ **£3,119** (£915; £457; £228)

Form				RPR
004-	1		**Rosslyn Castle**[20] 4305 5-10-11 105............................ DominicElsworth (Jonjo O'Neill) *hld up trcking ldrs: chal appr 3 out: dropped to 3rd and hit next: stl travelling wl whn swtchd to stands' side 2f run-in: taken lft and qcknd to trck ldr fnl 150yds: led fnl 40yds: readily* 9/2	110+
655-	2	¾	**Kaki Island (IRE)**[13] 4444 6-10-7 101............................... MarcGoldstein (Chris Gordon) *led: jnd 3 out and nt fluent: asserted again fr 2 out: wnt lft and nt fluent last: styd on wl: u.p: hdd and outpcd fnl 40yds* 4/1[3]	103
61P-	3	7	**Going Concern (IRE)**[76] 3225 7-11-7 115.............................. PaulMoloney (Evan Williams) *in tch: hdwy 3 out and wnt 2nd sn after: rdn and j. slow last: no imp: wknd into 3rd fnl 150yds* 7/2[2]	108
552-	4	17	**King Rolfe (IRE)**[19] 4324 6-11-4 115..........................(t) MichaelByrne(3) (Tim Vaughan) *in rr: sme hdwy appr 3 out: sn hanging lft and no ch* 6/1	91
1UP-	5	89	**Batu Ferringhi (FR)**[67] 3429 8-11-6 117...................(p) GavinSheehan(3) (Jamie Snowden) *j. slowly and bhd fr 2nd: t.o fr 1/2-way* 7/1	4
/4P-	P		**Roudoudou Ville (FR)**[49] 3786 9-11-9 120.................. GilesHawkins(3) (Victor Dartnall) *chsd ldr tl wknd appr 3 out: t.o whn p.u bef last* 3/1[1]	

4m 12.1s (1.50) **Going Correction** +0.30s/f (Yiel) **6** Ran SP% **112.2**
Speed ratings (Par 105): **108,107,104,96,54**
CSF £22.51 TOTE £4.40: £1.60, £1.60; EX 29.90 Trifecta £189.20.
Owner Chanelle Medical UK Limited **Bred** Carwell Equities Ltd **Trained** Cheltenham, Gloucs
■ Stewards' Enquiry : Marc Goldstein two-day ban: used whip above permitted level (Mar 22-23)

FOCUS
Just a modest event but it saw a fascinating three-horse battle in the final stages. The winner looked to have a bit in hand.

4675 BETVICTOR NON-RUNNER NO BET AT CHELTENHAM H'CAP CHASE (16 fncs) 2m 3f 110y
3:55 (3:55) (Class 3) (0-140,140) 5-Y-0+ **£6,498** (£1,908; £954; £477)

Form				RPR
622-	1		**Consigliere (FR)**[14] 4430 11-11-0 135.........................(p) MikeyEnnis(7) (David Pipe) *mde all: gng clr whn hit 3 out: in n.d after: v easily* 11/8[1]	147+
UF5-	2	11	**Quincy Des Pictons (FR)**[21] 4269 10-11-9 140.............. JamesBest(3) (Alan Jones) *chsd wnr fr 6th and chal fr 8th to 11th: rdn 4 out and no ch fr next but clr of 3rd* 7/1	137
556-	3	8	**Get It On (IRE)**[14] 4414 9-10-12 126.................................. PaulMoloney (Evan Williams) *in tch: rdn after 11th and wl in rr next: styd on fr 2 out to take 3rd after last but no ch w ldng duo* 8/1	115
001-	4	4 ½	**Kilcrea Asla (IRE)**[68] 3414 13-10-3 122........................ KillianMoore(5) (Graeme McPherson) *chsd ldrs: hit 9th: rdn after 11th: disp 2nd 12th: chsd ldrs in 3rd 4 out: wknd fr 3 out and dropped to 4th after last* 11/2[3]	107
23P-	5	1 ½	**Simply Wings (IRE)**[70] 3362 10-10-13 130.................. MichealNolan(3) (Richard Lee) *chsd ldrs: chal 10th to 12th: wknd fr 12th: wl btn whn wnt rt last* 5/2[2]	113

5m 12.19s (0.89) **Going Correction** +0.30s/f (Yiel) **5** Ran SP% **109.7**
Speed ratings: **110,105,102,100,100**
CSF £10.53 TOTE £2.40: £1.30, £3.50; EX 12.60 Trifecta £52.10.
Owner E A P Scouller **Bred** Erick Bec De La Motte **Trained** Nicholashayne, Devon

FOCUS
The early pace wasn't strong, and the five runners ran in a pack for a long time. It paid to race handy. The easy winner was well in and is rated back to the best of last season's form.

4676 VICTOR'S LIVE CASINO MARES' H'CAP HURDLE (9 hdls 2 omitted) 2m 4f
4:30 (4:30) (Class 4) (0-120,115) 4-Y-0+ **£3,119** (£915; £457; £228)

Form				RPR
005-	1		**Pyleigh Lass**[15] 4393 8-11-5 108..(t) IanPopham (Martin Keighley) *in rr early: hdwy to press ldrs 6th: wnt 2nd 3 out: drvn to take slt ld whn mstke last: drvn and styd on 2f run-in* 11/4[1]	116+
020-	2	6	**Lights Of Broadway (IRE)**[68] 3420 8-10-7 101.......... RobertWilliams(5) (Bernard Llewellyn) *in rr: hdwy to press ldrs 6th: rdn and dropped to mod 3rd 3 out: styd on again after 2 out to chse wnr after last on 2f run-in but no imp* 7/2[2]	102
636-	3	12	**Marie Deja La (FR)**[12] 4472 8-10-6 95...............................(b) TomCannon (Chris Gordon) *chsd ldrs: led after 4th: rdn 2 out: narrowly hdd last: no ex 2f run-in and wknd into 3rd* 7/1	85
P5P-	4	25	**Amber Flush**[29] 4132 5-9-9 89 oh4...................................(p) BenPoste(5) (Tom Symonds) *in tch: chsd ldrs 6th: wknd sn after* 13/2	52
P2P-	5	dist	**Clara Peggotty**[21] 4276 7-10-5 94.. FelixDeGiles (Tom Gretton) *t.k.h: chsd ldrs to 6th: wknd sn after and qckly t.o* 4/1[3]	
PP3-	P		**Dreambrook Lady (IRE)**[19] 4328 8-11-9 115............. GavinSheehan(3) (Warren Greatrex) *t.k.h: led and sn clr: hdd & wknd qckly after 4th: sn t.o: p.u after 6th* 5/1	

5m 9.73s (7.93) **Going Correction** +0.30s/f (Yiel) **6** Ran SP% **111.4**
Speed ratings (Par 105): **96,93,88,78,**
CSF £12.70 TOTE £2.90: £1.90, £1.30; EX 14.30 Trifecta £46.80.
Owner F D Popham **Bred** Mrs H Pudd **Trained** Condicote, Gloucs

FOCUS
This looks really weak form. The winner was well in on her best form and the second ran to her mark.

4677 CHELTENHAM 2014 NRNB AT BETVICTOR.COM H'CAP HURDLE (10 hdls 2 omitted) 3m
5:05 (5:07) (Class 4) (0-120,120) 4-Y-0+ **£3,119** (£915; £457; £228)

Form				RPR
323-	1		**Minella On Line (IRE)**[14] 4423 5-10-13 114..................... PaulO'Brien(7) (Rebecca Curtis) *trckd ldr fr 3rd: hit 4th: led appr 3 out and nt fluent: sn clr: readily* 2/1[1]	127+
336-	2	4 ½	**Westerly Breeze (IRE)**[28] 4161 6-10-8 102......................... IanPopham (Martin Keighley) *chsd ldrs: rdn and outpcd 3 out: styd on again fr 2 out: rallied on 2f run-in to take 2nd fnl 75yds: no imp on wnr* 9/2[3]	103
/P2-	3	1 ¼	**Mobaasher (USA)**[10] 4501 11-10-5 104................. MissLucyGardner(5) (Patricia Shaw) *in tch tl lost pl and struggling in rr 7th: stl wl bhd 3 out and only 5th whn styng on last: kpt on wl on 2f run-in and fin wl to take 3rd clsng stages and gaining on 2nd: no ch w wnr* 16/1	104
012-	4	¾	**Heavenstown (IRE)**[18] 4338 8-11-4 117................(b) MauriceLinehan(5) (John Spearing) *led tl hdd appr 3 out: sn no ch w wnr: no ex on 2f run-in and dropped 2 pls clsng stages* 7/2[2]	117
P46-	5	15	**One In A Milan (IRE)**[14] 4415 9-11-12 120........................ PaulMoloney (Evan Williams) *chsd ldrs: hit 6th: rdn 5th and after 7th: wknd bef 3 out* 8/1	104
/P4-	6	71	**Tenby Jewel (IRE)**[16] 4377 9-10-4 105................ ThomasCheesman(7) (Mark Gillard) *in tch: rdn 7th and sme hdwy: sn wknd* 14/1	18
44-	P		**Paddy The Oscar (IRE)**[15] 4393 11-10-3 102............... CharlieWallis(5) (Grace Harris) *chsd ldrs to 5th: wknd next: t.o whn p.u after 7th* 14/1	
1P2-	P		**Bendant**[52] 3717 9-11-3 116.. PatrickCorbett(5) (Debra Hamer) *in tch: hdwy 4th: chsd ldrs 6th: rdn 7th: wknd sn after: t.o whn p.u bef last* 10/1	

6m 19.85s (17.65) **Going Correction** +0.30s/f (Yiel) **8** Ran SP% **113.2**
Speed ratings (Par 105): **82,80,80,79,74 51,,**
CSF £11.52 CT £107.76 TOTE £2.10: £1.40, £2.10, £3.10; EX 10.30 Trifecta £126.30.
Owner AHB Racing Partnership **Bred** R Cotton & S Lannigan O'Keeffe **Trained** Newport, Dyfed

FOCUS
Probably just a modest event. The early pace wasn't particularly quick and one got the impression the gallop was steadily increased on the final circuit. A step up from the winner, who was value for further.

4678 BACK OF THE NET AT BETVICTOR.COM CONDITIONAL JOCKEYS' H'CAP CHASE (18 fncs) 3m
5:35 (5:41) (Class 4) (0-115,114) 5-Y-0+ **£3,768** (£1,106; £553; £276)

Form				RPR
P1U-	1		**Barton Gift**[15] 4399 7-10-13 101.................................(b) MauriceLinehan (John Spearing) *chsd ldrs fr 7th: outpcd 4 out: rallied after next to chse ldr 2 out: styd on wl u.p to ld fnl 50yds: won gng away* 9/4[1]	121+
PP3-	2	3	**Camden (IRE)**[18] 4339 8-11-9 114...........................(p) ThomasGarner(3) (Oliver Sherwood) *chsd ldrs: trckd ldr 14th: chal 4 out: sn led: 5 l clr 2 out: rdn last: hdd and no ex fnl 50yds* 10/1	132
/03-	3	23	**Victory Gunner (IRE)**[15] 4396 16-11-4 106........................ MichealNolan (Richard Lee) *mde most tl jnd 4 out: sn hdd: wknd into mod 3rd 2 out* 8/1[3]	103
/4F-	4	18	**Master Neo (FR)**[44] 3858 8-11-10 112..................................(t) JamesBest (Nigel Hawke) *in tch drvn and sme hdwy after 13th: nvr rchd ldrs and wknd next* 6/1[2]	88
344-	5	12	**Ballylifen (IRE)**[14] 4412 7-11-4 114.............................. JamesHuxham(8) (Jonjo O'Neill) *chsd ldrs fr 7th: wknd after 13th* 6/1[2]	78
3P2-	6	25	**Rocky Bender (IRE)**[27] 4176 9-10-13 104..............(b) CallumWhillans(3) (Venetia Williams) *chsd ldrs: rdn after 13th: blnd and btn next* 17/2	43
/56-	7	¾	**Requin (FR)**[37] 3990 9-11-8 113..................................(p) GilesHawkins(3) (Victor Dartnall) *in rr whn hmpd 4th: j. slowly 9th: t.o fr13th* 14/1	51
305-	F		**Mauricetheathlete (IRE)**[19] 4326 11-10-11 107.............. OllieGarner(8) (Martin Keighley) *pressed ldr tl fell 4th* 25/1	
232-	P		**Present To You (IRE)**[12] 4470 9-11-1 111....................... JakeHodson(8) (David Bridgwater) *prom early: in rr fr 7th: t.o whn p.u bef 4 out* 12/1	
534-	P		**Cornish Ice**[53] 3696 10-10-6 102..............................(p) JosephPalmowski(8) (Robin Dickin) *a in rr: t.o whn p.u bef 11th* 16/1	

6m 27.84s (5.84) **Going Correction** +0.30s/f (Yiel) **10** Ran SP% **114.2**
Speed ratings: **102,101,93,87,83 75,74,,,**
CSF £24.72 CT £152.89 TOTE £2.90: £1.30, £4.00, £3.70; EX 26.90 Trifecta £213.70.
Owner Mercy Rimell & Kate Ive **Bred** Mrs Mercy Rimell **Trained** Kinnersley, Worcs

FOCUS
Only a few of these held any chance entering the home straight. The form looks believable.
T/Plt: £137.90 to a £1 stake. Pool: £70,757.69 - 374.49 winning units. T/Qpdt: £24.30 to a £1 stake. Pool: 4706.36 - 142.91 winning units. ST

4659 SANDOWN (R-H)
Saturday, March 8

OFFICIAL GOING: Chase course - good to soft (soft in places; 6.0); hurdle course - soft (5.4)
Wind: strong breeze across Weather: sunny

4679 WILLIAM HILL JUVENILE H'CAP HURDLE (8 hdls) 2m 110y
1:30 (1:30) (Class 3) (0-125,123) 4-Y-O **£6,498** (£1,908; £954; £477)

Form				RPR
4-	1		**Dormello Mo (FR)**[27] 4171 4-11-8 119.................................. DarylJacob (Paul Nicholls) *patiently rdn trcking ldrs: led appr last where wnt rt: rdn clr: readily* 3/1[2]	123+
42-	2	7	**Astrum**[32] 4073 4-11-1 112... RichardJohnson (Neil King) *trckd ldrs: travelling wl enough whn nt clr run between last 2: r.o whn clr run fr last: wnt 2nd nring fin but nt pce of wnr* 7/2[3]	109+
255-	3	1	**Cafe Au Lait (GER)**[21] 4268 4-11-0 116......................(tp) JamesBanks(5) (Anthony Middleton) *j. sltly lft and nt a fluent: pressed ldr: rdn into v narrow advantage appr 2 out: hdd last: kpt on but no ex whn lost 2nd nring fin* 8/1	109
212-	4	1 ¾	**Carry On Sydney**[21] 4281 4-11-12 123............................. LeightonAspell (Oliver Sherwood) *led: rdn and v narrowly hdd appr 2 out: kpt pressing ldr w ev ch tl no ex fr last* 2/1[1]	115
022-	5	5	**Rayak (IRE)**[46] 3822 4-11-10 121.. APMcCoy (Jonjo O'Neill) *hld up last but in tch: travelling strly on heels of ldrs appr 2 out: shkn up bef last: fnd little* 13/2	107

266- **6** *6* **Mr Vendman (IRE)**[15] 4401 4-10-4 **106**........................ RobertMcCarth(5) 88
(Ian Williams) *j.lft thrght: hld up in last pair: struggling after 3 out: hld but stl in tch next: wknd last* **16/1**

4m 7.0s (-0.20) **Going Correction** -0.025s/f (Good) **6** Ran SP% **110.9**
Speed ratings: **99,95,95,94,92 89**
CSF £13.65 TOTE £3.70: £1.80, £1.90; EX 13.20 Trifecta £61.50.
Owner The Kyle & Stewart Families **Bred** E A R L Haras Du Taillis & H Poulsen **Trained** Ditcheat, Somerset

FOCUS
A fair juvenile handicap and a big step up from the easy winner.

4680 EUROPEAN BREEDERS' FUND WILLIAM HILL "NATIONAL HUNT" NOVICES' H'CAP HURDLE FINAL (GRADE 3) (8 hdls 1 omitted) 2m 4f

2:05 (2:05) (Class 1) 4-7-Y-0

£34,170 (£12,822; £6,420; £3,198; £1,608; £804)

Form RPR

233- **1** **Brave Vic (IRE)**[13] 4442 6-10-12 **123**.................................. JoshuaMoore 134
(Gary Moore) *trckd ldrs: led appr 2 out: sn rdn: styd on strly: rdn out* **20/1**

213- **2** *3 ½* **Saffron Wells (IRE)**[22] 4251 6-11-1 **126**.......................... LeightonAspell 133
(Neil King) *hld up bhd: gd hdwy by-passing omitted 3 out: chsd ldrs next: rdn to chse wnr last: kpt on but a being hld fr last* **25/1**

151- **3** *1 ½* **Doctor Harper (IRE)**[22] 4251 6-11-12 **137**...................... ConorO'Farrell 143
(David Pipe) *trckd ldr: rdn and ev ch appr 2 out: lost 2nd appr last: styd on same pce* **12/1**

513- **4** *¾* **Brother Brian (IRE)**[52] 3716 6-11-1 **126**................................ TomO'Brien 131
(Hughie Morrison) *mid-div: hdwy by-passing omitted 3 out: rdn to chse ldrs bef next: styd on same pce* **11/2**[1]

311- **5** *2 ¾* **Ceasar Milan (IRE)**[9] 4517 6-11-3 **131**.........................(t) HarryDerham(3) 133
(Paul Nicholls) *mid-div: swtchd lft and hdwy to chse ldrs appr 2 out: sn rdn: styd on same pce* **9/1**

4- **6** *¾* **Boondooma (IRE)**[21] 4280 7-10-5 **116**.................... SamTwiston-Davies 118
(Dr Richard Newland) *mid-div: hdwy into cl 4th appr 2 out: rdn between last 2: sn hld: no ex run-in* **16/1**

321- **7** *7* **Goohar (IRE)**[68] 3415 5-10-4 **118**..................................... JakeGreenall(3) 114
(Henry Daly) *towards rr of midfield: rdn and hdwy appr 2 out: sn chsng ldrs: no ex fr last* **14/1**

213- **8** *13* **Strollawaynow (IRE)**[29] 4130 7-11-7 **132**.......................... TomCannon 113
(David Arbuthnot) *mid-div tl outpcd after by-passing 3 out: sme minor late prog past wkng horses but nt any danger after* **33/1**

123- **9** *nk* **Gone Too Far**[30] 4102 6-11-0 **125**.. APMcCoy 106
(Alan King) *mid-div whn squeezed out after 1st: towards rr: sme hdwy into midfield after omitted 3 out: swtchd lft and rdn bef next: wknd between last 2* **13/2**[3]

313- **10** *6* **Panama Petrus (IRE)**[14] 4428 6-11-1 **126**...................... LiamTreadwell 101
(Venetia Williams) *mid-div: nt fluent 4th: sn pushed along: rdn bef 2 out: sn wknd* **12/1**

324- **11** *16* **Theatrebar**[20] 4308 6-10-9 **120**.. FelixDeGiles 79
(Tom Symonds) *trckd ldrs: rdn appr 2 out: sn wknd* **16/1**

114- **12** *4* **Vice Et Vertu (FR)**[36] 4005 5-11-5 **130**............................ AndrewTinkler 85
(Henry Daly) *hit 3rd: struggling 5th: a towards rr* **33/1**

211- **13** *11* **Horizontal Speed (IRE)**[49] 3782 6-11-7 **132**............... RichardJohnson 76
(Philip Hobbs) *trckd ldrs: hit 2nd: rdn bef 2 out: sn wknd: eased whn btn* **6/1**[2]

F11- **14** *3 ½* **Knight Of Noir (IRE)**[21] 4280 5-11-10 **135**.................(t) TomScudamore 75
(David Pipe) *hld up towards rr: pushed along after 6th: rdn and little prog appr 2 out: sn wknd: eased whn btn* **13/2**[3]

213- **P** **Steel City**[53] 3694 6-10-11 **122**...................................... AndrewThornton
(Seamus Mullins) *mid-div: hit 1st: struggling 5th: wknd by-passing omitted 3 out: t.o whn p.u bef next: b.b.v* **33/1**

311- **F** **Classic Move (IRE)**[36] 4005 5-11-6 **131**........................... JasonMaguire
(Donald McCain) *t.k.h: led: rdn: hdd and fading in 7th whn fell 2 out* **11/1**

5m 1.6s (2.00) **Going Correction** -0.025s/f (Good) **16** Ran SP% **125.9**
Speed ratings: **95,93,92,91 91,88,83,83,80 74,72,68,66,**
CSF £433.85 CT £6126.52 TOTE £21.70: £4.30, £5.50, £3.40, £1.80; EX 987.00 Trifecta £20686.70.
Owner R Henderson **Bred** Mervyn Chamney **Trained** Lower Beeding, W Sussex

FOCUS
Traditionally a competitive handicap, there was no hanging around, with Jason Maguire aboard Classic Move, charging into the lead, and it proved a thorough test at the trip, with many of them not getting home. The third-last had to be bypassed on the final circuit. A massive step up from the surprise winner.

4681 WILLIAMHILL.COM MOBILE CHELTENHAM MONEY BACK 2ND H'CAP CHASE (22 fncs) 3m 110y

2:40 (2:41) (Class 3) (0-135,135) 5-Y-0+

£11,260 (£3,326; £1,663; £831; £415; £208)

Form RPR

0PF- **1** **Chartreux (FR)**[29] 4134 9-11-5 **128**................................(t) PaddyBrennan 138+
(Tom George) *j.w: trckd ldr: led 12th: rdn 3 l clr after 3 out: styd on wl: rdn out* **9/2**[2]

2/1- **2** *4* **Kasbadali (FR)**[104] 2692 9-11-8 **131**.................................. LeightonAspell 136
(Oliver Sherwood) *hld up last but in tch: rdn to dispute 3rd after 19th: chsd wnr bef last: styd on but a being hld by wnr: hld on gamely for 2nd* **5/1**[3]

16P- **3** *½* **De La Bech**[35] 4026 7-11-5 **128**...(p) TomO'Brien 133
(Philip Hobbs) *reminders and encouraged along fr the s: chsd ldrs: drvn to press wnr after 19th tl after next: lost 2nd appr last: styd on run-in* **11/2**

343- **4** *3 ¾* **Goring One (IRE)**[44] 3853 9-10-4 **113**................................ AdamWedge 113
(Anna Newton-Smith) *trckd ldrs: cl up 19th: sn rdn: hld after next: styd on same pce* **10/1**

540- **5** *1 ¾* **Soll**[21] 4270 9-11-11 **134**..(p) MarkGrant 134
(Jo Hughes) *led: jnd 11th: hdd next: sn rdn along: dropped to last after 19th: styd on again fr 2 out but nvr a danger after* **3/1**[1]

24P- **6** *29* **Howard's Legacy (IRE)**[30] 4104 8-11-6 **129**................ LiamTreadwell 108
(Venetia Williams) *hld up in tch: nt fluent 13th: pckd bdly 17th: rdn to dispute cl 3rd after 19th: wknd last* **16/1**

1P2- **P** **Noble Legend**[23] 4244 7-11-12 **135**................................ AndrewThornton
(Caroline Bailey) *trckd ldrs: squeezed up on rails and lost pl w a circ to run: stmbld 14th: lost tch qckly and p.u bef next* **8/1**

02F- **F** **Merrion Square (IRE)**[71] 3321 8-11-3 **133**........................(t) MrADoyle(7)
(Paul Nicholls) *trcking ldrs whn mstke 2nd: in last pair but wl in tch whn fell 11th* **6/1**

6m 27.2s (-0.60) **Going Correction** +0.225s/f (Yiel) **8** Ran SP% **115.6**
Speed ratings: **109,107,107,106,105 96, ,**
CSF £27.89 CT £126.22 TOTE £6.30: £2.20, £2.10, £1.50; EX 31.50 Trifecta £139.50.
Owner R S Brookhouse **Bred** Jean-Pierre Hebrard **Trained** Slad, Gloucs

■ Stewards' Enquiry : Mark Grant six-day ban: improper riding (Mar 22-27)

FOCUS
A fair handicap chase. The winner is rated back to his best.

4682 WILLIAM HILL IMPERIAL CUP H'CAP HURDLE (GRADE 3) (8 hdls) 2m 110y

3:15 (3:15) (Class 1) 4-Y-0+

£39,865 (£14,959; £7,490; £3,731; £1,876; £938)

Form RPR

121- **1** **Baltimore Rock (IRE)**[17] 4353 5-10-12 **125**................... TomScudamore 134+
(David Pipe) *hld up towards rr: smooth prog whn gap appeared kindly appr 2 out and sn chalng gng best: qcknd up wl whn rdn to ld after last: edgd rt: rdn out* **7/1**[3]

435- **2** *1* **Gassin Golf**[98] 2813 5-10-8 **121**... JamieMoore 128
(Richard Lee) *mid-div: hdwy after 3 out to dispute next: narrow advantage sn after: hdd sn after last: keeping on but hld whn swtchd lft fnl 75yds* **14/1**

221- **3** *4 ½* **Vibrato Valtat (FR)**[27] 4173 5-11-3 **130**...............................(t) DarylJacob 134+
(Paul Nicholls) *mid-div: gng wl enough but nt clr run bhd ldrs appr 2 out tl appr last: r.o to take 3rd run-in but nt pce to get on terms w front pair* **3/1**[1]

212- **4** *nk* **Regal Encore (IRE)**[87] 3017 6-11-3 **130**.................................. APMcCoy 132+
(Anthony Honeyball) *hld up towards rr: hdwy on outer after 3 out: ev ch next: sn rdn and sltly outpcd by front pair: no ex fr last* **9/2**[2]

244- **5** *1* **Chesil Beach Boy**[2] 4634 11-10-10 **130**...................... LouisMuspratt(7) 131
(John Coombe) *hld up towards rr: rdn and stdy hdwy appr 2 out: disp 3rd at the last: edging rt: no ex fnl 100yds* **66/1**

202- **6** *5* **Little Jon**[28] 4143 6-11-6 **133**...................................... SamTwiston-Davies 129
(Nigel Twiston-Davies) *led: rdn and hdd 2 out: wknd last* **33/1**

0/5- **7** *nk* **Swing Bowler**[28] 4147 7-11-12 **139**.................................... ConorO'Farrell 135
(David Pipe) *j.lft at times: trckd ldr: disp ld briefly 2 out: sn rdn: wknd run-in* **9/1**

622- **8** *1 ¼* **Somemothersdohavem**[9] 4517 5-10-10 **123**................. LiamTreadwell 117
(Venetia Williams) *trckd ldrs: rdn and ev ch but hanging rt appr 2 out: sn hld: wknd last* **12/1**

263- **9** *3 ¼* **Skint**[91] 2958 8-10-5 **118**..(b[1]) DenisO'Regan 111
(Ali Brewer) *in tch: ev ch after 3 out: rdn and looking hld whn mstke 2 out: sn wknd* **33/1**

011- **10** *8* **New Year's Eve**[20] 4306 6-11-0 **130**.................................. JackQuinlan(3) 113
(John Ferguson) *in tch: cl up after 3 out: rdn bef next: wknd between last 2* **11/1**

331- **11** *2 ¾* **Harristown**[30] 4111 4-10-6 **130**..(p) KielanWoods(3) 102
(Charlie Longsdon) *trckd ldrs: rdn appr 3 out: wknd bef next* **20/1**

/P0- **12** *28* **First Avenue**[23] 3648 9-11-3 **137**...................................... PaddyBradley(7) 89
(Laura Mongan) *bhd: nvr really travelling: wl detached 3rd: nvr any danger: t.o* **40/1**

4/2- **P** **Fourth Estate (IRE)**[103] 2717 8-10-11 **124**.......................... AndrewTinkler
(Nicky Henderson) *in tch: rdn after 3 out: wknd bef next: p.u bef last* **8/1**

120- **P** **Knight Of Pleasure**[49] 3771 5-11-2 **129**............................ JoshuaMoore
(Gary Moore) *mid-div: rdn and wknd after 3 out: t.o whn p.u bef 2 out* **20/1**

4m 2.5s (-4.70) **Going Correction** -0.025s/f (Good)
WFA 4 from 5yo+ 7lb **14** Ran SP% **118.8**
Speed ratings (Par 113): **110,109,107,107,106 104,104,103,102,98 97,83, ,**
CSF £89.04 CT £359.74 TOTE £8.50: £2.70, £4.10, £1.60; EX 89.40 Trifecta £286.90.
Owner R S Brookhouse **Bred** Lynn Lodge Stud And Foxtale Farm **Trained** Nicholashayne, Devon

FOCUS
Probably the strongest edition of this race in a while, the pace was an even one and those held up early came to the fore late on. It was a clean sweep for novices. Steps up from the first two and the third can improve on the bare form.

4683 EBF STALLIONS/TBA MARES' STANDARD OPEN NATIONAL HUNT FLAT RACE (LISTED) 2m 110y

3:50 (3:50) (Class 1) 4-7-Y-0

£14,237 (£5,342; £2,675; £1,332; £670; £335)

Form RPR

1 **Gaillimh A Chroi (IRE)**[21] 4288 5-11-0 0................................ NoelFehily 116
(John Queally, Ire) *trckd ldrs: led 3f out: hrd rdn whn strly pressed sn after: styd on v gamely to edge ahd fnl 120yds* **9/2**[2]

12- **2** *¾* **Tara Mist**[65] 3507 5-11-0 0.. RichardJohnson 115
(Henry Daly) *trckd ldrs: disp ld wl over 2f out: sn rdn: styd on gamely tl hdd and no ex fnl 120yds* **7/2**[1]

521- **3** *6* **Ballyhollow**[79] 3181 7-11-0 0.. APMcCoy 109
(Rebecca Curtis) *disp ld for 2f: trckd ldr: cl 3rd over 4f out: rdn over 2f out: nt pce to get on terms but kpt on for 3rd* **10/1**

41- **4** *8* **Avispa**[30] 4114 5-11-0 0.. RobertThornton 101
(Alan King) *hld up bhd ldrs: tk clsr order over 3f out: effrt over 2f out: sn hld in disp 3rd: no ex fnl f* **7/2**[1]

2- **5** *3 ¾* **Pressies Girl (IRE)**[18] 4335 6-11-0 0...................................... DarylJacob 97
(Paul Nicholls) *hld up bhd ldrs: rdn 4f out: wnt 5th over 2f out: nvr finding pce to get involved* **11/1**

31- **6** *½* **Pectora (IRE)**[255] 842 5-11-0 0.. LeightonAspell 97
(Oliver Sherwood) *hld up in last pair of bunch: struggling 6f out but styd in tch tl outpcd 3f out: sme late prog: nvr a threat* **25/1**

4/4- **7** *1 ¾* **Graffiti Art**[36] 4016 5-11-0 0.. BrendanPowell 95
(Brendan Powell) *hld up in last pair of bunch: effrt 3f out: sn outpcd: nvr threatened* **33/1**

11- **8** *6* **Pitter Patter**[52] 3719 4-10-1 0.................................... ConorShoemark(5) 81
(Fergal O'Brien) *disp ld: clr ldr after 2f: rdn and hdd 3f out: sn hld: grad fdd fr 2f out* **11/2**[3]

31- **9** *28* **Side Step**[42] 3898 5-11-0 0.. AndrewTinkler 61
(Nicky Henderson) *trckd ldrs: rdn 4f out: wknd 3f out: t.o* **7/1**

4m 2.9s (1.30) **Going Correction** -0.025s/f (Good)
WFA 4 from 5yo+ 7lb **9** Ran SP% **114.7**
Speed ratings: **95,94,91,88,86 86,85,82,69**
CSF £20.49 TOTE £4.30: £1.90, £1.60, £2.70; EX 22.80 Trifecta £182.80.
Owner Ms Eileen O'Brien/John A Harrington **Bred** Sean Galwey **Trained** Dungarvan, Co Waterford

■ Stewards' Enquiry : Noel Fehily four-day ban: used whip above permitted level (Mar 22-25)

The Form Book Jumps, Raceform Ltd, Compton, RG20 6NL.

FOCUS
Traditionally a good mares' bumper but this was robably an average renewal. The front pair duelled throughout the final 2f.

4684 WILLIAM HILL MOBILE BET ANYWHERE NOVICES' CHASE (FOR BURNT OAK AND SPECIAL CARGO CHALLENGE TROPHY) (13 fncs) 2m
4:25 (4:25) (Class 3) 5-Y-0+ **£6,498** (£1,908; £954)

Form RPR
521- **1** **Sound Investment (IRE)**9 4515 6-11-7 135 (t) DarylJacob 145+
(Paul Nicholls) *mde all: rchd for 9th: blnd 10th: qcknd clr after 2 out: readily* **4/11**1
P14- **2** 13 **Witness In Court (IRE)**34 4055 7-11-7 132 JasonMaguire 130
(Donald McCain) *pressed wnr tl after 3rd: dropped to 3rd and sltly detached after 5th: pushed along bk into contention after 10th: wnt 2nd after next: wnt lft 2 out: readily hld after* **3/1**2
263- **3** 2 3/4 **Roger Beantown (IRE)**35 4036 9-11-7 126 (p) DaveCrosse 126
(Zoe Davison) *trckd ldrs: chsd wnr fr 4th tl rdn after 3 out: kpt on same pce fr next* **11/1**3
4m 3.2s (1.40) **Going Correction** +0.225s/f (Yiel) **3** Ran SP% **106.6**
Speed ratings: **105,98,97**
CSF £1.85 TOTE £1.30; EX 2.00 Trifecta £1.40.
Owner Andrea & Graham Wylie **Bred** Mrs Jacinta McGeough **Trained** Ditcheat, Somerset

FOCUS
With neither of his rivals appearing to run up to their best, Sound Investment won with ease. The easy winner confirmed the merit of his much improved recent win.

4685 WILLIAM HILL CHELTENHAM DAILY PRICE BOOSTS H'CAP CHASE (JOCKEY CLUB GRASSROOTS JUMPS QUALIFIER) (17 fncs) 2m 4f 110y
5:00 (5:02) (Class 3) (0-130,130) 5-Y-0+ **£7,797** (£2,289; £1,144; £572)

Form RPR
5/6- **1** **Midnight Sail**103 2714 11-11-12 **130** RobertThornton 141+
(Alan King) *hld up in tch: hdwy to join ldr 8th: led after 10th: clr 2 out: r.o wl fr last: pushed out* **12/1**
130- **2** 11 **Tempest River (IRE)**42 3886 8-11-10 **128** DarylJacob 130+
(Ben Case) *hld up: rdn in cl enough 5th after 14th: wnt 4th after 3 out: styd on same pce fr next* **10/1**
236- **3** 1 **Denali Highway (IRE)**51 3742 7-11-8 **126** AndrewThornton 124
(Caroline Bailey) *trckd ldrs: rdn after 3 out: sn chsng wnr but nvr threatened: styd on same pce: lost 2nd nring fin* **7/1**3
30P- **4** 3/4 **Ballyallia Man (IRE)**72 3293 9-11-4 **122** (t) PaddyBrennan 119
(Tom George) *trckd ldr: led after 6th: narrowly hdd after 10th: kpt pressing wnr tl rdn3 out: sn hld and lost 2nd: one pce fr next* **15/2**
/24- **5** 30 **Ice 'N' Easy (IRE)**35 4039 8-11-5 **123** (tp) NoelFehily 90
(Charlie Longsdon) *j.ft thrght progively worse: towards rr: struggling 10th: no ch fr 14th: t.o* **3/1**1
P52- **6** 4 1/2 **Overclear**29 4131 12-11-2 **120** JackDoyle 83
(Victor Dartnall) *trckd ldrs: rdn in cl 4th after 3 out: wknd qckly: t.o* **12/1**
320- **7** 8 **Flaming Gorge (IRE)**14 4418 9-11-11 **129** LeightonAspell 84
(Fleur Hawes) *trckd ldrs tl 11th: wknd 14th: t.o* **25/1**
0/2- **8** 1 **Hit The Headlines (IRE)**48 3807 8-11-12 **130** HarrySkelton 84
(Caroline Fryer) *hld up in last pair: struggling 8th: wknd 14th: t.o* **20/1**
416- **P** **Aachen**17 4346 10-11-8 **126** LiamTreadwell
(Venetia Williams) *trckd ldrs: mstke 4th: stl in tch whn p.u after 10th* **5/1**2
/P6- **P** **Arbeo (IRE)**29 4134 8-10-13 **117** SamThomas
(Diana Grissell) *led tl after 6th: sn drvn and dropped to rr: tailing off whn p.u bef 7th* **5/1**2
5m 18.1s (-0.30) **Going Correction** +0.225s/f (Yiel) **10** Ran SP% **115.7**
Speed ratings: **109,104,104,104,92 91,87,87, ,**
CSF £122.23 CT £909.41 TOTE £13.00: £3.40, £2.70, £3.60; EX 132.40 Trifecta £1829.40.
Owner A R W Marsh **Bred** G W Sivell **Trained** Barbury Castle, Wilts

FOCUS
Poor jumping was the theme of this handicap, and it's perhaps no surprise that the winner was one of few who actually put in a fluent round. A small personal best from the decisive winner.
T/Jkpt: Not won. T/Plt: £130.60 to a £1 stake. Pool: £197,904.52 - 1105.49 winning units.
T/Qpdt: £8.50 to a £1 stake. Pool: £13,711.69 - 1184.78 winning units. TM

4686 - 4692a (Foreign Racing) - See Raceform Interactive

4304 MARKET RASEN (R-H)
Sunday, March 9

OFFICIAL GOING: Good to soft (good in places on hurdle course; chs 6.4, hdl 6.8)
Wind: Light; half behind Weather: Fine; sunny and mild

4693 LINCS LOOS "NATIONAL HUNT" NOVICES' HURDLE (8 hdls) 2m 1f
2:10 (2:10) (Class 4) 4-Y-0+ **£3,249** (£954; £477; £238)

Form RPR
211- **1** **Kilcooley (IRE)**21 4307 5-11-8 0 NoelFehily 127+
(Charlie Longsdon) *t.k.h: trckd ldrs: 2nd at 2nd: lft in ld bnd after next: rdn rt out* **1/2**1
1/0- **2** 2 **Such A Legend**79 3182 6-11-1 0 JasonMaguire 118
(Kim Bailey) *trckd ldrs: lft cl 2nd bnd after 3rd: effrt and upsides 2 out and last: styd on same pce* **6/1**3
6P- **3** 24 **Flash Tommie (IRE)**80 3177 6-10-12 0 JonathanEngland(3) 96
(Michael Appleby) *prom: outpcd and modest 3rd 4th: one pce* **100/1**
/43- **4** 3 1/4 **Pair Of Jacks (IRE)**99 2823 6-11-1 0 BrianHughes 110+
(Malcolm Jefferson) *t.k.h: led: hung violently lft: hdd: lost pl and virtually p.u bnd after 3rd: continued t.o: hdwy and poor 4th whn mstke 2 out: kpt on* **4/1**2
024- **5** 4 1/2 **Jac The Legend**73 3271 5-11-1 0 RichardJohnson 89
(Steve Gollings) *chsd ldrs to 3rd: outpcd next: wknd 2 out* **12/1**
0/6- **6** 17 **Sedano (FR)**242 948 8-10-10 0 ColmMcCormack(5) 74
(Sara Ender) *mid-div: outpcd 4th: poor 5th whn mstke 3 out: wknd appr next: sn bhd* **100/1**
/63- **7** 18 **Royal Macnab (IRE)**94 2900 6-11-1 0 (t) BrendanPowell 58
(Jamie Snowden) *in rr: outpcd whn mstke 4th: bhd fr 3 out: t.o whn eased run-in* **10/1**
0/0- **8** 18 **Master Malt**18 4343 6-11-1 0 RichieMcLernon 42
(Jonjo O'Neill) *prom: drvn and outpcd after 3rd: bhd and reminders 5th: t.o 2 out* **20/1**
4m 8.6s (1.90) **Going Correction** +0.075s/f (Yiel) **8** Ran SP% **124.5**
Speed ratings (Par 105): **98,97,85,84,82 74,65,57**
CSF £5.14 TOTE £1.40: £1.10, £1.90, £10.00; EX 5.30 Trifecta £245.40.
Owner J H & S M Wall **Bred** Fergal O'Mahoney **Trained** Over Norton, Oxon

FOCUS
Noel Fehily felt the ground was good down the back straight and good to soft up the straight. A fair novice hurdle and, even after his main market rival effectively exited the race with a circuit to run. The winner didn't need to improve and is rated a bit below the level of his recent C&D win.

4694 ROY MOLYNEUX 80TH BIRTHDAY NOVICES' HURDLE (10 hdls) 2m 3f
2:40 (2:41) (Class 4) 4-Y-0+ **£3,249** (£954; £477; £238)

Form RPR
341- **1** **No No Mac (IRE)**62 3567 5-11-9 121 NoelFehily 126
(Charlie Longsdon) *chsd ldrs: wnt 2nd appr 2 out: upsides last: sn led: fnd ex towards fin* **11/4**2
134- **2** 1/2 **Kilgefin Star (IRE)**87 3036 6-11-4 116 AdamNicol(5) 126
(Michael Smith) *led: jnd last: sn narrowly hdd: no ex last 50yds* **13/2**3
/21- **3** 4 **Act Alone**60 3600 5-11-4 0 NicodeBoinville(5) 124
(Nicky Henderson) *chsd ldrs: drvn along 6th: wnt 3rd appr 2 out: abt 3 l down whn mstke last: kpt on one pce* **11/8**1
25- **4** 22 **Jimmy The Jetplane (IRE)**44 3877 6-11-2 0 JasonMaguire 100
(Kim Bailey) *chsd ldr: drvn 6th: mstke 3 out: wknd appr next: bhd whn eased run-in* **13/2**3
4/1- **5** 7 **Cape York**303 207 6-11-2 0 BrianHughes 89
(Malcolm Jefferson) *chsd ldrs: outpcd whn blnd 7th: bhd after* **14/1**
065- **6** 28 **Lemons Ground**52 3747 5-11-2 0 BrendanPowell 64
(Jamie Snowden) *in rr 4th: sme hdwy 3 out: sn wknd: t.o whn eased clsng stages* **16/1**
PP3- **P** **Classical Chloe**20 4324 6-10-2 0 (t) MrRWinks(7)
(Sara Ender) *in rr: outpcd 4th: bhd fr 6th: t.o 3 out: p.u bef next* **100/1**
404- **P** **Supari**20 4329 5-11-2 0 WillKennedy
(Sarah-Jayne Davies) *nt fluent in rr: bhd and reminders 5th: t.o 7th: p.u bef 2 out* **80/1**
4m 36.8s (-2.60) **Going Correction** +0.075s/f (Yiel) **8** Ran SP% **110.2**
Speed ratings (Par 105): **108,107,106,96,93 82, ,**
CSF £19.45 TOTE £3.50: £1.10, £1.90, £1.10; EX 22.20 Trifecta £40.00.
Owner R Jenner & J Green **Bred** Mrs Kathleen McKeever **Trained** Over Norton, Oxon

FOCUS
No hanging around here, Kilgefin Star setting a really good gallop, and the majority of them were off the bridle early in the back straight. Fair novice form for the track, rated around the first three.

4695 LOWMANS H'CAP CHASE (17 fncs) 3m 1f
3:10 (3:11) (Class 4) (0-115,114) 5-Y-0+ **£3,994** (£1,240; £667)

Form RPR
123- **1** **Orange Nassau (FR)**73 3267 8-11-12 **114** NoelFehily 128+
(Charlie Longsdon) *mde all: j.lft 4 out: 20 l ahd last: eased clsng stages* **11/4**1
325- **2** 25 **Palos Conti (FR)**51 3759 11-11-6 **108** DougieCostello 105
(Brian Ellison) *hld up in rr: hdwy 8th: sn trcking ldrs: 2nd 4 out: effrt appr next: sn btn: hit last* **5/1**3
/43- **3** 44 **Airmen's Friend (IRE)**73 3265 8-10-11 **99** (tp) MarkGrant 51
(Charlie Mann) *chsd ldrs: 2nd 7th: wknd 4 out: bhd whn mstke next: sn t.o* **11/4**1
36P- **P** **Honest John**33 4078 10-10-12 **107** PaulBohan(7)
(Steve Gollings) *chsd ldrs: drvn 11th: lost pl 13th: sn bhd: t.o whn p.u after 4 out* **7/1**
042- **P** **Around A Pound (IRE)**52 3739 9-10-12 **100** HenryBrooke
(Nick Kent) *chsd ldrs: reminders 3rd: drvn 7th: bhd and reminders 9th: t.o whn p.u after 11th* **9/2**2
P50- **P** **Ballyhilty Bridge**22 4275 8-10-7 **95** TomO'Brien
(Paul Henderson) *in rr: hit 2nd: drvn 7th: hit 9th: sn bhd: t.o whn p.u bef 12th: b.b.v* **10/1**
6m 44.0s (12.70) **Going Correction** +0.65s/f (Soft) **6** Ran SP% **109.8**
Speed ratings: **105,97,82, ,**
CSF £15.81 TOTE £2.90: £1.90, £3.50; EX 13.70 Trifecta £29.00.
Owner The Ferandlin Peaches **Bred** E A R L La Dariole **Trained** Over Norton, Oxon

FOCUS
Little got into this. Possibly a big step forward from the winner but not one to be too confident about.

4696 LOWMANS YE OLDE HOG ROAST H'CAP CHASE (A JOCKEY CLUB GRASSROOTS JUMPS SERIES QUALIFIER) (14 fncs) 2m 4f
3:40 (3:43) (Class 4) (0-120,119) 5-Y-0+ **£3,898** (£1,144; £572; £286)

Form RPR
1UB- **1** **Highbury High (IRE)**82 3150 7-10-11 **104** TomO'Brien 111+
(Paul Henderson) *chsd ldrs: cl 2nd 10th: upsides 3 out: lft in ld last: kpt on* **6/1**
4F4- **2** 1 1/2 **Hatters River (IRE)**81 3158 7-11-9 **116** JackDoyle 124+
(Ali Brewer) *led 1st: hit 3rd: jnd 3 out: narrow advantage whn blnd and hdd last: kpt on same pce* **5/2**1
034- **3** 10 **Munsaab (IRE)**52 3738 8-11-10 **117** (t) NoelFehily 115
(Charlie Longsdon) *chsd ldrs: 4th whn blnd 10th: modest 3rd sn after next: one pce* **4/1**2
520- **4** 17 **O'Callaghan Strand (AUS)**21 4302 8-11-2 **119** TommieMO'Brien(10) 103
(Jonjo O'Neill) *sn chsng ldrs: hit 7th: outpcd 8th: poor 4th sn after 4 out: wknd between last 2* **10/1**
064- **5** 32 **Riguez Dancer**67 3478 10-11-4 **111** (bt) JasonMaguire 63
(Donald McCain) *led to 1st: w ldr: reminders 9th: wknd qckly 11th: sn bhd: t.o next* **4/1**2
3PU/ **P** **Sunsetten (IRE)**645 547 10-11-3 **110** BrianHughes
(Hugh Burns) *hld up towards rr: last but in tch whn p.u bef 9th: lame* **22/1**
33P- **U** **Ballywatt (IRE)**80 3172 8-11-11 **118** (tp) DougieCostello
(Kim Bailey) *hld up in rr: hit 8th: modest 6th but keeping on whn blnd and uns rdr 10th* **9/2**3
5m 20.6s (14.90) **Going Correction** +0.65s/f (Soft) **7** Ran SP% **114.5**
Speed ratings: **96,95,91,84,71 ,**
CSF £22.20 CT £67.06 TOTE £6.60: £3.10, £2.20; EX 30.20 Trifecta £187.90.
Owner The Affordable Partnership **Bred** Sean Deu Burca **Trained** Whitsbury, Hants

FOCUS
Jumping was the only difference between the front pair in this modest handicap chase. The winner is rated similar to his previous win.

4697 RASE VETERINARY EQUINE H'CAP HURDLE (12 hdls) 3m
4:10 (4:11) (Class 3) (0-130,130) 4-Y-0+ **£6,498** (£1,908; £954; £477)

Form RPR
613- **1** **Kaysersberg (FR)**18 4347 7-11-12 **130** RichardJohnson 133
(Neil King) *trckd ldrs: t.k.h: led appr 2 out: hld on towards fin* **10/3**1
506- **2** nk **Azure Fly (IRE)**79 3186 6-11-0 **125** (tp) CharlieDeutsch(7) 128
(Charlie Longsdon) *in rr: hdwy to chse ldrs 7th: 2nd run-in: no ex clsng stages* **5/1**3

400- **3** 3 ¾ **Invicta Lake (IRE)**[21] 4300 7-10-13 **117**............................(p) DarylJacob 117
(Suzy Smith) *t.k.h: sn trcking ldrs: ev ch last: kpt on one pce* **17/2**

3U2- **4** 1 ½ **Phare Isle (IRE)**[21] 4308 9-10-4 **115**.....................(tp) MrMJPKendrick(7) 113
(Ben Case) *hld up: hdwy 5th: sn trcking ldrs: hung rt and one pce run-in* **5/1[3]**

14- **5** 6 **Dream Flyer (IRE)**[67] 3453 7-10-10 **119**............................ AdamNicol(5) 112
(Michael Smith) *w ldr: wknd 2 out* **20/1**

6/0- **6** 1 **Mubrook (USA)**[21] 4306 9-10-7 **118**............................ CraigGallagher(7) 111
(Brian Ellison) *led: hdd appr 2 out: wknd last* **25/1**

421- **7** 5 **Five In A Row (IRE)**[21] 4297 6-11-5 **123**........................ DougieCostello 112
(Brian Ellison) *chsd ldrs 3rd: nt fluent and reminders 8th: j.lft 3 out: lost pl bef next* **9/2[2]**

/2P- **8** 34 **Allthekingshorses (IRE)**[67] 3455 8-11-9 **127**.................(tp) TomO'Brien 84
(Philip Hobbs) *in rr: sn drvn along: reminders 4th: bhd fr 3 out: t.o* **7/1**

563- **9** 43 **Abnaki (IRE)**[31] 4105 9-11-3 **126**..............................(p) MauriceLinehan(5) 44
(Jonjo O'Neill) *mid-div: nt fluent 3rd: lost pl 7th: sn bhd: t.o 9th* **12/1**

6m 0.3s (9.80) **Going Correction** +0.075s/f (Yiel) **9** Ran SP% **113.9**
Speed ratings (Par 107): **86,85,84,84,82 81,80,68,54**
CSF £20.44 CT £128.20 TOTE £4.10: £1.40, £2.20, £3.00; EX 23.50 Trifecta £223.10.
Owner Mrs Julien Turner & Andrew Merriam **Bred** Mme Marquerite De Tarragon **Trained** Newmarket, Suffolk

FOCUS
A decent handicap hurdle. The in-form winner is rated to a similar mark as his good recent Doncaster run.

4698 WEIGHTLIFTER MARES' H'CAP HURDLE (8 hdls) 2m 1f
4:40 (4:40) (Class 4) (0-120,120) 4-Y-0+ **£3,898** (£1,144; £572; £286)

Form RPR

232- **1** **Lily Waugh (IRE)**[62] 3570 7-11-4 **112**..........................(t) RobertThornton 116+
(Anthony Honeyball) *chsd ldr: led 5th: jnd whn hit last: drvn rt out* **13/8[1]**

532- **2** 3 ¼ **Fine Moment**[33] 4074 6-10-11 **105**..............................(t) BrianHughes 104
(Kevin Frost) *trckd ldrs: cl 2nd 3 out: 1 l down last: kpt on same pce* **9/2[3]**

234- **3** 6 **Phase Shift**[12] 4483 6-11-5 **120**................................(t) NathanMoscrop(7) 114
(Brian Ellison) *in rr: hdwy and cl 3rd 3 out: one pce fr next* **13/2**

464- **4** 17 **Buxom (IRE)**[20] 4324 7-11-0 **108**....................................(v) BrendanPowell 86
(Jamie Snowden) *led: nt fluent and hdd 5th: wknd bef 2 out: sn wl bhd* **11/1**

0/3- **5** 1 ½ **Ussee (FR)**[17] 4377 6-10-10 **104**...(t) RyanMahon 81
(Ben Case) *in rr: lost pl and reminders 5th: sn bhd: t.o 2 out* **9/4[2]**

4m 10.9s (4.20) **Going Correction** +0.075s/f (Yiel) **5** Ran SP% **108.7**
Speed ratings (Par 105): **93,91,88,80,79**
CSF £8.92 TOTE £2.00: £1.10, £2.30; EX 7.90 Trifecta £16.50.
Owner Go To War **Bred** F Boyd **Trained** Mosterton, Dorset

FOCUS
Modest form for the grade, rated through the runner-up.

4699 WATCH RACING UK ON CHANNEL 432 CONDITIONAL JOCKEYS' H'CAP HURDLE (10 hdls) 2m 3f
5:10 (5:10) (Class 4) (0-105,106) 4-Y-0+ **£3,249** (£954; £477; £238)

Form RPR

134- **1** **Crookstown (IRE)**[23] 4249 7-11-11 **102**............................. KielanWoods 112+
(Ben Case) *trckd ldrs: led appr 2 out: styd on wl: eased clsng stages* **10/1**

063- **2** 2 ½ **The Wealerdealer (IRE)**[22] 4275 7-11-10 **101**.................(b) MattGriffiths 107+
(David Pipe) *nt fluent detached in last: hdwy 3 out: modest 3rd 2 out: styd on to take 2nd last 100yds* **4/1[2]**

315- **3** 5 **Kayfrou**[67] 3451 9-10-5 **88**... CraigGallagher(6) 88
(Brian Ellison) *chsd ldr: led 6th: hdd next: led 3 out: hdd appr next: hld whn hit last* **13/2[3]**

040- **4** 12 **Bally Braes (IRE)**[44] 3880 6-11-1 **98**............................(p) RyanHatch(6) 86
(Nigel Twiston-Davies) *chsd ldrs: pushed along 3rd: outpcd 7th: lost pl bef 2 out* **4/1[2]**

P05- **5** 10 **Balinderry (IRE)**[33] 4076 7-10-4 **87**..............................(tp) PaulBohan(6) 69
(Steve Gollings) *led to 6th: wknd 3 out* **20/1**

033- **6** ½ **Edmaaj (IRE)**[37] 4022 6-11-9 **103**............................. MauriceLinehan(3) 87
(Jonjo O'Neill) *trckd ldrs: effrt appr 2 out: sn wknd* **3/1[1]**

/00- **7** 22 **Minsky Mine (IRE)**[46] 3839 7-11-4 **95**........................ JonathanEngland 54
(Michael Appleby) *chsd ldrs: lost pl after 4th: sn bhd: t.o 7th* **12/1**

/55- **P** **Tayarat (IRE)**[21] 4305 9-10-3 **80**..................................(t) JoeCornwall
(Michael Chapman) *in rr: bhd and drvn 4th: t.o whn p.u bef 6th* **50/1**

30/- **P** **Spanish Cruise (IRE)**[280] 10-11-6 **100**........................ NathanMoscrop(3)
(Lucinda Egerton) *in rr: hdwy 3rd: lost pl 7th: sn bhd: t.o whn p.u bef 2 out* **80/1**

53P- **P** **In The Gate (IRE)**[30] 4132 6-11-1 **100**.......................(t) CharlieDeutsch(8)
(Charlie Longsdon) *w ldr: mstke 6th: led next: hdd 3 out: sn lost pl: bhd whn p.u bef last* **7/1**

4m 39.3s (-0.10) **Going Correction** +0.075s/f (Yiel) **10** Ran SP% **115.6**
Speed ratings (Par 105): **103,101,99,94,90 90,81,,,**
CSF £49.61 CT £284.10 TOTE £6.60: £2.90, £2.90, £2.80; EX 33.70 Trifecta £427.30.
Owner Case Racing Partnership **Bred** Vincent Walsh **Trained** Edgcote, Northants

FOCUS
Moderate form, but the front pair pulled clear late on. They are rated better than the bare result and are on the upgrade.
T/Plt: £16.70 to a £1 stake. Pool: £101,107.90 - 4,408.80 winning units T/Qpdt: £14.20 to a £1 stake. Pool: £5,305.78 - 274.90 winning units WG

[4397]WARWICK (L-H)
Sunday, March 9

OFFICIAL GOING: Good to soft (soft in places on hurdle course; chs 6.3, hdl 5.7)
Wind: Light; across Weather: Dry and sunny

4700 32RED FREE £10 BONUS H'CAP HURDLE (THE JOCKEY CLUB GRASSROOTS JUMPS SERIES QUALIFIER (11 hdls) 2m 5f
2:20 (2:20) (Class 4) (0-115,115) 4-Y-0+ **£3,898** (£1,144; £572; £286)

Form RPR

434- **1** **Wily Fox**[21] 4306 7-11-9 **115**.. JackQuinlan(3) 119
(James Eustace) *wl in tch in midfield: hdwy to chse ldrs 5th: jnd ldr sn after 3 out: rdn to ld next: looked to be getting on top whn lft clr last: kpt on u.p and a holding runner-up* **14/1**

/00- **2** ¾ **Miss Lucky Penny**[44] 3872 8-10-6 **100**........................ RobertMcCarth(5) 104
(Ian Williams) *wl in tch in midfield: hdwy 7th: rdn and chsd ldrs bef 2 out: chsd clr wnr fnl 100yds: styd on strly u.p but nvr quite getting to wnr* **10/1**

/3P- **3** 3 **Peterbrown (IRE)**[67] 3473 6-11-2 **105**.............................. LeightonAspell 106
(Nick Gifford) *wl in tch in midfield: rdn along after 6th: 6th and outpcd sn after 3 out: rallied between last 2: styd on to go 3rd towards fin* **12/1**

220- **4** ¾ **Canuspotit**[18] 4347 7-11-2 **110**... MattCrawley(5) 113
(Lucy Wadham) *mstkes: t.k.h: hld up in midfield: hmpd 1st: hdwy 6th: rdn to chal 2 out: stl ev ch whn mstke last: lost 2nd and wknd fnl 100yds* **12/1**

254- **5** 3 ½ **Squire Trelawney**[92] 2936 8-11-6 **109**............................(tp) HarrySkelton 107
(Dan Skelton) *w ldr tl led 2nd: hrd pressed and drvn after 3 out: hdd next: 4th and btn whn mstke last: wknd flat* **7/1[3]**

4/0- **6** 15 **Vico (IRE)**[101] 2755 10-11-7 **110**.......................................(p) AidanColeman 96
(Ali Brewer) *hld up in tch in midfield: effrt and mstke 3 out: sn outpcd and wl hld bef next: plugged on* **25/1**

443- **7** 10 **The Game Is A Foot (IRE)**[14] 4444 7-10-10 **106**...... JosephAkehurst(7) 80
(Gary Moore) *in tch in midfield: rdn and mstke 7th: sn drvn and struggling: wl btn 3 out* **5/1[2]**

245- **8** 3 ¼ **Nicky Nutjob (GER)**[86] 3060 8-10-6 **102**......................... CiaranMckee(7) 73
(John O'Shea) *hld up in last pair: lost tch bef 3 out* **33/1**

222- **9** 2 **Sweet Boy Vic (IRE)**[22] 4275 6-10-0 **89** oh1........................ TomCannon 59
(Chris Gordon) *chsd ldrs: rdn 7th: lost pl u.p next: wl btn after 3 out: t.o* **7/2[1]**

220- **10** ½ **Georgian King**[37] 4021 11-11-11 **114**.................................... IanPopham 83
(Martin Keighley) *led tl 2nd: styd w ldr: mstke 8th: rdn and btn after 3 out: wkng whn mstke 2 out: t.o* **7/1[3]**

/0P- **11** 3 ½ **Reyno**[73] 3280 6-11-2 **105**..(tp) JamieMoore 71
(Renee Robeson) *in tch in midfield: rdn along after 6th: lost pl 8th: bhd after next: t.o* **25/1**

004- **12** 73 **Unknown Legend (IRE)**[77] 3225 7-11-0 **103**...................[1] PaulMoloney 3
(Anthony Middleton) *taken down early: t.k.h: hld up in rr: lost tch 8th: t.o after next* **12/1**

221/ **P** **Littledean Jimmy (IRE)**[16] 620 9-11-3 **106**.................... PaddyBrennan
(John O'Shea) *t.k.h: hld up in tch in last trio: mstke 4th: rdn and lost tch 8th: t.o whn p.u 2 out* **16/1**

5m 6.5s (-8.50) **Going Correction** -0.425s/f (Good) **13** Ran SP% **119.2**
Speed ratings (Par 105): **99,98,97,97,95 90,86,85,84,84 82,55,**
CSF £143.44 CT £1742.79 TOTE £10.30: £3.20, £4.70, £6.00; EX 207.50 Trifecta £2413.70 Part won. Pool: £3,218.61 - 0.58 winning units..
Owner Blue Peter Racing 10 **Bred** Juddmonte Farms Ltd **Trained** Newmarket, Suffolk

FOCUS
One would imagine that this isn't much more than modest form, although it makes sense. The early gallop wasn't overly strong.

4701 EBF STALLIONS/TBA MARES' NOVICES' LIMITED H'CAP CHASE (17 fncs) 2m 4f 110y
2:50 (2:51) (Class 3) (0-125,121) 5-Y-0+ **£7,528** (£2,194; £1,097)

Form RPR

332- **1** **Stone Light (FR)**[9] 4536 6-11-1 **115**................................. AidanColeman 125+
(Venetia Williams) *hld up in cl 3rd: wnt 2nd sn after 3 out: rdn to ld next: fnd ex u.p and almost 1 l ahd whn lft clr last: doing little in front and drvn out fnl 100yds* **6/4[1]**

132- **2** 2 ½ **Spirit Oscar (IRE)**[23] 4248 6-11-3 **117**........................... LeightonAspell 123+
(Oliver Sherwood) *led: jnd and pushed along bef 11th: outj. rival and def advantage again 12th: rdn and hdd 2 out: almost 1 l down whn stmbld bdly on landing last: rallied as wnr idled fnl 100yds eased nr fin* **2/1[2]**

3/0- **3** 18 **Miss Ballantyne**[93] 2928 7-11-7 **121**............................... AndrewTinkler 115
(Nicky Henderson) *j. deliberately: chsd ldr tl jnd ldr bef 11th: outj. 12th: mstke and rdn next: stl cl 3rd and drvn sn after 3 out: wknd next* **2/1[2]**

5m 13.2s (-7.80) **Going Correction** -0.20s/f (Good) **3** Ran SP% **106.7**
Speed ratings: **106,105,98**
CSF £4.53 TOTE £1.90; EX 4.60 Trifecta £2.50.
Owner Kate & Andrew Brooks **Bred** Patrick Boiteau **Trained** Kings Caple, H'fords

FOCUS
Only the three runners, but the pace looked decent from the outset. The winner is rated similar to her recent Newbury run.

4702 32RED CASINO NOVICES' HURDLE (12 hdls) 3m 1f
3:20 (3:20) (Class 4) 4-Y-0+ **£3,898** (£1,144; £572; £286)

Form RPR

122- **1** **Algernon Pazham (IRE)**[29] 4163 5-11-3 124.......... SamTwiston-Davies 126+
(Nigel Twiston-Davies) *chsd ldrs: wnt 2nd 3rd tl led 5th: drvn and hdd bef 2 out: stl ev ch whn j.rt and cannoned into runner-up last: carried lft flat: led fnl 50yds: styd on* **15/8[1]**

514- **2** nk **Walk On Al (IRE)**[43] 3896 6-11-9 129........................... HarrySkelton 129
(Dan Skelton) *chsd ldr tl 3rd: chsd ldrs after tl wnt 2nd 3 out: rdn to ld and wandered rt bef 2 out: hrd drvn between last 2: j.lft and cannoned into wnr last: hung lft flat: hdd fnl 50yds: no ex* **2/1[2]**

P32- **3** 45 **Island Cruise (IRE)**[18] 4356 6-11-3 110..............................(t) ColinBolger 94
(Pat Murphy) *led tl 5th: chsd wnr after tl 3rd and rdn 3 out: wknd bef next: t.o* **8/1**

430- **4** 35 **By The Boardwalk (IRE)**[50] 3774 6-11-3 120...............(t) NickScholfield 51
(Kim Bailey) *j.rt and mstkes: chsd ldng trio: lost tch 8th: t.o next* **11/4[3]**

0- **5** 3 ¾ **Carn Rock**[45] 3850 6-11-0 0..................................... PeterCarberry(3) 47
(Michael Gates) *a off the pce: rdn and struggling after 7th: t.o after next* **80/1**

00- **6** 1 ¾ **Mr Lennygreengrass (IRE)**[21] 4297 7-11-3 0............... PaddyBrennan 46
(Fergal O'Brien) *hld up wl off the pce in rr: hdwy and in tch 7th: wknd bef next: t.o 9th* **40/1**

63U- **P** **Spike Mac (IRE)**[23] 4248 9-11-3 0................................ AndrewThornton
(Richard Harper) *racd off the pce in midfield: dropped to last and rdn 7th: sn lost tch: t.o whn p.u next* **200/1**

6m 17.35s (2.35) **Going Correction** -0.425s/f (Good) **7** Ran SP% **110.1**
Speed ratings (Par 105): **79,78,64,53,52 51,**
CSF £5.68 TOTE £2.40: £1.30, £1.20; EX 5.00 Trifecta £16.50.
Owner Graham And Alison Jelley **Bred** Ms Cecily Purcell **Trained** Naunton, Gloucs
■ Stewards' Enquiry : Harry Skelton one-day ban: careless riding (Mar 23)

FOCUS
Three were clear from some way out, but that soon became two. The winner was a bit better than the bare result.

4703 32RED THUNDERSTRUCK II SLOT CONDITIONAL JOCKEYS' H'CAP HURDLE (8 hdls) 2m
3:50 (3:51) (Class 4) (0-105,105) 4-Y-0+ **£3,898** (£1,144; £572; £286)

Form RPR

363- **1** **Good Of Luck**[44] 3062 5-10-12 **94**..............................(p) GavinSheehan(3) 103
(Warren Greatrex) *chsd ldrs tl led 5th: drew clr w rival but hdd 2 out: ev ch after: drvn to ld again flat: styd on wl* **8/1**

The Form Book Jumps, Raceform Ltd, Compton, RG20 6NL.

000- **2** *1* **Mr Fickle (IRE)**[17] 4371 5-11-1 **102**........................(v[1]) JosephAkehurst[(8)] 111
(Gary Moore) *chsd ldrs: swtchd rt and rdn to bef 2 out: drew clr w wnr and led despite mstke 2 out: mstke last: sn hdd: wnt lft u.p flat: kpt on but hld whn rn in bhd wnr and hmpd cl home* **8/1**

006- **3** *20* **Grand March**[81] 3163 5-11-6 **102**.. EdCookson[(3)] 93
(Kim Bailey) *led tl 5th: styd pressing wnr tl 3rd and btn bef 2 out: wknd between last 2 but battled on to hold 3rd flat* **7/1[3]**

500- **4** *2 ¾* **Tempuran**[16] 4398 5-10-10 **97**... JakeHodson[(8)] 85
(David Bridgwater) *hld up in rr: hmpd 5th: clsd after 3 out: no ch w ldng pair but pushed along between last 2: wnt 4th on post* **14/1**

300/ **5** *nse* **Sambulando (FR)**[659] 345 11-11-8 **101**..........................(p) GilesHawkins 91
(Richard Hobson) *hld up in tch in midfield: hmpd 5th: stll cl enough and travelling wl bef 2 out: outpcd and btn whn pushed along between last 2: lost battle for modest 4th flat* **66/1**

F05- **6** *7* **Maxdelas (FR)**[68] 3428 8-10-0 **79** oh1...............................(t) PeterCarberry 60
(Roy Brotherton) *taken down early: hld up in rr: clsd to trck ldrs after 5th: rdn and fnd nil bef 2 out: disp 3rd and wl btn 2 out: wknd last* **25/1**

F05- **7** *16* **Etania**[32] 4091 6-10-10 **89**.. JakeGreenall 59
(Ian Williams) *hld up in last quartet: hdwy 4th: cl enough in 6th whn blnd 3 out: sn rdn and wkng whn mstke next: t.o* **8/1**

603/ **8** *6* **The Boogeyman (IRE)**[393] 4130 8-10-13 **92**.................... MichaelByrne 53
(Anthony Middleton) *t.k.h: hld up in midfield early: dropped to rr after 3rd and nvr on terms after: t.o* **12/1**

02F- **9** *3 ¼* **Who Am I**[199] 1342 8-11-2 **100**... PaulO'Brien[(5)] 59
(Debra Hamer) *chsd ldrs: mstke 4th and lost pl: bhd 3 out: t.o* **33/1**

162- **F** **Dungeness**[13] 4469 6-11-9 **105**..................................... CallumWhillans[(3)]
(Venetia Williams) *chsd ldr tl 4th: cl 3rd and rdn whn fell next* **5/1[2]**

/22- **B** **Voltchesko (FR)**[94] 2898 5-11-10 **103**................................ HarryDerham
(Robert Walford) *wl in tch in midfield tl b.d 5th: fatally injured* **2/1[1]**

3m 48.5s (-8.00) **Going Correction** -0.425s/f (Good) **11** Ran SP% **118.5**
Speed ratings (Par 105): **103,102,92,91,91 87,79,76,74,**
CSF £69.86 CT £476.13 TOTE £9.00: £2.80, £3.10, £2.40; EX 86.00 Trifecta £630.10.
Owner Mr & Mrs Bernard Panton **Bred** Mrs G Slater **Trained** Upper Lambourn, Berks

FOCUS
There was no hanging about in this, and plenty were in trouble early. The winner is rated to his best.

4704 32RED IMMORTAL ROMANCE SLOT H'CAP CHASE (22 fncs) 3m 5f
4:20 (4:22) (Class 3) (0-125,122) 5-Y-0+ **£7,797** (£2,289; £1,144; £572)

Form RPR

261- **1** **Loughalder (IRE)**[16] 4402 8-10-12 **108**............................(tp) CharliePoste 128+
(Matt Sheppard) *w ldrs tl led 6th: mstke 14th: drew clr bef 3 out and in command after: fiddled last: heavily eased towards fin* **5/1[2]**

UU2- **2** *9* **Jaunty Journey**[11] 4489 11-10-7 **103**....................(v) SamTwiston-Davies 112
(Nigel Twiston-Davies) *chsd ldrs: led 3rd tl hdd and mstke 5th: chsd ldrs: rdn and lost pl 14th: rallied u.p 16th: chsd clr wnr 2 out: kpt on but no imp* **9/1**

444- **3** *6* **Handsome Buddy (IRE)**[12] 4481 7-9-11 **96** oh7.......(v) PeterCarberry[(3)] 100+
(Michael Gates) *s.i.s: steadily rcvrd and in tch in rr 6th: hdwy after 15th: rdn and btn 19th: no ch w wnr but styd on last to go 3rd towards fin* **33/1**

322- **4** *1 ¼* **Bally Sands (IRE)**[16] 4402 10-10-4 **103** ow3..............(v) RobertDunne[(3)] 101
(Robin Mathew) *chsd ldrs: wnt 2nd 13th: rdn and struggling 19th: wl hld after next: lost 2nd 2 out: plugged on but lost 3rd towards fin* **7/2[1]**

4/P- **5** *1 ¼* **Trigger The Light**[16] 4402 13-11-9 **119**.......................... WayneHutchinson 116
(Alan King) *chsd ldrs: rdn and lost pl15th: rallied u.p to chse ldrs 19th: wknd bef 2 out* **14/1**

114- **6** *4 ½* **High Ron**[14] 4448 9-11-0 **110**.. AndrewThornton 105
(Caroline Bailey) *mstkes: mstke 1st: pushed along and hdwy to press ldr 3rd: led 5th tl next: pressed wnr after tl 13th: dropped to rr 16th: wl btn 19th* **16/1**

1U3- **7** *¾* **Union Jack D'Ycy (FR)**[16] 4402 6-11-12 **122**.................. AidanColeman 115
(Venetia Williams) *in tch in last pair: sme hdwy 14th: rdn 16th: struggling next: wl btn 3 out* **6/1[3]**

2P6- **8** *19* **Winds And Waves (IRE)**[53] 3717 8-11-9 **122**................. JakeGreenall[(3)] 97
(Henry Daly) *in tch in midfield: rdn 13th: rallied u.p and chsd ldrs 18th tl wknd after 3 out: t.o and eased flat* **6/1[3]**

51F- **9** *29* **Leg Iron (IRE)**[63] 3554 9-11-3 **113**.. MarcGoldstein 62
(Sheena West) *led tl 3rd: chsd ldrs: mstke11th: rdn after 15th: wknd 19th: t.o and eased flat* **8/1**

4U3- **P** **Fourovakind**[15] 4412 9-11-9 **122**...........................(b) JeremiahMcGrath[(3)]
(Harry Whittington) *in tch towards rr: hdwy to chse ldrs 14th: wknd and lost pl qckly 16th: t.o whn p.u 19th* **7/1**

7m 37.7s (-3.30) **Going Correction** -0.20s/f (Good) **10** Ran SP% **116.6**
Speed ratings: **96,93,91,91,91 89,89,84,76,**
CSF £49.06 CT £1340.48 TOTE £4.70: £1.90, £3.40, £8.30; EX 47.20 Trifecta £2608.70 Part won. Pool: £3,478.35 - 0.36 winning units..
Owner Simon Gegg & Tony Scrivin **Bred** Tom Burns **Trained** Eastnor, H'fords

FOCUS
A marathon contest, which contained the last two winners of this. The easy winner built on his recent C&D win.

4705 CGA FOXHUNTER OPEN HUNTERS' CHASE (FOR THE AIR WEDDING CHALLENGE TROPHY) (17 fncs) 2m 4f 110y
4:50 (4:52) (Class 6) 5-Y-0+ **£935** (£290; £145; £72)

Form RPR

0U6- **1** **Pentiffic (NZ)**[22] 4274 11-12-3 **114**................................(p) MrJHamilton[(3)] 124+
(Venetia Williams) *chsd clr ldr tl clsd and pressed ldr 8th: led after 10th: rdn and jnd 2 out: outj. and hdd last: edgd lft u.p but r.o gamely to ld again towards fin* **8/1[3]**

/45- **2** *½* **Shrewd Investment**[14] 8-11-9 **106**............................(t) MrSamPainting[(7)] 121+
(Miss L Thomas) *chsd ldrs: bmpd 1st: clsd and wl in tch 8th: wnt and mstke 13th: hit next and 3 out: effrt on inner to chal 2 out: outj. wnr and led last: drvn flat: kpt on tl hdd and no ex towards fin* **33/1**

/12- **3** *25* **Nowurhurlin (IRE)**[33] 4079 7-11-9 **111**..............................(p) MissETodd[(7)] 103
(Mrs S J Stilgoe) *mstkes: j.rt and bmpd rival 1st: racd in midfield mostly: clsd and in tch 8th: rdn to chse ldng pair bef 3 out: wknd 2 out* **12/1**

224- **4** *11* **Rob Conti (FR)**[18] 4355 9-12-1 **131**.................................... MrDMaxwell[(5)] 91
(Philip Hobbs) *racd off the pce in midfield: clsd and chsd ldrs 8th: wnt 2nd 10th tl mstke and pckd 13th: 5th and wl btn 3 out* **11/10[1]**

100- **5** *12* **Moon Over Miami (GER)**[8] 4554 13-11-9 **110**................ MrDHolmes[(7)] 76
(D Holmes) *led: clr tl 8th: hdd bef 10th: 6th and struggling whn mstke and nrly uns rdr 12th: n.d after: t.o after 3 out* **12/1**

1PP- **6** *1 ¾* **Rebel Alliance (IRE)**[15] 9-11-9 0..................................(t) MrWMaskill[(7)] 74
(Richard A Thomas) *t.k.h: hld up off the pce in last pair: clsd and wl in tch 8th: wnt 3rd 13th: rdn and btn after next: wknd bef 2 out: t.o* **40/1**

/54- **P** **Chiquilline (FR)**[22] 4274 8-11-13 **107**.......................... MrSDrinkwater[(3)]
(T Lacey) *hld up off the pce in last pair: clsd and in tch 8th: mstke 12th: pushed along and no rspnse bef next: lost tch 14th: t.o whn p.u 2 out* **9/4[2]**

5m 13.85s (-7.15) **Going Correction** -0.20s/f (Good) **7** Ran SP% **110.3**
Speed ratings: **105,104,95,91,86 85,**
CSF £144.73 TOTE £8.30: £2.50, £5.10; EX 155.70 Trifecta £541.40.
Owner P Sinn, P Lawrence, L Sutcliffe, M Smith **Bred** C Devine,L & S Hampton & L Stevenson **Trained** Kings Caple, H'fords

FOCUS
They went a decent pace in this thanks to Moon Over Miami, who shot clear over the first few fences. Pentiffic can probably win another of these.

4706 CGA HUNTERS' CHASE (FOR THE CRUDWELL CHALLENGE CUP) (20 fncs) 3m 2f
5:20 (5:20) (Class 6) 5-Y-0+ **£935** (£290; £145; £72)

Form RPR

3/U- **1** **Golan Way**[25] 4225 10-11-7 **142**... MrBGibbs[(5)] 135+
(Tim Vaughan) *led 2nd: mde rest in clr ld: hit 9th: in n.d after 3 out: eased flat: v easily* **5/6[1]**

221- **2** *14* **Gunmoney (IRE)**[12] 4485 9-11-9 **113**..............................(p) MrJRussell[(7)] 119
(G T H Bailey) *chsd wnr after 3rd: nr enough 17th: rdn and wl btn after next: plugged on* **4/1[2]**

P43- **3** *4 ½* **Schindler's Prince (IRE)**[18] 4348 9-11-7 **96**.................. MrJMRidley[(5)] 109
(Mrs H S M Ridley) *hld up in rr: hdwy into midfield 5th: nvr on terms wirh wnr: rdn and no imp 17th: wnt modest 3rd 2 out: plugged on* **5/1[3]**

4- **4** *75* **Bob Almighty (IRE)**[291] 430 9-11-5 0........................ MrSamPainting[(7)] 41
(Mrs Gaye Williams) *chsd ldrs 5th: mstke 14th: 3rd and wl btn 17th: dropped to last and t.o bef 2 out* **25/1**

U52/ **P** **Sona Sasta (IRE)**[35] 11-11-13 0............................ MrJJackson-Stops[(7)]
(S J Gilmore) *j.rt: a wl off the pce in rr: lost tch 12th: t.o whn p.u 15th* **10/1**

P/P- **P** **Departed (IRE)**[15] 10-11-7 **66**... MrJMartin[(5)]
(S G Allen) *led tl 2nd: chsd ldrs after: rdn and struggling after 14th: t.o whn p.u 16th* **100/1**

P25- **P** **Beggar's Velvet (IRE)**[25] 4225 8-11-13 **129**.................. MrDHolmes[(7)]
(D Holmes) *a wl off the pce in rr: lost tch 12th: t.o and p.u 14th* **10/1**

6m 53.4s (0.70) **Going Correction** -0.20s/f (Good) **7** Ran SP% **114.2**
Speed ratings: **90,85,84,61, ,**
CSF £4.85 TOTE £2.20: £2.00, £2.00; EX 4.80 Trifecta £18.20.
Owner W R B Racing 58 **Bred** Lewis Caterers **Trained** Aberthin, Vale of Glamorgan

FOCUS
An uncompetitive race. The easy winner was a 151 chaser at best and will be tough to beat in this grade. The next two were close to their marks.
T/Plt: £6,946.60 to a £1 stake. Pool: £91,828.81 - 9.65 winning units T/Qpdt: £215.90 to a £1 stake. Pool: £7,879.71 - 27.00 winning units SP

4707 - (Foreign Racing) - See Raceform Interactive

4453 NAAS (L-H)
Sunday, March 9

OFFICIAL GOING: Hurdle course - yielding to soft; chase course - soft

4708a IRISH RACING WRITERS KINGSFURZE NOVICE HURDLE (LISTED RACE) (8 hdls) 2m
3:00 (3:00) 4-Y-0+ **£13,541** (£3,958; £1,875; £625)

RPR

1 **Empire Of Dirt (IRE)**[14] 4456 7-11-6 **130**.......................... BryanCooper 138
(C A Murphy, Ire) *chsd ldrs: clsr in 2nd after 2nd: led narrowly bef 4th: qckd wl fr 2 out and wnt clr between last 2: strly pressed fr after last: kpt on wl towards fin: all out* **5/1[3]**

2 *2* **The Game Changer (IRE)**[43] 3910 5-11-9 **125**......................... DJCasey 139
(C F Swan, Ire) *chsd ldrs: 6th 1/2-way: hdwy gng wl bhd ldr bef 2 out: rdn in 2nd and clsd u.p fr last: kpt on wl towards fin wout matching wnr* **20/1**

3 *2 ½* **Sizing Codelco (IRE)**[46] 3845 5-11-6 .... AELynch 134
(Henry De Bromhead, Ire) *hld up in tch: clsr in 3rd 1/2-way: pushed along in 6th bef 2 out where nt fluent: clsd into nvr threatening 3rd at last: kpt on same pce* **10/1**

4 *1 ½* **Martello Tower (IRE)**[316] 5583 6-11-2 .... DavyRussell 128+
(Ms Margaret Mullins, Ire) *w.w towards rr: 11th 1/2-way: tk clsr order bef 2 out: sn rdn in 9th and qcknd bef last where lft 4th: kpt on wl run-in wout ever threatening principals* **16/1**

5 *11* **Shantou Ed (IRE)**[17] 4386 5-11-6 .... MarkWalsh 121
(P A Fahy, Ire) *chsd ldrs: 8th 1/2-way: pushed along 2 out and no imp on ldrs bef last: kpt on run-in into mod 5th fnl stride* **33/1**

6 *hd* **The Pounds (IRE)**[10] 4523 8-11-6 **123**.......................(t) RogerLoughran 121
(Thomas Foley, Ire) *chsd ldrs: 5th 1/2-way: wnt 3rd after 3 out: sn rdn and no ex u.p in 5th between last 2: one pce run-in and dropped to 6th fnl stride* **20/1**

7 *1 ¾* **Champagne James (IRE)**[29] 4166 6-11-6 **130**................. DannyMullins 119
(T M Walsh, Ire) *led: mstke 2nd: sn restrained and hdd: 4th 1/2-way: wnt 2nd fr 3 out: rdn and no ex u.p fr next: dropped to 5th whn nt fluent last: one pce run-in* **4/1[2]**

8 *1 ½* **The Big Apple (IRE)** 4-10-4 .... AlanCrowe 102
(C Roche, Ire) *towards rr: last 1/2-way: pushed along and no imp bef 3 out: kpt on fr last* **50/1**

9 *1 ½* **Pink Hat (IRE)**[35] 4059 6-10-9 .... PaulTownend 105
(W P Mullins, Ire) *hld up: slt mstke in 10th at 4th: clsd bhd ldrs into cl 7th bef 2 out: short of room between last 2 and checked on inner: no imp after* **20/1**

10 *28* **Kick On Boss (IRE)**[50] 3792 8-11-6 **129**.......................... BarryGeraghty 88
(W McCreery, Ire) *chsd ldrs: slt mstke disputing 2nd at 1st: led after next: nt fluent 3rd and hdd narrowly bef next: slt mstke 3 out and lost pl: sn wknd* **12/1**

11 *22* **Best Of Bocelli (IRE)**[215] 1226 11-11-2 .... RobbieColgan 62
(Peter Croke, Ire) *a towards rr: 12th 1/2-way: no imp 3 out: t.o* **100/1**

12 *2 ½* **Carriganog (IRE)**[73] 3312 5-11-9 **130**.............................. RobbiePower 67
(A P O'Brien, Ire) *chsd ldrs: nt fluent in 7th at 3rd: no imp bef 2 out where eased: t.o* **7/1**

U **Quickpick Vic (IRE)**[28] 4180 7-11-6 **139**............................. PCarberry 132+
(A J Martin, Ire) *w.w in rr of mid-div: 9th 1/2-way: hdwy on outer to chse ldrs 4 out: rdn into 3rd fr 2 out and no imp on ldrs u.p whn blnd and uns rdr last* **2/1[1]**

3m 52.1s (-11.40)
WFA 4 from 5yo+ 7lb **13** Ran SP% **125.3**
CSF £106.01 TOTE £8.40: £2.20, £6.50, £3.10; DF 151.20 Trifecta £1958.60.
Owner Gigginstown House Stud **Bred** Sean Harnedy **Trained** Gorey, Co Wexford

FOCUS
There looked to be no pace concerns beforehand with several potential front-runners in the line-up but, when the tape rose, nothing wanted to make it and the favourite was restrained.

4709a NAAS DIRECTORS PLATE NOVICE CHASE (GRADE 3) (13 fncs) 2m 4f
3:30 (3:30) 5-Y-0+ £16,250 (£4,750; £2,250)

RPR

1 **Bright New Dawn (IRE)**[21] 4314 7-11-10 144 BryanCooper 152+
(D T Hughes, Ire) *mde all: j. sltly rt and mstke 3rd: brought wd bef 6th and jnd briefly: extended advantage bef 5 out: slt mstke 3 out: strly pressed bef next where slt mstke and lft clr: styd on wl fr last* 8/11[1]

2 7 1/2 **Letter Of Credit (IRE)**[10] 4521 9-11-5 141 PhillipEnright 140
(James Joseph Mangan, Ire) *chsd ldrs in 3rd: nt fluent 3 out: lft mod 2nd 2 out where slt mstke: no imp on wnr between last 2: kpt on same pce* 7/1[3]

3 43 **Owega Star (IRE)**[140] 1996 7-11-5 134 (t) AndrewLeigh 97
(Peter Fahey, Ire) *in rr: nt fluent 5th: tk clsr order in mod 4th bef 6th: detached whn mstke 4 out: lft remote 3rd 2 out: j.lft last: kpt on one pce* 7/1[3]

P **Coldstonesober (IRE)**[146] 1910 8-11-2 108 EddieO'Connell
(J R Finn, Ire) *w.w towards rr: nt fluent 1st and dropped to rr bef 6th: trailing whn p.u after 7th* 50/1

U **Mullaghanoe River (IRE)**[43] 3908 6-11-2 136 PCarberry 142+
(Noel Meade, Ire) *chsd ldr in 2nd: on terms briefly bef 6th: nt fluent in 2nd next and 5 out: clsd stl gng wl to strly press wnr whn blnd and uns rdr 2 out* 3/1[2]

5m 51.1s (22.10) 5 Ran SP% **109.9**
CSF £6.32 TOTE £1.50: £1.02, £2.20; DF 4.90 Trifecta £9.80.
Owner Gigginstown House Stud **Bred** Mrs Marilyn Syme **Trained** The Curragh, Co Kildare

FOCUS
Given Flemenstar clashed with Bog Warrior in 2012, there was a rather disappointing feel to this year's renewal. It looked at the mercy of the odds-on favourite beforehand, but one wonders what might have happened had Mullaghanoe River not departed at the second-last. The winner is rated to his best.

4467 PLUMPTON (L-H)
Monday, March 10

OFFICIAL GOING: Soft (good to soft in places; hdl 5.1, chs 5.7)
Wind: half behind, light Weather: dry and bright

4715 ASPEN INSURANCE "NATIONAL HUNT" NOVICES' HURDLE (12 hdls) 2m 5f
2:00 (2:00) (Class 4) 5-Y-0+ £3,249 (£954; £477; £238)

Form RPR

3/1- 1 **Sergeant Mattie (IRE)**[150] 1853 6-10-12 0 CharlieDeutsch(7) 130+
(Charlie Longsdon) *led 2nd: mde rest: shkn up and readily c clr bef 2 out: heavily eased flat* 5/6[1]

3- 2 4 **Cove (IRE)**[56] 3689 7-10-5 0 LeightonAspell 102+
(Nick Gifford) *hld up in rr: stdy prog 7th: wnt 2nd bef last: kpt on but no ch w wnr* 25/1

3 3 1/2 **Ballyheigue Bay (IRE)**[29] 7-10-12 0 TomCannon 107
(Chris Gordon) *led tl 2nd: chsd wnr after: rdn bef 3 out: brushed aside and btn bef 2 out: lost 2nd bef last and plugged on same pce flat* 33/1

004- 4 19 **Wunfurlez**[64] 3552 6-10-12 0 SamThomas 87
(Diana Grissell) *chsd ldrs: chsd ldng pair 3 out: sn no imp and wknd bef next* 100/1

0/6- 5 2 1/4 **Call Carlo**[31] 4130 7-10-12 0 AidanColeman 85
(Venetia Williams) *hld up in midfield: rdn 8th: no imp whn blnd next: no ch whn j.rt last 3* 16/1

223- 6 9 **Major Milborne**[55] 3697 6-10-12 118 BrendanPowell 75
(Jamie Snowden) *t.k.h: chsd ldrs: rdn and lost 3rd 3 out: wknd bef next* 9/4[2]

606- 7 32 **Electric Mayhem**[23] 4281 7-10-12 0 WayneHutchinson 43
(Nick Mitchell) *racd in midfield: lost tch 9th: t.o 3 out* 20/1

/0F- P **Steepleofcopper (IRE)**[46] 3850 8-10-5 106 JosephAkehurst(7)
(Alan Jessop) *racd in midfield: u.p after 7th: lost tch after next: t.o bef 3 out tl p.u 2 out* 50/1

35P- P **Tigridia (IRE)**[112] 2566 7-10-5 0 MarcGoldstein
(Sarah Wall) *chsd ldrs tl 6th: steadily lost pl and bhd 8th: t.o after next tl p.u 2 out* 100/1

F- P **Billeragh Milan (IRE)**[11] 4514 7-10-12 0 AlainCawley
(David Bridgwater) *a bhd: lost tch 7th: t.o after 8th tl p.u 3 out* 50/1

003- P **Bow Quest**[14] 4467 7-10-5 0 JamieMoore
(Gary Moore) *hld up in rr: hdwy after 5th: mstke and rdn 8th: lost tch qckly next: t.o 3 out tl p.u next* 8/1[3]

5- P **Kikili**[98] 2864 6-10-12 0 AndrewThornton
(Nick Gifford) *a bhd: lost tch 7th: t.o next tl p.u 2 out* 50/1

5m 32.3s (15.30) **Going Correction** +1.025s/f (Soft) 12 Ran SP% **121.7**
Speed ratings: **111,109,108,100,100 96,84,, , ,**
CSF £30.63 TOTE £2.00: £1.20, £3.20, £5.40; EX 28.10 Trifecta £635.60.
Owner Swanee River Partnership **Bred** Miss Patricia Kirke **Trained** Over Norton, Oxon

FOCUS
A mixed bunch, with the winner proving to be in a different class. The pace was solid and few were still in contention in the final mile. The easy winner was value for further and is rated to his mark.

4716 ASPEN INSURANCE NOVICES' H'CAP CHASE (14 fncs) 2m 4f
2:30 (2:30) (Class 4) (0-110,109) 5-Y-0+ £3,898 (£1,144; £572; £286)

Form RPR

/03- 1 **Dont Do Mondays (IRE)**[25] 4242 7-11-12 109 AlainCawley 120+
(David Bridgwater) *j.rt: mde all: mstke 3 out: drvn bef next: edgd rt between last 2: styd on wl flat: rdn out* 15/8[1]

442- 2 2 1/2 **Mia's Vic (IRE)**[59] 3637 9-10-12 98 (t) RobertDunne(3) 104
(Edward Creighton) *in tch in midfield: hdwy 7th: chsd ldng pair after 10th: hmpd 3 out: chsd wnr next: swtchd lft bef last: styd on same pce flat* 8/1[3]

C3F- 3 1 **Bobbits Way**[84] 3139 9-9-11 83 oh5 (p) JamesBest(3) 88
(Alan Jones) *chsd wnr: rdn after 3 out: cl 3rd next: styd on same pce flat* 8/1[3]

U4P- 4 16 **Roparta Avenue**[15] 4451 7-10-3 86 MarcGoldstein 74
(Diana Grissell) *hld up in tch in last pair: hdwy 6th: 6th and rdn after 10th: outpcd 3 out: wnt 4th bef next: no imp* 16/1

/P4- 5 4 1/2 **Scuderia (IRE)**[45] 3880 7-10-7 95 ThomasGarner(5) 81
(Jamie Snowden) *hld up in tch in last pair: rdn after 9th: no imp after next and n.d after* 8/1[3]

P3P- 6 15 **Marble Walk (IRE)**[84] 3138 9-10-4 87 LeightonAspell 55
(Richard Rowe) *chsd ldr tl after 10th: struggling after next: wknd bef 2 out: wl btn and mstke last: t.o* 16/1

/40- 7 19 **Whispering Bob (IRE)**[121] 2369 7-11-8 105 AidanColeman 54
(Charlie Longsdon) *chsd ldrs tl wknd u.p after 3 out: bhd and heavily eased flat: t.o* 7/2[2]

P/P- P **Sherreb (IRE)**[86] 3093 8-10-12 95 (t) AndrewThornton
(Anna Newton-Smith) *in tch in rr: struggling 10th: lost tch after next: wl bhd whn p.u 2 out* 28/1

0P0- F **See More Power (IRE)**[23] 4275 9-10-0 83 oh1 (b[1]) JamieMoore
(Paul Henderson) *fell 1st* 33/1

/00- P **Witchesintune**[90] 3009 7-10-5 88 AdamWedge
(Helen Nelmes) *in tch in midfield: mstke 7th: lost pl and bhd next: tailing off whn p.u bef 10th: b.b.v* 50/1

04P- F **Brians Well (IRE)**[64] 3553 7-10-12 95 (t) BrendanPowell
(Brendan Powell) *hld up in tch in last pair tl fell 10th* 10/1

5m 19.1s (11.80) **Going Correction** +0.70s/f (Soft) 11 Ran SP% **119.5**
Speed ratings: **104,103,102,96,94 88,80,, ,**
CSF £18.00 CT £101.70 TOTE £3.40: £1.10, £2.50, £2.60; EX 13.90 Trifecta £83.60.
Owner F W K Griffin **Bred** NIALL RADFORD **Trained** Icomb, Gloucs

FOCUS
Despite being run at an ordinary pace, this routine handicap chase proved to be a good test of stamina at the trip. The winner was rated similar to his Leicester level with the next two pretty much to their marks.

4717 ASPEN INSURANCE MARES' H'CAP HURDLE (10 hdls) 2m 2f
3:00 (3:01) (Class 4) (0-115,114) 4-Y-0+ £6,498 (£1,908; £954; £477)

Form RPR

/31- 1 **Our Phylli Vera (IRE)**[84] 3140 5-11-1 103 WayneHutchinson 107+
(Alan King) *in tch in midfield: chsd ldrs 7th: rdn after next: ev ch 2 out: dived but j. into ld last: forged ahd u.p fnl 100yds: rdn out* 11/10[1]

5P3- 2 1 **Was My Valentine**[20] 4332 7-10-4 92 (bt[1]) LeightonAspell 93
(Jo Davis) *chsd ldr tl led 3 out: rdn bef next: hdd last: no ex u.p flat: eased last strides* 12/1

24P- 3 nk **Goochypoochyprader**[15] 4444 7-10-9 97 (t) GerardTumelty 100
(Nick Lampard) *chsd ldrs: reminders after 6th: drvn and outpcd bef 2 out: 4th and looked wl hld last: rallied and styd on strly fnl 100yds* 8/1

113- 4 2 1/2 **Truckers Darling (IRE)**[18] 4381 7-11-7 114 ConorShoemark(5) 113
(Don Cantillon) *hld up in tch in last pair: hedgway to go cl 2nd 3 out: rdn and nt qckn bef next: outpcd between last 2: no imp flat* 11/2[3]

42U- 5 4 1/2 **Lindsay's Dream**[73] 3318 8-10-3 98 (p) MrHGMiller(7) 93
(Zoe Davison) *hld up in tch in rr: rdn after 6th: plugged on fr 2 out but no threat to ldrs* 5/1[2]

P0P- 6 9 **Flora Lea**[53] 3729 7-10-0 88 oh4 TomCannon 73
(Andrew Price) *led tl 3 out: lost pl u.p bef next: wknd between last 2* 33/1

/60- F **Miss Tique (FR)**[19] 4353 6-11-8 110 AidanColeman
(Venetia Williams) *wl in tch in midfield: hdwy to chse ldrs 7th: rdn and wknd after next: last whn fell 2 out* 13/2

4m 51.6s (20.70) **Going Correction** +1.025s/f (Soft)
WFA 4 from 5yo+ 7lb 7 Ran SP% **114.7**
Speed ratings (Par 105): **95,94,94,93,91 87,**
CSF £14.81 CT £74.44 TOTE £1.90: £1.20, £4.70; EX 15.30 Trifecta £116.50.
Owner Let's Live Racing **Bred** Awbeg Stud **Trained** Barbury Castle, Wilts

FOCUS
Run at a routine pace, and with question marks against many of these, this didn't have much depth. The winner is progressing the most. Ordinary form rated around the second to fourth.

4718 BERNARD O'BRIEN MEMORIAL H'CAP CHASE (12 fncs) 2m 1f
3:30 (3:30) (Class 4) (0-110,104) 5-Y-0+ £4,223 (£1,240; £620; £310)

Form RPR

544- 1 **Nozic (FR)**[31] 4131 13-11-12 104 (p) WayneHutchinson 115
(Zoe Davison) *chsd ldr 3rd tl led after 3 out: rdn and fnd ex bef 2 out: r.o wl flat: rdn out* 5/2[2]

51/- 2 2 3/4 **Dynamic Idol (USA)**[419] 3671 7-11-11 103 JamieMoore 115+
(Gary Moore) *chsd ldrs: mstke 9th and 3 out: rdn and effrt to chse wnr bef 2 out: kpt on but no imp flat* 13/8[1]

F60- 3 7 **Sportsreport (IRE)**[18] 4371 6-10-8 86 (p) AndrewThornton 87
(Seamus Mullins) *hld up in tch in rr: clsd to press ldrs bef 2 out: 3rd and outpcd whn wnt lft between last 2: wknd flat* 9/2[3]

/PP- 4 hd **Red Anchor (IRE)**[98] 2861 10-11-2 94 TomCannon 96
(Linda Jewell) *led: rdn bef 3 out: drvn and hdd after 3 out: 4th and btn whn hit 2 out: plugged on* 11/2

135- 5 6 **Zhukov (IRE)**[48] 3817 12-10-7 92 (b) MrLKilgarriff(7) 90
(Kevin Tork) *chsd ldr tl 3rd: styd prom: mstke 6th and 7th and given reminders: swtchd rt and hdwy to chsd ldrs 9th: wknd 2 out: mstke last* 10/1

4m 35.4s (12.40) **Going Correction** +0.70s/f (Soft) 5 Ran SP% **109.3**
Speed ratings: **98,96,93,93,90**
CSF £7.18 TOTE £4.40: £2.00, £1.20; EX 7.40 Trifecta £37.30.
Owner The Lump O'Clock Syndicate **Bred** Patrick Le Gloannec **Trained** Hammerwood, E Sussex

FOCUS
The five runners, none of whom had shown much in recent months, went a modest pace and were all in contention until the tempo increased three out. Modest form. The winner had slipped to a good mark.

4719 ASPEN INSURANCE H'CAP HURDLE (14 hdls) 3m 1f 110y
4:00 (4:00) (Class 4) (0-110,110) 4-Y-0+ £3,249 (£954; £477; £238)

Form RPR

005- 1 **Solstice Son**[78] 3226 5-10-10 94 (t) RobertThornton 108+
(Anthony Honeyball) *t.k.h: jnd ldr 2nd tl led 4th: mde rest: gng best after 3 out: clr and pushed along between last 2: styd on wl: comf* 5/2[1]

023- 2 3 **Brantingham Breeze**[20] 4330 6-10-6 100 RichardO'Dea(10) 107
(Emma Lavelle) *hld up in rr: hdwy to go 3rd after 7th: trckd wnr after 10th: rdn and effrt bef 2 out: kpt on same pce after* 11/4[2]

310- 3 33 **Royal Chatelier (FR)**[17] 4396 9-11-9 110 (p) MichealNolan(3) 84
(Michael Blake) *chsd ldr tl 2nd: chsd ldrs: rdn 8th: styd in tch tl wknd after 3 out* 10/1

/35- 4 27 **Grace And Fortune**[98] 2860 7-11-2 100 LeightonAspell 47
(Richard Rowe) *in tch: mstke 7th: rdn next: wknd bef 3 out: t.o* 4/1[3]

PFP- P **Dom Lukka (FR)**[69] 3435 6-11-12 110 AidanColeman
(Charlie Longsdon) *led tl 4th: chsd wnr tl after 10th: sn rdn: wknd qckly 3 out: bhd whn eased and p.u bef next* 11/4[2]

6m 57.25s (32.25) **Going Correction** +1.025s/f (Soft) 5 Ran SP% **111.0**
Speed ratings (Par 105): **91,90,79,71,**
CSF £9.95 TOTE £4.00: £2.30, £1.30; EX 10.20 Trifecta £50.10.
Owner The Summer Solstice **Bred** R W Russell **Trained** Mosterton, Dorset

The Form Book Jumps, Raceform Ltd, Compton, RG20 6NL.

FOCUS
The two market leaders dominated a race which lacked depth. The pace was sedate but the result makes sense. A big step up from the winner on his hurdles form.

4720 ANISE CATERING H'CAP CHASE (16 fncs 2 omitted) 3m 2f
4:30 (4:30) (Class 5) (0-100,91) 5-Y-O+ £2,662 (£826; £445)

Form RPR

U42- 1 **Tarraco (FR)**[67] 3502 7-11-10 89 AidanColeman 116+
(Venetia Williams) *chsd ldr tl 3rd: chsd ldrs tl wnt 2nd again after 7th: led after 12th: drew clr bypassing 14th: wl clr fr next: easily* 7/4[1]

F22- 2 28 **Flugzeug**[56] 3688 6-10-0 72 KevinJones(7) 69
(Seamus Mullins) *hld up in tch: hdwy to chse ldrs 9th: 3rd and no imp 15th: chsd clr wnr bef 2 out: no prog: j.v.slowly last* 4/1[2]

321- 3 9 **Alteranthela (IRE)**[74] 3250 10-11-4 83 (b) ColinBolger 73
(Richard Rowe) *chsd ldr 3rd tl after 7th: 5th and drvn after 13th: no prog and wl btn after: plugged on* 5/1[3]

P61- P **According To Them (IRE)**[14] 4470 10-11-2 88 (t) MrFMitchell(7)
(Daniel Steele) *in tch towards rr: rdn and struggling after 11th: lost tch u.p after next: t.o whn p.u 15th* 8/1

/2P- P **Beware Chalk Pit (IRE)**[56] 3688 10-11-12 91 GerardTumelty
(Jonathan Geake) *chsd ldrs tl 3rd: steadily lost pl: reminders after 7th: lost tch 10th: t.o and p.u 13th* 20/1

5FP- P **Goring Two (IRE)**[32] 4109 9-11-2 81 (p) AndrewThornton
(Anna Newton-Smith) *a bhd: lost tch 11th: t.o whn p.u 13th* 25/1

P63- P **Ballyvoneen (IRE)**[14] 4470 9-11-3 82 (b) TomMessenger
(Neil King) *chsd ldrs: rdn and struggling after 13th: poor 4th whn blnd bdly 3 out: t.o whn p.u next* 7/1

425- F **Budsson**[98] 2861 8-10-0 65 oh9 AdamWedge
(Anna Newton-Smith) *hld up in last pair tl fell 2nd* 33/1

0PP- P **Dushy Valley (IRE)**[10] 4471 7-10-11 76 (b[1]) JamieMoore
(Paul Henderson) *led: hdd and rdn after 12th: lost tch w wnr bef 15th: lost poor 2nd bef 2 out: 4th and t.o whn p.u last* 8/1

7m 10.2s (19.50) **Going Correction** +0.70s/f (Soft) 9 Ran SP% 119.3
Speed ratings: **98,89,86, , , ,**
CSF £9.81 CT £30.26 TOTE £3.40: £1.30, £2.10, £1.80; EX 10.30 Trifecta £49.00.
Owner Mrs Vida Bingham **Bred** Pascal Mahe **Trained** Kings Caple, H'fords

FOCUS
A respectable pace made this a good test, but with the top weight rated just 91, the form doesn't amount to much. The winner is rated back to the level of his French form.

4721 ASPEN INSURANCE SUPPORTS THE H'CAP HURDLE (9 hdls) 2m
5:00 (5:00) (Class 5) (0-100,99) 4-Y-O+ £2,395 (£698; £349)

Form RPR

521- 1 **Hold The Bucks (USA)**[14] 4469 8-10-12 92 MrFMitchell(7) 97
(Daniel Steele) *chsd ldrs tl rdn to ld bef 2 out: clr between last 2: edgd lft but styd on wl flat: rdn out* 13/2[2]

453- 2 2 1/4 **Little Roxy (IRE)**[14] 4469 9-10-4 77 AdamWedge 80
(Anna Newton-Smith) *led: rdn after 3 out: hdd bef next: unable qck and lost 2nd last: chsd wnr again flat: kpt on gamely but a hld* 12/1

322- 3 2 1/4 **Qasser (IRE)**[18] 4371 5-10-11 91 RyanHatch(7) 93
(Harry Whittington) *hld up in tch towards rr: hdwy after 6th: trckd ldrs and n.m.r after 3 out: effrt bef next: wnt 2nd and mstke last: lost 2nd and wknd fnl 150yds* 7/2[1]

034- 4 7 **Juicy Legend**[51] 3788 7-9-10 79 LouisMuspratt(10) 73
(Chris Gordon) *chsd ldrs: cl 4th and drvn after 3 out: outpcd and btn next: wknd bef last* 13/2[2]

211- 5 nse **Clonusker (IRE)**[15] 4444 6-11-7 94 (t) GerardTumelty 88
(Linda Jewell) *chsd ldr tl after 3 out: outpcd u.p and btn 5th 2 out: wknd bef last* 8/1[3]

203- 6 7 **Jaja De Jau**[56] 3692 5-11-3 90 (t) RobertThornton 77
(Anthony Honeyball) *hld up in tch towards rr: clsd to chse ldrs 3 out: rdn and btn bef 2 out: wknd 2 out* 13/2[2]

000- 7 hd **Just Beware**[84] 3140 12-9-7 73 oh6 (p) MissTWorsley(7) 60
(Zoe Davison) *in tch in midfield: rdn after 5th: outpcd after 3 out: n.d after* 40/1

6PP- 8 1/2 **Cranky Corner**[41] 3960 10-11-5 99 (p) ChrisDavies(7) 85
(Helen Nelmes) *in tch in midfield: rdn and effrt after 3 out: wknd bef next* 66/1

064- 9 5 **Maccabees**[14] 4471 5-9-10 76 MrFTett(7) 57
(Roger Curtis) *hld up in tch towards rr: lost pl and rdn alonfg after 5th: wknd after 3 out* 12/1

66P- 10 12 **Si Bien (FR)**[150] 1860 9-10-0 73 BrendanPowell 42
(Ali Brewer) *hld up in tch in last pair: clsd after 6th: rdn and little rspnse after 3 out: sn wknd* 7/2[1]

/PP- 11 7 **Whatagoa (IRE)**[14] 4467 7-10-7 80 LeightonAspell 42
(Richard Rowe) *in tch in midfield: rdn and struggling whn mstke 3 out: sn wknd: t.o* 66/1

0P0- 12 3 1/2 **Arcas (IRE)**[51] 3783 5-10-1 77 (t) JamesBest(3) 36
(Alan Jones) *midfield whn mstke 1st: dropped to rr after next: in tch: rdn after 5th: wknd after 3 out: t.o* 28/1

4m 16.2s (15.40) **Going Correction** +1.025s/f (Soft) 12 Ran SP% 119.0
Speed ratings (Par 103): **102,100,99,96,96 92,92,92,89,83 80,78**
CSF £79.29 CT £319.74 TOTE £6.20: £1.90, £2.50, £1.60; EX 87.00 Trifecta £371.20.
Owner D Steele **Bred** David E Hager II **Trained** Henfield, W Sussex

FOCUS
A solid pace suggests a credible result, although the general quality was modest. Straightforward form.
T/Plt: £4.20 to a £1 stake. Pool: £85958.60 - 14648.41 winning tickets T/Qpdt: £2.60 to a £1 stake. Pool: £5581.12 - 1539.4 winning tickets SP

2175 STRATFORD (L-H)
Monday, March 10

OFFICIAL GOING: Hurdle course - good to soft (soft in places); chase course - soft (7.2)
Wind: Almost nil Weather: Warm and sunny; 10 degrees

4722 FOLLOW @ATTHERACES ON TWITTER JUVENILE HURDLE (6 hdls 2 omitted) 2m 110y
2:10 (2:10) (Class 3) 4-Y-O £5,380 (£1,589; £794; £397; £198)

Form RPR

0- 1 **Agreement (IRE)**[16] 4419 4-10-7 0 PatrickCorbett(5) 108+
(Rebecca Curtis) *racd keenly: j. slowly 2nd: cl up in chsng gp: effrt 2 out: jnd ldr 2f out: cl 2nd at last: sn lft in front and readily drew clr* 2/1[2]

240- 2 1 1/2 **Mandy's Boy (IRE)**[19] 4345 4-10-7 116 (p) RobertMcCarth(5) 108+
(Ian Williams) *settled midfield: effrt in last of five gng clr 2 out: rdn and slt ld 2f out tl mstke last: immediately hdd and outpcd* 6/1[3]

215- 3 2 3/4 **Forced Family Fun**[26] 4224 4-11-1 120 DeanPratt(7) 115
(John Quinn) *racd keenly and cl up in chsng gp: wnt 2nd bef 2 out: rdn and ev ch whn squeezed for room home turn: sn outpcd: 10 l 3rd at last: rallied and kpt on wl cl home* 6/4[1]

4 17 **King Muro**[145] 4-10-5 0 NickSlatter(7) 88
(Fergal O'Brien) *led after 1st: sn 8 l clr: wnt bdly rt 4th: wnt rt again next: rdn and hdd by three rivals 2f out: immediately fdd* 10/1

5 10 **Polvere D'Oro**[21] 4-10-7 0 JamesBanks(5) 79
(Michael Mullineaux) *disp modest 3rd tl rdn and clsd 3 out: 3rd at next: dropped out qckly* 150/1

6 16 **Secret Beau**[46] 4-10-12 0 TomSiddall 69
(David Evans) *mstkes: bhd: pckd 4th: effrt and blnd bdly next: struggling whn j. slowly 2 out: t.o* 25/1

006- 7 7 **Ronnie Rockcake**[11] 4506 4-10-12 0 DavidBass 59
(Ben Pauling) *led tl 1st: chsd clr ldr tl after 3 out: fdd bdly: t.o* 66/1

8 3 1/2 **Markami (FR)**[275] 4-10-12 0 IanPopham 55
(Johnny Farrelly) *midfield: rdn and btn 3 out: t.o after next* 20/1

00- 9 nk **Hidden Link**[22] 4307 4-10-12 0 FelixDeGiles 55
(Tom Symonds) *pushed along in midfield after 3rd: fdd u.p 3 out: t.o after next* 40/1

40- 10 hd **Maxi Mac (IRE)**[116] 2466 4-10-5 0 JoshWall(7) 55
(Trevor Wall) *12 l 3rd at 3rd: hit next: fdd rapidly after 3 out: t.o after next* 66/1

50- 11 3 1/4 **Super Cookie**[71] 3385 4-10-2 0 JackQuinlan(3) 45
(Noel Quinlan) *mstkes in rr: sme hdwy 4th: 7th and rdn and struggling bef 2 out: sn t.o* 33/1

PU- 12 69 **Bobtail**[10] 4534 4-10-5 0 JakeHodson(7)
(Mark Gillard) *j.v.slowly: dropped bk last at 2nd and hopelessly t.o fr next* 150/1

13 2 **Aster's Approval**[217] 4-10-12 0 SeanQuinlan
(David Bridgwater) *sn bhd: t.o bef 3 out: eased wl bef last and crashed over flight* 150/1

4m 15.8s (19.80) **Going Correction** +1.275s/f (Heav) 13 Ran SP% 115.7
Speed ratings: **104,103,102,94,89 81,78,76,76,76 75,42,41**
CSF £13.03 TOTE £3.20: £1.20, £1.90, £1.30; EX 14.70 Trifecta £19.90.
Owner Carl Hinchy **Bred** Lynch Bages Ltd **Trained** Newport, Dyfed

FOCUS
Two hurdle bends at widest configuration added about half a furlong per circuit to distances. A modest juvenile affair, rated around the winner and third.

4723 VISIT AT THE RACES VIRGIN 354 NOVICES' H'CAP CHASE (10 fncs 2 omitted) 2m 1f 110y
2:40 (2:40) (Class 4) (0-110,109) 5-Y-O+ £4,548 (£1,335; £667; £333)

Form RPR

250- 1 **Sonofagun (FR)**[22] 4298 8-11-6 108 RobertMcCarth(5) 131+
(Ian Williams) *pressed ldr tl led 4th: 4 l clr but gng best whn j. awkwardly 2 out: drew rt away bef last and eased flat* 11/2[2]

3/0- 2 20 **Marleno (GER)**[35] 4072 8-10-12 95 (t) CharliePoste 97
(Anthony Middleton) *j. slowly 3rd: chsd ldrs: rdn whn mstke 3 out: 4th next: chsd wnr vainly bef last where 15 l bhd and no ch* 12/1

350- 3 6 **Johnnys Legacy (IRE)**[13] 4482 7-10-4 90 PeterCarberry(3) 86
(Conor Dore) *chsd ldrs: nt fluent 6th: disp 2nd and rdn 2 out: plugged on same pce and wl hld after* 9/1

241- 4 1 **Riddleofthesands (IRE)**[19] 4352 10-11-7 104 (t) SamTwiston-Davies 98
(Nigel Twiston-Davies) *led tl 4th: rdn next: lost pl 3 out: poor 5th after next: consented to run on again after last but no ch* 6/1[3]

P24- 5 1/2 **Malibu Sun**[45] 3876 7-10-12 95 DavidBass 88
(Ben Pauling) *mstkes in chsng bunch: drvn 8th: plugged on and n.d fr 2 out* 4/1[1]

04P- 6 18 **Wah Wah Taysee (IRE)**[13] 4482 7-11-3 100 SeanQuinlan 77
(David Bridgwater) *towards rr: impeded 6th: hit next: drvn 3 out: t.o* 13/2

454- P **Radsoc De Sivola (FR)**[7] 4592 9-9-9 83 oh33 JoeCornwall(5)
(John Cornwall) *chsd ldrs tl rdn 6th: lost tch after 8th: t.o next: p.u 2 out* 150/1

/3F- P **Cody Wyoming**[9] 4560 8-11-12 109 FelixDeGiles
(Heather Main) *j. slowly 1st and 2nd: t.k.h: hdwy to press ldrs 4th: drvn 8th: v slow next: lost all ch and eased: t.o and p.u 2 out* 4/1[1]

042- P **Kyles Faith (IRE)**[13] 4475 6-11-5 102 TomSiddall
(Martin Keighley) *j. v poorly in detached last: t.o fr 3rd tl p.u 2 out* 8/1

4m 31.7s (24.60) **Going Correction** +1.35s/f (Heav) 9 Ran SP% 112.5
Speed ratings: **99,90,87,87,86 78, , ,**
CSF £63.92 CT £578.42 TOTE £7.70: £1.80, £4.80, £2.70; EX 80.20 Trifecta £425.20.
Owner The Piranha Partnership **Bred** Dora Bloodstock Ltd **Trained** Portway, Worcs

FOCUS
A moderate handicap. A big step up from the impressive winner under a claimer.

4724 TRY THE NEW CARVERY (S) HURDLE (7 hdls 2 omitted) 2m 3f
3.10 (3.10) (Class 5) 4-Y-O+ £2,599 (£763; £381; £190)

Form RPR

153- 1 **Lamps**[11] 4517 7-11-7 129 (v) NickScholfield 118+
(Michael Blake) *trckd ldrs: rdn 5th: led bef next: 4 l clr whn hit 2 out: idling and pushed along whn clr between last two: nvr in any danger* 13/8[2]

/05- 2 23 **Scribe (IRE)**[19] 4350 6-11-2 107 (v) SeanQuinlan 97
(David Evans) *trckd ldrs: wnt 2nd bef 3 out: rdn and outpcd fr next: gng slowly in 15 l 2nd whn hit last* 11/2[3]

513- 3 16 **Gigondas**[89] 3025 5-11-7 108 (b) TomO'Brien 83
(Gary Moore) *led or disp ld tl drvn and hdd bef 3 out: nt run on: remote 3rd fr next* 6/4[1]

54- 4 26 **Double U Dot Ede'S**[67] 3508 5-10-6 0 PaddyBradley(10) 54
(Pat Phelan) *trckd ldrs: hit 3rd: stopped to nthing bef 3 out and sn hopelessly t.o* 14/1

P64- 5 7 **Collingbourneducis (IRE)**[24] 4247 4-10-4 93 (v[1]) PeterCarberry(3) 39
(Michael Gates) *mstke 2nd: struggling whn nt fluent 3rd: hopelessly t.o bef 3 out* 14/1

PPP- P **Alfie Alexander (IRE)**[14] 4471 6-10-11 69 (b) JamesBanks(5)
(Mark Hoad) *reluctant and mostly off bridle: hit 3rd: w ldr tl after 4th: dropped bk last bef next: sn t.o: plld himself up bef 3 out* 100/1

5m 0.6s (29.10) **Going Correction** +1.275s/f (Heav)
WFA 4 from 5yo+ 7lb 6 Ran SP% 107.8
Speed ratings: **89,79,72,61,58**
CSF £10.02 TOTE £2.10: £1.30, £2.70; EX 8.00 Trifecta £14.10.The winner was bought in for 7,000gns.
Owner The Moonlighters **Bred** Kilboy Estate **Trained** Trowbridge, Wilts

FOCUS
A very weak seller, particularly with the favourite running poorly. The winner stood out in this grade.

4725 AT THE RACES SKY 415 H'CAP CHASE (17 fncs) 2m 7f
3:40 (3:40) (Class 3) (0-125,122) 5-Y-0+ £7,596 (£2,244; £1,122; £561; £280)

Form RPR
411- **1** **Caulfields Venture (IRE)**[38] 4021 8-10-3 **99**.......... SamTwiston-Davies 115+
(Emma Lavelle) *2nd tl led at 13th: rdn clr bef last where 6 l ahd: styd on wl and eased fnl 100yds* **2/1**[1]
051- **2** 2 ½ **Fredo (IRE)**[3] 4663 10-11-4 **119** 7ex..........................(v) RobertMcCarth(5) 128
(Ian Williams) *drvn to begin: chsd ldrs: outpcd 3 out: 4 l 4th and drvn 2 out: chsd wnr fr last and fin stoutly but wnr wl in command* **7/1**[3]
405- **3** 13 **Mister Grez (FR)**[74] 3287 8-11-12 **122**..............................(b) HarrySkelton 120
(Dan Skelton) *hld up trcking ldrs: effrt gng wl 3 out: disputing 2nd next: rdn and no rspnse between last two: lost 2nd and hit last* **8/1**
P51- **4** 7 **Keltic Rhythm (IRE)**[13] 4484 7-11-0 **110**.............................. NoelFehily 103
(Neil King) *hit 9th: led tl hdd and mstke 13th: chsd wnr tl 2 out: drvn and sn wknd* **11/4**[2]
P2P- **5** 66 **That's The Deal (IRE)**[46] 3853 10-9-11 **98**...................... JoeCornwall(5) 29
(John Cornwall) *cl up tl rdn and lost tch bef 13th: hopelessly t.o fr 2 out* **33/1**
026- **P** **Passato (GER)**[106] 2694 10-11-10 **120**.................................(t) SamJones
(Jo Davis) *blnd 1st: cl up tl dropped to rr and rdn 8th: t.o and p.u 14th* **25/1**
1PP- **P** **Castle Conflict (IRE)**[37] 4031 9-11-9 **119**............................ TomO'Brien
(Henry Daly) *mstkes in rr and nvr travelling: rdn 5th: blnd 12th: t.o and p.u next* **9/1**
2U3- **P** **Mentalist (FR)**[15] 4448 6-11-3 **113**...............................(b[1]) LiamTreadwell
(Venetia Williams) *mstkes: rdn 7th: struggling whn clouted 12th and next: t.o and p.u 3 out* **9/1**

6m 6.2s (27.00) **Going Correction** +1.35s/f (Heavy) 8 Ran SP% **110.4**
Speed ratings: **107,106,101,99,76 , ,**
CSF £15.41 CT £84.43 TOTE £3.10: £1.20, £1.70, £2.80; EX 16.50 Trifecta £75.80.
Owner C F Colquhoun **Bred** Michael Crean **Trained** Hatherden, Hants
FOCUS
A modest handicap. The form is rated around the second.

4726 VISIT ATTHERACES.COM/CHELTENHAM H'CAP HURDLE (4 hdls 4 omitted) 2m 110y
4:10 (4:10) (Class 3) (0-125,125) 4-Y-0+ £6,498 (£1,908; £954; £477)

Form RPR
41F- **1** **Leviathan**[20] 4333 7-11-12 **125**.. LiamTreadwell 131+
(Venetia Williams) *racd keenly: trckd ldrs gng wl: led briefly passing 2 out: 3rd and rdn home turn: led again passing last: hld on gamely after: all out* **10/1**
302- **2** hd **Canadian Diamond (IRE)**[19] 4353 7-11-7 **125**............... JamesBanks(5) 130
(Brendan Powell) *prom: lft in ld 3rd: hdd briefly passing 2 out: drvn and hdd passing last: kpt on w ev ch but a jst being hld* **4/1**[2]
455- **3** 6 **Right Step**[58] 3648 7-10-4 **113**...............................(t) PaddyBradley(10) 113
(Pat Phelan) *pressed ldr: rdn and ev ch bef omitted last: fdd fnl 100yds* **10/1**
105- **4** 10 **Red Admirable (IRE)**[74] 3269 8-11-1 **119**...................... KillianMoore(5) 110
(Graeme McPherson) *chsd ldrs: 4th and rdn passing 2 out: wl btn 5th on home turn* **20/1**
3F5- **5** 2 **Owen Na View (IRE)**[34] 4075 6-11-6 **119**.....................(t) PaddyBrennan 108
(Fergal O'Brien) *hld up: effrt 3 out: sn drvn: 4th and btn home turn* **22/1**
54/- **6** 9 **Red Skipper (IRE)**[21] 10 9-11-7 **120**................................ TomO'Brien 101
(John O'Shea) *nvr bttr than midfield: rdn and btn bef omitted 2 out* **16/1**
030- **7** 7 **Toubab (FR)**[135] 2087 8-11-11 **124**...................................... HarrySkelton 98
(Dan Skelton) *hld up and bhd: rdn and struggling bef 3 out* **14/1**
306- **8** 1 ½ **Tidal Way (IRE)**[22] 4306 5-11-3 **119**...........................(p) KielanWoods(3) 94
(Charlie Longsdon) *hmpd 2nd: effrt in 6th and rdn passing 2 out: sn btn* **16/1**
50P- **9** 11 **Ubaldo Des Menhies (FR)**[23] 4278 6-11-4 **117**.......... RichieMcLernon 80
(Jonjo O'Neill) *hld up in rr: hmpd 3rd: rdn after next: sn lost tch: t.o* **33/1**
0/1- **10** 19 **Presenting Arms (IRE)**[22] 4300 7-11-2 **115**........................(t) NoelFehily 61
(Harry Fry) *towards rr: hmpd 3rd: n.d after: t.o* **7/2**[1]
320- **11** nk **Bedouin Bay**[41] 3959 7-10-6 **105**.. IanPopham 51
(Johnny Farrelly) *bhd: bdly hmpd 3rd: sn last and rdn: nvr rcvrd: t.o* **11/1**
240- **F** **Descaro (USA)**[26] 1867 8-10-12 **118**.............................. CiaranMckee(7)
(John O'Shea) *led tl fell 3rd* **50/1**
0/0- **B** **Sonoran Sands (IRE)**[38] 4022 6-11-3 **116**............................ SamJones
(Brendan Powell) *plld hrd: pressed ldrs tl b.d 3rd* **33/1**
3P3- **U** **Scots Gaelic (IRE)**[36] 4058 7-11-7 **120**.............................. JasonMaguire
(John Quinn) *pressed ldrs tl hit 2nd and uns rdr* **11/2**[3]

4m 14.7s (18.70) **Going Correction** +1.275s/f (Heavy) 14 Ran SP% **119.5**
Speed ratings (Par 107): **107,106,104,99,98 94,90,90,85,76 75, , ,**
CSF £47.42 CT £422.18 TOTE £10.90: £4.50, £1.50, £3.70; EX 42.70 Trifecta £2081.40.
Owner Harry Ansell **Bred** Laundry Cottage Stud Farm **Trained** Kings Caple, H'fords
■ Stewards' Enquiry : Liam Treadwell two-day ban: used whip above permitted level (Mar 24-25)
FOCUS
A fair handicap. The winner is entitled to be at least this good on Flat form.

4727 CGA FOXHUNTER NOVICES' HUNTERS' CHASE (FOR THE CREDIT CALL CUP) (8 fncs 6 omitted) 2m 4f
4:40 (5:20) (Class 6) 5-Y-0+ £1,871 (£580; £290; £145)

Form RPR
1 **Shales Rock**[36] 8-11-7 0.......................................(p) MissImmyRobinson(7) 121+
(Mrs C J Robinson) *2nd or 3rd tl led 7th: hdd briefly passing last (normal 3 out): 2 l clr home turn: urged along thrght fnl f: jst clung on fnl strides* **80/1**
/36- **2** hd **Chosen Milan (IRE)**[8] 7-11-0 0..(t) MrEDavid(7) 115+
(R E Luke) *mstkes: chsd ldrs: wnt 2nd ent bk st: led briefly passing 3 out (normal last): outpcd home turn: rallied and ev ch and urged along fr over 1f out: looked hld tl desperate late lunge: jst failed* **5/2**[2]
05/ **3** 17 **Warwickshire (IRE)**[43] 7-11-7 0.. MrBRivett(7) 107
(A Pennock) *led 2nd: hdd 7th: sn outpcd by ldng pair: 12 l 3rd passing omitted 2 out* **16/1**
F/5- **4** ¾ **Bermuda Boy (FR)**[19] 4355 9-11-11 114.......................(p) MrJHamilton(3) 104
(S Flook) *midfield: effrt 6f out: 5 l 4th ent bk st: 15 l 4th and struggling passing normal 2 out* **18/1**
/P0- **5** 3 **Ballyjames (IRE)**[15] 9-11-7 100.. MrPGerety(7) 101
(Miss H Brookshaw) *chsd ldrs: outpcd by ldng trio 6f out: plodded on* **7/1**[3]
000/ **6** 11 **Dona**[15] 10-11-7 0.. MrSamPainting(7) 91
(Miss L Thomas) *outpcd whn mstke 7th: sn t.o* **16/1**
6/0- **7** 10 **The Rubber Man (IRE)**[296] 10-11-11 0..............................(t) MrRJarrett(3) 82
(Patrick J Hanly) *chsd ldrs: pushed along after 5th: t.o fnl 6f* **66/1**
506/ **8** 9 **Cashwell**[36] 7-11-7 0.. MrWTelfer(7) 74
(S Flook) *mstkes in rr: t.o fnl 6f* **40/1**
9 48 **Gallaflynn (IRE)**[268] 9-11-9 0.................................. MrMatthewBarber(5) 31
(M Barber) *plld hrd: prom: blnd 2nd: fading whn mstke 6th: t.o after: virtually p.u* **12/1**
0/2- **10** 15 **Mister Chancer (IRE)**[24] 4252 9-11-9 114........................... MrPMann(5) 17
(Richard J Bandey) *midfield: drvn 6th: no rspnse: t.o fnl 5f: virtually p.u* **11/1**
/46- **11** 5 **Risk (IRE)**[44] 11-11-11 102.. MissAGoschen(3) 13
(Miss A Goschen) *blnd 4th and rdr lost irons: no ch in rr after: t.o fr 6th: virtually p.u* **22/1**
323- **12** 2 ¼ **Midnight Tuesday (FR)**[138] 2025 9-12-0 114........(t) MrJoshuaGuerriero
(Dan Skelton) *plld hrd and wd: a hopelessly plcd: t.o fnl 6f: virtually p.u over 2f out* **2/1**[1]
250/ **13** 41 **Squinch**[22] 10-11-9 0...(t) MrJMartin(5)
(Mrs David Plunkett) *t.o fr 1/2-way: virtually p.u fnl 4f* **100/1**
/6P- **P** **Zipit (IRE)**[270] 726 9-11-7 103.. MrRDPotter(7)
(Mrs Laura Gretton) *nt jump wl in rr: t.o and p.u 2 out (normal 4 out)* **66/1**

5m 17.3s (27.30) **Going Correction** +1.35s/f (Heavy) 14 Ran SP% **119.5**
Speed ratings: **99,98,92,91,90 86,82,78,59,53 51,50,34,**
CSF £280.91 TOTE £47.60: £7.90, £2.00, £4.60; EX 1006.80 Trifecta £3463.70 Part won..
Owner Mrs Caroline Robinson **Bred** J G Beasley **Trained** Shifnal, Shropshire
FOCUS
A novice hunter in which few ever threatened, the leading pair having it between themselves from a long way out. The two fences in the home straight weren't jumped due to the low sun and the normal third-last was also omitted on the final circuit, leaving a run-in of around 6f. The fourth is probably the best guide.

4728 COMPARE TODAY'S PRICES AT ATTHERACES.COM/ODDS MAIDEN OPEN NATIONAL HUNT FLAT RACE 2m 110y
5:10 (5:45) (Class 5) 4-6-Y-O £2,599 (£572; £572; £190)

Form RPR
4- **1** **Chieftain's Choice (IRE)**[122] 2347 5-11-4 0.................. LiamTreadwell 118+
(John Quinn) *trckd ldrs: wnt 2nd gng best 3f out: rdn to ld over 1f out: styd on wl ins fnl f* **4/1**[2]
5- **2** 2 ¾ **The Wexfordian (IRE)**[23] 4267 5-11-4 0.......................... IanPopham 113
(Martin Keighley) *unruly bef r: chsd ldr: led 3f out: sn drvn: hdd over 1f out: wl hld by wnr after: jnd for 2nd on line* **6/1**[3]
62- **2** dht **Colin's Brother**[16] 4424 4-10-10 0.......................... SamTwiston-Davies 105
(Nigel Twiston-Davies) *t.k.h on outer: chsd ldrs: last of five gng clr and rdn 4f out: edgd lft and racd awkwardly whn drvn up st: kpt on wl cl home to join 2nd on line* **15/8**[1]
25- **4** 6 **Go Odee Go (IRE)**[38] 4016 6-11-4 0.................................. HarrySkelton 108
(Dan Skelton) *hld up: effrt 6f out: 4th 4f out: rdn and no imp fnl 2f* **10/1**
0- **5** 13 **Polamco (IRE)**[128] 2216 5-11-4 0...(t) NoelFehily 97
(Harry Fry) *hld up: effrt 1/2-way: rdn and lost tch w ldng quintet 4f out: t.o* **10/1**
4- **6** nk **Southsea Island (IRE)**[37] 4030 6-10-11 0....................... PaulO'Brien(7) 96
(Rebecca Curtis) *led at brisk pce: racd keenly: hdd 3f out: dropped out qckly: t.o* **14/1**
6- **7** 23 **Killshannon (IRE)**[14] 4473 5-11-4 0.................................. SeanQuinlan 75
(David Bridgwater) *rdn and struggling 6f out: t.o* **50/1**
3- **8** 2 **Arden Denis (IRE)**[22] 4310 5-11-4 0.................................... FelixDeGiles 74
(Tom Symonds) *prom early: lost pl 6f out: t.o fnl 3f* **16/1**
54- **9** ¾ **Rock On Rocky**[16] 4417 6-11-4 0....................................... CharliePoste 73
(Matt Sheppard) *last and rdn 1/2-way: sn t.o* **33/1**
5- **10** 12 **Henrybrowneyes (IRE)**[38] 4017 5-10-13 0............... RobertMcCarth(5) 62
(Ian Williams) *bhd: t.o fnl 6f* **7/1**
0/0- **11** 30 **Sammy Blade**[53] 3734 6-11-4 0.. JamesBanks 35
(Alan Phillips) *lost tch 1/2-way: t.o fnl 5f* **150/1**
12 nk **Herr Larry Hewis** 6-10-13 0.. BenPoste(5) 35
(Sarah-Jayne Davies) *t.o fnl 6f* **100/1**
13 10 **Flaming King** 6-10-11 0... MrMatthewBarber(7) 26
(Marc Barber) *bhd: t.o fnl 6f* **150/1**
0- **14** 23 **Brean Play Percy**[31] 4135 4-10-10 0.................................... TomO'Brien
(Philip Hobbs) *rdn in rr after 6f: a struggling: t.o fnl 6f* **50/1**

4m 7.4s (17.00) **Going Correction** +1.275s/f (Heavy)
WFA 4 from 5yo+ 7lb 14 Ran SP% **121.5**
Speed ratings: **111,109,109,106,100 100,89,88,88,82 68,68,63,53**
WIN: 7.30; PL: CC 2.70, TW 2.90, CB 1.10; EX: CC/TW 23.90, CC/CB 9.80; CSF: CC/TW 14.12, CC/CB 5.91; TF: CC/TW/CB 105.40, CC/CB/TW 81.70;.
Owner Distillery Stud **Bred** Frank Motherway **Trained** Settrington, N Yorks
FOCUS
Not a bad bumper.
T/Jkpt: Not won. T/Plt: £100.30 to a £1 stake. Pool: £93382.52 - 679.00 winning tickets T/Qpdt: £19.70 to a £1 stake. Pool: £6915.69 - 259.1 winning tickets IM

4513 TAUNTON (R-H)
Monday, March 10

OFFICIAL GOING: Soft (good to soft in places; 4.8)
Wind: virtually nil Weather: overcast

4729 BARLEY MOW AT ROCKWELL GREEN H'CAP HURDLE (10 hdls 2 omitted) 3m 110y
2:20 (2:20) (Class 5) (0-100,99) 4-Y-0+ £2,737 (£798; £399)

Form RPR
614- **1** **The Last Bridge**[25] 4243 7-10-7 **80**................................. RichardJohnson 87+
(Susan Johnson) *trckd ldrs: rdn after 9th: styd on to ld at the last: edgd lft run-in: drvn out* **9/2**[2]
040- **2** 4 **Chill Factor (IRE)**[101] 2802 5-11-4 **94**...........................(t) RachaelGreen(3) 97
(Anthony Honeyball) *mid-div: trcking ldrs whn rdn appr 8th: ev ch last: styd on same pce* **11/4**[1]
212- **3** shd **Comical Red**[11] 4516 6-11-1 **95**..........................(b) ThomasCheesman(7) 97
(Mark Gillard) *in tch: trcking ldrs whn reminders after 9th: led and hung rt appr 2 out: hdd last: styd on same pce* **6/1**[3]
000- **4** 6 **Nash Point (IRE)**[72] 3357 5-10-13 **86**............................(t) DougieCostello 84
(Tim Vaughan) *hld up towards rr: midfield 3 out: sn rdn: styd on fr next: nvr threatened ldrs* **20/1**

The Form Book Jumps, Raceform Ltd, Compton, RG20 6NL.

/4P- **5** *shd* **Radical Impact (IRE)**[78] 3227 6-10-0 **73** oh1...........(b[1]) TomScudamore 70
(Venetia Williams) *trckd ldr: rdn after 8th: styd chsng ldrs but nvr quite finding pce to chal: kpt on same pce fr 2 out* **10/1**

132- **6** *1 ½* **Over My Head**[20] 4330 6-10-7 **87**...................................(t) GeraldQuinn[(7)] 81
(Claire Dyson) *led: rdn after 8th: hdd appr 2 out: styd on same pce* **9/2**[2]

P5P- **7** *1 ½* **Best Boy Barney (IRE)**[84] 3129 8-11-9 **99**..................(tp) MattGriffiths[(3)] 92
(Jeremy Scott) *chsd ldrs: rdn after 8th: nvr got on terms to chal: styd on same pce fr 2 out* **16/1**

223- **8** *5* **Tin Pot Man (IRE)**[41] 3958 8-11-0 **87**..............................(vt) PaulMoloney 76
(Evan Williams) *hld up towards rr: rdn after 8th: nvr any real imp* **10/1**

600- **9** *1 ¼* **Russian Song (IRE)**[23] 4275 10-11-1 **95**.........................(p) MrMLegg[(7)] 82
(Fiona Shaw) *mid-div: rdn after 4th: kpt on but n.d fr 3 out* **25/1**

/UP- **P** **Poppy Gregg**[81] 3179 9-9-11 **73** oh4.......................(v) WayneKavanagh[(3)]
(Dr Jeremy Naylor) *hld up towards rr: rdn along fr 7th: wknd 9th: t.o whn p.u bef 2 out* **100/1**

P5P- **P** **Bobbisox (IRE)**[74] 3277 9-10-1 **74**..(t) AndrewTinkler
(Alex Hales) *a towards rr: t.o whn p.u bef 2 out* **40/1**

6m 10.8s (6.80) **Going Correction** +0.30s/f (Yiel) **11** Ran SP% **113.4**
Speed ratings (Par 103): **101,99,99,97,97 97,96,95,94,**
CSF £16.42 CT £73.28 TOTE £4.60: £2.00, £1.30, £2.20; EX 18.80 Trifecta £70.50.
Owner I K Johnson **Bred** I K Johnson **Trained** Madley, H'fords

FOCUS
Hurdle bends moved since last meeting along with chase bend into home straight. Racing line moved where possible. A competitive handicap for the grade, with the market leaders pulling clear to give the form a solid look. The winner has the potential to rate higher over hurdles.

4730 SOWERBY GOLDEN WEDDING FILLIES' JUVENILE HURDLE (7 hdls 2 omitted) 2m 1f
2:50 (2:50) (Class 4) 4-Y-O **£3,764** (£1,097; £548)

Form RPR

04- **1** **Flute Bowl**[54] 3719 4-10-10 0... JoshuaMoore 106+
(Gary Moore) *trckd ldrs: led appr 2 out: shkn up and r.o wl fr last: comf* **14/1**

P- **2** *7* **Sea Claria (FR)**[23] 4268 4-10-10 0................................. TomScudamore 98+
(Venetia Williams) *in tch: wnt cl 3rd after 3 out: rdn to chse wnr fr next: kpt on same pce* **11/2**[3]

13- **3** *3 ¼* **Red Four**[46] 3857 4-11-2 115..(v[1]) AndrewTinkler 99
(George Baker) *led: rdn and hdd appr 2 out: kpt on same pce* **8/1**

4 *24* **Double Accord**[144] 4-10-10 0.. RyanMahon 69
(Anthony Honeyball) *in tch tl rdn after 3 out: plugged on into modest 4th run-in* **50/1**

222- **5** *4 ½* **Haatefina**[17] 4401 4-10-10 113... DaveCrosse 65
(Mark Usher) *prom: rdn after 4th: wknd after 3 out: mstke last: lost modest 4th run-in* **7/4**[1]

6 *6* **Lady Garvagh** 4-10-10 0.. ConorO'Farrell 59
(Richard Woollacott) *racd green: nt fluent: a in rr* **66/1**

7 *58* **Lemon Grove** 4-10-3 0.. MrZBaker[(7)] 1
(Martin Bosley) *j.rt: mid-div tl wknd after 3 out: t.o whn tried to duck out last* **66/1**

8 *34* **Sureness (IRE)**[163] 4-10-10 0..(t) MarkGrant
(Charlie Mann) *a towards rr: t.o* **12/1**

0- **P** **Attente De Sivola (FR)**[82] 3167 4-10-7 0....................... HarryDerham[(3)]
(Paul Nicholls) *mid-div: rdn appr 3 out: sn wknd: t.o whn p.u bef 2 out* **5/2**[2]

4m 10.4s (2.40) **Going Correction** +0.30s/f (Yiel) **9** Ran SP% **110.7**
Speed ratings: **106,102,101,89,87 84,57,41,**
CSF £83.31 TOTE £19.60: £3.80, £2.30, £2.00; EX 96.20 Trifecta £959.60.
Owner C E Stedman **Bred** C E Stedman **Trained** Lower Beeding, W Sussex

FOCUS
The market leaders proved disappointing in this ordinary event, but the first two look potentially quite useful nevertheless.

4731 SIS H'CAP HURDLE (7 hdls 2 omitted) 2m 1f
3:20 (3:20) (Class 4) (0-120,118) 4-Y-O+ **£3,764** (£1,097; £548)

Form RPR

/05- **1** **Dovils Date**[11] 4512 5-11-2 **111**.............................. MichaelByrne[(3)] 117+
(Tim Vaughan) *prom: led 3rd: r.o wl and in command appr last: readily* **5/1**[3]

320- **2** *7* **Foggy's Wall (IRE)**[22] 4297 6-11-9 **118**........................... HarryDerham[(3)] 118
(Paul Nicholls) *trckd ldrs: veered lft appr 3 out: rdn and ev ch appr 2 out: hld bef last: kpt on same pce* **11/10**[1]

506- **3** *3* **Minella Definitely (IRE)**[9] 4555 7-11-9 **115**............(bt[1]) RichardJohnson 114
(Neil Mulholland) *led tl 3rd: hung bdly lft thereafter: chsd ldng pair: rdn after 3 out: styd on same pce* **13/8**[2]

1P0- **4** *47* **Big John Cannon (IRE)**[22] 4301 4-10-10 **110**................(b[1]) WillKennedy 51
(Sarah-Jayne Davies) *chsd ldrs: struggling bef 4th: sn lost tch: t.o* **16/1**

4m 10.5s (2.50) **Going Correction** +0.30s/f (Yiel)
WFA 4 from 5yo+ 7lb **4** Ran SP% **108.3**
Speed ratings (Par 105): **106,102,101,79**
CSF £11.26 TOTE £6.30; EX 11.00 Trifecta £17.80.
Owner Itsfuninit **Bred** Cranford Stud **Trained** Aberthin, Vale of Glamorgan

FOCUS
A fair handicap hurdle. The winner is rated in line with the best of his juvenile form.

4732 BATHWICK TYRES H'CAP CHASE (21 fncs) 3m 5f
3:50 (3:50) (Class 3) (0-140,140) 5-Y-O+ **£6,657** (£2,067; £1,113)

Form RPR

1F1/ **1** **Gotoyourplay (IRE)**[734] 4686 10-10-3 **117**...................... TomScudamore 131+
(Venetia Williams) *trckd ldrs: chal 4 out: led after 3 out: styd on wl: rdn out* **5/2**[1]

44P- **2** *7* **Poungach (FR)**[68] 3457 8-11-12 **140**..................................(b) RyanMahon 144
(Paul Nicholls) *trckd ldrs: rdn along briefly after 14th: drvn in cl 3rd after 4 out: styd on into 2nd after 2 out: kpt on but a being readily hld by wnr* **7/2**[2]

1/0- **3** *15* **Massini's Maguire (IRE)**[19] 4346 13-11-10 **138**.......... RichardJohnson 129
(Tim Vaughan) *led: rchd for 4th: rdn and hdd after 3 out: sn hld: wknd bef last* **8/1**

PPP/ **P** **Giles Cross (IRE)**[387] 4249 12-11-8 **136**........................... DenisO'Regan
(Victor Dartnall) *j. sltly lft: nt a fluent: disp most of way: mstke 11th: wknd qckly and p.u bef 17th* **9/2**[3]

3PP- **F** **Well Refreshed**[23] 4270 10-11-11 **139**................................. JoshuaMoore
(Gary Moore) *trcking ldrs and travelling wl enough whn fell 16th* **5/1**

060- **P** **Whispering Jack**[38] 4021 9-9-11 **114** oh2..................(p) GavinSheehan[(3)]
(Keiran Burke) *chsd ldrs: struggling and detached after 11th: losing tch 15th: p.u bef next* **13/2**

7m 50.6s (16.60) **Going Correction** +0.525s/f (Soft) **6** Ran SP% **110.1**
Speed ratings: **98,96,91,,**
CSF £11.40 TOTE £2.70: £2.00, £1.30; EX 10.60 Trifecta £46.70.
Owner Miss S Douglas-Pennant **Bred** Frank McKevitt **Trained** Kings Caple, H'fords

FOCUS
A tricky long-distance contest, mainly because none of the runners came into this in much form. Only half the field finished. The winner is rated to his novice form, with the second to his mark.

4733 IRL INDEPENDENT RACECOURSES H'CAP HURDLE (8 hdls 2 omitted) 2m 3f 110y
4:20 (4:20) (Class 5) (0-100,100) 4-Y-O+ **£2,737** (£798; £399)

Form RPR

000- **1** **Area Access (IRE)**[93] 2947 6-9-12 **79**........................ MrHAABannister[(7)] 86+
(Charlie Mann) *trckd ldrs: led appr 2 out: r.o wl fr last: rdn out* **9/2**[2]

544- **2** *4* **Captain Sharpe**[15] 4447 6-11-1 **89**...................................(t) HaddenFrost 91
(Bernard Llewellyn) *trckd ldrs: led after 3 out tl rdn next: kpt on same pce fr last* **12/1**

213- **3** *¾* **The Happy Warrior**[20] 4334 6-11-1 **96**............................ GaryDerwin[(7)] 98
(Bob Buckler) *led: rdn and hdd after 3 out: styd on same pce fr next* **3/1**[1]

/00- **4** *13* **Calusa Star**[23] 4281 5-11-4 **92**....................................(b[1]) RichardJohnson 80
(Philip Hobbs) *mid-div: pushed along and stdy prog after 3 out: rdn into 5th whn wnt lft 2 out: wnt 4th at the last: nvr threatened ldrs* **12/1**

10P- **5** *3 ½* **Little Eaglet (IRE)**[191] 1477 10-11-4 **92**................................. LiamHeard 77
(Colin Heard) *mid-div: rdn after 3 out: kpt on but nvr finding pce to get involved* **20/1**

300- **6** *3* **Keep The Cash (IRE)**[204] 1306 6-11-9 **97**................(bt[1]) TomScudamore 79
(David Pipe) *trcking ldrs whn hmpd 1st: in tch: hdwy appr 3 out: rdn and briefly ch bef 2 out: wknd between last 2* **6/1**[3]

045- **7** *2 ¼* **Going Nowhere Fast (IRE)**[70] 3426 9-10-8 **87**......(p) RobertWilliams[(5)] 66
(Bernard Llewellyn) *hld up towards rr: hdwy to chse ldrs whn pckd 3 out: sn rdn: wknd bef next* **10/1**

5P6- **8** *1 ¼* **Landenstown Star (IRE)**[20] 4330 9-9-7 **74** oh5(b) ThomasCheesman[(7)] 52
(Mark Gillard) *racd keenly: sn trcking ldr: nt fluent 5th: wknd after next* **12/1**

003- **9** *18* **Businessmoney Judi**[12] 4504 8-11-5 **100**......(tp) MrMatthewHampton[(7)] 60
(Keiran Burke) *in tch: rdn after 5th: btn bef next: t.o* **8/1**

000- **10** *1* **Spunky**[17] 4398 5-10-11 **85**..(t) DaveCrosse 44
(Marc Barber) *mid-div: rdn after 3 out: sn wknd: t.o* **50/1**

6P0- **11** *60* **Goodacres Garden (IRE)**[18] 4371 7-10-8 **82**............. DominicElsworth
(Shaun Lycett) *bever travelling and a bhd: wl t.o* **16/1**

000- **P** **Kill Van Kull (IRE)**[108] 2648 5-10-1 **75**.........................(t) DonalDevereux
(Marc Barber) *nt fluent 4th: a towards rr: t.o whn p.u bef 2 out* **50/1**

005- **P** **Clear Mix**[20] 4330 6-10-0 **74** oh5...(t) WillKennedy
(Sue Gardner) *prom: nt fluent 1st: rdn after 5th: wknd next: t.o whn p.u bef 2 out* **20/1**

4m 51.8s (5.80) **Going Correction** +0.525s/f (Soft) **13** Ran SP% **120.1**
Speed ratings (Par 103): **100,98,98,92,91 90,89,88,81,81 57,,**
CSF £54.97 CT £188.85 TOTE £8.40: £2.80, £3.20, £1.40; EX 84.00 Trifecta £703.60.
Owner Edwyn Good & Bryan Beacham **Bred** James Silk **Trained** Upper Lambourn, Berks

FOCUS
A steadily-run handicap with the field still bunched down the back until four pulled clear, dwindling to two from the home turn. The winner was the last of the leading quartet to make his move. The second and third set the level.

4734 TAUNTON CIVIL SERVICE SPORTS ASSOCIATION H'CAP CHASE (12 fncs) 2m 110y
4:50 (4:50) (Class 5) (0-100,93) 5-Y-O+ **£3,422** (£997; £499)

Form RPR

2/1- **1** **Capisci (IRE)**[88] 3048 9-11-7 **88**... WillKennedy 102+
(Sarah-Jayne Davies) *mde all: sn clr: looked wl in command whn stmbld last: sn rdn: hld on: all out* **3/1**[1]

50F- **2** *nk* **Wicklewood**[18] 4373 8-10-1 **75**..............................(t) ThomasCheesman[(7)] 88
(Mark Gillard) *chsd ldrs: clsd on wnr after 4 out: sn rdn: looked hld bef last: r.o fnl 140yds: jst hld* **14/1**

5P4- **3** *23* **Ashcott Boy**[16] 4416 6-11-4 **88**.. MichaelByrne[(3)] 81
(Neil Mulholland) *mid-div: hit 2nd: nt fluent next: struggling after 7th: btn after 4 out: lft modest 4th at the last: snatched 3rd towards fin* **5/1**[3]

/3P- **4** *½* **Kirbys Glen (IRE)**[74] 3281 12-11-2 **83**............................... AndrewTinkler 72
(Keiran Burke) *hld up: hdwy after 8th: rdn after 4 out: wnt hld 5th 3 out: lft 3rd at the last: lost 3rd towards fin* **12/1**

2F5- **5** *37* **Think Its All Over (USA)**[19] 4352 7-11-12 **93**.................... PaulMoloney 45
(Evan Williams) *nt a fluent: trckd wnr tl after 6th: rdn after 8th: wknd next: t.o* **6/1**

4F4- **F** **Fintan**[13] 4486 11-11-10 **91**.. DougieCostello 98
(Laura Young) *hld up: smooth hdwy after 4 out: wnt 3rd next: no further imp and hld whn fell last* **5/1**[3]

/46- **U** **Beauchamp Viking**[16] 4416 10-10-2 **76**...........................(t) MikeyEnnis[(7)] 75
(Hugo Froud) *hld up: trckd ldrs 5th: wnt 2nd 4 out: sn rdn: wknd bef next: lft 3rd whn bdly hmpd and uns rdr last* **14/1**

4P2- **P** **Regal Park (IRE)**[45] 3883 7-10-13 **80**..............................(v) JoshuaMoore
(Gary Moore) *trckd ldrs: pushed along to cl on wnr after 6th: rdn appr 4 out: sn wknd: bhd whn p.u bef 3 out* **4/1**[2]

4m 22.5s (8.50) **Going Correction** +0.525s/f (Soft) **8** Ran SP% **113.6**
Speed ratings: **101,100,90,89,72 ,,**
CSF £40.15 CT £202.43 TOTE £3.00: £1.10, £5.60, £2.10; EX 47.30 Trifecta £466.00.
Owner Keith Stait **Bred** Danny Doran **Trained** Leominster, H'fords

FOCUS
The winner stole a lead at the start and was never headed, though it was a close-run thing at the finish. The winner has the potential to rate a lot higher on old bumper form.

4735 JOIN AT THE RACES ON FACEBOOK MARES' STANDARD OPEN NATIONAL HUNT FLAT RACE 2m 1f
5:20 (5:27) (Class 6) 4-6-Y-O **£2,053** (£598; £299)

Form RPR

1 **Miss Estela (IRE)** 4-10-3 0..................................... GavinSheehan[(3)] 107+
(Warren Greatrex) *trckd ldrs: led over 2f out: sn in command: comf* **6/1**[3]

2 *7* **Mistress Mole (IRE)** 5-11-0 0.. DarylJacob 103
(Paul Nicholls) *mid-div: hdwy to ld briefly over 2f out: sn rdn and hld by wnr: jst hld on for 2nd* **9/4**[1]

3 *nse* **Cara Carlotta** 5-11-0 0.. RichardJohnson 103
(Philip Hobbs) *hld up towards rr: hdwy over 4f out: rdn to chse ldrs over 2f out: styd on fnl f: jst failed to snatch 2nd* **11/4**[2]

	4	2 1/4	**One Big Love** 6-11-0 0 ... AndrewTinkler	100
			(Keiran Burke) *mid-div: rdn over 2f out: styd on fr over 1f out: wnt 4th ins fnl f* **20/1**	
4-	5	3 1/4	**Holy Veil**[111] 2583 5-10-7 0 ... MrsAlexDunn(7)	97
			(Alexandra Dunn) *mid-div: hdwy over 4f out: rdn and ev ch over 2f out: kpt on same pce fr over 1f out* **10/1**	
-	6	1 1/2	**Tara For Lilly** 5-10-9 0 ... MissLucyGardner(5)	96
			(Sue Gardner) *hld up towards rr: hdwy over 4f out: rdn and ev ch over 2f out: sn one pce* **14/1**	
	7	9	**Inside Out** 4-10-3 0 ... RachaelGreen(3)	79
			(Anthony Honeyball) *hld up towards rr: rdn over 2f out: nvr threatened* **6/1**[3]	
0-	8	nk	**Pearly Legend**[22] 4296 6-10-11 0 ... MichaelByrne(3)	86
			(Neil Mulholland) *mid-div: trckd ldrs 1/2-way: rdn over 3f out: ev ch over 2f out: wknd over 1f out* **16/1**	
5-	9	11	**Orchard Mist**[16] 4417 5-10-9 0 ... RobertWilliams(5)	79
			(Bernard Llewellyn) *trckd ldr: led over 7f out: rdn and hdd over 2f out: wknd over 1f out* **20/1**	
0-	10	8	**Kayf Charmer**[139] 2015 4-10-3 0 ... GilesHawkins(3)	59
			(Stuart Howe) *mid-div tl wknd 3f out* **66/1**	
0-	11	39	**Pomegranate**[12] 4499 6-10-7 0 ... JWStevenson(7)	28
			(Tracey Barfoot-Saunt) *sn led: hdd over 7f out: sn dropped to rr: t.o fnl 3f* **100/1**	

4m 10.3s (7.90) **Going Correction** +0.525s/f (Soft)
WFA 4 from 5yo+ 7lb **11** Ran SP% **119.7**
Speed ratings: **93,89,89,88,87 86,82,82,76,73 54**
CSF £19.62 TOTE £7.60: £2.00, £1.30, £1.80; EX 27.80 Trifecta £64.80.
Owner Mrs L Suenson-Taylor **Bred** Mrs L Suenson-Taylor **Trained** Upper Lambourn, Berks

FOCUS
A fair bumper. The winner is probably an above-average mare.
T/Plt: £1,033.60 to a £1 stake. Pool: £86016.39 - 60.75 winning tickets T/Qpdt: £61.50 to a £1 stake. Pool: £7058.40 - 84.88 winning tickets TM

3885 CHELTENHAM (L-H)

Tuesday, March 11

OFFICIAL GOING: Good to soft (good in places; 6.9)
Wind: Moderate, half behind Weather: fine

4736 SKY BET SUPREME NOVICES' HURDLE GRADE 1 (8 hdls) 2m 110y

1:30 (1:30) (Class 1) 4-Y-0+

£68,340 (£25,644; £12,840; £6,396; £3,216; £1,608)

Form				RPR
11-	1		**Vautour (FR)**[30] 4180 5-11-7 155 ... RWalsh	158+
			(W P Mullins, Ire) *str: mde most: qcknd between last 2: big jump last: r.o wl to draw clr run-in: impressive* **7/2**[1]	
112-	2	6	**Josses Hill (IRE)**[59] 3644 6-11-7 148 ... AndrewTinkler	150
			(Nicky Henderson) *lw: in tch: pushed along to chal for pls appr last: styd on to take 2nd fnl 110yds: no ch w wnr* **14/1**	
141-	3	1/2	**Vaniteux (FR)**[33] 4102 5-11-7 143 ... BarryGeraghty	150
			(Nicky Henderson) *lw: midfield: in tch 3rd: effrt to chse ldrs appr 2 out: styd on u.p run-in: no threat to wnr* **11/1**	
131-	4	1	**Sgt Reckless**[39] 4022 7-11-7 130 ... DominicElsworth	150+
			(Mick Channon) *lw: hld up in rr: stl last abt 13 l off the pce appr 3 out: rdn and hdwy whn hung lft bef last: edgd lft run-in whn styng on: fin wl* **33/1**	
1FF-	5	1	**Wilde Blue Yonder (IRE)**[24] 4266 5-11-7 0 ... RobertThornton	148
			(Alan King) *lw: hld up: hdwy appr 3 out: chsd ldrs 2 out: kpt on u.p run-in* **25/1**	
	6	1	**Wicklow Brave**[37] 4060 5-11-7 142 ... PaulTownend	149+
			(W P Mullins, Ire) *in tch: trcking ldrs 3 out: wnt 2nd appr last: no imp on wnr: lost 2nd 110yds out: wknd towards fin* **8/1**[2]	
2-	7	3/4	**Western Boy (IRE)**[59] 3667 5-11-7 141 ... DavyRussell	146
			(P A Fahy, Ire) *athletic: hld up in midfield: hdwy appr 3 out: styng on to chse ldrs whn j. sltly rt last: one pce fnl 100yds* **20/1**	
0/1-	8	3/4	**Un Ace (FR)**[20] 4343 6-11-7 0 ... AidanColeman	145
			(Kim Bailey) *hld up: pushed along to go pce appr 2 out: styd on fnl 100yds: nt quite get to ldrs* **40/1**	
111-	9	nk	**Irving**[17] 4421 6-11-7 149 ... NickScholfield	145
			(Paul Nicholls) *midfield: lost pl 3rd: outpcd and towards rr after 5th: styd on fnl 110yds: nvr able to chal* **7/2**[1]	
1-	10	nk	**Valseur Lido (FR)**[80] 3215 5-11-7 142 ... BryanCooper	145
			(W P Mullins, Ire) *trckd ldrs: niggled along appr 2 out: outpcd between last 2: checked sltly after last: kpt on run-in* **16/1**	
115-	11	1/2	**The Liquidator**[59] 3644 6-11-7 142 ... TomScudamore	145
			(David Pipe) *prom: trckd wnr 3rd: ev ch 2 out: rdn and wknd appr last* **12/1**	
311-	12	1/2	**Three Kingdoms (IRE)**[74] 3322 5-11-7 140 ... DenisO'Regan	144
			(John Ferguson) *hld up: nt fluent 3rd: pushed along and no imp appr 2 out: kpt on run-in: nvr able to trble ldrs* **33/1**	
1-	13	3 1/2	**Gilgamboa (IRE)**[45] 3910 6-11-7 140 ... APMcCoy	143+
			(E Bolger, Ire) *tall: lw: in tch: nt fluent 4th: shkn up whn trcking ldrs abt 2 l off the pce whn blnd 2 out: sn wknd* **9/1**[3]	
124-	14	2 1/2	**Garde La Victoire (FR)**[59] 3644 5-11-7 138 ... RichardJohnson	140
			(Philip Hobbs) *hld up: niggled along and struggling to go pce after 5th: gng nowhere whn blnd 2 out: nvr a threat* **33/1**	
331-	15	1 1/2	**Splash Of Ginge**[31] 4147 6-11-7 142 ... SamTwiston-Davies	136
			(Nigel Twiston-Davies) *w wnr: led briefly after 1st: remained prom: rdn and wknd bef last* **20/1**	
215-	16	6	**Sky Khan**[3] 3758 5-11-7 123 ... (e) JakeGreenall	130
			(Richard Guest) *towards rr: struggling appr 3 out: nvr a threat* **100/1**	
325-	17	12	**Germany Calling (IRE)**[17] 4421 5-11-7 0 ... (t) NoelFehily	118
			(Charlie Longsdon) *lw: tall: midfield tl wknd bef 3 out* **100/1**	
	18	4	**Fantasy King**[15] 1882 8-11-7 120 ... BrianHughes	114
			(James Moffatt) *lw: towards rr: struggling after 5th: mstke 3 out: nvr on terms* **150/1**	

3m 46.4s (-15.60) **Going Correction** -0.425s/f (Good) course record **18** Ran SP% **121.4**
Speed ratings: **119,116,115,115,115 114,114,113,113,113 113,113,111,110,109 106,101,99**
CSF £50.20 CT £503.21 TOTE £4.60: £2.80, £4.40, £3.40; EX 62.50 Trifecta £620.60.
Owner Mrs S Ricci **Bred** Haras De Saint Voir & Patrick Joubert **Trained** Muine Beag, Co Carlow

FOCUS
All races on Old Course. The festival weather reverted to type in the past week and the going dried out quickly. Clerk of the course Simon Claisse reported beforehand it may ride on the slow side still due to the vast amount of rainfall since the turn of the year. However, respected figures who walked the track beforehand were very complimentary about it and it appeared in excellent nick through the Supreme Novice. A strong field made up the opener and one should be positive about the form. While the pace suited those racing handily, it was fair and the first seven home are promising performers. Vautour rates a well above average winner, the fifth best in the last 20 years. The time was good too.

4737 RACING POST ARKLE CHALLENGE TROPHY CHASE GRADE 1 (13 fncs) 2m

2:05 (2:05) (Class 1) 5-Y-0+

£85,425 (£32,055; £16,050; £7,995; £4,020; £2,010)

Form				RPR
261-	1		**Western Warhorse (IRE)**[62] 3601 6-11-4 135 ...[1] TomScudamore	161
			(David Pipe) *led tl after 1st: chsd ldrs tl pushed along and outpcd after 4 out: drvn and styd on fr 3 out: str run u.p fr last to chse ldr: chal fnl 110yds: led last stride: gamely* **33/1**	
3/3-	2	hd	**Champagne Fever (IRE)**[75] 3308 7-11-4 158 ... RWalsh	161
			(W P Mullins, Ire) *led after 1st: pushed along appr 2 out: rdn appr last: hrd pressed fnl 110yds: kpt on gamely: hdd last stride* **11/4**[1]	
/21-	3	4	**Trifolium (FR)**[44] 3928 7-11-4 157 ... BryanCooper	158
			(C Byrnes, Ire) *lw: chsd ldrs: nt fluent 3rd: trckd ldr fr 4th: rdn appr 2 out: no imp on wnr appr last: styd on same pce into 3rd run-in* **11/4**[1]	
112-	4	3/4	**Dodging Bullets**[31] 4146 6-11-4 156 ... DarylJacob	157
			(Paul Nicholls) *t.k.h: chsd ldrs: rdn after 3 out: kpt on same pce u.p fr 2 out* **6/1**[3]	
111-	5	1 3/4	**Valdez**[45] 3893 7-11-4 153 ... RobertThornton	156
			(Alan King) *in tch: hit 4th: hdwy to cl on ldrs appr 4 out: rdn appr 2 out: outpcd u.p run-in* **10/1**	
U22-	6	2 3/4	**Grandouet (FR)**[74] 3318 7-11-4 153 ... BarryGeraghty	153
			(Nicky Henderson) *lw: in tch: nvr really jumping fluently: effrt to cl on ldrs 3 out: rdn and no imp 2 out: wknd run-in* **9/1**	
312-	7	1	**Brick Red**[31] 4159 7-11-4 143 ... AidanColeman	153
			(Venetia Williams) *in rr: hit 6th: sme prog 3 out: nvr rchd ldrs: bhd whn hmpd 2 out* **66/1**	
211-	8	42	**Rock On Ruby (IRE)**[33] 4101 9-11-4 167 ... (t) NoelFehily	121
			(Harry Fry) *lw: trcking ldrs whn blnd bdly 3rd and rdr lost whip: styd in tch but nvr jumping w any real fluency after: hit 5th: bhd whn blnd 9th: no ch whn hit 4 out* **5/1**[2]	
354-	F		**Ted Veale (IRE)**[44] 3928 7-11-4 146 ... DavyRussell	153
			(A J Martin, Ire) *in rr: hit 1st: sme hdwy whn blnd 3 out: styng on same pce in 7th and hld whn fell 2 out* **25/1**	

3m 47.04s (-10.96) **Going Correction** -0.325s/f (Good) **9** Ran SP% **111.7**
Speed ratings: **114,113,111,111,110 109,108,87,**
CSF £121.67 CT £338.63 TOTE £40.90: £7.30, £1.60, £1.50; EX 189.80 Trifecta £523.40.
Owner R S Brookhouse **Bred** Harry Kavanagh **Trained** Nicholashayne, Devon

FOCUS
One certainly got the impression beforehand that this was not a vintage edition of the race, with several of the runners having question marks hanging over them (in part due to the extremely wet winter which had limited the amount of times we'd seen them on the track) and the result, which was a genuine shocker, only seemed to confirm those initial thoughts. Considering they went a decent gallop, it was disappointing that under not much more than 10l covered the first seven to finish. A massive step up from Western Warhorse, but the time compares well and it's hard to argue this was a fluke. Champagne Fever was 2lb off last season's Supreme mark.

4738 BAYLIS & HARDING AFFORDABLE LUXURY H'CAP CHASE GRADE 3 (19 fncs) 3m 110y

2:40 (2:41) (Class 1) 5-Y-0+

£51,255 (£19,233; £9,630; £4,797; £2,412; £1,206)

Form				RPR
U11-	1		**Holywell (IRE)**[20] 4344 7-11-6 **145** ... (b) RichieMcLernon	162+
			(Jonjo O'Neill) *trckd ldrs: nt fluent 12th: gng wl upsides after 3 out: rdn after last: led fnl 110yds: r.o wl and in command towards fin* **10/1**[3]	
3P1-	2	1 3/4	**Ma Filleule (FR)**[74] 3321 6-10-13 **143** ... NicodeBoinville(5)	157+
			(Nicky Henderson) *in tch: tk clsr order appr 9th: chalng whn blnd 3 out: rdr lost iron for a spell: led appr 2 out: rdn after last: hdd fnl 110yds: outpcd by wnr towards fin* **33/1**	
4PP/	3	7	**The Package**[364] 4721 11-11-2 **141** ... (t) TomScudamore	148
			(David Pipe) *midfield: j. slowly 11th: sn towards rr: hdwy appr 3 out: chsd ldrs bef 2 out: styd on same pce run-in and no ch w front two* **16/1**	
12U-	4	2 3/4	**Green Flag (IRE)**[38] 4041 7-11-4 **143** ... PeterBuchanan	146
			(Lucinda Russell) *lw: midfield: lost pl 8th: bhd bef 12th: outpcd gng nowhere appr 3 out: hdwy bef 2 out: styd on run-in: nvr able to chal* **16/1**	
6P3-	5	nk	**Tour Des Champs (FR)**[17] 4422 7-10-4 **129** ... (v) SamTwiston-Davies	132
			(Nigel Twiston-Davies) *prom: led appr 2nd: hdd 13th: remained prom: rdn and outpcd bef 2 out: styd on again run-in wout threatening* **11/1**	
100-	6	1/2	**Standing Ovation (IRE)**[17] 4422 7-10-6 **131** ... (tp) ConorO'Farrell	133
			(David Pipe) *racd keenly: prom: led 13th: rdn and hdd appr 2 out: no ex bef last* **20/1**	
26P-	7	1 3/4	**Ackertac (IRE)**[69] 3458 9-11-4 **143** ... (b) RichardJohnson	145
			(Tim Vaughan) *hld up in rr: pckd 12th: hdwy 4 out: rdn in midfield appr 3 out: outpcd bef 2 out: kpt on run-in* **20/1**	
4/4-	8	nk	**Alfie Sherrin**[108] 2672 11-10-9 **134** ... (p) APMcCoy	135
			(Jonjo O'Neill) *lw: hld up towards rr: mstke 2nd: hdwy appr 12th: sn in midfield: rdn to chse ldrs appr 2 out: no imp: one pce after* **7/1**[1]	
403-	9	1/2	**Renard (FR)**[10] 4544 9-11-2 **141** ... AidanColeman	142
			(Venetia Williams) *trckd ldrs: nt fluent 6th: outpcd whn hit 2 out: n.d after* **33/1**	
0/6-	10	1/2	**Pacha Du Polder (FR)**[296] 392 7-11-9 **148** ... DarylJacob	148
			(Paul Nicholls) *lw: trckd ldrs: hmpd 6th: lost pl 11th: in midfield 14th: hdwy 3 out: rdn and chsng ldrs bef 2 out: one pce appr last: n.d after* **50/1**	
550-	11	2	**Fruity O'Rooney**[20] 4346 11-10-7 **132** ... (v) JoshuaMoore	131
			(Gary Moore) *trckd ldrs: rdn after 4 out: outpcd bef 2 out: wl btn whn mstke last* **25/1**	
151-	12	6	**Restless Harry**[24] 4263 10-11-7 **146** ... CharliePoste	137
			(Robin Dickin) *in tch: rdn appr 3 out: sn wknd* **28/1**	
1PP-	13	6	**Vino Griego (FR)**[31] 4145 9-11-10 **149** ... (v) JamieMoore	135
			(Gary Moore) *bhd: blnd 7th: brief effrt on outer 15th: no hdwy: wl btn* **33/1**	
2U1-	14	1/2	**Hadrian's Approach (IRE)**[83] 3165 7-11-7 **146** ... BarryGeraghty	131
			(Nicky Henderson) *in tch: pushed along appr 15th: wknd 4 out: n.d whn mstke 2 out* **8/1**[2]	

The Form Book Jumps, Raceform Ltd, Compton, RG20 6NL.

1/5- **15** *11* **Golden Chieftain (IRE)**[24] 4279 9-11-7 **146**...............(tp) BrendanPowell 123
(Colin Tizzard) *in rr: blnd 15th: struggling whn mstke 3 out: nvr on terms*
33/1

543- **16** *5* **Solix (FR)**[4] 4661 8-10-4 **129**...(v) WillKennedy 98
(Ian Williams) *midfield: steadily lost pl fr 12th: bhd whn blnd 3 out: wl btn*
33/1

/6P- **17** *31* **Shakalakaboomboom (IRE)**[20] 4347 10-11-1 **140**............... DavidBass 78
(Nicky Henderson) *led: hdd appr 2nd: remained prom: mstke 15th: wknd 16th: bhd whn mstke 3 out: t.o*
50/1

402- **18** *2* **Time For Rupert (IRE)**[20] 4346 10-10-13 **138**...............(p) DenisO'Regan 74
(Paul Webber) *midfield: hmpd 6th: lost pl 12th: sn struggling: t.o 4 out*
10/1[3]

113- **P** **Muldoon's Picnic (IRE)**[63] 3594 8-10-10 **135**................. NickScholfield
(Kim Bailey) *bhd: nvr on terms: t.o whn p.u after 11th*
33/1

012- **F** **Cantlow (IRE)**[87] 3082 9-11-5 **151**... GerFox[(7)]
(Paul Webber) *hld up towards rr: fell 10th*
16/1

262- **F** **Vintage Star (IRE)**[52] 3780 8-11-4 **143**................................ DavyRussell
(Sue Smith) *hld up: fell 5th*
16/1

211- **F** **King Massini (IRE)**[83] 3158 8-10-6 **131**................................ AdamWedge
(Evan Williams) *racd keenly in tch: fell 6th*
16/1

P **Wrong Turn (IRE)**[44] 3932 8-10-6 **131**................................ DannyMullins
(A J Martin, Ire) *nt fluent: hld up: bhd whn hmpd 10th: t.o whn p.u sn after*
12/1

6m 1.8s (-16.50) **Going Correction** -0.325s/f (Good) **23** Ran SP% **125.6**
Speed ratings: **113,112,110,109,109 109,108,108,108,108 107,105,103,103,99 98,88,87, , , ,**
CSF £310.17 CT £5172.00 TOTE £9.70: £3.00, £8.50, £4.00, £4.10; EX 469.70 TRIFECTA Not won..
Owner Mrs Gay Smith **Bred** Patrick Doyle **Trained** Cheltenham, Gloucs
■ New sponsors for this race, previously run as the JLT Specialty Handicap Chase.

FOCUS
As ever this looked one of the most competitive handicaps of the season, let alone the festival, and having been run at a good gallop, it was two of the least-exposed runners who came clear. Holywell improved to the level of his best hurdles form and Ma Filleule rates a smart mare.

4739 STAN JAMES CHAMPION HURDLE CHALLENGE TROPHY GRADE 1 (8 hdls) 2m 110y

3:20 (3:20) (Class 1) 4-Y-0+

£238,051 (£89,326; £44,726; £22,279; £11,202; £5,601)

Form RPR

124- **1** **Jezki (IRE)**[44] 3930 6-11-10 165...[1] BarryGeraghty 173+
(Mrs John Harrington, Ire) *t.k.h: trckd ldrs: nt fluent 4 out: slt ld 2 out: edgd lft and rdn appr last: styd on wl u.p run-in: all out*
9/1

111- **2** *nk* **My Tent Or Yours (IRE)**[23] 4302 7-11-10 167........................ APMcCoy 173+
(Nicky Henderson) *tk str hold: trckd ldrs: nt fluent 4 out: trckd ldrs 2 out: chsd wnr last: str run u.p run-in: fin wl: jst failed*
3/1[2]

112- **3** *2 ½* **The New One (IRE)**[75] 3261 6-11-10 167............... SamTwiston-Davies 173+
(Nigel Twiston-Davies) *lw: trcking ldrs whn bdly hmpd and dropped to 7th 3rd: effrt to cl after 3 out: rdn appr 2 out and one pce: rallied u.p appr last: styd on wl for 3rd fnl 50yds: clsng on ldng duo but a hld*
10/3[3]

111- **4** *2 ¼* **Hurricane Fly (IRE)**[44] 3930 10-11-10 173................................ RWalsh 168
(W P Mullins, Ire) *nt fluent 1st: trcking ldrs whn lft in cl 2nd 3rd: str chal 2 out: styd upsides tl edgd lft and no ex into 3rd appr last: outpcd into 4th fnl 50yds*
11/4[1]

343- **5** *7* **Captain Cee Bee (IRE)**[44] 3930 13-11-10 154..................... MarkWalsh 160
(Edward P Harty, Ire) *pressed ldr tl lft in ld 3rd: narrowly hdd 2 out: wknd bef last*
100/1

122- **6** *2 ½* **Ptit Zig (FR)**[52] 3779 5-11-10 159... DarylJacob 160
(Paul Nicholls) *hit 1st: in tch: blnd 4 out: wknd bef 2 out*
28/1

511- **7** *4 ½* **Melodic Rendezvous**[24] 4279 8-11-10 163..................... NickScholfield 155
(Jeremy Scott) *nvr travelling and sn pushed along: a towards rr*
20/1

353- **8** *11* **Grumeti**[24] 4279 6-11-10 149.. WayneHutchinson 145
(Alan King) *in rr: hdwy after 4 out: pushed along and styng on whn hit 3 out: sn btn*
66/1

/32- **F** **Our Conor (IRE)**[44] 3930 5-11-10 164............................... DannyMullins
(D T Hughes, Ire) *led tl jnd and fell 3rd: fatally injured*
5/1

3m 45.25s (-16.75) **Going Correction** -0.425s/f (Good) course record **9** Ran SP% **112.1**
Speed ratings: **122,121,120,119,116 115,113,107,**
CSF £34.92 CT £108.55 TOTE £11.00: £2.10, £1.70, £1.40; EX 41.60 Trifecta £171.10.
Owner John P McManus **Bred** Gerard M McGrath **Trained** Moone, Co Kildare
■ A 1-2 for owner J. P. McManus.

FOCUS
The most highly anticipated Champion Hurdle in recent years as it was a completely absorbing race, with possible tactics long debated. The early pace did not look overly generous, and there was high drama at the third, leaving it as a three-horse race as those who avoided the drama asserted, unfortunately spoiling the spectacle as a whole. With the pace not appearing break-neck, most took a keen early hold and the leaders wound up the dash for home after the penultimate flight, resulting a tight finish. It rates a vintage renewal with the first three all worthy of ratings on a par with the best winning performance in the last ten years. The fifth to seventh set the level, with Hurricane Fly rated 5lb off last season's mark.

4740 OLBG MARES' HURDLE (REGISTERED AS THE DAVID NICHOLSON MARES' HURDLE RACE) GRADE 2 (9 hdls) 2m 4f

4:00 (4:00) (Class 1) 4-Y-0+

£47,829 (£18,020; £9,018; £4,505; £2,261; £1,130)

Form RPR

111/ **1** **Quevega (FR)**[320] 5529 10-11-5 167.. RWalsh 145+
(W P Mullins, Ire) *hld up sltly worse than midfield: hdwy appr 3 out: trckd ldrs bef 2 out: rdn to go 2nd bef last: r.o gamely to ld fnl 75yds: in command cl home*
8/11[1]

311- **2** *¾* **Glens Melody (IRE)**[31] 4158 6-11-5 142........................... PaulTownend 144
(W P Mullins, Ire) *hld up: hdwy whn blnd 3 out: qcknd to ld appr last: hdd fnl 75yds: hld cl home*
14/1

603- **3** *¾* **L'Unique (FR)**[31] 4158 5-11-5 135.................................. RobertThornton 142
(Alan King) *lw: hld up: hdwy 4 out: rdn after 2 out: styd on to chse ldrs and cl up appr last: nt qckn run-in: kpt on but hld by front two*
25/1

134- **4** *3* **Hidden Identity (IRE)**[31] 4158 8-11-0 135..................... RichardJohnson 134
(Tim Vaughan) *hld up in rr: hdwy bef 3 out: j. slowly 2 out: sn outpcd: styd on run-in: no imp on front trio*
66/1

12F- **5** *shd* **Cockney Sparrow**[45] 3895 5-11-5 145.. APMcCoy 141+
(John Quinn) *midfield: hdwy 6th: shkn up and lost pl 2 out: rallied last but no no imp on ldrs: one pce fnl 100yds*
8/1[2]

612- **6** *1 ¼* **Top Totti**[34] 4090 6-11-0 132.. JakeGreenall 134
(Henry Daly) *chsd ldrs: hit 6th: rdn and outpcd after 2 out: kpt on u.p run-in but hld*
66/1

141- **7** *¾* **Pass The Time**[11] 4531 5-11-0 127..(p) DarylJacob 132
(Neil Mulholland) *hld up in rr: hdwy whn sltly hmpd 2 out: styd on approachng last: no imp on ldrs: one pce fnl 100yds*
100/1

111- **8** *¾* **Highland Retreat**[52] 3770 7-11-5 144.................................. NoelFehily 137
(Harry Fry) *lw: chsd ldr: w ldr after 4th: lost 2nd 3 out: stl wl there 2 out: rdn and outpcd sn after: kpt on same pce u.p run-in but wl hld*
14/1

324- **9** *6* **Little King Robin (IRE)**[130] 2205 6-11-0 124......................(t) MarkWalsh 126
(Colin Bowe, Ire) *swtg: racd keenly: chsd ldrs: lft in ld 2 out: sn rdn and hdd: wknd run-in*
100/1

10 *½* **Uddy (FR)**[27] 6-11-5 125.. HubertTerrien 131
(Alain Couetil, France) *in tch: nt fluent 4 out: stl there 2 out: rdn and dropped away qckly bef last*
66/1

324- **11** *2* **Jennies Jewel (IRE)**[23] 4312 7-11-5 139........................... IanMcCarthy 129
(Jarlath P Fahey, Ire) *chsd ldrs: n.m.r and hmpd 3 out: sn lost pl and n.d*
50/1

2/1- **12** *10* **Cailin Annamh (IRE)**[145] 1948 6-11-5 139.....................(t) BarryGeraghty 118
(Mrs John Harrington, Ire) *midfield: lost pl appr 3 out: sn outpcd and n.d*
10/1[3]

111- **13** *6* **Down Ace (IRE)**[71] 3423 7-11-5 128...................................... DenisO'Regan 112
(Fergal O'Brien) *lw: hld up sltly worse than midfield: outpcd and struggling bef 2 out: nvr a threat*
20/1

224- **14** *5* **Doyly Carte**[26] 4237 6-11-5 138.. HenryBrooke 107
(Donald McCain) *hld up: struggling after 4 out: wl bhd after*
40/1

513- **15** *36* **Epee Celeste (FR)**[14] 4481 8-11-0 86...................................(b) JoeCornwall 66
(Michael Chapman) *midfield: lost pl qckly bef 6th: sn bhd and t.o*
200/1

12/ **F** **Sirene D'Ainay (FR)**[37] 8-11-5 141..(t) DavidCottin 142
(Emmanuel Clayeux, France) *led: hit 3rd: jst less than 1 l ahd whn fell 2 out*
11/1

4m 44.6s (-5.40) **Going Correction** -0.425s/f (Good) **16** Ran SP% **119.7**
Speed ratings (Par 115): **93,92,92,91,91 90,90,90,87,87 86,82,80,78,63**
CSF £11.24 CT £160.23 TOTE £1.80: £1.50, £3.10, £4.30; EX 13.20 Trifecta £197.20.
Owner Hammer & Trowel Syndicate **Bred** Pierre Rives **Trained** Muine Beag, Co Carlow
■ Quevega became the first two to win the same festival race six times. Willie Mullins had the runner-up too.

FOCUS
Once again a race that revolved around the legendary Quevega. She is rated up 5lb on last year but again a stone+ off her best on softer ground.

4741 TERRY BIDDLECOMBE NATIONAL HUNT CHASE AMATEUR RIDERS' NOVICES' CHASE (LISTED RACE) (25 fncs) 4m

4:40 (4:40) (Class 1) 5-Y-0+

£50,966 (£15,920; £7,956; £3,978; £1,989; £1,003)

Form RPR

U21- **1** **Midnight Prayer**[31] 4162 9-11-6 139........................... MrJoshuaNewman 138+
(Alan King) *chsd ldrs: hit 14th: wnt 2nd 4 out: led appr 2 out: hld on wl*
8/1

321- **2** *nk* **Shotgun Paddy (IRE)**[59] 3655 7-11-6 151.................. MrDerekO'Connor 142+
(Emma Lavelle) *lw: in rr: hit 14th: mstke 15th: drvn and hdwy whn hit 21st: chsd ldrs 3 out: wnt 2nd last: styd on wl u.p: jst failed*
7/2[2]

3 *1 ¼* **Suntiep (FR)**[38] 4048 8-11-6 136.. MrPWMullins 138+
(W P Mullins, Ire) *hit 1st: in rr: hdwy fr 3 out: styng on whn mstke 2 out: str run fr last to take 3rd clsng stages: nt rch ldng duo*
9/1

2P3- **4** *¾* **Adrenalin Flight (IRE)**[32] 4134 8-11-6 114......................... MrBO'Neill 136
(Seamus Mullins) *in rr: hdwy fr 3 out: styng on whn mstke 2 out: fin wl to take 4th clsng stages: gng on at fin*
100/1

F- **5** *½* **Living Next Door (IRE)**[45] 3909 8-11-6 126.......................... MrJJCodd 135
(A J Martin, Ire) *in rr: hdwy and mstke 20th: styd on wl fr 21st to chse ldrs fr 3 out: rdn 2 out: styd on same pce run-in*
33/1

124- **6** *½* **Shutthefrontdoor (IRE)**[87] 3079 7-11-6 146.................(tp) MsNCarberry 138+
(Jonjo O'Neill) *lw: in rr: blnd 17th: mstke 18th and 21st: hdwy 4 out: chsd ldrs 3 out and sn rdn: styd on same pce fr 2 out*
4/1[3]

/34- **7** *1 ¼* **Rogue Angel (IRE)**[52] 3791 6-11-6 134..........................(b) MrSClements 132
(M F Morris, Ire) *chsd ldrs: led appr 15th: kpt slt ld tl hdd appr 2 out: wknd last*
16/1

1F2- **8** *4* **Milborough (IRE)**[38] 4041 8-11-6 131...................................... MrBGibbs 130
(Tim Vaughan) *mid-div: hit 7th: lost pl 13th: hdwy 14th: hit 3 out: styd on same pce*
40/1

311- **9** *5* **Foxrock (IRE)**[23] 4315 6-11-6 143.. MsKWalsh 129+
(T M Walsh, Ire) *str: mid-div: hdwy and nt fluent 14th: hdwy to chse ldrs 3 out: blnd and wknd 2 out*
3/1[1]

50P- **10** *4* **American Spin**[74] 3321 10-11-6 122.............................. MrJoshuaGuerriero 121
(Luke Dace) *chsd ldrs: mstke 15th: wknd 21st*
100/1

323- **11** *34* **Beeves (IRE)**[46] 3873 7-11-6 132.......................................(b) MrOHarding 85
(Donald McCain) *led to 10th: led again appr 14th: hdd appr next: upsides to 21st: wknd qckly bef 3 out*
25/1

423- **P** **Firm Order (IRE)**[20] 4344 9-11-6 129..................................(p) MrFMitchell
(Paul Webber) *chsd ldrs: hit 21st: wknd fr 4 out: blnd next: p.u bef 2 out*
25/1

112- **F** **Merlin's Wish**[61] 3617 9-11-6 126... MrRPQuinlan
(Martin Keighley) *pressed ldrs early: losing position whn fell 12th*
33/1

261- **P** **Herdsman (IRE)**[29] 4190 9-11-6 132.................................. MrRPMcNamara
(Sue Smith) *chsd ldrs: led 12th: hdd appr 14th: hit 20th: blnd 21st and wknd: t.o whn p.u bef 3 out*
25/1

3FP- **P** **According To Trev (IRE)**[45] 3897 8-11-6 129.................(vt) MrJBargary
(Nigel Twiston-Davies) *pressed ldr fr 6th tl led 10th: hdd 12th: rdn 18th: sn wknd: t.o whn p.u bef 4 out*
28/1

8m 7.62s (-14.18) **Going Correction** -0.325s/f (Good) **15** Ran SP% **119.5**
Speed ratings: **104,103,103,103,103 103,102,101,100,99 91, , , ,**
CSF £33.51 CT £263.54 TOTE £8.90: £2.70, £1.90, £2.50; EX 35.50 Trifecta £360.00.
Owner The Legends Partnership **Bred** J P L Reynolds **Trained** Barbury Castle, Wilts
■ The name of Terry Biddlecombe, who died in January, was added to this historic event. Josh Newman's first festival winner.

FOCUS
On the face of it this didn't look the most competitive National Hunt Chase. The drying surface had a significant bearing on the race, though, and there were a bunch still in with a chance nearing the final fence. Midnight Prayer is rated 8lb off his best with the runner-up a stone+ off.

4742 REWARDS4RACING NOVICES' H'CAP CHASE (LISTED RACE) (16 fncs) 2m 4f 110y

5:15 (5:16) (Class 1) (0-140,140) 5-Y-0+

£34,170 (£12,822; £6,420; £3,198; £1,608; £804)

Form RPR

121- **1** **Present View**[17] 4418 6-11-7 **137**... BrendanPowell 146+
(Jamie Snowden) *lw: midfield: hdwy 9th: chsd ldrs 12th: wnt cl 2nd 4 out: led after 3 out: edgd lft whn rdn run-in: hld on wl towards fin*
8/1[2]

405- **2** ½ **Attaglance**[37] 4051 8-11-7 **137**..(t) BrianHughes 146+
(Malcolm Jefferson) *trckd ldrs: rdn after 3 out: wnt 2nd run-in: swtchd lft to rail and tried to chal fnl 150yds: sn nt clr run and swtchd rt: r.o for press and clsd on wnr fnl strides: unlucky* **10/1**

110- **3** 3 **Pendra (IRE)**[80] 3197 6-11-7 **137**.. APMcCoy 143+
(Charlie Longsdon) *lw: trckd ldrs: mstke 6th: mstke 8th: hit 3 out: swtchd lft to go 2nd appr 2 out: chalng whn hit last: nt qckn run-in: kpt on u.p towards fin but no imp on front two* **8/1**[2]

231- **4** ½ **Ahyaknowyerself (IRE)**[49] 3819 8-11-5 **135**.......(b) SamTwiston-Davies 139
(Dr Richard Newland) *midfield: hdwy 11th: trckd ldrs appr 3 out: effrt whn wl there 2 out: nt qckn bef last: kpt on u.p run-in: no imp on front two towards fin* **33/1**

111- **5** 3 **Buywise (IRE)**[34] 4089 7-11-4 **134**...................................... PaulMoloney 140+
(Evan Williams) *lw: hld up: blnd 5th: sme hdwy whn hanging lft whn mstke 3 out: 7th abt 5 l off the pce whn blnd 2 out: lost grnd: styd on again towards fin* **16/1**

121- **6** 2 **Persian Snow (IRE)**[18] 4400 8-11-8 **138**.....................(t) RichardJohnson 140+
(Philip Hobbs) *midfield: pushed along and hdwy appr 3 out: effrt whn n.m.r and hmpd on bnd bef 2 out: one pce in 5th whn hit last: btn run-in* **20/1**

162- **7** 1¼ **Manyriverstocross (IRE)**[38] 4033 9-11-8 **138**............... RobertThornton 135
(Alan King) *in tch: pushed along after 3 out: wknd bef 2 out* **17/2**[3]

330- **8** 2 **Tony Star (FR)**[143] 1969 7-11-4 **134**...................................... TomO'Brien 131+
(Philip Hobbs) *hld up: bhd 10th: styd on fr 2 out: nvr trbld ldrs* **20/1**

P31- **9** 6 **Festive Affair (IRE)**[55] 3715 6-11-4 **134**................................ MarkWalsh 125
(Jonjo O'Neill) *chsd ldr fr 3rd: led appr 11th: rdn and hdd after 3 out: btn 2 out* **20/1**

1/ **10** 7 **King Vuvuzela (IRE)**[45] 3909 7-11-1 **131**................................ PCarberry 113
(Paul Nolan, Ire) *hld up: blnd 5th: nvr on terms* **20/1**

245- **11** nse **Up To Something (FR)**[46] 3873 6-11-10 **140**.....................(tp) NoelFehily 122
(Charlie Longsdon) *led: hdd appr 2nd: remained prom: rdn after 3 out: sn wknd* **33/1**

013- **12** 1¼ **Grandads Horse**[122] 2365 8-11-7 **140**...........................(p) KielanWoods(3) 121
(Charlie Longsdon) *trckd ldrs: pushed along after 4 out: stl in tch whn mstke 3 out: sn wknd* **33/1**

154- **13** 6 **Art Of Logistics (IRE)**[75] 3308 6-11-9 **139**....................(v[1]) BryanCooper 117
(D T Hughes, Ire) *hld up: nt fluent 5th: hmpd 8th: struggling appr 4 out: nvr on terms* **13/2**[1]

421- **14** 6 **Buthelezi (USA)**[99] 2859 6-11-4 **134**...............................(p) DenisO'Regan 103
(John Ferguson) *racd keenly: prom: led appr 2nd: reminder bef 9th: hdd bef 11th: wknd 12th* **25/1**

U22- **15** 24 **Dursey Sound (IRE)**[14] 4474 6-11-7 **137**...................... RichieMcLernon 82
(Jonjo O'Neill) *hld up in rr: hdwy into midfield 11th: rdn and outpcd appr 3 out: no imp* **33/1**

424- **P** **Ohio Gold (IRE)**[45] 3886 8-11-2 **132**....................................(t) JoeTizzard
(Colin Tizzard) *midfield: blnd and lost pl 5th: bhd after: t.o whn p.u bef 9th* **14/1**

F34- **P** **Close House**[40] 3992 7-11-5 **135**...............................(bt[1]) TomScudamore
(David Pipe) *hld up in midfeld: mstke 8th: blnd 9th: stl gng okay in midfield whn blnd 3 out: nt rcvr: t.o whn p.u bef 2 out* **12/1**

251- **P** **Ericht (IRE)**[37] 4055 8-11-10 **140**....................................... BarryGeraghty
(Nicky Henderson) *midfield: blnd 8th: lost pl next: bhd 10th: t.o whn p.u bef 3 out* **13/2**[1]

P- **F** **Gardefort (FR)**[24] 4273 5-11-1 **132**.................................... AidanColeman
(Venetia Williams) *hld up: hdwy 12th: in midfield whn blnd 4 out: lost pl: wl bhd whn fell 2 out* **33/1**

5m 0.1s (-10.90) **Going Correction** -0.325s/f (Good) **19** Ran SP% **126.3**
Speed ratings: **107,106,105,105,104 103,103,102,100,97 97,96,94,92,83 , , ,**
CSF £75.42 CT £660.92 TOTE £9.40: £2.60, £3.20, £2.70, £7.70; EX 110.20 Trifecta £816.30.
Owner Sir Chips Keswick **Bred** Richard Mathias **Trained** Lambourn, Berks
■ Jamie Snowden's first festival winner.

FOCUS
Just 9lb separated the 20 runners on ratings in what looked a wide-open handicap that was run at a true gallop, and it produced a dramatic finish. Present View is rated similar to his recent win in a solid renewal which should produce plenty of winners.
T/Jkpt: Not won. T/Plt: £153.00 to a £1 stake. Pool: £1,173,212.12 - 5595.08 winning units.
T/Qpdt: £24.80 to a £1 stake. Pool: £42,925.80 - 1276.71 winning units. ST

4576 SEDGEFIELD (L-H)

Tuesday, March 11

OFFICIAL GOING: Good to soft (soft in places) changing to good to soft after race 1 (1.45)
Wind: Almost nil Weather: Sunny

4743 BETFRED MARES' NOVICES' HURDLE QUALIFIER (BETFRED HURDLE SERIES QUALIFIER) (10 hdls) 2m 4f

1:45 (1:45) (Class 4) 4-Y-0+ **£3,378** (£992; £496; £248)

Form RPR

631- **1** **Maison De Ville (GER)**[23] 4304 6-11-5 115..................... JamesReveley 106+
(Brian Ellison) *led to 2nd: cl up: stdy hdwy and led 2 out: clr whn flattened last: easily* **8/15**[1]

4- **2** 11 **Midnight Streaker**[43] 3934 5-10-12 0.............................. PaddyBrennan 84
(B Arthey, Ire) *cl up: led 2nd to 4 out: regained ld next: nt fluent and hdd 2 out: sn outpcd: hld whn nt fluent last* **11/4**[2]

2- **3** 1½ **Miss Mohawk (IRE)**[14] 4479 5-10-12 0............................. DavidEngland 81
(Alan Brown) *cl up: led 4 out to next: drvn and outpcd bef 2 out: rallied bef last: no imp* **9/1**[3]

153- **4** 8 **Falcon's Present**[74] 3329 6-10-12 0.............................. RichieMcGrath 74
(John Weymes) *t.k.h: prom: drvn and outpcd bef 3 out: n.d after* **16/1**

6- **5** nk **Simmply Sam**[14] 4479 7-10-9 0.............................. KyleJames(3) 74
(Marjorie Fife) *hld up in tch: drvn and outpcd whn nt fluent 3 out: nt fluent and no imp fr next* **66/1**

0/5- **P** **Squealy Keely**[9] 4576 6-10-12 0.............................. BarryKeniry
(James Turner) *hld up bhd ldng gp: struggling 1/2-way: t.o whn p.u 3 out* **150/1**

P **Rubyminx** 8-10-12 0... TomSiddall
(Lynn Siddall) *nt fluent: bhd and detached: struggling fnl circ: no ch whn p.u 3 out* **80/1**

4m 58.6s (5.90) **Going Correction** +0.025s/f (Yiel) **7** Ran SP% **111.2**
Speed ratings (Par 105): **89,84,84,80,80 ,**
CSF £2.20 TOTE £1.40: £1.20, £1.90; EX 2.30 Trifecta £6.10.
Owner Mrs J A Martin & Mrs C L Ellison **Bred** Gestut Etzean **Trained** Norton, N Yorks

FOCUS
Divided bends. Hurdles sited off outer rail towards centre. After this race the going was changed to good to soft. James Reveley described it as being 'on the dead side of good'. This was an uncompetitive mares' novice hurdle in which only two looked to have a chance. The pace was fair. The easy winner was value for further but didn't need to improve.

4744 ENJOY THE CHELTENHAM FESTIVAL WITH BOOKMAKERS.CO.UK NOVICES' H'CAP CHASE (16 fncs) 2m 4f

2:20 (2:20) (Class 4) (0-110,110) 5-Y-0+ **£4,028** (£1,182; £591; £295)

Form RPR

212- **1** **Tiny Dancer (IRE)**[6] 4613 6-11-10 **108**............................ PaddyBrennan 119+
(Alan Swinbank) *t.k.h: hld up in tch: nt fluent 8th: hdwy to ld 11th: hrd pressed fr 4 out: edgd lft u.p after last: drvn out* **9/5**[1]

603- **2** 1¾ **One In A Row (IRE)**[11] 4530 7-9-11 **84**........................... JohnKington(3) 90
(Andrew Crook) *prom: hit 8th: drvn and outpcd 4 out: rallied to chse wnr bef last: kpt on u.p run-in* **12/1**

3P3- **3** 1½ **Talkin Thomas (IRE)**[89] 3041 8-11-12 **110**........................ BrianHarding 117
(Nicky Richards) *led: mstke 7th: nt fluent and hdd next: led 9th tl blnd and hdd 11th: outpcd 3 out: rallied bef last: nt fluent last: kpt on same pce run-in* **11/4**[2]

000- **4** 15 **Uppercut De L'Orne (FR)**[34] 4082 6-10-12 **96**.................... AdrianLane 90
(Donald McCain) *prom: hdwy to chal 11th: rdn after 3 out: wknd bef last* **7/1**

41P- **5** 38 **Ravens Brook (IRE)**[59] 3662 8-11-6 **107**.....................(p) MichealNolan(3) 64
(Richard Lee) *cl up: hit 7th: led next to 9th: lost pl 11th: lost tch fr 3 out: t.o* **4/1**[3]

P20- **P** **Teo Vivo (FR)**[89] 3041 7-11-2 **100**....................................... RichieMcGrath
(James Ewart) *nt fluent bhd ldng gp: lost tch 9th: t.o whn p.u bef 5 out* **11/1**

5m 5.0s (2.00) **Going Correction** -0.10s/f (Good) **6** Ran SP% **110.9**
Speed ratings: **92,91,90,84,69**
CSF £20.13 TOTE £2.20: £1.10, £5.00; EX 27.20 Trifecta £63.30.
Owner Ms A Findlay **Bred** John Blake **Trained** Melsonby, N Yorks

FOCUS
A fair pace to this modest novice handicap chase. The winner built on his Ayr win and the next two were close to their marks.

4745 GET CHELTENHAM FREE BETS AT BOOKMAKERS.CO.UK H'CAP HURDLE (7 hdls 1 omitted) 2m 1f

2:55 (2:55) (Class 3) (0-130,124) 4-Y-0 **£5,697** (£1,683; £841; £421; £210)

Form RPR

045- **1** **Bygones Of Brid (IRE)**[26] 4237 11-11-8 **120**...............(v) PaddyBrennan 130+
(Karen McLintock) *mde all: clr bef omitted 2 out: styd on strly fr last: unchal* **4/1**[3]

643- **2** 3 **Bob's World**[22] 4327 5-11-1 **113**..(tp) SeanQuinlan 119
(Jennie Candlish) *hld up in tch: pushed along 3 out (usual 4 out): hdwy to chse wnr bef last: kpt on: no imp* **7/2**[2]

213/ **3** 7 **Looking On**[320] 5519 6-11-6 **118**.................................... DougieCostello 118
(Steve Gollings) *chsd wnr: rdn after 2 out (usual 3 out): no imp and lost 2nd bef last* **12/1**

135- **4** 2 **Grate Fella (IRE)**[17] 4426 6-11-1 **113**.................................... RyanMania 112
(Sue Smith) *chsd ldrs: outpcd 2 out (usual 3 out): 5th and hld whn hit last: no imp* **2/1**[1]

132- **5** ½ **It's A Mans World**[137] 2068 8-11-2 **124**.............................. GLavery(10) 122
(Brian Ellison) *prom: pushed along after 2 out (usual 3 out): no imp passing omitted 2 out* **12/1**

342- **P** **Sud Pacifique (IRE)**[37] 4058 6-11-0 **119**.........................(b) NickSlatter(7)
(Donald McCain) *in tch: mstke and broke down 2nd: fatally injured* **4/1**[3]

4m 4.1s (-2.80) **Going Correction** +0.025s/f (Yiel) **6** Ran SP% **110.9**
Speed ratings (Par 107): **107,105,102,101,101**
CSF £17.95 TOTE £4.80: £2.40, £4.60; EX 23.70 Trifecta £98.70.
Owner James Callow **Bred** Oliver Brennan **Trained** Ingoe, Northumberland

FOCUS
This wasn't the strongest of handicap hurdles. The winner's best run since Ayr last year.

4746 COMPARE HORSE RACING ODDS AT BOOKMAKERS.CO.UK "NATIONAL HUNT" NOVICES' H'CAP HURDLE (8 hdls) 2m 1f

3:35 (3:35) (Class 4) (0-105,105) 4-Y-0+ **£3,508** (£1,030; £515; £257)

Form RPR

511- **1** **Be Bop Boru (IRE)**[7] 4607 7-11-0 **96**.............................. MichaelByrne(3) 106+
(Tim Vaughan) *cl up: hit 2nd: led after next: hrd pressed fr 3 out: styd on strly fr last to go clr towards fin* **8/11**[1]

403- **2** 2½ **Lebanna**[38] 4037 4-10-3 **90**..(t) BrianHarding 87
(Tim Easterby) *in tch: pushed along after 3 out: hdwy to press wnr next: effrt and ev ch last: one pce towards fin* **12/1**

050- **3** 3¾ **Sleep In First (FR)**[27] 4224 8-11-5 **105**................................ DaleIrving(7) 107
(James Ewart) *led to after 3rd: cl up: rdn and outpcd bef 2 out: rallied appr last: kpt on: nt pce of first two* **4/1**[2]

045- **4** 1½ **Dalstontosiloth (IRE)**[46] 3871 6-10-9 **93**........................... CraigNichol(5) 93
(Barry Murtagh) *in tch: smooth hdwy and ev ch bef 2 out: sn rdn: no ex appr last* **16/1**

030- **5** 16 **Mister Jones**[10] 4553 6-11-4 **100**.............................. JonathanEngland(3) 86
(Sue Smith) *w ldrs: lost pl 3 out: sn n.d: btn 2 out* **7/1**[3]

FP6- **6** 7 **Two Oscars (IRE)**[73] 3353 8-9-11 **79** oh10..................(p) JohnKington(3) 59
(Andrew Crook) *in tch: pushed along and outpcd after 4 out: struggling fr next* **66/1**

UPP- **7** 4½ **Fling Me (IRE)**[92] 2997 7-10-5 **84**................................... WilsonRenwick 60
(Rose Dobbin) *hld up bhd ldng gp: rdn and outpcd 3 out: btn bef next* **25/1**

4m 14.6s (7.70) **Going Correction** +0.025s/f (Yiel)
WFA 4 from 6yo+ 7lb **7** Ran SP% **109.3**
Speed ratings (Par 105): **82,80,79,78,70 67,65**
CSF £9.25 TOTE £1.50: £1.10, £4.60; EX 6.60 Trifecta £38.10.
Owner The Oak Syndicate **Bred** Robert McCarthy **Trained** Aberthin, Vale of Glamorgan

FOCUS
Just an ordinary gallop to this handicap hurdle. There's still more to come from the winner.

4747 CHELTENHAM FESTIVAL FREE BETS WITH BOOKMAKERS.CO.UK H'CAP CHASE (12 fncs 4 omitted) 2m 4f

4:15 (4:19) (Class 5) (0-100,88) 5-Y-0+ **£2,599** (£763; £381; £190)

Form RPR

4U2- **1** **Solway Dornal**[7] 4607 9-9-13 **66**....................................(p) GrantCockburn(5) 77+
(Lisa Harrison) *trckd ldrs: led 9th: rdn 2 out: styd on strly fr last* **3/1**[2]

The Form Book Jumps, Raceform Ltd, Compton, RG20 6NL.

456- **2** 3 3/4 **Samtheman**[19] 4380 9-11-12 **88**.. WilsonRenwick 96
(Micky Hammond) *hld up: stdy hdwy 7th: effrt and chsd wnr bef last: kpt on same pce run-in* **5/1**

52U- **3** 3 1/4 **Cara Court (IRE)**[9] 4581 8-11-7 **88**..............................(p) JohnDawson(5) 93
(Joanne Foster) *w ldrs: led 8th to next: pressed wnr tl rdn and nt qckn bef last* **7/1**

30F- **4** 26 **Western Bound (IRE)**[98] 2870 13-10-7 **69**..................(t) DougieCostello 51
(Barbara Butterworth) *bhd: hdwy 7th: rdn and outpcd bypassing omitted 4 out: lost tch after next* **28/1**

012- **F** **Ancient Times (USA)**[28] 4201 7-11-6 **85**........................(p) KyleJames(3)
(Philip Kirby) *led: hdd whn blnd 8th: sn drvn: rallied: 4 l 3rd and keeping on same pce whn fell heavily 3 out: fatally injured* **2/1**[1]

411- **P** **Prince Blackthorn (IRE)**[44] 3925 8-11-8 **84**..................... BrianHarding
(William Amos) *hld up in tch: mstke 6th: rdn and struggling next: p.u bef 8th* **7/2**[3]

5m 3.7s (0.70) **Going Correction** -0.10s/f (Good) **6 Ran SP% 113.2**
Speed ratings: **94,92,91,80,**
CSF £18.23 TOTE £4.10: £2.00, £2.60; EX 21.70 Trifecta £88.60.
Owner David Alan Harrison **Bred** D A Harrison **Trained** Aldoth, Cumbria

FOCUS
A low-grade handicap chase in which two of the market leaders failed to complete. The pace was fair. The first two were rated to their marks.

4748 COMPARE BOOKMAKERS AND ODDS WITH BOOKMAKERS.CO.UK H'CAP CHASE (7 fncs 6 omitted) 2m 110y
4:55 (4:59) (Class 5) (0-100,100) 5-Y-0+ **£2,599** (£763; £381; £190)

Form RPR

F2P- **1** **Hotgrove Boy**[28] 4203 7-10-6 **87**.................................... DaraghBourke(7) 103+
(Stuart Coltherd) *mde all: sn clr: pushed along and styd on strly after 2 out: unchal* **11/4**[2]

054- **2** 8 **Dropzone (USA)**[26] 4242 5-11-4 **95**..............................(p) MichealNolan(3) 101
(Richard Lee) *prom: hdwy to chse (clr) wnr 4th: effrt whn nt fluent 3 out: rdn and no imp fr next* **9/4**[1]

/64- **3** 14 **Mister Wall Street (FR)**[21] 4341 9-11-9 **100**..................... TonyKelly(3) 97
(Rebecca Menzies) *chsd (clr) wnr to 4th: cl up: drvn and outpcd 3 out: n.d after* **9/1**

353- **4** 20 **Forestside (IRE)**[28] 4203 9-10-4 **78**................................. LucyAlexander 53
(Barry Murtagh) *cl up: lost pl 3rd: struggling fr next: n.d after* **9/2**[3]

P02- **5** 27 **Force Of Habit**[6] 4616 8-10-6 **85**..............................(p) JohnDawson(5) 36
(Joanne Foster) *nt fluent: bhd: struggling fr 4th: t.o* **5/1**

316- **P** **Bob's Dream (IRE)**[84] 3143 12-11-9 **97**............................(t) BrianHarding
(William Amos) *hld up: pushed along and outpcd bef omitted 4 out: sn btn: t.o whn p.u bef last* **10/1**

4m 5.8s (-2.80) **Going Correction** -0.10s/f (Good) **6 Ran SP% 111.4**
Speed ratings: **102,98,91,82,69**
CSF £9.59 TOTE £4.10: £2.10, £1.20; EX 11.60 Trifecta £63.70.
Owner Coltherd Cawkwell **Bred** John James **Trained** Selkirk, Borders

FOCUS
Four fences on each circuit were omitted due to the low sun so it wasn't much of a jumping test with only seven obstacles. In addition not many came into this in much form and that included the winner. He was thrown in on the level promised by his Catterick fall.

4749 BOOKMAKERS FREE BETS WITH BOOKMAKERS.CO.UK MARES' STANDARD OPEN NATIONAL HUNT FLAT RACE 2m 1f
5:25 (5:26) (Class 6) 4-6-Y-0 **£1,559** (£457; £228; £114)

Form RPR

1 **Jennys Melody (IRE)** 5-11-0 0.. PaddyBrennan 110+
(B Arthey, Ire) *t.k.h: mde all: clr over 4f out: rdn and kpt on wl fnl 2f: unchal* **10/1**

3- **2** 9 **Bespoke Lady (IRE)**[26] 4240 5-11-0 0.............................. AdrianLane 101
(Donald McCain) *chsd wnr: outpcd and hung rt over 4f out: rallied over 2f out: kpt on fnl f: no imp* **8/13**[1]

3 53 **Looking Glass** 5-11-0 0.. DougieCostello 53
(Tim Easterby) *hld up: rdn and outpcd 1/2-way: plugged on fnl f: no ch w first two* **8/1**[3]

4 1 1/4 **Falcon's Legend** 4-10-6 0.. RichieMcGrath 44
(John Weymes) *t.k.h: in tch tl rdn and wknd over 4f out* **12/1**

5 6 **It's Time To Dance (FR)** 4-10-6 0.................................... RyanMania 39
(Tim Easterby) *in tch: drvn and outpcd over 4f out: btn over 2f out* **4/1**[2]

4m 7.4s (6.10) **Going Correction** +0.025s/f (Yiel)
WFA 4 from 5yo 7lb **5 Ran SP% 109.8**
Speed ratings: **86,81,56,56,53**
CSF £17.03 TOTE £9.90: £3.30, £1.10; EX 18.00 Trifecta £32.60.
Owner Richard W Gilchrist **Bred** Miss M Byrne **Trained** Kells, Ballymena

FOCUS
Probably an ordinary mares' bumper, but the winner looks above average.
T/Plt: £57.50 to a £1 stake. Pool: £53,554.70 - 678.81 winning units. T/Qpdt: £22.60 to a £1 stake. Pool: £3034.89 - 99.20 winning units. RY

4736 CHELTENHAM (L-H)
Wednesday, March 12

OFFICIAL GOING: Chase & hurdle courses - good (good to soft in places; 7.5); cross country - good to soft (soft in places; 7.2)
Wind: Almost nil Weather: Fine

4750 NEPTUNE INVESTMENT MANAGEMENT NOVICES' HURDLE (REGISTERED AS BARING BINGHAM NOVICES' HURDLE) GRADE 1 (10 hdls) 2m 5f
1:30 (1:32) (Class 1) 4-Y-0+ **£68,340** (£25,644; £12,840; £6,396; £3,216; £1,608)

1- **1** **Faugheen (IRE)**[74] 3380 6-11-7 152.. RWalsh 155+
(W P Mullins, Ire) *prom: trckd ldr after 6th: nt fluent next: led and mstke 3 out: drew clr bef last: rdn out* **6/4**[1]

114- **2** 4 1/2 **Ballyalton (IRE)**[70] 3454 7-11-7 140.................................. WillKennedy 149
(Ian Williams) *hld up towards rr: prog 6th: mstke next but sn prom: drvn to chse wnr bef last: kpt on but no ch* **20/1**

F2- **3** 1/2 **Rathvinden (IRE)**[46] 3889 6-11-7 151.............................. PaulTownend 149+
(W P Mullins, Ire) *lost midfield pl 4th and sn in rr: prog 7th: chsd ldrs 3 out: drvn and forced way through bef last: pressed runner-up flat but no ch w wnr* **11/2**[3]

01P- **4** 1 **Killala Quay**[60] 3654 7-11-7 142.................................... RichardJohnson 149+
(Charlie Longsdon) *hld up towards rr: nt fluent 2nd: prog 7th: rdn and wl in tch 3 out: outpcd after next: styd on again bef last: pressed for a pl nr fin* **25/1**

240- **5** 3 3/4 **Twelve Roses**[76] 3263 6-11-7 130............................ SamTwiston-Davies 142
(Kim Bailey) *lw: hld up in last trio: prog 7th: chsd ldrs in 9th bef 3 out but nt on terms: hdwy u.p after 2 out: no ex fr last* **66/1**

6 3 1/2 **Lieutenant Colonel**[38] 4060 5-11-7 135.............................. BryanCooper 139
(D T Hughes, Ire) *trckd ldrs: wl in tch fr 3 out: nt qckn after 2 out: edgd lft and wknd last* **10/1**

112- **7** 1 1/2 **Cole Harden (IRE)**[25] 4261 5-11-7 135...........................(t) GavinSheehan 139
(Warren Greatrex) *led: j.lft 1st: blnd 7th: hdd 3 out: steadily wknd bef last* **40/1**

8 2 **Shanahan's Turn (IRE)**[73] 3401 6-11-7 0................................. AELynch 136
(Henry De Bromhead, Ire) *t.k.h: prom: hit 7th: cl up 3 out: n.m.r and lost grnd sn after 2 out: wknd last* **50/1**

111- **9** 7 **Red Sherlock**[46] 3889 5-11-7 151.................................... TomScudamore 130
(David Pipe) *lw: prog 4th: trckd ldng pair 7th: wnt 2nd and chal 2 out: losing pl whn sandwiched between rivals bef last: wknd* **7/2**[2]

/23- **10** 21 **Cup Final (IRE)**[18] 4421 5-11-7 0.. APMcCoy 107
(Nicky Henderson) *lw: hld up towards rr: nt fluent 6th: lost tch sn after next: t.o 3 out* **16/1**

4/3- **11** 8 **Cocktails At Dawn**[89] 3070 6-11-7 119.............................. BarryGeraghty 99
(Nicky Henderson) *in tch: nt fluent 3rd: struggling after 7th: sn bhd: t.o* **33/1**

11- **12** 3/4 **Fennell Bay (IRE)**[28] 4221 5-11-7 135................................. DenisO'Regan 99
(John Ferguson) *trckd ldrs: losing pl on inner whn mstke 7th: t.o 3 out* **28/1**

312- **13** 8 **Knock House (IRE)**[53] 3774 5-11-7 132.......................... DominicElsworth 91
(Mick Channon) *a in last trio: lost tch 7th: sn t.o* **50/1**

U55- **14** 2 3/4 **Creepy (IRE)**[46] 3889 6-11-7 135..[1] IanPopham 88
(Martin Keighley) *nt fluent 1st: chsd ldr tl after 6th: sn wknd: t.o 3 out* **40/1**

223- **15** dist **Midnight Thunder (IRE)**[14] 4503 5-11-7 110................. BrendanPowell
(Colin Tizzard) *nt fluent: a in last trio: wl t.o* **150/1**

4m 54.8s (-18.60) **Going Correction** -0.375s/f (Good) **15 Ran SP% 118.5**
Speed ratings: **120,118,118,117,116 114,114,113,110,102 99,99,96,95,**
CSF £36.46 TOTE £2.30: £1.60, £4.40, £2.00; EX 42.90 Trifecta £299.40.
Owner Mrs S Ricci **Bred** Dr John Waldron **Trained** Muine Beag, Co Carlow
■ Stewards' Enquiry : Will Kennedy three-day ban: careless riding (Mar 26-28)

FOCUS
All races on Old course except Cross country race 5. Following a dry night the going was left unchanged, and the jockeys reported the ground to be good. A race with a fine track record of producing future stars, and it's highly likely it did so again. It was strong run and in a comparatively good time compared with the Coral Cup. Faugheen is well up to standard and can rate higher.

4751 RSA CHASE (GRADE 1) (19 fncs) 3m 110y
2:05 (2:05) (Class 1) 5-Y-0+
£85,425 (£32,055; £16,050; £7,995; £4,020; £2,010)

Form RPR

2P1- **1** **O'Faolains Boy (IRE)**[25] 4262 7-11-4 144........................ BarryGeraghty 163+
(Rebecca Curtis) *lw: in rr: hdwy 4 out: chsd ldrs next: drvn to chse ldr appr 2 out: str chal last and run-in: slt ld u.p fnl 110yds: all out* **12/1**

U11- **2** nk **Smad Place (FR)**[32] 4148 7-11-4 148.............................. RobertThornton 163+
(Alan King) *lw: mid-div: hdwy 9th: sn chsng ldrs: chal 3 out: slt ld appr 2 out: hrd pressed last: kpt slt advantage tl narrowly hdd fnl 110yds: no ex last strides* **13/2**[1]

/12- **3** 6 **Morning Assembly (IRE)**[73] 3404 7-11-4 146.................. DavyRussell 156
(P A Fahy, Ire) *rangy: in tch: hdwy 12th: chsd ldrs fr 4 out: styd on u.p fr 2 out to take 3rd fnl 110yds: no ch w ldng duo* **9/1**[3]

3/1- **4** 2 1/4 **Ballycasey (IRE)**[31] 4181 7-11-4 157.. RWalsh 154
(W P Mullins, Ire) *chsd ldrs: led 3 out: sn rdn: hdd appr 2 out: no ex last: one pce into 4th fnl 110yds* **13/2**[1]

312- **5** nk **Sam Winner (FR)**[32] 4148 7-11-4 147.................................... DarylJacob 153
(Paul Nicholls) *chsd ldrs: chal 4 out: sn led: narrowly hdd next: styd chsng ldrs: no ex and one pce bef last* **12/1**

21U- **6** 1 **Carlingford Lough (IRE)**[31] 4181 8-11-4 150......................... APMcCoy 154
(John E Kiely, Ire) *lw: blnd 1st: in rr: nt fluent 3rd: hit 5th: hmpd 14th: hdwy 4 out: chsd ldrs 3 out: one pce fr 2 out* **7/1**[2]

214- **7** 9 **Just A Par (IRE)**[76] 3260 7-11-4 148.................................... NoelFehily 147
(Paul Nicholls) *in rr: hdwy 14th: chsd ldrs fr 4 out: drvn along next: wknd qckly after 2 out* **16/1**

212- **8** 23 **Annacotty (IRE)**[46] 3886 6-11-4 146...................................(b) IanPopham 125
(Martin Keighley) *lw: chsd ldr tl blnd 14th: wknd and blnd 4 out: no ch whn mstke 3 out* **20/1**

/1P- **9** 3/4 **Gevrey Chambertin (FR)**[25] 4262 6-11-4 147............(t) TomScudamore 119
(David Pipe) *in rr: j. slowly 4th: j. slowly 11th: hmpd 12th: no ch whn hit 15th* **25/1**

111- **10** 16 **Corrin Wood (IRE)**[60] 3651 7-11-4 156........................ RichardJohnson 113
(Donald McCain) *led: hit 4th and 11th: blnd 15th: jnd 4 out and sn hdd: wknd qckly: no ch whn j. slowly 3 out* **10/1**

112- **F** **Black Thunder (FR)**[60] 3651 7-11-4 153.......................... NickScholfield
(Paul Nicholls) *trckd ldrs: stl travelling ok whn fell 12th* **16/1**

212- **F** **Don Cossack (GER)**[31] 4181 7-11-4 152..........................(t) BryanCooper
(Gordon Elliott, Ire) *tall: lengthy: lw: in tch hdwy 9th: travelling ok in bhd ldrs whn fell 14th* **11/1**

112- **F** **Le Bec (FR)**[88] 3079 6-11-4 149... AidanColeman
(Emma Lavelle) *trckd ldrs: stl travelling ok whn fell 4 out* **10/1**

212- **B** **Many Clouds (IRE)**[25] 4262 7-11-4 145.............................. LeightonAspell
(Oliver Sherwood) *lw: in rr: stl bhd but gng ok whn mstke: hmpd and b.d 14th* **16/1**

115- **P** **Samingarry (FR)**[46] 3886 7-11-4 126..................................... PaulMoloney
(Nigel Hawke) *sn wl bhd: blnd 8th: t.o whn p.u bef 12th* **100/1**

6m 0.32s (-17.98) **Going Correction** -0.275s/f (Good) **15 Ran SP% 118.3**
Speed ratings: **117,116,114,114,114 113,110,103,103,98 , , , ,**
CSF £86.02 TOTE £13.30: £4.20, £2.20, £3.00; EX 92.80 Trifecta £1322.10.
Owner Trembath, Hyde, Outhart & Hill **Bred** Tom And P Phelan **Trained** Newport, Dyfed

FOCUS
The betting suggested that this year's RSA was open and competitive, but perhaps lacking a true Gold Cup prospect of the future. There was plenty of pace in the race, and only the strongest stayers were there at the finish. O'Faolains Boy built on his Ascot run, and the form is solid.

4752 CORAL CUP (A H'CAP HURDLE) GRADE 3 (10 hdls) 2m 5f
2:40 (2:40) (Class 1) 4-Y-0+
£45,560 (£17,096; £8,560; £4,264; £2,144; £1,072)

Form RPR

312- **1** **Whisper (FR)**[39] 4025 6-11-6 **153**.................................... NicodeBoinville(5) 159
(Nicky Henderson) *a in ldng gp: rdn to ld bef last: hrd pressed flat: jst hld on* **14/1**

/00- **2** *shd* **Get Me Out Of Here (IRE)**[115] 2533 10-11-6 **148**..............(tp) APMcCoy 154
(Jonjo O'Neill) *hld up in midfield: stdy prog fr 7th: trckd ldrs 3 out: hdwy after 2 out to chal last: upsides flat: jst denied* **12/1**[3]

112- **3** *2 ¼* **Bayan (IRE)**[129] 1970 5-10-10 **138**..............(tp) DavyCondon 142
(Gordon Elliott, Ire) *wl in tch on inner: mstke 7th: trckd ldrs gng strly whn nt fluent 3 out and next: rdn to chal bef last: kpt on same pce flat* **11/1**[2]

0- **4** *1 ¼* **Smashing (FR)**[32] 4147 5-11-1 **143**.. AELynch 145
(W P Mullins, Ire) *hld up in rr: blnd 1st: prog on inner fr 7th: mstke 3 out: hdwy after 2 out: chsd ldrs and nt clr run bef last: kpt on one pce after* **25/1**

1U2- **5** *shd* **Dell' Arca (IRE)**[32] 4147 5-10-13 **141**............................ TomScudamore 143
(David Pipe) *lw: wl plcd bhd ldrs: brought to chal 2 out: upsides bef last: no ex flat* **8/1**[1]

226- **6** *1 ¾* **Timesremembered (IRE)**[46] 3896 6-11-1 **143**................ LeightonAspell 143
(Emma Lavelle) *t.k.h: hld up in midfield: prog and in tch 3 out: tried to cl after 2 out: one pce* **33/1**

4/4- **7** *hd* **Noble Prince (GER)**[87] 3123 10-10-9 **137**..........................(p) MPFogarty 137
(Paul Nolan, Ire) *hld up in rr: stdy prog fr 7th: wl in tch and gng wl 3 out: mstke 2 out: tried to rally bef last: one pce* **66/1**

235- **8** *1 ½* **Sametegal (FR)**[38] 4056 5-11-8 **150**...................................... DarylJacob 148
(Paul Nicholls) *lw: wl plcd on inner in ldng gp: stl wl there 2 out: fdd jst bef last* **25/1**

060- **9** *2 ½* **Edgardo Sol (FR)**[89] 3069 7-11-0 **145**.................... HarryDerham(3) 141
(Paul Nicholls) *wl plcd bhd ldrs: cl up fr 3 out tl nt qckn after next: fdd last* **40/1**

010- **10** *1 ¾* **Vendor (FR)**[32] 4147 6-10-10 **138**.. JackDoyle 132
(Alan King) *hld up and in last early: prog after 7th: in tch after 3 out but hanging: no imp whn mstke last* **11/1**[2]

424- **11** *shd* **Son Of Flicka**[21] 4346 10-10-7 **135**............................ DougieCostello 129
(Tony Coyle) *mde most: rdn and hdd 2 out: steadily wknd* **25/1**

020/ **12** *½* **Clerk's Choice (IRE)**[27] 5352 8-11-5 **147**........................ AidanColeman 141
(William Jarvis) *hld up wl in rr: sme prog bef 3 out but nvr really on terms w ldrs: no hdwy bef last* **40/1**

/P2- **13** *½* **Meister Eckhart (IRE)**[17] 4441 8-11-7 **149**................... RobertThornton 142
(Alan King) *in tch in midfield: sme prog to chse ldrs after 7th: in tch 3 out: wknd after 2 out* **16/1**

/03- **14** *½* **Clondaw Kaempfer (IRE)**[95] 2935 6-10-10 **138**........... RichardJohnson 133
(Donald McCain) *w ldr: rdn to ld and mstke 2 out: hdd & wknd qckly bef last* **14/1**

125- **15** *3 ½* **Ifandbutwhynot (IRE)**[53] 3779 8-10-12 **140**.....................[1] BryanCooper 129
(David O'Meara) *hld up wl in rr: tried to make prog after 7th but nt on terms w main gp 3 out: no hdwy after* **20/1**

/1F- **16** *4* **Magnifique Etoile**[109] 2665 7-11-6 **148**.................................. NoelFehily 133
(Charlie Longsdon) *hld up towards rr on outer: prog fr 7th and in tch in main gp 3 out: wknd after 2 out* **20/1**

2P0/ **17** *1* **Sadler's Risk (IRE)**[38] 4061 6-11-3 **145**................................. PCarberry 129
(Henry De Bromhead, Ire) *lw: a wl in rr: nt in tch after 7th: no ch after* **33/1**

/24- **18** *2 ¾* **Oscars Well (IRE)**[38] 4061 9-11-0 **149**.......................... SAShortall(7) 134
(A J Martin, Ire) *blnd 2nd: in rr: trying to make prog but u.p whn blnd bdly 2 out: wknd* **25/1**

/44- **18** *dht* **Cotton Mill**[102] 2821 7-11-6 **148**.......................................(b) DenisO'Regan 129
(John Ferguson) *lw: t.k.h: pressed ldng pair tl wknd qckly after 2 out* **20/1**

22F/ **20** *½* **Waaheb (USA)**[67] 3543 7-11-0 **142**......................................(p) MarkWalsh 123
(D K Weld, Ire) *in tch tl mstke and wknd 3 out* **20/1**

24F- **21** *21* **Far West (FR)**[32] 4147 5-11-6 **148**................................... NickScholfield 108
(Paul Nicholls) *lw: wl in tch: trckd ldrs after 7th: lost pl qckly 3 out: sn eased* **20/1**

061- **22** *4* **Calculated Risk**[76] 3273 5-10-8 **136**...................................... BrianHughes 92
(John Quinn) *mstke 2nd: nvr beyond midfield: struggling whn mstke 7th: sn bhd: t.o* **33/1**

160- **23** *15* **Foxcub (IRE)**[25] 4264 6-10-7 **135**... FelixDeGiles 76
(Tom Symonds) *j.rt: racd wd: prom: sing to lose pl whn blnd and hmpd 3 out: t.o* **80/1**

/31- **P** **Dunguib (IRE)**[24] 4312 11-11-12 **154**................................ BrianO'Connell
(Philip Fenton, Ire) *j. bdly: trckd ldrs tl wknd after 7th: wl bhd whn p.u bef 3 out: lame* **14/1**

312- **P** **Yesyoucan (IRE)**[47] 3881 9-10-11 **139**...................... WayneHutchinson
(Brian Ellison) *lw: pressed ldrs tl wknd qckly 7th: t.o whn p.u bef last* **40/1**

651- **F** **Kaylif Aramis**[25] 4264 7-10-10 **138**.......................(t) SamTwiston-Davies
(Nigel Twiston-Davies) *hld up towards rr: mstke 3rd: prog 7th: in tch on outer whn fell 3 out* **20/1**

1F4- **P** **Indevan**[116] 2505 6-10-9 **137**... RWalsh
(W P Mullins, Ire) *mstke 3rd: a wl in rr: mstke 7th: t.o whn p.u bef 2 out* **16/1**

6P6- **P** **Party Rock (IRE)**[34] 4112 7-10-12 **140**................................. DavyRussell
(Jennie Candlish) *lost tch after 4th: t.o whn p.u bef 6th* **28/1**

4m 58.7s (-14.70) **Going Correction** -0.375s/f (Good) **28** Ran SP% **133.5**
Speed ratings (Par 113): **113,112,112,111,111 110,110,110,109,108 108,108,108,108,106 105,104,103,103,103 95,94,88, ,**
CSF £134.29 CT £1962.47 TOTE £17.00: £4.60, £2.60, £2.90, £7.60; EX 262.30 Trifecta £5861.30.
Owner Walters Plant Hire Ltd **Bred** Hubert & Sandra Hosselet **Trained** Upper Lambourn, Berks
■ The first festival win for amateur Nico de Boinville.
■ Stewards' Enquiry : S A Shortall five-day ban: used whip when out of contention (Mar 26-30)
Davy Condon two-day ban: used whip above permitted level (Mar 26-27)

FOCUS
The first of the week's big-field handicap hurdles was predictably an impossible-looking puzzle to work out, with so many of the field holding claims on bits and pieces of form in the past. The early gallop didn't appear overly strong (the winning time was almost four seconds slower than the Neptune) and it paid to be in mid-division at worst. The time was relatively slow compared with the earlier novice event but the form looks solid enough.

4753 BETVICTOR QUEEN MOTHER CHAMPION CHASE GRADE 1 (13 fncs) 2m
3:20 (3:20) (Class 1) 5-Y-O+

£199,325 (£74,795; £37,450; £18,655; £9,380; £4,690)

Form RPR

111- **1** **Sire De Grugy (FR)**[53] 3773 8-11-10 **169**............................. JamieMoore 173+
(Gary Moore) *lw: hld towards rr and confidently rdn: stdy hdwy fr 4 out to trck ldrs 3 out: travelling wl whn chal next: led sn after: drvn clr run-in* **11/4**[1]

12U- **2** *6* **Somersby (IRE)**[53] 3773 10-11-10 **164**......................(p) DominicElsworth 167
(Mick Channon) *trckd ldrs: lft in narrow ld 4th: hdd bef next: led after 8th: hdd after 4 out: hit 3 out: led again appr 2 out: sn jnd: hdd sn after: styd on same pce run-in* **14/1**

241- **3** *nk* **Module (FR)**[32] 4146 7-11-10 **157**...................................... PaddyBrennan 166
(Tom George) *in tch: hit 5th: hdwy 9th: sn pushed along: outpcd 3 out: rallied u.p fr 2 out: fin wl to press for 2nd clsng stages but nvr any ch w wnr* **20/1**

124- **4** *3 ¼* **Sizing Europe (IRE)**[75] 3338 12-11-10 **168**..........................(p) AELynch 162
(Henry De Bromhead, Ire) *lw: chsd ldrs: chal fr 4 out to next: stl upsides u.p 2 out: no ex last* **11/1**

621- **5** *3 ½* **Wishfull Thinking**[46] 3887 11-11-10 **162**.....................(t) RichardJohnson 160
(Philip Hobbs) *lw: in rr: stl plenty to do and u.p after 3 out: styd on wl fr last but nt rch ldrs* **18/1**

U34- **6** *2 ½* **Special Tiara**[38] 4062 7-11-10 **155**.. DavyRussell 160+
(Henry De Bromhead, Ire) *led: hit 3rd: blnd and hdd 4th: led again bef next: hdd 6th: styd pressing ldrs tl led again after 4 out: hdd appr 3 out: wknd 2 out* **16/1**

/10- **7** *29* **Kid Cassidy (IRE)**[75] 3338 8-11-10 **160**................................... APMcCoy 127
(Nicky Henderson) *in rr and j.rt at times: mstke 3rd: j.big 4th: stl off pce but nt asked for serious effrt whn bdly hmpd 4 out and no ch after* **10/1**

131- **P** **Arvika Ligeonniere (FR)**[38] 4062 9-11-10 **166**.......................... RWalsh
(W P Mullins, Ire) *pressed ldrs led 6th: blnd 8th: hdd sn after: wknd qckly after 4 out: t.o whn p.u bef 2 out* **8/1**[3]

252- **F** **Baily Green (IRE)**[31] 4182 8-11-10 **154**..................................... DJCasey
(M F Morris, Ire) *in tch: mstke 3rd: stdy hdwy 9th: trcking ldrs: travelling ok and disputing 3 l 4th whn fell 4 out* **14/1**

/11- **U** **Hinterland (FR)**[95] 2950 6-11-10 **154**...................................... NoelFehily
(Paul Nicholls) *lw: t.k.h: stdy hdwy to cl on ldrs and nt asked serious question whn bdly hmpd and uns rdr 4 out* **11/1**

1/3- **P** **Captain Conan (FR)**[95] 2952 7-11-10 **161**........................ BarryGeraghty
(Nicky Henderson) *nt fluent 2nd: in rr: j. slowly 5th and nvr travelling after: p.u bef 7th: lame* **7/2**[2]

3m 48.49s (-9.51) **Going Correction** -0.275s/f (Good) **11** Ran SP% **115.0**
Speed ratings: **112,109,108,107,105 104,89, , ,**
CSF £40.57 TOTE £3.50: £1.70, £3.90, £5.60; EX 45.40 Trifecta £786.40.
Owner The Preston Family & Friends Ltd **Bred** La Grugerie **Trained** Lower Beeding, W Sussex
■ Jamie Moore's first festival winner.

FOCUS
No Sprinter Sacre, so this year's race certainly had a "best of the rest" feel to it. Sire De Grugy is rated to his Ascot mark in a strongly renewal with Somersby to the level of his Tingle Creek run.

4754 GLENFARCLAS H'CAP CHASE (A CROSS COUNTRY CHASE) (32 fncs) 3m 7f
4:00 (4:00) (Class 2) 5-Y-O+

£31,280 (£9,240; £4,620; £2,310; £1,155; £580)

Form RPR

111- **1** **Balthazar King (IRE)**[117] 2491 10-11-12 **150**............... RichardJohnson 156
(Philip Hobbs) *prom: trckd ldr 27th: led next: hrd pressed fr last: hld on gamely nr fin* **4/1**[2]

325- **2** *shd* **Any Currency (IRE)**[60] 3655 11-10-8 **132**..........................(p) IanPopham 138
(Martin Keighley) *trckd ldr 5th: pckd 20th urged along 23rd: rdn to ld 25th: hdd 27th: rallied to chal last: upsides and edgd rt flat: jst failed* **10/1**

421/ **3** *3* **Big Shu (IRE)**[38] 4063 9-11-9 **147**...(t) PCarberry 149
(Peter Maher, Ire) *patiently rdn in rr: stdy prog fr 25th: jnd ldrs 3 out: chal bef last: one pce flat* **3/1**[1]

026- **4** *5* **Duke Of Lucca (IRE)**[89] 3067 9-10-10 **134**.....................(bt) TomO'Brien 133
(Philip Hobbs) *pressed ldr to 5th: styd prom: clr of rest in ldng quartet fr 3 out: drvn and one pce on long run bef last* **25/1**

5/U- **5** *16* **Sizing Australia (IRE)**[24] 4316 12-10-13 **137**.........................(p) AELynch 120
(Henry De Bromhead, Ire) *pressed ldrs: lost pl fr 18th: no hdwy 25th: tk poor 5th last* **20/1**

6 *4 ½* **A Stray Shot (IRE)**[38] 4063 7-10-7 **131**................................ MsKWalsh 110
(G M O'Neill, Ire) *towards rr: sme prog fr 23rd: rchd poor 5th 3 out: no hdwy after* **25/1**

/2P- **7** *3 ¾* **Uncle Junior (IRE)**[38] 4064 13-11-10 **148**........................ MrPWMullins 124
(W P Mullins, Ire) *swtg: nvr gng wl: a towards rr: no ch fr 4 out* **25/1**

061- **8** *½* **Sire Collonges (FR)**[89] 3068 8-11-7 **145**..........................(p) RyanMahon 121
(Paul Nicholls) *led at gd pce: hdd 25th: lost 2nd 27th: steadily wknd* **9/1**

F/0- **9** *nk* **Quiscover Fontaine (FR)**[38] 4063 10-10-9 **133**.........(p) RichieMcLernon 108
(E Bolger, Ire) *hld up towards rr: trying to make prog but plenty to do whn blnd 28th: no ch after* **25/1**

00/ **10** *19* **Love Rory (IRE)**[38] 4063 6-11-7 **145**.. APHeskin 103
(E Bolger, Ire) *lw: trckd ldng gp: no prog 25th: wknd after next: t.o* **10/1**

1PP- **11** *23* **Hey Big Spender (IRE)**[60] 3655 11-11-7 **145**......................... JoeTizzard 82
(Colin Tizzard) *wl in tch in midfield: wknd 24th: t.o* **33/1**

006/ **12** *3 ½* **Star Neuville (FR)**[18] 4434 8-10-6 **130**............................ DannyMullins 64
(E Bolger, Ire) *hld up in rr: mstke and hmpd 2nd: trying to make prog whn mstke 20th: no hdwy after: wl btn fr 27th: t.o* **7/1**[3]

/20- **13** *15* **Quantitativeeasing (IRE)**[45] 9-11-8 **146**............................ MarkWalsh 67
(E Bolger, Ire) *a in rr: wl bhd fr 25th: t.o* **16/1**

34F- **P** **Diamond Harry**[62] 3617 11-10-9 **133**......................................(t) DarylJacob
(Nick Williams) *swtg: nvr on terms w ldrs: wknd and p.u bef 23rd* **20/1**

U/4- **P** **Bishopsfurze (IRE)**[38] 4063 9-10-12 **136**.................................. DJCasey
(W P Mullins, Ire) *blnd bdly 2nd: nvr a factor: t.o whn p.u after 24th* **14/1**

50- **P** **Sin Palo (IRE)**[75] 3341 10-10-7 **131**...................................... PaulTownend
(W P Mullins, Ire) *chsd ldrs early: lost pl fr 18th: wl bhd whn clambered over 24th and p.u* **66/1**

8m 19.2s (-18.80) **Going Correction** -0.275s/f (Good) **16** Ran SP% **127.6**
Speed ratings: **113,112,112,110,106 105,104,104,104,99 93,92,88, ,**
CSF £40.71 CT £143.13 TOTE £4.70: £1.80, £2.70, £1.40, £6.50; EX 52.20 Trifecta £197.20.
Owner The Brushmakers **Bred** Sunnyhill Stud **Trained** Withycombe, Somerset
■ Stewards' Enquiry : Ian Popham four-day ban: used whip above permitted level (Mar 26-29)
Richard Johnson four-day ban: used whip above permitted level (Mar 26-29)

FOCUS
The form of this event usually has little relevance in conventional races, but it has produced plenty of specialists down the years, mainly based in Ireland, and the last three winners of the contest all took their chance again. It was one of the previous winners who got the job done. A personal best from the winner to beat the very solid Any Currency.

4755 FRED WINTER JUVENILE H'CAP HURDLE GRADE 3 (8 hdls) 2m 110y
4:40 (4:40) (Class 1) 4-Y-O

£42,712 (£16,027; £8,025; £3,997; £2,010; £1,005)

Form RPR

216- **1** **Hawk High (IRE)**[25] 4268 4-11-1 **130**................................(p) BrianHughes 128
(Tim Easterby) *trckd ldrs: drvn to press ldr last: led sn after: styd on strly clsng stages* **33/1**

The Form Book Jumps, Raceform Ltd, Compton, RG20 6NL.

2 ¾ **Katgary (FR)**[119] 4-11-1 **130** DarylJacob 130+
(Paul Nicholls) *w'like: chsd ldrs: rdn appr last to dispute 2nd: chsd wnr fnl 50yds: kpt on but a hld* **8/1**

36- **3** 1¾ **Orgilgo Bay (IRE)**[31] 4178 4-10-9 **127** [1] MarkBolger(3) 122
(John C McConnell, Ire) *athletic: lw: chsd ldr fr 2nd: lef in ld 2 out: sn rdn: jnd last: hdd sn after: styd on one pce and dropped to 3rd fnl 50yds* **16/1**

142- **4** ½ **Keltus (FR)**[90] 3031 4-10-13 **128** NickScholfield 124+
(Paul Nicholls) *t.k.h: hmpd 2nd: wl in tch: hdwy after 2 out: styd on wl appr last: fin strly: nt rch ldrs* **25/1**

612- **5** 2 **Baradari (IRE)**[34] 4111 4-11-4 **133** AidanColeman 126
(Venetia Williams) *in rr: stl plenty to do after fr 2 out: hdwy appr last: fin wl: gng on cl home* **16/1**

321- **6** nk **Raven's Tower (USA)**[19] 4401 4-10-13 **128** DavidBass 121
(Ben Pauling) *in rr: hdwy after 3 out: styd on wl appr last: kpt on clsng stages* **40/1**

43- **7** nk **Solar Impulse (FR)**[18] 4419 4-11-3 **135** (t) HarryDerham(3) 128
(Paul Nicholls) *hmpd 2nd: in tch: hdwy fr 3 out: rdn to chse ldrs appr last: one pce run-in* **25/1**

43- **8** 1 **Gerdago (IRE)**[18] 4432 4-11-9 **138** (t) EddieO'Connell 129
(K J Condon, Ire) *in rr: hdwy after 3 out: chsd ldrs u.p after 2 out: one pce fr last* **40/1**

124- **9** nk **Handiwork**[25] 4268 4-11-1 **130** (p) SamTwiston-Davies 120
(Steve Gollings) *in rr: drvn along fr 2 out: styd u.p appr last: gng on clsng satges* **33/1**

134- **10** 2¼ **Violet Dancer**[34] 4111 4-11-1 **130** JamieMoore 120
(Gary Moore) *lw: hmpd 2nd: sn in tch: chsd ldrs and nt fluent 3 out: wknd bef last* **20/1**

2- **11** 1¾ **Noble Inn (FR)**[48] 3864 4-11-10 **139** PaulTownend 128
(W P Mullins, Ire) *hmpd 2nd: in tch: blnd 3rd: wknd fr 2 out* **20/1**

4- **12** ¾ **Ivan Grozny (FR)**[31] 4178 4-11-7 **136** (t) RWalsh 123
(W P Mullins, Ire) *in tch: hdwy 3 out: wknd after 2 out* **7/1**[2]

112- **13** 2 **Dawalan (FR)**[40] 4023 4-11-4 **133** (p) BarryGeraghty 118
(Nicky Henderson) *in rr: hdwy 4 out: in tch and rdn 2 out: sn wknd* **7/2**[1]

133- **14** 3¼ **Vandross (IRE)**[34] 4112 4-10-13 **128** LeightonAspell 108
(Neil King) *in rr: sme hdwy 3 out: wknd next* **100/1**

312- **15** 1¼ **Certification (IRE)**[24] 4307 4-10-13 **128** (b1) DenisO'Regan 108
(John Ferguson) *hmpd 2nd: in tch fr 3rd: wknd: 2 out* **28/1**

4- **16** ½ **Arzembouy Premier (FR)**[48] 3864 4-11-6 **135** PCarberry 115
(Gordon Elliott, Ire) *hmpd 2nd: in rr: sme hdwy appr 2 out: sn btn* **20/1**

13- **17** 2½ **Azza (FR)**[116] 2500 4-11-0 **129** (t) TomScudamore 107
(David Pipe) *led tl hdd 2 out: sn wknd* **16/1**

252- **18** 23 **Cadoudoff (FR)**[74] 3364 4-11-3 **132** NoelFehily 85
(Charlie Longsdon) *lw: in rr: sme hdwy 4 out: wknd after 3 out* **40/1**

19 3¼ **Le Fin Bois (FR)**[122] 4-11-8 **137** RichardJohnson 87
(Tim Vaughan) *lw: sn chsng ldrs: wknd bef 2 out* **25/1**

314- **P** **Ballyglasheen (IRE)**[46] 3885 4-11-6 **135** (v1) PaulMoloney
(Evan Williams) *in tch whn bdly hmpd 2nd: t.o whn p.u after 3rd* **25/1**

321- **B** **Akdam (IRE)**[11] 3851 4-10-7 **127** (p) JoshHamer(5) 119
(Tony Carroll) *chsd ldrs: stl travelling ok and wl there whn b.d 2 out: fatally injured* **40/1**

165- **B** **Goodwood Mirage (IRE)**[18] 4419 4-11-3 **132** APMcCoy
(Jonjo O'Neill) *lw: mid-div whn hmpd and b.d 2nd* **15/2**[3]

322- **F** **Clarcam (FR)**[38] 4054 4-11-4 **133** (t) BryanCooper 128+
(Gordon Elliott, Ire) *chsd ldrs: tk slt advantage and travelling ok whn fell 2 out* **16/1**

41- **F** **Astre De La Cour (FR)**[53] 3768 4-11-1 **130** WayneHutchinson
(Robert Walford) *lw: chsng ldrs whn fell 2nd* **20/1**

3m 52.19s (-9.81) **Going Correction** -0.375s/f (Good) course record **24** Ran SP% **135.6**
Speed ratings: **108,107,106,106,105 105,105,104,104,103 102,102,101,100,99 99,98,87,85, , , ,EM**
CSF £253.33 CT £4444.64 TOTE £55.00: £9.30, £2.40, £4.30, £8.00; EX 642.60 Trifecta £9340.10.
Owner Trevor Hemmings **Bred** Gleadhill House Stud Ltd **Trained** Great Habton, N Yorks
■ Brian Hughes's first Cheltenham festival winner.

FOCUS
This was always going to be a difficult race to work out, but the drying ground added an extra element of confusion considering most of the hurdling form on offer had come in deep winter going. It also saw a couple of significant incidents at the second flight and the second-last, which meant plenty of horses were hampered to some degree. A solid enough renewal if lacking future stars. Hawk High improved towards the leevl of his Flat form.

4756 WEATHERBYS CHAMPION BUMPER (A STANDARD OPEN NATIONAL HUNT FLAT RACE) GRADE 1 2m 110y
5:15 (5:15) (Class 1) 4-6-Y-O
£34,170 (£12,822; £6,420; £3,198; £1,608; £804)

Form RPR

1 **Silver Concorde**[74] 3377 6-11-5 119 MrRPMcNamara 140+
(D K Weld, Ire) *lengthy: hld up in midfield: stdy prog on inner over 3f out: clsd to chal over 1f out: rdn to ld jst ins fnl f: edgd rt but styd on wl* **16/1**

2 1½ **Shaneshill (IRE)**[102] 2837 5-11-5 128 RWalsh 137
(W P Mullins, Ire) *lw: wl plcd bhd ldrs: clsd 3f out on inner: rdn to ld over 1f out: hdd jst ins fnl f: styd on but hld after* **7/2**[1]

2- **3** 1¾ **Joshua Lane (IRE)**[82] 3187 5-11-5 121 BarryGeraghty 135
(Edward P Harty, Ire) *athletic: hld up towards rr: prog 6f out: trckd ldrs over 2f out: sn rdn: styd on fnl f to take 3rd nr fin* **33/1**

1- **4** ½ **Black Hercules (IRE)**[48] 3870 5-11-5 130 MrPWMullins 135
(W P Mullins, Ire) *str: lengthy: lw: led at gd pce: drvn and hdd over 1f out: one pce after* **13/2**[3]

5 ½ **Vigil (IRE)**[31] 4185 5-11-5 128 PatSmullen 134
(D K Weld, Ire) *wl plcd bhd ldrs: prog and disp 2nd over 2f out: rdn and one pce wl over 1f out* **5/1**[2]

6 ¾ **Killultagh Vic (IRE)**[17] 4459 5-11-5 136 PaulTownend 136+
(W P Mullins, Ire) *wl in tch: n.m.r 5f out: rdn wl over 2f out: nt qckn and kpt on same pce after* **8/1**

11- **7** 3¾ **Definitly Red (IRE)**[32] 4149 5-11-5 124 APMcCoy 130
(Steve Gollings) *tall: chsd ldr to over 2f out: steadily fdd* **25/1**

11- **8** 1¾ **Modus**[70] 3460 4-10-11 130 TomO'Brien 120+
(Robert Stephens) *athletic: racd wd: hld up: prog into midfield 6f out: hdwy to dispute 2nd over 2f out: wknd over 1f out* **10/1**

4- **9** 2¾ **Royal Vacation (IRE)**[25] 4267 4-10-11 112 PaddyBrennan 117
(Colin Tizzard) *tall: wl in rr: rdn and stl towards rr over 3f out: kpt on fnl 2f: n.d* **50/1**

215- **10** shd **Oscarteea (IRE)**[82] 3187 5-11-5 115 (t) AidanColeman 125
(Anthony Honeyball) *mostly in last quartet: shkn up and outpcd fr 4f out: styd on fr over 1f out* **66/1**

3/ **11** 1 **Golantilla (IRE)**[17] 4459 6-11-5 129 DannyMullins 124
(A J Martin, Ire) *trckd ldrs: wl there over 2f out: sn rdn and steadily wknd* **16/1**

0- **12** 1¼ **Neck Or Nothing (GER)**[115] 2534 5-11-5 117 RichardJohnson 123
(Philip Hobbs) *t.k.h: hld up in rr: sme prog fr 3f out: no hdwy wl over 1f out: hanging and wknd* **20/1**

13 1 **Value At Risk**[73] 3405 5-11-5 122 BrianO'Connell 123
(Philip Fenton, Ire) *str: trckd ldrs: trbld passage fr over 5f out to over 3f out: wknd 2f out* **22/1**

1- **14** ½ **El Namoose**[54] 3760 5-11-5 118 DenisO'Regan 122
(John Ferguson) *well-made: t.k.h: hld up in midfield: sme prog 3f out and gng wl: rdn and no rspnse 2f out: wknd* **16/1**

211- **15** 1½ **Zeroeshadesofgrey (IRE)**[21] 4349 5-11-5 120 JamieMoore 120
(Neil King) *lengthy: a towards rr: rdn and brief effrt over 2f out: sn wknd* **66/1**

110- **16** 1½ **Coyaba**[70] 3460 4-10-11 121 IanPopham 111
(Martin Keighley) *str: hld up in last quartet: rdn and no prog 3f out* **100/1**

13- **17** ½ **Our Kaempfer (IRE)**[115] 2534 5-11-5 127 NoelFehily 118
(Charlie Longsdon) *lw: t.k.h: chsd ldr to 3f out: lost pl rapidly and wknd over 2f out* **25/1**

111/ **18** 2¾ **Izzini (IRE)**[325] 5429 6-10-12 115 MrSCrawford 108
(S R B Crawford, Ire) *leggy: athletic: hld up in last quartet: shkn up and no prog over 2f out* **50/1**

/21- **19** hd **Assam Black (IRE)**[118] 2479 6-11-5 118 RyanMahon 115
(Harry Fry) *t.k.h in midfield: wknd over 2f out* **66/1**

/21- **20** 9 **Third Act (IRE)**[33] 4135 5-11-5 122 JoeTizzard 106
(Colin Tizzard) *tall: str: prom: rdn over 4f out: wknd 3f out* **33/1**

213- **21** 70 **Mountain Of Mourne (IRE)**[32] 4149 5-11-5 114 MrCSmith 36
(Linda Blackford) *str: prom tl rdn and wknd 6f out: wl t.o* **150/1**

P **Stack The Deck (IRE)**[48] 3870 5-11-5 119 DavyRussell
(P A Fahy, Ire) *in tch 10f: t.o whn p.u over 3f out: fatally injured* **33/1**

3m 43.4s (-13.00) **Going Correction** -0.375s/f (Good)
WFA 4 from 5yo+ 7lb **22** Ran SP% **125.7**
Speed ratings: **115,114,113,113,113 112,110,110,108,108 108,107,107,106,106 105,105,104,103,99 66,**
CSF £62.86 TOTE £21.10: £5.00, £2.30, £7.70; EX 124.30 Trifecta £4084.90.
Owner Dr R Lambe **Bred** Mrs Anne Coughlan **Trained** The Curragh, Co Kildare
■ A first festival winner for Robbie McNamara.

FOCUS
Unsurprisingly for a race full of lightly raced horses doing something most have never tried before (racing at pace on good ground) there have been plenty of shock results in this event. Even the last two winners, both trained by Willie Mullins, were sent off at generous odds and were not the stable's first string. Not for the first time, Irish-trained runners dominated. This looked a pretty deep renewal, well up to standard.
T/Jkpt: Not won. T/Plt: £193.20 to a £1 stake. Pool: £1219633.10 - 4607.30 winning tickets
T/Qpdt: £56.20 to a £1 stake. Pool: £36117.49 - 475.42 winning tickets JN

4569 HUNTINGDON (R-H)
Wednesday, March 12

OFFICIAL GOING: Good to soft (chs 6.7; hdl 7.3)
Wind: Light across Weather: Hazy

4757 32RED LADY RIDERS' H'CAP HURDLE (8 hdls) 2m 110y
1:45 (1:45) (Class 5) (0-100,100) 4-Y-O+ **£2,274** (£667; £333; £166)

Form RPR

4FP- **1** **Delphi Mountain (IRE)**[43] 3959 9-11-5 **100** (bt) MissEKelly(7) 105
(Richard Woollacott) *hld up: hdwy after 3rd: chsd ldr after 3 out: led last: rdn out* **8/1**

634- **2** ¾ **Daliance (IRE)**[22] 3871 5-11-4 **99** MissBAndrews(7) 103
(Neil King) *hld up: pushed along and hdwy appr 3 out: rdn after next: r.o: nt quite rch wnr* **10/3**[1]

500- **3** 1½ **Drummond**[17] 4447 5-9-7 **74** (bt) MissJodieHughes(7) 78
(Bernard Llewellyn) *chsd ldrs: led 3 out: wnt lft next: rdn and hdd last: styd on same pce towards fin* **22/1**

31P- **4** 9 **Allerton (IRE)**[80] 3223 7-11-0 **95** (t) MissAEStirling(7) 90
(Fergal O'Brien) *hld up: pushed along after 5th: styd on to go 4th nr fin: nvr nrr* **9/2**[3]

36P- **5** ¾ **The Sneezer (IRE)**[43] 3960 11-10-12 **93** MrsAlexDunn(7) 87
(Alexandra Dunn) *racd keenly: disp ld tl wnt on after 3rd: hdd 3 out: wknd appr last* **12/1**

0P6- **6** 11 **Orlittlebylittle**[15] 4475 8-11-0 **95** (b) MissKYoung(7) 79
(Donald McCain) *trckd ldrs: j.lft 5th: rdn and wknd after 3 out* **14/1**

554- **7** 11 **Stag Hill (IRE)**[35] 3188 5-11-0 **93** (t) MissGAndrews(5) 67
(Bernard Llewellyn) *hld up: hdwy and j.lft 5th: wknd after next* **7/2**[2]

1PP- **8** 2¼ **Bathwick Junior**[58] 3692 7-11-3 **91** LucyAlexander 63
(Michael Blake) *prom: lost pl 4th: rdn after next: wknd 3 out* **7/1**

/PP **U** **Graylyn Amber**[65] 3570 9-10-0 **81** [1] MissCareyWilliamson(7)
(Robert Eddery) *plld hrd: disp ld tl after 3rd: jnd ldr agin 5th: wknd after 3 out: in rr whn blnd and uns rdr next* **20/1**

3m 55.4s (0.50) **Going Correction** +0.10s/f (Yiel) **9** Ran SP% **110.6**
Speed ratings (Par 103): **102,101,100,96,96 91,86,84,**
CSF £33.30 CT £535.10 TOTE £11.00: £3.00, £1.10, £5.90; EX 39.30 Trifecta £1092.40.
Owner D Stevens & Mrs S Stevens **Bred** Tim Hegarty **Trained** South Molton, Devon

FOCUS
They went a good clip in this very modest handicap.

4758 32RED CASINO MAIDEN HURDLE (8 hdls) 2m 110y
2:20 (2:20) (Class 4) 4-Y-O+ **£3,249** (£954; £477; £238)

Form RPR

000/ **1** **Speedy Tunes (IRE)**[325] 5438 7-11-1 0 AndrewTinkler 113
(Nicky Henderson) *chsd ldr: led 3rd to next: led 5th: rdn appr last: edgd rt flat: r.o* **7/2**[2]

2 ½ **Unex Modigliani (IRE)**[320] 5-11-1 0 (t) HarrySkelton 112
(Dan Skelton) *hld up: racd keenly: hdwy 5th: chsd wnr 2 out: rdn and ev ch last: r.o* **11/1**

6- **3** 2¾ **May Be Some Time**[90] 3034 6-11-1 0 (t) ConorO'Farrell 112+
(Stuart Kittow) *in rr: hdwy 3 out: rdn appr last: r.o* **5/1**[3]

P- **4** 1 **Shubaat**[69] 3506 7-10-12 0 JackQuinlan(3) 110
(John Ferguson) *trckd ldrs: racd keenly: chsd wnr 3 out: mstke next: sn rdn: styd on same pce flat* **9/4**[1]

5 21 **Capitol Gain (IRE)**[69] 5-11-1 0 GerardTumelty 90
(George Baker) *chsd ldrs: pushed along 4th: wknd 2 out* **25/1**

30U- **6** 1¾ **Warrant Officer**[16] 4469 4-10-7 110 MarcGoldstein 81
(Sheena West) *chsd ldrs: ev ch 3 out: sn rdn: wknd next* **12/1**

64P- **7** *8* **Eastern Witness (IRE)**[18] 4411 7-11-1 0........................ LiamTreadwell 81
(Venetia Williams) *mid-div: hdwy 5th: rdn and wknd appr 2 out* **14/1**

54- **8** *4 ½* **Ilewindelilah**[234] 1064 6-10-8 0.. JamesDavies 70
(Gary Brown) *hld up: pushed along 5th: wknd next* **100/1**

/0P- **9** *4* **Royalracket (IRE)**[84] 3163 6-10-12 0................................ JamesBest(3) 74
(Paul Webber) *mid-div: hdwy 5th: rdn and wknd appr 2 out* **50/1**

4/0- **10** *¾* **Jackthejourneyman (IRE)**[299] 359 5-11-1 0................ JamesReveley 73
(Tom Gretton) *hld up: hdwy after 5th: rdn and hung lft after 3 out: sn wknd* **25/1**

00- **11** *10* **Offherocker**[10] 4569 7-10-1 0... JWStevenson(7) 57
(Claire Dyson) *hld up: wknd appr 3 out* **150/1**

500- **12** *nk* **Veyranno (FR)**[49] 3838 5-11-1 0...(t) AlainCawley 64
(Tom George) *hld up: wknd after 5th* **100/1**

00- **13** *1 ½* **Flobury**[24] 4310 6-10-8 0.. SamJones 55
(Barry Leavy) *in rr whn j.rt 2nd: bhd fr 4th* **125/1**

14 *4 ½* **Run Rabbit Run**[997] 6-10-12 0.. PeterCarberry(3) 58
(Tim McCarthy) *prom: hit 1st: rdn and wknd after 5th* **25/1**

30- **15** *20* **The Selector**[97] 2906 5-10-8 0.. TomCannon 33
(Chris Gordon) *led to 3rd: led again next: hdd 5th: wknd 3 out* **100/1**

/P4- **16** *29* **Classic Rally (IRE)**[20] 4379 8-11-1 0.................................. CharliePoste 14
(Malcolm Jefferson) *chsd ldrs: j.rt 2nd: rdn and wknd after 5th: b.b.v* **9/1**

3m 54.5s (-0.40) **Going Correction** +0.10s/f (Yiel)
WFA 4 from 5yo+ 7lb **16** Ran SP% **120.3**
Speed ratings (Par 105): **104,103,102,102,92 91,87,85,83,83 78,78,77,75,66 52**
CSF £38.64 TOTE £3.80: £1.60, £3.40, £2.70; EX 37.60 Trifecta £211.40.
Owner Jimmy Hack Racing Partners **Bred** Neil R Tector **Trained** Upper Lambourn, Berks

FOCUS
A modest maiden hurdle in which the first four finished well clear. Nicky Henderson has now won three of the last four runnings. The winner stepped up on his previous hurdles form.

4759 BOB BROWN MEMORIAL H'CAP CHASE (19 fncs) 3m
2:55 (2:55) (Class 5) (0-100,100) 5-Y-0+ **£2,599** (£763; £381; £190)

Form RPR

343- **1** **Long Wave (IRE)**[107] 2722 7-11-7 **98**.........................(tp) KielanWoods(3) 113+
(Charlie Longsdon) *chsd ldr tl led 11th: mstke 14th: rdn appr 2 out: styd on* **15/8**[1]

U46- **2** *3 ¼* **Faith Keeper (IRE)**[15] 4481 9-11-7 **100**..................... ConorShoemark(5) 112
(Fergal O'Brien) *chsd ldrs: mstke 8th: wnt 2nd 15th: rdn appr 2 out: hung rt flat: styd on same pce* **9/2**[2]

5P0- **3** *3* **Riddlestown (IRE)**[15] 4482 7-11-7 **95**................................ HarrySkelton 105
(Caroline Fryer) *hld up: hdwy 12th: rdn to go 3rd appr 2 out: styd on: nt rch ldrs* **13/2**[3]

P3P- **4** *8* **Phoenix Des Mottes (FR)**[15] 4486 11-9-9 **74** oh6.......... JoeCornwall(5) 76
(John Cornwall) *led to 11th: chsd wnr to 15th: rdn 3 out: styd on same pce* **33/1**

600/ **5** *30* **Trifollet**[317] 29 9-11-1 **96**... MrJMartin(7) 78
(Andrew J Martin) *prom: outpcd 7th: bhd fr 13th: n.d after* **12/1**

556- **6** *2* **Salut Honore (FR)**[49] 3834 8-11-0 **93**...........................(t) KillianMoore(5) 65
(Alex Hales) *hld up: drvn along 13th: wknd 15th* **12/1**

13F- **7** *2 ¾* **Midnight Charmer**[48] 3855 8-11-2 **95**................................ JamesBanks(5) 65
(Emma Baker) *hld up: sme hdwy 9th: wknd 13th* **9/2**[2]

PUP- **8** *12* **Thorncliffer**[50] 3817 10-10-0 **74** oh2.................................(t) JamesDavies 33
(Derek Shaw) *prom tl wknd 15th* **16/1**

P/P- **P** **Celts Espere**[20] 4383 11-10-3 **77** oh24 ow3......................(p) DaveCrosse
(Trevor Wall) *in rr whn blnd 2nd: bhd fr 4th: p.u bef 7th: b.b.v* **100/1**

0/5- **P** **Rudinero (IRE)**[313] 100 12-10-0 **74** oh21.....................(tp) TommyPhelan
(Barry Brennan) *hld up: bhd fr 9th: p.u bef 11th* **80/1**

6m 2.6s (-7.70) **Going Correction** -0.25s/f (Good) **10** Ran SP% **110.9**
Speed ratings: **102,100,99,97,87 86,85,81, ,**
CSF £10.46 CT £41.30 TOTE £2.40: £1.10, £1.90, £2.10; EX 9.40 Trifecta £55.40.
Owner Neysauteur Partnership **Bred** Michael Long **Trained** Over Norton, Oxon

FOCUS
A moderate handicap chase, but they went a good gallop and the form looks sound if ordinary.

4760 32RED FREE £10 BONUS H'CAP HURDLE (10 hdls) 2m 5f 110y
3:35 (3:35) (Class 4) (0-105,107) 4-Y-0+ **£3,249** (£954; £477; £238)

Form RPR

061- **1** **Drombeg West**[17] 4447 7-10-6 **84**....................................... AndrewTinkler 91
(Anna Brooks) *hld up: hdwy and wnt lft 7th: led 2 out: rdn out* **10/1**

5/0- **2** *3 ¼* **High Kite (IRE)**[24] 4299 8-11-1 **103**.........(p) WilliamFeatherstone(10) 107
(Warren Greatrex) *chsd ldr 2nd tl led 5th: hdd 2 out: no ex flat* **11/2**[3]

6P0- **3** *2* **Hot Whiskey (IRE)**[24] 4299 6-11-8 **100**...........................(t) LiamTreadwell 103
(Brendan Powell) *a.p: rdn after 3 out: styd on same pce appr last* **10/1**

1/5- **4** *1 ¼* **Laughton Park**[313] 89 9-11-3 **98**.................................... MichealNolan(3) 99
(Suzy Smith) *chsd ldrs: rdn appr 2 out: no ex last* **20/1**

006- **5** *½* **Ereyna**[71] 3438 5-11-2 **94**.. SamJones 96
(Renee Robeson) *chsd ldrs: rdn appr 3 out: no ex last* **66/1**

041- **6** *4* **Ghost Of A Smile (IRE)**[10] 4571 6-11-10 **107** 7ex...... RobertMcCarth(5) 106
(Ian Williams) *hld up: mstke 5th: hdwy appr 3 out: wknd after next* **5/2**[1]

343- **7** *11* **El Indio (IRE)**[10] 4571 7-11-5 **104**.................................... GeraldQuinn(7) 91
(Claire Dyson) *led to 5th: remained handy: rdn and wknd appr 2 out* **12/1**

4/4- **8** *5* **Kingsfold Flare**[66] 3556 7-10-12 **90**..................................... JoshuaMoore 77
(Gary Moore) *hld up: nt fluent 2nd: hdwy 7th: wknd 2 out* **14/1**

PPP- **9** *6* **Zelos Diktator**[13] 3553 8-10-3 **81**... MarkGrant 58
(Sean Curran) *hld up: drvn after 6th: sn wknd* **33/1**

055- **10** *nk* **Expanding Universe (IRE)**[13] 4510 7-11-11 **103**.............. LeeEdwards 80
(Tony Carroll) *chsd ldr to 2nd: remained handy tl rdn and wknd after 7th* **20/1**

000- **11** *14* **Dalmo**[33] 4129 5-11-1 **98**.. ChristopherWard(5) 62
(Dr Richard Newland) *hld up: bhd fr 6th* **33/1**

021- **12** *4 ½* **Rugged Jack (FR)**[8] 4604 7-11-2 **99**.........................(t) ConorShoemark(5) 59
(Victor Dartnall) *chsd ldrs tl rdn and wknd after 3 out* **4/1**[2]

06P- **13** *12* **Gilanto (IRE)**[65] 3569 7-11-6 **98**...................................... ConorO'Farrell 48
(Michael Blake) *prom: pushed along and lost pl after 1st: sme hdwy after 5th: rdn and wknd bef next* **50/1**

0/0- **14** *14* **Generous Spender**[12] 4527 8-11-3 **95**.............................. MarcGoldstein 32
(Heather Cobb) *hld up: bhd fr 6th* **80/1**

5m 13.7s (3.10) **Going Correction** +0.10s/f (Yiel) **14** Ran SP% **116.6**
Speed ratings (Par 105): **98,96,96,95,95 94,90,88,86,85 80,79,74,69**
CSF £58.98 CT £571.58 TOTE £10.70: £3.70, £1.70, £1.90; EX 90.40 Trifecta £2186.70.
Owner Mrs J M Owen **Bred** Steve Hadley **Trained** Alderton, Northants

FOCUS
A moderate handicap hurdle. The form is rated around the balance of the second to fourth.

4761 32RED.COM MAIDEN HURDLE (12 hdls) 3m 2f
4:15 (4:15) (Class 4) 4-Y-0+ **£3,249** (£954; £477; £238)

Form RPR

02- **1** **Many Stars (IRE)**[99] 2874 6-11-3 0....................................(t) HarrySkelton 113+
(Dan Skelton) *a.p: led after 3 out: clr last: styd on wl* **5/4**[1]

540- **2** *12* **Royal Palladium (FR)**[89] 3061 6-11-3 104....................... LiamTreadwell 102+
(Venetia Williams) *trckd ldrs: racd keenly: wnt 2nd 7th: hit 9th: led 3 out: sn hdd: styd on same pce fr next: eased whn btn flat* **6/1**[3]

36P- **3** *13* **Tiller Belle**[50] 3816 6-10-10 0.. AndrewTinkler 79
(Nicky Henderson) *hld up: pushed along appr 9th: sn outpcd: wnt 3nd and j.lft 2 out* **14/1**

02- **4** *8* **Mercers Court (IRE)**[16] 4473 6-11-3 0............................ TomMessenger 81
(Neil King) *hld up: hit 5th: hdwy 8th: rdn and wknd after 3 out* **8/1**

52- **5** *10* **The Backup Plan (IRE)**[70] 3448 5-11-3 0........................ HenryBrooke 74
(Donald McCain) *led: racd keenly: mstke 9th: hdd 3 out: sn rdn and wknd* **9/4**[2]

/46- **6** *23* **Arfur Didit (IRE)**[48] 3850 6-11-0 0..................................... JackQuinlan(3) 49
(Sarah Humphrey) *trckd ldr: nt fluent 3rd: lost 2nd 7th: pushed along next: rdn and wknd 9th* **50/1**

06P/ **P** **Montys Cash**[319] 8-11-3 0... JoshuaMoore
(Heather Cobb) *hld up: hdwy 4th: rdn and wknd appr 9th: bhd whn p.u bef 2 out* **125/1**

6m 34.5s (11.60) **Going Correction** +0.10s/f (Yiel) **7** Ran SP% **110.0**
Speed ratings (Par 105): **86,82,78,75,72 65,**
CSF £8.83 TOTE £2.30: £1.10, £3.60; EX 7.80 Trifecta £31.60.
Owner James Hughes,John Hughes,Charles Hughes **Bred** Aidan Aherne **Trained** Alcester, Warwicks

FOCUS
An uncompetitive maiden hurdle run at a steady pace. The first two are rated pretty much to their marks.

4762 32RED ON THE APP STORE H'CAP CHASE (16 fncs) 2m 4f 110y
4:55 (4:55) (Class 5) (0-100,100) 5-Y-0+ **£2,599** (£763; £381; £190)

Form RPR

324- **1** **Bertie's Desire**[91] 3027 6-10-13 **92**................................ ThomasGarner(5) 106+
(Oliver Sherwood) *a.p: chsd ldr 9th: led appr 2 out: clr last: eased nr fin* **11/8**[1]

603- **2** *15* **Topaze Collonges (FR)**[17] 4440 7-11-9 **100**................. KielanWoods(3) 100
(Charlie Longsdon) *led: rdn appr 12th: hdd bef 2 out: wkng whn lft 2nd last* **5/1**[3]

/31- **3** *8* **Orang Outan (FR)**[283] 600 12-11-5 **98**............................ EdCookson(5) 88
(Laura Hurley) *chsd ldr to 11th: remained handy: rdn and wknd after 2 out: lft 3rd last* **14/1**

45P- **4** *7* **Mad Professor (IRE)**[26] 4247 11-9-9 **74** oh12.............(p) JoeCornwall(5) 61
(John Cornwall) *hld up: hdwy 6th: wknd 13th* **66/1**

120- **5** *47* **Osmosia (FR)**[24] 4303 9-11-7 **95**......................................(p) TomCannon 37
(Chris Gordon) *prom: lost pl 9th: wknd 13th* **14/1**

/63- **5** *dht* **Egypt Mill Spirit (IRE)**[15] 4486 8-11-8 **96**........................ AlainCawley 84+
(Tom George) *hld up: nt fluent 1st: mstke next: bhd 8th: hdwy 11th: rdn and wknd 2 out: bhd whn hmpd last* **9/4**[2]

0U0- **F** **Ilewin Kim**[18] 4416 8-10-0 **74** oh4....................................(b[1]) JamesDavies 76
(Gary Brown) *hld up: mstke 1st: hdwy 9th: rdn after 3 out: wnt 7 l 2nd and looked hld whn fell last* **14/1**

5m 4.7s (-0.60) **Going Correction** -0.25s/f (Good) **7** Ran SP% **111.0**
Speed ratings: **91,85,82,79,61 61,**
CSF £8.48 TOTE £2.50: £1.40, £3.20; EX 9.60 Trifecta £42.60.
Owner Tim Syder **Bred** Patrick Burling Developments Ltd **Trained** Upper Lambourn, Berks

FOCUS
They went a fair pace in this very modest handicap chase. The winner is on the upgrade.

4763 32RED CASINO STANDARD OPEN NATIONAL HUNT FLAT RACE 2m 110y
5:25 (5:28) (Class 6) 4-6-Y-0 **£1,559** (£457; £228; £114)

Form RPR

5- **1** **Destiny's Gold (IRE)**[86] 3133 4-10-8 0............................ AndrewTinkler 90
(George Baker) *chsd ldrs: rdn to ld over 1f out: r.o* **33/1**

112- **2** *1 ¼* **Fly Home Harry**[76] 3276 5-11-12 0................................ BrendanPowell 107
(Alan Swinbank) *led: rdn and hdd over 1f out: styd on* **11/4**[2]

21- **3** *nk* **Blue Heron (IRE)**[84] 3160 6-11-2 0.............................. MissBAndrews(7) 104
(Dan Skelton) *trckd ldrs: plld hrd: wnt 2nd 10f out: rdn and ev ch 2f out: swtchd rt 1f out: styd on* **11/2**

- **4** *¾* **Border Breaker (IRE)**[157] 5-10-9 0.................................. MikeyEnnis(7) 96
(David Pipe) *hld up: hdwy 1/2-way: rdn and ev ch 2f out: styd on same pce ins fnl f* **10/3**[3]

/31- **5** *4 ½* **River Deep (IRE)**[69] 3508 5-11-2 0........................ ThomasCheesman(7) 99
(Philip Hobbs) *prom: pushed along 1/2-way: rdn over 2f out: styd on same pce appr fnl f* **9/4**[1]

2- **6** *3 ½* **Beaufort Boy (IRE)**[17] 4445 5-11-2 0.................................. JoshuaMoore 88
(Gary Moore) *hld up: hdwy 7f out: rdn over 3f out: wknd over 1f out* **14/1**

7 *1 ¾* **Red Hott Robbie** 5-10-11 0.. CharlieWallis(5) 86
(Giuseppe Fierro) *hld up: hdwy over 6f out: rdn over 3f out: wknd 2f out* **100/1**

8 *50* **Robin Brook (IRE)** 4-9-11 0 ow1.................................... MissGAndrews(5) 22
(Pam Sly) *racd keenly: trckd ldr 6f: wknd over 5f out* **20/1**

9 *½* **Arthamint** 6-11-2 0.. ConorO'Farrell 36
(Nicholas Pomfret) *hld up: plld hrd: rdn and wknd over 4f out* **100/1**

3m 55.9s (6.80) **Going Correction** +0.10s/f (Yiel)
WFA 4 from 5yo+ 7lb **9** Ran SP% **112.2**
Speed ratings: **88,87,87,86,84 83,82,58,58**
CSF £117.85 TOTE £29.60: £4.70, £1.20, £2.00; EX 106.20 Trifecta £2698.60.
Owner Delancey & Mrs V Finegold **Bred** Janet, Rachel And Susan Kinsella **Trained** Manton, Wilts

FOCUS
A decent little bumper, but they didn't go much of a pace. A step up from the winner.

T/Plt: £115.00 to a £1 stake. Pool: £62358.05 - 395.61 winning tickets T/Qpdt: £25.00 to a £1 stake. Pool: £4053.54 - 119.84 winning tickets CR

[4750]CHELTENHAM (L-H)

Thursday, March 13

OFFICIAL GOING: Good (good to soft in places; 7.0)

Race 7 charity Flat race over 1m5f, not under rules, won by Vicky Laing riding Gifted Leader.

Wind: almost nil Weather: foggy early on, clearing during the day

4764 JLT NOVICES' CHASE (REGISTERED AS THE GOLDEN MILLER NOVICES' CHASE) GRADE 1 (16 fncs) 2m 4f

1:30 (1:30) (Class 1) 5-Y-0+

£68,340 (£25,644; £12,840; £6,396; £3,216; £1,608)

Form RPR

321- **1** **Taquin Du Seuil (FR)**[54] 3777 7-11-4 147 APMcCoy 164+
(Jonjo O'Neill) *lw: hld up in rr: j. slowly 4th and 12th: hdwy to trck ldrs after 4 out: drvn to dispute cl 2nd 2 out: chal last and styd upsides tl led u.p fnl 75yds: styd on wl* **7/1**

115- **2** ¾ **Uxizandre (FR)**[20] 4400 6-11-4 148 (p) RobertThornton 160
(Alan King) *led: rdn after 3 out: hrd pressed after 2 out: jnd last: gamely hld slt ld tl hdd fnl 75yds: kpt on: nt gng pce of wnr* **33/1**

112- **3** 1 ¼ **Double Ross (IRE)**[47] 3887 8-11-4 152 SamTwiston-Davies 159
(Nigel Twiston-Davies) *lw: chsd ldr: rdn after 3 out: jnd for cl 2nd 2 out: chal u.p last: nt gng pce of ldng duo fnl 110yds* **11/1**

122- **4** 7 **Felix Yonger (IRE)**[46] 3928 8-11-4 154 RWalsh 156+
(W P Mullins, Ire) *towards rr: hdwy and blnd 4 out: rcvrd to trck ldrs and hit next: chsd ldrs but no imp 2 out: one pce run-in and hld on all out for 4th* **7/2**[1]

112- **5** hd **Wonderful Charm (FR)**[90] 3064 6-11-4 158 (t) DarylJacob 155+
(Paul Nicholls) *in tch tl lost pl 10th: hdwy and hmpd 4 out: styd on again fr 2 out: kpt on to press for 4th run-in but no imp on ldng trio* **5/1**[3]

5/2- **6** 15 **Sizing Gold (IRE)**[54] 3791 7-11-4 140 AELynch 142
(Henry De Bromhead, Ire) *chsd ldrs: rdn 3 out: wknd bef next* **12/1**

21- **7** 16 **Vukovar (FR)**[75] 3368 5-11-3 152 (t) NoelFehily 127
(Harry Fry) *hmpd 1st and bhd: nt fluent 7th: hdwy to trck ldrs 12th: wknd 3 out* **11/1**

311- **8** 7 **Off The Ground (IRE)**[89] 3090 8-11-4 147 AidanColeman 126
(Emma Lavelle) *in tch: chsd ldrs fr 7th: hit 4 out: wknd next* **25/1**

111- **F** **Oscar Whisky (IRE)**[40] 4033 9-11-4 156 (t) BarryGeraghty
(Nicky Henderson) *fell 1st* **9/2**[2]

40- **P** **Captain Ocana (IRE)**[25] 4298 9-11-4 114 TomO'Brien
(Paul Henderson) *swtg: sn bhd: t.o whn p.u bef 3 out* **200/1**

/31- **F** **Mozoltov**[18] 4455 8-11-4 150 DavyRussell
(W P Mullins, Ire) *mstke, hmpd and fell 1st* **11/1**

4/1- **F** **Djakadam (FR)**[47] 3908 5-11-3 142 PaulTownend
(W P Mullins, Ire) *big: str: lw: chsd ldrs: nt fluent 3rd: hit 9th: disputing 3 l 2nd and gng ok whn fell 4 out* **14/1**

4m 56.72s (-7.48) **Going Correction** +0.10s/f (Yiel) 12 Ran SP% **116.2**
Speed ratings: **118,117,117,114,114 108,101,99, , ,**
CSF £191.83 CT £2496.74 TOTE £7.10: £2.10, £9.40, £2.70; EX 271.20 Trifecta £8826.40.

Owner Martin Broughton & Friends 1 **Bred** Marc Boudot **Trained** Cheltenham, Gloucs

■ New sponsors for this race, replacing Jewson.

FOCUS

All races on New Course. Switching to the New Course and with it drying up all the time, officials took the decision to water around two-thirds of the track after day two, between 3mm and 5mm, to ensure good, good to soft going. The thick morning fog took an age to lift and was still very evident in the opener, but visibility was fine. Promoted to Grade 1 status since last season, this novice chase over the intermediate distance looked a wide-open contest. They went a brisk early gallop, although it did seem to ease off after four fences, and those racing handily held an advantage when it lifted again from five out. The principals dominated in the home straight, resulting in a first success since the race's inception for the domestic team, and it was a quick winning time.\nTaquin Du Seuil looks well up to standard and Uxizandre ran a personal best in defeat.

4765 PERTEMPS NETWORK FINAL (A H'CAP HURDLE) (LISTED RACE) (12 hdls) 3m

2:05 (2:05) (Class 1) 5-Y-0+

£45,560 (£17,096; £8,560; £4,264; £2,144; £1,072)

Form RPR

0/1- **1** **Fingal Bay (IRE)**[32] 4174 8-11-12 **148** RichardJohnson 154+
(Philip Hobbs) *lw: trckd ldrs: wnt 2nd after 2 out: chalng whn blnd last: r.o for press whn duelled for ld run-in: led post* **9/2**[1]

435- **2** nse **Southfield Theatre (IRE)**[41] 4021 6-11-11 **147** DarylJacob 152
(Paul Nicholls) *lw: midfield: hdwy on outer appr 2 out: led bef last: hrd pressed run-in: hdd post* **20/1**

201- **3** nk **Pineau De Re (FR)**[58] 3698 11-11-4 **140** SamTwiston-Davies 146+
(Dr Richard Newland) *hld up towards rr: hdwy appr 2 out: chsng ldrs whn mstke last: r.o for press: fin strly* **33/1**

033- **4** nk **Trustan Times (IRE)**[54] 3776 8-11-8 **144** RyanMania 150
(Tim Easterby) *trckd ldrs: mstke 3rd: tried to chal fr last: r.o for press run-in: hld fnl strides* **33/1**

253- **5** 1 ¾ **Jetson (IRE)**[39] 4061 9-11-3 **144** PaddyKennedy(5) 148
(Mrs John Harrington, Ire) *midfield: hdwy appr 9th: rdn whn chsng ldrs bef last: styd on same pce fnl 100yds* **11/1**[3]

234- **6** 1 ¼ **On The Bridge (IRE)**[146] 1956 9-11-4 **140** NickScholfield 144+
(Jeremy Scott) *lw: hld up: mstke 7th: in last pl 8th: mstke 9th: hdwy whn nt clr run and swtchd rt and lft appr last: r.o run-in: fin wl* **16/1**

512- **7** 1 ¼ **Mister Dillon**[39] 4051 7-11-4 **140** BarryGeraghty 142
(Nicky Henderson) *hmpd 1st: towards rr: hdwy u.p 2 out: styd on after last: nvr able to chal ldrs* **20/1**

445- **8** 1 **Broadway Buffalo (IRE)**[32] 4174 6-11-1 **137** (t) TomScudamore 137
(David Pipe) *hld up: hdwy into midfield appr 2 out: hung lft bef last: styd on run-in: nt rch ldrs* **20/1**

122- **9** 2 **If In Doubt (IRE)**[32] 4174 6-11-4 **140** APMcCoy 138
(Philip Hobbs) *lw: hld up: niggled along briefly after 5th: hdwy appr 2 out: rdn to chse ldrs bef last: sn no imp and wknd* **13/2**[2]

404- **10** ½ **Cross Kennon (IRE)**[26] 4269 10-11-3 **139** (v) SeanQuinlan 137
(Jennie Candlish) *j.rt a few times: w ldr: led 7th: rdn and hdd bef last: sn btn* **33/1**

545- **11** 2 ¼ **Utopie Des Bordes (FR)**[54] 3770 6-11-2 **138** DavidBass 134
(Nicky Henderson) *midfield: pushed along after 8th: outpcd whn nt fluent 2 out: nvr able to trble ldrs* **20/1**

132- **12** ½ **Mickie**[26] 4269 6-11-4 **143** JakeGreenall(3) 139
(Henry Daly) *hld up: hmpd 1st: outpcd and struggling appr 2 out: styd on fr bef last: nvr rchd ldrs* **25/1**

220- **13** ½ **Pateese (FR)**[33] 4144 9-10-10 **139** (p) ChrisDavies(7) 134
(Philip Hobbs) *midfield: hdwy appr 3 out: rdn bef 2 out: one pce bef last* **50/1**

P35/ **14** hd **Seefood (IRE)**[75] 3372 7-11-7 **143** (b) RWalsh 139
(D T Hughes, Ire) *midfield: hit 6th: hdwy appr 3 out: in tch bef 2 out: rdn bef last: no imp: wknd* **14/1**

163- **15** shd **Crowning Jewel**[39] 4051 8-11-2 **138** JamesReveley 133
(Keith Reveley) *trckd ldrs tl wknd appr 2 out* **20/1**

303- **16** 1 ¾ **So Fine (IRE)**[90] 3069 8-10-13 **135** TomO'Brien 128
(Philip Hobbs) *midfield: hdwy appr 2 out: one pce and no imp bef last: sn wknd* **25/1**

341- **17** 10 **Uncle Jimmy (IRE)**[61] 3653 7-10-11 **140** ThomasCheesman(7) 129+
(Philip Hobbs) *hld up: hdwy on outer appr 9th: rdn after 3 out: rdn whn chsng ldrs disputing 4th and blnd 2 out: sn wknd* **20/1**

546- **18** 3 **Quartz De Thaix (FR)**[26] 4269 10-11-9 **145** (b) AidanColeman 126
(Venetia Williams) *prom tl wknd after 9th* **50/1**

2/1- **19** 7 **Top Wood (FR)**[26] 4271 7-11-4 **140** (t[1]) ConorO'Farrell 115
(David Pipe) *trckd ldrs tl pushed along and wknd after 9th* **16/1**

P23- **20** 2 ½ **Grand Vision (IRE)**[40] 4025 8-11-6 **142** BrendanPowell 115
(Colin Tizzard) *led: hit 4th: hdd 7th: pushed along and stl w ldr whn mstke 2 out: sn wknd* **12/1**

060- **21** 32 **First Fandango**[25] 4303 7-10-7 **139** (t) AlanJohns(10) 83
(Tim Vaughan) *midfield: lost pl bef 7th: sn towards rr and n.d: t.o* **50/1**

311- **22** 5 **Josies Orders (IRE)**[48] 3882 6-10-9 **136** (b) MauriceLinehan(5) 75
(Jonjo O'Neill) *hld up: rdn after 6th: hdwy 9th: in tch 3 out: rdn and wknd 2 out: t.o* **14/1**

S4/ **F** **Vics Canvas (IRE)**[39] 4061 11-11-4 **140** (p) RobbieColgan
(Dermot Anthony McLoughlin, Ire) *trckd ldrs: fell 1st* **50/1**

5m 49.4s (-11.60) **Going Correction** -0.15s/f (Good) **23** Ran SP% **125.6**
Speed ratings: **113,112,112,112,112 111,111,111,110,110 109,109,109,109,109 108,105,104,101,100 90,88,**
CSF £92.84 CT £2658.44 TOTE £4.70: £2.20, £5.40, £8.70, £7.70; EX 121.20 Trifecta £6974.40.

Owner Mrs R J Skan **Bred** James Kinsella **Trained** Withycombe, Somerset

■ Stewards' Enquiry : Paddy Kennedy four-day ban: used whip above permitted level (Mar 27-30)
Richard Johnson three-day ban: used whip without giving gelding time to respond (Mar 30-31,Apr 1)

FOCUS

A typically competitive edition of this race, run at a good gallop, and the form looks strong, with four of the five at the head of the weights being involved in the finish. Fingal Bay was a 156 novice and can still at least match that, and Southfield Theatre ran a personal best.

4766 RYANAIR CHASE (REGISTERED AS THE FESTIVAL TROPHY CHASE) GRADE 1 (17 fncs) 2m 5f

2:40 (2:40) (Class 1) 5-Y-0+

£156,612 (£58,767; £29,425; £14,657; £7,370; £3,685)

Form RPR

/25- **1** **Dynaste (FR)**[77] 3262 8-11-10 169 TomScudamore 168+
(David Pipe) *hld up towards rr: impr fr 4 out: pushed along and qcknd to chse ldrs appr 2 out: str run to go cl 2nd last: led sn after: fnd plenty for press and kpt on wl* **3/1**[1]

322- **2** 2 ¼ **Hidden Cyclone (IRE)**[54] 3773 9-11-10 156 (p) AndrewJMcNamara 166+
(John Joseph Hanlon, Ire) *lw: trckd ldr to 3rd: styd prom: wnt 2nd again 12th: slt ld 13th: drvn and styd on appr 2 out: hdd after last and wandered run-in but kpt on wl: nt gng pce of wnr* **10/1**

1/5- **3** 2 ¼ **Rajdhani Express**[117] 2503 7-11-10 155 MrSWaley-Cohen 162
(Nicky Henderson) *in rr: hdwy 7th: trckd ldrs fr 13th: wnt 2nd 3 out: rdn bef 2 out: chsd ldrs last: sltly hmpd sn after and styd on same pce* **18/1**

3/3- **4** 2 ¾ **Hunt Ball (IRE)**[26] 4265 9-11-10 155 BarryGeraghty 161
(Nicky Henderson) *in rr: hdwy 12th: chsd ldrs and drvn 3 out: styng on same pce whn hit 2 out* **14/1**

132- **5** ½ **Al Ferof (FR)**[33] 4145 9-11-10 165 DarylJacob 160
(Paul Nicholls) *bmpd 1st: chsd ldrs tl lost position 13th: rdn after 3 out: styd on u.p appr last: kpt on in clsng stages: nt rch ldrs* **5/1**[3]

F/6- **6** 1 ¼ **Boston Bob (IRE)**[47] 3890 9-11-10 154 RWalsh 158
(W P Mullins, Ire) *in rr: pushed along after 3 out: styd on fr 2 out: kpt on run-in: nt rch ldrs* **8/1**

153- **7** 13 **Rathlin**[39] 4062 9-11-10 158 (t) DJCasey 146
(M F Morris, Ire) *lw: chsd ldrs: rdn 3 out: wknd and hit 2 out* **20/1**

4/4- **8** 1 ¾ **Medermit (FR)**[26] 4265 10-11-10 154 RobertThornton 146
(Alan King) *in rr: j. slowly 2nd: shkn up after 5th: hit 6th: drvn fr 11th: no prog u.p 4 out: no ch fr next* **20/1**

535- **9** 30 **Kauto Stone (FR)**[26] 4265 8-11-10 150 SamTwiston-Davies 128
(Paul Nicholls) *lw: led: hdd 13th: hit 4 out and wknd* **50/1**

2/P- **10** 17 **Menorah (IRE)**[77] 3262 9-11-10 169 (p) RichardJohnson 102
(Philip Hobbs) *in tch to 10th: wknd 12th* **15/2**

/41- **P** **Benefficient (IRE)**[76] 3338 8-11-10 157 DavyRussell
(A J Martin, Ire) *lw: chsd ldr 3rd to 12th: nt fluent 3 out: wknd u.p bef next: p.u bef last* **9/2**[2]

5m 9.13s (-10.27) **Going Correction** +0.10s/f (Yiel) **11** Ran SP% **115.2**
Speed ratings: **123,122,121,120,120 119,114,113,102,96**
CSF £32.01 CT £460.15 TOTE £3.50: £1.70, £3.00, £4.60; EX 36.80 Trifecta £428.80.

Owner A J White **Bred** Paul Chartier **Trained** Nicholashayne, Devon

FOCUS

This year's Ryanair Chase was another open-looking affair and not the strongest race for the class. There was no hanging about, yet as was the case in the earlier JLT Novice Chase, it didn't prove easy to make up ground from off the pace. The placed horses rate the best guide for the form. Dynaste is rated 7lb off his Betfair second and Hidden Cyclone is rated to his best.

4767 LADBROKES WORLD HURDLE GRADE 1 (12 hdls) 3m

3:20 (3:20) (Class 1) 4-Y-0+

£156,612 (£58,767; £29,425; £14,657; £7,370; £3,685)

Form RPR

111- **1** **More Of That (IRE)**[89] 3084 6-11-10 160 BarryGeraghty 172+
(Jonjo O'Neill) *lengthy: lw: hld up: hdwy appr 2 out: sn trckd ldrs: disp ld bef last where tk narrow advantage: rdn run-in: styd on wl and in command fnl 75yds* **15/2**[3]

111- **2** 1 ½ **Annie Power (IRE)**[47] 3895 6-11-3 165 RWalsh 164+
(W P Mullins, Ire) *hld up racing w zest: swtchd rt and hdwy appr 2 out: big effrt to chal and draw level bef last where hdd narrowly: rdn run-in: nt qckn and hld fnl 75yds* **11/8**[1]

4U2- **3** *5* **At Fishers Cross (IRE)**[47] 3890 7-11-10 157......................(p) APMcCoy 166
(Rebecca Curtis) *in tch: clsd 3 out: cl up on outer appr 2 out: led between last 2: hdd bef last: sn drifted lft: outpcd by front two run-in: kpt on same pce whn no ch* **9/1**

222- **4** *2* **Zarkandar (IRE)**[26] 4279 7-11-10 162...................................... NoelFehily 165
(Paul Nicholls) *hld up in rr: mstke 4th: carried rt sltly appr 2 out: rdn and hdwy to go 4th appr last: kpt on run-in but unable to chal* **14/1**

1/3- **5** *5* **Big Buck's (FR)**[47] 3890 11-11-10 170........................ SamTwiston-Davies 160
(Paul Nicholls) *trckd ldrs: pushed along appr 2 out: unable to go w ldrs u.p bef last: wl hld after* **7/2**[2]

421- **6** *nk* **Rule The World**[54] 3790 7-11-10 158................................ BrianO'Connell 160
(M F Morris, Ire) *lw: trckd ldrs: wnt 2nd appr 2 out: sn upsides: rdn and btn appr last* **14/1**

/22- **7** *4* **Medinas (FR)**[103] 2814 7-11-10 154.......................... WayneHutchinson 156
(Alan King) *midfield: pushed along and lost pl appr 2 out: sn btn and outpcd* **25/1**

314- **8** *½* **Reve De Sivola (FR)**[47] 3890 9-11-10 161.................. RichardJohnson 158
(Nick Williams) *led: mstke 7th and 8th: niggled along appr 3 out: rdn and hdd between last 2: sn btn* **33/1**

222- **9** *10* **Salubrious (IRE)**[82] 3198 7-11-10 153.............................. NickScholfield 147
(Paul Nicholls) *in rr: pushed along and outpcd after 2 out: nvr a threat* **25/1**

613- **10** *9* **Celestial Halo (IRE)**[26] 4269 10-11-10 161.......................(bt) DarylJacob 141
(Paul Nicholls) *racd in 2nd pl tl appr 2 out: wknd u.p after flight* **20/1**

5m 49.5s (-11.50) **Going Correction** -0.15s/f (Good) **10 Ran SP% 114.8**
Speed ratings: **113,112,110,110,108 108,107,106,103,100**
CSF £17.72 CT £96.16 TOTE £8.40: £1.90, £1.50, £2.10; EX 21.10 Trifecta £150.40.
Owner John P McManus **Bred** Mrs Eleanor Hadden **Trained** Cheltenham, Gloucs

FOCUS
The deepest edition of this race in some years, with the inclusion of Annie Power creating a lot of excitement, and although the Champion Hurdle had widely been billed as the race of the week leading up to the festival, there's little doubt this event trumped it. Run at a good, even pace, all the major players, with the exception of the driven along Big Buck's, began to mass in behind travelling strongly on the run downhill, and a cracking duel between a pair of unbeaten, potentially top-class youngsters unfolded from before the last. Excellent form. More Of That maintained his relentless improvement and Annie Power is rated right up to her best.

4768 BYRNE GROUP PLATE (A H'CAP CHASE) GRADE 3 (16 fncs) 2m 4f
4:00 (4:01) (Class 1) 5-Y-0+

£51,255 (£19,233; £9,630; £4,797; £2,412; £1,206)

Form RPR

0/P- **1** **Ballynagour (IRE)**[117] 2503 8-10-9 **140**.......................(t) TomScudamore 156+
(David Pipe) *hld up towards rr: stdy hdwy fr 4 out: trckd ldrs gng wl fr 3 out: slt ld 2 out: qcknd last: pushed clr: comf* **12/1**

/23- **2** *8* **Colour Squadron (IRE)**[89] 3082 8-11-1 **146**........................... APMcCoy 153
(Philip Hobbs) *chsd ldrs: str chal 2 out: rdn to chse wnr last: readily outpcd but kpt on wl for clr 2nd* **5/1**[1]

/12- **3** *6* **Tatenen (FR)**[40] 4034 10-10-9 **140**.................................. AndrewThornton 142
(Richard Rowe) *sn chsng ldrs: wnt 2nd 11th: slt ld u.p 3 out: narrowly hdd but upside next: jst wkng into 3rd whn mstke last and no ex* **33/1**

115- **4** *1 ½* **Johns Spirit (IRE)**[89] 3082 7-11-3 **148**.......................... RichieMcLernon 147
(Jonjo O'Neill) *lw: in rr: hit 9th: hdwy appr 3 out: chsd ldrs u.p 2 out: one pce appr last* **9/1**

233- **5** *1 ¼* **Third Intention (IRE)**[26] 4262 7-10-12 **143**.......................(tp) JoeTizzard 143+
(Colin Tizzard) *lw: chsd ldrs: disp ld 3 out: rdn and stl chalng 2 out: wknd last* **7/1**[2]

/31- **6** *nk* **Giorgio Quercus (FR)**[108] 2714 9-9-13 **135**............... NicodeBoinville[(5)] 134
(Nicky Henderson) *sn chsng ldrs: hit 4 out: rdn fr 3 out: wknd after 2 out* **16/1**

U26- **7** *½* **Champion Court (IRE)**[47] 3888 9-11-5 **157**....................... RyanHatch[(7)] 154
(Martin Keighley) *lw: led to 4th: led again 5th: hdd 3 out: wknd after 2 out* **12/1**

5/ **8** *shd* **Sraid Padraig (IRE)**[103] 2833 8-10-8 **139**........................ DannyMullins 139+
(A J Martin, Ire) *chsd ldrs 5th: blnd and lost pl 9th: hdwy 4 out: chsd ldrs after 3 out and rdn: wknd after 2 out: blnd last* **11/1**

/6F- **9** *hd* **Wetak (FR)**[26] 4263 7-10-7 **138**..(t) ConorO'Farrell 135
(David Pipe) *in tch early: bhd 7th: effrt and hit 3 out: styd on same pce* **33/1**

113- **10** *8* **Firth Of The Clyde**[28] 4235 9-10-6 **137**.............................. BrianHughes 129
(Malcolm Jefferson) *stdd in mid-div: hdwy appr 3 out and sn trcking ldrs: wknd appr 2 out* **16/1**

521- **11** *4 ½* **Shangani (USA)**[12] 4559 8-10-6 **137** 5ex......................... AidanColeman 123
(Venetia Williams) *chsd ldrs tl wknd after 4 out* **14/1**

/4P- **12** *3 ½* **Tartak (FR)**[82] 3205 11-10-0 **131** oh2................................(t) PaulMoloney 114
(Victor Dartnall) *prom early: dropped towards rr 6th: sme prog appr 3 out: no ch after* **33/1**

113- **13** *1* **Bennys Mist (IRE)**[20] 4400 8-10-9 **140**............................ LiamTreadwell 124
(Venetia Williams) *chsd ldrs: hit 12th: wknd and mstke 3 out* **33/1**

013- **14** *nk* **King Edmund**[40] 4034 11-10-8 **139**.. TomCannon 122
(Chris Gordon) *hit 2nd and 6th: chsd ldrs to 4 out* **66/1**

64P- **15** *12* **Bless The Wings (IRE)**[19] 4422 9-10-9 **140**.........(b[1]) WayneHutchinson 113
(Alan King) *in tch: chsd ldrs fr 7th: blnd and wknd 4 out* **20/1**

641- **16** *4* **Sew On Target (IRE)**[40] 4036 9-10-3 **134**....................... BrendanPowell 101
(Colin Tizzard) *t.k.h: chsd ldrs to 12th* **25/1**

331- **17** *24* **Highway Code (USA)**[104] 2797 8-10-0 **131** oh2...............(t) JamieMoore 76
(Richard Lee) *hit 10th a towards rr* **25/1**

/0P- **P** **Mr Cracker (IRE)**[33] 4160 9-10-2 **136**............................ MichaelByrne[(3)]
(Tim Vaughan) *blnd 1st: in rr: hit 8th: blnd 9th: t.o whn p.u bef 4 out* **66/1**

1U0- **P** **Act Of Kalanisi (IRE)**[33] 4147 8-10-4 **135**..........(bt) SamTwiston-Davies
(Dr Richard Newland) *led 4th to 5th: chsd ldrs to 4 out: btn whn blnd 2 out: p.u bef last* **33/1**

125- **P** **Christopher Wren (USA)**[41] 4022 7-9-9 **131** oh3..(p) MauriceLinehan[(5)]
(Nick Gifford) *a in rr: t.o whn p.u bef 4 out* **40/1**

14P- **F** **Gallox Bridge**[36] 4089 9-10-1 **132**.......................................(t) IanPopham
(Tim Vaughan) *j. poorly in rr tl fell 4 out* **66/1**

030- **P** **Nadiya De La Vega (FR)**[61] 3647 8-10-7 **138**............(v[1]) AndrewTinkler
(Nicky Henderson) *a in rr: t.o whn p.u bef 3 out* **20/1**

003- **P** **Tap Night (USA)**[47] 3887 7-11-0 **145**................................. BarryGeraghty
(Lucinda Russell) *in tch hit 5th: dropped in rr 10th: j. slowly 11th: no ch after: p.u bef 4 out* **8/1**[3]

4m 59.34s (-4.86) **Going Correction** +0.10s/f (Yiel) **23 Ran SP% 131.3**
Speed ratings: **113,109,107,106,106 106,105,105,105,102 100,99,99,98,94 92,82,, ,** ,,
CSF £65.65 CT £1999.20 TOTE £15.50: £3.80, £2.00, £7.00, £2.60; EX 105.00 Trifecta £4394.10.
Owner Allan Stennett **Bred** G T Morrow **Trained** Nicholashayne, Devon

FOCUS
At the third time of asking (seven jumped the first during the initial false start), they took off in what again looked on paper to be a fiercely competitive handicap. The easy winner is rated back to the level of his Warwick win, with the next two to their marks.

4769 FULKE WALWYN KIM MUIR CHALLENGE CUP H'CAP CHASE (AMATEUR RIDERS) (21 fncs) 3m 1f 110y
4:40 (4:40) (Class 2) (0-145,144) 5-Y-0+

£35,976 (£11,238; £5,616; £2,808; £1,404; £708)

Form RPR

320- **1** **Spring Heeled (IRE)**[76] 3341 7-11-8 **140** ow2..........(p) MrRPMcNamara 151+
(J H Culloty, Ire) *sweating: w ldr: led 4th: pckd 4 out: pressed last: sn lft over 3 l clr: drvn out and styd on wl: weighed in 2lb over* **12/1**

100/ **2** *1 ¾* **Cause Of Causes (USA)**[76] 3341 6-11-8 **140**.................. MsNCarberry 151+
(Gordon Elliott, Ire) *lw: midfield: hdwy appr 4 out: wnt 2nd 2 out: chalng whn blnd last and lost grnd: rallied towards fin but no imp on wnr* **13/2**[2]

406- **3** *17* **Roberto Goldback (IRE)**[47] 3897 12-11-12 **144**........ MrSWaley-Cohen 138
(Nicky Henderson) *hld up: hdwy and in tch 10th: mstke whn outpcd 16th: styd on to take 3rd run-in: no ch w front two* **16/1**

534- **4** *2 ¾* **Balnaslow (IRE)**[49] 3868 7-11-4 **136**................................ MrPWMullins 128
(W P Mullins, Ire) *trckd ldrs: mstke 12th: big effrt and ev ch appr 2 out: no ex bef last: wl btn run-in* **9/1**[3]

00P- **5** *8* **Same Difference (IRE)**[61] 3655 8-11-2 **141**..................(v) MrJBargary[(7)] 129+
(Nigel Twiston-Davies) *chsd ldrs: blnd and lost pl 8th: nt bttr than midfield after: pushed along whn blnd 16th: struggling whn sltly hmpd 4 out: styd on after last wout threatening* **16/1**

014- **6** *1 ½* **Pickamus (FR)**[71] 3458 11-10-12 **135**.......................... MissJCWilliams[(5)] 119
(Henry Daly) *trckd ldrs: nt fluent 9th: chalng whn blnd 3 out: wknd 2 out* **66/1**

121- **7** *5* **Indian Castle (IRE)**[47] 3886 6-11-8 **140**........................ MrDerekO'Connor 130+
(Donald McCain) *lw: midfield: hdwy 14th: trckd ldrs appr 4 out: effrt whn wnt 2nd briefly appr 2 out: disputing 3rd and hld whn blnd bdly last: nt rcvr: wknd* **7/2**[1]

134- **8** *¾* **Gas Line Boy (IRE)**[85] 3162 8-10-8 **133**......................... MrCGethings[(7)] 112
(Philip Hobbs) *hld up: hdwy 8th: mstke 9th: rdn and outpcd whn hit 4 out: wknd bef 2 out* **25/1**

/05- **9** *2* **Our Father (IRE)**[26] 4270 8-11-7 **142**..........................(b[1]) MrDEdwards[(3)] 125+
(David Pipe) *midfield: mstke 2nd: hdwy and in tch w ldrs 9th: pckd 4 out and sn sltly outpcd: 6th and one pce whn blnd bdly 2 out: nt rcvr: wknd* **11/1**

P05- **10** *½* **Problema Tic (FR)**[82] 3199 8-10-8 **131**................................(bt) MrSFox[(5)] 107
(David Pipe) *trckd ldrs: lost pl 4th: struggling 10th: tried to make hdwy whn mstke 3 out: sn no imp* **25/1**

6/5- **11** *6* **Swing Bill (FR)**[96] 2937 13-10-13 **138**................................ MrMHeard[(7)] 110
(David Pipe) *s.s: bhd: sme hdwy 9th: nvr bttr than midfield: no imp fr 3 out* **33/1**

P05- **12** *36* **Quinz (FR)**[71] 3455 10-10-7 **132**.. MrCSmith[(7)] 69
(Philip Hobbs) *midfield: mstke 7th: sn lost pl: toiling whn blnd 16th: n.d: t.o* **28/1**

001- **P** **Mumbles Head (IRE)**[226] 1146 13-10-11 **136**..............(p) MrSPBowen[(7)]
(Peter Bowen) *bhd: nt gng wl after 11th: nt fluent 12th: wl bhd whn p.u bef 17th* **80/1**

231- **P** **Tranquil Sea (IRE)**[22] 4346 12-11-12 **144**................................ MrJJCodd
(Warren Greatrex) *hld up: sme hdwy appr 3 out: nvr able to get nr ldrs and no imp: wl bhd whn p.u bef last* **25/1**

115- **P** **Fine Parchment (IRE)**[40] 4034 11-10-12 **135**.......(tp) MrHAABannister[(5)]
(Charlie Mann) *s.s and bustled along: sn in midfield: hdwy to chse ldrs 9th: wknd after 15th: t.o whn p.u after 3 out* **50/1**

P51- **P** **There's No Panic (IRE)**[96] 2953 9-11-2 **134**....................... MrWBiddick
(Paul Nicholls) *a bhd: struggling fr 12th: t.o whn p.u bef 3 out* **20/1**

F1P- **P** **Night Alliance (IRE)**[54] 3780 9-11-2 **134**...........................(b) MrTWeston
(Dr Richard Newland) *hld up: hdwy into midfield 7th: rdn and sme hdwy whn mstke 3 out: sn wl btn: t.o whn p.u bef 2 out* **28/1**

30P- **P** **Lost Glory (NZ)**[89] 3091 9-11-0 **139**..................................(t) MrMWalton[(7)]
(Jonjo O'Neill) *bhd: blnd 8th: t.o whn p.u bef 17th* **50/1**

010- **U** **Twirling Magnet (IRE)**[131] 2214 8-11-10 **142**....................(tp) MrBO'Neill
(Jonjo O'Neill) *lw: chsd ldrs: mstke 2nd: prom 16th: over 4 l down and niggled whn blnd 3 out: sn wknd: bhd whn blnd and uns rdr 2 out* **16/1**

/04- **P** **Saint Are (FR)**[110] 2674 8-10-13 **136**............................... MrBGibbs[(5)]
(Tim Vaughan) *midfield: lost pl 5th: bhd 7th: blnd 8th: t.o whn p.u bef 2 out* **33/1**

061- **F** **Buddy Bolero (IRE)**[19] 4415 8-11-10 **142**..........................(b[1]) MsKWalsh
(David Pipe) *led after 1st: hdd 4th: remained prom: pckd bdly 8th: pushed along abt 4 l off the pce disputing 5th whn fell 4 out* **9/1**[3]

U **Tabhachtach (IRE)**[46] 3932 7-10-10 **133**......................... MrMTSlevin[(5)]
(S Slevin, Ire) *led: hdd after 1st: remained prom: 2nd after 10th: blnd and uns rdr 14th* **40/1**

0- **P** **Hunting Party (IRE)**[49] 3868 8-11-0 **132**................................. MrJJKing
(D T Hughes, Ire) *in tch: lost pl after 2nd: nvr bttr than midfield after: struggling whn hmpd 4 out: t.o whn p.u bef 3 out* **25/1**

6m 35.1s (-3.10) **Going Correction** +0.10s/f (Yiel) **23 Ran SP% 131.2**
Speed ratings: **108,107,102,101,98 98,96,96,96,95 94,83,, ,** ,,,,
CSF £79.53 CT £1301.48 TOTE £14.50: £3.70, £2.10, £3.80, £2.60; EX 117.40 Trifecta £2060.50.
Owner Dr R Lambe **Bred** Isidore And Padraic Murtagh **Trained** Mallow, Co Cork

■ Stewards' Enquiry : Mr R P McNamara two-day ban: used whip above permitted level (Mar 27-28); three-day ban: weighed in 2lb heavy (Mar 30,Apr 1-2)

Mr J J King Fine: £290, changed boots after weighing-out.

FOCUS
As with all the handicaps at the meeting, this looked an open contest, despite the presence of a relatively short-priced favourite, and it was run at a fair gallop, no more. The front pair pulled clear late on. Jumping was an issue for many of the runners, and indeed played a crucial role in the outcome of the race. Spring Heeled produced a big step forward and the second improved to the level of his best hurdles form.

T/Jkpt: Not won. T/Plt: £496.80 to a £1 stake. Pool of £1260652.50 - 1852.12 winning tickets. T/Qpdt: £18.80 to a £1 stake. Pool of £69470.71 - 2723.40 winning tickets. ST

[3017] HEXHAM (L-H)

Thursday, March 13

OFFICIAL GOING: Chase course - soft; hurdle course - good to soft (soft in places; chs 5.4; hdl 5.7)

Wind: Breezy, half against Weather: Overcast

4770 BHEST CONDITIONAL JOCKEYS' MARES' H'CAP HURDLE (8 hdls) 2m 110y
1:45 (1:45) (Class 4) (0-110,105) 4-Y-0+ **£3,285** (£957; £479)

Form RPR

343- **1** **Be My Present**[17] 4466 7-11-8 **100**........................ CraigNichol 106
(Rose Dobbin) *prom: hdwy to ld bef last: drvn and hld on wl towards fin* **7/1**

054- **2** *nk* **Politelysed**[8] 4615 8-9-11 **78** oh5........................ DeanPratt[(3)] 84
(Robert Johnson) *hld up: hdwy and in tch bef 2 out: effrt and wnt 2nd last: kpt on run-in: jst hld* **8/1**

044- **3** *3 ¾* **Bobs Lady Tamure**[21] 4364 7-11-0 **95**........................(t) DaraghBourke[(3)] 97
(Maurice Barnes) *t.k.h: hld up in tch: hdwy to ld bef 3 out: rdn and hdd bef last: one pce run-in* **14/1**

/4U- **4** *5* **Dante's Frolic**[17] 4463 6-11-12 **104**........................ AdamNicol 101
(Michael Smith) *hld up: hdwy and prom 2 out: drvn and outpcd whn nt fluent last: no imp* **6/1**[3]

/20- **5** *3 ¼* **High Fair**[57] 3723 8-10-7 **88**........................ NathanMoscrop[(3)] 82
(Sandy Forster) *hld up in midfield: rdn and outpcd 2 out: rallied last: kpt on: no imp* **66/1**

2P2- **6** *8* **Pixie Cut (IRE)**[21] 4364 4-11-5 **105**........................ JonathanEngland 83
(Alistair Whillans) *t.k.h: led: hdd whn hit 3 out: rallied: wknd between last 2* **11/2**[2]

5P5- **7** *16* **Sparkling Hand**[13] 4531 8-11-7 **99**........................(p) HarryChalloner 69
(Peter Atkinson) *chsd ldrs tl wknd 2 out* **4/1**[1]

\- **P** **Personal Shopper**[60] 3682 7-10-10 **88**........................ PatrickCorbett
(H Smyth, Ire) *chsd ldrs tl rdn and wknd 2 out: p.u bef last* **8/1**

454- **P** **Ellistrin Belle**[29] 4223 6-10-11 **89**........................ CallumWhillans
(Donald Whillans) *hld up: mstke 3rd: rdn after 3 out: lost tch after next: p.u bef last* **15/2**

P56- **P** **Flogarose (FR)**[69] 3518 5-10-2 **83**........................ GrantCockburn[(3)]
(Lucy Normile) *t.k.h: cl up: chal 4th to bef 3 out: wkng whn mstke next: p.u bef last* **10/1**

4m 26.0s (8.60) **Going Correction** +0.60s/f (Soft)
WFA 4 from 5yo+ 7lb **10** Ran SP% **113.4**
Speed ratings (Par 105): **103,102,101,98,97 93,85,,,**
CSF £60.04 CT £758.49 TOTE £4.50: £2.20, £3.20, £4.90; EX 53.30 Trifecta £450.80.
Owner Miss J Matterson & Mrs R Dobbin **Bred** Mrs L Suenson-Taylor **Trained** South Hazelrigg, Northumbria

FOCUS
The winning jockey described the going as 'soft and tacky'.This was an ordinary mares' handicap run at a medium gallop. The winner and third set the level.

4771 RACING TO SCHOOL NOVICES' H'CAP CHASE (19 fncs) 3m 1f
2:20 (2:20) (Class 4) (0-110,110) 5-Y-0+ **£3,768** (£1,106; £553; £276)

Form RPR

4F3- **1** **Lady Of Verona (IRE)**[12] 4551 7-10-2 **91**........................ CraigNichol[(5)] 98
(Lucinda Russell) *mde all: qcknd clr bef 3 out: rdn and kpt on wl run-in: unchal* **9/4**[1]

0P0- **2** *7* **Solis (GER)**[12] 4553 11-10-11 **100**........................ ColmMcCormack[(5)] 100
(Dianne Sayer) *hld up in tch: outpcd 1/2-way: rallied after 2 out: styd on to take 2nd cl home: nt rch wnr* **14/1**

P44- **3** *hd* **Royal Sam (IRE)**[36] 4086 9-11-1 **99**........................(t) WilsonRenwick 99
(Martin Todhunter) *chsd wnr to 4 out: rallied u.p to regain 2nd bef 2 out: clsd bef last: no ex last 150yds: lost 2nd cl home* **7/2**[3]

F33- **4** *16* **Forty Crown (IRE)**[23] 4338 8-11-7 **110**........................ JohnDawson[(5)] 98
(John Wade) *nt fluent on occasions: prom: wnt 2nd 4 out to bef 2 out: rdn and wknd between last 2* **11/4**[2]

136- **5** *33* **Maggie Blue (IRE)**[95] 2974 6-10-13 **97**........................ LucyAlexander 48
(Harriet Graham) *in tch: drvn and outpcd after 4 out: rallied next: wknd 2 out: t.o* **17/2**

656- **P** **Danebrook Lad (IRE)**[102] 2843 8-9-10 **87**........................ MrTHamilton[(7)]
(Sandy Thomson) *nt fluent in rr: struggling fnl circ: t.o whn p.u bef 2 out* **6/1**

6m 57.7s (25.50) **Going Correction** +0.725s/f (Soft) **6** Ran SP% **111.1**
Speed ratings: **88,85,85,80,70**
CSF £27.05 TOTE £2.30: £1.10, £3.20; EX 18.50 Trifecta £47.60.
Owner Peter K Dale Ltd **Bred** Peter K Dale **Trained** Arlary, Perth & Kinross

FOCUS
This novice handicap chase, which was run at a decent pace, didn't take a great deal of winning. A step up from the winner formwise.

4772 BECOME A HEXHAM MEMBER NOVICES' HURDLE (8 hdls) 2m 110y
2:55 (2:55) (Class 4) 4-Y-0+ **£3,285** (£957; £479)

Form RPR

334- **1** **Tikkandemickey (IRE)**[57] 3724 8-11-0 117........................ DaraghBourke[(7)] 117+
(Raymond Shiels) *chsd ldr: smooth hdwy to ld bef last: edgd lft run-in: rdn clr* **7/2**[2]

/6P- **2** *8* **Wilde Pastures (IRE)**[76] 3333 9-10-8 0........................(p) DaleIrving[(7)] 101
(James Ewart) *led: rdn and hdd bef last: kpt on same pce run-in* **5/1**[3]

450- **3** *2 ¼* **Factor Fifty (IRE)**[41] 4018 5-11-1 0........................ RichieMcGrath 99
(Philip Kirby) *prom: rdn and outpcd 2 out: rallied bef last: no imp run-in* **15/2**

0- **4** *12* **Kings Folly (IRE)**[40] 4043 6-11-1 0........................ PeterBuchanan 87
(Lucinda Russell) *bhd: outpcd 4 out: styd on fr 2 out: shkn up run-in: nvr nr ldrs* **40/1**

5 *4* **Safe Home (IRE)**[144] 4-10-7 0........................ DougieCostello 75
(John Quinn) *t.k.h: trckd ldrs: mstke and outpcd 2 out: btn bef last* **11/5**[1]

0/P- **6** *4 ½* **Bollin Line**[77] 3271 7-10-8 0........................ NathanMoscrop[(7)] 79
(Lucinda Egerton) *hld up: stdy hdwy after 3 out: rdn and wknd fr 2 out* **50/1**

P0- **7** *nk* **March Seventeenth (IRE)**[12] 4546 6-11-1 0........................ BarryKeniry 78
(Brian Ellison) *nt fluent on occasions: hld up: outpcd 3 out: btn next* **33/1**

0- **8** *28* **Casual Cavalier (IRE)**[140] 2037 6-10-10 0........................ JohnDawson[(5)] 50
(John Wade) *nt fluent: sn bhd: struggling on fnl circ: nvr on terms* **150/1**

0- **P** **Ihtikar (USA)**[158] 1786 4-10-7 0........................ AdrianLane
(Lucy Normile) *bhd: struggling bef 3 out: t.o whn p.u bef last* **66/1**

23- **F** **Lawsons Thorns (IRE)**[55] 3760 5-11-1 0........................ HarrySkelton
(Dan Skelton) *plld hrd: prom tl wknd 2 out: no ch whn fell heavily last* **7/2**[2]

4m 26.5s (9.10) **Going Correction** +0.60s/f (Soft)
WFA 4 from 5yo+ 7lb **10** Ran SP% **113.6**
Speed ratings (Par 105): **102,98,97,91,89 87,87,74,,**
CSF £20.36 TOTE £4.60: £1.70, £1.40, £2.20; EX 11.80 Trifecta £71.60.
Owner R Shiels **Bred** Alistair Thompson **Trained** Jedburgh, Borders

FOCUS
With the former useful Flat performer Safe Home disappointing and Lawson Thorns racing too keenly, this didn't take as much winning as expected. The pace was fair. The winner was the form pick and is rated to his mark.

4773 HEXHAM H'CAP CHASE (25 fncs) 4m
3:35 (3:35) (Class 4) (0-110,107) 5-Y-0+ **£3,768** (£1,106; £553; £276)

Form RPR

051- **1** **Boris The Blade**[11] 4577 12-9-13 **85**........................(b) SamanthaDrake[(5)] 99
(Tina Jackson) *led to 7th: regained ld 9th: clr w runner-up fr 20th: hrd pressed and pushed along fr 4 out: hdd briefly bef last: styd on gamely run-in* **6/5**[1]

135- **2** *7* **Mansonien L'As (FR)**[21] 4382 8-11-1 **96**........................(p) AdrianLane 104
(Donald McCain) *a cl up: led 7th to 9th: clr w wnr fr 20th: chal 4 out: led briefly bef last: kpt on same pce run-in* **13/2**

P04- **3** *39* **Outlaw Tom (IRE)**[21] 4368 10-11-9 **104**........................(p) PeterBuchanan 72
(Lucinda Russell) *nt fluent on occasions: in tch: pushed along 18th: tk mod 3rd 4 out: no imp fr next* **5/1**[2]

550- **4** *4* **More Equity**[17] 4461 12-11-7 **107**........................ ColmMcCormack[(5)] 71
(Dianne Sayer) *hld up bhd ldng gp: pushed along and outpcd fr 11th: struggling fnl circ: nvr on terms* **20/1**

/00- **P** **Desert Tommy**[62] 3639 13-10-0 **81** oh1........................(p) DougieCostello
(Lucinda Egerton) *nt fluent in rr: struggling 1/2-way: t.o whn p.u after 20th* **33/1**

0/5- **U** **Rojo Vivo**[36] 4082 8-10-8 **89**........................ RichieMcGrath
(Henry Hogarth) *trckd ldrs: cl 3rd and stl gng wl whn blnd bdly and uns rdr 18th* **8/1**

10P- **P** **Fozy Moss**[7] 4630 8-10-1 **89** ow2........................(vt[1]) DaraghBourke[(7)]
(Stuart Coltherd) *in tch: pushed along fr 1/2-way: rallied after 18th: struggling fr 4 out: t.o whn p.u bef last* **11/2**[3]

9m 14.9s (19.50) **Going Correction** +0.725s/f (Soft) **7** Ran SP% **109.7**
Speed ratings: **104,102,92,91,** ,
CSF £8.88 TOTE £2.00: £1.50, £3.90; EX 7.00 Trifecta £27.70.
Owner Simon Bodsworth & Howard Thompson **Bred** R Robinson **Trained** Liverton, Cleveland

FOCUS
A 4m handicap chase run at a fair gallop it went to a thorough stayer. The winner was still 12lb off last season's best.

4774 SIS H'CAP HURDLE (12 hdls) 3m
4:15 (4:15) (Class 5) (0-100,100) 4-Y-0+ **£2,053** (£598; £299)

Form RPR

050- **1** **Pierrers Bounty (IRE)**[16] 4478 7-11-9 **100**........................(p) TonyKelly[(3)] 104+
(Henry Hogarth) *midfield: stdy hdwy 4 out: rdn to ld bef last: hld on wl towards fin* **16/1**

6B3- **2** *hd* **Bollin Fiona**[6] 4649 10-10-11 **95**........................ RyanNichol[(10)] 99+
(Donald Whillans) *chsd ldrs: nt fluent 5th: drvn and outpcd 2 out: rallied bef last: wnt 2nd run-in: kpt on u.p: jst hld* **12/1**

630- **3** *5* **Master Murphy (IRE)**[12] 4553 9-10-8 **89**........................ AlistairFindlay[(7)] 86
(Jane Walton) *led to bef 7th: styd upsides: rdn and led briefly bef last: outpcd last 150yds* **9/1**

FR0- **4** *8* **Dun To Perfection**[8] 4615 7-10-0 **84**........................ JamesCorbett[(10)] 73
(Susan Corbett) *hld up: hdwy to chse ldrs after 3 out: rdn and outpcd bef last* **50/1**

U44- **5** *1 ¼* **Yukon Delta (IRE)**[17] 4461 7-10-11 **85**........................ KennyJohnson 73
(Robert Johnson) *cl up: led 3 out to bef last: sn rdn and wknd* **9/1**

320- **6** *2* **Stickleback**[23] 4338 5-10-11 **90**........................(v[1]) JoeColliver[(5)] 76
(Micky Hammond) *hld up: stdy hdwy 7th: hit and rdn 4 out: rallied after next: no imp fr 2 out* **8/1**[3]

S02- **7** *10* **Millers Reef (IRE)**[18] 4446 8-11-9 **97**........................ WilsonRenwick 76
(Keith Dalgleish) *t.k.h: hld up: smooth hdwy bef 2 out: rdn between last 2: sn btn* **7/2**[1]

/P0- **8** *16* **Double Whammy**[12] 4553 8-11-2 **90**........................(b[1]) AdrianLane 50
(Iain Jardine) *cl up tl rdn and wknd bef 2 out* **12/1**

310- **9** *12* **Rocky Stone (IRE)**[17] 4461 6-11-12 **100**........................ HenryBrooke 48
(Donald McCain) *prom: lost pl 4 out: struggling after next* **7/1**[2]

00- **10** *11* **Pairc Na Leasa (IRE)**[17] 4465 8-11-0 **91**........................(tp) HarryChalloner[(3)] 28
(Martin Todhunter) *hld up on outside: rdn whn mstke 3 out: sn struggling* **14/1**

F64- **11** *21* **Auberge (IRE)**[12] 4553 10-11-3 **96**........................(p) ColmMcCormack[(5)] 12
(Evelyn Slack) *sn towards rr on ins: struggling bef 4 out: nvr on terms* **7/1**[2]

40P- **12** *15* **Amethyst Rose (IRE)**[30] 4201 7-10-7 **88**........................ DaraghBourke[(7)]
(Stuart Coltherd) *chsd ldrs: led bef 7th to 3 out: rdn and wknd bef next* **16/1**

P/5- **P** **Patriot (IRE)**[17] 4465 10-10-6 **87**........................(p) GrahamWatters[(7)]
(Barry Murtagh) *midfield: struggling 8th: t.o whn p.u bef 2 out* **66/1**

605- **P** **The Boozy Bishop (IRE)**[8] 4612 9-9-10 **75** oh5 ow1(p) MissCWalton[(5)]
(Sheena Walton) *towards rr: stdy hdwy 7th: struggling bef 4 out: t.o whn p.u bef 2 out* **33/1**

004- **P** **Marlee Massie (IRE)**[40] 4038 5-10-6 **80**........................ LucyAlexander
(N W Alexander) *nt fluent in rr: outpcd whn hit 4 out: sn btn: t.o whn p.u bef last* **25/1**

6m 30.1s (21.10) **Going Correction** +0.60s/f (Soft) **15** Ran SP% **122.4**
Speed ratings (Par 103): **88,87,86,83,83 82,79,73,69,66 59,54,,,**
CSF £192.06 CT £1853.32 TOTE £20.10: £5.70, £4.00, £3.40; EX 367.90 Trifecta £1664.60.
Owner Hogarth Racing **Bred** S W Simmons **Trained** Stillington, N Yorks

FOCUS
A big field of mainly exposed staying handicappers, and run at just an ordinary gallop, with the majority still in contention going to the fourth-last. There's probably more to come the winner.

4775 SIS H'CAP CHASE (19 fncs) 3m 1f
4:55 (4:55) (Class 5) (0-100,99) 5-Y-0+ **£2,258** (£658; £329)

Form RPR

2PU- **1** **Samson Collonges (FR)**[6] 4652 8-9-13 **75**........................ TonyKelly[(3)] 82
(Rebecca Menzies) *hld up: smooth hdwy and cl up 15th: effrt and ev ch bef last: led run-in: drvn out* **5/1**[3]

5PP- **2** *nk* **Filbert Fox (IRE)**[11] 4577 8-10-0 **73**........................(p) PeterBuchanan 80
(Alistair Whillans) *led to 8th: led 10th: rdn and hrd pressed fr 3 out: drifted rt and hdd run-in: rallied: hld nr fin* **12/1**

414- **3** *6* **Esme Rides A Gaine**[50] 3834 12-10-6 **79**.......................... BrianHarding 81
(Christopher Wilson) *hld up bhd ldng gp: drvn and outpcd 13th: plenty to do 4 out: gd hdwy to chse ldng pair bef last: no further imp run-in* **14/1**

342- **4** *23* **Soul Angel**[6] 4652 10-10-1 **74**..(v) AdrianLane 52
(Sandy Forster) *cl up: ev ch after 4 out to 2 out: outpcd whn nt fluent last: sn wknd* **13/2**

604- **5** *27* **Trouble In Paris (IRE)**[75] 3355 7-10-4 **77**.....................(t) LucyAlexander 28
(Barry Murtagh) *w ldr: led 8th to 10th: drvn and outpcd after 4 out: struggling fr next* **10/1**

534- **6** *33* **Wave Breaker (IRE)**[21] 4380 7-10-0 **73**.....................(bt[1]) DougieCostello
(Robert Johnson) *prom: outpcd whn blnd 13th: struggling bef next: t.o* **7/1**

P42- **F** **Sam Patch**[21] 4380 11-9-9 **73**...................................(b[1]) CallumWhillans[(5)]
(Donald Whillans) *hld up: hdwy and prom 13th: nt fluent 15th: struggling after next: sixth and btn whn fell 2 out* **3/1**[1]

P/P- **P** **Reland (FR)**[17] 4465 9-10-6 **84**...................................... GrantCockburn[(5)]
(Mrs Jackie Stephen) *bhd: lost tch 10th: t.o whn p.u bef 12th* **40/1**

PP3- **U** **Beau Dandy (IRE)**[11] 4580 9-11-5 **99**...................(b) DiarmuidO'Regan[(7)]
(Chris Grant) *t.k.h: prom tl rdn and outpcd after 4 out: seventh and no ch whn hmpd and uns rdr 2 out* **4/1**[2]

0PP/ **P** **Master Conor (IRE)**[437] 3385 8-9-11 **73** oh23............. HarryChalloner[(3)]
(Henry Hogarth) *sn wl bhd: no ch whn p.u after 12th* **40/1**

6m 56.0s (23.80) **Going Correction** +0.725s/f (Soft) **10** Ran SP% **115.8**
Speed ratings: **90,89,87,80,71 61,,,,**
CSF £61.14 CT £781.10 TOTE £5.80: £1.70, £4.80, £3.50; EX 63.00 Trifecta £638.00.
Owner Premier Racing Partnerships **Bred** Gaec Delorme Freres **Trained** Stearsby, N Yorks
■ Stewards' Enquiry : Peter Buchanan one-day ban: careless riding (Mar 27)

FOCUS
A decent gallop to this handicap chase, but it was a low-grade affair. The winner and third set the level.

4776 FOLLOW US ON FACEBOOK "NATIONAL HUNT" MAIDEN HURDLE (10 hdls) 2m 4f 110y
5:25 (5:29) (Class 5) 4-Y-0+ **£2,053** (£598; £299)

Form RPR

35/- **1** **Bop Along (IRE)**[453] 3058 7-10-11 0.................................. AdamNicol[(5)] 105
(Michael Smith) *prom: rdn 2 out: rallied bef last: styd on wl to ld cl home* **9/1**

223- **2** *shd* **Greensalt (IRE)**[54] 3781 6-11-2 115..................................(t) HenryBrooke 105
(Donald McCain) *trckd ldrs: hdwy to ld after 2 out: rdn bef last: kpt on run-in: hdd cl home* **1/1**[1]

0- **3** *1 ¾* **Rascal (IRE)**[72] 3440 5-11-2 0.................................. HarrySkelton 103
(Dan Skelton) *plld hrd in midfield: hdwy and prom 3 out: rdn and rn green next: rallied bef last: kpt on run-in: bttr for r* **9/2**[3]

544- **4** *nk* **Sheilas Lady**[57] 3727 6-10-6 0.. JohnKington[(3)] 96
(Andrew Crook) *cl up: led 1/2-way: rdn and hdd after 2 out: rallied: one pce run-in* **16/1**

P56- **5** *21* **Mrs Grass**[17] 4465 7-10-4 69.. JoeColliver[(5)] 76
(Jonathan Haynes) *hld up in midfield: effrt and pushed along 2 out: sn outpcd* **150/1**

/P6- **6** *7* **Master Bud**[208] 1281 9-10-6 73.................................... JamesCorbett[(10)] 75
(Susan Corbett) *hld up: stdy hdwy and in tch 3 out: n.m.r and lost pl bef next: n.d after* **150/1**

/35- **7** *6* **Isaacstown Lad (IRE)**[17] 4460 7-11-2 111.......................... BrianHarding 69
(William Amos) *hld up: effrt on outside after 3 out: struggling fr next* **22/1**

050- **8** *1* **Westend Theatre (IRE)**[28] 4234 5-10-9 0.................... AlistairFindlay[(7)] 68
(Jane Walton) *led to 1/2-way: cl up tl rdn and wknd bef 2 out* **66/1**

024- **9** *¾* **Conjola**[36] 4083 7-10-9 0.. PeterBuchanan 61
(Geoffrey Harker) *hld up: hdwy and in tch bef 2 out: sn rdn and wknd* **33/1**

430- **10** *9* **Lilly's Legend**[37] 4074 4-10-0 0.. DougieCostello 42
(Mark Walford) *hld up in midfield on outside: rdn after 3 out: wknd bef next* **20/1**

66- **11** *27* **Lachlan Mor**[69] 3522 5-10-9 0....................................... DaraghBourke[(7)] 31
(Stuart Coltherd) *nt fluent in rr: struggling 4 out: nvr on terms* **100/1**

- **12** *33* **Probably Not (IRE)**[40] 4046 7-10-11 0......................... PatrickCorbett[(5)]
(H Smyth, Ire) *bhd: lost tch after 4 out: t.o* **100/1**

15- **P** **Ocean Waves (IRE)**[61] 3657 5-11-2 0............................ WilsonRenwick
(Jedd O'Keeffe) *prom: hdwy and ev ch bef 4 out: wknd qckly after next: t.o whn p.u bef last* **7/2**[2]

0- **P** **Dunleer Dixie**[91] 3042 6-11-2 0...(t) AdrianLane
(Lucy Normile) *bhd: lost tch fr 6th: t.o whn p.u after 2 out* **150/1**

5m 27.8s (15.30) **Going Correction** +0.60s/f (Soft)
WFA 4 from 5yo+ 8lb **14** Ran SP% **123.8**
Speed ratings (Par 103): **94,93,93,93,85 82,80,79,79,76 65,53,,**
CSF £19.10 TOTE £10.90: £1.80, £1.20, £1.60; EX 30.30 Trifecta £170.80.
Owner East-West Partnership **Bred** Mrs O O'Driscoll **Trained** Kirkheaton, Northumberland
■ Stewards' Enquiry : Adam Nicol seven-day ban: used whip above permitted level without giving gelding time to respond (Mar 27-31,Apr 1-2)

FOCUS
The first four finished clear in this 2m4f novice hurdle. The first pair are rated below their best.
T/Plt: £898.40 to a £1 stake. Pool of £68428.84 - 55.60 winning tickets. T/Qpdt: £143.70 to a £1 stake. Pool of £5687.07 - 29.27 winning tickets. RY

4446 TOWCESTER (R-H)
Thursday, March 13

OFFICIAL GOING: Good to soft (soft in places on hurdle course)
Wind: virtually nil Weather: fog clearing, sunny

4777 32RED THUNDERSTRUCK II SLOT MARES' NOVICES' HURDLE (11 hdls) 2m 5f
1:55 (1:55) (Class 4) 5-Y-0+ **£3,195** (£992; £534)

Form RPR

412- **1** **Rosa Fleet (IRE)**[15] 4487 6-11-3 119................................ LiamTreadwell 117+
(Venetia Williams) *mde all: mstke 5th: rdn and mstke 2 out: kpt on wl u.p flat* **10/11**[1]

4P2- **2** *¾* **Cabaret Girl**[21] 4375 7-10-10 0... LeightonAspell 108
(John O'Neill) *hld up in tch: clsd to chse wnr 8th: effrt and hit 2 out: ev ch between last 2: edgd lft and nt qckn flat* **5/4**[2]

4- **3** *11* **Our Cat (IRE)**[35] 4114 6-10-10 0...................................... PaddyBrennan 99
(Fergal O'Brien) *chsd wnr tl 8th: cl 3rd and rdn whn hit 2 out: wknd between last 2* **11/1**[3]

P- **P** **Teeton Blackvelvet**[15] 4487 5-10-10 0........................... TomMessenger
(Caroline Bailey) *wl in tch: mstke 2nd: rdn and mstke 8th: wknd bef next: t.o whn p.u 2 out* **66/1**

5m 29.7s (2.50) **Going Correction** -0.40s/f (Good) **4** Ran SP% **106.7**
Speed ratings: **79,78,74,**
CSF £2.38 TOTE £2.00; EX 2.00 Trifecta £2.20.
Owner Mezzone Family **Bred** J F C Maxwell **Trained** Kings Caple, H'fords

FOCUS
Chase course dolled out wide on separate bends. Hurdle course on inside line. The first two are rated to their marks in this modest event.

4778 32RED FREE £10 BONUS H'CAP CHASE (18 fncs) 3m 110y
2:30 (2:30) (Class 5) (0-100,94) 5-Y-0+ **£2,144** (£629; £314; £157)

Form RPR

5/4- **1** **Cosway Spirit (IRE)**[16] 4484 7-10-10 **78**......................(p) JamesDavies 91+
(Ben Pauling) *w ldr tl led 14th: rdn and j.rt 2 out: forged ahd between last 2: j.rt again last: styd on wl: rdn out* **3/1**[2]

035- **2** *6* **Witch's Hat (IRE)**[16] 4486 11-10-13 **81**................................(t) MarkGrant 90
(Jim Old) *mde most tl mstke and hdd 14th: rdn bef 2 out: no ex between last 2: swtchd lft last: plugged on same pce flat* **6/1**

233- **3** *17* **Craiglands (IRE)**[6] 4663 12-11-1 **83**................................(v) WillKennedy 76
(Ian Williams) *in tch in midfield: 4th and drvn after 3 out: sn btn: wnt modest 3rd between last 2: plugged on* **5/2**[1]

45P- **4** *12* **Top Benefit (IRE)**[28] 4243 12-10-3 **76**............................ JamesBanks[(5)] 58
(Richard Harper) *chsd ldrs: mstke 11th: rdn and no hdwy sn after 3 out: btn on uphill run to next: lost 3rd and wknd between last 2* **12/1**

06- **5** *7* **Caspian Piper (IRE)**[84] 3180 7-11-5 **94**.......................(b) MikeyEnnis[(7)] 70
(Hugo Froud) *chsd ldrs: rdn 11th: btn whn blnd 3 out: wknd wl bef next: t.o* **8/1**

503- **P** **I Know The Code (IRE)**[18] 4451 9-11-4 **86**......................... TomSiddall
(Lynn Siddall) *hld up in tch in last pair: short-lived effrt 15th: mstke and wknd next: t.o whn p.u 2 out* **4/1**[3]

P50- **P** **My Silver Lilly**[16] 4481 7-10-3 **74**...................................... JackQuinlan[(3)]
(Clive Drew) *mstkes: hld up in tch in last pair: mstke 12th: rdn: blnd and pckd 15th: sn lost tch and p.u next: dismntd* **20/1**

6m 31.4s (-5.50) **Going Correction** -0.175s/f (Good) **7** Ran SP% **111.4**
Speed ratings: **101,99,93,89,87 ,**
CSF £19.98 TOTE £4.20: £1.60, £3.80; EX 19.30 Trifecta £46.00.
Owner Alan Marsh & Partners **Bred** James Lawler **Trained** Bourton-On-The-Water, Gloucs

FOCUS
This was desperately weak but there were positives to be taken from the performances of the first two home. The form is rated around the second.

4779 32RED.COM H'CAP HURDLE (12 hdls) 3m
3:05 (3:05) (Class 5) (0-100,101) 4-Y-0+ **£1,949** (£572; £286; £143)

Form RPR

001- **1** **Warsaw Pact (IRE)**[7] 4636 11-9-9 **76** 7ex....................... MrLKilgarriff[(7)] 82
(Steven Dixon) *in tch in last pair: rdn and effrt in 4th after 3 out: led next: hung lft u.p flat: hld on* **9/2**[3]

/06- **2** *nk* **Cropley (IRE)**[26] 4275 5-10-6 **90**.........................(b[1]) TommieMO'Brien[(10)] 95
(Jonjo O'Neill) *t.k.h: chsd ldrs on outer: 3rd and nt qckn 2 out: wnt 2nd last: styd st as wnr hung and ev ch towards fin: a jst hld* **4/1**[2]

P23- **3** *7* **Earcomesthedream (IRE)**[18] 4446 11-11-7 **95**.................(b) JackDoyle 94
(Peter Pritchard) *w ldr tl led after 3 out: hdd next: lost 2nd last: wknd flat* **13/2**

462- **4** *14* **Burnthill (IRE)**[64] 3605 9-9-13 **80**..............................(tp) GeraldQuinn[(7)] 66
(Claire Dyson) *mde most: rdn and hdd after 3 out: 4th and btn whn j.rt 2 out: wknd between last 2* **8/1**

0/P- **5** *34* **Round The Horn (IRE)**[53] 3798 14-11-12 **100**.....................(t) MarkGrant 55
(Jim Old) *wl in tch in midfield: rdn and lost pl bef 3 out: lost tch on uphill run to 2 out: t.o* **16/1**

0F1- **P** **Newton Thistle**[18] 4446 7-11-0 **88**.. FelixDeGiles
(Ben Pauling) *chsd ldrs: rdn and sttruggling 3 out: wknd on uphill run to 2 out: t.o whn p.u last* **5/2**[1]

434- **P** **Blue Cove**[18] 4446 9-10-1 **75**.. TomSiddall
(Lynn Siddall) *hld up in tch in rr: rdn 7th: struggling after next: lost tch bef 3 out: t.o whn p.u 2 out* **11/2**

6m 6.6s (-8.40) **Going Correction** -0.40s/f (Good) **7** Ran SP% **112.5**
Speed ratings (Par 103): **98,97,95,90,79 ,**
CSF £22.21 CT £114.16 TOTE £5.60: £3.30, £1.80; EX 46.40 Trifecta £190.00.
Owner S Dixon **Bred** Saad Bin Mishrif **Trained** Winterslow, Wilts

FOCUS
A fair race for the grade. There's a case for rating the form a bit higher.

4780 32REDPOKER.COM FESTIVAL FREEROLLS NOVICES' CHASE (14 fncs) 2m 3f 110y
3:45 (3:45) (Class 4) 5-Y-0+ **£3,768** (£1,106; £553; £276)

Form RPR

421- **1** **Headly's Bridge (IRE)**[12] 4560 8-11-5 130...................... PaddyBrennan 133+
(Simon Earle) *mde all: j.rt at times: gng best and j.rt last: r.o wl flat: rdn out* **2/5**[1]

/15- **2** *1 ½* **Valid Point (IRE)**[93] 3011 8-10-12 112.................................(t) MarkGrant 121
(Jim Old) *trckd ldrs: wnt 2nd 6th: rdn and ev ch after 2 out: mstke last: r.o but nt gng pce of wnr fnl 100yds* **11/4**[2]

4RR- **3** *31* **Duaiseoir (IRE)**[21] 4373 8-10-9 109................................ RobertDunne[(3)] 99
(Venetia Williams) *j.lft and several slow jumps: chsd ldrs: reminders after 3rd: ev ch 3 out: wknd sn after next: eased flat* **12/1**[3]

340- **4** *28* **Ata Boy (IRE)**[83] 3188 8-10-5 0...................................... DanielHiskett[(7)] 62
(Richard Phillips) *chsd wnr tl 6th: styd chsng ldrs tl wknd sn after 3 out: t.o between last 2* **66/1**

5m 18.7s (0.50) **Going Correction** -0.175s/f (Good) **4** Ran SP% **107.3**
Speed ratings: **92,91,79,67**
CSF £1.94 TOTE £1.20; EX 2.10 Trifecta £2.30.
Owner Mrs P L Bridel **Bred** Islanmore Stud **Trained** Tytherington, Wilts

FOCUS
This was nothing more than a match on paper and that proved to be the case in the race itself. It was steadily run and the first three are rated to their marks.

4781 32RED TOMB RAIDER SLOT H'CAP HURDLE (8 hdls) 2m
4:25 (4:26) (Class 4) (0-120,120) 4-Y-0+ **£3,119** (£915; £457; £228)

Form RPR

P3U- **1** **Scots Gaelic (IRE)**[3] 4726 7-11-12 **120**......................... LeightonAspell 125+
(John Quinn) *chsd ldrs: chal bef 2 out: j. into ld 2 out: qckng clr bef last: r.o wl: comf* **11/10**[1]

The Form Book Jumps, Raceform Ltd, Compton, RG20 6NL.

133- **2** *4* **Helium (FR)**[7] 4634 9-11-1 **116**........ MrsAlexDunn[(7)] 114
(Alexandra Dunn) *chsd ldr tl led bef 2 out: outj. and hdd 2 out: r.o same pce between last 2* **7/2**[2]

204- **3** *1 ¼* **Rasheed**[7] 4020 6-10-9 **108**........(v) MattCrawley[(5)] 105
(Lucy Wadham) *in tch in rr: clsd and wl in tch 5th: effrt in cl 3rd 2 out: outpcd by wnr and styd on same pce between last 2* **7/2**[2]

15- **4** *8* **Great Link**[6] 4659 5-11-6 **114**........(t) LeeEdwards 104
(Tony Carroll) *chsd ldrs: nt fluent 4th: rdn and effrt sn after 3 out: wknd next* **11/2**[3]

/05- **5** *15* **Asker (IRE)**[15] 4494 6-9-13 **100**........(p) MrHGMiller[(7)] 74
(Zoe Davison) *led tl rdn and hdd bef 2 out: sn btn: wknd between last 2* **33/1**

3m 59.0s (-8.90) **Going Correction** -0.40s/f (Good) **5** Ran SP% **110.4**
Speed ratings (Par 105): **106,104,103,99,91**
CSF £5.53 TOTE £1.80: £1.10, £3.50; EX 5.80 Trifecta £11.50.
Owner Carl Hinchy **Bred** Alan MacAlister **Trained** Settrington, N Yorks

FOCUS
The cosy winner has the potential to rate higher on Flat form.

4782 32RED CASINO OPEN HUNTERS' CHASE (14 fncs) 2m 3f 110y
5:05 (5:07) (Class 6) 5-Y-0+ **£935** (£290; £145; £72)

Form RPR

/14- **1** **Penmore Mill (IRE)**[39] 4057 9-12-1 119........ MrTEllis[(5)] 129+
(F A Hutsby) *hld up in rr: gd hdwy to chse ldrs 6th: wnt 2nd 10th: led next: readily c clr after 3 out: v easily* **8/11**[1]

423/ **2** *22* **Stonethrower (IRE)**[533] 1642 9-11-13 124........(t) MrEDavid[(7)] 107
(Tim Vaughan) *in tch in midfield: hdwy to chse ldr after 5th: led 9th tl 11th: mstke 3 out: sn rdn and brushed aside by wnr: j.rt last: kpt on for 2nd flat* **15/8**[2]

4/P- **3** *nk* **Bell On Bike (IRE)**[11] 11-11-5 90........(p) MrTAMcclorey[(7)] 98
(Mrs Jackie Hunt) *in tch towards rr: hdwy to chse ldrs after 3 out: no ch w wnr but battling for 2nd last: kpt on* **80/1**

040- **4** *13* **Priceless Art (IRE)**[18] 9-11-9 113........ MrSDavies-Thomas[(7)] 90
(Tommy Morgan) *chsd ldrs: lost pl and rdn after 7th: wknd bef 3 out* **10/1**[3]

/24- **5** *18* **Orfeo Conti (FR)**[284] 597 12-11-5 87........ MrOWedmore[(7)] 70
(Miss Rose Grissell) *chsd ldrs: rdn and wknd after 3 out: t.o last* **25/1**

0P5/ **P** **Karasakal (IRE)**[12] 11-11-5 87........ MrHStock[(7)]
(Mrs Kim Sly) *chsd ldrs: lost pl and mstke 5th: t.o and p.u 2 out* **50/1**

PFP/ **P** **Samenerve (FR)**[25] 7-11-9 102........(tp) MrJDocker[(7)]
(Stuart Morris) *led tl 9th: wknd qckly bef 3 out: t.o and p.u 2 out* **50/1**

5m 12.4s (-5.80) **Going Correction** -0.175s/f (Good) **7** Ran SP% **110.8**
Speed ratings: **104,95,95,89,82** ,
CSF £2.30 TOTE £1.70: £1.10, £1.90; EX 2.30 Trifecta £63.20.
Owner K Hutsby **Bred** P Power **Trained** Stratford-Upon-Avon, Warwicks
■ Stewards' Enquiry : Mr T A Mcclorey two-day ban: used whip above permitted level (Mar 27-28)

FOCUS
This hunter chase was lacking in depth and it played out exactly as the market suggested. The winner is a decent hunter.

4783 32RED IMMORTAL ROMANCE SLOT CONDITIONAL JOCKEYS' H'CAP HURDLE (10 hdls) 2m 3f 110y
5:35 (5:35) (Class 5) (0-100,100) 4-Y-0+ **£1,949** (£572; £286; £143)

Form RPR

4P5- **1** **Fidelor (FR)**[18] 4447 8-11-1 **89**........(t) KillianMoore 90
(Alex Hales) *led tl rdn and hdd bef 2 out: looked in 3rd whn lft cl 2nd last: styd on u.p to ld last strides* **5/1**

656- **2** *hd* **Thinger Licht (FR)**[9] 4607 5-11-12 **100**........ ConorShoemark 101
(Tony Carroll) *hld up in tch in last pair: rdn and effrt to chse ldng pair bef 2 out: wnt 2nd between last 2: lft in ld and hmpd last: hung rt flat: hdd last strides* **3/1**[2]

00P- **3** *27* **Gainsborough's Art (IRE)**[53] 2427 9-9-9 **74** oh19.....(p) DanielHiskett[(5)] 51
(Harry Chisman) *chsd ldrs: wnt 2nd 6th tl 7th: wknd after 3 out: lft 3rd last* **66/1**

0P0- **4** *nk* **Photogenique (FR)**[20] 4398 11-10-0 **74** oh10........[1] JamesBest 50
(Rob Summers) *chsd ldr tl 4th: styd handy tl rdn and struggling after 3 out: sn wknd: lft 4th last* **33/1**

P60/ **U** **Aviador (GER)**[677] 98 8-11-3 **98**........ LukeIngram[(7)] 101+
(Lucy Wadham) *chsd ldrs: wnt 2nd 4th tl 6th: chsd ldr again 7th: led bef 2 out: keeping on and looked in command whn mstke, rdr unbalanced and uns last* **10/3**[3]

236- **F** **Caught By Witness (IRE)**[35] 4107 9-10-0 **79**........(t) CharlieDeutsch[(5)]
(Anthony Middleton) *hld up in last pair: clsd and wl in tch whn mstke 7th: nt rcvr and wknd after next: bhd whn fell last* **11/8**[1]

5m 3.6s (-6.00) **Going Correction** -0.40s/f (Good) **6** Ran SP% **111.3**
Speed ratings (Par 103): **96,95,85,85,**
CSF £20.16 TOTE £3.70: £2.10, £3.00; EX 12.40 Trifecta £123.30.
Owner Edging Ahead **Bred** Pascal Deshayes And Jean-Paul Deshayes **Trained** Edgcote, Northants
■ Stewards' Enquiry : Killian Moore two-day ban: used whip above permitted level (Mar 27-28)

FOCUS
As poor a handicap hurdle as you'll see. The first two set the level.
T/Plt: £40.90 to a £1 stake. Pool of £46572.94 - 831.08 winning tickets. T/Qpdt: £9.50 to a £1 stake. Pool of £3386.27 - 263.40 winning tickets. SP

4764 CHELTENHAM (L-H)
Friday, March 14

OFFICIAL GOING: Good (good to soft in places; 7.0)
Wind: Almost nil Weather: Fine

4784 JCB TRIUMPH HURDLE GRADE 1 (8 hdls) 2m 1f
1:30 (1:31) (Class 1) 4-Y-0 **£68,340** (£25,644; £12,840; £6,396; £3,216; £1,608)

Form RPR

12- **1** **Tiger Roll (IRE)**[33] 4178 4-11-0 0........ DavyRussell 144+
(Gordon Elliott, Ire) *lengthy: hld up: midfield: hdwy after 3 out: travelled wl: led appr last: r.o wl to draw clr fnl 75yds* **10/1**

222- **2** *3 ¼* **Kentucky Hyden (IRE)**[48] 3885 4-11-0 139........ DavidBass 141
(Nicky Henderson) *mstkes: prom: hmpd 2nd: led briefly between last 2: edgd lft appr last where stl cl 2nd: continued to go lft run-in: outpcd by wnr fnl 100yds: edgd rt whn wl hld towards fin* **20/1**

211- **3** *1 ¾* **Guitar Pete (IRE)**[33] 4178 4-11-0 142........(v) PCarberry 138
(D T Hughes, Ire) *lw: prom: led 3rd to 4th: remained prom: led again appr 2 out: hdd between last 2: stl cl 3rd last: styd on same pce run-in* **7/1**

11- **4** *3 ¾* **Calipto (FR)**[34] 4143 4-11-0 149........ DarylJacob 139+
(Paul Nicholls) *in tch: hmpd 2nd: trcking ldrs whn stirrup leather broke appr 2 out: rdr rode wout irons after flight whn stl cl up chsng ldrs: rdn between last 2: one pce whn mstke last: no imp after* **11/2**[1]

111- **5** *3 ¾* **Rutherglen**[29] 3474 4-11-0 135........ NoelFehily 132
(John Quinn) *swtg: midfield: sltly hmpd 2nd: rdn after 2 out: plugged on but nvr able to trble ldrs* **10/1**

113- **6** *4* **Royal Irish Hussar (IRE)**[90] 3089 4-11-0 145........ BarryGeraghty 129
(Nicky Henderson) *racd keenly on outer wout cover: midfield: prom bef 2nd: nt fluent 5th: rdn and wknd after 2 out* **6/1**[2]

311- **7** *4* **Pearl Castle (IRE)**[23] 4345 4-11-0 136........ BrianHughes 126
(John Quinn) *midfield: mstke 4th: n.m.r on inner appr 3 out: lost pl bef 2 out and u.p: n.d after* **12/1**

21- **8** *4 ½* **Broughton (GER)**[40] 4054 4-11-0 138........ DenisO'Regan 122
(John Ferguson) *hld up: hmpd appr 3 out: pushed along after 2 out: nvr picked-up: wl btn* **13/2**[3]

21- **9** *2* **Lindenhurst (IRE)**[160] 1772 4-11-0 134........(t) MarkBolger 122+
(John C McConnell, Ire) *racd keenly: hld up in midfield: hmpd and lost pl 2nd: struggling after 2 out: wl btn* **16/1**

4- **10** *30* **Amoruccio (FR)**[21] 4401 4-11-0 0........ JamesBest 91
(Paul Webber) *str: hld up: hmpd 2nd: hdwy into midfield 5th: pushed along after 3 out: wknd 2 out* **150/1**

0- **11** *19* **Achtung**[13] 4562 4-11-0 0........(t) PeterBuchanan 74
(Luke Comer, Ire) *in rr: sn niggled along: j. slowly 5th: lost tch bef 3 out: t.o* **250/1**

3- **12** *4* **Plinth (IRE)**[33] 4178 4-11-0 0........(p) APMcCoy 71
(A P O'Brien, Ire) *w'like: lw: a.p: lft in ld 2nd: hdd 3rd: led again 4th: mstke 5th: hdd appr 2 out where stl chsng ldrs whn mstke: sn rdn and wknd: t.o* **12/1**

F0- **R** **Cherry Tiger**[8] 4632 4-11-0 0........ WayneKavanagh
(Graeme McPherson) *racd keenly: hld up in rr: hdwy but no bttr than midfield 3rd: struggling next: j. slowly 5th: lost tch bef 3 out: t.o whn ref last* **250/1**

2- **B** **Adriana Des Mottes (FR)**[20] 4432 4-10-7 136........ PaulTownend
(W P Mullins, Ire) *lengthy: hld up: b.d 2nd* **20/1**

31- **F** **Abbyssial (IRE)**[20] 4432 4-11-0 143........ RWalsh
(W P Mullins, Ire) *led tl fell 2nd* **8/1**

4m 1.0s (-10.30) **Going Correction** -0.30s/f (Good) **15** Ran SP% **117.0**
Speed ratings: **112,110,109,107,106 104,102,100,99,85 76,74,,,**
CSF £191.47 CT £1491.51 TOTE £10.80: £3.20, £6.60, £2.00; EX 328.80 Trifecta £2016.90.
Owner Gigginstown House Stud **Bred** G O'Brien **Trained** Trim, Co Meath

FOCUS
All races on New course and chases reduced by about 36yds per circuit from Thursday. The consensus from the jockeys after the opener was that the ground, at that stage at any rate on a sunny day, was riding on the slow side of good. They didn't go what looked a great pace and the time was 6.5sec outside the standard. This championship event lacked leading juveniles Le Rocher, winner of the Finale Hurdle at Chepstow but ruled out through injury, and Adonis winner Activial, who is being kept for Aintree. It has to rate as very much a lesser renewal, although Tiger Roll and the unlucky Calipto can rate higher. The third is probably the best guide.

4785 VINCENT O'BRIEN COUNTY H'CAP HURDLE GRADE 3 (8 hdls) 2m 1f
2:05 (2:08) (Class 1) 5-Y-0+ **£45,560** (£17,096; £8,560; £4,264; £2,144; £1,072)

Form RPR

141- **1** **Lac Fontana (FR)**[48] 3891 5-10-11 **139**........ DarylJacob 149+
(Paul Nicholls) *lw: in tch: n.m.r: rdn and lost position after 3 out: hdwy u.p after 2 out: edgd lft bef last: styd on wl to ld clsng stages* **11/1**

34- **2** *½* **Arctic Fire (GER)**[77] 3339 5-10-13 **141**........ DJCasey 150
(W P Mullins, Ire) *lw: in rr: stdy hdwy fr 2 out: qcknd to trck ldrs appr last: drvn to ld w 1f to run: hdd clsng stages* **7/1**[2]

4/0- **3** *1* **Montbazon (FR)**[34] 4147 7-10-12 **140**........ RobertThornton 148
(Alan King) *in tch: lost position after 4 out: gd hdwy 2 out: led appr last: hdd w 1f to run: kpt on for 3rd clsng stages but nt pce of ldng duo* **20/1**

113- **4** *3 ¼* **Diakali (FR)**[103] 2855 5-11-12 **154**........ DannyMullins 160
(W P Mullins, Ire) *in rr: gd hdwy appr 2 out: bmpd appr last: kpt on run-in: nt pce of ldng trio* **25/1**

432- **5** *2 ½* **Flaxen Flare (IRE)**[48] 3910 5-11-7 **149**........(b) DavyCondon 152
(Gordon Elliott, Ire) *chsd ldrs: rdn after 2 out: ev ch u.p appr last: no ex run-in* **20/1**

103- **6** *½* **Minella Foru (IRE)**[19] 4456 5-10-11 **139**........ APMcCoy 142
(Edward P Harty, Ire) *lw: in tch: hdwy 3 out: chsd ldrs 2 out: one pce u.p last* **12/1**

120- **7** *2 ½* **Deep Trouble (IRE)**[34] 4147 7-10-10 **138**........ LeightonAspell 138+
(Ben Case) *lw: in rr: hit 2nd: hdwy but stl plenty to do fr 2 out: styd on run-in: nt rch ldrs* **33/1**

214- **8** *hd* **Lyvius**[40] 4056 6-10-11 **139**........(b[1]) BarryGeraghty 139
(Nicky Henderson) *mid-div: hdwy after 3 out: chsd ldrs next: btn appr last* **20/1**

026- **9** *¾* **Alaivan (IRE)**[34] 4147 8-9-13 **132**........(p) MauriceLinehan[(5)] 131
(Jonjo O'Neill) *chsd ldrs: rdn 2 out: styd on same pce* **10/1**

/10- **10** *nk* **Barizan (IRE)**[237] 1046 8-10-8 **136**........(bt) SamTwiston-Davies 135
(Donald McCain) *chsd ldrs: wl there 2 out: styng on whn hmpd bef last: kpt on again fnl 120yds* **50/1**

0/0- **11** *2 ¼* **Cash And Go (IRE)**[117] 2533 7-10-7 **138**........ PeterCarberry[(3)] 135
(Nicky Henderson) *chsd ldrs: rdn and outpcd 3 out: styd on again run-in* **25/1**

412- **12** *shd* **Rainbow Peak (IRE)**[29] 4234 8-10-10 **138**........ DenisO'Regan 135
(John Ferguson) *chsd ldrs: chal after 3 out and slt ld appr next: hdd & wknd appr last* **25/1**

B/B- **13** *1 ¼* **Thomas Edison (IRE)**[117] 2533 7-10-10 **138**........(t[1]) MarkWalsh 136
(A J Martin, Ire) *hit 2nd: in rr: hdwy appr 2 out: chsng ldrs but one pce u.p whn mstke last* **20/1**

/41- **14** *4* **Dunraven Storm (IRE)**[112] 2647 9-10-9 **137**........ TomO'Brien 130
(Philip Hobbs) *swtg: chsd ldrs hit 3rd: outpcd 3 out: sme hdwy again appr last* **33/1**

534- **15** *nk* **Morning Royalty (IRE)**[55] 3779 7-10-7 **135**........ PaddyBrennan 127
(James Moffatt) *hit 1st: in rr: sme prog after 2 out* **66/1**

301- **16** *1* **Jumps Road**[13] 4558 7-10-8 **136** 5ex........(p) BrendanPowell 127
(Colin Tizzard) *chsd ldrs: wknd after 2 out* **66/1**

101- **17** *5* **Makari**[90] 3088 7-10-8 **136**........ DavidBass 122
(Nicky Henderson) *towards rr most of way* **33/1**

P11- **18** *½* **Anay Turge (FR)**[39] 4069 9-10-5 **133**........(tp) TomScudamore 119
(Nigel Hawke) *towards rr most of way* **33/1**

211- **19** *2 ½* **Strongpoint (IRE)**[72] 3477 10-10-9 **137**........ PeterBuchanan 121
(S R B Crawford, Ire) *chsd ldrs: rdn after 3 out: wknd qckly after 2 out* **33/1**

P- **20** *14* **Lough Kent**[27] 4264 5-10-0 **133** NicodeBoinville(5) 104
(Nicky Henderson) *in tch: rdn 3 out: wknd sn after* **50/1**

1F2- **21** *nk* **Tzora**[26] 4303 9-10-7 **135** HaddenFrost 106
(Martin Hill) *swtg: in tch: sme hdwy after 3 out: wknd qckly next* **33/1**

3- **22** *7* **Upazo (FR)**[62] 3644 6-11-0 **142** PaulTownend 107
(W P Mullins, Ire) *hit 1st: in rr: nt fluent 3rd: sme hdwy appr 2 out: sn wknd* **33/1**

100- **23** *2 1/2* **Citizenship**[48] 3891 8-10-5 **133** AidanColeman 95
(Venetia Williams) *in tch: hdwy 3 out: wknd sn after* **66/1**

0/ **24** *1* **Never Enough Time (IRE)**[33] 4182 6-10-6 **141** GerFox(7) 102
(Thomas Foley, Ire) *chsd ldrs: wknd 2 out* **9/1**[3]

/01- **25** *1 1/4* **Master Of The Game (IRE)**[48] 3892 8-10-8 **136** (t) AndrewTinkler 96
(Nicky Henderson) *led after 1st: hdd after 3 out: sn wknd* **33/1**

/14- **P** **Cheltenian (FR)**[34] 4147 8-10-9 **137** RichardJohnson
(Philip Hobbs) *led tl after 1st: t.k.h: and trckd ldrs: chal 3 out: sn slt ld: narrowly hdd appr 2 out: styd pressing ldr: wknd qckly and p.u bef last* **5/1**[1]

25P/ **P** **Cinders And Ashes**[367] 4722 7-11-7 **149** NoelFehily
(Donald McCain) *in rr: mstke and btn 3 out: t.o whn p.u bef last* **28/1**

4F1- **P** **Runswick Royal (IRE)**[29] 4237 5-11-1 **143** BrianHughes
(Ann Hamilton) *chsd ldrs: hit 4 out: wknd next: t.o whn p.u bef last* **33/1**

3m 58.49s (-12.81) **Going Correction** -0.30s/f (Good) **28** Ran SP% **133.2**
Speed ratings: **118,117,117,115,114 114,113,113,112,112 111,111,110,109,108 108,106,105,104,98 97,94,93,92,92**
CSF £66.26 CT £1572.01 TOTE £12.40: £3.30, £2.50, £5.40, £7.20; EX 109.40 Trifecta £3468.70.

Owner Potensis Limited **Bred** S C A La Perrigne **Trained** Ditcheat, Somerset

■ Stewards' Enquiry : Robert Thornton four-day ban: used whip above permitted level (Mar 28-31)

FOCUS
A typically competitive renewal of this hot handicap hurdle. Irish trainers had been responsible for six of the last seven winners of this, but Paul Nicholls had the best recent record in the race, having won three of the last ten runnings and improved his record here. Strong handicap form, with the first two on the upgrade.

4786 ALBERT BARTLETT NOVICES' HURDLE (REGISTERED AS THE SPA NOVICES' HURDLE) GRADE 1 (12 hdls) 3m
2:40 (2:53) (Class 1) 4-Y-0+

£68,340 (£25,644; £12,840; £6,396; £3,216; £1,608)

Form RPR

253- **1** **Very Wood (FR)**[68] 3559 5-11-7 137 (p) PCarberry 153+
(Noel Meade, Ire) *hld up: stdy hdwy after 3 out: rdn and swtchd lft to go cl 2nd appr last: led sn after flight: styd on wl to draw clr clr fnl 110yds* **33/1**

211- **2** *4 1/2* **Deputy Dan (IRE)**[62] 3654 6-11-7 145 LeightonAspell 151+
(Oliver Sherwood) *trckd ldrs: wnt 2nd travelling wl appr 2 out: led after 2 out: sn kicked abt 3 l clr: rdn whn j. slowly w reduced advantage last: sn hdd: unable to go w wnr run-in: all out to hold on for 2nd* **10/1**

0/2- **3** *shd* **Apache Jack (IRE)**[68] 3559 6-11-7 136 BarryGeraghty 149
(D T Hughes, Ire) *in tch: nt fluent 3 out: effrt and wnt 2nd abt 3 l down between last 2: lost 2nd appr last where nt fluent: nt qckn run-in: kpt on u.p fnl 100yds and chal for 2nd: no imp on wnr* **20/1**

111- **4** *5* **Champagne West (IRE)**[55] 3774 6-11-7 145 RichardJohnson 143
(Philip Hobbs) *hld up: nt fluent 5th: stdy hdwy 8th: chsd ldrs 3 out: rdn after 2 out: one pce bef last: no imp after* **14/1**

P22- **5** *21* **Masters Hill (IRE)**[62] 3654 8-11-7 135 JoeTizzard 125
(Colin Tizzard) *trckd ldrs: pushed along and lost pl after 3 out: wknd next* **66/1**

115- **6** *9* **Sausalito Sunrise (IRE)**[48] 3896 6-11-7 140 TomO'Brien 119
(Philip Hobbs) *midfield: hdwy 8th: chsd ldrs 3 out: wknd 2 out: n.d whn hmpd last* **50/1**

211- **7** *10* **Urban Hymn (FR)**[48] 3896 6-11-7 142 BrianHughes 107
(Malcolm Jefferson) *racd keenly: prom: led after 4th: nt fluent and hdd 8th: wknd appr 2 out* **14/1**

311- **8** *2 3/4* **Cogry**[21] 4397 5-11-7 129 SamTwiston-Davies 105
(Nigel Twiston-Davies) *hld up: niggled along and bhd after 5th: rdn after 7th: nvr a threat: wl btn* **66/1**

1F6- **P** **Prince Siegfried (FR)**[62] 3644 8-11-7 138 DenisO'Regan
(John Ferguson) *edgy bef r: a bhd: hmpd 8th: t.o whn p.u bef last* **100/1**

3F3- **P** **Saint Roque (FR)**[42] 4019 8-11-7 144 (t) NoelFehily
(Paul Nicholls) *midfield: hdwy 7th: effrt affter 3 out: cl up disputing 4th whn hit 2 out: stopped qckly: wl bhd whn p.u bef last* **50/1**

111- **P** **Captain Cutter (IRE)**[76] 3367 7-11-7 147 APMcCoy
(Nicky Henderson) *lw: midfield: mstke 8th: hdwy 9th: chsd ldrs 2 out: 6th wkng and eased whn p.u bef last: dismntd* **7/1**[3]

/12- **F** **Rydon Pynes**[34] 4144 6-11-7 128 HaddenFrost
(Martin Hill) *in tch: pushed along and lost pl bef 7th: fell 8th* **66/1**

12P- **P** **The Job Is Right**[22] 4386 6-11-7 136 (b) APHeskin
(Michael Hourigan, Ire) *prom: nt fluent 1st: wknd appr 3 out: t.o whn p.u bef last* **80/1**

111- **F** **Kings Palace (IRE)**[90] 3081 6-11-7 156 TomScudamore 133
(David Pipe) *lw: led: hdd after 4th: remained chsng ldr tl regained ld 8th: hdd after 2 out: sn wknd: 5th and wl btn whn fell last* **5/2**[2]

/11- **F** **Briar Hill (IRE)**[68] 3559 6-11-7 147 DJCasey
(W P Mullins, Ire) *in tch: fell 7th* **2/1**[1]

11P- **P** **Madness Light (FR)**[48] 3889 5-11-7 132 (t) GavinSheehan
(Warren Greatrex) *midfield: lost pl and rdn after 6th: t.o 3 out: p.u bef 2 out* **100/1**

24P- **P** **Regal Diamond (IRE)**[23] 4356 6-11-7 125 JamieMoore
(Peter Bowen) *trckd ldrs: lost pl appr 2nd: bhd and struggling 6th: t.o whn p.u bef last* **100/1**

111- **P** **Mosspark (IRE)**[22] 4374 6-11-7 138 AidanColeman
(Emma Lavelle) *midfield: lost pl bef 6th: pushed along towards rr sn after: bhd whn p.u bef 2 out* **20/1**

5m 50.7s (-10.30) **Going Correction** -0.30s/f (Good) **18** Ran SP% **121.9**
Speed ratings: **105,103,103,101,94 91,88,87, , , , , , , , ,**
CSF £315.12 CT £6656.10 TOTE £51.90: £8.30, £2.60, £4.40; EX 661.30 Trifecta £4910.40.

Owner Gigginstown House Stud **Bred** C Jacquemont, J Gronfier, A Gronfier **Trained** Castletown, Co Meath

FOCUS
The tenth edition of this event, the seventh with Grade 1 status. Bobs Worth, in 2011, heads an impressive roll of honour. This looked a high-quality renewal, and it was run at a solid pace. Many of these will make nice chasers. It was delayed after an incident when Port Melon, who had to be withdrawn, threw Daryl Jacob, the rider sustaining serious injuries. Very Wood looks up to race standard, with another step forward from Deputy Dan.

4787 BETFRED CHELTENHAM GOLD CUP CHASE GRADE 1 (22 fncs) 3m 2f 110y
3:20 (3:35) (Class 1) 5-Y-0+

£327,325 (£122,826; £61,499; £30,634; £15,403; £7,701)

Form RPR

006- **1** **Lord Windermere (IRE)**[33] 4183 8-11-10 152 DavyRussell 170
(J H Culloty, Ire) *in rr and detached 10th: drvn 4 out: stl plenty to do next: hdwy u.p appr 2 out: chsd ldrs last: led and hung bdly rt fnl 110yds: hld on all out* **20/1**

611- **2** *shd* **On His Own (IRE)**[20] 4435 10-11-10 161 DJCasey 170
(W P Mullins, Ire) *led 4th: narrowly hdd 8th: styd chalng: led 11th: jnd 4 out: narrowly hdd: rdn 3 out: wnt rt and bmpd 2 out: rallied last: str chal and carried rt fnl 110yds: jst failed* **16/1**

U51- **3** *3/4* **The Giant Bolster**[48] 3888 9-11-10 160 (v) TomScudamore 170
(David Bridgwater) *in rr: tended to run in snatches: j. slowly 8th: 11th and 12th: rdn 13th: hit 15th: hdwy 3 out: bmpd 2 out: styd on wl to chse ldrs: carried rt fnl 110yds: kpt on wl cl home* **14/1**

/31- **4** *1* **Silviniaco Conti (FR)**[78] 3262 8-11-10 177 NoelFehily 169
(Paul Nicholls) *lw: towards rr but in tch: stdy hdwy 18th: chal 4 out and sn led: rdn appr 2 out: wnt lft and then wandered rt u.p run-in: hdd fnl 110yds: nt rcvr* **11/4**[2]

/61- **5** *2 1/4* **Bobs Worth (IRE)**[76] 3376 9-11-10 180 BarryGeraghty 167
(Nicky Henderson) *in rr: nt fluent 4th and 9th: impr 16th: chsd ldrs fr 4 out: nt fluent 3 out: styd on u.p appr next to chse ldr last: pushed lft sn after: wandered flat: no ex fnl 110yds* **6/4**[1]

/55- **6** *2 3/4* **Lyreen Legend (IRE)**[33] 4183 7-11-10 153 PCarberry 165
(D T Hughes, Ire) *in tch: blnd 6th: dropped to rr 8th: hdwy to chse ldrs fr 16th: wl there whn hit 2 out: wknd run-in* **33/1**

512- **7** *11* **Knockara Beau (IRE)**[29] 4238 11-11-10 146 JanFaltejsek 154
(George Charlton) *led to 4th: chsd ldrs: dropped to rr 14th: styd on again fr 2 out* **66/1**

/02- **8** *3 1/4* **Teaforthree (IRE)**[27] 4263 10-11-10 153 NickScholfield 152
(Rebecca Curtis) *lw: pressed ldrs: stl upsides appr 4 out whn dropped to 3rd: one pce 3 out: wknd fr 2 out: nt fluent last* **33/1**

143- **9** *3* **Houblon Des Obeaux (FR)**[27] 4263 7-11-10 158 LiamTreadwell 149
(Venetia Williams) *chsd ldrs: mstke 18th: mstke and wnt rt 4 out: sn wknd* **50/1**

/31- **10** *6* **Triolo D'Alene (FR)**[104] 2815 7-11-10 158 APMcCoy 148
(Nicky Henderson) *in rr: hdwy to chse ldrs 4 out: rdn next: one pce and hld whn bdly bmpd 2 out* **10/1**

443- **11** *4 1/2* **Katenko (FR)**[34] 4145 8-11-10 155 AidanColeman 140
(Venetia Williams) *lw: hit 3rd: in rr but in tch: blnd 13th: wknd and hit 4 out: no ch whn blnd 3 out* **66/1**

/31- **U** **Last Instalment (IRE)**[33] 4183 9-11-10 170 BrianO'Connell
(Philip Fenton, Ire) *w ldrs: led 8th: hdd 11th: styd prom tl wknd 16th: blnd and uns rdr next* **15/2**[3]

012- **U** **Cloudy Too (IRE)**[27] 4265 8-11-10 157 JonathanEngland 135
(Sue Smith) *chsd ldrs: rdn 16th: wknd 4 out: t.o whn blnd and uns rdr last* **50/1**

6m 43.88s (-9.92) **Going Correction** +0.075s/f (Yiel) **13** Ran SP% **117.6**
Speed ratings: **117,116,116,116,115 114,111,110,109,108 106, ,**
CSF £272.86 CT £4559.62 TOTE £23.40: £4.50, £3.60, £2.50; EX 358.20 Trifecta £5628.50.

Owner Dr R Lambe **Bred** Edmond Coleman **Trained** Mallow, Co Cork

■ Jim Culloty is the fifth man to win the Gold Cup as both a jockey and trainer.

■ Stewards' Enquiry : D J Casey seven-day ban: used whip above permitted level (Mar 28-Apr 3)
Noel Fehily two-day ban: used whip above permitted level (Mar 28-29)
Davy Russell one-day ban: careless riding (Mar 28)

FOCUS
They finally got away at the third attempt and, with the pace not that strong, this was a dramatic race with no less than six still in with a chance on the run-in. They wandered all over the place after the last and there was a lengthy stewards' enquiry before the placings were confirmed. The form is rated below standard, but the first two produced steps up. Silviniaco Conti and Bobs Worth both underperformed.

4788 CGA FOXHUNTER CHASE CHALLENGE CUP (22 fncs) 3m 2f 110y
4:00 (4:13) (Class 2) 5-Y-0+

£23,984 (£7,492; £3,744; £1,872; £936; £472)

Form RPR

2/6- **1** **Tammys Hill (IRE)**[20] 4437 9-12-0 134 MrJJSmyth 141+
(Liam Lennon, Ire) *midfield: hdwy 16th: prom 18th: wnt 2nd appr 2 out: led fnl 150yds: styd on wl to draw clr* **15/2**[3]

46F/ **2** *3 1/4* **Carsonstown Boy (IRE)**[20] 10-12-0 109 MrNMcParlan 136
(C A McBratney, Ire) *led: hdd 11th: remained prom: led again 12th: mstke 18th: rdn whn pressed appr 2 out: hdd fnl 150yds: no ex cl home* **40/1**

14/ **3** *1 3/4* **On The Fringe (IRE)**[33] 4184 9-12-0 133 MsNCarberry 133
(E Bolger, Ire) *midfield: hdwy appr 3 out: big effrt to chal fr 2 out: styd on same pce fnl 150yds* **11/2**[2]

/11- **4** *5* **Pearlysteps**[37] 4092 11-12-0 133 MrOGreenall 130
(Henry Daly) *hld up: hdwy appr 3 out: chsd ldrs 2 out: kpt on same pce u.p: no imp run-in* **8/1**

11U- **5** *1 1/2* **Harbour Court**[20] 8-12-0 120 MrJETudor 127+
(Alan Hill) *hld up in rr: hdwy to chse ldrs appr 3 out: swtchd lft and styd on whn effrt on heels of ldrs bef 2 out: one pce bef last* **5/1**[1]

140/ **6** *3 1/2* **Minella Stars (IRE)**[26] 9-12-0 115 (p) MrRGHenderson 126+
(Guy Henderson) *hld up: hdwy 15th: chsd ldrs 17th: rdn appr 3 out: stl on heels of ldrs bef 2 out: edgd lft whn one pce bef last: fdd run-in* **66/1**

/12- **7** *3/4* **Doctor Kingsley**[41] 4042 12-12-0 120 MrPMann 123
(Mrs Pauline Harkin) *chsd ldrs tl lost pl 17th: plugged on fr 2 out but n.d* **28/1**

/11- **8** *8* **Shy John**[29] 4246 8-12-0 124 MrPMason 116
(P W Mason) *hld up in rr: sme hdwy appr 3 out: one pce and no imp bef 2 out* **25/1**

5/ **9** *7* **Boxing Along (IRE)**[19] 10-12-0 109 MrPPower 115+
(Vincent Laurence Halley, Ire) *in tch: clsr 12th: chsd ldrs: outpcd and looking hld whn hmpd 2 out: wl btn* **100/1**

30U/ **10** *5* **Oscar Delta (IRE)**[27] 11-12-0 133 MissJMMangan 111
(James Joseph Mangan, Ire) *prom: lost pl 7th: in midfield 12th: blnd 13th: sn struggling: bhd 16th* **11/2**[2]

1/4- **11** ½ **Lucette Annie**[26] 10-11-7 107 .... MrDEdwards 98
(S J Partridge) *midfield early: bhd 11th: nvr a threat* **150/1**

P05/ **12** 59 **Berties Dream (IRE)**[40] 11-12-0 125 .... (b) MissGAndrews 52
(Mrs L Braithwaite) *in tch: mstke 2nd: trckd ldrs 9th: rdn after 12th: u.p and lost pl 16th: bhd after: virtually p.u run-in* **10/1**

1- **13** 6 **Certain Flight (IRE)**[22] 4376 9-12-0 0 .... MrWBiddick 46
(K J Cumings) *hld up: hdwy 17th: sn in tch: wknd appr 2 out: virtually p.u run-in* **20/1**

640/ **14** 3¾ **The Hollinwell**[19] 11-12-0 105 .... MrEMO'Sullivan 43
(Eugene M O'Sullivan, Ire) *prom: lost pl after 12th: bhd 18th: virtually p.u run-in* **50/1**

111- **P** **That's Rhythm (FR)**[40] 4057 14-12-0 129 .... (v) MissPFuller
(Miss Sally Duckett) *prom: pckd bdly 13th: wknd appr 4 out: hmpd 3 out: t.o whn p.u bef last* **25/1**

/01- **U** **Double Bank (IRE)**[16] 4505 11-12-0 108 .... MrMWoodward
(Ms Emma Oliver) *midfield whn mstke and uns rdr 1st* **66/1**

0/1- **U** **Ockey De Neulliac (FR)**[27] 4274 12-12-0 119 .... MissCWalton
(N Mechie) *hld up: mstke and uns rdr 2nd* **66/1**

/21- **F** **Made In Time (IRE)**[23] 4355 9-12-0 129 .... (t) MissLeandaTickle 115
(Rebecca Curtis) *prom on outer: led 11th to 12th: stl ev ch 3 out: 7th and wkng whn fell 2 out* **14/1**

141- **U** **Divine Intavention (IRE)**[17] 4477 10-12-0 122 .... MrMWall 116
(Martin Keighley) *hld up: hdwy 12th: prom 17th: outpcd whn blnd 4 out: no imp whn hmpd and uns rdr 3 out* **9/1**

3/P- **P** **Ravethebrave (IRE)**[19] 10-12-0 114 .... MrJoeHill
(Alan Hill) *hld up in midfield early: towards rr after: mstke whn bhd 16th: t.o whn p.u bef 3 out* **100/1**

054- **P** **Croan Rock (IRE)**[23] 4348 9-12-0 93 .... (p) MrJLyttle
(R A Owen) *prom: mstke and lost pl 15th: t.o whn p.u bef 3 out* **100/1**

P **Gale Force Oscar (IRE)**[12] 9-12-0 0 .... MissBHampson
(L M Power) *in rr: sn u.p and nt travelling: t.o whn p.u bef 10th* **150/1**

1P2- **P** **Foundry Square (IRE)**[23] 4348 8-12-0 114 .... (p) MrWTelfer
(S Flook) *trckd ldrs: lost pl after 13th: struggling 18th: t.o whn p.u bef 2 out* **50/1**

F **Ganbei**[19] 8-12-0 0 .... MrHAABannister 123
(Mrs Stephanie Easterby) *hld up: mstke 1st: pckd 9th: hdwy 16th: in tch and abt 5 l off the pce whn fell 3 out* **66/1**

6m 50.5s (-3.30) **Going Correction** +0.075s/f (Yiel) **24** Ran SP% **128.6**
Speed ratings: **107,106,105,104,103 102,102,99,97,96 96,78,77,75, , , , , , ,**
CSF £281.37 CT £1812.28 TOTE £8.80: £3.00, £14.70, £2.50; EX 548.30 Trifecta £4230.10.
Owner Patrick J Smyth **Bred** Patrick J Smyth **Trained** Newry, Co. Down

■ Liam Lennon's and James Smyth's first festival winner.

■ Stewards' Enquiry : Mr N McParlan four-day ban: used whip above permitted level (Mar 28,30,Apr 1-2)

FOCUS

A typically competitive running of the season's most prestigious hunter chase. Dual winner Salsify was missing through injury, as was costly buy Mossey Joe who'll wait for Aintree, but Irish stables still held a strong hand and were responsible for the first three home.

4789 MARTIN PIPE CONDITIONAL JOCKEYS' H'CAP HURDLE (10 hdls) 2m 4f 110y
4:40 (4:46) (Class 2) (0-145,146) 4-Y-0+

£31,280 (£9,240; £4,620; £2,310; £1,155; £580)

Form RPR

1- **1** **Don Poli (IRE)**[22] 4386 5-11-5 **143** .... MPFogarty(3) 153+
(W P Mullins, Ire) *hld up in rr: hdwy 3 out: drvn to chal after 2 out: slt ld last: drvn clr fnl 110yds* **12/1**

104- **2** 4½ **Thomas Crapper**[55] 3771 7-10-5 **134** .... JosephPalmowski(8) 141
(Robin Dickin) *hld up in rr: stdy hdwy after 3 out to ld appr 2 out: jnd wl bef last whn narrowly hdd: styd on wl but nt gng pce of wnr fnl 110yds* **10/1**

215- **3** 1¼ **Caid Du Berlais (FR)**[48] 3893 5-11-5 **143** .... HarryDerham(3) 147
(Paul Nicholls) *in rr: hdwy 3 out: rdn after 2 out: styd on to cl on 2nd nr fin but no ch w wnr* **9/1**[3]

/23- **4** 1¾ **Urbain De Sivola (FR)**[78] 3259 6-10-6 **135** .... (t) AndriasGuerin(8) 142+
(Paul Nicholls) *lw: slowly away and bhd: latched on to main gp after 2nd: stdy hdwy fr 3 out to trck ldrs travelling wl 2 out: rdn and one pce bef last* **33/1**

421- **5** 14 **One Lucky Lady**[16] 4494 6-10-9 **133** .... PeterCarberry(3) 123
(Nicky Henderson) *lw: pressed ldrs: rdn after 2 out: wknd bef last* **33/1**

311- **6** 1 **Virak (FR)**[24] 4333 5-11-5 **146** .... JackSherwood(6) 135
(Paul Nicholls) *chsd ldrs: rdn 2 out: wknd wl bef last* **25/1**

032- **7** 1 **Local Hero (GER)**[40] 4056 7-11-1 **142** .... (p) PaulBohan(6) 130
(Steve Gollings) *hld up towards rr: stdy hdwy 3 out to trck ldrs 2 out: chal sn after: wknd bef last* **33/1**

121- **8** 3¼ **Une Artiste (FR)**[35] 4133 6-11-2 **140** .... JeremiahMcGrath(3) 125
(Nicky Henderson) *swtg: in tch: chsd ldrs 4th: wknd after 2 out* **16/1**

F12- **9** ¾ **Princely Player (IRE)**[90] 3087 7-10-9 **138** .... ThomasCheesman(8) 123
(Philip Hobbs) *lw: towards rr: hdwy 5th: chsd ldrs 3 out: wknd fr next* **33/1**

115- **10** 1½ **Royal Regatta (IRE)**[72] 3454 6-10-9 **133** .... MichealNolan(3) 117
(Philip Hobbs) *in tch: hit 6th: sme hdwy after 3 out: wknd next* **12/1**

121- **11** ¾ **Full Shift (FR)**[20] 4423 5-10-11 **135** .... NicodeBoinville(3) 117
(Nicky Henderson) *chsd ldrs: dropped in rr after 4 out: detached after 2 out: mod prog run-in* **9/2**[1]

045- **12** hd **Ruacana**[48] 3891 5-11-2 **140** .... JackQuinlan(3) 122
(John Ferguson) *chsd ldrs tl wknd appr 2 out* **50/1**

11F- **13** 1 **Junction Fourteen (IRE)**[62] 3646 5-11-2 **137** .... MichaelByrne 118
(Emma Lavelle) *towards rr most of way* **20/1**

144- **14** ¾ **Shantou Magic (IRE)**[43] 3989 7-10-13 **137** .... KielanWoods(3) 118
(Charlie Longsdon) *chsd ldrs tl wknd appr 2 out* **33/1**

/63- **15** 2¼ **Leo Luna**[27] 4264 5-10-11 **135** .... JoshuaMoore(3) 113
(Gary Moore) *in rr: sme hdwy appr 2 out: sn wknd* **16/1**

115- **16** hd **The Skyfarmer**[55] 3771 6-11-1 **139** .... JamesBest(3) 117
(Philip Hobbs) *lw: hit 2nd: chsd ldrs: wknd 3 out* **10/1**

P22- **17** 7 **Art Professor (IRE)**[27] 4264 10-10-10 **134** .... HarryChalloner(3) 106
(Venetia Williams) *hit 1st: bhd fr 6th* **33/1**

P/3- **18** 13 **Carlito Brigante (IRE)**[139] 2072 8-11-5 **140** .... (p) JakeGreenall 100
(Karen McLintock) *in tch: chsd ldrs and rdn 3 out: wknd qckly bef 2 out* **40/1**

031- **19** 12 **Hazy Tom (IRE)**[25] 4328 8-10-10 **137** .... CharlieDeutsch(6) 87
(Charlie Longsdon) *in tch: rdn 3 out: btn sn after* **66/1**

132- **20** nk **Dolatulo (FR)**[25] 4325 7-11-1 **139** .... (b) GavinSheehan(3) 88
(Warren Greatrex) *chsd ldrs: led 5th: hdd & wknd bef 2 out* **40/1**

111- **21** 7 **Vieux Lion Rouge (FR)**[22] 4379 5-10-12 **139** .... TomBellamy(6) 82
(David Pipe) *prssed ldrs: chal 5th to next: wknd qckly bef 2 out* **5/1**[2]

014- **22** 7 **The Disengager (IRE)**[167] 1686 10-10-13 **134** .... MattGriffiths 71
(Philip Hobbs) *led: hit 3rd: hdd 5th: wknd qckly 3 out* **66/1**

122- **23** 23 **Rum And Butter (IRE)**[147] 1954 6-11-6 **144** .... (p) MauriceLinehan(3) 60
(Jonjo O'Neill) *prom early: bhd fr 4 out: t.o* **20/1**

/25- **P** **Open Day (IRE)**[27] 4271 8-10-6 **135** .... (p) JamesHuxham(8)
(Jonjo O'Neill) *in tch: dropped to rr 4 out: t.o whn p.u bef last* **33/1**

4m 48.58s (-12.42) **Going Correction** -0.30s/f (Good) **24** Ran SP% **134.0**
Speed ratings (Par 109): **111,109,108,108,102 102,102,100,100,99 99,99,99,98,98 97,95,90,85,85 83,80,71,**
CSF £113.83 CT £1169.04 TOTE £14.10: £3.50, £2.70, £3.00, £6.80; EX 241.10 Trifecta £1960.00.
Owner Gigginstown House Stud **Bred** Brian J Griffiths And John Nicholson **Trained** Muine Beag, Co Carlow

■ Michael Fogarty's first festival win.

■ Stewards' Enquiry : Andrias Guerin one-day ban: failed to obey starters' instructions (Mar 28)

FOCUS

This competitive conditionals' handicap, with a weight range of just 13lb covering the entire field, featured several unexposed types taking on more battle-hardened performers. The first four came from well off the pace. The winner looks a smart novice and the form could be rated higher.

4790 JOHNNY HENDERSON GRAND ANNUAL CHASE CHALLENGE CUP H'CAP GRADE 3 (14 fncs) 2m 110y
5:15 (5:25) (Class 1) 5-Y-0+

£51,255 (£19,233; £9,630; £4,797; £2,412; £1,206)

Form RPR

/40- **1** **Savello (IRE)**[54] 3806 8-11-5 **147** .... DavyRussell 157+
(A J Martin, Ire) *nt a fluent: hld up in midfield: hdwy 3 out: rdn bef last: styd on to ld fnl 100yds: on top cl home* **16/1**

3/ **2** 1¼ **Ned Buntline**[68] 3558 6-10-10 **138** .... [1] PCarberry 146
(Noel Meade, Ire) *lw: hld up: nt fluent 9th: gd hdwy appr 2 out: chsd ldrs bef last: styd on to take 2nd cl home: nt pce to get to wnr* **6/1**[1]

124- **3** nk **Claret Cloak (IRE)**[97] 2950 7-11-0 **142** .... NoelFehily 152+
(Emma Lavelle) *hld up: stdy hdwy 4 out: wnt 2nd appr 2 out where blnd whn chalng: stl str chal fnl 100yds: no ex cl home* **6/1**[1]

1U1- **4** nk **Next Sensation (IRE)**[75] 3386 7-11-0 **142** .... (t) RichardJohnson 149
(Michael Scudamore) *led: clr fr 4th: reduced advantage appr 3 out: rdn bef last: kpt on gamely tl hdd fnl 100yds: one pce cl home* **7/1**[2]

220- **5** 3 **French Opera**[42] 4020 11-11-7 **154** .... NicodeBoinville(5) 160
(Nicky Henderson) *lw: chsd ldrs: hit 3 out: effrt and wl there 2 out: nt qckn appr last: styd on same pce run-in* **33/1**

314- **6** 9 **Eastlake (IRE)**[41] 4032 8-11-0 **147** .... MauriceLinehan(5) 144
(Jonjo O'Neill) *in tch: rdn to chse ldrs after 3 out: outpcd appr last: kpt on run-in but no imp* **20/1**

021- **7** 3¾ **Dare Me (IRE)**[62] 3652 10-11-0 **142** .... AidanColeman 135
(Venetia Williams) *midfield: pushed along after 9th: rdn after 3 out: no imp after* **14/1**

310- **8** 1¾ **Lucky Landing (IRE)**[13] 4543 8-10-8 **136** .... DougieCostello 129
(Tony Coyle) *hld up bhd: hmpd 7th: struggling on get on terms after: nvr a threat* **66/1**

P61- **9** 2½ **Tanks For That (IRE)**[26] 4303 11-11-2 **144** .... BarryGeraghty 135
(Nicky Henderson) *swtg: in tch: nt fluent 1st: hit 2nd: pushed along and wknd appr 2 out: eased whn wl btn bef last* **12/1**[3]

550- **10** ½ **Anquetta (IRE)**[90] 3080 10-10-8 **139** .... MrSWaley-Cohen(3) 134+
(Nicky Henderson) *handy: chsd clr ldr after 4th: stl wl there whn mstke 2 out: btn last* **50/1**

662- **11** nk **Viva Colonia (IRE)**[72] 3476 9-11-2 **144** .... NickScholfield 138
(Brian Ellison) *bhd: hmpd 5th: keeping on but nowhere nr ldrs whn bdly hmpd and stopped to walk last: n.d* **40/1**

130- **12** 3¾ **Changing The Guard**[27] 4264 8-10-9 **137** .... (t) WayneHutchinson 124
(Dr Richard Newland) *chsd ldrs: blnd 2nd: mstke 7th: wknd 4 out* **25/1**

0P6- **13** 5 **Drumshambo (USA)**[34] 4160 8-11-2 **144** .... (p) LiamTreadwell 126
(Venetia Williams) *hld up: pckd bdly 1st: niggled along 6th (water): struggling appr 9th: bhd after* **40/1**

F62- **14** nse **His Excellency (IRE)**[40] 4053 6-11-0 **142** .... (b) TomScudamore 131+
(David Pipe) *midfield: stdy hdwy appr 2 out: no imp and wl hld whn bdly hmpd and stopped to walk last: wl btn* **14/1**

216- **15** 2½ **Lancetto (FR)**[55] 3773 9-10-6 **141** .... (v[1]) ConorRing(7) 123
(Evan Williams) *in tch: hit 2nd: mstke 7th: lost pl 8thg: bhd and outpcd 4 out* **50/1**

0P3- **16** 13 **Shooters Wood (IRE)**[16] 4495 10-10-6 **137** .... (t) HarryDerham(3) 104
(Paul Nicholls) *chsd ldrs: rdn after 3 out: sn wknd* **40/1**

425- **F** **Oiseau De Nuit (FR)**[55] 3773 12-11-11 **153** .... (t) BrendanPowell 140
(Colin Tizzard) *midfield: hdwy 8th: chsd ldrs: rdn and wkng whn fell 2 out* **28/1**

033- **P** **Astracad (FR)**[77] 3320 8-11-1 **143** .... (vt) SamTwiston-Davies
(Nigel Twiston-Davies) *prom: sn chsd ldrs: hit 3rd: blnd 5th: nt fluent 8th: lost pl 9th: p.u qckly appr 4 out* **33/1**

F26- **B** **Easter Meteor**[90] 3082 8-10-10 **148** .... RichardO'Dea(10)
(Emma Lavelle) *hld up: hit 1st: niggled along in rr appr 10th: b.d 4 out* **25/1**

223- **F** **Raya Star (IRE)**[34] 4146 8-11-7 **149** .... RobertThornton
(Alan King) *hld up: blnd 2nd: fell 5th: fatally injured* **7/1**[2]

2/3- **F** **Passage Vendome (FR)**[97] 2965 8-10-10 **138** .... DJCasey
(W P Mullins, Ire) *hld up: fell 1st* **33/1**

P/2- **F** **Competitive Edge (IRE)**[15] 4521 7-10-12 **140** .... MarkWalsh
(Conor O'Dwyer, Ire) *hld up: hmpd 5th: fell 4 out* **40/1**

132- **F** **Mr Mole (IRE)**[36] 4101 6-11-5 **147** .... (t) APMcCoy 144
(Paul Nicholls) *lw: midfield: nt fluent and lost pl 4th: nt fluent 3 out: hdwy appr 2 out: keeping but no imp on ldrs disputing 7th whn fell last* **7/1**[2]

4m 1.3s (-5.40) **Going Correction** +0.075s/f (Yiel) **23** Ran SP% **134.3**
Speed ratings: **115,114,114,114,112 108,106,105,104,104 104,102,100,100,99 92, , , , ,E**
CSF £102.54 CT £674.60 TOTE £21.10: £4.40, £2.20, £2.30, £2.40; EX 165.00 Trifecta £1540.30.
Owner Gigginstown House Stud **Bred** Anthony Walsh **Trained** Summerhill, Co. Meath

FOCUS

This was another hugely competitive edition of the top 2m handicap chase in the calendar. There was a delay at the start as Oscar Hill bolted. As expected, it was run at a very strong pace, with habitual front runner Next Sensation quickly compiling a clear lead. The form is strong, with steps up from the first three.

T/Jkpt: Not won. T/Plt: £44,616.30 to a £1 stake. Pool: £1295966.10 - 21.20 winning tickets
T/Qpdt: £2,700.20 to a £1 stake. Pool: £62580.81 - 17.15 winning tickets ST

[4247]FAKENHAM (L-H)

Friday, March 14

OFFICIAL GOING: Good (6.9)

Wind: very light across Weather: bright and sunny; 11 degrees

4791 TOTEPOOL (S) HURDLE (9 hdls) 2m

1:45 (1:52) (Class 5) 4-Y-O+ **£2,053** (£598; £299)

Form RPR

406- **1** **Regal D'Estruval (FR)**[41] 4036 9-10-10 0................ ChristopherWard(5) 103+
(Dr Richard Newland) *mde all: set fast pce: 15 l clr at 6th: hit 2 out: drvn between last two: nt fluent last: unchal* **15/2**

036- **2** *14* **Monroe Park (IRE)**[50] 3852 9-10-8 75...................(p) JosephAkehurst(7) 89
(Alan Blackmore) *lost pl and dropped to rr 3rd: wl bhd 6th: drvn and plugged on fr 2 out: wnt poor 2nd cl home* **66/1**

5/3- **3** *3/4* **Mister Frosty (IRE)**[19] 4450 8-10-10 95.......................... MattCrawley(5) 89
(Michael Squance) *hld up and t.k.h: hdwy bef 3 out: 14 l 2nd and rdn 2 out: no imp after: mstke last: lost 2nd nr fin* **4/1[3]**

000- **4** *9* **Minsky Mine (IRE)**[5] 4699 7-11-1 95.......................................(p[1]) RyanMahon 80
(Michael Appleby) *chsd ldrs: reminder 2nd: rdn and outpcd 3 out: lost mod 3rd sn after next* **13/2**

5U5- **5** *1 1/4* **Akula (IRE)**[16] 4497 7-11-1 114... ColinBolger 79
(Mark H Tompkins) *nvr bttr than midfield: rdn 3 out: sn struggling: no ch next* **3/1[2]**

55P- **6** *3* **Tayarat (IRE)**[5] 4699 9-10-10 80...................................(bt) JoeCornwall(5) 76
(Michael Chapman) *in rr and str reminders 3rd: wl bhd 6th: plugging on fr 2 out but no ch* **66/1**

2P5- **7** *26* **County Zen (FR)**[28] 4247 11-10-13 87.....................(b) MissBAndrews(7) 58
(Caroline Fryer) *chsd wnr: rdn fr 4th: lost pl bef 3 out and nt run on: t.o* **16/1**

P12- **P** **Arrayan**[15] 4513 9-11-10 122...(b) PaulMoloney
(Alexandra Dunn) *hld up in midfield: lost pl rapidly bef 3 out and stopping to nil: t.o and p.u after next: b.b.v* **11/4[1]**

P04- **P** **Big John Cannon (IRE)**[4] 4731 4-10-12 110...................(b) WillKennedy
(Sarah-Jayne Davies) *prom: rn wd bef 2nd: drvn and lost pl next: nt keen: t.o and p.u 2 out* **18/1**

3m 57.4s (-8.00) **Going Correction** -0.35s/f (Good)
WFA 4 from 7yo+ 7lb **9** Ran SP% **110.9**
Speed ratings (Par 103): **106,99,98,94,93 92,79, ,**
CSF £266.81 TOTE £9.20: £2.10, £7.30, £1.80; EX 155.30 Trifecta £1444.90.There was no bid for the winner.
Owner Paul Jenkins **Bred** Mme Bernard Le Gentil **Trained** Claines, Worcs

FOCUS
Fresh strip of ground whole way around on Hurdles course. This pretty ordinary seller was delayed by five minutes when the subsequently withdrawn Spessartine completed a circuit after an initial false start.

4792 PRINCE CARLTON H'CAP CHASE (FOR THE PRINCE CARLTON CHALLENGE CUP) (18 fncs) 3m 110y

2:20 (2:20) (Class 3) (0-130,130) 5-Y-O+ **£6,498** (£1,908; £954; £477)

Form RPR

120- **1** **Baile Anrai (IRE)**[20] 4422 10-11-12 130..........................(b) HarrySkelton 136+
(Dan Skelton) *led: hit 15th: hrd drvn and jnd 2 out where outj. rival: jnd again last: jst prevailed u.p: all out* **7/2[2]**

01P- **2** *hd* **Wiesentraum (GER)**[112] 2646 8-11-7 130....................(p) MattCrawley(5) 137+
(Lucy Wadham) *settled in 3rd: wnt 2nd at 14th: 3 l down at next: jnd wnr and outj. next: rdn and upsides again last: kpt on wl but rdr sn dropped rt hand side rein: jst pipped* **7/2[2]**

F/F- **3** *60* **Roving Lad (IRE)**[208] 1303 7-10-10 114..................................(t) AELynch 65
(Paul John Gilligan, Ire) *chsd ldrs: 9 l 3rd whn mstke 15th: fdd rapidly next: sn t.o* **9/1**

/20- **4** *56* **Hit The Headlines (IRE)**[6] 4685 8-11-7 130................(p) KillianMoore(5) 30
(Caroline Fryer) *chsd wnr tl blnd 14th: dropped out alarmingly qckly and climbed over fnl three: fin eventually* **14/1**

/31- **P** **Chapolimoss (FR)**[12] 4572 10-10-12 116 7ex...................(t) TomCannon
(Lawney Hill) *j. poorly: nvr really travelling in last pair: pushed along and blnd 7th: poor 5th whn p.u at 13th* **13/8[1]**

1P4- **P** **Flemi Two Toes (IRE)**[23] 4354 8-10-0 104 oh3................(p) IanPopham
(Sarah Humphrey) *j. slowly and getting progively worse: reminder 6th: last at 8th: t.o whn clambered over next three and p.u at 12th* **8/1[3]**

6m 28.4s (-7.30) **Going Correction** -0.075s/f (Good) **6** Ran SP% **110.3**
Speed ratings: **108,107,88,70,**
CSF £15.70 TOTE £5.40: £2.10, £2.80; EX 17.40 Trifecta £69.90.
Owner Massive **Bred** Fred Williams **Trained** Alcester, Warwicks

FOCUS
Quite competitive for the grade, with half of the field bang on the 130 rating ceiling. The early pace was fair.

4793 ROBERT CASE MEMORIAL NOVICES' CHASE (18 fncs) 3m 110y

2:55 (3:00) (Class 3) 5-Y-O+ **£7,213** (£2,623)

Form RPR

/32- **1** **Dreamy George (IRE)**[49] 3873 8-11-0 121........................ TomCannon 125+
(John Ferguson) *led 3rd and mde plenty of gd jumps: lft virtually solo at 14th: eased almost to a trot after last* **4/6[1]**

P56- **2** *dist* **Misty Mornin**[108] 2725 6-10-7 0..(p) MarkGrant
(Zoe Davison) *blnd 2nd where lft last: tended to jump indifferently: struggling 9th: abt to pull up whn rdr saw ch of gd prize whn lft v remote 2nd at 14th: hacked on to fin 30sec after wnr* **50/1**

353- **F** **Harry Hunt**[16] 4494 7-11-2 127.. KillianMoore(5)
(Graeme McPherson) *led tl outj. 3rd: j. slowly next two: pressed wnr but lacked fluency: bad mstke 8th: 3 l 2nd whn fell 14th* **15/8[2]**

4/- **F** **Our Ollie (IRE)**[55] 3794 8-11-0 89.. AELynch
(Paul John Gilligan, Ire) *trckd ldng pair tl fell 12th* **9/1[3]**

/0P- **U** **First Lad**[17] 4484 7-11-0 0.. TommyPhelan
(Nicholas Pomfret) *last whn terrible mstke and uns rdr 2nd* **100/1**

6m 40.4s (4.70) **Going Correction** -0.075s/f (Good) **5** Ran SP% **107.7**
Speed ratings: **89, , , ,**
CSF £17.86 TOTE £1.50: £1.10, £6.40; EX 15.80 Trifecta £16.90.
Owner Bloomfields **Bred** T J Foley **Trained** Cowlinge, Suffolk

FOCUS
This looked a two-horse contest on paper and didn't even prove to be that in the race proper.

4794 TOTEPOOL FAKENHAM SILVER CUP H'CAP HURDLE (9 hdls) 2m

3:35 (3:44) (Class 3) (0-125,125) 4-Y-O+ **£7,797** (£2,289; £1,144; £572)

Form RPR

3/5- **1** **Fujin Dancer (FR)**[16] 93 9-10-11 117......................... MissHBethell(7) 118
(Brian Ellison) *t.k.h in rr: hdwy after 3 out: 4th and drvn up on inner between last two: led last: kpt on stoutly* **4/1[2]**

416- **2** *3/4* **My Guardian Angel**[8] 2932 5-11-6 119................................ ColinBolger 120
(Mark H Tompkins) *led: hrd drvn between last two: hdd and hit last: nt qckn flat* **16/1**

4/6- **3** *1* **St Ignatius**[7] 2432 7-10-6 105.. JamesDavies 104
(Alan Bailey) *pressed ldrs: 3rd and drvn bef 3 out: stl on terms appr last: no imp after* **12/1**

306- **4** *5* **The Stig (FR)**[16] 4493 6-10-13 112...................................... PaulMoloney 107
(Nick Littmoden) *midfield: 6th and rdn 2 out: one pce after: wnt wrong and p.u jst after fin* **20/1**

0FP- **5** *1 1/4* **Occasionally Yours (IRE)**[72] 3471 10-10-1 107....... JosephAkehurst(7) 100+
(Alan Blackmore) *pressed ldr tl pushed along and lost pl 5th: last bef 3 out: plugged on again to pass btn horses* **25/1**

105- **6** *3* **Dresden (IRE)**[91] 3066 6-11-8 121.. WillKennedy 114+
(Sarah-Jayne Davies) *prom: pressed ldr fr 5th tl drvn between last two: 4th and btn whn mstke last* **14/1**

050- **7** *shd* **Taaresh (IRE)**[92] 3031 9-10-9 108.....................................(p) AdamWedge 100
(Kevin Morgan) *settled in rr: nt fluent 6th: effrt to trck ldrs and hit 3 out: wl hld fr next* **11/1**

221- **8** *3 1/4* **Pass Muster**[42] 4023 7-10-3 107.. AdamNicol(5) 95
(Philip Kirby) *midfield: shkn up whn effrt 6th: 3rd but u.p 2 out: sn btn* **11/8[1]**

210- **9** *1/2* **Town Mouse**[30] 4224 4-11-4 125..................................... TomMessenger 105
(Neil King) *awkward s then tk str hold: a bhd: rdn and brief effrt 3 out: little rspnse: btn next: hit last* **33/1**

03F- **10** *16* **Seventh Sky (GER)**[13] 4558 7-11-12 125............................(t) MarkGrant 104
(Charlie Mann) *midfield: nt fluent 6th: rdn and btn next: last whn mstke 2 out: sn eased* **15/2[3]**

3m 56.9s (-8.50) **Going Correction** -0.35s/f (Good)
WFA 4 from 5yo+ 7lb **10** Ran SP% **114.0**
Speed ratings (Par 107): **107,106,106,103,103 101,101,99,99,91**
CSF £59.24 CT £702.27 TOTE £6.30: £2.00, £4.40, £5.30; EX 61.30 Trifecta £355.30.
Owner W A Bethell **Bred** Loughtown Stud Ltd **Trained** Norton, N Yorks

FOCUS
Usually a fair handicap, but this year's renewal lost some of its intrigue when Grams And Ounces, backed from 16-1 into 3-1 in the morning for last year's winning connections, injured himself in his box before racing. Few got involved.

4795 MARHAM H'CAP CHASE (FOR THE WALTER WALES MEMORIAL CUP) (16 fncs) 2m 5f 110y

4:15 (4:21) (Class 5) (0-100,100) 5-Y-O+ **£2,599** (£763; £381; £190)

Form RPR

561- **1** **Lord Fox (IRE)**[17] 4482 7-11-1 91... BenPoste(5) 95+
(Shaun Harris) *led at v slow pce attended by loose horse tl 1/2-way: j.rt 13th: jnd between last two: plugged on gamely to gain upper hand flat* **1/1[1]**

U52- **2** *3/4* **King Ozzy (IRE)**[8] 4633 10-11-4 94.......................(tp) ConorShoemark(5) 96
(Lawney Hill) *chsd wnr: j. slowly 5th: effrt 2 out: kidded upsides between last two: ev ch last: outbattled flat* **9/2[3]**

1- **3** *3* **Martin Cash (IRE)**[8] 4633 8-12-1 100 7ex.................... DominicElsworth 99
(Paul Henderson) *tended to jump rt: hld up trcking ldng pair: disp 2 l 3rd 2 out: rdn and wknd bef last* **7/2[2]**

4 *2* **Manogue Supreme (IRE)**[115] 2588 8-11-5 97...............(p) RyanHatch(7) 96
(Neil Mulholland) *nt a fluent: trckd ldng pair: effrt 3 out: ev ch 2 out: drvn and wknd bef last* **8/1**

45P- **U** **Tchang Goon (FR)**[20] 4420 10-9-9 73 oh9 ow2.............(p) MrHGMiller(7)
(Zoe Davison) *hmpd and uns rdr 2nd* **12/1**

5m 54.9s (13.10) **Going Correction** -0.075s/f (Good) **5** Ran SP% **109.2**
Speed ratings: **73,72,71,70,**
CSF £5.92 TOTE £1.80: £1.10, £1.70; EX 6.00 Trifecta £12.20.
Owner Miss H Ward **Bred** Miss Violet Sweeney **Trained** Carburton, Notts

FOCUS
A gentler tempo to this modest handicap chase than in any of the preceding contests, which may have contributed to what was often some wayward jumping early on.

4796 COLKIRK CONDITIONAL JOCKEYS' MAIDEN HURDLE (9 hdls) 2m

4:55 (4:55) (Class 4) 4-Y-O+ **£3,119** (£915; £457; £228)

Form RPR

46- **1** **Boondooma (IRE)**[6] 4680 7-10-9 116........................ ChristopherWard(6) 118+
(Dr Richard Newland) *mde all: drew clr between last two: hrd hld* **4/5[1]**

045- **2** *6* **Focail Maith**[12] 4573 6-11-1 112.................................(p) ConorShoemark 109
(Neil King) *settled trcking ldrs: rdn in 5th whn n.m.r bnd bnd bef 2 out: drvn into 2nd bef last: wnr in total command* **8/1**

00- **3** *6* **Ever Fortune (USA)**[77] 3330 5-10-9 0.......................... CraigGallagher(6) 103
(Brian Ellison) *prom: wnt 2nd bef 2 out: drvn and nt qckn: lost 2nd bef last* **7/1[3]**

6P3- **4** *9* **Flash Tommie (IRE)**[5] 4693 6-11-1 0.. RyanWhile 92
(Michael Appleby) *hld up and bhd: kpt on past btn horses fr 2 out: wnt wl hld 4th at last* **14/1**

00- **5** *3 1/4* **Choral Bee**[94] 3005 5-10-3 0.......................................(t) JosephAkehurst(5) 84
(Alan Jessop) *chsd wnr tl 3 out: 4th and rdn and wkng whn blnd next* **100/1**

0- **6** *8* **Isdaal**[43] 3034 7-10-8 0... AdamWedge 74
(Kevin Morgan) *tk str hold: hld up and nvr bttr than midfield: rdn and fdd 2 out* **66/1**

220- **7** *1 1/2* **Aglaophonos**[57] 3161 4-10-4 114.......................................(v) RyanHatch(3) 71
(Ian Williams) *prom tl 3rd and drvn after 6th: no rspnse: wl btn 2 out* **5/2[2]**

4/6- **8** *hd* **Hortense Mancini**[16] 4499 5-10-5 0..............................(p) MattCrawley(3) 72
(Lucy Wadham) *bhd: mstke 5th and rdn: struggling after* **20/1**

0/6- **9** *2 1/2* **Simplified**[311] 161 11-10-8 59...(t) JoeCornwall 70
(Michael Chapman) *a towards rr: rdn and struggling 3 out* **100/1**

0- **10** *99* **Randall**[57] 3734 6-11-1 0... RobertWilliams
(Martin Bosley) *a last: shkn up 3rd: lost tch u.p 5th: hopelessly t.o after next* **150/1**

4m 2.2s (-3.20) **Going Correction** -0.35s/f (Good)
WFA 4 from 5yo+ 7lb **10** Ran SP% **123.3**
Speed ratings (Par 105): **94,91,88,83,81 77,77,77,75,26**
CSF £9.37 TOTE £2.10: £1.10, £3.00, £2.10; EX 9.70 Trifecta £48.90.
Owner P Jenkins & C E Stedman **Bred** Colm Griffin **Trained** Claines, Worcs

The Form Book Jumps, Raceform Ltd, Compton, RG20 6NL.

FOCUS
The slowest of the three 2m hurdles on the afternoon, clocking in over five seconds slower than the 117-rated winner of the feature handicap managed, and little strength in depth either.
T/Plt: £70.20 to a £1 stake. Pool: £69007.75 - 717.12 winning tickets T/Qpdt: £9.00 to a £1 stake. Pool: £5087.11 - 414.87 winning tickets IM

4439 FONTWELL (L-H)
Saturday, March 15

OFFICIAL GOING: Good to soft (soft in places; 6.7)
Wind: light, across Weather: dry and sunny

4797 EBF STALLIONS MARES' "NATIONAL HUNT" NOVICES' HURDLE (11 hdls) 2m 6f 110y
1:55 (1:55) (Class 4) 4-Y-0+ **£3,768** (£1,106; £553; £276)

Form RPR
32- **1** **Cove (IRE)**[5] 4715 7-11-3 0 .... TomCannon 104+
(Nick Gifford) *hld up in tch in rr: hdwy after 7th: effrt to chse ldr bef 2 out: led and mstke last: edgd rt but forged ahd flat: styd on wl: rdn out* **15/8**[2]
313- **2** *2 ¼* **Shuil Gealach (IRE)**[17] 4487 6-11-3 0 .... PaulMoloney 100+
(Paul Webber) *chsd ldrs tl wnt 2nd after 7th: led bef 2 out: rdn and hdd last: styd on same pce and swtchd lft flat* **11/8**[1]
50/- **3** *9* **Shine In Time (IRE)**[338] 5249 6-11-3 0 .... JamieMoore 91
(Laura Mongan) *chsd ldrs: mstke 7th: drvn next: 5th and btn 3 out: plugged on and wnt 3rd cl home* **14/1**
344- **4** *¾* **Dahteste**[112] 2675 6-10-12 0 .... NicodeBoinville[(5)] 90
(Mark Bradstock) *led: j.big 1st: rdn and hdd bef 3 out: 3rd and wl hld between last: plugged on but lost 3rd cl home* **14/1**
6- **5** *hd* **Lily Little Legs (IRE)**[49] 3898 5-10-12 0 .... RobertMcCarth[(5)] 90
(Ian Williams) *t.k.h: hld up in tch in last pair: hdwy to chse ldrs after 7th: rdn after 3 out: outpcd and btn next: plugged on* **11/2**[3]
044- **6** *51* **Delineate (IRE)**[11] 4600 5-11-3 0 .... GerardTumelty 39
(G C Maundrell) *chsd ldr: mstke 6th: rdn and lost pl qckly after 7th: bhd whn hmpd 3 out: t.o* **33/1**
6/6- **F** **She's Noble**[89] 3136 7-11-0 0 .... MichealNolan[(3)]
(Suzy Smith) *t.k.h: hld up in tch in midfield: hmpd 4th: mstke 7th: hdwy to chse ldrs bef next: 6th and struggling whn fell 3 out* **20/1**
P/0- **F** **Redinga**[27] 4298 8-10-10 0 ....(t) KevinJones[(7)]
(Linda Jewell) *hld up in tch in midfield: j.lft cannoned into rival and fell 4th* **100/1**

5m 49.4s (6.90) **Going Correction** +0.225s/f (Yiel) **8** Ran SP% **114.3**
Speed ratings (Par 105): **97,96,93,92,92 75, ,**
CSF £4.93 TOTE £2.40: £1.10, £1.10, £2.70; EX 4.70 Trifecta £21.00.
Owner Nick Gifford Racing Club **Bred** Maurice And Anthony Smiddy **Trained** Findon, W Sussex

FOCUS
Hurdles on outer and bends on fresh ground. Dry overnight and a sunny afternoon with perfect jumping ground. Very little strength in depth, and the pace was ordinary. The winner can rate higher.

4798 32RED CASINO H'CAP CHASE (19 fncs) 3m 2f 110y
2:30 (2:30) (Class 4) (0-120,119) 5-Y-0+ **£3,861** (£1,198; £645)

Form RPR
4U1- **1** **Itoldyou (IRE)**[20] 4440 8-11-2 **109** ....(t) AndrewThornton 119
(Linda Jewell) *hld up in tch in rr wnt 3rd 12th and chsd ldr after next: rdn and mstke 3 out: pressing ldr last: led flat: hung lft but kpt on fnl 100yds* **7/4**[2]
/U2- **2** *nse* **West Cork Flash (IRE)**[20] 4440 10-10-8 **101** ....(p) JamieMoore 111
(Paul Henderson) *led: rdn bef 3 out: hdd after last: kpt on wl u.p: jst hld* **6/4**[1]
546- **3** *19* **Princely Hero (IRE)**[20] 4441 10-10-0 **93** ....(b) TomCannon 88
(Chris Gordon) *chsd ldrs: wnt 2nd 3rd tl after 13th: 3rd and drvn after 16th: wknd 3 out* **9/1**
4PU- **P** **Ringa Bay**[22] 4396 9-11-5 **119** ....(p) JakeHodson[(7)]
(David Bridgwater) *chsd ldr tl 3rd: blnd 7th: mstke 11th: dropped to last next: lost tch after 16th: t.o whn p.u last* **4/1**[3]

7m 6.75s (5.65) **Going Correction** +0.325s/f (Yiel) **4** Ran SP% **106.4**
Speed ratings: **104,103,98,**
CSF £4.77 TOTE £2.30; EX 3.80 Trifecta £9.50.
Owner Valence Racing Too **Bred** James O'Leary **Trained** Sutton Valence, Kent
■ Stewards' Enquiry : Jamie Moore two-day ban: used whip above permitted level (Mar 29-30)

FOCUS
A paucity of runners for this fair staying handicap, although it was run at a decent pace. The first two are rated in line with their recent course form over shorter.

4799 32RED TOMB RAIDER II SLOT H'CAP HURDLE (9 hdls) 2m 2f 110y
3:05 (3:07) (Class 3) (0-135,129) 4-Y-0+ **£5,393** (£1,583; £791; £395)

Form RPR
23F- **1** **Phantom Prince (IRE)**[66] 3599 5-10-12 **115** .... AndrewTinkler 124+
(Brendan Powell) *chsd ldrs: cl 3rd and hit 3 out: led bef next: hdd 2 out and carried rt: swtchd lft between last 2: led again fnl 75yds: styd on: rdn out* **8/1**
222- **2** *2 ¾* **Ourmanmassini (IRE)**[17] 4496 6-10-7 **110** ....(t) GerardTumelty 117
(Suzy Smith) *in tch in midfield: hdwy to chse ldr 3 out: led 2 out: sn hung rt and racing against stands' rail between last 2: kpt hanging rt u.p and hitting rail flat: hdd and no ex fnl 75yds* **2/1**[1]
140- **3** *19* **Tuscan Gold**[43] 4022 7-11-2 **119** ....(p) TomCannon 108
(Laura Mongan) *led into s: wl in tch in midfield: drvn after 5th: dropped to rr bef 3 out: no ch w ldng trio after 3 out: plugged on to go modest 3rd flat* **14/1**
530- **4** *8* **Chemistry Master**[27] 4301 6-11-5 **122** ....(t) FelixDeGiles 107
(Harry Fry) *led: rdn and hdd 2 out: 3rd and btn whn blnd last: wknd and lost 3rd flat* **8/1**
5 *6* **Vision Des Champs (FR)**[77] 5-11-11 **128** .... JamieMoore 103
(Gary Moore) *hld up wl in tch in rr: rdn and btn after 3 out: wknd bef next* **7/1**[3]
1S6- **6** *11* **Hawkhill (IRE)**[91] 3083 8-11-5 **129** ....(t) JPKiely[(7)] 94
(Tim Vaughan) *w ldr tl after 6th: 4th and btn u.p after 3 out: wknd bef next: t.o* **10/1**
210- **7** *13* **Uhlan Bute (FR)**[44] 3989 6-11-5 **125** .... RobertDunne[(3)] 79
(Venetia Williams) *chsd ldrs: mstke 6th: sn rdn dropped to rr next: wknd and bhd bef 2 out: t.o* **5/2**[2]

4m 37.05s (2.75) **Going Correction** +0.225s/f (Yiel) **7** Ran SP% **112.4**
Speed ratings (Par 107): **103,101,93,90,87 83,77**
CSF £24.27 CT £220.48 TOTE £10.70: £3.80, £1.50; EX 23.70 Trifecta £175.10.
Owner Con Harrington **Bred** Mrs Chris Harrington **Trained** Upper Lambourn, Berks
■ Stewards' Enquiry : Gerard Tumelty four-day ban: used whip above permitted level (Mar 29-Apr 1)

FOCUS
They went a decent pace and a trio drew clear entering the home straight. Useful form with a big step up from the winner.

4800 32RED IMMORTAL ROMANCE SLOT H'CAP CHASE (13 fncs) 2m 2f
3:40 (3:40) (Class 3) (0-130,130) 5-Y-0+ **£6,330** (£1,870; £935; £468)

Form RPR
511- **1** **Umberto D'Olivate (FR)**[15] 4536 6-11-12 **130** .... FelixDeGiles 136+
(Robert Walford) *in tch in rr: reminders and clsd after 7th: chsd ldr 10th: rdn to ld bef 3 out: hdd last: led again on inner flat: styd on: rdn out* **1/1**[1]
340- **2** *1 ¾* **Last Shot (FR)**[21] 4414 7-11-5 **126** .... RobertDunne[(3)] 131
(Venetia Williams) *led tl hdd 10th: rallied u.p and ev ch 2 out: led last: hdd flat: no ex and btn fnl 75yds* **3/1**[2]
52P- **3** *11* **Speedy Bruere (FR)**[20] 4448 8-10-13 **117** .... SeanQuinlan 113
(David Bridgwater) *chsd ldrs: wnt 2nd 3rd tl 6th: wnt 2nd again 8th tl led 10th: rdn and hdd bef next: 3rd and btn 2 out: wknd last* **9/2**[3]
UP2- **4** *40* **Elsafeer (IRE)**[12] 4592 9-10-10 **114** .... JamieMoore 73
(Tim Vaughan) *chsd ldr tl 3rd: wnt 2nd again 6th tl 8th: lost tch after 10th: t.o* **5/1**

4m 36.7s (2.00) **Going Correction** +0.325s/f (Yiel) **4** Ran SP% **109.8**
Speed ratings: **108,107,102,84**
CSF £4.51 TOTE £1.70; EX 4.20 Trifecta £10.30.
Owner Mrs S De Wilde **Bred** J P Rivoire **Trained** Child Okeford, Dorset

FOCUS
The pace was genuine and this form can be rated as useful. The first two ran pretty much to their marks.

4801 32RED.COM H'CAP HURDLE (10 hdls) 2m 4f
4:15 (4:15) (Class 4) (0-120,120) 4-Y-0+ **£3,119** (£915; £457; £228)

Form RPR
203- **1** **Henryville**[27] 4299 6-11-10 **118** .... FelixDeGiles 127+
(Harry Fry) *nt a fluent: hld up in tch in rr: hdwy to trck ldrs and mstke 3 out: wnt 2nd and mstke 2 out: led and mstke last: immediately hung rt to stands' rail: styd on u.p* **4/1**[2]
243- **2** *2* **Coup De Grace (IRE)**[16] 4132 5-9-12 **102** .... PaddyBradley[(10)] 109+
(Pat Phelan) *chsd ldrs: wnt 2nd after 4th tl led bef 2 out: mstke 2 out: hdd last: swtchd lft and styd on same pce u.p flat* **9/4**[1]
100- **3** *22* **Sinbad The Sailor**[29] 3186 9-11-12 **120** ....(t) AndrewTinkler 105
(George Baker) *wl in tch in midfield: hdwy to chse ldrs 7th: 4th and btn 2 out: mstke last: plugged on to go modest 3rd fnl 75yds* **10/1**
345- **4** *6* **Auld Sthock (IRE)**[25] 4332 6-11-5 **113** .... JamieMoore 93
(Gary Moore) *hld up in tch: hdwy to ld after 4th: rdn and hdd bef 2 out: 3rd and btn between last 2: wknd flat and lost 3rd fnl 75yds* **8/1**
UP2- **5** *91* **Curtain Razer (IRE)**[29] 4249 8-11-2 **110** .... TomCannon 8
(Chris Gordon) *led tl after 4th: dropped to rr and drvn after 6th: losing tch whn j.lft 3 out: t.o next* **12/1**
/15- **P** **No No Bingo (IRE)**[50] 3884 8-11-0 **111** ....(p) KielanWoods[(3)]
(Charlie Longsdon) *chsd ldr tl after 4th: styd prom tl wknd u.p after 3 out: t.o whn p.u last* **5/1**[3]
40- **F** **Stay In My Heart (IRE)**[43] 4023 5-10-2 **101** .... NicodeBoinville[(5)]
(Laura Mongan) *wl in tch in midfield: pushed along whn fell 7th* **16/1**
304- **B** **Saffron Prince**[24] 4350 6-11-2 **110** .... SeanQuinlan
(David Bridgwater) *hld up in tch tl brought 7th* **8/1**

5m 0.5s (1.10) **Going Correction** +0.225s/f (Yiel) **8** Ran SP% **112.3**
Speed ratings (Par 105): **106,105,96,94,57 , ,**
CSF £13.32 CT £80.50 TOTE £4.60: £1.80, £1.10, £4.10; EX 12.20 Trifecta £108.90.
Owner R P B Michaelson & E M Thornton **Bred** Karen George **Trained** Seaborough, Dorset

FOCUS
Ordinary pace for this fair handicap and the front pair drew well clear. The winner built on a good bumper run.

4802 32RED FREE £10 BONUS H'CAP CHASE (13 fncs) 2m 2f
4:50 (4:50) (Class 5) (0-100,92) 5-Y-0+ **£2,144** (£629; £314; £157)

Form RPR
324- **1** **Benny The Swinger (IRE)**[46] 3960 9-11-12 **92** .... TomCannon 99+
(Chris Gordon) *j.rt at times: hld up in tch in last pair: clsd to press ldrs on inner whn j.rt and bmpd rival 2 out: ev ch last: rdn to ld fnl 100yds: fnd enough and r.o* **15/8**[1]
355- **2** *1* **Zhukov (IRE)**[5] 4718 12-11-5 **92** .... MrLKilgarriff[(7)] 96
(Kevin Tork) *chsd ldrs: wnt 2nd 9th: led after next: drvn last: hdd flat: r.o but no ex towards fin* **10/1**
224- **3** *6* **Morestead (IRE)**[68] 3564 9-11-9 **89** ....(t) JamieMoore 88
(Brendan Powell) *led: rdn 9th: hdd after next: stl pressing ldr and swtchd lft bef 2 out: ev ch last: outpcd flat* **7/2**[3]
P15- **4** *2 ¾* **The Informant**[21] 4416 8-11-0 **80** ....(p) AndrewThornton 77
(Seamus Mullins) *chsd ldr tl 9th: styd chsng ldrs: rdn in st 3rd whn bmpd 2 out: wknd flat* **11/4**[2]
3U4- **F** **Enchanting Smile (FR)**[9] 4633 7-11-7 **87** ....(t) TommyPhelan
(Mark Gillard) *mstkes: hld up in last pair tl fell 9th* **5/1**

4m 44.1s (9.40) **Going Correction** +0.325s/f (Yiel) **5** Ran SP% **109.4**
Speed ratings: **92,91,88,87,**
CSF £17.05 TOTE £2.80: £1.40, £4.30; EX 23.40 Trifecta £27.10.
Owner L Gilbert **Bred** Patrick J Walsh **Trained** Morestead, Hants

FOCUS
A moderate handicap chase run at a steady pace and there were three in a line jumping the last. The cosy winner is rated to his mark.

4803 32RED CONDITIONAL JOCKEYS' H'CAP HURDLE (13 hdls) 3m 3f
5:25 (5:25) (Class 5) (0-100,101) 4-Y-0+ **£1,949** (£572; £286; £143)

Form RPR
051- **1** **Solstice Son**[5] 4719 5-11-12 **101** 7ex ....(t) GaryDerwin[(5)] 114+
(Anthony Honeyball) *hld up: hdwy to ld and travelling wl 3 out: clr w runner-up and dived next: forged ahd and edgd rt u.p flat: styd on* **1/1**[1]
034- **2** *3 ¾* **Marmalade Man**[40] 4071 8-10-11 **87** ....(p) KevinJones[(6)] 94
(Seamus Mullins) *t.k.h: pressed ldr: wnt clr w wnr after 3 out: rdn between last 2: no ex and swtchd lft flat: styd on same pce after* **7/2**[2]
045- **3** *13* **Kapricorne (FR)**[9] 4636 7-10-6 **76** .... JamesBest 73
(Sophie Leech) *wl in tch in midfield: 3rd and drvn after 3 out: no imp next: btn whn mstke last: wknd flat* **10/1**
322- **4** *22* **Absolute Shambles**[89] 3138 10-11-0 **92** ....(p) LouisMuspratt[(8)] 68
(Chris Gordon) *in tch in last pair: pushed along after 1st: rdn and outpcd 3 out: wl btn next: plugged on to go poor 4th flat: t.o* **8/1**[3]

U/0- **5** *4 1/2* **Pimbury (IRE)**[28] 4275 12-10-0 **70** oh1[1] ThomasGarner 41
(Fiona Shaw) *hld up in tch in last pair: rdn and effrt after 3 out: sn outpcd and wl btn 4th whn mstke next: wknd and lost 4th flat: t.o* **33/1**

454- **6** *17* **Leith Hill Legasi**[23] 4375 5-11-9 **96** KielanWoods(3) 52
(Charlie Longsdon) *led tl 3rd: styd pressing ldrs tl wknd u.p after 3 out: t.o between last 2* **14/1**

541- **7** *1 1/4* **Strange Bird (IRE)**[19] 4471 9-11-6 **90** JeremiahMcGrath 45
(Richard Rowe) *w ldr tl led 3rd: mstke 7th: hdd 3 out: sn dropped out and bhd: t.o whn mstke last* **8/1**[3]

5/3- **8** *6* **Converti**[20] 4447 10-10-1 **76** JPKiely(5) 26
(Carroll Gray) *chsd ldr after 3rd tl bef 3 out: wknd u.p wl bef 2 out: t.o between last 2* **20/1**

6m 57.1s (4.30) **Going Correction** +0.225s/f (Yiel) **8** Ran SP% **117.9**
Speed ratings (Par 103): **102,100,97,90,89 84,83,82**
CSF £5.52 CT £22.09 TOTE £2.70: £1.30, £1.20, £2.60; EX 4.60 Trifecta £49.60.
Owner The Summer Solstice **Bred** R W Russell **Trained** Mosterton, Dorset

FOCUS
A moderate handicap with little depth and the front two in the market dominated, drawing well clear of the remainder. The winner was well in on his recent win and there is probably more to come.
T/Plt: £45.40 to a £1 stake. Pool: £72,422.00 - 1,163.71 winning tickets. T/Qpdt: £12.40 to a £1 stake. Pool: £2,881.07 - 170.57 winning tickets. SP

4418 KEMPTON (R-H)

Saturday, March 15

OFFICIAL GOING: Good to soft (good in places; chs 6.8, hdl 6.3)
Wind: Moderate, half against Weather: Fine, warm

4804 BETDAQ THE SPORTS BETTING EXCHANGE NOVICES' LIMITED H'CAP CHASE (12 fncs) 2m

2:20 (2:20) (Class 3) (0-125,125) 5-Y-0+ **£9,747** (£2,862; £1,431; £715)

Form RPR

5/0- **1** **Kitegen (IRE)**[154] 1867 8-11-0 **120** CharliePoste 127+
(Robin Dickin) *trckd ldrs: shkn up bef 3 out: clsd to ld 2 out: rdn and kpt on wl* **7/1**

324- **2** *2* **Able Deputy**[123] 2434 7-11-2 **122** (t) SamTwiston-Davies 128+
(Kim Bailey) *tended to jump lft: hld up in 5th: loomed up on outer after 3 out: upsides next: sn rdn and fnd nil: kpt on fr last* **6/1**

124- **3** *nk* **Easily Pleased (IRE)**[17] 4503 8-11-0 **120** HaddenFrost 125
(Martin Hill) *t.k.h: hld up in last pair: mstke 1st: cl up 3 out: nt qckn next: styd on again bef last* **5/1**[3]

U21- **4** *1* **Arkaim**[8] 4653 6-11-0 **123** KielanWoods(3) 129
(Pam Sly) *mde most: slow jump 4 out and briefly hdd: rdn and hdd 2 out: one pce* **7/1**

443- **5** *1/2* **Noche De Reyes (FR)**[56] 3787 5-10-12 **118** AlainCawley 121
(Tom George) *mostly chsd ldr: led briefly 4 out: chal again 2 out: one pce after* **4/1**[2]

410- **6** *2 3/4* **Doynosaur**[76] 3386 7-11-5 **125** TomScudamore 125
(K R Burke) *trckd ldrs: c lose up 3 out: sn shkn up and nt qckn: wknd after 2 out* **8/1**

/P0- **7** *21* **Tante Sissi (FR)**[98] 2948 7-11-0 **120** RobertThornton 102
(Alan King) *t.k.h: hld up in last pair: mstke 3rd: nt fluent 6th: rdn and struggling sn after 4 out: t.o* **7/2**[1]

(-0.30) **Going Correction** -0.225s/f (Good) **7** Ran SP% **109.3**
Speed ratings: **91,90,89,89,89 87,77**
CSF £42.99 TOTE £8.20: £4.30, £2.90; EX 42.60 Trifecta £465.80.
Owner R G Whitehead **Bred** Michael Coughlan **Trained** Alcester, Warwicks

FOCUS
All rails moved out 3yds and all distances as advertised. Despite the pace looking solid enough in this fair novice handicap chase, all bar the favourite were in a line across the track with every chance coming to two out. A small step up from the winner.

4805 KEMPTON PARK BETDAQ SILVER PLATE (A H'CAP HURDLE) (10 hdls) 2m 5f

2:55 (2:55) (Class 2) 4-Y-0+

£21,896 (£6,468; £3,234; £1,617; £808; £406)

Form RPR

210- **1** **Carole's Destrier**[34] 4174 6-11-6 **129** MichaelByrne 133
(Neil Mulholland) *wl in tch: prog to trck ldrs 3 out: clsd fr next: chsd ldr last: styd on to ld post* **14/1**

21- **2** *shd* **Marcilhac (FR)**[69] 3552 5-11-7 **130** LiamTreadwell 134
(Venetia Williams) *prom: clsd to ld bef 2 out: rdn bef last: kpt on wl but hdd post* **14/1**

112- **3** *1 1/2* **Portway Flyer (IRE)**[37] 4102 6-11-3 **129** GavinSheehan(3) 132
(Ian Williams) *prom: tried to chal on long run bef 2 out: nt qckn bef last: kpt on* **12/1**

111- **4** *3/4* **Legacy Gold (IRE)**[22] 4394 6-11-10 **133** TomScudamore 138+
(David Pipe) *t.k.h: hld up wl in rr: mstke 6th: prog fr next to trck ldrs 3 out: chsd ldr 2 out: n.m.r and lost 2nd last: one pce* **7/2**[1]

244- **5** *8* **Benbane Head (USA)**[27] 4299 10-11-11 **134** (tp) IanPopham 130
(Martin Keighley) *led: rdn and hdd bef 2 out: steadily fdd* **33/1**

061- **6** *nk* **Seventh Sign**[24] 4347 5-11-5 **135** (b) StephenO'Donovan(7) 129
(Alan King) *hld up in midfield: effrt fr 3 out: rdn and no prog on long run to 2 out: fdd* **16/1**

435- **7** *nk* **Bygones Sovereign (IRE)**[28] 4264 8-10-8 **124** (p) MikeyEnnis(7) 118
(David Pipe) *chsd ldr: mstke 6th: rdn bef next: lost 2nd and steadily fdd bef 2 out* **33/1**

221- **8** *5* **Another Hero (IRE)**[123] 2443 5-10-13 **127** MauriceLinehan(5) 120+
(Jonjo O'Neill) *hld up in rr: mstke 1st: gd prog fr 7th to trck ldrs 3 out: rdn and wkng whn mstke 2 out* **9/1**[3]

151- **9** *3 3/4* **Lord Protector (IRE)**[21] 4413 7-11-4 **127** TomO'Brien 114
(Philip Hobbs) *hld up towards rr: prog into midfield after 3 out and gng bttr than many: rdn and fnd nil after 2 out* **25/1**

264- **10** *3 1/4* **Drum Valley**[76] 3387 6-11-8 **131** LeightonAspell 114
(Oliver Sherwood) *nvr bttr than midfield: rdn and struggling 3 out: sn lost tch: plugged on after 2 out* **16/1**

125- **11** *1 3/4* **Carrigmorna King (IRE)**[91] 3091 8-11-6 **132** (t) JamesBest(3) 114
(Philip Hobbs) *trckd ldrs: wl there 3 out: rdn and wknd bef next* **33/1**

131- **12** *2 3/4* **Prideofthecastle (IRE)**[37] 4112 7-11-2 **132** TomBellamy(7) 111
(David Pipe) *prom: rdn and lost pl rapidly jst bef 3 out: no ch after* **20/1**

2/0- **13** *12* **Golden Hoof (IRE)**[112] 2668 6-11-7 **130** BarryGeraghty 98
(Nicky Henderson) *racd on outer: hld up in midfield: shkn up after 3 out: sn lost tch w ldrs* **11/1**

313- **14** *2* **Special Catch (IRE)**[30] 4237 7-11-12 **135** JamesReveley 102
(Keith Reveley) *hld up and last early: prog on inner to rch midfield 3 out: sn rdn: no hdwy bef 2 out: wknd* **12/1**

023- **15** *2* **Imperial Leader (IRE)**[34] 4174 6-11-5 **128** (t) SamTwiston-Davies 93
(Nigel Twiston-Davies) *hld up in midfield: blnd 5th: dropped to rr and nvr on terms after* **7/1**[2]

36P/ **16** *hd* **Traditional Bob (IRE)**[457] 3024 9-10-5 **121** ConorRing(7) 86
(Evan Williams) *mstke 1st: hld up wl in rr: rdn after 7th: sn struggling* **40/1**

205- **17** *2* **Home Run (GER)**[42] 4025 6-11-0 **130** (b) MrEBarrett(7) 93
(David Pipe) *mstke 2nd: nvr gng wl after and a in rr* **25/1**

422- **18** *3 3/4* **Cannon Fodder**[14] 4542 7-11-6 **129** MarcGoldstein 89
(Sheena West) *in tch in midfield: rdn and lost pl after 7th: sn toiling* **25/1**

352- **P** **Empire Levant (USA)**[17] 4497 7-11-6 **132** HarryDerham(3)
(Paul Nicholls) *racd wd: hld up: blnd 4th: wknd after 6th: t.o whn p.u bef 2 out* **25/1**

3- **P** **Lord Of Scotland (FR)**[27] 4307 5-11-7 **130** RobertThornton
(Alan King) *wl in tch in midfield tl wknd rapidly and p.u bef 7th* **25/1**

5m 4.5s (-13.00) **Going Correction** -0.375s/f (Good) **20** Ran SP% **128.8**
Speed ratings (Par 109): **109,108,108,108,105 104,104,102,101,100 99,98,93,93,92 92,91,90, ,**
CSF £178.29 CT £2453.59 TOTE £17.40: £3.90, £3.50, £3.50, £1.60; EX 306.60 Trifecta £1288.20.
Owner Mrs C Skipworth **Bred** Larkinglass Ltd **Trained** Limpley Stoke, Wilts
■ Stewards' Enquiry : Liam Treadwell two-day ban: used whip above permitted level (Mar 29-30)

FOCUS
This competitive event was open to horses that were eliminated at the declaration stage from any handicap hurdle at this year's Cheltenham Festival. The first four are all on the upgrade and the form should work out.

4806 KEMPTON PARK BETDAQ SILVER BOWL (A H'CAP CHASE) (16 fncs) 2m 4f 110y

3:30 (3:30) (Class 2) 5-Y-0+

£24,760 (£7,352; £3,676; £1,832; £920; £464)

Form RPR

646- **1** **Lost Legend (IRE)**[21] 4418 7-11-2 **124** (p) RichieMcLernon 137+
(Jonjo O'Neill) *hld up: mstke 6th: prog 10th: sltly impeded 11th: clsd to ld bef 3 out gng easily: jnd bef 2 out: rdn to assert last: styd on wl: readily* **9/1**

26/ **2** *3/4* **Nearest The Pin (IRE)**[43] 1651 9-11-7 **134** (t) BrianHayes(5) 146+
(John Joseph Hanlon, Ire) *hld up in rr but wl in tch: mstke 12th: prog fr next: chal gng wl after 3 out: jnd wnr bef 2 out: hanging between last 2: styd on but hld fr last* **20/1**

333- **3** *6* **Cloudy Bob (IRE)**[30] 4244 7-11-3 **125** ColinBolger 131
(Pat Murphy) *led to 5th: led again 8th: rdn and hdd bef 3 out: steadily outpcd* **9/1**

332- **4** *4 1/2* **The Romford Pele (IRE)**[38] 4088 7-11-2 **129** PatrickCorbett(5) 133
(Rebecca Curtis) *hld up: blnd 6th: wl in tch 4 out: rdn and outpcd bef next* **4/1**[1]

1U4- **5** *3* **Top Of The Range (IRE)**[24] 4344 7-11-9 **131** BarryGeraghty 130
(Nicky Henderson) *racd wd: hld up in rr: urged along after 9th: prog to join ldrs 4 out: wknd after next* **7/1**[3]

255- **6** *15* **Saved By John (IRE)**[21] 4414 9-10-13 **131** (t) AlanJohns(10) 118
(Tim Vaughan) *prom: disp ld 5th to 8th: wknd bef 3 out* **14/1**

243- **7** *2 1/2* **Elenika (FR)**[14] 4559 6-11-1 **123** LiamTreadwell 106
(Venetia Williams) *wl in tch tl wknd 4 out* **7/1**[3]

312- **8** *27* **Bar De Ligne (FR)**[41] 4055 8-11-10 **132** (p) RobertThornton 91
(Steve Gollings) *prom: disp ld 5th to 8th: lost pl qckly after 12th: t.o* **11/1**

44F- **F** **The Cockney Mackem (IRE)**[84] 3197 8-11-8 **130**(vt) SamTwiston-Davies
(Nigel Twiston-Davies) *wl in tch: mstke 9th: in rr whn fell 12th* **16/1**

213- **F** **Al Alfa**[21] 4414 7-11-2 **124** TomO'Brien
(Philip Hobbs) *prom: fell 2nd* **8/1**

244- **U** **Royal Guardsman (IRE)**[76] 3386 7-11-1 **123** TomScudamore
(Ali Brewer) *hld up: uns rdr 1st* **11/2**[2]

5m 6.9s (-9.70) **Going Correction** -0.225s/f (Good) **11** Ran SP% **117.1**
Speed ratings: **109,108,106,104,103 97,96,86, ,**
CSF £161.06 CT £1665.76 TOTE £7.50: £2.80, £4.00, £4.20; EX 190.30 Trifecta £1875.70 Part won..
Owner Mrs Gay Smith **Bred** Highfort Stud **Trained** Cheltenham, Gloucs

FOCUS
This race was open to horses that were eliminated at the declaration stage from any handicap chase at this year's Cheltenham Festival. The field were soon thinned out with Royal Guardsman unseating at the first and Al Alfa falling at the second. Solid handiacp form.

4807 SOCCER AM NOVICES' HURDLE (8 hdls) 2m

4:05 (4:05) (Class 4) 4-Y-0+ **£3,898** (£1,144; £572; £286)

Form RPR

/21- **1** **Oscar Hoof (IRE)**[76] 3388 6-11-7 131 BarryGeraghty 135+
(Nicky Henderson) *prom: trckd ldr 5th: led bef 2 out: rdn bef last: styd on wl flat* **5/4**[1]

/23- **2** *3 1/4* **Fair Loch**[37] 4103 6-11-1 125 TomScudamore 122
(K R Burke) *trckd ldrs: wnt 2nd 2 out gng strly: nt rdn tl after last whn wnr had asserted: nt qckn* **5/1**[3]

16- **3** *2 1/4* **Fitzwilly**[21] 4419 4-10-10 0 GavinSheehan(3) 118
(Mick Channon) *w ldr: led 4th: hdd bef 2 out: outpcd but styd on* **16/1**

14- **4** *3 1/2* **First Mohican**[21] 4421 6-11-7 129 RobertThornton 123
(Alan King) *trckd ldrs: cl 4th 2 out: shkn up bef last: outpcd but styd on* **5/2**[2]

5 *8* **Solar Sky**[318] 6-11-1 0 DavidBass 111
(David Elsworth) *hld up towards rr: pushed along 5th: gd prog to chse ldrs 3 out: hld whn awkward 2 out: fdd* **20/1**

/26- **6** *3 1/4* **Devon Drum**[22] 2783 6-11-1 0 DenisO'Regan 107
(Paul Webber) *hld up wl in rr: stdy prog fr 5th: rchd 6th on long run bef 2 out: shkn up and no imp bef last: fdd* **16/1**

3- **7** *2 1/4* **Gun Shy (IRE)**[161] 1764 6-11-1 0 JoshuaMoore 108+
(Gary Moore) *trckd ldrs: shkn up after 3 out: outpcd fr next: wl btn whn hung bdly lft after last* **25/1**

P- **8** *8* **Here I Am (IRE)**[131] 2266 7-11-1 0 SamThomas 97
(Diana Grissell) *led to 4th: lost 2nd next: wknd on long run bef 2 out* **100/1**

9 *9* **Money Talks**[234] 4-10-7 0 MarcGoldstein 81
(Michael Madgwick) *hld up towards rr: stl in tch after 3 out: shkn up and wknd bef next* **100/1**

5- **10** *nk* **Markttag**[27] 4307 4-10-2 0 MauriceLinehan(5) 81
(Jonjo O'Neill) *racd wd: hld up towards rr: in tch 3 out: pushed along and fdd bef next* **66/1**

The Form Book Jumps, Raceform Ltd, Compton, RG20 6NL.

11 3¾ **Miracle Cure (IRE)**268 5-11-1 0 LiamTreadwell 86
(Venetia Williams) *plld hrd: mstke 1st: hld up in tch: wknd on long run bef 2 out* **16/1**

06- 12 ¾ **Gold Carrot**27 4297 6-11-1 0 LeightonAspell 85
(Gary Moore) *hld up and mostly in last trio: lost tch fr 5th: nudged along after 3 out: nvr remotely involved* **66/1**

045- 13 shd **Parting Way (IRE)**8 4664 6-11-1 0 MichaelByrne 85
(Tim Vaughan) *t.k.h: hld up towards rr: struggling fr 5th: wl btn after 3 out* **100/1**

P/5- 14 1 **Hung Parliament (FR)**113 2644 6-11-1 0 JackDoyle 84
(Alan King) *t.k.h: in tch to 3 out: wknd bef next* **66/1**

234- 15 4½ **Mr Shantu (IRE)**20 4450 5-11-1 0 RichieMcLernon 80
(Jonjo O'Neill) *nt fluent 3rd: a towards rr: mstke 3 out: no ch after* **66/1**

1- 16 38 **No Such Number**11 2876 6-11-7 0 TomMessenger 52
(Julia Feilden) *chsd ldrs tl wknd rapidly and mstke 3 out: t.o* **40/1**

050- 17 1¼ **Katie's Massini (IRE)**128 2317 6-10-8 0 JamesDavies 38
(Henry Oliver) *struggling fr 4th: sn btn: t.o* **100/1**

3m 49.0s (-9.10) **Going Correction** -0.375s/f (Good)
WFA 4 from 5yo+ 7lb 17 Ran SP% **128.3**
Speed ratings (Par 105): **107,105,104,102,98 96,95,91,87,87 85,84,84,84,82 63,62**
CSF £8.11 TOTE £2.10: £1.40, £2.80, £3.50; EX 12.20 Trifecta £132.40.
Owner The Hoof Partnership **Bred** John Bergin **Trained** Upper Lambourn, Berks

FOCUS
This novice hurdle wasn't as competitive as the size of the field would suggest and three dominated the market. The pace was fair. A few winners should come out of the race.

4808 MOLSON COORS NOVICES' HURDLE (10 hdls) 2m 5f
4:40 (4:40) (Class 4) 4-Y-0+ **£3,898** (£1,144; £572; £286)

Form RPR

42F- 1 **Andy Kelly (IRE)**35 4144 5-10-12 130 RichardO'Dea(10) 122+
(Emma Lavelle) *led at mod pce to 2nd: styd cl up: led again bef 2 out: sn drew clr: comf* **4/6**1

50- 2 9 **Withoutdefavourite (IRE)**15 4535 6-11-2 0 JamesDavies 105
(Henry Oliver) *led 2nd to 3rd: styd prom: urged along fr 6th: rdn and rallied to go 2nd after 2 out: no ch w wnr* **50/1**

3 nk **Generous Helpings (IRE)** 5-11-2 0 JoshuaMoore 108+
(Gary Moore) *hld up: bdly hmpd 2nd: prog after 3 out: rdn and styd on bef last: pressed runner-up flat: no ch w wnr* **14/1**

046- 4 4½ **Royal Ripple (IRE)**43 4017 6-10-9 0 MrGBranton(7) 101
(Paul Henderson) *hld up in tch: urged along and outpcd bef 2 out: styd on again fr last* **50/1**

313- 5 nse **Masquerade (IRE)**48 3920 5-11-5 121 GavinSheehan(3) 109
(Warren Greatrex) *tended to jump lft: t.k.h: led 3rd: hdd bef 2 out: fdd* **4/1**2

620- 6 2½ **Lemony Bay**76 3388 5-11-2 123 LeightonAspell 100
(Oliver Sherwood) *trckd ldrs: mstke 5th: cl up after 3 out: wnt 2nd briefly 2 out: sn wknd* **6/1**3

0- 7 8 **Road To Freedom**24 4349 5-11-2 0 TomO'Brien 93
(Lucy Wadham) *hld up in tch: shkn up and wknd on long run bef 2 out* **33/1**

304- 8 35 **Blue Bear (IRE)**117 2566 5-11-2 0 MarcGoldstein 60
(Diana Grissell) *trckd ldrs: wnt 2nd briefly 3 out: sn wknd rapidly: t.o* **33/1**

400- F **Couldhavehaditall (IRE)**27 4300 6-11-2 0 DenisO'Regan
(Paul Webber) *fell 2nd* **12/1**

5m 14.8s (-2.70) **Going Correction** -0.375s/f (Good) 9 Ran SP% **118.4**
Speed ratings (Par 105): **90,86,86,84,84 83,80,67,**
CSF £52.37 TOTE £1.50: £1.20, £6.30, £2.20; EX 42.40 Trifecta £1735.40.
Owner The Optimists **Bred** Grace Leahy **Trained** Hatherden, Hants

FOCUS
The absence of Ned Stark robbed this novice hurdle of much of its interest. They went a modest pace. The form is rated around the first two.

4809 BETDAQ £25 NO LOSE MOBILE BET H'CAP CHASE (THE JOCKEY CLUB GRASSROOTS JUMPS SERIES QUALIFIER) (18 fncs) 3m
5:15 (5:17) (Class 4) (0-115,115) 5-Y-0+ **£6,498** (£1,908; £954; £477)

Form RPR

424- 1 **Badgers Cove (IRE)**22 4399 10-11-1 **104** CharliePoste 115+
(Robin Dickin) *mde all: gng best after 4 out: shkn up after 2 out: a in command: comf* **5/2**1

452- 2 3 **Mic Aubin (FR)**9 4637 11-10-6 **95** DavidBass 100+
(Jennifer Mason) *chsd ldrs: rdn 14th: prog to chse wnr whn blnd 3 out: styd on but nvr able to chal* **5/1**3

325- 3 18 **Venetian Lad**20 4440 9-11-4 **107** MarcGoldstein 94
(Lydia Richards) *chsd ldng pair 6th: rdn 14th: no imp 3 out: wknd 2 out* **14/1**

336- 4 2¾ **Billy Dutton**22 4396 8-11-5 **108** (p) JamesDavies 92
(Chris Down) *in tch: urged along fr 11th: rdn and no imp 4 out: no ch whn mstke 3 out* **10/3**2

/14- 5 4 **Campbonnais (FR)**43 4006 9-11-12 **115** (p) JackDoyle 99
(Ali Brewer) *nt fluent: hld up in rr: rdn 14th: wknd 4 out: sn bhd* **7/1**

P06- 6 9 **Midnight Macarena**24 4354 9-11-0 **103** (p) LeightonAspell 76
(Lucy Wadham) *nt a fluent: mostly chsd wnr: rdn and wknd after 4 out: tired and eased fr last* **8/1**

60P- P **Whispering Jack**5 4732 9-11-9 **112** (p) TomO'Brien
(Keiran Burke) *j.lft: lost prom pl 6th: last and struggling 8th: t.o whn p.u after 11th* **8/1**

6m 8.8s (-6.60) **Going Correction** -0.225s/f (Good) 7 Ran SP% **109.7**
Speed ratings: **102,101,95,94,92 89,**
CSF £14.27 TOTE £3.40: £2.10, £2.50; EX 13.50 Trifecta £126.30.
Owner E R C Beech & B Wilkinson **Bred** Miss Lillian Barry **Trained** Alcester, Warwicks

FOCUS
A weak handicap chase in which the form looks moderate. The winner is rated to form.

4810 FAMILY FUN AT KEMPTON PARK 19.04.14 MAIDEN OPEN NATIONAL HUNT FLAT RACE 2m
5:50 (5:50) (Class 5) 4-6-Y-0 **£2,599** (£763; £381; £190)

Form RPR

1 **Miles To Memphis (IRE)** 5-11-4 0 RobertThornton 109+
(Alan King) *hld up in midfield: prog over 4f out: trckd ldr over 2f out: shkn up to ld over 1f out: qckly drew clr* **6/1**2

6- 2 8 **Run On Sterling**107 2759 5-11-4 0 DenisO'Regan 101+
(Paul Webber) *trckd ldrs: lost pl fr 5f out: pushed along in rr over 3f out: rdn over 2f out: r.o wl fr over 1f out to take 2nd last strides* **40/1**

2- 3 1 **Dancing Shadow (IRE)**34 4177 5-11-4 0 JackDoyle 100
(Victor Dartnall) *prom: chsd ldr 9f out to over 2f out: sn outpcd: kpt on nr fin* **9/1**

4 nse **Kayf Blanco**128 2325 5-11-4 0 SamTwiston-Davies 100
(Graeme McPherson) *racd wd most of way: t.k.h: led after 4f: shkn up and hdd over 1f out: wknd ins fnl f* **7/1**3

5 2 **Vinnie The Pooh (IRE)** 6-11-4 0 LeightonAspell 98
(Nick Gifford) *hld up in rr: outpcd and pushed along 4f out: prog over 2f out: kpt on fr over 1f out: nrst fin* **20/1**

0/ 6 2¾ **Scarlett Lady**695 5470 6-10-11 0 1 TomScudamore 89
(Ali Brewer) *prom: disp 2nd pl fr 1/2-way to 3f out: shkn up and steadily outpcd* **50/1**

- 7 11 **Ryde By Knight** 6-11-4 0 DavidBass 88
(Nicky Henderson) *hld up in midfield: prog over 4f out: shkn up over 2f out: sn wknd* **8/1**

8 shd **Loves Blind (IRE)** 5-11-4 0 ColinBolger 86
(Pat Murphy) *plld hrd: hld up in tch: pushed along and wknd 3f out* **33/1**

6- 9 1¼ **Manhattan Mead**59 3719 4-10-10 0 MarcGoldstein 77
(Michael Madgwick) *t.k.h: hld up in rr: outpcd and rn green over 3f out: no ch after* **66/1**

5- 10 6 **Free Of Charge (IRE)**79 3295 5-11-4 0 TomO'Brien 79
(Philip Hobbs) *t.k.h: hld up in rr: shkn up and outpcd over 3f out: wknd* **14/1**

11 5 **Oficial Ben (IRE)**104 5-11-4 0 RichieMcLernon 75
(Jonjo O'Neill) *hld up in last early: prog 5f out: 6th over 3f out: sn shkn up and wknd* **1/1**1

12 5 **Bo's Return** 4-10-10 0 MichaelByrne 62
(Tim Vaughan) *led 4f: prom tl wknd 4f out* **33/1**

3m 57.4s (4.90) **Going Correction** -0.375s/f (Good)
WFA 4 from 5yo+ 7lb 12 Ran SP% **121.1**
Speed ratings: **72,68,67,67,66 65,59,59,58,55 53,50**
CSF £236.15 TOTE £8.70: £2.50, £6.50, £3.10; EX 206.10 Trifecta £612.20.
Owner Mrs Lesley Field & Jules Sigler **Bred** Maurice And Anthony Smiddy **Trained** Barbury Castle, Wilts

FOCUS
While there were no obstacles, the runners did have to negotiate a few swans. Probably just ordinary bumper form for the track but the winner could be useful.
T/Plt: £220.80 to a £1 stake. Pool: £106,075.34 - 350.69 winning tickets. T/Qpdt: £18.90 to a £1 stake. Pool: £6,523.94 - 254.20 winning tickets. JN

4605 NEWCASTLE (L-H)
Saturday, March 15

OFFICIAL GOING: Home straight - good (good to firm in places); back straight - good (good to soft in places)
Wind: Fresh, half behind Weather: Overcast

4811 MTREC.CO.UK NOVICES' HURDLE (9 hdls) 2m
2:15 (2:15) (Class 4) 4-Y-0+ **£3,285** (£957; £479)

Form RPR

2FF- 1 **Master Red (IRE)**30 4234 5-11-1 0 HenryBrooke 111+
(Donald McCain) *t.k.h: chsd ldr: led on bit after 2 out: mstke last: hdd briefly last 150yds: rdn and r.o wl towards fin* **5/6**1

443- 2 ½ **Ride The Range (IRE)**21 4429 5-10-8 0 DiarmuidO'Regan(7) 105
(Chris Grant) *chsd ldrs: drvn and outpcd bef 3 out: rallied bef last: kpt on to take 2nd towards fin* **7/1**

3- 3 ¾ **Aneedh**160 1786 4-10-7 0 BrianHarding 97
(Jedd O'Keeffe) *t.k.h: hld up: hdwy to chse ldrs 3 out: swtchd rt and led briefly last 150yds: no ex towards fin* **6/1**3

064- 4 4½ **Utopian**14 4548 5-10-10 0 CraigNichol(5) 102+
(Rose Dobbin) *cl up: led 4 out: rdn next: hdd after 2 out: rallied and ev ch after last: outpcd last 150yds* **5/1**2

P3- 5 13 **Flawless Filly (IRE)**10 4614 4-10-0 0 WilsonRenwick 72
(Rose Dobbin) *prom: gng wl 3out: nt fluent and shkn uo briefly next: sn btn* **14/1**

6- 6 4½ **Golan Sun (IRE)**8 4647 6-10-10 0 DerekFox(5) 83
(Paul Stafford, Ire) *mstkes in rr: struggling 4 out: nvr able to chal* **100/1**

0- 7 1¾ **Vision De La Vie (FR)**84 3214 4-10-4 0 TonyKelly(3) 73
(Pauline Robson) *hld up: stdy hdwy 4 out: rdn and wknd next* **33/1**

040- 8 2¼ **Moheebb (IRE)**10 4612 10-11-1 92 (p) KennyJohnson 79
(Robert Johnson) *t.k.h: led to 4 out: rdn and wknd bef next* **66/1**

P **Syrian**368 7-10-12 0 PeterCarberry(3)
(Barry Murtagh) *bhd: struggling 1/2-way: t.o whn j. slowly last: sn p.u* **66/1**

250/ U **Viking Chief (IRE)**353 4976 7-10-10 0 JohnDawson(5)
(John Wade) *hld up in tch: hit and outpcd 4th: jinked and uns rdr next* **28/1**

4m 7.7s (-2.30) **Going Correction** -0.65s/f (Firm)
WFA 4 from 5yo+ 7lb 10 Ran SP% **116.0**
Speed ratings (Par 105): **79,78,78,76,69 67,66,65, ,**
CSF £7.05 TOTE £2.00: £1.10, £2.00, £1.30; EX 8.40 Trifecta £40.00.
Owner Paul & Clare Rooney **Bred** Colin Kennedy **Trained** Cholmondeley, Cheshire

FOCUS
Hurdles re-sited on best ground available. Rail at 3mile bend moved in 4m, bend into home straight moved in 3m, no dividing rail between hurdlers and chases in final furlong. Essentially an ordinary novice. The pace was on the steady side and the winner would have done it easily but for a mistake at the last. The winner was value for further.

4812 MTREC SPECIALISTS IN INDUSTRIAL RECRUITMENT H'CAP CHASE (19 fncs) 3m
2:50 (2:50) (Class 4) (0-110,105) 5-Y-0+ **£3,768** (£1,106; £553; £276)

Form RPR

144- 1 **Sharney Sike**14 4551 8-11-5 **105** DaraghBourke(7) 115+
(Stuart Coltherd) *chsd ldrs: led 10th: mde rest: clr 3 out: hit last: r.o wl* **7/2**2

503/ 2 3½ **Definite Appeal (IRE)**395 4188 11-10-1 **90** JamesCorbett(10) 98+
(Susan Corbett) *t.k.h: hld up: stdy hdwy whn blnd bdly 13th: rallied bef 4 out: chsd wnr run-in: styd on: no imp* **4/1**3

621- 3 ¾ **Gibbstown (IRE)**8 4652 8-10-10 **94** (p) DerekFox(5) 97
(Paul Stafford, Ire) *hld up in tch: hdwy to chse wnr bef 2 out: one pce and lost 2nd run-in* **11/2**

F12- 4 8 **Dingo Bay**19 4462 8-11-3 **96** WilsonRenwick 92
(John Wade) *chsd ldrs: drvn bef 4 out: rallied: wknd after last* **3/1**1

12P- 5 nk **Baltic Pathfinder (IRE)**13 4578 10-11-10 **103** ShaneByrne 101
(Sue Smith) *led to 10th: pressed wnr tl rdn and wknd bef 2 out* **10/1**

23P- **6** *8* **War On (IRE)**21 4427 7-11-9 **102** HenryBrooke 90
(Chris Grant) *w ldr to 10th: drvn and outpcd next: rallied: struggling fr 4 out* **7/2**2
6m 12.7s (-9.80) **Going Correction** -0.65s/f (Firm) **6** Ran SP% **113.9**
Speed ratings: **90,88,88,85,85 83**
CSF £18.21 TOTE £5.50: £2.30, £2.30; EX 34.90 Trifecta £182.00.
Owner John Hogg **Bred** John Hogg **Trained** Selkirk, Borders

FOCUS
Not a particularly competitive race for the grade. A modest pace increased after halfway.

4813 MTREC RECRUITMENT & TRAINING H'CAP HURDLE (9 hdls) 2m
3:25 (3:25) (Class 3) (0-130,128) 4-Y-0+ **£5,393** (£1,583; £791; £395)

Form RPR
502- **1** **Satanic Beat (IRE)**102 2868 5-10-12 **114** BrianHarding 121
(Jedd O'Keeffe) *chsd ldr: led bef 3 out: sn clr: pushed along after next: hld on wl run-in* **9/1**
3/0- **2** *1 3/4* **Fisher**31 4224 5-11-4 **127** (t) DeanPratt(7) 133
(John Quinn) *prom: hdwy to chse (clr) wnr 3 out: clsng whn nt fluent next: rallied bef last: kpt on same pce run-in* **9/1**
331- **3** *23* **Cool Sky**19 4463 5-11-1 **117** HenryBrooke 103
(Donald McCain) *hld up: hdwy u.p 4 out: disp 2nd pl next: wknd bef 2 out* **5/2**1
112- **4** *1* **Circus Star (USA)**70 3527 6-10-9 **118** MrJDixon(7) 101
(John Dixon) *led at decent gallop: rdn and hdd bef 3 out: wknd bef next* **10/3**2
004- **5** *27* **Stormy Weather (FR)**17 4497 8-11-5 **128** (p) NathanMoscrop(7) 87
(Brian Ellison) *hld up in tch: pushed along after 4 out: wknd bef next* **8/1**
3F3- **6** *5* **Lone Foot Laddie (IRE)**19 4463 5-10-3 **110** DerekFox(5) 65
(Lucinda Russell) *hld up: struggling 4 out: btn bef next* **7/1**
000- **7** *17* **Dumbarton (IRE)**41 4056 6-11-1 **122** CraigNichol(5) 61
(James Moffatt) *mstkes in rr: lost tch 1/2-way: t.o* **11/2**3
3m 56.1s (-13.90) **Going Correction** -0.65s/f (Firm) **7** Ran SP% **110.6**
Speed ratings (Par 107): **108,107,95,95,81 79,70**
CSF £75.62 TOTE £8.00: £3.60, £3.00; EX 119.50 Trifecta £612.40.
Owner Caron & Paul Chapman **Bred** Patrick Gleeson **Trained** Middleham Moor, N Yorks

FOCUS
A few clearly ran below form here but the leading pair still deserve some credit for pulling so far clear. They are both on the upgrade.

4814 MTREC SEARCH & SELECTION H'CAP HURDLE (13 hdls) 3m
4:00 (4:00) (Class 3) (0-135,130) 4-Y-0+ **£5,680** (£1,655; £828)

Form RPR
1F2- **1** **Wayward Glance**20 4449 6-11-4 **122** (p) WilsonRenwick 129+
(Keith Dalgleish) *hld up: hit 3rd: pushed along 8th: rallied u.p after 4 out: led next: drvn out* **6/1**3
1/F- **2** *1 1/4* **Lackamon**8 4651 9-11-0 **125** DaraghBourke(7) 130
(Sue Smith) *cl up: led 2nd: rdn and nt fluent whn hdd 3 out: rallied: kpt on fr last: nt rch wnr* **13/2**
531- **3** *6* **Ryton Runner (IRE)**19 4461 6-9-9 **104** (p) CraigNichol(5) 104
(Lucinda Russell) *in tch: hit 6th: chsng ldrs whn hit 4 out: rallied: kpt on same pce fr last* **9/2**1
31- **4** *6* **Masterleaderman (IRE)**76 3392 6-10-8 **115** PeterCarberry(3) 113
(Michael Smith) *prom: blnd 9th: effrt bef 3 out: hung lft next: no imp whn mstke last* **9/2**1
243/ **5** *22* **Merrydown (IRE)**320 24 11-10-11 **115** BrianHarding 89
(Nicky Richards) *bhd: outpcd 1/2-way: rallied bef 3 out: wknd bef next* **14/1**
/05- **6** *1 1/2* **Hollow Tree**26 4327 6-11-5 **130** NickSlatter(7) 103
(Donald McCain) *chsd ldrs: drvn along 9th: wknd bef 3 out* **11/1**
001- **7** *67* **Timeshisard (IRE)**91 3085 7-11-6 **129** (p) KillianMoore(5) 42
(Graeme McPherson) *prom: hdwy to chal 7th: rdn and wknd bef 3 out: t.o* **5/1**2
133- **P** **Moscow Presents (IRE)**43 4006 6-10-10 **119** (p) AdamNicol(5)
(Philip Kirby) *led to 2nd: cl up: blnd 7th: rallied: wknd after 4 out: t.o whn p.u bef 2 out* **5/1**2
5m 54.8s (-19.20) **Going Correction** -0.65s/f (Firm) **8** Ran SP% **112.3**
Speed ratings (Par 107): **106,105,103,101,94 93,71,**
CSF £42.59 CT £189.93 TOTE £4.40: £1.10, £2.60, £3.20; EX 39.50 Trifecta £501.10.
Owner Straightline Construction Ltd **Bred** The Queen **Trained** Carluke, S Lanarks

FOCUS
A fairly useful handicap. The gallop looked sound enough. The form looks solid.

4815 MTREC FOR ALL YOUR AGENCY LABOUR H'CAP CHASE (13 fncs) 2m 110y
4:35 (4:35) (Class 4) (0-110,107) 5-Y-0+ **£3,861** (£1,198; £645)

Form RPR
163- **1** **Pamak D'Airy (FR)**25 4341 11-11-5 **103** (p) TonyKelly(3) 108
(Henry Hogarth) *chsd ldrs: hdwy to chal 3 out: led after last: rdn and styd on wl* **9/1**
F22- **2** *1/2* **Little Jimmy**13 4570 7-10-3 **84** (p) SamJones 89
(Tom Gretton) *pressed ldr: rdn to ld 3 out: hdd after last: rallied: hld towards fin* **2/1**1
343- **3** *22* **Inoogoo (IRE)**14 4549 9-11-12 **107** WilsonRenwick 99
(Brian Ellison) *led: hdd whn hit 3 out: mstke and wknd next* **2/1**1
2F2- **F** **Cloverhill Lad (IRE)**9 4628 10-11-5 **107** DaraghBourke(7)
(Stuart Coltherd) *in tch whn fell heavily 4th: fatally injured* **5/1**2
243- **F** **Bocamix (FR)**13 4581 8-10-9 **93** JohnKington(3)
(Andrew Crook) *hld up in tch: fell heavily 6th: fatally injured* **6/1**3
664- **P** **Lillioftheballet (IRE)**22 3519 7-10-0 **81** (p) LucyAlexander
(Jim Goldie) *bhd: lost tch bef 4th: t.o whn p.u bef 5 out* **14/1**
4m 8.3s (-12.80) **Going Correction** -0.65s/f (Firm) **6** Ran SP% **114.3**
Speed ratings: **104,103,93,,**
CSF £29.05 TOTE £12.00: £3.80, £2.40; EX 42.30 Trifecta £109.40.
Owner Hogarth Racing **Bred** Claude Yves Pelsy **Trained** Stillington, N Yorks

FOCUS
A weak handicap, particularly with a couple departing, but it did least provide a tight finish.

4816 MTREC ENGINEERING, MANUFACTURING & DISTRIBUTION H'CAP HURDLE (11 hdls) 2m 4f
5:10 (5:11) (Class 4) (0-110,108) 4-Y-0+ **£3,119** (£915; £457; £228)

Form RPR
030- **1** **Nexius (IRE)**50 3872 5-11-2 **98** WilsonRenwick 103+
(Keith Dalgleish) *hld up in tch: smooth hdwy bef 3 out: led between last 2: drvn clr run-in: readily* **15/8**1
034- **2** *13* **Another Dimension (IRE)**66 3605 8-10-8 **95** CraigNichol(5) 88
(Rose Dobbin) *chsd ldrs: hdwy to ld 3 out: hdd between last 2: kpt on: no ch w ready wnr* **5/1**3
44P- **3** *8* **Foot The Bill**50 3876 9-10-12 **94** BrianHarding 80
(Patrick Holmes) *led tl rdn and hdd 3 out: rdn and edgd lft next: no imp whn nt fluent last* **33/1**
223- **4** *nse* **Bonnet's Vino**33 4189 6-11-7 **108** MissGAndrews(5) 95
(Pam Sly) *chsd ldr: rdn bef 3 out: drifted lft bef next: sn one pce* **6/1**
/02- **5** *21* **Mootabar (IRE)**18 4478 7-10-3 **85** BarryKeniry 52
(Chris Fairhurst) *hld up: rdn after 4 out: hung lft next: sn btn* **9/2**2
5/4- **6** *3 1/2* **Jasper Massini (IRE)**59 3723 9-11-2 **98** HenryBrooke 62
(Philip Kirby) *hld up in tch: drvn and outpcd after 4 out: btn next* **17/2**
6F6- **7** *1 1/2* **Northern Acres**47 3940 8-10-8 **90** LucyAlexander 53
(N W Alexander) *hld up: nt fluent 6th: rdn and outpcd 4 out: n.d after* **7/1**
U30- **8** *34* **Allez Cool (IRE)**94 3017 5-10-11 **98** JohnDawson(5) 30
(John Wade) *mstkes: in tch: struggling whn hit 4 out: t.o* **20/1**
5m 5.1s (-16.00) **Going Correction** -0.65s/f (Firm) **8** Ran SP% **114.6**
Speed ratings (Par 105): **106,100,97,97,89 87,87,73**
CSF £12.11 CT £225.06 TOTE £3.70: £1.10, £1.60, £3.70; EX 16.10 Trifecta £463.60.
Owner Straightline Construction Ltd **Bred** Juergen Imm **Trained** Carluke, S Lanarks

FOCUS
A one-sided handicap. The winner was well in on Flat form and there's probably more to come.

4817 MTREC TECHNICAL & PERMANENT PLACEMENTS "HANDS & HEELS" H'CAP HURDLE (CONDITIONALS/AMATEURS) (9 hdls) 2m
5:45 (5:45) (Class 5) (0-100,99) 4-Y-0+ **£1,949** (£572; £286; £143)

Form RPR
32P- **1** **Some Lad (IRE)**31 4223 9-10-10 **86** MrTHamilton(3) 89+
(Alison Hamilton) *trckd ldrs: rdn 3 out: led bef last: styd on wl run-in* **5/1**2
05B- **2** *1 1/2* **Vodka Red (IRE)**15 4527 6-10-8 **81** (b) DeanPratt 84+
(Robert Johnson) *t.k.h: hld up in tch: stdy hdwy bef 3 out: effrt whn nt fluent 2 out and last: kpt on: nt pce of wnr* **9/2**1
05P- **3** *1 3/4* **Right To Rule (IRE)**33 4189 5-11-12 **99** (b1) JamesCowley 98
(Donald McCain) *led at stdy pce: hit 1st: rdn 3 out: hdd bef last: kpt on same pce* **7/1**
640- **4** *hd* **Tweedo Paradiso (NZ)**31 4223 7-10-11 **89** MissHHarper(5) 88
(Rose Dobbin) *t.k.h: in tch: nt fluent 4th: hdwy 2 out: shkn up run-in: kpt on steadily* **6/1**3
424- **5** *1 1/2* **Baraboy (IRE)**25 4336 4-11-0 **95** DiarmuidO'Regan 84
(Barry Murtagh) *t.k.h: hld up in tch: nt fluent 4 out: pushed along bef next: kpt on same pce fr 2 out* **8/1**
000- **6** *nk* **Triple Eight (IRE)**15 4529 6-11-8 **98** MrPDennis(3) 95
(Philip Kirby) *hld up: nt fluent 2nd: effrt 3 out: no imp fr next* **7/1**
/05- **7** *nse* **Regal Ramirez**267 788 6-10-10 **88** MrLHall(5) 85
(Chris Grant) *t.k.h: hld up: stdy hdwy bef 3 out: pushed along next: no imp* **12/1**
/P0- **8** *1/2* **So Bazaar (IRE)**50 3871 7-9-9 **73** oh2 (t) MrJNuttall(5) 69
(Andrew Wilson) *t.k.h: hld up: hdwy on outside bef 3 out: outpcd bef next: n.d after* **12/1**
06- **9** *13* **Gunner Lindley (IRE)**33 3937 7-11-8 **95** DaraghBourke 78
(Stuart Coltherd) *cl up tl rdn and wknd fr 2 out* **6/1**3
4m 7.1s (-2.90) **Going Correction** -0.65s/f (Firm)
WFA 4 from 5yo+ 7lb **9** Ran SP% **114.9**
Speed ratings (Par 103): **81,80,79,79,78 78,78,78,71**
CSF £28.06 CT £157.18 TOTE £4.50: £1.70, £2.20, £2.20; EX 18.60 Trifecta £137.70.
Owner J P G Hamilton **Bred** W Tanner **Trained** Denholm, Borders

FOCUS
A modest conditionals/amateur event which was steadily run, the race developing into a bit of a sprint up the straight. They finished in a heap and this isn't form to take seriously.
T/Plt: £979.90 to a £1 stake. Pool: £60,473.42 - 45.05 winning tickets. T/Qpdt: £83.60 to a £1 stake. Pool: £3,921.10 - 34.70 winning tickets. RY

3427 UTTOXETER (L-H)
Saturday, March 15

OFFICIAL GOING: Good to soft (some soft places on chase course; 5.1) changing to good to soft after race 2 (2.40)
Wind: fresh 1/2 against Weather: fine but breezy

4818 BETFRED FUN AND FRIENDLY NOVICES' H'CAP HURDLE (8 hdls 1 omitted) 2m
2:05 (2:05) (Class 4) (0-115,112) 4-Y-0+
£6,256 (£1,848; £924; £462; £231; £116)

Form RPR
125/ **1** **Pure Style (IRE)**139 2121 6-11-10 **110** NoelFehily 115+
(Charlie Longsdon) *hld up: steadway hdwy 5th: trcking ldrs next: upsides last: led last 75yds: drvn out* **11/4**1
555- **2** *1 1/4* **Bold Adventure**23 4371 10-10-6 **95** JackQuinlan(3) 98
(Willie Musson) *chsd ldrs 3rd: led 3 out: hdd and no ex run-in* **8/1**
041- **3** *3 3/4* **Rosslyn Castle**7 4674 5-11-10 **110** DominicElsworth 111
(Jonjo O'Neill) *nt fluent in rr: hdwy 4th: chsng ldrs after 3 out: upsides last: kpt on one pce* **4/1**2
353- **4** *12* **Tracking Time**23 4371 7-10-12 **105** MrJMartin(7) 92
(Andrew J Martin) *in rr: drvn 5th: outpcd 3 out* **13/2**3
P03- **5** *2 1/2* **The Perfect Crime (IRE)**15 4529 5-11-5 **105** WillKennedy 90
(Ian Williams) *chsd ldrs: wknd 3 out* **20/1**
505- **6** *6* **Poetic Power (IRE)**12 4597 5-9-11 **90** GeraldQuinn(7) 74
(Claire Dyson) *hld up towards rr: bdly hmpd and lost pl 4th: bhd fr 2 out: hit last* **9/1**
24F- **P** **Broughtons Bandit**13 4573 7-11-5 **105** AidanColeman
(Willie Musson) *sn trcking ldrs: lft in ld 4th: hdd 3 out: 5th and wkng whn hmpd 2 out: sn eased: t.o whn p.u bef last* **10/1**
534- **F** **Ossie's Dancer**21 4411 5-11-12 **112** PaddyBrennan 97
(Martin Smith) *led tl fell 4th* **10/1**
4F5- **F** **Bawden Rocks**19 4467 5-10-12 **98** RichardJohnson 83
(David Bridgwater) *w ldrs: mstke 3 out: 4th and one pce whn fell next* **7/1**
4m 1.3s (9.30) **Going Correction** +0.025s/f (Yiel) **9** Ran SP% **116.6**
Speed ratings (Par 105): **77,76,74,68,67 64,,,**
CSF £25.45 CT £87.94 TOTE £3.70: £1.50, £2.90, £1.80; EX 35.90 Trifecta £169.10.
Owner Pat Curtin **Bred** Clody E Norton & Robert Norton **Trained** Over Norton, Oxon

The Form Book Jumps, Raceform Ltd, Compton, RG20 6NL.

FOCUS
Hurdles on inside and course at its shortest. Divided bends on fresher ground. Noel Fehily reported after his win in the first that the ground was on the slow side, more dead than good to soft. The pace wasn't strong in this modest event. The winner improved to the level of his bumper form, with the second and third to their marks.

4819 BETFRED MOBILE NOVICES' LIMITED H'CAP CHASE (18 fncs) 3m
2:40 (2:40) (Class 3) (0-140,138) 5-Y-0+
£12,512 (£3,696; £1,848; £924; £462; £232)

Form RPR
110- **1** **Bold Chief (IRE)**[168] 1686 9-11-8 **138**....(tp) NoelFehily 149+
(Harry Fry) *mde all: styd on strly to forge clr run-in* **9/1**
P31- **2** *6* **Knock A Hand (IRE)**[30] 4245 9-11-8 **138**....(b) NickScholfield 143
(Richard Lee) *chsd ldrs: outpcd after 4 out: rallied to chse wnr 2 out: styd on same pce run-in* **10/1**
523- **3** *7* **Lamb Or Cod (IRE)**[20] 4439 7-10-12 **128**....(t) RichardJohnson 129+
(Philip Hobbs) *nt fluent in rr: hit 7th: drvn 12th: hdwy 14th: outpcd whn j.lft and hit 3 out: modest 3rd whn blnd last* **11/2**[1]
161- **4** *1 ¼* **Bobcatbilly (IRE)**[28] 4273 8-10-11 **127**.... WillKennedy 125
(Ian Williams) *hld up in rr: hdwy 13th: hit 4 out: one pce* **8/1**
F42- **5** *1 ½* **Toby Lerone (IRE)**[42] 4031 7-10-9 **125**.... HarrySkelton 120
(Dan Skelton) *hld up in rr: hdwy 5th: chsng wnr 3 out: wknd appr last* **9/1**
U33- **6** *¾* **Renard D'Irlande (FR)**[30] 4245 9-10-10 **126**.... AidanColeman 121
(Venetia Williams) *chsd ldrs: outpcd 4 out: no threat after* **15/2**[3]
PPF- **7** *4* **Green Wizard (IRE)**[12] 4593 8-10-5 **124**.... JonathanEngland[(3)] 116
(Sue Smith) *chsd ldrs: pushed along 10th: wknd 3 out* **8/1**
311- **P** **Pinerolo**[21] 4425 8-11-4 **134**.... RyanMania
(Sue Smith) *nt fluent in last: reminders 2nd: mstke 6th: bhd fr 11th: sn t.o: p.u bef 3 out* **15/2**[3]
121- **P** **Kris Cross (IRE)**[19] 4464 7-10-8 **129**....(tp) GrantCockburn[(5)]
(Lucinda Russell) *chsd ldrs: mstke 8th: lost pl and hit 14th: sn bhd: t.o whn p.u bef 2 out* **10/1**
211- **P** **Dare To Endeavour**[22] 4395 7-11-3 **133**.... PaddyBrennan
(Tom George) *t.k.h towards rr: drvn and lost pl 11th: sn bhd: t.o whn p.u bef 4 out* **6/1**[2]

6m 12.3s (-2.80) **Going Correction** +0.15s/f (Yiel) **10** Ran SP% **113.6**
Speed ratings: **110,108,105,105,104 104,103, , ,**
CSF £91.19 CT £541.32 TOTE £10.30: £3.00, £3.30, £2.40; EX 112.20 Trifecta £439.80.
Owner The Eyre Family **Bred** Patrick Carroll **Trained** Seaborough, Dorset

FOCUS
An open and competitive novice handicap run at a good pace, and the form looks solid. A step up from the winner.

4820 BETFRED GOALS GALORE H'CAP HURDLE (10 hdls) 2m 4f 110y
3:15 (3:15) (Class 3) (0-135,135) 4-Y-0+
£10,009 (£2,956; £1,478; £739; £369; £185)

Form RPR
21- **1** **Liberty One (IRE)**[22] 4391 8-10-13 **122**.... NoelFehily 126
(Richard Woollacott) *trckd ldrs: led 3 out: styd on gamely run-in* **9/1**
065- **2** *1* **Swnymor (IRE)**[21] 4413 5-10-11 **127**....(t) PaulO'Brien[(7)] 130
(Rebecca Curtis) *hld up towards rr: hdwy 7th: rdn next: 4th last: styd on to take 2nd run-in* **9/1**
0/2- **3** *1 ½* **Songsmith**[21] 4423 6-11-0 **123**.... WayneHutchinson 125
(Lucy Wadham) *hld up in rr: j.rt: hdwy bef 3 out: chsd wnr 2 out: kpt on same pce run-in* **9/1**
112- **4** *¾* **Twoways (IRE)**[17] 4503 8-11-2 **125**.... ConorO'Farrell 126
(Mark Rimell) *hld up in rr: gd hdwy bef 2 out: styd on same pce between last 2: tk 4th nr fin* **8/1**[3]
212/ **5** *¾* **Irish Buccaneer (IRE)**[333] 5340 7-10-13 **122**.... RichardJohnson 123
(Philip Hobbs) *hld up in mid-div: hdwy 7th: chsng ldrs 2 out: kpt on one pce appr last* **10/3**[1]
515- **6** *hd* **Saphir River (FR)**[56] 3775 8-11-5 **128**....(tp) PeterBuchanan 129
(Lucinda Russell) *mid-div: hdwy 7th: chsng ldrs next: one pce fr 2 out* **10/1**
1P2- **7** *13* **Vivaccio (FR)**[40] 4069 5-10-13 **122**.... AidanColeman 110
(Venetia Williams) *w ldrs: lost ploace bef 2 out* **12/1**
2PF- **8** *½* **Sunny Ledgend**[21] 4418 9-10-13 **129**.... MrJMartin[(7)] 117
(Andrew J Martin) *chsd ldrs: drvn 3 out: wknd qckly last* **14/1**
P06- **9** *6* **Seymour Eric**[28] 4264 9-10-11 **127**....(b) RyanHatch[(7)] 111
(Martin Keighley) *led to 4th: blnd 6th: led next: hdd 3 out: sn wknd* **11/1**
312- **10** *3 ¼* **Bob Tucker (IRE)**[28] 4277 7-10-6 **120**.... JamesBanks[(5)] 100
(Brendan Powell) *chsd ldrs: pushed along 5th: lost pl bef 3 out* **7/1**[2]
13/- **11** *22* **Indian Daudaie (FR)**[118] 7-10-8 **120**....(v[1]) JackQuinlan[(3)] 80
(Sarah Humphrey) *w ldrs: led 4th to 7th: wknd next: sn bhd: t.o* **25/1**
3P0- **12** *6* **Prompter**[27] 4302 7-11-2 **125**.... DominicElsworth 79
(Jonjo O'Neill) *in rr: mstke 6th: sme hdwy 3 out: sn lost pl and bhd: eased run-in: t.o* **16/1**

4m 55.0s (-4.00) **Going Correction** +0.025s/f (Yiel) **12** Ran SP% **118.2**
Speed ratings (Par 107): **108,107,107,106,106 106,101,101,98,97 89,87**
CSF £87.39 CT £757.97 TOTE £7.80: £2.60, £3.90, £2.40; EX 121.60 Trifecta £1551.00 Part won..
Owner D G Staddon **Bred** John O'Doherty **Trained** South Molton, Devon

FOCUS
A decent handicap hurdle run at just a fair pace. The first six finished in something of a heap, which tempers enthusiasm for the form. The winner built on his recent win.

4821 BETFRED MIDLANDS GRAND NATIONAL CHASE (A H'CAP) (LISTED RACE) (24 fncs) 4m 1f 110y
3:50 (3:50) (Class 1) 5-Y-0+
£56,950 (£21,370; £10,700; £5,330; £2,680; £1,340)

Form RPR
/0P- **1** **Goulanes (IRE)**[77] 3361 8-10-3 **138**....(bt) RichardJohnson 152+
(David Pipe) *hld up in rr: stdy hdwy 17th: sn trcking ldrs: cl 3rd whn hit 3 out: led appr last: hit last: drvn out* **13/2**[1]
1R1- **2** *2 ½* **Alpha Victor (IRE)**[17] 4489 9-10-0 **135** oh5.... PeterBuchanan 146
(William Kinsey) *chsd ldrs 4th: cl 2nd 4 out: upsides between last 2: styd on same pce last 50yds* **33/1**
P03/ **3** *11* **West End Rocker (IRE)**[388] 4317 12-10-0 **135**.... WayneHutchinson 136
(Alan King) *chsd ldrs: led 13th: hdd between last 2: sn wknd* **20/1**
341- **4** *16* **Summery Justice (IRE)**[14] 4557 10-9-12 **136**.... HarryChalloner[(3)] 122
(Venetia Williams) *in rr: hdwy 6th: drvn and lost pl 18th: kpt on fr 4 out: tk poor 4th run-in* **20/1**
PPU- **5** *6* **Red Rocco (IRE)**[28] 4270 7-9-7 **135** oh8....(v) MrJBargary[(7)] 116
(Nigel Twiston-Davies) *chsd ldrs: wknd bef 3 out* **20/1**
0P1- **6** *6* **Wyck Hill (IRE)**[21] 4427 10-10-6 **141**....(t) MarkWalsh 120
(David Bridgwater) *chsd ldrs: 5th whn mstke 4 out: lost pl bef next* **9/1**[3]
441- **7** *nk* **Fill The Power (IRE)**[25] 4339 8-9-11 **135**.... JonathanEngland[(3)] 111
(Sue Smith) *chsd ldrs: lost pl appr 4 out* **10/1**
11F- **8** *12* **Sun Cloud (IRE)**[21] 4427 7-10-0 **135**.... BrianHughes 99
(Malcolm Jefferson) *hld up in rr: mstke 14th: sme hdwy 17th: lost pl 19th: sn bhd* **7/1**[2]
340- **9** *8* **Junior**[21] 4427 11-10-7 **142**....(b) ConorO'Farrell 99
(David Pipe) *led: hdd 6th: drvn 16th: lost pl after 20th: sn bhd* **20/1**
3PU- **F** **Pete The Feat (IRE)**[14] 4557 10-10-6 **141**.... NoelFehily
(Charlie Longsdon) *hld up towards rr: hdwy 12th: mid-div whn fell 14th* **7/1**[2]
42P- **P** **Alfie Spinner (IRE)**[42] 4026 9-10-0 **135** oh8.... BrendanPowell
(Nick Williams) *chsd ldrs: lost pl 19th: t.o whn p.u bef 2 out* **25/1**
0P1- **P** **Bradley**[8] 4661 10-9-9 **135** oh3.... ConorShoemark[(5)]
(Fergal O'Brien) *mid-div: lost pl 19th: sn bhd: t.o whn p.u last* **16/1**
243- **P** **Loch Ba (IRE)**[28] 4270 8-9-7 **135** oh9....(v[1]) MrHAABannister[(7)]
(Mick Channon) *chsd ldrs: lost pl 11th: bhd 16th: t.o whn p.u bef 20th* **12/1**
012- **P** **Emperor's Choice (IRE)**[28] 4270 7-10-1 **136**.... AidanColeman
(Venetia Williams) *in rr: drvn 10th: bhd fr 17th: t.o whn p.u bef 20th* **12/1**
P **Are Ya Right Chief (IRE)**[41] 4064 9-10-0 **135** oh5.... DJCasey
(W P Mullins, Ire) *in rr: sn bhd: t.o whn p.u bef 20th* **10/1**
331- **P** **Harry Topper**[35] 4145 7-11-12 **161**....(p) NickScholfield
(Kim Bailey) *nt fluent: w ldrs: blnd 2nd: mstke 14th: lost pl 18th: bhd whn p.u bef 20th* **7/1**[2]

8m 41.3s (-2.30) **Going Correction** +0.15s/f (Yiel) course record **16** Ran SP% **126.1**
Speed ratings: **108,107,104,101,99 98,98,95,93, , , , ,**
CSF £217.21 CT £4081.45 TOTE £6.60: £2.50, £5.30, £3.60, £5.50; EX 228.10 Trifecta £5749.00.
Owner R S Brookhouse **Bred** Ray Townsend **Trained** Nicholashayne, Devon

FOCUS
The second longest chase of the year, and a real stamina test in a well-run race on ground that, although drying, was still tacky. David Pipe has now won this prize for four successive years. Goulanes is rated back to the level of his best novice form.

4822 BETFRED GOALS GALORE EXTRA H'CAP CHASE (15 fncs) 2m 4f
4:25 (4:29) (Class 4) (0-115,114) 5-Y-0 **£6,330** (£1,870; £935; £468; £234)

Form RPR
3FP- **1** **Crystal Swing**[23] 4372 7-11-3 **105**.... AdamWedge 115
(Richard Phillips) *chsd ldrs: led 2 out: all out* **33/1**
/P6- **2** *shd* **Tiquer (FR)**[95] 3015 6-10-7 **95**.... WillKennedy 105
(Alan Jones) *t.k.h: hld up: in mid-div: mstke 10th: chsng ldrs next: cl 2nd 3 out: upsides last: styd on: jst failed* **6/1**[3]
542- **3** *12* **Pensnett Bay**[20] 4448 9-11-8 **110**....(b) MarkGrant 108
(Shaun Lycett) *w ldr: led after 7th: hdd 2 out: wknd appr last* **11/2**[2]
221- **4** *7* **Hollins**[85] 3190 10-11-0 **109**.... JoshWall[(7)] 101
(Tony Forbes) *hld up in rr: hdwy 9th: chsng ldrs 11th: wknd between last 2* **6/1**[3]
24U- **5** *10* **Kingcora (FR)**[20] 4440 6-11-9 **111**.... AidanColeman 96
(Venetia Williams) *chsd ldrs: wknd appr 2 out* **5/4**[1]
44P- **6** *13* **Material Boy**[97] 2979 7-10-13 **101**.... LiamHeard 72
(Barry Leavy) *in rr: drvn along 7th: sme hdwy 4 out: sn wknd* **20/1**
363- **7** *38* **Lord Of Drums (IRE)**[31] 4222 8-11-4 **106**.... PeterBuchanan 43
(Lucinda Russell) *led: hdd after 7th: lost pl bef 4 out: sn bhd: t.o 2 out* **10/1**
54- **P** **Itsuptoyou (IRE)**[16] 4515 10-11-5 **107**....[1] NickScholfield
(Arthur Whiting) *chsd ldrs: nt fluent 8th: hung lft and lost pl next: sn bhd: t.o whn p.u bef 11th* **16/1**

5m 10.2s (4.70) **Going Correction** +0.15s/f (Yiel) **8** Ran SP% **111.1**
Speed ratings: **96,95,91,88,84 79,63,**
CSF £204.72 CT £1235.19 TOTE £29.50: £4.90, £2.50, £1.60; EX 280.90 Trifecta £1852.70.
Owner Enjoy The Journey **Bred** Alan A Wright **Trained** Adlestrop, Gloucs

FOCUS
A modest handicap chase in which the first two drew clear as they fought out the finish. The winner improved to his hurdle mark.

4823 BETFRED TV NOVICES' H'CAP HURDLE (10 hdls) 2m 4f 110y
5:00 (5:02) (Class 5) (0-100,98) 4-Y-0+ **£3,249** (£954; £477; £238)

Form RPR
P40- **1** **Silver Dragon**[19] 4461 6-11-9 **95**....(p) DougieCostello 102
(Tony Coyle) *hld up in rr: hdwy 6th: sn chsng ldrs: led 2 out: narrowly hdd sn after last: styd on to ld towards fin* **9/2**[2]
630- **2** *nk* **Icanmotor**[85] 3192 7-10-6 **78**....(tp) NickScholfield 85
(Claire Dyson) *hld up in rr: hdwy 7th: handy 3rd appr 2 out: upsides last: sn led narrowly: hdd and no ex in clsng stages* **8/1**[3]
000- **3** *15* **Forget And Forgive (IRE)**[100] 2906 6-10-2 **79**....(p) JamesBanks[(5)] 73
(Anthony Middleton) *chsd ldrs: led 3 out: hdd next: wknd between last 2* **7/2**[1]
0P5- **4** *18* **First Of Never (IRE)**[17] 4496 8-10-0 **72** oh3.... TomSiddall 49
(Lynn Siddall) *in rr: drvn 6th: hdwy next: chsng ldrs bef 3 out: outpcd bef 2 out: tk modest 4th between last 2* **33/1**
F40- **5** *2 ¼* **Wheelavher**[66] 3605 8-9-7 **72** oh2....(t) GeraldQuinn[(7)] 47
(Claire Dyson) *led: hdd 3 out: sn wknd* **16/1**
/UP- **6** *25* **Mysula**[12] 4595 7-10-0 **72** oh3....(t) WillKennedy 25
(Claire Dyson) *chsd ldrs 2nd: lost pl after 7th: sn bhd* **50/1**
44P- **7** *11* **Seas Of Green**[51] 3854 7-11-8 **94**.... AdamWedge 37
(Paul Cowley) *in rr: hdwy 6th: sn chsng ldrs: wknd appr 2 out* **16/1**
002- **8** *3 ¼* **Swing State**[27] 4309 9-10-6 **78**.... LeeEdwards 18
(Tom Gretton) *chsd ldrs: lost pl sn after 7th* **9/1**
053- **9** *2* **La Belle Sauvage**[85] 3188 7-11-6 **97**.... EdCookson[(5)] 35
(Kim Bailey) *in rr: sme hdwy 6th: lost pl after next: sn bhd* **9/2**[2]
P36- **10** *25* **Wayne Manor (IRE)**[32] 4201 5-11-12 **98**.... PeterBuchanan 14
(Lucinda Russell) *in rr: t.o 7th* **8/1**[3]
00P- **11** *1* **Ricketyrock**[89] 3138 8-10-0 **72** oh3.... DaveCrosse
(Nick Mitchell) *prom: reminders 5th: lost pl next: sn bhd: t.o 3 out* **40/1**
0/P- **F** **Whichever**[56] 3788 8-11-9 **95**.... RichardJohnson
(Richard Phillips) *hld up in rr: hdwy after 6th: 7th and in tch and styng on whn fell 3 out* **16/1**
650- **P** **Oscar's Pet (IRE)**[19] 4472 6-11-4 **95**....(p) BenPoste[(5)]
(Tom Symonds) *chsd ldrs: lost pl 7th: sn bhd: t.o whn p.u bef 2 out* **20/1**

4m 57.8s (-1.20) **Going Correction** +0.025s/f (Yiel) **13** Ran SP% **120.6**
Speed ratings (Par 103): **103,102,97,90,89 79,75,74,73,64 63, ,**
CSF £39.67 CT £143.12 TOTE £4.90: £1.90, £2.80, £2.10; EX 34.40 Trifecta £370.70.
Owner Twenty Four Seven Recruitment **Bred** D L Pearcy **Trained** Norton, N Yorks
■ Stewards' Enquiry : James Banks caution: careless riding.

FOCUS
A very modest event run at a sound pace thanks to the runner-up's stablemate Wheelavher. The winner was well in on his Wetherby form.

4824 BETFRED "RACING'S BIGGEST SUPPORTER" STANDARD OPEN NATIONAL HUNT FLAT RACE 2m
5:35 (5:36) (Class 5) 4-6-Y-0 **£2,599** (£763; £381; £190)

Form RPR
12- **1** **Relic Rock (IRE)**[24] 4349 6-11-11 0 RichardJohnson 125
(Steve Gollings) *chsd ldrs: drvn over 5f out: led 3f out: rdn rt out* **9/2**[3]
2 *1 1/4* **Fletchers Flyer (IRE)**[370] 6-11-4 0 (t) NoelFehily 117
(Harry Fry) *led: hdd 3f out: rallied over 1f out: styd on same pce last 50yds* **2/1**[1]
F2- **3** *12* **Relentless Dreamer (IRE)**[95] 3016 5-10-11 0 PaulO'Brien(7) 106
(Rebecca Curtis) *chsd ldr: drvn 4f out: outpcd over 2f out: kpt on to take modest 3rd nr fin* **8/1**
4 *hd* **Some Plan (IRE)**[79] 3302 6-11-4 0 PaddyBrennan 106
(Tom George) *hld up in rr: hdwy 6f out: trcking ldrs and effrt over 3f out: modest 3rd over 1f out: fdd towards fin* **10/3**[2]
3/ **5** *16* **Master Vintage**[338] 5247 6-10-11 0 DanielHiskett(7) 91
(Richard Phillips) *s.s: t.k.h in rr: sme hdwy and modest 5th over 3f out: nvr on terms* **33/1**
6 *20* **Paskalis** 5-11-4 0 AidanColeman 73
(Emma Lavelle) *in rr: drvn 7f out: lost pl over 5f out: sn bhd* **14/1**
6- **7** *3 1/4* **Periquest**[27] 4310 5-11-4 0 DougieCostello 70
(Alex Hales) *chsd ldrs: drvn 6f out: lost pl 4f out: sn bhd* **40/1**
8 *8* **King Kayf** 5-10-13 0 JamesBanks(5) 63
(Noel Williams) *chsd ldrs: drvn 6f out: lost pl over 4f out: sn bhd* **16/1**
9 *12* **Tiger Feat** 4-10-10 0 WayneHutchinson 44
(Alan King) *mid-div: drvn and lost pl over 4f out: sn bhd* **8/1**
10 *25* **Minnie Mustang** 6-10-4 0 MrJMartin(7) 23
(Andrew J Martin) *in rr: drvn 7f out: sn lost pl and bhd: t.o 3f out* **33/1**

3m 56.8s (10.40) **Going Correction** +0.025s/f (Yiel)
WFA 4 from 5yo+ 7lb **10** Ran SP% **117.7**
Speed ratings: **75,74,68,68,60 50,48,44,38,26**
CSF £13.84 TOTE £4.40: £1.40, £1.70, £2.40; EX 20.20 Trifecta £88.50.
Owner P J Martin **Bred** Sean O'Loughlin **Trained** Scamblesby, Lincs

FOCUS
This bumper has been won by smart sorts in Cape Tribulation, Raya Star and Deputy Dan, and winners should come from this renewal. The pace was relatively sound. The winner looks a decent prospect.
T/Jkpt: Not won. T/Plt: £467.90 to a £1 stake. Pool of £201188.05 - 313.85 winning tickets. T/Qpdt: £270.60 to a £1 stake. Pool of £9472.88 - 25.9 winning tickets. WG

4825 - 4831a (Foreign Racing) - See Raceform Interactive

4625 CARLISLE (R-H)
Sunday, March 16

OFFICIAL GOING: Good to soft (chs 7.2; hdl 6.8)
Wind: Fresh, across Weather: Overcast

4832 APOLLOBET FREE DOWNLOAD APP NOVICES' HURDLE (8 hdls) 2m 1f
2:00 (2:00) (Class 4) 4-Y-0+ **£3,898** (£1,144; £572; £286)

Form RPR
052- **1** **Voyage A New York (FR)**[33] 4199 5-11-0 0 WilsonRenwick 111
(Lucinda Russell) *chsd clr ldr: lft in ld 4th: rdn and hdd 2 out: rallied to regain ld run-in: drifted lft u.p: hld on wl* **8/13**[1]
556- **2** *1/2* **Quick Brew**[80] 3274 6-10-7 102 (t) DaraghBourke(7) 111
(Maurice Barnes) *in tch: stdy hdwy whn lft cl 3rd 4th: led gng wl 2 out: rdn and hdd run-in: drifted lft and rallied: hld nr fin* **28/1**
3 *3 1/2* **Russborough (FR)**[126] 5-11-0 125 LiamTreadwell 107
(Venetia Williams) *chsd ldrs: lft 2nd 4th: drvn and outpcd after 3 out: rallied next: kpt on run-in: nt rch first two* **9/2**[2]
0/5- **4** *37* **Ballyvoque (IRE)**[54] 3826 8-11-0 0 RyanMania 81
(George Charlton) *in tch: rdn after 3 out: wknd next: 4th and no ch whn mstke and sprawled last* **11/1**[3]
/PP- **5** *77* **Knockcairn (IRE)**[33] 4199 7-10-7 0 BrianHughes
(Ian Duncan) *hld up in tch: struggling bef 4 out: lost tch fr next: t.o* **300/1**
560- **6** *19* **The Village (IRE)**[15] 4548 5-11-0 0 PeterBuchanan
(Lucinda Russell) *nt fluent on occasions: hld up: struggling 4th: lost tch fr next: t.o* **100/1**
14- **F** **Uppertown Cave (IRE)**[33] 4205 5-11-0 0 HenryBrooke
(Donald McCain) *t.k.h: led and sn clr: fell heavily 4th: fatally injured* **9/2**[2]

4m 18.8s (-10.40) **Going Correction** -0.40s/f (Good) **7** Ran SP% **111.4**
Speed ratings (Par 105): **108,107,106,88,52 43,**
CSF £15.46 TOTE £1.60: £1.20, £6.10; EX 14.00 Trifecta £56.40.
Owner Straightline Construction Ltd **Bred** Mme A Ouvry & Dr V Benoit Grosfils **Trained** Arlary, Perth & Kinross

FOCUS
Hurdles on New Hurdles course. On a blustery day, the ground had dried out and the going was reported to be riding tacky and slow on the new inner hurdle-race track. The complexion changed when pacesetter Uppertown Cave took a crashing fall at the first flight on the final circuit.

4833 APOLLOBET MOBILE GAMES NOVICES' CHASE (11 fncs 1 omitted) 2m
2:30 (2:30) (Class 3) 5-Y-0+ **£7,147** (£2,098; £1,049; £524)

Form RPR
411- **1** **Mitchell's Way**[14] 4578 7-11-5 120 TomScudamore 128
(Alan Swinbank) *trckd ldrs: led 4 out: rdn and flashed tail run-in: hld on wl* **9/2**[3]
414- **2** *1 1/4* **Indian Voyage (IRE)**[24] 4367 6-10-12 103 (t) DaraghBourke(7) 127
(Maurice Barnes) *hld up last but in tch: stdy hdwy after 3 out: effrt and chsd wnr run-in: kpt on: hld towards fin* **33/1**
331- **3** *1* **Un Guet Apens (FR)**[80] 3272 6-11-5 125 BrianHughes 127
(James Ewart) *j.lft on occasions: led: rdn and hdd 4 out: rallied: kpt on same pce and lost 2nd run-in* **5/1**
5FP- **4** *7* **Rockawango (FR)**[24] 4367 8-10-12 130 (tp) DaleIrving(7) 121
(James Ewart) *trckd ldrs: effrt bef 2 out: rdn and hung lft after last: sn outpcd* **25/1**
442- **5** *2 3/4* **Up And Go (FR)**[24] 4367 6-10-12 127 HenryBrooke 112
(Donald McCain) *nt fluent on occasions: pressed ldr: hit 5th: drvn 5 out: rallied: outpcd bef 2 out: 5th and btn whn hit last* **9/4**[2]
123- **F** **Hit The Top (IRE)**[15] 4550 7-10-12 0 RyanMania
(Sue Smith) *hld up in tch: 3 l down and stl gng wl whn hmpd and fell 4 out* **13/8**[1]

4m 7.1s (-9.00) **Going Correction** -0.60s/f (Firm) **6** Ran SP% **110.5**
Speed ratings: **98,97,96,93,92**
CSF £76.85 TOTE £5.30: £2.90, £5.60; EX 70.60 Trifecta £231.80.
Owner Ontoawinner 2 **Bred** Mrs P M Grainger **Trained** Melsonby, N Yorks

FOCUS
The fence in the dip going away from the stands was again omitted. Quite an interesting 2m novice chase and the first four were still in with a good shout jumping the final fence. The pace was very steady until the foot of the final hill.

4834 APOLLOBET £50 FREE BETS NOVICES' H'CAP HURDLE (THE JOCKEY CLUB GRASSROOTS JUMPS SERIES QUALIFIER) (10 hdls) 2m 3f 110y
3:05 (3:05) (Class 4) (0-120,120) 4-Y-0+ **£4,223** (£1,240; £620; £310)

Form RPR
101- **1** **Granaruid (IRE)**[10] 4625 11-11-4 **119** (p) MrTHamilton(7) 123+
(Alison Hamilton) *prom: hdwy to ld 2 out: rdn last: hld on wl towards fin* **8/1**
421- **2** *nk* **Island Heights (IRE)**[9] 4648 5-11-6 **114** WilsonRenwick 117
(Lucinda Russell) *hld up: stdy hdwy 3 out: effrt next: rdn and chsd wnr appr last: kpt on towards fin* **4/1**[2]
110- **3** *2* **Mr Utah**[25] 4347 7-11-9 **120** TonyKelly(3) 121
(Henry Hogarth) *hld up: hdwy on outside bef 2 out: styd on wl fr last: nt rch first two* **12/1**
P05- **4** *1/2* **Baileys Concerto (IRE)**[14] 4579 8-10-2 **96** BrianHughes 96
(Dianne Sayer) *hld up in tch: effrt and rdn 2 out: kpt on same pce fr last* **11/1**
112- **5** *2 1/2* **Mudita Moment (IRE)**[18] 4491 9-11-12 **120** LiamTreadwell 119
(Venetia Williams) *t.k.h: cl up: led bef 6th: rdn and hdd 2 out: rallied: outpcd fr last* **5/2**[1]
146- **6** *3 1/2* **Most Honourable**[42] 4054 4-10-9 **116** AdamNicol(5) 103
(Michael Smith) *cl up: rdn and hung rt after 2 out: wknd last* **10/1**
603- **7** *16* **Vasco Pierji (FR)**[39] 4081 5-10-8 **102** AdrianLane 83
(Donald McCain) *led to bef 6th: nt fluent and rdn 3 out: wknd bef next* **10/1**
1P5- **8** *3* **Vinny Gambini (IRE)**[24] 4365 7-11-4 **117** CraigNichol(5) 95
(Rose Dobbin) *in tch on ins: drvn along bef 4 out: rallied: wknd bef 2 out* **5/1**[3]

4m 57.7s (-11.10) **Going Correction** -0.40s/f (Good)
WFA 4 from 5yo+ 7lb **8** Ran SP% **110.6**
Speed ratings (Par 105): **106,105,105,104,103 102,96,94**
CSF £37.84 CT £363.22 TOTE £8.40: £2.90, £1.50, £3.40; EX 28.60 Trifecta £261.90.
Owner J P G Hamilton **Bred** S Donohoe And R Donohoe **Trained** Denholm, Borders

FOCUS
A competitive handicap hurdle, run at a sound pace, and plenty still in with a chance up the home straight.

4835 APOLLOBET ONLINE CASINO H'CAP CHASE (17 fncs 2 omitted) 3m 2f
3:35 (3:35) (Class 3) (0-130,130) 5-Y-0+ **£8,122** (£2,385; £1,192; £596)

Form RPR
065- **1** **Ballyoliver**[17] 4509 10-11-3 **121** LiamTreadwell 130+
(Venetia Williams) *trckd ldrs: pushed along 12th: led after 3 out: hrd pressed fr next: styd on gamely run-in* **8/1**
3/3- **2** *3* **Markadam**[312] 169 8-10-6 **115** ColmMcCormack(5) 122
(Dianne Sayer) *hld up: stdy hdwy after 5 out: effrt and ev ch between last 2: edgd rt u.p run-in: kpt on same pce* **16/1**
111- **3** *7* **Tutchec (FR)**[60] 3725 7-11-12 **130** BrianHarding 130
(Nicky Richards) *led to 2nd: cl up: led 10th to after 3 out: kpt on same pce between last 2* **5/1**[3]
411- **4** *1/2* **Nail 'M (IRE)**[14] 4580 6-10-10 **114** (p) TomScudamore 116
(Nigel Hawke) *mstkes: chsd ldrs: drvn and outpcd 5 out: rallied u.p bef 3 out: no imp fr next* **11/4**[1]
/5U- **5** *1 3/4* **You Know Yourself (IRE)**[26] 4338 11-11-3 **121** RyanMania 119
(Sue Smith) *cl up: led 2nd to 10th: chsd ldrs: drvn and outpcd after 5 out: no imp fr 3 out* **10/1**
2F5- **6** *nse* **Dreams Of Milan (IRE)**[52] 3860 6-11-5 **123** HenryBrooke 122
(Donald McCain) *hld up: stdy hdwy and prom whn nt fluent 5 out: sn outpcd: rallied 3 out: sn no imp* **14/1**
U12- **7** *60* **Count Guido Deiro (IRE)**[36] 4162 7-11-6 **127** (p) GavinSheehan(3) 71
(Nigel Twiston-Davies) *prom: lost pl 9th: struggling fr next: lost tch bef 4 out: t.o* **7/2**[2]
131- **P** **The Friary (IRE)**[24] 4368 7-10-8 **117** (tp) DerekFox(5)
(Lucinda Russell) *sn bhd and pushed along: lost tch 1/2-way: t.o whn p.u 5 out* **6/1**

6m 46.4s (-20.80) **Going Correction** -0.60s/f (Firm) **8** Ran SP% **112.6**
Speed ratings: **108,107,104,104,104 104,85,**
CSF £107.56 CT £700.59 TOTE £10.50: £5.10, £3.90, £1.60; EX 86.60 Trifecta £785.70.
Owner Richard Britten-Long **Bred** R R Evans **Trained** Kings Caple, H'fords

FOCUS
A competitive and quite valuable 3m2f handicap chase run at a sound pace.

4836 APOLLOBET BEST ODDS GUARANTEED H'CAP HURDLE (8 hdls) 2m 1f
4:10 (4:10) (Class 4) (0-115,112) 4-Y-0+ **£4,223** (£1,240; £620; £310)

Form RPR
212- **1** **Short Takes (USA)**[16] 4533 6-11-3 **110** (b) NickSlatter(7) 116+
(Donald McCain) *chsd ldrs: hdwy to ld 2 out: pushed clr fr last* **3/1**[2]
652- **2** *7* **Copt Hill**[53] 3830 6-10-2 **88** BrianHughes 88
(Tracy Waggott) *pressed ldr: rdn and led briefly appr 2 out: kpt on same pce bef last* **5/1**
366- **3** *2 1/4* **Snowed In (IRE)**[69] 3569 5-10-7 **93** (p) SeanQuinlan 94+
(Barbara Butterworth) *prom: blnd bdly and lost pl 3 out: rallied whn nt fluent next: no imp fr last* **9/1**
302- **4** *6* **Choisan (IRE)**[24] 4378 5-11-5 **105** (p) DougieCostello 97
(Tim Easterby) *hld up in tch: rdn and outpcd bef 4 out: sme hdwy bef last: nvr able to chal* **7/2**[3]
531- **5** *6* **Rosquero (FR)**[24] 4366 9-10-0 **86** (v) AdrianLane 73
(Robert Johnson) *t.k.h: led to appr 2 out: wknd qckly between last 2* **11/4**[1]
544- **6** *36* **Rupert Bear**[39] 4084 8-11-7 **112** MissCWalton(5) 66
(James Walton) *nt fluent in rr: hit 3rd: struggling fr next: nvr on terms* **12/1**

06P/ 7 14 **Vinomore**[506] 2027 8-10-6 **92**... RyanMania 33
(Dianne Sayer) *hld up in tch: nt fluent 2nd: struggling bef 3 out: eased whn btn bef next* **33/1**

4m 21.3s (-7.90) **Going Correction** -0.40s/f (Good) 7 Ran SP% **111.2**
Speed ratings (Par 105): **102,98,97,94,92 75,68**
CSF £17.36 TOTE £3.20: £1.90, £2.80; EX 16.40 Trifecta £125.00.
Owner T P McMahon and D McMahon **Bred** Rosa Colasanti **Trained** Cholmondeley, Cheshire

FOCUS
The two leaders took each other on and set the race up for the strong-travelling winner.

4837 APOLLOBET IN-PLAY BETTING OPEN HUNTERS' CHASE (18 fncs) 3m 110y
4:40 (4:42) (Class 6) 5-Y-0+ **£1,646** (£506; £253)

Form RPR
5/0- **1** **Viking Rebel (IRE)**[14] 12-11-5 78.................................(p) MrWHRReed(7) 111
(W T Reed) *t.k.h: w ldr: led bef 10th: mde rest: hrd pressed fr 4 out: hld on gamely fr last* **100/1**

/22- **2** 1 ½ **Moscow Menace (IRE)**[15] 4554 7-11-9 101................... MrTHamilton(7) 114
(Miss K Scott) *prom: hdwy to chal 4 out: kpt on run-in: hld towards fin* **13/2**

2- **3** 6 **Walden (IRE)**[42] 4057 7-11-5 121...............................(p) MrWThompson(7) 108+
(I R Ferguson, Ire) *nt fluent on occasions: hld up: stdy hdwy and in tch whn mstke 4 out: pushed along and hung rt bef 2 out: no imp run-in: eased towards fin* **4/6**[1]

421- **4** 2 ½ **Pena Dorada (IRE)**[15] 4554 7-11-13 107.................. MissRMcDonald(7) 111
(Alan J Brown) *nt fluent: hld up bhd ldng gp: pushed along after 5 out: hit 2 out: kpt on run-in: no imp* **11/2**[3]

S/5- **5** 4 ½ **Sacred Mountain**[31] 4239 13-12-2 105.................................(t) MissCWalton 102
(James Walton) *led to bef 10th: cl up tl rdn and outpcd 3 out: n.d after* **14/1**

P13- **6** ½ **Tartan Snow**[15] 4554 14-12-3 122.................................... MrJHamilton(3) 107
(Stuart Coltherd) *prom: hit 3rd: rdn 5 out: outpcd fr 3 out* **5/1**[2]

0P5- **7** 12 **Ballycolin**[15] 4554 11-11-7 104.. MrSFox(5) 87
(Ian Duncan) *hld up in tch: rdn and outpcd bef 4 out: btn after next* **16/1**

P/R- **8** 46 **Sammy Spiderman**[31] 4239 11-11-9 65....................... MissEDunkley(7) 50
(Miss K Scott) *nt fluent: t.k.h: hld up on outside: struggling 10th: lost tch 5 out: t.o* **100/1**

000/ **P** **Mardood**[91] 9-11-5 68.. MrCSmith(7)
(P Wilson) *hld up: struggling 10th: btn after 5 out: t.o whn p.u 2 out* **80/1**

6m 28.5s (-14.10) **Going Correction** -0.60s/f (Firm) 9 Ran SP% **121.1**
Speed ratings: **98,97,95,94,93 93,89,74,**
CSF £683.75 TOTE £22.90: £5.80, £1.70, £1.30; EX 1197.30 Trifecta £1956.20 Part won..
Owner W T Reed **Bred** Michael Goff **Trained** Haydon Bridge, Northumberland

FOCUS
The first seven home still had a shout at the foot of the hill, but in the end the first two pulled clear.
T/Plt: £245.60 to a £1 stake. Pool: £66,638.37 - 198.01 winning units. T/Qpdt: £19.20 to a £1 stake. Pool: 5945.98 - 228.90 winning units. RY

4024 FFOS LAS (L-H)
Sunday, March 16

OFFICIAL GOING: Soft (good to soft in places)
Wind: light across Weather: cloudy

4838 CENTERPLATE.CO.UK "NATIONAL HUNT" MAIDEN HURDLE (10 hdls) 2m 4f
2:15 (2:15) (Class 4) 4-Y-0+ **£3,119** (£915; £457; £228)

Form RPR
23- **1** **Ashford Wood (IRE)**[43] 4030 6-11-1 0.. RichardJohnson 119
(Tim Vaughan) *racd wd: wl in tch: led 6th: sn crossed to inner: rdn 3 out: jnd next where bttr jump than rival: drvn out to hold advantage* **4/1**[2]

444- **2** 2 **Gate Please (IRE)**[43] 4024 9-10-10 117...................(tp) PatrickCorbett(5) 117
(Rebecca Curtis) *trckd ldrs: wnt cl 2nd after 7th: rdn 3 out: chalng whn stepped into next: kpt on u.p after but a being hld* **9/2**[3]

/45- **3** 33 **Bar A Mine (FR)**[43] 4024 5-11-1 0............................ SamTwiston-Davies 84
(Paul Nicholls) *in tch: nt fluent 5th: rdn next: struggling after 7th: styd on u.p to take remote 3rd flat* **10/1**

/06- **4** 3 ½ **Fuse Wire**[14] 4569 7-10-12 102... RobertDunne(3) 81
(Dai Burchell) *wnt to post early: mid-div: clsd 4th: rdn after next: sn no ch w ldrs: lft mod 3rd 3 out: relegated a pl flat* **66/1**

5 11 **Gair Loat (IRE)**[1061] 10 11 1 0.. TomO'Brien 70
(Liam Corcoran) *in rr: mstke 7th: plugged on past btn rivals fr 3 out: t.o* **66/1**

P/0- **6** 12 **Serious Mixture**[77] 3388 7-11-1 95... JackDoyle 58
(Hilary Parrott) *prom: led 5th to next: wknd appr 3 out: t.o* **50/1**

6/0- **7** 6 **Lightning Moley (IRE)**[16] 4535 11-10-10 0.......................(t) BenPoste(5) 52
(Tracey Watkins) *a in rr: wknd after 7th: t.o* **100/1**

062- **8** 9 **Vermouth Bleu (FR)**[25] 4350 5-10-5 118............... TommieMO'Brien(10) 43
(Jonjo O'Neill) *racd keenly: trckd ldrs: hit 2nd: wknd qckly after 7th: t.o* **3/1**[1]

- **P** **Pelcomb Bridge**[1385] 9-11-1 0...(t) DaveCrosse
(Marc Barber) *in rr: awkward jump 3rd: wknd 7th: t.o whn p.u bef next* **100/1**

0- **P** **Thomastown (IRE)**[28] 4298 7-10-10 0........................ RobertMcCarth(5)
(Ian Williams) *led tl hdd and mstke 4th: wknd rapidly: p.u bef next* **33/1**

633- **P** **Dream Deal**[76] 3422 6-11-1 113.. NickScholfield
(Jeremy Scott) *hld up in tch: drvn appr 7th: sn struggling: t.o whn p.u bef 2 out* **3/1**[1]

212- **U** **Flying Eagle (IRE)**[24] 4370 6-11-1 0................................... JamieMoore 117
(Peter Bowen) *mid-div: hdwy 7th: 3 l 3rd whn stmbld bdly and uns rdr 3 out* **7/1**

5m 18.5s (27.60) **Going Correction** +1.675s/f (Heav) 12 Ran SP% **119.6**
Speed ratings (Par 105): **111,110,97,95,91 86,84,80,, ,**
CSF £22.56 TOTE £6.00: £2.80, £2.60, £3.90; EX 21.00 Trifecta £173.50.
Owner David & Susan Luke **Bred** Ms Debbie O'Neill **Trained** Aberthin, Vale of Glamorgan
■ Stewards' Enquiry : Patrick Corbett four-day ban: used whip above permitted level (Mar 30-Apr 2)

FOCUS
As much fresh ground as possible provided including all bends. The going was still on the soft side (described by the jockeys as 'tacky') and looked testing as the field came home well strung out. An ordinary maiden hurdle with a couple of locally trained bumper performers making their hurdling debuts and one of those came out on top.

4839 WALTERS LAND NOVICES' HURDLE (12 hdls) 3m
2:45 (2:45) (Class 4) 4-Y-0+ **£3,195** (£992; £534)

Form RPR
22P- **1** **Knockanrawley (IRE)**[29] 4272 6-11-3 130.....................(p) EdCookson(5) 129+
(Kim Bailey) *trckd ldng pair: reminder after 9th: wnt 2nd 3 out: sn led and wnt 4 l up: idled appr 2 out and jnd: sn asserted again: idling flat and drvn out to hold on* **2/1**[2]

165- **2** nk **Ashes House (IRE)**[68] 3592 8-11-8 124.............................(t) JamieMoore 125
(Rebecca Curtis) *led: jnd 6th: mstke 9th: hdd and rdn after 3 out: jnd idling wnr next: sn one pce: kpt on wl u.p flat* **5/1**[3]

235- **3** 52 **Tidal Dance (IRE)**[22] 4415 7-11-8 132................................ AidanColeman 73
(Venetia Williams) *trckd ldr: chal 6th tl after 9th: wknd 3 out: t.o* **1/1**[1]

P **Treliver Manor (IRE)**[286] 624 6-10-6 0........................ RichardO'Dea(10)
(Emma Lavelle) *a last: reminder 8th: mstke next and sn lost tch: t.o whn p.u bef 2 out* **9/1**

6m 33.5s (44.50) **Going Correction** +1.675s/f (Heav) 4 Ran SP% **110.0**
Speed ratings (Par 105): **92,91,74,**
CSF £10.94 TOTE £2.40; EX 8.40 Trifecta £12.20.
Owner Kim Bailey Racing Partnership VIII **Bred** Joe Fogarty **Trained** Andoversford, Gloucs

FOCUS
A small field for this better-than-average staying novices' hurdle and they went very steadily early. Despite that, they were all struggling leaving the back for the last time and it became attritional in the straight.

4840 BURNS HEALTHY PET H'CAP CHASE (17 fncs) 2m 5f
3:20 (3:20) (Class 4) (0-110,107) 5-Y-0+ **£3,768** (£1,106; £553; £276)

Form RPR
335- **1** **Cloudingstar (IRE)**[21] 4451 7-11-5 **105**...................(t) MauriceLinehan(5) 113+
(Jonjo O'Neill) *in tch: trckd wnr 10th tl led gng best 2 out: sn in command: rdn out flat* **2/1**[1]

525- **2** 3 **Tuskar Rock (FR)**[23] 4396 11-11-3 **98**.........................(b[1]) AidanColeman 100
(Venetia Williams) *j.w: cl up: led 3rd: drvn appr 4 out: hdd 2 out: kpt on same pce* **4/1**[2]

644- **3** 5 **Supreme Bob (IRE)**[23] 4396 8-11-9 **104**................................. WillKennedy 103
(Lucy Jones) *hld up in tch: hdwy 9th: disp 2nd 4 out: rdn next: 3rd and one pce whn mstke last* **7/1**

/45- **4** 57 **Accordingtopalm (IRE)**[296] 457 8-11-12 **107**................(t) PaulMoloney 47
(David Rees) *in rr: clsd 11th: wnt 4th next: sn no imp: wknd 4 out: t.o* **16/1**

145- **P** **Rossa Parks (IRE)**[10] 4637 8-11-12 **107**................................ NoelFehily
(Neil Mulholland) *in rr: pushed along fr 10th: wknd 13th: t.o whn p.u bef 4 out* **7/1**

040- **P** **Amaury De Lusignan (IRE)**[28] 4299 8-10-6 **87**................... TomO'Brien
(Paul Henderson) *led to 3rd: styd cl up tl 10th: struggling 12th: t.o whn p.u bef 4 out* **8/1**

P- **P** **Milans Well (IRE)**[62] 3691 8-11-9 **104**..........................(p) BrendanPowell
(Brendan Powell) *chsd ldrs: j.lft at times and niggled along: dropped to rr 9th: sn lost tch: wl bhd whn p.u bef 13th* **5/1**[3]

5m 47.6s (19.00) **Going Correction** +1.025s/f (Soft) 7 Ran SP% **112.0**
Speed ratings: **104,102,100,79, ,**
CSF £10.33 TOTE £3.10: £1.30, £3.00; EX 10.00 Trifecta £64.10.
Owner Mrs Peter Bond **Bred** Donal Barnwell **Trained** Cheltenham, Gloucs

FOCUS
A moderate contest, but competitive-looking on paper. However, there were only three in with a chance in the straight.

4841 REGISTER FOR WEARAHAT DAY 2014 H'CAP HURDLE (10 hdls) 2m 4f
3:50 (3:50) (Class 3) (0-125,129) 4-Y-0+ **£5,848** (£1,717; £858; £429)

Form RPR
100- **1** **Cawdor House Bert**[56] 3802 7-10-11 **110**.......................... PaulMoloney 117+
(David Rees) *hld up in rr: stdy hdwy fr 6th: hit 7th: led after 2 out: all out towards fin* **16/1**

124- **2** 1 ¾ **Heavenstown (IRE)**[8] 4677 8-10-13 **117**..................(b) NicodeBoinville(5) 121
(John Spearing) *led: rdn appr 3 out where 4 l up: j.lft 2 out: sn hdd: kpt on same pce* **5/1**[3]

211- **3** 20 **Carlton Jack**[136] 2172 7-11-12 **125**................................. RichieMcLernon 109
(Jonjo O'Neill) *t.k.h: prom: rdn after 7th: wknd 3 out: plugged on flat to take mod 3rd cl home* **6/1**

032- **4** hd **Big Casino**[17] 4510 8-11-12 **125**................................ SamTwiston-Davies 109
(Nigel Twiston-Davies) *in tch: rdn after 7th: wnt modest 3rd 2 out: no ch w 1st 2: ct for 3rd cl home* **11/4**[2]

310- **5** 9 **Still Believing (IRE)**[17] 4508 6-10-13 **119**............................ ConorRing(7) 94
(Evan Williams) *towards rr: hdwy 4th: wknd appr 3 out* **16/1**

441- **6** 28 **The Clock Leary (IRE)**[34] 4189 6-11-5 **118**....................... AidanColeman 65
(Venetia Williams) *racd keenly: prom: chsd ldr 7th: sn rdn: mstke 3 out: wknd qckly: t.o* **9/4**[1]

/P5- **7** 63 **Fishing Bridge (IRE)**[43] 4028 9-11-3 **116**........................ RichardJohnson
(David Rees) *prom: hit 2nd: niggled along fr 4th: mstke next: sn struggling: wl t.o fr 7th* **8/1**

P06- **8** ½ **Lava Lamp (GER)**[22] 4413 7-11-4 **117**................................ AdamWedge
(Evan Williams) *a in rr: rdn 6th: lost tch next: wl t.o* **16/1**

5m 20.9s (30.00) **Going Correction** +1.675s/f (Heav) 8 Ran SP% **117.1**
Speed ratings (Par 107): **107,106,98,98,94 83,58,58**
CSF £95.97 CT £546.41 TOTE £21.50: £4.80, £2.70, £1.10; EX 173.10 Trifecta £2130.80 Part won..
Owner A J & Dai Rees **Bred** Michael S Davies **Trained** Clarbeston, Pembrokes

FOCUS
Withdrawals reduced the field by a third in this fair handicap hurdle and only two mattered in the straight.

4842 32RED.COM H'CAP CHASE (18 fncs) 3m
4:25 (4:25) (Class 3) (0-135,129) 5-Y-0+ **£6,498** (£1,908; £954; £477)

Form RPR
205- **1** **Tullyraine (IRE)**[31] 4245 10-11-4 **121**......................... SamTwiston-Davies 129
(Nigel Twiston-Davies) *racd in last: rdn along fr 10th: reminders 13th: mstke next: styd on to go 2nd 3 out where hmpd: 2 l down last: r.o u.p to ld last 25yds* **6/1**

540- **2** 1 **Our Island (IRE)**[22] 4427 9-10-12 **115**..........................(v) RichardJohnson 123
(Tim Vaughan) *j.lft at times: led to 6th: styd cl up: led 4 out: j.lft next: 2 l up last: r.o u.p: hdd fnl 25yds* **9/4**[2]

435- **3** *34* **Raduis Bleu (FR)**[102] 2889 9-10-2 **112**.......................... MissLBrooke(7) 83
(Lady Susan Brooke) *trckd ldrs tl led 6th: hdd 4 out: 3rd and hld whn mstke next: wknd: t.o* **10/1**

31P- **4** *12* **Boyfromnowhere (IRE)**[64] 3655 7-11-7 **129**............(p) PatrickCorbett(5) 88
(Rebecca Curtis) *cl up: reminders after 2nd: rdn appr 4 out: wknd 3 out* **7/4**[1]

242- **U** **Titchwood (IRE)**[31] 4245 6-11-10 **127**.......................... RichieMcLernon
(Jonjo O'Neill) *hld up: blnd bdly and uns rdr 1st* **4/1**[3]

6m 44.5s (27.10) **Going Correction** +1.025s/f (Soft) **5** Ran SP% **110.5**
Speed ratings: **95,94,83,79,**
CSF £20.17 TOTE £6.70: £4.10, £1.10; EX 20.80 Trifecta £33.40.
Owner Geoffrey & Donna Keeys **Bred** Mrs Judith Todd **Trained** Naunton, Gloucs

FOCUS
The feature race and the best finish of the day.

4843 HERITAGE PORTFOLIO CONDITIONAL JOCKEYS' H'CAP CHASE (18 fncs) 3m
4:55 (4:58) (Class 5) (0-100,99) 5-Y-0+ **£2,144** (£629; £314; £157)

Form RPR

1U4- **1** **Tom Bach (IRE)**[106] 2829 10-10-0 **73** oh1..........................(b) JamesBest 95+
(Hywel Evans) *cl up: led 2nd: pckd 3 out: drew clr next: styd on strly* **8/1**[2]

3/P- **2** *22* **Night Safe (IRE)**[25] 4354 13-11-4 **97**............................(v[1]) RyanHatch(6) 98
(Nigel Twiston-Davies) *prom: chsd wnr fr 3rd: rdn after 14th: mstke 3 out: sn one pce and hld* **12/1**

355- **3** *8* **Chasers Chance (IRE)**[19] 4481 11-10-11 **84**................(p) JoshuaMoore 75
(Paul Henderson) *towards rr: rdn and sme hdwy 10th: no ch w ldrs fr 4 out: plugged on to take mod 3rd last* **10/1**[3]

421- **4** *4 1/2* **Tarraco (FR)**[6] 4720 7-11-6 **96** 7ex.............................. HarryChalloner(3) 87
(Venetia Williams) *chsd ldrs: mstke 5th: blnd and reminders 7th: drvn after 14th: hld whn mstke 4 out: sn wknd: lost 3rd last* **8/11**[1]

035- **5** *3/4* **Jump Up**[25] 4354 8-11-5 **92**...(v) MichaelByrne 78
(Peter Bowen) *in tch: rdn after 9th: wknd after 14th* **12/1**

FR2- **6** *30* **Jim Job Jones**[65] 3635 10-10-0 **73** oh4....................(tp) ConorShoemark 29
(Neil Mulholland) *chsd ldrs tl lost pl after 4th: clsd again 9th: drvn 14th: wknd 3 out: t.o* **20/1**

4/F- **P** **No More Whispers (IRE)**[9] 4654 9-10-0 **73** oh3................ KillianMoore
(Marc Barber) *towards rr: blnd 6th: rdn after 9th: lost tch 13th: t.o whn p.u bef 4 out* **14/1**

123- **P** **Glenwood Prince (IRE)**[62] 3688 8-11-9 **99**..................(t) MattGriffiths(3)
(Jeremy Scott) *led to 2nd: cl up tl dropped towards rr 6th: tried to rally u.p after 9th: struggling 12th: t.o whn p.u bef 14th* **8/1**[2]

6m 47.5s (30.10) **Going Correction** +1.025s/f (Soft) **8** Ran SP% **116.0**
Speed ratings: **90,82,80,78,78 68, ,**
CSF £91.81 CT £970.97 TOTE £9.70: £2.60, £3.00, £3.30; EX 122.60 Trifecta £648.70.
Owner Hywel Evans **Bred** Carthage Molloy **Trained** Kidwelly, Carmarthens

FOCUS
A moderate conditionals' handicap chase with three of the runners racing from out of the weights.

4844 32RED FREE £10 BONUS STANDARD OPEN NATIONAL HUNT FLAT RACE 2m
5:25 (5:25) (Class 6) 4-6-Y-0 **£1,559** (£457; £228; £114)

Form RPR

2- **1** **Princess Tara (IRE)**[126] 2391 4-10-3 0.......................... DonalDevereux 99+
(Peter Bowen) *in tch: racd alone on ins home st: pushed along over 3f out: led wl over 2f out: r.o strly* **8/1**

2 *7* **Quinlandio (IRE)** 4-10-5 0.. JamesBanks(5) 94
(Brendan Powell) *towards rr: dropped to last and rdn along 6f out: hdwy over 4f out: chsesd wnr 2f out: sn edgd lft: kpt on one pce* **7/1**[3]

3 *2* **Blown Cover** 5-11-3 0.. AidanColeman 99
(Emma Lavelle) *in tch: hdwy to chse ldrs over 3f out: one pce fnl 2f* **8/1**

4- **4** *15* **City Supreme (IRE)**[74] 3460 4-10-10 0........................ RobertThornton 77
(Anthony Honeyball) *towards rr: rdn over 5f out: outpcd by ldrs over 3f out: styd on fnl 2f* **3/1**[2]

5 *2 3/4* **Stonemadforspeed (IRE)**[168] 6-11-0 0........................ RobertDunne(3) 81
(Sirrell Griffiths) *racd keenly: led after 1f tl hdd over 5f out: sn dropped towards rr: styd on u.p fnl 2f* **66/1**

6 *3 1/4* **Ethelred (IRE)** 6-11-3 0.. BrendanPowell 78
(Jamie Snowden) *in tch: hdwy after 5f: led 4f out tl wl over 2f out: sn wknd* **16/1**

0- **7** *3 1/2* **Tinos Tank (IRE)**[15] 4547 5-11-3 0.................................. JackDoyle 75
(Hilary Parrott) *racd keenly: hld up: hdwy after 6f: rdn 3f out: wknd over 1f out* **25/1**

8 *2 1/2* **Mac Bertie** 5-11-3 0.. AdamWedge 72
(Evan Williams) *towards rr: sme hdwy 6f out: wknd over 3f out* **33/1**

9 *5* **Vodkaontherocks (IRE)** 6-11-3 0................................ RichardJohnson 67
(Philip Hobbs) *towards rr: racd wd in bk st: chsd ldrs over 4f out: rdn over 3f out: wknd 2f out* **6/4**[1]

0- **10** *7* **Crowd Control (IRE)**[113] 2681 5-11-3 0........................ JamieMoore 60
(Rebecca Curtis) *led 1f: trckd ldr tl led over 5f out: hdd 4f out: sn wknd* **16/1**

3- **11** *51* **Essteepee**[35] 4177 5-11-3 0...................................... MichaelByrne 9
(Tim Vaughan) *prom tl rdn and wknd 6f out: eased 4f out: t.o* **20/1**

4m 5.2s (22.30) **Going Correction** +1.675s/f (Heav)
WFA 4 from 5yo+ 7lb **11** Ran SP% **124.5**
Speed ratings: **111,107,106,99,97 96,94,93,90,87 61**
CSF £64.35 TOTE £10.20: £2.00, £4.70, £3.20; EX 42.20 Trifecta £579.00.
Owner David Perkins & Kate Becton **Bred** Brendan Fitzpatrick & Timmy Hillman **Trained** Little Newcastle, Pembrokes

FOCUS
An inexperienced bunch contested this bumper and they finished well strung out.
T/Plt: £1115.40 to a £1 stake. Pool: £72,074.23 - 47.17 winning units. T/Qpdt: £102.80 to a £1 stake. Pool: £5,679.95 - 40.85 winning units. RL

4845 - (Foreign Racing) - See Raceform Interactive

4825 LIMERICK (R-H)
Sunday, March 16

OFFICIAL GOING: Heavy

4846a KERRY GROUP EUROPEAN BREEDERS FUND MARES NOVICE HURDLE (GRADE 3) (9 hdls) 2m
2:40 (2:40) 4-Y-0+ **£17,875** (£5,225; £2,475; £825)

RPR

1 **Katie T (IRE)**[21] 4453 5-10-12 121.................................. APHeskin 131
(Kevin Prendergast, Ire) *hld up in tch: slt mstke in 6th 4 out: rdn to chal disputing 3rd bef 2 out: styd on wl u.p fr last between horses to ld nr fin* **13/2**[2]

2 *1/2* **Urticaire (FR)**[25] 4359 6-10-12 .... PatrickMangan 130+
(W P Mullins, Ire) *hld up: 7th 1/2-way: tk clsr order in 5th fr 3 out: clsd on outer gng wl to chal into st: led narrowly bef 2 out: strly pressed u.p fr after last and hdd nr fin* **9/10**[1]

3 *1* **Que Pasa (IRE)**[135] 2205 6-11-5 130.............................. DavyCondon 136+
(David Harry Kelly, Ire) *hld up towards rr: last 1/2-way: tk clsr order fr 3 out: rdn to chal next: wnt 2nd between last 2: no ex u.p fr last and dropped to 3rd: kpt on same pce* **9/1**

4 *5* **Love On Top (IRE)**[80] 3313 6-10-12 120.......................... MrAMcCurtin 124
(John J Walsh, Ire) *chsd ldr tl led bef 2nd: hdd briefly bef next: narrow advantage appr st and hdd bef 2 out: no ex in 4th bef last: kpt on one pce* **33/1**

5 *1* **Emily Gray (IRE)**[35] 4179 6-11-5 117.............................. MartinFerris 130
(T E Hyde, Ire) *hld up bhd ldrs: 4th 1/2-way: cl 3rd appr st: rdn and lost pl bef 2 out: kpt on one pce in 5th fr bef last* **7/1**[3]

6 *3 1/4* **Sunday Serenade (IRE)**[42] 4060 6-10-12 .... DavyRussell 120
(Peter Fahey, Ire) *hld up in tch: 5th 1/2-way: tk clsr order bhd ldrs 3 out: rdn and wknd 2 out* **13/2**[2]

7 *2 3/4* **Railway Zira (IRE)**[24] 4386 6-10-12 .... SeanFlanagan 117
(David Harry Kelly, Ire) *led and clr early: reduced advantage bef 1st and hdd bef next where nt fluent: regained advantage briefly bef 3rd: pushed along in 4th after 3 out and sn wknd: kpt on one pce fr next* **10/1**

8 *16* **The Cookie Jar (IRE)**[84] 3234 7-10-12 116.................... JodyMcGarvey 101
(C A Murphy, Ire) *chsd ldrs: 3rd 1/2-way: rdn and no ex 3 out: wknd bef st* **20/1**

4m 13.3s (253.30) **8** Ran SP% **118.6**
CSF £13.80 TOTE £6.40: £2.50, £1.02, £1.02; DF 17.00 Trifecta £60.80.
Owner Barrywhite Partnership **Bred** Long Acre Syndicate **Trained** Friarstown, Co Kildare

FOCUS
The improving Katie T proved too good with her turn of foot proving the key at the end of a steadily run contest. The first and fifth have been rated as running personal bests, with the runner-up just off her mark back in trip.

4848a I.N.H. STALLION OWNERS EUROPEAN BREEDERS FUND DAWN RUN MARES NOVICE CHASE (GRADE 2) (14 fncs) 2m 6f
3:40 (3:40) 5-Y-0+ **£24,375** (£7,125; £3,375; £1,125)

RPR

1 **Caoimhe's Delight (IRE)**[23] 4408 8-11-0 128................(p) DavyCondon 134
(Sean O'Brien, Ire) *chsd ldrs: 4th 1/2-way: rdn appr st and clsd u.p into 2nd between last 2: clsng on ldr whn lft w narrow advantage last: kpt on wl run-in* **5/1**[3]

2 *1 3/4* **Civena (IRE)**[28] 4315 8-11-0 123.. AFO'Neill 132
(J A Berry, Ire) *hld up in tch: 5th 1/2-way: rdn in 6th after 3 out and clsd u.p into 3rd between last 2: lft cl 2nd at last and kpt on wl run-in wout matching wnr* **14/1**

3 *6* **Backinthere (IRE)**[23] 4408 9-11-0 119.............................. APHeskin 126
(Eamonn Francis Gallagher, Ire) *chsd ldr in 2nd tl disp 1/2-way: narrow advantage bef 8th: hdd 3 out tl regained advantage bef st: hdd u.p 2 out: sn no ex in 4th: lft mod 3rd at last: kpt on one pce* **12/1**

4 *1 3/4* **Byerley Babe (IRE)**[36] 4165 7-11-5 134........................ PhillipEnright 130
(Robert Tyner, Ire) *w.w: slt mstke in 7th at 6th: clsr in 6th 1/2-way: slt mstke 8th: wnt 3rd after 3 out: sn no ex u.p and dropped to 5th 2 out: lft mod 4th last: kpt on one pce* **1/1**[1]

5 *26* **Kilitlane Rose (IRE)**[17] 4520 9-11-0 107.......................... DavidSplaine 99
(W Harney, Ire) *led: jnd 1/2-way and hdd bef 8th: remained prom tl rdn and wknd 3 out* **33/1**

6 *3/4* **Liz's D'Estruval (IRE)**[23] 4408 6-11-0 112...................... DavyRussell 98
(John Joseph Murphy, Ire) *hld up: slt mstke in 7th at 2nd: last 1/2-way: no imp bef 3 out: one pce* **16/1**

7 *nk* **Lisrose (IRE)**[23] 4408 9-11-0 114................................ JodyMcGarvey 97
(Ms Alice Curran, Ire) *hld up: j.lft at times: slt mstke in mod 7th at 9th: rdn and no imp bef 3 out* **16/1**

F **Baby Shine (IRE)**[20] 4468 8-11-0 131............................ LeightonAspell 136+
(Lucy Wadham) *hld up in tch: clsr in 3rd bef 3rd where nt fluent: nt fluent 8th: clsd between horses into 2nd 4 out and ld next tl hdd appr st: regained advantage 2 out and 1 l clr whn fell last* **3/1**[2]

6m 13.3s (373.30) **8** Ran SP% **120.7**
CSF £68.18 TOTE £5.90: £1.30, £2.90, £2.90; DF 53.40 Trifecta £201.30.
Owner Mrs Caroline O'Brien **Bred** Sean O'Brien **Trained** Kilworth, Co. Cork

FOCUS
It is arguable whether Caoimhe's Delight would have won anyway but she stayed on dourly and was bearing down on the last-fence faller at the time. The standard in set around the winner and third.

4849 - 4860a (Foreign Racing) - See Raceform Interactive

4592 SOUTHWELL (L-H)
Monday, March 17

OFFICIAL GOING: Good (good to soft in places) changing to good after race 1 (2:35)
Wind: Light half-behind Weather: Cloudy

4861 BET TOTEPLACEPOT WITH TOTEPOOL H'CAP CHASE (13 fncs) 2m
2:05 (2:05) (Class 4) (0-120,120) 5-Y-0+ **£3,768** (£1,106; £553; £276)

Form RPR

P21/ **1** **Memorabilia**[403] 4079 6-11-7 **115**.................................. DenisO'Regan 130+
(John Ferguson) *hld up in rr: smooth hdwy to trck ldrs after 4 out: a travelling strly: led bef last: easily drew clr flat* **7/1**

1PP- **2** *5* **George Nympton (IRE)**[30] 4278 8-11-12 **120**.................(tp) DaveCrosse 125
(Brian Barr) *chsd ldr most of way tl rdn to ld 2 out: hdd bef last: no ch and unable to go w wnr flat* **20/1**

F25- **3** *3 ½* **Pearls Legend**[23] 4418 7-11-12 **120**...................................... JamieMoore 124
(John Spearing) *in tch: effrt to chal fr 3 out: looking hld whn hit last: one pce flat* **5/4**[1]

045- **4** *3 ¾* **Le Bacardy (FR)**[80] 3323 8-11-7 **115**.................................(p) LeeEdwards 113
(Tony Carroll) *in tch: outpcd after 4 out: kpt on but n.d flat* **6/1**[3]

03P- **5** *1* **Fiftyonefiftyone (IRE)**[162] 1780 10-11-0 **113**.............(tp) JoeCornwall[(5)] 112
(John Cornwall) *led: pressed 3 out: rdn and hdd bef 2 out: wknd bef last* **20/1**

325- **6** *5* **Shadrack (IRE)**[16] 4543 10-11-11 **119**..........................(b[1]) JamesReveley 115+
(Keith Reveley) *hld up: blnd 2nd: hdwy 7th: blnd 8th: chsd ldrs tl fdd 2 out* **11/4**[2]

6/P- **7** *5* **Playing With Fire (IRE)**[10] 4653 10-10-6 **100**.................... CharliePoste 91
(Robin Dickin) *handily plcd tl wknd after 4 out* **16/1**

3m 54.6s (-7.40) **Going Correction** -0.30s/f (Good) course record **7** Ran SP% **113.3**
Speed ratings: **106,103,101,99,99 96,94**
CSF £102.42 TOTE £5.80: £3.50, £6.40; EX 46.20 Trifecta £105.40.
Owner Bloomfields **Bred** Whitley Stud **Trained** Cowlinge, Suffolk
■ Stewards' Enquiry : Lee Edwards 14-day ban: failed to obtain best possible placing (31- Mar - 8 April and 10-14 April)

FOCUS
Fences sited 7yds outside line utilised on March 3rd. An average handicap chase but it featured a very easy winner. The second and third set the level.

4862 TOTEPOOL.COM HOME OF POOL BETTING H'CAP CHASE (16 fncs) 2m 4f 110y
2:35 (2:35) (Class 4) (0-120,120) 5-Y-0+ **£3,768** (£1,106; £553; £276)

Form RPR

P26- **1** **Great Value (IRE)**[68] 3599 9-11-12 **120**....................(t) WayneHutchinson 133+
(Graeme McPherson) *mstkes: hld up: reminders after 9th: smooth hdwy 3 out: wnt 2nd 2 out: led last: readily drew clr fnl 75yds* **7/2**[2]

014- **2** *2 ¾* **Proud Times (USA)**[22] 4444 8-11-4 **112**.............................(p) JackDoyle 118
(Ali Brewer) *chsd ldr: lft in ld 4 out: rdn appr 2 out: hdd last: outpcd and no ch w wnr fnl 75yds* **4/1**[3]

2P5- **3** *6* **That's The Deal (IRE)**[7] 4725 10-9-13 **98**....................... JoeCornwall[(5)] 99
(John Cornwall) *chsd ldrs: pushed along after 10th: wknd bef last* **13/2**

342- **4** *3 ½* **Carpincho (FR)**[20] 4486 10-10-8 **102**...........................[1] RichardJohnson 103
(Sarah Humphrey) *led: mstke and hdd 4 out: stl cl up 3 out: lost 2nd 2 out: outpcd by ldrs and hld whn mstke last: wknd run-in* **5/4**[1]

223- **5** *3 ¼* **Father Shine (IRE)**[74] 3113 11-10-11 **110**.......................... BenPoste[(5)] 105
(Shaun Harris) *hld up: hdwy to chse ldrs 10th: rdn and outpcd bef 3 out: wl btn whn hit last* **10/1**

5m 11.0s (-6.00) **Going Correction** -0.30s/f (Good) **5** Ran SP% **109.1**
Speed ratings: **99,97,95,94,93**
CSF £16.77 TOTE £4.10: £2.60, £1.80; EX 22.00 Trifecta £102.90.
Owner The Martins Hill Racing Partnership **Bred** Bernie Breen **Trained** Upper Oddington, Gloucs

FOCUS
A modest handicap chase which again produced another easy winner. The second ran close to his mark.

4863 BET TOTEQUADPOT WITH TOTEPOOL "NATIONAL HUNT" MAIDEN HURDLE (11 hdls) 2m 4f 110y
3:10 (3:10) (Class 4) 4-Y-0+ **£3,119** (£915; £457; £228)

Form RPR

22- **1** **At Reception (IRE)**[29] 4304 7-10-10 0........................ MauriceLinehan[(5)] 104+
(Jonjo O'Neill) *hld up: nt fluent 1st: hdwy into midfield 4th: effrt to chse ldrs appr 2 out: wnt 2nd bef last: styd on to ld towards fin* **5/1**[3]

5U- **2** *½* **Troufion (FR)**[23] 5-10-8 101.................................... MissBAndrews[(7)] 102
(Caroline Fryer) *led: nt fluent 5th: abt 5 l clr 2 out: rdn bef last: hdd towards fin* **20/1**

/FF- **3** *2 ½* **Ready Token (IRE)**[37] 4163 6-11-1 0.................................(t[1]) NoelFehily 101
(Charlie Longsdon) *midfield: hdwy 7th: wnt 2nd 4 out: rdn and lost 2nd appr last: nt qckn: styd on same pce run-in* **2/1**[1]

0/4- **4** *¾* **Liars Poker (IRE)**[40] 4091 7-10-10 0............................ ThomasGarner[(5)] 98
(Oliver Sherwood) *hld up in rr: hdwy appr 2 out: rdn bef last: one pce run-in* **16/1**

/43- **5** *2 ¼* **Troyan (IRE)**[18] 4506 7-11-1 0... CharliePoste 96
(Robin Dickin) *prom tl rdn and wknd appr 2 out* **11/4**[2]

3- **6** *14* **Super Lunar (IRE)**[24] 4397 5-11-1 0.................................. RobertThornton 83
(Alan King) *hld up: nt fluent 1st: hdwy appr 7th: mstke 3 out: rdn and wknd bef 2 out* **11/4**[2]

0- **7** *18* **Vaillant Creek (FR)**[52] 3872 5-11-1 0............................. DougieCostello 67
(Alex Hales) *midfield: lost pl 6th: rdn and wknd after 3 out* **50/1**

60- **8** *10* **Rattleandrun (IRE)**[10] 4664 6-11-1 0............................... BrendanPowell 58
(Brendan Powell) *hld up: nt fluent 6th: mstke 3 out: sn wknd* **50/1**

65P- **P** **Ballycracken (IRE)**[85] 3227 10-10-10 77........................... JoeCornwall[(5)]
(David Pearson) *chsd ldrs: wknd 7th: rdn and bhd 4 out: t.o whn p.u bef 2 out* **50/1**

066- **P** **High Holloa**[19] 4487 5-10-8 0.. AndrewThornton
(Caroline Bailey) *midfield: lost pl 5th: bhd 6th: t.o whn p.u bef 4 out* **100/1**

64- **U** **Western Dolly**[31] 4253 5-10-5 0.. JackQuinlan[(3)]
(Caroline Fryer) *chsd ldrs: wnt 2nd 3rd tl pushed along and wkng whn blnd and uns rdr 7th* **100/1**

5m 2.6s (-10.40) **Going Correction** -0.625s/f (Firm) **11** Ran SP% **121.8**
Speed ratings (Par 105): **94,93,92,92,91 86,79,75,,**
CSF £90.24 TOTE £6.20: £2.10, £5.90, £1.80; EX 80.50 Trifecta £309.40.
Owner Mrs R D Hodgson & G & P Barker Ltd **Bred** Gerald McStay **Trained** Cheltenham, Gloucs

FOCUS
There were a number in with a chance heading into the straight. The first two ran pretty much to their marks.

4864 FOLLOW TOTEPOOL ON FACEBOOK AND TWITTER CLAIMING HURDLE (11 hdls) 2m 4f 110y
3:40 (3:40) (Class 5) 4-Y-0+ **£2,053** (£598; £299)

Form RPR

531- **1** **Lamps**[7] 4724 7-11-12 129..(v) NickScholfield 125
(Michael Blake) *chsd ldrs: wnt 2nd 7th: led after 3 out: styd on run-in* **7/4**[2]

1P1- **2** *1 ¾* **Waltz Darling (IRE)**[12] 4612 6-11-10 117.......................... JamesReveley 121
(Keith Reveley) *hld up: clsd after 3 out: wnt 2nd appr 2 out: rdn bef last: nt qckn run-in* **6/4**[1]

PP4- **3** *29* **Maller Tree**[18] 4517 7-11-12 133..(v) NoelFehily 101
(David Dennis) *led: hdd after 3 out: wkng whn mstke 2 out* **5/2**[3]

P34- **4** *62* **Captain Cardington (IRE)**[10] 4659 5-11-6 105........(b) RichardJohnson 35
(John O'Shea) *chsd ldr: pushed along after 6th: lost pl 7th: wknd 3 out: t.o* **10/1**

4m 58.4s (-14.60) **Going Correction** -0.625s/f (Firm) **4** Ran SP% **114.0**
Speed ratings (Par 103): **102,101,90,66**
CSF £5.20 TOTE £2.80; EX 5.50 Trifecta £7.80.
Owner The Moonlighters **Bred** Kilboy Estate **Trained** Trowbridge, Wilts

FOCUS
This four-runner seller came down to two of them in the straight. The second has been rated to his mark.

4865 BEST ODDS GUARANTEED AT TOTEPOOL.COM H'CAP HURDLE (11 hdls) 2m 4f 110y
4:10 (4:10) (Class 5) (0-100,100) 4-Y-0+ **£2,053** (£598; £299)

Form RPR

2P4- **1** **Speckled Door**[53] 3850 6-11-10 **98**............................... AndrewThornton 105+
(Caroline Bailey) *hld up: hdwy to trck ldrs after 3 out: led last: styd on gamely* **16/1**

001- **2** *¾* **Area Access (IRE)**[7] 4733 6-10-5 **86** 7ex.................. MrHAABannister[(7)] 94+
(Charlie Mann) *in tch: led 2 out: nt fluent and hdd last: kpt on: hld towards fin* **7/4**[1]

0/0- **3** *2 ¼* **On The Record (IRE)**[121] 2511 6-11-7 **95**.................... RichieMcLernon 101
(Jonjo O'Neill) *hld up: hdwy 3 out: rdn whn chsng ldrs appr last: styd on same pce run-in* **10/1**

055- **4** *5* **Balinderry (IRE)**[8] 4699 7-10-6 **87**.................................(tp) PaulBohan[(7)] 88
(Steve Gollings) *prom: led after 4th: hdd 5th: ev ch appr 2 out: no ex bef last* **16/1**

005- **5** *7* **Hand On Bach (IRE)**[97] 3015 6-11-7 **98**....................(b) GavinSheehan[(3)] 92
(Warren Greatrex) *in tch: led after 3 out: hdd 2 out: wknd appr last* **8/1**[3]

/PP- **6** *nk* **Valrene**[18] 4508 8-11-2 **100**................................. JosephPalmowski[(10)] 93
(Robin Dickin) *in tch tl rdn and wknd appr 2 out* **20/1**

34P- **7** *7* **Tisfreetdream (IRE)**[22] 4447 13-11-4 **92**...............................(b) JackDoyle 81
(Peter Pritchard) *midfield: mstke 4th: wknd bef 2 out* **25/1**

F6P- **8** *18* **Nomadic Storm**[81] 3265 8-10-6 **80**............................. WayneHutchinson 51
(Graeme McPherson) *midfield: nt fluent 4th: towards rr after 6th: n.d after* **16/1**

01U- **9** *22* **Lord Landen (IRE)**[10] 4654 9-11-5 **98**....................(t) ConorShoemark[(5)] 49
(Fergal O'Brien) *midfield: hdwy to trck ldrs after 4th: led 5th: hit 3 out: sn hdd: wknd bef 2 out* **4/1**[2]

/40- **10** *25* **Boosha**[102] 2896 9-10-8 **85**... HarryChalloner[(3)] 14
(John Bryan Groucott) *chsd ldrs tl rdn and wknd after 3 out* **50/1**

500- **11** *1* **Shinooki (IRE)**[60] 3735 7-11-6 **94**.............................. DougieCostello 22
(Alex Hales) *hld up: niggled along bef 5th: struggling to keep up after 6th: nvr a threat* **8/1**[3]

P53- **12** *27* **Weston Lodge (IRE)**[85] 3222 8-11-7 **95**..........................(b[1]) DaveCrosse
(Christopher Kellett) *led: hdd after 4th: lost pl after 6th: t.o 3 out* **50/1**

42P- **P** **Around A Pound (IRE)**[8] 4695 9-11-5 **100**.............(p) CharlieDeutsch[(7)]
(Nick Kent) *hld up: t.o whn p.u bef 2 out* **16/1**

433/ **P** **Doyenne Dream**[23] 7-11-0 **88**..(p) HarrySkelton
(Caroline Fryer) *in tch: lost pl after 4th: bhd after 6th: t.o whn p.u bef 4 out* **50/1**

54P- **P** **Snow Alert**[108] 2787 8-10-8 **82**... AdrianLane
(John Norton) *hld up: struggling 5th: t.o 6th: p.u bef 7th* **33/1**

4m 58.5s (-14.50) **Going Correction** -0.625s/f (Firm) **15** Ran SP% **128.6**
Speed ratings (Par 103): **102,101,100,98,96 96,93,86,78,68 68,58,,,**
CSF £45.80 CT £323.63 TOTE £15.90: £3.10, £1.20, £3.80; EX 60.10 Trifecta £504.40.
Owner A & Mrs P Hurn **Bred** Mrs L M Pestell **Trained** Holdenby, Northants

FOCUS
This was a moderate handicap hurdle. The time was good for the grade and the first three should still all be competitive when reassessed.

4866 GRAND NATIONAL ANTE POST AT TOTEPOOL.COM H'CAP HURDLE (9 hdls) 2m
4:40 (4:40) (Class 4) (0-110,110) 4-Y-0+ **£3,119** (£915; £457; £228)

Form RPR

246- **1** **Yes Daddy (IRE)**[77] 3420 6-11-5 **103**.............................. RichardJohnson 109+
(Tim Vaughan) *hld up: hdwy 3 out: led bef 2 out: r.o and kpt finding more run-in* **6/1**[3]

631- **2** *2 ¼* **Good Of Luck**[8] 4703 5-10-7 **94**...................................(p) GavinSheehan[(3)] 97
(Warren Greatrex) *hld up: hdwy to chse ldrs appr 2 out: wnt 2nd bef last: one pce and no imp towards fin* **5/4**[1]

342- **3** *6* **Daliance (IRE)**[5] 4757 5-11-1 **99**...(p) JamieMoore 98
(Neil King) *in rr: pushed along after 4th: styd on bef last: nt trble front two* **4/1**[2]

52B- **4** *1 ½* **Ergo Sum**[17] 4527 7-10-8 **95**... RobertDunne[(3)] 94+
(Robin Mathew) *j.rt: led: hdd 4 out: led again after 3 out: hdd appr 2 out: wknd bef last* **8/1**

65F- **5** *5* **No No Charlie (IRE)**[15] 4573 7-11-12 **110**.............................(t[1]) NoelFehily 103
(Charlie Longsdon) *prom: dived at 2nd: sn lost pl: towards rr and struggling bef 3 out: no imp after* **12/1**

/04- **6** *4* **Allusive Power (IRE)**[25] 4371 5-10-4 **88**..........................(p) CharliePoste 78
(Anna Brooks) *prom: mstke 4 out: sn wknd* **16/1**

34P- **7** *4 ½* **Ballygrooby Bertie (IRE)**[18] 4510 6-11-7 **110**........(t) ConorShoemark[(5)] 96
(Fergal O'Brien) *sn prom: led 4 out: hdd after 3 out: rdn whn hung lft and wknd after 2 out* **8/1**

3m 50.3s (-6.70) **Going Correction** -0.625s/f (Firm) **7** Ran SP% **114.5**
Speed ratings (Par 105): **91,89,86,86,83 81,79**
CSF £14.54 TOTE £7.20: £3.30, £1.60; EX 17.60 Trifecta £53.80.
Owner Paul Cooper **Bred** Mrs S Brennan **Trained** Aberthin, Vale of Glamorgan

FOCUS
This was a fair race for the grade, and the finish was fought out by two progressive horses. The winner has been rated as running a small personal best, with the second below the level of his recent soft-ground win.

4867 COLLECT TOTEPOOL WINNINGS AT BETFRED SHOPS MARES' STANDARD NH FLAT RACE (CONDITIONALS/AMATEURS) 2m
5:10 (5:10) (Class 6) 4-6-Y-0 **£1,642** (£478; £239)

Form RPR

1 **Amberkatann (IRE)** 5-10-7 0...................................... MissBAndrews[(7)] 97+
(Dan Skelton) *racd keenly: hld up: hdwy on outer over 3f out: led over 1f out: r.o to draw away ins fnl f* **14/1**

2 *2 ¾* **Belle De Londres (IRE)** 4-10-0 0........................ MrJoshuaNewman[(7)] 87
(Alan King) *hld up: hdwy over 2f out: rdn and nt qckn over 1f out: styd on to take 2nd nr fin: nt trble wnr* **5/2**[2]

2- 3 *nk* **Mighty Minnie**[107] 2809 5-10-11 0 .... JakeGreenall(3) 94
(Henry Daly) *prom: led over 4f out: rdn and hdd over 1f out: kpt on uinder press ins fnl f* **2/1**[1]

4 *nk* **Stand 'N' Boogie** 4-10-4 0 .... KielanWoods(3) 87
(Pam Sly) *prom: rdn over 2f out: chal over 1f out: nt qckn ins fnl f: no ex towards fin* **12/1**

5 *2* **Come On Harriet** 5-10-7 0 .... (t) MrNicholasMeek(7) 92
(Alex Hales) *hld up in rr: rdn over 3f out: styd on fr over 1f out: nvr trbld ldrs* **50/1**

6 *6* **First Page** 4-10-2 0 .... NicodeBoinville(5) 80
(Paul Cowley) *prom: rdn and ch 3f out: wknd 2f out* **20/1**

0- 7 *¾* **Over The Air**[48] 3961 6-11-0 0 .... JoshuaMoore 86
(John Spearing) *midfield: effrt bhd ldrs over 2f out: sn wknd* **50/1**

1- 8 *½* **Dog Or Divorce**[93] 3098 5-11-2 0 .... MauriceLinehan(5) 92
(Paul Webber) *led: hdd over 4f out: wknd over 1f out* **5/1**[3]

9 *2 ¾* **Wild At Midnight** 5-10-9 0 .... ConorShoemark(5) 83
(Fergal O'Brien) *uns rdr and broke loose bef r: hld up: hdwy 6f out: wknd over 2f out* **8/1**

10 *¾* **Polly Wiggle** 5-10-11 0 .... JackQuinlan(3) 82
(Caroline Fryer) *trckd ldrs: effrt 3f out: wknd 2f out* **50/1**

0- 11 *2 ½* **Radmores Jewel**[16] 4561 4-10-4 0 .... MrFMitchell(3) 73
(John O'Shea) *midfield: rdn and lost pl over 5f out: n.d* **50/1**

0- 12 *39* **Tarantelle**[29] 4296 5-10-11 0 .... JeremiahMcGrath(3) 45
(John Spearing) *midfield: pushed along 6f out: wknd 4f out* **25/1**

13 *18* **Sprogzilla** 5-10-9 0 .... BenPoste(5) 29
(Alan Phillips) *racd keenly: midfield: pushed along and lost pl 6f out: sn bhd* **50/1**

14 *24* **Sirnita** 5-10-11 0 .... JonathanEngland(3) 7
(Richard Guest) *racd keenly: hld up in rr: struggling 6f out: nvr a threat* **33/1**

3m 48.7s (-2.70) **Going Correction** -0.625s/f (Firm)
WFA 4 from 5yo+ 7lb 14 Ran SP% **125.4**
Speed ratings: **81,79,79,79,78 75,74,74,73,72 71,52,43,31**
CSF £48.37 TOTE £19.40: £5.40, £1.40, £1.60; EX 108.50 Trifecta £292.60.
Owner Miss Charlotte Smith **Bred** D J Sweeney **Trained** Alcester, Warwicks
■ Stewards' Enquiry : Jack Quinlan £80 fine: passport irregularity

FOCUS
This was an average bumper that produced a surprise winner. It's been rated around the third and eighth.
T/Plt: £172.90 to a £1 stake. Pool: £70503.97 - 297.61 winning tickets T/Qpdt: £16.30 to a £1 stake. Pool: £7176.37 - 324.00 winning tickets DO

4868 - 4881a (Foreign Racing) - See Raceform Interactive

[4599] EXETER (R-H)
Tuesday, March 18

OFFICIAL GOING: Good (good to soft in places; chs 7.8, hdl 7.4)
Wind: Quite strong; across Weather: Sunny periods

4882 MARLEY ETERNIT RIDGEFAST NOVICES' (S) HURDLE (8 hdls) 2m 1f
2:00 (2:00) (Class 5) 4-Y-0+ **£1,949** (£572; £286; £143)

Form RPR

004- 1 **Karl Marx (IRE)**[20] 4504 4-10-0 86 .... (b) ThomasCheesman(7) 93+
(Mark Gillard) *trckd ldrs: rdn after 5th: chal 3 out: narrow advantage whn lft in clr ld 2 out: sn idling: r.o whn pressed run-in: rdn out* **9/1**

63- 2 *1 ½* **Fruity Bun**[19] 4513 4-9-9 0 .... (t) JamesBanks(5) 81
(Keiran Burke) *racd keenly: trckd ldrs: rdn after 5th: disputing 3rd whn pckd 3 out: lft 3rd 2 out: r.o fr last: hld* **16/1**

506- 3 *1 ¾* **To The Sky (IRE)**[104] 2886 6-11-0 98 .... RichardJohnson 93
(John O'Shea) *racd keenly: hld up: hdwy into 2nd 4th tl rdn appr 3 out: lft 2nd 2 out: rallied to press idling wnr last: no ex run-in* **3/1**[2]

004- 4 *36* **Sedgemoor Top Bid (IRE)**[19] 4513 6-11-0 93 ..(b[1]) SamTwiston-Davies 61
(Nigel Hawke) *trckd ldrs: rdn after 4th: sn hld: lft modest 4th 2 out: t.o* **8/1**[3]

052- P **Scribe (IRE)**[8] 4724 6-11-0 107 .... (b) SeanQuinlan
(David Evans) *trckd ldrs: rdn in 5th after 5th: wknd appr 3 out: t.o whn p.u run-in* **2/1**[1]

P- P **Studfarmer**[54] 1473 4-10-2 0 .... CharlieWallis(5)
(John Panvert) *hld up: nt fluent 1st: lost tch qckly after 2nd: p.u bef 4th* **100/1**

220- F **Slaney Star (IRE)**[12] 4636 6-11-0 105 .... (v) RhysFlint 100
(Jim Best) *led: rdn appr 3 out: sn jnd: narrowly hdd whn fell 2 out* **3/1**[2]

4m 15.4s (-0.10) **Going Correction** -0.275s/f (Good)
WFA 4 from 6yo+ 7lb 7 Ran SP% **111.3**
Speed ratings (Par 103): **89,88,87,70, ,**
CSF £113.91 TOTE £10.50: £3.50, £5.70; EX 199.10 Trifecta £386.40.There was no bid for the winner
Owner Sam Bartlett **Bred** George S O'Malley **Trained** Holwell, Dorset

FOCUS
Richard Johnson described the ground as "good with good to soft patches" Not an overly competitive selling hurdle and it's given a guessy rating around the first three and the faller.

4883 TRIFLEX NOVICES' H'CAP HURDLE (12 hdls) 2m 7f 110y
2:30 (2:30) (Class 4) (0-105,102) 4-Y-0+ **£3,249** (£954; £477; £238)

Form RPR

436- 1 **Bob Keown (IRE)**[49] 3955 6-11-1 98 .... (p) PaulO'Brien(7) 112+
(Rebecca Curtis) *a.p: led appr 9th: styd on strly to draw clr after 3 out: pushed out* **7/2**[1]

046/ 2 *15* **Noble Perk**[468] 2856 9-10-12 88 .... AidanColeman 88
(Adrian Wintle) *mid-div: hdwy to chse wnr 9th: sn rdn: styd on but comf hld fr 3 out* **14/1**

5P5- 3 *2 ½* **Langarve Lady (IRE)**[15] 4595 6-10-2 83 .... (p) ConorShoemark(5) 82
(Neil Mulholland) *j.lft at times: mid-div: hdwy after 9th: rdn into 3rd bef 3 out: nt fluent 2 out: styd on same pce* **13/2**

140- 4 *3* **Kings Apollo**[27] 4351 5-10-12 93 .... BenPoste(5) 87
(Tom Symonds) *trckd ldrs: nt fluent 7th: rdn after 9th: one pce fr next* **6/1**[3]

0/P- 5 *5* **Applause For Amy (IRE)**[28] 4331 7-10-2 85 .... MrJBargary(7) 75
(Mary Sanderson) *in tch: rdn to chse ldrs after 9th: one pce fr next* **33/1**

100- 6 *38* **Monderon (FR)**[14] 4599 7-11-5 102 .... MrRobertHawker(7) 58
(Richard Hawker) *hld up towards rr: nt fluent 4th and pushed along briefly: nt fluent 7th: sn drvn: hld in 6th whn mstke 3 out: sn wknd: t.o* **12/1**

050- 7 *hd* **Henwood (IRE)**[31] 4275 6-11-8 98 .... JoeTizzard 53
(Colin Tizzard) *trckd ldrs: rdn after 9th: wknd bef next: t.o* **10/1**

444- 8 *36* **General Girling**[12] 4636 7-10-0 76 oh1 .... (b[1]) IanPopham
(Caroline Keevil) *mid-div: rdn after 9th: sn wknd: t.o* **17/2**

050- 9 *13* **Luckster**[16] 4569 4-11-1 100 .... SeanQuinlan 2
(David Evans) *mid-div tl 6th: sn bhd: t.o* **33/1**

/03- 10 *9* **I'm So Special (IRE)**[15] 4595 8-10-7 83 .... (t) RichardJohnson
(Susan Johnson) *hld up towards rr: nt fluent 6th: drvn 9th: nvr any imp: wknd bef next: t.o* **5/1**[2]

000- P **Miles Of Sunshine**[29] 3788 9-10-7 83 .... JamieMoore
(Ron Hodges) *towards rr of midfield: rdn after 9th: no imp whn p.u bef next: dismntd* **14/1**

/3P- P **Social Overdrive (IRE)**[27] 4344 8-11-4 99 .... (b[1]) JamesBanks(5)
(Emma Baker) *led tl rdn appr 9th: wknd qckly sn after: tailing off whn p.u bef 3 out* **20/1**

4- P **Alizari (IRE)**[25] 3839 5-11-5 102 .... MikeyHamill(7)
(Barry Brennan) *nvr fluent in rr: a towards rr: lost tch 7th: t.o whn p.u after 9th* **50/1**

5m 50.1s (-8.90) **Going Correction** -0.275s/f (Good)
WFA 4 from 5yo+ 8lb 13 Ran SP% **119.8**
Speed ratings (Par 105): **103,98,97,96,94 81,81,69,65,62 , ,**
CSF £49.95 CT £312.47 TOTE £4.80: £2.10, £4.70, £3.10; EX 72.50 Trifecta £515.50.
Owner C R Trembath **Bred** Peter Molony & Mrs Ethel Browne **Trained** Newport, Dyfed

FOCUS
Modest form, but a progressive winner. The third helps set the level.

4884 ECIC INSURANCE NOVICES' H'CAP CHASE (18 fncs) 3m
3:00 (3:00) (Class 4) (0-110,110) 5-Y-0+ **£3,898** (£1,144; £572; £286)

Form RPR

111- 1 **Caulfields Venture (IRE)**[8] 4725 8-11-8 106 7ex .... AidanColeman 120+
(Emma Lavelle) *trckd ldrs: mstke 6th: shkn up in cl 3rd 4 out: chsd wnr next: hit 2 out: chal last: keeping on wl whn short of room run-in: led nring fin* **1/1**[1]

34P- 2 *shd* **Regal Presence (IRE)**[79] 3389 7-11-11 109 .... (b) JackDoyle 120
(Victor Dartnall) *led: clr tl 4th: nt fluent 8th (water): rdn and hrd pressed fr 4 out: stuck to task v gamely: drifted lft between last 2: jnd last: kpt on wl: hdd nring fin* **10/1**

142/ 3 *19* **Oscarslad (IRE)**[674] 246 8-11-2 107 .... (t) GaryDerwin(7) 104
(Harry Fry) *trckd ldr: prom fr 4th: rdn and ev ch whn nt fluent 4 out: cl 3rd next: styd on same pce tl no ex fr last* **5/1**[2]

4P5- 4 *¾* **Comeonginger (IRE)**[25] 4399 7-11-6 104 .... TomCannon 98
(Chris Gordon) *mid-div: hdwy 12th: rdn in 4th appr 4 out: styd on same pce* **6/1**[3]

23P- 5 *11* **Just Benny (IRE)**[31] 4275 9-10-11 95 .... RichardJohnson 78
(Richard Phillips) *hld up towards rr: nt fluent 2nd and 3rd: hdwy fr after 12th: rdn in 5th appr 4 out: sn wknd* **16/1**

054- 6 *1 ¾* **Lady From Geneva**[15] 4595 7-10-5 89 .... BrendanPowell 71
(Brendan Powell) *hld up towards rr: struggling 14th: plugged on fr 4 out: nvr a factor* **14/1**

43P- 7 *14* **Uncle Pettit (IRE)**[49] 3955 6-10-0 84 oh2 .... JamieMoore 58
(Jonathan Portman) *in tch: rdn appr 4 out: sn wknd* **50/1**

0/S- 8 *10* **Ballycassel (IRE)**[121] 2536 9-11-12 110 .... FelixDeGiles 70
(Tom Symonds) *hld up towards rr: midfield 14th: sn rdn: wknd next* **25/1**

/6P- 9 *9* **Lupita (IRE)**[132] 2290 10-10-0 84 oh22 .... (t) IanPopham 36
(Derrick Scott) *mid-div: trckd ldrs briefly 11th: lost pl fr next: bhd and no ch after 14th* **66/1**

450- 10 *26* **Nicene Creed**[63] 3699 9-10-13 97 .... (tp) PaulMoloney 25
(Sophie Leech) *nt a fluent: a towards rr: struggling whn hit 14th: sn t.o* **16/1**

060- 11 *7* **Cool Fantasy (IRE)**[120] 2568 5-10-0 85 oh10 .... AdamWedge 6
(Caroline Keevil) *mid-div: struggling in rr whn nt fluent 14th: sn wknd: t.o* **80/1**

000- F **Ask The Boss**[78] 3425 9-9-9 84 oh3 ow2 .... MikeyEnnis(7)
(Tim Dennis) *hld up towards rr: rdn after 13th: sme prog into 6th whn stmbld bdly and fell appr 4 out: fatally injured* **50/1**

3PP- P **Bravo Bravo**[24] 4412 7-11-2 105 .... (p) NicodeBoinville(5)
(Mark Gillard) *chsd ldrs: pushed along bef 10th: grad lost pl fr 11th: t.o whn p.u bef 4 out* **12/1**

5m 59.9s (-9.40) **Going Correction** -0.375s/f (Good)
WFA 5 from 6yo+ 1lb 13 Ran SP% **126.7**
Speed ratings: **100,99,93,93,89 89,84,81,78,69 67, ,**
CSF £13.13 CT £42.62 TOTE £1.80: £1.10, £3.60, £2.60; EX 13.40 Trifecta £53.70.
Owner C F Colquhoun **Bred** Michael Crean **Trained** Hatherden, Hants
■ Stewards' Enquiry : Jack Doyle caution: careless riding.

FOCUS
The front pair drew clear late on and the form looks reasonable for the level. The winner was well in and is rated to a similar level as his last couple of runs.

4885 ROCKWOOL MULTI FIX NOVICES' CHASE (15 fncs) 2m 3f 110y
3:35 (3:35) (Class 3) 5-Y-0+ **£6,498** (£1,908; £954; £477)

Form RPR

U11- 1 **Freckle Face**[23] 4448 7-11-12 123 .... TommyPhelan 136+
(Bill Turner) *hld up: nt fluent 9th: hdwy into cl 3rd 11th: chal 4 out: led 2 out: drew clr: comf* **11/1**

13P- 2 *8* **Gores Island (IRE)**[66] 3646 8-10-12 115 .... JoshuaMoore 111
(Gary Moore) *trckd ldrs: tk ld whn awkward 8th: rdn and strly pressed fr 4 out: mstke whn hdd 2 out: sn hld: kpt on same pce* **9/2**[3]

154- 3 *1* **Seebright**[31] 4277 7-10-12 0 .... JackDoyle 107
(Victor Dartnall) *trckd ldrs: pushed along in 4th 11th: rdn to dispute 3rd 4 out: nvr quite got on terms w ldrs: styd on same pce* **10/11**[1]

3F3- 4 *7* **Flaming Charmer (IRE)**[26] 4373 6-11-5 122 .... JoeTizzard 108
(Colin Tizzard) *led tl 8th: chsd ldr: rdn and ev ch briefly appr 4 out: sn hld: hit 3 out: lost 3rd next* **3/1**[2]

/56- 5 *11* **Simply Charles (IRE)**[98] 3011 7-10-12 0 .... WillKennedy 90
(Hilary Parrott) *prom: hit 2nd: lost pl after 11th: sn btn* **66/1**

062- 6 *12* **Lady Bridget**[14] 4604 6-9-12 0 .... (t) ThomasCheesman(7) 70
(Mark Gillard) *trckd ldrs: rdn after 11th: wknd bef next* **25/1**

006- 7 *74* **Ravens Secret**[21] 4484 9-10-13 90 ow1 .... MrGBarfoot-Saunt 4
(Tracey Barfoot-Saunt) *hld up: hit 3rd: t.o fr 10th* **100/1**

4m 51.0s (-6.30) **Going Correction** -0.375s/f (Good) 7 Ran SP% **110.2**
Speed ratings: **97,93,93,90,86 81,51**
CSF £53.76 TOTE £9.40: £2.90, £2.40; EX 38.60 Trifecta £75.90.
Owner Mrs Christine Goldsmith **Bred** B J Goldsmith **Trained** Sigwells, Somerset

FOCUS
A modest novice chase, with the favourite disappointing, but hard not to be taken with the performance of the winner. He's on the upgrade and the type to rate higher yet.

4886 ICB INTERNATIONAL CONSTRUCTION BUREAU INTERACTIVE H'CAP CHASE (17 fncs 1 omitted) 3m
4:10 (4:10) (Class 3) (0-130,128) 5-Y-0 **£6,330** (£1,870; £935; £468; £234)

Form RPR
P40- **1** **On Trend (IRE)**[45] 4035 8-11-2 118 ....(b[1]) TomCannon 130
(Nick Gifford) *trckd ldr: led after 14th: qcknd clr by-passing omitted 4 out: tiring appr last but enough in hand to hold on run-in: drvn out* **11/2[3]**
20P- **2** *2 ½* **Lamboro Lad (IRE)**[19] 4509 9-11-5 121 ....(tp) JamieMoore 131
(Peter Bowen) *hld up: pushed along briefly after 2nd: hdwy 14th: sn rdn to chse wnr: j.rt last 3: rallied to cl on wnr last but a being hld run-in* **12/1**
5/3- **3** *10* **Max Bygraves**[95] 3065 11-11-4 120 .... SamTwiston-Davies 121
(Kim Bailey) *in tch: rdn into 3rd after 14th: styd on but nvr finding pce to get on terms fr 3 out* **9/2[2]**
20U- **4** *11* **Qianshan Leader (IRE)**[102] 2923 10-11-8 124 ....(p) AidanColeman 114
(Emma Lavelle) *led: rdn and hdd after 14th: sn outpcd: plugged on to regain 4th at the last* **8/1**
541- **5** *3* **Woodford County**[24] 4412 7-11-6 122 ....(p) TomO'Brien 112
(Philip Hobbs) *mid-div: dropped to rr and reminders after 5th: slow 9th and sltly detached: plugged on past btn horses fr 3 out but nvr any danger* **7/1**
P0P- **6** *5* **Handy Andy (IRE)**[62] 3717 8-11-12 128 ....(t) JoeTizzard 113
(Colin Tizzard) *nt fluent 7th: slow 10th: nvr travelling in rr sn after: plugged on by-passing omitted 4 out but nvr any danger* **12/1**
104- **7** *4 ½* **Imperial Circus (IRE)**[95] 3068 8-11-9 125 ....(p) RichardJohnson 108
(Philip Hobbs) *hld up: hdwy whn hit 11th: effrt in 4th after 14th: sn btn: wknd last* **4/1[1]**
130- **P** **Aimigayle**[95] 3067 11-11-3 119 .... ColinBolger
(Suzy Smith) *trckd ldrs: blnd 4th (broke fence): rdn after 14th: wknd after next: p.u bef last* **7/1**
434- **P** **Goring One (IRE)**[10] 4681 9-10-10 112 .... AndrewThornton
(Anna Newton-Smith) *trckd ldrs tl 11th: grad lost pl: tailing off whn p.u after 14th* **10/1**

5m 55.2s (-14.10) **Going Correction** -0.375s/f (Good) **9** Ran SP% **114.2**
Speed ratings: **108,107,103,100,99 97,96, ,**
CSF £65.11 CT £320.45 TOTE £8.30: £2.90, £4.00, £1.80; EX 82.50 Trifecta £364.30.
Owner Ham Manor Farms Ltd **Bred** Jonathan Murphy **Trained** Findon, W Sussex

FOCUS
Quite a decent staying handicap that saw the front pair pull clear. The winner is rated back to something like his best.

4887 NFRC SOUTH WESTERN COMMITTEE H'CAP HURDLE (DIV I) (10 hdls) 2m 3f
4:40 (4:40) (Class 4) (0-110,109) 4-Y-0+ **£3,249** (£954; £477; £238)

Form RPR
210- **1** **Rugged Jack (FR)**[6] 4760 7-11-4 **101** .... JackDoyle 112+
(Victor Dartnall) *a.p: led 5th: rdn clr after 3 out: readily* **13/2[2]**
505- **2** *12* **Trillerin Minella (IRE)**[69] 3602 6-11-10 **107** .... WayneHutchinson 105
(Graeme McPherson) *in tch: rdn and hdwy after 7th: disp 2nd fr next: hld by wnr 2 out: kpt on same pce* **13/2[2]**
10P- **3** *¾* **Boss In Boots (IRE)**[39] 4132 6-11-7 **104** .... AndrewThornton 101
(Seamus Mullins) *in tch: sltly hmpd 6th: rdn to dispute 2nd fr 3 out: kpt on same pce fr next* **9/4[1]**
256- **4** *¾* **Back In June**[66] 3643 6-11-12 **109** .... TomO'Brien 105
(Paul Henderson) *hld up: effrt to cl on ldrs appr 3 out: nvr gng pce to get involved but styd on into 4th run-in* **11/1**
1/1- **5** *1 ¾* **Fuzzy Logic (IRE)**[228] 482 5-11-6 **108** .... RobertWilliams[(5)] 103
(Bernard Llewellyn) *trckd ldrs: rdn to dispute 2nd fr 3 out tl no ex fr last* **12/1**
200- **6** *5* **Bedouin Bay**[8] 4726 7-11-8 **105** .... BrendanPowell 95
(Johnny Farrelly) *hld up: rdn and sme prog after 7th: nvr finding pce to get involved fr 3 out: wknd last* **8/1[3]**
226- **7** *10* **Jigsaw Financial (IRE)**[198] 1488 8-10-4 **87** .... DougieCostello 72
(Laura Young) *hld up: sme prog u.p whn mstke 3 out: wknd next* **9/1**
553- **8** *¾* **La Madonnina (IRE)**[22] 4472 6-10-2 **85** .... IanPopham 65
(Caroline Keevil) *led tl 5th: prom tl rdn appr 3 out: sn wknd* **9/1**
4P0- **9** *16* **Trumix**[118] 2598 6-11-5 **102** .... SamTwiston-Davies 68
(Kim Bailey) *in tch tl pushed along appr 4th: sn towards rr: sltly hmpd 6th: wknd after next: t.o* **12/1**
P45- **F** **Aroseforoscar**[20] 4500 5-10-7 **90** .... JamesDavies
(Chris Down) *trckd ldrs: cl 3rd whn fell 6th* **20/1**

4m 38.4s (-4.30) **Going Correction** -0.275s/f (Good) **10** Ran SP% **117.0**
Speed ratings (Par 105): **98,92,92,92,91 89,85,84,78,**
CSF £48.86 CT £125.03 TOTE £7.10: £2.20, £2.30, £1.40; EX 54.50 Trifecta £200.90.
Owner G D Hake **Bred** Breeding & Racing Enterprise Ltd **Trained** Brayford, Devon

FOCUS
Run at a steady gallop, the winner was always well placed. The second to fourth set the level.

4888 NFRC SOUTH WESTERN COMMITTEE H'CAP HURDLE (DIV II) (10 hdls) 2m 3f
5:15 (5:15) (Class 4) (0-110,108) 4-Y-0+ **£3,249** (£954; £477; £238)

Form RPR
536- **1** **Generous Ransom (IRE)**[30] 4301 6-11-12 **108** .... RichardJohnson 113+
(Nick Gifford) *trckd ldr: led 4th: rdn after 2 out: r.o wl fr last: rdn out* **4/1[2]**
341- **2** *2 ¾* **Crookstown (IRE)**[9] 4699 7-11-3 **102** .... KielanWoods[(3)] 106+
(Ben Case) *in tch: tk clsr order after 7th: rdn in disp 2nd fr 3 out: kpt on same pce fr last* **13/8[1]**
3PP- **3** *5* **Redlynch Rock (IRE)**[49] 3955 6-10-8 **90** ....(t) SamJones 87
(Bob Buckler) *trckd ldr: rdn and ev ch appr 3 out: disp cl 2nd bef 2 out: kpt on but no ex fr last* **50/1**
U/0- **4** *nse* **Winning Spark (USA)**[319] 97 7-11-7 **106** .... JamesBest[(3)] 103
(Jackie Du Plessis) *hld up: rdn to chse ldrs appr 3 out: kpt on but nt pce to chal: wnt 4th run-in* **40/1**
U46- **5** *1* **Bandol (IRE)**[28] 4334 6-10-0 **83** ow2 .... RobertDunne[(3)] 81
(Laura Young) *hld up: rdn and hdwy to chse ldrs appr 3 out: kpt on but nt pce to threaten* **12/1**
500- **6** *8* **Silent Knight (IRE)**[19] 4506 5-10-7 **92** ....(p) GavinSheehan[(3)] 81
(Warren Greatrex) *trckd ldrs tl lost pl 6th: rdn appr 3 out: sn one pce* **16/1**
245/ **7** *6* **Revani**[504] 2118 7-11-4 **107** .... MrRobertHawker[(7)] 102+
(Johnny Farrelly) *racd keenly: hld up: hdwy after 7th: rdn to dispute 2nd 3 out: hld in disp 3rd whn blnd last: eased* **4/1[2]**
040- **8** *15* **Xaarcet (IRE)**[31] 4278 7-11-9 **105** ....(b[1]) BrendanPowell 75
(Colin Tizzard) *in tch: rdn after 7th: wknd after 3 out* **12/1**
413- **9** *11* **Shadarpour (IRE)**[60] 3029 5-11-8 **104** .... JamieMoore 64
(Gary Moore) *led tl 4th: pressed ldr tl rdn after 7th: wknd after 3 out* **8/1[3]**

4m 37.4s (-5.30) **Going Correction** -0.275s/f (Good) **9** Ran SP% **114.9**
Speed ratings (Par 105): **100,98,96,96,96 92,90,84,79**
CSF £11.18 CT £273.04 TOTE £4.70: £1.40, £1.20, £8.20; EX 11.80 Trifecta £346.50.
Owner Sir Christopher Wates **Bred** Sir Christopher Stephen Wates **Trained** Findon, W Sussex

FOCUS
As in the first division, there was little pace on and the winner was up there throughout. He's on the upgrade.
T/Jkpt: Not won. T/Plt: £1,832.60 to a £1 stake. Pool: £90,252.39 - 35.95 winning units T/Qpdt: £29.10 to a £1 stake. Pool: £9,084.75 - 230.70 winning units TM

[4336]WETHERBY (L-H)
Tuesday, March 18

OFFICIAL GOING: Good (good to soft in places)
Wind: Strong; half behind Weather: Overcast; very breezy; cold

4889 WATCH RACING UK ON SKY 432 MAIDEN HURDLE (9 hdls) 2m 110y
2:10 (2:10) (Class 5) 4-Y-0+ **£1,949** (£572; £286; £143)

Form RPR
 1 **Oliver's Hill (IRE)**[141] 2140 5-11-0 0 .... AndrewTinkler 122
(Charlie Longsdon) *w ldr: led appr 3 out: hung lft: styd on towards fin* **7/1**
403- **2** *1 ¼* **Rock A Doodle Doo (IRE)**[21] 4476 7-10-9 110 ....(p) AdamNicol[(5)] 121
(Sally Hall) *trckd ldrs: upsides 3 out: kpt on same pce last 50yds* **7/1**
434- **3** *15* **Pair Of Jacks (IRE)**[9] 4693 6-11-0 0 .... BrianHughes 110
(Malcolm Jefferson) *led: hdd appr 3 out: wknd bef 2 out: lft modest 3rd last* **4/1[2]**
3F/ **4** *18* **Eltheeb**[249] 3967 7-11-0 0 .... BarryKeniry 95
(Philip Kirby) *trckd ldrs: 5th and wkng whn blnd 2 out: lft poor 4th last* **7/1**
060- **5** *15* **Be A Dreamer**[31] 4267 6-11-0 0 .... RyanMania 78
(Sue Smith) *mid-div: outpcd 6th: kpt on and lft distant 5th last* **66/1**
00- **6** *4* **Bold And Free**[14] 3332 4-10-4 0 .... TonyKelly[(3)] 67
(David Thompson) *nt fluent in rr: sme hdwy 5th: nvr a factor* **100/1**
 7 *1 ¼* **Artifice Sivola (FR)**[147] 4-10-2 0 ....[1] MattCrawley[(5)] 66
(Lucy Wadham) *hld up in rr: kpt on appr 3 out: nvr on terms* **66/1**
 8 *¾* **Red Joker (IRE)**[94] 4-10-4 0 .... JohnKington[(3)] 65
(Andrew Crook) *in rr: sme hdwy 3 out: nvr on terms* **100/1**
0- **9** *9* **Mighty Cliche (IRE)**[14] 4611 5-10-9 0 .... ColmMcCormack[(5)] 64
(Dianne Sayer) *in rr: nvr on terms* **100/1**
 10 *1 ¼* **Sunblazer (IRE)**[144] 4-10-7 0 .... NickScholfield 56
(Kim Bailey) *j.lft 1st: trckd ldrs 4th: wknd appr 3 out* **9/2[3]**
465- **11** *7* **Khelac**[21] 4476 4-10-2 0 .... JoeColliver[(5)] 50
(Micky Hammond) *mid-div: lost pl after 5th* **100/1**
650- **12** *26* **Interior Minister**[25] 4401 4-10-7 0 .... RichieMcLernon 26
(Jonjo O'Neill) *chsng ldrs whn hmpd 1st: mid-div: lost pl 5th: sn bhd* **20/1**
0P4- **13** *91* **Teatreids (IRE)**[22] 4466 6-10-7 0 .... DavidEngland
(Brian Ellison) *mid-div: drvn 3rd: lost pl 5th: sn wl bhd: t.o 3 out: eventually completed* **100/1**
6- **P** **Martin Chuzzlewit (IRE)**[34] 4221 5-11-0 0 .... WilsonRenwick
(Martin Todhunter) *in rr: bhd fr 6th: t.o whn p.u bef 2 out: b.b.v* **40/1**
0/ **P** **Its A Story**[381] 4514 7-10-7 0 .... LucyAlexander
(Mairi Wilson) *j.lft in last: t.o 3rd: p.u bef 5th* **100/1**
424- **F** **I Got Power**[17] 4546 5-11-0 115 .... JamesReveley 117
(Keith Reveley) *trckd ldrs: effrt and cl 4th whn nt fluent 3 out: 3 l 3rd and wl hld whn fell last* **3/1[1]**
F50- **P** **Lacocodanza**[21] 4476 5-10-7 0 .... BrianHarding
(George Moore) *in rr: bhd fr 5th: t.o whn p.u bef 3 out* **100/1**

3m 51.4s (-4.40) **Going Correction** -0.125s/f (Good)
WFA 4 from 5yo+ 7lb **17** Ran SP% **117.8**
Speed ratings (Par 103): **105,104,97,88,81 79,79,79,74,74 70,58,15, , ,**
CSF £51.75 TOTE £8.50: £2.90, £2.90, £1.90; EX 60.10 Trifecta £187.10.
Owner Charlie Longsdon **Bred** John J Brennan **Trained** Over Norton, Oxon

FOCUS
They finished strung out behind the first pair in this opening maiden and it was evident the course had been selectively watered as they kicked up the turf. Fair novice form.

4890 WETHERBYRACING.CO.UK NOVICES' H'CAP CHASE (13 fncs) 2m
2:40 (2:41) (Class 5) (0-100,95) 5-Y-0+ **£2,258** (£658; £329)

Form RPR
014- **1** **Have You Had Yours (IRE)**[118] 2591 8-10-2 **78** .... AlistairFindlay[(7)] 91
(Jane Walton) *chsd ldrs: led appr 4 out: clr appr 2 out: 5 l ahd last: drvn rt out* **11/2[3]**
05U- **2** *4 ½* **Teenage Dream (IRE)**[6] 3564 6-11-8 **91** ....(vt) CharliePoste 99
(Derek Shaw) *in rr: j. slowly 6th: chsng ldrs whn blnd 9th: 2nd appr 4 out: j.lft 2 out: styd on same pce* **14/1**
406- **3** *½* **Tom Sang (FR)**[28] 4336 7-10-2 **76** ....(t) ThomasGarner[(5)] 84
(Jamie Snowden) *hld up: hdwy 9th: cl 3rd next: kpt on one pce* **5/1[2]**
050- **4** *1 ¾* **Mac's Grey (IRE)**[46] 4019 7-10-4 **73** .... MarkGrant 79
(Zoe Davison) *hld up in rr: hdwy 9th: chsng ldrs next: one pce* **66/1**
032- **5** *7* **One In A Row (IRE)**[7] 4744 7-10-12 **84** .... JohnKington[(3)] 84
(Andrew Crook) *in rr: hdwy to chse ldrs 9th: drvn bef next: fdd 2 out* **8/1**
325- **6** *4* **Miss Sunflower**[34] 4220 12-9-10 **70** ....(p) SamanthaDrake[(5)] 66
(Tina Jackson) *chsd ldrs: drvn 9th: fdd 3 out* **25/1**
31F- **7** *51* **Turf Trivia**[21] 4477 7-11-12 **95** ....(b) BarryKeniry 45
(George Moore) *chsd ldrs: blnd 2nd: wknd after 9th: sn bhd: t.o 2 out: virtually p.u* **12/1**
2P1- **P** **Hotgrove Boy**[7] 4748 7-11-4 **94** 7ex .... DaraghBourke[(7)]
(Stuart Coltherd) *led: rdr lost iron 1st: blnd 2nd: sn clr: rdr regained iron after 4th: jnd 9th: hdd: lost pl and 5th whn blnd 4 out: eased and bhd whn p.u bef next: b.b.v* **1/1[1]**

3m 57.1s (1.30) **Going Correction** +0.125s/f (Yiel) **8** Ran SP% **112.9**
Speed ratings: **101,98,98,97,94 92,66,**
CSF £69.33 CT £405.92 TOTE £5.40: £1.70, £4.60, £1.40; EX 96.80 Trifecta £552.90.
Owner Highly Recommended Partnership **Bred** Margaret McKenna **Trained** Otterburn, Northumberland

FOCUS
An eventful handicap. Modest form, rated through the second.

4891 WETHERBY RACECOURSE FAMILY SUNDAY - 13TH APRIL NOVICES' HURDLE (12 hdls) 2m 6f
3:15 (3:16) (Class 4) 4-Y-0+ **£3,119** (£915; £457; £228)

Form RPR
12P- **1** **Askamore Darsi (IRE)**[35] 4200 5-11-1 0 ....(p) HenryBrooke 108+
(Donald McCain) *led to 2nd: w ldrs: drvn to ld appr 3 out: hdd narrowly appr last: styd on to ld towards fin* **7/2**[2]

5- **2** ¾ **Almost Gemini (IRE)**[24] 4411 5-11-1 0 .... MarkGrant 107+
(Charlie Mann) *hld up: hdwy to trck ldrs 6th: cl 2nd 3 out: narrow ld appr last: hdd and no ex clsng stages* **7/1**

264- **3** 5 **Rendezvous Peak**[43] 4069 5-10-10 0 .... MattCrawley(5) 102
(Lucy Wadham) *hld up in rr: hdwy 7th: trcking ldrs 9th: cl 3rd next: upsides 2 out: kpt on same pce run-in* **4/1**[3]

034- **4** 11 **Cinnomhor**[18] 4528 6-10-1 97 .... DiarmuidO'Regan(7) 85
(Chris Grant) *chsd ldrs 5th: outpcd 3 out: kpt on to take modest 4th last* **16/1**

653- **5** 12 **Native Spa (IRE)**[14] 4609 6-10-10 0 .... AdamNicol(5) 83
(Michael Smith) *w ldrs: led 2nd: hdd next: led 9th: hdd appr next: wknd appr 2 out* **3/1**[1]

P00- **6** 33 **Frosty Dawn**[21] 4479 6-10-5 0 .... JonathanEngland(3) 44
(Mike Sowersby) *in rr: hdwy 7th: drvn 9th: sn lost pl and bhd: t.o* **100/1**

0- **7** 4 **The Purchaser (IRE)**[40] 4102 6-11-1 0 .... TomMessenger 48
(Chris Bealby) *w ldrs: led 3rd to 9th: lost pl bef next: sn bhd t.o* **7/2**[2]

P/5- **8** 77 **Henry Jenkins**[45] 4038 7-11-1 0 .... BrianHughes
(Malcolm Jefferson) *in rr: reminders 4th: bhd fr 7th: t.o 9th: eventually completed* **20/1**

5m 26.2s (-0.60) **Going Correction** -0.125s/f (Good) **8** Ran SP% **113.6**
Speed ratings (Par 105): **96,95,93,89,85 73,72,44**
CSF £27.59 TOTE £4.80: £1.70, £1.70, £1.50; EX 18.10 Trifecta £80.50.
Owner Deva Racing Darsi Partnership **Bred** William McGladdery **Trained** Cholmondeley, Cheshire

FOCUS
Not a bad novice hurdle, and the form makes sense, with the third and fourth rated close to their marks.

4892 NEW RACING UK ANYWHERE AVAILABLE NOW H'CAP CHASE (16 fncs) 2m 4f 110y
3:50 (3:51) (Class 4) (0-115,112) 5-Y-0+ **£3,768** (£1,106; £553; £276)

Form RPR
1/4- **1** **Work Boy**[16] 4578 13-11-2 107 .... SamanthaDrake(5) 114+
(Richard Drake) *chsd ldrs: drvn whn hit 11th: cl 2nd 4 out: swtchd rt appr 2 out: styd on to ld towards fin* **7/1**

P13- **2** ½ **Whiskey Ridge (IRE)**[16] 4578 8-10-11 97 .... RyanMania 102
(Sue Smith) *led: reminder 3rd: drvn appr 4 out: hdd and no ex clsng stages* **7/4**[1]

244- **3** 27 **Desgrey**[17] 4549 6-11-12 112 ....(p) WilsonRenwick 97
(Peter Niven) *chsd ldr: j.rt 4th: drvn along 11th: stmbld on landing 4 out: wknd appr 2 out* **11/4**[2]

/P3- **4** 32 **Mister Stickler (IRE)**[21] 4477 10-11-2 102 .... BrianHughes 53
(Chris Grant) *trckd ldrs: outpcd 12th: lost pl appr next: t.o 2 out* **8/1**

0P5- **5** 42 **Champagne Agent (IRE)**[28] 4341 8-11-12 112 ....(p) PeterBuchanan 26
(Lucinda Russell) *chsd ldrs: pushed along 8th: lost pl 10th: sn bhd: t.o 4 out* **14/1**

251- **P** **Alpha One (IRE)**[34] 4222 8-11-9 109 .... DenisO'Regan
(Chris Grant) *trckd ldrs: p.u bef 9th: lame* **6/1**[3]

5m 11.5s (3.70) **Going Correction** +0.125s/f (Yiel) **6** Ran SP% **107.6**
Speed ratings: **97,96,86,74,58**
CSF £18.86 TOTE £7.20: £3.20, £1.70; EX 17.90 Trifecta £61.70.
Owner Mrs J Drake **Bred** Mrs M Parker **Trained** Ilkley, W Yorks

FOCUS
A moderate handicap. The winner is rated 3lb off his 2011 mark.

4893 WATCH RACING UK ON CHANNEL 432 H'CAP HURDLE (11 hdls) 2m 4f
4:20 (4:22) (Class 4) (0-120,118) 4-Y-0+ **£3,119** (£915; £457; £228)

Form RPR
043- **1** **Feast Of Fire (IRE)**[21] 4478 7-10-8 100 .... BrianHughes 104+
(Mike Sowersby) *hld up: hdwy appr 3 out: sn upsides: level last: styd on to ld run-in: drvn out* **8/1**

0/0- **2** 2½ **Parc Des Princes (USA)**[18] 4533 8-10-10 102 .... DenisO'Regan 105
(Nicky Richards) *w ldr: shkn up and led narrowly appr last: hdd and no ex last 50yds* **16/1**

P53- **3** 8 **Divers (FR)**[76] 3475 10-11-5 118 ....(b) NickSlatter(7) 114
(Donald McCain) *t.k.h: trckd ldrs 6th: led narrowly 3 out: hdd appr last: fdd* **6/1**[3]

032- **4** 5 **Hartside (GER)**[16] 4573 5-11-4 117 .... MrRWinks(7) 107
(Peter Winks) *chsd ldrs: upsides 3 out: wknd between last 2* **8/1**

5/F- **5** nk **Hurraboru (IRE)**[318] 114 7-11-4 113 .... TonyKelly(3) 103
(David Thompson) *in rr: detached last and drvn 8th: kpt on appr 2 out: nvr a factor* **25/1**

2P4- **6** ½ **Murtys Delight (IRE)**[27] 4351 7-10-10 107 ....(t) ChristopherWard(5) 98
(Dr Richard Newland) *trckd ldrs: hung lft appr 3 out: j.rt and wknd 2 out* **11/4**[1]

221- **7** ¾ **Summerlea (IRE)**[21] 4475 8-11-1 107 .... WilsonRenwick 96
(Micky Hammond) *in tch: drvn and outpcd 3 out: no threat after* **9/2**[2]

503- **8** 5 **Kent Street (IRE)**[15] 4596 9-10-7 102 .... JonathanEngland(3) 86
(Sue Smith) *set v stdy pce: reminders 5th: sn increased pce: hdd next: lost pl after 8th* **6/1**[3]

/24- **9** 22 **South Stack**[146] 2025 9-11-9 115 .... NickScholfield 80
(Kim Bailey) *chsd ldrs: nt fluent and lost pl 7th: lost pl bef 3 out: sn bhd: t.o* **8/1**

5m 14.9s (15.40) **Going Correction** -0.125s/f (Good) **9** Ran SP% **116.5**
Speed ratings (Par 105): **64,63,59,57,57 57,57,55,46**
CSF £119.63 CT £824.59 TOTE £9.10: £2.60, £2.90, £2.30; EX 152.60 Trifecta £2474.50 Part won. Pool: £3,299.36 - 0.92 winning units..
Owner Mrs E A Verity **Bred** Patrick Joyce **Trained** Goodmanham, E Yorks

FOCUS
A modest and slowly run handicap. The first two are rated back to their best.

4894 FOLLOW @WETHERBYRACES ON TWITTER H'CAP CHASE (18 fncs) 3m 1f
4:55 (4:55) (Class 4) (0-120,118) 5-Y-0+ **£3,768** (£1,106; £553; £276)

Form RPR
402- **1** **Fiddlers Reel**[17] 4551 11-11-7 113 ....(p) RyanMania 127+
(Jane Clark) *trckd ldrs: led 8th: 3 l ahd whn blnd 3 out: drvn and styd on wl to forge clr run-in* **7/2**[2]

512- **2** 9 **Everaard (USA)**[36] 4190 8-10-11 103 ....(tp) JamesReveley 109
(Philip Kirby) *rn in snatches: reminders 3rd outpcd 14th: kpt on and 3rd next: 2 l 2nd appr 2 out: kpt on same pce run-in* **11/4**[1]

/32- **3** 32 **Harris Hawk**[28] 4339 9-11-3 109 ....(p) BrianHughes 84
(John Wade) *chsd ldrs: hit 7th: reminders next: drvn 9th: outpcd bef 4 out: tk modest 3rd last* **5/1**[3]

31P- **4** nk **Settledoutofcourt (IRE)**[50] 3939 8-11-8 114 .... PeterBuchanan 89
(Lucinda Russell) *led: hdd 8th: lost pl appr 4 out* **7/1**

2FP- **5** 2 **Deise Dynamo (IRE)**[103] 2901 6-11-11 117 ....(p) HenryBrooke 90
(Donald McCain) *chsd ldrs: nt fluent 12th: outpcd next: lost pl appr 4 out* **10/1**

562- **F** **Saints And Sinners (IRE)**[42] 4077 6-11-6 115 .... JakeGreenall(3) 119+
(Michael Easterby) *sn chsng ldrs: 2nd 11th: 3 l down overall in 3rd and looking hld whn fell 2 out* **7/2**[2]

6m 8.6s (-0.80) **Going Correction** +0.125s/f (Yiel) **6** Ran SP% **109.4**
Speed ratings: **106,103,92,92,92**
CSF £13.16 CT £41.54 TOTE £4.10: £1.90, £3.30; EX 13.50 Trifecta £55.80.
Owner Mrs Jane Clark **Bred** Mrs Jane Clark **Trained** Kelso, Borders

FOCUS
A modest staying handicap. There's probably more to come from the winner.

4895 RACING AGAIN ON 28TH MARCH STANDARD OPEN NATIONAL HUNT FLAT RACE 2m 110y
5:25 (5:27) (Class 6) 4-6-Y-0 **£1,711** (£498; £249)

Form RPR
1 **Supasundae** 4-10-9 0 .... AndrewTinkler 105+
(Tim Fitzgerald) *trckd ldrs: styd on to ld over 1f out: forged clr* **9/2**[3]

2 2½ **Azure Glamour (IRE)** 5-11-2 0 .... BrianHarding 109
(Nicky Richards) *hld up in rr: hdwy 7f out: sn chsng ldrs: pushed along over 4f out: styd on to take 2nd nr fin* **8/1**

3 1 **Along Came Theo (IRE)** 4-10-6 0 .... JohnKington(3) 101
(Andrew Crook) *mid-div: hdwy to chse ldrs 5f out: led over 2f out: hdd over 1f out: kpt on same pce* **14/1**

4 1 **Special Wells** 5-11-2 0 .... RyanMania 108
(Sue Smith) *trckd ldrs: upsides over 2f out: kpt on one pce fnl f* **9/1**

2- **5** 4½ **Hitman Harry**[112] 2738 6-11-2 0 .... DenisO'Regan 104
(Tina Jackson) *hld up in mid-div: hdwy to chse ldrs 4f out: edgd rt and one pce over 1f out* **7/2**[2]

4- **6** 5 **Orby's Man (IRE)**[30] 4310 5-11-2 0 ....(t[1]) NickScholfield 99
(Charlie Longsdon) *w ldr: led after 5f: hdd over 2f out: wknd over 1f out* **9/4**[1]

0- **7** 1¾ **Teescomponents Max**[27] 4349 5-11-2 0 .... JamesReveley 97
(Keith Reveley) *hld up in rr: gd hdwy 6f out: chsng ldrs over 3f out: wknd over 1f out: sn eased* **16/1**

4/5- **8** 14 **Lucky Emily**[98] 3016 5-10-9 0 .... BrianHughes 78
(John Mackie) *trckd ldrs: effrt over 4f out: lost pl 3f out* **20/1**

9 1¾ **Tomorrow's Legend** 4-10-9 0 .... BarryKeniry 76
(George Moore) *in rr: bhd fnl 5f* **20/1**

10 3 **Riquet The King (FR)** 5-11-2 0 .... DavidEngland 81
(Alan Brown) *in rr: drvn 6f out: sn bhd* **66/1**

0- **11** 2 **New Zafeen (IRE)**[87] 3214 4-10-6 0 .... TonyKelly(3) 72
(Rebecca Menzies) *trckd ldrs: lost pl 3f out* **100/1**

0- **12** 10 **One Act**[13] 4618 5-10-6 0 .... JakeGreenall(3) 63
(Michael Easterby) *mid-div: lost pl 5f out: sn bhd* **40/1**

13 3½ **Dicky Shore** 6-10-9 0 .... DiarmuidO'Regan(7) 67
(Ashley Dodgson) *led 5f: lost pl 4f out: sn bhd* **66/1**

3m 48.1s (-2.10) **Going Correction** -0.125s/f (Good)
WFA 4 from 5yo+ 7lb **13** Ran SP% **120.8**
Speed ratings: **99,97,97,96,94 92,91,85,84,82 81,77,75**
CSF £38.43 TOTE £5.50: £1.90, £2.70, £4.50; EX 45.50 Trifecta £587.20.
Owner T J Fitzgerald **Bred** Newsells Park Stud **Trained** Norton, N Yorks

FOCUS
Not a bad bumper with the first four all newcomers. The form is rated around the next two home.
T/Plt: £170.10 to a £1 stake. Pool: £89,706.66 - 384.89 winning units T/Qpdt: £18.20 to a £1 stake. Pool: £6,913.74 - 280.40 winning units WG

4268 HAYDOCK (L-H)
Wednesday, March 19

OFFICIAL GOING: Good (good to soft in places on chase course; chs 6.6, hdl 6.0)
Wind: fresh 1/2 against Weather: fine and sunny but very breezy

4896 32RED CASINO H'CAP CHASE (THE JOCKEY CLUB GRASSROOTS JUMPS SERIES QUALIFIER) 3m
2:10 (2:11) (Class 4) (0-115,115) 5-Y-0+ **£4,873** (£1,431; £715; £357)

Form RPR
212- **1** **Bennys Well (IRE)**[17] 4580 8-11-0 106 .... JonathanEngland(3) 117+
(Sue Smith) *led to 4th: led 6th: styd on gamely fr 2 out* **11/1**

216- **2** 3¾ **Presented (IRE)**[25] 4427 7-11-8 111 ....(p) APMcCoy 119
(Brian Ellison) *chsd ldrs: cl 2nd and drvn 14th: hung lft 3 out: swtchd rt appr next: styd on same pce* **9/2**[2]

/P4- **3** 10 **Blenheim Brook (IRE)**[100] 3001 9-11-12 115 .... PeterBuchanan 115
(Lucinda Russell) *hld up in rr: hdwy 14th: handy 3rd next: one pce* **14/1**

P44- **4** 6 **Purcell's Bridge (FR)**[17] 4580 7-11-6 109 .... WilsonRenwick 103
(Rose Dobbin) *hld up in rr: hdwy 14th: modest 4th 3 out: one pce* **11/2**[3]

141- **5** 1¾ **Carli King (IRE)**[22] 4481 8-11-10 113 ....(p) TomMessenger 106
(Caroline Bailey) *w ldr: led 4th to 6th: hit 8th: drvn 14th: lost pl next* **9/2**[2]

/62- **P** **Dancing Art (IRE)**[74] 3524 8-11-7 110 .... JamesReveley
(Keith Reveley) *in rr: nt fluent 9th: drvn 14th: sn lost pl: bhd whn p.u bef 3 out: b.b.v* **9/2**[2]

The Form Book Jumps, Raceform Ltd, Compton, RG20 6NL.

121- **P** **Harris (IRE)**[14] 4613 7-11-12 **115**.....(p) TomScudamore
(William Kinsey) *chsd ldrs: hit 7th: drvn 9th: lost pl 12th: sn bhd: t.o whn p.u bef 4 out* **3/1**[1]

6m 5.4s (-8.60) **Going Correction** -0.675s/f (Firm) 7 Ran SP% **109.9**
Speed ratings: **87,85,82,80,79** ,
CSF £55.00 TOTE £10.10: £3.70, £1.30; EX 35.60 Trifecta £394.80.
Owner Mrs A Ellis **Bred** J Costello **Trained** High Eldwick, W Yorks

FOCUS
Shared bends. Stable bend out 16yds, increasing race distances by about 50yds per circuit. Bend out of back straight at innermost configuration. The opening 3m chase was run over roughly half a furlong extra as a result. It was run at a fair gallop and the drying ground was evident in the home straight. A step up from the winner with the second to his mark.

4897 32RED BURNING DESIRE SLOT H'CAP HURDLE 2m 4f
2:40 (2:40) (Class 3) (0-135,131) 4-Y-0+ **£7,147** (£2,098; £1,049; £524)

Form RPR
000- **1** **Hidden Justice (IRE)**[25] 4423 5-10-13 **125**..... DeanPratt(7) 131+
(John Quinn) *hld up towards rr: hdwy to chse ldrs 7th: hmpd 3 out: styd on to chse ldrs between last 2: swtchd rt 100yds out: r.o to ld post* **8/1**

512- **2** *shd* **Rumble Of Thunder (IRE)**[31] 4306 8-11-4 **128**..... AdamNicol(5) 130
(Philip Kirby) *led to 4th: w ldrs: led 2 out: tired and hdd post* **6/1**[3]

P4P- **3** *1 ¼* **The Knoxs (IRE)**[32] 4271 11-10-10 **122**..... DaraghBourke(7) 123
(Sandy Thomson) *hld up in rr: hdwy to chse ldrs whn slt;ly hmpd 3 out: kpt on to take 3rd nr fin* **20/1**

403- **4** *hd* **Kayaan**[31] 4306 7-10-12 **120**..... KielanWoods(3) 121
(Pam Sly) *t.k.h in rr: hdwy to trck ldrs 7th: cl 3rd whn hit 2 out: hung lft and kpt on same pce run-in* **10/1**

330- **5** *8* **Dartford Warbler (IRE)**[18] 4549 7-11-6 **125**..... RyanMania 121
(Sue Smith) *w ldrs: led after 7th: hdd 2 out: wknd last 75yds* **12/1**

6 *20* **Moveable Asset (IRE)**[187] 1453 6-11-9 **128**..... HaddenFrost 103
(Roger Curtis) *hld up in rr: hdwy to trck ldrs 6th: lost pl 3 out* **33/1**

221- **7** *3* **Cloud Creeper (IRE)**[16] 4594 7-11-4 **123**..... TomO'Brien 103+
(Philip Hobbs) *chsd ldrs: hmpd 3 out: lost pl bef next* **4/1**[2]

P54- **8** *14* **Master Of The Hall (IRE)**[11] 4670 10-11-3 **122**.....[1] WilsonRenwick 82
(Micky Hammond) *chsd ldrs: drvn 6th: lost pl bef next: sn bhd* **22/1**

1/P- **9** *7* **Shalone**[109] 2807 10-11-4 **123**.....(p) GerardTumelty 77
(Adrian Wintle) *chsd ldrs: lost pl and behibnd whn hmpd 3 out: sn eased* **33/1**

/0F- **F** **Top Gamble (IRE)**[38] 4174 6-11-12 **131**.....(t) TomScudamore
(David Pipe) *trckd ldrs: led 4th: hit 6th: hdd after next: upsides whn fell 3 out* **15/8**[1]

4m 40.2s (-12.80) **Going Correction** -0.525s/f (Firm) 10 Ran SP% **112.0**
Speed ratings (Par 107): **104,103,103,103,100 92,90,85,82,**
CSF £50.37 CT £916.79 TOTE £8.70: £2.10, £2.60, £5.00; EX 44.00 Trifecta £1486.50.
Owner Highfield Racing 2 **Bred** Ballylinch Stud **Trained** Settrington, N Yorks
■ Stewards' Enquiry : Kielan Woods caution: careless riding.

FOCUS
A fair handicap. They went a sound enough gallop and, after drama three out, it saw a very tight finish. A hurdles best from the winner with the second to his mark.

4898 32RED FREE £10 BONUS NOVICES' LIMITED H'CAP CHASE 2m 4f
3:10 (3:11) (Class 3) (0-125,125) 5-Y-0+ **£6,498** (£1,908; £954; £477)

Form RPR
431- **1** **Bincombe**[19] 4539 6-10-9 **112**..... TomO'Brien 126+
(Philip Hobbs) *w ldr: drvn 11th: upsides 3 out: narrow ld next: drvn rt out* **11/4**[1]

123- **2** *3 ¼* **Alderbrook Lad (IRE)**[37] 4188 8-10-10 **118**..... JoeCollivér(5) 128
(Micky Hammond) *led: jnd 3 out: hdd next: styd on same pce* **10/1**

313- **3** *10* **Clondaw Knight (IRE)**[41] 4106 6-11-5 **122**..... PeterBuchanan 125
(Lucinda Russell) *chsd ldng pair: drvn 8th: handy 3rd whn nt fluent 4 out: wkng whn hit 2 out* **11/4**[1]

240/ **4** *dist* **Ballymacahillcross (IRE)**[404] 4108 6-10-7 **110**..... PaulMoloney
(Evan Williams) *trckd ldrs: nt fluent 1st: lost pl 6th: bhd 8th: t.o whn j.lft 11th: j. bdly lft last* **11/2**[3]

231- **P** **Rocking Blues (FR)**[18] 4551 9-10-10 **113**..... WilsonRenwick
(Rose Dobbin) *hld up in rr: hit 7th: drvn to chse ldrs 11th: wknd bef next: bhd whn p.u bef 3 out* **9/2**[2]

/P2- **P** **Oscatara (IRE)**[19] 4530 7-11-8 **125**..... APMcCoy
(Donald McCain) *t.k.h: trckd ldng pair: hit 6th: drvn 11th: wknd appr next: bhd whn p.u bef 3 out* **6/1**

4m 53.0s (-17.00) **Going Correction** -0.675s/f (Firm) 6 Ran SP% **110.3**
Speed ratings: **107,105,101,** ,
CSF £25.62 TOTE £3.00: £2.70, £2.00; EX 28.20 Trifecta £38.30.
Owner Martin Short **Bred** R D And Mrs J S Chugg **Trained** Withycombe, Somerset

FOCUS
There was no hanging about in this modest novice handicap yet the first pair were always up there and dominated. They should still be competitive when reassessed.

4899 32RED.COM H'CAP HURDLE 2m
3:40 (3:40) (Class 3) (0-140,130) 4-Y-0+ **£7,147** (£2,098; £1,049; £524)

Form RPR
/46- **1** **Kudu Country (IRE)**[25] 4426 8-11-4 **122**..... DougieCostello 126
(Tom Tate) *led to 4th: nt fluent 6th: rallied 2 out: 3rd last: styd on to ld towards fin* **14/1**

206- **2** *¾* **Discovery Bay**[61] 3758 6-11-10 **128**..... APMcCoy 133+
(Brian Ellison) *t.k.h: trckd ldrs 3rd: led appr 2 out: drvn 3 l clr appr last: hdd and no ex clsng stages* **5/1**[2]

F2U- **3** *¾* **Roman Flight (IRE)**[18] 4558 6-11-12 **130**.....(v) WayneHutchinson 131
(David Dennis) *hld up in rr: hdwy 3 out: styd on run-in* **6/1**[3]

503- **4** *5* **Aazif (IRE)**[31] 4300 5-11-11 **129**.....(t) WillKennedy 126
(Ian Williams) *sn w ldr: led 4th: hdd appr 2 out: one pce* **9/1**

232- **5** *¾* **Sleepy Haven (IRE)**[42] 4081 4-10-12 **123**..... SeanQuinlan 112
(Jennie Candlish) *in rr: kpt on fr 3 out: nvr a threat* **16/1**

2U3- **6** *4 ½* **Smart Ruler (IRE)**[61] 3758 8-11-0 **118**..... BrianHughes 110
(James Moffatt) *hld up: hdwy 6th: chsng ldrs next: wknd appr 2 out* **8/1**

1/4- **7** *5* **Karazhan**[97] 3031 6-11-11 **129**..... DavidBass 116
(Nicky Henderson) *hld up in rr: pushed wd bnd bef 3 out: sn wknd* **11/4**[1]

635- **8** *32* **Moscow Me (IRE)**[91] 3157 7-10-1 **105**..... PaulMoloney 64
(Henry Oliver) *trckd ldrs: hit 2nd: lost pl appr 3 out: t.o last: virtually p.u* **6/1**[3]

603- **F** **Robbie**[19] 4532 10-11-12 **130**..... JamesReveley
(Keith Reveley) *chsd ldrs: lost pl sn after 6th: bhd whn fell next* **14/1**

3m 52.5s (-11.70) **Going Correction** -0.525s/f (Firm)
WFA 4 from 5yo+ 7lb 9 Ran SP% **112.2**
Speed ratings (Par 107): **108,107,107,104,104 102,99,83,**
CSF £80.37 CT £468.56 TOTE £13.00: £3.80, £1.80, £2.30; EX 57.90 Trifecta £233.00.
Owner The Flat Cap Syndicate **Bred** Roger A Ryan **Trained** Tadcaster, N Yorks

FOCUS
A competitive handicap, run at a routine gallop, and the principals were clear at the finish. The winner is rated to last season's C&D mark, and the second should have won.

4900 32RED THUNDERSTRUCK II SLOT H'CAP CHASE 2m 4f
4:15 (4:15) (Class 3) (0-135,135) 5-Y-0+ **£8,122** (£2,385; £1,192; £596)

Form RPR
F61- **1** **Shadows Lengthen**[19] 4532 8-11-6 **129**..... BrianHughes 132
(Michael Easterby) *hld up in rr: hdwy 10th: effrt 4 out: 3rd last: n.m.r clsng stages: styd on to ld post* **5/1**[2]

42P- **2** *shd* **Real Milan (IRE)**[18] 4544 9-11-4 **127**.....(bt[1]) HenryBrooke 131+
(Donald McCain) *w ldr: led after 6th: drvn over 3 l clr run-in: faultered and edgd rt last 50yds: hdd post* **11/2**[3]

015- **3** *hd* **Granville Island (IRE)**[19] 4532 7-11-4 **127**..... SeanQuinlan 131+
(Jennie Candlish) *hld up in rr: hit 9th: hdwy on outer to trck ldrs 11th: styd on and 2nd last: kpt on towards fin* **9/1**

255- **4** *18* **Gansey (IRE)**[25] 4430 12-11-4 **127**..... RyanMania 115
(Sue Smith) *chsd ldrs: mstke 7th: wknd appr last* **8/1**

P2P- **5** *3 ¼* **Noble Legend**[11] 4681 7-11-12 **135**..... AndrewThornton 120
(Caroline Bailey) *led: hdd after 6th: wknd between last 2* **6/1**

14P- **6** *13* **Rudemeister (IRE)**[61] 3759 8-11-0 **123**.....(t) PeterBuchanan 94
(Lucinda Russell) *mid-div: chsd ldrs 10th: lost pl appr 4 out* **9/2**[1]

1/P- **7** *10* **Tiptoeaway (IRE)**[25] 4418 9-11-4 **127**..... BrianHarding 89
(Tim Easterby) *chsd ldrs: drvn 11th: lost pl appr next* **7/1**

13P- **F** **Reaping The Reward (IRE)**[45] 4055 10-11-2 **130**..... CraigNichol(5)
(Lucinda Russell) *hld up in rr: hdwy 10th: chsng ldrs 4 out: 6th and one pce whn fell next* **20/1**

544- **P** **Ros Castle (IRE)**[34] 4236 8-10-8 **117**.....(p) WilsonRenwick
(Rose Dobbin) *prom: lost pl and reminders 6th: lost pl next: bhd fr 9th: t.o whn p.u bef 4 out* **8/1**

4m 54.5s (-15.50) **Going Correction** -0.675s/f (Firm) 9 Ran SP% **114.0**
Speed ratings: **104,103,103,96,95 90,86,** ,
CSF £32.65 CT £239.16 TOTE £5.80: £1.80, £2.40, £3.40; EX 21.40 Trifecta £379.10.
Owner T A F Frost **Bred** London Thoroughbred Services Ltd **Trained** Sheriff Hutton, N Yorks
■ Stewards' Enquiry : Henry Brooke caution: careless riding.

FOCUS
Not a bad handicap and another race that saw changing fortunes on the run-in. The winner is rated to his mark.

4901 32RED "FIXED BRUSH" NOVICES' HURDLE 2m 4f
4:50 (4:51) (Class 4) 4-Y-0+ **£3,898** (£1,144; £572; £286)

Form RPR
P46- **1** **Garrahalish (IRE)**[20] 4510 6-11-8 128..... CharliePoste 125
(Robin Dickin) *t.k.h: trckd ldng pair: drvn 7th: lft handy 3rd next: styd on run-in: led last 75yds* **9/2**[3]

32P- **2** *1 ¼* **Straidnahanna (IRE)**[32] 4272 5-11-1 121..... RyanMania 120+
(Sue Smith) *led to 3rd: w ldr: drvn whn lft in ld 3 out: 4 l ahd whn landed awkwardly last: sn rdn: fdd and hdd last 75yds* **1/1**[1]

3P- **3** *10* **Spiculas (IRE)**[28] 4343 5-11-1 0..... JamesReveley 109
(Keith Reveley) *hld up: trckd ldrs 5th: lft handy 2nd 3 out hit next: wknd between last 2* **16/1**

0/ **4** *14* **Present Lodger (IRE)**[458] 3098 6-11-1 0..... PeterBuchanan 95
(Lucinda Russell) *chsd ldrs: drvn 7th: lost pl bef next: lft modest 4th 3 out* **12/1**

/65- **5** *29* **Queen Olivia**[109] 2824 6-10-8 0.....[1] AndrewThornton 62
(Caroline Bailey) *hld up in rr: mstke 1st: sme hdwy 7th: sn lost pl and bhd* **28/1**

01- **F** **Count Danilo (IRE)**[92] 3148 5-11-8 0..... TomScudamore 125+
(David Pipe) *sn w ldr: led 3rd: 2 l clr and travelling strly whn fell 3 out* **11/4**[2]

50- **P** **Prairie Lad**[80] 3392 6-11-1 0..... DougieCostello
(Sandy Thomson) *j. slowly 1st: nt fluent and sn bhd: t.o 5th: p.u bef 3 out* **66/1**

4m 46.0s (-7.00) **Going Correction** -0.525s/f (Firm) 7 Ran SP% **113.4**
Speed ratings (Par 105): **93,92,88,82,71** ,
CSF £9.62 TOTE £4.80: £2.20, £1.10; EX 12.30 Trifecta £71.60.
Owner Just 4 Fun **Bred** Godfrey Moylan **Trained** Alcester, Warwicks

FOCUS
For the third contest running, this novice event saw a leader capitulate after the last. It was run at a fair gallop and the form is straightforward enough, with the fortunate winner rated to his mark.

4902 32RED TOMB RAIDER SLOT STANDARD OPEN NATIONAL HUNT FLAT RACE 2m
5:20 (5:21) (Class 5) 4-5-Y-0 **£1,949** (£572; £286; £143)

Form RPR
3- **1** **Palermo Don**[63] 3719 4-10-9 0..... APMcCoy 106+
(Donald McCain) *set slow pce: t.k.h and green: increased pce 6f out: wnt for home wl over 3f out: pushed clr over 1f out: readily* **8/11**[1]

2 *3* **Pied Du Roi (IRE)** 4-10-2 0..... CharlieDeutsch(7) 99
(Charlie Longsdon) *trckd ldrs: upsides 8f out: drvn over 3f out: kpt on same pce* **5/1**[2]

3 *3 ½* **Crinkle Crags (IRE)** 4-10-9 0..... BrianHarding 96
(Nicky Richards) *hld up in rr: effrt over 2f out: styd on to take 3rd nr fin* **7/1**

1- **4** *1* **Grove Silver (IRE)**[25] 4431 5-11-4 0..... KillianMoore(5) 109
(Jennie Candlish) *trckd ldrs: t.k.h: one pce fnl 2f* **6/1**[3]

3- **5** *¾* **Varene De Vauzelle (FR)**[110] 2795 5-11-2 0..... BrianHughes 101
(James Ewart) *trckd ldrs: one pce fnl 2f* **20/1**

0- **6** *12* **Red Hott Robbie**[7] 4763 5-10-11 0..... CharlieWallis(5) 89
(Giuseppe Fierro) *hld up in rr: drvn over 5f out: sn wl outpcd* **66/1**

7 *1 ½* **The Lady Maggi (FR)** 4-9-11 0..... CraigNichol(5) 74
(Lucinda Russell) *hld up in rr: hdwy to trck ldrs 6f out: lost pl 2f out* **20/1**

4m 31.6s (33.00)
WFA 4 from 5yo 7lb 7 Ran SP% **112.4**
CSF £4.45 TOTE £1.50: £1.10, £4.00; EX 7.10 Trifecta £27.70.
Owner T G Leslie **Bred** Pendley Farm **Trained** Cholmondeley, Cheshire

FOCUS
This usually falls the way of a promising sort. It was very slowly run and is rated around those with previous experience.
T/Plt: £501.60 to a £1 stake. Pool: £94,950.71 - 138.17 winning tickets. T/Qpdt: £22.80 to a £1 stake. Pool: £7,327.44 - 237.00 winning tickets. WG

[4700]WARWICK (L-H)

Wednesday, March 19

OFFICIAL GOING: Good changing to good (good to firm in places) after race 1 (2:20)

Wind: Light behind Weather: Cloudy with sunny spells

4903 MHM ONE CALL MAIDEN HURDLE (11 hdls) 2m 5f
2:20 (2:20) (Class 4) 4-Y-0+ **£3,249** (£954; £477; £238)

Form RPR

163- **1** **Ulzana's Raid (IRE)**[101] 2978 5-11-1 0 RobertThornton 124+
(Alan King) *a.p: chsd ldr whn n.m.r after 3 out: mstke next: led appr last: r.o* **13/8**[1]

/24- **2** 2 ¼ **Java Rose**[20] 3153 5-10-8 0 SamTwiston-Davies 112
(Charlie Longsdon) *a.p: ev ch fr 2 out: tl rdn and styd on same pce flat* **20/1**

/P3- **3** 4 **Master Todd (IRE)**[11] 4672 9-11-1 115 (t) NickScholfield 115
(Grant Cann) *a.p: chsd ldr 4th: led 6th: rdn and hdd appr last: no ex flat* **14/1**

342- **4** 11 **Broadway Symphony (IRE)**[28] 4351 7-11-1 122 MarkGrant 104
(Tracey L Bailey) *hld up: hdwy 6th: rdn and wknd 2 out* **3/1**[2]

00F- **5** 1 **Couldhavehaditall (IRE)**[4] 4808 6-11-1 0 DenisO'Regan 102
(Paul Webber) *hld up: pushed along and hdwy after 3 out: wknd next* **10/1**

/44- **6** 4 ½ **Presenting The Way**[111] 2761 7-11-1 0 RyanMahon 98
(Harry Fry) *led to 6th: rdn and wknd appr 2 out* **12/1**

644- **7** 1 **Sukiyaki (IRE)**[47] 4019 5-11-1 98 NoelFehily 99
(Charlie Longsdon) *prom tl rdn and wknd appr 2 out* **14/1**

060- **8** 11 **Carpies Boy**[20] 4506 5-10-5 0 (t) WilliamFeatherstone(10) 86
(Warren Greatrex) *mid-div: hdwy 5th: wknd 3 out* **100/1**

434- **9** ¾ **Rio Milan (IRE)**[16] 4596 8-10-10 115 (t) ConorShoemark(5) 85
(Fergal O'Brien) *hld up: hdwy 7th: wknd 3 out* **6/1**[3]

0- **10** ¾ **Diamond Pro (IRE)**[50] 2886 5-11-1 0 JamesDavies 84
(Christopher Kellett) *prom: rdn after 8th: wknd next* **200/1**

05- **11** 1 ¾ **Carn Rock**[10] 4702 6-10-12 0 PeterCarberry(3) 82
(Michael Gates) *hld up: bhd fr 7th* **150/1**

000- **12** hd **Moorlands George**[38] 4175 6-10-12 0 MattGriffiths(3) 82
(Jeremy Scott) *hld up: hdwy 5th: wknd 7th* **100/1**

4- **13** hd **Buckontupence (IRE)**[21] 4492 6-11-1 0 LiamTreadwell 82
(James Evans) *hld up: rdn and wknd 3 out* **100/1**

000- **14** 6 **Top Show**[25] 4424 5-11-1 0 AlainCawley 76
(Dean Ivory) *bhd fr 4th* **100/1**

F- **15** 19 **London Skolar**[26] 4401 4-10-4 0 JackQuinlan(3) 49
(James Eustace) *hld up: a in rr: wknd 8th* **100/1**

00- **16** ½ **Gaye Memories**[119] 2600 6-10-8 0 HarrySkelton 49
(Dan Skelton) *chsd ldr to 4th: mstke and lost pl next: bhd fr 6th* **100/1**

6- **P** **Flinstone (IRE)**[38] 4177 5-11-1 0 RichieMcLernon
(Jonjo O'Neill) *hld up: plld hrd: nt fluent: hdwy 5th: wknd appr 7th: bhd whn p.u bef 2 out* **50/1**

4m 52.5s (-22.50) **Going Correction** -1.00s/f (Hard)
WFA 4 from 5yo+ 8lb **17** Ran SP% **121.3**
Speed ratings (Par 105): **102,101,99,95,95 93,92,88,88,88 87,87,87,85,77 77,**
CSF £37.19 TOTE £2.60: £1.60, £2.90, £3.50; EX 27.30 Trifecta £482.30.
Owner Thomas Barr **Bred** M Brennan **Trained** Barbury Castle, Wilts

FOCUS
Following the first, the going was changed to good, good to firm in places (from good), with some jockeys describing the ground as "rough". The last hurdle was less than a furlong from the post, which was closer than usual. Not form to go overboard about, especially as the early pace wasn't particularly quick, but the winner looks a fair prospect.

4904 BRANDON HIRE GROUP NOVICES' HURDLE (8 hdls) 2m
2:50 (2:52) (Class 4) 4-Y-0+ **£3,249** (£954; £477; £238)

Form RPR

31- **1** **Saint Jerome (IRE)**[21] 2466 4-10-13 117 JackDoyle 120+
(Jamie Osborne) *mde all and sn clr: hit 2 out and last: unchal* **7/1**[3]

1F2- **2** 6 **Long Lunch**[56] 3838 5-11-6 125 NoelFehily 122+
(Charlie Longsdon) *a.p: chsd wnr after 3rd: rdn appr 2 out: styd on same pce* **11/10**[1]

3 3 ¼ **Worthy Award (IRE)**[101] 6-10-9 0 MauriceLinehan(5) 112
(Jonjo O'Neill) *prom: rdn after 3 out: styd on same pce* **25/1**

0F- **4** 1 ¾ **Storm Of Swords (IRE)**[96] 3061 6-11-0 0 HarrySkelton 109
(Dan Skelton) *prom: rdn appr 2 out: styd on same pce* **7/1**[3]

5/2- **5** 11 **Yabadabadoo**[136] 2252 6-11-0 0 AidanColeman 99
(Emma Lavelle) *hld up: plld hrd: hdwy 4th: rdn and wknd after 3 out* **7/1**[3]

U- **6** 13 **The Yank**[72] 2563 5-10-11 0 RobertDunne(3) 87
(Richard Lee) *hld up: hdwy 4th: rdn and wknd after 3 out* **66/1**

54- **7** nk **Less Time (IRE)**[16] 4598 6-11-0 0 RichieMcLernon 87
(Jonjo O'Neill) *chsd ldrs: pushed along 5th: wknd next* **25/1**

62- **8** 13 **Neighbourhood (USA)**[24] 4450 6-11-0 0 LiamTreadwell 75
(James Evans) *chsd clr ldr tl after 3rd: wknd 5th* **13/2**[2]

/46- **9** 22 **Lotus Pond (IRE)**[106] 2876 6-11-0 0 RobertThornton 56
(Alan King) *hld up: sme hdwy 4th: sn rdn and wknd* **20/1**

23- **10** 5 **Lucky Thirteen**[112] 2745 6-11-0 0 RichardJohnson 51
(Richard Phillips) *bhd fr 3rd: hmpd next* **25/1**

5- **11** 1 **Saint John Henry (FR)**[17] 4569 4-10-7 0 ConorO'Farrell 43
(David Pipe) *hld up: bhd fr 3rd* **25/1**

0- **P** **Emiratesdotcom**[105] 2886 8-10-7 0 ChrisDavies(7)
(Milton Bradley) *hld up: hit 2nd: bhd whn hmpd 4th: p.u bef 2 out* **100/1**

U **Egotist (IRE)**[6] 6-10-9 0 (t) CharlieWallis(5)
(Milton Bradley) *nt fluent: bhd whn j.lft and uns rdr 4th* **100/1**

P **Just Gets Better (IRE)**[222] 5-10-4 0 (t[1]) MikeyHamill(10)
(Sean Curran) *sn behind: p.u bef 2 out* **100/1**

0- **F** **L Stig**[103] 2926 4-10-4 0 JakeGreenall(3)
(Henry Daly) *hld up: a in rr: bhd whn fell 4th* **66/1**

3m 35.1s (-21.40) **Going Correction** -1.00s/f (Hard)
WFA 4 from 5yo+ 7lb **15** Ran SP% **124.6**
Speed ratings (Par 105): **113,110,108,107,102 95,95,88,77,75 74, , ,**
CSF £14.86 TOTE £8.20: £3.10, £1.20, £6.70; EX 17.70 Trifecta £394.00.
Owner Mrs F Walwyn **Bred** P Turley **Trained** Upper Lambourn, Berks

FOCUS
This was an extremely impressive performance by the winner, who looks a fair juvenile.

4905 FAIRPORT TRELAWNY H'CAP CHASE (22 fncs) 3m 5f
3:20 (3:20) (Class 4) (0-105,99) 5-Y-0+ **£3,898** (£1,144; £572; £286)

Form RPR

443- **1** **Handsome Buddy (IRE)**[10] 4704 7-10-13 89 (v) PeterCarberry(3) 102+
(Michael Gates) *hld up: nt fluent 12th: hdwy 17th: chsd ldr 3 out: sn rdn: led last: styd on wl* **11/4**[1]

/34- **2** 2 ¼ **Get Ready To Go (IRE)**[35] 4220 10-9-12 74 (p) HarryChalloner(3) 83
(Richard Ford) *plld hrd: led: j.w: clr 5th tl after 15th: hdd last: styd on same pce flat* **7/2**[2]

63P- **3** 10 **Ballyvoneen (IRE)**[9] 4720 9-10-9 82 NoelFehily 81
(Neil King) *hld up: hdwy appr 16th: chsd ldr 4 out to next: sn rdn: styd on same pce fr 2 out* **7/2**[2]

516- **4** 8 **Volio Vincente (FR)**[24] 4446 7-10-0 73 IanPopham 67
(Carroll Gray) *chsd ldr to 11th: wnt 2nd again 16th tl 4 out: sn rdn: wknd 2 out* **15/2**

P0P- **5** 9 **Bishophill Jack (IRE)**[59] 3797 8-11-6 93 (p) NickScholfield 78
(Kim Bailey) *hld up: rdn and wknd appr 16th* **8/1**

34P- **6** 20 **Cornish Ice**[11] 4678 10-11-12 99 RichardJohnson 77
(Robin Dickin) *chsd ldrs: wnt 2nd 11th to 16th: wknd next: eased flat* **9/2**[3]

7m 15.3s (-25.70) **Going Correction** -1.00s/f (Hard) **6** Ran SP% **112.2**
Speed ratings: **95,94,91,89,86 81**
CSF £12.97 TOTE £3.20: £1.60, £2.00; EX 10.00 Trifecta £36.90.
Owner Michael Gates **Bred** Edward Burns **Trained** Clifford Chambers, Warwicks

FOCUS
A weak contest, rated around the second.

4906 GENSET H'CAP HURDLE (12 hdls) 3m 1f
3:55 (3:55) (Class 4) (0-110,110) 4-Y-0+ **£3,249** (£954; £477; £238)

Form RPR

531- **1** **Winged Crusader (IRE)**[27] 4371 6-11-10 108 SamTwiston-Davies 117+
(Nigel Twiston-Davies) *a.p: trckd ldr after 3 out: led last: shkn up and styd on wl* **11/4**[1]

545- **2** ½ **Squire Trelawney**[10] 4700 8-11-11 109 (tp) HarrySkelton 114
(Dan Skelton) *chsd ldrs: led after 8th: rdn and hdd last: styd on* **9/2**[3]

/0P- **3** 15 **Lisheen Hill (IRE)**[97] 3044 8-11-7 105 RichardJohnson 96
(Richard Phillips) *chsd ldr: ev ch whn mstke 3 out: sn rdn: wknd after next* **8/1**

000/ **4** 1 ¾ **Dixie Bull (IRE)**[673] 284 9-10-10 94 FelixDeGiles 82
(Tom Symonds) *hld up: hdwy appr 8th: rdn and wknd appr 2 out* **20/1**

003- **5** 1 **Grand Gigolo (FR)**[19] 4533 5-10-9 98 RobertMcCarth(5) 85
(Ian Williams) *hld up: mstke 7th: hdwy next: rdn and wknd appr 2 out* **7/2**[2]

510- **6** 2 **Dancing Daffodil**[125] 2470 9-9-8 88 JosephPalmowski(10) 73
(Robin Dickin) *hld up: nvr on terms* **8/1**

0PF- **7** 44 **Estates Recovery (IRE)**[12] 4661 9-11-8 109 JamesBest(3) 50
(Luke Dace) *led and clr to 5th: mstke next: hdd after 8th: sn wknd* **33/1**

15/- **8** 14 **John's Gem**[428] 3674 9-10-0 91 (p) MrHGMiller(7) 18
(Zoe Davison) *prom: nt fluent 3rd: pushed along 5th: wknd appr 8th* **50/1**

P06- **9** 30 **Go Amwell**[28] 3151 11-10-13 97 (v) LeightonAspell
(J R Jenkins) *hld up: a in rr: bhd fr 6th* **16/1**

/26- **P** **Val D'Allier (FR)**[27] 4377 5-11-12 110 MarkGrant
(Jim Old) *hld up: hdwy 9th: wknd after 3 out: p.u and dismntd bef last* **9/1**

6m 1.4s (-13.60) **Going Correction** -1.00s/f (Hard) **10** Ran SP% **114.8**
Speed ratings (Par 105): **81,80,76,75,75 74,60,55,46,**
CSF £15.32 CT £86.84 TOTE £3.60: £1.60, £1.80, £2.30; EX 16.60 Trifecta £113.00.
Owner Imperial Racing Partnership No 6 **Bred** Mrs Hugh Baird **Trained** Naunton, Gloucs

FOCUS
Quite a good race for the level, and it produced a tight finish. A step up from the winner.

4907 EXECUTIVE HIRE NEWS MARES' H'CAP HURDLE (11 hdls) 2m 5f
4:30 (4:31) (Class 4) (0-120,120) 4-Y-0+ **£3,249** (£954; £477; £238)

Form RPR

1/5- **1** **Polly Peachum (IRE)**[89] 3186 6-11-4 117 NicodeBoinville(5) 138+
(Nicky Henderson) *trckd ldrs: led after 3 out: clr next: comf* **3/1**[1]

145- **2** 14 **Woodland Walk**[32] 4276 6-11-6 114 AidanColeman 118
(Emma Lavelle) *prom: rdn after 3 out: styd on same pce: wnt 2nd and hit last* **10/1**

561- **3** 2 ½ **Iron Butterfly**[80] 3391 5-11-1 112 JackQuinlan(3) 113
(James Eustace) *hld up: hdwy 6th: rdn after 3 out: wknd appr last* **12/1**

120- **4** 1 ¾ **Weather Babe**[62] 3741 6-11-12 120 ConorO'Farrell 119
(David Pipe) *mde most tl after 3 out: rdn and wknd appr last* **8/1**

45P- **5** 6 **Lady Kathleen**[82] 3319 7-11-3 111 DenisO'Regan 104
(Paul Webber) *hld up: effrt after 3 out: sn wknd* **9/1**

522- **6** nk **Queen Spud**[70] 3604 5-10-0 94 (p) AndrewTinkler 86
(Henry Daly) *chsd ldrs tl rdn and wknd appr 2 out* **10/1**

4/P- **7** 51 **Dancingtilmidnight**[20] 4508 7-11-6 114 (t) NoelFehily 55
(Harry Fry) *w ldr tl after 7th: rdn and wknd after 3 out* **4/1**[2]

200- **P** **Dreams And Songs**[104] 2907 6-10-11 105 (t) RichardJohnson
(Philip Hobbs) *hld up: wknd 3 out: bhd whn p.u bef last* **16/1**

615- **P** **A Shade Of Bay**[26] 4392 6-11-7 115 NickScholfield
(Kim Bailey) *a in rr: j. slowly 2nd: p.u bef 6th* **33/1**

411- **P** **Barton Rose**[16] 4595 5-11-5 113 MichaelByrne
(Neil Mulholland) *hld up: hdwy 6th: blnd next: jnd ldr 8th tl wknd after 3 out: sn p.u* **6/1**[3]

4m 53.9s (-21.10) **Going Correction** -1.00s/f (Hard) **10** Ran SP% **115.1**
Speed ratings (Par 105): **100,94,93,93,90 90,71, , ,**
CSF £32.67 CT £314.77 TOTE £4.40: £2.20, £3.20, £3.60; EX 40.70 Trifecta £295.00.
Owner Lady Tennant **Bred** Colman O'Flynn **Trained** Upper Lambourn, Berks

■ Miss Lucky Penny was withdrawn. Price at time of withdrawal 7-1. Rule 4 applies to bets placed prior to withdrawal but not to SP bets - Deduction 10p in the pound. New market formed.

FOCUS
The early gallop wasn't strong, so this developed into a bit of a sprint in the final stages. A big step up from the easy winner with the second to her mark.

4908 EXECUTIVE HIRE SHOW H'CAP CHASE (FOR THE STEPHEN ALLDAY PERPETUAL PLATE) (17 fncs) 2m 4f 110y
5:00 (5:00) (Class 4) (0-120,118) 5-Y-0+ **£3,898** (£1,144; £572; £286)

Form RPR

/50- **1** **Speed Master (IRE)**[110] 2797 8-11-12 118 (v[1]) SamTwiston-Davies 132+
(Nigel Twiston-Davies) *chsd ldrs: pushed along appr 11th: led next: rdn appr last: styd on u.p* **5/1**[3]

The Form Book Jumps, Raceform Ltd, Compton, RG20 6NL.

014- **2** 3 ¾ **Rockchasebullett (IRE)**[119] 2599 6-11-4 **110**................ PaddyBrennan 121+
(Fergal O'Brien) *hld up: hdwy 13th: chsd wnr and nt clr run appr 2 out: rdn whn mstke last: styd on same pce* **7/2**[1]
265- **3** 2 ¼ **The Nephew (IRE)**[21] 4493 6-11-9 **115**.......................(t) RichieMcLernon 122
(Jonjo O'Neill) *hld up: hdwy 12th: rdn appr 2 out: styd on same pce* **7/1**
244- **4** 24 **Free World (FR)**[28] 4352 10-10-6 **105**............................ MissLBrooke(7) 97
(Lady Susan Brooke) *prom tl wknd after 3 out* **14/1**
06P- **5** 22 **Wessex King (IRE)**[82] 3323 10-11-8 **117**......................... JakeGreenall(3) 83
(Henry Daly) *led to 12th: rdn and wknd after 3 out* **14/1**
326- **6** 4 ½ **Entertain Me**[80] 3391 10-10-13 **110**.................................... BenPoste(5) 72
(Robin Dickin) *sn outpcd: hdwy appr 11th: wknd next* **14/1**
/1P- **7** 26 **Alpancho**[91] 3162 8-11-11 **117**.......................................(t) LeightonAspell 55
(Ben Case) *prom: lost pl whn hmpd 13th: sn bhd* **4/1**[2]
P34- **F** **Brody Bleu (FR)**[25] 4418 7-11-10 **116**................................ FelixDeGiles
(Robert Walford) *chsd ldr: pushed along and ev ch whn fell 13th* **7/2**[1]

4m 56.8s (-24.20) **Going Correction** -1.00s/f (Hard) 8 Ran SP% **113.6**
Speed ratings: **106,104,103,94,86 84,74,**
CSF £23.22 CT £121.18 TOTE £4.40: £2.00, £1.80, £2.40; EX 27.00 Trifecta £304.00.
Owner Walters Plant Hire Spiers & Hartwell **Bred** J Keegan And J Hamilton **Trained** Naunton, Gloucs
■ Roll The Dice was withdrawn. Price at time of withdrawal 6-1. Rule 4 applies to bets placed prior to withdrawal but not to SP bets - Deduction 10p in the pound. New market formed.

FOCUS
Probably decent form for the grade and the time was quick. The winner improved to the level of his hurdles form.

4909 EXECUTIVE HIRE SHOW STANDARD OPEN NATIONAL HUNT FLAT RACE 2m
5:30 (5:30) (Class 6) 4-6-Y-O **£1,559** (£457; £228; £114)

Form RPR
1 **King's Tempest** 5-11-4 0.. SamTwiston-Davies 107+
(Nigel Twiston-Davies) *hld up: hdwy over 4f out: led over 1f out: rdn out* **6/4**[1]
2 2 ¾ **Max The Minister** 4-10-11 0.. TomO'Brien 94
(Hughie Morrison) *trckd ldrs: led over 3f out: rdn and hdd over 1f out: styd on same pce ins fnl f* **13/2**[3]
60- **3** 4 **Caldey**[81] 3363 5-10-11 0..(p) JackDoyle 90
(Keith Goldsworthy) *hld up: pushed along over 6f out: hdwy over 2f out: styd on same pce fr over 1f out* **50/1**
4 3 ½ **Carole's Lord** 5-11-4 0...(t) LeightonAspell 94
(Robert Walford) *trckd ldr to 1/2-way: rdn over 2f out: styd on same pce* **7/2**[2]
5 2 ½ **Fingers Crossed (IRE)** 4-10-11 0.................................. DenisO'Regan 84
(Paul Webber) *prom: rdn over 2f out: sn outpcd* **8/1**
06- **6** 6 **Say When**[106] 2878 6-11-4 0.. RobertThornton 85
(Alan King) *hld up: hdwy over 3f out: wknd over 1f out* **8/1**
7 1 ½ **Verve Argent (FR)** 5-11-4 0... LiamTreadwell 84
(Paul Webber) *led at stdy pce tl pushed along and hdd over 3f out: wknd over 2f out* **10/1**
8 11 **Point Of Attack (IRE)**[150] 5-10-8 0.....................(t) JosephPalmowski(10) 73
(Robin Dickin) *hld up: plld hrd: hdwy to chse ldr 1/2-way: wknd over 3f out* **12/1**

3m 46.7s (-4.20) **Going Correction** -1.00s/f (Hard) 8 Ran SP% **116.5**
WFA 4 from 5yo+ 7lb
Speed ratings: **70,68,66,64,63 60,59,54**
CSF £12.24 TOTE £2.10: £1.10, £2.30, £8.00; EX 14.20 Trifecta £190.90.
Owner Mrs R Vaughan **Bred** Mrs R I Vaughan **Trained** Naunton, Gloucs

FOCUS
Plenty of non-runners trimmed this field down. Ordinary form but the winner should go on to rate lot higher.
T/Jkpt: Not won. T/Plt: £27.20 to a £1 stake. Pool: £79,530.85 - 2,134.18 winning tickets. T/Qpdt: £10.10 to a £1 stake. Pool: £5,158.98 - 375.46 winning tickets. CR

4672 CHEPSTOW (L-H)
Thursday, March 20

OFFICIAL GOING: Good (good to firm in places; chs 6.7, hdl 7.2)
Wind: fresh across Weather: raining from race 3

4910 32RED ON THE APP STORE MARES' NOVICES' HURDLE (8 hdls) 2m 110y
2:00 (2:04) (Class 4) 4-Y-0+ **£3,249** (£954; £477; £238)

Form RPR
/62- **1** **Ginger Fizz**[22] 4493 7-10-9 0...(t) KielanWoods(3) 98+
(Ben Case) *racd keenly: chsd clr ldr and clr of main gp: led after 2 out: drvn out* **8/1**[3]
2 1 ½ **Northern Meeting (IRE)**[166] 4-10-5 0.............................. TomO'Brien 88
(Robert Stephens) *in tch in chsng gp: trckd ldrs gng wl fr 4 out: pushed along appr last where edgd rt: unable qck flat* **16/1**
0- **3** nk **Reillys Daughter**[29] 2907 6-10-9 0..............................(b) GavinSheehan(3) 96
(Richard Mitchell) *jinked lft as tapes rose: racd keenly: led: clr after 1st to 4 out: rdn 3 out: hit 2 out: sn hdd: edgd lft appr last: kpt on once pce* **100/1**
205- **4** 3 **Makadamia**[51] 3961 5-10-12 0.. TomScudamore 94+
(David Pipe) *mid-div: hdwy after 4th: chsd ldrs 3 out where nt fluent: 4th and pushed along whn hmpd appr last: unable qck flat* **4/1**[2]
- **5** 1 ½ **Danisa**[37] 5-10-12 0.. SeanQuinlan 91
(David Bridgwater) *mid-div: clsd 4 out: rdn 3 out: outpcd by ldrs next: r.o flat* **40/1**
002- **6** 4 ½ **Goldie Horn**[18] 4569 6-10-12 0...............................(t) SamTwiston-Davies 87
(Nigel Twiston-Davies) *prom in chsng gp: outpcd by ldrs 3 out: kpt on u.p* **10/1**
1- **7** nk **Churchtown Love (IRE)**[22] 4487 6-11-0 0.................... PatrickCorbett(5) 95
(Rebecca Curtis) *uns rdr in false s and rn loose 1f: hmpd s: prom in chsng gp: rdn 3 out: one pce fr next* **4/5**[1]
/55- **8** 4 **Taffy Dare (IRE)**[22] 4487 5-10-12 0............................. WayneHutchinson 83
(Alan King) *hld up towards rr: hdwy 3 out: one pce fr next* **20/1**
300- **9** 6 **According To Sarah (IRE)**[100] 3005 6-10-12 0........... RichardJohnson 78
(Philip Hobbs) *a mid-div* **16/1**
10 4 **Goldray** 8-10-9 0.. RobertDunne(3) 74
(Richard Lee) *a towards rr* **66/1**
006- **11** ½ **Langarve Lass (IRE)**[24] 4467 5-10-12 0............................... NoelFehily 74
(Neil Mulholland) *in tch in chsng gp tl wknd 2 out: bhd whn j.lft last* **66/1**
0/0- **12** nk **My Space**[14] 4632 8-10-12 0...(t) IanPopham 73
(Fiona Shaw) *taken to post early: mstke 2nd: a in rr* **100/1**
5- **13** 1 **Nordic Nymph**[106] 2892 5-10-9 0...................................... JakeGreenall(3) 73
(Henry Daly) *mid-div tl wknd after 3 out* **33/1**
300- **14** 7 **Dream Destiny**[14] 4632 5-10-7 0.................................(t) NicodeBoinville(5) 66
(Mark Gillard) *a in rr: wknd 3 out* **100/1**

3m 59.4s (-11.20) **Going Correction** -0.925s/f (Hard) 14 Ran SP% **123.6**
WFA 4 from 5yo+ 7lb
Speed ratings (Par 105): **89,88,88,86,86 83,83,81,79,77 76,76,76,73**
CSF £118.45 TOTE £9.40: £2.40, £3.80, £15.20; EX 166.30 Trifecta £2465.80 Part won..
Owner Itchen Valley Stud **Bred** Mrs A D Bourne **Trained** Edgcote, Northants

FOCUS
A windy day and the going was changed to good, good to firm in places. The hot favourite unseated her rider in the false start for this novice hurdle and she was lacklustre in the race. They finished in heap off a steady pace and the form looks modest.

4911 32RED CASINO H'CAP HURDLE (8 hdls) 2m 110y
2:30 (2:32) (Class 5) (0-100,107) 4-Y-0+ **£2,014** (£591; £295; £147)

Form RPR
400- **1** **Take The Crown**[22] 4504 5-10-4 **78**................................ RobertThornton 94+
(Henry Oliver) *trckd ldrs: led narrowly 4 out: drew clr appr last: r.o wl flat* **4/1**[1]
P46- **2** 8 **Tenby Jewel (IRE)**[12] 4677 9-11-5 **100**.........................(p) RyanHatch(7) 105
(Mark Gillard) *mid-div: hdwy 4th: rdn 3 out: wnt 2nd appr last: outpcd by wnr flat but kpt on* **25/1**
1F2- **3** 2 ½ **Straits Of Messina (IRE)**[32] 4305 5-11-12 **100**.................. FelixDeGiles 102
(Tom Symonds) *towards rr: hdwy 4th: rdn 3 out: kpt on same pce fr next* **6/1**[3]
6F0- **4** ¾ **Chance Encounter (IRE)**[61] 3788 8-11-0 **95**...................... MrCSmith(7) 98
(Linda Blackford) *chsd ldr to 4 out: styd prom: swtchd rt appr 3 out: one pce after 2 out* **14/1**
0U4- **5** 1 ¾ **Benefitofhindsight**[20] 4527 5-10-7 **86**......................(t) NicodeBoinville(5) 86
(Ben Pauling) *led tl rdn and hdd 4 out: stl ev ch 2 out: wknd last* **5/1**[2]
/P6- **6** 7 **Out Of Nothing**[98] 3047 11-10-9 **86**................................ RobertDunne(3) 81
(Dai Burchell) *mid-div: hdwy 4th: sn chsng ldrs: wknd after 2 out* **14/1**
FP1- **7** 3 **Delphi Mountain (IRE)**[8] 4757 9-11-12 **107** 7ex(bt) ThomasCheesman(7) 98
(Richard Woollacott) *towards rr: hdwy 4th: one pce fr 3 out* **9/1**
336- **8** 8 **Pennant Dancer**[80] 3426 7-10-5 **79**...................................(p) TomO'Brien 63
(Debra Hamer) *nt far away: rdn 4 out: outpcd by ldrs next and no ch after* **20/1**
303- **9** 6 **Crackerjack**[21] 4519 7-10-12 **91**.. JamesBanks(5) 69
(Emma Baker) *racd keenly: hld up in rr: rdn 4 out: passed btn rivals but nvr trbld ldrs* **10/1**
/U0- **10** hd **Mister Fantastic**[31] 3157 8-10-7 **86**.................................. CharlieWallis(5) 64
(Dai Burchell) *racd keenly: mid-div tl n.m.r and lost pl bnd after 1st: no ch fr 4 out* **33/1**
06F- **11** 8 **Drumgooland (IRE)**[32] 4309 7-11-2 **97**................................ MrJMahot(7) 68
(Sarah-Jayne Davies) *mid-div: dropped to rr 4th: lost tch next* **16/1**
2P6- **12** 1 ½ **Lodgician (IRE)**[45] 4072 12-11-4 **92**......................(vt) SamTwiston-Davies 62
(Nigel Twiston-Davies) *prom: j.rt 2nd: rdn and wknd after 4th* **14/1**
03F- **13** 17 **Billy My Boy**[51] 3956 5-11-1 **92**...(t) GilesHawkins(3) 46
(Chris Down) *in rr: sme hdwy after 4th: rdn and wknd 4 out: t.o* **11/1**
0/P- **14** 67 **Generous Bob**[22] 4504 7-10-7 **84**................................... WayneKavanagh(3)
(Seamus Mullins) *towards rr: reminder after 2nd: hit next: hdwy 4th: wknd 4 out: t.o* **33/1**
404/ **P** **Donnachas Chant (USA)**[565] 1458 9-11-9 **97**............. RichardJohnson
(Tim Vaughan) *in rr: struggling bef 2nd: mstke next: sn t.o: p.u after 4th* **16/1**
/24- **F** **Oscar Rainbow**[67] 8-10-5 **79**... LiamTreadwell
(Tracey Barfoot-Saunt) *in tch: grad lost pl fr 4th: bhd whn fell 3 out* **25/1**

3m 53.9s (-16.70) **Going Correction** -0.925s/f (Hard) 16 Ran SP% **128.5**
Speed ratings (Par 103): **102,98,97,96,95 92,91,87,84,84 80,80,72,40,**
CSF £114.10 CT £618.03 TOTE £6.60: £1.40, £3.80, £2.10, £4.80; EX 174.50 Trifecta £2113.70 Part won..
Owner R G Whitehead **Bred** R D M Sharp **Trained** Broomhall, Worcs

FOCUS
The well-backed favourite scored in good style in this handicap hurdle. A big step up from the easy winner who should go in again.

4912 32RED.COM H'CAP CHASE (16 fncs) 2m 3f 110y
3:05 (3:05) (Class 4) (0-115,115) 5-Y-0+ **£4,548** (£1,335; £667)

Form RPR
222- **1** **Overnight Fame (IRE)**[74] 3555 10-10-11 **105**......(p) AodhaganConlon(5) 111+
(Tom George) *led to 4th: trckd ldr tl led 8th: rdn along 4 out: 3 l up whn lft in command last: r.o wl* **5/2**[3]
612- **2** 11 **Barenger (IRE)**[23] 4483 7-11-10 **113**..................................(p) JackDoyle 114+
(Ali Brewer) *racd in 3rd: cl up fr 9th: wnt 2nd 5 out: pushed along fr next: 3 l down and hld whn blnd last: nt rcvr* **1/1**[1]
032- **3** 25 **Picaroon**[22] 4505 10-11-5 **115**.. MrsAlexDunn(7) 99
(Alexandra Dunn) *j.rt: racd in 2nd tl led 4th: hdd 8th: styd cl up: mstke 10th: wknd 4 out: t.o* **9/4**[2]

5m 0.1s (-11.20) **Going Correction** -0.575s/f (Firm) 3 Ran SP% **109.3**
Speed ratings: **99,94,84**
CSF £5.47 TOTE £2.30; EX 3.20 Trifecta £3.30.
Owner Mr & Mrs R Cornock **Bred** Malachy And Anne Hanley **Trained** Slad, Gloucs

FOCUS
It was raining. There was a tight market for this small-field handicap but the winner put in a professional display and scored with some authority. The first two ran pretty much to their marks.

4913 32RED H'CAP HURDLE (12 hdls) 3m
3:40 (3:40) (Class 4) (0-120,120) 4-Y-0+ **£3,898** (£1,144; £572; £286)

Form RPR
511- **1** **Solstice Son**[5] 4803 5-10-7 **101** 7ex.............................(t) RobertThornton 117+
(Anthony Honeyball) *trckd ldrs: led after 8th: c clr fr 2 out: eased nr fin* **10/11**[1]
F45- **2** 7 **Midnight Oscar (IRE)**[81] 3387 7-11-12 **120**................(p) NickScholfield 123
(Kim Bailey) *in tch in rr: pushed along 7th: hdwy 4th: wnt 2nd appr 2 out: kpt on but no ch w easy wnr* **3/1**[2]
/5P- **3** 9 **Milo Milan (IRE)**[55] 3874 9-11-6 **114**...............................(p) CharliePoste 110
(Richard Lee) *in tch: nt fluent 4th: pushed along and lost pl 8th: struggling in rr 4 out: styd on wl fr 2 out: tk 3rd nr fin* **20/1**
223- **4** 1 ½ **Cash Injection**[14] 4636 5-10-6 **100**................................(t) ConorO'Farrell 93
(Richard Woollacott) *racd keenly: hld up in rr: hdwy 4 out: rdn 3 out: sn one pce: lost 3rd nr fin* **8/1**
554- **5** 6 **Rich Buddy**[115] 2715 8-11-9 **117**.. IanPopham 106
(Richard Phillips) *in tch: rdn along fr 8th: hit 4 out: outpcd by ldrs fr next* **7/1**[3]

/PP- 6 1 1/2 **Addiction**[116] 2693 9-11-2 **113**.......................(tp) MattGriffiths(3) 99
(Jeremy Scott) *cl up: led 6th tl after 8th: rdn 4 out: lost 2nd after next: wknd* **40/1**
05F- 7 8 **Mauricetheathlete (IRE)**[12] 4678 11-10-12 **113**............... NickSlatter(7) 92
(Martin Keighley) *led to 6th: styd cl up tl rdn 4 out: wknd 3 out* **20/1**
5m 59.7s (-2.50) **Going Correction** -0.575s/f (Firm) 7 Ran SP% **113.0**
Speed ratings (Par 105): **81,78,75,75,73 72,70**
CSF £4.08 CT £27.08 TOTE £2.10: £1.30, £2.00; EX 4.40 Trifecta £35.80.
Owner The Summer Solstice **Bred** R W Russell **Trained** Mosterton, Dorset
FOCUS
The hot favourite had no trouble taking advantage of a golden opportunity in this handicap hurdle. The easy winner was value for further and should still be competitive when his new mark kicks in.

4914 £32 BONUS AT 32RED.COM H'CAP CHASE (18 fncs) 3m
4:15 (4:15) (Class 4) (0-120,120) 5-Y-O+ **£4,548** (£1,335; £667; £333)

Form RPR
350- 1 **Barlow (IRE)**[48] 4020 7-11-12 **120**..........................(p) NoelFehily 131+
(Warren Greatrex) *j.w: mde virtually all: jnd 5 out: lost shoe 2 out: asserted bef last: in command whn stride shortened towards fin* **11/4[1]**
1P4- 2 3 1/4 **Dark Glacier (IRE)**[27] 4395 9-11-5 **113**.......................(v) JamieMoore 122+
(Peter Bowen) *chsd ldrs: nt fluent 8th or 10th: trckd wnr 13th: chal and hung lft 5 out: mstke 3 out: 2 l down whn j.rt last: no ex* **7/2[2]**
053- 3 1 1/4 **Rebeccas Choice (IRE)**[102] 2979 11-11-7 **118**..........(p) RobertDunne(3) 124
(Dai Burchell) *towards rr: hdwy 11th: outpcd by ldng pair 3 out: styd on flat* **7/2[2]**
4F4- 4 33 **The Musical Guy (IRE)**[99] 3026 8-11-9 **117**........(v) SamTwiston-Davies 103
(Nigel Twiston-Davies) *chsd ldrs: nt fluent 13th: rdn 5 out: wknd 3 out: no ch whn mstke last: t.o* **9/2[3]**
446- 5 12 **Counting House (IRE)**[27] 4402 11-11-9 **117**......................(t) MarkGrant 82
(Jim Old) *trckd wnr to 13th and disp ld at times: wknd appr 5 out: t.o: b.b.v* **6/1**
45P- P **Special Account (IRE)**[91] 3172 9-11-9 **117**..................... NickScholfield
(Jeremy Scott) *hld up in last: struggling 11th: lost tch 13th: t.o whn p.u bef 5 out* **8/1**
6m 12.9s (-9.10) **Going Correction** -0.225s/f (Good) 6 Ran SP% **114.7**
Speed ratings: **106,104,104,93,89**
CSF £13.40 TOTE £3.30: £1.90, £1.90; EX 12.20 Trifecta £49.70.
Owner Gdm Partnership **Bred** Mrs R H Lalor **Trained** Upper Lambourn, Berks
FOCUS
The pace was not very strong in this staying handicap but the winner put in a fluent display to record his first win over fences. He is rated back to his best.

4915 32REDBINGO.COM OPEN HUNTERS' CHASE (18 fncs) 3m
4:50 (4:50) (Class 6) 5-Y-O+ **£987** (£303; £151)

Form RPR
P60/ 1 **Vincitore (FR)**[26] 8-11-2 0...............................(p) MissCVHart(7) 102+
(Miss C V Hart) *racd keenly: led to 6th: styd cl up: disp ld 4 out tl led w bttr jump last: drvn out* **11/2[2]**
24P/ 2 1/2 **Catspan (FR)**[19] 8-11-2 0................................... MissHLewis(7) 101
(Miss H Lewis) *chsd ldrs: led 10th: jnd 4 out: stl ev ch whn landed flat-footed last: kpt on u.p flat: jst hld* **20/1**
2P3- 3 2 3/4 **Ski Sunday**[31] 4325 9-11-4 115...............................(t) MrBGibbs(5) 103+
(Tim Vaughan) *mid-div: mstke 11th: clsd after 13th: rdn whn sltly hmpd 4 out and outpcd by ldrs: styd on wl flat to go 3rd cl home* **3/1[1]**
3/2- 4 hd **Swansbrook (IRE)**[21] 4518 11-11-4 108........................ MrMLegg(5) 98
(Mrs Sue Popham) *in rr: mstkes 1st and 2nd: hdwy 4th: lost pl 8th: clsd again 11th: rdn 3 out: one pce fr next: lost 3rd cl home* **13/2[3]**
3/ 5 3 **Nipper John (IRE)**[12] 13-11-2 0............................... MissBHampson(7) 95
(L M Power) *chsd ldrs: rdn 5 out: keeping on whn blnd 4 out: sn outpcd by ldrs: styd on fr 2 out* **8/1**
5P0/ 6 1 **Wogan**[19] 14-11-2 0.. MrDLordan(7) 98+
(Mrs Dawn Woolf) *in tch: blnd and lost pl 9th: mstke next: rallied u.p 4 out: outpcd by ldrs 3 out: styd on* **50/1**
/6P- 7 18 **Interpleader**[18] 9-11-2 88......................................(tp) MrCWest(7) 79
(Mrs S W Lewis) *prom: led 5th to 10th: wknd 4 out: t.o* **14/1**
165- 8 24 **Findlay's Find (IRE)**[286] 658 8-11-10 103........................ MrGCrow(3) 60
(Mrs Myfanwy Miles) *dropped to rr 3rd: pushed along 9th: lost tch 5 out: t.o* **10/1**
6/4- 9 7 **Coup Royale (FR)**[21] 4518 10-11-9 113................(t) MrJoshuaGuerriero 50
(Mrs Claire Hitch) *in rr: mstke 11th: wknd 5 out: t.o* **8/1**
/2P- U **Pathian Prince**[43] 4092 11-11-2 100........................ MissJodieHughes(7)
(E R Clough) *hld up towards rr: hdwy 8th: 3rd whn blnd and uns rdr 4 out* **15/2**
3- F **Meilyr**[21] 4518 11-11-4 0.................................... MrMatthewHampton(5)
(Mrs C Lawrence) *mid-div tl fell 4th* **20/1**
6m 18.7s (-3.30) **Going Correction** -0.225s/f (Good) 11 Ran SP% **114.9**
Speed ratings: **96,95,94,94,93 93,87,79,77,**
CSF £101.81 TOTE £7.50: £2.50, £6.40, £2.20; EX 211.00 Trifecta £2280.90 Part won..
Owner DWD Partnership **Bred** Mme Isabelle Garcon **Trained** Chipping Campden, Glos
FOCUS
A big gamble was landed in this ordinary hunters' chase. The winner didn't have to be near his best.

4916 32REDBET.COM MARES' INTERMEDIATE OPEN NATIONAL HUNT FLAT RACE 2m 110y
5:20 (5:22) (Class 6) 4-6-Y-O **£1,559** (£457; £228; £114)

Form RPR
24- 1 **Meetmeatthemoon (IRE)**[27] 4403 5-11-0 0................ RichardJohnson 102+
(Philip Hobbs) *disp ld: pushed along 4f out: def advantage 2f out: styd on wl fnl f* **7/2[2]**
2 1 1/4 **Carnival Flag (FR)** 5-11-0 0.................................. AndrewTinkler 101+
(Nicky Henderson) *mid-div: rdn and clsd 4f out: styd on u.p to chse wnr 1f out: kpt on* **5/4[1]**
3- 3 2 **Coco Shambhala**[166] 1771 6-10-9 0.......................... ThomasGarner(5) 99
(Oliver Sherwood) *racd keenly: prom: chsd ldng pair 5f out: edgd lft u.p 1f out: one pce* **14/1**
4 1 1/4 **Aces Over Eights (IRE)** 5-11-0 0................................. CharliePoste 98
(Richard Lee) *mid-div: hdwy to chse ldrs 5f out: rdn 3f out: styd on one pce* **25/1**
22- 5 nk **Etheridge Annie**[20] 4540 5-10-7 0.............................. MikeyEnnis(7) 98
(Hugo Froud) *disp ld: rdn 3f out: dropped to 2nd 2f out: grad wknd* **8/1[3]**
6 2 1/4 **Pinamar** 4-10-4 0.. JamesBest(3) 89
(Paul Webber) *prom: outpcd by ldrs over 2f out: styd on u.p* **11/1**
3- 7 3 1/4 **Bel Esprit (IRE)**[27] 4403 5-11-0 0................................... TomO'Brien 93
(Robert Stephens) *chsd ldrs: pushed along 5f out: one pce fnl 3f* **16/1**
8 6 **Tambura** 4-10-0 0... MrZBaker(7) 80
(G C Maundrell) *towards rr: struggling 5f out: styd on wl fnl 2f: nrst fin* **66/1**
9 15 **Poetic Presence (IRE)** 4-10-7 0..................................... NoelFehily 67
(Adrian Wintle) *towards rr: struggling 5f out: styd on fnl 2f: nvr trbld ldrs* **33/1**
10 3 1/2 **Margaret Baker** 4-10-2 0....................................... CharlieWallis(5) 64
(Ronald Harris) *in rr: bustled along 1/2-way: struggling 5f out: modest late prog* **100/1**
4- 11 3/4 **Bus Named Desire**[22] 4499 6-11-0 0.............................. SeanQuinlan 70
(David Bridgwater) *mid-div: wknd 3f out* **40/1**
5- 12 17 **Bellucia**[126] 2472 5-11-0 0.. LeightonAspell 55
(Oliver Sherwood) *towards rr: sme hdwy 5f out: wknd 2f out: t.o* **12/1**
0- 13 hd **Florabury**[267] 842 5-11-0 0....................................... WillKennedy 54
(Sarah-Jayne Davies) *chsd ldrs tl wknd 3f out: t.o* **100/1**
5- 14 nk **Cloudbusting**[20] 4540 6-11-0 0.................................. GerardTumelty 54
(Zoe Davison) *mid-div: hdwy after 3f: wknd over 4f out: t.o* **50/1**
15 3 1/2 **Red Legend** 6-10-7 0.. MrHGMiller(7) 51
(Zoe Davison) *a towards rr: wknd 5f out: t.o* **66/1**
4- 16 5 **Eaton Louie**[88] 3228 5-11-0 0... FelixDeGiles 47
(Tom Symonds) *mid-div: rdn and wknd 5f out: t.o* **66/1**
4m 4.5s (-0.50) **Going Correction** -0.225s/f (Good)
WFA 4 from 5yo+ 7lb 16 Ran SP% **124.0**
Speed ratings: **92,91,90,89,89 88,87,84,77,75 75,67,67,67,65 63**
CSF £7.91 TOTE £3.60: £1.20, £1.50, £3.60; EX 13.20 Trifecta £85.00.
Owner Mrs Caren Walsh **Bred** Patrick Cullinan And Sandra Bromley **Trained** Withycombe, Somerset
FOCUS
A well-backed newcomer was just held by her main market rival in this interesting mares' bumper. Ordinary form, and the fifth and seventh help set the level.
T/Jkpt: Not won. T/Plt: £767.90 to a £1 stake. Pool: £104,239.00 - 99.09 winning units. T/Qpdt: £12.90 to a £1 stake. Pool: £8905.67 - 510.60 winning units. RL

4506 LUDLOW (R-H)
Thursday, March 20

OFFICIAL GOING: Good (good to soft in places; 7.8)
Wind: Fresh, behind Weather: Cloudy

4917 BITTERLEY MARES' NOVICES' HURDLE (11 hdls) 2m 5f
2:20 (2:20) (Class 4) 4-Y-O+ **£3,898** (£1,144; £572; £286)

Form RPR
4/2- 1 **Fabrika**[111] 2801 6-10-12 0... APMcCoy 118+
(Nicky Henderson) *mde all: a travelling wl and in command: j.lft last: shkn up to draw clr run-in: comf* **1/7[1]**
440- 2 7 **Maypole Lass**[20] 4531 4-10-4 105......................(tp) JoshuaMoore 96
(Renee Robeson) *hld up in rr: hdwy 6th: chalng for 2nd bef 3 out: rdn bef 2 out: wnt 2nd fnl 110yds: no ch w wnr* **16/1**
003- 3 1 3/4 **Wyfield Rose**[20] 4528 5-10-12 0................................ BrendanPowell 102
(Jamie Snowden) *hld up: hdwy to trck ldrs 3rd: wnt 2nd appr 7th: rdn bef 2 out: no imp on wnr: lost 2nd fnl 110yds: one pce cl home* **10/1[3]**
500- 4 6 **Princess Bella (IRE)**[17] 4594 5-10-12 0...................... PaddyBrennan 97
(Fergal O'Brien) *hld up: j. slowly and mstke 2nd: pushed along appr 4 out: styd on to chse ldrs bef 3 out: no ex fr 2 out* **33/1**
22U- 5 21 **Playhara (IRE)**[73] 3570 5-10-9 0............................ PeterCarberry(3) 78
(Nicky Henderson) *trckd ldrs tl j. slowly 7th: wknd after 4 out* **7/1[2]**
00- 6 58 **Glacial Roes (IRE)**[92] 3159 6-10-5 0...........................[1] PaulJohn(7) 26
(Sarah-Jayne Davies) *trckd ldrs tl lost pl 5th: niggled along and struggling 6th: t.o after 4 out* **100/1**
7 15 **Minella Duchess (IRE)**[67] 7-10-12 0............................. PaulMoloney 12
(Grace Harris) *racd keenly: chsd wnr tl appr 7th: wknd qckly: t.o after 4 out* **66/1**
5m 15.8s (1.00) **Going Correction** +0.125s/f (Yiel)
WFA 4 from 5yo+ 8lb 7 Ran SP% **120.4**
Speed ratings (Par 105): **103,100,99,97,89 67,61**
CSF £5.46 TOTE £1.10: £1.10, £5.20; EX 4.60 Trifecta £14.90.
Owner Mr & Mrs R Kelvin-Hughes **Bred** Goldford Stud **Trained** Upper Lambourn, Berks
FOCUS
Tony McCoy described the ground as "good and a bit rough in places". A race with little depth. The easy winner stood out in this grade.

4918 EUROPEAN BREEDERS' FUND/THOROUGHBRED BREEDERS' ASSOCIATION MARES' NOVICES' CHASE (17 fncs) 2m 4f
2:55 (2:55) (Class 4) 5-Y-O+ **£5,198** (£1,526; £763; £381)

Form RPR
244- 1 **Prima Porta**[61] 3770 8-10-12 0..................................... PaulMoloney 110+
(Evan Williams) *chsd ldr: led appr last: drvn out and kpt on wl run-in* **8/11[1]**
600- 2 1 3/4 **September Blaze**[35] 4242 7-10-12 103........................ DominicElsworth 104
(Paul Webber) *hld up: wl adrift bef 10th: hdwy after 13th: chalng whn hit 2 out: stl ev ch whn bmpd rival last: no ex towards fin* **16/1**
4F1- 3 3 **She Ranks Me (IRE)**[24] 4468 7-11-4 0...........................(p) APMcCoy 108
(Donald McCain) *mostly j.lft: led: hdd appr last where hmpd: no ex fnl 100yds* **6/4[2]**
244- 4 113 **Floral Spinner**[29] 4356 7-10-12 0................................ TommyPhelan
(Bill Turner) *chsd ldrs tl blnd 2nd: bhd after: lost tch after 9th (water): t.o* **12/1[3]**
5m 14.8s (10.40) **Going Correction** +0.125s/f (Yiel) 4 Ran SP% **111.5**
Speed ratings: **84,83,82,**
CSF £9.39 TOTE £2.00; EX 10.20 Trifecta £19.00.
Owner D P Barrie & H A F Parshall **Bred** Haras De Bourgeauville **Trained** Llancarfan, Vale Of Glamorgan
FOCUS
The rain had set in prior to this contest. A muddling mares' chase that was run at a stop-start gallop, and it's been rated through the second to her hurdles mark.

4919 BROMFIELD NOVICES' LIMITED H'CAP CHASE (13 fncs) 2m
3:30 (3:30) (Class 3) (0-125,122) 5-Y-£7,596 (£2,244; £1,122; £561; £280)

Form RPR
435- 1 **Noche De Reyes (FR)**[5] 4804 5-11-3 **118**....................... PaddyBrennan 128+
(Tom George) *prom: chsd ldr 4th to 9th and again appr 3 out: led bef 2 out: r.o wl and stormed clr run-in* **3/1[1]**
432- 2 4 **Bullet Street (IRE)**[13] 4660 6-11-0 **115**....................... PaulMoloney 120
(Evan Williams) *hld up: hdwy and in tch w ldrs 6th: mstke 4 out: effrt 2 out: wnt 2nd appr last: nt trble wnr* **10/3[2]**

The Form Book Jumps, Raceform Ltd, Compton, RG20 6NL.

443- **3** 2 ¾ **Blackwater King (IRE)**^{48} [4004] 6-10-7 **108**........................ HenryBrooke 112
(Donald McCain) *chsd ldr: nt fluent 2nd: lost 2nd 4th: chsd ldr 9th: hit 4 out: sn lost 2nd: rdn bef 2 out: nt qckn appr last: kpt on and wnt 3rd fnl 100yds but wl hld* **6/1**

111- **4** 2 ¼ **Lord Navits (IRE)**^{17} [4592] 6-11-4 **119**..............................(vt) AlainCawley 121+
(David Bridgwater) *j.lft several times: led: hdd appr 2 out where blnd: lost 2nd bef last: no ex and wl btn run-in* **7/2**^{3}

655- **5** *14* **Ted Dolly (IRE)**^{41} [4131] 10-11-0 **120**.................................... BenPoste$^{(5)}$ 107
(Tom Symonds) *racd keenly: hld up: outpcd fr 3 out: no imp* **50/1**

513- **6** *nk* **Edlomond (IRE)**^{43} [4087] 8-10-2 **108** oh1..........................(t) RyanWhile$^{(5)}$ 96
(Bill Turner) *hld up: hdwy to chse ldrs 3rd: lost pl 7th: outpcd 9th: n.d after* **10/1**

10P- **7** 1 ½ **Strongly Suggested**^{126} [2469] 7-11-7 **122**.............................. APMcCoy 107
(Jonjo O'Neill) *midfield: rdn and outpcd bef 2 out: no imp on ldrs: wknd run-in* **8/1**

110- **8** 3 ¼ **Come On Annie**^{43} [4090] 8-10-12 **113**............................... AidanColeman 95
(Alexandra Dunn) *hld up in rr: outpcd after 9th: nvr a threat* **8/1**

3m 59.2s (0.70) **Going Correction** +0.125s/f (Yiel) **8** Ran SP% **117.9**
Speed ratings: **103,101,99,98,91 91,90,88**
CSF £14.48 CT £56.59 TOTE £4.00: £1.80, £1.80, £2.20; EX 15.10 Trifecta £115.80.
Owner D W Fox **Bred** Dr Vet R Y Simon & N Simon **Trained** Slad, Gloucs

FOCUS
Run at a fair gallop, little got into what was an ordinary race for the level. The second, third and fourth have been rated pretty much to their marks.

4920 BARRELS MARES' H'CAP HURDLE (9 hdls) 2m
4:05 (4:05) (Class 3) (0-135,120) 4-Y-0+ **£6,646** (£1,963; £981; £491)

Form RPR

214- **1** **Loyaute (FR)**^{27} [4392] 7-11-12 **120**...................................... JamesDavies 132+
(Chris Down) *racd keenly: w ldr tl after 3rd: racd in 2nd pl tl led 4 out: shkn up bef 3 out: grad wnt clr fr 2 out: eased down towards fin* **5/2**^{2}

355- **2** *15* **Springinherstep (IRE)**^{98} [3031] 7-11-9 **117**................................^{1} APMcCoy 112
(Nicky Henderson) *hld up in rr: hit 4th: nt fluent 5th: j.lft 4 out: wnt 2nd bef 3 out and tried to chal: sn unable qck and no imp: no ch whn nt fluent last* **1/1**^{1}

1P1- **3** *9* **Bobble Boru (IRE)**^{16} [4600] 6-11-10 **118**.......................... AidanColeman 103
(Venetia Williams) *racd keenly: led: dived 1st: hdd 4 out: rdn and wknd appr 3 out* **3/1**^{3}

436- **4** 3 ¼ **Bollin Judith**^{34} [2894] 8-11-3 **114**...................................(t) TrevorWhelan$^{(3)}$ 99
(Chris Nenadich) *chsd ldrs: hit 2nd: rdn and wknd bef 3 out: wl btn whn mstke last: eased towards fin* **16/1**

3m 48.8s (-0.70) **Going Correction** +0.125s/f (Yiel) **4** Ran SP% **109.5**
Speed ratings (Par 107): **106,98,94,92**
CSF £5.68 TOTE £4.30; EX 6.10 Trifecta £15.70.
Owner Upton Racing 2 **Bred** Haras De Mezeray **Trained** Mutterton, Devon

FOCUS
A race that ultimately took little winning, with a couple of the key contenders failing to run to their best. It's been rated around the first two.

4921 WYE VALLEY BREWERY H'CAP CHASE (13 fncs) 2m
4:40 (4:40) (Class 3) (0-140,137) 5-Y-0+ **£6,077** (£3,272; £1,636; £819; £409)

Form RPR

501- **1** **Sonofagun (FR)**^{10} [4723] 8-10-4 **115** 7ex...................... RobertMcCarth$^{(5)}$ 123+
(Ian Williams) *in tch: mstke 2nd: outpcd after 4 out: rallied 2 out sn in 2nd: styd on to ld fnl 100yds: on top cl home* **7/2**^{2}

231- **2** *1* **Oyster Shell**^{126} [2469] 7-11-0 **128**...................................... JakeGreenall$^{(3)}$ 132
(Henry Daly) *chsd ldrs: mikstake 8th: effrt appr 4 out: bmpd in 2nd and abt 1 l down whn lft in ld 3 out: hdd fnl 100yds: hld cl home* **6/1**

300- **3** 1 ¾ **Changing The Guard**^{6} [4790] 8-11-12 **137**....................(t) BrendanPowell 140
(Dr Richard Newland) *led: mstke 1st: clr fr 5th (water) tl 7th: mstke 8th: hdd appr 4 out: rdn bef 3 out: styd on same pce run-in* **6/1**

310- **4** *1* **Highway Code (USA)**^{7} [4768] 8-11-4 **129**........................(t) JoshuaMoore 130
(Richard Lee) *hld up: mstke 1st: outpcd briefly after 9th: rallied and ch 4 out: nt qckn appr last: kpt on same pce run-in* **11/1**

4F3- **5** *3* **Zarzal (IRE)**^{21} [4507] 6-10-9 **127**.. ConorRing$^{(7)}$ 127
(Evan Williams) *hld up: mstke 1st: outpcd 4 out: j.lft 3 out: plugged on but nvr able to chal* **6/1**

024- **6** *5* **Parsnip Pete**^{96} [3080] 8-11-11 **136**..................................... PaddyBrennan 131
(Tom George) *hld up in last pl: mstke 1st: pushed along appr 4 out: effrt bhd ldrs after: one pce and no imp bef last* **10/3**^{1}

503- **P** **Gracchus (USA)**^{254} [929] 8-10-3 **114**......................... WayneHutchinson
(Richard Price) *chsd ldrs: stmbld 1st: wknd bef 9th: t.o whn p.u bef 4 out* **33/1**

402- **U** **Last Shot (FR)**^{5} [4800] 7-11-1 **126**..................................... AidanColeman 130
(Venetia Williams) *chsd ldr: j. slowly 5th (water): led appr 4 out: pushed along abt 1 l up whn blnd and uns rdr 3 out* **11/2**^{3}

4m 0.3s (1.80) **Going Correction** +0.125s/f (Yiel) **8** Ran SP% **114.8**
Speed ratings: **100,99,98,98,96 94, ,**
CSF £25.01 CT £121.23 TOTE £3.10: £1.20, £2.00, £2.30; EX 17.70 Trifecta £75.60.
Owner The Piranha Partnership **Bred** Dora Bloodstock Ltd **Trained** Portway, Worcs

FOCUS
This was run in horrible conditions with the rain really hammering it down, and they finished quite tired with Changing The Guard having set a strong gallop. Sloppy jumping was the theme. The second, third and faller help set the level.

4922 2C'S ANTIQUES FAIRS OPEN HUNTERS' CHASE (17 fncs) 2m 4f
5:10 (5:13) (Class 5) 5-Y-0+ **£2,495** (£774; £386; £193)

Form RPR

612- **1** **Rockiteer (IRE)**^{162} [1815] 11-11-9 127.....................(p) MissJCWilliams$^{(5)}$ 118+
(Henry Daly) *led: hdd narrowly 3 out: regained ld last: r.o wl to draw clr towards fin* **11/4**^{2}

353- **2** 2 ½ **Chief Heckler (IRE)**^{21} [4511] 8-11-5 93........................ MrAlexEdwards$^{(5)}$ 110
(Philip Rowley) *racd keenly: prom: pressed wnr fnl circ: led narrowly 3 out: hdd last: no ex towards fin* **8/1**

141- **3** *14* **Penmore Mill (IRE)**^{7} [4782] 9-12-1 119............................... MrTEllis$^{(3)}$ 109
(F A Hutsby) *hld up: blnd 4th: hdwy appr 5th: sn prom: rdn appr 2 out: unable to go w front pair bef last: wl btn run-in* **8/11**^{1}

634- **4** *14* **Tiermore (IRE)**^{194} [1521] 10-11-7 105.................................... MrEDavid$^{(7)}$ 90
(R E Luke) *hld up: hdwy 6th: sn prom: mstke 11th: nt fluent 4 out: wknd appr 2 out* **16/1**

0/4- **5** 1 ¾ **Areuwitmenow (IRE)**^{13} [4658] 9-11-7 94..................... MissAEStirling$^{(3)}$ 83
(S Rea) *chsd ldrs: outpcd bef 4 out: n.d after* **20/1**

6 *20* **Music Of The Morn**^{19} 7-11-3 0.. MrDMansell 58
(Mrs Julie Mansell) *hld up: mstke 10th: in tch tl rdn after 13th: wknd bef 4 out* **66/1**

/P- **7** *34* **Rockers Field (IRE)**^{11} 12-11-3 96.................................(p) MrBFurnival$^{(7)}$ 34
(B A Furnival) *prom: blnd 4th: blnd and lost pl 6th: bhd 7th: blnd 8th: t.o fr 12th* **66/1**

622/ **8** *10* **Logans Run (IRE)**^{53} 11-11-10 0..................................(p) MissGAndrews 25
(Mrs S E Busby) *a bhd: lost tch 13th: t.o* **5/1**^{3}

5m 12.2s (7.80) **Going Correction** +0.125s/f (Yiel) **8** Ran SP% **126.0**
Speed ratings: **89,88,82,76,76 68,54,50**
CSF £26.34 TOTE £4.00: £1.40, £1.90, £1.10; EX 23.00 Trifecta £73.80.
Owner Michael O'Flynn & John Nesbitt **Bred** R C A Latta **Trained** Stanton Lacy, Shropshire

FOCUS
A decent hunter chase. There's a case for rating the race 10lb higher.

4923 LUDLOW POINT TO POINT ON 12TH APRIL STANDARD OPEN NATIONAL HUNT FLAT RACE 2m
5:40 (5:40) (Class 5) 4-6-Y-0 **£2,599** (£763; £381; £190)

Form RPR

1 **Brownville**^{39} 5-10-11 0.. RyanHatch$^{(7)}$ 96+
(Nigel Twiston-Davies) *mde all: rdn whn edgd lft over 1f out: kpt on wl towards fin* **10/11**^{1}

5- **2** 1 ¼ **Turkey Creek (IRE)**^{126} [2479] 5-11-4 0.................................. APMcCoy 95+
(Paul Webber) *racd keenly: chsd ldrs: rdn over 2f out: sn wnt 2nd: ev ch ins fnl f: nt qckn towards fin* **3/1**^{2}

3 *nk* **Score Card (IRE)** 4-10-8 0.. JakeGreenall$^{(3)}$ 87+
(Henry Daly) *racd keenly: chsd ldrs: effrt over 2f out: ch ins fnl f: kpt on u.p: nvr quite able to get to wnr* **4/1**^{3}

0- **4** *9* **Solitairy Girl**^{90} [3194] 5-10-11 0.................................... RichieMcLernon 78
(Harry Dunlop) *chsd wnr: pushed along over 3f out: rdn and lost 2nd 2f out: wknd fnl f* **16/1**

5 *4* **Spinning Scooter** 4-10-11 0.. JackDoyle 74
(Hilary Parrott) *hld up in rr: outpcd over 3f out: nvr a threat* **16/1**

3m 57.6s (13.70) **Going Correction** +0.125s/f (Yiel)
WFA 4 from 5yo 7lb **5** Ran SP% **109.1**
Speed ratings: **70,69,69,64,62**
CSF £3.79 TOTE £1.70: £1.50, £1.30; EX 4.90 Trifecta £4.60.
Owner N A Twiston-Davies **Bred** Paul Brewer **Trained** Naunton, Gloucs

FOCUS
A fair bumper that turned into a bit of a dash for home.
T/Plt: £23.40 to a £1 stake. Pool: £59,222.25 - 1844.95 winning units. T/Qpdt: £10.20 to a £1 stake. Pool: £4384.23 - 315.10 winning units. DO

4924 - 4930a (Foreign Racing) - See Raceform Interactive

4555 NEWBURY (L-H)
Friday, March 21

OFFICIAL GOING: Good (good to soft in places; hdl 6.9, chs 7.2)
Wind: Brisk ahead Weather: Sunny spells

4931 EMMA LAVELLE RACING MAIDEN HURDLE (10 hdls) 2m 5f
2:10 (2:10) (Class 3) 4-Y-0+ **£5,848** (£1,717; £858; £429)

Form RPR

2F3- **1** **My Wigwam Or Yours (IRE)**^{85} [3278] 5-11-1 126........... BarryGeraghty 139+
(Nicky Henderson) *trckd ldrs: wnt 2nd after 3 out: chal next: led sn after: pushed clr lear: easily* **3/1**^{2}

12- **2** *16* **Call Me Vic (IRE)**^{56} [3877] 7-11-1 0.................................. PaddyBrennan 127+
(Tom George) *trckd ldr: led after 3rd: jnd fr 6th but kpt slt ld tl hdd sn after 2 out: no ch w wnr fr last but kpt on for clr 2nd* **8/11**^{1}

/40- **3** *13* **Audacious Plan (IRE)**^{116} [2720] 5-10-8 0.......................... PaulO'Brien$^{(7)}$ 113+
(Rebecca Curtis) *chsd ldrs: chal 6th: chsd ldr 3 out: btn in to wl-hld 3rd after 2 out* **50/1**

/23- **4** *3* **Our Pollyanna (IRE)**^{34} [4261] 7-10-8 0........................... RobertThornton 102
(Alan King) *chsd ldrs: hit 3 out: btn after 2 out* **8/1**^{3}

02- **5** 2 ½ **Tsar Alexandre (FR)**^{20} [4546] 7-10-12 0......................(t) GavinSheehan$^{(3)}$ 106
(Warren Greatrex) *chsd ldrs: chal 6th to 4 out: wknd appr next* **8/1**^{3}

254- **6** 4 ½ **Jimmy The Jetplane (IRE)**^{12} [4694] 6-11-1 0................. NickScholfield 103
(Kim Bailey) *slt ld tl hdd after 3rd: styd pressing ldrs and chal fr 6th tl wknd appr 3 out* **33/1**

/40- **7** *10* **Money For Nothing**^{104} [2947] 5-11-1 0........................ WayneHutchinson 93
(Alan King) *in tch 4th: sme hdwy 6th: wknd 3 out: no ch whn hit 2 out* **14/1**

654- **8** 2 ¼ **Max Ward (IRE)**^{18} [4594] 5-10-8 0................................. MrSDrinkwater$^{(7)}$ 91
(Charlie Brooks) *rr: sme prog after 4 out: sn wknd* **50/1**

030- **9** *34* **Stella's Fella**^{131} [2393] 6-11-1 0.. DavidEngland 60
(Giles Smyly) *j. slowly 2nd: hit 5th: a bhd* **100/1**

600- **10** *6* **Paddocks Lounge (IRE)**^{15} [4632] 7-11-1 0..................... MattieBatchelor 55
(Jim Best) *t.k.h early: a bhd: t.o* **100/1**

/00- **P** **Sleepy (FR)**^{30} [4350] 8-11-1 0...(t) PaulMoloney
(Sophie Leech) *tk ken hold: early: sn bhd: t.o whn p.u bef 2 out* **100/1**

4m 57.47s (-21.53) **Going Correction** -0.85s/f (Firm) **11** Ran SP% **121.6**
Speed ratings (Par 107): **107,100,95,94,93 92,88,87,74,72**
CSF £5.93 TOTE £4.80: £1.40, £1.20, £10.50; EX 7.50 Trifecta £140.30.
Owner The Happy Campers **Bred** Geoffrey Thompson **Trained** Upper Lambourn, Berks

FOCUS
Rails on both courses moved in. After the first Barry Geraghty said the ground was "on the easy side of good - I'm pleased they put on some water". Robert Thornton described it as "dead". Recent Midlands National winner Goulanes won this race two years ago. This edition, a fairly modest event, was run in a time 3.47sec outside standard. A step up from the winner on the better ground.

4932 PHEASANT INN H'CAP CHASE (17 fncs) 2m 6f 110y
2:40 (2:40) (Class 3) (0-125,124) 5-Y-0 **£6,330** (£1,870; £935; £468; £234)

Form RPR

50P- **1** **Doctor Foxtrot (IRE)**^{93} [3158] 9-11-2 **114**..................(b) RichardJohnson 120
(Philip Hobbs) *in tch fr 7th: chsd ldrs 13th: slt ld fr 3 out: styd on wl u.p run-in: drvn out* **25/1**

P66- **2** ¾ **Savant Bleu (FR)**^{82} [3389] 8-11-11 **123**............................. NickScholfield 128
(Kim Bailey) *chsd ldrs: ev ch fr 4 out: chal next: and chsd wnr run-in: styd on wl u.p but a hld* **16/1**

44U- **3** 1 ½ **Royal Guardsman (IRE)**^{6} [4806] 7-11-11 **123**......... SamTwiston-Davies 127
(Ali Brewer) *chsd ldrs: drvn and styd on fr 3 out to disp 2nd last: styd on same pce u.p* **3/1**^{1}

2- **4** 1 ¼ **Ziga Boy (FR)**^{21} [4535] 5-11-6 **119**.................................... RobertThornton 121
(Alan King) *chsd ldrs: chal 13th to 4 out: stl ev ch next: one pce 2 out: styd on again run-in and gng on clsng stages* **3/1**^{1}

UF2- **5** *1* **Shockingtimes (IRE)**^{85} [3266] 7-11-8 **120**............................... NoelFehily 123
(Charlie Mann) *hit 2nd: rr: hdwy fr 3 out: rdn and one pce fr 3 out: styd on again run-in* **8/1**^{3}

2/1- **6** *3 ½* **Deciding Moment (IRE)**[145] 2107 8-11-7 **119**.....................(t) JackDoyle 119
(Ben De Haan) *hit 1st: rr: hdwy fr 13th: ev ch 3 out: rdn 2 out: wknd bef last* **8/1**[3]

140- **7** *5* **Le Grand Chene (FR)**[30] 4354 8-10-1 **98** oh2 ow1.........(t) PaulMoloney 93
(Sophie Leech) *rr: j. slowly 11th hdwy and hit 4 out: wknd after 3 out* **66/1**

P04- **8** *nk* **Super Villan**[17] 4602 9-10-9 **112**.........................(b) NicodeBoinville(5) 106
(Mark Bradstock) *led: jnd fr 13th: hdd 3 out: wknd sn after* **8/1**[3]

233- **9** *3 ½* **Mic's Delight (IRE)**[27] 4418 10-11-5 **117**.......................(b) DenisO'Regan 113
(Victor Dartnall) *rr: hit 5th: blnd 6th: sme hdwy after 13th: wknd 4 out* **6/1**[2]

310- **10** *16* **Sheriff Hutton (IRE)**[201] 1485 11-11-12 **124**...................... HaddenFrost 113
(Martin Hill) *chsd ldr to 3rd: styd chsng ldrs: blnd and wknd 12th* **16/1**

5m 46.88s (-0.12) **Going Correction** -0.25s/f (Good) **10** Ran SP% **114.7**
Speed ratings: **90,89,89,88,88 87,85,85,84,78**
CSF £343.87 CT £1554.11 TOTE £21.20: £4.60, £4.50, £2.00; EX 462.50 Trifecta £1853.70 Part won..
Owner Dr V M G Ferguson **Bred** Highfort Stud **Trained** Withycombe, Somerset

FOCUS
A fair handicap chase run in a rainstorm. They didn't go a great pace and all ten were still in with a chance at the first up the home straight, so this may not be form to treat too literally. The third and fifth help set the level.

4933 HILDON 25TH ANNIVERSARY H'CAP HURDLE (12 hdls) 3m 110y
3:10 (3:11) (Class 4) (0-115,115) 4-Y-0+ **£3,249** (£954; £477; £238)

Form RPR

054- **1** **Mister Newby (IRE)**[72] 3600 8-11-9 **112**.....................[1] RichardJohnson 118
(Richard Phillips) *hld up in rr: stdy hdwy fr 3 out to ld appr last: drvn and styd on wl run-in* **16/1**

264- **2** *1 ½* **Dundee**[30] 4347 6-11-7 **110**.................................... RobertThornton 115
(Alan King) *stdd towards rr: impr 7th: drvn and styd on fr 2 out: kpt on wl run-in to chse wnr fnl 110yds but a hld* **5/1**[1]

304- **3** *1 ½* **Even If**[82] 3390 6-11-4 **107**.. APMcCoy 111
(Jonjo O'Neill) *rr: drvn and styd on fr 2 out: kpt on to take 3rd run-in: nt rch ldng duo* **13/2**[3]

432- **4** *1 ¼* **Thomas Junior (FR)**[19] 4571 5-11-7 **110**...................(p) TomScudamore 114+
(David Pipe) *hit 1st: chsd ldrs: pushed rt 2nd: led appr 2 out and sn drvn hdd appr last: styd on same pce into 4th run-in* **5/1**[1]

603- **5** *1 ¾* **Darkestbeforedawn (IRE)**[17] 4599 7-11-6 **109**................. TomO'Brien 110
(Caroline Keevil) *rr: hdwy 4 out: chsd ldrs fr 3 out: one pce u.p appr last* **33/1**

545- **6** *7* **Premier Portrait (IRE)**[20] 4555 7-11-8 **111**...................(p) NickScholfield 106
(Kim Bailey) *chsd ldrs: led after 4 out: jnd next: hdd bef 2 out: btn sn after* **12/1**

402- **7** *2 ¼* **Royal Palladium (FR)**[9] 4761 6-11-1 **104**...................... AidanColeman 97
(Venetia Williams) *rr but in tch: hdwy appr 3 out: chsd ldrs u.p 2 out: wknd sn after* **12/1**

0/U- **8** *2 ¼* **Aviador (GER)**[8] 4783 8-10-4 **98**............................. MattCrawley(5) 89
(Lucy Wadham) *chsd ldrs: led 5th: hdd after 4 out: chal next: btn 2 out* **20/1**

000- **9** *8* **Russian Song (IRE)**[11] 4729 10-9-13 **95**.........................(p) MrMLegg(7) 78
(Fiona Shaw) *rr: drvn 4 out: styd on fr 2 out: kpt on run-in: nvr any threat* **66/1**

610- **10** *shd* **Fix It Right (IRE)**[97] 3085 6-11-2 **115**......................... RichardO'Dea(10) 98
(Emma Lavelle) *chsd ldrs to 3 out* **6/1**[2]

F44- **11** *2* **Milarrow (IRE)**[43] 4109 7-10-12 **101**............................. PaddyBrennan 83
(Colin Tizzard) *chsd ldrs to 4 out: wknd bef next* **16/1**

430- **12** *3 ¼* **I Am Colin**[113] 2755 5-11-7 **110**................................ SamTwiston-Davies 89
(Nigel Twiston-Davies) *hit 3rd: rr: hdwy to cl on ldrs after 4 out: wknd after 3 out* **10/1**

410- **13** *1 ¼* **Top Billing**[43] 4105 5-10-11 **100**..(p) DenisO'Regan 77
(Nicky Richards) *towards rr most of way* **25/1**

554- **14** *5* **Promised Wings (GER)**[20] 4556 7-11-12 **115**.................(v) TomCannon 88
(Chris Gordon) *led to 5th: styd pressing ldrs u.p: wknd after 4 out* **33/1**

413- **15** *22* **Fountains Mary**[74] 3566 6-11-2 **105**...................................(b) RyanMahon 58
(Anthony Honeyball) *tendency to jump rt: hit 2nd: wknd after 4 out* **16/1**

UP5- **16** *6* **Batu Ferringhi (FR)**[13] 4674 8-11-10 **113**...................(p) BrendanPowell 61
(Jamie Snowden) *chsd ldrs to 4 out* **66/1**

P46- **17** *3* **Colebrooke**[27] 4423 6-11-4 **114**..(b) RyanHatch(7) 59
(Renee Robeson) *rr but in tch: hdwy to chse ldrs 4 out: wknd qckly bef next* **14/1**

6m 0.66s (-7.64) **Going Correction** -0.35s/f (Good) **17** Ran SP% **127.2**
Speed ratings (Par 105): **98,97,97,96,96 93,93,92,89,89 89,88,87,86,79 77,76**
CSF £93.56 CT £596.82 TOTE £19.10: £3.70, £1.70, £2.50, £1.90; EX 143.80 Trifecta £2758.30 Part won..
Owner Colin Pocock **Bred** John Joe Shaughnessy **Trained** Adlestrop, Gloucs

FOCUS
A competitive handicap hurdle which should work out. The winner is rated back to his best.

4934 OAKLEY COACHBUILDERS NOVICES' LIMITED H'CAP CHASE (FOR THE BROWN CHAMBERLIN TROPHY) (18 fncs) 3m
3:45 (3:46) (Class 3) (0-125,125) 5-Y-0+ **£7,147** (£2,098; £1,049; £524)

Form RPR

1P3- **1** **Thanks For Coming**[234] 1155 8-11-8 **125**......................... BarryGeraghty 137+
(Nicky Henderson) *hit 4th: trckd ldrs: wnt 2nd 7th tl after 13th: wnt 2nd again after 4 out: chal fr 3 out hit last: drvn to ld fnl 50yds: kpt on wl* **5/1**[3]

411- **2** *nk* **Ifyousayso (IRE)**[72] 3603 7-11-8 **125**.............................(t) PaddyBrennan 136
(Tom George) *led: hrd pressed fr 3 out: kpt slt advantage tl hdd fnl 50yds: kpt on but nt quite pce of wnr* **3/1**[1]

202- **3** *20* **Dunlough Bay (IRE)**[21] 4537 8-11-3 **120**......................... DenisO'Regan 114
(Paul Webber) *chsd ldrs: wnt 2nd after 13th: mstke 4 out: lost position 3 out: styd on u.p to take wl-hld 3rd last strides* **6/1**

4U2- **4** *shd* **De Blacksmith (IRE)**[67] 3690 6-11-5 **122**........................ JamieMoore 115
(Gary Moore) *rr: hdwy 8th: chsd ldrs in 3rd fr 3 out: no imp and lost wl-hld 3rd last strides* **4/1**[2]

405- **5** *4 ½* **Lookout Mountain (IRE)**[30] 4347 6-11-5 **122**..............(t) APMcCoy 111
(Jonjo O'Neill) *rr: rdn 9th: hdwy to chse ldrs 4 out: wknd next* **10/1**

30- **6** *21* **Twice Returned (IRE)**[128] 2458 8-11-0 **117**..................... HarrySkelton 87
(Dan Skelton) *tendency to jump rt: chsd ldrs: blnd 5th: j. bdly rt and wknd fr 4 ou* **7/1**

F11- **7** *19* **Farbreaga (IRE)**[21] 4537 8-11-3 **123**......................... JeremiahMcGrath(3) 76
(Jamie Poulton) *chsd ldrs: dropped rrnd mstke 12th: blnd 14th: jumping wnt pieces after no ch fr 4 oit* **5/1**[3]

5m 55.63s (-10.37) **Going Correction** -0.25s/f (Good) **7** Ran SP% **114.2**
Speed ratings: **107,106,100,100,98 91,85**
CSF £20.91 CT £91.11 TOTE £5.70: £2.20, £2.10; EX 21.30 Trifecta £214.50.
Owner Seven Barrows Limited **Bred** The National Stud **Trained** Upper Lambourn, Berks

FOCUS
The first two came well clear in this decent novice handicap. The winner is rated to his best, with another step up from the second.

4935 CARTER JONAS H'CAP HURDLE (8 hdls) 2m 110y
4:20 (4:20) (Class 2) (0-145,138) 4-Y-0+ **£9,747** (£2,862; £1,431; £715)

Form RPR

112- **1** **Volnay De Thaix (FR)**[91] 3184 5-11-12 **138**..................... BarryGeraghty 143+
(Nicky Henderson) *mde all at modest pce tl drvn and qcknd fr 2 out: styd on wl u.p run-in* **5/4**[1]

P03/ **2** *3 ½* **Kings Lad (IRE)**[341] 5318 7-10-13 **125**........................... BrendanPowell 127
(Colin Tizzard) *chsd ldrs: rdn and one pce whn pce qckdn 2 out: chsd wnr sn after: styd on u.p run-in but no imp on wnr* **20/1**

/35- **3** *1 ½* **Ted Spread**[20] 3088 7-11-4 **130**..................................(t) PaddyBrennan 130
(Suzy Smith) *rr but in tch: one pce whn pce qckdn 2 out: styd on to cl on 2nd u.p last: nt qckn run-in* **7/1**

164- **4** *8* **Shammick Boy (IRE)**[52] 3957 9-11-4 **130**............................ JackDoyle 122
(Victor Dartnall) *chsd ldrs: rdn after 3 out: wknd bef next* **16/1**

41- **5** *2 ¼* **Dormello Mo (FR)**[13] 4679 4-10-9 **131**.......................... HarryDerham(3) 114
(Paul Nicholls) *trckd wnr rdn and sn btn whn pce qckdn 2 out* **5/2**[2]

1/2- **6** *5* **Kuda Huraa (IRE)**[20] 4558 6-10-11 **123**........................ WayneHutchinson 109
(Alan King) *rr but in tch: chsd ldrs 3 out: rdn and wknd next* **6/1**[3]

3m 59.72s (-10.28) **Going Correction** -0.35s/f (Good)
WFA 4 from 5yo+ 7lb **6** Ran SP% **110.4**
Speed ratings (Par 109): **110,108,107,103,102 100**
CSF £21.11 TOTE £2.10: £1.10, £6.10; EX 23.10.
Owner Mrs Judy Wilson **Bred** Michel Bourgneuf **Trained** Upper Lambourn, Berks

FOCUS
A decent handicap hurdle in which the winner dictated. He's a smart novice.

4936 BJP INSURANCE BROKERS OPEN HUNTERS' CHASE (18 fncs) 3m
4:55 (4:56) (Class 6) 6-Y-0+ **£987** (£303; £151)

Form RPR

11P/ **1** **Paint The Clouds**[371] 4772 9-11-12 0......................... MrSWaley-Cohen 134+
(Warren Greatrex) *trckd ldr: led 6th: hdd after 8th: led again 10th: jnd 4 out: clr next: easily* **6/4**[1]

2F5- **2** *19* **Seigneur Des Bois (FR)**[22] 4518 8-11-13 110...................(b) MrTEllis(3) 114
(D Buckett) *chsd ldrs: lost pl and wl bhd 13th: styd on fr 3 out to take wl hld 2nd appr last* **20/1**

112/ **3** *9* **Maurisca (FR)**[1061] 46 9-11-5 0.. MissCVHart(7) 106
(Richard J Bandey) *chsd ldrs: wnt 2nd 12th: blnd 14th: chal 4 out: sn no ch w wnr: wknd and lost poor 2nd appr last* **12/1**

P/3- **4** *44* **Offshore Account (IRE)**[33] 14-11-13 117..........(tp) MrDominicSutton(7) 82
(Tracey L Bailey) *rdn 13th: a wl bhd* **7/1**[3]

B/5- **P** **Prince Tom**[264] 851 10-12-6 135................................... MrNickWilliams
(Alexandra Dunn) *chse ldrs: wknd appr 14th: t.o whn blnd 3 out: p.u bef 2 out* **10/3**[2]

020- **F** **Larks Lad (IRE)**[153] 1972 10-11-9 117......................... MrSamPainting(7)
(M Foley) *fell 2nd* **20/1**

132/ **P** **Johnny's Way**[19] 10-11-11 0..(p) MrMLegg(5)
(G B Foot) *led: hdd 6th: led again after 8th: hdd 10th: wknd 14th: t.o whn p.u bef last* **7/1**[3]

\- **U** **Hudson Gunner (IRE)**[47] 7-11-7 0................................(p) MrJMRidley(5)
(Francesca Nimmo) *in tch: hdwy 11th: wnt 3rd 14th: rdn: 10l 3rd and no imp on wnr whn mstke and uns rdr 3 out* **14/1**

5m 58.74s (-7.26) **Going Correction** -0.25s/f (Good) **8** Ran SP% **112.0**
Speed ratings: **102,95,92,78, , ,**
CSF £29.06 TOTE £2.40: £1.10, £6.00, £2.30; EX 30.90 Trifecta £260.90.
Owner Peter Deal & Jill & Robin Eynon **Bred** Guy Reed And Mrs A H Daniels **Trained** Upper Lambourn, Berks

FOCUS
Not a strong hunter chase, but an emphatic winner. He was a 139 chaser in 2011 and may still be able to better that.

4937 HAWK INN "HANDS AND HEELS" NOVICES' H'CAP HURDLE (FOR CONDITIONAL JOCKEYS AND AMATEUR RIDERS) (10 hdls) 2m 3f
5:25 (5:26) (Class 4) (0-120,118) 4-Y-0+ **£3,249** (£954; £477; £238)

Form RPR

/1P- **1** **Horatio Hornblower (IRE)**[34] 4271 6-11-11 **117**................. MissEKelly 129+
(Nick Williams) *chsd ldrs: chal 3 out: led 2 out: c clr appr last and nt fluent: easily* **9/2**[1]

413- **2** *12* **Should I Stay (FR)**[14] 4659 6-10-11 **108**........................ MrVAdam(5) 108
(Gary Moore) *chsd ldrs: rdn appr 3 out: hld in 3rd whn lft 2nd last* **20/1**

1P5- **3** *2 ¼* **Easydoesit (IRE)**[21] 4527 6-10-12 **104**........................... CharlieDeutsch 104
(Tony Carroll) *chsd ldrs: rdn 4 out and lost pl hmpd 3 out: mstke 2 out: styd on and lft in wl hld 3rd last* **20/1**

330- **4** *2 ¼* **Golanova**[64] 3741 6-11-3 **112**.. MrGGorman(3) 108
(Gary Moore) *rr: drvn and sme hdwy after 4 out: outpcd 3 out: modearte prog again run-in* **7/1**[2]

324- **5** *3 ¾* **Red Devil Lads (IRE)**[20] 4555 5-11-7 **113**....................... PaulO'Brien 109
(Rebecca Curtis) *led to 2nd: styd w ldr: led again 4th: narrowly hdd after 4 out: outpcd 3 out: wknd 2 out: no ch whn blnd last* **9/2**[1]

554- **6** *26* **West End (IRE)**[106] 2897 7-10-9 **101**.......................... MrHAABannister 70
(Kim Bailey) *a in rr* **20/1**

062- **7** *2 ¾* **Steel Summit (IRE)**[50] 3988 5-11-1 **107**............................ JakeHodson 74
(David Dennis) *nt fluent: a in rr* **14/1**

033- **8** *10* **Mission To Mars (IRE)**[19] 4573 5-11-2 **108**...................... RyanHatch 66
(Nigel Twiston-Davies) *led 2nd to 4th: rdn after 4 out: wknd next* **10/1**[3]

133- **9** *46* **Mount Vesuvius (IRE)**[155] 1943 6-11-0 **109**...................(t) MrGTreacy(3) 25
(Paul Henderson) *a in rr* **20/1**

020- **P** **Backhomeinderry (IRE)**[112] 2802 9-10-5 **100**.............(t) MrSPBowen(3)
(Kate Buckett) *a in rr: t.o whn p.u bef 6th* **33/1**

312- **F** **Good Of Luck**[4] 4866 5-10-6 **101** 7ex................(p) WilliamFeatherstone(3) 65
(Warren Greatrex) *chsd ldrs to 3 out: sn wknd: whn fell last* **9/2**[1]

202- **F** **Foggy's Wall (IRE)**[11] 4731 6-11-12 **118**...................(p) JackSherwood 122
(Paul Nicholls) *chsd ldrs: slt ld after 4 out: jnd 3 out: hdd 2 out: 6l off wnr and hld but clr 2nd whn fell last* **10/1**[3]

600- **F** **Bayley's Dream**[33] 4301 5-11-4 **110**.................................(t) MrFMitchell
(Paul Webber) *rr: hdwy after 4 out: shalen up and styng on to dispute 4l 4th whn fell 3 out* **50/1**

4m 38.33s (-9.67) **Going Correction** -0.35s/f (Good) **13** Ran SP% **115.8**
Speed ratings (Par 105): **106,100,100,99,97 86,85,81,61, , ,**
CSF £94.89 CT £1628.06 TOTE £5.60: £1.70, £5.80, £7.30; EX 116.40 Trifecta £1806.90 Part won..
Owner Huw & Richard Davies **Bred** H Davies & R Davies **Trained** George Nympton, Devon

FOCUS
They went a fair gallop in this modest handicap and finished strung out. A step up from the winner with the next two to their marks.
T/Jkpt: £71,811.40 to a £1 stake. Pool: £101142.87 - 1.00 winning tickets T/Plt: £24.50 to a £1 stake. Pool: £137730.47 - 4094.74 winning tickets T/Qpdt: £9.30 to a £1 stake. Pool: £7916.54 - 626.58 winning tickets ST

4743 SEDGEFIELD (L-H)
Friday, March 21

OFFICIAL GOING: Good (good to soft in places; 7.5)
Wind: fairly strong half behind Weather: Sunny

4938 BETFRED TV CONDITIONAL JOCKEYS' TRAINING SERIES H'CAP HURDLE (THE RACING EXCELLENCE INITIATIVE) (9 hdls 1 omitted) 2m 4f
1:50 (1:50) (Class 5) (0-100,100) 4-Y-0+ **£2,209** (£648; £324; £162)

Form RPR
U21- **1** **Solway Dornal**[10] 4747 9-10-1 **75**..........(p) GrantCockburn 83
(Lisa Harrison) *trckd ldrs: led bef 2 out: pressed by runner-up between last 2: kpt on wl* **6/1**[2]
032- **2** 3 ¼ **Lebanna**[10] 4746 4-10-8 **90**..........(t) CraigNichol 87
(Tim Easterby) *in tch: hdwy to chse ldr bef 2 out: rdn to chal 2 out: no ex and hld towards fin* **5/2**[1]
/P6- **3** 13 **De Chissler (IRE)**[16] 4615 7-11-6 **94**..........GrahamWatters 87
(Martin Todhunter) *led narrowly: hdd jst after 7th but remained prom: rdn bef 2 out: sn one pce in 3rd* **11/1**
041- **4** 3 **Patavium (IRE)**[16] 4615 11-11-10 **98**..........CraigGallagher 91
(Edwin Tuer) *in tch: hdwy to ld narrowly jst after 7th: rdn whn hdd bef 2 out: hit 2 out: no ex* **6/1**[2]
00P- **5** 11 **Rozener (IRE)**[59] 3828 8-11-3 **94**..........DiarmuidO'Regan(3) 75
(Henry Hogarth) *hld up: rdn after 7th: nvr threatened ldrs* **13/2**[3]
022- **6** ½ **Saddlers Mot**[121] 2596 10-11-12 **100**..........(p) JohnDawson 80+
(Karen Tutty) *hld up: rdn bef 2 out: nvr threatened* **12/1**
4/P- **7** ¾ **Sea Cliff (IRE)**[121] 2596 10-9-12 **77**..........RyanDClark(5) 57
(Andrew Crook) *hld up:reminders 1/2-way: nvr threatened* **40/1**
30- **8** 7 **Beyondtemptation**[16] 4615 6-10-0 **74** oh2..........NickSlatter 47
(Jonathan Haynes) *prom: wknd after 7th* **66/1**
0/P- **9** 6 **Spanish Cruise (IRE)**[12] 4699 10-11-12 **100**..........NathanMoscrop 68
(Lucinda Egerton) *w ldr: rdn after 7th: wknd bef 2 out* **100/1**
R04- **10** 7 **Dun To Perfection**[8] 4774 7-10-0 **81**..........JamesCorbett(7) 43
(Susan Corbett) *trckd ldrs on outer: hit 7th: sn wknd* **7/1**
343- **U** **Blue Sea Of Ibrox (IRE)**[24] 4475 6-10-0 **74** oh3..........(p) KevinJones
(Alan Brown) *trckd ldrs: uns jst after 3rd* **10/1**

4m 55.7s (3.00) **Going Correction** +0.15s/f (Yiel)
WFA 4 from 6yo+ 8lb 11 Ran SP% **113.0**
Speed ratings (Par 103): **100,98,93,92,87 87,87,84,82,79**
CSF £20.91 CT £159.36 TOTE £4.60: £1.40, £1.80, £3.90; EX 16.80 Trifecta £232.50.
Owner David Alan Harrison **Bred** D A Harrison **Trained** Aldoth, Cumbria
■ Stewards' Enquiry : John Dawson 14-day ban: failed to take all reasonable and permissable measures to obtain best possible placing (Apr 4-8,10-17,19)

FOCUS
Common bends and hurdles sited off outer rail towards centre. A weak handicap, confined to conditional riders. It's rated through the second.

4939 BETFRED MOBILE CASINO NOVICES' HURDLE (8 hdls) 2m 1f
2:20 (2:22) (Class 4) 4-Y-0+ **£3,378** (£992; £496; £248)

Form RPR
2U1- **1** **Dark Dune (IRE)**[27] 4429 6-11-6 115..........RyanMania 128+
(Tim Easterby) *in tch: wnt 2nd appr 3 out: led bef 2 out: c clr on bit: eased nr fin* **11/4**[2]
301- **2** 21 **Benzanno (IRE)**[24] 4476 5-11-6 126..........HenryBrooke 105
(Donald McCain) *led: rdn whn hdd bef 2 out: sn no ch w wnr* **10/11**[1]
15- **3** 7 **Rockabilly Riot (IRE)**[20] 4548 4-10-13 0..........WilsonRenwick 89
(Martin Todhunter) *in tch: rdn 3 out: sn hld in modest 3rd* **12/1**
/P6- **4** ¾ **Bollin Line**[8] 4772 7-10-7 0..........NathanMoscrop(7) 89
(Lucinda Egerton) *hld up: wnt 4th after 3 out: plugged on: nvr threatened* **100/1**
332- **5** 21 **Bulas Belle**[49] 4008 4-9-11 0..........TonyKelly(3) 56
(Edwin Tuer) *hld up: hit 2nd: sn wl bhd: t.o tl minor hdwy fr appr 2 out* **20/1**
422- **6** 3 ½ **Kolonel Kirkup**[24] 4476 4-10-7 107..........BarryKeniry 60
(Michael Dods) *in tch: wknd 3 out* **9/1**
15P/ **7** 15 **Brave Spartacus (IRE)**[349] 5176 8-11-0 0..........[1] JamesReveley 54
(Keith Reveley) *hld up in rr: pushed along bef 3 out: nvr threatened* **6/1**[3]
/60- **8** 16 **Hope For Glory**[24] 4476 5-10-9 0..........JoeColliver(5) 39
(Jason Ward) *chsd ldr: wknd after 5th* **125/1**
06- **P** **Tara Springs**[17] 4605 5-10-7 0..........BrianHarding
(Barry Murtagh) *hld up: sn wl bhd: p.u bef 5th* **200/1**

4m 10.5s (3.60) **Going Correction** +0.15s/f (Yiel)
WFA 4 from 5yo+ 7lb 9 Ran SP% **118.1**
Speed ratings (Par 105): **97,87,83,83,73 71,64,57,**
CSF £5.96 TOTE £3.70: £1.30, £1.10, £2.50; EX 6.00 Trifecta £36.30.
Owner Ryedale Partners No 5 **Bred** P Turley **Trained** Great Habton, N Yorks

FOCUS
A novice hurdle that rather fell apart. The winner improved in line with his Flat form.

4940 BETFRED MOBILE LOTTO NOVICES' H'CAP CHASE (16 fncs) 2m 4f
2:50 (2:50) (Class 4) (0-110,104) 5-Y-0+ **£3,898** (£1,144; £572; £286)

Form RPR
562- **1** **Samtheman**[10] 4747 9-10-10 **88**..........(p) WilsonRenwick 97+
(Micky Hammond) *hld up in tch: trckd ldrs 12th: led on bit between last 2: j.rt last: rdn clr run-in* **9/4**[1]
253- **2** 5 **Indigo Island (IRE)**[16] 4616 5-10-10 **88**..........(p) HenryBrooke 87
(Robert Bewley) *led narrowly: hdd 5th: remained prom: hit 8th: led again 4 out: rdn whn hdd between last 2: one pce and no ch w wnr after last* **15/2**
5/0- **3** 1 ¼ **Roseville Cottage (IRE)**[59] 3824 7-10-12 **90**..........BrianHughes 88
(John Wade) *w ldr: led 5th: hdd 4 out: rdn 3 out: one pced in 3rd after 2 out* **7/1**
4P5- **4** ½ **Gleann Na Ndochais (IRE)**[90] 3213 8-11-6 **98**..........BrianHarding 95
(Alistair Whillans) *hld up: slow 1st: reminders after 7th: rdn after 3 out: one pce and nvr threatened ldrs* **5/1**[3]
036- **5** 3 ½ **Runswick Days (IRE)**[25] 4461 7-10-7 **90**..........JohnDawson(5) 86
(John Wade) *trckd ldrs: rdn after 3 out: sn btn* **11/2**
12F- **6** 1 ¾ **Presenting Junior (IRE)**[148] 2036 7-10-12 **90**..........LucyAlexander 86
(Martin Todhunter) *hld up: nt a fluent: rdn after 3 out: sn no imp* **7/2**[2]

5m 17.3s (14.30) **Going Correction** +0.775s/f (Soft) 6 Ran SP% **109.3**
Speed ratings: **102,100,99,99,97 97**
CSF £17.28 CT £90.15 TOTE £3.60: £2.00, £2.70; EX 12.60 Trifecta £68.90.
Owner The Rat Pack Racing Club **Bred** P H Nash And M Jackson **Trained** Middleham Moor, N Yorks

FOCUS
A weak novice handicap. The easy winner is rated similar to his recent C&D run.

4941 BETFRED NOVICES' H'CAP HURDLE RACE FINAL (10 hdls) 2m 4f
3:25 (3:25) (Class 2) 4-Y-0+
£12,432 (£3,678; £1,838; £918; £460; £232)

Form RPR
11F- **1** **Getabuzz**[27] 4428 6-11-10 **125**..........(b) DougieCostello 131+
(Tim Easterby) *hld up in tch: slow 6th: hdwy 3 out: sn upsides: hit 2 out: led jst bef last: kpt on* **15/2**
23F- **2** 4 ½ **Hit The Top (IRE)**[5] 4833 7-11-12 **127**..........RyanMania 129
(Sue Smith) *prom: led 4th: hit 6th: jnd after 3 out: rdn appr 2 out: jst hdd whn hit last: no ex* **3/1**[1]
332- **3** 7 **Oscar Tanner (IRE)**[85] 3273 6-11-7 **122**..........WilsonRenwick 117
(Martin Todhunter) *hld up: pushed along 6th: hdwy 3 out: rdn to chse ldng pair appr 2 out: kpt on one pce* **3/1**[1]
112- **4** 14 **Cloudy Joker (IRE)**[22] 4507 6-11-1 **123**..........NickSlatter(7) 105
(Donald McCain) *trckd ldrs: rdn after 3 out: sn wknd* **11/2**[3]
130- **5** hd **Maybe I Wont**[20] 4550 9-11-4 **119**..........BrianHughes 101
(James Moffatt) *in tch: pushed along and lost pl after 7th: already struggling whn sltly hmpd by faller 3 out* **14/1**
532- **6** ½ **Riskier**[15] 4627 9-10-1 **107**..........JohnDawson(5) 88
(John Wade) *led: hdd 4th: nt fluent 7th: wknd after 3 out* **16/1**
034- **7** 15 **Marlborough House**[25] 4460 4-9-7 **109** oh4..........(p) DiarmuidO'Regan(7) 69
(Chris Grant) *prom: wknd after 3 out* **28/1**
251- **F** **Knightly Escapade**[14] 4301 6-10-11 **112**..........JamesReveley
(Brian Ellison) *hld up: fell 3 out* **4/1**[2]

4m 55.8s (3.10) **Going Correction** +0.15s/f (Yiel)
WFA 4 from 6yo+ 8lb 8 Ran SP% **113.1**
Speed ratings (Par 109): **99,97,94,88,88 88,82,**
CSF £30.30 CT £82.25 TOTE £6.10: £1.70, £1.60, £1.40; EX 40.40 Trifecta £115.20.
Owner Langham Hall Stud Three **Bred** Peter Botham **Trained** Great Habton, N Yorks

FOCUS
A fair handicap in which two pulled clear. They are on the upgrade, while the third helps set the level.

4942 BETFRED "RACING'S BIGGEST SUPPORTER" H'CAP CHASE (21 fncs) 3m 3f
3:55 (3:56) (Class 4) (0-110,96) 5-Y-0+ **£3,833** (£1,157; £596; £315)

Form RPR
644- **1** **Heez A Steel (IRE)**[19] 4577 13-11-2 **93**..........AlistairFindlay(7) 105+
(Jane Walton) *trckd ldr: led bef 3 out: pushed clr after 2 out: easily* **4/1**[3]
3P- **2** 25 **Debt To Society (IRE)**[37] 4220 7-11-4 **91**..........(t) HarryChalloner(3) 81
(Richard Ford) *hld up: wnt 2nd after 11th: rdn after 4 out: wknd after 2 out* **9/2**
F31- **3** 6 **Snuker**[15] 4626 7-11-12 **96**..........(p) BrianHughes 84
(James Ewart) *in tch: slow 16th and sn outpcd in 4th: hit 3 out: wnt poor 3rd bef 2 out* **9/4**[1]
P5P- **4** 80 **Thats Ben (IRE)**[25] 4470 9-10-13 **83**..........(tp) FelixDeGiles
(Tom Gretton) *led: rdn 5 out: hdd bef 3 out: wknd* **8/1**
313- **P** **Tears From Heaven (USA)**[14] 4652 8-10-6 **83**..(p) DiarmuidO'Regan(7)
(Chris Grant) *hld up: struggling fr 13th: slow 14th: t.o whn p.u bef 16th* **5/2**[2]

7m 10.7s (21.70) **Going Correction** +0.775s/f (Soft) 5 Ran SP% **108.6**
Speed ratings: **98,90,88,65,**
CSF £20.27 TOTE £3.30: £1.40, £4.00; EX 28.80 Trifecta £87.30.
Owner Mrs J M Walton **Bred** James J Whelan **Trained** Otterburn, Northumberland

FOCUS
A very moderate marathon handicap. The winner is rated in line with the best of his form from last year.

4943 BETFRED MOBILE SPORTS H'CAP HURDLE (4 hdls 4 omitted) 2m 1f
4:30 (4:34) (Class 4) (0-110,110) 4-Y-0+ **£3,249** (£954; £477; £238)

Form RPR
055- **1** **Stanley Bridge**[58] 3830 7-10-3 **92**..........CraigNichol(5) 98+
(Barry Murtagh) *midfield: smooth hdwy passing omitted 3 out: led 2 out: pushed along to assert between last 2: hit last: drvn run in: hld on towards fin* **15/2**
11B- **2** 1 ½ **Ben Cee Pee M (IRE)**[171] 1717 9-11-5 **110**..........(v) CraigGallagher(7) 113
(Brian Ellison) *trckd ldr: hit 2 out: sn rdn: kpt on: wnt 2nd fnl 75 yds* **11/2**[3]
040- **3** 1 **Amir Pasha (UAE)**[16] 4615 9-11-0 **98**..........(b) WilsonRenwick 100
(Micky Hammond) *led bef 2nd: rdn whn hdd 2 out: no ex and lost 2nd fnl 75 yds* **20/1**
522- **4** 1 ¼ **Copt Hill**[5] 4836 6-10-4 **88**..........DougieCostello 88
(Tracy Waggott) *led: hdd bef 2nd: trckd ldr: rdn bef 2 out: sn one pced in 4th* **7/2**[2]
501- **5** ½ **Polstar (FR)**[21] 4527 5-11-2 **105**..........JamesBanks(5) 105
(Harry Whittington) *hld up: rdn 2 out: kpt on: nvr threatened ldrs* **2/1**[1]
503- **6** 15 **Danby's Legend**[21] 4527 7-10-10 **94**..........BrianHughes 83
(Malcolm Jefferson) *trckd ldrs: wknd 2 out* **6/1**
4P4- **7** 34 **Indepub**[13] 4667 5-11-0 **98**..........LucyAlexander 53
(Martin Todhunter) *sn pushed along in rr: a bhd* **25/1**
5P5- **8** 8 **Lordenshaws (IRE)**[17] 4605 7-10-11 **95**..........KennyJohnson 43
(Robert Johnson) *hld up in rr: a bhd* **100/1**
065- **P** **Pertemps Networks**[32] 3527 10-11-6 **107**..........JakeGreenall(3)
(Michael Easterby) *hld up: rdn passing omitted 3 out: sn btn: p.u bef 2 out* **12/1**

4m 7.4s (0.50) **Going Correction** +0.15s/f (Yiel) 9 Ran SP% **114.3**
Speed ratings (Par 105): **104,103,102,102,102 94,78,75,**
CSF £46.96 CT £790.96 TOTE £13.60: £3.10, £2.10, £5.50; EX 51.50 Trifecta £554.40.
Owner Michael A Proudfoot **Bred** Slatch Farm Stud **Trained** Low Braithwaite, Cumbria

FOCUS
Not a bad handicap for the class, and the form looks sound rated around the second to his C&D mark and the third and fourth close to their form.

4944 BETFRED TV STANDARD OPEN NATIONAL HUNT FLAT RACE 2m 1f
5:05 (5:05) (Class 6) 4-6-Y-O **£1,559** (£457; £228; £114)

Form RPR
130- **1** **Oleohneh (IRE)**[27] 4431 6-11-4 0 [1] BrianHughes 106+
(Malcolm Jefferson) *hld up: smooth hdwy 5f out: pushed along to ld over 1f out: drvn ins fnl f: edgd lft: a holding on* **7/1**
412- **2** *1 ¼* **Georgian Firebird**[16] 4618 4-10-11 0 RichieMcLernon 98
(Alan Swinbank) *trckd ldrs: rdn to ld over 2f out: hdd over 1f out: kpt on but a jst hld* **4/1**[3]
3- **3** *6* **Palm Grey (IRE)**[24] 4480 6-11-4 0 RyanMania 100
(Sue Smith) *in tch: rdn and ev ch over 2f out: one pced in 3rd fnl 2f* **3/1**[2]
0- **4** *16* **Sir Tommy**[38] 4205 5-10-11 0 (t) DaraghBourke(7) 85
(Maurice Barnes) *hld up: bhd tl styd on fnl 3f: wnt 4th fnl 100 yds* **33/1**
5- **5** *6* **Bouggietopieces**[111] 2830 4-10-8 0 KielanWoods(3) 73
(Pam Sly) *w ldr: led 4f out: hdd over 2f out: sn wknd* **20/1**
6 *19* **Pegasus Walk (IRE)** 5-10-13 0 CraigNichol(5) 63
(Rose Dobbin) *hld up: rdn and outpcd over 6f out: nvr threatened* **13/2**
0/0- **7** *7* **Hi Bob**[19] 4582 6-10-11 0 NathanMoscrop(7) 56
(Lucinda Egerton) *led narrowly: hdd 4f out: sn wknd* **100/1**
8 *45* **Colonial Style (IRE)** 4-10-11 0 BarryKeniry 9
(George Moore) *trckd ldrs: wknd 5f out: t.o* **14/1**
22- **P** **Diaktoros (IRE)**[65] 3719 4-10-11 0 AndrewTinkler
(Ben Haslam) *trckd ldrs: lost pl qckly 5f out: sn bhd: p.u 1f out* **5/2**[1]

4m 3.2s (1.90) **Going Correction** +0.15s/f (Yiel)
WFA 4 from 5yo+ 7lb **9** Ran SP% **114.8**
Speed ratings: **101,100,97,90,87 78,75,53,**
CSF £34.35 TOTE £8.90: £2.40, £1.50, £1.10; EX 26.50 Trifecta £101.30.
Owner T A Stephenson & Mrs S Jefferson **Bred** Miss Mary O'Sullivan **Trained** Norton, N Yorks
FOCUS
This was run at a fair gallop and the second and third set the level.
T/Plt: £127.10 to a £1 stake. Pool: £81408.98 - 467.37 winning tickets T/Qpdt: £73.80 to a £1 stake. Pool: £5032.24 - 50.40 winning tickets AS

[4487] BANGOR-ON-DEE (L-H)
Saturday, March 22
OFFICIAL GOING: Good to soft (soft in places on paddock bend; chs 6.4, hdl 6.9)
Wind: Fresh half-against Weather: Overcast turning to rain after race 5

4945 STELLA ARTOIS "NATIONAL HUNT" NOVICES' HURDLE (9 hdls) 2m 1f
2:15 (2:16) (Class 4) 4-Y-O+ **£3,249** (£954; £477; £238)

Form RPR
114- **1** **Irish Cavalier (IRE)**[35] 4261 5-11-7 135 PatrickCorbett(5) 133+
(Rebecca Curtis) *chsd ldr tl lft in ld 5th: rdn appr last: styd on u.p* **9/4**[2]
221- **2** *½* **Desoto County**[21] 4548 5-11-6 120 HenryBrooke 128+
(Donald McCain) *a.p: lft chsng wnr 5th: nt fluent 3 out: rdn and hung lft appr last: styd on* **6/4**[1]
332- **3** *20* **Chebsey Beau**[22] 4529 4-10-0 117 DeanPratt(7) 99
(John Quinn) *mid-div: hdwy 4th: rdn and wknd appr 2 out* **4/1**[3]
466- **4** *15* **River Clare (IRE)**[31] 4350 6-10-9 0 AodhaganConlon(5) 92
(John O'Shea) *hld up: hmpd 3rd: hdwy next: wknd 6th* **50/1**
0U0- **5** *shd* **Sir Harry Hotspur**[73] 3598 6-11-0 0 (t) DonalDevereux 88
(John Mackie) *chsd ldrs tl rdn and wknd 3 out* **100/1**
036- **6** *nk* **Grey Earl**[28] 4411 7-11-0 0 JamieMoore 88
(Richard Lee) *hld up: hmpd 5th: effrt appr 3 out: sn wknd* **16/1**
4P- **7** *10* **Money Maid (IRE)**[32] 4331 6-10-7 0 AndrewThornton 72
(Simon Earle) *hld up: a in rr: bhd fr 6th* **66/1**
54- **8** *6* **I'm A Rocker (IRE)**[29] 4397 5-10-7 0 NickSlatter(7) 74
(Donald McCain) *hld up: rdn appr 5th: sn wknd* **25/1**
044- **9** *4* **Wing Mira (IRE)**[23] 4506 6-11-0 0 LiamTreadwell 70
(Venetia Williams) *hld up: wknd after 5th* **40/1**
3P0- **R** **Shays River (IRE)**[16] 4632 9-11-0 0 PaulMoloney
(Evan Williams) *mde most tl rn out 5th* **100/1**
262- **F** **Serenity Now (IRE)**[25] 4480 6-11-0 0 DenisO'Regan
(Brian Ellison) *hld up: fell 3rd* **12/1**

4m 5.7s (-5.20) **Going Correction** -0.075s/f (Good)
WFA 4 from 5yo+ 7lb **11** Ran SP% **116.1**
Speed ratings (Par 105): **109,108,99,92,92 92,87,84,82,**
CSF £5.95 TOTE £3.70: £1.20, £1.10, £1.40; EX 5.00 Trifecta £11.80.
Owner A McIver **Bred** Limetree Stud **Trained** Newport, Dyfed
FOCUS
The going was eased to good to soft, soft in places (mainly on the paddock bend) before this opening novice hurdle, which was dominated by the two market leaders from four out. The third and fourth have been rated to their marks.

4946 STELLA ARTOIS CIDRE NOVICES' CHASE (18 fncs) 3m 110y
2:45 (2:46) (Class 4) 5-Y-O+ **£3,898** (£1,144; £572; £286)

Form RPR
232- **1** **Sixty Something (FR)**[35] 4273 8-10-11 129 JakeGreenall(3) 140+
(Paul Webber) *chsd ldr tl led and pckd 5th: clr fr 15th: hit last: easily* **2/1**[2]
43- **2** *35* **Colonel Iain**[80] 3450 8-11-0 0 DenisO'Regan 108
(John Ferguson) *hld up: hdwy 5th: chsd wnr 12th: rdn and wknd after 3 out* **20/1**
410- **3** *4 ½* **Lienosus (IRE)**[35] 4269 8-11-0 0 PaulMoloney 100
(Evan Williams) *chsd ldrs: pushed along 7th: outpcd 12th: bhd whn nt fluent 15th: stmbld 2 out* **6/4**[1]
/4P- **4** *6* **Awesome Freddie**[63] 3784 9-11-0 0 RyanMahon 94
(Dan Skelton) *hld up: hdwy 13th: wknd next* **12/1**
353- **5** *33* **My Dads Horse**[21] 4541 8-11-0 0 AdamWedge 64
(Evan Williams) *hld up: mstke 9th: hdwy 11th: wknd appr 3 out* **20/1**
033- **P** **Midnight Mustang**[25] 4484 7-10-7 80 MrJMartin(7)
(Andrew J Martin) *hld up: mstke 3rd: rdn and wknd after 12th: bhd whn p.u bef next* **50/1**
PP1- **P** **Bob Ford (IRE)**[14] 4673 7-11-2 123 (t) PatrickCorbett(5)
(Rebecca Curtis) *led to 5th: chsd wnr to 12th: rdn and wknd after next: bhd whn p.u bef 3 out* **9/2**[3]

6m 27.1s (7.30) **Going Correction** +0.50s/f (Soft) **7** Ran SP% **110.7**
Speed ratings: **108,96,95,93,82** ,
CSF £32.73 TOTE £2.60: £1.70, £10.70; EX 26.90 Trifecta £159.90.
Owner Mrs A Timpson **Bred** Marc Trinquet **Trained** Mollington, Oxon
FOCUS
A fair staying novice chase in which there was a sound gallop on. The winner has been rated as running a small personal best, and there's a case for rating the race higher through the second and third.

4947 ANNO 1366 H'CAP HURDLE (9 hdls) 2m 1f
3:20 (3:21) (Class 4) (0-120,120) 4-Y-O+ **£3,249** (£954; £477; £238)

Form RPR
/00- **1** **Chat Room**[100] 3031 6-11-12 **120** DenisO'Regan 122+
(John Ferguson) *led tl after 1st: trckd ldr tl led appr 2 out: shkn up bef last: r.o wl* **3/1**[2]
003- **2** *3 ¾* **The Pier (IRE)**[23] 4512 8-11-4 **112** (t) AndrewTinkler 110
(Anna Brooks) *a.p: chsd wnr 2 out: sn rdn: styd on same pce flat* **5/1**
33- **3** *1 ¾* **Nordic Quest (IRE)**[73] 3598 5-11-11 **119** DavidBass 118+
(Nicky Henderson) *hld up: racd keenly: outpcd and mstke 3 out: hdwy next: sn rdn: styd on same pce flat* **9/4**[1]
4/6- **4** *8* **Red Skipper (IRE)**[12] 4726 9-11-5 **118** AodhaganConlon(5) 107
(John O'Shea) *led after 1st: hit 3rd: rdn and hdd appr 2 out: wknd bef last* **12/1**
605- **5** *14* **Tom Wade (IRE)**[26] 4463 7-11-1 **114** BenPoste(5) 92
(Shaun Harris) *chsd ldrs: mstke 5th: rdn and wknd appr last* **8/1**
42P/ **6** *3 ¾* **Absinthe (IRE)**[539] 1673 8-11-12 **120** (t) HenryBrooke 93
(Donald McCain) *hld up: hdwy 3 out: rdn and wknd after next* **4/1**[3]

4m 15.1s (4.20) **Going Correction** +0.225s/f (Yiel) **6** Ran SP% **111.2**
Speed ratings (Par 105): **99,97,96,92,86 84**
CSF £17.63 TOTE £3.90: £1.80, £4.00; EX 26.20 Trifecta £105.00.
Owner Bloomfields **Bred** Saleh Al Homaizi & Imad Al Sagar **Trained** Cowlinge, Suffolk
FOCUS
This modest handicap looked a tight affair. They went a fair enough gallop early yet each of the runners held a chance of sorts at the penultimate flight. The winner has been rated as running a personal best, but the time was slow compared with the earlier novice hurdle.

4948 STELLA ARTOIS BLACK H'CAP CHASE (15 fncs) 2m 4f 110y
3:55 (3:59) (Class 4) (0-120,117) 5-Y-O+ **£3,898** (£1,144; £572; £286)

Form RPR
312- **1** **King's Grace**[26] 4464 8-11-10 **115** HenryBrooke 124+
(Donald McCain) *chsd clr ldr: tk clsr order 10th: rdn after 3 out: led appr last: styd on wl* **10/3**[2]
046- **2** *6* **Arctic Ben (IRE)**[50] 4007 10-11-9 **117** JakeGreenall(3) 122
(Henry Daly) *led: clr 2nd: nt fluent 7th: c bk to the field to 10th: rdn and hdd appr last: no ex flat* **7/2**[3]
351- **3** *55* **Cloudingstar (IRE)**[6] 4840 7-11-2 **112** 7ex (t) MauriceLinehan(5) 67
(Jonjo O'Neill) *chsd ldrs: mstke and lost pl 8th: rdn and wknd after next* **1/1**[1]
P5P- **4** *20* **Marie Des Anges (FR)**[29] 4392 6-11-3 **108** (t) RyanMahon 45
(Anthony Honeyball) *hld up: plld hrd: hdwy 8th: wknd 12th* **7/1**

5m 26.1s (17.00) **Going Correction** +0.80s/f (Soft) **4** Ran SP% **107.8**
Speed ratings: **99,96,75,68**
CSF £13.80 TOTE £4.20; EX 7.70 Trifecta £17.70.
Owner T G Leslie **Bred** R T Crellin **Trained** Cholmondeley, Cheshire
FOCUS
Another tight-looking handicap, but only two mattered leaving the back straight. The second has been rated as running to his mark.

4949 STELLA ARTOIS H'CAP HURDLE (12 hdls) 3m
4:30 (4:31) (Class 3) (0-135,132) 4-Y-O+ **£6,498** (£1,908; £954; £477)

Form RPR
242- **1** **Heavenstown (IRE)**[6] 4841 8-10-6 **117** (b) NicodeBoinville(5) 121
(John Spearing) *mde all: clr fr 2nd tl 8th: rdn appr last: styd on gamely* **7/2**[1]
013- **2** *nk* **Warden Hill (IRE)**[56] 3896 6-11-10 **130** DominicElsworth 134
(Mick Channon) *hld up: hdwy 7th: chsd wnr 2 out: rdn and ev ch last: styd on* **7/2**[1]
125- **3** *3* **Templebraden (IRE)**[19] 4594 7-11-0 **120** DenisO'Regan 122
(Henry Oliver) *hld up: nt fluent 1st: mstke next: hdwy 9th: rdn to chse wnr after 3 out tl next: nt clr run appr last: styd on same pce flat* **16/1**
150- **4** *8* **Alderley Rover (IRE)**[50] 4006 10-10-10 **123** NickSlatter(7) 117
(Donald McCain) *hld up: hdwy 3 out: nt trble ldrs* **22/1**
332- **5** *8* **Ivy Gate (IRE)**[28] 4428 6-10-10 **121** MauriceLinehan(5) 108
(Jonjo O'Neill) *hld up in tch: rdn after 9th: wknd next* **10/1**
PF0- **6** *1 ¾* **Sunny Ledgend**[7] 4820 9-10-12 **125** MrJMartin(7) 112
(Andrew J Martin) *chsd wnr tl rdn and wknd after 3 out* **12/1**
2PF- **7** *5* **American Life (FR)**[15] 4662 7-10-3 **109** (bt) PaulMoloney 90
(Anthony Middleton) *hld up: nvr on terms* **16/1**
030- **8** *3 ½* **Red Not Blue (IRE)**[99] 3069 11-11-5 **125** AndrewThornton 102
(Simon Earle) *hld up: hdwy after 7th: wknd appr 3 out* **10/1**
330- **9** *9* **Bourne**[35] 4264 8-11-4 **124** (b) HenryBrooke 93
(Donald McCain) *prom: pushed along appr 8th: wknd 3 out* **7/1**[2]
P00- **10** *7* **Cyrien Star**[28] 4415 7-11-2 **125** JakeGreenall(3) 88
(Henry Daly) *chsd ldrs tl rdn and wknd appr 3 out* **15/2**[3]
214- **11** *3 ½* **Beauboreen (IRE)**[49] 4040 7-11-6 **126** SeanQuinlan 86
(Jennie Candlish) *prom tl rdn and wknd after 9th* **14/1**

5m 51.1s (0.10) **Going Correction** +0.225s/f (Yiel) **11** Ran SP% **117.4**
Speed ratings (Par 107): **108,107,106,104,101 100,99,98,95,92 91**
CSF £16.29 CT £173.29 TOTE £5.60: £1.70, £1.20, £5.40; EX 16.90 Trifecta £222.20.
Owner Malcolm Page **Bred** Thistletown Stud **Trained** Kinnersley, Worcs
■ Stewards' Enquiry : Dominic Elsworth two-day ban: used whip in incorrect place (Apr 6-7)
FOCUS
There was no hanging about in this fair staying handicap. The second ran a personal best in defeat.

4950 A CUT ABOVE NOVICES' HURDLE (11 hdls) 2m 4f
5:05 (5:05) (Class 4) 4-Y-O+ **£3,249** (£954; £477; £238)

Form RPR
0/1- **1** **Monkey Kingdom**[28] 4411 6-11-2 0 (t) PatrickCorbett(5) 134+
(Rebecca Curtis) *mde all: clr after 3 out: pushed out* **4/1**[3]
21- **2** *3 ½* **Big Hands Harry**[22] 4535 5-11-7 137 AndrewTinkler 132
(Nicky Henderson) *hld up in tch: pushed along after 6th: rdn 8th: chsd wnr 2 out: nt fluent last: styd on same pce flat* **1/2**[1]
654- **3** *13* **Shantou Tiger (IRE)**[25] 4480 5-10-8 0 JamesCowley(7) 112
(Donald McCain) *hld up: hdwy appr 7th: rdn 3 out: styd on same pce: wnt 3rd last* **33/1**
41- **4** *11* **Take The Cash (IRE)**[20] 4576 5-11-7 0 HenryBrooke 110
(Donald McCain) *trckd wnr to 5th: wnt 2nd again next: rdn appr 3 out: wknd next* **7/2**[2]
0- **5** *30* **Garton Star (IRE)**[44] 4102 5-11-1 0 RyanMahon 75
(Harry Fry) *trckd ldrs: racd keenly: rdn appr 6th: wknd next* **25/1**

The Form Book Jumps, Raceform Ltd, Compton, RG20 6NL.

P05- **P** **Izza Diva**[22] [4528] 6-10-8 0 ....(t) PaulMoloney
(John Holt) *hld up: bhd fr 6th: p.u bef 8th* **100/1**

00- **P** **Alfie Moone**[13] 6-10-8 0 .... MrCSmith(7)
(Barry Leavy) *hld up: bhd fr 6th: p.u bef 8th* **100/1**

000- **P** **Flobury**[10] [4758] 6-10-8 0 .... LiamHeard
(Barry Leavy) *trckd ldrs: wnt 2nd 5th tl hit next: sn rdn and wknd: bhd whn mstke next: sn p.u* **100/1**

4m 58.9s (6.90) **Going Correction** +0.225s/f (Yiel) **8** Ran SP% **118.6**
Speed ratings (Par 105): **95,93,88,84,72 , ,**
CSF £7.00 TOTE £8.50: £1.30, £1.02, £8.10; EX 13.00 Trifecta £56.30.
Owner Carl Hinchy **Bred** R Aston **Trained** Newport, Dyfed

FOCUS
An above-average novice hurdle. The second has been rated to his best.

4951 STELLA ARTOIS INTERMEDIATE OPEN NATIONAL HUNT FLAT RACE 2m 1f
5:40 (5:40) (Class 5) 4-6-Y-O **£2,053** (£598; £299)

Form RPR

410- **1** **Thomas Brown**[42] [4149] 5-11-10 0 .... RyanMahon 122
(Harry Fry) *trckd ldr tl over 6f out: rdn over 3f out: wnt 2nd again over 2f out: r.o u.p to ld towards fin* **11/10**[1]

31- **2** *2* **Otago Trail (IRE)**[27] [4445] 6-11-10 0 .... LiamTreadwell 120
(Venetia Williams) *led: rdn over 1f out: hdd towards fin* **15/8**[2]

3 *11* **Super Sam** 5-10-12 0 .... NicodeBoinville(5) 103
(John Spearing) *sn pushed along to chse ldrs: wnt 2nd over 6f out tl rdn over 2f out: wknd fnl f* **16/1**

- **4** *23* **Heresmynumber (IRE)** 4-10-7 0 .... JakeGreenall(3) 75
(Henry Daly) *hld up: hdwy over 6f out: rdn and wknd over 3f out* **9/1**[3]

5 *17* **Raise A Spark** 4-10-10 0 .... HenryBrooke 60
(Donald McCain) *hld up: hdwy 11f out: rdn and wknd 3f out* **9/1**[3]

0- **6** *15* **Tea In Marrakech (IRE)**[141] [2195] 6-11-3 0 .... DenisO'Regan 54
(William Kinsey) *prom: rdn 1/2-way: sn wknd* **50/1**

60- **7** *3 1/2* **Midnight Memories**[34] [4310] 4-10-3 0 .... AndrewTinkler 36
(Steph Hollinshead) *hld up: rdn and wknd 1/2-way* **66/1**

4m 5.0s (-0.30) **Going Correction** +0.225s/f (Yiel)
WFA 4 from 5yo+ 7lb **7** Ran SP% **111.7**
Speed ratings: **109,108,102,92,84 77,75**
CSF £3.14 TOTE £1.40: £1.10, £1.60; EX 3.40 Trifecta £17.90.
Owner The Corse Lawners **Bred** Elms Stud Co Ltd **Trained** Seaborough, Dorset

FOCUS
The two penalised winners dominated the market and the finish of this interesting little bumper. They have been rated pretty close to their previous bests.
T/Plt: £81.00 to a £1 stake. Pool: £50,993.96 - 459.04 winning units. T/Qpdt: £30.90 to a £1 stake. Pool: £2379.90 - 56.90 winning units. CR

4548 KELSO (L-H)
Saturday, March 22

OFFICIAL GOING: Good (good to soft in places; 7.7)
Wind: Fresh, half against Weather: Cloudy, bright

4952 ABBEY TOOL & GAUGE H'CAP HURDLE (8 hdls) 2m 110y
1:30 (1:30) (Class 4) (0-120,116) 4-Y-0+ **£3,249** (£954; £477; £238)

Form RPR

1/6- **1** **Keeneland (IRE)**[20] [4579] 7-11-11 **114** .... AdrianLane 114
(Donald McCain) *trckd ldrs: wnt 2nd 3 out: rdn bef next: 5 l 2nd and keeping on whn lft over 3 l clr last: hld on wl* **12/1**

0U0- **2** *hd* **Overpriced**[91] [3212] 8-11-5 **115** ....(t) DaraghBourke(7) 115
(Maurice Barnes) *hld up: stdy hdwy prom after 4 out: rdn after next: jst over 3 l down and keeping on whn lft 2nd last: kpt on wl run-in: jst hld* **33/1**

356- **3** *2 1/2* **Spitz (FR)**[21] [4548] 6-11-4 **107** .... WilsonRenwick 105
(Rose Dobbin) *hld up: rdn and hdwy bef 3 out: lft 3rd last: kpt on wl towards fin* **9/1**

6P0- **4** *8* **Damascus Steel (IRE)**[80] [3475] 6-11-5 **108** .... BrianHarding 100
(Alison Hamilton) *t.k.h: in tch: rdn and outpcd after 3 out: no imp fr next* **12/1**

606- **5** *7* **Rhymers Ha**[37] [4235] 7-11-6 **114** ....(p) CraigNichol(5) 99
(Lucinda Russell) *cl up: lost pl 3rd: outpcd bef 4 out: styd on fr 2 out: nvr rchd ldrs* **20/1**

63P- **6** *1 1/2* **Pulpitarian (USA)**[85] [3330] 6-11-8 **111** .... PeterBuchanan 94
(Lucinda Russell) *hld up: rdn along bef 3 out: no imp bef next* **10/1**

324- **7** *3/4* **Trust Thomas**[38] [4224] 6-10-13 **109** ....(t) GrahamWatters(7) 91
(Ann Hamilton) *hld up: rdn along bef 3 out: effrt u.p bef next: sn no imp* **10/3**[1]

/23- **8** *2 1/2* **Bright Applause**[109] [2868] 6-10-9 **103** .... AdamNicol(5) 85
(Tracy Waggott) *midfield: blnd 3rd: drvn and outpcd bef 3 out: btn bef next* **7/2**[2]

31- **9** *34* **War Lord (IRE)**[142] [2168] 4-11-6 **116** .... BarryKeniry 58
(Philip Kirby) *nt fluent: chsd ldrs: mstke 2nd: sn chsng ldr: nt fluent and lost 2nd 3 out: sn struggling: t.o* **8/1**

205- **F** **Captain Brown**[83] [3398] 6-11-12 **115** .... BrianHughes 117
(James Moffatt) *led: qcknd clr 3 out: 5 l in front next: rdn and hung lft bef last: stl 5 l up and keeping on whn fell and down for sme time last* **11/2**[3]

4m 4.6s (2.80) **Going Correction** +0.20s/f (Yiel)
WFA 4 from 6yo+ 7lb **10** Ran SP% **114.0**
Speed ratings (Par 105): **101,100,99,95,92 91,91,90,74,**
CSF £296.66 CT £3673.08 TOTE £12.00: £3.60, £7.20, £4.50; EX 190.00 Trifecta £534.00.
Owner Paul & Clare Rooney **Bred** Whisperview Trading Ltd **Trained** Cholmondeley, Cheshire

FOCUS
All bends moved to best ground available. Hurdle race distances increased by about 15yds. A few of these had something to prove, and there was drama at the final hurdle when Captain Brown, who was looking tired after attempting to make all, came down when holding an advantage. The first two have been rated to their marks.

4953 LIZ ADAM MEMORIAL H'CAP CHASE (19 fncs) 3m 2f
2:00 (2:00) (Class 2) 5-Y-0+ **£16,245** (£4,770; £2,385; £1,192)

Form RPR

324- **1** **Scotswell**[21] [4552] 8-10-5 **121** .... JamesReveley 130+
(Harriet Graham) *cl up: led 6th to 11th: led 13th: rdn and hrd pressed bef 2 out: styd on gamely fr last* **7/1**

23P- **2** *2* **Fentara**[14] [4669] 9-10-7 **123** ....(t) PeterBuchanan 129
(Mark Walford) *nt fluent on occasions: hld up: smooth hdwy to press ldrs bef 2 out: rdn and edgd lft bef last: styd on to take 2nd nr fin: nt rch wnr* **12/1**

53P- **3** *nk* **Gullinbursti (IRE)**[56] [3897] 8-11-12 **142** .... ConorO'Farrell 147
(Emma Lavelle) *hld up in tch: stdy hdwy to chse wnr bef 5 out: effrt and ev ch 2 out to last: rdn and hung lft run-in: kpt on same pce and lost 2nd towards fin* **9/2**[2]

333- **4** *13* **Imperial Vic (IRE)**[66] [3725] 9-10-13 **129** .... DannyCook 125
(Michael Smith) *led to 3rd: cl up: drvn along fr 14th: nt fluent and outpcd 4 out: plugged on fr 2 out: no ch w first three* **11/4**[1]

116- **5** *19* **The Panama Kid (IRE)**[37] [4236] 10-10-8 **124** ....(b) BrianHughes 100
(Malcolm Jefferson) *trckd ldrs: rdn 5 out: wknd bef 2 out* **12/1**

314- **6** *34* **No Planning**[29] [4400] 7-11-10 **140** .... RyanMania 86
(Sue Smith) *nt fluent on occasions: hld up bhd ldng gp: stdy hdwy after 5 out: rdn and wknd 3 out* **7/1**

013- **P** **Isla Pearl Fisher**[37] [4238] 11-10-13 **129** .... LucyAlexander
(N W Alexander) *bhd: outpcd fr 5th: lost tch and p.u after 12th* **16/1**

003- **U** **Sergeant Pink (IRE)**[18] [4610] 8-9-13 **118** ....(p) TonyKelly(3)
(Dianne Sayer) *hld up in tch: lost pl and struggling bef 12th: losing tch whn tried to refuse and uns rdr next* **18/1**

1P5- **P** **Sydney Paget (IRE)**[63] [3780] 7-11-8 **138** .... BrianHarding
(Donald McCain) *cl up: led 3rd to 6th: led 11th to 13th: rdn and wknd 5 out: tailing off whn p.u next* **13/2**[3]

6m 53.7s (6.50) **Going Correction** +0.425s/f (Soft) **9** Ran SP% **109.7**
Speed ratings: **107,106,106,102,96 85, , ,**
CSF £76.66 CT £388.17 TOTE £9.30: £2.90, £2.70, £1.80; EX 72.40 Trifecta £520.20.
Owner H G Racing **Bred** Mrs H O Graham **Trained** Philip Law, Borders

FOCUS
A classy handicap run at a decent gallop. The second has been rated in line with her recent form and the third close to his mark.

4954 BENTLEY HOMES H'CAP HURDLE (13 hdls) 3m 3f
2:30 (2:32) (Class 2) 4-Y-0+ **£16,245** (£4,770; £2,385; £1,192)

Form RPR

136- **1** **Lie Forrit (IRE)**[97] [3108] 10-11-12 **140** .... PeterBuchanan 141
(Lucinda Russell) *mde all: pushed along whn edgd rt and idled bef last: kpt on wl run-in* **5/1**[3]

536- **2** *3/4* **Neptune Equester**[15] [4661] 11-10-4 **118** .... RyanMania 118
(Sandy Thomson) *hld up in tch: rdn and outpcd after 4 out: rallied bef 2 out: styd on wl run-in to take 2nd nr fin* **14/1**

/F2- **3** *1/2* **Lackamon**[7] [4814] 9-10-9 **130** .... DaraghBourke(7) 131
(Sue Smith) *in tch: stdy hdwy to chse wnr bef 3 out: effrt and cl 2nd bef next: sn rdn: nt fluent last: edgd lft run-in: no ex and lost 2nd nr fin* **3/1**[1]

243- **4** *6* **Quel Elite (FR)**[24] [4489] 10-10-0 **114** oh3 ....(v) BrianHughes 109
(James Moffatt) *hld up in tch: stdy hdwy to chse ldrs 3 out: sn rdn: kpt on same pce fr next* **9/1**

14P- **5** *3/4* **Arctic Court (IRE)**[48] [4051] 10-10-9 **123** .... WilsonRenwick 118
(Jim Goldie) *hld up: stdy hdwy after 4 out: rdn after next: no imp fr 2 out* **8/1**

221- **6** *30* **Hellorboston (IRE)**[24] [4491] 6-10-7 **121** ....(b) AdrianLane 88
(Donald McCain) *prom: drvn and outpcd bef 7th: rallied after next: wknd 3 out: t.o* **10/1**

513- **7** *3 3/4* **Wolf Shield (IRE)**[35] [4271] 7-10-4 **118** ....(p) BarryKeniry 82
(George Moore) *nt fluent on occasions: chsd ldrs: wnt 2nd 8th: rdn after 4 out: nt fluent and wknd next: t.o* **9/1**

012- **P** **Who Owns Me (IRE)**[21] [4556] 8-11-5 **133** ....(b) JamesReveley
(Charlie Mann) *bhd: struggling fnl circ: t.o whn p.u bef 3 out* **10/1**

232- **P** **Drop Out Joe**[21] [4545] 6-11-3 **131** .... BrianHarding
(Charlie Longsdon) *chsd wnr to 8th: drvn and lost pl next: struggling 4 out: tailing off whn p.u bef next* **9/2**[2]

6m 38.5s (-1.50) **Going Correction** +0.20s/f (Yiel) **9** Ran SP% **115.8**
Speed ratings (Par 109): **110,109,109,107,107 98,97, ,**
CSF £69.03 CT £245.89 TOTE £7.30: £2.10, £3.50, £1.10; EX 81.00 Trifecta £745.80 Part won..
Owner JW McNeill C McNeill Ms L Gillies **Bred** Niall McGrady **Trained** Arlary, Perth & Kinross

FOCUS
There was a decent gallop for this staying event. Solid form. The winner has been rated to his season's best, and the third similar to his good recent run.

4955 ASHLEYBANK INVESTMENTS REG & BETTY TWEEDIE H'CAP CHASE (11 fncs 1 omitted) 2m 1f
3:05 (3:08) (Class 3) (0-135,134) 5-Y-0+ **£6,498** (£1,908; £954; £477)

Form RPR

321- **1** **Jet Master (IRE)**[21] [4549] 8-11-10 **132** ....(t) LucyAlexander 139+
(N W Alexander) *hld up in last pl: stdy hdwy whn nt fluent 3 out (usual 4 out): swtchd wd and hdwy appr omitted 2 out: led and hung lft bef last: idled run-in: drvn out* **7/2**[1]

313- **2** *nk* **Un Guet Apens (FR)**[6] [4833] 6-11-3 **125** ....(p) BrianHughes 130
(James Ewart) *prom: hdwy to ld bef omitted 2 out: hdd bef last: swtchd rt and rallied run-in: kpt on: hld nr fin* **7/2**[1]

443- **3** *18* **Stormin Exit (IRE)**[15] [4651] 11-10-10 **118** .... JamesReveley 111
(Jim Goldie) *chsd ldrs: lft 2nd 3rd: mstkes 6th and 8th: led 2 out (usual 3 out) to bef omitted 2 out: sn outpcd by first two* **8/1**

262- **4** *3/4* **Imjoeking (IRE)**[15] [4646] 7-11-6 **128** .... PeterBuchanan 118
(Lucinda Russell) *hld up in tch: blnd bdly 4 out (usual 5 out) rallied bef omitted 2 out: sn outpcd* **5/1**[2]

055- **5** *5* **Stagecoach Pearl**[105] [2957] 10-11-7 **129** .... RyanMania 115
(Sue Smith) *led at decent gallop: hdd 2 out (usual 3 out): wknd passing omitted 2 out* **7/2**[1]

FP4- **P** **Rockawango (FR)**[6] [4833] 8-11-1 **130** ....(tp) DaleIrving(7)
(James Ewart) *towards rr: struggling fr 5th: t.o whn p.u after 2 out (usual 3 out)* **16/1**

/03- **U** **Kie (IRE)**[48] [4053] 6-11-12 **134** .... WilsonRenwick
(Donald McCain) *chsd ldr: blnd bdly and uns rdr 3rd* **15/2**[3]

4m 21.4s (3.40) **Going Correction** +0.425s/f (Soft) **7** Ran SP% **112.1**
Speed ratings: **109,108,100,100,97 ,**
CSF £15.90 TOTE £3.50: £2.20, £1.90; EX 17.90 Trifecta £76.70.
Owner H W Turcan & Sir Simon Dunning **Bred** Roger G English **Trained** Kinneston, Perth & Kinross

FOCUS
With a couple of front-runners in attendance, this was always going to be run at a good gallop but Kie, one of the pace-setters, ploughed through the third and jettisoned his jockey out of the saddle. That fence was missed out on the final circuit due to damage. The winner is on the upgrade and the second has been rated back to his best.

4956 D G PRYDE LTD NOVICES' HURDLE (10 hdls) 2m 2f
3:40 (3:54) (Class 4) 4-Y-0+ **£3,249** (£954; £477; £238)

Form RPR

342- 1 **Kilgefin Star (IRE)**[13] 4694 6-11-6 121 DannyCook 129+
(Michael Smith) *mde all: lft 5 l clr 3 out: pushed along and styd on strly fr next* **11/8**[1]

2- 2 *5* **One For Arthur (IRE)**[28] 4431 5-11-0 0 PeterBuchanan 119
(Lucinda Russell) *hld up in tch: stdy hdwy whn lft 5 l 2nd 3 out: effrt and pushed along after next: one pce appr last* **9/2**[2]

04- 3 *23* **Just Chilly**[17] 4614 5-10-2 0 DerekFox(5) 91
(Lucinda Russell) *hld up and bhd: stdy hdwy after 3 out: shkn up bef next: kpt on fr last: nvr nr ldrs* **50/1**

060- 4 *6* **Neville Woods**[21] 4548 7-10-7 0 AlistairFindlay(7) 93
(J L Gledson) *midfield: mstke 1st: stdy hdwy after 3 out: no imp fr next* **50/1**

322- 5 *6* **Cousin Guillaume (FR)**[78] 3522 5-11-0 0 BrianHughes 90
(James Ewart) *prom: lft 3rd and hmpd 3 out: rdn and wknd bef next* **9/1**

4P- 6 *6* **Doubledisdoubledat (IRE)**[14] 4665 7-10-7 0 DaraghBourke(7) 82
(Stuart Coltherd) *cl up tl rdn and wknd bef 3 out* **50/1**

54- 7 *3* **Elfego Baca (IRE)**[38] 4221 5-10-7 0 GrahamWatters(7) 79
(Lucinda Russell) *hld up: outpcd after 4 out: n.d after* **28/1**

/13- 8 *8* **Plan Again (IRE)**[38] 4221 7-11-6 121 AdrianLane 80
(Donald McCain) *prom: pushed along whn swvd to avoid faller 3 out: sn wknd* **5/1**[3]

P00- 9 *22* **March Seventeenth (IRE)**[9] 4772 6-11-0 0 BarryKeniry 52
(Brian Ellison) *midfield: outpcd whn mstke 4 out: sn btn* **80/1**

334- 10 *7* **Proud Jack**[16] 4631 6-10-9 0 CraigNichol(5) 46
(Ann Hamilton) *hld up: struggling whn nt fluent 4 out: sn n.d* **40/1**

P **Taxiformissbyron**[58] 4-10-0 0 BrianHarding
(Iain Jardine) *mstkes in rr: struggling fnl circ: t.o whn p.u bef 4 out* **50/1**

146- F **Tough Trade**[21] 4550 5-11-6 120 RyanMania
(Chris Grant) *cl up: 3 l 2nd and niggled along whn fell 3 out* **11/2**

0PP- P **Wind Echo**[104] 2968 6-10-11 0 JohnKington(3)
(Rayson Nixon) *nt fluent in rr: struggling fnl circ: t.o whn p.u bef 4 out* **250/1**

4m 33.2s (6.20) **Going Correction** +0.20s/f (Yiel)
WFA 4 from 5yo+ 7lb **13** Ran SP% **117.7**
Speed ratings (Par 105): **94,91,81,78,76 73,72,68,58,55 , ,**
CSF £7.27 TOTE £2.30: £1.10, £2.50, £14.90; EX 10.30 Trifecta £229.10.
Owner J Stephenson, S Smith **Bred** John F Gibbons **Trained** Kirkheaton, Northumberland

FOCUS
A big field but not many of these could be seriously fancied on previous form. The third and fourth set the level.

4957 JEDFOREST DEER PARK H'CAP HURDLE (11 hdls) 2m 4f 110y
4:15 (4:19) (Class 4) (0-115,110) 4-Y-0+ **£3,249** (£954; £477; £238)

Form RPR

006- 1 **Bellorophon (IRE)**[19] 4595 5-10-11 **95** RyanMania 111+
(Keith Dalgleish) *trckd ldrs: led after 3 out: drew clr fr next: easily* **9/2**[1]

506- 2 *23* **Funky Munky**[21] 4553 9-11-0 **98** (p) BrianHarding 91
(Alistair Whillans) *chsd ldrs: drvn and outpcd 3 out: rallied to chse (clr) wnr bef last: kpt on: no imp* **12/1**

544- 3 *1 ½* **Knight Valliant**[54] 3940 11-9-13 **90** MissEButterworth(7) 82
(Barbara Butterworth) *hld up and bhd: stdy hdwy after 3 out: pushed along and kpt on fr last: nt pce to chal* **12/1**

166- 4 *1 ¼* **Our Boy Ben**[55] 3920 5-11-12 **110** BrianHughes 101
(Malcolm Jefferson) *hld up: stdy hdwy and in tch 3 out: pushed along whn nt fluent next: sn one pce* **12/1**

312- 5 *nk* **Newdane Dancer (IRE)**[17] 4615 7-10-7 **96** (b) ColmMcCormack(5) 86
(Dianne Sayer) *mde most to after 3 out: sn rdn and rallied: outpcd bef last* **13/2**[3]

110- 6 *5* **Markem (IRE)**[32] 4338 7-11-5 **108** (t) CraigNichol(5) 94
(Rose Dobbin) *prom: rdn 3 out: wknd between last 2* **9/1**

4P5- 7 *16* **Northern Oscar (IRE)**[22] 4533 6-11-3 **106** GrantCockburn(5) 82
(Mark Walford) *midfield: stdy hdwy 4 out: blnd bdly next: sn btn* **5/1**[2]

1U6- 8 *1* **I'Ll Be Frank**[95] 3145 9-10-9 **100** (t) DaraghBourke(7) 70
(Maurice Barnes) *hld up in midfield: outpcd whn blnd 7th: struggling fr next* **11/1**

113- 9 *¾* **Too Cool To Fool (IRE)**[14] 4666 11-11-3 **101** JamesReveley 71
(Jim Goldie) *nt fluent on occasions: hld up: bmpd 7th: struggling fr next* **12/1**

/66- 10 *½* **Benmadigan (IRE)**[113] 2789 12-10-1 **88** HarryChalloner(3) 57
(Nicky Richards) *hld up: outpcd bef 4 out: sn btn* **16/1**

/P0- 11 *26* **Bow School (IRE)**[21] 4553 13-11-0 **105** MrJHamilton(7) 51
(Alison Hamilton) *sn cl up: rdn and wknd bef 3 out* **11/1**

213/ P **Everdon Brook (IRE)**[400] 4228 9-11-9 **110** TonyKelly(3)
(David Thompson) *hld up: mstke 6th: struggling bef 4 out: t.o whn p.u and dismntd bef 2 out* **25/1**

5m 19.4s (11.40) **Going Correction** +0.20s/f (Yiel) **12** Ran SP% **115.3**
Speed ratings (Par 105): **86,77,76,76,76 74,68,67,67,67 57,**
CSF £55.86 CT £605.84 TOTE £5.40: £1.90, £3.80, £5.00; EX 66.60 Trifecta £1631.60 Part won..
Owner Straightline Construction Ltd **Bred** Paul Barden **Trained** Carluke, S Lanarks

FOCUS
A moderate event run at a decent gallop. The second has been rated in line with his recent runs.

4958 KELSO RACES A GREAT DAY OUT STANDARD OPEN NATIONAL HUNT FLAT RACE 2m 110y
4:50 (4:53) (Class 6) 4-6-Y-0 **£1,624** (£477; £238; £119)

Form RPR

1 **Sir Vinski (IRE)** 5-11-3 0 BrianHarding 112+
(Nicky Richards) *hld up: niggled along 1/2-way: hdwy over 4f out: led and hrd pressed over 2f out: pushed clr fnl f* **5/1**[2]

2 *10* **Major Ivan (IRE)** 5-11-3 0 BrianHughes 100
(Malcolm Jefferson) *hld up: pushed along and rn green 1/2-way: hdwy over 4f out: styd on to chse (clr) wnr wl ins fnl f: bttr for r* **8/1**

3 *¾* **Shades Of Midnight** 4-10-5 0 CallumWhillans(5) 92
(Donald Whillans) *prom: drvn to ld 4f out: hdd over 2f out: kpt on same pce fr over 1f out* **25/1**

41- 4 *½* **Wolf Sword (IRE)**[86] 3276 5-11-10 0 BarryKeniry 106
(George Moore) *t.k.h: in tch: hdwy to chal over 2f out to over 1f out: no ex ins fnl f* **3/1**[1]

5- 5 *10* **Head Of The Class (IRE)**[21] 4547 5-10-10 0 NathanMoscrop(7) 90
(Brian Ellison) *hld up: stdy hdwy over 5f out: shkn up and no imp fr over 2f out* **8/1**

2- 6 *3 ¼* **Fearless Tunes (IRE)**[24] 4492 6-11-3 0 AdrianLane 87
(Donald McCain) *cl up: chal over 5f out: rdn and n.m.r briefly over 2f out: sn btn* **7/1**[3]

7 *19* **Fight Away Boys (IRE)**[118] 6-10-12 0 CraigNichol(5) 70
(Lucinda Russell) *cl up: led 7f out to over 4f out: rdn and wknd 3f out* **12/1**

4- 8 *39* **Touch Of Steel (IRE)**[79] 3500 5-10-10 0 DaleIrving(7) 35
(James Ewart) *prom on ins: rdn over 4f out: wknd over 2f out: t.o* **18/1**

9 *2 ½* **Meet Henry** 5-11-0 0 JohnKington(3) 33
(Rayson Nixon) *t.k.h: hld up: struggling over 4f out: sn btn: t.o* **100/1**

10 *6* **Golans Choice (IRE)**[76] 5-10-10 0 DaraghBourke(7) 27
(Rose Dobbin) *t.k.h: in tch: lost pl 1/2-way: struggling fnl 4f: t.o* **14/1**

11 *34* **Jacaranda Star** 6-10-12 0 AdamNicol(5)
(Geoffrey Harker) *sddle slipped and loose bef s: hld up on outside: struggling over 6f out: sn btn: t.o* **50/1**

12 *¾* **Lunar Legend** 5-10-5 0 GrantCockburn(5)
(Lucinda Russell) *rn green in rr: drvn along fr 1/2-way: nvr on terms: t.o* **20/1**

13 *7* **Theatre One (IRE)**[140] 2237 5-11-0 0 PeterCarberry(3)
(Sarah Dawson, Ire) *led to 7f out: sn rdn and struggling: t.o* **8/1**

00- 14 *43* **Ceilidh (IRE)**[66] 3727 6-10-10 0 LucyAlexander
(N W Alexander) *in tch on outside: stdy hdwy 1/2-way: wknd over 4f out: t.o* **33/1**

3m 59.0s (2.80) **Going Correction** +0.20s/f (Yiel)
WFA 4 from 5yo+ 7lb **14** Ran SP% **121.6**
Speed ratings: **101,96,95,95,91 89,80,62,61,58 42,41,38,18**
CSF £43.10 TOTE £4.80: £1.80, £2.90, £8.50; EX 27.50 Trifecta £1219.80 Part won..
Owner Langdale Bloodstock **Bred** James F Barry **Trained** Greystoke, Cumbria

FOCUS
Lots of these were bunched heading into the closing stages. The third and sixth help set the level.
T/Plt: £376.90 to a £1 stake. Pool: £70,696.19 - 136.91 winning units. T/Qpdt: £13.20 to a £1 stake. Pool: £4938.88 - 275.90 winning units. RY

4931 NEWBURY (L-H)
Saturday, March 22

OFFICIAL GOING: Good to soft (soft in places on hurdle course; chs 7.0; hdl 6.3)
Wind: mild breeze across Weather: sunny periods

4959 ULTIMA MARK ELLIOTT AND JARED JOHNSTON NOVICES' HURDLE (8 hdls) 2m 110y
1:50 (1:50) (Class 4) 4-Y-0+ **£3,898** (£1,144; £572; £286)

Form RPR

411- 1 **Sign Of A Victory (IRE)**[22] 4529 5-11-0 134 BarryGeraghty 137+
(Nicky Henderson) *travelled strly: mid-div: hdwy 3 out: sn trcking ldr: led last: qcknd clr: impressive* **4/9**[1]

52- 2 *6* **Huff And Puff**[44] 4103 7-11-0 0 AidanColeman 126
(Venetia Williams) *trckd ldrs: led 3 out: sn rdn: rn green: hdd bef last: kpt on but nt pce of wnr* **7/2**[2]

3 *16* **Laser Blazer**[108] 6-11-0 0 RobertThornton 112
(Alan King) *mid-div: hdwy 3 out: sn rdn: wnt 3rd after next but nvr gng pce to threaten front pair* **20/1**

344- 4 *2 ¾* **Fred Le Macon (FR)**[24] 4495 5-11-0 0 WayneHutchinson 109
(Alan King) *mid-div: hdwy to chse ldrs 3 out: sn rdn: nvr threatened ldng pair: one pce fr next* **33/1**

4- 5 *9* **She's Late**[31] 4345 4-10-7 0 RichieMcLernon 93
(Jonjo O'Neill) *w ldr: nt fluent 1st: ev ch 3 out: sn rdn: grad fdd fr next* **8/1**[3]

0/5- 6 *¾* **Herecomesthehollow (IRE)**[23] 4506 8-10-7 0 MrJBargary(7) 99
(Nigel Twiston-Davies) *trckd ldrs tl after 5th: sn struggling: no ch fr next* **66/1**

060- 7 *11* **Gold Carrot**[7] 4807 6-11-0 0 JoshuaMoore 89
(Gary Moore) *hld up towards rr: sme prog into midfield 3 out: sn rdn: wknd next* **66/1**

00P- 8 *2 ½* **Matripajo (IRE)**[22] 4535 5-11-0 0 APMcCoy 87
(Jonjo O'Neill) *j.rt progively worse: led tl 3 out: sn wknd* **33/1**

F0P- 9 *29* **Upham Running (IRE)**[22] 4535 6-11-0 0 BrendanPowell 61
(Kate Buckett) *struggling 5th: a towards rr: t.o* **100/1**

10 *13* **Kiama Bay (IRE)**[71] 8-11-0 0 MattieBatchelor 49
(Jim Best) *a towards rr: lost tch fr 3 out: t.o* **33/1**

F **Devils Paintbrush (IRE)**[169] 1758 6-11-0 0 SamTwiston-Davies
(Kim Bailey) *mid-div: rdn after 3 out: hld in 5th whn fell 2 out: fatally injured* **20/1**

400- F **Miller's Maverick**[16] 4632 6-11-0 0 NickScholfield
(Grant Cann) *mid-div tl after 3rd: bhd whn fell 5th* **100/1**

4m 0.7s (-9.30) **Going Correction** -0.425s/f (Good)
WFA 4 from 5yo+ 7lb **12** Ran SP% **125.9**
Speed ratings (Par 105): **104,101,93,92,88 87,82,81,67,61 ,**
CSF £2.32 TOTE £1.50: £1.10, £1.30, £4.50; EX 3.00 Trifecta £23.50.
Owner Matt & Lauren Morgan **Bred** John Hore **Trained** Upper Lambourn, Berks

FOCUS
Hurdle bends moved in from Friday and chase bends moved out. 9mm of rain overnight led to the ground easing a little, with Barry Geraghty describing it as "good to soft" and Robert Thornton feeling it to be "very dead". Little depth to this novice hurdle, but it was won in impression fashion by red-hot favourite. The second has been rated similar to his Doncaster mark, with the fourth in line with his bumper form.

4960 ULTIMA'S MATT HUDSON H'CAP CHASE (16 fncs) 2m 4f
2:20 (2:21) (Class 2) 5-Y-0+ **£12,660** (£3,740; £1,870; £936; £468)

Form RPR

140- 1 **Pepite Rose (FR)**[49] 4032 7-11-12 **145** AidanColeman 154+
(Venetia Williams) *travelled wl: mid-div: hdwy after 11th: gng best upsides after 4 out: led bef 2 out: clr last: pushed out* **8/1**

300- 2 *12* **Tony Star (FR)**[11] 4742 7-11-0 **133** RichardJohnson 136+
(Philip Hobbs) *nvr fluent: j.lft thrght: hld up: pushed along and hdwy after 12th: rdn into 3rd 3 out: chsd wnr 2 out: styd on same pce* **4/1**[1]

421- 3 *12* **Bally Legend**[28] 4422 9-11-11 **144** IanPopham 132
(Caroline Keevil) *chsd ldrs tl after 10th: rdn in last pair after next: 6th and plenty to do 2 out: styd on wl fr last: wnt 3rd towards fin* **15/2**

505- **4** 2 1/4 **Ulck Du Lin (FR)**[21] 4559 6-10-10 **129**................................(bt[1]) APMcCoy 114
(Paul Nicholls) *prom: led 4 out: sn rdn: hdd bef 2 out: hld between last 2: pckd last: no ex whn lost 3rd towards fin* **8/1**

/32- **5** 2 3/4 **Balzaccio (FR)**[19] 4593 9-10-1 **120**.................................. PaddyBrennan 102
(Fergal O'Brien) *trckd ldrs: rdn appr 4 out: kpt on same pce tl no ex fr last* **11/2[3]**

021- **6** 5 **Greywell Boy**[15] 4660 7-10-5 **124**................................... TomScudamore 101
(Nick Williams) *mid-div: trckd ldrs 8th tl rdn after 11th: nt a danger after* **5/1[2]**

064- **7** 3 **Tara Rose**[21] 4559 9-10-4 **123**................................(t) SamTwiston-Davies 100
(Nigel Twiston-Davies) *hld up towards rr: rdn after 11th: nvr any imp* **7/1**

130- **8** 22 **Grandads Horse**[11] 4742 8-11-2 **138**..........................(p) KielanWoods(3) 103
(Charlie Longsdon) *j.rt thrght: led tl 4 out: sn rdn: wknd after next: t.o* **7/1**

5m 1.1s (-1.90) **Going Correction** +0.10s/f (Yiel) **8** Ran SP% **111.0**
Speed ratings: **107,102,97,96,95 93,92,83**
CSF £38.45 CT £241.25 TOTE £10.10: £2.70, £2.00, £2.30; EX 43.60 Trifecta £393.20.
Owner Falcon's Line Ltd **Bred** Pegasus Breeding Ltd **Trained** Kings Caple, H'fords

FOCUS
A decent handicap that saw the front pair draw clear. Sound form, with the winner rated back to her best.

4961 EBF STALLIONS & TBA MARES' "NATIONAL HUNT" NOVICES' HURDLE FINALE (A LIMITED H'CAP) (LISTED RACE) (10 hdls) 2m 5f

2:55 (2:55) (Class 1) 4-Y-0+

£22,780 (£8,548; £4,280; £2,132; £1,072; £536)

Form RPR

121- **1** **Run Ructions Run (IRE)**[34] 4305 5-10-7 **126**............(p) DougieCostello 131
(Tim Easterby) *trckd ldrs: rdn after 3 out: styd on to chal last: tk narrow ld fnl 100yds: hld on: all out* **11/2[1]**

224- **2** shd **The Pirate's Queen (IRE)**[35] 4276 5-10-9 **128**............. RobertThornton 132
(Alan King) *mid-div: hdwy after 7th: led 2 out: sn drvn: jnd last: narrowly hdd fnl 100yds: kpt on gamely: jst hld* **13/2[3]**

321- **3** 9 **Lily Waugh (IRE)**[13] 4698 7-10-1 **123** oh5..................(t) RachaelGreen(3) 120
(Anthony Honeyball) *trckd ldrs: led after 7th: rdn and hdd 2 out: sn hld: styd on same pce* **7/1**

135- **4** 1 1/4 **Molly's A Diva**[23] 4508 7-10-4 **123** oh8......................(v[1]) RichieMcLernon 118
(Kim Bailey) *hld up bhd: hdwy 3 out: sn rdn: styd on but nt pce to get on terms* **16/1**

531- **5** 3 **Midnight Cataria**[23] 4508 5-10-4 **123** oh1.................. WayneHutchinson 115
(Alan King) *mid-div: hdwy after 7th: rdn to chse ldrs after 3 out: styd on same pce tl no ex fr last* **12/1**

211- **6** 6 **Fairytale Theatre (IRE)**[24] 4500 7-10-11 **130**.......(t) SamTwiston-Davies 119
(Paul Nicholls) *trckd ldrs: rdn 3 out: styd on same pce tl no ex appr last* **10/1**

110- **7** 6 **Down Ace (IRE)**[11] 4740 7-10-2 **128**............................ MissAEStirling(7) 111
(Fergal O'Brien) *trckd ldrs: rdn after 3 out: wknd after 2 out* **8/1**

113- **8** 15 **Toubeera**[21] 4542 8-11-10 **143**.. AidanColeman 111
(Venetia Williams) *led tl after 7th: sn rdn: wknd after 3 out* **20/1**

234- **9** 1/2 **Luci Di Mezzanotte**[21] 4542 6-10-4 **123** oh3...............(p) LeightonAspell 90
(Oliver Sherwood) *hld up towards rr of mid-div: rdn 3 out: nvr any imp: wknd after 2 out* **16/1**

P22- **10** 5 **Cabaret Girl**[9] 4777 7-9-11 **123** oh11............................ CharlieDeutsch(7) 86
(John O'Neill) *mid-div tl wknd appr 3 out* **33/1**

126- **11** 4 1/2 **Joanne One (IRE)**[34] 4298 6-10-4 **123**.........................(t) BrendanPowell 82
(Jamie Snowden) *towards rr of mid-div: rdn 3 out: sn wknd* **10/1**

245- **12** 17 **Mrs Peachey (IRE)**[85] 3319 7-10-11 **130**................................. APMcCoy 74
(Kim Bailey) *mid-div: rdn and sme prog after 7th: wknd after next: t.o* **6/1[2]**

F22- **P** **Massannie (IRE)**[18] 4600 6-10-11 **130**........................(p) TomScudamore
(David Pipe) *hld up towards rr: reluctant and drvn after 4th: sn lost tch: p.u bef 3 out* **16/1**

5m 4.1s (-14.90) **Going Correction** -0.425s/f (Good) **13** Ran SP% **117.8**
Speed ratings (Par 111): **111,110,107,107,105 103,101,95,95,93 91,85,**
CSF £40.87 CT £256.20 TOTE £6.80: £2.70, £2.70, £2.70; EX 41.90 Trifecta £458.90.
Owner Tom Ford **Bred** Minch Bloodstock & AV Bloodstock **Trained** Great Habton, N Yorks

FOCUS
A typically open edition of this race, it was run at a fair gallop and the front pair drew clear. Decent form, with the third rated to her best, and the fifth and sixth rated close to their marks.

4962 ULTIMA - PROUD SPONSORS OF ALAN KING RACING H'CAP CHASE (21 fncs) 3m 2f 110y

3:30 (3:30) (Class 3) (0-140,137) 5-Y-0+

£12,512 (£3,696; £1,848; £924; £462; £232)

Form RPR

/P3- **1** **Roalco De Farges (FR)**[23] 4509 9-11-2 **127**................ RichardJohnson 139+
(Philip Hobbs) *hld up bhd: stdy prog fr 13th: led gng best 3 out: in command bef last: styd on strly: rdn out* **7/2[1]**

/45- **2** 2 3/4 **No Secrets (IRE)**[82] 3424 10-11-3 **128**........................(tp) TomScudamore 137+
(David Pipe) *j.rt thrght: led: rdn hdd 3 out: styd on but hld by wnr fr next: hld on gamely for 2nd run-in* **8/1**

15P- **3** 3/4 **Samingarry (FR)**[10] 4751 7-11-1 **126**....................................... APMcCoy 133
(Nigel Hawke) *mid-div: gd hdwy 17th: rdn bef 4 out: dropped to 6th but stl in tch: styd on u.p fr last to chal for hld 2nd: no ex nring fin* **14/1**

P33- **4** 1 1/2 **Ballypatrick (IRE)**[28] 4427 8-10-10 **124**..................... GavinSheehan(3) 129
(Mick Channon) *trckd ldrs: ev ch 4 out: sn rdn: styd on same pce fr 3 out* **6/1[3]**

356- **5** 6 **What A Warrior (IRE)**[29] 4400 7-11-2 **127**...........(p) SamTwiston-Davies 128
(Nigel Twiston-Davies) *mid-div: trckd ldrs 11th: chal gng wl 4 out: sn hung lft u.p: styd on same pce* **12/1**

556- **6** 3 1/2 **Niceonefrankie**[28] 4422 8-11-11 **136**................................. AidanColeman 134
(Venetia Williams) *in tch: hdwy after 16th: rdn and ev ch appr 4 out: hld in 4th whn hit 2 out: fdd* **10/1**

01P- **7** 4 **Major Malarkey (IRE)**[70] 3655 11-10-8 **126**..................(v) MrJBargary(7) 119
(Nigel Twiston-Davies) *towards rr: hit 2nd: reminders after 7th: drvn after 15th: nvr threatened* **33/1**

4P6- **8** 14 **Highland Lodge (IRE)**[35] 4263 8-11-12 **137**.................... LeightonAspell 117
(Emma Lavelle) *prom early: mid-div 5th: impr to trck ldr 10th tl after 12th: mid-div and outpcd after 17th: nt a threat after* **11/2[2]**

0F4- **9** 11 **Upham Atom**[23] 4516 11-11-0 **125**..................................(p) BrendanPowell 95
(Kate Buckett) *trckd ldrs tl 10th: mid-div: j.rt fr 12th: wkng whn wnt bdly rt 4 out* **66/1**

1F3- **10** nse **Bertie Boru (IRE)**[29] 4395 7-10-11 **125**.......................... JamesBest(3) 95
(Philip Hobbs) *hld up: mid-div: rdn along fr 16th: nvr threatened: btn 4 out* **16/1**

611- **11** 15 **Loughalder (IRE)**[13] 4704 8-10-11 **122**...........................(tp) CharliePoste 78
(Matt Sheppard) *trckd ldrs: reminders after 13th: rdn after 16th: wknd after 4 out* **12/1**

611- **12** 10 **Reblis (FR)**[76] 3554 9-11-5 **130**.. JoshuaMoore 77
(Gary Moore) *towards rr: rdn after 16th: sn btn* **20/1**

130- **13** 24 **Sivola De Sivola (FR)**[83] 3387 8-11-8 **133**....................... PaddyBrennan 59
(Tom George) *trckd ldrs tl rdn after 16th: sn wknd: t.o* **10/1**

6m 40.8s (-5.20) **Going Correction** +0.10s/f (Yiel) **13** Ran SP% **118.3**
Speed ratings: **111,110,109,109,107 106,105,101,98,98 93,90,83**
CSF £31.36 CT £353.90 TOTE £4.20: £2.10, £3.50, £3.80; EX 39.00 Trifecta £671.80.
Owner The Brushmakers **Bred** Regine Bollet **Trained** Withycombe, Somerset

FOCUS
Good staying handicap form. The winner was well in on his old form and has been rated back to the level of his novice form, with the second running a personal best, and the third rated to his mark.

4963 JOHN HAINE MEMORIAL JUVENILE H'CAP HURDLE (10 hdls) 2m 3f

4:05 (4:06) (Class 3) (0-130,130) 4-Y-O **£5,848** (£1,717; £858; £429)

Form RPR

431- **1** **Aldopicgros (FR)**[35] 4278 4-11-5 **126**............................ HarryDerham(3) 135+
(Paul Nicholls) *mid-div: hdwy after 7th: w.w bhd ldng pair: led on bit after 2 out: sn drew clr: v easily* **7/2[2]**

044- **2** 9 **Dolores Delightful (FR)**[82] 3423 4-10-6 **110**............... RichardJohnson 107
(Nick Williams) *travelled wl in rr: hdwy after 7th: outpcd bef 3 out: styd on wl fr bef 2 out: wnt 2nd bef last: nvr any ch w wnr* **10/3[1]**

455- **3** 5 **Refer**[106] 2932 4-10-6 **113**...(p) KielanWoods(3) 106
(Phil Middleton) *hld up towards rr: hdwy after 7th: rdn next: styd on into 3rd gng to last: kpt on same pce* **20/1**

163- **4** 11 **Fitzwilly**[7] 4807 4-11-12 **130**.. APMcCoy 114
(Mick Channon) *prom: rdn and ev ch after 3 out tl after next: fdd run-in* **15/2**

5 nk **Seeyouallincoppers (IRE)**[168] 1772 4-11-1 **119**............ BarryGeraghty 102
(Paul W Flynn, Ire) *trckd ldrs: pushed along whn nt fluent 3 out: sn one pce: disputing btn 4th whn awkward 2 out* **5/1[3]**

41- **6** nse **Stiff Upper Lip (IRE)**[22] 4534 4-11-2 **120**........................ LeightonAspell 104
(Oliver Sherwood) *mid-div: mstke 6th: rdn bef 3 out: nvr any real imp on ldrs* **11/1**

553- **7** 1/2 **Cafe Au Lait (GER)**[14] 4679 4-10-12 **116**...................(tp) TomScudamore 98
(Anthony Middleton) *led: strly pressed fr 3 out: rdn and hdd after 2 out: sn hld by wnr: fdd last* **10/1**

350- **8** 27 **Andi'Amu (FR)**[94] 3161 4-10-7 **114**..........................(p) GavinSheehan(3) 71
(Warren Greatrex) *hld up towards rr: rdn after 7th: wknd after next: t.o* **16/1**

410- **9** 34 **Keychain (IRE)**[106] 2932 4-10-9 **113**................................ BrendanPowell 39
(Brendan Powell) *in tch: wnt 4th 7th: sn rdn: wknd bef next: t.o* **40/1**

2F6- **10** 3 **Brave Helios**[31] 3161 4-10-13 **117**................................. RobertThornton 41
(Jonathan Portman) *mid-div tl wknd appr 3 out: t.o* **16/1**

053- **11** 56 **Shalianzi (IRE)**[38] 3245 4-9-7 **104** oh3..........................(v) MrGGorman(7)
(Gary Moore) *in tch: mstke 5th: rdn after 7th: qckly wknd: t.o* **12/1**

4m 40.0s (-8.00) **Going Correction** -0.425s/f (Good) **11** Ran SP% **117.8**
Speed ratings: **99,95,93,88,88 88,88,76,62,61 37**
CSF £16.02 CT £204.36 TOTE £4.30: £1.60, £1.80, £4.80; EX 18.40 Trifecta £282.80.
Owner Million In Mind Partnership **Bred** S C I De Cercy & Maurice Goin **Trained** Ditcheat, Somerset

FOCUS
A fair juvenile handicap. The second and third set the level.

4964 DBS SPRING SALES BUMPER (A STANDARD OPEN NATIONAL HUNT FLAT RACE) 2m 110y

4:40 (4:40) (Class 2) 4-5-Y-O

£29,505 (£9,840; £4,920; £2,455; £1,480; £985)

Form RPR

1 **Gaitway** 4-10-9 0.. BarryGeraghty 125+
(Nicky Henderson) *mid-div: hdwy 4f out: sn trcking ldr: drew wl clr of remainder fr over 2f out: shkn up to ld jst ins fnl f: rn green but kpt on nicely: readily* **7/2[2]**

1/2- **2** 1 **Tea For Two**[42] 4149 5-10-13 0... MissEKelly(7) 134+
(Nick Williams) *led after 3f: drew wl clr w wnr over 2f out: rdn over 1f out: hdd jst ins fnl f: kpt on wl to draw wl clr of remainder but nt quite pce of wnr* **10/3[1]**

4- **3** 34 **Hurricane Vic**[28] 4424 4-10-9 0... GerardTumelty 92
(Alan King) *mid-div: rdn and stdy prog fr over 3f out: styd on fnl 2f but nvr any ch: wnt 3rd nring fin* **25/1**

4- **4** 3/4 **L'Amiral David (FR)**[21] 4561 4-10-9 0............................ RobertThornton 91
(Alan King) *hld up towards rr: stdy prog fr 4f out: rdn and styd on fnl 2f: wnt 4th nring fin but nvr any ch w ldng pair* **14/1**

5- **5** nk **Rainy City (IRE)**[34] 4296 4-10-6 0..................................... HarryDerham(3) 91
(Paul Nicholls) *in tch: wnt 3rd over 3f out: sn rdn: no ch w front pair fr over 2f out: no ex whn lost 2 pls nring fin* **16/1**

6 7 **Sassanova (FR)** 4-9-9 0.. CharlieDeutsch(7) 78
(Charlie Longsdon) *mid-div: styd on same pce fr 3f out but nvr any imp on ldrs* **33/1**

7 1 **Midnight Spin** 4-10-9 0... RichardJohnson 84
(Philip Hobbs) *mid-div: hdwy on outer over 4f out: sn pushed along into 4th: wknd over 1f out* **5/1[3]**

40- **8** 4 1/2 **Knight's Reward**[50] 4017 4-10-9 0...................................... AidanColeman 80
(Tim Vaughan) *trckd ldrs tl wknd over 2f out* **66/1**

9 2 1/2 **Storming Strumpet** 4-10-2 0.. PaddyBrennan 71
(Tom George) *hld up towards rr: rdn into midfield 3f out but nvr any imp on ldrs* **20/1**

10 6 **Alfiboy** 4-10-9 0.. RichieMcLernon 72
(Paul Webber) *t.k.h: a towards rr* **50/1**

0- **11** 3 1/4 **Terra Firma**[50] 4017 4-10-9 0.. LeightonAspell 69
(Brendan Powell) *a towards rr* **66/1**

12 1 1/2 **Springboks (IRE)** 4-10-9 0... WayneHutchinson 68
(Alan King) *a towards rr* **8/1**

3/5- **13** 1 1/2 **Apachee Prince (IRE)**[38] 4226 5-10-13 0.......................... EwanWhillans(3) 74
(Alistair Whillans) *in tch: rdn over 3f out: wknd over 2f out* **20/1**

14 2 1/2 **Murray Mount (IRE)** 4-10-9 0..................................... SamTwiston-Davies 64
(Charlie Mann) *mid-div on outer tl wknd over 2f out* **50/1**

0- **15** 8 **Sandy Beach**[80] 3460 4-10-9 0... BrendanPowell 57
(Colin Tizzard) *mid-div tl wknd 4f out* **50/1**

16 8 **Another Bygones (IRE)** 5-11-2 0... APMcCoy 57
(Karen McLintock) *mid-div tl wknd over 3f out* **8/1**

0- **17** *4 ½* **Ticinese**[21] 4561 4-10-9 0.. FelixDeGiles 46
(Heather Main) *led tl jinked rt on bnd by paddock entrnce after 2f: pushed along 1/2-way: wknd 4f out* **100/1**

18 *10* **Domino King** 4-10-6 0.. KielanWoods(3) 37
(Charlie Longsdon) *mid-div tl wknd over 3f out* **33/1**

3m 51.4s (-12.90) **Going Correction** -0.425s/f (Good)
WFA 4 from 5yo 7lb **18** Ran SP% **125.8**
Speed ratings: **113,112,96,96,96 92,92,90,88,86 84,83,83,82,78 74,72,67**
CSF £14.15 TOTE £3.80: £2.10, £1.70, £6.30; EX 14.80 Trifecta £699.80.
Owner Mrs J K Powell **Bred** The Hon Mrs E J Wills **Trained** Upper Lambourn, Berks

FOCUS

This looked a good, open bumper, so the fact the front pair drew so far clear bodes well for their futures. The winner looks a smart 4yo, and the third, fourth and fifth have been rated pretty much to their marks.

4965 ULTIMA'S DAVID GARDINER AND JOHN ARMSTRONG H'CAP CHASE (13 fncs) 2m 1f

5:15 (5:15) (Class 3) (0-125,122) 5-Y-0+ **£6,498** (£1,908; £954; £477)

Form RPR

U20- **1** **Prince Of Dreams**[21] 4543 7-11-12 **122**.. FelixDeGiles 136+
(Ed de Giles) *trckd ldrs: wnt 2nd after 5th: led 9th: pushed clr after 4 out: in command after: wnt rt last: rdn out* **7/2**[3]

643- **2** *15* **Sands Cove (IRE)**[15] 4660 7-11-10 **120**...............(t) SamTwiston-Davies 123
(Charlie Mann) *trckd ldrs: rdn appr 4 out: wnt 2nd 3 out: kpt on but nvr threatened wnr* **2/1**[1]

001- **3** *6* **Dark And Dangerous (IRE)**[17] 4616 6-10-13 **109**......(v) BrendanPowell 103
(Brendan Powell) *led tl 9th: sn rdn: lost 2nd 3 out: kpt on same pce fr next* **5/2**[2]

406- **4** *1 ¼* **Olympian Boy (IRE)**[100] 3039 10-11-2 **112**.................. RichieMcLernon 106
(Sophie Leech) *hld up 5th: rdn after 9th: wnt hld 4th after 3 out: kpt on same pce fr next* **8/1**

034- **5** *18* **Alwaystheoptimist**[114] 2762 11-11-7 **120**...................... KielanWoods(3) 105
(Phil Middleton) *trckd ldr tl rchd for 5th: rdn in disp 3rd after 9th: hld in 4th whn mstke 3 out* **11/2**

4m 11.0s (3.00) **Going Correction** +0.10s/f (Yiel) **5** Ran SP% **110.6**
Speed ratings: **96,88,86,85,77**
CSF £11.29 TOTE £5.30: £2.00, £1.50; EX 10.80 Trifecta £21.50.
Owner Jennifer & Alex Viall **Bred** D J Bloodstock, G Roddick & Wrottesley Ltd **Trained** Ledbury, H'fords

■ Stewards' Enquiry : Felix De Giles two-day ban: used whip when clearly winning (Apr 6-7)

FOCUS

Ordinary form for the track. The winner has been rated as running a personal best, and there's a case for rating it higher through the second.

T/Jkpt: £3,550.00 to a £1 stake. Pool: £25,000.00 - 5.0 winning units. T/Plt: £17.70 to a £1 stake. Pool: £168,938.50 - 6,947.24 winning units. T/Qpdt: £8.90 to a £1 stake. Pool: £8352.64 - 687.13 winning units. TM

4722 STRATFORD (L-H)

Saturday, March 22

OFFICIAL GOING: Good (good to soft in places on chase course)

Wind: blustery Weather: sunny with showers; 9 degrees

4966 STRATFORD BOOKMAKERS DAY MARES' H'CAP CHASE (14 fncs) 2m 4f

1:55 (1:55) (Class 4) (0-120,114) 5-Y-0+ **£3,768** (£1,106; £553; £276)

Form RPR

454- **1** **My Flora**[73] 3603 10-11-12 **114**.. HarrySkelton 121+
(Dan Skelton) *racd keenly in 2nd: jnd ldr on inner and gng best between last two: led last: sn asserted* **5/4**[1]

034- **2** *2 ¼* **Carhue Princess (IRE)**[65] 3729 8-10-2 **90** ow2.................. FelixDeGiles 92
(Tom Symonds) *led at v stdy pce: drvn and jnd between last two: hdd last: sn outpcd* **7/1**

462- **3** *1 ½* **Me And Ben (IRE)**[25] 4482 7-11-3 **105**..............................(t) AlainCawley 107
(Fergal O'Brien) *nt fluent 2nd: shkn up 6th and again 7th: wnt 3rd at 10th: 6 l 3rd 2 out: drvn and v one pce after: mstke last* **15/8**[2]

343/ **4** *29* **Queen's Bay**[430] 3682 8-11-12 **114**.. TomO'Brien 89
(Jamie Snowden) *j. slowly 3rd: 3rd but nvr really looked to be travelling wl: dropped bk last and rdn 10th: lost tch 3 out* **11/2**[3]

5m 2.6s (12.60) **Going Correction** +0.40s/f (Soft) **4** Ran SP% **107.1**
Speed ratings: **90,89,88,76**
CSF £8.62 TOTE £2.10; EX 10.50 Trifecta £20.50.
Owner W D Edwards & J Whitfield **Bred** Edward Crow **Trained** Alcester, Warwicks

FOCUS

All bends split and hurdle course rail on inner with distances more or less as advertised on both courses. A modest mares' handicap in which they went an honest gallop. The cosy winner was a 129 chaser at her best and was well in here. The third has been rated to form.

4967 BET WITH RAILS BOOKMAKERS (S) H'CAP HURDLE (8 hdls) 2m 110y

2:25 (2:27) (Class 5) (0-100,97) 4-7-Y-0 **£2,144** (£629; £314; £157)

Form RPR

0/6- **1** **Osgood**[26] 4469 7-10-12 **90**.. JosephAkehurst(7) 96
(Gary Moore) *t.k.h: prom: rdn and outpcd briefly after 2 out: kpt on to go 2nd bef last: sn lft in ld flat: idling and all out* **11/1**

60P- **2** *¾* **Echoes Of Joy**[27] 4447 5-10-4 **82**.. RyanHatch(7) 88
(David Evans) *wore a nosenet: sn prom: wnt 2nd at 5th: hit next: rdn to ld between last two: abt 2 l clr whn clouted last: sn hdd: no ex fnl 100yds* **33/1**

245- **3** *9* **Douchkirk (FR)**[17] 4615 7-11-6 **91**..(b) WillKennedy 90
(John Berry) *led: rdn and hdd between last two: fnd little: wl btn 3rd whn awkward jump last* **9/2**[2]

442- **4** *1 ¼* **Captain Sharpe**[12] 4733 6-11-5 **90**..(t) HaddenFrost 87
(Bernard Llewellyn) *towards rr: rdn after 4th: brief effrt bef 2 out: sn btn* **11/4**[1]

50F- **5** *3 ¾* **Tallulah Mai**[5] 4482 7-11-7 **97**.. JamesBanks(5) 90
(Alastair Lidderdale) *j. slowly 1st: cl up tl rdn and j. slowly 2 out: immediately btn* **6/1**

540- **6** *½* **Stag Hill (IRE)**[10] 4757 5-11-0 **90**..............................(tp) RobertWilliams(5) 83
(Bernard Llewellyn) *mstke 1st: bhd: rdn bef 3 out: no ch fr next* **15/2**

003- **7** *18* **Drummond**[10] 4757 5-9-13 **77**..............................(bt) MissJodieHughes(7) 53
(Bernard Llewellyn) *hmpd 1st: towards rr: rdn 4th: effrt 3 out: lost tch tamely fr next* **5/1**[3]

640- **8** *3* **Maccabees**[12] 4721 5-9-10 **74**.. MrFTett(7) 47
(Roger Curtis) *t.k.h: wnt 2nd at 2nd: hit next: lost 2nd and mstke 5th: lost tch qckly after 3 out: mstke next* **10/1**

004- **9** *5* **Cash For Steel (IRE)**[142] 2176 7-10-13 **84**.. AlainCawley 53
(Richard Phillips) *a in last: rdn fr 3rd: lost tch 5th: t.o after next* **14/1**

3m 54.2s (-1.80) **Going Correction** -0.10s/f (Good) **9** Ran SP% **114.6**
Speed ratings: **100,99,95,94,93 92,84,82,80**
CSF £262.73 CT £1861.24 TOTE £12.90: £3.20, £4.10, £1.50; EX 147.60 Trifecta £692.10 Part won..There was no bid for the winner.
Owner G L Moore **Bred** Eurostrait Ltd **Trained** Lower Beeding, W Sussex

FOCUS

A moderate selling handicap in which they went a proper gallop. The third has been rated close to his mark.

4968 BET WITH TATTERSALLS BOOKMAKERS H'CAP CHASE (20 fncs) 3m 4f

3:00 (3:00) (Class 4) (0-120,119) 5-Y-0+ **£3,768** (£1,106; £553; £276)

Form RPR

043- **1** **Talkonthestreet (IRE)**[82] 3424 7-11-9 **116**........................(p) TomO'Brien 130
(Philip Hobbs) *mde all: drvn and drew clr w one rival 2 out: hung on gamely to narrow advantage after* **7/2**[2]

130- **2** *nk* **Royale Knight**[28] 4427 8-11-7 **119**.............................. ChristopherWard(5) 133
(Dr Richard Newland) *settled towards rr: hit 13th (water): wnt 2nd at 17th: drew clr w wnr 2 out: hrd rdn and kpt trying: a jst hld* **3/1**[1]

224- **3** *16* **Bally Sands (IRE)**[13] 4704 10-10-2 **100**..........................(v) EdCookson(5) 100
(Robin Mathew) *nt fluent 3rd and 12th: pressed wnr tl rdn 17th: 6 l 4th 2 out: racd v awkwardly and no ch after: plodded on* **11/2**

630- **4** *1 ¼* **Sail And Return**[73] 3603 10-11-6 **113**..............................(t) TomCannon 110
(Phil Middleton) *t.k.h in last pair: hdwy 13th: hit 3 out: 5 l 3rd and rdn next: sn lost tch w ldng pair* **15/2**

222- **5** *12* **Lough Coi (IRE)**[15] 4657 8-9-11 **95**..............................(vt) JamesBanks(5) 82
(Anthony Middleton) *a abt same pl: 7 l 5th and rdn 2 out: struggling after* **10/1**

1P4- **6** *11* **Allerton (IRE)**[10] 4757 7-10-10 **103**..............................(t) AlainCawley 80
(Fergal O'Brien) *prom: rdn 17th: sn btn: 10 l 6th 2 out: t.o* **11/1**

23P- **P** **Stormhoek (IRE)**[24] 4490 9-10-2 **102**..............................(vt) RyanHatch(7)
(Nigel Twiston-Davies) *j. slowly: nt keen and nvr travelling: last fr 3rd: struggling fr 11th: t.o and p.u 2 out* **5/1**[3]

/PP- **P** **The Clyda Rover (IRE)**[125] 2537 10-10-9 **109**..............(p) ChrisDavies(7)
(Helen Nelmes) *wl plcd early: dropped bk 8th and mstke 10th: struggling and jumping poorly after: t.o 15th: climbed over 17th and p.u* **25/1**

7m 11.9s (8.90) **Going Correction** +0.40s/f (Soft) **8** Ran SP% **112.3**
Speed ratings: **103,102,98,97,94 91, ,**
CSF £14.44 CT £54.38 TOTE £4.90: £1.60, £1.70, £1.50; EX 15.40 Trifecta £63.80.
Owner Mrs Diana L Whateley **Bred** Edward Kelly **Trained** Withycombe, Somerset

FOCUS

The feature race of the day and it didn't disappoint. The winner and runner-up have been rated in line with their previous chase best.

4969 BET WITH COURSE BOOKMAKERS H'CAP HURDLE (11 hdls) 2m 6f 110y

3:35 (3:37) (Class 4) (0-120,119) 4-Y-0+ **£3,119** (£915; £457; £228)

Form RPR

0P0- **1** **Decimus (IRE)**[29] 4393 7-11-2 **112**.. MattGriffiths(3) 113
(Jeremy Scott) *midfield: mstke 6th: nt fluent 7th: looked outpcd fr 2 out: 5th home turn: styd on stoutly bef last: led flat: drvn and hld on wl* **12/1**

6P6- **2** *½* **Halifax (IRE)**[22] 4533 6-11-2 **109**..(v) TomCannon 111
(Tony Newcombe) *2nd tl led bef 3 out: 4 l clr next: rdn and idling whn mstke last: sn hdd: kpt on again nr fin* **6/1**[2]

335- **3** *½* **Unowhatimeanharry**[27] 4441 6-10-13 **113**........................ ChrisDavies(7) 113
(Helen Nelmes) *hld up in last pair: effrt but stl plenty to do 2 out: 6th and wd st: r.o gamely and threatened briefly after last: nt qckn fnl 75yds* **7/1**

226- **4** *2 ¾* **Scales (IRE)**[49] 4028 8-11-0 **110**.. RobertDunne(3) 108
(Richard Lee) *hld up towards rr: effrt 3 out: 4th at next: hrd rdn between last two: no ex flat* **12/1**

FP5- **5** *¾* **Occasionally Yours (IRE)**[8] 4794 10-10-7 **107**......... JosephAkehurst(7) 104+
(Alan Blackmore) *prom: drvn and lost pl bef 2 out: styng on again after last: fin strly* **9/2**[1]

432- **6** *¾* **Sky Watch (IRE)**[19] 4596 7-11-2 **119**..............(tp) WilliamFeatherstone(10) 116
(Warren Greatrex) *settled towards rr: effrt 3 out: drvn into 3rd at next: nt qckn bef last* **9/2**[1]

2P4- **7** *¾* **Yazdi (IRE)**[10] 4309 5-10-0 **98**.. ChristopherWard(5) 94
(Henry Oliver) *prom: pressed ldr 3 out: rdn next: lost pl bef last: eased cl home* **10/1**

541- **8** *20* **Moss On The Mill**[58] 3850 6-11-8 **115**.. WillKennedy 93
(Ben Case) *settled midfield: rdn and effrt on outer whn hit 3 out: btn next: eased last* **10/1**

100- **P** **Kilflora**[22] 4533 11-10-6 **106**..(p) GeraldQuinn(7)
(Claire Dyson) *led: drvn and hdd bef 3 out: lost pl rapidly: t.o and p.u last: lame* **33/1**

/05- **P** **Minella Special (IRE)**[28] 4423 8-11-7 **114**.. TomO'Brien
(Paul Henderson) *towards rr: rdn after 8th: t.o next: p.u last* **13/2**[3]

5m 21.8s (-6.30) **Going Correction** -0.10s/f (Good) **10** Ran SP% **113.0**
Speed ratings (Par 105): **106,105,105,104,104 104,103,96, ,**
CSF £80.33 CT £545.30 TOTE £15.20: £4.80, £2.60, £2.80; EX 114.20 Trifecta £613.20 Part won..
Owner The Ten 2 One Gang **Bred** Mrs Sheila Kelleher **Trained** Brompton Regis, Somerset

FOCUS

A modest staying handicap hurdle. The winner, second and fifth have all been better than this in the past but look high enough in the weights.

4970 SUPPORT YOUR ON COURSE BOOKMAKER NOVICES' H'CAP CHASE (15 fncs) 2m 5f 110y

4:10 (4:10) (Class 4) (0-110,108) 5-Y-0+ **£3,768** (£1,106; £553; £276)

Form RPR

260- **1** **Ballincurrig (IRE)**[67] 3693 8-11-12 **108**..............................(t) HarrySkelton 118+
(Dan Skelton) *racd keenly: pressed ldr fr 3rd: sustained effrt fr 2 out: led last: kpt on gamely and in command fnl 100yds but all out* **3/1**[1]

/22- **2** *1 ¼* **Sure Thing (FR)**[270] 833 8-11-12 **108**.. TomO'Brien 117
(Henry Daly) *led: 2 l clr 2 out: sn drvn: hdd last: outpcd fnl 100yds: eased cl home* **5/1**[2]

423- **3** *15* **Daliance (IRE)**[5] 4866 5-11-5 **104**.. TrevorWhelan(3) 101
(Neil King) *towards rr: mstke 8th (water): u.p bef 11th: blnd next: stl poor 7th 2 out: decided to run on after 2 and snatched poor 3rd* **8/1**

055- **4** *shd* **Market Option (IRE)**[31] 4351 8-11-5 **104**........................ RobertDunne(3) 99
(Venetia Williams) *midfield: rdn bef 12th: effrt next: 8 l 3rd 2 out: struggling bhd ldng pair after: lost mod 3rd fnl strides* **7/1**[3]

U3P- **5** *3 ¼* **What A Good Night (IRE)**[47] 4066 6-10-3 **92**.................. RyanHatch(7) 84
(Nigel Twiston-Davies) *nvr bttr than midfield: rdn bef 10th: little rspnse: no ch fr 3 out* **5/1**[2]

/02- **6** *1 1/4* **Marleno (GER)**[12] 4723 8-10-8 **95**..............................(t) JamesBanks(5) 86
(Anthony Middleton) *chsd ldrs: rdn bef 12th: 4th and btn 2 out: wknd after* **10/1**

6P3- **7** *11* **One For The Boss (IRE)**[114] 2772 7-10-0 **82** oh7...........(p) DaveCrosse 63
(Dai Burchell) *chsd ldng pair fr 3rd tl rdn and fdd bef 2 out* **12/1**

F4P- **8** *hd* **Tinelyra (IRE)**[60] 3817 8-10-6 **88**...........................(t) AlainCawley 69
(Fergal O'Brien) *settled in last trio trio: rdn and btn 3 out* **12/1**

3P0- **9** *1 3/4* **Marju King (IRE)**[50] 4020 8-10-11 **100**......................(p) TomBellamy(7) 79
(Phil Middleton) *last trio: rdn bef 12th: no ch after* **14/1**

24F- **10** *19* **Oscar Rainbow**[2] 4911 8-9-9 **82** oh3.......................... KillianMoore(5) 44
(Tracey Barfoot-Saunt) *last trio: mstke 5th: struggling in last whn mstke 3 out: t.o after* **33/1**

5m 21.6s (6.60) **Going Correction** +0.40s/f (Soft) **10** Ran SP% **116.0**
Speed ratings: **104,103,98,98,96 96,92,92,91,84**
CSF £18.94 CT £108.57 TOTE £4.20: £1.20, £1.90, £2.70; EX 19.20 Trifecta £144.50.

Owner H B Hodge **Bred** Dick White **Trained** Alcester, Warwicks

FOCUS
A modest novices' handicap chase. The second is a better chaser than hurdler and should win over fences.

4971 STRATFORD BOOKMAKERS DAY MAIDEN HURDLE (9 hdls) 2m 3f
4:45 (4:45) (Class 5) 4-Y-0+ **£2,144** (£629; £314; £157)

Form RPR

000- **1** **Gaye Memories**[3] 4903 6-10-8 0.. HarrySkelton 95
(Dan Skelton) *mde all: running green at times and nt a fluent: u.p between last two: 3 l clr whn mstke last: in command after* **9/2**

360- **2** *4 1/2* **All Riled Up**[83] 3388 6-10-1 0.................................... DanielHiskett(7) 90
(Harry Chisman) *hld up: wnt 3rd bef 3 out and 2nd bef next: hrd rdn and tried to cl fr home turn: plugging on same pce whn j.rt last* **16/1**

3 *24* **Willow Island (IRE)**[17] 3884 5-10-8 0.............................. RyanHatch(7) 75
(David Evans) *nvr looked dangerous: rdn bef 3 out: 4th and btn next: tk poor 3rd at last* **10/3**[2]

00- **4** *6* **Master Wickham (IRE)**[31] 4343 5-11-1 0.......................... TomO'Brien 70
(Paul Webber) *dropped out last: brief effrt 3 out: 7 l 3rd and rdn whn stmbld next: struggling after* **10/1**

0U0- **5** *25* **Back By Midnight**[31] 4343 5-10-10 0.......................... JamesBanks(5) 48
(Emma Baker) *t.k.h: nt jump wl: 2nd or 3rd tl fdd bdly after 3 out: t.o after next* **11/4**[1]

6P/ **6** *6* **Freddie Mael Duin**[344] 5279 5-11-1 0................................ AlainCawley 42
(David Bridgwater) *t.k.h in 2nd or 3rd: lacked fluency: blnd 5th: lost pl rapidly bef 3 out: t.o next* **8/1**

/00- **P** **Sammyman**[96] 3128 7-11-1 0... WillKennedy
(Michael Blanshard) *midfield: rdn and fdd after hitting 3 out: p.u bef next: fatally injured* **7/2**[3]

4m 35.1s (3.60) **Going Correction** -0.10s/f (Good) **7** Ran SP% **116.2**
Speed ratings (Par 103): **88,86,76,73,62 60,**
CSF £64.38 TOTE £5.30: £3.00, £4.30; EX 83.40 Trifecta £171.00.

Owner Mrs Jacky Allen **Bred** Mrs Mercy Rimell **Trained** Alcester, Warwicks

FOCUS
A moderate maiden hurdle. The first two have both been rated as improving, although the level is guessy.

4972 GET VALUE ON COURSE AT STRATFORD CONDITIONAL JOCKEYS' H'CAP HURDLE (9 hdls) 2m 3f
5:20 (5:21) (Class 5) (0-100,100) 4-Y-0+ **£2,144** (£629; £314; £157)

Form RPR

F22- **1** **Watt Broderick (IRE)**[17] 4301 5-11-12 **100**...................(t) MichaelByrne 117+
(Ian Williams) *on his toes: set off last and v patiently rdn: smooth prog bef 3 out: led on bit bef last: sn clr: hrd hld* **15/8**[1]

P/0- **2** *5* **Polo Springs**[73] 3605 7-9-11 **74** oh3...........................(t) KillianMoore(3) 79
(Graeme McPherson) *led: nt a fluent: hit 2 out: rdn and hdd bef last: immediately outpcd by wnr: hit last but gamely hld off the rest* **25/1**

/64- **3** *3/4* **Florida Quays (IRE)**[18] 4604 6-10-11 **90**........................ JakeHodson(5) 92
(David Dennis) *chsd ldr: rdn and ev ch 2 out: nt qckn in 3rd bef last* **9/1**

064- **4** *7* **Drussell (IRE)**[19] 4597 8-11-5 **96**................................. RyanHatch(3) 95
(Martin Bosley) *midfield: hrd drvn bef 3 out: 4th next: no ex bef last where pckd bdly* **8/1**[3]

230- **5** *1/2* **Wom**[132] 2397 6-11-9 **100**...(b) TrevorWhelan(3) 95
(Neil King) *a chsng ldrs: 5th and gng clr of rest 2 out: rdn and no imp after* **15/2**[2]

031- **6** *10* **Ruby Valentine (FR)**[123] 2571 11-10-2 **76**................. JeremiahMcGrath 62
(Jim Wilson) *settled in rr: rdn and brief effrt bef 3 out: wl btn next* **8/1**[3]

000- **7** *nk* **Baksheesh**[41] 4175 5-10-11 **85**... MattGriffiths 71
(Sue Gardner) *bhd: pushed along bef 3 out: no ch after* **14/1**

46P/ **8** *23* **Abayaan**[810] 3553 8-10-9 **83**... AdamWedge 48
(Richenda Ford) *cl up tl rdn 3 out: dropped out qckly: t.o* **25/1**

F0P- **9** *2 1/2* **Genuine Art**[96] 3128 7-10-0 **74** oh3.................................. ThomasGarner 37
(Lucy Jones) *last whn mstke 4th: no ch fr 3 out: t.o* **40/1**

3/0- **10** *3 1/2* **The Boogeyman (IRE)**[13] 4703 8-11-0 **88**......................(t) JackQuinlan 48
(Anthony Middleton) *prom tl rdn 6th: sn floundering: t.o whn mstke 2 out* **9/1**

P/P- **P** **Final Flyer (IRE)**[99] 3062 10-9-9 **74** oh5.........................(b) OllieGarner(5)
(Nikki Evans) *chsd ldrs: hrd drvn bef 6th: sn stopped to almost nil: t.o and p.u 3 out* **66/1**

450- **U** **Going Nowhere Fast (IRE)**[12] 4733 9-10-8 **85**......(p) RobertWilliams(3)
(Bernard Llewellyn) *midfield: effrt in 3rd briefly bef 3 out: 9th and fading rapidly whn mstke and uns rdr 2 out* **8/1**[3]

4m 34.6s (3.10) **Going Correction** -0.10s/f (Good) **12** Ran SP% **118.2**
Speed ratings (Par 103): **89,86,86,83,83 79,79,69,68,66 ,**
CSF £54.29 CT £354.62 TOTE £2.60: £1.40, £4.20, £2.80; EX 68.20 Trifecta £443.10.

Owner Patrick Kelly **Bred** Joe Fogarty **Trained** Portway, Worcs

FOCUS
A modest handicap hurdle for conditional jockeys. The third has been rated to his mark.

T/Plt: £2,571.90 to a £1 stake. Pool of £66766.09 - 18.95 winning tickets. T/Qpdt: £440.50 to a £1 stake. Pool of £4881.75 - 8.20 winning tickets. IM

4973 - 4979a (Foreign Racing) - See Raceform Interactive

4693 MARKET RASEN (R-H)
Sunday, March 23

OFFICIAL GOING: Good (good to firm in places) changing to good after race 1 (2:00)
Wind: moderate 1/2 against Weather: overcast, showers, rain race 4 to 6

4980 32RED THUNDERSTRUCK II SLOT "NATIONAL HUNT" MAIDEN HURDLE (8 hdls) 2m 1f
2:00 (2:01) (Class 5) 4-Y-0+ **£2,274** (£667; £333; £166)

Form RPR

544- **1** **Vinstar (FR)**[45] 4102 5-11-0 115......................................(t) APMcCoy 110
(Donald McCain) *w ldr: led 4th: hrd drvn between last 2: kpt on: all out* **8/15**[1]

63- **2** *1/2* **Broughtons Warrior**[21] 4569 6-11-0 0.......................... LeightonAspell 110
(Willie Musson) *t.k.h: trckd ldrs: clr 2nd appr 2 out: kpt on run-in: no ex nr fin* **8/1**

100- **3** *19* **Wymeswold**[87] 3270 7-10-4 0.. KielanWoods(3) 86
(Michael Mullineaux) *prom: drvn and outpcd 3 out: kpt on between last 2: tk modest 3rd run-in* **28/1**

245- **4** *14* **Jac The Legend**[14] 4693 5-11-0 0.......................... SamTwiston-Davies 80
(Steve Gollings) *led to 4th: drvn after 3 out: wknd last* **4/1**[2]

4- **5** *4 1/2* **King's Opus (IRE)**[308] 389 5-11-0 0.........................(t) TomScudamore 79
(Kim Bailey) *chsd ldrs: drvn after 3 out: lft modest 5th last* **5/1**[3]

0/ **6** *44* **Fine Jewellery**[334] 5469 5-11-0 0.................................... DougieCostello 36
(Tom Gretton) *swvd bdly lft s: sn t.o* **66/1**

P0P- **7** *dist* **Secret Island**[81] 3469 5-10-7 0... CharliePoste
(Anthony Day) *in rr: bhd fr 3rd: t.o 2 out: virtually p.u run-in: eventually fin* **150/1**

/66- **F** **Sedano (FR)**[14] 4693 8-11-0 0... BrianHughes 88
(Sara Ender) *hld up: stdy hdwy 4th: effrt appr 2 out: 10 l down and disputing 3rd whn fell last* **66/1**

4m 4.4s (-2.30) **Going Correction** 0.0s/f (Good) **8** Ran SP% **120.1**
Speed ratings (Par 103): **105,104,95,89,87 66, ,**
CSF £6.51 TOTE £1.40: £1.10, £2.50, £3.80; EX 6.00 Trifecta £50.00.

Owner T G Leslie **Bred** Andre Marcel Pommerai **Trained** Cholmondeley, Cheshire

FOCUS
This is ordinary form. Two came clear late on. The winner has been rated to his mark.

4981 32RED CASINO H'CAP HURDLE (10 hdls) 2m 5f
2:30 (2:30) (Class 5) (0-100,100) 4-Y-0+ **£2,274** (£667; £333; £166)

Form RPR

152- **1** **Jack Albert (IRE)**[39] 4223 7-10-13 **87**.............................(b) BrianHarding 100+
(Dianne Sayer) *mde all: drvn appr 2 out: styd on strly to forge clr between last 2* **11/2**[2]

P/0- **2** *15* **Barnack**[23] 4533 8-10-10 **87**...(t) KielanWoods(3) 85
(Pam Sly) *prom: 2nd after 3 out: kpt on same pce appr 2 out* **12/1**

500- **3** *4 1/2* **Galley Slave (IRE)**[34] 4327 9-10-1 **80**............................ JoeCornwall(5) 74
(Michael Chapman) *chsd ldrs: outpcd 3 out: kpt on to take modest 3rd last* **12/1**

365- **4** *1 1/2* **Iktiview**[39] 4223 6-10-12 **91**..(bt) AdamNicol(5) 84
(Philip Kirby) *hld up towards rr: hdwy 6th: kpt on to take modest 4th run-in* **15/2**

212- **5** *25* **Alaccordion**[20] 4595 9-11-0 **88**.. WillKennedy 58
(Violet M Jordan) *in rr: nvr on terms* **6/1**[3]

U53- **6** *6* **Solway Sam**[141] 2218 11-11-4 **95**................................... EwanWhillans(3) 60
(Lisa Harrison) *chsd ldr: drvn 7th: wknd bef 2 out* **6/1**[3]

266- **7** *6* **Spiekeroog**[26] 4478 8-11-12 **100**..................................(p) DavidEngland 59
(Alan Brown) *in rr: sme hdwy whn hit 7th: sn wknd* **25/1**

400- **8** *3/4* **Siksika (IRE)**[123] 2602 6-11-4 **92**.. HarrySkelton 51
(Dan Skelton) *in rr: drvn 5th: sn bhd* **7/2**[1]

/06- **9** *20* **Jawaab (IRE)**[75] 933 10-11-7 **98**......................................(e) KyleJames(3) 39
(Philip Kirby) *chsd ldrs: lost pl after 5th: wl bhd 3 out: sn t.o* **20/1**

050/ **P** **Jaunty Dove**[33] 12-10-0 **74** oh10... JamieMoore
(Miss Imogen Pickard) *chsd ldrs to 6th: wknd next: bhd whn p.u between last 2: lame* **100/1**

6/0- **P** **Gunpoint (IRE)**[18] 4615 10-9-9 **74** oh6........................ SamanthaDrake(5)
(Richard Drake) *in rr: nt fluent 1st: bhd fr 6th: t.o whn p.u bef 2 out* **50/1**

000- **P** **Amazingreyce**[96] 3141 9-9-11 **74** oh9......................... JonathanEngland(3)
(Christopher Kellett) *detached in last: bhd fr 5th: t.o whn p.u bef 2 out* **80/1**

35U- **P** **Midnight Choice**[24] 4507 9-10-0 **74**.................................. LiamTreadwell
(James Evans) *trckd ldrs: 3rd and one pce whn hit 2 out: 4th whn heavily eased sn after last: p.u and dismntd nr fin: fatally injured* **9/1**

5m 7.7s (-1.10) **Going Correction** 0.0s/f (Good) **13** Ran SP% **116.1**
Speed ratings (Par 103): **102,96,94,94,84 82,79,79,72, ,**
CSF £63.65 CT £761.10 TOTE £5.30: £1.70, £6.20, £6.00; EX 84.70 Trifecta £1075.20.

Owner E G Tunstall **Bred** Miss Marie Harding **Trained** Hackthorpe, Cumbria

FOCUS
A moderate contest. The second and third were well in on old form and could be rated higher, but the fourth has been rated in line with his latest run.

4982 32RED FREE £10 BONUS H'CAP CHASE (17 fncs) 3m 1f
3:00 (3:01) (Class 5) (0-100,93) 5-Y-0+ **£2,599** (£763; £381; £190)

Form RPR

3P4- **1** **Phoenix Des Mottes (FR)**[11] 4759 11-9-10 **68**.............. JoeCornwall(5) 79+
(John Cornwall) *led to 2nd: w ldr: led after 10th: drvn clr between last 2: styd on* **11/1**

211- **2** *8* **Solway Dornal**[2] 4938 9-10-1 **73**.............................(p) GrantCockburn(5) 80+
(Lisa Harrison) *chsd ldrs: blnd 5th: mstke 10th: chsd wnr appr 3 out: one pce whn j.lft last* **6/5**[1]

1P4- **3** *2 1/2* **Over And Above (IRE)**[18] 4613 8-10-8 **78**...................(bt) TonyKelly(3) 79
(Henry Hogarth) *in rr: pushed along 6th: hdwy appr 3 out: one pce and modest 3rd last* **12/1**

2P4- **4** *9* **Winter Alchemy (IRE)**[168] 1789 9-11-12 **93**...................... BrianHarding 86
(Nicky Richards) *chsd ldrs: reminders and lost pl 10th: rallied 12th: lost pl appr 3 out* **3/1**[2]

411- **5** *hd* **Quayside Court (IRE)**[110] 2872 10-10-1 **75**................(vt) GeraldQuinn(7) 69
(Claire Dyson) *w ldr: led 2nd: hdd after 10th: 3rd and one pce whn mstke 3 out: wknd last* **6/1**[3]

/50- **6** *1 3/4* **Killfinnan Castle (IRE)**[26] 4486 11-10-8 **75**.......................... WillKennedy 67
(Violet M Jordan) *hld up: nt fluent 3rd: hdwy 9th: sn chsng ldrs: wknd between last 2* **20/1**

256- 7 1 3/4 **Miss Sunflower**[5] 4890 12-9-12 **70**..........................(p) SamanthaDrake(5) 60
(Tina Jackson) *chsd ldrs 3rd: pushed along 6th: reminders after 10th: outpcd whn hit next: lost pl appr 3 out* **18/1**

6m 18.3s (-13.00) **Going Correction** -0.425s/f (Good) 7 Ran SP% **110.8**
Speed ratings: **103,100,99,96,96 96,95**
CSF £24.52 TOTE £12.30: £2.90, £1.70; EX 30.10 Trifecta £125.10.
Owner J R Cornwall **Bred** Mme Claudie Poirier & Yann Poirier **Trained** Long Clawson, Leics

FOCUS
An uncompetitive race. The second and third have been rated pretty much to their marks.

4983 32RED.COM MARES' H'CAP HURDLE (12 hdls) 3m
3:30 (3:30) (Class 4) (0-110,110) 4-Y-0+ **£3,249** (£954; £477; £238)

Form RPR
320- 1 **Emerald Rose**[134] 2371 7-11-12 **110**.......................... SamTwiston-Davies 113+
(Julian Smith) *trckd ldng pair: nt fluent 8th: hit 3 out: cl 4th whn swtchd lft appr next: led: j.rt and hit last: drvn clr fnl 150yds* **11/8**[1]

333- 2 6 **Dewala**[24] 3390 5-11-4 **105**.......................... JonathanEngland(3) 102
(Michael Appleby) *t.k.h: led: mstke 4th: j.lft and hdd next: led 8th: j.lft 3 out: hdd: j.lft and bmpd last: kpt on same pce* **3/1**[2]

336- 3 3 **Belle De Fontenay (FR)**[21] 4573 9-11-4 **105**.............(p) PeterCarberry(3) 98
(Conor Dore) *trckd ldr: led 5th: hit 7th: hdd next: drvn 3 out: one pce run-in* **5/1**[3]

053- 4 4 **Dream Mistress**[26] 4479 5-10-10 **94**.......................... TomMessenger 85
(Chris Bealby) *nt fluent2nd: hld up in rr: hdwy 9th: 2nd appr 2 out: cl 3rd whn hmpd and blnd last: wknd clsng stages* **7/1**

644- 5 78 **Buxom (IRE)**[14] 4698 7-11-7 **105**..........................(v) AndrewTinkler 63
(Jamie Snowden) *hld up in rr: sme hdwy 8th: drvn next: lost pl appr 2 out: bhd whn heavily eased run-in: virtually p.u: hopelessly t.o* **8/1**

5m 56.7s (6.20) **Going Correction** 0.0s/f (Good) 5 Ran SP% **107.4**
Speed ratings (Par 105): **72,70,69,67,41**
CSF £5.69 TOTE £1.70: £1.10, £2.30; EX 4.60 Trifecta £18.50.
Owner Grand Jury Partnership **Bred** Grand Jury Partnership **Trained** Tirley, Gloucs

FOCUS
A fair mares' race. The winner was the only one with proven stamina and it's doubtful any of the rest got home.

4984 32RED TOMB RAIDER II SLOT NOVICES' H'CAP CHASE (17 fncs) 3m 1f
4:00 (4:00) (Class 4) (0-110,106) 5-Y-0+ **£3,898** (£1,144; £572; £286)

Form RPR
1U5- 1 **Smart Catch (IRE)**[26] 4482 8-11-1 **95**.......................... LeeEdwards 110+
(Tony Carroll) *in rr: nt fluent 9th: drvn 11th: hdwy 4 out: led appr next: j.lft last 2: forged clr run-in* **7/1**

113- 2 12 **Oh Right (IRE)**[27] 4462 10-10-1 **84**..........................(b) HarryChalloner(3) 86
(Dianne Sayer) *w ldr: led 10th: hdd appr 3 out: tired appr last* **4/1**[2]

2/F- 3 4 1/2 **Swingbridge (IRE)**[18] 4613 6-11-12 **106**.......................... BrianHughes 106
(Chris Grant) *nt fluent: chsd ldrs: hit 10th: handy 3rd appr 3 out: sn outpcd: kpt on last 100yds* **3/1**[1]

535- 4 10 **Flichity (IRE)**[26] 4484 9-9-9 **80** oh22.......................... JoeCornwall(5) 68
(John Cornwall) *led to 10th: lost pl 3 out* **16/1**

3P3/ 5 1 **Dancing Dude (IRE)**[523] 1880 7-11-12 **106**.......................... LiamHeard 94
(Barry Leavy) *chsd ldrs: nt fluent 4th: drvn 12th: lost pl 3 out* **6/1**[3]

P00- P **Le Pergolese (FR)**[24] 4514 8-10-0 **80** oh1..................(t) TomScudamore
(Nigel Hawke) *nt fluent: t.k.h early: hit 5th: sn chsng ldrs: j.lft 7th: pushed along 11th: wknd: eased and p.u bef 3 out* **4/1**[2]

600- F **Ziggie (IRE)**[22] 4546 7-11-11 **105**..........................(t) HenryBrooke
(Donald McCain) *trckd ldrs: fell 3rd* **7/1**

6m 21.0s (-10.30) **Going Correction** -0.425s/f (Good) 7 Ran SP% **110.2**
Speed ratings: **99,95,93,90,90** ,
CSF £32.78 TOTE £12.60: £3.20, £1.60; EX 40.00 Trifecta £229.40.
Owner Cover Point Racing **Bred** His Highness The Aga Khan's Studs S C **Trained** Cropthorne, Worcs

FOCUS
Not strong form for a number of reasons. The winner was a 118 hurdler at his best and may be capable of a bit better than this, while the second was again below his best, but similar to his latest run.

4985 32REDPOKER.COM H'CAP CHASE (14 fncs) 2m 4f
4:30 (4:32) (Class 4) (0-105,105) 5-Y-0+ **£3,898** (£1,144; £572; £286)

Form RPR
5P0- 1 **Book'Em Danno (IRE)**[109] 2887 8-11-12 **105**.......................... JamieMoore 115+
(Peter Bowen) *chsd ldr: led 8th: drvn 3 out: forged clr last 200yds* **4/1**[2]

503- 2 8 **Johnnys Legacy (IRE)**[13] 4723 7-10-6 **88**..........................(p) PeterCarberry(3) 91
(Conor Dore) *chsd ldrs: cl 2nd 9th: drvn bef 3 out: styd on same pce appr last* **12/1**

663- 3 3 **Spoil Me (IRE)**[25] 4496 7-11-12 **105**.......................... APMcCoy 107
(Jonjo O'Neill) *trckd ldrs: reminders 10th: handy 3rd and hrd drvn next: hit 2 out: swtchd lft appr last: kpt on one pce* **5/4**[1]

214- 4 1/2 **Croco Mister (IRE)**[122] 2626 7-10-3 **87**.......................... BenPoste(5) 89
(Rosemary Gasson) *in rr: drvn 9th: sn outpcd: handy 4th appr 3 out: swtchd rt and hit last: one pce* **14/1**

514- 5 18 **River Purple**[85] 3352 7-10-10 **89**..........................(t) BrianHughes 75
(John Mackie) *chsd ldrs: wknd appr 3 out* **7/1**

P35- 6 27 **Mister Wiseman**[21] 4578 12-10-8 **87**..........................(vt) TomScudamore 56
(Nigel Hawke) *led to 8th: lost pl after next: sn bhd: t.o 4 out* **12/1**

255- P **Peachey Moment (USA)**[22] 4551 9-11-11 **104**.......................... DenisO'Regan
(Nicky Richards) *in rr: blnd 7th: sn drvn: lost pl next: bhd whn p.u bef 9th: b.b.v* **11/2**[3]

4m 55.4s (-10.30) **Going Correction** -0.425s/f (Good) 7 Ran SP% **114.4**
Speed ratings: **103,99,98,98,91 80,**
CSF £45.00 CT £91.44 TOTE £12.30: £4.40, £6.40; EX 171.00 Trifecta £554.60.
Owner Roddy Owen & Paul Fullagar **Bred** Gerard Mullins **Trained** Little Newcastle, Pembrokes

FOCUS
Weak form. There's a case for rating the race higher through the second and third, while the fourth helps set the level.

4986 32RED IMMORTAL ROMANCE SLOT STANDARD OPEN NATIONAL HUNT FLAT RACE 2m 1f
5:00 (5:00) (Class 6) 4-6-Y-0 **£1,559** (£457; £228; £114)

Form RPR
2- 1 **Its A Sting (IRE)**[34] 4329 5-11-3 0.......................... DougieCostello 107+
(Tony Coyle) *mid-div: hdwy to trck ldrs on inner over 3f out: swtchd lft and chal 1f out: sn led: drvn out* **10/1**[3]

42- 2 1 1/2 **The Grey Taylor (IRE)**[22] 4547 5-11-3 0.......................... APMcCoy 105
(Steve Gollings) *led: drvn over 2f out: hdd and no ex last 150yds* **7/2**[2]

0- 3 2 1/2 **Acertain Circus**[22] 4547 4-10-7 0.......................... KielanWoods(3) 96
(Pam Sly) *trckd ldrs: chal over 2f out: kpt on same pce appr fnl f* **22/1**

2- 4 2 **Maestro Royal**[115] 2759 5-11-3 0.......................... AndrewTinkler 102
(Nicky Henderson) *trckd ldrs: hdwy 4f out: chal over 2f out: kpt on one pce appr fnl f* **5/4**[1]

25- 5 12 **Rock On Bollinski**[50] 4043 4-10-10 0.......................... BrianHughes 83
(Tim Fitzgerald) *mid-div: outpcd over 4f out: lost pl over 2f out* **11/1**

221- 6 shd **Rons Dream**[37] 4253 4-10-10 0.......................... DonalDevereux 83
(Peter Bowen) *chsd ldr: drvn over 4f out: wknd over 2f out* **7/2**[2]

7 11 **Scutsisland (IRE)**[126] 5-10-12 0.......................... BenPoste(5) 80
(Rosemary Gasson) *in rr: drvn 7f out: lost pl over 3f out* **33/1**

6- 8 25 **Diego Suarez (FR)**[144] 2160 4-10-10 0.......................... TomMessenger 51
(Chris Bealby) *in rr: drvn and lost pl 8f out: bhd fnl 6f: t.o* **50/1**

0- 9 1/2 **Robin The Rich (IRE)**[106] 2960 4-10-10 0.......................... DenisO'Regan 50
(Richard Guest) *hld up in rr: bhd fnl 6f: t.o* **50/1**

3m 59.9s (-1.20) **Going Correction** 0.0s/f (Good)
WFA 4 from 5yo 7lb 9 Ran SP% **117.5**
Speed ratings: **102,101,100,99,93 93,88,76,76**
CSF £44.56 TOTE £5.10: £3.20, £2.30, £6.50; EX 72.60 Trifecta £505.10.
Owner Mrs Alurie O'Sullivan **Bred** Peter Byrne **Trained** Norton, N Yorks

FOCUS
This had the look of a decent contest. It's rated around the balance of the second, third and fourth.
T/Jkpt: Part won. £7,169.00 to a £1 stake. Pool: £10,097.31 - 0.50 winning tickets. T/Plt: £216.40 to a £1 stake. Pool: £98,057 - 330.73 winning tickets T/Qpdt: £41.40 to a £1 stake. Pool: £6,024 - 107.60 winning tickets WG

4632 WINCANTON (R-H)
Sunday, March 23

OFFICIAL GOING: Good to soft (good in places; chs 8.0, hdl 7.7)
Wind: quite strong behind Weather: sunny periods

4987 FINISHING POST @ WHITE POST RIMPTON NOVICES' HURDLE (DIV I) (7 hdls 1 omitted) 2m
2:15 (2:15) (Class 4) 4-Y-0+ **£3,249** (£954; £477; £238)

Form RPR
/41- 1 **Attwaal (IRE)**[21] 4569 5-11-3 120.......................... TrevorWhelan(3) 115+
(Neil King) *hld up: hdwy after 3 out to ld next: sn clr: easily* **11/10**[1]

2 14 **Knave Of Clubs (IRE)**[541] 5-10-11 0.......................... MattGriffiths(3) 89
(Jeremy Scott) *hld up: rdn and hdwy after 3 out: styd on same pce fr next: lft 2nd whn hmpd last: no ch w wnr* **25/1**

005- 3 2 1/2 **Ma'Ire Rua (IRE)**[52] 3988 7-11-0 0.......................... JackDoyle 84
(Alan Jones) *hld up: hdwy appr 2 out: sn rdn: styd on same pce: wnt 3rd run-in* **33/1**

P- 4 3 3/4 **Vauban Du Seuil (FR)**[64] 3783 5-11-0 0..........................(t) RyanMahon 82
(Harry Fry) *trckd ldrs: led after 3 out: rdn and hdd bef next: sn one pce: lost 3rd run-in* **8/1**

0- 5 73 **Markami (FR)**[13] 4722 4-10-7 0.......................... IanPopham 8
(Johnny Farrelly) *in tch: rdn after 3 out: sn wknd: t.o* **80/1**

6/ P **Franco Is My Name**[74] 1393 8-11-0 0.......................... TomCannon
(Peter Hedger) *hld up: wknd after 3 out: t.o whn p.u bef next* **50/1**

P **Wyoyo (IRE)**[174] 4-10-7 0..........................(t) RichardJohnson
(Tim Vaughan) *hld up in tch: rdn after 3 out: wkng whn virtually ref 2 out: p.u bef last* **6/1**[3]

4- U **King Muro**[13] 4722 4-10-7 0.......................... AlainCawley
(Fergal O'Brien) *led: j. bdly rt: awkward on landing whn uns rdr after 4th* **10/1**

/0P- P **Starship Trouper**[64] 3782 6-11-0 0.......................... MichaelByrne
(Neil Mulholland) *chsd clr ldr: lft in ld 4th: rdn and hdd after 3 out: wknd qckly: p.u bef next* **100/1**

416- U **Buckhorn Timothy**[43] 4149 5-11-0 0.......................... BrendanPowell
(Colin Tizzard) *wnt v bdly rt and uns rdr 1st* **7/2**[2]

00P- F **Genson**[36] 4280 5-11-0 0.......................... ConorO'Farrell 89
(Richard Woollacott) *in tch: rdn after 3 out: wnt 2nd next: styng on at same pce in wl hld 2nd whn fell last* **100/1**

3m 47.2s (-1.70) **Going Correction** +0.025s/f (Yiel)
WFA 4 from 5yo+ 7lb 11 Ran SP% **116.3**
Speed ratings (Par 105): **105,98,96,94,58** , , , ,
CSF £34.31 TOTE £1.80: £1.10, £5.00, £6.30; EX 36.00 Trifecta £1272.30.
Owner Dr & Mrs Clive Layton **Bred** Darley **Trained** Newmarket, Suffolk

FOCUS
Ryan Mahon described the ground as "good to soft". This looked the stronger of the two divisions on paper. The winner was value for further and the third has been rated to his mark.

4988 FINISHING POST @ WHITE POST RIMPTON NOVICES' HURDLE (DIV II) (7 hdls 1 omitted) 2m
2:45 (2:46) (Class 4) 4-Y-0+ **£3,249** (£954; £477; £238)

Form RPR
U56- 1 **Benbecula**[25] 4503 5-11-0 110.......................... RobertThornton 114
(Richard Mitchell) *mde all: sn clr: kpt on wl: rdn out* **10/3**[3]

/10- 2 2 3/4 **Fair Dreamer**[45] 4102 6-11-0 0..........................(t) RyanMahon 111
(Harry Fry) *in tch in chsng gp: rdn into 2nd gng to 2 out: kpt on but a being hld* **11/4**[2]

4- 3 17 **Verano (GER)**[23] 4529 5-10-11 0..........................(t) GavinSheehan(3) 97
(Charlie Mann) *chsd ldrs: rdn appr 2 out: sn one pce: wnt 3rd towards fin: nvr a threat* **7/2**

00P- 4 1 **Home For Tea**[27] 4467 5-11-0 0.......................... FelixDeGiles 95
(Tom Symonds) *chsd clr ldr tl rdn appr 2 out: grad fdd: lost 3rd towards fin* **50/1**

452- 5 3/4 **Focail Maith**[9] 4796 6-10-11 110.......................... TrevorWhelan(3) 94
(Neil King) *hld up in chsng gp: rdn and sme prog gng to 2 out: nvr threatened to get involved* **9/4**[1]

00- 6 20 **Rocket Scientist**[51] 4017 5-11-0 0.......................... BrendanPowell 76
(Colin Tizzard) *in tch in chsng gp tl wknd appr 2 out: t.o* **25/1**

P00- 7 4 1/2 **Sarahs Doll**[32] 4350 6-10-4 0.......................... RobertDunne(3) 65
(Dai Burchell) *hld up in chsng gp: nvr a factor: t.o* **150/1**

P- 8 14 **Medal Of Valour (JPN)**[54] 3956 6-11-0 0..........................(t) TomO'Brien 60
(Mark Gillard) *chsd ldrs tl wknd appr 2 out: tauled off* **40/1**

/00- 9 16 **Indiana Oscar**[36] 4281 6-10-8 0 ow1.......................... JonPark(7) 46
(Carroll Gray) *a towards rr: t.o 2 out* **50/1**

- 10 1 **Beauchamp Sunset**[24] 4-10-7 0.......................... JamesDavies 37
(Paul Fitzsimons) *chsd ldrs tl wknd after 3 out: t.o* **50/1**

00/ 11 12 **Loxley Mezile**[443] 3489 5-10-7 0.......................... AndrewThornton 27
(Simon Earle) *a towards rr: t.o* **66/1**

3m 44.4s (-4.50) **Going Correction** +0.025s/f (Yiel)
WFA 4 from 5yo+ 7lb 11 Ran SP% **117.1**
Speed ratings (Par 105): **112,110,102,101,101 91,89,82,74,73 67**
CSF £12.81 TOTE £4.00: £1.50, £1.30, £1.80; EX 14.60 Trifecta £64.50.

Owner Mr And Mrs Andrew May **Bred** Floors Farming And Christopher J Heath **Trained** Piddletrenthide, Dorset

FOCUS

Little got into this. The winner has stepped up for the better ground and the third has been rated as building on his recent hurdling debut.

4989 32RED BURNING DESIRE SLOT NOVICES' H'CAP CHASE (13 fncs) 2m

3:15 (3:16) (Class 4) (0-110,107) 5-Y-0+ **£3,994** (£1,240; £667)

Form				RPR
00/-	1		**General Ross (IRE)**[112] 7-10-6 **87** BrendanPowell (Colin Tizzard) *trckd ldrs: nt fluent 1st: bmpd 2nd and 3rd: lft in ld 3 out: kpt on: rdn out* **3/1**[2]	95+
423-	2	6	**Looks Like Slim**[87] 3268 7-11-8 **103** JackDoyle (Ben De Haan) *led: clr tl 9th: hdd next: sn rdn and hld: lft 2nd 3 out: kpt on same pce* **5/2**[1]	104
1U3-	3	38	**Lamb's Cross**[94] 3170 8-11-5 **107** RyanHatch(7) (Mark Gillard) *hld up: cl up whn rdn into 3rd after 9th: wknd after next: lft modest 3rd 3 out: t.o* **7/1**[3]	79
RR3-	U		**Duaiseoir (IRE)**[10] 4780 8-11-9 **107** (b) RobertDunne(3) (Venetia Williams) *chsd ldr: wnt lft 3rd: led 4 out: 3 l up and pushed along whn wnt lft: knuckled on landing and uns rdr 3 out* **8/1**	115
426-	F		**Shady Lane**[123] 2598 7-11-7 **102** RobertThornton (Alan King) *trcking ldrs whn fell 4th* **5/2**[1]	
00P-	U		**No No Cardinal (IRE)**[36] 4281 5-9-7 **81** oh6 (t) ThomasCheesman(7) (Mark Gillard) *hld up: bdly hmpd and uns rdr 4th* **25/1**	

4m 11.2s (11.30) **Going Correction** +0.40s/f (Soft) 6 Ran SP% **109.6**

Speed ratings: **87,84,65, ,**

CSF £10.74 TOTE £3.90: £1.70, £1.60; EX 15.00 Trifecta £72.90.

Owner Mrs S Tainton **Bred** Brian Gallivan **Trained** Milborne Port, Dorset

FOCUS

A messy race and the form is worth little. The second has been rated 4lb off his season's best.

4990 32RED CASINO H'CAP CHASE (21 fncs) 3m 1f 110y

3:45 (3:45) (Class 4) (0-115,114) 5-Y-0+ **£3,994** (£1,240; £572)

Form				RPR
411-	1		**Kentford Legend**[16] 4657 7-11-12 **114** AndrewThornton (Seamus Mullins) *mde all: nt fluent 4 out: hit 3 out: styd on wl: rdn out* **5/4**[1]	128+
213-	2	7	**Jayandbee (IRE)**[107] 2923 7-11-9 **111** (p) RichardJohnson (Philip Hobbs) *trckd ldrs: rchd for 8th: pushed along after 15th: wnt 3rd next: rdn to chse wnr 3 out: styd on but a being hld fr next* **15/8**[2]	116
F1P-	3	11	**Trojan Sun**[31] 4372 8-11-10 **112** (t) FelixDeGiles (Tom Symonds) *trckd ldrs: wnt 2nd gng wl 15th tl rdn appr 3 out: fnd little* **8/1**	106
/23-	P		**Nom De Guerre (IRE)**[112] 2847 12-11-5 **107** (p) JackDoyle (Ben De Haan) *hld up 5th: struggling after 12th: wknd after 14th: tailing off whn p.u bef 16th* **7/1**[3]	
505-	P		**Musical Wedge**[19] 4601 10-11-8 **110** NickScholfield (Claire Dyson) *trckd ldr: pushed along after 12th: lost 2nd 15th: sn wknd: t.o whn p.u bef 3 out* **18/1**	

6m 46.2s (6.70) **Going Correction** +0.40s/f (Soft) 5 Ran SP% **108.1**

Speed ratings: **105,102,99, ,**

CSF £4.00 TOTE £2.20: £1.30, £1.40; EX 5.70 Trifecta £11.40.

Owner D I Bare **Bred** D I Bare **Trained** Wilsford-Cum-Lake, Wilts

FOCUS

A race that took a bit of getting and fair form for the level. The second has been rated to his mark.

4991 32RED FREE £10 BONUS CONDITIONAL JOCKEYS' H'CAP HURDLE (9 hdls 1 omitted) 2m 4f

4:15 (4:15) (Class 3) (0-135,129) 4-Y-0 **£6,330** (£1,870; £935; £468; £234)

Form				RPR
42-	1		**Vicente (FR)**[24] 4514 5-11-6 **126** HarryDerham(3) (Paul Nicholls) *trckd ldrs: pushed into ld appr 2 out where lft clr: easily* **11/2**[3]	133+
/10-	2	10	**Gold Ingot**[154] 1991 7-10-12 **118** TomBellamy(3) (Alan King) *hld up bhd ldrs: pushed along after 3 out: rdn whn lft 2rd next: styd on into 2nd bef last: no ch w wnr* **14/1**	110
350-	3	6	**Castlemorris King**[35] 4300 6-11-5 **122** NicodeBoinville (Brian Barr) *trckd ldrs: nt fluent 2 out: rdn after 3 out: kpt on same pce: wnt 3rd nring fin* **16/1**	110
P14-	4	nk	**Alder Mairi (IRE)**[29] 4413 7-11-9 **126** JeremiahMcGrath (Seamus Mullins) **9/2**[2]	112
663-	5	5	**Old Tricks (IRE)**[30] 4393 7-10-2 **115** (p) LewisGordon(10) (Colin Tizzard) *trckd ldrs: rdn after 3 out: 5th and hld whn hmpd 2 out* **7/1**	100
54P-	6	34	**Falcon Island**[66] 3742 9-10-5 **113** MartinMcIntyre(5) (Colin Tizzard) *pressed ldr: nudged along after 4th: rdn 3 out: sn btn: t.o* **33/1**	74
12B-	F		**Tiqris**[22] 4558 6-11-9 **129** (t) JamesBest(3) (Philip Hobbs) *hld up bhd ldrs: travelling strly and abt to mount chal whn fell 2 out: fatally injured* **1/1**[1]	136+
6F-	P		**Ballinalacken (IRE)**[135] 2337 6-10-11 **117** CharlieDeutsch(3) (Anthony Middleton) *hld up bhd ldrs: struggling whn nt fluent 5th: lost tch next: p.u bef 2 out* **16/1**	

4m 53.0s (-3.80) **Going Correction** +0.025s/f (Yiel) 8 Ran SP% **117.4**

Speed ratings (Par 107): **108,104,101,101,99 85, ,**

CSF £74.60 CT £1163.82 TOTE £6.80: £2.00, £2.80, £3.90; EX 36.70 Trifecta £426.40.

Owner Ian Fogg & John Hales **Bred** Thierry Cypres & Jean-Francois Naudin **Trained** Ditcheat, Somerset

FOCUS

Ordinary form for the level. It would have been an interesting duel between Vicente and Tiqris had the latter not taken a horrible fall two out. There's a case for rating the form 3lb higher through the third.

4992 32RED MEGA MOOLAH SLOT H'CAP CHASE (17 fncs) 2m 5f

4:45 (4:45) (Class 4) (0-120,117) 5-Y-0+ **£5,198** (£1,526; £763; £381)

Form				RPR
121-	1		**Ratify**[21] 4570 10-11-0 **108** RobertDunne(3) (Dai Burchell) *trckd ldrs: stmbld 6th: led 12th: nt fluent 4 out: j.rt but in command last 3: easily* **7/4**[1]	122+
312-	2	6	**Time To Think**[25] 4502 9-11-12 **117** AndrewThornton (Seamus Mullins) *disp ld: nt fluent 5th: nt fluent and hdd 11th: sn rdn: chsd wnr after 4 out: hld fr next: styd on same pce fr next* **7/2**[3]	121+
140-	3	19	**Fitandproperjob**[26] 4486 8-9-9 **91** oh2 (vt) JamesBanks(5) (Anthony Middleton) *hld up in 4th: disp 2nd briefly after 13th: sn rdn: wknd 3 out: lft in 3rd at the last* **8/1**	76
305-	4	dist	**Wait No More (IRE)**[17] 4633 9-10-7 **98** (p) MichaelByrne (Neil Mulholland) *hld up bhd ldrs: struggling and getting detached 9th: lost tch after next: t.o whn virtually p.u to catch loose horse run-in* **8/1**	
0P3-	F		**Webberys Dream**[17] 4637 11-10-4 **98** (p) MattGriffiths(3) (Jeremy Scott) *disp ld tl 12th: rdn in cl 3rd after 4 out: disputing hld 2nd whn fell last: fatally injured* **11/4**[2]	102

5m 35.9s (10.70) **Going Correction** +0.40s/f (Soft) 5 Ran SP% **107.5**

Speed ratings: **95,92,85, ,**

CSF £7.89 TOTE £3.50: £3.30, £1.40; EX 4.80 Trifecta £14.60.

Owner J J King **Bred** Mrs R Lyon **Trained** Briery Hill, Blaenau Gwent

FOCUS

A modest handicap that didn't take much winning. The second is better on softer ground and has been rated below her best.

4993 32RED.COM NOVICES' HURDLE (10 hdls 1 omitted) 2m 6f

5:15 (5:15) (Class 4) 4-Y-0+ **£3,249** (£954; £477; £238)

Form				RPR
50P-	1		**Saddlers Encore (IRE)**[36] 4280 5-11-1 0 RichardJohnson (Philip Hobbs) *in tch: hdwy appr 2 out: sn rdn: led bef last: styd on wl: rdn out* **20/1**	121+
250-	2	1	**Southfield Vic (IRE)**[51] 4016 5-11-1 0 NickScholfield (Paul Nicholls) *trckd ldr: led after 3 out: rdn and hdd bef last: styd on same pce* **5/6**[1]	119
0/6-	3	12	**Monksgold (IRE)**[22] 4546 6-11-1 0 JackDoyle (Alan King) *hld up towards rr: hdwy 7th: rdn appr 2 out: styd on but nt pce to get terms w front pair* **20/1**	108
40-	4	½	**Kudu Shine**[42] 4175 8-11-1 0 ConorO'Farrell (Richard Woollacott) *led: j.lft 4th: pushed along on stable bnd: hdd after 3 out: sn rdn: styd on same pce fr next* **13/2**[3]	109
/40-	5	4 ½	**Malibu Rock**[35] 4296 6-11-1 0 TomO'Brien (Suzy Smith) *in tch: rdn appr 2 out: kpt on same pce* **50/1**	105
P12-	6	9	**Saint Breiz (FR)**[19] 4603 8-11-0 114 MrRobertHawker(7) (Carroll Gray) *mid-div: hdwy 3 out: sn rdn: wknd next* **16/1**	101
/04-	7	½	**Fourth Act (IRE)**[44] 4130 5-11-1 0 PaddyBrennan (Colin Tizzard) *trckd ldr: hmpd 4th: rdn and ev ch after 3 out: hld in 4th whn blnd 2 out: wknd* **4/1**[2]	99+
/06-	8	15	**Absolutely Bygones (IRE)**[119] 2695 6-10-12 0 JamesBest(3) (Jackie Du Plessis) *a towards rr: wknd bef 2 out* **20/1**	81
000-	9	1 ¼	**Bostin (IRE)**[35] 4297 6-11-1 0 DaveCrosse (Brian Barr) *a towards rr: wknd bef 2 out* **100/1**	80
/62-	10	1 ¼	**Demographic (USA)**[101] 3046 5-10-6 0 ow1 RichardO'Dea(10) (Emma Lavelle) *trckd ldrs tl 3 out: sn rdn and wknd* **8/1**	80

5m 28.8s (2.30) **Going Correction** +0.025s/f (Yiel) 10 Ran SP% **122.1**

Speed ratings (Par 105): **96,95,91,91,89 86,86,80,80,79**

CSF £39.02 TOTE £23.40: £6.10, £1.10, £4.40; EX 95.20 Trifecta £567.80.

Owner Robert & Janet Gibbs **Bred** Kevin Neville **Trained** Withycombe, Somerset

FOCUS

The front pair drew clear in what looked a fair novice hurdle. They went just a steady gallop. The second, fourth and fifth have been rated in line with their bumper form.

T/Plt: £48.30 to a £1 stake. Pool: £90000.69 - 1360.04 winning tickets T/Qpdt: £9.20 to a £1 stake. Pool: £5586.38 - 446.00 winning tickets TM

4994 - 5000a (Foreign Racing) - See Raceform Interactive

4729 TAUNTON (R-H)

Monday, March 24

OFFICIAL GOING: Good (good to soft in places; 6.2)

Wind: strong half across Weather: rain

5001 RURAL LIVING SHOW 12TH APRIL CLAIMING HURDLE (9 hdls) 2m 1f

2:20 (2:20) (Class 5) 4-Y-0+ **£2,395** (£698; £349)

Form				RPR
121-	1		**Stow**[25] 4513 9-11-1 125 (p) JoshWall(7) (Michael Blake) *trckd ldng pair: pushed along after 3 out: chal next: led bef last: r.o wl* **4/6**[1]	117+
061-	2	4 ½	**Regal D'Estruval (FR)**[10] 4791 9-11-4 110 ChristopherWard(5) (Dr Richard Newland) *led: jnd 2 out: rdn and hdd whn mstke last: no ex and drifted lft run-in* **6/4**[2]	115+
00-	3	14	**Kagouillot (FR)**[33] 4350 5-10-12 0 (t) PaulJohn(7) (Reginald Brown) *trckd ldr tl rdn appr 2 out: sn one pce* **28/1**[3]	95
/PP-	4	63	**Final Flyer (IRE)**[2] 4972 10-11-5 69 (b) JamesDavies (Nikki Evans) *chsd ldng trio tl pushed along after 5th: wknd 3 out: t.o* **100/1**	32

3m 52.3s (-15.70) **Going Correction** -0.725s/f (Firm) 4 Ran SP% **104.4**

Speed ratings (Par 103): **107,104,98,68**

CSF £1.86 TOTE £1.40; EX 1.70 Trifecta £2.00.

Owner Mrs J M Haines **Bred** Plantation Stud **Trained** Trowbridge, Wilts

FOCUS

Shared bends and hurdles moved onto fresher line. The wind was behind them up the straight, but as a consequence was in their faces running down the back. It began to rain following this opening contest. This was left looking a straight match following the withdrawals. The first two are decent in this grade and were close to their marks.

5002 MENTAL HEALTH CHALLENGE MARES' NOVICES' HURDLE (10 hdls) 2m 3f 110y

2:50 (2:50) (Class 4) 4-Y-0+ **£3,422** (£997; £499)

Form				RPR
12F-	1		**Blue Buttons (IRE)**[37] 4276 6-11-5 126 (t) RyanMahon (Harry Fry) *mde all: in command fr 2 out: readily* **2/9**[1]	98+
600/	2	6	**Bright Intervals (IRE)**[347] 5256 6-10-12 0 RichardJohnson (Henry Daly) *trckd ldrs: wnt 2nd after 5th: rdn appr 2 out: kpt on but sn hld by wnr* **12/1**[3]	83+
/F0-	3	7	**Diddypurptoon**[165] 1832 8-10-9 0 JamesBest(3) (Jackie Du Plessis) *trckd ldrs: rdn after 3 out: styd on same pce fr next* **50/1**	73
/F4-	4	1 ¼	**Rosa Imperialis**[26] 4496 5-10-12 0 FelixDeGiles (Robert Walford) *hld up towards rr: hit 2nd: hdwy after 5th: rdn into 4th 2 out: styd on same pce* **25/1**	72
P00-	5	2	**Canarbino Girl**[36] 4297 7-10-5 0 MrLDrowne(7) (Caroline Keevil) *trckd ldrs: rdn whn outpcd after 3 out: styd on again after next* **100/1**	70
50-	6	1	**Kentford Myth**[55] 3961 4-10-1 0 WayneKavanagh(3) (Seamus Mullins) *hld up towards rr: styd on fr 2 out: nvr threatened* **16/1**	61
0/0-	7	2	**Nowweareseven**[33] 4350 7-10-12 0 SamTwiston-Davies (Nigel Twiston-Davies) *hld up towards rr: rdn and sme late prog: nvr any danger* **20/1**	67

/P0- **8** 1 ¾ **Ifits A Fiddle**[75] 3602 5-10-12 0.. TomO'Brien 65
(Richard Phillips) *mid-div: hdwy 3 out: wknd between last 2* **16/1**

000- **9** *hd* **Miss Dimples (IRE)**[48] 4074 5-10-12 0.............................. WillKennedy 65
(Sarah-Jayne Davies) *trckd ldr tl after 5th: pushed along after mstke next: rdn after 3 out: fdd fr next* **100/1**

32U- **10** ¾ **Buckboru (IRE)**[20] 4600 6-10-12 0.................................. DougieCostello 64
(Laura Young) *a in rr* **8/1**[2]

0/6- **11** 7 **Tamarton Tansy**[326] 85 7-10-12 0................................ PaddyBrennan 57
(Fergal O'Brien) *mid-div tl 7th: sn in rr* **20/1**

4m 39.2s (-6.80) **Going Correction** -0.725s/f (Firm)
WFA 4 from 5yo+ 7lb **11** Ran SP% **129.7**
Speed ratings (Par 105): **84,81,78,78,77 77,76,75,75,75 72**
CSF £5.05 TOTE £1.10: £1.10, £3.20, £11.80; EX 6.50 Trifecta £120.70.
Owner Richard Barber **Bred** Miss Annette McMahon **Trained** Seaborough, Dorset

FOCUS
No depth to this mares' hurdle.

5003 SOMERSET CHAMBER OF COMMERCE NOVICES' HURDLE (9 hdls) 2m 1f
3:20 (3:20) (Class 4) 4-Y-0+ **£3,764** (£1,097; £548)

Form RPR

314- **1** **Hint Of Mint**[43] 4173 5-11-6 124..................................... RichardJohnson 126+
(Nick Williams) *trckd ldr: led sn after 2 out: hung towards paddock whn in command run-in: kpt on: rdn out* **3/1**[3]

112- **2** 1 ¼ **Massena (IRE)**[25] 4515 7-11-0 128.................................. AidanColeman 118+
(Venetia Williams) *led: rdn whn nt fluent 2 out: sn hdd: kpt on to regain 2nd fr last but a being hld* **11/4**[2]

501- **3** 1 ¼ **Very Noble (FR)**[26] 4493 5-11-0 0....................................(t) NickScholfield 116
(Paul Nicholls) *trckd ldrs: rdn appr 2 out: chsd wnr between last 2: no ex whn lost 2nd run-in* **9/2**

/60- **4** 6 **Roberto Pegasus (USA)**[102] 3031 8-11-0 115............. RobertThornton 109
(Alan King) *trckd ldrs: rdn appr 2 out: sn outpcd* **2/1**[1]

/03- **5** 11 **Cape Breton**[31] 2265 8-10-11 0.................................... NicodeBoinville(3) 99
(Patrick Chamings) *mid-div: rdn after 3 out: nvr gng pce to get on terms* **20/1**

6 27 **Tide Runner**[21] 513 8-11-0 0.. TomO'Brien 75
(Liam Corcoran) *in tch tl after 5th: wknd after 3 out: t.o* **150/1**

20- **7** 1 **Obistar (FR)**[18] 4632 4-10-7 0... ConorO'Farrell 67
(David Pipe) *bhd and struggling 4th: nvr any danger: t.o* **28/1**

F/- **8** 9 **Suffice (IRE)**[268] 4740 5-11-0 0.. DougieCostello 66
(Laura Young) *a in rr: t.o* **33/1**

50U- **9** ½ **Sand Artist (IRE)**[31] 4391 6-10-11 0........................... HarryChalloner(3) 66
(Venetia Williams) *a in rr: t.o* **100/1**

10 68 **Shining Cross (IRE)**[412] 4-10-7 0...................................... PaulMoloney
(Richard Woollacott) *a towards rr: t.o* **100/1**

3m 51.0s (-17.00) **Going Correction** -0.725s/f (Firm)
WFA 4 from 5yo+ 7lb **10** Ran SP% **117.0**
Speed ratings (Par 105): **111,110,109,107,101 89,88,84,84,52**
CSF £11.52 TOTE £3.20: £1.70, £1.10, £1.30; EX 13.40 Trifecta £41.40.
Owner Sandie & David Newton **Bred** Mrs J S Newton **Trained** George Nympton, Devon

FOCUS
The market leaders were clear from some way out in this fair novice hurdle. The winner ran to his mark.

5004 BATHWICK TYRES NOVICES' H'CAP CHASE (17 fncs) 2m 7f 110y
3:50 (3:50) (Class 4) (0-110,109) 5-Y-0+ **£4,548** (£1,335; £667; £333)

Form RPR

12P- **1** **Milosam (IRE)**[33] 4354 7-10-10 93.......................................(b) TomO'Brien 109+
(Philip Hobbs) *led tl after 3rd: trckd ldr: hit 4th: pushed along after 10th: led after 4 out: sn rdn: wnt lft whn jnd last: styd on: drvn out* **7/2**[1]

P26- **2** *nk* **Rocky Bender (IRE)**[16] 4678 9-11-2 99........................(b) AidanColeman 111
(Venetia Williams) *led after 3rd: rdn and hdd after 4 out: rallied to hold ev ch at the last where bmpd: styd on* **9/1**

233- **3** 13 **Possibly Flora**[27] 4482 9-10-6 89......................................(t) DougieCostello 88
(Richard Woollacott) *hld up in last pair: stdy hdwy u.p after 4 out: wnt 3rd bef last: nvr threatened ldrs* **7/2**[1]

004- **4** 8 **Tresor De La Vie (FR)**[25] 4514 7-10-11 94..........................(p) JackDoyle 86
(Victor Dartnall) *mid-div: smooth hdwy after 4 out to trck ldng pair gng wl: rdn bef 2 out: fnd little: wknd and lost 3rd between last 2* **4/1**[2]

31P- **5** 1 ¼ **He's The Daddy**[44] 4161 7-11-12 109..................(vt[1]) SamTwiston-Davies 102
(Nigel Twiston-Davies) *trckd ldrs: mstke 12th: rdn after 4 out: wknd 2 out* **6/1**

320/ **P** **Southway Star**[357] 5080 9-10-13 103....................................(t) PaulJohn(7)
(Sue Gardner) *a in rr: nt fluent 11th: losing tch whn p.u bef next* **33/1**

/6P- **P** **Spanish Optimist (IRE)**[109] 2901 8-11-11 108..........(t) RichardJohnson
(Tim Vaughan) *j.lft: mid-div: pckd bdly 1st: wknd after 11th: p.u bef 13th* **9/2**[3]

5m 54.9s (-21.10) **Going Correction** -0.825s/f (Firm) **7** Ran SP% **109.9**
Speed ratings: **102,101,97,94,94** ,
CSF £30.07 TOTE £3.30: £1.90, £4.60; EX 22.80 Trifecta £77.50.
Owner Rob Croker **Bred** James Canty **Trained** Withycombe, Somerset

FOCUS
Little got into this modest handicap, with the front pair drawing clear. The winner can probably rate higher.

5005 SOUTHWEST RACING CLUB H'CAP HURDLE (9 hdls) 2m 1f
4:20 (4:20) (Class 4) (0-115,115) 4-Y-0+ **£3,422** (£997; £499)

Form RPR

230- **1** **Superciliary**[20] 4599 5-10-12 101.. GerardTumelty 107+
(Chris Gordon) *mde all: jnd 2 out: kpt on v gamely fr last: asserted fnl 120yds: rdn out* **28/1**

000- **2** 4 ½ **Frozen Over**[72] 3650 6-10-7 96...(t) JamesDavies 98
(Chris Down) *mid-div: hdwy to chal 2 out: sn rdn: ev ch last: kpt on but no ex fnl 120yds* **20/1**

221- **3** 1 ¼ **Watt Broderick (IRE)**[2] 4972 5-10-11 100.......................(t) MichaelByrne 102+
(Ian Williams) *hld up towards rr: nudged along briefly after 5th: hdwy after 3 out: rdn to chse ldrs next: kpt on but nvr gng pce to get on terms* **10/11**[1]

044- **4** 7 **King's Warrior (FR)**[22] 4569 7-11-4 107.............................. PaddyBrennan 100
(Tom George) *hld up towards rr: hdwy after 3 out to trck ldrs: rdn bef next: nt pce to mount chal: no ex fnl 120yds* **8/1**

143- **5** 1 **Taste The Wine (IRE)**[49] 831 8-11-3 111................... RobertWilliams(5) 103
(Bernard Llewellyn) *mid-div: hdwy to trck ldrs 3 out: rdn bef next: kpt on but nt pce to chal: no ex fr last* **28/1**

502- **6** *nk* **Noble Friend (IRE)**[26] 4494 6-11-4 107................................ TomCannon 100
(Chris Gordon) *mid-div: hdwy 3 out: rdn to chse wnr briefly appr 2 out: kpt on same pce fr last* **25/1**

002- **7** 6 **Quite By Chance**[29] 4444 5-11-5 115............................... MrMLegg(7) 101
(Colin Tizzard) *hld up towards rr: cl enough after 3 out: sn rdn: wknd between last 2* **6/1**[3]

556- **8** 53 **Silvergrove**[25] 4514 6-11-8 111...(t) PaulMoloney 44
(Richard Woollacott) *chsd ldr tl after 3rd: wknd 3 out: sn t.o* **33/1**

402- **F** **August Hill (IRE)**[88] 3289 6-11-0 103...............................(t) RichardJohnson 96
(Philip Hobbs) *racd keenly: trckd ldrs: wnt 2nd after the 3rd: hit 6th: rdn after 3 out: disputing 4th and hld whn fell last* **9/2**[2]

3m 55.3s (-12.70) **Going Correction** -0.725s/f (Firm) **9** Ran SP% **114.4**
Speed ratings (Par 105): **100,97,97,94,93 93,90,65,**
CSF £407.75 CT £1043.73 TOTE £42.40: £5.60, £5.50, £1.10; EX 771.50 Trifecta £3608.90 Part won..
Owner David Henery **Bred** Prince Of Wales And Duchess Of Cornwall **Trained** Morestead, Hants

FOCUS
There was a bit of a turn up in this moderate handicap. The form is rated around the second.

5006 SOUTHWEST RACING CLUB H'CAP CHASE (17 fncs) 2m 7f 110y
4:50 (4:50) (Class 4) (0-120,120) 5-Y-0+ **£4,327** (£1,343; £723)

Form RPR

125- **1** **Duneen Point (IRE)**[197] 1526 10-10-11 105.................. RichardJohnson 109+
(Tim Vaughan) *hld up last but wl in tch: hdwy 4 out: rdn to chal after 3 out: led after 2 out: styd on wl: drvn out* **8/1**

2P2- **2** 1 ¼ **Sin Bin (IRE)**[35] 4326 8-11-11 119.....................................(t) NickScholfield 120
(Paul Nicholls) *trckd ldr: led after 4 out: rdn whn pressed after 3 out: hdd after 2 out: ev ch last: styd on but no ex* **9/2**[2]

330- **3** 38 **Mic's Delight (IRE)**[3] 4932 10-11-9 117................................(b) JackDoyle 94
(Victor Dartnall) *led: rdn and hdd after 4 out: wknd 2 out: t.o* **9/4**[1]

0PP- **P** **Arthur's Pass**[21] 4593 10-11-12 120...............................(p) PaddyBrennan
(Tom George) *trckd ldr: reminders after 10th: wkng whn mstke 4 out: sn p.u* **5/1**[3]

113- **P** **Browns Brook (IRE)**[39] 4243 8-11-4 112.............................. AidanColeman
(Venetia Williams) *trckd ldrs: hit 9th: pushed along whn nt fluent 12th: reminders: losing grnd whn p.u bef 4 out* **9/4**[1]

5m 52.4s (-23.60) **Going Correction** -0.825s/f (Firm) **5** Ran SP% **107.5**
Speed ratings: **106,105,92**, ,
CSF £38.37 TOTE £6.50: £2.00, £1.90; EX 22.80 Trifecta £71.00.
Owner Robin Clay **Bred** Con Troy And David Fenton **Trained** Aberthin, Vale of Glamorgan

FOCUS
Questionable form, with the two joint-favourites failing to run up to their best. The first two ran pretty much to their marks.

5007 LADIES DAY 3RD APRIL H'CAP HURDLE (12 hdls) 3m 110y
5:20 (5:21) (Class 5) (0-100,100) 4-Y-0+ **£2,737** (£798; £399)

Form RPR

000- **1** **On The Move**[70] 3686 6-10-8 89..(t) MrMLegg(7) 91
(Anthony Honeyball) *hld up towards rr: stdy prog fr 8th: rdn to chse ldrs 2 out: styd on strly to ld fnl 100yds: all out* **25/1**

4P6- **2** *nk* **Tara Tavey (IRE)**[43] 4176 9-10-7 91...................................... JonPark(10) 93
(Kevin Bishop) *disp ld most of way: rdn after 8th: tk narrow advantage after 2 out: strly pressed fr last: kpt on whn hdd fnl 100yds* **20/1**

532- **3** *hd* **Frontier Vic**[119] 2723 7-11-5 93............................... SamTwiston-Davies 96
(Nigel Twiston-Davies) *hld up towards rr: stmbld 7th: pushed along and hdwy after 3 out: rdn to chse ldrs next: ev ch last: kpt on strly fnl 100yds* **4/1**[2]

304- **4** ½ **Taradrewe**[77] 3569 7-11-7 95..(t) RobertThornton 98
(Anthony Honeyball) *disp ld: nt fluent 6th: narrow advatage after 3 out: nt fluent and narrowly hdd next: sn rdn: ev ch fr last: no ex fnl 75yds* **11/4**[1]

004- **5** 1 ¾ **Calusa Star**[14] 4733 5-11-2 90..(b) RichardJohnson 90
(Philip Hobbs) *mid-div: hdwy after 3 out: rdn to chse ldrs next: styd on w ev ch run-in: no ex fnl 75yds* **10/1**

66P- **6** 2 ¼ **High Aspirations (IRE)**[77] 3567 6-11-0 88........................ NickScholfield 86
(Michael Blake) *trckd ldrs: rdn appr 2 out: kpt on same pce* **20/1**

006- **7** *nk* **Keep The Cash (IRE)**[14] 4733 6-11-6 94.......................(bt) ConorO'Farrell 92
(David Pipe) *hld up towards rr: pushed along after 7th: rdn and hdwy after 3 out: chsd ldrs next: nvr quite chal: no ex fnl 100yds* **10/1**

P35- **8** 7 **Ballyegan (IRE)**[43] 4176 9-10-0 74 oh2..........................(t) GerardTumelty 65
(Bob Buckler) *trckd ldrs: rdn bef 3 out: sn one pce* **40/1**

531- **9** 48 **Thedeboftheyear**[26] 4501 10-11-2 90...............................(p) JamesDavies 63
(Chris Down) *disp ld tl after 3 out: sn rdn: wknd between last 2: dismntd* **9/1**

123- **10** 11 **Comical Red**[14] 4729 6-11-0 95..........................(b) ThomasCheesman(7) 33
(Mark Gillard) *in tch: rdn after 8th: wknd after 3 out: t.o* **8/1**

004- **11** 8 **Two Mile Bridge (IRE)**[26] 4500 8-11-4 92............................ TomO'Brien 23
(Paul Henderson) *mid-div tl after 8th: sn struggling in rr: t.o* **33/1**

4P5- **P** **Radical Impact (IRE)**[14] 4729 6-10-0 74 oh4..................(b) AidanColeman
(Venetia Williams) *trckd ldrs: nudged along fr 5th: rdn after 8th: wknd after 3 out: p.u bef next* **7/1**[3]

5m 51.9s (-12.10) **Going Correction** -0.725s/f (Firm) **12** Ran SP% **117.2**
Speed ratings (Par 103): **90,89,89,89,89 88,88,86,70,67 64,**
CSF £407.32 CT £2420.27 TOTE £28.10: £6.60, £4.70, £1.80; EX 772.00 Trifecta £2337.40 Part won..
Owner John and Heather Snook **Bred** J M Dare, T Hamlin, J W Snook **Trained** Mosterton, Dorset

FOCUS
Lowly handicap form and they finished in a heap. The winner was entitled to be at least this good on bumper form.
T/Plt: £22.40 to a £1 stake. Pool: £86538.00 - 2809.43 winning tickets T/Qpdt: £14.80 to a £1 stake. Pool: £5283.17 - 263.70 winning tickets TM

4777 TOWCESTER (R-H)
Monday, March 24
OFFICIAL GOING: Good to soft (good in places; 9.1)
Wind: medium, half against Weather: dry

5008 TOWCESTER RACECOURSE NEW GREYHOUND TRACK DEVELOPMENT NOVICES' HURDLE (8 hdls) 2m
2:00 (2:00) (Class 4) 4-Y-0+ **£3,119** (£915; £457; £228)

Form RPR

2- **1** **Spyder**[49] 4068 6-11-0 0.. LeightonAspell 121+
(Lucy Wadham) *hld up in midfield: j.lft 1st: hdwy to chse ldng pair: 5th: rdn after 3 out: chsd ldr next: led between last 2: drvn clr flat* **9/2**

The Form Book Jumps, Raceform Ltd, Compton, RG20 6NL.

/02- **2** 2 1/4 **Such A Legend**15 4693 6-11-0 0 TomScudamore 118
(Kim Bailey) *chsd ldrs: wnt 2nd 4th: led sn after 3 out: rdn and dived next: hdd between last 2: no ex and outpcd flat* **5/2**1

213- **3** 5 **Master Dee (IRE)**33 4343 5-11-0 0 APMcCoy 112
(Donald McCain) *chsd ldr tl led and blnd 2nd: rdn and hdd after 3 out: 3rd and no ex next: styd on same pce between last 2* **3/1**2

244- **4** 5 **Rhapando**33 4343 5-11-0 114 DenisO'Regan 107
(Paul Webber) *hld up in tch in midfield: hdwy to chse ldng trio bef 3 out: rdn and no imp bef 2 out: plugged on* **4/1**3

311- **5** 6 **Son Of Suzie**29 4450 6-11-1 0 ConorShoemark(5) 108
(Fergal O'Brien) *led tl 2nd: chsd ldr tl 4th: rdn and lost pl bef 3 out: wknd bef 2 out: wl hld whn hmpd and swtchd lft flat* **13/2**

00P- **6** 1/2 **Hollywood All Star (IRE)**76 3592 5-10-9 0 KillianMoore(5) 101
(Graeme McPherson) *in tch in towards rr: blnd 2nd: hdwy into midfield after 5th: rdn and no hdwy bef 2 out: wknd and wl hld whn mstke last* **150/1**

7 13 **Maria's Choice (IRE)**75 5-11-0 0 MattieBatchelor 88
(Jim Best) *in tch in midfield: rdn sn after 5th: wknd wl bef 2 out* **66/1**

FP- **8** 2 **Billeragh Milan (IRE)**14 4715 7-10-7 0 JakeHodson(7) 86
(David Bridgwater) *chsd ldrs: rdn and lost pl sn after 5th: lost tch and bhd after next* **150/1**

30- **9** 8 **Wasabi (IRE)**28 4467 5-10-7 0 DaveCrosse 71
(John Berry) *hld up in tch in last trio: rdn and btn 3 out: sn wknd and bhd next: t.o* **100/1**

00- **10** 4 1/2 **Revouge**120 2703 5-10-7 0 MrHAABannister(7) 73
(Jim Old) *a towards rr: in tch: blnd 2nd: nt fluent 4th: rdn 3 out: sn lost tch and bhd next: t.o* **100/1**

3m 56.2s (-11.70) **Going Correction** -1.00s/f (Hard) 10 Ran SP% **109.9**
Speed ratings (Par 105): **89,87,85,82,79 79,73,72,68,65**
CSF £15.29 TOTE £6.70: £2.00, £1.20, £1.50; EX 17.30 Trifecta £51.90.
Owner Miss KJ Austin & Miss Christina Blockley **Bred** Graham Aldrich & Miss Tracy Robinson **Trained** Newmarket, Suffolk

FOCUS
Chase course out wide on separate bends. Hurdle course on inside line as utilised on March 13th. A fair novice hurdle in which they went a steady gallop. The first two are rated pretty much to their marks.

5009 HAPPY BIRTHDAY JANET H'CAP CHASE (14 fncs) 2m 3f 110y
2:30 (2:31) (Class 5) (0-100,100) 5-Y-0+ **£2,144** (£629; £314; £157)

Form RPR

P03- **1** **Riddlestown (IRE)**12 4759 7-11-6 94 HarrySkelton 110+
(Caroline Fryer) *chsd ldrs: pressed ldr 9th: j.rt and mstke next: nt fluent next: rdn and ev ch 3 out: drvn ahd bef next: battled on gamely u.p flat: a jst holding on* **3/1**1

323- **2** nk **Todareistodo**32 4372 8-11-5 100 MrHAABannister(7) 113
(Jim Old) *hld up in rr: stdy prog 6th: trckd ldrs 11th: cl 3rd and effrt bef 2 out: gd jump and pressed wnr last: kpt on u.p: a jst hld* **3/1**1

253- **3** 6 **Fair Bramble**34 4337 8-11-12 100 (b1) LeightonAspell 109+
(Oliver Sherwood) *j.rt and mstkes: pressed ldrs tl led 6th: rdn and hdd after 3 out: stl ev ch and j.rt last: wknd flat* **5/1**2

134- **4** 12 **Bill The Lad (IRE)**60 3855 7-11-0 88 AdamWedge 87
(Paul Cowley) *hld up in last pair: struggling and mstke 9th: plugged on past btn horses to go 4th 2 out: no imp and wl hld whn wandered lft flat* **3/1**1

UP0- **5** 7 **Thorncliffer**12 4759 10-9-7 74 oh8 (t) OllieGarner(7) 64
(Derek Shaw) *pressed ldrs tl led 2nd: hdd: dived and mstke 6th: nvr jumping fluently after: rdn and struggling 10th: wknd after 3 out* **25/1**

6P4- **6** 9 **Trozulon (FR)**26 4488 7-11-8 99 RobertDunne(3) 87
(Venetia Williams) *hld up towards rr: hdwy into midfield 5th: mstke 10th: cl 5th and rdn 3 out: wknd bef next* **10/1**3

133- **P** **Shantou Breeze (IRE)**207 1432 7-11-4 92 MarcGoldstein
(Michael Madgwick) *in tch in midfield: cl 4th 3 out: rdn and btn whn j.lft and mstke next: sn wknd: bhd whn p.u last* **20/1**

00F- **P** **Saudi Pearl (IRE)**114 2825 6-10-8 89 (v) RyanHatch(7)
(Nigel Twiston-Davies) *led tl after 2nd: styd pressing ldrs tl lost pl qckly after 11th: bhd next: t.o whn p.u 2 out* **25/1**

5m 6.15s (-12.05) **Going Correction** -0.575s/f (Firm) 8 Ran SP% **113.2**
Speed ratings: **101,100,98,93,90 87, ,**
CSF £12.39 CT £41.28 TOTE £3.80: £1.30, £1.30, £1.70; EX 13.20 Trifecta £55.10.
Owner J Ward **Bred** Jeremiah O'Brien **Trained** Wymondham, Norfolk

FOCUS
A moderate handicap chase. The winner was a bit better than the bare form and is rated to his mark.

5010 MICK & SHEILA 50TH WEDDING ANNIVERSARY MARES' H'CAP HURDLE (12 hdls) 3m
3:00 (3:00) (Class 3) (0-130,124) 4-Y-0+ **£5,393** (£1,583; £791; £395)

Form RPR

021- **1** **Bull And Bush (IRE)**24 4528 5-11-9 121 WayneHutchinson 128+
(Alan King) *hld up in tch in midfield: 5th and clsng on ldrs after 3 out: rdn to ld between last 2: looked in command whn blnd last: rdn and asserted flat: styd on wl* **4/1**1

321- **2** 3/4 **Cove (IRE)**9 4797 7-10-6 104 AndrewThornton 107+
(Nick Gifford) *t.k.h: hld up in tch in rr: hdwy to chse ldrs 3 out: ev ch next: drew w wnr between last 2: looked hld last: lft upsides again flat: no ex u.p fnl 75yds* **6/1**3

/32- **3** 3 1/4 **Miss Milborne**27 4484 8-11-8 120 (v1) BrendanPowell 120
(Jamie Snowden) *chsd ldrs: wnt 2nd 3rd tl bef 2 out: outpcd whn short of room and swtchd lft between last: kpt on u.p: no threat to ldng pair* **8/1**

104- **4** 1 3/4 **Tea Caddy**34 4337 8-10-9 107 (t) AndrewTinkler 106
(Jamie Snowden) *chsd ldrs: n.m.r bef 3 out: lost pl and last pair whn nt fluent 3 out: rallied and kpt on between last 2: no threat to ldng pair* **50/1**

051- **5** 4 **Pyleigh Lass**16 4676 8-11-2 114 (t) IanPopham 110
(Martin Keighley) *in tch: j.lft 5th: rdn and outpcd bef 2 out: plugged on same pce between last 2* **12/1**

134- **6** 8 **Truckers Darling (IRE)**14 4717 7-10-10 113 ConorShoemark(5) 106+
(Don Cantillon) *in tch in midfield: j. awkwardly 8th: jnd ldrs next: rdn to ld bef 2 out: hdd wl bef last: sn hung rt and btn: wkng whn blnd last* **16/1**

246- **7** 2 1/2 **Teochew (IRE)**72 3649 6-11-3 118 GavinSheehan(3) 105
(Warren Greatrex) *led tl rdn and hdd bef 2 out: wknd between last 2* **9/2**2

154- **8** 4 1/2 **Coronea Lilly (IRE)**155 1989 10-11-12 124 (tp) APMcCoy 105
(Neil Mulholland) *chsd ldr tl 3rd: styd chsng ldrs: rdn bef 8th: wknd after 3 out* **11/1**

241- **P** **Mistral Reine**38 4249 5-10-12 110 LeightonAspell
(Lucy Wadham) *hld up in rr: dived at 2nd and immediately eased and p.u* **15/2**

132- **P** **Dardanella**25 4508 7-10-13 111 JamieMoore
(Richard Lee) *in tch in midfield: struggling and dropped to rr 3 out: sn wknd: t.o whn p.u last* **13/2**

6m 6.4s (-8.60) **Going Correction** -1.00s/f (Hard) 10 Ran SP% **112.5**
Speed ratings (Par 107): **74,73,72,72,70 68,67,65, ,**
CSF £27.52 CT £180.01 TOTE £3.80: £2.00, £2.10, £4.00; EX 16.50 Trifecta £120.90.
Owner W A Harrison-Allan **Bred** M Conaghan **Trained** Barbury Castle, Wilts

FOCUS
Not a bad mares' handicap. A big step up from the unexposed winner.

5011 PAUL HARDICK MEMORIAL H'CAP CHASE (18 fncs) 3m 110y
3:30 (3:30) (Class 5) (0-100,98) 5-Y-0+ **£2,144** (£629; £314; £157)

Form RPR

/41- **1** **Cosway Spirit (IRE)**11 4778 7-11-0 86 (p) DavidBass 106+
(Ben Pauling) *rn green: w ldr: gng best 3 out: led and drew clr bef next: in command and wandering whn mstke last: wnt lft u.p flat: eased towards fin* **9/4**1

/01- **2** 9 **Classic Case (IRE)**114 2825 7-11-6 92 LeightonAspell 98
(Sean Curran) *hld up in tch towards rr: hdwy to chse ldrs 14th: 3rd and effrt 3 out: chsd clr wnr between last 2: plugged on but no imp* **8/1**

332- **3** 6 **Basford Ben**18 4630 6-11-9 95 (p) SeanQuinlan 98+
(Jennie Candlish) *in tch in midfield: 6th and struggling u.p 3 out: no prog and wl btn next: plugged on u.p to go 3rd towards fin* **4/1**2

0P5- **4** 1 1/4 **Bishophill Jack (IRE)**5 4905 8-11-7 93 (v) AndrewThornton 96+
(Kim Bailey) *mde most: mstke 13th: rdn and hdd after 3 out: btn 2 out: 3rd and wl hld last: wknd and lost 3rd towards fin* **10/1**

565- **5** 1 1/4 **Ultra Klass (FR)**17 4663 6-11-4 90 (p) AndrewTinkler 89
(Jamie Snowden) *chsd ldrs: 4th and drvn after 3 out: no hdwy and btn next: wknd between last 2* **16/1**

54P- **6** 14 **Jolly Boys Outing (IRE)**88 3277 11-10-8 85 BenPoste(5) 71
(Rosemary Gasson) *t.k.h: hld up in tch in midfield: rdn and struggling 14th: wknd 3 out* **10/1**

0/5- **7** 9 **Trifollet**12 4759 9-10-8 87 MrJMartin(7) 65
(Andrew J Martin) *in tch towards rr: mstke 8th: pushed along next: rdn 12th: struggling after next: wknd bef 3 out: t.o* **20/1**

362- **8** 4 1/2 **Doubletoilntrouble (IRE)**48 4078 8-11-3 94 (bt) ConorShoemark(5) 68
(Fergal O'Brien) *in tch towards rr: hdwy into midfield 13th: drvn and btn whn j.rt 3 out: sn wknd: t.o* **7/1**3

13U- **9** shd **Royaume Bleu (FR)**28 4471 9-11-7 98 KillianMoore(5) 72
(Alex Hales) *t.k.h: chsd ldrs tl dropped to rr and rdn after 11th: wknd bef 3 out: t.o* **14/1**

33P- **P** **Overton Lad**99 3114 13-9-11 72 oh8 (bt) GavinSheehan(3)
(Peter Pritchard) *in tch tl lost pl 8th: detached and rdn 10th: nvr on terms after: t.o whn p.u 3 out* **25/1**

PP0- **P** **Zelos Diktator**12 4760 8-9-10 78 ow3 MikeyHamill(10)
(Sean Curran) *nt jump wl and nvr gng wl: a in rr: reminders after several fences: lost tch after 9th: t.o and p.u 11th* **50/1**

6m 20.9s (-16.00) **Going Correction** -0.575s/f (Firm) 11 Ran SP% **115.7**
Speed ratings: **102,99,97,96,96 91,89,87,87,**
CSF £20.22 CT £68.47 TOTE £3.10: £1.60, £2.10, £1.70; EX 20.60 Trifecta £51.70.
Owner Alan Marsh & Partners **Bred** James Lawler **Trained** Bourton-On-The-Water, Gloucs

FOCUS
A moderate handicap won by a progressive chaser. The form is rated around the second to fourth.

5012 HAPPY 90TH BIRTHDAY MICHAEL FINN H'CAP HURDLE (8 hdls) 2m
4:00 (4:00) (Class 5) (0-100,99) 4-Y-0+ **£1,949** (£572; £286; £143)

Form RPR

001- **1** **Take The Crown**4 4911 5-10-12 85 7ex DenisO'Regan 96+
(Henry Oliver) *in tch and a gng wl: trckd ldr bef 2 out: led 2 out: sn clr and r.o wl: easily* **4/5**1

004- **2** 6 **El Toreros (USA)**88 3251 6-10-10 88 (t) ConorShoemark(5) 91
(Lawney Hill) *t.k.h: hld up in last trio: hdwy bef 3 out: rdn to chse ldng trio bef 2 out: kpt on u.p to go 2nd towards fin: no ch w wnr* **12/1**

332- **3** 1/2 **Walter De La Mare (IRE)**21 4597 7-11-9 96 APMcCoy 98
(Anabel K Murphy) *hld up in rr: stdy hdwy 5th: rdn to chse ldng pair 2 out: no ch w wnr and kpt on same pce between last 2* **11/2**2

00P- **4** shd **Sun Quest**34 4334 10-10-9 89 (t) MrLKilgarriff(7) 93+
(Steven Dixon) *in tch in midfield: hdwy to chse ldr bef 3 out: led bef 2 out: rdn and hdd 2 out: sn brushed aside by wnr: blnd last: lost 2 pls flat* **25/1**

04P- **5** 9 **Hurricane Ivan (IRE)**84 3425 6-11-0 94 (t) MrHBeswick(7) 87
(Fergal O'Brien) *bhd: detached in last pair and rdn 4th: styd on past btn horses 2 out: nvr trbld ldrs* **33/1**

404- **6** 2 1/2 **Hellesbelles (IRE)**35 4328 6-11-1 98 (p) AlanJohns(10) 88
(Tim Vaughan) *in tch in midfield: mstke 5th: rdn and effrt after 3 out: 5th and wl hld 2 out: wknd* **20/1**

055- **7** 11 **Asker (IRE)**11 4781 6-11-0 94 (p) MrHGMiller(7) 73
(Zoe Davison) *chsd ldrs: rdn and btn bef 2 out: fdd between last 2* **50/1**

060- **8** 3/4 **Houseparty**22 4573 6-11-5 99 1 MissTWorsley(7) 78
(Zoe Davison) *hld up in rr: steadily clsd fr 4th: chsd ldrs 3 out: rdn and btn bef next: fdd between last 2* **50/1**

/32- **9** 9 **Grand Article (IRE)**60 3856 10-10-1 74 AdamWedge 44
(Paul Cowley) *led tl 2nd: chsd ldr tl lost pl u.p bef 3 out: bhd 2 out: t.o* **12/1**

660- **10** 8 **Prime Contender**24 4533 12-11-8 95 (vt) SamThomas 57
(Jennie Candlish) *dropped to rr 2nd and nvr gng wl after: detached last after 3rd: t.o fr next* **25/1**

05P- **11** 26 **Torgamah Lad (IRE)**18 4636 6-11-5 95 (b1) RobertDunne(3) 31
(Venetia Williams) *t.k.h: chsd ldrs tl led 2nd: rdn and hdd bef 2 out: sn fdd: wl bhd and heavily eased flat: t.o* **8/1**3

3m 50.95s (-16.95) **Going Correction** -1.00s/f (Hard) 11 Ran SP% **116.8**
Speed ratings (Par 103): **102,99,98,98,94 92,87,87,82,78 65**
CSF £9.78 CT £35.24 TOTE £1.50: £1.10, £3.00, £1.70; EX 11.00 Trifecta £54.10.
Owner R G Whitehead **Bred** R D M Sharp **Trained** Broomhall, Worcs

FOCUS
A weak handicap hurdle in which they went a decent gallop. The winner was well in and is rated to his Chepstow level.

5013 BARRY R JOHNSON 65 ISN'T OLD H'CAP CHASE (12 fncs) 2m 110y
4:30 (4:30) (Class 4) (0-115,115) 5-Y-0+ **£3,768** (£1,106; £553; £276)

Form RPR

454- **1** **Le Bacardy (FR)**7 4861 8-11-12 115 (p) LeeEdwards 126+
(Tony Carroll) *chsd ldr: nt fluent 6th: pushed into ld bef 2 out: clr and in command between last 2: kpt on: comf* **2/1**2

2P3- **2** 4 1/2 **Speedy Bruere (FR)**9 4800 8-11-12 115 TomScudamore 123+
(David Bridgwater) *led: rdn and hdd after 3 out: blnd next: lost 2nd between last 2: wnt 2nd again and mstke last: no imp* **6/4**1

44F- **3** *2* **Missionaire (USA)**[123] 2615 7-10-0 **92**........................ TrevorWhelan(3) 96
(Tony Carroll) *in tch in 3rd: effrt 2 out: outpcd by wnr between last 2: battling for 2nd flat: no ex fnl 100yds* **7/2**[3]

122- **4** *10* **Bennys Quest (IRE)**[175] 1696 11-11-7 **115**............(p) ConorShoemark(5) 112
(Neil Mulholland) *hld up in tch in rr: clsd to trck ldrs 3 out: effrt next: chsd clr wnr but no rspnse whn rdn between last 2: mstke and lost 2nd last: wknd* **7/1**

4m 6.5s (-9.60) **Going Correction** -0.575s/f (Firm) **4** Ran SP% **108.1**
Speed ratings: **99,96,95,91**
CSF £5.53 TOTE £2.50; EX 7.40 Trifecta £11.70.
Owner Carl Hodgson **Bred** Jean-Charles Coude **Trained** Cropthorne, Worcs

FOCUS
A modest small-field handicap chase in which they went a proper gallop. The winner was well in on form from this time last year and ran to a similar level.

5014 HAYGAIN HAY STEAMERS CLEAN HEALTHY FORAGE STANDARD OPEN NATIONAL HUNT FLAT RACE 2m

5:00 (5:00) (Class 6) 4-6-Y-O **£1,559** (£457; £228; £114)

Form RPR

1- **1** **Ballybolley (IRE)**[111] 2878 5-11-3 0.................................. RyanHatch(7) 116+
(Nigel Twiston-Davies) *t.k.h: chsd ldrs tl led 5f out: rdn clr 2f out: styd on strly: readily* **10/1**

2 *3 ½* **Scooter Boy** 5-10-12 0.................................... KillianMoore(5) 105
(Alex Hales) *hld up in tch in midfield: nt clr run 3f out: rdn and hdwy to go 3rd 2f out: styd on to chse wnr ins fnl f: kpt on but no threat to wnr* **50/1**

3 *1 ¼* **Gamain (IRE)**[64] 5-11-0 0.................................... KielanWoods(3) 104
(Ben Case) *t.k.h: chsd ldrs: wnt 2nd wl over 2f out: rdn and outpcd over 2f out: kpt on same pce after: lost 2nd ins fnl f* **10/1**

/2S- **4** *6* **Western Diva (IRE)**[31] 4403 5-10-10 0.........................[1] TomScudamore 91
(David Pipe) *t.k.h: hld up in tch in rr: hdwy and nt clr run 3f out: swtchd lft and effrt over 2f out: kpt on to go 4th cl home: no ch w wnr* **7/2**[2]

5 *½* **Thedrinkymeister (IRE)**[64] 5-11-3 0.................................... APMcCoy 98
(Kim Bailey) *chsd ldrs: wnt 2nd 5f out: rdn and no ex over 2f out: 4th and wknd over 1f out* **11/4**[1]

1- **6** *2* **So Oscar (IRE)**[120] 2703 6-11-5 0...........................(t) ConorShoemark(5) 103
(Lawney Hill) *in tch in midfield: effrt to go 4th over 2f out: outpcd ent fnl 2f: wknd over 1f out* **5/1**[3]

7 *1 ¾* **War On The Rocks (IRE)** 5-11-3 0.................................. AlainCawley 94
(Fergal O'Brien) *in tch in midfield: nt clr run over 3f out: hdwy over 2f out: kpt on but no threat to ldrs* **14/1**

3/ **8** *4 ½* **Tuffstuff**[345] 5287 6-11-3 0.................................... DaveCrosse 90
(Brian Barr) *in toouch in midfield: hdwy to chse ldrs: rdn and no ex over 2f out: wknd 2f out* **14/1**

6- **9** *1 ½* **Krackatoa King**[18] 4638 6-10-12 0.................................. JamesBanks(5) 89
(Noel Williams) *rn green and pushed along thrght: in tch in midfield: lost pl and rdn over 4f out: plugged on but n.d fnl 2f* **50/1**

04- **10** *2 ½* **Izzy Piccolina (IRE)**[24] 4540 6-10-10 0.............. WayneHutchinson 80
(Geoffrey Deacon) *hld up in rr: hdwy on outer into midfield over 4f out: rdn and btn 3f out: sn wknd* **66/1**

11 *nk* **Irish Octave (IRE)** 4-10-5 0.. BenPoste(5) 80
(Rosemary Gasson) *hld up in tch in last trio: swtchd to outer over 4f out: rdn 3f out: sn outpcd and wknd* **100/1**

4- **12** *9* **Dawson City**[72] 3656 5-11-3 0....................................... AndrewThornton 78
(Polly Gundry) *in tch in midfield on outer: rdn and btn over 2f out: sn wknd and bhd 1f out* **20/1**

13 *1* **Global Bonus (IRE)** 5-11-3 0.................................... JamieMoore 78
(Caroline Bailey) *t.k.h: chsd ldrs tl btn over 2f out: sn wknd and bhd 1f out* **16/1**

30- **14** *14* **Goneinaglance**[31] 4403 5-10-3 0... MrJMartin(7) 58
(Andrew J Martin) *in tch in midfield: rdn and struggling over 3f out: sn wknd: t.o 1f out* **66/1**

0/0- **15** *6* **Winneys Boy**[22] 4575 6-11-0 0....................................... PeterCarberry(3) 60
(Shaun Lycett) *chsd ldr tl 5f out: sn rdn: wknd over 3f out: bhd fnl 2f: t.o fnl f* **150/1**

6- **16** *67* **Primitive Sam**[21] 4598 6-11-3 0..................................... TomMessenger
(Chris Bealby) *led tl 5f out: dropped out rapidly and sn bhd: t.o over 2f out* **100/1**

3m 43.7s (-18.60) **Going Correction** -1.00s/f (Hard)
WFA 4 from 5yo+ 7lb **16** Ran SP% **117.3**
Speed ratings: **106,104,103,100,100 99,98,96,95,94 94,89,89,82,79 45**
CSF £447.24 TOTE £8.10: £2.50, £11.60, £3.20; EX 696.40 Trifecta £1274.20 Part won..
Owner N A Twiston-Davies **Bred** The Red Marble Syndicate **Trained** Naunton, Gloucs

FOCUS
A competitive bumper in which they went a respectable tempo after furlong or so. The winner looks decent and should win more races.
T/Jkpt: £456.50 to a £1 stake. Pool: £14467.08 - 22.50 winning tickets T/Plt: £8.90 to a £1 stake. Pool: £102074.29 - 8279.72 winning tickets T/Qpdt: £8.20 to a £1 stake. Pool: £5246.20 - 473.40 winning tickets SP

4910 CHEPSTOW (L-H)

Tuesday, March 25

OFFICIAL GOING: Soft (chs 4.3; hdl 5.3)
Wind: Moderate behind Weather: Overcast

5015 PLAY BURNING DESIRE AT 32RED NOVICES' HURDLE (10 hdls 1 omitted) 2m 4f

2:00 (2:00) (Class 4) 4-Y-0+ **£3,249** (£954; £477; £238)

Form RPR

21- **1** **Fayette County (IRE)**[26] 4514 7-11-7 129......................... DougieCostello 130+
(Tim Vaughan) *hld up in rr: stdy hdwy 4 out: trckd ldr after 3 out: drvn and qcknd bypassed 2 out: chal last: styd upsides tl led u.p last stride* **7/4**[2]

314- **2** *shd* **Call The Cops (IRE)**[66] 3774 5-11-7 125......................... AndrewTinkler 129
(Nicky Henderson) *trckd ldrs in 3rd: slt ld 4 out: drvn bypassed 2 out: jnd last: hrd pressed u.p run-in: hdd last stride* **11/8**[1]

423- **3** *11* **Cool George**[32] 4391 6-10-12 121.................................. JamesBest(3) 113
(Jackie Du Plessis) *chsd ldrs: chal 4 out: wnt 2nd 3 out: outpcd into 3rd bypassed 2 out* **4/1**[3]

4 *24* **Kilcullen Article (IRE)**[72] 6-11-1 0................................ LiamTreadwell 88
(Michael Scudamore) *chsd ldrs: chal and rdn 4 out: wknd sn after* **28/1**

000- **5** *10* **Bonds Conquest**[70] 3695 5-11-1 0................................ AndrewThornton 78
(Seamus Mullins) *hit 7th: in rr: lost tch 4 out* **100/1**

04- **6** *½* **The Bogman's Ball**[17] 4672 8-11-1 0................................ PaulMoloney 78
(Grace Harris) *led to 5th: wknd qckly after 4 out* **50/1**

/0F- **F** **Milanese (IRE)**[108] 2942 6-11-1 0.................................. RichardJohnson
(Emma Lavelle) *in rr whn fell 3rd* **8/1**

000- **F** **Hot Pepper**[32] 4391 6-10-12 0.. GilesHawkins(3) 78
(Chris Down) *chsd ldr: led 5th: narrowly hdd 4 out: sn wknd: no ch whn fell last* **100/1**

4m 59.15s (-2.65) **Going Correction** -0.05s/f (Good) **8** Ran SP% **117.0**
Speed ratings (Par 105): **103,102,98,88,84 84, ,**
CSF £4.83 TOTE £2.30: £1.10, £1.30, £1.60; EX 5.30 Trifecta £9.60.
Owner John P McManus **Bred** T G Mooney **Trained** Aberthin, Vale of Glamorgan

FOCUS
The second-last flight was bypassed. Dougie Costello's take on the ground after winning the opener was: "good to soft and goodish in places." They went a very steady gallop in this ordinary novice hurdle, the race not starting in earnest until they'd turned for home. The first two quickly pulled clear as they contested a tight finish, and are useful novices, but the bare form may not be wholly reliable and could be 5lb out either way.

5016 32RED WELCOMES MICROGAMING PLAYERS "NATIONAL HUNT" MAIDEN HURDLE (7 hdls 1 omitted) 2m 110y

2:30 (2:30) (Class 5) 4-Y-0+ **£1,949** (£572; £286; £143)

Form RPR

213- **1** **Blue Heron (IRE)**[13] 4763 6-11-0 0.................................... HarrySkelton 125+
(Dan Skelton) *mde all: c clr fr 3 out: eased fr by bypassed fnl flight* **9/4**[1]

53- **2** *17* **El Macca (IRE)**[93] 3226 5-11-0 0.................................... DougieCostello 104
(Rebecca Curtis) *t.k.h: in rr: hdwy fr 4 out: chsd easy wnr wl bef bypassed fnl flight but nvr any ch* **5/1**[3]

336- **3** *1 ½* **Mrs Jordan (IRE)**[48] 4090 6-10-7 108.............................. LiamTreadwell 94
(Venetia Williams) *in rr: shkn up after 4th: sn in tch: rdn bef 4 out and outpcd: styd on agin fr bypassed fnl flight but nvr any ch* **5/2**[2]

540- **4** *½* **Rock On Rocky**[15] 4728 6-11-0 0.. CharliePoste 101
(Matt Sheppard) *chsd wnr tl after 4th: styd in tch: outpcd 3 out: styd on appr bypassed fnl flight: kpt on cl home but nvr any ch* **66/1**

50- **5** *4* **Knight ofthe Realm**[54] 3994 5-11-0 0................................... IanPopham 98
(Caroline Keevil) *j. slowly 2nd: hit 4th: rdn and outpcd 4 out: styd on again fr bypassed fnl flight: nvr any ch* **66/1**

/03- **6** *10* **When Ben When (IRE)**[48] 4091 5-10-7 0................... MrSamPainting(7) 91
(Colin Tizzard) *chsd ldrs: wnt 2nd after 4th: rdn and no ch w wnr after 4 out: wknd wl bef bypassed fnl flight* **8/1**

0- **7** *6* **Alberto's Dream**[34] 4350 5-11-0 0.. FelixDeGiles 81
(Tom Symonds) *in tch: rdn after 4th: nvr any ch after* **50/1**

0/0- **8** *¾* **Follow The Master**[121] 2689 8-10-7 0............................. ChrisDavies(7) 80
(Brian Forsey) *a in rr* **100/1**

600- **9** *1 ¾* **Viacometti (FR)**[76] 3602 5-11-0 0.................................. PaddyBrennan 78
(Tom George) *t.k.h: chsd ldrs to 4th* **12/1**

500- **B** **Western Movie**[19] 4632 6-11-0 0.. TomO'Brien
(Philip Hobbs) *in rr whn b.d 1st* **20/1**

06- **F** **Monart Diamond**[84] 3433 5-11-0 0................................ RichardJohnson
(Tim Vaughan) *towards rr whn fell 1st* **16/1**

P **Lord Carrigross (IRE)**[314] 7-10-7 0.................................. MrCSmith(7)
(Linda Blackford) *a in rr: t.o 4th: sn p.u* **100/1**

60- **B** **Greybougg**[53] 4017 5-11-0 0.................................... SamTwiston-Davies
(Nigel Hawke) *in rr whn b.d 1st* **50/1**

2- **B** **Eaton Rock (IRE)**[30] 4452 5-10-9 0.. BenPoste(5)
(Tom Symonds) *in rr whn b.d 1st* **16/1**

4m 7.74s (-2.86) **Going Correction** -0.05s/f (Good) **14** Ran SP% **120.2**
Speed ratings (Par 103): **104,96,95,95,93 88,85,85,84, , , ,**
CSF £13.67 TOTE £3.20: £1.90, £1.20, £1.50; EX 15.00 Trifecta £29.40.
Owner Horwood Harriers Partnership **Bred** Louise Cooper-Joyce **Trained** Alcester, Warwicks

FOCUS
The last flight was bypassed on the final circuit. A weak maiden hurdle with little depth, in which the field was thinned out by a four-horse pile-up at the first. The impressive winner should go on to rate higher.

5017 PLAY IMMORTAL ROMANCE AT 32RED H'CAP CHASE (12 fncs) 2m 110y

3:00 (3:00) (Class 4) (0-110,110) 5-Y-0+ **£3,898** (£1,144; £572; £286)

Form RPR

321- **1** **Tokyo Javilex (FR)**[23] 4581 7-11-1 99..................(t) SamTwiston-Davies 110+
(Nigel Hawke) *chsd ldrs: mstke 7th: rdn along 8th: chsd ldrs 4 out: disp 2nd and hit 3 out: chsd ldr next: chal fr last: led u.p fnl 50yds: styd on wl* **5/4**[1]

354- **2** *1 ½* **Mon Chevalier (IRE)**[19] 4637 11-11-1 102.................(p) MichealNolan(3) 108
(Carroll Gray) *in tch: hdwy and mstke 8th: chsd ldr 4 out: led appr next: jnd u.p last: hdd and no ex fnl 50yds* **12/1**

023- **3** *10* **Islandmagee (IRE)**[19] 4633 7-11-4 102...........................(t) AdamWedge 100
(Evan Williams) *led: pressed fr 4th to 7th jnd again 8th: hdd appr 3 out: dropped to 3rd next: wknd last* **13/2**

4F2- **4** *5* **Walden Prince (IRE)**[247] 1063 7-11-1 99......................... RichardJohnson 90
(Richard Lee) *in tch: drvn and hdwy to chse ldrs 4 out: j. slowly 3 out: sn wknd* **11/4**[2]

441- **5** *2 ¼* **Nozic (FR)**[15] 4718 13-11-12 110...............................(p) WayneHutchinson 102
(Zoe Davison) *chsd ldr: chal fr 4th to 7th: btn next* **6/1**[3]

4m 16.53s (-0.57) **Going Correction** +0.075s/f (Yiel) **5** Ran SP% **106.4**
Speed ratings: **104,103,98,96,95**
CSF £12.83 TOTE £1.60: £1.10, £4.10; EX 11.80 Trifecta £43.50.
Owner D R Mead **Bred** Scea Ecurie Jc Laisis **Trained** Stoodleigh, Devon

FOCUS
A modest handicap chase, but the form seems sound enough. The winner is steadily progressive.

5018 32RED FOR MICROGAMING GAMES MARES' H'CAP HURDLE (8 hdls) 2m 110y

3:35 (3:35) (Class 4) (0-115,109) 4-Y-0+ **£3,119** (£915; £457; £228)

Form RPR

40- **1** **Madame De Guise (FR)**[125] 2600 5-11-12 109..................... DavidBass 110+
(Nicky Henderson) *trckd ldrs in 4th: hdwy 4 out: pushed along to chse ldr 2 out: chal last: sn led: drvn out* **3/1**[3]

/2P- **2** *2* **Ruby Glow**[100] 3117 6-11-11 108.................................. AndrewThornton 108
(Seamus Mullins) *led: drvn and styd on fr 3 out: jnd u.p last: sn hdd: styd on same pce* **6/1**

2U5- **3** *1 ¼* **Lindsay's Dream**[15] 4717 8-10-6 96..............................(p) MrHGMiller(7) 94
(Zoe Davison) *hit 2nd: racd in 5th: effrt 4 out: chsd ldrs in 3rd 2 out: hit last: kpt on run-in but nt pce of ldng duo* **14/1**

51F- **4** *13* **Lady Charisma**[54] 3988 5-11-11 108............................ RichardJohnson 96
(Philip Hobbs) *chsd ldr: rdn 3 out: mstke and wknd 2 out* **7/4**[1]

311- 5 7 **Our Phylli Vera (IRE)**[15] 4717 5-11-10 **107**............... WayneHutchinson 95
(Alan King) *in tch: hdwy appr 4 out: 5 l 4th and drvn whn bad mstke and wknd 3 out* **5/2**[2]

4m 11.53s (0.93) **Going Correction** -0.05s/f (Good) **5** Ran SP% **110.9**
Speed ratings (Par 105): **95,94,93,87,84**
CSF £19.41 TOTE £3.70: £2.10, £2.70; EX 18.90 Trifecta £85.00.
Owner Million In Mind Partnership **Bred** Jean-Pierre Roussel & Diego Roussel **Trained** Upper Lambourn, Berks

FOCUS
A tight little mares' handicap. The first three are rated pretty much to their marks.

5019 SWITCH TO 32RED FOR £10 FREE H'CAP HURDLE (11 hdls) 2m 4f
4:10 (4:10) (Class 4) (0-115,115) 4-Y-O+ **£3,119** (£915; £457; £228)

Form RPR
/52- 1 **Pilgreen (FR)**[24] 4555 9-11-2 **105**................................ WayneHutchinson 116+
(Robert Walford) *chsd ldrs: wnt 2nd 3 out: rdn to chal last: sn led: drvn out* **13/2**[2]
361- 2 ¾ **Bob Keown (IRE)**[7] 4883 6-10-9 **105** 7ex......................(b[1]) PaulO'Brien[(7)] 115+
(Rebecca Curtis) *led: hit 2 out: jnd last: hdd sn after: kpt on u.p: nt pce of wnr* **11/8**[1]
6PP- 3 11 **Mister Snowball (FR)**[66] 3784 7-11-7 **110**.................... RichardJohnson 109
(Chris Down) *chsd ldrs: stdd after 7th: hdwy to chsd ldrs fr 4 out: btn whn j. slowly 2 out and no ch after: kpt on for 3rd* **11/1**
00P- 4 2 **Look For Love**[35] 4333 6-10-13 **107**......................... MissLucyGardner[(5)] 104
(Sue Gardner) *in rr: hit 6th: rdn fr 4 out: styd on fr 2 out: kpt on run-in but nvr any ch w ldrs* **20/1**
220- 5 1 **Midnight Request**[37] 4309 5-10-8 **97**................................... FelixDeGiles 95
(Tom Symonds) *chsd ldrs: rdn 4 out: hit 3 out: no ch w ldrs whn hit 2 out* **8/1**[3]
/40- 6 8 **King Helissio (IRE)**[128] 2529 6-11-9 **112**........................ DougieCostello 100
(Neil Mulholland) *in rr: hit 6th and 7th: hdwy 4 out: nvr rchd ldrs and one pce fr 3 out* **17/2**
404- 7 6 **Thundering Home**[23] 4573 7-10-9 **105**........................... TomBellamy[(7)] 87
(Richard Mitchell) *in rr: hit 6th: hdwy fr next: wknd after 4 out* **20/1**
223- 8 hd **Ray Diamond**[70] 3693 9-10-13 **105**...................................... JamesBest[(3)] 87
(Jackie Du Plessis) *pressed ldr: stl upsides u.p 4 out: wknd next* **14/1**
/30- 9 6 **Switched Off**[45] 4157 9-11-5 **115**................................ JakeHodson[(7)] 91
(Kevin Frost) *hit 1st: in tch: sme hdwy appr 4 out: sn wknd* **33/1**
450- 10 ¾ **Nicky Nutjob (GER)**[16] 4700 8-10-3 **99**.......................... MikeyHamill[(7)] 74
(John O'Shea) *in rr: rdn along 6th: hdwy next: wknd 4 out* **50/1**
323- 11 17 **Buckhorn Tom**[34] 4351 6-11-8 **111**.................................(p) TomO'Brien 69
(Colin Tizzard) *chsd ldrs: hit 5th: rdn after 7th: wknd bef 4 out* **10/1**
1/P- 12 20 **Littledean Jimmy (IRE)**[16] 4700 9-10-11 **105**................ JamesBanks[(5)] 43
(John O'Shea) *in rr: hit 5th: lost tch after 7th* **50/1**

4m 58.11s (-3.69) **Going Correction** -0.05s/f (Good) **12** Ran SP% **117.6**
Speed ratings (Par 105): **105,104,100,99,99 95,93,93,91,90 83,75**
CSF £15.26 CT £98.38 TOTE £7.10: £2.10, £1.30, £4.20; EX 18.00 Trifecta £147.60.
Owner Mrs S De Wilde **Bred** Earl Detouillon Raphael & Frederique **Trained** Child Okeford, Dorset

FOCUS
A moderate handicap where two pulled clear. A big step up from the winner, and sound form.

5020 PLAY AVALON AT 32RED H'CAP CHASE (16 fncs) 2m 3f 110y
4:45 (4:46) (Class 4) (0-120,118) 5-Y-O+ **£3,898** (£1,144; £572; £286)

Form RPR
3PU- 1 **Ballywatt (IRE)**[16] 4696 8-11-12 **118**..............................(tp) NickScholfield 129+
(Kim Bailey) *stdd in rr and mstke 6th: blnd 12th: hdwy fr 4 out to chse ldr next: chal travelling best 2 out: upsides last: sn drvn ld fnl 110yds: readily* **5/2**[2]
241- 2 1 ¾ **Cruchain (IRE)**[248] 1039 11-11-6 **115**...........................(p) RobertDunne[(3)] 122
(Dai Burchell) *led: rdn 2 out: jnd 2 out: hrd ppressed last: hdd and outpcd fnl 110yds* **5/1**[3]
051- 3 12 **Tolkeins Tango (IRE)**[19] 4637 6-11-6 **112**............................ JackDoyle 110
(Victor Dartnall) *t.k.h: chsd ldr to 9th: racd in cl 3rd: rdn appr 12th: no ch w ldng duo after 3 out* **11/10**[1]
4U0- 4 14 **Gud Day (IRE)**[37] 4300 6-11-12 **118**............................(tp) PaddyBrennan 104
(Fergal O'Brien) *racd in cl 4th tl chsd ldr fr 7th to 4 out: sn wknd* **11/2**

5m 19.08s (7.78) **Going Correction** +0.075s/f (Yiel) **4** Ran SP% **108.2**
Speed ratings: **87,86,81,75**
CSF £13.00 TOTE £2.80; EX 14.40 Trifecta £18.80.
Owner Mrs David Johnson **Bred** Oak Lodge Bloodstock **Trained** Andoversford, Gloucs

FOCUS
An ordinary handicap chase. The tricky winner is rated to form, through the second.

5021 32RED MICROGAMING CASINO MAIDEN OPEN NATIONAL HUNT FLAT RACE 2m 110y
5:15 (5:15) (Class 6) 4-6-Y-O **£1,559** (£457; £228; £114)

Form RPR
3- 1 **Minella Present (IRE)**[103] 3035 5-11-4 0........................ DougieCostello 120+
(Neil Mulholland) *mde all: sn clr: in n.d fr 1/2-way: v easily: unchal* **3/1**[1]
4- 2 11 **Nightline**[115] 2830 4-10-11 0...................................... RichardJohnson 100
(Henry Daly) *t.k.h: prom but nvr nr clr wnr: tk wl-hld 2nd fr 3f out* **10/1**
223- 3 5 **Flamenco Lad**[37] 4296 4-10-11 0... HaddenFrost 96
(Martin Hill) *in rr: drvn and hdwy fr 5f out: styd on to take wl-hld 3rd wl over 2f out* **5/1**[2]
4 6 **Sonny The One** 4-10-4 0.. MrMLegg[(7)] 89
(Colin Tizzard) *in rr: sn pushed along: styd on fnl 3f: nvr any ch* **25/1**
05- 5 1 **Are We There**[35] 4335 5-10-11 0............................. MrRobertHawker[(7)] 95
(Carroll Gray) *mid-div and rdn along over 5f out: mod prog fnl 2f* **100/1**
2- 6 6 **Theunnamedsoldier**[31] 4417 6-11-4 0................... SamTwiston-Davies 89
(Nigel Hawke) *in rr: rdn and no prog fr 5f out* **10/1**
5- 7 4 ½ **Mister Chairman (IRE)**[23] 4575 6-10-11 0..................... MrFMitchell[(7)] 85
(Nicky Henderson) *chsd ldrs: wnt mod 2nd over 6f out: no imp on easy wnr u.p 6f out: wknd 3f out* **16/1**
- 8 26 **Mystical Flame (IRE)** 5-10-11 0.................................. NickScholfield 52
(David Pipe) *pushed along in mid-div 1/2-way: disp 2nd 7f out: wknd qckly 6f out* **8/1**
35- 9 99 **Keep Presenting (IRE)**[34] 4349 5-10-13 0................. PatrickCorbett[(5)]
(Rebecca Curtis) *chsd wnr tl rdn and wknd qckly 1/2-way: sn wl t.o: virtually p.u fnl 6f* **3/1**[1]
P **Sid's Topper (FR)** 4-10-11 0.. PaddyBrennan
(Tom George) *prom tl wknd over 5f out: wl t.o whn p.u fnl f* **13/2**[3]

4m 3.85s (-1.15) **Going Correction** -0.05s/f (Good)
WFA 4 from 5yo+ 7lb **10** Ran SP% **120.0**
Speed ratings: **100,94,92,89,89 86,84,72,25,**
CSF £36.33 TOTE £4.70: £1.40, £3.50, £1.40; EX 37.30 Trifecta £275.10.
Owner Lady Clarke **Bred** Paddy Kennedy **Trained** Limpley Stoke, Wilts

FOCUS
The useful winner took this bumper apart. The winner looks a fair prospect.
T/Plt: £55.40 to a £1 stake. Pool: £94,149.48 - 1239.44 winning units. T/Qpdt: £63.90 to a £1 stake. Pool: £3981.62 - 46.10 winning units. ST

[4797]FONTWELL (L-H)
Tuesday, March 25

OFFICIAL GOING: Good to soft (6.7)
Wind: strong breeze behind Weather: light rain

5022 PREMIER ROULETTE AT 32RED.COM "HANDS AND HEELS" H'CAP HURDLE (CONDITIONALS & AMATEURS) (11 hdls 2 omitted) 3m 3f
2:10 (2:12) (Class 4) (0-105,105) 4-Y-O+ **£3,119** (£915; £457; £228)

Form RPR
234- 1 **Sea Cadet**[99] 3138 12-10-0 **79** oh1...................................(p) JackSherwood 80
(Laura Mongan) *cl up: led 2 out: styd on wl fr last: pushed out* **12/1**
625- 2 1 ¾ **Miss Mayfair (IRE)**[30] 4446 7-10-9 **88**........................ CharlieDeutsch 86
(Lawney Hill) *cl up: trckd ldrs after 8th: rdn and ev ch 2 out: hld last: kpt on same pce* **15/2**[2]
224- 3 nk **Absolute Shambles**[10] 4803 10-10-10 **92**.................(p) LouisMuspratt[(3)] 90
(Chris Gordon) *led at crawl: hdd after 7th: trckd ldr: disp bypassed 3 out: sn rdn: narrowly hdd next: hld last: styd on same pce* **9/1**
052- 4 nse **Cool Bob (IRE)**[18] 4656 11-9-9 **79** oh1....................(t) MrStanSheppard[(5)] 78
(Matt Sheppard) *hld up but wl in tch: pushed along whn nt fluent 2 out: styd on into 4th run-in: nvr finding pce to get on terms* **8/1**[3]
06P- 5 4 ½ **Jazz Man (IRE)**[89] 3284 7-11-7 **100**.................................... DanielHiskett 95
(Mark Rimell) *racd keenly trcking ldr: led after 7th: continued slow pce tl upped tempo 9th: rdn and hdd 2 out: hld whn nt fluent last: kpt on same pce* **20/1**
342- 6 1 **Marmalade Man**[10] 4803 8-10-8 **92**..............................(p) MrDSansom[(5)] 85
(Seamus Mullins) *trckd ldrs: stmbld on bnd after 7th: rdn after bypassed 3 out: sltly outpcd next: nvr able to mount chal* **11/8**[1]
/54- 7 nk **Mystic Appeal (IRE)**[27] 4501 8-11-9 **105**...................(p) ChrisMeehan[(3)] 98
(Jeremy Scott) *trckd ldr: rdn after bypassed 3 out: one pce fr next* **8/1**[3]
P23- 8 3 **Mobaasher (USA)**[17] 4677 11-11-6 **104**........................ MrDGNoonan[(5)] 94
(Patricia Shaw) *hld up wl in tch: effrt bef 2 out but nvr pce to get on terms* **10/1**
P41- U **Elegant Olive**[122] 2680 11-11-4 **100**.. MrFTett[(3)]
(Roger Curtis) *hld up but wl in tch: stmbld bdly and uns rdr 3rd* **20/1**

7m 41.2s (48.40) **Going Correction** +0.65s/f (Soft) **9** Ran SP% **112.4**
Speed ratings (Par 105): **54,53,53,53,52 51,51,50,**
CSF £94.75 CT £847.35 TOTE £11.80: £2.20, £2.10, £2.80; EX 99.60 Trifecta £803.60.
Owner Mrs P J Sheen **Bred** M H Easterby **Trained** Epsom, Surrey

FOCUS
Bends moved in from last meeting, hurdles on middle to inner. The third-last flight was bypassed on the last two circuits. After 6.7mm of overnight rain the going was eased to good to soft. This moderate handicap, confined to conditional and amateur riders, was run at a very steady gallop. The first three were all close to their marks.

5023 32RED FOR MICROGAMING GAMES H'CAP CHASE (16 fncs) 2m 6f
2:40 (2:42) (Class 4) (0-110,110) 5-Y-O+ **£3,994** (£1,240; £667)

Form RPR
514- 1 **Keltic Rhythm (IRE)**[15] 4725 7-11-9 **110**........................ TrevorWhelan[(3)] 123
(Neil King) *disp ld tl clr ldr after 7th: pushed along after 12th: rdn after 4 out: pckd 2 out: styd on gamely: rdn out* **6/4**[1]
253- 2 1 ¾ **Venetian Lad**[10] 4809 9-11-4 **102**... MarcGoldstein 113
(Lydia Richards) *trckd ldrs: pushed along into 2nd after 4 out: rdn after 3 out: styd on but a being hld fr last* **13/2**
252- 3 30 **Tuskar Rock (FR)**[9] 4840 11-11-0 **98**.............................(b) AidanColeman 91
(Venetia Williams) *trckd ldrs: wnt 2nd after 7th: pushed along after 11th: rdn after 4 out: lost 2nd and hld fr next: wknd after 2 out: t.o* **3/1**[2]
/PP- P **Autumn Day (IRE)**[71] 3687 9-10-0 **84** oh9.............................. JamieMoore
(Luke Dace) *disp ld tl after 7th: struggling 9th: losing tch whn p.u after next* **50/1**
662/ F **Rivermouth**[586] 1243 9-10-5 **89**......................................(v) TomCannon
(Laura Mongan) *cl up whn fell 7th* **12/1**
PP4- F **Red Anchor (IRE)**[15] 4718 10-10-6 **90**.............................. LeightonAspell
(Linda Jewell) *fell 2nd* **10/1**
1/2- P **Dynamic Idol (USA)**[15] 4718 7-11-7 **105**........................... JoshuaMoore
(Gary Moore) *j.lft: nt travelling in last whn p.u on bnd bef 5th; b.b.v* **5/1**[3]

5m 46.5s (3.50) **Going Correction** +0.275s/f (Yiel) **7** Ran SP% **113.7**
Speed ratings: **104,103,92, , ,**
CSF £11.81 CT £26.82 TOTE £2.60: £2.60, £2.00; EX 12.10 Trifecta £40.00.
Owner Stephen Lower Insurance Services Ltd **Bred** Michael Fennessy **Trained** Newmarket, Suffolk
■ Stewards' Enquiry : Trevor Whelan two-day ban: jsed whip above permitted level (Apr 8,10)

FOCUS
They went an honest gallop in this eventful contest.

5024 DOCKER HUGHES MEMORIAL NOVICES' HURDLE (11 hdls) 2m 6f 110y
3:10 (3:11) (Class 4) 4-Y-O+ **£3,508** (£1,030; £515; £257)

Form RPR
1- 1 **Virtuel D'Oudon (FR)**[29] 4473 5-11-2 0........................... ConorO'Farrell 114+
(David Pipe) *trckd ldr: drvn after 8th: led after 3 out: 6 l clr last: tiring and wandering fnl 150yds: a holding on: all out* **2/1**[2]
3- 2 ¾ **Ballyheigue Bay (IRE)**[15] 4715 7-11-2 0............................. TomCannon 109
(Chris Gordon) *trckd ldng pair: nt fluent 6th: rdn whn wnt rt 3 out: sn outpcd: 17 l down 2 out: 12 l down last: styd on wl: nvr quite getting there* **4/1**[3]
241- 3 15 **Arthur's Oak**[44] 4171 6-11-8 **124**.. AidanColeman 104+
(Venetia Williams) *sn led: hdd after 3 out: rdn whn blnd 2 out: wkng whn lost 2nd run-in: jst hld on for 3rd* **10/11**[1]
544- 4 nk **Double U Dot Ede'S**[15] 4724 5-10-6 0........................ PaddyBradley[(10)] 95
(Pat Phelan) *trckd ldng trio: rdn after 8th: nvr any threat but styd on fr last to nrly snatch 3rd fnl strides* **33/1**
5- 5 49 **Eddy**[171] 1771 5-10-11 0.. CharlieWallis[(5)] 51
(John Panvert) *racd keenly: hld up: lost tch 8th: t.o* **33/1**
065- 6 29 **A Keen Sense (GER)**[32] 4397 5-11-2 0............................ LeightonAspell 25
(David Dennis) *in tch tl 6th: sn t.o* **12/1**
P/P- P **Montys Cash**[13] 4761 8-11-2 0.. JoshuaMoore
(Heather Cobb) *in tch tl 6th: sn t.o: p.u bef 8th* **66/1**

/0F- P Redinga[10] 4797 8-10-9 0 ....(t) GerardTumelty
(Linda Jewell) *sn struggling in rr: hit 2nd: t.o 5th: p.u bef next* 150/1

5m 53.0s (10.50) **Going Correction** +0.65s/f (Soft) **8** Ran SP% **121.4**
Speed ratings (Par 105): **107,106,101,101,84 74,,**
CSF £11.28 TOTE £3.40: £1.10, £1.80, £1.10; EX 13.80 Trifecta £18.60.
Owner Stephen Quinlan **Bred** Mme F Marionneau & Mlle V Dasque **Trained** Nicholashayne, Devon
FOCUS
An uncompetitive novice hurdle run at a sound gallop. The winner is sure to rate higher.

5025 SWITCH TO 32RED FOR £10 FREE H'CAP CHASE (19 fncs) 3m 2f 110y
3:45 (3:45) (Class 4) (0-110,107) 5-Y-0+ **£3,768** (£1,106; £553; £276)

Form RPR
214- **1** **Tarraco (FR)**[9] 4843 7-11-10 105 .... AidanColeman 118+
(Venetia Williams) *disp ld: hit 7th: clr ldr 14th: rdn after 3 out: edgd lft sn after last: hld on: all out* **11/4**[1]

642- **2** *shd* **Danners (IRE)**[17] 4673 8-11-7 107 .... MrMWall(5) 121+
(Giles Smyly) *chsd ldrs fr 4th: pushed along fr 10th: rdn after 4 out: chsd wnr next: tried to mount chal up ins rail after 2 out: hit last: swtchd rt run-in: ev ch fnl 75yds: drifted rt nr fin: jst hld* **4/1**[3]

5P0- **3** *11* **Best Boy Barney (IRE)**[15] 4729 8-10-6 90 ....(tp) MattGriffiths(3) 93
(Jeremy Scott) *rn in snatches: chsd ldrs: pushed along after 6th: reminders after next: plugged on fr 3 out but nvr threatened to get involved* **3/1**[2]

214- **4** *13* **Smart Exit (IRE)**[30] 4451 7-11-9 104 ....(v[1]) JoshuaMoore 94
(Renee Robeson) *disp ld tl 14th: rdn after 15th: lost 2nd after next: wknd after 3 out* **11/4**[1]

463- **5** *1 ½* **Princely Hero (IRE)**[10] 4798 10-10-10 91 ....(v) TomCannon 80
(Chris Gordon) *chsd ldrs: pushed along after 8th: detached after 13th: plenty to do after 4 out: styd on again after 2 out but nvr any danger* **8/1**

7m 6.2s (5.10) **Going Correction** +0.275s/f (Yiel) **5** Ran SP% **109.4**
Speed ratings: **103,102,99,95,95**
CSF £13.50 TOTE £3.40: £1.50, £2.20; EX 10.10 Trifecta £44.80.
Owner Mrs Vida Bingham **Bred** Pascal Mahe **Trained** Kings Caple, H'fords
FOCUS
They went a fair gallop with the first two home fighting out a thrilling finish. The winner was back to the level of his Plumpton win.

5026 PLAY TOMB RAIDER AT 32RED MARES' MAIDEN HURDLE (9 hdls) 2m 2f 110y
4:20 (4:20) (Class 4) 4-Y-0+ **£3,119** (£915; £457; £228)

Form RPR
06- **1** **Norfolk Sky**[19] 4632 5-11-0 0 .... DaveCrosse 115+
(Brian Barr) *mde virtually all: kicked clr 6th: in command after 2 out: mstke last where nrly unshipped jockey: kpt on wl: rdn out* **5/1**[2]

03P- **2** *17* **Bow Quest**[15] 4715 7-11-0 0 .... JoshuaMoore 96
(Gary Moore) *hld up towards rr: hdwy after 6th: rdn in midfield after 3 out: styd on fr next: wnt 3rd at last: kpt on to go 2nd towards fin* **14/1**

0/5- **3** *½* **Midnight Minx**[163] 1885 7-10-11 0 ....(t) RachaelGreen(3) 98
(Anthony Honeyball) *trckd wnr most of way: pushed along whn nt fluent 2 out: sn rdn and hld: no ex whn lost 2nd towards fin* **4/6**[1]

6P3- **4** *2 ¼* **Tiller Belle**[13] 4761 6-10-11 0 .... JeremiahMcGrath(3) 94
(Nicky Henderson) *mid-div tl outpcd 6th: styd on again fr after 3 out: wnt 4th run-in* **12/1**

344/ **5** *1 ¼* **Sapphire Moon**[289] 7-11-0 0 .... RobertThornton 93
(Alan King) *mid-div: rdn in midfield whn wnt rt 3 out: styd on same pce fr next* **10/1**

4- **6** *2 ¾* **Double Accord**[15] 4730 4-10-6 0 .... RyanMahon 84
(Anthony Honeyball) *trckd ldrs: rdn after 3 out: 3rd and hld 2 out: nt fluent last: no ex* **25/1**

504- **7** *6* **Hermosa Vaquera (IRE)**[71] 3686 4-10-3 94 .... NicodeBoinville(3) 78
(Anna Newton-Smith) *led tl 1st where nt fluent: led again but nt fluent and hdd 2nd: chsd ldrs: rdn appr 6th: hld in 3rd after 3 out tl next: fdd run-in* **33/1**

FF- **8** *8* **Miss Fortywinks**[32] 4394 5-10-11 0 .... WayneKavanagh(3) 77
(Seamus Mullins) *a towards rr* **50/1**

24- **9** *53* **Lily Mars (IRE)**[37] 4297 7-11-0 0 .... MichaelByrne 30
(Neil Mulholland) *mid-div tl wknd after 3 out: t.o* **8/1**[3]

10 *16* **Bell'Arte (IRE)**[20] 4-10-6 0 .... LeightonAspell
(Laura Mongan) *mid-div tl wknd after 3 out: t.o* **100/1**

00- **P** **The Selector**[13] 4758 5-11-0 0 .... TomCannon
(Chris Gordon) *a towards rr: reminders after 3rd: lost tch 5th: sn p.u* **100/1**

005- **P** **Todoistodare**[25] 4534 4-10-6 0 .... RichieMcLernon
(Brendan Powell) *lost tch after 6th: t.o whn p.u 3 out* **100/1**

4m 45.7s (11.40) **Going Correction** +0.65s/f (Soft)
WFA 4 from 5yo+ 7lb **12** Ran SP% **122.9**
Speed ratings (Par 105): **102,94,94,93,93 92,89,86,63,57 ,**
CSF £67.59 TOTE £6.70: £1.70, £4.20, £1.10; EX 107.20 Trifecta £323.40.
Owner Miss Daisy Hitchins **Bred** Farmers Hill Stud **Trained** Longburton, Dorset
■ Norfolk Sky's win broke a losing run of just over a year for rider Dave Crosse.
FOCUS
The gallop was sound for this mares' maiden. A step up from the winner but she can do better yet.

5027 32RED WELCOMES MICROGAMING PLAYERS H'CAP CHASE (13 fncs) 2m 2f
4:55 (4:55) (Class 5) (0-100,100) 5-Y-0+ **£2,144** (£629; £314; £157)

Form RPR
245- **1** **Malibu Sun**[15] 4723 7-11-1 92 .... NicodeBoinville(3) 110+
(Ben Pauling) *disp ld: clr ldr 3rd: hdd after 7th: led 9th: r.o wl to draw clr fom last: eased towards fin* **9/4**[1]

243- **2** *11* **Morestead (IRE)**[10] 4802 9-11-1 89 ....(v) LeightonAspell 96
(Brendan Powell) *disp tl 3rd: trckd wnr: led after 7th tl 9th: sn rdn: kpt chsng wnr but a being hld fr 3 out* **14/1**

033- **3** *13* **Moulin De La Croix**[34] 4352 10-11-5 100 ....(t) JackSherwood(7) 94
(Oliver Sherwood) *mid-div: rdn after 4 out: styd on fr next: wnt 3rd at last: nvr gng pce to get involved* **12/1**

0F2- **4** *1 ½* **Wicklewood**[15] 4734 8-10-0 81 ....(t) ThomasCheesman(7) 75
(Mark Gillard) *hld up: reminders after 6th: midfield 8th whn pckd: rdn after next: nvr pce to get involved: wnt 4th towards fin* **16/1**

U22- **5** *1 ¾* **Sablazo (FR)**[31] 4416 8-10-5 79 .... GerardTumelty 71
(Andy Turnell) *chsd ldrs: nt fluent 5th: wnt 3rd 4 out tl last: no ex* **14/1**

12P- **6** *8* **Red Rock (FR)**[68] 3729 9-11-9 100 .... GavinSheehan(3) 84
(Emma Lavelle) *mid-div: rdn after 4 out: wnt lft next: nvr any imp* **11/4**[2]

43P- **7** *22* **Meirig's Dream (IRE)**[77] 3595 8-10-2 76 .... JamesDavies 40
(Philip Hobbs) *struggling in last pair fr 4th: t.o 9th* **11/2**[3]

/P4- **P** **West Bay Hoolie**[105] 3008 8-10-2 76 oh6 ow2 ....(p) PaulMoloney
(Helen Nelmes) *sn outpcd in rr: t.o 9th: p.u bef last* **33/1**

203- **P** **Asian Prince (IRE)**[142] 2249 5-11-10 98 ....(bt) WillKennedy
(Alastair Lidderdale) *disp tl 3rd: chsd ldrs: rdn after 9th: wknd after 4 out: p.u next* **8/1**

4m 42.3s (7.60) **Going Correction** +0.275s/f (Yiel) **9** Ran SP% **113.8**
Speed ratings: **94,89,83,82,81 78,68,,**
CSF £31.93 CT £309.91 TOTE £3.70: £1.30, £3.80, £3.20; EX 38.80 Trifecta £460.90.
Owner Easy Going Racing **Bred** N Shutts **Trained** Bourton-On-The-Water, Gloucs
FOCUS
A moderate handicap run at a fair pace. It paid to race handy. The runner-up sets the level.

5028 PLAY THUNDERSTRUCK AT 32RED STANDARD OPEN NATIONAL HUNT FLAT RACE 2m 2f 110y
5:25 (5:25) (Class 6) 4-6-Y-0 **£1,559** (£457; £228; £114)

Form RPR
414- **1** **Justanother Muddle**[45] 4149 5-11-11 0 .... MarcGoldstein 117
(Sheena West) *mde all: rdn whn strly pressed fr over 2f out: kpt on v gamely to edge ahd again fnl 75yds: drvn out* **4/1**

254- **2** *½* **Go Odee Go (IRE)**[15] 4728 6-11-4 0 .... HarrySkelton 110
(Dan Skelton) *hld up: hdwy 1/2-way: rdn to chal over 2f out: sn hung rt: kpt on fnl 75yds to go 2nd* **9/4**[1]

3- **3** *4* **Frampton (IRE)**[110] 2905 5-11-4 0 ....(p) AidanColeman 107
(Charlie Longsdon) *trckd ldrs: rdn for str chal fr over 2f out: ev ch ins fnl f: no ex whn lost 2nd fnl 75yds: drifted rt towards fin* **3/1**[2]

4 *15* **Chill In The Wood** 5-10-4 0 .... BenFfrenchDavis(7) 87
(Dominic Ffrench Davis) *hld up: hdwy over 4f out: sn rdn and hld: wnt 4th fnl 2f: nvr threatened ldrs* **40/1**

/3- **5** *16* **Exitas (IRE)**[20] 4473 6-11-4 0 .... LeightonAspell 80
(Oliver Sherwood) *in tch: rdn 3f out: wknd 2f out* **7/2**[3]

6 *1* **Ice Cool Curler** 5-11-1 0 .... GavinSheehan(3) 77
(Ali Brewer) *in tch tl dropped to last pair after 8f: pushed along over 6f out: sn outpcd and bhd* **16/1**

4- **7** *26* **Family Motto**[27] 4498 5-11-4 0 .... TomCannon 54
(Chris Gordon) *trckd ldrs: rdn over 3f out: wknd over 2f out* **14/1**

/0- **8** *85* **Ragtime Lady**[198] 1531 6-10-4 0 .... MrLKilgarriff(7)
(Steven Dixon) *struggling in rr 1/2-way: t.o 6f out* **100/1**

4m 39.6s (10.90) **Going Correction** +0.65s/f (Soft) **8** Ran SP% **114.0**
Speed ratings: **103,102,101,94,88 87,76,40**
CSF £13.34 TOTE £4.30: £1.60, £1.10, £1.30; EX 12.60 Trifecta £24.80.
Owner Saloop **Bred** Saloop Ltd **Trained** Falmer, E Sussex
FOCUS
They went an honest gallop. The first three are rated pretty much to their marks in a decent bumper for the track.
T/Jkpt: Not won. T/Plt: £53.10 to a £1 stake. Pool: £99,558.14 - 1366.93 winning units. T/Qpdt: £3.50 to a £1 stake. Pool: £7955.70 - 1662.55 winning units. TM

4882 EXETER (R-H)
Wednesday, March 26

OFFICIAL GOING: Good to soft (good in places; chs 8.1, hdl 7.9)
Wind: mild breeze across Weather: overcast with sunny periods

5029 HIGOS FOR YOUR COMMERCIAL INSURANCE NOVICES' (S) HURDLE (10 hdls) 2m 3f
2:10 (2:10) (Class 5) 4-Y-0+ **£1,949** (£572; £286; £143)

Form RPR
4/0- **1** **While You Wait (IRE)**[27] 2628 5-11-1 97 .... JamieMoore 100+
(Gary Moore) *in tch: trckd ldrs 4th: rdn bef by-passed 3 out: led sn after 2 out: kpt on wl fr last* **2/1**[1]

660- **2** *4* **Y A Bon (IRE)**[27] 4514 6-11-1 0 ....(b[1]) HaddenFrost 94
(Martin Hill) *trckd ldrs: lft disputing 2nd 7th: rdn and ev ch appr 2 out: hld whn hmpd last: kpt on same pce* **4/1**[3]

632- **3** *4 ½* **Fruity Bun**[8] 4882 4-9-9 0 ....(t) JamesBanks(5) 77
(Keiran Burke) *trckd ldrs: lft in ld appr 7th: rdn by-passing 3 out: hdd sn after next: wnt lft and bmpd last: no ex* **6/1**

044- **4** *31* **Sedgemoor Top Bid (IRE)**[8] 4882 6-11-1 93 ....(b) TomScudamore 68
(Nigel Hawke) *led tl 5th: chsd ldrs: u.p whn hmpd after 7th: sn btn: t.o* **16/1**

P00- **P** **Trumix**[8] 4887 6-11-1 102 ....(b[1]) NickScholfield
(Kim Bailey) *sn struggling in rr: reminders after 2nd and 3rd: lost tch after 4th: t.o whn p.u bef 2 out* **15/2**

20F- **R** **Slaney Star (IRE)**[8] 4882 6-11-1 105 ....(v) MattieBatchelor
(Jim Best) *trckd ldr: led 5th: rn out 7th* **11/4**[2]

60- **P** **Ruby's From Milan (IRE)**[252] 1016 6-10-8 0 .... JamesDavies
(Mark Shears) *lost tch 4th: sn t.o: p.u 7th* **66/1**

00P- **U** **Castanum (IRE)**[39] 4281 5-11-1 0 ....(b[1]) TomCannon
(Laura Young) *in tch: awkward 4th: wnt bdly lft and uns rdr next* **100/1**

06- **U** **War Treaty (IRE)**[114] 2864 6-11-1 0 ....(p) DaveCrosse
(Mark Shears) *blnd and uns rdr 1st* **80/1**

4m 39.5s (-3.20) **Going Correction** -0.375s/f (Good)
WFA 4 from 5yo+ 7lb **9** Ran SP% **115.6**
Speed ratings (Par 103): **91,89,87,74, , ,**
CSF £10.65 TOTE £3.10: £1.10, £2.20, £1.90; EX 13.30 Trifecta £48.80.There was no bid for the winner.
Owner Galloping On The South Downs Partnership **Bred** Redmondstown Stud **Trained** Lower Beeding, W Sussex
FOCUS
The third-last was bypassed in this opening event. Weak selling form, but big steps up from the first two. The race wasn't without incident.

5030 HIGOS INSURANCE SERVICES PLYMSTOCK H'CAP HURDLE (JOCKEY CLUB GRASSROOTS JUMPS SERIES QUALIFIER) (10 hdls) 2m 3f
2:40 (2:44) (Class 3) (0-125,125) 4-Y-0+ **£6,498** (£1,908; £954; £477)

Form RPR
521- **1** **Here's Herbie**[22] 4599 6-10-10 114 .... MissLucyGardner(5) 121+
(Sue Gardner) *trckd ldrs: led and j.rt fr 3 out: rdn clr bef last: strly chal run-in: asserted cl home* **9/1**

031- **2** *1 ½* **Henryville**[11] 4801 6-11-12 125 .... NoelFehily 130+
(Harry Fry) *hld up bhd: j.lft 1st 3: pushed along and hdwy fr 6th: rdn to chse ldrs 3 out: styd on to hold ev ch after last: no ex fnl 50yds* **9/2**[1]

/U0- **3** 8 **Hollow Penny**[139] 2314 6-11-4 **117** RobertThornton 114
(Alan King) *mid-div: hdwy after 7th: rdn bef next: styd on same pce: wnt 3rd run-in* **10/1**

442- **4** ½ **Dragon's Den (IRE)**[20] 4634 7-11-1 **114** LeightonAspell 112+
(Chris Down) *hld up towards rr: hdwy 7th: chsd ldrs 3 out: rdn whn bdly hmpd 2 out: styd on to go 4th run-in: nt rch ldrs* **14/1**

151/ **5** 2 **Grand Gold**[28] 1676 5-11-11 **124** (t) ConorO'Farrell 118
(Seamus Durack) *disp ld most of way tl after 7th: ev ch 3 out: sn rdn: no ex fr last: lost 2 pls run-in* **25/1**

426- **6** 1¾ **Tinker Time (IRE)**[39] 4277 6-11-4 **117** LiamHeard 110
(Bob Buckler) *in tch: rdn to chse ldrs 3 out: styd on same pce fr 2 out* **20/1**

160- **7** hd **Quick Decisson (IRE)**[39] 4278 6-11-9 **122** TomO'Brien 115
(Philip Hobbs) *trckd ldrs: rdn appr 3 out: styd chsng ldrs tl no ex appr last* **14/1**

402- **8** shd **Fond Memory (IRE)**[26] 4538 6-10-13 **112** SamTwiston-Davies 104
(Nigel Twiston-Davies) *disp ld tl led after 7th: rdn and hdd whn pckd 3 out: fdd appr last* **6/1**[2]

0U5- **9** ½ **Quaddick Lake (IRE)**[20] 4634 11-10-9 **118** ChrisMeehan(10) 110
(Jeremy Scott) *hld up towards rr: sme hdwy on outer appr 3 out: sn rdn: no further imp fr bef 2 out* **25/1**

0/5- **10** 1 **Phoenix Flight (IRE)**[23] 1972 9-11-1 **114** (p) LiamTreadwell 106
(James Evans) *mid-div on outer: rdn after 7th: nvr any imp* **33/1**

242- **11** 9 **Sun Wild Life (FR)**[33] 4391 4-10-13 **120** FelixDeGiles 97
(Robert Walford) *trckd ldrs: rdn after 7th: wknd 3 out: blnd last* **20/1**

260- **12** 4½ **Angles Hill (IRE)**[39] 4277 7-11-9 **125** MichealNolan(3) 104
(Richard Woollacott) *in tch: rdn to chse ldrs 3 out: wknd 2 out* **13/2**[3]

041- **13** 16 **Agincourt Reef (IRE)**[106] 3007 5-11-4 **117** JamieMoore 81
(Gary Moore) *mid-div: rdn appr 3 out: wkng whn bdly hmpd 2 out* **16/1**

P00- **14** 10 **Golden Gael**[38] 4303 8-11-6 **119** NickScholfield 74
(Jeremy Scott) *trckd ldrs tl rdn and wknd appr 3 out: t.o* **33/1**

P/0- **15** 5 **Jackies Solitaire**[32] 4418 6-11-11 **124** AidanColeman 75
(Anthony Honeyball) *mid-div tl 4th: sn struggling in rr: t.o* **16/1**

506- **P** **Decoy (FR)**[57] 3957 8-10-10 **116** (p) MrEBarrett(7)
(David Pipe) *mid-div: pushed along after 4th: sn bhd: t.o whn p.u after 2 out* **20/1**

5PP- **P** **Pasture Bay (IRE)**[96] 3183 8-10-6 **110** ConorShoemark(5)
(Fergal O'Brien) *hld up towards rr: struggling 6th: sn lost tch: t.o whn p.u bef 3 out* **50/1**

P32- **P** **Phone Home (IRE)**[19] 4662 7-11-5 **118** DominicElsworth
(Nick Mitchell) *a in rr: t.o whn p.u bef last* **20/1**

F06- **F** **Urcalin (FR)**[74] 3648 6-11-0 **113** TomCannon 105
(David Arbuthnot) *mid-div: rdn appr 3 out: no imp whn fell 2 out* **11/1**

4m 32.2s (-10.50) **Going Correction** -0.375s/f (Good)
WFA 4 from 5yo+ 7lb **19** Ran SP% **132.9**
Speed ratings (Par 107): **107,106,103,102,101 101,101,101,100,100 96,94,88,83,81 , , ,**
CSF £46.39 CT £439.92 TOTE £9.70: £2.40, £2.10, £3.40, £2.40; EX 45.90 Trifecta £678.30.
Owner D V Gardner **Bred** D V Gardner Woodhayes Stud **Trained** Longdown, Devon

FOCUS
A wide-open handicap in which two last-time-out winners dominated the finish. Fair form which should work out.

5031 HIGOS INSURANCE SERVICES NOVICES' LIMITED H'CAP CHASE (15 fncs) 2m 3f 110y
3:10 (3:10) (Class 3) (0-125,125) 5-Y-0 **£6,330** (£1,870; £935; £468; £234)

Form RPR

223- **1** **Daymar Bay (IRE)**[38] 4303 8-10-11 **115** (v¹) AidanColeman 128+
(Emma Lavelle) *j.w: hld up in tch: hdwy to dispute 8th: led 10th: in command and drew clr fr 3 out: readily* **3/1**[1]

3P2- **2** 12 **Gores Island (IRE)**[8] 4885 8-10-11 **115** JoshuaMoore 117
(Gary Moore) *j.rt at times: hld up: hdwy 8th: rdn to chse wnr 4 out: styd on but nvr any ch w wnr fr 3 out* **12/1**

243- **3** 4½ **Easily Pleased (IRE)**[11] 4804 8-11-2 **120** HaddenFrost 118
(Martin Hill) *hld up: hdwy after 11th: rdn after 4 out: wnt 3rd next: kpt on same pce fr 2 out* **12/1**

423- **4** 3 **Gorsky Island**[53] 4029 6-11-2 **120** PaddyBrennan 116
(Tom George) *in tch: rchd for 7th: rdn after 11th: styd on same pce fr 4 out* **20/1**

425- **5** 22 **Toby Lerone (IRE)**[11] 4819 7-11-7 **125** HarrySkelton 104
(Dan Skelton) *trckd ldr: disp 8th tl 10th: rdn after next: hld in 5th whn mstke 3 out: wkng whn blnd 2 out: t.o* **7/2**[2]

/03- **6** 8 **Atlantic Roller (IRE)**[61] 3875 7-11-7 **125** (t) NickScholfield 93
(Paul Nicholls) *trckd ldrs: disp 8th tl rchd for 10th: rdn after 11th btn bef next: j.rt last 4: t.o* **9/2**[3]

445- **7** 4½ **Tour D'Argent (FR)**[41] 4235 7-11-4 **122** SamTwiston-Davies 86
(Donald McCain) *hld up: struggling 10th: wknd after 4 out: t.o* **16/1**

222- **8** 5 **Sure Thing (FR)**[4] 4970 8-10-7 **111** oh3 TomO'Brien 71
(Henry Daly) *led 2nd: jnd 8th: hdd 9th: rdn after 11th: sn btn: t.o* **9/2**[3]

/34- **9** 5 **Mcvicar**[111] 2910 5-11-5 **123** RobertThornton 78
(Alan King) *chsd ldrs: rdn after 11th: wknd bef next: t.o* **18/1**

4m 40.6s (-16.70) **Going Correction** -0.65s/f (Firm) **9** Ran SP% **114.9**
Speed ratings: **107,102,100,99,90 87,85,83,81**
CSF £37.22 CT £377.84 TOTE £3.70: £1.10, £3.70, £2.50; EX 40.70 Trifecta £260.10.
Owner The Hawk Inn Syndicate 2 **Bred** Barry Noonan **Trained** Hatherden, Hants

FOCUS
A couple of the key contenders were disappointing. A step up from the winner with the second to his mark.

5032 HIGOS INSURANCE SERVICES EXETER H'CAP CHASE (18 fncs) 3m
3:40 (3:40) (Class 4) (0-115,115) 5-Y-0+ **£4,548** (£1,335; £667; £333)

Form RPR

33P- **1** **Miss Saffron**[66] 3797 11-10-3 **92** PaulMoloney 102+
(Sue Gardner) *hld up: hdwy appr 4 out: chal between last 2: led last: drifted lft briefly: styd on wl to assert towards fin: pushed out* **5/1**[3]

/3P- **2** 1 **Off The Wall (IRE)**[79] 3565 7-11-5 **108** (bt) TomScudamore 118+
(David Pipe) *hld up: hdwy after 11th: led 3 out: narrowly hdd last: carried sltly lft: styd on: hld towards fin* **7/1**

325- **3** 7 **Susquehanna River (IRE)**[87] 3389 7-11-12 **115** SamTwiston-Davies 117
(Nigel Twiston-Davies) *led tl 7th: prom: led 12th tl after 14th: rdn w ev ch next tl 3 out: styd on same pce* **9/1**

462- **4** nk **Faith Keeper (IRE)**[14] 4759 9-10-11 **100** NoelFehily 103
(Fergal O'Brien) *j. sltly lft at times: trckd ldr: led 7th tl 14th: led again bef 4 out: rdn and hdd 3 out* **4/1**[2]

563- **5** nk **Knockraheen (IRE)**[22] 4602 6-10-13 **107** (b) MauriceLinehan(5) 110
(Jonjo O'Neill) *racd keenly most of way: in tch: trckd ldrs 14th: pushed along and ch whn nt fluent 4 out: sn rdn: disp 3rd fr 3 out: kpt on same pce fr next* **8/1**

F56- **6** 14 **Robin Will (FR)**[67] 3784 9-11-7 **115** MrJoshuaGuerriero(5) 104
(Richard Woollacott) *hld up: sme prog 4 out: sn rdn: nvr threatened: wkng whn mstke 2 out* **16/1**

340- **7** nk **Rio Milan (IRE)**[7] 4903 8-11-7 **115** (t) ConorShoemark(5) 104
(Fergal O'Brien) *hld up: pushed along bef 11th: effrt 4 out: wknd 3 out* **25/1**

356- **8** 21 **Pistol (IRE)**[26] 4537 5-11-9 **113** (b) TomO'Brien 82
(Philip Hobbs) *trckd ldrs: nudged along fr 10th: mstke 11th: sn lost pl and struggling: nvr any danger fr 4 out* **16/1**

442- **P** **Nodebateaboutit**[33] 4396 9-11-8 **111** (tp) PaddyBrennan
(Tom George) *in tch: tk clsr order 11th: rdn appr 4 out: wknd 3 out: p.u bef 2 out* **85/40**[1]

6m 10.7s (1.40) **Going Correction** -0.65s/f (Firm)
WFA 5 from 6yo+ 1lb **9** Ran SP% **117.9**
Speed ratings: **71,70,68,68,68 63,63,56,**
CSF £40.66 CT £309.79 TOTE £8.80: £2.90, £2.50, £2.30; EX 70.70 Trifecta £310.20.
Owner P A Tylor **Bred** P A Tylor **Trained** Longdown, Devon

FOCUS
A decent staying handicap that was run at a sound pace. The winner might still be competitive when reassessed.

5033 HIGOS INSURANCE SERVICES PLATINUM H'CAP HURDLE (12 hdls) 2m 7f 110y
4:10 (4:10) (Class 4) (0-105,108) 4-Y-0+ **£3,249** (£954; £477; £238)

Form RPR

/52- **1** **Pertinent (FR)**[90] 3290 11-11-3 **103** (t) MissAliceMills(5) 109+
(Charles Whittaker) *travelled wl: mde all: styd on wl fr last: rdn out* **22/1**

12P- **2** 2 **Night Of Passion (IRE)**[46] 4161 6-11-12 **105** (p) NickScholfield 109
(Jeremy Scott) *trckd wnr: rdn after 9th: styd on but a being hld fr 2 out* **10/1**[3]

101- **3** 5 **Rugged Jack (FR)**[8] 4887 7-11-8 **108** 7ex MrMatthewHampton(7) 110
(Victor Dartnall) *mid-div: hdwy 9th: rdn to dispute 2nd 2 out tl after next: no ex fr last* **4/1**[1]

0P5- **4** 5 **Little Eaglet (IRE)**[16] 4733 10-10-11 **90** LiamHeard 85
(Colin Heard) *in tch: trckd ldrs 7th: rdn appr 3 out: styd on same pce* **25/1**

530- **5** 10 **La Belle Sauvage**[11] 4823 7-11-4 **97** (p) SamTwiston-Davies 83
(Kim Bailey) *mid-div: rdn after 9th: styd on same pce fr next: nvr threatened* **20/1**

2P5- **6** 2 **Clouds Of Mist**[27] 4516 9-10-13 **97** MissLucyGardner(5) 83
(Sue Gardner) *trckd wnr tl rdn appr 3 out: sn hld: fdd fr 2 out* **4/1**[1]

P11- **7** 4 **Admiral Blake**[63] 3842 7-10-10 **89** DougieCostello 70
(Laura Young) *hld up and a towards rr* **8/1**[2]

362- **8** 14 **Westerly Breeze (IRE)**[18] 4677 6-11-10 **103** TomSiddall 71
(Martin Keighley) *trckd wnr tl rdn after 9th: sn wknd: hmpd 3 out: t.o* **8/1**[2]

43- **9** 3¼ **Minella Gathering (IRE)**[28] 4501 5-11-2 **95** TomO'Brien 60
(Paul Henderson) *sn struggling in rr: no ch whn hmpd 3 out: t.o* **12/1**

534- **10** ¾ **Tracking Time**[11] 4818 7-11-4 **104** MrJMartin(7) 68
(Andrew J Martin) *mid-div: rdn after 8th: sn btn: hmpd 3 out: t.o* **25/1**

232- **U** **Brantingham Breeze**[16] 4719 6-10-11 **100** RichardO'Dea(10)
(Emma Lavelle) *hld up towards rr: making hdwy whn awkward and uns rdr 8th* **4/1**[1]

656- **F** **Lemons Ground**[17] 4694 5-11-4 **100** GavinSheehan(3)
(Jamie Snowden) *mid-div: rdn after 9th: styng on at same pce whn fell 3 out* **12/1**

5m 52.4s (-6.60) **Going Correction** -0.375s/f (Good) **12** Ran SP% **123.5**
Speed ratings (Par 105): **96,95,93,92,88 88,86,82,80,80 ,**
CSF £223.58 CT £1077.10 TOTE £23.80: £9.40, £2.50, £3.00; EX 291.00 Trifecta £1869.50.
Owner C R Whittaker **Bred** Haras De St Voir **Trained** Radstock, Somerset
■ Charles Whittaker's first winner under rules.

FOCUS
A moderate handicap. The winner was well in on old form.

5034 HIGOS INSURANCE SERVICES BRAUNTON NOVICES' H'CAP HURDLE (8 hdls) 2m 1f
4:40 (4:40) (Class 4) (0-110,110) 4-Y-0+ **£3,573** (£1,049; £524; £262)

Form RPR

15P- **1** **Withy Mills**[36] 4334 9-10-0 **87** (bt) JamesBest(3) 91
(Kevin Bishop) *trckd ldrs: chal after 5th: led bef 3 out: styd on wl: rdn out* **50/1**

664- **2** 3½ **Comte D'Anjou**[19] 4664 5-11-10 **108** (p) PaddyBrennan 109
(Nick Williams) *hld up towards rr: stdy prog after 3rd: trckd ldrs after 5th: rdn to chse wnr 3 out: kpt on but a being hld fr next* **10/1**

065- **3** 2¾ **Rafafie**[33] 4391 6-10-7 **96** MissLucyGardner(5) 95
(Sue Gardner) *mid-div: hdwy after 5th: disp 3rd 3 out where wnt rt: sn rdn: styd on same pce fr next* **7/2**[1]

045- **4** nk **Dan's Wee Man**[88] 3357 5-11-6 **109** (p) JamesBanks(5) 107
(Andy Turnell) *mid-div: hdwy after 5th: rdn to dispute 3rd fr 3 out: kpt on same pce fr 2 out* **25/1**

324- **5** hd **Daveron (IRE)**[26] 4538 6-11-12 **110** NickScholfield 109
(Jeremy Scott) *trckd ldrs: nt clr run bhd wkng horse and lost pl on bnd bef 3 out: rdn to dispute 3rd 2 out: styd on same pce* **9/1**

415- **6** 8 **Ivanhoe**[70] 3714 4-11-4 **109** NoelFehily 94
(Michael Blanshard) *mid-div: rdn appr 3 out: styd on but nvr gng pce to get involved* **15/2**

55P- **7** 11 **River Dancing (IRE)**[57] 3959 7-9-13 **90** MrMLegg(7) 74
(Andy Turnell) *towards rr: struggling after 2nd: sme prog bef 3 out: nvr any danger* **10/1**

604- **8** 1½ **Lady Fingers**[79] 3566 6-10-11 **95** SamTwiston-Davies 76
(Nigel Twiston-Davies) *mid-div tl 5th: sn bhd* **14/1**

042/ **9** 1¾ **No Likey (IRE)**[356] 5148 7-11-7 **105** (t) TomO'Brien 83
(Philip Hobbs) *trckd ldrs: chal after 5th: rdn bef next: sn wknd* **7/1**[3]

/21- **10** ½ **The Darling Boy**[27] 4519 9-11-5 **103** (tp) TomScudamore 80
(David Pipe) *led tl rdn bef 3 out: sn wknd* **5/1**[2]

250- **11** 14 **Castle Beach (IRE)**[24] 5-11-4 **105** (t) MichealNolan(3) 70
(Robert Stephens) *trckd ldrs tl rdn after 5th: sn wknd: t.o* **25/1**

060- **12** 4½ **Electric Mayhem**[16] 4715 7-11-7 **105** WayneHutchinson 66
(Nick Mitchell) *a in rr: t.o* **33/1**

310- **13** 12 **Exemplary**[37] 4324 7-11-8 **106** AidanColeman 56
(Alexandra Dunn) *trckd ldrs tl wknd after 5th: t.o* **16/1**

050- **P** **Berkeley Avenue**[38] 4302 5-11-3 **104** (bt¹) GavinSheehan(3)
(Warren Greatrex) *a towards rr: t.o whn p.u 3 out* **14/1**

065- **F** **Dream Lucky**[27] 4514 9-10-4 **91**........................ MattGriffiths(3)
(Richard Woollacott) *fell 1st* **40/1**

4m 7.8s (-7.70) **Going Correction** -0.375s/f (Good)
WFA 4 from 5yo+ 7lb **15** Ran SP% **125.6**
Speed ratings (Par 105): **103,101,100,99,99 96,90,90,89,89 82,80,74, ,**
CSF £494.63 CT £2242.93 TOTE £51.00: £7.10, £5.20, £1.90; EX 896.20 Trifecta £2033.40 Part won..
Owner Slabs And Lucan **Bred** K Bishop **Trained** Spaxton, Somerset

FOCUS
A steadily run race and there was a bit of a turn up. Still, it's a race that should produce winners. The fourth and fifth help with the standard.

5035 HIGOS FOR YOUR TRAVEL INSURANCE OPEN HUNTERS' CHASE (15 fncs) 2m 3f 110y
5:10 (5:10) (Class 6) 5-Y-O+ **£935** (£290; £145; £72)

Form RPR

452- **1** **Shrewd Investment**[17] 4705 8-11-9 109..................(tp) MrSamPainting(7) 121+
(Miss L Thomas) *trckd ldrs: nudged along after 7th: chal 4 out: led 2 out: drew clr last: r.o wl* **7/2**[2]

10- **2** *5* **King Of Alcatraz (IRE)**[11] 8-11-9 0.................................. MissVWade(7) 117+
(N Harris) *disp ld tl clr ldr after 11th: awkward 4 out: rdn and hdd 2 out: no ex appr last* **13/2**

232- **3** *12* **Delta Borget (FR)**[19] 4658 9-11-5 103..................... MissLeandaTickle(7) 101
(L Jefford) *trckd ldrs: rdn in cl 4th after 4 out: styd on same pce fr next: wnt 3rd run-in* **5/1**[3]

/0P- **4** *3* **Noble Ben (IRE)**[27] 4511 12-11-7 93.............................(p) MrJMRidley(5) 97
(Mrs H S M Ridley) *hld up: hdwy after 11th: ev ch 4 out tl after 3 out: hld next: fdd and lost 3rd run-in* **33/1**

335- **5** *4* **Sound Stage**[17] 11-11-12 107..................................... MrJoshuaGuerriero 94
(Miss S Berry) *disp ld tl rdn after 11th: hld next: grad fdd fr 3 out* **8/1**

/P4- **6** *1 ¼* **Restezen D'Armor (FR)**[28] 4505 9-11-5 108........(p) MrRobertHawker(7) 93
(Mrs O C Jackson) *disp ld tl rdn after 11th: grad fdd fr 4 out* **33/1**

P15- **7** *32* **Spock (FR)**[161] 1921 9-12-3 118....................................(p) MrsAlexDunn(3) 72
(Alexandra Dunn) *trckd ldrs: rdn after 11th: wknd bef 4 out: t.o* **14/1**

61- **P** **Siro Demur (FR)**[19] 4658 8-11-11 107......................... MrAlexEdwards(5)
(Philip Rowley) *trckd ldrs tl lost pl 10th: wknd after next: p.u bef 4 out* **6/4**[1]

4m 45.7s (-11.60) **Going Correction** -0.65s/f (Firm) **8** Ran SP% **115.9**
Speed ratings: **97,95,90,89,87 86,74,**
CSF £26.83 TOTE £5.90: £1.90, £2.50, £1.10; EX 21.30 Trifecta £89.30.
Owner Norman Thomas **Bred** A W Buller **Trained** Wroughton, Oxon

FOCUS
Fair hunter chase form. The winner can win more of these.
T/Jkpt: Not won. T/Plt: £216.80 to a £1 stake. Pool of £112364.24 - 378.22 winning tickets.
T/Qpdt: £203.50 to a £1 stake. Pool of £7673.08 - 27.90 winning tickets. TM

4838 FFOS LAS (L-H)
Thursday, March 27

OFFICIAL GOING: Soft (6.0)
Wind: moderate across Weather: sunny spells

5036 VICTORIAN HOUSE WINDOW GROUP MAIDEN HURDLE (10 hdls) 2m 4f
1:50 (1:50) (Class 4) 4-Y-O+ **£3,573** (£1,049; £524; £262)

Form RPR

12U- **1** **Flying Eagle (IRE)**[11] 4838 6-11-1 0.................................. JamieMoore 130+
(Peter Bowen) *towards rr: tk clsr order 2nd: trckd ldrs 6th: chal 3 out: sn led: styd on to draw clr 2 out: drvn out* **2/1**[1]

\- **2** *9* **Lookslikerainted (IRE)**[403] 7-10-8 0.............................. PaulO'Brien(7) 122+
(Rebecca Curtis) *prom: trckd ldr 5th: led appr 7th tl rdn and hdd appr 2 out: one pce and hld whn mstke last* **12/1**

321- **3** *12* **Onenightinvienna (IRE)**[37] 4335 5-11-1 0........................... TomO'Brien 109
(Philip Hobbs) *in tch: clsd 6th: drvn in 4th and outpcd by ldrs after 7th: no ch after but styd on to take mod 3rd last* **11/4**[2]

/62- **4** *5* **King Of Glory**[37] 4332 6-11-1 112..................................... AidanColeman 107
(Venetia Williams) *racd alone on ins: in tch: cl up fr 4th tl stmbld and wknd 3 out: lost mod 3rd last* **7/2**[3]

30/ **5** *25* **Tipsy Gypsy (IRE)**[354] 5195 7-11-1 0.............................. DougieCostello 78
(Tim Vaughan) *a towards rr: lost tch after 7th: modest prog past btn rivals: t.o* **33/1**

62- **6** *23* **Always Archie**[19] 4672 7-11-1 0.. MichaelByrne 55
(Tim Vaughan) *led tl after 1st: led 3rd tl appr 7th: sn wknd: t.o* **16/1**

7 *18* **King Of Jazz (IRE)**[169] 6-11-1 0...................................... DonalDevereux 37
(Peter Bowen) *in rr: hdwy after 6th: wknd appr 3 out: t.o* **50/1**

/00- **8** *75* **Pennies And Pounds**[107] 3010 7-10-8 0................. WayneHutchinson
(Julian Smith) *a bhd: reminder after 1st: lost tch 5th: wl t.o* **100/1**

620- **P** **Master Rajeem (USA)**[114] 2874 5-11-1 124.......(v[1]) SamTwiston-Davies
(Nigel Twiston-Davies) *racd keenly: led after 1st to 3rd: styd in 2nd to 5th: drvn and wknd next: t.o whn p.u bef 2 out* **6/1**

0P5- **P** **Pru**[247] 1082 6-10-1 0.. ConorRing(7)
(Mary Evans) *in tch tl mstke and dropped to rr 3rd: struggling after next: t.o whn p.u bef 7th* **100/1**

5m 31.2s (40.30) **Going Correction** +1.725s/f (Heav) **10** Ran SP% **117.0**
Speed ratings (Par 105): **88,84,79,77,67 58,51,21, ,**
CSF £27.07 TOTE £3.50: £1.40, £3.50, £1.40; EX 27.40 Trifecta £90.40.
Owner West Coast Haulage Limited **Bred** Dion Egan **Trained** Little Newcastle, Pembrokes

FOCUS
Aidan Coleman said of the ground "it's worse than the last meeting, it's very heavy". The runners finished tired in this ordinary maiden hurdle. The winner built on the promise of his recent run.

5037 WALTERS UK H'CAP HURDLE (12 hdls) 3m
2:20 (2:20) (Class 4) (0-115,115) 4-Y-O+ **£3,119** (£915; £457; £228)

Form RPR

640- **1** **Garde Fou (FR)**[47] 4161 8-11-1 **104**..............................(t) TomO'Brien 118+
(Paul Henderson) *hld up: hdwy 8th: led gng wl 3 out: sn drew clr: in command whn j.lft last 2: v easily* **5/2**[2]

323- **2** *13* **Island Cruise (IRE)**[18] 4702 6-11-7 **110**............................(t) ColinBolger 105
(Pat Murphy) *hld up: mstke 5th: clsd 8th: rdn after next: wnt mod 2nd bef 2 out: styd on but no ch w easy wnr* **6/1**

20P- **3** *7* **Ifyouthinkso**[52] 4070 7-10-13 **102**..........................(v[1]) NickScholfield 89
(Lucy Jones) *chsd clr ldr: clsd 6th: led next tl hdd and nt fluent 3 out: one pce and no ch after* **9/4**[1]

P- **4** *33* **Sandanski (IRE)**[155] 2024 6-11-12 **115**..........................(tp) FelixDeGiles 93
(Tom Gretton) *racd in 3rd: hit 3rd: trckd ldr 7th: rdn after 9th: wknd 3 out: t.o* **14/1**

/06- **P** **Cygnet**[78] 3130 8-11-7 **110**.. DonalDevereux
(Peter Bowen) *racd keenly: led: clr after 2nd to 6th: hdd 7th: struggling whn nt fluent 9th: t.o whn p.u bef 2 out* **10/1**

202- **P** **Lights Of Broadway (IRE)**[19] 4676 8-10-7 **101**.......(t) RobertWilliams(5)
(Bernard Llewellyn) *hld up in last: mstke 6th: sn rdn along: sme hdwy after 9th: wknd 3 out: wl bhd whn p.u bef next* **7/2**[3]

6m 53.3s (64.30) **Going Correction** +1.725s/f (Heav) **6** Ran SP% **111.6**
Speed ratings (Par 105): **61,56,54,43,**
CSF £17.08 CT £36.11 TOTE £4.20: £1.40, £2.40; EX 18.00 Trifecta £61.70.
Owner Ray Antell **Bred** Mme Edwige Le Metayer **Trained** Whitsbury, Hants

FOCUS
A modest handicap.

5038 DAVIES CHEMISTS H'CAP CHASE (17 fncs) 2m 5f
2:55 (2:55) (Class 5) (0-100,100) 5-Y-O+ **£2,274** (£667; £333; £166)

Form RPR

U41- **1** **Tom Bach (IRE)**[11] 4843 10-9-11 **74** oh2...........................(b) JamesBest(3) 86+
(Hywel Evans) *tended to jump rt: mde all: rdn 4 out: reduced ld 2 out: styd on wl u.p* **11/10**[1]

5/4- **2** *1 ¾* **No Through Road**[30] 4482 7-10-0 **74** oh4....................(t) TomScudamore 83
(Michael Scudamore) *hld up bhd ldrs: rdn 4 out: chsd wnr next: clsd 2 out: kpt on u.p but a being hld* **6/1**[3]

PPP- **3** *12* **Big News**[21] 4630 8-11-9 **100**..(t) MichealNolan(3) 103+
(Richard Lee) *trckd ldrs: rdn after 13th: disputing 2nd whn blnd bdly 3 out: one pce after* **4/1**[2]

611- **4** *6* **Lord Fox (IRE)**[13] 4795 7-11-2 **95**.. BenPoste(5) 86
(Shaun Harris) *chsd ldrs: rdn along after 13th: lost tch 4 out: tk mod 4th last* **6/1**[3]

230- **5** *2 ¾* **Tin Pot Man (IRE)**[17] 4729 8-11-5 **93**...................................(t) PaulMoloney 81
(Evan Williams) *a in rr: pushed along 10th: no ch fr 13th* **10/1**

/0P- **6** *38* **Bens Moor (IRE)**[152] 2088 9-10-13 **87**................................ MichaelByrne 50
(Tim Vaughan) *racd keenly: mainly trckd wnr fr 4th: rdn after 13th: lost 2nd and mstke 3 out: wknd next: t.o* **14/1**

6m 0.5s (31.90) **Going Correction** +1.50s/f (Heav) **6** Ran SP% **111.9**
Speed ratings: **99,98,93,91,90 75**
CSF £8.30 TOTE £2.50: £1.10, £2.60; EX 11.90 Trifecta £46.70.
Owner Hywel Evans **Bred** Carthage Molloy **Trained** Kidwelly, Carmarthens

FOCUS
Weak handicap chase form. The winner was below the level of his easy course win over further.

5039 TANNERS WINES H'CAP CHASE (18 fncs) 3m
3:30 (3:30) (Class 4) (0-120,116) 5-Y-O+ **£4,223** (£1,240; £620; £310)

Form RPR

520- **1** **Royal Riviera**[30] 4486 8-10-11 **101**......................(vt[1]) SamTwiston-Davies 111
(Nigel Twiston-Davies) *hld up in last: clsd 12th: nt fluent 14th: wnt 3rd 3 out: trckd wnr and pushed along next: led narrowly last: drvn out* **9/2**

033- **2** *nk* **Victory Gunner (IRE)**[19] 4678 16-10-12 **105**................ MichealNolan(3) 115
(Richard Lee) *trckd ldr tl led 6th: tended to jump rt after: rdn 4 out: narrowly hdd last: kpt on gamely: jst hld* **7/2**[3]

12P- **3** *18* **Take The Mick**[29] 4490 7-11-12 **116**................................. AidanColeman 110
(Venetia Williams) *led to 1st: chsd ldrs: mainly 2nd fr 9th: rdn appr 4 out: lost 2nd 3 out: wknd after next* **5/2**[2]

402- **4** *6* **Our Island (IRE)**[11] 4842 9-11-11 **115**.............................(v) DougieCostello 101
(Tim Vaughan) *led 1st: j. slowly 5th: hdd 6th: sn rdn along: reminders after 9th: u.p but styd prom tl wknd 4 out* **2/1**[1]

353- **5** *42* **Raduis Bleu (FR)**[11] 4842 9-11-1 **112**................................ MissLBrooke(7) 56
(Lady Susan Brooke) *in tch in 4th: rdn after 14th: wknd 4 out: t.o* **16/1**

6m 52.5s (35.10) **Going Correction** +1.50s/f (Heav) **5** Ran SP% **108.2**
Speed ratings: **101,100,94,92,78**
CSF £19.22 TOTE £7.10: £3.50, £2.70; EX 19.60 Trifecta £113.30.
Owner N A Twiston-Davies **Bred** J L C Pearce **Trained** Naunton, Gloucs
■ Stewards' Enquiry : Micheal Nolan two-day ban: use of whip (10-11 Apr)

FOCUS
Not form to get excited about, with the two at the head of the market disappointing and the runner-up, beaten just a neck, being a 16yo. The winner is rated to his mark.

5040 HUGH JAMES SOLICITORS H'CAP HURDLE (8 hdls) 2m
4:00 (4:01) (Class 4) (0-120,117) 4-Y-O+ **£3,119** (£915; £457; £228)

Form RPR

222- **1** **Lac Sacre (FR)**[22] 4612 5-11-10 **115**.................................(bt[1]) TomO'Brien 127+
(John Flint) *hld up bhd ldrs: wnt 2nd 3 out: chal 2 out: led on bit last: easily drew clr flat* **3/1**[2]

/2P- **2** *5* **Explained (IRE)**[91] 3249 7-11-8 **113**................................... MichaelByrne 114
(Tim Vaughan) *led: rdn 3 out: jnd next: hdd and nt fluent last: kpt on but no ch w easy wnr* **7/1**

234- **3** *6* **Santo Thomas (FR)**[28] 4512 8-10-12 **103**......................... AidanColeman 98
(Venetia Williams) *prom: trckd ldr 4th tl rdn 3 out: one pce after* **7/4**[1]

1P3- **4** *9* **Going Concern (IRE)**[19] 4674 7-11-10 **115**....................... PaulMoloney 103
(Evan Williams) *hld up: hdwy 5th: cl 4th and stl gng wl 3 out: sn outpcd by ldrs: rdn next: no imp* **4/1**[3]

0P0- **5** *17* **Ubaldo Des Menhies (FR)**[17] 4726 6-11-12 **117**......... RichieMcLernon 85
(Jonjo O'Neill) *hld up in last: shkn up after 3rd: rdn 5th: sn lost tch: t.o* **7/1**

/15- **6** *27* **Fuzzy Logic (IRE)**[9] 4887 5-10-12 **108**........................ RobertWilliams(5) 49
(Bernard Llewellyn) *trckd ldr: nt fluent and lost pl 4th: rdn and wknd after next: t.o* **14/1**

4m 13.7s (25.20) **Going Correction** +1.725s/f (Heav) **6** Ran SP% **113.0**
Speed ratings (Par 105): **106,103,100,96,87 74**
CSF £23.12 TOTE £2.80: £1.70, £4.10; EX 24.30 Trifecta £73.00.
Owner L H & Mrs T Evans **Bred** Mlle Francoise Perree **Trained** Kenfig Hill, Bridgend

FOCUS
Moderate handicap form, with a big step up from the easy winner.

5041 LLEWELLYN HUMPHREYS NOVICES' HUNTERS' CHASE (17 fncs) 2m 5f
4:35 (4:35) (Class 6) 5-Y-O+ **£1,580** (£486; £243)

Form RPR

104/ **1** **Silver Token**[32] 9-11-12 102....................................(tp) MrTomDavid 118+
(David Brace) *hld up in tch: hdwy after 8th: led 10th: drew clr fr 4 out: easily* **5/4**[1]

/54- **2** *16* **Bermuda Boy (FR)**[17] 4727 9-11-9 109.........................(tp) MrJHamilton(3) 98
(S Flook) *cl up: led 4th to 6th: rdn in 3rd after 13th: chsd wnr appr 4 out: plugged on but no imp: mstke last* **8/1**[3]

513- **3** *18* **Qualviro (FR)**[35] 4376 10-11-11 120.................................(v) MrBGibbs(5) 81
(Tim Vaughan) *towards rr: j. slowly 5th: struggling 9th and sn rdn along: mstke 12th: no ch after: wnt poor 3rd last* **6/4**[2]

50P/ **4** *8* **Kingspark Boy (IRE)**[389] 7-11-5 65........................ MissJodieHughes(7) 69
(E R Clough) *racd keenly: trckd ldrs: led 6th to 10th: lost 2nd appr 4 out: sn wknd* **50/1**
P **Red Watch (IRE)**[348] 12-11-12 70................................(p) MrNickWilliams
(L Price) *led to 4th: styd cl up tl after 8th: lost tch 10th: t.o whn p.u bef 3 out* **10/1**
P/ **P** **Coole Abbey Major (IRE)**[304] 10-11-5 0............................... MrGBall(7)
(Robert J Evans) *in tch to 9th: struggling whn j. slowly next: t.o whn p.u bef 12th* **100/1**
416/ **U** **Surprise Us**[516] 2052 7-11-5 0.................................. MrRichardPatrick(7)
(Richard Hambleton) *hld up in last: blnd and uns rdr 7th* **20/1**
5m 59.1s (30.50) **Going Correction** +1.50s/f (Heavy) 7 Ran SP% **112.4**
Speed ratings: **101,94,88,85, ,**
CSF £11.13 TOTE £2.20: £1.60, £1.70; EX 10.20 Trifecta £24.40.
Owner David Brace **Bred** David Brace **Trained** Pyle, Bridgend
FOCUS
A lowly hunters' chase that looked a match. The winner looks a fair hunter.

5042 GLYN ABBEY STANDARD OPEN NATIONAL HUNT FLAT RACE 2m
5:05 (5:06) (Class 6) 4-5-Y-0 **£1,624** (£477; £238; £119)

Form RPR
1 **Blaklion**[81] 5-11-0 0.. SamTwiston-Davies 123+
(Nigel Twiston-Davies) *in tch: hmpd bnd after 4f: clsd 7f out: led 5f out: coasted clr 4f out: v easily* **5/2**[1]
2- **2** *15* **Hughesie (IRE)**[99] 3160 5-10-7 0.. ConorRing(7) 98
(Evan Williams) *t.k.h: trckd ldrs: hrd drvn to go 2nd 3f out: kpt on but no ch w easy wnr* **11/4**[2]
13- **3** *2 ¾* **Bennachie (IRE)**[39] 4297 5-10-11 0.................................. AlanJohns(10) 102
(Tim Vaughan) *hld up in tch: rdn over 4f out: wnt 3rd over 2f out: one pce whn wandered u.p over 1f out* **6/1**
4 *1 ¾* **Ballybough Andy (IRE)**[81] 5-11-0 0................................ AidanColeman 94
(David Dennis) *prom tl lost pl 5f out: sn drvn: plugged on one pce: wnt mod 4th over 1f out* **25/1**
5 *13* **Shanaderry Kin (IRE)**[109] 5-11-0 0............................. AndrewThornton 81
(Simon Earle) *hld up: hdwy 6f out: chsd wnr 4f out to 3f out: nudged along and grad wknd* **20/1**
53- **6** *16* **Con Forza (IRE)**[60] 3926 5-10-11 0.............................. GavinSheehan(3) 65
(Warren Greatrex) *cl up: rdn 6f out: wknd 4f out: t.o* **7/1**
4- **7** *89* **Our Chief (IRE)**[21] 4638 5-11-0 0................................... TomScudamore
(David Pipe) *led tl rdn and hdd 5f out: wknd rapidly: t.o fnl 4f* **7/2**[3]
4m 10.7s (27.80) **Going Correction** +1.725s/f (Heavy) 7 Ran SP% **112.9**
Speed ratings: **99,91,90,89,82 74,30**
CSF £9.39 TOTE £3.90: £1.60, £2.60; EX 11.20 Trifecta £39.80.
Owner N A Twiston-Davies **Bred** Mrs M D W Morrison **Trained** Naunton, Gloucs
FOCUS
This had the look of a reasonable bumper beforehand. The impressive winner should win more races, and the second and third set the level.
T/Jkpt: £3060.60 to a £1 stake. Pool: £45,263.52 - 10.50 winning units. T/Plt: £145.30 to a £1 stake. Pool: £81,702.13 - 410.36 winning units. T/Qpdt: £35.80 to a £1 stake. Pool: £5828.80 - 120.20 winning units. RL

5043 - 5049a (Foreign Racing) - See Raceform Interactive

4811 NEWCASTLE (L-H)
Friday, March 28

OFFICIAL GOING: Soft (heavy in places)
Hurdles re-sited and rails on best ground available. Middle and penultimate fences in back straight omitted in all chases.
Wind: Light, half behind Weather: Overcast, showers

5050 IJF 50TH ANNIVERSARY NOVICES' HURDLE (11 hdls) 2m 4f
2:10 (2:11) (Class 4) 4-Y-0+ **£3,119** (£915; £457; £228)

Form RPR
461- **1** **Boondooma (IRE)**[14] 4796 7-11-1 123.................... SamTwiston-Davies 113+
(Dr Richard Newland) *mde all: qcknd clr bef 3 out: v easily* **1/5**[1]
635- **2** *6* **Itstimeforapint (IRE)**[21] 4647 6-11-1 0.......................... PeterBuchanan 97
(Lucinda Russell) *hld up in tch: smooth hdwy to chse wnr 7th: effrt and rdn bef 3 out: plugged on fr next: no ch w wnr* **5/1**[2]
0/U- **3** *6* **Viking Chief (IRE)**[13] 4811 7-10-10 0............................ JohnDawson(5) 91
(John Wade) *t.k.h: hld up in tch: mstke 6th: hdwy bef 3 out: hung lft bef next: sn rdn and no imp* **25/1**
660- **4** *5* **Lachlan Mor**[15] 4776 5-11-1 0.. JamesReveley 86
(Stuart Coltherd) *chsd ldrs tl rdn and wknd bef 2 out* **66/1**
34- **5** *2 ¾* **Silver Vogue**[24] 4605 6-11-1 0... RyanMania 83
(Sue Smith) *chsd wnr to 7th: rdn and outpcd bef 3 out: n.d after* **10/1**[3]
665- **6** *2* **Cadgers Hole**[77] 3634 7-11-1 0.. TomSiddall 81
(Lynn Siddall) *nt fluent in rr: struggling after 4 out: n.d after* **66/1**
64- **7** *20* **Blue Bellini**[24] 4609 6-10-1 0..................................... DiarmuidO'Regan(7) 54
(Chris Grant) *chsd ldrs: mstke and lost pl 6th: hit and struggling next: lost tch after 4 out: t.o* **33/1**
5m 20.0s (-1.10) **Going Correction** -0.175s/f (Good) 7 Ran SP% **118.9**
Speed ratings (Par 105): **95,92,90,88,87 86,78**
CSF £2.03 TOTE £1.10: £1.10, £2.00; EX 2.10 Trifecta £13.00.
Owner P Jenkins & C E Stedman **Bred** Colm Griffin **Trained** Claines, Worcs
FOCUS
Hurdles re-sited and rails on best ground available. There was a plethora of non-runners through the card, following an unexpected deluge of rain falling on ground that had already been watered in the expectation of a sound surface. It rode soft, but they were getting through it.

5051 IJF JACK BERRY HOUSE H'CAP CHASE (11 fncs 2 omitted) 2m 110y
2:40 (2:41) (Class 5) (0-100,98) 5-Y-0+ **£2,144** (£629; £314; £157)

Form RPR
F24- **1** **Edmund (IRE)**[22] 4628 7-11-12 98...............................(t) WilsonRenwick 108+
(Ann Hamilton) *cl up: pushed along 4 out: rallied to ld appr next: pushed clr fr 2 out* **11/8**[1]
2P1- **2** *8* **Some Lad (IRE)**[13] 4817 9-11-1 94.................................. MrTHamilton(7) 95
(Alison Hamilton) *t.k.h: mde most tl rdn and hdd 3 out: kpt on same pce fr next* **7/2**[3]
/24- **3** *8* **Sambelucky (IRE)**[114] 2880 9-10-11 83........................(b) JamesReveley 75
(Keith Reveley) *chsd ldrs tl rdn and outpcd after 4 out: btn after next* **2/1**[2]
45P- **4** *8* **Crackerjack Lad (IRE)**[107] 3020 11-10-4 76.................[1] PeterBuchanan 63
(Lucinda Russell) *chsd ldrs: chal after 3rd to bef next: cl up: outpcd whn nt fluent 5 out: sn struggling: btn fr next* **8/1**
4m 21.9s (0.80) **Going Correction** -0.175s/f (Good) 4 Ran SP% **108.8**
Speed ratings: **91,87,83,79**
CSF £6.36 TOTE £2.30; EX 5.70 Trifecta £6.20.
Owner Ian Hamilton **Bred** Raymond Murphy **Trained** Great Bavington, Northumbland
FOCUS
A pretty weak handicap chase. The winner is rated to his best.

5052 NOW CAREERS SUPPORTING THE CONSTRUCTION INDUSTRY H'CAP HURDLE (11 hdls) 2m 4f
3:10 (3:10) (Class 5) (0-100,102) 4-Y-0+ **£1,949** (£572; £286; £143)

Form RPR
5B2- **1** **Vodka Red (IRE)**[13] 4817 6-10-11 83...........................(b) KennyJohnson 99+
(Robert Johnson) *t.k.h: hld up: smooth hdwy to trck ldrs after 4 out: led on bit appr last: shkn up briefly and qcknd clr run-in: readily* **6/1**[3]
112- **2** *12* **Solway Dornal**[5] 4982 9-9-13 76...............................(p) GrantCockburn(5) 72
(Lisa Harrison) *cl up: rdn to ld 3 out: hdd appr last: no ch w easy wnr* **11/8**[1]
P54- **3** *2 ¾* **First Of Never (IRE)**[13] 4823 8-10-0 72 oh3.......................... TomSiddall 64
(Lynn Siddall) *prom: blnd bdly 4 out: given time to rcvr: rdn after 2 out: no imp* **20/1**
/56- **4** *hd* **Dissidancer (IRE)**[90] 3351 6-11-7 98............................ JohnDawson(5) 91
(John Wade) *t.k.h: led at stdy pce: rdn and hdd 3 out: outpcd fr next* **6/1**[3]
3U5- **5** *21* **Doyenthedecenthing**[66] 3828 6-10-4 76.............................. HenryBrooke 47
(John Davies) *chsd ldrs: effrt and rdn bef 3 out: wknd bef next* **5/2**[2]
400- **6** *13* **Cigalas**[117] 2844 9-9-7 72 oh7....................................... MissAMcGregor(7) 30
(Jean McGregor) *hld up: hdwy and in tch whn hit 5th: rdn and struggling bef 3 out: sn btn* **20/1**
5m 21.0s (-0.10) **Going Correction** -0.175s/f (Good) 6 Ran SP% **108.8**
Speed ratings (Par 103): **93,88,87,87,78 73**
CSF £14.32 CT £133.73 TOTE £5.70: £2.50, £1.50; EX 13.80 Trifecta £76.50.
Owner Ontoawinner,R Johnson,Carter Thomson **Bred** Gerard Mullins **Trained** Newburn, Tyne & Wear
FOCUS
Six of the top seven in the weights were absent from this weak handicap hurdle. A step up from the easy winner, with the third and fourth helping to set the level.

5053 IJF JOHN OAKSEY MEMORIAL H'CAP CHASE (13 fncs 3 omitted) 2m 4f
3:40 (3:40) (Class 3) (0-135,130) 5-Y-0+ **£6,498** (£1,908; £954; £477)

Form RPR
521- **1** **Galway Jack (IRE)**[25] 4593 9-11-10 128........................ AndrewThornton 139+
(Caroline Bailey) *mde virtually all: rdn and styd on wl fr 2 out* **7/2**[1]
332- **2** *2 ½* **Badger Foot (IRE)**[20] 4666 9-10-1 110.......................(t) CraigNichol(5) 116
(Lucinda Russell) *hld up in tch: hdwy to chse wnr 8th: led briefly bef 4 out: kpt on fr 2 out: nt pce of wnr* **9/2**[3]
111- **3** *nk* **Mitchell's Way**[12] 4833 7-11-9 127 7ex.............................. PaddyBrennan 134
(Alan Swinbank) *hld up in tch: stdy hdwy bef 5 out: rdn and outpcd appr next: styd on fr 2 out: nt gng pce to chal* **4/1**[2]
501- **4** *6* **Categorical**[24] 4610 11-11-2 120.. JamesReveley 121
(Keith Reveley) *cl up: nt fluent 2nd: lost pl next: rdn and struggling after 5 out: sme late hdwy: n.d* **13/2**
5U5- **5** *25* **You Know Yourself (IRE)**[12] 4835 11-11-3 121.................. RyanMania 102
(Sue Smith) *chsd ldrs: drvn bef 5 out: wknd fr next: t.o* **8/1**
633- **P** **Rossini's Dancer**[55] 4039 9-11-4 129.......................(p) MrKitAlexander(7)
(N W Alexander) *nt fluent on occasions: hld up: struggling 5 out: sn btn: t.o whn p.u bef 2 out* **18/1**
612- **U** **Zaru (FR)**[97] 3211 8-11-5 130.. DaleIrving(7) 126
(James Ewart) *nt fluent: prom: pushed along 5 out: sn outpcd: struggling fr next: 5th and hld whn nt fluent and uns rdr last* **7/2**[1]
5m 19.7s (-7.50) **Going Correction** -0.175s/f (Good) 7 Ran SP% **112.3**
Speed ratings: **108,107,106,104,94 ,**
CSF £19.07 CT £63.55 TOTE £4.10: £3.00, £1.80; EX 24.70 Trifecta £78.40.
Owner Mrs M E Moody **Bred** John O'Mahony **Trained** Holdenby, Northants
FOCUS
An open race for this fair handicap chase. Solid handicap form.

5054 IJF FARRELL/BROOKSHAW MEMORIAL H'CAP HURDLE (9 hdls) 2m
4:15 (4:15) (Class 3) (0-140,140) 4-Y-0+ **£5,393** (£1,583; £791; £395)

Form RPR
451- **1** **Bygones Of Brid (IRE)**[17] 4745 11-10-12 126.............(v) PaddyBrennan 135+
(Karen McLintock) *mde all: rdn and qcknd clr bef 3 out: idled run-in: drvn out* **2/1**[1]
03F- **2** *1 ½* **Robbie**[9] 4899 10-11-2 130.. JamesReveley 133
(Keith Reveley) *in tch: shkn up and hdwy bef 3 out: chsd (clr) wnr next: kpt on fr last: flattered by proximity to idling wnr* **16/1**
025- **3** *4 ½* **Rock Relief (IRE)**[20] 4670 8-10-6 120................................. HenryBrooke 120
(Chris Grant) *nt fluent in rr: outpcd 1/2-way: styd on fr 2 out: nvr rchd ldrs* **4/1**[3]
305- **4** *2* **Dartford Warbler (IRE)**[9] 4897 7-10-11 125.......................... RyanMania 124
(Sue Smith) *chsd ldrs: drvn along 4 out: wnt 2nd next to 2 out: sn one pce* **3/1**[2]
U0P- **5** *33* **Act Of Kalanisi (IRE)**[15] 4768 8-11-12 140.........(bt) SamTwiston-Davies 119
(Dr Richard Newland) *pressed wnr: nt fluent 4th: rdn and wknd bef 2 out* **3/1**[2]
4m 2.9s (-7.10) **Going Correction** -0.175s/f (Good) 5 Ran SP% **109.2**
Speed ratings (Par 107): **110,109,107,106,89**
CSF £24.11 TOTE £2.60: £1.40, £5.00; EX 19.70 Trifecta £46.60.
Owner James Callow **Bred** Oliver Brennan **Trained** Ingoe, Northumberland
FOCUS
A decent handicap hurdle run at a searching gallop. The winner is rated a bit better than the bare result and in line with the best of last season's form.

5055 IJF ALMONERS H'CAP CHASE (15 fncs 4 omitted) 3m
4:50 (4:50) (Class 4) (0-105,103) 5-Y-0+ **£3,768** (£1,106; £553; £276)

Form RPR
023- **1** **Mr Supreme (IRE)**[24] 4606 9-11-7 98................................ JamesReveley 114+
(Keith Reveley) *led to 7th: regained ld next: rdn and drew clr 2 out: styd on wl run-in* **7/2**[1]
2P5- **2** *3 ¾* **Baltic Pathfinder (IRE)**[13] 4812 10-11-4 102.......... DiarmuidO'Regan(7) 110
(Sue Smith) *chsd ldrs: wnt 2nd after 10th: effrt 4 out: hit 2 out: sn one pce* **7/1**[3]
565- **3** *2* **Chicago Outfit (IRE)**[111] 2959 9-10-12 94.................(p) JohnDawson(5) 100
(John Wade) *hld up: outpcd 1/2-way: rallied bef 4 out: styd on wl fr 2 out: nt rch first two* **20/1**
233- **4** *½* **Ballyben (IRE)**[45] 4202 6-11-7 103...................................... CraigNichol(5) 107
(Lucinda Russell) *hld up: stdy hdwy and in tch 9th: effrt and rdn bef 4 out: one pce fr 2 out* **7/2**[1]
/PP- **P** **Shadow Boxer**[21] 4652 9-10-1 83...........................(b[1]) CallumWhillans(5)
(Donald Whillans) *in tch: rdn and outpcd whn hit 8th: outpcd whn blnd 10th: lost tch and p.u after 5 out* **9/2**[2]

0P6- P Runswick Relax[61] 3925 8-10-1 78 .... WilsonRenwick
(John Wade) *nt fluent: sn bhd: lost tch and p.u bef 8th* 9/2[2]
465- P Notonebuttwo (IRE)[27] 4553 7-10-0 77 oh17 .... (vt) HenryBrooke
(Chris Grant) *cl up: led 7th to next: pressed wnr to after 10th: 4th and outpcd whn blnd 5 out: sn p.u* 7/1[3]
6m 24.5s (2.00) **Going Correction** -0.175s/f (Good) 7 Ran SP% **110.6**
Speed ratings: **89,87,87,86,** ,
CSF £25.41 CT £398.13 TOTE £3.40: £1.60, £2.70; EX 21.90 Trifecta £66.10.
Owner Mrs Susan Granger **Bred** James Cousins **Trained** Lingdale, Redcar & Cleveland
FOCUS
A very ordinary handicap chase which proved quite a slog. The winner improved towards his hurdles mark.

5056 IJF JOHN FRANCOME PRESIDENT CONDITIONAL JOCKEYS' NOVICES' H'CAP HURDLE (13 hdls) 3m
5:25 (5:25) (Class 5) (0-100,99) 4-Y-0+ **£1,949** (£572; £286; £143)

Form RPR
644- 1 Bollin Julie[24] 4607 7-10-1 74 .... CallumWhillans 82+
(Donald Whillans) *hld up in tch: smooth hdwy 1/2-way: led gng wl 3 out: rdn and wandered whn hit last: kpt on wl run-in* 4/1[2]
55U- 2 3 Heron's Mill (IRE)[109] 2997 6-11-0 95 .... (p) DaleIrving(8) 97
(James Ewart) *t.k.h: prom: wnt 2nd 7th: effrt and ev ch whn mstke 3 out: kpt on fr last: nt pce of wnr* 13/2[3]
P42- 3 11 Highlander Ted[32] 4461 6-11-3 90 .... (p) JakeGreenall 81
(Mark Walford) *led and clr to 1/2-way: rdn and hdd 3 out: outpcd fr next* 11/4[1]
65P- 4 5 Thorlak (FR)[45] 4201 7-11-8 95 .... (p) CraigNichol 82
(James Ewart) *chsd ldrs: drvn bef 3 out: outpcd bef next* 17/2
/0P- 5 26 Solway Legend[24] 4607 7-10-3 76 .... GrantCockburn 35
(Lisa Harrison) *nt fluent in rr: pushed along 1/2-way: struggling 4 out: btn next* 25/1
565- 6 1 1/4 Mrs Grass[15] 4776 7-10-0 73 oh4 .... JoeColliver 31
(Jonathan Haynes) *bhd: shortlived effrt after 4 out: struggling fr next* 18/1
321- 7 3 W Six Times[45] 4201 8-10-11 89 .... JamesCowley(5) 44
(Alistair Whillans) *hld up: pushed along 8th: struggling fr 4 out: btn next* 11/4[1]
05P- P Thurnham[79] 3605 8-10-11 90 .... (p) DaraghBourke(6)
(Stuart Coltherd) *nt fluent: chsd ldr to 7th: struggling fr next: t.o whn p.u bef 2 out* 28/1
P66- P Master Bud[15] 4776 9-10-0 83 .... JamesCorbett(10)
(Susan Corbett) *mstkes in rr: struggling fr 1/2-way: t.o whn p.u bef 3 out* 33/1
6m 16.4s (2.40) **Going Correction** -0.175s/f (Good) 9 Ran SP% **112.7**
Speed ratings (Par 103): **89,88,84,82,74 73,72,** ,
CSF £28.61 CT £81.44 TOTE £5.60: £2.00, £2.00, £1.70; EX 23.70 Trifecta £168.20.
Owner Chas N Whillans **Bred** Sir Neil & Exors Of Late Lady Westbrook **Trained** Hawick, Borders
FOCUS
A low-grade handicap run in gloomy conditions. The pace was fair. A step up from the winner, who was value for further.
T/Plt: £23.60 to a £1 stake. Pool: £83774.86 - 2590.62 winning tickets T/Qpdt: £9.60 to a £1 stake. Pool: £5352.46 - 408.88 winning tickets RY

4889 WETHERBY (L-H)
Friday, March 28
OFFICIAL GOING: Good to soft (soft in places; 5.9)
Wind: fresh 1/2 against Weather: overcast

5057 WEAR A HAT DAY SUPPORTING BRAINTUMOURRESEARCH.ORG CONDITIONAL JOCKEYS' NOVICES' HURDLE (9 hdls) 2m 110y
2:20 (2:20) (Class 4) 4-Y-0+ **£3,285** (£957; £479)

Form RPR
144- 1 Nesterenko (GER)[62] 3891 5-11-3 125 .... NicodeBoinville(3) 128+
(Nicky Henderson) *nt fluent: chsd ldr: effrt 3 out: led sn after 2 out: drvn out: fnd ex clsng stages* 1/1[1]
3- 2 1 1/2 Villoresi (IRE)[28] 2933 5-10-8 0 .... DeanPratt(6) 119
(John Quinn) *trckd ldrs: chsd wnr appr last: kpt on: no ex clsng stages* 5/1[3]
135- 3 8 Masquerade (IRE)[13] 4808 5-11-3 120 .... GavinSheehan(3) 116
(Warren Greatrex) *led: drvn 3 out: hdd sn after next: hung lft and one pce run-in* 7/1
041- 4 2 1/4 Flute Bowl[18] 4730 4-10-3 0 .... JoshuaMoore(3) 102
(Gary Moore) *trckd ldrs: mstke 4th: wknd last* 7/2[2]
562- 5 6 Quick Brew[12] 4832 6-10-11 102 .... (t) DaraghBourke(3) 101
(Maurice Barnes) *hld up in rr: hdwy appr 3 out: one pce fr next* 14/1
5- 6 30 Mr Maynard[28] 4529 5-10-11 0 .... TomBellamy(3) 71
(Renee Robeson) *mid-div: drvn appr 3 out: wknd 2 out* 66/1
5/ 7 hd Catchthemoonlight[734] 5061 6-10-7 0 .... JoeColliver 64
(Lucinda Russell) *mid-div: hdwy 6th: lost pl next: sn bhd* 100/1
5P0- 8 14 Pennine Josie[43] 4234 5-10-7 0 .... TonyKelly 50
(James Moffatt) *in rr: drvn 5th: wl bhd fr 3 out* 100/1
2- P Waddingstown (IRE)[20] 4671 5-10-11 0 .... DerekFox(3)
(Lucinda Russell) *in rr: t.o whn p.u immediately after 3 out: fatally injured* 20/1
00- U Mighty Cliche (IRE)[10] 4889 5-11-0 0 .... ColmMcCormack
(Dianne Sayer) *in rr: uns rdr 1st* 100/1
3m 59.2s (3.40) **Going Correction** +0.80s/f (Soft)
WFA 4 from 5yo+ 7lb 10 Ran SP% **117.3**
Speed ratings (Par 105): **105,104,100,99,96 82,82,75,** ,
CSF £6.55 TOTE £1.80: £1.10, £1.50, £1.60; EX 8.40 Trifecta £29.00.
Owner Juergen Meyer **Bred** A Pereira **Trained** Upper Lambourn, Berks
FOCUS
A competitive looking novices hurdle run at an ordinary pace with the four principals in the market holding every chance at the second-last. The winner set a decent standard and is rated pretty much to his mark.

5058 PERMIT TRAINERS ASSOCIATION H'CAP CHASE (16 fncs) 2m 4f 110y
2:50 (2:50) (Class 4) (0-120,127) 5-Y-0+ **£3,768** (£1,106; £553; £276)

Form RPR
142- 1 Indian Voyage (IRE)[12] 4833 6-10-3 104 ow1 .... (t) DaraghBourke(7) 118+
(Maurice Barnes) *trckd ldrs: 2nd 6th: led 3 out: 5 l clr last: drvn rt out* 11/10[1]
444- 2 5 Free World (FR)[9] 4908 10-10-4 105 .... MissLBrooke(7) 112
(Lady Susan Brooke) *t.k.h: led: j. boldly: jnd whn hit 4 out: hdd next: kpt on same pce fr 2 out* 20/1
001- 3 2 3/4 Groomed (IRE)[28] 4533 6-11-0 111 .... JonathanEngland(3) 114
(Sue Smith) *chsd ldrs: pushed along and lost pl 7th: hdwy appr 4 out: 3rd sn after next: one pce fr 2 out* 5/1[3]
121- 4 9 Tiny Dancer (IRE)[17] 4744 6-11-5 113 .... BrianHughes 111
(Alan Swinbank) *chsd ldrs 4th: stmbld on landing 12th: 3rd and drvn whn mstke 4 out: sn wknd* 3/1[2]
P/2- 5 2 Safari Journey (USA)[26] 4579 10-11-0 115 .... NathanMoscrop(7) 110
(Lucinda Egerton) *hdwy to chse ldrs 4th: outpcd 8th: hdwy 12th: 4th and wkng whn hit 3 out* 16/1
035- 6 19 Allow Me[22] 4628 9-10-8 107 .... (p) ColmMcCormack(5) 80
(Dianne Sayer) *chsd ldrs: lost pl 8th: sn bhd: t.o 4 out* 8/1
5m 14.7s (6.90) **Going Correction** +0.80s/f (Soft) 6 Ran SP% **111.0**
Speed ratings: **99,97,96,92,91 84**
CSF £18.69 TOTE £2.00: £1.70, £2.50; EX 19.60 Trifecta £67.50.
Owner D Carr & M Carlyle **Bred** Victor Stud Bloodstock Ltd **Trained** Farlam, Cumbria
FOCUS
A tight handicap run at just a reasonable pace, and the jumping proved the deciding factor. The winner was well in on his recent run but is rated below that level here, with the second to his mark.

5059 WATCH ON 3 DEVICES RACINGUK.COM/ANYWHERE H'CAP HURDLE (12 hdls) 2m 6f
3:20 (3:21) (Class 4) (0-115,115) 4-Y-0+ **£3,285** (£957; £479)

Form RPR
642- 1 Bescot Springs (IRE)[21] 4649 9-11-0 110 .... (b[1]) GrahamWatters(7) 114
(Lucinda Russell) *w ldrs: led 9th: 5 l clr last: jst lasted* 14/1
/02- 2 3/4 High Kite (IRE)[16] 4760 8-10-6 105 .... (p) WilliamFeatherstone(10) 107
(Warren Greatrex) *chsd ldrs 5th: led next: hdd 9th: 3rd whn hit 2 out: styd on run-in: jst hld* 7/1[2]
6P- 3 1/2 Trafords Hero[33] 4446 6-10-6 95 .... DougieCostello 96
(Tony Coyle) *mid-div: pushed along 8th: styd on and 7th 3 out: 4th last: kpt on wl clsng stages* 9/2[1]
0/1- 4 2 Lua De Itapoan[36] 4381 9-11-3 106 .... BrianHughes 106
(Malcolm Jefferson) *chsd ldrs: 2nd whn mstke 2 out: one pce run-in* 8/1[3]
432- 5 1 Bob's World[17] 4745 5-11-12 115 .... (tp) SeanQuinlan 115
(Jennie Candlish) *nt fluent and in rr 4th: hdwy 7th: chsng ldrs 3 out: kpt on same pce run-in* 10/1
253- 6 4 1/2 Big Sound[26] 4577 7-10-8 102 .... (p) MauriceLinehan(5) 95
(Mark Walford) *led to 6th: outpcd appr 3 out: rallied 2 out: fdd last 100yds* 8/1[3]
046- 7 1 3/4 Willpower (IRE)[21] 4664 5-10-11 103 .... PeterCarberry(3) 95
(Nicky Henderson) *mid-div: hdwy 7th: sn chsng ldrs: outpcd 3 out: hit next: kpt on run-in* 9/1
/P1- 8 7 Luctor Emergo (IRE)[52] 2999 5-11-0 110 .... (p) RyanNichol(7) 95
(Keith Dalgleish) *mid-div: chsd ldrs 6th: drvn 3 out: hung lft and wknd appr next* 8/1[3]
501- 9 6 Pierrers Bounty (IRE)[15] 4774 7-11-0 106 .... (p) TonyKelly(3) 85
(Henry Hogarth) *chsd ldrs: lost pl 9th* 12/1
/F5- 10 10 Hurraboru (IRE)[10] 4893 7-11-10 113 .... DenisO'Regan 82
(David Thompson) *in rr: drvn 7th: bhd fr 9th* 25/1
005- 11 6 Frizzo (FR)[27] 4556 7-11-12 115 .... (b) WayneHutchinson 78
(Alan King) *prom: drvn 9th: wknd appr next* 10/1
030- 12 9 Kent Street (IRE)[10] 4893 9-10-10 102 .... JonathanEngland(3) 56
(Sue Smith) *in rr: bhd fr 3 out* 20/1
3PP/ P Awareiness (IRE)[817] 3489 8-10-9 98 .... TomMessenger
(Chris Bealby) *w ldrs: j.lft 1st: lost pl 6th: sn bhd: t.o 9th: p.u bef next* 100/1
043- P Vasco D'Ycy (FR)[26] 4579 5-11-6 112 .... JackQuinlan(3)
(Sarah Humphrey) *in rr: drvn 7th: bhd fr 9th: t.o whn p.u bef last* 14/1
5m 31.9s (5.10) **Going Correction** +0.80s/f (Soft) 14 Ran SP% **122.8**
Speed ratings (Par 105): **103,102,102,101,101 99,99,96,94,90 88,85,** ,
CSF £110.22 CT £525.59 TOTE £14.30: £4.50, £1.90, £2.20; EX 108.60 Trifecta £1986.60.
Owner Mirror Punters Club **Bred** Pat Tobin **Trained** Arlary, Perth & Kinross
■ Stewards' Enquiry : Graham Watters two-day ban; used whip above permitted level (11th, 12th Apr)
FOCUS
A wide-open handicap. The winner is on a decent mark and is rated back to form.

5060 EVANS HALSHAW HARROGATE H'CAP CHASE (18 fncs) 2m 6f 110y
3:55 (3:55) (Class 4) (0-120,120) 5-Y-0+ **£3,768** (£1,106; £553; £276)

Form RPR
325- 1 My Idea[54] 4055 8-10-8 105 .... (p) JonathanEngland(3) 112
(Maurice Barnes) *in rr: chsd ldrs 9th: 2nd 14th: drvn 3 out: styd on run-in: led nr fin* 9/2[2]
213- 2 nk Foundation Man (IRE)[112] 2928 7-11-12 120 .... (v[1]) RichieMcLernon 128+
(Jonjo O'Neill) *led: drvn 4 out: 3 l ahd whn blnd last: hdd nr fin* 5/4[1]
343- 3 7 Indigo Rock (IRE)[89] 3397 8-11-9 117 .... BrianHughes 116
(Malcolm Jefferson) *chsd ldrs: mstke 9th: one pce fr 4 out* 6/1[3]
02P- 4 7 Be My Deputy (IRE)[34] 4430 9-11-3 116 .... (bt) DerekFox(5) 110
(Lucinda Russell) *chsd ldrs: drvn 9th: lost pl 12th: kpt on and modest 4th sn after 3 out* 10/1
2P0- 5 17 Balinroab (IRE)[70] 3759 7-11-5 113 .... DenisO'Regan 91
(Richard Guest) *hld up: racd wd: hdwy to trck ldrs 9th: lost pl bef 4 out: sn bhd* 7/1
P/P- P New Shuil (IRE)[44] 4222 10-10-1 95 .... AdrianLane
(John Wade) *nt fluent in rr: hdwy to chse ldrs 9th: lost pl next: sn bhd: t.o whn p.u bef 13th* 33/1
/41- U Work Boy[10] 4892 13-11-1 114 7ex .... SamanthaDrake(5)
(Richard Drake) *chsd ldrs: blnd and uns rdr 13th* 8/1
5m 50.9s (13.90) **Going Correction** +0.80s/f (Soft) 7 Ran SP% **112.6**
Speed ratings: **107,106,104,102,96** ,
CSF £10.78 CT £32.22 TOTE £7.20: £3.00, £1.10; EX 14.70 Trifecta £62.30.
Owner The Whisperers **Bred** Mrs P M Grainger **Trained** Farlam, Cumbria
■ Stewards' Enquiry : Jonathan England two-day ban; used whip above permitted level (11th,12th Apr)
FOCUS
A fair handicap run at an ordinary pace, and fortunes turned in the latter stages. The winner and third set the lvel, with the runner-up unlucky.

5061 ROA OWNERS JACKPOT H'CAP HURDLE (9 hdls) 2m 110y
4:30 (4:31) (Class 4) (0-120,118) 4-Y-0+ **£3,285** (£957; £479)

Form RPR
213- 1 Watt Broderick (IRE)[4] 5005 5-10-4 100 .... (t) RobertMcCarth(5) 117+
(Ian Williams) *hld up: wnt 2nd 4th: led on bit 3 out: pushed clr between last 2: comf* 5/4[1]
032- 2 6 Rock A Doodle Doo (IRE)[10] 4889 7-11-0 110 .... (p) MauriceLinehan(5) 118+
(Sally Hall) *trckd ldr: nt fluent 3 out: 5 l 2nd whn hit last: no imp* 3/1[2]

3/3- **3** 2 ½ **Looking On**[17] 4745 6-11-10 **115** ...... DougieCostello 117
(Steve Gollings) *reluctant ldr: wnt clr 2nd to 6th: hdd 3 out: one pce fr next* **11/2**[3]

324- **4** 23 **Hartside (GER)**[10] 4893 5-11-5 **117** ...... MrRWinks(7) 96
(Peter Winks) *in rr: bhd fr 4th: tk distant 4th run-in* **14/1**

000- **5** 1 ¼ **Dumbarton (IRE)**[13] 4813 6-11-12 **117** ...... BrianHughes 95
(James Moffatt) *t.k.h: trckd ldrs: wknd appr 2 out* **25/1**

/06- **6** 1 **Mubrook (USA)**[19] 4697 9-11-11 **116** ...... DannyCook 93
(Brian Ellison) *in rr: drvn and lost tch 6th* **10/1**

225- **F** **Rayak (IRE)**[20] 4679 4-11-6 **118** ...... RichieMcLernon 107
(Jonjo O'Neill) *hld up: hdwy to trck ldrs 6th: abt 5 l down overall in 4th whn fell 2 out* **9/1**

4m 8.0s (12.20) **Going Correction** +0.80s/f (Soft)
WFA 4 from 5yo+ 7lb 7 Ran SP% **114.4**
Speed ratings (Par 105): **103,100,99,88,87 87,**
CSF £5.72 CT £14.07 TOTE £2.80: £1.20, £2.00; EX 6.30 Trifecta £20.20.

Owner Patrick Kelly **Bred** Joe Fogarty **Trained** Portway, Worcs

FOCUS
With no confirmed pacesetter this was run at a steady early pace before Looking On upped the tempo at the third and soon went 20 lengths clear. The winner confirmed the merit of his recent easy win.

5062 READ AIDAN COLEMAN EVERY FRIDAY RACINGUK.COM MARES' HUNTERS' CHASE (18 fncs) 3m 1f
5:05 (5:05) (Class 6) 5-Y-O+ **£987** (£303; £151)

Form RPR

054/ **1** **Radharc Na Mara (IRE)**[26] 10-11-1 96 ...... MissHHarper(7) 104+
(Miss H Harper) *hdwy 5th: sn chsng ldrs: led 8th: mde rest: styd on wl* **10/1**

2- **2** 3 ½ **Spotthestripe**[43] 4246 9-11-1 0 ...... MrRGSpencer(7) 101
(G J Tarry) *t.k.h: trckd ldrs: handy 2nd 10th: hit 13th: 3 l down and effrt 3 out: hung lft and one pce between last 2* **2/1**[2]

650/ **3** 26 **Rowan Road**[13] 10-11-1 0 ...... MissJWalton(7) 73
(Mrs D Walton) *t.k.h: trckd ldrs: lost pl 7th: hdwy to chse ldrs 10th: outpcd 12th: tk modest 3rd appr 4 out: distant 3rd whn j.rt last* **7/1**[3]

420/ **4** dist **Gers Benefit (IRE)**[33] 10-11-1 0 ...... MrSDavies-Thomas(7) 23
(Tommy Morgan) *chsd ldrs: led 7th: hdd next: lost pl after 14th: sn bhd: distant 4th bef 2 out: t.o* **33/1**

/PP- **P** **Melua Maid (IRE)**[19] 12-11-5 86 ......(p) MrRLindsay(7)
(Mrs B Ewart) *ledto 7th: drvn and lost pl 9th: sn bhd: t.o next: p.u bef last* **33/1**

044/ **P** **Gwyre (IRE)**[19] 8-11-3 86 ......(b) MrWEasterby(5)
(Mrs Sarah Easterby) *in rr: hdwy to chse ldrs 9th: drvn 14th: lost pl appr next: sn bhd: t.o whn p.u bef last* **25/1**

1- **F** **Rosie Du Berlais (IRE)**[23] 4617 8-11-5 0 ...... MrPDennis(7)
(Philip Kirby) *t.k.h: trckd ldrs 5th: fell 7th* **11/10**[1]

6m 27.6s (18.20) **Going Correction** +0.80s/f (Soft) 7 Ran SP% **112.3**
Speed ratings: **102,100,92,76, ,**
CSF £30.33 TOTE £13.90: £3.80, £1.40; EX 36.40 Trifecta £148.40.

Owner Grant Harper **Bred** Eugene Matthews **Trained** Chatton, Northumberland
■ Holly Harper's first winner under rules.

FOCUS
A fairly uncompetitive mares' hunters' chase, especially after the favourite Rosie Du Berlais crashed out. They went a fair pace.

5063 WETHERBY RACECOURSE FAMILY DAY - SUNDAY 13TH APRIL STANDARD OPEN NATIONAL HUNT FLAT RACE 2m 110y
5:40 (5:40) (Class 6) 4-6-Y-O **£1,711** (£498; £249)

Form RPR

1 **Up The Bees** 4-10-11 0 ...... BarryKeniry 106
(Philip Kirby) *hld up in mid-div: hdwy to trck ldrs after 7f: effrt 3f out: led over 1f out: drvn out* **7/2**[2]

2 1 **Grande Antarctique (FR)** 4-10-11 0 ...... SeanQuinlan 105
(Jennie Candlish) *hld up in rr: hdwy 6f out: sn chsng ldrs: n.m.r and swtchd lft over 1f out: styd on to take 2nd last 50yds* **10/1**

13- **3** 1 **Bandit Country (IRE)**[87] 3440 5-11-11 0 ...... RichieMcLernon 118
(Jonjo O'Neill) *hld up in rr: hdwy after 6f: sn trcking ldrs: swtchd rt 2f out: sn upsides and hung lft: kpt on same pce last 75yds* **4/6**[1]

4 6 **Karisma King** 5-11-1 0 ...... JonathanEngland(3) 105
(Sue Smith) *jnd ldr after 1f: upsides over 1f out: wknd fnl 200yds* **20/1**

422- **5** nk **Gilnockie**[85] 3500 6-11-4 0 ...... BrianHughes 105
(James Ewart) *led: increased pce 6f out: hdd over 1f out: edgd lft and sn wknd* **6/1**[3]

0- **6** 12 **Silver Crossing**[24] 4611 5-11-4 0 ...... AdrianLane 93
(John Wade) *mid-div: hdwy to chse ldrs 7f out: drvn and lost pl 5f out* **100/1**

7 3 **Remedio (IRE)** 4-10-8 0 ...... JohnKington(3) 83
(Andrew Crook) *chsd ldrs: drvn and lost pl 3f out* **33/1**

4- **8** shd **Falcon's Legend**[17] 4749 4-10-4 0 ...... DougieCostello 76
(John Weymes) *t.k.h: trckd ldrs: drvn over 5f out: lost pl over 3f out* **33/1**

9 21 **William Wild** 6-10-13 0 ...... SamanthaDrake(5) 69
(Tina Jackson) *hld up in rr: drvn 6f out: sn lost pl: bhd whn eased clsng stages: t.o* **66/1**

4m 11.2s (21.00) **Going Correction** +0.80s/f (Soft)
WFA 4 from 5yo+ 7lb 9 Ran SP% **118.7**
Speed ratings: **82,81,81,78,78 72,71,70,61**
CSF £35.35 TOTE £2.80: £1.10, £2.40, £1.10; EX 42.90 Trifecta £159.60.

Owner Colin W German **Bred** Jenny Hall Bloodstock Ltd **Trained** Middleham, N Yorks

FOCUS
A very slow time and the form is suspect, but there were plenty of likeable sorts for this fair bumper.

T/Jkpt: Not Won. T/Plt: £39.60 to a £1 stake. Pool: £80032.43 - 1473.67 winning tickets T/Qpdt: £13.40 to a £1 stake. Pool: £5603.05 - 308.20 winning tickets WG

4966 STRATFORD (L-H)
Saturday, March 29

OFFICIAL GOING: Good to soft (good in places on hurdle course; soft in places on chase course)
Wind: fresh behind Weather: very sunny; 16 degrees

5064 BORDEAUX-UNDISCOVERED.CO.UK NOVICES' HURDLE (8 hdls) 2m 110y
1:55 (1:55) (Class 4) 4-Y-O+ **£3,249** (£954; £477; £238)

Form RPR

1 **Kelvingrove (IRE)**[168] 4-10-2 0 ...... MauriceLinehan(5) 116+
(Jonjo O'Neill) *prom but racing idly and often off bridle: rdn bef 3 out: wnt 2nd next: sn led: drvn 4 l clr last: stl idling but kpt on strly* **5/1**[2]

122- **2** 8 **Massena (IRE)**[5] 5003 7-11-0 128 ...... AidanColeman 113
(Venetia Williams) *led: drvn and hdd 2 out: sn outpcd in 3rd: plugged on gamely to chse wnr vainly fr last* **4/7**[1]

4/1- **3** ½ **Prouts Pub (IRE)**[137] 2439 5-11-0 0 ...... TomCannon 113
(Nick Gifford) *a ldng quartet: led briefly 2 out: sn rdn and outpcd by wnr: lost 2nd at last but kpt on steadily* **10/1**[3]

40- **4** 5 **John Louis**[34] 4450 6-11-0 0 ...... LiamTreadwell 108
(Venetia Williams) *settled chsng ldrs: lost tch w front rnk 3 out: kpt on nicely wout threatening fr after next* **10/1**[3]

62F- **5** 3 ½ **Serenity Now (IRE)**[7] 4945 6-11-0 0 ...... DannyCook 106
(Brian Ellison) *bhd: str reminders after 2nd: virtually t.o after 3 out: kpt on steadily but no ch after* **14/1**

6 1 **Breaking The Bank**[159] 5-10-11 0 ...... KielanWoods(3) 105
(Ben Case) *nt a fluent: chsd ldrs tl 3 out: 7 l 4th and rdn and wkng next* **11/1**

7 nk **Florida Beat**[177] 4-10-7 0 ...... DonalDevereux 98
(Dai Burchell) *hmpd 1st: wl bhd: sme hdwy fr 2 out but nvr nr ldrs* **50/1**

0- **8** 8 **Webbswood (IRE)**[57] 4016 5-10-4 0 ...... MikeyHamill(10) 97
(Sean Curran) *racd keenly and prom: hrd rdn and fdd rapidly bef 2 out* **100/1**

0- **9** 19 **Kiama Bay (IRE)**[7] 4959 8-11-0 0 ...... MattieBatchelor 80
(Jim Best) *rdn after 4th: nvr gng wl enough after: t.o after 3 out* **50/1**

10 4 ½ **Paddy's Saltantes (IRE)**[45] 4-10-2 0 ...... KillianMoore(5) 69
(Alex Hales) *bhd: j. slowly 3rd and pushed along: t.o 3 out* **50/1**

540- **11** 5 **Ilewindelilah**[17] 4758 6-10-7 0 ...... JoshuaMoore 64
(Gary Brown) *sltly hmpd 1st: bhd: struggling fr 5th: t.o after next* **66/1**

12 2 ¾ **Kelpie Blitz (IRE)**[16] 5-11-0 0 ......(t) RichieMcLernon 69
(Paul Morgan) *hmpd 1st: in last pair: t.o 3 out* **66/1**

U- **U** **Egotist (IRE)**[10] 4904 6-10-9 0 ...... CharlieWallis(5)
(Milton Bradley) *j. bdly rt 1st and uns rdr* **100/1**

(4.00) **Going Correction** +0.375s/f (Yiel)
WFA 4 from 5yo+ 7lb 13 Ran SP% **124.3**
Speed ratings (Par 105): **105,101,101,98,97 96,96,92,83,81 79,77,**
CSF £8.77 TOTE £6.50: £1.40, £1.10, £3.70; EX 13.00 Trifecta £78.70.

Owner The All In Syndicate **Bred** Mark Johnston Racing Ltd **Trained** Cheltenham, Gloucs

FOCUS
An ordinary novices' hurdle but fair form for the track. The principals were always prominent and not many got into it. The winner looks a fair recruit and should win more races.

5065 BORDEAUX UNDISCOVERED 1855 CLASSIFICATION H'CAP CHASE (14 fncs) 2m 4f
2:30 (2:30) (Class 4) (0-105,103) 5-Y-O+ **£3,898** (£1,144; £572; £286)

Form RPR

222- **1** **Little Jimmy**[14] 4815 7-10-7 **84** ......(p) FelixDeGiles 88+
(Tom Gretton) *trckd ldrs: led 12th: hrd rdn fr between last two: 2 l clr last: idling flat but a jst doing enough* **5/4**[1]

P41- **2** nk **Phoenix Des Mottes (FR)**[6] 4982 11-9-9 **77** 7ex ...... JoeCornwall(5) 79
(John Cornwall) *nrly a 2nd: drew clr w wnr after 3 out: ev ch tl rdn and jst outpcd bef last where nt fluent: rallied and tried hrd flat but a jst hld* **11/2**[3]

42P- **3** 16 **Kyles Faith (IRE)**[19] 4723 6-11-2 **100** ...... OllieGarner(7) 88
(Martin Keighley) *chsd ldr tl rdn and outpcd 12th: u.p to go 10 l 3rd bef 2 out: no ch after* **16/1**

405- **4** 4 ½ **Wheelavher**[14] 4823 8-9-7 **77** oh7 ......(t) GeraldQuinn(7) 61
(Claire Dyson) *nt fluent in rr: lost tch and hit 12th: plugged on to remote 4th flat* **14/1**

066- **5** 1 ½ **Midnight Macarena**[14] 4809 9-11-10 **101** ......(tp) LeightonAspell 83
(Lucy Wadham) *mstkes in rr: drvn 8th: struggling fr 12th* **8/1**

414- **6** 2 **Riddleofthesands (IRE)**[19] 4723 10-11-12 **103** ...(t) SamTwiston-Davies 83
(Nigel Twiston-Davies) *tk str hold: led tl 12th: rapidly lost interest: poor 4th after next: eased flat* **7/2**[2]

530- **P** **Weston Lodge (IRE)**[12] 4865 8-10-6 **83** ...... SamJones
(Christopher Kellett) *j. bdly lft: last and rdn 5th: lost tch next: t.o fr 8th tl p.u 12th* **33/1**

5m 9.5s (19.50) **Going Correction** +1.05s/f (Soft) 7 Ran SP% **108.7**
Speed ratings: **103,102,96,94,94 93,**
CSF £7.93 TOTE £1.90: £1.30, £2.50; EX 8.10 Trifecta £41.10.

Owner T R Gretton **Bred** Mrs Marigold West **Trained** Inkberrow, Worcestershire

FOCUS
A moderate handicap chase in which the first two came well clear. The winner is rated in line with recent runs.

5066 BORDEAUX UNDISCOVERED FOR A GOOD TIPPLE (S) HURDLE (9 hdls) 2m 3f
3:05 (3:05) (Class 5) 4-Y-O+ **£2,599** (£763; £381; £190)

Form RPR

503- **1** **Bob's Legend (IRE)**[188] 1633 8-11-1 93 ...... RyanMahon 115+
(Michael Appleby) *trckd ldrs: led after 3 out: drew clr w one rival after next: hrd drvn bef last where small advantage: styd on wl flat* **8/1**[3]

633/ **2** 2 ¼ **Alsadaa (USA)**[593] 1479 11-11-1 128 ...... TomCannon 112
(Laura Mongan) *chsd ldrs: effrt to go 2nd after 3 out: hrd drvn between last two: stl had a ch whn outj. last: nt qckn after* **22/1**

211- **3** 5 **Stow**[5] 5001 9-11-4 125 ......(p) JoshWall(7) 117
(Michael Blake) *mstke 2nd: wl in rr early: gd prog in 4th bef 3 out: drvn to chal in 2 l 3rd next: racd quirkily and wl hld after: plugged on* **6/4**[1]

1UP- **4** 16 **Full Ov Beans**[32] 4486 10-10-12 0 ...... PeterCarberry(3) 93
(Michael Gates) *chsd ldrs: wnt 2nd at 6th: led bef 3 out: hdd sn after flight and drvn: nt run on: poor 4th at next* **16/1**

U6P- **5** 7 **Viking Blond (FR)**[42] 4271 9-11-1 120 ......(v) SamTwiston-Davies 87
(Nigel Twiston-Davies) *mstke 2nd: wknd and j. slowly 3rd: drvn and nt keen 4th: stoked along and kpt gng reluctantly w no ch after* **9/4**[2]

P00- **6** ½ **Marju King (IRE)**[7] 4970 8-10-10 103........................(p) ThomasGarner(5) 86
(Phil Middleton) *settled in rr: effrt and trckd ldrs briefly 3 out: u.p and no rspnse bef next: sn btn* **12/1**

4P5- **7** 10 **Regal One (IRE)**[33] 4469 6-10-8 103................................ JakeHodson(7) 77
(David Bridgwater) *cl up: 3rd at 6th: hrd rdn and no rspnse 3 out: sn dropped rt out: t.o* **12/1**

362- **8** 45 **Monroe Park (IRE)**[15] 4791 9-10-8 85....................(p) JosephAkehurst(7) 37
(Alan Blackmore) *pressed ldr tl hrd drvn and dropped out rapidly bef 6th: sn hopelessly t.o: fin eventually* **50/1**

64P- **P** **Dontpaytheferryman (USA)**[11] 1886 9-10-12 117........(v) KyleJames(3)
(Peter Hiatt) *led tl hdd and lost pl v rapidly bef 3 out: hopelessly t.o whn p.u next* **20/1**

0P3- **P** **Gainsborough's Art (IRE)**[16] 4783 9-11-1 55.............(p) LeightonAspell
(Harry Chisman) *bhd: reminder after 4th: nvr travelling after: hopelessly t.o whn p.u after 3 out* **100/1**

00P- **P** **Amazingreyce**[6] 4981 9-10-5 65.................................(b[1]) GavinSheehan(3)
(Christopher Kellett) *wl bhd: rdn after 4th: t.o 6th: p.u 3 out* **150/1**

000- **P** **Elixir Du Lac**[105] 3092 7-10-8 0.. SamJones
(Jo Davis) *wl bhd: last and rdn 5th: t.o next: p.u 3 out* **100/1**

4m 34.5s (3.00) **Going Correction** +0.375s/f (Yiel) **12** Ran SP% **116.9**
Speed ratings (Par 103): **108,107,104,98,95 95,90,71,, ,**
CSF £158.32 TOTE £8.70: £2.30, £3.00, £1.30; EX 59.90 Trifecta £231.40.The winner bought in 10,000gns. Stow was subject to a friendly claim. Viking Blond was claimed by S. V. O. Leech for £6000.
Owner C L Bacon **Bred** R Guiry **Trained** Danethorpe, Notts

FOCUS
A decent race for the class, run at a good clip. A big step up from the winner.

5067 BORDEAUX UNDISCOVERED CLARET H'CAP HURDLE (8 hdls) 2m 110y
3:40 (3:40) (Class 3) (0-135,130) 4-Y-0+ **£5,523** (£1,621; £810; £405)

Form RPR

500- **1** **Vulcanite (IRE)**[98] 3200 7-11-11 **129**.. NoelFehily 140+
(Charlie Longsdon) *trckd ldrs: wnt 3rd 3 out: 6 l 3rd and cajoled and sltly outpcd 2 out: styd on to ld bef last: racd lazily in front but sn in command* **10/3[2]**

0/0- **2** 2 ½ **Gifted Leader (USA)**[41] 4302 9-10-6 **115**................(vt) RobertMcCarth(5) 122
(Ian Williams) *pressed ldr: stl clr of rest whn nt fluent 2 out: drvn to ld between last two: sn hdd: 2 l 2nd and hld at last* **10/1**

231- **3** 7 **Red Seventy**[23] 4634 5-10-13 **124**..................................(p) TomBellamy(7) 125
(David Pipe) *led: rdn 2 out: hdd between last two: sn wknd* **7/1[3]**

325- **4** 1 **It's A Mans World**[18] 4745 8-10-6 **120**.......................... GLavery(10) 121
(Brian Ellison) *chsd ldrs: wnt 4th but rdn and outpcd bef 2 out: n.d after: hit last* **20/1**

/U6- **5** 1 **Get Back In Line (IRE)**[70] 3771 6-11-2 **125**.............. MauriceLinehan(5) 125
(Jonjo O'Neill) *hld up and bhd: hdwy to midfield 3 out: rdn and no imp in 8 l 5th whn hit next: wl hld after* **3/1[1]**

3F0- **6** 3 ¼ **Seventh Sky (GER)**[15] 4794 7-11-6 **124**.............(t[1]) SamTwiston-Davies 120
(Charlie Mann) *settled in rr: sme prog to chse ldrs bef 3 out: drvn and wl btn bef next* **7/1[3]**

553- **7** 8 **Right Step**[19] 4726 7-9-13 **113**.................................. PaddyBradley(10) 102
(Pat Phelan) *nvr bttr than midfield: struggling fr 3 out* **12/1**

022- **8** 5 **Canadian Diamond (IRE)**[19] 4726 7-11-7 **130**............. JamesBanks(5) 115
(Brendan Powell) *t.k.h: pressed ldrs tl rdn and fdd tamely after 3 out* **17/2**

006- **9** 4 ½ **Grams And Ounces**[38] 4353 7-10-3 **107**......................(t) AndrewTinkler 88
(John Flint) *in rr and drvn and struggling at 5th: wl bhd after* **10/1**

4PU- **10** 20 **Next Exit (IRE)**[155] 2063 9-10-5 **114**..............................(t) JoeCornwall(5) 77
(John Cornwall) *towards rr: lost tch bef 3 out: hit next: t.o between last two* **100/1**

345- **P** **Alwaystheoptimist**[7] 4965 11-11-1 **122**.............................. KielanWoods(3)
(Phil Middleton) *sn last: nt travelling 5th: t.o and p.u 2 out* **40/1**

3m 58.7s (2.70) **Going Correction** +0.375s/f (Yiel) **11** Ran SP% **117.7**
Speed ratings (Par 107): **108,106,103,103,102 101,97,94,92,83**
CSF £36.04 CT £222.56 TOTE £5.30: £2.30, £2.70, £2.00; EX 42.20 Trifecta £422.00.
Owner John P McManus **Bred** Barouche Stud Ireland Ltd **Trained** Over Norton, Oxon

FOCUS
A fair handicap hurdle. The first two were very well in on old old form.

5068 GREAT VALUE WINES FROM BORDEAUX UNDISCOVERED H'CAP CHASE (17 fncs) 2m 7f
4:15 (4:15) (Class 3) (0-135,137) 5-Y-0+ **£6,498** (£1,908; £954; £477)

Form RPR

320- **1** **Dolatulo (FR)**[15] 4789 7-11-8 **134**.............................(p) GavinSheehan(3) 139
(Warren Greatrex) *wnt 2nd at 5th: hit 10th (water): rdn and lft in ld 2 out: v hrd pressed and all out and edging rt whn rival was lft short of room and brushed into rail cl home: fin first: disqualified and plcd 2nd* **9/1**

211- **2** 2 ¼ **Benbens (IRE)**[23] 4635 9-11-7 **130**......................... SamTwiston-Davies 136+
(Nigel Twiston-Davies) *chsd ldrs: effrt 13th: wnt 3rd but nt fluent next: v vigorously drvn fr 2 out: tried to chal and hit last: clsng whn rail dolling off water and rival c up to greet him: lost all momentum fnl 50yds: fin 2nd: plcd 1st* **15/8[1]**

024- **3** ½ **Majorica King (FR)**[53] 4077 8-10-8 **117**......................... LeightonAspell 121
(Oliver Sherwood) *settled in rr: clsd bef 14th: led after next: j. slowly 2 out and hdd: rdn and ev ch between last two: one pce fr last* **16/1**

0F2- **4** 10 **Forgotten Gold (IRE)**[30] 4509 8-11-9 **137**............... AodhaganConlon(5) 132
(Tom George) *led tl after 3rd: hmpd 7th and lost grnd: rcvrd to press ldrs tl hmpd again 13th: nt fluent next: rdn and btn after* **11/2[2]**

326- **5** 20 **Court By Surprise (IRE)**[28] 4544 9-11-8 **131**............... RichieMcLernon 106
(Emma Lavelle) *trckd ldrs: effrt 14th: led briefly next: rdn and dropped out qckly bef 2 out* **8/1**

16P- **6** 1 **Dashing George (IRE)**[26] 4593 12-10-9 **125**....................... MrRWinks(7) 99
(Peter Winks) *led after 3rd: often hassled by loose horse but mde nrly all tl hmpd 14th: nt fluent next: sn rdn and dropped out* **50/1**

500- **U** **Fruity O'Rooney**[18] 4738 11-11-6 **129**.............................(v) JoshuaMoore
(Gary Moore) *lunged at 1st and uns rdr* **6/1[3]**

336- **F** **Renard D'Irlande (FR)**[14] 4819 9-11-2 **125**......................... AidanColeman
(Venetia Williams) *cl up on outer whn bmpd and fell 7th* **8/1**

341- **P** **Little Chip (IRE)**[108] 3026 7-11-1 **124**.. NoelFehily
(Charlie Longsdon) *in last whn hit 6th: hmpd 7th: stl last whn hit 11th and rdn: sn lost tch: t.o and p.u 14th* **9/1**

5m 57.2s (18.00) **Going Correction** +1.05s/f (Soft) **9** Ran SP% **114.5**
Speed ratings: **110,109,109,105,98 98,, ,**
CSF £19.28 CT £207.09 TOTE £2.50: £1.10, £3.30, £6.00; EX 27.80 Trifecta £579.10.
Owner Chasemore Farm **Bred** Claude Michel **Trained** Upper Lambourn, Berks

FOCUS
A decent handicap chase with a dramatic and controversial finish. Dolatulo is rated to his best hurdles figure, while Benbens is rated pretty much to his mark.

5069 BU GRAND CRU CLASSES H'CAP HURDLE (8 hdls 3 omitted) 2m 6f 110y
4:50 (4:52) (Class 5) (0-100,100) 4-Y-0+ **£3,249** (£954; £477; £238)

Form RPR

012- **1** **Area Access (IRE)**[12] 4865 6-10-11 **92**...................... MrHAABannister(7) 99
(Charlie Mann) *chsd ldrs: mstke 4th: effrt ent bk st: wnt 2nd last (normal 2 out): rdn to ld over 1f out: sn in command* **3/1[1]**

PF0- **2** 1 ¼ **Killegney**[34] 4447 10-10-8 **85**......................................(p) PeterCarberry(3) 90
(Michael Gates) *prom: led 2 out (normal 3 out): hrd rdn and clr w wnr home turn: hdd over 1f out: nt qckn after* **50/1**

032- **3** 3 ¾ **Gorey Lane (IRE)**[28] 4553 8-11-3 **98**.........................(v) DaraghBourke(7) 100
(John Norton) *midfield: rdn and effrt in 4th at last (normal 2 out): styd on fr home turn: no imp fnl 100yds* **11/2[3]**

060- **4** 3 **Sterling Gent (IRE)**[114] 2908 7-11-7 **95**........................ PaddyBrennan 95
(Liam Corcoran) *hit 2nd: bhd: hdwy 3 out (normal 2 out): rdn to chal next: hanging lft and wl hld fr wl over 1f out* **14/1**

063- **5** 17 **Clues And Arrows (IRE)**[65] 3856 6-10-10 **84**............. RichieMcLernon 68
(Jonjo O'Neill) *midfield: struggling after 1/2-way* **7/1**

0P0- **6** 3 ¾ **Royalracket (IRE)**[17] 4758 6-11-1 **92**.................................. JamesBest(3) 72
(Paul Webber) *towards rr: sn drvn along: laboured prog bef 2 out (normal 3 out): sn wl btn* **28/1**

430- **7** 13 **Dougalstar (FR)**[26] 4595 5-10-11 **95**............................ MikeyHamill(10) 64
(Sean Curran) *t.k.h: cl up on outer: drvn after 5th: lost tch after 2 out (normal 3 out): t.o* **25/1**

550- **8** ½ **Landenstown Pearl (IRE)**[26] 4595 8-10-6 **80**................. ConorO'Farrell 48
(Sarah Humphrey) *struggling in rr 1/2-way: t.o* **25/1**

/02- **9** 1 ¼ **Barnack**[6] 4981 8-10-10 **87**...(t) KielanWoods(3) 54
(Pam Sly) *cl up: mstke 5th: rdn bef 2 out (normal 3 out): sn btn: t.o* **5/1[2]**

P51- **10** 3 ¼ **Fidelor (FR)**[16] 4783 8-10-13 **92**...................................(t) KillianMoore(5) 56
(Alex Hales) *2nd tl led after 4th: drvn and hdd 2 out (normal 3 out): 4th and losing tch qckly after next: t.o* **16/1**

500- **11** 60 **Agent Fedora**[114] 2896 6-10-7 **86**.................................(t) EdCookson(5)
(Kim Bailey) *struggling 1/2-way: hopelessly t.o* **9/1**

050- **P** **Romney Marsh**[83] 3553 13-10-11 **85**....................................... HaddenFrost
(Roger Curtis) *trckd ldrs tl 1/2-way: nt run on: t.o and p.u last (normal 2 out)* **50/1**

05P/ **P** **Ovthenight (IRE)**[758] 4605 9-11-0 **95**...............................(p) MrFTett(7)
(Roger Curtis) *last whn nrly fell 3rd: continued t.o tl p.u next: dismntd* **100/1**

004- **P** **Petit Fleur**[104] 3117 12-11-7 **95**................................... SamTwiston-Davies
(Julian Smith) *towards rr: nt travelling fr 1/2-way: t.o and p.u last (normal 2 out)* **20/1**

6PP- **P** **Hassadin**[39] 4334 8-10-7 **88**...(b[1]) JoshWall(7)
(Michael Blake) *a wl bhd: t.o and p.u last (normal 2 out)* **12/1**

040- **P** **Unknown Legend (IRE)**[20] 4700 7-11-7 **100**................... JamesBanks(5)
(Anthony Middleton) *kpt wl away fr rest at s: plld v hrd: led tl after 4th: lost pl rapidly: t.o and p.u last (normal 2 out)* **33/1**

5m 33.0s (4.90) **Going Correction** +0.375s/f (Yiel) **16** Ran SP% **123.5**
Speed ratings (Par 103): **106,105,104,103,97 96,91,91,90,89 68,, , ,**
CSF £171.59 CT £824.11 TOTE £3.60: £1.30, £9.60, £1.70, £2.80; EX 158.70 Trifecta £1278.90 Part won..
Owner Edwyn Good & Bryan Beacham **Bred** James Silk **Trained** Upper Lambourn, Berks

FOCUS
A low-grade handicap hurdle. The flight in the home straight was omitted on each circuit due to the low sun. Another step up from the progressive winner.

5070 LA FLEUR MORANGE MATHILDE STANDARD OPEN NATIONAL HUNT FLAT RACE 2m 110y
5:25 (5:25) (Class 5) 4-6-Y-0 **£2,599** (£763; £381; £190)

Form RPR

1 **Broughtons Rhythm** 5-11-3 0... LeightonAspell 106+
(Willie Musson) *settled in rr: hdwy 4f out: chal wd home turn: led 1f out: sn rdn clr* **16/1**

133- **2** 4 **Henllan Harri (IRE)**[72] 3734 6-11-10 0............................ DonalDevereux 109
(Peter Bowen) *cl 2nd tl led 10f out: drvn and hdd 1f out: kpt on gamely* **6/1[3]**

3 2 **Well Rewarded (IRE)** 4-10-10 0.. AidanColeman 93
(Emma Lavelle) *chsd ldrs: drvn and outpcd fr 6f out tl styd on strly ins fnl f: snatched 3rd: promising* **8/1**

- **4** ½ **Mazurati (IRE)** 5-11-0 0... KielanWoods(3) 100
(Ben Case) *bhd: hdwy 4f out: wnt 3rd 2f out: drvn and nt qckn fr over 1f out* **16/1**

3- **5** 1 ¼ **Superior Fire (IRE)**[77] 3656 4-10-10 0.................................... NoelFehily 92
(Charlie Longsdon) *t.k.h: set stdy pce on outer: hdd 10f out: 3rd home turn: no ex* **5/1[2]**

2- **6** ½ **Quinlandio (IRE)**[13] 4844 4-10-5 0.................................. JamesBanks(5) 91
(Brendan Powell) *chsd ldrs: rdn wl over 1f out: one pce after* **5/1[2]**

7 4 ½ **Grand Introduction (IRE)** 4-10-10 0............................... PaddyBrennan 87
(Fergal O'Brien) *t.k.h: midfield: rdn and btn wl over 1f out* **15/8[1]**

8 7 **Singh Is King** 6-11-3 0.. SamTwiston-Davies 88
(Marc Barber) *cl up tl rdn and fdd 2f out* **33/1**

00- **9** 1 ½ **Tinos Tank (IRE)**[13] 4844 5-10-12 0............................ RobertMcCarth(5) 86
(Hilary Parrott) *unbalanced on turns: nvr bttr than midfield: lost tch 3f out: t.o* **100/1**

6- **10** 17 **Catcharose (IRE)**[60] 3961 4-10-3 0.. FelixDeGiles 57
(Jennifer Mason) *struggling 6f out: t.o fnl 3f* **100/1**

11 2 **Westbrooke (IRE)** 4-10-10 0.. MarkGrant 62
(Charlie Mann) *n.d: t.o fnl 3f* **25/1**

6- **12** 1 ¾ **Johns Luck (IRE)**[35] 4417 5-11-3 0..................................... MichaelByrne 68
(Neil Mulholland) *prom: rdn and fdd over 2f out: heavily eased fnl f: t.o* **25/1**

13 20 **Carnaross** 5-10-10 0...(t) CharlieDeutsch(7) 50
(Anthony Middleton) *bhd: t.o fnl 3f* **40/1**

06- **14** 12 **Foolsandorses (IRE)**[114] 2912 6-10-10 0........... WilliamFeatherstone(7) 39
(W De Best-Turner) *a last: bdly t.o fr 1/2-way* **100/1**

4m 0.4s (10.00) **Going Correction** +0.375s/f (Yiel)
WFA 4 from 5yo+ 7lb **14** Ran SP% **121.3**
Speed ratings: **91,89,88,87,87 87,85,81,81,73 72,71,61,56**
CSF £106.18 TOTE £27.50: £5.70, £1.30, £4.40; EX 82.60 Trifecta £1059.00 Part won..
Owner Broughton Thermal Insulation **Bred** Michael E Broughton **Trained** Newmarket, Suffolk

FOCUS
Ordinary bumper form, rated around the second, fifth and sixth.
T/Plt: £11.30 to a £1 stake. Pool: £89083.57 - 5740.88 winning tickets. T/Qpdt: £10.70 to a £1 stake. Pool of £5976.06 - 411.77 winning tickets. IM

4818 UTTOXETER (L-H)

Saturday, March 29

OFFICIAL GOING: Good to soft (soft in places on chase course and in the chute; chs 4.9, hdl 5.1)

Wind: Moderate, behind Weather: Sunny

5071 BETFRED TV CONDITIONAL JOCKEYS' TRAINING SERIES MAIDEN HURDLE (THE RACING EXCELLENCE INITIATIVE) (10 hdls) 2m 4f 110y

1:40 (1:40) (Class 5) 4-Y-0+ **£2,339** (£686; £343; £171)

Form RPR

P4- **1** **Shubaat**[17] 4758 7-10-12 0 .... CharlieDeutsch[(3)] 123+
(John Ferguson) *in tch: travelling wl bef 3 out: wnt 2nd long bef 2 out: led between last 2: dived at last: sn rdn: r.o wl to draw clr fnl 100yds* **4/1**[2]

420- **2** *5* **Sir Pitt**[45] 4224 7-11-1 115 .... CraigNichol 115
(John Bryan Groucott) *trckd ldrs: led appr 3 out where nt fluent: rdn 2 out: hdd between last 2: kpt on same pce and unable to go w wnr run-in* **5/1**[3]

3- **3** *4½* **Yasir (USA)**[8] 4304 6-10-12 0 .... (p) JackSherwood[(3)] 111
(Conor Dore) *hld up in midfield: hdwy appr 3 out: sn wl there: rdn bef 2 out: outpcd bef last: kpt on to take 3rd fnl 75yds but no imp* **7/1**

P5F- **4** *1* **Allow Dallow (IRE)**[21] 4672 7-10-7 122 .... (t) TommieMO'Brien[(8)] 111
(Jonjo O'Neill) *in tch on outer: wl there fr 3 out: ev ch 2 out: rdn and nt pick-up sn after: hld whn mstke last: kpt on same pce run-in* **7/4**[1]

25- **5** *16* **Silver Gent (IRE)**[27] 4574 6-10-9 0 .... NickSlatter[(6)] 96
(Donald McCain) *led: hit 6th: rdn and hdd appr 3 out: wknd bef 2 out* **12/1**

6- **6** *57* **Golden Milan (IRE)**[42] 4267 6-10-7 0 .... PaulO'Brien[(8)] 44
(Rebecca Curtis) *prom: rdn and losing pl in 6th whn blnd 3 out: wl btn: t.o* **16/1**

6- **7** *13* **Hinton Magic**[36] 4403 5-10-0 0 .... JamesHuxham[(8)] 26
(Jonjo O'Neill) *hld up: struggling after 7th: nvr a threat: t.o* **66/1**

4- **8** *3¾* **Maxilian (IRE)**[109] 3016 5-10-12 0 .... TomBellamy[(3)] 29
(Emma Lavelle) *prom: pushed along after 4 out: wknd bef 3 out: t.o* **40/1**

323- **9** *5* **Fruity Bun**[3] 5029 4-9-11 92 .... (t) RyanHatch[(3)] 10
(Keiran Burke) *midfield: mstke 3rd: struggling bef 6th: bhd after: t.o* **25/1**

/60- **10** *20* **Do Be Dashing**[101] 3159 6-10-3 0 .... ThomasCheesman[(5)]
(Graeme McPherson) *towards rr: pushed along after 5th: t.o after 7th* **100/1**

106- **P** **Minella Hero (IRE)**[123] 2732 6-11-1 0 .... PatrickCorbett
(Sarah Humphrey) *midfield: j. slowly 2nd: struggling bef 4 out: t.o whn p.u bef 3 out* **25/1**

\- **P** **Sing Alone** 8-10-10 0 .... PaulJohn[(5)]
(Christopher Kellett) *bhd: sn detached: struggling early: t.o whn p.u bef 4 out* **125/1**

5m 3.6s (4.60) **Going Correction** +0.30s/f (Yiel)
WFA 4 from 5yo+ 8lb 12 Ran SP% **112.5**
Speed ratings (Par 103): **103,101,99,99,92 71,66,64,62,55 ,**
CSF £22.15 TOTE £5.30: £2.00, £1.50, £2.20; EX 20.90 Trifecta £107.20.
Owner Bloomfields **Bred** Darley **Trained** Cowlinge, Suffolk

FOCUS
Divided bends, hurdles moved out 4-6m on to fresher ground. The going had dried out a little after minimal overnight rain. A maiden hurdle for conditional jockeys and the market leaders had it between them from the third-last. Fair novice form for the track, with a step up from the winner.

5072 BETFRED SUPPORTS JACK BERRY HOUSE H'CAP HURDLE (8 hdls 1 omitted) 2m

2:10 (2:13) (Class 5) (0-100,100) 4-Y-0+ **£2,599** (£763; £381; £190)

Form RPR

212- **1** **Wintered Well (IRE)**[99] 3192 6-11-12 100 .... SeanQuinlan 112+
(Jennie Candlish) *midfield: hdwy 4th: reminder sn after: led 3 out: rdn appr 2 out: mstke last: pressed run-in: styd on wl and fnd ex towards fin* **4/1**[1]

036- **2** *1½* **Jaja De Jau**[19] 4721 5-10-10 87 .... (t) RachaelGreen[(3)] 93
(Anthony Honeyball) *hld up in rr: hdwy appr 3 out: wnt 2nd bef 2 out: tried to chal run-in: nt qckn and hld towards fin* **10/1**

0/5- **3** *½* **Sambulando (FR)**[20] 4703 11-11-8 99 .... (p) GilesHawkins[(3)] 106
(Richard Hobson) *hld up: hdwy 4 out: chsng ldrs whn mstke 3 out: rdn bef 2 out: nt qckn appr last: styd on towards fin* **14/1**

006- **4** *2¼* **Un Bleu A L'Aam (FR)**[31] 4504 6-11-7 95 .... JackDoyle 99
(Victor Dartnall) *in tch: mstke 4th: rdn whn chsng ldrs appr 2 out: kpt on same pce run-in: no imp towards fin* **7/1**[2]

35P- **5** *16* **Ghaabesh (IRE)**[34] 4447 7-9-12 79 .... (t) ConorRing[(7)] 69
(Barry Leavy) *bhd: niggled along appr 4 out: plugged on fr 3 out: nvr a threat* **16/1**

3/4- **6** *1¾* **Theredballoon**[31] 4493 8-11-10 98 .... TomMessenger 86
(David Elsworth) *midfield: hdwy and pushed along appr 3 out: no imp and one pce* **9/1**

25P- **7** *½* **Prince Freddie**[39] 4334 6-9-11 75 ow3 .... (b[1]) RyanHatch[(7)] 66
(Roy Brotherton) *in tch: rdn and ev ch appr 3 out: btn bef 2 out* **14/1**

/33- **8** *3* **Mister Frosty (IRE)**[15] 4791 8-11-4 95 .... (p) JackQuinlan[(3)] 80
(Michael Squance) *prom: led appr 4 out: mstke and hdd 3 out: sn wknd* **22/1**

013- **9** *17* **Powertakeoff (IRE)**[26] 4597 6-10-10 84 .... (t) DenisO'Regan 54
(Henry Oliver) *bhd: reminder after 4th: hdwy after 4 out: nvr able to trble ldrs* **8/1**[3]

030- **10** *2¼* **Table Bluff (IRE)**[100] 3175 5-11-4 95 .... NicodeBoinville[(3)] 63
(John Spearing) *trckd ldrs: lost pl briefly 4th: pushed along appr 3 out: sn wknd* **14/1**

005- **11** *½* **Femme D'Espere**[37] 4379 8-10-0 74 .... AdamWedge 41
(Trevor Wall) *midfield: wknd 4 out* **100/1**

/00- **12** *1¼* **Quinola Des Obeaux (FR)**[54] 4072 10-10-7 84 .... JamesBest[(3)] 50
(Rob Summers) *prom tl rdn and lost pl appr 4 out: sn wknd* **50/1**

305- **13** *11* **Wom**[7] 4972 6-11-8 99 .... (b) TrevorWhelan[(3)] 55
(Neil King) *towards rr: pushed along 4th: nvr a threat* **12/1**

00P- **14** *2½* **Heurtevent (FR)**[37] 4366 5-11-7 95 .... (t) LeeEdwards 49
(Tony Carroll) *hld up in midfield: hdwy after 3rd: sn prom: pushed along after 4 out: wknd appr 3 out* **7/1**[2]

P66- **15** *3¼* **Orlittlebylittle**[17] 4757 8-11-4 92 .... (b) HenryBrooke 43
(Donald McCain) *led: hdd appr 4 out: wknd after flight* **25/1**

3m 55.9s (3.90) **Going Correction** +0.30s/f (Yiel) 15 Ran SP% **119.9**
Speed ratings (Par 103): **102,101,101,99,91 91,90,89,80,79 79,78,73,72,70**
CSF £42.12 CT £519.52 TOTE £4.50: £2.20, £4.10, £7.00; EX 52.60 Trifecta £380.80.
Owner Mrs Kristene Hunter **Bred** Mrs Kathleen Leahy **Trained** Basford Green, Staffs

FOCUS
The hurdle in the cute was omitted. A big field for this moderate but competitive handicap hurdle, but once again four came clear of the rest. A big step up from the winner with the second to his 2013 best.

5073 BETFRED FOLLOW US ON FACEBOOK NOVICES' CHASE (12 fncs) 2m

2:45 (2:45) (Class 4) 5-Y-0+ **£6,256** (£1,848; £924; £462)

Form RPR

24P- **1** **Ohio Gold (IRE)**[18] 4742 8-11-0 132 .... BrendanPowell 129+
(Colin Tizzard) *prom: chsd ldr 4th: led appr 7th: rdn and jnd 3 out: tk advantage and asserted fnl 75yds: styd on gamely* **7/4**[2]

130- **2** *3* **Ut Majeur Aulmes (FR)**[42] 4278 6-11-0 0 .... JackDoyle 126
(Victor Dartnall) *hld up in rr: wnt 3rd 5th: wnt 2nd gng wl appr 4 out: drew level on bit 3 out: shkn up appr last: rdn run-in: defly hdd and unable to go w wnr fnl 75yds: no ex* **11/2**[3]

021- **3** *11* **Shotavodka (IRE)**[37] 4373 8-11-7 139 .... TomScudamore 125+
(David Pipe) *prom: led 3rd: hdd appr 7th: mstke 8th: sn lost 2nd: outpcd fr 3 out: no imp after* **10/11**[1]

5P6- **4** *15* **Tayarat (IRE)**[15] 4791 9-10-9 0 .... JohnDawson[(5)] 100
(Michael Chapman) *j.lft a few times: led: hdd 3rd: j. slowly and dropped to rr 5th: lft bhd fr 8th* **100/1**

4m 13.0s (18.00) **Going Correction** +0.45s/f (Soft) 4 Ran SP% **105.1**
Speed ratings: **73,71,66,58**
CSF £9.59 TOTE £2.90; EX 8.20 Trifecta £12.60.
Owner P M Warren **Bred** J R Weston **Trained** Milborne Port, Dorset

FOCUS
An interesting novices' chase that produced a good finish. The form could be rated nearly a stone higher using the winner and third.

5074 BETFRED "RACING'S BIGGEST SUPPORTER" H'CAP HURDLE (12 hdls) 3m

3:20 (3:20) (Class 4) (0-120,120) 4-Y-0 **£3,798** (£1,122; £561; £280; £140)

Form RPR

364- **1** **Billy Dutton**[14] 4809 8-11-5 113 .... JamesDavies 119+
(Chris Down) *midfield: hdwy after 7th: rdn and wnt 2nd appr 2 out: led bef last: styd on wl run-in* **16/1**

63F- **2** *1¾* **Karinga Dandy (IRE)**[122] 2747 8-11-1 109 .... RyanMania 112
(Sue Smith) *hld up: pushed along appr 4 out to go pce: hdwy 3 out: effrt to chse ldrs bef 2 out: kpt on to take 2nd fnl 75yds: no imp on wnr towards fin* **9/1**[3]

111- **3** *1¼* **Solstice Son**[9] 4913 5-11-4 115 .... (t) RachaelGreen[(3)] 117
(Anthony Honeyball) *prom: led appr 4 out: rdn bef 2 out: hdd bef last: lost 2nd fnl 75yds: no ex* **13/8**[1]

F44- **4** *7* **Mohi Rahrere (IRE)**[93] 3267 11-11-4 112 .... LiamHeard 108
(Barry Leavy) *trckd ldrs: ev ch appr 3 out: rdn and outpcd bef 2 out: kpt on run-in: tk 4th fnl 75yds but no imp after* **50/1**

052- **5** *2* **Barton Stacey (IRE)**[54] 4070 9-11-8 116 .... (b) TomScudamore 110
(David Pipe) *in tch: prom 4 out: ev ch 3 out: rdn whn chalng appr 2 out: one pce bef last: fdd fnl 75yds* **7/1**[2]

520- **6** *11* **Alberobello (IRE)**[88] 3435 6-11-8 116 .... (t) NickScholfield 100
(Jeremy Scott) *hld up: sltly detached after 7th: plugged on fr 3 out: nvr a threat* **9/1**[3]

PP6- **7** *nse* **Duke Of Monmouth (IRE)**[57] 4006 7-11-4 112 .... DominicElsworth 96
(Charlie Mann) *hld up: struggling 4 out: plugged on fr 3 out: nvr a threat* **16/1**

P/2- **8** *31* **Lundy Sky**[36] 4393 9-11-12 120 .... AndrewThornton 76
(Tony Newcombe) *led: hdd appr 4 out: rdn bef 3 out: sn wknd* **12/1**

245- **9** *13* **Ice 'N' Easy (IRE)**[21] 4685 8-11-8 116 .... (t) TommyPhelan 60
(Charlie Longsdon) *in tch: rdn and wknd appr 3 out* **16/1**

200- **10** *3¼* **Georgian King**[20] 4700 11-11-5 113 ....[1] TomO'Brien 54
(Martin Keighley) *prom tl rdn and wknd after 4 out* **20/1**

64U- **11** *16* **Know More Oats (IRE)**[36] 4391 6-11-0 108 .... JackDoyle 35
(Victor Dartnall) *hld up: rdn appr 4 out: nvr a threat: t.o* **20/1**

416- **12** *21* **Jojabean (IRE)**[121] 2755 7-11-9 117 .... WayneHutchinson 25
(Alan King) *midfield: hdwy 4 out: rdn and wknd bef 3 out: t.o* **7/1**[2]

3PP- **P** **No Principles**[103] 3137 11-11-0 108 .... MarkGrant
(Julian Smith) *hld up: struggling after 8th: t.o after 4 out: p.u bef 3 out* **40/1**

5m 58.8s (8.80) **Going Correction** +0.30s/f (Yiel) 13 Ran SP% **122.4**
Speed ratings (Par 105): **97,96,96,93,93 89,89,78,74,73 68,61,**
CSF £150.11 CT £369.19 TOTE £28.00: £6.10, £3.10, £1.10; EX 297.70 Trifecta £916.60 Part won..
Owner W A Bromley **Bred** Wood Farm Stud **Trained** Mutterton, Devon

FOCUS
A competitive staying handicap hurdle featuring several switching back from a spell over fences, and it was one of those that triumphed. The winner is rated back to his 2013 hurdling form.

5075 BETFRED GOALS GALORE EXTRA H'CAP HURDLE (10 hdls) 2m 4f 110y

3:55 (3:55) (Class 4) (0-120,120) 4-Y-0 **£3,798** (£1,122; £561; £280; £140)

Form RPR

521- **1** **Jack Albert (IRE)**[6] 4001 7-10-0 94 7ex .... (b) BrianHarding 105+
(Dianne Sayer) *led: hdd after 2nd: remained prom: led again 5th: nt fluent 2 out: drew clr appr last: styd on wl: comf* **3/1**[1]

002- **2** *11* **Miss Lucky Penny**[20] 4700 8-10-10 104 .... WillKennedy 104
(Ian Williams) *handy: hit 5th: effrt whn chsng ldrs 3 out: kpt on u.p to take 2nd last: no ch w wnr* **8/1**

203/ **3** *¾* **Leader Of The Gang**[340] 5468 8-11-10 118 .... (tp) TomScudamore 117
(David Pipe) *in tch: lft 2nd after 4 out: tried to chal 3 out: rdn bef 2 out: sn no imp on wnr: lost 2nd last: kpt on u.p* **6/1**

265- **4** *20* **Rattlin**[21] 4668 6-11-7 118 .... JonathanEngland[(3)] 99
(Sue Smith) *prom tl rdn and wknd after 4 out* **10/1**

341- **5** *27* **Wily Fox**[20] 4700 7-11-9 120 .... JackQuinlan[(3)] 77
(James Eustace) *hld up: rdn and wknd appr 4th* **8/1**

42F- **6** *24* **King Zeal (IRE)**[41] 4305 10-10-11 105 .... (t) LiamHeard 40
(Barry Leavy) *hld up: struggling bef 4 out: t.o whn mstke last* **20/1**

655- **P** **Six One Away (IRE)**[106] 3061 5-10-12 106 .... DenisO'Regan
(Paul Webber) *led after 2nd: hdd 5th: rdn and wknd appr 6th: t.o whn p.u bef 4 out* **20/1**

/03- **R** **Go West Young Man (IRE)**[28] 4546 6-10-12 109 .... JakeGreenall[(3)]
(Henry Daly) *hld up: hdwy appr 6th and hung rt: continued to hang rt after and wnt 2nd appr 4 out: rn out after 4 out* **9/2**[2]

220- **P** **Make Me A Fortune (IRE)**[38] 4347 6-10-11 112 .... (p) PaulBohan[(7)]
(Steve Gollings) *hld up: bhd and struggling 5th: t.o whn p.u bef 6th* **5/1**[3]

5m 4.3s (5.30) **Going Correction** +0.30s/f (Yiel) 9 Ran SP% **115.0**
Speed ratings (Par 105): **101,96,96,88,78 69, , ,**
CSF £27.17 CT £132.58 TOTE £3.80: £1.70, £2.60, £1.90; EX 33.00 Trifecta £124.70.
Owner E G Tunstall **Bred** Miss Marie Harding **Trained** Hackthorpe, Cumbria

FOCUS
An ordinary handicap hurdle. The winner was well in on his recent win but this looks another step up, with the next two close to their marks.

5076 BETFRED 4 X ODDS ON LUCKY 31'S H'CAP CHASE (15 fncs) 2m 4f
4:30 (4:30) (Class 4) (0-115,115) 5-Y-0+

£5,004 (£1,478; £739; £369; £184; £92)

Form RPR
445- **1** **Ballylifen (IRE)**[21] 4678 7-10-12 **111**.......................... JamesHuxham(10) 121+
(Jonjo O'Neill) *in tch: wnt 2nd appr 10th: led after 11th: asserted 3 out and hung lft after: styd on run-in* **7/2**[2]
343- **2** *3 ½* **Munsaab (IRE)**[20] 4696 8-11-10 **113**..........................(t) TomScudamore 118
(Charlie Longsdon) *chsd ldrs: wnt 2nd after 11th: ev ch 4 out: rdn bef 2 out: no imp on wnr bef last: one pce run-in* **7/2**[2]
214- **3** *29* **Hollins**[14] 4822 10-10-13 **109**.. OllieGarner(7) 88
(Tony Forbes) *in rr: blnd 6th: struggling 8th and bhd 8th: kpt on fr bef 2 out: tk poor 3rd appr last: no ch w front two* **14/1**
/42- **4** *8* **Gentle Bob (IRE)**[37] 4372 9-11-11 **114**.............................. AlainCawley 86
(Tom George) *led: mstke 1st: sn hdd: chsd ldr tl appr 10th: niggled along and losing pl whn mstke 11th: sn btn* **3/1**[1]
4P3/ **5** *8* **Prince Du Seuil (FR)**[696] 58 11-11-2 **112**.................. DanielHiskett(7) 77
(Richard Phillips) *racd keenly: led after 1st: clr after 3rd: mstke 5th: reduced advantage 10th: nt fluent 11th: sn hdd: wknd 4 out* **14/1**
136- **6** *33* **Ballycool (IRE)**[28] 4549 7-10-9 **103**..........................(t) DerekFox(5) 38
(Lucinda Russell) *chsd ldrs: lost pl after 7th: struggling and bhd 8th: t.o* **7/1**
FP1- **P** **Crystal Swing**[14] 4822 7-11-9 **112**.................................... AdamWedge
(Richard Phillips) *hld up: tk clsr order 4th: blnd 5th: lost pl bef 11th: t.o whn p.u bef 4 out* **5/1**[3]

5m 12.0s (6.50) **Going Correction** +0.45s/f (Soft) **7** Ran SP% **111.9**
Speed ratings: **105,103,92,88,85 72,**
CSF £15.85 CT £146.51 TOTE £5.10: £2.60, £2.50; EX 17.00 Trifecta £190.70.
Owner Toby Cole **Bred** J Mangan **Trained** Cheltenham, Gloucs

FOCUS
Another tightly knit contest, this time over fences, but it concerned just two in the straight. The winner was nicely in on the best of his form from the autumn.

5077 BETFRED "DOUBLE DELIGHT" MARES' STANDARD OPEN NATIONAL HUNT FLAT RACE 2m
5:05 (5:05) (Class 6) 4-6-Y-0 **£1,559** (£457; £228; £114)

Form RPR
1 **Molo** 4-10-10 0.. TomScudamore 100+
(David Pipe) *prom: rdn 3f out: led over 2f out: clr 1f out: styd on* **9/2**[2]
2 *4* **Vicky's Charm (IRE)** 5-11-3 0.. RyanMania 103
(Barry Brennan) *trckd ldrs: led 5f out: rdn 3f out: hdd over 2f out: one pce and hld by wnr ins fnl f* **25/1**
4- **3** *3* **One Big Love**[19] 4735 6-11-3 0.. NickScholfield 100
(Keiran Burke) *hld up: hdwy 6f out: in tch: outpcd over 3f out: kpt on fr 2f out: styd on and hung lft ins fnl f: tk 3rd fnl strides: no ch w front two* **12/1**
5- **4** *½* **Glamorous Sister (IRE)**[28] 4561 4-10-10 0......................... TomO'Brien 93
(Robert Stephens) *hld up in rr: hdwy 4f out: rdn to chse ldrs over 2f out: styd on same pce fnl f* **20/1**
5 *½* **Samedi Soir** 4-10-10 0.. JamesReveley 92
(Keith Reveley) *hld up in rr: stdy hdwy 4f out: rdn whn chsng ldrs 2f out: styd on same pce ins fnl fulong tl no ex fnl strides* **13/2**
6 *½* **Gabriella Rose** 4-10-10 0.. WayneHutchinson 92
(Alan King) *hld up: hdwy over 3f out: styd on steadily ins fnl f: nvr able to trble ldrs* **4/1**[1]
0- **7** *4* **Eastern Calm**[124] 2724 5-10-12 0................................ ThomasGarner(5) 95
(Oliver Sherwood) *trckd ldrs: rdn 3f out: outpcd 2f out: kpt on one pce after* **25/1**
5- **8** *11* **Well Connected**[63] 3898 5-11-3 0.. JackDoyle 85
(Emma Lavelle) *midfield: pushed along 1/2-way: outpcd 5f out: n.d after* **16/1**
2- **9** *¾* **Gwendoliner (IRE)**[26] 4598 5-10-12 0............................ BenPoste(5) 84
(Tom Symonds) *plld hrd: in tch: wknd 3f out* **12/1**
10 *6* **Call Me Kate** 4-10-7 0... JakeGreenall(3) 72
(Henry Daly) *midfield: rdn over 6f out: bhd and struggling 4f out* **10/1**
11 *20* **Maxford Lady (IRE)**[111] 5-11-3 0.................................... BrendanPowell 61
(Jamie Snowden) *led: hdd 5f out: rdn and wknd 3f out* **14/1**
/40- **12** *nk* **Graffiti Art**[21] 4683 5-11-3 0.. LiamTreadwell 61
(Brendan Powell) *midfield: hdwy to trck ldrs after 5f: rdn and wknd over 3f out* **11/2**[3]
13 *dist* **Eagles Road** 4-10-3 0.. RyanHatch(7)
(Harry Whittington) *in tch: pushed along and lost pl 1/2-way: bhd 6f out: woefully t.o* **28/1**

3m 55.1s (8.70) **Going Correction** +0.30s/f (Yiel)
WFA 4 from 5yo+ 7lb **13** Ran SP% **119.8**
Speed ratings: **90,88,86,86,86 85,83,78,77,74 64,64,**
CSF £119.85 TOTE £6.30: £2.60, £8.50, £2.50; EX 78.30.
Owner R J H Geffen **Bred** R D Chugg & Lady J Fowler **Trained** Nicholashayne, Devon

FOCUS
Mostly inexperienced mares in this bumper and the finish was dominated by debutantes. Ordinary form.
T/Plt: £205.80 to a £1 stake. Pool of £84784.82 - 300.74 winning tickets. T/Qpdt: £27.10 to a £1 stake. Pool of £5751.61 - 156.70 winning tickets. DO

4852 NAVAN (L-H)
Saturday, March 29
OFFICIAL GOING: Hurdle course - soft to heavy; chase course - heavy

5082a WEBSTER CUP CHASE (GRADE 2) (14 fncs) 2m 4f
4:35 (4:35) 5-Y-0+ **£20,312** (£5,937; £2,812; £937)

RPR
1 **Bog Warrior (IRE)**[12] 4871 10-11-5 .... PCarberry 156+
(A J Martin, Ire) *chsd ldrs in 3rd tl wnt 2nd after 4th: racd keenly: mod 2nd after 4 out: tk clsr order fr next and clsd u.p 2 out to ld bef last: kpt on wl run-in* **5/2**[2]
2 *3* **Baily Green (IRE)**[17] 4753 8-11-10 **152**.......................(t) MarkEnright 157
(M F Morris, Ire) *trckd ldr tl gd jump to ld 2nd: stl gng wl and clr fr 4 out: reduced advantage next: rdn between last 2 and hdd bef last: no ex run-in* **6/4**[1]
3 *34* **Down In Neworleans (IRE)**[531] 1866 9-11-8 .... DannyMullins 121
(Ms Margaret Mullins, Ire) *w.w in rr of quartet: trailing fr 6th: wnt remote 3rd bef 10th: no imp on ldrs 4 out: kpt on one pce* **7/1**[3]
4 *¾* **Roi Du Mee (FR)**[35] 4435 9-11-12 154............................(tp) DavyRussell 124
(Gordon Elliott, Ire) *led 1st tl hdd 2nd: dropped to 3rd after 4th: slt mstkes 6th and next whn wl bhd ldrs: dropped to rr of quartet bef 10th: no imp on ldrs 4 out: kpt on one pce* **5/2**[2]

5m 37.3s (-3.00) **4** Ran SP% **109.6**
CSF £6.90 TOTE £2.70; DF 5.70 Trifecta £42.00.
Owner Gigginstown House Stud **Bred** John Furlong **Trained** Summerhill, Co. Meath

FOCUS
The winner was the clear pick if anywhere near his best. The second helps the standard.

4261 ASCOT (R-H)
Sunday, March 30
OFFICIAL GOING: Good (chs 7.7, hdl 7.8)
Wind: Moderate, behind Weather: Fine, warm

5088 COLTS & FILLIES CLUB MAIDEN HURDLE (11 hdls) 2m 3f 110y
2:00 (2:02) (Class 4) 4-Y-0+

£5,004 (£1,478; £739; £369; £184; £92)

Form RPR
262- **1** **Simply A Legend**[31] 4506 5-11-1 116........................[1] WayneHutchinson 127
(Alan King) *sltly hmpd 2nd: hld up and last to 5th: stdy prog fr next: trckd ldrs 3 out: chal next: lft in ld after last: drvn out* **14/1**
/2- **2** *¾* **Shelford (IRE)**[55] 477 5-11-1 0.. HarrySkelton 127+
(Dan Skelton) *prom: led 3 out: j.lft 2 out: hrd pressed whn blnd last: sn hdd: rallied nr fin* **10/1**
352- **3** *1 ¼* **Gassin Golf**[22] 4682 5-11-1 127.. JamieMoore 128+
(Richard Lee) *hld up in midfield: prog 7th: cl up 3 out: hmpd bnd bef 2 out: sn on terms: rdn to chal whn hmpd last: one pce flat* **2/1**[1]
FFP- **4** *4* **Milord (GER)**[58] 4022 5-11-1 124.............................. SamTwiston-Davies 124
(Kim Bailey) *hld up in midfield: blnd bdly 6th: prog to chse ldrs 3 out: rdn 2 out: kpt on same pce* **8/1**[3]
152- **5** *10* **Tara Road**[53] 4093 6-11-1 0.. APMcCoy 113
(Rebecca Curtis) *prom: chsd ldr 3 out to next: shkn up and steadily wknd fr last* **8/1**[3]
36- **6** *3 ½* **Benenden (IRE)**[27] 4594 6-11-1 0.................................. TomScudamore 109
(Michael Scudamore) *hld up wl in rr: stdy prog bef 8th: in tch after 3 out: pushed along and outpcd after 2 out: hanging and wknd last: shaped w sme promise* **25/1**
6- **7** *14* **Sacramento King (IRE)**[100] 3182 5-11-1 0.............................. MarkGrant 97
(Jonathan Geake) *hld up wl in rr: stl in last pair after 7th: prog 3 out: shkn up after: nvr on terms w ldrs: nt disgracd* **150/1**
334- **8** *6* **Black Cow (IRE)**[58] 4017 6-11-1 0...................................... NickScholfield 91
(Paul Nicholls) *cl up: wl on terms 3 out: wkng whn mstke 2 out* **25/1**
442- **9** *6* **Gallic Warrior (FR)**[26] 4599 7-11-1 115.............................. PaddyBrennan 86
(Fergal O'Brien) *prom: mstke 5th: led after 7th to 3 out: wknd qckly bef 2 out* **16/1**
10 *½* **Jay Are (IRE)**[50] 5-11-1 0.. JoshuaMoore 86
(Gary Moore) *a towards rr: shkn up and lost tch 3 out* **80/1**
33- **11** *3 ¼* **Fight Commander (IRE)**[23] 4664 5-11-1 0....................... LeightonAspell 83
(Oliver Sherwood) *hld up in midfield: wl in tch whn mstke 3 out: stl chsng ldrs whn trapped bhd wkng rival bnd bef 2 out: no ch after* **33/1**
5U2- **12** *8* **Troufion (FR)**[13] 4863 5-10-8 110...................................... RyanHatch(7) 75
(Caroline Fryer) *pressed ldr: led 4th and sn clr: hdd & wknd 3 out* **66/1**
13 *15* **Minerfortyniner (IRE)**[112] 5-11-1 0.................................... DavidEngland 62
(Giles Smyly) *sweating: in tch: mstke 5th: wkng whn mstke 3 out: t.o* **100/1**
0- **14** *3 ½* **Now Ben (IRE)**[141] 2375 6-11-1 0...................................... BarryGeraghty 59
(Nicky Henderson) *mstke 2nd: nvr j. w any fluency after and sn dropped to rr: t.o after 3 out* **11/4**[2]
0- **15** *41* **Bahumbug**[37] 4401 4-10-7 0... AndrewThornton 14
(Seamus Mullins) *j.lft 2nd: a bhd: t.o after 7th* **150/1**
/54- **P** **Spring Steel (IRE)**[65] 3872 5-11-1 0.. DavidBass
(Ben Pauling) *fractious bef r: led to 4th: wknd rapidly 7th: t.o whn p.u bef 2 out* **20/1**

4m 35.4s (-9.30) **Going Correction** -0.675s/f (Firm)
WFA 4 from 5yo+ 7lb **16** Ran SP% **124.3**
Speed ratings (Par 105): **91,90,90,88,84 83,77,75,72,72 71,68,62,60,44**
CSF £139.59 TOTE £15.60: £4.00, £4.50, £1.40; EX 160.90 Trifecta £1018.30.
Owner Mrs Peter Prowting **Bred** G Staniek **Trained** Barbury Castle, Wilts

FOCUS
A decent race of its type, run at a fair pace. Winners should come from it. A big step up from Simply A Legend.

5089 A.P. SECURITY NOVICES' CHASE (17 fncs) 2m 5f 110y
2:30 (2:33) (Class 3) 5-Y-0+ **£7,576** (£2,286; £1,178; £623)

Form RPR
21P- **1** **Benefit Cut (IRE)**[45] 4244 8-11-4 135....................(t) SamTwiston-Davies 137+
(Renee Robeson) *racd enthusiastically: mde all: j.lft on occasions but soundly: rdn after 2 out: hrd pressed nr fin: hld on* **5/2**[2]
246- **2** *½* **Superior Quality (IRE)**[73] 3737 9-10-12 129.......................... NoelFehily 132+
(Charlie Longsdon) *hld up in last: chsd ldng pair 13th: creeping clsr whn mstke 2 out: rallied to go 2nd last: drvn and clsd on wnr flat: jst hld* **4/1**[3]
/01- **3** *7* **Kitegen (IRE)**[15] 4804 8-11-4 123.. CharliePoste 130
(Robin Dickin) *prom: chsd wnr 10th: rdn 4 out: cl enough 2 out: one pce and lost 2nd last* **6/1**
/21- **4** *37* **Farmer Matt (IRE)**[26] 4602 8-11-4 118...........................(t) PaddyBrennan 108
(Fergal O'Brien) *nt that fluent: hld up in last 4th: chsd ldng pair 11th to 13th: wknd 3 out: eased whn no ch last* **8/1**
1PP- **P** **The Italian Yob (IRE)**[37] 4395 6-11-4 131............................ BarryGeraghty
(Nick Williams) *chsd wnr to 10th: lost pl qckly and last fr next: bhd whn p.u bef 13th* **15/8**[1]

5m 17.5s (-8.50) **Going Correction** -0.35s/f (Good) **5** Ran SP% **108.8**
Speed ratings: **101,100,98,84,**
CSF £12.21 TOTE £3.30: £1.90, £2.60; EX 13.50 Trifecta £41.30.
Owner Howard Cooke & Terence Jenner **Bred** B Kendellen **Trained** Tyringham, Bucks

The Form Book Jumps, Raceform Ltd, Compton, RG20 6NL.

FOCUS
Quite a good novices' chase.

5090 A.P. SECURITY JUVENILE H'CAP HURDLE (9 hdls) 2m
3:00 (3:02) (Class 3) (0-135,131) 4-Y-O
£9,384 (£2,772; £1,386; £693; £346; £174)

Form RPR
216- **1** **Raven's Tower (USA)**[18] 4755 4-11-9 **128**............................ DavidBass 125+
(Ben Pauling) *hld up in last pair: prog 6th: rdn after 3 out: chsd ldng pair and mstke 2 out: clsd to ld immediately after last: drvn clr* **13/2**
232- **2** 3 ¼ **The Green Ogre**[24] 4632 4-11-6 **125**.............................. JoshuaMoore 118
(Gary Moore) *hmpd s: wl in tch: chsd ldrs 3 out: drvn next: kpt on fr last to take 2nd fnl stride* **25/1**
453- **3** shd **Ronaldinho (IRE)**[39] 4345 4-11-1 **120**.....................(b) WayneHutchinson 113
(Alan King) *t.k.h: allowed to ld after 2nd: mstke 5th: jnd 2 out: hdd immediately after last: kpt on but lost 2nd fnl stride* **7/1**
100- **4** nk **Town Mouse**[16] 4794 4-11-3 **125**.................................... TrevorWhelan[(3)] 118
(Neil King) *taken down early: fractious bef s: pressed ldr: chal and upsides 2 out to jst after last: nt qckn* **40/1**
211- **5** 4 ½ **Aalim**[58] 4003 4-11-7 **126**..(b[1]) DenisO'Regan 115
(John Ferguson) *hld up in last pair: stl last 3 out: prog and shkn up 2 out: tk 5th bef last: no imp after* **5/1**[2]
160- **6** 1 ¼ **Kitchapoly (FR)**[46] 4224 4-11-3 **122**.. NoelFehily 110
(Donald McCain) *racd wd: hld up in rr: prog 5th: on terms 3 out: fdd fr 2 out* **16/1**
402- **7** 1 **Mandy's Boy (IRE)**[20] 4722 4-10-11 **116**..........................(p) WillKennedy 103
(Ian Williams) *hld up in tch: gng wl enough 3 out: rdn and no imp on ldrs bef 2 out: plugged on* **25/1**
124- **8** 3 ¾ **Carry On Sydney**[22] 4679 4-11-2 **121**................................ LeightonAspell 105
(Oliver Sherwood) *hmpd s: hld up in rr: rdn 3 out: no prog and btn next* **8/1**
13- **9** 2 **Baltic Blade (IRE)**[203] 1524 4-10-9 **114**................................ JamieMoore 96
(Gary Moore) *in tch: rdn 3 out: no prog and btn next* **33/1**
120- **10** 2 ¼ **Dawalan (FR)**[18] 4755 4-11-12 **131**...................................(t) BarryGeraghty 111
(Nicky Henderson) *cl up: mstke 4th: nvr gng wl after: styd prom: nt fluent 3 out: drvn and wknd bef 2 out* **11/4**[1]
332- **11** 23 **Zamoyski**[39] 4345 4-11-5 **124**.. APMcCoy 83
(Steve Gollings) *led at modest pce to after 2nd: prom tl wknd and mstke 3 out: sn btn: eased after last* **11/2**[3]
330- **U** **Vandross (IRE)**[18] 4755 4-11-4 **126**................................... JackQuinlan[(3)]
(Neil King) *jinked and uns rdr s* **33/1**

3m 48.5s (1.10) **Going Correction** -0.675s/f (Firm) **12** Ran SP% **117.6**
Speed ratings: **70,68,68,68,65 65,64,62,61,60 49,**
CSF £155.71 CT £1174.85 TOTE £7.30: £2.40, £4.80, £2.20; EX 205.00 Trifecta £2110.70.
Owner Faithful Friends **Bred** Darley **Trained** Bourton-On-The-Water, Gloucs

FOCUS
A decent juvenile hurdle but one with a ragged start in which Vandross unseated his rider. The early pace was steady and the race developed into a dash for home from the second-last.

5091 COUNTRYSIDE ALLIANCE NOVICES' H'CAP CHASE (13 fncs) 2m 1f
3:35 (3:35) (Class 2) 5-Y-0+ **£25,992** (£7,632; £3,816; £1,908)

Form RPR
620- **1** **Manyriverstocross (IRE)**[19] 4742 9-11-7 **138**........... WayneHutchinson 148
(Alan King) *t.k.h: trckd ldrs: led bef 2 out where pressed: drvn after last: jnd 50yds out: battled on wl* **10/3**[1]
162- **2** shd **Bellenos (FR)**[38] 4373 6-11-3 **134**..(t) HarrySkelton 144
(Dan Skelton) *hld up in last pair: prog after 7th: trckd ldng trio after 3 out: clsd fr next: drvn to take 2nd flat: jnd wnr 50yds out: jst denied* **10/1**
120- **3** 2 ¾ **Brick Red**[19] 4737 7-11-12 **143**... AidanColeman 152
(Venetia Williams) *trckd ldrs: gng strly 3 out: produced to chal bef 2 out: rdn and stl in w a ch last: one pce* **7/1**[3]
242- **4** 1 ¾ **Able Deputy**[15] 4804 7-10-5 **122**.....................................(t) TomScudamore 128
(Kim Bailey) *hld up in last pair: prog but only 7th after 3 out: coaxed along to cl on ldrs after 2 out: rdn and one pce flat* **14/1**
312- **5** 4 ½ **Oyster Shell**[10] 4921 7-10-10 **130**.................................... JakeGreenall[(3)] 132
(Henry Daly) *w.w in midfield: chsd ldrs in 5th after 3 out: rdn bef next: one pce and no imp* **10/1**
142- **6** 1 ¾ **Witness In Court (IRE)**[22] 4684 7-10-13 **130**........................ APMcCoy 130
(Donald McCain) *led to 3rd: led again 6th: drvn 9th: hdd & wknd bef 2 out* **12/1**
351- **7** nk **Noche De Reyes (FR)**[10] 4919 5-10-10 **127**..................... PaddyBrennan 131+
(Tom George) *hld up towards rr: terrible blunder 7th and dropped to last: rallied 9th: 6th and in tch after 3 out: one pce* **9/2**[2]
113- **8** 21 **Funny Star (FR)**[56] 4055 6-11-9 **140**.................................(t) NickScholfield 123
(Paul Nicholls) *hld up in tch: j. slowly 4th and dropped to rr: nt fluent 8th and lost tch: bhd after: t.o* **14/1**
5- **9** 4 ½ **Vision Des Champs (FR)**[15] 4799 5-10-8 **125**.................. JamieMoore 102
(Gary Moore) *pressed ldr: led 3rd to 6th: wknd qckly 4 out: t.o* **33/1**
314- **P** **Ahyaknowyerself (IRE)**[19] 4742 8-11-7 **138**.......(b) SamTwiston-Davies
(Dr Richard Newland) *sn prom on outer: shkn up and lost pl fr 9th: rdn and bhd 3 out: p.u bef next* **8/1**
/15- **P** **Definite Dream (IRE)**[121] 2797 7-10-3 **120**.......................... PaulMoloney
(Evan Williams) *pressed ldng pair: lost pl fr 8th and nudged along: bhd whn shkn up after 3 out: eased and p.u bef next* **8/1**

4m 3.7s (-10.90) **Going Correction** -0.35s/f (Good) **11** Ran SP% **118.1**
Speed ratings: **111,110,109,108,106 105,105,95,93,**
CSF £37.02 CT £223.10 TOTE £3.60: £1.60, £3.40, £2.60; EX 40.90 Trifecta £506.20.
Owner Mrs M C Sweeney **Bred** Crone Stud Farms Ltd **Trained** Barbury Castle, Wilts

FOCUS
The second running of this valuable event, and a suitably competitive field. Steps up from the first two, and solid form, backed up by a good time.

5092 IRON STAND VETERANS' H'CAP CHASE (20 fncs) 3m
4:10 (4:10) (Class 2) (0-150,143)
10-Y-0+
£11,573 (£3,418; £1,709; £854; £427; £214)

Form RPR
PP0- **1** **Hey Big Spender (IRE)**[18] 4754 11-11-12 **143**.............. BrendanPowell 149
(Colin Tizzard) *wl plcd bhd ldrs: cl up 3 out: rdn to chse ldr next: drvn and styd on gamely to ld last 100yds* **22/1**
020- **2** ¾ **Time For Rupert (IRE)**[19] 4738 10-11-7 **138**.............(v[1]) DenisO'Regan 143
(Paul Webber) *trckd ldrs: wnt 2nd after 14th: led 4 out: drvn bef last: kpt on wl but hdd last 100yds* **5/1**[1]
512- **3** 2 ½ **Fredo (IRE)**[20] 4725 10-9-11 **119**.................................(v) RobertMcCarth[(5)] 123
(Ian Williams) *wl in tch: clsd on ldrs fr 15th: rdn to dispute 2nd 2 out: nt qckn and hld bef last: styd on again flat* **6/1**[3]
605- **4** ¾ **Gauvain (GER)**[90] 3414 12-11-8 **139**.....................................(t) TomO'Brien 141
(Philip Hobbs) *j. slowly 1st: towards rr: prog 16th: rdn in 6th after 3 out: clsd on ldrs 2 out: one pce bef last* **14/1**
P1P- **5** 4 **Bradley**[15] 4821 10-11-1 **132**.. PaddyBrennan 133
(Fergal O'Brien) *wl in rr and nt a fluent: hanging lft after 14th: wl adrift in 9th after 3 out: styd on fr next: nrst fin* **16/1**
400- **6** 5 **Junior**[15] 4821 11-11-8 **139**...(b) ConorO'Farrell 134
(David Pipe) *tried to ld but unable to and sn in rr: prog fr 15th: cl 5th 3 out and drvn: wknd bef next* **5/1**[1]
254- **7** 4 **Tullamore Dew (IRE)**[29] 4557 12-10-9 **126**........................ TomCannon 117
(Nick Gifford) *a in rr: rdn 16th and no prog: plugged on fr 2 out* **8/1**
F13- **8** 2 ¼ **Coole River (IRE)**[114] 2931 10-10-11 **128**............................ NoelFehily 119
(Emma Lavelle) *blnd 4th and dropped to rr: prog after 14th: wnt 2nd 4 out gng strly: wknd rapidly bef 2 out* **10/1**
/33- **9** 99 **Max Bygraves**[12] 4886 11-10-2 **119**......................... SamTwiston-Davies 19
(Kim Bailey) *trckd ldrs: steadily lost pl after 15th: wl btn 3 out: disputing poor 9th whn virtually p.u after last* **11/2**[2]
146- **P** **Pickamus (FR)**[17] 4769 11-11-2 **133**.................................. AndrewTinkler
(Henry Daly) *alternated ld tl advantage after 14th: hdd 4 out: sn wknd: bhd whn p.u and dismntd after last* **9/1**
15P- **P** **Fine Parchment (IRE)**[17] 4769 11-10-11 **135**.......(tp) MrHAABannister[(7)]
(Charlie Mann) *alternated ld at gd pce: exvagant leaps 13th and 14th: wknd next: bhd whn p.u bef 2 out* **28/1**
PPF- **P** **Well Refreshed**[20] 4732 10-11-8 **139**................................... JoshuaMoore
(Gary Moore) *nt fluent in rr: last whn blnd 9th: lost tch after mstke 12th: wl bhd whn p.u bef 4 out* **22/1**

5m 56.9s (-6.60) **Going Correction** -0.35s/f (Good) **12** Ran SP% **117.9**
Speed ratings: **97,96,95,95,94 92,91,90,57, ,**
CSF £128.42 CT £762.14 TOTE £23.70: £6.00, £2.60, £2.20; EX 143.30 Trifecta £1126.90.
Owner Brocade Racing **Bred** Oliver Brennan **Trained** Milborne Port, Dorset

FOCUS
Plenty of old favourites in a well contested race of its type. The first two are rated to their season's best.

5093 MOTHER'S DAY CONDITIONAL JOCKEYS' H'CAP HURDLE (13 hdls) 3m
4:45 (4:45) (Class 3) (0-135,135) 4-Y-0+
£5,630 (£1,663; £831; £415; £207; £104)

Form RPR
P23- **1** **Heronry (IRE)**[58] 4021 6-11-2 **128**................................ NicodeBoinville[(3)] 137
(Nicky Henderson) *wl plcd: cl up bhd ldrs 9th: led after next: drvn and jnd last: sustained battle flat: jst prevailed* **7/1**[1]
212- **2** nse **Kris Spin (IRE)**[36] 4415 6-11-9 **132**.. JakeGreenall 142+
(Richard Lee) *wl plcd: jnd ldrs after 9th: wnt 2nd bef 2 out: upsides whn mstke last: sustained chal again flat: jst pipped* **10/1**
062- **3** 10 **Azure Fly (IRE)**[21] 4697 6-11-0 **129**........................(tp) CharlieDeutsch[(6)] 129
(Charlie Longsdon) *hld up towards rr: prog fr 8th: trckd ldrs after 10th: rdn bef 2 out: wnt 3rd last but outpcd: hung bdly rt flat* **12/1**
322- **4** 1 **Howlongisafoot (IRE)**[35] 4442 5-10-13 **125**.................. HarryDerham[(3)] 124
(Paul Nicholls) *hld up in rr: stdy prog fr 8th: jnd ldng gp 10th: chsd ldng pair 2 out and in tch: drvn and nt qckn after* **7/1**[1]
501- **5** nk **Billy Twyford (IRE)**[29] 4556 7-11-4 **127**............................(t) AdamWedge 127
(Lawney Hill) *wl in tch: trckd ldrs fr 9th: cl up after 3 out: rdn whn mstke 2 out: fdd and awkward jump last* **20/1**
6F5- **6** 3 **Monetary Fund (USA)**[32] 4489 8-10-13 **125**............... HarryChalloner[(3)] 121
(Venetia Williams) *mostly in midfield: dropped to rr and rdn 9th: struggling after: poor 11th after 3 out: styd on wl fr next* **9/1**[3]
030- **7** ½ **So Fine (IRE)**[17] 4765 8-11-9 **135**.. JamesBest[(3)] 131
(Philip Hobbs) *wl in tch: rdn after 10th: cl up 3 out: wd bnd bef next and lost grnd: wknd after 2 out* **20/1**
120- **8** 5 **Bob Tucker (IRE)**[15] 4820 7-10-6 **120**............................. MikeyHamill[(5)] 113
(Brendan Powell) *wl plcd: chal fr 4 out tl wknd jst bef 2 out* **33/1**
150- **9** 3 ¼ **Moorlands Mist**[50] 4144 7-10-13 **130**.................... ThomasCheesman[(8)] 120
(Philip Hobbs) *hld up towards rr: bdly hmpd on inner bnd after 4th: rdn 7th: wl in rr 10th: sme prog fr 3 out: no hdwy after next* **9/1**[3]
025- **10** 10 **Silver Eagle (IRE)**[106] 3086 6-11-4 **130**..........................(t) EdCookson[(3)] 110
(Kim Bailey) *hld up in rr: nt fluent 7th: no prog after 9th: nt on terms fr next* **9/1**[3]
350- **11** 2 ¼ **Bygones Sovereign (IRE)**[15] 4805 8-10-7 **122**..........(p) TomBellamy[(6)] 101
(David Pipe) *unable to ld: chsd ldr tl blnd 4th: dropped rapidly to rr after 6th: struggling after* **12/1**
160- **12** 4 ½ **Staigue Fort**[42] 4300 6-11-6 **129**...................................... GavinSheehan 102
(Emma Lavelle) *in tch: lost pl sltly 8th: effrt fr 10th: chsd ldrs in 8th after 3 out and shkn up: wknd and eased 2 out* **22/1**
431- **13** 25 **Mysteree (IRE)**[23] 4650 6-10-13 **125**................................ CraigNichol[(3)] 76
(Lucinda Russell) *nt fluent 2nd: a in rr: lost tch u.p after 9th: t.o* **14/1**
060- **14** 7 **Seymour Eric**[15] 4820 9-10-8 **125**......................................(b) OllieGarner[(8)] 69
(Martin Keighley) *mde most and drvn into hurdles: hdd & wknd after 10th: t.o* **20/1**
23P- **15** 2 **Ugly Bug**[36] 4415 8-11-0 **123**.. JeremiahMcGrath 66
(Seamus Mullins) *a in rr: urged along after 6th: nvr a factor: t.o* **20/1**
230- **16** 4 ½ **Champagne Rian (IRE)**[71] 3775 6-10-7 **124**................... PaulO'Brien[(8)] 63
(Rebecca Curtis) *j.lft: prom: chsd ldr 4th tl bef 10th: wknd rapidly: t.o* **8/1**[2]
363- **P** **San Telm (IRE)**[23] 4662 9-10-10 **122**.................................. RyanHatch[(3)]
(Renee Robeson) *nt jump wl and a struggling in last: t.o fr 9th: p.u bef 2 out* **14/1**

5m 34.1s (-21.90) **Going Correction** -0.675s/f (Firm) **17** Ran SP% **130.3**
Speed ratings (Par 107): **109,108,105,105,105 104,104,102,101,97 97,95,87,85,84 82,**
CSF £71.38 CT £859.05 TOTE £8.20: £2.60, £2.40, £3.00, £1.80; EX 43.50 Trifecta £835.50.
Owner The Ten From Seven **Bred** John Morgan **Trained** Upper Lambourn, Berks

FOCUS
A competitive handicap hurdle. The first two drew clear as they contested a terrific finish. Steps up from the first two.

5094 FLEMING FAMILY & PARTNERS OPEN HUNTERS' CHASE (17 fncs) 2m 5f 110y
5:15 (5:16) (Class 5) 5-Y-0+ **£2,807** (£870; £435; £217)

Form RPR
123- **1** **Nowurhurlin (IRE)**[21] 4705 7-11-9 107.....................(v[1]) MrGSpencer[(7)] 122+
(Mrs S J Stilgoe) *trckd ldr: led after 11th: bounded clr fr next: in n.d after: nt fluent last: pushed out* **7/1**[3]

244- **2** *29* **Rob Conti (FR)**[21] 4705 9-12-1 130 MrDMaxwell[(5)] 100
(Philip Hobbs) *trckd ldng pair: nt fluent 7th: chal 11th: sn lft bhd by wnr and urged along: won battle for remote 2nd after last* **2/1**[2]
206- **3** *4* **Buck Mulligan**[172] 1815 9-12-6 127 MrJETudor 96
(Evan Williams) *led to after 11th: sn no ch w wnr: lost remote 2nd after last* **1/1**[1]
F21- **4** *24* **Martys Mission (IRE)**[31] 4518 12-12-3 109 MrDavidPrichard[(3)] 75
(Miss Becky Furber) *a last: lost tch 8th: sn wl t.o* **7/1**[3]
5m 20.4s (-5.60) **Going Correction** -0.35s/f (Good) 4 Ran SP% **108.3**
Speed ratings: **96,85,84,75**
CSF £20.72 TOTE £5.70; EX 17.40 Trifecta £31.50.
Owner Mrs S J Stilgoe **Bred** Thomas Meagher **Trained** Hutton-Le-Hole, North Yorks

FOCUS
A step up from the winer, and a case for rating the form higher through the second and third.
T/Jkpt: Not won. T/Plt: £153.30 to a £1 stake. Pool: £155,772.28 - 741.70 winning units. T/Qpdt: £42.60 to a £1 stake. Pool: £10,305.97 - 178.85 winning units. JN

5095 - 5098a (Foreign Racing) - See Raceform Interactive

4845 LIMERICK (R-H)

Sunday, March 30

OFFICIAL GOING: Hurdle course - heavy; chase course - soft to heavy

5099a HUGH MCMAHON MEMORIAL NOVICE CHASE (GRADE 2) (16 fncs) 3m
4:35 (4:36) 5-Y-0+ **£20,312** (£5,937; £2,812; £937)

RPR

1 **Touch The Eden (FR)**[29] 4565 7-11-3 136 PaulTownend 149+
(W P Mullins, Ire) *trckd ldrs: led briefly 3rd and at 6th: in front again 7 out: mstke 4 out: reasserted bef 2 out: styd on wl run-in* **2/1**[1]
2 *2 ½* **Letter Of Credit (IRE)**[21] 4709 9-11-3 139 PhillipEnright 145
(James Joseph Mangan, Ire) *hld up in rr tl tk clsr order to trck ldrs after 3 out: pushed along to chse ldr in 2nd after 2 out: no imp last: kpt on same pce* **7/1**
3 *1* **Folsom Blue (IRE)**[21] 4712 7-11-3 135 PCarberry 144+
(Conor O'Dwyer, Ire) *chsd ldrs: on terms whn slow at 3rd: prog into 2nd w a circ to r and sn led: slow 7 and 6 out where hdd and dropped bk to 4th: clsd again into 2nd bef 2 out: nt qckn appr last: kpt on same pce* **10/3**[3]
4 *18* **Rogue Angel (IRE)**[19] 4741 6-11-3 130 (b) BrianO'Connell 128
(M F Morris, Ire) *chsd ldrs in 3rd: prog into 2nd after 7 out and on terms 4 out: led after next but sn hdd and nt qckn bef 2 out: one pce* **9/2**
5 *16* **Domination**[14] 4849 7-11-3 DavyRussell 114
(C Byrnes, Ire) *w.w in 5th whn mstke 3rd: tk clsr order 5 out in 3rd: pressed ldrs after 3 out: sn rdn and no imp: eased* **3/1**[2]
6 *16* **Carrigeen Lonicera (IRE)**[14] 4856 8-10-10 109 (b) MissEALalor 87
(R H Lalor, Ire) *led: briefly hdd 3rd: extended advantage 5th but hdd next and dropped to 4th w a circ to r: sn no ex* **28/1**
7m 1.2s (26.20) 6 Ran SP% **115.5**
CSF £16.49 TOTE £2.20: £1.02, £4.30; DF 13.80 Trifecta £40.60.
Owner Mrs S Ricci **Bred** Earl Detouillon Raphael & Frederique **Trained** Muine Beag, Co Carlow

FOCUS
There was five grouped up travelling well three out. The second and third help set the standard.

5100 - 5101a (Foreign Racing) - See Raceform Interactive

4770 HEXHAM (L-H)

Monday, March 31

OFFICIAL GOING: Soft (heavy in places; 4.9)
Wind: Almost nil Weather: Overcast

5102 SIS NOVICES' HURDLE (8 hdls) 2m 110y
2:10 (2:11) (Class 4) 4-Y-0+ **£3,285** (£957; £479)

Form RPR

312- **1** **Mohawk Ridge**[30] 4548 8-11-6 120 BrianHughes 123+
(James Moffatt) *cl up: led after 2 out: drvn clr bef last: styd on wl* **13/2**[3]
341- **2** *6* **Tikkandemickey (IRE)**[18] 4772 8-11-5 120 DaraghBourke[(7)] 123
(Raymond Shiels) *nt fluent on occasions: chsd ldrs: mstke 3 out: drvn to chse wnr bef last: no imp* **4/1**[2]
124- **3** *6* **Circus Star (USA)**[16] 4813 6-11-5 116 MrJDixon[(7)] 116
(John Dixon) *led and clr to 1/2-way: rdn and hdd after 2 out: outpcd bef last* **14/1**
540- **4** *10* **Elfego Baca (IRE)**[9] 4956 5-10-7 0 [1] GrahamWatters[(7)] 94
(Lucinda Russell) *hld up: pushed along and hdwy bef 2 out: styd on fr last: nvr able to chal* **66/1**
1- **5** *¾* **Volcanic (FR)**[25] 4627 5-11-6 125 APMcCoy 99
(Donald McCain) *prom: drvn bef 2 out: wknd between last 2* **8/15**[1]
53F- **6** *5* **Marrakech Trader (NZ)**[39] 4364 7-11-0 0 WilsonRenwick 88
(Rose Dobbin) *midfield: rdn and outpcd after 3 out: btn after next* **66/1**
66- **7** *7* **Purple Harry**[37] 4431 6-10-9 0 SamanthaDrake[(5)] 81
(Tina Jackson) *midfield: outpcd 3 out: no imp bef next* **100/1**
00U- **8** *1 ¾* **Mighty Cliche (IRE)**[3] 5057 5-10-9 0 ColmMcCormack[(5)] 80
(Dianne Sayer) *hld up: struggling 4 out: btn bef 2 out* **200/1**
4/2- **9** *1 ¾* **Garth (IRE)**[25] 4631 6-10-9 0 DerekFox[(5)] 78
(Lucinda Russell) *hld up: mstke 3rd: struggling after 4 out: nvr on terms* **33/1**
4U0/ **10** *14* **Taxi Des Obeaux (FR)**[444] 3601 7-10-11 0 KyleJames[(3)] 64
(Philip Kirby) *hld up: outpcd after 4 out: btn after next* **50/1**
504- **11** *17* **Zuileka**[33] 4487 5-10-4 0 TonyKelly[(3)] 40
(James Moffatt) *hld up: struggling 4 out: sn btn* **100/1**
23- **P** **Miss Mohawk (IRE)**[20] 4743 5-10-7 95 DavidEngland
(Alan Brown) *in tch to 1/2-way: struggling 3 out: t.o whn p.u bef last* **33/1**
563- **P** **Boruma (IRE)**[25] 4627 4-10-7 0 JamesReveley
(Dianne Sayer) *hld up: blnd 2nd: struggling and p.u 4 out* **100/1**
04- **P** **Kings Folly (IRE)**[18] 4772 6-11-0 0 PeterBuchanan
(Lucinda Russell) *bhd: struggling 4 out: t.o whn p.u bef last* **40/1**
4m 29.9s (12.50) **Going Correction** +0.925s/f (Soft)
WFA 4 from 5yo+ 7lb 14 Ran SP% **122.0**
Speed ratings (Par 105): **107,104,101,96,96 93,90,89,89,82 74,,,**
CSF £32.86 TOTE £9.80: £2.70, £1.40, £2.10; EX 36.90 Trifecta £80.40.
Owner K Bowron **Bred** Old Mill Stud Ltd And Oomswell Ltd **Trained** Cartmel, Cumbria

FOCUS
Bends moved onto fresher line. The mist and fog meant precious little of the action could be seen. Any price bar the four previous winners in the line-up and they were out of their own with a circuit to run. The first two are on the upgrade in a well run race.

5103 CHOLLERFORD NOVICES' HURDLE (12 hdls) 3m
2:40 (2:40) (Class 4) 5-Y-0+ **£3,285** (£957; £479)

Form RPR

/10- **1** **Tonvadosa**[100] 3203 6-10-12 0 APMcCoy 125+
(Donald McCain) *hld up in tch: hdwy to press ldr after 3 out: led on bit between last 2: qcknd clr bef last: easily* **10/3**[3]
34P- **2** *8* **Strike Fast (IRE)**[23] 4673 9-10-9 0 HarryChalloner[(3)] 110
(William Kinsey) *chsd ldrs: drvn and outpcd bef 2 out: rallied bef last: styd on to take 2nd towards fin: no ch w easy wnr* **100/1**
523- **3** *nk* **Kilbree Chief (IRE)**[23] 4670 6-11-0 127 CraigNichol[(5)] 117
(Lucinda Russell) *chsd ldrs: drvn and outpcd after 3 out: rallied bef last: kpt on u.p run-in* **11/10**[1]
31- **4** *¾* **The Ramblin Kid**[37] 4428 6-11-5 125 WilsonRenwick 116
(Micky Hammond) *led: clr whn nt fluent 8th: jnd after 3 out: hdd between last 2: kpt on same pce run-in* **2/1**[2]
0- **P** **Messina Straights**[37] 4431 6-10-7 0 JonathonBewley[(5)]
(George Bewley) *in tch: struggling 7th: lost tch next: t.o whn p.u after 3 out* **100/1**
P- **P** **Rubyminx**[20] 4743 8-10-5 0 TomSiddall
(Lynn Siddall) *hld up: drvn and struggling 1/2-way: t.o whn p.u bef 4 out* **200/1**
6m 41.0s (32.00) **Going Correction** +1.55s/f (Heav) 6 Ran SP% **106.5**
Speed ratings: **108,105,105,104,**
CSF £77.81 TOTE £3.70: £1.90, £5.70; EX 36.50 Trifecta £120.80.
Owner T Meehan & D J Burke **Bred** Whitley Stud **Trained** Cholmondeley, Cheshire

FOCUS
Visibility was again very limited. A big step up from the easy winner, who looks decent.

5104 PRIMARY WEBSITES H'CAP CHASE (19 fncs) 3m 1f
3:10 (3:10) (Class 5) (0-100,99) 5-Y-0+ **£2,144** (£629; £314; £157)

Form RPR

213- **1** **Gibbstown (IRE)**[16] 4812 8-11-1 **93** (p) DerekFox[(5)] 97+
(Paul Stafford, Ire) *nt fluent early: hld up in tch: hdwy and prom 13th: effrt and led appr last: drvn and styd on wl run-in* **11/2**[3]
PU1- **2** *3* **Samson Collonges (FR)**[18] 4775 8-10-7 **83** TonyKelly[(3)] 82
(Rebecca Menzies) *prom: nt fluent 8th: pushed along 3 out: rallied after next: effrt and chsd wnr last: kpt on same pce run-in* **6/1**
3/P- **3** *5* **Mr Chippy (IRE)**[86] 3528 10-11-5 **92** (b[1]) HenryBrooke 86
(Donald McCain) *cl up: hit 12th: led bef 3 out to appr last: rdn and outpcd run-in* **10/1**
143- **4** *17* **Esme Rides A Gaine**[18] 4775 12-10-6 **79** BrianHarding 55
(Christopher Wilson) *bhd and sn pushed along: plenty to do 4 out: plugged on fr 2 out: no ch w first three* **15/2**
324- **5** *28* **Farm Pixie (IRE)**[27] 4606 8-11-3 **97** GrahamWatters[(7)] 45
(Ann Hamilton) *hld up in tch: drvn and outpcd after 4 out: struggling fr next* **7/1**
3U0- **6** *9* **Mannered**[29] 4577 9-11-0 **92** JohnDawson[(5)] 31
(John Wade) *t.k.h: led to bef 3 out: rdn and wknd next* **16/1**
PP2- **P** **Filbert Fox (IRE)**[18] 4775 8-10-6 **79** (p) PeterBuchanan
(Alistair Whillans) *chsd ldrs: lost pl 8th: struggling and p.u bef 13th* **7/2**[1]
124- **F** **Dingo Bay**[16] 4812 8-11-9 **96** BrianHughes
(John Wade) *hld up in tch: rdn along and outpcd after 4 out: nrly 6 l down and no imp whn fell next* **4/1**[2]
7m 17.9s (45.70) **Going Correction** +1.90s/f (Heav) 8 Ran SP% **111.1**
Speed ratings: **102,101,99,94,85 82,,**
CSF £36.09 CT £308.43 TOTE £6.40: £2.00, £1.90, £3.20; EX 33.60 Trifecta £523.40.
Owner Mrs L Skelly **Bred** John And Ann Goold **Trained** Oldtown, Co. Dublin

FOCUS
A low-grade staying handicap chase. The first two are rated in line with recent runs.

5105 ST JOHN LEE H'CAP HURDLE (10 hdls) 2m 4f 110y
3:40 (3:41) (Class 4) (0-120,118) 4-Y-0+ **£3,119** (£915; £457; £228)

Form RPR

42P- **1** **One For Harry (IRE)**[88] 3499 6-11-12 **118** BrianHarding 123+
(Nicky Richards) *disp ld: nt fluent 3rd and 6th: led whn nt fluent last: drvn and styd on wl* **11/8**[1]
432- **2** *2 ¼* **Persian Herald**[27] 4608 6-10-9 **108** DaraghBourke[(7)] 109
(Sue Smith) *led to bef last: rallied u.p and ev ch run-in: kpt on same pce towards fin* **5/2**[2]
2FF- **3** *3 ¼* **Romany Ryme**[37] 4428 8-11-5 **116** JonathonBewley[(5)] 114
(George Bewley) *t.k.h: chsd ldrs: pushed along and outpcd bef last: no imp run-in* **4/1**[3]
540- **4** *23* **Master Of The Hall (IRE)**[12] 4897 10-11-11 **117** (p) WilsonRenwick 92
(Micky Hammond) *prom tl rdn and wknd between last 2* **11/1**
315- **P** **Morning Time (IRE)**[131] 2597 8-11-1 **107** PeterBuchanan
(Lucinda Russell) *hld up in tch: drvn and outpcd appr 2 out: sn btn: t.o whn p.u bef last* **11/1**
5m 41.4s (28.90) **Going Correction** +1.55s/f (Heav) 5 Ran SP% **107.3**
Speed ratings (Par 105): **106,105,103,95,**
CSF £5.05 TOTE £2.60: £2.60, £1.10; EX 5.70 Trifecta £13.00.
Owner The Fife Boys + 1 **Bred** Berry Farms **Trained** Greystoke, Cumbria

FOCUS
The visbility had improved a good deal ahead of this weak-looking handicap hurdle. The first two matched strides much of the way. The form is rated around the third.

5106 HEXHAM INTERACTIVE H'CAP HURDLE (12 hdls) 3m
4:10 (4:10) (Class 5) (0-100,100) 4-Y-0+ **£1,949** (£572; £286; £143)

Form RPR

303- **1** **Master Murphy (IRE)**[18] 4774 9-10-8 **89** AlistairFindlay[(7)] 96+
(Jane Walton) *cl up: hit 3rd: led 8th: mstke next: pushed along after 2 out: styd on wl fr last* **11/4**[1]
025- **2** *5* **Mootabar (IRE)**[16] 4816 7-10-8 **85** JonathanEngland[(3)] 85
(Chris Fairhurst) *hld up: smooth hdwy to chse ldrs 3 out: stl gng wl after next: effrt and chsd wnr bef last: rdn: edgd lft and one pce run-in* **8/1**
B32- **3** *2 ½* **Bollin Fiona**[18] 4774 10-11-2 **100** RyanNichol[(10)] 98
(Donald Whillans) *prom: hdwy and ev ch fr 4 out: rdn and one pce bef last* **6/1**[3]
354- **4** *10* **Amore Mio (GER)**[24] 4649 9-11-12 **100** (tp) PeterBuchanan 90
(Lucinda Russell) *mde most to 8th: styd upsides: drvn bef 2 out: wknd appr last* **5/1**[2]

226- **5** *73* **Saddlers Mot**[10] 4938 10-11-5 **98**.................................(b) JohnDawson(5) 13
(Karen Tutty) *nt fluent in rr: struggling 4 out: t.o fnl 2* **8/1**

654- **P** **Easement**[289] 751 11-10-10 **89**..............................(p) JonathonBewley(5)
(George Bewley) *cl up tl rdn and wknd after 3 out: t.o whn p.u between last 2* **12/1**

F60- **P** **Northern Acres**[16] 4816 8-10-13 **87**................................. LucyAlexander
(N W Alexander) *hld up: nt fluent 7th: mstke 3 out: rdn and wknd next: t.o whn p.u bef last* **17/2**

350- **F** **Isaacstown Lad (IRE)**[18] 4776 7-11-7 **100**....................(p) CraigNichol(5)
(William Amos) *in tch: fell 1st* **10/1**

34P- **P** **Blue Cove**[18] 4779 9-10-0 **74** oh4... TomSiddall
(Lynn Siddall) *hld up in tch: stdy hdwy and cl up 4 out: rdn and wknd appr 2 out: p.u bef last* **16/1**

6m 50.0s (41.00) **Going Correction** +1.55s/f (Heavy) **9** Ran SP% **113.0**
Speed ratings (Par 103): **93,91,90,87,62** , , ,
CSF £24.55 CT £120.14 TOTE £3.70: £2.20, £1.60, £2.00; EX 19.10 Trifecta £152.30.
Owner Mrs J M Walton **Bred** R Ryan **Trained** Otterburn, Northumberland

FOCUS
An unrelenting gallop and a true test in the conditions. The whole course was now in view from the stands. The form is rated around the second and third.

5107 SIS H'CAP CHASE (15 fncs) 2m 4f 110y
4:40 (4:40) (Class 5) (0-100,96) 5-Y-O+ **£2,258** (£658; £329)

Form RPR

054- **1** **Baileys Concerto (IRE)**[15] 4834 8-11-12 **96**.................. JamesReveley 104+
(Dianne Sayer) *hld up: smooth hdwy to chse ldrs 4 out: effrt and rdn appr last: styd on to ld last 50yds: drvn out* **9/2**[2]

P00- **2** *1* **Double Whammy**[18] 4774 8-11-6 **95**..............................(b) CraigNichol(5) 102
(Iain Jardine) *cl up: led after 9th: rdn and hrd pressed fr 2 out: hdd last 50yds: kpt on same pce* **18/1**

03P- **3** *2* **I Know The Code (IRE)**[18] 4778 9-10-10 **80**........................ TomSiddall 84
(Lynn Siddall) *hld up in tch: stdy hdwy 4 out: chal 2 out to run-in: kpt on: hld last 75yds* **10/1**

534- **4** *7* **Forestside (IRE)**[20] 4748 9-10-5 **75**.................................... BrianHughes 73
(Barry Murtagh) *cl up: rdn 2 out: outpcd bef last* **6/1**[3]

4P3- **5** *12* **Alexander Oats**[39] 4380 11-9-11 **70** oh3...................(b) HarryChalloner(3) 58
(Robert Goldie) *hld up in tch: stdy hdwy after 4 out: rdn and wknd after next* **11/1**

344- **P** **Panthers Run**[29] 4581 14-9-13 **72** oh10 ow2.................(t) JohnKington(3)
(Jonathan Haynes) *led to after 9th: sn struggling: p.u next* **50/1**

325/ **P** **Pen Gwen (FR)**[393] 4548 11-10-4 **77**.................................... KyleJames(3)
(Philip Kirby) *chsd ldrs: lost pl 8th: struggling and p.u 10th* **22/1**

020- **P** **Millers Reef (IRE)**[18] 4774 8-11-11 **95**.............................. WilsonRenwick
(Keith Dalgleish) *prom tl rdn and wknd after 4 out: p.u bef next* **9/2**[2]

PPP- **P** **Heart O Annandale (IRE)**[24] 4652 7-10-4 **77**.............. EwanWhillans(3)
(Alistair Whillans) *j. bdly in rr: lost tch 9th: p.u next* **3/1**[1]

532- **P** **Indigo Island (IRE)**[10] 4940 5-11-5 **89**............................(p) HenryBrooke
(Robert Bewley) *in tch: hit 9th: sn rdn and outpcd next: wknd and p.u bef 4 out* **9/1**

5m 54.1s (40.60) **Going Correction** +1.90s/f (Heavy) **10** Ran SP% **114.6**
Speed ratings: **98,97,96,94,89** , , , ,
CSF £74.98 CT £766.98 TOTE £5.10: £1.50, £7.10, £4.60; EX 106.80 Trifecta £1238.80.
Owner United Five Racing & Andrew Sayer **Bred** Ronan Keane **Trained** Hackthorpe, Cumbria

FOCUS
The fog and mist had returned ahead of this low-grade, strongly run handicap chase. The winner should still be competitive when reassessed.

5108 HEXHAM FOR TOURISTS MAIDEN OPEN NATIONAL HUNT FLAT RACE (DIV I) 2m 110y
5:10 (5:20) (Class 6) 4-6-Y-O **£1,711** (£498; £249)

Form RPR

1 **Aniknam (FR)** 4-10-11 0.. BarryKeniry 109+
(Philip Kirby) *t.k.h: hld up: smooth hdwy and prom 1/2-way: led gng wl over 2f out: qcknd clr on bit: readily* **6/4**[1]

34- **2** *10* **Redkalani (IRE)**[37] 4431 6-11-4 0.. JamesReveley 101
(Keith Reveley) *hld up in tch: rdn and outpcd 1/2-way: rallied over 4f out: effrt and rdn 3f out: chsd (clr) wnr ins fnl f: no imp* **7/2**[3]

3 *2* **Smooth Stepper** 5-11-1 0.. JonathanEngland(3) 99
(Sue Smith) *midfield on outside: stdy hdwy 1/2-way: effrt and chsd wnr over 2f out to ins fnl f: kpt on same pce* **11/1**

05- **4** *23* **Bossy Beccy**[26] 4618 5-10-6 0.. MissCWalton(5) 69
(James Walton) *midfield: lost pl after 6f: sn struggling: rallied over 2f out: styd on: nvr able to chal* **22/1**

0- **5** *3* **Alwaysrecommended (IRE)**[109] 3042 5-10-11 0.......... AlistairFindlay(7) 73
(Jane Walton) *led to over 2f out: sn rdn and wknd* **16/1**

00- **6** *3 ¼* **New Zafeen (IRE)**[13] 4895 4-10-8 0...................................... TonyKelly(3) 63
(Rebecca Menzies) *hld up: stdy hdwy and in tch 1/2-way: rdn and wknd over 2f out* **66/1**

7 *3 ¼* **Daring Exit** 5-11-4 0.. HenryBrooke 67
(Robert Bewley) *prom: rdn over 4f out: wknd over 2f out* **14/1**

P0/ **8** *12* **Jasani**[362] 5125 6-11-4 0.. DavidEngland 55
(Alan Brown) *cl up tl rdn and wknd over 3f out* **20/1**

3- **9** *99* **Dreamisi (IRE)**[95] 3276 5-11-4 0.. BrianHughes
(James Ewart) *chsd ldrs: struggling fr 1/2-way: virtually p.u fnl 3f* **11/4**[2]

4m 36.0s (23.30) **Going Correction** +1.55s/f (Heavy)
WFA 4 from 5yo+ 7lb **9** Ran SP% **120.4**
Speed ratings: **107,102,101,90,89 87,86,80,33**
CSF £7.19 TOTE £3.10: £1.30, £1.20, £2.30; EX 7.70 Trifecta £44.20.
Owner W A Bethell **Bred** Daniel Pironneau & Mme Daniel Pironneau **Trained** Middleham, N Yorks

FOCUS
A soundly run bumper but probably a weak one, although the winner could be decent.

5109 HEXHAM FOR TOURISTS MAIDEN OPEN NATIONAL HUNT FLAT RACE (DIV II) 2m 110y
5:40 (5:45) (Class 6) 4-6-Y-O **£1,711** (£374; £374)

Form RPR

1 **Never Never (IRE)**[29] 4589 4-10-11 0.. APMcCoy 97
(Donald McCain) *t.k.h: led to over 4f out: rallied and regained ld over 2f out: sn hrd pressed: drvn and hld on gamely fnl f* **6/4**[1]

2 *1 ¾* **Present Flight (IRE)**[92] 5-10-13 0.................................. CraigNichol(5) 102
(Lucinda Russell) *prom: smooth hdwy to ld over 4f out: rdn and hdd over 2f out: rallied and upsides over 1f out: one pce last 75yds: jnd for 2nd on line* **3/1**[2]

2 *dht* **Toarmandowithlove (IRE)** 6-10-1 0......................... JamesCorbett(10) 95
(Susan Corbett) *hld up: rdn and outpcd over 5f out: rallied over 2f out: edgd lft and styd on on fnl f to dead-heat for 2nd on line* **66/1**

4- **4** *7* **Transient Bay (IRE)**[29] 4582 4-10-8 0.................................. KyleJames(3) 88
(Philip Kirby) *chsd ldrs: drvn and outpcd over 4f out: rallied 2f out: no imp fnl f* **10/1**[3]

5- **5** *4* **Major Ridge (IRE)**[23] 4671 5-11-4 0...................................... HenryBrooke 91
(Robert Bewley) *prom: rdn and outpcd over 3f out: no imp fr 2f out* **22/1**

24- **6** *3 ¼* **Warriors Tale**[73] 3760 5-11-4 0... WilsonRenwick 88
(Nicky Richards) *prom tl rdn and wknd fr over 2f out* **3/1**[2]

7 *55* **Fort Canning** 5-11-4 0.. BrianHarding 33
(William Amos) *hld up in tch: drvn and outpcd over 4f out: sn btn: t.o* **28/1**

8 *80* **Golden Orchid (IRE)** 5-10-11 0......................................[1] BrianHughes
(Miss Clare Louise Cannon, Ire) *hld up: struggling over 4f out: t.o* **33/1**

P **Clan Legend** 4-10-11 0... LucyAlexander
(N W Alexander) *bhd: lost tch 1/2-way: p.u 5f out* **12/1**

4m 49.1s (36.40) **Going Correction** +1.55s/f (Heavy)
WFA 4 from 5yo+ 7lb **9** Ran SP% **119.0**
Speed ratings: **76,75,75,71,70 68,42,4,**
WIN: 2.20 Never Never; PL: 1.10 Never Never, 2.00 Present Flight, 7.60 Toarmandowithlove; EX: 39.20, 3.90; CSF: 3.07, 71.09; TC: ; TF: 116.80, 162.30;.
Owner Paul & Clare Rooney **Bred** Grangemore Stud **Trained** Cholmondeley, Cheshire

FOCUS
Very little could be seen of division two of this bumper, which was run in a very slow time. The winner is rated below the level of his Irish form.
T/Plt: £439.40 to a £1 stake. Pool: £83,628.28 - 138.93 winning units. T/Qpdt: £19.80 to a £1 stake. Pool: £8585.81 - 319.35 winning units. RY

4715 PLUMPTON (L-H)
Monday, March 31

OFFICIAL GOING: Good (chs 7.6, hdl 7.8)
Wind: virtually nil Weather: overcast, dry

5110 GEORGE DIGWEED SPORTING AGENCY LTD. NOVICES' HURDLE (12 hdls) 2m 5f
2:20 (2:20) (Class 4) 4-Y-O+ **£3,249** (£954; £477; £238)

Form RPR

314- **1** **Ellnando Queen**[43] 4301 6-10-5 0.................................. GavinSheehan(3) 117
(Warren Greatrex) *chsd ldrs: bmpd and lost pl 1st: in tch in midfield: 4th and outpcd 9th: rallied and chsd ldng pair after 3 out: wandered and chal 2 out: led last: forged ahd flat: styd on strly* **9/2**

/11- **2** *2* **Sergeant Mattie (IRE)**[21] 4715 6-11-6 130................ CharlieDeutsch(7) 134
(Charlie Longsdon) *chsd ldr tl 3rd: j.rt and bmpd rival 1st: chsd ldng pair after tl jnd ldr 3 out: sn led: rdn and pressed 2 out: hdd last: no ex and outpcd fnl 100yds* **7/4**[1]

130- **3** *11* **Strollawaynow (IRE)**[23] 4680 7-11-7 130.............................. TomCannon 119
(David Arbuthnot) *led tl hdd and drvn bef 3 out: wknd bef 2 out: lft disputing 3rd 2 out: plugged on but no ch w ldng pair* **5/2**[2]

024- **4** *nse* **Mercers Court (IRE)**[19] 4761 6-10-12 0........................ TrevorWhelan(3) 113
(Neil King) *t.k.h: hld up off the pce in last quartet: sme hdwy but only modest 6th after 8th: no imp on ldrs fr 3 out: lft disputing 3rd and hmpd 2 out: plugged on but no ch w ldng pair* **33/1**

5PP- **5** *49* **Tigridia (IRE)**[21] 4715 7-10-8 89.. MarcGoldstein 61
(Sarah Wall) *in tch in midfield: struggling 6th: 6th and losing tch 9th: t.o 3 out* **150/1**

0- **6** *43* **Wilde And Willing (IRE)**[50] 4171 6-11-1 0........................ AndrewThornton 29
(Seamus Mullins) *hld up off the pce in last quartet: rdn and struggling after 7th: t.o after next* **100/1**

P **Yajber (USA)**[234] 5-11-1 0..(t) MattieBatchelor
(Sheena West) *a wl off the pce in last quartet: struggling and rdn after 5th: t.o and p.u 8th* **66/1**

/0P- **P** **Harlequins Gleams**[35] 4467 6-11-1 0..................................... AdamWedge
(Anna Newton-Smith) *hld up off the pce in last quartet: mstke 5th: j.lft and struggling 7th: t.o after next tl p.u 2 out* **100/1**

01F- **F** **Count Danilo (IRE)**[12] 4901 5-11-7 0.............................. TomScudamore 124
(David Pipe) *j.big at sme flights: chsd ldr 3rd tl led bef 3 out: hdd and drvn wl bef 2 out: 3rd and btn whn fell heavily 2 out* **3/1**[3]

5m 2.3s (-14.70) **Going Correction** -0.35s/f (Good) **9** Ran SP% **115.2**
Speed ratings (Par 105): **114,113,109,109,90 73**, , ,
CSF £13.24 TOTE £9.60: £1.50, £1.30, £1.10; EX 16.20 Trifecta £39.20.
Owner Mrs R Vaughan **Bred** Mrs R I Vaughan **Trained** Upper Lambourn, Berks

FOCUS
A brisk gallop, which soon had the field strung out, sorted out the better-class runners from the rest. The winner improved to the level of his bumper win.

5111 SIS CONDITIONAL JOCKEYS' H'CAP CHASE (14 fncs) 2m 4f
2:50 (2:51) (Class 5) (0-100,100) 5-Y-O+ **£2,924** (£858; £429; £214)

Form RPR

P52- **1** **Kastani Beach (IRE)**[24] 4659 8-11-12 **100**...................... JeremiahMcGrath 107+
(Seamus Mullins) *hld up towards rr: stdy hdwy 7th: jnd ldrs 11th: wnt clr w rival and rdn after 3 out: blnd and lft 5 l clr next: drvn flat: kpt on and a holding on* **8/1**

422- **2** *1 ¼* **Mia's Vic (IRE)**[21] 4716 9-11-7 **100**......................(t) ThomasCheesman(5) 104
(Edward Creighton) *in tch in midfield: hdwy to chse ldrs after 9th: 3rd and outpcd u.p after 3 out: lft 5 l 2nd next: kpt on u.p flat* **7/1**

404- **3** *8* **Ata Boy (IRE)**[18] 4780 8-9-7 **75**.. DanielHiskett(8) 72
(Richard Phillips) *chsd ldrs tl 9th: outpcd and u.p 11th: lft 5th 2 out: wnt 3rd between last 2: styd on but no threat to ldng pair* **33/1**

542- **4** *4* **Bit Of A Clown (IRE)**[89] 3472 8-11-2 **90**........................(b[1]) JoshuaMoore 83
(Nick Gifford) *chsd ldr tl after 4th: styd chsng ldrs tl 5th and outpcd after 10th: no imp u.p 3 out: lft 4th next: plugged on* **7/2**[1]

3F3- **5** *1 ¼* **Bobbits Way**[21] 4716 9-10-10 **84**..(p) JamesBest 78
(Alan Jones) *t.k.h: chsd ldrs: wnt 2nd 8th tl mstke 3 out: sn rdn and outpcd: btn whn lft 4th next: plugged on* **9/1**

032- **6** *12* **Topaze Collonges (FR)**[19] 4762 7-11-6 **97**...................... KielanWoods(3) 81
(Charlie Longsdon) *led tl after 4th: rdn after next: mstke 7th: sn drvn and lost pl: no ch whn mstke 11th: plugged on* **13/2**[3]

063- **7** *6* **Tom Sang (FR)**[13] 4890 7-10-2 **76**..................................(t) ThomasGarner 57
(Jamie Snowden) *hld up in rr: blnd bdly 1st: blnd again 4th: sme hdwy: blnd and btn 10th: no ch fr next* **8/1**

4PF- **8** *11* **Brians Well (IRE)**[21] 4716 7-11-7 **95**..........................(t) ConorShoemark 61
(Brendan Powell) *midfield whn mstke 1st: dropped to rr 3rd: wknd after 10th: t.o 3 out* **12/1**

032- **U** **Johnnys Legacy (IRE)**[8] 4985 7-11-0 **88**......................(p) PeterCarberry 95
(Conor Dore) *j.lft: chsd ldrs tl led after 4th: jnd 11th: rdn and wnt clr w wnr after 3 out: blnd: pckd and uns rdr 2 out* **5/1**[2]

065- P **Caspian Piper (IRE)**[18] 4778 7-10-8 **85**..........................(b) ConorRing(3)
(Hugo Froud) *reminders sn after s: a in rr: rdn and struggling 7th: t.o 11th tl p.u 2 out* **9/1**

5m 0.9s (-6.40) **Going Correction** -0.55s/f (Firm) **10** Ran SP% **117.6**
Speed ratings: **90,89,86,84,84 79,77,72, ,**
CSF £63.72 CT £1757.36 TOTE £12.70: £2.80, £2.10, £6.00; EX 61.20 Trifecta £679.40.
Owner G B Balding & Philippa Downing **Bred** Harold McGahern **Trained** Wilsford-Cum-Lake, Wilts

FOCUS
The pace was only respectable, but it looked a fair tempo for all, with the hold-up horses having every chance. The second and third set the level.

5112 HOWDEN INSURANCE BROKING GROUP H'CAP HURDLE (12 hdls) 2m 5f
3:20 (3:20) (Class 4) (0-115,114) 4-Y-O+ **£4,548** (£1,335; £667; £333)

Form RPR

/54- **1** **Laughton Park**[19] 4760 9-10-7 **98**.................................... MichealNolan(3) 107+
(Suzy Smith) *hld up in tch: hdwy to join ldrs 9th: led sn after 3 out: clr and in command next: r.o wl: eased towards fin* **13/2**[2]

/35- **2** *5* **Ussee (FR)**[22] 4698 6-10-13 **104**.................................... KielanWoods(3) 106
(Ben Case) *t.k.h: wl in tch in midfield: chsd ldrs after 4th: drvn and chsd clr wnr bef 2 out: r.o but no ch w wnr* **9/1**

065- **3** *12* **Pembroke House**[28] 4596 7-11-3 **105**.................................... WillKennedy 96
(Sarah-Jayne Davies) *led tl rdn and hdd after 3 out: no ex and btn 3rd bef next: wknd between last 2* **14/1**

34P- **4** *1 3/4* **Torero**[30] 4555 5-11-6 **108**..(p) JoshuaMoore 98
(Diana Grissell) *in tch in midfield: hdwy 8th: 4th and no imp u.p after 3 out: plugged on* **14/1**

40F- **5** *3* **Stay In My Heart (IRE)**[16] 4801 5-10-13 **101**...................... TomCannon 88
(Laura Mongan) *chsd ldr tl after 2nd: styd prom: wnt 2nd again tl bef 3 out: drvn and btn after 3 out: wknd next* **16/1**

453- **6** *1* **Mr Muddle**[31] 4539 7-11-12 **114**.. MarcGoldstein 102
(Sheena West) *jnd ldr after 2nd tl rdn and lost pl after 8th: mstke 9th: n.d but plugged on again after 3 out* **12/1**

130- **7** *6* **Fountains Mary**[10] 4933 6-11-2 **104**................................(t) AidanColeman 85
(Anthony Honeyball) *chsd ldrs tl 3rd: steadily lost pl: towards rr and drvn w no rspnse after 8th: plugged on but n.d fr 3 out* **13/2**[2]

5P3- **8** *hd* **Amazing Scenes (IRE)**[60] 3988 5-10-12 **100**...............(t) BrendanPowell 82
(Brendan Powell) *t.k.h: wl in tch in midfield: mstke 6th: rdn and btn 3 out: wknd bef next* **7/1**[3]

304- **9** *1* **Amazing D'Azy (IRE)**[103] 3159 6-11-3 **105**............. SamTwiston-Davies 86
(Kim Bailey) *in tch in midfield: hdwy after 8th: btn 3 out: wknd and no ch whn mstke next* **5/1**[1]

444- **10** *7* **Garde Ville (FR)**[25] 4629 4-10-5 **106**.........................(p) ThomasGarner(5) 71
(Lisa Williamson) *in tch in last trio: clsd after 8th: btn 3 out: wknd wl bef next* **14/1**

/0P- **11** *nk* **Ctappers**[33] 4501 5-10-12 **100**..(p) TomO'Brien 73
(Michael Madgwick) *in tch in rr: effrt after 9th: sn btn and wknd next* **33/1**

12 *31* **Lord Lir (IRE)**[188] 1653 8-11-1 **103**.................................... MichaelByrne 48
(Tim Vaughan) *a towards rr: in tch: drvn and no hdwy after 8th: wl bhd after 3 out: t.o* **20/1**

50P- **P** **Berkeley Avenue**[5] 5034 5-10-13 **104**.......................(tp) GavinSheehan(3)
(Warren Greatrex) *j.rt and racd wd: chsd ldrs tl lost pl rapidly bef 3 out: t.o whn p.u 2 out* **8/1**

5m 6.6s (-10.40) **Going Correction** -0.35s/f (Good)
WFA 4 from 5yo+ 8lb **13** Ran SP% **118.2**
Speed ratings (Par 105): **105,103,98,97,96 96,94,93,93,90 90,79,**
CSF £63.55 CT £798.30 TOTE £5.00: £1.90, £3.90, £6.80; EX 73.10 Trifecta £1351.40 Part won..
Owner The Sams Partnership **Bred** R Bowers **Trained** Lewes, E Sussex

FOCUS
A solid pace made this a decent test, and the form should work out at this modest level. A personal best from the winner with the second close to her best.

5113 UNDERWRITING EXCHANGE H'CAP CHASE (18 fncs) 3m 2f
3:50 (3:53) (Class 5) (0-100,95) 5-Y-O+ **£3,249** (£954; £477; £238)

Form RPR

3P3- **1** **Ballyvoneen (IRE)**[12] 4905 9-10-6 **78**..........................(p) TrevorWhelan(3) 94
(Neil King) *chsd ldrs: effrt after 3 out: drvn and styd on between last 2: gd jump and chsd ldr last: led fnl 100yds: drvn out* **7/2**[1]

PPP- **2** *1 1/4* **Dushy Valley (IRE)**[21] 4720 7-10-0 **69** oh1......................(b) JamieMoore 84
(Paul Henderson) *mde most: drvn and wnt clr w rival after 3 out: battled on and forged ahd last: hdd and no ex fnl 100yds* **7/1**[3]

222- **3** *6* **Flugzeug**[21] 4720 6-9-11 **69** oh5.............................. WayneKavanagh(3) 79
(Seamus Mullins) *t.k.h: hld up in tch in midfield: hdwy to join ldr 15th: wnt clr w ldr after 3 out: drvn and j.rt next: j. bdly rt last: wknd flat* **4/1**[2]

4P4- **4** *1/2* **Roparta Avenue**[21] 4716 7-11-0 **83**.................................... MarcGoldstein 93
(Diana Grissell) *chsd ldrs: mstke 3rd: rdn after 3 out: 3rd whn j.rt next: rallied between last 2: no ex last: wknd flat* **16/1**

253- **5** *8* **Roseneath (IRE)**[24] 4657 10-11-7 **95**..........................(tp) KillianMoore(5) 100
(Alex Hales) *in tch in midfield: clsd and wl in tch 13th: cl 5th whn blnd 15th: mstke next: drvn and btn after 3 out* **12/1**

213- **6** *5* **Alteranthela (IRE)**[21] 4720 10-11-0 **83**................................(b) ColinBolger 80
(Richard Rowe) *chsd ldr tl 15th: wknd u.p bef 2 out* **8/1**

3P0- **7** *22* **Uncle Pettit (IRE)**[13] 4884 6-10-8 **80**............................ GavinSheehan(3) 70
(Jonathan Portman) *racd wd: chsd ldrs: blnd 5th: cl 7th and mstke 15th: wknd u.p after next: t.o* **7/1**[3]

5PU- **P** **Tchang Goon (FR)**[17] 4795 10-9-9 **71** oh7 ow2.............(p) MrHGMiller(7)
(Zoe Davison) *a in rr: rdn and lost tch after 12th: t.o whn p.u 14th* **33/1**

433- **P** **Airmen's Friend (IRE)**[22] 4695 8-11-12 **95**.........................(tp) NoelFehily
(Charlie Mann) *in tch in last trio: mstke 7th: rdn and struggling after 12th: lost tch after next: t.o whn p.u 15th* **4/1**[2]

600- **P** **Cool Fantasy (IRE)**[13] 4884 5-10-5 **75**.................................... AdamWedge
(Caroline Keevil) *in tch in rr: drvn and lost tch after 12th: t.o after next tl p.u 15th* **50/1**

6m 35.5s (-15.20) **Going Correction** -0.55s/f (Firm)
WFA 5 from 6yo+ 1lb **10** Ran SP% **116.8**
Speed ratings: **101,100,98,98,96 94,87, , ,**
CSF £28.75 CT £102.40 TOTE £5.40: £1.40, £2.40, £1.70; EX 33.40 Trifecta £205.30.
Owner Across The Pond Partnership **Bred** James Flood **Trained** Newmarket, Suffolk

FOCUS
This was a low-grade chase in which the first two hadn't shown anything for a long time. The pace was average for a race of this distance. The first three were all very well in on their best form and the race could be rated a fair bit higher.

5114 FRIENDS OF RACING WELFARE H'CAP HURDLE (14 hdls) 3m 1f 110y
4:20 (4:22) (Class 5) (0-100,100) 4-Y-O+ **£2,737** (£798; £399)

Form RPR

044- **1** **Taradrewe**[7] 5007 7-11-7 **95**..(t) AidanColeman 117+
(Anthony Honeyball) *w ldr tl led 6th: clr and in command bef 3 out: drew wl clr bef 2 out: v easily* **2/1**[1]

P03- **2** *20* **Hot Whiskey (IRE)**[19] 4760 6-11-5 **100**......................(t) CharlieDeutsch(7) 99
(Brendan Powell) *hld up in tch towards rr: stdy hdwy 8th: 3rd and shkn up bef 3 out: no real prog: wnt 2nd but no ch w wnr 2 out: plugged on* **3/1**[2]

0/0- **3** *12* **Vicator**[329] 140 6-10-4 **81**...(t) RachaelGreen(3) 69
(Anthony Honeyball) *t.k.h: chsd ldrs: chsd clr wnr after 10th: rdn and btn after 3 out: lost 2nd 2 out: wknd* **10/1**

011- **4** *1 1/2* **Warsaw Pact (IRE)**[18] 4779 11-10-1 **82**............................ MrLKilgarriff(7) 69
(Steven Dixon) *in tch in rr: rdn and hdwy into midfield after 10th: no ch w wnr but plugged on into modest 4th 2 out* **10/1**

624- **5** *7* **Burnthill (IRE)**[18] 4779 9-9-8 **75**.....................................(tp) GeraldQuinn(7) 56
(Claire Dyson) *led tl mstke and hdd 6th: lost pl after 9th: struggling whn mstke 11th: lost poor 4th and j.rt 2 out: t.o* **18/1**

243- **6** *18* **Absolute Shambles**[6] 5022 10-11-4 **92**...............................(p) TomCannon 56
(Chris Gordon) *in tch in midfield tl rdn and dropped to rr after 6th: lost tch u.p 9th: t.o fr 11th* **9/1**

555- **7** *28* **Always Smiling (IRE)**[109] 3030 7-11-5 **100**............(t) MrHAABannister(7) 39
(Charlie Mann) *racd wd: nt fluent 1st: in tch in rr: rdn and btn after 9th: lost tch next and t.o bef 3 out* **20/1**

F1P- **8** *nk* **Newton Thistle**[18] 4779 7-10-12 **86**.. DavidBass 25
(Ben Pauling) *chsd ldrs: wnt 2nd after 7th tl after 10th: 4th and wknd bef 3 out: t.o* **7/1**[3]

0/3- **P** **Shine In Time (IRE)**[16] 4797 6-11-7 **95**................................ JamieMoore
(Laura Mongan) *in tch in midfield: rdn and lost pl bef 8th: bhd and lost tch after next: t.o whn p.u 11th* **16/1**

6m 14.3s (-10.70) **Going Correction** -0.35s/f (Good) **9** Ran SP% **114.9**
Speed ratings (Par 103): **102,95,92,91,89 84,75,75,**
CSF £8.70 CT £46.14 TOTE £2.80: £1.10, £2.30, £3.00; EX 10.30 Trifecta £100.40.
Owner Frosties Friends II **Bred** T C Frost **Trained** Mosterton, Dorset

FOCUS
In a weak race, the pace was ordinary for two circuits, but the winner then increased the tempo to such good effect that the final mile was a formality. This was a massive step up from the winner, but it looks believable.

5115 HARWOODS GROUP H'CAP CHASE (12 fncs) 2m 1f
4:50 (4:51) (Class 5) (0-100,97) 5-Y-O+ **£3,249** (£954; £477; £238)

Form RPR

154- **1** **The Informant**[16] 4802 8-10-7 **78**......................................(b1) RyanMahon 87+
(Seamus Mullins) *mde all: j. 5th: drvn and forged ahd 2 out: styd on strly: rdn out* **4/1**[2]

603- **2** *3* **Sportsreport (IRE)**[21] 4718 6-10-11 **82**.....................(p) AndrewThornton 87
(Seamus Mullins) *t.k.h: hld up in tch: gd hdwy to chse ldrs 9th: chsd wnr 2 out: rdn and no imp between last 2* **4/1**[2]

225- **3** *1 1/2* **Sablazo (FR)**[6] 5027 8-10-8 **79**.. LiamTreadwell 83
(Andy Turnell) *wl in tch in midfield: chsd ldrs 9th: drvn after 3 out: 3rd between last 2: edgd lft and kpt on same pce flat* **8/1**[3]

552- **4** *2* **Zhukov (IRE)**[16] 4802 12-11-2 **94**.................................... MrLKilgarriff(7) 96
(Kevin Tork) *chsd ldrs: drvn and unable qck after 3 out: styd on same pce between last 2* **14/1**

00P- **5** *2 3/4* **Star Presenter (IRE)**[46] 4242 6-11-7 **92**..........................(p) DenisO'Regan 91
(Paul Webber) *t.k.h: pressed ldr: ev ch rdn bef 2 out: lost 2nd next: sn btn and wknd bef last* **7/2**[1]

41- **6** *5* **Benny The Swinger (IRE)**[16] 4802 9-11-11 **96**................. TomCannon 97+
(Chris Gordon) *j.rt: hld up in rr: mstke 1st: clsd and mstke 9th: cl 5th and blnd bdly 2 out: nt rcvr and n.d after* **4/1**[2]

522- **7** *2 1/4* **King Ozzy (IRE)**[17] 4795 10-11-7 **97**.......................(tp) ConorShoemark(5) 90
(Lawney Hill) *wl in tch in midfield: mstke 8th: mstke and lost pl 9th: wknd u.p bef 2 out* **12/1**

040- **8** *2 1/2* **Petit Ecuyer (FR)**[24] 4658 8-11-10 **95**................................ JoshuaMoore 86
(Barry Brennan) *hld up in last pair: clsd and wl in tch 9th: effrt and wd after 3 out: wknd 2 out* **16/1**

4m 17.0s (-6.00) **Going Correction** -0.55s/f (Firm) **8** Ran SP% **113.6**
Speed ratings: **92,90,89,88,87 85,84,83**
CSF £20.62 CT £120.04 TOTE £4.60: £2.00, £1.80, £2.00; EX 29.20 Trifecta £247.50.
Owner Dr & Mrs John Millar **Bred** Mrs J D Richards, Mrs C L Shaw & Mrs V Gilmou **Trained** Wilsford-Cum-Lake, Wilts

FOCUS
The winner was able to dictate his own pace but he won on merit. The form looks pretty solid.

5116 EPDS RACING WELFARE BTO SERIES 2014 H'CAP HURDLE (10 hdls) 2m 2f
5:20 (5:26) (Class 5) (0-100,100) 4-Y-O+ **£2,737** (£798; £399)

Form RPR

400- **1** **Al Amaan**[161] 2008 9-10-4 **78**.. MattieBatchelor 86+
(Sheena West) *hld up off the pce in rr: stdy hdwy 5th: chsd ldrs 3 out: rdn to ld and wnt clr bef 2 out: styd on wl: rdn out* **9/1**[3]

3/0- **2** *3* **Galiotto (IRE)**[26] 3140 8-11-7 **95**..(v) JamieMoore 99
(Gary Moore) *in tch in midfield: drvn and no hdwy after 7th: styd on u.p and chsd wnr between last 2: styd on but no imp* **5/1**[1]

526- **3** *3 3/4* **Recway Lass**[190] 1630 6-9-13 **76**..................................(p) TrevorWhelan(3) 77
(Des Donovan) *hld up off the pce in rr: clsd and in tch whn stmbld after 6th: kpt on wl u.p after 3 out: no threat to wnr* **12/1**

205- **4** *7* **Osmosia (FR)**[19] 4762 9-10-12 **86**..(p) TomCannon 81
(Chris Gordon) *w ldrs tl lft in ld 2nd: drvn and hdd bef 2 out: 3rd and btn between last 2: wknd flat* **20/1**

656- **5** *3 1/2* **Celebrian**[16] 1176 7-10-4 **83**...(t) KillianMoore(5) 75
(Alex Hales) *wl in tch in midfield: hdwy after 5th: chsd ldr 7th: ev ch next tl drvn and btn bef 2 out: wknd between 2* **20/1**

060- **6** *3/4* **Mariet**[33] 4493 5-10-10 **87**.. GavinSheehan(3) 78
(Suzy Smith) *racd off the pce in midfield: hdwy after 6th: in tch whn mstke 3 out: kpt on same pce u.p fr bef 2 out: j.rt last* **8/1**[2]

0P2- **7** *5* **Landerbee (IRE)**[25] 4636 7-10-2 **79**............................ WayneKavanagh(3) 68
(Seamus Mullins) *t.k.h: hld up off the pce in rr: stdy hdwy after 5th: n.m.r after 3 out: sn rdn and no hdwy: 6th and wl hld whn blnd bdly last* **5/1**[1]

The Form Book Jumps, Raceform Ltd, Compton, RG20 6NL.

344- **8** 3 1/2 **Chankillo**[56] 4072 5-11-2 **90**.................................... SamTwiston-Davies 75
(Sarah-Jayne Davies) *w ldrs tl drvn and no ex after 3 out: wknd bef next* **16/1**

U53- **9** 6 **Lindsay's Dream**[6] 5018 8-11-1 **96**.................................(p) MrHGMiller(7) 73
(Zoe Davison) *wl in tch in midfield: hdwy to chse ldrs 6th: rdn and outpcd after 3 out: wknd bef next* **8/1**[2]

PP0- **10** 7 **Whatagoa (IRE)**[21] 4721 7-10-1 **75**...................................... ColinBolger 46
(Richard Rowe) *wl off the pce in rr: mstke 11th: styd on to pass btn horses fr 2 out: n.d: t.o* **100/1**

532- **11** 1 **Little Roxy (IRE)**[21] 4721 9-10-5 **79**.................................... AdamWedge 49
(Anna Newton-Smith) *led tl mstke and hdd 2nd: styd prom tl wknd u.p after 3 out: t.o* **10/1**

000- **12** 10 **Just Beware**[21] 4721 12-9-8 **75** oh7 ow1....................(p) MissTWorsley(7) 36
(Zoe Davison) *wl in tch in midfield: hit 6th: sn rdn and lost pl: bhd 3 out: t.o* **33/1**

0P6- **13** 4 1/2 **Flora Lea**[21] 4717 7-10-6 **83**.. JamesBest(3) 40
(Andrew Price) *chsd ldrs tl lost pl qckly and mstke 11th: bhd next: t.o* **50/1**

U66- **14** 14 **Major Martin (IRE)**[121] 2826 5-11-12 **100**........................ JoshuaMoore 45
(Gary Moore) *in tch in midfield: rdn and lost pl after 6th: bhd 3 out: t.o* **5/1**[1]

4m 24.5s (-6.40) **Going Correction** -0.35s/f (Good) **14** Ran SP% **120.3**
Speed ratings (Par 103): **100,98,97,93,92 92,89,88,85,82 82,77,75,69**
CSF £51.65 CT £555.31 TOTE £13.70: £5.30, £1.90, £3.90; EX 60.30 Trifecta £1273.10 Part won..
Owner Mark Waters **Bred** Compagnia Generale S R L **Trained** Falmer, E Sussex
■ Mattie Batchelor's first winner in Britain since December 2012.

FOCUS
The pace was just a medium one, but it was good enough to bring out the class of the rejuvenated winner, who had been rated 125 in his early days. The form is rated around the second and third.
T/Jkpt: £34,204.10 to a £1 stake. Pool: £48,174.83 - 0.5 winning units. T/Plt: £359.40 to a £1 stake. Pool: £108,818.45 - 221.0 winning units. T/Qpdt: £23.90 to a £1 stake. Pool: £9599.28 - 296.80 winning units. SP

1855 NEWTON ABBOT (L-H)
Tuesday, April 1

OFFICIAL GOING: Soft (heavy in places; 4.3)
Wind: mild breeze across Weather: sunny

5117 LADIES DAY 24 JUNE MAIDEN HURDLE (8 hdls) 2m 1f
2:10 (2:10) (Class 4) 4-Y-0+ **£3,508** (£1,030; £515; £257)

Form RPR

2/ **1** **Sail By The Sea (IRE)**[409] 4257 6-11-0 0...................... TomScudamore 138+
(David Pipe) *trckd ldr: led after 4th: drew wl clr after 3 out: v easily* **9/4**[2]

4- **2** 25 **Star Date (IRE)**[28] 3501 5-11-0 0........................... LeightonAspell 111+
(Oliver Sherwood) *trckd ldr in chsng gp: plenty to do after 5th: styd on fr after 3 out: wnt 3rd between last 2: no ch w wnr* **25/1**

32F- **3** 7 **Revaader**[28] 4604 6-10-7 105.. TommyPhelan 99
(Mark Gillard) *led tl after 4th: chsd wnr tl after next: sn rdn: styd on same pce fr after 3 out* **5/2**[3]

4 7 **Remiluc (FR)**[132] 5-11-0 0.....................................(t) SamTwiston-Davies 99
(Paul Nicholls) *trckd ldng pair: trckd wnr after 5th: rdn after 3 out: wknd 2 out: lost 2 pls gng to the last* **7/4**[1]

000- **5** 11 **According To Sarah (IRE)**[12] 4910 6-10-4 0..................... JamesBest(3) 80
(Philip Hobbs) *towards rr of chsng gp: no ch fr after 5th: plugged on* **33/1**

460- **6** 2 1/4 **The Snappy Poet**[60] 4017 5-10-11 0............................... MattGriffiths(3) 83
(Jeremy Scott) *mid-div in chsng gp: no ch fr after 5th: plugged on after 3 out* **33/1**

7 shd **Kept**[90] 5-11-0 0... JoshuaMoore 83
(Alison Batchelor) *mid-div in chsng gp: no ch fr after 5th: plugged on* **66/1**

00B- **8** 4 1/2 **Western Movie**[7] 5016 6-11-0 0.. TomO'Brien 78
(Philip Hobbs) *mid-div in chsng gp: nvr any danger* **40/1**

440- **9** 2 **Wing Mira (IRE)**[10] 4945 6-11-0 0....................................... AidanColeman 76
(Venetia Williams) *trckd ldrs in chsng gp: no ch fr after 5th: t.o* **33/1**

00F- **10** 14 **Miller's Maverick**[10] 4959 6-11-0 0..................................... NickScholfield 62
(Grant Cann) *hmpd 1st: a in rr: t.o* **100/1**

P0P- **11** 11 **Saint Helena (IRE)**[36] 4467 6-10-7 0.............................. MattieBatchelor 44
(Jim Best) *mid-div in chsng gp tl 5th: t.o* **150/1**

05- **12** 10 **Markami (FR)**[9] 4987 4-10-8 0.. IanPopham 35
(Johnny Farrelly) *hld up in chsng gp: nerv any danger: t.o* **100/1**

P- **13** 5 **Lord Carrigross (IRE)**[7] 5016 7-10-7 0.............................[1] MrCSmith(7) 36
(Linda Blackford) *trckd ldng 3 tl after 4th: wknd after next: t.o* **200/1**

0- **14** 17 **Hi Bronco**[117] 2912 7-11-0 0.. JamesDavies 19
(John Ryall) *a towards rr: t.o after 4th* **150/1**

340- **U** **Mr Shantu (IRE)**[17] 4807 5-11-0 0.................................... RichieMcLernon
(Jonjo O'Neill) *awkward: wnt rt and uns rdr 1st* **18/1**

4m 16.0s (10.30) **Going Correction** +0.725s/f (Soft)
WFA 4 from 5yo+ 5lb **15** Ran SP% **121.4**
Speed ratings (Par 105): **104,92,88,85,80 79,79,77,76,69 64,59,57,49,**
CSF £58.05 TOTE £3.90: £1.20, £6.60, £1.50; EX 55.20 Trifecta £324.80.
Owner R S Brookhouse **Bred** Michael McSweeney **Trained** Nicholashayne, Devon

FOCUS
Rail and hurdles sited in wide positions. The promising winner totally took this apart and looks a decent winner.

5118 NEWTONABBOTRACING.COM H'CAP HURDLE (8 hdls) 2m 1f
2:40 (2:41) (Class 4) (0-105,105) 4-Y-0+ **£3,508** (£1,030; £515; £257)

Form RPR

U00- **1** **Mister Fantastic**[12] 4911 8-10-0 **81** ow1......................... RobertDunne(3) 91+
(Dai Burchell) *in tch: hdwy 5th: led after 3 out: shkn up and sn drew clr: comf* **11/2**

211- **2** 7 **Hold The Bucks (USA)**[22] 4721 8-11-3 **99**.................. GavinSheehan(3) 97
(Daniel Steele) *in tch: rdn bef 5th: styd on into 3rd appr 2 out: kpt on to snatch 2nd towards fin: no ch w wnr* **3/1**[1]

F2U- **3** nk **Lucky Sunny (IRE)**[35] 4477 11-11-12 **105**.......................[1] AidanColeman 102
(Venetia Williams) *w ldr tl after 2nd: led after 5th: rdn and hdd bef 2 out: sn hld: no ex whn lost 2nd towards fin* **4/1**[3]

006- **4** 4 **Bedouin Bay**[14] 4887 7-11-10 **103**.. BrendanPowell 96
(Johnny Farrelly) *hld up: rdn bef 5th: styd on same pce after 3 out: wnt 4th 2 out: nvr threatened ldrs* **17/2**

1/0- **P** **Cridda Boy**[92] 3420 8-11-12 **105**...(t) TomO'Brien
(Richard Woollacott) *trckd ldrs: rdn after 5th: wknd sn after next: p.u bef 2 out* **5/1**

040- **P** **Special Report (IRE)**[112] 3003 4-11-3 **102**............................ NoelFehily
(Neil Mulholland) *hld up in last pair: struggling after 4th: t.o whn p.u after 3 out* **22/1**

552- **F** **Kaki Island (IRE)**[24] 4674 6-11-11 **104**.............................. TomCannon 90
(Chris Gordon) *led: nt a fluent: rdn and hdd after 5th: wknd bef 2 out: fell last* **7/2**[2]

4m 25.8s (20.10) **Going Correction** +0.725s/f (Soft)
WFA 4 from 6yo+ 5lb **7** Ran SP% **114.1**
Speed ratings (Par 105): **81,77,77,75, ,**
CSF £22.69 TOTE £6.40: £3.20, £1.90; EX 29.40 Trifecta £154.80.
Owner Mrs J K Bradley **Bred** Mascalls Stud **Trained** Briery Hill, Blaenau Gwent

FOCUS
A weak handicap. The easy winner may still be competitive when reassessed.

5119 NEWTONABBOTRACE ON TWITTER H'CAP CHASE (20 fncs) 3m 2f 110y
3:10 (3:10) (Class 3) (0-130,128) 5-Y-0+ **£7,027** (£2,121; £1,092; £579)

Form RPR

P32- **1** **Camden (IRE)**[24] 4678 8-11-3 **119**.................................(p) LeightonAspell 133+
(Oliver Sherwood) *mde all: clr ldr 15th: rdn after 3 out: styd on wl to assert fr next: awkward last: pushed out* **5/2**[2]

205- **2** 12 **Seven Woods (IRE)**[38] 4427 8-11-10 **126**...................(tp) PaddyBrennan 129
(Tom George) *trckd ldrs: pushed along to chse wnr fr 15th tl rdn after 4 out: styd on to regain 2nd at the last: no ch w wnr* **9/4**[1]

3P3- **3** hd **Cnoc Seoda (IRE)**[53] 4133 9-11-1 **117**................................(t) TomO'Brien 118
(Paul Henderson) *hld up in last pair but wl in tch: wnt 3rd 15th: rdn to chse wnr 3 out: hld fr next: lost 2nd narrowly last: kpt on but no ex* **12/1**

1/1- **4** 16 **Gotoyourplay (IRE)**[22] 4732 10-11-12 **128**....................... AidanColeman 118
(Venetia Williams) *trckd ldrs: stmbld 14th: sn rdn in cl 4th: wknd after 3 out: j.rt last 2* **4/1**[3]

100- **P** **Sheriff Hutton (IRE)**[11] 4932 11-11-4 **120**.......................... HaddenFrost
(Martin Hill) *hld up in last pair but wl in tch: pushed along 10th: mstke 13th: sn rdn: losing tch whn p.u bef 15th* **12/1**

/26- **P** **My Boy Paddy (IRE)**[68] 3858 10-10-12 **114**.......(v[1]) SamTwiston-Davies
(Nigel Twiston-Davies) *disp ld tl rdn appr 15th: wknd 4 out: p.u after next* **9/2**

6m 58.3s (13.70) **Going Correction** +0.725s/f (Soft) **6** Ran SP% **112.9**
Speed ratings: **108,104,104,99,**
CSF £9.04 TOTE £4.00: £1.90, £1.60; EX 9.40 Trifecta £58.80.
Owner Tim Syder **Bred** Fran Kavanagh **Trained** Upper Lambourn, Berks

FOCUS
This modest handicap was run at a routine gallop, but still served up a decent test. The winner is rated close to his best.

5120 SIS LIVE "NATIONAL HUNT" NOVICES' HURDLE (9 hdls) 2m 3f
3:40 (3:40) (Class 4) 4-Y-0+ **£3,508** (£1,030; £515; £257)

Form RPR

455- **1** **Volt Face (FR)**[26] 4632 5-11-0 0.. TomScudamore 114+
(David Pipe) *hld up in last pair: hdwy 6th: led bef 2 out: sn in command: eased run-in* **9/4**[2]

4- **2** 3 3/4 **St Dominick (IRE)**[115] 2946 7-10-11 0.............................. JamesBest(3) 103
(Jackie Du Plessis) *hld up in last pair in tch: wnt 3rd after 3 out: sn rdn: styd on to go 2nd run-in: no ch w wnr* **25/1**

PP0- **3** 1 **Rody (FR)**[38] 4414 9-10-9 130................................(t) AodhaganConlon(5) 102
(Tom George) *led: rdn appr 6th: hdd bef 2 out: sn hld by wnr: no ex whn lost 2nd towards fin* **8/1**[3]

16U- **4** 20 **Buckhorn Timothy**[9] 4987 5-11-0 0.............................. BrendanPowell 82
(Colin Tizzard) *trckd ldrs: rdn after 3 out: sn outpcd: wknd next* **9/1**

5 23 **Rothman (FR)**[67] 4-10-13 132...................................... NickScholfield 65+
(Paul Nicholls) *w ldr: nt fluent 4th: rdn after 3 out: qckly btn: t.o* **5/6**[1]

000- **6** 24 **Revouge**[8] 5008 5-11-0 0.. MarkGrant 35
(Jim Old) *trckd ldrs: rdn after 6th: wknd next: t.o* **150/1**

/0P- **P** **Morebutwhen**[38] 4411 7-10-7 0.. TomCannon
(Richard King) *trckd ldrs: pushed along after 3rd: reminders next: drvn after 5th: wknd next: t.o whn p.u after 3 out* **66/1**

4m 53.43s (23.43) **Going Correction** +0.725s/f (Soft)
WFA 4 from 5yo+ 5lb **7** Ran SP% **112.4**
Speed ratings (Par 105): **79,77,77,68,58 48,**
CSF £36.41 TOTE £2.60: £1.60, £6.40; EX 28.40 Trifecta £128.40.
Owner R S Brookhouse **Bred** S Hamon & Mme C Hamon **Trained** Nicholashayne, Devon

FOCUS
A modest novice hurdle. A step up from the easy winner and there should be more to come.

5121 AT THE RACES SKY415 H'CAP CHASE (16 fncs) 2m 5f 110y
4:10 (4:10) (Class 4) (0-115,115) 5-Y-0+ **£3,898** (£1,144; £572; £286)

Form RPR

6PP **1** **Special Account (IRE)**[12] 4914 9-11-12 **115**........................ LiamHeard 114
(Jeremy Scott) *hld up: hdwy after 9th: wnt 4th next: j.rt 12th: sn struggling w plenty to do: looked 4th and hld 3 out: lft 3rd 2 out: kpt on to ld run-in where hmpd by loose horse: rdn out* **16/1**

513- **2** 2 **Tolkeins Tango (IRE)**[7] 5020 6-11-9 **112**.............................(t) JackDoyle 116+
(Victor Dartnall) *j.rt at times: trckd ldrs: chsd wnr u.p after 4 out: hld whn lft in ld 2 out: 8 l clr whn slowed into last: no ex whn hdd run-in* **4/1**[2]

635- **3** 5 **Old Tricks (IRE)**[9] 4991 7-11-6 **109**.................................(p) BrendanPowell 100
(Colin Tizzard) *trckd ldrs: reminders after 6th: drvn after 9th: wl bhd 12th: styd on fr after 3 out: lft 4th 2 out: r.o to snatch 3rd run-in* **11/2**

152- **4** 2 1/4 **Valid Point (IRE)**[19] 4780 8-11-9 **112**.................................(t) MarkGrant 113+
(Jim Old) *in tch: hmpd 1st: wnt 2nd at the 9th tl nt fluent 4 out: sn rdn: lft hld 2nd whn blnd 2 out: wknd* **7/2**[1]

142- **P** **Proud Times (USA)**[15] 4862 8-11-9 **112**........................(p) AidanColeman
(Ali Brewer) *led tl 4th: trckd ldr: pushed along after 6th: rdn after 9th: wknd after next: p.u bef 12th* **11/2**

F54- **F** **Tony Dinozzo (FR)**[25] 4657 7-11-2 **105**...........................(p) JamieMoore 114
(Peter Bowen) *w ldr: led 4th: pushed along but wl in command whn fell 2 out* **9/2**[3]

1/4- **P** **Roll The Dice (IRE)**[34] 4502 8-11-7 **110**................................ TomO'Brien
(Philip Hobbs) *trckd ldrs: reminders after 5th: lost pl and rdn after 9th: losing tch whn p.u bef 12th* **6/1**

5m 42.3s (20.90) **Going Correction** +0.725s/f (Soft) **7** Ran SP% **111.3**
Speed ratings: **91,90,88,87, ,**
CSF £74.89 TOTE £23.20: £7.40, £2.40; EX 96.20 Trifecta £601.30.
Owner Mrs Jenny Perry **Bred** M Murphy **Trained** Brompton Regis, Somerset

FOCUS
A dramatic finish dictates this is form to take with a pinch of salt. The winner was probably only the fourth best horse in the race.

5122 INDEPENDENT RACECOURSES LIMITED IRL H'CAP HURDLE (11 hdls 1 omitted) 3m 3f
4:40 (4:41) (Class 5) (0-100,100) 4-Y-0+ £2,737 (£798; £399)

Form RPR
U22- 1 **Jaunty Journey**[23] 4704 11-11-12 **100**....................(v) SamTwiston-Davies 107+
(Nigel Twiston-Davies) *led 2nd: reminders after 4th: hit 7th: pushed along but in command 2 out: styd on wl: rdn out* **5/2**[2]
060- 2 3 ¾ **Brunette'Sonly (IRE)**[77] 3699 9-10-6 **80**....................... AndrewThornton 81
(Seamus Mullins) *trckd ldrs on outer: rdn after 7th: nt fluent next: sn chsng wnr: styd on but a being hld fr 2 out* **15/8**[1]
5P6- 3 ¾ **Acosta**[92] 3425 10-9-11 **74** oh5.............................(b) WayneKavanagh(3) 73
(Dr Jeremy Naylor) *in tch: wnt 3rd u.p bef 3 out: chal for 2nd fr 2 out: styd on same pce fr last* **20/1**
0PB- 4 34 **Hobb's Dream (IRE)**[183] 1701 10-10-10 **84**....................(p) MichaelByrne 58
(Neil Mulholland) *hld up: nudged along after 6th: hdwy 8th: sn rdn: cl enough 4th 3 out: wknd bef next: t.o* **20/1**
61P- 5 35 **According To Them (IRE)**[22] 4720 10-10-11 **88**....(tp) GavinSheehan(3) 18
(Daniel Steele) *hld up: rdn after 7th: wknd bef next: t.o* **16/1**
4P2/ P **Fortification (USA)**[30] 11-11-10 **98**...............................(p) LeightonAspell
(Stephen Hughes) *prom: pushed along to chse ldrs 6th: wknd bef 8th: t.o 3 out: p.u bef 2 out* **8/1**
605- P **Award Winner**[33] 4519 11-11-5 **93**..(v) APMcCoy
(Brendan Powell) *led tl 2nd: prom tl rdn and wknd after 8th: t.o whn p.u bef 2 out* **7/2**[3]
41U- P **Elegant Olive**[7] 5022 11-11-12 **100**.. HaddenFrost
(Roger Curtis) *hld up: struggling after 6th: wknd after next: p.u bef 8th* **14/1**

7m 12.5s (31.50) **Going Correction** +0.725s/f (Soft) 8 Ran SP% **118.8**
Speed ratings (Par 103): **82,80,80,70,60** , ,
CSF £8.26 CT £70.34 TOTE £3.60: £1.60, £1.10, £5.90; EX 10.90 Trifecta £124.20.
Owner Colin Roberts **Bred** B J Eckley **Trained** Naunton, Gloucs

FOCUS
An ordinary staying handicap. The well-in winner is rated similar to his Bangor hurdles run.

5123 TOTNES & BRIDGETOWN RACES COMPANY NOVICES' HUNTERS' CHASE (16 fncs) 2m 5f 110y
5:10 (5:11) (Class 6) 5-Y-0+ £1,317 (£405; £202)

Form RPR
362- 1 **Chosen Milan (IRE)**[22] 4727 7-10-12 0..............................(t) MrEDavid(7) 125+
(R E Luke) *trckd ldrs: prom 5th: led 8th: drrw wl clr after 3 out: v easily* **2/1**[2]
F- 2 31 **Little Cornham (IRE)**[30] 7-11-5 0.................................... MrCGethings(7) 99
(Mrs C Fear) *prom early: trckd ldrs fr 4th: rdn in 3rd after 3 out: sn hld: kpt on to go 2nd run-in: no ch w v easy wnr* **14/1**
10- 3 1 ½ **Certain Flight (IRE)**[18] 4788 9-12-2 0.................................. MrWBiddick 104
(K J Cumings) *hld up bhd ldrs: tk clsr order after 9th: wnt 2nd 4 out: nt fluent next: sn rdn and wl hld: no ex whn lost 2nd run-in* **13/8**[1]
01U- 4 13 **Double Bank (IRE)**[9] 11-11-9 108.............................. MrMWoodward(7) 89
(Ms Emma Oliver) *trckd ldrs: led 6th tl next: rdn after 10th: no ch fr 12th: regained modest 4th after 2 out* **7/2**[3]
/30- 5 6 **Sangfroid**[10] 10-11-7 0.. MrMatthewBarber(5) 79
(Andrew Quick) *nvr travelling: drvn along most of way: in tch tl 11th: t.o* **14/1**
6 6 **Ladfromhighworth**[9] 9-11-5 0.. MissVWade(7) 77
(Mrs Camilla Scott) *trckd ldrs: led briefly 5th: rdn after 12th: sn wknd: blnd 2 out: t.o* **40/1**
0P/ P **Mt Kintyre (IRE)**[37] 8-11-5 0.................................... MissLeandaTickle(7)
(J Tickle) *hld up: sme prog into 5th 12th: wknd after next: t.o whn p.u bef 2 out* **66/1**
F/ P **Reliable Richie (IRE)**[16] 8-11-5 0....................................... MrMHeard(7)
(R G Chapman) *led tl 5th: led 7th tl blnd next: wknd bef 11th: t.o whn p.u bef 4 out* **20/1**
U **Waddingtown Hero (IRE)**[58] 7-11-5 0.................(tp) MissBHampson(7)
(L M Power) *in tch tl mstke and uns rdr 10th* **33/1**

5m 34.7s (13.30) **Going Correction** +0.725s/f (Soft) 9 Ran SP% **118.6**
Speed ratings: **104,92,92,87,85 83**, , ,
CSF £26.95 TOTE £2.70: £1.10, £3.30, £1.20; EX 31.00 Trifecta £85.10.
Owner D H Morgan **Bred** Mrs Ann Jenkins **Trained** Haverfordwest, Pembrokeshire

FOCUS
Not a bad hunter chase. The winner's effort could be rated higher.
T/Plt: £217.30 to a £1 stake. Pool of £76229.47 - 256.04 winning tickets. T/Qpdt: £35.70 to a £1 stake. Pool of £6859.40 - 141.80 winning tickets. TM

4987 WINCANTON (R-H)
Wednesday, April 2

OFFICIAL GOING: Good to soft (soft in places; chs 8.4, hdl 8.8)
Hurdle on stable bend omitted due to ground.
Wind: virtually nil Weather: occassional light showers

5124 32RED £10 FREE BONUS MARES' NOVICES' HURDLE (10 hdls 1 omitted) 2m 6f
2:15 (2:15) (Class 4) 4-Y-0+ £3,249 (£954; £477; £238)

Form RPR
102- 1 **Koolala (IRE)**[33] 4531 6-11-5 115....................................... DenisO'Regan 122+
(Paul Webber) *travelled stly thrght: mid-div: hit 1st: smooth hdwy after 3 out to trck ldrs: led appr last: sn clr: easily* **5/2**[1]
25- 2 5 **Pressies Girl (IRE)**[25] 4683 6-10-12 0.................. SamTwiston-Davies 106
(Paul Nicholls) *trckd ldrs: rdn to dispute 2nd 2 out: styd on fr last to go 2nd fnl 75yds: no ch w wnr* **3/1**[2]
322- 3 2 ¾ **Spirit Oscar (IRE)**[24] 4701 6-11-7 121......................... ThomasGarner(5) 118
(Oliver Sherwood) *led: rdn appr 2 out: hdd appr last: kpt on tl no ex whn lost 2nd fnl 75yds* **4/1**[3]
054- 4 1 ¾ **Makadamia**[13] 4910 5-10-12 0.. TomScudamore 101
(David Pipe) *hld up towards rr: hdwy after 5th: trckd ldrs after 3 out: rdn to dispute 2nd 2 out: no ex fr last* **5/1**
/65- 5 4 ½ **Easter Dancer**[84] 3598 7-10-12 0... AidanColeman 97
(Emma Lavelle) *trckd ldr: rdn appr 2 out: no ex appr last* **16/1**
4P0- 6 12 **Money Maid (IRE)**[11] 4945 6-10-12 0.............................. AndrewThornton 86
(Simon Earle) *hld up towards rr: nt fluent 1st: stdy prog into midfield 7th: sn rdn: styd on wout ever threatening to get involved* **100/1**
15P- 7 ¾ **A Shade Of Bay**[14] 4907 6-11-0 114.................................[1] EdCookson(5) 93
(Kim Bailey) *trckd ldrs: rdn after 3 out: sn hld: one pce fr next* **14/1**
446- 8 16 **Delineate (IRE)**[18] 4797 5-10-5 0.. MrZBaker(7) 77
(G C Maundrell) *mid-div: struggling to hold pl 4th: nvr any imp: wknd 2 out: hmpd last* **100/1**
3- 9 66 **Theionlady (IRE)**[33] 4534 4-10-5 0...................................... ConorO'Farrell 5
(Richard Woollacott) *struggling 5th: a towards rr: t.o* **50/1**
06- 10 ½ **Pandy Wells**[104] 3181 5-10-12 0... CharliePoste 11
(Graeme McPherson) *towards rr: midfield 5th: wknd after 7th: t.o* **100/1**
/6F- 11 6 **She's Noble**[18] 4797 7-10-9 0.. MichealNolan(3) 6
(Suzy Smith) *nt fluent early: a towards rr: t.o 7th* **66/1**
00- 12 4 ½ **Tomorrow Night**[27] 4632 4-10-5 0... FelixDeGiles
(Jennifer Mason) *mid-div tl wknd after 7th: t.o* **200/1**
P/0- 13 41 **Affiliate**[140] 2463 6-10-12 0... MarkGrant
(Geoffrey Deacon) *a bhd: t.o 7th* **200/1**
43- F **Our Cat (IRE)**[20] 4777 6-10-7 0................................ ConorShoemark(5) 91
(Fergal O'Brien) *mid-div: nt fluent 1st: hdwy 3 out: rdn to chse ldrs appr 2 out: hld in 6th whn fell last* **25/1**

5m 17.6s (-8.90) **Going Correction** -0.15s/f (Good)
WFA 4 from 5yo+ 6lb 14 Ran SP% **114.1**
Speed ratings (Par 105): **110,108,107,106,104 100,100,94,70,70 68,66,51,**
CSF £9.47 TOTE £3.90: £1.50, £1.40, £2.00; EX 10.80 Trifecta £26.80.
Owner Lady Richard Wellesley **Bred** Marston Stud **Trained** Mollington, Oxon

FOCUS
After riding in the first Tom Scudamore felt the ground was soft, while Sam Twiston-Davies gave it as being "dead". This was probably just a modest event, although a case could be made for a few of them, and the form looks solid enough.

5125 LAND VALUE ALLIANCES LLP H'CAP HURDLE (7 hdls 1 omitted) 2m
2:45 (2:45) (Class 4) (0-115,115) 4-Y-0+ £3,249 (£954; £477; £238)

Form RPR
301- 1 **Superciliary**[9] 5005 5-10-9 **108** 7ex................................ LouisMuspratt(10) 114+
(Chris Gordon) *trckd ldr: chal 3 out: led appr 2 out: sn clr: kpt on gamely: rdn out* **11/2**[3]
021- 2 6 **Breaking Bits (IRE)**[230] 1270 7-11-12 **115**........................... TomO'Brien 115
(Jamie Snowden) *racd keenly early: trckd ldr: rdn appr 2 out: wnt 2nd sn after: styd on but a being hld by wnr* **6/1**
/31- 3 1 ½ **Seven Summits (IRE)**[70] 3830 7-11-5 **108**......................... PaulMoloney 107
(Sophie Leech) *hld up towards rr: hdwy after 3 out: wnt 3rd next: sn rdn: edgd lft: kpt on same pce* **14/1**
015- 4 nk **Vikekhal (FR)**[58] 4069 5-11-9 **112**.. JamieMoore 111
(Gary Moore) *hld up towards rr: rdn after 3 out: no real imp tl styd on fr last: nrly snatched 3rd* **12/1**
5P1- 5 7 **Withy Mills**[7] 5034 9-10-2 **94** 7ex....................................(bt) JamesBest(3) 87
(Kevin Bishop) *mid-div: nt fluent 2nd: wnt 4th after 3 out: sn rdn: nt pce to get on terms: fdd run-in* **8/1**
046/ 6 ¾ **All The Winds (GER)**[16] 1159 9-10-13 **105**................(t) PeterCarberry(3) 97
(Shaun Lycett) *mid-div: rdn after 3 out: kpt on but nvr threatened* **25/1**
504- 7 nk **Ladies Dancing**[30] 3043 8-11-2 **105**...................................... JamesDavies 97
(Chris Down) *mid-div: rdn after 3 out: no imp: fdd between last 2* **5/1**[2]
063- 8 1 **Minella Definitely (IRE)**[23] 4731 7-11-10 **113**..................... NoelFehily 105
(Neil Mulholland) *trckd ldrs: rdn after 3 out: sn one pce* **7/1**
165- 9 17 **Kettlewell**[57] 4023 5-11-10 **113**..(tp) APMcCoy 95
(Warren Greatrex) *racd keenly: led: rdn and hdd appr 2 out: sn wknd* **3/1**[1]
041- 10 35 **Karl Marx (IRE)**[15] 4882 4-10-2 **104**....................(b) ThomasCheesman(7) 42
(Mark Gillard) *mid-div tl after 2nd: lost tch fr 4th: t.o* **50/1**

3m 44.3s (-4.60) **Going Correction** -0.15s/f (Good)
WFA 4 from 5yo+ 5lb 10 Ran SP% **115.1**
Speed ratings (Par 105): **105,102,101,101,97 97,97,96,88,70**
CSF £38.35 CT £438.13 TOTE £6.90: £1.50, £2.40, £2.90; EX 44.30 Trifecta £262.80.
Owner David Henery **Bred** Prince Of Wales And Duchess Of Cornwall **Trained** Morestead, Hants

FOCUS
A fairly competitive handicap, run at a decent gallop. The form looks solid.

5126 32RED THUNDERSTRUCK II SLOT H'CAP CHASE (17 fncs) 2m 5f
3:15 (3:16) (Class 3) (0-130,130) 5-Y-0 **£6,330** (£1,870; £935; £468; £234)

Form RPR
/00- 1 **Hector's Choice (FR)**[123] 2812 10-11-11 **129**........................ JamieMoore 138+
(Richard Lee) *trckd ldr: led after 8th: rdn clr 3 out: styd on: rdn out* **6/1**[3]
13F- 2 2 **Al Alfa**[18] 4806 7-11-6 **124**... RichardJohnson 129
(Philip Hobbs) *led tl after 8th: trckd wnr: rdn appr 3 out: swtchd lft bef last: styd on but a being hld* **5/1**[2]
260- 3 1 ¾ **Jump City (FR)**[39] 4422 8-11-9 **130**...............................(p) HarryDerham(3) 133
(Paul Nicholls) *trckd ldrs: rdn after 4 out: styd on same pce* **7/1**
0P4- 4 6 **Ballyallia Man (IRE)**[25] 4685 9-11-2 **120**........................(t) PaddyBrennan 119
(Tom George) *trckd ldrs: rdn after 13th: hld after next: styd on same pce: regained 4th last* **9/2**[1]
0P1- 5 8 **Vif Argent (FR)**[35] 4502 5-11-7 **125**...............................(b) TomScudamore 116
(David Pipe) *trckd ldrs: cl 3rd 13th: rdn after 4 out: kpt chsng ldrs but nvr threatened: fdd fr last* **5/1**[2]
313- 6 6 **Balbriggan (IRE)**[112] 3026 7-11-4 **122**.......................... DominicElsworth 108
(Mick Channon) *hld up: pushed along between 10th and 11th: making hdwy whn stmbld bdly 4 out: sn rdn: fdd fr 2 out* **15/2**
40P- 7 1 ¼ **Captain Ocana (IRE)**[20] 4764 9-10-10 **114**.......................... TomO'Brien 98
(Paul Henderson) *sn pushed along towards rr: plugged on fr after 3 out: nvr any danger* **66/1**
155- 8 29 **Miss Tenacious**[35] 4502 7-11-4 **122**.. JackDoyle 80
(Ron Hodges) *hld up: wknd after 4 out: t.o* **50/1**
52P- 9 2 ½ **Lord Of The Dunes**[41] 4372 6-10-0 **104**.........................(t) BrendanPowell 60
(Colin Tizzard) *trckd ldrs: rdn after 11th: wknd after 4 out: t.o* **9/1**
/P6- P **Velator**[167] 1944 7-11-7 **125**... DenisO'Regan
(Anthony Honeyball) *hld up: nt travelling fr 6th and reminders: wknd after 4 out: p.u after next* **7/1**

5m 24.7s (-0.50) **Going Correction** +0.20s/f (Yiel) 10 Ran SP% **116.0**
Speed ratings: **108,107,106,104,101 98,98,87,86,**
CSF £36.71 CT £215.86 TOTE £9.30: £2.60, £2.20, £1.90; EX 51.00 Trifecta £355.60.
Owner James and Jean Potter **Bred** Mme Marie Prod'Homme **Trained** Byton, H'fords

FOCUS
A fair handicap, run at a sound gallop in which it paid to be handy. The winner is rated in line with the best of his 2013 form but was a 150+ horse at his peak.

5127 ROYAL ARTILLERY GOLD CUP (CHASE FOR AMATEUR RIDERS) (21 fncs) 3m 1f 110y
3:45 (3:47) (Class 3) 6-Y-0+ **£6,070** (£1,896; £948; £474; £237)

Form RPR

662- **1** **Savant Bleu (FR)**[12] 4932 8-11-12 125 .... CaptHarryWallace(7) 131+
(Kim Bailey) *trckd ldrs: pckd 6th: chal briefly after 4 out: hmpd next: 3 l 2nd jumping last: styd on wl to ld nring fin* **9/2**

/33- **2** *nk* **Benedictus (IRE)**[26] 4655 9-11-9 126 .... MajorAlexMichael(5) 126+
(Jack Barber) *cl up: pckd 7th: trckd ldrs 9th: led appr 3 out: j.lft last 3: 3 l up last: no ex whn hdd nring fin* **3/1**[2]

/10- **3** *2 3/4* **Jack Bene (IRE)**[26] 4661 8-11-7 115 ....(p) MrAVaughan-Jones(7) 122
(Miss Louise Allan) *j.rt at tmes: led 2nd: rdn whn hdd and hmpd 3 out: styd chalng for 2nd tl no ex fr last* **28/1**

/6F- **4** *9* **Danimix (IRE)**[276] 851 9-11-12 127 ....(t) MrRGSpencer(7) 119
(Anthony Honeyball) *led: wnt lft 1st: cl up tl struggling 14th: effrt 4 out: one pce fr next* **2/1**[1]

51P- **5** *11* **Buck's Bond (FR)**[97] 3293 8-12-2 124 ....(bt) MrJSole(3) 105
(Paul Nicholls) *trckd ldrs: wnt 2nd 7th tl rdn after 4 out: fdd fr next* **4/1**[3]

6/2- **6** *hd* **Bolachoir (IRE)**[335] 84 12-11-7 94 .... LtColEricaBridge(7) 102
(Patrick Chamings) *trckd ldrs tl lost pl 15th: short-lived effrt after 4 out: fdd fr next: chalng for wl-hld 5th whn rdr lost irons last* **66/1**

/34- **P** **Offshore Account (IRE)**[12] 4936 14-11-7 110..(vt[1]) MrDominicSutton(7)
(Tracey L Bailey) *in tch: trckd ldrs 10th: nt fluent next: wknd after 4 out: p.u bef 2 out* **33/1**

126/ **P** **Vintage Class (IRE)**[17] 11-11-7 99 ....(bt[1]) CaptCharlieO'Shea(7)
(Mrs Kayley Woollacott) *virtually ref to r: j. off 3 fences bhd: styd there tl p.u bef 10th* **100/1**

605- **U** **Marley Roca (IRE)**[26] 4661 10-11-7 119 .... CaptMaxChenery(7)
(Paul Webber) *hld up: blnd and uns rdr 6th* **16/1**

4/P- **U** **Qualypso D'Allier (FR)**[26] 4661 10-11-10 89 ow3... MrRobertSkinner(7)
(Richard Woollacott) *sn in tch: mstke 2nd: nt fluent next: awkward whn unseating rdr 8th* **100/1**

6m 54.8s (15.30) **Going Correction** +0.20s/f (Yiel) 10 Ran SP% **112.3**
Speed ratings: **84,83,83,80,76 76,,,,**
CSF £17.87 TOTE £8.20: £1.80, £1.40, £2.30; EX 19.20 Trifecta £236.70.

Owner Don Churston **Bred** Marc Trinquet And Olivier Trinquet **Trained** Andoversford, Gloucs

■ Stewards' Enquiry : Capt Charlie O'Shea six-day ban: hit horse at start, improper riding (Apr 16,21-25)

FOCUS
This was the first time in 83 years that the Royal Artillery Gold Cup had not taken place at Sandown. It had been move here after the original fixture at the Esher track was abandoned in February. It's unlikely that this is anything other than modest form for the class. The winner is rated to his mark.

5128 32RED WELCOMES MICROGAMING PLAYERS H'CAP HURDLE (JOCKEY CLUB GRASSROOTS JUMPS SERIES QUALIFIER) (10 hdls 1 omitted) 2m 6f
4:15 (4:17) (Class 3) (0-125,125) 4-Y-0+ **£5,848** (£1,717; £858; £429)

Form RPR

361- **1** **Generous Ransom (IRE)**[15] 4888 6-11-3 116 .... RichardJohnson 123+
(Nick Gifford) *mde all: set stdy pce tl 4th where qcknd sltly: rdn into clr ld appr 2 out: nt fluent last: kpt on gamely: rdn out* **11/2**[3]

312- **2** *3 1/4* **Henryville**[7] 5030 6-11-12 125 .... NoelFehily 130+
(Harry Fry) *hld up towards rr on outer: pushed along and hdwy after 3 out: nt clr run bef next: rdn between last 2: styd on to go 2nd run-in: nvr rching wnr* **5/2**[1]

235- **3** *1 1/2* **Kalmbeforethestorm**[151] 2210 6-11-1 114 .... PaulMoloney 115
(Helen Nelmes) *in tch: rdn appr 2 out: styd on fr last: wnt 3rd towards fin* **33/1**

22- **4** *1/2* **V Neck (IRE)**[104] 3173 5-11-7 120 .... APMcCoy 124+
(Paul Nicholls) *hld up towards rr: hdwy after 7th: shkn up appr 2 out: cld and clsng on wnr whn stmbld bdly last: sn hld whn hung bdly lft and lost 2 pls run-in* **5/1**[2]

U24- **5** *1/2* **Phare Isle (IRE)**[24] 4697 9-10-9 115 ....(tp) MrMJPKendrick(7) 115
(Ben Case) *trckd ldrs: rdn appr 2 out: kpt on same pce fr last* **16/1**

564- **6** *9* **Back In June**[15] 4887 6-10-9 108 .... TomO'Brien 99
(Paul Henderson) *disp ld most of way: rdn after 3 out: hdd bef next: fdd fr last* **33/1**

003- **7** *5* **Sinbad The Sailor**[18] 4801 9-11-2 118 ....(t) TrevorWhelan(3) 104
(George Baker) *hld up towards rr: pushed along and hdwy after 3 out: rdn to chse ldrs next: wknd last* **28/1**

003- **8** *shd* **Invicta Lake (IRE)**[24] 4697 7-11-4 117 ....(p) PaddyBrennan 103
(Suzy Smith) *mid-div: hdwy to trck ldrs after 3 out: sn rdn: wknd bef last* **10/1**

42P- **9** *5* **Patsys Castle (IRE)**[102] 3195 7-11-6 119 .... SamTwiston-Davies 100
(Kim Bailey) *trckd ldrs: rdn after 3 out: wknd bef 2 out* **25/1**

1F5- **10** *4 1/2* **Rior (IRE)**[33] 4538 7-10-6 105 .... JamieMoore 81
(Paul Henderson) *a towards rr* **14/1**

113- **11** *6* **Carlton Jack**[17] 4841 7-11-12 125 .... RichieMcLernon 95
(Jonjo O'Neill) *trckd ldrs: rdn after 3 out: wknd bef next* **14/1**

620- **12** *3 3/4* **Steel Summit (IRE)**[12] 4937 5-10-6 105 .... DougieCostello 72
(David Dennis) *mid-div: rdn after 3 out: sn wknd* **40/1**

4/3- **13** *7* **Kings Bayonet**[32] 4555 7-11-4 117 .... RobertThornton 77
(Alan King) *mid-div: hdwy appr 3 out: rdn bef 2 out: sn wknd* **8/1**

1/6- **14** *11* **Fountains Flypast**[112] 3028 10-11-9 122 ....(t) AidanColeman 71
(Anthony Honeyball) *mid-div: rdn after 3 out: sn wknd* **33/1**

5m 32.1s (5.60) **Going Correction** -0.15s/f (Good) 14 Ran SP% **118.6**
Speed ratings (Par 107): **83,81,81,81,80 77,75,75,73,72 70,68,66,62**
CSF £18.32 CT £423.02 TOTE £6.30: £1.80, £1.10, £16.20; EX 26.60 Trifecta £1430.50.

Owner Sir Christopher Wates **Bred** Sir Christopher Stephen Wates **Trained** Findon, W Sussex

FOCUS
Surprisingly when considering the field size, there was little pace on early here. Another step forward from the winner, but suspect form.

5129 RED & YELLA MICKEY BOWLEY MEMORIAL H'CAP CHASE (21 fncs) 3m 1f 110y
4:45 (4:45) (Class 4) (0-115,115) 5-Y-0+ **£4,873** (£1,431; £715; £357)

Form RPR

426- **1** **Water Wagtail**[40] 4399 7-10-9 101 .... GavinSheehan(3) 112+
(Emma Lavelle) *hld up: pushd along after 15th: hdwy after 17th: rdn to chse ldr appr 3 out: wnt lft and nt fluent 2 out: led sn after last: styd on: rdn out* **5/4**[1]

262- **2** *2 1/4* **Rocky Bender (IRE)**[9] 5004 9-10-10 99 ....(b) AidanColeman 111+
(Venetia Williams) *wnt sltly rt at times: led: clr after 3rd: wnt rt 5th: blnd 15th: mstke 17th: rdn after next: nt fluent last: sn hdd: no ex* **10/1**

U22- **3** *23* **West Cork Flash (IRE)**[18] 4798 10-10-12 101 ....(p) RichardJohnson 93
(Paul Henderson) *trckd ldrs: wnt 2nd 15th tl rdn after 4 out: wknd after next* **6/1**[3]

1P3- **4** *32* **Trojan Sun**[10] 4990 8-11-9 112 ....(t) FelixDeGiles 71
(Tom Symonds) *hld up: hdwy after 9th to dispute 2nd tl mstke 15th: sn rdn: wknd 17th: t.o* **25/1**

522- **F** **Mic Aubin (FR)**[18] 4809 11-10-6 95 .... SamTwiston-Davies
(Jennifer Mason) *prom tl trckd ldng pair after 3rd: fell 12th* **10/1**

P25- **P** **Curtain Razer (IRE)**[18] 4801 8-11-3 106 .... TomCannon
(Chris Gordon) *last: nt fluent 6th: nvr travelling fr 8th and detached: p.u after 12th* **33/1**

3P2- **P** **Off The Wall (IRE)**[7] 5032 7-11-5 108 ....(bt) TomScudamore
(David Pipe) *hld up: rdn after 15th: mstke 17th: sn wknd: t.o whn p.u bef 3 out* **3/1**[2]

4P2- **P** **Regal Presence (IRE)**[15] 4884 7-11-12 115 ....(b) JackDoyle
(Victor Dartnall) *prom: hit 2nd: trckd ldr fr next: mstke 9th: lost pl and pushed along after 13th: grad lost tch: p.u bef 16th* **10/1**

6m 46.8s (7.30) **Going Correction** +0.20s/f (Yiel) 8 Ran SP% **117.8**
Speed ratings: **96,95,88,78,,,,**
CSF £15.14 CT £58.84 TOTE £2.70: £1.20, £2.00, £2.30; EX 17.90 Trifecta £69.30.

Owner D I Bare **Bred** D I Bare **Trained** Hatherden, Hants

FOCUS
Lots of these were struggling a long way from home thanks to the pace set by Rocky Bender. The winner was again below the level of his Taunton second.

5130 32RED TOMB RAIDER SLOT "NEWCOMERS" STANDARD OPEN NATIONAL HUNT FLAT RACE 2m
5:15 (5:17) (Class 6) 4-6-Y-0 **£1,624** (£477; £238; £119)

Form RPR

1 **Jollyallan** 5-11-4 0 .... NoelFehily 118+
(Harry Fry) *mde all: qcknd clr over 2f out: impressive* **9/4**[1]

- **2** *15* **Abitofbob** 5-11-4 0 .... AidanColeman 103
(Emma Lavelle) *pressed wnr tl readily outpcd over 2f out but kpt on wl for clr 2nd* **20/1**

3 *11* **Starlight Sonata** 4-10-2 0 .... GavinSheehan(3) 79
(Emma Lavelle) *mid-div: hdwy over 3f out: rdn in 4th over 2f out: styd on to go 3rd ent fnl f: nvr any danger to ldng pair* **40/1**

4 *2* **Horace Hazel** 5-11-1 0 .... RachaelGreen(3) 90
(Anthony Honeyball) *mid-div: styd on but nvr gng pce to get on terms: wnt 4th ent fnl f* **5/1**

5 *3 3/4* **Abuelo (FR)** 4-10-12 0 .... JoshuaMoore 80
(Gary Moore) *trckd ldng pair tl otpced over 2f out: wknd ent fnl f* **25/1**

- **6** *3* **George Arthur** 6-11-4 0 .... LeightonAspell 83
(Nick Gifford) *bhd: styd on past btn horses fnl 2f: nvr any danger* **33/1**

- **7** *2 1/2* **Strictly The One (IRE)** 4-10-12 0 .... APMcCoy 75
(Neil Mulholland) *chsd ldrs: rdn over 3f out: wknd over 2f out* **20/1**

8 *4* **Mylittlemouse (IRE)** 6-10-11 0 .... PaulMoloney 70
(Helen Nelmes) *mid-div tl wknd over 2f out* **100/1**

9 *1/2* **Zanstra (IRE)** 4-10-12 0 .... BrendanPowell 70
(Colin Tizzard) *mid-div tl wknd over 2f out* **16/1**

10 *1* **Kerry Maur** 5-11-4 0 .... TomCannon 75
(Chris Gordon) *rn wd on bnd leaving bk st: a towards rr* **66/1**

11 *7* **Praetura (IRE)** 4-10-12 0 .... NickScholfield 62
(Paul Nicholls) *chsd ldrs for 4f: sn in rr* **9/2**[3]

12 *14* **Lanta's Legacy** 4-10-2 0 .... MattGriffiths(3) 41
(Jeremy Scott) *plld hrd: trckd ldrs after 3f: wknd wl over 2f out* **33/1**

13 *13* **Bilbrook Blaze** 4-10-12 0 ....(t) RichardJohnson 35
(Philip Hobbs) *mid-div tl wknd over 2f out* **4/1**[2]

14 *7* **Bears Rails** 4-10-12 0 .... RyanMahon 28
(Colin Tizzard) *sn struggling in rr: t.o* **16/1**

3m 38.6s (-4.70) **Going Correction** -0.15s/f (Good)
WFA 4 from 5yo+ 5lb 14 Ran SP% **121.6**
Speed ratings: **55,47,42,41,39 37,36,34,34,33 30,23,16,13**
CSF £56.50 TOTE £3.50: £1.40, £6.80, £8.10; EX 52.90 Trifecta £1019.00.

Owner Richard Barber **Bred** Jethro Bloodstock **Trained** Seaborough, Dorset

FOCUS
None of these had run before, so it is total guesswork how strong this form will turn out to be. The time was slow.

5131 JOHN DUFOSEE MEMORIAL OPEN HUNTERS' CHASE (21 fncs) 3m 1f 110y
5:45 (5:45) (Class 6) 5-Y-0+ **£987** (£303; £151)

Form RPR

4P3- **1** **Coombe Hill**[31] 13-11-13 115 .... MrDEdwards(3) 120+
(Mrs C Fear) *trckd ldrs: disputing 3rd whn stmbld bdly 4 out and dropped to hld looking 4th: styd on fr after 3 out: led after 2 out: drifted rt fnl 40yds: drvn rt out* **9/2**[3]

/04- **2** *3/4* **How's My Friend**[18] 9-11-5 108 .... MissABush(7) 115
(Grant Cann) *hld up: sltly detached and pushed along after 13th: hdwy after 4 out: disp 4th 2 out: styd on wl fr last: clsng qckly and into 2nd whn short of room fnl strides* **16/1**

P50/ **3** *1/2* **Iron Chancellor (IRE)**[24] 9-11-7 0 .... MrMLegg(5) 115
(Mrs Sue Popham) *trckd ldrs: hit 2nd: chal 17th: led appr 3 out: sn rdn: hdd sn after 2 out: styd on* **4/1**[2]

110- **4** *5* **Shy John**[19] 4788 8-11-13 121 .... MrPMason(7) 120
(P W Mason) *hld up: pckd 1st: hdwy after 14th: rdn in 3rd appr 3 out: ch 2 out: no ex appr last* **10/11**[1]

/00- **5** *7* **Marufo (IRE)**[42] 4348 12-11-5 108 ....(tp) MrDominicSutton(7) 102
(Tracey L Bailey) *led: rdn and hdd appr 3 out: kpt chsng ldrs tl wknd appr last* **12/1**

4/P- **P** **Special Occasion**[10] 10-11-5 0....................................(p) MissLGould(7)
(Miss S L Gould) *trckd ldrs: pckd 1st: lost pl and reminders after 6th: styd in tch tl wknd after 17th: p.u bef 3 out* **50/1**

/53- **P** **Captain Marlon (IRE)**[224] 1336 13-11-5 85.................... MrJBargary(7)
(Mrs Claire Hitch) *trckd ldrs: hmpd 8th: hit 10th: wknd qckly 4 out: p.u bef next* **66/1**

3F- **P** **Meilyr**[13] 4915 11-11-5 0.. MrMWoodward(7)
(Mrs C Lawrence) *trckd ldrs: j.lft and bmpd 8th: wknd 17th: p.u bef 3 out* **33/1**

443- **P** **Latest Trend (IRE)**[18] 8-11-7 98.................................. MissBAndrews(5)
(S Penny) *hld up: nvr threatened: wknd 4 out: p.u bef next* **16/1**

6m 58.8s (19.30) **Going Correction** +0.20s/f (Yiel) **9** Ran SP% **116.4**
Speed ratings: **78,77,77,76,73** , , ,
CSF £64.86 TOTE £5.50: £1.70, £3.90, £1.10; EX 53.40 Trifecta £288.80.
Owner G Thompson **Bred** A Kirtley **Trained** Sherborne, Dorset

FOCUS
All the major players came to the fore in the final stages, and it saw a repeat of last year's outcome. It was also the slowest of the three races run over this distance on the card.
T/Jkpt: Not won. T/Plt: £42.90 to a £1 stake. Pool: £104,965.57 - 1784.33 winning units. T/Qpdt: £17.70 to a £1 stake. Pool: £6342.44 - 264.64 winning units. TM

2933 AINTREE (L-H)
Thursday, April 3

OFFICIAL GOING: Mildmay course - good (7.1); hurdle course - good (good to soft in places; 6.8); national course - good to soft (good in places; 6.6)
Wind: light 1/2 against Weather: fine

5132 INJURED JOCKEYS FUND 50TH ANNIVERSARY 4-Y-O JUVENILE HURDLE (GRADE 1) (9 hdls) 2m 1f
2:00 (2:00) (Class 1) 4-Y-O

£56,270 (£21,200; £10,610; £5,300; £2,660; £1,330)

Form RPR

113- **1** **Guitar Pete (IRE)**[20] 4784 4-11-0 144..................................(v) PCarberry 141+
(D T Hughes, Ire) *hld up: mstke 6th: rdn bef 3 out: 9th and stl plenty to do 2 out: 4th last: styd on wl: squeezed through gap 100yds out: led 50yds out* **13/2**

22F- **2** 1 3/4 **Clarcam (FR)**[22] 4755 4-11-0 133.....................................(t[1]) DavyRussell 138
(Gordon Elliott, Ire) *midfield: hdwy bef 3 out: sn chsd ldrs: led narrowly last: kpt on: hdd 50yds out* **14/1**

114- **3** 2 1/4 **Calipto (FR)**[20] 4784 4-11-0 148............................... SamTwiston-Davies 138+
(Paul Nicholls) *prom: led 5th: nt fluent 3 out: sn rdn and strly pressed: jst hdd whn nt fluent last: no ex fnl 75yds* **7/2**[1]

32- **4** 3/4 **Commissioned (IRE)**[40] 4419 4-11-0 131.....................(b) DenisO'Regan 135
(John Ferguson) *racd keenly: prom: led 3rd: hdd 5th: remained cl up: rdn after 3 out: ev ch whn hit last: sn edgd lft: wknd fnl 75yds* **16/1**

12- **5** 5 **Aurore D'Estruval (FR)**[47] 4268 4-10-7 137..................... TomScudamore 124
(John Quinn) *trckd ldrs: hit 5th: rdn bef 3 out: wknd after last* **10/1**

421- **6** shd **Fox Norton (FR)**[110] 3089 4-11-0 146............................ RichardJohnson 130
(Nick Williams) *midfield: hdwy on outer to chse ldrs 3 out: wknd after last* **5/1**[2]

146- **7** 5 **Dispour (IRE)**[46] 4302 4-11-0 124...........................(b[1]) WayneHutchinson 125
(Donald McCain) *midfield: rdn bef 3 out: sn no imp on ldrs: wknd bef last* **100/1**

21- **8** 1 3/4 **Activial (FR)**[40] 4419 4-11-0 137.. NoelFehily 124
(Harry Fry) *in tch: rdn 3 out: wknd after 2 out* **11/2**[3]

340- **9** 3/4 **Violet Dancer**[22] 4755 4-11-0 130.. JamieMoore 124
(Gary Moore) *midfield: hit 4th: wknd 2 out* **40/1**

161- **10** 3 1/4 **Hawk High (IRE)**[22] 4755 4-11-0 138..................................(p) BrianHughes 124+
(Tim Easterby) *in tch: rdn 3 out: 4th whn mstke 2 out: wknd* **10/1**

210- **11** 5 **Broughton (GER)**[20] 4784 4-11-0 138.......................................[1] APMcCoy 119
(John Ferguson) *trckd ldr: led after 1st: hdd 3rd: remained cl up: nt fluent 6th and qckly lost pl: btn whn hmpd 3 out* **9/1**

01- **12** 9 **Agreement (IRE)**[24] 4722 4-11-0 0................................... PatrickCorbett 108
(Rebecca Curtis) *trckd ldrs: pushed along and lost pl after 6th: wknd bef 3 out* **66/1**

240- **13** 4 **Handiwork**[22] 4755 4-11-0 130...(p) NickScholfield 108
(Steve Gollings) *led tl slow and j.rt 1st: sn dropped to rr: bhd and btn whn hmpd by faller 6th* **66/1**

14 9 **Rhamnus**[103] 4-11-0 0... DavidBass 96
(Ben Pauling) *hld up: a towards rr* **100/1**

125- **F** **Baradari (IRE)**[22] 4755 4-11-0 134.................................... AidanColeman
(Venetia Williams) *midfield on inner: fell 6th* **25/1**

4m 9.8s (-3.90) **Going Correction** +0.10s/f (Yiel) **15** Ran SP% **119.6**
Speed ratings: **113,112,111,110,108 108,106,105,104,103 100,96,94,90,**
CSF £88.29 CT £373.03 TOTE £6.40: £2.10, £5.00, £1.80; EX 98.20 Trifecta £688.50.
Owner Mrs P Sloan **Bred** P J Burke **Trained** The Curragh, Co Kildare

FOCUS
The ground was changed to good on both the hurdle and chase track prior to racing, while it remained good to soft, good in places on the National course. Mildmay bends were at outermost configuration increasing advertised distances by about 40yds per circuit. Hurdles and bends were also on outermost line increasing advertised distances by about 90yds per circuit. The Triumph Hurdle form was upheld courtesy of the first and third, but this was probably just an ordinary renewal in what looks an ordinary year for juveniles, with a small step up from Guitar Pete.

5133 BETFRED BOWL CHASE (GRADE 1) (19 fncs) 3m 1f
2:30 (2:32) (Class 1) 5-Y-0+

£84,405 (£31,800; £15,915; £7,950; £3,990; £1,995)

Form RPR

314- **1** **Silviniaco Conti (FR)**[20] 4787 8-11-7 177.............................. NoelFehily 171+
(Paul Nicholls) *w ldrs: led 3rd: hit 13th: hdd briefly after 4 out: hung lft after 2 out: wandered appr last: styd on wl* **9/4**[2]

251- **2** 1 1/2 **Dynaste (FR)**[21] 4766 8-11-7 169............................... TomScudamore 168
(David Pipe) *hld up in tch: hdwy to trck ldrs 7th: handy 3rd 15th: carried rt between last 2: upsides last: styd on same pce* **13/8**[1]

F61- **3** 1 1/2 **Argocat (IRE)**[47] 4283 6-11-7 149.. APMcCoy 167
(T J Taaffe, Ire) *in tch in last: outpcd 14: chsng ldrs 4 out: kpt on same pce to take 3rd sn after last* **25/1**

423- **4** 3/4 **First Lieutenant (IRE)**[53] 4183 9-11-7 164...................(p) BarryGeraghty 165
(M F Morris, Ire) *w ldrs: led briefly after 4 out: edgd rt between last 2: kpt on one pce run-in* **10/3**[3]

/P0- **5** 10 **Menorah (IRE)**[21] 4766 9-11-7 166................................ RichardJohnson 158
(Philip Hobbs) *trckd ldrs 4th: cl 3rd whn hit 15th: sn drvn: nt fluent 2 out: wknd between last 2* **12/1**

430- **6** 9 **Houblon Des Obeaux (FR)**[20] 4787 7-11-7 158............. AidanColeman 152
(Venetia Williams) *led to 3rd: nt fluent after: hit 7th: lost pl 9th: reminders 14th: sn bhd* **25/1**

6m 21.8s (-8.20) **Going Correction** 0.0s/f (Good) **6** Ran SP% **107.3**
Speed ratings: **113,112,112,111,108 105**
CSF £6.01 TOTE £3.10: £1.80, £1.40; EX 6.50 Trifecta £49.80.
Owner Potensis Limited & Chris Giles **Bred** Patrick Joubert **Trained** Ditcheat, Somerset
■ Stewards' Enquiry : Barry Geraghty one-day ban: careless riding (Apr 17)

FOCUS
The three main protagonists in this Grade 1 were all previous C&D winners, and they filled first and second places. Silviniaco Conti probably ran to a similar level as in last year's race, and was a bit better than the bare result but rated 8lb off his King George mark. Dynaste is rated in line with his his Ryanair win.

5134 DOOM BAR AINTREE HURDLE (GRADE 1) (11 hdls) 2m 4f
3:05 (3:08) (Class 1) 4-Y-O+

£112,540 (£42,400; £21,220; £10,600; £5,320; £2,660)

Form RPR

123- **1** **The New One (IRE)**[23] 4739 6-11-7 167................... SamTwiston-Davies 166
(Nigel Twiston-Davies) *trckd ldrs: effrt appr 3 out: led between last 2: j.rt last: all out* **4/9**[1]

110- **2** hd **Rock On Ruby (IRE)**[23] 4737 9-11-7 163..............................(t) NoelFehily 165
(Harry Fry) *trckd ldrs: upsides 6th: led 8th: hdd between last 2: styd on wl: jst hld* **10/1**[3]

134- **3** nse **Diakali (FR)**[20] 4785 5-11-7 158.. APMcCoy 165
(W P Mullins, Ire) *t.k.h in last: hdwy appr 3 out: disp cl 2nd last: r.o wl: jst hld* **13/2**[2]

226- **4** 10 **Ptit Zig (FR)**[23] 4739 5-11-7 159.. NickScholfield 158
(Paul Nicholls) *led: mstke 1st: hdd 3rd: cl 3rd whn nt fluent 2 out: wknd last* **14/1**

530- **5** 21 **Grumeti**[23] 4739 6-11-7 148... RobertThornton 137
(Alan King) *chsd ldrs: drvn appr 3 out: lost pl appr 2 out* **66/1**

013- **6** 9 **Irish Saint (FR)**[54] 4147 5-11-7 151..............................(t) TomScudamore 130
(Paul Nicholls) *w ldr: led 3rd: hdd 8th: lost pl appr 2 out* **16/1**

226- **7** 16 **Grandouet (FR)**[23] 4737 7-11-7 160....................................... BarryGeraghty 121
(Nicky Henderson) *hld up towards rr: hit 7th: lost pl 3 out: bhd whn mstke next* **20/1**

4m 54.8s (-5.90) **Going Correction** +0.10s/f (Yiel) **7** Ran SP% **110.5**
Speed ratings (Par 117): **115,114,114,110,102 98,92**
CSF £5.45 TOTE £1.50: £1.20, £2.30; EX 4.40 Trifecta £13.70.
Owner Mrs S Such **Bred** R Brown & Ballylinch Stud **Trained** Naunton, Gloucs
■ This event has previously been run on the Saturday.
■ Stewards' Enquiry : A P McCoy four-day ban: used whip above permitted level (Apr 17,19-21)

FOCUS
A race that lacked the depth of recent years, but it produced an enthralling finish, with the first three separated by just a head and a nose. It was run at an even gallop. Ther New One is rated up 2lb on his form in this last year but, like Rock On Ruby, was below his best 2m form.

5135 CRABBIE'S SUPPORTING THE HILLSBOROUGH FAMILIES FOX HUNTERS' CHASE (18 fncs) 2m 5f 110y
3:40 (3:40) (Class 2) 6-Y-0+

£23,984 (£7,492; £3,744; £1,872; £936; £472)

Form RPR

004/ **1** **Warne (IRE)**[40] 4437 10-12-0 135................................ MrSWaley-Cohen 138+
(B R Hamilton, Ire) *mde all: clr 8th tl after 3 out: styd on strly to forge clr run-in* **7/2**[2]

136- **2** 13 **Tartan Snow**[18] 4837 14-12-0 120................................ MrDerekO'Connor 126
(Stuart Coltherd) *in rr div: hdwy 10th (Becher's): 3rd 3 out: chsd ldng pair next: wnt 2nd at elbow: kpt on same pce* **25/1**

U/1- **3** 4 1/2 **Mossey Joe (IRE)**[17] 11-12-0 152.. MrDSkehan 125+
(E Bolger, Ire) *trckd ldrs: 2nd 3rd (Chair): cl up appr 3 out: 3 l 2nd and drvn last: hrd rdn after elbow* **11/8**[1]

10P/ **4** 8 **Earth Dream (IRE)**[95] 11-12-0 117............................ MrJamesFerguson 116
(John Ferguson) *chsd ldrs: 3rd fr 4th (Water): mstke 13th (Valentine's): one pce fr 3 out* **33/1**

130/ **5** 3 3/4 **Cottage Oak (IRE)**[97] 11-12-0 130.. MrGCrow 114
(J J O'Shea) *mid-div: outpcd whn mstke 14th: one pce fr 3 out* **20/1**

3/2- **6** 8 **Court Red Handed (IRE)**[27] 4655 9-12-0 117...............(t) MrMJPKendrick 108
(Mrs S Case) *prom: 4th 10th (Becher's): fdd appr last* **25/1**

P21- **7** 8 **Richard's Sundance (IRE)**[39] 4443 12-12-0 127(p) MrMatthewHampton 100
(Victor Dartnall) *prom: hit 11th (Foinavon): outpcd 13th (Valentine's): one pce fr 3 out: mstke last* **16/1**

0P0- **8** 1/2 **Himalayan Express**[27] 4658 10-12-0 110................................ MrJMartin 102
(Mrs David Plunkett) *mid-div: hit 11th (Foinavon) and 14th: kpt on fr 3 out: nvr a factor* **100/1**

433- **9** 3 1/2 **Swallows Delight (IRE)**[27] 4658 9-12-0 100........................ MrDMansell 93
(Mrs Julie Mansell) *towards rr: msitake 1st: sme hdwy 13th (Valentine's): kpt on fr 3 out: nvr a factor* **100/1**

626/ **10** 29 **Sizing America (IRE)**[12] 13-12-0 109..................................... MrWTelfer 67
(Miss S Randell) *mstkes: prom: lost pl 8th: bhd whn blnd 14th: t.o 3 out* **66/1**

/3P- **11** shd **Douglas Julian**[33] 4554 12-12-0 112..............................(p) MrTHamilton 67
(Miss K Scott) *sn bhd: drvn along 5th: t.o 3 out* **66/1**

/2P- **12** 3 1/2 **Island Life (IRE)**[27] 4655 11-12-0 109..........................(p) MissGAndrews 64
(S Flook) *in rr: bhd whn mstke 12th (Becher's): t.o 3 out* **100/1**

30P- **13** 3 1/4 **Keenan's Future (IRE)**[11] 13-12-0 91..........................(p) MissAEStirling 61
(S Rea) *in rr: bhd fr5th: t.o 3 out* **100/1**

/56- **14** 1 1/4 **Cool Friend (IRE)**[43] 4355 11-11-7 114................................ MrOGreenall 53
(Oliver Greenall) *in rr: bhd fr 7th: t.o 3 out* **20/1**

245- **15** 12 **Orfeo Conti (FR)**[21] 4782 12-12-0 87................................ MrOWedmore 49
(Miss Rose Grissell) *mid-div: bhd whn mstke 10th (Becher's): blnd 12th (Canal Turn) t.o 2 out* **200/1**

/24- **16** dist **Harry Flashman**[312] 496 13-12-0 107................................ MrNOrpwood
(Greg Aitken) *chsd ldrs: wkng whn blnd 13th (Valentine's): sn bhd: t.o 3 out: virtually p.u run-in: eventually completed* **50/1**

5/2- **P** **Dead Or Alive (IRE)**[42] 4376 11-12-0 113................................ MrGWheeler
(Miss Rose Grissell) *sn bhd: t.o after 4th (water): p.u bef 7th* **100/1**

033- **U** **Fresh Air And Fun (IRE)**[43] 4355 11-12-0 108.................. MrWBiddick
(Alastair Ralph) *mid-div: in tch whn blnd and uns rdr 11th (Foinavon)* **50/1**

000/ **U** **Boxer Georg (IRE)**[25] 12-12-0 122.. MrPWMullins
(W P Mullins, Ire) *chsd ldrs: lost pl 5th: in rr whn blnd and uns rdr 7th* **16/1**

F/5- **U** **Supreme Doc (IRE)**[200] 1589 9-12-0 139..............................(p) MrJJCodd
(M T O'Donovan, Ire) *in rr whn blnd and uns rdr 1st* **11/1**[3]

The Form Book Jumps, Raceform Ltd, Compton, RG20 6NL.

U61- **U** **Pentiffic (NZ)**[25] 4705 11-12-0 114....................................(p) MrJHamilton
(Venetia Williams) *mid-div: blnd bdly 2nd: sn uns rdr* **14/1**
5m 29.4s (-7.60) **Going Correction** 0.0s/f (Good) **21** Ran SP% **123.6**
Speed ratings: **113,108,106,103,102 99,96,96,95,84 84,83,82,81,77 , , , ,**
CSF £91.09 CT £179.76 TOTE £4.40: £1.70, £5.50, £1.80; EX 104.10 Trifecta £245.90.
Owner R Waley-Cohen C Fenwick M Hankin C Noell **Bred** J Wesley Trimble **Trained** Downpatrick, Co Down
■ Brunswick Gold was withdrawn after running loose before the start.
■ Brunswick Gold was withdrawn. Price at time of withdrawal 25/1. Rule 4 does not apply.
■ Stewards' Enquiry : Mr D Skehan 11-day ban: used whip above permitted level (tbn)

FOCUS
This proved to be remarkably uncompetitive for a 21-runner contest over the National fences, with the two clear market leaders taking control from an early stage. Warne ran to his mark but has the potential to rate higher, and is well up to standard for this race. Tartan Snow ran to last year's winning mark and Mossey Joe was 2st+ off his best.

5136 SILVER CROSS RED RUM H'CAP CHASE (GRADE 3) (12 fncs) 2m
4:15 (4:15) (Class 1) 5-Y-0+
£45,560 (£17,096; £8,560; £4,264; £2,144; £1,072)

Form RPR
246- **1** **Parsnip Pete**[14] 4921 8-10-10 **134**.................................... PaddyBrennan 145+
(Tom George) *midfield: hdwy 6th: trckd ldr 8th: led 3 out: sn rdn: 4 l up whn hit last: drvn out* **16/1**
232- **2** *1 ½* **Turn Over Sivola (FR)**[33] 4543 7-10-10 **134**................. RobertThornton 142+
(Alan King) *hld up: mstke 5th: nt fluent 8th: rdn and gd hdwy after 2 out: 3rd bef last: styd on: wnt 2nd towards fin* **13/2**[3]
243- **3** *1 ½* **Claret Cloak (IRE)**[20] 4790 7-11-8 **146**................................... NoelFehily 152
(Emma Lavelle) *hld up: stdy hdwy fr 7th: hit 3 out: rdn to chse ldr between last 2: one pce run-in: lost 2nd towards fin* **7/2**[1]
33P- **4** *5* **Astracad (FR)**[20] 4790 8-11-2 **140**.......................(vt) SamTwiston-Davies 141
(Nigel Twiston-Davies) *trckd ldrs: led 8th: hdd 3 out: sn rdn: edgd lft and dropped to 4th bef last: no ex run-in* **16/1**
20P- **5** *9* **Gus Macrae (IRE)**[40] 4414 10-9-12 **127**....................(tp) PatrickCorbett[(5)] 119
(Rebecca Curtis) *sn in tch: drvn and outpcd after 4 out: plugged on after 2 out* **20/1**
25F- **6** *nk* **Oiseau De Nuit (FR)**[20] 4790 12-11-12 **150**..................(t) BrendanPowell 142
(Colin Tizzard) *midfield: briefly n.m.r after 8th: rdn after 4 out: plugged on: nvr threatened ldrs* **16/1**
210- **7** *1 ¼* **Dare Me (IRE)**[20] 4790 10-11-4 **142**.................................. AidanColeman 135
(Venetia Williams) *hld up: hit 7th: bhd tl styd on after 2 out: nvr threatened* **16/1**
003- **8** *shd* **Changing The Guard**[14] 4921 8-10-13 **137**..................(tp) DenisO'Regan 131+
(Dr Richard Newland) *mstkes in rr: sme hdwy 3 out: blnd 2 out: styng on whn another mstke last* **16/1**
0/2- **9** *1* **Arnaud (IRE)**[68] 3893 6-11-3 **148**.. GerFox[(7)] 140
(C Byrnes, Ire) *mde most tl 8th: trckd ldr: rdn 3 out: wknd last* **5/1**[2]
410- **10** *6* **Sew On Target (IRE)**[21] 4768 9-10-9 **133**..................... TomScudamore 118
(Colin Tizzard) *prom: led briefly 5th: lost pl after 8th: wl btn 4 out* **20/1**
354- **11** *2 ¼* **Kings Grey (IRE)**[33] 4543 10-10-11 **135**............................. JamesReveley 121
(Keith Reveley) *trckd ldrs: rdn after 3 out: wknd between last 2: eased* **16/1**
110- **12** *1 ¼* **Anay Turge (FR)**[20] 4785 9-10-3 **134**..........................(bt[1]) TomBellamy[(7)] 115
(Nigel Hawke) *midfield: lost pl after 4th: rdn bef 4 out and brief hdwy: wknd 3 out* **20/1**
211- **13** *14* **Sound Investment (IRE)**[26] 4684 6-11-2 **140**..............(t) NickScholfield 109
(Paul Nicholls) *chsd ldrs: lost pl 7th: wknd after 4 out* **8/1**
110- **14** *30* **Off The Ground (IRE)**[21] 4764 8-11-9 **147**...................... LeightonAspell 89
(Emma Lavelle) *hld up: sme hdwy on outer 7th: wknd after 4 out* **20/1**
500- **P** **Anquetta (IRE)**[20] 4790 10-10-10 **137**......................... MrSWaley-Cohen[(3)]
(Nicky Henderson) *in tch on outer: hit 1st: wknd after 4 out: p.u bef last* **25/1**
02U- **P** **Last Shot (FR)**[14] 4921 7-10-2 **126**.................................... LiamTreadwell
(Venetia Williams) *hld up: a bhd: p.u bef 3 out* **25/1**
3m 54.5s (-5.50) **Going Correction** 0.0s/f (Good) **16** Ran SP% **125.4**
Speed ratings: **113,112,111,109,104 104,103,103,103,100 99,98,91,76,**
CSF £108.74 CT £458.80 TOTE £16.10: £2.60, £1.90, £1.50, £3.70; EX 131.30 Trifecta £502.90.

Owner The Parsnips **Bred** A E Smith And Co **Trained** Slad, Gloucs

FOCUS
This is invariably a hot 2m handicap and, despite four of the last ten winners being market leaders, there have been several shocks as well. The pace was good with a couple taking each other on for the lead. A personal best from Parsnip Pete and Turn Over Sivola is on the upgrade too.

5137 PINSENT MASONS MANIFESTO NOVICES' CHASE (GRADE 1) (16 fncs) 2m 4f
4:50 (4:50) (Class 1) 5-Y-0+ **£50,643** (£19,080; £9,549; £4,770; £2,394)

Form RPR
152- **1** **Uxizandre (FR)**[21] 4764 6-11-4 153.......................................(p) APMcCoy 162+
(Alan King) *trckd ldr: led 6th: rdn bef 2 out: 5 l up between last 2: wandered and reduced advantage last: drvn out run-in* **11/4**[2]
11F- **2** *1 ½* **Oscar Whisky (IRE)**[21] 4764 9-11-4 156...........................(t) BarryGeraghty 162+
(Nicky Henderson) *hld up: nt fluent 10th and 12th: pushed along bef 4 out: rdn to go 2nd jst after 2 out: 2 1/2 l down last: kpt on but a hld* **7/4**[1]
611- **3** *26* **Western Warhorse (IRE)**[23] 4737 6-11-4 161............. TomScudamore 137
(David Pipe) *edgy befhand: led: hdd 6th: remained cl up tl wknd qckly 2 out: hit last* **4/1**[3]
133- **4** *shd* **Fox Appeal (IRE)**[40] 4420 7-11-4 151.................................. AidanColeman 138
(Emma Lavelle) *in tch: nt fluent: mstke 9th: rdn bef 4 out: wknd 2 out* **11/2**
124- **5** *5* **Dodging Bullets**[23] 4737 6-11-4 156..................... SamTwiston-Davies 135
(Paul Nicholls) *hld up in tch: mstke 4 out: drvn bef 3 out: sn btn* **9/1**
4m 59.4s (-4.60) **Going Correction** 0.0s/f (Good) **5** Ran SP% **108.4**
Speed ratings: **109,108,98,97,95**
CSF £8.03 TOTE £3.80: £2.00, £1.30; EX 8.70 Trifecta £22.40.
Owner John P McManus **Bred** Frederic Aimez **Trained** Barbury Castle, Wilts

FOCUS
Ordinary form for the level, but another really likeable effort from Uxizandre, who confirm the merit of his Cheltenham run. A chase best from Oscar Whisky.

5138 DOMINICAN REPUBLIC H'CAP HURDLE (GRADE 3) (13 hdls) 3m 110y
5:25 (5:25) (Class 1) 4-Y-0+
£28,475 (£10,685; £5,350; £2,665; £1,340; £670)

Form RPR
513- **1** **Doctor Harper (IRE)**[26] 4680 6-11-3 **138**....................... TomScudamore 145+
(David Pipe) *hld up in mid-div: hdwy 8th: chsng ldrs 3 out: cl 2nd last: sn led: drvn out* **8/1**[2]
51F- **2** *1 ¾* **Kaylif Aramis**[22] 4752 7-11-3 **138**...........................(t) SamTwiston-Davies 141
(Nigel Twiston-Davies) *rr-div: hdwy appr 3 out: styd on and 5th last: kpt on to take 2nd last 75yds* **12/1**[3]
P20- **3** *½* **Meister Eckhart (IRE)**[22] 4752 8-11-12 **147**.................. RobertThornton 150
(Alan King) *chsd ldrs: cl 3rd last: styd on same pce last 75yds* **20/1**
535- **4** *1 ¼* **Jetson (IRE)**[21] 4765 9-11-5 **145**..................................... PaddyKennedy[(5)] 147
(Mrs John Harrington, Ire) *chsd ldrs: cl 4th last: kpt on same pce* **14/1**
450- **5** *2 ¾* **Utopie Des Bordes (FR)**[21] 4765 6-11-1 **136**............... DavidBass 136
(Nicky Henderson) *led: hdd sn after last: wknd last 75yds* **20/1**
061/ **6** *1 ¾* **Big Easy (GER)**[173] 5362 7-10-12 **136**........................... MichealNolan[(3)] 135
(Philip Hobbs) *chsd ldrs: hit 9th: one pce fr 2 out* **14/1**
346- **7** *1 ½* **On The Bridge (IRE)**[21] 4765 9-11-2 **140**....................... MattGriffiths[(3)] 137
(Jeremy Scott) *in rr: hdwy 3 out: hit wing next: styd on run-in* **12/1**[3]
442- **8** *hd* **Spirit Of Shankly**[42] 4374 6-11-0 **135**................................(tp) NoelFehily 133
(Charlie Longsdon) *mid-div: kpt on fr 3 out: nvr a threat* **8/1**[2]
1U6- **9** *5* **Riverside Theatre**[47] 4265 10-11-10 **145**......................... BarryGeraghty 137
(Nicky Henderson) *in rr: blnd 1st: kpt on fr 3 out: nvr on terms* **20/1**
312/ **10** *¾* **Busty Brown (IRE)**[32] 4584 8-11-5 **140**.................................. PCarberry 131
(Noel Meade, Ire) *mid-div: rdn 3 out: sn outpcd* **7/1**[1]
200- **11** *2* **Pateese (FR)**[21] 4765 9-10-8 **136**...................................(p) ChrisDavies[(7)] 125
(Philip Hobbs) *hld up towards rr: hdwy 3 out: wknd between last 2* **40/1**
12F- **12** *4 ½* **Cantlow (IRE)**[23] 4738 9-11-8 **143**............................ DominicElsworth 128
(Paul Webber) *hld up in rr: sme hdwy 3 out: nvr on terms* **25/1**
600- **13** *1 ¾* **Edgardo Sol (FR)**[22] 4752 7-11-9 **144**.......................... NickScholfield 128
(Paul Nicholls) *hld up in rr: sme hdwy appr 3 out: nvr a factor* **33/1**
/0F- **14** *9* **Two Rockers (IRE)**[47] 4264 7-11-7 **142**..................... WayneHutchinson 118
(Alan King) *in rr-div: effrt appr 3 out: sn btn* **12/1**[3]
110- **15** *1* **Josies Orders (IRE)**[21] 4765 6-11-1 **136**...........................(b) APMcCoy 115
(Jonjo O'Neill) *chsd ldrs: wknd appr 2 out* **14/1**
630- **16** *3 ¾* **Crowning Jewel**[21] 4765 8-11-3 **138**................................ JamesReveley 110
(Keith Reveley) *hld up in last: mstke 5th: sme hdwy 3 out: sn wknd* **33/1**
5/0- **17** *6* **Seefood (IRE)**[21] 4765 7-11-8 **143**...................................(b) DavyCondon 109
(D T Hughes, Ire) *chsd ldrs: lost pl appr 3 out: eased appr last* **20/1**
101- **18** *¾* **Carole's Destrier**[19] 4805 6-11-0 **135**................................ MichaelByrne 100
(Neil Mulholland) *chsd ldrs: wknd appr 2 out: eased last* **14/1**
34P- **19** *8* **Close House**[23] 4742 7-10-10 **138**..............................(tp) TomBellamy[(7)] 96
(David Pipe) *a towards rr: bhd fr 3 out* **28/1**
410- **20** *3 ¼* **Uncle Jimmy (IRE)**[21] 4765 7-10-12 **140**.............. ThomasCheesman[(7)] 95
(Philip Hobbs) *mid-div: hdwy 8th: wknd appr 3 out* **33/1**
210- **21** *8* **Return Spring (IRE)**[53] 4174 7-11-6 **141**........................ RichardJohnson 89
(Philip Hobbs) *chsd ldrs: drvn 10th: lost pl next: bhd whn eased last* **20/1**
121- **22** *21* **Any Given Day (IRE)**[45] 4325 9-11-5 **140**....................... HenryBrooke 69
(Donald McCain) *chsd ldrs: lost pl 3 out: sn bhd: t.o last* **28/1**
6m 18.7s (2.40) **Going Correction** +0.10s/f (Yiel) **22** Ran SP% **130.3**
Speed ratings (Par 113): **100,99,99,98,98 97,96,96,95,95 94,92,92,89,89 88,86,85,83,82 79,72**
CSF £84.14 CT £1903.54 TOTE £9.60: £3.10, £4.30, £5.30, £4.20; EX 138.70 Trifecta £2481.30.

Owner The Johnson Family **Bred** Stephen O'Flynn **Trained** Nicholashayne, Devon

FOCUS
A competitive staying handicap hurdle with just 12lb covering the whole field. Several of these were returning from a spell over fences, but none of them could make a serious impression. The race was relatively steadily run. The first two are on the upgrade with the next two setting the level.
T/Jkpt: Part won. £29041.00 to a £1 stake. Pool £40902.84 - 0.50 winning units. T/Plt: £9.60 to a £1 stake. Pool of £464970.50 - 35040.68 winning tickets. T/Qpdt: £4.30 to a £1 stake. Pool of £19013.04 - 3270.01 winning tickets. WG

5001 TAUNTON (R-H)
Thursday, April 3

OFFICIAL GOING: Good changing to good (good to soft in places) after race 4 (3.55)
Wind: mild breeze across Weather: light rain becoming heavier

5139 TAUNTON JAGUAR ALL NEW F-TYPE COUPE (S) H'CAP HURDLE (9 hdls) 2m 1f
2:10 (2:10) (Class 5) (0-100,98) 4-7-Y-0 **£2,053** (£598; £299)

Form RPR
424- **1** **Captain Sharpe**[12] 4967 6-11-1 **90**................................(t) RobertDunne[(3)] 94+
(Bernard Llewellyn) *in tch: hdwy after 3 out: led narrowly next: kpt on wl to assert run-in: rdn out* **9/4**[1]
544- **2** *2 ¼* **Moneymix**[35] 4519 7-10-3 **75** ow1.......................................(b) TomO'Brien 78
(Ali Brewer) *trckd ldrs: rdn whn nt clr run 2 out: hung lft between last 2: stmbld last: kpt on to go 2nd run-in* **9/4**[1]
063- **3** *1 ½* **To The Sky (IRE)**[16] 4882 6-11-7 **98**....................(p[1]) AodhaganConlon[(5)] 99
(John O'Shea) *led: clr 3rd tl 3 out: sn rdn: narrowly hdd 2 out: ev ch whn hit last: kpt on but no ex* **13/2**[3]
453- **4** *2 ½* **Douchkirk (FR)**[12] 4967 7-11-5 **91**.......................................(b) WillKennedy 90
(John Berry) *hld up: nt fluent 3rd: dropped to last but in tch next: rdn after 3 out: styd on but nt gng pce to get involved* **4/1**[2]
/01- **5** *1 ½* **Kozmina Bay**[45] 3188 5-10-7 **84**..................................(b) RobertWilliams[(5)] 81
(Bernard Llewellyn) *in tch: rdn to chal 2 out: hld bef last: kpt on same pce* **16/1**
000- **6** *1 ¼* **Spunky**[24] 4733 5-10-8 **80**...(t) DonalDevereux 78
(Marc Barber) *trckd ldr: chal 3 out: rdn after 2 out: ev ch last: no ex* **16/1**
0F0- **7** *31* **Pullmen**[43] 3697 6-10-7 **86**.. MrGBranton[(7)] 54
(Paul Henderson) *hld up but in tch: nt fluent 6th: wknd after 3 out: t.o* **33/1**
3m 59.9s (-8.10) **Going Correction** -0.40s/f (Good) **7** Ran SP% **109.6**
Speed ratings: **103,101,101,100,99 98,84**
CSF £7.28 TOTE £2.00: £2.90, £1.30; EX 10.70 Trifecta £43.30.The winner was bought in for 5,200gns.
Owner B J Llewellyn **Bred** Bumble Bloodstock & Mrs S Nicholls **Trained** Fochriw, Caerphilly

FOCUS
Bends moved out 2-3 metres. A desperately weak opener. The winner was on a good mark and is rated in line with the best of his recent form.

5140 DEBRA SPURWAY CELEBRATION NOVICES' HURDLE (10 hdls) 2m 3f 110y
2:45 (2:45) (Class 4) 4-Y-0+ **£4,106** (£1,197; £598)

Form RPR
240- **1** **Garde La Victoire (FR)**[23] 4736 5-11-12 138.......................... TomO'Brien 125+
(Philip Hobbs) *trckd ldrs: looked to be hanging lft most of way: lft in ld after 3 out: nt fluent next: kpt on wl: rdn out* **4/9**[1]
66- **2** *1 ¼* **Vesperal Dream (FR)**[148] 2287 5-10-11 0.......................... HarryDerham[(3)] 109
(Paul Nicholls) *mid-div: hdwy after 7th: trckd wnr gng to 2 out: looking hld whn rdn between last 2: kpt on wl in clsng stages* **7/1**[3]

52- **3** 23 **Almost Gemini (IRE)**[16] 4891 5-11-0 0..............................(p) MarkGrant 88
(Charlie Mann) *mid-div: hdwy 7th: rdn in cl 3rd appr 2 out: nt gng pce to get on terms: hld whn nt fluent last: wknd* **5/1**[2]

600- **4** 1 **Rattleandrun (IRE)**[17] 4863 6-11-0 0.............................. AndrewTinkler 85
(Brendan Powell) *hld up towards rr: struggling 3 out: hdwy bef next: wnt 4th between last 2: styd on w out ever threatening ldrs* **100/1**

0F- **5** 2 ½ **Ernest Speak (IRE)**[149] 2280 5-11-0 0.............................. HaddenFrost 82
(Martin Hill) *hld up towards rr: sme prog in chsng bunch after 3 out: nvr any danger to ldrs* **100/1**

2U5- **6** 2 ¼ **Playhara (IRE)**[14] 4917 5-10-4 0.............................. PeterCarberry(3) 78+
(Nicky Henderson) *mid-div: rdn after 3 out: wnt wl hld 4th whn blnd 2 out: fdd* **16/1**

0- **7** 2 **Italian Symphony (IRE)**[62] 4016 4-10-0 0.............................. WillKennedy 64
(Brendan Powell) *hld up towards rr: sme late minor prog in chsng gp: nvr a factor* **66/1**

8 2 **Ring Eye (IRE)**[41] 1676 6-10-7 107.............................. CiaranMckee(7) 78
(John O'Shea) *a towards rr* **12/1**

000- **9** *nk* **Dream Destiny**[14] 4910 5-10-7 0..............................(t) TommyPhelan 69
(Mark Gillard) *trckd ldr: stmbld 5th: wknd bef 2 out* **100/1**

05- **10** 3 ¾ **Garton Star (IRE)**[12] 4950 5-11-0 0..............................(t) RyanMahon 72
(Harry Fry) *trckd ldrs: rdn after 3 out: sn wknd* **14/1**

0P- **11** 20 **Strategic Exit**[108] 3128 6-11-0 0.............................. TomCannon 52
(James Frost) *trckd ldrs: rdn after 3 out: wknd bef next: t.o* **100/1**

300- **R** **Stella's Fella**[13] 4931 6-11-0 0..............................(p) DavidEngland
(Giles Smyly) *led: hung/j.lft thrght: unsteerable and hung off crse after 3 out* **50/1**

5- **P** **Ollisu Lad (IRE)**[39] 4445 5-11-0 0.............................. DougieCostello
(Tim Vaughan) *hld up towards rr: struggling 6th: p.u after next* **66/1**

4m 38.2s (-7.80) **Going Correction** -0.40s/f (Good)
WFA 4 from 5yo+ 5lb **13** Ran SP% **127.6**
Speed ratings (Par 105): **99,98,89,88,87 87,86,85,85,83 75, ,**
CSF £5.13 TOTE £1.60: £1.02, £1.30, £2.30; EX 6.70 Trifecta £15.00.
Owner Mrs Diana L Whateley **Bred** Mlle Laure Godet **Trained** Withycombe, Somerset

FOCUS
The winner stood out in this modest novice hurdle.

5141 RETAIL THERAPY HERE COME THE GIRLS H'CAP CHASE (12 fncs) 2m 110y
3:20 (3:20) (Class 4) (0-120,122) 5-Y-0+ **£4,223** (£1,240; £620; £310)

Form RPR

541- **1** **Le Bacardy (FR)**[10] 5013 8-11-11 122 7ex..............................(p) TrevorWhelan(3) 133+
(Tony Carroll) *trckd ldrs: chal 4 out: led next: drew clr after 2 out: readily* **6/4**[1]

526- **2** 14 **Overclear**[26] 4685 12-11-11 119.............................. JackDoyle 120
(Victor Dartnall) *trckd ldr: led 4 out: hdd next: sn rdn: kpt on but sn hld by wnr* **5/1**[3]

3P3- **3** 19 **Workbench (FR)**[31] 4592 6-11-12 120..............................(tp) HarrySkelton 99
(Dan Skelton) *led: reminders appr 6th: rdn and hdd 4 out: btn bef next* **9/4**[2]

154- **4** 1 ¾ **Engai (GER)**[49] 4241 8-11-7 115.............................. SeanQuinlan 94
(David Bridgwater) *hld up bhd ldrs: short-lived effrt 4 out: sn btn* **9/1**

23P- **5** 4 ½ **Takeroc (FR)**[106] 3156 11-11-9 117..............................(t) TomO'Brien 93
(Alexandra Dunn) *trckd ldr tl after 7th: last but in tch tl btn after 4 out* **15/2**

4m 4.1s (-9.90) **Going Correction** -0.40s/f (Good) **5** Ran SP% **109.2**
Speed ratings: **107,100,91,90,88**
CSF £9.01 TOTE £2.10: £1.10, £2.70; EX 3.80 Trifecta £10.10.
Owner Carl Hodgson **Bred** Jean-Charles Coude **Trained** Cropthorne, Worcs

FOCUS
The in-form winner is arguably on the upgrade but this was not a strong race.

5142 C & D SOUTHWEST H'CAP HURDLE (10 hdls) 2m 3f 110y
3:55 (3:55) (Class 3) (0-140,137) 4-Y-0+ **£5,523** (£1,621; £810; £405)

Form RPR

410- **1** **Dunraven Storm (IRE)**[20] 4785 9-11-10 135.............................. TomO'Brien 141+
(Philip Hobbs) *hld up: hdwy after 7th: led appr 2 out: kpt on wl: pushed out* **4/1**[2]

3F1- **2** 2 ¼ **Phantom Prince (IRE)**[19] 4799 5-10-11 122.............................. AndrewTinkler 124
(Brendan Powell) *hld up: hdwy appr 2 out: sn rdn: kpt on wl fr last: wnt 2nd fnl 110yds: nt rch wnr* **11/1**

051- **3** 2 ¾ **Dovils Date**[24] 4731 5-9-12 119.............................. AlanJohns(10) 120
(Tim Vaughan) *trckd ldrs: chsd wnr appr 2 out: rdn between last 2: hld whn stmbld last: no ex whn lost 2nd fnl 110yds* **9/1**

424- **4** 1 ¾ **Dragon's Den (IRE)**[8] 5030 7-10-3 114..............................[1] PaulMoloney 114
(Chris Down) *hld up: rdn after 3 out: styd on but nt pce to get on terms: wnt 4th run-in* **11/2**[3]

430- **5** ¾ **Solar Impulse (FR)**[22] 4755 4-11-0 135..............................(t) HarryDerham(3) 125
(Paul Nicholls) *travelled wl: j. sltly lft: trckd ldr: lft in ld 3 out: rdn and hdd bef next: fnd little and wandered u.p between last 2: lost 4th run-in* **15/8**[1]

600- **6** 11 **Foxcub (IRE)**[22] 4752 6-11-7 132.............................. FelixDeGiles 124
(Tom Symonds) *trckd ldrs: reminders after 2nd: bdly hmpd 3 out: sn rdn and btn* **14/1**

644- **7** ¾ **Shammick Boy (IRE)**[13] 4935 9-11-4 129.............................. JackDoyle 116
(Victor Dartnall) *kpt wd: chsd ldrs tl after 7th: btn after next* **20/1**

1/2- **F** **Fiendish Flame (IRE)**[328] 204 10-11-12 137.............................. SeanQuinlan
(Jennie Candlish) *led tl fell 3 out* **20/1**

351- **P** **Sporting Boy (IRE)**[185] 1699 6-11-4 129..............................(t) TomCannon
(Johnny Farrelly) *chsd ldrs tl lost tch qckly 6th: p.u bef next* **8/1**

4m 37.4s (-8.60) **Going Correction** -0.40s/f (Good)
WFA 4 from 5yo+ 5lb **9** Ran SP% **115.8**
Speed ratings (Par 107): **101,100,99,98,98 93,93, ,**
CSF £46.29 CT £367.68 TOTE £4.40: £1.90, £3.00, £3.60; EX 48.80 Trifecta £830.90.
Owner Mrs Karola Vann **Bred** Miss Violet Sweeney **Trained** Withycombe, Somerset

FOCUS
Fair form that makes sense.

5143 MANOR HOUSE SOMERSET H'CAP HURDLE (10 hdls) 2m 3f 110y
4:30 (4:30) (Class 5) (0-100,100) 4-Y-0+ **£2,053** (£598; £299)

Form RPR

133- **1** **The Happy Warrior**[24] 4733 6-11-1 96.............................. GaryDerwin(7) 111+
(Bob Buckler) *a.p: pushed along after 5th: led 7th: drew clr after 3 out: nt fluent next: easily* **3/1**[1]

000- **2** 23 **Until The Man (IRE)**[15] 2105 7-10-3 77..............................(b) MarcGoldstein 69
(Natalie Lloyd-Beavis) *trckd ldrs: blnd 2nd: rdn to chse wnr after 3 out: sn no ch: a holding on for 2nd fr next* **14/1**

/40- **3** 1 ¼ **Kingsfold Flare**[22] 4760 7-10-11 85.............................. JoshuaMoore 76
(Gary Moore) *mid-div: pushed along and hdwy after 7th: disp wl hld 3rd after 3 out: kpt on same pce* **11/2**[3]

20P- **4** 2 ¾ **Key To Milan**[141] 2460 8-11-7 98..............................(tp) GilesHawkins(3) 87
(Chris Down) *prom: hit 5th: led next: hdd 7th: sn rdn: disp wl hld 3rd u.p after 3 out* **10/1**

F4F- **5** 8 **Fintan**[24] 4734 11-11-0 91.............................. RobertDunne(3) 73
(Laura Young) *mid-div: hdwy after 7th to trck ldrs: rdn after 3 out: fdd fr next* **25/1**

/P5- **6** 17 **Applause For Amy (IRE)**[16] 4883 7-9-13 80.............................. MrJBargary(7) 49
(Mary Sanderson) *mid-div: rdn after 5th: btn 3 out: t.o* **18/1**

133- **7** *nk* **Shaddaii (FR)**[36] 4493 8-10-8 82..............................(t) IanPopham 51
(Caroline Keevil) *mid-div tl wknd after 3 out: t.o* **17/2**

500- **8** 2 ¼ **Henwood (IRE)**[16] 4883 6-10-11 95.............................. LewisGordon(10) 62
(Colin Tizzard) *nvr bttr than mid-div: t.o after 3 out* **17/2**

F23- **9** 1 ½ **Straits Of Messina (IRE)**[14] 4911 5-11-12 100.............................. FelixDeGiles 66
(Tom Symonds) *hld up towards rr: struggling in midfield 3 out: sn wknd: t.o* **5/1**[2]

546- **10** 2 ¾ **Vexillum (IRE)**[36] 3290 5-11-6 94..............................[1] JamesDavies 57
(Simon Hodgson) *a towards rr: t.o 3 out* **33/1**

/P0- **11** 20 **Cnoc Moy (IRE)**[302] 635 10-10-4 78..............................(t) SamJones 25
(Helen Rees) *mid-div: rdn after 6th: wknd after next: t.o* **40/1**

0P0- **12** *hd* **Genuine Art**[12] 4972 7-9-7 74 oh6.............................. ThomasGarner(5) 21
(Lucy Jones) *a towards rr: t.o 3 out* **100/1**

00P- **13** 30 **Top Chief**[98] 3280 6-11-1 94.............................. KillianMoore(5) 17
(Mark Rimell) *led: hdd 6th: sn rdn: wknd bef 3 out: t.o* **33/1**

535- **P** **Free Falling**[38] 4472 8-10-2 76..............................(v) WillKennedy
(Alastair Lidderdale) *nvr travelling towards rr: nt fluent 2nd: lost tch after 6th: p.u bef 3 out* **14/1**

2F0- **P** **Who Am I**[25] 4703 8-11-7 95.............................. TomO'Brien
(Debra Hamer) *hit 3rd: rdn after 5th: a in rr: t.o 6th: p.u next* **33/1**

4m 41.5s (-4.50) **Going Correction** -0.40s/f (Good) **15** Ran SP% **121.9**
Speed ratings (Par 103): **93,83,83,82,79 72,72,71,70,69 61,61,49, ,**
CSF £42.81 CT £229.27 TOTE £3.20: £1.90, £6.00, £2.30; EX 70.60 Trifecta £995.30.
Owner Nick Elliott **Bred** H G Llewellyn **Trained** Henley, Somerset

FOCUS
The official going description was changed to good, good to soft in places following the 3.55. They got racing a long way out. The easy winner stood out in a modest handicap but this does look a step forward.

5144 PORTER DODSON SOLICITORS AND ADVISORS H'CAP CHASE (14 fncs) 2m 3f
5:05 (5:05) (Class 5) (0-100,99) 5-Y-0+ **£3,422** (£997; £499)

Form RPR

451- **1** **Malibu Sun**[9] 5027 7-11-11 99 7ex.............................. NicodeBoinville(3) 113+
(Ben Pauling) *trckd ldr: jnd ldr 8th: led next: in command fr 3 out: comf* **1/1**[1]

220- **2** 14 **Finch Flyer (IRE)**[136] 2562 7-9-9 73..............................(p) MrAlexEdwards(7) 79
(Aytach Sadik) *hld up in tch: hdwy fr 9th: rdn after 4 out: sn chsng wnr: hld fr 3 out: eased up fnl 70yds but a holding on for 2nd* **20/1**

F24- **3** ½ **Wicklewood**[9] 5027 8-10-3 81..............................(t) RyanHatch(7) 85
(Mark Gillard) *trckd ldrs: rdn in 4th 4 out: styd on same pce fr next: nrly snatched 2nd fnl strides* **12/1**

PP3- **4** 2 **Redlynch Rock (IRE)**[16] 4888 6-11-9 94..............................(t) SamJones 95
(Bob Buckler) *trckd ldrs: rdn after 4 out: hld fr next: kpt on same pce* **8/1**

6P0- **P** **Si Bien (FR)**[24] 4721 9-11-3 88..............................(t) JackDoyle
(Ali Brewer) *trckd ldrs tl 9th: sn wknd: t.o whn p.u after 4 out* **25/1**

/11- **P** **Capisci (IRE)**[24] 4734 9-11-11 96.............................. WillKennedy
(Sarah-Jayne Davies) *led: narrowly hdd whn hit 9th: sn wknd: t.o whn p.u bef 3 out* **13/2**[3]

P43- **P** **Ashcott Boy**[24] 4734 6-10-10 86.............................. ConorShoemark(5)
(Neil Mulholland) *blnd 5th and next: sn struggling in last: wknd 4 out: p.u bef next* **9/1**

4P6- **F** **Wah Wah Taysee (IRE)**[24] 4723 7-11-12 97..............................(tp) SeanQuinlan
(David Bridgwater) *hld up in tch: fell 9th* **6/1**[2]

4m 53.2s (1.20) **Going Correction** -0.40s/f (Good) **8** Ran SP% **115.0**
Speed ratings: **81,75,74,74, , ,**
CSF £20.71 CT £161.66 TOTE £1.70: £1.10, £3.70, £3.20; EX 22.10 Trifecta £139.40.
Owner Easy Going Racing **Bred** N Shutts **Trained** Bourton-On-The-Water, Gloucs

FOCUS
A weak handicap. The winner is on the upgrade and there's probably more to come.

5145 SOMERSET COUNTY GAZETTE STANDARD OPEN NATIONAL HUNT FLAT RACE 2m 1f
5:35 (5:36) (Class 5) 4-6-Y-0 **£2,053** (£598; £299)

Form RPR

05- **1** **Polamco (IRE)**[24] 4728 5-11-3 0..............................(t) RyanMahon 110+
(Harry Fry) *trckd ldrs: led over 3f out: rdn and hrd pressed over 2f out: styd on strly to assert ent fnl f: rdn out* **12/1**

2 3 ½ **Days Of Heaven (FR)** 4-10-11 0.............................. AndrewTinkler 102+
(Nicky Henderson) *mid-div: hdwy 5f out: chal 3f out: sn rdn: kpt on w ev ch tl no ex ent fnl f* **1/2**[1]

1- **3** 2 **Earthmoves (FR)**[28] 4638 4-11-1 0.............................. HarryDerham(3) 106
(Paul Nicholls) *trckd ldrs: rdn over 2f out: kpt on same pce* **4/1**[2]

30- **4** 15 **Rough Fighter (USA)**[62] 4017 5-10-12 0.............................. JamesBanks(5) 92
(Neil Mulholland) *trckd ldrs: rdn over 2f out: sn outpcd* **14/1**

36- **5** 7 **Swincombe Star**[46] 4296 5-11-3 0.............................. FelixDeGiles 85
(Robert Walford) *hld up: rdn 3f out: passed btn horses fr over 2f out: nvr any danger to ldrs* **16/1**

6 15 **Bobonyx**[19] 4-10-11 0.............................. JoshuaMoore 66
(Barry Brennan) *led tl over 3f out: wknd over 2f out: t.o* **66/1**

3- **7** 3 **Kublai (FR)**[28] 4638 4-10-11 0.............................. TomO'Brien 63
(Philip Hobbs) *racd keenly: sn mid-div: wknd 3f out: t.o* **8/1**[3]

8 10 **Looking For Mick** 5-11-0 0.............................. GilesHawkins(3) 60
(Victor Dartnall) *hld up towards rr: hdwy 1/2-way: wknd 4f out: t.o* **22/1**

9 ¾ **Posh Millie (IRE)** 4-10-1 0.............................. JamesBest(3) 46
(Ron Hodges) *a towards rr: t.o* **50/1**

- **10** 48 **Over The Bridge** 4-10-11 0.............................. TommyPhelan 10
(Mark Gillard) *chsd ldrs tl wknd over 5f out: t.o* **50/1**

4m 5.4s (3.00) **Going Correction** -0.40s/f (Good)
WFA 4 from 5yo 5lb **10** Ran SP% **127.8**
Speed ratings: **76,74,73,66,63 56,54,49,49,26**
CSF £20.10 TOTE £15.80: £2.40, £1.10, £1.30; EX 43.50 Trifecta £226.90.
Owner Andrew Polson **Bred** Shane Crawley **Trained** Seaborough, Dorset

FOCUS
Some big yards represented in this bumper and the likelihood that the first three home will go on to better things. A big step up from the winner.

The Form Book Jumps, Raceform Ltd, Compton, RG20 6NL.

T/Plt: £29.80 to a £1 stake. Pool of £58866.50 - 1441.30 winning tickets. T/Qpdt: £16.80 to a £1 stake. Pool of £3554.60 - 156.20 winning tickets. TM

5146 - 5152a (Foreign Racing) - See Raceform Interactive

5132 AINTREE (L-H)

Friday, April 4

OFFICIAL GOING: Mildmay course - good (good to soft in places; 7.1); hurdle course - good to soft (6.8); national course - good to soft (good in places; 6.6)

Wind: light 1/2 against Weather: fine

5153 INTERNATIONAL FESTIVAL FOR BUSINESS 2014 TOP NOVICES' HURDLE (GRADE 2) (9 hdls) 2m 110y

2:00 (2:00) (Class 1) 4-Y-0+

£34,170 (£12,822; £6,420; £3,198; £1,608; £804)

Form RPR

122- **1** **Josses Hill (IRE)**[24] 4736 6-11-4 148 BarryGeraghty 148+
(Nicky Henderson) *in tch: hdwy to ld bef 2 out: rdn and strly pressed between last 2: styd on wl: drew clr fnl 150yds* **6/4**[1]

314- **2** *6* **Sgt Reckless**[24] 4736 7-11-4 146 APMcCoy 142
(Mick Channon) *hld up: gd hdwy after 3 out: upsides 2 out: sn rdn: stl ev ch last: sn outpcd by wnr run-in: no ex fnl 75yds* **9/2**[2]

323- **3** *3 1/4* **King Of The Picts (IRE)**[54] 4180 5-11-4 140 PaulTownend 138
(John Patrick Shanahan, Ire) *trckd ldrs: rdn and outpcd after 3 out: styd on fr bef last: wnt 3rd fnl 75yds* **25/1**

211- **4** *1/2* **Baltimore Rock (IRE)**[27] 4682 5-11-4 134 TomScudamore 138
(David Pipe) *hld up: mstke 3 out: rdn and hdwy bef 2 out: wnt 3rd after 2 out: sn one pce and no imp on ldng pair: lost 3rd 75yds out* **8/1**

1F- **5** *2 1/4* **Mijhaar**[92] 3501 6-11-4 0 DenisO'Regan 136
(John Ferguson) *hld up in tch towards outer: rdn 3 out: no imp on ldrs fr bef last: edgd lft run-in* **16/1**

45- **6** *3* **Art Of Payroll (GER)**[33] 4585 5-11-4 142 PCarberry 134
(D T Hughes, Ire) *hld up in tch: n.m.r bef 2 out: rdn after 2 out: sn no imp on ldrs* **13/2**[3]

141- **7** *6* **Irish Cavalier (IRE)**[13] 4945 5-11-4 135 JamieMoore 127
(Rebecca Curtis) *prom: rdn bef 3 out: wknd after 2 out* **25/1**

602- **8** *5* **The Game Changer (IRE)**[26] 4708 5-11-4 142 DJCasey 127
(C F Swan, Ire) *hld up in tch: stl gng wl whn short of room and shuffled to rr 2 out: no ch after* **16/1**

051- **9** *9* **Gentleman Jon**[29] 4632 6-11-4 0 BrendanPowell 117
(Colin Tizzard) *trckd ldr: nt fluent 3rd and 5th: pushed along to chal appr 3 out: mstke 2 out: wknd* **50/1**

132- **10** *8* **Amore Alato**[41] 4421 5-11-4 137 RichardJohnson 115
(Nick Williams) *led: rdn whn hdd jst after 3 out: wknd after 2 out: eased* **10/1**

3m 59.6s (-6.60) **Going Correction** -0.15s/f (Good) **10 Ran SP% 113.1**
Speed ratings (Par 115): **109,106,104,104,103 101,99,96,92,88**
CSF £7.66 CT £112.22 TOTE £2.50: £1.20, £2.00, £5.70; EX 8.50 Trifecta £78.00.
Owner A D Spence **Bred** I W Moore **Trained** Upper Lambourn, Berks

FOCUS
The bends had been moved in 5yds, resulting in there being an extra 25yds per circuit on the Mildmay Course (40yds the previous day) and 60yds per circuit on the hurdles track (95yds previous day). The ground had eased slightly following 1.5mm of rain overnight, with it appearing to be riding slightly softer on the hurdles track. Probably an ordinary renewal of this race, with the runner-up and fourth from the Supreme clashing once again, and that pair started to draw clear from two out. It was run at a fair pace and the form looks solid. Josses Hill is rated similar to his Cheltenham mark.

5154 BETFRED MOBILE MILDMAY NOVICES' CHASE (GRADE 1) (19 fncs) 3m 1f

2:30 (2:30) (Class 1) 5-Y-0+

£50,643 (£19,080; £9,549; £4,770; £2,394; £1,197)

Form RPR

111- **1** **Holywell (IRE)**[24] 4738 7-11-4 157 (b) APMcCoy 165+
(Jonjo O'Neill) *w ldr: led 8th: nt fluent next: drvn clr appr 2 out: styd on strly* **7/2**[2]

12F- **2** *10* **Don Cossack (GER)**[23] 4751 7-11-4 152 (t) DavyRussell 155
(Gordon Elliott, Ire) *trckd ldrs: clr 2nd appr 2 out: no imp* **4/1**[3]

125- **3** *7* **Wonderful Charm (FR)**[22] 4764 6-11-4 158 (t) SamTwiston-Davies 149
(Paul Nicholls) *chsd ldrs: drvn appr 3 out: kpt on one pce: modest 3rd appr last* **4/1**[3]

12B- **4** *3 1/2* **Many Clouds (IRE)**[23] 4751 7-11-4 145 LeightonAspell 148
(Oliver Sherwood) *chsd ldrs: drvn appr 3 out: kpt on one pce: modest 4th last* **6/1**

P11- **5** *3 3/4* **O'Faolains Boy (IRE)**[23] 4751 7-11-4 156 BarryGeraghty 143
(Rebecca Curtis) *chsd ldrs: nt fluent 4th: upsides 12th: drvn after 16th: wknd appr last* **3/1**[1]

140- **6** *28* **Just A Par (IRE)**[23] 4751 7-11-4 146 NickScholfield 117
(Paul Nicholls) *led to 8th: drvn 12th: lost pl 15th: sn bhd* **12/1**

6m 14.8s (-15.20) **Going Correction** -0.25s/f (Good) **6 Ran SP% 109.2**
Speed ratings: **114,110,108,107,106 97**
CSF £16.82 TOTE £3.00: £1.80, £2.50; EX 21.10 Trifecta £87.80.
Owner Mrs Gay Smith **Bred** Patrick Doyle **Trained** Cheltenham, Gloucs

FOCUS
The first running as a Grade 1 of a contest that has fallen to some classy chasers in recent times and this looked a good running of the race, with two festival winners taking part. Although having a more workmanlike way about him than some, it was hard not to be impressed with the performance of Holywell. He improved from Cheltenhanm, and Don Cossack ran to his best.

5155 BETFRED MELLING CHASE (GRADE 1) (16 fncs) 2m 4f

3:05 (3:06) (Class 1) 5-Y-0+

£112,540 (£42,400; £21,220; £10,600; £5,320; £2,660)

Form RPR

/66- **1** **Boston Bob (IRE)**[22] 4766 9-11-10 154 PaulTownend 163+
(W P Mullins, Ire) *hld up in rr: hdwy 3f out: chsng ldrs and swtchd lft between last 2: upsides whn nt fluent last: led run-in: forged clr* **5/1**[3]

12P- **2** *3 1/4* **Rolling Aces (IRE)**[48] 4265 8-11-10 149 (tp) NickScholfield 157
(Paul Nicholls) *led 1st: hdd 6th: w ldrs: led narrowly sn after last: sn hdd: styd on same pce* **16/1**

/P1- **3** *1 1/4* **Ballynagour (IRE)**[22] 4768 8-11-10 155 (t) TomScudamore 156
(David Pipe) *hld up in rr: hdwy 11th: chsng ldrs 13th: led narrowly appr last: sn hdd: kpt on same pce* **5/1**[3]

222- **4** *1 3/4* **Toner D'Oudairies (FR)**[40] 4457 7-11-10 150 (tp) DavyRussell 154
(Gordon Elliott, Ire) *hld up in rr: hdwy 3 out: chsng ldrs between last 2: kpt on same pce run-in* **14/1**

530- **5** *2* **Rathlin**[22] 4766 9-11-10 155 (t) BrianO'Connell 153
(M F Morris, Ire) *w ldrs: led 6th: hdd 2 out: one pce whn n.m.r appr last* **16/1**

401- **6** *shd* **Pepite Rose (FR)**[13] 4960 7-11-3 154 AidanColeman 145
(Venetia Williams) *chsd ldrs: led narrowly 2 out: hdd appr last: kpt on one pce* **9/1**

/53- **7** *7* **Rajdhani Express**[22] 4766 7-11-10 158 MrSWaley-Cohen 148
(Nicky Henderson) *hld up in rr: hdwy to chse ldrs 8th: drvn appr 3 out: wknd last* **7/2**[1]

215- **8** *4* **Wishfull Thinking**[23] 4753 11-11-10 162 (t) RichardJohnson 144
(Philip Hobbs) *chsd ldrs 3rd: nt fluent 9th: drvn 11th: lost pl appr 3 out* **9/2**[2]

205- **9** *3* **French Opera**[21] 4790 11-11-10 154 BarryGeraghty 141
(Nicky Henderson) *chsd ldrs: lost pl bef 13th: sn bhd* **25/1**

341- **10** *14* **Days Hotel (IRE)**[40] 4457 9-11-10 154 AELynch 127
(Henry De Bromhead, Ire) *led to 1st: t.k.h: trckd ldrs outpcd whn hit 13th: wknd next* **9/1**

4m 58.1s (-5.90) **Going Correction** -0.25s/f (Good) **10 Ran SP% 116.0**
Speed ratings: **101,99,99,98,97 97,94,93,92,86**
CSF £76.48 CT £421.53 TOTE £5.50: £2.20, £4.60, £2.30; EX 77.50 Trifecta £978.40.
Owner Andrea & Graham Wylie **Bred** Burgage Stud **Trained** Muine Beag, Co Carlow

FOCUS
This already had the look of a below-par edition of the race prior to Module becoming a late withdrawal, but it was certainly competitive and, having been run at an ordinary gallop until Rathlin took over, there were no fewer than seven horses in with a chance between the last two fences. There's probably more to come from Boston Bob, and the next three are rated to their best.

5156 CRABBIE'S SUPPORTING EVERTON IN THE COMMUNITY TOPHAM CHASE (H'CAP) (GRADE 3) (18 fncs) 2m 5f 110y

3:40 (3:40) (Class 1) 5-Y-0+

£67,524 (£25,440; £12,732; £6,360; £3,192; £1,596)

Form RPR

P12- **1** **Ma Filleule (FR)**[24] 4738 6-11-7 **150** BarryGeraghty 164+
(Nicky Henderson) *trckd ldrs: led 13th: stmbld on landing next: drew clr run-in: v readily* **9/1**[2]

130- **2** *8* **Bennys Mist (IRE)**[22] 4768 8-10-9 **138** [1] AidanColeman 143
(Venetia Williams) *chsd ldrs: outpcd and 5th last: styd on wl to take 2nds last 75yds* **33/1**

146- **3** *1* **Eastlake (IRE)**[21] 4790 8-11-3 **146** APMcCoy 149
(Jonjo O'Neill) *in rr: hdwy 9th: chsng ldrs 12th (Canal Turn): handy 3rd 2 out: styd on to take 3rd last 25yds* **25/1**

123- **4** *1 1/4* **Tatenen (FR)**[22] 4768 10-10-11 **140** AndrewThornton 142
(Richard Rowe) *in rr: hdwy 13th (Valentine's): chsng ldrs 3 out: styd on strly run-in: tk 4th post* **25/1**

123- **5** *hd* **Double Ross (IRE)**[22] 4764 8-11-9 **152** SamTwiston-Davies 154
(Nigel Twiston-Davies) *w ldrs: led 8th: hdd 13th (Valentine's): chsd wnr after: kpt on same pce fr elbow* **6/1**[1]

5/3- **6** *2* **You Must Know Me (IRE)**[94] 3441 8-10-11 **140** AELynch 143
(Henry De Bromhead, Ire) *in rr: mstke 4th (Water): mstke 10th (Becher's): hdwy 14th: chsng ldrs 3 out: styd on fr elbow* **14/1**

065- **7** *11* **Big Fella Thanks**[44] 4346 12-10-12 **141** (tp) PaddyBrennan 135
(Tom George) *chsd ldrs: hmpd 9th: wknd appr last* **10/1**[3]

0/0- **8** *nk* **He'llberemembered (IRE)**[33] 4587 11-11-0 **143** DavyCondon 133
(P G Fahey, Ire) *rr-div: hdwy 15th: rdn appr 2 out: kpt on one pce* **33/1**

260- **9** *1* **Champion Court (IRE)**[22] 4768 9-11-12 **155** IanPopham 145
(Martin Keighley) *chsd ldrs: hit 12th (Canal Turn): one pce fr 3 out* **33/1**

226- **10** *2* **Cedre Bleu (FR)**[69] 3887 7-10-12 **141** (bt) NickScholfield 128
(Paul Nicholls) *hdwy to chse ldrs 5th: wknd between last 2* **20/1**

405- **11** *1* **Soll**[27] 4681 9-10-3 **132** MarkGrant 120
(Jo Hughes) *in rr: hmpd 12th (Canal Turn): styd on fr 2 out: nvr on terms* **25/1**

411- **12** *2* **Poole Master**[41] 4414 9-11-0 **143** (b) TomScudamore 127
(David Pipe) *prom: lost pl 6th: sn in rr: hdwy 14th: chsng ldrs 3 out: wknd run-in* **20/1**

/03- **13** *31* **Massini's Maguire (IRE)**[25] 4732 13-10-5 **134** RichardJohnson 91
(Tim Vaughan) *in rr: hmpd 12th (Canal Turn): mstke 14th: hdwy 3 out: chsng ldrs next: wknd between last 2: eased run-in* **33/1**

162- **14** *6* **Your Busy (IRE)**[33] 4587 11-10-1 **130** (t) DJCasey 81
(J A Nash, Ire) *chsd ldrs: outpcd whn hmpd 14th: sn lost pl* **16/1**

132- **15** *1 1/2* **Rebel Rebellion (IRE)**[34] 4559 9-11-7 **150** (bt) RyanMahon 100
(Paul Nicholls) *in rr: hdwy 9th: hmpd 12th (Canal Turn): chsng ldrs 14th: wknd between last 2* **16/1**

100- **16** *11* **Lucky Landing (IRE)**[21] 4790 8-10-5 **134** DougieCostello 74
(Tony Coyle) *mid-div: lost pl 9th: hit 11th (Foinavon): bhd fr 3 out* **66/1**

P54- **17** *2 1/2* **Dunowen Point (IRE)**[68] 3923 8-10-1 **130** BrianHarding 68
(Donald McCain) *chsd ldrs: wknd qckly appr 2 out: sn wl bhd* **14/1**

130- **U** **King Edmund**[22] 4768 11-10-8 **137** (t) TomCannon
(Chris Gordon) *in rr whn blnd and uns rdr 3rd (Chair)* **66/1**

610- **F** **Tanks For That (IRE)**[21] 4790 11-10-13 **142** AndrewTinkler
(Nicky Henderson) *towards rr: mid-div whn fell 12th (Canal Turn)* **50/1**

521- **F** **Doeslessthanme (IRE)**[34] 4543 10-10-12 **144** (tp) HarryChalloner(3)
(Richard Ford) *led to 8th: chsng ldrs whn fell 13th (Valentine's)* **33/1**

316- **F** **Giorgio Quercus (FR)**[22] 4768 9-10-5 **134** DavidBass
(Nicky Henderson) *in rr: stdy hdwy and in tch whn fell 13th (Valentine's)* **20/1**

620- **U** **Viva Colonia (IRE)**[21] 4790 9-11-0 **143** DannyCook
(Brian Ellison) *chsd ldrs: blnd and uns rdr 9th* **33/1**

350- **U** **Kauto Stone (FR)**[22] 4766 8-11-2 **145** (t) PCarberry
(Paul Nicholls) *mid-div: blnd and uns rdr 8th* **25/1**

221- **U** **Tahiti Pearl (IRE)**[68] 3923 10-10-9 **138** RyanMania
(Sue Smith) *w ldrs: blnd and uns rdr 10th (Becher's)* **25/1**

/4P- **F** **Bishopsfurze (IRE)**[23] 4754 9-10-5 **134** ow1 MPFogarty
(W P Mullins, Ire) *mid-div: fell 7th* **40/1**

1P0- **P** **Mart Lane (IRE)**[34] 4544 9-10-10 **139** (b) WayneHutchinson
(Dr Richard Newland) *in rr: bdly hmpd 13th (Valentine's): bhd whn p.u bef next* **50/1**

P16- **P** **Swift Arrow (IRE)**[34] 4543 8-10-7 **136** HenryBrooke
(Donald McCain) *in rr: hmpd 13th (Valentine's): sn bhd: t.o 3 out: p.u bef next* **100/1**

006- **U** **Standing Ovation (IRE)**[24] 4738 7-10-0 **129** (t[1]) ConorO'Farrell
(David Pipe) *in rr hmpd and uns rdr 12th (Canal Turn)* **12/1**

154- **F** **Fago (FR)**[41] 4414 6-11-5 **148** NoelFehily
(Paul Nicholls) *hld up in rr: hdwy 9th: prom whn fell 15th* **33/1**

461- **P** **Lost Legend (IRE)**[20] 4806 7-10-2 **131**........................(p) RichieMcLernon
(Jonjo O'Neill) *prom: lost pl 9th: mstke 13th (Valentine's): sn bhd: t.o 3 out: p.u bef next* **14/1**

5m 23.2s (-13.80) **Going Correction** -0.25s/f (Good) **30** Ran SP% **137.3**
Speed ratings: **115,112,111,111,111 110,106,106,106,105 104,104,92,90,90 86,85,, , , , ,**
CSF £280.13 CT £7105.60 TOTE £11.20: £3.20, £11.70, £4.70, £8.00; EX 763.40 Trifecta £2973.40.
Owner Simon Munir **Bred** Serge Dubois **Trained** Upper Lambourn, Berks

FOCUS
Quite a classy running of the race, with seven horses rated 145-plus, and it was one of those, Ma Filleule, who won convincingly, in the process defying of a mark of 150. She took another step forward and the mares' allowance brings her into the Gold Cup picture.

5157 DOOM BAR SEFTON NOVICES' HURDLE (GRADE 1) (13 hdls) 3m 110y
4:15 (4:15) (Class 1) 4-Y-0+

£56,270 (£21,200; £10,610; £5,300; £2,660; £1,330)

Form RPR
/12- **1** **Beat That (IRE)**[119] 2929 6-11-4 142.................................. BarryGeraghty 159+
(Nicky Henderson) *midfield: hdwy after 8th: trckd ldrs whn nt fluent 4 out: hit 2 out but sn led gng wl: rdn clr after last* **6/1**[3]

120- **2** *4* **Cole Harden (IRE)**[23] 4750 5-11-4 135..........................(t) GavinSheehan 152
(Warren Greatrex) *led: rdn whn hdd jst after 2 out: kpt on but no ch w wnr after last* **16/1**

111- **3** *25* **Seeyouatmidnight**[48] 4269 6-11-4 155.................................. RyanMania 135
(Sandy Thomson) *trckd ldr: nt fluent 9th and 4 out: rdn after 3 out: hit 2 out: nt fluent last: wknd* **7/2**[1]

11- **4** *7* **Capote (IRE)**[31] 4603 6-11-4 135.. APMcCoy 126
(Jonjo O'Neill) *hld up: hdwy into midfield after 8th: rdn 3 out: wl btn in 4th whn blnd 2 out* **8/1**

1P4- **5** *1 ¼* **Killala Quay**[23] 4750 7-11-4 143.................................. RichardJohnson 123
(Charlie Longsdon) *trckd ldrs: rdn after 4 out: wknd after 3 out* **11/2**[2]

132- **6** *11* **Racing Pulse (IRE)**[61] 4052 5-11-4 140........................ TomScudamore 113
(John Quinn) *midfield: mstke 1st: rdn after 4 out: btn whn mstke 3 out* **9/1**

142- **7** *5* **Walk On Al (IRE)**[26] 4702 6-11-4 129..............................(p) HarrySkelton 108
(Dan Skelton) *hld up: rdn and btn whn hmpd by faller 3 out* **25/1**

111- **8** *9* **Tagrita (IRE)**[48] 4276 6-10-11 135................................ NickScholfield 93
(Paul Nicholls) *midfield towards outer: rdn after 4 out: wknd 3 out* **16/1**

111- **9** *9* **The Last Samuri (IRE)**[72] 3829 6-11-4 131..................... HenryBrooke 92
(Donald McCain) *hld up: nvr threatened* **25/1**

3- **10** *13* **Port Melon (IRE)**[139] 2505 6-11-4 0........................ SamTwiston-Davies 80
(Paul Nicholls) *midfield: pushed along whn n.m.r on inner after 4 out: btn 3 out* **17/2**

4- **11** *½* **Flatfoot Boogie (FR)**[198] 1603 9-11-4 136.............. AndrewJMcNamara 80
(N F Glynn, Ire) *in tch: rdn after 4 out: wknd appr 3 out* **50/1**

1- **12** *38* **Giantofaman (IRE)**[36] 4523 6-11-4 140............................(b) DavyCondon 46
(D T Hughes, Ire) *trckd ldr: rdn after 4 out: wknd appr 3 out and eased* **14/1**

2U2- **13** *64* **Mondo Cane (IRE)**[32] 4594 7-11-4 0.................................. AdamPogson
(Charles Pogson) *midfield: lost pl after 8th: sn btn* **150/1**

130- **P** **Toubeera**[13] 4961 8-10-11 141.. AidanColeman
(Venetia Williams) *hld up: mstke 2nd: sn struggling: p.u bef 7th* **33/1**

121- **P** **Tistory (FR)**[34] 4546 7-11-4 132.. DavidBass
(Nicky Henderson) *hld up: mstke 7th: hdwy towards outer after 8th: rdn after 4 out: wknd bef 3 out: p.u bef 2 out* **16/1**

110- **F** **Cogry**[21] 4786 5-11-4 129..(p) RyanHatch
(Nigel Twiston-Davies) *midfield: hdwy and in tch after 8th: rdn after 4 out: wkng whn fell 3 out* **80/1**

631- **P** **Themanfrom Minella (IRE)**[33] 4574 5-11-4 128..........(t) LeightonAspell
(Ben Case) *midfield: wknd bef 4 out: p.u bef last* **50/1**

/14- **P** **Deadly Sting (IRE)**[47] 4304 5-11-4 0.............................. DougieCostello
(Jonjo O'Neill) *hld up: nt fluent 4th and reminders: sn bhd: p.u after 4 out* **100/1**

6m 2.9s (-13.40) **Going Correction** -0.15s/f (Good) **18** Ran SP% **125.3**
Speed ratings (Par 117): **115,113,105,103,103 99,97,95,92,88 87,75,55,, , ,**
CSF £93.76 CT £397.41 TOTE £6.20: £2.60, £7.40, £2.10; EX 140.00 Trifecta £1306.40.
Owner Michael Buckley **Bred** John O'Brien **Trained** Upper Lambourn, Berks

FOCUS
More quantity than quality in this staying hurdle for novices, but it was run at a decent gallop and produced a ready winner.

5158 ALDER HEY CHILDREN'S CHARITY H'CAP HURDLE (GRADE 3) (11 hdls) 2m 4f
4:50 (4:50) (Class 1) 4-Y-0+

£28,475 (£10,685; £5,350; £2,665; £1,340; £670)

Form RPR
030- **1** **Clondaw Kaempfer (IRE)**[23] 4752 6-11-4 **137**.......... WayneHutchinson 145+
(Donald McCain) *in tch: trckd ldrs bef 3 out: upsides 2 out: sn rdn: 2 1/2 l down in 3rd last: styd on: led towards fin* **10/1**

153- **2** *nk* **Caid Du Berlais (FR)**[21] 4789 5-11-9 **145**...................... HarryDerham[(3)] 152+
(Paul Nicholls) *midfield: swtchd to outer and gd hdwy 3 out: led 2 out: sn rdn: idled run-in: hdd towards fin* **8/1**[2]

/00- **3** *¾* **Cash And Go (IRE)**[21] 4785 7-11-2 **135**........................ TomScudamore 141
(Nicky Henderson) *hld up: nt fluent 3 out: sn hdwy: rdn to chse ldrs appr last: styd on: wnt 3rd towards fin* **12/1**

14P- **4** *1 ¼* **Cheltenian (FR)**[21] 4785 8-11-4 **137**.......................... RichardJohnson 142
(Philip Hobbs) *midfield: gd hdwy 3 out: rdn to chal after 2 out: hit last: no ex fnl 75yds: lost 3rd towards fin* **8/1**[2]

0- **5** *7* **Zabana (IRE)**[69] 3911 5-10-13 **132**............................... RobbieColgan 131
(Andrew Lynch, Ire) *racd keenly: midfield: hit 4th: hdwy to chse ldrs after 3 out: rdn 2 out: no ex and edgd lft run-in* **8/1**[2]

260- **6** *7* **Alaivan (IRE)**[21] 4785 8-10-8 **132**....................(p) MauriceLinehan[(5)] 125
(Jonjo O'Neill) *midfield: nt fluent 3 out: sn rdn: one pce and nvr threatened ldrs* **12/1**

230- **7** *3 ½* **Grand Vision (IRE)**[22] 4765 8-11-7 **140**....................... BrendanPowell 128
(Colin Tizzard) *trckd ldrs: rdn and outpcd 3 out: no threat after* **40/1**

/00- **8** *¾* **Golden Hoof (IRE)**[20] 4805 6-10-11 **130**............................ DavidBass 118
(Nicky Henderson) *prom: led bef 3 out: hdd 2 out: grad wknd* **50/1**

410- **9** *2 ½* **Pass The Time**[24] 4740 5-10-6 **130**.....................(p) ConorShoemark[(5)] 115
(Neil Mulholland) *hld up: rdn and sme hdwy 3 out: no imp fr 2 out* **25/1**

000- **10** *4 ½* **Citizenship**[21] 4785 8-11-0 **133**................................. AidanColeman 114
(Venetia Williams) *midfield: rdn and outpcd bef 3 out: no threat after* **66/1**

0/ **11** *1 ¾* **Mister Hotelier (IRE)**[18] 4878 7-10-12 **131**.................(t) BrianO'Connell 111
(C A Murphy, Ire) *hld up: rdn bef 2 out: nvr threatened* **33/1**

052- **12** *¾* **Attaglance**[24] 4742 8-11-12 **145**..(t) BrianHughes 124
(Malcolm Jefferson) *in tch on outer: wknd after 4 out* **9/1**[3]

034- **13** *1 ¾* **Aazif (IRE)**[16] 4899 5-10-9 **128**...(t) WillKennedy 105
(Ian Williams) *trckd ldrs: rdn 3 out: wknd after 2 out* **33/1**

311- **14** *5* **Stonebrook (IRE)**[31] 4605 6-10-12 **131**...................................... APMcCoy 116+
(Donald McCain) *midfield on inner: rdn after 3 out: bdly hmpd by faller 2 out: eased* **4/1**[1]

026- **15** *shd* **Little Jon**[27] 4682 6-10-13 **132**................................... SamTwiston-Davies 115+
(Nigel Twiston-Davies) *led 2nd: hdd bef 3 out: wknd 2 out* **28/1**

130- **16** *1 ½* **Like Minded**[48] 4264 10-11-4 **137**..(t) HarrySkelton 117+
(Dan Skelton) *hld up in midfield: rdn 3 out: no imp whn hmpd by faller 2 out* **20/1**

140- **17** *8* **Lyvius**[21] 4785 6-11-5 **138**..(b) BarryGeraghty 102
(Nicky Henderson) *hld up towards outer: nvr threatened* **12/1**

12P- **18** *18* **Yesyoucan (IRE)**[23] 4752 9-11-1 **134**...................................... DannyCook 82
(Brian Ellison) *hld up: a towards rr* **66/1**

220- **19** *9* **Art Professor (IRE)**[21] 4789 10-11-1 **134**........................ LiamTreadwell 74
(Venetia Williams) *midfield: lost pl whn mstke 4 out: wknd* **50/1**

310- **U** **Hazy Tom (IRE)**[21] 4789 8-10-8 **134**............................ CharlieDeutsch[(7)]
(Charlie Longsdon) *midfield: clipped heels, stmbld and uns rdr after 5th* **50/1**

340- **P** **Morning Royalty (IRE)**[21] 4785 7-10-13 **132**..................... BrianHarding
(James Moffatt) *midfield: lost pl after 5th: sn strruggling in rr: p.u bef 3 out* **66/1**

P6P- **F** **Party Rock (IRE)**[23] 4752 7-11-2 **135**................................ SeanQuinlan 128
(Jennie Candlish) *led tl 2nd: trckd ldr: rdn 3 out: ev ch whn fell 2 out* **16/1**

4m 53.5s (-7.20) **Going Correction** -0.15s/f (Good) **22** Ran SP% **132.1**
Speed ratings (Par 113): **108,107,107,107,104 101,100,99,98,97 96,96,95,93,93 92,89,82,78,**
CSF £83.70 CT £1004.10 TOTE £13.00: £3.50, £2.40, £3.40, £2.70; EX 124.30 Trifecta £1655.70.
Owner T Leslie & D Gorton **Bred** P Hore **Trained** Cholmondeley, Cheshire

FOCUS
The first four pulled clear late on in what was a wide-open handicap, run at an ordinary early gallop, with the picture changing late on. The winner was back to the level promised by his novice form and there's probably more to come.

5159 CONCERTO GROUP MARES' STANDARD OPEN NATIONAL HUNT FLAT RACE (LISTED) 2m 1f
5:25 (5:25) (Class 1) 4-6-Y-0

£17,085 (£6,411; £3,210; £1,599; £804; £402)

Form RPR
414- **1** **Avispa**[27] 4683 5-11-0 105.. RobertThornton 116
(Alan King) *mid-div: hdwy 6f out: w ldrs over 2f out: led jst ins fnl f: hld on towards fin* **25/1**

101- **2** *hd* **Lady Buttons**[45] 4342 4-10-3 117... AdamNicol[(5)] 110
(Philip Kirby) *trckd ldrs: styd on to take 2nd last 100yds: no ex nr fin* **8/1**

122- **3** *1 ¼* **Tara Mist**[27] 4683 5-11-0 117.. RichardJohnson 115
(Henry Daly) *trckd ldrs: effrt 4f out: narrow ld over 2f out: hdd jst ins fnl f: styd on same pce* **13/2**[3]

/51- **4** *2 ½* **The Govaness**[139] 2506 5-11-4 121...................................... PaddyBrennan 116
(Fergal O'Brien) *hld up in rr: hdwy 7f out: chal over 2f out: kpt on same pce appr fnl f* **13/2**[3]

5 *1 ¼* **Queen Alphabet (IRE)**[180] 1805 5-11-0 103.....................(t) DavyRussell 111
(Peter Fahey, Ire) *rr-div: hdwy 4f out: chsng ldrs over 2f out: kpt on one pce over 1f out* **20/1**

11- **6** *¾* **Hannah's Princess (IRE)**[143] 2442 5-10-11 113.......... GavinSheehan[(3)] 110
(Warren Greatrex) *in rr: hdwy 4f out: chsng ldrs over 2f out: one pce over 1f out* **11/2**[2]

323- **7** *nk* **Ebony Empress (IRE)**[69] 3898 5-11-0 104....................... MichaelByrne 110
(Neil Mulholland) *mid-div: hdwy 4f out: chsng ldrs over 2f out: kpt on same pce over 1f out* **100/1**

21- **8** *¾* **Princess Tara (IRE)**[19] 4844 4-10-8 106......................... DonalDevereux 103
(Peter Bowen) *trckd ldrs: upsides over 2f out: wknd over 1f out* **11/1**

9 *2 ½* **Kayf Hampshire (IRE)**[20] 4831 5-10-7 107............................ JJBurke[(7)] 107
(W J Burke, Ire) *hld up in rr: hdwy 4f out: chsng ldrs over 2f out: wknd over 1f out* **33/1**

11- **10** *2* **Miss Sassypants**[228] 1317 5-11-0 115.................................... RyanMahon 105
(Seamus Mullins) *in rr: hdwy 4f out: chsng ldrs over 2f out: wknd over 1f out* **16/1**

23- **11** *1* **Tara Mac**[33] 4582 5-11-0 105.. WilsonRenwick 104
(Keith Dalgleish) *trckd ldrs: upsides over 2f out: wknd over 1f out* **40/1**

12- **12** *½* **Molly Cat**[63] 4017 4-10-8 116.. APMcCoy 97
(Alan Swinbank) *t.k.h: mde most at stdy pce: increased gallop over 4f out: hdd over 2f out: sn lost pl* **5/1**[1]

12- **13** *4 ½* **Millicent Silver**[45] 4342 5-11-0 103....................... SamTwiston-Davies 99
(Nigel Twiston-Davies) *w ldrs: lost pl over 1f out* **66/1**

301- **14** *nk* **Oleohneh (IRE)**[14] 4944 6-11-0 114..................................... BrianHughes 98
(Malcolm Jefferson) *hld up in rr: sme hdwy over 3f out: nvr on terms* **25/1**

1- **15** *4* **Amberkatann (IRE)**[18] 4867 5-11-0 109............................... HarrySkelton 94
(Dan Skelton) *hld up in rr: hdwy 4f out: wknd over 2f out* **25/1**

3/1- **16** *1 ½* **Roll On Ruby (IRE)**[327] 250 6-10-7 109.......................... CharlieDeutsch[(7)] 93
(Alan Phillips) *t.k.h: trckd ldrs: lost pl over 2f out* **50/1**

0/6- **17** *4* **Diligent**[30] 4618 6-11-0 114... HenryBrooke 89
(Donald McCain) *mid-div: drvn 6f out: lost pl over 3f out* **100/1**

01- **18** *½* **Midnight Jazz**[42] 4403 4-10-5 114.................................... KielanWoods[(3)] 82
(Ben Case) *trckd ldrs: lost pl over 2f out* **20/1**

1- **19** *12* **Plum Stone**[136] 2583 5-11-0 109.. BarryGeraghty 76
(Charlie Mann) *hld up in rr: hdwy after 4f: drvn over fourth 3f out: sn lost pl: bhd whn eased fnl f* **12/1**

/21- **20** *9* **No Pushover**[35] 4540 5-11-0 108.. DavidBass 67
(Nicky Henderson) *chsd ldrs: drvn 6f out: lost pl over 3f out: bhd whn eased over 1f out* **20/1**

4m 9.6s (2.20) **Going Correction** -0.15s/f (Good)
WFA 4 from 5yo+ 5lb **20** Ran SP% **128.4**
Speed ratings: **88,87,87,86,85 85,85,84,83,82 82,81,79,79,77 77,75,74,69,65**
CSF £197.64 CT £1491.07 TOTE £26.30: £6.80, £3.70, £2.60; EX 352.10 Trifecta £2311.60.
Owner The Wasp Partnership **Bred** R D And Mrs J S Chugg **Trained** Barbury Castle, Wilts

FOCUS
The big mares' bumper of the season was run at a fairly steady pace and plenty had their chance in the straight. Not for the first time in recent years the race threw up a big-price winner. They finished in a heap and the second to fourth set the level.

T/Jkpt: £34,630.00 to a £1 stake. Pool: £48,774.69 - 1.00 winning ticket. T/Plt: £386.70 to a £1 stake. Pool: £594,515.25 - 1,122.30 winning tickets. T/Qpdt: £95.90 to £1 stake. Pool: £25,872.09 - 199.60 winning tickets. WG

[4938]SEDGEFIELD (L-H)

Friday, April 4

OFFICIAL GOING: Chase course - soft (good to soft in places; 5.8); hurdle course - good to soft (soft in places; 6.3)

Wind: Almost nil Weather: Overcast

5160 COMPARE BOOKMAKERS AT BOOKMAKERS.CO.UK AMATEUR RIDERS' NOVICES' HURDLE (8 hdls) 2m 1f

2:10 (2:10) (Class 4) 4-Y-0+ **£3,369** (£1,044; £522; £261)

Form RPR

0F0- 1 **Franciscan**[34] 4550 6-11-11 126.....(b) MrHStock(7) 128+
(Donald McCain) *j.w: mde all: qcknd bef 2 out: kpt on wl fr last* **9/4**[2]

432- 2 2 ¼ **Ride The Range (IRE)**[20] 4811 5-10-13 0..... MrLHall(7) 114
(Chris Grant) *chsd ldrs: wnt 2nd after 3rd: effrt bef 2 out: lost 2nd bef last: rallied to chse (clr) wnr run-in: kpt on* **8/1**[3]

U11- 3 1 ½ **Dark Dune (IRE)**[14] 4939 6-11-13 132..... MrWEasterby(5) 125
(Tim Easterby) *t.k.h: chsd wnr to after 3rd: rdn and sltly outpcd after 3 out: rallied to regain 2nd bef last to run-in: no ex* **4/7**[1]

0/ 4 59 **Grandiloquent**[28] 3941 5-11-3 0..... MissHBethell(3) 70
(Brian Ellison) *in tch: drvn and struggling after 3 out: lost tch bef next: t.o* **33/1**

4m 14.2s (7.30) **Going Correction** +0.60s/f (Soft) 4 Ran SP% **108.5**
Speed ratings (Par 105): **106,104,104,76**
CSF £15.43 TOTE £3.10; EX 17.50 Trifecta £30.60.
Owner T G Leslie **Bred** Fittocks Stud **Trained** Cholmondeley, Cheshire
■ Harry Stock's first winner under rules.

FOCUS
Just the four runners for this novice hurdle and they went no more than a medium gallop. Common bends and hurdles were sited off the outer rail towards centre. The winner is rated back to form with the second on the upgrade.

5161 SEDGEFIELD RACECOURSE BOOKMAKERS H'CAP HURDLE (10 hdls) 2m 5f 110y

2:45 (2:48) (Class 5) (0-100,100) 4-Y-0+ **£2,339** (£686; £343; £171)

Form RPR

0P0- 1 **Rayadour (IRE)**[45] 4336 5-9-13 78..... CraigNichol(5) 81
(Micky Hammond) *hld up in midfield: stdy hdwy 1/2-way: pushed along 4 out: hdwy on outside bef 2 out: led and edgd lft between last 2: edgd rt run-in: drvn out* **9/2**[2]

U6/- 2 nk **Highland Cathedral**[33] 10-10-10 89..... MissCWalton(5) 91
(James Walton) *cl up: led 1/2-way to 3 out: rallied and ev ch next: kpt on wl fr last: jst hld* **50/1**

433- 3 2 ½ **Generous Chief (IRE)**[39] 4461 6-11-2 97..... DiarmuidO'Regan(7) 96+
(Chris Grant) *prom: reminders 3rd: drvn and outpcd after 3 out: rallied bef last: kpt on run-in: nt rch first two* **8/1**

242/ 4 ½ **George Fernbeck**[27] 4688 6-10-9 93..... GLavery(10) 94
(Brian Ellison) *midfield: rdn and outpcd bef 4 out: rallied and cl up appr 2 out: kpt on same pce fr last* **11/4**[1]

542- 5 1 **Politelysed**[22] 4770 8-10-10 84..... KennyJohnson 83
(Robert Johnson) *bhd and detached: nt fluent 4th: gd hdwy to chse ldrs 3 out: rdn next: one pce last* **16/1**

604- 6 16 **Agent Louise**[38] 4479 6-10-10 91..... DaraghBourke(7) 78
(Mike Sowersby) *prom: wnt 2nd after 4 out: mstke and outpcd next: btn fnl 2* **20/1**

P64- 7 6 **Bollin Line**[14] 4939 7-11-5 100..... NathanMoscrop(7) 78
(Lucinda Egerton) *hld up: hdwy and in tch 1/2-way: rdn and wknd after 3 out* **22/1**

322- 8 1 ½ **Lebanna**[14] 4938 4-10-13 94.....(t) LucyAlexander 64
(Tim Easterby) *hld up: hdwy to ld 3 out: rdn and hdd bef next: wknd bef last* **9/2**[2]

/5P- 9 4 ½ **Patriot (IRE)**[22] 4774 10-10-1 82 ow2..... GrahamWatters(7) 55
(Barry Murtagh) *led to 1/2-way: cl up tl rdn and wknd bef 2 out* **66/1**

342- 10 1 ¾ **Another Dimension (IRE)**[20] 4816 8-11-2 95..... DerekFox(5) 66
(Rose Dobbin) *in tch: drvn and outpcd after 4 out: struggling fr next* **6/1**[3]

440- 11 11 **Native Optimist (IRE)**[39] 4461 7-10-4 83..... JoeColliver(5) 44
(Sheena Walton) *prom tl rdn and wknd bef 3 out* **9/1**

006- 12 nk **Frosty Dawn**[17] 4891 6-9-11 74 oh5..... JonathanEngland(3) 35
(Mike Sowersby) *hld up: struggling bef 4 out: lost tch after next* **100/1**

5m 32.9s (18.30) **Going Correction** +0.60s/f (Soft)
WFA 4 from 5yo+ 6lb 12 Ran SP% **117.9**
Speed ratings (Par 103): **90,89,88,88,88 82,80,79,78,77 73,73**
CSF £211.83 CT £1756.72 TOTE £6.90: £2.20, £4.80, £2.50; EX 346.70 Trifecta £2382.20 Part won. Pool: £3,176.20 - 0.55 winning tickets..
Owner Straightline Construction Ltd **Bred** His Highness The Aga Khan's Studs S C **Trained** Middleham Moor, N Yorks

FOCUS
In essence a low-grade handicap hurdle run at no more than a fair pace, but there was plenty of market activity with two in particular well supported. The fourth to sixth help set the level.

5162 HAPPY 40TH BIRTHDAY MR TALLENTIRE H'CAP CHASE (14 fncs 2 omitted) 2m 4f

3:20 (3:20) (Class 4) (0-120,117) 5-Y-0+ **£4,260** (£1,322; £712)

Form RPR

2U3- 1 **Cara Court (IRE)**[24] 4747 8-9-11 91 oh3.....(p) JonathanEngland(3) 94
(Joanne Foster) *j.rt: mde virtually all: rdn after 3 out: asserted after next: edgd lft and idled bef last: drvn out run-in* **2/1**[2]

U54- 2 3 ¼ **Kykate**[27] 4668 8-11-9 117.....(t) JakeGreenall(3) 117
(William Kinsey) *w wnr: effrt and rdn 2 out: one pce appr last* **5/4**[1]

41U- 3 11 **Work Boy**[7] 5060 13-11-1 111..... SamanthaDrake(5) 107
(Richard Drake) *chsd ldrs: drvn and outpcd 4 out (usual 5 out): no imp bef 2 out* **4/1**[3]

/54- P **Apache Blue (IRE)**[182] 1756 10-11-0 105..... AdrianLane
(John Wade) *in tch: drvn and outpcd 1/2-way: lost tch 10th: t.o whn p.u bef 2 out* **11/1**

5m 11.6s (8.60) **Going Correction** +0.60s/f (Soft) 4 Ran SP% **106.1**
Speed ratings: **106,104,100,**
CSF £4.91 TOTE £3.10; EX 5.90 Trifecta £10.20.
Owner The Golden Syndicate **Bred** L W Doran **Trained** Menston, W Yorks

FOCUS
Just four runners in this uncompetitive 0-120 handicap chase. The first two are rated in line with the best of their 2014 form.

5163 BOOKMAKERS FREE BETS WITH BOOKMAKERS.CO.UK H'CAP HURDLE (8 hdls) 2m 1f

3:55 (3:55) (Class 4) (0-110,107) 4-Y-0+ **£3,638** (£1,068; £534; £267)

Form RPR

121- 1 **Wintered Well (IRE)**[6] 5072 6-11-6 107 7ex..... ConorRing(7) 116+
(Jennie Candlish) *chsd ldrs: pushed along after 3 out: rallied: led bef last: rdn clr* **4/6**[1]

224- 2 6 **Copt Hill**[14] 4943 6-10-8 88..... LucyAlexander 91
(Tracy Waggott) *disp ld to 2nd: chsd ldr: rdn after 3 out: rallied: hit last: wnt 2nd run-in: nt pce of wnr* **12/1**

6P2- 3 1 ¼ **Wilde Pastures (IRE)**[22] 4772 9-11-5 106.....(p) DaleIrving(7) 107
(James Ewart) *led: rdn bef 2 out: hdd bef last: outpcd and lost 2nd run-in* **7/1**[2]

443- 4 2 ¾ **Bobs Lady Tamure**[22] 4770 7-10-10 97.....(t) DaraghBourke(7) 96
(Maurice Barnes) *hld up: nt fluent 4th: hdwy after 3 out: in tch and rdn next: one pce bef last* **8/1**[3]

245- 5 12 **Baraboy (IRE)**[20] 4817 4-10-2 95..... GrahamWatters(7) 78
(Barry Murtagh) *in tch: pushed along and outpcd after 3 out: no imp bef next* **22/1**

403- 6 1 ¼ **Amir Pasha (UAE)**[14] 4943 9-11-0 99.....(b) JoeColliver(5) 85
(Micky Hammond) *in tch: drvn after 4 out: rallied: wknd bef 2 out* **16/1**

340- 7 nk **Marlborough House**[14] 4941 4-10-11 104.....(p) DiarmuidO'Regan(7) 84
(Chris Grant) *in tch: drvn and outpcd after 3 out: wknd bef next* **33/1**

05P- 8 1 ¾ **The Boozy Bishop (IRE)**[22] 4774 9-9-10 81 oh4 ow1(p) MissCWalton(5) 66
(Sheena Walton) *hld up: hdwy and prom 3 out: rdn and wknd bef next* **80/1**

426- 9 1 **Brunello**[31] 3284 6-11-8 105.....(p) KyleJames(3) 89
(Philip Kirby) *hld up: drvn and edgd rt bef 3 out: nvr on terms* **16/1**

050- 10 2 ¾ **Politeness (FR)**[30] 4615 5-10-12 97.....[1] CraigNichol(5) 78
(Rose Dobbin) *hld up: rdn after 3 out: btn next: no ch whn mstke last* **33/1**

044- 11 11 **Pink Mischief**[38] 4476 4-10-0 89..... JohnKington(3) 54
(Andrew Crook) *hld up: hdwy and in tch bef 3 out: rdn and wknd bef next* **100/1**

P- 12 ½ **Beau Ballistic (IRE)**[12] 4996 6-10-2 85..... PeterCarberry(3) 56
(Sarah Dawson, Ire) *hld up: struggling after 4 out: btn bef 2 out* **12/1**

4m 16.9s (10.00) **Going Correction** +0.60s/f (Soft)
WFA 4 from 5yo+ 5lb 12 Ran SP% **123.2**
Speed ratings (Par 105): **100,97,96,95,89 89,88,88,87,86 81,80**
CSF £10.31 CT £40.07 TOTE £1.50: £1.10, £2.90, £2.60; EX 10.50 Trifecta £49.20.
Owner Mrs Kristene Hunter **Bred** Mrs Kathleen Leahy **Trained** Basford Green, Staffs

FOCUS
A fair gallop to this handicap hurdle. The winner is rated in line with his recent win but can do better.

5164 ALBERT HILL COMMERCIALS OPEN HUNTERS' CHASE (18 fncs 3 omitted) 3m 3f

4:30 (4:32) (Class 6) 5-Y-0+ **£1,871** (£580; £290; £145)

Form RPR

/55- 1 **Sacred Mountain**[19] 4837 13-12-4 99.....(t) MissCWalton 103+
(James Walton) *chsd ldrs: outpcd 1/2-way: rallied after 3 out (usual 4 out): led bef last: pushed out run-in* **14/1**

16P- 2 2 **Special Portrait (IRE)**[34] 4554 10-12-3 109.....(t) MrPGerety(5) 105
(Mark Hughes) *hld up: pushed along and hdwy 1/2-way: rdn to ld after 2 out: hdd bef last: kpt on same pce run-in* **4/1**[3]

14P/ 3 22 **Eyre Square (IRE)**[19] 11-11-7 117..... MrCMO'Mahony(7) 77
(John Wade) *prom: wnt 2nd 4th: rdn after 3 out (usual 4 out): outpcd fr next* **7/1**

4/1- 4 1 ½ **Radharc Na Mara (IRE)**[7] 5062 10-11-4 96..... MissHHarper(7) 76
(Miss H Harper) *t.k.h: led: rdn whn mstke 2 out: sn hdd & wknd* **3/1**[2]

/3P- 5 27 **Playing The Field (IRE)**[12] 9-12-0 86..... MissJCoward 52
(Mrs Alison Christmas) *sn towards rr: struggling fr 1/2-way: nvr on terms* **20/1**

240- 6 34 **Gin Cobbler**[13] 8-11-11 100..... MrTSpeke(7) 25
(Victor Thompson) *hld up in tch: rdn after 12th: struggling after next: t.o* **16/1**

42P- P **Loose Preformer (IRE)**[34] 8-11-7 111..... MrRobertHawker(7)
(Michael Hawker) *in tch tl nt fluent and outpcd 13th: struggling bef 3 out (usual 4 out): t.o whn p.u bef next* **18/1**

1F- U **Rosie Du Berlais (IRE)**[7] 5062 8-11-4 0..... MrPDennis(7)
(Philip Kirby) *nt fluent on occasions: hld up: hit 4th: hdwy and cl up 6th: disputing 2nd pl whn hit and uns rdr 10th* **2/1**[1]

7m 26.1s (37.10) **Going Correction** +0.60s/f (Soft) 8 Ran SP% **113.4**
Speed ratings: **69,68,61,61,53 43,,**
CSF £69.24 TOTE £14.60: £2.90, £1.30, £2.60; EX 79.50 Trifecta £490.00.
Owner Messrs F T Walton **Bred** Messrs F T Walton **Trained** Thropton, Northumberland
■ Stewards' Enquiry : Miss J Coward one-day ban: careless riding (21 Apr)

FOCUS
Not a particularly competitive hunter chase, but the pace was strong and two veterans fought out the finish. The winner is rated to his mark.

5165 BE PREMIERE HAIR NOVICES' HUNTERS' CHASE (14 fncs 2 omitted) 2m 4f

5:05 (5:07) (Class 6) 5-Y-0+ **£1,280** (£419; £225)

Form RPR

1- 1 **Shales Rock**[25] 4727 8-11-9 0.....(p) MissImmyRobinson(7) 121+
(Mrs C J Robinson) *chsd ldr: hmpd 7th: led 10th: hrd pressed bef 2 out to last: styd on gamely to draw clr run-in* **3/1**[2]

4/1- 2 7 **Silver Token**[8] 5041 9-12-2 102.....(tp) MrTomDavid 116
(David Brace) *hld up: hdwy to chse ldrs 1/2-way: wnt 2nd 3 out: disp ld bef next tl hit last: sn outpcd* **10/11**[1]

036/ 3 dist **Ballymartin King (IRE)**[26] 8-11-7 0..... MrWEasterby(5) 66
(Mrs Sarah Easterby) *mstkes in rr: struggling fnl circ: tk poor 3rd 2 out: nvr on terms* **22/1**

PP3/ P **Bayfirth (IRE)**[6] 11-11-7 79..... MrTHamilton(5)
(A B Hamilton) *in tch: struggling 8th: t.o whn p.u after 3 out (usual 4 out)* **33/1**

0/ P **Can't Call It (IRE)**[13] 9-11-9 0..... MrHAABannister(3)
(Ms J Andrews) *in tch: struggling fr 9th: blnd 3 out (usual 4 out): sn p.u* **14/1**

4/0- P **Blackthirteen (IRE)**[13] 10-11-5 0 MissJGillam(7)
(Michael B Jones) *hld up in tch: lost pl 7th: struggling fr next: t.o whn p.u after 3 out (usual 4 out)* **25/1**

5/5- P **Sharivarry (FR)**[13] 8-11-5 97 MrTSpeke(7)
(Victor Thompson) *bhd and detached: lost tch and p.u after 8th* **14/1**

6/ R **Wacket Willie**[54] 8-11-9 0 MrJHamilton(3)
(J M B Cookson) *t.k.h: j.rt: led at decent gallop to 10th: lost 2nd 3 out: sn struggling: 4th and no ch whn ref last* **5/1**[3]

5m 19.7s (16.70) **Going Correction** +0.60s/f (Soft) **8** Ran SP% **118.5**
Speed ratings: **90,87,67,** , ,
CSF £6.60 TOTE £3.60: £1.60, £1.10, £5.50; EX 6.80 Trifecta £53.20.
Owner Mrs Caroline Robinson **Bred** J G Beasley **Trained** Shifnal, Shropshire

FOCUS
A novice hunter chase run at a good gallop in which only three finished and the closing stages were dominated by the two previous winners. The winner is rated in line with his Stratford win, the second similar to his Ffos Las win.

5166 COMPARE BOOKIES FREE BETS WITH BOOKMAKERS.CO.UK STANDARD OPEN NATIONAL HUNT FLAT RACE 2m 1f

5:35 (5:35) (Class 6) 4-6-Y-0 **£1,559** (£457; £228; £114)

Form RPR

0- **1** **Dubai Sonnet**[162] 2037 5-11-4 0 AlainCawley 112+
(Alan Swinbank) *hld up: smooth hdwy 1/2-way: wnt 2nd and poised to chal fr 4f out: led on bit over 1f out: qcknd clr: canter* **3/1**[2]

6- **2** *8* **Ardenlee Lad (IRE)**[31] 4611 4-10-5 0 GrahamWatters(7) 89
(Philip Kirby) *prom: hdwy to ld over 4f out: drvn and hdd over 1f out: no ch w v easy wnr* **4/1**[3]

0- **3** *28* **Riquet The King (FR)**[17] 4895 5-11-4 0 DavidEngland 70
(Alan Brown) *in tch: drvn and struggling 1/2-way: styd on fr 2f out: no ch w first two* **66/1**

5- **4** *nk* **Chiron (IRE)**[31] 4611 5-10-13 0 CraigNichol(5) 70
(Keith Dalgleish) *chsd clr ldr: rdn and outpcd over 4f out: btn fnl 2f* **4/5**[1]

5 *52* **Morgans Rock (IRE)**[12] 5000 6-11-1 0 PeterCarberry(3) 23
(Sarah Dawson, Ire) *t.k.h: led and clr: hdd over 4f out: wknd over 3f out: t.o* **12/1**

4m 11.7s (10.40) **Going Correction** +0.60s/f (Soft)
WFA 4 from 5yo+ 5lb **5** Ran SP% **109.7**
Speed ratings: **99,95,82,81,57**
CSF £14.78 TOTE £3.30: £1.30, £2.30; EX 16.70 Trifecta £109.00.
Owner Solway Stayers **Bred** R G Percival And Mrs A Lockhart **Trained** Melsonby, N Yorks

FOCUS
A good gallop to this bumper.
T/Plt: £350.60 to a £1 stake. Pool: £57,519.92 - 119.75 winning tickets. T/Qpdt: £12.30 to a £1 stake. Pool: £4,926.58 - 294.10 winning tickets. RY

5153 AINTREE (L-H)

Saturday, April 5

OFFICIAL GOING: Mildmay course - good; hurdle course - good to soft (good in places); national course - good to soft (good in places; mildmay 7.1, hurdle 6.8, national 6.6)
Wind: moderate 1/2 against Weather: overcast, breezy, light showers

5167 PERTEMPS NETWORK MERSEY NOVICES' HURDLE (GRADE 1) (11 hdls) 2m 4f

1:30 (1:30) (Class 1) 4-Y-0+

£42,202 (£15,900; £7,957; £3,975; £1,995; £997)

Form RPR

411- **1** **Lac Fontana (FR)**[22] 4785 5-11-4 148 APMcCoy 149+
(Paul Nicholls) *lw: midfield: hdwy to trck ldrs after 6th: wnt 2nd bef 3 out: rdn after 3 out: drvn between last 2: led 110yds out: styd on wl* **9/2**[1]

310- **2** *1 1/2* **Splash Of Ginge**[25] 4736 6-11-4 142 SamTwiston-Davies 146
(Nigel Twiston-Davies) *trckd ldr: led after 4 out: rdn after 3 out: hdd 110yds out: kpt on but a hld by wnr* **12/1**

U25- **3** *1/2* **Dell' Arca (IRE)**[24] 4752 5-11-4 143 TomScudamore 145
(David Pipe) *trckd ldrs: rdn and outpcd in 4th after 3 out: styd on run-in: wnt 3rd towards fin* **13/2**[3]

FF5- **4** *1/2* **Wilde Blue Yonder (IRE)**[25] 4736 5-11-4 145 RobertThornton 148+
(Alan King) *lw: midfield: short of room after 4 out and shuffled bk sltly: rcvrd to chse ldng pair bef 3 out: rdn bef 2 out: hit last: one pce run-in: lost 3rd towards fin* **11/2**[2]

121- **5** *3 3/4* **Volnay De Thaix (FR)**[15] 4935 5-11-4 145 RichardJohnson 143
(Nicky Henderson) *lw: in tch: lost pl after 5th: sme hdwy u.p bef 3 out: plugged on after 2 out: nvr threatened ldrs* **9/1**

112- **6** *17* **Sea Lord (IRE)**[139] 2530 7-11-4 150 DenisO'Regan 127
(John Ferguson) *hld up: pushed along after 7th: sme hdwy u.p bef 3 out: wknd after last* **8/1**

212- **7** *3* **No No Romeo (IRE)**[34] 4575 5-11-4 0 AidanColeman 124
(Charlie Longsdon) *str: hld up: rdn 4 out: sn btn* **66/1**

111- **8** *3* **Kayf Moss**[41] 4441 6-11-4 143 (b) TomO'Brien 122
(John Flint) *trckd ldrs: pushed along and lost pl 7th: sn struggling in rr* **16/1**

/11- **9** *25* **Monkey Kingdom**[14] 4950 6-11-4 135 (t) JamieMoore 98
(Rebecca Curtis) *led: hdd after 4 out: sn wknd* **25/1**

111- **10** *5* **Kilcooley (IRE)**[27] 4693 5-11-4 137 NoelFehily 94
(Charlie Longsdon) *hld up in midfield: pushed along after 7th: sn btn* **25/1**

211- **F** **Oscar Hoof (IRE)**[21] 4807 6-11-4 138 BarryGeraghty
(Nicky Henderson) *lw: midfield: hdwy to trck ldrs 6th: rdn whn fell 3 out* **11/2**[2]

/10- **P** **Un Ace (FR)**[25] 4736 6-11-4 0 NickScholfield
(Kim Bailey) *hld up: already struggling whn sltly short of room after 4 out: wl bhd whn p.u bef last: b.b.v* **8/1**

4m 50.6s (-10.10) **Going Correction** -0.075s/f (Good) **12** Ran SP% **117.3**
Speed ratings (Par 117): **117,116,116,116,114 107,106,105,95,93** ,
CSF £57.04 CT £352.64 TOTE £4.60: £2.50, £2.00, £2.70; EX 62.00 Trifecta £272.30.
Owner Potensis Limited **Bred** S C A La Perrigne **Trained** Ditcheat, Somerset
■ The first running of this event as a Grade 1.

FOCUS
The ground was Good to soft, good in places on the hurdles course. The jockeys said the ground was "on the slow side of good" and "a bit dead". Hurdles, all rails and bends on inside line. This event has been won by such as Tidal Bay, Peddlers Cross and Simonsig in recent seasons. Despite several front-runners, the pace was solid, but not hectic, and the first three positions were filled by horses that had won big handicaps earlier in the season. Solid form.

5168 DOOM BAR MAGHULL NOVICES' CHASE (GRADE 1) (12 fncs) 2m

2:05 (2:05) (Class 1) 5-Y-0+

£61,897 (£23,320; £11,671; £5,830; £2,926; £1,463)

Form RPR

511- **1** **Balder Succes (FR)**[42] 4420 6-11-4 153 WayneHutchinson 162+
(Alan King) *trckd ldrs: led 2 out: drvn and styd on strly run-in* **7/2**[2]

213- **2** *4* **Simply Ned (IRE)**[35] 4543 7-11-4 148 BrianHarding 157
(Nicky Richards) *hld up in rr: hdwy to chse ldrs whn hit 8th: kpt on and 2nd last: no imp* **12/1**

213- **3** *1/2* **Trifolium (FR)**[25] 4737 7-11-4 156 APMcCoy 158
(C Byrnes, Ire) *chsd ldr: hit 9th: led next: hdd 2 out: kpt on same pce run-in* **11/4**[1]

44/ **4** *10* **Moscow Mannon (IRE)**[34] 4586 8-11-4 146 DavyRussell 151+
(Henry De Bromhead, Ire) *lw: chsd ldrs to 6th: outpcd and modest 5th whn blnd 3 out: kpt on run-in: tk modest 4th nr fin* **9/2**[3]

U14- **5** *hd* **Next Sensation (IRE)**[22] 4790 7-11-4 145 (t) TomScudamore 148
(Michael Scudamore) *led: t.k.h: hit 8th: hdd 3 out: wknd between last 2: fin tired* **6/1**

54F- **6** *6* **Ted Veale (IRE)**[25] 4737 7-11-4 146 BarryGeraghty 143
(A J Martin, Ire) *j.rt in rr: hit 5th: outpcd and bhd fr 8th* **12/1**

11U- **7** *63* **Hinterland (FR)**[24] 4753 6-11-4 154 NoelFehily 85
(Paul Nicholls) *lw: t.k.h: in rr: lost pl 9th: sn bhd: j.rt and hit 2 out: t.o whn eased last: eventually completed* **11/2**

3m 48.4s (-11.60) **Going Correction** -0.30s/f (Good) **7** Ran SP% **112.1**
Speed ratings: **117,115,114,109,109 106,75**
CSF £38.34 TOTE £4.00: £2.40, £3.00; EX 43.60 Trifecta £160.00.
Owner Masterson Holdings Limited **Bred** Damien Bellanger Et Al **Trained** Barbury Castle, Wilts

FOCUS
The ground on the chase course had dried out to Good all over. A race boasting a rich heritage since it was promoted to Grade 1 status in 1995, with winners including Flagship Uberalles, Well Chief, Twist Magic, Finian's Rainbow and Sprinter Sacre. With established trailblazer Next Sensation in the field, this was always going to be run at a rapid pace. Balder Success moves to the head of the 2m novice chase ratings, with another step forward from the progressive Simply Ned.

5169 SILVER CROSS STAYERS' HURDLE (REGISTERED AS THE LIVERPOOL HURDLE) (GRADE 1) (13 hdls) 3m 110y

2:50 (2:50) (Class 1) 4-Y-0+

£67,524 (£25,440; £12,732; £6,360; £3,192; £1,596)

Form RPR

121- **1** **Whisper (FR)**[24] 4752 6-11-7 159 BarryGeraghty 157+
(Nicky Henderson) *hld up: hdwy appr 3 out: sn chsng ldrs: led last: hld on wl* **4/1**[3]

U23- **2** *1* **At Fishers Cross (IRE)**[23] 4767 7-11-7 162 (p) APMcCoy 156+
(Rebecca Curtis) *j.rt: w wnr: led 9th: hdd last: no ex last 50yds* **11/8**[1]

405- **3** *3 3/4* **Thousand Stars (FR)**[34] 4584 10-11-7 158 PaulTownend 150
(W P Mullins, Ire) *swtg: in rr: drvn and outpcd 10th: styd on fr 2 out: 6th last: swtchd lft: styd on to take 3rd last 150yds* **11/1**

224- **4** *5* **Zarkandar (IRE)**[23] 4767 7-11-7 162 (b) NoelFehily 146
(Paul Nicholls) *led to 9th: hit next: 3rd last: wknd fnl 150yds* **10/3**[2]

220- **5** *5* **Salubrious (IRE)**[23] 4767 7-11-7 153 [1] HarryDerham 143
(Paul Nicholls) *hld up: hdwy appr 3 out: chsng ldrs whn hmpd and swtchd rt 2 out: 4th whn hit last: wknd fnl 150yds* **16/1**

4P3- **6** *6* **The Knoxs (IRE)**[17] 4897 11-11-7 123 RyanMania 135
(Sandy Thomson) *hld up in rr: effrt appr 3 out: sn prom: 6th and wkng whn hit last* **66/1**

110- **7** *53* **Melodic Rendezvous**[25] 4739 8-11-7 163 NickScholfield 81
(Jeremy Scott) *lw: chsd ldng pair: drvn 10th: wknd 3 out: sn bhd: t.o whn eased after 2 out: eventually completed* **8/1**

6m 6.8s (-9.50) **Going Correction** -0.075s/f (Good) **7** Ran SP% **112.0**
Speed ratings (Par 117): **112,111,110,108,107 105,88**
CSF £9.85 TOTE £4.70: £2.30, £1.60; EX 11.80 Trifecta £53.50.
Owner Walters Plant Hire Ltd **Bred** Hubert & Sandra Hosselet **Trained** Upper Lambourn, Berks
■ A new identity for this race.

FOCUS
A competitive renewal of this stayers' hurdle, if lacking a real top-notcher such as recent winners Big Buck's and Solwhit. In fact the last five winners of this race had taken the World Hurdle on their previous start, but that was not to be the case this time with More of That bypassing this contest. The pace was steady early, but then the market leaders pushed on a little after a mile. The runners looked pretty tired in the closing stages, suggesting the ground was quite holding. Whisper is rated similar to his Cheltenham form, with A t Fishers Cross 10lb off.

5170 BETFRED TV H'CAP CHASE (LISTED RACE) (19 fncs) 3m 1f

3:25 (3:25) (Class 1) 5-Y-0+

£34,170 (£12,822; £6,420; £3,198; £1,608; £804)

Form RPR

264- **1** **Duke Of Lucca (IRE)**[24] 4754 9-10-7 **134** (bt) RichardJohnson 147
(Philip Hobbs) *mid-div: chsd ldrs 7th: handy 4th whn hit 3 out: led last: jst hld on* **12/1**

PP0- **2** *hd* **Vino Griego (FR)**[25] 4738 9-11-5 **146** (v) JamieMoore 158
(Gary Moore) *chsd ldrs: led between last 2: hdd last: styd on towards fin: jst hld* **25/1**

3P3- **3** *8* **Gullinbursti (IRE)**[14] 4953 8-11-1 **142** (v[1]) NoelFehily 147
(Emma Lavelle) *lw: chsd ldrs: 3rd and keeping on same pce whn j.lft last* **10/1**

630- **4** *3* **Kian's Delight**[168] 1971 6-10-1 **128** BrianHughes 131
(Peter Bowen) *chsd ldrs: blnd 6th: outpcd after 15th: 7th last: styd on run-in* **14/1**

/50- **5** *1 3/4* **Golden Chieftain (IRE)**[25] 4738 9-11-1 **142** (p) BrendanPowell 142
(Colin Tizzard) *lw: chsd ldrs: one pce fr 3 out* **33/1**

P3P- **6** *1/2* **Our Mick**[70] 3887 8-10-10 **137** WayneHutchinson 138
(Donald McCain) *led 2nd: blnd 14th: hdd between last 2: n.m.r last: sn fdd* **14/1**

6/4- **7** *8* **Minella For Value (IRE)**[169] 1957 8-10-9 **136** DavyRussell 129
(John Butler) *chsd ldrs: outpcd 15th: wknd 2 out* **14/1**

103- **8** *1 1/4* **Unioniste (FR)**[70] 3897 6-11-12 **153** SamTwiston-Davies 146
(Paul Nicholls) *nt fluent in mid-div: effrt 15th: nvr nr ldrs* **6/1**[2]

24P- **9** 1¼ **Sir Du Bearn (FR)**[63] 4026 8-10-2 **129** DonalDevereux 120
(Peter Bowen) *in rr: blnd 11th: nvr on terms* **33/1**
154- **10** 2¼ **Johns Spirit (IRE)**[23] 4768 7-11-7 **148** RichieMcLernon 141
(Jonjo O'Neill) *lw: in rr: hdwy 13th: hit 15th: wknd appr 2 out* **8/1**[3]
030- **11** 1 **Renard (FR)**[25] 4738 9-11-0 **141** AidanColeman 130
(Venetia Williams) *prom: outpcd 4 out: sn lost pl* **16/1**
31P- **12** 1¾ **Tranquil Sea (IRE)**[23] 4769 12-11-0 **144** (t) GavinSheehan(3) 129
(Warren Greatrex) *in rr: jumperd rt: bhd whn hmpd 12th: sme hdwy 2 out: nvr on terms* **50/1**
/26- **U** **Carruthers**[35] 4557 11-11-4 **148** (t) NicodeBoinville(3)
(Mark Bradstock) *uns rdr s* **33/1**
04P- **F** **Saint Are (FR)**[23] 4769 8-10-2 **129** (v) DougieCostello
(Tim Vaughan) *mid-div: bhd whn fell 12th* **10/1**
6F0- **P** **Wetak (FR)**[23] 4768 7-10-10 **137** (t) TomScudamore
(David Pipe) *in rr: bhd fr 15th: t.o whn p.u bef last* **9/1**
1P2- **P** **Wiesentraum (GER)**[22] 4792 8-10-3 **130** (b1) LeightonAspell
(Lucy Wadham) *in rr: bhd whn hit 15th: t.o whn p.u bef 2 out* **18/1**
121- **P** **Victor Hewgo**[35] 4541 9-10-12 **139** JamesReveley
(Keith Reveley) *in rr: nt fluent: reminders 6th: bhd whn blnd 8th: p.u bef next* **5/1**[1]

6m 19.8s (-10.20) **Going Correction** -0.075s/f (Good) **17** Ran SP% **123.7**
Speed ratings: **113,112,110,109,108 108,106,105,105,104 104,103,,,**
CSF £286.80 CT £3110.92 TOTE £15.50: £3.60, £4.40, £2.60, £4.30; EX 444.60 Trifecta £5107.30.
Owner Mrs Lesley Field **Bred** Liam Gilsenan **Trained** Withycombe, Somerset

FOCUS
A red-hot handicap chase in which Our Mick set a decent gallop. A solid handicap, the winner rated back to the best of his 2012 form.

5171 CRABBIE'S GRAND NATIONAL CHASE (H'CAP) (GRADE 3) (30 fncs) 4m 3f 110y

4:15 (4:17) (Class 1) 7-Y-O+

£561,300 (£211,100; £105,500; £52,700; £26,500; £13,200)

Form RPR

013- **1** **Pineau De Re (FR)**[23] 4765 11-10-6 143 LeightonAspell 157+
(Dr Richard Newland) *mid-div: hdwy whn hit 13th: chsng ldrs 16th (Water): led appr 2 out: drew clr run-in* **25/1**
111- **2** 5 **Balthazar King (IRE)**[24] 4754 10-10-13 150 RichardJohnson 156
(Philip Hobbs) *prom: chsng ldrs 4 out: drvn next: 2nd at last: styd on same pce* **14/1**[3]
/11- **3** 1¼ **Double Seven (IRE)**[34] 4587 8-10-11 148 (tp) APMcCoy 155
(Martin Brassil, Ire) *mid-div: mstke 5th: hdwy to chse ldrs: drvn appr 2 out: 3rd last: kpt on same pce* **10/1**[1]
51P- **4** 10 **Alvarado (IRE)**[94] 3455 9-10-2 139 PaulMoloney 135
(Fergal O'Brien) *lw: in rr: hdwy 19th: chsng ldrs 3 out: 8th last: styd on to take 4th in clsng stages* **33/1**
/22- **5** 2½ **Rocky Creek (IRE)**[70] 3888 8-11-5 156 NoelFehily 150
(Paul Nicholls) *lw: chsd ldrs: led 18th: hdd 22nd (2nd Becher's): led 4 out: hdd appr 2 out: wknd appr elbow* **16/1**
1P4- **6** shd **Chance Du Roy (FR)**[49] 4263 10-10-6 143 (p) TomO'Brien 138
(Philip Hobbs) *mid-div: hmpd 9th (1st Valentine's): hdwy 26th: one pce appr 2 out* **33/1**
415- **7** 3 **Monbeg Dude (IRE)**[35] 4544 9-10-9 146 PCarberry 139
(Michael Scudamore) *lw: in rr: hdwy whn blnd 22nd (2nd Becher's): hit 24th (2nd Canal Turn): chsng ldrs 26th: one pce appr 2 out* **16/1**
1/P- **8** 16 **Raz De Maree (FR)**[19] 4871 9-10-3 140 (v1) DavyCondon 117
(D T Hughes, Ire) *mid-div: hit 2nd: lost pl 9th: bhd fr 25th (2nd Valentine's): kpt on run-in: nvr on terms* **50/1**
/50- **9** shd **Swing Bill (FR)**[23] 4769 13-10-1 138 ConorO'Farrell 114
(David Pipe) *mid-div: hdwy 25th (2nd Valentine's): chsng ldrs 3 out: wknd appr next* **66/1**
103- **10** 4½ **Kruzhlinin (GER)**[35] 4552 7-10-6 143 WilsonRenwick 120
(Donald McCain) *in rr: sme hdwy whn mstke 25th (2nd Valentine's): nvr on terms* **100/1**
053- **11** 2½ **Buckers Bridge (IRE)**[42] 4435 8-10-10 147 AELynch 120
(Henry De Bromhead, Ire) *hld up in rr: mstke 18th: hdwy into mid-div next: mstke and outpcd 23rd (2nd Foinavon): hit 26th: wknd after 3 out* **66/1**
P/3- **12** 18 **The Package**[25] 4738 11-10-4 141 (tp) TomScudamore 97
(David Pipe) *mid-div: chsd ldrs 12th: wknd appr 2 out* **14/1**[3]
FU0- **13** 6 **Vesper Bell (IRE)**[72] 3868 8-10-5 142 MsKWalsh 90
(W P Mullins, Ire) *lw: mstkes: mid-div: blnd 6th (1st Becher's): hdwy 13th: wknd after 3 out* **40/1**
01U- **14** 2 **Across The Bay (IRE)**[49] 4270 10-10-11 148 (bt) HenryBrooke 125+
(Donald McCain) *led tl hdd whn carried v wd by loose horse on bnd after water: no ch after* **50/1**
112- **15** 7 **Mr Moonshine (IRE)**[35] 4552 10-10-12 149 RyanMania 89
(Sue Smith) *w ldrs: hit 12th: led 22nd (2nd Becher's): hdd 4 out: lost pl bef 2 out* **20/1**
004- **16** 37 **Prince De Beauchene (FR)**[79] 3751 11-10-10 147 PaulTownend 54
(W P Mullins, Ire) *chsd ldrs: wknd 26th: bhd fr 2 out: eased run-in: virtually p.u* **20/1**
/34- **17** 33 **Hunt Ball (IRE)**[23] 4766 9-11-7 158 AndrewTinkler 35
(Nicky Henderson) *hld up in rr: mid-div whn hit 21st: bhd fr 26th: t.o* **50/1**
426- **18** 1 **Hawkes Point**[49] 4270 9-10-6 143 RyanMahon 19
(Paul Nicholls) *hld up in rr: outpcd 22nd (2nd Becher's): bhd fr 25th (2nd Valentine's): t.o* **50/1**
532- **U** **Tidal Bay (IRE)**[55] 4183 13-11-10 161 SamTwiston-Davies
(Paul Nicholls) *hld up in mid-div: hmpd and uns rdr 8th (1st Canal Turn)* **16/1**
/U1- **F** **Golan Way**[27] 4706 10-10-5 142 MichaelByrne
(Tim Vaughan) *s.s: hdwy 7th (1st Foinavon): in tch whn fell next (1st Canal Turn)* **66/1**
P/4- **P** **Lion Na Bearnai (IRE)**[42] 4435 12-10-10 147 DavyRussell
(Thomas Gibney, Ire) *s.i.s: mid-div whn blnd 6th (1st Becher's): sddle slipped and lost pl 23rd (2nd Foinavon): t.o whn p.u bef 4 out* **33/1**
261- **U** **The Rainbow Hunter**[70] 3897 10-10-7 144 AidanColeman
(Kim Bailey) *in tch whn hmpd and uns rdr 9th (1st Valentine's)* **25/1**
P02- **U** **Burton Port (IRE)**[35] 4557 10-10-8 145 (tp) BrianHarding
(Jonjo O'Neill) *mid-div: blnd and uns rdr 2nd* **16/1**
F0P- **P** **Quito De La Roque (FR)**[42] 4435 10-11-1 152 (p) BrianO'Connell
(C A Murphy, Ire) *lw: sn in rr: bhd whn blnd 16th (Water): sn t.o: p.u bef 21st: b.b.v* **40/1**
033/ **U** **Last Time D'Albain (FR)**[14] 4975 10-10-2 139 RobbieColgan
(Liam P Cusack, Ire) *hld up in rr: blnd and uns rdr 6th (1st Becher's)* **50/1**
4U1- **F** **Long Run (FR)**[51] 4238 9-11-9 160 (p) MrSWaley-Cohen
(Nicky Henderson) *chsd ldrs: 2nd whn fell 9th (1st Valentine's)* **12/1**[2]
/U4- **P** **Walkon (FR)**[56] 4145 9-11-0 151 (p) WayneHutchinson
(Alan King) *mid-div: hmpd 2nd: lost pl 25th (2nd Valentine's): t.o whn p.u bef 2 out* **33/1**
U/3- **P** **Colbert Station (IRE)**[34] 4587 10-11-0 151 (t) MarkWalsh
(T M Walsh, Ire) *chsd ldrs: lft in ld bef 17th: hdd 18th: mid-div whn blnd 23rd (2nd Foinavon): bhd whn p.u bef 25th (2nd Valantine's)* **33/1**
2P0- **F** **Wayward Prince**[35] 4544 10-10-13 150 (t) JackDoyle
(Hilary Parrott) *chsd ldrs: hit 17th: lost pl 19th: bhd whn fell 3 out* **66/1**
1/3- **F** **Big Shu (IRE)**[24] 4754 9-10-8 145 (t) PeterBuchanan
(Peter Maher, Ire) *in rr whn hmpd by loose horse and fell 3rd* **14/1**[3]
PRP- **R** **Battle Group**[105] 3199 9-10-10 147 (p) BrendanPowell
(Johnny Farrelly) *reluctant to line-up: ref to r: lft at s* **40/1**
6P0- **P** **Shakalakaboomboom (IRE)**[25] 4738 10-10-3 140 (p) DavidBass
(Nicky Henderson) *mid-div: hmpd 2nd: lost pl 6th (1st Becher's): bhd fr 19th: t.o whn p.u bef 20th* **16/1**
020- **U** **Teaforthree (IRE)**[22] 4787 10-10-12 149 NickScholfield
(Rebecca Curtis) *hld up: hdwy 13th: in tch whn blnd and uns rdr 15th (Chair)* **10/1**[1]
465- **F** **One In A Milan (IRE)**[28] 4677 9-10-2 139 (v1) AdamWedge
(Evan Williams) *lw: mid-div: hdwy 17th: chsng ldrs whn mstke 19th: in tch whn fell 22nd (2nd Becher's)* **40/1**
315- **F** **Mountainous (IRE)**[63] 4026 9-10-7 144 JamieMoore
(Richard Lee) *chsd ldrs: 3rd whn fell 9th (1st Valentine's)* **40/1**
/01- **F** **Rose Of The Moon (IRE)**[74] 3825 9-10-3 140 (p) JakeGreenall
(David O'Meara) *chsd ldrs: hmpd 9th (1st Canal Turn): mstke 23rd (2nd Foinavon): outpcd whn fell 26th: b.b.v* **50/1**
10U- **F** **Twirling Magnet (IRE)**[23] 4769 8-10-5 142 (tp) RichieMcLernon
(Jonjo O'Neill) *prom: fell 1st* **100/1**
050- **U** **Our Father (IRE)**[23] 4769 8-10-8 145 (b) DenisO'Regan
(David Pipe) *mid-div: whn blnd and uns rdr 8th (1st Canal Turn)* **25/1**
62F- **P** **Vintage Star (IRE)**[25] 4738 8-10-7 144 BrianHughes
(Sue Smith) *lw: mstkes in rr: drvn 10th: sme hdwy 17th: lost pl 22nd (2nd Becher's): sn bhd: t.o whn p.u bef 26th* **50/1**
310- **P** **Triolo D'Alene (FR)**[22] 4787 7-11-6 157 BarryGeraghty
(Nicky Henderson) *mid-div: lost pl 17th: sn bhd fr 18th: blnd 21st: p.u bef next (2nd Becher's)* **16/1**

9m 9.9s (-3.10) **Going Correction** +0.35s/f (Yiel) **40** Ran SP% **150.8**
Speed ratings: **117,115,115,113,112 112,112,108,108,107 107,103,101,101,99 91,84,83,,,,,**
CSF £316.27 CT £3790.64 TOTE £32.80: £8.80, £3.90, £3.60, £10.30; EX 580.30 Trifecta £16720.40.
Owner J A Provan **Bred** Michel Hardy **Trained** Claines, Worcs
■ New sponsors for the Grand National and a lot of the supporting events at the meeting, Crabbie's replacing John Smith's.
■ Stewards' Enquiry : Jack Doyle twelve-day ban: continued to race when horse appeared exhausted (19-26 Apr)

FOCUS
The ground was good to soft, good in places on the National course. One of the classiest recent renewals of the most famous steeplechase in the world, evidenced by the fact that last year's winner, who was not bottom weight then, would have not got a run this time, and with the weights headed by a pair of multiple Grade 1 winners. The race was delayed by Battle Group, who contributed to a false start. Pineau De Re had previously threatened this sort of rating, and Balthazar King and Double Seven ran to their marks.

5172 MAXILEAD METALS H'CAP HURDLE (FOR CONDITIONAL JOCKEYS AND AMATEUR RIDERS) (9 hdls) 2m 110y

5:10 (5:10) (Class 2) 4-Y-O+

£25,024 (£7,392; £3,696; £1,848; £924; £464)

Form RPR

004- **1** **Court Minstrel (IRE)**[112] 3083 7-11-12 **147** AdamWedge 153+
(Evan Williams) *hld up in rr: smooth hdwy fr after 6th: trckd ldrs gng wl 2 out: led jst after last: sn rdn: edgd lft fnl 100yds: kpt on* **16/1**
120- **2** 1¼ **Rainbow Peak (IRE)**[22] 4785 8-11-0 **135** JoshuaMoore 140
(John Ferguson) *lw: trckd ldrs: rdn 2 out: ev ch last: kpt on but a jst hld* **8/1**[2]
60/ **3** 4 **Glen Beg (IRE)**[20] 4853 7-10-0 **126** (p) KevinSexton(5) 126
(Miss Elizabeth Doyle, Ire) *in tch on outer: hdwy 3 out: led 2 out: hdd jst after last: wknd* **25/1**
441- **4** shd **Nesterenko (GER)**[8] 5057 5-10-4 **128** NicodeBoinville(3) 128
(Nicky Henderson) *trckd ldrs: rdn after 3 out: kpt on* **9/1**[3]
110- **5** ½ **Strongpoint (IRE)**[22] 4785 10-10-10 **134** MrSCrawford(3) 134
(S R B Crawford, Ire) *hld up towards outer: tk clsr order 6th: cl up 3 out: stl ev ch between last 2: grad wknd* **16/1**
2- **6** 2¼ **Katgary (FR)**[24] 4755 4-10-7 **137** HarryDerham(3) 130
(Paul Nicholls) *lw: in tch: rdn after 3 out: one pce* **5/2**[1]
2U3- **7** 1½ **Roman Flight (IRE)**[17] 4899 6-10-3 **131** (b1) JakeHodson(7) 128
(David Dennis) *lw: midfield: rdn 3 out: kpt on one pce* **25/1**
50/- **8** 1¼ **Vasco Du Ronceray (FR)**[366] 5135 5-11-1 **139** PeterCarberry(3) 134
(Nicky Henderson) *midfield: rdn after 3 out: one pce and nvr threatened* **12/1**
161- **9** 3 **Yorkist (IRE)**[42] 4426 6-10-10 **138** NathanMoscrop(7) 131
(Brian Ellison) *in tch on outer: wnt prom after 6th: stl ev ch 2 out: wknd* **18/1**
652- **10** 1¼ **Swnymor (IRE)**[21] 4820 5-10-2 **130** (t) PaulO'Brien(7) 122
(Rebecca Curtis) *midfield: rdn bef 3 out: sn no imp* **20/1**
5/0- **11** nk **Somethingwonderful (IRE)**[20] 4853 6-10-7 **131** MarkEnright(3) 122
(D T Hughes, Ire) *led narrowly: hdd 2 out: wknd* **12/1**
0/0- **12** 1½ **Kashmir Peak (IRE)**[36] 2533 5-10-9 **133** JakeGreenall(3) 123
(John Quinn) *midfield: rdn bef 3 out: no imp* **25/1**
010- **13** nk **Jumps Road**[22] 4785 7-10-9 **135** ConorShoemark(5) 124
(Colin Tizzard) *midfield: rdn after 6th: nvr threatened ldrs* **66/1**
3U1- **14** nse **Scots Gaelic (IRE)**[23] 4781 7-9-12 **126** DeanPratt(7) 115
(John Quinn) *hld up in midfield: reminders after 5th: nvr threatened* **20/1**
2/0- **15** ¾ **Rocky Wednesday (IRE)**[41] 4454 7-11-1 **136** MichaelByrne 125
(Gordon Elliott, Ire) *hld up towards outer: rdn 3 out: nvr threatened* **40/1**
010/ **16** 1 **Bordoni (USA)**[388] 4737 5-10-4 **128** (p) JackQuinlan(3) 119
(John Ferguson) *trckd ldrs: mstke 3 out: wknd bef last* **33/1**
0/ **17** 11 **Drumlee (IRE)**[20] 4853 6-9-13 **127** GerFox(7) 105
(C F Swan, Ire) *hld up: nvr threatened* **14/1**
113- **18** 2¾ **Ubaltique (FR)**[42] 4426 6-10-13 **137** (b) GavinSheehan(3) 112
(Donald McCain) *hld up: a towards rr* **40/1**
440- **19** 5 **Massini's Trap (IRE)**[70] 3910 5-10-13 **134** [1] MsKWalsh 105
(J A Nash, Ire) *hld up in rr: a bhd* **14/1**
123/ **20** 18 **Bold Henry**[507] 2420 8-10-0 **128** ThomasCheesman(7) 88
(Philip Hobbs) *midfield: mstke 5th and lost pl: sn struggling* **22/1**

1F1- **21** *43* **Leviathan**[26] 4726 7-10-7 **131**.. HarryChalloner(3) 47
(Venetia Williams) *w ldr: mstke 5th: wknd qckly after 6th: t.o* **33/1**

124- **P** **Twoways (IRE)**[21] 4820 8-10-0 **126**.. KillianMoore(5)
(Mark Rimell) *hld up in midfield: wnt wrong and p.u bef 4th* **50/1**

4m 1.9s (-4.30) **Going Correction** +0.075s/f (Yiel)
WFA 4 from 5yo+ 5lb **22** Ran SP% **135.1**
Speed ratings (Par 109): **113,112,110,110,110 109,108,107,106,105 105,105,104,104,104 104,98,97,95,86 66,**
CSF £129.09 CT £3263.99 TOTE £20.10: £4.70, £2.70, £7.40, £2.50; EX 144.60 Trifecta £2098.10.
Owner Mrs Janet Davies **Bred** William Flood **Trained** Llancarfan, Vale Of Glamorgan

FOCUS
A competitive handicap hurdle, confined to conditional and amateur riders, in which they went a solid pace thanks to a disputed lead. Decent handicap form, with steps up from the first two.

5173 WEATHERBYS PRIVATE BANKING CHAMPION STANDARD OPEN NATIONAL HUNT FLAT RACE (GRADE 2) 2m 1f
5:45 (5:46) (Class 1) 4-6-Y-0

£17,085 (£6,411; £3,210; £1,599; £804; £402)

Form RPR

11- **1** **Ballybolley (IRE)**[12] 5014 5-11-4 123........................ SamTwiston-Davies 129+
(Nigel Twiston-Davies) *in tch: trckd ldrs over 4f out: rdn to chse ldr 2f out: drvn and hung lft over 1f out: kpt on: led post* **14/1**

121- **2** *hd* **Relic Rock (IRE)**[21] 4824 6-11-4 122.. APMcCoy 129
(Steve Gollings) *lengthy: trckd ldrs: led over 3f out: stl gng wl 2f out: pushed along over 1f out: drvn ins fnl f: sn one pce: hdd post* **12/1**

11- **3** *2 1/2* **Aqalim**[42] 4424 4-10-12 117.. DenisO'Regan 120
(John Ferguson) *str: trckd ldrs: rdn over 3f out: hung lft fr over 1f out: kpt on* **16/1**

1- **4** *1 3/4* **Ordo Ab Chao (IRE)**[34] 4575 5-11-4 121........................ RobertThornton 124
(Alan King) *str: lw: midfield: pushed along over 3f out: rdn and hdwy 2f out: kpt on* **11/1**

130- **5** *1 1/4* **Our Kaempfer (IRE)**[24] 4756 5-11-4 125........................ AidanColeman 123
(Charlie Longsdon) *hld up in midfield: rdn over 3f out: styd on: nt rch ldrs* **14/1**

311- **6** *2 1/4* **Battle Born**[38] 4492 5-11-4 121.. NoelFehily 121
(Charlie Longsdon) *lengthy: led: rdn whn hdd over 3f out: grad wknd over 1f out* **11/2**[2]

126- **7** *3/4* **Hurricane Hollow**[35] 4561 4-10-12 111........................ WilsonRenwick 114
(Keith Dalgleish) *hld up in rr: rdn over 2f out: kpt on: nvr threatened* **66/1**

21- **8** *1 1/2* **It's High Time (IRE)**[117] 3002 6-10-13 109........................ CraigNichol(5) 119
(Lucinda Russell) *lengthy: hld up: stdy hdwy on outside fr 1/2-way: rdn over 3f out: stl ev ch 2f out: wknd* **50/1**

2/1- **9** *1 1/2* **Aiaam Al Namoos**[35] 4547 5-11-4 108........................ BrianHughes 117
(John Wade) *tall: in tch: rdn and outpcd over 3f out: no threat after* **66/1**

1- **10** *nk* **Puisque Tu Pars (FR)**[35] 4561 4-10-12 117........................ JamieMoore 111
(Gary Moore) *tall: lengthy: in tch: pushed along and lost pl over 3f out: no threat after* **10/1**[3]

110- **11** *nk* **Modus**[24] 4756 4-10-12 124.. TomO'Brien 110
(Robert Stephens) *racd keenly: trckd ldrs: pushed along and lost pl over 3f out: no threat after* **9/2**[1]

62- **12** *1 1/4* **Hunters Hoof (IRE)**[127] 2788 5-11-4 116........................ AndrewTinkler 115
(Nicky Henderson) *str: midfield: rdn over 3f out: sn no imp* **40/1**

4/1- **13** *nk* **Bringithomeminty**[48] 4296 5-11-4 120........................ BarryGeraghty 116
(Nicky Henderson) *athletic: midfield: pushed along over 3f out: grad wknd* **9/2**[1]

13- **14** *15* **Clondaw Banker (IRE)**[42] 4424 5-11-1 116........................ NicodeBoinville(3) 100
(Nicky Henderson) *prom: rdn and lost pl over 3f out: sn wknd* **16/1**

2- **15** *4* **McCabe Creek (IRE)**[35] 4561 4-10-12 111........................ WayneHutchinson 90
(Alan King) *athletic: hld up: pushed along and brief hdwy 3f out: wknd fnl 2f* **25/1**

31- **16** *6* **Beatu (IRE)**[109] 3147 5-11-4 116.. PCarberry 90
(Donald McCain) *racd keenly: hld up: a towards rr* **25/1**

122- **17** *5* **Fly Home Harry**[24] 4763 5-11-4 114.. PaulMoloney 85
(Alan Swinbank) *lengthy: midfield on inner: pushed along and lost pl over 4f out: sn wknd* **20/1**

1- **18** *9* **Royal Supreme (IRE)**[69] 3926 4-10-12 114........................ DougieCostello 70
(Alex Hales) *str: hld up: rdn over 4f out: a towards rr* **50/1**

11- **19** *57* **Uncle Muf (USA)**[104] 3229 4-10-12 117.. JackDoyle 13
(Ali Brewer) *hld up: a bhd* **25/1**

4m 12.5s (5.10) **Going Correction** +0.075s/f (Yiel)
WFA 4 from 5yo+ 5lb **19** Ran SP% **127.6**
Speed ratings: **91,90,89,88,88 87,86,86,85,85 85,84,84,77,75 72,70,66,39**
CSF £162.16 CT £2741.90 TOTE £13.50: £4.10, £3.90, £5.20; EX 203.70 Trifecta £3912.80 Part won..
Owner Simon Munir & Isaac Souede **Bred** The Red Marble Syndicate **Trained** Naunton, Gloucs

FOCUS
This year's Aintree Champion bumper looked well up to scratch, even though the pace didn't lift appreciably until almost halfway. They finished in a heap but the first three are rated on the upgrade.
T/Jkpt: Not won. T/Plt: £1,633.80 to a £1 stake. Pool: £567369.56 - 253.49 winning tickets
T/Qpdt: £215.20 to a £1 stake. Pool: £36758.59 - 126.35 winning tickets WG

5015 CHEPSTOW (L-H)
Saturday, April 5

OFFICIAL GOING: Good to soft (soft in places) changing to soft after race 4 (3.05)
Wind: light, half against Weather: overcast, rain threatening

5174 UNIBET OFFERING 5 PLACES IN NATIONAL NOVICES' HURDLE (DIV I) (8 hdls) 2m 110y
1:20 (1:20) (Class 4) 4-Y-0+ **£3,249** (£954; £477; £238)

Form RPR

11- **1** **Dubawi Island (FR)**[90] 3550 5-11-11 131........................ LiamTreadwell 130+
(Venetia Williams) *chsd ldrs: lft 2nd bnd after 1st: led jst bef 5th: rdn and wnt clr between last 2: hit last: styd on wl: rdn out* **6/4**[1]

63- **2** *3 1/2* **May Be Some Time**[24] 4758 6-10-13 0........................(t) PaddyBrennan 112+
(Stuart Kittow) *hld up towards rr: hdwy into midfield 2nd: cl 3rd and wnt clr 5th: rdn and outpcd whn swtchd rt between last 2: swtchd lft and styd on same pce flat* **7/2**[3]

556- **3** *10* **Morning Reggie**[45] 4343 5-10-8 0........................ ThomasGarner(5) 104
(Oliver Sherwood) *t.k.h: hld up in tch in midfield: mstke 2nd: hdwy to chse ldrs 4th: pressed wnr 5th: 3rd and btn 2 out: wknd bef last* **11/4**[2]

420- **4** *11* **Barney Rubble**[106] 3189 5-10-13 0.. CharliePoste 91
(Richard Lee) *chsd ldrs: lft 3rd bnd after 1st: rdn and struggling bef 5th: wknd 3 out* **16/1**

00- **5** *2 3/4* **Kiama Bay (IRE)**[7] 5064 8-10-13 0........................ MattieBatchelor 88
(Jim Best) *chsd ldrs tl distracted: hung rt and lft in ld bnd after 1st: blnd 3rd: hdd jst bef 5th: sn struggling: wknd 3 out* **66/1**

44- **6** *11* **Chicoria (IRE)**[35] 4547 5-10-13 0........................ DominicElsworth 85+
(Henry Daly) *chsd ldr tl carried bdly rt and dropped to last pair bnd after 1st: nvr on terms after: mstke 2nd and 3rd: t.o 5th* **8/1**

060- **7** *6* **Ronnie Rockcake**[26] 4722 4-10-7 0.. JamesDavies 65
(Ben Pauling) *in tch in midfield: rdn and btn on long run after 4th: wknd 5th: t.o* **66/1**

2B- **8** *nk* **Eaton Rock (IRE)**[11] 5016 5-10-13 0.. FelixDeGiles 70
(Tom Symonds) *in tch in midfield: rdn and struggling on long run after 4th: wknd next: t.o* **25/1**

/00- **F** **Nowweareseven**[12] 5002 7-9-13 0.. RyanHatch(7)
(Nigel Twiston-Davies) *in tch in midfield: struggling 5th: 6th and wl hld whn fell next* **33/1**

0- **P** **Aster's Approval**[26] 4722 4-10-7 0.. SeanQuinlan
(David Bridgwater) *rn green: led wandered 1st: hung bdly rt and hdd bnd after 1st: wl bhd next: t.o after next tl p.u 3 out* **100/1**

4m 7.2s (-3.40) **Going Correction** -0.225s/f (Good)
WFA 4 from 5yo+ 5lb **10** Ran SP% **116.6**
Speed ratings (Par 105): **99,97,92,87,86 81,78,78, ,**
CSF £7.00 TOTE £2.50: £1.50, £1.30, £1.10; EX 6.10 Trifecta £7.50.
Owner Andrew Brooks & Julian Taylor **Bred** Darley Stud Management Co Ltd **Trained** Kings Caple, H'fords

FOCUS
The ground had dried out slightly overnight, changing the going stick readings from 5.6 to 5.9 on the hurdles course and from 4.6 to 5.8 on the chase course. This looked a reasonable novice hurdle with the main players coming clear.

5175 UNIBET OFFERING 5 PLACES IN NATIONAL NOVICES' HURDLE (DIV II) (8 hdls) 2m 110y
1:55 (1:55) (Class 4) 4-Y-0+ **£3,249** (£954; £477; £238)

Form RPR

022- **1** **Such A Legend**[12] 5008 6-10-8 0.. EdCookson(5) 118+
(Kim Bailey) *hld up in tch in midfield: hdwy to chse ldrs 5th: rdn and effrt to ld last: styd on: rdn out* **4/7**[1]

404- **2** *1 1/2* **Rock On Rocky**[11] 5016 6-10-13 0.. CharliePoste 116
(Matt Sheppard) *chsd ldr tl led on long run after 4th: dived but wnt clr 5th: blnd next: drvn: hdd and out j. last: styd on same pce flat* **14/1**

0F4- **3** *7* **Storm Of Swords (IRE)**[17] 4904 6-10-13 0........................ HarrySkelton 110
(Dan Skelton) *chsd ldrs: wnt 2nd bef 5th: rdn bef 2 out: cl 3rd last: no ex and wknd fnl 100yds* **2/1**[2]

0- **4** *13* **Mr Fitzroy (IRE)**[108] 3161 4-10-7 0.. SamJones 92
(Jo Davis) *in tch in midfield: mstke 2nd: 4th and rdn 5th: outpcd and btn next: plugged on but n.d after* **33/1**

P- **5** *12* **Ice Nelly (IRE)**[100] 3289 6-10-6 0..(t) PaddyBrennan 82
(Stuart Kittow) *hld up in last trio: clsd on long run after 4th: mstke next: sn rdn and wknd bef 3 out* **33/1**

00- **6** *6* **Alberto's Dream**[11] 5016 5-10-13 0.. FelixDeGiles 81
(Tom Symonds) *hld up in last trio: hdwy into midfield and mstke 2nd: rdn on long run after 4th: wknd u.p bef 3 out: t.o* **50/1**

03- **7** *1 1/2* **Reillys Daughter**[16] 4910 6-10-3 0..(b) JamesBest(3) 73
(Richard Mitchell) *led and sn clr: rdn 4th: sn hdd: dropped out bef next: wl bhd bef 2 out: t.o* **10/1**[3]

F5F- **8** *4* **Bawden Rocks**[21] 4818 5-10-13 98.. SeanQuinlan 76
(David Bridgwater) *nt fluent: in tch in midfield: reminders after 2nd and 3rd: sme hdwy bef 5th: 6th and btn after 5th: wknd next: t.o* **20/1**

0- **9** *dist* **Maria's Choice (IRE)**[12] 5008 5-10-13 0........................ MattieBatchelor
(Jim Best) *plld hrd in rr: lost tch 3rd: wl t.o on long run after next* **20/1**

4m 4.0s (-6.60) **Going Correction** -0.225s/f (Good)
WFA 4 from 5yo+ 5lb **9** Ran SP% **130.1**
Speed ratings (Par 105): **106,105,102,95,90 87,86,84,**
CSF £12.02 TOTE £1.50: £1.02, £3.00, £1.10; EX 12.30 Trifecta £13.30.
Owner The Real Partnership **Bred** Mrs S Steer-Fowler **Trained** Andoversford, Gloucs

FOCUS
This looked the weaker of the two divisions, especially once the 119-rated Bodega became a non-runner. The overall time was quicker, thanks to a strong early pace.

5176 CHECK OUT GRAND NATIONAL SPECIALS AT UNIBET.CO.UK H'CAP CHASE (16 fncs) 2m 3f 110y
2:30 (2:30) (Class 4) (0-120,120) 5-Y-0+ **£3,898** (£1,144; £572; £286)

Form RPR

266- **1** **Entertain Me**[17] 4908 10-10-13 **107**.. CharliePoste 128+
(Robin Dickin) *chsd ldr tl led 12th: clr and in command bef 2 out: heavily eased towards fin* **22/1**

053- **2** *23* **Mister Grez (FR)**[26] 4725 8-11-12 **120**........................(b) HarrySkelton 123+
(Dan Skelton) *j.rt: chsd ldrs: chsd wnr sn after 12th: mstke 3 out: sn drvn and no imp: wl btn last: heavily eased towards fin* **6/4**[1]

634- **3** *5* **The Mumper (IRE)**[127] 2784 7-11-2 **110**........................ GerardTumelty 101
(Alan King) *in tch in midfield: mstke 3rd: wnt 4th 11th: chsd clr ldng pair 13th: no imp on ldrs: plugged on* **4/1**[2]

064- **4** *5* **Olympian Boy (IRE)**[14] 4965 10-11-2 **110**........................ PaddyBrennan 98
(Sophie Leech) *t.k.h: hld up in last trio: blnd bdly 7th: rallied and sme hdwy after 11th: no hdwy next: wnt modest 4th 3 out* **10/1**

204- **5** *4 1/2* **O'Callaghan Strand (AUS)**[27] 4696 8-11-5 **118**....... MauriceLinehan(5) 100
(Jonjo O'Neill) *chsd ldng trio tl after 11th: rdn and lost pl bef next: wl btn 3 out* **10/1**

PP2- **6** *6* **George Nympton (IRE)**[19] 4861 8-11-5 **120**................(tp) RyanHatch(7) 99
(Brian Barr) *led tl 12th: 3rd and btn next: wknd: t.o* **8/1**

312- **7** *9* **Jeanry (FR)**[38] 4488 11-10-0 **101**.. JoshWall(7) 70
(Arthur Whitehead) *t.k.h: hld up in last trio: effrt after 11th: btn next: sn wknd: t.o whn blnd last* **13/2**[3]

U33- **P** **Lamb's Cross**[13] 4989 8-10-11 **105**.. AndrewThornton
(Mark Gillard) *in tch in midfield tl dropped to rr 9th: lost tch 11th: wl t.o whn p.u next* **25/1**

100- **P** **Come On Annie**[16] 4919 8-10-13 **110**.. RobertDunne(3)
(Alexandra Dunn) *hld up in rr: rdn and shortlived effrt after 11th: lost tch after next: wl t.o whn p.u last* **14/1**

5m 0.9s (-10.40) **Going Correction** -0.225s/f (Good) **9** Ran SP% **117.5**
Speed ratings: **111,101,99,97,96 93,90, ,**
CSF £59.34 CT £172.27 TOTE £32.10: £8.50, £1.30, £2.70; EX 98.40 Trifecta £370.90 Part won..
Owner Mrs A L Merry **Bred** Mrs A L Merry **Trained** Alcester, Warwicks

The Form Book Jumps, Raceform Ltd, Compton, RG20 6NL.

FOCUS
Not many really got into this as the winner came right away.

5177 NEW HORSE RACING ODDS AT UNIBET.CO.UK NOVICES' H'CAP HURDLE (11 hdls) 2m 4f
3:05 (3:06) (Class 5) (0-100,100) 4-Y-0+ **£2,274** (£667; £333; £166)

Form RPR

/03- **1** **On The Record (IRE)**[19] 4865 6-11-6 **99**.................. MauriceLinehan(5) 104+
(Jonjo O'Neill) *t.k.h: trckd ldrs: rdn to chse ldr 2 out: gd jump to ld last: styd on flat: rdn out* **5/2**[1]

040- **2** *1 ¼* **Lady Fingers**[10] 5034 6-10-11 **92**.................................. MrJBargary(7) 95+
(Nigel Twiston-Davies) *led and set stdy gallop: hrd pressed and rdn after 3 out: blnd next: out j. and hdd last: styd on same pce flat* **16/1**

/00- **3** *¾* **Follow The Master**[11] 5016 8-10-13 **94**............................ ChrisDavies(7) 95
(Brian Forsey) *t.k.h: chsd ldr tl 7th: shifting lft u.p but stl chsng ldrs between last 2: kpt on same pce flat* **66/1**

064- **4** *5* **Fuse Wire**[20] 4838 7-11-6 **97**.. RobertDunne(3) 94
(Dai Burchell) *hld up in tch: hdwy on long run after 7th: chsd ldr 8th tl 2 out: no ex bef last: wknd flat* **16/1**

P5P- **5** *¾* **Almadan (IRE)**[153] 2253 6-10-8 **87**.................................(tp) EdCookson(5) 83
(Kim Bailey) *hld up in tch in midfield: hdwy 8th: unable qck between last 2: plugged on same pce after* **7/1**[3]

543- **6** *1 ¼* **Milor De La Borie (FR)**[32] 4604 5-11-4 **92**........................(p) LiamHeard 87
(David Pipe) *hld up in tch towards rr: rdn and effrt after 3 out: edging lft and no imp between last 2* **10/1**

003- **7** *4 ½* **Lecale Lad (IRE)**[89] 3567 7-10-12 **96**............................... AlanJohns(10) 87
(Tim Vaughan) *t.k.h: hld up in tch in rr: hdwy 7th: chsd ldrs and mstke next: rdn next: wknd bef last* **16/1**

500- **8** *8* **Katie's Massini (IRE)**[21] 4807 6-11-2 **90**....................... DominicElsworth 74
(Henry Oliver) *chsd ldrs: rdn after 3 out: no ex between last 2: btn whn mstke last: wknd flat* **25/1**

/56- **9** *1* **Herecomesthehollow (IRE)**[14] 4959 8-11-5 **100**............ RyanHatch(7) 83
(Nigel Twiston-Davies) *chsd ldrs: mstke 3rd: lost pl and rdn 8th: wknd bef 2 out* **9/1**

/00- **10** *nk* **Lightning Moley (IRE)**[20] 4838 11-10-7 **86**........................(t) BenPoste(5) 69
(Tracey Watkins) *hld up in tch towards rr: rdn and effrt 8th: no hdwy and wl hld fr next* **66/1**

45F- **11** *1 ¼* **Aroseforoscar**[18] 4887 5-11-2 **90**...................................... JamesDavies 71
(Chris Down) *wl in tch in midfield: lost pl on long run after 7th: wknd bef 3 out* **33/1**

004- **12** *1 ½* **Definitely Better (IRE)**[99] 3329 6-11-4 **92**...................... PaddyBrennan 72
(Tom George) *t.k.h: chsd ldrs tl 4th: steadily lost pl but stl in tch: rdn and btn after 8th: wkng whn j.rt 2 out* **10/1**

U00- **13** *23* **Unefille De Guye (FR)**[121] 2906 6-10-10 **87**.............(p[1]) GilesHawkins(3) 46
(Victor Dartnall) *in tch in midfield: hdwy to chse ldrs 7th tl rdn and lost pl bef next: wknd bef 3 out: t.o* **10/1**

223- **14** *1* **Perfect Timing**[170] 1945 6-11-1 **96**............................ MrRobertHawker(7) 55
(Johnny Farrelly) *in tch in midfield: rdn and lost pl bef 8th: wknd bef 3 out: t.o* **10/1**

F04- **15** *7* **Chance Encounter (IRE)**[16] 4911 8-10-13 **94**.................... MrCSmith(7) 46
(Linda Blackford) *in tch in midfield: hdwy to chse ldr 7th tl rdn and lost pl bef next: wknd bef 3 out: t.o* **6/1**[2]

5m 9.6s (7.80) **Going Correction** +0.05s/f (Yiel) **15 Ran SP% 129.1**
Speed ratings (Par 103): **86,85,85,83,82 82,80,77,77,76 76,75,66,66,63**
CSF £46.40 CT £2235.88 TOTE £3.30: £1.10, £7.30, £26.30; EX 53.30 Trifecta £420.90 Part won..
Owner John P McManus **Bred** S O Berry & C J Berry **Trained** Cheltenham, Gloucs

FOCUS
It was raining steadily by this stage and the going was changed to soft. They went slowly in the conditions and the bunch did not thin out much before the last.

5178 UNIBET OFFERING 5 PLACES IN NATIONAL NOVICES' LIMITED H'CAP CHASE (18 fncs) 3m
3:45 (3:45) (Class 3) (0-140,137) 5-Y-0+ **£7,147** (£2,098; £1,049; £524)

Form RPR

5P3- **1** **Samingarry (FR)**[14] 4962 7-10-9 **127**................................ JamesBest(3) 141+
(Nigel Hawke) *chsd ldrs: wnt 2nd 11th tl after 13th: rdn to chal 15th: led and j.rt next: clr between last 2: styd on strly* **5/2**[1]

4P1- **2** *9* **Ohio Gold (IRE)**[7] 5073 8-11-3 **132**.................................... IanPopham 138
(Colin Tizzard) *t.k.h: wl in tch in midfield: wnt 2nd 8th tl 11th: chsng ldrs whn blnd 15th: chsd clr wnr bef 2 out: kpt on but no imp* **9/2**[3]

13P- **3** *½* **Financial Climate (IRE)**[42] 4427 7-10-5 **125**.................. ThomasGarner(5) 128
(Oliver Sherwood) *wl in tch in rr: cl 5th and rdn bef 14th: wnt 3rd 2 out: kpt on u.p but no threat to wnr* **9/2**[3]

520- **4** *3 ¼* **Whats Happening (IRE)**[42] 4422 7-11-8 **137**................(t) PaddyBrennan 138
(Tom George) *hld up wl in tch: mstke 8th: hdwy to press ldr after 13th: ev ch next: struggling whn hmpd and mstke next: 5th and btn between last 2* **8/1**

312- **5** *2 ¼* **Saroque (IRE)**[10] 4393 7-10-12 **127**................................. LiamTreadwell 130+
(Venetia Williams) *led tl hdd and sltly hmpd 3 out: wknd 2 out: 4th and wl hld whn blnd last: eased towards fin* **7/2**[2]

031- **6** *40* **Dont Do Mondays (IRE)**[26] 4716 7-10-3 **118** oh3............. AlainCawley 80
(David Bridgwater) *chsd ldr tl mstke 8th: dropped to last 11th: lost tch 14th: t.o* **11/2**

6m 20.7s (-1.30) **Going Correction** +0.05s/f (Yiel) **6 Ran SP% 113.7**
Speed ratings: **104,101,100,99,99 85**
CSF £14.41 CT £46.65 TOTE £2.90: £2.20, £2.50; EX 14.90 Trifecta £57.30.
Owner D R Mead **Bred** Isabelle Garcon & Jean-Pierre Garcon **Trained** Stoodleigh, Devon

FOCUS
A competitive and solid-looking novice handicap chase.

5179 UNIBET - BY PLAYERS FOR PLAYERS H'CAP HURDLE (8 hdls) 2m 110y
4:50 (4:52) (Class 4) (0-120,120) 4-Y-0+ **£3,249** (£954; £477; £238)

Form RPR

34F- **1** **Ossie's Dancer**[21] 4818 5-11-4 **112**.................................... ColinBolger 116+
(Martin Smith) *chsd ldrs tl led 5th: clr next: 4 l clr 2 out: hit last and sn hrd pressed: battled on gamely and forged ahd towards fin: rdn out* **20/1**

000- **2** *½* **Radmores Revenge**[63] 4028 11-11-7 **120**............................ CharlieWallis(5) 122
(Sophie Leech) *hld up in rr: stdy prog on long run after 4th: chsd ldrs 3 out: rdn between last 2: gd jump last and sn ev ch: edging lft and hld towards fin* **20/1**

P40- **3** *1 ½* **Yazdi (IRE)**[14] 4969 5-10-3 **97**... LiamTreadwell 99
(Henry Oliver) *in tch in midfild: hdwy to chse ldrs bef 5th: pressed ldrs briefly flat: styd on same pce fnl 100yds* **8/1**[3]

P62- **4** *2 ½* **Halifax (IRE)**[14] 4969 6-11-4 **112**.....................................(v) TomCannon 110
(Tony Newcombe) *led tl 5th: drvn and unable qck bef 3 out: 4th and kpt on same pce between last 2* **7/1**[2]

5F5- **5** *24* **No No Charlie (IRE)**[19] 4866 7-10-12 **109**..................... KielanWoods(3) 93
(Charlie Longsdon) *in tch in midfield: mstke and lost pl 3rd: towards rr and nt clr run on long run after 4th: hdwy after 5th: no hdwy 3 out* **12/1**

423- **6** *2 ¾* **Reverb**[120] 2932 5-11-6 **117**.. JeremiahMcGrath(3) 96
(Nicky Henderson) *chsd ldrs: cl 3rd and travelling wl 5th: dived next and immediately btn: wknd bef 2 out* **15/8**[1]

20P- **7** *hd* **Boston Blue**[29] 4659 7-11-1 **112**...................................... TrevorWhelan(3) 86
(Tony Carroll) *sn niggled along in last trio: sme hdwy u.p bef 5th: plugged on: nvr trbld ldrs* **20/1**

03P- **8** *4* **Gracchus (USA)**[16] 4921 8-10-10 **104**......................[1] DominicElsworth 75
(Richard Price) *hld up in last trio: sme hdwy on inner bef 5th: sn no imp: wknd bef 2 out* **50/1**

435- **9** *7* **Taste The Wine (IRE)**[12] 5005 8-10-11 **110**.............. RobertWilliams(5) 74
(Bernard Llewellyn) *in tch in midfield: drvn and no ex bef 5th: wknd 3 out: t.o* **16/1**

462- **10** *16* **James Pollard (IRE)**[19] 2760 9-11-2 **113**..................(tp) RobertDunne(3) 63
(Bernard Llewellyn) *in tch in midfield: mstke 3rd: rdn and struggling bef 5th: sn wknd: t.o* **25/1**

304- **11** *½* **Chemistry Master**[21] 4799 6-11-11 **119**..............................(t) FelixDeGiles 68
(Harry Fry) *in tch in midfield: mstke 3rd: sn rdn and lost pl: lost tch bef 5th: t.o* **7/1**[2]

/65- **12** *2 ¾* **Orabora**[106] 3183 8-11-9 **120**.. MichealNolan(3) 67
(Philip Hobbs) *chsd ldr tl 5th: wkng rapidly whn mstke next: t.o* **12/1**

24P- **P** **Upton Wood**[57] 4132 8-10-11 **105**.. JamesDavies
(Chris Down) *chsd ldrs tl rdn and lost pl qckly on long run after 4th: wl t.o whn p.u 5th* **8/1**[3]

4m 7.7s (-2.90) **Going Correction** +0.05s/f (Yiel) **13 Ran SP% 123.4**
Speed ratings (Par 105): **108,107,107,105,94 93,93,91,88,80 80,78,**
CSF £348.54 CT £3458.66 TOTE £16.40: £4.20, £8.30, £3.20; EX 481.60 Trifecta £756.90 Part won..
Owner Mrs V Garner **Bred** Verity Garner **Trained** Newmarket, Suffolk

FOCUS
An ordinary handicap hurdle.

5180 BET ON UK & IRISH RACING - UNIBET.CO.UK H'CAP CHASE (18 fncs) 3m
5:25 (5:25) (Class 4) (0-115,114) 5-Y-0+ **£3,898** (£1,144; £572; £286)

Form RPR

4F4- **1** **Master Neo (FR)**[28] 4678 8-11-3 **108**................................(t) JamesBest(3) 121+
(Nigel Hawke) *chsd ldrs: wnt 2nd bef 8th: rdn to ld after 14th: forged ahd last: styd on strly: rdn out* **3/1**[1]

242- **2** *9* **Mighty Mobb (IRE)**[43] 4399 7-11-12 **114**......................(v[1]) AndrewThornton 121+
(Seamus Mullins) *t.k.h: in tch in midfield: hdwy to chse ldrs after 7th: ev ch bef 14th tl no ex bef last: wknd fnl 100yds* **11/2**[2]

230- **3** *8* **Green Bank (IRE)**[167] 1988 8-11-9 **114**.......................(tp) KielanWoods(3) 113
(Charlie Longsdon) *in tch in last pair: hdwy into midfield after 7th: 4th and outpcd u.p bef 14th: wnt 3rd after 3 out: no imp* **12/1**

312- **4** *3* **Thomas Wild**[30] 4635 9-11-9 **114**.................................(p) MichealNolan(3) 110
(Philip Hobbs) *in tch in midfield: 5th and outpcd u.p bef 14th: no threat to ldrs after: wnt modest 4th and j.lft 2 out* **3/1**[1]

560- **5** *17* **Requin (FR)**[28] 4678 9-11-1 **106**...................................(p) GilesHawkins(3) 91
(Victor Dartnall) *led tl hdd after 14th: 3rd and wl btn whn j.rt 3 out: sn wknd* **10/1**

442- **P** **Be Definite (IRE)**[36] 4539 10-11-9 **111**................................(p) AlainCawley
(Tom George) *nt jump fluently a in rr: pushed along and clsd after 7th: struggling after next: bhd whn p.u 10th* **10/1**

F44- **P** **The Musical Guy (IRE)**[16] 4914 8-11-4 **113**.......................(v) RyanHatch(7)
(Nigel Twiston-Davies) *in tch in midfield: dropped to rr 8th: blnd 9th and struggling next: t.o whn p.u 15th* **14/1**

FPP- **P** **Chac Du Cadran (FR)**[86] 3617 8-11-5 **107**.......................(p) TomMessenger
(Chris Bealby) *chsd ldr tl rdn and lost pl qckly bef 8th: sn bhd: t.o whn p.u 13th* **6/1**[3]

P4- **P** **Sandanski (IRE)**[9] 5037 6-11-10 **112**..................................(tp) FelixDeGiles
(Tom Gretton) *in tch on outer tl 9th: sn struggling and bhd after next: t.o bef 14th tl p.u 2 out* **33/1**

6m 26.5s (4.50) **Going Correction** +0.325s/f (Yiel) **9 Ran SP% 115.2**
Speed ratings: **105,102,99,98,92 , , ,**
CSF £20.32 CT £171.72 TOTE £6.40: £1.30, £2.00, £3.00; EX 22.00 Trifecta £104.30.
Owner W E Donohue & Pearce Bros **Bred** Jean-Marie Vergnaud **Trained** Stoodleigh, Devon

FOCUS
An ordinary staying handicap chase.

5181 DOWNLOAD THE UNIBET PRO APP STANDARD OPEN NATIONAL HUNT FLAT RACE 2m 110y
5:55 (5:55) (Class 6) 4-6-Y-0 **£1,559** (£457; £228; £114)

Form RPR

1 **Simon Squirrel (IRE)** 4-10-12 0.................................... LiamTreadwell 102+
(Charlie Brooks) *chsd ldrs: wnt 2nd 4f out tl led ent fnl 3f: fnd ex u.p and forged ahd ent fnl f: r.o wl: readily* **12/1**

2 *4 ½* **Rock The Kasbah (IRE)** 4-10-9 0................................ MichealNolan(3) 97
(Philip Hobbs) *in tch in rr: hdwy into midfield 12f out: effrt and rdn to chal 3f out: unable qck ent fnl f: styd on same pce after* **13/8**[1]

12- **3** *1 ¼* **Sidbury Hill**[133] 2667 6-11-11 0.. AndrewThornton 109
(Seamus Mullins) *hld up in tch in rr: gd hdwy and rdn to chal 3f out: no ex ent fnl f: 3rd and one pce fnl f* **5/2**[2]

01- **4** *2* **Trickaway (IRE)**[55] 4177 6-11-8 0..................................... JamesBest(3) 107
(Philip Hobbs) *led tl rdn and hdd ent fnl 3f: 4th and outpcd wl over 1f out: styd on same pce after* **9/2**[3]

34- **5** *¾* **Dashaway (IRE)**[65] 3994 5-11-4 0.. IanPopham 99
(Jeremy Scott) *in tch in midfield: rdn and effrt over 3f out: no imp tl styd on ins fnl f* **12/1**

3/0- **6** *½* **Tuffstuff**[12] 5014 6-10-11 0... RyanHatch(7) 99
(Brian Barr) *in tch in midfield: rdn over 3f out: outpcd over 2f out: no threat to wnr but kpt on again ins fnl f* **20/1**

50- **7** *5* **Henrybrowneyes (IRE)**[26] 4728 5-11-4 0............................ WillKennedy 94
(Ian Williams) *in tch in midfield: lost pl and rdn over 4f out: hdwy over 3f out: outpcd and btn 3f out* **25/1**

3/5- **8** *hd* **Master Vintage**[21] 4824 6-10-11 0..........................[1] DanielHiskett(7) 94
(Richard Phillips) *t.k.h: hld up in last trio: hdwy over 4f out: outpcd and btn over 2f out* **40/1**

0- **9** *8* **Loves Blind (IRE)**[21] 4810 5-11-4 0.................................... ColinBolger 86
(Pat Murphy) *chsd ldr tl 4f out: sn lost pl u.p: bhd fnl 2f* **50/1**

0- **10** 1 1/4 **Darloa (IRE)**[57] 4135 5-11-1 0 GilesHawkins(3) 84
(Victor Dartnall) *chsd ldrs: ev ch and rdn over 3f out: btn 3f out: sn wknd: bhd fnl f* **20/1**

11 8 **Quick N' Easy (IRE)** 4-10-7 0 MissLucyGardner(5) 70
(Sue Gardner) *in tch in rr: rdn 4f out: sn struggling and bhd 2f out* **25/1**

4m 10.3s (5.30) **Going Correction** +0.325s/f (Yiel)
WFA 4 from 5yo+ 5lb **11** Ran SP% **121.8**
Speed ratings: **100,97,97,96,96 95,93,93,89,88 85**
CSF £30.78 TOTE £12.20: £2.60, £1.40, £1.70; EX 45.80 Trifecta £326.30 Part won..
Owner T Lacey **Bred** John O'Dwyer **Trained** Sarsden, Oxon

FOCUS
They crawled until a sprint developed halfway up the home straight, as two newcomers finished ahead of two previous winners.
T/Plt: £104.60 to a £1 stake. Pool of £64968.99 - 453.17 winning tickets. T/Qpdt: £149.60 to a £1 stake. Pool of £3740.20 - 18.50 winning tickets. SP

5036 FFOS LAS (L-H)
Sunday, April 6

OFFICIAL GOING: Heavy (5.2)
Wind: half against, medium to fresh Weather: rain and breezy

5182 TOTEPLACEPOT MAIDEN HURDLE (10 hdls) 2m 4f
2:00 (2:00) (Class 4) 4-Y-0+ **£3,328** (£1,033; £556)

Form RPR
2- **1** **Lookslikerainted (IRE)**[10] 5036 7-10-7 0 PaulO'Brien(7) 130+
(Rebecca Curtis) *trckd ldrs tl hdwy to join ldr 6th: led and mstke next: drew wl clr bef 3 out: easily* **5/4**[2]

- **2** 81 **Tetralogy (IRE)**[28] 5-11-0 0 SamTwiston-Davies 49
(Tom Gretton) *chsd ldr tl 7th: chsd wnr after 7th: rdn and wl btn bef next: t.o 3 out* **25/1**

0- **3** 49 **King Of Jazz (IRE)**[10] 5036 6-11-0 0 DonalDevereux
(Peter Bowen) *in tch in rr: effrt to go 3rd after 7th: sn rdn and wknd: wl t.o 3 out* **33/1**

324- **P** **Thomas Junior (FR)**[16] 4933 5-11-0 112 (tp) TomScudamore
(David Pipe) *led tl 7th: sn dropped out: 4th and fading whn eased and p.u bef 3 out* **10/11**[1]

P **Shady Glen (IRE)**[119] 5-11-0 0 WayneHutchinson
(Graeme McPherson) *chsd ldrs: rdn 5th: rapidly lost tch after 7th: wl t.o whn p.u bef 3 out* **16/1**[3]

P **Milburn**[295] 8-10-9 0 ow2 MissEKelly(7)
(Gail Haywood) *wl in tch: chsd ldrs 4th: reminder after next: rdn and rapidly lost tch after 7th: wl t.o and p.u bef 3 out* **33/1**

5m 46.6s (55.70) **Going Correction** +2.90s/f (Heav) **6** Ran SP% **112.4**
Speed ratings (Par 105): **104,71,52, ,**
CSF £24.98 TOTE £2.30: £1.20, £9.00; EX 33.70 Trifecta £189.20.
Owner A J Rhead **Bred** Joseph Scallan **Trained** Newport, Dyfed

FOCUS
Hurdles were sited at innermost positions on fresh ground. All bends moved. Following 22mm of rain, the ground was officially heavy. The rider of the runner-up in the opener described conditions as "Heavy, heavy. It's very wet, but it's very deep, which makes it hard work." As one-sided a race as you are ever likely to see with only the winner still galloping from the home bend.

5183 BET ON ALL UK RACING WITH TOTEPOOL CONDITIONAL JOCKEYS' (S) HURDLE (12 hdls) 3m
2:30 (2:30) (Class 5) 4-Y-0+ **£1,949** (£572; £286; £143)

Form RPR
6P5- **1** **Viking Blond (FR)**[8] 5066 9-11-1 114 JamesBest 105
(Sophie Leech) *in tch in midfield: hdwy to press ldrs and mstke 9th: drvn and looked hld in 3rd bef next: 5 l down and rallying 2 out: styd on dourly u.p flat to ld fnl 50yds* **11/4**[1]

P43- **2** 1 **Maller Tree**[20] 4864 7-11-0 130 (b[1]) JakeHodson(5) 109
(David Dennis) *chsd ldr tl led sn after 9th: 4 l clr next: rdn bef next: hit 2 out: almost jnd last: kpt on u.p tl hdd and no ex fnl 50yds* **6/1**[3]

150- **3** nk **Gap Of Dunloe (IRE)**[187] 1707 6-11-5 106 (tp) MichaelByrne 109
(Peter Bowen) *hld up in tch in last pair: hdwy to chse clr ldr and rdn bef 3 out: styd on u.p and chal last: one pce fnl 150yds* **7/1**

106- **4** 15 **Extreme Impact**[39] 4489 8-11-2 118 (b) AdamWedge(3) 93
(Evan Williams) *chsd ldrs tl rdn and dropped to last after 9th: wl btn next: plugged on* **11/4**[1]

44P- **5** 28 **Paddy The Oscar (IRE)**[29] 4677 11-10-12 99 (p) ConorRing(3) 61
(Grace Harris) *ld tl hdd after 9th: sn rdn and wknd bef next: t.o* **10/1**

UU0- **P** **What An Oscar (IRE)**[36] 4555 9-10-9 110 (v) RyanHatch(6)
(Nigel Twiston-Davies) *in tch in last pair tl struggling 7th: sn rdn: lost tch after next: tailing off whn j.lft and mstke 9th: sn p.u* **4/1**[2]

7m 18.4s (89.40) **Going Correction** +3.00s/f (Heav) **6** Ran SP% **109.2**
Speed ratings (Par 103): **71,70,70,65,56**
CSF £18.08 TOTE £3.00: £1.50, £2.40; EX 15.30 Trifecta £64.50.Viking Blond was bought by Peter Bowen for 9,000gns
Owner C J Leech **Bred** Dominique Le Baron **Trained** Elton, Gloucs

FOCUS
This moderate seller was almost as exhausting to watch as to take part in. Understandably they went very steady in the conditions and it became a war of attrition.

5184 TOTEPOOL SUPPORTS THE SPORT YOU LOVE H'CAP CHASE (13 fncs 6 omitted) 3m 1f 110y
3:05 (3:05) (Class 3) (0-135,128) 5-Y-0+ **£7,797** (£2,289; £1,144; £572)

Form RPR
122- **1** **Beforeall (IRE)**[33] 4602 6-11-4 125 ThomasGarner(5) 135
(Oliver Sherwood) *j.rt at times: led tl bef 7th: led again 9th: rdn and hdd bef 2 out: rallied gamely and gd jump to ld again last: styd on wl to forge ahd fnl 100yds* **4/1**[2]

0P2- **2** 2 **Lamboro Lad (IRE)**[19] 4886 9-11-7 123 (tp) DonalDevereux 131
(Peter Bowen) *racd wd: in tch in midfield: trckd ldrs 9th: wnt clr w wnr on long run after 11th: led and looked to be gng best bef 2 out: rdn between last 2: outj. and hdd last: no ex fnl 100yds* **10/1**

1P4- **3** 15 **Boyfromnowhere (IRE)**[21] 4842 7-11-7 128 (b[1]) PatrickCorbett(5) 124
(Rebecca Curtis) *j.rt: chsd wnr tl led bef 7th: hdd 9th: 3rd and drvn on long run after 11th: wknd 2 out* **12/1**

031- **4** 14 **Makethe Mostofnow (IRE)**[39] 4490 9-11-7 123 PaulMoloney 102
(Evan Williams) *chsd ldrs: rdn and wknd on long run after 11th: no ch 2 out* **9/1**

051- **5** 8 **Tullyraine (IRE)**[21] 4842 10-11-8 124 (v[1]) SamTwiston-Davies 95
(Nigel Twiston-Davies) *chsd ldrs: blnd 9th: sn rdn and struggling: wknd on long run to 2 out* **8/1**[3]

U30- **U** **Union Jack D'Ycy (FR)**[28] 4704 6-11-5 121 AidanColeman
(Venetia Williams) *in tch in last pair tl cannoned into by loose horse and uns rdr bef 6th* **10/1**

1U1- **U** **Barton Gift**[29] 4678 7-10-6 111 (b) NicodeBoinville(3)
(John Spearing) *uns rdr 1st* **7/4**[1]

42U- **P** **Titchwood (IRE)**[21] 4842 6-11-11 127 (p) RichieMcLernon
(Jonjo O'Neill) *in tch in last pair: cannoned into by loose horse and hmpd bef 6th: sn rcvrd: blnd 9th: wknd sn after 11th: t.o whn p.u bef 2 out* **10/1**

7m 26.2s (45.20) **Going Correction** +1.95s/f (Heav) **8** Ran SP% **112.4**
Speed ratings: **108,107,102,98,96 , ,**
CSF £40.02 CT £435.02 TOTE £5.40: £1.60, £4.20, £2.80; EX 37.60 Trifecta £281.90.
Owner Beforeall Partnership **Bred** Ms Barbara Johnston **Trained** Upper Lambourn, Berks

FOCUS
The first fence in the back straight and the first two fences in the home straight were omitted in all chases, meaning that only 13 fences were jumped in this rather than the usual 19. This proved a real slog and there was early drama when the favourite Barton Gift ejected his rider at the first. The gelding wasn't finished, though, as after running loose he ploughed his way back into the field before halfway, badly hampering Titchwood and causing Union Jack d'Ycy's rider to be knocked out of the saddle.

5185 TOTEEXACTA H'CAP CHASE (11 fncs 8 omitted) 3m 1f 110y
3:40 (3:40) (Class 4) (0-105,102) 5-Y-0+ **£3,768** (£1,106; £553; £276)

Form RPR
411- **1** **Tom Bach (IRE)**[10] 5038 10-10-4 83 (b) JamesBest(3) 99+
(Hywel Evans) *mde virtually all: gng best on long run after 9th: blnd 2 out: rdn and styd on wl flat: readily* **9/4**[1]

141- **2** 6 **The Last Bridge**[27] 4729 7-10-13 89 (p) RichardJohnson 97
(Susan Johnson) *trckd ldrs: rdn 7th: 3rd and one pce u.p on long run to 2 out: chsd wnr sn after last: no imp* **9/4**[1]

454- **3** 5 **Accordingtopalm (IRE)**[21] 4840 8-11-12 102 (t) PaulMoloney 105
(David Rees) *hld up in tch in rr: stdy hdwy on long run after 9th: wnt 2nd bef 2 out: rdn and no imp between last 2: mstke and lost 2nd last: wknd flat* **16/1**

355- **4** 21 **Jump Up**[21] 4843 8-10-11 87 DonalDevereux 68
(Peter Bowen) *in tch in midfield: rdn and after 7th: wknd on long run after 9th: wl btn 2 out* **6/1**[2]

/P2- **5** 3 1/2 **Night Safe (IRE)**[21] 4843 13-11-4 94 (v) SamTwiston-Davies 72
(Nigel Twiston-Davies) *pressed ldrs tl 6th: styd chsng ldrs: stl cl 5th and drvn bef 2 out: wknd and btn whn mstke 2 out* **6/1**[2]

4P6- **F** **Material Boy**[22] 4822 7-11-8 98 (bt[1]) LiamHeard
(Barry Leavy) *pressed wnr tl after 11th: 4th and wkng whn j. slowly 2 out: wl btn and fell last* **10/1**[3]

P45- **P** **Scuderia (IRE)**[27] 4716 7-11-2 92 (t) BrendanPowell
(Jamie Snowden) *in tch: rdn and lost pl 7th: rallied u.p after next: wknd sn after 11th: t.o whn p.u 2 out* **16/1**

7m 37.1s (56.10) **Going Correction** +2.05s/f (Heav) **7** Ran SP% **111.0**
Speed ratings: **95,93,91,85,84 ,**
CSF £7.61 TOTE £3.00: £1.70, £1.50; EX 8.50 Trifecta £83.50.
Owner Hywel Evans **Bred** Carthage Molloy **Trained** Kidwelly, Carmarthens

FOCUS
A more modest handicap chase than the previous event over the same trip and, with the open ditch in the back straight also being taken out here, they only jumped 11 fences.

5186 TOTEPOOL SUPPORTS THE IJF 50TH ANNIVERSARY H'CAP HURDLE (11 hdls) 2m 6f
4:10 (4:11) (Class 3) (0-135,128) 4-Y-0+ **£5,523** (£1,621; £810; £405)

Form RPR
0/U- **1** **Double Double (FR)**[116] 3024 8-11-7 123 DonalDevereux 124
(Peter Bowen) *hld up in tch in rr: hdwy to join ldr 7th: led and mstke 8th: gng best after: shkn up bef 2 out: drvn flat: a jst holding on: all out* **20/1**

520- **2** nk **Rev It Up (IRE)**[46] 4347 8-11-9 125 (v) RichardJohnson 126
(Tim Vaughan) *chsd ldrs: mstke 5th: drvn after 8th: 4th and looked btn 2 out: rallied and mstke last: chsd wnr flat: styd on wl u.p: nvr quite getting to wnr* **7/1**

426- **3** 11 **Astigos (FR)**[44] 4393 7-11-5 121 AidanColeman 110
(Venetia Williams) *in tch in midfield: pushed along after 5th: chsd ldrs and rdn bef 3 out: no ex last: wknd flat* **7/2**[1]

/00- **4** 1 1/2 **Jackies Solitaire**[11] 5030 6-11-3 119 SamTwiston-Davies 107
(Anthony Honeyball) *in tch: hdwy to chse wnr 3 out: rdn and no imp 2 out: lost 2nd sn after last: wknd flat* **16/1**

421- **5** 10 **Heavenstown (IRE)**[15] 4949 8-11-4 123 (b) NicodeBoinville(3) 101
(John Spearing) *led tl 8th: sn rdn: stl cl 3rd next: wknd after 2 out* **5/1**[3]

060- **6** 68 **Lava Lamp (GER)**[21] 4841 7-10-12 114 PaulMoloney 24
(Evan Williams) *a bhd: t.o 6th* **20/1**

313/ **P** **King Of Dubai**[882] 2354 9-10-2 111 JPKiely(7)
(Tim Vaughan) *chsd ldr tl 7th: blnd 5th: wknd next: t.o whn p.u 3 out* **12/1**

P50- **P** **Fishing Bridge (IRE)**[21] 4841 9-10-11 113 (p) AdamWedge
(David Rees) *in tch in midfield: rdn and 7th: tailing off whn p.u next* **25/1**

001- **P** **Touch Back (IRE)**[72] 3884 8-11-8 124 (p) RichieMcLernon
(Jonjo O'Neill) *chsd ldrs: rdn bef 8th: wknd and t.o whn p.u 3 out* **11/1**

401- **P** **Garde Fou (FR)**[10] 5037 8-11-2 118 (t) TomO'Brien
(Paul Henderson) *a in rr: rdn and lost tch sn after 5th: tailing off whn p.u next* **6/1**

210- **P** **Tullyesker Hill (IRE)**[43] 4415 5-11-12 128 (p) TomScudamore
(David Pipe) *chsd ldrs: mstke 5th: sn lost pl: in rr and losing tch whn p.u 7th* **9/2**[2]

6m 35.75s (75.75) **Going Correction** +3.10s/f (Heav) **11** Ran SP% **119.1**
Speed ratings (Par 107): **86,85,81,81,77 52, , , ,**
CSF £152.69 CT £619.09 TOTE £20.40: £4.60, £2.90, £2.00; EX 120.20 Trifecta £2086.30 Part won..
Owner Roddy Owen & Paul Fullagar **Bred** Le Thenney S A **Trained** Little Newcastle, Pembrokes
■ Stewards' Enquiry : Richard Johnson two-day ban: use of whip (20-21 Apr)

FOCUS
They went a good pace early in this decent handicap hurdle considering the conditions and it proved too much for several of these.

5187 TOTEPOOL "IT'S ALL ABOUT THE HORSE" H'CAP CHASE (10 fncs 7 omitted) 2m 5f
4:45 (4:45) (Class 5) (0-100,100) 5-Y-0+ **£2,144** (£629; £314; £157)

Form RPR
333- **1** **Possibly Flora**[13] 5004 9-11-1 89 (t) ConorO'Farrell 109+
(Richard Woollacott) *w ldrs on inner: led on long run after 8th: rdn and asserted 2 out: sn clr: styd on wl* **10/3**[3]

443- **2** 15 **Supreme Bob (IRE)**[21] 4840 8-11-12 100 WillKennedy 103
(Lucy Jones) *in tch in last pair: wnt 3rd on long run after 8th: 3rd and no imp wl bef 2 out: plugged on to go 2nd flat* **2/1**[2]

The Form Book Jumps, Raceform Ltd, Compton, RG20 6NL.

22P- **3** 1 1/4 **Billybo**[101] 3277 11-10-0 **84**.......... AlanJohns(10) 86
(Tim Vaughan) *w ldrs: drew clr w wnr on long run after 8th: rdn jst bef 2 out: no rspnse and sn btn: wl hld between last 2: lost 2nd flat* **15/8**[1]

400- **4** 21 **Le Grand Chene (FR)**[16] 4932 8-11-7 **95**.......... (t) PaulMoloney 76
(Sophie Leech) *in tch in last pair: rdn after 8th: wknd on long run to next* **7/1**

500- **P** **Nicene Creed**[19] 4884 9-11-7 **95**.......... (tp) RichieMcLernon
(Sophie Leech) *mde most tl sn after 8th: sn wknd u.p: t.o whn p.u 2 out* **16/1**

6m 21.1s (52.50) **Going Correction** +2.15s/f (Heav) 5 Ran SP% **109.6**
Speed ratings: **86,80,79,71,**
CSF £10.62 TOTE £3.80: £1.70, £1.50; EX 10.10 Trifecta £13.00.
Owner R Mitford-Slade & Lucy Johnson **Bred** D A G And Mrs Billington **Trained** South Molton, Devon

FOCUS
A modest handicap chase, in which they jumped just the ten fences. They went a sensible pace and all five runners were still within a couple of lengths of each other jumping the final fence in the back straight (three out).

5188 TOTETRIFECTA INTERMEDIATE OPEN NATIONAL HUNT FLAT RACE 2m
5:15 (5:18) (Class 6) 4-5-Y-O **£1,642** (£478; £239)

Form RPR

6- **1** **At First Light**[48] 4329 5-10-8 0.......... NicodeBoinville(3) 94
(Jonathan Geake) *mde all: 5 l clr and gng best over 3f out: rdn over 1f out: kpt on* **14/1**

03- **2** 6 **Millanisi Boy**[47] 4335 5-11-4 0.......... ConorO'Farrell 95
(Richard Woollacott) *hld up in tch in last: 3rd and effrt over 3f out: edging lft and chsd wnr jst over 1f out: no imp* **8/1**[3]

3 7 **Titans Approach (IRE)**[375] 5-11-4 0.......... WayneHutchinson 90
(Graeme McPherson) *chsd wnr: rdn over 3f out: edging lft and no imp wl over 1f out: 3rd and btn 1f out: wknd* **5/2**[2]

4 37 **Royal Salute** 4-10-12 0.......... RichardJohnson 45
(Anthony Honeyball) *chsd ldng pair: pushed along over 4f out: dropped to last over 3f out and sn lost tch: t.o* **4/6**[1]

4m 34.9s (52.00) **Going Correction** +3.20s/f (Heav)
WFA 4 from 5yo 5lb 4 Ran SP% **106.3**
Speed ratings: **98,95,91,73**
CSF £84.67 TOTE £6.30; EX 14.90 Trifecta £72.40.
Owner Miss E J Tanner **Bred** D J Weston **Trained** Marlborough, Wilts

FOCUS
A steadily run, small-field bumper run in bad ground, so there was always the chance of a turn up and so it proved.
T/Plt: £63.90 to a £1 stake. Pool: £82,513.30 - 942.17 winning units. T/Qpdt: £20.70 to a £1 stake. Pool: £8119.33 - 289.52 winning units. SP

4980 MARKET RASEN (R-H)
Sunday, April 6

OFFICIAL GOING: Good (good to soft in places on chase course; hdl 7.7, chs 8.1)
Wind: fresh 1/2 across Weather: overcast, very breezy

5189 RACING UK LADY RIDERS' (S) H'CAP HURDLE (8 hdls) 2m 1f
1:45 (1:45) (Class 5) (0-100,95) 4-Y-0+ **£2,053** (£598; £299)

Form RPR

000- **1** **Dalmo**[25] 4760 5-11-0 **90**.......... (b) MissAEStirling(7) 101+
(Dr Richard Newland) *mde virtually all: drvn and drew clr run-in* **13/8**[1]

644- **2** 6 **Drussell (IRE)**[15] 4972 8-11-5 **95**.......... MissAliceMills(7) 100
(Martin Bosley) *in rr: pushed along 3rd: chsd ldrs 3 out: 1 l 2nd last: kpt on same pce* **3/1**[3]

056- **3** 7 **Vertueux (FR)**[9] 2898 9-11-2 **85**.......... (p) LucyAlexander 84
(Tony Carroll) *trckd wnr: upsides 3 out: wknd appr last* **5/2**[2]

P/0- **4** 46 **Vinomore**[21] 4836 8-10-13 **87**.......... (tp) EmmaSayer(5) 44
(Dianne Sayer) *t.k.h: trckd ldrs: upsides after 1st: lost pl 4th: bhd fr 5th: tk distant 4th 2 out: t.o* **16/1**

00U- **5** 17 **Devil At Midnight (IRE)**[46] 4343 6-10-0 **74**.......... SamanthaDrake(5) 16
(Richard Drake) *in rr: hdwy to chse ldrs 3 out: sn drvn: lost pl bef next: sn bhd: t.o* **8/1**

/60- **U** **Simplified**[23] 4796 11-9-7 **69** oh10.......... (t) MissGSwan(7)
(Michael Chapman) *handy 4th whn uns rdr 4th* **66/1**

4m 11.7s (5.00) **Going Correction** +0.40s/f (Soft) 6 Ran SP% **110.2**
Speed ratings (Par 103): **104,101,97,76,68**
CSF £6.84 TOTE £2.60: £1.30, £3.60; EX 6.30 Trifecta £11.20.
Owner J A Provan **Bred** Sir Eric Parker **Trained** Claines, Worcs

FOCUS
Both tracks moved onto fresher ground on Summer lines. A weak handicap.

5190 DOUBLE M NOVICES' HURDLE (8 hdls) 2m 1f
2:15 (2:15) (Class 4) 4-Y-0+ **£3,249** (£954; £477; £238)

Form RPR

P30- **1** **Dubai Prince (IRE)**[43] 4421 6-11-5 127.......... DenisO'Regan 121+
(John Ferguson) *t.k.h: trckd ldrs: led 4th: wnt 6 l clr last: drvn out* **13/8**[1]

244- **2** 1 1/4 **Herecomestrouble**[85] 3657 7-10-13 0.......... BrianHughes 113
(Malcolm Jefferson) *t.k.h in rr: hdwy 5th: 3rd 2 out: styd on to take 2nd run-in: edgd lft and kpt on: nt rch wnr* **20/1**

335- **3** hd **In The Rough (IRE)**[46] 4343 5-10-13 0.......... DominicElsworth 113
(Jonjo O'Neill) *mid-div: outpcd 4th: hdwy and modest 5th appr 2 out: 4th between last 2: swtchd rt then lft sn after last: styd on wl: n.m.r nr fin* **13/2**

325- **4** 4 1/2 **Sleepy Haven (IRE)**[18] 4899 4-10-13 122.......... SeanQuinlan 109
(Jennie Candlish) *chsd ldrs: drvn and cl 2nd 3 out: wknd run-in* **7/2**[3]

34- **5** 25 **Grey Blue (IRE)**[17] 4300 4-10-7 0.......... DavidBass 84
(Nicky Henderson) *chsd ldrs: clr 3rd 3 out: wknd qckly appr next* **11/4**[2]

6 3 1/4 **Don Padeja**[180] 4-10-2 0.......... MauriceLinehan(5) 77
(Jonjo O'Neill) *in tch: j.lft 1st: outpcd 3rd: drvn and lost pl next* **20/1**

0- **7** 7 **Artifice Sivola (FR)**[19] 4889 4-10-7 0.......... LeightonAspell 70
(Lucy Wadham) *led: t.k.h: hdd 4th: lost pl bef 2 out* **50/1**

/34- **8** 23 **Frankie Four Feet**[164] 2053 6-10-10 0.......... KielanWoods(3) 56
(Michael Mullineaux) *nt fluent: chsd ldrs to 4th: bhd fr 3 out: t.o* **33/1**

00- **9** 12 **Vision De La Vie (FR)**[22] 4811 4-10-4 0.......... TonyKelly(3) 39
(Pauline Robson) *in rr: bhd fr 4th: t.o 3 out* **100/1**

P/6- **P** **Monzino (USA)**[11] 383 6-10-8 0.......... JoeCornwall(5)
(Michael Chapman) *in rr: lost tch 8th: sn t.o and p.u* **100/1**

P **Maygo's Joy**[81] 4-10-7 0.......... LiamTreadwell
(Suzy Smith) *chsd ldrs: lost pl 5th: sn bhd: t.o whn p.u bef last* **100/1**

4m 14.8s (8.10) **Going Correction** +0.40s/f (Soft)
WFA 4 from 5yo+ 5lb 11 Ran SP% **117.7**
Speed ratings (Par 105): **96,95,95,93,81 79,76,65,60,**
CSF £35.65 TOTE £2.40: £1.10, £4.20, £2.80; EX 34.30 Trifecta £175.40.
Owner Bloomfields **Bred** Mrs Eithne Hamilton **Trained** Cowlinge, Suffolk

FOCUS
A fair novice event. They went a truer gallop than is sometimes the case in these events, the field was well strung out a long way from home. The second and third closed as the leaders tied up and are possibly a shade flattered by the bare result.

5191 EASTER MONDAY IS NEXT H'CAP HURDLE (JOCKEY CLUB GRASSROOTS SERIES QUALIFIER) (10 hdls) 2m 5f
2:45 (2:46) (Class 4) (0-115,115) 4-Y-0+ **£3,249** (£954; £477; £238)

Form RPR

1B2- **1** **Ben Cee Pee M (IRE)**[16] 4943 9-11-2 **112**.......... (v) CraigGallagher(7) 113
(Brian Ellison) *hld up in rr: hdwy 6th: cl 2nd sn after 3 out: led appr last: hung lft: drvn rt out* **10/1**

030- **2** 1 1/2 **Go West Young Man (IRE)**[8] 5075 6-11-3 **109**.......... JakeGreenall(3) 110
(Henry Daly) *hld up in mid-div: hdwy 6th: hmpd 3 out: 3rd appr next: cl 2nd last: edgd lft and fnd little clsng stages* **15/2**[3]

502- **3** 5 **Withoutdefavourite (IRE)**[22] 4808 6-11-6 **109**.......... DenisO'Regan 105
(Henry Oliver) *chsd ldrs: outpcd appr 2 out: styd on to take 3rd nr fin* **16/1**

240- **4** 1/2 **South Stack**[19] 4893 9-11-4 **112**.......... EdCookson(5) 107
(Kim Bailey) *mid-div: hdwy 6th: 4th appr 2 out: kpt on same pce: tk 4th cl home* **33/1**

130- **5** hd **Epee Celeste (FR)**[26] 4740 8-9-9 **89** oh3.......... (b) JoeCornwall(5) 85
(Michael Chapman) *chsd ldng pair: upsides 7th: cl 3rd last: one pce* **25/1**

334- **6** 1 3/4 **Letemgo (IRE)**[122] 2908 6-11-8 **111**.......... DavidEngland 104
(Giles Smyly) *in rr: sme hdwy 3 out: styd on fr next: nt rch ldrs* **9/1**

050- **7** 2 1/2 **Church Field (IRE)**[127] 2828 6-11-2 **115**.......... PatrickCowley(10) 106
(Jonjo O'Neill) *prom: drvn and outpcd 6th: hmpd 3 out: lost pl appr next: rallied between last 2: kpt on one pce* **7/2**[1]

611- **8** 25 **Drombeg West**[25] 4760 7-10-6 **95**.......... AndrewTinkler 69
(Anna Brooks) *s.i.s: in rr: hdwy whn hmpd 3 out: lost pl appr next: sn bhd* **10/1**

306- **9** 37 **Tenmoku**[137] 2600 5-11-0 **108**.......... MauriceLinehan(5) 43
(Jonjo O'Neill) *t.k.h in mid-div: hmpd and lost pl 3 out: sn bhd: eased whn t.o run-in* **25/1**

00- **10** 7 **Diamond Pro (IRE)**[18] 4903 5-10-6 **95**.......... JamesDavies 24
(Christopher Kellett) *chsd ldrs: drvn 5th: sn lost pl and bhd: t.o 7th* **100/1**

000- **P** **Nether Stream (IRE)**[78] 3788 10-10-8 **97**.......... TomMessenger
(David Dennis) *in rr: bhd 8th: t.o 3 out: p.u bef next* **20/1**

303- **P** **Halucha (IRE)**[42] 4449 9-11-2 **105**.......... (p) LiamTreadwell
(Paul Webber) *sn drvn in mid-div: lost pl 2nd: sn bhd: t.o 4th: sn p.u* **20/1**

401- **P** **Madame De Guise (FR)**[12] 5018 5-11-9 **112**.......... DavidBass
(Nicky Henderson) *in rr: outpcd 6th: bhd and eased 3 out: t.o whn p.u bef last* **9/1**

211- **F** **Jack Albert (IRE)**[8] 5075 7-11-2 **105**.......... (b) BrianHarding
(Dianne Sayer) *led early: w ldr: led 3rd: fell 3 out* **5/1**[2]

000- **P** **Rocky Island (IRE)**[142] 2493 6-10-13 **102**.......... SeanQuinlan
(Jennie Candlish) *sn led: hdd 4th: lost pl bef 3 out: sn eased and t.o: p.u bef 2 out* **12/1**

5m 14.09s (5.29) **Going Correction** +0.40s/f (Soft) 15 Ran SP% **123.6**
Speed ratings (Par 105): **105,104,102,102,102 101,100,91,77,74 , , , ,**
CSF £78.26 CT £1216.78 TOTE £8.30: £2.50, £4.50, £4.20; EX 71.10 Trifecta £1199.50 Part won..
Owner CPM Group Limited **Bred** Daniel Fogarty **Trained** Norton, N Yorks

FOCUS
A fair handicap which was run at a good pace and it should prove solid form for the level.

5192 DOUBLE M NOVICES' CHASE (17 fncs) 3m 1f
3:20 (3:20) (Class 3) 5-Y-0+ **£7,797** (£2,289; £1,144; £572)

Form RPR

125- **1** **Ardkilly Witness (IRE)**[43] 4422 8-11-4 136.......... LeightonAspell 140+
(Dr Richard Newland) *j.rt: trckd ldrs: led 3rd to 5th: led 10th: stmbld on landing 3 out: 5 l ahd last: drvn rt out* **8/11**[1]

F20- **2** 3/4 **Milborough (IRE)**[26] 4741 8-11-4 131.......... JamieMoore 136
(Tim Vaughan) *chsd ldrs: lft cl 3rd 10th: sn chsng wnr: drvn 4 out: mstke next: styd on last 100yds* **7/2**[2]

0FP- **3** 60 **Steepleofcopper (IRE)**[27] 4715 8-10-9 0.......... (t) JackQuinlan(3) 75
(Alan Jessop) *in rr: outpcd 8th: lft 4th 10th: drvn and lost tch next: t.o 3rd whn j.lft 13th* **100/1**

354- **4** 1 **Flichity (IRE)**[14] 4984 9-10-7 66.......... JoeCornwall(5) 74
(John Cornwall) *led to 3rd: led 5th: hdd 10th: reminders and outpcd next: sn lost tch w 1st 2: t.o 13th* **100/1**

240- **U** **Son Of Flicka**[25] 4752 10-10-12 123.......... DougieCostello
(Tony Coyle) *chsd ldrs: hit 10th then bdly hmpd and uns rdr* **7/2**[2]

4PP- **F** **Lucky Cody (IRE)**[43] 4428 5-10-12 0.......... (b[1]) DannyCook
(Brian Ellison) *t.k.h: mstke 2nd: w ldrs: fell 10th* **25/1**[3]

6m 23.9s (-7.40) **Going Correction** -0.575s/f (Firm) 6 Ran SP% **108.2**
Speed ratings: **88,87,68,68,**
CSF £3.48 TOTE £1.40: £1.10, £2.00; EX 3.20 Trifecta £82.10.
Owner C E Stedman & Dr R D P Newland **Bred** F Tierney **Trained** Claines, Worcs

FOCUS
A race which effectively developed into a match.

5193 WATCH RACING UK ON SKY CHANNEL 432 H'CAP CHASE (14 fncs) 2m 6f 110y
3:55 (3:55) (Class 4) (0-110,105) 5-Y-0+ **£3,898** (£1,144; £572; £286)

Form RPR

142- **1** **Roc De Guye (FR)**[122] 2895 9-11-4 **97**.......... (p) LiamTreadwell 106+
(James Evans) *t.k.h: jnd ldrs 8th: led 3 out: j.rt next: hung rt and drvn clr run-in* **8/1**

412- **2** 8 **Phoenix Des Mottes (FR)**[8] 5065 11-9-9 **79** oh1.......... JoeCornwall(5) 79
(John Cornwall) *w ldrs: upsides 5th: drvn 9th: kpt on same pce fr 2 out* **8/1**

P44- **3** 7 **Xenophon**[112] 3119 6-9-7 **79** oh10.......... MissAliceMills(7) 73
(Michael Chapman) *chsd ldrs: lost pl 8th: drvn and bhd 10th: kpt on and modest 5th last: styd on to take 3rd last 50yds* **16/1**

U34- **4** 3 **Taffy Thomas**[30] 4656 10-11-3 **96**.......... (t) JamieMoore 88
(Peter Bowen) *chsd ldrs 8th: almost upsides 3 out: one pce* **2/1**[1]

005- **5** 1 **Ifonlyalfie**[150] 2313 9-10-5 **84**.......... (bt) TomMessenger 75
(Chris Bealby) *led: hit 2nd: hdd 3 out: wknd between last 2* **6/1**[3]

643- **6** *9* **Mister Wall Street (FR)**[26] 4748 9-10-13 **95**...................... TonyKelly(3) 77
(Rebecca Menzies) *chsd ldrs: drvn 8th: sn outpcd: wknd 11th* **7/1**

252- **7** *6* **Palos Conti (FR)**[28] 4695 11-11-12 **105**.............................. DannyCook 82
(Brian Ellison) *in rr: nt fluent 8th: sn drvn: bhd fr 10th: b.b.v* **10/3**[2]

5m 38.1s (-7.90) **Going Correction** -0.575s/f (Firm) **7** Ran SP% **111.3**
Speed ratings: **90,87,84,83,83 80,78**
CSF £62.00 TOTE £4.70: £3.20, £4.10; EX 22.30 Trifecta £237.90.
Owner S Crawley, T Crawley **Bred** G A E C Delorme Gerard & Vincent **Trained** Broadwas, Worcs

FOCUS
A modest handicap. It was run at no more than a fair gallop.

5194 WET WET WET PERFORMING 16TH AUGUST H'CAP CHASE (11 fncs 1 omitted) 2m 2f

4:25 (4:25) (Class 4) (0-115,115) 5-Y-0+ **£4,288** (£1,259; £629; £314)

Form RPR

P64- **1** **Tayarat (IRE)**[8] 5073 9-9-9 **89** oh9.................................. JoeCornwall(5) 100+
(Michael Chapman) *chsd ldrs: drvn 6th: outpcd after 9th: rallied and cl 2nd omitted last: led last 150yds: drvn clr* **40/1**

325- **2** *2 3/4* **Un Anjou (FR)**[64] 4036 6-11-9 **115**.............................. MichealNolan(3) 124
(David Dennis) *hld up: t.k.h: trckd ldrs 7th: led last: (normal 2 out): hdd and no ex last 150yds* **9/2**[2]

6P5- **3** *3 3/4* **Wessex King (IRE)**[18] 4908 10-11-8 **114**........................ JakeGreenall(3) 119
(Henry Daly) *trckd ldrs: led 8th: hdd last (normal 2 out): one pce* **12/1**

P01- **4** *29* **Book'Em Danno (IRE)**[14] 4985 8-11-11 **114**...................... JamieMoore 101
(Peter Bowen) *w ldr 3rd: nt fluent 7th: reminders 9th: wknd 2 out (normal 3 out)* **11/8**[1]

306- **5** *60* **Twice Returned (IRE)**[16] 4934 8-11-12 **115**..................... HarrySkelton 40
(Dan Skelton) *chsd ldrs: reminders after 5th: drvn and lost pl next: t.o 8th: eventually completed* **5/1**[3]

612- **F** **Regal D'Estruval (FR)**[13] 5001 9-11-11 **114**.................... LeightonAspell 108
(Dr Richard Newland) *led to 8th: sn outpcd: lost pl 3 out: poor 5th whn fell last (normal 2 out)* **11/2**

043- **F** **Rasheed**[24] 4781 6-10-13 **105**..(v) JackQuinlan(3)
(Lucy Wadham) *in rr: fell 5th; fatally injured* **11/1**

4m 22.2s (-12.80) **Going Correction** -0.575s/f (Firm) **7** Ran SP% **110.8**
Speed ratings: **105,103,102,89,62** ,
CSF £196.36 CT £2238.32 TOTE £39.10: £6.10, £2.30; EX 139.20 Trifecta £357.10.
Owner Mrs M Chapman **Bred** Golden Garden Stud **Trained** Market Rasen, Lincs

FOCUS
A fair handicap. A few of the market leaders were well below form.

5195 EASTER BUNNY MARES' STANDARD OPEN NATIONAL HUNT FLAT RACE (DIV I) 2m 1f

5:00 (5:00) (Class 6) 4-6-Y-O **£1,559** (£457; £228; £114)

Form RPR

1/ **1** **Spartan Angel (IRE)**[663] 705 6-11-5 0.................................. DavidBass 116+
(Nicky Henderson) *hld up towards rr: hdwy after 6f: sn trcking ldrs: led 2f out: drvn and styd on* **9/4**[1]

3- **2** *1 3/4* **There Is No Point (IRE)**[65] 4016 5-10-7 0................ MauriceLinehan(5) 107+
(Jonjo O'Neill) *t.k.h in mid-div: effrt over 4f out: sn chsng ldrs: chsd wnr over 1f out: kpt on same pce* **9/2**[3]

4- **3** *10* **Toola Boola**[32] 4618 4-10-1 0... AdamNicol(5) 92
(Philip Kirby) *w ldr: led 6f out: hdd 2f out: wknd fnl f* **10/3**[2]

4 *2* **Glenarm** 5-10-12 0.. AndrewThornton 96
(Seamus Mullins) *led: narrowly hdd 6f out: wknd over 1f out* **20/1**

343- **5** *2 1/2* **Donna's Pride**[32] 4618 5-10-12 0.. JamesReveley 94
(Keith Reveley) *trckd ldrs: drvn 3f out: wknd over 1f out* **8/1**

6 *4 1/2* **Ishusharella** 5-10-9 0.. JackQuinlan(3) 90
(J R Jenkins) *in rr: outpcd 6f out: rallied 4f out: lost pl over 2f out* **33/1**

7 *1* **Blast Martha (IRE)** 5-10-12 0... DannyCook 89
(Michael Smith) *trckd ldrs: t.k.h: drvn over 5f out: edgd lft and wknd 2f out* **14/1**

8 *3/4* **Grandma Smith** 6-10-7 0.. EdCookson(5) 88
(Kim Bailey) *in rr: hdwy over 7f out: sn chsng ldrs: drvn and lost pl over 5f out: in rr whn carried wd bnd over 3f out* **16/1**

0- **9** *16* **Inside Out**[27] 4735 4-10-3 0... RachaelGreen(3) 68
(Anthony Honeyball) *mid-div: pushed along after 6f: in rr whn rn wd bnd over 3f out* **14/1**

3- **10** *48* **Tyre Hill Lady**[37] 4540 5-10-12 0...................................... LeightonAspell 31
(David Dennis) *sn trcking ldrs: drvn over 4f out: lost pl 3f out: sn bhd: t.o whn eased over 1f out: virtually p.u* **20/1**

4m 8.2s (7.10) **Going Correction** -0.575s/f (Firm)
WFA 4 from 5yo+ 5lb **10** Ran SP% **114.8**
Speed ratings: **99,98,93,92,91 89,88,88,80,58**
CSF £11.74 TOTE £3.60: £1.30, £1.60, £2.00; EX 13.10 Trifecta £38.40.
Owner Sir Eric Parker & Mary Anne Parker **Bred** Niall Delany **Trained** Upper Lambourn, Berks

FOCUS
The leading pair pulled well clear in the final 2f and both look useful, particularly the winner.

5196 EASTER BUNNY MARES' STANDARD OPEN NATIONAL HUNT FLAT RACE (DIV II) 2m 1f

5:30 (5:31) (Class 6) 4-6-Y-O **£1,559** (£457; £228; £114)

Form RPR

1 **Chilly Miss** 5-10-12 0.. BrianHughes 104+
(Malcolm Jefferson) *in rr: green and pushed along after 6f: hdwy 7f out: chsng ldrs over 3f out: chal over 1f out: carried lft ins fnl f: styd on to ld last 50yds* **7/1**[3]

3- **2** *nk* **Prettyasapicture**[39] 4499 5-10-12 0................................ RobertThornton 104+
(Alan King) *trckd ldrs: smooth hdwy to ld narrowly over 2f out: edgd lft fnl f: hdd and no ex clsng stages* **10/11**[1]

3 *13* **Daisie Raymond** 6-10-9 0.. WayneKavanagh(3) 92
(Charles Smith) *hdwy to chse ldrs after 4f: pushed along over 6f out: w ldrs over 2f out: 3rd and one pce over 1f out* **25/1**

4 *2 3/4* **Tapaidh Frankie (IRE)** 5-10-7 0.. JoeColliver(5) 89
(Simon West) *hld up in last: hdwy to chse ldrs over 3f out: styd on same pce fnl 2f* **14/1**

0- **5** *2 3/4* **Annies Idea**[284] 841 5-10-12 0.. AdamPogson 87
(Mandy Rowland) *led: hdd 6f out: w ldrs tl wknd over 1f out* **14/1**

4- **6** *11* **Stand 'N' Boogie**[20] 4867 4-10-3 0................................... KielanWoods(3) 71
(Pam Sly) *w ldr: led 6f out: hdd over 2f out: lost pl over 1f out* **10/3**[2]

7 *6* **Vinaigrette** 5-10-5 0.. DanielHiskett(7) 72
(Richard Phillips) *hdwy to chse ldrs after 4f: drvn 6f out: outpcd over 4f out: sn lost pl* **11/1**

8 *75* **Dream's Park** 4-10-6 0... LiamTreadwell
(Sarah-Jayne Davies) *t.k.h: hdwy to trck ldrs after 4f: drvn 6f out: lost pl over 4f out: sn bhd: virtually p.u: hopelessly t.o* **40/1**

4m 17.8s (16.70) **Going Correction** -0.575s/f (Firm)
WFA 4 from 5yo+ 5lb **8** Ran SP% **115.9**
Speed ratings: **76,75,69,68,67 61,59,23**
CSF £14.00 TOTE £6.60: £1.10, £1.30, £5.80; EX 11.80 Trifecta £141.10.
Owner Racegoers Club Owners Group **Bred** Lesley Winn And Reveley Farms **Trained** Norton, N Yorks

FOCUS
This was weaker than the first division. Once again two pulled clear when the race really began in earnest.
T/Jkpt: Not won. T/Plt: £195.10 to a £1 stake. Pool: £81,868.36 - 6306.22 winning units. T/Qpdt: £40.40 to a £1 stake. Pool: £5303.46 - 96.95 winning units. WG

4432 FAIRYHOUSE (R-H)

Sunday, April 6

OFFICIAL GOING: Soft

5197a NORMANS GROVE CHASE (GRADE 2) (13 fncs) 2m 1f

2:10 (2:10) 5-Y-0+ **£20,312** (£5,937; £2,812; £937)

RPR

1 **Arvika Ligeonniere (FR)**[25] 4753 9-11-12 166................. PaulTownend 166+
(W P Mullins, Ire) *mde all: extended advantage fr 5th and over 4 l clr 1/2-way: stl gng wl into st: easily* **1/2**[1]

2 *3 1/4* **Twinlight (FR)**[42] 4457 7-11-10 157.................................. BarryGeraghty 160
(W P Mullins, Ire) *settled bhd ldr: nt fluent in 2nd at 2nd: niggled along bef 3 out and no imp on wnr bef next where j. sltly rt: kpt on same pce fr last* **5/1**[2]

3 *17* **Foildubh (IRE)**[84] 3680 10-11-10 153....................................... PCarberry 145
(John Patrick Ryan, Ire) *w.w: sme hdwy into 3rd bef 4 out: no imp on easy bef 2 out where nt fluent: sn rdn and no ex: kpt on one pce* **16/1**

4 *5 1/2* **Kates Benefit (IRE)**[15] 4977 8-10-11 130.......................... DannyMullins 126
(David Kenneth Budds, Ire) *settled bhd ldrs: mod 3rd 1/2-way: dropped to rr bef 4 out and no imp appr st: kpt on one pce* **20/1**

F **Turban (FR)**[50] 4283 7-11-4 151.. DJCasey
(W P Mullins, Ire) *in rr whn fell 1st* **11/2**[3]

4m 22.9s (-8.10) **Going Correction** -0.225s/f (Good) **5** Ran SP% **109.4**
Speed ratings: **110,108,100,97,**
CSF £3.59 TOTE £1.40: £1.02, £1.70; DF 3.50 Trifecta £11.00.
Owner Mrs S Ricci **Bred** Yves Lepage **Trained** Muine Beag, Co Carlow

FOCUS
Soft and hard enough work was how the going was described by the riders after the opening race of this new fixture. The five that started became four when Turban got rid of David Casey at the first and the odds-on favourite does what he normally does going right-handed – galloped and jumped his rivals into submission.

5199a IRISH STALLION FARMS EUROPEAN BREEDERS FUND MARES NOVICE HURDLE CHAMPIONSHIP FINAL (GRADE 1) (12 hdls) 2m 4f

3:15 (3:16) 4-Y-0+ **£48,750** (£14,250; £6,750; £2,250)

RPR

1 **Adriana Des Mottes (FR)**[23] 4784 4-10-10 127............... PaulTownend 131+
(W P Mullins, Ire) *mde all: j.big 2nd: over 3 l clr 1/2-way: reduced advantage bef 4 out: in command stl gng wl bef 2 out: sn wl clr: easily* **15/8**[1]

2 *7* **Beluckyagain (IRE)**[7] 5098 6-11-7 .... DJCasey 132
(W P Mullins, Ire) *hld up in tch: clsd into mod 3rd after 3 out: rdn into mod 2nd at last and no imp on easy wnr: kpt on same pce* **20/1**

3 *6* **Urticaire (FR)**[21] 4846 6-11-7 127....................................... DavyRussell 128
(W P Mullins, Ire) *hld up: tk clsr order in 3rd after 4 out: wnt 2nd appr st: rdn and no imp on wnr 2 out where nt fluent: dropped to mod 3rd at last: kpt on one pce* **3/1**[3]

4 *20* **Little King Robin (IRE)**[26] 4740 6-11-7 116......................(t[1]) MarkWalsh 106
(Colin Bowe, Ire) *hld up: nt fluent in 5th at 2nd: racd keenly: rdn and no imp on easy wnr 3 out: kpt on one pce* **16/1**

5 *16* **The Cookie Jar (IRE)**[21] 4846 7-11-7 115....................... JodyMcGarvey 90
(C A Murphy, Ire) *w.w in rr: niggled along fr 6th and sn no imp: one pce fr 3 out* **66/1**

6 *45* **Elsie (IRE)**[85] 3668 7-11-7 .... DannyMullins 45
(Thomas Mullins, Ire) *chsd ldrs: nt fluent in 4th at 2nd: lft 3rd at 4th: lost pl fr 4 out: rdn in 5th after next and no imp: wknd: completely t.o* **50/1**

7 *2 1/2* **Florishwells D'Ete (FR)**[50] 4286 4-10-10 .... APMcCoy 32
(W P Mullins, Ire) *chsd ldr in 2nd: nt fluent 3rd and 6th: tk clsr order bhd ldr bef 4 out: rdn after next and no imp on wnr appr st: wknd qckly and eased bef 2 out: completely t.o* **7/1**

U **Layla Joan (IRE)**[36] 4542 6-11-7 ....(t) PCarberry
(Gordon Elliott, Ire) *chsd ldrs: slt mstke in 3rd at 3rd: slt mstke again and uns rdr next* **11/4**[2]

5m 16.8s (-6.20) **Going Correction** -0.30s/f (Good)
WFA 4 from 5yo+ 6lb **8** Ran SP% **113.0**
Speed ratings: **100,97,94,86,80 62,61,**
CSF £34.83 TOTE £2.20: £1.20, £3.10, £1.10; DF 47.50 Trifecta £200.70.
Owner Mrs S Ricci **Bred** E A R L Ecurie Des Mottes **Trained** Muine Beag, Co Carlow

FOCUS
Willie Mullins certainly won't be complaining given that it was a clean sweep for the champion trainer but this was a substandard Grade 1.

5200a COOLMORE N.H. SIRES FAME AND GLORY & SANS FRONTIERES NOVICE HURDLE (GRADE 2) (12 hdls) 2m 4f

3:50 (3:52) 4-Y-0+ **£21,666** (£6,333; £3,000; £1,000)

RPR

1 **Lieutenant Colonel**[25] 4750 5-11-5 133............................ BrianO'Connell 151+
(D T Hughes, Ire) *chsd ldrs: 5th 1/2-way: tk clsr order bef 3 out: sn disp gng best and led fr 2 out: sn rdn and drew clr run-in* **5/1**

2 *10* **Le Vent D'Antan (FR)**[21] 4854 5-11-5 130.......................... BarryGeraghty 141
(Miss Elizabeth Doyle, Ire) *chsd ldrs: clsr in 3rd 1/2-way: slt mstke 6th: disp fr 3 out tl hdd u.p next: swtchd lft in 2nd bef last where slt mstke and no imp on wnr: kpt on same pce* **3/1**[1]

3 *5 1/2* **Azorian (IRE)**[56] 4180 6-11-5 134.......................................[1] DavyRussell 136
(Eoin Griffin, Ire) *w.w: tk clsr order in 6th bef 1/2-way: clsd u.p fr 3 out into mod 3rd 2 out: kpt on one pce: nt trble principals* **20/1**

The Form Book Jumps, Raceform Ltd, Compton, RG20 6NL.

4 4 ½ **Apache Stronghold (IRE)**[133] 2706 6-11-10 144.................. PCarberry 136
(Noel Meade, Ire) *hld up in rr of mid-div: 9th 1/2-way: hdwy into cl 5th bef 3 out: pushed along in 3rd into st and sn no imp on ldrs: kpt on one pce in mod 4th fr 2 out where nt fluent* **4/1**[2]

5 3 ¾ **Rightdownthemiddle (IRE)**[21] 4855 6-11-5 121.................. JohnCullen 127
(Michael Mulvany, Ire) *chsd ldrs: 4th 1/2-way: rdn in 6th and no ex u.p after 3 out: kpt on one pce fr next* **66/1**

6 4 ½ **Balbir Du Mathan (FR)**[140] 5-11-5 .... DannyMullins 123
(Gordon Elliott, Ire) *disp early: cl 2nd bef 2nd: mstke next: gained narrow advantage bef 6th: jnd after 4 out: rdn and wknd after next* **20/1**

7 13 **Urano (FR)**[38] 4523 6-11-5 130.. MsKWalsh 110
(W P Mullins, Ire) *racd in mid-div: 10th 1/2-way: tk clsr order bef 3 out: sn rdn in 8th and no imp bef next: kpt on one pce* **12/1**

8 13 **Moonshine Lad (IRE)**[29] 4665 6-11-5 135......................... DavyCondon 97
(Gordon Elliott, Ire) *racd in mid-div: dropped towards rr bef 5th: rdn and no imp 3 out: t.o* **14/1**

9 1 **Gallant Tipp (IRE)**[38] 4523 6-11-5 131..................................... APMcCoy 96
(E J O'Grady, Ire) *hld up in tch: 7th 1/2-way: rdn and no imp 3 out: wknd: t.o* **16/1**

10 4 ½ **Festive Felon (IRE)**[21] 4855 7-11-5 135........................... RobbieColgan 91
(Noel Meade, Ire) *disp early: narrow advantage bef 2nd: dropped to cl 2nd bef 6th: pushed along on terms bef 3 out and sn wknd: t.o* **20/1**

P **Upazo (FR)**[23] 4785 6-11-5 139.. DJCasey
(W P Mullins, Ire) *hld up in tch: slt mstkes 4th and next: 8th 1/2-way: rdn and no ex fr 3 out: sn wknd and eased: p.u bef 2 out* **14/1**

R **Renneti (FR)**[100] 3344 5-11-5 142... PaulTownend
(W P Mullins, Ire) *ref to r* **9/2**[3]

P **Feenakilmeedy (IRE)**[7] 5098 6-10-12 .... AndrewJMcNamara
(C Byrnes, Ire) *racd in rr: rdn and no ex fr 3 out: sn wknd and eased: p.u bef 2 out* **25/1**

5m 10.3s (-12.70) **Going Correction** -0.30s/f (Good) **13** Ran SP% **123.5**
Speed ratings: **113,109,106,105,103 101,96,91,90,89 , ,**
CSF £19.38 TOTE £5.90: £2.50, £1.30, £4.30; DF 22.60 Trifecta £299.70.
Owner Gigginstown House Stud **Bred** Mrs H I S Calzini **Trained** The Curragh, Co Kildare

FOCUS
A contest deserving of its Grade 2 status. The early pace was only even but it quickened considerably with a mile to run. The winner put up a very professional performance. This could be a race that will throw up some Grade 1 staying chasers in years to come.

5201a RATHBARRY & GLENVIEW STUDS NOVICE HURDLE (GRADE 2) (10 hdls) 2m
4:20 (4:22) 4-Y-0+ **£21,666** (£6,333; £3,000; £1,000)

RPR

1 **Valseur Lido (FR)**[26] 4736 5-11-4 142................................. DavyRussell 145
(W P Mullins, Ire) *hld up in tch: slt mstke in 6th at 2nd: 7th 1/2-way: clsd fr 3 out to chse ldrs in 3rd into st: effrt in 2nd fr 2 out and led gng best bef last: kpt on wl* **5/2**[2]

2 4 ¼ **Real Steel (IRE)**[42] 4456 6-11-10 135............................ BrianO'Connell 147
(Philip Fenton, Ire) *led: wnt sltly lft at 2nd and next: 2 l clr 1/2-way: reduced advantage 4 out: pushed along 2 out where nt fluent and wnt sltly lft again: hdd u.p bef last where nt fluent: no ex* **8/1**[3]

3 14 **Double Irish (IRE)**[45] 4386 6-11-4 .... DannyMullins 128
(Gordon Elliott, Ire) *chsd ldrs: clsr in 2nd 1/2-way: rdn bef 2 out and sn no imp on ldr: dropped to 3rd fr 2 out and no ex: one pce after* **14/1**

4 6 **Draycott Place (IRE)**[38] 4523 5-11-4 124........................... DavyCondon 121
(John Patrick Ryan, Ire) *hld up in tch: 8th 1/2-way: tk clsr order 3 out: sn rdn in mod 6th and no imp on ldrs in mod 4th bef next where mstke: kpt on one pce* **66/1**

5 1 ½ **Empire Of Dirt (IRE)**[28] 4708 7-11-4 131......................... BarryGeraghty 120
(C A Murphy, Ire) *chsd ldrs: 3rd 1/2-way: pushed along bef 3 out and sn no imp on ldrs in 5th: kpt on one pce fr next* **12/1**

6 11 **Wicklow Brave**[26] 4736 5-11-4 145.................................. PaulTownend 109
(W P Mullins, Ire) *hld up: 6th 1/2-way: clsr in 4th bef 3 out: sn pushed along in 3rd and no imp on ldrs bef st: dropped to mod 6th next: wknd* **5/4**[1]

7 34 **Quickpick Vic (IRE)**[28] 4708 7-11-4 138............................ PCarberry 75
(A J Martin, Ire) *chsd ldr in 2nd: dropped to 5th bef 1/2-way: rdn in 6th and no ex fr 3 out: wknd and eased: t.o* **12/1**

P **City Slicker (IRE)**[42] 4456 6-11-7 138..................................... DJCasey
(W P Mullins, Ire) *w.w in rr: last 1/2-way: pushed along and no imp 3 out: sn wknd and eased into st: p.u bef last* **28/1**

P **Waxies Dargle**[77] 3803 5-11-4 131...(t) APMcCoy
(Noel Meade, Ire) *chsd ldrs: 4th 1/2-way: pushed along bef 3 out and sn no ex u.p: sn wknd and eased: p.u bef last* **16/1**

4m 1.2s (-10.80) **Going Correction** -0.30s/f (Good)
WFA 4 from 5yo+ 5lb **9** Ran SP% **117.0**
Speed ratings: **115,112,105,102,102 96,79, ,**
CSF £23.41 TOTE £3.70: £1.10, £2.20, £4.80; DF 26.30 Trifecta £400.80.
Owner Gigginstown House Stud **Bred** M Contignon & Mme N Contignon **Trained** Muine Beag, Co Carlow

FOCUS
Supreme form was turned on its head here.

5198 - 5204a (Foreign Racing) - See Raceform Interactive

[4952]KELSO (L-H)
Monday, April 7

OFFICIAL GOING: Soft (good to soft in places; 6.2)
Wind: Light, half against Weather: Overcast

5205 DUNCAN SINCLAIR MEMORIAL NOVICES' HURDLE (DIV I) (10 hdls) 2m 2f
2:00 (2:01) (Class 4) 4-Y-0+ **£3,249** (£954; £477; £238)

Form RPR

331- 1 **Katachenko (IRE)**[42] 4460 5-11-6 127.................................. APMcCoy 132+
(Donald McCain) *t.k.h: mde all: nt fluent 3rd: pushed clr fr 2 out* **4/9**[1]

223- 2 7 **Another Mattie (IRE)**[46] 4369 7-10-13 114.............(t) LucyAlexander 112
(N W Alexander) *hld up: stdy hdwy and in tch 1/2-way: rdn and outpcd after 3 out: rallied bef last: kpt on to take 2nd nr fin: nt rch wnr* **3/1**[2]

2F5- 3 ¾ **Serenity Now (IRE)**[9] 5064 6-10-13 0.............................. DannyCook 113+
(Brian Ellison) *prom: lft 2nd 1st: effrt whn carried rt by loose horse appr 2 out: one pce fr last: lost 2nd nr fin* **8/1**[3]

4 14 **Maraweh (IRE)**[168] 4-10-7 0.................................. PeterBuchanan 93
(Lucinda Russell) *nt fluent in rr: hmpd 1st: hdwy to chse ldrs after 3 out: wknd after next* **12/1**

PP- 5 99 **Apache Pilot**[54] 4221 6-10-6 0.......................................(t) DaraghBourke[(7)]
(Maurice Barnes) *in tch to 1/2-way: sn lost tch: t.o* **150/1**

00P- 6 4 **Alkali (IRE)**[31] 4647 4-9-7 0...................................... JonathanMoore[(7)]
(S R B Crawford, Ire) *in tch: struggling bef 6th: t.o* **40/1**

06/- F **Crofton Lane**[541] 1845 8-10-6 0...[1] MrJDixon[(7)]
(John Dixon) *t.k.h: chsd wnr tl fell 1st* **150/1**

P **Overpresently** 6-10-6 0.. RyanMania
(Simon Waugh) *nt fluent: hld up bhd ldng gp: lost tch and p.u bef 6th* **40/1**

35- F **Varene De Vauzelle (FR)**[19] 4902 5-10-13 0.................... BrianHughes
(James Ewart) *chsd ldrs: fell 1st* **16/1**

4m 51.8s (24.80) **Going Correction** +1.275s/f (Heav)
WFA 4 from 5yo+ 5lb **9** Ran SP% **125.1**
Speed ratings (Par 105): **95,91,91,85,41 39, , ,**
CSF £2.56 TOTE £1.50: £1.10, £1.10, £1.60; EX 2.40 Trifecta £7.70.
Owner Trevor Hemmings **Bred** Charles Harte **Trained** Cholmondeley, Cheshire

FOCUS
Bends moved onto fresh ground. Hurdle track on outside line increasing distances by about 20yds per circuit. The easy winner is on the upgrade.

5206 DUNCAN SINCLAIR MEMORIAL NOVICES' HURDLE (DIV II) (10 hdls) 2m 2f
2:30 (2:30) (Class 4) 4-Y-0+ **£3,249** (£954; £477; £238)

Form RPR

010- 1 **Landecker (IRE)**[37] 4550 6-11-6 128.............................. LucyAlexander 121+
(N W Alexander) *in tch: nt fluent and pushed along 3 out: hdwy to ld next: pushed out fr last* **2/1**[1]

443- 2 2 ¼ **Lord Brendy**[46] 4379 6-10-13 105.................................. KennyJohnson 111
(Robert Johnson) *taken early to post: t.k.h: hld up in tch: stdy hdwy bef 2 out: effrt and chsd wnr last: kpt on run-in: hld towards fin* **10/3**[2]

63P- 3 4 **Boruma (IRE)**[7] 5102 4-10-7 0.. JamesReveley 101
(Dianne Sayer) *hld up in tch on outside: hdwy and ev ch whn nt fluent 3 out: kpt on same pce bef last* **50/1**

604- 4 7 **Neville Woods**[16] 4956 7-10-6 0.................................... AlistairFindlay[(7)] 100
(J L Gledson) *cl up: mstke 2nd: led briefly bef 2 out: sn rdn: outpcd between last 2* **10/1**

/U5- 5 6 **Whiskey Chaser (IRE)**[76] 3816 6-10-13 0............................. APMcCoy 93
(Donald McCain) *chsd ldrs: hit 3rd: pushed along bef 2 out: sn wknd* **9/2**

543- 6 5 **Il Testone (FR)**[34] 4605 5-10-13 0..................................... HenryBrooke 88
(Chris Grant) *hld up in tch: struggling after 3 out: btn next* **25/1**

225- 7 11 **Cousin Guillaume (FR)**[16] 4956 5-10-13 0......................... BrianHughes 77
(James Ewart) *led to bef 2 out: sn rdn and btn* **4/1**[3]

P- P **Syrian**[23] 4811 7-10-13 0...[1] BrianHarding
(Barry Murtagh) *hld up: struggling after 4 out: lost tch and p.u bef 2 out* **150/1**

P35- P **Flawless Filly (IRE)**[23] 4811 4-10-0 0.......................... WilsonRenwick
(Rose Dobbin) *t.k.h: hld up in tch: struggling after 3 out: t.o whn p.u bef next* **20/1**

0- P **Lunar Legend**[16] 4958 5-10-6 0.................................... PeterBuchanan
(Lucinda Russell) *hld up bhd ldng gp: struggling bef 4 out: lost tch and p.u bef 2 out* **100/1**

4m 52.5s (25.50) **Going Correction** +1.275s/f (Heav)
WFA 4 from 5yo+ 5lb **10** Ran SP% **115.9**
Speed ratings (Par 105): **94,93,91,88,85 83,78, , ,**
CSF £8.61 TOTE £2.40: £1.20, £1.40, £9.60; EX 8.80 Trifecta £585.60.
Owner Mrs N Hodge **Bred** Mrs Patricia Furlong **Trained** Kinneston, Perth & Kinross

FOCUS
This was a deal more competitive than the first division but the form is only ordinary.

5207 BORDERS CARERS CENTRE H'CAP CHASE (12 fncs) 2m 1f
3:00 (3:02) (Class 4) (0-115,115) 5-Y-0+ **£5,198** (£1,526; £763; £381)

Form RPR

053- 1 **Sudski Star (IRE)**[32] 4628 6-10-2 **91**.............................(vt[1]) BrianHughes 108+
(Patrick Griffin, Ire) *chsd ldr: blnd 5th: drvn and outpcd 4 out: rallied bef 2 out: styd on u.p to ld last 50yds: kpt on* **3/1**[1]

241- 2 1 ¾ **Edmund (IRE)**[10] 5051 7-11-2 **105**.................................(t) WilsonRenwick 119
(Ann Hamilton) *hld up in tch: smooth hdwy to chse ldr 5 out: rdn to ld bef last: edgd lft run-in: hdd and no ex last 50yds* **10/3**[2]

256- 3 6 **Shadrack (IRE)**[21] 4861 10-11-12 **115**............................... JamesReveley 124
(Keith Reveley) *led at ordinary gallop: mstke 2nd: qcknd 3 out: rdn and hdd bef last: outpcd run-in* **7/2**[3]

4P1- 4 23 **Prosecco (IRE)**[32] 4628 12-11-11 **114**............................ PeterBuchanan 98
(Lucinda Russell) *hld up in tch: pushed along and outpcd 5th: rallied after 5 out: wknd appr 2 out* **5/1**

055- 5 25 **Prince Tam**[82] 3722 10-9-11 **89** oh2.......................... JonathanEngland[(3)] 48
(Harriet Graham) *in tch on outside: nt fluent 6th: rdn and wknd after 3 out* **10/1**

344- P **Endeavor**[33] 4616 9-10-12 **101**.. RyanMania
(Dianne Sayer) *nt fluent: chsd ldrs: mstke 5 out: rdn and wknd bef 2 out: p.u bef last* **5/1**

4m 33.6s (15.60) **Going Correction** +0.95s/f (Soft) **6** Ran SP% **112.7**
Speed ratings: **101,100,97,86,74**
CSF £13.76 TOTE £4.40: £2.20, £1.90; EX 16.60 Trifecta £64.80.
Owner Patrick Griffin **Bred** Mrs J P Duffy **Trained** Oldtown, Co Dublin
■ Stewards' Enquiry : Wilson Renwick two-day ban: used whip above permitted level (Apr 21-22)

FOCUS
A competitive handicap chase run at a fair pace, and a small step up from the winner.

5208 KIDS GO FREE AT BERWICK SPEEDWAY H'CAP HURDLE (11 hdls) 2m 6f 110y
3:30 (3:30) (Class 4) (0-120,120) 4-Y-0+ **£3,898** (£1,144; £572; £286)

Form RPR

243- 1 **Sealous Scout (IRE)**[39] 4510 6-11-1 **109**.............................. APMcCoy 118+
(Donald McCain) *cl up: led 7th to next: regained ld 4 out: rdn and styd on strly fr 2 out* **7/4**[1]

356- 2 3 ¾ **Allow Me**[10] 5058 9-10-13 **107**......................................(b[1]) JamesReveley 109
(Dianne Sayer) *led to 7th: regained ld next: hdd 4 out: effrt and rdn bef 2 out: kpt on same pce* **12/1**

2F5- 3 32 **The Orange Rogue (IRE)**[55] 4199 7-11-2 **110**................ LucyAlexander 80
(N W Alexander) *nt fluent in rr: outpcd 1/2-way: rallied to chse clr ldng pair 2 out: no imp* **10/1**

263- 4 11 **Walser (IRE)**[82] 3724 7-11-5 **113**.......................................(b) BrianHughes 72
(John Wade) *hld up in tch: stdy hdwy to chse ldrs 1/2-way: rdn and outpcd fr 3 out: btn next* **7/1**

032- 5 25 **Caerlaverock (IRE)**[36] 4577 9-10-11 **105**.....................(b) WilsonRenwick 39
(Rose Dobbin) *nt fluent on occasions: hld up in tch: rdn and outpcd after 5 out: struggling fr 3 out: t.o* **7/2**[2]

212- **6** *3 ¼* **Makhzoon (USA)**[46] 4365 10-11-5 **120**.................(v) DiarmuidO'Regan(7) 51
(N W Alexander) *chsd ldrs: struggling fnl circ: t.o* **6/1**[3]

065- **7** *39* **Rhymers Ha'**[16] 4952 7-10-13 **112**.................... CraigNichol(5) 4
(Lucinda Russell) *hld up: pushed along bef 5 out: lost tch after next: t.o* **10/1**

6m 6.7s (25.70) **Going Correction** +1.275s/f (Heav) 7 Ran SP% **111.2**
Speed ratings (Par 105): **106,104,93,89,81 79,66**
CSF £20.56 CT £156.60 TOTE £2.40: £1.50, £6.60; EX 29.90 Trifecta £256.00.
Owner T G Leslie **Bred** Mervyn Chamney **Trained** Cholmondeley, Cheshire

FOCUS
A modest handicap. The winner finally built on the promise of his bumper form.

5209 CAZENOVE CAPITAL MANAGEMENT BUCCLEUCH CUP (A MAIDEN HUNTERS' CHASE) (19 fncs) 3m 2f
4:00 (4:00) (Class 5) 5-Y-O+ **£3,119** (£967; £483; £242)

Form RPR

/ **1** **Present Potential (IRE)**[16] 7-11-9 0.....................(p) MrKitAlexander(5) 105+
(N W Alexander) *cl up: led 11th to 3 out: rallied and regained ld bef last: styd on gamely u.p run-in* **9/2**[3]

UP- **2** *2 ¼* **Just Awake**[23] 7-11-11 0.................................... MrJHamilton(3) 103+
(Mrs A M Thomson) *hld up: blnd 3rd: hit 10th: stdy hdwy to chse ldrs after 12th: led 3 out to bef last: rallied: kpt on same pce run-in* **4/1**[2]

33F- **3** *1 ¼* **Barachois Silver**[23] 10-11-2 79................................ MrSFox(5) 93
(Mrs J M Hollands) *nt fluent: hld up: hdwy bef 4 out: hrd rdn and styd on fr last: nt rch first two* **11/8**[1]

/P5- **4** *22* **Senor Alco (FR)**[9] 8-11-7 94................................ MrTSpeke(7) 79
(Victor Thompson) *hld up in tch: stdy hdwy to chse wnr bef 13th: rdn bef 3 out: wknd bef next* **15/2**

P/3- **5** *14* **Silk And Roses**[16] 11-11-2 67.............................(t) MrTHamilton(5) 56
(Mrs Wendy Hamilton) *prom: pushed along thrght: lost pl 1/2-way: no imp fr 4 out* **14/1**

4FP- **6** *5* **Raifteiri (IRE)**[16] 7-11-7 76.................................. MrJDixon(7) 58
(William Young Jnr) *hld up on outside: blnd 10th: rdn and outpcd 5 out: n.d after* **33/1**

04P/ **P** **Treacle Moon**[428] 11-11-0 0.................................. MrMJohnson(7)
(Mrs Sarah L Dent) *hld up: bmpd 3rd: stdy hdwy and prom 8th: rdn and wknd bef 5 out: t.o whn p.u bef next* **25/1**

45P/ **P** **Coole Murphy (IRE)**[449] 3649 10-11-7 0...................... MrNOrpwood(7)
(Mrs Clare Moore) *led to 11th: lost pl after next: lost tch and p.u bef 13th* **50/1**

P **Raid Stane (IRE)**[23] 8-11-9 0.............................(p) MissKBryson(5)
(Miss K Scott) *bhd: lost tch and p.u bef 11th* **28/1**

P **Darsi Dancer (IRE)**[9] 6-11-9 0................................ MrRSmith(5)
(Stuart Coltherd) *hld up: j.lft and bmpd 3rd: sn struggling: t.o whn p.u bef 10th* **16/1**

7m 23.9s (36.70) **Going Correction** +0.95s/f (Soft) 10 Ran SP% **116.8**
Speed ratings: **81,80,79,73,68 67,,,,**
CSF £22.70 TOTE £4.70: £2.40, £1.90, £1.10; EX 29.00 Trifecta £74.10.
Owner Nicholas Alexander **Bred** Michael Murphy **Trained** Kinneston, Perth & Kinross
■ Stewards' Enquiry : Mr S Fox 19-day ban: used whip above permitted level (Apr 21-25,30,May 2-3,5-6,8,12-15,21,25-27)

FOCUS
They went plenty hard enough in this maiden hunters' chase and stamina very much won the day. The winner was a 110 horse in Ireland and there's probably more to come.

5210 SHEENA COCHRANE CELEBRATION H'CAP CHASE (17 fncs) 2m 7f 110y
4:30 (4:30) (Class 3) (0-125,124) 5-Y-O+ **£6,564** (£2,104; £1,169)

Form RPR

3P2- **1** **Fentara**[16] 4953 9-11-8 123.............................(t) JakeGreenall(3) 135+
(Mark Walford) *in tch: stdy hdwy 11th: wnt 2nd bef 4 out: 2 l down and gng wl whn lft 4 l clr next: pushed along and kpt on strly* **11/4**[1]

10P- **2** *18* **Chavoy (FR)**[44] 4427 9-11-7 122.............................(t) TonyKelly(3) 112
(Rebecca Menzies) *hld up: pushed along 1/2-way: hdwy and lft 6 l 3rd 3 out: tk modest 2nd between last 2: no imp* **15/2**

323- **3** *5* **Harris Hawk**[20] 4894 9-10-9 107.............................(b[1]) BrianHughes 91
(John Wade) *prom: hdwy to chse ldr bef 11th to bef 4 out: rdn whn lft 4 l 2nd next: sn outpcd: lost 2nd and btn between last 2* **13/2**[3]

512- **P** **Or De Grugy (FR)**[53] 4236 12-11-1 113...................... LucyAlexander
(N W Alexander) *in tch: lost pl 1/2-way: struggling fnl circ: t.o whn p.u bef 5 out* **3/1**[2]

1PP- **P** **Kealigolane (IRE)**[30] 4669 10-11-7 124...................... CraigNichol(5)
(Barry Murtagh) *led to 11th: cl up: wknd after 13th: t.o whn p.u bef 4 out* **22/1**

P4P- **F** **Rockawango (FR)**[16] 4955 8-11-4 123.......................(tp) DaleIrving(7)
(James Ewart) *hld up: pushed along 10th: no imp whn fell next* **28/1**

021- **U** **Fiddlers Reel**[20] 4894 11-11-8 120.............................(p) RyanMania 125
(Jane Clark) *t.k.h: cl up on outside: led 7th: 2 l in front and gng wl whn blnd bdly and uns rdr 3 out* **3/1**[2]

6m 26.1s (18.10) **Going Correction** +0.95s/f (Soft) 7 Ran SP% **109.6**
Speed ratings: **107,101,99,,,**
CSF £20.94 CT £109.89 TOTE £2.90: £1.90, £4.60; EX 18.90 Trifecta £142.60.
Owner Chasing Gold Racing Club **Bred** Mrs A E And Miss S J Dixon **Trained** Sherriff Hutton, N Yorks
■ Mark Walford's first winner over jumps.

FOCUS
A competitive handicap chase. The winner is rated back to last season's C&D mark.

5211 GREEN TREE HOTEL PEEBLES MARES' H'CAP CHASE (BETFAIR SCOTTISH CHASE SERIES QUALIFIER) (16 fncs) 2m 5f 110y
5:00 (5:00) (Class 4) (0-120,120) 5-Y-O+ **£3,994** (£1,240; £667)

Form RPR

F31- **1** **Lady Of Verona (IRE)**[25] 4771 7-10-2 **101**...................... CraigNichol(5) 98
(Lucinda Russell) *chsd clr ldr: effrt bef 4 out: 15 l 2nd and plugging on whn lft 16 l clr last* **5/6**[1]

43P- **2** *14* **The Flaming Matron (IRE)**[48] 4337 8-10-9 **103**..........(t) LucyAlexander 86
(N W Alexander) *in tch: outpcd fr 1/2-way: wnt poor 3rd after 3 out: no imp whn lft 16 l 2nd last* **7/1**[3]

541- **3** *85* **My Flora**[16] 4966 10-11-12 **120**.............................. HarrySkelton 18
(Dan Skelton) *in tch: outpcd fr 10th: no imp whn blnd 3 out: sn lost 3rd pl: continued: no ch whn lft poor 3rd last* **15/8**[2]

F5U- **U** **Harrys Whim**[55] 4202 9-10-0 **94** oh32..........................(t) HenryBrooke 98+
(Maurice Barnes) *led and sn clr: pushed along and 15 l in front whn blnd last and uns ride* **18/1**

6m 6.1s (36.90) **Going Correction** +0.95s/f (Soft) 4 Ran SP% **107.1**
Speed ratings: **70,64,34,**
CSF £6.25 TOTE £2.50; EX 6.00 Trifecta £7.80.
Owner Peter K Dale Ltd **Bred** Peter K Dale **Trained** Arlary, Perth & Kinross

FOCUS
Only four lined up for this mares' handicap chase, but there was no shortage of drama. The lucky winner is rated to her mark.

5212 MCMILLANFINEART.COM CONDITIONAL JOCKEYS' H'CAP HURDLE (10 hdls) 2m 2f
5:30 (5:30) (Class 4) (0-115,115) 4-Y-O+ **£3,249** (£954; £477; £238)

Form RPR

F24- **1** **Hunters Belt (IRE)**[32] 4625 10-11-4 **113**................(vt) JonathonBewley(6) 121+
(George Bewley) *hld up: rdn and outpcd bef 4 out: rallied next: led 2 out: pushed along and styd on strly* **11/1**

240- **2** *5* **Trust Thomas**[16] 4952 6-11-2 **108**.............................. NickSlatter(3) 109
(Ann Hamilton) *hld up in midfield: hdwy to chse wnr after 2 out: kpt on same pce fr last* **8/1**

423- **3** *4 ½* **Scimon Templar (FR)**[30] 4667 6-10-8 **97**...................... TonyKelly 93
(Pauline Robson) *prom: rdn and outpcd 6th: rallied bef 2 out: kpt on to take 3rd run-in: nt rch first two* **4/1**[2]

524- **4** *1 ½* **King Of Strings (IRE)**[94] 3516 5-11-5 **108**...................... JakeGreenall 102
(Mark Walford) *hld up: smooth hdwy and ev ch bef 2 out: sn rdn and outpcd* **3/1**[1]

54P- **5** *3 ¾* **Ellistrin Belle**[25] 4770 6-10-0 **89** oh4.......................... CallumWhillans 82+
(Donald Whillans) *led: rdn 3 out: hdd whn blnd next: sn btn* **25/1**

213- **6** *16* **Bernardelli (IRE)**[117] 3021 6-11-12 **115**...................... HarryChalloner 89
(Nicky Richards) *hld up: struggling bef 4 out: sme late hdwy: nvr able to chal* **5/1**[3]

4U4- **7** *1 ¾* **Dante's Frolic**[25] 4770 6-11-0 **103**.............................. AdamNicol 76
(Michael Smith) *hld up: hdwy on ins and in tch 6th: rdn and wknd bef 2 out* **9/1**

004- **8** *37* **Cool Baranca (GER)**[42] 4463 8-11-4 **110**...................... EmmaSayer(3) 46
(Dianne Sayer) *chsd ldrs tl rdn and wknd appr 3 out: t.o* **20/1**

P12- **P** **Some Lad (IRE)**[10] 5051 9-10-2 **91**.............................. ConorShoemark
(Alison Hamilton) *in tch: hdwy to chse ldr bef 3 out to bef next: sn wknd: p.u appr last* **8/1**

100- **P** **Roc De Prince**[53] 4234 5-11-0 **111**.............................(t) DaleIrving(8)
(James Ewart) *in tch: stdy hdwy bef 4th: rdn 3 out: wknd and p.u bef next* **16/1**

4m 57.4s (30.40) **Going Correction** +1.275s/f (Heav) 10 Ran SP% **116.7**
Speed ratings (Par 105): **83,80,78,78,76 69,68,52,,**
CSF £95.62 CT £417.23 TOTE £12.60: £3.50, £2.00, £2.30; EX 114.30 Trifecta £1338.80.
Owner R A Fisher **Bred** Charlie Purcell **Trained** Bonchester Bridge, Borders

FOCUS
Easily the most competitive race on the card, but with conditions proving more gruelling than anticipated, they finished well strung out. The winner is rated back to form on his return to his old yard.
T/Plt: £11.60 to a £1 stake. Pool: £67507.49 - 4213.79 winning tickets T/Qpdt: £10.20 to a £1 stake. Pool: £4551.83 - 327.30 winning tickets RY

4832 CARLISLE (R-H)
Tuesday, April 8

OFFICIAL GOING: Soft changing to good to soft on hurdle course after race 2 (2.50)
Wind: Fairly strong, half against Weather: Cloudy, bright

5213 APOLLOBET ENHANCED DAILY RACING SPECIALS NOVICES' CHASE (12 fncs) 2m
2:20 (2:20) (Class 4) 5-Y-O+ **£3,768** (£1,106; £553; £276)

Form RPR

132- **1** **Un Guet Apens (FR)**[17] 4955 6-11-5 128.....................(p) BrianHughes 132+
(James Ewart) *trckd ldrs: effrt after 2 out: led last 100yds: pushed clr* **3/1**[2]

321- **2** *4 ½* **Supreme Asset (IRE)**[62] 4084 6-11-5 130...................... APMcCoy 128
(Donald McCain) *t.k.h: in tch: stdy hdwy 1/2-way: led gng wl bef last: rdn and hdd last 100yds: no ex* **8/11**[1]

F13- **3** *¾* **Little Glenshee (IRE)**[31] 4668 8-10-12 120...................... LucyAlexander 121
(N W Alexander) *led tl j. path and hdd bef 4th: chsd ldr: drvn and outpcd 3 out: styd on fr last: nt rch first two* **4/1**[3]

00- **4** *nk* **Boric**[132] 2748 6-10-12 0.. RyanMania 121
(Simon Waugh) *nt fluent on occasions: chsd ldr: led bef 4th: clr 5 out to next: rdn whn mstke 2 out: hdd bef last: rallied: outpcd run-in* **250/1**

315- **5** *11* **Rosquero (FR)**[23] 4836 9-10-12 0.............................. KennyJohnson 110
(Robert Johnson) *in tch: rdn and outpcd 1/2-way: n.d after* **100/1**

52B/ **6** *34* **Heliopsis (IRE)**[689] 341 9-10-7 100.............................(t) DerekFox(5) 75
(Lucinda Russell) *hld up: outpcd after 4th: struggling fr 1/2-way: t.o* **20/1**

4m 7.1s (-9.00) **Going Correction** -0.75s/f (Firm) 6 Ran SP% **109.1**
Speed ratings: **92,89,89,89,83 66**
CSF £5.58 TOTE £3.40: £2.20, £1.10; EX 6.80 Trifecta £9.80.
Owner Drew, Sperling, Graham, Carruthers **Bred** Pierre De Maleissye Melun **Trained** Langholm, Dumfries & G'way

FOCUS
All hurdle races on Inner track. The first three were close to their marks in a fair novice for the track.

5214 APOLLOBET ONLINE GAMES AND CASINO NOVICES' H'CAP HURDLE (8 hdls) 2m 1f
2:50 (2:50) (Class 4) (0-120,118) 4-Y-O+ **£3,119** (£915; £457; £228)

Form RPR

663- **1** **Snowed In (IRE)**[23] 4836 5-10-1 **93**.............................(p) SeanQuinlan 101+
(Barbara Butterworth) *mde virtually all: clr after 4 out: rdn and 10 l in front whn mstke last: eased nr fin: unchal* **13/8**[1]

405- **2** *6* **Badea**[47] 4366 5-10-0 **92**.. WilsonRenwick 89
(Martin Todhunter) *t.k.h: prom: outpcd 4 out: rallied after next: wnt 2nd last 100yds: no ch w eased down wnr* **16/1**

/14- **3** *2 ¼* **Moss Cloud (IRE)**[128] 2838 7-11-12 **118**...................... APMcCoy 115
(Donald McCain) *in tch: niggled bef 2nd: drvn and outpcd after next: rallied to chse (clr) wnr after 4 out: rdn and hung rt bef 2 out: no imp whn mstke last: lost 2nd fnl 100yds* **5/1**

P22- **4** *7* **Hallmark Star**[33] 4629 5-10-13 **110**.............................. CraigNichol(5) 100
(Lucinda Russell) *w ldr to 2nd: cl up tl outpcd 3 out: no imp bef next* **5/2**[2]

503- **5** *51* **Sleep In First (FR)**[28] 4746 8-10-13 **105**.....................(p) BrianHughes 42
(James Ewart) *trckd ldrs: flattened 4th: struggling fr next: lost tch fnl 3: t.o* **10/3**[3]

4m 19.1s (-10.10) **Going Correction** -0.65s/f (Firm) 5 Ran SP% **112.3**
Speed ratings (Par 105): **97,94,93,89,65**
CSF £21.01 TOTE £2.50: £1.30, £7.10; EX 24.80 Trifecta £199.40.
Owner Miss E J Butterworth **Bred** T Cahalan & D Cahalan **Trained** Bolton, Cumbria

The Form Book Jumps, Raceform Ltd, Compton, RG20 6NL.

FOCUS
A modest novice handicap, racing on ground described as good to soft on the hurdle track. The cosy winner is rated to his best.

5215 APOLLOBET £50 FREE BET H'CAP CHASE (19 fncs) 3m 2f
3:20 (3:20) (Class 4) (0-120,120) 5-Y-O+ **£4,678** (£1,373; £686; £343)

Form RPR
4P1- **1** **Frank The Slink**^{35} 4606 8-11-1 **109**................................ WilsonRenwick 118
(Micky Hammond) *nt fluent on occasions: led tl mstke and hdd 7th: led after 9th: mde rest: hrd drvn and hld on gamely run-in* **10/3**^{2}
642- **2** *shd* **Lively Baron (IRE)**^{37} 4572 9-11-9 **117**..........................(bt) HenryBrooke 124
(Donald McCain) *t.k.h: cl up: effrt and rdn after 4 out: styd on wl fr last: jst hld* **8/1**
P42- **3** *10* **Dark Glacier (IRE)**^{19} 4914 9-11-6 **114**............................(v) JamieMoore 116
(Peter Bowen) *prom: blnd 10th: rallied after 5 out: one pce whn hit 3 out: no imp fr next* **11/8**^{1}
055- **4** *39* **Lookout Mountain (IRE)**^{18} 4934 6-11-12 **120**................(bt^{1}) APMcCoy 98
(Jonjo O'Neill) *nt fluent on occasions: in tch: drvn and outpcd 5 out: lost tch bef 2 out: t.o* **4/1**^{3}
P3U- **P** **Beau Dandy (IRE)**^{26} 4775 9-10-0 **94** oh1.......................(b) BrianHarding
(Chris Grant) *cl up: lost pl 8th: struggling fr 10th: t.o whn p.u 2 out* **8/1**

6m 55.1s (-12.10) **Going Correction** -0.75s/f (Firm) **5** Ran SP% **107.4**
Speed ratings: **88,87,84,72,**
CSF £23.90 TOTE £4.10: £2.40, £3.40; EX 24.50 Trifecta £38.50.
Owner M H O G **Bred** G A Greaves **Trained** Middleham Moor, N Yorks
■ Stewards' Enquiry : Henry Brooke four-day ban: used whip above permitted level (Apr 22-25)
Wilson Renwick four-day ban: used whip above permitted level (Apr 23-25,May 1)

FOCUS
A modest staying handicap. The winner was a 121 horse here in 2012 and may still match that.

5216 APOLLOBET FREE DOWNLOAD APP NOVICES' H'CAP CHASE (17 fncs) 2m 5f
3:50 (3:50) (Class 4) (0-110,110) 5-Y-O+ **£3,768** (£1,106; £553; £276)

Form RPR
4P6- **1** **Doubledisdoubledat (IRE)**^{17} 4956 7-10-9 **93**.................... RyanMania 109+
(Stuart Coltherd) *mde all: rdn and hrd pressed fr 2 out: kpt on wl run-in* **8/1**
P54- **2** *2 1/4* **Gleann Na Ndochais (IRE)**^{18} 4940 8-10-10 **97**.......... EwanWhillans$^{(3)}$ 109
(Alistair Whillans) *hld up in tch: hdwy to chse ldrs 5 out: effrt and wnt 2nd 3 out: swtchd lft and rdn bef last: kpt on same pce run-in* **4/1**^{3}
600- **3** *30* **Azerodegree (IRE)**^{38} 4553 5-11-2 **100**.................... JamesReveley 82
(Harriet Graham) *bhd: outpcd 1/2-way: mstke 3 out: styd on fr next: nvr able to chal* **40/1**
P55- **4** *2 1/2* **Champagne Agent (IRE)**^{21} 4892 8-11-4 **107**.............(v^{1}) CraigNichol$^{(5)}$ 87
(Lucinda Russell) *cl up: wnt 2nd 10th to 3 out: drvn and wknd fr next* **14/1**
441- **5** *11* **Sharney Sike**^{24} 4812 8-11-5 **110**.................... DaraghBourke$^{(7)}$ 87
(Stuart Coltherd) *prom: rdn and outpcd 11th: rallied after next: mstke 4 out: sn struggling* **9/4**^{1}
/PP- **6** *18* **Picks Milan (IRE)**^{83} 3724 8-11-8 **109**.................... JohnKington$^{(3)}$ 60
(Philip Kirby) *pressed wnr to 10th: struggling 5 out: wknd next* **14/1**
/0P- **7** *2 1/2* **Irish By Name (IRE)**^{102} 3335 8-10-4 **88**.................... BrianHughes 36
(John Wade) *hld up in tch: drvn and outpcd 11th: btn whn mstke 3 out* **33/1**
P/P- **P** **Caught In The Act (IRE)**^{38} 4553 7-10-0 **84** oh3..........(t) LucyAlexander
(N W Alexander) *nt fluent: bhd and detached: t.o whn p.u after 10th* **8/1**
461- **U** **Ben Akram (IRE)**^{43} 4462 6-11-6 **104**.................... PeterBuchanan
(Lucinda Russell) *hld up in tch: outpcd 11th: no ch whn mstke and uns rdr 4 out* **7/2**^{2}

5m 27.0s (-18.10) **Going Correction** -0.75s/f (Firm) **9** Ran SP% **113.9**
Speed ratings: **104,103,91,90,86 79,78,,**
CSF £40.51 CT £1204.51 TOTE £8.50: £3.10, £1.60, £6.50; EX 54.80 Trifecta £737.30.
Owner Mr & Mrs Mark J Gilbert **Bred** John Joe Ronayne **Trained** Selkirk, Borders

FOCUS
An ordinary novice handicap. The winner can probably rate higher and win again.

5217 APOLLOBET FOLLOW ON TWITTER AND FACEBOOK H'CAP HURDLE (9 hdls 1 omitted) 2m 3f 110y
4:25 (4:25) (Class 4) (0-110,110) 4-Y-O+ **£3,119** (£915; £457; £228)

Form RPR
062- **1** **Funky Munky**^{17} 4957 9-10-11 **98**..............................(p) EwanWhillans$^{(3)}$ 103+
(Alistair Whillans) *chsd ldrs: stmbld bef 4th: drvn after 3 out: rallied to ld next: sn edgd rt: kpt on wl fr last* **17/2**
641- **2** *2 1/4* **Omid**^{128} 2842 6-10-9 **93**..............................(tp) HenryBrooke 96
(Evelyn Slack) *nt fluent on occasions: in tch: rdn after 3 out: rallied bef next: styd on to take 2nd last 50yds: kpt on* **15/2**
413- **3** *1 1/4* **Rosslyn Castle**^{24} 4818 5-11-12 **110**.............................. APMcCoy 111
(Jonjo O'Neill) *nt fluent: prom: smooth hdwy bef 3 out: ev ch next: sn rdn: one pce fr last: lost 2nd last 50yds* **7/4**^{1}
P40- **4** *15* **Indepub**^{18} 4943 5-10-8 **92**.............................. WilsonRenwick 82
(Martin Todhunter) *chsd ldr: led 3 out: rdn and hdd next: sn btn* **22/1**
443- **P** **Knight Valliant**^{17} 4957 11-10-5 **89**.............................. SeanQuinlan
(Barbara Butterworth) *led tl hdd 3 out: lost tch and p.u next* **13/2**^{3}
2FF- **F** **Dickie Henderhoop (IRE)**^{47} 4365 9-10-13 **104**.............. MrRWilson$^{(7)}$
(Lucy Normile) *bhd whn fell 2nd: fatally injured* **13/2**^{3}
60P- **U** **Agesilas (FR)**^{92} 3569 6-10-3 **90**.............................. JohnKington$^{(3)}$
(Andrew Crook) *in tch: outpcd whn flashed tail, faltered and uns rdr after 5th* **4/1**^{2}

4m 53.6s (-15.20) **Going Correction** -0.65s/f (Firm) **7** Ran SP% **109.7**
Speed ratings (Par 105): **104,103,102,96,**
CSF £61.67 TOTE £9.10: £4.40, £3.20; EX 41.10 Trifecta £198.40.
Owner The Twelve Munkys **Bred** Mrs S Corbett **Trained** Newmill-On-Slitrig, Borders

FOCUS
A moderate handicap. The first three are rated pretty much to their marks.

5218 APOLLOBET HORSE RACING BEST ODDS GUARANTEED H'CAP CHASE (16 fncs) 2m 4f
4:55 (4:55) (Class 4) (0-120,117) 5-Y-O+ **£4,678** (£1,373; £686; £343)

Form RPR
421- **1** **Indian Voyage (IRE)**^{11} 5058 6-11-2 **114**....................(t) DaraghBourke$^{(7)}$ 130+
(Maurice Barnes) *pressed ldr: led 7th: mde rest: blnd 5 out: styd on wl fr 2 out* **6/4**^{1}
U55- **2** *2 1/2* **Ultra Du Chatelet (FR)**^{96} 3498 6-11-0 **105**................(t) TomScudamore 112
(Lucinda Russell) *hld up in tch: stdy hdwy bef 4 out: chsd wnr and effrt next: kpt on same pce fr last* **11/4**^{2}
P13- **3** *3* **Etxalar (FR)**^{31} 4669 11-11-7 **112**..............................(t) PeterBuchanan 117
(Lucinda Russell) *led to 7th: cl up: effrt and rdn 4 out: nt fluent 2 out: kpt on same pce fr last* **13/2**^{3}
P3U- **4** *22* **Hawaii Klass**^{43} 4464 9-11-4 **114**..............................(b) CallumWhillans$^{(5)}$ 96
(Donald Whillans) *in tch: drvn and outpcd 1/2-way: plugged on fr 2 out: no ch w first three* **9/1**
03U- **5** *2 3/4* **Sergeant Pink (IRE)**^{17} 4953 8-11-11 **116**...................... LucyAlexander 97
(Dianne Sayer) *in tch: stdy hdwy 7th: rdn and outpcd 5 out: n.d after* **20/1**
F42- **6** *2 3/4* **Whats Up Woody (IRE)**^{37} 4578 9-11-12 **117**.................... BrianHughes 97
(John Wade) *prom: wnt 2nd 5 out: lost 2nd and hit 3 out: sn btn* **7/1**
011/ **P** **Five Rivers (IRE)**^{372} 5080 8-10-9 **110**......................(p) JamesCorbett$^{(10)}$
(Susan Corbett) *bhd and detached: clsd briefly after 7th: struggling fr next: t.o whn p.u bef 2 out* **40/1**

5m 14.5s (-12.90) **Going Correction** -0.75s/f (Firm) **7** Ran SP% **109.7**
Speed ratings: **95,94,92,84,82 81,**
CSF £5.80 TOTE £2.20: £1.30, £2.80; EX 6.30 Trifecta £19.20.
Owner D Carr & M Carlyle **Bred** Victor Stud Bloodstock Ltd **Trained** Farlam, Cumbria

FOCUS
A modest handicap. The winner was value for further and is probably capable of a bit better yet.

5219 APOLLOBET IN PLAY BETTING STANDARD OPEN NATIONAL HUNT FLAT RACE 2m 1f
5:25 (5:26) (Class 6) 4-6-Y-O **£1,559** (£457; £228; £114)

Form RPR
1 **Go Conquer (IRE)**^{100} 5-11-3 0.. APMcCoy 116+
(Donald McCain) *mde all at ordinary gallop: qcknd 2f out: rdn: edgd lft and r.o wl fnl f* **10/11**^{1}
2 *2 1/4* **Joffrey (IRE)** 5-10-10 0.. MissJRRichards$^{(7)}$ 113+
(Nicky Richards) *hld up: stdy hdwy on outside 1/2-way: effrt and chsd wnr 2f out: kpt on ins fnl f: improve* **20/1**
3 *8* **For Instance (IRE)** 4-10-11 0.. BrianHughes 100
(Tony Coyle) *chsd wnr to 2f out: sn rdn: outpcd by first two fnl f* **16/1**
22- **4** *2 1/2* **Bryden Boy (IRE)**^{37} 4582 4-10-4 0.................................... ConorRing$^{(7)}$ 98
(Jennie Candlish) *hld up: stdy hdwy and prom over 6f out: effrt and rdn over 2f out: outpcd over 1f out* **7/4**^{2}
5 *14* **Un Noble (FR)** 4-10-11 0.. BrianHarding 85
(Nicky Richards) *hld up: hdwy and prom over 5f out: rdn and wknd fr over 2f out* **12/1**^{3}
6 *7* **Jepeck (IRE)**^{310} 5-10-12 0.. AdamNicol$^{(5)}$ 85
(Karen Tutty) *in tch: rdn over 4f out: rallied: wknd over 2f out* **50/1**
7 *24* **Thedfactor (IRE)**^{310} 5-10-10 0.................................... AlistairFindlay$^{(7)}$ 64
(Jane Walton) *bhd: rdn and outpcd 6f out: n.d after* **80/1**
- **8** *12* **Dutch Canyon (IRE)** 4-10-11 0.. LucyAlexander 47
(N W Alexander) *t.k.h: in tch: drvn and struggling over 5f out: btn fnl 3f* **50/1**
9 *2 1/4* **Micky Fingers** 5-11-0 0.. KyleJames$^{(3)}$ 51
(Philip Kirby) *chsd ldrs: lost pl 6f out: sn struggling* **20/1**
- **10** *29* **Noble Bell** 4-10-11 0.. PeterBuchanan 19
(Lucinda Russell) *midfield: outpcd 1/2-way: no ch whn drifted to stands' side ent st* **33/1**

4m 15.5s (-8.70) **Going Correction** -0.65s/f (Firm)
WFA 4 from 5yo 5lb **10** Ran SP% **119.9**
Speed ratings: **94,92,89,88,81 78,66,61,60,46**
CSF £28.34 TOTE £2.30: £1.10, £4.80, £3.00; EX 32.60 Trifecta £217.80.
Owner Paul & Clare Rooney **Bred** Ben Furney **Trained** Cholmondeley, Cheshire

FOCUS
Probably not a bad bumper. The first two look above average and should win more races.
T/Plt: £414.90 to a £1 stake. Pool of £60454.85 - 106.35 winning tickets. T/Qpdt: £108.00 to a £1 stake. Pool of £4810.72 - 32.95 winning tickets. RY

5220 - 5226a (Foreign Racing) - See Raceform Interactive

4917 LUDLOW (R-H)
Thursday, April 10

OFFICIAL GOING: Good (7.0)
Wind: slight across Weather: cloudy

5227 LUDLOW RACING PARTNERSHIP NOVICES' HURDLE (9 hdls) 2m
2:30 (2:30) (Class 4) 4-Y-O+ **£4,223** (£1,240; £620; £310)

Form RPR
311- **1** **Saint Jerome (IRE)**^{22} 4904 4-11-6 **129**.......................... RobertThornton 131+
(Jamie Osborne) *mde all: clr fr 3rd: increased advantage appr 3 out: unchal* **8/13**^{1}
03- **2** *22* **Rascal (IRE)**^{28} 4776 5-10-13 0.. HarrySkelton 103
(Dan Skelton) *t.k.h early: in tch in chsng gp: wnt 2nd after 3 out: no ch w easy wnr* **10/3**^{2}
/FF- **3** *12* **Sparville (IRE)**^{313} 585 8-10-13 0........................... SamTwiston-Davies 90
(Kim Bailey) *sn prom in chsng gp: nt fluent 4th: rdn after 6th: kpt on one pce* **6/1**^{3}
45- **4** *1 1/2* **King's Opus (IRE)**^{18} 4980 5-10-13 0............................(t) AidanColeman 91
(Kim Bailey) *chsd clr ldr: rdn after 6th: mstke 3 out and lost 2nd: wkng whn hit last* **14/1**
5- **5** *4* **Capitol Gain (IRE)**^{29} 4758 5-10-13 0.......................... AndrewTinkler 85
(George Baker) *in tch: rdn after 6th: no ch in 5th whn mstke 3 out* **14/1**
FP0- **6** *10* **Billeragh Milan (IRE)**^{17} 5008 7-10-6 0.......................... JakeHodson$^{(7)}$ 76
(David Bridgwater) *prom in chsng gp tl wknd after 5th* **66/1**
7 *1* **Dancing Ecco (IRE)**^{266} 720 5-10-13 0.......................... AdamWedge 75
(Evan Williams) *in rr: hdwy after 5th: one pce and no ch fr 3 out* **40/1**
0P0- **8** *1 1/4* **Kilfinichen Bay (IRE)**^{41} 3598 6-10-13 0.......................... WillKennedy 74
(Violet M Jordan) *prom in chsng gp: wknd appr 3 out* **66/1**
64- **9** *7* **Major Parkes**^{162} 2154 4-10-7 0.......................... AdrianLane 62
(Donald McCain) *racd keenly: in rr: sme hdwy 6th: wknd appr 3 out* **28/1**
3- **10** *23* **Private Jones**^{191} 1539 5-10-13 0.......................... MichaelByrne 47
(Miss Imogen Pickard) *racd keenly: hld up towards rr: lost tch after 6th: t.o* **100/1**
/00- **P** **Sammy Blade**^{31} 4728 6-10-13 0.......................... DonalDevereux
(Alan Phillips) *a bhd: pushed along after 3rd: t.o fr 5th: p.u bef 3 out* **100/1**
00- **P** **Randall**^{27} 4796 6-10-8 0..........................(t) AnthonyFreeman$^{(5)}$
(Martin Bosley) *towards rr: struggling 4th: t.o fr next: p.u bef 3 out* **100/1**

3m 44.3s (-5.20) **Going Correction** -0.075s/f (Good) **12** Ran SP% **124.5**
Speed ratings (Par 105): **110,99,93,92,90 85,84,84,80,69 ,**
CSF £3.15 TOTE £1.70: £1.02, £1.70, £2.00; EX 3.10 Trifecta £9.10.
Owner Mrs F Walwyn **Bred** P Turley **Trained** Upper Lambourn, Berks

FOCUS
Hurdles track on outside in back straight and inside on home straight, fresh bends. The winner dominated at a solid pace and outclassed his opponents. He's closing in on his Flat form.

5228 ALFA AGGREGATES PRODUCTS NOVICES' LIMITED H'CAP CHASE (17 fncs) 2m 4f
3:00 (3:00) (Class 3) (0-120,125) 5-Y-O+ **£7,596** (£2,244; £1,122; £561; £280)

Form / RPR

3/0- **1** **Lamool (GER)**[181] 7-10-11 **114** .... MichaelByrne 127+
(Tim Vaughan) *hld up in rr: clsd 12th: pushed along after next: chal 3 out: led last: drvn out* **10/1**

501- **2** *1 ¼* **Speed Master (IRE)**[22] 4908 8-11-8 **125** ....(v) SamTwiston-Davies 136+
(Nigel Twiston-Davies) *cl up: w ldr fr 8th: pushed along after 13th: def advantage appr 4 out: jnd next: nt fluent and hdd last: kpt on u.p* **5/4**[1]

P00- **3** *10* **Tante Sissi (FR)**[26] 4804 7-11-3 **120** .... RobertThornton 122
(Alan King) *racd keenly: trckd ldrs: rdn 3 out: 3rd whn mstke 2 out: sn no ex* **8/1**

0/4- **4** *19* **Ballymacahillcross (IRE)**[22] 4898 6-10-4 **107** .... PaulMoloney 91
(Evan Williams) *tended to jump lft: led: jnd 8th: blnd 13th: hdd appr 4 out: sn wknd* **5/1**[2]

13P- **5** *6* **Tresor De Bontee (FR)**[40] 4560 7-11-3 **120** .... JamieMoore 99
(Richard Lee) *in tch: rdn after 13th: wknd 4 out* **7/1**

F25- **6** *2 ¾* **Shockingtimes (IRE)**[20] 4932 7-11-3 **120** .... MarkGrant 96
(Charlie Mann) *chsd ldrs: drvn 12th: wknd after next* **13/2**[3]

343- **7** *20* **Phase Shift**[32] 4698 6-11-1 **118** ....(t) DannyCook 76
(Brian Ellison) *in tch in rr: mstke 2nd: wknd appr 4 out: t.o* **12/1**

5m 0.3s (-4.10) **Going Correction** -0.025s/f (Good) **7** Ran SP% **114.8**
Speed ratings: **107,106,102,94,92 91,83**
CSF £24.50 TOTE £12.00: £5.10, £1.10; EX 46.70 Trifecta £189.20.
Owner J H Frost **Bred** Frau M U W Lohmann **Trained** Aberthin, Vale of Glamorgan

FOCUS
The pace was modest, but the first two set a decent standard and should win more races. The third is closing in on her hurdles mark.

5229 ROBERT HOLDEN LTD MARES' NOVICES' HURDLE (11 hdls) 2m 5f
3:30 (3:30) (Class 4) 4-Y-0+ **£4,223** (£1,240; £620; £310)

Form / RPR

13P- **1** **Magic Money**[133] 2764 6-11-5 106 .... SamTwiston-Davies 113+
(Kim Bailey) *mde virtually all: pushed along 2 out: comf* **10/3**[3]

/4P- **2** *3 ½* **Pandy**[113] 3159 5-10-12 0 ....(tp) AndrewTinkler 103+
(George Baker) *trckd ldrs: hit 3 out: sn chsng wnr: kpt on u.p flat but a being hld* **16/1**

402- **3** *28* **Maypole Lass**[21] 4917 4-10-5 105 ....(tp) JamieMoore 72
(Renee Robeson) *chsd ldrs: nt fluent 8th: sn rdn: wknd 2 out* **11/4**[2]

121- **4** *1 ¾* **Rosa Fleet (IRE)**[28] 4777 6-11-12 120 .... AidanColeman 91
(Venetia Williams) *racd keenly: nt a fluent: cl up fr 2nd: rdn appr 3 out where mstke and lost 2nd: sn wknd* **6/4**[1]

600- **5** *35* **Do Be Dashing**[12] 5071 6-10-12 0 .... RichieMcLernon 44
(Graeme McPherson) *chsd ldrs tl rdn and wknd after 8th: t.o* **100/1**

55- **6** *7* **Harriet's Ark**[325] 412 7-10-12 0 .... MarkGrant 37
(Julian Smith) *in rr: nt fluent 5th: lost tch 8th: t.o* **25/1**

006- **7** *48* **Glacial Roes (IRE)**[21] 4917 6-10-12 0 .... WillKennedy
(Sarah-Jayne Davies) *in tch tl lost pl after 5th: bhd fr next: t.o* **100/1**

0- **8** *6* **Cloudy Smith**[47] 4411 5-10-12 0 .... DonalDevereux
(Brian Eckley) *in rr: pushed along 6th: lost tch next: t.o* **66/1**

10- **U** **Dog Or Divorce**[24] 4867 5-10-12 0 .... DenisO'Regan
(Paul Webber) *midfield whn j.lft and uns rdr 1st* **8/1**

5m 9.5s (-5.30) **Going Correction** -0.075s/f (Good)
WFA 4 from 5yo+ 6lb **9** Ran SP% **114.1**
Speed ratings (Par 105): **107,105,95,94,81 78,60,57,**
CSF £46.93 TOTE £5.70: £1.70, £3.50, £1.10; EX 32.60 Trifecta £243.70.
Owner David Jenks **Bred** Hartshill Stud **Trained** Andoversford, Gloucs

FOCUS
There wasn't much experience among the runners, and the pace was just a medium one, but the first two are going the right way. The form could be rated higher using the third and fourth, but both were below par.

5230 BROMFIELD SAND & GRAVEL H'CAP CHASE (FOR THE OAKLY PARK CHALLENGE CUP) (16 fncs 1 omitted) 2m 4f
4:00 (4:00) (Class 3) (0-135,129) 5-Y-O+ **£9,495** (£2,805; £1,402; £702; £351)

Form / RPR

3/2- **1** **Stonethrower (IRE)**[28] 4782 9-10-9 **122** ....(t) AlanJohns[(10)] 135+
(Tim Vaughan) *led to 2nd: styd prom: mstke 11th: led again after 13th: hit 2 out: j.rt last: drvn out* **16/1**

41U- **2** *3 ¼* **Divine Intavention (IRE)**[27] 4788 10-11-0 **122** .... MrMWall[(5)] 134+
(Martin Keighley) *prom: trckd ldr fr 4th tl lft in ld 8th: mstke and rdr lost whip 11th: hdd after 13th: wnt 2nd again 2 out: kpt on flat* **7/4**[1]

104- **3** *5* **Highway Code (USA)**[21] 4921 8-11-11 **128** ....(t) JamieMoore 133
(Richard Lee) *towards rr: hmpd 3rd: rdn along 8th: hdwy 11th: chsd wnr 4 out to 2 out: no ex* **8/1**

200- **4** *16* **Flaming Gorge (IRE)**[33] 4685 9-11-3 **127** .... MikeyEnnis[(7)] 117
(Fleur Hawes) *in rr: hmpd 3rd: pushed along 9th: tk mod 4th 4 out: nvr nr ldrs* **25/1**

640- **5** *17* **Tara Rose**[19] 4960 9-11-4 **121** ....(vt[1]) SamTwiston-Davies 98
(Nigel Twiston-Davies) *cl up: led 2nd: blnd 7th: hmpd by loose horse and hdd next: wknd after 13th: t.o* **6/1**[2]

PF- **6** *12* **Gardefort (FR)**[30] 4742 5-11-12 **129** .... AidanColeman 100
(Venetia Williams) *in tch: hdwy to chse ldrs 9th: rdn appr 4 out: wknd 3 out: t.o* **15/2**

261- **U** **Great Value (IRE)**[24] 4862 9-11-10 **127** ....(t) RichieMcLernon
(Graeme McPherson) *chsd ldrs tl blnd bdly and uns rdr 3rd* **12/1**

P/0- **F** **Traditional Bob (IRE)**[26] 4805 9-10-12 **115** .... AdamWedge
(Evan Williams) *hld up towards rr: hdwy after 12th: disputing 3 l 3rd and keeping on whn fell 4 out* **8/1**

4/4- **P** **Cayman Islands**[56] 4235 6-11-6 **123** .... DenisO'Regan
(John Ferguson) *trckd ldrs tl lost pl 10th: styd in tch tl wknd 4 out: t.o whn p.u bef 2 out* **7/1**[3]

5m 1.2s (-3.20) **Going Correction** -0.025s/f (Good) **9** Ran SP% **114.6**
Speed ratings: **105,103,101,95,88 83, , ,**
CSF £46.18 CT £251.76 TOTE £16.90: £2.90, £1.10, £2.40; EX 49.10 Trifecta £958.40.
Owner M & S Clarke **Bred** J Harding **Trained** Aberthin, Vale of Glamorgan

FOCUS
The third fence in the back straight was bypassed on the second circuit. Horses who had run in hunter chase company last time filled the first two places in a race run at an average tempo. The winner is rated back to the level of his novice form.

5231 EFG HARRIS ALLDAY STOCKBROKERS H'CAP HURDLE (9 hdls) 2m
4:30 (4:30) (Class 3) (0-125,125) 4-Y-O+ **£9,495** (£2,805; £1,402; £702; £351)

Form / RPR

503- **1** **Castlemorris King**[18] 4991 6-11-7 **120** .... DaveCrosse 126+
(Brian Barr) *mid-div: hdwy 6th: chal 3 out: led 2 out: sn jnd: nt fluent last: drvn out to hold narrow advantage* **33/1**

552- **2** *hd* **Springinherstep (IRE)**[21] 4920 7-11-4 **117** .... AndrewTinkler 122
(Nicky Henderson) *trckd keenly: trckd ldrs: rdn to chal 2 out: ev ch last: kpt on flat: jst hld* **10/1**

/51- **3** *3 ¾* **Fujin Dancer (FR)**[27] 4794 9-11-2 **122** .... MissHBethell[(7)] 124
(Brian Ellison) *hld up in rr: stdy hdwy appr 3 out: wnt 3rd last: rdn and no further imp* **12/1**

313- **4** *3 ¾* **Red Seventy**[12] 5067 5-11-4 **124** ....(p) MikeyEnnis[(7)] 124
(David Pipe) *cl up: led 5th: jnd 3 out: hdd and n.m.r next: sn one pce* **9/1**[3]

220- **5** *7* **Somemothersdohavem**[33] 4682 5-11-10 **123** .... AidanColeman 115
(Venetia Williams) *chsd ldrs tl lost pl 5th: rallied u.p 3 out: kpt on one pce* **10/3**[1]

146- **6** *1 ¾* **Zafranagar (IRE)**[12] 4278 9-10-6 **110** ....(p) RobertMcCarth[(5)] 101
(Ian Williams) *chsd ldrs: rdn 3 out: sn one pce* **10/3**[1]

003- **7** *4 ½* **Ever Fortune (USA)**[27] 4796 5-10-6 **105** .... JamieMoore 91
(Brian Ellison) *hld up in rr: hdwy after 6th: rdn appr 3 out: sn one pce* **14/1**

300- **8** *1* **Toubab (FR)**[31] 4726 8-11-9 **122** .... HarrySkelton 107
(Dan Skelton) *chsd ldrs: rdn appr 3 out: wknd 2 out* **10/1**

/40- **9** *7* **Tiger O'Toole (IRE)**[47] 4413 9-11-2 **115** .... PaulMoloney 94
(Evan Williams) *a in rr: lost tch after 6th* **25/1**

001- **10** *8* **Chat Room**[19] 4947 6-11-12 **125** .... DenisO'Regan 97
(John Ferguson) *led to 5th: styd cl up tl rdn and wknd 3 out* **4/1**[2]

6- **11** *17* **Moveable Asset (IRE)**[22] 4897 6-11-5 **125** ....(p) MrFTett[(7)] 82
(Roger Curtis) *in tch tl rdn and wknd appr 3 out: no ch whn blnd 2 out: t.o* **50/1**

3m 45.4s (-4.10) **Going Correction** -0.075s/f (Good) **11** Ran SP% **117.4**
Speed ratings (Par 107): **107,106,105,103,99 98,96,96,92,88 80**
CSF £325.74 CT £4167.96 TOTE £17.80: £4.70, £3.80, £3.70; EX 174.30 Trifecta £773.20.
Owner Miss Daisy Hitchins **Bred** Peter Storey **Trained** Longburton, Dorset

FOCUS
This competitive event was run at a medium pace. A snmall step up from the winner with the second back to form in a hood.

5232 ABBERLEY HALL OLD PUPILS ASSOCIATION OPEN HUNTERS' CHASE (19 fncs) 3m
5:00 (5:00) (Class 5) 5-Y-0+ **£2,495** (£774; £386; £193)

Form / RPR

121- **1** **Rockiteer (IRE)**[21] 4922 11-11-13 127 ....(p) MissJCWilliams[(5)] 140+
(Henry Daly) *led 2nd to 12th: led 15th: pushed along fr 2 out: comf* **9/4**[1]

P2P- **2** *5* **Foundry Square (IRE)**[27] 4788 8-11-9 114 ....(p) MrMatthewBarber[(5)] 130
(S Flook) *racd mainly in 4th: clsd 11th: chsd wnr after 15th: rdn 4 out: one pce fr 2 out* **7/1**

61U- **3** *10* **Pentiffic (NZ)**[7] 5135 11-12-1 118 ....(p) MrJHamilton[(3)] 126
(Venetia Williams) *led to 2nd: styd cl up: led 12th to 15th: wknd 4 out: plugged on to take 3rd flat* **4/1**

063- **4** *7* **Buck Mulligan**[11] 5094 9-11-10 127 .... MrJETudor 111
(Evan Williams) *hld up in last but in tch: wnt 3rd 4 out: sn no imp on ldrs: lost 3rd flat* **7/2**[3]

600- **5** *2* **First Fandango**[28] 4765 7-11-5 0 ....(vt) MrBGibbs[(5)] 112
(Tim Vaughan) *trckd ldrs: mstke 9th: rdn appr 4 out: wkng whn mstke 3 out* **3/1**[2]

53P- **U** **Captain Marlon (IRE)**[8] 5131 13-11-3 85 .... MrJBargary[(7)]
(Mrs Claire Hitch) *towards rr tl blnd and uns rdr 4th* **66/1**

6m 3.5s (-4.80) **Going Correction** -0.025s/f (Good) **6** Ran SP% **112.0**
Speed ratings: **107,105,102,99,99**
CSF £17.51 TOTE £2.30: £2.10, £4.20; EX 15.00 Trifecta £42.60.
Owner Michael O'Flynn & John Nesbitt **Bred** R C A Latta **Trained** Stanton Lacy, Shropshire

FOCUS
They went an undemanding gallop, which wouldn't have suited some of the runners, but the winner responded generously when asked. He's rated to his best.

5233 LUDLOW FOOD CENTRE H'CAP HURDLE (11 hdls) 2m 5f
5:30 (5:30) (Class 4) (0-120,117) 4-Y-0+ **£4,548** (£1,335; £667; £333)

Form / RPR

004- **1** **Hold Court (IRE)**[50] 4353 7-11-10 **115** .... PaulMoloney 125+
(Evan Williams) *trckd ldrs: wnt 2nd appr 3 out: led after 2 out: j.rt and mstke last: all out* **3/1**[1]

0/1- **2** *nk* **Speedy Tunes (IRE)**[29] 4758 7-11-9 **114** .... AndrewTinkler 123+
(Nicky Henderson) *prom: chsd ldr 6th: led appr 3 out: mstke 2 out: sn hdd: carried rt after last: ev ch flat: jst hld* **5/1**[2]

PPP- **3** *25* **Castle Conflict (IRE)**[31] 4725 9-11-10 **115** ....(p) RobertThornton 100
(Henry Daly) *chsd ldrs: mstke 8th: sn drvn: no ch fr 3 out: tk mod 3rd flat* **20/1**

154- **4** *1* **Mini Muck**[42] 4508 8-11-9 **114** .... SamTwiston-Davies 98
(Nigel Twiston-Davies) *chsd ldr tl steadily lost pl after 6th: no ch fr 3 out: plugged on to take mod 4th flat* **7/1**[3]

264- **5** *2 ¾* **Scales (IRE)**[19] 4969 8-11-5 **110** .... JamieMoore 92
(Richard Lee) *t.k.h: hld up: hdwy to chse ldrs 6th: rdn and wknd 3 out: lost mod 3rd flat* **12/1**

416- **6** *shd* **Ghost Of A Smile (IRE)**[29] 4760 6-10-12 **108** .... RobertMcCarth[(5)] 93
(Ian Williams) *hld up in rr: clsd 3rd: rdn after 8th: wkng whn blnd 3 out* **3/1**[1]

62F- **7** *6* **Dungeness**[32] 4703 6-11-0 **105** .... AidanColeman 81
(Venetia Williams) *led tl rdn and wknd appr 3 out* **8/1**

332- **8** *43* **Helium (FR)**[28] 4781 9-11-5 **117** .... MrsAlexDunn[(7)] 55
(Alexandra Dunn) *in tch tl wknd after 8th: t.o* **20/1**

P53- **P** **Easydoesit (IRE)**[20] 4937 6-10-6 **104** .... CharlieDeutsch[(7)]
(Tony Carroll) *j. slowly at times: in rr: lost tch 7th: t.o whn p.u bef 3 out* **9/1**

5m 9.6s (-5.20) **Going Correction** -0.075s/f (Good) **9** Ran SP% **117.5**
Speed ratings (Par 105): **106,105,96,95,94 94,92,76,**
CSF £19.19 CT £247.06 TOTE £4.30: £1.30, £2.20, £6.80; EX 18.20 Trifecta £444.50.
Owner Edwards & Howell **Bred** Jim Ruane **Trained** Llancarfan, Vale Of Glamorgan

The Form Book Jumps, Raceform Ltd, Compton, RG20 6NL.

FOCUS
There were some horses with fair form and potential in the line-up, but the pace was ordinary and the first two sprinted away from the others off the final bend. The winner, who survived a stewards' enquiry, is rated back in line with last season's form.
T/Plt: £69.40 to a £1 stake. Pool of £56508.64 - 594.17 winning tickets. T/Qpdt: £24.10 to a £1 stake. Pool of £3727.0 - 114.10 winning tickets. RL

5139 TAUNTON (R-H)

Thursday, April 10

OFFICIAL GOING: Good (good to soft in places; 6.1)
Wind: mild breeze Weather: cloudy with sunny periods

5234 TOTEJACKPOT GO FOR THE BIG ONE CONDITIONAL JOCKEYS' TRAINING SERIES H'CAP HURDLE (12 hdls) 3m 110y
2:20 (2:21) (Class 5) (0-100,103) 4-Y-0+ **£2,737** (£798; £399)

Form RPR
PP- **1** **Milans Well (IRE)**[25] 4840 8-11-7 **100**.......................(p) PaulO'Brien(5) 107+
(Brendan Powell) *a.p: hit 3 out: sn led: styd on wl fr last: rdn out* **28/1**
331- **2** 1 3/4 **The Happy Warrior**[7] 5143 6-11-10 **103** 7ex.................. GaryDerwin(5) 108
(Bob Buckler) *slowly away: trckd ldrs after 2nd: rdn along fr 7th: kpt chsng ldrs: styd on to go 2nd run-in: a being hld by wnr* **9/4**[1]
055- **3** 1 3/4 **Hand On Bach (IRE)**[24] 4865 6-10-12 **94**.......(bt) WilliamFeatherstone(8) 97
(Warren Greatrex) *mid-div: smooth hdwy 3 out: wnt 2nd 2 out: sn rdn: nt gng pce to chal: no ex whn lost 2nd run-in* **12/1**
233- **4** 3/4 **Torran Sound**[45] 4471 7-11-5 **96**.......................(p) CharlieDeutsch(3) 98
(Lawney Hill) *mid-div: rdn and stdy prog after 3 out: styd on into 4th run-in wout ever threatening* **6/1**[2]
PF0- **5** 1 **Brians Well (IRE)**[10] 5111 7-11-7 **95**.......................(t[1]) PatrickCorbett 96
(Brendan Powell) *mid-div: rdn after 3 out: styd on after next: nvr trbld ldrs* **33/1**
P62- **6** 1 3/4 **Tara Tavey (IRE)**[17] 5007 9-10-12 **94**.............................. JonPark(8) 95
(Kevin Bishop) *mid-div: nt fluent 3rd: lost pl and rdn after 7th: styd on fr 2 out but nvr any danger* **12/1**
004- **7** 2 1/2 **Nash Point (IRE)**[31] 4729 5-10-2 **84**.............................(tp) JPKiely(8) 81
(Tim Vaughan) *nvr travelling in rr: reminders after 5th: sme late prog: nvr any threat* **12/1**
436- **8** 5 **Milor De La Borie (FR)**[5] 5177 5-10-12 **92**.............(b[1]) TomBellamy(6) 85
(David Pipe) *racd keenly most of way tl jst after 3 out: towards rr: hdwy 3 out: rdn bef next: sn one pce* **9/1**
6P6- **9** nk **High Aspirations (IRE)**[17] 5007 6-10-10 **87**.................... JoshWall(3) 80
(Michael Blake) *sme late prog u.p: mainly towards rr* **6/1**[2]
045- **10** 10 **Calusa Star**[17] 5007 5-10-8 **90**.......................(b) ThomasCheesman(8) 76
(Philip Hobbs) *mid-div: hdwy whn short of room on bnd after 7th: rdn after 3 out: wknd 2 out* **8/1**[3]
/30- **11** 8 **Converti**[26] 4803 10-9-9 **74** oh5.................................. MartinMcIntyre(5) 50
(Carroll Gray) *a towards rr* **40/1**
060- **12** 2 1/2 **Keep The Cash (IRE)**[17] 5007 6-11-0 **93**...................(bt) PaulJohn(5) 74
(David Pipe) *led: rdn and hdd after 3 out: wknd next* **18/1**
UP6- **13** 21 **Mysula**[26] 4823 7-9-8 **74** oh5.......................................(t) GeraldQuinn(6) 29
(Claire Dyson) *trckd ldrs tl wknd after 8th: t.o* **150/1**
/04- **14** 20 **Pearl (IRE)**[133] 2760 10-10-4 **81**.................................. JackSherwood(3) 18
(Ron Hodges) *mid-div tl wknd 3 out: t.o* **25/1**
5P4- **P** **Amber Flush**[33] 4676 5-10-5 **84**...................................(p) OllieGarner(5)
(Tom Symonds) *trckd ldrs tl 7th: wknd after next: in rr whn p.u bef 9th* **66/1**

5m 51.4s (-12.60) **Going Correction** -0.55s/f (Firm) **15** Ran SP% **123.6**
Speed ratings (Par 103): **98,97,96,96,96 95,94,93,93,90 87,86,79,73,**
CSF £92.08 CT £858.37 TOTE £29.80: £6.60, £1.60, £8.70; EX 157.10 Trifecta £1184.70 Part won..
Owner Tony Head **Bred** Hugh Fitzpatrick **Trained** Upper Lambourn, Berks

FOCUS
Bends moved out 2-3 metres, Hurdles moved out two sections. They went a fair pace in this staying handicap hurdle and it was dominated by those at the top of the weights. The third to sixth set the level.

5235 INJURED JOCKEYS FUND 50TH ANNIVERSARY MAIDEN HURDLE (DIV I) (10 hdls) 2m 3f 110y
2:50 (2:53) (Class 5) 4-Y-0+ **£2,737** (£798; £399)

Form RPR
0/0- **1** **Liberty Court (IRE)**[124] 2949 7-11-0 120.....................(t) RichardJohnson 107+
(Tim Vaughan) *trckd ldrs: led 2 out: sn pushed clr: eased towards fin* **5/4**[1]
026- **2** 8 **Badger Wood**[116] 3115 5-11-0 110.................................. DavidEngland 96
(Giles Smyly) *trckd ldr tl rdn appr 2 out: styd on fr last: snatched 2nd fnl stride* **16/1**
/30- **3** hd **Accordingtojodie (IRE)**[76] 3877 8-11-0 0.......................... FelixDeGiles 97
(Tom Symonds) *led: rdn whn hit and hdd after 2 out: sn hld by wnr: kpt on but no ex whn lost 2nd fnl strides* **33/1**
530- **4** shd **La Madonnina (IRE)**[23] 4887 6-10-7 81.............................. IanPopham 89
(Caroline Keevil) *chsd ldrs: rdn after 3 out: styd on fr last: nrly snatched 3rd fnl stride* **100/1**
4/0- **5** 4 1/2 **Sea Wall (FR)**[156] 2279 6-11-0 0...................................... NickScholfield 91
(Paul Nicholls) *racd keenly in tch: effrt after 3 out: nt gng pce to chal: no ex fnl 120yds* **11/2**[2]
40U- **6** nk **Mr Shantu (IRE)**[9] 5117 5-11-0 0... APMcCoy 91
(Jonjo O'Neill) *mid-div on outer: rdn after 3 out: chsng ldrs in hld 6th whn nt fluent 2 out: styd on same pce* **12/1**
363- **7** 4 1/2 **Mrs Jordan (IRE)**[16] 5016 6-10-7 107.............................. LiamTreadwell 80
(Venetia Williams) *trckd ldr tl 7th: sn rdn and lost pl: nt a threat after* **13/2**[3]
0F3- **8** 2 **Somerset Lias (IRE)**[54] 4281 6-11-0 111.............................. SamJones 85
(Bob Buckler) *mid-div: rdn after 6th: outpcd after 3 out: nvr threatened* **15/2**
2- **9** 3/4 **Knave Of Clubs (IRE)**[18] 4987 5-10-11 0.......................... MattGriffiths(3) 84
(Jeremy Scott) *towards rr: pushed along after 5th: nvr any danger* **14/1**
200- **10** 20 **Obistar (FR)**[17] 5003 4-10-7 0.. ConorO'Farrell 57
(David Pipe) *reminders after 3rd: a towards rr: t.o bef 2 out* **28/1**
0P0- **11** 7 **Strategic Exit**[7] 5140 6-11-0 0... TomO'Brien 57
(James Frost) *mid-div: rdn after 6th: wknd 3 out: t.o* **150/1**
PFP- **12** 11 **Party Girls (FR)**[37] 4600 6-10-0 0...........................(t) MrMHeard(7) 39
(David Pipe) *hld up and a in rr* **80/1**

4m 35.2s (-10.80) **Going Correction** -0.55s/f (Firm)
WFA 4 from 5yo+ 5lb **12** Ran SP% **114.4**
Speed ratings (Par 103): **99,95,95,95,93 93,91,91,90,82 80,75**
CSF £22.50 TOTE £2.20: £1.50, £4.70, £8.40; EX 24.80 Trifecta £287.60.
Owner Passant & Butt **Bred** Alistair Thompson **Trained** Aberthin, Vale of Glamorgan

FOCUS
This maiden hurdle went very much the way the market predicted. The form could be rated up to 10lb higher through the first two.

5236 INJURED JOCKEYS FUND 50TH ANNIVERSARY MAIDEN HURDLE (DIV II) (10 hdls) 2m 3f 110y
3:20 (3:20) (Class 5) 4-Y-0+ **£2,737** (£798; £399)

Form RPR
540- **1** **Max Ward (IRE)**[20] 4931 5-11-0 0................................ LiamTreadwell 115+
(Charlie Brooks) *trckd ldrs: led 7th: styd on strly to draw wl clr after 2 out: comf* **9/1**
3- **2** 20 **Willow Island (IRE)**[19] 4971 5-11-0 0.............................. SeanQuinlan 98
(David Evans) *trckd ldrs: rdn after 3 out: styd on to go 2nd nring fin: no ch w wnr* **66/1**
5- **3** nk **Solar Sky**[26] 4807 6-11-0 0.. DavidBass 98
(David Elsworth) *trckd ldrs: rdn to dispute 2nd after 3 out: lft clr 2nd next: sn hld by wnr: no ex whn lost 2nd nring fin: b.b.v* **2/1**[2]
50- **4** 4 **Saint John Henry (FR)**[22] 4904 4-10-0 0........................ MrMHeard(7) 86
(David Pipe) *hld up towards rr: sme prog whn rdn after 7th: styd on fr last but nvr any danger* **33/1**
0F5- **5** 1 1/4 **Ernest Speak (IRE)**[7] 5140 5-11-0 0................................ BrendanPowell 95
(Martin Hill) *hld up wl in tch: hdwy after 6th: travelling wl upsides wnr whn bad mstke 3 out: nt rcvr and sn hld: lft 4th next* **33/1**
3/5- **6** 3 1/2 **Morito Du Berlais (FR)**[124] 2940 5-11-0 0.....................(t) NickScholfield 89
(Paul Nicholls) *sn prom: rdn after 3 out: sn btn* **4/1**[3]
060- **7** 15 **Absolutely Bygones (IRE)**[18] 4993 6-10-11 0..............(t) JamesBest(3) 75
(Jackie Du Plessis) *disp ld tl rdn after 6th: wknd after next: t.o* **18/1**
006- **8** 16 **Mrs Winchester (IRE)**[41] 4540 5-10-0 0.......................... MrLDrowne(7) 54
(Caroline Keevil) *hld up in last pair: rdn after 6th: sn lost tch: t.o* **150/1**
400- **9** 15 **Ilewindelilah**[12] 5064 6-10-7 0.. JamesDavies 40
(Gary Brown) *trckd ldrs on outer: rdn after 6th: sn wknd: t.o* **100/1**
0- **P** **Run Rabbit Run**[29] 4758 6-11-0 0.. TomO'Brien
(Tim McCarthy) *plld v hrd: trckd ldrs tl dropped away tamely bef 6th: t.o whn p.u after 3 out: b.b.v* **50/1**
253- **U** **Great Choice (IRE)**[42] 4514 5-11-0 0.........................(t) ConorO'Farrell 98
(David Pipe) *disp ld tl 7th: rdn to dispute 2nd after 3 out: stmbld bdly and uns rdr next* **15/8**[1]

4m 36.9s (-9.10) **Going Correction** -0.55s/f (Firm)
WFA 4 from 5yo+ 5lb **11** Ran SP% **114.4**
Speed ratings (Par 103): **96,88,87,86,85 84,78,71,65,**
CSF £420.74 TOTE £11.50: £2.50, £4.80, £1.10; EX 256.30 Trifecta £850.70.
Owner Mrs H M Haddock **Bred** J And J Lawler **Trained** Sarsden, Oxon

FOCUS
They went a moderate early pace in this leg and the winning time was 1.7sec slower than division one. A step up from the easy winner.

5237 DOWNLOAD TOTEPOOL LIVE INFO APP NOVICES' H'CAP CHASE (12 fncs) 2m 110y
3:50 (3:50) (Class 4) (0-110,108) 5-Y-0+ **£4,548** (£1,335; £667; £333)

Form RPR
54P- **1** **Itsuptoyou (IRE)**[26] 4822 10-11-7 **103**.......................(t) NickScholfield 117+
(Arthur Whiting) *travelled wl thrght: in tch: hdwy after 4 out: chal after 3 out: led bef last: qcknd clr: readily* **22/1**
433- **2** 4 **Blackwater King (IRE)**[21] 4919 6-11-12 **108**........................ NoelFehily 112
(Donald McCain) *trckd ldr: hit 6th: rdn to take narrow advantage after 3 out: hdd sn after 2 out: nt gng pce of wnr* **11/4**[1]
0PU- **3** 5 **No No Cardinal (IRE)**[18] 4989 5-10-0 **82** oh7..............(t) TommyPhelan 82
(Mark Gillard) *hld up: hdwy into cl 5th after 4 out: rdn bef next: styd on same pce: wnt 3rd at the last* **66/1**
0/1- **4** 7 **General Ross (IRE)**[18] 4989 7-10-12 **94**........................ BrendanPowell 89
(Colin Tizzard) *trckd ldrs: rdn after 6th: led bef 3 out: hdd bef 2 out: sn outpcd: fdd last* **5/1**[2]
130- **5** 3 1/4 **Powertakeoff (IRE)**[12] 5072 6-10-2 **84**.......................... LiamTreadwell 74
(Henry Oliver) *hld up: rdn in cl 6th after 4 out: one pce fr next* **14/1**
430- **6** 21 **Railway Vic (IRE)**[51] 4334 7-10-0 **82**............................ ConorO'Farrell 53
(James Frost) *nt fluent and wl bhd 5th: nvr any threat* **11/2**[3]
30/- **7** 1/2 **Ilewin For Hannah**[477] 3143 7-10-7 **89**............................ JamesDavies 60
(Gary Brown) *mid-div: hit 5th: lost pl sn after: t.o fr after 7th* **40/1**
044- **8** 7 **Tresor De La Vie (FR)**[17] 5004 7-10-12 **94**....................(tp) JackDoyle 59
(Victor Dartnall) *led: rdn and hdd bef 3 out: wknd qckly: t.o* **7/1**
633- **U** **Spoil Me (IRE)**[16] 4985 7-11-8 **104**...................................... APMcCoy
(Jonjo O'Neill) *trckd ldr: wnt lft 1st: wnt lft on landing after rching for 7th and uns rdr* **11/4**[1]

4m 8.3s (-5.70) **Going Correction** -0.55s/f (Firm) **9** Ran SP% **112.8**
Speed ratings: **91,89,86,83,81 72,71,68,**
CSF £82.40 CT £3964.69 TOTE £13.20: £4.10, £1.40, £8.20; EX 64.40 Trifecta £1602.50.
Owner A J Whiting **Bred** John P Kiely **Trained** North Nibley, Gloucs

FOCUS
An ordinary novices' handicap chase and questionable form with a few near the head of the market not performing. The easy winner should win again.

5238 TOTETRIFECTA AVAILABLE ON ALL RACES NOVICES' H'CAP HURDLE (8 hdls 1 omitted) 2m 1f
4:20 (4:20) (Class 4) (0-110,108) 4-Y-0+ **£3,764** (£1,097; £548)

Form RPR
015- **1** **Polstar (FR)**[20] 4943 5-11-9 **105**.. APMcCoy 113+
(Harry Whittington) *led tl 4th: led next: rdn and hdd after 2 out (usual 3 out): led by-passing omitted 2 out: kpt on wl fr last: rdn out* **7/4**[1]
002- **2** 2 1/2 **Frozen Over**[17] 5005 6-11-4 **100**.................................(t[1]) JamesDavies 104
(Chris Down) *trckd ldrs: rdn to chal after 2 out (usual 3 out): ev ch last: kpt on but no ex: jst hld on for 2nd* **4/1**[2]
002- **3** nk **Mr Fickle (IRE)**[32] 4703 5-11-5 **108**.........................(v) JosephAkehurst(7) 111+
(Gary Moore) *cl up tl rdn along fr 5th: kpt on into 4th at the last: styd on wl fnl 120yds: nrly snatched 2nd fnl strides* **11/2**[3]
056- **4** 3 1/4 **Poetic Power (IRE)**[26] 4818 5-9-12 **87**............................ GeraldQuinn(7) 88
(Claire Dyson) *hld up: hdwy after 4th: led 2 out (usual 3 out): rdn and hdd by-passing omitted 2 out: one pce after* **12/1**
P12- **5** 3 1/4 **Join The Navy**[42] 4519 9-11-8 **104**................................ LiamTreadwell 102
(Kate Buckett) *hld up: rdn after 6th: styd on but nvr gng pce to get involved* **7/1**
0P2- **6** 6 **Echoes Of Joy**[19] 4967 5-10-6 **88**...................................... SeanQuinlan 81
(David Evans) *racd keenly: trckd ldrs: rdn after 2 out (usual 3 out): nt gng pce to chal: fdd fr last* **14/1**
004- **7** 2 1/2 **Iguacu**[127] 2886 10-10-13 **95**.. NickScholfield 85
(Richard Price) *in last pair but in tch: struggling to hold pl after 6th: nvr any threat to ldrs* **33/1**

400- **8** *19* **Maxi Mac (IRE)**[31] 4722 4-10-13 **108** JoshWall(7) 75
(Trevor Wall) *racd keenly: trckd ldr: nt fluent 3rd: led next tl 5th: rdn and wknd 2 out (usual 3 out) t.o* **66/1**

/03- **F** **Waving**[34] 2085 5-11-8 **104** (t) RichardJohnson
(Tony Carroll) *hld up in tch: fell 3rd: fatally injured* **7/1**

4m 0.7s (-7.30) **Going Correction** -0.55s/f (Firm)
WFA 4 from 5yo+ 5lb **9** Ran SP% **115.5**
Speed ratings (Par 105): **95,93,93,92,90 87,86,77,**
CSF £9.59 CT £31.37 TOTE £2.20: £1.10, £2.30, £2.40; EX 12.50 Trifecta £56.30.
Owner Dixon,Ellis,Lynds,Travers,Watkins **Bred** Comte Jean-Jacques De La Rochette **Trained** Sparsholt, Oxfordshire

FOCUS
An ordinary novices' handicap and they went no pace early, causing a few to take a grip. The race was marred by the terrible fall of Waving at the third, causing that flight (would have been the second-last) to be omitted on the final circuit.

5239 TOTEEXACTA PICK 1ST AND 2ND H'CAP HURDLE (9 hdls) 2m 1f
4:50 (4:50) (Class 3) (0-135,131) 4-Y-0+ **£6,173** (£1,812; £906; £453)

Form RPR

141- **1** **Hint Of Mint**[17] 5003 5-11-9 **128** RichardJohnson 133+
(Nick Williams) *prom: rdn to chse ldr after 3 out: led bef next: kpt on wl: drvn out* **5/1**[2]

142- **2** *½* **Purple Bay (IRE)**[117] 3088 5-11-9 **131**[1] JackQuinlan(3) 137+
(John Ferguson) *in tch: lost pl 5th: mstke 6th: rdn and hdwy on outer after 3 out: mounting chal whn nt fluent 2 out: kpt on fr last but a looking jst hld* **7/4**[1]

221- **3** *3¾* **Lac Sacre (FR)**[14] 5040 5-11-6 **125** (bt) TomO'Brien 125
(John Flint) *hld up: hdwy after 6th: rdn in 3rd after 3 out: kpt on same pce fr next* **8/1**

222- **4** *3½* **Ourmanmassini (IRE)**[26] 4799 6-10-6 **114** (t) MichealNolan(3) 111
(Suzy Smith) *trckd ldrs: rdn after 3 out: styd on same pce fr next* **6/1**[3]

036- **5** *4* **Moujik Borget (FR)**[35] 4634 6-11-4 **123** (b) LiamTreadwell 116
(Venetia Williams) *trckd ldrs: rdn after 3 out: kpt on but nt gng pce to get on terms* **16/1**

200- **6** *7* **Della Sun (FR)**[144] 2529 8-10-8 **120** JoshWall(7) 107
(Arthur Whitehead) *hld up: pushed along after 4th: nvr gng pce to get involved* **20/1**

555- **7** *1¼* **Brinestine (USA)**[53] 4301 5-11-4 **123** NickScholfield 113+
(Paul Nicholls) *trckd ldrs: dived for 6th and hmpd sn after where rdr lost reins briefly: nt rcvr and hld after* **13/2**

/0B- **8** *2¼* **Sonoran Sands (IRE)**[31] 4726 6-10-11 **116** BrendanPowell 100
(Brendan Powell) *hld up in tch: rdn after 3 out: sn one pce* **28/1**

332- **9** *5* **Purple 'n Gold (IRE)**[183] 1697 5-10-6 **111** (p) ConorO'Farrell 92
(David Pipe) *led: rdn after 3 out: hdd bef next: wknd* **14/1**

100- **10** *1½* **Ashdown Lad**[105] 3263 5-10-10 **115** FelixDeGiles 96
(Tom Symonds) *prom: mstke and wnt lft 6th: rdn after 3 out: btn bef next* **50/1**

3m 55.2s (-12.80) **Going Correction** -0.55s/f (Firm) **10** Ran SP% **114.5**
Speed ratings (Par 107): **108,107,106,104,102 99,98,97,95,94**
CSF £14.00 CT £68.09 TOTE £8.90: £2.50, £1.10, £2.90; EX 10.60 Trifecta £55.70.
Owner Sandie & David Newton **Bred** Mrs J S Newton **Trained** George Nympton, Devon

FOCUS
A decent handicap hurdle, run at a decent pace in a time 5.5sec quicker than the preceding novices' handicap. A step up from the progressive winner though the second was arguably unlucky.

5240 FOLLOW TOTEPOOL ON FACEBOOK AND TWITTER H'CAP CHASE (17 fncs) 2m 7f 110y
5:20 (5:20) (Class 5) (0-100,100) 5-Y-0+ **£3,422** (£997; £499)

Form RPR

P03- **1** **Best Boy Barney (IRE)**[16] 5025 8-10-10 **87** (bt[1]) MattGriffiths(3) 108+
(Jeremy Scott) *mde all: clr at times: hit 5th: rdn after 4 out: hit next: clr 2 out: styd on wl: rdn out* **5/1**[2]

2P1- **2** *12* **Milosam (IRE)**[17] 5004 7-11-12 **100** (v[1]) TomO'Brien 109
(Philip Hobbs) *chsd wnr: rdn after 13th: clsd on wnr appr 3 out: hld 2 out: styd on same pce to regain 2nd run-in* **85/40**[1]

635- **3** *nk* **Egypt Mill Spirit (IRE)**[29] 4762 8-11-0 **93** AodhaganConlon(5) 102
(Tom George) *mid-div: hdwy after 11th: rdn after 4 out in disp 2nd: clsng on wnr whn mstke 3 out: sn hld: no ex fr last* **15/2**[3]

/PU- **4** *19* **Qualypso D'Allier (FR)**[8] 5127 10-10-12 **89** MichealNolan(3) 82
(Richard Woollacott) *mid-div: u.p in disp 5th whn mstke 4 out: sn wknd* **10/1**

P34- **5** *1* **Double Chocolate**[46] 4440 11-11-5 **93** (p) BrendanPowell 83
(John O'Shea) *mid-div: disp 2nd briefly 10th: rdn after next: wknd after 4 out* **10/1**

350- **6** *26* **Ballyegan (IRE)**[17] 5007 9-10-8 **82** (t) SamJones 48
(Bob Buckler) *mid-div: rdn after 11th: wknd 4 out: t.o* **17/2**

/33- **7** *1¾* **Cypress Grove (IRE)**[105] 3250 11-10-8 **82** (v) IanPopham 47
(John Ryall) *nvr travelling: a in rr: t.o* **20/1**

0/P- **8** *1¼* **Southway Star**[17] 5004 9-11-4 **99** (t) PaulJohn(7) 63
(Sue Gardner) *a bhd: struggling 6th: t.o fr 12th* **33/1**

054- **9** *½* **Wheelavher**[12] 5065 8-9-7 **74** oh4 (t) GeraldQuinn(7) 37
(Claire Dyson) *chsd ldrs: lost pl and pushed along after 10th: nvr a danger after: wknd bef 4 out: t.o* **25/1**

P/4- **P** **Starburst Diamond (IRE)**[126] 2911 12-10-9 **90** (b) MissAliceMills(7)
(Charles Whittaker) *struggling in rr after 3rd: t.o whn p.u bef 11th* **20/1**

523- **P** **Tuskar Rock (FR)**[16] 5023 11-11-9 **97** (b) LiamTreadwell
(Venetia Williams) *chsd wnr: rdn after 11th: sn dropped to hld 4th: wknd after 4 out: p.u bef 2 out* **8/1**

5m 58.5s (-17.50) **Going Correction** -0.55s/f (Firm) **11** Ran SP% **116.6**
Speed ratings: **107,103,102,96,96 87,86,86,86,**
CSF £15.70 CT £79.54 TOTE £6.20: £2.20, £1.10, £2.50; EX 21.80 Trifecta £158.20.
Owner G T Lever **Bred** Michael Kennedy **Trained** Brompton Regis, Somerset

FOCUS
A modest staying handicap chase and the order didn't change that much. There was no hanging about thanks to the attacking ride given to the winner. The form is rated around the runner-up.

5241 COLLECT TOTEPOOL WINNINGS AT BETFRED SHOPS STANDARD OPEN NATIONAL HUNT FLAT RACE 2m 1f
5:55 (5:55) (Class 6) 4-6-Y-0 **£2,053** (£598; £299)

Form RPR

12- **1** **One For The Guv'Nr (IRE)**[43] 4495 5-11-9 0 DavidBass 112+
(Nicky Henderson) *racd keenly in mid-div: hdwy over 3f out: led over 2f out: kpt on but edgd lft fnl f: rdn out* **7/4**[2]

2 *1* **The Outlaw (IRE)** 4-10-3 0 MrADoyle(7) 98+
(Paul Nicholls) *hld up: gd hdwy fr 3f out: rdn to chse wnr 2f out: kpt on but a being hld ins fnl f* **14/1**

3 *1½* **Sir Ivan** 4-10-10 0 NoelFehily 97+
(Harry Fry) *trckd ldrs: hmpd on bnd after winning post: led briefly over 2f out: sn rdn: kpt on same pce fnl f* **13/8**[1]

6- **4** *5* **Murrayana (IRE)**[47] 4424 4-10-10 0 BrendanPowell 92
(Colin Tizzard) *trckd ldrs: rdn over 4f out: styd on same pce fnl 2f* **7/1**[3]

5 *nk* **Dry Ol'Party** 4-10-3 0 RichardJohnson 85
(Philip Hobbs) *mid-div: hdwy to chse ldrs 3f out: sn rdn: kpt on same pce fnl 2f* **12/1**

6 *2¼* **Shanty Town (IRE)**[179] 5-10-13 0 (t) MichealNolan(3) 96
(Suzy Smith) *disp ld tl clr ldr over 4f out: rdn and hdd over 2f out: sn one pce* **14/1**

7 *8* **Alderley Heights** 5-10-9 0 TomO'Brien 82
(Polly Gundry) *mid-div: rdn 3f out: sn outpcd* **40/1**

0- **8** *21* **Mystical Flame (IRE)**[16] 5021 5-10-9 0 (t) ConorO'Farrell 63
(David Pipe) *disp ld: slowed up on bnd after winning post: sn rdn: hdd over 4f out: sn btn: t.o* **33/1**

4- **P** **Harry Partridge**[60] 4177 5-10-13 0 MattGriffiths(3)
(Sue Gardner) *trckd ldr tl rdn 1/2-way: hung bdly lft towards stable and lost tch qckly: sn p.u* **50/1**

3m 54.8s (-7.60) **Going Correction** -0.55s/f (Firm)
WFA 4 from 5yo 5lb **9** Ran SP% **115.3**
Speed ratings: **95,94,93,91,91 90,86,76,**
CSF £26.07 TOTE £2.70: £1.30, £3.20, £1.10; EX 23.10 Trifecta £45.70.
Owner Bradley Partnership **Bred** Chris Kinane **Trained** Upper Lambourn, Berks

FOCUS
Probably not a bad little bumper in which previous experience may have made all the difference.
T/Plt: £86.40 to a £1 stake. Pool of £78532.65 - 662.79 winning tickets. T/Qpdt: £20.70 to a £1 stake. Pool of £5844.92 - 208.15 winning tickets. TM

5008 TOWCESTER (R-H)
Thursday, April 10

OFFICIAL GOING: Good (good to soft in places; 9.0)
Wind: light breeze Weather: fairly sunny; 16 degrees

5242 HAYGAIN HAY STEAMERS CLEAN HEALTHY FORAGE CONDITIONAL JOCKEYS' H'CAP HURDLE (8 hdls) 2m
2:10 (2:10) (Class 5) (0-100,100) 4-Y-0+ **£1,949** (£572; £286; £143)

Form RPR

001- **1** **Dalmo**[4] 5189 5-11-9 **97** 7ex (b) GavinSheehan 107+
(Dr Richard Newland) *ldng trio: led 4th: drew clr between last two: kpt on wl and unchal after* **9/2**[2]

5/4- **2** *4½* **Buddy Love**[269] 997 7-10-6 **86** RyanHatch(6) 90
(Nigel Twiston-Davies) *settled in midfield: effrt 3 out: wnt 2nd bef next: sn drvn: 4 l 2nd and wl hld at last* **4/1**[1]

260- **3** *3* **Jigsaw Financial (IRE)**[23] 4887 8-10-12 **86** MauriceLinehan 87
(Laura Young) *settled in midfield: effrt 3 out: drvn bef next: chsd ldng pair vainly appr last* **22/1**

5P0- **4** *¾* **Prince Freddie**[12] 5072 6-10-1 **75** (b) KillianMoore 75
(Roy Brotherton) *t.k.h: towards rr: hdwy 3 out: disp 2nd and rdn home turn: kpt on same pce* **33/1**

562- **5** *3¼* **Thinger Licht (FR)**[28] 4783 5-11-12 **100** (v[1]) TrevorWhelan 97
(Tony Carroll) *chsd ldrs: drvn after 3 out: 7th at last: plugged on wout threatening flat* **5/1**[3]

U03- **6** *hd* **Celtic Charlie (FR)**[90] 2862 9-9-8 **76** (t) PaddyBradley(8) 73
(Pat Phelan) *in rr gp: styd on fr 3 out: rdn and nt qckn bef next* **20/1**

/P6- **7** *1* **Pistolet Noir (FR)**[115] 3132 8-11-9 **97** (bt) NicodeBoinville 93
(Richard Woollacott) *prom tl 3 out: rdn and lost pl on long uphill run bef next* **14/1**

40P- **8** *shd* **Unknown Legend (IRE)**[12] 5069 7-11-7 **95** HarryChalloner 91
(Anthony Middleton) *wore ear plugs: taken down late and kpt away fr rest: last away: struggling and racing awkwardly bef 3 out: plugged on past btn horses fr next* **66/1**

/61- **9** *8* **Osgood**[19] 4967 7-11-6 **97** JoshuaMoore(3) 87
(Gary Moore) *pressed ldrs: drvn wl bef 2 out where mstke whn btn: n.d after* **20/1**

003- **10** *nse* **Galley Slave (IRE)**[18] 4981 9-10-4 **78** JoeCornwall 68
(Michael Chapman) *a in midfield: no ch after 3 out* **33/1**

5/6- **11** *4½* **Seymour Legend**[327] 368 8-10-9 **83**[1] JakeGreenall 68
(Jim Wilson) *chsd ldrs: hrd drvn bef 3 out: struggling after* **66/1**

042- **12** *5* **El Toreros (USA)**[17] 5012 6-11-1 **89** (t) ConorShoemark 69
(Lawney Hill) *chsd ldrs tl 1/2-way: drvn after 4th: no rspnse: struggling fr next* **7/1**

0P4- **13** *12* **Home For Tea**[18] 4988 5-11-1 **92** BenPoste(3) 62
(Tom Symonds) *mde most tl 4th: w ldr tl 3 out: fdd qckly bef 2 out: t.o* **16/1**

165- **14** *¾* **Lucys Girl (IRE)**[183] 1824 7-11-2 **90** ThomasGarner 59
(Jamie Snowden) *a wl bhd: t.o after 3 out* **20/1**

0F5- **15** *2¾* **Tallulah Mai**[19] 4967 7-11-0 **93** MikeyHamill(5) 59
(Alastair Lidderdale) *wl in rr early: struggling 3 out: fin tired and t.o* **33/1**

040- **16** *12* **Cash For Steel (IRE)**[19] 4967 7-10-5 **79** KielanWoods 35
(Richard Phillips) *chsd ldrs tl 1/2-way: dropped out rapidly bef 3 out: sn t.o* **40/1**

645- **17** *17* **Collingbourneducis (IRE)**[31] 4724 4-10-9 **89** PeterCarberry 23
(Michael Gates) *wl bhd: last whn mstke 3rd: sn drvn and no rspnse: t.o bef 3 out* **50/1**

600- **P** **Early Bonnet (IRE)**[70] 3988 6-10-8 **85** EdCookson(3)
(Kim Bailey) *chsd ldrs and t.k.h: wknd bef 3 out: struggling in midfield whn blnd 2 out: p.u last* **16/1**

3m 48.1s (-19.80) **Going Correction** -1.175s/f (Hard)
WFA 4 from 5yo+ 5lb **18** Ran SP% **120.6**
Speed ratings (Par 103): **102,99,98,97,96 96,95,95,91,91 89,86,80,80,79 73,64,**
CSF £19.31 CT £363.68 TOTE £6.80: £1.60, £1.60, £3.00, £6.20; EX 27.30 Trifecta £239.20.
Owner J A Provan **Bred** Sir Eric Parker **Trained** Claines, Worcs

The Form Book Jumps, Raceform Ltd, Compton, RG20 6NL.

FOCUS
Chase course dolled out wide, Hurdles course on inside line. An open handicap, confined to conditional riders, run at an honest gallop. A step up from Dalmo on his recent win.

5243 HAYGAIN HAY STEAMERS CLEAN HEALTHY FORAGE H'CAP CHASE (12 fncs) 2m 110y
2:40 (2:41) (Class 5) (0-100,91) 5-Y-0+ **£2,144** (£629; £314; £157)

Form RPR
4P0- **1** **Tinelyra (IRE)**[19] 4970 8-11-0 **84**.................................... ConorShoemark[(5)] 95
(Fergal O'Brien) *dropped out in rr: hdwy 7th: shkn up 3 out: no imp at next and stl 5 l 4th at last: swtchd lft and r.o u.p to ld 1/2-way up run-in: v gd ride* **8/1**

/0P- **2** 1 ¼ **On The Case**[76] 3876 6-11-0 **79**.. PaddyBrennan 89
(Tom George) *racd keenly and prom: wnt 2nd at 7th: slt ld 3 out: drvn and jst hdd after jumping lft next: stl ev ch after last: outpcd fnl 100yds* **11/1**

P03- **3** shd **Bally Lagan (IRE)**[34] 4656 6-10-11 **76**..............................(tp) CharliePoste 86
(Robin Dickin) *chsd ldrs: disp 2nd fr 6th: rdn to ld after 2 out: racing idly whn nt fluent last: sn jnd: nt qckn fnl 100yds* **4/1**[2]

533- **4** 13 **Rebel High (IRE)**[126] 2895 10-11-7 **86**........................(p) TomScudamore 88
(Derek Frankland) *j.big in ld: rdn 9th: hdd and mstke 3 out: 3rd and btn next: 4th whn blnd last and nrly lost rdr* **8/1**

4F5- **5** 1 ¾ **Fintan**[7] 5143 11-11-9 **91**.. RobertDunne[(3)] 87
(Laura Young) *taken down early: cl up: ev ch tl drvn 3 out: sn wknd* **7/1**[3]

46U- **6** 8 **Beauchamp Viking**[31] 4734 10-10-10 **75**..............................(t) ColinBolger 65
(Hugo Froud) *towards rr: rdn and btn after 9th* **20/1**

4F3- **7** ¾ **Missionaire (USA)**[17] 5013 7-11-9 **91**......................... TrevorWhelan[(3)] 79
(Tony Carroll) *nvr bttr than midfield: rdn and btn after 3 out* **10/1**

P30- **8** 6 **One For The Boss (IRE)**[19] 4970 7-10-5 **75**...............(p) CharlieWallis[(5)] 57
(Dai Burchell) *prom tl 5th: j. slowly next and reminder: sn detached in last: nvr looked like regaining tch* **10/3**[1]

026- **U** **Marleno (GER)**[19] 4970 8-11-7 **91**.................................(t) JamesBanks[(5)]
(Anthony Middleton) *pressed ldrs tl appeared unsighted and uns rdr 4th* **8/1**

4m 6.6s (-9.50) **Going Correction** -0.95s/f (Hard) 9 Ran SP% **111.1**
Speed ratings: **84,83,83,77,76 72,72,69,**
CSF £83.53 CT £390.75 TOTE £7.00: £3.00, £3.40, £2.70; EX 126.00 Trifecta £304.50.
Owner M R Costello **Bred** Mrs Norah Valentine **Trained** Coln St. Dennis, Gloucs

FOCUS
The gallop was steady for this very modest handicap. The winner is rated 5lb off this season's best.

5244 BEST RACING BLOGS ON GG.COM MARES' MAIDEN HURDLE (DIV I) (8 hdls) 2m
3:10 (3:10) (Class 5) 4-Y-0+ **£1,949** (£572; £286; £143)

Form RPR
3/P- **1** **Doyenne Dream**[24] 4865 7-10-7 86.........................(vt[1]) MissBAndrews[(7)] 97
(Caroline Fryer) *3rd early: 2nd at 4th: hmpd next: cajoled along to ld after 2 out: drew clr bef last* **50/1**

2 4 ½ **Cailin (IRE)** 6-11-0 0... TomScudamore 92
(Grant Cann) *midfield: shkn up and styd on fr after 3 out: 6 l 3rd at last: wnt 2nd fnl 100yds: no ch w wnr but encouraging debut* **33/1**

203- **3** 1 ¾ **Shanendou (IRE)**[51] 4331 5-11-0 0.................................... PaddyBrennan 92
(Tom George) *led: j.lft 5th: tending to hang after: rdn and hdd after 2 out: wl hld in 2nd whn blnd last and caused rdr to become v unbalanced* **9/2**[2]

P06- **4** 6 **Money Maid (IRE)**[8] 5124 6-11-0 0....................................... HaddenFrost 86
(Simon Earle) *wl bhd and mstke 2nd: nvr threatened ldrs after: impeded 3 out: styng on wl after last: snatched 4th: too much to do* **5/1**[3]

46- **5** ¾ **Multiview**[225] 1427 5-10-9 0.. BenPoste[(5)] 84
(Tom Symonds) *mstke 3rd: chsd ldrs: rdn and no ex 3 out: lost 4th cl home* **50/1**

505- **6** 4 **Banreenahreenkah (IRE)**[123] 2975 4-10-8 104............. DougieCostello 76
(Jennie Candlish) *bhd: nt a fluent: mstke 3rd: btn bef 3 out* **8/1**

/30- **7** 1 ½ **Indiefront**[155] 2286 5-11-0 0.. LeightonAspell 81
(Jo Davis) *bhd: mod prog whn impeded 3 out: no ch after* **25/1**

0- **8** 3 ½ **Lemon Grove**[31] 4730 4-10-2 0 ow1..................................(p) MrZBaker[(7)] 71
(Martin Bosley) *chsd ldrs tl 5th: struggling next* **100/1**

U56- **9** 12 **Playhara (IRE)**[7] 5140 5-10-11 0...................................... PeterCarberry[(3)] 65
(Nicky Henderson) *midfield: rdn 5th: a gng bdly after and last by next* **2/1**[1]

0/0- **P** **Just Satisfaction**[149] 2442 5-11-0 0.................................. GerardTumelty
(Nick Lampard) *t.o and p.u 4th* **100/1**

0/2- **U** **Bright Intervals (IRE)**[17] 5002 6-10-11 0......................... JakeGreenall[(3)]
(Henry Daly) *t.k.h: prom: stl on terms in 5th whn bdly hmpd and uns rdr 3 out* **9/2**[2]

66P- **P** **High Holloa**[24] 4863 5-11-0 0.. AndrewThornton
(Caroline Bailey) *bhd: t.o and p.u 5th* **100/1**

6- **F** **Lady Garvagh**[31] 4730 4-10-8 0..................................... WayneHutchinson
(Richard Woollacott) *prom: stl 3rd and ev ch whn fell 3 out* **40/1**

3m 53.6s (-14.30) **Going Correction** -1.175s/f (Hard)
WFA 4 from 5yo+ 5lb 13 Ran SP% **113.6**
Speed ratings (Par 103): **88,85,84,81,81 79,78,77,71, , ,**
CSF £1048.37 TOTE £33.40: £5.20, £4.60, £1.80; EX 498.90 Trifecta £2025.00 Part won..
Owner Hockham Lodge Stud **Bred** Mrs R Wilson **Trained** Wymondham, Norfolk

FOCUS
A modest mares' maiden hurdle run at a fair gallop. It paid to race handily. The winner is rated in line with her old form.

5245 BEST RACING BLOGS ON GG.COM MARES' MAIDEN HURDLE (DIV II) (8 hdls) 2m
3:40 (3:41) (Class 5) 4-Y-0+ **£1,949** (£572; £286; £143)

Form RPR
322- **1** **Fine Moment**[32] 4698 6-11-0 107......................................(bt[1]) BrianHughes 104+
(Kevin Frost) *cl up: led bef 2 out: in command whn hit flight: drew rt away and heavily eased flat* **6/4**[1]

602- **2** 9 **All Riled Up**[19] 4971 6-10-7 0... DanielHiskett[(7)] 90
(Harry Chisman) *t.k.h: chsd ldrs: effrt in 3rd and rdn at 5th: chsd wnr vainly fr 2 out* **25/1**

00P- **3** 2 ¼ **Flobury**[19] 4950 6-11-0 0.. LiamHeard 90+
(Barry Leavy) *bhd: stdy prog after 3 out: mstke next: kpt on gamely after but nvr able to chal* **100/1**

33P- **4** 1 ¼ **Rising Teal**[45] 4472 5-11-0 103... LeightonAspell 87
(Lucy Wadham) *prom: 2nd at 5th: drvn and lost pl after 3 out: consented to plug on again after last* **3/1**[2]

054- **5** hd **Present Trend (IRE)**[87] 3689 5-10-11 0............................ KielanWoods[(3)] 86
(Charlie Longsdon) *led at v slow pce: nt fluent 3 out: rdn and hdd bef 2 out: sn btn: plodded on* **14/1**

P- **6** ½ **Simmons**[123] 2978 6-10-9 0.. JamesBanks[(5)] 86
(Alastair Lidderdale) *nvr bttr than midfield: rdn and wl hld after jumping lft 3 out: plugged on* **100/1**

5- **7** 1 ¼ **Danisa**[21] 4910 5-11-0 0... TomScudamore 85
(David Bridgwater) *t.k.h: chsd ldrs: effrt after 3 out: sn no imp* **4/1**[3]

0- **8** 7 **Bell'Arte (IRE)**[16] 5026 4-10-8 0.. TomCannon 72
(Laura Mongan) *nvr bttr than midfield: btn bef 3 out* **100/1**

0/0- **9** 29 **Loxley Mezile**[18] 4988 5-11-0 0.. AndrewThornton 49
(Simon Earle) *bhd: nt fluent 3rd: struggling 5th: hmpd next: t.o bef 2 out* **66/1**

10 hd **Sakhee's Alround**[22] 4-10-8 0.. DougieCostello 42
(K F Clutterbuck) *t.k.h early: bhd: lost tch tamely 3 out: t.o* **66/1**

F **Diamond Gesture (IRE)**[109] 3234 6-11-0 98................... PaddyBrennan
(Fergal O'Brien) *chsd ldrs: 7th whn fell 5th* **8/1**

PP- **B** **Teeton Blackvelvet**[28] 4777 5-11-0 0..........................(t) TomMessenger
(Caroline Bailey) *pressed ldr tl j. slowly 4th and dropped out rapidly: b.d next: fatally injured* **100/1**

4m 0.5s (-7.40) **Going Correction** -1.175s/f (Hard)
WFA 4 from 5yo+ 5lb 12 Ran SP% **113.6**
Speed ratings (Par 103): **71,66,65,64,64 64,63,60,45,45 ,**
CSF £38.19 TOTE £2.10: £1.10, £5.80, £8.50; EX 27.00 Trifecta £350.90.
Owner The Ferandlin Peaches **Bred** Cheveley Park Stud Ltd **Trained** Stratford-upon-Avon

FOCUS
An uncompetitive mares' maiden hurdle run at a steady pace. The easy winner was value for further.

5246 EBF STALLIONS/TBA MARES' NOVICES' H'CAP CHASE (14 fncs) 2m 3f 110y
4:10 (4:11) (Class 4) (0-110,105) 5-Y-0 **£3,671** (£1,084; £542; £271; £135)

Form RPR
533- **1** **Fair Bramble**[17] 5009 8-11-7 **100**..................................(b) LeightonAspell 110+
(Oliver Sherwood) *t.k.h: 2nd or 3rd tl led bef 6th: rdn and drew clr w runner-up bef 2 out: idling after but a doing enough: kpt up to work* **4/1**[2]

455- **2** 2 **Genstone Trail**[53] 4308 8-11-2 **95**................................... DougieCostello 104+
(Alan King) *settled in midfield: wnt 2nd after 3 out: sn clr of rest: drvn and kpt trying to chal fr next but a jst hld* **7/2**[1]

365- **3** 15 **Vinnieslittle Lamb (IRE)**[76] 3878 6-11-7 **100**....................... AlainCawley 94
(David Bridgwater) *towards rr: lost tch 10th: 10 l 9th and rdn bef 3 out: rallied to pass faders and tk 3rd after next: 12 l 3rd and nt fluent last: nvr nr ldrs* **16/1**

623- **4** 5 **Me And Ben (IRE)**[19] 4966 7-11-11 **104**.........................(t) PaddyBrennan 93
(Fergal O'Brien) *hld up and bhd: effrt bef 3 out: 8 l 3rd next: rdn and one pce: nvr able to chal ldng pair* **15/2**[3]

006- **5** 1 ½ **Upbeat Cobbler (FR)**[42] 4508 6-11-7 **103**...................... JakeGreenall[(3)] 90
(Henry Daly) *chsd ldrs: rdn and wknd after 3 out* **15/2**[3]

342- **6** 1 ¾ **Carhue Princess (IRE)**[19] 4966 8-10-6 **90**............................ BenPoste[(5)] 77
(Tom Symonds) *led and t.k.h: hdd bef 6th: w wnr tl mstke 3 out: sn fdd* **14/1**

444- **7** 9 **Floral Spinner**[21] 4918 7-11-2 **102**.................................. ChrisDavies[(7)] 79
(Bill Turner) *mstkes in rr: last and struggling 8th: plugged on* **16/1**

60F- **8** 15 **Miss Tique (FR)**[31] 4717 6-11-9 **105**............................ RobertDunne[(3)] 69
(Venetia Williams) *hdwy to chse ldrs 6th: disp 3rd and rdn home turn: wknd bef 2 out: t.o* **20/1**

F63- **9** 10 **The Absent Mare**[24] 2349 6-9-9 **79** oh2......................... MauriceLinehan[(5)] 34
(Robin Dickin) *a bhd: struggling 3 out: t.o* **12/1**

UP1- **10** 3 ¾ **Legendary Hop**[51] 4337 8-11-6 **102**................................ TrevorWhelan[(3)] 54
(Chris Bealby) *prom tl 3 out: rdn and fdd bef next: t.o* **10/1**

4P3- **11** ½ **Goochypoochyprader**[31] 4717 7-11-5 **98**.........................(t) GerardTumelty 49
(Nick Lampard) *lost tch 9th: t.o 11th* **25/1**

106- **P** **Dancing Daffodil**[22] 4906 9-11-1 **94**.. CharliePoste
(Robin Dickin) *sn struggling in rr: lost tch 8th: t.o and p.u 2 out* **14/1**

4m 57.5s (-20.70) **Going Correction** -0.95s/f (Hard) 12 Ran SP% **116.2**
Speed ratings: **103,102,96,94,93 92,89,83,79,77 77,**
CSF £18.65 CT £201.52 TOTE £4.00: £1.70, £2.30, £5.80; EX 26.80 Trifecta £939.60.
Owner Weatherbys Racing Club & P Deal **Bred** Simon And Helen Plumbly **Trained** Upper Lambourn, Berks

FOCUS
A wide-open mares' handicap run at a fair pace. The winner built on a good recent C&D run.

5247 TRY GG.COM ON YOUR MOBILE H'CAP CHASE (14 fncs) 2m 3f 110y
4:40 (4:41) (Class 4) (0-110,110) 5-Y-0+ **£3,768** (£1,106; £553; £276)

Form RPR
031- **1** **Riddlestown (IRE)**[17] 5009 7-11-3 **101**.........................(b[1]) LeightonAspell 112+
(Caroline Fryer) *rn in snatches: dropped to rr 10th: 8th whn j.rt and bmpd next: 4th and rallying 3 out: wnt 2nd bef next where wnt rt and bmpd: led 2 out: rdn 5 l clr and idling last: eased nr fin and had a bit in hand* **5/1**[2]

3P2- **2** 1 **Russe Blanc (FR)**[35] 4626 7-11-7 **105**.........................(p) TomScudamore 113
(Richard Lee) *settled in rr: hdwy 9th: sn rdn: wnt 2nd u.p after 2 out: j.rt last: styd on gamely but a hld* **6/1**[3]

626- **3** 14 **Got Attitude (IRE)**[44] 4486 11-10-3 **90**.....................(vt[1]) TrevorWhelan[(3)] 89
(Tony Carroll) *midfield: wnt 3rd at 9th: j. ahd 3 out: rdn whn j.lft next and hdd: fnd nil and wl btn 3rd at last* **11/1**

144- **4** 7 **Croco Mister (IRE)**[18] 4985 7-9-11 **86**.................................. BenPoste[(5)] 75
(Rosemary Gasson) *hld up in rr: effrt 3 out: mod 5th bef next: no imp after* **12/1**

263- **5** 2 ¼ **Moleskin (IRE)**[63] 4109 11-10-12 **103**..............(bt) MrMatthewHampton[(7)] 90
(Victor Dartnall) *cl up: wnt 2nd after 7th: led 8th tl drvn and hdd 3 out: wknd bef next* **8/1**

415- **6** 5 **Carli King (IRE)**[22] 4896 8-11-5 **110**......................................(p) MrPMann[(7)] 93
(Caroline Bailey) *chsd ldrs: rdn 9th: fdd after 3 out* **9/4**[1]

/S0- **7** 29 **Ballycassel (IRE)**[23] 4884 9-11-4 **105**............................ NicodeBoinville[(3)] 61
(Tom Symonds) *nvr trbld ldrs: struggling fr 3 out: t.o* **12/1**

3/P- **8** 5 **Bally Gunner**[319] 504 9-11-11 **109**...................................... HaddenFrost 61
(Roger Curtis) *bhd: sme prog 9th: struggling after 3 out: t.o* **22/1**

/P0- **9** 2 ¼ **Playing With Fire (IRE)**[24] 4861 10-10-12 **96**.......................... CharliePoste 46
(Robin Dickin) *taken down early: led tl 8th: w ldr tl 10th: wknd 3 out: climbed 2 out and virtually p.u after* **33/1**

FUP- **10** 44 **Keltic Crisis (IRE)**[86] 3696 10-10-12 **96**............................. DougieCostello 6
(Sophie Leech) *a bhd: struggling 9th: t.o after 3 out* **25/1**

313- **U** **Orang Outan (FR)**[29] 4762 12-10-6 **95**................................... EdCookson[(5)]
(Laura Hurley) *chsd ldr tl 6th: rdn bef 11th: sn wknd: wl bhd whn blnd and uns rdr 2 out* **20/1**

110- **P** **Take Of Shoc'S (IRE)**[123] 2977 10-11-4 **107**......................(t) CharlieWallis[(5)]
(Sophie Leech) *prom: wnt lft 6th and 7th and rapidly lost pl bef next: t.o bef 11th: p.u bef next* **25/1**

4m 59.3s (-18.90) **Going Correction** -0.95s/f (Hard) 12 Ran SP% **116.3**
Speed ratings: **99,98,93,90,89 87,75,73,72,55 ,**
CSF £31.99 CT £316.46 TOTE £6.40: £2.40, £2.60, £3.00; EX 19.50 Trifecta £533.40.

Owner J Ward **Bred** Jeremiah O'Brien **Trained** Wymondham, Norfolk
FOCUS
A competitive handicap run at a fair pace. The winner is rated to the level of his recent C&D win.

5248 VISIT THE FORUM ON GG.COM MAIDEN HUNTERS' CHASE (14 fncs) 2m 3f 110y
5:10 (5:11) (Class 6) 6-Y-0+ **£987** (£303; £151)

Form RPR
5/3- **1** **Warwickshire (IRE)**[11] 7-11-7 0 MrBRivett(7) 107+
(A Pennock) *v keen to s: nt a fluent: mde all: wnt 8 l clr fr 8th tl bef 3 out: hit next hrd: rdn and kpt finding enough after* **10/11**[1]
2 3/4 **Done A Runner (IRE)**[11] 8-11-11 0 MrTEllis(3) 105+
(Alan Hill) *hld up: wnt 8 l 2nd at 8th: clsd to win 4 l of wnr 3 out: sn drvn: making no imp whn v awkward at last* **5/2**[2]
3 15 **Big Georgie (IRE)**[11] 7-11-9 0 MrJMRidley(5) 90
(Mrs H S M Ridley) *chsd ldrs: rdn and outpcd 3 out: poor 3rd at next* **10/1**
/45- **4** 37 **Areuwitmenow (IRE)**[21] 4922 9-11-11 94 MissAEStirling(3) 57
(S Rea) *chsd wnr tl 8th: 3rd and outpcd 3 out: struggling bdly after: t.o* **13/2**[3]
6- **U** **Music Of The Morn**[21] 4922 7-11-7 0 MrDMansell
(Mrs Julie Mansell) *detached in last whn blnd and uns rdr 1st* **28/1**
P **Rise Before Dawn (IRE)**[33] 7-11-7 0 MrWHickman(7)
(M Kehoe) *cl up tl 5th: hanging bdly lft after and sn poor last: t.o and p.u 9th* **28/1**

5m 3.9s (-14.30) **Going Correction** -0.95s/f (Hard) **6** Ran SP% **110.3**
Speed ratings: **90,89,83,68,**
CSF £3.55 TOTE £1.60: £1.10, £1.90; EX 4.10 Trifecta £12.70.
Owner Mrs K Exall **Bred** Walter Purcell **Trained** Scalby, N Yorks
FOCUS
A modest maiden hunters' chase run at a fair pace. The winner is rated to his mark.

5249 FREE TIPS EVERY DAY ON GG.COM MAIDEN OPEN NATIONAL HUNT FLAT RACE 2m
5:45 (5:45) (Class 6) 4-6-Y-0 **£1,559** (£457; £228; £114)

Form RPR
1 **Hel Tara** 5-10-7 0 JeremiahMcGrath(3) 100+
(Nicky Henderson) *midfield: rdn and hdwy wl over 2f out: styd on after: led 100yds out: grad asserted* **11/4**[2]
2 1 1/2 **Truckers Highway (IRE)**[137] 5-11-0 0 HarryChalloner(3) 103+
(John Bryan Groucott) *plld hrd and trckd ldrs in slowly run r: led wl over 1f out: rdn and hdd 100yds out: nt qckn* **9/1**
40- **3** 6 **Dawson City**[17] 5014 5-11-3 0 AndrewThornton 97
(Polly Gundry) *mde most tl rdn and hdd wl over 1f out: kpt on same pce and btn 1f out* **14/1**
0- **4** 2 **Wild At Midnight**[24] 4867 5-10-5 0 ConorShoemark(5) 88
(Fergal O'Brien) *hld up: hdwy over 3f out: rdn and unable to chal fnl 2f* **20/1**
0- **5** nk **Be My Witness (IRE)**[69] 4016 5-10-0 0 JosephPalmowski(10) 88
(Robin Dickin) *w ldng pair tl rdn and btn over 2f out: plugged on* **66/1**
4- **6** 3 **Border Breaker (IRE)**[29] 4763 5-11-3 0 TomScudamore 92
(David Pipe) *w ldr tl rdn 2f out: wknd tamely fnl f* **15/8**[1]
60- **7** 1 3/4 **Periquest**[26] 4824 5-11-3 0 PaddyBrennan 90
(Alex Hales) *midfield: rdn and btn over 2f out* **33/1**
00- **8** 12 **Dan's Quest**[85] 3719 4-10-11 0 CharliePoste 72
(Robin Dickin) *chsd ldrs tl rdn and wknd wl over 2f out: t.o* **20/1**
9 3/4 **Ginja Ninja** 6-10-3 0 JakeHodson(7) 70
(Rob Summers) *rdn and struggling over 3f out: t.o* **50/1**
06- **10** 26 **Red Hott Robbie**[22] 4902 5-10-12 0 CharlieWallis(5) 51
(Giuseppe Fierro) *cl up tl rdn 4f out: t.o over 2f out* **33/1**
64- **11** 1 1/4 **Nimbus Gale (IRE)**[39] 4575 5-11-3 0 LeightonAspell 50
(Oliver Sherwood) *midfield: shkn up 1/2-way: dropped out qckly over 4f out and sn t.o* **9/2**[3]
- **R** **Black Bizarre (IRE)** 4-10-1 0 (p) MikeyHamill(10)
(Sean Curran) *kpt hanging bdly lft: dropped bk: detached in last ent bk st: rallied on outer 4f out and chsd ldrs: unsteerable fr home turn and fnlly rn off crse over 1f out* **66/1**

3m 49.0s (-13.30) **Going Correction** -1.175s/f (Hard)
WFA 4 from 5yo+ 5lb **12** Ran SP% **116.6**
Speed ratings: **86,85,82,81,81 79,78,72,72,59 58,**
CSF £25.00 TOTE £3.70: £1.20, £3.00, £3.30; EX 28.60 Trifecta £253.10.
Owner Racegoers Club Owners Group **Bred** Steve Molloy **Trained** Upper Lambourn, Berks
FOCUS
A moderate bumper run at a steady pace. The first two are fair prospects but overall the form is ordinary.
T/Jkpt: Not won. T/Plt: £174.60 to a £1 stake. Pool of £65743.59 - 274.73 winning tickets.
T/Qpdt: £23.60 to a £1 stake. Pool of £6297.84 - 197.46 winning tickets. IM

4665 AYR (L-H)
Friday, April 11

OFFICIAL GOING: Good to soft (soft in places on chase course; chs 8.4, hdl 8.5)
Wind: Fresh, half against Weather: Cloudy

5250 WEST SOUND NOVICES' HURDLE (9 hdls) 2m
2:10 (2:10) (Class 3) 4-Y-0+ **£6,657** (£2,067; £1,113)

Form RPR
213- **1** **Vibrato Valtat (FR)**[34] 4682 5-11-10 131 (t) SamTwiston-Davies 126+
(Paul Nicholls) *hld up in tch: smooth hdwy 2 out: shkn up whn lft cl 2nd at last: sn lft in ld: pushed clr last 100yds* **5/2**[2]
111- **2** 4 1/2 **Sign Of A Victory (IRE)**[20] 4959 5-11-6 139 BarryGeraghty 122+
(Nicky Henderson) *t.k.h: chsd ldrs: stdy hdwy and jst over 1 l down whn lft in ld and hmpd last: sn hdd and persistently carried lft by loose horse: no ex last 100yds: eased nr fin* **4/9**[1]
/04- **3** 10 **Molly Milan**[147] 2495 6-10-7 0 JamesReveley 94
(Jim Goldie) *chsd ldr tl lost pl after 3 out: struggling fr next: no imp whn lft 3rd last* **100/1**
/65- **U** **Mister Nibbles (IRE)**[41] 4550 6-11-7 126 MrSCrawford(3) 126
(S R B Crawford, Ire) *t.k.h: led at stdy pce: rdn and jst over 1 l in front whn blnd and uns rdr last* **10/1**[3]

3m 58.7s (-4.40) **Going Correction** -0.725s/f (Firm) **4** Ran SP% **107.9**
Speed ratings (Par 107): **82,79,74,**
CSF £4.20 TOTE £2.30; EX 3.80 Trifecta £24.00.
Owner Axom XLIII **Bred** Mme C Duperret & Mlle A-M Duperret **Trained** Ditcheat, Somerset

FOCUS
Rails about 6 metres from innermost line on hurdles track and Chase bends increasing advertised distances by about 24yds per circuit. A dramatic event, with leader Mister Nibbles departing at the last and effectively putting Sign Of A Victory out of the race. It had been a slowly run affair that had become a sprint, and this isn't form to take literally. The race is rated as a triple dead-heat, with the first two around a stone off.

5251 ALAN SHEARER'S SPEEDFLEX H'CAP HURDLE (9 hdls) 2m
2:40 (2:40) (Class 3) (0-130,130) 4-Y-0+ **£7,797** (£2,289; £1,144; £572)

Form RPR
254- **1** **It's A Mans World**[13] 5067 8-10-5 119 GLavery(10) 124
(Brian Ellison) *hld up: hdwy and in tch on outside whn nt fluent 4 out: sn rdn: rallied next: led run-in: rdn out* **20/1**
351- **2** 2 3/4 **Just Cameron**[36] 4629 7-11-3 121 JamesReveley 124
(Philip Kirby) *led: rdn and hrd pressed 2 out: hdd run-in: kpt on same pce* **6/1**[3]
U02- **3** 6 **Overpriced**[20] 4952 8-10-7 118 (t) DaraghBourke(7) 115
(Maurice Barnes) *chsd ldr to after 4 out: drvn next: edgd lft after 2 out: kpt on same pce run-in* **25/1**
611- **4** 1 1/2 **Plus Jamais (FR)**[34] 4667 7-10-7 111 BrianHughes 107
(Jim Goldie) *prom: drvn and outpcd 4 out: rallied 2 out: styd on run-in: no imp* **6/1**[3]
232- **5** 1/2 **Fair Loch**[27] 4807 6-11-9 127 TomScudamore 124+
(K R Burke) *in tch: smooth hdwy to chse ldr after 4 out: effrt and ev ch next: upsides and rdn whn stmbld last: wknd last 100yds* **6/1**[3]
2P0/ **6** 10 **Sir Tantallus Hawk**[488] 2942 10-9-13 106 oh1 ow2 EwanWhillans(3) 92
(Alistair Whillans) *bhd: struggling 4th: rallied 2 out: kpt on: nvr able to chal* **40/1**
/2P- **7** nk **Fourth Estate (IRE)**[34] 4682 8-11-5 123 BarryGeraghty 109
(Nicky Henderson) *hld up bhd ldng gp: nt fluent and pushed along 4th: rdn after next: struggling bef 3 out: sn btn* **11/4**[1]
/53- **8** 6 **Veloce (IRE)**[80] 3819 6-11-2 120 (bt[1]) APMcCoy 104
(Donald McCain) *in tch tl rdn and wknd fr 3 out* **9/1**
211/ **9** 54 **Ballybogey (IRE)**[48] 4436 8-11-12 130 RichardJohnson 62
(J J Lambe, Ire) *chsd ldrs to 4 out: sn lost pl: t.o fr next* **14/1**
2F5- **F** **Fascino Rustico**[44] 4503 6-11-8 126 (t[1]) SamTwiston-Davies 124+
(Paul Nicholls) *hld up: smooth hdwy bef 3 out: nrly 4 l 4th and styng on whn fell next* **5/1**[2]

3m 48.2s (-14.90) **Going Correction** -0.725s/f (Firm) **10** Ran SP% **113.9**
Speed ratings (Par 107): **108,106,103,102,102 97,97,94,67,**
CSF £130.97 CT £3008.06 TOTE £15.70: £3.50, £2.40, £5.80; EX 69.40 Trifecta £1607.00.
Owner David Foster & Brian Ellison **Bred** Cheveley Park Stud Ltd **Trained** Norton, N Yorks
FOCUS
Quite a competitive handicap, run in a time 10.5sec quicker than the four-runner novice event and 9.2 sec over the standard, suggesting the ground was no worse than good to soft. The winner is rated to his hurdles best.

5252 ABBOTT RISK CONSULTING NOVICES' H'CAP HURDLE (12 hdls) 3m 110y
3:15 (3:15) (Class 3) (0-135,134) 4-Y-0+ **£7,797** (£2,289; £1,144; £572)

Form RPR
631- **1** **Ulzana's Raid (IRE)**[23] 4903 5-11-6 128 RobertThornton 133+
(Alan King) *in tch: smooth hdwy to chal bef 3 out: led next: rdn and hdd briefly last: styd on gamely u.p towards fin* **11/4**[1]
0/ **2** nk **Quickasyoucan (IRE)**[33] 4711 6-10-7 115 BrianHughes 119+
(C A McBratney, Ire) *hld up: smooth hdwy to chse ldrs appr 3 out: rdn and led briefly last: kpt on u.p: hld cl home* **7/2**[2]
114- **3** 6 **Hartforth**[41] 4545 6-10-2 115 CallumWhillans(5) 115
(Donald Whillans) *cl up: led 7th to next: drvn 4 out: rallied: kpt on same pce fr 2 out* **16/1**
2P2- **4** 8 **Straidnahanna (IRE)**[23] 4901 5-10-13 121 RyanMania 113
(Sue Smith) *hld up on outside: hdwy to ld 8th: drvn and hdd 2 out: sn outpcd* **8/1**
123- **5** 18 **Portway Flyer (IRE)**[27] 4805 6-11-11 133 APMcCoy 111
(Ian Williams) *in tch: lost pl 4 out: shortlived effrt bef next: sn btn* **9/2**[3]
233- **6** 39 **Kilbree Chief (IRE)**[11] 5103 6-11-5 127 PeterBuchanan 67
(Lucinda Russell) *led to 7th: drvn and lost pl after next: lost tch bef 3 out: t.o* **18/1**
114- **P** **Waldorf Salad**[35] 4662 6-11-3 125 LiamTreadwell
(Venetia Williams) *t.k.h: cl up tl wknd after 4 out: t.o whn p.u bef next* **9/1**
421- **P** **Vicente (FR)**[19] 4991 5-11-12 134 SamTwiston-Davies
(Paul Nicholls) *prom: mstke 4th: nt fluent: lost pl and drvn next: nt fluent 6th: sn lost tch: p.u bef next* **6/1**

6m 10.9s (-20.90) **Going Correction** -0.725s/f (Firm) **8** Ran SP% **113.6**
Speed ratings (Par 107): **104,103,101,99,93 81, ,**
CSF £12.99 CT £125.02 TOTE £3.90: £1.10, £1.90, £3.60; EX 16.30 Trifecta £208.10.
Owner Thomas Barr **Bred** M Brennan **Trained** Barbury Castle, Wilts
FOCUS
A fair handicap in which the first two pulled clear. The progressive winner looks a decent prospect.

5253 HILLHOUSE QUARRY H'CAP CHASE (17 fncs) 2m 4f
3:50 (3:50) (Class 2) 5-Y-0+
£15,640 (£4,620; £2,310; £1,155; £577; £290)

Form RPR
216- **1** **Scotch Warrior**[198] 1659 10-10-8 127 WilsonRenwick 135
(R Mike Smith) *cl up: lost 2nd whn hit and outpcd 4 out: edgd lft bef next: rallied after 2 out: styd on wl u.p to ld nr fin* **22/1**
305- **2** nk **Quito Du Tresor (FR)**[68] 4053 10-10-3 122 (p) TomScudamore 130
(Lucinda Russell) *chsd ldrs: led 10th: nrly 4 l clr whn nt fluent 3 out: rdn bef next: kpt on run-in: hdd nr fin* **11/1**
211- **3** 2 1/2 **Headly's Bridge (IRE)**[29] 4780 8-10-11 130 AndrewThornton 136
(Simon Earle) *prom: nt fluent 5 out: chsd ldr next: effrt whn nt fluent 3 out: lost 2nd last: one pce* **6/1**
03P- **4** 13 **Tap Night (USA)**[29] 4768 7-11-12 145 APMcCoy 139
(Lucinda Russell) *nt fluent: hld up bhd ldng gp: stead hdwy whn hit 11th: drvn and effrt bef 4 out: hit next: sn no imp* **10/3**[1]
433- **5** 4 **Stormin Exit (IRE)**[20] 4955 11-10-0 119 oh3 HenryBrooke 109
(Jim Goldie) *hld up: mstke 5th: rdn whn nt fluent 5 out: no imp fr next* **18/1**
4P0- **6** 3 **Bless The Wings (IRE)**[29] 4768 9-11-4 137 (b) RobertThornton 125
(Alan King) *hld up in tch on outside: blnd 4th: nt fluent 11th: sn pushed along: rdn and wknd bef 4 out* **4/1**[3]
20U- **7** 6 **Viva Colonia (IRE)**[7] 5156 9-11-10 143 RichardJohnson 125
(Brian Ellison) *hld up: smooth hdwy and prom 5 out: rdn and wknd qckly after next* **9/1**

The Form Book Jumps, Raceform Ltd, Compton, RG20 6NL.

21U- **P** **Tahiti Pearl (IRE)**[7] 5156 10-11-5 **138**.................................. RyanMania
(Sue Smith) *prom: nt fluent and lost pl 7th: drvn 6 out: wknd bef 4 out: no ch whn p.u bef last* **12/1**
430- **P** **Solix (FR)**[31] 4738 8-10-5 **124**..(b[1]) WillKennedy
(Ian Williams) *led to 9th: rdn and lost pl 12th: lost tch and p.u bef 4 out* **7/2**[2]

5m 14.6s (-8.30) **Going Correction** -0.125s/f (Good) 9 Ran SP% **115.2**
Speed ratings: **111,110,109,104,103 101,99, ,**
CSF £230.26 CT £1642.50 TOTE £17.80: £3.90, £4.60, £2.40; EX 167.40 Trifecta £2693.40.
Owner R Michael Smith **Bred** Miss Jayne Butler **Trained** Galston, E Ayrshire

FOCUS
A decent handicap chase. A personal best from the winner, with the second rated to form.

5254 PORCELANOSA SCOTLAND NOVICES' LIMITED H'CAP CHASE (12 fncs) 2m
4:25 (4:25) (Class 3) (0-125,129) 5-Y-0+ **£9,747** (£2,862; £1,431; £715)

Form				RPR
130-	**1**		**Too Cool To Fool (IRE)**[20] 4957 11-9-10 **106** oh11........... DaleIrving(7) (Jim Goldie) *chsd ldr to 1/2-way: drvn and outpcd 5 out: rallied bef 3 out: styd on wl fr last to ld towards fin* **9/1**	112
411-	**2**	*3/4*	**Le Bacardy (FR)**[8] 5141 8-11-9 **129** 7ex......................(p) TrevorWhelan(3) (Tony Carroll) *trckd ldrs: hdwy to ld bef last: rdn and kpt on run-in: hdd and no ex towards fin* **11/4**[1]	135+
	3	*14*	**Araglen Lad (IRE)**[119] 3076 8-10-10 **113**........................... APMcCoy (J J Lambe, Ire) *led: rdn bef 2 out: hdd bef last: sn outpcd* **11/2**	104
	4	*3 3/4*	**Back To Balloo (IRE)**[33] 4707 8-11-8 **125**......................... BrianHughes (C A McBratney, Ire) *nt fluent: hld up: stdy hdwy and in tch bef 4 out: rdn and outpcd after next: no imp whn blnd last* **5/1**[3]	116
106-	**5**	*2*	**Doynosaur**[27] 4804 7-11-5 **122**... HenryBrooke (K R Burke) *prom: blnd 1st: chsd ldr 6th: hit next: effrt and rdn bef 2 out: 3rd and one pce whn mstke last: sn btn* **10/3**[2]	115+
630-	**U**		**Claragh Native (IRE)**[68] 4053 9-10-12 **115**................(tp) WilsonRenwick (Martin Todhunter) *nt fluent: hld up in tch: outpcd whn bdly hmpd and uns rdr 5 out* **16/1**	
/6-	**F**		**Ellaway Rose (IRE)**[20] 4977 6-10-7 **110**........................ RichardJohnson (J P Kenny, Ire) *hld up: stdy hdwy and prom whn hit 7th: fell heavily next* **11/2**	

4m 5.5s (-5.20) **Going Correction** -0.125s/f (Good) 7 Ran SP% **113.1**
Speed ratings: **108,107,100,98,97 ,**
CSF £34.17 CT £150.06 TOTE £12.10: £4.30, £2.00; EX 44.20 Trifecta £283.10.
Owner Johnnie Delta Racing **Bred** Simon Young **Trained** Uplawmoor, E Renfrews

FOCUS
A fair novice handicap chase in which there were four with a chance heading down to the last, plus the loose Claragh Native whose presence didn't help matters. A personal best from the winner.

5255 CORAL BACKING POPPYSCOTLAND MARES' H'CAP HURDLE (12 hdls) 3m 110y
4:55 (4:58) (Class 2) 4-Y-0+
£12,512 (£3,696; £1,848; £924; £462; £232)

Form				RPR
115-	**1**		**Land Of Vic**[41] 4542 6-10-9 **125**.. DonalDevereux (Peter Bowen) *mde all: rdn bef 2 out: styd on gamely fr last* **9/1**	133+
	2	*2*	**Clara Mc Cloud (IRE)**[2] 5223 6-10-4 **120** 6ex..................(t) DavyCondon (Gordon Elliott, Ire) *hld up: smooth hdwy to press wnr bef 2 out: effrt and rdn bef last: kpt on same pce last 50yds* **11/4**[1]	126
542-	**3**	*7*	**Golden Sparkle (IRE)**[34] 4668 8-9-8 **117**................. DiarmuidO'Regan(7) (Ian Duncan) *hld up: stdy hdwy whn hit 3 out: rdn and kpt on fr last: nt rch first two* **20/1**	117
320-	**4**	*3 1/4*	**Mickie**[29] 4765 6-11-12 **142**... RichardJohnson (Henry Daly) *prom: effrt and drvn along 3 out: kpt on same pce between last 2* **3/1**[2]	139
352-	**5**	*3 1/4*	**Micro Mission (IRE)**[35] 4650 8-10-0 **116** oh8................(p[1]) HenryBrooke (Chris Grant) *prom: drvn and outpcd 3 out: kpt on run-in: nvr able to chal* **28/1**	110
341-	**6**	*1/2*	**Romantic Fashion (IRE)**[34] 4668 7-10-4 **120**......... SamTwiston-Davies (Mrs Prunella Dobbs, Ire) *t.k.h: sn pressing wnr: rdn 3 out: wknd fr next* **17/2**[3]	113
11/	**7**	*6*	**Twin Plan (IRE)**[19] 4995 9-10-7 **123**.. APMcCoy (J J Lambe, Ire) *nt fluent on occasions: hld up: effrt whn nt fluent 3 out: wknd next* **12/1**	112
P22-	**8**	*1 3/4*	**Gulf Punch**[36] 4625 7-9-7 **116**..(p) NickSlatter(7) (Donald McCain) *hld up in tch: stdy hdwy after 4 out: rdn and wknd after next* **25/1**	102
211-	**P**		**Bull And Bush (IRE)**[18] 5010 5-10-11 **127**......................... RobertThornton (Alan King) *prom: pushed along fr 5th: struggling 4 out: wknd and p.u bef next* **3/1**[2]	

6m 11.1s (-20.70) **Going Correction** -0.725s/f (Firm) 9 Ran SP% **116.9**
Speed ratings (Par 109): **104,103,101,100,99 90,90,90,**
CSF £34.48 CT £493.43 TOTE £10.40: £2.90, £1.20, £4.80; EX 47.30 Trifecta £1507.10.
Owner W Hill **Bred** Stewart Pike **Trained** Little Newcastle, Pembrokes

FOCUS
A decent handicap confined to mares. The winner dictated but this has to rate a step up.

5256 NEWTON ARMS BISTRO H'CAP HURDLE (12 hdls) 3m 110y
5:25 (5:26) (Class 3) (0-125,125) 4-Y-0+ **£7,797** (£2,289; £1,144; £572)

Form				RPR
263-	**1**		**Vivaldi Collonges (FR)**[62] 4163 5-11-6 **119**.......... SamTwiston-Davies (Paul Nicholls) *hld up: smooth hdwy bef 3 out: led appr next: rdn and qcknd clr run-in: readily* **10/1**	132+
/21-	**2**	*8*	**See Double You (IRE)**[34] 4666 11-10-9 **115**............. MrRMPMcNally(7) (Ronan M P McNally, Ire) *hld up: smooth hdwy to chse wnr after 2 out: rdn and edgd lft run-in: sn outpcd* **8/1**	120+
0/F-	**3**	*2 1/2*	**Jim Bowie (IRE)**[19] 4998 9-10-6 **105**..............................(b) BrianHughes (J J Lambe, Ire) *hld up: hdwy bef 3 out: rdn and kpt on fr last: nt rch first two* **40/1**	105
311-	**4**	*1 3/4*	**Forward Flight (IRE)**[34] 4670 8-11-5 **118**................................. APMcCoy (Sue Smith) *nt fluent on occasions: hld up in midfield: rdn after 4 out: rallied whn checked after 2 out: one pce fr last* **7/1**[3]	118
421-	**5**	*nk*	**Bescot Springs (IRE)**[14] 5059 9-10-9 **115**..........(b) GrahamWatters(7) (Lucinda Russell) *cl up: led 4 out to appr 2 out: sn rdn and one pce* **28/1**	113
050-	**6**	*7*	**Problema Tic (FR)**[29] 4769 8-11-11 **124**...................(bt) TomScudamore (David Pipe) *led to 4 out: drvn and outpcd next: n.d after* **20/1**	116
3/5-	**7**	*12*	**Merrydown (IRE)**[27] 4814 11-11-2 **115**............................ BrianHarding (Nicky Richards) *hld up: mstke 6th: drvn next: no imp fr 4 out* **33/1**	98
021-	**8**	*nk*	**Many Stars (IRE)**[30] 4761 6-11-12 **125**...............................(t) HarrySkelton (Dan Skelton) *in tch tl rdn and wknd bef 3 out* **18/1**	106
642-	**9**	*29*	**Dundee**[21] 4933 6-11-2 **115**.. RobertThornton (Alan King) *hld up in midfield: stdy hdwy 1/2-way: effrt and rdn next: one pce whn hmpd 2 out: sn btn and eased: t.o* **8/1**	100
314-	**10**	*9*	**Masterleaderman (IRE)**[27] 4814 6-11-1 **114**....................... DannyCook (Michael Smith) *prom tl rdn and wknd 4 out: t.o* **12/1**	61
531-	**11**	*20*	**Finaghy Ayr (IRE)**[35] 4649 6-10-7 **106**.......................... RichardJohnson (Ian Duncan) *w ldr: drvn and outpcd 4 out: sn btn: t.o* **16/1**	35
/44-	**P**		**Lieutenant Miller**[125] 2935 8-11-8 **121**............................ BarryGeraghty (Nicky Henderson) *hld up: stdy hdwy 1/2-way: outpcd 8th: lost tch and p.u after next* **3/1**[1]	
54P-	**F**		**Howizee**[117] 3108 8-11-2 **122**..(t) DaraghBourke(7) (Maurice Barnes) *prom: hdwy to chse ldr bef 3 out: effrt and ev ch whn fell next* **5/1**[2]	127

6m 9.0s (-22.80) **Going Correction** -0.725s/f (Firm) 13 Ran SP% **117.9**
Speed ratings (Par 107): **107,104,103,103,102 100,96,96,87,84 78, ,**
CSF £83.35 CT £3058.98 TOTE £13.40: £4.20, £2.70, £14.50; EX 103.30 Trifecta £1850.10 Part won..
Owner The Gi Gi Syndicate **Bred** G A E C Delorme Freres **Trained** Ditcheat, Somerset

FOCUS
The principals came from the rear in this reasonable handicap hurdle, which was the quickest of the three races over the trip. A big step up from the unexposed winner.
T/Plt: £1,578.50 to a £1 stake. Pool: £76678.73 - 35.46 winning tickets T/Qpdt: £66.20 to a £1 stake. Pool: £8270.94 - 92.45 winning tickets RY

5022 FONTWELL (L-H)
Friday, April 11

OFFICIAL GOING: Good (7.3)
Wind: almost nil Weather: sunny; 16 degrees

5257 MALCOLM "HAIRY" ROBERTS MEMORIAL NOVICES' HURDLE (DIV I) (10 hdls) 2m 4f
1:20 (1:20) (Class 4) 4-Y-0+ **£3,119** (£915; £457; £228)

Form				RPR
30-	**1**		**Gun Shy (IRE)**[27] 4807 6-11-0 0.. JoshuaMoore (Gary Moore) *mde all: j. sltly rt at times: gng best 2 out: 5 l clr and drvn last: edgd rt flat but kpt on wl* **11/2**[3]	123+
F22-	**2**	*9*	**Long Lunch**[23] 4904 5-11-6 122...(t) NoelFehily (Charlie Longsdon) *prom and racd keenly: chsd wnr fr 7th: 4 l down and rdn bef 2 out: no imp after* **11/8**[1]	120
	3	*4 1/2*	**Taggia (FR)**[882] 7-10-7 0.. TomCannon (Alison Batchelor) *hld up: hdwy after 7th: wnt 4th and drvn after 3 out: tk 3rd bef last: no imp whn hung rt flat* **100/1**	103
3-	**4**	*5*	**Generous Helpings (IRE)**[27] 4808 5-11-0 0..................... JamieMoore (Gary Moore) *nt fluent: sn last pair: pushed along 3rd: outpcd 5th tl began to stay on after 3 out: nvr nr ldrs* **6/1**	108+
405-	**5**	*3 1/4*	**Malibu Rock**[19] 4993 6-11-0 0... PaddyBrennan (Suzy Smith) *last pair: rdn and sme prog after 3 out: btn whn impeded by faller next* **33/1**	104
614-	**6**	*8*	**Houndscourt (IRE)**[125] 2955 7-11-6 124.....................(t[1]) BrendanPowell (Jamie Snowden) *prom: drvn bef 7th: fnd nil: lost pl and struggling next* **16/1**	102
464-	**7**	*nk*	**Royal Ripple (IRE)**[27] 4808 6-11-0 0.................................. TomO'Brien (Paul Henderson) *prom on outer: rdn and wknd 3 out: no ch whn j. faller next* **33/1**	98
0-	**8**	*9*	**Langham Lily (USA)**[70] 2514 5-10-4 0........................... JackQuinlan(3) (Sarah Humphrey) *cl up tl rdn and dropped out qckly bef 7th: t.o after being impeded by faller 2 out* **100/1**	80
	9	*66*	**Capitano Lento** 6-11-0 0.. IanPopham (Caroline Keevil) *midfield tl lost pl 6th: last next: t.o after 3 out* **100/1**	28
21-	**F**		**Spyder**[18] 5008 6-11-6 124... LeightonAspell (Lucy Wadham) *t.k.h in midfield: effrt after 3 out: 6 l 3rd and drvn and hld whn fell 2 out* **11/4**[2]	116

4m 42.8s (-16.60) **Going Correction** -0.725s/f (Firm) 10 Ran SP% **113.2**
Speed ratings (Par 105): **104,100,98,96,95 92,91,88,61,**
CSF £13.41 TOTE £6.10: £2.10, £1.10, £11.50; EX 14.40 Trifecta £625.90.
Owner Paul Chapman **Bred** Pat Fenlon **Trained** Lower Beeding, W Sussex

FOCUS
A dry morning caused the good to soft places in the overnight going description to be dropped, and racing took place on good ground. The rails on the bends were moved to their innermost positions. A medium gallop in this novice hurdle, which was dictated throughout by the front-running winner. A big step up from him, with the second and fourth pretty much to their marks.

5258 MALCOLM "HAIRY" ROBERTS MEMORIAL NOVICES' HURDLE (DIV II) (10 hdls) 2m 4f
1:50 (1:51) (Class 4) 4-Y-0+ **£3,119** (£915; £457; £228)

Form				RPR
262-	**1**		**Mcllhatton (IRE)**[76] 3892 6-11-6 125................................. NickScholfield (Paul Nicholls) *settled in 2nd or 3rd: rdn and effrt and wnt rt bef last: led 120yds out: styd on wl and sn in command* **9/4**[2]	126+
P41-	**2**	*2 1/4*	**Shubaat**[13] 5071 7-11-0 122.. DenisO'Regan (John Ferguson) *prom: ev ch and cajoled along bef 2 out: swtchd lft bef last: outbattled flat* **1/1**[1]	118+
1-	**3**	*1*	**Oliver's Hill (IRE)**[24] 4889 5-11-6 120.................................... NoelFehily (Charlie Longsdon) *racd keenly in ld: lft 6 l clr 2nd: rdn between last two: hdd and hung rt after last: no ex* **7/2**[3]	122
05-	**4**	*3 3/4*	**Candyman Can (IRE)**[66] 3364 4-10-7 0...............................[1] MarkGrant (Dominic Ffrench Davis) *midfield: effrt 3 out: rdn and on heels of ldrs next: nt qckn bef last* **20/1**	106
5-	**5**	*16*	**Shanaderry Kin (IRE)**[15] 5042 5-11-0 0.......................... PaddyBrennan (Simon Earle) *mstkes: anchored in last tl bef 7th: qcknd and on heels of ldrs 3 out tl next: eased bef last: promising* **25/1**	101+
600-	**6**	*27*	**Gold Carrot**[20] 4959 6-11-0 0... JamieMoore (Gary Moore) *in tch tl rdn and struggling after 3 out: t.o* **20/1**	74
005-	**7**	*10*	**Canarbino Girl**[18] 5002 7-10-0 0...................................... MrLDrowne(7) (Caroline Keevil) *midfield: pushed along after 6th: blnd next whn fading: rdn and t.o 3 out* **50/1**	58
5-	**8**	*21*	**Gair Leat (IRE)**[26] 4838 10-11-0 0.. TomO'Brien (Liam Corcoran) *bhd: reminder 5th: rdn and t.o 3 out* **50/1**	46
5/P-	**F**		**Lord Aldervale (IRE)**[116] 3138 7-11-0 64.....................(p) MarcGoldstein (Steve Woodman) *w ldr tl crashing fall 2nd* **100/1**	

00P- **U** **The Selector**[17] 5026 5-10-7 0 .... TomCannon
(Chris Gordon) *hit 1st and uns rdr* **100/1**

4m 42.0s (-17.40) **Going Correction** -0.725s/f (Firm)
WFA 4 from 5yo+ 6lb **10** Ran SP% **122.3**
Speed ratings (Par 105): **105,104,103,102,95 85,81,72, ,**
CSF £5.09 TOTE £4.00: £1.10, £1.10, £1.80; EX 6.00 Trifecta £12.50.
Owner Giles, Donlon & MacDonald **Bred** Maurice O'Brien **Trained** Ditcheat, Somerset

FOCUS
A slightly stronger gallop in this second division of the novice hurdle. The winner and third set the level.

5259 CHANCELLOR OF FORM CHECKER CLUB NOVICES' CHASE (16 fncs) 2m 6f
2:20 (2:20) (Class 4) 5-Y-0+ **£3,768** (£1,106; £553; £276)

Form RPR
543- **1** **Seebright**[24] 4885 7-10-12 0 .... JackDoyle 111+
(Victor Dartnall) *pressed ldr: led 2 out: 3 l clr last: rdn out and a in control after* **10/11**[1]
PF5- **2** *1 ¾* **Wilton Milan (IRE)**[49] 4395 6-10-12 129 .... NickScholfield 111+
(Paul Nicholls) *led: mstke 12th: rdn and hdd and hit 2 out: edgd rt sn after last: drvn and kpt on but flattered by proximity to wnr* **11/10**[2]
/06- **3** *12* **Serious Mixture**[26] 4838 7-10-12 0 .... DougieCostello 99
(Hilary Parrott) *a 3rd: 6 l 3rd bef 3 out: wl hld fr next: eased flat* **33/1**
00F/ **4** *13* **Zigzaga (IRE)**[327] 8-10-12 68 .... MarcGoldstein 84
(Lydia Richards) *last pair: rdn and outpcd 12th: lost tch bef 3 out* **50/1**
20P- **P** **Backhomeinderry (IRE)**[21] 4937 9-10-12 0 .... BrendanPowell
(Kate Buckett) *last pair and nt a fluent: rdn and struggling 8th: t.o and p.u 11th* **20/1**[3]

5m 24.2s (-18.80) **Going Correction** -0.925s/f (Hard) **5** Ran SP% **109.7**
Speed ratings: **97,96,92,87,**
CSF £2.29 TOTE £1.60: £1.10, £1.20; EX 2.60 Trifecta £11.10.
Owner Mrs D J Fleming **Bred** R Johnson **Trained** Brayford, Devon

FOCUS
This novice chase looked a match on paper. The first two are rated more in line with their previous chase form than their much better hurdle form.

5260 TOM CANNON, FONTWELL'S CHAMPION JOCKEY 2013 H'CAP HURDLE (10 hdls) 2m 4f
2:50 (2:50) (Class 4) (0-120,120) 4-Y-0+ **£3,119** (£915; £457; £228)

Form RPR
441- **1** **Taradrewe**[11] 5114 7-10-10 104 7ex .... (t) AidanColeman 112+
(Anthony Honeyball) *hld up: 6th and effrt after 3 out: rdn and gd prog bef next: led last: sn urged clr: comf* **5/4**[1]
3/3- **2** *6* **Leader Of The Gang**[13] 5075 8-11-9 117 .... (bt[1]) ConorO'Farrell 120
(David Pipe) *hld up and bhd: gd hdwy u.p on outer bef 2 out: drvn to chal and ev ch last: sn outpcd by wnr flat* **15/2**[2]
363- **3** *2* **Marie Deja La (FR)**[34] 4676 8-10-0 94 oh1 .... (b) TomCannon 96
(Chris Gordon) *sweating profusely: sn prom: rdn after 3 out: led and hit next: hdd last: btn whn edgd rt flat* **10/1**[3]
660- **4** *1 ½* **Dollar Bill**[106] 3288 5-11-1 109 .... (tp) LeightonAspell 111
(Nick Gifford) *settled towards rr: bdly hmpd 7th and continued in 14th pl: styd on fr 2 out: passed two rivals after last but nt rch ldrs: did v wl to get so cl* **12/1**
P55- **5** *nk* **Occasionally Yours (IRE)**[20] 4969 10-10-6 107 .... JosephAkehurst[(7)] 107
(Alan Blackmore) *led: hrd drvn after 3 out: hdd next: no ex and btn bef last: plugged on* **10/1**[3]
260- **6** *2* **Murcar**[77] 2314 9-10-13 107 .... DougieCostello 105
(Liam Corcoran) *hld up: outpcd in rr 3 out: drvn and effrt 2 out: pressed ldrs briefly: no ex fr last* **28/1**
4P4- **7** *6* **Torero**[11] 5112 5-11-0 108 .... (p) MarcGoldstein 101
(Diana Grissell) *prom and racd keenly: drvn after 3 out: lft 3rd and hmpd next: no imp whn hung rt flat* **50/1**
1F6- **8** *¾* **Chilworth Screamer**[139] 2663 6-11-2 110 .... BrendanPowell 104
(Chris Gordon) *nvr bttr than midfield: hmpd 3 out: rdn and btn after* **20/1**
05P- **9** *5* **Minella Special (IRE)**[20] 4969 8-11-6 114 .... TomO'Brien 101
(Paul Henderson) *nvr trbld ldrs: rdn and btn 3 out* **33/1**
33- **10** *½* **Yasir (USA)**[13] 5071 6-11-0 111 .... (p) PeterCarberry[(3)] 98
(Conor Dore) *jinked rt s and sn last: nvr on terms: drvn and btn 3 out* **14/1**
/64- **11** *7* **Red Skipper (IRE)**[20] 4947 9-11-7 115 .... PaddyBrennan 98
(John O'Shea) *plld hrd and prom: disp 3rd and rdn after 3 out: lost pl next: being eased whn bungled last* **33/1**
060- **12** *2* **Tidal Way (IRE)**[32] 4726 5-11-8 116 .... (p) NoelFehily 95
(Charlie Longsdon) *hld up: prog to trck ldrs 6th: drvn and wknd after 3 out* **14/1**
3/2- **F** **Alsadaa (USA)**[13] 5066 11-11-5 120 .... JackSherwood[(7)]
(Laura Mongan) *prom: 3rd at 6th: losing pl whn fell 3 out* **20/1**
5/0- **P** **John's Gem**[23] 4906 9-10-0 94 oh4 .... (p) GerardTumelty
(Zoe Davison) *mstke 3rd: dropped to rr and rdn 5th: sn struggling: t.o 7th: p.u next* **100/1**
410- **F** **Agincourt Reef (IRE)**[16] 5030 5-11-9 117 .... JamieMoore
(Gary Moore) *midfield tl fell 7th* **14/1**

4m 41.7s (-17.70) **Going Correction** -0.725s/f (Firm) **15** Ran SP% **123.9**
Speed ratings (Par 105): **106,103,102,102,102 101,98,98,96,96 93,92, , ,**
CSF £10.56 CT £73.68 TOTE £2.50: £1.10, £1.90, £3.60; EX 12.90 Trifecta £61.10.
Owner Frosties Friends II **Bred** T C Frost **Trained** Mosterton, Dorset

FOCUS
A good gallop for a race won by the handicap snip. She id rated 5lb off her recent win over further.

5261 NEIL MADGWICK/CLIP SCAFFOLDING SOUTHERN H'CAP CHASE (16 fncs) 2m 6f
3:25 (3:25) (Class 3) (0-140,140) 5-Y-0 **£6,330** (£1,870; £935; £468; £234)

Form RPR
00U- **1** **Fruity O'Rooney**[13] 5068 11-11-1 129 .... (v) JamieMoore 139+
(Gary Moore) *j. v boldly: mde all at str gallop: hrd drvn bef 3 out: pressed all way fr last but kpt pulling out ex: v game* **7/2**[2]
111- **2** *½* **Caulfields Venture (IRE)**[24] 4884 8-10-0 114 .... ConorO'Farrell 124+
(Emma Lavelle) *prom early: dropped towards rr of bunch 10th: nvr v fluent fr 12th: effrt home turn: wnt 2nd and hit 2 out: rdn to chal last: kpt on stoutly after but a jst hld* **11/4**[1]
215- **3** *12* **Domtaline (FR)**[54] 4303 7-11-9 140 .... HarryDerham[(3)] 140
(Paul Nicholls) *chsd ldrs: nt fluent 12th: rdn and btn bef 3 out: wnt modest 3rd cl home* **8/1**
4PP- **4** *½* **Roudoudou Ville (FR)**[34] 4674 9-11-12 140 .... JackDoyle 138
(Victor Dartnall) *settled chsng ldrs: nt fluent 11th: effrt to go 2nd bef 3 out: tl rdn next: wknd last* **25/1**
566- **5** *2 ¼* **Niceonefrankie**[20] 4962 8-11-6 134 .... AidanColeman 131
(Venetia Williams) *prom: rdn whn mstke 13th: sn dropped out* **9/2**[3]
201- **6** *nk* **Dolatulo (FR)**[13] 5068 7-11-7 138 .... (p) GavinSheehan[(3)] 134
(Warren Greatrex) *prom: 3rd and rdn bef 3 out: sn wknd* **5/1**
210- **7** *1* **Buthelezi (USA)**[31] 4742 6-11-5 133 .... DenisO'Regan 127
(John Ferguson) *plld hrd for two ms: a in last: j.lft 9th: drvn bef 13th: sn btn* **8/1**

5m 16.7s (-26.30) **Going Correction** -0.925s/f (Hard) **7** Ran SP% **109.8**
Speed ratings: **110,109,105,105,104 104,103**
CSF £12.90 TOTE £4.50: £3.20, £1.10; EX 16.30 Trifecta £143.40.
Owner Heart Of The South Racing **Bred** R W Russell **Trained** Lower Beeding, W Sussex

FOCUS
A decent handicap chase, and the winner's best figure since a C&D win last year.

5262 ALWAYS A CHANCE H'CAP HURDLE (9 hdls) 2m 2f 110y
4:00 (4:00) (Class 5) (0-100,100) 4-Y-0+ **£1,949** (£572; £286; £143)

Form RPR
406- **1** **Mighty Mambo**[25] 3434 7-10-9 83 .... (tp) DavidBass 95+
(Lawney Hill) *settled midfield: clsd fr 5th: tk 3rd gng strly after 3 out: led bef next: 6 l clr whn hit last: edgd rt flat but nvr in danger* **4/1**[2]
040- **2** *2* **Hermosa Vaquera (IRE)**[17] 5026 4-10-10 91 .... AdamWedge 91
(Anna Newton-Smith) *midfield: effrt 6th: wnt 3rd and nt fluent 3 out: chsd wnr fr last: edgd rt and no imp* **33/1**
344- **3** *8* **Juicy Legend**[32] 4721 7-10-3 77 .... TomCannon 77
(Chris Gordon) *a ldng quartet: pushed along after 5th: led briefly bef 2 out: drvn and no ex bef last* **15/2**
/01- **4** *hd* **While You Wait (IRE)**[16] 5029 5-11-12 100 .... JamieMoore 100
(Gary Moore) *midfield: hrd rdn and effrt after 3 out: kpt on same pce and wl hld fr next: drvn into modest 4th cl home: v one pce* **8/1**
6F0- **5** *¾* **Drumgooland (IRE)**[22] 4911 7-11-0 95 .... MrJMahot[(7)] 94
(Sarah-Jayne Davies) *sweating profusely: prom: lost pl and mstke 6th: kpt on again after 2 out: no ch w ldrs* **40/1**
001- **6** *1 ¼* **Al Amaan**[11] 5116 9-10-11 85 7ex .... MattieBatchelor 85
(Sheena West) *bhd: drvn bef 6th and nvr gng wl enough: laboured prog in 5th home turn: no further imp: nt fluent last* **7/2**[1]
020- **7** *¾* **Regal Flow**[132] 2827 7-11-5 100 .... MrLDrowne[(7)] 97
(Caroline Keevil) *in rr and rdn 4th: struggling after next: pluged on fr 2 out but no ch* **13/2**
13P- **8** *2* **Windpfeil (IRE)**[53] 3650 8-10-8 89 .... (p) MissCBoxall[(7)] 85
(Dominic Ffrench Davis) *bhd: outpcd after 5th: hit 2 out* **16/1**
0P0- **9** *1 ½* **Ricketyrock**[27] 4823 8-10-1 75 oh5 ow1 .... (v[1]) DaveCrosse 68
(Nick Mitchell) *led and racd freely: hrd drvn after 3 out: hdd bef next: sn dropped bk to midfield: hanging rt bef last* **66/1**
506- **10** *¾* **Superstiction**[67] 2907 5-10-12 86 .... MarcGoldstein 80
(Michael Madgwick) *towards rr: rdn and btn bef 2 out* **28/1**
100- **11** *1 ¾* **Sylvan Legend**[102] 3426 6-10-7 81 .... IanPopham 73
(Caroline Keevil) *sn lost gd pl: rdn and struggling after 3 out: blnd last* **6/1**[3]
500- **12** *2 ¼* **Nicky Nutjob (GER)**[17] 5019 8-11-1 96 .... (p) CiaranMckee[(7)] 86
(John O'Shea) *a wl bhd: struggling bef 6th: blnd next* **14/1**
0P0- **13** *10* **Upham Running (IRE)**[20] 4959 6-11-7 95 .... BrendanPowell 76
(Kate Buckett) *cl up tl drvn and fdd bef 2 out* **20/1**
P2P- **P** **Formedable (IRE)**[239] 1272 12-9-10 77 oh14 ow3 ... (p) CharlieDeutsch[(7)]
(Violet M Jordan) *last and drvn and struggling 3rd: nvr travelling: t.o and p.u 2 out* **66/1**
PP5- **U** **Tigridia (IRE)**[11] 5110 7-11-1 89 .... JoshuaMoore
(Sarah Wall) *towards rr whn blnd bdly and uns rdr 5th* **66/1**

4m 21.2s (-13.10) **Going Correction** -0.725s/f (Firm)
WFA 4 from 5yo+ 5lb **15** Ran SP% **123.3**
Speed ratings (Par 103): **98,97,93,93,93 92,92,91,91,90 90,89,84, ,**
CSF £135.68 CT £971.14 TOTE £5.60: £2.40, £7.60, £3.10; EX 205.10 Trifecta £1586.10 Part won..
Owner Fortnum Racing **Bred** Norcroft Park Stud **Trained** Aston Rowant, Oxon
■ Stewards' Enquiry : Dave Crosse one-day ban: weighed in 2lb heavy (Apr 25)

FOCUS
A competitive, if low-level handicap produced a comfortable winner. He was well in on his best Flat form.

5263 CHANCELLOR'S TROPHIES PROVIDED BY TROPHYSTORE.CO.UK H'CAP CHASE (15 fncs) 2m 4f
4:35 (4:35) (Class 5) (0-100,100) 5-Y-0+ **£2,144** (£629; £314; £157)

Form RPR
P54- **1** **Comeonginger (IRE)**[24] 4884 7-11-12 100 .... (t) TomCannon 111+
(Chris Gordon) *mde most fr 4th: hrd drvn bef 3 out: kpt finding a bit ex after: all out but game* **7/4**[1]
32U- **2** *1 ¼* **Johnnys Legacy (IRE)**[11] 5111 7-10-11 88 .... (p) PeterCarberry[(3)] 98
(Conor Dore) *led tl 4th: w wnr tl 1 l 2nd home turn: drvn and continued to press hrd tl no imp fnl 100yds* **7/1**[3]
334- **3** *½* **Harris Garden (IRE)**[187] 1800 7-10-12 86 .... (p) AdamWedge 96
(Paul Cowley) *bhd: hdwy 10th: 3 l 3rd home turn: effrt u.p whn n.m.r and hit last: kpt on but a hld after* **10/1**
565- **4** *7* **Simply Charles (IRE)**[24] 4885 7-10-8 82 .... DougieCostello 86
(Hilary Parrott) *mstkes and wl bhd: looked struggling w a lot to do after 7th: kpt plugging on fnl circ and wnt modest 4th at last: nvr rchd ldrs* **11/2**[2]
33P- **5** *12* **Shantou Breeze (IRE)**[18] 5009 7-11-3 91 .... MarcGoldstein 82
(Michael Madgwick) *cl up: drvn after 11th: no rspnse: lost tch bef 3 out* **33/1**
2PP- **6** *½* **Pod**[102] 3421 6-10-0 74 oh1 .... IanPopham 66
(Caroline Keevil) *mstke 6th: midfield and pushed along after 9th: effrt and last of five w ch but drvn home turn: sn wknd* **12/1**
432- **7** *nk* **Morestead (IRE)**[17] 5027 9-11-1 89 .... (p) LeightonAspell 80
(Brendan Powell) *midfield: pushed along 9th: struggling fr 11th* **12/1**
506- **8** *2 ½* **Killfinnan Castle (IRE)**[19] 4982 11-9-11 74 oh4 .... JamesBest[(3)] 62
(Violet M Jordan) *chsd ldrs: rdn after 9th: lost tch 11th* **14/1**
336- **9** *7* **Ballyman (IRE)**[116] 3139 13-10-5 79 .... (v) MarkGrant 61
(Jonathan Geake) *chsd ldrs: rdn whn mstke 12th: sn lost tch* **50/1**
/54- **10** *18* **Abbey Dore (IRE)**[96] 3555 11-9-12 75 .... NicodeBoinville[(3)] 41
(Jonathan Geake) *v erratic early: nrly uns rdr 2nd: in last pair: lost tch 7th: t.o 9th* **16/1**
P4F- **11** *9* **Red Anchor (IRE)**[17] 5023 10-11-2 90 .... JamieMoore 48
(Linda Jewell) *a rdn in rr and nvr gng wl: t.o fr 10th* **16/1**
PUP- **P** **Tchang Goon (FR)**[11] 5113 10-10-0 74 oh12 .... (p) GerardTumelty
(Zoe Davison) *bhd and nvr looked hopeful: mstke 5th: tailing off whn mstke 11th: p.u 3 out* **100/1**

424- **P** **Carpincho (FR)**[25] 4862 10-11-12 **100** AidanColeman
(Sarah Humphrey) *a bhd: struggling 9th: t.o and p.u 12th* **9/1**
4m 47.9s (-19.40) **Going Correction** -0.925s/f (Hard) 13 Ran SP% **123.0**
Speed ratings: **101,100,100,97,92 92,92,91,88,81 77,,**
CSF £15.73 CT £102.75 TOTE £3.30: £1.70, £2.20, £3.50; EX 15.40 Trifecta £249.20.
Owner Mr & Mrs Michael Coates **Bred** Miss Annette McMahon **Trained** Morestead, Hants

FOCUS
A strongly run affair but modest form. The first three were all on decent marks.

5264 CHANCELLOR SUPPORTS ALWAYS A CHANCE STANDARD OPEN NATIONAL HUNT FLAT RACE 1m 6f
5:05 (5:06) (Class 6) 4-6-Y-0 **£1,559** (£457; £228; £114)

Form RPR
1- **1** **Rhythm Star**[73] 3961 4-10-10 0 BrendanPowell 102+
(Jamie Snowden) *settled trcking ldrs: effrt in 3 l 3rd home turn: rdn to ld over 2f out: edgd lft 1f out: styd on wl fnl f* **7/1**
2 *3* **He's A Bully (IRE)**[19] 5-11-2 0 NickScholfield 105
(Polly Gundry) *tk str hold in 2nd: outpcd v briefly home turn: ev ch over 2f out: chsd wnr and rdn after: rn green: edgd rt 1f out: no ex ins fnl f* **7/1**
3 *5* **Golan Silk** 4-10-7 0 RachaelGreen(3) 94
(Anthony Honeyball) *hld up: prog in 5th home turn: sn pushed along and no imp wl over 1f out* **10/3**[1]
2- **4** *½* **Max The Minister**[23] 4909 4-10-10 0 TomO'Brien 94
(Hughie Morrison) *a ldng quartet: 2 l 2nd and rdn home turn: no ex wl over 1f out* **9/2**[3]
1- **5** *7* **Bjornlucky (IRE)**[141] 2634 4-11-0 0 HarryDerham(3) 95
(Dan Skelton) *chsd ldrs: rdn and wknd over 2f out* **11/1**
6 *2¼* **Bonnie Major** 4-9-12 0 MauriceLinehan(5) 79
(Gerry Enright) *rdn 1/2-way: nvr nr ldrs* **50/1**
7 *4½* **Primo Blue** 4-10-10 0 GerardTumelty 82
(Noel Williams) *rn green in rr: struggling 4f out: t.o* **20/1**
30- **8** *1½* **Seas The Moment (IRE)**[44] 4499 5-10-9 0 TomCannon 79
(Chris Gordon) *chsd ldrs 10f: sn dropped out: t.o* **16/1**
13- **9** *7* **Two Jabs**[132] 2830 4-11-3 0 JamieMoore 81+
(Mark Brisbourne) *tk ferocious hold: led and sn 7 l clr: hdd over 2f out and stopped to virtually nil: t.o* **4/1**[2]
10 *9* **Sir Hubert** 4-10-10 0 LeightonAspell 66
(Richard Rowe) *unruly paddock: mounted on crse: a bhd: struggling 1/2-way: bdly t.o: v green* **40/1**
11 *24* **Quest For Caviar** 4-10-10 0 AdamWedge 44
(Anna Newton-Smith) *bdly t.o fr 1/2-way* **100/1**
40- **P** **Little Louie**[46] 4473 5-11-2 0 JoshuaMoore
(Gary Moore) *midfield: struggling whn p.u sharply 4f out: fatally injured* **14/1**
3m 11.4s (-19.70) 12 Ran SP% **117.3**
CSF £53.33 TOTE £6.80: £2.10, £2.30, £1.40; EX 61.50 Trifecta £371.40.
Owner ValueRacingClub.co.uk **Bred** Mrs J A Thomas **Trained** Lambourn, Berks

FOCUS
A competitive bumper, but it was was run at an uneven gallop. Ordinary form, the winner building on her debut win.
T/Plt: £15.80 to a £1 stake. Pool: £61075.97 - 2807.20 winning tickets T/Qpdt: £10.20 to a £1 stake. Pool: £5683.60 - 411.57 winning tickets IM

5265 - 5271a (Foreign Racing) - See Raceform Interactive

5250 AYR (L-H)
Saturday, April 12

OFFICIAL GOING: Good to soft (soft in placess; chs 8.5 hdl 8.7)
Wind: Fresh, half against Weather: Cloudy

5272 CLYDE AND SOLWAY SYSTEMS LIMITED RACING EXCELLENCE "HANDS & HEELS" FINALE H'CAP HURDLE (CONS/AMS) (11 hdls) 2m 4f
1:30 (1:31) (Class 3) (0-130,128) 4-Y-0+ **£7,797** (£2,289; £1,144; £572)

Form RPR
222- **1** **Silsol (GER)**[55] 4300 5-11-8 **124** (tp) JackSherwood 140+
(Paul Nicholls) *prom: led 7th: clr after next: rdr dropped reins and swvd rt bef 2 out: sn rcvrd and kpt on strly: unchal* **7/2**[1]
152- **2** *14* **Final Assault (IRE)**[35] 4667 5-10-11 **113** [1] MrSFox 113
(Lucinda Russell) *bhd and detached: hdwy 4 out: chsd (clr) wnr next: no imp fr 2 out* **15/2**[0]
312- **3** *13* **Titus Bolt (IRE)**[36] 4647 5-11-1 **117** ConorRing 106
(Jim Goldie) *hld up: stdy hdwy 7th: effrt and rdn bef 3 out: no imp fr next* **9/1**
066- **4** *14* **Mubrook (USA)**[15] 5061 9-10-9 **111** (b) CraigGallagher 86
(Brian Ellison) *led to 2nd: cl up: regained ld after 5th: hdd 7th: chsd wnr tl wknd 3 out* **8/1**
054- **5** *14* **Dartford Warbler (IRE)**[15] 5054 7-11-6 **122** DaraghBourke 84
(Sue Smith) *prom: drvn along after 4 out: wknd fr next* **12/1**
533- **6** *6* **Divers (FR)**[25] 4893 10-11-1 **117** (b) JamesCowley 74
(Donald McCain) *hld up: rdn along bef 4 out: sn btn* **14/1**
P50- **7** *11* **Northern Oscar (IRE)**[21] 4957 6-10-0 **105** (p[1]) MrJoshuaNewman(3) 52
(Mark Walford) *in tch: drvn and outpcd 6th: struggling fr next* **8/1**
361- **8** *6* **Call Box (IRE)**[101] 3475 9-11-9 **128** (p) MrBGCrawford(3) 69
(S R B Crawford, Ire) *pressed ldr: led 2nd to after 5th: chsd ldrs tl wknd bef 2 out* **8/1**
011- **9** *2¼* **Granaruid (IRE)**[27] 4834 11-11-8 **124** (p) ThomasCheesman 63
(Alison Hamilton) *prom: drvn and outpcd 7th: struggling fr next* **20/1**
115- **U** **Aalim**[13] 5090 4-11-3 **126** (p) CharlieDeutsch
(John Ferguson) *hld up in midfield: stmbld and uns rdr after 5th* **5/1**[2]
4- **P** **Haughtons Bridge (IRE)**[14] 5081 6-10-0 **102** oh3 LiamMcKenna
(J J Lambe, Ire) *bhd and detached: drvn fr 1/2-way: nvr on terms: lost tch and p.u after 4 out* **33/1**
4m 56.6s (-15.40) **Going Correction** -0.65s/f (Firm)
WFA 4 from 5yo+ 6lb 11 Ran SP% **116.0**
Speed ratings (Par 107): **104,98,93,87,82 79,75,72,71,,**
CSF £29.87 CT £218.51 TOTE £3.90: £1.50, £2.60, £2.50; EX 29.20 Trifecta £175.10.
Owner Michelle And Dan MacDonald **Bred** Gestut Hof Iserneichen **Trained** Ditcheat, Somerset

FOCUS
All rails and bends on inside line and distances as advertised. The winning jockey in the first said the ground was "on the dead side" while fourth-placed Craig Gallagher said: "walking it you'd think it's better than it is, but it's tacky in a fair few places". Silsol's trainer Paul Nicholls added: "You can see it is a lot softer than yesterday - he is a soft-ground horse and it suited him." A fair "hands and heels" handicap run at a decent gallop. They finished at wide intervals.

5273 ARCADIA CONSULTING WILLIAM DICKIE & MARY ROBERTSON FUTURE CHAMPION NOVICES' CHASE (THE VULMIDAS CUP) (17 fncs) 2m 4f
2:05 (2:05) (Class 1) 5-Y-0+ **£26,748** (£10,017; £5,004; £2,497)

Form RPR
211- **1** **Eduard (IRE)**[36] 4646 6-11-4 144 BrianHarding 158+
(Nicky Richards) *j.w: chsd ldr: chal 6th: led after 5 out: drew clr bef 2 out: readily* **7/4**[2]
115- **2** *20* **Valdez**[32] 4737 7-11-7 153 RobertThornton 146
(Alan King) *j.rt thrght: t.k.h early: cl up: hdwy to ld 6th: hdd after 5 out: rdn along next: outpcd fr 3 out* **5/6**[1]
/PP- **3** *21* **Aibrean (IRE)**[86] 3750 10-10-11 130 PCarberry 119
(S R B Crawford, Ire) *hld up in last but in tch: stdy hdwy to chse clr ldrs 9th: nt fluent next: mstke and rdn 5 out: 3rd and hld whn nt fluent next* **14/1**
3PF- **4** *28* **Reaping The Reward (IRE)**[24] 4900 10-11-0 125 PeterBuchanan 92
(Lucinda Russell) *in tch: niggled along 11th: struggling fr 5 out: t.o* **28/1**
0/0- **P** **Miley Shah (IRE)**[9] 5150 9-11-4 140 (p) BarryGeraghty
(J P Kenny, Ire) *led: mstke 5th: nt fluent and hdd next: chsng clr ldrs whn blnd and lost pl 9th: j. slowly and p.u next* **8/1**[3]
5m 14.1s (-8.80) **Going Correction** -0.55s/f (Firm) 5 Ran SP% **112.1**
Speed ratings: **95,87,78,67,**
CSF £3.88 TOTE £2.90: £1.80, £1.10; EX 3.70 Trifecta £12.60.
Owner Kingdom Taverns Ltd **Bred** Cecil And Martin McCracken **Trained** Greystoke, Cumbria

FOCUS
The likes of Monet's Garden and French Opera have taken this race within the past ten years and today's winner looks a very nice prospect. The pace was fair and the race looked like it would develop into the duel the betting had predicted exiting the back straight, but it wasn't long before it became a one-horse race.

5274 QTS SCOTTISH CHAMPION HURDLE (LIMITED H'CAP) GRADE 2 (9 hdls) 2m
2:40 (2:40) (Class 1) 4-Y-0+
£39,865 (£14,959; £7,490; £3,731; £1,876; £938)

Form RPR
2F5- **1** **Cockney Sparrow**[32] 4740 5-9-11 **148** oh4 DeanPratt(7) 153+
(John Quinn) *hld up: pushed along after 4 out: hdwy next: rdn and nrly 4 l down last: qcknd to ld last 75yds: r.o* **12/1**
041- **2** *2¼* **Court Minstrel (IRE)**[7] 5172 7-10-8 **152** 5ex AdamWedge 154
(Evan Williams) *hld up: stdy hdwy 3 out: rdn to ld briefly run-in: kpt on: nt pce of wnr* **8/1**[3]
112- **3** *1¾* **My Tent Or Yours (IRE)**[32] 4739 7-11-10 **168** [1] APMcCoy 169
(Nicky Henderson) *plld hrd in midfield: hdwy to chse ldrs whn hit 4 out: led and rdn after 2 out: hdd run-in: kpt on same pce* **1/1**[1]
/50- **4** *3¼* **Swing Bowler**[35] 4682 7-9-11 **148** oh9 MikeyEnnis(7) 146
(David Pipe) *hld up: stdy hdwy 1/2-way: effrt and chsng ldr whn hung lft bef last: outpcd run-in* **33/1**
250- **5** *3¾* **Ifandbutwhynot (IRE)**[31] 4752 8-10-4 **148** oh9 RichardJohnson 142
(David O'Meara) *hld up: hdwy and prom after 3rd: led 4 out to 2 out: rallied: wknd after last* **33/1**
325- **6** *3¼* **Flaxen Flare (IRE)**[29] 4785 5-10-6 **150** (b) DavyCondon 143
(Gordon Elliott, Ire) *hld up in midfield: nt fluent 4th: outpcd next: drvn along bef 3 out: no imp fr next* **12/1**
/03- **7** *1½* **Montbazon (FR)**[29] 4785 7-10-4 **148** oh1 RobertThornton 139
(Alan King) *hld up: hdwy and prom bef 4 out: rdn whn nt fluent next: sn outpcd: n.d after* **7/1**[2]
111- **8** *9* **Clever Cookie**[42] 4550 6-10-4 **148** oh4 WilsonRenwick 130
(Peter Niven) *hld up: stdy hdwy on outside bef 3 out: rdn and wknd bef next* **7/1**[2]
100- **9** *¾* **Barizan (IRE)**[29] 4785 8-10-4 **148** oh12 (bt) SamTwiston-Davies 129
(Donald McCain) *led and clr to 4th: hdd 4 out: rdn and wknd fr next* **50/1**
/01- **10** *86* **Silk Hall (UAE)**[13] 1383 9-10-4 **148** oh10 (b) BrianHughes 52
(J J Lambe, Ire) *prom: pld 1/2-way: lost tch after 4 out: t.o* **100/1**
440- **P** **Cotton Mill**[31] 4752 7-10-1 **148** oh1 (b) JackQuinlan(3)
(John Ferguson) *chsd clr ldr: rdn and struggling bef 4 out: pulling up whn crashed through stands' rail and collapsed bef next: fatally injured* **16/1**
3m 45.9s (-17.20) **Going Correction** -0.65s/f (Firm) 11 Ran SP% **116.2**
Speed ratings (Par 115): **117,115,115,113,111 109,109,104,104,61**
CSF £100.10 CT £103.00 TOTE £14.10: £2.70, £2.00, £1.10; EX 90.10 Trifecta £260.00.
Owner Mr & Mrs Paul Gaffney **Bred** P Cunningham **Trained** Settrington, N Yorks

FOCUS
A fascinating edition of this event, with the presence of Champion Hurdle runner-up My Tent Or Yours off 168 meaning all except three of the field, the winner included, were out of the handicap proper. The pace, initially set by Barizan, was solid until it slowed a little down the back.

5275 SCOTTY BRAND H'CAP CHASE (LISTED RACE) (12 fncs) 2m
3:15 (3:15) (Class 1) 5-Y-0+ **£20,804** (£7,791; £3,892; £1,942)

Form RPR
112- **1** **Le Bacardy (FR)**[1] 5254 8-10-1 **130** (p) TrevorWhelan(3) 137+
(Tony Carroll) *trckd ldrs: stdy hdwy and ev ch fr 3 out: led run-in: rdn and r.o wl* **7/1**
124- **2** *nk* **Desert Cry (IRE)**[63] 4146 8-11-12 **152** APMcCoy 160+
(Donald McCain) *t.k.h: hld up in tch: stdy hdwy to ld 4 out: hit and rdn 2 out: sn hrd pressed: hdd run-in: kpt on: hld nr fin* **8/1**
422- **3** *13* **Upsilon Bleu (FR)**[58] 4237 6-11-0 **140** [1] WilsonRenwick 138
(Pauline Robson) *nt fluent on occasions: prom: hit 7th: hdwy and cl up after 5 out: drvn next: outpcd by first two fr after 3 out* **5/2**[1]
620- **4** *6* **His Excellency (IRE)**[29] 4790 6-11-0 **140** (bt) TomScudamore 132
(David Pipe) *hld up: stdy hdwy 5 out: rdn and hung lft after next: sn no imp* **6/1**
201- **5** *7* **Manyriverstocross (IRE)**[13] 5091 9-11-4 **144** RobertThornton 131
(Alan King) *cl up: led 7th to 4 out: rdn and wknd fr next* **3/1**[2]
045- **P** **Stormy Weather (FR)**[28] 4813 8-10-0 **126** (b) JamieMoore
(Brian Ellison) *bhd: struggling 1/2-way: t.o whn p.u after 4 out* **22/1**

123- **F** **Valco De Touzaine (FR)**[63] 4159 5-11-2 **142**.......(t) SamTwiston-Davies
(Paul Nicholls) *nt fluent on occasions: led to 7th: lost pl after 5 out: sn struggling: sixth and btn whn fell 3 out* **5/1**[3]

3m 56.4s (-14.30) **Going Correction** -0.55s/f (Firm) **7** Ran SP% **112.5**
Speed ratings: **113,112,106,103,99** ,
CSF £55.66 CT £176.88 TOTE £7.90: £3.60, £2.60; EX 54.00 Trifecta £267.30.
Owner Carl Hodgson **Bred** Jean-Charles Coude **Trained** Cropthorne, Worcs

FOCUS
A decent handicap chase and a pulsating finish.

5276 CORAL SCOTTISH GRAND NATIONAL H'CAP CHASE GRADE 3 (27 fncs) 4m 110y

3:50 (3:52) (Class 1) 5-Y-O+
£113,900 (£42,740; £21,400; £10,660; £5,360; £2,680)

Form RPR

020- **1** **Al Co (FR)**[104] 3387 9-10-0 **140** oh2....................................... JamieMoore 151+
(Peter Bowen) *hld up: stdy hdwy 1/2-way: chal 5 out: led next: jst over 4 l clr last: drvn and keeping on whn jinked rt twice nr fin* **40/1**

5PP- **2** *1 ½* **Godsmejudge (IRE)**[42] 4544 8-10-5 **145**.......................... AidanColeman 153
(Alan King) *prom: pckd 5 out: rdn and outpcd after next: rallied to chse (clr) wnr last: styd on wl towards fin* **16/1**

334- **3** *nk* **Trustan Times (IRE)**[30] 4765 8-10-0 **140** oh6................. WilsonRenwick 148
(Tim Easterby) *blnd 1st: hld up: hdwy and in tch 6 out: effrt and edgd lft 3 out: styd on fr last: nt pce to chal* **10/1**[2]

53P- **4** *14* **Merry King (IRE)**[56] 4270 7-9-9 **140** oh2..................... MauriceLinehan(5) 137
(Jonjo O'Neill) *hld up: stdy hdwy 1/2-way: effrt and drvn bef 4 out: no imp fr next* **16/1**

414- **5** *7* **Summery Justice (IRE)**[28] 4821 10-10-0 **140** oh6......(p) LiamTreadwell 131
(Venetia Williams) *hld up: stdy hdwy whn nt fluent 15th: blnd 20th: plugged on fr 3 out: no ch w ldrs* **50/1**

2U4- **6** *2 ¾* **Green Flag (IRE)**[32] 4738 7-10-2 **142**.............................. PeterBuchanan 130
(Lucinda Russell) *hld up: stdy hdwy and in tch 1/2-way: effrt and ev ch 4 out: rdn and hung lft after 2 out: lost 2nd and wkng whn mstke last* **9/1**[1]

32U- **7** *2* **Tidal Bay (IRE)**[7] 5171 13-11-12 **166**...................... SamTwiston-Davies 150
(Paul Nicholls) *hld up: pushed along and effrt after 6 out: outpcd fr 4 out* **11/1**[3]

F23- **8** *14* **Lackamon**[21] 4954 9-9-11 **140** oh1............................ JonathanEngland(3) 111
(Sue Smith) *cl up: led 6th to 5 out: rdn and wknd next: no ch whn j. bdly rt last* **33/1**

343/ **9** *24* **Yes Tom (IRE)**[26] 4871 9-10-0 **140**... PCarberry 89
(S R B Crawford, Ire) *hld up: stdy hdwy to ld 5 out: hdd next: wknd qckly bef 3 out* **12/1**

361- **P** **Lie Forrit (IRE)**[21] 4954 10-9-9 **140** oh5............................ CraigNichol(5)
(Lucinda Russell) *in tch: hit and outpcd 21st: no ch whn p.u bef 3 out* **14/1**

3U3- **P** **Mcmurrough (IRE)**[52] 4346 10-10-0 **140** oh1..................(b) BrianHughes
(Malcolm Jefferson) *in tch on outside: stdy hdwy after 18th: rdn and wknd after 5 out: p.u bef 3 out* **50/1**

P12- **P** **Mister Marker (IRE)**[36] 4651 10-10-0 **140** oh5.................. BrianHarding
(Nicky Richards) *hld up in midfield: outpcd 1/2-way: t.o whn p.u bef 20th* **25/1**

/06- **P** **Sole Witness (IRE)**[42] 4566 10-9-11 **140** oh9...................... BenDalton(3)
(C A McBratney, Ire) *towards rr: struggling fr 18th: t.o whn p.u bef next* **100/1**

063- **P** **Roberto Goldback (IRE)**[30] 4769 12-10-2 **142**.................... DavidBass
(Nicky Henderson) *in tch: mstke 7th: struggling bef 19th: t.o whn p.u after 5 out* **25/1**

P/1- **P** **Rigadin De Beauchene (FR)**[56] 4270 9-10-4 **147**........ RobertDunne(3)
(Venetia Williams) *chsd ldrs: blnd and lost pl 17th: struggling and p.u after next* **28/1**

024- **F** **Midnight Appeal**[49] 4422 9-10-3 **143** ow2..................(b) RobertThornton
(Alan King) *hld up: fell 18th* **25/1**

100- **P** **Pure Faith (IRE)**[168] 2071 10-10-0 **140** oh3.....................(t) JoshuaMoore
(Peter Bowen) *in tch: struggling fr 18th: wknd and p.u bef 20th* **80/1**

RPR- **P** **Battle Group**[7] 5171 9-10-7 **147**...................................(b) BrendanPowell
(Johnny Farrelly) *virtually ref to r: t.o whn consented to jump off: p.u bef 8th* **33/1**

125- **P** **Sam Winner (FR)**[31] 4751 7-10-7 **147**............................... NickScholfield
(Paul Nicholls) *in tch: pushed along fr 1/2-way: outpcd 20th: no ch whn p.u bef 2 out* **12/1**

201- **P** **Baile Anrai (IRE)**[29] 4792 10-10-0 **140** oh8......................(b) HarrySkelton
(Dan Skelton) *cl up: outpcd whn hit and struggling 6 out: sn btn: t.o whn p.u bef 4 out* **40/1**

4P0- **P** **Sir Du Bearn (FR)**[7] 5170 8-10-0 **140** oh11..................(p) DonalDevereux
(Peter Bowen) *led to 6th: hit 12th: struggling fr next: lost tch and p.u after 18th* **100/1**

1P4- **P** **Nuts N Bolts**[56] 4270 8-10-0 **140** oh4.............................(t) LucyAlexander
(Lucinda Russell) *towards rr: struggling fr 1/2-way: t.o whn p.u bef 21st* **20/1**

R12- **P** **Alpha Victor (IRE)**[28] 4821 9-10-0 **140** oh2...................... DougieCostello
(William Kinsey) *towards rr: outpcd whn hmpd 18th: sn btn: t.o whn p.u bef 20th* **20/1**

P31- **P** **Roalco De Farges (FR)**[21] 4962 9-10-0 **140** oh5.......... RichardJohnson
(Philip Hobbs) *hld up on outside: nt fluent 9th: hdwy and prom 20th: rdn and wknd bef 4 out: p.u bef 2 out* **9/1**[1]

410- **P** **Fill The Power (IRE)**[28] 4821 8-10-3 **143** oh5 ow3.............. RyanMania
(Sue Smith) *towards rr: struggling fr 15th: t.o whn p.u after 18th* **40/1**

113- **P** **Mendip Express (IRE)**[63] 4148 8-10-7 **147**........................(t) NoelFehily
(Harry Fry) *mstkes in rr: struggling fnl circ: t.o whn p.u bef 4 out* **9/1**[1]

04P- **P** **Ballybough Gorta (IRE)**[97] 3554 7-9-9 **140** oh11..(p) ConorShoemark(5)
(Peter Bowen) *nt fluent: towards rr: struggling and p.u bef 16th* **100/1**

P34- **P** **Adrenalin Flight (IRE)**[32] 4741 8-10-0 **140** oh10............... RyanMahon
(Seamus Mullins) *in tch: drvn and outpcd bef 6 out: sn btn: p.u bef 2 out* **25/1**

113- **P** **Edmund Kean (IRE)**[49] 4425 7-10-0 **140** oh3............. TomScudamore
(David Pipe) *towards rr: blnd 15th: bdly hmpd by faller 18th: sn btn: p.u bef 20th* **25/1**

8m 35.7s (-17.30) **Going Correction** -0.55s/f (Firm) **29** Ran SP% **134.8**
Speed ratings: **98,97,97,94,92 91,91,87,82,** , , , , , , , , , , ,**E**
CSF £527.53 CT £6778.67 TOTE £50.60: £9.70, £4.70, £4.30, £7.20; EX 1374.40 Trifecta £11121.50 Part won..
Owner F Lloyd **Bred** Jacky Rauch & Mme Colette Rauch **Trained** Little Newcastle, Pembrokes
■ Stewards' Enquiry : Brendan Powell five-day ban: improper, excessive and rapid use of the whip (May 3,5-8)

FOCUS
A competitive edition of this historic event. With the classy Tidal Bay in the line-up, well over half the field were out of the handicap, although this isn't a bar to success in this race as a dozen winners since 1982 had been wrong at the weights. As at Aintree there was a false start, with Battle Group again making a nuisance of himself. They went a sound gallop and it proved a thorough test of stamina.

5277 AYRSHIRE HOSPICE MAKING TODAY MATTER H'CAP HURDLE (12 hdls) 2m 5f 110y

4:25 (4:27) (Class 2) (0-155,137) 4-Y-O+ **£12,996** (£3,816; £1,908; £954)

Form RPR

2- **1** **Brother Du Berlais (FR)**[56] 4280 5-11-7 **132**.......... SamTwiston-Davies 137+
(Paul Nicholls) *trckd ldrs: led between last 2: drvn out* **5/1**[3]

122- **2** *3 ¼* **Rumble Of Thunder (IRE)**[24] 4897 8-11-0 **130**................ AdamNicol(5) 130
(Philip Kirby) *hld up towards rr: hdwy to trck ldrs 7th: tk 2nd run-in: kpt on same pce* **10/1**

/01- **3** *1 ¼* **Wyse Hill Teabags**[69] 4051 9-11-10 **135**......................... JamesReveley 134
(Jim Goldie) *led tl after 2nd: chsd ldrs: outpcd appr 2 out: kpt on run-in: tk 3rd nr fin* **5/1**[3]

3F2- **4** *nk* **Hit The Top (IRE)**[22] 4941 7-11-4 **129**.................................. RyanMania 128
(Sue Smith) *chsd ldrs: led narrowly 3 out: hdd between last 2: one pce* **8/1**

121- **5** *8* **Fine Rightly (IRE)**[53] 4340 6-11-6 **134**..........................[1] MrSCrawford(3) 128
(S R B Crawford, Ire) *trckd ldr: t.k.h: j.lft: led after 2nd: hdd 3 out: wknd appr last* **7/2**[2]

100- **6** *49* **Vendor (FR)**[31] 4752 6-11-12 **137**.. JackDoyle 84
(Alan King) *nt fluent in rr: shkn up 7th: drvn and nt fluent 9th: sn lost pl and bhd: t.o 2 out: virtually p.u* **2/1**[1]

4P5- **P** **Arctic Court (IRE)**[21] 4954 10-10-11 **122**........................ WilsonRenwick
(Jim Goldie) *chsd ldrs: reminders 5th and after next: lost pl 7th: sn bhd: t.o whn p.u bef 9th* **16/1**

5m 23.1s (-17.20) **Going Correction** -0.65s/f (Firm) **7** Ran SP% **115.0**
Speed ratings (Par 109): **105,103,103,103,100 82,**
CSF £50.19 CT £262.49 TOTE £4.60: £2.30, £3.20; EX 30.70 Trifecta £174.90.
Owner John Hales & Ian Fogg **Bred** J M Lucas, L Collet & C Collet **Trained** Ditcheat, Somerset

FOCUS
A decent handicap hurdle, run at just a fair pace.

5278 WEATHERBYS PRIVATE BANKING NOVICES' H'CAP CHASE (19 fncs) 3m 1f

5:00 (5:00) (Class 2) 5-Y-O+ **£19,494** (£5,724; £2,862; £1,431)

Form RPR

422- **1** **Samstown**[35] 4669 7-10-5 **116**.. EwanWhillans(3) 136+
(Alistair Whillans) *chsd ldrs: led 4 out: drew clr 2 out* **7/2**[1]

244- **2** *19* **King Of The Wolds (IRE)**[43] 4532 7-11-5 **127**.................. BrianHughes 132
(Malcolm Jefferson) *hld up in rr: hdwy 12th: 5th whn hit 14th and next: kpt on and chse wnr 2 out: no imp* **15/2**

111- **3** *13* **Kentford Legend**[20] 4990 7-11-0 **122**.......................... AndrewThornton 118
(Seamus Mullins) *chsd ldr: led 9th: j.rt and hit 12th: mstke 14th: hdd 4 out: modest 3rd and tired whn blnd last* **5/1**[2]

2- **4** *9* **Butney Boy (IRE)**[20] 4997 8-9-11 **108**............................(p) BenDalton(3) 92
(C A McBratney, Ire) *led to 9th: outpcd 15th: wknd next* **14/1**

002- **5** *¾* **Tony Star (FR)**[21] 4960 7-11-11 **133**............................. RichardJohnson 114
(Philip Hobbs) *hld up in rr: hdwy 10th: sn chsng ldrs: wkng whn mstke 15th: sn bhd* **5/1**[2]

241- **6** *8* **Scotswell**[21] 4953 8-11-2 **124**.. JamesReveley 98
(Harriet Graham) *chsd ldrs: mstke 10th: lost pl 14th: t.o 4 out* **6/1**[3]

11P- **P** **Pinerolo**[28] 4819 8-11-12 **134**.. RyanMania
(Sue Smith) *reminders 2nd and 4th: lost pl and blnd 6th: bhd after 10th: t.o whn p.u bef 13th* **16/1**

162- **P** **Presented (IRE)**[24] 4896 7-10-4 **112**..........................(p) TomScudamore
(Brian Ellison) *in rr: chsd ldrs 6th: drvn 11th: sn lost pl: t.o whn p.u bef 14th* **8/1**

211- **P** **Bit Of A Jig (IRE)**[46] 4474 7-11-10 **132**.................................(p) APMcCoy
(Donald McCain) *chsd ldrs: nt fluent and reminders 5th: lost pl and reminders after 10th: t.o whn p.u bef next* **6/1**[3]

6m 33.6s (-16.30) **Going Correction** -0.55s/f (Firm) **9** Ran SP% **119.6**
Speed ratings: **104,97,93,90,90 88,** , ,
CSF £31.11 CT £133.66 TOTE £5.60: £1.80, £3.00, £2.20; EX 43.00 Trifecta £321.50.
Owner Mrs Elizabeth Ferguson **Bred** Cheveley Park Stud Ltd **Trained** Newmill-On-Slitrig, Borders

FOCUS
This valuable event has quite a role of honour, with Merigo (who beat Ballabriggs), Auroras Encore and On His Own all winning it in recent seasons. This looked a decent edition, but not many passed the stamina test.

5279 JORDAN ELECTRICS LTD STANDARD OPEN NATIONAL HUNT FLAT RACE 2m

5:35 (5:35) (Class 3) 4-6-Y-O **£6,498** (£1,908; £954; £477)

Form RPR

1- **1** **Miles To Memphis (IRE)**[28] 4810 5-11-9 0.................. RobertThornton 118+
(Alan King) *hld up: smooth hdwy 3 out: rdn to ld over 1f out: drvn and styd on wl fnl f* **3/1**[2]

21- **2** *1* **The Unsub (IRE)**[35] 4671 6-11-9 0..................................... DavyCondon 116
(Gordon Elliott, Ire) *hld up in tch: rdn over 4f out: rallied over 2f out: chsd wnr ins fnl f: kpt on* **7/1**

/50- **3** *¾* **Apachee Prince (IRE)**[21] 4964 5-10-13 0..................... EwanWhillans(3) 109
(Alistair Whillans) *hld up: rdn and hdwy over 2f out: kpt on ins fnl f: nrst fin* **25/1**

4- **4** *¾* **Special Wells**[25] 4895 5-11-2 0.. RyanMania 108
(Sue Smith) *cl up: led 6f out: rdn and edgd lft over 2f out: hdd over 1f out: kpt on same pce ins fnl f* **33/1**

5 *3 ¼* **Wish In A Well (IRE)**[21] 5-10-13 0.............................. MrSCrawford(3) 105
(S R B Crawford, Ire) *hld up: pushed along 1/2-way: outpcd 4f out: rallied over 2f out: kpt on fnl f: nvr able to chal* **16/1**

41- **6** *¾* **Chieftain's Choice (IRE)**[33] 4728 5-11-9 0...................... BrianHughes 111
(John Quinn) *prom: drvn and outpcd 2f out: n.d after* **11/2**[3]

7 *1 ¾* **Shanroe Santos (IRE)**[26] 4874 5-11-2 0.................. RichardJohnson 103
(J J Lambe, Ire) *in tch: drvn along and outpcd over 2f out: no imp over 1f out* **33/1**

551- **8** *½* **Donna's Diamond (IRE)**[59] 4226 5-11-2 0............. DiarmuidO'Regan(7) 109
(Chris Grant) *led to 6f out: drvn and outpcd over 2f out: sn n.d* **16/1**

9 *2* **Superior Command (IRE)**[14] 5-11-2 0...................... TomScudamore 101
(Lucinda Russell) *trckd ldr: effrt and ev ch wl over 2f out: rdn and wknd over 1f out* **16/1**

10 *1* **California Desert (IRE)**[28] 6-10-6 0.................................. BenDalton(3) 93
(C A McBratney, Ire) *cl up tl rdn and outpcd over 3f out: n.d after* **66/1**

11 8 **Saint Charles (FR)**[48] 4-10-10 0 APMcCoy 86
(Nicky Henderson) *plld hrd: hld up towards rr: effrt and rdn wl over 2f out: sn btn* **15/8**[1]

5- 12 3 ½ **Buzzard Flight**[41] 4582 5-10-13 0 JonathanEngland(3) 89
(Sue Smith) *hld up: rdn and outpcd over 3f out: sn struggling* **50/1**

2- 13 4 ½ **Azure Glamour (IRE)**[25] 4895 5-11-2 0 BrianHarding 85
(Nicky Richards) *t.k.h: hld up: rdn and struggling over 6f out: sn btn* **16/1**

13- 14 1 ½ **Seldom Inn**[35] 4671 6-11-9 0 PeterBuchanan 91
(Sandy Thomson) *hld up: drvn and struggling over 6f out: nvr on terms* **25/1**

6- 15 26 **Bengairn**[35] 4671 6-11-2 0 JamesReveley 61
(Jim Goldie) *towards rr: struggling 6f out: sn btn: t.o* **50/1**

3m 50.0s (-7.50) **Going Correction** -0.65s/f (Firm)
WFA 4 from 5yo+ 5lb **15** Ran SP% **130.2**
Speed ratings: **92,91,91,90,89 88,87,87,86,86 82,80,78,77,64**
CSF £25.18 TOTE £3.60: £1.70, £3.20, £6.50; EX 34.00 Trifecta £641.60.
Owner Mrs Lesley Field & Jules Sigler **Bred** Maurice And Anthony Smiddy **Trained** Barbury Castle, Wilts
■ Stewards' Enquiry : Davy Condon four-day ban: used whip above permitted level (May 8-11)

FOCUS
A decent bumper which looks sure to have contained winners.
T/Jkpt: Not won. T/Plt: £465.80 to a £1 stake. Pool: £175,986.75 - 275.80 winning tickets.
T/Qpdt: £187.80 to a £1 stake. Pool: £11,883.32 - 46.80 winning tickets. RY

4945 BANGOR-ON-DEE (L-H)

Saturday, April 12

OFFICIAL GOING: Good to soft (soft in places on paddock bend; 6.8)
Wind: Strong, across Weather: Cloudy

5280 LARRY PRYDE 70TH BIRTHDAY CELEBRATION NOVICES' HURDLE (12 hdls) 3m
1:55 (1:55) (Class 4) 4-Y-0+ **£3,898** (£1,144; £572; £286)

Form RPR

156- 1 **Sausalito Sunrise (IRE)**[29] 4786 6-11-13 135 TomO'Brien 143+
(Philip Hobbs) *trckd ldrs: led appr 4 out: drew clr bef 3 out: unchal after* **10/11**[1]

0- 2 12 **Billy Biscuit (IRE)**[163] 2181 6-11-1 0 GerardTumelty 113
(Alan King) *hld up: mstke 4th: niggled along after 6th: shkn up bef 4 out: outpcd: wnt mod 2nd appr 2 out: no ch w wnr* **25/1**

124- 3 26 **Sir Mangan (IRE)**[45] 4489 6-11-7 125 HenryBrooke 106
(Donald McCain) *led: blnd 6th and sn hdd briefly: rdn and hdd appr 4 out where blnd: sn lft bhd by wnr: lost 2nd bef 2 out where blnd bdly: wl btn* **5/1**[3]

422- 4 24 **Glowinginthedark (IRE)**[41] 4574 6-11-1 119 (b) AndrewTinkler 78
(Charlie Longsdon) *chsd ldr: nt fluent 5th: led briefly after 6th: w ldr: mstke 8th: wknd appr 4 out* **7/1**

5 37 **Trafficker (IRE)**[97] 7-10-10 0 KillianMoore(5) 35
(Graeme McPherson) *in rr: rdn after 4th: struggling after next: lost tch after 6th: t.o* **66/1**

652- P **Ashes House (IRE)**[27] 4839 8-11-2 125 (t) PatrickCorbett(5)
(Rebecca Curtis) *trckd ldrs: rdn appr 8th: wknd sn after: t.o whn p.u bef 2 out* **7/2**[2]

5m 49.6s (-1.40) **Going Correction** +0.175s/f (Yiel) **6** Ran SP% **109.1**
Speed ratings (Par 105): **109,105,96,88,76**
CSF £20.91 TOTE £1.80: £2.20, £3.90; EX 10.60 Trifecta £116.50.
Owner Mrs Diana L Whateley **Bred** Thomas Corish **Trained** Withycombe, Somerset

FOCUS
A fair novice hurdle run at an honest gallop.

5281 RACING UK NOVICES' CHASE (15 fncs) 2m 4f 110y
2:30 (2:32) (Class 4) 5-Y-0+ **£3,994** (£1,239; £667)

Form RPR

121- 1 **King's Grace**[21] 4948 8-11-12 122 HenryBrooke 135
(Donald McCain) *racd in cl 2nd pl: led appr 4th: hdd 8th: remained w ldr: led again 11th: rdn and hdd narrowly bef 2 out: continued to chal: led again last: kpt on and on top fnl 100yds* **3/1**[3]

320- 2 1 ¼ **Swaledale Lad (IRE)**[164] 2159 7-10-9 122 HarryChalloner(3) 121
(Richard Ford) *led: hdd appr 4th: led again 8th tl hdd 11th: rdn to ld narrowly appr 2 out: nt fluent and hdd last: rdn on same pce fnl 100yds* **11/8**[1]

/30- 3 73 **The Bear Trap (IRE)**[133] 2813 7-10-12 0 (t) DominicElsworth 54
(Rebecca Curtis) *hld up: lost tch w front two fr 8th: 3rd and no ch after 3 out* **2/1**[2]

630- P **Royal Macnab (IRE)**[34] 4693 6-10-12 0 (t[1]) AndrewTinkler
(Jamie Snowden) *hld up: lost tch w front two fr 8th: eased and wl btn whn p.u after 3 out* **12/1**

5m 19.1s (10.00) **Going Correction** +0.725s/f (Soft) **4** Ran SP% **108.1**
Speed ratings: **109,108,80,**
CSF £7.72 TOTE £3.40; EX 6.00 Trifecta £5.90.
Owner T G Leslie **Bred** R T Crellin **Trained** Cholmondeley, Cheshire

FOCUS
Not a bad contest despite the small field.

5282 BROXTON GATES H'CAP HURDLE (DIV I) (11 hdls) 2m 4f
3:05 (3:05) (Class 5) (0-100,100) 4-Y-0+ **£3,422** (£997; £499)

Form RPR

/02- 1 **Polo Springs**[21] 4972 7-9-10 75 (t) KillianMoore(5) 84+
(Graeme McPherson) *mde all: mstke 4 out: rdn clr appr last: eased down cl home* **7/1**

/04- 2 7 **Fiddleesticks (IRE)**[41] 4579 6-11-5 96 (t) HarryChalloner(3) 96
(William Kinsey) *midfield: lost pl bef 6th: sn pushed along: struggling 7th: tried to make hdwy appr 4 out: sn outpcd: styd on bef last: tk 2nd fnl 100yds: no ch w wnr* **10/3**[1]

063- 3 2 ¼ **Grand March**[34] 4703 5-11-7 100 EdCookson(5) 100
(Kim Bailey) *hld up in midfield: hdwy to chse ldrs 7th: hit 4 out: wnt 2nd appr 2 out: no imp on wnr whn nt fluent last: lost 2nd and no ex fnl 100yds* **4/1**[2]

302- 4 10 **Icanmotor**[28] 4823 7-10-11 85 (tp) AndrewTinkler 75
(Claire Dyson) *prom: wnt 2nd after 5th: lost 2nd appr 2 out: wknd between last 2* **5/1**[3]

0/P- 5 1 ½ **Vintage Vixon (IRE)**[139] 2701 7-11-2 90 MichaelByrne 80
(Tim Vaughan) *hld up: pushed along appr 5th: tried to make hdwy bef 7th: sn struggling again: j. slowly 3 out: n.d after* **16/1**

P/6- 6 ¾ **Lucky Prince**[102] 3428 7-10-12 93 GaryDerwin(7) 80
(Brian Eckley) *hld up in rr: niggled along after 6th: hdwy 3 out: rdn and no imp bef 2 out* **20/1**

5P3- 7 7 **Right To Rule (IRE)**[28] 4817 5-11-11 99 (b) AdrianLane 81
(Donald McCain) *prom: nt fluent 6th: rdn and wknd after 3 out* **8/1**

316- 8 108 **Ruby Valentine (FR)**[21] 4972 11-10-2 76 PaulMoloney
(Jim Wilson) *hld up: rdn appr 4 out: wl btn: t.o* **12/1**

000- P **Siksika (IRE)**[20] 4981 6-11-2 90 (b[1]) IanPopham
(Dan Skelton) *midfield: sn pushed along: losing pl whn mstke 5th: t.o whn p.u sn after* **12/1**

600- P **Carpies Boy**[24] 4903 5-10-11 95 (t) WilliamFeatherstone(10)
(Warren Greatrex) *prom: pushed along after 5th: rdn and losing pl whn nt fluent 7th: bhd after: t.o whn p.u bef 2 out* **16/1**

4m 58.5s (6.50) **Going Correction** +0.175s/f (Yiel) **10** Ran SP% **115.3**
Speed ratings (Par 103): **94,91,90,86,85 85,82,,,**
CSF £30.89 CT £106.80 TOTE £7.40: £2.90, £1.20, £2.50; EX 42.00 Trifecta £248.60.
Owner Denarius Consulting Ltd **Bred** J C Boher **Trained** Upper Oddington, Gloucs

FOCUS
A weak handicap.

5283 BROXTON GATES H'CAP HURDLE (DIV II) (11 hdls) 2m 4f
3:40 (3:40) (Class 5) (0-100,100) 4-Y-0+ **£3,422** (£997; £499)

Form RPR

100- 1 **Rocky Stone (IRE)**[30] 4774 6-11-11 99 HenryBrooke 99
(Donald McCain) *trckd ldrs: wnt 2nd appr 3 out: rdn nrly 4 l down and looking hld whn lft in ld last: kpt on* **7/2**[2]

PP6- 2 2 ½ **Valrene**[26] 4865 8-11-7 95 CharliePoste 93
(Robin Dickin) *hld up: hdwy to chse ldrs 7th: one pce whn lft in 2nd pl last: no imp on wnr run-in* **9/2**[3]

5PP- 3 4 **Ballycracken (IRE)**[26] 4863 10-9-11 76 (b[1]) JoeCornwall(5) 69
(David Pearson) *in tch: rdn after 5th: kpt on same pce u.p fr 2 out: lft 3rd at last* **33/1**

0F0- 4 18 **Miller's Maverick**[11] 5117 6-11-6 94 TomO'Brien 71
(Grant Cann) *hld up: rdn and struggling after 5th: tried to make hdwy whn mstke 7th: wknd bef 2 out* **10/1**

050- 5 9 **Femme D'Espere**[14] 5072 8-9-8 75 oh5 ow1 JoshWall(7) 44
(Trevor Wall) *hld up: pushed along after 4 out: sn no ch* **66/1**

460- 6 3 **Delineate (IRE)**[10] 5124 5-10-8 89 MrZBaker(7) 55
(G C Maundrell) *bhd: niggled along bef 4th: struggling after 5th: nvr a threat* **22/1**

554- 7 45 **Tribal Dance (IRE)**[36] 4663 8-11-5 100 CiaranMckee(7) 26
(John O'Shea) *midfield: lost pl after 5th: struggling and bhd after: t.o* **10/1**

50/- P **Blazing Desert**[32] 4590 10-10-12 91 ThomasGarner(5)
(William Kinsey) *racd keenly: w ldrs: rdn and lost pl qckly after 6th: t.o whn p.u bef 7th* **7/1**

100- U **Peqeno Diablo (IRE)**[48] 4447 9-9-7 74 oh2 (tp) GeraldQuinn(7)
(Claire Dyson) *led: hdd 6th: mstke 7th: lost 2nd appr 3 out where nrly 3 l down whn blnd and uns rdr* **12/1**

420- F **Mist The Boat**[197] 1673 6-11-2 90 MichaelByrne 95+
(Tim Vaughan) *w ldrs: led 6th: styng on and looking in command nrly 4 l clr whn fell last: unlucky* **11/4**[1]

4m 58.5s (6.50) **Going Correction** +0.175s/f (Yiel) **10** Ran SP% **114.2**
Speed ratings (Par 103): **94,93,91,84,80 79,61,,,**
CSF £19.25 CT £437.36 TOTE £4.50: £1.80, £2.50, £5.10; EX 23.10 Trifecta £388.40.
Owner Penketh And Sankey Jech Racing Club **Bred** James Cregan **Trained** Cholmondeley, Cheshire

FOCUS
The second division of the weak 2m4f handicap and it saw a dramatic conclusion.

5284 BANGOR ON DEE H'CAP CHASE (18 fncs) 3m 110y
4:15 (4:15) (Class 4) (0-120,120) 5-Y-0+ **£6,498** (£1,908; £954; £477)

Form RPR

4U5- 1 **Kingcora (FR)**[28] 4822 6-10-12 111 CallumWhillans(5) 124+
(Venetia Williams) *chsd ldrs: mstke 3rd: wnt cl 2nd after 12th: blnd 4 out: led appr 2 out: rdn bef last: styd on: in command towards fin* **10/3**[2]

P35- 2 6 **Young Hurricane (IRE)**[43] 4537 8-11-4 112 (bt) PaulMoloney 119
(Dr Richard Newland) *led to 9th: led again 10th: mstke 4 out: hdd appr 2 out: one pce u.p fr last* **11/2**

26P- 3 16 **My Boy Paddy (IRE)**[11] 5119 10-10-8 109 (p) RyanHatch(7) 106
(Nigel Twiston-Davies) *chsd ldrs: pushed along appr 10th: prom 12th: mstke 4 out: last 3 out: outpcd after: tk 3rd bef last but no ch* **7/1**

16P- 4 30 **Lough Derg Way (IRE)**[211] 1759 8-11-9 120 GavinSheehan(3) 105
(Jamie Snowden) *bhd: nt fluent 8th: j. slowly 12th: effrt bhd ldrs 13th: wnt 3rd 3 out: wknd after 2 out* **15/2**

023- P **Dunlough Bay (IRE)**[22] 4934 8-11-10 118 (p) DenisO'Regan
(Paul Webber) *prom: nt fluent 5th: led 9th to 10th: lost pl after 12th: bhd whn p.u after 13th* **7/2**[3]

P31- P **No Duffer**[50] 4399 7-11-9 117 AndrewTinkler
(Henry Daly) *chsd ldrs: nt travel wl after 4th: bhd after 9th: p.u bef 11th* **3/1**[1]

6m 33.6s (13.80) **Going Correction** +0.725s/f (Soft) **6** Ran SP% **110.0**
Speed ratings: **106,104,98,89,**
CSF £20.26 TOTE £3.90: £1.20, £2.80; EX 22.00 Trifecta £89.60.
Owner Mrs Julian Blackwell **Bred** Richard Corveller **Trained** Kings Caple, H'fords

FOCUS
A modest handicap.

5285 ALFA AGGREGATE PRODUCTS H'CAP HURDLE (12 hdls) 3m
4:50 (4:51) (Class 4) (0-120,120) 4-Y-0+ **£5,198** (£1,526; £763; £381)

Form RPR

035- 1 **Darkestbeforedawn (IRE)**[22] 4933 7-11-1 109 TomO'Brien 115
(Caroline Keevil) *trckd ldrs: led 7th: rdn appr last: pressed briefly fnl 75yds: fnd ex towards fin* **9/1**

460- 2 1 ¼ **Teochew (IRE)**[19] 5010 6-11-5 116 (t) GavinSheehan(3) 123+
(Warren Greatrex) *in tch: effrt 4 out: bdly hmpd 3 out: lost grnd: rdn and styd on to take 2nd appr 2 out: over 2 l down whn mstke last: rallied and ev ch fnl 75yds: no ex cl home* **7/1**[3]

P01- 3 6 **Decimus (IRE)**[21] 4969 7-11-5 116 MattGriffiths(3) 118
(Jeremy Scott) *in rr: mstke 7th: hdwy whn nt fluent 4 out: styd on fr 2 out: tk 3rd towards fin: nt trble front two* **9/1**

452- 4 1 ¼ **Midnight Oscar (IRE)**[23] 4913 7-11-7 120 (v) EdCookson(5) 118
(Kim Bailey) *in tch: effrt whn lft 2nd 3 out: lost 2nd appr 2 out: kpt on same pce bef last* **9/4**[1]

PP3- 5 8 **Mister Snowball (FR)**[18] 5019 7-11-2 110 PaulMoloney 101
(Chris Down) *midfield: hdwy to go handy 3rd: rdn appr 2 out: wknd bef last* **12/1**

640- **6** *6* **Welsh Bard (IRE)**[46] 4478 5-10-13 **107**..........(b) HenryBrooke 93
(Donald McCain) *midfield: hdwy 7th: sn chsd ldrs: rdn and wknd after 3 out* **22/1**

0P3- **7** *9* **Lisheen Hill (IRE)**[24] 4906 8-10-4 **105**.......... DanielHiskett[(7)] 83
(Richard Phillips) *w ldr tl after 8th: rdn and wkng whn mstke 4 out: no ch whn hmpd 3 out* **16/1**

633- **8** *13* **Master Butcher (IRE)**[52] 4356 7-10-12 **113**.......... PaulO'Brien[(7)] 79
(Rebecca Curtis) *prom: dropped to midfield 4th: rdn after 7th: wknd appr 4 out: hmpd 3 out: wl btn* **12/1**

052- **9** *20* **Trillerin Minella (IRE)**[25] 4887 6-10-8 **107**.......... KillianMoore[(5)] 55
(Graeme McPherson) *midfield: rdn appr 7th: struggling whn hmpd 3 out* **14/1**

102- **10** *3 ¾* **Gold Ingot**[20] 4991 7-11-3 **118**.......... TomBellamy[(7)] 63
(Alan King) *hld up: pushed along after 7th: bhd whn hmpd 3 out: no ch after* **11/2**[2]

/P0- **U** **Shalone**[24] 4897 10-11-5 **120**..........(p) RyanHatch[(7)]
(Adrian Wintle) *midfield: rdn and outpcd bef 4 out: hmpd and uns rdr next* **33/1**

430- **F** **El Indio (IRE)**[31] 4760 7-10-2 **103**.......... GeraldQuinn[(7)]
(Claire Dyson) *led: hdd 7th: stl chalng 4 out: ev ch whn fell 3 out* **20/1**

4B0- **U** **Kukurudu (IRE)**[124] 2999 7-9-10 **95**..........(p) JoeColliver[(5)]
(Simon West) *in rr: rdn after 7th: stdy hdwy into midfield whn hmpd and uns rdr 3 out* **33/1**

5m 52.9s (1.90) **Going Correction** +0.175s/f (Yiel) **13** Ran SP% **121.6**
Speed ratings (Par 105): **103,102,100,100,97 95,92,88,81,80 , ,**
CSF £69.26 CT £592.12 TOTE £9.20: £2.80, £3.70, £2.70; EX 101.90 Trifecta £1071.80 Part won..
Owner The Jago Family Partnership **Bred** Miss Fay Clarke **Trained** Motcombe, Dorset
FOCUS
A competitive handicap for the class.

5286 BANGORBET STANDARD NATIONAL HUNT FLAT RACE (CONDITIONAL JOCKEYS' AND AMATEUR RIDERS' RACE) 2m 1f
5:25 (5:26) (Class 5) 4-6-Y-0 **£2,053** (£598; £299)

Form RPR

1 **Bells 'N' Banjos (IRE)** 4-10-9 0.......... GavinSheehan[(3)] 105+
(Warren Greatrex) *hld up in rr: hdwy 6f out: wnt 2nd over 4f out: led 3f out: drew clr over 1f out: readily* **9/4**[2]

2 *7* **Final Pass (IRE)**[132] 6-10-11 0.......... MrHStock[(7)] 101+
(Donald McCain) *led: rdn and hdd 3f out: no ch w wnr fr over 1f out* **2/1**[1]

0- **3** *8* **Call Me Emma (IRE)**[102] 3440 6-10-4 0.......... DanielHiskett[(7)] 86
(Richard Phillips) *hld up: niggled along after 7f: hdwy 6f out: kpt on one pce fnl 3f: no imp* **20/1**

00- **4** *8* **Crowd Control (IRE)**[27] 4844 5-10-13 0..........(p) PatrickCorbett[(5)] 86
(Rebecca Curtis) *hld up in tch: pushed along 5f out: sn outpcd* **14/1**

5 *3 ¾* **Rain Down (FR)**[83] 5-10-11 0.......... NickSlatter[(7)] 82
(Donald McCain) *prom: pushed along over 4f out: sn wknd* **11/2**[3]

6 *23* **Pyrshan (IRE)**[146] 5-10-13 0.......... KillianMoore[(5)] 62
(Graeme McPherson) *racd keenly: trckd ldrs: rdn 6f out: wknd 5f out* **20/1**

7 *52* **Earl The Pearl** 4-10-9 0.......... HarryDerham[(3)] 9
(Dan Skelton) *midfield: pushed along bef 1/2-way: wknd 7f out: t.o* **8/1**

8 *125* **Bumble Bay** 4-10-9 0.......... MichealNolan[(3)]
(Robert Stephens) *trckd ldrs: pushed along and wknd 6f out: t.o* **16/1**

4m 4.2s (-1.10) **Going Correction** +0.175s/f (Yiel)
WFA 4 from 5yo+ 5lb **8** Ran SP% **112.7**
Speed ratings: **109,105,101,98,96 85,61,**
CSF £6.91 TOTE £2.60: £1.10, £1.60, £3.30; EX 8.90 Trifecta £89.20.
Owner The Maple Hurst Partnership **Bred** Beech Hill Stud **Trained** Upper Lambourn, Berks
FOCUS
A modest bumper.

5287 COUNTRYSIDE ALLIANCE OPEN HUNTERS' CHASE (18 fncs) 3m 110y
5:55 (5:55) (Class 6) 6-Y-0+ **£1,317** (£405; £202)

Form RPR

/U5- **1** **King Fontaine (IRE)**[13] 11-11-11 111.......... MrGCrow[(3)] 120+
(J J O'Shea) *hld up: hdwy 12th: wnt 2nd appr 14th: led 3 out: styd on wl to draw clr run-in* **2/1**[1]

042- **2** *3 ½* **How's My Friend**[10] 5131 9-11-7 108.......... MissABush[(7)] 115
(Grant Cann) *chsd ldr tl appr 14th: outpcd after 3 out: kpt on after last: tk 2nd fnl strides: nt trble wnr* **3/1**[2]

P33- **3** *nk* **Ski Sunday**[23] 4915 9-11-9 112..........(t) MrADoyle[(5)] 115
(Tim Vaughan) *chsd ldrs: rdn after 4 out: wnt 2nd appr last: no imp on wnr: lost 2nd fnl strides* **7/2**[3]

2P0- **4** *7* **Island Life (IRE)**[9] 5135 11-11-7 104..........(p) MrDerekSmith[(7)] 111
(S Flook) *in tch: led appr 11th: rdn and hdd 3 out: u.p and hld in 3rd whn blnd last: no ex run-in* **16/1**

54P- **P** **Croan Rock (IRE)**[29] 4788 9-11-7 93..........(p) MrJLyttle[(7)]
(R A Owen) *hld up in rr: rdn after 13th: lft bhd fr 4 out: t.o whn p.u bef 2 out* **6/1**

5/4- **U** **Best Served Cold**[13] 8-11-7 115.......... MrCSmith[(7)]
(J J O'Shea) *led: hdd appr 11th: pushed along bef 12th: u.p in 5th but stl in tch whn blnd and uns rdr 14th* **8/1**

6m 33.3s (13.50) **Going Correction** +0.725s/f (Soft) **6** Ran SP% **111.8**
Speed ratings: **107,105,105,103,**
CSF £8.57 TOTE £2.90: £1.50, £1.50; EX 9.80 Trifecta £20.20.
Owner R J Hewitt **Bred** Peter McCarthy **Trained** Farnworth, Gt Manchester
FOCUS
An ordinary hunter chase.
T/Plt: £510.60 to a £1 stake. Pool: £43,776.16 - 62.58 winning tickets. T/Qpdt: £77.30 to a £1 stake. Pool: £3,617.09 - 34.58 winning tickets. DO

5064 STRATFORD (L-H)
Sunday, April 13

OFFICIAL GOING: Hurdle course - good changing to good (good to firm in places) after race 1 (2.00); chase course - good (good to soft in places) changing to good (good to firm in places) after race 2 (2.30)
Wind: Fresh across Weather: Cloudy with sunny spells

5288 TOTEJACKPOT GO FOR THE BIG ONE NOVICES' HURDLE (11 hdls) 2m 6f 110y
2:00 (2:00) (Class 4) 4-Y-0+ **£4,548** (£1,335; £667; £333)

Form RPR

122- **1** **Call Me Vic (IRE)**[23] 4931 7-11-1 129.......... PaddyBrennan 119+
(Tom George) *mde all: clr fr 3 out: nt fluent last: easily* **1/4**[1]

050- **2** *3 ½* **Carn Rock**[25] 4903 6-10-12 93.......... PeterCarberry[(3)] 106
(Michael Gates) *a.p: chsd wnr 6th: rdn appr last: styd on same pce flat* **40/1**

00- **3** *16* **Road To Freedom**[29] 4808 5-11-1 0.......... TomO'Brien 92
(Lucy Wadham) *hld up: hdwy 3 out: rdn and wknd appr last* **12/1**[3]

4 *28* **Rock Me Zippo (IRE)**[329] 6-10-5 0.......... MikeyHamill[(10)] 62
(Sean Curran) *prom: nt fluent 2nd: rdn and wknd after 2 out* **14/1**

30/ **5** *18* **Millers Pudsey**[520] 2305 8-11-1 0.......... SeanQuinlan 44
(David Bridgwater) *hld up: wknd 3 out* **14/1**

0/6- **6** *1 ½* **Fine Jewellery**[21] 4980 5-11-1 0..........(t) DougieCostello 43
(Tom Gretton) *hld up: plld hrd: wknd 3 out: bhd whn j.rt 2 out and last* **40/1**

621- **P** **Robbers Roost (IRE)**[36] 4672 6-10-11 120.......... AlanJohns[(10)]
(Tim Vaughan) *chsd ldrs tl wnt wrong bnd after 5th and sn p.u: fatally injured* **7/2**[2]

006- **P** **Mr Lennygreengrass (IRE)**[35] 4702 7-10-10 0.....(t) ConorShoemark[(5)]
(Fergal O'Brien) *chsd wnr 2nd to 6th: wnt wrong and p.u bef next: fatally injured* **33/1**

5m 27.1s (-1.00) **Going Correction** -0.15s/f (Good) **8** Ran SP% **131.1**
Speed ratings (Par 105): **95,93,88,78,72 71, ,**
CSF £25.59 TOTE £1.20: £1.02, £13.20, £2.80; EX 38.50 Trifecta £405.50.
Owner C B Compton **Bred** R P Walshe **Trained** Slad, Gloucs
FOCUS
Double bends throughout and all on fresh ground. The jockeys agreed that the ground was on the firm side, and the official going on the hurdles track was amended to good, good to firm in places after the opener. A modest and uncompetitive novice hurdle which was marred by the fatal injuries suffered by both Robbers Roost and Mr Lennygreengrass.

5289 TOTEPLACEPOT RACING'S FAVOURITE BET NOVICES' CHASE (12 fncs) 2m 1f 110y
2:30 (2:31) (Class 4) 5-Y-0+ **£4,548** (£1,335; £667; £333)

Form RPR

622- **1** **Bellenos (FR)**[14] 5091 6-11-5 139..........(t) HarrySkelton 147+
(Dan Skelton) *trckd ldrs: wnt 2nd 7th: led appr last: rdn out* **4/6**[1]

426- **2** *3 ¼* **Witness In Court (IRE)**[14] 5091 7-11-5 128.......... APMcCoy 142
(Donald McCain) *led to 2nd: led again 6th: drvn along after 2 out: hdd bef last: styd on same pce flat* **15/8**[2]

330- **3** *dist* **Mission To Mars (IRE)**[23] 4937 5-10-12 107.......... SamTwiston-Davies 96
(Nigel Twiston-Davies) *hld up: wknd 3 out: b.b.v* **17/2**[3]

35U- **4** *nk* **Red Whisper**[255] 1175 10-10-5 85.......... JakeHodson[(7)] 97
(Rob Summers) *led 2nd to 6th: wkng whn pckd 9th: mstke next* **66/1**

4m 13.1s (6.00) **Going Correction** +0.275s/f (Yiel) **4** Ran SP% **106.8**
Speed ratings: **97,95,77,77**
CSF £2.31 TOTE £1.80; EX 2.20 Trifecta £2.90.
Owner Mr And Mrs J D Cotton **Bred** Pierre De Maleissye Melun **Trained** Alcester, Warwicks
FOCUS
This novice chase was won 12 months ago by a certain Sire De Grugy.

5290 TOTETRIFECTA AVAILABLE ON ALL RACES H'CAP CHASE (14 fncs) 2m 4f
3:05 (3:05) (Class 3) (0-130,129) 5-Y-£7,596 (£2,244; £1,122; £561; £280)

Form RPR

601- **1** **Ballincurrig (IRE)**[22] 4970 8-10-13 **116**..........(t) HarrySkelton 127+
(Dan Skelton) *led 2nd: sn hdd: chsd ldrs: rdn whn nt fluent last: r.o u.p to ld towards fin* **7/1**

425- **2** *½* **Wings Of Smoke (IRE)**[37] 4660 9-11-8 **125**..........(vt) MichaelByrne 134
(Tim Vaughan) *hld up: hdwy 3 out: led appr last: rdn flat: hdd towards fin* **20/1**

231- **3** *4* **Daymar Bay (IRE)**[18] 5031 8-11-10 **127**..........(v) AidanColeman 132
(Emma Lavelle) *led to 2nd: chsd ldrs: led again 11th: rdn: hung lft and hdd appr last: styd on same pce flat* **7/2**[1]

54F- **4** *10* **Tony Dinozzo (FR)**[12] 5121 7-10-5 **108**..........(p) JamieMoore 104
(Peter Bowen) *chsd ldrs: led after 2nd tl 4th: remained handy: chal 11th tl rdn after 2 out: sn wknd* **4/1**[2]

05U- **5** *4* **Marley Roca (IRE)**[11] 5127 10-11-2 **119**..........(p) SamTwiston-Davies 112
(Paul Webber) *hld up: hdwy 3 out: rdn and wknd after next* **10/1**

422- **6** *14* **Smadynium (FR)**[43] 4549 6-11-4 **121**.......... TomO'Brien 101
(Philip Hobbs) *chsd ldrs: nt fluent 2nd: wknd 10th* **9/2**[3]

3P5- **7** *3* **Fiftyonefiftyone (IRE)**[27] 4861 10-10-2 **110**..........(tp) JoeCornwall[(5)] 90
(John Cornwall) *prom: lost pl bef 3rd: hdwy after 11th: wknd next* **33/1**

442- **8** *14* **Free World (FR)**[16] 5058 10-9-10 **106** ow1.......... MissLBrooke[(7)] 78
(Lady Susan Brooke) *chsd ldrs: led 4th to 11th: wknd next: b.b.v* **12/1**

FPP- **P** **Havingotascoobydo (IRE)**[105] 3389 9-10-9 **112**.......... AlainCawley
(Martin Keighley) *hld up: pushed along 8th: bhd fr next: p.u bef 2 out* **11/2**

4m 51.3s (1.30) **Going Correction** +0.275s/f (Yiel) **9** Ran SP% **112.8**
Speed ratings: **108,107,106,102,100 95,93,88,**
CSF £116.94 CT £568.13 TOTE £9.30: £3.10, £3.80, £1.10; EX 139.40 Trifecta £937.20.
Owner H B Hodge **Bred** Dick White **Trained** Alcester, Warwicks
FOCUS
The official ground on the chase course was changed after this race to mirror that on the hurdles track. They went a decent gallop in this ordinary handicap chase, and the form has a sound look to it.

5291 TOTEEXACTA PICK THE 1ST AND 2ND MARES' H'CAP HURDLE (9 hdls) 2m 3f
3:40 (3:40) (Class 4) (0-120,115) 4-Y-0+ **£3,898** (£1,144; £572; £286)

Form RPR

226- **1** **Queen Spud**[25] 4907 5-10-5 **94**..........(p) TomO'Brien 98
(Henry Daly) *w ldr tl led 2nd: rdn appr last: styd on wl* **7/2**[2]

203- **2** *5* **In By Midnight**[105] 3391 6-11-6 **109**.......... PaddyBrennan 108
(Tom George) *a.p: racd keenly: hmpd 1st: rdn to chse wnr and hung lft appr last: styd on same pce flat* **11/2**[3]

143- **3** *2 ¼* **Favorite Girl (GER)**[87] 3736 6-11-3 **106**.......... APMcCoy 103
(Michael Appleby) *hld up: plld hrd: rdn bef 3 out: hdwy appr next: styd on to go 3rd flat: nt rch ldrs* **5/2**[1]

4P0- **4** *1* **Seas Of Green**[29] 4823 7-10-1 **90**..........[1] AdamWedge 86
(Paul Cowley) *chsd ldrs: rdn appr 2 out: no ex flat* **8/1**

001- **5** *2 ¾* **Gaye Memories**[22] 4971 6-11-2 **105**.......... HarrySkelton 99
(Dan Skelton) *wnt prom 2nd: rdn appr 2 out: styd on same pce* **9/1**

230- **6** *9* **Candelita**[171] 2050 7-11-6 **109**.......... SamTwiston-Davies 95
(Jo Hughes) *hld up: racd keenly: nvr on terms* **12/1**

62P- **7** *12* **Definite Ruby (IRE)**[119] 3117 6-11-12 **115**.......... DavidBass 92
(Nicky Henderson) *led to 2nd: pushed along after next: ev ch 3 out: rdn whn nt fluent next: sn wknd* **8/1**

The Form Book Jumps, Raceform Ltd, Compton, RG20 6NL.

003- **P** **Wymeswold**[21] 4980 7-10-1 **90**.. DougieCostello
(Michael Mullineaux) *prom: j.rt 1st: wknd after 6th: bhd whn p.u bef last* **20/1**

4m 31.7s (0.20) **Going Correction** -0.15s/f (Good) **8** Ran SP% **110.9**
Speed ratings (Par 105): **93,90,89,89,88 84,79,**
CSF £21.74 CT £52.44 TOTE £4.40: £1.40, £1.80, £1.30; EX 26.10 Trifecta £56.60.
Owner Barlow, Brindley, Hanley & Russell **Bred** Mickley Stud **Trained** Stanton Lacy, Shropshire

FOCUS
An ordinary handicap for mares.

5292 FOLLOW @TOTEPOOL ON TWITTER HUNTERS' CHASE (FOR THE JOHN AND NIGEL THORNE MEMORIAL CUP) (17 fncs) 2m 7f
4:10 (4:10) (Class 6) 6-Y-0+ **£1,871** (£580; £290; £145)

Form RPR
P/1- **1** **Paint The Clouds**[23] 4936 9-12-0 130.......................... MrSWaley-Cohen 139+
(Warren Greatrex) *trckd ldrs: plld hrd: wnt 2nd 13th: led next: clr fr 2 out: easily* **8/15**[1]
542- **2** *19* **Bermuda Boy (FR)**[17] 5041 9-11-5 104........................(tp) MrPGerety(5) 112
(S Flook) *hld up: hdwy 14th: chsd wnr 3 out: wknd next* **12/1**[3]
/6P- **3** *13* **Archie Boy (IRE)**[22] 12-11-3 124..................................(tp) MrDLordan(7) 100
(R D Potter) *chsd ldrs: rdn appr 3 out: wknd bef next* **66/1**
114- **4** *16* **Little Legend**[22] 10-11-13 117......................................(p) MissCHaydon(5) 97
(Miss C M E Haydon) *led to 14th: mstke next: wknd appr 2 out* **5/2**[2]
P/2- **5** *22* **Catspan (FR)**[24] 4915 8-11-3 103..................................... MissHLewis(7) 66
(Miss H Lewis) *chsd ldr tl mstke 13th: wknd after 3 out* **12/1**[3]
P/ **6** *95* **Duc De Normandie (IRE)**[22] 10-11-3 67............(tp) MissRPLeyshon(7)
(Andrew Leyshon) *nt fluent: bhd fr 5th* **100/1**
/40- **P** **Coup Royale (FR)**[24] 4915 10-11-3 109....................(t[1]) MrCGethings(7)
(Mrs Claire Hitch) *hld up: mstke 3rd: wknd after 12th: bhd whn p.u bef last* **33/1**

5m 42.4s (3.20) **Going Correction** +0.275s/f (Yiel) **7** Ran SP% **114.6**
Speed ratings: **105,98,93,88,80 47,**
CSF £8.26 TOTE £1.70: £1.10, £5.30; EX 6.10 Trifecta £234.90.
Owner Peter Deal & Jill & Robin Eynon **Bred** Guy Reed And Mrs A H Daniels **Trained** Upper Lambourn, Berks

FOCUS
There wasn't much strength in depth to this.

5293 BEST ODDS GUARANTEED AT TOTEPOOL.COM H'CAP CHASE (20 fncs) 3m 4f
4:45 (4:47) (Class 5) (0-100,99) 5-Y-0+ **£3,898** (£1,144; £572; £286)

Form RPR
620- **1** **Doubletoilntrouble (IRE)**[20] 5011 8-11-0 **87**..............(bt) PaddyBrennan 94
(Fergal O'Brien) *a.p: chsd ldr 3 out: r.o u.p to ld nr fin* **8/1**
333- **2** *1 ½* **Craiglands (IRE)**[31] 4778 12-10-8 **81**................................(v) WillKennedy 87
(Ian Williams) *hld up: hdwy 7th: led 17th: rdn appr last: idled flat: hdd nr fin* **11/1**
344- **3** *12* **Bill The Lad (IRE)**[20] 5009 7-11-0 **87**.................................. AdamWedge 82
(Paul Cowley) *hld up: hdwy 16th: sn pushed along: wknd last* **12/1**
323- **4** *28* **Basford Ben**[20] 5011 6-11-7 **94**..................................(p) DougieCostello 65
(Jennie Candlish) *chsd ldrs: hit 2nd: lost pl 9th: n.d after* **4/1**[1]
122- **5** *1* **Phoenix Des Mottes (FR)**[7] 5193 11-10-0 **78**............... JoeCornwall(5) 47
(John Cornwall) *led 3rd to 10th: led 14th to 17th: wknd appr 2 out* **10/1**
60P- **6** *¾* **Very Stylish (IRE)**[129] 2902 10-11-12 **99**.............................(p) APMcCoy 69
(Jonjo O'Neill) *prom: drvn along 17th: hit 3 out: sn wknd* **6/1**[3]
050- **7** *22* **Bruslini (FR)**[47] 4481 9-11-1 **95**....................................... JWStevenson(7) 44
(Tracey Barfoot-Saunt) *sn pushed along in rr: bhd whn hmpd 4th* **33/1**
253- **P** **Timpo (FR)**[119] 3114 11-11-4 **91**......................................(p) TomO'Brien
(Henry Daly) *mid-div: sn pushed along: hdwy 13th: rdn and wknd 15th: bhd whn p.u bef 17th* **10/1**
012- **P** **Classic Case (IRE)**[20] 5011 7-11-7 **94**.................... SamTwiston-Davies
(Sean Curran) *led to 3rd: led 10th tl hit hdd and hit 14th: rdn and weakemned 16th: hit next: bhd whn p.u bef 3 out* **6/1**[3]
431- **F** **Handsome Buddy (IRE)**[25] 4905 7-11-5 **95**.............(v) PeterCarberry(3)
(Michael Gates) *hld up: fell 4th* **5/1**[2]
2P3- **P** **Kyles Faith (IRE)**[15] 5065 6-11-3 **97**.................................. OllieGarner(7)
(Martin Keighley) *prom tl rdn and wknd 15th: bhd whn p.u bef 2 out* **20/1**

7m 6.8s (3.80) **Going Correction** +0.275s/f (Yiel) **11** Ran SP% **118.3**
Speed ratings: **105,104,101,93,92 92,86,, ,**
CSF £91.62 CT £1057.81 TOTE £10.50: £3.90, £4.10, £4.30; EX 122.60 Trifecta £1374.40.
Owner Peter & Lisa Hall **Bred** H Rothwell **Trained** Coln St. Dennis, Gloucs

FOCUS
A very modest staying chase, and not form to get interested in.

5294 COLLECT TOTEPOOL WINNINGS AT BETFRED SHOPS NOVICES' H'CAP HURDLE (8 hdls) 2m 110y
5:15 (5:15) (Class 4) (0-120,120) 4-Y-0+ **£3,898** (£1,144; £572; £286)

Form RPR
/24- **1** **Calaf**[65] 3851 6-11-1 **114**.. MauriceLinehan(5) 119+
(Jonjo O'Neill) *plld hrd: trckd ldr: wnt upsides 3rd: led 6th: rdn appr last: styd on u.p* **25/1**
031- **2** *¾* **Bob's Legend (IRE)**[15] 5066 8-10-11 **105**............. SamTwiston-Davies 109
(Michael Appleby) *prom: rdn appr 2 out: r.o* **7/2**[1]
22/- **3** *¾* **Stevie Thunder**[46] 2136 9-10-6 **100**.................................(t) WillKennedy 103
(Ian Williams) *prom: chsd wnr 2 out: sn rdn: styd on* **7/1**
524- **4** *1 ½* **Dont Take Me Alive**[144] 2601 5-11-4 **112**.....................(tp) AidanColeman 114
(Charlie Longsdon) *hld up: hdwy appr 2 out: sn rdn: styd on same pce flat* **20/1**
204- **5** *6* **Canuspotit**[35] 4700 7-11-2 **110**... TomO'Brien 107
(Lucy Wadham) *hld up: pushed along 4th: rdn appr 2 out: nt trble ldrs* **8/1**
006- **6** *½* **Honour System (IRE)**[60] 4224 7-11-7 **118**........................ JackQuinlan(3) 114
(John Ferguson) *trckd ldrs: rdn after 2 out: wknd bef last* **13/2**
154- **7** *nk* **Great Link**[31] 4781 5-11-0 **113**...................................(t) ConorShoemark(5) 109
(Tony Carroll) *hld up: rdn bef 6th: hdwy 2 out: wknd bef last* **18/1**
005- **P** **Vedani (IRE)**[45] 3597 5-10-10 **104**... PaddyBrennan
(Tony Carroll) *hld up: hmpd 5th: sn wknd: bhd whn p.u bef last* **16/1**
012- **P** **Benzanno (IRE)**[23] 4939 5-11-11 **119**...................................... APMcCoy
(Donald McCain) *led: hung rt appr 4th: hdd 3 out: sn wknd and eased: bhd whn p.u bef last* **6/1**[3]
411- **F** **Attwaal (IRE)**[21] 4987 5-11-9 **120**................................... TrevorWhelan(3)
(Neil King) *hld up: fell 5th* **4/1**[2]

3m 50.8s (-5.20) **Going Correction** -0.15s/f (Good) **10** Ran SP% **113.2**
Speed ratings (Par 105): **106,105,105,104,101 101,101, , ,**
CSF £110.06 CT £694.18 TOTE £10.80: £5.40, £1.20, £2.60; EX 118.90 Trifecta £394.50.
Owner Local Parking Security Limited **Bred** Norcroft Park Stud **Trained** Cheltenham, Gloucs

FOCUS
Just fair form.
T/Plt: £77.50 to a £1 stake. Pool: £70,557.42 - 663.88 winning units. T/Qpdt: £53.20 to a £1 stake. Pool: £5324.50 - 73.95 winning units. CR

5057 WETHERBY (L-H)
Sunday, April 13

OFFICIAL GOING: Good to soft (good in places; 6.5)
Wind: strong 1/2 behind Weather: fine, very breezy

5295 NATIONAL FESTIVAL CIRCUS IS HERE TODAY NOVICES' HURDLE (DIV I) (9 hdls) 2m 110y
2:10 (2:11) (Class 4) 4-Y-0+ **£4,106** (£1,197; £598)

Form RPR
/41- **1** **Kings Bandit (IRE)**[45] 4506 6-11-6 0.. NoelFehily 117+
(Donald McCain) *mde all: drvn and hung bdly lft between last 2: kpt on run-in* **10/11**[1]
621- **2** *1 ¼* **Ginger Fizz**[24] 4910 7-10-10 0...(t) KielanWoods(3) 108
(Ben Case) *chsd ldrs: 2nd 4th: 1/2 l down whn nt fluent last: no ex last 50yds* **3/1**[2]
U36- **3** *5* **Smart Ruler (IRE)**[25] 4899 8-11-7 116.............................. CraigNichol(5) 116
(James Moffatt) *chsd ldrs: kpt on same pce fr 3 out* **9/2**[3]
/U3- **4** *21* **Viking Chief (IRE)**[16] 5050 7-10-13 0.................................... BrianHughes 84
(John Wade) *mid-div: hdwy 6th: drvn and modest 4th 3 out: one pce* **12/1**
55- **5** *5* **Laird Of Monksford (IRE)**[52] 4384 5-10-13 0...................... AdrianLane 79
(Donald McCain) *hld up in rr: mstke 6th: drvn and sme hdwy next: nvr a factor* **33/1**
0- **6** *1 ½* **Red Joker (IRE)**[26] 4889 4-10-0 0.................................... RyanDClark(7) 72
(Andrew Crook) *chsd ldrs: drvn appr 3 out: sn wknd* **80/1**
006- **7** *15* **Bold And Free**[26] 4889 4-10-4 0...................................... TonyKelly(3) 59
(David Thompson) *in rr-div: mstke 2nd: reminders 5th: bhd fr next* **33/1**
00- **8** *13* **Teescomponents Max**[26] 4895 5-10-13 0......................... JamesReveley 53
(Keith Reveley) *hld up in rr: gd hdwy 3rd: sn chsng ldrs: lost pl 6th* **22/1**
325- **9** *26* **Bulas Belle**[23] 4939 4-10-0 0... BrianHarding 16
(Edwin Tuer) *in rr: drvn 4th: bhd whn mstke 6th: t.o 2 out* **25/1**
P **Mcmonagle (USA)**[94] 500 6-10-13 0..............................(t) DavidEngland
(Alan Brown) *j.rt: w ldrs: lost pl after 3rd: bhd fr 6th: t.o whn p.u bef next* **50/1**

3m 51.7s (-4.10) **Going Correction** +0.025s/f (Yiel)
WFA 4 from 5yo+ 5lb **10** Ran SP% **120.5**
Speed ratings (Par 105): **110,109,107,97,94 94,87,80,68,**
CSF £3.80 TOTE £1.90: £1.10, £1.40, £1.30; EX 5.00 Trifecta £13.30.
Owner Mrs Diana L Whateley **Bred** Rathbarry Stud **Trained** Cholmondeley, Cheshire

FOCUS
Bend after Winning post restored to split bend with Chasers on Inner and Hurdles on Outer. The going was good to soft, good in places following watering on the two preceding days. The jockeys reported it was riding mostly as described but quicker in the straight. There was a strong tailwind in the home straight but conversely a strong headwind down the far side. The first division of an ordinary novices' hurdle was dominated by those at the head of the market, who came clear.

5296 NATIONAL FESTIVAL CIRCUS IS HERE TODAY NOVICES' HURDLE (DIV II) (9 hdls) 2m 110y
2:40 (2:41) (Class 4) 4-Y-0+ **£4,106** (£1,197; £598)

Form RPR
FF1- **1** **Master Red (IRE)**[29] 4811 5-11-6 128................................... NoelFehily 125+
(Donald McCain) *w ldr: led appr 5th: hit 2 out: pushed out* **15/8**[1]
0- **2** *8* **Fantasy King**[33] 4736 8-11-6 120....................................... BrianHughes 116
(James Moffatt) *trckd ldng pair: chsd wnr appr 3 out: hit 3 out: rdn between last 2: no imp* **7/2**[3]
33- **3** *7* **Aneedh**[29] 4811 4-10-7 0.. BrianHarding 97
(Jedd O'Keeffe) *mid-div: hdwy 4th: 3rd appr 3 out: one pce* **6/1**
320- **4** *16* **Zamoyski**[14] 5090 4-10-7 122..(p) DenisO'Regan 81
(Steve Gollings) *led: hdd and swtchd outside appr 5th: reminders after next: wknd appr 3 out* **3/1**[2]
F0P- **5** *5* **Dibdabs (IRE)**[67] 4081 6-10-6 0.................................(t) DaraghBourke(7) 83
(Maurice Barnes) *in rr: hit 4th: nvr on terms* **40/1**
345- **6** *10* **Silver Vogue**[16] 5050 6-10-13 0.. RyanMania 76
(Sue Smith) *chsd ldrs: lost pl 6th* **20/1**
7 *1* **Verko (FR)**[57] 5-10-8 0... CraigNichol(5) 73
(Micky Hammond) *a in rr: bhd fr 6th* **40/1**
8 *5* **Woodstock (IRE)**[206] 4-10-7 0.................................... WilsonRenwick 62
(Ann Hamilton) *t.k.h: hdwy 5th: lost pl after next: sn bhd* **25/1**
0- **9** *1* **Verdasco (FR)**[71] 4043 5-10-13 0.. AdrianLane 67
(Donald McCain) *nt fluent in rr: t.k.h: bhd fr 6th* **50/1**

3m 52.5s (-3.30) **Going Correction** +0.025s/f (Yiel)
WFA 4 from 5yo+ 5lb **9** Ran SP% **111.7**
Speed ratings (Par 105): **108,104,100,93,91 86,85,83,83**
CSF £7.95 TOTE £2.80: £1.40, £1.60, £1.90; EX 10.40 Trifecta £26.90.
Owner Paul & Clare Rooney **Bred** Colin Kennedy **Trained** Cholmondeley, Cheshire

FOCUS
The second leg of the novices' hurdle and a stronger race on paper, with three of the runners rated in the 120s.

5297 RACINGUK.COM/ANYWHERE: 3DEVICES, 1PRICE NOVICES' LIMITED H'CAP CHASE (16 fncs) 2m 4f 110y
3:15 (3:15) (Class 3) (0-125,125) 5-Y-0+ **£7,213** (£2,623)

Form RPR
/1P- **1** **Diocles (IRE)**[62] 4188 8-11-8 **125**....................................... NoelFehily 135
(Donald McCain) *hld up: trckd ldrs 9th: disputing 3rd whn lft cl 2nd 4 out: led and lft 30 l clr 2 out: eased run-in* **13/2**
2 *37* **Rory's Brother (IRE)**[10] 5148 7-10-3 **106** oh2.................(p) BrianHughes 83
(Denis Gerard Hogan, Ire) *t.k.h: trckd ldrs: hit 10th: lost pl 12th: lft poor 3rd next: lft distant 2nd 2 out* **12/1**
/16- **U** **Deciding Moment (IRE)**[23] 4932 8-11-2 **119**....................(t) JackDoyle
(Ben De Haan) *hld up: hdwy 8th: trcking ldrs 12th: 5th whn bdly hmpd and uns rdr next* **11/1**
251- **B** **My Idea**[16] 5060 8-10-6 **112**.....................................(p) JonathanEngland(3)
(Maurice Barnes) *chsd ldrs: disputing cl 3rd whn b.d 4 out* **9/1**
04F- **P** **See What Happens (IRE)**[42] 4578 8-10-10 **113**................. WilsonRenwick
(Martin Todhunter) *prom: drvn 9th: bhd 11th: t.o next: p.u bef 4 out* **5/1**[3]
321- **P** **Dreamy George (IRE)**[30] 4793 8-11-4 **121**........................ DenisO'Regan
(John Ferguson) *chsd ldrs: lost pl 4th: reminders next: lost pl after 7th: j. slowly next: t.o whn p.u bef 11th* **9/2**[2]

PF0- **F** **Green Wizard (IRE)**[29] 4819 8-11-4 **121**................ RyanMania
(Sue Smith) *trckd ldrs: drvn 12th: led narrowly and fell next* **10/3**[1]

232- **F** **Alderbrook Lad (IRE)**[25] 4898 8-10-12 **120**.................. JoeColliver(5) 125
(Micky Hammond) *led: hdd and lft in ld 4 out: narrowly hdd whn fell 2 out* **11/2**

4m 58.0s (-9.80) **Going Correction** -0.275s/f (Good) **8** Ran SP% **112.7**
Speed ratings: **107,92,** , , , ,
CSF £72.48 TOTE £7.10: £4.20, £5.10; EX 145.50 Trifecta £121.30.
Owner L G M Racing **Bred** Eric Watson **Trained** Cholmondeley, Cheshire

FOCUS
Not bad prizemoney and a fair novices' handicap chase but there was plenty of drama in the closing stages.

5298 BOOK YOUR LADIES DAY HOSPITALITY MARQUEE PACKAGE (S) H'CAP HURDLE (11 hdls) 2m 4f
3:50 (3:50) (Class 5) (0-100,100) 4-Y-O+ **£2,737** (£798; £399)

Form RPR

4P0- **1** **Exit To Freedom**[93] 3636 8-9-10 **77** ow3.................(p) GLavery(7) 79
(John Wainwright) *w ldr: led appr 8th: hung rt run-in: jst hld on* **9/1**[2]

265- **2** *nk* **Saddlers Mot**[13] 5106 10-11-0 **95**..................(b) DiarmuidO'Regan(7) 96
(Karen Tutty) *in rr: hdwy 8th: chsng ldrs next: 3rd last: keeping on whn carried rt and hmpd nr fin* **10/1**[3]

046- **3** *nk* **Inside Knowledge (USA)**[9] 4447 8-10-12 **86**.............. AdamPogson 88
(Garry Woodward) *in rr: hdwy 8th: hit next: 7th last: styd on strly to take 3rd nr fin* **9/1**[2]

5B3- **4** *¾* **Stand Clear**[191] 1751 9-11-0 **88**.......................... PeterBuchanan 87
(David Thompson) *hld up in rr: hdwy 6th: chsng ldrs next: 2nd last: kpt on same pce* **11/1**

43U- **5** *½* **Blue Sea Of Ibrox (IRE)**[23] 4938 6-10-0 **74** oh3..........(b) DavidEngland 74
(Alan Brown) *chsd ldrs: 5th last: one pce* **12/1**

P00- **6** *2* **Bow School (IRE)**[22] 4957 13-11-5 **100**................... MrJHamilton(7) 97
(Alison Hamilton) *chsd ldrs: drvn appr 3 out: sn outpcd: 6th last: kpt on* **16/1**

000- **7** *1* **Katie's Massini (IRE)**[8] 5177 6-10-12 **86**................. DenisO'Regan 82
(Henry Oliver) *hld up in mid-div: hdwy 6th: trcking ldrs 8th: 5th last: one pce* **9/1**[2]

660- **8** *1 ½* **Benmadigan (IRE)**[22] 4957 12-10-8 **85**................. HarryChalloner(3) 80
(Nicky Richards) *in rr: hdwy 8th: 8th last: one pce* **14/1**

04/- **9** *14* **Rexmehead (IRE)**[751] 5043 13-10-0 **74** oh5.................. BrianHarding 56
(Andrew Wilson) *mid-div: lost pl 8th: sme hdwy next: sn wknd* **66/1**

404- **10** *3 ¾* **Executive's Hall (IRE)**[220] 1506 10-11-1 **92**..............(p) JakeGreenall(3) 71
(Ben Haslam) *hld up in mid-div: nt fluent 4th: hdwy 6th: trcking ldrs next: lost pl bef 3 out* **12/1**

5P5- **11** *3 ¼* **Ghaabesh (IRE)**[15] 5072 7-9-11 **78**.........................(t) ConorRing(7) 54
(Barry Leavy) *mid-div: lost pl 5th: bhd next* **6/1**[1]

346- **12** *10* **Wave Breaker (IRE)**[31] 4775 7-10-0 **74** oh1..................... AdrianLane 41
(Robert Johnson) *chsd ldrs: hit 5th: lost pl 8th: sn bhd* **25/1**

640- **13** *12* **Hi Candy (IRE)**[41] 4595 4-10-4 **95**........................(p) RyanDClark(10) 44
(Ben Haslam) *led: reminders after 1st: hdd 8th: sn lost pl and bhd* **25/1**

444- **14** *15* **Sedgemoor Top Bid (IRE)**[18] 5029 6-10-12 **89**..........(bt) JamesBest(3) 32
(Nigel Hawke) *chsd ldrs: reminders 2nd: hrd drvn 6th: lost pl after 8th: sn bhd: t.o: b.b.v* **16/1**

144/ **P** **Secret Desert**[497] 2815 8-9-11 **74**................................ TonyKelly(3)
(Rebecca Menzies) *in rr: bhd fr 6th: t.o whn p.u bef 2 out* **14/1**

305- **P** **Mister Jones**[33] 4746 6-11-7 **98**......................... JonathanEngland(3)
(Sue Smith) *in rr: reminders 4th: drvn after next: sn chsng ldrs: lost pl after 7th: bhd whn p.u bef 3 out* **6/1**[1]

5m 3.0s (3.50) **Going Correction** +0.025s/f (Yiel) **16** Ran SP% **125.7**
WFA 4 from 6yo+ 6lb
Speed ratings (Par 103): **94,93,93,93,93 92,92,91,85,84 83,79,74,68,**
CSF £97.77 CT £855.10 TOTE £10.10: £2.90, £2.30, £3.30, £3.10; EX 110.80 Trifecta £716.10.
Owner I Barran **Bred** J S Wainwright **Trained** Kennythorpe, N Yorks

FOCUS
A big field for this seller and something of a blanket finish.

5299 NEW RACINGUK ANYWHERE AVAILABLE NOW H'CAP CHASE (16 fncs 2 omitted) 3m 1f
4:20 (4:22) (Class 3) (0-130,124) 5-Y-O+ **£6,498** (£1,908; £954; £477)

Form RPR

122- **1** **Everaard (USA)**[26] 4894 8-10-5 **103**.....................(tp) JamesReveley 115+
(Philip Kirby) *chsd ldrs: lost pl after 10th: rallied bef 4 out: cl up whn blnd 2 out: upsides last: led last 50yds: all out* **10/3**[1]

3PP- **2** *hd* **The Magic Bishop**[42] 4580 9-10-5 **103**...................... BrianHughes 113
(Malcolm Jefferson) *hld up: trcking ldrs 9th: swtchd lft appr 2 out: upsides last: no ex nr fin* **11/1**

21P- **3** *nse* **Goodtoknow**[50] 4412 6-11-7 **122**........................... JakeGreenall(3) 132
(Richard Lee) *w ldrs 2nd: led after 4th: hdd 11th: led bef 4 out: j.rt 3 out: hdd last 50yds: styd on: jst hld* **11/1**

334- **4** *5* **Ballypatrick (IRE)**[22] 4962 8-11-12 **124**...................... BrianHarding 129
(Mick Channon) *led to 3rd: chsd ldrs: cl 2nd 4 out: n.m.r next: 4th last: sn fdd* **9/2**[3]

F41- **5** *5* **Master Neo (FR)**[8] 5180 8-11-2 **117**........................(t) JamesBest(3) 118
(Nigel Hawke) *chsd ldrs: drvn 9th: outpcd 4 out: no threat after* **4/1**[2]

P05- **6** *16* **Balinroab (IRE)**[16] 5060 7-10-12 **110**....................... DenisO'Regan 101
(Richard Guest) *trckd ldrs 6th: cl 4th whn hit 4 out: 5th whn hit next: wknd appr 2 out* **16/1**

U55- **P** **You Know Yourself (IRE)**[16] 5053 11-11-3 **118**...... JonathanEngland(3)
(Sue Smith) *in rr: pushed along 8th: bhd fr 11th: t.o whn p.u bef 2 out* **14/1**

443- **P** **Royal Sam (IRE)**[31] 4771 9-10-1 **99**....................(tp) WilsonRenwick
(Martin Todhunter) *jnd ldrs 2nd: led next: hdd after 4th: reminders and lost pl next: drvn 8th: chsd ldrs next: led 11th: hdd bef 4 out: sn lost pl and bhd: t.o whn p.u bef 3 out* **15/2**

/01- **F** **Nodform Richard**[130] 2884 8-11-10 **122**........................(b) NoelFehily
(Donald McCain) *hld up towards rr: fell 2nd* **6/1**

6m 1.7s (-7.70) **Going Correction** -0.275s/f (Good) **9** Ran SP% **116.5**
Speed ratings: **101,100,100,99,97 92,** , ,
CSF £38.93 CT £365.02 TOTE £3.50: £1.30, £3.10, £3.50; EX 36.80 Trifecta £354.70.
Owner Tennant, Sharpe & Boston **Bred** F & F Investments **Trained** Middleham, N Yorks

FOCUS
A fair handicap chase although the top weight was rated 6lb below the race ceiling and it produced another close finish. The final fence in the back straight was omitted.

5300 DM KEITH SKODA & SEAT MAIDEN HURDLE (12 hdls) 2m 6f
4:55 (4:56) (Class 5) 4-Y-O+ **£2,737** (£798; £399)

Form RPR

533- **1** **Ballythomas**[37] 4650 7-10-11 105..............................(p) TonyKelly(3) 107
(David Thompson) *mde all: lft 1 1/2 l ahd last: drvn out* **10/1**

FF3- **2** *2* **Ready Token (IRE)**[27] 4863 6-11-0 114.............................(t) NoelFehily 105
(Charlie Longsdon) *trckd ldrs 5th: lft handy 2nd last: kpt on same pce* **11/4**[2]

55- **3** *4* **Head Of The Class (IRE)**[22] 4958 5-11-0 0.....................[1] DannyCook 101
(Brian Ellison) *in rr-div: outpcd and drvn 9th: kpt on fr next: lft 4th last: tk 3rd run-in* **8/1**

FF3- **4** *¾* **Romany Ryme**[13] 5105 8-10-9 115........................ JonathonBewley(5) 99
(George Bewley) *chsd ldrs: drvn appr 3 out: one pce whn lft 3rd last* **13/8**[1]

/5P- **5** *1 ¾* **Alaplee**[163] 2197 6-11-0 0.. DenisO'Regan 99
(Chris Grant) *hld up in rr: hdwy 9th: chsng ldrs next: outpcd appr 2 out: lft 5th last: kpt on* **40/1**

U6- **6** *13* **The Yank**[25] 4904 5-10-11 0.................................... RobertDunne(3) 87
(Richard Lee) *hld up in rr: hdwy to chse ldrs 9th: wknd 2 out* **20/1**

4PP- **7** *3 ¼* **Snow Alert**[27] 4865 8-11-0 80... AdrianLane 84
(John Norton) *chsd ldrs 5th: outpcd 9th: rallied next: wknd after 2 out* **50/1**

656- **8** *39* **Cadgers Hole**[16] 5050 7-11-0 0.....................................[1] GerardTumelty 49
(Lynn Siddall) *hld up in rr: lost pl 9th: t.o and j. bdly last 3* **100/1**

006- **9** *3 ¼* **Viking Mistress**[137] 2752 6-10-7 0................................... TomSiddall 39
(Martin Keighley) *t.k.h in mid-div: trckd ldrs in 5th: lost pl after 8th: sn bhd: t.o next: blnd 2 out* **28/1**

00- **10** *44* **Backforce**[50] 4431 6-11-0 0.. BarryKeniry 6
(Noel Wilson) *chsd ldrs: drvn 8th: lost pl next: t.o and j. bdly fr3 out* **100/1**

/00- **P** **Hi Bob**[23] 4944 6-10-7 0.. NathanMoscrop(7)
(Lucinda Egerton) *s.s: detached in last: hmpd 7th: sn t.o: p.u bef 3 out* **100/1**

543- **U** **Shantou Tiger (IRE)**[22] 4950 5-10-7 0......................... JamesCowley(7) 105
(Donald McCain) *chsd ldrs: 2nd 9th: cl 2nd whn wandered and uns rdr last* **5/1**[3]

5- **F** **Fiddler's Flight (IRE)**[171] 2049 8-10-7 0...................... DaraghBourke(7)
(John Norton) *in rr: mstke 1st: fell 7th* **80/1**

5m 22.9s (-3.90) **Going Correction** +0.025s/f (Yiel) **13** Ran SP% **118.4**
Speed ratings (Par 103): **108,107,105,105,104 100,99,84,83,67** , ,
CSF £36.94 TOTE £6.20: £2.40, £1.50, £3.60; EX 32.20 Trifecta £238.10.
Owner Alan Moore & Tony Livingston **Bred** Fiona Williams-Jones **Trained** Bolam, Co Durham

FOCUS
A modest maiden hurdle.

5301 DOWNLOAD NEW RACINGUK IPAD APP H'CAP CHASE (13 fncs 3 omitted) 2m 4f 110y
5:30 (5:31) (Class 5) (0-100,95) 5-Y-O+ **£3,249** (£954; £477; £238)

Form RPR

145- **1** **River Purple**[21] 4985 7-11-4 **87**.................................(t) BrianHughes 102+
(John Mackie) *hld up towards rr: trckd ldrs 6th: 2nd appr 4 out: led 2 out: drvn rt out* **10/1**

045- **2** *4 ½* **Trouble In Paris (IRE)**[31] 4775 7-10-0 **69** oh4...........(tp) LucyAlexander 79
(Barry Murtagh) *led: hdd and mstke 2 out: one pce* **8/1**[3]

445- **3** *7* **Yukon Delta (IRE)**[31] 4774 7-10-8 **77**.......................... KennyJohnson 80
(Robert Johnson) *in rr: reminders after 6th: hdwy to chse ldrs next: drvn and 3rd appr 4 out: fdd appr 2 out* **11/4**[1]

00P- **4** *11* **Le Pergolese (FR)**[21] 4984 8-10-1 **73**.........................(t) JamesBest(3) 66
(Nigel Hawke) *chsd ldrs: drvn 7th: outpcd 9th: modest 4th whn j.rt 3 out* **12/1**

560- **5** *7* **Miss Sunflower**[21] 4982 12-9-9 **69** oh6..................(p) SamanthaDrake(5) 56
(Tina Jackson) *chsd ldrs: outpcd and lost pl 9th: bhd next: kpt on fr 2 out* **33/1**

400- **6** *3 ¼* **Petit Ecuyer (FR)**[13] 5115 8-11-8 **91**.......................... JamesReveley 75
(Barry Brennan) *in rr: bhd 7th: sme hdwy 9th: wknd 3 out* **25/1**

325- **7** *7* **One In A Row (IRE)**[26] 4890 7-11-2 **85**........................ DenisO'Regan 68
(Andrew Crook) *in rr: reminders 4th and 6th: hdwy to chse ldrs 7th: lost pl bef 4 out: sn bhd: heavily eased run-in* **14/1**

31P- **8** *2* **Pistol Basc (FR)**[60] 4222 10-11-7 **93**............................ TonyKelly(3) 69
(Rebecca Menzies) *t.k.h: trckd ldrs: mstke 6th: sn lost pl: bhd fr 9th* **12/1**

114- **9** *18* **Lord Fox (IRE)**[17] 5038 7-11-7 **95**............................... BenPoste(5) 55
(Shaun Harris) *chsd ldrs: drvn 9th: sn lost pl: bhd fr 3 out: t.o: heavily eased run-in: b.b.v* **17/2**

PP3- **F** **Big News**[17] 5038 8-11-12 **95**....................................(t) PaulMoloney
(Richard Lee) *in rr: fell 2nd* **10/3**[2]

/03- **P** **Roseville Cottage (IRE)**[23] 4940 7-11-7 **90**.................. WilsonRenwick
(John Wade) *nt fluent in rr: mstke 5th: bhd whn p.u after next* **14/1**

4m 58.0s (-9.80) **Going Correction** -0.275s/f (Good) **11** Ran SP% **116.0**
Speed ratings: **107,105,102,98,95 94,91,91,84,**
CSF £86.61 CT £282.27 TOTE £9.00: £3.10, £3.50, £1.80; EX 127.80 Trifecta £1395.20.
Owner Sotby Farming Company Limited **Bred** Wood Farm Stud **Trained** Church Broughton , Derbys

FOCUS
A very moderate handicap chase and both open ditches in the back straight were omitted.

5302 ROYAL PIGEON RACING ASSOCIATION LADY RIDERS' H'CAP HURDLE (9 hdls) 2m 110y
6:00 (6:04) (Class 5) (0-100,96) 4-Y-O+ **£2,737** (£798; £399)

Form RPR

P01- **1** **Rayadour (IRE)**[9] 5161 5-10-6 **81**.............................(p) MissCWalton(5) 93+
(Micky Hammond) *mid-div: j.lft 1st: hdwy to trck ldrs 6th: 3rd apprroaching next: led last: drvn out* **5/2**[1]

/60- **2** *2 ½* **Carters Rest**[62] 4187 11-10-10 **87**.......................[1] MissJWalton(7) 94
(George Bewley) *trckd clr ldr: led 2 out: hdd last: kpt on same pce* **11/1**

323- **3** *11* **Walter De La Mare (IRE)**[20] 5012 7-11-5 **96**........ MissJoannaMason(7) 93
(Anabel K Murphy) *in rr: modest 5th appr 3 out: stl 5th last: kpt on to take 3rd nr fin* **8/1**

0/ **4** *nk* **My Old Lady (IRE)**[17] 5045 9-10-8 **85**.......(p) MissEvannaMcCutcheon(7) 83
(Denis Gerard Hogan, Ire) *in rr: hdwy 5th: handy 4th and drvn 3 out: 3rd appr last: one pce* **14/1**

1/0- **5** *4* **Goodlukin Lucy**[18] 879 7-10-10 **87**............................ MissAEStirling(7) 82
(Keith Dalgleish) *led: hit 1st: clr next tl appr 3 out: hdd 2 out: wknd appr last* **7/2**[2]

125- **6** *2 1/4* **Newdane Dancer (IRE)**[22] 4957 7-11-6 **95**..................(b) EmmaSayer(5) 86
(Dianne Sayer) *mid-div: drvn 4th: outpcd 6th: lost pl bef next* **8/1**

0PP- **7** *10* **Samizdat (FR)**[141] 2679 11-9-7 **70** oh4.............................. MissGSwan(7) 52
(John Upson) *mid-div: hmpd 1st: outpcd 4th: sme hdwy 9th: drvn and lost pl bef next: sn bhd* **40/1**

0/0- **P** **Hydrant**[18] 3838 8-11-0 **84**.. LucyAlexander
(Richard Guest) *stdd s: t.k.h: hdwy to trck ldrs 2nd: drvn and wknd qckly 6th: sn bhd: t.o whn p.u bef next: b.b.v* **4/1**[3]

454- **P** **Dalstontosiloth (IRE)**[33] 4746 6-11-0 **91**........................ MissHHarper(7)
(Barry Murtagh) *in rr: bhd fr 3 out: t.o whn p.u bef next* **9/1**

3m 52.8s (-3.00) **Going Correction** +0.025s/f (Yiel) **9** Ran SP% **120.5**
Speed ratings (Par 103): **108,106,101,101,99 98,93, ,**
CSF £31.31 CT £199.85 TOTE £3.60: £1.40, £3.50, £2.10; EX 30.70 Trifecta £332.80.
Owner Straightline Construction Ltd **Bred** His Highness The Aga Khan's Studs S C **Trained** Middleham Moor, N Yorks

FOCUS
A moderate lady riders' hurdle.
T/Plt: £215.90 to a £1 stake. Pool: £68,459.59 - 231.39 winning units. T/Qpdt: £146.40 to a £1 stake. Pool: 3799.40 - 19.20 winning units. WG

5124 WINCANTON (R-H)
Sunday, April 13

OFFICIAL GOING: Good (good to soft in places; chs 8.3, hdl 8.2)
Wind: strong breeze behind Weather: sunny

5303 32RED £10 FREE BONUS MAIDEN HURDLE (DIV I) (8 hdls) 2m
1:50 (1:50) (Class 4) 4-Y-0+ **£3,249** (£954; £477; £238)

Form RPR

333- **1** **Nordic Quest (IRE)**[22] 4947 5-11-0 **119**.......................... AndrewTinkler 124+
(Nicky Henderson) *racd keenly: trckd ldrs: wnt 2nd bef 2 out: led between last 2: hit last: easily* **2/1**[1]

000- **2** *8* **Stella's Fella**[10] 5140 6-11-0 0.. TomCannon 113
(Giles Smyly) *led: rdn appr 2 out: hdd between last 2: hld whn hit last: kpt on same pce* **50/1**

2F3- **3** *1 1/4* **Revaader**[12] 5117 6-10-7 105.. TommyPhelan 106
(Mark Gillard) *trckd ldr tl rdn appr 2 out: sn hld: kpt on same pce* **6/1**[3]

300- **4** *31* **Thats Yer Man (IRE)**[50] 4417 6-10-7 0.............................. MrCSmith(7) 84
(Linda Blackford) *trckd ldrs: wnt lft 1st: nt fluent 3 out: sn rdn: wkng whn lft btn 4th 2 out: t.o* **50/1**

102- **5** *1/2* **Fair Dreamer**[21] 4988 6-11-0 0..(t) RyanMahon 83
(Harry Fry) *in tch: rdn after 3 out: sn wknd: t.o* **11/4**[2]

6 *9* **Mrs Burbidge**[43] 4-9-10 0.. JamesBanks(5) 61
(Neil Mulholland) *hld up: rdn after 3 out: sn wknd: t.o* **50/1**

P/ **7** *17* **Artful Dodger**[433] 2834 7-10-7 0... ChrisDavies(7) 59
(Helen Nelmes) *in tch: rdn after 3 out: sn wknd: t.o* **100/1**

0P0- **8** *7* **Saint Helena (IRE)**[12] 5117 6-10-7 0................................ MattieBatchelor 46
(Jim Best) *hld up: hit 4th: sn struggling: wknd after 3 out: t.o* **50/1**

210- **U** **Third Act (IRE)**[32] 4756 5-11-0 0.. BrendanPowell 88
(Colin Tizzard) *trckd ldrs: bmpd 1st: rdn after 3 out: sn btn: awkward: stmbld and uns rdr next* **2/1**[1]

3m 32.6s (-16.30) **Going Correction** -1.00s/f (Hard)
WFA 4 from 5yo+ 5lb **9** Ran SP% **116.5**
Speed ratings (Par 105): **100,96,95,79,79 75,66,63,**
CSF £85.84 TOTE £3.60: £1.30, £6.60, £1.60; EX 79.20 Trifecta £175.80.
Owner A D Spence **Bred** Gestut Wittekindshof **Trained** Upper Lambourn, Berks

FOCUS
Both tracks moved in onto fresher ground not used since November. This didn't look a bad maiden, but with two of the three clear market leaders failing to fire it was a messy race.

5304 CHILDREN'S TRUST CONDITIONAL JOCKEYS' H'CAP HURDLE (8 hdls) 2m
2:20 (2:21) (Class 4) (0-105,105) 4-Y-0+ **£3,249** (£954; £477; £238)

Form RPR

02F- **1** **August Hill (IRE)**[20] 5005 6-11-7 **103**..........................(t[1]) MichealNolan(3) 118+
(Philip Hobbs) *mid-div: hdwy appr 2 out: led bef last: r.o: rdn out* **9/2**[2]

U4F- **2** *3* **Enchanting Smile (FR)**[29] 4802 7-10-2 **86**..........(t) ThomasCheesman(5) 97+
(Mark Gillard) *trckd ldr: chal 2 out: sn rdn: ev ch whn nt fluent last: kpt on same pce* **25/1**

100- **3** *1 1/4* **Nothing Is Forever (IRE)**[273] 977 10-10-8 **87**............ NicodeBoinville 95
(Chris Down) *led: rdn after 2 out: hdd bef last: kpt on same pce* **7/2**[1]

253- **4** *5* **Cappielow Park**[58] 4247 5-11-5 **98**................................... GavinSheehan 101
(Ali Brewer) *mid-div: hdwy after 3 out: rdn in cl 4th 2 out: kpt on same pce* **5/1**[3]

P10- **5** *4* **Delphi Mountain (IRE)**[24] 4911 9-11-12 **105**..................(bt) MattGriffiths 105
(Richard Woollacott) *trckd ldr: c wd into st: sn wandered u.p: hld bef last: kpt on same pce* **16/1**

643- **6** *7* **Reggie Perrin**[108] 3249 6-11-0 **101**.................................. PaddyBradley(8) 94
(Pat Phelan) *hld up: sme hdwy 5th: rdn after 3 out: plugged on but nvr finding pce to get on terms w ldrs* **10/1**

124- **7** *4 1/2* **Acapulco Bay**[284] 812 10-11-8 **101**................................ RobertWilliams 90
(Dai Burchell) *mid-div: hdwy after 3 out: rdn in cl 6th bef 2 out: wknd bef last* **12/1**

2P0- **8** *6* **Lord Of The Dunes**[11] 5126 6-11-6 **102**......................(t) JackSherwood(3) 88
(Colin Tizzard) *mid-div: rdn after 3 out: wknd next* **10/1**

026- **9** *8* **Noble Friend (IRE)**[20] 5005 6-11-4 **105**......................... LouisMuspratt(8) 82
(Chris Gordon) *hld up towards rr: rdn after 3 out: nvr any real imp on ldrs: wknd bef next* **6/1**

600- **10** *20* **Electric Mayhem**[18] 5034 7-11-8 **101**.............................. ThomasGarner 60
(Nick Mitchell) *trckd ldrs tl 5th: wknd after 3 out* **33/1**

/60- **11** *1/2* **Whileaway (USA)**[103] 3427 5-11-4 **100**..........................(p) RyanHatch(3) 58
(Neil Mulholland) *mid-div: rdn after 3 out: sn wknd* **16/1**

PP0- **P** **Cranky Corner**[34] 4721 10-11-2 **95**.................................. JoshuaMoore
(Helen Nelmes) *mid-div: rdn after 3 out: sn wknd: p.u bef next: b.b.v* **33/1**

3m 32.1s (-16.80) **Going Correction** -1.00s/f (Hard) **12** Ran SP% **118.7**
Speed ratings (Par 105): **102,100,99,97,95 91,89,86,82,72 72,**
CSF £109.78 CT £438.56 TOTE £4.60: £1.80, £9.70, £1.30; EX 78.20 Trifecta £900.20.
Owner Mrs Caren Walsh & Mrs Kathleen Quinn **Bred** Thomas James **Trained** Withycombe, Somerset

FOCUS
They went a sound gallop in this moderate conditional riders' handicap and the form looks fair enough.

5305 32RED £10 FREE BONUS MAIDEN HURDLE (DIV II) (8 hdls) 2m
2:50 (2:51) (Class 4) 4-Y-0+ **£3,249** (£954; £477; £238)

Form RPR

23- **1** **Paradise Valley (IRE)**[81] 3841 5-11-0 0......................... DominicElsworth 115+
(Mick Channon) *mde all: j. sltly lft thrght: in command fr after 2 out: r.o strly: comf* **11/4**[2]

013- **2** *9* **Very Noble (FR)**[20] 5003 5-11-0 117................................(t) NickScholfield 105+
(Paul Nicholls) *trckd ldrs: wnt 2nd after 3 out: rdn between last 2: kpt on for clr 2nd but nvr finding pce to get on terms w wnr* **7/4**[1]

50- **3** *12* **Free Of Charge (IRE)**[29] 4810 5-11-0 0...................... RichardJohnson 91
(Philip Hobbs) *trckd ldr tl rdn after 3 out: sn one pce: nt fluent last* **18/1**

0- **4** *2* **King's Ciel**[38] 4632 5-11-0 0.. MarkGrant 90
(Sean Curran) *hld up: sme hdwy after 3 out: sn rdn: chsng hld 3rd after next: kpt on same pce* **100/1**

P4- **5** *4 1/2* **Vauban Du Seuil (FR)**[21] 4987 5-11-0 0............................(t) RyanMahon 85
(Harry Fry) *t.k.h: hld up: sme hdwy after 3 out: no further imp fr next* **8/1**

00- **6** *1/2* **Italian Symphony (IRE)**[10] 5140 4-10-1 0.................... AndrewTinkler 71
(Brendan Powell) *hld up towards rr: rdn after 3 out: sme minor late prog: nvr a danger* **66/1**

56- **7** *1 1/4* **Smart Motive**[53] 4349 4-10-8 0...................................... RobertThornton 77
(Alan King) *hld up towards rr: rdn after 3 out: nvr any imp* **14/1**

8 *1* **Mutashabek (USA)**[179] 4-10-8 0... IanPopham 76
(Caroline Keevil) *in tch: rdn after 3 out: sn hld: wknd between last 2* **66/1**

006- **9** *3 3/4* **Rocket Scientist**[21] 4988 5-11-0 0................................ BrendanPowell 78
(Colin Tizzard) *trckd ldrs: rdn after 3 out: wknd bef next* **80/1**

0/F- **U** **The Wonga Coup (IRE)**[39] 427 7-10-4 0.................. PaddyBradley(10)
(Pat Phelan) *a towards rr: untidy whn uns rdr 2 out* **100/1**

/13- **P** **Prouts Pub (IRE)**[15] 5064 5-11-0 0................................... TomCannon
(Nick Gifford) *hld up: rdn after 3 out: no imp whn p.u bef next: lame* **3/1**[3]

3m 39.4s (-9.50) **Going Correction** -1.00s/f (Hard)
WFA 4 from 5yo+ 5lb **11** Ran SP% **117.3**
Speed ratings (Par 105): **83,78,72,71,69 69,68,67,66,**
CSF £8.23 TOTE £3.10: £1.70, £1.10, £4.50; EX 12.40 Trifecta £85.20.
Owner Mrs T P Radford **Bred** William McCarthy **Trained** West Ilsley, Berks

FOCUS
Only two mattered from the penultimate flight in this second division of the maiden hurdle.

5306 32RED THUNDERSTRUCK II SLOT H'CAP CHASE (13 fncs) 2m
3:25 (3:25) (Class 3) (0-135,135) 5-Y-0 **£6,330** (£1,870; £935; £468; £234)

Form RPR

03U- **1** **Kie (IRE)**[22] 4955 6-11-11 **134**.. HenryBrooke 141
(Donald McCain) *mde all: rdn after 3 out: kpt on wl* **7/2**[3]

150- **2** *3* **Spock (FR)**[18] 5035 9-10-2 **118**......................................(b) MrsAlexDunn(7) 122
(Alexandra Dunn) *chsd ldrs: wnt 2nd 3 out: hit 2 out: sn rdn: kpt on but nt pce to get on terms* **16/1**

222- **3** *3 1/4* **Massena (IRE)**[15] 5064 7-11-12 **135**............................... LiamTreadwell 135
(Venetia Williams) *chsd ldrs: rdn after 4 out: kpt on same pce fr next* **3/1**[2]

0U4- **4** *3/4* **Qianshan Leader (IRE)**[26] 4886 10-10-10 **122**.........(v) GavinSheehan(3) 122
(Emma Lavelle) *prom: chsd wnr fr 9th tl appr 3 out: kpt on same pce: nt fluent last* **4/1**

201- **5** *43* **Prince Of Dreams**[22] 4965 7-11-7 **130**................................. FelixDeGiles 91
(Ed de Giles) *detached 4th: struggling but clsd on ldrs sltly 6th: nvr threatened: wknd after 4 out: sn eased: t.o: lame* **7/4**[1]

3m 47.9s (-12.00) **Going Correction** -0.525s/f (Firm) **5** Ran SP% **109.5**
Speed ratings: **109,107,105,105,84**
CSF £37.67 TOTE £5.60: £3.50, £4.00; EX 40.80 Trifecta £60.90.
Owner Allan Stennett **Bred** Azienda Agricola La Selvatica **Trained** Cholmondeley, Cheshire

FOCUS
A tight little handicap and, as expected, it was run at a solid gallop.

5307 YEOVIL TOWN FOOTBALL CLUB H'CAP HURDLE (11 hdls) 2m 6f
4:00 (4:00) (Class 4) (0-110,110) 4-Y-0+ **£3,898** (£1,144; £572; £286)

Form RPR

546- **1** **Jimmy The Jetplane (IRE)**[23] 4931 6-11-4 **107**.............. EdCookson(5) 116+
(Kim Bailey) *trckd ldrs: chal 2 out: ldng whn nt fluent last: styd on wl: pushed out* **13/2**[3]

521- **2** *3 1/4* **Pertinent (FR)**[18] 5033 11-11-5 **110**...........................(t) MissAliceMills(7) 115
(Charles Whittaker) *prom: led 7th: rdn appr 2 out: hdd jst bef last: kpt on same pce* **8/1**

032- **3** *5* **Hot Whiskey (IRE)**[13] 5114 6-11-2 **100**.........................(t) BrendanPowell 102
(Brendan Powell) *in tch: hdwy 3 out: rdn in 3rd bef 2 out: kpt on same pce* **5/1**[2]

035- **4** *6* **Cape Breton**[20] 5003 8-11-6 **107**.................................... NicodeBoinville(3) 102
(Patrick Chamings) *hld up towards rr: hdwy after 7th: rdn in 4th appr 2 out: styd on same pce* **12/1**

UP- **5** *2 1/2* **Friendly Society (IRE)**[76] 3958 9-11-2 **105**..................(p) JamesBanks(5) 98
(Noel Williams) *mid-div: rdn and hdwy to chse ldrs after 3 out: one pce fr next* **16/1**

632- **6** *6* **The Wealerdealer (IRE)**[35] 4699 7-11-6 **104**.............(b) TomScudamore 93
(David Pipe) *mid-div: rdn along fr 8th: nvr threatened ldrs: wknd bef last* **4/1**[1]

0U6- **7** *24* **The Kings Assassin (IRE)**[203] 1625 6-10-6 **90**.................. TomCannon 56
(Chris Gordon) *a towards rr: wknd bef 2 out: t.o* **14/1**

25P- **8** *5* **Curtain Razer (IRE)**[11] 5129 8-11-7 **105**........................(v[1]) MarcGoldstein 66
(Chris Gordon) *led tl 7th: rdn bef 3 out: wknd bef 2 out: t.o* **33/1**

040- **9** *45* **Admiral Boom (IRE)**[126] 2980 8-10-4 **88**...................... RichardJohnson 9
(Paul Henderson) *rdn after 3 out: a towards rr: t.o* **10/1**

36P/ **10** *4 1/2* **Caminero (IRE)**[377] 7-10-11 **102**....................................... MissEKelly(7) 19
(Jamie Snowden) *a towards rr: t.o after 3 out* **33/1**

444- **P** **Prince Pippin (IRE)**[182] 1887 8-10-12 **103**....................(t) MsLucyJones(7)
(Lucy Jones) *mid-div: rdn after 3 out: wknd bef next: p.u bef last* **20/1**

P34- **S** **Tiller Belle**[19] 5026 6-11-1 **99**... AndrewTinkler
(Nicky Henderson) *chsd ldrs: pushed along and losing pl whn stmbld and uns rdr on bnd after 3 out* **9/1**

533- **P** **Miner Distraction**[51] 4392 6-11-7 **105**............................... NickScholfield
(Jeremy Scott) *hung lft thrght: a towards rr: losing tch whn p.u after 8th* **8/1**

5m 1.9s (-24.60) **Going Correction** -1.00s/f (Hard) **13** Ran SP% **122.2**
Speed ratings (Par 105): **104,102,101,98,97 95,87,85,68,67 , ,**
CSF £58.25 CT £285.67 TOTE £5.70: £3.10, £2.30, £2.00; EX 45.00 Trifecta £792.70 Part won..
Owner The Cool Silk Partnership **Bred** A Buchanan **Trained** Andoversford, Gloucs

FOCUS
This looked wide open. It was run at a fair gallop and they finished well strung out.

5308 32RED WELCOMES MICROGAMING PLAYERS "NATIONAL HUNT" NOVICES' HURDLE (10 hdls) 2m 4f
4:30 (4:30) (Class 4) 4-Y-0+ **£3,898** (£1,144; £572; £286)

Form RPR
311- **1** **Aldopicgros (FR)**[22] 4963 4-11-2 143 .... HarryDerham(3) 115+
(Paul Nicholls) *trckd ldr: shkn up to chal last: hrd rdn into narrow advantage sn after: hld on: all out* **1/5**[1]

446- **2** *hd* **Presenting The Way**[25] 4903 7-10-4 0 .... MartinMcIntyre(10) 110+
(Harry Fry) *j.rt: led: rdn whn pressed appr last: narrowly hdd run-in: rallied wl fnl 120yds: jst hld* **10/3**[2]

00- **3** *13* **Webbswood (IRE)**[15] 5064 5-11-0 0 .... MarkGrant 97
(Sean Curran) *hld up: hdwy after 3 out: rdn to chse ldng pair after next: sn outpcd* **33/1**

55- **4** *12* **Eddy**[19] 5024 5-11-0 0 .... ConorO'Farrell 86
(John Panvert) *hld up: hdwy after 3 out: sn rdn: outpcd fr next* **33/1**

240- **5** *7* **Lily Mars (IRE)**[19] 5026 7-10-7 0 .... MattieBatchelor 72
(Neil Mulholland) *trckd ldr tl rdn appr 2 out: sn wknd* **14/1**[3]

600- **6** *9* **Brogeen Boy (IRE)**[45] 4514 6-11-0 0 .... CharliePoste 69
(Alan Jones) *hld up bhd ldrs: wnt lft 1st: tk clsr order 3 out: sn rdn: wkng whn mstke 2 out* **50/1**

060- **7** *45* **Foolsandorses (IRE)**[15] 5070 6-10-7 0 .... WilliamFeatherstone(7) 24
(W De Best-Turner) *kpt wd: trckd ldr: hit 6th: sn lost pl: wknd after 3 out: t.o* **50/1**

4m 39.4s (-17.40) **Going Correction** -1.00s/f (Hard) 7 Ran SP% **122.9**
Speed ratings (Par 105): **94,93,88,83,81 77,59**
CSF £1.67 TOTE £1.10: £1.02, £2.30; EX 1.40 Trifecta £11.30.
Owner Million In Mind Partnership **Bred** S C I De Cercy & Maurice Goin **Trained** Ditcheat, Somerset

FOCUS
This was hard work for the favourite.

5309 32RED TOMB RAIDER SLOT NOVICES' H'CAP CHASE (21 fncs) 3m 1f 110y
5:05 (5:05) (Class 4) (0-110,107) 5-Y-0+ **£4,548** (£1,335; £667; £333)

Form RPR
U33- **1** **Ruapehu (IRE)**[108] 3291 8-10-11 **92** .... NickScholfield 112+
(Charles Whittaker) *mde all: j.w: in command fr 3 out: pushed out* **7/2**[2]

2/3- **2** *13* **Oscarslad (IRE)**[26] 4884 8-11-5 **107** ....(t) GaryDerwin(7) 120+
(Harry Fry) *trckd wnr thrght: hit 11th: reminders whn nt fluent 14th: chal briefly 4 out: sn rdn: hld fr next: styd on same pce* **7/4**[1]

554- **3** *11* **Market Option (IRE)**[22] 4970 8-11-7 **102** .... LiamTreadwell 103
(Venetia Williams) *hld up 4th: struggling 16th: pckd 4 out: wnt 3rd but no ch w front pair whn pckd bdly 3 out* **10/1**

353- **4** *6* **Old Tricks (IRE)**[12] 5121 7-11-11 **106** ....(p) BrendanPowell 97
(Colin Tizzard) *trckd ldrs: rdn after 16th: losing tch whn slow 4 out: no ch whn lost 3rd bef 3 out* **9/1**

424- **F** **Bit Of A Clown (IRE)**[13] 5111 8-10-8 **89** ....(b) TomCannon
(Nick Gifford) *trcking ldrs whn fell 1st* **7/1**

404- **U** **Kings Apollo**[26] 4883 5-10-7 **91** .... NicodeBoinville(3)
(Tom Symonds) *cl up whn bdly hmpd and uns rdr 1st* **9/2**[3]

440- **P** **General Girling**[26] 4883 7-10-0 **81** oh8 ....(p) IanPopham
(Caroline Keevil) *hld up 5th: pckd 7th: nt fluent after: lost tch fr 9th: p.u bef 15th* **22/1**

6m 21.8s (-17.70) **Going Correction** -0.525s/f (Firm) 7 Ran SP% **112.7**
Speed ratings: **106,102,98,96, ,**
CSF £10.25 TOTE £4.40: £2.10, £1.70; EX 12.90 Trifecta £112.30.
Owner C R Whittaker **Bred** Miss Mary McCabe **Trained** Radstock, Somerset

FOCUS
This moderate novice handicap saw early drama as Bit Of A Clown came down at the first and badly hampered Kings Apollo, causing his rider to unseat. Despite that, though, this form still looks fair for the class.

5310 32RED PREMIER ROULETTE STANDARD OPEN NATIONAL HUNT FLAT RACE 2m
5:40 (5:40) (Class 6) 4-6-Y-0 **£1,624** (£477; £238; £119)

Form RPR
3/ **1** **Thistlecrack**[364] 5323 6-10-9 0 .... MrMLegg(7) 106+
(Colin Tizzard) *in tch: jnd ldrs over 5f out: led over 3f out: r.o strly to assert ent fnl f: pushed out* **14/1**

00- **2** *3* **Neck Or Nothing (GER)**[32] 4756 5-11-9 0 .... RichardJohnson 111+
(Philip Hobbs) *hld up towards rr: smooth hdwy fr 4f out: wnt 2nd wl over 2f out: sn rdn: kpt on but nt pce of wnr fnl f* **8/11**[1]

46- **3** *11* **Picodean**[71] 4030 6-11-2 0 .... LiamTreadwell 94
(Robert Stephens) *trckd ldrs: rdn over 2f out: styd on but nt pce of front pair* **50/1**

4 *2 1/2* **Do We Like Him (IRE)** 4-10-7 0 .... HarryDerham(3) 85
(Paul Nicholls) *hld up: hdwy 3f out: sn rdn: kpt on same pce fnl 2f* **6/1**[3]

0- **5** *2 3/4* **Singh Is King**[15] 5070 6-10-9 0 .... MrMatthewBarber(7) 89
(Marc Barber) *hld up towards rr: rdn into midfield over 3f out: sn hung lft: one pce after* **50/1**

6 *5* **Loukhaar (IRE)** 6-11-2 0 .... MarkGrant 85
(Jonathan Geake) *in tch: effrt 3f out: one pce fnl 2f* **50/1**

02- **7** *6* **The Cider Maker**[38] 4638 4-10-10 0 .... BrendanPowell 73
(Colin Tizzard) *trckd ldrs: rdn and ev ch over 3f out: wknd over 2f out* **5/1**[2]

4- **8** *13* **Carole's Lord**[25] 4909 5-11-2 0 ....(t) AndrewTinkler 67
(Robert Walford) *disp ld: hdd over 3f out: sn rdn: wknd over 2f out* **18/1**

9 *8* **Charming Charlie (IRE)** 4-10-7 0 .... GavinSheehan(3) 54
(Emma Lavelle) *disp ld tl over 5f out: sn wknd* **9/1**

0/- **10** *15* **Southfield Belle (IRE)**[410] 4459 5-10-9 0 ....(t) IanPopham 40
(Caroline Keevil) *trckd ldrs: jnd ldrs over 5f out tl wknd qckly over 3f out* **50/1**

3m 26.6s (-16.70) **Going Correction** -1.00s/f (Hard)
WFA 4 from 5yo+ 5lb 10 Ran SP% **118.6**
Speed ratings: **101,99,94,92,91 88,85,79,75,67**
CSF £25.05 TOTE £11.00: £3.10, £1.10, £4.70; EX 40.00 Trifecta £560.10.
Owner John and Heather Snook **Bred** R F And S D Knipe **Trained** Milborne Port, Dorset

FOCUS
The first pair dominated off the home turn in this modest bumper and there was something of a turn up.

T/Jkpt: £4449.80 to a £1 stake. Pool: £71,009.50 - 11.33 winning units. T/Plt: £79.70 to a £1 stake. Pool: £64,360.07 - 588.80 winning units. T/Qpdt: £16.80 to a £1 stake. Pool: £3536.65 - 155.20 winning units. TM

5311 - 5317a (Foreign Racing) - See Raceform Interactive

[5102] HEXHAM (L-H)
Monday, April 14

OFFICIAL GOING: Good to soft (soft in places; good in the home straight; 6.5)
Wind: Fresh, half against Weather: Cloudy, bright

5318 VISIT HADRIAN'S WALL H'CAP CHASE (10 fncs 2 omitted) 2m 110y
2:00 (2:00) (Class 4) (0-115,107) 5-Y-0+ **£3,898** (£1,144; £572; £286)

Form RPR
531- **1** **Sudski Star (IRE)**[7] 5207 6-11-3 **98** 7ex ....(vt) BrianHughes 108+
(Patrick Griffin, Ire) *cl up: lft 2nd 7th: shkn up to ld last: rdn and edgd lft run-in: drew clr last 100yds* **15/8**[1]

631- **2** *5* **Pamak D'Airy (FR)**[30] 4815 11-11-9 **107** ....(p) TonyKelly(3) 110
(Henry Hogarth) *prom: effrt and rdn bef last: wnt 2nd last 50yds: nt rch wnr* **7/1**

630- **3** *1 1/4* **Lord Of Drums (IRE)**[30] 4822 8-11-9 **104** .... PeterBuchanan 106
(Lucinda Russell) *led to 3rd: lft in ld 7th: rdn and hdd last: kpt on same pce and lost 2nd last 50yds* **7/2**[3]

/PP- **4** *25* **Barnevelder (IRE)**[82] 3834 9-10-0 **81** oh5 ....(bt) AdrianLane 62
(Sandy Forster) *nt fluent in rr: niggled along fr 3rd: drvn and outpcd fr 3 out: lost tch after next* **9/1**

U31- **P** **Cara Court (IRE)**[10] 5162 8-10-11 **95** ....(p) JonathanEngland(3)
(Joanne Foster) *cl up: led 3rd: j.rt 6th: jst in front whn hesitated, blnd and hdd next: sn p.u* **11/4**[2]

4m 11.9s (2.10) **Going Correction** +0.075s/f (Yiel) 5 Ran SP% **106.2**
Speed ratings: **98,95,95,83,**
CSF £12.85 TOTE £3.10: £1.80, £1.30; EX 7.30 Trifecta £18.80.
Owner Patrick Griffin **Bred** Mrs J P Duffy **Trained** Oldtown, Co Dublin

FOCUS
After a dry night the going was changed to good to soft, soft in places. Three last-time-out winners lined up in this small-field handicap. The pace was not very not very strong but the favourite scored in good style. The form is rated around the second and third. Bends moved onto best ground available.

5319 CORBRIDGE H'CAP HURDLE (8 hdls 2 omitted) 2m 4f 110y
2:30 (2:30) (Class 4) (0-120,117) 4-Y-0+ **£3,249** (£954; £477; £238)

Form RPR
334- **1** **Forty Crown (IRE)**[32] 4771 8-11-5 **110** .... WilsonRenwick 115+
(John Wade) *w ldr: led bef 2 out: clr last: drvn out* **4/1**[2]

5/1- **2** *4* **Bop Along (IRE)**[32] 4776 7-11-5 **110** .... DannyCook 109+
(Michael Smith) *t.k.h early: prom: rdn and outpcd appr 2 out: rallied bef last: chsd (clr) wnr run-in: kpt on: no imp* **4/1**[2]

431/ **3** *1 1/4* **Vuvuzela**[517] 2404 8-11-2 **110** .... TonyKelly(3) 107
(Rebecca Menzies) *t.k.h: hld up in tch: smooth hdwy to chse wnr bef 2 out: rdn bef last: sn no imp: lost 2nd run-in* **10/1**[3]

300- **4** *17* **Kent Street (IRE)**[17] 5059 9-10-3 **97** .... JonathanEngland(3) 79
(Sue Smith) *t.k.h: prom: effrt on outside whn nt fluent 2 out: rdn and wknd bef last* **4/1**[2]

121- **5** *10* **Short Takes (USA)**[29] 4836 6-11-12 **117** ....(b) APMcCoy 90
(Donald McCain) *plld hrd: hld up in tch: rdn and outpcd after 2 out: sn btn* **2/1**[1]

032- **6** *14* **Sam Lord**[38] 4648 10-11-2 **107** .... BrianHughes 67
(James Moffatt) *led tl hdd bef 2 out: sn rdn and lost pl: t.o* **16/1**

5m 13.3s (0.80) **Going Correction** -0.075s/f (Good) 6 Ran SP% **108.3**
Speed ratings (Par 105): **95,93,93,86,82 77**
CSF £18.72 TOTE £5.40: £2.40, £1.80; EX 23.40 Trifecta £123.50.
Owner Miss Maria D Myco **Bred** Declan Little **Trained** Mordon, Co Durham

FOCUS
They went a stop-start gallop in this handicap. The winner was always prominent and the favourite was disappointing. The first two are rated to form.

5320 THORNTON-FIRKIN "NATIONAL HUNT" NOVICES' HURDLE (6 hdls 2 omitted) 2m 110y
3:00 (3:00) (Class 4) 4-Y-0+ **£3,422** (£997; £499)

Form RPR
2U1- **1** **Frankie's Promise (IRE)**[41] 4609 6-11-6 120 ....(p) LucyAlexander 122+
(N W Alexander) *in tch: nt fluent 4th: hdwy to ld appr 2 out: clr bef last: kpt on strly: eased nr fin* **4/1**[3]

/32- **2** *10* **Wild Card**[41] 4609 7-11-6 118 .... APMcCoy 110
(Donald McCain) *pressed ldr: led after 3 out to appr next: sn rdn: kpt on fr last* **10/3**[2]

412- **3** *hd* **Tikkandemickey (IRE)**[14] 5102 8-11-6 120 .... DaraghBourke(7) 117
(Raymond Shiels) *led to after 3 out: cl up tl outpcd appr next: rallied bef last: kpt on same pce run-in* **6/4**[1]

212- **4** *1 3/4* **Howwoulduno (IRE)**[164] 2207 6-11-13 122 .... GrahamWatters(7) 123
(Liam Lennon, Ire) *hld up: hdwy and in tch after 3 out: effrt and rdn next: kpt on same pce fr last* **13/2**

5 *7* **Where's Malachy (IRE)** 6-10-13 0 .... WilsonRenwick 95
(Rose Dobbin) *midfield: hdwy and prom 3 out: rdn and outpcd appr next: n.d after* **40/1**

660- **6** *6* **Purple Harry**[14] 5102 6-10-8 0 .... SamanthaDrake(5) 90
(Tina Jackson) *prom: outpcd whn hit 3 out: rallied last: kpt on: no imp* **100/1**

605- **7** *3/4* **Be A Dreamer**[27] 4889 6-10-10 0 .... JonathanEngland(3) 89
(Sue Smith) *hld up towards rr: drvn and outpcd 3 out: sme late hdwy: nvr on terms* **80/1**

300- **8** *2 3/4* **Lilly's Legend**[32] 4776 4-10-0 0 .... DougieCostello 73
(Mark Walford) *prom tl drvn and outpcd 3 out: n.d after* **33/1**

0/4- **9** *3 1/2* **Present Lodger (IRE)**[26] 4901 6-10-13 0 .... PeterBuchanan 83
(Lucinda Russell) *prom tl drvn and outpcd bef 2 out: sn no imp* **12/1**

0U0- **10** *1/2* **Mighty Cliche (IRE)**[14] 5102 5-10-8 0 .... ColmMcCormack(5) 83
(Dianne Sayer) *nt fluent towards rr: outpcd after 3 out: btn after next* **150/1**

0- **11** *50* **Always Summat**[42] 4598 4-10-7 0 .... BrianHarding 32
(Michael Easterby) *bhd: struggling bef 3 out: lost tch bef next: t.o* **80/1**

66F- **12** *34* **Sedano (FR)**[22] 4980 8-10-13 0 .... BrianHughes 7
(Sara Ender) *midfield: effrt after 3 out: wknd qckly appr next: t.o* **50/1**

6/F- **U** **Crofton Lane**[7] 5205 8-10-6 0 .... MrJDixon(7)
(John Dixon) *nt fluent in rr: lost tch whn j. slowly and uns rdr 3 out* **250/1**

00- U Diamond Native (IRE)62 4205 6-10-6 0 MrJHamilton(7)
(Brian Storey) bhd: struggling bef 3 out: t.o whn j. slowly and uns rdr 2 out 250/1
4m 13.5s (-3.90) **Going Correction** -0.075s/f (Good)
WFA 4 from 5yo+ 5lb **14** Ran SP% **116.4**
Speed ratings (Par 105): **106,101,101,100,97 94,93,92,90,90 67,51, ,**
CSF £17.30 TOTE £4.20: £1.70, £1.80, £1.10; EX 24.10 Trifecta £33.40.
Owner Brian Castle **Bred** Sean And Batt Leahy **Trained** Kinneston, Perth & Kinross
FOCUS
The winner powered clear from the two market leaders in this decent novices' hurdle for the track, and took another step up.

5321 COHORT H'CAP CHASE (17 fncs 2 omitted) 3m 1f
3:30 (3:30) (Class 5) (0-100,100) 5-Y-0+ **£2,274** (£667; £333; £166)

Form RPR
043- 1 **Outlaw Tom (IRE)**32 4773 10-11-5 **93** (p) PeterBuchanan 109+
(Lucinda Russell) cl up: outpcd briefly after 12th: rallied next: hdwy to ld bef last: sn clr 15/2
P0P- 2 12 **Almond Court (IRE)**51 4428 11-10-10 **84** KennyJohnson 89+
(Robert Johnson) led: mstke 3rd: hdd 10th: upsides whn mstke 12th: rdn and sltly outpcd between last 2: rallied to chse wnr run-in: kpt on: no imp 40/1
U06- 3 hd **Mannered**14 5104 9-11-0 **88** BrianHughes 91
(John Wade) t.k.h early: prom: stdy hdwy bef 4 out: effrt and rdn between last 2: one pce 14/1
131- 4 4 **Gibbstown (IRE)**14 5104 8-11-5 **98** (p) DerekFox(5) 97
(Paul Stafford, Ire) cl up: led 10th: rdn and hdd bef last: drvn and outpcd run-in 9/2[1]
64P- 5 1 3/4 **Daasij (IRE)**103 3478 9-11-7 **95** LucyAlexander 93
(N W Alexander) bhd: drvn and struggling 1/2-way: styd on fr 2 out: nvr rchd ldrs 8/1
P2P- 6 1 3/4 **Filbert Fox (IRE)**14 5104 8-10-2 **79** (p) EwanWhillans(3) 75
(Alistair Whillans) prom: drvn along 1/2-way: outpcd after 4 out: no imp fr next 11/2[3]
P/0- 7 3/4 **Finbin (IRE)**326 444 12-10-5 **82** TonyKelly(3) 78
(Henry Hogarth) towards rr: drvn along fnl circ: no imp fr 4 out 8/1
8 69 **Ravensdale Lady (IRE)**22 4997 8-11-2 **97** (p) GrahamWatters(7) 30
(Mark Michael McNiff, Ire) towards rr: drvn along 1/2-way: wknd after 4 out: t.o 16/1
4PP- 9 18 **Fog Patches (IRE)**61 4220 8-11-6 **99** (p) CraigNichol(5) 16
(Lucinda Russell) mstkes: prom to 12th: struggling fr next: t.o 16/1
3/2- P **Definite Appeal (IRE)**30 4812 11-10-6 **90** JamesCorbett(10)
(Susan Corbett) bhd: shortlived effrt appr 12th: struggling fr next: no ch whn p.u bef last 5/1[2]
3P6- P **War On (IRE)**30 4812 7-11-12 **100** (p) HenryBrooke
(Chris Grant) towards rr: struggling and p.u after 9th 6/1
6m 32.41s (0.21) **Going Correction** +0.075s/f (Yiel) **11** Ran SP% **119.4**
Speed ratings: **102,98,98,96,96 95,95,73,67,**
CSF £223.47 CT £4068.44 TOTE £8.70: £2.80, £7.20, £4.20; EX 212.70 Trifecta £369.00.
Owner Milnathort Racing Club **Bred** N J Connors **Trained** Arlary, Perth & Kinross
FOCUS
There was an emphatic winner in this fair handicap chase for the grade. The winner's best figure since 2012.

5322 RIDING MARES' MAIDEN HURDLE (9 hdls 3 omitted) 3m
4:00 (4:00) (Class 5) 5-Y-0+ **£2,395** (£698; £349)

Form RPR
32- 1 **Bespoke Lady (IRE)**34 4749 5-10-12 0 APMcCoy 109+
(Donald McCain) cl up: led 6th: hit 3 out: rdn after next: edgd lft and drvn clr fr last 9/4[2]
22- 2 7 **Nosey Box (IRE)**54 4361 8-10-7 105 (bt[1]) DerekFox(5) 103
(Noel C Kelly, Ire) hld up in tch: hdwy bef 2 out: effrt and chsd wnr bef last: kpt on same pce run-in 5/1[3]
3 1 1/2 **Waltz Legend (IRE)**23 4977 8-10-5 0 (t) GrahamWatters(7) 102
(Liam Lennon, Ire) t.k.h: trckd ldrs: effrt and drvn after 2 out: kpt on same pce fr last 15/8[1]
444- 4 1 1/4 **Sheilas Lady**32 4776 6-10-12 0 BrianHughes 101
(Andrew Crook) cl up: disp ld 6th to bef 2 out: rdn and outpcd fr last 9/1
42- 5 27 **Midnight Streaker**34 4743 5-10-12 97 PaddyBrennan 79
(B Arthey, Ire) hld up in tch: effrt after 3 out: nt fluent and wknd fr next 11/2
656- 6 22 **Mrs Grass**17 5056 7-10-12 69 HenryBrooke 56
(Jonathan Haynes) hld up: pushed along after 3 out: wknd bef next: t.o 100/1
P **Castle Goer (IRE)**23 5-10-12 0 (p) PeterBuchanan
(B Arthey, Ire) led to 6th: cl up tl lost pl bef 3 out: struggling bef next: t.o whn p.u bef last 33/1
06P- P **Tara Springs**24 4939 5-10-12 0 (t) BrianHarding
(Barry Murtagh) t.k.h: hld up in tch: struggling after 7th: t.o whn p.u bef last 80/1
6m 12.1s (3.10) **Going Correction** -0.075s/f (Good) **8** Ran SP% **112.8**
Speed ratings: **91,88,88,87,78 71, ,**
CSF £13.65 TOTE £2.40: £1.10, £2.10, £1.10; EX 13.20 Trifecta £32.60.
Owner Paul & Clare Rooney **Bred** David Fenton **Trained** Cholmondeley, Cheshire
FOCUS
They went a steady pace in this mares' maiden hurdle. Four runners were tightly grouped around the final turn but the unexposed winner powered clear in the closing stages. The form is rated around the second and fourth.

5323 LINNELS BRIDGE OPEN HUNTERS' CHASE (16 fncs 3 omitted) 3m 1f
4:30 (4:30) (Class 6) 5-Y-0+ **£1,497** (£464; £232; £116)

Form RPR
/21- 1 **Current Exchange (IRE)**16 9-12-3 119 MrPGerety(5) 117+
(Mrs Sheila Crow) t.k.h: cl up: led gng wl bef last: drew clr run-in 5/6[1]
3P0- 2 9 **Douglas Julian**11 5135 12-11-9 107 MrTHamilton(5) 101
(Miss K Scott) pressed ldr: drvn and outpcd after 2 out: rallied last: tk 2nd last 50yds 18/1
/20- 3 1 **A New Rising (IRE)**16 12-11-7 73 (p) MrJLyttle(7) 100
(M E Ellwood) mde most tl hdd bef last: rallied: kpt on same pce and lost 2nd last 50yds 50/1
P36- 4 12 **Back On The Road (IRE)**30 12-11-11 104 MrJamieAlexander(7) 95
(N W Alexander) nt fluent: hld up in tch: outpcd 1/2-way: rallied after 4 out: no imp fr next 20/1
P31/ 5 10 **Ocarina (FR)**16 12-11-13 0 (p) MrKitAlexander(5) 87
(N W Alexander) chsd ldrs: drvn and outpcd 8th: rallied 4 out: struggling after next 4/1[2]
/14- 6 54 **Radharc Na Mara (IRE)**10 5164 10-11-4 105 MissHHarper(7) 59
(Miss H Harper) hld up: hdwy and prom 1/2-way: rdn and wknd fr 5 out 7/1[3]
5/P- P **Pen Gwen (FR)**14 5107 11-11-7 75 (tp) MrPDennis(7)
(Philip Kirby) prom: drvn and outpcd 12th: struggling after 4 out: t.o whn p.u bef last 50/1
6P2- P **Special Portrait (IRE)**10 5164 10-12-5 109 (t) MrGCrow(3)
(Mark Hughes) hld up: outpcd 1/2-way: sn struggling: t.o whn p.u bef last 7/1[3]
4/ F **Page One Two Nine (IRE)**16 11-11-7 105 MrNOrpwood(7)
(Miss J Luton) hld up in tch: fell 3rd 20/1
6m 36.1s (3.90) **Going Correction** +0.075s/f (Yiel) **9** Ran SP% **118.3**
Speed ratings: **96,93,92,88,85 68, , ,**
CSF £16.54 TOTE £1.80: £1.10, £3.50, £12.80; EX 13.30 Trifecta £445.60.
Owner Alastair Crow **Bred** R Guiry **Trained** Shrewsbury, Shropshire
FOCUS
The hot favourite was a clear-cut winner in this hunters' chase. The winner didn't need to reproduce his mark.

5324 VALLUM STANDARD OPEN NATIONAL HUNT FLAT RACE 2m 110y
5:00 (5:02) (Class 6) 4-5-Y-0 **£1,642** (£478; £239)

Form RPR
3- 1 **Shades Of Midnight**23 4958 4-10-5 0 CallumWhillans(5) 99+
(Donald Whillans) in tch: hdwy to ld over 3f out: rdn clr fnl f 11/4[2]
33- 2 8 **Pithivier (FR)**51 4431 4-10-10 0 WilsonRenwick 92
(Peter Niven) trckd ldrs: led over 4f out to over 3f out: effrt and pushed along 2f out: kpt on same pce fnl f 5/4[1]
3 1 1/2 **Apples And Trees (IRE)** 5-11-2 0 AdrianLane 97
(Donald McCain) hld up on outside: stdy hdwy and prom 1/2-way: effrt and ch over 3f out: rdn and outpcd wl over 1f out 9/2[3]
4 11 **Charlie Snow Angel** 5-10-9 0 MrTHamilton(7) 87
(Sandy Forster) hld up: pushed along fr over 4f out: plugged on fr 3f out: no imp 33/1
P- 5 5 **Clan Legend**14 5109 4-10-10 0 LucyAlexander 78
(N W Alexander) t.k.h: led to over 4f out: rdn and wknd over 2f out 10/1
0- 6 19 **Valnamixe Du Mee (FR)**41 4611 5-11-2 0 KennyJohnson 65
(Robert Johnson) t.k.h: cl up tl rdn and wknd over 3f out 50/1
0- 7 10 **Meet Henry**23 4958 5-10-9 0 DaleIrving(7) 56
(Rayson Nixon) hld up: rdn and outpcd over 5f out: sn btn 100/1
55- 8 13 **Major Ridge (IRE)**14 5109 5-10-9 0 CallumBewley(7) 44
(Robert Bewley) hld up in tch: stdy hdwy after 7f: drvn along and outpcd over 4f out: sn btn 18/1
6- 9 34 **Pegasus Walk (IRE)**24 4944 5-10-11 0 CraigNichol(5) 14
(Rose Dobbin) trckd ldrs: drvn and outpcd 1/2-way: struggling fr over 4f out: t.o 16/1
4m 6.2s (-6.50) **Going Correction** -0.075s/f (Good)
WFA 4 from 5yo 5lb **9** Ran SP% **115.4**
Speed ratings: **112,108,107,102,100 91,86,80,64**
CSF £6.48 TOTE £3.50: £1.10, £1.10, £2.40; EX 8.40 Trifecta £28.10.
Owner The Potassium Partnership **Bred** Potassium Partnership II **Trained** Hawick, Borders
FOCUS
There was a decisive winner in this modest bumper which was run at a steady pace. The form is rated around the first two.
T/Plt: £80.60 to a £1 stake. Pool: £74411.58 - 673.29 winning tickets T/Qpdt: £16.00 to a £1 stake. Pool: £7484.58 - 344.78 winning tickets RY

5029 EXETER (R-H)
Tuesday, April 15

OFFICIAL GOING: Good (chs 7.8, hdl 7.5)
Wind: fresh across Weather: sunny

5332 FINLAKE HOLIDAY PARK NOVICES' HURDLE (12 hdls) 2m 7f 110y
2:00 (2:00) (Class 4) 4-Y-0+ **£3,249** (£954; £477; £238)

Form RPR
0P1- 1 **Saddlers Encore (IRE)**23 4993 5-11-7 0 RichardJohnson 126+
(Philip Hobbs) trckd ldrs: nodded 7th: sn pushed along: chal 3 out: sn drvn: narrow ld 2 out: mstke last: veered lft towards fin: hld on: all out 6/1
11- 2 hd **Virtuel D'Oudon (FR)**21 5024 5-11-7 0 TomScudamore 124
(David Pipe) trckd ldrs: jnd ldrs 8th: rdn to ld 3 out: hdd 2 out: ev ch last: kpt on wl fnl 70yds: jst hld 5/1[3]
303- 3 18 **Strollawaynow (IRE)**15 5110 7-11-7 128 APMcCoy 110
(David Arbuthnot) led tl 5th: led bef next: rdn and hdd appr 3 out: sn hld: lft 3rd 2 out: wknd 9/4[2]
231- 4 20 **Ashford Wood (IRE)**30 4838 6-11-7 0 MichaelByrne 89
(Tim Vaughan) j.lft: nvr travelling in last trio: wl hld after 9th: lft btn 4th 2 out: wknd: t.o 7/1
0FF- 5 15 **Milanese (IRE)**21 5015 6-10-12 0 GavinSheehan(3) 69
(Emma Lavelle) prom: led 5th tl bef next: rdn after 9th: wknd bef next: t.o 16/1
B14- F **Sego Success (IRE)**59 4272 6-11-7 128 RobertThornton 123
(Alan King) trckd ldrs: rdn after 9th: nt clrest of runs 3 out: mounting chal but short of room whn fell 2 out 2/1[1]
/60- P **Tamarton Tansy**22 5002 7-10-8 0 PaddyBrennan
(Fergal O'Brien) hld up: wknd after 9th: tailing off whn p.u bef 3 out 100/1
06U- P **War Treaty (IRE)**20 5029 6-11-1 0 TommyPhelan
(Mark Shears) hld up: detached whn p.u on long run bef 6th 250/1
5m 38.1s (-20.90) **Going Correction** -1.075s/f (Hard) **8** Ran SP% **114.8**
Speed ratings (Par 105): **91,90,84,78,73 , ,**
CSF £36.34 TOTE £9.60: £2.10, £2.10, £1.10; EX 31.10 Trifecta £140.20.
Owner Robert & Janet Gibbs **Bred** Kevin Neville **Trained** Withycombe, Somerset
FOCUS
Hurdle course moved onto ground not used since November. Both Richard Johnson and Tony McCoy concluded the ground was riding as per the official description. A fair novice hurdle featuring several promising chasing types. The first two are on the upgrade.

5333 CITY OF EXETER CHALLENGE CUP H'CAP HURDLE (12 hdls) 2m 7f 110y
2:30 (2:30) (Class 3) (0-130,130) 4-Y-0+ **£5,523** (£1,621; £810; £405)

Form RPR
641- 1 **Billy Dutton**17 5074 8-11-1 **119** JamesDavies 127
(Chris Down) in tch: rdn to chal 3 out: 2 l down last: r.o strly to ld towards fin 12/1
61P- 2 nk **Join The Clan (IRE)**51 4449 5-11-7 **125** APMcCoy 134+
(Jonjo O'Neill) hld up towards rr: hdwy after 7th: chal 3 out: led 2 out: sn drvn: hung lft: 2 l up last: no ex whn hdd nring fin 9/1

12F- **3** *6* **Rydon Pynes**[32] 4786 6-11-10 **128** .... HaddenFrost 130
(Martin Hill) *mid-div: hdwy appr 3 out: wnt 4th whn nt fluent 2 out: sn rdn: kpt on to go 3rd sn after last* **11/2**[1]

114- **4** *6* **Royal Player**[52] 4423 5-11-5 **130** .... MrCGethings(7) 127
(Philip Hobbs) *in tch: trckd ldrs 5th: rdn to dispute 3 out tl next: kpt on same pce fr last* **7/1**[2]

361- **5** *nk* **Storm Alert**[53] 4393 7-10-8 **117** .... MissLucyGardner(5) 116
(Sue Gardner) *trckd ldrs: rdn and ev ch appr 3 out: styd on same pce fr 2 out* **10/1**

231- **6** *nk* **King Boru (IRE)**[138] 2764 6-11-4 **122** .... RichardJohnson 118
(Emma Lavelle) *hld up towards rr: hdwy after 9th: rdn next: styd on same pce* **7/1**[2]

5/P- **7** *3¼* **Sir Kezbaah (IRE)**[117] 3172 10-11-2 **120** .... (t) ConorO'Farrell 113
(Richard Woollacott) *mid-div: rdn after 9th: no imp tl styd on appr last* **20/1**

545- **8** *5* **Rich Buddy**[26] 4913 8-10-11 **115** .... SamTwiston-Davies 106
(Richard Phillips) *in tch: rdn after 9th: sn one pce* **14/1**

413- **9** *5* **Oscar Prairie (IRE)**[59] 4277 9-11-0 **128** .... (b) WilliamFeatherstone(10) 112
(Warren Greatrex) *towards rr: struggling 8th: no ch after next: r.o fr last* **16/1**

000- **10** *3½* **Georgian King**[17] 5074 11-9-13 **110** .... OllieGarner(7) 91
(Martin Keighley) *led tl 6th: styd prom: rdn after 9th: wknd bef next* **33/1**

040- **11** *hd* **Super Villan**[25] 4932 9-10-8 **115** .... NicodeBoinville(3) 97
(Mark Bradstock) *prom: led 6th tl rdn appr 3 out: grad fdd* **28/1**

160- **12** *1¾* **Jojabean (IRE)**[17] 5074 7-10-10 **114** .... RobertThornton 94
(Alan King) *mid-div: rdn after 9th: no imp: wknd after next* **16/1**

515- **13** *½* **Pyleigh Lass**[22] 5010 8-10-9 **113** .... (t) IanPopham 92
(Martin Keighley) *trckd ldrs: rdn after 8th: wknd bef 3 out* **33/1**

5PP- **14** *4½* **Bathwick Brave (IRE)**[65] 4174 7-11-6 **124** .... (t) DougieCostello 99
(Johnny Farrelly) *j.lft: nvr travelling: a towards rr* **66/1**

433- **F** **Brackloon High (IRE)**[45] 4556 9-11-1 **119** .... (p) BrendanPowell 115
(Brendan Powell) *mid-div: rdn after 9th: styng on at same pce in hld 7th whn fell last* **14/1**

525- **P** **Barton Stacey (IRE)**[17] 5074 9-10-12 **116** .... (b) TomScudamore
(David Pipe) *mid-div: hit 7th: sn pushed along: wknd after 9th: p.u bef next* **8/1**[3]

4FP- **P** **Forresters Folly**[126] 3004 8-11-6 **124** .... (p) JackDoyle
(Alan King) *in tch: trckd ldrs 5th: hit 9th: rdn appr 3 out: sn wknd: p.u bef last* **28/1**

5m 35.5s (-23.50) **Going Correction** -1.075s/f (Hard) **17** Ran SP% **122.4**
Speed ratings (Par 107): **96,95,93,91,91 91,90,88,87,86 86,85,85,83,** ,
CSF £108.00 CT £675.40 TOTE £13.50: £3.40, £2.20, £2.20, £2.20; EX 151.80 Trifecta £1516.60 Part won..
Owner W A Bromley **Bred** Wood Farm Stud **Trained** Mutterton, Devon

FOCUS
Quite a decent staying handicap, in which they got racing a fair way out, and there were changing fortunes late on, with Join The Clan, who had travelled well and readily asserted, doing little in front and throwing away what had seemed a certain victory (traded at 1.01 on Betfair), being worn down close home by Billy Dutton, who was making it back-to-back wins in the race. Steps up from the first two.

5334 HAULFRYN HOLIDAYS MARATHON H'CAP CHASE (21 fncs) 3m 6f 110y
3:00 (3:00) (Class 3) (0-125,125) 5-Y-O **£6,330** (£1,870; £935; £468; £234)

Form RPR

F40- **1** **Upham Atom**[24] 4962 11-11-10 **123** .... LiamTreadwell 131
(Kate Buckett) *mid-div: in last trio 14th: rdn and hdwy appr 4 out: sn chsng ldr: j.rt last 4: chal last: sn led: styd on dourly* **20/1**

2P0- **2** *4* **Allthekingshorses (IRE)**[37] 4697 8-11-6 **122** .... (tp) JamesBest(3) 126
(Philip Hobbs) *hld up: hdwy to trck ldr 4th: rdn after 17th: led bef 4 out: jnd last: sn hdd: no ex* **9/1**

132- **3** *10* **Jayandbee (IRE)**[23] 4990 7-10-12 **111** .... (p) RichardJohnson 106
(Philip Hobbs) *sn trcking ldrs: lost pl 10th: hdwy 14th: rdn after 17th: wnt 3rd after 4 out: styd on same pce fr next* **5/1**[2]

114- **4** *13* **Nail 'M (IRE)**[30] 4835 6-11-1 **114** .... (p) TomScudamore 101
(Nigel Hawke) *in tch: trckd ldrs 10th: mstke 13th: rdn after 17th: styd on same pce fr 4 out: wnt 4th towards fin* **6/1**[3]

012- **5** *¾* **Sarika (FR)**[157] 2384 8-10-1 **107** .... (b) MissEKelly(7) 90
(Nick Williams) *hld up: mid-div 5th: wnt 3rd 14th: rdn after 17th: grad fdd fr 3 out: lost 4th towards fin* **20/1**

363- **6** *37* **Inside Dealer (IRE)**[131] 2909 10-11-3 **116** .... (p) BrendanPowell 66
(Colin Tizzard) *trckd ldrs tl lost pl 10th: bhd after 14th: t.o* **12/1**

221- **P** **Jaunty Journey**[14] 5122 11-10-1 **100** .... (p) SamTwiston-Davies
(Nigel Twiston-Davies) *chsd ldrs: rdn 14th: grad lost pl fr next: t.o whn p.u after 17th* **9/2**[1]

231- **P** **Orange Nassau (FR)**[37] 4695 8-11-12 **125** .... NoelFehily
(Charlie Longsdon) *trckd ldr tl 3rd: in tch tl dropped to last pair 12th: struggling after next: t.o whn p.u bef 4 out* **5/1**[2]

624- **S** **Faith Keeper (IRE)**[20] 5032 9-10-1 **100** .... (b[1]) PaddyBrennan
(Fergal O'Brien) *mid-div whn slipped up on bnd bef 7th* **9/1**

3P1- **U** **Miss Saffron**[20] 5032 11-10-3 **102** .... PaulMoloney
(Sue Gardner) *hld up: v bdly hmpd and uns rdr on bnd bef 7th* **10/1**

566- **P** **Robin Will (FR)**[20] 5032 9-10-12 **111** .... ConorO'Farrell
(Richard Woollacott) *detached in last: bdly hmpd on bnd bef 7th: nvr rcvrd: continued t.o tl p.u bef 4 out* **33/1**

P2P- **P** **Regal Presence (IRE)**[13] 5129 7-11-2 **115** .... (b) JackDoyle
(Victor Dartnall) *led: rdn and hdd appr 4 out: wknd rapidly: p.u bef 2 out* **16/1**

7m 32.8s (-15.80) **Going Correction** -0.775s/f (Firm) **12** Ran SP% **120.9**
Speed ratings: **89,87,85,82,81 72,** , , , ,
CSF £188.86 CT £1057.61 TOTE £24.30: £5.20, £3.00, £1.50; EX 300.40 Trifecta £1474.60.
Owner Mrs D Buckett **Bred** M J Le May **Trained** Upham, Hants

FOCUS
Although run on a sound surface, stamina was still at a premium in this marathon chase. The winner is rated back to his best.

5335 SOUTH WEST RACING CLUB H'CAP HURDLE (8 hdls) 2m 1f
3:35 (3:35) (Class 4) (0-115,115) 4-Y-O+ **£3,898** (£1,144; £572; £286)

Form RPR

5/0- **1** **Revani**[28] 4888 7-11-4 **107** .... RichardJohnson 115+
(Johnny Farrelly) *mde all: rdn after 3 out: kpt on wl: drvn out* **12/1**

040- **2** *2* **Ladies Dancing**[13] 5125 8-11-0 **103** .... JamesDavies 109
(Chris Down) *in tch: hdwy 3rd: pressed wnr after 5th: rdn bef next: styd on but hld fr 2 out* **14/1**

011- **3** *3½* **Take The Crown**[22] 5012 5-10-6 **95** .... DenisO'Regan 97
(Henry Oliver) *mid-div: pushed along after 5th: rdn into disp 3rd 3 out: kpt on wout getting on terms w front pair* **11/8**[1]

/10- **4** *2* **Presenting Arms (IRE)**[36] 4726 7-11-12 **115** .... (t) NoelFehily 115
(Harry Fry) *mid-div: hdwy 4th: rdn in cl 3rd appr 3 out: kpt on tl no ex appr last* **8/1**[3]

400- **5** *11* **Money For Nothing**[25] 4931 5-11-9 **112** .... RobertThornton 102
(Alan King) *hld up: hdwy fr 3rd: trckd ldrs after 5th: rdn bef next: fdd fr 2 out* **9/1**

060- **6** *nse* **Grams And Ounces**[17] 5067 7-10-13 **102** .... (t) AndrewTinkler 92
(Tony Newcombe) *a in mid-div* **22/1**

013- **7** *1¾* **Rugged Jack (FR)**[20] 5033 7-11-10 **113** .... JackDoyle 103
(Victor Dartnall) *trckd ldrs: reminders after 3rd: nt fluent next: rdn after 5th: wknd 2 out* **7/1**[2]

561- **8** *4½* **Benbecula**[23] 4988 5-11-10 **113** .... SamTwiston-Davies 97
(Richard Mitchell) *j.lft 1st: trckd ldr tl dropped to last pair 2nd: sn struggling: hdwy u.p appr 3 out: wknd 2 out* **8/1**[3]

U50- **9** *½* **Quaddick Lake (IRE)**[20] 5030 11-11-12 **115** .... (t) ConorO'Farrell 99
(Richard Woollacott) *hld up: rdn appr 3 out: nvr any imp* **25/1**

100- **10** *17* **Keychain (IRE)**[24] 4963 4-11-4 **113** .... BrendanPowell 76
(Brendan Powell) *trckd ldrs: pushed along fr 2nd: rdn after 5th: wknd bef next* **66/1**

420- **11** *1¼* **Gallic Warrior (FR)**[16] 5088 7-11-5 **113** ....[1] ConorShoemark(5) 81
(Fergal O'Brien) *hld up: rdn after 5th: wknd bef 3 out: t.o* **14/1**

3m 55.0s (-20.50) **Going Correction** -1.075s/f (Hard)
WFA 4 from 5yo+ 5lb **11** Ran SP% **117.5**
Speed ratings (Par 105): **105,104,102,101,96 96,95,93,93,85 84**
CSF £159.10 CT £379.50 TOTE £13.70: £3.80, £4.30, £1.10; EX 170.00 Trifecta £625.10.
Owner Mrs Sarah Faulks **Bred** Mr And Mrs N Faulks **Trained** Bridgwater, Somerset

FOCUS
The winner belatedly built on the promise of his novice form.

5336 DARTMOUTH TERM OF 65 H'CAP CHASE (15 fncs) 2m 3f 110y
4:10 (4:10) (Class 4) (0-120,119) 5-Y-O+ **£3,898** (£1,144; £572; £286)

Form RPR

1P0- **1** **Midnight Lira**[58] 4299 7-10-8 **104** .... JamesBest(3) 108+
(Caroline Keevil) *trckd ldrs: rdn along fr 10th: hdwy appr 4 out: sn chsng wnr: styd on in 2 l 2nd whn lft in ld and hmpd 2 out: drvn rt out* **8/1**

323- **2** *¾* **Picaroon**[26] 4912 10-10-10 **110** .... MrsAlexDunn(7) 112
(Alexandra Dunn) *led: rdn and hdd appr 4 out: looked hld in 4th whn lft 3rd 2 out: kpt on fr last but nvr quite rching wnr* **25/1**

303- **3** *4½* **Mic's Delight (IRE)**[22] 5006 10-11-7 **114** .... (b) JackDoyle 111
(Victor Dartnall) *trckd ldrs: rdn appr 4 out: lft w ev ch between last 2: no ex fr last* **9/1**

P32- **4** *5* **Speedy Bruere (FR)**[22] 5013 8-11-8 **115** .... TomScudamore 107
(David Bridgwater) *trckd ldr tl 11th: sn rdn: styd on same pce fr 4 out* **9/2**[3]

512- **5** *5* **Morgan's Bay**[39] 4653 9-11-6 **113** .... PaulMoloney 100
(Tom George) *hld up in tch: hdwy 8th: rdn after 11th: sn one pce* **12/1**

P22- **F** **Gores Island (IRE)**[20] 5031 8-11-8 **115** .... JoshuaMoore 119
(Gary Moore) *hld up in tch: hdwy 9th: upsides 11th: led sn after: j.rt fr next: 2 l up but rdn whn fell 2 out* **5/2**[1]

P46- **P** **Allerton (IRE)**[24] 4968 7-10-3 **101** .... (t) ConorShoemark(5)
(Fergal O'Brien) *nvr travelling and sn detached: t.o whn p.u bef 4 out* **8/1**

34P- **P** **Mr Watson (IRE)**[64] 4190 7-11-12 **119** .... APMcCoy
(Jonjo O'Neill) *trckd ldrs tl 8th: sn struggling in last pair: t.o whn p.u after 11th* **10/3**[2]

4m 38.5s (-18.80) **Going Correction** -0.775s/f (Firm) **8** Ran SP% **113.6**
Speed ratings: **106,105,103,101,99** , ,
CSF £145.19 CT £1818.35 TOTE £10.10: £3.00, £3.30, £2.20; EX 258.50 Trifecta £1359.40.
Owner Brian Derrick **Bred** B Derrick And P R Rodford **Trained** Motcombe, Dorset

FOCUS
Not form to take much notice of going forward with the complexion of the race changing late on. The winner is rated to his mark.

5337 TOTNES AND BRIDGETOWN NOVICES' HUNTERS' CHASE (18 fncs) 3m
4:40 (4:40) (Class 6) 5-Y-O+ **£935** (£290; £145; £72)

Form RPR

24- **1** **Alskamatic**[17] 8-11-5 105 .... (p) MissCVHart(5) 122+
(Richard J Bandey) *mde all: strly pressed and shkn up after 14th: nt fluent 3 out: styd on gamely to edge ahd gng to last: rdn out* **14/1**

621- **2** *5* **Chosen Milan (IRE)**[14] 5123 7-11-0 115 .... (t) MrEDavid(7) 116+
(R E Luke) *trckd wnr thrght: str chal fr after 14th: ev ch whn rdn 2 out: no ex fr last* **5/6**[1]

332- **3** *2¾* **Hameldown Tor**[37] 10-11-7 112 .... MrRGHenderson(3) 114
(E Walker) *hld up: hdwy 11th: outpcd 12th: plenty to do after 14th: stdy prog fr 4 out: styd on strly fr 2 out: wnt 3rd at the last: fin wl* **5/1**[3]

2- **4** *7* **Indiana Bay (IRE)**[30] 7-11-10 0 .... MrJoshuaGuerriero 109
(Mrs Jill Dennis) *mid-div: wnt 4th 11th: rdn after 14th: nvr threatened front pair: one pce fr 4 out* **3/1**[2]

236/ **5** *shd* **Perfectly Willing (IRE)**[17] 8-11-10 0 .... MrMWall 111+
(T F Sage) *trckd ldrs: prom 5th tl 11th: hit 13th: sn rdn: hld by ldng pair bef 4 out: pckd 3 out: no ex fr last* **10/1**

00P/ **P** **Bernshaw**[30] 9-11-10 0 .... (b) MrWBiddick
(Mrs Claire Hitch) *led tl 4th: chsd ldrs tl wknd 12th: t.o whn p.u after 14th* **50/1**

R0/- **P** **Furmagiatt**[2] 10-11-3 0 .... MrJCole(7)
(J Cole) *hld up: hdwy 5th: wknd 12th: t.o whn p.u after 14th* **100/1**

4/2- **P** **Blinding Lights (IRE)**[16] 9-11-3 102 .... MrJBargary(7)
(Mary Sanderson) *hld up: pushed along after 10th: wknd 12th: t.o whn p.u after 14th* **33/1**

4/4- **P** **Ned The Post (IRE)**[9] 10-11-3 103 .... MrJoshuaNewman(7)
(E Walker) *hld up: reminders after 7th: rdn appr 11th: wknd 12th: t.o whn p.u after 14th* **25/1**

5m 56.3s (-13.00) **Going Correction** -0.775s/f (Firm) **9** Ran SP% **121.7**
Speed ratings: **90,88,87,85,85** , , ,
CSF £29.10 TOTE £13.90: £2.40, £1.10, £1.70; EX 31.40 Trifecta £139.10.
Owner The Plantation Picnic Club **Bred** P L And Mrs Southcombe **Trained** Tadley, Hants

FOCUS
Bit of a turn up in this novice hunters' chase. The third and fourth help set the level.

5338 CONNOLLY'S RED MILLS BUMPER CHALLENGE INTERMEDIATE OPEN NATIONAL HUNT FLAT RACE (DIV I) 2m 1f
5:10 (5:10) (Class 6) 4-6-Y-O **£1,624** (£477; £238; £119)

Form RPR

/22- **1** **Tea For Two**[24] 4964 5-11-2 0 .... MissEKelly(7) 120+
(Nick Williams) *prom: led narrowly 1/2-way: rdn over 2f out: sn strly pressed: kpt on wl fnl f: hld on* **30/100**[1]

/56- **2** *hd* **Arthur Mc Bride (IRE)**[45] 4547 5-11-2 0................ SamTwiston-Davies 113
(Fergal O'Brien) *hld up in tch: disp cl 3rd 4f out: pressed wnr over 2f out: sn rdn: kpt on wl fnl f: jst hld* **8/1**[3]

23- **3** *15* **Dancing Shadow (IRE)**[31] 4810 5-10-11 0.............. ConorShoemark(5) 99
(Victor Dartnall) *led tl 1/2-way: pressed wnr tl rdn over 2f out: 3rd and hld 2f out: no ex fnl f* **8/1**[3]

2- **4** *2 1/4* **Mad Jack Mytton (IRE)**[154] 2436 4-10-10 0.......................... APMcCoy 91
(Jonjo O'Neill) *racd keenly bhd ldrs: wnt cl 3rd 4f out: sn rdn: wknd ent fnl f* **6/1**[2]

4- **5** *7* **Sonny The One**[21] 5021 4-10-10 0.................................. BrendanPowell 85
(Colin Tizzard) *trckd ldrs: rdn 5f out: fdd fnl 2f* **20/1**

6 *12* **Damby's Star (IRE)** 4-10-7 0..................................... NicodeBoinville(3) 74
(Mark Bradstock) *hld up in tch: rdn over 5f out: wknd wl over 2f out* **18/1**

7 *30* **Berwick Bassett** 5-10-13 0...................................... GavinSheehan(3) 53
(Warren Greatrex) *rn green in rr but in tch tl wknd over 3f out: t.o* **10/1**

50- **8** *24* **Wolftrap (IRE)**[75] 3994 5-11-2 0....................................... DougieCostello 31
(Laura Young) *prom tl over 4f out: sn wknd: t.o* **50/1**

3m 49.7s (-19.10) **Going Correction** -1.075s/f (Hard)
WFA 4 from 5yo 5lb 8 Ran SP% **134.5**
Speed ratings: **101,100,93,92,89 83,69,58**
CSF £5.63 TOTE £1.20: £1.02, £2.80, £2.00; EX 6.20 Trifecta £24.50.
Owner Mrs Jane Williams & Len Jakeman **Bred** Mrs P G Lewin **Trained** George Nympton, Devon

FOCUS
The front pair drew clear in what was undoubtedly the stronger of the two divisions. The form is rated around the first two.

5339 CONNOLLY'S RED MILLS BUMPER CHALLENGE INTERMEDIATE OPEN NATIONAL HUNT FLAT RACE (DIV II) 2m 1f
5:45 (5:45) (Class 6) 4-6-Y-O **£1,624** (£477; £238; £119)

Form RPR

1 **More Buck'S (IRE)** 4-10-7 0.. HarryDerham(3) 95+
(Paul Nicholls) *hld up: hdwy whn nt clr run briefly over 2f out: sn mounting str chal: rn green: tk narrow advantage ent fnl f: rdn out* **13/8**[2]

2 *nk* **Spring Wolf** 6-11-2 0... DaveCrosse 101
(John Ryall) *disp ld tl clr ldr 3f out: sn drvn and strly pressed: narrowly hdd ent fnl f: kpt on gamely* **40/1**

0- **3** *3* **Kincora Fort (IRE)**[74] 4016 5-11-2 0.............................. RobertThornton 98
(Noel Williams) *trckd ldrs: rdn over 2f out: swtchd lft over 1f out: styd on fnl f* **8/1**[3]

- **4** *1/2* **Handsome Horace (IRE)** 4-10-10 0.......................... RichardJohnson 92
(Philip Hobbs) *hld up: nudged along over 4f out: hdwy whn nt clr run wl over 2f out: sn rdn: kpt on but nt gng pce to get on terms* **6/5**[1]

5 *4 1/2* **Alfstar**[24] 6-11-2 0.. DenisO'Regan 94
(Henry Oliver) *trckd ldrs: rdn over 2f out: kpt on tl no ex ent fnl f* **14/1**

6 *2 1/2* **Precious Ground** 4-10-7 0... JamesBest(3) 85
(Kevin Bishop) *trckd ldrs: rdn over 3f out: kpt on same pce fnl 2f* **16/1**

- **7** *20* **Rebel Island (IRE)** 5-10-9 0... ConorO'Farrell 66
(John Panvert) *disp ld tl rdn 3f out: wknd over 1f out* **25/1**

4m 5.9s (-2.90) **Going Correction** -1.075s/f (Hard)
WFA 4 from 5yo+ 5lb 7 Ran SP% **113.5**
Speed ratings: **63,62,61,61,59 57,48**
CSF £54.64 TOTE £2.60: £1.20, £7.20; EX 82.30 Trifecta £279.50.
Owner The Stewart Family **Bred** Philip Hore Jnr **Trained** Ditcheat, Somerset

FOCUS
The weaker of the two divisions, it was run at a steady gallop and proved quite messy, with a couple of the runners, including the favourite, finding trouble. It's been given a token rating through the third.
T/Jkpt: Not won. T/Plt: £176.50 to a £1 stake. Pool of £91488.11 - 378.23 winning tickets. T/Qpdt: £45.60 to a £1 stake. Pool of £6815.76 - 110.49 winning tickets. TM

4804 KEMPTON (R-H)
Tuesday, April 15

OFFICIAL GOING: Good (chs 7.4, hdl 7.2)
Wind: Moderate, half behind Weather: Fine

5340 SIKA LIQUID PLASTICS SEAMLESS H'CAP CHASE (12 fncs) 2m
2:10 (2:10) (Class 4) (0-120,120) 5-Y-0+ **£4,548** (£1,335; £667; £333)

Form RPR

0/1- **1** **The Last Night (FR)**[125] 3027 7-11-4 **112**.............................. AidanColeman 119
(Emma Lavelle) *j.w: mde all: drvn 2 out: hrd pressed last: hld on wl* **3/1**[2]

432- **2** *1/2* **Sands Cove (IRE)**[24] 4965 7-11-12 **120**.........................(t) BarryGeraghty 126
(Charlie Mann) *chsd clr ldng pair: wl in tch fr 1/2-way: wnt 2nd bef 3 out: drvn and nt fluent 2 out: chal last: styd on but a jst hld* **4/1**[3]

416- **3** *2 1/2* **Benny The Swinger (IRE)**[15] 5115 9-10-2 **96**.................. TomCannon 100
(Chris Gordon) *hld up in rr: trckd ldrs fr 7th: prog and nt fluent 3 out: wnt 3rd next and tried to cl: one pce fr last* **8/1**

252- **4** *5* **Un Anjou (FR)**[9] 5194 6-11-4 **115**................................... MichealNolan(3) 115
(David Dennis) *hld up in tch: trckd ldrs fr 6th: disp 2nd bef 3 out where nt fluent: shkn up and no rspnse sn after: wl btn fr 2 out* **9/4**[1]

50- **5** *18* **Vision Des Champs (FR)**[16] 5091 5-11-12 **120**..............(t) JamieMoore 105
(Gary Moore) *chsd wnr and clr of rest to 1/2-way: wknd and lost 3rd bef 3 out* **10/1**

6UP- **6** *13* **Marcus Antonius**[26] 3690 7-11-4 **112**.............................. LeightonAspell 84
(Jim Boyle) *hld up: nt fluent 5th: lost tch 7th: sn wl bhd* **16/1**

262- **P** **Overclear**[12] 5141 12-11-11 **119**.. TomO'Brien
(Victor Dartnall) *blnd 1st: lost tch in last pl 6th: sn t.o: p.u bef 3 out* **7/1**

3m 53.1s (-7.20) **Going Correction** -0.60s/f (Firm) 7 Ran SP% **114.4**
Speed ratings: **94,93,92,90,81 74,**
CSF £15.75 TOTE £3.00: £1.50, £2.60; EX 14.10 Trifecta £64.10.
Owner Tim Syder **Bred** I Kellit, N Madamet & Ann Thomlinson **Trained** Hatherden, Hants

FOCUS
A fair handicap chase, in which the pace was even throughout. The first three are rated pretty much to their marks.

5341 MARLEY ETERNIT "NATIONAL HUNT" NOVICES' HURDLE (8 hdls) 2m
2:40 (2:40) (Class 4) 4-Y-0+ **£3,898** (£1,144; £572; £286)

Form RPR

212- **1** **Desoto County**[24] 4945 5-11-5 123.................................... BarryGeraghty 116+
(Donald McCain) *prom: trckd ldr 3 out: led next: sn pressed and rdn: narrowly hdd last: styd on to ld again fnl 100yds* **4/7**[1]

332- **2** *3/4* **Tiradia (FR)**[232] 1400 7-10-13 94.................................... JamieMoore 107
(J R Jenkins) *t.k.h: hld up: hmpd 2nd: prog to trck ldrs 5th: chal gng wl after 2 out: narrow ld last: hdd and nt qckn fnl 100yds* **14/1**

/25- **3** *7* **Yabadabadoo**[27] 4904 6-10-13 0...................................... AidanColeman 100
(Emma Lavelle) *t.k.h: hld up in rr: prog to trck ldrs 5th: cl up gng strly bef 2 out: shkn up and nt qckn bef last* **6/1**[3]

60- **4** *32* **Manhattan Mead**[31] 4810 4-10-7 0.................................... MarcGoldstein 65
(Michael Madgwick) *mstke 2nd: in tch to 5th: nt on terms w ldrs after: pushed along and wknd 2 out* **100/1**

0P0- **5** *11* **Matripajo (IRE)**[24] 4959 5-10-8 0............................... MauriceLinehan(5) 61
(Jonjo O'Neill) *in tch: prog to chse ldr after 4th to 3 out: shkn up and wknd bef 2 out* **33/1**

6- **6** *5* **Primo Milano**[89] 3734 5-10-6 0... ConorRing(7) 62
(Evan Williams) *hld up: last whn mstke 3rd: brief rally whn nt fluent 5th: sn struggling: t.o* **33/1**

206- **P** **Lemony Bay**[31] 4808 5-10-13 120.......................................[1] LeightonAspell
(Oliver Sherwood) *trckd ldr: hanging bdly bnd after 4th: rapidly dropped to last and lost tch: t.o 2 out: p.u bef last* **11/4**[2]

6P- **F** **Flinstone (IRE)**[27] 4903 5-10-3 0...............................[1] PatrickCowley(10) 98
(Jonjo O'Neill) *led: j.rt 2nd: rdn and hdd 2 out: nt qckn and wl hld in 5 l 4th whn fell last* **33/1**

3m 50.9s (-7.20) **Going Correction** -0.475s/f (Good)
WFA 4 from 5yo+ 5lb 8 Ran SP% **121.1**
Speed ratings (Par 105): **99,98,95,79,73 71,,**
CSF £11.20 TOTE £1.60: £1.02, £3.30, £1.80; EX 8.20 Trifecta £26.80.
Owner Paul & Clare Rooney **Bred** Miss K Rausing **Trained** Cholmondeley, Cheshire

FOCUS
Little depth to this novices' hurdle, with the favourite prevailing in a thrilling finish. The form's rated around the first two.

5342 SIKA-TROCAL FLEXIBLE NOVICES' H'CAP CHASE (16 fncs) 2m 4f 110y
3:15 (3:15) (Class 4) (0-110,109) 5-Y-0+ **£4,548** (£1,335; £667; £333)

Form RPR

241- **1** **Bertie's Desire**[34] 4762 6-11-5 **102**................................... LeightonAspell 113+
(Oliver Sherwood) *mde virtually all: pressed thrght: rdn and jnd 3 out: gained upper hand next: drvn out* **9/4**[1]

14F- **2** *2* **Lemon's Gent**[131] 2895 7-11-6 **103**.......................................(tp) SamJones 110
(Paul Webber) *pressed wnr thrght: upsides 3 out: rdn and nt qckn next: hld after but kpt on* **5/1**[3]

222- **3** *2* **Mia's Vic (IRE)**[15] 5111 9-11-2 **102**..............................(t) RobertDunne(3) 106
(Edward Creighton) *in tch: trckd ldrs fr 7th: cl up and clr of rest fr 10th: chal on outer after 4 out: rdn bef next: kpt on same pce* **10/1**

0PP- **4** *21* **Captain Sully (IRE)**[170] 2107 9-11-8 **105**............................ NickScholfield 90
(Jim Wilson) *hld up in rr: lost tch bef 10th: no ch after: kpt on to take remote 4th last* **33/1**

13- **5** *5* **Martin Cash (IRE)**[32] 4795 8-11-3 **100**.............................. TomO'Brien 83
(Paul Henderson) *hld up in rr: lost tch w ldrs bef 10th: pushed along next: wnt remote 4th 3 out tl j. bdly lft last* **16/1**

0P3- **6** *19* **Boss In Boots (IRE)**[28] 4887 6-11-7 **104**...................... AndrewThornton 68
(Seamus Mullins) *chsd ldng pair tl mstke 7th: lost tch w ldng quartet 10th: nvr on terms after: wknd 3 out* **3/1**[2]

F/5- **P** **Grey Wulff (IRE)**[84] 3820 9-11-11 **108**.............................. AidanColeman
(Emma Lavelle) *hld up in rr: lost tch bef 10th: t.o whn p.u bef 2 out* **7/1**

3FP- **P** **Cody Wyoming**[36] 4723 8-11-12 **109**.............................. DominicElsworth
(Heather Main) *racd wd: nt a fluent: hld up in rr: lost tch bef 10th: j. slowly 11th: t.o whn p.u bef 2 out* **10/1**

05P- **U** **June French (FR)**[77] 3955 6-10-0 **83** oh14........................... TomCannon
(Kevin Tork) *in tch: trckd ldng pair 7th: cl up whn stmbld and uns rdr 10th* **66/1**

5m 3.2s (-13.40) **Going Correction** -0.60s/f (Firm) 9 Ran SP% **113.4**
Speed ratings: **101,100,99,91,89 82,,,**
CSF £14.17 CT £90.92 TOTE £3.70: £1.30, £2.70, £2.70; EX 15.70 Trifecta £69.40.
Owner Tim Syder **Bred** Patrick Burling Developments Ltd **Trained** Upper Lambourn, Berks

FOCUS
A modest novices' handicap chase, in which few got into contention and the front three pulled a long way clear. Straightforward form, with the winner on the upgrade.

5343 KLOBER ROOFING ACCESSORIES NOVICES' HURDLE (10 hdls) 2m 5f
3:50 (3:50) (Class 4) 4-Y-0+ **£3,898** (£1,144; £572; £286)

Form RPR

110- **1** **Boogie In The Barn (IRE)**[46] 4535 6-11-6 0.................[1] NickScholfield 115+
(Jeremy Scott) *mde all: jinked lft briefly bnd after 4th: gng best bef 2 out: in command whn stuttered into last and almost jnd: rdn and r.o to assert again flat* **2/1**[2]

213- **2** *1* **Act Alone**[37] 4694 5-11-6 127.. BarryGeraghty 112
(Nicky Henderson) *mostly trckd wnr: rdn and nt qckn bef 2 out: lft w ch last: styd on but readily outpointed* **11/10**[1]

36- **3** *6* **Super Lunar (IRE)**[29] 4863 5-11-0 0............................... AidanColeman 102
(Alan King) *hld up: chsd ldrs fr 7th: shkn up to go 3rd 2 out: kpt on but nt gng pce to threaten* **8/1**

064- **4** *12* **Money Maid (IRE)**[5] 5244 6-10-7 0............................. AndrewThornton 86
(Simon Earle) *hld up and mostly in tch: outpcd and pushed along 3 out: kpt on steadily at one pce fr 2 out: nt disgracd* **28/1**

016- **5** *1 1/4* **Gallery Exhibition (IRE)**[118] 3166 7-11-1 125................. EdCookson(5) 95
(Kim Bailey) *prom: disp 2nd pl fr 5th tl rdn after 3 out: steadily wknd fr next* **5/1**[3]

/P0- **6** *35* **Cinematique (IRE)**[74] 4023 6-11-0 103........................(p) TomCannon 57
(Laura Mongan) *hld up: rdn and wknd 3 out: t.o* **66/1**

5m 7.8s (-9.70) **Going Correction** -0.475s/f (Good) 6 Ran SP% **113.7**
Speed ratings (Par 105): **99,98,96,91,91 77**
CSF £4.88 TOTE £2.40: £1.70, £1.20; EX 5.20 Trifecta £15.90.
Owner Bradley Partnership **Bred** Patrick Gardiner **Trained** Brompton Regis, Somerset

FOCUS
A fair novices' hurdle, in which the two principals pulled clear off a steady pace. They are rated a stone below their marks.

5344 SIKA SARNAFIL LEADERS H'CAP CHASE (18 fncs) 3m
4:20 (4:21) (Class 3) (0-135,133) 5-Y-0+ **£6,498** (£1,908; £954; £477)

Form RPR

/03- **1** **Miss Ballantyne**[37] 4701 7-10-10 **117**.............................. BarryGeraghty 127
(Nicky Henderson) *nt a fluent: trckd ldng pair fr 9th: rdn 3 out: wnt 2nd bef next: drvn to ld last: kpt on* **13/2**[3]

3/4- **2** *3/4* **Brass Tax (IRE)**[47] 4509 8-11-1 **129**........................(p) MrMJPKendrick(7) 138
(Ben Case) *led 3rd: mostly after: rdn and hrd pressed 2 out: hdd last: hung lft flat but styd on: jst hld* **5/2**[1]

U11- **3** *6* **Itoldyou (IRE)**[31] 4798 8-10-4 **111**..............................(t) AndrewThornton 117
(Linda Jewell) *trckd ldrs: prog and cl up 13th: nt fluent next and reminder: nt qckn 3 out: one pce after* **8/1**

0P1- **4** 1¼ **Doctor Foxtrot (IRE)**[25] 4932 9-10-10 **117**........................(b) TomO'Brien 120
(Philip Hobbs) *w.w in last pair: in tch at bk of main gp after 4 out: rdn and no imp 3 out: plugged on* **5/1**[2]

130- **5** 6 **Coole River (IRE)**[16] 5092 10-11-7 **128**........................... AidanColeman 127
(Emma Lavelle) *led 2nd to 3rd: pressed ldr: rdn and lost 2nd bef 2 out: wknd tamely* **7/1**

2FF- **6** 6 **Merrion Square (IRE)**[38] 4681 8-11-12 **133**..................(t) NickScholfield 125
(Paul Nicholls) *w.w in tch: prog 4 out and looked a threat: rdn and wknd tamely after 3 out* **8/1**

300- **7** 18 **Nataani (IRE)**[39] 4662 11-11-5 **126**.......................................(bt) SamJones 101
(Jo Davis) *led to 2nd: nt fluent 9th and reminder: mstke 11th: wknd 4 out: mstke next: t.o* **16/1**

PF0- **P** **Estates Recovery (IRE)**[27] 4906 9-10-2 **109**...................... JamieMoore
(Luke Dace) *last whn j. slowly 3rd: nvr on terms after: t.o whn p.u after 11th* **33/1**

13P- **F** **Muldoon's Picnic (IRE)**[35] 4738 8-11-12 **133**................. LeightonAspell
(Kim Bailey) *trckd ldrs: 5th and in tch whn fell 11th* **5/1**[2]

5m 55.3s (-20.10) **Going Correction** -0.60s/f (Firm) **9** Ran SP% **118.8**
Speed ratings: **109,108,106,106,104 102,96, ,**
CSF £24.82 CT £135.68 TOTE £7.50: £2.70, £1.90, £1.80; EX 31.00 Trifecta £279.30.
Owner Mr & Mrs R Kelvin-Hughes **Bred** R D And Mrs J S Chugg **Trained** Upper Lambourn, Berks

FOCUS
A useful staying handicap with a step up from the lightly raced winner.

5345 TOR COATINGS LIQUID WATERPROOFING H'CAP HURDLE (10 hdls) 2m 5f

4:50 (4:52) (Class 3) (0-130,130) 4-Y-0+ **£5,848** (£1,717; £858; £429)

Form RPR

/30- **1** **Cocktails At Dawn**[34] 4750 6-11-1 **119**........................... BarryGeraghty 133+
(Nicky Henderson) *j. fluently: cl up: trckd ldr 5th: led 3 out: cruised home fr next: nvr extended* **5/4**[1]

324- **2** 3¼ **Kilmurvy (IRE)**[66] 4144 6-11-7 **125**................................(tp) NickScholfield 126
(Jeremy Scott) *chsd ldr to 5th: mstke 7th: rdn and struggling to hold pl after 3 out: rallied fr 2 out: wnt 2nd again nr fin: no ch w wnr* **9/2**[3]

611- **3** 1 **Homer Run (IRE)**[116] 3192 7-10-6 **110**........................ AndrewThornton 110
(Simon Earle) *in tch: prog to chse wnr bef 2 out: nvr any ch: kpt on but lost 2nd nr fin* **20/1**

315- **4** 7 **Chasse En Mer (FR)**[54] 4374 4-10-9 **120**........................... JamieMoore 107
(Caroline Bailey) *hld up but in tch: rdn and prog bef 2 out: no hdwy and btn sn after* **25/1**

53F- **5** ½ **Harry Hunt**[32] 4793 7-11-10 **128**....................................... AidanColeman 122
(Graeme McPherson) *chsd ldr tl mstke 5th and reminder: nt fluent 7th: rdn and btn on long run bef 2 out* **25/1**

P00- **6** 3¼ **First Avenue**[38] 4682 9-11-12 **130**... TomCannon 121
(Laura Mongan) *hld up in last but wl in tch: prog to go 3rd on long run bef 2 out: sn pushed along and wknd after 2 out* **40/1**

500- **7** 3½ **Bygones Sovereign (IRE)**[16] 5093 8-11-2 **120**................(p) LiamHeard 109
(David Pipe) *led: jnd 7th: hdd next: wknd on long run bef 2 out* **8/1**

0/0- **P** **Spanish Treasure (GER)**[74] 4023 8-11-0 **123**............... JamesBanks(5)
(Andy Turnell) *wl in tch tl wknd 3 out: t.o whn p.u bef last* **25/1**

2/5- **F** **Irish Buccaneer (IRE)**[31] 4820 7-11-4 **122**........................ TomO'Brien
(Philip Hobbs) *hld up: in tch whn stmbld and fell on bnd after 2nd* **11/4**[2]

5m 3.1s (-14.40) **Going Correction** -0.475s/f (Good)
WFA 4 from 6yo+ 6lb **9** Ran SP% **119.1**
Speed ratings (Par 107): **108,106,106,103,103 102,100, ,**
CSF £7.18 CT £77.27 TOTE £2.50: £1.40, £1.10, £4.30; EX 8.10 Trifecta £80.80.
Owner R J H Geffen & Sir John Ritblat **Bred** Mrs J Way **Trained** Upper Lambourn, Berks

FOCUS
A handicap dominated by an impressive winner, who looks to have a big future. The form is rated around the second and third.

5346 FREDDIE FARMER FOUNDATION OPEN HUNTERS' CHASE (16 fncs) 2m 4f 110y

5:20 (5:21) (Class 5) 6-Y-0+ **£2,495** (£774; £386; £193)

Form RPR

61P- **1** **Siro Demur (FR)**[20] 5035 8-11-9 107........................... MrAlexEdwards(5) 117
(Philip Rowley) *hld up in rr: prog on outer after 4 out: rdn to chse ldr bef 2 out: narrow ld last: drvn and hld on wl* **25/1**

01P/ **2** ½ **Shoreacres (IRE)**[23] 11-11-3 0....................................... MissHLewis(7) 114
(Ms Gillian Jones) *hld up towards rr: prog 10th: trckd ldrs 12th: led bef 3 out and sent for home: rdn and narrowly hdd last: styd on but jst hld* **5/2**[1]

332- **3** ½ **Benedictus (IRE)**[13] 5127 9-11-13 124................................. MrJBarber(5) 120+
(Jack Barber) *hld up in last trio: stl in last pair bef 3 out: rapid prog on outer bef 2 out: rdn last: styd on to take 3rd nr fin: too much to do* **5/2**[1]

336- **4** ½ **Milgen Bay**[177] 1988 8-11-7 105............................. MrLeoMahon(7) 116
(Oliver Sherwood) *led to 2nd: grad lost pl and in midfield fr 7th: prog again bef 3 out: tried to cl on ldrs last: kpt on flat: a hld* **25/1**

/0P- **5** 7 **King's Legacy (IRE)**[37] 10-11-10 127.......................................(t) MrJETudor 106
(Alan Hill) *hld up in last trio: rdn and prog on inner 3 out: wandered u.p after 2 out: no imp on ldrs after* **5/1**[2]

F/P- **6** 4 **Bold Addition (FR)**[45] 9-11-13 128.. MrADoyle(5) 109
(Mrs F J Browne) *trckd ldrs: lft disputing 2nd pl 10th: cl up after 4 out: wknd tamely after 3 out* **20/1**

442- **7** nk **Rob Conti (FR)**[16] 5094 9-11-5 128.................................. MrDMaxwell(5) 101
(Philip Hobbs) *trckd ldrs: moved up to ld 8th: hdd bef 3 out: bmpd along and wknd next* **8/1**[3]

11- **8** 1¼ **Shales Rock**[11] 5165 8-11-11 0.........................(p) MissImmyRobinson(7) 107
(Mrs C J Robinson) *fractious bef s: led 2nd to 8th: styd prom tl wknd after 3 out* **10/1**

323- **9** ¾ **Delta Borget (FR)**[20] 5035 9-11-3 103..................... MissLeandaTickle(7) 98
(L Jefford) *w.w towards rr: sme prog 10th: no hdwy after 4 out: wl btn after 3 out* **33/1**

21/- **10** 39 **Commander Kev (IRE)**[471] 13-11-3 97.............................(p) MrCSmith(7) 59
(Mrs K Hobbs) *j. slowly 2nd: chsd ldrs: mstke 5th: in tch tl wknd rapidly after 3 out: t.o* **50/1**

331- **P** **Run Along Boy**[186] 1860 9-11-3 105.................(tp) MrSDavies-Thomas(7)
(Miss H Cumbley) *a in rr and racd wd: mstke 6th: t.o whn p.u bef 10th* **50/1**

102- **U** **King Of Alcatraz (IRE)**[20] 5035 8-11-7 0................................ MissVWade(7)
(N Harris) *pressed ldr fr 2nd tl mstke and uns rdr 10th* **10/1**

5m 4.2s (-12.40) **Going Correction** -0.60s/f (Firm) **12** Ran SP% **122.4**
Speed ratings: **99,98,98,98,95 94,94,93,93,78 ,**
CSF £88.94 TOTE £33.40: £7.50, £1.80, £1.10; EX 196.30 Trifecta £1527.50.
Owner Philip Rowley **Bred** Serge Hamon **Trained** Bridgnorth, Shorpshire

FOCUS
The pace was steady in this hunter chase and several were still in contention jumping the last. The winner is rated to his mark.

T/Plt: £11.60 to a £1 stake. Pool of £67978.53 - 4277.51 winning tickets. T/Qpdt: £5.60 to a £1 stake. Pool of £5095.41 - 664.45 winning tickets. JN

4784 CHELTENHAM (L-H)

Wednesday, April 16

OFFICIAL GOING: Good changing to good (good to firm in places) after race 5 (4.25)
Wind: mild breeze Weather: sunny

5347 CITIPOST NOVICES' HURDLE (10 hdls) 2m 4f 110y

2:05 (2:05) (Class 2) 4-Y-0+

£10,009 (£2,956; £1,478; £739; £369; £185)

Form RPR

401- **1** **Garde La Victoire (FR)**[13] 5140 5-11-4 138.................. RichardJohnson 140+
(Philip Hobbs) *trckd ldrs: led appr last where wnt sltly lft: styd on strly to assert run-in: rdn out* **13/8**[1]

/11- **2** 6 **Oscars Den (IRE)**[122] 3110 6-11-4 125............................. MichaelByrne 133
(Tim Vaughan) *nt a fluent: hld up bhd ldrs: hdwy after 3 out: rdn to ld after 2 out tl jst bef last: sn hld by wnr: drifted lft fnl 75yds: jst hld on for 2nd* **16/1**

110- **3** hd **Vieux Lion Rouge (FR)**[33] 4789 5-11-8 139.................. TomScudamore 137
(David Pipe) *cl up: rdn after 2 out: nt gng pce to chal: kpt on fr last: nrly snatched 2nd fnl strides* **13/2**[3]

F31- **4** 1½ **My Wigwam Or Yours (IRE)**[26] 4931 5-11-8 134........... BarryGeraghty 136
(Nicky Henderson) *trckd ldr: t.k.h early: nt fluent 4th: rdn to ld briefly after 2 out: styd on but no ex fr last* **15/8**[2]

131- **5** 2¾ **Blue Heron (IRE)**[22] 5016 6-11-4 0.................................... HarrySkelton 128
(Dan Skelton) *led: wnt rt 2 out: sn rdn and hdd: no ex fr last* **12/1**

052- **6** 42 **Muckle Roe (IRE)**[90] 3728 5-11-0 0......................... SamTwiston-Davies 82
(Nigel Twiston-Davies) *hld up in last: struggling 6th: wknd after 3 out: t.o* **50/1**

21- **7** 12 **Lookslikerainted (IRE)**[10] 5182 7-11-4 0.................................. APMcCoy 74
(Rebecca Curtis) *prom: hit 5th: wknd after 3 out: t.o* **12/1**

5m 2.7s (1.70) **Going Correction** -0.175s/f (Good) **7** Ran SP% **109.4**
Speed ratings (Par 109): **89,86,86,86,85 69,64**
CSF £23.95 TOTE £2.40: £1.90, £3.40; EX 24.00 Trifecta £100.70.
Owner Mrs Diana L Whateley **Bred** Mlle Laure Godet **Trained** Withycombe, Somerset

FOCUS
All races on the New Course. Watered ground and a drying day brought down the curtain on Cheltenham's jumps campaign. Senior jockey Richard Johnson said it was "good all over" but Barry Geraghty felt it was quicker in places. This is traditionally a good-quality opening novice hurdle and was won last year by subsequent Grade 1 winner Whisper. They went steadily through the first half of the race, and the entire field ran freely to varying degrees, but the form still looks well up to scratch.

5348 RUNDLE AND CO H'CAP CHASE (24 fncs) 3m 4f 110y

2:40 (2:40) (Class 3) (0-130,129) 5-Y-0+

£6,256 (£1,848; £924; £462; £231; £116)

Form RPR

533- **1** **Rebeccas Choice (IRE)**[27] 4914 11-10-12 **118**..........(p) RobertDunne(3) 127
(Dai Burchell) *hld up: hdwy fr 15th: chal after 4 out: led sn after 3 out: rdn 3 l clr sn after: hdd and hmpd on landing last: nk down tl rallied bravely cl home: led fnl strides* **8/1**

1P0- **2** nk **Major Malarkey (IRE)**[25] 4962 11-11-7 **124**.........(v) SamTwiston-Davies 133
(Nigel Twiston-Davies) *mid-div: trckd ldrs 11th: lost pl and pushed along 18th: rdn whn outpcd after 4 out: gd hdwy appr 2 out: slt ld whn mstke and wnt rt after last: kpt on w nk advantage tl no ex fnl strides* **12/1**

123- **3** 9 **Fredo (IRE)**[17] 5092 10-10-11 **119**.............................(p) RobertMcCarth(5) 119
(Ian Williams) *mid-div: hit 17th: rdn fr 4 out: hdwy after 3 out to chal for 2nd next: styd on same pce appr last: wnt 3rd run-in* **7/1**

0P6- **4** ½ **Handy Andy (IRE)**[29] 4886 8-11-1 **125**...................................(p) MrMLegg(7) 125
(Colin Tizzard) *trckd ldrs: hit 8th and 17th: wnt 2nd next: rdn and ev ch whn wnt lft 3 out: 3rd and hld whn hit 2 out: styd on same pce: lost 3rd run-in* **13/2**[3]

110- **5** 26 **Reblis (FR)**[25] 4962 9-11-11 **128**.. JoshuaMoore 103
(Gary Moore) *sn struggling in rr: drvn along fr 8th: sme hdwy 4 out: wknd after 3 out: t.o* **28/1**

160- **6** 10 **Top Smart**[130] 2953 8-11-7 **124**.. RyanMahon 90
(Seamus Mullins) *mid-div: reminders after 14th: in tch and rdn 18th: wknd after 3 out: t.o* **15/2**

6P3- **7** 20 **De La Bech**[39] 4681 7-11-11 **128**...(b[1]) TomO'Brien 76
(Philip Hobbs) *chsd ldr: pushed along briefly 6th: lft in ld after 11th: rdn and hdd sn after 3 out: wknd bef next: t.o* **5/1**[1]

253- **8** 1½ **Susquehanna River (IRE)**[21] 5032 7-10-5 **115**............(v[1]) RyanHatch(7) 62
(Nigel Twiston-Davies) *led tl mstke and stmbld bdly 11th: trckd ldr: hit 14th: rdn and losing pl whn hit 4 out: wknd next: t.o* **6/1**[2]

243- **F** **Bally Sands (IRE)**[25] 4968 10-9-9 **103** oh5.......................(v) EdCookson(5)
(Robin Mathew) *mid-div: in last pair 10th: struggling 14th: no ch whn fell 4 out* **14/1**

1P1- **P** **Flying Award (IRE)**[43] 4601 10-11-7 **129**................ MissLucyGardner(5)
(Sue Gardner) *hld up bhd: detached 10th: rdn after 15th: t.o whn p.u bef 18th* **8/1**

21P- **U** **Kris Cross (IRE)**[32] 4819 7-11-12 **129**............................(tp) TomScudamore
(Lucinda Russell) *trckd ldr: blnd 7th: stl cl up whn blnd bdly and uns rdr 17th* **14/1**

7m 21.3s (-3.70) **Going Correction** -0.175s/f (Good) **11** Ran SP% **115.2**
Speed ratings: **98,97,95,95,88 85,79,79, ,**
CSF £95.80 CT £705.67 TOTE £9.70: £3.40, £3.40, £2.30; EX 156.90 Trifecta £1508.40.
Owner J E Mutch **Bred** D Adair **Trained** Briery Hill, Blaenau Gwent

FOCUS
A competitive marathon handicap. It was run at a proper gallop and served up a cracking finish. The first two are rated to their marks.

5349 LONGCROFT BUILDING SERVICES H'CAP HURDLE (10 hdls) 2m 4f 110y

3:15 (3:15) (Class 2) 4-Y-0+

£12,512 (£3,696; £1,848; £924; £462; £232)

Form RPR

134- **1** **Brother Brian (IRE)**[39] 4680 6-10-7 **127**............................ TomO'Brien 135+
(Hughie Morrison) *trckd ldrs: chal after 2 out: led bef last where wnt bdly lft and dived: r.o wl: rdn out* **11/2**[2]

210- **2** 3 3/4 **Another Hero (IRE)**[32] 4805 5-10-6 **126**................................ APMcCoy 129
(Jonjo O'Neill) *mid-div: rdn and hdwy after 2 out: wnt 2nd sn after last: swtchd rt: nt gng pce to get on terms w wnr: jst hld on for 2nd* **9/1**

000- **3** *hd* **Edgardo Sol (FR)**[13] 5138 7-11-5 **142**........................(p) HarryDerham(3) 145
(Paul Nicholls) *hld up: rdn and hdwy after 2 out: 4th whn nt fluent last: kpt on wl run-in: nrly snatched 2nd* **14/1**

116- **4** 3/4 **Virak (FR)**[33] 4789 5-11-5 **146**.. JackSherwood(7) 148
(Paul Nicholls) *trckd ldrs tl dropped to midfield 3 out: rdn and hdwy after 2 out: styd on run-in* **20/1**

611- **5** 1 1/2 **Boondooma (IRE)**[19] 5050 7-10-3 **123**.................... SamTwiston-Davies 124
(Dr Richard Newland) *led after 1st: rdn and hdd appr last: no ex fnl 120yds* **8/1**[3]

324- **6** 2 **The Romford Pele (IRE)**[32] 4806 7-10-6 **126**................. BarryGeraghty 127+
(Rebecca Curtis) *mid-div: hit 4th: nt fluent next: outpcd after 2 out: styd on run-in* **12/1**

324- **7** 1/2 **Big Casino**[31] 4841 8-10-5 **125**... NoelFehily 124
(Nigel Twiston-Davies) *racd keenly: led tl after 1st: trckd ldr: ev ch 2 out: sn rdn: wknd bef last* **33/1**

450- **8** 2 3/4 **Broadway Buffalo (IRE)**[34] 4765 6-10-9 **136**..............(t) TomBellamy(7) 132
(David Pipe) *trckd ldrs: rdn after 3 out: outpcd after next* **10/1**

520- **9** 5 **Swnymor (IRE)**[11] 5172 5-10-3 **130**................................(t) PaulO'Brien(7) 122
(Rebecca Curtis) *mid-div: hdwy on outer after 3rd: sn trcking ldrs: ev ch 2 out: wknd bef last* **25/1**

042- **10** 9 **Thomas Crapper**[33] 4789 7-11-5 **139**................................. CharliePoste 124
(Robin Dickin) *hld up towards rr: hdwy on outer after 6th: rdn appr 2 out: wknd bef last* **5/1**[1]

551- **11** 16 **Volt Face (FR)**[15] 5120 5-10-7 **127**................................. TomScudamore 106
(David Pipe) *hld up towards rr: short-lived effrt after 2 out: eased whn btn* **25/1**

0/1- **P** **Softsong (FR)**[62] 3598 6-11-0 **134**..................................... LiamTreadwell
(James Evans) *racd keenly: mid-div: wknd sn after 3 out: t.o whn p.u bef next* **25/1**

150- **P** **Royal Regatta (IRE)**[33] 4789 6-10-13 **133**.................... RichardJohnson
(Philip Hobbs) *hld up towards rr: hdwy 4th: swtchd out to chal 2 out: wknd rapidly whn rdn: p.u bef last* **11/2**[2]

211- **P** **Wintered Well (IRE)**[12] 5163 6-9-7 **120** oh1...................... ConorRing(7)
(Jennie Candlish) *hld up towards rr: pushed along fr 4th: short-lived effrt 2 out: sn wknd: p.u bef last* **16/1**

4m 53.5s (-7.50) **Going Correction** -0.175s/f (Good) **14 Ran SP% 117.1**
Speed ratings (Par 109): **107,105,105,105,104 103,103,102,100,97 91,,,**
CSF £48.72 CT £661.50 TOTE £6.90: £2.70, £1.90, £5.30; EX 64.90 Trifecta £766.60.
Owner L A Garfield **Bred** Daniel N O'Donovan **Trained** East Ilsley, Berks

FOCUS
A fair handicap, run at a solid gallop. Solid handicap form.

5350 WOODEN SPOON CHARITY SILVER TROPHY CHASE (LIMITED H'CAP) (GRADE 2) (17 fncs) 2m 5f
3:50 (3:50) (Class 1) 5-Y-0+

£28,475 (£10,685; £5,350; £2,665; £1,340; £670)

Form RPR

115- **1** **Buywise (IRE)**[36] 4742 7-10-12 **134**................................... PaulMoloney 151+
(Evan Williams) *nvr that fluent in rr: sme prog after 4 out: gd hdwy after 3 out: led between last 2: nt fluent last: drifted rt whn rdn but r.o strly fnl 200yds: readily* **5/2**[1]

3P4- **2** 9 **Astracad (FR)**[13] 5136 8-11-4 **140**....................(vt) SamTwiston-Davies 146
(Nigel Twiston-Davies) *disp decent pce fr 3rd tl 10th: trckd ldr: rdn after 3 out: lost 2nd between last 2: styd on to regain 2nd run-in but nt gng pce of wnr* **10/1**

2P2- **3** 4 1/2 **Real Milan (IRE)**[28] 4900 9-10-7 **129**..............................(bt) NoelFehily 130
(Donald McCain) *disp decent pce: clr ldr 10th: rdn after 2 out: hdd bef last: drifted rt and no ex fnl 200yds* **7/1**

213- **4** *hd* **Bally Legend**[25] 4960 9-11-8 **144**... IanPopham 146
(Caroline Keevil) *mid-div: struggling to go pce early: hdwy after 4 out: wnt 3rd next tl 2 out: hld in 4th whn hit last: edgd rt: styd on same pce* **16/1**

300- **5** 19 **Kumbeshwar**[74] 4032 7-11-1 **137**.......................................(p) JackDoyle 121
(Alan King) *in tch: trckd ldrs 8th: rdn to dispute 3rd sn after 3 out tl wknd next* **12/1**

/60- **6** 9 **Pacha Du Polder (FR)**[36] 4738 7-11-10 **146**................(p) NickScholfield 122
(Paul Nicholls) *sn trcking ldrs: pushed along after 10th: rdn after 4 out: wknd next* **6/1**[3]

216- **7** 5 **Persian Snow (IRE)**[36] 4742 8-11-2 **138**....................(t) RichardJohnson 109
(Philip Hobbs) *a struggling to go pce: towards rr: in tch 8th: outpcd after 4 out: wknd next* **5/1**[2]

F0P- **8** 23 **Wetak (FR)**[11] 5170 7-11-0 **136**..................................(bt[1]) TomScudamore 87
(David Pipe) *sn trcking ldrs: rdn after 13th: wknd bef 3 out: t.o* **16/1**

2P5- **P** **Noble Legend**[28] 4900 7-10-11 **133**.................................. AndrewThornton
(Caroline Bailey) *towards rr: struggling 8th: lost tch next: p.u bef 4 out* **25/1**

0P3- **P** **Carrickboy (IRE)**[76] 3990 10-11-4 **140**................................ LiamTreadwell
(Venetia Williams) *disp decent pce tl after 3rd: chsd ldrs: mstke 8th: wknd 11th: tailing off whn p.u after 4 out* **12/1**

5m 9.7s (-9.70) **Going Correction** -0.175s/f (Good) **10 Ran SP% 112.1**
Speed ratings: **111,107,105,105,98 95,93,84,,**
CSF £26.66 CT £152.33 TOTE £3.70: £1.50, £2.90, £2.20; EX 25.50 Trifecta £154.20.
Owner T Hywel Jones **Bred** Mrs A Stack **Trained** Llancarfan, Vale Of Glamorgan

FOCUS
Although the race this year perhaps lacked the smart performer or two often associated, it was very competitive. There was no hanging about and it provided a real test. Buywise continues on the upgrade and is better than the bare result. The next three were better than the bare result.

5351 MESSIER-BUGATTI-DOWTY NOVICES' H'CAP HURDLE (12 hdls) 3m
4:25 (4:26) (Class 3) (0-125,125) 4-Y-0+

£6,256 (£1,848; £924; £462; £231; £116)

Form RPR

266- **1** **Tinker Time (IRE)**[21] 5030 6-11-2 **115**................................... LiamHeard 122
(Bob Buckler) *in tch: sltly outpcd whn rdn sn after 2 out: styd on wl appr last: chal sn after: led run-in: drvn out* **33/1**

111- **2** 1 1/4 **Be Bop Boru (IRE)**[36] 4746 7-10-6 **105**....................... RichardJohnson 111
(Tim Vaughan) *hld up towards rr: hdwy whn hit 5th: trckd ldrs 3 out: rdn after 2 out: led bef last: hdd run-in: kpt on but hld fnl 100yds* **9/1**

612- **3** 1 3/4 **Bob Keown (IRE)**[22] 5019 6-10-7 **113**..........................(b) PaulO'Brien(7) 118
(Rebecca Curtis) *trckd ldr: led 3 out: sn clr: hit 2 out: rdn: idling and hdd nt long after: rallied last: ev ch run-in: no ex fnl 100yds* **10/1**

043- **4** 3 1/4 **Even If**[26] 4933 6-10-11 **110**...(p) APMcCoy 111
(Jonjo O'Neill) *hld up towards rr: stdy hdwy after 3 out: rdn after 2 out: ev ch briefly sn after last: sn no ex* **15/2**[2]

404- **5** 1 1/2 **Kudu Shine**[24] 4993 8-11-1 **114**.. ConorO'Farrell 114
(Richard Woollacott) *in tch: outpcd 2 out: styng on wl whn swtchd lft appr last: kpt on wout threatening ldrs* **66/1**

211- **6** 3/4 **Here's Herbie**[21] 5030 6-11-4 **122**..........................(t) MissLucyGardner(5) 123
(Sue Gardner) *mid-div: hdwy after 3 out: rdn and ev ch after 2 out: hld last: no ex flat* **14/1**

022- **7** 2 **Miss Lucky Penny**[18] 5075 8-10-0 **104**...................... RobertMcCarth(5) 101
(Ian Williams) *mid-div: hdwy 3 out: rdn to chse ldrs sn after next: styd on same pce* **14/1**

/56- **8** 8 **Pay The King (IRE)**[73] 4051 7-10-13 **115**....................... HarryDerham(3) 105
(Paul Nicholls) *hld up towards rr: rdn into midfield 2 out: no further imp* **10/3**[1]

32- **9** 9 **Ballyheigue Bay (IRE)**[22] 5024 7-11-1 **114**........................ TomCannon 98
(Chris Gordon) *trckd ldr: pressed ldr 6th: mstke 8th: led next tl 3 out: sn rdn: wknd bef last* **16/1**

212- **10** 1/2 **Cove (IRE)**[23] 5010 7-10-8 **107**.. LiamTreadwell 88
(Nick Gifford) *mid-div tl outpcd appr 2 out: nt a danger after* **14/1**

541- **11** 6 **Mister Newby (IRE)**[26] 4933 8-11-6 **119**............................. SeanQuinlan 97
(Richard Phillips) *hld up bhd: hdwy after 3 out: rdn after 2 out: nvr threatened: wknd bef last* **20/1**

32P- **12** 9 **Phone Home (IRE)**[21] 5030 7-11-5 **118**........................ RobertThornton 86
(Nick Mitchell) *mid-div: hdwy 3 out to trck ldrs: sn rdn: wknd after 2 out* **50/1**

452- **13** 22 **Squire Trelawney**[28] 4906 8-11-2 **115**..........................(tp) HarrySkelton 63
(Dan Skelton) *hld up towards rr: sme hdwy into midfield u.p appr 2 out: wknd bef last: t.o* **20/1**

P21- **14** 19 **Cadeau George**[52] 4449 5-11-7 **120**..................................(p) DavidBass 51
(Ben Pauling) *led tl 9th: sn rdn: wknd after 3 out: t.o* **20/1**

354- **15** 25 **Grace And Fortune**[37] 4719 7-10-0 **99** oh4........................ JamesDavies 8
(Richard Rowe) *a towards rr: wknd bef 2 out: t.o* **66/1**

2P0- **P** **Patsys Castle (IRE)**[14] 5128 7-11-2 **115**......................... NickScholfield
(Kim Bailey) *struggling 6th: a in rr: sn bhd: t.o whn p.u after 2 out* **20/1**

222- **P** **Bebinn (IRE)**[51] 4472 7-10-3 **105**.................................(p) KielanWoods(3)
(Ben Case) *trckd ldrs: pushed along and prom fr 7th tl rdn after 3 out: sn wknd: p.u bef last* **33/1**

311- **P** **Winged Crusader (IRE)**[28] 4906 6-11-4 **117**.......... SamTwiston-Davies
(Nigel Twiston-Davies) *a towards rr: struggling 8th: nvr any imp whn p.u bef last* **8/1**[3]

023- **P** **Withoutdefavourite (IRE)**[10] 5191 6-10-10 **109**.............. DenisO'Regan
(Henry Oliver) *in tch: pushed along after 5th: wknd 7th: t.o 3 out: p.u after next* **16/1**

5m 53.5s (-7.50) **Going Correction** -0.175s/f (Good) **19 Ran SP% 126.7**
Speed ratings (Par 107): **105,104,104,102,102 102,101,98,95,95 93,90,83,77,68 ,,,,**
CSF £289.31 CT £3220.22 TOTE £41.30: £9.60, £2.70, £2.10, £2.00; EX 651.10 Trifecta £1690.60 Part won. Pool of £2254.16 - 0.01 winning units..
Owner Golden Cap **Bred** Patrick Moore **Trained** Henley, Somerset

FOCUS
This modest novice handicap was another race that proved a real test at the distance. Solid handicap form, with the first two on the upgrade.

5352 WEATHERITE NOVICES' CHASE (17 fncs) 2m 5f
4:55 (4:55) (Class 2) 5-Y-0+ **£12,512** (£3,696; £1,848; £924; £462)

Form RPR

12P- **1** **Pantxoa (FR)**[158] 2373 7-11-8 139.................................... RobertThornton 146+
(Alan King) *j.rt quite bdly at times thrght: mde all: rdn appr 2 out: strly chal gng to last: kpt on v gamely: all out to hold on on nod* **11/4**[3]

F3P- **2** *shd* **Saint Roque (FR)**[33] 4786 8-11-0 0.......................(t) SamTwiston-Davies 137+
(Paul Nicholls) *trckd wnr: looked to be gng best whn mounting str chal gng to last: rdn run-in: kpt on w ev ch: jst hld on nod* **13/8**[2]

513- **3** 4 1/2 **Karinga Dancer**[98] 3601 8-11-5 140......................................(t) NoelFehily 138
(Harry Fry) *trckd ldng pair: hit 11th: chal for 2nd after 3 out tl short of room next: sn rdn: nt gng pce to get bk on terms* **6/4**[1]

PFP- **4** 98 **Next Oasis (IRE)**[158] 2370 8-11-5 113............................. NickScholfield 39
(Paul Henderson) *hld up: wnt 4th 11th but nvr on terms: lost tch 5 out: t.o* **33/1**

540- **5** 5 **Wheelavher**[6] 5240 8-10-7 70..(t) GerardTumelty 22
(Claire Dyson) *racd in 4th tl 11th: sn wknd: t.o* **100/1**

5m 16.2s (-3.20) **Going Correction** -0.175s/f (Good) **5 Ran SP% 108.7**
Speed ratings: **99,98,97,59,58**
CSF £7.75 TOTE £3.00: £1.70, £1.20; EX 9.30 Trifecta £12.20.
Owner Mrs June Watts **Bred** Pierre De Maleissye Melun **Trained** Barbury Castle, Wilts

FOCUS
The winner dictated and was close to his mark.

5353 ENDSLEIGH INSURANCE PONY RACING AUTHORITY GRADUATES' H'CAP HURDLE (CONDITIONALS/AMATEURS) (8 hdls) 2m 1f
5:30 (5:30) (Class 3) (0-140,130) 4-Y-0+

£6,256 (£1,848; £924; £462; £231; £116)

Form RPR

F01- **1** **Franciscan**[12] 5160 6-11-5 **130**..(b) NickSlatter(7) 137+
(Donald McCain) *trckd ldrs: lost pl 3 out: pushed along and hdwy after 2 out: led last: r.o wl to assert fnl 120yds: rdn out* **14/1**

553- **2** 2 3/4 **Refer**[25] 4963 4-9-11 **113**..(p) CharlieDeutsch(7) 113
(Phil Middleton) *in tch: hdwy 5th: rdn to disputen ld 2 out: hdd last: kpt on but no ex fnl 120yds* **10/1**

21P- **3** 6 **Figaro**[53] 4426 6-10-9 **120**...(t) MrBGibbs(7) 120
(Tim Vaughan) *mid-div tl after 5th: in tch in last whn nt fluent 3 out: hdwy on outer to ld bef next: sn rdn: hdd last: no ex* **6/1**[2]

340- **4** *nk* **Aazif (IRE)**[12] 5158 5-11-4 **125**...............................(t) JakeGreenall(3) 124
(Ian Williams) *trckd ldrs: rdn after 2 out: kpt on same pce* **15/2**

/U1- **5** 3/4 **Double Double (FR)**[10] 5186 8-11-5 **130** 7ex................. MrSPBowen(7) 130+
(Peter Bowen) *hld up: awkward 1st: nt fluent 5th: hdwy on outer appr 2 out: sn rdn: styng on at same pce in hld 5th whn hit last* **12/1**

/34- **6** *hd* **For Two (FR)**[180] 1960 5-11-6 **127**..............................(t) HarryDerham(3) 125
(Paul Nicholls) *hld up: hdwy 2 out: sn rdn: nt pce to get involved: styd on fr last* **9/2**[1]

600- **7** 4 1/2 **Quick Decisson (IRE)**[21] 5030 6-11-0 **121**......................... JamesBest(3) 115
(Philip Hobbs) *trckd ldrs: pushed along after 5th: rdn after 2 out: fdd run-in* **13/2**[3]

113- **8** *4* **Dark Dune (IRE)**[12] 5160 6-11-5 **130**.............................. MrWEasterby(7) 120
(Tim Easterby) *hld up: sme hdwy to get in tch on outer 2 out: sn rdn: nt pce to threaten: wknd bef last* **16/1**

202- **9** *13* **Sir Pitt**[18] 5071 7-10-8 **115**.. GilesHawkins(3) 94
(John Bryan Groucott) *mid-div: hdwy on outer 5th: rdn and wknd after 2 out* **12/1**

461- **10** *15* **Yes Daddy (IRE)**[30] 4866 6-10-1 **115**.............................. AlanJohns(10) 80
(Tim Vaughan) *mid-div: cl enough 2 out: sn rdn and wknd* **12/1**

656- **11** *¾* **Mister Matt (IRE)**[172] 2081 11-10-3 **114**................ MrJoshuaNewman(7) 78
(Tom Symonds) *diputed ld tl appr 2 out: sn wknd* **40/1**

011- **P** **Superciliary**[14] 5125 5-10-13 **117**.............................. JoshuaMoore
(Chris Gordon) *led tl rdn and hdd appr 2 out: wknd qckly: p.u bef last* **14/1**

265- **P** **Johnny Og**[97] 3614 5-10-2 **113**.............................. JackSherwood(7)
(Martin Keighley) *towards rr but in tch: rdn after 3 out: sn wknd: p.u bef last* **20/1**

4m 3.7s (-7.60) **Going Correction** -0.175s/f (Good)
WFA 4 from 5yo+ 5lb **13** Ran SP% **116.2**
Speed ratings (Par 107): **110,108,105,105,105 105,103,101,95,88 87, ,**
CSF £143.21 CT £937.21 TOTE £12.70: £3.50, £3.10, £2.50; EX 170.10 Trifecta £1189.60 Part won. Pool of £1586.16 - 0.50 winning units..
Owner T G Leslie **Bred** Fittocks Stud **Trained** Cholmondeley, Cheshire

FOCUS
Although the top weight was 10lb below the race ceiling this was a competitive-looking handicap for conditional/amatuer riders graduating from approved pony races. The winner has the potential to rate higher yet on Flat form.
T/Jkpt: Not won. T/Plt: £208.90 to a £1 stake. Pool of £125629.20 - 439.0 winning tickets.
T/Qpdt: £26.70 to a £1 stake. Pool of £8564.93 - 236.79 winning tickets. TM

5160 SEDGEFIELD (L-H)

Wednesday, April 16

OFFICIAL GOING: Hurdle course - good (good to soft in places) changing to good after race 1 (4.45); chase course - good (good to soft in places)
The third last fence was omitted in all chases; ground under repair.
Wind: fresh behind Weather: Fine

5354 ELLEN TIMNEY FOUNDATION "NATIONAL HUNT" NOVICES' HURDLE (10 hdls) 2m 4f

4:45 (4:47) (Class 4) 4-Y-0+ **£3,249** (£954; £477; £238)

Form RPR

/15- **1** **Cape York**[38] 4694 6-10-13 0.. BrianHughes 112+
(Malcolm Jefferson) *trckd ldr: pressed ldr whn nt fluent 7th: rdn appr 2 out: led jst after 2 out: styd on wl and sn in command run-in* **3/1**[3]

521- **2** *3 ¼* **Voyage A New York (FR)**[31] 4832 5-11-6 **122**.............. WilsonRenwick 118+
(Lucinda Russell) *trckd ldr: hit 7th: led after 3 out: gng wl in narrow ld whn blnd 2 out and sn hdd: rdn and ev ch last: one pce and sn hld in 2nd run-in* **7/4**[1]

525- **3** *21* **The Backup Plan (IRE)**[35] 4761 5-10-13 0...................... HenryBrooke 89
(Donald McCain) *led: hdd jst after 3 out: sn no ch w ldng pair* **7/1**

0- **4** *8* **Verko (FR)**[3] 5296 5-10-8 0.. CraigNichol(5) 81
(Micky Hammond) *hld up: pushed along and sme hdwy after 3 out: wnt 4th between last 2: nvr threatened ldrs* **33/1**

5 *2 ½* **Steady Progress (IRE)**[193] 6-10-10 0.............................. HarryChalloner(3) 79
(Richard Ford) *in tch: rdn and sn no ch w ldng trio after 7th: lost 4th betwwen last 2* **100/1**

00P- **6** *13* **Hi Bob**[3] 5300 6-10-13 0.. BrianHarding 67
(Lucinda Egerton) *hld up: nvr threatened* **200/1**

0/0- **7** *½* **Jasani**[16] 5108 6-10-13 0.. DavidEngland 67
(Alan Brown) *hld up: blnd 1st: nvr threatened* **200/1**

00- **8** *nse* **Casual Cavalier (IRE)**[34] 4772 6-10-13 0.............................. AdrianLane 66
(John Wade) *midfield: nt fluent 4th and reminders: wknd after 3 out* **125/1**

0PP- **9** *1 ¼* **Manyshadesofblack (IRE)**[50] 4479 6-10-1 0........... SamanthaDrake(5) 58
(Tina Jackson) *midfield: wknd after 7th* **200/1**

3- **10** *1 ¾* **Looking Glass**[36] 4749 5-10-6 0.. DannyCook 57
(Tim Easterby) *midfield: mstke 3rd: wknd after 7th* **25/1**

604- **11** *49* **Lachlan Mor**[19] 5050 5-10-13 0.. JamesReveley 20
(Stuart Coltherd) *hld up: a bhd* **25/1**

426- **P** **Maxed Out King (IRE)**[71] 4075 6-10-6 0...................... DaraghBourke(7)
(Sue Smith) *in tch: wknd after 7th: t.o whn p.u bef 2 out* **5/2**[2]

4m 50.0s (-2.70) **Going Correction** -0.075s/f (Good) **12** Ran SP% **116.3**
Speed ratings (Par 105): **102,100,92,89,88 82,82,82,82,81 61,**
CSF £8.55 TOTE £2.40: £1.10, £1.20, £2.90; EX 9.70 Trifecta £48.90.
Owner J David Abell **Bred** J M Jefferson **Trained** Norton, N Yorks

FOCUS
Hurdles sited on outside, common bends dolled off the inner. A dry run up to a meeting that saw water applied to the back straight. The cross fence at the top of the hill was omitted in all chases. An uncompetitive event in which the first two pulled clear in the last half mile. The gallop was reasonable. A big step up from the winner but the form looks reasonable.

5355 FURLONGS RACING NOVICES' H'CAP CHASE (11 fncs 2 omitted) 2m 110y

5:15 (5:17) (Class 5) (0-100,93) 5-Y-0+ **£2,599** (£763; £381; £190)

Form RPR

054/ **1** **Grey Life**[66] 8-11-5 **86**.. BrianHughes 108+
(Malcolm Jefferson) *trckd ldr: rdn to ld between last 2: mstke last: kpt on* **4/1**[3]

555- **2** *2 ¼* **Robin's Command (IRE)**[126] 3020 7-9-13 **71**................ CraigNichol(5) 90
(Rose Dobbin) *led: rdn whn hdd between last 2: kpt on but a hld* **3/1**[2]

1F0- **3** *38* **Turf Trivia**[29] 4890 7-11-12 **93**.............................(b) BarryKeniry 81
(George Moore) *in tch in 3rd: readily outpcd by ldng pair after 9th: wl hld whn blnd last* **15/2**

225- **4** *12* **Shan Valley (IRE)**[43] 4607 8-10-11 **85**.............................. DaraghBourke(7) 59
(Stuart Coltherd) *slowly away: hld up: remote 4th whn mstke 2 out* **11/4**[1]

460- **5** *6* **Mister D (IRE)**[63] 4223 8-11-5 **91**.............................. JonathonBewley(5) 60
(George Bewley) *trckd ldrs: wknd after 9th* **5/1**

45P- **P** **Cloudy Deal (IRE)**[106] 3428 7-11-9 **90**.............................. WilsonRenwick
(Martin Todhunter) *hld up: bhd after 8th: p.u bef 2 out* **11/1**

4m 6.6s (-2.00) **Going Correction** -0.075s/f (Good) **6** Ran SP% **108.4**
Speed ratings: **101,99,82,76,73**
CSF £15.54 TOTE £3.20: £1.20, £2.70; EX 27.30 Trifecta £113.10.
Owner D T Todd **Bred** Mrs C Teanby **Trained** Norton, N Yorks

FOCUS
A moderate and uncompetitive handicap in which the first two pulled clear in the last half mile. The gallop was fair. The winner is rated up a stone on his old mark.

5356 MULTIBOND SOLUTIONS H'CAP CHASE (15 fncs 2 omitted) 2m 6f

5:50 (5:50) (Class 4) (0-115,112) 5-Y-0 **£3,798** (£1,122; £561; £280; £140)

Form RPR

P52- **1** **Baltic Pathfinder (IRE)**[19] 5055 10-10-9 **102**.......... DiarmuidO'Regan(7) 110+
(Sue Smith) *hld up in tch: mstke 2nd: rdn and hdwy to chse ldr appr 2 out: styd on: led nr fin* **9/1**

352- **2** *½* **Young Hurricane (IRE)**[4] 5284 8-11-12 **112**...................(bt) JamieMoore 119
(Dr Richard Newland) *w ldr: led after 8th: stl gng wl appr 2 out: rdn between last 2: slowed into last: one pce run-in: hdd nr fin* **2/1**[1]

2F6- **3** *1* **Presenting Junior (IRE)**[26] 4940 7-10-3 **89**.................. WilsonRenwick 94
(Martin Todhunter) *hld up: rdn after 11th hdwy u.p on extended run to 2 out: wnt 3rd between last 2: kpt on* **12/1**

P33- **4** *6* **Talkin Thomas (IRE)**[36] 4744 8-11-10 **110**.............................. BrianHarding 112
(Nicky Richards) *led narrowly: hdd 8th: remained prom: rdn and outpcd appr 2 out: hld in 4th fr between last 2* **7/2**[2]

653- **5** *11* **Chicago Outfit (IRE)**[19] 5055 9-10-6 **92**.....................(p) BrianHughes 83
(John Wade) *trckd ldr: rdn appr 2 out: wknd between last 2* **11/2**[3]

336- **6** *10* **Attycran (IRE)**[129] 2969 9-10-10 **103**.............................(t) DaraghBourke(7) 85
(Maurice Barnes) *in tch: rdn on extended run to 2 out: wknd after 2 out* **10/1**

245- **7** *3 ½* **Farm Pixie (IRE)**[16] 5104 8-10-1 **92**.............................. CraigNichol(5) 72
(Ann Hamilton) *in tch on outer: mstke 3rd: lost pl after 8th: struggling fr 10th* **11/1**

645- **8** *2* **Riguez Dancer**[38] 4696 10-11-11 **111**.............................(b) HenryBrooke 86
(Donald McCain) *hld up: reminders after 11th: a bhd* **12/1**

5m 31.9s (-1.10) **Going Correction** -0.075s/f (Good) **8** Ran SP% **113.7**
Speed ratings: **99,98,98,96,92 88,87,86**
CSF £28.36 CT £220.05 TOTE £6.20: £2.40, £1.02, £4.10; EX 20.60 Trifecta £191.00.
Owner John Regan & John Conroy **Bred** Christopher Maye **Trained** High Eldwick, W Yorks

FOCUS
A fair handicap in which the gallop picked up setting out on the final circuit. Straightforward form.

5357 BOOKMAKERS ON YOUR MOBILE AT BOOKMAKERS.CO.UK H'CAP HURDLE (9 hdls) 2m 2f 110y

6:25 (6:25) (Class 4) (0-120,115) 4-Y-0+ **£3,249** (£954; £477; £238)

Form RPR

343- **1** **Pair Of Jacks (IRE)**[29] 4889 6-11-12 **115**.............................. BrianHughes 124+
(Malcolm Jefferson) *trckd ldr: led after 3rd: mde rest: pushed clr between last 2: eased towards fin* **3/1**[2]

530- **2** *6* **Grand Vintage (IRE)**[50] 4475 8-10-2 **96**.................. ColmMcCormack(5) 96
(Evelyn Slack) *hld up: pushed along after 5th: stl only 6th 2 out: styd on wl: wnt 2nd nr fin* **13/2**[3]

241- **3** *½* **Hunters Belt (IRE)**[9] 5212 10-11-5 **113**................(vt) JonathonBewley(5) 113
(George Bewley) *led tl after 1st: trckd ldr: briefly lost pl 5th: hdwy to chse wnr after 3 out: one pce and sn no ch w wnr after 2 out: lost 2nd nr fin* **11/8**[1]

/25- **4** *2 ½* **Safari Journey (USA)**[19] 5058 10-11-5 **115**.............. NathanMoscrop(7) 113
(Lucinda Egerton) *hld up: rdn after 3 out: one pce and nvr threatened* **20/1**

2U6- **5** *2 ¼* **Andreo Bambaleo**[111] 3269 10-11-8 **111**.........................(b) FelixDeGiles 106
(Brian Ellison) *led after 1st: hdd after 3rd: trckd ldr: rdn appr 2 out: wknd run-in* **10/1**

104- **6** *1* **Muwalla**[138] 2791 7-10-8 **104**.................................(tp) DiarmuidO'Regan(7) 98
(Chris Grant) *trckd ldrs: rdn 2 out: wknd run-in* **16/1**

644- **7** *38* **Utopian**[32] 4811 5-11-4 **112**.. CraigNichol(5) 72
(Rose Dobbin) *hld up: nt fluent 4th: hit 3 out: wknd 2 out* **8/1**

4m 29.9s (1.20) **Going Correction** -0.075s/f (Good) **7** Ran SP% **111.3**
Speed ratings (Par 105): **94,91,91,90,89 88,72**
CSF £21.17 TOTE £4.60: £2.10, £2.20; EX 20.00 Trifecta £59.90.
Owner Mrs Rita Williams **Bred** Mary And Mrs Letty O'Sullivan **Trained** Norton, N Yorks

FOCUS
A fair handicap but a steady pace to the home turn means the bare form isn't reliable. A step up from the winner.

5358 JACK HIRST MEMORIAL H'CAP CHASE (18 fncs 3 omitted) 3m 3f

6:55 (6:58) (Class 5) (0-100,100) 5-Y-0+ **£2,599** (£763; £381; £190)

Form RPR

3P2- **1** **Debt To Society (IRE)**[26] 4942 7-10-11 **88**..............(t) HarryChalloner(3) 100+
(Richard Ford) *hld up: hdwy and in tch fr 11th: led narrowly on extended run to 2 out: rdn between last 2: stl strly pressed last: hld on wl run-in* **12/1**

224- **2** *1 ½* **Twice Lucky**[89] 3755 10-10-2 **83**.............................. DaraghBourke(7) 93
(Sue Smith) *trckd ldrs: led 15th: hdd narrowly on extended run to 2 out: stl upsides last: one pce and a jst hld run-in* **7/1**

424- **3** *18* **Soul Angel**[34] 4775 10-10-0 **74** oh8.......................................(v) AdrianLane 69
(Sandy Forster) *trckd ldrs: rdn 15th: hld in 3rd fr extended run to 2 out* **20/1**

P43- **4** *nk* **Over And Above (IRE)**[24] 4982 8-10-0 **77**......................(bt) TonyKelly(3) 71
(Henry Hogarth) *hld up: rdn 15th: styd on to go modest 4th between last 2: nvr threatened* **12/1**

122- **5** *3 ½* **Solway Dornal**[19] 5052 9-9-9 **74**.................................(p) GrantCockburn(5) 64
(Lisa Harrison) *trckd ldrs: rdn 16th: wknd 2 out* **9/2**[2]

441- **6** *1 ¾* **Heez A Steel (IRE)**[26] 4942 13-11-5 **100**.............................. AlistairFindlay(7) 92
(Jane Walton) *hld up: slow 13th: sn rdn: nvr threatened* **5/1**[3]

3UP- **7** *¾* **Beau Dandy (IRE)**[8] 5215 9-10-12 **93**.................(v[1]) DiarmuidO'Regan(7) 81
(Chris Grant) *hld up: rdn 15th: sn btn* **10/1**

13P- **8** *½* **Tears From Heaven (USA)**[26] 4942 8-10-8 **82**.................. BrianHughes 70
(Chris Grant) *midfield: rdn 14th: sn btn* **16/1**

324- **9** *3 ½* **The Shrimp (IRE)**[41] 4630 7-9-7 **74**.............................(b[1]) MrJHamilton(7) 61
(Sandy Thomson) *led: hdd 15th: mstke 2 out: wknd* **4/1**[1]

511- **P** **Boris The Blade**[34] 4773 12-11-1 **94**.........................(b) SamanthaDrake(5)
(Tina Jackson) *trckd ldr: nt fluent 11th: lost pl next: sn struggling: p.u bef 2 out* **8/1**

6m 54.11s (5.11) **Going Correction** -0.075s/f (Good) **10** Ran SP% **113.6**
Speed ratings: **89,88,83,83,82 81,81,81,80,**
CSF £91.30 CT £1661.78 TOTE £13.10: £3.20, £4.10, £4.80; EX 137.00 Trifecta £1602.80 Part won. Pool of £2137.11 - 0.15 winning units..
Owner Mr & Mrs G E Pickering **Bred** Brett Merry **Trained** Garstang, Lancs

FOCUS
A moderate handicap in which the gallop was fair and the first two pulled a long way clear turning for home. The winner is well in on the best of his Irish form and is rated back to that level.

5359 SEDGEFIELD RACECOURSE BOOKMAKERS H'CAP HURDLE (13 hdls) 3m 3f 110y
7:25 (7:27) (Class 5) (0-100,100) 4-Y-0+ **£2,339** (£686; £343; £171)

Form RPR
2/4- **1** **George Fernbeck**[12] 5161 6-11-5 **93**....................[1] DannyCook 104+
(Brian Ellison) *prom: led 4th: mde rest: rdn clr after 2 out: comf* **4/1**[2]
524- **2** *6* **Phar Away Island (IRE)**[150] 2535 6-9-13 **78**..........(p) KillianMoore(5) 79
(Graeme McPherson) *trckd ldrs: chsd wnr after 3 out: rdn 2 out: no ex run-in* **10/1**
333- **3** *hd* **Generous Chief (IRE)**[12] 5161 6-11-2 **97**............ DiarmuidO'Regan(7) 98
(Chris Grant) *midfield: rdn after 3 out: styd on: wnt 3rd nr fin* **5/1**[3]
654- **4** *½* **Iktiview**[8] 4981 6-10-10 **89**..........................(p) AdamNicol(5) 89
(Philip Kirby) *led: hdd 4th: remained prom: rdn and outpcd after 3 out: plugged on after 2 out* **12/1**
640- **5** *1* **Auberge (IRE)**[34] 4774 10-10-13 **94**...................... CallumBewley(7) 93
(Evelyn Slack) *hld up: rdn and sme hdwy after 3 out: styd on after 2 out* **14/1**
536- **6** *5* **Big Sound**[19] 5059 7-11-7 **100**............................ GrantCockburn(5) 96
(Mark Walford) *prom: sltly hmpd and lost pl after 8th: rdn 3 out: no imp* **3/1**[1]
0P5- **7** *7* **Solway Legend**[19] 5056 7-10-0 **74** oh2.................... BrianHarding 62
(Lisa Harrison) *hld up: hdwy after 3 out: disp 3rd 2 out: wknd last* **33/1**
400- **8** *3 ¾* **Native Optimist (IRE)**[12] 5161 7-10-0 **79**............ MissCWalton(5) 64
(Sheena Walton) *hld up: nvr threatened* **25/1**
660- **9** *1 ¼* **Spiekeroog**[24] 4981 8-11-8 **96**.............................. DavidEngland 79
(Alan Brown) *midfield: rdn after 4 out: sn btn* **33/1**
0F4- **10** *21* **Western Bound (IRE)**[36] 4747 13-9-9 **74** oh10..........(bt) CraigNichol(5) 38
(Barbara Butterworth) *racd keenly: trckd ldrs: wknd qckly after 3 out* **40/1**
252- **11** *1* **Mootabar (IRE)**[16] 5106 7-10-7 **86**........................ JoeColliver(5) 50
(Chris Fairhurst) *hld up: nt fluent 10th: wknd after 3 out* **8/1**
/P0- **12** *13* **Sea Cliff (IRE)**[26] 4938 10-10-0 **74** oh1....................(p) BrianHughes 26
(Andrew Crook) *midfield: wknd after 3 out* **28/1**
0P0- **P** **Well Related**[50] 4476 7-9-12 **75**............................ TonyKelly(3)
(Henry Hogarth) *hld up: hdwy into midfield whn wnt wrong and p.u after 3 out* **14/1**

6m 48.2s (-3.80) **Going Correction** -0.075s/f (Good) **13 Ran SP% 118.5**
Speed ratings (Par 103): **102,100,100,100,99 98,96,95,94,88 88,84,**
CSF £40.61 CT £206.82 TOTE £6.80: £2.80, £5.50, £3.10; EX 49.50 Trifecta £114.90.
Owner Mrs Claire Ellison **Bred** Gestut Ammerland **Trained** Norton, N Yorks

FOCUS
A moderate handicap in which the gallop was no more than fair. The second and third set the level.

5360 WILLS PROPERTY SERVICES H'CAP HURDLE (6 hdls 2 omitted) 2m 1f
7:55 (7:57) (Class 5) (0-100,97) 4-Y-0+ **£2,209** (£648; £324; £162)

Form RPR
011- **1** **Dalmo**[6] 5242 5-11-7 **97** 7ex..........................(b) ChristopherWard(5) 106+
(Dr Richard Newland) *w ldr: hit 2nd: led passing omitted 3 out: nt fluent 2 out: sn hdd: rallied u.p to ld again 75yds out* **4/6**[1]
551- **2** *3 ¾* **Stanley Bridge**[26] 4943 7-11-7 **97**.......................... CraigNichol(5) 101
(Barry Murtagh) *in tch: hdwy to trck ldr appr 2 out: rdn to ld narrowly after 2 out: hdd 75yds out: no ex* **10/1**
P00- **3** *4 ½* **So Bazaar (IRE)**[32] 4817 7-10-0 **71**..........................(t) BrianHarding 72
(Andrew Wilson) *midfield: hdwy passing omitted 3 out: ev ch whn nt fluent 2 out: sn one pce and hld in 3rd* **25/1**
242- **4** *nk* **Copt Hill**[12] 5163 6-11-1 **91**...................................... AdamNicol(5) 91
(Tracy Waggott) *led narrowly: hdd passing omitted 3 out: rdn and one pce in 4th fr 2 out* **7/1**[3]
315- **5** *11* **Dynamic Drive (IRE)**[155] 2449 7-10-13 **91**..............(t) DaraghBourke(7) 83
(Maurice Barnes) *midfield: hdwy and in tch appr 2 out: wknd appr last* **12/1**
036- **6** *22* **Danby's Legend**[26] 4943 7-11-4 **89**.............................. BrianHughes 59
(Malcolm Jefferson) *hld up in rr: hit 3rd: nvr threatened* **5/1**[2]
45P/ **7** *3 ¼* **Emirate Isle**[380] 5073 10-10-5 **83**......................(v) DiarmuidO'Regan(7) 50
(Chris Grant) *midfield: hit 2nd: rdn after 3rd: sn struggling* **50/1**
5P0- **8** *16* **The Boozy Bishop (IRE)**[12] 5163 9-10-0 **76**..........(bt[1]) MissCWalton(5) 29
(Sheena Walton) *hld up: nvr threatened* **33/1**
000- **9** *13* **On The Buckle**[138] 2783 6-11-5 **90**.......................... WilsonRenwick 31
(Rose Dobbin) *trckd ldrs: wknd passing omitted 3 out* **28/1**
P40- **10** *½* **Teaatreids (IRE)**[29] 4889 6-10-9 **80**..........................(b[1]) DannyCook 21
(Brian Ellison) *trckd ldrs: mstke 3rd: wknd passing omitted 3 out* **40/1**

4m 1.2s (-5.70) **Going Correction** -0.275s/f (Good) **10 Ran SP% 120.6**
Speed ratings (Par 103): **102,100,98,97,92 82,80,73,67,67**
CSF £8.27 CT £102.25 TOTE £1.50: £1.10, £2.80, £6.40; EX 11.20 Trifecta £65.90.
Owner J A Provan **Bred** Sir Eric Parker **Trained** Claines, Worcs

FOCUS
A moderate handicap in which the two hurdles in the back straight were omitted. The gallop was reasonable and the form is solid enough.
T/Plt: £105.90 to a £1 stake. Pool of £53981.28 - 371.86 winning tickets. T/Qpdt: £20.80 to a £1 stake. Pool of £6295.26 - 223.80 winning tickets. AS

4861 SOUTHWELL (L-H)
Wednesday, April 16

OFFICIAL GOING: Good (7.8)
Wind: moderate 1/2 against Weather: fine and sunny

5361 MICHAELTOWERS.CO.UK MASTER OF SECTIONAL TIMING H'CAP CHASE (16 fncs) 2m 4f 110y
4:30 (4:32) (Class 4) (0-105,102) 5-Y-0+ **£3,768** (£1,106; £553; £276)

Form RPR
233- **1** **Daliance (IRE)**[25] 4970 5-11-9 **102**........................(p) TrevorWhelan(3) 107
(Neil King) *in rr: reminders 3rd: sn drvn: gd hdwy 4 out: chsd ldr after 2 out: 2 l down last: styd on to ld last 30yds* **4/1**[2]
6/P- **2** *1 ¼* **Mr Goofy (IRE)**[240] 1314 13-10-9 **85**.......................... AndrewTinkler 89
(Michael Scudamore) *trckd ldrs: l2nd 4 out: led 2 out: hdd and no ex in clsng stages* **16/1**
443- **3** *4* **Xenophon**[10] 5193 6-9-7 **76** oh7.............................. MissAliceMills(7) 76
(Michael Chapman) *in rr: chsd ldrs 10th: outpcd 4 out: styd on fr next: tk 3rd last: kpt on* **8/1**
24P- **4** *12* **Carpincho (FR)**[5] 5263 10-11-10 **100**.......................... AidanColeman 92
(Sarah Humphrey) *led: mstke 2nd: drvn 4 out: hdd 2 out: sn wknd* **6/1**[3]
211- **5** *14* **Mr Bachster (IRE)**[149] 2562 9-10-6 **85**.................... MichealNolan(3) 62
(Richard Lee) *j.rt: chsd ldrs: drvn 4 out: sn wknd* **5/2**[1]
202- **6** *12* **Finch Flyer (IRE)**[13] 5144 7-9-7 **76** oh3..................(p) MrAlexEdwards(7) 42
(Aytach Sadik) *in rr: hit 4th: drvn 9th: reminders 12th: sn bhd* **8/1**
P53- **P** **That's The Deal (IRE)**[30] 4862 10-11-0 **95**.................. JoeCornwall(5)
(John Cornwall) *chsd ldr: drvn 9th: lost pl and bhd next: t.o whn p.u bef 11th: b.b.v* **4/1**[2]

5m 19.9s (2.90) **Going Correction** +0.225s/f (Yiel) **7 Ran SP% 111.0**
Speed ratings: **103,102,101,96,91 86,**
CSF £51.50 CT £466.77 TOTE £3.20: £1.80, £7.70; EX 51.60 Trifecta £406.30.
Owner The St Gatien Racing For Fun Partnership **Bred** Societa Agricola Gem Srl **Trained** Newmarket, Suffolk

FOCUS
Fences sited 7yds off outside rail, bend into home straight was on the outside and Gold Club bend was on the inside. A modest handicap chase got proceedings underway on a sundrenched evening, racing on watered ground officially described as good, and they went a decent gallop. A step up from the winner on his recent run.

5362 MICHAELTOWERS.CO.UK MAKING BOOKIES SAD NOVICES' CHASE (19 fncs) 3m 110y
5:00 (5:02) (Class 4) 5-Y-0+ **£3,861** (£1,198; £645)

Form RPR
3F2- **1** **Karinga Dandy (IRE)**[18] 5074 8-10-12 0.......................... RyanMania 93+
(Sue Smith) *chsd ldrs: lft clr 2nd 6th: drvn 4 out: styd on fr next: led last: kpt on wl* **2/1**[2]
544- **2** *4 ½* **Flichity (IRE)**[10] 5192 9-10-7 66.............................. JoeCornwall(5) 83
(John Cornwall) *t.k.h: led: hdd last: kpt on same pce* **50/1**
0PU- **3** *66* **First Lad**[33] 4793 7-10-9 0.................................... TrevorWhelan(3) 17
(Nicholas Pomfret) *t.k.h: j.lft 1st: lft modest 3rd 6th: jnd other pair 13th: wknd 4 out: bhd next: sn t.o: eventually completed* **50/1**
40U- **U** **Son Of Flicka**[10] 5192 10-10-12 123.............................. DougieCostello
(Tony Coyle) *j.lft: trckd ldrs: mstke 4th: handy 4th whn bdly hmpd and uns rdr 6th* **5/2**[3]
035- **R** **Zafaraban (IRE)**[51] 4471 7-10-12 88..............................(b) LeeEdwards
(Aytach Sadik) *j. bdly and lft-handed: in rr: lft poor 4th 6th: t.o 11th: dived lft and ref 4 out* **33/1**
340- **U** **Gas Line Boy (IRE)**[34] 4769 8-10-12 131...................... MrCGethings(7)
(Philip Hobbs) *trckd ldrs: cl 2nd 5th: blnd and uns rdr next* **5/4**[1]

6m 39.3s (16.30) **Going Correction** +0.225s/f (Yiel) **6 Ran SP% 113.2**
Speed ratings: **82,80,59, ,**
CSF £54.68 TOTE £3.00: £1.70, £5.80; EX 48.60 Trifecta £333.60.
Owner Mrs M B Scholey & Mrs S J Smith **Bred** Edwin Carlisle **Trained** High Eldwick, W Yorks

FOCUS
A fair small-field staying novice chase and very guessy form.

5363 MICHAELTOWERS.CO.UK PROFESSIONAL ADVICE H'CAP CHASE (13 fncs) 2m
5:35 (5:35) (Class 4) (0-105,105) 5-Y-0+ **£3,768** (£1,106; £553; £276)

Form RPR
641- **1** **Tayarat (IRE)**[10] 5194 9-10-3 **87** 7ex.......................... JoeCornwall(5) 99+
(Michael Chapman) *led: j.lft 1st: j. slowly and hdd 7th: led next: hdd appr 2 out: led appr last: drvn out* **3/1**[1]
360- **2** *1* **Umustbejoking (FR)**[260] 1149 6-10-9 **88**..................[1] AidanColeman 97
(Michael Blake) *hld up: hdwy to chse ldrs 4 out: outpcd next: styd on to take 2nd last 50yds* **3/1**[1]
652- **3** *4 ½* **Apache Dawn**[246] 1260 10-10-6 **85**..........................(t) LeeEdwards 91
(Aytach Sadik) *j.lft: chsd wnr: led 7th: hdd next: led appr 2 out: hdd appr last: fdd last 50yds* **7/1**
542- **4** *2 ¼* **Mon Chevalier (IRE)**[22] 5017 11-11-9 **105**..............(p) MichealNolan(3) 108
(Carroll Gray) *chsd ldrs: one pce fr 3 out* **4/1**[2]
124- **5** *6* **Hopeand**[84] 3837 9-11-12 **105**..............................(t) AdamPogson 103
(Charles Pogson) *trckd ldrs: outpcd 4 out: kpt on fr next: wknd last* **8/1**
10P- **6** *28* **Alba King (IRE)**[232] 1417 8-10-10 **92**.................. JonathanEngland(3) 64
(Sue Smith) *in rr: nt fluent 6th: sn pushed along: bhd fr 9th: t.o* **9/2**[3]

4m 10.9s (8.90) **Going Correction** +0.225s/f (Yiel) **6 Ran SP% 111.8**
Speed ratings: **86,85,83,82,79 65**
CSF £12.61 TOTE £5.00: £2.90, £1.20; EX 16.90 Trifecta £73.00.
Owner Mrs M Chapman **Bred** Golden Garden Stud **Trained** Market Rasen, Lincs

FOCUS
A modest handicap chase. The winner was nicely in and is rated similar to his recent win.

5364 MICHAELTOWERS.CO.UK WORKING HARD GETTING YOU MONEY OPEN HUNTERS' CHASE (19 fncs) 3m 110y
6:05 (6:05) (Class 6) 5-Y-0+ **£1,063** (£379)

Form RPR
15P- **1** **Bay To Go (IRE)**[10] 8-11-9 107...................... MrSDavies-Thomas(7) 116+
(Mrs H M Kemp) *mde all: hit 9th: shkn up appr 3 out: wl clr bef 2 out: easily* **9/2**[2]
520/ **2** *21* **Jack's The Lad (IRE)**[18] 10-11-5 105..................(p) MrJBargary(7) 86
(Mrs Alice Campbell) *trckd wnr: j.rt: hit 11th: drvn 15th: outpcd and hit next: rallied and 5 l down whn mstke 3 out: sn btn* **7/1**[3]
U1F- **L** **Golan Way**[11] 5171 10-11-9 142.................................. MrEDavid(7)
(Tim Vaughan) *ref to r: lft at s* **2/7**[1]

6m 46.1s (23.10) **Going Correction** +0.225s/f (Yiel) **3 Ran SP% 108.4**
Speed ratings: **72,65,**
CSF £19.16 TOTE £3.30; EX 7.40 Trifecta £7.60.
Owner Mrs Heather Kemp **Bred** Brett Merry **Trained** Banbury, Oxon

FOCUS
A fair small-field hunter chase which lost its main player when the long odds-on favourite refused to race. Pretty meaningless form, with the winner given a token rating.

5365 GET ON MICHAELTOWERS.CO.UK PROFIT TRAIN H'CAP HURDLE (9 hdls) 2m
6:35 (6:37) (Class 4) (0-115,115) 4-Y-0+ **£3,119** (£915; £457; £228)

Form RPR
336- **1** **Edmaaj (IRE)**[38] 4699 6-10-7 **101**.......................... MauriceLinehan(5) 106+
(Jonjo O'Neill) *w ldr: led 2nd: drvn and hdd 2 out: styd on to ld last: drvn rt out* **7/4**[1]
655- **2** *1* **Queen Olivia**[28] 4901 6-10-9 **98**.............................. AndrewThornton 103
(Caroline Bailey) *hld up towards rr: hdwy into mid-div 4th: effrt 3 out: chsng ldrs appr next: led between last 2: hdd last: kpt on same pce* **20/1**
500- **3** *3 ¾* **Taaresh (IRE)**[33] 4794 9-11-4 **107**..........................[1] AdamWedge 109
(Kevin Morgan) *chsd ldrs 4th: slt ld 2 out: hdd between last 2: kpt on same pce* **10/1**

032- **4** 3 1/4 **The Pier (IRE)**[25] 4947 8-11-9 **112**.....................................(t) CharliePoste 110
(Anna Brooks) *hld up in mid-div: hdwy to chse ldrs 3 out: styd on same pce fr next* **8/1**[3]

460- **5** nk **Marju's Quest (IRE)**[119] 3161 4-11-1 **112**.......................... MichealNolan(3) 105
(David Dennis) *in rr: gd hdwy to chse ldrs 3 out: one pce fr next* **20/1**

055- **6** 1 1/4 **Tom Wade (IRE)**[25] 4947 7-11-11 **114**...................................(tp) DaveCrosse 111
(Shaun Harris) *led to 2nd: chsd ldrs: kpt on one pce fr 2 out* **20/1**

246/ **7** 3 **Alta Rock (IRE)**[372] 5224 9-11-5 **108**.................................. RyanMania 102
(Sue Smith) *chsd ldrs: one pce fr 2 out* **20/1**

233- **8** 1 1/4 **Spin Cast**[89] 3756 6-11-0 **110**.. MissHBethell(7) 103
(Brian Ellison) *chsd ldrs: one pce fr 2 out* **16/1**

404- **9** 2 **Pippa Greene**[142] 2717 10-11-12 **115**..............................[1] AndrewTinkler 106
(Nicky Henderson) *chsd ldrs: drvn 3 out: one pce appr next* **6/1**[2]

4P0- **10** 8 **Ballygrooby Bertie (IRE)**[30] 4866 6-11-4 **107**....................(t) AlainCawley 91
(Fergal O'Brien) *in rr: hmpd 5th: bhd after* **14/1**

0/0- **11** 25 **Tornade D'Estruval (FR)**[310] 697 7-11-3 **109**.............[1] JackQuinlan(3) 71
(Sarah Humphrey) *in rr: bhd fr 6th: t.o whn hung bdly lft 2 out* **33/1**

231- **B** **Hi Tide (IRE)**[188] 1840 10-11-8 **111**...................................... AidanColeman
(J R Jenkins) *hld up towards rr: b.d 5th* **12/1**

644- **P** **Tealissio**[51] 4469 8-11-6 **109**.. DougieCostello
(Lucy Wadham) *chsd ldrs: hit 4th: lost pl 6th: sn bhd: t.o whn p.u bef 2 out* **8/1**[3]

244- **F** **Hartside (GER)**[19] 5061 5-11-5 **115**...................................... MrRWinks(7)
(Peter Winks) *chsd ldrs: fell 5th* **20/1**

3m 56.5s (-0.50) **Going Correction** -0.375s/f (Good)
WFA 4 from 5yo+ 5lb **14** Ran SP% **129.0**
Speed ratings (Par 105): **86,85,83,82,81 81,79,79,78,74 61,,,**
CSF £47.41 CT £310.27 TOTE £2.90: £1.50, £7.80, £5.50; EX 70.00 Trifecta £377.80.
Owner John P McManus **Bred** Airlie Stud **Trained** Cheltenham, Gloucs

FOCUS
A modest handicap hurdle. The winner was potentially thrown in on Flat form but is rated only in line with his previous hurdle best.

5366 SMIS LTD NIGHT OR DAY DELIVERING WINNERS NOVICES' H'CAP HURDLE (11 hdls) 2m 4f 110y
7:05 (7:05) (Class 4) (0-105,105) 4-Y-0+ **£3,119** (£915; £457; £228)

Form RPR

041- **1** **Catching On (IRE)**[85] 3828 6-11-6 **104**.......................... MauriceLinehan(5) 114+
(Jonjo O'Neill) *led after 1st: mde rest: blnd 8th: styd on fr 2 out: hld on wl run-in* **7/2**[1]

643- **2** 1 1/2 **Florida Quays (IRE)**[25] 4972 6-10-11 **90**.......................... AidanColeman 97
(David Dennis) *mid-div: hdwy to chse wnr sn after 3 out: 2 l down last: styd on same pce* **8/1**

604- **3** 7 **Sterling Gent (IRE)**[18] 5069 7-11-0 **93**............................(t) TomO'Brien 95
(Liam Corcoran) *hld up in rr: hdwy 8th: 3rd appr 2 out: one pce* **6/1**[3]

554- **4** 1 1/4 **Balinderry (IRE)**[30] 4865 7-10-8 **87**..............................(tp) AndrewTinkler 87
(Steve Gollings) *chsd ldrs: drvn 3 out: 4th and one pce appr next* **12/1**

401- **5** 21 **Silver Dragon**[32] 4823 6-11-10 **103**..............................(p) DougieCostello 84
(Tony Coyle) *in rr: kpt on fr 2 out: nvr a factor* **7/1**

503- **6** 2 1/4 **Oorayvic (IRE)**[42] 4615 7-10-11 **90**................................... RyanMania 70
(Sue Smith) *chsd ldrs: wknd bef 2 out* **5/1**[2]

004- **7** 1 **Princess Bella (IRE)**[27] 4917 5-11-5 **98**............................. AlainCawley 76
(Fergal O'Brien) *chsd ldrs: nt fluent 3rd: lost pl 6th* **33/1**

460- **8** 2 1/4 **Willpower (IRE)**[19] 5059 5-11-5 **101**............................ PeterCarberry(3) 78
(Nicky Henderson) *chsd ldrs: drvn 3 out: sn btn* **8/1**

035- **9** 21 **The Perfect Crime (IRE)**[32] 4818 5-11-10 **103**..................... WillKennedy 60
(Ian Williams) *in rr: hdwy 4th: reminders next: lost pl 3 out: sn bhd* **25/1**

P34- **10** nk **Flash Tommie (IRE)**[33] 4796 6-11-4 **100**................ JonathanEngland(3) 57
(Michael Appleby) *in rr: nt fluent 4th: bhd fr 7th* **16/1**

U05- **11** hd **Sir Harry Hotspur**[25] 4945 6-10-11 **90**........................(t) DonalDevereux 46
(John Mackie) *chsd ldrs: lost pl 8th: sn bhd* **20/1**

P0- **12** 60 **Here I Am (IRE)**[32] 4807 7-11-9 **102**.................................... SamThomas 4
(Diana Grissell) *led tl after 1st: chsd ldrs: lost pl after 7th: sn bhd: t.o 3 out: eventually completed* **16/1**

P **Sea Rocket (IRE)**[41] 4641 6-11-12 **105**.................................. PaulMoloney
(Dominic Ffrench Davis) *in rr: hdwy to chse ldrs 4th: lost pl after next: sn bhd: t.o whn j.rt 7th: p.u bef 2 out* **16/1**

5m 3.5s (-9.50) **Going Correction** -0.375s/f (Good) **13** Ran SP% **124.8**
Speed ratings (Par 105): **103,102,99,99,91 90,90,89,81,81 81,58,**
CSF £32.86 CT £170.66 TOTE £4.50: £2.00, £3.20, £2.40; EX 36.40 Trifecta £380.40 Part won. Pool of £507.29 - 0.37 winning units..
Owner Mrs Gay Smith **Bred** Gareth Adair **Trained** Cheltenham, Gloucs

FOCUS
A modest novices' handicap hurdle. The winner is back on the upgrade and there's probably more to come.

5367 MICHAELTOWERS.CO.UK GETTING YOUR WINNERS HOME STANDARD NH FLAT RACE (CONDITIONALS/AMATEURS) 2m
7:35 (7:35) (Class 6) 4-6-Y-0 **£1,642** (£478; £239)

Form RPR

1 **Horsted Valley** 4-10-9 0... GavinSheehan(3) 106+
(Warren Greatrex) *sn mid-div: drvn along after 5f: hdwy to chse ldrs 5f out: led 1f out: styd on* **5/2**[2]

03- **2** 1 **Acertain Circus**[24] 4986 4-10-9 0.................................... KielanWoods(3) 104
(Pam Sly) *trckd ldrs: 2nd over 3f out: led briefly over 1f out: kpt on same pce* **7/1**

6/5- **3** 4 **Carmino (IRE)**[111] 3282 5-11-0 0..............................(p) NicodeBoinville(3) 105
(Mark Bradstock) *chsd ldrs: drvn 6f out: rallied over 2f out: kpt on to take 3rd nr fin* **33/1**

422- **4** 1/2 **The Grey Taylor (IRE)**[24] 4986 5-10-10 0.......................... PaulBohan(7) 105
(Steve Gollings) *led: drvn over 3f out: hdd over 1f out: wknd last 150yds* **3/1**[3]

01- **5** 4 **Dubai Sonnet**[12] 5166 5-11-5 0..................................... MauriceLinehan(5) 108
(Alan Swinbank) *hld up in rr: hdwy 8f out: chsng ldrs and drvn over 4f out: wknd over 1f out* **15/8**[1]

5- **6** 19 **Ruaraidh Hugh (IRE)**[58] 4329 5-11-3 0................................ AdamWedge 84
(Chris Bealby) *chsd ldrs: drvn over 5f out: lost pl over 4f out* **50/1**

7 9 **Justcallhimbilly** 4-10-7 0.. BenPoste(5) 71
(Shaun Harris) *in rr-div: lost pl over 4f out* **50/1**

0- **8** 2 1/4 **Dicky Shore**[29] 4895 6-10-10 0....................................... DeanPratt(7) 74
(Ashley Dodgson) *in rr: drvn over 7f out: bhd fnl 5f* **66/1**

4- **9** hd **Karisma King**[19] 5063 5-11-0 0.................................... JonathanEngland(3) 74
(Sue Smith) *chsd ldrs: lost pl over 4f out: sn bhd* **16/1**

0- **10** 7 **Wabanaki Legend**[97] 3619 5-10-3 0.................................... MrJTeal(7) 60
(Malcolm Jefferson) *in rr: sn pushed along: bhd after 6f: t.o 4f out* **33/1**

0/0- **11** dist **Foreverbest (IRE)**[342] 187 5-10-6 0 ow3.............................. MrLTorbitt(7)
(Roger Teal) *sn chsng ldrs: drvn 6f out: sn lost pl and bhd: t.o 3f out: eventually fin* **66/1**

3m 48.9s (-2.50) **Going Correction** -0.375s/f (Good)
WFA 4 from 5yo+ 5lb **11** Ran SP% **119.5**
Speed ratings: **91,90,88,88,86 76,72,71,71,67**
CSF £19.86 TOTE £4.30: £1.50, £3.60, £7.40; EX 21.50 Trifecta £414.00.
Owner The Broadwell Fox Partnership **Bred** G Deren **Trained** Upper Lambourn, Berks

FOCUS
An ordinary bumper for conditional/amateur riders in which they went a proper gallop. The winner should go on to rate higher.
T/Plt: £1,074.20 to a £1 stake.Pool of £40837.39 - 27.75 winning tickets. T/Qpdt: £62.50 to a £1 stake. Pool of £5183.30 - 61.30 winning tickets. WG

5347 CHELTENHAM (L-H)
Thursday, April 17

OFFICIAL GOING: Good (7.5)

5368 THOROUGHBRED BREEDERS' ASSOCIATION MARES' NOVICES' HURDLE (LISTED RACE) (8 hdls) 2m 1f
2:05 (2:05) (Class 1) 4-Y-0+ **£11,888** (£4,452; £2,224; £1,110)

Form RPR

123- **1** **As I Am (IRE)**[108] 3423 6-11-3 139.............................. ConorShoemark 140+
(Don Cantillon) *mde all: clr after 2nd tl 3 out: kicked on again appr last: styd on gamely: rdn out* **7/2**[2]

5- **2** 3 **Emily Gray (IRE)**[32] 4846 6-10-12 127............................ BarryGeraghty 131
(T E Hyde, Ire) *trckd ldrs: hit 4th: chsd wnr after 2 out: sn rdn: kpt on but a being hld* **7/1**

242- **3** 11 **The Pirate's Queen (IRE)**[26] 4961 5-10-12 134........... RobertThornton 124
(Alan King) *hld up: short of room on bnd bef 3 out: sme hdwy appr 2 out: rdn into 3rd bef last: nvr threatening to rch ldng pair* **9/4**[1]

061- **4** 7 **Norfolk Sky**[23] 5026 5-10-12 118.. DaveCrosse 115
(Brian Barr) *hld up: hdwy 3 out: sn disputing 2nd: rdn after 2 out: wknd bef last* **33/1**

211- **5** 5 **Run Ructions Run (IRE)**[26] 4961 5-11-1 133............(p) DougieCostello 114
(Tim Easterby) *in tch: wnt cl 3rd 3 out: rdn and lost pl bef next where wnt rt: nt a threat after* **9/2**[3]

411- **6** 1 1/2 **Cloudante (IRE)**[51] 4479 6-10-12 128.................................... NoelFehily 109
(Donald McCain) *trckd clr ldr tl rdn after 3 out: readily sn after hld 2 out: regained 6th run-in past tiring horse* **12/1**

162- **7** 1/2 **Free Thinking**[48] 4528 6-10-12 125................................ MrSWaley-Cohen 109
(Nicky Henderson) *mid-div: wnt 5th 2 out: sn rdn: wknd bef last* **8/1**

50F- **8** 19 **Roja Dove (IRE)**[48] 4531 5-11-1 121................................ TrevorWhelan 95
(Neil King) *in tch tl struggling after 3 out: wknd bef next* **50/1**

10P- **9** 43 **Gambling Girl (IRE)**[111] 3339 5-11-3 130............................. RobbiePower 58
(Mrs John Harrington, Ire) *mid-div: mstke 2nd: nt fluent next: dropped to last 5th: rdn after 3 out: wknd bef next: eased bef last: t.o* **14/1**

4m 8.0s (-3.30) **Going Correction** +0.075s/f (Yiel) **9** Ran SP% **114.0**
Speed ratings (Par 111): **110,108,103,100,97 97,96,87,67**
CSF £27.96 TOTE £3.60: £1.70, £2.40, £1.20; EX 27.20 Trifecta £101.30.
Owner Don Cantillon **Bred** Don Cantillon **Trained** Newmarket, Suffolk

FOCUS
All races on New Course. The jockeys reported that the overnight watering had affected the ground, which was riding quite tacky and dead. The third running of this Listed event, in which the winner set a decent gallop and recorded a time 13.5sec outside the standard. The first two are rated pretty much to their marks.

5369 EBF/THOROUGHBRED BREEDERS' ASSOCIATION MARES' NOVICES' CHASE FINALE (A H'CAP) (LISTED RACE) (17 fncs) 2m 5f
2:40 (2:40) (Class 1) 5-Y-0+
£22,508 (£8,480; £4,244; £2,120; £1,064; £532)

Form RPR

234- **1** **Me And Ben (IRE)**[7] 5246 7-9-9 **108** oh4.................(t) ConorShoemark(5) 115+
(Fergal O'Brien) *hld up: hdwy 11th: disp 2nd 3 out: led narrowly next: 3 l clr last: edgd lft: styd on wl: rdn out* **9/1**[3]

331- **2** 2 **Possibly Flora**[11] 5187 9-10-0 **108** 6ex oh13..................(t) ConorO'Farrell 112
(Richard Woollacott) *led tl 5th: w ldr: led 11th: rdn after 3 out: narrowly hdd next: 3 l down last: styd on but a being hld* **14/1**

42F- **3** 10 **Baby Shine (IRE)**[32] 4848 8-11-10 **132**............................ AidanColeman 128
(Lucy Wadham) *trckd ldrs: j.w: rdn in cl 3rd after 3 out: no ex appr last* **15/8**[1]

302- **4** 8 **Tempest River (IRE)**[40] 4685 8-11-2 **127**....................(p) KielanWoods(3) 124+
(Ben Case) *trckd ldrs: mstke 10th: rdn after 13th: nodded on landing and nrly uns rdr 4 out: lost pl: styd on again appr 2 out but no ch* **15/8**[1]

3/4- **5** 7 **Queen's Bay**[26] 4966 8-10-4 **112**...................................... BrendanPowell 95
(Jamie Snowden) *trckd ldrs: hit 11th and dropped to last pair but in tch: rdn bef 3 out: styd on same pce tl fdd appr last* **25/1**

F13- **6** 5 **She Ranks Me (IRE)**[28] 4918 7-11-7 **129**...........................(p) NoelFehily 108
(Donald McCain) *nt a fluent: tended to jump lft: prom: hit 3rd: led 5th whn t.k.h: hdd 11th: w ldr tl rdn appr 3 out: wknd bef 2 out* **8/1**[2]

044- **7** 12 **Tea Caddy**[24] 5010 8-9-12 **109** oh1 ow1........................(t) GavinSheehan(3) 79
(Jamie Snowden) *trckd ldrs on outer tl dropped to last pair 7th: sn nudged along: rdn after 4 out: wknd after next* **10/1**

5m 21.2s (1.80) **Going Correction** +0.125s/f (Yiel) **7** Ran SP% **110.3**
Speed ratings: **101,100,96,93,90 88,84**
CSF £99.41 TOTE £9.70: £3.10, £4.50; EX 81.20 Trifecta £185.60.
Owner M C Fahy **Bred** Micheal Fahy **Trained** Coln St. Dennis, Gloucs

FOCUS
The second running of this race since it was switched from Newbury, and a slightly disappointing turnout for such a decent prize. The pace was only modest. A step up from the winner and there's a case for rating the form up to 7lb higher.

5370 OLBG.COM SUPPORTS MARES' JUMP RACING MARES' H'CAP HURDLE (LISTED RACE) (10 hdls) 2m 5f 110y
3:15 (3:15) (Class 1) 4-Y-0+
£11,390 (£4,274; £2,140; £1,066; £536; £268)

Form RPR

/51- **1** **Polly Peachum (IRE)**[29] 4907 6-11-4 **135**........................ BarryGeraghty 145+
(Nicky Henderson) *hld up towards rr: hdwy 5th: pushed along in midfield whn mstke 2 out: gd hdwy sn after: led sn after last: r.o strly to draw clr: rdn out* **9/1**

033- **2** 5 **L'Unique (FR)**[37] 4740 5-11-10 **141** .... RobertThornton 144
(Alan King) *mid-div: hdwy 6th: chsd ldrs 2 out: sn rdn: ch last: styd on to go 2nd fnl 120yds but no ch w wnr* **8/1**[3]

141- **3** ¾ **Loyaute (FR)**[28] 4920 7-11-1 **132** .... JamesDavies 134
(Chris Down) *mid-div: hdwy 6th: rdn to chse ldrs after 2 out: styd on wl fr last to go 3rd towards fin* **33/1**

021- **4** ¾ **Koolala (IRE)**[15] 5124 6-10-8 **125** .... DenisO'Regan 126
(Paul Webber) *trckd ldrs: chal 2 out: led briefly bef last: sn rdn: ev ch after last: no ex and lost 2 pls fnl 120yds* **12/1**

2F1- **5** 1 ½ **Blue Buttons (IRE)**[24] 5002 6-10-9 **126** .... (t) NoelFehily 126
(Harry Fry) *mid-div: hdwy on wd outer appr 2 out: rdn to chse ldrs sn after: disputing cl 3rd whn nt clr run appr last: swtchd lft run-in: styd on but hld after* **7/1**[2]

/10- **6** 1 ½ **Cailin Annamh (IRE)**[37] 4740 6-11-7 **138** .... (t) RobbiePower 138
(Mrs John Harrington, Ire) *in tch: hdwy to ld appr last where mstke: sn rdn and hdd: no ex fnl 120yds* **12/1**

340- **7** ½ **Luci Di Mezzanotte**[26] 4961 6-9-11 **119** .... (b1) ThomasGarner(5) 117
(Oliver Sherwood) *towards rr of midfield: hdwy appr 3 out: rdn and ev ch appr last: fdd run-in* **33/1**

213- **8** 9 **Lily Waugh (IRE)**[26] 4961 7-10-0 **120** .... (t) RachaelGreen(3) 110
(Anthony Honeyball) *trckd ldrs: led 2 out: sn rdn: hdd bef last: wknd run-in* **4/1**[1]

043- **9** 2 ½ **Beyeh (IRE)**[48] 4531 6-10-8 **125** .... RyanMahon 113
(Michael Appleby) *mid-div: hdwy appr 3 out: rdn to chse ldrs after 2 out: wknd after last* **28/1**

424- **10** 9 **Brijomi Queen (IRE)**[48] 4531 7-10-0 **117** oh5 .... BrianHarding 97
(Nicky Richards) *mid-div tl 5th: sn in rr and rdn: hdwy on outer after 3 out: wknd bef last* **28/1**

215- **11** 1 ¼ **One Lucky Lady**[34] 4789 6-10-13 **133** .... NicodeBoinville(3) 112
(Nicky Henderson) *hld up towards rr: hdwy after 6th: rdn after 3 out: wknd after next* **14/1**

126- **12** 30 **Top Totti**[37] 4740 6-10-12 **132** .... JakeGreenall(3) 84
(Henry Daly) *trckd ldrs: hit 4th: rdn after 3 out: wknd after next: t.o* **10/1**

450- **13** 4 ½ **Mrs Peachey (IRE)**[26] 4961 7-10-11 **128** .... AidanColeman 76
(Kim Bailey) *a towards rr: t.o after 2 out* **16/1**

116- **14** 16 **Fairytale Theatre (IRE)**[26] 4961 7-10-11 **128** .... (t) SamTwiston-Davies 61
(Paul Nicholls) *mid-div tl 3 out: sn in rr: t.o* **25/1**

100- **15** 3 ¾ **Down Ace (IRE)**[26] 4961 7-10-9 **126** .... DougieCostello 56
(Fergal O'Brien) *led tl 3rd: led 5th tl 3 out: sn rdn: cl up but hld whn squeezed up bef last: sn wknd and eased: t.o* **25/1**

144- **16** 12 **Alder Mairi (IRE)**[25] 4991 7-10-8 **125** .... AndrewThornton 44
(Seamus Mullins) *hld up towards rr: hdwy into midfield after 3 out: wknd bef last: eased: t.o* **28/1**

/11- **P** **Lovey Dovey (IRE)**[207] 1634 10-9-11 **117** oh2 .... HarryDerham(3)
(Simon West) *trckd ldr: led 3rd tl 5th: styd chsng ldrs: rdn appr 2 out: sn wknd: p.u bef last* **20/1**

4/ **P** **Point The Toes (IRE)**[171] 2145 9-9-13 **119** ow2 .... (p) RobertDunne(3)
(Mark Fahey, Ire) *mid-div: rdn after 7th: wknd bef 2 out: p.u bef last* **33/1**

344- **P** **Hidden Identity (IRE)**[37] 4740 8-11-4 **135** .... RichardJohnson
(Tim Vaughan) *a towards rr: struggling after 3 out: wkng whn mstke next: p.u bef last* **16/1**

5m 23.7s (7.10) **Going Correction** +0.075s/f (Yiel) **19** Ran SP% **128.1**
Speed ratings (Par 111): **90,88,87,87,87 86,86,83,82,78 78,67,65,60,58 54,,,**
CSF £72.26 CT £2298.31 TOTE £8.00: £2.20, £2.50, £7.70, £2.70; EX 49.20 Trifecta £1406.20.
Owner Lady Tennant **Bred** Colman O'Flynn **Trained** Upper Lambourn, Berks

FOCUS
Any number were in with a chance heading down to two out in this highly competitive mares' handicap. Another big step up from the impressive winner, who rates a useful mare, and pretty solid form overall.

5371 AURIGA NETWORK H'CAP CHASE (21 fncs) 3m 1f 110y
3:50 (3:50) (Class 2) (0-150,145) 5-Y-0+

£12,512 (£3,696; £1,848; £924; £462; £232)

Form RPR

/P0- **1** **Mon Parrain (FR)**[47] 4544 8-11-4 **137** .... (tp) NickScholfield 145
(Paul Nicholls) *prom hugging ins: lost pl 13th: outpcd whn nt fluent 18th: only 7th and u.p 3 out: rallied next: swtchd rt and stormed through fr last to squeeze between two rivals: led fnl stride: fine ride* **14/1**

F24- **2** shd **Forgotten Gold (IRE)**[19] 5068 8-11-4 **137** .... BarryGeraghty 145
(Tom George) *cl up on outer: ev ch fr 3 out: drvn ahd after last: kpt on gamely but pipped on post* **11/2**[2]

610- **3** 9 **Sire Collonges (FR)**[36] 4754 8-11-12 **145** .... (p) SamTwiston-Davies 145
(Paul Nicholls) *led tl 2nd: pressed ldr: rdn and ev ch last: nt qckn after* **12/1**

040- **4** ½ **Imperial Circus (IRE)**[30] 4886 8-10-4 **123** .... (b) RichardJohnson 123
(Philip Hobbs) *settled chsng ldrs: mstke 8th: wnt prom 16th: rdn to ld after 2 out: hdd after last: edgd rt and idled: wknd fnl 100yds* **7/1**

1P5- **5** 7 **Bradley**[18] 5092 10-10-13 **132** .... NoelFehily 127
(Fergal O'Brien) *towards rr: rdn and effrt 18th: 6th and stl jst in front of wnr 3 out: nt qckn fr next* **13/2**[3]

505- **6** 7 **Golden Chieftain (IRE)**[12] 5170 9-11-6 **139** .... (tp) BrendanPowell 129
(Colin Tizzard) *towards rr: blnd 11th: nvr really threatened after: rdn 17th: nt fluent next: plugged on after last* **8/1**

054- **7** nk **Gauvain (GER)**[18] 5092 12-11-5 **138** .... (tp) TomO'Brien 128
(Philip Hobbs) *hld up in tch: rdn 16th: struggling whn in last whn mstke next* **16/1**

202- **8** nse **Time For Rupert (IRE)**[18] 5092 10-11-7 **140** .... (v) DenisO'Regan 131
(Paul Webber) *led fr 2nd: mstke 18th: rdn 3 out: hit next and sn hdd: immediately btn and floundered up hill after* **7/1**

6P0- **9** 18 **Ackertac (IRE)**[37] 4738 9-11-6 **139** .... (b) AidanColeman 117
(Tim Vaughan) *trckd ldrs gng wl: 5th and wl on terms 3 out: rdn and dropped out qckly next* **4/1**[1]

460- **P** **Quartz De Thaix (FR)**[35] 4765 10-11-6 **139** .... (b) LiamTreadwell
(Venetia Williams) *pushed along to begin: nvr travelling and sluggish in rr: lost tch 9th: t.o and p.u 13th* **14/1**

6m 36.8s (-1.40) **Going Correction** +0.125s/f (Yiel) **10** Ran SP% **111.7**
Speed ratings: **107,106,104,104,101 99,99,99,94,**
CSF £86.83 CT £946.24 TOTE £13.20: £4.50, £2.40, £2.60; EX 116.10 Trifecta £990.10.
Owner Mr And Mrs J D Cotton **Bred** Serge Dubois **Trained** Ditcheat, Somerset
■ Stewards' Enquiry : Nick Scholfield two-day ban: used whip above permitted level (May 1-2)

FOCUS
A decent handicap chase, but not many arrived with progressive profiles. There was a terrific finish, with the lead changing twice on the run-in. Mon Parrain was a 160 horse in 2011 and could be interesting if building on this, and the second is rated to his best.

5372 BARBURY INTERNATIONAL SUPPORTING THE IJF H'CAP HURDLE (12 hdls) 3m
4:25 (4:25) (Class 2) (0-145,145) 4-Y-0+

£10,009 (£2,956; £1,478; £739; £369; £185)

Form RPR

/06- **1** **Kingsmere**[151] 2529 9-10-0 **119** oh1 .... AndrewTinkler 133+
(Henry Daly) *kpt wd: hld up towards rr: smooth hdwy after 3 out: led bef last: rdn clr: easily* **12/1**

145- **2** 10 **Ballyculla (IRE)**[96] 3653 7-10-11 **133** .... (p) GavinSheehan(3) 136
(Warren Greatrex) *kpt to inner: hld up bhd: gd hdwy after 2 out: sn rdn to chse ldrs: styd on to go 2nd towards fin: no ch w easy wnr* **20/1**

120- **3** ½ **Mister Dillon**[35] 4765 7-11-7 **140** .... BarryGeraghty 143
(Nicky Henderson) *kpt wd: mid-div: smooth hdwy 2 out: rdn to briefly chal appr last: sn hld: styd on same pce: lost 2nd towards fin* **5/1**[1]

600- **4** 1 ¼ **Angles Hill (IRE)**[22] 5030 7-10-4 **123** .... TomO'Brien 126
(Richard Woollacott) *in tch: hit 8th: wnt 3rd 3 out: rdn and ev ch after 2 out tl last: no ex fnl 100yds* **16/1**

401- **5** 5 **Berkeley Barron (IRE)**[41] 4662 6-11-1 **134** .... (t) RichardJohnson 133
(Philip Hobbs) *hld up towards rr: rdn after 3 out: hdwy after 2 out to chse ldrs: styd on same pce fr last* **8/1**

230- **6** 8 **Imperial Leader (IRE)**[33] 4805 6-10-0 **126** .... (t) RyanHatch(7) 117
(Nigel Twiston-Davies) *mid-div: pushed along 9th: rdn and hdwy appr 2 out: chsd ldrs bef last: fdd run-in* **6/1**[2]

040- **7** 8 **Cross Kennon (IRE)**[35] 4765 10-11-4 **137** .... (v) SeanQuinlan 120
(Jennie Candlish) *rdr's helmet hit tape leaving s: trckd ldr: led sn after 3 out: rdn and hdd after 2 out: wknd last* **12/1**

641- **8** 3 **Minellahalfcentury (IRE)**[61] 4277 6-10-9 **128** .... (tp) SamTwiston-Davies 108
(Paul Nicholls) *mid-div: rdn after 2 out: nvr any imp* **7/1**[3]

231- **9** hd **Heronry (IRE)**[18] 5093 6-11-1 **137** .... NicodeBoinville(3) 117
(Nicky Henderson) *mid-div: hdwy 3 out: rdn bef next: wknd bef last* **10/1**

010- **10** 4 ½ **Timesishard (IRE)**[33] 4814 7-10-5 **129** .... KillianMoore(5) 105
(Graeme McPherson) *in tch: rdn after 8th: wknd bef last* **25/1**

300- **11** nk **Red Not Blue (IRE)**[26] 4949 11-10-4 **123** .... BrendanPowell 100
(Simon Earle) *towards rr of mid-div: rdn 2 out: no imp: wknd bef last* **25/1**

220- **12** hd **Cannon Fodder**[33] 4805 7-10-11 **130** .... MarcGoldstein 108
(Sheena West) *trckd ldrs: rdn after 3 out: wknd after 2 out* **33/1**

540- **13** 5 **Coronea Lilly (IRE)**[24] 5010 10-10-2 **121** .... (tp) AidanColeman 92
(Neil Mulholland) *towards rr of mid-div: struggling 8th: wknd after 2 out* **66/1**

215- **14** 17 **Heavenstown (IRE)**[11] 5186 8-10-4 **123** .... (b) JamieMoore 79
(John Spearing) *rdr's helmet hit tape leaving s: led tl after 3 out: rdn and wknd after 2 out: t.o* **33/1**

623- **15** 2 ¾ **Azure Fly (IRE)**[18] 5093 6-10-10 **129** .... (tp) NoelFehily 82
(Charlie Longsdon) *hld up towards rr: hdwy appr 7th: chsd ldrs 2 out: sn rdn and wknd* **10/1**

131- **P** **Kaysersberg (FR)**[39] 4697 7-11-2 **135** .... TomScudamore
(Neil King) *mid-div: struggling 6th: bhd 8th: t.o whn p.u after 3 out* **14/1**

215- **P** **Up For An Oscar (IRE)**[181] 1956 7-9-13 **123** .... (t) EdCookson(5)
(Kim Bailey) *rdr's helmet hit tape leaving s: trckd ldr: hit 5th: lost pl 8th: sn in rr: t.o whn p.u bef last* **18/1**

5m 56.1s (-4.90) **Going Correction** +0.075s/f (Yiel) **17** Ran SP% **125.8**
Speed ratings (Par 109): **111,107,107,107,105 102,100,99,99,97 97,97,95,90,89 ,**
CSF £241.56 CT £1376.32 TOTE £17.60: £4.40, £4.20, £1.50, £4.30; EX 319.70 Trifecta £1783.10 Part won..
Owner Evan-Robert Hanbury **Bred** E R Hanbury **Trained** Stanton Lacy, Shropshire

FOCUS
A competitive handicap hurdle on paper, but it was taken apart by the winner. He showed big improvement on his hurdles besy but the form looks pretty solid.

5373 NICHOLSON HOLMAN NOVICES' LIMITED H'CAP CHASE (21 fncs) 3m 1f 110y
5:00 (5:00) (Class 3) (0-135,130) 5-Y-0 **£6,279** (£1,871; £947; £485; £254)

Form RPR

233- **1** **Lamb Or Cod (IRE)**[33] 4819 7-11-8 **128** .... (bt1) RichardJohnson 146+
(Philip Hobbs) *mid-div: wnt 3rd and mstke 4 out: dropped to 4th and rdn: hdwy appr 2 out: led last: styd on strly to draw clr run-in* **8/1**[3]

321- **2** 18 **Sixty Something (FR)**[26] 4946 8-11-6 **129** .... JakeGreenall(3) 132+
(Paul Webber) *trckd ldrs: led 4 out where stmbld: strly pressed after next: wnt rt and hdd last: wknd* **7/2**[1]

304- **3** 7 **Sail And Return**[26] 4968 10-10-1 **110** .... (t) KielanWoods(3) 104
(Phil Middleton) *slow 1st: hld up: hdwy after 4 out: chal 3 out: sn rdn: hld next: wknd last* **12/1**

1F0- **4** 8 **Leg Iron (IRE)**[39] 4704 9-10-6 **112** .... MarcGoldstein 98
(Sheena West) *in tch tl 5th: sn nudged along in last pair: rdn after 10th: wnt 5th after 4 out: styd on into 4th bef last: nvr any ch w ldrs* **33/1**

501- **5** 8 **Barlow (IRE)**[28] 4914 7-11-6 **126** .... (p) NoelFehily 107
(Warren Greatrex) *led tl 4 out: sn rdn: wknd after next* **10/1**

35P- **P** **Civil Disobedience**[132] 2923 10-10-8 **114** .... ConorO'Farrell
(Richard Woollacott) *sn in last pair: struggling 12th: lost tch 15th: p.u after 17th* **16/1**

012- **P** **Speed Master (IRE)**[7] 5228 8-11-5 **125** .... (v) SamTwiston-Davies
(Nigel Twiston-Davies) *nvr fluent: in last pair whn nt fluent 2nd: reminders: in tch whn blnd 5th: rdn fr 13th: mstke 15th: wknd next: p.u jst bef 17th* **9/2**[2]

112- **P** **Ifyousayso (IRE)**[27] 4934 7-11-10 **130** .... (t) AlainCawley
(Tom George) *trckd ldrs: rdn after 17th: wknd after next: t.o whn p.u after 3 out* **9/2**[2]

322- **P** **Whistling Senator (IRE)**[132] 2923 7-10-12 **123** ..... (v) MauriceLinehan(5)
(Jonjo O'Neill) *sn in tch: mstke 11th: struggling next: sn lost tch: t.o whn p.u bef 16th* **17/2**

122- **P** **The Potting Shed (IRE)**[137] 2847 7-11-0 **120** .... (v1) AidanColeman
(Emma Lavelle) *trckd ldrs: rdn after 15th: wknd next: p.u jst bef 17th* **14/1**

6m 35.2s (-3.00) **Going Correction** +0.125s/f (Yiel) **10** Ran SP% **112.5**
Speed ratings: **109,103,101,98,96 ,,,,**
CSF £36.01 CT £333.50 TOTE £9.10: £2.60, £1.80, £4.00; EX 42.40 Trifecta £528.30.
Owner Terry Warner **Bred** T Horgan **Trained** Withycombe, Somerset

FOCUS
This decent novice handicap proved a searching test of stamina, and not many saw it out. A big step up from the winner.

5374 "KINGSWAY CLAIMS" MARES' STANDARD OPEN NATIONAL HUNT FLAT RACE — 2m 1f

5:30 (5:34) (Class 4) 4-6-Y-O **£4,873** (£1,431; £715; £357)

Form — RPR

1- **1** **Miss Estela (IRE)**[38] 4735 4-10-11 0 GavinSheehan(3) 121+
(Warren Greatrex) *settled in midfield: prog towards outside over 3f out: str run home turn to ld 1f out: readily drew clr: gamely* **9/2**[2]

33- **2** *2 1/2* **Coco Shambhala**[28] 4916 6-10-7 0 ThomasGarner(5) 115
(Oliver Sherwood) *led: drvn 2f out: hdd 1f out: sn outpcd by wnr but remained clr of rest* **25/1**

\- **3** *5* **Taylor (IRE)**[144] 2710 5-10-12 0 BarryGeraghty 111
(Nicky Henderson) *towards rr and hld up: wnt cl up 6f out: ev ch over 2f out: rn green and btn 3rd 1f out: do bttr* **10/3**[1]

4 *1/2* **Ardnahoe (IRE)**[33] 4831 4-11-0 0 TomScudamore 112
(David A Kiely, Ire) *t.k.h: cl up: effrt gng wl 4f out: rdn and outpcd by ldng pair over 1f out* **16/1**

5 *11* **Presenting Newmill (IRE)**[32] 6-10-12 0 NoelFehily 101
(Harry Whittington) *bhd: last 7f out: hdwy 5f out: chsd ldrs 3f out: rdn and wknd over 2f out* **25/1**

43- **6** *1/2* **One Big Love**[19] 5077 6-10-7 0 JamesBanks(5) 100
(Keiran Burke) *wore ear plugs: chsd ldrs: rdn 5f out: drvn and wknd over 2f out* **33/1**

6- **7** *shd* **Gabriella Rose**[19] 5077 4-10-7 0 RobertThornton 95
(Alan King) *hld up: effrt 3f out: wl btn 2f out* **17/2**

8 *8* **Vera's Article (IRE)** 6-10-7 0 MrPYork(5) 94
(Raymond York) *last early: prog on outside 6f out: chsd ldrs 3f out tl wknd 2f out: t.o* **100/1**

3- **9** *17* **Cara Carlotta**[38] 4735 5-10-12 0 RichardJohnson 82
(Philip Hobbs) *bhd early: rdn 6f out: sme hdwy to midfield 3f out: sn btn: t.o* **5/1**[3]

350- **10** *1 1/4* **Morello Royale (IRE)**[55] 4403 4-10-0 0 MrMLegg(7) 71
(Colin Tizzard) *towards rr: rdn 6f out: no ch 3f out: t.o* **50/1**

2- **11** *9* **Mistress Mole (IRE)**[38] 4735 5-10-12 0 NickScholfield 68
(Paul Nicholls) *midfield: rdn 6f out: no rspnse: btn 3f out: t.o* **8/1**

12 *2 3/4* **The Scarlett Woman** 5-10-12 0 AidanColeman 66
(Kim Bailey) *chsd ldrs tl lost pl 6f out: t.o* **14/1**

0- **13** *2 1/4* **Alizee De Janeiro (FR)**[44] 4611 4-10-2 0 GrantCockburn(5) 59
(Lucinda Russell) *chsd ldrs tl rdn 6f out: sn struggling: t.o* **100/1**

54- **14** *77* **Glamorous Sister (IRE)**[19] 5077 4-10-7 0 TomO'Brien
(Robert Stephens) *t.k.h: sn w ldr: rdn and lost pl 5f out: fdd rapidly home turn and virtually p.u* **33/1**

P **Kilronan High (IRE)**[130] 5-10-12 0 SamTwiston-Davies
(Nigel Twiston-Davies) *prom tl sed to hang and r awkwardly whn drvn 6f out: t.o 3f out: p.u over 1f out* **12/1**

4m 3.8s (-1.90) **Going Correction** +0.075s/f (Yiel) **15** Ran SP% **117.3**
Speed ratings: **107,105,103,103,98 97,97,94,86,85 81,79,78,42,**
CSF £118.31 TOTE £6.90: £2.60, £5.60, £2.10; EX 132.00 Trifecta £650.90.
Owner Mrs L Suenson-Taylor **Bred** Mrs L Suenson-Taylor **Trained** Upper Lambourn, Berks

FOCUS
A fair race of its type, won by a useful prospect who looks decent. The next three are all above average.

T/Jkpt: Not won. T/Plt: £2414.40 to a £1 stake. Pool: £149,496.52 - 45.20 winning units. T/Qpdt: £130.50 to a £1 stake. Pool: 14,153.26 - 80.22 winning units. TM

[5213]CARLISLE (R-H)

Saturday, April 19

OFFICIAL GOING: Good (good to soft in places down the hill on the chase course) changing to good (good to firm in places on the hurdle course after race 2 (1.55))
Wind: Breezy, half against Weather: Sunny

5375 BET TOTEPLACEPOT NOVICES' H'CAP HURDLE (10 hdls) — 2m 3f 110y

1:20 (1:21) (Class 4) (0-115,114) 4-Y-O+ **£3,573** (£1,049; £524; £262)

Form — RPR

301- **1** **Nexius (IRE)**[35] 4816 5-11-11 **112** WilsonRenwick 117+
(Keith Dalgleish) *trckd ldr gng wl: smooth hdwy to ld 2 out: nt fluent last: shkn up and edgd rt run-in: kpt on wl: comf* **4/5**[1]

323- **2** *2 1/2* **Chebsey Beau**[28] 4945 4-11-0 **114** DeanPratt(7) 110+
(John Quinn) *chsd ldrs: nt fluent 3 out: effrt and chsd wnr appr last: n.m.r and swtchd rt run-in: kpt on: nt gng pce of wnr* **5/1**[3]

631- **3** *3 1/2* **Snowed In (IRE)**[11] 5214 5-10-12 **104** (p) CraigNichol(5) 100
(Barbara Butterworth) *led: rdn and hdd 2 out: rallied: lost 2nd appr last: kpt on same pce run-in* **4/1**[2]

050- **4** *49* **Young Jay**[59] 4345 4-9-11 **97** RyanDClark(7) 38
(Andrew Crook) *nt fluent on occasions: in tch: drvn and outpcd bef 4 out: rallied and cl up next: wknd bef 2 out: t.o* **28/1**

P04- **P** **Damascus Steel (IRE)**[28] 4952 6-11-5 **106** LucyAlexander
(Alison Hamilton) *t.k.h: hld up in tch: drvn and outpcd 1/2-way: struggling whn mstke 3 out: lost tch and p.u bef next* **17/2**

4m 45.1s (-23.70) **Going Correction** -1.05s/f (Hard) course record
WFA 4 from 5yo+ 5lb **5** Ran SP% **106.2**
Speed ratings (Par 105): **105,104,102,83,**
CSF £4.86 TOTE £1.60: £1.10, £2.30; EX 3.60 Trifecta £9.20.
Owner Straightline Construction Ltd **Bred** Juergen Imm **Trained** Carluke, S Lanarks
■ Stewards' Enquiry : Wilson Renwick one-day ban: careless riding (May 3)

FOCUS
Hurdles races on Inner course with hurdles and bends moved out three metres. An uncompetitive handicap, and favourite backers had few worrying moments. The winner has more to offer given his Flat form.

5376 £3 MILLION TOTESCOOP6 TODAY NOVICES' CHASE (15 fncs 1 omitted) — 2m 4f

1:55 (1:55) (Class 3) 5-Y-O+ **£6,498** (£1,908; £954; £477)

Form — RPR

P1P- **1** **Clondaw Hero (IRE)**[76] 4052 6-10-12 0 WilsonRenwick 122
(Donald McCain) *chsd clr ldr: clsd after 7th: rdn along after 5 out: rallied next: led 3 out: drvn and styd on wl fr last* **9/4**[2]

113- **2** *1 1/2* **Mitchell's Way**[22] 5053 7-11-8 128 AlainCawley 133
(Alan Swinbank) *nt fluent in rr: hdwy whn mstke 9th: effrt and clsng whn hit 3 out: rallied to chse wnr bef last: drifted lft and kpt on run-in: nt gng pce to chal* **4/7**[1]

00F- **3** *36* **Ziggie (IRE)**[27] 4984 7-10-12 105 (t) HenryBrooke 97+
(Donald McCain) *nt fluent on occasions: led and clr: pckd 2nd: rdn and hdd 3 out: nt fluent next: 3rd and outpcd whn blnd last* **25/1**

PP6- **4** *70* **Picks Milan (IRE)**[11] 5216 8-10-12 105 (t) JamesReveley 24
(Philip Kirby) *chsd clr ldng pair: struggling bef 8th: lost tch 5 out: t.o* **12/1**[3]

5m 5.9s (-21.50) **Going Correction** -0.925s/f (Hard) **4** Ran SP% **106.0**
Speed ratings: **106,105,91,63**
CSF £4.00 TOTE £2.90; EX 4.10 Trifecta £8.30.
Owner D McCain Jnr **Bred** P J Fortune **Trained** Cholmondeley, Cheshire
■ Stewards' Enquiry : Wilson Renwick two-day ban: used whip above permitted level (May 5-6)

FOCUS
A novice which effectively developed into a match. The winner is rated to his hurdles mark.

5377 DOWNLOAD THE TOTEPOOL LIVE INFO APP H'CAP HURDLE (8 hdls) — 2m 1f

2:30 (2:30) (Class 4) (0-115,115) 4-Y-O+ **£3,573** (£1,049; £524; £262)

Form — RPR

F36- **1** **Lone Foot Laddie (IRE)**[35] 4813 5-10-11 **107** GrahamWatters(7) 107
(Lucinda Russell) *hld up in tch: smooth hdwy to ld 2 out: rdn and sn hrd pressed: kpt on wl to assert towards fin* **5/1**[3]

650- **2** *1* **Super Collider**[222] 1544 7-10-9 **108** (bt) JamesCorbett(10) 107
(Susan Corbett) *t.k.h: led at stdy gallop: rdn and hdd whn hit 2 out: sn rdn and ev ch tl no ex towards fin* **18/1**

42- **3** *3 1/4* **May's Boy**[131] 2998 6-10-12 **106** CraigNichol(5) 104
(James Moffatt) *in tch: nt fluent 3 out: rdn and sltly outpcd bef next: rallied bef last: kpt on run-in* **7/1**

441- **4** *9* **Vinstar (FR)**[27] 4980 5-11-5 **115** (t) NickSlatter(7) 105
(Donald McCain) *pressed ldr: hit 4th: rdn and ev ch whn hit 2 out: sn outpcd* **11/8**[1]

625- **5** *1* **Quick Brew**[22] 5057 6-11-0 **110** (t) DaraghBourke(7) 97
(Maurice Barnes) *chsd ldrs: effrt and rdn appr 2 out: wknd between last 2* **5/2**[2]

120/ **6** *13* **Bivouac (UAE)**[18] 10-10-13 **102** AlainCawley 80
(Alan Swinbank) *nt fluent on occasions: plld hrd: in tch: struggling after 3 out: btn bef next* **28/1**

4m 13.2s (-16.00) **Going Correction** -1.05s/f (Hard) **6** Ran SP% **108.6**
Speed ratings (Par 105): **95,94,93,88,88 82**
CSF £63.78 CT £559.71 TOTE £7.70: £3.30, £5.10; EX 71.10 Trifecta £273.90.
Owner Dr John Wilson **Bred** Mountarmstrong Stud **Trained** Arlary, Perth & Kinross

FOCUS
Just an ordinary handicap, but it provided Lucinda Russell with the victory she needed to set a new record for the number of wins in a season by a Scottish-based trainer. The first three are rated pretty much to their marks.

5378 TOTEPOOL HOME OF POOL BETTING H'CAP CHASE (15 fncs 1 omitted) — 2m 4f

3:05 (3:05) (Class 3) (0-135,132) 5-Y-O+ **£7,147** (£2,098; £1,049; £524)

Form — RPR

/30- **1** **Carlito Brigante (IRE)**[36] 4789 8-11-8 **128** JamesReveley 140+
(Karen McLintock) *chsd ldr to after 7th: cl up: smooth hdwy to ld after 3 out: drew clr fr next: easily* **9/4**[1]

555- **2** *8* **Stagecoach Pearl**[28] 4955 10-11-0 **127** DaraghBourke(7) 129
(Sue Smith) *taken early to post: cl up: led 7th to after 3 out: rdn and kpt on same pce fr next* **4/1**[3]

1P3- **3** *19* **Billy Cuckoo (IRE)**[47] 4593 8-11-1 **121** (b) WilsonRenwick 108
(Tony Coyle) *led to 8th: cl up tl rdn and outpcd 4 out: plugged on to take modest 3rd run-in: no imp* **11/4**[2]

000- **4** *1/2* **Lucky Landing (IRE)**[15] 5156 8-11-5 **132** MrJHamilton(7) 116
(Tony Coyle) *hld up in tch: stdy hdwy 5 out: rdn and outpcd next: no imp fr 3 out* **4/1**[3]

2F4- **5** *8* **Storming Gale (IRE)**[46] 4610 8-11-1 **121** (tp) HenryBrooke 101
(Donald McCain) *mstkes: in tch: rdn along whn hit 3 out: no imp: no ch whn lost 3rd run-in* **8/1**

5m 4.8s (-22.60) **Going Correction** -0.925s/f (Hard) **5** Ran SP% **108.5**
Speed ratings: **108,104,97,97,93**
CSF £11.04 TOTE £2.70: £1.40, £2.40; EX 8.10 Trifecta £32.50.
Owner 06 Zoo Ltd **Bred** Ballylinch Stud **Trained** Ingoe, Northumberland

FOCUS
A weak race for the money, and three of the five ran well below form. The first two were thrown in on old form.

5379 LIVE SCOOP6 INFORMATION AT TOTEPOOL.COM H'CAP HURDLE (12 hdls) — 3m 1f

3:40 (3:40) (Class 3) (0-130,122) 4-Y-O+ **£5,685** (£1,669; £834; £417)

Form — RPR

103- **1** **Mr Utah**[34] 4834 7-11-8 **121** TonyKelly(3) 126+
(Henry Hogarth) *led to bef 6th: cl up: smooth hdwy to regain ld whn nt fluent 2 out: rdn and styd on wl fr last* **6/1**[3]

4PF- **2** *1* **Howizee**[8] 5256 8-11-5 **122** (t) DaraghBourke(7) 127+
(Maurice Barnes) *hld up in tch: pushed along after 3 out: n.m.r bef next: hdwy between last 2: styd on fr last to take 2nd nr fin* **15/8**[1]

PF0- **3** *shd* **American Life (FR)**[28] 4949 7-10-6 **107** (vt) JamesBanks(5) 110
(Anthony Middleton) *hld up: rdn after 3 out: hdwy next: ev ch and hung rt after last: sn chsng wnr: no ex and lost 2nd nr fin* **17/2**

/PU- **4** *3 1/4* **Aggie's Lad (IRE)**[143] 2746 12-10-2 **105** MrJHamilton(7) 105
(Alison Hamilton) *t.k.h: cl up: led bef 6th to bef 2 out: rallied: drvn and outpcd fr last* **50/1**

313/ **5** *1 1/2* **Tartan Tiger (IRE)**[687] 524 8-10-11 **107** JamesReveley 108
(John Quinn) *plld hrd: cl up: rdn along whn nt fluent 2 out: nt fluent last: kpt on same pce* **4/1**[2]

504- **6** *1/2* **Alderley Rover (IRE)**[28] 4949 10-11-12 **122** HenryBrooke 120
(Donald McCain) *hld up: rdn and outpcd bef 3 out: rallied next: rdn and no further imp bef last* **11/1**

305- **7** *29* **Maybe I Wont**[29] 4941 9-11-2 **117** (p) CraigNichol(5) 89
(James Moffatt) *nt fluent in rr: struggling fnl circ: nvr on terms* **18/1**

8 *20* **Maple Valley Gold (IRE)**[27] 4996 6-10-1 **104** MissRBlackmore(7) 58
(Liam Lennon, Ire) *chsd ldrs tl rdn and wknd qckly bef 2 out: t.o* **20/1**

404- **9** *10* **Master Of The Hall (IRE)**[19] 5105 10-11-2 **112** WilsonRenwick 57
(Micky Hammond) *prom tl rdn and wknd qckly bef 2 out: t.o* **12/1**

/35- **10** *62* **Devotion To Duty (IRE)**[161] 2357 8-11-12 **122**................(tp) BarryKeniry 11
(Philip Kirby) *midfield on ins: drvn and outpcd 8th: lost tch after next: eased whn no ch fnl 2: t.o* **25/1**

6m 13.7s (-25.30) **Going Correction** -1.05s/f (Hard) **10** Ran SP% **111.5**
Speed ratings (Par 107): **98,97,97,96,96 95,86,80,77,57**
CSF £16.93 CT £91.91 TOTE £5.60: £2.00, £1.60, £2.30; EX 20.50 Trifecta £168.20.
Owner Hogarth Racing **Bred** Dr B Mayoh **Trained** Stillington, N Yorks

FOCUS
A fair staying event. A good effort from the winner to beat a well-in rival.

5380 BEST ODDS GUARANTEED AT TOTEPOOL.COM H'CAP CHASE (11 fncs 1 omitted) 2m

4:10 (4:10) (Class 4) (0-120,120) 5-Y-0+ **£4,223** (£1,240; £620; £310)

Form RPR

541- **1** **Baileys Concerto (IRE)**[19] 5107 8-10-6 **100**.................... JamesReveley 111+
(Dianne Sayer) *chsd ldrs: sltly outpcd after 5 out: shkn up and rallied next: wnt 2nd bef 2 out: led last: pushed along and sn clr* **7/4**[2]

332- **2** *6* **Blackwater King (IRE)**[9] 5237 6-11-0 **108**.............. HenryBrooke 112
(Donald McCain) *t.k.h: cl up: led after 5 out: rdn bef 2 out: hdd last: no ch w wnr* **11/8**[1]

466- **3** *24* **Star In Flight**[78] 4020 7-11-12 **120**.................................. WilsonRenwick 106
(Donald McCain) *nt fluent on occasions: t.k.h: led to after 5 out: rdn and wknd appr 2 out* **5/1**[3]

26U- **4** *50* **Marleno (GER)**[9] 5243 8-9-9 **94** oh3...............................(t) JamesBanks[(5)] 51
(Anthony Middleton) *nt fluent in rr: struggling fr 5th: t.o* **7/1**

3m 57.8s (-18.30) **Going Correction** -0.925s/f (Hard) **4** Ran SP% **107.6**
Speed ratings: **108,105,93,68**
CSF £4.67 TOTE £3.60; EX 5.10 Trifecta £12.90.
Owner United Five Racing & Andrew Sayer **Bred** Ronan Keane **Trained** Hackthorpe, Cumbria

FOCUS
An uncompetitive handicap chase, though the winner is on a bit of a roll all of a sudden. Baileys Concerto built on his recent win.

5381 FOLLOW @TOTEPOOL ON TWITTER MARES' STANDARD OPEN NATIONAL HUNT FLAT RACE 2m 1f

4:40 (4:40) (Class 6) 4-6-Y-0 **£1,559** (£457; £228; £114)

Form RPR

1 **Chezzy (IRE)** 5-10-12 0.. AlainCawley 114+
(Fergal O'Brien) *chsd ldr: hdwy to ld 2f out: rdn clr fnl f* **4/1**[2]

1- **2** *12* **Jennys Melody (IRE)**[39] 4749 5-11-2 0........................ MrSCrawford[(3)] 113+
(B Arthey, Ire) *led: rdn and hdd 2f out: kpt on same pce fnl f* **7/4**[1]

3 *17* **Little Posh (IRE)** 5-10-12 0.. WilsonRenwick 88
(Peter Niven) *hld up: pushed along over 6f out: styd on fnl 2f: no ch w first two* **8/1**[3]

4 *25* **Tara Dee (IRE)** 5-10-9 0.. HarryChalloner[(3)] 65
(Andrew Wilson) *towards rr: pushed along 1/2-way: sme hdwy 2f out: nvr rchd ldrs* **33/1**

2- **5** *½* **Toarmandowithlove (IRE)**[19] 5109 6-10-2 0............. JamesCorbett[(10)] 65
(Susan Corbett) *t.k.h: hld up on outside: stdy hdwy over 6f out: rdn and no imp fr over 3f out* **14/1**

6 *nk* **Overtoyoulou** 6-10-5 0.. DiarmuidO'Regan[(7)] 64
(Chris Grant) *towards rr: drvn and struggling over 6f out: sme late hdwy: nvr on terms* **9/1**

7 *¾* **Dizoard** 4-10-7 0.. LucyAlexander 59
(Ollie Pears) *bhd: rdn along 1/2-way: plugged on fnl f: nvr on terms* **8/1**[3]

8 *3 ¼* **Broadway Belle** 4-10-7 0.. HenryBrooke 56
(Chris Grant) *hld up: hdwy to chse ldrs 6f out: rdn and wknd over 2f out* **20/1**

9 *12* **South Circle (IRE)**[42] 6-10-5 0................................... MissRBlackmore[(7)] 50
(Liam Lennon, Ire) *prom tl rdn and wknd over 4f out* **12/1**

4- **10** *15* **Silver Songstress**[144] 2731 4-10-2 0.............................. CraigNichol[(5)] 32
(John Weymes) *midfield: drvn and outpcd 1/2-way: struggling fnl 4f* **33/1**

11 *58* **Just Bee (IRE)** 5-10-5 0... DaleIrving[(7)]
(Rayson Nixon) *uns rdr bef s: prom: lost pl after 5f: sn struggling: virtually p.u fnl 2f: t.o* **50/1**

4m 7.3s (-16.90) **Going Correction** -1.05s/f (Hard)
WFA 4 from 5yo+ 5lb **11** Ran SP% **115.5**
Speed ratings: **97,91,83,71,71 71,70,69,63,56 29**
CSF £10.69 TOTE £7.30: £2.50, £1.40, £3.10; EX 15.60 Trifecta £95.50.
Owner Masterson Holdings Limited **Bred** Miss Margaret Masterson **Trained** Coln St. Dennis, Gloucs

FOCUS
No depth to this bumper and they finished well strung out, off what was a stronger gallop than you often get in these events. The winner looks decent.
T/Plt: £593.30 to a £1 stake. Pool: £42848.03 - 52.72 winning tickets T/Qpdt: £193.90 to a £1 stake. Pool: £2961.79 - 11.30 winning tickets RY

4890 HAYDOCK (L-H)

Saturday, April 19

OFFICIAL GOING: Good (good to soft in places; chs 6.0, hdl 6.1)
Wind: moderate 1/2 behind Weather: overcast

5382 MARIE TURNER EASTER BONNET MEMORIAL NOVICES' LIMITED H'CAP CHASE 2m

1:30 (1:30) (Class 3) (0-140,129) 5-Y-0+ **£6,498** (£1,908; £954; £477)

Form RPR

262- **1** **Witness In Court (IRE)**[6] 5289 7-11-7 **128**............................ NoelFehily 145+
(Donald McCain) *t.k.h: trckd ldrs: led sn after 9th: clr fr 3 out: easily* **7/2**[2]

013- **2** *13* **Kitegen (IRE)**[20] 5089 8-11-2 **123**...................................... CharliePoste 126
(Robin Dickin) *chsd ldrs 6th: drvn and 3rd appr 4 out: 2nd 2 out: no ch w wnr* **4/1**[3]

125- **3** *4* **Oyster Shell**[20] 5091 7-11-5 **129**................................ JakeGreenall[(3)] 130
(Henry Daly) *chsd ldrs 6th: 2nd appr 4 out: one pce* **4/1**[3]

2P5- **4** *27* **Un Bon P'Tit Gars (FR)**[49] 4560 6-10-13 **120**.......(t) SamTwiston-Davies 95
(Nick Williams) *led to 2nd: reminders 7th: drvn and lost pl 9th: poor 4th and hit 3 out: t.o* **7/2**[2]

5 *15* **Val D'Arc (FR)**[224] 5-11-6 **127**.. RichardJohnson 89
(Philip Hobbs) *w ldr: led 2nd: hdd sn after 9th: wknd qckly bef next: last whn hit 2 out: sn eased: t.o* **3/1**[1]

3m 52.3s (-18.70) **Going Correction** -0.975s/f (Hard) **5** Ran SP% **109.4**
Speed ratings: **107,100,98,85,77**
CSF £16.87 TOTE £3.50: £1.80, £2.40; EX 18.10 Trifecta £45.20.
Owner T G Leslie **Bred** Michael Ronayne **Trained** Cholmondeley, Cheshire

FOCUS
Course at innermost configuration and distances as advertised. Sam Twiston-Davies said after riding in the first that the ground was "just good." A fair race of its type with a step up from the impressive winner.

5383 BET AT CORBETTSPORTS.COM LEVY BOARD H'CAP CHASE 3m

2:05 (2:05) (Class 2) 5-Y-0+
£31,280 (£9,240; £4,620; £2,310; £1,155; £580)

Form RPR

146- **1** **No Planning**[28] 4953 7-10-6 **137**.. RyanMania 148+
(Sue Smith) *chsd ldrs: cl 2nd whn hit 14th: led 3 out: blnd next: drvn out* **16/1**

213- **2** *3* **Shotavodka (IRE)**[21] 5073 8-10-6 **137**............................ TomScudamore 142
(David Pipe) *hld up: hdwy to trck ldrs 10th: chsd wnr 2 out: kpt on same pce run-in* **12/1**

421- **3** *3 ½* **Firebird Flyer (IRE)**[51] 4509 7-9-7 **131** oh3......................... ConorRing[(7)] 136
(Evan Williams) *in rr: hdwy 9th: sn chsng ldrs: outpcd 3 out: mstke next: 4th last: styd on wl to take 3rd last 75yds* **5/1**[2]

101- **4** *3 ½* **Bold Chief (IRE)**[35] 4819 9-11-1 **146**................................(tp) NoelFehily 149+
(Harry Fry) *led: mstke 12th: hdd 3 out: modest 3rd whn hit last: wknd last 100yds* **4/1**[1]

P01- **5** *4 ½* **Hey Big Spender (IRE)**[20] 5092 11-11-2 **147**................ BrendanPowell 143
(Colin Tizzard) *trckd ldrs: lost pl after 4 out: kpt on run-in* **18/1**

12U- **6** *shd* **Cloudy Too (IRE)**[36] 4787 8-11-9 **157**........................ JonathanEngland[(3)] 156+
(Sue Smith) *j.rt and nt fluent in rr: bhd whn blnd 7th: sme hdwy 4 out: kpt on run-in* **10/1**

221- **7** *28* **Beforeall (IRE)**[13] 5184 6-9-9 **131** oh2........................... ThomasGarner[(5)] 110
(Oliver Sherwood) *chsd ldr: drvn 14th: sn lost pl and bhd: t.o 2 out: eased run-in: t.o* **7/1**[3]

304- **8** *6* **Kian's Delight**[14] 5170 6-10-0 **131** oh4.................................... JamieMoore 95
(Peter Bowen) *in rr: hdwy 9th: sn chsng ldrs: drvn and lost pl appr 4 out: sn bhd: t.o 2 out: eased last* **10/1**

665- **P** **Niceonefrankie**[8] 5261 8-10-1 **132**...................................... AidanColeman
(Venetia Williams) *chsd ldrs: drvn and lost pl bef 9th: sn bhd: t.o whn p.u bef 12th* **12/1**

3P6- **P** **Our Mick**[14] 5170 8-10-3 **134**... RichardJohnson
(Donald McCain) *chsd ldrs: drvn 9th: lost pl next: sn t.o: p.u bef 12th* **5/1**[2]

P0P- **P** **Mart Lane (IRE)**[15] 5156 9-10-6 **137**...................(b) SamTwiston-Davies
(Dr Richard Newland) *in rr: bmpd 5th: bhd 7th: p.u bef next* **25/1**

5m 41.5s (-32.50) **Going Correction** -0.975s/f (Hard) **11** Ran SP% **114.4**
Speed ratings: **115,114,112,111,110 110,100,98,,**
CSF £184.75 CT £1103.40 TOTE £16.80: £4.90, £3.50, £2.20; EX 256.00 Trifecta £1648.10.
Owner Mrs Jacqueline Conroy **Bred** Mrs S Johnson **Trained** High Eldwick, W Yorks

FOCUS
They went a strong pace in this valuable new race. Solid form, with the second to fourth all close to their marks.

5384 £3 MILLION TOTESCOOP6 TODAY H'CAP HURDLE (JOCKEY CLUB GRASSROOTS SERIES FINAL) 2m 4f

2:40 (2:40) (Class 2) 4-Y-0+
£31,280 (£9,240; £4,620; £2,310; £1,155; £580)

Form RPR

130- **1** **Carlton Jack**[17] 5128 7-10-11 **122**............................ MauriceLinehan[(5)] 129+
(Jonjo O'Neill) *t.k.h early: trckd ldrs: upsides last: styd on to ld last 50yds* **9/1**

114- **2** *1 ¾* **Heath Hunter (IRE)**[63] 4264 7-11-5 **125**...............(p) TomScudamore 131
(David Pipe) *trckd ldrs: cl 2nd whn hit 2 out: led between last 2: hdd and no ex last 50yds* **5/1**[1]

611- **3** *4* **Generous Ransom (IRE)**[17] 5128 6-11-3 **123**..................... JamieMoore 126
(Nick Gifford) *nt fluent: led tl after 1st: w ldr: led 5th: hit 2 out: hdd between last 2: kpt on same pce* **17/2**[3]

/23- **4** *shd* **Songsmith**[35] 4820 6-11-5 **125**.. AidanColeman 127
(Lucy Wadham) *hld up in mid-div: hdwy 7th: handy 5th whn hit 3 out: 4th last: kpt on* **14/1**

232- **5** *6* **Mojolika**[56] 4426 6-11-7 **127**.. BrianHarding 124
(Tim Easterby) *in rr: hdwy 7th: styd on fr next: nt rch ldrs* **14/1**

40R- **6** *7* **Ultimate**[77] 4039 8-11-3 **123**.. DannyCook 112
(Brian Ellison) *led after 1st: hdd 7th: hrd drvn appr 3 out: one pce* **20/1**

B21- **7** *nk* **Ben Cee Pee M (IRE)**[13] 5191 9-10-7 **120**...............(v) CraigGallagher[(7)] 109
(Brian Ellison) *nt fluent in last: kpt on fr 3 out: nvr on terms* **11/1**

415- **8** *nk* **Wily Fox**[21] 5075 7-10-11 **120**...(b[1]) JackQuinlan[(3)] 109
(James Eustace) *trckd ldrs: one pce fr 3 out* **40/1**

240- **9** *1 ½* **All That Remains (IRE)**[11] 4303 9-11-1 **121**.........(t) SamTwiston-Davies 108
(Brian Ellison) *in rr: kpt on fr 3 out: nvr on terms* **25/1**

300- **10** *¾* **Bourne**[28] 4949 8-11-1 **121**..(b) AdrianLane 108
(Donald McCain) *trckd ldrs: outpcd appr 3 out: sn wknd* **20/1**

211- **11** *1 ¾* **Keel Haul (IRE)**[52] 4503 6-11-5 **125**.................................. DenisO'Regan 110
(Henry Oliver) *trckd ldrs: effrt appr 3 out: sn wknd* **11/1**

411- **12** *3 ¼* **No No Mac (IRE)**[41] 4694 5-11-7 **127**.................................... NoelFehily 109
(Charlie Longsdon) *mid-div: hdwy 5th: lost pl appr 3 out* **7/1**[2]

510- **13** *1 ¼* **Lord Protector (IRE)**[35] 4805 7-11-6 **126**...................... RichardJohnson 107
(Philip Hobbs) *in rr: sme hdwy 7th: sn lost pl* **16/1**

1F1- **14** *3 ¾* **Getabuzz**[29] 4941 6-11-12 **132**..(b) DougieCostello 110
(Tim Easterby) *t.k.h: hdwy to trck ldrs 4th: lost pl and nt fluent 7th* **14/1**

040- **15** *1* **Orsippus (USA)**[76] 4056 8-11-5 **130**................................... AdamNicol[(5)] 107
(Michael Smith) *in rr: hdwy 4th: chsng ldrs next: lost pl 7th* **11/1**

041- **16** *6* **Hold Court (IRE)**[9] 5233 7-11-7 **127**..................................... PaulMoloney 98
(Evan Williams) *t.k.h in rr: hdwy 5th: lost pl after 7th: sn bhd* **14/1**

4m 33.0s (-20.00) **Going Correction** -0.975s/f (Hard) **16** Ran SP% **123.1**
Speed ratings (Par 109): **101,100,98,98,96 93,93,93,92,92 91,90,89,88,87 85**
CSF £52.09 CT £409.47 TOTE £12.60: £2.20, £1.80, £2.50, £3.60; EX 76.80 Trifecta £1197.90.
Owner John P McManus **Bred** A J Wall **Trained** Cheltenham, Gloucs

FOCUS
A good prize and a suitably competitive field for this series final. Not many got into it from the rear. Solid form, with the winner back on the upgrade.

5385 TOTESCOOP6 THE MILLIONAIRE MAKER H'CAP CHASE (JOCKEY CLUB GRASSROOTS SERIES FINAL) 2m 6f

3:15 (3:15) (Class 2) 5-Y-0+
£31,280 (£9,240; £4,620; £2,310; £1,155; £580)

Form RPR

F64- **1** **Streams Of Whiskey (IRE)**[48] 4572 7-10-10 **122**.............. BrianHarding 130+
(Nicky Richards) *mid-div: hdwy to trck ldrs 11th: styd on run-in: led clsng stages* **18/1**

62P- 2 ½ **Forest Walker (IRE)**[73] 4089 7-10-12 **124**........................(t) HarrySkelton 131
(Dan Skelton) *mid-div: hdwy 14th: sn chsng ldrs: led last 100yds: hdd towards fin* **12/1**

341- 3 ¾ **Hollow Blue Sky (FR)**[58] 4372 7-10-5 **117**.............. SamTwiston-Davies 124
(Nigel Twiston-Davies) *mid-div: hdwy 14th: hit next: chsng ldrs 3 out: led between last 2: hdd last 100yds: styd on same pce* **8/1**[2]

P2P- 4 4 ½ **Frontier Spirit (IRE)**[48] 4572 10-9-12 **117**........................(v) RyanHatch(7) 119
(Nigel Twiston-Davies) *chsd ldrs: led after 14th: hdd between last 2: one pce* **28/1**

62F- 5 11 **Saints And Sinners (IRE)**[32] 4894 6-10-0 **115**............(t) JakeGreenall(3) 109
(Michael Easterby) *chsd ldrs: drvn 14th: outpcd next: modest 6th whn mstke last* **8/1**[2]

/61- 6 hd **Midnight Sail**[42] 4685 11-11-11 **137**................................ RobertThornton 130
(Alan King) *chsd ldrs: one pce fr 3 out* **16/1**

61P- 7 nk **Lost Legend (IRE)**[15] 5156 7-11-0 **131**...........................(p) MauriceLinehan(5) 125
(Jonjo O'Neill) *mid-div: hdwy 5th: chsd ldrs 10th: one pce fr 4 out* **12/1**

133- 8 hd **Ultimatum Du Roy (FR)**[50] 4537 6-10-4 **116**................. DougieCostello 108
(Alex Hales) *in rr: kpt on fr 4 out: nvr on terms* **25/1**

333- 9 ½ **Cloudy Bob (IRE)**[35] 4806 7-10-13 **125**................................ ColinBolger 116
(Pat Murphy) *w ldr: led 8th to 10th: rdn 14th: lost pl appr next* **10/1**[3]

11F- 10 6 **King Massini (IRE)**[39] 4738 8-11-5 **131**.............................. AdamWedge 123
(Evan Williams) *mid-div: mstke 12th: hdwy 14th: one pce whn hmpd 3 out* **8/1**[2]

432- 11 6 **Munsaab (IRE)**[21] 5076 8-10-3 **115**..(t) PaulMoloney 105
(Charlie Longsdon) *mid-div: chsd ldrs 9th: lost pl bef 4 out: in rr whn bdly hmpd 3 out* **18/1**

PP1- 12 11 **Special Account (IRE)**[18] 5121 9-10-3 **115**.................... BrendanPowell 86
(Jeremy Scott) *in rr: hmpd 5th: bhd fr 4 out* **25/1**

430- 13 4 **Elenika (FR)**[35] 4806 6-10-9 **121**.. LiamTreadwell 88
(Venetia Williams) *in rr: drvn 10th: bhd fr 14th* **16/1**

F06- 14 4 ½ **Sunny Ledgend**[28] 4949 9-10-3 **122**.. MrJMartin(7) 85
(Andrew J Martin) *nt fluent in rr: mstke 2nd: bhd whn blnd 14th* **20/1**

210- P **Shangani (USA)**[37] 4768 8-11-12 **138**................................ AidanColeman
(Venetia Williams) *in rr: hmpd 5th: bhd fr 14th: t.o whn p.u bef 3 out* **25/1**

114- F **Wood Yer (IRE)**[60] 4339 8-10-5 **117**................................(bt[1]) BrianHughes
(Nigel Twiston-Davies) *in tch: fell 5th* **33/1**

/P0- F **Tiptoeaway (IRE)**[31] 4900 9-10-11 **123**................................(t) DannyCook
(Tim Easterby) *mde most to 8th: led 10th: hdd after 14th: 4th and looking hld whn fell 3 out* **20/1**

311- P **Bincombe**[31] 4898 6-10-7 **119**... RichardJohnson
(Philip Hobbs) *hld up in mid-div: lost pl bef 4 out: t.o whn p.u bef last* **6/1**[1]

P15- F **Vif Argent (FR)**[17] 5126 5-10-13 **125**...............................(b) TomScudamore
(David Pipe) *mid-div whn hit 1st and rdr briefly lost iron: chsd ldrs 6th: wkng whn fell 3 out* **25/1**

5m 23.2s (-17.80) **Going Correction** -0.975s/f (Hard) **19** Ran SP% **125.7**
Speed ratings: **93,92,92,90,86 86,86,86,86,84 82,78,76,75, , , ,**
CSF £196.74 CT £1891.99 TOTE £26.80: £5.80, £4.00, £2.10, £7.80; EX 405.90 Trifecta £3986.40.
Owner Mr & Mrs R Kelvin-Hughes **Bred** Miss Ann Hennessy **Trained** Greystoke, Cumbria
■ Stewards' Enquiry : Harry Skelton two-day ban: used whip above permitted level (May 3,5)

FOCUS
A very well contested series final, and solid handicap form, for all that some of these weren't at their best. There was a bunch finish. The winner is rated in line with his autumn falls.

5386 FOLLOW TOTESCOOP6 AT TOTEPOOLLIVEINFO.COM TIM MOLONY H'CAP CHASE 3m 4f
3:50 (3:50) (Class 3) (0-130,130) 5-Y-0+ **£8,122** (£2,385; £1,192; £596)

Form RPR

P43- 1 **Blenheim Brook (IRE)**[31] 4896 9-10-8 **112**......................... PeterBuchanan 119+
(Lucinda Russell) *hld up in rr: outpcd and pushed along 12th: hdwy to chse ldrs 15th: 2nd 17th: 6 l down whn j.rt 3 out: rallied and 4 l down 3rd whn nt fluent last: styd on wl to ld last strides* **13/2**

415- 2 nk **Woodford County**[32] 4886 7-11-4 **122**..........................(p) RichardJohnson 128
(Philip Hobbs) *chsd ldng pair: lft cl 2nd 13th: lft in ld 16th: edgd lft run-in: hdd post* **11/2**

P21- 3 7 **Fentara**[12] 5210 9-11-9 **130**...(t) JakeGreenall(3) 135+
(Mark Walford) *pckd 1st: nt fluent and reminders 3rd: chsd ldrs 13th: hmpd 16th: 2nd 5 out: upsides whn nt fluent next: rdn 2 out: wknd last 75yds* **9/2**[3]

014- 4 57 **Kilcrea Asla (IRE)**[42] 4675 13-10-11 **120**.......................... KillianMoore(5) 68
(Graeme McPherson) *in rr: drvn 11th: lft 4th 13th: drvn and nt fluent next: lost pl and hmpd 16th: sn bhd: t.o 4 out* **16/1**

PU5- P **Red Rocco (IRE)**[35] 4821 7-11-9 **127**....................(v) SamTwiston-Davies
(Nigel Twiston-Davies) *led to 6th: led 9th to 11th: chsng ldr whn p.u bef 13th: fatally injured* **2/1**[1]

121- F **Bennys Well (IRE)**[31] 4896 8-10-5 **112**......................... JonathanEngland(3)
(Sue Smith) *nt fluent: w ldr: reminders 5th: led next: hdd 9th: led 11th: fell 16th* **11/4**[2]

7m 7.7s (-8.30) **Going Correction** -0.975s/f (Hard) **6** Ran SP% **112.8**
Speed ratings: **72,71,69,53,**
CSF £39.97 TOTE £7.40: £2.70, £3.10; EX 46.20 Trifecta £304.10.
Owner The County Set Three **Bred** Richard Frisby **Trained** Arlary, Perth & Kinross

5387 BET ON YOUR MOBILE AT CORBETTSPORTS.COM "FIXED BRUSH" NOVICES' H'CAP HURDLE 2m 4f
4:20 (4:20) (Class 3) (0-135,132) 4-8-Y-0 **£8,122** (£2,385; £1,192; £596)

Form RPR

110- 1 **Horizontal Speed (IRE)**[42] 4680 6-11-12 **132**.............. RichardJohnson 138+
(Philip Hobbs) *trckd ldr: led appr 3 out: 3 l clr last: hrd drvn: hld on* **6/1**[3]

1P1- 2 2 **Horatio Hornblower (IRE)**[29] 4937 6-11-2 **129**................. MissEKelly(7) 132
(Nick Williams) *nt fluent: mstke 1st: shkn up and chsd ldrs 6th: reminders and 2nd 3 out: kpt on same pce run-in* **9/4**[1]

511- 3 6 **Wake Your Dreams (IRE)**[231] 1467 6-11-5 **125**................ SeanQuinlan 123
(Jennie Candlish) *lft 4th 3rd: chsd ldrs 5th: 3rd and outpcd 3 out: hit next: one pce* **12/1**

421- 4 25 **Kilgefin Star (IRE)**[28] 4956 6-11-10 **130**....................... BrianHughes 105
(Michael Smith) *chsd ldrs: drvn and lost pl 7th: sn wl bhd: t.o whn hit 2 out: distant 4th run-in* **11/1**

11F- 5 7 **Classic Move (IRE)**[42] 4680 5-11-9 **129**............................ NoelFehily 101
(Donald McCain) *t.k.h: nt fluent: led: hdd appr 3 out: sn lost pl: distant 4th whn hit 2 out: t.o* **7/2**[2]

461- B **Garrahalish (IRE)**[31] 4901 6-11-8 **128**........................... CharliePoste
(Robin Dickin) *in tch whn b.d 3rd* **14/1**

12F- F **It's A Doddle (IRE)**[70] 4161 6-10-6 **117**.......................(t) MauriceLinehan(5)
(Jonjo O'Neill) *hld up: trcking ldrs whn fell 3rd* **7/2**[2]

4m 32.1s (-20.90) **Going Correction** -0.975s/f (Hard) course record **7** Ran SP% **112.2**
Speed ratings: **102,101,98,88,86 ,**
CSF £19.67 TOTE £5.70: £2.20, £1.60; EX 24.20 Trifecta £113.90.
Owner Favourites Racing **Bred** Dick White **Trained** Withycombe, Somerset

FOCUS
A decent little race. The form makes sense.

5388 FOLLOW US ON TWITTER @HAYDOCKPARKRACES STANDARD OPEN NATIONAL HUNT FLAT RACE 2m
4:50 (4:50) (Class 5) 4-6-Y-O **£1,949** (£572; £286; £143)

Form RPR

1- 1 **Blaklion**[23] 5042 5-11-9 0... SamTwiston-Davies 118+
(Nigel Twiston-Davies) *led at v stdy pce: increased gallop 7f out: rdn and narrowly hdd over 1f out: kpt on gamely to regain ld last 100yds: styd on* **5/4**[1]

221- 2 1 ¼ **Degooch (IRE)**[48] 4582 5-11-9 0... NoelFehily 117
(Donald McCain) *trckd ldr: 2nd over 4f out: chal over 2f out: led narrowly over 1f out: rdn and edgd lft: hdd and no ex ins fnl f* **5/1**[2]

/05- 3 3 **Allbarnone**[83] 3926 6-11-2 0... DougieCostello 107
(William Kinsey) *hld up in mid-div: chsd ldrs over 3f out: one pce fnl 2f* **22/1**

4 1 ¾ **Allysson Monterg (FR)** 4-10-11 0.................................. RichardJohnson 100
(Victor Dartnall) *trckd ldrs: drvn 4f out: hung lft 2f out: one pce* **7/1**[3]

5 1 **Howwrongcanyoube** 5-11-2 0.. RobertThornton 104
(Alan King) *sn trcking ldrs: drvn 4f out: one pce fnl 2f* **5/1**[2]

5- 6 4 **Beautiful Gem (FR)**[57] 4403 4-10-4 0.................................. HarrySkelton 88
(Dan Skelton) *hld up in rr: drvn over 3f out: lost pl 2f out* **14/1**

7 1 ½ **Kwo Neshe (IRE)** 4-10-11 0.. BrianHughes 94
(Malcolm Jefferson) *hld up in rr: sme hdwy over 3f out: lost pl over 1f out* **12/1**

8 24 **Barrow Nook** 4-10-11 0... RyanMania 70
(Chris Grant) *hld up in rr: effrt on outer 6f out: sn lost pl: bhd fnl 4f: t.o 2f out* **22/1**

3m 40.6s (-18.00) **Going Correction** -0.975s/f (Hard)
WFA 4 from 5yo+ 5lb **8** Ran SP% **113.3**
Speed ratings: **106,105,103,103,102 100,99,87**
CSF £7.50 TOTE £2.20: £1.02, £1.80, £5.00; EX 5.90 Trifecta £59.20.
Owner Mrs S Such **Bred** Mrs M D W Morrison **Trained** Naunton, Gloucs

FOCUS
This bumper was won by the ill-fated Darlan three years ago. They stood still for quite a while once the tapes went up. The winner is rated below the level of his Ffos Las win.
T/Jkpt: Not won. T/Plt: £1,287.00, to a £1 stake. Pool of £151683.45 - 86.03 winning tickets.
T/Qpdt: £188.60 to a £1 stake. Pool of £12557.30 - 49.25 winning tickets. WG

[5117]NEWTON ABBOT (L-H)
Saturday, April 19
OFFICIAL GOING: Good (good to firm in places; 7.0)
Wind: fresh behind Weather: sunny

5389 AT THE RACES VIRGIN 534 "NATIONAL HUNT" NOVICES' HURDLE (9 hdls) 2m 3f
2:10 (2:11) (Class 4) 4-Y-0+ **£3,508** (£1,030; £515; £257)

Form RPR

224- 1 **Howlongisafoot (IRE)**[20] 5093 5-10-13 125...................... NickScholfield 124+
(Paul Nicholls) *trckd ldrs: rdn bef 3 out: squeezed through on inner to ld 2 out: styd on: rdn out* **4/7**[1]

233- 2 9 **Cool George**[25] 5015 6-10-10 118.. JamesBest(3) 116
(Jackie Du Plessis) *diputed ld tl rdn after 3 out: ch next: styng on at same pce whn lft 2nd at the last* **5/2**[2]

P0- 3 83 **Lord Carrigross (IRE)**[18] 5117 7-10-6 0................................ MrCSmith(7) 41
(Linda Blackford) *trckd ldrs: hit 3rd: rdn appr 6th: sn wknd: t.o* **80/1**

05- 4 14 **Wolfe Mountain (IRE)**[69] 4177 5-10-10 0..................... MichealNolan(3) 29
(Linda Blackford) *hld up: lost tch 6th: t.o* **16/1**

P03- F **Rody (FR)**[18] 5120 9-10-8 122..................................(t) AodhaganConlon(5) 118
(Tom George) *led: rdn and hdd 2 out: styng on at same pce in hld 2nd whn fell heavily last* **7/2**[3]

006- P **Brogeen Boy (IRE)**[6] 5308 6-10-13 0...................................... LiamHeard
(Alan Jones) *t.k.h: lost tch after 5th: t.o whn p.u bef 2* **33/1**

060- P **Mrs Winchester (IRE)**[9] 5236 5-10-6 0................................... IanPopham
(Caroline Keevil) *hit 1st: sn hld up last: lost tch 6th: t.o whn p.u 2 out* **50/1**

00- F **Kayf Charmer**[40] 4735 4-9-11 0.. GavinSheehan(3)
(Stuart Howe) *hld up: lost tch w front 3 bef 6th: modest 4th whn stmbld and fell between last 2* **50/1**

4m 30.1s (0.10) **Going Correction** 0.0s/f (Good)
WFA 4 from 5yo+ 5lb **8** Ran SP% **128.4**
Speed ratings (Par 105): **99,95,60,54, , ,**
CSF £3.00 TOTE £1.50: £1.02, £1.10, £15.40; EX 2.60 Trifecta £87.00.
Owner P J Vogt **Bred** G Merrigan **Trained** Ditcheat, Somerset
■ Stewards' Enquiry : Nick Scholfield three-day ban: careless riding (May 3,5,6)

FOCUS
All rails moved but impact on distances not quantified. A modest novice hurdle that went to the hot favourite. The form is rated around the front two.

5390 ST AUSTELL BREWERY H'CAP CHASE (20 fncs) 3m 2f 110y
2:45 (2:46) (Class 4) (0-110,110) 5-Y-0+ **£3,898** (£1,144; £572; £286)

Form RPR

331- 1 **Ruapehu (IRE)**[6] 5309 8-11-1 99 7ex................................ NickScholfield 115+
(Charles Whittaker) *mde virtually all: clr fr 15th: nt fluent 3 out (water): unchal* **8/11**[1]

320- 2 14 **Tickatack (IRE)**[101] 3603 9-11-0 **101**........................ GavinSheehan(3) 103
(Graeme McPherson) *trckd ldrs: rdn whn short of room after 16th: kpt pressing for hld 2nd fr next: wnt 2nd after 2 out: no ch w wnr* **9/2**[2]

251- 3 10 **Duneen Point (IRE)**[26] 5006 10-11-12 **110**...................... MichaelByrne 106
(Tim Vaughan) *trckd ldrs: disp 2nd 11th: blnd 14th: rdn after next: hld by wnr fr 3 out: blnd 2 out: sn lost 2nd and wknd* **8/1**[3]

32P- 4 19 **Present To You (IRE)**[42] 4678 9-11-5 **110**....................... JakeHodson(7) 86
(David Bridgwater) *trckd wnr: nudged along fr 6th: lost pl 11th: bhd and rdn 13th: got bk amongst chsng gp 15th: wknd 3 out: t.o* **14/1**

130- P **Health Is Wealth (IRE)**[191] 1830 9-11-0 **103**..........(p) ConorShoemark(5)
(Colin Tizzard) *trckd ldrs: rdn after 13th: wknd 15th: t.o whn p.u bef 3 out* **9/1**

1P5- **P** **He's The Daddy**[26] 5004 7-11-2 **107**................................(v) MrJBargary(7)
(Nigel Twiston-Davies) *trckd ldrs: nt fluent 1st and 5th: hit 12th: rdn after 15th: wknd after next: t.o whn p.u after 3 out* **11/1**

6m 26.6s (-18.00) **Going Correction** -0.45s/f (Good) **6** Ran SP% **112.2**
Speed ratings: **108,103,100,95,**
CSF £4.79 TOTE £2.00: £1.30, £2.20; EX 4.20 Trifecta £13.70.
Owner C R Whittaker **Bred** Miss Mary McCabe **Trained** Radstock, Somerset

FOCUS
A low-grade and uncompetitive handicap that was won in dominant fashion. There's probably more to come from the winner.

5391 SOUTH WEST RACING CLUB H'CAP HURDLE (10 hdls) 2m 6f
3:20 (3:21) (Class 4) (0-115,115) 4-Y-0+ **£3,508** (£1,030; £515; £257)

Form RPR

12P- **1** **The Rattler Obrien (IRE)**[69] 4172 8-10-13 **102**.................. HaddenFrost 108
(Martin Hill) *trckd ldrs: chal after 3 out: led bef next: sn in command: kpt on wl: rdn out* **13/2**[3]

345- **2** *7* **My Legal Lady**[46] 4599 9-11-2 **105**..............................(v) AndrewThornton 106
(Stuart Howe) *trckd ldrs: rdn after 3 out: wnt 2nd and nt fluent 2 out: styd on but a being hld by wnr* **10/1**

0P4- **3** *2 ½* **Look For Love**[25] 5019 6-10-13 **107**.......................... MissLucyGardner(5) 107+
(Sue Gardner) *hld up: hdwy 4th: nodded on landing 7th: rdn to chse ldrs after 3 out: wnt 3rd next: styng on at same pce in hld 3rd whn hit last* **9/2**[2]

646- **4** *shd* **Back In June**[17] 5128 6-11-4 **107**... TomO'Brien 105
(Paul Henderson) *hld up: pushed along after 6th: rdn after next: mo imp tl styd on fr 2 out: nvr threatened ldrs* **8/1**

440- **5** *10* **The Good Guy (IRE)**[184] 1945 11-10-7 **99**................... GavinSheehan(3) 89
(Graeme McPherson) *in tch: in last pair whn hit 5th: rdn after 3 out: plugged on: nvr any threat* **25/1**

454- **6** *nk* **Dan's Wee Man**[24] 5034 5-11-6 **109**..........................(p) DominicElsworth 98
(Andy Turnell) *hld up: pushed along after 6th: sme hdwy 3 out: sn rdn: wknd bef next* **8/1**

524- **7** *6* **King Rolfe (IRE)**[42] 4674 6-11-9 **112**..............................(t) MichaelByrne 98
(Tim Vaughan) *led tl after 2nd: trckd ldr: led 6th tl next: led 3 out: rdn and hdd bef 2 out: sn wknd* **14/1**

222- **8** *3 ¾* **Lumpys Gold**[135] 2908 6-11-12 **115**...............................(t) NickScholfield 97
(Paul Nicholls) *plld hrd: led after 2nd: mstke and hdd 6th: led next: hdd whn hit 3 out: sn rdn: wknd bef next* **7/4**[1]

63P- **P** **Russie With Love**[93] 3731 8-11-5 **108**................................ JamesDavies
(Chris Down) *in tch: reminders after 5th: rdn after 6th: wknd next: t.o whn p.u after 3 out: b.b.vs* **14/1**

5m 17.2s (-3.00) **Going Correction** 0.0s/f (Good) **9** Ran SP% **116.4**
Speed ratings (Par 105): **105,102,101,101,97 97,95,94,**
CSF £68.31 CT £323.95 TOTE £6.20: £2.00, £2.30, £1.70; EX 60.20 Trifecta £471.80.
Owner Spirit Of Devon **Bred** James Maher **Trained** Littlehempston, Devon

FOCUS
Moderate form, with the favourite disappointing. A personal best from the winner.

5392 SIS TOP ATA DELIVERY H'CAP CHASE (13 fncs) 2m 110y
3:55 (3:58) (Class 2) (0-150,148) 5-Y-0+ **£12,660** (£3,740; £1,870; £936; £468)

Form RPR

030- **1** **Changing The Guard**[16] 5136 8-11-1 **137**........................(tp) TomO'Brien 149+
(Dr Richard Newland) *mde all: nt fluent 3 out: in command whn mstke 2 out: hit last: kpt on wl* **5/2**[2]

011- **2** *4* **Sonofagun (FR)**[30] 4921 8-9-9 **122**............................... RobertMcCarth(5) 129+
(Ian Williams) *trckd ldrs: lft 2nd 5th: rdn after 9th: looking hld whn mstke and stmbld bdly 2 out: kpt on same pce* **9/4**[1]

5F6- **3** *6* **Oiseau De Nuit (FR)**[16] 5136 12-11-5 **148**........................... MrMLegg(7) 149
(Colin Tizzard) *chsd ldrs: dropped to last pair and nudged along: rdn after 7th: wnt 3rd 3 out: styd on same pce fr next* **4/1**[3]

200- **4** *12* **Lidar (FR)**[49] 4543 9-10-8 **137**...............................(b) StephenO'Donovan(7) 128
(Alan King) *hld up: lft 3rd at the 5th: rdn after 8th: dropped to 4th whn nt fluent 3 out: sn wknd* **14/1**

P30- **5** *4* **Shooters Wood (IRE)**[36] 4790 10-10-8 **133**................(t) HarryDerham(3) 117
(Paul Nicholls) *trckd ldr tl nt fluent 3rd: in last pair and pushed alng after 6th: nvr gng pce to get bk on terms: wknd 3 out* **10/1**

556- **F** **Saved By John (IRE)**[35] 4806 9-9-11 **129**......................(t) AlanJohns(10)
(Tim Vaughan) *trcking wnr whn fell 5th* **9/2**

3m 53.7s (-12.80) **Going Correction** -0.45s/f (Good) **6** Ran SP% **113.3**
Speed ratings: **112,110,107,101,99**
CSF £9.08 TOTE £3.50: £1.80, £1.80; EX 10.80 Trifecta £35.30.
Owner Jim Stewart **Bred** R A Bonnycastle And Marston Stud **Trained** Claines, Worcs

FOCUS
Little got into this decent handicap. A biggish personal best from the winner.

5393 HAPPY 60TH BIRTHDAY GEOFF LANG MARES' MAIDEN HURDLE (7 hdls 1 omitted) 2m 1f
4:25 (4:25) (Class 5) 4-Y-0+ **£2,737** (£798; £399)

Form RPR

4F2- **1** **Enchanting Smile (FR)**[6] 5304 7-10-7 86...........(t) ThomasCheesman(7) 97+
(Mark Gillard) *mde all: clr whn rn wd by paddock entrnce after 4th: clr again by-passing omitted 5th: kpt on gamely fr 2 out: rdn out* **3/1**[2]

2- **2** *3 ½* **Northern Meeting (IRE)**[30] 4910 4-10-9 0.............................. TomO'Brien 86
(Robert Stephens) *in tch: wnt 2nd bef 3 out: rdn and j. sltly lft: last 2: kpt on but a being readily hld* **11/4**[1]

FF0- **3** *6* **Miss Fortywinks**[25] 5026 5-10-11 0.......................... WayneKavanagh(3) 86
(Seamus Mullins) *hld up towards rr: midfield 4th: rdn after 3 out: styd on fr next: wnt 3rd at the last* **20/1**

4 *3 ½* **Rainbow Beauty**[155] 4-10-4 0.................................. AodhaganConlon(5) 79
(Tom George) *trckd ldrs: rdn to chse ldng pair after 3 out tl no ex fr last* **5/1**[3]

P5- **5** *16* **Ice Nelly (IRE)**[14] 5175 6-10-7 0......................................(t) MikeyEnnis(7) 69
(Stuart Kittow) *hld up towards rr: wnt modest 5th bef 2 out: nvr any threat* **20/1**

0- **6** *14* **Maxford Lady (IRE)**[21] 5077 5-11-0 0.............................. AndrewTinkler 55
(Jamie Snowden) *trckd ldrs: rdn after 3 out: sn wknd: t.o* **33/1**

545- **7** *15* **Present Trend (IRE)**[9] 5245 5-10-11 0.......................... KielanWoods(3) 42
(Charlie Longsdon) *trckd ldrs: rdn appr 3 out: sn wknd: t.o* **12/1**

3/U- **8** *7* **Dance**[33] 2906 5-11-0 0.. JamesDavies 36
(Rod Millman) *mid-div: hit 2nd: wknd after 3 out: t.o* **14/1**

9 *11* **Marishi Ten (IRE)**[44] 4-10-9 0.. SamJones 21
(Jo Davis) *trckd wnr tl rdn 3 out: sn wknd: t.o* **50/1**

050- **10** *62* **Colin's Nightmare**[318] 631 6-11-0 0.................................. DaveCrosse
(Nick Mitchell) *a towards rr: t.o bef omitted 5th* **66/1**

11 *1 ¾* **Morgana**[18] 6-11-0 0.. NickScholfield
(Simon Hodgson) *hmpd 1st: nvr fluent after: t.o bef omitted 5th* **50/1**

030- **P** **Reillys Daughter**[14] 5175 6-10-11 105.......................(b) GavinSheehan(3)
(Richard Mitchell) *nvr fluent: mid-div: struggling whn mstke 3 out: sn p.u (lame)* **11/1**

005- **F** **According To Sarah (IRE)**[18] 5117 6-10-11 95................ JamesBest(3)
(Philip Hobbs) *sltly hmpd whn fell heavily 1st* **8/1**

P **Miss Siskin** 5-11-0 0.. HaddenFrost
(James Frost) *bdly hmpd 1st: a in rr: t.o bef omitted 5th: p.u after 3 out* **40/1**

4m 1.1s (-4.60) **Going Correction** 0.0s/f (Good)
WFA 4 from 5yo+ 5lb **14** Ran SP% **122.5**
Speed ratings (Par 103): **110,108,105,103,96 89,82,79,74,45 44, , ,**
CSF £11.39 TOTE £5.30: £2.30, £1.20, £5.30; EX 15.70 Trifecta £241.90.
Owner N J McMullan **Bred** Sunny Days Limited & Michael Jarvis **Trained** Holwell, Dorset

FOCUS
Quite a lowly mares' hurdle that was dominated by the two at the head of the market. The winner will prove very well handicapped if left alone for this.

5394 NEWTONABBOTRACING.COM H'CAP CHASE (16 fncs) 2m 5f 110y
5:00 (5:00) (Class 5) (0-100,100) 5-Y-0+ **£3,079** (£897; £449)

Form RPR

1U0- **1** **Lord Landen (IRE)**[33] 4865 9-11-7 **100**.....................(t) ConorShoemark(5) 112
(Fergal O'Brien) *mid-div: hdwy 8th: rdn in cl 4th after 4 out: chal 2 out: led bef last: kpt on: rdn out* **8/1**

P6P- **2** *2 ½* **Shades Of Autumn (IRE)**[110] 3421 9-10-7 **84**...........(v) MichealNolan(3) 94
(Linda Blackford) *in tch: hit 1st: trckd ldrs 6th: led after 3 out: rdn whn jnd next: hdd bef last: kpt on but no ex* **20/1**

P00- **3** *7* **Uncle Pettit (IRE)**[19] 5113 6-9-11 **74**...........................(t) GavinSheehan(3) 77
(Jonathan Portman) *hld up towards rr: pushed along and stdy prog fr 11th: rdn after 4 out: wnt 4th 2 out: wnt 3rd at the last: styd on but nvr any threat* **10/1**

054- **4** *12* **Wait No More (IRE)**[27] 4992 9-11-7 **95**..........................(p) MichaelByrne 87
(Neil Mulholland) *led tl 4 out: sn rdn: wknd after next* **12/1**

52P- **5** *3* **Ring Bo Ree (IRE)**[72] 4109 11-11-7 **100**..............(p) AodhaganConlon(5) 92
(Tom George) *prom: mstke 8th: led 4 out: rdn and hdd after next: wknd 2 out* **5/1**[2]

230- **6** *14* **Ray Diamond**[25] 5019 9-11-12 **100**...................................... JamesDavies 77
(Jackie Du Plessis) *trckd ldrs tl 8th: sn struggling: no ch fr 4 out* **4/1**[1]

243- **7** *5* **Rusty Nail (IRE)**[128] 3048 9-9-7 **74** oh8.................................. MrFTett(7) 46
(James Frost) *mid-div: rdn after 11th: wknd 4 out* **11/1**

352- **8** *13* **Witch's Hat (IRE)**[37] 4778 11-10-7 **81**..................................(t) MarkGrant 48
(Jim Old) *trckd ldrs tl 10th: sn rdn and wknd* **11/2**[3]

/14- **9** *16* **General Ross (IRE)**[9] 5237 7-11-5 **93**.................................. RyanMahon 39
(Colin Tizzard) *towards rr of mid-div: rdn after 11th: sn wknd: t.o* **8/1**

243- **P** **Wicklewood**[16] 5144 8-9-12 **79**..............................(t) ThomasCheesman(7)
(Mark Gillard) *mid-div tl 8th: sn struggling in rr: awkward 10th: wknd next: t.o whn p.u bef 2 out* **9/1**

50P- **P** **Ballyhilty Bridge**[41] 4695 8-10-7 **81**..................................... TomO'Brien
(Paul Henderson) *a last: losing tch whn p.u after 9th* **8/1**

5m 11.3s (-10.10) **Going Correction** -0.45s/f (Good) **11** Ran SP% **125.3**
Speed ratings: **100,99,96,92,91 86,84,79,73,**
CSF £152.67 CT £1640.90 TOTE £11.50: £3.30, £5.80, £5.20; EX 171.80 Trifecta £1399.10 Part won..
Owner The B Lucky Partnership **Bred** Richard And Marie Hennessy **Trained** Coln St. Dennis, Gloucs

FOCUS
The front pair pulled clear late on in a race where the leaders probably went off too quickly. The winner fulfilled the promise of his Leicester win.

5395 PAIGNTON ZOO NOVICES' H'CAP HURDLE (10 hdls) 2m 6f
5:35 (5:35) (Class 5) (0-100,99) 4-Y-0+ **£2,737** (£798; £399)

Form RPR

021- **1** **Polo Springs**[7] 5282 7-10-9 **85**....................................(t) GavinSheehan(3) 95+
(Graeme McPherson) *mde all: pushed ahd appr 2 out: styd on: rdn out* **6/1**[2]

000- **2** *2 ½* **Bostin (IRE)**[27] 4993 6-11-3 **90**... DaveCrosse 99
(Brian Barr) *a.p: rdn and ev ch after 3 out tl mstke next: kpt on but hld after* **25/1**

121- **3** *1 ¾* **Area Access (IRE)**[21] 5069 6-11-4 **98**........................ MrHAABannister(7) 104
(Charlie Mann) *in tch: trckd ldng pair fr 6th: rdn after 3 out: kpt on same pce fr next* **2/1**[1]

402- **4** *7* **Lady Fingers**[14] 5177 6-11-2 **96**.. MrJBargary(7) 97
(Nigel Twiston-Davies) *mid-div: hdwy 3 out: sn rdn to chse ldrs: one pce fr next* **9/1**

P34- **5** *2 ½* **Redlynch Rock (IRE)**[16] 5144 6-11-3 **90**...............................(t) SamJones 87
(Bob Buckler) *mid-div: rdn after 3 out: styd on but nvr gng pce to get involved* **10/1**

440- **6** *1 ½* **Sukiyaki (IRE)**[31] 4903 5-11-12 **99**...................................... TomO'Brien 95
(Charlie Longsdon) *mid-div: rdn after 3 out: sn one pce* **8/1**[3]

336/ **7** *7* **Its Ruby**[627] 1141 8-11-3 **90**... AndrewTinkler 82
(Robert Walford) *mid-div: hit 4th and lost pl: rdn and hdwy after 3 out: wknd bef last* **16/1**

0- **8** *8* **Whatwillwedonext (IRE)**[121] 3173 8-11-4 **91**..................... HaddenFrost 74
(Martin Hill) *mid-div: pushed along after 3 out: wkng whn nt fluent 2 out* **20/1**

5P0- **9** *12* **River Dancing (IRE)**[24] 5034 7-10-7 **87**.................................. MrMLegg(7) 59
(Andy Turnell) *trckd ldrs: rdn and wknd after 3 out* **9/1**

163- **10** *½* **Isthereadifference (IRE)**[156] 2478 7-11-3 **95**........(p) ConorShoemark(5) 66
(Neil Mulholland) *hld up towards rr: hdwy after 6th: rdn after 3 out: sn wknd* **14/1**

F05- **11** *3* **Drumgooland (IRE)**[8] 5262 7-11-1 **95**..................................... MrJMahot(7) 64
(Sarah-Jayne Davies) *mid-div: hdwy 4th to trck ldrs: nt fluent 6th: wknd after 7th: t.o* **20/1**

40P- **12** *15* **Special Report (IRE)**[18] 5118 4-11-4 **97**.............................. MichaelByrne 46
(Neil Mulholland) *a bhd: struggling 6th: t.o* **40/1**

4P- **13** *16* **Toe To Toe (IRE)**[53] 4482 6-11-6 **93**................................... NickScholfield 34
(Lucy Jones) *hld up towards rr: hdwy appr 7th: rdn bef 3 out: sn wknd: t.o* **16/1**

/50- **P** **Romany Quest**[56] 4411 7-11-3 **97**.. MrCSmith(7)
(Linda Blackford) *trckd ldrs tl rdn after 7th: wknd after 3 out: t.o whn p.u bef next* **25/1**

000- **P** **Baksheesh**[28] 4972 5-10-6 **82**.......... MattGriffiths(3)
(Sue Gardner) *reminders after 3rd: a towards rr: t.o whn p.u after 3 out* **16/1**

5m 19.1s (-1.10) **Going Correction** 0.0s/f (Good)
WFA 4 from 5yo+ 6lb **15** Ran SP% **131.8**
Speed ratings (Par 103): **102,101,100,97,97 96,93,91,86,86 85,79,74, ,**
CSF £160.69 CT £419.13 TOTE £5.60: £3.00, £11.00, £1.10; EX 321.40 Trifecta £1375.20 Part won..
Owner Denarius Consulting Ltd **Bred** J C Boher **Trained** Upper Oddington, Gloucs
■ Stewards' Enquiry : Mr H A A Bannister three-day ban: careless riding (tbn)

FOCUS
Few got into what was quite a weak handicap. The form has a solid look.
T/Plt: £85.20 to a £1 stake. Pool: £76386.33 - 653.92 winning tickets T/Qpdt: £99.80 to a £1 stake. Pool: £4572.85 - 33.90 winning tickets TM

5110 PLUMPTON (L-H)
Sunday, April 20

OFFICIAL GOING: Good (good to firm in places) changing to good after race 1 (2:25) changing to good to soft after race 3 (3:25)
Wind: Light, half behind Weather: Murky, raining until race 4, then becoming bright

5396 TOTEPLACEPOT RACING'S FAVOURITE BET NOVICES' HURDLE (12 hdls) 2m 5f
2:25 (2:25) (Class 4) 4-Y-0+ **£4,223** (£1,240; £620; £310)

Form RPR
141- **1** **Ellnando Queen**[20] 5110 6-10-13 120.......... GavinSheehan 122+
(Warren Greatrex) *cl up: trckd ldr 7th: rdn after 3 out: clsd to ld 2 out: r.o wl fr last* **4/7**[1]

301- **2** *15* **Gun Shy (IRE)**[9] 5257 6-11-6 125.......... JoshuaMoore 123+
(Gary Moore) *led at gd pce: j.rt 8th: gng bttr than wnr 3 out: shkn up and hdd 2 out: sn btn: mstke last and wknd* **7/4**[2]

0PU- **3** *47* **The Selector**[9] 5258 5-10-7 0.......... TomCannon 60
(Chris Gordon) *hld up in last: lost tch 8th: no ch fr next: kpt on to take remote 3rd 2 out* **100/1**

P5U- **4** *9* **Tigridia (IRE)**[9] 5262 7-10-7 85.......... MarcGoldstein 52
(Sarah Wall) *hld up: gng bttr than sme but outpcd after 8th: wnt 3rd next: no imp on ldng pair: wknd after 3 out* **100/1**

444- **5** *59* **Dahteste**[36] 4797 6-10-4 92.......... NicodeBoinville(3)
(Mark Bradstock) *in tch: bmpd 4th: rdn 6th: wknd after 8th: wl t.o* **20/1**[3]

050- **P** **Classic Art**[99] 3641 4-10-8 98.......... (p) ColinBolger
(Roger Teal) *chsd ldr: j.lft 4th: lost 2nd 7th: wknd and mstke 9th: t.o whn p.u bef 2 out* **50/1**

5m 9.0s (-8.00) **Going Correction** -0.20s/f (Good)
WFA 4 from 5yo+ 6lb **6** Ran SP% **108.7**
Speed ratings (Par 105): **107,101,83,79,57**
CSF £1.75 TOTE £1.90: £1.10, £1.40; EX 1.90 Trifecta £15.80.
Owner Mrs R Vaughan **Bred** Mrs R I Vaughan **Trained** Upper Lambourn, Berks

FOCUS
The rain, which had fallen for several hours before racing, was beginning to get into the top of the ground for this first race but the going remained good, as reported overnight. In a race predictably dominated by two horses, there was no strength in depth.

5397 BEST ODDS GUARANTEED AT TOTEPOOL.COM H'CAP CHASE (14 fncs) 2m 4f
2:55 (2:55) (Class 5) (0-100,89) 5-Y-0+ **£3,249** (£954; £477; £238)

Form RPR
3P5- **1** **Shantou Breeze (IRE)**[9] 5263 7-11-12 **89**.......... MarcGoldstein 97
(Michael Madgwick) *mde most: rdn 3 out: narrowly hdd next: sn led again: drvn and kpt on gamely* **12/1**

442- **2** *4 ½* **Moneymix**[17] 5139 7-10-13 **76**.......... (b) TomO'Brien 80
(Ali Brewer) *trckd ldrs: wnt 2nd 10th: bmpd 3 out: drvn to ld narrowly 2 out: sn hdd and fnd nil: wl hld fr last* **11/4**[2]

P31- **3** *1* **Ballyvoneen (IRE)**[20] 5113 9-11-7 **87**.......... (p) TrevorWhelan(3) 90+
(Neil King) *w wnr: led briefly 3rd: lost 2nd pl 10th: rdn after 4 out: one pce after: kpt on fr last* **3/1**[3]

032- **4** *18* **Sportsreport (IRE)**[20] 5115 6-11-7 **84**.......... (p) AndrewThornton 81+
(Seamus Mullins) *hld up in last: blnd 1st and j. slowly 3rd: bhd tl clsd fr 7th: prog 10th: wnt 2nd briefly 3 out where bmpd rival: rdn and nt qckn after 2 out: wknd rapidly last: eased* **7/4**[1]

P40- **5** *28* **Curragh Dancer (FR)**[131] 3008 11-9-7 **63** oh3.......... (e[1]) LouisMuspratt(7) 25
(Paddy Butler) *trckd ldrs: lost pl 6th: toiling in rr fr 9th: t.o* **33/1**

016- **6** *7* **Al Amaan**[9] 5262 9-11-12 **89**.......... MattieBatchelor 44
(Sheena West) *hld up in last pair: mstke 5th: prog and prom 9th: sn rdn and nt run on: dropped away qckly: t.o 3 out: mstke last* **8/1**

5m 12.0s (4.70) **Going Correction** +0.30s/f (Yiel) **6** Ran SP% **109.8**
Speed ratings: **102,100,99,92,81 78**
CSF £43.68 TOTE £9.40: £4.30, £1.80; EX 41.00 Trifecta £122.60.
Owner Ian M McGready **Bred** Miss E Harrington **Trained** Denmead, Hants

FOCUS
The pace was fair enough in this weak race.

5398 TOTEEXACTA PICK THE 1ST AND 2ND NOVICES' H'CAP CHASE (12 fncs) 2m 1f
3:25 (3:27) (Class 4) (0-110,108) 5-Y-0+ **£4,873** (£1,431; £715; £357)

Form RPR
541- **1** **The Informant**[20] 5115 8-10-2 **84**.......... (b) RyanMahon 87
(Seamus Mullins) *mde virtually all: hrd pressed and rdn 3 out: kpt on wl u.p after last* **9/4**[1]

5PU- **2** *¾* **June French (FR)**[5] 5342 6-10-1 **83** oh13 ow1.......... TomCannon 85
(Kevin Tork) *trckd wnr: chal 4 out: upsides bef 2 out tl outbattled fr last* **10/1**

6P0- **3** *1 ½* **Nomadic Storm**[34] 4865 8-10-0 **82** oh8.......... (tp) TomScudamore 83
(David Bridgwater) *wl in tch: rdn to chse ldng pair 3 out: 3 l down next: kpt on but nvr able to chal* **7/2**[2]

P50- **4** *23* **Regal One (IRE)**[22] 5066 6-10-13 **102**.......... JakeHodson(7) 82
(David Bridgwater) *tended to jump rt: chsd ldng pair tl lunged at 3 out: wknd bef next* **6/1**

232- **5** *12* **Looks Like Slim**[28] 4989 7-11-7 **103**.......... (p) NoelFehily 72
(Ben De Haan) *hld up in last pair: in tch 8th: pushed along and outpcd bef next: no ch after: wknd* **9/2**[3]

013- **6** *4 ½* **Dark And Dangerous (IRE)**[29] 4965 6-11-12 **108**.......... (v) BrendanPowell 73
(Brendan Powell) *nt fluent: pushed along fr 3rd: stl in tch 8th: wknd fr next (4 out)* **5/1**

504- **U** **Mac's Grey (IRE)**[33] 4890 7-10-0 **82** oh10.......... GerardTumelty
(Zoe Davison) *hld up: last tl prog 4 out: abt 5 l bhd in 5th and gng wl enough whn blnd bdly and uns rdr 3 out* **25/1**

4m 26.8s (3.80) **Going Correction** +0.30s/f (Yiel) **7** Ran SP% **115.1**
Speed ratings: **103,102,101,91,85 83,**
CSF £23.82 TOTE £2.60: £1.60, £6.30; EX 24.50 Trifecta £172.90.
Owner Dr & Mrs John Millar **Bred** Mrs J D Richards, Mrs C L Shaw & Mrs V Gilmou **Trained** Wilsford-Cum-Lake, Wilts

FOCUS
They went a good gallop in this routine Plumpton chase.

5399 TOTEPOOL SUSSEX CHAMPION HURDLE (A H'CAP HURDLE RACE) (9 hdls) 2m
3:55 (3:55) (Class 2) 4-Y-0+ **£19,494** (£5,724; £2,862; £1,431)

Form RPR
162- **1** **Fergall (IRE)**[50] 4550 7-11-3 **136**.......... WayneKavanagh(3) 140+
(Seamus Mullins) *trckd ldrs: prog and mstke 5th: trckd ldng pair next: led sn after 3 out and sent for home: clr next: rdn out* **7/1**[3]

322- **2** *4 ½* **The Green Ogre**[21] 5090 4-10-5 **126**.......... JoshuaMoore 121
(Gary Moore) *hld up in last pair: gd prog after 6th: chsd ldng pair sn after 3 out: rdn and kpt on to take 2nd last strides* **8/1**

60P- **3** *shd* **Dan Breen (IRE)**[64] 4264 9-10-12 **128**.......... (bt) TomScudamore 127
(David Pipe) *pressed ldr: led briefly 3 out: outpcd by wnr after: kpt on but lost 2nd last stride* **10/1**

F35- **4** *5* **Zarzal (IRE)**[31] 4921 6-10-7 **123**.......... PaulMoloney 119
(Evan Williams) *set off promly but short of room bef 1st and dropped to rr: effrt 6th: outpcd fr 3 out: lft in 4th pl and hmpd 2 out: kpt on* **10/1**

162- **5** *3 ¼* **My Guardian Angel**[37] 4794 5-10-6 **122**.......... ColinBolger 114
(Mark H Tompkins) *prom: wl in tch whn sltly hmpd 6th: hit 3 out: fdd bef next* **25/1**

F10- **6** *11* **Leviathan**[15] 5172 7-10-12 **128**.......... LiamTreadwell 110
(Venetia Williams) *t.k.h: hld up in rr: brief effrt bef 5th: sn pushed along: in tch bef 3 out: wknd* **12/1**

320- **P** **Local Hero (GER)**[37] 4789 7-11-5 **142**.......... (p) PaulBohan(7)
(Steve Gollings) *hld up: mstke 3rd: dropped to last and immediately lost tch: t.o whn p.u bef 6th* **7/1**[3]

353- **F** **Ted Spread**[30] 4935 7-11-0 **130**.......... (t) TomO'Brien 130
(Suzy Smith) *hld up in tch: hmpd 6th and dropped to rr: rallied after 3 out: wnt 3rd but no ch w wnr whn fell 2 out* **6/1**[2]

513- **F** **Alfraamsey**[53] 4497 6-10-10 **126**.......... MarcGoldstein 108
(Sheena West) *led to 3 out: wknd: bhd whn fell next: winded* **16/1**

5/3- **F** **Dildar (IRE)**[169] 2213 6-10-13 **132**.......... (t) HarryDerham(3)
(Paul Nicholls) *trckd ldrs: disputing 4th and cl up whn fell 6th* **5/1**[1]

200- **P** **Specialagent Alfie**[114] 3322 8-10-9 **125**.......... (t) TomCannon
(Nick Gifford) *hld up in tch: stl chsng ldrs 3 out: wknd sn after: bhd whn p.u bef 2 out* **6/1**[2]

3m 53.1s (-7.70) **Going Correction** -0.20s/f (Good)
WFA 4 from 5yo+ 5lb **11** Ran SP% **117.0**
Speed ratings (Par 109): **111,108,108,106,104 99, , , ,**
CSF £61.80 CT £563.21 TOTE £10.20: £2.70, £2.00, £4.80; EX 91.10 Trifecta £1219.40.
Owner Andrew Cocks And Tara Johnson **Bred** Mrs Gail C List **Trained** Wilsford-Cum-Lake, Wilts

FOCUS
A lively gallop made this valuable race a good test and it had sorted out a decent field by the home turn.

5400 DOWNLOAD THE TOTEPOOL LIVE INFO APP MAIDEN HURDLE (9 hdls) 2m
4:25 (4:25) (Class 5) 4-Y-0+ **£2,599** (£763; £381; £190)

Form RPR
1 **Azabitmour (FR)**[76] 4-10-9 0.......... TomO'Brien 108+
(Suzy Smith) *t.k.h: trckd ldr after 1st tl 3 out: styd in tch: rallied to go 2nd last: styd on to ld post* **25/1**

500- **2** *nse* **Andi'Amu (FR)**[29] 4963 4-10-9 114.......... (t) GavinSheehan 109+
(Warren Greatrex) *led 1st: hit 5th: clattered 3 out: rdn and pressed bef next: kpt on fr last: hdd post* **11/4**[2]

2- **3** *7* **Unex Modigliani (IRE)**[39] 4758 5-11-0 0.......... (t) HarrySkelton 109+
(Dan Skelton) *trckd ldng pair fr 2nd: chsd ldr 3 out: drvn bef next whn trying to mount a chal: looked hld whn mstke last: wknd* **4/7**[1]

060- **4** *23* **Spartilla**[55] 4467 5-10-7 0.......... MrJPearce(7) 86
(Daniel O'Brien) *in tch tl nudged along and lft bhd fr 5th: poor 6th bef 3 out: kpt on to take remote 4th last: capable of bttr* **25/1**

00- **5** *3* **Heading To First**[67] 2272 7-10-7 0.......... LouisMuspratt(7) 83
(Paddy Butler) *chsd ldrs: jst in tch bef 6th: rdn and lft bhd sn after: steadily wknd* **66/1**

55/ **6** *20* **Bert The Alert**[18] 5345 6-11-0 0.......... TomCannon 65
(Laura Mongan) *chsd ldrs: in tch bef 6th: rdn and lft bhd sn after: wknd qckly bef 2 out* **10/1**[3]

7 *67* **Make A Fuss**[18] 5-10-7 0.......... MarcGoldstein
(Gerry Enright) *hld up and immediately detached in lat trio: t.k.h: nvr involved: poor 7th bef 3 out: blnd last and allowed to walk in* **66/1**

6/P- **P** **Franco Is My Name**[28] 4987 8-11-0 0.......... (t) LiamTreadwell
(Peter Hedger) *hld up and immediately detached in last trio: j. poorly and a bhd: gng v slowly whn t.o 3 out: p.u bef next* **25/1**

F **Lexington Blue**[237] 4-10-6 0.......... WayneKavanagh(3)
(Seamus Mullins) *hld up and immediately detached in last trio: t.k.h: nvr on terms: remote 9th whn fell 6th* **10/1**[3]

0PP- **U** **Harlequins Gleams**[20] 5110 6-11-0 0.......... AndrewThornton
(Anna Newton-Smith) *led to 1st: lost pl next: reminder 3rd: wknd next: remote 8th whn j. wildly 2 out and uns rdr* **66/1**

4m 0.2s (-0.60) **Going Correction** -0.20s/f (Good)
WFA 4 from 5yo+ 5lb **10** Ran SP% **124.5**
Speed ratings (Par 103): **93,92,89,77,76 66,32, , ,**
CSF £97.55 TOTE £29.00: £3.00, £1.70, £1.10; EX 108.70 Trifecta £365.20.
Owner G Jones & B Malt **Bred** Mathieu Daguzan-Garros Et Al **Trained** Lewes, E Sussex

FOCUS
A strong gallop soon had the field strung out, and the presence of the third suggests the form is solid for the track.

5401 TOTETRIFECTA AVAILABLE ON ALL RACES NOVICES' H'CAP CHASE (18 fncs) 3m 2f
4:55 (4:56) (Class 5) (0-100,97) 5-Y-0+ **£3,249** (£954; £477; £238)

Form RPR
223- **1** **Flugzeug**[20] 5113 6-9-11 **71** oh2.......... WayneKavanagh(3) 82+
(Seamus Mullins) *lost pl 5th: mostly in last pair fr 8th tl prog after 14th: chsd ldng pair 3 out: rdn and clsd 2 out: led last: styd on* **5/1**[2]

The Form Book Jumps, Raceform Ltd, Compton, RG20 6NL.

PP4- **2** *2* **Hinton Indiana**[175] 2110 9-10-6 **77**..............................(t) HarrySkelton 85
(Dan Skelton) *w.w: prog 13th: trckd ldr next: mstke 4 out: clsd to ld narrowly 2 out and looked to be gng strly: sn rdn: hdd and nt qckn last* **11/10**[1]

001- **3** *3 ½* **Leeroar (IRE)**[44] 4654 6-11-4 **89**.............................. SamJones 94
(Jo Davis) *led: gng wl enough whn blnd 4 out: hdd 2 out: fdd after last* **20/1**

P6F- **4** *29* **Wah Wah Taysee (IRE)**[17] 5144 7-11-12 **97**..............(t) TomScudamore 75
(David Bridgwater) *tended to jump rt: hld up in rr: 5th and in tch whn mstke 14th: no hdwy next (4 out): wknd* **12/1**

164- **5** *8* **Volio Vincente (FR)**[32] 4905 7-10-1 **72**.............................. BrendanPowell 43
(Carroll Gray) *chsd ldr to 12th: styd cl up tl wknd qckly 3 out* **12/1**

24F- **P** **Bit Of A Clown (IRE)**[7] 5309 8-11-4 **89**..............................(p) TomCannon
(Nick Gifford) *prom: chsd ldr 12th to 14th: sn wknd: wl bhd whn p.u bef 2 out* **6/1**[3]

043- **P** **Ata Boy (IRE)**[20] 5111 8-9-11 **75**.............................. DanielHiskett[(7)]
(Richard Phillips) *chsd ldrs: struggling fr 12th: sn wknd: t.o whn p.u bef 3 out* **12/1**

F/4- **P** **Zigzaga (IRE)**[9] 5259 8-10-0 **71** oh3.............................. MarcGoldstein
(Lydia Richards) *jumping lacked conviction: hld up and mostly in last: lost tch after 13th: t.o whn p.u bef 3 out* **8/1**

6m 57.7s (7.00) **Going Correction** +0.30s/f (Yiel) **8** Ran SP% **117.5**
Speed ratings: **101,100,99,90,87 , ,**
CSF £11.89 CT £102.84 TOTE £6.70: £1.70, £1.10, £2.70; EX 19.70 Trifecta £207.50.
Owner New Forest Racing Partnership **Bred** Mrs J N Humphreys **Trained** Wilsford-Cum-Lake, Wilts

FOCUS
These modest chasers went a sensible pace in the rain-softened ground.

5402 FOLLOW @TOTEPOOL ON TWITTER CONDITIONAL JOCKEYS' H'CAP HURDLE (12 hdls) 2m 5f
5:25 (5:25) (Class 5) (0-100,100) 4-Y-0+ **£2,599** (£763; £381; £190)

Form RPR

6F0- **1** **She's Noble**[18] 5124 7-10-8 **82**.............................. MichealNolan 88+
(Suzy Smith) *hld up in midfield: prog to press ldrs 9th: rdn bef 2 out: clsd last: led fnl 150yds: styd on strly* **20/1**

403- **2** *3 ¾* **Kingsfold Flare**[17] 5143 7-10-8 **85**.............................. JoshuaMoore[(3)] 86
(Gary Moore) *trckd ldrs: wnt 2nd bef 3 out: led after 3 out: hrd pressed and drvn next: hdd and outpcd last 150yds* **5/1**[2]

633- **3** *½* **Marie Deja La (FR)**[9] 5260 8-10-11 **93**..............(b) LouisMuspratt[(8)] 95
(Chris Gordon) *mostly pressed ldr: led 8th: rdn and hdd after 3 out: stl chalng whn sltly unbalanced bef last: one pce* **7/2**[1]

6P5- **4** *1 ¾* **Jazz Man (IRE)**[26] 5022 7-11-5 **98**.............................. DanielHiskett[(5)] 97
(Mark Rimell) *hld up in rr: rdn and prog after 8th: chsd ldrs after next: in tch but no imp 2 out: kpt on* **12/1**

0F5- **5** *1* **Stay In My Heart (IRE)**[20] 5112 5-11-4 **95**..............(p) JackSherwood[(3)] 93
(Laura Mongan) *trckd ldrs: shkn up and nt qckn bef 3 out: tried to rally bef 2 out: one pce u.p* **16/1**

400- **6** *10* **Maccabees**[29] 4967 5-9-9 **69**..............................(p[1]) ThomasCheesman[(5)] 63
(Roger Curtis) *hld up and mostly in last tl prog after 9th: no hope of rching ldrs but kpt on steadily: nvr involved* **20/1**

606- **7** *16* **Mariet**[20] 5116 5-10-11 **85**.............................. GavinSheehan 60
(Suzy Smith) *pressed ldrs: chal and upsides after 8th: wknd bef 3 out: eased after 2 out* **6/1**[3]

006- **P** **Marju King (IRE)**[22] 5066 8-11-9 **100**..............................(p) TomBellamy[(3)]
(Phil Middleton) *hld up towards rr: prog after 8th: tried to cl on ldrs bef 3 out: sn wknd: poor 8th whn p.u bef last* **12/1**

320- **P** **Little Roxy (IRE)**[20] 5116 9-10-5 **79**.............................. NicodeBoinville
(Anna Newton-Smith) *hld up in midfield: trying to make prog on inner whn no room bnd after 8th: no hdwy after next: wknd 3 out: poor 9th whn p.u bef 2 out* **12/1**

4/0- **P** **Lisahane Bog**[32] 177 7-10-10 **84**..............................(v) CallumWhillans
(Peter Hedger) *hld up: a in rr: rdn and wknd after 8th: t.o whn p.u after 3 out* **33/1**

423/ **P** **Easter Lad**[574] 1620 10-11-0 **88**..............................(b) TrevorWhelan
(Paddy Butler) *wl in rr: wknd 5th: p.u bef next* **20/1**

/P0- **P** **Generous Bob**[31] 4911 7-10-3 **77**.............................. JeremiahMcGrath
(Seamus Mullins) *pressed ldng pair: blnd 7th: drvn next: n.m.r sn after and wknd: t.o whn p.u bef 3 out* **6/1**[3]

546- **P** **Leith Hill Legasi**[36] 4803 5-10-13 **93**.............................. CharlieDeutsch[(6)]
(Charlie Longsdon) *led to 8th: losing pl whn n.m.r sn after: wknd: t.o whn p.u bef 2 out* **12/1**

5m 21.1s (4.10) **Going Correction** -0.20s/f (Good) **13** Ran SP% **121.3**
Speed ratings (Par 103): **84,82,82,81,81 77,71, , , , , ,**
CSF £115.66 CT £447.76 TOTE £22.30: £9.40, £1.30, £1.80; EX 149.20 Trifecta £1183.00 Part won..
Owner N L Crawford-Smith **Bred** O D Plunkett **Trained** Lewes, E Sussex

FOCUS
A competitive conditionals' race in which the pace was just medium. Mares filled the first three places.
T/Plt: £100.20 to a £1 stake. Pool: £83097.48 - 604.98 winning tickets T/Qpdt: £15.50 to a £1 stake. Pool: £5385.41 - 256.40 winning tickets JN

5242 TOWCESTER (R-H)
Sunday, April 20

OFFICIAL GOING: Good (good to firm in places)
Wind: fresh behind Weather: very overcast; 11 degrees

5403 BET TOTEJACKPOT NOVICES' HURDLE (8 hdls) 2m
2:15 (2:15) (Class 4) 4-Y-0+ **£3,119** (£915; £457; £228)

Form RPR

416- **1** **Stiff Upper Lip (IRE)**[29] 4963 4-10-9 117.............................. ThomasGarner[(5)] 114+
(Oliver Sherwood) *trckd ldrs: rdn to ld bef 2 out and clipped flight: sn drvn clr: wl in command last* **9/2**[3]

340- **2** *7* **Tracking Time**[25] 5033 7-10-5 101..............................(b[1]) MrJMartin[(7)] 106
(Andrew J Martin) *settled handy: effrt after 3 out: rdn and wnt 2nd after 2 out: 4 l down whn landed awkwardly last: wl hld after* **12/1**

424- **3** *4* **Broadway Symphony (IRE)**[32] 4903 7-10-12 120.............................. MarkGrant 101
(Tracey L Bailey) *hld up trcking ldrs: chal 3 out: wnt 2nd and rdn bef 2 out: sn v one pce* **13/8**[1]

/00- **4** *1 ½* **Master Malt**[42] 4693 6-10-9 0.............................. MauriceLinehan[(3)] 100
(Jonjo O'Neill) *t.k.h and prom: coaxed along home turn: btn between last two: 4th whn nt fluent last* **11/4**[2]

56- **5** *5* **Mr Maynard**[23] 5057 5-10-12 0.............................. JamieMoore 97
(Renee Robeson) *bhd: rdn 5th: outpcd next: rallied and clsd to trck ldrs between last two: sn no imp: eased flat* **25/1**

4U- **6** *9* **King Muro**[28] 4987 4-10-2 0.............................. ConorShoemark[(5)] 82
(Fergal O'Brien) *led: sn stdy pce: 8 l clr after 2nd tl next: pressed fr 4th: rdn and hdd bef 2 out: dropped out qckly* **8/1**

0- **7** *29* **Florida Beat**[22] 5064 4-10-5 0 ow1..............................(t) RobertDunne[(3)] 57
(Dai Burchell) *a bhd: rdn and lost tch qckly and hit 3 out: t.o next* **14/1**

300- **8** *29* **Indiefront**[10] 5244 5-10-5 0.............................. FelixDeGiles 28
(Jo Davis) *bhd: j. slowly 5th: drvn and lost tch next: t.o 2 out* **50/1**

P **Trust Me Boy**[334] 6-10-9 0.............................. PeterCarberry[(3)]
(John E Long) *towards rr: shkn up 5th: stopped rapidly 3 out and sn t.o: p.u next* **100/1**

3m 43.4s (-24.50) **Going Correction** -1.375s/f (Hard)
WFA 4 from 5yo+ 5lb **9** Ran SP% **115.2**
Speed ratings (Par 105): **106,102,100,99,97 92,78,63,**
CSF £53.21 TOTE £5.80: £2.00, £3.00, £1.10; EX 40.50 Trifecta £122.70.
Owner Richard Hitchcock Alan King **Bred** B Kennedy **Trained** Upper Lambourn, Berks

FOCUS
Shared bends and hurdle track dolled out to middle position. A race significantly weakened by a couple of well-fancied horses coming out during the morning. After riding in the first, most jockeys reported the ground as on the fast side of good, but Maurice Linehan reckoned it was "good".

5404 BEST ODDS GUARANTEED AT TOTEPOOL.COM H'CAP CHASE (12 fncs) 2m 110y
2:45 (2:45) (Class 5) (0-100,99) 5-Y-0+ **£2,144** (£629; £314; £157)

Form RPR

320- **1** **Grand Article (IRE)**[27] 5012 10-10-0 **73** oh1.............................. AdamWedge 81
(Paul Cowley) *led: hdd 3 out: drvn to ld again bef next: 4 l clr last: kpt on steadily* **14/1**

P01- **2** *1 ½* **Tinelyra (IRE)**[10] 5243 8-10-12 **90**.............................. ConorShoemark[(5)] 99+
(Fergal O'Brien) *settled towards rr: bdly hmpd 4th: effrt 9th: 3rd and u.p home turn: chsd wnr but racing awkwardly fr after 2 out: fnd little and no imp fr last* **7/2**[2]

064- **3** *7* **Minellaforlunch (IRE)**[110] 3439 7-11-12 **99**..............................(p) DenisO'Regan 100
(Henry Oliver) *2nd tl lost pl 4th: 10 l 4th 3 out tl next: drvn to snatch mod 4th nr fin* **11/4**[1]

033- **4** *¾* **Bally Lagan (IRE)**[10] 5243 6-10-6 **79**..............................(tp) CharliePoste 80
(Robin Dickin) *cl up: wnt 2nd at 6th: led 3 out: drvn and hdd bef next: plodded on and btn bef last: lost 3rd cl home* **7/2**[2]

444- **5** *14* **Croco Mister (IRE)**[10] 5247 7-10-6 **84**.............................. BenPoste[(5)] 71
(Rosemary Gasson) *wnt 2nd at 3rd: losing pl whn mstke 7th: wl btn 3 out* **6/1**[3]

264- **6** *15* **Mr Robinson (FR)**[173] 2152 7-10-0 **73** oh4.............................. IanPopham 47
(Rob Summers) *chsd ldrs: wkng whn mstke 9th: wl bhd fr next* **12/1**

2P0- **P** **Moscow Mule**[79] 4021 11-10-11 **89**.............................. EdCookson[(5)]
(Laura Hurley) *bhd: rdn and struggling 6th: t.o and p.u 3 out* **10/1**

/05- **U** **Chicago Alley**[100] 3637 13-10-4 **77**.............................. LeeEdwards
(Dave Roberts) *trckd ldrs: blnd and uns rdr 4th* **25/1**

P3P- **P** **Gainsborough's Art (IRE)**[22] 5066 9-9-11 **73** oh18(p) MauriceLinehan[(3)]
(Harry Chisman) *nt jump wl in rr: t.o 6th: p.u 9th* **100/1**

3m 55.8s (-20.30) **Going Correction** -1.325s/f (Hard) **9** Ran SP% **113.7**
Speed ratings: **94,93,90,89,83 76, , ,**
CSF £63.49 CT £177.64 TOTE £15.10: £3.00, £1.60, £1.30; EX 71.20 Trifecta £218.50.
Owner Stan West **Bred** Mrs Lorraine Castle **Trained** Culworth, Northants

FOCUS
A moderate contest. The stewards gave permission for the open ditch going down the hill (fence 4) to be omitted following this race due to the frame being broken.

5405 BET TOTETRIFECTA MARES' H'CAP HURDLE (8 hdls) 2m
3:15 (3:16) (Class 4) (0-120,115) 4-Y-0+ **£3,119** (£915; £457; £228)

Form RPR

305- **1** **Epee Celeste (FR)**[14] 5191 8-9-9 **89**..............................(b) JoeCornwall[(5)] 88+
(Michael Chapman) *pressed ldr: rdn 3 out: led wl bef next: drvn and styd on v gamely to outbattle rivals fr bef last* **3/1**[3]

221- **2** *4 ½* **Fine Moment**[10] 5245 6-11-12 **115**..............................(bt) BrianHughes 110
(Kevin Frost) *trckd ldng pair: hit 4th: wnt 2nd bef 2 out: edging rt and fnd nil whn rdn after: wl hld fr last* **7/4**[1]

3PP- **3** *3* **Definitely Glad (IRE)**[146] 2713 7-11-7 **110**..............................(t) DenisO'Regan 102
(Paul Webber) *led and t.k.h: rdn and hdd after 3 out: plodded on between last two* **8/1**

050- **4** *3 ½* **Etania**[42] 4703 6-9-9 **89** oh4.............................. RobertMcCarth[(5)] 78
(Ian Williams) *t.k.h in last: nt fluent: rdn and no rspnse bef 2 out: sn btn* **2/1**[2]

3m 46.5s (-21.40) **Going Correction** -1.375s/f (Hard) **4** Ran SP% **105.8**
Speed ratings (Par 105): **98,95,94,92**
CSF £8.35 TOTE £4.60; EX 6.70 Trifecta £16.10.
Owner Mrs S M Richards **Bred** E A R L Haras De Trefontaine **Trained** Market Rasen, Lincs

FOCUS
All of these had some sort of chance off the final bend.

5406 DOWNLOAD THE TOTEPOOL LIVE INFO APP H'CAP CHASE (16 fncs 2 omitted) 3m 110y
3:45 (3:46) (Class 4) (0-120,118) 5-Y-0+ **£3,768** (£1,106; £553; £276)

Form RPR

24P- **1** **Arkose (IRE)**[56] 4449 10-11-1 **112**..............................(v) ThomasGarner[(5)] 122
(Oliver Sherwood) *mde all: rdn and jnd home turn: drew 5 l clr and mstke 2 out: idling and wandering after: jnd 100yds out: hung on cl home* **5/2**[2]

303- **2** *hd* **Green Bank (IRE)**[15] 5180 8-11-3 **112**..............................(t) KielanWoods[(3)] 121
(Charlie Longsdon) *pressed wnr: pushed along bef 10th: cl home turn: rdn and sn outpcd: lft w ev ch by idling rival after last: drew upsides 100yds out but hld fnl strides* **11/4**[3]

451- **3** *7* **Ballylifen (IRE)**[22] 5076 7-11-2 **118**.............................. JamesHuxham[(10)] 121
(Jonjo O'Neill) *last pair: mstke 10th: rdn to go 7 l 3rd 2 out: racd lazily and nvr making any imp after* **15/8**[1]

4P6- **4** *12* **Jolly Boys Outing (IRE)**[27] 5011 11-9-9 **92** oh19.............. BenPoste[(5)] 84
(Rosemary Gasson) *j. deliberately 6th: pressed ldrs tl rdn 3 out: 4th and wkng bef next* **10/1**

465- **5** *shd* **Counting House (IRE)**[31] 4914 11-11-9 **115**.............................. MarkGrant 107
(Jim Old) *last pair: struggling 11th: nvr looked like clsng after* **9/1**

5m 59.8s (-37.10) **Going Correction** -1.325s/f (Hard) **5** Ran SP% **109.1**
Speed ratings: **106,105,103,99,99**
CSF £9.71 TOTE £3.10: £1.60, £1.80; EX 8.90 Trifecta £22.50.
Owner D P Barrie & Partners 'A' **Bred** Stephen Eustace **Trained** Upper Lambourn, Berks
■ Stewards' Enquiry : Thomas Garner nine-day ban: used whip above permitted level (May 5-13)

FOCUS
A modest contest that produced a terrific finish.

5407 BET TOTEEXACTA NOVICES' H'CAP CHASE (14 fncs 2 omitted) 2m 6f
4:15 (4:17) (Class 5) (0-100,100) 5-Y-O+ **£2,144** (£629; £314; £157)

Form RPR
42- **1** **Typhon De Guye (FR)**[122] 3179 7-11-9 **97**.......................... IanPopham 108
(Martin Keighley) *j. soundly: 2nd mostly and gng wl: led 11th: 2 l clr 2 out: rdn and styd on wl after: readily* **4/1**[3]

0P4- **2** *3 1/4* **Le Pergolese (FR)**[7] 5301 8-10-0 **74** oh1......................(t) DougieCostello 84
(Nigel Hawke) *trckd ldrs: t.k.h: nt fluent 12th: rdn to chse wnr 2 out: no imp whn pckd last* **15/2**

433- **3** *2* **Xenophon**[4] 5361 6-9-9 **74** oh3.. JoeCornwall(5) 81
(Michael Chapman) *t.k.h: pressed ldrs: hit 7th: wnt 2nd 12th tl 3rd and u.p bef 2 out: sn outpcd: rallied and styng on wl after last* **10/3**[1]

655- **4** *4* **Ultra Klass (FR)**[27] 5011 6-10-11 **85**..............................(p) AndrewTinkler 88
(Jamie Snowden) *cl up in rr: mstke 7th: rdn and effrt after 3 out: 4th and rdn home turn: one pce and nt trble ldrs after* **7/2**[2]

31F- **5** *21* **Handsome Buddy (IRE)**[7] 5293 7-11-4 **95**.............(b[1]) PeterCarberry(3) 79
(Michael Gates) *cl up in rr: mstkes 10th and next: clsd to 3rd at next: drvn and fdd bef 2 out* **4/1**[3]

432- **6** *5* **Badb Catha (IRE)**[44] 4654 8-9-7 **74** oh10............................... MrFTett(7) 53
(Roger Curtis) *nt a fluent: in rr but wl in tch tl rdn and wknd 3 out* **25/1**

04P- **P** **Cash In Hand (IRE)**[115] 3277 14-10-1 **75** oh23 ow1.......... DaveCrosse
(Christopher Kellett) *mde most tl 11th: set modest pce: rdn 12th: fdd qckly up hill after 3 out: t.o and p.u 2 out* **66/1**

0/P- **P** **Green Hackle (IRE)**[82] 3959 9-11-7 **100**................(b[1]) ThomasGarner(5)
(Oliver Sherwood) *wnt 3rd at 8th: led bef next but pckd bdly and hdd: tried to rally and mstke 12th: struggling after: t.o and p.u 2 out* **10/1**

5m 23.9s (-29.10) **Going Correction** -1.325s/f (Hard) 8 Ran SP% **111.5**
Speed ratings: **99,97,97,95,88 86, ,**
CSF £31.70 CT £106.58 TOTE £5.50: £1.10, £3.40, £1.70; EX 35.30 Trifecta £154.70.
Owner Daydream Believers **Bred** G A E C Delorme Gerard & Vincent **Trained** Condicote, Gloucs

FOCUS
Quite a competitive-looking event.

5408 TOTEPOOL BETTING AT BETFRED.COM MAIDEN HURDLE (11 hdls) 2m 5f
4:45 (4:47) (Class 5) 4-Y-O+ **£1,949** (£572; £286; £143)

Form RPR
65- **1** **Lily Little Legs (IRE)**[36] 4797 5-10-2 0....................... RobertMcCarth(5) 95+
(Ian Williams) *rrd and uns rdr leaving paddock: chsd ldr fr 3rd tl led 6th: edgd rt coming up hill and squeezed rivals: drvn 2 out: kpt finding ex after and r.o gamely flat* **11/2**

0F5- **2** *3/4* **Couldhavehaditall (IRE)**[32] 4903 6-11-0 118.................. DenisO'Regan 102+
(Paul Webber) *settled in rr: smooth prog 3 out: squeezed for room bef st: wnt 2 l 2nd and drvn 2 out: tried to chal last: outbattled flat* **15/8**[1]

643- **3** *10* **Rendezvous Peak**[33] 4891 5-11-0 108........................... DougieCostello 90
(Lucy Wadham) *hld up in last pair: effrt 3 out: rdn and no rspnse fr next: wl hld 3rd and edging rt bef last* **7/2**[3]

00- **4** *3 1/4* **The Purchaser (IRE)**[33] 4891 6-11-0 0............................. AdamWedge 88
(Chris Bealby) *led tl 2nd: prom: 2nd whn squeezed for room home turn: rdn after: lost 3rd and wl btn 2 out* **20/1**

000- **5** *10* **Top Show**[32] 4903 5-11-0 0... AlainCawley 78
(Dean Ivory) *last pair: effrt 7th: rdn and wkng whn nt fluent 3 out: hit next* **33/1**

006- **6** *14* **Revouge**[19] 5120 5-11-0 0..(t) MarkGrant 63
(Jim Old) *pressed ldrs: rdn and nt fluent 3 out: fdd tamely up hill* **33/1**

5/0- **7** *7* **Turoyal (FR)**[87] 3863 6-10-9 0.. EdCookson(5) 56
(Laura Hurley) *wnt prom at 5th: 2nd at 7th: rdn and wknd rapidly after next* **50/1**

/26- **P** **Rossoneri (IRE)**[49] 4574 7-11-0 0........................... SamTwiston-Davies
(Nigel Twiston-Davies) *led 2nd tl 6th: j. slowly next and sn struggling in last: t.o and p.u last* **11/4**[2]

5m 10.7s (-16.50) **Going Correction** -1.375s/f (Hard) 8 Ran SP% **111.7**
Speed ratings (Par 103): **76,75,71,70,66 61,58,**
CSF £15.81 TOTE £6.20: £1.80, £1.20, £1.20; EX 16.40 Trifecta £55.00.
Owner Jim Hanifin **Bred** James Wickham **Trained** Portway, Worcs
■ Stewards' Enquiry : Robert McCarth two-day ban: careless riding (May 5-6)

FOCUS
The absence of the likely short-priced favourite Ned Stark (among plenty of non-runners) opened this up a bit.

5409 FOLLOW @TOTEPOOL ON TWITTER STANDARD OPEN NATIONAL HUNT FLAT RACE (DIV I) 2m
5:15 (5:15) (Class 6) 4-6-Y-O **£1,559** (£457; £228; £114)

Form RPR
1 **Warrantor (IRE)**[56] 5-11-2 0... AidanColeman 102+
(Warren Greatrex) *dropped out last: smooth prog on inner 3f out: led over 1f out and qcknd clr: impressive* **7/4**[1]

10- **2** *2 1/4* **Mont Royale**[60] 4349 6-11-6 0... MauriceLinehan(3) 104+
(Jonjo O'Neill) *a 2nd or 3rd: 2nd and rdn home turn: ev ch 1f out: sn edgd lft and outpcd by wnr fnl f* **2/1**[2]

3 *8* **Seacon Beg (IRE)**[29] 5-11-2 0................................ SamTwiston-Davies 91
(Nigel Twiston-Davies) *led at decent pce: rdn 2f out: hdd over 1f out: wknd ins fnl f* **5/1**[3]

6- **4** *10* **Borguy (FR)**[129] 3049 4-10-11 0.. AndrewTinkler 76
(Jamie Snowden) *t.k.h: chsd ldrs: rdn and wknd qckly over 2f out: t.o* **14/1**

5 *2 1/2* **Queen Of The Stage (IRE)** 4-9-8 0.................... JosephPalmowski(10) 67
(Robin Dickin) *trckd ldrs: rdn over 3f out: struggling wl over 2f out: t.o* **14/1**

5- **6** *hd* **Anwyl House**[180] 2015 4-10-11 0.. MarkGrant 73
(Jo Hughes) *towards rr: rdn and fdd wl over 2f out: t.o* **14/1**

0- **7** *16* **Verve Argent (FR)**[32] 4909 5-11-2 0.................................. DenisO'Regan 64
(Paul Webber) *pressed ldr tl over 3f out: dropped out rapidly: bdly t.o* **20/1**

0- **8** *21* **Arthamint**[39] 4763 6-10-13 0...[1] JackQuinlan(3) 45
(Nicholas Pomfret) *taken down early: in last pair: fdd rapidly wl over 2f out: edgd lft home turn: hopelessly t.o* **80/1**

3m 42.6s (-19.70) **Going Correction** -1.375s/f (Hard)
WFA 4 from 5yo+ 5lb 8 Ran SP% **112.4**
Speed ratings: **94,92,88,83,82 82,74,64**
CSF £5.22 TOTE £3.00: £1.10, £1.10, £1.70; EX 5.30 Trifecta £19.20.
Owner Mrs Sarah Drysdale **Bred** Jim Lanigan **Trained** Upper Lambourn, Berks

FOCUS
The field stood still for a good few seconds before setting off.

5410 FOLLOW @TOTEPOOL ON TWITTER STANDARD OPEN NATIONAL HUNT FLAT RACE (DIV II) 2m
5:45 (5:45) (Class 6) 4-6-Y-O **£1,559** (£457; £228; £114)

Form RPR
1 **Belmount (IRE)**[36] 5-11-2 0....................................... SamTwiston-Davies 99+
(Nigel Twiston-Davies) *big str: hld up last tl smooth prog on inner to ld 2f out: in command fnl f: rdn out* **5/4**[1]

2 *3 1/2* **Danvinnie** 5-10-11 0... ThomasGarner(5) 92+
(Oliver Sherwood) *trckd ldrs: rdn and outpcd in 4th 2f out: styd on steadily after and wnt 2nd cl home: no ch w wnr* **6/4**[2]

3 *nk* **Brigstock Seabra** 6-10-9 0.. DavidEngland 86
(Caroline Bailey) *cl up: rdn to go 2nd wl over 1f out: rn green and no imp on wnr fnl f: lost 2nd nr fin* **17/2**[3]

4 *4 1/2* **Youngdocgallagher (IRE)** 5-10-11 0.................................. BenPoste(5) 88
(Michael Mullineaux) *2nd tl led over 2f out: hdd 2f out: rdr immediately dropped whip: one pce and btn 4th 1f out* **11/1**

0- **5** *16* **Minnie Mustang**[36] 4824 6-10-2 0.. MrJMartin(7) 65
(Andrew J Martin) *t.k.h to post: led tl rdn and hdd over 2f out: sn dropped rt out: t.o* **20/1**

3m 53.0s (-9.30) **Going Correction** -1.375s/f (Hard)
WFA 4 from 5yo+ 5lb 5 Ran SP% **108.1**
Speed ratings: **68,66,66,63,55**
CSF £3.24 TOTE £1.80: £1.20, £1.70; EX 3.70 Trifecta £8.30.
Owner N A Twiston-Davies **Bred** Pamela Sweeney **Trained** Naunton, Gloucs

FOCUS
Half of the declared field were withdrawn in this division of the bumper.
T/Plt: £39.40 to a £1 stake. Pool: £82853.54 - 1531.29 winning tickets T/Qpdt: £13.90 to a £1 stake. Pool: £4093.53 - 217.41 winning tickets IM

5411 - 5414a (Foreign Racing) - See Raceform Interactive

5043 CORK (R-H)
Sunday, April 20

OFFICIAL GOING: Soft changing to yielding to soft after race 1 (2.30) changing to yielding after race 4 (4.00)

5415a IMPERIAL CALL CHASE (GRADE 3) (16 fncs) 3m
4:30 (4:33) 5-Y-O+ **£16,250** (£4,750; £2,250; £750)

RPR
1 **Toner D'Oudairies (FR)**[16] 5155 7-11-8 150..................(tp) DavyCondon 151
(Gordon Elliott, Ire) *chsd ldrs in 3rd tl slow at 9th and 10th: clsd again appr 3 out: sn chsd ldr in 2nd and on terms last: styd on wl stands' rails to ld in clsng strides* **9/10**[1]

2 *1/2* **Noble Prince (GER)**[39] 4752 10-11-2 149..........................(p) AlanCrowe 144
(Paul Nolan, Ire) *chsd ldrs in 4th tl wnt 3rd after 9th: gd hdwy to ld 3 out: jnd last: styd on wl on far side: hdd in clsng strides* **3/1**[2]

3 *11* **Caim Hill (IRE)**[17] 5150 11-11-2 130...................................(p) APHeskin 133
(Philip Fenton, Ire) *chsd ldr in 2nd tl nt qckn appr 3 out: kpt on at one pce bef last* **5/1**[3]

4 *1/2* **Carrigeen Lechuga (IRE)**[21] 5098 9-10-9 123.................. MissEALalor 125
(R H Lalor, Ire) *sn clr ldr: jst hdd whn pckd bdly 3 out: no imp whn mstke 2 out: kpt on again into 4th run-in* **11/1**

5 *1/2* **Liz's D'Estruval (IRE)**[35] 4848 6-10-5 111........................ PhillipEnright 121
(John Joseph Murphy, Ire) *racd in 5th tl dropped to rr 5 out: hdwy to cl on inner whn short of room and snatched up after 4 out: prog into 4th 2 out: sn no imp and dropped to 5th run-in* **20/1**

6 *7 1/2* **Supreme Doc (IRE)**[17] 5135 9-11-5 133.......................(p) PatrickMangan 127
(M T O'Donovan, Ire) *hld up in rr tl tk clsr order 5 out: nt qckn after 3 out: sn no ex* **10/1**

6m 24.6s (28.20) 6 Ran SP% **116.5**
CSF £4.48 TOTE £1.40: £1.40, £1.30; DF 2.90 Trifecta £6.90.
Owner Gigginstown House Stud **Bred** Comte Michel De Gigou **Trained** Trim, Co Meath

FOCUS
There was only a couple of lengths between the field two out. The fifth helps set the standard.

5416 - 5419a (Foreign Racing) - See Raceform Interactive

5197 FAIRYHOUSE (R-H)
Sunday, April 20

OFFICIAL GOING: Good to yielding

5420a BOYLESPORTS EASTER FESTIVAL H'CAP HURDLE (GRADE B) (10 hdls) 2m
3:40 (3:41) 4-Y-O+ **£27,083** (£7,916; £3,750; £1,250)

RPR
1 **Daneking**[63] 4313 5-10-12 **128**.. PaulTownend 141+
(W P Mullins, Ire) *sn chsd ldrs: racd keenly early: clsr in 3rd 1/2-way: hdwy into 2nd bef 2 out: gng best: led travelling wl between last 2 and kpt on wl u.p run-in* **6/1**[2]

2 *3* **Darwins Fox (FR)**[49] 4586 8-11-1 **131**.............................. BrianO'Connell 140
(Henry De Bromhead, Ire) *chsd ldrs tl disp and led fr 2nd: nt fluent 3rd: 1 l clr 1/2-way: reduced advantage 3 out and strly pressed bef next: hdd between last 2: kpt on wl run-in wout matching wnr* **33/1**

3 *2 3/4* **False Economy (IRE)**[44] 2553 9-11-1 **136**......................... ShaneButler(5) 142
(Michael Hourigan, Ire) *hld up in tch: 9th 1/2-way: prog to chse ldrs bef 2 out: rdn in 4th between last 2 and clsd u.p into mod 3rd fr last: kpt on same pce* **33/1**

4 *1 1/4* **Bally Longford (IRE)**[214] 1603 6-10-9 **125**................................. AELynch 130
(W P Mullins, Ire) *chsd ldrs: j. sltly lft 3rd: 6th 1/2-way: clsd into 3rd bef 2 out and no imp on ldrs between last 2: slt mstke last and dropped to 4th: kpt on one pce* **12/1**

5 *shd* **Stocktons Wing (IRE)**[176] 5581 5-10-5 **128**.............................. GerFox(7) 133
(Charles O'Brien, Ire) *hld up towards rr: prog fr bef 3 out: tk clsr order bef next where hmpd by faller: rdn into mod 5th between last 2: kpt on one pce* **16/1**

6 *5* **Art Of Payroll (GER)**[16] 5153 5-11-7 **137**............................. MarkEnright 138
(D T Hughes, Ire) *in rr of mid-div: sltly hmpd 3rd: 10th 1/2-way: hdwy 4 out to chse ldrs after next: rdn and no imp on ldrs 2 out: kpt on one pce* **6/1**[2]

The Form Book Jumps, Raceform Ltd, Compton, RG20 6NL.

7 6 1/2 **Bishopslough (IRE)**[29] 4975 6-10-5 121 DannyMullins 114
(Anthony Mullins, Ire) *racd in mid-div: 11th 1/2-way: no imp whn hmpd by faller 2 out: kpt on again in 11th fr between last 2* **16/1**

8 1 1/4 **Aladdins Cave**[265] 1140 10-10-2 118 (p) MarkBolger 110
(C A Murphy, Ire) *hld up towards rr: hdwy to chse ldrs in 8th after 3 out: sn no ex u.p: kpt on one pce fr next* **14/1**

9 3 3/4 **Sailors Warn (IRE)**[21] 4584 7-11-6 136 BarryGeraghty 124
(E J O'Grady, Ire) *hld up: clsr in 7th 1/2-way: rdn bef 2 out and nt clr run bhd horses: hmpd by faller and no imp after: kpt on one pce* **9/2**[1]

10 4 1/2 **To Choose (IRE)**[21] 3803 5-10-3 119 AndrewPThornton 103
(Thomas Gibney, Ire) *led tl jnd and hdd fr 2nd: rdn in 2nd after 3 out and wknd bef next* **25/1**

11 6 1/2 **Steps To Freedom (IRE)**[233] 1460 8-11-10 140 (t) RobbiePower 117
(Mrs John Harrington, Ire) *w.w in rr: sme hdwy bef 4 out: rdn in 11th on outer bef next and no imp whn hmpd by faller: kpt on one pce* **14/1**

12 4 1/2 **Midnight Game**[49] 4584 7-11-4 139 BrianHayes(5) 112
(W P Mullins, Ire) *hld up in tch: 5th 1/2-way: rdn and wknd fr 3 out* **33/1**

13 3 3/4 **Wooly Tom (IRE)**[21] 5096 10-10-3 119 ow2 (tp) MartinMooney 86
(Patrick Mooney, Ire) *chsd ldrs: j.big 2nd: 4th 1/2-way: rdn in 4th after 3 out and wknd bef next where mstke* **14/1**

14 43 **Ally Cascade (IRE)**[126] 3123 6-11-5 135 PCarberry 61
(Noel Meade, Ire) *hld up towards rr: sltly hmpd 3rd: rdn and no imp after 3 out: wknd and eased: t.o* **7/1**[3]

15 1 1/2 **Passage Vendome (FR)**[28] 4995 8-10-12 128 ow1 EmmetMullins 52
(W P Mullins, Ire) *hld up in rr of mid-div: sme hdwy bef 4 out: rdn and no ex fr next: wknd and eased: t.o* **12/1**

P **Coffee (IRE)**[274] 1046 7-11-5 135 MarkWalsh
(Jonjo O'Neill) *in rr of mid-div: rdn in rr fr 3 out and no ex: trailing whn p.u bef next* **12/1**

F **Kylestyle (IRE)**[56] 4456 5-10-12 128 AndrewJMcNamara
(F Flood, Ire) *chsd ldrs early: 8th 1/2-way: tk clsr order bhd ldrs and in tch whn fell 2 out* **14/1**

4m 3.5s (-8.50) **17 Ran SP% 133.4**
CSF £208.54 CT £6046.18 TOTE £7.20: £1.70, £10.10, £7.90, £4.30; DF 265.00.
Owner Mrs S Ricci **Bred** Sir Eric Parker **Trained** Muine Beag, Co Carlow

FOCUS
Competitive, a reasonably generous early gallop and no hard luck stores. The winner looked like fulfilling that role from a long way out and won comfortably. Those who raced near the pace were suited.

5422a POWERS GOLD CUP (GRADE 1) (16 fncs) 2m 4f
4:40 (4:42) 5-Y-0+ **£48,750** (£14,250)

RPR

1 **Rebel Fitz (FR)**[24] 5044 9-11-10 151 BarryGeraghty 157+
(Michael Winters, Ire) *hld up: clsr in 3rd fr 6th: niggled along fr 4 out: clsr in 2nd bef 2 out where lft in front: sn pushed clr of remaining rival: kpt on wl* **2/1**[2]

2 15 **Bright New Dawn (IRE)**[42] 4709 7-11-10 145 PCarberry 144
(D T Hughes, Ire) *chsd ldr: racd keenly: mstke in 2nd at 2nd: nt fluent 10th: pushed along into st and no imp on ldr in 3rd whn lft 2nd 2 out: no ex between last 2: kpt on one pce* **5/1**[3]

F **Ballycasey (IRE)**[39] 4751 7-11-10 155 PaulTownend 156+
(W P Mullins, Ire) *attempted to make all: stl gng wl bef 3 out: gng best and over 1 l clr whn fell 2 out* **11/8**[1]

U **Mozoltov**[22] 5081 8-11-10 150 DavyRussell
(W P Mullins, Ire) *chsd ldrs: mstke in 3rd at 2nd: dropped to rr fr 6th: stl in tch in rr whn blnd and uns rdr 8th* **11/2**

5m 5.1s (-18.90) **4 Ran SP% 107.5**
CSF £10.63 TOTE £2.40; DF 8.40 Trifecta £11.10.
Owner Brian Sweetnam **Bred** Pierre De Maleissye Melun Et Al **Trained** Kanturk, Co Cork

FOCUS
Disappointing numbers for this Grade 1 novices' chase but the quartet who turned up were all rated above 145, which speaks volumes about the quality of the race. Indeed, three of the four had marks in the 150s. The problem is that we were left with more questions than answers due to the fall of Ballycasey two fences from home.

5424a TATTERSALLS IRELAND GEORGE MERNAGH MEMORIAL SALES BUMPER 2m
5:40 (5:40) 4-5-Y-0
£49,166 (£15,833; £7,500; £3,333; £1,666; £833)

RPR

1 **Moon Racer (IRE)** 5-11-7 MrMJLynch(7) 118+
(Michael Ronayne, Ire) *hld up in rr: last over 5f out: gd hdwy to chse ldrs in 5th into st: clsd gng wl between horses and rdn to ld over 1f out: styd on strly* **50/1**

2 7 1/2 **Sir Scorpion (IRE)** 5-11-7 MrDJMullins(7) 111
(Thomas Mullins, Ire) *chsd ldrs: 5th 1/2-way: tk clsr order in 3rd 3f out: disp gng wl 2f out: sn rdn in 2nd and no imp on wnr ins fnl f: kpt on same pce* **10/1**

3 3 1/2 **Turcagua (FR)** 4-11-4 MrPWMullins 97
(W P Mullins, Ire) *hld up in tch: 8th 1/2-way: prog to chse ldrs in 4th under 3f out: rdn and sn outpcd: kpt on u.p in 6th fr over 1f out into mod 3rd nr fin* **4/5**[1]

4 1/2 **Tycoon Prince (IRE)** 4-11-1 MrRPQuinlan(3) 97
(P M J Doyle, Ire) *w.w towards rr: hdwy over 5f out to chse ldrs in 6th 3f out: rdn into 3rd 1 1/2f out and no imp on ldrs ins fnl f: dropped to mod 4th nr fin* **12/1**

5 1 1/2 **Motown Bob (IRE)**[60] 4363 4-10-13 MrDRoche(5) 95
(Henry De Bromhead, Ire) *chsd ldr in 2nd: tk clsr order gng wl 5f out: led over 3f out tl rdn and jnd 2f out: sn hdd and no ex u.p in 4th ent fnl f: kpt on one pce* **4/1**[2]

6 nk **Kilkishen (IRE)** 4-10-13 MrRJKiely(5) 95
(John Joseph Hanlon, Ire) *hld up in tch: 6th 1/2-way: hdwy to chse ldrs in 3rd 5f out: wnt 2nd 3f out: sn rdn and no ex u.p: wknd fnl 2f* **25/1**

7 6 1/2 **Rufino (IRE)** 4-10-13 MrDGLavery(5) 88
(P J Rothwell, Ire) *hld up in tch: 7th 1/2-way: rdn in 6th into st and sn no imp: kpt on one pce* **40/1**

8 nk **Barossa Pearl (IRE)** 4-10-11 MsNCarberry 81
(Noel Meade, Ire) *w.w towards rr: tk clsr order over 3f out: rdn in 8th over 2f out and sn no ex u.p: kpt on one pce* **8/1**[3]

9 4 1/4 **Gotadime (IRE)**[36] 4827 5-11-7 MrBGCrawford(7) 94
(P J Rothwell, Ire) *led and sn clr: 10 l in front at 1/2-way: reduced advantage 5f out: rdn and hdd over 3f out: wknd* **50/1**

10 58 **Rock This Town (IRE)** 5-11-7 [1] MrJPDowling(7) 36
(Brendan W Duke, Ire) *hld up in tch: tk clsr order into 3rd bef 1/2-way: rdn and wknd 4f out: t.o* **50/1**

11 4 3/4 **Chasing Waterfalls (IRE)** 4-11-4 MrSCrawford 21
(C F Swan, Ire) *chsd ldrs: 4th 1/2-way: rdn and wknd 4f out: t.o* **16/1**

12 dist **Tapaidh Frankie (IRE)**[14] 5196 5-11-2 MrNMcParlan(5)
(Simon West) *chsd ldrs early: rdn in 8th over 5f out and sn wknd: completely t.o* **25/1**

13 94 **Barren Hill (IRE)** 5-11-7 MissKHarrington(7)
(Mrs John Harrington, Ire) *hld up: rdn in 9th 5f out and sn no ex u.p: wknd 4f out: completely t.o* **20/1**

4m 3.5s (-2.90)
WFA 4 from 5yo 5lb **13 Ran SP% 130.1**
Pick Six: Not Won. Pool of 7,942.05 carried forward to Fairyhouse on Monday 21st April. Tote Aggregate: 2013: 399,003.00, 2014: 214,433.00 CSF £505.67 TOTE £40.00: £11.00, £4.10, £1.10; DF 630.50 Trifecta £1816.30.
Owner Michael Ronayne **Bred** Denis And Mrs Teresa Bergin **Trained** Dungarvan, Co Waterford

FOCUS
One of the rank outsiders went off a good gallop. The rest were reasonably well bunched. The complete rank outsider (on the exchanges) won.
T/Jkpt: @1,166.60. Pool: @4,560.00 - 6 winning units. T/Plt: @104.80. Pool: @243.61 - 36,485.50 winning units. BF

5421 - 5424a (Foreign Racing) - See Raceform Interactive

5085 AUTEUIL (L-H)
Sunday, April 20

OFFICIAL GOING: Turf: very soft

5425a PRIX DU PRESIDENT DE LA REPUBLIQUE (CHASE) (GRADE 3 H'CAP) (5YO+) (TURF) 2m 7f 110y
2:08 (12:00) 5-Y-0+
£84,375 (£41,250; £24,375; £16,875; £9,375; £6,562)

RPR

1 **Tzar's Dancer (FR)**[28] 6-10-6 0 WilfridDenuault 143
(E Leenders, France) **47/10**[2]

2 6 **Sidi Bouknadel (FR)**[28] 6-11-4 0 ThomasBeaurain 149
(J-L Guillochon, France) **15/1**

3 snk **Pearse (FR)**[28] 10-9-11 0 PACarberry 128
(Louisa Carberry, France) **13/1**

4 1 1/4 **Urkashe (FR)**[28] 6-9-11 0 (b) MorganRegairaz 127
(E Lecoiffier, France) **72/1**

5 1 **Extreme Sud (FR)**[49] 6-10-10 0 DavidCottin 139
(N Bertran De Balanda, France) **4/1**[1]

6 4 **Sundream (GER)**[28] 6-10-6 0 ArnaudDuchene 131
(G Macaire, France) **19/1**

7 5 **Vent Sombre (FR)**[16] 5-10-7 0 (p) AlainDeChitray 127
(G Cherel, France) **33/1**

8 snk **Very Heaven (FR)**[28] 5-10-3 0 (p) JacquesRicou 122
(G Cherel, France) **39/1**

9 7 **Pierrot Bay (FR)**[35] 4859 7-10-6 0 BertrandBourez 118
(T Trapenard, France) **31/1**

10 10 **Kipour'son (FR)**[28] 6-9-11 0 (b) RegisSchmidlin 99
(M Seror, France) **14/1**

11 3 **Tito Dela Barriere (FR)**[49] 4591 7-10-10 0 ThierryMajorcryk 109
(E Lecoiffier, France) **17/1**

12 hd **Estoril (FR)**[22] 7-10-3 0 (p) CyrilleGombeau 102
(G Cherel, France) **26/1**

13 20 **Biloute De Houelle (FR)**[22] 6-10-3 0 FrancoisPamart 82
(A Chaille-Chaille, France) **11/2**[3]

P **Savigne (FR)**[49] 9-9-11 0 (b) WilfriedLajon
(Mali Droueche, France) **75/1**

P **Alberto De Ballon (FR)**[25] 7-10-10 0 BertrandLestrade
(Y-M Porzier, France) **20/1**

F **Sundahia (FR)**[28] 7-10-10 0 (b) KevinNabet
(J-D Marion, France) **13/1**

F **Don Alejandro (FR)**[28] 6-9-13 0 ow2 SylvainDehez
(J Ortet, France) **41/1**

F **Yellow Ball (FR)**[45] 4635 6-10-1 0 (p) LudovicPhilipperon
(Venetia Williams) *prom early: midfield fr 8th: niggled along to hold pl whn fell 4 out* **25/1**

F **Saint Val (FR)**[35] 5-9-13 0 ow2 AnthonyLecordier
(J Bertran De Balanda, France) **57/1**

P **Chardonnay (FR)**[91] 5-10-10 0 (p) KevinGuignon
(G Cherel, France) **42/1**

5m 58.21s (358.21) **20 Ran SP% 120.7**
PARI-MUTUEL (all including 1 euro stake): WIN 5.70; PLACE 2.20, 4.70, 3.70; DF 36.90; SF 62.50.
Owner Mlle Marie-Cecile De Saint-Seine **Bred** Mlle M C De Saint-Seine **Trained** France

5174 CHEPSTOW (L-H)
Monday, April 21

OFFICIAL GOING: Good (good to soft in places)
Wind: mild across Weather: sunny

5426 CHILLIMINT "NATIONAL HUNT" NOVICES' HURDLE (8 hdls) 2m 110y
1:30 (1:30) (Class 4) 4-Y-0+ **£3,119** (£915; £457; £228)

Form RPR

305- 1 **Solar Impulse (FR)**[18] 5142 4-11-1 135 (t) SamTwiston-Davies 125+
(Paul Nicholls) *trckd ldr: led 4 out: r.o wl: comf* **8/11**[1]

424- 2 3 3/4 **Anteros (IRE)**[116] 3278 6-11-0 122 PaulMoloney 117
(Sophie Leech) *hld up: hdwy after 4th: tended to jump lft fr 4 out: trckd wnr after 3 out: rdn after 2 out: kpt on but nt gng pce to chal* **7/2**[3]

353- 3 7 **Masquerade (IRE)**[24] 5057 5-11-6 120 LiamTreadwell 116
(Warren Greatrex) *led tl 4 out: sn rdn: kpt on same pce fr 2 out* **3/1**[2]

P0- 4 13 **Memberof (FR)**[74] 4111 4-11-1 0 RobertThornton 98
(Alan King) *hld up in tch: wnt 3rd at the 3rd: rdn after 4 out: wknd between last 2* **11/1**

45/ 5 16 **C J Mackintosh**[710] 199 8-10-2 0 RobertMcCarth(5) 74
(Ian Williams) *trckd ldrs: rdn appr 4 out: sn wknd: t.o* **50/1**

55- 6 10 **Farasi Kubwa**[71] 4175 6-10-9 0 CallumWhillans(5) 71
(Venetia Williams) *trckd ldrs: nt fluent 2nd: wknd bef 4 out: blnd 2 out: t.o* **33/1**

0- **7** *19* **Point Of Attack (IRE)**^{33} 4909 5-11-0 0..............................(t) CharliePoste 52
(Robin Dickin) *racd keenly: hld up: lost tch after 4th: t.o* **33/1**

PU0- **8** *140* **Bobtail**^{42} 4722 4-10-2 0.. ThomasCheesman$^{(7)}$
(Mark Gillard) *in tch: pushed along after 3rd: lost tch after next: continued t.o* **100/1**

3m 58.9s (-11.70) **Going Correction** -0.45s/f (Good)
WFA 4 from 5yo+ 5lb **8** Ran SP% **122.3**
Speed ratings (Par 105): **109,107,103,97,90 85,76,**
CSF £4.22 TOTE £1.80: £1.10, £1.70, £1.10; EX 4.70 Trifecta £8.40.
Owner Andrea & Graham Wylie **Bred** Paul Nataf **Trained** Ditcheat, Somerset

FOCUS

An uncompetitive novices' hurdle run at a steady gallop. The cosy winner was value for a bit further.

5427 JENKINS OF NANTYFYLLON MARES' NOVICES' HURDLE (11 hdls) 2m 4f

2:05 (2:05) (Class 4) 4-Y-0+ **£3,119** (£915; £457; £228)

Form RPR

252- **1** **Pressies Girl (IRE)**^{19} 5124 6-10-12 0..................... SamTwiston-Davies 114+
(Paul Nicholls) *trckd ldrs: wnt clr 2nd appr 4 out: led bef 2 out: styd on wl: pushed out* **7/2^{2}**

22P- **2** *7* **Hopstrings**^{193} 1829 6-11-5 102.. LiamTreadwell 113+
(Charlie Brooks) *hld up towards rr of mid-div: outpcd after 7th: styd on fr 3 out: wnt 2nd run-in: fin strly but no ch w wnr* **20/1**

2P2- **3** *7* **Ruby Glow**^{27} 5018 6-10-12 108..................................... AndrewThornton 102
(Seamus Mullins) *in tch: nt fluent 5th: hdwy after 6th: cl up but rdn whn mstke 4 out: sn outpcd: mstke 2 out: styd on to go 3rd run-in* **12/1**

354- **4** *1 1/2* **Molly's A Diva**^{30} 4961 7-11-5 119..........................(v) RichardJohnson 105
(Kim Bailey) *hld up towards rr: mstke 3rd: hdwy after 5th: outpcd after 7th: styd on fr 3 out: wnt 4th towards fin* **7/2^{2}**

43F- **5** *hd* **Our Cat (IRE)**^{19} 5124 6-10-12 0.. AlainCawley 102+
(Fergal O'Brien) *set decent pce: clr after 4th tl after 7th: kicked clr again 4 out: hdd bef 2 out: wkng in btn 2nd whn mstke last: lost 3 pls run-in* **33/1**

234- **6** *24* **Our Pollyanna (IRE)**^{31} 4931 7-10-12 110..................(p) RobertThornton 76
(Alan King) *trckd ldr: rdn appr 4 out: wknd after 3 out: t.o* **11/2^{3}**

060- **7** *58* **Pandy Wells**^{19} 5124 5-10-12 0.. CharliePoste 24
(Graeme McPherson) *mid-div tl after 5th: t.o after 7th* **100/1**

512- **P** **Flementime (IRE)**^{59} 4392 6-11-5 129.................................. IanPopham
(Martin Keighley) *trckd ldrs: rdn appr 4 out: mstke and stmbld bdly 3 out: nt rcvr and sn p.u* **2/1^{1}**

0/F- **P** **Abigail Lynch (IRE)**^{103} 3600 6-10-12 0........................(t) AndrewTinkler
(George Baker) *a towards rr: t.o whn p.u bef 4 out* **33/1**

00/ **P** **Highway Joe**^{420} 4432 7-10-7 0...................................... RobertMcCarth$^{(5)}$
(Ian Williams) *a towards rr: t.o whn p.u bef 4 out* **66/1**

00- **F** **Over The Air**^{35} 4867 6-10-9 0.. RobertDunne$^{(3)}$
(John Spearing) *fell 1st* **100/1**

00- **P** **Cloudy Smith**^{11} 5229 5-10-5 0... ConorRing$^{(7)}$
(Brian Eckley) *struggling 5th: a in rr: t.o whn p.u after 7th* **100/1**

4m 52.2s (-9.60) **Going Correction** -0.45s/f (Good)
WFA 4 from 5yo+ 6lb **12** Ran SP% **116.0**
Speed ratings (Par 105): **101,98,95,94,94 85,61,, ,**
CSF £65.51 TOTE £4.50: £1.90, £4.10, £3.80; EX 64.60 Trifecta £545.00.
Owner W A Harrison-Allan **Bred** Donal Murphy **Trained** Ditcheat, Somerset

FOCUS

The gallop was sound for this mares' novices' hurdle. The winner is on the upgrade, with a bigger step up from the second.

5428 FINE WINES DIRECT NOVICES' H'CAP CHASE (16 fncs) 2m 3f 110y

2:40 (2:42) (Class 4) (0-110,106) 5-Y-0+ **£3,768** (£1,106; £553; £276)

Form RPR

211- **1** **Tokyo Javilex (FR)**^{27} 5017 7-11-12 106...............(t) SamTwiston-Davies 115+
(Nigel Hawke) *nt travelling early but in tch: trckd ldr after 5th: rdn whn lft 6 l 2nd 4 out: 4 l down last: styd on wl to ld towards fin: drvn out* **7/4^{1}**

233- **2** *1/2* **Islandmagee (IRE)**^{27} 5017 7-11-1 102...........................(t) ConorRing$^{(7)}$ 110
(Evan Williams) *led: lft 6 l clr 4 out: rdn after next: 4 l up last: no ex whn hdd towards fin* **15/2**

6PP/ **3** *3 1/2* **Push The Trigger**^{441} 4029 7-10-0 80 oh4............................. IanPopham 85
(Caroline Keevil) *trckd ldrs: shkn up briefly after 7th: rdn after 5 out: kpt on same pce fr 2 out* **12/1**

542- **4** *10* **Dropzone (USA)**^{41} 4748 5-10-12 95................................... RobertDunne$^{(3)}$ 92
(Richard Lee) *trckd ldr: reminder after 6th: rdn along to hold pce after 10th: kpt chsng ldrs but nvr threatened: wknd last* **9/2^{3}**

4/3- **5** *3 3/4* **Wishes And Stars (IRE)**^{341} 317 8-11-5 106................ MikeyEnnis$^{(7)}$ 97
(Tim Dennis) *in tch: tk clsr order after 11th: rdn after 5 out: nvr threatened: wknd 2 out* **16/1**

462- **P** **Tenby Jewel (IRE)**^{32} 4911 9-11-8 102.................................... LiamHeard
(Mark Gillard) *j.lft: chsd ldrs: nt fluent 3rd: losing pl whn mstke 10th: sn bhd: p.u bef 5 out* **8/1**

432- **U** **Supreme Bob (IRE)**^{15} 5187 8-10-11 98......................... TomBellamy$^{(7)}$
(Lucy Jones) *in tch: tk clsr order 10th: travelling wl enough in 4 l 2nd whn blnd and uns rdr 4 out* **7/2^{2}**

5m 1.8s (-9.50) **Going Correction** -0.325s/f (Good) **7** Ran SP% **113.2**
Speed ratings: **106,105,104,100,98 ,**
CSF £14.91 CT £118.55 TOTE £2.20: £1.40, £1.80; EX 8.30 Trifecta £464.70.
Owner D R Mead **Bred** Scea Ecurie Jc Laisis **Trained** Stoodleigh, Devon

FOCUS

They went an honest gallop for this novices' handicap. Improvement for the first two.

5429 K.N.M. H'CAP HURDLE (11 hdls) 2m 4f

3:15 (3:15) (Class 3) (0-140,126) 4-Y-0+ **£5,393** (£1,583; £791; £395)

Form RPR

0/4- **1** **Fear Glic (IRE)**^{336} 409 8-11-9 123.................................. RichardJohnson 127
(Jackie Du Plessis) *mde all: kpt on gamely: rdn out* **12/1^{3}**

301- **2** *3 1/4* **Cocktails At Dawn**^{6} 5345 6-11-12 126 7ex....................... AndrewTinkler 129+
(Nicky Henderson) *travelled wl bhd ldrs: wnt clr 2nd after 4 out: hit 2 out: sn rdn: nt qckn and sn hung in bhd wnr: mstke last: hld after* **4/11^{1}**

002- **3** *3 3/4* **Radmores Revenge**^{16} 5179 11-11-5 124............................ CharlieWallis$^{(5)}$ 122
(Sophie Leech) *hld up last: hdwy into cl 5th after 7th: rdn bef next: kpt on but nt pce to threaten* **12/1^{3}**

440- **4** *shd* **Shammick Boy (IRE)**^{18} 5142 9-11-9 126........................ GilesHawkins$^{(3)}$ 125
(Victor Dartnall) *trckd ldr: hit 4th: rdn after 4 out: kpt on but nt pce to get on terms* **8/1^{2}**

054- **5** *5* **Red Admirable (IRE)**^{42} 4726 8-10-13 118....................... KillianMoore$^{(5)}$ 112
(Graeme McPherson) *trckd ldrs: disp 2nd after 7th tl rdn after 3 out: kpt on same pce fr next* **12/1^{3}**

606- **6** *110* **Lava Lamp (GER)**^{15} 5186 7-10-13 113.................................. PaulMoloney
(Evan Williams) *trckd wnr tl 5th: sn struggling in rr: t.o after 7th: continued* **20/1**

4m 52.2s (-9.60) **Going Correction** -0.45s/f (Good)
WFA 4 from 6yo+ 6lb **6** Ran SP% **112.3**
Speed ratings (Par 107): **101,99,98,98,96**
CSF £17.95 TOTE £10.90: £4.70, £1.10; EX 16.80 Trifecta £135.20.
Owner Du Plessis, Martin & Waterman **Bred** Jay Leahy **Trained** Trehan, Cornwall

FOCUS

A weak race for the grade and, with the odds-on favourite appearing to run well below the form he'd showed when winning easily at Kempton. The winner is rated in line with the best of his 2012 form.

5430 PROSTATE CYMRU H'CAP CHASE (18 fncs) 3m

3:50 (3:51) (Class 3) (0-140,137) 5-Y-0+ **£9,747** (£2,862; £1,431; £715)

Form RPR

621- **1** **Savant Bleu (FR)**^{19} 5127 8-11-0 125.......................... SamTwiston-Davies 133+
(Kim Bailey) *cl up: hdwy 5 out: wnt 2nd 3 out: sn rdn: led between last 2: all out to hold on to diminishing advantage* **7/2^{2}**

4P6- **2** *nk* **Howard's Legacy (IRE)**^{44} 4681 8-10-13 127................. RobertDunne$^{(3)}$ 136+
(Venetia Williams) *hld up bhd ldrs: hdwy 12th: led appr 5 out: rdn after 4 out: hdd after 2 out: rallied wl fnl 100yds: nt quite get bk up* **12/1**

651- **3** *2* **Ballyoliver**^{36} 4835 10-11-2 127.. LiamTreadwell 132
(Venetia Williams) *cl up: trckd ldrs 9th: rdn appr 3 out: styd on same pce fr 2 out* **5/1**

211- **4** *9* **Galway Jack (IRE)**^{24} 5053 9-11-9 134.......................... AndrewThornton 131
(Caroline Bailey) *led: rchd for 4th: rdn and hdd appr 5 out: lost 2nd 3 out: styd on same pce tl no ex fr last* **4/1^{3}**

03P- **5** *5* **Harry The Viking**^{51} 4544 9-10-13 127........................(p^{1}) HarryDerham$^{(3)}$ 123
(Paul Nicholls) *trckd ldr: pushed along after 12th: rdn and looking hld in 5th whn mstke and stmbld 5 out: btn after* **9/4^{1}**

314- **6** *1 1/4* **Makethe Mostofnow (IRE)**^{15} 5184 9-10-11 122............. PaulMoloney 114
(Evan Williams) *trckd ldr tl 13th: sn rdn: wl hld fr next* **7/1**

6m 8.6s (-13.40) **Going Correction** -0.325s/f (Good) **6** Ran SP% **109.9**
Speed ratings: **109,108,108,105,103 103**
CSF £35.56 TOTE £3.30: £1.60, £6.80; EX 45.30 Trifecta £301.60.
Owner Kim Bailey Racing Partnership III **Bred** Marc Trinquet And Olivier Trinquet **Trained** Andoversford, Gloucs

FOCUS

Some in-form staying handicap chasers locked horns, but it was steadily run. The first two are rated to their best.

5431 REAL RADIO BREAKFAST WITH JAGGER AND WOODY H'CAP HURDLE (DIV I) (12 hdls) 3m

4:25 (4:26) (Class 5) (0-100,100) 4-Y-0+ **£1,949** (£572; £286; £143)

Form RPR

233- **1** **Earcomesthedream (IRE)**^{39} 4779 11-11-0 95...........(b) TomBellamy$^{(7)}$ 102
(Peter Pritchard) *trckd ldrs: rdn after 4 out: led after 3 out: 2 l up last: hld on: rdn out* **11/2**

400- **2** *nk* **Power Of God (IRE)**^{77} 4068 6-11-2 90........................... RichardJohnson 97
(Tim Vaughan) *trckd ldrs: rdn after 4 out: wnt 2nd after 2 out: styd on wl fnl 75yds: a being jst hld* **3/1^{1}**

453- **3** *2* **Kapricorne (FR)**^{37} 4803 7-10-2 76...................................... PaulMoloney 82+
(Sophie Leech) *hld up towards rr: hdwy after 7th: rdn after 4 out: wnt 4th after 4 out: sn rdn: wnt 3rd after 2 out: kpt on but nt pce to mount chal* **7/2^{2}**

4/P- **4** *5* **Silent Cliche (IRE)**^{337} 10-10-12 89.............................. RobertDunne$^{(3)}$ 90
(Ms N M Hugo) *disp ld tl advantage 4 out: sn rdn: nt fluent and hdd next: styd chsng wnr tl appr last: no ex run-in* **20/1**

UU6- **5** *1* **Hector's House**^{46} 4636 8-10-0 74..................................... DonalDevereux 73
(Nikki Evans) *hld up: rdn in tch after 7th: styd on same pce fr 3 out* **16/1**

114- **6** *1 3/4* **Warsaw Pact (IRE)**^{21} 5114 11-10-1 82.......................... MrLKilgarriff$^{(7)}$ 79
(Steven Dixon) *trckd ldrs tl 5th: in tch and sn pushed along: rdn after 8th: outpcd 4 out: kpt on fr 2 out* **7/1**

046- **7** *19* **The Bogman's Ball**^{27} 5015 8-11-4 99..............................(p) ConorRing$^{(7)}$ 79
(Grace Harris) *disp ld tl rdn appr 4 out: wknd 3 out* **14/1**

0U0- **8** *36* **Canadian Dreamer (IRE)**^{46} 4636 7-11-3 96................. KillianMoore$^{(5)}$ 44
(Graeme McPherson) *trckd ldrs: rdn after 7th: wknd bef next: t.o* **5/1^{3}**

660- **9** *9* **Orlittlebylittle**^{23} 5072 8-10-11 85.......................................(b) AdrianLane 24
(Donald McCain) *hld up: struggling 7th: sn bhd: t.o* **14/1**

6m 6.8s (4.60) **Going Correction** -0.45s/f (Good) **9** Ran SP% **115.8**
Speed ratings (Par 103): **74,73,73,71,71 70,64,52,49**
CSF £22.98 CT £66.04 TOTE £5.20: £2.10, £1.40, £1.30; EX 30.90 Trifecta £157.20.
Owner Woodland Generators & D R Pritchard **Bred** Cornelius O'Riordan **Trained** Whatcote, Warwicks

FOCUS

Moderate form. The winenr is rated to a similar level as last year's C&D win.

5432 REAL RADIO BREAKFAST WITH JAGGER AND WOODY H'CAP HURDLE (DIV II) (12 hdls) 3m

5:00 (5:00) (Class 5) (0-100,100) 4-Y-0+ **£1,949** (£572; £286; £143)

Form RPR

360- **1** **Pennant Dancer**^{32} 4911 7-10-1 75.. PaulMoloney 86+
(Debra Hamer) *hld up towards rr: smooth hdwy after 8th: trckd ldr after next: rdn whn mstke 2 out: led last: styd on wl* **16/1**

5PP- **2** *2 1/2* **Bobbisox (IRE)**^{42} 4729 9-10-0 74 oh5........................(p) LiamTreadwell 81
(Alex Hales) *racd keenly: led after 1st: rdn after 2 out: hdd last: kpt on but no ex* **33/1**

0P3- **3** *9* **Ifyouthinkso**^{25} 5037 7-11-5 100....................................(t) TomBellamy$^{(7)}$ 98
(Lucy Jones) *chsd ldrs tl lost pl and rdn after 6th: towards rr: stdy hdwy fr 4 out: wnt 3rd sn after last: styd on* **8/1**

000- **4** *1 3/4* **Lightning Moley (IRE)**^{16} 5177 11-10-2 81.........................(t) BenPoste$^{(5)}$ 77
(Tracey Watkins) *mid-div: hdwy after 8th: rdn after next: wnt 3rd after 3 out: styd on same pce: lost 3rd sn after last* **25/1**

404- **5** *5* **Bally Braes (IRE)**^{43} 4699 6-11-8 96.......................(p) SamTwiston-Davies 88
(Nigel Twiston-Davies) *mid-div: nt fluent 6th: hdwy 8th: effrt 4 out: sn one pce* **4/1^{1}**

626- **6** *5* **Tara Tavey (IRE)**^{11} 5234 9-10-12 93........................ ThomasCheesman$^{(7)}$ 80
(Kevin Bishop) *nvr travelling in rr: plugged on fr 4 out: n.d* **7/1**

04P- **7** *24* **Duke's Affair**^{65} 4275 6-10-13 90..................................... MattGriffiths$^{(3)}$ 55
(Jeremy Scott) *racd keenly: mid-div: hdwy 7th: prom after 8th: rdn and ev ch appr 4 out: wknd 2 out* **8/1**

34S- **8** *18* **Tiller Belle**^{8} 5307 6-11-8 99.. JeremiahMcGrath$^{(3)}$ 48
(Nicky Henderson) *mid-div: pushed along after 4th: wknd bef 4 out: t.o* **12/1**

PP4- **P** **Radetsky March (IRE)**[37] 11-11-12 **100**..................(p) AndrewThornton
(Geoffrey Deacon) *led tl after 1st: prom: rdn after 8th: wknd next: p.u bef 3 out* **25/1**

101- **P** **Safferano (IRE)**[153] 2575 8-11-7 **95**.............................. RichardJohnson
(Tim Vaughan) *hld up bhd: hdwy after 7th: rdn bef 4 out: wknd bef 3 out: p.u bef 2 out* **6/1**[3]

6/2- **P** **Noble Perk**[34] 4883 9-11-0 **88**.. RobertThornton
(Adrian Wintle) *mid-div: hdwy 7th: effrt 4 out: sn wknd: p.u bef 2 out* **5/1**[2]

000- **P** **Agent Fedora**[23] 5069 6-10-5 **82**..................................(tp) RobertDunne[(3)]
(Kim Bailey) *racd wout declared tongue-strap: prom: hit 8th: sn rdn: wknd bef next: bhd whn p.u bef 2 out* **10/1**

6m 1.5s (-0.70) **Going Correction** -0.45s/f (Good) **12** Ran SP% **119.0**
Speed ratings (Par 103): **83,82,79,78,76 75,67,61, ,**
CSF £443.91 CT £4476.59 TOTE £16.90: £6.10, £8.20, £1.80; EX 743.80.
Owner P J Woolley **Bred** P J Woolley **Trained** Nantycaws, Carmarthens

FOCUS
Many of the market principals failed to run up to expectations. The cosy winner is rated back to the level of his surprise Ludlow third.

5433 BATH ALES H'CAP CHASE (18 fncs) 3m
5:35 (5:35) (Class 5) (0-100,97) 5-Y-0+ **£2,144** (£629; £314; £157)

Form RPR

42P- **1** **Bringewood Belle**[104] 3595 11-9-7 **71** oh16........................ PaulJohn[(7)] 84+
(John Needham) *trckd ldrs: reminder 11th: led 5 out: rdn after 3 out: styd on wl fr last: rdn out* **33/1**

412- **2** *3 ¾* **The Last Bridge**[15] 5185 7-11-4 **89**...................(p) RichardJohnson 98
(Susan Johnson) *in tch: wnt 3rd 11th: rdn appr 5 out: wnt 2nd 4 out: ch after last: no ex fnl 100yds* **9/2**[1]

004- **3** *13* **Le Grand Chene (FR)**[15] 5187 8-11-7 **92**........................(t) PaulMoloney 90
(Sophie Leech) *hld up towards rr: hdwy after 13th: rdn after next: wnt 3rd 3 out: styd on but nvr any threat to front pair* **16/1**

654- **4** *1* **Simply Charles (IRE)**[10] 5263 7-10-11 **82**................... RobertThornton 81
(Hilary Parrott) *trckd ldrs tl blnd 4th: mid-div: pushed along fr 7th: rdn after 13th: styd on same pce fr 4 out: nvr any threat to ldrs* **5/1**[2]

P/P- **5** *1 ¼* **Ovthenight (IRE)**[23] 5069 9-11-9 **94**.................................... HaddenFrost 89
(Roger Curtis) *hld up towards rr: rdn and hdwy after 13th: hmpd 4 out: wnt 4th bef last: styd on but nvr any danger to ldrs* **50/1**

305- **6** *12* **Tin Pot Man (IRE)**[25] 5038 8-10-13 **91**..............................(t) ConorRing[(7)] 79
(Evan Williams) *mid-div: hdwy after 13th: lft 3rd briefly whn rdn and bdly hmpd 4 out: nt a threat after: wknd after 2 out* **16/1**

6P0- **7** *17* **Lupita (IRE)**[34] 4884 10-10-0 **71** oh12..................................(t) IanPopham 40
(Derrick Scott) *chsd ldrs tl rdn after 12th: sn towards rr: wknd 4 out: t.o* **50/1**

332- **8** *2* **Craiglands (IRE)**[8] 5293 12-10-5 **81**.......................(v) RobertMcCarth[(5)] 48
(Ian Williams) *in tch: rdn after 13th: wknd next: t.o* **6/1**[3]

P46- **9** *33* **Trozulon (FR)**[28] 5009 7-11-10 **95**.................................... LiamTreadwell 33
(Venetia Williams) *a towards rr: t.o fr 5 out* **20/1**

554- **10** *1* **Jump Up**[15] 5185 8-10-7 **78**...(v) DonalDevereux 15
(Peter Bowen) *led tl 3rd: chsd ldrs tl 9th: sn struggling in rr: t.o 5 out* **6/1**[3]

P54- **P** **Bishophill Jack (IRE)**[28] 5011 8-11-4 **89**.................(v) AndrewThornton
(Kim Bailey) *in tch: trckd ldrs 4th: rdn after 13th: fading whn mstke 5 out: p.u bef next* **11/1**

665- **F** **Midnight Macarena**[23] 5065 9-11-9 **97**......................(v[1]) RobertDunne[(3)]
(Lucy Wadham) *j.rt: prom: led 3rd: hdd 5 out: sn rdn: 3rd and fading whn fell heavily next* **16/1**

/42- **P** **No Through Road**[25] 5038 7-10-8 **79**...........................(t) AndrewTinkler
(Michael Scudamore) *mid-div tl 12th: wknd after next: t.o whn p.u bef 5 out* **14/1**

3P5- **P** **What A Good Night (IRE)**[30] 4970 6-11-3 **88**........ SamTwiston-Davies
(Nigel Twiston-Davies) *nvr travelling: a in rr: t.o whn p.u bef 5 out* **7/1**

6m 11.2s (-10.80) **Going Correction** -0.325s/f (Good) **14** Ran SP% **120.2**
Speed ratings: **105,103,99,99,98 94,89,88,77,77 , , ,**
CSF £177.40 CT £2516.86 TOTE £30.30: £10.10, £2.00, £4.80; EX 299.20.
Owner J L Needham **Bred** John Needham **Trained** Ludlow, Shropshire

FOCUS
An upset in the finale, with a big chase best from the winner.
T/Plt: £21.70 to a £1 stake. Pool: £57587.28 - 1934.77 winning tickets T/Qpdt: £6.30 to a £1 stake. Pool: £3572.38 - 414.52 winning tickets TM

[4791]FAKENHAM (L-H)
Monday, April 21

OFFICIAL GOING: Good (6.6)
All rail moved.
Wind: light breeze Weather: warm and sunny; 18 degrees

5434 FAKENHAM LADIES RACEDAY 1ST JUNE (S) HURDLE (11 hdls) 2m 4f
1:55 (1:55) (Class 5) 4-Y-0+ **£2,737** (£798; £399)

Form RPR

432- **1** **Maller Tree**[15] 5183 7-11-9 125....................................(b) MichealNolan[(3)] 116+
(David Dennis) *hit 1st: pushed along 4th: prom: wnt 5 l 2nd bef 3 out: drvn to ld on home turn bef last: sn clr* **9/4**[1]

23P- **2** *8* **Neverownup (IRE)**[206] 1668 9-11-0 0.................................. DaveCrosse 97
(K F Clutterbuck) *led tl 7th: 8 l 3rd and rdn and outpcd bef 3 out: bmpd along fr next: wnt 6 l 2nd at last: no ch w wnr* **14/1**

136- **3** *5* **Edlomond (IRE)**[32] 4919 8-11-2 119..............................(t) ChrisDavies[(7)] 103
(Bill Turner) *trckd ldrs: led 7th: wnt 5 l clr bef 3 out: rdn wl bef next: hdd 120yds bef last where lost 2nd: fin v weakly* **6/1**

B34- **4** *20* **Stand Clear**[8] 5298 9-10-9 88... TonyKelly[(3)] 73
(David Thompson) *hld up in last pair tl 6th: lost tch w ldrs bef 3 out and sn remote* **10/1**

P50- **5** *1 ¾* **County Zen (FR)**[38] 4791 11-10-12 87.........................(v[1]) MissAEStirling[(7)] 78
(Caroline Fryer) *2nd or 3rd tl rdn and lost interest after 7th: remote fr 3 out* **25/1**

12F- **P** **Regal D'Estruval (FR)**[15] 5194 9-11-0 110.............. ChristopherWard[(5)]
(Dr Richard Newland) *taken down early: 2nd or 3rd tl rdn 5th: sn downed tools: t.o fr 8th tl p.u 3 out* **11/4**[2]

4FP- **P** **Broughtons Bandit**[37] 4818 7-11-0 104.................................. RyanMania
(Willie Musson) *towards rr: rdn and struggling after 8th: bdly t.o whn p.u 2 out* **9/2**[3]

555/ **P** **Celtic Legacy**[294] 1881 7-10-3 0 ow3..........................(b[1]) JakeHodson[(7)]
(Michael Murphy) *last pair: mstke 7th and drvn: t.o next: p.u 3 out* **50/1**

4m 59.0s (-13.60) **Going Correction** -0.50s/f (Good) **8** Ran SP% **111.5**
Speed ratings (Par 103): **107,103,101,93,93 , ,**
CSF £31.65 TOTE £3.50: £1.30, £2.50, £2.20; EX 29.10 Trifecta £138.30.The winner was bought in for 5,200gns.

Owner Favourites Racing **Bred** Phil Toft **Trained** Hanley Swan, Worcestershire

FOCUS
A moderate seller. The winner is rated a stone+ below his best.

5435 ROBERT HOARE NOVICES' HUNTERS' CHASE (FOR THE ROBERT HOARE MEMORIAL TROPHY) (15 fncs 1 omitted) 2m 5f 110y
2:30 (2:30) (Class 6) 5-Y-0+ **£1,247** (£387; £193; £96)

Form RPR

215/ **1** **Utopian (FR)**[29] 6-11-10 0... MrDHDunsdon 115+
(David Dunsdon) *detached in last early and under plenty of restraint: j. slowly 5th: wnt 4th at 8th: blnd next: tk 3rd and nt fluent 2 out: clsd readily to ld last: rdn to qckn clr* **7/2**[3]

P/ **2** *3 ¼* **Master Workman (IRE)**[29] 8-11-7 0.................................. MrDKemp[(3)] 107
(David Kemp) *pckd 1st: led tl 4th: 2nd tl led again 3 out: 5 l clr next: rdn and hdd last: immediately outpcd* **8/1**

2/5- **3** *19* **Volcan Surprise (FR)**[16] 6-11-3 109...............................(p) MrRStearn[(7)] 88
(Caroline Fryer) *lacked fluency: hld up: wnt 3rd and j. slowly 8th: blnd 13th and rdn: chal briefly next: lost 2nd between last two and wknd qckly* **6/4**[1]

P/0- **4** *9* **Irish Rebel (IRE)**[9] 10-11-7 0..(t) MrFMitchell[(3)] 83
(Miss Clare Hobson) *led 4th: pushed along 10th: drvn and j.v.slowly and hdd 3 out: floundering in 4th whn mstke next* **20/1**

21P/ **F** **Lion On The Prowl (IRE)**[15] 10-11-7 114................(tp) MrsAlexDunn[(3)]
(Alexandra Dunn) *j.lft and t.k.h: pressed ldrs tl fell 6th* **3/1**[2]

F **Baltic Blue**[15] 7-11-5 0....................................(p) MissCareyWilliamson[(5)]
(B Dowling) *trckd ldrs tl fell heavily 6th* **50/1**

PP5/ **P** **Pericoloso (IRE)**[36] 8-11-7 0..(b) MrJSole[(3)]
(Ms A E Embiricos) *j. slowly and reluctantly in last pair: nvr wnt a yard: u.p 5th: climbed over 7th and crashed over 11th: t.o bef 13th: p.u 2 out* **16/1**

5m 37.3s (-4.50) **Going Correction** -0.30s/f (Good) **7** Ran SP% **110.9**
Speed ratings: **96,94,87,84, ,**
CSF £28.18 TOTE £6.70: £2.30, £2.90; EX 35.60 Trifecta £185.60.
Owner Coldunell Limited **Bred** Mlle Katherine Aalen **Trained** Shere, Surrey

FOCUS
A modest novice hunter chase run at a steady pace. The winner is rated in line with last year's hurdles form.

5436 CECIL AND SHEILA BUTTIFANT MEMORIAL NOVICES' H'CAP HURDLE (11 hdls) 2m 4f
3:05 (3:17) (Class 4) (0-105,105) 4-Y-0+ **£3,898** (£1,144; £572; £286)

Form RPR

/06- **1** **Vico (IRE)**[43] 4700 10-11-12 **105**....................................(p) AdamWedge 107
(Ali Brewer) *sn pressing ldr: led 7th: u.p bef 2 out: looked to be abt to assert after last: edgd rt and only jst hld on* **10/1**

00- **2** *shd* **Artifice Sivola (FR)**[15] 5190 4-10-4 **92**.......................... MichealNolan[(3)] 88
(Lucy Wadham) *settled midfield: clsd to 2nd gng wl bef 3 out: coaxed upsides last: looked abt to be outbattled flat but almost ct idling wnr* **10/1**

0P0- **3** *1 ½* **Unknown Legend (IRE)**[11] 5242 7-10-11 **95**................. JamesBanks[(5)] 94
(Anthony Middleton) *settled in rr: pushed along 7th: clsd to 4th bef 3 out where mstke and drvn: 2nd bef next: racd awkwardly whn ev ch on home turn: nt qckn fr last* **8/1**[3]

200- **4** *2 ¾* **Steel Summit (IRE)**[19] 5128 5-11-5 **103**................... AnthonyFreeman[(5)] 100+
(David Dennis) *sn bhd: mstke 4th: lost tch and mstke 6th: sn rdn: stl last and 15 l fr wnr 3 out: styng on strly after last: too much to do* **5/1**[2]

300- **5** *3* **Dougalstar (FR)**[23] 5069 5-10-13 **92**...............................(b[1]) FelixDeGiles 87
(Sean Curran) *prom: hit 6th: disp 2nd and hrd drvn 3 out: sn btn: plugged on* **16/1**

/P1- **6** *20* **Doyenne Dream**[11] 5244 7-11-3 **103**.........................(vt) MissAEStirling[(7)] 79
(Caroline Fryer) *trckd ldrs: mstke 7th: rdn bef 3 out: sn lost tch and nt run on* **16/1**

044- **7** *13* **Wunfurlez**[42] 4715 6-11-2 **95**... SamThomas 60
(Diana Grissell) *midfield: fdd tamely bef 3 out: t.o* **8/1**[3]

F02- **U** **Killegney**[23] 5069 10-10-6 **88**..(p) PeterCarberry[(3)]
(Michael Gates) *led tl blnd 1st and eventually uns rdr* **5/1**[2]

12F- **P** **Good Of Luck**[31] 4937 5-11-9 **102**................................(p) GavinSheehan
(Warren Greatrex) *lft in ld 1st: hdd 7th: mstke 8th and lost 2nd: stopped rapidly and sn t.o: p.u 2 out* **5/2**[1]

5m 3.0s (-9.60) **Going Correction** -0.50s/f (Good)
WFA 4 from 5yo+ 6lb **9** Ran SP% **114.1**
Speed ratings (Par 105): **99,98,98,97,96 88,82, ,**
CSF £101.28 CT £839.48 TOTE £10.10: £3.90, £5.60, £3.70; EX 76.30 Trifecta £345.50.
Owner Mrs V M Verdin **Bred** Sunnyhill Stud **Trained** Eastbury, Berks
■ Stewards' Enquiry : Adam Wedge caution: careless riding.

FOCUS
An ordinary novice handicap. The winner was very well in on old form.

5437 DAVID KEITH MEMORIAL H'CAP CHASE (14 fncs 2 omitted) 2m 5f 110y
3:40 (3:48) (Class 4) (0-110,108) 5-Y-0+ **£6,324** (£1,963; £1,057)

Form RPR

UP4- **1** **Full Ov Beans**[23] 5066 10-10-13 **98**............................... PeterCarberry[(3)] 105+
(Michael Gates) *mde all at fast gallop: sn 6 l clr: mstke 4th: dived at next: mstke 6th: pressed whn outj. rival 2 out: drvn bef last: responded generously and a in command* **7/2**[2]

221- **2** *7* **Little Jimmy**[23] 5065 7-10-5 **87**..(p) FelixDeGiles 89
(Tom Gretton) *blnd 2nd: nt a fluent: chsd wnr after 5th: drvn to chal and 2 l down whn outj. 2 out: a hld after* **11/8**[1]

45P- **3** *8* **Rossa Parks (IRE)**[36] 4840 8-11-9 **105**........................(t) GavinSheehan 99
(Neil Mulholland) *last pair: 12 l in last and pushed along at 9th: struggling whn pckd 11th: rallied bef last and kpt on v wl flat* **5/1**[3]

P03- **P** **Ballybach (IRE)**[55] 4483 10-11-12 **108**................................(t) AdamWedge
(Nick Gifford) *nvr travelling: 2nd tl mstke 5th: blnd next: dropped bk last at 8th: p.u and dismntd next* **7/1**

403- **U** **Fitandproperjob**[29] 4992 8-10-0 **87**.............................(vt) JamesBanks[(5)]
(Anthony Middleton) *last but in tch whn blnd bdly and uns rdr 7th* **6/1**

5m 32.8s (-9.00) **Going Correction** -0.30s/f (Good) **5** Ran SP% **107.8**
Speed ratings: **104,101,98, ,**
CSF £8.76 TOTE £4.10: £2.10, £1.10; EX 7.90 Trifecta £35.00.
Owner Michael Gates **Bred** Miss A Thompson **Trained** Clifford Chambers, Warwicks

FOCUS
A weak handicap, and a small personal best from the winner.

5438 WELLS COMMUNITY HOSPITAL H'CAP HURDLE (13 hdls) 2m 7f 110y
4:15 (4:15) (Class 4) (0-110,110) 4-Y-0+ **£3,573** (£1,049; £524; £262)

Form RPR
145- **1** **Campbonnais (FR)**[37] 4809 9-11-12 **110**..........................(p) AdamWedge 112
(Ali Brewer) *settled trcking ldrs: 4 l 4th and drvn and outpcd 3 out tl next: urged through on inner to chal last: sn led: hld on gamely: all out* **8/1**
004- **2** *hd* **Armedandbeautiful**[52] 4533 6-10-13 **97**.............................. FelixDeGiles 100
(Tom Gretton) *prom: cl 3rd and bmpd along bef 2 out: chal bef last where led briefly: kpt on wl but jst hld* **9/2**[2]
546- **3** *1 ¾* **West End (IRE)**[31] 4937 7-10-10 **99**..........................(p) EdCookson[(5)] 99
(Kim Bailey) *hld up trcking ldrs: effrt 9th: 2nd next: led 2 out: 2 l clr and rdn bef last where hdd: wknd cl home* **8/1**
000- **4** *2 ¼* **Diamond Pro (IRE)**[15] 5191 5-9-13 **88**..................... JamesBanks[(5)] 86
(Christopher Kellett) *last trio tl mstke 8th: drvn next: outpcd 3 out: 12 l 5th whn hopped through flattened next: styng on stoutly after last* **50/1**
321- **5** *15* **Storm To Pass**[323] 598 6-10-7 **98**..............................(t) MissAEStirling[(7)] 82
(Caroline Fryer) *towards rr: hdwy to ld after 8th: sn 4 l clr: drvn and hdd and mstke 2 out: dropped out qckly* **5/1**[3]
363- **P** **Belle De Fontenay (FR)**[29] 4983 9-11-6 **104**....................(p) BarryKeniry
(Conor Dore) *bhd: rdn 5th: nvr travelling: t.o 9th: p.u 2 out* **16/1**
F50- **P** **Hurraboru (IRE)**[24] 5059 7-11-8 **109**..............................(b) TonyKelly[(3)]
(David Thompson) *led: hdd after 8th: sn hrd drvn and trying to pull himself up: t.o and p.u after 3 out* **8/1**
41P- **P** **Mistral Reine**[28] 5010 5-11-9 **110**.................................... MichealNolan[(3)]
(Lucy Wadham) *virtually ref to r and lost 25l: clambered over first two and p.u* **8/1**
3P3- **P** **Peterbrown (IRE)**[43] 4700 6-11-5 **106**..........................(p) PeterCarberry[(3)]
(Nick Gifford) *prom tl drvn and lost pl bef 7th: blnd next: t.o bef 3 out: p.u 2 out* **11/4**[1]

6m 6.1s (-0.30) **Going Correction** -0.50s/f (Good) **9** Ran SP% **113.8**
Speed ratings (Par 105): **80,79,79,78,73 , , ,**
CSF £43.81 CT £298.20 TOTE £8.40: £2.80, £2.70, £3.10; EX 64.60 Trifecta £281.40.
Owner Robert Tyrrell & Ian Mason **Bred** Patrick Lemarie & Patrick Le Gougouec **Trained** Eastbury, Berks

FOCUS
A competitive staying handicap hurdle and there were three upsides at the last. The form seems sound.

5439 QUEEN'S CUP, AN EASTERN COUNTIES HUNTERS' CHASE (16 fncs 2 omitted) 3m 110y
4:50 (4:50) (Class 6) 5-Y-0+ **£1,646** (£506; £253)

Form RPR
1 **Thornleigh Ben (IRE)**[36] 9-11-5 0...................................... MrAWright[(7)] 115+
(N R W Wright) *hld up: tk clsr order 8th: wnt 2nd at 12th: pressing ldr whn lft w big advantage 2 out: sn rdn: unchal after: eased flat* **7/1**
P22/ **2** *20* **Benheir (IRE)**[36] 8-11-5 0...(p) MrRStearn[(7)] 97
(S J Stearn) *blnd 2nd: w ldr tl 4th: sn lost pl: lost tch and blnd 9th: hit next: kpt plodding out: lft 25 l 4th and hit 2 out: wnt remote 2nd flat* **7/1**
312- **3** *6* **Otto The Great (FR)**[8] 6-11-9 132.................... MrGeorgeHenderson[(7)] 94
(Mrs Antonia Bealby) *cl up: disp 2nd fr 10th: ev ch 13th: wkng whn lft poor 2nd next: tired whn lost 2nd after last* **3/1**[2]
3PP/ **4** *11* **Picabo Kid (USA)**[29] 11-11-5 99..(p) MissSLKlug[(7)] 77
(Miss S L Klug) *rn in snatches first circ: sn rdn: dropped bk last and j. slowly 7th: t.o 10th* **25/1**
103- **5** *37* **Jack Bene (IRE)**[19] 5127 8-11-9 115.................(p) MrAVaughan-Jones[(7)] 47
(Miss Louise Allan) *prom: dropped bk 4th at 13th and qckly lost tch: j. bdly rt and crashed over 2 out: t.o and v tired after* **4/1**[3]
U **Moroman (IRE)**[30] 7-11-9 0.. MrDKemp[(3)] 115+
(David Kemp) *uns rdr bef s: j.rt: w ldr tl led fr 4th: 2 l clr and stl gng wl whn lunged rt and uns rdr 2 out* **15/8**[1]

6m 30.7s (-5.00) **Going Correction** -0.30s/f (Good) **6** Ran SP% **108.6**
Speed ratings: **96,89,87,84,72**
CSF £46.93 TOTE £8.50: £5.20, £7.80; EX 46.50 Trifecta £228.70.
Owner Mrs Angela Wright **Bred** Gerald McPolin **Trained** Chippenham, Wiltshire

FOCUS
Not much rules form to go on, and very guessy ratings.

5440 LADIES DAY 1ST JUNE MARES' MAIDEN OPEN NATIONAL HUNT FLAT RACE 2m
5:25 (5:25) (Class 5) 4-6-Y-0 **£2,395** (£698; £349)

Form RPR
1 **Caitys Joy (GER)** 4-10-10 0.. GavinSheehan 109+
(Warren Greatrex) *wnt 2nd after 4f: drew clr w ldr wl over 2f out: sn rdn: led 1f out: readily asserted* **1/1**[1]
542- **2** *2 ¾* **Ellin's Tower**[54] 4499 5-10-10 0..(t) EdCookson[(5)] 107
(Kim Bailey) *led: rdn over 1f out: hdd 1f out: one pce and no match for wnr but wl clr of rest* **7/2**[2]
0/6- **3** *20* **Scarlett Lady**[37] 4810 6-11-1 0.. AdamWedge 89
(Ali Brewer) *dropped out last tl 1/2-way: prog 5f out: 5 l 3rd 3f out: rdn and qckly lost tch w ldng pair* **14/1**
30- **4** *24* **Tyre Hill Lady**[15] 5195 5-10-12 0...................................... MichealNolan[(3)] 67
(David Dennis) *settled in rr: effrt 5f out: 12 l 5th and rdn 3f out: sn struggling: t.o* **25/1**
6- **5** *2 ½* **Ishusharella**[15] 5195 5-10-8 0.. MrFMitchell[(7)] 65
(J R Jenkins) *midfield: pushed along 6f out: 17 l 5th 3f out: t.o after* **20/1**
03- **6** *10* **Ella's Promise**[66] 4253 5-11-1 0.. RyanMania 56
(Barry Brennan) *cl up for 11f: hopelessly t.o fnl 3f* **20/1**
5- **7** *9* **Come On Harriet**[35] 4867 5-10-12 0..............................(t) PeterCarberry[(3)] 48
(Alex Hales) *plld hrd: pressed ldr 4f: wknd 5f out: hopelessly t.o fnl 3f* **12/1**[3]
20- **8** *17* **Sirrah Star (IRE)**[80] 4016 6-10-10 0...................................... JamesBanks[(5)] 33
(Neil Mulholland) *bhd: in last and struggling 7f out: hopelessly t.o 5f out* **12/1**[3]
0- **9** *1 ¾* **Polly Wiggle**[35] 4867 5-10-8 0.. MissAEStirling[(7)] 31
(Caroline Fryer) *midfield: fdd rapidly 6f out: hopelessly t.o 5f out* **33/1**
10 *37* **Full Of Mischief (IRE)**[148] 2710 6-11-1 0.............................. DaveCrosse
(K F Clutterbuck) *bhd: hopelessly t.o 5f out: virtually p.u 3f out* **14/1**

3m 55.1s (-4.70) **Going Correction** -0.50s/f (Good)
WFA 4 from 5yo+ 5lb **10** Ran SP% **117.3**
Speed ratings: **91,89,79,67,66 61,56,48,47,29**
CSF £4.03 TOTE £2.10: £1.10, £2.00, £4.00; EX 5.10 Trifecta £46.30.
Owner Mrs Tessa Greatrex **Bred** Gestut Erlenhof **Trained** Upper Lambourn, Berks

FOCUS
Most of the mares in this bumper had previous experience but it looked a two-horse race according to the market, and so it proved. The winner looks a decent recruit.
T/Plt: £1,048.40 to a £1 stake. Pool: £40583.07 - 28.25 winning tickets T/Qpdt: £140.40 to a £1 stake. Pool: £3112.90 - 16.40 winning tickets IM

4757 HUNTINGDON (R-H)
Monday, April 21

OFFICIAL GOING: Good (7.6)
Wind: Light across Weather: Hazy sunshine

5441 WIN A RIO ON LADIES NIGHT CONDITIONAL JOCKEYS' TRAINING SERIES H'CAP HURDLE (RACING EXCELLENCE) (10 hdls) 2m 5f 110y
2:00 (2:00) (Class 4) (0-110,108) 4-Y-0+ **£3,119** (£915; £457; £228)

Form RPR
132- **1** **Should I Stay (FR)**[31] 4937 6-11-9 **108**....................(p) JosephAkehurst[(3)] 115+
(Gary Moore) *chsd ldr tl led appr 6th: clr whn nt fluent 3 out: wnt lft next: rdn and hung lft flat: styd on* **9/4**[1]
065- **2** *4* **Thoresby (IRE)**[130] 3029 8-11-9 **105**....................................(p) RyanHatch 106
(Ben Case) *a.p: mstke 7th: rdn to chse wnr after 2 out: hung lft flat: styd on* **6/1**
620- **3** *2 ¼* **Westerly Breeze (IRE)**[26] 5033 6-11-4 **103**...................(p) OllieGarner[(3)] 102
(Martin Keighley) *led: pushed along and hdd appr 6th: chsd wnr: hit 7th: sn rdn: lost 2nd after 2 out: no ex flat* **5/1**[3]
225- **4** *10* **Thornton Alice**[202] 1707 9-11-3 **102**................................ DanielHiskett[(3)] 91
(Richard Phillips) *hld up: rdn 7th: hdwy u.p after 3 out: styd on same pce fr next* **14/1**
004- **5** *11* **Rattleandrun (IRE)**[18] 5140 6-11-3 **102**.............................. PaulO'Brien[(3)] 81
(Brendan Powell) *hld up: rdn whn hit 7th: wknd next* **14/1**
442- **6** *6* **Drussell (IRE)**[15] 5189 8-11-3 **99**.. JoshWall 73
(Martin Bosley) *hld up: hdwy 7th: rdn and wknd after 3 out* **10/1**
544- **7** *36* **Balinderry (IRE)**[5] 5366 7-10-5 **87**..................................(tp) CharlieDeutsch 28
(Steve Gollings) *chsd ldrs: pushed along appr 6th: wknd bef 3 out* **5/2**[2]

5m 4.3s (-6.30) **Going Correction** -0.35s/f (Good) **7** Ran SP% **112.7**
Speed ratings (Par 105): **97,95,94,91,87 84,71**
CSF £15.68 TOTE £2.60: £2.30, £2.20; EX 16.20 Trifecta £85.30.
Owner M L Bloodstock Ltd **Bred** M L Bloodstock Limited **Trained** Lower Beeding, W Sussex

FOCUS
A modest handicap, confined to conditional riders. The winner rates a bit better than the bare result.

5442 ROY KELLEHER BIRTHDAY CELEBRATION H'CAP CHASE (16 fncs) 2m 4f 110y
2:35 (2:37) (Class 5) (0-100,95) 5-Y-0+ **£2,144** (£629; £314; £157)

Form RPR
03P- **1** **Asian Prince (IRE)**[27] 5027 5-11-12 **95**..........................(bt) DenisO'Regan 110+
(Alastair Lidderdale) *led 2nd: rdn clr appr 2 out: hung rt flat: styd on u.p* **6/1**
320- **2** *7* **Morestead (IRE)**[10] 5263 9-11-4 **87**.................................... BrendanPowell 95
(Brendan Powell) *led to 2nd: chsd ldrs: mstke 10th: wnt 2nd 3 out: sn rdn: styd on same pce appr last* **12/1**
263- **3** *1* **Got Attitude (IRE)**[11] 5247 11-10-13 **89**..........................(vt) RyanHatch[(7)] 96
(Tony Carroll) *hld up: hdwy 13th: rdn bef 2 out: styd on same pce appr last* **11/4**[1]
243- **4** *8* **Sambelucky (IRE)**[24] 5051 9-10-12 **81**...........................(v[1]) JamesReveley 80
(Keith Reveley) *hld up: bhd and pushed along 8th: styd on to go 4th last: nvr nrr* **5/1**[3]
220- **5** *17* **King Ozzy (IRE)**[21] 5115 10-11-7 **95**......................(tp) ConorShoemark[(5)] 79
(Lawney Hill) *hld up: mstke 4th: rdn after 9th: wknd 11th* **10/1**
2U2- **6** *9* **Johnnys Legacy (IRE)**[10] 5263 7-11-9 **92**................................(p) DavidBass 67
(Conor Dore) *prom: chsd wnr 4th tl rdn appr 3 out: wknd bef next* **7/2**[2]
5P4- **P** **Mad Professor (IRE)**[40] 4762 11-9-9 **69** oh7...............(p) JoeCornwall[(5)]
(John Cornwall) *prom: lost pl 1st: pushed along 6th: wknd 11th: bhd whn p.u bef last* **25/1**
P03- **P** **Silver Steel (FR)**[50] 4570 11-10-12 **84**...........................(t) HarryChalloner[(3)]
(Richard Ford) *prom: lost pl 3rd: wknd 10th: bhd whn p.u bef 3 out* **9/1**
444- **P** **Chapel House**[50] 4570 11-9-7 **69** oh5.................................. MrMJPKendrick[(7)]
(Richard Harper) *chsd ldrs tl rdn and wknd 3 out: bhd whn p.u bef next* **16/1**

4m 59.2s (-6.10) **Going Correction** -0.225s/f (Good) **9** Ran SP% **116.4**
Speed ratings: **102,99,98,95,89 86, , ,**
CSF £71.95 CT £242.61 TOTE £6.90: £1.80, £3.40, £1.80; EX 74.90 Trifecta £374.60.
Owner Lidderdale Racing LLP **Bred** Michael O'Dwyer **Trained** Lambourn, Berks

FOCUS
A moderate handicap chase in which they went a decent gallop. The winner comfirmed the merit of his previous C&D run but this looks a step up.

5443 M&D FLOORING, HOME SELECT SERVICE H'CAP HURDLE (8 hdls) 2m 110y
3:10 (3:10) (Class 4) (0-120,120) 4-Y-0+ **£3,119** (£915; £457; £228)

Form RPR
525- **1** **Focail Maith**[29] 4988 6-11-0 **108**......................................(v[1]) HarrySkelton 113+
(Neil King) *hld up in tch: shkn up to ld after 2 out: nt fluent last: r.o wl* **8/1**
212- **2** *3 ¾* **Breaking Bits (IRE)**[19] 5125 7-11-9 **117**.............................. BrendanPowell 118
(Jamie Snowden) *chsd ldr tl led 4th: rdn and hdd after 2 out: styd on same pce flat* **4/1**[2]
555- **3** *2 ¼* **Occasionally Yours (IRE)**[10] 5260 10-10-5 **106**....... JosephAkehurst[(7)] 105
(Alan Blackmore) *chsd ldrs: ev ch 3 out: sn rdn: styd on same pce last* **13/2**
050- **4** *1 ½* **Dormouse**[64] 4300 9-11-7 **115**...(p) RyanMahon 114
(Anabel K Murphy) *hld up: mstke 5th: hdwy after 3 out: sn rdn: no ex last* **9/1**
P12- **5** *4* **Waltz Darling (IRE)**[12] 4864 6-11-12 **120**........................... JamesReveley 116
(Keith Reveley) *hld up: hdwy after 3 out: rdn and wknd appr last* **6/1**[3]
U55- **6** *8* **Akula (IRE)**[38] 4791 7-10-12 **106**... ColinBolger 95
(Mark H Tompkins) *led to 4th: chsd ldr tl appr 3 out: wknd next* **12/1**
050- **7** *9* **Wom**[23] 5072 6-9-10 **95**...(b) ConorShoemark[(5)] 74
(Neil King) *hld up: nt fluent 3rd: sn given reminders: drvn along and wknd next* **9/4**[1]
/63- **8** *8* **St Ignatius**[20] 4794 7-10-13 **107**.. JamesDavies 79
(Alan Bailey) *chsd ldrs: rdn appr 3 out: sn wknd* **7/1**

3m 46.2s (-8.70) **Going Correction** -0.35s/f (Good) **8** Ran SP% **119.7**
Speed ratings (Par 105): **106,104,103,102,100 96,92,88**
CSF £42.41 CT £226.39 TOTE £13.90: £3.10, £1.50, £2.26; EX 35.60 Trifecta £244.40.
Owner Ken Lawrence, Bob Smith, Michael Gibbons **Bred** D Robb **Trained** Newmarket, Suffolk

The Form Book Jumps, Raceform Ltd, Compton, RG20 6NL.

FOCUS
An ordinary handicap. The second and fourth set the level.

5444 M&D FLOORING, CARPETS, VINYLS AND WOODS H'CAP CHASE (19 fncs) 3m
3:45 (3:45) (Class 3) (0-125,125) 5-Y-O+ **£6,498** (£1,908; £954; £477)

Form RPR
004- **1** **Flaming Gorge (IRE)**[11] 5230 9-11-9 **125**.................. NicodeBoinville[(3)] 137+
(Fleur Hawes) *w ldr tl wnt on 13th: pushed clr appr 2 out: easily* **13/2**
136- **2** *9* **Balbriggan (IRE)**[19] 5126 7-11-8 **121**........................... DominicElsworth 124
(Mick Channon) *led: nt fluent 3rd: mstke 10th: hdd 13th: chsd wnr: hit 3 out: sn rdn: styd on same pce fr next* **5/2**[2]
6P6- **3** *1 ½* **Dashing George (IRE)**[23] 5068 12-11-3 **123**...................... MrRWinks[(7)] 123
(Peter Winks) *hld up: pushed along 12th: hdwy 14th: rdn appr 2 out: styd on same pce* **8/1**
325- **4** *9* **Balzaccio (FR)**[30] 4960 9-11-0 **118**............................ ConorShoemark[(5)] 112
(Fergal O'Brien) *chsd ldrs: blnd 15th: rdn after 3 out: wknd next* **11/8**[1]
41P- **5** *29* **Little Chip (IRE)**[23] 5068 7-11-11 **124**..................... DenisO'Regan 98
(Charlie Longsdon) *hld up: mstke 9th: rdn and wknd appr 13th* **5/1**[3]
6m 0.6s (-9.70) **Going Correction** -0.225s/f (Good) **5** Ran SP% **111.8**
Speed ratings: **107,104,103,100,90**
CSF £23.41 TOTE £6.60: £2.80, £2.30; EX 25.30 Trifecta £136.20.
Owner A Fool & His Money **Bred** Alastair Pim **Trained** Diss, Norfolk

FOCUS
Not a strong race for the grade. The second sets the level.

5445 M&D FLOORING DOMESTIC AND COMMERCIAL NOVICES' HURDLE (8 hdls) 2m 110y
4:20 (4:20) (Class 4) 4-Y-O+ **£3,119** (£915; £457; £228)

Form RPR
231- **1** **Paradise Valley (IRE)**[8] 5305 5-11-5 0........................ DominicElsworth 126+
(Mick Channon) *led to 2 out: led again last: rdn out* **7/4**[2]
230- **2** *3 ¼* **Gone Too Far**[44] 4680 6-11-5 125..................................[1] DenisO'Regan 124+
(Alan King) *trckd wnr: wnt upsides 4th: nt fluent next: rdn to ld 2 out: hdd and mstke last: styd on same pce flat* **1/1**[1]
24F- **3** *23* **I Got Power**[34] 4889 5-10-12 115...................................... JamesReveley 95
(Keith Reveley) *chsd ldrs tl rdn and wknd after 3 out* **9/2**[3]
/50- **4** *3 ¼* **Hung Parliament (FR)**[37] 4807 6-10-12 0.................... GerardTumelty 92
(Alan King) *hld up and bhd: mstke and wknd 3 out* **16/1**
4- **5** *3* **Bermacha**[146] 2725 9-10-7 0 ow2.. ColinBolger 86
(John E Long) *plld hrd and prom: hit 3rd: rdn and wknd after 3 out* **33/1**
/60- **P** **Cool Chief**[50] 4569 5-10-5 0..................................... JosephAkehurst[(7)]
(Alan Blackmore) *hld up: rdn and wknd after 4th: bhd whn p.u bef 2 out* **66/1**
3m 46.6s (-8.30) **Going Correction** -0.35s/f (Good) **6** Ran SP% **114.9**
Speed ratings (Par 105): **105,103,92,91,89**
CSF £4.18 TOTE £3.50: £1.60, £1.10; EX 4.30 Trifecta £7.20.
Owner Mrs T P Radford **Bred** William McCarthy **Trained** West Ilsley, Berks
■ Stewards' Enquiry : Colin Bolger one-day ban: weighed in 2lb heavy (May 5)

FOCUS
A fair novice hurdle. The winner built on his recent win and can rate higher.

5446 BOONGATE KIA 7 YEAR WARRANTY NOVICES' CHASE (12 fncs) 2m 110y
4:55 (4:55) (Class 4) 5-Y-O+ **£3,768** (£1,106; £553)

Form RPR
22F- **1** **Woodbank**[128] 3087 7-11-0 123..................................... HarrySkelton 133+
(Dan Skelton) *mde all: rdn after 2 out: nt fluent last: styd on wl* **11/8**[2]
264- **2** *7* **Dark Lover (GER)**[58] 4420 9-11-7 139.......................... BrendanPowell 134
(Jamie Snowden) *hld up in tch: lft trcking wnr after 4th: rdn appr last: no ex flat* **4/6**[1]
PU0- **3** *82* **Next Exit (IRE)**[23] 5067 9-10-9 104................................(t) JoeCornwall[(5)] 53
(John Cornwall) *racd keenly: trckd wnr tl slipped on landing 4th: wknd 6th* **18/1**[3]
4m 5.4s (-4.80) **Going Correction** -0.225s/f (Good) **3** Ran SP% **107.4**
Speed ratings: **102,98,60**
CSF £2.76 TOTE £2.50; EX 2.70 Trifecta £2.00.
Owner James and Jean Potter **Bred** James And Jean Potter **Trained** Alcester, Warwicks

FOCUS
A quite decent small-field novice chase in which they went a solid pace. The form could be rated up to 7lb higher through the second.

5447 RED MILLS BUMPER CHALLENGE INTERMEDIATE OPEN NATIONAL HUNT FLAT RACE 2m 110y
5:30 (5:30) (Class 6) 4-6-Y-O **£1,559** (£457; £228; £114)

Form RPR
62- **1** **Run On Sterling**[37] 4810 5-11-3 0...................................... DenisO'Regan 97
(Paul Webber) *mde all: rdn over 1f out: styd on u.p* **3/1**[1]
446- **2** *¾* **Closest Friend**[128] 3098 5-11-3 0.................................. BrendanPowell 96
(J R Jenkins) *a.p: racd keenly: rdn and ev ch over 1f out: styd on* **14/1**
3 *½* **Mr Beatle** 5-11-3 0.. JamesReveley 95
(Keith Reveley) *trckd ldrs: wnt 2nd 9f out: rdn and ev ch fr over 1f out: unable qck towards fin* **5/1**[3]
4 *1* **Benissimo (IRE)** 4-10-12 0... HarrySkelton 89
(Dan Skelton) *hld up: hdwy over 2f out: rdn over 1f out: r.o* **4/1**[2]
4- **5** *shd* **Mazurati (IRE)**[23] 5070 5-11-0 0...................................... KielanWoods[(3)] 94
(Ben Case) *trckd ldr over 7f: remained handy: rdn over 1f out: styd on* **13/2**
36- **6** *2 ¼* **Kibo**[136] 2926 4-10-12 0.. RyanMahon 87
(Kim Bailey) *hld up: hdwy over 5f out: rdn over 1f out: styd on same pce fnl f* **20/1**
44- **7** *5* **L'Amiral David (FR)**[30] 4964 4-10-12 0.......................... GerardTumelty 82
(Alan King) *trckd ldrs: rdn over 2f out: wknd fnl f* **3/1**[1]
0- **8** *18* **Global Bonus (IRE)**[28] 5014 5-11-3 0............................. DominicElsworth 69
(Caroline Bailey) *hld up: bhd fnl 6f* **33/1**
9 *7* **Bold Achiever** 4-10-12 0.. DavidBass 57
(John Butler) *hld up: wknd over 3f out* **14/1**
0- **10** *22* **Singapore Story (FR)**[64] 4310 5-10-12 0.................. ConorShoemark[(5)] 40
(Neil King) *hld up in tch: rdn over 3f out: wknd over 2f out* **33/1**
3m 48.8s (-0.30) **Going Correction** -0.35s/f (Good)
WFA 4 from 5yo 5lb **10** Ran SP% **124.0**
Speed ratings: **86,85,85,84,84 83,81,73,69,59**
CSF £50.05 TOTE £3.70: £1.60, £3.50, £2.60; EX 56.30 Trifecta £1112.50.
Owner Andrew Rowland **Bred** Juddmonte Farms Ltd **Trained** Mollington, Oxon

FOCUS
A modest bumper which was steadily run. The form is rated around the first two.

T/Plt: £120.70 to a £1 stake. Pool: £32310.26 - 195.26 winning tickets T/Qpdt: £15.70 to a £1 stake. Pool: £1708.86 - 80.15 winning tickets CR

5189 MARKET RASEN (R-H)
Monday, April 21

OFFICIAL GOING: Good (chs 8.2; hdl 8.3)
Wind: Light; half behind Weather: Fine, becoming overcast; light rain Race 4

5448 GARNETTS SWEETS NOVICES' HURDLE (10 hdls) 2m 3f
1:45 (1:46) (Class 4) 4-Y-O+ **£3,249** (£954; £477; £238)

Form RPR
2S4- **1** **Western Diva (IRE)**[28] 5014 5-10-6 0........................... TomScudamore 104+
(David Pipe) *tk fierce hold in last: hdwy to trck ldrs 7th: upsides on bit 2 out: sn led: 2 l ahd last: rdn clr* **5/2**[2]
1- **2** *7* **Kelvingrove (IRE)**[23] 5064 4-10-10 0........................ MauriceLinehan[(3)] 104+
(Jonjo O'Neill) *trckd ldrs: upsides 7th: led briefly appr 2 out: kpt on same pce run-in* **2/5**[1]
006- **3** *28* **Escape To The West**[55] 4476 6-10-8 0.................... SamanthaDrake[(5)] 76
(Joanne Foster) *led to 3rd: w ldrs: lost pl 2 out: sn bhd* **33/1**[3]
0/0- **4** *37* **Sab Le Beau (FR)**[304] 389 5-10-13 0.............................. DavidEngland 39
(Alan Brown) *w ldr: led 3rd: nt fluent 6th: hdd appr 2 out: sn wknd: t.o* **33/1**[3]
4m 51.7s (12.30) **Going Correction** +0.30s/f (Yiel)
WFA 4 from 5yo+ 5lb **4** Ran SP% **105.9**
Speed ratings (Par 105): **86,83,71,55**
CSF £3.94 TOTE £5.50; EX 3.60 Trifecta £8.80.
Owner R S Brookhouse **Bred** J F C Maxwell **Trained** Nicholashayne, Devon

FOCUS
The going was good on a watered track and the rail was moved out three metres on the hurdles course to provide fresh ground. They went a very steady pace in this novice and the hot favourite was turned over by an impressive hurdles debutante, who posted a fast finishing split. The race has been given a token rating.

5449 RACING UK ANYWHERE AVAILABLE NOW MARES' H'CAP HURDLE (12 hdls) 3m
2:20 (2:20) (Class 4) (0-120,117) 4-Y-O+ **£3,422** (£997; £499)

Form RPR
654- **1** **Rattlin**[23] 5075 6-11-3 **115**.. DaraghBourke[(7)] 122
(Sue Smith) *trckd ldrs: cl 2nd appr 2 out: styd on run-in: led clsng stages* **3/1**[2]
452- **2** *½* **Woodland Walk**[33] 4907 6-11-9 **114**............................ TomScudamore 121
(Emma Lavelle) *trckd ldrs: led bef 2 out: hdd and no ex clsng stages* **9/4**[1]
051- **3** *10* **Carolina Wren**[60] 4375 5-11-7 **117**............................ ThomasGarner[(5)] 115
(Renee Robeson) *chsd ldrs: drvn 3 out: modest 3rd appr next: one pce* **9/2**[3]
201- **4** *10* **Emerald Rose**[29] 4983 7-11-12 **117**.. MarkGrant 108
(Julian Smith) *chsd ldrs: pushed along after 7th: outpcd appr 2 out: sn lost pl: poor 4th whn mstke last* **8/1**
060- **5** *19* **Tenmoku**[15] 5191 5-10-11 **105**.................................... MauriceLinehan[(3)] 80
(Jonjo O'Neill) *t.k.h: led 2nd: hit 7th: hdd bef 2 out: sn lost pl and bhd* **12/1**
352- **P** **Ussee (FR)**[21] 5112 6-11-0 **108**...................................... KielanWoods[(3)]
(Ben Case) *chsd ldrs: pushed along after 7th: lost pl next: wl bhd whn p.u bef 9th* **6/1**
23P- **P** **Miss Mohawk (IRE)**[21] 5102 5-10-4 **95**........................(p) DavidEngland
(Alan Brown) *led to 2nd: lost pl bef 9th: sn bhd: t.o whn p.u bef 2 out* **20/1**
344- **P** **Cinnomhor**[34] 4891 6-9-13 **97**................................... DiarmuidO'Regan[(7)]
(Chris Grant) *nt fluent in rr: pushed along 5th: mstke 7th: bhd fr 9th: t.o whn p.u bef 2 out* **33/1**
5m 53.0s (2.50) **Going Correction** +0.30s/f (Yiel) **8** Ran SP% **114.7**
Speed ratings (Par 105): **107,106,103,100,93 , ,**
CSF £10.57 CT £28.74 TOTE £3.60: £1.30, £1.10, £2.30; EX 11.60 Trifecta £43.10.
Owner Broadband Partnership **Bred** R F Broad **Trained** High Eldwick, W Yorks

FOCUS
The two market leaders had a good battle and pulled clear in this mares' handicap. A personal best from the winner.

5450 KEITH SHARPE MEMORIAL H'CAP CHASE (17 fncs) 3m 1f
2:55 (2:55) (Class 4) (0-115,114) 5-Y-O+ **£4,106** (£1,197; £598)

Form RPR
421- **1** **Roc De Guye (FR)**[15] 5193 9-11-1 **106**........................(p) MarkQuinlan[(3)] 119+
(James Evans) *trckd ldrs: upsides 2 out: rdn to ld appr last: forged clr run-in* **10/3**[2]
141- **2** *13* **Keltic Rhythm (IRE)**[27] 5023 7-11-9 **114**........................ TrevorWhelan[(3)] 116
(Neil King) *led to 3rd: led 8th to 12th: swtchd outside and drvn sn after 4 out: upsides next: kpt on same pce run-in* **6/5**[1]
U51- **3** *5* **Smart Catch (IRE)**[28] 4984 8-11-6 **108**............................... LeeEdwards 100
(Tony Carroll) *j.lft: nt fluent 3rd: jnd ldr 12th: led appr 3 out: hdd and hit last: one pce* **4/1**[3]
6PP- **4** *32* **Spanish Optimist (IRE)**[28] 5004 8-11-0 **102**..................(t) MichaelByrne 84
(Tim Vaughan) *w ldr: led 3rd to 8th: led again 12th: hdd appr 3 out: 4th and wkng whn stmbld on landing 2 out: bhd whn eased run-in: t.o* **9/2**
6m 15.3s (-16.00) **Going Correction** -0.55s/f (Firm) **4** Ran SP% **106.7**
Speed ratings: **103,98,97,87**
CSF £7.86 TOTE £4.50; EX 4.50 Trifecta £10.10.
Owner S Crawley, T Crawley **Bred** G A E C Delorme Gerard & Vincent **Trained** Broadwas, Worcs

FOCUS
Three last-time-out winners line-up in this interesting small-field handicap. The pace was not strong but the winner scored with authority and the form looks fairly solid. The winner can probably rate higher.

5451 WATCH RACING UK SKY CHANNEL 432 NOVICES' LIMITED H'CAP CHASE (14 fncs) 2m 4f
3:30 (3:31) (Class 3) (0-125,125) 5-Y-O+ **£7,797** (£2,289; £1,144; £572)

Form RPR
2P2- **1** **Explained (IRE)**[25] 5040 7-10-10 **113**.............................. MichaelByrne 121
(Tim Vaughan) *trckd ldrs: 2nd 10th: lft in ld 3 out: wnt rt sn after last: edgd lft run-in: hld on* **9/2**
16U- **2** *¾* **Deciding Moment (IRE)**[8] 5297 8-11-2 **119**....................(t) MarkGrant 127
(Ben De Haan) *hld up: trckd ldrs 4th: lft cl 2nd 3 out: 1 1/2 l down whn hit last and sn swtchd lft: styd on towards fin: a jst hld* **7/2**[3]
443- **3** *3 ½* **Desgrey**[34] 4892 6-10-7 **110**......................................(p) BrianHughes 116
(Peter Niven) *led: stmbld on landing and hdd 3 out: kpt on same pce* **3/1**[2]

600- **4** *39* **Staigue Fort**[22] 5093 6-11-5 **125** .... MauriceLinehan(3) 94
(Emma Lavelle) *t.k.h: trckd ldrs: j.rt 2nd: lost pl appr 4 out: hung rt and sn bhd: t.o* **5/1**

434- **5** *2* **Walkabout Creek (IRE)**[103] 3601 7-11-8 **125** .... TomScudamore 92
(Steve Gollings) *chsd ldrs: nt fluent 2nd: drvn 4 out: sn lost pl and bhd: t.o* **5/2**[1]

4m 57.5s (-8.20) **Going Correction** -0.55s/f (Firm) **5** Ran SP% **110.6**
Speed ratings: **94,93,92,76,75**
CSF £19.99 TOTE £3.80: £1.10, £2.60; EX 20.20 Trifecta £67.20.
Owner D N V Churton & Mrs C Wilson **Bred** Mrs Patricia Doarn **Trained** Aberthin, Vale of Glamorgan
■ Stewards' Enquiry : Michael Byrne caution: careless riding

FOCUS
Most of the runners had a bit to prove in this handicap. There was a tight market and a close finish, and the form does not look very strong. The winner is rated in line with his hurdle mark.

5452 RACINGUK.COM/ANYWHERE: 3 DEVICES, 1 PRICE H'CAP HURDLE (8 hdls) 2m 1f
4:05 (4:05) (Class 3) (0-130,130) 4-Y-0+ **£8,122** (£2,385; £1,192; £596)

Form RPR

/02- **1** **Gifted Leader (USA)**[23] 5067 9-11-2 **120** .... (t) TomScudamore 124
(Ian Williams) *mde all: increased gallop 4th: 4 l ahd last: styd on* **13/2**

U30- **2** *1 3/4* **Roman Flight (IRE)**[16] 5172 6-11-12 **130** .... (v) BrianHughes 132+
(David Dennis) *t.k.h: hld up: trckd ldrs 3rd: n.m.r after 3 out: hdwy on ins and 4th 2 out: chsd wnr sn after last: kpt on: nt rch wnr* **5/1**[3]

244- **3** *4 1/2* **King Of Strings (IRE)**[14] 5212 5-10-4 **108** .... DougieCostello 107
(Mark Walford) *chsd ldng pair: 2nd 2 out: kpt on same pce* **3/1**[2]

F06- **4** *3/4* **Seventh Sky (GER)**[23] 5067 7-11-4 **122** .... (tp[1]) MarkGrant 119
(Charlie Mann) *chsd wnr: kpt on same pce appr 2 out* **8/1**

U65- **5** *5* **Get Back In Line (IRE)**[23] 5067 6-11-2 **123** .... MauriceLinehan(3) 117
(Jonjo O'Neill) *j.lft 1st: hld up in rr: swtchd lft and sme hdwy appr 2 out: sn outpcd: j.lft last 2: kpt on run-in* **11/4**[1]

004- **6** *shd* **Town Mouse**[22] 5090 4-10-13 **125** .... TrevorWhelan(3) 113
(Neil King) *hld up towards rr: hdwy 4th: drvn and outpcd appr 2 out* **8/1**

P/6- **7** *80* **Absinthe (IRE)**[30] 4947 8-11-2 **120** .... (t) HenryBrooke 41
(Donald McCain) *mid-div: hdwy 5th: rdn and lost pl next: sn bhd: t.o 2 out: eventually fin: lame* **9/1**

4m 8.4s (1.70) **Going Correction** +0.30s/f (Yiel)
WFA 4 from 5yo+ 5lb **7** Ran SP% **113.9**
Speed ratings (Par 107): **108,107,105,104,102 102,64**
CSF £38.11 TOTE £6.10: £3.30, £2.60; EX 30.00 Trifecta £180.80.
Owner The Ferandlin Peaches **Bred** Juddmonte Farms Inc **Trained** Portway, Worcs

FOCUS
They went a stop-start gallop in this decent handicap and the winner made all. He rated 128 in 2011 and might still match that.

5453 WATCH ON 3 DEVICES RACINGUK.COM/ANYWHERE CONDITIONAL JOCKEYS' H'CAP CHASE (14 fncs) 2m 4f
4:40 (4:41) (Class 4) (0-120,114) 5-Y-0+ **£3,768** (£1,106; £553; £276)

Form RPR

P53- **1** **Wessex King (IRE)**[15] 5194 10-11-9 **114** .... JakeGreenall(3) 128+
(Henry Daly) *led to 2nd: w ldr: led 8th: styd on wl fr 3 out: drvn out* **10/3**[3]

013- **2** *6* **Groomed (IRE)**[24] 5058 6-11-5 **110** .... DaraghBourke(3) 120
(Sue Smith) *trckd ldng pair 5th: 2nd 9th: 2 l down whn blnd 4 out: hit next: kpt on same pce* **3/1**[2]

225- **3** *27* **Lough Coi (IRE)**[30] 4968 8-10-1 **92** .... (vt) CharlieDeutsch(3) 75
(Anthony Middleton) *nt fluent 2nd: chsd ldrs 5th: pushed along next: lost pl bef 3 out: tk distant 3rd clsng stages* **3/1**[2]

31P- **4** *1 1/4* **Cara Court (IRE)**[7] 5318 8-10-4 **95** .... (p) JohnDawson(3) 77
(Joanne Foster) *led 2nd to 8th: drvn next: lost pl bef 3 out* **10/1**

331- **F** **Fair Bramble**[11] 5246 8-11-3 **108** .... (b) ThomasGarner(3)
(Oliver Sherwood) *chsd ldng pair: 3rd whn fell 3rd: rn loose and completed over 4 laps of trck* **5/2**[1]

4m 52.2s (-13.50) **Going Correction** -0.55s/f (Firm) **5** Ran SP% **110.7**
Speed ratings: **105,102,91,91,**
CSF £13.73 TOTE £2.80: £1.60, £1.10; EX 4.90 Trifecta £55.60.
Owner Mrs D P G Flory **Bred** Peter McCutcheon **Trained** Stanton Lacy, Shropshire

FOCUS
They went a reasonable pace in this fair handicap. The winner scored with something in hand under a prominent ride and favourite Fair Bramble made a bad mistake and fell at the third. The winner is rated in line with his best 2013 form.

5454 DOWNLOAD NEW RACING UK IPAD APP STANDARD OPEN NATIONAL HUNT FLAT RACE 2m 1f
5:15 (5:15) (Class 6) 4-6-Y-0 **£1,559** (£457; £228; £114)

Form RPR

622- **1** **Countersign**[179] 2052 5-11-3 0 .... AdamPogson 105+
(Charles Pogson) *t.k.h in last: hld up: stdy hdwy on outer over 5f out: trcking ldrs over 2f out: qcknd to ld over 1f out: smoothly* **3/1**[2]

3- **2** *1 1/4* **Bigindie (IRE)**[146] 2731 4-10-12 0 .... BrianHarding 94
(John Weymes) *trckd ldrs: 2nd and drvn over 2f out: chsd wnr over 1f out: styd on same pce* **14/1**

60/ **3** *6* **Days Gone By**[358] 4 6-11-3 0 .... TomScudamore 94
(Emma Lavelle) *chsd ldrs: 2nd over 5f out: kpt on one pce fnl 2f: tk 3rd nr fin* **6/1**[3]

/35- **4** *1 1/4* **Exitas (IRE)**[27] 5028 6-10-12 0 .... ThomasGarner(5) 92
(Oliver Sherwood) *led: drvn over 3f out: hdd over 1f out: one pce* **3/1**[2]

0- **5** *20* **Royal Roo**[86] 3898 5-10-10 0 .... DougieCostello 67
(Mark Rimell) *hld up in mid-div: effrt over 4f out: chsng ldrs over 3f out: sn wknd* **10/1**

6 *4 1/2* **Krasnodar (IRE)** 4-10-12 0 .... BrianHughes 65
(Malcolm Jefferson) *in rr: drvn 6f out: short-lived effrt 4f out: sn lost pl and bhd* **5/2**[1]

0- **7** *52* **Remedio (IRE)**[24] 5063 4-10-5 0 .... RyanDClark(7) 19
(Andrew Crook) *chsd ldrs: drvn 6f out: lost pl over 4f out: sn bhd: t.o over 2f out: eventually completed* **28/1**

4m 6.8s (5.70) **Going Correction** +0.30s/f (Yiel)
WFA 4 from 5yo+ 5lb **7** Ran SP% **112.1**
Speed ratings: **98,97,94,94,84 82,58**
CSF £40.26 TOTE £2.80: £1.10, £11.00; EX 27.20 Trifecta £45.40.
Owner C T Pogson **Bred** Hesmonds Stud Ltd **Trained** Farnsfield, Notts

FOCUS
This looked an ordinary bumper but the winner scored with much more in hand than the winning margin and looks a fair prospect. He may not have needed to improve.
T/Plt: £173.10 to a £1 stake. Pool: £28,697.28 - 120.98 winning units T/Qpdt: £39.50 to a £1 stake. Pool: £1,404.82 - 26.30 winning units WG

5396 PLUMPTON (L-H)
Monday, April 21

OFFICIAL GOING: Good to soft (hdl 6.4, chs 7.0)
Wind: Light, behind Weather: Fine but cloudy

5455 WIN BIG WITH THE TOTEJACKPOT JUVENILE HURDLE (9 hdls) 2m
2:20 (2:20) (Class 4) 4-Y-0 **£3,898** (£1,144; £572; £286)

Form RPR

414- **1** **Flute Bowl**[24] 5057 4-10-12 0 .... JoshuaMoore 111+
(Gary Moore) *racd wd: trckd ldr to 5th: styd w ldrs: chal 3 out: narrow ld and j.lft 2 out: j.lft and hdd last: drvn to ld flat* **3/1**[2]

0- **2** *1/2* **Money Talks**[37] 4807 4-10-12 0 .... MarcGoldstein 109
(Michael Madgwick) *racd wd: hld up in last: prog to trck ldr and mstke 5th: led next: rdn and narrowly hdd 2 out: led last: edgd rt and hdd flat: kpt on* **20/1**[3]

12- **3** *8* **Mystery Drama**[135] 2934 4-10-12 124 .... AidanColeman 101
(Alan King) *hld up: in last fr 5th: nt fluent 3 out: rdn to chse ldng pair 2 out: nt qckn and wl hld after* **5/6**[1]

30U- **4** *1/2* **Vandross (IRE)**[22] 5090 4-11-2 126 .... JackQuinlan(3) 108
(Neil King) *led at modest pce: hit 6th and hdd: upsides 3 out: sn rdn and nt qckn: wl hld after* **3/1**[2]

4m 2.7s (1.90) **Going Correction** +0.025s/f (Yiel) **4** Ran SP% **109.3**
Speed ratings: **96,95,91,91**
CSF £29.21 TOTE £3.30; EX 29.20 Trifecta £67.30.
Owner C E Stedman **Bred** C E Stedman **Trained** Lower Beeding, W Sussex

FOCUS
Quite a competitive event despite the small field, but it was steadily run with a sprint finish. Questionable form.

5456 TRY A TOTETRIFECTA NOVICES' LIMITED H'CAP CHASE (14 fncs) 2m 4f
2:50 (2:50) (Class 3) (0-125,124) 5-Y-0+ **£7,797** (£2,289; £1,144; £572)

Form RPR

363- **1** **Suerte Al Salto (IRE)**[21] 2977 7-11-2 **118** .... TomCannon 125+
(Chris Gordon) *w.w: last to 9th: steadily clsd fr 4 out: chsd ldr after 2 out: j. into ld last: drvn out* **7/1**

/0P- **2** *3/4* **No Substitute (IRE)**[73] 4130 9-11-4 **120** .... AidanColeman 126
(Alan King) *trckd ldng pair fr 4th: wnt 2nd 3 out: shkn up to ld bef 2 out: outj. and hdd last: styd on but hld nr fin* **4/1**[3]

U24- **3** *3* **De Blacksmith (IRE)**[31] 4934 6-11-4 **120** .... JamieMoore 124
(Gary Moore) *led: pushed into fences: urged along fr 10th: hdd and one pce bef 2 out* **6/4**[1]

521- **4** *7* **Kastani Beach (IRE)**[21] 5111 8-10-0 **105** .... WayneKavanagh(3) 102
(Seamus Mullins) *chsd ldng pair to 4th: last fr 9th and nt gng wl: struggling next: rallied bef 2 out: wknd last* **7/2**[2]

633- **5** *31* **Roger Beantown (IRE)**[44] 4684 9-11-8 **124** .... (p) NickScholfield 99
(Zoe Davison) *pressed wnr gng wl: disputing 2nd whn j.rt and stmbld 3 out: wknd rapidly* **6/1**

5m 7.9s (0.60) **Going Correction** -0.075s/f (Good) **5** Ran SP% **109.0**
Speed ratings: **95,94,93,90,78**
CSF £32.24 TOTE £8.00: £2.80, £2.20; EX 36.50 Trifecta £116.50.
Owner David Henery **Bred** M McCabe **Trained** Morestead, Hants

FOCUS
A moderate novice handicap in which the favourite tried to pinch the race on the final circuit. The winner is rated to his mark.

5457 DOWNLOAD THE TOTEPOOL LIVE INFO APP H'CAP HURDLE (12 hdls) 2m 5f
3:25 (3:25) (Class 3) (0-125,117) 4-Y-0+ **£5,848** (£1,717; £858; £429)

Form RPR

454- **1** **Auld Sthock (IRE)**[37] 4801 6-11-5 **110** .... JamieMoore 124+
(Gary Moore) *racd wdr than rivals thrght: hld up in tch: mstke 8th: prog to ld 3 out: clr next: eased fnl 100yds* **5/1**[3]

030- **2** *9* **Invicta Lake (IRE)**[19] 5128 7-11-5 **117** .... JackSherwood(7) 117
(Suzy Smith) *trckd ldrs: effrt to ld briefly bef 3 out: sn outpcd: kpt on to chse wnr bef 2 out: no imp* **7/2**[2]

U03- **3** *7* **Hollow Penny**[26] 5030 6-11-12 **117** .... AidanColeman 112
(Alan King) *trckd ldrs: pushed along and nt qckn bef 3 out: kpt on to take 3rd after 2 out: n.d* **6/4**[1]

F50- **4** *4 1/2* **Rior (IRE)**[19] 5128 7-10-12 **103** .... TomO'Brien 93
(Paul Henderson) *led after nthing else would: hit 9th: hdd bef 3 out: sn wl outpcd* **7/1**

P40- **5** *3 1/2* **Torero**[10] 5260 5-11-0 **105** .... (p) JoshuaMoore 92
(Diana Grissell) *hld up in tch: rdn after 8th: prog on outer to chal 3 out: wknd qckly bef 2 out* **10/1**

20P- **6** *15* **The Master Remover (IRE)**[88] 3851 5-10-6 **97** .... (p) TomCannon 70
(Chris Gordon) *nt fluent: chsd ldr: rdn after 8th: lost 2nd and wknd bef 3 out: t.o* **16/1**

112- **P** **Hold The Bucks (USA)**[20] 5118 8-10-5 **99** .... JackQuinlan(3)
(Daniel Steele) *hld up in last: blnd 3rd: nvr gng wl after: lost tch 6th: t.o whn p.u bef 3 out* **8/1**

5m 13.9s (-3.10) **Going Correction** +0.025s/f (Yiel) **7** Ran SP% **117.5**
Speed ratings (Par 107): **106,102,99,98,96 91,**
CSF £24.10 CT £38.75 TOTE £6.60: £2.80, £2.40; EX 24.80 Trifecta £119.50.
Owner Mark Albon & Chris Stedman **Bred** Michael Queally **Trained** Lower Beeding, W Sussex

FOCUS
A fair handicap hurdle. A personal best from the easy winner with the second rated to his mark.

5458 BEST ODDS GUARANTEED AT TOTEPOOL.COM H'CAP CHASE (12 fncs) 2m 1f
4:00 (4:00) (Class 3) (0-130,127) 5-Y-0+ **£9,747** (£2,862; £1,431; £715)

Form RPR

5/ **1** **Fair Dilemma (IRE)**[43] 9-11-5 **120** .... (t) TomO'Brien 127+
(Paul Henderson) *prog to press ldr 2nd: led next: mde rest: shkn up and in command after 3 out: readily* **10/1**

054- **2** *6* **Ulck Du Lin (FR)**[30] 4960 6-11-12 **127** .... (bt) NickScholfield 128
(Paul Nicholls) *wl in tch: trckd wnr 7th: rdn and nt qckn after 3 out: wl hld fr next* **5/4**[1]

505- **3** *21* **Vision Des Champs (FR)**[6] 5340 5-11-5 **120** .... (t) JamieMoore 105
(Gary Moore) *t.k.h: hld up: chsd ldng pair 7th: wl in tch next tl rdn and outpcd 3 out: wknd next* **9/2**

2P6- **4** *25* **Marky Bob (IRE)**[111] 3431 9-10-13 **114** .... AidanColeman 73
(Hugo Froud) *led to 3rd: chsd wnr to 7th: sn wknd: t.o* **7/2**[2]

415- **P** **Nozic (FR)**[27] 5017 13-10-8 **109**..........................(p) TomCannon
(Zoe Davison) *nt fluent: struggling to keep in tch 5th: wknd 7th: t.o whn p.u bef next* **4/1**[3]

4m 18.3s (-4.70) **Going Correction** -0.075s/f (Good) **5** Ran SP% **113.9**
Speed ratings: **108,105,95,83,**
CSF £24.93 TOTE £10.90: £5.20, £1.30; EX 35.60 Trifecta £194.00.
Owner D S Dennis **Bred** Liam Brennan **Trained** Whitsbury, Hants

FOCUS
This was run at a good pace and the winner burned them all off. The runner-up was 20lb off his best.

5459 HARRY AND BETTY SAVILL MEMORIAL NOVICES' H'CAP HURDLE (10 hdls) 2m 2f
4:35 (4:35) (Class 5) (0-100,100) 4-Y-O+ **£2,599** (£763; £381; £190)

Form				RPR
014-	**1**		**While You Wait (IRE)**[10] 5262 5-11-12 **100**.......... JamieMoore (Gary Moore) *hld up towards rr: prog 7th: clsd w others 3 out: led 2 out: pushed clr: comf* **5/1**[1]	114+
P30-	**2**	9	**Amazing Scenes (IRE)**[21] 5112 5-11-7 **95**..........(t) JoshuaMoore (Brendan Powell) *led to 3rd: chsd ldr: clsd w others to ld sn after 3 out: hdd 2 out: one pce and no ch w wnr after* **6/1**[2]	96
443-	**3**	2	**Juicy Legend**[10] 5262 7-10-3 **77**..........(v[1]) TomCannon (Chris Gordon) *chsd clr ldng pair: clsd 3 out: chal bef next: sn outpcd and btn* **6/1**[2]	77
060-	**4**	12	**Comedy House**[26] 3007 6-10-8 **82**..........(v) MarcGoldstein (Michael Madgwick) *settled in midfield: clsd w others 3 out: rdn to go 4th bef 2 out but no imp: wknd bef last* **10/1**	70
402-	**5**	1 3/4	**Hermosa Vaquera (IRE)**[10] 5262 4-11-3 **96**.......... NickScholfield (Anna Newton-Smith) *trckd clr ldrs: nt fluent 2nd: mstke 7th: clsd 3 out: sn rdn: wknd bef 2 out* **10/1**	78
660-	**6**	4	**Major Martin (IRE)**[21] 5116 5-11-9 **97**.......... AidanColeman (Gary Moore) *hld up in last pair: lost tch and pushed along 7th: no ch after: modest late prog: nvr involved* **6/1**[2]	80
036-	**7**	1/2	**Celtic Charlie (FR)**[11] 5242 9-9-13 **76**..........(t) JackQuinlan[(3)] (Pat Phelan) *hld up towards rr: rdn and nt on terms w ldng gp bef 3 out: no real prog after* **8/1**[3]	59
564-	**8**	10	**Poetic Power (IRE)**[11] 5238 5-10-12 **86**.......... TommyPhelan (Claire Dyson) *only runner to r on inner: t.k.h: trckd ldr: led 3rd: clr 7th: hdd & wknd qckly after 3 out* **10/1**	60
600-	**9**	44	**Houseparty**[28] 5012 6-11-0 **95**.......... MrHGMiller[(7)] (Zoe Davison) *hld up in last pair: pushed along and lost tch 7th: no ch after: t.o* **16/1**	29
233-	**P**		**Walter De La Mare (IRE)**[8] 5302 7-11-8 **96**.......... TomO'Brien (Anabel K Murphy) *hld up in rr: struggling fr 7th: btn whn blnd 3 out and p.u* **5/1**[1]	

4m 30.9s **Going Correction** +0.025s/f (Yiel)
WFA 4 from 5yo+ 5lb **10** Ran SP% **120.5**
Speed ratings (Par 103): **101,97,96,90,90 88,88,83,64,**
CSF £36.71 CT £188.10 TOTE £7.20: £2.10, £3.30, £2.90; EX 48.50 Trifecta £105.80.
Owner Galloping On The South Downs Partnership **Bred** Redmondstown Stud **Trained** Lower Beeding, W Sussex

FOCUS
The betting suggested this was an open contest, and the form looks fair. A big step up from the easy winner.

5460 LIKE TOTEPOOL ON FACEBOOK H'CAP CHASE (18 fncs) 3m 2f
5:10 (5:10) (Class 5) (0-100,89) 5-Y-O+ **£2,995** (£930; £500)

Form				RPR
313-	**1**		**Ballyvoneen (IRE)**[1] 5397 9-11-10 **87**..........(p) JamieMoore (Neil King) *hld up in last: j. slowly 8th: trckd ldr bef 14th where mstke: led bef 2 out: sn clr: 15 l ahd last: eased* **7/4**[2]	100+
635-	**2**	9	**Princely Hero (IRE)**[27] 5025 10-11-12 **89**..........(tp) TomCannon (Chris Gordon) *led 4th to 7th: sn pushed along: dropped to 3rd u.p after 13th: no imp after: kpt on to take 2nd again sn after last* **6/1**	88
342-	**3**	8	**Get Ready To Go (IRE)**[33] 4905 10-11-0 **77**..........(p) JoshuaMoore (Richard Ford) *led to 4th: led 7th: rdn and hdd bef 2 out: wknd qckly and lost 2nd sn after last* **6/4**[1]	69
115-	**P**		**Quayside Court (IRE)**[29] 4982 10-10-12 **75**..........(vt) TomO'Brien (Claire Dyson) *chsd ldng pair: mstke 5th: rdn and wknd 11th: t.o whn p.u bef 14th* **9/2**[3]	

6m 57.9s (7.20) **Going Correction** -0.075s/f (Good) **4** Ran SP% **108.8**
Speed ratings: **85,82,79,**
CSF £10.61 TOTE £2.90; EX 7.80 Trifecta £21.50.
Owner Across The Pond Partnership **Bred** James Flood **Trained** Newmarket, Suffolk

FOCUS
A very moderate affair. The winner was very well in on the best of his form from a year ago.

5461 COLLECT TOTEPOOL WINNINGS AT BETFRED SHOPS H'CAP HURDLE (14 hdls) 3m 1f 110y
5:45 (5:45) (Class 5) (0-100,100) 4-Y-O+ **£2,274** (£667; £333; £166)

Form				RPR
500-	**1**		**Landenstown Pearl (IRE)**[23] 5069 8-9-13 **76**..........(t) JackQuinlan[(3)] (Sarah Humphrey) *in tch: prog to trck ldr 11th: led next gng wl: clr after 2 out: rdn out* **14/1**	85+
F05-	**2**	10	**Brians Well (IRE)**[11] 5234 7-11-7 **95**..........(t) JoshuaMoore (Brendan Powell) *hld up in rr: prog to chse ldrs 11th: drvn 3 out: chsd wnr bef next: sn lft bhd: hld on for 2nd* **5/1**[2]	96
602-	**3**	1 1/4	**Brunette'Sonly (IRE)**[20] 5122 9-10-7 **81**.......... TomO'Brien (Seamus Mullins) *pressed ldr: led 7th: rdn and hdd 3 out: steadily fdd bef 2 out* **9/4**[1]	81
436-	**4**	2	**Absolute Shambles**[21] 5114 10-10-7 **91**..........(p) LouisMuspratt[(10)] (Chris Gordon) *wl in tch tl rdn and outpcd after 10th: n.d after: wnt modest 4th after 3 out: kpt on to cl on plcd horses fr 2 out* **8/1**	88
341-	**5**	53	**Sea Cadet**[27] 5022 12-10-0 **81**..........(p) JackSherwood[(7)] (Laura Mongan) *racd on inner: hld up in tch: prog and prom 9th: wknd qckly bef 3 out: t.o* **5/1**[2]	30
245-	**6**	31	**Burnthill (IRE)**[21] 5114 9-10-0 **74**..........(tp) JamieMoore (Claire Dyson) *mde most to 7th: drvn next: lost 2nd and mstke 11th: wknd qckly: t.o* **12/1**	
P63-	**7**	21	**Acosta**[20] 5122 10-9-11 **74**..........(b) WayneKavanagh[(3)] (Dr Jeremy Naylor) *hld up in last: lost tch fr 6th: continued wl t.o* **12/1**	
0P0-	**P**		**Ctappers**[21] 5112 5-11-7 **95**..........(p) MarcGoldstein (Michael Madgwick) *t.k.h early: prom to 6th: wknd u.p next: bhd whn blnd 9th and p.u* **20/1**	

002- **P** **Twopoundsofbutter (IRE)**[56] 4471 7-11-12 **100**..........(t) AidanColeman
(Tim Vaughan) *racd on inner: in tch tl rdn and wknd 10th: t.o whn p.u bef 3 out* **7/1**[3]

6m 24.1s (-0.90) **Going Correction** +0.025s/f (Yiel) **9** Ran SP% **114.5**
Speed ratings (Par 103): **102,98,98,97,81 72,65,,**
CSF £82.48 CT £219.20 TOTE £15.80: £6.30, £3.30, £1.10; EX 110.30 Trifecta £260.80.
Owner A A Whyte **Bred** Mrs Valerie Dalgetty **Trained** West Wratting, Cambs

FOCUS
Four came clear in a moderate contest. Straightforward form.
T/Plt: £704.00 to a £1 stake. Pool of £42213.68, 43.77 winning tickets. T/Qpdt: £42.70 to a £1 stake. Pool of £3427.70, 59.30 winning tickets. JN

5462 - 5469a (Foreign Racing) - See Raceform Interactive

5418 FAIRYHOUSE (R-H)
Monday, April 21

OFFICIAL GOING: Good to yielding

5470a TAYTO HURDLE (GRADE 3) (10 hdls) 2m
2:45 (2:45) 4-Y-0 **£16,250** (£4,750; £2,250; £750)

			RPR
1		**Ivan Grozny (FR)**[40] 4755 4-11-0 132..........[1] PaulTownend (W P Mullins, Ire) *chsd ldrs: 4th 1/2-way: clsd far side 2 out to ld between last 2: rdn clr bef last: strly pressed u.p nr fin and all out to jst hold on* **5/1**[3]	134
2	hd	**Kitten Rock (FR)**[36] 4845 4-11-4 125.......... BarryGeraghty (E J O'Grady, Ire) *hld up in tch: pushed along in 7th into st where nt clr run far side bef 2 out and swtchd lft: sn rdn in 4th and clsd into 2nd bef last: styd on wl towards fin: jst failed* **3/1**[2]	138+
3	3 1/2	**Lindenhurst (IRE)**[38] 4784 4-11-4 130..........(t) MarkBolger (John C McConnell, Ire) *chsd ldr: cl 2nd 1/2-way: disp briefly 3 out: rdn in 2nd appr st and sn no ex u.p: kpt on one pce in 3rd fr 2 out* **8/1**	135
4	1/2	**Clarcam (FR)**[18] 5132 4-11-0 141..........(t) NoelFehily (Gordon Elliott, Ire) *hld up in mid-div: 6th 1/2-way: tk clsr order bef 4 out: nt fluent in 4th 2 out and sn no imp on ldrs: kpt on one pce* **5/2**[1]	130
5	3/4	**Plinth (IRE)**[38] 4784 4-11-0 132.......... RobbiePower (A P O'Brien, Ire) *racd in mid-div: 8th 1/2-way: rdn in 9th after 3 out and no imp on ldrs bef next: kpt on wl fr last* **8/1**	129
6	1/2	**Indian Icon (FR)**[22] 4045 4-11-0 116.......... PCarberry (D T Hughes, Ire) *hld up: 10th 1/2-way: tk clsr order in 8th after 3 out: rdn on outer fr 2 out and no imp on ldrs: kpt on same pce* **25/1**	129
7	1 1/4	**Florishwells D'Ete (FR)**[15] 5199 4-10-7..........[1] DJCasey (W P Mullins, Ire) *attempted to make all: narrow advantage 1/2-way: jnd briefly 3 out: rdn w narrow advantage whn mstke 2 out: hdd between last 2 and no ex whn mstke in 4th at last: one pce run-in* **33/1**	121
8	3/4	**Gerdago (IRE)**[40] 4755 4-11-0 132..........(t) EddieO'Connell (K J Condon, Ire) *chsd ldrs: nt fluent in 3rd at 2nd: rdn in 5th after 3 out and no ex bef next* **10/1**	127
9	3 1/2	**Bertimont (FR)**[8] 4432 4-11-4 127.......... RobbieColgan (J J Lambe, Ire) *chsd ldrs: clsr in 3rd bef 4 out: disp briefly 3 out: sn rdn in 3rd and no ex fr 2 out: wknd* **33/1**	127
10	4 3/4	**Rundell**[306] 4-11-0 .... MarkWalsh (D T Hughes, Ire) *w.w in rr: rdn in 11th and no imp fr 3 out: kpt on one pce* **50/1**	119
11	9	**Sardinia (IRE)**[35] 4875 4-11-0 115..........(p) DavyCondon (Paul Nolan, Ire) *hld up in rr of mid-div: 9th 1/2-way: rdn in 10th and no imp fr after 3 out* **20/1**	110
12	14	**Cape Glory (IRE)**[38] 4-11-0 ....(t) BrianO'Connell (Gordon Elliott, Ire) *hld up: 11th 1/2-way: rdn and no imp 3 out* **33/1**	96
13	1 3/4	**Time For Action (IRE)**[190] 4-11-0 .... AndrewJMcNamara (David Wachman, Ire) *a towards rr: rdn and no imp fr 3 out* **20/1**	94

4m 0.8s (-11.20) **Going Correction** -1.15s/f (Hard) **13** Ran SP% **125.7**
Speed ratings: **82,81,80,79,79 79,78,78,76,74 69,62,61**
CSF £20.34 TOTE £10.00: £2.50, £1.60, £2.40; DF 34.20 Trifecta £621.60.
Owner Andrea & Graham Wylie **Bred** Mme Larissa Kneip **Trained** Muine Beag, Co Carlow

FOCUS
The best of the four-year-olds were not here and the favourite was a shade disappointing.

5471a KEELINGS IRISH STRAWBERRY HURDLE (GRADE 2) (12 hdls) 2m 4f
3:15 (3:17) 5-Y-0+ **£27,083** (£7,916; £3,750; £1,250)

			RPR
1		**Thousand Stars (FR)**[16] 5169 10-11-10 158..........(p) PaulTownend (W P Mullins, Ire) *mde virtually all: 1 l clr bef 4 out: stl gng wl into st and in command between last 2 gng best: styd on wl* **4/1**[2]	158+
2	10	**Get Me Out Of Here (IRE)**[40] 4752 10-11-8 152..........(tp) BarryGeraghty (Jonjo O'Neill) *hld up in tch: pushed along in 4th fr 4 out and wnt 3rd u.p after next: rdn into 2nd bef 2 out and sn no imp on wnr: kpt on same pce* **5/4**[1]	146
3	2	**Upsie (FR)**[25] 5044 6-10-13 140.......... DJCasey (W P Mullins, Ire) *w.w in rr: no imp bef 3 out: wnt mod 5th under hands and heels bef next where mstke: styd on wl fr last: nrst fin* **8/1**[3]	135+
4	2 1/2	**Un Beau Matin (IRE)**[29] 4995 6-11-3 136.......... NoelFehily (Gordon Elliott, Ire) *chsd ldrs in 3rd: j. sltly rt 2nd: wnt 2nd after 3 out: sn no imp on wnr and dropped to 3rd u.p bef 2 out: kpt on one pce* **4/1**[2]	137
5	27	**Mourad (IRE)**[32] 4928 9-11-3 150..........(b[1]) MsKWalsh (W P Mullins, Ire) *sweated up befhand: trckd ldr in cl 2nd: nt fluent 3rd and next: nt fluent again in 2nd at 6th and 3 out: rdn and sn no ex u.p in 4th: wknd* **20/1**	110
6	6 1/2	**Busty Brown (IRE)**[18] 5138 8-11-8 138.......... PCarberry (Noel Meade, Ire) *hld up in tch: rdn in 5th after 4 out and no imp on ldrs: one pce after* **9/1**	108
7	41	**Silk Hall (UAE)**[9] 5274 9-11-6 135..........(b) EddieO'Connell (J J Lambe, Ire) *towards rr: nt fluent in 6th at 4th: hit 6th: rdn in 6th after 4 out and dropped to rr whn slt mstke 3 out: t.o* **50/1**	65

4m 52.6s (-30.40) **Going Correction** -1.15s/f (Hard) **7** Ran SP% **112.3**
Speed ratings: **114,110,109,108,97 94,78**
CSF £9.41 TOTE £4.70: £2.60, £1.80; DF 8.30 Trifecta £37.90.
Owner Hammer & Trowel Syndicate **Bred** Mlle Camille & Mlle Ophelie Demercastel **Trained** Muine Beag, Co Carlow

FOCUS
This had the feeling of a veterans' race in some respects. The pace was even and they wound it up down the back.

5474a BOYLESPORTS IRISH GRAND NATIONAL CHASE (EXTENDED H'CAP CHASE) (GRADE A) (24 fncs) 3m 5f
5:00 (5:00) 5-Y-0+

£117,500 (£40,416; £19,583; £7,083; £5,000; £2,916)

RPR

1 **Shutthefrontdoor (IRE)**[41] 4741 7-10-13 **142**............(tp) BarryGeraghty 155+
(Jonjo O'Neill) *chsd ldrs: 4th after 11th: tk clsr order in 2nd fr 4 out: rdn in 3rd between last 2 and wnt 2nd fr last: styd on wl u.p to ld ins fnl 100yds* **8/1**[1]

2 *3/4* **Golden Wonder (IRE)**[15] 5202 8-10-6 **135**.................... RogerLoughran 147
(D T Hughes, Ire) *chsd ldrs: tk clsr order bef 15th where slt mstke: led narrowly bef 3 out: strly pressed w narrow advantage whn j. sltly rt last: hdd u.p ins fnl 100yds* **16/1**

3 *nk* **Saoirse Dun (IRE)**[43] 4712 8-9-7 **129**..........................(t) AndrewRing(7) 141+
(P J Rothwell, Ire) *hld up: hdwy on outer 4f out to chal in 3rd fr next: wnt 2nd stl gng wl between last 2: rdn in 3rd fr last and kpt on wl towards fin: hld* **20/1**

4 *3 3/4* **Jamsie Hall (IRE)**[23] 5083 11-9-13 **135**..............................(tp) GerFox(7) 143
(Gordon Elliott, Ire) *in rr of mid-div: hdwy in 13th after 3 out to chse ldrs in 4th between last 2: kpt on same pce fr last: nt trble ldrs* **40/1**

5 *2* **Folsom Blue (IRE)**[22] 5099 7-10-3 **135**............................ BenDalton(3) 142+
(Conor O'Dwyer, Ire) *in tch: hdwy in 11th fr after 3 out to chse ldrs on outer bef next where nt fluent: no imp on ldrs in 5th bef last: kpt on same pce* **20/1**

6 *3 3/4* **Heaney (IRE)**[115] 3341 7-10-0 **129**.................................. ConorO'Farrell 131
(T J Taaffe, Ire) *hld up: mstke 5th: tk clsr order in 14th 3 out: kpt on wl fr after 2 out: nvr nrr* **20/1**

7 *3/4* **Goonyella (IRE)**[60] 4386 7-10-6 **135**.. AELynch 136
(J T R Dreaper, Ire) *chsd ldrs: 3rd after 11th: rdn in 5th after 3 out and sn no imp on ldrs: slt mstke in 6th at last: kpt on one pce* **10/1**[2]

8 *2 3/4* **Cantlow (IRE)**[18] 5138 9-11-7 **150**........................... AndrewJMcNamara 149
(Paul Webber) *racd in mid-div: hdwy to chse ldrs fr 3 out: rdn and no ex u.p fr next: kpt on same pce* **40/1**

9 *4 1/2* **Away We Go (IRE)**[359] 5576 11-10-10 **139**......................(t) MsKWalsh 133
(W P Mullins, Ire) *hld up towards rr: tk clsr order fr 5 out: rdn into 6th after 3 out: no imp on ldrs fr next: kpt on one pce* **25/1**

10 *4 1/2* **Pendra (IRE)**[41] 4742 6-10-11 **140**.. NoelFehily 130
(Charlie Longsdon) *hld up: hdwy to chse ldrs fr 3 out: rdn in 9th bef next and no imp on ldrs: kpt on one pce* **22/1**

11 *1 3/4* **Lion Na Bearnai (IRE)**[16] 5171 12-10-11 **140**........................ APHeskin 128
(Thomas Gibney, Ire) *chsd ldrs: 5th after 11th: rdn in 4th after 3 out and no ex bef next: wknd* **33/1**

12 *4 3/4* **Cause Of Causes (USA)**[39] 4769 6-11-3 **146**......................... MarkWalsh 129
(Gordon Elliott, Ire) *w.w in rr of mid-div: nt fluent 3rd: tk clsr order bef 3 out: rdn in 11th appr st and no imp on ldrs fr next: kpt on one pce* **14/1**

13 *2 3/4* **Sraid Padraig (IRE)**[39] 4768 8-10-6 **135**.......................... DannyMullins 115
(A J Martin, Ire) *racd in mid-div: racd keenly: tk clsr order bef 5 out: rdn in 9th and no ex after 3 out: one pce fr next* **16/1**

14 *2* **Alfie Sherrin**[41] 4738 11-10-0 **129**..............................(p) WillKennedy 107
(Jonjo O'Neill) *hld up in mid-div: slt mstke 1st: tk clsr order 4 out: rdn and no ex fr next: kpt on one pce* **14/1**

15 *21* **Letter Of Credit (IRE)**[22] 5099 9-10-8 **137**.....................[1] PatrickMangan 94
(James Joseph Mangan, Ire) *w.w: stmbld in rr after 3rd: tk clsr order fr 5 out: rdn into st and no imp on ldrs 2 out: kpt on one pce* **33/1**

16 *59* **Rogue Angel (IRE)**[22] 5099 6-9-10 **130**.......................(b) KevinSexton(5) 28
(M F Morris, Ire) *racd in mid-div: hdwy bef 15th: tk clsr order 5 out: rdn bef 3 out and no ex: wknd: completely t.o* **16/1**

P **Toon River (IRE)**[44] 4690 9-10-3 **132**.................................. MarkEnright
(Miss Mary Louise Hallahan, Ire) *chsd ldrs tl led fr 1st: jnd 10th where slt mstke: hdd narrowly next: remained prom tl rdn and wknd 4 out: p.u bef next* **33/1**

P **Oscars Well (IRE)**[40] 4752 9-11-0 **143**.............................(t) MartinFerris
(A J Martin, Ire) *hld up towards rr: racd keenly: sltly hmpd by faller at 13th: trailing 4 out and p.u bef next* **50/1**

U **Gallant Oscar (IRE)**[43] 4712 8-10-3 **132**............................ DavyCondon
(A J Martin, Ire) *hld up: towards rr whn blnd and uns rdr 13th* **14/1**

P **Daring Article (IRE)**[50] 4587 8-10-0 **129**.....................(tp) PhillipEnright
(Robert Tyner, Ire) *in rr of mid-div: bad mstke 14th and dropped to rr: p.u bef 2 out* **14/1**

P **My Murphy (IRE)**[36] 4856 8-10-12 **141**............................. RobbiePower
(W J Burke, Ire) *hld up towards rr: tk clsr order on outer 3 out where slt mstke: rdn and no ex u.p: wknd and p.u bef 2 out* **14/1**

P **Make A Track (IRE)**[35] 4871 8-10-11 **145**.................(p) BrianCawley(5)
(C F Swan, Ire) *led tl hdd fr after 1st: mstke 9th: chsd ldrs tl slt mstkes 6 out and next: wknd and trailing whn p.u bef 2 out* **66/1**

P **Home Farm (IRE)**[50] 4587 7-10-13 **142**................................(t) DJCasey
(A L T Moore, Ire) *racd in mid-div: wknd bef 5 out where mstke: p.u bef next* **12/1**

P **Touch The Eden (FR)**[22] 5099 7-10-12 **141**..................... PaulTownend
(W P Mullins, Ire) *chsd ldrs early: wknd fr 15th and p.u bef 5 out* **11/1**[3]

P **Clar Na Mionn (IRE)**[36] 4856 7-10-2 **131**........................ RobbieColgan
(V T O'Brien, Ire) *chsd ldrs tl disp 10th and led narrowly next: j.lft 16th: mstke 5 out and hdd after next: wknd and slt mstke 3 out: p.u bef next* **33/1**

F **Mullaghanoe River (IRE)**[43] 4709 6-10-7 **136**...........(b[1]) MsNCarberry
(Noel Meade, Ire) *chsd ldrs: 6th after 11th: wl in tch whn fell 5 out* **18/1**

7m 40.2s (-25.80) **Going Correction** -0.70s/f (Firm) **26** Ran SP% **135.0**
Speed ratings: **107,106,106,105,105 104,103,103,101,100 100,98,98,97,91 75,,,, ,,,**
CSF £115.87 CT £2540.51 TOTE £7.40: £1.90, £4.40, £5.10, £8.90; DF 189.10 Trifecta £4386.70.
Owner John P McManus **Bred** Ms Deirdre Connolly **Trained** Cheltenham, Gloucs
■ Barry Geraghty's first Irish National winner.
■ Stewards' Enquiry : Andrew Ring three-day ban: used whip without giving gelding time to respond (tbn)

FOCUS
Probably an average renewal and the pace was such that it was possible to be handy and win or come from behind to score. There were around ten in with a shout at the second-last. The winner was on a fair mark on his novice form.

5475a JOHN & CHICH FOWLER MEMORIAL EUROPEAN BREEDERS FUND MARES CHASE (GRADE 3) (16 fncs) 2m 4f
5:35 (5:39) 5-Y-0+ **£18,958** (£5,541; £2,625; £875)

RPR

1 **Une Artiste (FR)**[38] 4789 6-11-0 134................................ BarryGeraghty 134
(Nicky Henderson) *chsd ldrs: pushed along in 4th bef 2 out and sn clsd to chal: rdn to ld between last 2: strly pressed u.p nr fin: all out to hold on* **2/1**[1]

2 *1/2* **Nadiya De La Vega (FR)**[39] 4768 8-11-3 135....................(v) MarkWalsh 136+
(Nicky Henderson) *chsd ldrs: pushed along in 4th after 5 out: bmpd 2 out: sn qcknd into 3rd bef last and clsd u.p run-in to strly press wnr cl home: jst hld* **12/1**

3 *2 3/4* **Burn And Turn (IRE)**[50] 4584 8-10-11 129.....................(t) RobbiePower 127
(Mrs John Harrington, Ire) *in tch: clsr in 3rd bef 5 out: effrt 2 out: rdn in 2nd between last 2 and no imp on wnr in 3rd fr last: kpt on same pce* **9/1**

4 *6* **Twin Plan (IRE)**[10] 5255 9-11-0 114.. APHeskin 124
(J J Lambe, Ire) *hld up towards rr: prog bef 4 out: tk clsr order in 5th after next: cl up whn j.lft and mstke 2 out: rdn and no imp after* **33/1**

5 *3* **Avondhu Lady (IRE)**[46] 4641 9-11-3 134............................. MarkEnright 124
(David Fenton, Ire) *chsd ldrs: slt mstke in 4th 5 out and lost pl: rdn in 7th into st and no imp on ldrs fr 2 out: kpt on one pce* **7/1**[3]

6 *3/4* **Blazing Sonnet (IRE)**[71] 4179 8-10-11 118............ AndrewJMcNamara 120
(W J Austin, Ire) *in tch: mstke 2nd: rdn in 7th bef 2 out and no imp in mod 6th between last 2: kpt on one pce* **33/1**

7 *1 3/4* **Pestal And Mortar (IRE)**[61] 4360 9-10-11 109.................... MarkBolger 116
(F G Hand, Ire) *hld up: rdn in 8th after 3 out and no imp on ldrs next where slt mstke: kpt on one pce* **66/1**

8 *3* **Tarla (FR)**[25] 5044 8-11-3 142.. PaulTownend 119
(W P Mullins, Ire) *led tl jnd and hdd after 3rd: disp 4 out: hdd fr 2 out and dropped to 4th bef last where slow: wknd* **11/4**[2]

9 *17* **Caoimhe's Delight (IRE)**[22] 5098 8-11-5 128......................(p) AELynch 104
(Sean O'Brien, Ire) *chsd ldrs early: no imp in rr bef 3 out: t.o* **18/1**

P **Kates Benefit (IRE)**[15] 5197 8-10-11 130.......................... DannyMullins
(David Kenneth Budds, Ire) *trckd ldr tl led after 3rd: jnd 4 out: rdn in 3rd after next and no ex u.p bef 2 out: wknd and p.u bef last* **14/1**

U **Cinder Rua (IRE)**[10] 5266 7-10-11 .... PaddyKennedy
(D T Kelly, Ire) *towards rr: mstke and uns rdr 6th* **100/1**

P **Byerley Babe (IRE)**[36] 4848 7-11-5 134............................ PhillipEnright
(Robert Tyner, Ire) *hld up towards rr: wknd and p.u after 8th* **7/1**[3]

5m 5.3s (-18.70) **Going Correction** -0.70s/f (Firm) **12** Ran SP% **123.0**
Speed ratings: **109,108,107,105,104 103,103,101,95, ,**
CSF £28.18 TOTE £3.20: £1.50, £4.40, £2.30; DF 29.50 Trifecta £283.10.
Owner Simon Munir **Bred** E Clayeux & D Clayeux **Trained** Upper Lambourn, Berks
FOCUS
A decent mares' contest most memorable for the gutsy performance of the winner.

5476 - 5477a (Foreign Racing) - See Raceform Interactive

1827 LES LANDES
Monday, April 21

OFFICIAL GOING: Good (good to soft in places)

5478a MARK TWAIN H'CAP HURDLE 2m
2:30 (2:30) 4-Y-0+ **£950** (£345; £205)

RPR

1 **The Bay Bandit**[31] 1816 7-11-10 ....(p) MattieBatchelor
(Neil Mulholland) **1/3**[1]

2 *8* **Reach Out**[385] 5117 6-9-4 ow1.. HarryPoulton
(Mrs A Malzard, Jersey) **8/1**[3]

3 *1 1/2* **Azaria (FR)**[238] 1827 8-9-7 .... MrPCollington
(Mrs A Malzard, Jersey) **5/2**[2]

4m 8.0s (7.00) **3** Ran SP% **114.7**

Owner Neil Mulholland Racing Club **Bred** Darley **Trained** Limpley Stoke, Wilts

5205 KELSO (L-H)
Tuesday, April 22

OFFICIAL GOING: Good (good to firm in places) changing to good after race 4 (3.25)
All rail on innermost line reducing advertised distances by about 15yds per circuit.
Wind: Light, half behind Weather: Overcast

5479 LYNTOUN PRIVATE HIRE MAIDEN HURDLE (10 hdls) 2m 2f
1:45 (1:45) (Class 4) 4-Y-0+ **£3,249** (£954; £477; £238)

Form RPR

432- 1 **Lord Brendy**[15] 5206 6-11-0 113...................................... KennyJohnson 106+
(Robert Johnson) *taken early to post: in tch: n.m.r bnd bef 6th: effrt and led 2 out: rdn clr fr last* **1/1**[1]

000- 2 *5* **Amilliontimes (IRE)**[164] 2355 6-10-9 0..........................(t) CraigNichol(5) 98
(Mrs Jackie Stephen) *led: rdn and hdd 2 out: rallied and regained ld run-in: kpt on: nt pce of wnr* **100/1**

26- 3 *hd* **Fearless Tunes (IRE)**[31] 4958 6-11-0 0............................ AdrianLane 100+
(Donald McCain) *in tch: stdy hdwy gng wl bef 2 out: effrt and ch whn mstke last: kpt on same pce run-in* **6/1**[3]

0- 4 *3/4* **Fight Away Boys (IRE)**[31] 4958 6-11-0 0....................... PeterBuchanan 100
(Lucinda Russell) *chsd ldrs: hit 6th: effrt and rdn whn nt fluent and stmbld 2 out: edgd lft and kpt on same pce fr last* **20/1**

0- 5 *1 1/2* **Woodstock (IRE)**[9] 5296 4-10-6 0...................................... TonyKelly(3) 92
(Ann Hamilton) *hld up in midfield: blnd 2nd: rdn bef 2 out: kpt on same pce fr last* **28/1**

/54- 6 *7* **Ballyvoque (IRE)**[37] 4832 8-11-0 0................................... LucyAlexander 92
(George Charlton) *t.k.h: cl up: hit 3rd: rdn and wknd fr 2 out* **5/1**[2]

00- 7 *22* **Verdasco (FR)**[9] 5296 5-11-0 0... BrianHarding 70
(Donald McCain) *hld up: pushed along and effrt 3 out: wknd bef next* **33/1**

0/4- 8 *hd* **Grandiloquent**[18] 5160 5-11-0 0.. JamieMoore 70
(Brian Ellison) *t.k.h in midfield: drvn and outpcd after 3 out: n.d after* **16/1**

The Form Book Jumps, Raceform Ltd, Compton, RG20 6NL.

455/ **9** *3* **Wor Lass**[567] 1712 6-10-7 0 JamesReveley 60
(Iain Jardine) *hld up: hdwy on outside and in tch bef 3 out: rdn and wknd bef next* **40/1**

04P- **10** *6* **Kings Folly (IRE)**[22] 5102 6-10-9 0 DerekFox(5) 62
(Lucinda Russell) *hld up: shkn up after 4 out: no imp after next: nvr nr to chal* **22/1**

53- **11** *34* **Trackanais (FR)**[126] 3147 7-11-0 0 (t) BarryKeniry 31
(Simon Shirley-Beavan) *t.k.h: cl up: mstke 4 out: rdn and wknd bef next* **9/1**

0P- **12** *56* **Thatsmylot (IRE)**[52] 4548 5-10-7 0 DaraghBourke(7)
(Stuart Coltherd) *nt fluent in rr: struggling bef 4 out: t.o* **100/1**

PP/ **13** *6* **Fa'Side Castle (IRE)**[350] 5499 5-10-11 0 (t) JonathanEngland(3)
(Maurice Barnes) *nt fluent: bhd: struggling fnl circ: nvr on terms* **250/1**

4m 19.9s (-7.10) **Going Correction** -0.35s/f (Good)
WFA 4 from 5yo+ 5lb 13 Ran SP% **117.2**
Speed ratings (Par 105): **101,98,98,98,97 94,84,84,83,80 65,40,38**
CSF £182.87 TOTE £2.20: £1.10, £17.70, £2.70; EX 114.80 Trifecta £859.10.

Owner T L A & R A Robson **Bred** William Goldie **Trained** Newburn, Tyne & Wear

FOCUS
The ground was on the quicker side of good for this modest maiden hurdle with a sound gallop being set. The winner set the standard and is rated a bit better than the bare result.

5480 TIMEFORM NOVICES' LIMITED H'CAP CHASE (16 fncs) 2m 5f 110y
2:15 (2:15) (Class 3) (0-125,120) 5-Y-0+ **£6,498** (£1,908; £954; £477)

Form RPR

P61- **1** **Doubledisdoubledat (IRE)**[14] 5216 7-10-4 **102** JamesReveley 112+
(Stuart Coltherd) *nt fluent on occasions: mde all: rdn bef 2 out: hrd pressed whn nt fluent last: styd on wl u.p run-in* **2/1**[2]

214- **2** *¾* **Mandarin Sunset (IRE)**[126] 3142 7-11-3 **115** (p) JamieMoore 123
(James Ewart) *t.k.h: trckd ldrs: smooth hdwy 4 out: effrt 2 out: chsd wnr run-in: kpt on: hld nr fin* **8/1**

133- **3** *1 ¾* **Clondaw Knight (IRE)**[34] 4898 6-11-8 **120** PeterBuchanan 129
(Lucinda Russell) *pressed wnr: effrt and rdn whn hit 2 out: ev ch last: lost 2nd run-in: one pce* **13/8**[1]

50- **4** *8* **Tour D'Argent (FR)**[27] 5031 7-11-6 **118** BrianHarding 120
(Donald McCain) *t.k.h: hld up in tch: mstkes 8th and next: drvn bef 5 out: rallied next: rdn and wknd appr 2 out* **5/1**[3]

5P4- **5** *1 ¼* **Thorlak (FR)**[25] 5056 7-9-10 **101** oh9 (b[1]) DaleIrving(7) 99
(James Ewart) *trckd ldrs: hit and outpcd 10th: rallied after 5 out: rdn and wknd after 3 out* **10/1**

5m 24.9s (-4.30) **Going Correction** -0.35s/f (Good) 5 Ran SP% **108.3**
Speed ratings: **93,92,92,89,88**
CSF £15.41 TOTE £3.10: £2.10, £1.30; EX 14.90 Trifecta £20.70.

Owner Mr & Mrs Mark J Gilbert **Bred** John Joe Ronayne **Trained** Selkirk, Borders

FOCUS
A good finish in a tight limited handicap chase with the three principals in the market holding every chance at the last. The winner is on the upgrade.

5481 FIONA DALRYMPLE H'CAP CHASE (19 fncs) 3m 2f
2:50 (2:50) (Class 3) (0-125,125) 5-Y-0+ **£6,657** (£2,067; £1,113)

Form RPR

231- **1** **Mr Supreme (IRE)**[25] 5055 9-10-10 **109** ow2 JamesReveley 119+
(Keith Reveley) *j.w: mde all: qcknd after 3 out: pushed out fr last: rdr weighed in 2lb heavy* **1/1**[1]

13P- **2** *2 ¼* **Isla Pearl Fisher**[31] 4953 11-11-12 **125** (t[1]) LucyAlexander 130
(N W Alexander) *nt fluent: chsd wnr to after 12th: rallied and regained 2nd whn hit 4 out: nt fluent and outpcd next: styd on fr last: nt pce of wnr* **4/1**[3]

01F- **3** *46* **Nodform Richard**[9] 5299 8-11-9 **122** (bt) BrianHarding 105
(Donald McCain) *chsd ldrs: mstke 4th: wnt 2nd after 12th: blnd 5 out: lost 2nd bef next: wknd 3 out: t.o* **5/1**

144- **P** **Simarthur**[53] 4530 7-11-2 **115** (v) PeterBuchanan
(Lucinda Russell) *nt fluent: in tch: outpcd whn nt fluent 11th: struggling fr 13th: t.o whn p.u bef 3 out* **7/2**[2]

6m 34.9s (-12.30) **Going Correction** -0.35s/f (Good) 4 Ran SP% **108.9**
Speed ratings: **104,103,89,**
CSF £5.29 TOTE £1.90; EX 4.70 Trifecta £12.00.

Owner Mrs Susan Granger **Bred** James Cousins **Trained** Lingdale, Redcar & Cleveland

■ Stewards' Enquiry : James Reveley three-day ban: weighed in 2lb heavy (May 6-8)

FOCUS
Only the four runners, but a sound enough pace for this fairly uncompetitive staying handicap chase with question marks surrounding most of the field, apart from the winner. The form is rated around the second.

5482 ELLIOT HENDERSON LTD H'CAP HURDLE (11 hdls) 2m 6f 110y
3:25 (3:25) (Class 3) (0-130,125) 4-Y-0+ **£5,523** (£1,621; £810; £405)

Form RPR

12U- **1** **Zaru (FR)**[25] 5053 8-11-0 **120** DaleIrving(7) 124+
(James Ewart) *t.k.h: cl up: led 3rd: mde rest: hit 3 out: hrd pressed fr next: hld on gamely u.p run-in* **4/1**[3]

F15- **2** *½* **Embsay Crag**[51] 4571 8-10-8 **112** AdamNicol(5) 115+
(Philip Kirby) *cl up: mstke 3 out: sn drvn and sltly outpcd: rallied bef next: effrt and ev ch last: kpt on: hld nr fin* **15/8**[1]

/02- **3** *2 ½* **Parc Des Princes (USA)**[35] 4893 8-10-7 **106** BrianHarding 105
(Nicky Richards) *in tch: effrt bef 2 out: sn rdn: kpt on same pce fr last* **4/1**[3]

056- **4** *4* **Hollow Tree**[38] 4814 6-11-5 **125** NickSlatter(7) 120
(Donald McCain) *chsd ldrs: drvn and outpcd after 3 out: kpt on same pce fr next* **3/1**[2]

664- **5** *38* **Garleton (IRE)**[135] 2972 13-11-0 **120** (t) DaraghBourke(7) 91
(Maurice Barnes) *led to 3rd: cl up tl outpcd bef 3 out: lost tch bef next: t.o* **15/2**

5m 27.9s (-13.10) **Going Correction** -0.35s/f (Good) 5 Ran SP% **111.5**
Speed ratings (Par 107): **108,107,106,105,92**
CSF £12.37 TOTE £3.40: £1.40, £1.60; EX 14.00 Trifecta £21.30.

Owner Humbert, Drew **Bred** James Ewart & Mme Briony Ewart **Trained** Langholm, Dumfries & G'way

FOCUS
A very tricky 0-130 handicap hurdle with most of the runners coming here with a point to prove. A hurdles best from the winner.

5483 HOGG & THORBURN CHARTERED ACCOUNTANTS H'CAP CHASE (12 fncs) 2m 1f
3:55 (3:56) (Class 4) (0-105,98) 5-Y-0+ **£3,898** (£1,144; £572; £286)

Form RPR

552- **1** **Robin's Command (IRE)**[6] 5355 7-9-9 **72** oh1 CraigNichol(5) 87+
(Rose Dobbin) *j.w: cl up: led 1st: mde rest: qcknd after 3 out: drew clr fr next: edgd rt run-in* **7/4**[1]

P1P- **2** *10* **Hotgrove Boy**[35] 4890 7-11-3 **96** DaraghBourke(7) 103
(Stuart Coltherd) *hld up in tch: stdy hdwy and prom 1/2-way: chsd wnr 4 out: nt fluent 3 out: effrt whn nt fluent next: sn one pce* **13/2**

141- **3** *7* **Have You Had Yours (IRE)**[35] 4890 8-10-6 **85** AlistairFindlay(7) 85
(Jane Walton) *nt fluent on occasions: in tch: outpcd 1/2-way: plugged on fr 2 out: no ch w first two* **11/4**[2]

555- **4** *7* **Prince Tam**[15] 5207 10-10-9 **84** JonathanEngland(3) 79
(Harriet Graham) *chsd ldrs: wnt 2nd 1/2-way to 4 out: rdn whn hit next: wknd bef 2 out* **14/1**

411- **5** *18* **Soul Magic (IRE)**[239] 1395 12-11-5 **98** CallumBewley(7) 75
(Harriet Graham) *hld up: nt fluent 1st: struggling fr 5th: nvr on terms* **16/1**

F52- **6** *6* **Sendiym (FR)**[51] 4581 7-11-4 **90** (b) JamesReveley 62
(Dianne Sayer) *led to 1st: chsd wnr to 1/2-way: outpcd whn hit 4 out: struggling fr next* **7/2**[3]

00P- **P** **Snooze N You Lose**[198] 1789 9-9-7 **72** oh22 (p) MissAMcGregor(7)
(Jean McGregor) *hld up: shortlived effrt after 4th: struggling fr next: t.o whn p.u after 2 out* **150/1**

4m 9.3s (-8.70) **Going Correction** -0.35s/f (Good) 7 Ran SP% **111.8**
Speed ratings: **106,101,98,94,86 83,**
CSF £13.02 TOTE £2.70: £1.60, £2.80; EX 17.70 Trifecta £53.30.

Owner M Hunter, J Matterson & R Jacobs **Bred** Gregory Lawler **Trained** South Hazelrigg, Northumbria

FOCUS
The going had eased to good all round before a competitive 0-105 handicap chase where the pace was fair. The winner is rated similar to his Sedgefield level.

5484 ISLE OF SKYE BLENDED SCOTCH WHISKY H'CAP HURDLE (11 hdls) 2m 4f 110y
4:25 (4:25) (Class 4) (0-120,118) 4-Y-0+ **£3,249** (£954; £477; £238)

Form RPR

/61- **1** **Keeneland (IRE)**[31] 4952 7-11-12 **118** AdrianLane 122+
(Donald McCain) *t.k.h: chsd ldrs: wnt 2nd 3 out: rdn bef next: rallied to ld last: edgd lft: drvn out* **4/1**[3]

562- **2** *2 ½* **Allow Me**[15] 5208 9-11-6 **112** (b) JamesReveley 112
(Dianne Sayer) *led: gng wl bef 2 out: rdn and hdd whn nt fluent last: swtchd rt run-in: nt pce of wnr* **2/1**[1]

300/ **3** *2 ½* **Winstone (IRE)**[420] 4433 9-9-8 **93** CallumBewley(7) 92
(George Charlton) *t.k.h: chsd ldrs: mstke 6th: rdn and outpcd 3 out: rallied bef next: kpt on same pce between last 2* **11/2**

414- **4** *26* **Patavium (IRE)**[13] 4938 11-10-2 **97** TonyKelly(3) 71
(Edwin Tuer) *hld up in tch: drvn and outpcd after 4 out: no imp fr next* **10/1**

1/P- **5** *7* **Five Rivers (IRE)**[14] 5218 8-10-6 **108** (p) JamesCorbett(10) 76
(Susan Corbett) *nt fluent: hld up on outside: outpcd and hung lft after 4 out: struggling fr next* **28/1**

664- **6** *14* **Mubrook (USA)**[10] 5272 9-11-3 **109** (b) JamieMoore 64
(Brian Ellison) *nt fluent: cl up: rdn whn hit 3 out: wknd bef next* **3/1**[2]

634- **7** *18* **Walser (IRE)**[15] 5208 7-11-6 **112** (b) LucyAlexander 51
(John Wade) *nt fluent: hld up: struggling bef 4 out: lost tch fr next* **10/1**

4m 57.4s (-10.60) **Going Correction** -0.35s/f (Good) 7 Ran SP% **115.3**
Speed ratings (Par 105): **106,105,104,94,91 86,79**
CSF £13.08 TOTE £4.60: £3.10, £2.80; EX 10.80 Trifecta £100.80.

Owner Paul & Clare Rooney **Bred** Whisperview Trading Ltd **Trained** Cholmondeley, Cheshire

FOCUS
A decent pace for an ordinary handicap hurdle. The winner is rated on the upgrade with the second pretty much to his mark,.

5485 EILDON HILL STABLES NOVICES' HUNTERS' CHASE (FOR THE CHARLIE BROWN TROPHY) (19 fncs) 3m 2f
5:00 (5:00) (Class 5) 5-Y-0+ **£2,495** (£774; £386; £193)

Form RPR

P- **1** **Fruit Fayre**[16] 7-11-0 0 MrPGerety(5) 106+
(Mrs Sheila Crow) *hld up: stdy hdwy and cl up 13th: shkn up to ld between last 2: pushed clr run-in: readily* **10/11**[1]

/1- **2** *12* **Present Potential (IRE)**[15] 5209 7-11-11 102 (p) MrKitAlexander(5) 105
(N W Alexander) *chsd ldr: rdn and outpcd after 3 out: rallied to chse (clr) wnr run-in: no imp* **11/4**[2]

3 *4* **Ballyanrahan (IRE)**[10] 8-11-7 0 MrTHamilton(5) 97
(Miss A E Petch) *nt fluent on occasions: led: hmpd by loose horse appr 13th: blnd 5 out: rdn and hdd between last 2: sn no ex: lost 2nd run-in* **20/1**

1FU- **4** *4* **Rosie Du Berlais (IRE)**[18] 5164 8-11-9 0 MissCWalton 88
(Philip Kirby) *nt fluent in rr: outpcd whn mstke 14th: hdwy bef 3 out: kpt on fr last: no imp* **4/1**[3]

5P- **5** *dist* **Duhallowcountry (IRE)**[10] 8-11-5 94 MrCJMiller(7)
(Victor Thompson) *nt fluent: in tch: outpcd 1/2-way: struggling fr 5 out: t.o* **40/1**

PPP/ **F** **Slick Operator (IRE)**[31] 8-11-7 0 (t) MrRSmith(5)
(D J Dickenson) *in tch: fell 2nd* **14/1**

6m 47.5s (0.30) **Going Correction** -0.35s/f (Good) 6 Ran SP% **112.9**
Speed ratings: **85,81,80,78,65**
CSF £4.05 TOTE £2.40: £1.70, £1.60; EX 4.20 Trifecta £28.10.

Owner Robin Lewis **Bred** Edward Crow **Trained** Shrewsbury, Shropshire

FOCUS
This hunters' Chase revolved around how the prolific pointing winner Fruit Fayre would act back over regulation fences. She can probably rate higher. The time was slow.

T/Plt: £40.30 to a £1 stake. Pool: £36,654.97 - 663.50 winning units. T/Qpdt: £7.20 to a £1 stake. Pool: £2867.58 - 291.00 winning units. RY

5227 LUDLOW (R-H)
Tuesday, April 22

OFFICIAL GOING: Good (7.3)
Wind: slight behind Weather: overcast with showers

5486 FAMILY DAY ON 11TH MAY NOVICES' HURDLE (11 hdls) 2m 5f
1:55 (1:55) (Class 4) 4-Y-0+ **£3,898** (£1,144; £572; £286)

Form RPR
142- **1** **Call The Cops (IRE)**[28] 5015 5-11-6 128 BarryGeraghty 132+
(Nicky Henderson) *hld up: hdwy to trck ldrs 3rd: pushed along 3 out where pckd on landing: chsd ldr 2 out: drvn to ld flat: wl on top nr fin* **4/11**[1]
626- **2** 1 1/2 **Always Archie**[26] 5036 7-10-13 114 RichardJohnson 121
(Tim Vaughan) *trckd ldr: led 2 out: sn drvn: hdd and edgd lft after last: hld whn sltly hmpd nr fin* **20/1**
3P1- **3** 20 **Magic Money**[12] 5229 6-11-0 115 EdCookson(5) 112+
(Kim Bailey) *led tl hdd and blnd bdly 2 out: one pce and no ch after* **9/2**[2]
60- **4** 1 1/4 **Sacramento King (IRE)**[23] 5088 5-10-10 0 NicodeBoinville(3) 100
(Jonathan Geake) *hld up towards rr: hdwy 7th: rdn appr 3 out: sn outpcd by ldrs* **33/1**
3- **5** 3 **Russborough (FR)**[37] 4832 5-10-13 118 AidanColeman 97
(Venetia Williams) *trckd ldrs: rdn appr 3 out: wknd 2 out* **10/1**[3]
6 dist **Blazing Glen (IRE)**[93] 6-10-10 0 JackQuinlan(3)
(Alan Jessop) *hld up in tch: dropped to rr 3rd: wknd appr 3 out: t.o* **100/1**
0- **P** **Dancing Ecco (IRE)**[12] 5227 5-10-6 0 ConorRing(7)
(Evan Williams) *t.k.h early: in tch tl wknd after 8th: t.o whn p.u bef 3 out* **100/1**

5m 12.9s (-1.90) **Going Correction** +0.125s/f (Yiel) 7 Ran SP% **110.3**
Speed ratings (Par 105): **108,107,99,99,98 81,**
CSF £9.51 TOTE £1.20: £1.10, £2.50; EX 6.50 Trifecta £23.70.
Owner Matt & Lauren Morgan **Bred** Martin Donnellan **Trained** Upper Lambourn, Berks

FOCUS
A modest novice event, run at a steady early gallop. The winner and fourth set the level.

5487 EASTER TUESDAY H'CAP CHASE (13 fncs) 2m
2:25 (2:25) (Class 4) (0-115,113) 5-Y-0+ **£5,198** (£1,526; £763; £381)

Form RPR
42F- **1** **Another Flutter (IRE)**[172] 2191 10-11-7 108 (tp) CharliePoste 115+
(Matt Sheppard) *tended to jump lft: mde all: strly pressed whn nt fluent 2 out: hld on wl u.p flat* **12/1**
P24- **2** nk **Elsafeer (IRE)**[38] 4800 9-11-9 110 RichardJohnson 115
(Tim Vaughan) *last tl hdwy to r promly 3rd: chsd wnr fr 6th: chal after 3 out: sn swtchd rt and drvn: ev ch flat: jst hld* **5/1**[3]
5P3- **3** 4 **Kayalar (IRE)**[55] 4488 6-10-3 90 PaulMoloney 93
(Evan Williams) *hld up: clsd after 9th: blnd bdly 4 out: sn rdn and outpcd by ldng pair: kpt on to take 3rd flat* **5/1**[3]
426- **4** 3/4 **Carhue Princess (IRE)**[12] 5246 8-10-2 89 ow1 FelixDeGiles 89
(Tom Symonds) *in tch: hdwy to chse ldrs 6th: rdn appr 4 out: sn one pce: lost 3rd flat* **16/1**
544- **5** 16 **Engai (GER)**[19] 5141 8-11-12 113 TomScudamore 105
(David Bridgwater) *chsd ldrs: mstkes 9th and 4 out: wknd 3 out* **14/1**
146- **6** 18 **Riddleofthesands (IRE)**[24] 5065 10-11-1 102 SamTwiston-Davies 72
(Nigel Twiston-Davies) *t.k.h: trckd wnr to 6th: styd prom tl wknd appr 4 out: t.o* **8/1**
F00- **7** 3 3/4 **Topthorn**[135] 2977 8-10-6 98 AnthonyFreeman(5) 64
(Martin Bosley) *in rr: hmpd 1st: sme hdwy appr 4 out: wknd 3 out: t.o* **7/2**[1]
10P- **8** 31 **Take Of Shoc'S (IRE)**[12] 5247 10-10-11 103 (t) CharlieWallis(5) 42
(Sophie Leech) *chsd ldrs tl j.lft and dropped to rr 6th: continued to jump lft after and qckly lost tch: t.o* **14/1**
33U- **F** **Spoil Me (IRE)**[12] 5237 7-11-0 104 (b[1]) MauriceLinehan(3)
(Jonjo O'Neill) *mid-div whn fell 1st* **4/1**[2]

4m 1.7s (3.20) **Going Correction** +0.225s/f (Yiel) 9 Ran SP% **113.6**
Speed ratings: **101,100,98,98,90 81,79,64,**
CSF £70.73 CT £342.30 TOTE £13.00: £3.00, £2.00, £2.00; EX 46.00 Trifecta £635.40.
Owner Tony Scrivin **Bred** Eamon D Delany **Trained** Eastnor, H'fords

FOCUS
As expected the race was run at a fair gallop and the first pair had it to themselves from the third-last.

5488 H R SMITH GROUP LTD H'CAP CHASE (22 fncs) 3m 1f 110y
3:00 (3:00) (Class 3) (0-130,127) 5-Y-0+ **£12,660** (£3,740; £1,870; £936; £468)

Form RPR
1U2- **1** **Divine Intavention (IRE)**[12] 5230 10-11-5 125 MrMWall(5) 134+
(Martin Keighley) *in tch: modest 4th whn rdn 18th: wnt 2nd 2 out: led sn after last: idled and drvn out* **9/2**[2]
431- **2** 2 1/4 **Talkonthestreet (IRE)**[31] 4968 7-11-7 122 (p) RichardJohnson 133+
(Philip Hobbs) *cl up: mstke 14th (water): led next: drew clr appr 4 out: wnt lft 3 out: veered rt then wnt lft next: wnt lft last: sn hdd and no ex* **7/2**[1]
535- **3** 20 **Raduis Bleu (FR)**[26] 5039 9-9-12 106 MissLBrooke(7) 95
(Lady Susan Brooke) *chsd ldrs: outpcd by wnr fr 18th: wnt mod 2nd 4 out: one pce: tired and lost 2nd flat* **16/1**
233- **4** 1 **Charingworth (IRE)**[113] 3414 11-11-12 127 NickScholfield 113
(Kim Bailey) *hld up: mstke 12th: outpcd by ldrs 15th and no ch after: styd on u.p fr 2 out* **11/1**
163- **5** 1 3/4 **Bold Perk (IRE)**[281] 998 12-11-7 122 HaddenFrost 107
(Martin Hill) *a in rr: no ch fr 18th* **33/1**
P43- **6** shd **Boyfromnowhere (IRE)**[16] 5184 7-11-7 127 (b) PatrickCorbett(5) 111
(Rebecca Curtis) *narrow ld to 15th: styd cl up tl drvn and wknd after 18th: lost 2nd 4 out* **9/1**
3/2- **P** **Gambo (IRE)**[341] 334 8-11-5 120 PaulMoloney
(Evan Williams) *hld up: hdwy 13th: wkng whn mstke 17th: p.u bef next* **9/1**
565- **P** **What A Warrior (IRE)**[31] 4962 7-11-10 125 (p) SamTwiston-Davies
(Nigel Twiston-Davies) *mid-div: outpcd by ldrs 15th: wknd 18th: t.o whn p.u bef 4 out* **7/2**[1]
2P3- **P** **Take The Mick**[26] 5039 7-10-11 112 AidanColeman
(Venetia Williams) *chsd ldrs tl j. slowly and lost pl 7th: dropped to rr 13th: losing tch whn p.u bef 15th* **7/1**[3]

6m 40.1s (4.80) **Going Correction** +0.225s/f (Yiel) 9 Ran SP% **112.3**
Speed ratings: **101,100,94,93,93 93, , ,**
CSF £20.58 CT £225.56 TOTE £4.90: £1.10, £1.50, £3.80; EX 22.10 Trifecta £271.90.
Owner H Wilson **Bred** James Nolan **Trained** Condicote, Gloucs

FOCUS
This competitive staying handicap was run at a sound gallop and few managed to play a serious part, but it saw changing fortunes in the home straight. The winner is on a good mark and the second is capable of better the other way round.

5489 RACINGUK.COM/ANYWHERE: 3 DEVICES, 1 PRICE H'CAP HURDLE (12 hdls) 3m
3:35 (3:35) (Class 3) (0-125,125) 4-Y-0+ **£7,596** (£2,244; £1,122; £561; £280)

Form RPR
013- **1** **Decimus (IRE)**[10] 5285 7-11-1 116 MattGriffiths(3) 122
(Jeremy Scott) *a.p: led 3rd: pushed along 3 out: nt fluent 2 out: drvn out* **14/1**
061- **2** 1 1/4 **Kingsmere**[5] 5372 9-11-10 125 7ex JakeGreenall(3) 131+
(Henry Daly) *hld up: hdwy after 7th: 4th whn rdn appr 3 out: sn chal ldr: ev ch whn nt fluent 2 out: kpt on u.p: edgd lft and unable qck flat* **6/4**[1]
/FP- **3** 1 1/4 **One Conemara (IRE)**[75] 4105 6-11-8 120 BarryGeraghty 125
(Nicky Henderson) *chsd ldrs: chal 3 out: mstke last: kpt on same pce* **4/1**[2]
244- **4** 3 1/4 **Dragon's Den (IRE)**[19] 5142 7-11-1 113 RichardJohnson 115
(Chris Down) *in rr: hdwy 8th: mstke 2 out: styd on flat* **8/1**
245- **5** 10 **Phare Isle (IRE)**[20] 5128 9-10-10 115 (tp) MrMJPKendrick(7) 108
(Ben Case) *chsd ldrs: rdn 3 out: wknd after 2 out* **20/1**
615- **6** 9 **Storm Alert**[7] 5333 7-11-0 117 MissLucyGardner(5) 102
(Sue Gardner) *chsd ldrs: nt fluent 7th: wknd appr 3 out* **20/1**
PP0- **7** 6 **Bathwick Brave (IRE)**[7] 5333 7-11-12 124 NickScholfield 103
(Johnny Farrelly) *towards rr: sme hdwy 8th: wknd 3 out* **66/1**
315- **8** 43 **Midnight Cataria**[31] 4961 5-11-10 122 RobertThornton 62
(Alan King) *mid-div: tk clsr order 6th: rdn after 9th: wknd 3 out: t.o* **7/1**[3]
500- **9** 9 **Church Field (IRE)**[16] 5191 6-10-13 114 MauriceLinehan(3) 46
(Jonjo O'Neill) *in tch: tk clsr order 8th: rdn after next: sn wknd: t.o* **10/1**
21P- **10** 23 **Harris (IRE)**[34] 4896 7-11-0 112 (p) AndrewTinkler 23
(William Kinsey) *chsd ldrs tl lost pl after 6th: wknd 3 out: t.o* **25/1**
03P- **P** **Halucha (IRE)**[16] 5191 9-10-5 103 (p) LiamTreadwell
(Paul Webber) *led to 3rd: styd prom to 6th: struggling 8th: t.o whn p.u bef 3 out* **33/1**
35R- **R** **Zafaraban (IRE)**[6] 5362 7-10-0 98 oh10 (b) LeeEdwards
(Aytach Sadik) *a in rr: lost tch 8th: t.o whn ref at flattened hurdle and uns rdr 2 out* **66/1**

5m 52.6s (0.30) **Going Correction** +0.125s/f (Yiel) 12 Ran SP% **118.7**
Speed ratings (Par 107): **104,103,103,102,98 95,93,79,76,68 ,**
CSF £34.36 CT £106.38 TOTE £17.80: £4.30, £1.40, £1.80; EX 72.50 Trifecta £285.80.
Owner The Ten 2 One Gang **Bred** Mrs Sheila Kelleher **Trained** Brompton Regis, Somerset
■ Stewards' Enquiry : Jake Greenall two-day ban: used whip above permitted level (May 6-7)

FOCUS
A modest staying handicap, run at an ordinary gallop until around the fifth-last. Straightforward form.

5490 LUDLOW FESTIVAL NOVICES' H'CAP HURDLE (9 hdls) 2m
4:05 (4:05) (Class 4) (0-110,115) 4-Y-0+ **£4,548** (£1,335; £500; £500)

Form RPR
2F1- **1** **August Hill (IRE)**[9] 5304 6-11-2 103 (t) MichealNolan(3) 110+
(Philip Hobbs) *mid-div: hdwy after 6th: chal 3 out: rdn next: lft in ld last: rdn clr flat* **13/8**[1]
320- **2** 5 **Purple 'n Gold (IRE)**[12] 5239 5-11-12 110 (b) TomScudamore 110
(David Pipe) *chsd ldrs: pushed along 2 out: rdn last: sn chsng wnr: unable qck* **11/1**
022- **3** 3/4 **Frozen Over**[12] 5238 6-11-5 103 (t) JamesDavies 105+
(Chris Down) *in tch: hdwy 6th: led appr 3 out: strly pressed whn blnd bdly and hdd last: no ex* **12/1**
P21- **3** dht **Rolling Dough (IRE)**[125] 3157 6-10-1 85 (p) PaulMoloney 84
(Sophie Leech) *hld up in rr: hdwy 6th: rdn 3 out: sn outpcd by ldrs: r.o flat* **16/1**
325- **5** 1/2 **Knockgraffon Lad (USA)**[39] 1938 7-10-8 97 (t) JamesBanks(5) 96
(Brendan Powell) *hld up in rr: hdwy after 6th: styd on fr 2 out* **7/1**[3]
0P6- **6** 10 **Hollywood All Star (IRE)**[29] 5008 5-11-2 105 KillianMoore(5) 98
(Graeme McPherson) *towards rr: j. slowly 4th: clsd next: rdn appr 3 out: sn one pce* **40/1**
F44- **7** 3 1/4 **Cantony**[105] 3592 5-11-7 108 JakeGreenall(3) 95
(Henry Daly) *in tch: hdwy 5th: chsng ldrs whn nudged along 3 out: steadily wknd* **12/1**
653- **8** 18 **Pembroke House**[22] 5112 7-11-6 104 WillKennedy 75
(Sarah-Jayne Davies) *led tl rdn and hdd appr 3 out: wknd qckly: t.o* **20/1**
2/3- **9** 4 **Stevie Thunder**[9] 5294 9-11-2 100 (t) RichardJohnson 67
(Ian Williams) *cl up: hit 2nd: nt fluent 5th: wknd 2 out: t.o* **7/2**[2]
000- **10** nk **Maxi Mac (IRE)**[12] 5238 4-10-7 103 JoshWall(7) 65
(Trevor Wall) *a in rr: wl bhd whn mstke last: t.o* **80/1**
204- **11** 2 **Barney Rubble**[17] 5174 5-10-11 95 CharliePoste 60
(Richard Lee) *chsd ldrs tl rdn and wknd after 6th: t.o* **20/1**
F55- **12** 26 **Ernest Speak (IRE)**[12] 5236 5-11-3 101 HaddenFrost 43
(Martin Hill) *t.k.h: chsd ldrs tl wknd after 6th: t.o* **25/1**
540/ **P** **Rhinestone Rebel (IRE)**[78] 186 8-10-0 84 oh2 LiamTreadwell
(Peter Hiatt) *racd keenly: in tch: hdwy 3rd: dropped to rr 5th: sn struggling: t.o whn p.u bef 3 out* **50/1**

3m 49.9s (0.40) **Going Correction** +0.125s/f (Yiel)
WFA 4 from 5yo+ 5lb 13 Ran SP% **121.4**
Speed ratings (Par 105): **104,101,101,101,100 95,94,85,83,83 82,69,**
WIN: £3.00; PL: August Hill £1.10, Purple 'n Gold £2.10, Frozen Over £1.80, Rolling Dough £1.80; EX: £21.20; CSF: £18.95; TC: AH/PNG/FO £86.73, AH/PNG/RD £113.40; TF: AH/PNG/FO £153.30, AH/PNG/RD £63.80.
Owner Mrs Caren Walsh & Mrs Kathleen Quinn **Bred** Thomas James **Trained** Withycombe, Somerset

FOCUS
There was a modest gallop in this weak novice handicap and the winner did what she had to. She didn't quite need to be at her recent level.

5491 EDDIE MAPP MEMORIAL OPEN HUNTERS' CHASE (17 fncs) 2m 4f
4:35 (4:35) (Class 5) 5-Y-0+ **£2,495** (£774; £386; £193)

Form RPR
2P2- **1** **Foundry Square (IRE)**[12] 5232 8-12-0 114 (p) MissGAndrews 128+
(S Flook) *in rr: hdwy 10th: pushed along 13th: led 4 out: rdn next: drew clr appr last: comf* **11/4**[2]
521- **2** 11 **Shrewd Investment**[27] 5035 8-11-11 118 (tp) MrSamPainting(7) 123
(Miss L Thomas) *in tch: hdwy 7th: wnt 2nd and rdn 3 out: mstke next: one pce and sn no ch w wnr* **3/1**[3]

The Form Book Jumps, Raceform Ltd, Compton, RG20 6NL.

PP6- **3** *27* **Rebel Alliance (IRE)**[44] 4705 9-11-7 95........................(t) MrWHickman(7) 95
(Richard A Thomas) *chsd ldr tl appr 4 out: sn outpcd by ldrs: plugged on to take 3rd appr last* **50/1**

/31- **4** *nk* **Warwickshire (IRE)**[12] 5248 7-11-7 0.............................. MrBRivett(7) 93
(A Pennock) *led: j.lft 1st: clr to 4th: hdd 4 out: wknd 3 out* **8/1**

231- **5** *1 3/4* **Nowurhurlin (IRE)**[23] 5094 7-11-11 118....................(v) MrRGSpencer(7) 96
(Mrs S J Stilgoe) *chsd ldrs: rdn after 13th: wknd 3 out* **2/1**[1]

/51- **6** *38* **What Of It (IRE)**[16] 11-11-11 108.............................. MissLDocker(7) 62
(Mrs Sarah Ward) *a towards rr: lost tch 12th: t.o* **28/1**

06P/ **P** **Rebel Chief (IRE)**[37] 13-11-3 0.. MrCWest(7)
(Richard A Thomas) *a in rr: struggling 9th: t.o whn p.u bef 11th* **66/1**

344- **P** **Tiermore (IRE)**[16] 10-11-7 105... MrEDavid(7)
(R E Luke) *mstke 1st: a towards rr: struggling 10th: t.o whn p.u bef 12th* **12/1**

265- **P** **Up To The Mark**[10] 9-11-7 102..........................(p) MissHannahWatson(3)
(Miss V Collins) *in tch tl wknd 11th: t.o whn p.u bef 3 out* **20/1**

6/ **P** **Regal Reform (IRE)**[59] 9-11-3 69............................ MrRichardPatrick(7)
(Richard A Thomas) *in tch: mstke 2nd: dropped to rr 10th: t.o whn p.u bef 12th* **100/1**

5m 5.6s (1.20) **Going Correction** +0.225s/f (Yiel) **10** Ran SP% **116.5**
Speed ratings: **106,101,90,90,89 74,,,,**
CSF £11.42 TOTE £4.80: £1.90, £1.10, £9.80; EX 14.60 Trifecta £366.60.
Owner B J Mould **Bred** W H Neville **Trained** Leominster, Herefordshire

FOCUS
There was a generous gallop on in this modest hunter chase and they finished fairly strung out. The winner was the form pick.

5492 LADIES DAY ON 11TH MAY INTERMEDIATE OPEN NATIONAL HUNT FLAT RACE 2m
5:10 (5:10) (Class 5) 4-6-Y-O **£2,599** (£763; £381; £190)

Form RPR

1 **Gaelic Myth** 4-10-7 0.. EdCookson(5) 96+
(Kim Bailey) *cl up: led after 2f: jinked lft bnd over 2f out: rdn over 1f out: styd on wl* **8/1**

1- **2** *4 1/2* **Brownville**[33] 4923 5-11-10 0.................................... SamTwiston-Davies 103
(Nigel Twiston-Davies) *a.p: chsd wnr after 7f: rdn over 1f out: styd on same pce* **5/1**[3]

3 *3/4* **Nicolas Chauvin (IRE)** 6-11-3 0.................................... BarryGeraghty 95+
(Nicky Henderson) *hld up: hdwy after 6f: trcking ldrs whn sltly hmpd bnd over 2f out: rdn over 1f out: unable qck* **6/4**[1]

4 *3 3/4* **Green Winter (IRE)**[24] 6-11-3 0.................................... DenisO'Regan 92
(Henry Oliver) *in tch towards rr: hdwy 5f out: rdn 2f out: one pce* **16/1**

0- **5** *1* **Midnight Spin**[31] 4964 4-10-12 0.................................. RichardJohnson 86
(Philip Hobbs) *hld up: stdy hdwy 6f out: pushed along 2f out: styd on same pce* **11/4**[2]

0- **6** *10* **State The Blend**[182] 2015 4-10-5 0.................................. PaulMoloney 70
(Sue Gardner) *racd keenly: hld up: hdwy 7f out: rdn 3f out: sn one pce* **33/1**

0- **7** *3 3/4* **Poetic Presence (IRE)**[33] 4916 4-10-5 0........................ AidanColeman 67
(Adrian Wintle) *mid-div: rdn and struggling 4f out: pushed along and styd on fnl 2f* **40/1**

3- **8** *1/2* **Titans Approach (IRE)**[16] 5188 5-10-12 0........................ KillianMoore(5) 78
(Graeme McPherson) *mid-div: hdwy to trck ldrs 1/2-way: pushed along over 3f out: grad wknd fnl 2f* **16/1**

0- **9** *14* **Herr Larry Hewis**[43] 4728 6-11-3 0.................................. WillKennedy 66
(Sarah-Jayne Davies) *racd keenly: led 2f: styd prom tl rdn and wknd over 3f out: t.o* **100/1**

6- **10** *1 1/2* **Misirlou (FR)**[55] 4498 4-10-12 0.................................. MichaelByrne 59
(Tim Vaughan) *chsd ldrs tl wknd over 4f out: t.o* **40/1**

0- **11** *19* **Over The Bridge**[19] 5145 4-10-12 0................................ TommyPhelan 42
(Mark Gillard) *towards rr: rdn 6f out: wknd over 3f out: t.o* **100/1**

3m 46.6s (2.70) **Going Correction** +0.125s/f (Yiel)
WFA 4 from 5yo+ 5lb **11** Ran SP% **116.0**
Speed ratings: **98,95,95,93,93 88,86,85,78,78 68**
CSF £46.03 TOTE £8.90: £2.00, £1.70, £1.90; EX 70.40 Trifecta £407.90.
Owner A N Solomons **Bred** Megan Bates **Trained** Andoversford, Gloucs

FOCUS
Not a bad bumper, rated around the fifth and seventh.
T/Jkpt: Part won. £8800.20 to a £1 stake. Pool: £12,394.78 - 0.50 winning units. T/Plt: £21.90 to a £1 stake. Pool: £68,174.10 - 2268.91 winning units. T/Qpdt: £7.00 to a £1 stake. Pool: £4706.48 - 496.86 winning units. RL

5295 WETHERBY (L-H)
Tuesday, April 22

OFFICIAL GOING: Good (good to soft in places) changing to good to soft after race 1 (2.05)
Wind: moderate 1/2 against Weather: light rain at first, overcast and damp

5493 NEW RACING UK ANYWHERE AVAILABLE NOW (S) HURDLE (12 hdls) 2m 6f
2:05 (2:05) (Class 5) 4-8-Y-O **£2,053** (£598; £299)

Form RPR

321- **1** **Maller Tree**[1] 5434 7-11-10 125..................................(b) NoelFehily 116+
(David Dennis) *mde all: increased gallop 5th: drvn 2 out: rdn clr last 50yds* **8/13**[1]

133- **2** *5* **Rosslyn Castle**[14] 5217 5-11-6 110.. APMcCoy 107
(Jonjo O'Neill) *trckd ldrs: handy 2nd 8th: effrt 2 out: hung lft: 1 1/2 l down last: kpt on same pce* **7/4**[2]

320/ **3** *21* **Drummers Drumming (USA)**[29] 1613 8-11-0 0.............(t) BrianHughes 80
(Alan Berry) *chsd wnr: drvn appr 3 out: sn wl outpcd* **33/1**

0/0- **4** *1 3/4* **Taxi Des Obeaux (FR)**[22] 5102 7-10-11 0........................ KyleJames(3) 78
(Philip Kirby) *nt fluent 1st: hld up in last but wl in tch: pushed along 8th: outpcd and lost pl bef 3 out* **18/1**[3]

5m 46.0s (19.20) **Going Correction** +0.60s/f (Soft) **4** Ran SP% **106.5**
Speed ratings: **89,87,79,78**
CSF £1.98 TOTE £1.70; EX 2.10 Trifecta £5.50.The winner was bought in for 10,000gns. Rosslyn Castle was bought by Mr P J Mcbride for £6,000.
Owner Favourites Racing **Bred** Phil Toft **Trained** Hanley Swan, Worcestershire

FOCUS
After riding in the opener, Noel Fehily said it was good to soft, soft ground. A steadily run affair with the favourite making all. The winner is rated similar to his previous day's victory.

5494 WETHERBYRACING.CO.UK NOVICES' H'CAP HURDLE (11 hdls) 2m 4f
2:35 (2:36) (Class 5) (0-100,100) 4-Y-O+ **£2,053** (£598; £299)

Form RPR

011- **1** **Rayadour (IRE)**[9] 5302 5-11-3 88 7ex..........................(p) WilsonRenwick 98+
(Micky Hammond) *hld up in rr: hdwy 8th: trcking ldrs next: rdn to ld appr last: drvn clr clsng stages* **7/2**[1]

360- **2** *5* **Wayne Manor (IRE)**[38] 4823 5-11-5 95..................(tp) GrantCockburn(5) 100
(Lucinda Russell) *chsd ldrs: clr 2nd appr 3 out: led 2 out: hdd appr last: no ex* **8/1**

P64- **3** *1 3/4* **Thatildee (IRE)**[51] 4576 6-10-9 87............................ DiarmuidO'Regan(7) 91
(Chris Grant) *chsd ldrs: drvn 3 out: 4th whn mstke last: styd on to take 3rd nr fin* **20/1**

20P- **4** *shd* **Teo Vivo (FR)**[42] 4744 7-11-11 96.. BrianHughes 99
(Pauline Robson) *chsd ldrs: led after 8th: hdd 2 out: styd on same pce* **10/1**

002- **5** *8* **Double Whammy**[22] 5107 8-11-2 87............................(b) DominicElsworth 83
(Iain Jardine) *chsd ldrs: rdn 3 out: 6th and wkng whn j.lft last* **6/1**[3]

4P3- **6** *1 3/4* **Foot The Bill**[38] 4816 9-11-7 92.. DannyCook 89
(Patrick Holmes) *led: hdd after 8th: 7th whn mstke 2 out: sn wknd* **20/1**

220- **7** *1* **Lebanna**[18] 5161 4-10-10 94......................................(t) MrWEasterby(7) 83
(Tim Easterby) *hld up in rr: hdwy 5th: chsng ldrs next: wknd between last 2* **8/1**

205- **8** *hd* **High Fair**[40] 4770 8-10-8 86.. NathanMoscrop(7) 79
(Sandy Forster) *in rr: drvn 6th: styd on fr 2 out* **25/1**

666- **9** *4 1/2* **Mr Vendman (IRE)**[19] 4679 4-11-4 100...................(p) RobertMcCarth(5) 83
(Ian Williams) *mid-div: hdwy 5th: lost pl bef 3 out* **20/1**

534- **10** *13* **Falcon's Present**[42] 4743 6-11-6 91.. NoelFehily 74
(John Weymes) *in rr: sme hdwy 8th: wknd bef next: eased run-in* **20/1**

66P- **11** *2 1/2* **Master Bud**[25] 5056 9-10-0 78.. RyanHatch(7) 53
(Susan Corbett) *mid-div: drvn 8th: sn wknd* **66/1**

0/F- **12** *4 1/2* **Deportation**[334] 444 7-11-0 90...............................(v) ColmMcCormack(5) 61
(John Norton) *in rr: bhd and reminders 8th* **33/1**

060- **13** *7* **Daylan (IRE)**[75] 4103 6-11-10 95.. DougieCostello 60
(Tony Coyle) *mid-div: nt fluent 6th: sme hdwy 8th: lost pl bef next: struck into* **11/2**[2]

030- **14** *6* **Young Lou**[36] 4398 5-9-12 74..(b) BenPoste(5) 34
(Robin Dickin) *chsd ldrs: nt fluent 1st: lost pl bef 8th: t.o 3 out* **25/1**

0P5- **15** *4 1/2* **Rozener (IRE)**[32] 4938 8-11-3 91...........................[1] HarryChalloner(3) 47
(Henry Hogarth) *chsd ldrs: lost pl bef 3 out: sn bhd* **20/1**

240- **16** *14* **Monita Bonita**[88] 3871 5-11-12 97.. RyanMania 40
(Tim Easterby) *mid-div: hdwy and prom 7th: lost pl after next: sn bhd* **12/1**

046- **P** **Agent Louise**[18] 5161 6-11-4 89.. GavinSheehan
(Mike Sowersby) *in rr: drvn 3rd: bhd 5th: t.o whn p.u bef 7th* **25/1**

5m 11.2s (11.70) **Going Correction** +0.60s/f (Soft)
WFA 4 from 5yo+ 6lb **17** Ran SP% **130.7**
Speed ratings (Par 103): **100,98,97,97,94 93,92,92,91,85 84,83,80,77,76 70,**
CSF £28.68 CT £524.54 TOTE £3.90: £1.40, £3.30, £5.80, £2.80; EX 30.20 Trifecta £1253.00 Part won..
Owner Straightline Construction Ltd **Bred** His Highness The Aga Khan's Studs S C **Trained** Middleham Moor, N Yorks

FOCUS
After the first race the going was changed to good to soft. A modest handicap run at an honest gallop. The winner is on the upgrade over hurdles and can probably win another.

5495 DOWNLOAD NEW RACING UK IPAD APP NOVICES' CHASE (18 fncs) 3m 1f
3:10 (3:10) (Class 4) 5-Y-O+ **£3,768** (£1,106; £553)

Form RPR

3P3- **1** **Financial Climate (IRE)**[17] 5178 7-10-7 123.............. ThomasGarner(5) 138+
(Oliver Sherwood) *led 2nd to 5th: led travelling much the best after 9th: clr 14th: pushed along fr next: nvr in any danger* **5/2**[3]

334- **2** *15* **Imperial Vic (IRE)**[31] 4953 9-10-12 127..............................(p) DannyCook 122
(Michael Smith) *led 1st: hdd next: pushed along 9th: chsd wnr next: no imp* **5/4**[1]

11P- **3** *26* **Bit Of A Jig (IRE)**[10] 5278 7-10-12 132................................(b[1]) APMcCoy 108
(Donald McCain) *led: nt fluent and hdd 1st: led 5th: hrd drvn next: hdd after 9th: lost pl bef 4 out: bhd whn stmbld on landing 3 out: t.o whn eased clsng stages* **7/4**[2]

6m 14.0s (4.60) **Going Correction** +0.475s/f (Soft) **3** Ran SP% **109.4**
Speed ratings: **111,106,97**
CSF £5.94 TOTE £4.60; EX 6.90 Trifecta £6.00.
Owner Sara Fillery & Friends **Bred** Mrs E M Motherway **Trained** Upper Lambourn, Berks

FOCUS
This looked competitive enough, but it was turned into a procession by the winner.

5496 BOOK TICKETS ONLINE AT WETHERBYRACING.CO.UK H'CAP HURDLE (9 hdls) 2m 110y
3:45 (3:45) (Class 4) (0-120,118) 4-Y-O+ **£3,119** (£915; £457; £228)

Form RPR

110- **1** **Oliver's Gold**[39] 1378 6-10-11 103.................................... DougieCostello 111+
(Mark Walford) *trckd ldrs: led and mstke 3 out: hung lft: drvn rt out* **16/1**

433- **2** *3* **Bohemian Rhapsody (IRE)**[53] 4157 5-11-12 118.................. NoelFehily 122
(Seamus Durack) *mid-div: hdwy to chse ldrs 6th: 3rd between last 2: styd on to take 2nd nr fin* **11/4**[1]

630- **3** *1/2* **Skint**[45] 4682 8-11-12 118...(p) AdamWedge 122
(Ali Brewer) *hld up in rr: hdwy 6th: hit next: chsd wnr between last 2: kpt on same pce* **5/1**[3]

030- **4** *3/4* **Narcissist (IRE)**[147] 2732 5-11-0 106.................................. WilsonRenwick 109
(Michael Easterby) *hld up in rr: hdwy 3 out: styd on to take 4th appr last: kpt on same pce* **20/1**

135- **5** *3 1/2* **Weybridge Light**[166] 2311 9-10-2 101..............................(b) DeanPratt(7) 102
(David Thompson) *chsd ldrs: one pce fr 3 out* **12/1**

230- **6** *8* **Bright Applause**[31] 4952 6-10-8 100.. DannyCook 94
(Tracy Waggott) *mid-div: outpcd and lost pl appr 3 out: hit 2 out* **12/1**

125- **7** *3* **Blake Dean**[47] 4629 6-10-8 100.. RyanMania 92
(Sue Smith) *led: drvn 6th: hdd appr next: wknd between last 2: eased clsng stages* **8/1**

313- **8** *6* **Cool Sky**[38] 4813 5-11-10 116.. APMcCoy 100
(Donald McCain) *in rr: drvn and sme hdwy appr 3 out: lost pl bef 2 out* **3/1**[2]

330- **9** *4* **Spin Cast**[6] 5365 6-10-11 **110**..(p) MissHBethell(7) 95
(Brian Ellison) *chsd ldr: hit 2 out: wknd qckly between last 2: eased clsng stages* **14/1**

005- **10** *nk* **Dumbarton (IRE)**[25] 5061 6-11-6 **112**................................(p) BrianHughes 93
(James Moffatt) *hld up in rr: hdwy to chse ldrs 6th: lost pl appr 3 out* **16/1**

4m 3.2s (7.40) **Going Correction** +0.60s/f (Soft)
WFA 4 from 5yo+ 5lb **10** Ran SP% **118.0**
Speed ratings (Par 105): **106,104,104,104,102 98,97,94,92,92**
CSF £62.15 CT £262.97 TOTE £12.10: £3.40, £2.30, £1.40; EX 42.90 Trifecta £356.90.
Owner Quench Racing Partnership **Bred** Bearstone Stud **Trained** Sherriff Hutton, N Yorks

FOCUS
They went a fair gallop for this handicap. The second and third set the level.

5497 WETHERBY RACECOURSE & CONFERENCE CENTRE H'CAP CHASE (18 fncs) 2m 6f 110y
4:15 (4:15) (Class 4) (0-120,120) 5-Y-O+ **£3,768** (£1,106; £553; £276)

Form RPR

132- **1** **Whiskey Ridge (IRE)**[35] 4892 8-10-5 **99**.............................. RyanMania 112
(Sue Smith) *led to 6th: reminders 9th: sn regained ld: drvn 14th: drew clr fr 2 out* **11/4**[1]

532- **2** *17* **Mr Syntax (IRE)**[49] 4606 10-11-11 **119**...............................(t) BrianHughes 118
(Tim Fitzgerald) *trckd ldrs: 2nd 11th: drvn and upsides 4 out: fdd 2 out: 6 l down whn mstke last* **7/2**[2]

513- **3** *31* **Cloudingstar (IRE)**[31] 4948 7-11-2 **110**..................................(t) APMcCoy 89
(Jonjo O'Neill) *racd wd: hdwy to trck ldrs 10th: rdn and lost pl appr 4 out: mstke next: t.o whn j. slowly 2 out* **7/2**[2]

54P- **4** *8* **Apache Blue (IRE)**[18] 5162 10-10-4 **103**......................... JohnDawson(5) 65
(John Wade) *chsd ldrs: drvn along 9th: lost pl and hmpd 11th: t.o 13th* **20/1**

1U3- **U** **Work Boy**[18] 5162 13-10-11 **110**................................... SamanthaDrake(5)
(Richard Drake) *w ldr: led 6th: hdd after 9th: cl 4th whn mstke and uns rdr 11th* **14/1**

4P6- **P** **Rudemeister (IRE)**[34] 4900 8-11-12 **120**......................(t) WilsonRenwick
(Lucinda Russell) *hld up: hdwy to trck ldrs 10th: lost pl 12th: wknd qckly 14th: sn t.o: p.u bef next* **7/1**

243- **F** **Majorica King (FR)**[24] 5068 8-11-5 **118**....................... ThomasGarner(5)
(Oliver Sherwood) *hld up: hdwy to trck ldrs 10th: handy 4th whn fell 14th: fatally injured* **4/1**[3]

5m 50.9s (13.90) **Going Correction** +0.475s/f (Soft) **7** Ran SP% **115.0**
Speed ratings: **94,88,77,74, ,**
CSF £13.40 TOTE £3.70: £3.30, £1.90; EX 12.00 Trifecta £38.40.
Owner Widdop Wanderers **Bred** Tankardstown Stud **Trained** High Eldwick, W Yorks

FOCUS
A fair handicap run at a sound gallop. The winner was the only one to get home in a slow-motion finish.

5498 DOWNLOAD NEW RACING UK APP INTERACTIVE NOVICES' H'CAP CHASE (18 fncs) 2m 6f 110y
4:45 (4:45) (Class 5) (0-100,97) 5-Y-O+ **£2,144** (£629; £314; £157)

Form RPR

453- **1** **Yukon Delta (IRE)**[9] 5301 7-9-13 77.................................... DeanPratt(7) 92+
(Robert Johnson) *in rr 5th: drvn 8th: hdwy 14th: sn chsng ldrs: 2nd 3 out: upsides last: sn led: drvn out* **6/4**[1]

451- **2** *1 1/4* **River Purple**[9] 5301 7-11-9 94 7ex.......................................(t) BrianHughes 108+
(John Mackie) *trckd ldrs: led narrowly 3 out: hdd sn after last: no ex* **5/2**[2]

452- **3** *25* **Trouble In Paris (IRE)**[9] 5301 7-10-0 67 oh2............(tp) WilsonRenwick 63
(Barry Murtagh) *led: mstke 11th: hdd 14th: outpcd and modest 3rd 3 out: sn wknd: t.o* **7/2**[3]

U26- **4** *6* **Sir Lynx (IRE)**[56] 4482 7-11-12 97......................................(t) AdamWedge 83
(Chris Bealby) *trckd ldrs 4th: led narrowly appr 4 out: hdd 3 out: lost pl appr next: sn bhd: t.o* **16/1**

605- **P** **Miss Sunflower**[9] 5301 12-9-9 67 oh4.....................(p) SamanthaDrake(5)
(Tina Jackson) *chsd ldrs: outpcd 8th: sn drvn and lost tch: t.o 13th: p.u bef next* **25/1**

560- **P** **Ballyreesode (IRE)**[49] 4607 9-9-12 76...........................(p) RyanHatch(7)
(Susan Corbett) *nt fluent in rr: bhd and reminders 5th: t.o 7th: p.u after 9th* **20/1**

302- **P** **Hero's Call**[133] 3015 9-10-2 73.. MarkGrant
(Julian Smith) *trckd ldrs 6th: outpcd 10th: lost pl 12th: sn bhd: t.o whn p.u bef 3 out* **14/1**

4- **P** **Manogue Supreme (IRE)**[39] 4795 8-11-10 95..................(p) NoelFehily
(Neil Mulholland) *trckd ldrs: nt fluent 1st: led 14th: hdd and lost pl appr next: sn bhd: t.o whn p.u bef 3 out* **14/1**

5m 46.7s (9.70) **Going Correction** +0.475s/f (Soft) **8** Ran SP% **118.6**
Speed ratings: **102,101,92,90, , ,**
CSF £6.35 CT £11.01 TOTE £3.00: £1.30, £1.60, £1.20; EX 8.70 Trifecta £18.40.
Owner Magpie Racing **Bred** J McCabe & Pat Furlong **Trained** Newburn, Tyne & Wear

FOCUS
They went a steady pace for this weak novices' handicap. The winner improved in line with his hurdles form.

5499 WATCH ON 3 DEVICES RACINGUK.COM/ANYWHERE STANDARD OPEN NATIONAL HUNT FLAT RACE (DIV I) 2m 110y
5:20 (5:21) (Class 6) 4-6-Y-O **£1,642** (£478; £239)

Form RPR

1 **One Track Mind (IRE)** 4-10-13 0.................................... GavinSheehan 118+
(Warren Greatrex) *trckd ldr: handy 2nd 6f out: rdn to ld over 1f out: forged clr last 150yds* **7/2**[2]

2- **2** *6* **Grande Antarctique (FR)**[25] 5063 4-10-13 0........................ SeanQuinlan 110
(Jennie Candlish) *mid-div: hdwy 6f out: sn handy 4th: 3rd over 2f out: styd on to take 2nd last 50yds* **7/2**[2]

31- **3** *2 1/2* **Minella Present (IRE)**[28] 5021 5-11-6 0................... ConorShoemark(5) 120
(Neil Mulholland) *led: drvn 3f out: hdd over 1f out: kpt on same pce* **3/1**[1]

/ **4** *6* **Cyrus Darius** 5-11-4 0... DannyCook 108
(William Amos) *mid-div: hdwy to trck ldrs 7f out: 3rd over 5f out: drvn over 3f out: one pce* **33/1**

3- **5** *1 1/4* **Along Came Theo (IRE)**[35] 4895 4-10-13 0.................. DougieCostello 101
(Andrew Crook) *in tch: outpcd over 6f out: hdwy over 4f out: kpt on fnl 2f* **10/1**

6 *19* **Lewis** 5-11-4 0.. NoelFehily 89
(David Thompson) *hld up towards rr: sme hdwy 6f out: lost pl over 4f out* **7/1**

13- **7** *4* **Star Lily (IRE)**[71] 4191 5-10-13 0....................... ColmMcCormack(5) 86
(Keith Reveley) *in rr: drvn 6f out: nvr on terms* **6/1**[3]

0- **8** *17* **Tomorrow's Legend**[35] 4895 4-10-13 0................................ BarryKeniry 65
(George Moore) *chsd ldr: drvn 6f out: lost pl over 4f out: sn bhd* **66/1**

04- **9** *2* **Sir Tommy**[32] 4944 5-11-4 0...(t) RyanMania 69
(Maurice Barnes) *mid-div: lost pl 5f out: sn bhd* **33/1**

0- **P** **Jacaranda Star**[31] 4958 6-11-1 0.................................. HarryChalloner(3)
(Geoffrey Harker) *mid-div: drvn 7f out: sn lost pl and bhd: t.o 5f out: sn p.u* **66/1**

P **Norse Of Corse** 4-10-13 0...................................... BrianHughes
(Malcolm Jefferson) *in rr: drvn after 5f: sn bhd: t.o whn p.u 9f out: fatally injured* **14/1**

3m 55.0s (4.80) **Going Correction** +0.60s/f (Soft)
WFA 4 from 5yo+ 5lb **11** Ran SP% **120.9**
Speed ratings: **112,109,108,105,104 95,93,85,84,**
CSF £16.43 TOTE £7.70: £1.90, £1.40, £1.90; EX 24.40 Trifecta £110.30.
Owner Andy Weller **Bred** Tony Mullins **Trained** Upper Lambourn, Berks

FOCUS
Not a bad bumper, run at a fair pace. The winner looks a decent recruit.

5500 WATCH ON 3 DEVICES RACINGUK.COM/ANYWHERE STANDARD OPEN NATIONAL HUNT FLAT RACE (DIV II) 2m 110y
5:50 (5:51) (Class 6) 4-6-Y-O **£1,642** (£478; £239)

Form RPR

1 **Ma Du Fou (FR)** 4-10-13 0.. GavinSheehan 107+
(Warren Greatrex) *hld up in mid-div: hdwy 8f out: drvn and outpcd 6f out: hdwy over 3f out: chal over 2f out: led wl over 1f out: forged clr last 150yds: v readily* **4/5**[1]

401- **2** *10* **Bobs Lord Tara**[47] 4631 4-11-6 0.................................... APMcCoy 101
(Alan Swinbank) *hld up in rr: hdwy to trck ldrs after 6f: led narrowly over 2f out: hdd wl over 1f out: styd on same pce* **7/2**[2]

3 *2* **Stylish Chap (IRE)** 4-10-13 0.................................... DougieCostello 92
(John Quinn) *in tch: chsd ldrs 6f out: upsides over 2f out: kpt on same pce over 1f out* **14/1**

4- **4** *8* **Imperial Prince (IRE)**[49] 4611 5-11-4 0............................ DannyCook 89
(Michael Smith) *trckd ldrs: 2nd 8f out: fdd over 2f out* **8/1**[3]

63- **5** *3 1/4* **Ifonlywecud (IRE)**[230] 1499 5-11-4 0.............................. BrianHughes 86
(Clive Mulhall) *led: hdd over 2f out: sn wknd* **16/1**

6 *5* **Weather The Storm** 6-10-6 0.................................. ThomasGarner(5) 74
(Oliver Sherwood) *trckd ldrs: outpcd over 4f out* **12/1**

06- **7** *13* **Silver Crossing**[25] 5063 5-10-13 0.............................. JohnDawson(5) 68
(John Wade) *chsd ldr: hung lft and wknd fnl 3f* **100/1**

0- **8** *47* **William Wild**[25] 5063 6-10-13 0................................ SamanthaDrake(5) 21
(Tina Jackson) *in rr: chsd ldrs after 3f: lost pl 6f out: sn bhd: t.o* **100/1**

9 *2 1/4* **Ginger B** 5-10-11 0...(t) RyanMania 12
(Maurice Barnes) *hld up in rr: hdwy 9f out: drvn 6f out: sn lost pl and bhd: t.o* **50/1**

0- **10** *1 1/4* **Colonial Style (IRE)**[32] 4944 4-10-13 0.............................. BarryKeniry 12
(George Moore) *sn chsng ldrs: lost pl over 4f out: sn bhd: t.o* **100/1**

0- **11** *27* **Bold Prince Rupert (IRE)**[64] 4329 4-10-6 0.................. MrMJohnson(7)
(Sara Ender) *t.k.h in rr: drvn after 5f: reminders 7f out: sn bhd: t.o over 5f out: eventually completed* **100/1**

12 *29* **Big Frank (USA)** 5-10-13 0.. JoeColliver(5)
(Micky Hammond) *in rr-div: drvn after 6f: sn bhd: t.o 6f out: eventually completed* **33/1**

13 *dist* **Red Legacy** 6-10-8 0.. KyleJames(3)
(Sean Regan) *stdd s: sn in tch: lost pl after 5f: sn bhd: hopelessly t.o 7f out: hacked home: completed in own time* **66/1**

4m 2.5s (12.30) **Going Correction** +0.60s/f (Soft) **13** Ran SP% **119.5**
Speed ratings: **95,90,89,85,84 81,75,53,52,51 39,25,11**
CSF £3.45 TOTE £2.00: £1.10, £1.30, £2.20; EX 5.30 Trifecta £32.60.
Owner Lee Bolingbroke & Graeme Howard **Bred** Scea Ecurie Jc Laisis **Trained** Upper Lambourn, Berks

FOCUS
This looked weaker than the first division, and the time was slower, but the winner won in the style of a nice type.
T/Plt: £37.60 to a £1 stake. Pool: £50,184.20 - 972.16 winning units. T/Qpdt: £9.40 to a £1 stake. Pool: £2613.84 - 204.45 winning units. WG

5501 - 5507a (Foreign Racing) - See Raceform Interactive

1661 PERTH (R-H)
Wednesday, April 23

OFFICIAL GOING: Good to soft (good in places; 6.4)
Track at innermost configuration.
Wind: Light, half against Weather: Cloudy

5508 ABERDEEN ASSET MANAGEMENT PLC MAIDEN HURDLE (10 hdls) 2m 4f 110y
2:10 (2:10) (Class 4) 4-Y-O+ **£3,249** (£954; £477; £238)

Form RPR

255- **1** **Silver Gent (IRE)**[25] 5071 6-11-0 0............................ SamTwiston-Davies 108
(Donald McCain) *mde all: rdn bef 2 out: styd on gamely fr last* **11/2**[2]

45P- **2** *hd* **Mo Rouge (IRE)**[166] 2342 6-11-0 0................................ DenisO'Regan 108
(Mrs Jackie Stephen) *prom: drvn and sltly outpcd bef 2 out: rallied bef last: styng on wl whn drifted lft u.p towards fin* **80/1**

014- **3** *1 1/2* **Trickaway (IRE)**[18] 5181 6-11-0 0.......................... RichardJohnson 108+
(Philip Hobbs) *nt fluent: t.k.h: pressed ldr: effrt and ev ch 2 out: rdn and kpt on same pce run-in* **15/8**[1]

232- **4** *1/2* **Another Mattie (IRE)**[16] 5205 7-11-0 114.................(t) LucyAlexander 106+
(N W Alexander) *hld up: nt fluent and pushed along 4 out: effrt and drvn next: styd on fr last: nvr able to chal* **15/8**[1]

33- **5** *3 1/4* **Cobajayisland (IRE)**[209] 1662 6-11-0 0............................ PeterBuchanan 103
(Lucinda Russell) *hld up in tch: hdwy 3 out: ev ch and rdn next: outpcd fr last* **12/1**[3]

0- **6** *26* **Wicked Spice (IRE)**[50] 4611 5-11-0 0............................ BrianHarding 80
(Nicky Richards) *hld up: rdn after 3 out: sn outpcd: n.d after* **18/1**

00- **7** *10* **Badged**[127] 3144 5-11-0 0.. RyanMania 71
(Lucy Normile) *hld up: rdn and struggling 3 out: sn btn* **150/1**

- **8** *17* **Benefit In Kind (IRE)**[136] 6-11-0 0.................................. TomO'Brien 55
(Michael Smith) *midfield: drvn and struggling bef 3 out: sn btn* **28/1**

9 *2 1/2* **Tambour Major (FR)**[11] 7-11-0 0............................ TomScudamore 53
(Simon Shirley-Beavan) *chsd ldrs: nt fluent 2nd: mstke and struggling 4 out: wknd bef next* **12/1**[3]

0P- **10** *2 1/4* **Dr Paddy (IRE)**[193] 1875 7-11-0 0.................................. AdrianLane 51
(Lucy Normile) *midfield on outside: drvn after 4 out: wknd fr next* **150/1**

P- **11** *25* **Firth Of Bavard**[46] 4665 7-11-0 0 BrianHughes 29
(Robert Goldie) *bhd: lost tch 1/2-way: nvr on terms* **250/1**
4m 54.1s (-7.90) **Going Correction** -0.175s/f (Good) **11** Ran SP% **112.0**
Speed ratings (Par 105): **108,107,107,107,105 96,92,85,84,83 74**
CSF £308.80 TOTE £7.60: £1.80, £6.20, £1.20; EX 401.80 Trifecta £1026.00.

Owner Deva Racing Milan Partnership **Bred** Thomas K Geraghty **Trained** Cholmondeley, Cheshire

FOCUS
A cool and overcast afternoon. With 9mm of rainfall in the preceding 24 hours, the going had eased from good and rode as advertised according to the jockeys. A modest maiden hurdle produced a tight finish. The winner and third are rated in line with their bumper form.

5509 CRABBIE'S ALCOHOLIC GINGER BEER MARES' H'CAP HURDLE (10 hdls) 2m 4f 110y

2:40 (2:40) (Class 4) (0-120,117) 4-Y-0+ **£3,898** (£1,144; £572; £286)

Form RPR
423- **1** **Golden Sparkle (IRE)**[12] 5255 8-11-5 **117** GrahamWatters(7) 121+
(Ian Duncan) *t.k.h: prom: smooth hdwy to ld 2 out: rdn whn nt fluent last: styd on wl* **10/3**[2]

240- **2** *1 3/4* **Brijomi Queen (IRE)**[6] 5370 7-11-7 **112** BrianHarding 112
(Nicky Richards) *led tl rdn and hdd 2 out: rallied: kpt on fr last: nt gng pce of wnr* **2/1**[1]

032- **3** *2* **In By Midnight**[10] 5291 6-11-4 **109** AlainCawley 107
(Tom George) *trckd ldrs: effrt and ev ch 2 out: sn rdn and edgd lft: kpt on same pce fr last* **5/1**[3]

5P0- **4** *4 1/2* **A Shade Of Bay**[21] 5124 6-11-0 **110** EdCookson(5) 106
(Kim Bailey) *hld up in tch: hit and drvn 4 out: outpcd next: styd on wl fr last: nt rch first three* **6/1**

013- **5** *nk* **Rev Up Ruby**[136] 2973 6-11-1 **111** JonathonBewley(5) 105
(George Bewley) *taken early to post: nt fluent: hld up: hdwy after 4 out: nt fluent next: rdn and outpcd fr 2 out* **16/1**

040- **6** *1 3/4* **Definitely Better (IRE)**[18] 5177 6-10-0 **91** oh3 SamTwiston-Davies 83
(Tom George) *t.k.h: w ldr tl rdn and outpcd bef 2 out: n.d after* **5/1**[3]
5m 0.9s (-1.10) **Going Correction** -0.175s/f (Good) **6** Ran SP% **109.9**
Speed ratings (Par 105): **95,94,93,91,91 91**
CSF £10.28 TOTE £2.90: £1.90, £1.40; EX 11.00 Trifecta £27.30.

Owner Miss Helen Cross **Bred** Mrs H E Duncan **Trained** Coylton, Ayrshire

FOCUS
A fair mares' hurdle, run at a decent pace, but overall the form is not particularly strong. The winner is rated similar to last year's win.

5510 PENTLAND LAND ROVER EBF "FUTURE CHAMPIONS" "NATIONAL HUNT" NOVICES' HURDLE (FOR THE PERTHSHIRE CUP) (12 hdls) 3m 110y

3:15 (3:15) (Class 2) 5-Y-0+ **£9,747** (£2,862; £1,431; £715)

Form RPR
561- **1** **Sausalito Sunrise (IRE)**[11] 5280 6-11-6 140 TomO'Brien 142+
(Philip Hobbs) *trckd ldrs: hdwy to ld bef 2 out: clr whn hit last: styd on strly* **15/8**[2]

233- **2** *11* **Oscar Rock (IRE)**[67] 4272 6-11-3 138 BrianHughes 129
(Malcolm Jefferson) *pressed ldr: nt fluent 4 out: drvn and outpcd after next: rallied to chse (clr) wnr whn nt fluent last: no imp* **11/10**[1]

101- **3** *2 3/4* **Tonvadosa**[23] 5103 6-10-13 130 SamTwiston-Davies 120
(Donald McCain) *hld up in tch: rdn and outpcd bef 2 out: plugged on fr last: no imp* **16/1**

2U1- **4** *2 1/2* **Flying Eagle (IRE)**[27] 5036 6-11-3 JamieMoore 123
(Peter Bowen) *hld up in tch: stdy hdwy 3 out: drvn bef next: outpcd whn hit last* **8/1**[3]

114- **5** *nk* **Kilbree Kid (IRE)**[186] 1968 7-11-6 125 (t) AlainCawley 124
(Tom George) *led at ordinary gallop: rdn and hdd bef 2 out: outpcd between last 2* **25/1**

115- **6** *nk* **Son Of Suzie**[30] 5008 6-11-3 ConorShoemark 122
(Fergal O'Brien) *hld up: hdwy on outside and prom 1/2-way: drvn and outpcd after 3 out: styd on fr last: no imp* **50/1**

101- **P** **Landecker (IRE)**[16] 5206 6-11-6 128 LucyAlexander
(N W Alexander) *w.r.s: t.o whn jumped off: p.u 2nd* **33/1**
5m 56.9s (-8.10) **Going Correction** -0.175s/f (Good) **7** Ran SP% **108.1**
Speed ratings: **105,101,100,99,99 99,**
CSF £3.90 TOTE £2.90: £2.30, £1.10; EX 4.70 Trifecta £23.10.

Owner Mrs Diana L Whateley **Bred** Thomas Corish **Trained** Withycombe, Somerset

FOCUS
A fascinating contest that looked a decent heat. Monet's Garden took this race in 2004, and quite a few above-average chasers have emerged from this. There was a decent pace. The winner is rated in line with his recent win.

5511 ABERDEEN ASSET MANAGEMENT PLC NOVICES' LIMITED H'CAP CHASE (12 fncs) 2m

3:50 (3:50) (Class 3) (0-125,121) 5-Y-0+ **£7,147** (£2,098; £1,049; £524)

Form RPR
302- **1** **Ut Majeur Aulmes (FR)**[25] 5073 6-11-8 **121** DenisO'Regan 128+
(Victor Dartnall) *confidently rdn in last pl: smooth hdwy 3 out: led on bit after last: sn hrd pressed: pushed out towards fin* **5/4**[1]

321- **2** *nk* **Roc D'Apsis (FR)**[129] 3113 5-11-6 **119** AlainCawley 124+
(Tom George) *nt fluent on occasions: in tch: hdwy bef 4 out: effrt and shkn up 2 out: chalng whn sddle slipped and nrly uns rdr last: rdr rode wout irons but sn bk upsides: kpt on wl: jst hld* **10/3**[2]

U04- **3** *4* **Gud Day (IRE)**[29] 5020 6-10-11 **115** (bt) ConorShoemark(5) 115
(Fergal O'Brien) *nt fluent on occasions: chsd ldrs: effrt and ev ch 3 out: sn rdn: kpt on same pce after last* **8/1**

30F- **4** *1 1/4* **Castlelawn (IRE)**[159] 2496 7-11-5 **118** PeterBuchanan 118
(Lucinda Russell) *nt fluent on occasions: t.k.h early: led: rdn bef 2 out: hdd after last* **11/2**[3]

301- **5** *nk* **Too Cool To Fool (IRE)**[12] 5254 11-10-6 **112** DaleIrving(7) 112
(Jim Goldie) *chsd ldr to 4 out: sn drvn and outpcd: no imp fr next* **6/1**
3m 58.7s (1.70) **Going Correction** +0.275s/f (Yiel) **5** Ran SP% **108.3**
Speed ratings: **106,105,103,103,103**
CSF £5.76 TOTE £2.50: £1.60, £1.80; EX 6.70 Trifecta £17.70.

Owner Mrs S De Wilde **Bred** Emmanuel Bodard **Trained** Brayford, Devon

FOCUS
A fair handicap and the form looks solid. The winner comfirmed the merit of his recent chase debut.

5512 MCBOOKIE.COM BEST ODDS GUARANTEED H'CAP HURDLE (8 hdls) 2m 110y

4:25 (4:25) (Class 3) (0-135,134) 4-Y-0+ **£5,848** (£1,717; £858; £429)

Form RPR
105- **1** **Strongpoint (IRE)**[18] 5172 10-11-9 **134** MrSCrawford(3) 140+
(S R B Crawford, Ire) *t.k.h early: trckd ldrs: hdwy to ld after 2 out: rdn and edgd rt run-in: kpt on strly towards fin* **13/8**[1]

513- **2** *1 3/4* **Minella Reception (IRE)**[54] 4538 8-10-5 **113** SamTwiston-Davies 117
(Nigel Twiston-Davies) *in tch: smooth hdwy to chal between last 2: sn rdn: kpt on run-in: hld towards fin* **3/1**[2]

633- **3** *9* **Pas Trop Tard (FR)**[70] 4224 7-11-1 **130** (t) DaraghBourke(7) 125
(Maurice Barnes) *mde most tl rdn and hdd after 2 out: sn outpcd by first two* **6/1**

512- **4** *3 1/2* **Just Cameron**[12] 5251 7-11-3 **125** BrianHarding 118
(Philip Kirby) *t.k.h: cl up: chal after 3rd: rdn whn hit 2 out: sn btn* **7/2**[3]

040- **5** *11* **Cool Baranca (GER)**[16] 5212 8-9-9 **108** oh1 EmmaSayer(5) 90
(Dianne Sayer) *bhd: outpcd after 3rd: sn struggling: n.d after* **11/1**
3m 51.1s (-6.90) **Going Correction** -0.175s/f (Good) **5** Ran SP% **107.9**
Speed ratings (Par 107): **109,108,103,102,97**
CSF £6.70 TOTE £2.30: £1.30, £1.60; EX 6.50 Trifecta £24.60.

Owner S McAlister **Bred** Seamus Murphy **Trained** Larne, Co Antrim

FOCUS
Plenty of pace despite the paucity of runners and the form looks useful. The winner is rated back to the level of the best of his Musselburgh wins.

5513 ABERDEEN ASSET MANAGEMENT PLC H'CAP CHASE (FOR THE SCOTTISH MEMORIES CHALLENGE CUP) (18 fncs) 3m

5:00 (5:00) (Class 3) (0-140,132) 5-Y-0+ **£7,797** (£2,289; £1,144; £572)

Form RPR
P22- **1** **Lamboro Lad (IRE)**[17] 5184 9-11-3 **123** (tp) JamieMoore 131
(Peter Bowen) *in tch: smooth hdwy to ld 3 out: rdn next: hrd pressed fr last: styd on gamely to assert nr fin* **5/1**[2]

21U- **2** *1/2* **Fiddlers Reel**[16] 5210 11-11-0 **120** RyanMania 128
(Jane Clark) *prom: effrt and pushed along 3 out: hdwy to chal last: kpt on u.p: hld towards fin* **4/1**[1]

1F0- **3** *3 1/2* **Sun Cloud (IRE)**[39] 4821 7-11-12 **132** BrianHughes 136
(Malcolm Jefferson) *hld up: stdy hdwy and in tch 13th: rdn and sltly outpcd 3 out: styd on wl fr last: nt rch first two* **10/1**

506- **4** *2 1/2* **Problema Tic (FR)**[12] 5256 8-11-10 **130** (bt) TomScudamore 132
(David Pipe) *mde most tl rdn and hdd 3 out: outpcd fr last* **5/1**[2]

P03- **5** *7* **Pigeon Island**[53] 4557 11-11-3 **123** (vt) SamTwiston-Davies 119
(Nigel Twiston-Davies) *hld up towards rr: effrt and drvn along bef 3 out: no imp fr next* **7/1**

250- **6** *1/2* **Carrigmorna King (IRE)**[39] 4805 8-11-12 **132** (t) RichardJohnson 128
(Philip Hobbs) *hld up: shkn up and effrt whn nt fluent 2 out: no further imp* **11/2**[3]

313- **7** *6* **Oil Burner**[62] 4368 9-10-0 **106** oh1 BrianHarding 96
(William Amos) *t.k.h in midfield: drvn and outpcd 4 out: n.d after* **18/1**

/1P- **8** *8* **Good Order**[102] 3647 9-11-7 **127** (t) AlainCawley 110
(Tom George) *hld up on outside: drvn after 4 out: wknd fr next* **10/1**

16P- **9** *hd* **Aachen**[46] 4685 10-11-2 **125** RobertDunne(3) 112
(Venetia Williams) *cl up: ev ch whn blnd and lost pl 4 out: struggling fr next* **18/1**

33P- **10** *19* **Rossini's Dancer**[26] 5053 9-11-7 **127** (v) LucyAlexander 97
(N W Alexander) *w ldr tl drvn and outpcd 14th: struggling fr next: t.o* **28/1**
6m 7.1s (3.10) **Going Correction** +0.275s/f (Yiel) **10** Ran SP% **113.4**
Speed ratings: **105,104,103,102,100 100,98,95,95,89**
CSF £25.35 CT £190.33 TOTE £5.30: £1.90, £1.90, £2.90; EX 22.90 Trifecta £160.50.
Owner Margaret and Raymond John **Bred** Dan And Mrs Margaret O'Neill **Trained** Little Newcastle, Pembrokes

■ Stewards' Enquiry : Jamie Moore two-day ban: used whip above permitted level (May 7-8)

FOCUS
A thrilling finish to this this typically competitive handicap chase fought out by the market leaders. The form looks very useful. The first two are rated to their best in a solid handicap.

5514 FONAB CASTLE HOTEL AMATEUR RIDERS' H'CAP HURDLE (12 hdls) 3m 110y

5:35 (5:36) (Class 4) (0-105,105) 4-Y-0+ **£3,119** (£967; £483; £242)

Form RPR
406- **1** **Shooting Times**[70] 4223 9-10-7 **89** (b) MrHAABannister(3) 101+
(Lucinda Russell) *hld up in midfield: hdwy and prom 3rd: led appr 2 out: sn clr* **20/1**

U3P- **2** *10* **Milano Magic (IRE)**[53] 4551 8-11-7 **105** (p) MrKitAlexander(5) 108
(N W Alexander) *in tch: drvn and outpcd 3 out: rallied bef last: styd on to take 2nd towards fin: no ch w wnr* **12/1**

500- **3** *3/4* **Church Bray**[79] 4068 6-10-2 **88** MrJBargary(7) 90
(Nigel Twiston-Davies) *mstkes: in tch: hdwy to chal whn hit 8th: ev ch and rdn bef 2 out: one pce whn hung rt run-in: lost 2nd towards fin* **9/2**[1]

536- **4** *nk* **Solway Sam**[31] 4981 11-10-13 **92** MrSCrawford 94
(Lisa Harrison) *hld up: smooth hdwy and in tch bef 2 out: sn rdn: one pce between last 2* **14/1**

54P- **5** *3 1/2* **Easement**[23] 5106 11-9-13 **85** (v) MissJWalton(7) 83
(George Bewley) *hld up: stdy hdwy after 8th: rdn bef 3 out: no imp bef next* **16/1**

544- **6** *1/2* **Amore Mio (GER)**[23] 5106 9-10-12 **98** (tp) MrNOrpwood(7) 95
(Lucinda Russell) *cl up: drvn and lost pl bef 8th: rallied bef 2 out: nvr rchd ldrs* **12/1**

225- **7** *8* **Solway Dornal**[7] 5358 9-9-11 **83** (p) MrRDDay(7) 73
(Lisa Harrison) *hld up: drvn and outpcd 4 out: n.d after* **25/1**

P44- **8** *2 1/2* **Winter Alchemy (IRE)**[31] 4982 9-10-12 **94** (p) MissJRRichards(3) 82
(Nicky Richards) *t.k.h: mde most tl rdn and hdd appr 2 out: sn btn* **8/1**

313- **9** *4 1/2* **Ryton Runner (IRE)**[39] 4814 6-11-11 **104** (p) MissCWalton 88
(Lucinda Russell) *hld up: drvn along after 4 out: nvr on terms* **5/1**[2]

/PP- **10** *31* **Pen Gwen (FR)**[9] 5323 11-9-7 **79** oh10 (tp) MrPDennis(7) 35
(Philip Kirby) *in tch: rdn bef 4 out: wknd bef next: t.o* **40/1**

630- **11** *42* **Knight Woodsman**[145] 2789 10-9-11 **81** (p) MrTHamilton(5)
(R Mike Smith) *midfield: drvn and outpcd 1/2-way: lost tch fr 4 out: t.o* **20/1**

135/ **P** **Nelson Du Ronceray (FR)**[437] 13-11-3 **103** MissAMcGregor(7)
(Jean McGregor) *bhd: struggling fnl circ: t.o whn p.u bef 2 out* **66/1**

PPP- **P** **Heart O Annandale (IRE)**[23] 5107 7-9-12 **84**......(p) MrGaryBeaumont(7)
(Alistair Whillans) *hld up in midfield on outside: hdwy and in tch 4th: outpcd whn mstke 4 out: sn btn: t.o whn p.u bef 2 out* **25/1**

022- **P** **St Gregory (IRE)**[136] 2974 6-9-7 **79** oh1.................................... MrJNuttall(7)
(Nicky Richards) *bhd: struggling fnl circ: t.o whn p.u bef 2 out* **11/2**[3]

454- **P** **Jac The Legend**[31] 4980 5-11-8 **104**................................ MrJHamilton(3)
(Steve Gollings) *midfield: drvn and outpcd bef 8th: sn struggling: t.o whn p.u bef 2 out* **12/1**

65P- **P** **Allforthelove**[47] 4649 6-10-2 **88** ow1..............................(p) MrRLindsay(7)
(N W Alexander) *cl up: chal 5th to next: lost pl after 8th: sn struggling: t.o whn p.u bef 2 out* **20/1**

5m 56.7s (-8.30) **Going Correction** -0.175s/f (Good) **16** Ran SP% **122.9**
Speed ratings (Par 105): **106,102,102,102,101 101,98,97,96,86 73,,,,**
CSF £227.46 CT £1289.32 TOTE £21.60: £4.00, £3.80, £2.20, £3.00; EX 402.40 Trifecta £1188.50.
Owner Mrs I C Lancaster **Bred** Mrs J M Lancaster **Trained** Arlary, Perth & Kinross

FOCUS
A lowly staying handicap. The winner is rated in line with his hurdles form.
T/Plt: £12.80 to a £1 stake. Pool: £62224.55 - 3544.35 winning tickets T/Qpdt: £2.80 to a £1 stake. Pool: £4115.71 - 1076.12 winning tickets RY

5361 SOUTHWELL (L-H)
Wednesday, April 23

OFFICIAL GOING: Good (7.8; watered)
Wind: light 1/2 against Weather: overcast, light rain last 2

5515 BET TOTEPLACEPOT WITH TOTEPOOL NOVICES' H'CAP CHASE (21 fncs) 3m 2f
4:40 (4:40) (Class 4) (0-110,109) 5-Y-0+ **£3,768** (£1,106; £553; £276)

Form RPR

146- **1** **High Ron**[45] 4704 9-11-12 **109**.. AndrewThornton 118+
(Caroline Bailey) *chsd ldrs: hmpd 15th: led 17th: hung rt bnd bef 3 out: rdn out* **6/1**

311- **2** *3* **Riddlestown (IRE)**[13] 5247 7-11-12 **109**..........................(b) HarrySkelton 114
(Caroline Fryer) *hld up in rr: trckd ldrs 13th: cl 2nd 4 out: upsides next: 2 l down last: styd on same pce* **8/1**

431- **3** *26* **Long Wave (IRE)**[42] 4759 7-11-8 **105**..................................(tp) NoelFehily 90
(Charlie Longsdon) *trckd ldrs: lft in ld 15th: hdd 17th: 3rd and drvn 5 out: modest 3rd whn blnd 2 out* **2/1**[1]

00P- **4** *½* **Rocky Island (IRE)**[17] 5191 6-11-3 **100**.............................. SeanQuinlan 85
(Jennie Candlish) *led: blnd: wnt lft and hdd 15th: drvn 4 out: wknd appr next* **12/1**

622- **5** *10* **Rocky Bender (IRE)**[21] 5129 9-11-8 **105**......................(b) LiamTreadwell 83
(Venetia Williams) *j.rt: w ldrs: drvn 13th: lost pl 4 out: sn bhd* **5/1**[3]

635- **P** **Knockraheen (IRE)**[28] 5032 6-11-7 **107**.....................(b) MauriceLinehan(3)
(Jonjo O'Neill) *hld up in rr: trckd ldrs 11th: hit 14th and reminders: hung rt and lost pl next: sn bhd: t.o whn p.u bef 4 out* **9/2**[2]

/F3- **P** **Swingbridge (IRE)**[31] 4984 6-11-4 **104**......................... JonathanEngland(3)
(Chris Grant) *j.rt: chsd ldrs: reminders 9th: lost pl 12th: bhd fr 15th: t.o 4 out: sn p.u* **8/1**

6m 52.3s (6.30) **Going Correction** +0.275s/f (Yiel) **7** Ran SP% **112.4**
Speed ratings: **101,100,92,91,88 ,**
CSF £47.99 TOTE £6.50: £1.80, £2.60; EX 50.10 Trifecta £98.30.
Owner Mrs Gillian Burke **Bred** Gillian & Micheal Burke **Trained** Holdenby, Northants

FOCUS
Fences and the bend into the home straight were 5yds inside but the Golf Club bend was outside of the line raced on the 16th April. 20mm of water had been applied to the course since that last meeting and the ground was officially described as good. An ordinary staying chase. The winner is rated to his C&D best.

5516 TOTEPOOL.COM HOME OF POOL BETTING H'CAP CHASE (16 fncs) 2m 4f 110y
5:10 (5:10) (Class 4) (0-120,120) 5-Y-0+ **£3,768** (£1,106; £553; £276)

Form RPR

450- **1** **Ice 'N' Easy (IRE)**[25] 5074 8-11-12 **120**...........................(t) TommyPhelan 131+
(Charlie Longsdon) *chsd ldrs 4th: 3rd: drvn and outpcd after 4 out: upsides next: sn led: j.lft 2 out: sn drvn clr* **8/1**

412- **2** *8* **Cruchain (IRE)**[29] 5020 11-11-9 **117**...............................(p) DougieCostello 119
(Dai Burchell) *in rr: hdwy 10th: 4th sn after 4 out: kpt on to take modest 2nd last* **10/1**

462- **3** *6* **Arctic Ben (IRE)**[32] 4948 10-11-6 **117**.............................. JakeGreenall(3) 114
(Henry Daly) *led: hdd sn after 3 out: fdd last* **9/2**[3]

532- **4** *¾* **Mister Grez (FR)**[18] 5176 8-11-12 **120**...............................(b) HarrySkelton 116
(Dan Skelton) *hld up in rr: hdwy to trck ldrs 10th: cl 2nd 12th: upsides 3 out: one pce* **3/1**[2]

045- **5** *12* **O'Callaghan Strand (AUS)**[18] 5176 8-10-11 **115**.. TommieMO'Brien(10) 100
(Jonjo O'Neill) *in rr: chsd ldrs 10th: sn drvn: outpcd 4 out: sn lost pl* **14/1**

235- **6** *9* **Father Shine (IRE)**[24] 4862 11-10-8 **107**.............................. BenPoste(5) 84
(Shaun Harris) *chsd ldrs: outpcd 9th: lost pl 12th: sn bhd* **20/1**

636- **P** **Sergeant Dick (IRE)**[53] 4560 9-11-11 **119**.............................(t) FelixDeGiles
(Barry Brennan) *w ldrs: drvn 10th: wknd qckly 12th: t.o next: p.u bef 2 out* **8/1**

522- **P** **Young Hurricane (IRE)**[7] 5356 8-11-3 **111**.....................(bt) PaulMoloney
(Dr Richard Newland) *chsd ldrs: rdn and wknd 4 out: sn bhd: t.o whn p.u bef 2 out* **11/4**[1]

5m 19.6s (2.60) **Going Correction** +0.275s/f (Yiel) **8** Ran SP% **112.6**
Speed ratings: **106,102,100,100,95 92,,**
CSF £77.32 CT £402.11 TOTE £8.80: £2.30, £2.50, £1.80; EX 68.40 Trifecta £1100.70.
Owner R Jenner & J Green **Bred** Edward Curtin **Trained** Over Norton, Oxon

FOCUS
Just a modest race but it was competitive enough and they went a sound pace. The winner belatedly built on the promise of his Kempton second.

5517 BET TOTEEXACTA ON ALL RACES H'CAP CHASE (13 fncs) 2m
5:40 (5:42) (Class 3) (0-140,137) 5-Y-0+ **£6,498** (£1,908; £954; £477)

Form RPR

540- **1** **Kings Grey (IRE)**[20] 5136 10-11-8 **133**.............................. JamesReveley 139
(Keith Reveley) *hld up in rr: hdwy 9th: 3rd sn after 4 out: handy 3rd next: 1 1/2 l down and swtchd rt last: styd on to ld post* **7/2**[2]

112- **2** *shd* **Sonofagun (FR)**[4] 5392 8-10-6 **122**.............................. RobertMcCarth(5) 130+
(Ian Williams) *hmpd 1st: blnd 7th: hdwy to chse ldrs next: led 2 out: nt fluent and wnt lft landing last: hdd fnl stride* **6/4**[1]

10U- **3** *7* **Hazy Tom (IRE)**[19] 5158 8-11-12 **137**.. NoelFehily 139
(Charlie Longsdon) *hld up: hdwy on outside to ld 8th: hdd and blnd 2 out: wknd run-in* **5/1**

P50- **4** *42* **Fiftyonefiftyone (IRE)**[10] 5290 10-9-9 **111** oh1............(tp) JoeCornwall(5) 73
(John Cornwall) *led to 3rd: lost pl bef 4 out: t.o 3 out* **20/1**

30/- **P** **Uncle Tom Cobley (IRE)**[262] 1208 10-11-5 **130**...........(t) LiamTreadwell
(Michael Scudamore) *t.k.h: hdwy to ld after 3rd: clr 6th: wknd and hdd 8th: bhd whn p.u bef 4 out* **12/1**

642- **P** **Jack The Gent (IRE)**[54] 4532 10-10-4 **115**.......................... BarryKeniry
(George Moore) *w ldr: led briefly 3rd: lost pl 8th: sn bhd: t.o whn blnd 4 out: p.u bef next* **4/1**[3]

4m 3.8s (1.80) **Going Correction** +0.275s/f (Yiel) **6** Ran SP% **111.3**
Speed ratings: **106,105,102,81,**
CSF £9.49 TOTE £5.10: £2.00, £1.60; EX 11.10 Trifecta £38.80.
Owner John Wade **Bred** Fred Mackey **Trained** Lingdale, Redcar & Cleveland

FOCUS
Some decent performers clashed for the feature event on the card which was a fair race where they went a good pace. The winner is rated to his best.

5518 FOLLOW TOTEPOOL ON FACEBOOK AND TWITTER MARES' H'CAP HURDLE (9 hdls) 2m
6:15 (6:16) (Class 4) (0-120,117) 4-Y-0+ **£3,119** (£915; £457; £228)

Form RPR

552- **1** **Queen Olivia**[7] 5365 6-10-7 **98**...................................... AndrewThornton 107+
(Caroline Bailey) *trckd ldng pair: cl 2nd appr 2 out: sn led and wnt clr: nt fluent last: eased clsng stages* **11/10**[1]

332- **2** *14* **Dewala**[31] 4983 5-11-1 **106**... RyanMahon 95
(Michael Appleby) *led: hit 5th: hdd appr 2 out: 3rd whn hit 2 out: regained modest 2nd last* **2/1**[2]

321- **3** *2 ¼* **Nellie Forbush**[180] 2066 4-10-11 **107**................................ PaulMoloney 88
(Sophie Leech) *in tch: pushed along and wl outpcd 6th: sn poor 4th: styd on strly run-in: fin wl to take 3rd nr fin* **8/1**[3]

2P4- **4** *1* **Fairyinthewind (IRE)**[21] 2763 5-11-12 **117**..................... BrendanPowell 103
(Brendan Powell) *trckd ldr: led briefly appr 2 out: wknd last* **10/1**

056- **5** *43* **Banreenahreenkah (IRE)**[13] 5244 4-10-4 **100**................... SeanQuinlan 41
(Jennie Candlish) *t.k.h in last: nt jump wl 5th onwards: bhd fr 6th: t.o 2 out* **10/1**

3m 58.9s (1.90) **Going Correction** +0.275s/f (Yiel)
WFA 4 from 5yo+ 5lb **5** Ran SP% **110.2**
Speed ratings (Par 105): **106,99,97,97,75**
CSF £3.85 TOTE £2.40: £1.10, £1.30; EX 4.00 Trifecta £11.00.
Owner R S Hunnisett **Bred** R Chugg **Trained** Holdenby, Northants

FOCUS
A modest mares' handicap hurdle. Arguably another step up from the winner.

5519 BEST ODDS GUARANTEED AT TOTEPOOL.COM MAIDEN HURDLE (9 hdls) 2m
6:45 (6:45) (Class 5) 4-Y-0+ **£1,949** (£572; £286; £143)

Form RPR

F2F- **1** **Sir Valentino (FR)**[54] 4536 5-10-9 122..................... AodhaganConlon(5) 115+
(Tom George) *led tl after 2nd: led after 3rd: shkn up and wnt clr appr last: eased clsng stages* **4/5**[1]

42- **2** *5* **Star Date (IRE)**[22] 5117 5-10-9 0................................... ThomasGarner(5) 105+
(Oliver Sherwood) *trckd ldrs: cl 2nd 3 out: upsides appr next: styd on same pce between last 2* **7/2**[2]

6- **3** *1 ¼* **Don Padeja**[17] 5190 4-10-6 0.................................... MauriceLinehan(3) 98
(Jonjo O'Neill) *t.k.h: trckd ldrs: 3rd and outpcd 2 out: kpt on run-in* **8/1**[3]

245- **4** *¾* **Trapper Peak (IRE)**[51] 4598 5-11-0 0............................ AndrewThornton 102
(Caroline Bailey) *trckd ldrs: outpcd and 6th 2 out: modest 4th between last 2: styd on run-in* **16/1**

300- **5** *10* **Table Bluff (IRE)**[25] 5072 5-10-11 90.......................... NicodeBoinville(3) 92
(John Spearing) *chsd ldrs 4th: drvn 3 out: wknd between last 2* **20/1**

0- **6** *14* **Paddy's Saltantes (IRE)**[25] 5064 4-10-4 0....................... KillianMoore(5) 75
(Alex Hales) *chsd ldrs: drvn 3 out: wknd between last 2: eased run-in* **50/1**

55- **7** *4 ½* **Bouggietopieces**[33] 4944 4-10-6 0.................................. KielanWoods(3) 69
(Pam Sly) *in rr-div: chsd ldrs 4th: lost pl and j.rt 3 out* **33/1**

000- **8** *16* **Auto Mac**[116] 3350 6-10-9 85... AdamNicol(5) 58
(Mike Sowersby) *in rr: sme hdwy 4th: lost pl after next: j.lft 3 out: sn bhd* **100/1**

435- **9** *17* **Donna's Pride**[17] 5195 5-10-7 0.. JamesReveley 34
(Keith Reveley) *nt jump wl in last: blnd 3rd: bhd fr 5th: t.o 3 out* **8/1**[3]

P- **P** **Don't Tell**[49] 4614 4-10-2 0.. BarryKeniry
(George Moore) *w ldrs: t.k.h: led after 2nd: hdd after next: lost pl after 5th: t.o whn blnd 3 out: sn p.u* **100/1**

4m 1.3s (4.30) **Going Correction** +0.275s/f (Yiel)
WFA 4 from 5yo+ 5lb **10** Ran SP% **117.5**
Speed ratings (Par 103): **100,97,96,96,91 84,82,74,65,**
CSF £3.73 TOTE £1.80: £1.10, £1.70, £1.40; EX 4.90 Trifecta £14.60.
Owner Doone Hulse Susie Saunders & Lady Cobham **Bred** Mlle Camille Serveau & Roger Simon **Trained** Slad, Gloucs

FOCUS
Uncompetitive fare where it was 16/1 bar four. It was steadily run. The easy winner was value for further and close to her hurdles mark.

5520 TOTETRIFECTA PICK THE 1, 2, 3 H'CAP HURDLE (13 hdls) 3m 110y
7:15 (7:15) (Class 4) (0-115,115) 4-Y-0+ **£3,119** (£915; £457; £228)

Form RPR

/41- **1** **George Fernbeck**[7] 5359 6-10-11 **100** 7ex............................ DannyCook 104+
(Brian Ellison) *w ldrs: led after 3rd: hdd 7th: led 9th: hung lft and jnd last: rdn rt out* **7/2**[1]

/50- **2** *¾* **Phoenix Flight (IRE)**[28] 5030 9-11-7 **110**.....................(p) LiamTreadwell 114+
(James Evans) *hld up in rr: hdwy 3 out: cl 4th 2 out: 2nd appr last: upsides whn hit last: no ex clsng stages* **10/1**

221- **3** *6* **At Reception (IRE)**[37] 4863 7-11-5 **111**...................... MauriceLinehan(3) 109
(Jonjo O'Neill) *trckd ldrs: t.k.h: chsd wnr appr 2 out: kpt on same pce between last 2* **7/1**

351- **4** *½* **Darkestbeforedawn (IRE)**[11] 5285 7-11-12 **115**........... BrendanPowell 112
(Caroline Keevil) *chsd ldrs: kpt on same pce between last 2* **8/1**

00F- **5** *3 ¼* **Bayley's Dream**[33] 4937 5-11-7 **110**.................................(t) PaulMoloney 105
(Paul Webber) *in rr: hdwy 3 out: 6th and keeping on whn hmpd and lost pl 2 out: kpt on run-in* **14/1**

P03/ **6** *2 ½* **Carlicue (IRE)**[46] 9-11-7 **110**..(t) HarrySkelton 102
(Dan Skelton) *trckd ldrs: t.k.h: one pce fr 2 out* **16/1**

The Form Book Jumps, Raceform Ltd, Compton, RG20 6NL.

022- **7** *12* **High Kite (IRE)**[26] 5059 8-11-6 **109**...(p) GavinSheehan 91
(Warren Greatrex) *w ldrs: led 2nd tl after next: led 7th to 9th: wknd bef 2 out* **5/1**[2]

100- **8** *7* **Top Billing**[33] 4933 5-10-6 **98**...(p) HarryChalloner(3) 73
(Nicky Richards) *in rr: drvn 7th: sme hdwy after next: rdn and lost pl bef 3 out* **14/1**

P41- **9** *17* **Speckled Door**[37] 4865 6-11-7 **110**... AndrewThornton 70
(Caroline Bailey) *mid-div: hdwy 6th: drvn 3 out: lost pl appr next* **6/1**[3]

5F0- **10** *49* **Mauricetheathlete (IRE)**[34] 4913 11-11-0 **110**... NickSlatter(7) 25
(Martin Keighley) *chsd ldrs: reminders 9th: lost pl after 10th: t.o 2 out: eventually completed* **33/1**

FPP- **11** *6* **Dom Lukka (FR)**[44] 4719 6-11-4 **107**... NoelFehily 17
(Charlie Longsdon) *led to 2nd: lost pl and blnd bdly 6th: sn bhd: t.o 3 out: eventually completed* **16/1**

P1P- **F** **Crystal Swing**[25] 5076 7-11-7 **110**... AdamWedge 109
(Richard Phillips) *in rr: hdwy 6th: chsng ldrs 8th: cl 5th but looking hld whn fell 2 out* **33/1**

500- **P** **Northern Oscar (IRE)**[11] 5272 6-11-0 **103**...(b[1]) DougieCostello
(Mark Walford) *in rr: hdwy 6th: lost pl 10th: sn bhd: t.o whn p.u bef 2 out* **20/1**

6m 18.4s (3.40) **Going Correction** +0.275s/f (Yiel) **13** Ran SP% **121.6**
Speed ratings (Par 105): **105,104,102,102,101 100,97,94,89,73 71, ,**
CSF £38.79 CT £236.72 TOTE £4.50: £2.40, £4.70, £2.50; EX 48.00 Trifecta £503.80.
Owner Racing Management & Training Ltd **Bred** Gestut Ammerland **Trained** Norton, N Yorks
■ Stewards' Enquiry : Danny Cook two-day ban: used whip above permitted level (May 7-8)

FOCUS
Despite a few last-time-out winners opposing this looks to be only modest form. The winner is rated in line with his recent win but may be capable of a bit better.

5521 COLLECT TOTEPOOL WINNINGS AT BETFRED SHOPS CONDITIONAL JOCKEYS' H'CAP HURDLE (11 hdls) 2m 4f 110y
7:45 (7:45) (Class 4) (0-110,110) 4-Y-0+ **£3,119** (£915; £457; £228)

Form RPR

500- **1** **Surf And Turf (IRE)**[162] 2447 8-11-11 **109**... TrevorWhelan 116+
(Kevin Frost) *trckd ldrs: effrt and 4th 2 out: led appr last: rdn and hung bdly rt on run-in: drvn rt out* **25/1**

412- **2** *1 ¼* **Crookstown (IRE)**[36] 4888 7-11-12 **110**... KielanWoods 115
(Ben Case) *chsd ldr: hit 8th: led sn after 3 out: hdd appr last: kpt on same pce last 50yds* **5/1**[3]

460- **3** *4 ½* **Colebrooke**[33] 4933 6-11-12 **110**... JoshuaMoore 111
(Dan Skelton) *chsd ldrs: hit 7th: cl 5th 2 out: styd on run-in: tk 3rd nr fin* **7/1**

/46- **4** *nk* **Theredballoon**[25] 5072 8-10-11 **95**... AdamWedge 95
(David Elsworth) *in rr-div: hdwy to chse ldrs 4th: cl 3rd 2 out: upsides between last 2: kpt on one pce* **9/2**[2]

312- **5** *10* **Bob's Legend (IRE)**[10] 5294 8-11-7 **105**... NicodeBoinville 100
(Michael Appleby) *chsd ldrs: drvn and chsd ldr after 3 out: wknd appr last* **7/4**[1]

214- **6** *14* **Bold Tara**[91] 3842 7-9-12 **90**...(tp) OllieGarner(8) 69
(Martin Keighley) *led: drvn 6th: hdd sn after 3 out: lost pl appr next* **14/1**

P/P- **7** *1 ¼* **Uno Valoroso (FR)**[347] 221 6-10-0 **84**... TonyKelly 61
(Mark Walford) *in rr: sme hdwy and modest 7th whn mstke 3 out: wknd bef next* **16/1**

230- **8** *53* **Bold Raider (IRE)**[97] 3740 7-11-2 **110**... PatrickCowley(10) 39
(Jonjo O'Neill) *in rr: bhd fr 7th: t.o 2 out: eventually completed* **6/1**

400- **9** *1* **Not Another Monday (IRE)**[97] 3735 6-10-0 **84** oh6... JoeColliver 12
(George Moore) *in rr: sme hdwy 6th: lost pl next: bhd 3 out: t.o next: eventually completed* **33/1**

U20- **10** *2 ½* **Troufion (FR)**[24] 5088 5-11-12 **110**... JackQuinlan 36
(Caroline Fryer) *t.k.h in mid-div: trckd ldrs 4th: rdn 8th: sn lost pl: t.o 2 out: eventually completed* **20/1**

353/ **P** **The Society Man (IRE)**[418] 4495 7-10-8 **92**... JoeCornwall
(Michael Chapman) *t.k.h: hmpd and j.rt 1st: chsd ldrs: lost pl 4th: bhd and eased 3 out: sn t.o and p.u* **33/1**

060- **P** **Frosty Dawn**[19] 5161 6-10-0 **84** oh15... AdamNicol
(Mike Sowersby) *in rr: sme hdwy 6th: lost pl and bhd next: t.o 3 out: sn p.u* **100/1**

5m 16.2s (3.20) **Going Correction** +0.275s/f (Yiel) **12** Ran SP% **126.0**
Speed ratings (Par 105): **104,103,101,101,97 92,92,71,71,70 ,**
CSF £150.56 CT £1008.23 TOTE £9.10: £5.20, £1.50, £3.00; EX 165.60 Trifecta £1253.40.
Owner Kevin Frost **Bred** J P Murphy & M Barry Murphy **Trained** Stratford-upon-Avon

FOCUS
Not a bad race of its type. There were a few in contention as they turned for the home straight and the winner was a bit of a turn-up. The winner is rated in line with his old hurdles form.
T/Plt: £41.10 to a £1 stake. Pool: £59322.17 - 1052.95 winning tickets T/Qpdt: £2.70 to a £1 stake. Pool: £7275.88 - 1946.69 winning tickets WG

[5234]TAUNTON (R-H)
Wednesday, April 23

OFFICIAL GOING: Good (good to soft in places; 6.1)
Wind: mild across Weather: overcast

5522 BATHWICK TYRES BATH H'CAP HURDLE (9 hdls) 2m 1f
4:55 (4:55) (Class 5) (0-100,97) 4-Y-0+ **£2,566** (£748; £374)

Form RPR

322- **1** **Tiradia (FR)**[8] 5341 7-11-11 **94**... APMcCoy 110+
(J R Jenkins) *mid-div: hdwy after 6th: led 2 out: sn in command: pushed out* **5/2**[1]

410- **2** *7* **Karl Marx (IRE)**[21] 5125 4-11-2 **97**...(b) GaryDerwin(7) 98
(Mark Gillard) *sn chsng clr ldr: lft prom 4th: led after 5th: sn rdn: hdd 2 out: kpt on same pce* **50/1**

056- **3** *3 ½* **Maxdelas (FR)**[45] 4703 8-10-4 **76**...(t) PeterCarberry(3) 78
(Roy Brotherton) *mid-div: hdwy after 3 out to trck ldrs bef next: sn rdn: nt gng pce to chal but kpt on to go 3rd run-in* **18/1**

0P0- **4** *nk* **Heurtevent (FR)**[25] 5072 5-11-6 **89**... LeeEdwards 91
(Tony Carroll) *hld up towards rr: stdy hdwy after 3 out: sn rdn: styd on wl fr last: wnt 4th towards fin* **5/1**[2]

440- **5** *1* **Chankillo**[23] 5116 5-11-3 **86**... WillKennedy 87
(Sarah-Jayne Davies) *trckd clr ldr: lft in ld 4th: hdd bef 6th: sn rdn: kpt on same pce fr after 3 out* **5/1**[2]

060- **6** *1* **Midnight Thomas**[184] 2004 5-10-5 **74**...(t) IanPopham 75
(Martin Keighley) *hld up towards rr: hdwy after 3 out: sn rdn: styd on same pce fr next* **10/1**[3]

00P- **7** *4* **Kruseman**[317] 686 7-11-5 **88**... ConorO'Farrell 85
(Richard Woollacott) *trckd clr ldr: lft prom 4th: rdn and ev ch after 3 out tl bef next: one pce after* **40/1**

6F0- **8** *4* **Gizzit (IRE)**[56] 4504 8-11-7 **90**...(p) NickScholfield 83
(Karen George) *mid-div: rdn after 3 out: nvr any imp* **14/1**

440- **9** *nk* **Cruise In Style (IRE)**[114] 3426 8-11-9 **92**...(bt) AidanColeman 84
(Kevin Bishop) *in tch: effrt after 3 out: one pce fr next* **10/1**[3]

063/ **10** *2 ¾* **Hope Point**[693] 487 6-11-12 **95**... DaveCrosse 85
(Mark Usher) *t.k.h in rr: midfield after 3 out: sn rdn: wknd bef next* **25/1**

0P4- **11** *1 ¾* **Sun Quest**[30] 5012 10-10-13 **89**...(t) MrLKilgarriff(7) 79
(Steven Dixon) *chsd ldrs tl 3 out: sn in rr* **12/1**

/15- **12** *1* **Bach On Tow (IRE)**[325] 598 7-10-13 **87**... MissLucyGardner(5) 74
(Sue Gardner) *alway towards rr* **10/1**[3]

000- **13** *51* **Sarahs Doll**[31] 4988 6-10-1 **70**... DonalDevereux 11
(Dai Burchell) *in tch tl 6th: sn wknd: t.o* **33/1**

030- **U** **Crackerjack**[34] 4911 7-11-1 **89**... JamesBanks(5)
(Emma Baker) *led: sn clr: mstke: stmbld bdly and uns rdr 4th* **12/1**

2F0- **P** **Sea Island Pearl**[150] 2695 5-11-6 **92**... MichealNolan(3)
(Philip Hobbs) *dwlt: bhd: lost tch qckly 5th: p.u next* **16/1**

(-8.00) **Going Correction** -0.30s/f (Good)
WFA 4 from 5yo+ 5lb **15** Ran SP% **120.7**
Speed ratings (Par 103): **106,102,101,100,100 99,98,96,96,94 93,93,69, ,**
CSF £149.06 CT £1918.51 TOTE £2.50: £1.30, £11.10, £5.30; EX 73.40 Trifecta £549.40.
Owner B Dowling **Bred** Marc Trinquet And Olivier Trinquet **Trained** Royston, Herts

FOCUS
There was a strong gallop on in this weak handicap. The easy winner confirmed the merit of his much improved recent Kempton run.

5523 BATHWICK TYRES YEOVIL NOVICES' H'CAP HURDLE (12 hdls) 3m 110y
5:25 (5:25) (Class 5) (0-100,95) 4-Y-0+ **£2,566** (£748; £374)

Form RPR

635- **1** **Clues And Arrows (IRE)**[25] 5069 6-10-11 **80**... APMcCoy 92+
(Jonjo O'Neill) *travelled wl: trckd ldrs: disp 3 out: outrt ldr sn after 2 out: kpt on run-in: pressed fnl 75yds: drvn out* **7/2**[2]

323- **2** *nk* **Frontier Vic**[30] 5007 7-11-5 **95**... RyanHatch(7) 102
(Nigel Twiston-Davies) *hld up towards rr: nudged along and hdwy after 8th: chsd ldrs after 3 out: sn rdn: styd on wl run-in: hld nring fin* **5/1**[3]

001- **3** *7* **On The Move**[30] 5007 6-11-2 **92**...(t) MrMLegg(7) 94
(Anthony Honeyball) *trckd ldrs: disp ld 3 out tl rdn bef next: styd on same pce* **8/1**

502- **4** *9* **Carn Rock**[10] 5288 6-11-7 **93**... PeterCarberry(3) 87
(Michael Gates) *mid-div: rdn appr 2 out: styd on same pce to go 4th at the last: no ch w ldrs* **9/1**

432- **5** *4 ½* **Florida Quays (IRE)**[7] 5366 6-11-7 **90**... AidanColeman 79
(David Dennis) *trckd ldrs: disp ld 3 out: sn rdn: hdd sn after next: sn wknd: lost 4th at the last* **9/4**[1]

33P- **6** *2* **Midnight Mustang**[32] 4946 7-10-4 **80**... MrJMartin(7) 67
(Andrew J Martin) *mid-div: awkward 2nd: rdn after 3 out: wknd next* **14/1**

F0P- **7** *2 ½* **Puerto Azul (IRE)**[138] 2920 10-11-2 **85**...(t) IanPopham 70
(Bernard Scriven) *hld up towards rr: rdn into midfield after 3 out: wknd next* **50/1**

0P0- **8** *15* **Top Chief**[20] 5143 6-11-6 **89**... NickScholfield 60
(Mark Rimell) *a towards rr* **50/1**

600- **9** *¾* **Keep The Cash (IRE)**[13] 5234 6-11-1 **91**...(b) MrMHeard(7) 61
(David Pipe) *led: rdn after 8th: hdd after next: sn wknd* **9/1**

P00- **10** *58* **Strategic Exit**[13] 5235 6-10-6 **75**... ConorO'Farrell
(James Frost) *w ldr: awkward 4th: rdn after 9th: hdd sn after 3 out: qckly wknd: t.o* **33/1**

5m 57.2s (-6.80) **Going Correction** -0.30s/f (Good) **10** Ran SP% **114.3**
Speed ratings (Par 103): **98,97,95,92,91 90,89,85,84,66**
CSF £21.04 CT £127.40 TOTE £3.20: £1.80, £2.70, £1.02; EX 18.20 Trifecta £142.00.
Owner Peter Piller, Eric Brooke & John Wade **Bred** Liam Cosgrave **Trained** Cheltenham, Gloucs

FOCUS
A moderate, but competitive novice handicap which saw the first two come clear off the uneven gallop. A massive step up on his previous hurdles form from the winner.

5524 BATHWICK TYRES TAUNTON NOVICES' HURDLE (10 hdls) 2m 3f 110y
5:55 (5:55) (Class 4) 4-Y-0+ **£3,422** (£997; £499)

Form RPR

411- **1** **Kings Bandit (IRE)**[10] 5295 6-11-11 0... APMcCoy 135+
(Donald McCain) *mde all: rdn and wandered arnd appr 2 out: rdn bef last: hung lft run-in: rdn out* **1/2**[1]

30U- **2** *2 ¼* **King Edmund**[19] 5156 11-10-13 0...(t) TomCannon 118
(Chris Gordon) *pressed wnr tl rdn after 3 out: hld bef last but kpt on to fin wl clr of remainder* **5/2**[2]

606- **3** *37* **The Snappy Poet**[22] 5117 5-10-10 0... MattGriffiths(3) 86
(Jeremy Scott) *sn nudged along towards rr of midfield: wnt modest 3rd 2 out: nvr any danger: t.o* **16/1**

00F- **4** *2* **Nowweareseven**[18] 5174 7-10-6 0... DaveCrosse 76
(Nigel Twiston-Davies) *hld up towards rr: hdwy 3 out but no ch w ldrs: wnt modest 4th: t.o* **25/1**

4/ **5** *4 ½* **Geton Xmoor (IRE)**[702] 386 7-10-13 0... WillKennedy 79
(Miss Jessica Westwood) *trckd ldrs rdn after 7th: sn no ch w ldrs: wknd next: t.o* **14/1**[3]

0P0- **6** *1 ¾* **Driving Well (IRE)**[60] 4411 6-10-13 0... ConorO'Farrell 77
(Arthur Whiting) *chsd ldrs: rdn after 6th: wknd after 3 out: t.o* **50/1**

55- **7** *5* **Capitol Gain (IRE)**[13] 5227 5-10-13 0... AndrewTinkler 75
(George Baker) *in tch: rdn into 3rd after 3 out but no ch w ldng pair: wkng whn mstke 2 out: t.o* **14/1**[3]

600- **8** *50* **Foolsandorses (IRE)**[10] 5308 6-10-8 0... JamesBanks(5) 28
(W De Best-Turner) *a bhd: t.o* **125/1**

0P- **9** *2 ½* **Minister Of Mayhem**[11] 2466 4-10-8 0 ow1...(p) NickScholfield 21
(Nick Mitchell) *in tch tl wknd qckly after 7th: t.o* **50/1**

556- **10** *38* **Harriet's Ark**[13] 5229 7-10-6 0... MarkGrant
(Julian Smith) *mid-div tl 5th: sn in rr: t.o after next: continued* **100/1**

0- **P** **Gartan Boy**[56] 4498 6-10-13 0... CharliePoste
(Anabel K Murphy) *nvr fluent in rr: t.o 5th: p.u after next* **150/1**

00- **P** **Inside Out**[17] 5195 4-9-11 0... RachaelGreen(3)
(Anthony Honeyball) *a towards rr: t.o whn p.u bef 7th* **33/1**

4m 36.5s (-9.50) **Going Correction** -0.30s/f (Good)
WFA 4 from 5yo+ 5lb **12** Ran SP% **127.6**
Speed ratings (Par 105): **107,106,91,90,88 88,86,66,65,49 ,**
CSF £2.21 TOTE £1.30: £1.10, £1.20, £4.00; EX 3.20 Trifecta £19.50.
Owner Mrs Diana L Whateley **Bred** Rathbarry Stud **Trained** Cholmondeley, Cheshire

FOCUS
The two vastly superior market leaders predictably dominated this novice event. The winner is on the upgrade.

5525 BATHWICK TYRES NOVICES' CHASE (17 fncs) 2m 7f 110y
6:30 (6:30) (Class 4) 5-Y-0+ **£4,061** (£1,192; £596; £298)

Form RPR
102- 1 **Cowards Close (IRE)**[53] 4541 7-10-12 123..................(t) NickScholfield 136+
(Paul Nicholls) *led tl 3rd: styd disputing: clr ldr after 13th: drew wl clr fr 3 out: v easily* **6/4**[1]
1/1- 2 *18* **Gunna Be A Devil (IRE)**[113] 3435 10-10-9 120.............. MattGriffiths(3) 120
(Jeremy Scott) *trckd ldng pair: disp 4th tl 13th: pressed wnr tl rdn after 4 out: wknd after next* **4/1**[3]
100- 3 *36* **Fix It Right (IRE)**[33] 4933 6-10-12 0.................................. AidanColeman 88
(Emma Lavelle) *trckd ldng trio: nt that fluent early: wnt 3rd after 10th: reminder bef next: rdn after 13th: wknd after 4 out: t.o* **8/1**
230- 4 *38* **Beeves (IRE)**[43] 4741 7-11-5 131...(b) APMcCoy 60
(Donald McCain) *nt a fluent: w ldr: reminder after 2nd: led next: jnd 4th: reminder: bdly hmpd and nrly uns rdr 7th: drvn along to stay upsides after 10th: blnd bdly and rdr lost irons 12th: no ch after: sn t.o* **13/8**[2]
5m 58.2s (-17.80) **Going Correction** -0.55s/f (Firm) **4** Ran SP% **109.2**
Speed ratings: **107,101,89,76**
CSF £7.45 TOTE £2.70; EX 7.40 Trifecta £20.70.
Owner Barry Fulton & Paul K Barber **Bred** Mrs Nichola Kyle **Trained** Ditcheat, Somerset

FOCUS
An eventful staying novice chase. The winner should go on to rate higher.

5526 BATHWICK TYRES BRIDGWATER H'CAP HURDLE (10 hdls) 2m 3f 110y
7:00 (7:00) (Class 4) (0-120,120) 4-Y-0+ **£3,422** (£997; £499)

Form RPR
245- 1 **Daveron (IRE)**[28] 5034 6-10-6 **110**................................ ChrisMeehan(10) 116+
(Jeremy Scott) *trckd ldrs: led 7th: hung lft and rdn after 2 out: wnt rt and nt fluent last: hung lft run-in: r.o* **13/8**[1]
132- 2 *8* **Very Noble (FR)**[10] 5305 5-11-9 **117**..............................(t) NickScholfield 116
(Paul Nicholls) *trckd ldng trio: jnd ldr gng wl 3 out: rdn bef next: fnd little: hld whn nt fluent last* **9/4**[2]
006- 3 *2 1/4* **Della Sun (FR)**[13] 5239 8-11-4 **119**.. JoshWall(7) 116
(Arthur Whitehead) *trckd ldrs: pushed along in last after 5th: styd in tch: wnt 4th after 7th: wnt 3rd after 3 out: styd on same pce fr next* **7/1**
100- 4 *40* **Exemplary**[28] 5034 7-10-10 **104**..(p) APMcCoy 64
(Alexandra Dunn) *disp ld tl 7th: pressed wnr tl rdn after 3 out: sn wknd: t.o* **6/1**[3]
/60- P **Fountains Flypast**[21] 5128 10-11-12 **120**......................(t) RobertThornton
(Anthony Honeyball) *disp ld tl pushed along after 6th: wknd 3 out: t.o whn p.u bef next* **13/2**
4m 40.5s (-5.50) **Going Correction** -0.30s/f (Good) **5** Ran SP% **109.0**
Speed ratings (Par 105): **99,95,94,78,**
CSF £5.72 TOTE £2.00: £1.30, £1.70; EX 5.70 Trifecta £20.80.
Owner Nigel Holder **Bred** C B Poots **Trained** Brompton Regis, Somerset

FOCUS
Unsurprisingly this proved a tactical affair, but the form still looks straightforward enough through the runner-up.

5527 BATHWICK TYRES MIDSOMER NORTON H'CAP CHASE (12 fncs) 2m 110y
7:30 (7:30) (Class 4) (0-120,120) 5-Y-0+ **£4,061** (£1,192; £596; £298)

Form RPR
4P1- 1 **Itsuptoyou (IRE)**[13] 5237 10-11-4 **112**..........................(t) NickScholfield 129+
(Arthur Whiting) *travelled strly bhd ldrs: led 8th gng best: sn wl in command: j.lft last 2: hung lft run-in. easily* **15/8**[1]
550- 2 *5* **Miss Tenacious**[21] 5126 7-11-11 **119**.................................... IanPopham 124
(Ron Hodges) *disp ld: hit 3rd: nt fluent next: hdd 8th: sn rdn: kpt on for clr 2nd fr 4 out but sn readily hld* **11/1**
122- 3 *30* **Barenger (IRE)**[34] 4912 7-11-4 **112**..........................(p) AidanColeman 90
(Ali Brewer) *j.lft: disp ld tl 8th: sn rdn: wknd after 4 out: t.o* **9/4**[2]
0P0- 4 *1/2* **Strongly Suggested**[34] 4919 7-11-12 **120**............................ APMcCoy 98
(Jonjo O'Neill) *trckd ldrs: nt fluent 3rd: lost tch after 8th: t.o* **11/4**[3]
3P5- 5 *12* **Takeroc (FR)**[20] 5141 11-10-13 **114**..........................(tp) TomBellamy(7) 81
(Alexandra Dunn) *hld up last but in tch: hit 2nd: rdn after 7th: wknd 4 out: t.o* **10/1**
4m 6.5s (-7.50) **Going Correction** -0.55s/f (Firm) **5** Ran SP% **109.6**
Speed ratings: **95,92,78,78,72**
CSF £18.11 TOTE £2.40: £1.60, £4.70; EX 17.10 Trifecta £62.70.
Owner A J Whiting **Bred** John P Kiely **Trained** North Nibley, Gloucs

FOCUS
There was no hanging about in this modest handicap. The easy winner built on his recent impressive C&D win.

5528 BATHWICK TYRES SALISBURY MARES' STANDARD OPEN NATIONAL HUNT FLAT RACE 2m 1f
8:00 (8:00) (Class 5) 4-6-Y-0 **£2,395** (£698; £349)

Form RPR
1 **Tara Point**[375] 5-10-13 0.. HarryDerham(3) 119+
(Paul Nicholls) *trckd ldr: led 4f out: clr wl over 2f out: heavily eased ins fnl f* **3/1**[2]
2 *8* **Catherines Well** 5-10-13 0.. MichealNolan(3) 107
(Philip Hobbs) *mid-div: hdwy on outer 1/2-way: rdn to chse wnr over 2f out: kpt on but nvr any ch* **7/1**[3]
- 3 *11* **Cresswell Breeze** 4-10-8 0..(t) RachaelGreen(3) 92
(Anthony Honeyball) *hld up towards rr: pushed along after 7f: rdn 4f out: styd on fnl 2f: wnt 3rd ins fnl f* **3/1**[2]
32- 4 *2 1/2* **Prettyasapicture**[17] 5196 5-11-2 0.................................... RobertThornton 94
(Alan King) *mid-div: hdwy 1/2-way: rdn to chse wnr over 3f out tl over 2f out: sn one pce* **11/4**[1]
300- 5 *shd* **Goneinaglance**[30] 5014 5-10-9 0.. MrJMartin(7) 94
(Andrew J Martin) *trckd ldr tl 4f out: sn rdn: one pce fnl 2f* **33/1**
6 *nk* **Daisy Picker** 4-10-6 0... JamesBanks(5) 89
(Noel Williams) *a mid-div* **50/1**
603- 7 *9* **Caldey**[35] 4909 5-11-2 0..(p) APMcCoy 86
(Keith Goldsworthy) *mid-div: rdn over 7f out: wknd over 2f out* **14/1**
3- 8 *2 1/4* **Starlight Sonata**[21] 5130 4-10-11 0.................................... AidanColeman 79
(Emma Lavelle) *mid-div: rdn over 3f out: nvr any imp* **12/1**
4- 9 *3/4* **Chill In The Wood**[29] 5028 5-10-9 0........................ BenFfrenchDavis(7) 83
(Dominic Ffrench Davis) *hld up towards rr: rdn 1/2-way: midfield over 2f out: wknd over 1f out* **40/1**
00- 10 *17* **Crazy Train**[56] 4499 5-11-2 0......................................(t) NickScholfield 68
(Keiran Burke) *led tl 4f out: sn wknd: t.o* **100/1**
11 *21* **Native Explorer** 5-10-13 0.. PeterCarberry(3) 49
(John Gallagher) *mid-div: rdn over 6f out: sn wknd: t.o* **14/1**
0- P **Eagles Road**[25] 5077 4-10-11 0... JamesDavies
(Harry Whittington) *sn drvn along in rr: lost tch bef 1/2-way: sn p.u* **125/1**
3m 52.3s (-10.10) **Going Correction** -0.30s/f (Good)
WFA 4 from 5yo+ 5lb **12** Ran SP% **119.3**
Speed ratings: **111,107,102,100,100 100,96,95,95,87 77,**
CSF £24.14 TOTE £4.10: £2.50, £5.90, £2.20; EX 26.50 Trifecta £129.80.
Owner R J H Geffen **Bred** Miss A Gibson-Fleming **Trained** Ditcheat, Somerset

FOCUS
This didn't look a bad mare's bumper and so one has to be very positive about the style the winner did it in.
T/Plt: £8.00 to £1 stake. Pool: £58862.65 - 5322.55 winning tickets T/Qpdt: £3.90 to a £1 stake. Pool: £4253.32 - 791.72 winning tickets TM

5529 - (Foreign Racing) - See Raceform Interactive

5425 AUTEUIL (L-H)
Wednesday, April 23
OFFICIAL GOING: Turf: very soft

5530a PRIX GUILLAUME JAVOY (CHASE) (CONDITIONS) (5YO+) (TURF) 2m 2f 110y
3:10 (3:10) 5-Y-0+ **£22,000** (£11,000; £6,416; £4,354; £2,062)

RPR
1 **Tornade Precieuse (FR)**[31] 7-10-12 0.............................. AlbanDesvaux 126
(Mme M Desvaux, France) **9/5**[1]
2 *3* **Upepito (FR)**[80] 4053 6-10-8 0.. DavidCottin 119
(Venetia Williams) *sn led: pressed fr 5 out: hdd bnd appr 2 out: rdn and nt match pce of wnr between last 2: kpt on at same pce u.p run-in* **19/5**[3]
3 *1* **Rivaliste (FR)**[186] 9-11-3 0... AlexisAcker 127
(M Rolland, France) **84/10**
4 *20* **Complicated (FR)**[25] 6-10-8 0....................................... AngeloGasnier 98
(J-Y Artu, France) **248/10**
5 *6* **Tamberma (FR)** 7-11-0 0...................................... JonathanPlouganou 98
(P Journiac, France) **57/10**
6 *5* **Veinard De Ballon (FR)**[12] 6-10-3 0.................. Marc-AntoineBillard(5) 87
(D Retif, France) **34/1**
7 *dist* **Kauto D'Aloes (FR)**[150] 5-10-6 0.................................(p) ThomasGillet(4)
(Ferdy Murphy, France) **39/1**
F **Raphy De La Roche (FR)**[19] 9-10-8 0..................................... KevinNabet
(Yannick Fouin, France) **12/5**[2]
4m 38.39s (-6.61) **8** Ran SP% **120.8**
PARI-MUTUEL (all including 1 euro stake): WIN 2.80; PLACE 1.40, 1.80, 2.00; DF 7.40; SF 15.00.
Owner Mme Mireille Desvaux **Bred** Mme M Desvaux, M Gainche & E Desvaux **Trained** France

5508 PERTH (R-H)
Thursday, April 24
OFFICIAL GOING: Soft (good to soft in places; 6.2)
Wind: Almost nil Weather: Cloudy

5531 CRABBIE'S ALCOHOLIC GINGER BEER NOVICES' HURDLE (8 hdls) 2m 110y
2:20 (2:21) (Class 4) 4-Y-0+ **£3,249** (£954; £477; £238)

Form RPR
221- 1 **Such A Legend**[19] 5175 6-11-0 120................................. EdCookson(5) 126+
(Kim Bailey) *chsd ldr: hdwy to ld between last 2: pushed along and kpt on wl run-in* **6/5**[1]
311- 2 *3 1/2* **Katachenko (IRE)**[17] 5205 5-11-12 130.................................. APMcCoy 128
(Donald McCain) *t.k.h: j.lft: led: hung lft bef 2 out: hdd between last 2: kpt on same pce fr last* **5/4**[2]
1- 3 *10* **Mixed Message (IRE)**[16] 1920 4-10-7 0.............................. DannyCook 98
(Brian Ellison) *chsd ldrs: nt fluent 3 out: rdn and outpcd next* **28/1**
4 *28* **Carthaginian (IRE)**[270] 5-10-9 0................................ HarryChalloner(3) 75
(Martin Todhunter) *nt fluent in rr: struggling fr 3rd: nvr on terms* **100/1**
4- 5 *1 1/4* **Maraweh (IRE)**[17] 5205 4-10-7 0.................................... PeterBuchanan 69
(Lucinda Russell) *nt fluent: in tch: struggling fr 3rd: t.o* **28/1**
46F- U **Tough Trade**[33] 4956 5-11-5 120.. BrianHughes
(Chris Grant) *hld up: sprawled and uns rdr 1st* **17/2**[3]
3m 56.0s (-2.00) **Going Correction** -0.10s/f (Good)
WFA 4 from 5yo+ 5lb **6** Ran SP% **108.3**
Speed ratings (Par 105): **100,98,93,80,79**
CSF £2.87 TOTE £2.30: £1.20, £1.50; EX 3.40 Trifecta £17.30.
Owner The Real Partnership **Bred** Mrs S Steer-Fowler **Trained** Andoversford, Gloucs

FOCUS
There was 4mm of rain overnight and jockey Peter Buchanan confirmed the ground was riding softer than the previous day. Danny Cook described it as "patchy" and "tacky". The form is rated around the first two.

5532 RUNNER UP CASH BACK AT MCBOOKIE.COM H'CAP HURDLE (8 hdls) 2m 110y
2:50 (2:51) (Class 5) (0-100,100) 4-Y-0+ **£3,249** (£954; £477; £238)

Form RPR
60P- 1 **Northern Acres**[24] 5106 8-10-4 **85**................................ MrKitAlexander(7) 94+
(N W Alexander) *in tch: stmbld bdly 3rd: hdwy to ld 2 out: rdn and styd on wl fr last* **13/2**[3]
/2F- 2 *nk* **Solway Dandy**[294] 884 7-11-4 **95**................................ EwanWhillans(3) 104+
(Lisa Harrison) *hld up: nt fluent 1st: stdy hdwy 3 out: effrt and chsng wnr whn mstke last: styd on strly towards fin: jst hld* **7/2**[1]
56P- 3 *2 3/4* **Flogarose (FR)**[42] 4770 5-10-4 **83**.............................. GrantCockburn(5) 87
(Lucy Normile) *cl up: led 3 out to next: sn rdn: kpt on same pce fr last* **12/1**
455- 4 *1 3/4* **Baraboy (IRE)**[20] 5163 4-10-8 **94**............................. GrahamWatters(7) 92
(Barry Murtagh) *hld up in midfield: hdwy and prom 2 out: sn rdn: kpt on same pce after last* **11/1**
326- 5 *6* **Momkinzain (USA)**[136] 2997 7-11-7 **100**......................(p) CraigNichol(5) 97
(Lucinda Russell) *hld up: hit 2nd: hdwy into midfield after next: rdn after 3 out: outpcd fr next* **6/1**[2]
U45- 6 *5* **Claude Carter**[168] 2306 10-11-2 **97**.................................. RyanNichol(7) 89
(Alistair Whillans) *hld up: rdn bef 3 out: plugged on fr next: nvr able to chal* **12/1**

4P5- **7** 2 **Ellistrin Belle**[17] 5212 6-10-6 **85** CallumWhillans[(5)] 75
(Donald Whillans) *t.k.h: led to 2nd: led 4 out to next: rdn and wknd bef 2 out* **6/1**[2]

2F6- **8** 7 **Early Applause**[239] 1206 6-11-10 **98** BrianHarding 81
(Nicky Richards) *nt fluent in rr: drvn along bef 4 out: nvr able to chal* **25/1**

44P- **9** 2 ¾ **Endeavor**[17] 5207 9-11-12 **100** (p) RyanMania 80
(Dianne Sayer) *hld up in midfield on outside: hdwy and cl up 3 out: wknd next: eased whn no ch* **12/1**

/PP- **10** nk **Caught In The Act (IRE)**[16] 5216 7-10-7 **81** LucyAlexander 60
(N W Alexander) *bhd: drvn fr 3rd: shortlived effrt after 4 out: struggling fr next* **20/1**

0- **11** 4 **Ivanka (IRE)**[13] 5265 6-11-4 **97** (t) DerekFox[(5)] 72
(Noel C Kelly, Ire) *in tch tl rdn and wknd bef 2 out* **8/1**

006- **12** 18 **Cigalas**[27] 5052 9-9-7 **74** oh9 (v[1]) MissAMcGregor[(7)] 31
(Jean McGregor) *t.k.h: cl up: led 2nd: blnd 4th: hdd 4 out: wknd fr next: t.o* **50/1**

3m 55.3s (-2.70) **Going Correction** -0.10s/f (Good)
WFA 4 from 5yo+ 5lb **12** Ran SP% **117.2**
Speed ratings (Par 103): **102,101,100,99,96 94,93,90,89,88 87,78**
CSF £29.11 CT £270.62 TOTE £8.30: £2.50, £1.90, £4.80; EX 38.50 Trifecta £187.20.
Owner C Lysaght Media, Quandt & Cochrane **Bred** Darley **Trained** Kinneston, Perth & Kinross

FOCUS
A moderate handicap that was run at a decent gallop and the gamble of the race, Northern Acres, got his head in front for the first time in 13 months. He was well in on form from this time last year.

5533 BILL AND BUNNY CADOGAN MEMORIAL NOVICES' LIMITED H'CAP CHASE (18 fncs) 3m

3:20 (3:20) (Class 3) (0-125,125) 5-Y-0+ **£7,147** (£2,098; £1,049; £524)

Form RPR

431- **1** **Seebright**[13] 5259 7-11-8 **125** DenisO'Regan 138+
(Victor Dartnall) *trckd ldrs: hit 7th: hdwy to ld 4 out: asserting whn stmbld 2 out: rdn and r.o wl fr last* **13/2**

413- **2** 3 ¾ **Hollow Blue Sky (FR)**[5] 5385 7-11-0 **117** SamTwiston-Davies 124
(Nigel Twiston-Davies) *hld up: stdy hdwy after 4 out: chsng wnr and clsd appr last: rdn and hung rt run-in: kpt on same pce* **5/2**[1]

132- **3** 3 ¼ **Big Society (IRE)**[61] 4412 8-11-6 **123** AlainCawley 129
(Tom George) *chsd ldrs: blkd 4 out: rdn and outpcd bef 2 out: styd on wl fr last: nt rch first two* **9/2**[3]

/0F- **4** 1 ½ **Humphrey Bee (IRE)**[333] 504 11-10-4 **107** LucyAlexander 112
(N W Alexander) *nt fluent on occasions: w ldr: led 4th tl j.rt and hdd 4 out: drvn next: outpcd bef last* **28/1**

305- **5** 30 **Ballytober**[51] 4602 8-11-5 **122** (t[1]) RichardJohnson 94
(Philip Hobbs) *hld up: effrt and pushed along after 4 out: struggling fr next: t.o* **4/1**[2]

334- **6** nse **Ballyben (IRE)**[27] 5055 6-9-12 **106** oh5 CraigNichol[(5)] 78
(Lucinda Russell) *chsd ldrs: outpcd 13th: rallied u.p: wknd bef 3 out: t.o* **9/1**

3U4- **P** **Hawaii Klass**[16] 5218 9-10-4 **112** (b) CallumWhillans[(5)]
(Donald Whillans) *led to 4th: w ldr tl lost pl after 12th: struggling and p.u after next* **18/1**

142- **P** **Rockchasebullett (IRE)**[36] 4908 6-10-4 **112** ConorShoemark[(5)]
(Fergal O'Brien) *nt fluent: hld up on outside: outpcd 13th: struggling after next: p.u bef 3 out* **6/1**

6m 12.0s (8.00) **Going Correction** +0.50s/f (Soft) **8** Ran SP% **113.1**
Speed ratings: **106,104,103,103,93 93, ,**
CSF £23.53 CT £80.14 TOTE £6.60: £1.40, £1.40, £2.10; EX 18.30 Trifecta £68.70.
Owner Mrs D J Fleming **Bred** R Johnson **Trained** Brayford, Devon

FOCUS
A decent handicap and the form looks solid enough.

5534 LONMAR GLOBAL RISKS H'CAP HURDLE (FOR THE MARK BLACK MEMORIAL TROPHY) (10 hdls) 2m 4f 110y

3:50 (3:50) (Class 3) (0-140,141) 4-Y-0+ **£6,498** (£1,908; £954; £477)

Form RPR

123- **1** **Titus Bolt (IRE)**[12] 5272 5-10-9 **117** JamesReveley 123+
(Jim Goldie) *hld up: stdy hdwy 1/2-way: led 2 out: rdn and styd on strly fr last* **7/1**

2P1- **2** 3 ½ **One For Harry (IRE)**[24] 5105 6-10-12 **120** BrianHarding 123
(Nicky Richards) *nt fluent on occasions: cl up: led 4th: rdn and hdd 2 out: 2 l down and styng on whn mstke last: kpt on same pce* **5/1**[3]

/12- **3** 1 ¼ **Enchanted Garden**[53] 4576 6-10-12 **120** BrianHughes 121
(Malcolm Jefferson) *in tch: stdy hdwy bef 3 out: effrt and rdn next: kpt on same pce bef last* **11/4**[2]

531- **4** 6 **Pure Science (IRE)**[56] 4512 6-11-0 **122** (p) SamTwiston-Davies 119
(Nigel Twiston-Davies) *nt fluent on occasions: chsd ldrs: rdn and outpcd after 3 out: no imp fr next* **5/2**[1]

610- **5** ½ **Call Box (IRE)**[12] 5272 9-11-3 **128** MrSCrawford[(3)] 122
(S R B Crawford, Ire) *hld up in tch: stdy hdwy after 3 out: rdn bef next: btn bef last* **9/1**

000- **6** 6 **Citizenship**[20] 5158 8-11-7 **129** AidanColeman 118
(Venetia Williams) *in tch: rdn after 3 out: wknd fr next* **8/1**

126- **7** 47 **Makhzoon (USA)**[17] 5208 10-10-11 **119** (p) LucyAlexander 60
(N W Alexander) *led to 4th: lost pl after next: lost tch bef 4 out: t.o* **28/1**

5m 4.4s (2.40) **Going Correction** +0.325s/f (Yiel) **7** Ran SP% **109.0**
Speed ratings (Par 107): **108,106,106,103,103 101,83**
CSF £37.50 CT £107.43 TOTE £7.00: £3.60, £2.30; EX 40.40 Trifecta £209.30.
Owner Ian G M Dalgleish **Bred** Patrick Brady **Trained** Uplawmoor, E Renfrews

FOCUS
Ordinary handicap form, rated around the second.

5535 MCBOOKIE.COM FESTIVAL H'CAP CHASE (FOR THE KILMANY CHALLENGE CUP) (15 fncs) 2m 4f 110y

4:20 (4:20) (Class 2) (0-150,150) 5-Y-0+ **£16,245** (£4,770; £2,385; £1,192)

Form RPR

P50- **1** **Majala (FR)**[54] 4559 8-11-0 **138** (t) AlainCawley 146+
(Tom George) *hld up: smooth hdwy on outside bef 3 out: effrt and rdn bef last: styd on wl to ld towards fin* **10/1**

PP4- **2** nk **Roudoudou Ville (FR)**[13] 5261 9-10-13 **137** DenisO'Regan 145+
(Victor Dartnall) *hld up: smooth hdwy and prom 5 out: hit and rdn 2 out: ev ch fr last: kpt on u.p: hld cl home* **10/1**

100- **3** nk **Dare Me (IRE)**[21] 5136 10-11-2 **140** AidanColeman 147
(Venetia Williams) *hld up: blnd and pushed along 5 out: hdwy after 3 out: led last: kpt on: hdd towards fin* **14/1**

204- **4** 6 **His Excellency (IRE)**[12] 5275 6-11-0 **138** (p) TomScudamore 139
(David Pipe) *in tch: drvn and outpcd bef 3 out: styd on fr last: nt rch first three* **12/1**

005- **5** ½ **Conquisto**[89] 3894 9-11-12 **150** RichardJohnson 150
(Steve Gollings) *led to after 3 out: sn rdn: outpcd fr last* **20/1**

/1P- **6** 1 **Silver Roque (FR)**[131] 3082 8-11-0 **143** ConorShoemark[(5)] 142
(Fergal O'Brien) *prom: hdwy to ld after 3 out: rdn and hdd last: sn outpcd* **9/1**

161- **7** nk **Scotch Warrior**[13] 5253 10-10-8 **132** PeterBuchanan 131
(R Mike Smith) *chsd ldrs: drvn and outpcd bef 3 out: no imp fr next* **15/2**[3]

P0P- **8** 2 **Bobowen (IRE)**[208] 1686 8-11-2 **140** TomO'Brien 139
(Dr Richard Newland) *midfield: lost pl 10th: rdn after 4 out: nvr able to chal* **12/1**

3P4- **9** nk **Tap Night (USA)**[13] 5253 7-11-4 **142** APMcCoy 140
(Lucinda Russell) *nt fluent on occasions: hld up: rdn after 3 out: n.d* **7/1**[2]

F52- **10** 4 ½ **Quincy Des Pictons (FR)**[47] 4675 10-10-13 **137** SamTwiston-Davies 131
(Alan Jones) *cl up: hit 4th: hit and rdn 4 out: wknd fr next* **14/5**[1]

362- **11** 2 **Tartan Snow**[21] 5135 14-9-7 **124** oh2 MrJHamilton[(7)] 115
(Stuart Coltherd) *prom: hit and rdn 10th: rallied: wknd after 4 out* **20/1**

611- **12** 12 **Shadows Lengthen**[36] 4900 8-10-5 **132** JakeGreenall[(3)] 110
(Michael Easterby) *nt fluent on occasions: hld up: drvn along bef 4 out: wknd bef next* **14/1**

5m 8.9s (3.90) **Going Correction** +0.50s/f (Soft) **12** Ran SP% **117.0**
Speed ratings: **112,111,111,109,109 108,108,108,107,106 105,100**
CSF £104.32 CT £1389.32 TOTE £13.80: £5.50, £3.50, £5.20; EX 147.60 Trifecta £1202.20.
Owner Sharon Nelson Jayne Taylor Darren Taylor **Bred** Michel Langot, And Hubert Langot **Trained** Slad, Gloucs

FOCUS
A good, competitive handicap, that set up for the closers, highlighted by the fact there was four in a row taking the last. The winner is rated back to the best of this season's form.

5536 LANDROVER EXPERIENCE AT PERTH RACECOURSE HUNTERS' CHASE (FOR THE PERTH HUNT BALNAKEILY CUP) (20 fncs) 3m 2f 110y

4:55 (4:56) (Class 5) 5-Y-0+ **£2,495** (£774; £386; £193)

Form RPR

44P- **1** **Well Mett (IRE)**[32] 7-11-9 120 (bt) MissAEStirling[(3)] 115+
(Fergal O'Brien) *racd wd: prom: led after 14th: mde rest: drew clr fr 3 out: easily* **5/2**[2]

U/2- **2** 18 **Scrum V**[50] 4617 10-11-5 87 MrJLyttle[(7)] 97
(Mrs N Naughton) *chsd ldrs: lost pl bef 1/2-way: rallied bef 4 out: styd on fr last to take 2nd nr fin: no ch w wnr* **25/1**

222- **3** nse **Moscow Menace (IRE)**[39] 4837 7-11-13 101 MrJHamilton[(3)] 102
(Miss K Scott) *prom: hit 8th: hdwy to chse wnr 5 out: rdn and outpcd by wnr fr 2 out: lost 2nd nr fin* **11/4**[3]

214- **4** 24 **Pena Dorada (IRE)**[26] 7-11-9 107 MrNOrpwood[(7)] 77
(Alan J Brown) *cl up: rdn along after 5 out: struggling bef 3 out: sn btn* **9/4**[1]

FP6- **5** 3 ¾ **Raifteiri (IRE)**[17] 5209 7-11-5 70 MrJDixon[(7)] 69
(William Young Jnr) *nt fluent: bhd: struggling fnl circ: nvr on terms* **80/1**

364- **U** **Back On The Road (IRE)**[10] 5323 12-11-9 104 MrJamieAlexander[(7)]
(N W Alexander) *hld up: nt fluent and uns rdr 1st* **11/1**

44F- **F** **Captain Americo (IRE)**[12] 12-11-5 104 (b) MrRLindsay[(7)]
(Mrs B Ewart) *led: blnd 8th: mstke and hdd 14th: struggling 5 out: 4th and btn whn fell 3 out* **13/2**

7m 3.8s (21.80) **Going Correction** +0.975s/f (Soft) **7** Ran SP% **112.8**
Speed ratings: **106,100,100,93,92 ,**
CSF £46.12 TOTE £5.30: £2.70, £7.50; EX 53.00 Trifecta £188.40.
Owner Fergal O'Brien **Bred** Arctic Tack Stud **Trained** Coln St. Dennis, Gloucs

FOCUS
A modest hunter chase that was won with ease by Well Mett. He can win more of these.

5537 COUPON BUSTER CASHBACK AT MCBOOKIE.COM NOVICES' H'CAP HURDLE (10 hdls) 2m 4f 110y

5:30 (5:30) (Class 4) (0-120,119) 4-Y-0+ **£5,198** (£1,526; £763; £381)

Form RPR

136- **1** **Bernardelli (IRE)**[17] 5212 6-11-8 **115** BrianHarding 118
(Nicky Richards) *hld up: hdwy after 4 out: chsng ldrs and drvn bef 2 out: led last: styd on wl* **10/1**

130- **2** 2 **Rugged Jack (FR)**[9] 5335 7-11-6 **113** DenisO'Regan 114
(Victor Dartnall) *cl up: led 5th: jnd after 4 out: rdn bef 2 out: hdd last: rallied: hld nr fin* **9/1**

323- **3** 7 **Solidago (IRE)**[38] 4869 7-10-5 **105** (v) AnthonyFox[(7)] 101
(S R B Crawford, Ire) *in tch: smooth hdwy to chal after 4 out: rdn bef 2 out: outpcd after last* **15/2**

664- **4** 1 ½ **Our Boy Ben**[33] 4957 5-11-2 **109** BrianHughes 103
(Malcolm Jefferson) *hld up: smooth hdwy and prom 1/2-way: effrt and drvn after 3 out: outpcd after next* **9/1**

413- **5** 12 **Blue Kascade (IRE)**[59] 4465 7-10-7 **100** RyanMania 83
(Sandy Thomson) *cl up: nt fluent and outpcd 4 out: n.d after* **7/2**[1]

6 65 **Moyvic (IRE)**[91] 3867 5-11-1 **115** SAShortall[(7)] 31
(A J Martin, Ire) *hld up: rdn after 4 out: struggling bef 2 out: t.o* **16/1**

114- **F** **Plus Jamais (FR)**[13] 5251 7-11-4 **111** JamesReveley 107
(Jim Goldie) *hld up in tch: lost pl 1/2-way: rallied after 4 out: drvn next: 3 l 5th and styng on whn fell 2 out* **13/2**[3]

F55- **P** **Owen Na View (IRE)**[45] 4726 6-11-5 **117** ConorShoemark[(5)]
(Fergal O'Brien) *nt fluent on occasions: hld up on outside: drvn and outpcd after 4 out: struggling bef next: t.o whn p.u after 2 out* **12/1**

143- **P** **Moss Cloud (IRE)**[16] 5214 7-11-10 **117** (b[1]) APMcCoy
(Donald McCain) *chsd ldrs: nt fluent 3rd: reminders next: lost pl qckly bef 6th: lost tch and p.u bef 4 out* **5/1**[2]

P20- **P** **Vivaccio (FR)**[40] 4820 5-11-12 **119** AidanColeman
(Venetia Williams) *hld up in tch: drvn and outpcd after 4 out: struggling fr next: t.o whn p.u after 2 out* **10/1**

5m 8.0s (6.00) **Going Correction** +0.45s/f (Soft) **10** Ran SP% **115.7**
Speed ratings (Par 105): **106,105,102,102,97 72, , ,**
CSF £95.03 CT £717.26 TOTE £10.00: £3.20, £2.60, £3.00; EX 115.30 Trifecta £307.50.
Owner Henriques & LLoyd-Bakers **Bred** Minch Bloodstock **Trained** Greystoke, Cumbria

FOCUS
Run at a really good gallop, they finished tired. Ordinary handicap form with the winner to his best.

T/Plt: £584.20 to a £1 stake. Pool: £68,519.90 - 85.61 winning units. T/Qpdt: £156.50 to a £1 stake. Pool: £5,522.11 - 26.10 winning units. RY

5426 CHEPSTOW (L-H)

Friday, April 25

OFFICIAL GOING: Good to soft

Wind: Light across Weather: Raining clearing to leave sunny spells

5541 EVAN AND MEGAN BRACE MEMORIAL NOVICES' HURDLE (11 hdls) 2m 4f

5:00 (5:02) (Class 4) 4-Y-0+ **£3,119** (£915; £457; £228)

Form RPR

2- **1** **Ned Stark (IRE)**[163] 2457 6-10-13 0 RobertThornton 115+
(Alan King) *hld up in tch: nt fluent 3rd and 6th: jnd ldr 4 out: led next: clr last: styd on wl* **4/6**[1]

126- **2** *5* **Saint Breiz (FR)**[33] 4993 8-11-5 113 IanPopham 115
(Carroll Gray) *chsd ldrs: led 7th: hdd 3 out: sn rdn: styd on same pce last* **20/1**

/63- **3** *3/4* **Monksgold (IRE)**[33] 4993 6-10-13 0 AidanColeman 108
(Alan King) *hld up: hdwy 6th: rdn appr 2 out: styd on: nt rch ldrs* **7/1**[3]

21F- **4** *4 1/2* **Spyder**[14] 5257 6-11-5 124 RichardJohnson 110
(Lucy Wadham) *chsd ldrs: led appr 4th: hdd 7th: rdn 3 out: styd on same pce fr next* **3/1**[2]

340- **5** *8* **Black Cow (IRE)**[26] 5088 6-10-13 0 NickScholfield 97
(Paul Nicholls) *hld up: plld hrd: mstke 6th: hdwy appr 8th: rdn and wknd 3 out* **11/1**

4- **6** *20* **Rock Me Zippo (IRE)**[12] 5288 6-10-13 0 MarkGrant 79
(Sean Curran) *chsd ldr to 3rd: remained handy tl rdn and wknd 8th* **50/1**

P- **7** *9* **Shady Glen (IRE)**[19] 5182 5-10-8 0 KillianMoore(5) 71
(Graeme McPherson) *hld up: bhd fr 5th* **66/1**

6- **8** *16* **Mrs Burbidge**[12] 5303 4-9-9 0 JamesBanks(5) 43
(Neil Mulholland) *plld hrd and prom: rdn and wknd appr 8th* **100/1**

/60- **9** *8* **Seymour Legend**[15] 5242 8-10-13 81 TommyPhelan 49
(Jim Wilson) *mid-div: rdn and wknd after 7th* **100/1**

60- **10** *42* **Johns Luck (IRE)**[27] 5070 5-10-13 0 MichaelByrne 11
(Neil Mulholland) *led: j.lft 1st: hdd appr 4th: wknd bef 8th* **66/1**

40- **P** **Maxilian (IRE)**[27] 5071 5-10-13 0 GavinSheehan
(Emma Lavelle) *hld up: bhd fr 5th: p.u bef 8th* **50/1**

6- **P** **Ice Cool Curler**[31] 5028 5-10-13 0 NoelFehily
(Ali Brewer) *hld up: mstke 3rd: bhd fr 5th: p.u bef 8th* **66/1**

5m 3.1s (1.30) **Going Correction** +0.10s/f (Yiel)
WFA 4 from 5yo+ 6lb **12** Ran SP% **121.0**
Speed ratings (Par 105): **101,99,98,96,93 85,82,75,72,55 ,**
CSF £18.98 TOTE £1.80: £1.10, £5.80, £2.30; EX 14.10 Trifecta £61.70.
Owner The Dunkley & Reilly Partnership **Bred** Miss Susan Scott **Trained** Barbury Castle, Wilts

FOCUS
A fair novice hurdle.

5542 SUN TRADE WINDOWS H'CAP HURDLE (11 hdls) 2m 4f

5:30 (5:31) (Class 4) (0-115,114) 4-Y-0+ **£3,119** (£915; £457; £228)

Form RPR

1/5- **1** **Orangeaday**[120] 3286 7-11-7 112 (t) KielanWoods(3) 125+
(Ben Case) *a.p: nt fluent 5th: led 3 out: hit last: drvn out* **4/1**[2]

330- **2** *3/4* **Detroit Red**[207] 1699 8-11-2 104 HaddenFrost 117+
(Martin Hill) *hld up: plld hrd: hdwy 7th: chsd wnr after 3 out: styd on u.p* **14/1**

040- **3** *12* **Amazing D'Azy (IRE)**[25] 5112 6-10-12 105 EdCookson(5) 107
(Kim Bailey) *prom: rdn after 3 out: styd on same pce fr next* **12/1**

346- **4** *1 1/4* **Letemgo (IRE)**[19] 5191 6-11-8 110 (p) DavidEngland 111
(Giles Smyly) *w ldr tl led after 4th: hdd 6th: rdn and ev ch 3 out: wknd appr last* **7/2**[1]

44F- **5** *10* **It's Oscar (IRE)**[266] 1184 7-11-0 105 MarkQuinlan(3) 99
(James Evans) *hld up: nvr nrr* **25/1**

403- **6** *15* **Yazdi (IRE)**[20] 5179 5-10-11 99 JamesDavies 77
(Henry Oliver) *prom: hmpd 3 out: sn rdn and wknd* **7/1**

400- **7** *18* **Wing Mira (IRE)**[24] 5117 6-10-4 95 RobertDunne(3) 57
(Venetia Williams) *hld up: rdn and wknd 8th: bhd whn hit 2 out* **10/1**

313- **8** *1 1/2* **Seven Summits (IRE)**[23] 5125 7-11-6 108 PaulMoloney 69
(Sophie Leech) *hld up: hdwy 5th: rdn and wknd appr 3 out* **6/1**

01/- **9** *15* **Staccato Valtat (FR)**[370] 5410 8-11-5 114 CiaranMckee(7) 61
(John O'Shea) *hld up: wknd 7th* **25/1**

150- **F** **Pyleigh Lass**[10] 5333 8-11-11 113 (tp) IanPopham 114
(Martin Keighley) *led tl after 4th: led again 6th: rdn and hdd whn fell 3 out* **11/2**[3]

5m 0.4s (-1.40) **Going Correction** +0.10s/f (Yiel) **10** Ran SP% **115.5**
Speed ratings (Par 105): **106,105,100,100,96 90,83,82,76,**
CSF £56.55 CT £608.76 TOTE £4.90: £2.10, £3.90, £4.60; EX 77.30 Trifecta £1549.00 Part won..
Owner D Allen **Bred** R F And S D Knipe **Trained** Edgcote, Northants

FOCUS
A competitive race, despite some notable absentees.

5543 BRACEYS BUILDERS MERCHANT H'CAP CHASE (16 fncs) 2m 3f 110y

6:00 (6:00) (Class 3) (0-130,123) 5-Y-0+ **£6,498** (£1,908; £954; £477)

Form RPR

211- **1** **Ratify**[33] 4992 10-11-4 118 RobertDunne(3) 126+
(Dai Burchell) *chsd ldr tl led 4th: rdn appr 3 out: jst hld on* **11/4**[1]

661- **2** *nk* **Entertain Me**[20] 5176 10-11-11 122 CharliePoste 128
(Robin Dickin) *chsd ldrs: wnt 2nd 12th tl 3 out: sn rdn: styd on u.p* **11/2**

PU1- **3** *1/2* **Ballywatt (IRE)**[31] 5020 8-11-12 123 (tp) NickScholfield 130
(Kim Bailey) *hld up in tch: mstkes 5th and 9th: nt fluent 4 out: chsd wnr last: sn rdn and ev ch: styd on* **3/1**[2]

122- **4** *1 3/4* **Time To Think**[33] 4992 9-11-6 117 AndrewThornton 122
(Seamus Mullins) *led to 4th: chsd wnr to 6th: sn pushed along and lost pl: rallied 4 out: chsd wnr next tl rdn appr last: styd on same pce flat* **5/1**[3]

644- **5** *nk* **Olympian Boy (IRE)**[20] 5176 10-10-11 108 PaulMoloney 112
(Sophie Leech) *hld up: hdwy 9th: rdn after 2 out: styd on same pce flat* **8/1**

P2P- **6** *8* **Bendant**[48] 4677 9-11-5 116 RobertThornton 114
(Debra Hamer) *prom: chsd wnr 6th to 12th: sn rdn: styd on same pce fr 3 out* **11/2**

5m 9.6s (-1.70) **Going Correction** +0.10s/f (Yiel) **6** Ran SP% **110.2**
Speed ratings: **107,106,106,105,105 102**
CSF £17.03 TOTE £2.90: £1.60, £2.80; EX 15.30 Trifecta £23.90.
Owner J J King **Bred** Mrs R Lyon **Trained** Briery Hill, Blaenau Gwent

FOCUS
Some likeable, in-form types were on show in this handicap chase.

5544 DUNRAVEN WINDOWS H'CAP HURDLE (12 hdls) 3m

6:35 (6:36) (Class 2) 4-Y-0+ **£12,021** (£3,529; £1,764; £882)

Form RPR

2F3- **1** **Rydon Pynes**[10] 5333 6-11-5 128 HaddenFrost 132
(Martin Hill) *hld up: mstke 6th: hdwy after 8th: styd on u.p to ld fnl 75yds* **4/1**[1]

411- **2** *3/4* **Billy Dutton**[10] 5333 8-11-3 126 7ex JamesDavies 129
(Chris Down) *a.p: rdn to chse ldr 3 out: ev ch flat: r.o* **8/1**

000- **3** *shd* **Pateese (FR)**[22] 5138 9-11-11 134 (b) RichardJohnson 138
(Philip Hobbs) *hld up: mstke 6th: hdwy 8th: chsd ldr 2 out: rdn flat: r.o* **13/2**[2]

/10- **4** *1/2* **Top Wood (FR)**[43] 4765 7-11-12 135 (t) TomScudamore 138
(David Pipe) *led: rdn appr last: hdd and unable qck fnl 75yds* **4/1**[1]

F03- **5** *6* **American Life (FR)**[6] 5379 7-9-9 109 oh2 (vt) JamesBanks(5) 107
(Anthony Middleton) *hld up: hdwy and nt fluent 4 out: sn rdn: styd on same pce fr 2 out* **16/1**

F56- **6** *10* **Monetary Fund (USA)**[26] 5093 8-11-0 123 AidanColeman 112
(Venetia Williams) *mid-div: lost pl 5th: rdn appr 4 out: sn outpcd* **7/1**[3]

3P0- **7** *15* **Ugly Bug**[26] 5093 8-10-11 120 AndrewThornton 95
(Seamus Mullins) *chsd ldrs: wnt 2nd 7th tl rdn 3 out: wknd bef next* **16/1**

100- **8** *1/2* **Josies Orders (IRE)**[22] 5138 6-11-6 132 (b) MauriceLinehan(3) 106
(Jonjo O'Neill) *prom: rdn appr 9th: wknd after 3 out* **11/1**

616- **9** *29* **Seventh Sign**[41] 4805 5-11-12 135 (b) RobertThornton 83
(Alan King) *prom: chsd ldr 5th tl mstke 7th: sn rdn: wknd 9th* **8/1**

P04- **P** **Green Belt Elite (FR)**[52] 4599 10-9-12 109 ow1 RobertDunne(3)
(Venetia Williams) *hld up: rdn and wknd after 8th: bhd whn p.u bef next* **25/1**

12P- **P** **Who Owns Me (IRE)**[34] 4954 8-11-10 133 (b) NoelFehily
(Charlie Mann) *prom: pushed along and lost pl 4th: bhd fr 6th: p.u bef 9th* **25/1**

6m 6.9s (4.70) **Going Correction** +0.10s/f (Yiel) **11** Ran SP% **115.8**
Speed ratings (Par 109): **96,95,95,95,93 90,85,85,75,**
CSF £35.75 CT £200.09 TOTE £5.70: £2.80, £2.60, £3.70; EX 29.40 Trifecta £238.70.
Owner The Rydon Pynes Partnership **Bred** Jamie Donovan **Trained** Littlehempston, Devon

FOCUS
A pulsating finish to this competitive feature.

5545 DUNRAVEN BOWL NOVICES' HUNTERS' CHASE (DUNRAVEN WINDOWS SOUTH AND WEST WALES P-T-P CHAMPIONSHIP) (18 fncs) 3m

7:10 (7:10) (Class 5) 5-Y-0+ **£2,183** (£677; £338; £169)

Form RPR

P- **1** **Gale Force Oscar (IRE)**[42] 4788 9-11-9 82 (t) MrJFMathias(3) 115+
(L M Power) *hld up: hdwy 8th: hit next: led 14th: clr next: easily* **5/2**[1]

2 *20* **Supreme Regime (IRE)**[13] 8-11-5 0 MrJSKnox(7) 87
(Miss Katy Jane Price) *hld up: hdwy 11th: rdn and wknd 15th* **16/1**

530/ **3** *4* **Doc Wells (IRE)**[27] 11-11-12 0 MrNickWilliams 85
(Ms D C Faulkner) *chsd ldrs: led appr 14th: sn hdd: wknd bef next* **8/1**[3]

006- **4** *44* **Patricktom Boru (IRE)**[13] 7-11-5 87 MrEDavid(7) 44
(R W J Willcox) *prom: hit 3rd: rdn and wkng whn mstke 15th* **8/1**[3]

560/ **5** *15* **Awesome Bella**[19] 7-10-12 0 MrWMaskill(7) 23
(David Rees) *mid-div: hdwy 7th: wknd 10th* **9/1**

6 *1/2* **Our Differences (IRE)**[19] 7-11-7 0 MrMatthewBarber(5) 30
(M Barber) *chsd ldrs tl rdn and wknd 11th* **9/1**

0/ **P** **Skating Home (IRE)**[12] 8-11-5 0 (p) MrJAPonting(7)
(P Ponting) *mid-div: lost pl 6th: bhd fr 8th: p.u bef 11th* **25/1**

030/ **P** **Earth Tremor (IRE)**[19] 8-11-5 0 (t) MrCWest(7)
(E Parry) *hdwy 4th: chsd ldr 7th to 12th: rdn and wknd appr 14th: bhd whn p.u bef 3 out* **25/1**

60P/ **P** **Cool Steel (IRE)**[6] 8-11-7 86 (tp) MrBGibbs(5)
(David Brace) *hld up: bhd and rdn 7th: p.u bef 14th* **25/1**

P45- **P** **Rainbow Haze**[27] 8-11-9 0 (t) MrFMitchell(3)
(Mrs K M Dando) *chsd ldr tl led 6th: rdn and hdd appr 14th: sn wknd: bhd whn p.u bef 3 out* **14/1**

0/ **P** **Minellaformarriage (IRE)**[19] 8-11-5 0 MrKMHanmer(7)
(Neville Thomas) *led to 6th: mstke 10th: rdn and wknd after 13th: bhd whn p.u bef 4 out* **25/1**

P **Barney Dunne (IRE)**[13] 10-11-7 0 MrJMRidley(5)
(R Meyrick) *hld up: mstke 4th: bhd fr 9th: p.u bef 12th* **40/1**

P **Renta Gallery (IRE)**[389] 8-11-5 0 MrMWall
(Richard A Thomas) *mstke 1st: hld up: bhd fr 10th: p.u bef 14th* **7/1**[2]

0/ **P** **Bringinthebranston**[6] 6-11-12 0 (tp) MrJETudor
(David Brace) *hld up: sme hdwy 12th: rdn and wknd after next: bhd whn p.u bef 14th* **12/1**

6m 23.5s (1.50) **Going Correction** +0.10s/f (Yiel) **14** Ran SP% **121.4**
Speed ratings: **101,94,93,78,73 73,,,,, ,,,**
CSF £42.08 TOTE £2.70: £1.30, £7.40, £3.30; EX 69.30 Trifecta £830.30.
Owner L M Power **Bred** Patrick Moakley **Trained** Port Talbot, Neath

FOCUS
Plenty of winning point form on offer in this novices' hunters' chase but it was turned into a procession.

5546 SUN TRADE WINDOWS H'CAP CHASE (22 fncs) 3m 2f 110y

7:40 (7:40) (Class 5) (0-100,100) 5-Y-0+ **£2,144** (£629; £314; £157)

Form RPR

2P1- **1** **Bringewood Belle**[4] 5433 11-9-7 74 7ex oh5 PaulJohn(7) 87+
(John Needham) *a.p: chsd ldr 10th: led 13th: rdn appr 3 out: styd on wl* **9/2**[2]

122- **2** *5* **The Last Bridge**[4] 5433 7-11-1 89 (p) RichardJohnson 98
(Susan Johnson) *chsd ldr tl led 7th to 9th: remained handy: nt fluent 15th: chsd wnr appr 3 out: sn rdn: no imp flat* **2/1**[1]

PB4- **3** *38* **Hobb's Dream (IRE)**[24] 5122 10-10-7 81 (p) MichaelByrne 55
(Neil Mulholland) *hld up: hdwy 16th: chsd wnr 18th tl 3 out: sn wknd* **14/1**

366- **4** *14* **Kilcascan**[126] 3193 10-10-2 81 (p) BenPoste(5) 42
(Rosemary Gasson) *prom: lost pl 8th: tk clsr order 11th: outpcd 13th: rallied appr 18th: sn wknd* **16/1**

543- **5** *1 1/2* **Accordingtopalm (IRE)**[19] 5185 8-11-11 99 (t) PaulMoloney 59
(David Rees) *hld up: blnd 13th: n.d* **10/1**[3]

411- **6** *59* **Cosway Spirit (IRE)**[32] 5011 7-11-12 100 (p) DavidBass 7
(Ben Pauling) *led to 7th: led again 9th: hdd 13th: rdn and wknd appr 4 out* **9/2**[2]

/50- **7** *18* **Trifollet**[32] 5011 9-10-0 79 (b[1]) KillianMoore(5)
(Andrew J Martin) *prom: drvn along 12th: sn wknd* **25/1**

The Form Book Jumps, Raceform Ltd, Compton, RG20 6NL.

P25- P Night Safe (IRE)[19] 5185 13-10-8 89..............................(v) MrJBargary(7)
(Nigel Twiston-Davies) prom tl rdn and wknd after 17th: bhd whn p.u bef 3 out 14/1
22F- P Mic Aubin (FR)[23] 5129 11-11-2 95 ow2.............................. MrPMason(7)
(Jennifer Mason) prom to 15th: bhd whn p.u bef 17th 12/1
03P- P Ball Hopper (IRE)[61] 4451 10-10-12 86.......................(t) AndrewThornton
(Richenda Ford) hld up: a in rr: bhd whn p.u bef 16th 20/1
06P- P Dancing Daffodil[15] 5246 9-10-9 93..................... JosephPalmowski(10)
(Robin Dickin) hld up: pushed along 12th: bhd fr 14th: p.u bef 17th 28/1

7m 12.5s (10.50) **Going Correction** +0.10s/f (Yiel) 11 Ran SP% 117.8
Speed ratings: **88,86,75,71,70 53,47,,,**
CSF £14.16 CT £117.68 TOTE £4.80: £1.60, £1.60, £3.00; EX 15.80 Trifecta £123.40.
Owner J L Needham **Bred** John Needham **Trained** Ludlow, Shropshire
■ Stewards' Enquiry : Paul John three-day ban: used whip without giving mare time to respond (May 9-11)

FOCUS
Another solid handicap on the card.

5547 BRACEYS "THE FRIENDLY BUILDERS MERCHANT" "NATIONAL HUNT" MAIDEN HURDLE (8 hdls) 2m 110y
8:10 (8:11) (Class 5) 4-Y-0+ £1,949 (£572; £286; £143)

Form RPR
563- 1 Morning Reggie[20] 5174 5-11-0 110................................. GavinSheehan 107
(Oliver Sherwood) hld up: plld hrd: hdwy appr 5th: chsd ldr 3 out: led flat: r.o wl 5/2[2]
042- 2 2 Rock On Rocky[20] 5175 6-11-0 115.................................. CharliePoste 107
(Matt Sheppard) led: rdn whn hit last: sn hdd: styd on same pce 1/1[1]
3 8 Flying Bandit (IRE) 5-11-0 0.. NoelFehily 98
(Fergal O'Brien) hld up: hdwy appr 5th: wnt 3rd 2 out: styd on: nt trble ldrs 20/1
4- 4 3½ Ballybough Andy (IRE)[29] 5042 5-11-0 0.................. RichardJohnson 97
(David Dennis) chsd ldr to 5th: styd on same pce fr 3 out 16/1
0- 5 7 Scutsisland (IRE)[33] 4986 5-10-9 0.................................. BenPoste(5) 90
(Rosemary Gasson) prom: chsd ldr 5th to next: wknd 2 out 100/1
006- 6 2¼ Italian Symphony (IRE)[12] 5305 4-10-2 0..................... BrendanPowell 75
(Brendan Powell) hld up: rdn appr 5th: n.d 66/1
00- 7 4½ Bahumbug[26] 5088 4-10-9 0..................................... AndrewThornton 78
(Seamus Mullins) prom: racd keenly: rdn and wknd after 5th 100/1
022- 8 nk All Riled Up[15] 5245 6-10-0 101.................................. DanielHiskett(7) 76
(Harry Chisman) hld up: a in rr 25/1
405- 9 4 Lily Mars (IRE)[12] 5308 7-10-7 0.. MichaelByrne 72
(Neil Mulholland) hld up: a in rr 33/1
454- 10 2½ King's Opus (IRE)[15] 5227 5-10-9 0.................................. EdCookson(5) 77
(Kim Bailey) trckd ldrs: racd keenly: hit 3rd: rdn and wknd after 5th 20/1
26P- 11 10 Rouquine Sauvage[60] 4467 6-10-7 0............................(t) AidanColeman 61
(Anthony Honeyball) hld up: hmpd after 4th: sn bhd 10/1[3]
066- F Say When[37] 4909 6-11-0 0.. RobertThornton
(Alan King) hld up: stmbld and fell after 4th 25/1

4m 13.6s (3.00) **Going Correction** +0.10s/f (Yiel)
WFA 4 from 5yo+ 5lb 12 Ran SP% 117.2
Speed ratings (Par 103): **96,95,91,89,86 85,83,83,81,79 75,**
CSF £4.94 TOTE £3.00: £1.10, £1.10, £5.70; EX 7.50 Trifecta £53.80.
Owner Tim Syder **Bred** R D & Mrs J S Chugg **Trained** Upper Lambourn, Berks

FOCUS
The market leaders dominated the final jumps race of Chepstow's season.
T/Plt: £159.60 to a £1 stake. Pool: £67316.55 - 307.75 winning tickets T/Qpdt: £13.30 to a £1 stake. Pool: £6803.29 - 376.75 winning tickets CR

5389 NEWTON ABBOT (L-H)
Friday, April 25

OFFICIAL GOING: Good (good to firm in places) changing to good to soft after race 2 (5:45)
All rail moved since April 19th but effect on distances not quantified.
Wind: fresh across Weather: sunny

5548 NATIONAL COASTWATCH TEIGNMOUTH STATION MAIDEN HURDLE (9 hdls) 2m 3f
5:10 (5:10) (Class 5) 4-Y-0+ £2,737 (£798; £399)

Form RPR
02F- 1 Foggy's Wall (IRE)[35] 4937 6-10-10 120....................(b¹) HarryDerham(3) 123+
(Paul Nicholls) trckd ldrs: led appr 2 out: sn in command: comf 1/2[1]
065- 2 9 Twice Returned (IRE)[19] 5194 8-10-13 113....................(p) HarrySkelton 110
(Dan Skelton) led: rdn after 3 out: hdd bef next: sn hld by wnr: kpt on same pce 5/2[2]
0PF- 3 21 Genson[33] 4987 5-10-13 0.. ConorO'Farrell 95
(Richard Woollacott) trckd ldr: rdn after 3 out: dropped to 3rd bef next: fdd 10/1[3]
00- 4 23 Hi Bronco[24] 5117 7-10-13 0.. DaveCrosse 73
(John Ryall) reminders after 1st: sn in tch: modest 4th and struggling 6th: hit 3 out: t.o 66/1
5 6 Blue Grand (IRE)[54] 6-10-13 0...................................... DominicElsworth 65
(Adrian Wintle) sn towards rr: struggling 6th: nvr any danger: t.o 33/1
P- 6 7 Wansbeck[99] 3746 6-10-10 0... WayneKavanagh(3) 59
(James Frost) in tch tl bef 6th: sn wknd: t.o 50/1
P Sanctioned[59] 5-10-13 0...(t) LiamTreadwell
(Robert Stephens) towards rr: wknd after 5th: t.o whn p.u after next 12/1
66- P Primo Milano[10] 5341 5-10-6 0...................................... ConorRing(7)
(Evan Williams) hld up: wknd after 5th: t.o whn p.u after next 16/1
5P- P Ollisu Lad (IRE)[22] 5140 5-10-13 0...................................... JamieMoore
(Tim Vaughan) nt fluent 1st: a towards rr: struggling after 5th: t.o whn p.u after next 33/1

4m 32.5s (2.50) **Going Correction** +0.275s/f (Yiel) 9 Ran SP% 127.2
Speed ratings (Par 103): **105,101,92,82,80 77,,,**
CSF £2.44 TOTE £1.60: £1.02, £1.40, £2.60; EX 2.70 Trifecta £7.10.
Owner Mr & Mrs Mark Woodhouse **Bred** Denis Cummins **Trained** Ditcheat, Somerset
■ Stewards' Enquiry : Jamie Moore four-day ban: used whip with excessive force (May 9-12)

FOCUS
Run at a solid pace, this was an uncompetitive race in which the winner and runner-up were a class or more above the rest.

5549 OLIVE AND JACK OLIVER MEMORIAL H'CAP CHASE (13 fncs) 2m 110y
5:45 (5:45) (Class 4) (0-120,119) 5-Y-0+ £3,994 (£1,240; £667)

Form RPR
653- 1 The Nephew (IRE)[37] 4908 6-11-8 115..................................(t) APMcCoy 122+
(Jonjo O'Neill) j.rt at times: led 3rd: mde rest: reminders after 4 out: rdn 2 out: kpt on: rdn out 6/4[1]
105- 2 1¾ Delphi Mountain (IRE)[12] 5304 9-10-12 105...............(bt) ConorO'Farrell 110
(Richard Woollacott) trckd ldrs: wnt 2nd after 6th tl appr 4 out: sn rdn: kpt on into cl 2nd between last 2: styd on same pce flat 12/1
433- 3 12 Easily Pleased (IRE)[30] 5031 8-11-12 119.......................... JamieMoore 117
(Martin Hill) racd keenly: hld up: clsd on ldrs 6th: wnt 2nd bef 4 out: rdn after 3 out: cl up whn hit 2 out: fdd bef last 7/4[2]
120- P Jeanry (FR)[20] 5176 11-10-1 101.. JoshWall(7)
(Arthur Whitehead) hld up: clsd on ldrs 6th: pushed along next: rdn after 8th: wknd 4 out: p.u next 14/1
P26- U George Nympton (IRE)[20] 5176 8-11-5 119........... BenFfrenchDavis(7)
(Dominic Ffrench Davis) hld up: nudged along and clsd on ldrs 6th: rdn after 8th: wknd 4 out: modest 4th whn uns rdr last 14/1
2U3- P Lucky Sunny (IRE)[24] 5118 11-11-4 111........................... LiamTreadwell
(Venetia Williams) racd keenly: led tl 3rd: trckd wnr tl after 6th: blnd bdly next: sn p.u: b.b.v 6/1[3]

4m 5.8s (-0.70) **Going Correction** +0.125s/f (Yiel) 6 Ran SP% 111.7
Speed ratings: **106,105,99,,**
CSF £17.49 TOTE £1.60: £1.10, £6.40; EX 13.00 Trifecta £46.30.
Owner Geoff & Peter Bond **Bred** Nicholas Teehan **Trained** Cheltenham, Gloucs

FOCUS
The lively pace put pressure on the jumping of these middling chasers, and not all of them were up to it.

5550 NEWQUAY ZOO NOVICES' HURDLE (10 hdls) 2m 6f
6:20 (6:20) (Class 4) 4-Y-0+ £3,508 (£1,030; £515; £257)

Form RPR
221- 1 Silsol (GER)[13] 5272 5-10-10 136..............................(tp) HarryDerham(3) 131+
(Paul Nicholls) trckd ldrs: wnt 2nd 6th: chal 2 out: sn rdn into ld: r.o wl fr last 4/7[1]
122- 2 2¼ Kris Spin (IRE)[26] 5093 6-11-5 140.. JamieMoore 135+
(Richard Lee) disp ld: nt fluent 2nd: outight ldr 5th: nt fluent 7th: rdn after 3 out: hdd sn after 2 out: kpt on but nt gng pce of wnr 7/4[2]
P33- 3 41 Master Todd (IRE)[37] 4903 9-10-13 115..................(t) DominicElsworth 97
(Grant Cann) disp ld tl 5th: trckd ldng pair: rdn after 3 out: outpcd bef next: wknd bef last: t.o 12/1[3]
50- 4 18 Gair Leat (IRE)[14] 5258 10-10-13 0...................................... AdamWedge 70
(Liam Corcoran) trckd ldrs: rdn after 3 out: sn wknd: t.o 66/1
6UP- 5 7 War Treaty (IRE)[10] 5332 6-10-10 0.......................(p) WayneKavanagh(3) 63
(Mark Shears) trckd ldrs: rdn after 3 out: sn wknd: t.o 200/1

5m 27.3s (7.10) **Going Correction** +0.275s/f (Yiel) 5 Ran SP% 109.7
Speed ratings (Par 105): **98,97,82,75,73**
CSF £1.92 TOTE £1.30: £1.10, £1.30; EX 2.00 Trifecta £2.30.
Owner Michelle And Dan MacDonald **Bred** Gestut Hof Iserneichen **Trained** Ditcheat, Somerset

FOCUS
After advice from jockeys, the ground was changed from "good, good to firm in places" to "good to soft" before this race. As there had been no rain, it's fair to assume it was similar for the first two races. Dominated by the first two, it was run at a modest pace until the runner-up began to crank it up from the front at the third-last.

5551 VISIT US AT SIS.TV NOVICES' CHASE (16 fncs) 2m 5f 110y
6:50 (6:50) (Class 3) 5-Y-0+ £7,027 (£2,121; £1,092; £579)

Form RPR
32F- 1 Mr Mole (IRE)[42] 4790 6-11-4 146..(t) APMcCoy 115+
(Paul Nicholls) mde all: awkward 6th: idling but wl in command after 3 out: hit last: nudged out 1/5[1]
2 3½ Master Mariner (IRE)[33] 10-10-5 0.................................. MrGTreacy(7) 100
(Paul Henderson) chsd wnr thrght: rdn after 3 out: flattered briefly 2 out but a being readily hld 10/1[3]
644- 3 9 Fuse Wire[20] 5177 7-10-12 0.. DaveCrosse 95
(Dai Burchell) wnt to s early: trckd ldrs: rdn after 4 out: mstke next: one pce after 6/1[2]
626- 4 79 Lady Bridget[38] 4885 6-9-12 79.....................................(tp) GaryDerwin(7) 5
(Mark Gillard) trckd ldng 4: pushed along after 7th: rdn whn lft 4th 4 out: wknd next: t.o 16/1
65F- U Dream Lucky[30] 5034 9-10-12 0.. ConorO'Farrell
(Richard Woollacott) trckd ldrs: pushed along in 4th whn blnd bdly and uns rdr 4 out 16/1

5m 28.8s (7.40) **Going Correction** +0.125s/f (Yiel) 5 Ran SP% 118.5
Speed ratings: **91,89,86,57,**
CSF £4.13 TOTE £1.10: £1.02, £4.70; EX 3.00 Trifecta £13.70.
Owner John P McManus **Bred** Mrs Hugh Baird **Trained** Ditcheat, Somerset

FOCUS
This was a disappointingly poor turnout, both in quantity and quality, in return for a good prize. The talented-but-quirky winner, the only runner with an official chase rating, made all at an ordinary pace that tested neither himself nor his opponents, culminating in a misleading result.

5552 INDEPENDENT RACECOURSES LTD, IRL H'CAP HURDLE (8 hdls) 2m 1f
7:25 (7:25) (Class 4) (0-120,119) 4-Y-0+ £3,508 (£1,030; £515; £257)

Form RPR
513- 1 Dovils Date[22] 5142 5-11-2 119.. AlanJohns(10) 122
(Tim Vaughan) a.p: led after 3 out: sn rdn: jnd between last 2: hld on wl: rdn out 15/2[3]
441- 2 nk Chalk It Down (IRE)[58] 4496 5-11-5 112.................................. APMcCoy 116+
(Warren Greatrex) trckd ldrs: rdn after 3 out: chal between ast 2: ev ch whn nt fluent last: kpt on 10/11[1]
253- 3 13 Pearls Legend[39] 4861 7-11-11 118...................................... JamieMoore 109
(John Spearing) trckd ldrs: chal 5th: rdn and ev ch after 3 out tl bef next: one pce after 12/1
/53- 4 1 Sambulando (FR)[27] 5072 11-10-4 100.......................(p) GilesHawkins(3) 91
(Richard Hobson) hld up in tch: rdn into 4th bef 2 out: nt pce to get involved 11/2[2]
066- 5 6 Who's Jeff (IRE)[65] 4351 6-9-13 99.............................. MrCGethings(7) 84
(Philip Hobbs) led by handler to s: racd keenly bhd ldrs: effrt after 3 out: sn btn 11/2[2]
200- 6 3¼ Tamarillo Grove (IRE)[242] 1400 7-10-9 107.................(t) CharlieWallis(5) 89
(Sophie Leech) led: nt fluent 2nd: rdn after 3 out: hdd bef next: wknd 16/1

605- 7 3½ **Marju's Quest (IRE)**[9] 5365 4-11-0 112............................ WillKennedy 86
(David Dennis) *in tch: rdn after 3 out: sn btn* **14/1**
4m 7.8s (2.10) **Going Correction** +0.275s/f (Yiel)
WFA 4 from 5yo+ 5lb **7** Ran SP% **115.2**
Speed ratings (Par 105): **106,105,99,99,96 94,93**
CSF £15.64 TOTE £11.60: £4.50, £1.10; EX 19.40 Trifecta £46.30.
Owner Itsfuninit **Bred** Cranford Stud **Trained** Aberthin, Vale of Glamorgan

FOCUS
Run at a medium pace, this was competitive despite the small field and the presence of an odds-on favourite, but the two most progressive runners had the finish between them.

5553 TOTNES AND BRIDGETOWN RACES COMPANY NOVICES' HUNTERS' CHASE (16 fncs) 2m 5f 110y
7:55 (7:56) (Class 6) 5-Y-0+ **£1,317** (£405; £202)

Form RPR
422- 1 **Bermuda Boy (FR)**[12] 5292 9-11-7 104.......................(t) MrPGerety(5) 106
(S Flook) *in tch: hit 4 out: rdn and chsd ldrs next: chal bnetween last 2: styd on wl to ld nring fin* **9/2**[2]
1U4- 2 nk **Double Bank (IRE)**[24] 5123 11-11-9 105................ MrMWoodward(7) 110
(Ms Emma Oliver) *led tl 2nd: trckd ldrs: led after 4 out: rdn after 3 out: kpt on but no ex whn hdd nring fin* **6/1**[3]
/12- 3 ¾ **Silver Token**[6] 9-12-2 114.......................................(tp) MrTomDavid 110+
(David Brace) *hld up: hdwy whn squeezed up on bnd after 10th: hdwy after 4 out: rdn after 3 out to chse ldrs: wnt 3rd last: styd on* **11/8**[1]
4 5 **Turtle Tim (IRE)**[12] 10-11-12 0...................................... MrWBiddick 100
(Miss S L Pidsley) *hld up: rdn and hdwy after 4 out: chse ldrs after next: styd on same pce* **12/1**
125- 5 4 **Numbercruncher (IRE)**[19] 8-11-9 105................. MrRobertHawker(7) 100
(Michael Hawker) *trckd ldrs: rdn and ev ch after 4 out tl bef last: styd on same pce* **6/1**[3]
P44/ 6 ¾ **What Er Say**[422] 4462 9-11-7 0....................................... MrADoyle(5) 95
(Mrs O Bush) *mid-div: effrt afer 4 out: one pce fr 2 out* **33/1**
7 2¾ **Shanann Star (IRE)**[12] 8-11-5 0................................... MrDEdwards 84
(Gordon Edwards) *mid-div: rdn after 4 out: wknd 2 out* **20/1**
6- 8 6 **Ladfromhighworth**[24] 5123 9-11-5 0............................. MissVWade(7) 85
(Mrs Camilla Scott) *mid-div: rdn after 4 out: wknd after next* **66/1**
2/ 9 ½ **Firmount Beech (IRE)**[19] 10-11-5 0........................ MrDIJAndrews(7) 85
(Mrs E Scott) *a towards rr* **50/1**
P/ U **Derniere Dance (FR)**[33] 9-11-9 0........................ MrRGHenderson(3)
(Miss C Prouse) *hld up: mstke and uns rdr 2nd* **33/1**
564/ F **Rajamand (FR)**[54] 8-11-5 109.......................................(p) MrDLordan(7)
(Miss Chloe Roddick) *led 2nd: j.rt at times: blnd 12th: rdn and hdd after 4 out: sn wknd bhd whn fell 2 out* **8/1**
454- B **Diamond Eclipse (IRE)**[33] 8-11-12 83................ MissLucyGardner
(Mrs E J Loosemore) *pressed ldr: hit 2nd: rdn after 4 out: sn wknd: bhd whn b.d 2 out* **33/1**
5m 27.4s (6.00) **Going Correction** +0.125s/f (Yiel) **12** Ran SP% **124.7**
Speed ratings: **94,93,93,91,90 90,89,86,86,**
CSF £31.52 TOTE £4.30: £1.10, £3.70, £1.20; EX 41.70 Trifecta £79.00.
Owner Foxhunters In Mind **Bred** Douglas McIntyre **Trained** Leominster, Herefordshire
■ Stewards' Enquiry : Mr P Gerety four-day ban: used whip above permitted level (May 12-15)

FOCUS
A fair pace for a hunter chase, with two front-runners taking one another on and the rest biding their time, ensured that the finish involved both prominent runners and hold-up performers.
T/Plt: £3.40 to a £1 stake. Pool: £48896.82 - 10320.53 winning tickets T/Qpdt: £2.00 to a £1 stake. Pool: £4022.66 - 1480.0 winning tickets TM

5531 PERTH (R-H)
Friday, April 25

OFFICIAL GOING: Soft (6.2)
Stands bend moved out on to fresh ground.
Wind: Almost nil Weather: Overcast

5554 CRABBIE'S ALCOHOLIC GINGER BEER "NATIONAL HUNT" MAIDEN HURDLE (8 hdls) 2m 110y
2:00 (2:01) (Class 4) 4-Y-0+ **£3,249** (£954; £477; £238)

Form RPR
020- 1 **Fond Memory (IRE)**[30] 5030 6-11-0 112................ SamTwiston-Davies 101+
(Nigel Twiston-Davies) *prom: smooth hdwy to ld 2 out: hit last: drvn out: eased towards fin* **4/7**[1]
2- 2 1¾ **Final Pass (IRE)**[13] 5286 6-11-0 0..................................... AdrianLane 95
(Donald McCain) *t.k.h: cl up: led 3rd: rdn and hdd 2 out: kpt on fr last: no ch w wnr* **7/2**[2]
000- 3 13 **Vision De La Vie (FR)**[19] 5190 4-10-6 0............................ TonyKelly(3) 77
(Pauline Robson) *hld up: stdy hdwy bef 3 out: rdn and outpcd bef next: styd on fr last: no ch w first two* **33/1**
20- 4 ½ **This Thyne Jude**[201] 1792 6-10-7 0.............................. PeterBuchanan 76
(Lucinda Russell) *hld up: shkn up and outpcd bef 2 out: kpt on steadily fr last: nvr nrr* **16/1**
/00- 5 ½ **Mr Mansson (IRE)**[117] 3392 7-11-0 68.................................. RyanMania 81
(Lucy Normile) *set stdy pce to 3rd: cl up: ev ch bef 2 out: sn rdn: wknd fr last* **66/1**
35F- 6 shd **Varene De Vauzelle (FR)**[18] 5205 5-11-0 0..................... BrianHughes 81
(James Ewart) *prom: rdn after 3 out: wknd fr next* **12/1**
000- 7 19 **Ceilidh (IRE)**[34] 4958 6-10-7 0..................................(t) LucyAlexander 55
(N W Alexander) *nt fluent in rr: struggling bef 3 out: sn btn* **40/1**
5- F **Where's Malachy (IRE)**[11] 5320 6-10-9 0........................ CraigNichol(5)
(Rose Dobbin) *prom tl rdn and wknd after 3 out: no ch whn fell next* **8/1**[3]
4m 0.5s (2.50) **Going Correction** +0.275s/f (Yiel)
WFA 4 from 5yo+ 5lb **8** Ran SP% **117.4**
Speed ratings (Par 105): **105,104,98,97,97 97,88,**
CSF £3.07 TOTE £2.00: £1.10, £1.20, £7.30; EX 3.30 Trifecta £67.00.
Owner The Stirling Partnership **Bred** C Kenneally **Trained** Naunton, Gloucs

FOCUS
After more light rain the ground was changed to soft. A maiden hurdle lacking any strength in depth and the pace was just steady to past halfway. The winner didn't need to be at his best.

5555 TURNING OUT QUALITY H'CAP CHASE (BETFAIR SCOTTISH CHASE SERIES QUALIFIER) (12 fncs) 2m
2:30 (2:30) (Class 3) (0-125,125) 5-Y-0+ **£7,147** (£2,098; £1,049; £524)

Form RPR
433- 1 **Inoogoo (IRE)**[41] 4815 9-10-6 105...................................(t) DannyCook 112
(Brian Ellison) *in tch: stdy hdwy 1/2-way: chsng ldrs whn hit 4 out: rallied and led bef 2 out: drvn and hld on wl fr last* **7/2**[2]
/24- 2 shd **Coeur De Fou (FR)**[342] 377 9-10-6 105.......................(p) AlainCawley 112
(Tom George) *hld up in tch: stdy hdwy 5 out: swtchd lft and chsd wnr 2 out: rdn and edgd rt bef last: kpt on wl towards fin: jst hld* **8/1**
411- 3 1½ **Baileys Concerto (IRE)**[6] 5380 8-10-8 107 7ex.............. JamesReveley 113
(Dianne Sayer) *hld up: stdy hdwy 5 out: nt fluent and outpcd 3 out: rallied bef last: swtchd lft run-in: kpt on: hld nr fin* **13/8**[1]
303- 4 8 **Lord Of Drums (IRE)**[11] 5318 8-10-5 104..................... PeterBuchanan 102
(Lucinda Russell) *pressed ldr and clr of rest to 1/2-way: effrt and ev ch bef 2 out: rdn and wknd bef last* **6/1**
P23- 5 23 **Wilde Pastures (IRE)**[21] 5163 9-11-5 125......................(p) DaleIrving(7) 111
(James Ewart) *led at decent gallop: rdn and hdd bef 2 out: sn wknd* **4/1**[3]
163- 6 33 **Strobe**[168] 2346 10-10-7 106......................................(p) DougieCostello 48
(Lucy Normile) *cl up: lost pl 4th: struggling fr 6th: t.o* **18/1**
3m 59.2s (2.20) **Going Correction** +0.325s/f (Yiel) **6** Ran SP% **111.0**
Speed ratings: **107,106,106,102,90 74**
CSF £27.85 CT £57.87 TOTE £4.40: £2.30, £4.70; EX 35.50 Trifecta £92.30.
Owner EBB Racing **Bred** Hugh Douglas **Trained** Norton, N Yorks

FOCUS
The two pacesetters took each other on and finished well beaten. The form is rated around the second and third.

5556 MCBOOKIE.COM LIVE CASINO H'CAP HURDLE (10 hdls) 2m 4f 110y
3:05 (3:05) (Class 5) (0-100,100) 4-Y-0+ **£3,249** (£954; £477; £238)

Form RPR
F60- 1 **King's Chorister**[51] 4615 8-9-11 76...............................(t) CraigNichol(5) 78
(Barry Murtagh) *hld up: hdwy and cl up 1/2-way: lft 2nd 4 out: led bef 2 out: drvn and hld on wl fr last* **5/1**[2]
0P0- 2 1¼ **Amethyst Rose (IRE)**[43] 4774 7-10-12 86.......................... RyanMania 86
(Stuart Coltherd) *hld up: hdwy and in tch 3 out: effrt appr next: chsd wnr bef last: kpt on run-in* **11/1**
32P- 3 ¾ **Indigo Island (IRE)**[25] 5107 5-10-9 90......................(p) CallumBewley(7) 89
(Robert Bewley) *t.k.h: hld up: hdwy bef 3 out: effrt and ev ch next: kpt on run-in* **18/1**
60P- 4 1¼ **Master Cynk**[77] 4132 7-11-12 100...................................... AlainCawley 100
(Tom George) *hld up in tch: stdy hdwy and ev ch whn hit 2 out: rdn and one pce fr last* **10/1**
5/5- 5 6 **De Bee Keeper (IRE)**[211] 1665 6-11-7 95....................... PeterBuchanan 87
(Lucinda Russell) *hld up: stdy hdwy whn checked 4 out: rdn after next: styd on fr 2 out: nvr rchd ldrs* **5/1**[2]
04P- 6 4 **Marlee Massie (IRE)**[43] 4774 5-10-1 75.......................(p) LucyAlexander 63
(N W Alexander) *bhd: drvn and outpcd 1/2-way: kpt on u.p fr 2 out: n.d* **40/1**
132- 7 1 **Oh Right (IRE)**[33] 4984 10-9-13 78...............................(b) EmmaSayer(5) 65
(Dianne Sayer) *cl up: drvn after 4 out: wknd bef 2 out* **7/1**[3]
1U4- 8 6 **Cumbrian Farmer**[59] 4475 7-10-11 90....................(t) JonathonBewley(5) 71
(George Bewley) *in tch on outside: lost pl 1/2-way: sn struggling: n.d after* **16/1**
F60- 9 ¾ **Grey Area (IRE)**[66] 4338 9-11-5 100.................................. DaleIrving(7) 80
(Tristan Davidson) *led: mstke 3 out: hdd bef next: sn btn* **10/1**
404- F **Indepub**[17] 5217 5-11-0 88..(v[1]) DannyCook
(Martin Todhunter) *w ldr: fell 4 out* **11/1**
233- U **Scimon Templar (FR)**[18] 5212 6-11-4 95............................. TonyKelly(3)
(Pauline Robson) *in tch: gng wl whn hmpd and uns rdr 4 out* **7/2**[1]
5m 8.7s (6.70) **Going Correction** +0.275s/f (Yiel) **11** Ran SP% **116.5**
Speed ratings (Par 103): **98,97,97,96,94 92,92,90,90,**
CSF £57.96 CT £917.05 TOTE £6.70: £2.00, £3.80, £3.00; EX 56.60 Trifecta £694.40.
Owner Woodgate Partnership **Bred** Cheveley Park Stud Ltd **Trained** Low Braithwaite, Cumbria

FOCUS
Again the pace was generous given the underfoot conditions. The first four jumped the second-last flight almost in a line. The winner should still be well in when reassessed.

5557 OUT OF ORDINARY INVESTMENT CUP NOVICES' LIMITED H'CAP CHASE (15 fncs) 2m 4f 110y
3:35 (3:35) (Class 3) (0-140,133) 5-Y-0+ **£7,797** (£2,289; £1,144; £572)

Form RPR
11P- 1 **Dare To Endeavour**[41] 4819 7-11-8 133............................. AlainCawley 142+
(Tom George) *mde all: rdn bef 2 out: styd on wl run-in* **3/1**[2]
120- 2 2¼ **Bar De Ligne (FR)**[41] 4806 8-11-7 132...............(p) SamTwiston-Davies 138
(Steve Gollings) *prom: hdwy to chse wnr 5 out: effrt bef 2 out: kpt on fr last: no imp* **5/2**[1]
3F2- 3 2¾ **Robbie**[28] 5054 10-11-5 130... JamesReveley 134
(Keith Reveley) *hld up: hdwy and cl up bef 4 out: rdn next: kpt on same pce fr 2 out* **5/1**[3]
321- 4 1¼ **Un Guet Apens (FR)**[17] 5213 6-11-8 133.......................(p) BrianHughes 135
(James Ewart) *chsd ldrs: drvn and outpcd bef 3 out: kpt on fr last: no imp* **5/2**[1]
U10- 5 18 **Suprise Vendor (IRE)**[17] 4549 8-10-5 123.................. DaraghBourke(7) 113
(Stuart Coltherd) *pressed ldr: mstke and lost 2nd 5 out: wknd next: btn whn hit 3 out* **9/1**
5m 11.0s (6.00) **Going Correction** +0.325s/f (Yiel) **5** Ran SP% **108.8**
Speed ratings: **101,100,99,98,91**
CSF £10.80 TOTE £4.40: £1.80, £1.70; EX 12.00 Trifecta £42.10.
Owner J B Property Developments (Midlands) Ltd **Bred** Direct Sales (uk) Ltd **Trained** Slad, Gloucs

FOCUS
A decent handicap. The winner is rated back on the upgrade.

5558 G A ENGINEERING HIGHLAND NATIONAL H'CAP CHASE (FOR THE JULIAN LLEWELYN PALMER MEMORIAL TROPHY) (23 fncs) 3m 7f
4:10 (4:10) (Class 3) (0-125,124) 5-Y-0+ **£12,996** (£3,816; £1,908; £954)

Form RPR
356- 1 **Bertie Milan (IRE)**[79] 4086 9-10-0 98 oh2...................... LucyAlexander 112+
(N W Alexander) *chsd ldrs: led 14th: mde rest: hrd pressed fr 4 out: styd on wl u.p fr last* **15/2**

3U3- **2** *3* **Hidden Horizons (IRE)**[33] 4997 8-10-12 **117**..............(p) AnthonyFox(7) 126
(S R B Crawford, Ire) *hld up in midfield: stdy hdwy to chal after 5 out: rdn 3 out: kpt on same pce fr last* **13/2**[3]

302- **3** *14* **Royale Knight**[34] 4968 8-11-12 **124**........................ TomO'Brien 120
(Dr Richard Newland) *prom: effrt and rdn after 4 out: outpcd by first two fr next* **11/2**[2]

621- **4** *6* **Mister Philson (IRE)**[33] 4997 9-10-6 **109**......................(p) CraigNichol(5) 98
(S R B Crawford, Ire) *in tch: drvn along after 5 out: outpcd fr 3 out* **20/1**

433- **5** *24* **Indigo Rock (IRE)**[28] 5060 8-11-5 **117**.......................... BrianHughes 82
(Malcolm Jefferson) *towards rr: pushed along 1/2-way: hdwy and in tch 17th: rdn and wknd fr 3 out* **9/1**

416- **U** **Heez A Steel (IRE)**[9] 5358 13-9-11 **102** ow2................ AlistairFindlay(7)
(Jane Walton) *in tch on outside: lost pl and struggling whn blnd and uns rdr 17th* **20/1**

2UU- **P** **Five Star Wilsham (IRE)**[52] 4601 10-11-5 **117**...(p) SamTwiston-Davies
(Nigel Twiston-Davies) *t.k.h: hld up: hdwy to ld 6th: hdd 14th: cl up tl wknd bef 4 out: lost tch and p.u bef next* **9/2**[1]

362- **P** **Neptune Equester**[34] 4954 11-11-6 **118**.............................. RyanMania
(Sandy Thomson) *bhd: mstke 2nd: struggling fr 1/2-way: t.o whn p.u bef 4 out* **12/1**

42P- **P** **Nodebateaboutit**[30] 5032 9-10-13 **111**............................(tp) AlainCawley
(Tom George) *bhd and nvr gng wl: lost tch and p.u after 17th* **7/1**

P2F- **P** **Wild Geese (IRE)**[212] 1659 7-11-8 **120**........................(p) PeterBuchanan
(Lucinda Russell) *bhd: struggling fr 1/2-way: t.o whn p.u bef 5 out* **25/1**

/14- **F** **Gotoyourplay (IRE)**[24] 5119 10-11-12 **124**...................... DenisO'Regan
(Venetia Williams) *t.k.h: in tch: outpcd and drvn whn fell 5 out* **16/1**

141- **P** **Tarraco (FR)**[31] 5025 7-10-9 **112**.............................. CallumWhillans(5)
(Venetia Williams) *prom: drvn and outpcd 15th: struggling 18th: t.o whn p.u bef 4 out* **9/1**

8m 7.8s (17.80) **Going Correction** +0.325s/f (Yiel) 12 Ran SP% **118.1**
Speed ratings: **90,89,85,84,77** , , , , ,
CSF £54.59 CT £293.48 TOTE £9.70: £4.20, £3.30, £1.30; EX 77.10 Trifecta £619.00.
Owner Turcan Barber Douglas Miller Dunning **Bred** Brian Curley **Trained** Kinneston, Perth & Kinross

FOCUS
The Highland National proved a severe test and just getting round proved difficult. Probably not a race to get carried away with.

5559 BET ON ALL NON LEAGUE AT MCBOOKIE.COM CONDITIONAL JOCKEYS' H'CAP HURDLE (20 hdls) 3m 3f
4:45 (4:46) (Class 3) (0-130,121) 4-Y-0+ **£5,848** (£1,717; £858; £429)

Form RPR

241- **1** **Sybarite (FR)**[65] 4356 8-11-4 **116**.............................. RyanHatch(3) 125+
(Nigel Twiston-Davies) *hld up: hdwy bef 4 out: drvn and outpcd bef next: rallied after 3 out: led between last 2: styd on strly fr last* **3/1**[1]

21P- **2** *6* **Jaunty Journey**[10] 5334 11-10-13 **108**...........................(v) MichealNolan 110
(Nigel Twiston-Davies) *led: qcknd clr after 9th: rdn and hdd between last 2: kpt on same pce fr last* **12/1**

216- **3** *4* **Hellorboston (IRE)**[34] 4954 6-11-9 **121**..........................(b) NickSlatter(3) 120
(Donald McCain) *hld up: hdwy and prom bef 3 out: effrt and rdn bef next: sn one pce* **10/1**

323- **4** *11* **Bollin Fiona**[25] 5106 10-10-5 **100**................................ CallumWhillans 87
(Donald Whillans) *hld up: rdn bef 4 out: hdwy after next: no imp fr 2 out* **12/1**

244- **5** *nk* **Perfect Candidate (IRE)**[56] 4537 7-11-10 **119**............ ConorShoemark 107
(Fergal O'Brien) *hld up: hdwy to chse clr ldr 4 out: rdn and hung rt bef 2 out: sn outpcd: hld whn nt fluent last* **9/1**

130- **6** *14* **Ryton Runner (IRE)**[2] 5514 6-10-9 **104**..........................(p) CraigNichol 76
(Lucinda Russell) *hld up in tch: drvn and outpcd after 4 out: struggling fr next* **6/1**[2]

25P- **7** *5* **Los Nadis (GER)**[49] 4650 10-11-1 **115**............................ DaleIrving(5) 82
(Jim Goldie) *bhd: drvn and outpcd after 4 out: nvr on terms* **16/1**

350- **8** *42* **Magic Present**[55] 4553 7-10-3 **105**...............................(b) JakeHolliday(7) 30
(Malcolm Jefferson) *hld up in tch: hdwy to chse ldr 1/2-way to 4 out: rdn and struggling fr next: t.o* **9/1**

P02- **F** **Solis (GER)**[23] 4771 11-10-2 **100**.............................. CallumBewley(3)
(Dianne Sayer) *hld up on ins: rdn whn fell 9th* **20/1**

215- **P** **Bescot Springs (IRE)**[14] 5256 9-11-3 **115**.............(b) GrahamWatters(3)
(Lucinda Russell) *hld up in tch: struggling after 4 out: t.o whn p.u bef 2 out* **13/2**[3]

445- **P** **Merrydown Vintage (IRE)**[60] 4461 7-9-7 **95** oh3...(p) JonathanMoore(7)
(S R B Crawford, Ire) *prom: rdn along 9th: wknd next: t.o whn p.u bef 2 out* **8/1**

6m 44.5s (2.50) **Going Correction** +0.275s/f (Yiel) 11 Ran SP% **118.8**
Speed ratings (Par 107): **107,105,104,100,100 96,95,82,** ,
CSF £39.59 CT £327.02 TOTE £3.20: £1.30, £2.70, £2.90; EX 24.00 Trifecta £154.00.
Owner H R Mould **Bred** Mme Andre Vagne And Bruno Vagne **Trained** Naunton, Gloucs

FOCUS
The leader set an unremitting pace and this proved a severe test of stamina. The winner rates in line with his hurdles best.

5560 GO TO BALCORMO RACES TOMORROW STANDARD OPEN NATIONAL HUNT FLAT RACE 2m 110y
5:20 (5:20) (Class 5) 4-6-Y-0 **£2,053** (£598; £299)

Form RPR

1 **Looking Well (IRE)** 5-11-3 0.................................... BrianHarding 104
(Nicky Richards) *hld up: hdwy over 4f out: effrt and rn green 2f out: styd on wl fnl f to ld cl home* **15/2**

2- **2** *shd* **Major Ivan (IRE)**[34] 4958 5-11-3 0................................ BrianHughes 104
(Malcolm Jefferson) *midfield: smooth hdwy over 3f out: led and rdn 2f out: sn edgd rt: kpt on fnl f: hdd cl home* **3/1**[2]

3 *3 ½* **The Way It Works (IRE)** 4-10-0 0................................ DerekFox(5) 89
(Lucinda Russell) *hld up: stdy hdwy 4f out: shkn up 2f out: rdn and kpt on ins fnl f* **11/2**[3]

4 *nk* **Melbourne Lady**[371] 5396 6-10-10 0................................ AlainCawley 93
(P Fegan, Ire) *in tch: effrt and drvn over 2f out: one pce over 1f out* **25/1**

5- **5** *4 ½* **Wish In A Well (IRE)**[13] 5279 5-11-0 0........................ MrSCrawford(3) 97
(S R B Crawford, Ire) *t.k.h: prom: led over 3f out to 2f out: sn rdn and outpcd* **5/2**[1]

6 *10* **Mixboy (FR)** 4-10-5 0...[1] DaleIrving(7) 81
(James Ewart) *t.k.h: w ldrs tl rdn and wknd over 2f out* **14/1**

1- **7** *4 ½* **Clan Chief**[64] 4370 5-11-3 0.................................... MrKitAlexander(7) 88
(N W Alexander) *unruly to post: chsd ldrs tl rdn and wknd over 2f out* **11/2**[3]

05- **8** *5* **Alwaysrecommended (IRE)**[25] 5108 5-10-10 0.......... AlistairFindlay(7) 76
(Jane Walton) *t.k.h: led to over 3f out: sn rdn and wknd* **80/1**

00- **9** *3* **Bracing**[134] 3042 5-10-10 0.. LucyAlexander 66
(N W Alexander) *hld up: drvn along over 3f out: nvr on terms* **50/1**

10 *4 ½* **Solway Summer** 5-10-7 0.. EwanWhillans(3) 62
(Lisa Harrison) *in tch: rdn 1/2-way: wknd over 4f out* **66/1**

11 *10* **Quietude** 4-10-12 0...(t) SamTwiston-Davies 54
(Nigel Twiston-Davies) *bhd: drvn 1/2-way: struggling over 4f out: styd on wl* **10/1**

05- **12** *2* **Queens Regatta (IRE)**[50] 4631 5-10-5 0........................ CraigNichol(5) 50
(Bruce Mactaggart) *in tch on outside tl rdn and wknd over 4f out* **150/1**

3m 58.4s (6.00) **Going Correction** +0.275s/f (Yiel)
WFA 4 from 5yo+ 5lb 12 Ran SP% **121.1**
Speed ratings: **96,95,94,94,92 87,85,82,81,79 74,73**
CSF £30.53 TOTE £13.00: £4.30, £1.70, £2.30; EX 50.60 Trifecta £266.20.
Owner David Wesley Yates **Bred** J S Cullen **Trained** Greystoke, Cumbria
■ Stewards' Enquiry : Brian Hughes caution: careless riding.

FOCUS
A bumper run at a sound pace throughout and the first five home came clear of the remainder. The second and fourth set the level.
T/Plt: £144.90 to a £1 stake. Pool: £66390.26 - 334.36 winning tickets T/Qpdt: £43.00 to a £1 stake. Pool: £5042.66 - 86.70 winning tickets RY

5561 - 5567a (Foreign Racing) - See Raceform Interactive

4679 SANDOWN (R-H)
Saturday, April 26

OFFICIAL GOING: Good to soft (soft in places on hurdle course; chs 6.8, hdl 6.6)
Traditionally a mixed card, but now an enhanced all-jumps finale to the season.
Wind: Light to medium; half behind Weather: Dry; bright spells

5568 BET365 JUVENILE H'CAP HURDLE (8 hdls) 2m 110y
2:05 (2:05) (Class 2) 4-Y-O
£18,768 (£5,544; £2,772; £1,386; £693; £348)

Form RPR

460- **1** **Dispour (IRE)**[23] 5132 4-11-8 **131**..(b) APMcCoy 130+
(Donald McCain) *racd keenly: chsd ldr: nt fluent 3 out: drvn to ld btn last 2: clr flat: a holding on: drvn out* **14/1**

254- **2** *½* **Sleepy Haven (IRE)**[20] 5190 4-10-13 **122**........................(t) SeanQuinlan 120+
(Jennie Candlish) *hld up in tch in midfield: effrt bef 2 out: shifting rt but hdwy to go 3rd whn j. slowly and lft last: chsd clr wnr flat: styd on wl and steadily clsng fnl 150yds: nvr quite getting to wnr* **25/1**

111- **3** *3* **Saint Jerome (IRE)**[16] 5227 4-11-12 **135**............................ NoelFehily 129
(Jamie Osborne) *j.w: led: rdn and hdd after 2 out: styd on same pce after: lost 2nd flat* **10/1**

424- **4** *1* **Keltus (FR)**[45] 4755 4-11-8 **131**.................................. NickScholfield 124
(Paul Nicholls) *wl in tch in midfield: rdn and effrt to chse ldrs 2 out: unable qck between last 2: styd on same pce flat* **13/2**[2]

442- **5** *shd* **Dolores Delightful (FR)**[35] 4963 4-10-5 **114**................ RichardJohnson 107
(Nick Williams) *in tch in midfield: mstke 5th: hdwy to chse ldrs 3 out: rdn: fnd little and outpcd after 2 out: no threat to wnr but plugged on again flat* **5/1**[1]

14P- **6** *hd* **Ballyglasheen (IRE)**[45] 4755 4-11-12 **135**........................ PaulMoloney 129
(Evan Williams) *mstkes: in rr: pushed along after 5th: hdwy 2 out: 8th last: styd on strly flat: nvr trbld ldrs* **33/1**

161- **7** *1* **Raven's Tower (USA)**[27] 5090 4-11-11 **134**........................ DavidBass 126
(Ben Pauling) *hld up in tch in rr: effrt on inner bef 2 out: no imp between last 2: styd on same pce flat* **12/1**

533- **8** *1 ¼* **Ronaldinho (IRE)**[27] 5090 4-10-12 **121**..................(b) WayneHutchinson 114
(Alan King) *hld up wl in tch in midfield: mstke 3 out: effrt to chse ldrs next: no ex bef last: wknd flat* **9/1**

161- **9** *1 ¼* **Stiff Upper Lip (IRE)**[6] 5403 4-10-8 **122** 5ex............... ThomasGarner(5) 112
(Oliver Sherwood) *wl in tch in midfield: rdn and lost pl wl bef 2 out: no threat to ldrs but plugged on flat* **7/1**[3]

25F- **10** *8* **Baradari (IRE)**[23] 5132 4-11-11 **134**.............................. AidanColeman 119
(Venetia Williams) *chsd ldrs: mstke 4th: rdn and lost pl bef 2 out: wknd between last 2* **8/1**

11 *11* **Vodka Wells (FR)**[85] 4-11-5 **128**..[1] BarryGeraghty 101
(Brian Ellison) *wl in tch in midfield: effrt bef 2 out: sn no imp: wknd between last 2* **8/1**

225- **12** *9* **Stephen Hero (IRE)**[108] 3599 4-10-10 **119**....................(tp) HarrySkelton 87
(Dan Skelton) *in tch towards rr: effrt on inner but no real hdwy bef 2 out: wknd between last 2: wl bhd flat* **11/1**

634- **13** *3 ¾* **Fitzwilly**[7] 4963 4-11-7 **130**.. GavinSheehan 98
(Mick Channon) *in tch in midfield tl dropped to rr 3rd: nvr gng wl after: wl btn between last 2: t.o* **20/1**

4m 1.5s (-5.70) **Going Correction** -0.10s/f (Good) 13 Ran SP% **118.1**
Speed ratings: **109,108,107,106,106 106,106,105,105,101 96,91,90**
CSF £314.33 CT £3621.55 TOTE £15.60: £5.20, £6.90, £3.20; EX 390.30 Trifecta £1619.20 Part won..
Owner Paul & Clare Rooney **Bred** His Highness The Aga Khan's Studs S C **Trained** Cholmondeley, Cheshire

FOCUS
The ground looked to have dried out a little from the previous day and the time of this opening contest suggested it was just on the slow side. A good, competitive juvenile handicap that was run at a fair gallop, not the breakneck one anticipated. The winner built on his decent Aintree run.

5569 BET365 OAKSEY CHASE (LISTED RACE) 2m 6f
2:40 (2:40) (Class 1) 5-Y-0+ **£28,475** (£10,685; £5,350; £2,665; £1,340)

Form RPR

P05- **1** **Menorah (IRE)**[23] 5133 9-11-10 161.............................. RichardJohnson 172+
(Philip Hobbs) *a travelling wl and j.w: trckd ldrs tl wnt 2nd 11th: jnd ldr next: j. into ld 15th: readily wnt clr 3 out: pushed out: easily* **11/4**[2]

P33- **2** *17* **Gullinbursti (IRE)**[21] 5170 8-11-0 142..........................(v) AidanColeman 147
(Emma Lavelle) *led: jnd and nt fluent 12th: outj. and hdd 15th: drvn after 17th: no ch w wnr fr next: plugged on u.p for clr 2nd* **9/2**[3]

340- **3** *6* **Hunt Ball (IRE)**[21] 5171 9-11-4 155................................ BarryGeraghty 147
(Nicky Henderson) *nt a fluent early: hld up wl in tch: wnt 3rd 16th: effrt and c wd bef 3 out: no imp on wnr: 3rd and wl hld whn j. slowly last* **2/1**[1]

2P2- **4** *8* **Rolling Aces (IRE)**[22] 5155 8-11-10 156......................(tp) NickScholfield 143
(Paul Nicholls) *chsd ldr tl 11th: 4th and struggling whn mstke 15th: wknd u.p bef 3 out* **11/4**[2]

021- **5** *14* **Maggio (FR)**[56] 4552 9-11-10 143.......................................(t) BrianHughes 131
(Patrick Griffin, Ire) *trckd ldrs tl dropped to rr after 13th: struggling and rdn 15th: wknd after next: t.o* **20/1**

5m 44.4s **Going Correction** +0.05s/f (Yiel) **5** Ran SP% **109.6**
Speed ratings: **102,95,93,90,85**
CSF £14.59 TOTE £3.60: £2.10, £2.30; EX 13.20 Trifecta £59.70.
Owner Mrs Diana L Whateley **Bred** Mrs E Grant And Miss Anna Brislane **Trained** Withycombe, Somerset
■ The first running of this Listed chase.

FOCUS
This looked a tight affair but the winner proved in a different class. The winner was back to the level of his final run last season.

5570 BET365 CELEBRATION CHASE (GRADE 1) (13 fncs) 2m
3:15 (3:16) (Class 1) 5-Y-0+

£71,187 (£26,712; £13,375; £6,662; £3,350; £1,675)

Form RPR

111- **1** **Sire De Grugy (FR)**[45] 4753 8-11-7 171............................... JamieMoore 159+
(Gary Moore) *in tch: hdwy to trck ldrs and travelling wl 8th: upsides ldr after 3 out: led and rdr looking arnd between last 2: j. sltly lft last: rdn and readily asserted flat: rdn out* **2/7**[1]

016- **2** *3 ¼* **Pepite Rose (FR)**[22] 5155 7-11-0 154.............................. AidanColeman 147
(Venetia Williams) *chsd ldrs tl wnt 2nd 4th: led 3 out: clr w wnr next: rdn and hdd between last 2: sltly hmpd last: outpcd by wnr but battled on to hold 2nd flat* **9/1**[3]

346- **3** *1 ½* **Special Tiara**[45] 4753 7-11-7 155... AELynch 152
(Henry De Bromhead, Ire) *led tl hdd 3 out: rdn and outpcd whn mstke next: kpt on same pce u.p flat* **7/1**[2]

160- **4** *2 ½* **Lancetto (FR)**[43] 4790 9-11-7 140.. AdamWedge 150
(Evan Williams) *hld up in tch in last trio: effrt and cl enough 3 out: wnt 4th and styd on same pce fr bef 2 out* **50/1**

050- **5** *9* **French Opera**[22] 5155 11-11-7 154.................................... BarryGeraghty 143
(Nicky Henderson) *in tch in rr: moved wdr than rivals in bk st: struggling 8th: rdn and btn bef 3 out: wknd bef 2 out* **12/1**

50U- **6** *3 ¾* **Kauto Stone (FR)**[22] 5156 8-11-7 142..................(t[1]) SamTwiston-Davies 142
(Paul Nicholls) *chsd ldr tl 4th: styd chsng ldrs tl 4th and struggling 3 out: wknd bef next* **20/1**

3m 56.1s (-5.70) **Going Correction** +0.05s/f (Yiel) **6** Ran SP% **114.7**
Speed ratings: **116,114,113,112,107 106**
CSF £4.29 TOTE £1.30: £1.20, £1.70; EX 3.20 Trifecta £10.20.
Owner The Preston Family & Friends Ltd **Bred** La Grugerie **Trained** Lower Beeding, W Sussex

FOCUS
A race carrying Grade 1 status for the first time, but it was a weak contest for the level and lacked depth. Sire De Grugy is rated a stone off his best, with the second and third around 7lb off.

5571 BET365 GOLD CUP CHASE (H'CAP) (GRADE 3) (24 fncs) 3m 5f 110y
3:50 (3:51) (Class 1) 5-Y-0+

£85,425 (£32,055; £16,050; £7,995; £4,020; £2,010)

Form RPR

U10- **1** **Hadrian's Approach (IRE)**[46] 4738 7-11-0 **146**...........(p) BarryGeraghty 155
(Nicky Henderson) *hld up in tch: hdwy 17th: rdn to chse ldr bef 2 out: hrd drvn to ld flat: styd on wl: drvn out* **10/1**[3]

02U- **2** *¾* **Burton Port (IRE)**[21] 5171 10-10-9 **141**..............................(p) APMcCoy 149
(Jonjo O'Neill) *travelled strly: chsd ldrs: wnt 2nd 14th tl led 3 out: rdn between last 2: drvn and hdd flat: kpt on gamely but a hld fnl 100yds* **8/1**[1]

PP2- **3** *2 ½* **Godsmejudge (IRE)**[14] 5276 8-10-13 **145**................. WayneHutchinson 152
(Alan King) *in tch in midfield: hdwy to chse ldrs 6th: fiddled 13th and rdr briefly unbalanced: rdn and effrt after 21st: chsd ldng pair between last 2: styd on but no impon ldng pair flat* **10/1**[3]

510- **4** *hd* **Restless Harry**[46] 4738 10-11-0 **146**.................................... CharliePoste 154
(Robin Dickin) *in tch in midfield: mstke 4th and 16th: rdn 18th: hdwy bef 3 out: chsd ldng trio between last 2: styd on but no imp on ldng pair flat* **20/1**

201- **5** *12* **Spring Heeled (IRE)**[44] 4769 7-11-3 **149**........................(p) DavyRussell 146
(J H Culloty, Ire) *chsd ldr tl 3rd: styd prom tl losing pl and rdn 17th: lost tch w ldrs after 21st: n.d but styd on past btn rivals fr 2 out* **12/1**

145- **6** *6* **Summery Justice (IRE)**[14] 5276 10-10-2 **134**................ LiamTreadwell 128
(Venetia Williams) *mstkes: in rr: mstke 11th: reminders after 13th: wl bhd 21st: styd on past btn horses fr 2 out: n.d* **25/1**

31P- **7** *nk* **Roalco De Farges (FR)**[14] 5276 9-10-3 **135**................ RichardJohnson 125
(Philip Hobbs) *hld up in tch towards rr: stdy prog 15th: 3rd and rdn wl bef 3 out: 5th and btn between last 2: fdd flat* **8/1**[1]

4P2- **8** *3 ½* **Poungach (FR)**[47] 4732 8-10-6 138..................................(b) RyanMahon 124
(Paul Nicholls) *in tch in midfield: mstke 3rd: rdn and struggling 17th: no threat to ldrs but plugged on fr 3 out* **14/1**

26U- **9** *4 ½* **Carruthers**[21] 5170 11-10-13 **148**.............................(t) NicodeBoinville[(3)] 130
(Mark Bradstock) *pushed along and hdwy to chse ldr 3rd tl 14th: styd prom tl rdn and btn after 21st: wknd next* **25/1**

134- **10** *14* **Bally Legend**[10] 5350 9-10-12 **144**... IanPopham 118
(Caroline Keevil) *in tch in midfield: rdn 20th: struggling and btn after next: wknd after 3 out: t.o* **25/1**

251- **11** *21* **Ardkilly Witness (IRE)**[20] 5192 8-10-4 **136**......................... TomO'Brien 97
(Dr Richard Newland) *in tch in midfield: clsd to chse ldrs 17th: cl 4th 21st: rdn and btn bef 2 out: fading whn bmpd last: eased flat: t.o* **8/1**[1]

F05- **12** *7* **Opening Batsman (IRE)**[56] 4552 8-10-8 **140**............(b[1]) NickScholfield 84
(Harry Fry) *racd keenly: led tl 3 out: sn rdn and btn: fading whn bmpd last: eased flat: t.o* **33/1**

24F- **13** *19* **Midnight Appeal**[14] 5276 9-10-9 **141**...............................(b) JamieMoore 68
(Alan King) *in tch towards rr: hdwy 14th: rdn and effrt 18th: btn 3 out: eased fr next: t.o* **16/1**

/1P- **P** **Rigadin De Beauchene (FR)**[14] 5276 9-10-12 **147**...... RobertDunne[(3)]
(Venetia Williams) *in tch in midfield: dropped to rr and rdn w no rspnse 12th: tailing off whn p.u after next* **33/1**

01F- **P** **Rose Of The Moon (IRE)**[21] 5171 9-10-4 **139**...........(p) JakeGreenall[(3)]
(David O'Meara) *in tch in midfield: rdn and lost pl after 13th: bhd 16th: t.o whn p.u 3 out* **20/1**

306- **U** **Houblon Des Obeaux (FR)**[23] 5133 7-11-12 **158**........... AidanColeman
(Venetia Williams) *midfield whn stmbld and uns rdr 1st* **20/1**

12P- **P** **Emperor's Choice (IRE)**[42] 4821 7-10-2 **134**............... TomScudamore
(Venetia Williams) *mstkes: a bhd: tailing off whn p.u 14th* **33/1**

0P5- **P** **Same Difference (IRE)**[44] 4769 8-10-5 **137**........(v) SamTwiston-Davies
(Nigel Twiston-Davies) *chsd ldrs: mstke 6th: rdn and lost pl rapidly after 13th: tailing off whn p.u next* **8/1**[1]

R12- **P** **Bury Parade (IRE)**[63] 4422 8-11-10 **156**................................. NoelFehily
(Paul Nicholls) *in tch towards rr: struggling 15th: lost tch 18th: t.o whn p.u 3 out* **9/1**[2]

7m 35.1s (-8.90) **Going Correction** +0.05s/f (Yiel) **19** Ran SP% **127.5**
Speed ratings: **113,112,112,112,108 107,107,106,105,101 95,93,88,, , , ,**
CSF £78.58 CT £837.01 TOTE £15.30: £4.00, £2.20, £2.90, £5.50; EX 104.30 Trifecta £1662.20.

Owner Mr & Mrs R Kelvin-Hughes **Bred** Marie Gavin **Trained** Upper Lambourn, Berks
■ Stewards' Enquiry : Barry Geraghty nine-day ban: used whip above permitted level (May 10-18); Fine: £3,150.

FOCUS
A wide-open running of this end-of-season staying handicap. The first three are rated pretty much to their marks in a solid renewal.

5572 BET365 SELECT HURDLE (LISTED RACE) (11 hdls) 2m 6f
4:25 (4:26) (Class 1) 4-Y-0+ **£28,475** (£10,685; £5,350; £2,665; £1,340)

Form RPR

352- **1** **Southfield Theatre (IRE)**[44] 4765 6-11-0 150........ SamTwiston-Davies 148+
(Paul Nicholls) *mde all: clr tl 5th: mstke 7th and wl clr: edgd lft towards stands' rail bef 2 out: edgd bk rt u.p and hrd pressed last: flashed tail but battled on v gamely flat: all out* **15/8**[1]

511- **2** *shd* **Polly Peachum (IRE)**[9] 5370 6-10-11 150.......................... BarryGeraghty 143
(Nicky Henderson) *hld up in last pair: mstke 4th: clsd and wl in tch next: swtchd rt bef 2 out effrt to chal last: styd on wl u.p: jst hld* **10/3**[3]

0/0- **3** *2* **Clerk's Choice (IRE)**[45] 4752 8-11-0 145......................... TrevorWhelan 145
(William Jarvis) *chsd ldrs: clsd and wl in tch 5th: chsd ldr and nt fluent 2 out: stl ev ch last: no ex and one pce fnl 150yds* **28/1**

301- **4** *4* **Clondaw Kaempfer (IRE)**[22] 5158 6-11-4 144......................... APMcCoy 145
(Donald McCain) *hld up in rr: clsd and wl in tch 5th: effrt between last 2: no imp last: kpt on* **9/2**

220- **5** *4 ½* **Medinas (FR)**[44] 4767 7-11-4 154................................ WayneHutchinson 143
(Alan King) *chsd wnr: clsd 5th: lost 2nd: rdn and swtchd rt bef 2 out: outpcd and lost whn mstke last: wknd flat* **5/2**[2]

5m 24.7s (-5.30) **Going Correction** -0.10s/f (Good) **5** Ran SP% **108.1**
Speed ratings (Par 111): **105,104,104,102,101**
CSF £8.18 TOTE £2.70: £1.30, £1.80; EX 6.90 Trifecta £49.80.
Owner Mrs Angela Yeoman **Bred** Mrs Angela Yeoman **Trained** Ditcheat, Somerset
■ A new Listed event.

FOCUS
In what looked such a tight Listed hurdle, there was always a good chance the several-length lead Southfield Theatre was gifted at the start would prove decisive. The winner is rated 4lb off his best.

5573 BET365 JOSH GIFFORD NOVICES' H'CAP CHASE (17 fncs) 2m 4f 110y
5:00 (5:00) (Class 2) 5-Y-0+

£18,768 (£5,544; £2,772; £1,386; £693; £348)

Form RPR

011- **1** **Ballincurrig (IRE)**[13] 5290 8-10-8 **122**.................................(t) HarrySkelton 129
(Dan Skelton) *travelled strly and j.w: trckd ldrs fr 5th tl led 3 out: rdn between last 2: idling: drvn and turned hd towards rival whn jnd flat: sn hdd: battled bk u.p and led again towards fin: drvn out* **11/2**[3]

25P- **2** *nk* **Christopher Wren (USA)**[12] 4768 7-11-0 **128**..................(p) TomCannon 134
(Nick Gifford) *hld up in tch in rr: hdwy to trck ldrs bef 3 out: chsd wnr sn after 2 out: rdn to chal flat: sn led: hdd and no ex towards fin* **16/1**

110- **3** *2 ½* **Sound Investment (IRE)**[23] 5136 6-11-9 **140**............(t) HarryDerham[(3)] 143
(Paul Nicholls) *chsd ldrs: mstke 2nd: mstke 3 out: wnt 3rd between last 2: styd on same pce u.p flat* **13/2**

132- **4** *13* **Kitegen (IRE)**[7] 5382 8-10-9 **123**... CharliePoste 117
(Robin Dickin) *in tch in midfield: rdn 11th: clsd and jnd ldrs whn mstke 3 out: 2nd and drvn next: wknd between last 2* **8/1**

243- **5** *shd* **De Blacksmith (IRE)**[5] 5456 6-10-6 **120**...........................(b[1]) JamieMoore 115
(Gary Moore) *mstkes: in tch in rr: mstke 10th: rdn 11th: stl plenty cl enough 3 out: drvn and swtchd rt bef next: wknd between last 2* **6/1**

132- **6** *7* **Foundation Man (IRE)**[29] 5060 7-10-13 **127**.........................(v) APMcCoy 114
(Jonjo O'Neill) *t.k.h and j. boldly at times: chsd ldr: dived and mstke 8th: styd chsng ldrs tl btn and edgd lft bef 2 out: wknd between last 2* **7/2**[2]

662- **7** *18* **Vesperal Dream (FR)**[23] 5140 5-10-5 **119**............... SamTwiston-Davies 88
(Paul Nicholls) *in tch in midfield: stl cl enough and rdn bef 3 out: btn bef 2 out: fdd between last 2: t.o* **5/2**[1]

223- **8** *20* **Massena (IRE)**[13] 5306 7-11-6 **134**.................................... AidanColeman 85
(Venetia Williams) *mde most tl 3 out: sn lost pl u.p and bhd next: sn fdd: t.o* **20/1**

5m 17.5s (-0.90) **Going Correction** +0.05s/f (Yiel) **8** Ran SP% **115.6**
Speed ratings: **103,102,101,96,96 94,87,79**
CSF £78.65 CT £584.80 TOTE £6.70: £1.90, £2.40, £2.60; EX 108.00 Trifecta £946.00.
Owner H B Hodge **Bred** Dick White **Trained** Alcester, Warwicks

FOCUS
A couple of in-form novices had this between them in the closing stages. Steps up from the first two.

5574 BET365 H'CAP HURDLE (9 hdls) 2m 4f
5:30 (5:32) (Class 2) (0-145,142) 4-Y-0+

£18,768 (£5,544; £2,772; £1,386; £693; £348)

Form RPR

332- **1** **L'Unique (FR)**[9] 5370 5-11-12 **142**................................ WayneHutchinson 147+
(Alan King) *chsd ldrs: rdn to chal between last 2: led and lft clr last: styd on strly: rdn out* **8/1**

003- **2** *8* **Cash And Go (IRE)**[22] 5158 7-11-10 **140**....................... TomScudamore 138+
(Nicky Henderson) *wl in tch in midfield: mstke 4th: rdn and effrt 2 out: outpcd and lft 3rd last: kpt on to chse clr wnr flat: no imp* **5/1**[3]

115- **3** *4 ½* **Ceasar Milan (IRE)**[49] 4680 6-11-1 **134**.................(t) HarryDerham[(3)] 129
(Paul Nicholls) *led and set stdy gallop tl hdd 4th: chsd ldr after tl led again bef 2 out: hdd and rdn 2 out: outpcd and lft 2nd whn hmpd last: edgd rt and wknd flat* **4/1**[1]

0/0- **4** *1 ½* **Vasco Du Ronceray (FR)**[21] 5172 5-11-9 **139**............... BarryGeraghty 132
(Nicky Henderson) *wl in tch in midfield: effrt u.p 2 out: no ex between last 2: lft 4th last: plugged on same pce after* **5/1**[3]

630- **5** *1 ¾* **Leo Luna**[15] 4789 5-11-3 **133**..(v[1]) JamieMoore 124
(Gary Moore) *in tch in rr: cl enough and mstke 3 out: sn rdn: wknd after 2 out* **16/1**

6 *6* **Vaxalco (FR)**[23] 5148 5-9-9 **116** oh1..........................(t) ConorShoemark[(5)] 102
(J H Culloty, Ire) *hld up in last pair: rdn and effrt after 3 out: outpcd and btn next: wknd between last 2* **25/1**

122- **7** *10* **Henryville**[24] 5128 6-11-0 **130**.. NoelFehily 110
(Harry Fry) *in tch in midfield: effrt on inner bef 2 out: no prog 2 out and sn btn: wl hld and mstke last: wknd* **9/2**[2]

1F2- **P** **Kaylif Aramis**[23] 5138 7-11-11 **141**..........................(t) SamTwiston-Davies
(Nigel Twiston-Davies) *wl in tch in midfield tl hdwy to ld and qcknd gallop 4th: hdd bef 2 out: sn btn: bhd whn p.u last* **11/2**

F12- **F** **Phantom Prince (IRE)**[23] 5142 5-10-9 **125**..................... BrendanPowell 124
(Brendan Powell) *chsd ldr tl 4th: styd chsng ldrs tl effrt to ld 2 out: rdn and hdd whn fell last* **20/1**

5m 7.0s (7.40) **Going Correction** -0.10s/f (Good) **9** Ran SP% **112.5**
Speed ratings (Par 109): **81,77,76,75,74 72,68, ,**
CSF £46.73 CT £183.14 TOTE £6.20: £2.40, £2.10, £1.70; EX 44.00 Trifecta £427.70.
Owner Denis J Barry **Bred** S A R L Ecurie D **Trained** Barbury Castle, Wilts

FOCUS
A race hit by five non-runners, but it was still competitive. The pace was a steady one until Kaylif Aramis went on early down the back straight. A personal best from L'Unique.
T/Jkpt: £26,569.40 to a £1 stake. Pool: £205,820.06 - 5.50 winning units T/Plt: £463.10 to a £1 stake. Pool: £177,955.52 - 280.47 winning units T/Qpdt: £16.50 to a £1 stake. Pool: £13,889.69 - 619.72 winning units SP

5575 - 5578a (Foreign Racing) - See Raceform Interactive

5529 AUTEUIL (L-H)
Saturday, April 26

OFFICIAL GOING: Turf: heavy

5577a PRIX LEON RAMBAUD (HURDLE) (GRADE 2) (5YO+) (TURF) 2m 3f 110y
1:35 (12:00) 5-Y-0+

£65,625 (£32,083; £18,958; £13,125; £7,291; £5,104)

RPR

1 **Un De Sceaux (FR)**[28] 5087 6-10-8 0... RWalsh 157+
(W P Mullins, Ire) *tk a v t.k.h: led appr 1st: mde rest: 2 l ld whn c stands' side side 2 out: rdn and r.o run-in: wl on top cl home* **11/10**[1]

2 *2 ½* **Le Grand Luce (FR)**[157] 2613 5-10-6 0.......................... JonathanNattiez 152+
(J-P Gallorini, France) *towards rr: 5th and styng on appr 2 out: rdn and styd on run-in: wnt 2nd cl home: nvr on terms w wnr* **53/10**[3]

3 *1 ½* **Saint Du Chenet (FR)**[28] 5087 8-10-6 0....................(b) MorganRegairaz 151
(M Rolland, France) *a.p: 2 l 2nd in centre of crse 2 out: sn rdn: kpt on at one pce u.p run-in: lost 2nd cl home* **37/1**

4 *3* **Gemix (FR)**[28] 5087 6-11-0 0... DavidCottin 156
(N Bertran De Balanda, France) *settled in 5th: hdwy after 3 out: 3rd and rdn last: nt qckn run-in and fdd fnl 100yds* **17/10**[2]

5 *8* **Tir Au But (FR)**[28] 5087 7-10-3 0..................................(p) CyrilleGombeau 137
(G Cherel, France) *trckd ldr: lost pl 3 out: hrd rdn 2 out: plugged on at one pce* **23/1**

6 *15* **Lord Prestige (FR)**[28] 5087 7-10-12 0..................... JonathanPlouganou 131
(M Rolland, France) *w.w in 4th: chsd ldr fr 6 out: rdn and wknd appr 2 out* **43/5**

7 *¾* **Lamego (FR)**[28] 5087 7-10-6 0..................................... Jean-LucBeaunez 124
(Mme P Butel, France) *in rr: rdn and no imp fr 3 out: sn wl btn* **44/1**

4m 43.5s (-11.50) **7** Ran SP% **120.0**
PARI-MUTUEL (all including 1 euro stake): WIN 2.10; PLACE 1.60, 2.30; SF 10.50.
Owner E O'Connell **Bred** Haras De La Rousseliere Et Al **Trained** Muine Beag, Co Carlow

MAISONS-LAFFITTE (R-H)
Tuesday, April 22

OFFICIAL GOING: Turf: good to soft

5579a PRIX BANGO (AQPS) (CONDITIONS) (4YO NON-THOROUGHBREDS) (TURF) 1m 4f 110y
11:45 (12:00) 4-Y-0 **£11,666** (£4,666; £3,500; £2,333; £1,166)

RPR

1 **Adula (FR)**[28] 4-10-2 0... AdrienFouassier 7 113
(Alain Couetil, France) **3/5**[1]

2 *½* **Agha Des Mottes (FR)**[55] 4498 4-9-11 0..................... StevieDonohoe 5 107
(Ian Williams) *restrained and hld up in rr: hdwy on outer 3f out: rdn over 2f out: chal and wnt 2nd ent fnl f: styd on strly but a jst hld by wnr* **63/10**

3 *1* **Allee De Forme (FR)** 4-10-0 0............................... AlexandreRoussel 3 109
(J-P Bourdin, France) **5/1**[2]

4 *4* **Agate D'Estruval (FR)** 4-9-7 0.............................. StephanePasquier 1 95
(Y Rougegrez, France) **176/10**

5 *1 ½* **Arum De L'Argos (FR)** 4-9-13 0.................................... NicolasPerret 4 99
(Y Gourraud, France) **53/10**[3]

6 *3* **Ausone Kergador (FR)** 4-9-11 0..................................(p) TheoBachelot 6 92
(G Ridel, France) **26/1**

7 *3* **Alba Rosa (FR)** 4-9-7 0... RaphaelMarchelli 2 83
(Mme I Audon, France) **33/1**

2m 56.12s (176.12) **7** Ran SP% **120.8**
WIN (incl. 1 euro stake): 1.60. PLACES: 1.20, 2.10. SF: 8.10.
Owner Mlle P-M David & Couetil Elevage **Bred** A Couetil **Trained** France

INDEX TO MEETINGS JUMPS 2013-2014

*AW bumper meeting
† Abandoned
(M) Mixed meeting

INDEX TO STEEPLECHASING & HURDLE RACING

Figure underneath the horse's name indicates its age. The figures following the pedigree refer to the numbers of the races (steeplechases are in bold) in which the horse has run; parentheses () indicate a win; superscript figures denote other placings. Foreign races are denoted by the suffix 'a'. Horses withdrawn (not under orders) are shown with the suffix 'w'. The figures within arrows indicate Raceform Private Handicap MASTER ratings. The ratings are based on a scale of 0-175. The following symbols are used: 'h' hurdle rating, 'c' chase rating, '+' on the upgrade, 'd' disappointing, '?' questionable form. 't' tentative rating based on time.

Aachen *Venetia Williams* 142h 127c
10 b g Rainbow Quest(USA) Anna Of Saxony (Ela-Mana-Mou)
3825^{4} (4034)
4346^{6} 4685^{P} 5513^{9}

Aalim *John Ferguson* 115h
4 b g Nayef(USA) Anna Palariva (IRE) (Caerleon (USA))
2899^{2} (3351) (4003) 5090^{5} 5272^{U}

Aaly *Lydia Richards* 71h
7 b g Milan Leyaaly (Night Shift (USA))
711^{2}

Aazif (IRE) *Ian Williams* 130h
5 ch g Nayef(USA) Ayun (USA) (Swain (IRE))
(73) ◆ (278) 734^{2} ◆ (1082) 1290^{5} *4023^{15}*
4300^{3} 4899^{4} 5158^{13} 5353^{4}

Abayaan *Richenda Ford* 48h
8 gr g Sadler's Wells(USA) Showdown (Darshaan)
4972^{8}

Abbey Court (IRE) *Nicky Henderson*
6 b g Wareed(IRE) North Kerry Rose (IRE) (Un Desperado (FR))
4535^{P}

Abbey Dore (IRE) *Jonathan Geake* 14h 41c
11 ch g Alderbrook Bone Of Contention (IRE) (Buckskin (FR))
2578^{5} 3555^{4} 5263^{10}

Abbey Garth (IRE) *Nicky Richards* 104h
7 b g Dr Massini(IRE) Elegant Gale (IRE) (Strong Gale)
491^{P} 1785^{4} 2311^{9}

Abbey Storm (IRE) *Donald McCain* 115h 125c
8 br g Presenting Bobbies Storm (IRE) (Bob Back (USA))
1669^{P} 2099^{2} 3397^{2} 4236^{8}

Abbi Jicaro *Mark Shears* 79h
7 b m Passing Glance Makeover (Priolo (USA))
155^{3} 188^{P} 501^{P} 522^{6} 648^{9} 686^{6} 828^{7}

Abbraccio *Fergal O'Brien* 62h
6 b g Pivotal Embraced (Pursuit Of Love)
69^{3} 1330^{5}

Abbyssial (IRE) *W P Mullins* 148h
4 ch g Beneficial Mega D'Estruval (FR) (Garde Royale)
262a^{3} (4432a) 4784^{F}

Abel J Tasman (IRE) *James Moffatt* 78h
6 b g Aussie Rules(USA) Vin Santo (IRE) (Mujadil (USA))
1420^{2} 1877^{6} 2174^{11} 2968^{11}

Abigail Lynch (IRE) *George Baker*
6 b m Oscar(IRE) Tanit Lady (IRE) (Presenting)
3600^{F} 5427^{P}

Abijoe *Pam Sly* 70b
5 b m Fair Mix(IRE) Casewick Mist (Primitive Rising (USA))
2681^{3}

A Bit Breezy *Bill Turner* 43b
7 b m Emperor Fountain Ryewater Dream (Touching Wood (USA))
1317^{9}

Abitofbob *Emma Lavelle* 103b
5 b g Enrique My World (FR) (Lost World (IRE))
5130^{2} ◆

Able Deputy *Kim Bailey* 122h 128c
7 b g Lomitas Island Colony (USA) (Pleasant Colony (USA))
30^{2} 234^{3} 1990^{2} 2434^{4} 4804^{2} 5091^{4}

Abnaki (IRE) *Jonjo O'Neill* 131h 127c
9 b g Milan Laboc (Rymer)
2033^{P} (2170) 2388^{5} 3060^{6} 4105^{3} 4697^{9}

Abolitionist (IRE) *John Joseph Hanlon* 114h 89c
6 b g Flemensfirth(USA) All The Roses (IRE) (Roselier (FR))
590^{4} 3828^{3}

About Thyne (IRE) *Maurice Barnes* 108h
9 ch g Anshan Down The Garden (IRE) (Good Thyne (USA))
16^{P}

Abracadabra Sivola (FR) *Nick Williams* 130h
4 b g Le Fou(IRE) Pierrebrune (FR) (Cadoudal (FR))
1855^{2} 2500^{5} 2927^{3} 3778^{5} (4268)

A Bridge Too Far (IRE) *Donald McCain* 114h 113c
8 b g Oscar(IRE) Private Rose (IRE) (Roselier (FR))
45^{2} 370^{P} 604^{5} 884^{3} 1161^{4}

Abruzzi *Tom Symonds* 122h
6 b g Milan Shannon Native (IRE) (Be My Native (USA))
158^{5} 2006^{2} 2655^{3} 3069^{10} 3359^{P} 4105^{8}

Absinthe (IRE) *Donald McCain* 93h
8 b g King's Best(USA) Triple Try (IRE) (Sadler's Wells (USA))
4947^{6} 5452^{7}

Absolutely Bygones (IRE) *Jackie Du Plessis* 99h
6 b g Alderbrook Majella (IRE) (Fourstars Allstar (USA))
2011^{8} 2695^{6} 4993^{8} 5236^{7}

Absolute Return *Tom George* 26h
5 b g Kayf Tara Kitty Wong (IRE) (Supreme Leader)
3838^{9}

Absolute Shambles *Chris Gordon* 93h 93c
10 b g Shambo Brass Castle (IRE) (Carlingford Castle)
241^{8} 690^{10} 1105^{9} 1405^{8} (1675) (1768) 2541^{3}
2744^{2} 3138^{2} 4803^{4} 5022^{3} 5114^{6} 5461^{4}

Absolutlyfantastic *Henry De Bromhead* 129h 130c
7 b g Alhaarth(IRE) Persian Walk (FR) (Persian Bold)
1001a^{2}

Abuelo (FR) *Gary Moore* 80b
4 bl g Califet(FR) Quolcevyta (FR) (Ungaro (GER))
5130^{5}

Abundantly *Venetia Williams* 73h
5 b m Sakhee(USA) Composing (IRE) (Noverre (USA))
3733^{3}

Academy (IRE) *N W Alexander* 96h
6 br g Montjeu(IRE) Rock The Casbah (FR) (Lavirco (GER))
168^{2} 881^{P}

Academy General (IRE) *David Bridgwater* 115h 120c
8 b g Beneficial Discerning Air (Ezzoud (IRE))
(435) 747^{8}
861^{3} ◆ 1119^{U} 1262^{4} 1518^{6} 1598^{2} 1748^{6} 2024^{7}

Acapulco Bay *Dai Burchell* 102h
10 b g Pursuit Of Love Lapu-Lapu (Prince Sabo)
(376) 505^{2} 812^{4} 5304^{7}

Acapulco Gold (IRE) *Paul Nolan* 102h 126c
7 b g Azamour(IRE) El Rabab (USA) (Roberto (USA))
656^{2} 1291^{4} (1542)

Accessallareas (IRE) *Sarah-Jayne Davies* 58h 118c
9 ch g Swift Gulliver(IRE) Arushofgold (IRE) (Alphabatim (USA))
(84) **(183)**
377^{2} 585^{6} 693^{5} 947^{9}

Accordingtojodie (IRE) *Tom Symonds* 97h
8 b g Accordion La Fiamma (FR) (General Assembly (USA))
367^{3} 3877^{12} 5235^{3}

Accordingtopalm (IRE) *David Rees* 102h 105c
8 ch g Great Palm(USA) Supreme Accord (IRE) (Accordion)
143^{4} 457^{5} 4840^{4} 5185^{3} 5546^{5}

According To Sarah (IRE) *Philip Hobbs* 80h
6 ch m Golan(IRE) Miss Accordion (IRE) (Accordion)
1318^{3} 2602^{8} 3005^{9} 4910^{9} 5117^{5} 5393^{F}

According To Them (IRE) *Daniel Steele* 18h 98c
10 ch g Quws Any Old Music (IRE) (Montelimar (USA))
2441^{P} 2739^{2} 3139^{5} 3250^{2} 3554^{P} 4031^{6} (4470)
4720^{P} 5122^{5}

According To Trev (IRE) *Nigel Twiston-Davies* 132h 138c
8 ch g Accordion Autumn Sky (IRE) (Roselier (FR))
(1303)
(1494) 1957^{3} 2692^{3} 3162^{F} 3897^{P} 4741^{P}

Accordion Exhibit (IRE) *Fergal O'Brien* 95h 111c
8 ch g Accordion Curraghmeela (IRE) (Exhibitioner)
422^{4} 736^{F} 875^{4}

Accordion To Paddy (IRE) *Michael O'Hare* 76h 45c
10 b g Accordion Missymp (IRE) (Mi Selecto (USA))
2173^{P} 2772^{P} 4551^{P}

Ace Fighter Pilot *Jim Best* 128h 125c
8 b g Silver Patriarch(IRE) Vedra (IRE) (Carlingford Castle)
586^{4} (921)
3162^{3}

Ace High *David Pipe* 103h 136c
10 b g Kayf Tara Celtic Native (IRE) (Be My Native (USA))
1971^{13} 2670^{3} ◆ 3361^{P}

Acertain Circus *Pam Sly* 104b
4 ch g Definite Article Circus Rose (Most Welcome)
4547^{8} 4986^{3} 5367^{2}

Aces Over Eights (IRE) *Richard Lee* 101b
5 b m Old Vic Conjure Up (IRE) (Jurado (USA))
4916^{4}

Aces Over Kings (IRE) *Rebecca Curtis* 97b
7 b g Overbury(IRE) Aces Royale (IRE) (Accordion)
2216^{8} 2981^{5}

Achieved *Daniel O'Brien* 62h
11 b g Lahib(USA) Equity's Darling (IRE) (Law Society (USA))
264^{9}

Achimota (IRE) *Matt Sheppard* 98h 125c
8 b g Double Eclipse(IRE) Tullyfoyle (IRE) (Montelimar (USA))
92^{2} 2024^{6} 2450^{7}

Acht (GER) *Noel C Kelly* 84h
5 b m Big Shuffle(USA) Avanti Adda (GER) (Law Society (USA))
729^{5} 1043^{10}

Achtung *Luke Comer* 96h
4 b c Montjeu(IRE) Funsie (FR) (Saumarez)
4432a^{8} 4784^{11}

Ackertac (IRE) *Tim Vaughan* 130h 152c
9 ch g Anshan Clonsingle Native (IRE) (Be My Native (USA))
2365^{2} 2800^{6} 3458^{P} 4738^{7} 5371^{9}

Acordingtoscript (IRE) *Martin Todhunter* 96h 86c
8 ch g Accordion Jane Jones (IRE) (Beau Sher)
1870^{F} 2219^{5} 2518^{P} 3040^{10} 3356^{2} 3940^{7} 4366^{3}

Acosta *Dr Jeremy Naylor* 73h
10 b g Foxhound(USA) Dancing Heights (IRE) (High Estate)
2680^{5}
3114^{P} 3425^{6} 5122^{3} 5461^{7}

Acrai Rua (IRE) *Tim Fitzgerald* 112h 112c
11 ch g Rock Hopper Dontbelieveaword (IRE) (Be My Native (USA))
509^{P} 766^{P} 2201^{6} (2902)
4580^{U}

Across The Bay (IRE) *Donald McCain* 125h 160c
10 b g Bob's Return(IRE) The Southern (IRE) (Glacial Storm (USA))
2228^{5}
2937^{8} (3416)
4270^{U} 5171^{14}

Across The Tweed (IRE) *Maurice Barnes* 84h 59c
8 bb g Alderbrook Cash Chase (IRE) (Sexton Blake)
74^{P} 628^{P}

Act Alone *Nicky Henderson* 130h
5 b g Act One Figlette (Darshaan)
309^{2} (3600) 4694^{3} 5343^{2}

Action Front (USA) *Derek Shaw* 12h
6 bb g Aptitude(USA) Palisade (USA) (Gone West (USA))
2893^{11} 3034^{P}

Activial (FR) *Harry Fry* 128h
4 rg g Lord Du Sud(FR) Kissmirial (FR) (Smadoun (FR))
2796^{2} (4419) ◆ 5132^{8}

Actodos (IRE) *Richard Woollacott* 65h
10 ro g Act One Really Gifted (IRE) (Cadeaux Genereux)
390^{6} 633^{4} 2278^{6} 2696^{P}

Act Of Kalanisi (IRE) *Dr Richard Newland* 143h 140c
8 b g Kalanisi(IRE) Act Of The Pace (IRE) (King's Theatre (IRE))
1766^{5} 1956^{6} ◆ 2624^{3} 2949^{12} (3132) (3328)
3779^{U} 4147^{18} **4768^{P}** 5054^{5}

Act Of Supremacy (IRE) *Charles Egerton* 46b
4 b g Presenting Supreme Touch (IRE) (Supreme Leader)
4561^{9}

Adajarad (IRE) *Evan Williams* 80h
7 b g Tiger Hill(IRE) Adirika (IRE) (Miswaki (USA))
155^{P}

Addiction *Jeremy Scott* 99h 121c
9 b m Alflora(IRE) Premier Princess (Hard Fought)
294^{P} 2693^{P} 4913^{6}

Adelaide Square (FR) *G Macaire* 116c
8 b g Turgeon(USA) Nile Glorieuse (FR) (Le Glorieux)
(855a)
1214a^{4}

Adelar (GER) *Venetia Williams* 125h
9 b g Samum(GER) Arpista (GER) (Chief Singer)
(1185)

Adept Approach (IRE) *P G Hall* 120c
8 b g Milan Musical Approach (IRE) (Dry Dock)
(325) **658^{11}**
4443^{2}

Adeupas D'Ycy (FR) *Nicky Henderson* 108b
4 gr g Al Namix(FR) Jacady (FR) (Fill My Hopes (FR))
(2926) 3460^{2} 4054^{P} (Dead)

Adili (IRE) *Brian Ellison* 86h
5 ch g Dubai Destination(USA) Adirika (IRE) (Miswaki (USA))
2511^{6} 2827^{5} 3119^{P} (3335) 3824^{7}

Adios Alonso (IRE) *Rosemary Gasson* 95h
8 b g Saffron Walden(FR) Rosy Rockford (IRE) (Beneficial)
(67) 253^{3} 565^{2} 669^{U} 860^{7}

Adiynara (IRE) *Neil Mulholland* 113h
6 b m Halling(USA) Adirika (IRE) (Miswaki (USA))
3117^{6} *4022^{8}*

Ad Man (FR) *C A McBratney* 95h
9 b g Septieme Ciel(USA) Kelbelange (FR) (Ganges (USA))
880^{3}

Admirable Duque (IRE) *Dominic Ffrench Davis* 98h
8 b g Selkirk(USA) Stunning (USA) (Nureyev (USA))
2718^{7} 3174^{P}

Admiral Blake *Laura Young* 90h
7 b g Witness Box(USA) Brenda Bella (FR) (Linamix (FR))
2291^{P} (3699) (3842) 5033^{7}

Admiral Boom (IRE) *Paul Henderson* 91h
8 b g Beneficial Gleann Na Smaointe (IRE) (Kasmayo)
179^{P} 1945^{8} 2430^{4} 2980^{11} 5307^{9}

Admiral Hawke (IRE) *Brian Ellison* 121h
8 b g Stowaway Classical Rachel (IRE) (Shahanndeh)
2932^{11} 3448^{3}

Adrenalin Flight (IRE) *Seamus Mullins* 108h 136c
8 b g Dr Massini(IRE) Chapel Queen (IRE) (Jolly Jake (NZ))
40^{2} 245^{3} 656^{3} (871)
996^{5} (1316)
2177^{2} 2537^{2} 3554^{P} 4134^{3} 4741^{4} 5276^{P}

Adriana Des Mottes (FR) *W P Mullins* 131h
4 br f Network(GER) Daisy Des Mottes (FR) (Abdonski (FR))
4432a^{2} 4784^{B} (5199a)

Adula (FR) *Alain Couetil* 113b
4 b f Day Flight Lazary (FR) (Bobinski)
(5579a)

Advisor (FR) *Mark Gillard* 106h 29c
8 gr g Anabaa(USA) Armilina (FR) (Linamix (FR))
203^{5} 650^{3} 854^{6} (1110) 1171^{5} 2176^{8} 2760^{6}
3043^{6} 3744^{12} 4275^{7}

Aegean Dawn *Robert Walford* 132h 44c
9 b g Alflora(IRE) Wychnor Dawn (IRE) (Broken Hearted)
2813^{10} ◆ 3207^{3} **3642^{7}**

Aegean Destiny *John Mackie* 102h
7 b m Beat Hollow Starlist (Observatory (USA))
421^{5} 811^{5} 933^{7}

Aerial (FR) *Paul Nicholls* 111h 138c
8 b g Turgeon(USA) Fille Formidable (USA) (Trempolino (USA))
1968^{7} (3046) 3896^{7}

Affiliate *Geoffrey Deacon* 61h
6 ch m Nayef(USA) Allied Cause (Giant's Causeway (USA))
2463^{7} 5124^{13}

Aficionado *Chris Grant* 103h
4 ch g Halling(USA) Prithee (Barathea (IRE))
1394^{4} (1501) 1658^{5} 2417^{2} 2879^{2}

Afillycalledlily (IRE) *Lawney Hill* 15b
5 b m Gamut(IRE) Stefphonic (IRE) (Orchestra)
1264^{7} 1531^{6} 1770^{9}

African Gold (IRE) *Nigel Twiston-Davies* 148h 140c
6 b g King's Theatre(IRE) Mrs Dempsey (IRE) (Presenting)
2501^{4} 3011^{F} 3653^{P}

After Eight Sivola (FR) *Nick Williams* 106h
4 b g Shaanmer(IRE) Eva De Chalamont (FR) (Iron Duke (FR))
1862^{5} 3641^{5} 4111^{5} 4401^{7}

After The Storm *John O'Shea* 100h
5 b g Dylan Thomas(IRE) Inchiri (Sadler's Wells (USA))
2507^{4}

Against The Wind *Lucinda Russell* 66h 83c
11 b g Anshan Harvest Memories (Oats)
23^{6} 533^{6}

Agapanthus (GER) *Neil Mulholland* 85h
9 b g Tiger Hill(IRE) Astilbe (GER) (Monsun (GER))
2862^{2} 3290^{3}

Agate D'Estruval (FR) *Y Rougegrez* 95b
4 b f Le Fou(IRE) Mome D'Estruval (FR) (Cyborg (FR))
5579a^{4}

Agent Archie (USA) *Donald McCain* 127h 99c
7 b g Smart Strike(CAN) Dans La Ville (CHI) (Winning (USA))
1185^{3} 1504^{4} **1817^{3}**

Agent Fedora *Kim Bailey* 85h
6 b m Kayf Tara Flora Poste (Alflora (IRE))
70^{4} 2027^{5} 2432^{12} 2896^{10} 5069^{11} 5432^{P}

Agent Louise *Mike Sowersby* 86h
6 b m Alflora(IRE) Oso Special (Teenoso (USA))
567^{9} 754^{4} 970^{8} 3735^{6} 4075^{7} 4479^{4} 5161^{6}
5494^{P}

Agent Mimi (FR) *M Seror*
4 bb f Medecis Azucar (IRE) (Desert Prince (IRE))
2781a^{5}

Age Of Glory *D J Bunyan* 116h
5 b g Zamindar(USA) Fleeting Moon (Fleetwood (IRE))
3215a^{3}

Agesilas (FR) *Andrew Crook* 94h
6 gr g Ultimately Lucky(IRE) Aimessa Du Berlais (FR) (Nikos)
359^{6} 1924^{10} 2659^{6} 2954^{8} 3569^{P} 5217^{U}

Aggie's Lad (IRE) *Alison Hamilton* 105h 123c
12 b g Saddlers' Hall(IRE) Grangemills (Strong Gale)
2218^{P} 2746^{U} 5379^{4}

Agha Des Mottes (FR) *Ian Williams* 68h
4 b g Mister Sacha(FR) Java Des Mottes (FR) (Passing Sale (FR))
4498^{3} 5579a^{2}

Aghill (IRE) *Lawney Hill* 95h 114c
10 ch g Denel(FR) Hannah's Pet (IRE) (Fidel)
1402^{4} 1538^{8}

Agincourt Reef (IRE) *Gary Moore* 118h
5 b g Gold Well Hillside Native (IRE) (Be My Native (USA))
306^{3} 706^{3} 2210^{9} 2676^{4} (3007) 5030^{13} 5260^{F}

Agitation *Alan Hollingsworth*
10 b g Cloudings(IRE) Shadowgraff (Scorpio (FR))
374^{P}

Aglaophonos *Ian Williams* 110h
4 ch g Dutch Art Lasting Image (Zilzal (USA))
2038^{2} 2466^{2} 3161^{7} 4796^{7}

Agreement (IRE) *Rebecca Curtis* 110h
4 b g Galileo(IRE) Cozzene's Angel (USA) (Cozzene (USA))
4419^{7} (4722) 5132^{12}

Agricultural *Lucy Normile* 100h 102c
8 b g Daylami(IRE) Rustic (IRE) (Grand Lodge (USA))
27^{6} 283^{2} 581^{4}
798^{5} 957^{2} 1657^{2} 1870^{3} 2308^{F} 2791^{3}

A Hare Breath (IRE) *Nick Gifford* 124h
6 b g Alkaadhem Lady Willmurt (IRE) (Mandalus)
2644^{2} 3163^{4}

Ahcomeretome (IRE) *Lady Susan Brooke* 89h
9 ch g Oscar Schindler(IRE) Call Me Over (IRE) (Callernish)
649^{7} 946^{P}

Ahead Ahead (IRE) *David Rees* 108h
9 b g Heron Island(IRE) Lady Tenby (IRE) (Tenby)
254^{6} (590) 690^{2} 998^{4}

Ahhdehken *Alistair Whillans* 84h
9 b g Cloudings(IRE) Swazi Princess (IRE) (Brush Aside (USA))
750^{6}

Ahkel Vie (FR) *Yannick Fouin* 94h 53c
4 b f Khalkevi(IRE) Jour De Chance (FR) (Mollicone Junior (FR))
(2781a)

Ahyaknowyerself (IRE) *Dr Richard Newland* 148h 139c
8 b g Milan Summer Break (IRE) (Foxhound (USA))
1520^{4} (1685) 2372^{3} 2533^{F}
3057^{2} 3202^{3} (3819)
4742^{4} 5091^{P}

Aiaam Al Namoos *John Wade* 99h
5 b g Teofilo(IRE) Deveron (USA) (Cozzene (USA))
(4547) 5173^{9}

Aibrean (IRE) *S R B Crawford* 132h 126c
10 b m Winged Love(IRE) Bealtaine (IRE) (Zaffaran (USA))
358^{P}
3750a^{P} 5273^{3}

Aikideau (FR) *Paul Nicholls* 134h 118c
7 b g Le Balafre(FR) Kizitso (FR) (En Calcat (FR))
217^{5} 636^{4} 778^{4} 1055^{2} 1195^{P}

Aikman (IRE) *James Ewart* 103h 93c
10 b g Rudimentary(USA) Omas Lady (IRE) (Be My Native (USA))
2346^{5}

Ailanthus *Richard Woollacott* 84h
5 b m Trade Fair The Abbess (Bishop Of Cashel)
777^{9} 922^{3} 1107^{7} 1191^{4} 1259^{11}

Aim *Sean Curran* 98h
9 b g Weetman's Weigh(IRE) Ballet On Ice (FR) (Fijar Tango (FR))
178^{P}

Aimigayle *Suzy Smith* 118h 111c
11 b m Midnight Legend Cherrygayle (IRE) (Strong Gale)
1304^{P} (1628) 2860^{3} **3067^{8} 4886^{P}**

Ainm Spartacus (IRE) *S J Mahon* 22h 117c
7 b g Spartacus(IRE) Hasainm (IRE) (Grand Lodge (USA))
1319^{P}

Ainsi Fideles (FR) *David Pipe* 119h
4 ch g Dream Well(FR) Loya Lescribaa (FR) (Robin Des Champs (FR))
2200^{5} 2733^{F} 3989^{11}

Ainsivalanour (FR) *A Vetault* 109c
6 b g Valanour(IRE) Silicie (FR) (Risk Me (FR))
(198a)

Aintnosanityclause (IRE) *S R B Crawford* 88h
6 b m Definite Article Santa Suzanna (IRE) (Supreme Leader)
1145^{5} 2495^{6}

Air Chief *Andrew Crook* 106h 90c
9 ch g Dr Fong(USA) Fly For Fame (Shaadi (USA))
2198^{14}
2804^{3} 3272^{P}

Airedale Lad (IRE) *Zoe Davison* 68h
13 b g Charnwood Forest(IRE) Tamarsiya (USA) (Shahrastani (USA))
97^{U} 243^{5} 490^{3} 710^{5} 1438^{P} 2568^{10} 3140^{11}

Airmen's Friend (IRE) *Charlie Mann* 95h 103c
8 b g Craigsteel High Academy (IRE) (Insan (USA))
2764^{4} 3265^{3} **4695^{3} 5113^{P}**

Aitch Factor *Henry Hogarth* 65h
8 b g Beat All(USA) Farmers Girl (Classic Cliche (IRE))
750^{P}

Aiteen Thirtythree (IRE) *Paul Nicholls* 119b
10 b g Old Vic Prudent View (IRE) (Supreme Leader)
2373^{P} 2798^{P}

Ajman (IRE) *Evan Williams* 111h
9 b g Orpen(USA) Grand Madam (Grand Lodge (USA))
266^{3} 783^{2} 947^{5} 1342^{5} (1402) 1443^{2} 2150^{5} 2760^{9}

Ajzal (IRE) *Ed de Giles* 56h 59c
10 b g Alhaarth(IRE) Alkaffeyeh (IRE) (Sadler's Wells (USA))
1534^{U}

Akatara (IRE) *Michael J Bowe* 117h
7 b m Desert Style(IRE) Akdara (IRE) (Sadler's Wells (USA))
2552a^{5} 3804a^{P}

Akbabend *Chris Gordon* 123h 78c
8 b g Refuse To Bend(IRE) Akdariya (IRE) (Shirley Heights)
358^{16} 659^{10} **839^{6}** 2006^{8}

Akdam (IRE) *Tony Carroll* 119h
4 br g Dubai Destination(USA) Akdara (IRE) (Sadler's Wells (USA))
(582) 725^{2} 1193^{2} 1439^{3} 1658^{2} 1862^{3} (2307) 2500^{4} 3127^{3} 3245^{2} (3851) 4755^{B}

A Keen Sense (GER) *David Dennis* 89h
5 b g Sholokhov(IRE) All Our Luck (GER) (Spectrum (IRE))
3440^{8} 3988^{6} 4397^{5} 5024^{6}

Akula (IRE) *Mark H Tompkins* 120h 109c
7 ch g Soviet Star(USA) Danielli (IRE) (Danehill (USA))
176^{3} 447^{5} 734^{8} 877^{9} **1821^{3} 2558^{U} 2721^{5} 2782^{U}**
4497^{5} 4791^{5} 5443^{6}

Alabama Le Dun (FR) *J-P Gallorini* 130h
4 bl g Network(GER) Silvazeyra (FR) (Sheyrann (IRE))
2262a^{2}

Alaccordion *Violet M Jordan* 86h
9 br g Alflora(IRE) Song For Jess (IRE) (Accordion)
99^{3} 490^{2} (4071) 4595^{2} 4981^{5}

Aladdins Cave *C A Murphy* 128h
10 b g Rainbow Quest(USA) Flight Of Fancy (Sadler's Wells (USA))
5420a^{8}

Aladin Du Chenet (FR) *M Rolland* 126h
4 b g Poliglote Orthence (FR) (Epervier Bleu)
1741a^{F}

Alaivan (IRE) *Jonjo O'Neill* 135h
8 b g Kalanisi(IRE) Alaya (IRE) (Ela-Mana-Mou)
2958^{8} 3200^{14} 3744^{2} 4147^{6} 4785^{9} 5158^{6}

Al Alfa *Philip Hobbs* 109h 129c
7 ch g Alflora(IRE) Two For Joy (IRE) (Mandalus)
(1598)
1944^{U} 2086^{3} 2645^{5} 3065^{4} 3652^{2} (3960)
4414^{3} 4806^{F} 5126^{2}

Al Amaan *Sheena West* 86h 90c
9 b g Nayef(USA) Siobhan (Generous (IRE))
243^{3} 490^{6} 708^{4} 1438^{4} 1630^{9} 2008^{13} (5116) 5262^{6} **5397^{6}**

Alanco (GER) *O W Seiler*
13 b g Colon(GER) Alanaa (GER) (Northjet)
1424a^{4}

Alanjou (FR) *Jamie Snowden* 96h
4 b g Maresca Sorrento(FR) Partie Time (FR) (Nononito (FR))
1524^{2} 1743^{4} 3796^{4} 4659^{6}

Alaparo (FR) *G Macaire* 77h
4 b c Saint Des Saints(FR) Messine (FR) (Garde Royale)
614a^{7}

Alaplee *Chris Grant* 99h 73c
6 b g Alflora(IRE) Cloudy Pearl (Cloudings (IRE))
1924^{5} 2197^{P} 5300^{5}

Alasi *Paul Webber* 139h 143c
10 b m Alflora(IRE) Anamasi (Idiots Delight)
2226^{3}
(2666) 3032^{5} 3895^{3}

Alba King (IRE) *Sue Smith* 97h 97c
8 b g Beauchamp King Alba Dancer (Gran Alba (USA))
279^{9} 493^{7} 798^{7} (964)
1075^{7} 1417^{P} 5363^{6}

Alba Rosa (FR) *Mme L Audon* 83b
4 b f Special Kaldoun(IRE) Donatella II (FR) (Brezzo (FR))
5579a^{7}

Albatros Tresor (FR) *Lucinda Russell* 83b
4 b g Network(GER) Itiga (FR) (Djarvis (FR))
2160^{5} 4226^{8}

Alberobello (IRE) *Jeremy Scott* 118h
6 b g Old Vic Tourist Attraction (IRE) (Pollerton)
2020^{5} 2288^{5} 2715^{2} 3435^{8} 5074^{6}

Albert Bridge *Emma Lavelle* 128h
6 gr g Hernando(FR) Alvarita (Selkirk (USA))
4130^{5} (4467)

Albert Hall (USA) *A Chaille-Chaille* 132h
9 b g Stravinsky(USA) Albertine (FR) (Irish River (FR))
3083^{5}

Alberto *Alastair Lidderdale* 45h
4 b g Bertolini(USA) Al Awaalah (Mukaddamah (USA))
2975^{11}

Alberto De Ballon (FR) *Y-M Porzier* 124h 134c
7 b g Alberto Giacometti(IRE) Nile Palace (FR) (Crystal Palace (FR))
5425a^{P}

Alberto's Dream *Tom Symonds* 81h
5 b g Fantastic Spain(USA) Molly's Folly (My Lamb)
4350^{8} 5016^{7} 5175^{6}

Alborz (IRE) *Tim Vaughan* 112h
5 b g Dubai Destination(USA) Mount Elbrus (Barathea (IRE))
2617^{P}

Alcala (FR) *Paul Nicholls* 117h
4 gr g Turgeon(USA) Pail Mel (FR) (Sleeping Car (FR))
4419^{4}

Al Co (FR) *Peter Bowen* 130h 151c
9 ch g Dom Alco(FR) Carama (FR) (Tip Moss (FR))
358^{3} **1686^{5}**
(1868)
2214^{10} 2624^{2} 3387^{10} **(5276)**

Alco Baba (IRE) *Ferdy Murphy* 81b
6 ch m Dom Alco(FR) Aintree Baba (FR) (Robin Des Champs (FR))
567^{7}

Alco Sivola (FR) *Nick Williams* 106h
4 gr g Dom Alco(FR) Oeuvre Vive (FR) (Robin Des Champs (FR))
3161^{4} 4111^{6}

Aldeburgh *Jim Old* 81h
5 b g Oasis Dream Orford Ness (Selkirk (USA))
2286^{11} 2802^{11}

Alderbrook Lad (IRE) *Micky Hammond* 120h 128c
8 ch g Alderbrook Alone Tabankulu (IRE) (Phardante (FR))
920^{5} 1052^{7} **1184^{4} (1328)**
(1416) 1435^{2} 1629^{2} 2173^{5} 3143^{F} (3452)
(3615) 4084^{2} 4188^{3}
4898^{2} 5297^{F}

Alderley Heights *Polly Gundry* 82h
5 b m Windsor Heights Alderley Girl (Footloose Esquire)
5241^{7}

Alderley Rover (IRE) *Donald McCain* 124h 137c
10 gr g Beneficial St Anne's Lady (IRE) (Roselier (FR))
(2807) 3479^{5} 4006^{7} 4949^{4} 5379^{6}

Alderluck (IRE) *David Pipe* 131h 131c
11 ch g Alderbrook Cecelia's Charm (IRE) (Mister Lord (USA))
2283^{7} 2537^{4} 2923^{4} 3698^{5} 4402^{4} 4601^{3}

Alder Mairi (IRE) *Seamus Mullins* 129h
7 ch m Alderbrook Amari Queen (Nicholas Bill)
2352^{4} 2948^{7} 3319^{P} (3989) 4413^{4} 4991^{4} 5370^{16}

Alderwood (IRE) *Thomas Mullins* 148h 159c
10 b g Alderbrook Clamit Falls (IRE) (Homo Sapien)
2141a^{4}

Aldopicgros (FR) *Paul Nicholls* 135h
4 b g Tirwanako(FR) In'Challha (FR) (Bad Conduct (USA))
1985^{3} ◆ 2276^{2} 3003^{4} *4018^{3}* (4278) (4963) (5308)

Alelchi Inois (FR) *W P Mullins* 131h
6 b g Night Tango(GER) Witness Gama (FR) (Take Risks (FR))
2706a^{7} 2983a^{4}

Alexander Oats *Robert Goldie* 48h 95c
11 b g Insan(USA) Easter Oats (Oats)
311^{4} 2219^{4} 2818^{4} 3497^{4} 3936^{P} 4380^{3} 5107^{5}

Alfa Red *Sean Curran* 70b
4 b g Crosspeace(IRE) King's Jewel (King's Signet (USA))
2015^{9} 2391^{4} *2731^{8}*

Al Ferof (FR) *Paul Nicholls* 151h 168c
9 gr g Dom Alco(FR) Maralta (FR) (Altayan)
(2664)
3262^{3} 4145^{2} 4766^{5}

Alfiboy *Paul Webber* 72b
4 b g Alflora(IRE) Cloudy Pearl (Cloudings (IRE))
4964^{10}

Alfie Alexander (IRE) *Mark Hoad* 80h
6 b g Indian Danehill(IRE) Bella Galiana (ITY) (Don Roberto (USA))
417^{10} 2827^{P} 3138^{P} 4471^{P} 4724^{P}

Alfie Joe *Ron Hodges*
5 b g Bandmaster(USA) The Grey Bam Bam (Baryshnikov (AUS))
3422^{P}

Alfie Moone *Barry Leavy* 53b
6 b g Deploy Capricorn Princess (Nicholas Bill)
380^{7} 2513^{11} 4950^{P}

Alfies Gift *Dai Burchell* 73h
5 br m Helissio(FR) Scarvagh Solitaire (IRE) (Beauchamp King)
1523^{6} 1672^{10}

Alfie Sherrin *Jonjo O'Neill* 134h 135c
11 b g Kayf Tara Mandys Native (IRE) (Be My Native (USA))
2672^{4}
4738^{8} 5474a^{14}

Alfie Spinner (IRE) *Nick Williams* 125h 136c
9 b g Alflora(IRE) Little Red Spider (Bustino)
448^{6} 1868^{10} 2373^{2} 2953^{4} 3455^{2} 4026^{P} 4821^{P}

Alfinski *Clive Mulhall* 60b
9 b g Alflora(IRE) Auntie Alice (Uncle Pokey)
1007^{P}

Alfoisin (IRE) *Mrs C A Coward* 43b 98c
10 ch g Alflora(IRE) Alphacall (Forzando)
288^{P}

Alfraamsey *Sheena West* 123h 102c
6 b g Fraam Evanesce (Lujain (USA))
1520^{5} (1627) *4497^{3}* 5399^{F}

Alfred Oats *Robert Goldie* 89c
10 b g Alflora(IRE) Easter Oats (Oats)
2356^{8} 2820^{P} 3498^{6}

Alfstar *Henry Oliver* 94b
6 b g Alflora(IRE) Starboard Tack (FR) (Saddlers' Hall (IRE))
5339^{5}

Alf The Audacious *Sue Smith* 96h
8 gr g Alflora(IRE) Rua Ros (IRE) (Roselier (FR))
3021^{6} 3356^{7} **3658^{P}**

Algernon Pazham (IRE) *Nigel Twiston-Davies* 129h
5 b g Milan Kitty Star (IRE) (Montelimar (USA))
395^{3} 2563^{2} (3023) 3417^{2} 4163^{2} (4702)

Alibi De Sivola (FR) *Paul Nicholls*
4 bb g Shaanmer(IRE) Neva De Sivola (FR) (Blushing Flame (USA))
4296^{2}

Alicesam *Philip Kirby* 11h
5 b m Revoque(IRE) Hinton Grace (Vital Season)
15^{10}

Aliking *Peter Niven* 62b
7 b g Alflora(IRE) Kingennie (Dunbeath (USA))
19^{P} 449^{P} 554^{P}

Alimure *Clive Mulhall* 62h
8 b m Tamure(IRE) Auntie Alice (Uncle Pokey)
73^{9} 532^{5} 1188^{9}

Alistorm *Mark Campion* 33h
8 b m Bob Back(USA) Storm In Front (IRE) (Fourstars Allstar (USA))
748^{5} 2514^{P} 2900^{8}

A Little Bit Dusty *Conor Dore* 117h
6 ch g Needwood Blade Dusty Dazzler (IRE) (Titus Livius (FR))
2250^{4} 2559^{4} 2846^{2} 2898^{3} 3038^{2}

A Little Swifter (IRE) *Neil King* 110h 107c
8 ch m Noverre(USA) Swiftur (Snurge)
2352^{5}
2572^{2} 3058^{6}

Alizari (IRE) *Barry Brennan* 111h
5 b g Oratorio(IRE) Alaya (IRE) (Ela-Mana-Mou)
3839^{4} 4883^{P}

Alizee De Janeiro (FR) *Lucinda Russell* 62b
4 b f Network(GER) Katana (GER) (Funambule (USA))
4611^{10} 5374^{13}

Al Jaz (CZE) *J Blecha*
8 ch g Moonjaz Arani (SWI) (Law Society (USA))
1905a^{U}

Alkali (IRE) *S R B Crawford* 66h
4 gr f Dalakhani(IRE) Alambic (Cozzene (USA))
4199^{7} 4548^{8} 4647^{P} 5205^{6}

Allanard (IRE) *Martin Todhunter* 79h 110c
10 b g Oscar(IRE) Allatrim (IRE) (Montelimar (USA))
1872^{2} 2749^{6} 3355^{3} 3939^{3}

Allbarnone *William Kinsey* 107h
6 b g Alflora(IRE) What A Gem (Karinga Bay)
3598^{3} 3926^{5} 5388^{3}

All But Grey *Carroll Gray* 105h
8 ro g Baryshnikov(AUS) Butleigh Rose (Nicholas Bill)
2689^{4} 3163^{10} (3783) 3956^{6} 4599^{P}

Allee De Forme (FR) *J-P Bourdin* 109b
4 gr f Voix Du Nord(FR) Kinase (FR) (Kadrou (FR))
5579a^{3}

Alleged Vanity (IRE) *Chris Grant* 81h
8 ch g Flemensfirth(USA) Vanity Jane (IRE) (Revoque (IRE))
561^{8} 750^{P}

Allerford Jack *Richard Woollacott* 104h 118c
10 br g Overbury(IRE) Jiggiwithit (Distant Relative)
63^{8} 646^{P}

Allerton (IRE) *Fergal O'Brien* 93h 108c
7 b g Flemensfirth(USA) Bonny Hall (IRE) (Saddlers' Hall (IRE))
1914^{3} (2450) ◆ **3223^{P}** 4757^{4}
4968^{6} 5336^{P}

Alleu (FR) *Mme I Pacault* 107h 117c
4 b g Al Namix(FR) Quisait (FR) (Goldneyev (USA))
1741a^{6}

Allez Cool (IRE) *John Wade* 93h
5 ch g Flemensfirth(USA) La Fisarmonica (IRE) (Accordion)
2444^{U} 2593^{3} 3017^{7} 4816^{8}

Allez Zane *Giles Smyly* 81h
5 b m Sir Harry Lewis(USA) Gaspaisie (FR) (Beyssac (FR))
2027^{6} 2432^{9}

All For Free (IRE) *David Bridgwater* 110h 118c
8 b g Atraf Milain (IRE) (Unfuwain (USA))
2086^{4}

All For Lily *Charles Pogson* 56h
5 b m Alflora(IRE) Who Let The Foxout (Saddlers' Hall (IRE))
1317^{5} 1472^{5} 4074^{7} 4528^{6}

Allforthelove *N W Alexander* 85h
6 b g Alflora(IRE) Powerlove (FR) (Solon (GER))
2355^{P} 3018^{4} 3392^{6} 3721^{5} 4649^{P} 5514^{P}

All Great N Theory (IRE) *Mrs Julie Marles* 95b 107c
8 b g Old Vic Miss Compliance (IRE) (Broken Hearted)
4485^{2}

All Hope *Paul Davies* 74h
7 b m Beat All(USA) Spectacular Hope (Marju (IRE))
391^{F} 590^{P} 2016^{P}

Allied Answer *Steve Gollings* 116h
6 gr g Danehill Dancer(IRE) Hotelgenie Dot Com (Selkirk (USA))
3330^{2} ◆ (3659) 4103^{7} 4629^{3}

Allow Dallow (IRE) *Jonjo O'Neill* 118h
7 b g Gold Well Russland (GER) (Surumu (GER))
2850^{2} 3189^{2} 3697^{P} 4280^{5} 4672^{F} 5071^{4}

Allowed *John Ferguson* 107h
5 b g Authorized(IRE) Japanese Whisper (UAE) (Machiavellian (USA))
507^{4} 856^{9}

Allow Me *Dianne Sayer* 112h 117c
9 b g Daylami(IRE) Time Honoured (Sadler's Wells (USA))
3273^{5} 3661^{7} **4084^{3} 4628^{5} 5058^{6}** 5208^{2} 5484^{2}

All Pepper (GER) *W P Mullins* 122h
4 b c Peppershot(GER) Alkeste (GER) (Nebos (GER))
4432a^{7}

All Riled Up *Harry Chisman* 90h
6 b m Dr Massini(IRE) Martha Reilly (IRE) (Rainbows For Life (CAN))
760^{5} 970^{10} 1196^{3} 1472^{6} 3388^{15} 4971^{2} 5245^{2} 5547^{8}

Alls It Is *Donald McCain* 14h
7 b g Beat All(USA) Binny Bay (Karinga Bay)
116^{13}

Allterrain (IRE) *Gary Moore* 19h 41c
11 b g Almutawakel Queen Of Art (IRE) (Royal Academy (USA))
1300^{P} 1548^{10} 1644^{P}

All That Remains (IRE) *Brian Ellison* 120h 106c
9 b g King's Theatre(IRE) Morning Breeze (IRE) (Bigstone (IRE))
(27) 447^{6} 2064^{2} 2828^{4} *4303^{7}* 5384^{9}

All The Fashion (IRE) *Violet M Jordan* 54h 74c
10 br m Alflora(IRE) Fashion Day (Environment Friend)
1188^{P} 1635^{P}

Allthekingshorses (IRE) *Philip Hobbs* 133h 129c
8 b g King's Theatre(IRE) Penny Brae (IRE) (Montelimar (USA))
2909^{2} 3455^{P} 4697^{8}
5334^{2}

All The Winds (GER) *Shaun Lycett* 97h
9 ch g Samum(GER) All Our Luck (GER) (Spectrum (IRE))
5125^{6}

Allusive Power (IRE) *Anna Brooks* 94h
5 gr m Verglas(IRE) Fernanda (Be My Chief (USA))
3012^{8} 4371^{4} 4866^{6}

Ally Cascade (IRE) *Noel Meade* 141h
6 b g Golan(IRE) Nikkis Alstar (IRE) (Fourstars Allstar (USA))
5420a^{14}

Allysson Monterg (FR) *Victor Dartnall* 100b
4 b g Network(GER) Mellyssa (FR) (Panoramic)
5388^{4}

Almadan (IRE) *Kim Bailey* 85h
6 b g Azamour(IRE) Alamouna (IRE) (Indian Ridge)
595^{U} 750^{P} 1940^{5} 2253^{P} 5177^{5}

Almond Court (IRE) *Robert Johnson* 87h 97c
11 ch m Accordion Glencairn Fox (IRE) (Le Moss)
115^{3} **(580)**
751^{7} **1789^{P}**
3335^{8} 4428^{P} **5321^{2}**

Almost Gemini (IRE) *Charlie Mann* 107h
5 gr g Dylan Thomas(IRE) Streetcar (IRE) (In The Wings)
4411^{5} 4891^{2} ◆ 5140^{3}

Almutaham (USA) *Nicky Richards* 83h 60c
7 bb g Dynaformer(USA) Forest Lady (USA) (Woodman (USA))
2211^{11} 1188^{6} 1374^{10} 1874^{4} 2218^{P} 2680^{P}

Along Came Rosie *Andrew Crook* 78h 102c
10 b m Alflora(IRE) Seraphim (FR) (Lashkari)
20^{P} 626^{4} 751^{3}

Along Came Theo (IRE) *Andrew Crook* 101b
4 b g Vertical Speed(FR) Kachina (IRE) (Mandalus)
4895^{3} 5499^{5}

Alongthewatchtower (IRE) *Barry Brennan* 94b
6 b g Heron Island(IRE) Manesbil (IRE) (Fourstars Allstar (USA))
338^{4} 589^{5}

Alonso (SPA) *W P Mullins* 137h
5 ch g Green Tune(USA) Lady Cree (IRE) (Medicean)
2852a^{4}

Alpancho *Ben Case* 121h 123c
8 ch g Alflora(IRE) Run Tiger (IRE) (Commanche Run)
(2599)
3162^{P} 4908^{7}

Alpetetim *Stuart Kittow* 68b
5 gr g Proclamation(IRE) Krismick (IRE) (Orpen (USA))
874[9]

Alphabetical Order *Tim Vaughan* 111h
6 b g Alflora(IRE) Lady Turk (FR) (Baby Turk)
1839[2]

Alphanov (FR) *H Billot* 87h
4 b g Night Tango(GER) Prival (FR) (Valanour (IRE))
262a[P]

Alpha One (IRE) *Chris Grant* 98h 116c
8 b g Fruits Of Love(USA) Dunedin Lass (IRE) (Alphabatim (USA))
387[6] 470[5]
2496[B] 2751[3] 2996[2] 3275[5] (4222)
4892[P]

Alpha Victor (IRE) *William Kinsey* 144h 146c
9 b g Old Vic Harvest View (IRE) (Good Thyne (USA))
2357[4] 3108[P] (3921)
4162[R] (4489)
4821[2] 5276[P]

Al Qeddaaf (IRE) *Donald McCain* 114h 113c
8 b g Alhaarth(IRE) Just Special (Cadeaux Genereux)
343[3]

Alrafid (IRE) *Ms G Howell* 91h 80c
15 ch g Halling(USA) Ginger Tree (USA) (Dayjur (USA))
331[P]

Already Basking (CAN) *Simon Earle* 81h
6 ch g More Than Ready(USA) Basking (USA) (Alydar (USA))
2631[P] 2906[10]

Alsadaa (USA) *Laura Mongan* 112h 103c
11 b g Kingmambo(USA) Aljawza (USA) (Riverman (USA))
5066[2] 5260[F]

Alskamatic *Richard J Bandey* 126c
8 b g Systematic Alska (FR) (Leading Counsel (USA))
325[2] 3801[4] (5337)

Alta Rock (IRE) *Sue Smith* 102h 78c
9 b g Luso Princess Lulu (IRE) (Carroll House)
5365[7]

Alteranthela (IRE) *Richard Rowe* 102h 92c
10 br g Alderbrook Anthela (GER) (Orfano (GER))
712[3] 2743[2] (3250)
4720[3] 5113[6]

Alto Des Mottes (FR) *Paul Nicholls* 89b
4 b g Dream Well(FR) Omance (FR) (Video Rock (FR))
2926[5]

Alvarado (IRE) *Fergal O'Brien* 122h 140c
9 ch g Goldmark(USA) Mrs Jones (IRE) (Roselier (FR))
1868[5] ◆ (2502)
3455[P] 5171[4]

Always Archie *Tim Vaughan* 124h
7 b g Silver Patriarch(IRE) Angel Dust (FR) (Cadoudal (FR))
4304[6] 4672[2] 5036[6] 5486[2] ◆

Always Bold (IRE) *Martin Keighley* 107h 106c
9 ch g King's Best(USA) Tarakana (USA) (Shahrastani (USA))
120[4] 1010[2] 1055[3] 1340[5] 1634[6] 1936[2] 2275[4]

Alwayslookback (IRE) *Rosemary Gasson* 48h
5 b g Trans Island Malachy's Attic (IRE) (Old Vic)
1826[9] 2285[9] 2876[12] 3592[9]

Always Managing *Brendan Powell* 96b
5 b m Oscar(IRE) Sunshine Rays (Alflora (IRE))
2298[11] 2892[4]

Alwaysrecommended (IRE) *Jane Walton* 76b
5 ch g Gamut(IRE) Awbeg Beauty (IRE) (Supreme Leader)
3042[13] 5108[5] 5560[8]

Always Right (IRE) *John Wade* 147c
12 ch g Right Win(IRE) Kemal Brave (IRE) (Kemal (FR))
170[P] 4042[3] ◆ 4274[P]

Always Smiling (IRE) *Charlie Mann* 87h 92c
7 b m Dushyantor(USA) Aherlabeag (IRE) (Presenting)
2266[5] 2697[5] 3030[5] 5114[7]

Always Summat *Michael Easterby* 32h
4 b g Bollin Eric Amalfi Storm (Slip Anchor)
4598[7] 5320[11]

Alwaystheoptimist *Phil Middleton* 122h 130c
11 b g Muhtarram(USA) Miss Optimist (Relkino)
31[F] (247)
585[2] (674)
840[5] 1535[4] (1816) (1943) 2087[8] 2434[3] 2762[4]
4965[5] 5067[P]

Always Tipsy *N W Alexander* 92b
5 b g Dushyantor(USA) French Pick (USA) (Johannesburg (USA))
3522[3] 4226[7]

Alys Rock (IRE) *Michael Appleby* 77b
5 gr m Medaaly Rock Slide (IRE) (Bob Back (USA))
1719[4]

Amalric (FR) *Anabel K Murphy* 86h
7 b g Laveron Aimessa Du Berlais (FR) (Nikos)
417[11] 844[8] 1105[7]

Amana (USA) *P A Fahy* 97h
10 b m Diesis Ma-Arif (IRE) (Alzao (USA))
891a[P]

Amantius *Johnny Farrelly* 81h
5 b g Multiplex Ghana (GER) (Bigstone (IRE))
1191[5] 1255[10] 1832[4]

Amaragon (CZE) *S Popelka Jr*
9 b g Rainbows For Life(CAN) Amadara (CZE) (Dara Monarch)
1904a[F]

Amaury De Lusignan (IRE) *Paul Henderson* 64h 103c
8 b g Dushyantor(USA) Celtic Sails (IRE) (M Double M (USA))
236[11] 705[6] 859[P] 1263[7] 1444[4] 1767[7] 2387[2] 2727[9]
3174[7] 3883[4]
4299[11]
4840[P]

Amazing D'Azy (IRE) *Kim Bailey* 107h
6 br m Presenting Shuil Mavourneen (IRE) (Welsh Term)
1823[3] 2317[15] 3159[4] 5112[9] 5542[3]

Amazing Eight *Michael Easterby* 97b
5 b g Erhaab(USA) Harry's Bride (Sir Harry Lewis (USA))
3112[5] 3760[5]

Amazingreyce *Christopher Kellett* 49h
9 gr m Rainbow High Lightning Belle (Belfort (FR))
376[8] 2701[10] 3141[10] 4981[P] 5066[P]

Amazing Scenes (IRE) *Brendan Powell* 96h
5 bb g Desert King(IRE) Lady Leila (IRE) (Taipan (IRE))
(76) 2802[12] 3136[5] 3506[P] 3988[3] 5112[8] 5459[2]

Amber Beat *John Spearing* 85b
7 b m Beat All(USA) Running For Kerry (Le Moss)
649[P]

Amber Flush *Tom Symonds* 52h
5 b m Sir Harry Lewis(USA) Sari Rose (FR) (Vertical Speed (FR))
970[4] 2022[8] 2317[11] 2600[12] 3115[P] 3733[5] 4132[P]
4676[4] 5234[P]

Amberkatann (IRE) *Dan Skelton* 97b
5 b m Ivan Denisovich(IRE) Another Shadow (IRE) (Topanoora)
(4867) 5159[15]

Ambion Wood (IRE) *Victor Dartnall* 153h 127c
8 b g Oscar(IRE) Dorans Grove (Gildoran)
(586)

Amen (IRE) *Gary Moore* 93h 95c
6 b g Galileo(IRE) Kitza (IRE) (Danehill (USA))
240[5] 488[10] 634[8] 1401[5]

American Kiss (SWE) *Robin Dickin* 35h
5 b m American Post Power Kiss (SWE) (Richard Of York)
46[10] 1305[P]

American Legend (IRE) *Jonjo O'Neill* 115h 110c
6 b g Presenting Cool Eile (IRE) (King's Ride)
(998) 1304[3]

American Life (FR) *Anthony Middleton* 110h
7 bb g American Post Poplife (FR) (Zino)
2105[9] 2807[5] 3191[4] 3413[2] 3638[2] 3784[2] 4006[2]
4271[P] 4662[F] 4949[7] 5379[3] 5544[5]

American Spin *Luke Dace* 140h 139c
10 ch g Groom Dancer(USA) Sea Vixen (Machiavellian (USA))
302[3] (518)
1821[5] 2953[10] 3321[P] 4741[10]

American Trilogy (IRE) *Dan Skelton* 130h 126c
10 gr g Sendawar(IRE) Affaire Classee (FR) (Anabaa (USA))
1485[6] 1867[9]

Amethyst Rose (IRE) *Stuart Coltherd* 89h
7 ch m Beneficial Cap The Rose (IRE) (Roselier (FR))
313[7] 2156[11] (2596) 2974[8] 3396[4] 3940[8] 4201[P]
4774[12] 5556[2]

Am I Blue *Mrs D Thomas* 104h
8 b m Dubai Destination(USA) Seal Indigo (IRE) (Glenstal (USA))
83[3] 144[7] 237[5] 730[6] 1110[4] 1266[5]

Amigo (FR) *David Pipe* 133h 128c
7 b g Ballingarry(IRE) Allez Y (FR) (Pistolet Bleu (IRE))
2180[7] 2798[14]
3361[7]

Amilliontimes (IRE) *Mrs Jackie Stephen* 98h
6 b g Olden Times Miss Million (IRE) (Roselier (FR))
1667[11] 1875[9] 2355[10] 5479[2]

Aminah *Venetia Williams* 76h
4 b f Dubawi(IRE) Why Dubai (USA) (Kris S (USA))
2934[5] 3385[6]

Amirico (IRE) *Richard Rowe* 46h 103c
9 b g Lord Americo Maori's Delight (Idiots Delight)
99[P] 543[7]

Amir Pasha (UAE) *Micky Hammond* 102h
9 br g Halling(USA) Clarinda (IRE) (Lomond (USA))
(2449) (2736) 2879[7] 3451[8] 4378[4] 4615[9] 4943[3]
5163[6]

Amisfield Lad *Michael Smith* 87b
5 b g Zafeen(FR) Flying Wind (Forzando)
494[P]

Amistress *Renee Robeson* 105h
6 b m Kalanisi(IRE) Atwirl (Pivotal)
(292) (765)

Amok (IRE) *Tim Vaughan* 112h
6 b g Shirocco(GER) Alharmina (Linamix (FR))
2013[3] 2529[7] 2903[F]

Amore Alato *Nick Williams* 139h
5 b g Winged Love(IRE) Sardagna (FR) (Medaaly)
1864[4] (2369) (3258) 3891[3] 4421[2] 5153[10]

Amore Mio (GER) *Lucinda Russell* 107h 101c
9 b g Trempolino(USA) Amore (GER) (Lando (GER))
1873[4] (2218) 2843[3] 3413[6] 3938[3] 4577[5] 4649[4]
5106[4] 5514[6]

Amoruccio (FR) *Paul Webber* 99h
4 b g Le Fou(IRE) Mandchou (FR) (Mansonnien (FR))
4401[4] 4784[10] ◆

Amour Collonges (FR) *Chris Grant* 60h
4 b g Lavirco(GER) Kapucine Collonges (FR) (Dom Alco (FR))
2960[12] 3332[5]

Ampleforth *Ian Williams* 116h
6 ch g Pivotal Anna Amalia (IRE) (In The Wings)
2978[5] 3357[11] 3567[2] ◆ 3796[2] (4093) 4545[5]

Amtired *Marjorie Fife* 86h
8 gr g Beauchamp King Rising Talisker (Primitive Rising (USA))
3288[9]

Amuse Me *Jonjo O'Neill* 103h 118c
8 gr g Daylami(IRE) Have Fun (Indian Ridge)
175[3] 636[F] 756[9] 858[5] 966[4]
(1502) 1687[4] 2105[6] 2397[3] 3420[8]

Amy Farah Fowler (IRE) *Martin Todhunter*
5 b m Oratorio(IRE) Fay (IRE) (Polish Precedent (USA))
2883[P]

Analifet (FR) *W P Mullins* 137h
4 b f Califet(FR) Viana (FR) (Signe Divin (USA))
(130a) (2851a) ◆ 3305a[P]

Anay Turge (FR) *Nigel Hawke* 127h 138c
9 gr g Turgeon(USA) Anayette (FR) (Vaguely Pleasant (FR))
236[U] (631)
735[2] 1960[5]
2101[2] (2488)
2816[U] 2890[P] (3838) (4069) 4785[18]
5136[12]

An Capall Mor (IRE) *Donald McCain* 111h 104c
8 b g Flemensfirth(USA) Corravilla (IRE) (Yashgan)
733[P] 853[6] 1085[4] 1396[5]

Ancelotti (IRE) *Michael G Cleary* 90h
5 ch g Modigliani(USA) Dazilyn Lady (USA) (Zilzal (USA))
1139a[12]

Anchoretta Eyre (IRE) *Fergal O'Brien* 71h
8 ch m Endeavour(USA) Derry Lark (IRE) (Lancastrian)
1731[6] 2009[9] 2509[8] 2600[10]

Ancient Greece *George Baker* 89h
7 b g Pivotal Classicism (USA) (A.P. Indy (USA))
732[7]

Ancient Times (USA) *Philip Kirby* 94h 95c
7 bb g Smart Strike(CAN) Histoire Sainte (FR) (Kendor (FR))
220[5] 558[8]
749[7] 2336[6] 2511[9] 2736[4] 3040[8] (3940) 4201[2]
4747[F]

Anda De Grissay (FR) *Anthony Honeyball* 92b
4 b f Network(GER) Karima II (FR) (Luchiroverte (IRE))
2318[4] 2604[2]

Andhaar *Richard Phillips* 131h
8 b g Bahri(USA) Deraasaat (Nashwan (USA))
336[6] 606[P] 845[4] 1155[5] 1340[3]

Andi'Amu (FR) *Warren Greatrex* 109h
4 b g Walk In The Park(IRE) Sainte Parfaite (FR) (Septieme Ciel (USA))
2248[3] 2796[5] 3161[11] 4963[8] 5400[2]

Andreo Bambaleo *Brian Ellison* 113h 125c
10 ch g Silver Patriarch(IRE) Time And A Place (IRE) (Phardante (FR))
121[3] (205) 681[4] 801[7] 2625[2] 2903[U] 3269[6] 5357[5]

And The Man *Nicky Richards* 120h 130c
8 ch g Generous(IRE) Retro's Lady (IRE) (Zaffaran (USA))
3190[P] 3498[2] (3939)
(4204)

Andy Kelly (IRE) *Emma Lavelle* 132h
5 ch g Flemensfirth(USA) Fae Taylor (IRE) (Desert Style (IRE))
1991[4] (2181) 2755[4] ◆ 3186[2] 4144[F] (4808)

Andy Vic (IRE) *Ian Brown* 94h
11 b g Old Vic Garranard Ros (IRE) (Roselier (FR))
444[U]

Aneda Rose (IRE) *G D Hanmer*
10 b m Bob's Return(IRE) Strong Watch (IRE) (Strong Gale)
57[P]

Aneedh *Jedd O'Keeffe* 97h
4 b g Lucky Story(USA) Seed Al Maha (USA) (Seeking The Gold (USA))
1786[3] 4811[3] 5296[3]

A New Rising (IRE) *M E Ellwood* 102h 102c
12 b g New Frontier(IRE) Rising Sara (IRE) (The Parson)
112[2] 496[8] 5323[3]

Aneyeforaneye (IRE) *Malcolm Jefferson* 118h 134c
8 ch m Definite Article Resolute Approach (IRE) (Toulon)
204[8] 680[4] ◆ 900[P] 1659[3] 2065[F] 2358[3] 3287[6]
3759[6]

An Fear Glic (IRE) *Jo Davis* 71h
11 b g Marignan(USA) Nags Head (IRE) (Aristocracy I)
828[P]

Ange Du Lemo (FR) *T Boivin* 102c
7 gr g Maille Pistol(FR) Kiswa (FR) (Top Waltz (FR))
616a[2]

Angelot Du Berlais (FR) *Dr Richard Newland* 117h
5 b g Poliglote Afragha (IRE) (Darshaan)
4426[4]

Anger Management (IRE) *Rebecca Curtis* 83h
8 b g Spadoun(FR) Catherinestown (Warcraft (USA))
(1264) 1427[3] 1632[5] 1860[4]

Angles Hill (IRE) *Richard Woollacott* 126h
7 b g Heron Island(IRE) No Tails Told (IRE) (Glacial Storm (USA))
(1641) 2490[2] 3069[6] 4277[8] 5030[12] 5372[4]

Anglingforcharlie *Philip Hobbs* 10h
5 b g Catcher In The Rye(IRE) Annies Valentine (My Best Valentine)
250[8] 517[12]

Anglo Paddy (IRE) *Sean Curran*
5 ch m Mountain High(IRE) Hazel Sylph (IRE) (Executive Perk)
2153[8] *2583[7]*

Anik De Maspie (FR) *E Leray* 94h 129c
12 b g Panoramic Vagueline De Maspi (FR) (Vaguely Pleasant (FR))
1740a[3]

Aniknam (FR) *Philip Kirby* 109b
4 b g Nickname(FR) Kelle Home (FR) (Useful (FR))
(5108)

Aniri (FR) *F Nicolle* 117h 117c
5 ch g Panis(USA) Seinfeld (FR) (Solid Illusion (USA))
1199a[3]

Anjum (USA) *John Joseph Hanlon* 95h
6 ch m Forestry(USA) Asareer (USA) (Gone West (USA))
73[8]

Annacotty (IRE) *Martin Keighley* 127h 155c
6 b g Beneficial Mini Moo Min (Ardross)
1709[5] 2012[5] (2267)
2646[6] 2941[2] (3260)
3886[2] 4751[8]

Annaluna (IRE) *David Evans* 91h
5 b m Whipper(USA) Annaletta (Belmez (USA))
4351[7] 4571[4]

Annelko *Michael Blake* 105h
7 b g Sulamani(IRE) Creeking (Persian Bold)
140[11] 593[3] 846[4] 1120[2]

Annie Confidential (IRE) *Pam Ford* 78h 81c
11 b m Turtle Island(IRE) Black Ivor (USA) (Sir Ivor (USA))
330[3] 1769[2] 2044[P] 2829[8]

Annie Power (IRE) *W P Mullins* 164h
6 ch m Shirocco(GER) Anno Luce (Old Vic)
(2665) (3459) (3895) ◆ 4767[2]

Annie's Act *Joanne Foster*
5 b m Act One Nite Fox (IRE) (Anshan)
4582[9]

Annie's Daughter *Lynn Siddall* 9b
7 b m Danbird(AUS) Moondance (Siberian Express (USA))
2752[14]

Annies Idea *Mandy Rowland* 87b
5 ch m Yoshka Danum Diva (IRE) (Danehill Dancer (IRE))
841[7] 5196[5]

Annimation (IRE) *Lucy Jones* 100h 90c
10 b m Accordion Euro Breeze (IRE) (Roselier (FR))
3731[3] 4508[3]

Another Article (IRE) *Marc Barber* 61b
6 ch g Definite Article Shuil Ub (Le Moss)
146[7]

Another Brandy (IRE) *Neil Mulholland* 108h 86c
6 b g Oscar(IRE) Reapers Dream (IRE) (Electric)
544[4] 1861[3] 2570[2] 3422[10] 3695[11]
3861[3] 4171[9]

Another Bygones (IRE) *Karen McLintock* 57b
5 b g High-Rise(IRE) Little Chartridge (Anshan)
4964[16]

Another Dark Rum *S J Leadbetter* 70h 77c
10 br g Beat All(USA) Gourmet (IRE) (Homo Sapien)
4617[4]

Another Dimension (IRE) *Rose Dobbin* 91h
8 b g Overbury(IRE) Freshwater (IRE) (Commanche Run)
2447[10] 2879[3] 3605[4] 4816[2] 5161[10]

Another Flutter (IRE) *Matt Sheppard* 100h 115c
10 b g Lahib(USA) Golden Fizz (Carroll House)
853[3] 1050[3] 1263[2] 1390[4] 1566[3] 1711[4]
2025[2] 2191[F]
(5487)

Another Hero (IRE) *Jonjo O'Neill* 129h
5 b g Kalanisi(IRE) Storm Front (IRE) (Strong Gale)
(589) (760) (920) (1108) 1576[2] 1866[2] (2443)
4805[8] 5349[2]

Another Jewel (IRE) *Denis Paul Murphy* 108h 129c
12 b g Saddlers' Hall(IRE) Sapphire Eile (Mujtahid (USA))
199a[6]

Another Journey *Lisa Williamson* 69b
5 b g Rail Link Singasongosixpence (Singspiel (IRE))
760[10]

Another Kate (IRE) *David Richards* 107h 106c
10 gr m Norwich Cracking Kate (IRE) (Roselier (FR))
1518[2] 1594[2] 1865[5] 2618[F]

Another Mattie (IRE) *N W Alexander* 117h
7 b g Zagreb(USA) Silver Tassie (FR) (Kaldounevees (FR))
313[4] 1977[P] 2748[3] 3398[2] 3721[2] 4369[3] 5205[2]
5508[4]

Another Trump (NZ) *Jonjo O'Neill* 99h 109c
10 b g Montjeu(IRE) She's A Trump (NZ) (Centro (NZ))
426[5] 1073[9] 1266[6] 1580[8]

Anquetta (IRE) *Nicky Henderson* 119h 147c
10 b g Anshan Quetta (IRE) (Alphabatim (USA))
(249) (520)
◆ 672[U] 974[5] 1194[5] 3080[11] 4790[10] 5136[P]

Anrheg *Dai Burchell* 52h
6 b m Diktat Dim Ots (Alhijaz)
671[9] 848[P]

Anshantor (IRE) *Henry Daly* 97h
8 ch g Anshan Ephony Lady (IRE) (Lord Americo)
2850[F] 2978[8] 3506[5]

An Spailpin Fanach (USA) *John Joseph Hanlon* 98h
7 ch g Purge(USA) Wild Crazy Lady (USA) (Touch Gold (USA))
598[6]

Anteros (IRE) *Sophie Leech* 123h
6 b g Milan Sovereign Star (IRE) (Taufan (USA))
2018[3] 2471[4] 2876[2] 3278[4] 5426[2]

Antihero *David Thompson* 79h
7 b g Motivator Damsel (Danzero (AUS))
598[2] 1635[P]

Antirrhinum *Ferdy Murphy* 106h
7 b g Bollin Eric Artemesia (Teenoso (USA))
470[3]

Anton Chigurh *Brendan Powell* 108h
5 b g Oasis Dream Barathiki (Barathea (IRE))
3880[2] 4281[7] 4632[3]

Anton Dolin (IRE) *Dr Richard Newland* 102h
6 ch g Danehill Dancer(IRE) Ski For Gold (Shirley Heights)
436[9] 809[2] (844) 977[P] (1269) 1345[6] 1475[5]

Antonius Lad (IRE) *Paul Webber* 85h
7 b g Antonius Pius(USA) Fey Lady (IRE) (Fairy King (USA))
635[P]

Anwyl House *Jo Hughes* 86b
4 gr g Auction House(USA) Amwell Star (USA) (Silver Buck (USA))
2015[5] 5409[6]

Any Currency (IRE) *Martin Keighley* 119h 139c
11 b g Moscow Society(USA) Native Bavard (IRE) (Be My Native (USA))
317[P] **2108[5]**
2491[3] 3068[2] 3655[5] 4754[2]

Any Given Day (IRE) *Donald McCain* 142h 118c
9 gr g Clodovil(IRE) Five Of Wands (Caerleon (USA))
(279) **736[2]**
(4325) 5138[22]

Any Given Moment (IRE) *Sandy Thomson* 117h
8 b g Alhaarth(IRE) Shastri (USA) (Alleged (USA))
24[8] 310[2] 476[2] 2311[3] 2786[2] 3085[3] (3479) 4051[4]

Apache Blue (IRE) *John Wade* 89h 110c
10 b g Presenting La Eile (IRE) (Brief Truce (USA))
1502[5] 1756[4] 5162[P] 5497[4]

Apache Dawn *Aytach Sadik* 97h 91c
10 ch g Pursuit Of Love Taza (Persian Bold)
(65) **694[2]**
964[P] 1086[6] 1172[5] 1260[2] 5363[3]

Apachee Prince (IRE) *Alistair Whillans* 97h
5 b g Indian Danehill(IRE) Wheredidthemoneygo (IRE) (Anshan)
4226[5] 4964[13] 5279[3]

Apache Jack (IRE) *D T Hughes* 149h
6 bb g Oscar(IRE) Cailin Supreme (IRE) (Supreme Leader)
3559a[2] 4786[3]

Apache Pilot *Maurice Barnes* 71h
6 br g Indian Danehill(IRE) Annie-Jo (Presenting)
3657[P] 4221[P] 5205[5]

Apache Stronghold (IRE) *Noel Meade* 149h
6 b g Milan First Battle (IRE) (Un Desperado (FR))
(2706a) ◆ 5200a[4]

A Pint Ahead (IRE) *Donal Hassett* 78h
5 b g Golan(IRE) Reproche Orient (FR) (Garde Royale)
2995a[8]

Apollo Eleven (IRE) *Donald McCain* 105h
5 bb g Manduro(GER) Arlesienne (IRE) (Alzao (USA))
1578[3] 1958[3] 2217[8] 2932[8]

Apolskapart (IRE) *Michael Smith* 103h
6 b g Red Ransom(USA) Polska (USA) (Danzig (USA))
561[3] 1072[4] 1419[P]

Appeal Denied (IRE) *Sandy Forster* 79h 29c
12 ch g Lord Of Appeal Cothu Na Slaine (IRE) (Roselier (FR))
20[P]

Applause For Amy (IRE) *Mary Sanderson* 84h
7 b m King's Theatre(IRE) Amathea (FR) (Exit To Nowhere (USA))
4331[P] 4883[5] 5143[6]

Apples And Trees (IRE) *Donald McCain* 97b
5 b g Oscar(IRE) Native Bramble (IRE) (Be My Native (USA))
5324[3]

Apterix (FR) *Brian Ellison* 75h
4 b g Day Flight Ohe Les Aulmes (FR) (Lute Antique (FR))
3926[4] 4234[6]

Aqalim *John Ferguson* 120b
4 b g Raven's Pass(USA) Aviacion (BRZ) (Know Heights (IRE))
(3049) (4424) 5173[3]

Arabougg *Nikki Evans* 53h
4 b g Tobougg(IRE) Arabellas Homer (Mark Of Esteem (IRE))
1439[7] 1781[P]

Araglen Lad (IRE) *J J Lambe* 61h 109c
8 b g Chinook Eclipse(USA) Lovely Valley (IRE) (Glacial Storm (USA))
5254[3]

Arakelton *Mark H Tompkins* 81b
6 b m Largesse Sally Rainbow (Primitive Rising (USA))
1472[4] 2254[8]

Araldur (FR) *Alan King* 144h 155c
10 ch g Spadoun(FR) Aimessa (FR) (Tropular)
215[4] 2080[5] 2504[15]

Arbeo (IRE) *Diana Grissell* 87h 109c
8 b g Brian Boru Don't Waste It (IRE) (Mister Lord (USA))
2065[P] 4134[6] 4685[P]

Arbour Hill (IRE) *Miss Francesca Moller* 103c
12 b g Moonax(IRE) Croagh Lady (IRE) (Electric)
60[4] (328)

Arcas (IRE) *Alan Jones* 48h
5 br g Shamardal(USA) Callisto (IRE) (Darshaan)
1793[13] 2476[13] 3173[P] 3783[9] 4721[12]

Arcayo (IRE) *Gary Moore*
5 b g Arcadio(GER) Hindi (FR) (Cadoudal (FR))
2536[P]

Archie Boy (IRE) *R D Potter* 83h 100c
12 b g Basanta(IRE) Darial Mill (IRE) (Salluceva)
335[6] 718[P]
5292[3]

Archie Meade (IRE) *Daniel John Howard* 137h 131c
9 b g Beneficial Polar Charm (IRE) (Supreme Leader)
3868a[P]

Arctic Ben (IRE) *Henry Daly* 107h 126c
10 gr g Beneficial Hurst Flyer (Neltino)
2180[5] 2785[8] 3204[4] 4007[6] 4948[2] 5516[3]

Arctic Chief *Richard Phillips*
4 b g Sleeping Indian Neiges Eternelles (FR) (Exit To Nowhere (USA))
2731[2]

Arctic Court (IRE) *Jim Goldie* 123h
10 b g Arctic Lord Polls Joy (IRE) (Pollerton)
(24) 356[6] (2345) 3479[4] 4051[P] 4954[5] 5277[P]

Arctic Dixie *Rob Summers* 91b
6 ch m Desideratum Arctic Oats (Oats)
1317[3] 1671[8]

Arctic Fire (GER) *W P Mullins* 150h
5 b g Soldier Hollow Adelma (GER) (Sternkoenig (IRE))
2852a[3] 3339a[4] 4785[2]

Arctic Pond (IRE) *Jonjo O'Neill* 96h
6 bb g Presenting Bar Un'que (IRE) (Un Desperado (FR))
482[8] 854[P]

Arctic Trail (IRE) *Paul John Gilligan* 79h
8 b g Flemensfirth(USA) River Valley Lady (IRE) (Salt Dome (USA))
518[P]

Arc Warrior (FR) *William Amos* 100h 99c
10 b g Even Top(IRE) What The Hell (IRE) (Henbit (USA))
3022[3] (3497)
(3827) 4382[P]

Arden Denis (IRE) *Tom Symonds* 100b
5 ch g Generous(IRE) Christian Lady (IRE) (Mandalus)
4310[3] 4728[8]

Ardenlee Lad (IRE) *Philip Kirby* 89b
4 b g Westerner Little Elk (IRE) (Be My Native (USA))
4611[6] 5166[2]

Ardkilly Witness (IRE) *Dr Richard Newland* 135h 141c
8 b g Witness Box(USA) Ardkilly Angel (IRE) (Yashgan)
2459[2] 2756[3] (3291)
4035[2] 4422[5] (5192)
5571[11]

Ardlui (IRE) *Alan King* 129h
6 b g Galileo(IRE) Epping (Charnwood Forest (IRE))
2230[P]

Ardmaddy (IRE) *Sheena West* 94h
10 b g Generous(IRE) Yazmin (IRE) (Green Desert (USA))
243[8]

Ardnahoe (IRE) *David A Kiely* 112b
4 b f Brian Boru Queen Sophie (IRE) (Be My Native (USA))
5374[4]

Area Access (IRE) *Charlie Mann* 112h
6 b g Oscar(IRE) Lady Bramble (IRE) (Be My Native (USA))
2181[10] 2621[12] 2947[8] (4733) 4865[2] (5069) 5395[3]

Area Fifty One *Nicky Henderson* 107h
6 b g Green Desert(USA) Secret History (USA) (Bahri (USA))
3872[6]

Aregra (FR) *Peter Niven* 67b
4 gr g Fragrant Mix(IRE) Elisa De Mai (FR) (Video Rock (FR))
4582[6]

Are They Your Own (IRE) *Fergal O'Brien* 74h
6 b g Exit To Nowhere(USA) Carioca Dream (USA) (Diesis)
(412) 647[4] 760[7] 1007[5] 1176[8]

Areuwitmenow (IRE) *S Rea* 114h 102c
9 b g Beneficial Clonartic (IRE) (Be My Native (USA))
4658[4] 4922[5] 5248[4]

Are We There *Carroll Gray* 95b
5 ch g Needwood Blade Hayden Grace (In The Wings)
3994[12] 4335[5] 5021[5]

Are Ya Right Chief (IRE) *W P Mullins* 128h 134c
9 b g Flemensfirth(USA) River Clyde (IRE) (Presenting)
4821[P]

Arfur Didit (IRE) *Sarah Humphrey* 85h
6 b g Blueprint(IRE) Authentic Creature (IRE) (Beneficial)
3506[4] 3850[6] 4761[6]

Argaum (IRE) *Evan Williams* 97h
7 ch g Medicean Poppy Carew (IRE) (Danehill (USA))
184[4] 482[11] 977[3] 1285[4] 1428[2] (1643)

Argocat (IRE) *T J Taaffe* 130h 167c
6 b g Montjeu(IRE) Spirit Of South (AUS) (Giant's Causeway (USA))
2235a[F] 3751a[6] (4283a)
5133[3]

Arguidos (IRE) *Debra Hamer* 87h 72c
10 b g Winged Love(IRE) Open Meeting (IRE) (Maledetto (IRE))
335[P] 1267[P] 1342[6] 1887[9] 2571[4] 2921[5]

Ariane Nopolis (FR) *Gordon Elliott* 93h
4 b f Saint Des Saints(FR) Okawanga Royale (FR) (Lesotho (USA))
2066[3]

Arisda *Johnny Farrelly* 95h
6 b m Exit To Nowhere(USA) Clotted Cream (USA) (Eagle Eyed (USA))
450[6] 629[2] 1136[P]

Arizona River *Jason Ward* 81h
8 b m Fair Mix(IRE) Halo Flora (Alflora (IRE))
1977[P] 3141[P]

Arkaim *Pam Sly* 103h 129c
6 b g Oasis Dream Habariya (IRE) (Perugino (USA))
21[8] 384[5] **(2315)**
(2677) 3833[U] 4241[2] (4653)
4804[4]

Arkansas Dave (IRE) *Mark Michael McNiff* 86h
7 b g Dr Massini(IRE) Martinstown Lady (IRE) (Scribano)
290[3] 3636[5] 4527[7]

Arkendale (IRE) *Miss K L Mellor* 110b
12 b g Portrait Gallery(IRE) Baby Alice (IRE) (Top Of The World)
4443[P]

Arkose (IRE) *Oliver Sherwood* 129h 122c
10 b g Luso Endless Patience (IRE) (Miner's Lamp)
2283[3] 2678[2] 3505[4] 4449[P] **(5406)**

Arman (GER) *J Vana Jr*
9 b g Lando(GER) Ariane Zwei (GER) (Big Shuffle (USA))
1683a[4]

Armedandbeautiful *Tom Gretton* 100h
6 b m Oscar(IRE) Grey Mistral (Terimon)
2317[7] 3010[7] 3828[7] 4533[4] 5438[2] ◆

Armedanddangerous (IRE) *Tom Gretton* 104h 113c
9 b g Kris Kin(USA) Lucky Fountain (IRE) (Lafontaine (USA))
2650[2] 3178[3] 4601[4]

Armenian Boy (FR) *Jackie Du Plessis* 85h 129c
11 b g Simon Du Desert(FR) Jade D'Eau (IRE) (Lion Cavern (USA))
2458[11]

Armoury House *D Buckett* 91h 118c
13 ch g Gunner B Coire Vannich (Celtic Cone)
329[4]

Arnaud (IRE) *C Byrnes* 131h 152c
6 b g Chevalier(IRE) Jumbo Romance (IRE) (Tagula (IRE))
3893[2] ◆ 5136[9]

Aroseforoscar *Chris Down* 86h
5 b m Oscar(IRE) Made For A King (Roselier (FR))
3168[6] 3733[P] 3991[4] 4500[5] 4887[F] 5177[11]

Around A Pound (IRE) *Nick Kent* 104h 100c
9 b g Old Vic Mary Ellen Best (IRE) (Danehill (USA))
68[2] 421[10] 1205[8]
3268[4] 3739[2] 4695[P] 4865[P]

Arrayan *Alexandra Dunn* 125h 115c
9 b g Catcher In The Rye(IRE) Ganga (IRE) (Generous (IRE))
48[8] 2569[6] 3094[6]
3439[P] (4087) 4513[2] 4791[P]

Arrow Barrow (IRE) *John Wade* 94h 97c
9 b g Moscow Society(USA) Miss Nee (IRE) (Strong Gale)
20[3] (285)
600[3]

Arrowmint *Nicholas Pomfret* 72h
8 b m Executive Perk Araminta (Carlingford Castle)
67[P] 268[P]

Arte Del Calcio *Tony Carroll* 95h
5 b g Manduro(GER) Movie Queen (Danehill (USA))
2292[14] 3871[12]

Artful Dodger *Helen Nelmes* 59h
7 b g Josr Algarhoud(IRE) Artistic Belle (IRE) (Orpen (USA))
5303[7]

Arthamint *Nicholas Pomfret* 45b
6 b g Passing Glance Araminta (Carlingford Castle)
4763[9] 5409[8]

Arthurian Legend *Philip Hobbs* 135h 135c
9 b g Alflora(IRE) Be My Adelina (IRE) (Be My Native (USA))
2077[4] 2798[18]

Arthur Mc Bride (IRE) *Fergal O'Brien* 80h
5 bb g Royal Anthem(USA) Lucky Diverse (IRE) (Lucky Guest)
2759[5] 4547[6] 5338[2]

Arthur's Oak *Venetia Williams* 120h
6 b g Kayf Tara Myumi (Charmer)
4[3] 3501[2] 3735[4] (4171) 5024[3]

Arthur's Pass *Tom George* 106h 137c
10 b g Midnight Legend Bella Coola (Northern State (USA))
2086[P] 2812[P] 3090[4] 3642[8] 4104[P] 4593[P] 5006[P]

Artic Night (FR) *Nigel Twiston-Davies* 91h 78c
8 gr g Take Risks(FR) Just Win (FR) (Homme De Loi (IRE))
1266[P] 1406[5] (1673)
2088[2] 2473[3] 2680[6] 3227[8]
3797[F]

Artic Pride (IRE) *Mrs Emma Clark* 72h 100c
10 b g Definite Article Tricias Pride (IRE) (Broken Hearted)
58[DSQ] (388)
658[P]

Artifice Sivola (FR) *Lucy Wadham* 88h
4 gr g Dom Alco(FR) Kerrana (FR) (Cadoudal (FR))
4889[7] 5190[7] 5436[2]

Artiste Rochelais (FR) *Mme I Pacault*
4 b g Al Namix(FR) Neige Rochelaise (FR) (Goldneyev (USA))
262a[P]

Artists Boy *Chris Down* 15b
7 ch g Thank Heavens Night Bloomer (USA) (Told (USA))
3956[P]

Artiwork (FR) *S Foucher* 91h
4 bl f Network(GER) Ribertina (FR) (Rifapour (IRE))
130a[0]

Art Mauresque (FR) *Paul Nicholls* 122h
4 b g Policy Maker(IRE) Modeva (FR) (Valanour (IRE))
2500[7] 4266[3]

Art Of Logistics (IRE) *D T Hughes* 142h 146c
6 b g Exit To Nowhere(USA) Sanadja (IRE) (Slip Anchor)
(1950a)
2853a[5] 3308a[4] 4742[13]

Art Of Payroll (GER) *D T Hughes* 144h
5 b g Shirocco(GER) Anna Maria (GER) (Night Shift (USA))
2377a[4] 3339a[5] 5153[6] 5420a[6]

Art Professor (IRE) *Venetia Williams* 134h
10 b g In The Wings Itab (USA) (Dayjur (USA))
215[20] 3206[2] 3646[P] 4112[2] 4264[2] 4789[17] 5158[19]

Arty Campbell (IRE) *Bernard Llewellyn* 49h
4 b g Dylan Thomas(IRE) Kincob (USA) (Kingmambo (USA))
3127[0] 3360[5]

Arum De L'Argos (FR) *Y Gourraud* 99b
4 gr g Smadoun(FR) Onoleeta (FR) (Nononito (FR))
5579a[5]

Arumun (IRE) *Alan Phillips* 81h 101c
13 b g Posidonas Adwoa (IRE) (Eurobus)
287[P] 655[5]

Arvika Ligeonniere (FR) *W P Mullins* 146h 166c
9 b g Arvico(FR) Daraka (FR) (Akarad (FR))
(2483a)
(2991a) 3338a[3] (4062a)
4753[P] (5197a)

Arzembouy Premier (FR) *Gordon Elliott* 127h 109c
4 b g Lavirco(GER) Laurence (FR) (Hawker's News (IRE))
3305a[4] 4755[16]

Ascott Rock (FR) *Mme P Butel* 84h
4 b g Antarctique(IRE) Ascotte Royale (FR) (Cadoudal (FR))
1741a[P]

As De Mee (FR) *Paul Nicholls* 104b
4 bb g Kapgarde(FR) Koeur De Mee (FR) (Video Rock (FR))
4298[4]

As Du Bosc (FR) *F-M Cottin* 105h
4 b g Valanour(IRE) Fourmille (FR) (Rose Laurel)
614a[9]

A Shade Of Bay *Kim Bailey* 110h
6 b m Midnight Legend Pulling Strings (IRE) (Accordion)
2022[4] 2506[14] 3010[P] 3289[6] (3570) 4392[5] 4907[P] 5124[7] 5509[4]

Ashbrittle *Neil King* 126h
7 b g Rainbow Quest(USA) Caesarea (GER) (Generous (IRE))
1766[3]

Ashclyst (IRE) *L Jefford* 98c
12 b g Anshan Donegal Grey (IRE) (Roselier (FR))
523[4]

Ashcott Boy *Neil Mulholland* 94h 91c
6 ch g Lahib(USA) Last Ambition (IRE) (Cadeaux Genereux)
368[9] 810[2] 1120[7] 2004[10] 2568[5]
3785[P] 4416[4] 4734[3] 5144[P]

Ashdown Lad *Tom Symonds* 111h
5 ch g Sir Percy Antibes (IRE) (Grand Lodge (USA))
1779[5] 2040[2] (2272) 2561[11] 3263[10] 5239[10]

Ashes House (IRE) *Rebecca Curtis* 125h
8 b g Dushyantor(USA) Cailinclover (IRE) (Ajraas (USA))
1937[2] ◆ (2509) 3177[6] 3592[5] 4839[2] 5280[P]

Ashford Wood (IRE) *Tim Vaughan* 119h
6 b g Stowaway Shambala (IRE) (Imperial Ballet (IRE))
3363[2] 4030[3] (4838) 5332[4]

Ashmolian (IRE) *Zoe Davison* 86h
11 b g Grand Lodge(USA) Animatrice (USA) (Alleged (USA))
99[8]

Ashtonmore *Miss V Renwick* 67h 69c
11 b g Classic Cliche(IRE) Sillymore (Silly Prices)
4554[9]

As I Am (IRE) *Don Cantillon* 140h
6 b m Old Vic Faucon (Polar Falcon (USA))
(717) 878[4] (1090) (1187) (1265) (1321) 2371[3] (2810) 3203[2] 3423[3] (5368)

Asian Prince (IRE) *Alastair Lidderdale* 94h 110c
5 b g Strategic Prince Asian Alliance (IRE) (Soviet Star (USA))
177[3] 407[2] 844[12]
2249[3] 5027[P] (5442)

Askalott (IRE) *Jean McGregor* 44b
9 b g Ashkalani(IRE) Alottalady (IRE) (Mandalus)
114[P] 679[P] 959[4] 2792[P]

Askamore Darsi (IRE) *Donald McCain* 122h
5 b g Darsi(FR) Galamear (Strong Gale)
(3016) 3616[2] 4200[P] (4891)

Asker (IRE) *Zoe Davison* 74h
6 b g High Chaparral(IRE) Pay The Bank (High Top)
3151[7] *4494[5]* 4781[5] 5012[7]

Ask The Boss *Tim Dennis* 79h
9 b g Deploy Fermoy Lady (IRE) (Riot Helmet)
2076[8] 2457[12] 2689[9] 3425[9] **4884[F]**

Assam Black (IRE) *Harry Fry* 115b
6 b g Oscar(IRE) Contrasting Lady (Respect)
1861[2] (2479) 4756[19]

Assembly *Pat Phelan* 37h
4 ch g Kyllachy Constitute (USA) (Gone West (USA))
1985[8]

Astaroland (FR) *Jennie Candlish* 85b
4 b g Astarabad(USA) Orlandaise (FR) (Goldneyev (USA))
3640[3] 4310[5]

Aster's Approval *David Bridgwater*
4 b g With Approval(CAN) Aster (IRE) (Danehill (USA))
4722[13] 5174[P]

Astigos (FR) *Venetia Williams* 120h
7 b g Trempolino(USA) Astonishing (BRZ) (Vacilante (ARG))
3457[P] 3737[3] 3798[4] 4271[2] 4393[6] 5186[3]

Astracad (FR) *Nigel Twiston-Davies* 139h 150c
8 br g Cadoudal(FR) Astre Eria (FR) (Garde Royale)
249[4] 1969[5] 2071[2] 2503[11] 3080[3] 3320[3] 4790[P]
5136[4] 5350[2]

A Stray Shot (IRE) *G M O'Neill* 87h 115c
7 b g Great Palm(USA) Take Aim (Gunner B)
4754[6]

Astre De La Cour (FR) *Robert Walford* 115h
4 bb g Khalkevi(IRE) Gracieuse Delacour (FR) (Port Etienne (FR))
3317[4] (3768) 4755[F]

Astrogold *Mark H Tompkins* 85h
5 ch m Motivator Mega (IRE) (Petardia)
1561[P] 1793[5] 2190[11]

Astrum *Neil King* 109h
4 gr g Haafhd Vax Star (Petong)
3714[4] 4073[2] 4679[2] ◆

A Suivre (FR) *A Lamotte D'Argy* 97c
5 b m Lando(GER) Ulanowa (GER) (Kamiros (IRE))
1465a[6]

Ata Boy (IRE) *Richard Phillips* 76h 72c
8 br g Key Of Luck(USA) Atalina (FR) (Linamix (FR))
434[3] 716[4] 3188[10]
4780[4] 5111[3] 5401[P]

A Tail Of Intrigue (IRE) *Ian Williams* 118h
6 b g Tillerman Princess Commanche (IRE) (Commanche Run)
1499[2] 1732[2] 2509[2] 2826[5] 3226[2] *4297[5]* 4664[P]

At First Light *Jonathan Geake* 94b
5 b m Echo Of Light Bisaat (USA) (Bahri (USA))
4329[6] (5188)

At Fishers Cross (IRE) *Rebecca Curtis* 166h
7 b g Oscar(IRE) Fermoy Supreme (IRE) (Supreme Leader)
2814^4 3198^U 3890^2 4767^3 5169^2

Atherstone Hill (IRE) *Robin Dickin* 73h 66c
12 b g Presenting Mystic Madam (IRE) (Lafontaine (USA))
32^P 461^8

Atlanta Falcon (IRE) *Donald McCain* 120h 127c
9 b g Winged Love(IRE) Oneofmegirls (IRE) (Supreme Leader)
(500) **728^2**
(943) **1076^2**
1184^P 1787^2 2446^2 3065^F

Atlantic Roller (IRE) *Paul Nicholls* 127h 93c
7 b g Old Vic Tourist Attraction (IRE) (Pollerton)
2490^{11} 3875^3 **5031^6**

At Reception (IRE) *Jonjo O'Neill* 111h
7 b g Gamut(IRE) Receptionist (Reference Point)
2195^2 4304^2 (4863) 5520^3

Atriptomilan (IRE) *Jonjo O'Neill* 103h 85c
6 b g Milan Lady Of Sonas (IRE) (Lancastrian)
179^8 1010^P 3277^P

Attaglance *Malcolm Jefferson* 141h 146c
8 b g Passing Glance Our Ethel (Be My Chief (USA))
217^P 1663^2 2503^4 ◆ 3082^9 4051^5
4742^2 5158^{12}

Attansky (IRE) *Tim Easterby* 79h
4 b g Ivan Denisovich(IRE) Attanagh (IRE) (Darnay)
1920^7 2168^U

Attawo (FR) *A Lamotte D'Argy* 97h
4 b g Turtle Bowl(IRE) Maikawa (FR) (Green Tune (USA))
614a^4

Attente De Sivola (FR) *Paul Nicholls* 62b
4 gr f Dom Alco(FR) Gamine D'Ici (FR) (Cadoudal (FR))
3167^8 4730^P

Attila De Sivola (FR) *Y-M Porzier* 127h 135c
4 ch g Kapgarde(FR) Wild Rose Bloom (FR) (Kaldounevees (FR))
2262a^6

Attimo (GER) *Charlie Mann* 102h
5 ch g Nayef(USA) Alanda (GER) (Lando (GER))
2280^5 2661^5 3598^6

Attrapeur (FR) *Michael Easterby* 7h 97c
10 b g Raintrap Pampa Girl (FR) (Pampabird)
1109^7

Attwaal (IRE) *Neil King* 115h
5 b g Teofilo(IRE) Qasirah (IRE) (Machiavellian (USA))
4103^4 (4569) (4987) 5294^F

Attycran (IRE) *Maurice Barnes* 112h 107c
9 b g Snurge Baltimore Lass (IRE) (Anshan)
77^3 282^2 552^2 753^2 866^5 1715^2 1872^7 2224^3
2747^3 2969^6
5356^6

Auberge (IRE) *Evelyn Slack* 100h
10 ch m Blueprint(IRE) Castlegrace I (IRE) (Kemal (FR))
(628) (751) 804^2 1398^7 1565^4 1797^4 2035^3
2218^4 2789^2 3356^F 4308^6 4553^4 4774^{11} 5359^5
◆

Aubusson (FR) *Nick Williams* 137h
5 b g Ballingarry(IRE) Katioucha (FR) (Mansonnien (FR))
1199a^7 (2940) (3454) 3889^3

Audacious *Charles Pogson* 91h
6 b g Motivator Flash Of Gold (Darshaan)
69^U 560^8 2783^P 2876^P

Audacious Plan (IRE) *Rebecca Curtis* 113h
5 b g Old Vic North Star Poly (IRE) (Presenting)
2028^4 2720^7 4931^3

Aughcarra (IRE) *Harry Chisman* 80h
9 b g High Chaparral(IRE) Pearly Brooks (Efisio)
605^5 903^3 966^3 1206^P

Augher Castle (IRE) *Patrick Mooney* 90h
6 ch g Lahib(USA) Castlemartin (IRE) (Carlingford Castle)
3215a^5

Aughnacurraveel (IRE) *Thomas P Cummins* 140h 129c
10 b g Tajraasi(USA) Water Ore (IRE) (Ore)
1067a^5 3866a^5

August Hill (IRE) *Philip Hobbs* 119h
6 b m Presenting Nuit Des Chartreux (FR) (Villez (USA))
1861^5 2190^4 2767^7 3289^2 5005^F (5304) (5490)

Auld Sthock (IRE) *Gary Moore* 124h
6 ch g Definite Article Native Archive (IRE) (Be My Native (USA))
484^9 2002^2 ◆ 2272^2 2569^3 3136^4 4332^5 4801^4
(5457)

Aupcharlie (IRE) *Henry De Bromhead* 131h 153c
8 b g Daliapour(IRE) Lirfa (USA) (Lear Fan (USA))
4283a^F

Auroras Encore (IRE) *Sue Smith* 137h 152c
12 b g Second Empire(IRE) Sama Veda (IRE) (Rainbow Quest (USA))
3285^5 3897^9

Aurore D'Estruval (FR) *John Quinn* 127h
4 ch f Nickname(FR) Option D'Estruval (FR) (Epervier Bleu)
(4037) 4268^2 ◆ 5132^5

Ausone Kergador (FR) *G Ridel* 92b
4 b g Dark Moondancer Just In (FR) (Start Fast (FR))
5579a^6

Australia Day (IRE) *Paul Webber* 138h 154c
11 gr g Key Of Luck(USA) Atalina (FR) (Linamix (FR))
(81) 673^9 1046^7 2344^4

Authentic Act (IRE) *Martin Todhunter* 64h 74c
10 ch g Pivotal All In All (Halling (USA))
17^{11} **281^8**
627^7

Authorative (IRE) *Patrick O Brady* 65h
4 b g Refuse To Bend(IRE) Reasonably Devout (CAN) (St Jovite (USA))
2851a^7

Auto Mac *Mike Sowersby* 83h
6 b g Auction House(USA) Charlottevalentina (IRE) (Perugino (USA))
2900^7 3144^{11} 3350^8 5519^8

Autumm Spirit *Robin Dickin* 107c
10 ch m Kadastrof(FR) Dickies Girl (Saxon Farm)
457^2 689^P 844^P
1050^P 1914^P 2313^P

Autumn Day (IRE) *Luke Dace*
9 b g Milan Alice Freyne (IRE) (Lancastrian)
2727^P 3687^P 5023^P

Autumn Haze *Phillip Dando* 75h 85c
9 b g Chaddleworth(IRE) Kristal Haze (Krisinsky (USA))
43^P 478^P

Avanos (FR) *Philip Kirby* 85h 71c
9 b g Kaldounevees(FR) Annee De La Femme (IRE) (Common Grounds)
930^6

Avenging Ace (IRE) *Donald McCain* 119h 98c
8 b g Heron Island(IRE) How Provincial (IRE) (Be My Native (USA))
930^P

Aves (IRE) *Timothy Doyle* 81h
7 bb m Overbury(IRE) Anna Bird (IRE) (Be My Native (USA))
891a^{12}

Aviador (GER) *Lucy Wadham* 101h
8 b g Paolini(GER) Albarana (GER) (Sure Blade (USA))
4783^U 4933^8

Avidity *James Ewart* 116h
5 b g Passing Glance Epicurean (Pursuit Of Love)
2493^4 (4647)

Aviso (GER) *David Evans* 99h 126c
10 b g Tertullian(USA) Akasma (GER) (Windwurf (GER))
10^7

Avispa *Alan King* 116b
5 b m Kayf Tara Ladylliat (FR) (Simon Du Desert (FR))
2298^4 ◆ (4114) 4683^4 (5159)

Avoca Promise (IRE) *Tom Symonds* 121h 130c
9 b g Oscar(IRE) High Ace (IRE) (Good Thyne (USA))
(1916)
2212^{11} 3109^2 3690^P 4507^4

Avondhu Lady (IRE) *David Fenton* 127h 140c
9 ch m Beneficial Rag's Lady (IRE) (King's Ride)
2484a^3 5475a^5

A Vos Gardes (FR) *Charlie Longsdon* 118b
4 b g Kapgarde(FR) Miscia Nera (FR) (Panoramic)
(2456) (4267)

Award Winner *Brendan Powell* 105h 91c
11 b g Alflora(IRE) Blackwater Bay (IRE) (Supreme Leader)
421^8 730^{13} (1136) 1940^6 2253^7 4519^5 5122^P

Awareiness (IRE) *Chris Bealby*
8 b g Flemensfirth(USA) Special Case (IRE) (Be My Native (USA))
5059^P

Away We Go (IRE) *W P Mullins* 131h 146c
11 ch g Stowaway Margurites Pet (IRE) (Roselier (FR))
5474a^9

Awaywiththegreys (IRE) *Peter Bowen* 135h 129c
7 gr g Whipper(USA) Silver Sash (GER) (Mark Of Esteem (IRE))
779^2 861^4 1042^9
1150^2 2652^2 3060^3 (3359) 4025^4 4415^3 4545^3

Awesome Bella *David Rees* 100h 23c
7 b m Karinga Bay Awesome Aunt (IRE) (Vestris Abu)
5545^5

Awesome Freddie *Dan Skelton* 93h 94c
9 b g Karinga Bay Awesome Aunt (IRE) (Vestris Abu)
3286^4 3784^P **4946^4**

Aw Ripe China (IRE) *Simon Waugh* 93h
6 b g Bach(IRE) Karolena Bay (Karinga Bay)
284^7 629^6 1754^5 1975^5 2449^P

Azabitmour (FR) *Suzy Smith* 108h
4 b g Azamour(IRE) Brixa (FR) (Linamix (FR))
(5400)

Azaria (FR) *Mrs A Malzard*
8 b m Miesque's Son(USA) Polar Return (FR) (Polar Falcon (USA))
1827a^3 5478a^3

Azaro De La Mare (FR) *E Leray* 73c
6 b g Agnes Kamikaze(JPN) Love Love Kate (FR) (Saint Andrews (FR))
198a^8

Azerodegree (IRE) *Harriet Graham* 94h 82c
5 b g Azamour(IRE) Fairy (USA) (Gulch (USA))
223^2 313^6 2792^7 4553^{14} **5216^3**

Azolla De Sivola (FR) *T Trapenard* 86h
4 bb g Shaanmer(IRE) Histoire Des Ifs (FR) (Robin Des Champs (FR))
262a^P

Azorian (IRE) *Eoin Griffin* 143h
6 b g Westerner Eliane Di Rupette (Cosmonaut)
2706a^2 3122a^2 3380a^3 4180a^6 5200a^3

Azure Aware (IRE) *Kim Bailey* 125h
7 b g Milan Luck Penni (IRE) (Erdelistan (FR))
(140) **2024^F**

Azure Fly (IRE) *Charlie Longsdon* 129h
6 br g Blueprint(IRE) Lady Delight (IRE) (Be My Native (USA))
484^2 695^U (857) (1779) 1987^3 2454^5 2813^{14}
3186^6 4697^2 5093^3 5372^{15}

Azure Glamour (IRE) *Nicky Richards* 109b
5 br g Golan(IRE) Mirazur (IRE) (Good Thyne (USA))
4895^2 5279^{13}

Azza (FR) *David Pipe* 118h
4 bb f Great Pretender(IRE) Indecise (FR) (Cyborg (FR))
(2154) 2500^3 4755^{17}

Bab Al Salam (USA) *John Ferguson* 116h
8 b g Seeking The Gold(USA) Encandiladora (ARG) (Equalize (USA))
202^6

Baby Mix (FR) *Warren Greatrex* 139h 143c
6 gr g Al Namix(FR) Douchka (FR) (Fijar Tango (FR))
216^{15} **(634)**
◆ 830^2 2295^2 (2716)
3196^3

Baby Run (FR) *Nigel Twiston-Davies* 134h 148c
14 b g Baby Turk Run For Laborie (FR) (Lesotho (USA))
2937^2 3414^4

Baby Shine (IRE) *Lucy Wadham* 130h 139c
8 b m King's Theatre(IRE) Brambleshine (IRE) (Phardante (FR))
2019^F 2622^2 3030^2 (3279)
(3718) 4262^4 4468^2 4848a^F 5369^3

Baby's Hot (IRE) *D T Hughes* 107h 98c
10 b m Winged Love(IRE) Annaelaine (IRE) (Wood Chanter)
1163^P (Dead)

Baccalaureate (FR) *Sue Smith* 127h 101c
8 b g High Chaparral(IRE) Rose D'Or (IRE) (Polish Precedent (USA))
93^3 (581) (697) 850^4 1046^{10}
1301^2

Bachelor Lad (IRE) *C A McBratney* 112h 93c
10 ch g Bach(IRE) Saddlers Dawn (IRE) (Saddlers' Hall (IRE))
798^P

Bacher Son (IRE) *Paul Stafford*
9 b g Bach(IRE) Dillys Dawn (IRE) (Old Vic)
1074^P

Bach On Tow (IRE) *Sue Gardner* 86h
7 b g Bach(IRE) Handmade (IRE) (Supreme Leader)
(407) 598^5 5522^{12}

Back Bob Back (IRE) *Tom George* 101h 120c
9 b g Bob Back(USA) Joyney (Harlow (USA))
943^P

Back By Midnight *Emma Baker* 95h
5 ch g Midnight Legend Roberta Back (IRE) (Bob Back (USA))
1869^{10} 2472^7 4171^U 4343^7 4971^5

Backforce *Noel Wilson* 6h
6 b g Jelani(IRE) Scoffera (Scottish Reel)
4043^8 4431^8 5300^{10}

Backhomeinderry (IRE) *Kate Buckett* 98h
9 b g Oscar(IRE) Foyle Wanderer (IRE) (Supreme Leader)
193^U 484^4 2474^9 2628^2 2802^{13} 4937^P **5259^P**

Back In A Tic (IRE) *Colin Kidd* 114h 124c
8 b m Flemensfirth(USA) Wakt (Akarad (FR))
2986a^5

Back In June *Paul Henderson* 105h
6 b g Bach(IRE) Bathwick June (IRE) (Supreme Leader)
1856^2 2929^5 3643^6 4887^4 5128^6 5391^4

Backinthere (IRE) *Eamonn Francis Gallagher* 126h 126c
9 b m Flemensfirth(USA) Hester Hall (IRE) (Saddlers' Hall (IRE))
2484a^2 2986a^4 3750a^6 4848a^3

Back On The Road (IRE) *N W Alexander* 72h 110c
12 br g Broken Hearted Special Trix (IRE) (Peacock (FR))
(315) **496^3**
4057^P 4225^3 4554^6 5323^4 5536^U

Back To Balloo (IRE) *C A McBratney* 130h 131c
8 gr g Jimble(FR) Fleur Du Chenet (FR) (Northern Fashion (USA))
5254^4

Badb Catha (IRE) *Roger Curtis* 64h 67c
8 b m Flemensfirth(USA) Beann Ard (IRE) (Mandalus)
2003^6 2849^4 3555^3 4654^2 5407^6

Baddam *Martin Jones* 105h 98c
12 b g Mujahid(USA) Aude La Belle (FR) (Ela-Mana-Mou)
13^P

Badea *Martin Todhunter* 93h
5 b g Cockney Rebel(IRE) Gibraltar Bay (IRE) (Cape Cross (IRE))
2840^8 2968^6 3106^4 3527^8 4366^5 5214^2

Badged *Lucy Normile* 97h
5 b g High Chaparral(IRE) Meshhed (USA) (Gulch (USA))
1654^7 3144^8 5508^7

Badger *Mrs C Dennis* 68h 97c
14 b g Classic Cliche(IRE) Tyrilda (FR) (Saint Cyrien (FR))
328^P

Badger Foot (IRE) *Lucinda Russell* 101h 118c
9 br g Beneficial Droim Alton Gale (IRE) (Strong Gale)
1756^5 (2518)
2820^5 (3211)
3874^3 4236^3 4666^2 5053^2

Badgers Cove (IRE) *Robin Dickin* 127h 115c
10 b g Witness Box(USA) Celestial Rose (IRE) (Roselier (FR))
2267^U 2700^4 3836^2 4399^4 (4809)

Badgers Retreat *Ferdy Murphy* 106h 110c
8 b g Elusive City(USA) Heuston Station (IRE) (Fairy King (USA))
(203) **472^3**

Badger Wood *Giles Smyly* 108h
5 b g Overbury(IRE) Parlour Game (Petoski)
1771^4 2181^{12} 2761^2 3115^6 5235^2

Bad Girls (FR) *David Pipe* 70h
5 b m Astarabad(USA) Canadiane (FR) (Nikos)
324^6 715^7 841^5 920^8 994^P

Bad Made (IRE) *David Evans* 80h 83c
6 b g Well Made(GER) Altizaf (Zafonic (USA))
337^5 **645^U**

Bafana Choice *Chris Grant* 97c
8 b g Bollin Eric Lorna's Choice (Oats)
16^3 510^2 579^U 753^9

Bahira (IRE) *Donald McCain* 68h
7 b m Kalanisi(IRE) Biagiotti (GER) (Winged Love (IRE))
1017^4 1187^6 1517^5

Bahumbug *Seamus Mullins* 78h
4 b g Bahamian Bounty Stan's Smarty Girl (USA) (Smarty Jones (USA))
4401^9 5088^{15} 5547^7

Baile Anrai (IRE) *Dan Skelton* 116h 138c
10 b g Norwich Rose Ana (IRE) (Roselier (FR))
2433^3
2822^3 3091^4 (3323)
3897^2 4422^{11} (4792)
5276^P

Baile Atha Cliath (IRE) *Declan Carroll* 70h
5 b g Barathea(IRE) Danielli (IRE) (Danehill (USA))
2507^9 3330^P

Baileys Concerto (IRE) *Dianne Sayer* 96h 121c
8 b g Bach(IRE) None The Wiser (IRE) (Dr Massini (IRE))
3724^P 4338^7 4579^5 4834^4 **(5107)**
(5380) 5555^3

Baily Green (IRE) *M F Morris* 131h 158c
8 b g King's Theatre(IRE) Dream On Boys (IRE) (Anshan)
1776a^2 3338a^5 3751a^2 4753^F 5082a^2

Baily Storm (IRE) *Lawney Hill* 112h 112c
12 br g Anshan Euroblend (IRE) (The Parson)
712^7 (872)
1257^5 1403^2 1748^5 1988^9

Baizically (IRE) *John Joseph Hanlon* 106h 103c
11 ch g Galileo(IRE) Baize (Efisio)
74^5 942^3 1038^2 1327^3 1526^6 1655^6

Bajan Blu *David Brace* 104h
6 b g Generous(IRE) Bajan Girl (FR) (Emperor Jones (USA))
2286^7 ◆ 2614^6 3357^6 3878^6 4377^5

Bajan Sunshine (IRE) *Chris Dwyer* 30h 96c
13 b g Presenting Tina's Charm (IRE) (Hatim (USA))
875^9

Bakari *Graeme McPherson* 57b
6 bl g Trade Fair Wathbat Mtoto (Mtoto)
250^{12}

Baksheesh *Sue Gardner* 71h
5 b g Presenting Dancing Dasi (IRE) (Supreme Leader)
589^8 2761^{10} 3783^7 4175^7 4972^7 5395^P

Balady (IRE) *Dominic Ffrench Davis* 67h
5 b m Zamindar(USA) Faydah (USA) (Bahri (USA))
2027^9 3370^U

Balbir Du Mathan (FR) *Gordon Elliott* 123h
5 b g Saint Des Saints(FR) Jeapano (FR) (Panoramic)
5200a^6

Balbriggan (IRE) *Mick Channon* 102h 126c
7 gr g King's Theatre(IRE) Halfway Home (Presenting)
2394^3 (2847)
3026^3 5126^6 ◆ 5444^2

Bal Celtique (FR) *Mlle M-L Mortier* 100h 109c
5 b m Ballingarry(IRE) Aurore Celtique (FR) (Alamo Bay (USA))
1199a^9

Baldadash (IRE) *Barry Brennan* 109h 110c
9 b g Beneficial Balda Girl (IRE) (Mandalus)
394^5 726^5

Balder Succes (FR) *Alan King* 147h 162c
6 b g Goldneyev(USA) Frija Eria (FR) (Kadalko (FR))
(1865)
1973^F (2295)
2950^5 (4159)
(4420) ◆ (5168) ◆

Balding Banker (IRE) *Rebecca Menzies* 105h 128c
8 b g Accordion What A Breeze (IRE) (Naheez (USA))
(114) **625^4**
1750^2 1976^4 2171^P 3146^3

Balinderry (IRE) *Steve Gollings* 92h 96c
7 b g Flemensfirth(USA) Erins Love (IRE) (Double Bed (FR))
207^5 291^3 560^4 2429^3 2621^6
3033^5 3283^P 3605^7 4076^5 4699^5 4865^4 5366^4
5441^7

Balinroab (IRE) *Richard Guest* 109h 124c
7 b g Milan Gentle Eyre (IRE) (Aristocracy)
387^3 728^4 1135^P (1403)
2293^7 2623^2 3205^P 3759^8 5060^5 5299^6

Balistix (FR) *J-P Carnel* 77c
11 b g Manninamix Balisto (FR) (Caramo (FR))
616a^P

Ball Hopper (IRE) *Richenda Ford* 97c
10 ch g Rock Hopper Lady Vic (IRE) (Old Vic)
3696^7 4067^3 4451^P 5546^P

Ballinahow Lady (IRE) *David M O'Brien* 118h 129c
9 b m Beneficial Ballinahowliss (IRE) (Supreme Leader)
2123a^2 (2484a)

Ballinahow Star (IRE) *Jeremy Scott* 126h 124c
8 b m Definite Article Ballinahowliss (IRE) (Supreme Leader)
(379) **2769^2**
3011^3 3319^3

Ballinalacken (IRE) *Anthony Middleton* 114h
6 b g Fruits Of Love(USA) Miss Daisy (Daylami (IRE))
1991^6 2337^F 4991^P

Ballincurrig (IRE) *Dan Skelton* 112h 129c
8 b g Craigsteel Flora Rambler (Alflora (IRE))
2676^2
2928^6 3693^7 (4970)
(5290) (5573)

Ballinhassig (IRE) *Sarah Wall* 56h 92c
9 ch g Beneficial Dear Polly (IRE) (Germany (USA))
2863^3 3137^4

Ballinvarrig (IRE) *Tom George* 112h 134c
7 b g Beneficial Leos Holiday (IRE) (Commanche Run)
1796^4 2078^2 ◆ (3172)
(3769) 4418^2

Ballyadam Brook (IRE) *Terence O'Brien* 132h 136c
10 b g Alderbrook Luna Fleur (IRE) (Shardari)
2488^{15} 3910a^9

Ballyallia Man (IRE) *Tom George* 107h 119c
9 b g Flemensfirth(USA) Hatch Away (IRE) (Lord Americo)
2106[3]
2373[10] 3293[P] 4685[4] 5126[4]

Ballyalton (IRE) *Ian Williams* 149h
7 b g Pierre Almilto (IRE) (Mandalus)
(1793) (2819) (3070) 3454[4] 4750[2]

Ballyanrahan (IRE) *Miss A E Petch* 97c
8 b g Oscar Schindler(IRE) Camas North (IRE) (Muharib (USA))
5485[3]

Ballybach (IRE) *Nick Gifford* 103h 96c
10 b g Bach(IRE) Croom River (IRE) (Over The River (FR))
2210[14] 2764[P] *4021[7]* **4483[3] 5437[P]**

Ballybanks (IRE) *Robert Johnson* 97h 87c
10 b g Exit To Nowhere(USA) Incharder (IRE) (Slip Anchor)
2880[7]

Ballyben (IRE) *Lucinda Russell* 113h 108c
6 ch g Beneficial I'm Maggy (NZ) (Danseur Etoile (FR))
339[2] 1660[P] (1875) 2158[3] 2956[2] **3209[3] 4202[3] 5055[4] 5533[6]**

Ballybogey (IRE) *J J Lambe* 130h
8 b g Definite Article Beenaround (IRE) (King's Ride)
5251[9]

Ballybolley (IRE) *Nigel Twiston-Davies* 129b
5 b g Kayf Tara Gales Hill (IRE) (Beau Sher)
(2878) (5014) (5173) ◆

Ballybough Andy (IRE) *David Dennis* 97h
5 ch g City Honours(USA) Princess Ruth (IRE) (Weld)
5042[4] 5547[4]

Ballybough Gorta (IRE) *Peter Bowen* 72h 135c
7 b g Indian Danehill(IRE) Eyelet (IRE) (Satco (FR))
643[5] **923[4]**
(1040)
(1396) 1579[2] 2502[9] 2937[4] 3554[P] 5276[P]

Bally Braes (IRE) *Nigel Twiston-Davies* 91h
6 b g Old Vic Gaelic Stream (IRE) (Brush Aside (USA))
2104[2] 2978[9] 3568[4] 3880[7] 4699[4] 5432[5]

Ballybriggan (IRE) *Donald McCain* 130h 124c
10 b g Flemensfirth(USA) Shean Hill (IRE) (Bar Dexter (USA))
(78) 2101[5]
3039[3] 3452[P]

Bally Broadwell *Michael Madgwick* 47b
4 b f Kayf Tara Ballyhoo (IRE) (Supreme Leader)
2318[7] 3003[P]

Ballybroe (IRE) *Harriet Graham* 101h
7 b g Presenting Mini Minor (IRE) (Black Minstrel)
168[7] 537[3] 1785[P]

Ballycasey (IRE) *W P Mullins* 144h 156c
7 gr g Presenting Pink Mist (IRE) (Montelimar (USA))
(4181a)
4751[4] 5422a[F]

Ballycassel (IRE) *Tom Symonds* 114h 98c
9 ch g Presenting Sara's Gold (IRE) (Ashkalani (IRE))
2536[S]
4884[8] 5247[7]

Ballycolin *Ian Duncan* 106h 121c
11 ch g Alflora(IRE) Shift Changeover (Saxon Farm)
170[8] 4057[P] 4554[5] 4837[7]

Ballycool (IRE) *Lucinda Russell* 98h 110c
7 b g Helissio(FR) Carnoustie (USA) (Ezzoud (IRE))
15[3] 1635[U] **1870[5] 2219[U] 2361[4] (3395) 3517[3] 4549[6] 5076[6]**

Ballycracken (IRE) *David Pearson* 109h 82c
10 b g Flemensfirth(USA) Cons Dual Sale (IRE) (Tidaro (USA))
20[P] 120[6] 553[5] 3227[P] 4863[P] 5283[3]

Ballyculla (IRE) *Warren Greatrex* 136h
7 b g Westerner Someone Told Me (IRE) (Saddlers' Hall (IRE))
2006[3] (2458) (2652) 3207[4] 3653[5] 5372[2]

Ballyegan (IRE) *Bob Buckler* 65h 74c
9 b g Saddlers' Hall(IRE) Knapping Princess (IRE) (Prince Of Birds (USA))
1859[5] 2619[P] 3696[3] 4176[5] 5007[8] **5240[6]**

Ballyeightra Cross (IRE) *G D Hanmer* 64b 108c
10 ch g Anshan Riancoir Alainn (Strong Gale)
60[P]

Ballyfinboy (IRE) *J R Finn* 105h 126c
8 gr g Great Palm(USA) Tender Return (IRE) (Strong Gale)
1702a[3]

Ballygarvey (FR) *Philip Hobbs* 120h 144c
8 b g Laveron Vollore (FR) (Cadoudal (FR))
2488[4] ◆

Ballyglasheen (IRE) *Evan Williams* 137h
4 ch g Galileo(IRE) Luas Line (IRE) (Danehill (USA))
(1813) (2038) 2172[3] 2466[3] (3078) 3885[4] 4755[P] 5568[6]

Ballygrooby Bertie (IRE) *Fergal O'Brien* 119h
6 b g King's Theatre(IRE) Vigna Maggio (FR) (Starborough)
207[7] 2040[4] 2265[5] 2563[3] *4302[4]* 4510[P] 4866[7] 5365[10]

Bally Gunner *Roger Curtis* 96h 109c
9 br g Needle Gun(IRE) Rich Pickings (Dominion)
504[P] 5247[8]

Ballyheigue Bay (IRE) *Chris Gordon* 115h
7 b g Rudimentary(USA) Terinka (IRE) (Erins Isle)
4715[3] 5024[2] 5351[9]

Ballyhilty Bridge *Paul Henderson* 73h 82c
8 b g Exit To Nowhere(USA) Gemolly (IRE) (Be My Native (USA))
1942[U] 2431[P] 3174[5] 4275[13] **4695[P] 5394[P]**

Ballyhollow *Rebecca Curtis* 109b
7 ch m Beat Hollow Ballet-K (Gunner B)
324[5] 2892[2] ◆ (3181) 4683[3]

Ballyhooley Boy (IRE) *Robin Dickin* 111h
7 b g Oscar(IRE) Nivalf (Gildoran)
2426[5] 2642[8] 3070[4] 3390[7]

Ballyhoulihan (IRE) *David O'Meara* 20h
6 b g Golan(IRE) Dun Ar Aill (IRE) (Supreme Leader)
115[6]

Ballyjames (IRE) *Miss H Brookshaw* 110c
9 b g Winged Love(IRE) Lynina (IRE) (Bob Back (USA))
58[P] 658[8] 4727[5]

Bally Lagan (IRE) *Robin Dickin* 83h 88c
6 gr g Kalanisi(IRE) Rose Palma (FR) (Great Palm (USA))
2[10] 1820[3] **2599[5] 2849[3] 3180[P]** *4020[9]* **4656[3] 5243[3] 5404[4]**

Bally Legend *Caroline Keevil* 139h 146c
9 b g Midnight Legend Bally Lira (Lir)
(2020) 2504[14]
2714[2] (2925)
3321[4] *4021[2]* **(4422)**
4960[3] 5350[4] 5571[10]

Ballylifen (IRE) *Jonjo O'Neill* 122h 124c
7 b g Brian Boru Line Jade (FR) (Luchiroverte (IRE))
921[3] 2450[2] 2662[3] 3365[4] 4412[4] 4678[5] (5076) 5406[3]

Bally Longford (IRE) *W P Mullins* 132h
6 b g Gold Well Stay On Line (IRE) (Over The River (FR))
5420a[4]

Ballymacahillcross (IRE) *Evan Williams* 100h 91c
6 br g Presenting Topanberry (IRE) (Topanoora)
4898[4] 5228[4]

Ballymacduff (IRE) *George Charlton* 80h 92c
10 b g Strategic Choice(USA) Ashpark Rose (IRE) (Roselier (FR))
628[P]

Ballyman (IRE) *Jonathan Geake* 88b 88c
13 gr g Accordion Sliabhin Rose (Roselier (FR))
2277[3] 2861[3] 3139[6] 5263[9]

Ballymartin King (IRE) *Mrs Sarah Easterby* 100h 66c
8 b g King's Theatre(IRE) Lady Sipash (Erin's Hope)
5165[3]

Ballymoat *Tim Vaughan* 101h 111c
7 b g Grape Tree Road Frosty Mistress (Arctic Lord)
1497[3]
1765[3] 2308[2] 3065[14] 4578[6]

Ballynagour (IRE) *David Pipe* 133h 157c
8 b g Shantou(USA) Simply Deep (IRE) (Simply Great (FR))
2503[P] (4768)
5155[3]

Ballyoliver *Venetia Williams* 99h 135c
10 b g Kayf Tara Macklette (IRE) (Buckskin (FR))
2373[5] 3416[8] 3698[6] 4509[5] (4835) 5430[3]

Ballypatrick (IRE) *Mick Channon* 106h 136c
8 bb g Presenting Jewell For A King (IRE) (King's Ride)
1918[U] 2646[4] 2923[P] 3455[3] 4427[3] 4962[4] 5299[4]

Ballyreesode (IRE) *Susan Corbett* 112h
9 b g Waveney(UAE) Sinead's Joy (IRE) (Kambalda)
2034[P] 2311[8] 2842[P] 3356[5] 3525[6] 4607[7] **5498[P]**

Ballyrock (IRE) *Tim Vaughan* 144h
8 b g Milan Ardent Love (IRE) (Ardross)
358[5]

Ballyroe Rambler (IRE) *J A Berry* 121h
7 br g Lahib(USA) Victoria's Rose (IRE) (Be My Native (USA))
2983a[5]

Bally Rone (IRE) *Sarah Humphrey* 122h
6 br g Fruits Of Love(USA) Presenting Marble (IRE) (Presenting)
3544 2020[P]

Bally Sands (IRE) *Robin Mathew* 113h 114c
10 b g Luso Sandwell Old Rose (IRE) (Roselier (FR))
1988[7] 2297[U] 2678[6] 3193[5] 3502[3] 3858[2] 4402[2] 4704[4] 4968[3] 5348[F]

Ballythomas *David Thompson* 107h
7 b g Kayf Tara Gregale (Gildoran)
3453[3] 3850[5] 4340[3] 4650[3] (5300)

Ballytober *Philip Hobbs* 107h 132c
8 b g Kahyasi Full Of Birds (FR) (Epervier Bleu)
358[12]
2692[2] 2941[3] 3205[7] 4602[5] 5533[5]

Ballyvesey (IRE) *Peter Bowen* 53h 101c
9 ch g Anshan Bridgequarter Lady (IRE) (King's Ride)
1135[4] 1486[3] 1626[2] 1830[8]

Ballyvoneen (IRE) *Neil King* 84h 103c
9 b g Stowaway Miss Ira Zarad (IRE) (Darazari (IRE))
74[P] 242[5] 1403[4] 1626[6] 1798[P] 2047[4] 2313[2] 2425[2] 2678[P] 3267[P]
4220[6] 4470[3]
4720[P] 4905[3]
(5113) 5397[3]
(5460)

Ballyvoque (IRE) *George Charlton* 97h
8 b g Revoque(IRE) Timissa (IRE) (Kahyasi)
3826[5] 4832[4] 5479[6]

Ballywatt (IRE) *Kim Bailey* 103h 130c
8 b g Kayf Tara Lady Arpel (IRE) (Phardante (FR))
92[3] 2293[3] 2797[3] 3172[P] 4696[U] (5020) 5543[3]

Balmusette *Keith Reveley* 116b
5 b m Halling(USA) Tcherina (IRE) (Danehill Dancer (IRE))
372[3] (1138) 2298[3] 3898[2] ◆

Balnaslow (IRE) *W P Mullins* 136h 142c
7 b g Presenting Noble Choice (Dahar (USA))
2550a[5] 3314a[3] 3868a[4] ◆ **4769[4]**

Balthazar King (IRE) *Philip Hobbs* 138h 156c
10 b g King's Theatre(IRE) Afdala (IRE) (Hernando (FR))
(1532a)
(1971) (2491)
(4754) 5171[2]

Baltic Blade (IRE) *Gary Moore* 97h
4 b g Baltic King Anita's Contessa (IRE) (Anita's Prince)
(1335) 1524[3] 5090[9]

Baltic Blue *B Dowling*
7 b g Beat All(USA) Laced Up (IRE) (The Parson)
5435[F]

Baltic Pathfinder (IRE) *Sue Smith* 108h 113c
10 b g Alflora(IRE) Boro Bow (IRE) (Buckskin (FR))
1039[F] 1397[6] 1502[4] 1756[2] 2201[P] 3019[3] 3275[4] (3635)
4086[2] 4578[P] 4812[5]
5055[2] (5356)

Baltimore Rock (IRE) *David Pipe* 138h
5 b g Tiger Hill(IRE) La Vita E Bella (IRE) (Definite Article)
3128[3] (3746) 4129[2] (4353) (4682) 5153[4]

Balzaccio (FR) *Fergal O'Brien* 112h 126c
9 b g Marchand De Sable(USA) Baliyna (USA) (Woodman (USA))
2630[3]
4593[2] ◆ **4960[5] 5444[4]**

Bandalero (IRE) *Philip Kirby* 77b
6 b g Bandari(IRE) Cloudy Outlook (IRE) (Hubbly Bubbly (USA))
3042[10]

Banderitos *Tim Easterby* 53h
5 b g Revoque(IRE) Orchid (Orchestra)
2174[10] 2621[11]

Bandit Country (IRE) *Jonjo O'Neill* 119b
5 b g Flemensfirth(USA) Calomeria (Groom Dancer (USA))
(2905) 3440[3] 5063[3]

Band Of Blood (IRE) *Philip Fenton* 147h
6 b g King's Theatre(IRE) Cherry Falls (IRE) (Ali-Royal (IRE))
2983a[2] 4523a[7]

Band Of Thunder *Nick Mitchell* 87h
6 ch g Shirocco(GER) Black Opal (Machiavellian (USA))
710[2] (946)

Bandol (IRE) *Laura Young* 81h
6 b g Zagreb(USA) Formal Affair (Rousillon (USA))
250[4] 675[3] 2375[14] 2761[11] 3694[U] 3783[4] 4334[6] 4888[5]

Bangkok Pete (IRE) *Jamie Poulton* 88h 82c
9 b g Alflora(IRE) Kinnegads Pride (IRE) (Be My Native (USA))
2565[4] 3691[P] 4555[7]

Banks Road (IRE) *Geoffrey Deacon* 89h
9 b g Beneficial Cecelia's Charm (IRE) (Mister Lord (USA))
538[U] 849[P] 1201[6] 1431[3] 1561[9] 1837[3]

Banna Man (IRE) *T J O'Mara* 113h 111c
14 b g Zaffaran(USA) Next Adventure (IRE) (Denel (FR))
1001a[P]

Banreenahreenkah (IRE) *Jennie Candlish* 83h
4 b f Steppe Dancer(IRE) Carmencita (Rock Of Gibraltar (IRE))
2154[5] 2557[7] 2975[5] 5244[6] 5518[5]

Bantry Bere (IRE) *Fleur Hawes*
10 b g Distant Music(USA) Tirana (USA) (Fappiano (USA))
3471[P]

Baraboy (IRE) *Barry Murtagh* 92h
4 b g Barathea(IRE) Irina (IRE) (Polar Falcon (USA))
2168[7] 2592[3] 2881[4] 3210[4] 4107[2] 4336[4] 4817[5] 5163[5] 5532[4]

Barachois Silver *Mrs J M Hollands* 104c
10 gr m Silver Patriarch(IRE) Barachois Princess (USA) (Barachois (CAN))
112[3] 535[3] 4239[F] 5209[3]

Baradari (IRE) *Venetia Williams* 126h
4 br g Manduro(GER) Behra (IRE) (Grand Lodge (USA))
2796[6] (3364) 4111[2] 4755[5] 5132[F] 5568[10]

Barafundle (IRE) *Jennie Candlish* 145h
10 ch g Flemensfirth(USA) Different Dee (IRE) (Beau Sher)
2151[5]

Bar A Mine (FR) *Paul Nicholls* 84h
5 b g Martaline Treekle Toffee (FR) (Cadoudal (FR))
3363[4] 4024[5] 4838[3]

Bardeli (IRE) *Donald McCain* 75h
7 br g Overbury(IRE) Miss Denman (IRE) (Presenting)
218[7]

Bar De Ligne (FR) *Steve Gollings* 136h 138c
8 b g Martaline Treekle Toffee (FR) (Cadoudal (FR))
356[10] **562[5]**
(786) 2074[3]
2395[2] 2782[3] 3476[3] (3759)
4055[2] 4806[8] 5557[2]

Barel Of Laughs (IRE) *J H Culloty* 93h 103c
8 b g Milan Danette (GER) (Exit To Nowhere (USA))
1362[8]

Barenger (IRE) *Ali Brewer* 113h 114c
7 b g Indian Danehill(IRE) Build A Dream (USA) (Runaway Groom (CAN))
121[P] **2437[6]**
(3268)
4483[2] 4912[2] 5527[3]

Barista (IRE) *Brian Forsey* 101h
6 b g Titus Livius(FR) Cappuccino (IRE) (Mujadil (USA))
2476[4] 2910[6] ◆ 3043[3] ◆

Barizan (IRE) *Donald McCain* 138h 133c
8 b g Kalanisi(IRE) Behra (IRE) (Grand Lodge (USA))
(216) 1046[11] 4785[10] 5274[9]

Barlow (IRE) *Warren Greatrex* 128h 131c
7 br g Beneficial Carrigeen Kerria (IRE) (Kemal (FR))
6[6] 296[3] 2005[4] 2693[3] 3642[5] *4020[11]* **(4914) 5373[5]**

Barnaby Brook (CAN) *Nick Littmoden*
4 b g North Light(IRE) Mascara (USA) (Milwaukee Brew (USA))
1781[7]

Barnack *Pam Sly* 85h
8 b g Karinga Bay Ima Delight (Idiots Delight)
4533[7] 4981[2] 5069[9]

Barnevelder (IRE) *Sandy Forster* 50h 89c
9 ch g Old Vic Cluain-Ard (IRE) (Glacial Storm (USA))
2818[P] 3834[P] 5318[4]

Barney Cool *David Pipe* 117h
7 b g Bollin Eric Laurel Diver (Celtic Cone)
48[4]

Barney Dunne (IRE) *R Meyrick* 91b
10 gr g Heron Island(IRE) Coolraheen Rose (IRE) (Roselier (FR))
5545[P]

Barney Rubble *Richard Lee* 91h
5 b g Medicean Jade Chequer (Green Desert (USA))
291[4] 695[2] 3189[12] 5174[4] 5490[11]

Barneys Honour (IRE) *Gordon Elliott* 137h 129c
10 b g City Honours(USA) Ballyburn Lady (IRE) (Needle Gun (IRE))
4204[3] 4612[3]

Barossa Pearl (IRE) *Noel Meade* 81b
4 b f Milan What An Answer (IRE) (Executive Perk)
5424a[8]

Barrakilla (IRE) *Evan Williams* 131h 137c
7 b g Milan Kigali (IRE) (Torus)
2012[4] 2882[3] (3436)

Barren Hill (IRE) *Mrs John Harrington*
5 b g Mountain High(IRE) Great Cullen (IRE) (Simply Great (FR))
5424a[13]

Barr Head (IRE) *Lucy Normile* 59b 83c
10 b g Anshan Doolin Lake (IRE) (Salluceva)
315[7] 496[P]

Barrick's Hill (IRE) *Mrs Sarah J Bosley* 89c
9 b g Oscar(IRE) Lisnacunna Lord (IRE) (Mister Lord (USA))
62[6]

Barrow Nook *Chris Grant* 70b
4 b g Overbury(IRE) Rippling Brook (Phardante (FR))
5388[8]

Barrs Lane *Arthur Whiting* 94b
6 b m Sir Harry Lewis(USA) Cashel Dancer (Bishop Of Cashel)
462[2] 1836[3]

Barry The Barber (IRE) *Tracey Barfoot-Saunt* 53h 49c
8 b g Flemensfirth(USA) Dining Hall (IRE) (Saddlers' Hall (IRE))
5[P]

Bartered Bride *John Norton* 38b
6 b m Gentleman's Deal(IRE) Stolen Glance (Mujahid (USA))
5671[4]

Barton Antix *Neil Mulholland* 77b
5 b g Fair Mix(IRE) Barton Dante (Phardante (FR))
2026[6] *3098[4]*

Barton Gift *John Spearing* 99h 121c
7 b g Alflora(IRE) Marina Bird (Julio Mariner)
89[2] **2431[5]**
2897[5] 3277[P] (3696)
4399[U] (4678)
5184[U]

Barton Heather *Neil Mulholland* 96h
5 b m Midnight Legend Home From The Hill (IRE) (Jareer (USA))
644[3] 1836[4] 2767[11] 3189[11] 3746[5] 4500[3]

Barton Jubilee *Neil Mulholland* 110h
6 ch g Midnight Legend Home From The Hill (IRE) (Jareer (USA))
374[3] 1941[5] 2284[10]

Barton Rose *Neil Mulholland* 110h
5 b m Midnight Legend Barton Flower (Danzero (AUS))
1836[5] 2767[9] 3189[10] 3747[4] (4472) (4595) 4907[P]

Barton Stacey (IRE) *David Pipe* 117h 134c
9 b g Snurge Lifes Treasure (IRE) (Brush Aside (USA))
2715[9] 3741[5] 4070[2] ◆ 5074[5] 5333[P]

Basford Ben *Jennie Candlish* 104h 100c
6 b g Trade Fair Moly (FR) (Anabaa (USA))
322[7] 564[5]
713[3] 763[8] 872[8] 1010[4] 1172[3] (2959)
3283[P] 3827[2] 4082[3] 4399[3]
4630[2] 5011[3]
5293[4]

Basford Bob (IRE) *Jennie Candlish* 109h 108c
9 b g Bob's Return(IRE) El Monica (IRE) (Kahyasi)
2510[P] 2956[5] 3419[3] 3724[6]

Basil Fawlty (IRE) *David Pipe* 104h 113c
9 b g Balakheri(IRE) Laughing Lesa (IRE) (Bob Back (USA))
(713) 1015[F]
1257[2] 1486[U] 1830[4]

Basoda *Kim Bailey* 103h 117c
11 b g Karinga Bay Another Wag (Scallywag)
334[5] 712[2] 1015[P]

Bassett Road (IRE) *Keith Dalgleish* 84h
6 ch g Byron Topiary (IRE) (Selkirk (USA))
2968[9] 3516[11]

Bathcounty (IRE) *Barry Brennan* 112h 45c
7 ch g Tobougg(IRE) Seasons Estates (Mark Of Esteem (IRE))
784[6] 1391[10] 1551[5] 1938[F] 2561[7] 2771[6] **3152[5]**

Bathwick Brave (IRE) *Johnny Farrelly* 136h 111c
7 b g Westerner Dorans Grove (Gildoran)
2630[11]
3279[5] 3745[P] 4174[P] 5333[14] 5489[7]

Bathwick Junior *Michael Blake* 93h
7 b m Reset(AUS) Bathwick Babe (IRE) (Sri Pekan (USA))
(2291) 2581[P] 3692[P] 4757[8]

Bathwick Man *David Pipe* 121h
9 b g Mark Of Esteem(IRE) Local Abbey (IRE) (Primo Dominie)
591^{9} 782^{6} 877^{13} 1062^{5} 1273^{4} 1391^{2} 1488^{2} 1634^{3} 1828^{5}

Batonnier (FR) *Alan King* 126h 123c
8 ch g Spadoun(FR) La Bazine (FR) (Dreams To Reality (USA))
2813^{7} ◆ **4133^{4}**

Battle Born *Charlie Longsdon* 125b
5 b g Kayf Tara Realms Of Gold (USA) (Gulch (USA))
2660^{3} (3863) (4492) 5173^{6}

Battlecat *Evan Williams* 123h
7 b g Tiger Hill(IRE) Applecross (Glint Of Gold)
176^{4}

Battlecry *Nigel Twiston-Davies* 122b
13 bb g Accordion Miss Orchestra (IRE) (Orchestra)
1361^{P}

Battledancer *Peter Maddison* 77b
8 b g Baryshnikov(AUS) Cede Nullis (Primitive Rising (USA))
2954^{P}

Battle Group *Johnny Farrelly* 105b 151c
9 b g Beat Hollow Cantanta (Top Ville)
(215) **2503^{P}**
2814^{RR}
3199^{P} 5171^{RR} 5276^{P}

Batu Ferringhi (FR) *Jamie Snowden* 115h
8 b g Numerous(USA) Dara (IRE) (Danehill (USA))
60^{P} 2147^{3} (2385)
2977^{U} 3429^{P} 4674^{5} 4933^{16}

Bawden Rocks *David Bridgwater* 106h
5 b g Anabaa(USA) Late Night (GER) (Groom Dancer (USA))
116^{4} 434^{F} 4467^{5} 4818^{F} 5175^{8}

Bayan (IRE) *Gordon Elliott* 142h
5 b g Danehill Dancer(IRE) Kindling (Dr Fong (USA))
(865) (1288) 1970^{2} 4752^{3}

Bay Central (IRE) *Evan Williams* 91h 113c
10 b g Exit To Nowhere(USA) Pretty Beau (IRE) (Beau Charmeur (FR))
142^{5} 781^{4} 853^{2} (931) 1000^{4} **1122^{5} 1390^{2} 1503^{4}**

Bayfirth (IRE) *A B Hamilton* 77h 77c
11 b g Flemensfirth(USA) Baylough Lady (IRE) (Lancastrian)
5165^{P}

Bay Fortuna *Mark Usher* 57h
5 b g Old Vic East Rose (Keen)
588^{3} 3716^{7} *4297^{8}*

Bayley's Dream *Paul Webber* 105h
5 b g Presenting Swaythe (USA) (Swain (IRE))
2083^{7} 2471^{6} 3877^{13} *4301^{9}* 4937^{F} 5520^{5}

Bay To Go (IRE) *Mrs H M Kemp* 98h 118c
8 b g Moscow Society(USA) Lily Langtry (IRE) (Duky)
58^{5} (326)
656^{5} 4511^{P} (5364)

Bazart *Bernard Llewellyn* 90h
12 b g Highest Honor(FR) Summer Exhibition (Royal Academy (USA))
1428^{9} 1643^{2} 1833^{6} 2090^{P} 2766^{12}

B B Baloo *John Wainwright* 54b
5 b m Proclamation(IRE) Bellabaloo (Seymour Hicks (FR))
35^{10} 567^{13}

Beachfire *John Ferguson* 131h
7 ch g Indian Haven Maine Lobster (USA) (Woodman (USA))
1191^{3} (1404) 1915^{2} 2215^{2} 2630^{7}

Be A Dreamer *Sue Smith* 89h
6 ch g Dreams End Miss Fahrenheit (IRE) (Oscar (IRE))
3147^{7} 3619^{6} 4267^{9} 4889^{5} 5320^{7}

Be All Man (IRE) *Gary Moore* 115h 128c
7 b g Dubawi(IRE) Belle Allemande (CAN) (Royal Academy (USA))
48^{3} 244^{4} **1986^{4} (2042)**
(2440) 2762^{2} 3155^{P}

Beamazed *Malcolm Jefferson* 101b
10 ch g Silver Patriarch(IRE) Gotogeton (Le Moss)
3416^{P}

Bear Island Flint *Brendan Powell* 101b
6 br g Overbury(IRE) Chippewa (FR) (Cricket Ball (USA))
760^{3} 1124^{4} 1196^{2}

Bear's Affair (IRE) *Nicky Henderson* 152h 150c
8 br g Presenting Gladtogetit (Green Shoon)
1796^{7} 2003^{3} (2712)
3091^{6}

Bears Rails *Colin Tizzard* 28b
4 b g Flemensfirth(USA) Clandestine (Saddlers' Hall (IRE))
5130^{14}

Bear Witness (IRE) *Lady Susan Watson* 82c
12 b g Witness Box(USA) Anyone's Fancy (Callernish)
557^{P}

Beatrix Kiddo (IRE) *Dan Skelton* 59h
5 b m Scorpion(IRE) Garden City (IRE) (Shernazar)
1531^{4} 3159^{7} 3747^{F}

Beat That (IRE) *Nicky Henderson* 159h
6 b g Milan Knotted Midge (IRE) (Presenting)
(2642) 2929^{2} ◆ (5157)

Beat The Bounds *Martin Hill* 44h
5 b g Beat All(USA) Regally (Gildoran)
2375^{11} 3695^{10}

Beat The Shower *Peter Niven* 96h
8 b g Beat Hollow Crimson Shower (Dowsing (USA))
2198^{11} 2625^{5}

Beatu (IRE) *Donald McCain* 105b
5 b g Beat All(USA) Auntie Bob (Overbury (IRE))
2885^{3} (3147) 5173^{16}

Beau Ballistic (IRE) *Sarah Dawson* 86h
6 b g Silver Patriarch(IRE) Miniballist (IRE) (Tragic Role (USA))
4627^{P} 5163^{12}

Beauboreen (IRE) *Jennie Candlish* 128h
7 b g Revoque(IRE) Roseboreen (IRE) (Roselier (FR))
(2245) 2807^{2} (3505) 4040^{4} 4949^{11}

Beauchamp Sunset *Paul Fitzsimons* 37h
4 b g Tiger Hill(IRE) Orange Sunset (IRE) (Roanoke (USA))
4988^{10}

Beauchamp Viking *Hugo Froud* 68h 83c
10 b g Compton Admiral Beauchamp Jade (Kalaglow)
3799^{4} 4416^{6} 4734^{U} 5243^{6}

Beau Dandy (IRE) *Chris Grant* 75h 108c
9 b g Exit To Nowhere(USA) Northern Dandy (The Parson)
2201^{2} 2594^{P} 3825^{P} 4580^{3} 4775^{U} 5215^{P} 5358^{7}

Beau De Tabel (FR) *Nick Williams* 100h
6 b g Assessor(IRE) Garde Aux Armes (FR) (Garde Royale)
(380) 1856^{3} 2279^{U} 2457^{6} 3166^{13}

Beaufort Boy (IRE) *Gary Moore* 88b
5 b g Heron Island(IRE) What A Mewsment (IRE) (Persian Mews)
4445^{2} 4763^{6}

Beaujolais (IRE) *John Ferguson* 108h 93c
6 ch g Moscow Society(USA) Chirouble (IRE) (High Roller (IRE))
588^{4} 1915^{5} 2068^{3} 2369^{6} 2748^{4}
3176^{5}

Beaujolais Bob *Richard Hawker* 101b
6 gr g Grape Tree Road Charliebob (Nomadic Way (USA))
2375^{13} 2826^{P}

Beau Lake (IRE) *Suzy Smith* 109h
10 bb g Heron Island(IRE) Brennan For Audits (IRE) (Creative Plan (USA))
2581^{5} (3094) (3556)

Beaumont's Party (IRE) *Brian Ellison* 103h
7 b g High Chaparral(IRE) Miss Champagne (FR) (Bering)
2869^{3} 3288^{5}

Beautiful Gem (FR) *Dan Skelton* 88b
4 ch f Muhtathir Hunorisk (FR) (Mansonnien (FR))
4403^{5} 5388^{6}

Beau Traveller *Miss Bianca Dunk* 79c
11 b g Beauchamp King Steady Woman (IRE) (Aristocracy I)
112^{4} 315^{6}

Bebinn (IRE) *Ben Case* 103h
7 b m Brian Boru Windmill Star (IRE) (Orchestra)
2684 2193^{6} 2896^{11} 3280^{2} 4108^{2} 4472^{2} 5351^{P}

Be Bop Boru (IRE) *Tim Vaughan* 111h
7 b g Brian Boru Henrietta Howard (IRE) (King's Ride)
1958^{9} 2940^{11} 3783^{5} (4504) (4607) (4746) 5351^{2}

Becauseicouldntsee (IRE) *N F Glynn* 126h 135c
11 ch g Beneficial Ath Dara (Duky)
851^{10} 1971^{11} 2502^{11}

Becausewecan (USA) *Brian Ellison* 78h
8 b g Giant's Causeway(USA) Belle Sultane (USA) (Seattle Slew (USA))
2529^{17} 2625^{7}

Beckhani *Jonjo O'Neill* 106h 115c
7 b g Flemensfirth(USA) Nicklup (Netherkelly)
179^{2} 726^{3} 1088^{2} 1325^{4}

Bedale Lane (IRE) *Philip Kirby* 90b
5 b m Kayf Tara Misleain (IRE) (Un Desperado (FR))
4545^{7}

Be Definite (IRE) *Tom George* 114h 122c
10 b g Definite Article Etoile Margot (FR) (Garde Royale)
1988^{4} 2370^{2} 2847^{4} 3874^{4} 4539^{2} 5180^{P}

Bedibyes *Richard Mitchell* 56h
6 b m Sleeping Indian Aunt Sadie (Pursuit Of Love)
1925^{5} 2927 631^{9} 1270^{11} 3047^{P}

Bedouin Bay *Johnny Farrelly* 106h 27c
7 b g Dubai Destination(USA) Sahara Sonnet (USA) (Stravinsky (USA))
643^{4} 767^{P} 1833^{5} 2474^{8} 2696^{8} 2921^{3} 3174^{2} 3959^{7} 4726^{11} 4887^{6} 5118^{4}

Bedrock Fred *Miss E J Tanner* 92b 73c
8 ch g Monsieur Bond(IRE) Sea Mist (IRE) (Shalford (IRE))
388^{3}

Beeves (IRE) *Donald McCain* 133h 138c
7 b g Portrait Gallery(IRE) Camas North (IRE) (Muharib (USA))
(1851)
2074^{2} 2969^{3} 3327^{2} 3873^{3} 4741^{11} 5525^{4}

Beforeall (IRE) *Oliver Sherwood* 104h 135c
6 b g Spadoun(FR) Maggie Howard (IRE) (Good Thyne (USA))
(368) **2315^{2}**
(2567) ◆ **3004^{2} (3246)**
4110^{2} 4602^{2} (5184)
5383^{7}

Beggar's Velvet (IRE) *D Holmes* 87h 132c
8 b g Dr Massini(IRE) Lakelough (IRE) (Mandalus)
845^{P} **1060^{2}**
4225^{5} 4706^{P}

Beggers Belief *Zoe Davison*
6 ch g Bertolini(USA) Dropitlikeit's Hot (IRE) (Tagula (IRE))
3134^{P}

Behind The Scenes (IRE) *A Coveney* 67h 76c
12 br g Presenting Run For Cover (IRE) (Lafontaine (USA))
4443^{F}

Behtarini (IRE) *Richenda Ford* 105h
7 b g Dalakhani(IRE) Behkiyra (IRE) (Entrepreneur)
2641^{14} 2766^{13}

Beidh Tine Anseo (IRE) *Lucinda Russell* 118h 118c
8 b g Rock Of Gibraltar(IRE) Siamsa (USA) (Quest For Fame)
493^{3}

Be Kind *Tim Vaughan*
8 b m Generous(IRE) Aquavita (Kalaglow)
1631^{8}
1821^{7} 2023^{P} 4472^{8}

Bel Ami Rich *Barry Brennan* 49b
4 b g Black Sam Bellamy(IRE) Granny Rich (Ardross)
3719^{9}

Belanna *Tim Easterby* 82b
5 b m Bollin Eric Bollin Annabel (King's Theatre (IRE))
3835^{8} 4191^{6}

Belenien (FR) *Y-M Porzier* 119h
5 b g Anzillero(GER) Slew Dancer (Fabulous Dancer (USA))
(1199a)

Bel Esprit (IRE) *Robert Stephens* 93b
5 b m Presenting D Judge (IRE) (Strong Gale)
4403^{3} 4916^{7}

Belfastdarknstormy (IRE) *B Arthey* 41b
6 br g Storming Home Whatalady (IRE) (Executive Perk)
4671^{7}

Bella Cara (FR) *H Billot* 104h
6 b m Bernebeau(FR) La Kador (FR) (Kadounor (FR))
263a^{P}

Bella Montagna *Sharon Watt*
6 b m Dubai Destination(USA) Hagwah (USA) (Dancing Brave (USA))
956^{U}

Bell'Arte (IRE) *Laura Mongan* 72h
4 b f Zamindar(USA) Art Eyes (USA) (Halling (USA))
5026^{10} 5245^{8}

Belle De Fontenay (FR) *Conor Dore* 98h
9 b m Spadoun(FR) Friendly Hostess (Environment Friend)
(875) (1092) (1562) 1960^{9} (2250) 2698^{4} (2894) 3117^{5} 3324^{F} 3593^{5} 4002^{3} 4305^{3} 4573^{6} 4983^{3} 5438^{P}

Belle De Londres (IRE) *Alan King* 87b
4 b f King's Theatre(IRE) J'y Reste (FR) (Freedom Cry)
4867^{2}

Bellenos (FR) *Dan Skelton* 112h 147c
6 b g Apsis Palmeria (FR) (Great Palm (USA))
2785^{7} (3183)
3894^{6} 4373^{2} 5091^{2} ◆ **(5289)**

Belle Noverre (IRE) *John Carr* 55h
10 b m Noverre(USA) Belle Etoile (FR) (Lead On Time (USA))
1656^{8}

Bellgrove (IRE) *Ian Semple* 114h
6 b g Gold Well Less Hassle (IRE) (Strong Gale)
(1292) 1667^{4} 2341^{3} 2792^{2} 4463^{2}

Bellingo *Robert Johnson* 29b
7 b m Danroad(AUS) Rasin Luck (Primitive Rising (USA))
3147^{9} 3351^{P}

Bell On Bike (IRE) *Mrs Jackie Hunt* 98c
11 b g Oscar Schindler(IRE) Crystal Mover (IRE) (Eurobus)
62^{P} 4782^{3}

Bellorophon (IRE) *Keith Dalgleish* 111h
5 ch g Beneficial Mrs Kick (IRE) (Supreme Leader)
76^{8} 2174^{3} 2724^{6} 3128^{6} 3516^{10} 3877^{8} 4595^{6} (4957) ◆

Bellosguardo *Kate Buckett* 91h 97c
11 ch g Medicean Barsham (Be My Guest (USA))
29^{8}

Bells 'N' Banjos (IRE) *Warren Greatrex* 105b
4 b g Indian River(FR) Beechill Dancer (IRE) (Darnay)
(5286)

Bells Of Berlin *Tim Vaughan* 98h
5 ch g Pivotal Choirgirl (Unfuwain (USA))
(188) 482^{7} 833^{5} 2891^{P}

Bellucia *Oliver Sherwood* 71h
5 b m Kayf Tara L'Ultima (FR) (Verglas (IRE))
2472^{5} 4916^{12}

Belmount (IRE) *Nigel Twiston-Davies* 108b
5 b g Westerner Artist's Jewel (Le Moss)
(5410)

Beluckyagain (IRE) *W P Mullins* 132h
6 b m Old Vic Whizz (Salse (USA))
5199a^{2}

Be Marvellous (IRE) *Colin Tizzard* 87h
6 gr g Old Vic Kalamix (IRE) (Linamix (FR))
410^{4} 1764^{10} 1863^{6} 2008^{10}

Be My Deputy (IRE) *Lucinda Russell* 102h 122c
9 b g Oscar(IRE) Have A Myth (IRE) (Roselier (FR))
883^{3} 1142^{3}
1291^{5} 2785^{9} 3823^{2} 4430^{P} 5060^{4}

De My Light (IRE) *Charlie Longsdon* 112h 108c
8 b m Oscar(IRE) Simply Divine (IRE) (Be My Native (USA))
38^{P}

Be My Present *Rose Dobbin* 106h
7 b m Presenting Simply Divine (IRE) (Be My Native (USA))
46^{3} 4074^{4} 4466^{3} (4770)

Be My Witness (IRE) *Robin Dickin* 88b
5 b m Witness Box(USA) Smokey Firth (IRE) (Flemensfirth (USA))
4016^{14} 5249^{5}

Ben Akram (IRE) *Lucinda Russell* 99h 107c
6 b g Beneficial Ring Four (IRE) (Supreme Leader)
27^{8} **1981^{5}**
2308^{F} 2361^{2} 2791^{U} 3041^{4} 3528^{6} (4462)
5216^{U}

Benalex Park *Denis Gerard Hogan* 101h
5 b g Echo Of Light Dijital Power (Pivotal)
(3518)

Benbane Head (USA) *Martin Keighley* 136h 144c
10 ch g Giant's Causeway(USA) Prospectress (USA) (Mining (USA))
877^{10} 1195^{2} (1363) 1597^{2} 1956^{2} *4022^{4} 4299^{4}* 4805^{5}

Benbecula *Richard Mitchell* 114h
5 b g Motivator Isle Of Flame (Shirley Heights)
2695^{3} 3370^{U} 4281^{5} 4503^{6} (4988) 5335^{8}

Benbens (IRE) *Nigel Twiston-Davies* 119h 137c
9 ch g Beneficial Millicent Bridge (IRE) (Over The River (FR))
3155^{2} (4507) ◆ **(4635) 5068^{2}**

Ben Cee Pee M (IRE) *Brian Ellison* 113h
9 ch g Beneficial Supreme Magical (Supreme Leader)
564^{4} 966^{7} (1414) (1506) 1717^{8} 4943^{2} (5191) 5384^{7}

Bendant *Debra Hamer* 118h 122c
9 b g Beat All(USA) Rendita (IRE) (Waajib)
2014^{2} 2390^{F} (2650)
3455^{P} 3717^{2} 4677^{P}
5543^{6}

Benedictus (IRE) *Jack Barber* 132c
9 ch g Alderbrook Dante's Thatch (IRE) (Phardante (FR))
63^{3} 4655^{3} 5127^{2} 5346^{3}

Beneficient (IRE) *A J Martin* 147h 166c
8 ch g Beneficial Supreme Breda (IRE) (Supreme Leader)
2229^{4} (3338a)
4766^{P}

Beneficial Reform (IRE) *Mrs A Rucker*
9 ch g Beneficial Miss Performance (IRE) (Lancastrian)
170^{2} 4348^{U}

Beneficial Spirit (IRE) *P J Rothwell* 117h 126c
11 b g Beneficial Ballinard Sarah (IRE) (Phardante (FR))
3806a^{P}

Benefique Royale *Nick Williams* 107h
6 ch m Beneficial Royale De Vassy (FR) (Royal Charter (FR))
1885^{7} 2027^{2} 2602^{4} (2948) 4090^{5} 4392^{P}

Benefit Cut (IRE) *Renee Robeson* 117h 142c
8 b g Beneficial I'm Maggy (NZ) (Danseur Etoile (FR))
1688^{3} 2050^{2} **3769^{2} (4077)**
4244^{P} (5089)

Benefit Evening (IRE) *Noel Quinlan* 104h 70c
9 b g Beneficial She Is Promising (IRE) (Henbit (USA))
164^{P} 707^{3}

Benefit Game (IRE) *Richard Hawker* 86h 42c
10 b g Beneficial Glenarb Molly (IRE) (Phardante (FR))
43^{10} 478^{P} 522^{10} 661^{10} 1018^{10}

Benefit In Kind (IRE) *Michael Smith* 55h
6 b g Beneficial She's So Beautiful (IRE) (Bluebird (USA))
5508^{8}

Benefit Night (IRE) *Warren Greatrex* 73h 86c
14 b g Beneficial Broomhill Star (IRE) (Deep Society)
373^{3} 535^{P} 778^{6} 872^{B}

Benefitofhindsight *Ben Pauling* 86h
5 ch g Sir Harry Lewis(USA) Aoninch (Inchinor)
4334 2968^{12} 3278^{10} 3592^{6} 3877^{16} 4398^{U} 4527^{4} 4911^{5}

Benefit Of Youth (IRE) *Tim Vaughan* 117h
7 b g Beneficial Persian Avenue (IRE) (Persian Mews)
(1007) (1154) 1330^{2} 1440^{3} 1755^{4}

Benefits Well (IRE) *Brendan Powell* 112h
7 b g Beneficial Farran Lady (IRE) (The Parson)
(828) 2018^{11}

Bene Lad (IRE) *Jim Goldie* 90h 114c
12 bb g Beneficial Sandwell Old Rose (IRE) (Roselier (FR))
220^{P}

Benenden (IRE) *Michael Scudamore* 115h
6 b g Moscow Society(USA) Ashanti Dancer (IRE) (Dancing Dissident (USA))
3600^{3} 4594^{6} 5088^{6}

Benevolent (IRE) *Chris Bealby* 58h 59c
7 ch g Beneficial Bobs Lass (IRE) (Bob's Return (IRE))
2622^{4} 4077^{P}

Bengairn *Jim Goldie* 74b
6 ch g Zafeen(FR) Miss Hermione (Bahamian Bounty)
4671^{6} 5279^{15}

Benheir (IRE) *S J Stearn* 87h 143c
8 b g Beneficial Vicford (IRE) (Old Vic)
5439^{2}

Benidorm *John Wainwright* 29h
6 b g Bahamian Bounty Famcred (Inchinor)
3106^{P} 4307^{9}

Benissimo (IRE) *Dan Skelton* 89b
4 b g Beneficial Fennor Rose (IRE) (Kotashaan (FR))
5447^{4}

Benmadigan (IRE) *Nicky Richards* 86h 35c
12 ch g Presenting Dont Tell Nell (IRE) (Denel (FR))
2397^{6} 2789^{6} 4957^{10} 5298^{8}

Bennachie (IRE) *Tim Vaughan* 102b
5 b g Milan Stormy Lady (IRE) (Glacial Storm (USA))
(1094) *4297^{3}* 5042^{3}

Bennative (IRE) *Stephen Francis Magee* 76h
9 b g Beneficial Which Is Which (IRE) (Be My Native (USA))
471^{U}

Bennys Mist (IRE) *Venetia Williams* 119h 143c
8 b g Beneficial Dark Mist (IRE) (Mister Lord (USA))
2180^{6} 2937^{11} (3742)
(3990) 4400^{3} 4768^{13} 5156^{2}

Bennys Quest (IRE) *Neil Mulholland* 114h 118c
11 ch g Beneficial Wonder Winnie (IRE) (Be My Guest (USA))
632^{2} 853^{7} 931^{3} 1122^{2} (1352)
(1417) 1522^{2} 1696^{2} 5013^{4}

Bennys Well (IRE) *Sue Smith* 66h 117c
8 b g Beneficial Alure (IRE) (Carroll House)
74^{P} 1506^{12}
1798^{2} (1936)
2339^{5} 2872^{2} 3193^{2} 3834^{2} (4382)
4580^{2} (4896)
5386^{F}

Benny The Swinger (IRE) *Chris Gordon* 97h 103c
9 b g Beneficial The Olde Swinger (IRE) (Lord Americo)
308[2] **632[F]**
674[7] 1674[2] 2004[5] **2251[3] 2629[2] 3960[4] (4802)**
5115[6] 5340[3]

Benozzo Gozzoli *Simon Earle* 69h 39c
8 ch g Medicean Star Precision (Shavian)
67[8] **1104[5]**

Ben's Folly (IRE) *R A Owen* 95h 100c
9 ch g Beneficial Daddy's Folly (Le Moss)
3862[3] 4274[P]

Bens Moor (IRE) *Tim Vaughan* 71h 93c
9 b g Beneficial Moor Lady (Primitive Rising (USA))
1672[12]
2088[P] 5038[6]

Benvolio (IRE) *Paul Nicholls* 136h 147c
7 b g Beneficial Coumeenoole Lady (The Parson)
2539[F] (3162)
(3776) 4033[3] 4439[2]

Benzanno (IRE) *Donald McCain* 123h
5 b g Refuse To Bend(IRE) Crossanza (IRE) (Cape Cross (IRE))
3350[3] *4022[9]* (4476) 4939[2] 5294[P]

Benzel (IRE) *Jonjo O'Neill* 112h
6 b g Beneficial Jezel (IRE) (Accordion)
4102[5] 4574[3]

Berea Boru (IRE) *Peter Bowen* 136h
6 b g Brian Boru Wayward Venture (IRE) (Mister Mat (FR))
1561[7] 1672[5] (2147) (2386) 2649[2] 3081[6]

Berkeley Avenue *Warren Greatrex* 107h
5 ch g Needwood Blade Dropitlikeit's Hot (IRE) (Tagula (IRE))
2109[3] 2718[5] 3134[10] *4019[5] 4302[12]* 5034[P] 5112[P]

Berkeley Barron (IRE) *Philip Hobbs* 135h
6 b g Subtle Power(IRE) Roseabel (IRE) (Roselier (FR))
1864[2] 2079[4] 4174[9] (4662) 5372[5]

Bermacha *John E Long* 90h
9 ch m Bertolini(USA) Machaera (Machiavellian (USA))
2725[4] 5445[5]

Bermuda Boy (FR) *S Flook* 108h 112c
9 b g Anabaa Blue Fast Reema (IRE) (Fast Topaze (USA))
4355[6] 4727[4] 5041[2] 5292[2] (5553)

Bernardelli (IRE) *Nicky Richards* 118h
6 b g Golan(IRE) Beautiful Blue (IRE) (Xaar)
1975[2] 2241[2] (2676) 3021[3] 5212[6] (5537)

Bernburg (FR) *Mlle A Pelletant*
11 b g Cricket Ball(USA) Astrelia (FR) (Full Of Stars)
1279a[5]

Bernisdale *John Flint* 83h
6 ch m Bertolini(USA) Carradale (Pursuit Of Love)
407[8] 925[10] 1700[5]

Bernix *Julie Camacho* 26h
12 gr g Linamix(FR) Bernique (USA) (Affirmed (USA))
1848[9]

Bernshaw *Mrs Claire Hitch* 27b
9 b g Fantastic Light(USA) Lauren (GER) (Lightning (FR))
5337[P]

Bertie Boru (IRE) *Philip Hobbs* 121h 130c
7 b g Brian Boru Sleeven Lady (Crash Course)
1797[2]
2475[2] ◆ 2925[3] 3358[4] (3745)
3990[F] 4395[3] 4962[10]

Bertielicious *Jonathan Haynes* 62h
6 b g And Beyond(IRE) Pennepoint (Pennekamp (USA))
73[6] 278[4] 630[6] 1853[12] 2243[P] 2449[P] 2596[P]

Bertie Milan (IRE) *N W Alexander* 105h 112c
9 b g Milan Miss Bertaine (IRE) (Denel (FR))
312[2] 2036[2] 2416[5] 3001[3] 3526[5] 4086[6] (5558)

Berties Coin *Hilary Parrott* 24h
5 b g Sakhee(USA) Spinning Coin (Mujahid (USA))
2718[15]

Bertie's Desire *Oliver Sherwood* 99h 115c
6 b g King's Theatre(IRE) Temptation (FR) (Lando (GER))
290[5] **1834[3]**
2677[2] 3027[4] (4762) ◆ (5342)

Berties Dream (IRE) *Mrs L Braithwaite* 68h 135c
11 b g Golden Tornado(IRE) Orla's Pride (IRE) (Brush Aside (USA))
4788[12]

Bertimont (FR) *J J Lambe* 127h 112c
4 gr g Slickly(FR) Bocanegra (FR) (Night Shift (USA))
4432a[6] 5470a[9]

Bert The Alert *Laura Mongan* 65h
6 b g Proclamation(IRE) Megalex (Karinga Bay)
5400[6]

Berwick Bassett *Warren Greatrex* 53b
5 b g Beat All(USA) Hottentot (Sula Bula)
5338[7]

Bescot Springs (IRE) *Lucinda Russell* 116h 121c
9 b g Saddlers' Hall(IRE) Silver Glen (IRE) (Roselier (FR))
310[4] **733[5]**
1289[5] 1543[3] 1660[2]
1978[2] 2246[6] 2971[P] 3396[6] 3938[4] 4649[2] (5059)
5256[5] 5559[P]

Beside The Fire *Colin Tizzard* 123h 93c
9 b g Cois Na Tine(IRE) Champagne N Dreams (Rambo Dancer (CAN))
2111[9]
2370[F] 2945[P] 3096[P]

Bespoke Lady (IRE) *Donald McCain* 109h
5 ch m Presenting Coole Alainn (IRE) (Glacial Storm (USA))
4240[3] 4749[2] (5322)

Best Bette *Clarissa Caroe* 48h 57c
9 b m Bob Back(USA) Gavotte Du Cochet (FR) (Urbain Minotiere (FR))
461[U] 2175[6] 2312[10] 2541[6]

Best Boy Barney (IRE) *Jeremy Scott* 93h 116c
8 b g Rashar(USA) Graigue Lass (IRE) (Phardante (FR))
1941[10]
2315[P] 2730[5] 3129[P] 4729[7]
5025[3] (5240)

Best Excuse *Jennie Candlish* 85h
7 b g Lucky Owners(NZ) Zambia (IRE) (Zafonic (USA))
732[8] 860[15] 1379[P]

Best Lover (FR) *Laura Hurley* 80h 105c
12 ch g Great Palm(USA) Droid (FR) (Belgio (FR))
457[4] 2470[P]

Best Of Bocelli (IRE) *Peter Croke* 62h 73c
11 ch g Anshan Patience Of Angels (IRE) (Distinctly North (USA))
4708a[11]

Best Served Cold *J J O'Shea* 100h 93c
8 b g King's Theatre(IRE) Mirana (IRE) (Ela-Mana-Mou)
957[4] 5287[U]

Best Time Ever *Philip Hobbs*
6 b g Tobougg(IRE) Lucky Arrow (Indian Ridge)
155[8]

Be There In Five (IRE) *Mrs Sarah Easterby* 138h 135c
10 b g Indian Danehill(IRE) Marwa (IRE) (Shahrastani (USA))
62[8]

Between The Lines (IRE) *Anthony Middleton* 60h
5 gr g Dalakhani(IRE) Stage Struck (IRE) (Sadler's Wells (USA))
390[7]

Beuillac (FR) *G Macaire* 132c
11 b g Robin Des Champs(FR) Mazzina (FR) (Mad Captain)
(1279a)
1532a[3]

Beverley Beck *Bruce Mactaggart* 55h
11 b m Namaqualand(USA) Richards Kate (Fidel)
748[4]

Beware Chalk Pit (IRE) *Jonathan Geake* 88h 98c
10 b g Anshan Rakiura (IRE) (Good Thyne (USA))
2863[2] 3688[P] 4720[P]

Be Wise (IRE) *Harriet Graham* 5h
7 gr g Cloudings(IRE) Crashtown Lucy (Crash Course)
173[9] 1037[5] 1788[6] 1980[P]

Beyeh (IRE) *Michael Appleby* 127h
6 b m King's Best(USA) Cradle Rock (IRE) (Desert Sun)
2655[8] (3117) 3263[8] 3737[4] 4531[3] 5370[9]

Beyond (IRE) *David Pipe* 109h
7 ch g Galileo(IRE) Run To Jane (IRE) (Doyoun)
144[6] 1284[10] 1436[5]

Beyond Dreams (IRE) *Stephen Hughes* 54h
10 ch m Bob's Return(IRE) You'll Never Know (IRE) (Un Desperado (FR))
948[U] 1017[P]

Beyondtemptation *Jonathan Haynes* 71h
6 ch m And Beyond(IRE) Tempted (IRE) (Invited (USA))
225[7] 754[5] 800[8] 1415[5] 2593[4] 2869[7] 3523[4]
3934[5] 4336[3] 4615[12] 4938[8]

Beyond The Creek *George Bewley*
7 ch g And Beyond(IRE) Bearami Creek (IRE) (Henbit (USA))
110[P]

Bhakti (IRE) *Mark Rimell* 114h
7 b g Rakti Royal Bossi (IRE) (Spectrum (IRE))
185[6] 2954[2] ◆ 3326[2] 4510[4]

Big Benjie *Edwin Tuer*
6 ch g Lahib(USA) Bula Rose (IRE) (Alphabatim (USA))
76[11] 695[P]

Big Buck's (FR) *Paul Nicholls* 175h 146c
11 bb g Cadoudal(FR) Buck's (FR) (Le Glorieux)
3890[3] 4767[5]

Big Casino *Nigel Twiston-Davies* 125h
8 b g Court Cave(IRE) Migsy Malone (Afzal)
174[3] (2158) 2529[10] 3263[3] 4510[2] 4841[4] 5349[7]

Big Easy (GER) *Philip Hobbs* 141h
7 b g Ransom O'War(USA) Basilea Gold (GER) (Monsun (GER))
5138[6]

Big Fella Thanks *Tom George* 138h 156c
12 b g Primitive Rising(USA) Nunsdream (Derrylin)
2214[12] 2937[7] 3772[6] 4346[5] 5156[7]

Big Frank (USA) *Micky Hammond* 47b
5 bb g More Than Ready(USA) Salchow (USA) (Nijinsky (CAN))
5500[12]

Big Game Hunter (IRE) *Andrew Leyshon* 128h 120c
8 b g Sadler's Wells(USA) Hill Of Snow (Reference Point)
63[4] 413[4]

Biggar (IRE) *Lucinda Russell* 105h
6 b g Court Cave(IRE) Native Success (IRE) (Be My Native (USA))
497[2] 1853[5] 2340[2] 2792[4] 3475[5] 4527[F]

Big Generator *Paul Nolan* 126h 112c
8 ch g Generous(IRE) Frizzball (IRE) (Orchestra)
3910a[13]

Big George *Simon Waugh* 65h 92c
7 b g Alflora(IRE) Petrea (St Ninian)
1976[P] 2782[5]

Big Georgie (IRE) *Mrs H S M Ridley* 90c
7 b g Exit To Nowhere(USA) Afreen (IRE) (Entrepreneur)
5248[3]

Big Hands Harry *Nicky Henderson* 132h
5 b g Multiplex Harristown Lady (Muscatite)
3182[2] (4535) 4950[2]

Bigindie (IRE) *John Weymes* 99b
4 ch g Indian Haven Graceful Air (IRE) (Danzero (AUS))
2731[3] 5454[2]

Big Jim *Alex Hales* 96b
5 b g Revoque(IRE) Chilly Squaw (IRE) (Commanche Run)
(4452)

Big John Cannon (IRE) *Sarah-Jayne Davies* 101h
4 b g High Chaparral(IRE) Bakiya (USA) (Trempolino (USA))
1727[P] 2038[7] 2466[7] 2559[5] 3047[7] (3154) 3317[P]
4301[12] 4731[4] 4791[P]

Big Knickers *Neil Mulholland* 71h
9 b m Bob Back(USA) Island Hopper (Be My Native (USA))
543[P]

Big Mike (IRE) *Sarah Humphrey* 109b
6 b g Flemensfirth(USA) Minoras Return (IRE) (Bob's Return (IRE))
3835[2] 4480[6]

Big News *Richard Lee* 76h 103c
8 ch g Karinga Bay Welcome News (Bob Back (USA))
2945[F] 3158[P] 3730[P] 4630[P] 5038[3] 5301[F]

Big Night Out *Nigel Hawke* 89h
8 b m Midnight Legend Big Decision (Arzanni)
2463[4] 2940[P]

Big Shu (IRE) *Peter Maher* 110b 149c
9 b g Milan Straight 'n Furry (IRE) (Furry Glen)
4754[3] 5171[F]

Big Society (IRE) *Tom George* 129h 129c
8 b g Flemensfirth(USA) Choice Of Kings (IRE) (King's Ride)
2024[F] 2651[U] 2944[9] 3207[5] (3724) 3860[3]
4412[2] 5533[3]

Big Sound *Mark Walford* 102h 106c
7 b g Supreme Sound Tarbolton Moss (Le Moss)
428[4] (804) 2447[5] 2843[P] 3638[5] 3824[2] 4006[5]
4577[3] 5059[6] 5359[6]

Big Talk *David Bridgwater* 101h 120c
7 b g Selkirk(USA) Common Request (USA) (Lear Fan (USA))
(1594)

Big Time Billy (IRE) *Peter Bowen* 145h
8 b m Definite Article Zaratu (IRE) (Key Of Luck (USA))
(158) (780)

Big Water (IRE) *Alan Swinbank* 125h 130c
6 ch g Saffron Walden(FR) Magic Feeling (IRE) (Magical Wonder (USA))
1922[5] 2221[8] 3000[2]
3142[2] 3354[3]

Big Whitfield *David Thompson* 8h
8 b g Tobougg(IRE) Natalie Jay (Ballacashtal (CAN))
4225[P]

Bijou Plage (FR) *A Lamotte D'Argy*
4 ch f Martaline Onciale (FR) (Ultimately Lucky (IRE))
130a[0]

Bilbrook Blaze *Philip Hobbs* 35b
4 b g Kayf Tara Za Beau (IRE) (Beneficial)
5130[13]

Bilidn *Ben De Haan* 107h
6 b m Tiger Hill(IRE) Brightest Star (Unfuwain (USA))
2907[3] 3733[6]

Billeragh Milan (IRE) *David Bridgwater* 86h
7 bb g Milan Billeragh Thyne (IRE) (Good Thyne (USA))
4514[F] 4715[P] 5008[8] 5227[6]

Billericay Allstar *Susan Corbett* 22b
6 ch m Septieme Ciel(USA) Magical Day (Halling (USA))
73[U]

Billesley Road *Philip Hobbs* 102h
6 ch g Zafeen(FR) Doubletta (IRE) (Barathea (IRE))
488[5] 730[5]

Billfromthebar (IRE) *Donald McCain* 132h 129c
7 b g Morozov(USA) Eden Breeze (IRE) (Insan (USA))
(284) 588[2] 737[2] 847[3] (1019) (1142) (1755)

Billie Magern *Nigel Twiston-Davies* 128h 145c
10 b g Alderbrook Outfield (Monksfield)
6[3] (334)
787[2] 1302[4] 1476[4] 2373[6]

Billing (IRE) *Jonjo O'Neill* 75h
6 b g Milan Melodic Tune (IRE) (Roselier (FR))
67[2] 711[5]

Billsgrey (IRE) *William Amos* 70h 77c
12 gr g Pistolet Bleu(IRE) Grouse-N-Heather (Grey Desire)
2416[8]

Bill The Lad (IRE) *Paul Cowley* 62h 100c
7 b g Classic Cliche(IRE) Quilty's Rose Bud (IRE) (Executive Perk)
2432[10]
2719[6] (3180)
3281[3] 3855[4] 5009[4] 5293[3]

Billy Biscuit (IRE) *Alan King* 115h
6 b g Presenting Native Novel (IRE) (Be My Native (USA))
2181[11] 5280[2]

Billybo *Tim Vaughan* 83h 102c
11 b g Kayf Tara Pollys Perk (IRE) (Executive Perk)
2152[2] 2653[2] 3277[P] 5187[3]

Billy Cuckoo (IRE) *Tony Coyle* 79h 125c
8 b g Alderbrook First Battle (IRE) (Un Desperado (FR))
2035[7]
(2873) 3211[3] 3452[2] 4007[3] (4106)
4244[P] 4593[3] 5378[3]

Billy Dutton *Chris Down* 129h 107c
8 ch g Sir Harry Lewis(USA) Tinoforty (FR) (Saint Estephe (FR))
2267[F] 2460[3] 3358[3] 4396[6] 4809[4] (5074) (5333)
5544[2]

Billy My Boy *Chris Down* 88h
5 b g Volochine(IRE) Key West (FR) (Highest Honor (FR))
160[7] 3422[7] 3746[3] 3956[F] 4911[13]

Billy No Name (IRE) *Colin Tizzard* 120h 114c
6 b g Westerner Just Little (Mtoto)
1749[3] (1946) 2279[4] **2859[3]**

Billy Teal *C I Ratcliffe* 95h 66c
9 ch g Keen Morcat (Morston (FR))
565[P] **1301[4]**
1494[P]

Billy The Bandit (IRE) *Jennie Candlish* 85b
6 b g Beneficial Kilfane (IRE) (Hollow Hand)
2052[5] 2513[8]

Billy Twyford (IRE) *Lawney Hill* 127h
7 b g Brian Boru The Distaff Spy (Seymour Hicks (FR))
119[3] 3028[5] 3263[5] 3653[8] (4556) 5093[5]

Biloute De Houelle (FR) *A Chaille-Chaille* 129h 136c
6 b g Roli Abi(FR) Kassite (FR) (Courtroom (FR))
5425a[13]

Bincombe *Philip Hobbs* 99h 126c
6 gr g Indian Danehill(IRE) Siroyalta (FR) (Royal Charter (FR))
2088[P] (2911)
3172[4] 3729[3] (4539)
(4898) 5385[P]

Bin End *Barry Brennan* 104h 110c
8 b g King's Best(USA) Overboard (IRE) (Rainbow Quest (USA))
2045[8] 2250[3] **2887[6] 3318[3] 3596[3] 3819[2] 4242[B]**
4653[P]

Binge Drinker (IRE) *Rebecca Curtis* 111b
5 b g Spadoun(FR) Our Honey (IRE) (Old Vic)
2026[2] 3433[3] (4417)

Binowagh Bay (IRE) *Mark Michael McNiff* 89h
6 b m Flemensfirth(USA) Sarah O'Malley (IRE) (Bob Back (USA))
(506) 748[2] 932[11]

Birnies Boy *Brian Storey* 88h
10 b g Thowra(FR) Drumkilly Lilly (IRE) (Executive Perk)
881[P]

Birzali (FR) *John Joseph Hanlon* 98h 78c
7 gr g Kalanisi(IRE) Bernimixa (FR) (Linamix (FR))
72[F] 593[6]

Bishophill Jack (IRE) *Kim Bailey* 90h 110c
8 b g Tikkanen(USA) Kerrys Cross (IRE) (Phardante (FR))
7[5] 265[3] (420)
1830[5] 2498[P] 2700[P] 3193[8] 3797[P] 4905[5] 5011[4]
5433[P]

Bishopsfurze (IRE) *W P Mullins* 129h 118c
9 b g Broadway Flyer(USA) Supreme Dipper (IRE) (Supreme Leader)
3866a[4]
4754[P] 5156[F]

Bishops Gate (IRE) *Nicky Richards* 110h
8 br g Bishop Of Cashel Lischelle Star (IRE) (Broussard (USA))
3208[P] 3838[6]

Bishops Heir *James Ewart* 113h 129c
9 b g Turbo Speed Linns Heir (Leading Counsel (USA))
2357[2] **2971[P]**

Bishop's Lane (IRE) *Hugo Froud* 98b 107c
11 ch g Pierre Sophie Victoria (IRE) (Satco (FR))
3222[4]

Bishopslough (IRE) *Anthony Mullins* 128h 107c
6 b g Fruits Of Love(USA) Maid In Blue (IRE) (Bluebird (USA))
5420a[7]

Bit Of A Clown (IRE) *Nick Gifford* 83h 83c
8 b g Anshan Dead Right Too (IRE) (Good Thyne (USA))
(327) **2017[4]**
2437[5] 3139[4] 3472[2] 5111[4] 5309[F] 5401[P]

Bit Of A Jig (IRE) *Donald McCain* 114h 138c
7 ch g Alderbrook Ardower (IRE) (Montelimar (USA))
2494[2] (2867)
(4474) 5278[P] 5495[3]

Bit Of A Madam *F-M Cottin* 85h
6 b m Loup Sauvage(USA) Miss Gratis (IRE) (Supreme Leader)
863a[0]

Bitofapuzzle *Harry Fry* 116b
6 b m Tamure(IRE) Gaelic Gold (IRE) (Good Thyne (USA))
(2809) (3507)

Bit Of A Scruff (IRE) *Hilary Parrott* 39b
7 b g Westerner Collage (Ela-Mana-Mou)
4506[P]

Bittersweetheart *David Bridgwater* 109h
7 b m Storming Home Cruz Santa (Lord Bud)
(761) 1008[2] 1132[2] (1305)

Bivouac (UAE) *Alan Swinbank* 80h
10 b g Jade Robbery(USA) Tentpole (USA) (Rainbow Quest (USA))
5377[6]

Bjornlucky (IRE) *Dan Skelton* 95b
4 b g Key Of Luck(USA) Super Trouper (FR) (Nashwan (USA))
(2634) 5264[5]

Black Bizarre (IRE) *Sean Curran* 81b
4 br g Buster King Lady Delight (IRE) (Be My Native (USA))
5249[0]

Black Coffee *Richard Woollacott* 78h
9 br g Vettori(IRE) In The Woods (You And I (USA))
651[9]

Black Cow (IRE) *Paul Nicholls* 97h
6 br g Presenting Back Market Lass (IRE) (Bob Back (USA))
298[3] 2788[3] *4017[4]* 5088[8] 5541[5]

Blackdown Babe *Alexandra Dunn*
6 b m Weld Blackdown Beauty (Deltic (USA))
2912[10]

Black Hercules (IRE) *W P Mullins* 135b
5 b g Heron Island(IRE) Annalecky (IRE) (Bob's Return (IRE))
(2995a) 4756[4] ◆

Black Is Beautiful (FR) *Richard Lee* 113h 100c
6 b g Black Sam Bellamy(IRE) Queen's Theatre (FR) (King's Theatre (IRE))
2451[3] 3193[7] 3797[6]

Black Kit (FR) *G Macaire* 121h
6 b g Black Sam Bellamy(IRE) Kitara (GER) (Camp David (GER))
(863a)
Blacklough (IRE) *W J Austin* 143h
6 b g King's Theatre(IRE) Oh Susannah (FR) (Turgeon (USA))
3910a[5]
Blackmore *N W Alexander* 84h
7 b g Rainbow Quest(USA) Waki Music (USA) (Miswaki (USA))
2075[8] 2997[4] 3520[P] 3824[P]
Black Phantom (IRE) *Mark Gillard* 119h 73c
8 br g Alderbrook Blenheim Blinder (IRE) (Mandalus)
295[9] 637[11]
Black River (FR) *Paul Nicholls* 131h
5 b g Secret Singer(FR) Love River (FR) (Epervier Bleu)
2811[F] 3369[4] 4112[4]
Black Rock Lake (IRE) *T G McCourt* 91h 83c
8 gr m Daylami(IRE) God Speed (IRE) (Be My Guest (USA))
1074[2]
Black Sambuca *Chris Bealby* 84h
7 b g Samraan(USA) Derring Floss (Derring Rose)
122[P]
Blacksmiths Arms *Michael Easterby* 73b
4 b g Multiplex Kingsfold Blaze (Mazilier (USA))
3508[5] 3926[6]
Black Spirit (USA) *Nicky Henderson* 127h
7 b g Black Minnaloushe(USA) L'Extra Honor (USA) (Hero's Honor (USA))
235[4]
Blackstone Vegas *Derek Shaw* 92h
8 ch g Nayef(USA) Waqood (USA) (Riverman (USA))
561[4] 669[3] 1442[4] 1635[3] 1797[6] 1940[B]
Blackstown Flyer (IRE) *G T H Bailey* 105h 81c
7 b g King's Theatre(IRE) Brownlow Castle (IRE) (Supreme Leader)
4658[6]
Blackthirteen (IRE) *Michael B Jones* 51c
10 br g Key Of Luck(USA) Jenny May (IRE) (Orchestra)
557[8] 5165[P]
Black Thunder (FR) *Paul Nicholls* 141h 157c
7 bl g Malinas(GER) Blackmika (FR) (Subotica (FR))
2151[0]
(2019) (2658) ◆ (3095) ◆ 3651[2] 4751[F]
Black Velvet Belle (IRE) *Lucy Normile* 66h
7 br m Spadoun(FR) Shimla (IRE) (Rudimentary (USA))
223[5] 628[P]
Blackwater King (IRE) *Donald McCain* 107h 112c
6 bb g Beneficial Accordian Lady (IRE) (Accordion)
1922[8]
2159[4] 2804[4] 4004[3] 4919[3] 5237[2] 5380[2]
Blackwell Synergy (FR) *Jonjo O'Neill* 138h 94c
8 b g Antarctique(IRE) Pyu (GER) (Surumu (GER))
120[3] (606)
Blades Lad *Peter Niven* 115h
5 ch g Haafhd Blades Girl (Bertolini (USA))
1853[2] 2840[4] 3288[11]
Bladoun (FR) *David Pipe* 112h
6 gr g Smadoun(FR) Blabliramic (FR) (Panoramic)
2458[8] 2764[6] 3013[9]
Blake Dean *Sue Smith* 100h
6 b g Halling(USA) Antediluvian (Air Express (IRE))
1938[8] (2191) 2336[2] 3188[2] (3723) 4189[2] 4629[5] 5496[7]
Blakemount (IRE) *Sue Smith* 140h
6 br g Presenting Smashing Leader (IRE) (Supreme Leader)
2030[3] (2520) 2819[3] (3208) 3896[2] ◆
Blaklion *Nigel Twiston-Davies* 123b
5 b g Kayf Tara Franciscaine (FR) (Legend Of France (USA))
(5042) (5388) ◆
Blase Chevalier (IRE) *Seamus Mullins* 103h
8 b m Chevalier(IRE) Dancing Line (High Line)
(1823) 2371[11]
Blast Martha (IRE) *Michael Smith* 89b
5 b m Definite Article Calendula (Be My Guest (USA))
5195[7]
Blazing Bouncer *Richard Woollacott* 96h
9 b g Relief Pitcher Blazing Miracle (Shaab)
2076[4] 2649[4] 3014[2] 3179[P] 3955[3]
Blazing Bull (IRE) *John Wade* 79h 119c
10 b g Winged Love(IRE) Our Buttons (IRE) (Bulldozer)
18[F]
Blazing Desert *William Kinsey* 84b
10 b g Beat All(USA) Kingsfold Blaze (Mazilier (USA))
5283[P]
Blazing Glen (IRE) *Alan Jessop* 77h
6 ch g Beneficial Kofiyah's Rose (IRE) (Roselier (FR))
5486[6]
Blazing Sonnet (IRE) *W J Austin* 117h 120c
8 b m Oscar(IRE) Leading Duke (IRE) (Supreme Leader)
5475a[6]
Blazing Whale *E Walker* 105c
9 b g Classic Cliche(IRE) Baby Whale (IRE) (Supreme Leader)
4485[3]
Blazin White Face (IRE) *Lucinda Russell* 101h 113c
7 b m Noverre(USA) Watch The Clock (Mtoto)
341[3] 626[3]
Blenheim Brook (IRE) *Lucinda Russell* 122h 119c
9 br g Alderbrook Blenheim Blinder (IRE) (Mandalus)
2358[P] 3001[4] 4896[3] (5386)
Bless The Wings (IRE) *Alan King* 117h 152c
9 b g Winged Love(IRE) Silva Venture (IRE) (Mandalus)
2214[6] 3199[4] 4422[P] 4768[15] 5253[6]

Bleu Et Rose (FR) *E Leray* 123h 121c
9 b g Indian River(FR) Femme D'Honneur (FR) (Take Risks (FR))
263a[3]
Bleuvito (IRE) *S Turner* 54h 92c
10 b g Corrouge(USA) Clare Hogan (IRE) (Moscow Society (USA))
62[12] 658[P]
Blewit (IRE) *William Kinsey* 94h
6 b g Iffraaj Privileged Speech (USA) (General Assembly (USA))
333[B]
Blinding Lights (IRE) *Mary Sanderson* 92c
9 b g Snurge Tender Return (IRE) (Strong Gale)
159[2] 5337[P]
Blingless (FR) *J Bertran De Balanda*
6 b g Enrique Three Well (FR) (Sicyos (USA))
1901a[P]
Blondinabar *Philip Kirby* 50b
5 b m Beat All(USA) Kissinthepeach (IRE) (Witness Box (USA))
2174[7]
Blood Cotil (FR) *W P Mullins* 144h 128c
5 b g Enrique Move Along (FR) (Northern Crystal)
3910a[10]
Blowing A Hoolie (IRE) *Sophie Leech* 79h
6 b m Val Royal(FR) Moly (Inchinor)
1707[8] 3227[P]
Blown Cover *Emma Lavelle* 99b
5 b g Kayf Tara Cullen Bay (IRE) (Supreme Leader)
4844[3]
Blue Bear (IRE) *Diana Grissell* 100h
5 b g Blueprint(IRE) In For It (IRE) (Tale Quale)
544[3] 2002[10] 2566[4] 4808[8]
Blue Bellini *Chris Grant* 54h
6 b m Blueprint(IRE) Knysna Belle (Royal Fountain)
4240[6] 4609[4] 5050[7]
Blue Buttons (IRE) *Harry Fry* 126h
6 b m King's Theatre(IRE) Babet (IRE) (Mujadil (USA))
372[4] 2463[F] 2600[3] (3168) 3423[2] 4276[F] (5002) 5370[5]
Blue Clumber *Shaun Harris*
4 b f Sleeping Indian Blue Nile (IRE) (Bluebird (USA))
1044[P]
Blue Cove *Lynn Siddall* 80h
9 ch g Karinga Bay Meadow Blue (Northern State (USA))
89[6] 2509[9] 2827[3] 3179[3] 3334[4] 3842[3] 4446[4] 4779[P] 5106[P]
Blue Fashion (IRE) *Nicky Henderson* 150h
5 b g Scorpion(IRE) Moon Glow (FR) (Solar One (FR))
683a[4] 2671[2]
Blue Grand (IRE) *Adrian Wintle* 92h
6 ch g Blueprint(IRE) Grandolly (IRE) (The Parson)
5548[5]
Bluegun (IRE) *S R Andrews*
12 b g Pistolet Bleu(IRE) Supreme Spice (IRE) (Supreme Leader)
4376[P]
Blue Hell (FR) *Anthony Mullins* 126h
4 b g Russian Blue(IRE) Art Fair (FR) (Fairy King (USA))
4432a[4] ◆
Blue Heron (IRE) *Dan Skelton* 128h
6 b g Heron Island(IRE) American Chick (IRE) (Lord Americo)
2724[2] (3160) 4763[3] (5016) 5347[5]
Blue Kascade (IRE) *Sandy Thomson* 99h 101c
7 ch g Kaieteur(USA) Lydia Blue (IRE) (Eve's Error)
1790[7] 2035[4] (4223) 4465[3] 5537[5]
Blue Lodge (IRE) *James Moffatt*
8 b g Wareed(IRE) Glacial Air (IRE) (Glacial Storm (USA))
747[P]
Blue Ridge Lane (IRE) *John C McConnell* 101h
8 ch g Indian Ridge Upperville (IRE) (Selkirk (USA))
891a[5]
Blue Sea Of Ibrox (IRE) *Alan Brown* 74h
6 gr m Subtle Power(IRE) Jerpoint Rose (IRE) (Roselier (FR))
1848[4] 2360[4] 2701[6] 3040[9] 3265[4] 3605[3] 3840[4] 4475[3] 4938[U] 5298[5]
Blueside Boy (IRE) *Lucinda Russell* 93h 63c
6 b g Blueprint(IRE) Asidewager (IRE) (Brush Aside (USA))
3392[3]
4082[6] 4551[6]
Blue Signal (IRE) *Colin Heard* 91h 75c
9 b g Blueprint(IRE) Signal Lizzy (IRE) (Petorius)
83[4] **175[F]**
637[2] 946[9] 1339[9] 1477[5]
Blue Top *Tim Walford* 94h
5 b g Millkom Pompey Blue (Abou Zouz (USA))
2353[5]
Bob Almighty (IRE) *Mrs Gaye Williams* 81c
9 b g Bob's Return(IRE) Clashdermot Lass (Cardinal Flower)
430[4] 4706[4]
Bobbisox (IRE) *Alex Hales* 81h 94c
9 ch m Bob Back(USA) Swift Approach (IRE) (Dry Dock)
2[8] **786[3]**
1300[F] 1936[5] 2088[F] 2253[P]
2769[5] 3277[P] 4729[P] 5432[2]
Bobbits Way *Alan Jones* 89h 91c
9 b g Overbury(IRE) Bit Of A Chick (Henbit (USA))
1259[P] 1388[P] **1596[6] 2277[C] 2615[3] 3139[F] 4716[3] 5111[5]**
Bobble Boru (IRE) *Venetia Williams* 110h
6 b m Brian Boru Balreask Lady (IRE) (Shardari)
(2724) (3289) 4251[P] (4600) 4920[3]
Bobble Hat Bob (FR) *Lucinda Russell* 114h 130c
9 b g Lost World(IRE) Bisette (FR) (Star Maite (FR))
(169) (625)

Bob Bo Jangles (IRE) *Paul Stafford* 67h
6 b g Chevalier(IRE) Mossy Maze (Zamindar (USA))
1877[10]
Bobby Dove *Andrew Price* 78h 98c
7 b g Fraam Flakey Dove (Oats)
2251[6] 2653[3] 3048[P]
Bobcatbilly (IRE) *Ian Williams* 110h 130c
8 b g Overbury(IRE) Cush Jewel (IRE) (Executive Perk)
(2887)
3155[3] (3418)
3769[6] (4273)
4819[4]
Bob Ford (IRE) *Rebecca Curtis* 130h 133c
7 b g Vinnie Roe(IRE) Polar Lamb (IRE) (Brush Aside (USA))
2151[2] 2501[5] 2803[2] 3416[7] 4026[P] 4273[P] (4673)
4946[P]
Bob Keown (IRE) *Rebecca Curtis* 125h
6 b g Indian Danehill(IRE) Arteea Princess (IRE) (Oscar (IRE))
2181[4] 2942[4] 3227[3] 3955[6] (4883) 5019[2] 5351[3]
Bob Lewis *Anthony Middleton* 89h
8 b g Sir Harry Lewis(USA) Teelyna (Teenoso (USA))
29[2] 188[5] 264[2] 421[2] 456[5] 767[9] 1259[4] 1388[2]
Bob Lingo (IRE) *Thomas Mullins* 129h 135c
12 b g Bob's Return(IRE) Pharlingo (IRE) (Phardante (FR))
1168a[16] 1572a[3] 1613a[5] 1897a[14]
Bobonyx *Barry Brennan* 66b
4 b g Phoenix Reach(IRE) Twist The Facts (IRE) (Un Desperado (FR))
5145[6]
Bobowen (IRE) *Dr Richard Newland* 137h 145c
8 b g Bob Back(USA) Opus One (Slip Anchor)
205[F] 877[7] **(1047)**
1168a[P] 1476[8] 1686[P] 5535[8]
Bob's Dream (IRE) *William Amos* 86h 103c
12 b g Bob's Return(IRE) Back In Kansas (IRE) (Mister Lord (USA))
281[P] 2361[3] (2737)
3143[6] 4748[P]
Bobs Lady Tamure *Maurice Barnes* 101h
7 b m Tamure(IRE) Bob Back's Lady (IRE) (Bob Back (USA))
2037[6] 2748[12] 4199[4] 4364[4] 4770[3] 5163[4]
Bobs Law (IRE) *Mickey Bowen* 111h 111c
10 b g Bob Back(USA) Retinue (IRE) (Mister Lord (USA))
4274[P]
Bob's Legend (IRE) *Michael Appleby* 115h
8 b g Bob's Return(IRE) Pepsi Starlet (IRE) (Heavenly Manna)
333[3] 788[4] 1258[5] 1391[8] 1633[3] (5066) 5294[2] ◆ 5521[5]
Bobs Lord Tara *Alan Swinbank* 101b
4 b g Kayf Tara Bob Back's Lady (IRE) (Bob Back (USA))
4043[4] *4329[7]* (4631) 5500[2]
Bob's Ticket (IRE) *Philip Kirby* 89h
9 ch g Bob's Return(IRE) Some Ticket (IRE) (Montelimar (USA))
222[3] 628[4] 2333[4]
Bob's World *Jennie Candlish* 123h
5 b g Multiplex Vocation (IRE) (Royal Academy (USA))
2069[10] 2454[7] 2668[4] 3201[5] 3430[6] 4085[4] *4327[3]* 4745[2] 5059[5]
Bobs Worth (IRE) *Nicky Henderson* 153h 181c
9 b g Bob Back(USA) Fashionista (IRE) (King's Theatre (IRE))
2673[6] (3376a)
4787[5]
Bobtail *Mark Gillard* 36h
4 b g Nomadic Way(USA) Rabbit (Muhtarram (USA))
4030[P] 4534[U] 4722[12] 5426[8]
Bob Tucker (IRE) *Brendan Powell* 119h
7 b g Brian Boru Acumen (IRE) (Phardante (FR))
1082[3] 1256[5] 1348[7] 1672[3] (1838) 2458[6] 2908[6] 3195[3] (3741) 4277[2] 4820[10] 5093[8]
Bob Will (IRE) *Tim Vaughan* 57h 70c
9 b g Bob's Return(IRE) Mini Moo Min (Ardross)
172[8] 444[7]
753[5] 881[7] 2148[5] 3014[5]
Bocamix (FR) *Andrew Crook* 96h 102c
8 gr g Linamix(FR) Bocanegra (FR) (Night Shift (USA))
26[2] 167[5] 2173[4] 2445[3] 2734[2] 3039[U] 3449[2] 3833[4] 4681[3] 4815[F]
Bocciani (GER) *Brian Ellison* 120h 143c
9 b g Banyumanik(IRE) Baila (Lando (GER))
(204) 1047[5]
Bodega *Ian Williams* 117h
6 b g Grape Tree Road Gurleigh (IRE) (Pivotal)
2642[4] 2978[7] 3388[F] ◆ 3877[10] (4350) 4558[3]
Bodyguard (POL) *Michal Rocak*
8 b h Be My Chief(USA) Batalia (POL) (Wolver Heights)
1905a[P]
Bogside (IRE) *George Charlton* 110h 117c
10 ch g Commander Collins(IRE) Miss Henrietta (IRE) (Step Together I (USA))
273[3] 1979[3] 2311[4] (2970)
Bog Warrior (IRE) *A J Martin* 164h 156c
10 b g Strategic Choice(USA) Kilmac Princess (IRE) (King's Ride)
4283a[U] (5082a)
Bohemian Rhapsody (IRE) *Seamus Durack* 122h
5 b g Galileo(IRE) Quiet Mouse (USA) (Quiet American (USA))
2755[2] ◆ 3322[4] 3599[3] 4157[3] ◆ 5496[2]
Bois D'Auge (FR) *D Delorme* 77c
8 b g Sassanian(USA) La Sasline (FR) (Grand Pavois (USA))
1214a[7]
Bois Des Aigles (FR) *David Pipe* 96h
5 gr g Stormy River(FR) Silver Fun (FR) (Saumarez)
2105[14] 2691[15]

Bolachoir (IRE) *Patrick Chamings* 103c
12 b g Hubbly Bubbly(USA) Boolindrum Lady (IRE) (Meneval (USA))
84[2] 5127[6]
Bolberry Springs *Colin Tizzard* 88h
7 ch g Hamairi(IRE) Hand Out (Spare A Dime)
920[11] 994[F] 1348[4] 1700[6] 1941[9] 2289[6]
Bold Achiever *John Butler* 57b
4 b g Rail Link Achieve (Rainbow Quest (USA))
5447[9]
Bold Addition (FR) *Mrs F J Browne* 109h 138c
9 b g Cadoudal(FR) Kaldona (FR) (Kaldoun (FR))
3720[P] 5346[6]
Bold Adventure *Willie Musson* 98h
10 ch g Arkadian Hero(USA) Impatiente (USA) (Vaguely Noble)
2848[5] 3284[5] 4371[5] 4818[2]
Bold And Free *David Thompson* 67h
4 b g Bertolini(USA) Lady Broughton (IRE) (Grand Lodge (USA))
2899[8] 3332[7] 4889[6] 5295[7]
Bold Chief (IRE) *Harry Fry* 134h 149c
9 br g Oscar(IRE) Cottage Girl (IRE) (Actinium (FR))
(9) (861)
(1338)
1686[9] (4819)
5383[4]
Bold Cuffs *Colin Tizzard* 106h
5 b g Dutch Art Chambray (IRE) (Barathea (IRE))
1699[6] 1829[3] 2111[6] 2755[7] 3650[2]
Bold Henry *Philip Hobbs* 88h 88c
8 b g Kayf Tara Madam Min (Overbury (IRE))
5172[20]
Bold Perk (IRE) *Martin Hill* 102h 124c
12 ch g Executive Perk Mugazine (Kemal (FR))
(190) (487)
787[6] 998[3]
5488[5]
Bold Prince Rupert (IRE) *Sara Ender*
4 br g Royal Anthem(USA) Fortune And Favour (IRE) (Homo Sapien)
4329[9] 5500[11]
Bold Raider (IRE) *Jonjo O'Neill* 110h
7 b g Presenting Dato Fairy (IRE) (Accordion)
(997) 1121[3] (1434) 1707[7] 2105[2] 2786[3] 3740[8] 5521[8]
Bold Revenge (IRE) *John C McConnell* 107h
6 b g Oscar(IRE) Gala Festival (IRE) (Supreme Leader)
1183[3]
Bold Slasher (IRE) *Sue Smith* 87h
6 b g Millenary Witney Girl (Le Bavard (FR))
2035[6] 2202[7] 2746[4]
Bold Tara *Martin Keighley* 96h
7 b m Kayf Tara Bruley (Weld)
1169[6] 1351[11] 1517[4] 1675[F] 2008[4] 2278[5] 2696[5] 3119[2] (3569) 3842[4] 5521[6]
Boldwood *James Evans*
5 b g September Storm(GER) Christie (Environment Friend)
4296[14]
Bollin Across *Andrew Hollinshead* 86b
6 b m Bollin Eric Miss Lacroix (Picea)
1317[6] 1523[7] 1819[7]
Bollin Bob *Tim Easterby* 38b
5 b g Bollin Eric Bollin Roberta (Bob's Return (IRE))
76[7]
Bollin Dolly *James Moffatt* 107h
11 ch m Bien Bien(USA) Bollin Roberta (Bob's Return (IRE))
626[2] 1043[7]
Bollin Fiona *Donald Whillans* 99h 93c
10 ch m Silver Patriarch(IRE) Bollin Nellie (Rock Hopper)
224[2] 473[P] 2416[6] 3525[8] 4649[3] 4774[2] 5106[3] 5559[4]
Bollin Judith *Chris Nenadich* 116h
8 br m Bollin Eric Bollin Nellie (Rock Hopper)
(1009) 1562[2] (2271) 2477[4] 2760[3] 2894[6] 4920[4]
Bollin Julie *Donald Whillans* 82h
7 b m Bollin Eric Bollin Nellie (Rock Hopper)
1979[7] 2241[5] 3038[6] 3639[4] 4607[4] (5056)
Bollin Line *Lucinda Egerton* 89h
7 b g Bollin Eric Leading Line (Leading Man)
3271[P] 4772[6] 4939[4] 5161[7]
Bollin Sam *Sue Smith* 55h
8 b g Bollin Eric Cranborne (IRE) (King's Ride)
278[6] 695[3] 800[9]
Bollin Tahini *Neil King* 90h
8 b m Bollin Eric Cinnamon Club (Derrylin)
428[C] (595)
Bollywood (IRE) *Alison Batchelor* 40h 94c
11 ch g Indian Rocket La Fille De Cirque (Cadeaux Genereux)
860[14] 1051[P]
Bombadero (IRE) *Dr Richard Newland* 123h
7 b g Sadler's Wells(USA) Fantasy Girl (IRE) (Marju (IRE))
1564[6] 1708[2] 1840[2] (1889)
Bombel (IRE) *Evan Williams* 38h
6 b g Curtain Time(IRE) Approach The Ocean (IRE) (Shernazar)
810[8]
Bonds Conquest *Seamus Mullins* 78h
5 ch g Monsieur Bond(IRE) Another Conquest (El Conquistador)
2026[8] 2457[15] 3136[8] 3695[7] 5015[5]
Bonnet's Vino *Pam Sly* 106h
6 b m Grape Tree Road Bonnet's Pieces (Alderbrook)
36[2] 2317[8] 2621[3] (2883) 3151[2] 3657[2] 4189[3] 4816[4]
Bonnie Burnett (IRE) *Brian Rothwell* 104h
7 bb m Hawk Wing(USA) Chameleon (Green Desert (USA))
2597[9] 2868[9] 3659[9] 3924[P] 4615[8]
Bonnie Major *Gerry Enright* 79b
4 ch f Apple Tree(FR) Carly Bay (Carlton (GER))
5264[6]
Bonoman (IRE) *Evan Williams* 68h 97c
11 b g Aboo Hom Toreva (IRE) (Torus)
141[6]

Boogie Dancer *Jim Best* 88h
10 b m Tobougg(IRE) Bolero (Rainbow Quest (USA))
429^10

Boogie De Bispo *Stuart Kittow* 68h
4 b f Tobougg(IRE) Mellifluous (IRE) (Noverre (USA))
1855^5

Boogie In The Barn (IRE) *Jeremy Scott* 128h
6 b g Milan Presenting Mist (IRE) (Presenting)
2216^5 (2864) (4130) 4535^7 (5343)

Book'Em Danno (IRE) *Peter Bowen* 126h 124c
8 ch g Moscow Society(USA) Rifada (Ela-Mana-Mou)
1851^5 2389^P 2887^7 (4985)
5194^4

Books Review *D C Gibbs* 67h 88c
10 b g Karinga Bay In A Whirl (USA) (Island Whirl (USA))
658^10

Boomtown *Claire Dyson* 100h
9 b g Fantastic Light(USA) Ville D'Amore (USA) (Irish River (FR))
2771^7 3029^9 3192^3 (3503) 3828^2 4636^P

Boomtown Kat *Karen George* 97h 68c
10 b g Double Trigger(IRE) Storm Kitten (IRE) (Catrail (USA))
295^5 829^6 1153^5

Boondooma (IRE) *Dr Richard Newland* 124h
7 b g Westerner Kissantell (IRE) (Broken Hearted)
4280^4 4680^6 (4796) (5050) 5349^5

Boosha *John Bryan Groucott* 42h
9 ch m Sir Harry Lewis(USA) Musical Vocation (IRE) (Orchestra)
2723^4 2896^9 4865^10

Bop Along (IRE) *Michael Smith* 116h
7 b g Double Eclipse(IRE) Bob Girl (IRE) (Bob Back (USA))
(4776) 5319^2

Boracha (IRE) *Seamus Mullins* 91b
6 bb m Presenting Bacchonthebottle (IRE) (Bob Back (USA))
268^P

Border Breaker (IRE) *David Pipe* 96b
5 br g Indian Danehill(IRE) Flying Answer (IRE) (Anshan)
4763^4 ◆ 5249^6

Borderland (IRE) *S Popelka Jr*
8 b h Fasliyev(USA) Alcove (USA) (Valdez (USA))
1904a^4

Border Phoenix *Sandy Forster* 104h
7 b g Karinga Bay Dusky Dante (IRE) (Phardante (FR))
168^U 556^U (676) 2158^7 2655^13

Border Station (IRE) *Alison Batchelor* 104h 74c
8 b g Shantou(USA) Telemania (IRE) (Mujtahid (USA))
95^3 (708) 2274^6 2474^3 2932^13 **3139^P**

Border Tale *James Moffatt* 91h 94c
14 b g Selkirk(USA) Likely Story (IRE) (Night Shift (USA))
219^4 471^4

Bordoni (USA) *John Ferguson* 130h
5 b g Bernardini(USA) Argentina (IRE) (Sadler's Wells (USA))
5172^16 ◆

Borguy (FR) *Jamie Snowden* 76b
4 b g Irish Wells(FR) Bally Borg (FR) (Cyborg (FR))
3049^6 5409^4

Boric *Simon Waugh* 67h 121c
6 b g Grape Tree Road Petrea (St Ninian)
1980^8 2748^11 **5213^4**

Boris The Blade *Tina Jackson* 95h 99c
12 gr g Cloudings(IRE) Cherry Lane (Buckley)
2201^5 2818^6 3022^8 3497^5 (4577)
(4773) 5358^P

Borkum (IRE) *Philip Hobbs* 77b
6 b g Germany(USA) Lizabeth Glick (IRE) (Turtle Island (IRE))
1599^11 1712^12

Born To Benefit (IRE) *Fergal O'Brien* 105h 92c
8 b m Beneficial Sister Superior (IRE) (Supreme Leader)
1938^9 2190^3 2514^2 2824^2 **3171^4** 3570^3

Born To Shine (USA) *Alan Swinbank* 94h
6 b g Suave(USA) Sentimental Keep (USA) (Behrens (USA))
491^3 752^F 961^U 1078^5

Borolee (IRE) *Ferdy Murphy* 82b 101c
11 b g Taipan(IRE) Leeway (IRE) (Archway (IRE))
(172) 492^3
(601) 670^5

Boruma (IRE) *Dianne Sayer* 101h
4 b g Brian Boru Itlallendintears (IRE) (Lil's Boy (USA))
3214^5 4307^6 4627^3 5102^P 5206^3

Bo's Return *Tim Vaughan* 62b
4 b g Tobougg(IRE) Lamp's Return (Bob's Return (IRE))
4810^12

Boss In Boots (IRE) *Seamus Mullins* 109h 111c
6 gr g King's Theatre(IRE) Grey Mo (IRE) (Roselier (FR))
95^4 2430^5 (2920) 3195^7 4132^P 4887^3
5342^6

Boss's Star (IRE) *Peter Casey* 117h
5 b g Barathea(IRE) Palace Star (IRE) (Desert Style (IRE))
1139a^8

Bossy Beccy *James Walton* 91b
5 b m And Beyond(IRE) Merry Tina (Tina's Pet)
4240^8 4618^5 5108^4

Bostin (IRE) *Brian Barr* 105h
6 ch g Busy Flight Bustingoutallover (USA) (Trempolino (USA))
2912^5 3433^4 3694^8 3988^9 *4297^11* 4993^9 5395^2

Boston Blue *Tony Carroll* 113h
7 b g Halling(USA) City Of Gold (IRE) (Sadler's Wells (USA))
2617^2 3599^10 4659^P 5179^7

Boston Bob (IRE) *W P Mullins* 148h 165c
9 b g Bob Back(USA) Bavaway (Le Bavard (FR))
3890^6
4766^6 (5155)

Bostons Angel (IRE) *David Pipe* 113b
10 b g Winged Love(IRE) Lady Boston (FR) (Mansonnien (FR))
199a^P 2937^P

Bouggietopieces *Pam Sly* 69h
4 b g Tobougg(IRE) Bonnet's Pieces (Alderbrook)
2830^5 4944^5 5519^7

Bouggler *Emma Lavelle* 140h 151c
9 b g Tobougg(IRE) Rush Hour (IRE) (Night Shift (USA))
(1686)
2214^5

Boulevard Auteuil (FR) *T Civel* 107h 131c
6 ch g Discover D'Auteuil(FR) Nini Malta (FR) (Cyborg (FR))
1740a^5

Bound For Glory (IRE) *Donald McCain* 118h 120c
8 b g Witness Box(USA) Musical View (IRE) (Orchestra)
182^2 562^4

Bountiful Bess *Pam Sly* 77h
4 ch f Bahamian Bounty Saida Lenasera (FR) (Fasliyev (USA))
975^3

Bourne *Donald McCain* 139h
8 gr g Linamix(FR) L'Affaire Monique (Machiavellian (USA))
356^12 512^7 1926^6 2170^4 2454^3 2949^8 3286^3
3771^3 4264^10 4949^9 5384^10

Bournie (FR) *J-P Gallorini* 108h 120c
6 b m Kahyasi Ashbourne (FR) (Ashkalani (IRE))
2465a^4

Bow Badger *John Wade* 126h
8 b g Sadler's Wells(USA) Biloxi (Caerleon (USA))
(344) 734^F

Bow Fiddle (IRE) *Patrick Holmes* 84h
8 br m Anshan Elite Racing (Risk Me (FR))
552^P 800^5 1072^7 3518^8 4107^8 4479^5

Bowie (IRE) *Nick Kent* 115h
7 br g Pelder(IRE) La Fenice (IRE) (Krayyan)
280^2 (560) 2397^4 2828^3 3269^3

Bow Quest *Gary Moore* 96h
7 b m Rainbow High Fair Kai (IRE) (Fayruz)
544^7 3961^8 4467^3 4715^P 5026^2

Bow School (IRE) *Alison Hamilton* 106h 120c
13 b g New Frontier(IRE) Sallaghan (IRE) (Hays)
341^P 4553^10 4957^11 5298^6

Boxer Beat (IRE) *Paul W Flynn* 122h 128c
7 b g Xaar Pantoufle (Bering)
1702a^4 1804a^4 2101^4

Boxer Georg (IRE) *W P Mullins* 104c
12 b g Taipan(IRE) Country Course (IRE) (Crash Course)
5135^U

Boxing Along (IRE) *Vincent Laurence Halley* 123h 117c
10 b g Witness Box(USA) Ballybeg Rose (IRE) (Roselier (FR))
4788^9

Boyfromnowhere (IRE) *Rebecca Curtis* 127h 134c
7 br g Old Vic Eist Do Gale (IRE) (Strong Gale)
1728^3 2077^3 (2537) ◆ **3655^P 4842^4 5184^3**
5488^6

Boy Of Boru (IRE) *Diana Grissell* 60h
7 b g Brian Boru Don't Waste It (IRE) (Mister Lord (USA))
2535^8

Brabazon (IRE) *Emmet Michael Butterly* 109h
11 b g In The Wings Azure Lake (USA) (Lac Ouimet (USA))
891a^8

Bracing *N W Alexander* 80b
5 ch m Alflora(IRE) Sports Express (Then Again)
1719^8 3042^12 5560^9

Bracken House (IRE) *Graeme McPherson* 98h 120c
7 ch g Great Palm(USA) Carraig Aille (IRE) (Anshan)
854^2 1109^3 1266^4
(1375) 1851^4 2224^2

Brackloon High (IRE) *Brendan Powell* 123h 130c
9 b g Bob Back(USA) Homebird (IRE) (Be My Native (USA))
1747^5
2108^P 2646^U 2944^2 3359^3 3784^4 4144^3 4556^3
5333^F

Bradley *Fergal O'Brien* 86b 139c
10 ch g Karinga Bay Good Taste (Handsome Sailor)
355^10 1971^5 2502^3 2953^9 3455^P (4661)
4821^P 5092^5 ◆ **5371^5**

Brady (IRE) *Donald McCain* 109h 122c
8 ch g Albano(IRE) Quiet Sovereign (Supreme Leader)
114^2 603^2 1083^5 1916^P 2173^U

Brae On (IRE) *George Bewley* 98h
6 ch g Presenting Raphuca (IRE) (Be My Native (USA))
115^5 313^9 1791^7 2333^2 2842^6 (2974) (4478)
4577^P

Brampour (IRE) *Paul Nicholls* 161h 63c
7 b g Daylami(IRE) Brusca (USA) (Grindstone (USA))
45^5

Brandon Thomas (IRE) *Nick Gifford* 91h 97c
8 br g Norwich Last Sunrise (IRE) (Shahanndeh)
2765^3 3283^6 (3687)
3883^3 4416^P

Brandy And Pep (IRE) *R P Rath* 69h 75c
10 b g Lord Americo Furry Hope (Furry Glen)
540^6 **759^6**
1474^2

Brannoc (IRE) *Tony Newcombe* 89h 83c
9 b g Pilsudski(IRE) Ned's Choice (IRE) (Montelimar (USA))
602^2 1057^3 1328^6

Brantingham Breeze *Emma Lavelle* 107h
6 gr m Tamure(IRE) Absalom's Lady (Absalom)
2273^3 3005^8 3991^2 4330^3 4719^2 5033^U

Brasero (FR) *D Bressou* 113h
6 ch g Green Tune(USA) Behriya (IRE) (Kenmare (FR))
263a^8

Brasingaman Espee *George Moore* 74h
5 b h Silver Patriarch(IRE) Serene Pearl (IRE) (Night Shift (USA))
2075^9 2563^9 3144^12 4103^14

Brassbound (USA) *Caroline Bailey* 108h 112c
6 b g Redoute's Choice(AUS) In A Bound (AUS) (Ashkalani (IRE))
31^2 267^5 696^4 858^2 947^6 1400^4 1551^8
2315^3 2677^7 3596^5 4372^5 4653^3

Brassick *Mrs A Rucker* 129h 134c
7 b g Presenting No More Money (Alflora (IRE))
386^3 **645^3**
839^2 (1119)
1494^2 1709^2 4057^3 ◆

Brass Monkey (IRE) *Neil King* 104h
7 b g Craigsteel Saltee Great (IRE) (Fourstars Allstar (USA))
71^5 253^11 (661) 860^9 1018^6 1259^3 1405^7
1630^8 (2175) (2353) 2535^2 3249^2 3471^2 3821^6

Brass Tax (IRE) *Ben Case* 123h 138c
8 b g Morozov(USA) Cry Before Dawn (IRE) (Roselier (FR))
4509^4 5344^2

Brave Buck *Henry Daly* 104h
6 b g Bollin Eric Silken Pearls (Leading Counsel (USA))
(2148) (2289) 3195^10 3775^7 4338^4

Brave Decision *Suzy Smith* 65h
7 gr g With Approval(CAN) Brave Vanessa (USA) (Private Account (USA))
8^8 243^P

Brave Encounter (IRE) *Sue Gardner* 80h
6 br g Indian Danehill(IRE) Dartmeet (IRE) (Presenting)
2660^7 3173^8 3782^4 4029^6

Brave Helios *Jonathan Portman* 104h
4 b g High Chaparral(IRE) Renowned (IRE) (Darshaan)
2248^2 2466^F 3161^6 4963^10

Brave Mouse *Michael Easterby* 25b
6 b m Cape Town(IRE) Ela Aphrodite (Halling (USA))
754^8

Brave Spartacus (IRE) *Keith Reveley* 94h 142c
8 b g Spartacus(IRE) Peaches Polly (Slip Anchor)
4939^7

Brave Vic (IRE) *Gary Moore* 134h
6 b g Old Vic Baliya (IRE) (Robellino (USA))
3092^3 3552^2 4068^3 4442^3 (4680)

Bravo Belle (IRE) *Paddy Butler*
7 b m Bertolini(USA) Dazilyn Lady (USA) (Zilzal (USA))
240^P

Bravo Bravo *Mark Gillard* 115h
7 b g Sadler's Wells(USA) Top Table (Shirley Heights)
12^2 1707^10 1858^4 2020^P 3741^3 3989^P **4412^P**
4884^P

Bravo Riquet (FR) *Robin Mathew* 101h 60c
8 br g Laveron Jeroline (FR) (Cadoudal (FR))
2313^8 2680^P 3432^4 3824^5

Breaking Bits (IRE) *Jamie Snowden* 118h
7 br g Oscar(IRE) Lantern Lark (IRE) (Be My Native (USA))
8^F (484) 764^7 995^2 (1270) 5125^2 5443^2

Breaking The Bank *Ben Case* 113h
5 ch g Medicean Russian Dance (USA) (Nureyev (USA))
5064^6

Brean Play Percy *Philip Hobbs* 38b
4 b g Tobougg(IRE) Jenny From Brean (Commanche Run)
4135^11 4728^14

Bredon Hill Lad *Sue Gardner* 83h
7 ch g Kirkwall Persian Clover (Abutammam)
2535^3 ◆

Breeze With Ease (IRE) *Barry Murtagh* 96h 82c
10 b g Fourstars Allstar(USA) Roses Return (IRE) (Bob's Return (IRE))
75^6 1379^12 **1657^3** 1848^7
2361^7 2818^P 3353^P

Brians Well (IRE) *Brendan Powell* 96h 61c
7 b g Brian Boru Cons Dual Sale (IRE) (Tidaro (USA))
101^4 484^10 2018^10 2280^11 3029^4 3553^P **4716^F**
5111^8 5234^5 5461^2

Briar Hill (IRE) *W P Mullins* 150h
6 b g Shantou(USA) Backaway (IRE) (Bob Back (USA))
(3122a) (3559a) 4786^F

Brick Red *Venetia Williams* 126h 153c
7 ch g Dubawi(IRE) Duchcov (Caerleon (USA))
(3551)
3715^3 (3992)
4159^2 4737^7 5091^3

Bridgetown *Simon Hodgson* 64b
6 gr g Beat All(USA) Moon Magic (Polish Precedent (USA))
4135^10

Briefcase (IRE) *Gordon Edwards* 50h
9 b g Witness Box(USA) Another Tycoon (IRE) (Phardante (FR))
3044^8

Brieryhill Boy *William Amos* 92h 116c
7 gr g Terimon Bella Mary (Derrylin)
2356^7 2734^3 3275^2 4222^F

Bright Abbey *Dianne Sayer* 122h
6 ch g Halling(USA) Bright Hope (IRE) (Danehill (USA))
(758) ◆ 843^2 1054^3 1203^2 1289^2 1378^2 1467^2
(1714) 1788^4 2102^10

Bright Applause *Tracy Waggott* 102h
6 b g Royal Applause Sadaka (USA) (Kingmambo (USA))
1785^2 2868^3 4952^8 5496^6

Bright Intervals (IRE) *Henry Daly* 83h
6 b m Flemensfirth(USA) Sail By The Stars (Celtic Cone)
5002^2 5244^U

Bright Light *Richard Phillips* 66h
7 ch m Exit To Nowhere(USA) Lamp's Return (Bob's Return (IRE))
241^6 711^8 1267^7

Bright New Dawn (IRE) *D T Hughes* 132h 152c
7 br g Presenting Shuil Dorcha (IRE) (Bob Back (USA))
3404a^5 3908a^2 (4314a) ◆ **(4709a) 5422a^2**

Brighton Road (IRE) *R Mike Smith* 79h
7 b g Milan Grand Quest (Grand Lodge (USA))
1977^7 2217^9 2838^8

Brigstock Seabra *Caroline Bailey* 71h
6 b m Sea Freedom Inbra (Infantry)
5410^3

Brijomi Queen (IRE) *Nicky Richards* 113h
7 b m King's Theatre(IRE) Tempest Belle (IRE) (Glacial Storm (USA))
(2309) 2810^5 3757^4 4083^2 4531^4 5370^10 5509^2

Brilliant Barca *Sheena West* 115h
6 b g Imperial Dancer Fading Away (Fraam)
486^7 764^10

Brimham Boy *Martin Keighley* 93h 104c
12 ch g Minster Son Winnie Lorraine (St Columbus)
976^4 1174^4 1336^2 (1534)
1687^P

Brinestine (USA) *Paul Nicholls* 122h
5 b g Bernstein(USA) Miss Zafonic (FR) (Zafonic (USA))
2011^4 (2474) ◆ 2647^5 3744^5 *4301^5* 5239^7

Bringewood Belle *John Needham* 98h 87c
11 b m Kayf Tara Carlingford Belle (Carlingford Castle)
2872^4 3222^2 3595^P (5433)
(5546)

Bringinthebranston *David Brace* 81b
6 ch g Generous(IRE) Branston Lily (Cadeaux Genereux)
5545^P

Bringithomeminty *Nicky Henderson* 116b
5 gr g Presenting Rosie Redman (IRE) (Roselier (FR))
(4296) 5173^13

Bring It On Home *Sarah Kerswell*
10 b g Beat Hollow Dernier Cri (Slip Anchor)
709^F

Broadway Belle *Chris Grant* 56b
4 b f Lucarno(USA) Theatre Belle (King's Theatre (IRE))
5381^8

Broadway Buffalo (IRE) *David Pipe* 142h
6 ch g Broadway Flyer(USA) Benbradagh Vard (IRE) (Le Bavard (FR))
2080^4 ◆ 2433^4 4174^5 4765^8 5349^8

Broadway Cord (IRE) *Martin Hill* 60h
7 ch g Broadway Flyer(USA) Carraban Star (IRE) (Kahyasi)
920^9

Broadway Symphony (IRE) *Tracey L Bailey* 116h
7 ch g Broadway Flyer(USA) Flying Hooves (IRE) (Orchestra)
2467^5 3177^3 3877^4 4351^2 4903^4 5403^3

Brockwell Park *Jeremy Scott* 100h 96c
7 ch m Central Park(IRE) Little Brockwell (IRE) (Nestor)
179^5 2105^12
2462^P 2691^11

Broctune Papa Gio *Keith Reveley* 103h
7 b g Tobougg(IRE) Fairlie (Halling (USA))
605^8 2449^2 4608^4

Brody Bleu (FR) *Robert Walford* 111h 124c
7 b g Kotky Bleu(FR) Brodie Blue (FR) (Agent Bleu (FR))
(40) (245)
370^2 728^P 3859^3 4418^4 4908^F

Brogeen Boy (IRE) *Alan Jones* 69h
6 br g Golan(IRE) Brogeen Lady (IRE) (Phardante (FR))
3063^6 3695^12 4514^9 5308^6 5389^P

Bromhead (USA) *S Heard* 89h 57c
8 ch g Johannesburg(USA) Caramel Queen (NZ) (Turbulent Dancer (USA))
57^11

Brookland Breeze (IRE) *J J Lambe* 77h
4 b f Amadeus Wolf Gold Marie (IRE) (Green Desert (USA))
1786^4

Broomfield *Paul Nicholls* 126h
7 b g Selkirk(USA) Behera (IRE) (Mill Reef (USA))
2280^3 2755^3 3166^P

Brother Brian (IRE) *Hughie Morrison* 135h
6 b g Millenary Miner Detail (IRE) (Presenting)
1974^7 2642^5 (3166) 3716^3 4680^4 (5349)

Brother Du Berlais (FR) *Paul Nicholls* 137h
5 bb g Saint Des Saints(FR) King's Daughter (FR) (King's Theatre (IRE))
4280^2 (5277)

Brother Scott *Sue Smith* 91h
7 b g Kirkwall Crimson Shower (Dowsing (USA))
21^U (283) 561^6 630^2 803^P 1078^3 1306^8 1379^3

Brother Tedd *Philip Hobbs* 112b
5 gr g Kayf Tara Neltina (Neltino)
(3035) 3994^5

Brough Academy (IRE) *Lawney Hill* 93h 115c
8 b g Key Of Luck(USA) Cantaloupe (Priolo (USA))
422^5 1015^2 1316^4 1526^4 1637^4

Broughton (GER) *John Ferguson* 131h
4 b g Teofilo(IRE) Boccassini (GER) (Artan (IRE))
3089^2 (4054) 4784^8 5132^11

Broughtons Bandit *Willie Musson* 106h
7 b g Kyllachy Broughton Bounty (Bahamian Bounty)
427^2 856^4 4573^F 4818^P 5434^P

Broughtons Rhythm *Willie Musson* 106b
5 b g Araafa(IRE) Broughton Singer (IRE) (Common Grounds)
(5070)

Broughtons Star *Willie Musson* 108h
7 ch g Starcraft(NZ) Marrakech (IRE) (Barathea (IRE))
427^3

Broughtons Warrior *Willie Musson* 113h
6 b g Where Or When(IRE) Sleave Silk (IRE) (Unfuwain (USA))
3508[6] 4569[3] 4980[2]
Brousse En Feux (FR) *Nigel Twiston-Davies* 101h 99c
11 ch m April Night(FR) Antoniola (FR) (Kashneb (FR))
1314[2] 1936[4] 2387[3]
Browns Brook (IRE) *Venetia Williams* 83h 120c
8 b g Bob Back(USA) All Over Now (IRE) (Broken Hearted)
3015[10] 3555[S] (3883)
(4109) 4243[3] 5006[P]
Brownville *Nigel Twiston-Davies* 103b
5 b g Kayf Tara Cool Spice (Karinga Bay)
(4923) 5492[2]
Brunello *Philip Kirby* 104h
6 b g Leporello(IRE) Lydia Maria (Dancing Brave (USA))
2351[4] 2732[4] 2997[2] 3284[6] 5163[9]
Brunette'Sonly (IRE) *Seamus Mullins* 88h 102c
9 ch m Flemensfirth(USA) Pride Of St Gallen (IRE) (Orchestra)
420[P] 460[3] 2541[8] 3138[6] 3699[10] 5122[2] 5461[3]
Brunswick Gold (IRE) *Miss Rose Grissell* 123h 130c
9 ch g Moscow Society(USA) Tranbu (IRE) (Buckskin (FR))
(387) **900[P]**
(4113)
Brunton Blue *Lucy Wadham* 99h
9 b m Compton Place Persian Blue (Persian Bold)
(166) 423[2]
Bruslini (FR) *Tracey Barfoot-Saunt* 68h 75c
9 gr g Linamix(FR) Brusca (USA) (Grindstone (USA))
3603[9] *4328[5]* **4481[8] 5293[7]**
Bryden Boy (IRE) *Jennie Candlish* 105b
4 b g Craigsteel Cailin Vic Mo Cri (IRE) (Old Vic)
4043[2] ◆ 4582[2] 5219[4]
Buachaill Alainn (IRE) *Peter Bowen* 144h 134c
7 b g Oscar(IRE) Bottle A Knock (IRE) (Le Moss)
394[2] ◆ 553[3] (839)
2803[4] 3095[3] 3260[5]
Buachaill Tapa (IRE) *H Rogers* 69h
5 b g Windsor Knot(IRE) Hamsah (IRE) (Green Desert (USA))
3215a[4]
Bubbly Braveheart (IRE) *Phil McEntee* 77h
7 b g Cape Cross(IRE) Infinity (FR) (Bering)
2[7] 429[8]
Buckboru (IRE) *Laura Young* 64h
6 b m Brian Boru Buckland Filleigh (IRE) (Buckskin (FR))
2026[5] 2570[7] 3961[3] 4191[2] 4600[U] 5002[10]
Buckers Bridge (IRE) *Henry De Bromhead* 138b 152c
8 b g Pelder(IRE) La Fiere Dame (IRE) (Lafontaine (USA))
1168a[11] 2235a[5] 4435a[3] 5171[11]
Buckhorn Timothy *Colin Tizzard* 107h
5 b g Tamure(IRE) Waimea Bay (Karinga Bay)
760[4] (3734) 4149[6] 4987[U] 5120[4]
Buckhorn Tom *Colin Tizzard* 118h
6 b g Tamure(IRE) Waimea Bay (Karinga Bay)
1645[2] 1941[8] 2458[5] 2691[3] 3784[3] 4028[2] 4351[3]
5019[11]
Bucking The Trend *Tim Vaughan* 119h 135c
6 b g Kayf Tara Macklette (IRE) (Buckskin (FR))
1916[4] (3004)
4425[2]
Bucklemyshoe (IRE) *Robert Johnson* 62c
13 ch g Anshan Extra Chance (Pollerton)
474[5] 625[P] 798[6]
Buck Mulligan *Evan Williams* 128h 137c
9 b g Robellino(USA) Music Park (IRE) (Common Grounds)
11[2] 392[3] 680[2] 1047[9] 1362[7] 1476[7] 1636[2] 1686[13]
1815[6] 5094[3]
5232[4]
Buckontupence (IRE) *James Evans* 104h
6 b g Brian Boru Miss Od (IRE) (Good Thyne (USA))
4492[4] 4903[13]
Buck's Bond (FR) *Paul Nicholls* 118h 132c
8 gr g Turgeon(USA) Buck's Beauty (FR) (Lyphard's Wish (FR))
190[F] 2108[F] 2537[5] (2909)
3293[P] 5127[5]
Buckstruther (IRE) *Alastair Bell* 92h 107c
12 ch g Anshan Immediate Action (Roselier (FR))
28[2] 496[2] 4554[4]
Budapest (IRE) *J Vana Jr*
9 b g Montjeu(IRE) Run To Jane (IRE) (Doyoun)
1905a[U]
Buddy Bolero (IRE) *David Pipe* 148h 152c
8 b g Accordion Quinnsboro Ice (IRE) (Glacial Storm (USA))
2214[F] 2419[2] 2953[7] 3647[6] (4415)
4769[F]
Buddy Love *Nigel Twiston-Davies* 90h
7 gr m Silver Patriarch(IRE) O My Love (Idiots Delight)
997[4] 5242[2]
Budsson *Anna Newton-Smith* 60h 66c
8 b g Alflora(IRE) Little Bud (Lord Bud)
241[7] 543[4] **2580[2] 2861[5] 4720[F]**
Buffalo Pile (FR) *Patrice Quinton*
6 b g Fragrant Mix(IRE) La Courteillaise (FR) (Air De Cour (USA))
616a[3] 2384a[5]
Buffalo Stampede (IRE) *Miss V Collins* 103h
11 b g Accordion Killoughey Fairy (IRE) (Torus)
325[P]
Buffy Brosnan *Chris Gordon* 30h
6 b g Overbury(IRE) Materiality (Karinga Bay)
95[13] 306[7] 543[8]
Buffy The Beatle *Kim Bailey* 89h
6 b g Beat All(USA) Wishy (IRE) (Leading Counsel (USA))
3[5] 233[5]
Bugbug N Booboo *Mike Sowersby* 13h
5 b g Tobougg(IRE) Cryptogam (Zamindar (USA))
445[5]
Bugler's Dream (USA) *John Ferguson* 105h
6 bb g Medaglia d'Oro(USA) Marquet Rent (USA) (Marquetry (USA))
2265[4] 2876[7]
Bugsy *Seamus Durack* 99h
4 b g Dansili Maroussie (FR) (Saumarez)
1934[6] 2750[3] 3161[5]
Bugsy's Boy *George Baker* 86h 125c
10 b g Double Trigger(IRE) Bugsy's Sister (Aragon)
289[7]
Bugsy's Girl (IRE) *Jim Best* 101b
6 ch m Desert King(IRE) Icydora (FR) (Cyborg (FR))
(246) 841[3] *3230[2]*
Bulas Belle *Edwin Tuer* 93h
4 b f Rob Roy(USA) Bula Rose (IRE) (Alphabatim (USA))
2960[7] 3214[3] 3663[3] 4008[2] 4939[5] 5295[9]
Bull And Bush (IRE) *Alan King* 128h
5 br m Presenting Sound Of The Crowd (IRE) (Accordion)
2506[7] 3005[2] (4528) (5010) 5255[P]
Bullet Street (IRE) *Evan Williams* 113h 120c
6 ch g Arakan(USA) Play A Tune (IRE) (Fayruz)
251[6] **2469[4]**
2762[3] 4660[2] 4919[2]
Bullet Tooth (IRE) *G Cherel* 109h
4 b g Peintre Celebre(USA) Reynosa (IRE) (Montjeu (IRE))
1741a[4]
Bull Five *Nick Littmoden* 59h
7 b g Intikhab(USA) Digamist Girl (IRE) (Digamist (USA))
648[11]
Bumble Bay *Robert Stephens*
4 b g Trade Fair Amica (Averti (IRE))
5286[8]
Bunratty (IRE) *Dianne Sayer* 94h 81c
8 b g Rudimentary(USA) Miss Huff N Puff (IRE) (Grand Plaisir (IRE))
122[3] (558)
749[4] 803[5] 1471[3]
Bunty Boy *Philip Kirby*
8 b g Bollin Eric Dara's Course (IRE) (Crash Course)
280[P]
Burgoyne (USA) *C Von Der Recke*
4 b g Officer(USA) Married For Money (USA) (Not For Love (USA))
3078[6]
Burlington Bertie (IRE) *Sarah Humphrey* 86h
6 ch g Old Vic Clara's Dream (IRE) (Phardante (FR))
499[4]
Burmese Jewel *Martin Todhunter* 74b
6 b g Sulamani(IRE) Woodwind Down (Piccolo)
731[6]
Burn And Turn (IRE) *Mrs John Harrington* 117h 138c
8 b m Flemensfirth(USA) Pescetto Lady (IRE) (Toulon)
5475a[3]
Burnbrake *Richard Rowe* 48h
9 b g Mujahid(USA) Duena (Grand Lodge (USA))
307[8]
Burns Night *Philip Kirby* 98h
8 ch g Selkirk(USA) Night Frolic (Night Shift (USA))
184[7] 661[2] ◆ 1306[2] (1442) ◆ 1673[2] 2575[2]
2789[7] 3520[P]
Burnswood (IRE) *Marc Barber* 71h
10 b g Monsun(GER) Banaja (IRE) (Sadler's Wells (USA))
1345[7] 1551[10] 1890[P]
Burnt Again (IRE) *Jim Best* 39h 92c
10 b m Moscow Society(USA) Divebomb (Rudimentary (USA))
162[4] 710[6]
Burnthill (IRE) *Claire Dyson* 89h 47c
9 b g Winged Love(IRE) Kilcorig (IRE) (Niels)
1088[P] 1188[12] 1405[10] 1784[P] 2827[4] 3335[6] 3605[2]
4779[4] 5114[5] 5461[6]
Burton Port (IRE) *Jonjo O'Neill* 95h 149c
10 b g Bob Back(USA) Despute (IRE) (Be My Native (USA))
2100[5]
2502[12] 3067[9] 3457[P]
4346[8] 4557[2] 5171[U] 5571[2]
Bury Parade (IRE) *Paul Nicholls* 123h 160c
8 br g Overbury(IRE) Alexandra Parade (IRE) (Mister Lord (USA))
(2269)
3170[RR] (3772)
4422[2] ◆ 5571[P]
Bushel (USA) *John Ferguson* 103h
4 b g Street Cry(IRE) Melhor Ainda (USA) (Pulpit (USA))
3474[3]
Businessmoney Jive *Keiran Burke* 70b
7 b m Kayf Tara Cloverjay (Lir)
1861[9] 2022[10]
Businessmoney Judi *Keiran Burke* 104h
8 ch m Kirkwall Cloverjay (Lir)
3788[11] *4301[11]* 4504[3] 4733[9]
Business Mover (IRE) *Mark Bradstock* 90b
6 ch g Shantou(USA) Bit Of A Chance (Lord Ha Ha)
246[P]
Business Time *Hugh Burns* 70h
8 b g Definite Article Blue Shannon (IRE) (Be My Native (USA))
316[9] **579[P]**
Bus Named Desire *David Bridgwater* 56h
6 b m Alflora(IRE) Arctic Ring (Karinga Bay)
4499[4] 4916[11]
Busted Tycoon (IRE) *A J Martin* 129h
5 b m Marju(IRE) Khatela (IRE) (Shernazar)
(681) ◆ (764)
Busty Brown (IRE) *Noel Meade* 142h 128c
8 b g Mr Combustible(IRE) Misty Brown (IRE) (Aristocracy)
5138[10] 5471a[6]
Buthelezi (USA) *John Ferguson* 128h 130c
6 bb g Dynaformer(USA) Ntombi (USA) (Quiet American (USA))
2295[4] 2558[2] (2859)
4742[14] 5261[7]
Butney Boy (IRE) *C A McBratney* 107h 108c
8 ch g Posidonas Killultagh Dawn (IRE) (Phardante (FR))
1145[2] **5278[4]**
Butney Rock *C A McBratney* 112h 119c
7 br g Beat All(USA) Plaisance (GER) (Monsun (GER))
1288[2] 1654[2]
Buxom (IRE) *Jamie Snowden* 117h
7 b m Milan Bermuda Bay (IRE) (Be My Native (USA))
450[8] 2190[6] (2435) 2888[4] *4018[6] 4324[4]* 4698[4]
4983[5]
Buywise (IRE) *Evan Williams* 97h 151c
7 b g Tikkanen(USA) Greenogue Princess (IRE) (Rainbows For Life (CAN))
2614[5] ◆ 3128[8] **(3729)**
(3785) (4089)
4742[5] (5350)
Buzzard Flight *Sue Smith* 89b
5 b g Kayf Tara Im Busy (Busy Flight)
4582[5] 5279[12]
Buzz Me In (IRE) *R G Chapman* 8c
9 b g Moonax(IRE) Fanlahane June (IRE) (Supreme Leader)
159[5]
Byerley Babe (IRE) *Robert Tyner* 131h 141c
7 b m Beneficial I Can Imagine (IRE) (Husyan (USA))
(3750a) ◆ 4848a[4] 5475a[P]
Byerley Bear (IRE) *Jackie Du Plessis* 100h 105c
9 ch g Exit To Nowhere(USA) Miss Kamsy (Kambalda)
63[6]
Bygones For Coins (IRE) *Robert Johnson* 81h
6 ch m Danroad(AUS) Reservation (IRE) (Common Grounds)
506[F]
Bygones Of Brid (IRE) *Karen McLintock* 85h 137c
11 b g Alderbrook Glenadore (Furry Glen)
216[13] **(579)**
(798)
1077[3] 1849[R] 2069[2] 2665[3] 2935[9] 3477[9] 3832[4]
4237[5] (4745) (5054)
Bygones Sovereign (IRE) *David Pipe* 125h
8 b g Old Vic Miss Hollygrove (IRE) (King's Ride)
119[5] 1972[6] 2284[7] 2630[2] (3186) 3653[4] 3989[3]
4264[5] 4805[7] 5093[11] 5345[7]
Bypass *Tim Vaughan* 88b
5 br m Passing Glance Florida Heart (First Trump)
502[P]
Byronsprincess *Brian Eckley* 73b
6 b m Byron Sun Bonnet (Grand Lodge (USA))
146[8]
By The Boardwalk (IRE) *Kim Bailey* 115h
6 br g Presenting Peripheral Vision (IRE) (Saddlers' Hall (IRE))
1937[4] 2661[3] 3774[7] 4702[4]
Cabaret Girl *John O'Neill* 108h
7 ch m Karinga Bay Little Miss Prim (Gildoran)
2506[4] 3203[P] 4375[2] 4777[2] 4961[10]
Cabimas *Gary Moore* 121h
7 b g King's Best(USA) Casanga (IRE) (Rainbow Quest (USA))
1745[3] 2006[4]
Cabo Roche *Milton Bradley* 58h
7 ch m Alflora(IRE) Pougatcheva (FR) (Epervier Bleu)
45[F] 391[U]
Cabra Boy (IRE) *S McParlan* 75h
7 b g Winged Love(IRE) Mandalus Lady (IRE) (Mandalus)
880[P]
Caddells Row *Karen McLintock* 95b
6 b g Lahib(USA) Tartan Belle (Classic Cliche (IRE))
584[5] 944[6]
Cadeau George *Ben Pauling* 116h
5 b g Relief Pitcher Sovereign's Gift (Elegant Monarch)
2053[5] 2457[8] 3092[7] 3326[3] 3691[P] 4161[2] (4449)
5351[14]
Cadgers Hole *Lynn Siddall* 81h
7 b g Helissio(FR) Not So Prim (Primitive Rising (USA))
380[6] 3016[6] 3634[5] 5050[6] 5300[8]
Cadore (IRE) *Lucy Normile* 105h
6 b g Hurricane Run(IRE) Mansiya (Vettori (IRE))
342[6] 803[4] (1143) 1665[8] 2306[2] 2794[2] 3518[5]
4366[4]
Cadoudoff (FR) *Charlie Longsdon* 121h
4 gr g Davidoff(GER) Hera Du Berlais (FR) (Cadoudal (FR))
2200[2] 3078[5] 3364[2] 4755[18]
Cadspeed (FR) *W P Mullins* 127h 133c
11 b g Vertical Speed(FR) Cadmina (FR) (Cadoudal (FR))
3806a[P]
Caduceus (IRE) *P Hughes* 120h 121c
10 b g Luso Carrigeen Kerria (IRE) (Kemal (FR))
3868a[P]
Caerlaverock (IRE) *Rose Dobbin* 105h
9 br g Statue Of Liberty(USA) Daziyra (IRE) (Doyoun)
2447[P] 2956[7] 3396[3] 4577[2] 5208[5]
Cafe Au Lait (GER) *Anthony Middleton* 111h
4 b c Nicaron(GER) Cariera (GER) (Macanal (USA))
2294[2] 3089[5] 4268[5] 4679[3] 4963[7]
Cafe De Paris (FR) *S Foucher* 106c
9 b g Fly To The Stars Saint Patricia (FR) (Assert)
1424a[6] 1623a[6]
Caheronaun (IRE) *D T Hughes* 121h 125c
8 b m Milan Fair Present (IRE) (Presenting)
2484a[4]
Caid Du Berlais (FR) *Paul Nicholls* 152h 139c
5 b g Westerner Kenza Du Berlais (FR) (Kahyasi)
2206a[2]
(2922) 3893[5] 4789[3] 5158[2]
Cailin (IRE) *Grant Cann* 92h
6 b m Golan(IRE) Castle Arms Cailin (IRE) (Be My Native (USA))
5244[2]
Cailin Annamh (IRE) *Mrs John Harrington* 142h 128c
6 b m Definite Article Prairie Bell (IRE) (Sadler's Wells (USA))
(1948a) 4740[12] 5370[6]
Caim Hill (IRE) *Philip Fenton* 141h 136c
11 b g Deploy Glen's Gale (IRE) (Strong Gale)
5415a[3]
Cairanne *Tom Keddy* 75h
6 b m High Chaparral(IRE) Celestial Choir (Celestial Storm (USA))
166[6]
Caitys Joy (GER) *Warren Greatrex* 109b
4 b f Malinas(GER) Cassilera (GER) (Anzillero (GER))
(5440) ◆
Calaf *Jonjo O'Neill* 119h
6 b g Dubai Destination(USA) Tarandot (IRE) (Singspiel (IRE))
3043[2] 3851[4] (5294)
Calculaite *Richard Ford* 107h 107c
13 b g Komaite(USA) Miss Calculate (Mummy's Game)
343[4]
Calculated Risk *John Quinn* 137h
5 ch g Motivator Glen Rosie (IRE) (Mujtahid (USA))
2533[9] 2951[6] (3273) 4752[22]
Caldew Lad (IRE) *Barry Murtagh* 40b
6 b g Aahsaylad Princess Le Moss (IRE) (Le Moss)
2499[13] 2838[P]
Caldey *Keith Goldsworthy* 60h
5 b m Overbury(IRE) Barfleur (IRE) (Anshan)
3133[6] 3363[11] 4909[3] 5528[7]
Caledonia *Jim Goldie* 95h
7 b g Sulamani(IRE) Vanessa Bell (IRE) (Lahib (USA))
2819[7] 4272[5]
California Desert (IRE) *C A McBratney* 95b
6 b m Desert King(IRE) California Blue (FR) (Pebble (FR))
5279[10]
Calipto (FR) *Paul Nicholls* 139h
4 b g Califet(FR) Peutiot (FR) (Valanour (IRE))
(2796) (4143) 4784[4] 5132[3]
Call At Midnight *Sarah Humphrey* 89h 97c
9 b m Midnight Legend Second Call (Kind Of Hush)
712[P] 969[P] 1406[3]
Call A Truce (IRE) *Ben Case* 105h
6 b g Court Cave(IRE) No More Trouble (IRE) (Old Vic)
33[7] 318[3] 2105[3] 2755[14]
Call Back *Donald McCain* 126h
6 b g Beat Hollow Payphone (Anabaa (USA))
474[F]
Call Box (IRE) *S R B Crawford* 130h 101c
9 b g Witness Box(USA) Brown Willows (IRE) (Kemal (FR))
867[2] **1146[5]**
(1543) 1752[3] 2221[6] (3475) 5272[8] 5534[5]
Call Carlo *Venetia Williams* 87h
7 ch g Karinga Bay Lady Widd (IRE) (Commanche Run)
4130[6] 4715[5]
Call Him Something (IRE) *Sarah Humphrey* 98b
6 b g Heron Island(IRE) Stoned Imaculate (IRE) (Durgam (USA))
599[5]
Callhimwhatyouwant (IRE) *Dr Richard Newland* 103h 122c
9 b g Old Vic Jaynes Supreme (IRE) (Supreme Leader)
65[3] 202[F] 875[5] 1092[3] 1153[2] **1315[2] (1493)**
1566[4]
Callisto Moon *Jo Hughes* 113h 127c
10 b g Mujahid(USA) Nursling (IRE) (Kahyasi)
267[2] 1471[4] 1627[4] 1745[6] 2013[5]
Call It On (IRE) *Philip Kirby* 118h 118c
8 ch g Raise A Grand(IRE) Birthday Procont (Cadeaux Genereux)
224[U] 2447[9] 2786[5]
Call Me April *Karen George* 94h
6 b m Generous(IRE) Anyhow (IRE) (Distant Relative)
41[7] 292[4] 521[3] 729[4]
Call Me A Star *Alan King* 136h
7 b m Midnight Legend Second Call (Kind Of Hush)
2371[9]
Call Me Emma (IRE) *Richard Phillips* 86b
6 b m Beneficial Clody Girl (IRE) (Zaffaran (USA))
3440[10] 5286[3]
Call Me Kate *Henry Daly* 72b
4 b f Kalanisi(IRE) Last Of Her Line (Silver Patriarch (IRE))
5077[10]
Call Me Mulligan (IRE) *John Wade* 103h 106c
10 ch g Bach(IRE) They Call Me Molly (CAN) (Charlie Barley (USA))
495[4] 766[2] 2394[8] 2735[5] 3755[8]
Call Me Sir (IRE) *Sue Gardner* 101h
12 b g Lord Americo Crash Call (Crash Course)
643[P]
Call Me Vic (IRE) *Tom George* 129h
7 b g Old Vic Call Me Dara (IRE) (Arapahos (FR))
(3440) 3877[2] 4931[2] (5288)
Call Of Duty (IRE) *Dianne Sayer* 105h 110c
9 br g Storming Home Blushing Barada (USA) (Blushing Groom (FR))
1661[3] 1754[6] 2075[7]
2839[4] 3021[8] 3274[9] 3527[7] 3723[8]

Call The Cops (IRE) *Nicky Henderson* 132h
5 b g Presenting Ballygill Heights (IRE) (Symboli Heights (FR))
(291) 2351[3] (3175) 3774[4] 5015[2] (5486)

Calton Entry (IRE) *Ian Semple* 94b
5 b g Bahri(USA) Gaybrook (IRE) (Shernazar)
2795[4] 4631[6]

Calusa Star *Philip Hobbs* 93h 97c
5 b g Multiplex Pugnacious Lady (Hernando (FR))
3956[10] 4281[11] 4733[4] 5007[5] 5234[10]

Calverleigh Court (IRE) *Mary Sanderson* 25b
7 b m Presenting Alexandra Parade (IRE) (Mister Lord (USA))
160[9]

Calypso Bay (IRE) *Jonjo O'Neill* 116h 115c
8 b g Galileo(IRE) Poule De Luxe (IRE) (Cadeaux Genereux)
(485) **871[2]**
(1202)
1469[3] 1797[P]

Calypso Princess *Alan King* 83b
7 b m Helissio(FR) Marathea (FR) (Marathon (USA))
4[5]

Calypso Star (IRE) *Nigel Hawke* 42h
7 ch g Exceed And Excel(AUS) Reematna (Sabrehill (USA))
186[6] 810[9] 924[11]

Camden (IRE) *Oliver Sherwood* 126h 133c
8 b g Old Vic Electric View (IRE) (Electric)
2537[P] 3059[P] 4339[3] 4678[2] (5119)

Camden George (IRE) *Sue Smith* 78h 94c
13 b g Pasternak Triple Town Lass (IRE) (Camden Town)
2194[6] 2416[4] 2594[4] 3022[4] 3827[6]

Camden Vine *Victor Thompson* 60b
6 b m Grape Tree Road Camden Bella (Sir Harry Lewis (USA))
2738[8] 3529[6]

Camera Shy (IRE) *Kevin Morgan* 63h
10 ch g Pivotal Shy Danceuse (FR) (Groom Dancer (USA))
290[8] 651[6] 809[8]

Caminero (IRE) *Jamie Snowden* 19h
7 b g Cloudings(IRE) Sounds Confident (IRE) (Orchestra)
5307[10]

Campbonnais (FR) *Ali Brewer* 112h 109c
9 b g Sassanian(USA) Kries Du Berlais (FR) (Nikos)
11[6] (3852) 4006[4]
4809[5] (5438)

Camptown Lady *Laura Young* 83h
5 b m Doyen(IRE) Ballyquintet (IRE) (Orchestra)
380[5] 2354[7] 2614[U] 3092[8] 3427[3] 3788[P] 4072[3]

Canadian Diamond (IRE) *Brendan Powell* 130h
7 ch g Halling(USA) Six Nations (USA) (Danzig (USA))
304[4] **1426[P]**
1745[7] 1960[2] 2561[2] 3066[3] 3744[8] 4353[2] 4726[2]
5067[8]

Canadian Dreamer (IRE) *Graeme McPherson* 91h
7 b g Westerner Ride The Tide (IRE) (Long Pond)
2691[9] 3191[7] 4475[U] 4636[7] 5431[8]

Canaly (IRE) *D T Hughes* 128h 146c
9 b g Bob Back(USA) Starry Lady (IRE) (Marju (IRE))
1157a[5]

Canarbino Girl *Caroline Keevil* 70h
7 b m Beat All(USA) Peasedown Tofana (Teenoso (USA))
309[5] 3005[13] 3695[P] *4019[9] 4297[12]* 5002[5] 5258[7]

Candelita *Jo Hughes* 111h 113c
7 b m Trade Fair Gramada (IRE) (Cape Cross (IRE))
10[2] **1426[2]**
1503[3] 2050[7] 5291[6]

Candleford *Ashley Dodgson* 112h
9 b g Vettori(IRE) Second Affair (IRE) (Pursuit Of Love)
(222) (556)

Candyman Can (IRE) *Dominic Ffrench Davis* 106h
4 b g Holy Roman Emperor(IRE) Palwina (FR) (Unfuwain (USA))
3161[9] 3364[5] 5258[4]

Cane Cat (IRE) *Tony Carroll* 77h
7 bb m One Cool Cat(USA) Seven Wonders (USA) (Rahy (USA))
2040[8] 2770[6]

Canicallyouback *Evan Williams* 92b
6 b g Auction House(USA) Island Colony (USA) (Pleasant Colony (USA))
2724[4]

Canna (IRE) *Ali Brewer* 92h
6 b g High Chaparral(IRE) Brave Madam (IRE) (Invincible Spirit (IRE))
858[6] 1087[P]

Cannon Fodder *Sheena West* 128h
7 b m Nomadic Way(USA) Grace Dieu (Commanche Run)
484[5] 755[2] 920[6] 1436[2] (1529) 1628[3] (2006)
2860[2] 3319[2] 3882[4] 4276[2] 4542[2] 4805[18] 5372[12]

Cantabilly (IRE) *Ron Hodges* 94h 89c
11 b g Distant Music(USA) Cantaloupe (Priolo (USA))
83[5] 3047[12] 3420[13]

Can't Agree *Stuart Morris*
9 bb m Dansili Buck's Fizz (Kris)
331[P]

Can't Call It (IRE) *Ms J Andrews* 93b
9 ch g Bob's Return(IRE) Capincur Lady (Over The River (FR))
5165[P]

Cantlow (IRE) *Paul Webber* 128h 158c
9 b g Kayf Tara Winnowing (IRE) (Strong Gale)
2199[9] (2800)
3082[2] 4738[F] 5138[12]
5474a[8]

Cantony *Henry Daly* 104h
5 b m Fantastic Spain(USA) Cantique (IRE) (Danetime (IRE))
2190[F] 2824[F] 3010[4] ◆ 3592[4] 5490[7]

Cantridara (SLO) *J Papousek*
8 b m Security Risk(USA) Cantrida (CZE) (Dara Monarch)
1905a[U]

Canuspotit *Lucy Wadham* 116h
7 b g Nomadic Way(USA) Play Alone (IRE) (Mandalus)
2783[7] 3115[2] 3850[2] 4347[10] 4700[4] 5294[5]

Caoimhe's Delight (IRE) *Sean O'Brien* 132h 136c
8 b m Blueprint(IRE) Scintilla (Sir Harry Lewis (USA))
1804a[6] 2484a[P] 2986a[3] 3403a[2]
3750a[3] (4848a)
5475a[9]

Cape Breton *Patrick Chamings* 107h
8 b g Cape Cross(IRE) Red Bouquet (Reference Point)
235[7] 2265[3] 5003[5] 5307[4]

Cape Dutch (IRE) *John Ferguson* 134h 134c
7 b g Cape Cross(IRE) Rosia (IRE) (Mr Prospector (USA))
3045[2]

Cape Explorer *Brian Ellison* 115h
5 b g Cape Cross(IRE) Eve (Rainbow Quest (USA))
73[2] 507[2]

Cape Express (IRE) *Nicky Henderson* 137h
9 b g Cape Cross(IRE) Lilissa (IRE) (Doyoun)
673[10] 901[F]

Cape Glory (IRE) *Gordon Elliott* 113h
4 b c Cape Cross(IRE) Array Of Stars (IRE) (Barathea (IRE))
5470a[12]

Capellanus (IRE) *Brian Ellison* 127h 94c
8 b g Montjeu(IRE) Secret Dream (IRE) (Zafonic (USA))
(2050) 2345[2] 2935[8] 3479[3] 4051[7] *4302[3]*

Capel Le Ferne (IRE) *Robert Walford* 69b
6 ch g Anabaa Blue Lox Lane (IRE) (Presenting)
3994[13] *4498[5]*

Capellini *Charles Egerton* 98h
7 b g Cape Cross(IRE) Red Stella (FR) (Rainbow Quest (USA))
188[3] 243[7] (1137) 1275[2] (1630)

Cap Elorn (FR) *Lawney Hill* 87h 125c
8 b g Kapgarde(FR) Legretta (USA) (Al Nasr (FR))
942[9] (1014)
(1149) (1537)
(1780) 1990[3]

Cape Schanck *Alan Coogan* 62h
10 b g Observatory(USA) Sally Gardens (Alzao (USA))
593[P] 1915[P] 2292[13]

Cape Tribulation *Malcolm Jefferson* 161h 161c
10 b g Hernando(FR) Gay Fantastic (Ela-Mana-Mou)
2229[P] 2815[16] 3285[3]

Cape York *Malcolm Jefferson* 114h
6 ch g Revoque(IRE) Altogether Now (IRE) (Step Together I (USA))
(207) 4694[5] (5354) ◆

Capilla (IRE) *Evan Williams* 116b
6 gr g Beneficial Cap The Rose (IRE) (Roselier (FR))
(2153) 2654[2] 3363[7] 4030[7]

Capisci (IRE) *Sarah-Jayne Davies* 96h 105c
9 br g Tikkanen(USA) Dolce Notte (IRE) (Strong Gale)
(3048)
(4734) 5144[P]

Capital Venture (IRE) *N W Alexander* 104h 104c
8 b g Moscow Society(USA) Benrue Adventure (IRE) (Broken Hearted)
(1982)
2334[3]

Capitano Lento *Caroline Keevil* 28h
6 b g Overbury(IRE) Peasedown Tofana (Teenoso (USA))
5257[9]

Capitol Gain (IRE) *George Baker* 90h
5 b g Bahamian Bounty Emmas Princess (IRE) (Bahhare (USA))
4758[5] 5227[5] 5524[7]

Capote (IRE) *Jonjo O'Neill* 137h
6 b g Oscar(IRE) Kinsella's Rose (IRE) (Roselier (FR))
(4186) (4603) 5157[4]

Cappa Bleu (IRE) *Evan Williams* 136h 151c
12 b g Pistolet Bleu(IRE) Cappagale (IRE) (Strong Gale)
2419[4]

Cappacurry Zak (IRE) *L Young* 118h
5 ch g Arakan(USA) Girl From De North (IRE) (Flemensfirth (USA))
2995a[7]

Cappielow Park *Ali Brewer* 112h
5 b g Exceed And Excel(AUS) Barakat (Bustino)
3[6] 3149[7] 3469[2] 3736[2] 4072[5] 4247[3] 5304[4]

Captain Americo (IRE) *Mrs B Ewart* 111h 108c
12 b g Lord Americo Excitable Lady (Buckskin (FR))
25[3] 169[4] 509[4] 4042[4] 4239[F] 5536[F]

Captain Baldwin *Jim Goldie* 77h
5 b g Dubai Destination(USA) Tripti (IRE) (Sesaro (USA))
879[6] 961[4]

Captain Blonde (IRE) *Gerard O'Leary*
5 ch g Captain Rio Faithfulbond (IRE) (Elbio)
2995a[11]

Captain Brown *James Moffatt* 122h 109c
6 b g Lomitas Nicola Bella (IRE) (Sadler's Wells (USA))
118[6] 679[F] 929[4] 1398[F] 1979[2] 2668[7] 3398[5] 4952[F]

Captain Cardington (IRE) *John O'Shea* 112h
5 b g Strategic Prince Alkaffeyeh (IRE) (Sadler's Wells (USA))
1268[6] 2087[15] 2362[4] 2652[5] 2894[4] 3025[2] 4351[P]
4413[3] 4659[4] 4864[4]

Captain Cee Bee (IRE) *Edward P Harty* 161h 165c
13 b g Germany(USA) Elea Victoria (IRE) (Sharp Victor (USA))
(1801a) 2408a[3] 3402a[4] 3930a[3] 4739[5]

Captain Chris (IRE) *Philip Hobbs* 151h 176c
10 b g King's Theatre(IRE) Function Dream (IRE) (Strong Gale)
3032[3] (3645)
(4265)

Captain Clayton (IRE) *Simon West* 109h
7 b g Subtle Power(IRE) Dont Hurry (IRE) (Muroto)
2417[5] 2997[5] (4338) 4577[6]

Captain Conan (FR) *Nicky Henderson* 152h 162c
7 b g Kingsalsa(USA) Lavandou (Sadler's Wells (USA))
2952[3] 4753[P]

Captain Cutter (IRE) *Nicky Henderson* 150h
7 b g Westerner Hollygrove Samba (IRE) (Accordion)
(2266) (2900) (3367) 4786[P]

Captain Jinx (IRE) *Carroll Gray* 43h
7 b g Luso Gone To Town (IRE) (Camden Town)
250[9] 633[5]

Captain Kelly (IRE) *Paul Nicholls* 126h 127c
7 b g Oscar(IRE) Tri Folene (FR) (Nebos (GER))
79[2] (189) (638) 845[7] **(1150)**
1262[2] 1642[4]

Captain Marlon (IRE) *Mrs Claire Hitch* 50h 91c
13 b g Supreme Leader Marlonette (IRE) (Jareer (USA))
13[5] 180[5] 1336[3] 5131[P] 5232[U]

Captain Moonman (IRE) *Rebecca Curtis* 92h
9 b g Milan Bridgeofallen (IRE) (Torus)
1890[2] 2148[3]

Captain Ocana (IRE) *Paul Henderson* 111h 115c
9 b g Karinga Bay Jaystara (IRE) (Jurado (USA))
3064[4] *4298[9]* **4764[P] 5126[7]** ◆

Captainofthefleet (IRE) *Eamonn O'Connell* 130h
7 ch g Refuse To Bend(IRE) Darabaka (IRE) (Doyoun)
3667a[5] 4386a[4]

Captain Paulie (IRE) *Evan Williams* 93h 123c
11 b g Lahib(USA) Garvivonne (Belfalas)
(377) **1780[3]**
2618[5] 3183[4]

Captain P K (IRE) *Noel C Kelly* 83h
7 b g Turtle Island(IRE) Something Green (IRE) (Green Shoon)
19[7] 1982[7] 4446[P] (Dead)

Captain Reacher *Chris Bealby*
5 b g Phoenix Reach(IRE) Arctic Queen (Linamix (FR))
207[U]

Captain Scarlett (IRE) *John Flint* 115h 61c
8 b g Milan Count My Blessings (IRE) (Shernazar)
942[P] 1134[P]

Captain Sharpe *Bernard Llewellyn* 100h
6 ch g Tobougg(IRE) Helen Sharp (Pivotal)
409[6] 691[7] 833[3] 995[6] 2617[P] 2760[5] 2898[4] 4447[4]
4733[2] 4967[4] (5139)

Captain Sully (IRE) *Jim Wilson* 80h 115c
9 b g Pairumani Star(IRE) Ginger Lily (IRE) (Lucky Guest)
93[8] **411[6]**
656[4] 859[2] 1060[8] 1259[10] 1783[P] **2107[P] 5342[4]**

Captain Sunshine *Emma Lavelle* 142h
8 b g Oscar(IRE) Gaye Fame (Ardross)
1956[13] 2228[3]

Captain Wilson *Mark Rimell* 59h
7 b g Olden Times Competa (Hernando (FR))
186[P] 499[P]

Captive Moment *John Norton* 89h
8 b m Almaty(IRE) Captive Heart (Conquistador Cielo (USA))
450[U] 552[5] 2514[7] 3014[P]

Cara Carlotta *Philip Hobbs* 103b
5 br m Presenting Dara's Pride (IRE) (Darazari (IRE))
4735[3] 5374[9]

Cara Court (IRE) *Joanne Foster* 94h 98c
8 b g Court Cave(IRE) Tarasandy (IRE) (Arapahos (FR))
89[U] **206[5]**
471[7] 1506[9] **1716[2] 2047[U] 2562[4]** 3040[12]
(3449) 3637[F] 3834[5] 4383[2] 4581[U]
4747[3] (5162)
5318[P] 5453[4]

Caramack *Richard Lee* 15h
4 ch g Danehill Dancer(IRE) Oshiponga (Barathea (IRE))
2294[6]

Caravel (IRE) *Tim Vaughan* 103h 95c
10 ch g Medicean Caraiyma (IRE) (Shahrastani (USA))
594[4] 901[6]

Carbis Bay *Zoe Davison* 61h 49c
8 b g Deploy Hi Lily (Jupiter Island)
234[4] 2277[8]

Cardigan Island (IRE) *Dai Burchell* 116h 124c
9 br g Winged Love(IRE) Wollongong (IRE) (King Persian)
(92) **481[2]**
(728) 877[3] **1944[3]** 2288[8]

Cardinal Richelieu (IRE) *Tom Gretton* 26h
6 b g King's Theatre(IRE) Vol De Minuit (FR) (Loup Solitaire (USA))
192[6] 499[P]

Carheney River (IRE) *Colin Heard* 65h
9 b g Flemensfirth(USA) Odeeka (IRE) (Posen (USA))
431[P]

Carhue Princess (IRE) *Tom Symonds* 92h 92c
8 b m Desert Prince(IRE) Carhue Journey (IRE) (Barathea (IRE))
650[5] 932[6] 1106[8] 1269[8] 1799[7] 2193[5] (2312)
2771[9] 2896[3] **3729[4] 4966[2] 5246[6] 5487[4]** ◆

Cariflora *Nick Gifford* 85h
7 b m Alflora(IRE) Oso Special (Teenoso (USA))
240[7] 484[F] 765[7]

Carilo (IRE) *C Lerner* 129h
5 ch g Dubai Destination(USA) Coco (USA) (Storm Bird (CAN))
683a[7]

Carlain (FR) *C Aubert* 126h 118c
6 ch g Le Fou(IRE) Act Of Honor (FR) (Alhaarth (IRE))
455a[5] **838a[P]**

Carlicue (IRE) *Dan Skelton* 102h 98c
9 b g King's Theatre(IRE) Woodville Star (IRE) (Phardante (FR))
5520[6]

Carli King (IRE) *Caroline Bailey* 116c
8 br g Witness Box(USA) Abinitio Lady (IRE) (Be My Native (USA))
2192[3] 2558[3] 2782[4] 3180[2] (3595)
3820[4] (4481)
4896[5] 5247[6]

Carlingford Lough (IRE) *John E Kiely* 148h 158c
8 b g King's Theatre(IRE) Baden (IRE) (Furry Glen)
(1168a)
1604a[2] 2853a[2] (3404a)
4181a[U] 4751[6]

Carlito Brigante (IRE) *Karen McLintock* 100h 140c
8 b g Haafhd Desert Magic (IRE) (Green Desert (USA))
2072[3] 4789[18]
(5378)

Carlton Jack *Jonjo O'Neill* 129h
7 b g Erhaab(USA) Harry's Bride (Sir Harry Lewis (USA))
93[2] ◆ 1553[2] (1794) (2172) 4841[3] 5128[11]
(5384)

Carmela Maria *Mike Sowersby* 96h
9 b m Medicean Carmela Owen (Owington)
444[P] (969) 1498[4] 2956[6] 3145[5] 3356[3] 3824[P]
4108[6] 4478[8]

Carmino (IRE) *Mark Bradstock* 105b
5 ch g Stowaway Fiddlers Pal (IRE) (Pasternak)
3282[5] 5367[3]

Carmona (FR) *D Sourdeau De Beauregard* 104h 102c
7 b m Sleeping Car(FR) Blue Mona (FR) (Saint Estephe (FR))
616a[P]

Carnaross *Anthony Middleton* 50b
5 b g Norse Dancer(IRE) Miss Lewis (Sir Harry Lewis (USA))
5070[13]

Carningli (IRE) *Rebecca Curtis* 123b
5 b g Old Vic Name For Fame (USA) (Quest For Fame)
(1974) 2534[2] 3187[4]

Carnival Flag (FR) *Nicky Henderson* 101b
5 ch m Ballingarry(IRE) Run For Laborie (FR) (Lesotho (USA))
4916[2]

Carn Rock *Michael Gates* 106h
6 b g Tamure(IRE) Solent Sunbeam (Sovereign Water (FR))
3850[7] 4702[5] 4903[11] 5288[2] 5523[4]

Carobello (IRE) *Martin Bosley* 83h 86c
7 b g Luso Vic's Queen (IRE) (Old Vic)
318[7] 758[4] 1183[5] 1339[P] 1632[10]
2039[5] (2576)
3152[U]

Carole's Destrier *Neil Mulholland* 133h
6 b g Kayf Tara Barton May (Midnight Legend)
1991[2] 2566[F] 2940[2] (3506) 4174[7] (4805) ◆
5138[18]

Carole's Lord *Robert Walford* 94b
5 b g Hernando(FR) Carole's Crusader (Faustus (USA))
4909[4] 5310[8]

Carole's Spirit *Robert Walford* 146h
6 b m Hernando(FR) Carole's Crusader (Faustus (USA))
(2273) (2801) (3203) 3770[2]

Carolina Wren *Renee Robeson* 115h
5 b m Sir Harry Lewis(USA) Wren Warbler (Relkino)
1731[7] 3159[5] (4375) 5449[3]

Carolingian (USA) *Michael Blanshard* 67h
5 b g Empire Maker(USA) Shoogle (USA) (A.P. Indy (USA))
155[6] 633[P]

Carpies Boy *Warren Greatrex* 86h
5 b g Dreams End Bungar Belle (IRE) (Sea Raven (IRE))
2153[7] 2724[8] 3746[6] 4506[8] 4903[8] 5282[P]

Carpincho (FR) *Sarah Humphrey* 108h 120c
10 bb g Jimble(FR) La Rapaille (IRE) (Mandalus)
2567[3] 2805[4] 4486[2] 4862[4] 5263[P] 5361[4]

Carraig Mor (IRE) *Alan King* 145h
6 b g Old Vic Lynrick Lady (IRE) (Un Desperado (FR))
(2189) ◆ 2661[2] 4374[3]

Carraig Rock *Hughie Morrison* 79b
4 b g Beat Hollow Riverine (Risk Me (FR))
2015[6]

Carrickboy (IRE) *Venetia Williams* 130h 149c
10 b g Silver Patriarch(IRE) Alaskan Princess (IRE) (Prince Rupert (FR))
2071[9] 2503[12] 3458[P] 3990[3] 5350[P]

Carriganog (IRE) *A P O'Brien* 136h
5 ch g Shantou(USA) Penny Fiction (IRE) (Welsh Term)
2706a[3] 4708a[12]

Carrigdhoun (IRE) *Maurice Barnes* 122h 131c
9 gr g Goldmark(USA) Pet Tomjammar (IRE) (Accordion)
169[2] 495[2] ◆ 1750[5] (1787)
(2033)

Carrigeen Aspen (IRE) *Oliver Sherwood*
7 gr m Indian River(FR) Carrigeen Acer (IRE) (Lord Americo)
3177[P] 3567[P]

Carrigeen Kariega (IRE) *R H Lalor* 106h 115c
9 b m Luso Carrigeen Kerria (IRE) (Kemal (FR))
3827[P]

Carrigeen Lechuga (IRE) *R H Lalor* 122h 132c
9 b m Beneficial Carrigeen Lily (IRE) (Supreme Leader)
3617[P] 5415a[4]

Carrigeen Lonicera (IRE) *R H Lalor* 108h 115c
8 b m Old Vic Carrigeen Lily (IRE) (Supreme Leader)
3750a^{5} 5099a^{6}

Carrig Millie (IRE) *Michael Cullen* 97h 129c
9 b m Milan Stormy Skies (Strong Gale)
2123a^{6} 2708a^{P}

Carrigmorna King (IRE) *Philip Hobbs* 130h 135c
8 b g King's Theatre(IRE) Carrigmorna Flyer (IRE) (Bob Back (USA))
1867^{6} (2630)
2812^{2} 3091^{5} 4805^{11}
5513^{6}

Carronhills (IRE) *P J Tolman*
12 b g Old Vic Too Sharp (True Song)
3862^{P} 4274^{P}

Carruthers *Mark Bradstock* 147h 159c
11 b g Kayf Tara Plaid Maid (IRE) (Executive Perk)
3655^{2} 4557^{6} 5170^{U} 5571^{9}

Carrybridge (IRE) *S R B Crawford* 95b
7 bb m Milan Black Gayle (IRE) (Strong Gale)
2738^{3} 3634^{P} (Dead)

Carry On Sydney *Oliver Sherwood* 122h
4 ch g Notnowcato River Fantasy (USA) (Irish River (FR))
3714^{2} ◆ (4073) 4281^{2} 4679^{4} 5090^{8}

Carsonstown Boy (IRE) *C A McBratney* 133h 136c
10 b g Golden Tornado(IRE) Elbonne (IRE) (Supreme Leader)
4788^{2}

Carters Rest *George Bewley* 94h 96c
11 gr g Rock City Yemaail (IRE) (Shaadi (USA))
3723^{6} 4187^{8} 5302^{2}

Carthaginian (IRE) *Martin Todhunter* 75h
5 b g Azamour(IRE) Khayrat (IRE) (Polar Falcon (USA))
5531^{4}

Cash And Go (IRE) *Nicky Henderson* 141h
7 b g Sulamani(IRE) Calcida (GER) (Konigsstuhl (GER))
2533^{16} 4785^{11} 5158^{3} 5574^{2}

Cashback Dreamer (IRE) *Grace Harris*
6 b g Oscar(IRE) Our Dream (IRE) (Bob Back (USA))
4417^{P}

Cashed That *Dan Skelton* 49b
5 b m Presenting Cash 'N' Credit (Homo Sapien)
2752^{12}

Cash For Steel (IRE) *Richard Phillips* 76h
7 b m Craigsteel Neiges Eternelles (FR) (Exit To Nowhere (USA))
1599^{10} 1706^{9} 1958^{7} 2176^{4} 4967^{9} 5242^{16}

Cash In Hand (IRE) *Christopher Kellett*
14 b g Charente River(IRE) Fern Fields (IRE) (Be My Native (USA))
1547^{9} 2702^{4} 3277^{P} 5407^{P}

Cash Injection *Richard Woollacott* 103h
5 b g Halling(USA) Cape Siren (Warning)
37^{4} 407^{5} 1351^{8} 1517^{F} 1643^{4} 1833^{4} 2291^{8} 2690^{4} (3174) 3699^{2} 3852^{2} 4636^{3} 4913^{4}

Cashwell *S Flook* 92h 74c
7 b g Saddlers' Hall(IRE) Cashmere Lady (Hubbly Bubbly (USA))
4727^{8}

Caspian Piper (IRE) *Hugo Froud* 112h 86c
7 b g Millenary Pepsi Starlet (IRE) (Heavenly Manna)
2897^{8} 3180^{6} 4778^{5} 5111^{P}

Castanum (IRE) *Laura Young* 48b
5 ch g Kris Kin(USA) Persian Argument (IRE) (Persian Mews)
2472^{11} 2513^{10} 4030^{8} 4281^{P} 5029^{U}

Castarnie *Robert Walford* 67h
6 b g Alflora(IRE) Just Jenny (IRE) (King's Ride)
2457^{13} 3782^{8} 4280^{6}

Castell Avon *Milton Bradley* 41h
4 b f Avonbridge Castellina (USA) (Danzig Connection (USA))
1473^{3} 1524^{P}

Castle Beach (IRE) *Robert Stephens* 102h
5 b g Millenary Don't Fall (IRE) (Castle Keep)
1431^{2} 1519^{5} 1708^{7} 5034^{11}

Castle Cheetah (IRE) *Martin Keighley* 104h
6 br g Presenting Castle Crystal (IRE) (Beneficial)
3177^{4} *4019^{8} 4300^{15}*

Castle Conflict (IRE) *Henry Daly* 100h 125c
9 b g Close Conflict(USA) Renty (IRE) (Carlingford Castle)
2177^{3} (2805)
3365^{P} 4031^{P} 4725^{P} 5233^{3}

Castle Eden (IRE) *Colin Teague*
4 ch g Where Or When(IRE) Brilliant Trees (IRE) (Spectrum (IRE))
3214^{12} 4226^{P}

Castle Goer (IRE) *B Arthey* 13h
5 b m Helissio(FR) Hill Of Light (IRE) (Luso)
5322^{P}

Castlelawn (IRE) *Lucinda Russell* 98h 125c
7 b g Runyon(IRE) Pure Magic (IRE) (Flemensfirth (USA))
(627) **(749)**
864^{2} ◆ 1162^{3} 1921^{9} 2496^{F} 5511^{4}

Castlemorris King *Brian Barr* 127h
6 br g And Beyond(IRE) Brookshield Baby (IRE) (Sadler's Wells (USA))
42^{2} (267) 756^{2} (858) 973^{3} 1054^{5} *4300^{11}* 4991^{3} (5231)

Castletown (IRE) *Laura Young* 111h
6 b g Oscar(IRE) Closing Thyne (IRE) (Good Thyne (USA))
3363^{5} 4029^{4} 4171^{2} ◆ 4555^{9}

Castletown Bridge (IRE) *Gordon Elliott* 123h
7 ch g Bienamado(USA) Midnight Orchid (IRE) (Petardia)
(1661) 1960^{11}

Castle View (IRE) *Anna Brooks* 99h
7 b g Bach(IRE) Leefield Rose (IRE) (Parthian Springs)
1019^{4}

Castley Lane *Sara Ender* 33b 63c
8 b g Dapper Holly (Skyliner)
28^{4}

Casual Cavalier (IRE) *John Wade* 66h
6 br g Presenting Asklynn (IRE) (Beau Sher)
2037^{11} 4772^{8} 5354^{8}

Catawollow *Richard Guest* 90h
7 b m Beat Hollow Catalonia (IRE) (Catrail (USA))
(21) 184^{3}

Catcharose (IRE) *Jennifer Mason* 59b
4 b f Catcher In The Rye(IRE) Persian Flower (Persian Heights)
3961^{6} 5070^{10}

Catcher In The Bog (IRE) *S J Mahon* 90h
7 bb g Catcher In The Rye(IRE) Bogtown (IRE) (Nashamaa)
1331^{F} (Dead)

Catcher Star (IRE) *Nick Gifford* 91h
6 b g Catcher In The Rye(IRE) Drumdeels Star (IRE) (Le Bavard (FR))
(3284) 3699^{4}

Catching On (IRE) *Jonjo O'Neill* 114h
6 b g Milan Miracle Lady (Bob's Return (IRE))
2563^{7} 2893^{8} 3128^{10} 3428^{4} (3828) (5366)

Catch Me Up (IRE) *Brendan Powell* 78h
6 b g Brian Boru Hartwell Lake (IRE) (Pistolet Bleu (IRE))
948^{P}

Catch One (FR) *Mlle T Puitg* 125h 113c
6 b g Smadoun(FR) Nan's Catch (FR) (Loup Solitaire (USA))
455a^{3}

Catch Tammy (IRE) *Tom George* 116h 120c
8 br g Tamayaz(CAN) Bramble Orchard (IRE) (Orchestra)
(459) **853^{P}**
1197^{7} 1429^{6}
(1596) 2222^{4}

Catch The Fire *Peter Bowen* 101h
6 b g Motivator Salinova (FR) (Linamix (FR))
237^{8} 1488^{4}

Catch The Katt *Richard Mitchell*
7 b m Wared(USA) Kittenkat (Riverwise (USA))
2570^{9} 4171^{U}

Catchthemoonlight *Lucinda Russell* 64h
6 b m Generous(IRE) Moon Catcher (Kahyasi)
5057^{7}

Catch The Rhythm (IRE) *Charlie Longsdon* 109h
6 b g Bandari(IRE) Christys Wish (IRE) (Anshan)
(95)

Categorical *Keith Reveley* 98h 123c
11 b g Diktat Zibet (Kris)
312^{5} 2070^{3} ◆ 2884^{3} 3389^{2} 3603^{5} 4346^{9} (4610)
5053^{4}

Catherines Well *Philip Hobbs* 107b
5 b m Kayf Tara Dudeen (IRE) (Anshan)
5528^{2}

Catspan (FR) *Miss H Lewis* 108h 101c
8 gr g Turgeon(USA) Royale Pour Moi (FR) (Cadoudal (FR))
4915^{2} 5292^{5}

Caught By Witness (IRE) *Anthony Middleton* 78h
9 b g Witness Box(USA) Donegans Daughter (Auction Ring (USA))
289^{P} 833^{P} 2175^{4} 2571^{6} 3264^{5} 3639^{2} ◆ 3821^{3} 4107^{6} 4783^{F}

Caught In The Act (IRE) *N W Alexander* 60h
7 br g Overbury(IRE) Catch Those Kisses (Deploy)
4553^{P}
5216^{P} 5532^{10}

Caught Inthe Light *Nigel Hawke* 79h 89c
9 b g Old Vic Webb Find (IRE) (Over The River (FR))
431^{4}

Caulfields Venture (IRE) *Emma Lavelle* 103h 124c
8 b g Catcher In The Rye(IRE) Saddlers' Venture (IRE) (Saddlers' Hall (IRE))
64^{4} (1765) *(4021)* **(4725)**
(4884) 5261^{2}

Caulkin (IRE) *David Kemp* 103h 111c
11 b g King's Theatre(IRE) Alice Brennan (IRE) (Good Thyne (USA))
57^{P}

Caunay *Neil Mulholland* 95h
7 ch g Generous(IRE) Chantilly Lady (Rising)
179^{S} 485^{P}

Cause Of Causes (USA) *Gordon Elliott* 126h 151c
6 b g Dynaformer(USA) Angel In My Heart (FR) (Rainbow Quest (USA))
4769^{2} 5474a^{12}

Cavite Eta (IRE) *Barry Murtagh* 97h 110c
7 br g Spadoun(FR) Samarinnda (IRE) (Akarad (FR))
1258^{6} 1414^{5} 1785^{5}
1981^{U} (2173)
2595^{2} 2734^{4}

Cawdor House Bert *David Rees* 117h
7 b g Kayf Tara Lady Shanan (IRE) (Anshan)
(145) 3130^{7} 3802^{8} (4841)

Cayetina *Ali Brewer* 76b
5 b m Kayf Tara Princess Hotpot (IRE) (King's Ride)
35^{7} 372^{15} 2697^{P}

Cayman Islands *John Ferguson* 97h 124c
6 b g Shirocco(GER) Barbuda (Rainbow Quest (USA))
4235^{4} 5230^{P}

Ceasar Milan (IRE) *Paul Nicholls* 133h
6 br g Milan Standfast (IRE) (Supreme Leader)
2079^{7} 3357^{2} 3774^{3} (4332) (4517) 4680^{5} 5574^{3}

Ceasar's Palace (FR) *J-P Gallorini* 143h
7 b g Voix Du Nord(FR) Cardounika (FR) (Nikos)
(1901a) 2240a^{F}

Cedre Bleu (FR) *Paul Nicholls* 123h 145c
7 b g Le Fou(IRE) Arvoire (IRE) (Exit To Nowhere (USA))
2800^{7} 3199^{2} 3458^{2} 3887^{6} 5156^{10}

Cedrus Libani (IRE) *Mrs Libby Lawson* 104h 106c
13 b g Beneficial Cedar Castle (IRE) (Castle Keep)
331^{2} 655^{RR}

Ceevee *Tim Vaughan* 41b
4 ch g Vita Rosa(JPN) Calonnog (IRE) (Peintre Celebre (USA))
2015^{11} *3229^{3}*

Ceilidh (IRE) *N W Alexander* 55h
6 b m Tamure(IRE) Eyesabeatin (IRE) (Alphabatim (USA))
2660^{9} 3727^{7} 4958^{14} 5554^{7}

Celebrian *Alex Hales* 83h
7 b m Fasliyev(USA) Triplemoon (USA) (Trempolino (USA))
856^{6} 1090^{5} 1176^{6} 5116^{5}

Celestial Halo (IRE) *Paul Nicholls* 165h 129c
10 b g Galileo(IRE) Pay The Bank (High Top)
(406a) 685a^{6} (2814) 4269^{3} 4767^{10}

Celestial Island *John Gallagher* 106b
7 gr m Silver Patriarch(IRE) Celtic Island (Celtic Swing)
(35)

Celtic Abbey *Donald McCain* 105h
7 br g Overbury(IRE) Celtic Native (IRE) (Be My Native (USA))
1935^{7} 2868^{8}

Celtic Agent *Philip Kirby* 110b
6 b g Kayf Tara Poor Celt (Impecunious)
(4598)

Celtic Charlie (FR) *Pat Phelan* 73h 40c
9 ch g Until Sundown(USA) India Regalona (USA) (Dehere (USA))
1530^{U} 1630^{11} 2862^{3} 5242^{6} 5459^{7}

Celtic Fella (IRE) *Debra Hamer* 46h
7 gr g Kahtan Mens Buisiness (IRE) (Buckskin (FR))
777^{8} 1864^{10} **2389^{P} 3114^{P}**

Celtic Intrigue (IRE) *Tom George* 90h 97c
7 b g Celtic Swing Macca Luna (IRE) (Kahyasi)
43^{4} 314^{2} 707^{2}

Celtic Legacy *Michael Murphy* 95b
7 ch m Where Or When(IRE) An Cailin Rua (Aragon)
5434^{P}

Celtic Monarch (IRE) *Mark Michael McNiff* 112h
5 b g Celtic Swing Trim (IRE) (Ela-Mana-Mou)
(507) 1139a^{6} 1399^{2}

Celts Espere *Trevor Wall* 92b 43c
11 ch g Samraan(USA) Celtic Dream (Celtic Cone)
4383^{P} 4759^{P}

Centasia *David Pipe* 123h
7 b m Presenting Cent Prime (Hernando (FR))
(2190) ◆ 3168^{2} 3892^{4}

Centoria (IRE) *Jamie Snowden* 96b
6 ch m Generous(IRE) Cent Prime (Hernando (FR))
1531^{2} 2022^{3} 2892^{10}

Central Flame *James Walton* 99b 93c
6 ch g Central Park(IRE) More Flair (Alflora (IRE))
584^{7}

Certain Flight (IRE) *K J Cumings* 120c
9 b g Convinced Carole's Dove (Manhal)
(4376)
4788^{13} 5123^{3}

Certification (IRE) *John Ferguson* 110h
4 b g Authorized(IRE) Most Charming (FR) (Darshaan)
3161^{3} (3822) 4307^{2} 4755^{15}

Cesar De La Haulle (FR) *T Trapenard* 88h
4 b g Laveron Dear Shrimp (FR) (Pistolet Bleu (IRE))
614a^{5}

Cevaro (IRE) *Nicky Henderson* 108h
6 b m Milan Jollie Bollie (IRE) (Husyan (USA))
166^{3}

Chac Du Cadran (FR) *Chris Bealby* 131c
8 b g Passing Sale(FR) L'Indienne (FR) (Le Nain Jaune (FR))
2157^{F} 2670^{P} 3617^{P} 5180^{P}

Chadford *Claire Dyson* 56h 81c
6 b g Trade Fair Quiz Time (Efisio)
120^{F} 1267^{P}

Chain Of Beacons *Charlie Longsdon* 87b
5 b g Midnight Legend Millennium Girl (Skyliner)
3734^{7}

Chain Of Events *Sarah Humphrey* 104h
7 ch g Nayef(USA) Ermine (IRE) (Cadeaux Genereux)
384^{P} 593^{5}

Chalk It Down (IRE) *Warren Greatrex* 118h
5 b g Milan Feedthegoodmare (IRE) (Heron Island (IRE))
(1353) 1671^{4} 1935^{4} 2265^{6} 3034^{4} 3736^{4} 4157^{4} *(4496)* 5552^{2}

Chambray Dancer (IRE) *Seamus Mullins* 74h
6 b m Darsi(FR) Cotton Gale (Strong Gale)
2027^{6} 2579^{0}

Champagne Agent (IRE) *Lucinda Russell* 128h 103c
8 b g Smadoun(FR) Madame Jean (FR) (Cricket Ball (USA))
2159^{8} 3017^{P}
4341^{5} 4892^{5} 5216^{4}

Champagne At Tara *Jonjo O'Neill* 120h
5 gr g Kayf Tara Champagne Lil (Terimon)
(1861) 2534^{4} ◆ 2947^{3} 3258^{5}

Champagne Chaser *Tim Vaughan* 91b
4 b g Tobougg(IRE) Champagne Lil (Terimon)
4424^{5}

Champagne Fever (IRE) *W P Mullins* 145h 161c
7 gr g Stowaway Forever Bubbles (IRE) (Roselier (FR))
3308a^{3} 4737^{2}

Champagne James (IRE) *T M Walsh* 125h
6 b g Stowaway Champagne Lady (IRE) (Turtle Island (IRE))
4708a^{7}

Champagne Rian (IRE) *Rebecca Curtis* 122h
6 b g Dr Massini(IRE) Vul Gale (IRE) (Strong Gale)
2386^{2} 2942^{3} 3775^{8} 5093^{16}

Champagne West (IRE) *Philip Hobbs* 143h
6 b g Westerner Wyndham Sweetmarie (IRE) (Mister Lord (USA))
2279^{9} 2642^{2} (2978) (3292) (3774) 4786^{4} ◆

Champion Court (IRE) *Martin Keighley* 139h 161c
9 b g Court Cave(IRE) Mooneys Hill (IRE) (Supreme Leader)
2503^{7} 3032^{2} 3262^{U} 3645^{2} 3888^{6} 4768^{7} 5156^{9}

Chance Du Roy (FR) *Philip Hobbs* 123h 148c
10 ch g Morespeed La Chance Au Roy (FR) (Rex Magna (FR))
(2937)
3780^{P} 4263^{4} 5171^{6}

Chance Encounter (IRE) *Linda Blackford* 98h 96c
8 br g Anshan Glittering Grit (IRE) (Sheer Grit)
2906^{6} 3290^{F} 3788^{7} 4911^{4} 5177^{15}

Chanceofa Lifetime (IRE) *Victor Thompson* 72b
7 ch g Beneficial Bounty Queen (IRE) (King's Ride)
498^{6}

Chandler Bing *Eugene Stanford* 94b
5 b g Librettist(USA) Gina Tribbiani (Diktat)
3508^{8}

Chandler Jack *Derek Wellicome* 38h
7 b g Lujain(USA) Moonlight Seas (Sabrehill (USA))
716^{P} 971^{4}

Chandlers Cross (IRE) *David Rees* 95h 92c
12 ch g Rakaposhi King Tullow Lady (IRE) (Mazaad)
692^{P} 759^{10} (1010)
1103^{P}

Changing Lanes *David Rees* 95h 97c
11 b g Overbury(IRE) Snowdon Lily (Town And Country)
1051^{5}
1344^{P} 1565^{10} 1707^{6} 1890^{4} 2541^{2} 2620^{3} 2827^{2} 3179^{4}

Changing The Guard *Dr Richard Newland* 136h 149c
8 b g King's Best(USA) Our Queen Of Kings (Arazi (USA))
447^{8} 673^{7} **(830)**
(1053) 1178a^{3} 4264^{9}
4790^{12} 4921^{3} 5136^{8} (5392)

Chaninbar (FR) *Anthony Middleton* 50h 78c
11 b g Milford Track(IRE) Logicia (FR) (Homme De Loi (IRE))
1572a^{6} 1613a^{R}

Chankillo *Sarah-Jayne Davies* 92h
5 ch g Observatory(USA) Seasonal Blossom (IRE) (Fairy King (USA))
1404^{6} 1575^{2} 1643^{7} 1700^{2} 1938^{7} 2016^{7} 2291^{7} 2559^{3} 2766^{3} 3025^{4} 4072^{4} 5116^{8} 5522^{5}

Chantara Rose *Anthony Honeyball* 97b
5 br m Kayf Tara Fragrant Rose (Alflora (IRE))
3228^{2} 3507^{5}

Chapel House *Richard Harper* 68h 74c
11 b g Beneficial My Moona (Ballacashtal (CAN))
807^{P} 1437^{P} 1824^{P} 3261^{6} 3503^{4}
3817^{4} 4570^{4} 5442^{P}

Chapelle du Roi (USA) *Robert Stephens* 86h
5 ch g Danehill Dancer(IRE) Capilla Bonita (USA) (Pleasant Colony (USA))
857^{9} 1059^{4} 1348^{3} 1582^{4} 2016^{2} 2877^{14} 4336^{9}

Chapolimoss (FR) *Lawney Hill* 98h 125c
10 ch g Trempolino(USA) Chamoss (FR) (Tip Moss (FR))
3879^{3} (4572)
4792^{P}

Chapoturgeon (FR) *R Barber* 109h 147c
10 gr g Turgeon(USA) Chapohio (FR) (Script Ohio (USA))
(413) **660^{2}**

Chapter Five *Ian Williams* 83h
7 b m Grape Tree Road Northern Shadows (Rock Hopper)
2689^{6}

Chardonnay (FR) *G Cherel* 96h 125c
5 ch g Protektor(GER) Jolie Mome (FR) (Art Francais (USA))
2263a^{5} 5425a^{P}

Chargen (IRE) *Sean Curran* 113h 75c
11 b g Charente River(IRE) Blasgan (IRE) (Yashgan)
698^{P}

Charingworth (IRE) *Kim Bailey* 114h 135c
11 b g Supreme Leader Quinnsboro Guest (IRE) (Be My Guest (USA))
2487^{2} 2889^{3} 3414^{3} 5488^{4}

Charles Bruce (IRE) *A Campbell* 116c
11 br g Lord Americo Lissanuhig (Le Bavard (FR))
(62) **658^{P}**
3720^{P} 3801^{6} 4348^{6}

Charles Onze (FR) *Dave Roberts* 63b
7 b g Epalo(GER) Karmiva (FR) (Epervier Bleu)
1427^{9} 1671^{13}

Charlie Bucket *Donald Whillans* 87h 103c
11 ch g Sugarfoot Stoproveritate (Scorpio (FR))
2214^{4} 471^{5} (2333)

Charlies Lady *Anna Newton-Smith* 58h
7 b m Trade Fair Heavenly Waters (Celestial Storm (USA))
308^{5} 490^{P}

Charlie Snow Angel *Sandy Forster* 87b
5 b g Overbury(IRE) Sister Seven (IRE) (Henbit (USA))
5324^{4}

Charming Charlie (IRE) *Emma Lavelle* 54b
4 b g Beneficial Baile An Droichid (IRE) (King's Ride)
5310^{9}

Charming Knight (IRE) *Jane Walton* 48b 63c
13 b g Mohaajir(USA) Arctic Laura (Le Bavard (FR))
114^{4} 4239^{P}

Chartreux (FR) *Tom George* 133h 146c
9 gr g Colonel Collins(USA) Ruaha River (FR) (Villez (USA))
1604a^{15} 2937^{15} 3361^{P} 4134^{F} (4681)

Chase Gate *James Frost* 93h 105c
9 ch g Arkadian Hero(USA) Carlingford Lass (IRE) (Carlingford Castle)
(175) **689^{4}**
1349^{P} 2462^{5}

Chasers Chance (IRE) *Paul Henderson* 104h 106c
11 ch g Shernazar Lucy Walters (IRE) (King's Ride)
238^{5} 1526^{2} 1748^{4} 1959^{8} 2390^{2} 2730^{4} 3293^{3}
3879^{5} 4481^{5} 4843^{3}

Chase The Spud *Fergal O'Brien* 122h
6 b g Alflora(IRE) Trial Trip (Le Moss)
1919[3] (2252) 2507[2] 3884[4] 4374[4]

Chase The Wind (IRE) *Warren Greatrex* 117h
5 ch g Spadoun(FR) Asfreeasthewind (IRE) (Moscow Society (USA))
1974[2] 2802[10] 3134[4] ◆ *4298[5]*

Chasing Waterfalls (IRE) *C F Swan* 21b
4 b g Gold Well Tatiana (IRE) (Erins Isle)
5424a[11]

Chasse En Mer (FR) *Caroline Bailey* 107h
4 b f Protektor(GER) Cybertina (FR) (Cyborg (FR))
2066[2] 3212[3] (3604) 4374[5] 5345[4]

Chat Room *John Ferguson* 122h
6 ch g Dubawi(IRE) Contradictive (USA) (Kingmambo (USA))
2366[10] 3031[10] (4947) 5231[10]

Chatterbox (IRE) *Nicky Henderson* 148h
6 b g Poliglote Ney Will (FR) (Pistolet Bleu (IRE))
2758[2] 3200[P]

Chavoy (FR) *Rebecca Menzies* 127h 119c
9 br g Saint Des Saints(FR) Dictania (FR) (Iron Duke (FR))
3661[6] (3938) ◆ 4271[7] **4427[P] 5210[2]**

Cheat The Cheater (IRE) *Claire Dyson* 118h 86c
7 b g Flemensfirth(USA) Ballyclough Gale (IRE) (Strong Gale)
2451[5] 3358[5] 3696[6] 4399[7]

Chebsey Beau *John Quinn* 110h
4 b g Multiplex Chebsey Belle (IRE) (Karinga Bay)
2247[2] 2960[4] 3822[3] 4073[3] 4529[2] 4945[3] 5375[2]

Checkerboard (IRE) *Mrs Kayley Woollacott* 50h 66c
11 b g Alderbrook Jamie's Lady (Ashmore (FR))
4505[5]

Checkmate *Christopher Kellett* 77c
9 b g Needle Gun(IRE) Lady Of Spain (Aragon)
1133[7] 1303[4] 1550[8] 1668[8] 2423[5]

Checkpoint *Gary Moore*
5 ch g Zamindar(USA) Kalima (Kahyasi)
427[P]

Chegei Has (FR) *J-P Gallorini* 128h 132c
6 b m Kahyasi Nasou (FR) (Kaldounevees (FR))
406a[11]
1583a[2]

Cheltenian (FR) *Philip Hobbs* 142h
8 b g Astarabad(USA) Salamaite (FR) (Mansonnien (FR))
(3427) 4147[4] ◆ 4785[P] 5158[4]

Chemistry Master *Harry Fry* 122h
6 b g Doyen(IRE) Elemental (Rudimentary (USA))
2111[3] 2461[5] 3132[3] *4301[10]* 4799[4] 5179[11]

Chendiyr (FR) *Sarah Humphrey* 70h
5 gr g Red Ransom(USA) Cherryxma (FR) (Linamix (FR))
1749[8] 2016[10]

Cherie Gold (FR) *Patrice Quinton*
4 b f Goldneyev(USA) Bois Cherie (FR) (The Shadow (FR))
615a[P]

Chernik (IRE) *Micky Hammond* 70h 82c
13 b g Norwich Sue Pickering (IRE) (Tremblant)
580[2] 753[6] 1038[P]

Cherry's Bay *Sandy Forster* 19c
8 b m Helissio(FR) Buck Comtess (USA) (Spend A Buck (USA))
3496[2] 3936[P] 4337[P]

Cherry Tiger *Graeme McPherson* 25h
4 b g Tiger Hill(IRE) Lolla's Spirit (IRE) (Montjeu (IRE))
4534[F] 4632[15] 4784[R]

Chesil Beach Boy *John Coombe* 131h
11 b g Commanche Run Eatons (Daring March)
3292[7] 3744[4] 3957[2] 4333[4] 4634[4] 4682[5]

Chesnut Annie (IRE) *Beth Roberts* 47h 117c
13 ch m Weld Leaden Sky (IRE) (Roselier (FR))
61[2]

Chester Legend *Sue Taylor* 85b
7 ch g Pasternak Sally Smith (Alias Smith (USA))
497[5] 682[6] 2499[14]

Chestertern *Jennie Candlish* 117h 117c
7 ch g Karinga Bay My Tern (IRE) (Glacial Storm (USA))
12[7] **2031[3]**
2803[5] 3325[P] 4347[P]

Chestnut Ben (IRE) *Gary Brown* 78h 113c
9 ch g Ridgewood Ben Betseale (IRE) (Step Together I (USA))
43[3] 245[2] 426[3] 632[3] 807[3] 942[7] 1328[2] (1530)
1710[2] 2440[3] (3164)

Chezzy (IRE) *Fergal O'Brien* 114b
5 b m Chevalier(IRE) Mags Benefit (IRE) (Beneficial)
(5381)

Chiberta King *Andrew Balding* 130h
8 b g King's Best(USA) Glam Rock (Nashwan (USA))
2798[12]

Chicago (IRE) *John Patrick Shanahan* 130h
5 b g Montjeu(IRE) Lady Karr (Mark Of Esteem (IRE))
3667a[4] 4285a[3]

Chicago Alley *Dave Roberts* 20h 46c
13 br m Bob Back(USA) Winnetka Gal (IRE) (Phardante (FR))
3352[7] 3637[5] 5404[U]

Chicago Grey (IRE) *Gordon Elliott* 122h 153c
11 gr g Luso Carrigeen Acer (IRE) (Lord Americo)
2491[5] 3068[7]

Chicago Outfit (IRE) *John Wade* 100h 100c
9 b g Old Vic Lambourne Lace (IRE) (Un Desperado (FR))
279[3] 566[10] 802[4] 1502[2] (1789)
2036[5] 2445[6] 2959[5] 5055[3] 5356[5]

Chicklemix *Pam Sly* 114h 114c
8 gr m Fair Mix(IRE) Chichell's Hurst (Oats)
1821[4] 2315[5] 2895[4] (3176)
(3662) 4007[P]

Chicoria (IRE) *Henry Daly* 85h
5 ch g Presenting Coco Girl (Mystiko (USA))
2703[4] 4547[4] 5174[6]

Chidswell (IRE) *Nicky Richards* 109b
5 b g Gold Well Manacured (IRE) (Mandalus)
(2499)

Chief Heckler (IRE) *Philip Rowley* 82b 110c
8 b g Dushyantor(USA) Asidewager (IRE) (Brush Aside (USA))
94[3] 4246[5] 4511[3] 4922[2]

Chieftain's Choice (IRE) *John Quinn* 118b
5 b g King's Theatre(IRE) Fairly Native (IRE) (Be My Native (USA))
2347[4] (4728) 5279[6]

Chilbury Hill (IRE) *Tim Vaughan* 97h 107c
11 b g Bahhare(USA) Fire Goddess (Magic Ring (IRE))
17[P] **(873)**
(1057)
1086[2] 1364[7] (1428)
1537[2]

Chill Factor (IRE) *Anthony Honeyball* 97h
5 b g Oscar(IRE) Glacial Princess (IRE) (Glacial Storm (USA))
1974[15] 2280[10] 2385[4] 2802[14] 4729[2]

Chill In The Wood *Dominic Ffrench Davis* 80h
5 br m Desert King(IRE) Zaffaranni (IRE) (Zaffaran (USA))
5028[4] 5528[9]

Chilly Miss *Malcolm Jefferson* 104b
5 b m Iceman Fairlie (Halling (USA))
(5196)

Chiltern Hills (IRE) *W P Mullins* 119h 80c
7 ch m Beneficial Mirazur (IRE) (Good Thyne (USA))
3750a[P]

Chilworth Screamer *Chris Gordon* 124h
6 b m Imperial Dancer The Screamer (IRE) (Insan (USA))
29[5] 188[2] (293) 353[2] 1062[2] 1321[4] (1527) 1941[F] 2663[6] 5260[8]

China Reel (IRE) *Jonjo O'Neill* 86h
5 ch m Shantou(USA) Midnight Reel (IRE) (Accordion)
502[6]

Chinatown Boy (IRE) *Paul Nicholls* 110h
6 ch g Presenting Asian Maze (IRE) (Anshan)
4603[P]

Chinook Run (IRE) *P Cluskey* 99h
10 b g Chinook Eclipse(USA) Night Run (IRE) (Supreme Leader)
891a[4]

Chippy *John Holt* 57h
6 b g Diktat French Mannequin (IRE) (Key Of Luck (USA))
927[P]

Chiquilline (FR) *T Lacey* 97h 120c
8 bb g Kapgarde(FR) Sheyrinca (FR) (Sheyrann (IRE))
286[5] 4274[4] ◆ **4705[P]**

Chiron (IRE) *Keith Dalgleish* 89b
5 b g Celtic Swing Jane Digby (IRE) (Magical Strike (USA))
4611[5] 5166[4]

Chloe's Image *Philip Kirby* 68h
4 b f Lucky Story(USA) Iwunder (IRE) (King's Best (USA))
1658[6] 1786[5] 1920[9]

Chocala (IRE) *Alan King* 118h
4 b g Rock Of Gibraltar(IRE) Arbella (Primo Dominie)
2796[3] 4173[5]

Choisan (IRE) *Tim Easterby* 97h
5 b g Choisir(AUS) Attanagh (IRE) (Darnay)
2493[12] 2840[3] 3330[7] 4378[2] 4836[4]

Choisirez (IRE) *John Panvert* 60h
5 b m Choisir(AUS) Filimeala (IRE) (Pennekamp (USA))
925[6]

Choral Bee *Alan Jessop* 84h
5 b m Oratorio(IRE) Chief Bee (Chief's Crown (USA))
2190[12] 3005[12] 4796[5]

Chosen Dream (IRE) *Jonjo O'Neill* 87h
6 b g Well Chosen Peoples Dream (IRE) (Mandalus)
320[6] 590[8] 669[4] 844[7] 946[2] 1188[7]

Chosen Milan (IRE) *R E Luke* 88b 125c
7 b m Milan Grey Mistral (Terimon)
58[3] 658[6] 4727[2] (5123)
5337[2]

Chriseti (FR) *E Leenders* 120h 127c
14 gr g April Night(FR) L'Allier (FR) (Rose Laurel)
199a[F] 1532a[4]

Chris Pea Green *Gary Moore* 145h
5 b g Proclamation(IRE) Another Secret (Efisio)
2213[2] 2758[3] 3200[4] 4147[7] 4441[3]

Christopher Wren (USA) *Nick Gifford* 128h 134c
7 ch g D'Wildcat(USA) Ashley's Coy (USA) (Country Pine (USA))
66[5] (2025)
2469[9] (2845)
3323[2] *4022[5]* **4768[P] 5573[2]**

Chuchoteuse (FR) *L Postic* 140h 125c
9 b m Astarabad(USA) Belle Yepa (FR) (Mansonnien (FR))
406a[5]

Chunck *Edward Creighton*
7 ch g Alflora(IRE) Gaye Fame (Ardross)
4298[14]

Church Bray *Nigel Twiston-Davies* 90h
6 b g Kayf Tara Castle Lynch (IRE) (Castle Keep)
675[4] 3116[5] 3716[10] 4068[8] 5514[3]

Church Field (IRE) *Jonjo O'Neill* 117h
6 b g Heron Island(IRE) Dante's Thatch (IRE) (Phardante (FR))
(177) (333) (564) (1042) 1485[7] 1972[8] 2314[5] 2828[9] 5191[7] 5489[9]

Churchfield Champ (IRE) *Paul John Gilligan* 125h 129c
8 b g Norwich Ash Dame (IRE) (Strong Gale)
(385)

Church Hall (IRE) *Emma Baker* 108h
6 b g Craigsteel Island Religion (IRE) (Religiously (USA))
250[6] 1795[8] 1946[3] 2429[U] 2720[10]

Churchtown Love (IRE) *Rebecca Curtis* 113h
6 b m Beneficial Katie Murphy (IRE) (Over The River (FR))
(4487) 4910[7]

Churt *Christopher Kellett*
5 b g Namid Darayna (IRE) (Shernazar)
2068[P]

Cian Boy (IRE) *Nick Kent* 54h 51c
8 bb g Indian Danehill(IRE) Dotty Dee (IRE) (Hatim (USA))
264[15] **1416[4]**

Ciceron (IRE) *Venetia Williams* 136h 133c
8 b g Pivotal Aiglonne (USA) (Silver Hawk (USA))
217[P] 587[2] 787[4]

Cigalas *Jean McGregor* 70h
9 ch g Selkirk(USA) Langoustine (AUS) (Danehill (USA))
316[7] 630[5] 1143[4] 1374[11] 2844[7] 5052[6] 5532[12]

Cigliano (FR) *F Nicolle* 123h 125c
8 gr g Poliglote La Reine Chic (FR) (Balleroy (USA))
863a[6]

Cillian's Return (IRE) *W T Farrell* 130h
5 b g Diamond Green(FR) Sally Anne (ITY) (Scenic)
2995a[2]

Cilliseal (IRE) *Noel C Kelly* 96h 104c
9 b g Lahib(USA) Hyacinth Bucket (Lighter)
1505[4] 1655[7] 1873[6]
2339[3] 2594[5] 3497[6]

Cinder Rua (IRE) *D T Kelly* 111h
7 ch m Carroll House Scree (IRE) (Broken Hearted)
5475a[U]

Cinders And Ashes *Donald McCain* 120b
7 b g Beat Hollow Moon Search (Rainbow Quest (USA))
4785[P]

Cinematique (IRE) *Laura Mongan* 103h
6 br g King's Theatre(IRE) Chantoue Royale (FR) (Cadoudal (FR))
486[P] *4023[16]* 5343[6]

Cinevator (IRE) *Caroline Keevil* 130h 127c
7 b g Dr Massini(IRE) Hurricane Bella (IRE) (Taipan (IRE))
(38) **(1433)**
1709[8] 2107[2] 2267[P] 2504[17]

Cinnomhor *Chris Grant* 89h
6 b m Grape Tree Road Brass Buckle (IRE) (Buckskin (FR))
1871[U] 2196[8] 2495[7] 2865[3] 4528[4] 4891[4] 5449[P]

Circus Of Dreams *Oliver Sherwood* 116h 124c
11 b g Kayf Tara Foehn Gale (IRE) (Strong Gale)
2179[7]

Circus Star (USA) *John Dixon* 118h
6 b g Borrego(USA) Picadilly Circus (USA) (Fantastic Fellow (USA))
2241[7] 2597[6] (3021) (3288) 3527[2] 4813[4] 5102[3]

Cirrus Coin *Andrew Hollinshead* 87h
9 ch g Cloudings(IRE) Andy Coin (Andy Rew)
317[P] 649[5]

Citizenship *Venetia Williams* 138h
8 b g Beat Hollow Three More (USA) (Sanglamore (USA))
2813[15] (3169) 3771[9] 3891[9] 4785[23] 5158[10] 5534[6]

Citrus Mark *Paul Webber* 96h 113c
9 b g Mark Of Esteem(IRE) Lemon's Mill (USA) (Roberto (USA))
245[P] 714[3] 898[2] (1122)
1263[4] 1670[3]

City Line (IRE) *Karl Thornton* 116h 101c
7 b g Antonius Pius(USA) Indian Myth (USA) (Lear Fan (USA))
879[2]

City Nebula (FR) *J Bertran De Balanda* 74h
4 b f Astarabad(USA) Chicita Du Berlais (FR) (Nikos)
2781a[P]

City Of Doral *J J Lambe* 108h 105c
12 b g Double Trigger(IRE) Double Resolve (Gildoran)
3938[P]

City Press (IRE) *Warren Greatrex* 114h 124c
8 b g Presenting Phargara (IRE) (Phardante (FR))
(7) **96[F]**
596[3] (757)
923[P] 1062[3]

City Slicker (IRE) *W P Mullins* 150h
6 b g King's Theatre(IRE) Donna's Princess (IRE) (Supreme Leader)
3200[13] 4456a[6] 5201a[P]

City Supreme (IRE) *Anthony Honeyball* 98b
4 b g Milan Run Supreme (IRE) (Supreme Leader)
3460[4] 4844[4]

Civena (IRE) *J A Berry* 118h 132c
8 b m Oscar(IRE) The Village Merc (IRE) (Be My Native (USA))
4315a[5] 4848a[2]

Civil Disobedience *Richard Woollacott* 94h 120c
10 b g Roi De Rome(USA) Biddles (Norwick (USA))
1563[2] 1959[3] 2662[5] 2923[P] 5373[P]

Civil Unrest (IRE) *James Ewart* 109h 115c
8 ch g Blueprint(IRE) Yore (IRE) (Ore)
220[6] 693[4] 883[8] 1039[2] 1260[3] 1469[4] 1668[4] (1715)
(2306) (2360) 2879[4] **(3517)**
4222[2]

Civil War (IRE) *Gary Moore* 117h
5 b g Scorpion(IRE) Silvestre (ITY) (Unfuwain (USA))
3550[2] 4103[5] *4301[3]* 4467[2]

C J Mackintosh *Ian Williams* 90h
8 b m Beat All(USA) Fringe Benefit (IRE) (Executive Perk)
5426[5]

Claiming Benefits (IRE) *Ronald O'Leary* 113h
6 b g Beneficial Eurocurrency (IRE) (Brush Aside (USA))
856[7]

Clan Chief *N W Alexander* 106b
5 ch g Generous(IRE) Harrietfield (Nicholas Bill)
(4370) 5560[7]

Clancy's Cross (IRE) *Rebecca Curtis* 93b
5 b g Oscar(IRE) Murphys Lady (IRE) (Over The River (FR))
2513[4]

Clan Legend *N W Alexander* 78b
4 ch g Midnight Legend Harrietfield (Nicholas Bill)
5109[P] 5324[5]

Clan William (IRE) *Sue Smith* 106h
6 b g Antonius Pius(USA) Celebrated Smile (IRE) (Cadeaux Genereux)
(318) 2748[6] 3330[5] 3781[7]

Claragh Native (IRE) *Martin Todhunter* 98h 125c
9 ch g Beneficial Susy In The Summer (IRE) (Be My Native (USA))
(2793)
2957[2] 3090[6] 3452[3] 4053[7] 5254[U]

Clara Mc Cloud (IRE) *Gordon Elliott* 126h
6 b m Cloudings(IRE) Aoife Landers (IRE) (Zaffaran (USA))
5255[2]

Clara Peggotty *Tom Gretton* 96h
7 b m Beat All(USA) Clair Valley (Ardross)
2507[U] 2824[P] 4037[2] 4276[P] 4676[5]

Claraty *James Unett* 5b
4 b f Firebreak Claradotnet (Sri Pekan (USA))
3663[8]

Clarcam (FR) *Gordon Elliott* 138h
4 b g Califet(FR) Rose Beryl (FR) (Lost World (IRE))
2851a[3] 3305a[2] 4054[2] ◆ 4755[F] 5132[2] 5470a[4]

Clarence Beeks (IRE) *Brian Ellison* 80b
4 gr g Verglas(IRE) Dazzling Dancer (Nashwan (USA))
2960[9] 3619[9]

Claret Cloak (IRE) *Emma Lavelle* 141h 152c
7 b g Vinnie Roe(IRE) Bewildered (IRE) (Prince Sabo)
(1821)
2282[2] 2950[4] 4790[3] ◆ **5136[3]**

Clarion Call *Graeme McPherson* 112h
6 b g Beat Hollow Fanfare (Deploy)
252[11] 925[9] 1171[2] 1275[5] 1379[2] 1711[2] (1833)

Clar Na Mionn (IRE) *V T O'Brien* 135h 139c
7 b g Witness Box(USA) Playtime Girl (IRE) (Commanche Run)
1804a[3] 2116a[2] 2258a[2] 2853a[6] 3314a[4] 3791a[3]
4315a[3] 5474a[P]

Clash Duff (IRE) *Jeremy Scott*
9 gr g Great Palm(USA) Evnelu (IRE) (Old Vic)
2108[P]

Classical Chloe *Sara Ender*
6 b m Sleeping Indian Mana Pools (IRE) (Brief Truce (USA))
3329[P] 3840[P] *4324[3]* 4694[P]

Classical Twist (IRE) *Jonjo O'Neill* 78h
6 br g Oscar(IRE) Basically Supreme (IRE) (Supreme Leader)
490[11]

Classic Art *Roger Teal* 79h
4 ch g Excellent Art Sensibility (Halling (USA))
2927[7] 3317[5] 3641[8] 5396[P]

Classic Case (IRE) *Sean Curran* 79h 101c
7 b g Classic Cliche(IRE) Rashie (IRE) (Corrouge (USA))
1939[12] (2825)
5011[2] 5293[P]

Classic Cut *James Ewart* 90h 113c
10 b g Classic Cliche(IRE) Leading Line (Leading Man)
220[4]

Classic Move (IRE) *Donald McCain* 129h
5 b g Flying Legend(USA) Jennylee (IRE) (Lord Americo)
(2174) 2659[3] (3225) (4005) ◆ 4680[F] 5387[5]

Classic Orange *Simon Waugh*
4 ch f Assertive Classical Song (IRE) (Fayruz)
1786[10]

Classic Rally (IRE) *Malcolm Jefferson* 103h
8 b g Zagreb(USA) Classic Material (Classic Cliche (IRE))
3036[P] 4379[4] 4758[16]

Classinaglass *Mrs Stephanie Easterby* 54c
7 b g Grape Tree Road Sounds Familiar (IRE) (Orchestra)
4079[3]

Classy Chassis (IRE) *Iain Jardine*
6 br m Heron Island(IRE) Marika's King (IRE) (King's Ride)
4240[12]

Claude Carter *Alistair Whillans* 100h
10 b g Elmaamul(USA) Cruz Santa (Lord Bud)
344[4] 537[4] 961[5] 1206[3] 1285[3] 1419[U] 1567[4] 2306[5] 5532[6]

Clear Mix *Sue Gardner* 75h
6 b m Fair Mix(IRE) Nortonthorpe-Rose (Derrylin)
174[F] 410[5] 2027[10] 2291[12] 4330[5] 4733[P]

Cleetons Turn *Alan Hollingsworth*
7 b g Alflora(IRE) Indyana Run (Commanche Run)
380[P]

Cleeve Cloud (IRE) *Liam Grassick* 92h
8 b g Noverre(USA) La Galeisa (IRE) (Warning)
716[6] 844[P] 1061[P]

Clement (IRE) *John O'Shea* 27h
4 b g Clodovil(IRE) Winnifred (Green Desert (USA))
2466[8]

Clerk's Choice (IRE) *William Jarvis* 146h
8 b g Bachelor Duke(USA) Credit Crunch (IRE) (Caerleon (USA))
4752[12] 5572[3]

Cleve Cottage *Philip Kirby* 104h
6 ch g Presenting Reverse Swing (Charmer)
1794[4] 2202[6] 2786[7] 3569[5]

Clever Cookie *Peter Niven* 145h
6 b g Primo Valentino(IRE) Mystic Memory (Ela-Mana-Mou)
(790) 2341[2] ◆ 2823[2] (3758) (4056) (4550) 5274[8]

Cliff Lane (IRE) *Lucinda Russell* 71b
5 b g Scorpion(IRE) Susan's Dream (IRE) (Euphemism)
4631[3]

Clonbanan Lad (IRE) *Henry De Bromhead* 134h 139c
8 b g Rudimentary(USA) Flute Orchestra (IRE) (Deep Run)
2551a[3]

Clondaw Banker (IRE) *Nicky Henderson* 113b
5 b g Court Cave(IRE) Freya Alex (Makbul)
(4017) ◆ 4424[3] 5173[14]

Clondaw Draft (IRE) *Donald McCain* 136h
6 b g Shantou(USA) Glen Ten (IRE) (Mandalus)
675[2] 1118[2] (1329) (1576) 1954[3]

Clondaw Flicka (IRE) *Lucinda Russell* 100h 121c
6 ch g Stowaway Bealaha Essie (IRE) (Denel (FR))
1979[6]
2308[4] (2784)
(3283) 4610[2]

Clondaw Hero (IRE) *Donald McCain* 122h 122c
6 b g Milan Rose Of Winter (IRE) (Roselier (FR))
(1261) 1392[2] 1497[P] (2342) 4052[P]
(5376)

Clondaw Kaempfer (IRE) *Donald McCain* 145h
6 b g Oscar(IRE) Gra-Bri (IRE) (Rashar (USA))
2671[9] 2935[3] 4752[14] (5158) 5572[4]

Clondaw Knight (IRE) *Lucinda Russell* 105h 132c
6 b g Heron Island(IRE) Sarah Supreme (IRE) (Supreme Leader)
3133[3] **(2356)**
4106[3] 4898[3] 5480[3]

Clonusker (IRE) *Linda Jewell* 98h
6 b g Fasliyev(USA) Tamburello (IRE) (Roi Danzig (USA))
3[8] 308[4] 708[P] 2862[10] 3140[2] (3692) (4444) 4721[5]

Close House *David Pipe* 136h 133c
7 b g Generous(IRE) Not Now Nellie (Saddlers' Hall (IRE))
2504[9]
3064[F] 3456[3] 3992[4] 4742[P] 5138[19]

Closest Friend *J R Jenkins* 96b
5 b g Kayf Tara Princess Of War (Warrshan (USA))
2026[4] 2681[4] *3098[6]* 5447[2]

Closing Ceremony (IRE) *Emma Lavelle* 126h
5 b g Flemensfirth(USA) Supreme Von Pres (IRE) (Presenting)
2076[2] ◆ 2649[3] (3643) 4442[4]

Cloudante (IRE) *Donald McCain* 119h
6 b m Cloudings(IRE) Carrig Lucy (IRE) (Phardante (FR))
(3228) 3507[4] (3757) (4479) 5368[6]

Cloud Brook (IRE) *Rebecca Curtis* 130h
6 b g Cloudings(IRE) Stoney Brook (IRE) (Rich Charlie)
(1732) 1954[5] (2648)

Cloudbusting *Zoe Davison* 76b
6 b m Midnight Legend Minibelle (Macmillion)
4540[5] 4916[14]

Cloud Creeper (IRE) *Philip Hobbs* 123h
7 b g Cloudings(IRE) First Of April (IRE) (Presenting)
116[8] 2351[2] 2740[2] 3506[2] (4594) 4897[7]

Clouded Thoughts (IRE) *Venetia Williams* 117h 128c
8 br g Definite Article Native Design (IRE) (Be My Native (USA))
181[3]

Cloudgazer (IRE) *Giles Bravery* 119h
6 b g Dalakhani(IRE) City Zone (IRE) (Zafonic (USA))
1402[6]

Cloudingstar (IRE) *Jonjo O'Neill* 106h 113c
7 gr g Cloudings(IRE) Different Dee (IRE) (Beau Sher)
2284[5] 2771[4] 3413[3] 4108[3] **4451[5] (4840)**
4948[3] 5497[3]

Clouds Of Mist *Sue Gardner* 104h
9 b m Cloudings(IRE) Island Mist (Jupiter Island)
177[9] (511) 595[2] 4176[P] 4516[5] 5033[6]

Cloudy Bob (IRE) *Pat Murphy* 125h 131c
7 gr g Cloudings(IRE) Keen Supreme (IRE) (Bob Back (USA))
182[P] 1745[10] 1867[3] 2230[3] (2625) 3028[3] **3769[3]**
4244[3] 4806[3] 5385[9]

Cloudy Dawn *Sue Smith* 59h 80c
9 gr g Cloudings(IRE) Persistent Gunner (Gunner B)
172[7] 580[7] 802[2] 1038[6] 1300[4] 1376[3] 2047[3] 2423[3]
2735[6] 3925[2] 4071[P] 4383[P]

Cloudy Deal (IRE) *Martin Todhunter* 90h
7 b g Cloudings(IRE) Native Gift (IRE) (Be My Native (USA))
1850[7] 2156[7] 2453[4] ◆ 3210[5] 3428[P]
5355[P]

Cloudy Joker (IRE) *Donald McCain* 105h 132c
6 gr g Cloudings(IRE) Rosa View (IRE) (Roselier (FR))
962[3] 1145[4] 1418[4] 1500[2] 1714[2]
(2308) (3155)
(3833) 4507[2] 4941[4]

Cloudy Lady *Caroline Keevil* 62h
6 gr m Alflora(IRE) Cirrious (Cloudings (IRE))
715[4] 1695[5]

Cloudy Smith *Brian Eckley*
5 b m Cloudings(IRE) Poppy Smith (Busy Flight)
4411[9] 5229[8] 5427[P]

Cloudy Spirit *Andrew Hollinshead* 134h 110c
9 gr m Silver Patriarch(IRE) Miss Lacroix (Picea)
1195[10]
2719[2] 3327[F] 4090[7]

Cloudy Start *Violet M Jordan* 86h
8 b g Oasis Dream Set Fair (USA) (Alleged (USA))
758[7] 857[8] 927[10] 1259[9] 1406[P]

Cloudy Too (IRE) *Sue Smith* 134h 161c
8 b g Cloudings(IRE) Curra Citizen (IRE) (Phardante (FR))
(2244)
2815[12] (3285)
4265[2] 4787[U] 5383[6]

Cloverhill Lad (IRE) *Stuart Coltherd* 111h 111c
10 b g New Frontier(IRE) Flat Dutch (IRE) (Le Bavard (FR))
26[4] (314)
533[2] 627[3] (3020)
3213[3] 3395[U] (3524)
4341[2] 4477[F] 4628[2] 4815[F]

Clovers Boy *Sue Gardner* 71b
9 b g First Trump Persian Clover (Abutammam)
3697[11] 4029[P]

Clubs Are Trumps (IRE) *Jonjo O'Neill* 88h
5 b g Flemensfirth(USA) Pairtree (Double Trigger (IRE))
2354[4] 2695[9] 3061[10] 3278[8]

Clues And Arrows (IRE) *Jonjo O'Neill* 120h
6 b g Clerkenwell(USA) Ballela Girl (IRE) (Mandalus)
2444[5] 2933[5] 3144[9] 3415[6] 3856[3] 5069[5] (5523)

Clyffe Dancer *Emma Lavelle* 42b
6 b m Grape Tree Road Chandni (IRE) (Ahonoora)
2298[14] 3282[6]

Cmana (CZE) *V Luka Jr*
9 b g Magnus(POL) Cigyra (CZE) (Lancelot (CZE))
1904a[8]

Cnoc Moy (IRE) *Helen Rees* 69h
10 b g Mull Of Kintyre(USA) Ewar Sunrise (Shavian)
293[P] 635[8] 5143[11]

Cnoc Seoda (IRE) *Paul Henderson* 105h 120c
9 b m Dr Massini(IRE) Hill Diamond (IRE) (Acceglio)
1745[9]
2754[4] 3321[3] 3743[P] 4133[3] 5119[3]

Coax *Patrick Holmes* 88h 109c
6 b g Red Ransom(USA) True Glory (IRE) (In The Wings)
2356[4] (3143)
3517[2]

Cobajayisland (IRE) *Lucinda Russell* 103h
6 b g Heron Island(IRE) Shinora (IRE) (Black Minstrel)
584[3] 1662[3] 5508[5]

Cocacobana (IRE) *Graeme McPherson* 118h 114c
9 ch g Snurge Dun Dun (IRE) (Saddlers' Hall (IRE))
2020[3]
2508[5] 3131[3] 3662[3]

Coccinnelle (FR) *Ferdy Murphy* 74b
6 b m Caballo Raptor(CAN) Pierrebrune (FR) (Cadoudal (FR))
699[10] 754[6]

Cochinillo (IRE) *Ben Case*
5 b g Shantou(USA) Nut Touluze (IRE) (Toulon)
4016[6]

Cock And Hen (IRE) *Jonjo O'Neill* 125c
8 b g Flemensfirth(USA) Jodi (IRE) (Phardante (FR))
586[2] 963[P]

Cockney Class (USA) *Dave Roberts* 93h
7 rg g Speightstown(USA) Snappy Little Cat (USA) (Tactical Cat (USA))
848[5]

Cockney Lacey *Lucinda Russell* 75h
5 b g Prince Daniel(USA) Turtle Bay (Dr Fong (USA))
1854[6] 2420[6]

Cockney Sparrow *John Quinn* 153h
5 b m Cockney Rebel(IRE) Compose (Anabaa (USA))
(2226) 2821[2] 3895[F] 4740[5] (5274)

Cockney Trucker (IRE) *Philip Hobbs* 137h 146c
12 b g Presenting Kiltiernan Easter (IRE) (Broken Hearted)
356[9] 780[5] 1195[8] 1660[9]

Cocktails At Dawn *Nicky Henderson* 133h
6 b g Fair Mix(IRE) Fond Farewell (IRE) (Phardante (FR))
3070[3] 4750[11] (5345) 5429[2]

Cocoa Key (IRE) *Richard Ford* 100h 100c
10 br g Key Of Luck(USA) Renvyle Rose (IRE) (Rainbows For Life (CAN))
20[2] 183[4] 1039[P] 1086[5] 1548[9]

Coco Shambhala *Oliver Sherwood* 115b
6 b m Indian Danehill(IRE) Kohinor (Supreme Leader)
1771[3] 4916[3] 5374[2]

Codoor (GER) *Charlie Longsdon* 109h
7 b g Sabiango(GER) Codera (GER) (Zilzal (USA))
1840[3] ◆

Cody Wyoming *Heather Main* 115h 110c
8 b g Passing Glance Tenderfoot (Be My Chief (USA))
2437[3] 4560[F] 4723[P] 5342[P]

Coeur De Fou (FR) *Tom George* 106h 115c
9 ch g Limnos(JPN) Folly Lady (FR) (Saint Estephe (FR))
90[2] 377[4] 5555[2]

Coffee (IRE) *Jonjo O'Neill* 136h
7 bb g Beneficial Boro Cruise (IRE) (Accordion)
(202) (673) 1046[2] 5420a[P]

Coffers *Renee Robeson* 60h
4 ch g Bahamian Bounty Fabuleux Millie (IRE) (Noverre (USA))
2436[7] 2975[10]

Cogry *Nigel Twiston-Davies* 122h
5 b g King's Theatre(IRE) Wyldello (Supreme Leader)
(2053) 2534[6] 3189[3] (3816) (4397) 4786[8] 5157[F]

Coinage (IRE) *Tony Coyle* 99b
5 b g Westerner Sovereign Star (IRE) (Taufan (USA))
3002[4] 3282[2]

Coin Of The Realm (IRE) *S Flook* 98h 108c
9 b g Galileo(IRE) Common Knowledge (Rainbow Quest (USA))
13[3]

Coin River (IRE) *Bob Buckler* 52h
8 b g Beneficial Holly Lake (IRE) (Aylesfield)
459[P] 2628[8] 3009[P]

Cokydal (FR) *G Cherel* 107h 124c
9 b g Cadoudal(FR) Dominatrice (FR) (Dom Pasquini (FR))
1984a[P] 2415a[3]

Colbert Station (IRE) *T M Walsh* 117h 159c
10 b g Witness Box(USA) Laurenca's Girl (IRE) (Commanche Run)
2708a[3] 5171[P]

Cold Mountain (IRE) *Paul Blagg* 86h 76c
12 b g Inchinor Streak Of Silver (USA) (Dynaformer (USA))
62[17]

Coldstonesober (IRE) *J R Finn* 121h 118c
8 ch g Great Palm(USA) You Can Dance (IRE) (King's Theatre (IRE))
4709a[P]

Colebrooke *Dan Skelton* 122h 130c
6 b g Shamardal(USA) Shimna (Mr Prospector (USA))
2087[P]
(2539) 3097[7] 3853[P] 4105[4] 4423[6] 4933[17] 5521[3]

Cole Harden (IRE) *Warren Greatrex* 152h
5 b g Westerner Nosie Betty (IRE) (Alphabatim (USA))
(1427) 2018[4] (2536) ◆ (3716) 4261[2] 4750[7] 5157[2]

Colin's Brother *Nigel Twiston-Davies* 105b
4 b g Overbury(IRE) Dd's Glenalla (IRE) (Be My Native (USA))
3460[6] 4424[2] 4728[2]

Colin's Nightmare *Nick Mitchell* 73h
6 b m Wared(USA) Sarah's Destiny (Riverwise (USA))
85[7] 292[8] 519[5] 631[12] 5393[10]

Colleen Bawn (FR) *Dan Skelton* 87h
4 b f Cockney Rebel(IRE) Compose (Anabaa (USA))
3385[5] 3613[3]

Collingbourneducis (IRE) *Michael Gates* 88h
4 b g Bahamian Bounty Quickstyx (Night Shift (USA))
2294[5] 3134[P] 3796[6] 4247[4] 4724[5] 5242[17]

Collingwood (FR) *Philip Hobbs* 93h
8 b g Ocean Of Wisdom(USA) Libera (Turtle Island (IRE))
732[5] 856[8]

Collyns Avenue *Tristan Davidson* 48h 68c
11 ch g Bal Harbour Flower Of Dunblane (Ardross)
4551[7]

Colonel Iain *John Ferguson* 122c
8 gr g Alflora(IRE) Cheeky Mare (Derrylin)
3011[4] 3450[3] 4946[2]

Colonial Style (IRE) *George Moore* 12b
4 b g Gamut(IRE) The Dukes Pert (IRE) (Revoque (IRE))
4944[8] 5500[10]

Colorado Seven (FR) *J-L Gay* 117h 119c
7 b g Laveron Ronquerolles (FR) (Comrade In Arms)
1984a[P]

Colour Squadron (IRE) *Philip Hobbs* 148h 153c
8 b g Old Vic That's The Goose (IRE) (Be My Native (USA))
2503[2] ◆ 3082[3] 4768[2]

Combustible Kate (IRE) *Nick Kent* 98h
8 b m Mr Combustible(IRE) Aussie Hope (Gran Alba (USA))
564[6] 750[U] 1121[10] 1205[4] 1284[4] 1468[4] 3265[6]

Combustible Lady (IRE) *Seamus Mullins* 102h
9 b m Mr Combustible(IRE) Ladyogan (IRE) (Torus)
2029[4] ◆ 2477[7]

Comealong Cornwall *M J Wall* 21c
12 b m Kayf Tara Batease (Quiet Fling (USA))
4246[7]

Comeback Colin *Sue Smith* 116h
6 b g Beat Hollow Queen G (USA) (Matty G (USA))
2049[3] 2393[3] 3922[2] ◆

Comedinewithme *Jamie Snowden* 109h
6 b m Milan Skipcarl (IRE) (Carlingford Castle)
1318[5] 2579[2] 3247[2] 3840[3]

Comedy House *Michael Madgwick* 89h
6 b g Auction House(USA) Kyle Akin (Vettori (IRE))
307[4] 809[7] 2729[6] 3007[8] 5459[4]

Comehomequietly (IRE) *David Rees* 117h 134c
10 b g King's Theatre(IRE) Windswept Lady (IRE) (Strong Gale)
1268[7] 1345[8] 1551[7]

Come On Annie *Alexandra Dunn* 118h 95c
8 b m Karinga Bay Irish Ferry (Overbury (IRE))
3012[3] (3428) (3959) 4090[8] **4919[8] 5176[P]**

Comeonginger (IRE) *Chris Gordon* 114h 111c
7 b g King's Theatre(IRE) Miss Poutine (FR) (Chamberlin (FR))
38[5] **2024[5]**
2662[4] 3293[P] 4399[5] 4884[4] (5263)

Come On Harriet *Alex Hales* 92b
5 b m Kayf Tara Royal Musical (Royal Abjar (USA))
4867[5] 5440[7]

Come On Laurie (IRE) *Lawney Hill* 123h
6 b g Oscar(IRE) Megan's Magic (Blue Ocean (USA))
2570[3] 2868[2] 3278[2] 3816[3]

Comeragh King *Tim Fitzgerald* 72h 111c
10 b g Kayf Tara Velcro Girl (IRE) (Be My Native (USA))
566[F] 1205[P]

Comical Red *Mark Gillard* 97h
6 ch g Sulamani(IRE) Sellette (IRE) (Selkirk (USA))
407[P] 829[17] **1053[P]** 3174[6] 3699[6] 3955[2] (4330)
4516[2] 4729[3] 5007[10]

Commander Kev (IRE) *Mrs K Hobbs* 76h 59c
13 b g Needle Gun(IRE) Grange Park (IRE) (Warcraft (USA))
5346[10]

Commerce *Dai Burchell* 85h
7 b m Trade Fair Well Away (IRE) (Sadler's Wells (USA))
49[10]

Commissioned (IRE) *John Ferguson* 135h
4 b g Authorized(IRE) Zelda (IRE) (Caerleon (USA))
3078[3] ◆ 4419[2] ◆ 5132[4]

Commitment *Neil Mulholland* 112h
5 b g Motivator Courting (Pursuit Of Love)
479[4] 777[3] 1945[4] 2430[3]

Communicator *Andrew Balding* 128h
6 b g Motivator Goodie Twosues (Fraam)
3163[2]

Compassion *Emma Lavelle* 53h
6 b m Tiger Hill(IRE) Windmill (Ezzoud (IRE))
456[P]

Competitive Edge (IRE) *Conor O'Dwyer* 127h 149c
7 b g Presenting Sanghasta (IRE) (Un Desperado (FR))
3806a[2] 4790[F]

Complexity *Seamus Mullins* 73h
4 b g Multiplex Asinara (GER) (Big Shuffle (USA))
1473[4] 1624[4] 1855[6] 1985[P] 2276[5]

Complicated (FR) *J-Y Artu* 111h 125c
6 b g Anabaa Blue What Cheeky (FR) (Cadoudal (FR))
5530a[4]

Compton Blue *Alan King* 119h
8 b g Compton Place Blue Goddess (IRE) (Blues Traveller (IRE))
604[4] (902) 1123[4] 1498[2]
2107[F] 2625[6]

Comte D'Anjou *Nick Williams* 109h
5 b g Desert King(IRE) Delayed (FR) (Fijar Tango (FR))
1869[7] 2947[6] 4024[6] 4664[4] 5034[2]

Conellie *Rebecca Curtis* 125h
8 ch g Hernando(FR) Superstore (USA) (Blushing Groom (FR))
(782) 877[5]

Coney Choice (IRE) *John F O'Neill* 86h 65c
6 br g Strategic Choice(USA) Coney Ficial (IRE) (Beneficial)
878[P]

Con Forza (IRE) *Warren Greatrex* 107b
5 b g Milan Classic Track (Distant Music (USA))
3098[5] 3926[3] 5042[6]

Conigre *Ali Brewer* 99h 20c
7 b g Selkirk(USA) Mystify (Batshoof)
253[4] ◆ **459[3]** 651[10] 708[P] 2862[5] 3265[P]

Conjola *Geoffrey Harker* 61h
7 b m Grape Tree Road Conchita (St Ninian)
2752[3] 3042[9] 3529[2] 4083[4] 4776[9]

Connectivity (IRE) *Dr Richard Newland* 134h 123c
10 b g Flemensfirth(USA) Garden Town (IRE) (Un Desperado (FR))
358[8] **586[3]**
(1669)
1971[F] 2177[7] (2428) 2746[3]

Conn Man (IRE) *Geoffrey Deacon* 74h
9 ch g Whitmore's Conn(USA) Special Artist (IRE) (Rock Hopper)
241[4]

Conquering Spirit *David Evans* 9b
6 b g Beat All(USA) Malay (Karinga Bay)
2724[11]

Conquisto *Steve Gollings* 141h 156c
9 ch g Hernando(FR) Seal Indigo (IRE) (Glenstal (USA))
217[2] (2071)
2503[14] 3032[7] 3894[5] 5535[5]

Consigliere (FR) *David Pipe* 114h 147c
11 ch g Trempolino(USA) Gianna Nannini (ITY) (Fire Of Life (USA))
2212[7] 2488[14] 2816[6] 3197[6] 3923[2] 4430[2] (4675)

Consulate (IRE) *Gordon Edwards* 108h
10 b g Rock Of Gibraltar(IRE) Soha (USA) (Dancing Brave (USA))
3043[P]

Converti *Carroll Gray* 63h 52c
10 b g Averti(IRE) Conquestadora (Hernando (FR))
4447[3] 4803[8] 5234[11]

Cool Baranca (GER) *Dianne Sayer* 117h
8 b m Beat Hollow Cool Storm (IRE) (Rainbow Quest (USA))
563[3] 681[9] 870[3] (1665) 1689[2] 2069[7] 2221[4]
2970[6] 3212[8] 3398[8] 4463[4] 5212[8] 5512[5]

Coolbeg (IRE) *Heather Main* 101h 110c
8 b g Oscar(IRE) Dianeme (Primo Dominie)
2629[F] 2895[5] 3960[3] 4660[4]

Cool Bob (IRE) *Matt Sheppard* 78h 100c
11 b g Bob Back(USA) Rosie Jaques (Doyoun)
2470[10] 3188[7] **3730[5] 4656[2]** 5022[4]

Cool Cascade *Lawney Hill* 84h 87c
8 b m Alderbrook Miss Pout (Kris)
541[P] 2743[RR]

Cool Chief *Alan Blackmore* 28h
5 b g Sleeping Indian Be Bop Aloha (Most Welcome)
309[6] 4569[11] 5445[P]

Cooldine Run (IRE) *John Needham* 102h 103c
10 br g Shernazar Run A Fairy (IRE) (King's Ride)
2877[7] 3227[7] **3564[3] (3837)**
4080[4] 4352[6]

Coole Abbey Major (IRE) *Robert J Evans*
10 b g Marignan(USA) Coole Tide (IRE) (Rising)
5041[F]

Coole Murphy (IRE) *Mrs Clare Moore*
10 b g Humbel(USA) Coole Jasmine (IRE) (Good Thyne (USA))
5209[P]

Coole River (IRE) *Emma Lavelle* 144h 133c
10 ch g Carroll House Kyle Cailin (Over The River (FR))
81[2] 587[10] 2107[F] (2475)
2931[3] 5092[8] 5344[5]

Cool Fantasy (IRE) *Caroline Keevil* 83h 6c
5 b g One Cool Cat(USA) Regal Fantasy (IRE) (King's Theatre (IRE))
517[10] 631[P] 1191[6] 1270[12] 1643[10] 2083[6] 2568[9]
4884[11] 5113[P]

Cool Friend (IRE) *Oliver Greenall* 111h 117c
11 b m Anshan Glacial Friend (IRE) (Glacial Storm (USA))
63[5] 4355[6] 5135[14]

Cool George *Jackie Du Plessis* 119h
6 b g Pastoral Pursuits Magic Valentine (Magic Ring (IRE))
2279[U] 2457[4] 3169[4] 3695[2] 4391[3] 5015[3] 5389[2]

Cool Hand Luke (IRE) *Ian Williams* 107h
5 br g Le Vie Dei Colori Thelma Louise (IRE) (Desert Style (IRE))
592[2]

Coolking *Lawney Hill* 115h 122c
7 b g King's Theatre(IRE) Osocool (Teenoso (USA))
566[9] 3004[4] 3990[4] 4601[2]

Cool Macavity (IRE) *Nicky Henderson* 137h
6 b g One Cool Cat(USA) Cause Celebre (IRE) (Peintre Celebre (USA))
(69) 354[3] (843) (1183) 1350[4] 1987[4]

Cool Mission (IRE) *Donald McCain* 86h 86c
10 ch g Definite Article Mettlesome (Lomond (USA))
357[4] 535[6] 766[P]

Cool Sky *Donald McCain* 115h
5 b g Millkom Intersky High (USA) (Royal Anthem (USA))
1399[4] 3144[3] *4023[3]* ◆ (4463) 4813[3] 5496[8]

Cool Steel (IRE) *David Brace* 100b
8 br g Craigsteel Coolafinka (IRE) (Strong Statement (USA))
5545[P]

Coombe Hill *Mrs C Fear* 123c
13 b g Prince Daniel(USA) Betty Ann Pit VII (Damsire Unregistered)
59[4] 660[P] 3993[3] (5131)

Coosan Belle (IRE) *John Joseph Hanlon* 105h
8 b m Definite Article Princess Of Zurich (IRE) (Law Society (USA))
1529[5]

Cootamundra (IRE) *J A Berry* 140h 141c
11 ch g Broken Hearted Sigginstown (Kambalda)
1702a[2] (2708a)
3868a[5] 4315a[4]

Cootehill (IRE) *Nigel Twiston-Davies* 124h 133c
10 b g Alflora(IRE) Dancing Dove (IRE) (Denel (FR))
11[3] 672[5] 1397[3] 1815[5] 2468[3] 2889[2] 3158[3] 4089[3]
4509[P]

Coozan George *Malcolm Jefferson* 108b
5 b g Bollin Eric Pasja (IRE) (Posen (USA))
2347[5] (3522) 4226[3]

Copper Birch (IRE) *Evan Williams* 126h 118c
6 ch g Beneficial Givehertime (IRE) (Commanche Run)
2147[4] 2529[16] **3155[4]** (4029) 4272[P]

Copper Carroll (IRE) *Beth Roberts* 84h
10 b m Carroll House Edermine Sunset (IRE) (Red Sunset)
640[3] 860[13] 1364[11]

Copper's Gold (IRE) *R A Owen* 33b
10 b g Presenting West Hill Rose (IRE) (Roselier (FR))
172[P] 4079[P]

Copt Hill *Tracy Waggott* 91h
6 b g Avonbridge Lalique (IRE) (Lahib (USA))
283[6] 3723[5] 3830[2] 4836[2] 4943[4] 5163[2] 5360[4]

Coquet Head *James Walton* 97h 82c
8 br g Alflora(IRE) Coquet Gold (Rambling River)
2156[8]

Coral Point (IRE) *B Dowling* 69h 79c
8 ch g Hawkeye(IRE) Green Crystal (Green Dancer (USA))
165[2]

Corkage (IRE) *Keith Reveley* 126h 141c
11 b g Second Empire(IRE) Maslam (IRE) (Robellino (USA))
247 2428[3] **2785[10]** 3085[2] 3387[3]

Corky Dancer *Andrew Parker* 92h
9 b g Groom Dancer(USA) Cita Verda (FR) (Take Risks (FR))
17[4] (221) 628[2]

Cornas (NZ) *Nick Williams* 79h 117c
12 b g Prized(USA) Duvessa (NZ) (Sound Reason (CAN))
838a[P] 1583a[5] 2081[4] ◆ **2925[7]**

Cornish Ice *Robin Dickin* 112h 109c
10 b g Dolpour(IRE) Icelandic Poppy (Oats)
1925[4] 2179[2] 2582[2] 2979[5] 3176[3] 3696[4] 4678[P]
4905[6]

Coronea Lilly (IRE) *Neil Mulholland* 121h
10 ch m Busy Flight Aoife's Joy (IRE) (Electric)
811[9] 1205[2] 1284[2] (1468) 1818[5] 1989[4] 5010[8]
5372[13]

Corrin Wood (IRE) *Donald McCain* 131h 159c
7 gr g Garuda(IRE) Allstar Rose (IRE) (Fourstars Allstar (USA))
(2622)
(3146) (3651)
4751[10]

Corsair Prince *Keith Reveley* 86b
4 b g Black Sam Bellamy(IRE) Nobratinetta (FR) (Celtic Swing)
4611[3]

Corso Palladio (IRE) *Peter Bowen* 106h 84c
12 b g Montjeu(IRE) Falafil (FR) (Fabulous Dancer (USA))
1136[3] 1673[6] 1768[3]

Cossack Prince *Laura Mongan* 106h 81c
9 b g Dubai Destination(USA) Danemere (IRE) (Danehill (USA))
425[5] 1274[5] 1765[P]

Cosway Spirit (IRE) *Ben Pauling* 83h 106c
7 ch g Shantou(USA) Annalisa (IRE) (Rhoman Rule (USA))
4484[4] (4778)
(5011) ◆ **5546[6]**

Cottage Acre (IRE) *Colin Heard* 76h 99c
11 b g Shernazar Quits (IRE) (Brief Truce (USA))
40[4] 689[P] 844[10] 1641[3] 1829[4]

Cottage Oak (IRE) *J J O'Shea* 104h 137c
11 ch g Flemensfirth(USA) Native Thistle (IRE) (Ovac (ITY))
5135[5]

Cottam Maybel *Michael Easterby* 43h
5 b m Doyen(IRE) Northern Bird (Interrex (CAN))
3448[6] 3757[8] 3920[7]

Cottenwood (IRE) *Nicky Richards* 96b
6 br g Tillerman Chavi (JPN) (Carnegie (IRE))
4370[3]

Cottesmore (USA) *John Ferguson* 80h
5 b g Medaglia d'Oro(USA) Racing Heart (USA) (Fusaichi Pegasus (USA))
2904 593[9]

Cottiers Den (IRE) *Martin Todhunter* 88c
7 b g Snurge Silvretta (IRE) (Tirol)
2747[4] 3022[P] 3283[F] 3936[P] 4082[4] 4630[3]

Cotton Mill *John Ferguson* 152h
7 b g Tiger Hill(IRE) Mill Line (Mill Reef (USA))
2372[4] 2821[4] 4752[18] 5274[P]

Couldhavehaditall (IRE) *Paul Webber* 118h
6 b g Milan Night Leader (IRE) (Supreme Leader)
2215[4] 2718[11] *4300[12]* 4808[F] 4903[5] 5408[2]

Couloir Extreme (IRE) *Gary Moore* 64h
4 gr g Verglas(IRE) Chica Roca (USA) (Woodman (USA))
1684[7] 2577[7] 3003[11]

Counsel (IRE) *Donald McCain* 137h
5 b g Dansili Kitty O'Shea (Sadler's Wells (USA))
344[F]

Count Danilo (IRE) *David Pipe* 125h
5 b g Zagreb(USA) Miss Bobby Bennett (Kings Lake (USA))
2534[11] (3148) 4901[F] 5110[F]

Countersign *Charles Pogson* 105b
5 b g Authorized(IRE) Circle Of Love (Sakhee (USA))
790[6] 1826[2] 2052[2] (5454)

Countess Comet (IRE) *Chris Bealby* 117h 113c
7 b m Medicean Countess Sybil (IRE) (Dr Devious (IRE))
120[5]

Count Guido Deiro (IRE) *Nigel Twiston-Davies* 113h 131c
7 b g Accordion Ivy Lane (IRE) (Be My Native (USA))
2662[U] (3293)
4162[2] 4835[7]

Counting House (IRE) *Jim Old* 130h 122c
11 ch g King's Best(USA) Inforapenny (Deploy)
2459[4] 2941[4] 4402[6] 4914[5] 5406[5]

Countrywide City (IRE) *Sarah Robinson*
8 b g Elusive City(USA) Handy Station (IRE) (Desert Style (IRE))
631[P]

Count Vettori (IRE) *Kevin Bishop* 80h
8 br g Vettori(IRE) Alifandango (IRE) (Alzao (USA))
2458[10] 3699[8] 3955[P]

County Zen (FR) *Caroline Fryer* 97h 82c
11 bb g Lost World(IRE) Fair County (FR) (Armos)
161[2] 445[3] 3149[9] 3468[2] 3852[P] 4247[5] 4791[7]
5434[5]

Coup De Grace (IRE) *Pat Phelan* 109h
5 b g Elusive City(USA) No Way (IRE) (Rainbows For Life (CAN))
2004[4] 2210[2] 3195[4] 4132[3] 4801[2]

Coup Royale (FR) *Mrs Claire Hitch* 82h 97c
10 b g Balleroy(USA) Coup De Rouge (FR) (Quart De Vin (FR))
4518[4] 4915[9] 5292[P]

Courageous (IRE) *Milton Bradley*
8 ch g Refuse To Bend(IRE) Bella Bella (IRE) (Sri Pekan (USA))
1525[P]

Court Appeal (IRE) *Charlie Longsdon* 16h
7 b g Court Cave(IRE) Lady Braid (IRE) (Riverhead (USA))
1838[F] 2536[6] 3023[F]
3279[P]

Court By Surprise (IRE) *Emma Lavelle* 125h 135c
9 b g Beneficial Garryduff Princess (IRE) (Husyan (USA))
1868[3] 2373[3] 2953[2] 4544[6] 5068[5]

Courtesy Call (IRE) *Nicky Henderson* 119h
5 br g Manduro(GER) Three Wrens (IRE) (Second Empire (IRE))
(80)

Court In Session (IRE) *Martin Keighley* 109h 115c
9 b g Court Cave(IRE) Dangerous Dolly (IRE) (Jurado (USA))
236[8] 900[6] 1597[P]
1780[4] 1972[10] 2292[3] 2529[18]

Courtly Conduct (IRE) *W M Roper* 127h
9 b g Court Cave(IRE) Regency Charm (IRE) (Prince Regent (FR))
2206a[5]

Court Minstrel (IRE) *Evan Williams* 154h
7 b g Court Cave(IRE) Theatral (Orchestra)
2213[8] 2533[7] 3083[4] (5172) ◆ 5274[2]

Courtncatcher (IRE) *Patrick J Duffy* 134h
7 b g Catcher In The Rye(IRE) Tapneiram (IRE) (Kahyasi)
2256a[3]

Courtown Oscar (IRE) *Philip Kirby* 78h
5 b g Oscar(IRE) Courtown Bowe VII (Damsire Unregistered)
2420[5]

Court Red (IRE) *John Wade* 68h
8 b g Court Cave(IRE) An Bonnan Bui (IRE) (Riverhead (USA))
1870[U]

Court Red Handed (IRE) *Mrs S Case* 107h 120c
9 ch g Flemensfirth(USA) Desert Gail (IRE) (Desert Style (IRE))
4655[2] 5135[6]

Court Victory (IRE) *Emma Lavelle* 115c
9 b g Old Vic Sarah's Smile (Callernish)
3651[3] 4134[P]

Cousinade (FR) *Mrs Kim Thomas* 52c
7 b g Protektor(GER) Carmen Tonic (FR) (Double Bed (FR))
523[6]

Cousin Guillaume (FR) *James Ewart* 90h
5 bb g Kapgarde(FR) Tante Zoe (FR) (Danzero (AUS))
1792[3] 2052[3] 2871[2] 3522[2] 4956[5] 5206[7]

Cove (IRE) *Nick Gifford* 107h
7 b m Westerner Phillis Hill (Karinga Bay)
3689[3] 4715[2] (4797) 5010[2] 5351[10]

Coverholder (IRE) *Sue Smith* 119h 143c
7 b g Oscar(IRE) Lasado (IRE) (Jurado (USA))
1922[9] 2032[2] **(2446)**
(2969) 3362[P] 3777[2] 4041[P]

Cowards Close (IRE) *Paul Nicholls* 129h 136c
7 br g Presenting Parsee (IRE) (Persian Mews)
(163) 3387[7]
4541[2] (5525)

Cowbridge (IRE) *Peter Pritchard* 58h
8 b g Pilsudski(IRE) Clyde Goddess (IRE) (Scottish Reel)
122[P] 590[14] 2723[6] 2827[P]

Coyaba *Martin Keighley* 111b
4 b g Midnight Legend Peel Me A Grape (Gunner B)
(2391) (2830) 3460[8] 4756[16]

Crabbie's Cloudy (IRE) *Donald McCain* 90h
7 b g Cloudings(IRE) Santavino (IRE) (Be My Native (USA))
223[4]

Crack At Dawn (IRE) *Michael Gates* 73h 98c
13 bb g Insan(USA) Ten Quid Short (IRE) (Colonel Godfrey (USA))
34[3] 264[7]
(418) 694[5] 805[5] 976[2] 1172[9] (1314)
1547[2] 1638[P] 1835[P]

Crackerjack *Emma Baker* 92h
7 ch g Lahib(USA) Tidesong (Top Ville)
2770[5] 3047[3] ◆ *4298[7]* 4519[3] 4911[9] 5522[U]

Crackerjack Lad (IRE) *Lucinda Russell* 78h 74c
11 br g Exit To Nowhere(USA) Crowther Homes (Neltino)
314[4] 2338[5] 3020[P] 5051[4]

Crafty Roberto *Alex Hales* 120h
6 ch g Intikhab(USA) Mowazana (IRE) (Galileo (IRE))
202[2] 2366[7]

Craicneasy (IRE) *Bruce Mactaggart* 58h 73c
11 br g Anshan Craic Go Leor (Deep Run)
23[5] 172[P] 493[5] 753[P]

Craiganee (IRE) *Chris Down* 100b
7 b g Craigsteel Hows She Going (IRE) (Strong Statement (USA))
345[2] 1974[10]

Craiglands (IRE) *Ian Williams* 71h 87c
12 b g Dushyantor(USA) Fernhill (IRE) (Good Thyne (USA))
2980[10]
3439[6] 3879[2] 4354[3] 4663[3] 4778[3] 5293[2] 5433[8]

Crank Hill *Mrs H M Tory* 104h 99c
12 b g Shambo Mariner's Air (Julio Mariner)
62[15]

Cranky Corner *Helen Nelmes* 85h 82c
10 b g Classic Cliche(IRE) Pondimari (FR) (Marignan (USA))
40[6] 3093[P] 3960[P] 4721[8] 5304[P]

Crannaghmore Boy (IRE) *Jim Best* 96h 102c
9 b g Pilsudski(IRE) Glencairn Mist (IRE) (Roselier (FR))
143[2] 542[6] 642[7] 873[4] 942[2] 1103[F] 3139[2]

Crazy (GER) *David Bridgwater* 97h
5 b m Nicaron(GER) Chato's Girl (GER) (Chato (USA))
(1017) 1187[4] 1321[5]

Crazy Bold (GER) *Tony Carroll* 92h
11 ch g Erminius(GER) Crazy Love (GER) (Presto)
253[5] 661[6]

Crazy Chester (IRE) *Michael Easterby* 52h
5 b g Golan(IRE) Nosey Oscar (IRE) (Oscar (IRE))
862[4] 3225[6] 3388[16] 3920[8] 4038[P]

Crazy Jane (IRE) *Tom Gretton* 58h
5 br m Definite Article Blue Romance (IRE) (Bob Back (USA))
3818[4] 4074[6] 4479[8]

Crazy Train *Keiran Burke* 68b
5 ch m Sir Harry Lewis(USA) Vent D'Aout (IRE) (Imp Society (USA))
4017[15] 4499[8] 5528[10]

Creative Boru (IRE) *Rebecca Curtis* 81b
6 b g Brian Boru Ruths Rhapsody (IRE) (Creative Plan (USA))
4492[3]

Creekside *John Ferguson* 116h 125c
6 b g Dubai Destination(USA) Khubza (Green Desert (USA))
119[P] **587[4]**
859[P]

Creepy (IRE) *Martin Keighley* 137h
6 b g Westerner Prowler (IRE) (Old Vic)
(1706) 1968[2] (2505) 3367[U] 3654[5] 3889[5] 4750[14]

Crescent Beach (IRE) *Henry Oliver* 103h 99c
7 b g Presenting Angelas Choice (IRE) (Saddlers' Hall (IRE))
505[6] 648[8] **806[7] 942[6] 1014[F] 1149[3] 1315[3] 1401[3]**
1534[U] (2849)
3595[3] 3876[6]
4243[2]

Cresswell Breeze *Anthony Honeyball* 92b
4 b f Midnight Legend Cresswell Willow (IRE) (Witness Box (USA))
5528[3]

Cridda Boy *Richard Woollacott* 104h
8 ch g Mark Of Esteem(IRE) Second Affair (IRE) (Pursuit Of Love)
3420[12] 5118[P]

Crinkle Crags (IRE) *Nicky Richards* 96b
4 ch g Trans Island Ashanti Dancer (IRE) (Dancing Dissident (USA))
4902[3]

Crios (FR) *F-X De Chevigny* 122h 122c
7 b g Canyon Creek(IRE) Lespois (Sicyos (USA))
863a[0]

Crispo (IRE) *David Thompson* 68b
6 b g Byron Titania (Fairy King (USA))
885[10] 1420[6]

Croan Rock (IRE) *R A Owen* 111h 107c
9 b g Milan Fiddlers Bar (IRE) (Un Desperado (FR))
58[11] 4042[5] 4348[4] 4788[P] 5287[P]

Croco Bay (IRE) *Peter Atkinson* 124h 138c
7 b g Croco Rouge(IRE) April Thistle (IRE) (Alphabatim (USA))
278[2] (491) 737[P] **2882[5] (3354)**
4235[2] (4530)

Croco Mister (IRE) *Rosemary Gasson* 92c
7 ch g Croco Rouge(IRE) Nimrods Dream (IRE) (Orchestra)
930[4] 1800[2] (2277)
2626[4] 4985[4] 5247[4] 5404[5]

Crofton Lane *John Dixon* 17b
8 b g And Beyond(IRE) Joyful Imp (Import)
5205[F] 5320[U]

Crooked Arrow (IRE) *Marjorie Fife* 93h
6 b g Galileo(IRE) Mythologie (FR) (Bering)
449[7] 1853[6] 1924[9] 3659[7]

Crookstown (IRE) *Ben Case* 115h
7 b g Rudimentary(USA) Millview Lass (IRE) (Jurado (USA))
(880) 2507[8] 2826[7] (3265) 3432[3] 4249[4] (4699)
4888[5] 5521[2]

Cropley (IRE) *Jonjo O'Neill* 95h
5 gr g Galileo(IRE) Niyla (IRE) (Darshaan)
3650[7] 4275[6] 4779[2]

Cross Appeal (IRE) *Noel Meade* 120h 126c
8 b g Cape Cross(IRE) Hadeb (Unfuwain (USA))
2708a[9]

Cross Kennon (IRE) *Jennie Candlish* 146h 86c
10 b g Craigsteel Gaelic Million (IRE) (Strong Gale)
215[3] 1956[8] 2504[4] 3207[8] 4269[4] 4765[10] 5372[7]

Cross Of Honour (IRE) *Charlie Longsdon* 125h 132c
7 ch g Publisher(USA) Threecrossmammies (IRE) (Be My Native (USA))
66[4] 432[P] 591[P]

Crouching Harry (IRE) *Anabel K Murphy* 110h
5 b g Tiger Hill(IRE) Catwalk Dreamer (IRE) (Acatenango (GER))
3736[P]

Crowcombe Park *Kevin Bishop* 24h
6 b m Overbury(IRE) Just Jasmine (Nicholas Bill)
2027[11] 3697[P]

Crowd Control (IRE) *Rebecca Curtis* 86b
5 b g Oscar(IRE) Apollo Lady (Alflora (IRE))
2681[8] 4844[10] 5286[4]

Crow Down (IRE) *Charles Hills* 75b
5 b g Oratorio(IRE) Louve Sereine (FR) (Sadler's Wells (USA))
944[7]

Crown And Glory (IRE) *Karen Tutty* 83h
7 b g Turtle Island(IRE) Monteleena (IRE) (Montelimar (USA))
1854[3] 2037[7] 2838[7] 3270[7]

Crowning Jewel *Keith Reveley* 137h
8 b g Sulamani(IRE) Pennys Pride (IRE) (Pips Pride)
(2102) 2672[6] 4051[3] 4765[15] 5138[16]

Cruachan (IRE) *Lucy Normile* 107h
5 b g Authorized(IRE) Calico Moon (USA) (Seeking The Gold (USA))
313[5] 681[6] (801) 867[8] 1664[3] 2035[5]

Cruchain (IRE) *Dai Burchell* 118h 122c
11 ch g Shernazar Mack Tack (IRE) (Shardari)
175[2] 566[2] 757[4] (1039)
5020[2] 5516[2]

Cru Classe (FR) *F Lagarde* 74h 79c
8 b g Sin Kiang(FR) Champion's Sister (USA) (Spence Bay)
2569[5]

Cruise Control *John Bryan Groucott* 85h
8 b g Piccolo Urban Dancer (IRE) (Generous (IRE))
91[5] 332[3] 561[9] 729[6] 844[F]

Cruise In Luxury (IRE) *Kevin Bishop* 31h
9 ch m Definite Article Galvina (FR) (Northern Fashion (USA))
2312[P] 2628[0]

Cruise In Style (IRE) *Kevin Bishop* 99h 106c
8 b m Definite Article Henrietta Street (IRE) (Royal Academy (USA))
43[2] 585[3] 807[2] 931[8] 1596[3] (1696)
1939[5] 2474[4]
2629[4] 3426[9] 5522[9]

Cruising Bye *Peter Bowen* 94h 100c
8 b g Alflora(IRE) Althrey Flame (IRE) (Torus)
876[2] 1087[2] (1829) 2073[4] 2458[U] 2690[8]
(3129) 3855[5]

Crushed Ice *Malcolm Jefferson* 80h
8 gr g Silver Patriarch(IRE) Altogether Now (IRE) (Step Together I (USA))
91[7] 2680[3] 3334[6] 3525[8]

Cry Of Freedom (USA) *John Ferguson* 132h 117c
8 b g Street Cry(IRE) Tustarta (USA) (Trempolino (USA))
(82) 216[12]
446[2] 594[F] 831[8] 1520[7]

Crystal Swing *Richard Phillips* 109h 115c
7 b g Trade Fair Due West (Inchinor)
2314[15] 2771[3] **3729[F] 4372[P] (4822)**
5076[P] 5520[F]

Ctappers *Michael Madgwick* 73h
5 b g Imperial Dancer Stride Home (Absalom)
2510[12] 4501[P] 5112[11] 5461[P]

Cuckoo Rock (IRE) *Jonathan Portman* 87h
7 b g Refuse To Bend(IRE) Ringmoor Down (Pivotal)
2920[6] 3174[U]

Cucumber Run (IRE) *Nicky Henderson* 145h 139c
9 b g Oscar(IRE) Back To Roost (IRE) (Presenting)
215[16]

Cue Card *Colin Tizzard* 152h 180c
8 b g King's Theatre(IRE) Wicked Crack (IRE) (King's Ride)
2281[3] (2673)
3262[2]

Cumbrian Farmer *George Bewley* 91h
7 ch g Alflora(IRE) Quark Top (FR) (Perrault)
1375[U] 1662[4] 1850[6] 2497[P] (3141) 3525[U] 4475[4]
5556[8]

Cunning Plan (IRE) *Raymond York* 54h
7 ch g Bachelor Duke(USA) Madamaa (IRE) (Alzao (USA))
2912 903[9]

Cup Final (IRE) *Nicky Henderson* 125h
5 ch g Presenting Asian Maze (IRE) (Anshan)
2476[2] ◆ 4421[3] ◆ 4750[10] ◆

Curley Bill (IRE) *Noel Meade* 142h
6 b g Heron Island(IRE) In Excelsis (GER) (Tertullian (USA))
1802a[5]

Curragh Dancer (FR) *Paddy Butler* 83h 65c
11 ch g Grand Lodge(USA) Native Twine (Be My Native (USA))
305[P] 1272[P] 1769[4] 2003[5] 2702[P] 2739[4] 3008[7]
5397[5]

Current Climate (IRE) *Richard Rowe* 96h 100c
10 b g Luso Kambaya (IRE) (Kambalda)
100^6 460^5

Current Event (FR) *Paul Nicholls* 130h 141c
7 b g Muhtathir La Curamalal (IRE) (Rainbow Quest (USA))
157^3 (677)
2065^3 2939^6

Current Exchange (IRE) *Mrs Sheila Crow* 126c
9 ch g Beneficial Musical Millie (IRE) (Orchestra)
4274^2 (4655)
(5323)

Cursum Perficio *John Upson* 98h
12 b g Tagula(IRE) Simply Sooty (Absalom)
429^P

Curtain Razer (IRE) *Chris Gordon* 96h 28c
8 b g Old Vic Echo Creek (IRE) (Strong Gale)
2539^U 2740^5
3006^U 3691^P 4249^2 4801^5
5129^P 5307^8

Curvacious (IRE) *Edward Stanners* 129h 106c
8 ch m Anshan Tarqueen (IRE) (King's Ride)
2986a^6

Curzon Line *John Ferguson* 112h
5 b g Dubawi(IRE) Polska (USA) (Danzig (USA))
1793^2 (2040) 2351^6

Cusheen Bridge (IRE) *Charles Pogson* 99h
6 b h Oscar(IRE) One Hell Ofa Woman (IRE) (Fourstars Allstar (USA))
1919^6 2195^5 2621^5 3115^4 3567^6

Custer Of The West (IRE) *Alan King* 96h
9 ch g Shernazar Karlybelle (FR) (Sandhurst Prince)
295^6

Cute Court (IRE) *Liam Corcoran* 91h
7 b g Court Cave(IRE) Cute Play (Salluceva)
1013^6 1154^5 1552^4 1706^5 2284^4 2680^4

Cut'N'Shut *Zoe Davison* 62b
7 b g Motivator Millennium Dash (Nashwan (USA))
2745^5 3035^6 *4018^{10} 4495^6*

Cut The Cards (IRE) *Jonjo O'Neill* 129h
7 ch g Vinnie Roe(IRE) Mansonienne (FR) (Phantom Breeze)
201^5 691^4 (783) (968) (1093)

Cyclothymique (FR) *J Bigot*
10 b g Victory Note(USA) Ascensionna (FR) (Acteur Francais (USA))
855a^F

Cygnet *Peter Bowen* 82h
8 b g Dansili Ballet Princess (Muhtarram (USA))
2894^7 3130^6 5037^P

Cypress Grove (IRE) *John Ryall* 95h 82c
11 b g Windsor Castle Grecian Queen (Fairy King (USA))
3008^3 3250^3 5240^7

Cyprusormilan *Nikki Evans* 122h
7 b g Milan Persrolla (Persian Bold)
4076^P

Cyrien Star *Henry Daly* 128h
7 b g Bollin Eric Sainte Etoile (FR) (Saint Cyrien (FR))
121^8 (2202) (2655) (3060) 3191^P 3653^9 4415^7 4949^{10}

Cyrus Darius *William Amos* 108b
5 b g Overbury(IRE) Barton Belle (Barathea (IRE))
5499^4

Daasij (IRE) *N W Alexander* 102h 95c
9 b g Dalakhani(IRE) Alyakkh (IRE) (Sadler's Wells (USA))
2218^6
3213^4 3478^P 5321^5

Daddy'Slittlegirl *Claire Dyson* 68h
7 b m Midnight Legend Lochnagold (Lochnager)
269^P 423^8 932^P 1121^P

Dahteste *Mark Bradstock* 90h
6 b m Overbury(IRE) Sunday News'N'Echo (USA) (Trempolino (USA))
250^3 644^4 2675^4 4797^4 5396^5

Daisie Raymond *Charles Smith* 92b
6 br m Kayf Tara Santa Ana (Robellino (USA))
5196^3

Daisy Picker *Noel Williams* 89b
4 b f Piccolo Duly Noted (IRE) (Flemensfirth (USA))
5528^6

Daizy (IRE) *Hilary Parrott* 84h
5 ch g Presenting I Remember It Well (IRE) (Don't Forget Me)
1706^P 1832^8 2040^9 2432^P

Dakar Run *Jonjo O'Neill* 117h
5 gr g Dalakhani(IRE) Turn Of A Century (Halling (USA))
1795^3 2089^2 3877^6

Dalasiri (IRE) *Sabrina J Harty* 135h
5 gr g Dylan Thomas(IRE) Dalataya (IRE) (Sadler's Wells (USA))
683a^8 2377a^3

Dalavar (IRE) *Alan King* 112h
6 b g Dalakhani(IRE) Giant's Way (IRE) (Giant's Causeway (USA))
237^2 643^2

Daliance (IRE) *Neil King* 110h 107c
5 ch g Dalakhani(IRE) Everlasting Love (Pursuit Of Love)
186^2 ◆ 390^2 698^3 1206^2 1913^3 2492^{10} 2755^8 3195^6 3471^3 3871^4 4757^2 4866^3 **4970^3 (5361)**

Dalmo *Dr Richard Newland* 107h
5 b g Dalakhani(IRE) Morina (USA) (Lyphard (USA))
251^9 505^9 4129^8 4760^{11} (5189) (5242) (5360)

Dalrymple (IRE) *Nick Ayliffe* 97h
8 ch g Daylami(IRE) Dallaah (Green Desert (USA))
635^2 1110^6 1711^7 (2679) 2766^2 3426^2 4278^5 4519^6

Dalstontosiloth (IRE) *Barry Murtagh* 93h
6 b g Gamut(IRE) The Boss's Dance (USA) (Sword Dance)
962^4 1292^5 1420^3 2347^6 2823^8 2968^8 3110^4 3871^5 4746^3 5302^P

Damascus Steel (IRE) *Alison Hamilton* 104h
6 gr g Definite Article Diamarouna (FR) (Kouroun (FR))
(218) 2156^6 2970^P 3475^7 4952^4 5375^P

Damby's Star (IRE) *Mark Bradstock* 74b
4 b g Kayf Tara She Took A Tree (FR) (Sri Pekan (USA))
5338^6

Dammam *Fergal O'Brien* 95b 119c
9 b g Josr Algarhoud(IRE) Vanessa Bell (IRE) (Lahib (USA))
62^3 1959^9

Danandy (IRE) *Philip Hobbs* 114h 125c
7 b g Cloudings(IRE) Tower Princess (IRE) (King's Ride)
1052^2 (1118)
1197^8 2041^P (2179) ◆ **2651^F 3004^5 3603^{11}**

Dan Breen (IRE) *David Pipe* 127h 149c
9 b g Mull Of Kintyre(USA) Kunuz (Ela-Mana-Mou)
2212^{12} 2656^4 3066^6 3200^9 4264^P 5399^3

Danby's Legend *Malcolm Jefferson* 92h
7 b g Midnight Legend Miss Danbys (Charmer)
2393^5 2621^{13} 3616^5 3871^{10} 4527^3 4943^6 5360^6

Dance *Rod Millman* 36h
5 b m Erhaab(USA) Shi Shi (Alnasr Alwasheek)
2906^U 5393^8

Dance Floor King (IRE) *Nick Mitchell* 110h
7 b g Generous(IRE) Strawberry Fool (FR) (Tel Quel (FR))
592^3 764^P 2210^{11}

Danceintothelight *Micky Hammond* 106h
7 gr g Dansili Kali (Linamix (FR))
386^P **798^F**
1926^5 2516^6 2844^8 3145^7 3356^6

Dance Tempo *Kim Bailey* 125h 119c
7 b g Dansili Musical Twist (USA) (Woodman (USA))
118^3 431^P

Danceur Bresilien (FR) *Yannick Fouin* 121h 119c
5 b g Irish Wells(FR) Fille Du Bresil (FR) (Smadoun (FR))
1199a^4

Dancing Art (IRE) *Keith Reveley* 90h 123c
8 b g Definite Article Seductive Dance (Groom Dancer (USA))
2512^6 3524^2 4896^P

Dancing Daffodil *Robin Dickin* 97h 92c
9 ch m Kadastrof(FR) Whistling Song (True Song)
1890^5
(2348) 2470^9 4906^6 **5246^P 5546^P**

Dancing Dude (IRE) *Barry Leavy* 120h 94c
7 ch g Danehill Dancer(IRE) Wadud (Nashwan (USA))
4984^5

Dancing Ecco (IRE) *Evan Williams* 75h
5 b g Elnadim(USA) Ecco Mi (IRE) (Priolo (USA))
5227^7 5486^P

Dancing Emily (IRE) *Graeme McPherson* 99h
8 ch m Anshan Goodthyne Lady (IRE) (Good Thyne (USA))
41^2 511^4 932^9

Dancing Lancer *Tim Walford* 64h
5 b g Alhaarth(IRE) Mafatin (IRE) (Sadler's Wells (USA))
1794^{10} 1937^9 2732^9 3192^P

Dancing Royal *Jamie Snowden* 16h
6 ch g Tobougg(IRE) Just Kate (Bob's Return (IRE))
189^3 1749^9

Dancing Shadow (IRE) *Victor Dartnall* 100b
5 br g Craigsteel Be My Shadow (IRE) (Torus)
4177^2 4810^3 5338^3

Dancing Teasel *Emma Lavelle* 63h
7 ch m Snurge Cajole (IRE) (Barathea (IRE))
293^9 460^9

Dancingtilmidnight *Harry Fry* 117h
7 ch m Midnight Legend Solo Dancer (Sayaarr (USA))
4508^P 4907^7

Danebrook Lad (IRE) *Sandy Thomson* 89h
8 b g Indian Danehill(IRE) Lady Brookvale (IRE) (Montelimar (USA))
1875^6 2337^5 2843^6
4771^P

Dane Cottage *Richard Ford* 78h
7 ch m Beat Hollow Lady Soleas (Be My Guest (USA))
253^{10} 506^4 531^3

Danehill Dante (IRE) *Chris Gordon* 80h
6 ch g Danehill Dancer(IRE) En Garde (USA) (Irish River (FR))
758^5 928^5 1206^P 1643^P

Danehills Well (IRE) *Alison Hamilton* 106h
6 b g Indian Danehill(IRE) Collatrim Choice (IRE) (Saddlers' Hall (IRE))
2217^{10} 2493^3 3021^7

Daneking *W P Mullins* 141h
5 b g Dylan Thomas(IRE) Sadie Thompson (IRE) (King's Best (USA))
(5420a) ◆

Daneva (IRE) *Matt Sheppard* 102h 103c
10 b m Turtle Island(IRE) Testaway (IRE) (Commanche Run)
674^3 807^8 (976)
1174^9 1260^{10} 1547^5 2044^8

Daniel's Dream *John Dixon* 63h
14 b g Prince Daniel(USA) Amber Holly (Import)
630^9 752^7 1072^9

Danimix (IRE) *Anthony Honeyball* 122h 140c
9 b g Dr Massini(IRE) Spring Blend (IRE) (Persian Mews)
355^6 851^F 5127^4

Danisa *David Bridgwater* 91h
5 b m Shamardal(USA) Divisa (GER) (Lomitas)
4910^5 5245^7

Dannanceys Hill (IRE) *Donald McCain* 114h 121c
7 b g Revoque(IRE) Some Orchestra (IRE) (Orchestra)
1375^3

Danners (IRE) *Giles Smyly* 121c
8 bb g Old Vic The Great O'Malley (IRE) (Mandalus)
3279^3 3873^6 4148^4 4673^2 5025^2

Dannicourtney (IRE) *J A Nash* 93b
6 b m Definite Article Early Hours (IRE) (Un Desperado (FR))
3126a^6

Danser Encore (FR) *Mlle I Gallorini*
6 b g Dano-Mast Ainsi Soit Je (FR) (Nikos)
455a^P

Dan's Heir *Wilf Storey* 50h 67c
12 b g Dansili Million Heiress (Auction Ring (USA))
2169^{13}
2880^5

Dansili Dutch (IRE) *Andrew Crook* 39h
5 gr m Dutch Art Joyful Leap (Dansili)
391^U 578^5

Dan's Quest *Robin Dickin* 84b
4 b g Kalanisi(IRE) Piedmont (UAE) (Jade Robbery (USA))
2830^8 3719^7 5249^8

Dan's Wee Man *Andy Turnell* 107h
5 b g Kayf Tara Hazel Bank Lass (IRE) (Insan (USA))
4^6 2265^{13} 2924^4 3357^5 5034^4 5391^6

Dantari (IRE) *Evan Williams* 114h 116c
9 b g Alhaarth(IRE) Daniysha (IRE) (Doyoun)
(332) 1092^4 1402^2

Dantes Firth (IRE) *Thomas Foley* 123h
7 b m Flemensfirth(USA) Blue Dante (IRE) (Phardante (FR))
3804a^4

Dante's Frolic *Michael Smith* 104h
6 b m Overbury(IRE) Dusky Dante (IRE) (Phardante (FR))
3398^4 4463^U 4770^4 5212^7

Dantes King (IRE) *Gordon Elliott* 45h 138c
9 b g King's Theatre(IRE) Forecast Rain (IRE) (Phardante (FR))
(869) (956)
1157a^4

Danvilla *Paul Webber* 101h
7 b m Dansili Newtown Villa (Spectrum (IRE))
1689^4 **3171^P**

Danvinnie *Oliver Sherwood* 92b
5 b g Midnight Legend Top Gale (IRE) (Topanoora)
5410^2

Dapper's Dancer *Chris Grant*
5 b m Dapper Party Princess (IRE) (Orpen (USA))
1305^{11}

Darcey Diva *David Pipe* 64h
6 ch m Weld Tamar Lily (Lir)
187^2 567^4 1090^4 1176^F

Dardanella *Richard Lee* 110h
7 b m Alflora(IRE) Ella Falls (IRE) (Dancing Dissident (USA))
715^2 ◆ 841^2 (1056) 1387^5 1885^4 (2697) 3604^3 4508^2 5010^P

Dare Me (IRE) *Venetia Williams* 134h 147c
10 b g Bob Back(USA) Gaye Chatelaine (IRE) (Castle Keep)
217^7 474^2 (3652)
4790^7 5136^7 5535^3

Darenjan (IRE) *John Joseph Hanlon* 125h 133c
11 b g Alhaarth(IRE) Darariyna (IRE) (Shirley Heights)
563^5

Dare To Endeavour *Tom George* 110h 142c
7 b g Alflora(IRE) Miss Chinchilla (Perpendicular)
3189^5 3634^2 **(4110)**
(4395) 4819^P (5557)

D'Argent Cloud *Brian Ellison* 79h
6 gr g Tikkanen(USA) Sounds Familiar (IRE) (Orchestra)
91^6 2827^P 3141^{11} 3353^P

Daring Article (IRE) *Robert Tyner* 135h 137c
8 bb g Definite Article Daring Hen (IRE) (Henbit (USA))
5474a^P

Daring Exit *Robert Bewley* 102b
5 b g Exit To Nowhere(USA) Aberdare (Overbury (IRE))
5108^7

Dark And Dangerous (IRE) *Brendan Powell* 120h 120c
6 b g Cacique(IRE) Gilah (IRE) (Saddlers' Hall (IRE))
176^2 480^7 2461^8 2729^4 3599^9 4129^7 **(4616)**
4965^3 5398^6

Darkan Road *Sandy Forster* 71h 80c
9 bb g Beat All(USA) Sister Seven (IRE) (Henbit (USA))
879^{11}

Dark Caviar (IRE) *George Bewley* 87b
6 b g Indian Danehill(IRE) Whites Cross (IRE) (Lord Americo)
1667^8 1792^6

Dark Desire *Colin Tizzard* 91b
5 br g Generous(IRE) Diletia (Dilum (USA))
2018^P

Dark Dune (IRE) *Tim Easterby* 128h
6 b g Diamond Green(FR) Panpipes (USA) (Woodman (USA))
2783^5 3106^2 3351^2 3616^U (4429) (4939) 5160^3 5353^8

Dark Emerald (IRE) *Brendan Powell* 69h
4 gr g Dark Angel(IRE) Xema (Danehill (USA))
1985^6 2364^4

Dark Energy *Fergal O'Brien* 121h 129c
10 br g Observatory(USA) Waterfowl Creek (IRE) (Be My Guest (USA))
(419) 488^6
830^5 (1050)
(1204) 1302^5 1545^3 1659^5 1663^4 1944^4

Darkestbeforedawn (IRE) *Caroline Keevil* 117h 88c
7 br g Dr Massini(IRE) Camden Dolphin (IRE) (Camden Town)
304^8 **1857^7**
2107^P 2828^6 *4300^{14}* 4599^3 4933^5 (5285) 5520^4

Dark Glacier (IRE) *Peter Bowen* 133h 122c
9 b g Flemensfirth(USA) Glacier Lilly (IRE) (Glacial Storm (USA))
1925^5 2897^2 (3193)
3858^P 4395^4 4914^2 5215^3

Dark Justice (IRE) *Tim Pitt* 57h
4 b f Lawman(FR) Dark Raider (IRE) (Definite Article)
975^F 1271^4

Dark Lover (GER) *Jamie Snowden* 151h 141c
9 b g Zinaad Dark Lady (GER) (Lagunas)
(1973)
2282^F 3715^2 3886^6 4420^4 5446^2

Dark Mix *Pat Phelan*
6 bl g Fair Mix(IRE) Rose Marine (Handsome Sailor)
2439^5

Dark Oasis *Natalie Lloyd-Beavis* 102h 57c
8 b g Dubai Destination(USA) Silent Waters (Polish Precedent (USA))
1274^U 1443^7
1534^4 1598^4 1687^P 1825^4 2044^7

Dark Spirit (IRE) *Evan Williams* 111h
6 b m Whipper(USA) Dark Raider (IRE) (Definite Article)
193^2 1284^5 (1708) (1818)

Darley Sun (IRE) *John Ferguson* 130h
8 b g Tiger Hill(IRE) Sagamartha (Rainbow Quest (USA))
215^9 1195^{11}

Darlington County (IRE) *Donald McCain* 104h
6 b g Oscar(IRE) Laura's Native (IRE) (Be My Native (USA))
1924^{12}
2334^P 4223^P

Darloa (IRE) *Victor Dartnall* 78h
5 br g Darsi(FR) Lady Lola (IRE) (Supreme Leader)
4135^8 5181^{10}

Darnborough (IRE) *Tom Symonds* 74h 84c
8 b g Darnay Princesse Sharpo (USA) (Trempolino (USA))
112^P (602)
707^4 964^3 1149^8 1534^F 1914^4

Darroun (IRE) *Shaun Lycett* 130h 136c
6 gr g Dalakhani(IRE) Darayka (FR) (Dr Fong (USA))
2258a^4 2949^P

Darsi Dancer (IRE) *Stuart Coltherd*
6 b g Darsi(FR) Jaystara (IRE) (Jurado (USA))
5209^P

Dartbridge (IRE) *Mark Gillard*
8 b m Norwich Laurenca's Girl (IRE) (Commanche Run)
633^P 828^P

Dartford Warbler (IRE) *Sue Smith* 127h 119c
7 bb g Overbury(IRE) Stony View (IRE) (Tirol)
1042^7 1304^6 (1378) (1564)
1796^5 2955^5 3354^4 3615^3 4077^3 4549^7 4897^5 5054^4 5272^5

Darwins Fox (FR) *Henry De Bromhead* 140h 142c
8 bb g Kahyasi Parcelle De Sou (FR) (Ajdayt (USA))
(1702a)
1950a^3 5420a^2

Dasaint (FR) *G Macaire* 107h 125c
8 b g Saint Des Saints(FR) Damnation (FR) (Pistolet Bleu (IRE))
(559a)

Dashaway (IRE) *Jeremy Scott* 99b
5 ch g Shantou(USA) Backaway (IRE) (Bob Back (USA))
3133^3 3994^4 5181^5

Dashing Doc (IRE) *Evan Williams* 103h
7 ch g Dr Fong(USA) Dashiba (Dashing Blade)
421^P 691^8 833^{10}

Dashing George (IRE) *Peter Winks* 107h 132c
12 ch g Beneficial Here It Is (Stanford)
3802^5
4106^5 (4250)
4559^6 4593^P 5068^6 5444^3

Daveron (IRE) *Jeremy Scott* 116h
6 b g Winged Love(IRE) Double Doc (IRE) (Moonax (IRE))
3422^4 3686^3 4091^2 ◆ 4538^4 5034^5 (5526)

Dave The Dauphin *Mike Sowersby* 14b
5 b g Alflora(IRE) Ma Jolie (Shalford (IRE))
3147^{10}

David's Folly (IRE) *Tim Vaughan*
5 b m Asian Heights Dolphin Stamp (IRE) (Dolphin Street (FR))
450^F

Davy Doubt (IRE) *David Pipe* 108h
5 b g Kalanisi(IRE) Trompe L'Oeil (IRE) (Distant View (USA))
3994^2 4335^4

Dawalan (FR) *Nicky Henderson* 128h
4 gr g Azamour(IRE) Daltawa (IRE) (Miswaki (USA))
2796^4 (3161) (3714) *4023^2* 4755^{13} 5090^{10}

Dawerann (IRE) *Michael Hourigan* 121h 96c
5 b g Medicean Dawera (IRE) (Spinning World (USA))
1139a^4

Dawn Commander (GER) *Renee Robeson* 139h 125c
7 gr g Mamool(IRE) Dark Lady (GER) (Lagunas)
205^5 1628^2 **(1831)**
2065^P *4021^4 (4299)* (4545)

Dawn Twister (GER) *Lucy Wadham* 122h
7 br g Monsun(GER) Dawn Side (CAN) (Bold Forbes (USA))
2362^2 2798^{17} 3505^2 3882^2 4112^5

Dawson City *Polly Gundry* 58h
5 b g Midnight Legend Running For Annie (Gunner B)
3656^4 5014^{12} 5249^3

Day In Day Out *Seamus Mullins* 70h
4 b g Notnowcato Cockatrice (Petong)
1536^7 1743^9

Day In The Sun (IRE) *Jonjo O'Neill* 101h
7 b g Presenting Velsheda (IRE) (Royal Vulcan)
848^9

Daylan (IRE) *Tony Coyle* 93h
6 b g Darsi(FR) Mrs McClintock (IRE) (Arctic Lord)
3042^7 3602^{11} 3826^6 4103^{11} 5494^{13}

Daymar Bay (IRE) *Emma Lavelle* 112h 132c
8 b g Oscar(IRE) Sunset View (IRE) (Good Thyne (USA))
2469^2 2845^2 *4020^2 4303^3* **(5031)**
5290^3

Days Gone By *Emma Lavelle* 94b
6 b g Kayf Tara Nuzzle (Salse (USA))
4[11] 5454[3]

Days Hotel (IRE) *Henry De Bromhead* 133h 157c
9 b g Oscar(IRE) Call Catherine (IRE) (Strong Gale)
2410a[2] 2985a[3] 3773[4] (4457a)
5155[10]

Days Of Heaven (FR) *Nicky Henderson* 102b
4 bb g Saint Des Saints(FR) Daramour (FR) (Anabaa Blue)
5145[2]

Days Of Pleasure (IRE) *Chris Gordon* 100h 92c
9 b g Fraam Altizaf (Zafonic (USA))
541[P] 712[4] 1010[P] 1172[6] (2023)
(2275) 3137[P]

Dazinski *Sarah-Jayne Davies* 112h
8 ch g Sulamani(IRE) Shuheb (Nashwan (USA))
1255[4] 1440[2] 1672[4] 2073[5] 2285[F] 2936[8]

Dazzling Rita *Shaun Lycett* 82h
8 b m Midnight Legend Pytchley Dawn (Welsh Captain)
391[4] 711[6]

Dazzling Susie (IRE) *John F Phelan* 137h 106c
9 b m Stowaway Aunt Sue (IRE) (Shahanndeh)
2484a[6]

Dbanks (IRE) *Liam Corcoran* 85h 80c
11 ch g Blueprint(IRE) Smiles Again (IRE) (Brush Aside (USA))
1154[3] 1341[5] **1563[4]** 1673[9]
1825[8] 3174[8]

Dbobe *David Brace* 65b
5 br g Needle Gun(IRE) Braceys Girl (IRE) (Be My Native (USA))
1861[11]

Deadly Sting (IRE) *Jonjo O'Neill* 115h
5 b g Scorpion(IRE) Gaza Strip (IRE) (Hamas (IRE))
(2104) 4304[4] 5157[P]

Dead Or Alive (IRE) *Miss Rose Grissell* 82h 99c
11 b g Exit To Nowhere(USA) Avro Avian (Ardross)
4376[2] 5135[P]

Dealing River *Caroline Bailey* 96h
7 b g Avonbridge Greensand (Green Desert (USA))
1634[10] 1913[8] 2292[12] 2846[5] 3597[6]

De Bee Keeper (IRE) *Lucinda Russell* 87h
6 b g Milan Festival Leader (IRE) (Supreme Leader)
1665[5] 5556[5]

De Blacksmith (IRE) *Gary Moore* 122h 127c
6 b g Brian Boru Gift Of The Gab (IRE) (Orchestra)
2005[2] ◆ 2438[4] 3365[U] 3690[2] 4934[4] 4556[3] 5573[5]

De Boitron (FR) *Sue Smith* 90h 152c
10 b g Sassanian(USA) Pondiki (FR) (Sicyos (USA))
(170) **448[2]**
680[6] (2957) ◆ 3091[2] 3660[7]

Deb's Dasher *Richard Woollacott* 70c
9 b g Relief Pitcher Jentar Equilibra (IRE) (Miner's Lamp)
62[13] 923[P]

Deb's Town *Tony Carroll* 24b
7 b m Cape Town(IRE) Debbie's Darling (Baron Blakeney)
270[13] 502[P]

Debt To Society (IRE) *Richard Ford* 108h 102c
7 ch g Moscow Society(USA) Nobody's Darling (IRE) (Supreme Leader)
3635[3] 4220[P] 4942[2] (5358)

Decent Lord (IRE) *Jennie Candlish* 94h 96c
10 b g Lord Of Appeal Otorum (IRE) (Muroto)
536[5] **2591[5]**
3020[4] 3449[U] 3564[2] (3722)
3837[3] 4383[3]

Deceptive *Paul Webber* 93h
6 b m Red Ransom(USA) Fleeting Memory (Danehill (USA))
97[6] 708[7]

De Chissler (IRE) *Martin Todhunter* 110h
7 b g Zagreb(USA) Lady Lola (IRE) (Supreme Leader)
4189[P] 4615[6] 4938[3]

Deciding Moment (IRE) *Ben De Haan* 115h 132c
8 b g Zagreb(USA) Fontaine Jewel (IRE) (Lafontaine (USA))
(2107)
4932[6] 5297[U] 5451[2]

Decimus (IRE) *Jeremy Scott* 122h
7 b g Bienamado(USA) Catch Me Dreaming (IRE) (Safety Catch (USA))
2107[P] 2490[16]
3421[P] 4393[8] (4969) 5285[3] (5489)

Decoy (FR) *David Pipe* 126h
8 b g Della Francesca(USA) Vagualame (FR) (Saint Estephe (FR))
356[P] 877[4] 1042[3] 1485[11] 1752[2] 2020[6] 2630[8] 2910[3] 3169[5] 3744[13] 3957[6] 5030[P]

Dedigout (IRE) *A J Martin* 155h 154c
8 b g Bob Back(USA) Dainty Daisy (IRE) (Buckskin (FR))
(2408a) 2855a[5]

Dee Ayes Delight *David Bridgwater* 14h
7 gr g Beat All(USA) Copper Castle (Gran Alba (USA))
2509[10]

Deepika (IRE) *Mrs A Malzard*
6 b m Key Of Luck(USA) Soul Society (IRE) (Inchinor)
993a[4] 1827a[6]

Deepsand (IRE) *Tim Easterby* 129h
5 br g Footstepsinthesand Sinamay (USA) (Saint Ballado (CAN))
216[9] 2069[5] 2668[6] 2958[4] 3477[11] 4426[7]

Deep Trouble (IRE) *Ben Case* 148h
7 b g Shantou(USA) Out Of Trouble (IRE) (Mandalus)
116[2] (434) 2049[2] 2492[2] (2951) 3648[2] 4147[13] 4785[7]

Deer Park *Brendan Powell* 81b
7 b g Kier Park(IRE) Gazelle De Thou (FR) (Quart De Vin (FR))
862[6] 1056[4]

De Faoithesdream (IRE) *Evan Williams* 121h 134c
8 br g Balakheri(IRE) Cutteen Lass (IRE) (Tremblant)
634[4] 999[2] (1192)
1346[7] (1640)
1817[2] 2488[6]

Defi D'Anjou (FR) *L Viel* 122h 129c
6 b g Saint Des Saints(FR) Rosane (FR) (Sheyrann (IRE))
406a[P]

Defile De Mode (FR) *Mme V Seignoux* 107h
9 b g Ultimately Lucky(IRE) Naomie (FR) (Pistolet Bleu (IRE))
863a[7]

Definite Appeal (IRE) *Susan Corbett* 62h 104c
11 ch g Definite Article Marian's Wish (IRE) (Phardante (FR))
4812[2] 5321[P]

Definite Dream (IRE) *Evan Williams* 114h 127c
7 b g Definite Article Brooks Chariot (IRE) (Electric)
(2159) ◆ 2797[5] 5091[P]

Definite Elegance (IRE) *Denis Gerard Hogan* 110h
7 b m Vinnie Roe(IRE) Fair Conquest (IRE) (Be My Native (USA))
2407a[4]

Definite Future (IRE) *Dave Roberts* 105b
5 b g Definite Article Miss Marilyn (IRE) (Welsh Term)
699[3] 2375[9]

Definite Lady (IRE) *Mark Rimell* 98h
8 b m Definite Article Phillis Hill (Karinga Bay)
423[7] 738[2] 2568[7] 2980[2] 3334[2]

Definitely Better (IRE) *Tom George* 92h
6 ch m Definite Article Chevet Girl (IRE) (Roselier (FR))
2298[6] 2907[11] 3168[8] 3329[4] 5177[12] 5509[6]

Definitely Glad (IRE) *Paul Webber* 102h
7 b m Definite Article Gladys May (IRE) (Moscow Society (USA))
116[3] 450[2] 717[3] 2084[P] 2713[P] 5405[3]

Definite Maybe (IRE) *Martin Todhunter* 98h
6 b g Definite Article Nahla (Wassl)
498[4] ◆ 761[3] 1072[8]

Definite Memories (IRE) *David Bridgwater* 110h 124c
7 b m Definite Article Memories (FR) (Darshaan)
(2769)
3718[2] 4245[4]

Definite Row (IRE) *Gordon Elliott* 67h
5 b m Definite Article Be My Rainbow (IRE) (Be My Native (USA))
(754) 885[2] 962[2]

Definite Ruby (IRE) *Nicky Henderson* 122h
6 b m Definite Article Sunset Queen (IRE) (King's Theatre (IRE))
604[6] 2435[2] 3117[P] 5291[7]

Definitly Red (IRE) *Steve Gollings* 130b
5 ch g Definite Article The Red Wench (IRE) (Aahsaylad)
(3433) (4149) 4756[7]

Defying Gravity (IRE) *Mrs L Pomfret* 53h 59c
11 b g Old Vic Night Escape (IRE) (Satco (FR))
288[P]

Defy Logic (IRE) *Paul Nolan* 149h 154c
7 ch g Flemensfirth(USA) Osiery Girl (IRE) (Phardante (FR))
2550a[2] (3308a)
3928a[5]

Degas Art (IRE) *Lucinda Russell* 59h 46c
11 b g Danehill Dancer(IRE) Answer (Warning)
677[6]

Degenerate (FR) *Jeremy Scott* 82h 69c
7 b g Generous(IRE) Dancinginthedark (IRE) (Fasliyev (USA))
2009[6] 2181[8] 2457[10]
3015[9]

Degenerous (IRE) *Sarah Dawson* 100b
6 b m Generous(IRE) Brescia (FR) (Monsun (GER))
(4618)

Degooch (IRE) *Donald McCain* 111h
5 ch g Gamut(IRE) Blonde Ambition (IRE) (Old Vic)
2499[2] 2905[2] (4582) 5388[2]

De Grae Clouding (IRE) *Rebecca Curtis* 81b
5 gr m Cloudings(IRE) Half The Battle (IRE) (Bob Back (USA))
372[6]

Deia Sunrise (IRE) *Paul Webber* 108h
5 gr g Clodovil(IRE) Hedera (USA) (Woodman (USA))
8[F] 235[3] 3012[P]

Deireadh Re (IRE) *Paul Nicholls* 142h 130c
8 b g Old Vic Donaghmore Lady (IRE) (Orchestra)
(302) **851[P]**

Deise Dynamo (IRE) *Donald McCain* 116h 123c
6 br g Zagreb(USA) Magical Mist (IRE) (Be My Native (USA))
121[10]
2171[2] 2662[F] 2901[P] 4894[5]

De Kerry Man (IRE) *Fiona Kehoe* 97h
6 b g Westerner Fishy Fishy (IRE) (Mull Of Kintyre (USA))
3816[4] 4251[4]

De La Bech *Philip Hobbs* 123h 136c
7 ch g Karinga Bay Vallis Vale (St Columbus)
2373[7] (2943)
3455[6] 4026[P] 4681[3] 5348[7]

Delgany Demon *Neil King* 110h
6 b g Kayf Tara Little Twig (IRE) (Good Thyne (USA))
2981[2] (3282) 3774[5]

Delgany Gunner *Neil King* 95h 111c
10 b g Commanche Run No Grandad (Strong Gale)
96[2] 387[4]

Delightfully (FR) *Lucinda Russell* 102h
10 br m Sagacity(FR) Green House (FR) (Houston (FR))
751[P] 1873[5] 2497[7] 3335[5] 4338[6]

Delineate (IRE) *G C Maundrell* 77h
5 b m Definite Article New Line (IRE) (Roselier (FR))
2298[12] 3181[4] 4600[4] 4797[6] 5124[8] 5283[6]

Dell' Arca (IRE) *David Pipe* 145h
5 b g Sholokhov(IRE) Daisy Belle (GER) (Acatenango (GER))
(2533) 3200[U] 4147[2] 4752[5] 5167[3]

Della Sun (FR) *Arthur Whitehead* 121h
8 b g Della Francesca(USA) Algarve Sunrise (IRE) (Highest Honor (FR))
10[6] (1123) 1319[3] (1345) 1527[2] 1960[7] 2529[13] 5239[6] 5526[3]

Delphi Mountain (IRE) *Richard Woollacott* 105h 110c
9 b g Oscar(IRE) Summer Break (IRE) (Foxhound (USA))
764[9] **999[6]**
1352[5] 1699[5] 2274[4] 2696[F] 3959[P] (4757) 4911[7] 5304[5] **5549[2]**

Delta Borget (FR) *L Jefford* 108c
9 b g Kapgarde(FR) L'Oceane (FR) (Epervier Bleu)
159[4] 523[2] 655[3] 4658[2] 5035[3] 5346[9]

Delta Forty *Keith Reveley* 97h
6 b m Alflora(IRE) Northern Native (IRE) (Be My Native (USA))
2878[3] 3507[3] 4605[2]

Demographic (USA) *Emma Lavelle* 96h
5 b g Aptitude(USA) Private Line (USA) (Private Account (USA))
1794[6] 3046[2] 4993[10]

Denali Highway (IRE) *Caroline Bailey* 101h 133c
7 ch g Governor Brown(USA) Amaretto Flame (IRE) (First Trump)
2517[2] 3366[3] 3742[6] 4685[3]

Dence (FR) *Mlle C Comte*
4 b f Meshaheer(USA) Star Dancing (Danehill Dancer (IRE))
2781a[3]

Dennis *Tim Easterby* 78h
4 b g Mind Games Hetti Lewis (Sir Harry Lewis (USA))
2392[5]

Denton (NZ) *Polly Gundry* 112h
11 b g Montjeu(IRE) Melora (NZ) (Sir Tristram)
83[P]

Deny *Henry Hogarth* 82h
6 ch g Mr Greeley(USA) Sulk (IRE) (Selkirk (USA))
1120[4] (1419) 1495[3] 1848[3]

Departed (IRE) *S G Allen* 78b
10 b g Oscar(IRE) Same Token (IRE) (Cheval)
424[P] 4706[P]

Deportation *John Norton* 88h
7 b g Deportivo Kyle Rhea (In The Wings)
444[F] 5494[12]

Deputy Dan (IRE) *Oliver Sherwood* 151h
6 b g Westerner Louisas Dream (IRE) (Supreme Leader)
2243[2] 2978[2] (3357) ◆ (3654) 4786[2] ◆

Dermatologiste *Caroline Bailey* 94h 105c
11 b m Kayf Tara Poor Skin (IRE) (Lafontaine (USA))
2578[P] 3827[5] 4066[R] 4243[P]

Dermo's Dilemma *Chris Grant* 25h
4 b g Multiplex Gertrude Webb (Central Park (IRE))
2160[7] 2592[5] 4379[6] 4576[6]

Derniere Dance (FR) *Miss C Prouse*
9 ch g Colonel Collins(USA) Comedie Divine (FR) (Lesotho (USA))
5553[U]

Dervla (IRE) *Seamus Mullins* 71h
6 b m Definite Article Kennycourt Lady (IRE) (Persian Mews)
36[7] 391[5] 4331[F]

Derwen Pryde *Peter Bowen* 96h 91c
10 b m Hazaaf(USA) Landsker Pryde (Nearly A Hand)
248[8] 601[RR]

Descaro (USA) *John O'Shea* 120h
8 gr g Dr Fong(USA) Miarixa (FR) (Linamix (FR))
319[2] 332[2] 648[2] (727) 762[2] 799[2] 929[2] 1009[2] 1054[4] 1867[8] 4726[F]

Description (IRE) *Alan Hill* 85h 93c
12 b g Humbel(USA) Magic User (Deep Run)
657[5]

Desert Cry (IRE) *Donald McCain* 143h 160c
8 bb g Desert Prince(IRE) Hataana (USA) (Robellino (USA))
217[P] (3170)
(3660) 4032[2] 4146[4] 5275[2]

Desert Fairy *Trevor Wall*
8 b m Tobougg(IRE) Regal Fairy (IRE) (Desert King (IRE))
1017[U] 1632[U] 2043[P]

Desertmore Stream (IRE) *Philip Fenton* 137h
6 b g Celtic Swing Another Cross (FR) (Cape Cross (IRE))
3126a[3]

Desert Nova (IRE) *Mark Campion* 102h 73c
12 ch g Desert King(IRE) Assafiyah (IRE) (Kris)
368[5] 2787[13] 3335[9]

Desert Sting *Michael Easterby* 45h
5 b g Scorpion(IRE) Skipcarl (IRE) (Carlingford Castle)
318[U] 367[7] 747[9] 945[5]

Desert Tommy *Lucinda Egerton* 64h 40c
13 b g Desert King(IRE) Flambera (FR) (Akarad (FR))
3335[7] 3639[9] **4773[P]**

Desgrey *Peter Niven* 116h 116c
6 gr g Desideratum Briden (Minster Son)
1850[2] ◆ 2342[2] 2844[5] 3288[2] **3615[4] 4549[4] 4892[3]**
5451[3]

Desirer (FR) *E Lecoiffier*
8 gr g Slickly(FR) Bel Jade (FR) (Apeldoorn (FR))
855a[8]

Desoto County *Donald McCain* 128h
5 gr g Hernando(FR) Kaldounya (Kaldoun (FR))
(2660) ◆ 3063[2] 3415[2] (4548) 4945[2] (5341)

Desperate Dex (IRE) *Tom George* 100h 119c
14 b g Un Desperado(FR) Too Sharp (True Song)
2179[4] 2678[5]

Destiny Blue (IRE) *Brian Ellison*
7 b g Danehill Dancer(IRE) Arpege (IRE) (Sadler's Wells (USA))
2794[P]

Destiny's Gold (IRE) *George Baker* 90b
4 b g Millenary Knockhouse Rose (IRE) (Roselier (FR))
3133[5] (4763)

Destroyer Deployed *Tim Vaughan* 128h 131c
8 b g Deploy Supreme Cove (Supreme Leader)
358[11] 3069[9] **(4248)**
4484[U]

Detour Ahead *Jennie Candlish* 104h 98c
6 ch m Needwood Blade My Tern (IRE) (Glacial Storm (USA))
31[3] 111[3] **369[4] 2036[6] 2626[3] 2804[2] 3058[3]** 3428[3] 3821[8] 4071[5]

Detroit Red *Martin Hill* 124h
8 b m Hamairi(IRE) Kingston Black (Shaab)
178[5] (833) 925[2] 1321[3] 1488[3] 1699[8] 5542[2]

Deux Etoiles (IRE) *Gary Moore* 96h
7 b g Montjeu(IRE) Onereuse (Sanglamore (USA))
(2) (308)

Devenish Island *Karen McLintock* 108b
5 b g Multiplex Wahiba Reason (IRE) (Robellino (USA))
4267[7]

Devil At Midnight (IRE) *Richard Drake* 37h
6 b g Midnight Legend Obligee De Sivola (FR) (Video Rock (FR))
3826[13] 4005[7] 4103[13] 4343[U] 5189[5]

Devils Bride (IRE) *W P Mullins* 116h
7 b g Helissio(FR) Rigorous (Generous (IRE))
2706a[P]

Devil's Dyke (USA) *Evan Williams* 105h
6 bb g Redoute's Choice(AUS) Kotuku (A.P. Indy (USA))
2040[5] 2718[8] 3061[14] 3783[3]

Devils Paintbrush (IRE) *Kim Bailey* 119b
6 b g Shantou(USA) Back Log (IRE) (Bob Back (USA))
4959[F]

Devon Drum *Paul Webber* 109h
6 b g Beat Hollow West Devon (USA) (Gone West (USA))
2265[2] ◆ 2783[6] 4807[6]

Devotion To Duty (IRE) *Philip Kirby* 117h 129c
8 b g Montjeu(IRE) Charmante (USA) (Alydar (USA))
1926[3] 2357[5] 5379[10]

Dewala *Michael Appleby* 104h
5 b m Deportivo Fuwala (Unfuwain (USA))
2514[3] 2767[3] 3390[3] 4983[2] 5518[2]

D'Gigi *Nigel Twiston-Davies* 102h 102c
8 ch m Beat Hollow Strictly Cool (USA) (Bering)
32[2] 206[7] 763[6]

Dhaular Dhar (IRE) *Jim Goldie* 112h
12 b g Indian Ridge Pescara (IRE) (Common Grounds)
(1544) 1665[3] 2344[7] 2970[P]

Diable D'Enfer (FR) *P Peltier* 91h
4 b g Saint Des Saints(FR) Eyaelle (FR) (Green Tune (USA))
614a[3]

Diakali (FR) *W P Mullins* 165h
5 gr g Sinndar(IRE) Diasilixa (FR) (Linamix (FR))
(683a) (2377a) 2855a[3] 4785[4] 5134[3]

Diaktoros (IRE) *Ben Haslam* 108b
4 b g Red Clubs(IRE) Rinneen (IRE) (Bien Bien (USA))
2960[2] ◆ 3719[2] 4944[P]

Diamond Crescent (IRE) *Nigel Twiston-Davies*
7 b g Marignan(USA) Shaunies Nora (IRE) (Topanoora)
317[P]

Diamond Eclipse (IRE) *Mrs E J Loosemore* 84c
8 b g Double Eclipse(IRE) Glory-Glory (IRE) (Buckskin (FR))
926[4] 1174[5] 1474[4] 5553[8]

Diamond Frontier (IRE) *John Wade* 117h 126c
11 gr g Sadler's Wells(USA) Diamond Line (FR) (Linamix (FR))
508[10] 1921[7] 2346[4] 3065[13]

Diamond Gesture (IRE) *Fergal O'Brien* 104h
6 ch m Presenting Rare Gesture (IRE) (Shalford (IRE))
5245[F]

Diamond Harry *Nick Williams* 131h 136c
11 b g Sir Harry Lewis(USA) Swift Conveyance (IRE) (Strong Gale)
131a[4] 704a[3] 2491[4] 3617[F] 4754[P]

Diamond King (IRE) *Donald McCain* 136h
6 b g King's Theatre(IRE) Georgia On My Mind (FR) (Belmez (USA))
(2748) ◆ 3061[3] (3602)

Diamond Native (IRE) *Brian Storey* 51b
6 b g Alderbrook Native Sylph (IRE) (Supreme Leader)
3640[7] 4205[9] 5320[U]

Diamond Pro (IRE) *Christopher Kellett* 86h
6 b g Diamond Green(FR) Speedbird (USA) (Sky Classic (CAN))
2886[9] 4903[10] 5191[10] 5438[4]

Diamonds A Dancing *Rebecca Curtis* 66h
4 ch g Delta Dancer Zing (Zilzal (USA))
975[7] 1182[3]

Diamond's Return (IRE) *David Pipe* 121h
10 b g Bob's Return(IRE) Mitsubishi Diamond (Tender King)
421[9] 1319[5] 1345[3] (1565) 1581[P]

Diamond Sunrise (IRE) *Noel Wilson*
6 b m Diamond Green(FR) Sunrise (IRE) (Sri Pekan (USA))
506[P]

Diamond Tammy (IRE) *Anthony Middleton* 90h
8 b g Tamayaz(CAN) Mary Dont Be Long (IRE) (The Bart (USA))
49[11] 253[6] (501) 648[3] 1061[4]

Diamrock (FR) *E Leenders* 107c
9 b g Welkin(CAN) Diamarella (FR) (Rose Laurel)
200a[6]

Dibdabs (IRE) *Maurice Barnes* 101h
6 b g Royal Anthem(USA) Leadaro (IRE) (Supreme Leader)
3415[F] 3826[11] 4081[P] 5296[5]

Dica (FR) *Patrick Griffin* 85h 108c
8 ch g Kapgarde(FR) Easy World (FR) (Lost World (IRE))
752[5] **883[6]**

Dice (IRE) *Sirrell Griffiths* 78h
8 b g Kalanisi(IRE) Rain Dancer (IRE) (Sadler's Wells (USA))
1188[11]

Dicey Vows (USA) *Alan Jarvis*
6 b g Broken Vow(USA) Pretty Dicey (USA) (Cherokee Run (USA))
15[P]

Dick Dundee *Paul Nolan* 120h 139c
9 b g King's Theatre(IRE) Bayariyka (IRE) (Slip Anchor)
1286[4]

Dickie Henderhoop (IRE) *Lucy Normile* 104h
9 b g Milan Merry Breeze (Strong Gale)
310[5] 2034[F] (2417) 2844[2] 3396[F] 4365[F] 5217[F]

Dicky Shore *Ashley Dodgson* 74b
6 b g Iktibas Catton Lady (Chas Sawyer)
4895[13] 5367[8]

Diddley Dee *Lucy Normile* 97h 103c
10 b g Riverhead(USA) Ballydiddle (Abednego)
279[6] 580[9] 866[2] 1147[4] (1287)
1542[3]

Diddy Eric *Micky Hammond*
4 b g Oratorio(IRE) Amber Queen (IRE) (Cadeaux Genereux)
1394[P]

Diddypurptoon *Jackie Du Plessis* 73h
8 b m Lucky Story(USA) Dafne (Nashwan (USA))
1639[F] 1832[7] 5002[3]

Dido *Alexandra Dunn*
4 b g Killer Instinct Bowdlane Barb (Commanche Run)
3857[F] *4019[11]*

Diego Suarez (FR) *Chris Bealby* 71h
4 b g Astarabad(USA) Shabada (FR) (Cadoudal (FR))
2160[6] 4986[8]

Diesel Ten (IRE) *Patrick O Brady* 93h
4 b g Refuse To Bend(IRE) Zoudie (Ezzoud (IRE))
2851a[8]

Digger's Mate *Bob Buckler* 102b
6 b g General Gambul Miss Diskin (IRE) (Sexton Blake)
3163[P]

Digg Whitaker *John Wade* 83h 102c
9 b g Mounting Spendent Function Dreamer (Overbury (IRE))
(28) **535[F]**

Di Kaprio (FR) *Barry Leavy* 120h 132c
8 b g Kapgarde(FR) Miss Nousha (FR) (True Brave (USA))
394[P] (762) 1268[5] 1634[12] 2510[2] (3013) 3430[5]
4106[2]

Dildar (IRE) *Paul Nicholls* 133h
6 b g Red Ransom(USA) Diamond Tango (FR) (Acatenango (GER))
2213[3] 5399[F]

Diligent *Donald McCain* 93b
6 b m Generous(IRE) Diletia (Dilum (USA))
4618[6] 5159[17]

Dimpsy Time *Colin Tizzard* 97h 102c
8 b m Kayf Tara Cool Shuil (IRE) (Glacial Storm (USA))
541[2] 692[F]

Dineur (FR) *Peter Bowen* 124h 142c
8 ch g Discover D'Auteuil(FR) Sky Rocket (FR) (Sky Lawyer (FR))
(142) **432[6]**
(735) **(974)**
1047[4] (1194)
1346[3] (1484)

Ding Dong Dennis (IRE) *Laura Young* 58b
7 br g Zagreb(USA) Leighlinbridge (IRE) (Montelimar (USA))
2703[7] 2912[9]

Dingo Bay *John Wade* 56h 97c
8 b g Karinga Bay Do It On Dani (Weld)
2498[F] (3528)
4462[2] 4812[4] 5104[F]

Diocles (IRE) *Donald McCain* 126h 135c
8 b g Bob Back(USA) Ardrina (Ardross)
26[5] (3142)
4188[P] (5297)

Di'Philly's Dream *Lisa Day* 37h
6 b m Gentleman's Deal(IRE) Mia's Moll (IRE) (Flemensfirth (USA))
8081[0]

Diplomat (USA) *D K Weld* 131h
5 b g Kitten's Joy(USA) Waki Affair (USA) (Miswaki (USA))
(1139a) 3910a[18]

Direct Approach (IRE) *Lynn Siddall* 51h
10 b g Tel Quel(FR) Miss Telimar (IRE) (Montelimar (USA))
449[P] 3014[P] *(4324) 4493[8]*

Direct Flo (IRE) *Tony Carroll* 95h 78c
7 b m Mr Combustible(IRE) Direct Pursuit (IRE) (Hubbly Bubbly (USA))
2148[6]
2653[4] 2896[8]

Dirty Bertie (FR) *David Bridgwater* 108h 114c
8 ch g Dream Well(FR) Ma Reilly (FR) (Snurge)
1597[5] **1744[3]**

Discover Du Bourg (FR) *Mme F Gimmi Pellegrino* 108h
9 ch g Discover D'Auteuil(FR) Sekara (FR) (Grey Risk (FR))
863a[0]

Discoverie *Dianne Sayer* 74h 87c
6 b g Runyon(IRE) Sri (IRE) (Sri Pekan (USA))
279[7] 1791[2] 1982[12] **2335[3] 2880[2] 3020[3]**

Discovery Bay *Brian Ellison* 133h
6 b g Dansili Rainbow's Edge (Rainbow Quest (USA))
531[2] 2344[2] ◆ 2647[7] 3758[6] 4899[2]

Discussion Forum *Mrs C A Coward* 89c
8 gr m Fair Mix(IRE) Rosemoss (Le Moss)
287[5] 557[4]

Di's Gift *Richard Guest* 98b
5 b g Generous(IRE) Di's Dilemma (Teenoso (USA))
1826[3] 2053[3] 2878[4]

Dispour (IRE) *Donald McCain* 130h
4 ch g Monsun(GER) Dalataya (IRE) (Sadler's Wells (USA))
(1727) 2168[2] (2790) 3089[4] *4302[6]* 5132[7] (5568)

Dissidancer (IRE) *John Wade* 91h
6 b g Bishop Of Cashel Dancing At Lunasa (IRE) (Dancing Dissident (USA))
2792[5] 3351[6] 5052[4]

Distant Memories (IRE) *Tim Vaughan* 136h
8 b g Falbrav(IRE) Amathia (IRE) (Darshaan)
447[F]

Distime (IRE) *John Quinn* 122h 119c
8 b g Flemensfirth(USA) Technohead (IRE) (Distinctly North (USA))
2901[2] ◆ 3266[8]

District Attorney (IRE) *Chris Fairhurst* 65h
5 b g Lawman(FR) Mood Indigo (IRE) (Indian Ridge)
1713[8] 1853[9]

Divergont Quirec (FR) *Mlle M-L Mortier* 117h 127c
9 b g Denham Red(FR) Gwinidel Quirec (FR) (Turgeon (USA))
(131a)

Divers (FR) *Donald McCain* 122h 136c
10 gr g Highest Honor(FR) Divination (FR) (Groom Dancer (USA))
2448[P] 3000[5] 3475[3] 4893[3] 5272[6]

Divine Folly (IRE) *Lawney Hill* 91h 103c
9 b g Kotashaan(FR) Jennys Grove (IRE) (Strong Gale)
374[5] 671[7] (876) 1320[11]
2431[6] 2829[2]

Divine Intavention (IRE) *Martin Keighley* 102b 134c
10 b g Exit To Nowhere(USA) Merrill Gaye (IRE) (Roselier (FR))
59[2] 329[2] (4078) *4303[4]* **(4477)**
4788[U] 5230[2] (5488)

Dixie Bull (IRE) *Tom Symonds* 82h
9 br g Milan Calora (USA) (Private Account (USA))
4906[4]

Diyala (IRE) *Gordon Elliott* 109h
5 b m Tiger Hill(IRE) Daliya (IRE) (Giant's Causeway (USA))
1948a[5]

Dizoard *Ollie Pears* 59b
4 b f Desideratum Riviere (Meadowbrook)
5381[7]

Dizzy River (IRE) *Brian Ellison* 111h
9 ch g Flemensfirth(USA) Dizzy Dealer (IRE) (Le Bavard (FR))
(386) 476[4]

Djakadam (FR) *W P Mullins* 136h 146c
5 b g Saint Des Saints(FR) Rainbow Crest (FR) (Baryshnikov (AUS))
(3908a)
4764[F]

Dj Milan (IRE) *Donald McCain* 118h 104c
8 b g Milan Cafe Matisse (IRE) (Le Moss)
681[7] 867[3] **957[3] 1146[4] 1287[P]**

Do Be Dashing *Graeme McPherson* 82h
6 b m Doyen(IRE) Be Brave (FR) (Green Forest (USA))
2442[6] 3159[8] 5071[10] 5229[5]

Doberdan (USA) *Patrick Holmes* 102h 97c
9 b g Street Cry(IRE) Sophonisbe (Wollow)
205[P] 172[P]

Doctor Foxtrot (IRE) *Philip Hobbs* 113h 120c
9 b g Milan French Life (IRE) (Un Desperado (FR))
2362[5]
2928[9] 3158[P] (4932)
5344[4]

Doctor Harper (IRE) *David Pipe* 145h
6 b g Presenting Supreme Dreamer (IRE) (Supreme Leader)
(2280) (2689) 3070[5] (4251) 4680[3] (5138)

Doctor Kingsley *Mrs Pauline Harkin* 127c
12 ch g Classic Cliche(IRE) Query Line (High Line)
(60) **4042[2]**
◆ 4788[7]

Doctor Look Here (IRE) *Sue Gardner* 86b
4 b g Dr Massini(IRE) Eye Vision (IRE) (Taipan (IRE))
4417[3]

Doctor Ric (IRE) *Gerry Enright* 87h 98c
9 b g Dr Massini(IRE) Merric (IRE) (Electric)
242[8] 485[5] 709[P] (1272) 1434[3] **1526[3] 1626[5]**

Doc Wells (IRE) *Ms D C Faulkner* 111h 98c
11 b g Dr Massini(IRE) Palmrock Donna (Quayside)
5545[3]

Dodge The Bullet *Susan Corbett* 36h 37c
8 ch g Endoli(USA) Leighten Lass (IRE) (Henbit (USA))
109[6]

Dodging Bullets *Paul Nicholls* 113h 161c
6 b g Dubawi(IRE) Nova Cyngi (USA) (Kris S (USA))
(1986)
(2531) (3318)
4146[2] 4737[4] 5137[5]

Doeslessthanme (IRE) *Richard Ford* 126h 148c
10 ch g Definite Article Damemill (IRE) (Danehill (USA))
249[F] 3660[5] 4039[2] (4543)
5156[F]

Dog Or Divorce *Paul Webber* 33h
5 b m Midnight Legend Time For A Glass (Timeless Times (USA))
(3098) 4867[8] 5229[U]

Doheny Bar (IRE) *Paul Henderson* 73h 91c
11 b g Freddie's Star Old Fontaine (IRE) (Millfontaine)
1700[P]
2003[2] 2478[P] 2861[P] (3139)

Doing Fine (IRE) *Rebecca Curtis* 117h
6 b g Presenting Howaya Pet (IRE) (Montelimar (USA))
1770[2] 2076[3] (2661)

Doktor Glaz (FR) *Rose Dobbin* 98b
4 b g Mount Nelson Deviolina (IRE) (Dr Devious (IRE))
2960[3]

Dolatulo (FR) *Warren Greatrex* 140h 139c
7 ch g Le Fou(IRE) La Perspective (FR) (Beyssac (FR))
591[2] 2087[2] 2538[2] (3096)
3652[3] *4325[2]* 4789[20]
(5068) 5261[6]

Dolcetto (FR) *G Cherel* 130h 105c
7 b g Califet(FR) L'Inka (FR) (R B Chesne)
2415a[P]

Dollar Bill *Nick Gifford* 111h
5 ch g Medicean Jardin (Sinndar (IRE))
2087[6] 2717[6] 3288[7] 5260[4]

Dollar Mick (IRE) *James Moffatt* 90h 90c
9 b g Presenting Bula Beag (IRE) (Brush Aside (USA))
224[P] 473[4]

Dolores Delightful (FR) *Nick Williams* 107h
4 b f Saint Des Saints(FR) Us Et Coutumes (FR) (Shining Steel)
130a[7] 615a[4] 3423[4] 4963[2] 5568[5]

Domination *C Byrnes* 154h 132c
7 b g Motivator Soliza (IRE) (Intikhab (USA))
5099a[5]

Dominetta Vitali (IRE) *M P Sunderland* 101h 112c
8 ch m Beneficial Over The Pond (IRE) (Over The River (FR))
2973[2]

Domino King *Charlie Longsdon* 37b
4 br g Overbury(IRE) Parlour Game (Petoski)
4964[18]

Dom Lukka (FR) *Charlie Longsdon* 106h 106c
6 bb g Dom Alco(FR) Orlamonde Queen (FR) (Royal Charter (FR))
99[9] 490[4] **(709)**
872[F] 1673[3] (1917) 2253[P] 2744[F] 3435[P] 4719[P]
5520[11]

Domoly (FR) *Ferdy Murphy* 75h 95c
11 b g Varese(FR) Queen D'Ouilly (FR) (King Of Macedon)
580[6]

Domtaline (FR) *Paul Nicholls* 138h 146c
7 gr g Martaline Domna Noune (FR) (Dom Pasquini (FR))
2365[5] 2925[2] *(4020)* *4303[5]* **5261[3]**

Dona *Miss L Thomas* 92h 91c
10 b g Anabaa Blue Dominicana (FR) (King's Theatre (IRE))
4727[6]

Don Alejandro (FR) *J Ortet* 124c
6 b g Lost World(IRE) Shinobie (FR) (Le Nain Jaune (FR))
5425a[F]

Donapollo *Ian Williams* 8h
6 b g Kayf Tara Star Of Wonder (FR) (The Wonder (FR))
1991[12] 3182[P] 3600[P]

Don Cossack (GER) *Gordon Elliott* 146h 155c
7 br g Sholokhov(IRE) Depeche Toi (GER) (Konigsstuhl (GER))
2551a[2] (2853a) ◆ 4181a[2] 4751[F] 5154[2]

Done A Runner (IRE) *Alan Hill* 105c
8 b g Alderbrook Last Wager (IRE) (Strong Gale)
5248[2]

Dongarry (FR) *B Jollivet* 117h
7 gr g Ballingarry(IRE) Dona Honoria (FR) (Highest Honor (FR))
455a[9]

Donnachas Chant (USA) *Tim Vaughan* 76b
9 b g War Chant(USA) Super Supreme (IND) (Zafonic (USA))
4911[P]

Donna's Diamond (IRE) *Chris Grant* 112b
5 gr g Cloudings(IRE) Inish Bofin (IRE) (Glacial Storm (USA))
3002[5] ◆ 3640[5] (4226) 5279[8]

Donnas Palm (IRE) *Gary Moore* 128h 114c
10 gr g Great Palm(USA) Donna's Tarquin (IRE) (Husyan (USA))
432[3] 780[4]
1047[6] 1283[4] 2645[F] 3065[9] 3246[3] 3958[P] *4302[9]*

Donna's Pride *Keith Reveley* 76h
5 b m Beat All(USA) Pennys Pride (IRE) (Pips Pride)
1292[3] 2885[4] 4618[3] 5195[5] 5519[9]

Don Padeja *Jonjo O'Neill* 101h
4 br g Dansili La Leuze (IRE) (Caerleon (USA))
5190[6] 5519[3]

Don Poli (IRE) *W P Mullins* 153h
5 b g Poliglote Dalamine (FR) (Sillery (USA))
(4386a) (4789)

Don Pooleoni (IRE) *Harry Fry* 107h 122c
9 b g Catcher In The Rye(IRE) Liss Rua (IRE) (Bob Back (USA))
2474[2] ◆ 2598[4] 3650[U] 3839[5]

Don't Be Late (IRE) *Jonjo O'Neill* 131h 107c
6 b g Court Cave(IRE) Sylvella (Lear Fan (USA))
(436) 556[3] 764[4] (1020) 1123[2] (1268) 2813[3] ◆
3387[6]

Dont Call Me Oscar (IRE) *Mark Gillard* 90h
7 b g Oscar(IRE) Coolrua (IRE) (Commanche Run)
306[4] 1255[9] 1580[10] 1706[6] 1863[8] 2291[14] 2628[6]
2887[P] 3425[4]

Dont Do Mondays (IRE) *David Bridgwater* 111h 120c
7 b g Rashar(USA) Bit Of A Chance (Lord Ha Ha)
4023[13] **4242[3] (4716)**
5178[6]

Don't Hang About *F Lloyd* 87h 115c
9 ch g Alflora(IRE) Althrey Flame (IRE) (Torus)
1083[2]

Don't Look Bach (IRE) *Brian Barr* 94h
9 b g Bach(IRE) Buckalong (IRE) (Buckskin (FR))
1259[8] 1275[9]

Dontpaytheferryman (USA) *Peter Hiatt* 129h 111c
9 ch g Wiseman's Ferry(USA) Expletive Deleted (USA) (Dr Blum (USA))
850[8] 1520[6] **1698[4] 1886[P]** 5066[P]

Don't Stop Me Now (IRE) *John Joseph Hanlon* 122h 118c
9 b m Catcher In The Rye(IRE) Persian Flower (Persian Heights)
1527[P]

Dont Take Me Alive *Charlie Longsdon* 114h 107c
5 b g Araafa(IRE) Up At Dawn (Inchinor)
31[5] 651[5] (788) 924[4] 1093[2] 1471[2] 1627[5] **1821[2]**
2601[4] 5294[4]

Don't Tell *George Moore*
4 ch f Sakhee's Secret Starry Sky (Oasis Dream)
4614[P] 5519[P]

Donttellmother (IRE) *Richard Mathias* 112h
12 ch g Carroll House One Bid (IRE) (King Luthier)
373[P]

Dont Tell Sailor (IRE) *Jennie Candlish* 93h 124c
8 b g Saddlers' Hall(IRE) Pharlen's Dream (IRE) (Phardante (FR))
113[2] 504[2] 728[5] 933[11]
1060[9]

Dooney Rock (IRE) *John Butler* 127h
10 b g Luso Cormac Lady (IRE) (Simply Great (FR))
1564[4] 2746[5]

Door Boy (IRE) *John Wade* 48h 138c
11 bb g Dr Massini(IRE) Door Stopper (IRE) (Flemensfirth (USA))
355[P] 681[12]

Dorkas *J R Jenkins* 101b
5 b m Doyen(IRE) Jawwala (USA) (Green Dancer (USA))
842[2] 1064[2] 1317[2] (1445)

Dorlesh Way (IRE) *Patrick Holmes* 64h 78c
7 ch g Rakti Patalavaca (GER) (Acatenango (GER))
19[9] 558[5] **2595[4] 2880[6] 3352[5]**

Dormello Mo (FR) *Paul Nicholls* 123h
4 b g Conillon(GER) Neogel (USA) (Theatrical (IRE))
4171[4] (4679) 4935[5]

Dormouse *Anabel K Murphy* 118h
9 b g Medicean Black Fighter (USA) (Secretariat (USA))
97[4] 488[2] 719[4] 2397[7] 2598[3] 3269[7] 4157[5] *4300[9]*
5443[4]

Dorry K (IRE) *Jim Best* 88h
5 b m Ad Valorem(USA) Ashtaroute (USA) (Holy Bull (USA))
3163[16] (4398) 4504[2]

Dorset Dora *Maurice Barnes* 79b
6 b m Exit To Nowhere(USA) Pems Gift (Environment Friend)
76[4] 497[4]

Dorset Naga *Anthony Honeyball* 110h 127c
8 b g Alflora(IRE) Tellicherry (Strong Gale)
(1767)
1923[F] 2693[6] 3759[P]

Dorton (IRE) *Phil Middleton* 50b
4 b g Oratorio(IRE) Blue Reema (IRE) (Bluebird (USA))
2436[6] *2731[6]*

Dorton Lad (IRE) *Phil Middleton* 42b
5 b g Craigsteel Different Dee (IRE) (Beau Sher)
1919[U] 2472[8] 2681[7]

Do The Bookies *John Joseph Hanlon* 110h
10 b g Heron Island(IRE) Easter Morning (FR) (Nice Havrais (USA))
75[5] (Dead)

Dot Or Feather (IRE) *Graeme McPherson* 108h 108c
9 b g Indian Danehill(IRE) Gentian Blue (IRE) (Tirol)
117[P]

Dotties Dilema (IRE) *Lucinda Russell* 111h 106c
6 b g Pierre Tellarue (IRE) (Rhoman Rule (USA))
2595[3] 3524[3] 4626[5]

Double Accord *Anthony Honeyball* 84h
4 ch f Double Trigger(IRE) Got Tune (FR) (Green Tune (USA))
4730[4] 5026[6]

Double Bank (IRE) *Ms Emma Oliver* 110h 111c
11 b g Double Trigger(IRE) Misty Silks (Scottish Reel)
58[8] (4505)
4788[U] 5123[4] 5553[2]

Double Chocolate *John O'Shea* 95h 110c
11 b g Doubletour(USA) Matching Green (Green Ruby (USA))
189[2] **487[3]**
757[6] 923[P] 1060[7] 1135[6] 2017[2] 2297[3] 2540[4]
2923[P] 3817[3]
4440[4] 5240[5]

Double Dealites *Jamie Poulton*
4 b f Double Trigger(IRE) Linden Grace (USA) (Mister Baileys)
3229[4] (4499)

Doubledisdoubledat (IRE) *Stuart Coltherd* 82h 112c
7 ch g Vinnie Roe(IRE) Castle Graigue (IRE) (Aylesfield)
4200[4] 4665[P] 4956[6]
(5216) (5480)

Double Double (FR) *Peter Bowen* 130h
8 b g Sakhee(USA) Queen Sceptre (IRE) (Fairy King (USA))
3024[U] (5186) 5353[5]

Double Handful (GER) *Lawney Hill* 121h 124c
8 bl g Pentire Durania (GER) (Surumu (GER))
(97) **425[3]**
806[2] 3183[3]

Double Irish (IRE) *Gordon Elliott* 139h
6 b g King's Theatre(IRE) Palesa's Legacy (IRE) (Montelimar (USA))
4386a[F] 5201a[3]

Double Jeopardy *Dr Jon Scargill* 78h
4 b g Tobougg(IRE) Four-Legged Friend (Aragon)
975[P] 1536[5] 1684[P] 2248[6]

Double Mead *Alexandra Dunn* 82h 106c
12 b m Double Trigger(IRE) Normead Lass (Norwick (USA))
(330)

Double Ross (IRE) *Nigel Twiston-Davies* 142h 159c
8 ch g Double Eclipse(IRE) Kinross (Nearly A Hand)
215^6 **(1663)**
1865^3 2645^2 (3082)
(3458) 3887^2 4764^3 5156^5

Double Seven (IRE) *Martin Brassil* 144h 155c
8 b g Milan Bargante (IRE) (Phardante (FR))
(1897a)
(2123a) 5171^3

Double Silver *Fergal O'Brien* 109h 126c
7 gr m Silver Patriarch(IRE) Shadows Of Silver (Carwhite)
(431)

Doubletoilntrouble (IRE) *Fergal O'Brien* 86h 109c
8 b g Hubbly Bubbly(USA) Boolindrum Lady (IRE) (Meneval (USA))
2560^3 2754^6 4078^2 5011^8 (5293)

Double U Dot Ede'S *Pat Phelan* 95h
5 b g Rock Of Gibraltar(IRE) Reveuse De Jour (IRE) (Sadler's Wells (USA))
2570^5 3508^4 4724^4 5024^4

Double Whammy *Iain Jardine* 116h 117c
8 b g Systematic Honor Rouge (IRE) (Highest Honor (FR))
4366^P 4553^{11} 4774^8
5107^2 5494^5

Douchkirk (FR) *John Berry* 94h
7 b g Prince Kirk(FR) Douchka (FR) (Fijar Tango (FR))
252^{10} 1820^7 3009^2 3924^4 4615^5 4967^3 5139^4

Dougalstar (FR) *Sean Curran* 93h
5 b g Layman(USA) Concert House (IRE) (Entrepreneur)
33^5 307^3 2536^4 3878^3 4595^7 5069^7 5436^5

Douglas *Jo Hughes* 94h 99c
9 b g Beat All(USA) Cromaboo Crown (Crowning Honors (CAN))
1259^7
(1437) 1505^P 1626^4 1825^7 2047^6

Douglas Julian *Miss K Scott* 59h 132c
12 br g Overbury(IRE) Swing Quartet (IRE) (Orchestra)
4239^3 4554^P 5135^{11} 5323^2

Dover's Hill *Nigel Twiston-Davies* 112b
12 b g Pistolet Bleu(IRE) Classic Beauty (IRE) (Fairy King (USA))
1686^P 2065^P

Dovils Date *Tim Vaughan* 122h
5 gr g Clodovil(IRE) Lucky Date (IRE) (Halling (USA))
2848^9 4512^5 (4731) 5142^3 (5552)

Do We Like Him (IRE) *Paul Nicholls* 85b
4 b g Beneficial Pattern Queen (IRE) (Alderbrook)
5310^4

Down Ace (IRE) *Fergal O'Brien* 127h
7 ch m Generous(IRE) Full Of Birds (FR) (Epervier Bleu)
(372) (2317) (2725) (3423) 4740^{13} 4961^7 5370^{15}

Down In Neworleans (IRE) *Ms Margaret Mullins* 113h 129c
9 b g Saddlers' Hall(IRE) Miss Muppet (IRE) (Supreme Leader)
5082a^3

Down Time (USA) *John Joseph Hanlon* 89h 74c
4 b g Harlan's Holiday(USA) Frappay (USA) (Deputy Minister (CAN))
1524^4 1658^3

Downtown Boy (IRE) *Chris Grant* 116h
6 br g Kheleyf(USA) Uptown (IRE) (Be My Guest (USA))
1713^3 2340^3 2732^2 3144^2 3271^2

Downtown Manhattan (IRE) *Jonjo O'Neill* 80h
7 bb g Presenting La Speziana (IRE) (Perugino (USA))
2369^{10} 3094^8 3434^8 3878^7

Downward Spiral (IRE) *John Flint* 40h 120c
9 br g Windsor Castle Misty Links (IRE) (Hushang (IRE))
829^{14}

Doyenne Dream *Caroline Fryer* 97h
7 b m Doyen(IRE) Cribella (USA) (Robellino (USA))
4865^P (5244) 5436^6

Doyenthedecenthing *John Davies* 77h
6 gr m Doyen(IRE) Nearly Decent (Nearly A Hand)
75^4 2596^U 3040^3 3284^U 3828^5 5052^5

Doyly Carte *Donald McCain* 141h
6 b m Doyen(IRE) Generous Diana (Generous (IRE))
2226^5 2669^2 ◆ 3895^2 4237^4 4740^{14}

Doynosaur *K R Burke* 115h 125c
7 b m Doyen(IRE) Daring Destiny (Daring March)
2519^4
(3037) 3386^7 4804^6 5254^5

Dracula (CZE) *J Vana Jr*
6 ch g Jape(USA) Diva Bara (CZE) (Sectori (USA))
1904a^7

Dragon Mask (FR) *J-P Gallorini* 104h 131c
8 b g Turgeon(USA) Distant Meteor (Distant Relative)
1902a^{10} 2415a^P

Dragon's Den (IRE) *Chris Down* 117h
7 b g Antonius Pius(USA) Tallassee (Indian Ridge)
(12) 176^7 1858^3 1972^7 2461^4 4278^4 4634^2 5030^4 5142^4 5489^4

Dramatic Victory (IRE) *John Upson*
7 b g Old Vic Pinky The Nose (IRE) (Shardari)
16^4 422^P 2313^P 2603^P 3817^P

Drawn Free (IRE) *Colin Tizzard* 89h
6 b g Tagula(IRE) Mayfair (Green Desert (USA))
243^4 635^4 924^2 1137^4

Draycott Place (IRE) *John Patrick Ryan* 131h
5 b g Oscar(IRE) Power Again (GER) (Dashing Blade)
4180a^5 4523a^3 5201a^4

Dr Dalwhinny *Donald McCain* 108h
5 ch g Dr Fong(USA) Snow Polina (USA) (Trempolino (USA))
589^2 761^2 928^3 1072^6

Dr Dreamy (IRE) *Claire Dyson* 74h 97c
7 b g Dr Massini(IRE) Proud Aldi (IRE) (Cataldi)
117^8 385^3 759^8

Dreamabad (FR) *J Bertran De Balanda* 97h 92c
4 bl g Astarabad(USA) Premonitary Dream (FR) (Exit To Nowhere (USA))
614a^F

Dream Beat *G A Kingston* 18h
6 b m Beat All(USA) Function Dreamer (Overbury (IRE))
3126a^5

Dreambrook Lady (IRE) *Warren Greatrex* 57h
8 b m Alderbrook Easter Day (IRE) (Simply Great (FR))
176^6 2084^P 2352^P 3186^P *4328^3* 4676^P

Dream Deal *Jeremy Scott* 109h
6 b g Presenting Rowlands Dream (IRE) (Accordion)
2011^6 2614^3 3422^3 4838^P

Dream Destiny *Mark Gillard* 69h
5 b m King's Theatre(IRE) Queen's Banquet (Glacial Storm (USA))
2634^6 3295^3 3961^7 4632^{11} 4910^{14} 5140^9

Dream Flyer (IRE) *Michael Smith* 112h
7 ch g Moscow Society(USA) Bright Choice (IRE) (The Parson)
(2954) 3453^4 4697^5

Dream Honours (IRE) *Clarissa Caroe* 104h 59c
11 b g City Honours(USA) Kamstreampearl (IRE) (Kambalda)
34^8 805^P 969^P

Dreamisi (IRE) *James Ewart* 102b
5 b g Kalanisi(IRE) Marvellous Dream (FR) (Muhtathir)
3276^3 5108^9

Dream Lucky *Richard Woollacott* 78h
9 b g Bandmaster(USA) Sheilas Dream (Inca Chief (USA))
3988^8 4175^6 4514^5 5034^F **5551^U**

Dream Mistress *Chris Bealby* 85h
5 b m Doyen(IRE) Arcady (Slip Anchor)
36^9 2621^{15} 4074^5 4479^3 4983^4

Dreams And Songs *Philip Hobbs* 108h
6 ch m Presenting Karello Bay (Kahyasi)
1814^2 2471^{12} 2907^8 4907^P

Dreams Of Milan (IRE) *Donald McCain* 122h 122c
6 b g Milan Joe's Dream Catch (IRE) (Safety Catch (USA))
2955^2 ◆ 3266^F 3860^5
4835^6

Dreamsoftheatre (IRE) *Jonjo O'Neill* 126h 126c
6 gr g King's Theatre(IRE) Caroline Fontenail (IRE) (Kaldounevees (FR))
460^{12} 860^2 (1051) (1169) (1340) 1747^P (2715)

Dream's Park *Sarah-Jayne Davies*
4 b f Fictional Monty's Dream VII (Damsire Unregistered)
5196^8

Dreamy George (IRE) *John Ferguson* 90b 125c
6 b g Goldmark(USA) Killenard (IRE) (Un Desperado (FR))
3087^3 3873^2 (4793)
5297^P

Dresden (IRE) *Sarah-Jayne Davies* 126h
6 b g Diamond Green(FR) So Precious (IRE) (Batshoof)
(49) 251^4 (756) 2492^{13} 3066^5 4794^6

Dressedtothenines (IRE) *Edward P Harty* 132h 131c
7 b m Oscar(IRE) Regal Holly (Gildoran)
(2986a)

Drive The Bus (IRE) *Denis Gerard Hogan* 86h
5 b g Helissio(FR) Curraghs Annie (IRE) (Darazari (IRE))
2995a^9 4226^9

Driving Well (IRE) *Arthur Whiting* 80h
6 b g Oscar(IRE) Polly Anthus (Kahyasi)
1891^2 2703^6 3440^9 4029^P 4411^{10} 5524^6

Drom *Mrs C Drury* 113c
11 b g Gildoran Sabre Drom (Broadsword (USA))
(496) **660^P**

Drombeg West *Anna Brooks* 95h
7 b m Westerner Quinag (Tina's Pet)
717^5 1017^6 1152^{11} 2701^9 3014^6 (4447) (4760) 5191^8

Drop Anchor (IRE) *Edward Cawley* 101h 85c
11 b g King's Theatre(IRE) Ship's Twine (IRE) (Slip Anchor)
1660^{11}

Drop Out Joe *Charlie Longsdon* 131h
6 ch g Generous(IRE) La Feuillarde (FR) (Nikos)
(1632) (1850) 2505^6 3086^2 3653^3 4545^2 4954^P

Dropzone (USA) *Richard Lee* 94h 101c
5 b g Smart Strike(CAN) Dalisay (IRE) (Sadler's Wells (USA))
812^{10} 1020^7 1391^9
3729^5 4242^4 4748^2 5428^4

Dr Paddy (IRE) *Lucy Normile* 51h
7 b g Dr Massini(IRE) Tina Torus (IRE) (Torus)
1667^{10} 1875^P 5508^{10}

Dr Thistle (IRE) *Sarah-Jayne Davies* 82h 98c
7 b g Dr Massini(IRE) Thistle Thyne (IRE) (Good Thyne (USA))
303^4 541^6 946^{10}

Drumgooland (IRE) *Sarah-Jayne Davies* 117h 96c
7 b g Tikkanen(USA) Credora Storm (IRE) (Glacial Storm (USA))
2181^6 2467^{12} 2846^6 4309^F 4911^{11} 5262^5 5395^{11}

Drumlang (IRE) *Ian Williams* 106h 123c
8 b g Soviet Star(USA) Sherekiya (IRE) (Lycius (USA))
20^U 1638^3 (2039)
2469^5 2845^3 (2895)
3759^2 *4301^8*

Drumlee (IRE) *C F Swan* 129h
6 b g Helissio(FR) Wigwambrave (IRE) (Lord Americo)
5172^{17}

Drummers Drumming (USA) *Alan Berry* 80h
8 b g Stroll(USA) Afleet Summer (USA) (Afleet (CAN))
5493^3

Drummond *Bernard Llewellyn* 78h
5 b g Zamindar(USA) Alrisha (IRE) (Persian Bold)
1795^{11} 2011^{13} 2385^7 2898^5 3426^8 4447^7 4757^3 4967^7

Drumshambo (USA) *Venetia Williams* 119h 152c
8 b g Dynaformer(USA) Gossamer (USA) (Seattle Slew (USA))
(2212)
2666^3 3080^8 3458^P 4160^6 4790^{13}

Drum Valley *Oliver Sherwood* 132h 117c
6 b g Beat Hollow Euippe (Air Express (IRE))
(244) 356^4 2102^2 ◆ 2949^6 3387^4 4805^{10}

Drussell (IRE) *Martin Bosley* 115h 34c
8 b g Orpen(USA) Cahermee Queen (USA) (King Of Kings (IRE))
244^6 486^8 2561^6 3132^7 4129^6 4597^4 4972^4 5189^2 5441^6

Dry Ol'Party *Philip Hobbs* 85b
4 ch f Tobougg(IRE) Emergence (FR) (Poliglote)
5241^5

Dry Rein (IRE) *B Arthey* 85h
9 ch m Bold Fact(USA) Scherzo Impromptu (Music Boy)
799^P 1286^P

Duaiseoir (IRE) *Venetia Williams* 125h 115c
8 b g Bachelor Duke(USA) Masnada (IRE) (Erins Isle)
2719^4 3732^R 4373^R 4780^3 4989^U

Dubaianswer *Tony Coyle* 103h
6 b m Dubawi(IRE) Answered Prayer (Green Desert (USA))
450^3

Dubai Emerald (USA) *Chris Dwyer* 31h
5 bb m Henny Hughes(USA) Zanoubia (USA) (Our Emblem (USA))
875^8

Dubai Glory *Sheena West* 104h
6 b m Dubai Destination(USA) Rosse (Kris)
97^5 488^9 925^{12}

Dubai Kiss *Harry Whittington* 100b
5 b g Dubai Destination(USA) Smooch (Inchinor)
1688^8

Dubai Prince (IRE) *John Ferguson* 129h
6 b g Shamardal(USA) Desert Frolic (IRE) (Persian Bold)
(2563) 3258^P 3872^3 4421^7 (5190)

Dubai Sonnet *Alan Swinbank* 112b
5 b g Dubai Destination(USA) Twilight Sonnet (Exit To Nowhere (USA))
2037^{10} (5166) 5367^5

Dubawi Island (FR) *Venetia Williams* 130h
5 b g Dubawi(IRE) Housa Dancer (FR) (Fabulous Dancer (USA))
(3226) (3550) (5174)

Duc De Normandie (IRE) *Andrew Leyshon*
10 ch g Beneficial Droim Alton Gale (IRE) (Strong Gale)
5292^6

Duchess Of Dreams *Richard Guest* 67h
4 br f Royal Applause Wood Chorus (Singspiel (IRE))
1786^7 1920^8 2066^P

Duchess Theatre (IRE) *Michael Easterby* 95h
6 b m King's Theatre(IRE) Avitta (IRE) (Pennekamp (USA))
1187^3 1305^2 1495^4 1575^4

Dude Alert (IRE) *Anna Newton-Smith* 85h
4 b g Windsor Knot(IRE) Policy (Nashwan (USA))
1524^7 1743^8 2364^2 2927^P 3650^8 4444^6

Duhallowcountry (IRE) *Victor Thompson*
8 b g Beneficial Milltown Lass (IRE) (Mister Lord (USA))
491^5 **579^P**
5485^5

Dukeofchesterwood *Karen McLintock* 84h 88c
12 ch g Missed Flight Gale Storm (Midland Gayle)
(64) **473^5**
789^3 1038^4 1925^2 2310^2 2735^3 3283^3

Duke Of Kentford *Stuart Morris* 75h 97c
12 b g Shambo Kentford Duchess (Jupiter Island)
328^4

Duke Of Lucca (IRE) *Philip Hobbs* 149h 147c
9 b g Milan Derravaragh Native (IRE) (Be My Native (USA))
1868^6 2199^{10} 2646^2 3067^6 4754^4 (5170)

Duke Of Monmouth (IRE) *Charlie Mann* 122h 122c
7 b g Presenting Hayley Cometh (IRE) (Supreme Leader)
2267^P (2512)
2901^P 3717^P 4006^6 5074^7

Duke Of Navan (IRE) *Nicky Richards* 148h
6 bb g Presenting Greenfieldflyer (IRE) (Alphabatim (USA))
2821^6 3261^4 4237^F

Duke's Affair *Jeremy Scott* 83h
6 b g Fair Mix(IRE) Dunsfold Duchess (IRE) (Bustino)
2089^7 2280^8 2614^8 3290^4 4275^P 5432^7

Duke Special (IRE) *Miss Hannah James* 104h
10 ch g Snurge The Mighty Matron (IRE) (Montelimar (USA))
59^P

Dulce Leo (FR) *J-P Gallorini* 138h 131c
8 b g Priolo(USA) Danissima (FR) (Fabulous Dancer (USA))
1901a^3 2240a^7

Dumbarton (IRE) *James Moffatt* 130h
6 br h Danehill Dancer(IRE) Scottish Stage (IRE) (Selkirk (USA))
1185^4 1378^{11} 1922^3 2519^9 3273^7 4056^7 4813^7 5061^5 5496^{10}

Dumorazy (FR) *J-L Guillochon* 111c
11 b g Rasi Brasak School Teacher (Never So Bold)
2384a^F

Duncomplaining (IRE) *William Kinsey* 100b
5 b g Milan Notcomplainingbut (IRE) (Supreme Leader)
3640^2 ◆

Dundee *Alan King* 125h
6 ch g Definite Article Gardana (FR) (Garde Royale)
91^3 2103^5 2936^2 3419^6 4347^4 4933^2 5256^9

Dundock *Alistair Whillans* 94h
13 gr g Cloudings(IRE) Rakajack (Rakaposhi King)
1982^9

Duneen Dream (USA) *Nikki Evans* 70h
9 ch g Hennessy(USA) T N T Red (USA) (Explosive Red (CAN))
333^6 810^7 1269^F

Duneen Point (IRE) *Tim Vaughan* 92h 109c
10 b g Saddlers' Hall(IRE) Miss Ogan (IRE) (Supreme Leader)
500^2 (866)
1327^2 1526^5 (5006)
5390^3

Dune Island *John Upson* 28h
6 b m Compton Admiral Desert Island Disc (Turtle Island (IRE))
2467^{14} 2846^P

Dune Shine *Michael Blake* 112h
9 b g Karinga Bay Caipirinha (IRE) (Strong Gale)
522^U 1018^P

Dungarvan Lass (IRE) *Nicky Henderson* 63h
5 ch m Presenting Flying Iris (IRE) (Un Desperado (FR))
35^6 715^5 922^5

Dungeel (IRE) *Donald McCain* 124h 129c
8 b g Moscow Society(USA) Mis Fortune (IRE) (Be My Native (USA))
(3450)
4273^P

Dungeness *Venetia Williams* 107h 102c
6 b g Beat All(USA) Maydoo (IRE) (Mandalus)
3014^3 (3650) 4172^6 4469^2 4703^F 5233^7

Dunguib (IRE) *Philip Fenton* 156h
11 b g Presenting Edermine Berry (IRE) (Durgam (USA))
3790a^3 (4312a) ◆ 4752^P

Dunkelly Castle (IRE) *Brendan Powell* 66h 75c
10 ch g Old Vic Nanna's Joy (IRE) (Phardante (FR))
294^5 2744^6
3502^P

Dunkirk's First (IRE) *Rose Dobbin* 78h
6 b g Winged Love(IRE) Ball O'Fire (IRE) (Deploy)
1667^9 1877^4 2217^{13} 2443^3 2823^9 3040^P

Dunleer Dixie *Lucy Normile* 74b
6 b g Erhaab(USA) Andaleer (IRE) (Phardante (FR))
3042^{11} 4776^P

Dunlough Bay (IRE) *Paul Webber* 123h 126c
8 ch g Flemensfirth(USA) Loch Lomond (IRE) (Dry Dock)
2395^5 2712^2 3279^2 3717^7 4537^2 4934^3 5284^P

Dunluce Castle (IRE) *Steve Gollings* 102b
6 br g Secret Singer(FR) Royale Laguna (FR) (Cadoudal (FR))
2627^4

Dunmallet Belle *Tom Symonds* 67h
5 b m Kayf Tara Magic Mistress (Magic Ring (IRE))
2298^7 2767^{10}

Dun Masc (IRE) *James Moffatt* 102h 117c
9 b g Right Win(IRE) Timber Toes (IRE) (Mandalus)
355^P 1396^P 2033^P

Dunowen Point (IRE) *Donald McCain* 110h 126c
8 b g Old Vic Esbeggi (Sabrehill (USA))
2939^P 3652^5 3923^4 5156^{17}

Dunraven Prince (IRE) *David Brace* 86h 72c
7 b g Alderbrook Lost Prairie (IRE) (Be My Native (USA))
661^{13} **4246^6**

Dunraven Storm (IRE) *Philip Hobbs* 141h
9 br g Presenting Foxfire (Lord Americo)
2213^4 (2647) 4785^{14} (5142)

Dun To Perfection *Susan Corbett* 87h
7 ch g Endoli(USA) Dun To A Tern (Bay Tern (USA))
279^F 579^R 4615^{10} 4774^4 4938^{10}

Durham Express (IRE) *Tina Jackson* 72h
7 b g Acclamation Edwina (IRE) (Caerleon (USA))
2225^9 2493^{15} 2783^{10} 3040^P

Durian (IRE) *S Foucher*
9 b g Vettori(IRE) Nordican Inch (Inchinor)
616a^F

Duroble Man *Alan King* 104h
4 b g Manduro(GER) Jalousie (IRE) (Barathea (IRE))
1684^4 (1985) 2975^8 4419^8

Dursey Sound (IRE) *Jonjo O'Neill* 135h 144c
6 b g Milan Glendante (IRE) (Phardante (FR))
(1728)
2395^U 2574^U 3146^2 4474^2 4742^{15}

Dushybeag (IRE) *Michael Hourigan* 135h 132c
7 b g Dushyantor(USA) Bula Beag (IRE) (Brush Aside (USA))
3314a^5

Dushy Valley (IRE) *Paul Henderson* 46h 94c
7 b g Dushyantor(USA) Mum's Miracle (IRE) (Luso)
3425^7
3688^P 4471^P
4720^P 5113^2

Dusky Bob (IRE) *Brian Ellison* 111h 122c
9 br g Bob Back(USA) Sunsets Girl (IRE) (The Parson)
2157^P 2670^7 3662^6

Dusshera (IRE) *P York* 96c
9 b m Dushyantor(USA) Ganpati (IRE) (Over The River (FR))
327^2

Dustland Fairytale (IRE) *Ian Williams* 12h
6 b m Noverre(USA) Subtle Affair (IRE) (Barathea (IRE))
3175^P 3568^7

Dutch Canyon (IRE) *N W Alexander* 47b
4 bb g Craigsteel Chitabe (IRE) (Lord Of Appeal)
5219[8]

Dylan Ross (IRE) *Noel Meade* 114h 145c
8 b g Shantou(USA) Quit The Noise (IRE) (Un Desperado (FR))
2141a[U] 2985a[F] (Dead)

Dynamic Drive (IRE) *Maurice Barnes* 95h
7 b g Motivator Biriyani (IRE) (Danehill (USA))
865[6] 959[2] 1145[P] 1379[14] 1419[U] 1790[3] (2169) 2449[5] 5360[5]

Dynamic Idol (USA) *Gary Moore* 100h 115c
7 bb g Dynaformer(USA) El Nafis (USA) (Kingmambo (USA))
4718[2] 5023[P]

Dynaste (FR) *David Pipe* 162h 175c
8 gr g Martaline Bellissima De Mai (FR) (Pistolet Bleu (IRE))
2673[2] ◆ 3262[5] (4766)
5133[2]

Dysios (IRE) *Denis W Cullen* 134h
6 b g Invincible Spirit(IRE) Hataana (USA) (Robellino (USA))
3910a[15]

Eagles Road *Harry Whittington*
4 br f Grape Tree Road Look Of Eagles (Fraam)
5077[13] 5528[P]

Eanans Bay (IRE) *Mark H Tompkins* 58h
5 b g Tiger Hill(IRE) Gold Hush (USA) (Seeking The Gold (USA))
1795[13]

Earcomesthedream (IRE) *Peter Pritchard* 103h 82c
11 b g Marignan(USA) Play It By Ear (IRE) (Be My Native (USA))
68[4] 393[11] 2314[11] 2701[3] 2827[9] 3179[P] 3432[2] 4446[3] 4779[3] (5431)

Earl Grez (FR) *Alan Hill* 52h 67c
9 ch g Turgeon(USA) Yoruba (FR) (Cyborg (FR))
327[3] 4252[3]

Earls Quarter (IRE) *Ian Williams* 108h 118c
8 b g Shantou(USA) Par Street (IRE) (Dolphin Street (FR))
1986[3] 2811[4] *(4497)*

Earl The Pearl *Dan Skelton* 9b
4 b g Multiplex Colorado Pearl (IRE) (Anshan)
5286[7]

Early Applause *Nicky Richards* 102h
6 b g Royal Applause Early Evening (Daylami (IRE))
10[8] 371[3] 678[2] 870[F] 1206[6] 5532[8]

Early Bonnet (IRE) *Kim Bailey* 69h
6 b m Old Vic Superior Dawn (IRE) (Mandalus)
3427[6] 3728[11] 3988[10] 5242[P]

Earth Amber *Nicky Henderson* 114h
5 ch m Hurricane Run(IRE) Too Marvelous (FR) (Dansili)
3568[2] 3854[2]

Earth Dream (IRE) *John Ferguson* 100h 116c
11 b g Old Vic Barbaras Mews (IRE) (Persian Mews)
5135[4]

Earthmoves (FR) *Paul Nicholls* 106b
4 b g Antarctique(IRE) Red Rym (FR) (Denham Red (FR))
(4638) 5145[3]

Earth Planet (IRE) *Micky Hammond* 59h 111c
12 b g Kayf Tara Arctic Rose (IRE) (Jamesmead)
509[6] 766[7] 1039[P]

Earth Tremor (IRE) *E Parry* 96c
8 b g Definite Article Arctic Rose (IRE) (Jamesmead)
5545[P]

Easement *George Bewley* 89h
11 b g Kayf Tara Raspberry Sauce (Niniski (USA))
310[6] 476[5] 751[4] 5106[P] 5514[5]

Easily Pleased (IRE) *Martin Hill* 105h 125c
8 b g Beneficial Bro Ella (IRE) (Cataldi)
996[3] ◆ 1192[4] (1478)
1857[2] 4503[4]
4804[3] 5031[3] 5549[3]

Easter Dancer *Emma Lavelle* 97h
7 ch m Karinga Bay Easter Comet (Gunner B)
41[6] 3598[5] 5124[5]

Easter Day (FR) *Paul Nicholls* 142h 147c
6 b g Malinas(GER) Sainte Lea (FR) (Sirk)
1865[4] (2757) ◆ (3196)

Easter Hunt (IRE) *M F Morris* 118h
5 br g Kalanisi(IRE) Easter Day (IRE) (Simply Great (FR))
3667a[6]

Easter Lad *Paddy Butler* 69b
10 b g Shahrastani(USA) Frozen Pipe (Majestic Maharaj)
5402[P]

Easter Meteor *Emma Lavelle* 123h 151c
8 b g Midnight Legend Easter Comet (Gunner B)
1969[P] 2199[8] 2503[F] 2800[2] 3082[6] 4790[8]

Eastern Calm *Oliver Sherwood* 95b
5 b m Kayf Tara New Dawn (Rakaposhi King)
2724[9] 5077[7]

Eastern Witness (IRE) *Venetia Williams* 94h
7 b g Witness Box(USA) Eastertide (IRE) (Alphabatim (USA))
3173[6] 4093[4] 4411[P] 4758[7]

Eastlake (IRE) *Jonjo O'Neill* 126h 149c
8 b g Beneficial Guigone (FR) (Esprit Du Nord (USA))
(2101)
2488[3] (3080)
4032[4] 4790[6] 5156[3]

Eastwell Smiles *Sophie Leech* 95h
10 gr g Erhaab(USA) Miss University (USA) (Beau Genius (CAN))
376[3] 730[15] 1106[5]

Easy Beesy *Charles Egerton* 101h
6 b g Kalanisi(IRE) Queen Of The Bees (IRE) (Bob Back (USA))
(2016) 2175[2] (3179) 4132[6]

Easydoesit (IRE) *Tony Carroll* 104h
6 b g Iffraaj Fawaayid (USA) (Vaguely Noble)
812[11] (3871)
4004[P] 4527[5] 4937[3] 5233[P]

Easy Reach (IRE) *Mrs Gillian Callaghan* 114h
6 bz g High Chaparral(IRE) Cutting Reef (IRE) (Kris)
2311[6]

Eaton Louie *Tom Symonds* 48b
5 b m Rocamadour La Feuillarde (FR) (Nikos)
3228[4] 4916[16]

Eaton Rock (IRE) *Tom Symonds* 86h
5 b g Rocamadour Duchess Of Kinsale (IRE) (Montelimar (USA))
4452[2] 5016[8] 5174[8]

Ebazan (USA) *Conor O'Dwyer* 123h
5 ch g Lemon Drop Kid(USA) Ebaza (IRE) (Sinndar (IRE))
1139a[9]

Ebony Empress (IRE) *Neil Mulholland* 103h
5 br m Kris Kin(USA) Auditing Empress (IRE) (Accordion)
2216[3] 2946[2] 3898[3] 5159[7]

Ebony River (IRE) *Jennie Candlish* 85h 118c
8 b g Alderbrook Dishy (IRE) (Jurado (USA))
1940[7]

Ebony Roc (IRE) *Gordon Elliott* 65h
4 br g Shirocco(GER) Chia Laguna (IRE) (Ela-Mana-Mou)
4647[7]

Ebony Storm *H Edward Haynes* 58b
7 b g Zafeen(FR) Stormworthy Miss (IRE) (Glacial Storm (USA))
2981[10]

Echo Dancer *Trevor Wall* 78h 93c
8 br g Danehill Dancer(IRE) Entail (USA) (Riverman (USA))
369[5] (807)
1014[3] 1547[F] 1633[2] 1799[3]

Echoes Of Joy *David Evans* 88h
5 b g Echo Of Light Lambadora (Suave Dancer (USA))
1864[U] 2028[7] 2285[6] 2616[6] 3014[9] 4447[P] 4967[2] 5238[6]

Echo Foxtrot *Claire Dyson* 82h
5 b g Echo Of Light April Lee (USA) (Lyphard (USA))
2513[12] 2876[11] 3226[7] 3415[4] 3871[7] 4595[9]

Eddy *John Panvert* 100h
5 b g Exit To Nowhere(USA) Sharway Lady (Shareef Dancer (USA))
1771[5] 5024[5] 5308[4]

Edgardo Sol (FR) *Paul Nicholls* 148h 139c
7 ch g Kapgarde(FR) Tikiti Dancer (FR) (Fabulous Dancer (USA))
2071[7] 2671[6] 3069[11] 4752[9] 5138[13] 5349[3]

Edgar Jones *Peter Bowen* 90h
8 ch g Karinga Bay Chief Lady Nicola (Nicholas Bill)
482[5] 650[4] 1170[4]

Edgevine *Lisa Day* 72h
10 b m Grape Tree Road Vieille Russie (Kenmare (FR))
1673[P]

Edgeworth (IRE) *David Bridgwater* 84h
8 b g Pyrus(USA) Credibility (Komaite (USA))
1171[4] 1280[3] 1487[3]

Edgware Road *Sean Curran* 90h
6 ch g Selkirk(USA) Bayswater (Caerleon (USA))
1143[P]

Edlomond (IRE) *Bill Turner* 118h 96c
8 gr g Great Palm(USA) Samardana (IRE) (Hernando (FR))
2021[P] 2176[5] (2698) 4087[3] **4919[6]** 5434[3]

Edmaaj (IRE) *Jonjo O'Neill* 107h
6 ch g Intikhab(USA) Lady Angola (USA) (Lord At War (ARG))
2083[3] 2492[7] 3556[3] *4022[3]* 4699[6] (5365)

Edmund (IRE) *Ann Hamilton* 105h 123c
7 b g Indian River(FR) Awomansdream (IRE) (Beneficial)
3041[5] (3213)
3722[F] 4080[2] 4628[4] (5051)
5207[2]

Edmund Kean (IRE) *David Pipe* 133h 144c
7 b g Old Vic Baliya (IRE) (Robellino (USA))
2504[16]
(3594) (4088)
4425[3] 5276[P]

Edmundo (IRE) *R P Rath* 106h 107c
8 bb g Flemensfirth(USA) Carrigkem (IRE) (Kemal (FR))
1178a[5]

Eduard (IRE) *Nicky Richards* 131h 158c
6 b g Morozov(USA) Dinny Kenn (IRE) (Phardante (FR))
2031[7] (2830)
(4646) (5273)

Educated Son *Ben De Haan* 98h
6 br g Diktat Spring Sunrise (Robellino (USA))
1816[P]

Egotist (IRE) *Milton Bradley*
6 ch g Halling(USA) Devil's Imp (IRE) (Cadeaux Genereux)
4904[U] 5064[U]

Egypt Mill Spirit (IRE) *Tom George* 106h 102c
8 b g Overbury(IRE) Miss Tickill (IRE) (Mandalus)
3596[6] 4486[3] 4762[5] 5240[3]

Eighteen Carat (IRE) *John Cornwall* 4h 116c
10 b g Luso Jemma's Gold (IRE) (Buckskin (FR))
1913[9] 2051[P]

Eightfold *Seamus Durack* 109h 88c
5 b g Cadeaux Genereux Nirvana (Marju (IRE))
333[2] 605[6] 1816[6] 2045[4] **2677[6]**

Eila Wheeler *Maurice Barnes* 85h
7 b m Central Park(IRE) Only So Far (Teenoso (USA))
1500[5] 1853[7]

El Camino Real (IRE) *Barry Leavy* 53h
6 b g Dansili Soviet Artic (FR) (Bering)
332[4]

Eleazar (GER) *Lucy Wadham* 123h 125c
13 bb g Alkalde(GER) Eicidora (GER) (Surumu (GER))
487[2] (670)
1283[3] (1748)
3006[5]

Electric Mayhem *Nick Mitchell* 99h
7 b g Alflora(IRE) She's No Muppet (Teenoso (USA))
146[6] 3357[13] 4281[6] 4715[7] 5034[12] 5304[10]

Electric Tiger (GER) *David Bridgwater* 107h
7 b g Konigstiger(GER) Elle Plate (GER) (Platini (GER))
201[3] 486[3] 649[3] 762[3] 933[2] 1205[6] 1497[2]

Electrolyser (IRE) *Nicky Henderson* 123h
9 gr g Daylami(IRE) Iviza (IRE) (Sadler's Wells (USA))
(2858) 4103[9]

Elegant Olive *Roger Curtis* 100h
11 b m Alflora(IRE) Strong Cloth (IRE) (Strong Gale)
38[4] 428[5] 1917[P] 2253[4] (2680) 5022[U] 5122[P]

Elegant Stride (IRE) *Don Cantillon*
4 b f One Cool Cat(USA) Good Thought (IRE) (Mukaddamah (USA))
3898[10] *4017[10]*

Elenika (FR) *Venetia Williams* 102h 135c
6 gr g Martaline Nika Glitters (FR) (Nikos)
2179[9] 2488[5] 2816[5] 3197[4] 3660[3] 4089[2] 4250[4] 4559[3] 4806[7] 5385[13]

Eleven Fifty Nine *Anthony Honeyball* 121h
8 b m Midnight Legend Essex Bird (Primitive Rising (USA))
144[2]

Elfego Baca (IRE) *Lucinda Russell* 96h
5 br g Kalanisi(IRE) Lady Padivor (IRE) (Zaffaran (USA))
3522[5] 4221[4] 4956[7] 5102[4]

El Gran Torino (IRE) *A J Martin* 101h
6 b g Ad Valorem(USA) Silview (USA) (Saint Ballado (CAN))
10[P]

Eliades Run (IRE) *Ferdy Murphy* 71h 68c
8 b g Turtle Island(IRE) Chancy Gal (Al Sirat)
444[4] **597[2]**
802[P] 868[P]

El Indio (IRE) *Claire Dyson* 106h
7 b g Flemensfirth(USA) Final Bond (IRE) (Supreme Leader)
2386[3] 3417[3] 4068[4] 4571[3] 4760[7] 5285[F]

Elishpour (IRE) *A J Martin* 110h
4 b g Oasis Dream Elbasana (IRE) (Indian Ridge)
2851a[6] 4432a[9]

Elite Beneficial (IRE) *Rosemary Gasson* 97c
9 ch g Beneficial A Fine Romance (IRE) (Air Display (USA))
2290[P] 2603[2] 2979[4] 3437[4]

Elixir Du Lac *Jo Davis* 67h
7 gr m Fair Mix(IRE) Hutcel Loch (Lochnager)
671[10] 2563[8] 3092[11] 5066[P]

Ellandshe (IRE) *William Young Jnr*
14 bb g Topanoora Fox Glen (Furry Glen)
957[P]

Ella's Promise *Barry Brennan* 74b
5 ch m Doyen(IRE) Sweet N' Twenty (High Top)
3181[8] 4253[3] 5440[6]

Ellaway Rose (IRE) *J P Kenny* 111h 111c
6 b m Beneficial Going My Way (Henbit (USA))
3403a[6]
5254[F]

Ellin's Tower *Kim Bailey* 107h
5 b m Kayf Tara Lucia Forte (Neltino)
372[5] 3898[4] *4499[2]* 5440[2]

Ellistrin Belle *Donald Whillans* 82h
6 b m Helissio(FR) Hannah Park (IRE) (Lycius (USA))
1975[4] 2243[5] 4223[4] 4770[P] 5212[5] 5532[7]

Ellnando Queen *Warren Greatrex* 122h
6 b m Hernando(FR) Queen Of Spades (IRE) (Strong Gale)
2043[3] *(4018) 4301[4]* (5110) (5396)

El Lobo (FR) *David Pipe* 115c
7 b g Loup Solitaire(USA) Mirage Du Simbeu (FR) (Mansonnien (FR))
44[6]

Ellymac *Richard Mitchell* 22b
6 b m Deltic(USA) Or Aibrean (Commanche Run)
2634[7]

El Macca (IRE) *Rebecca Curtis* 104h
5 ch g Old Vic Cluain-Ard (IRE) (Glacial Storm (USA))
2285[5] 3226[3] 5016[2]

El Massivo (IRE) *Brian Ellison* 110h
4 b g Authorized(IRE) Umthoulah (IRE) (Unfuwain (USA))
3616[F]

Elmore Back (IRE) *Charlie Mann* 125h
5 b g Wareed(IRE) Katie Buckers (IRE) (Yashgan)
2701[2] 3000[3] ◆ 3092[P]

El Namoose *John Ferguson* 122b
5 b g Authorized(IRE) Hashimiya (USA) (Gone West (USA))
(3760) ◆ 4756[14]

Elsafeer (IRE) *Tim Vaughan* 108h 123c
9 b g Sakhee(USA) Nabadhaat (USA) (Mr Prospector (USA))
1689[3]
2363[3] 2762[U] 3272[P] 4592[2] 4800[4] 5487[2] ◆

Elsie (IRE) *Thomas Mullins* 115h
7 b m Milan Notcomplainingbut (IRE) (Supreme Leader)
5199a[6]

Eltheeb *Philip Kirby* 95h
7 gr g Red Ransom(USA) Snowdrops (Gulch (USA))
4889[4]

Elton Fox *John Needham* 49h
9 br g Bob Back(USA) Leinthall Fox (Deep Run)
48[9]

El Toreros (USA) *Lawney Hill* 91h
6 b g El Prado(IRE) Soul Reason (USA) (Seeking The Gold (USA))
605[4] 854[9] 2169[14] 3251[4] 5012[2] 5242[12]

Ely Brown (IRE) *Charlie Longsdon* 144h 148c
9 b g Sunshine Street(USA) Browneyed Daughter (IRE) (Broken Hearted)
(2100) 2672[15]
(3327) (4041)
4262[5]

Elysian Heights (IRE) *David Brace* 57h
6 b g Galileo(IRE) Ziffany (Taufan (USA))
2285[10] 2614[12]

E Major *Renee Robeson* 115h
9 ch g Singspiel(IRE) Crystal Cavern (USA) (Be My Guest (USA))
386[5]

Embsay Crag *Philip Kirby* 115h
8 b g Elmaamul(USA) Wigman Lady (IRE) (Tenby)
27[P] 2447[3] 3286[F] (3661) ◆ 4571[5] 5482[2]

Emeebee *Willie Musson* 81h
8 b g Medicean Broughtons Motto (Mtoto)
809[4]

Emerald Glade (IRE) *Jim Best* 107h
7 b m Azamour(IRE) Woodland Glade (Mark Of Esteem (IRE))
(809) (852) 927[3] (1280) 1400[P]

Emerald Rose *Julian Smith* 113h
7 b m Sir Harry Lewis(USA) Swiss Rose (Michelozzo (USA))
46[4] 252[2] ◆ 502[3] (811) 922[2] 1529[3] 1818[2] 2371[10] (4983) 5449[4]

Emily Gray (IRE) *T E Hyde* 131h
6 b m Flemensfirth(USA) Rose Island (Jupiter Island)
4846a[5] 5368[2]

Emily's Flyer (IRE) *Fergal O'Brien* 119h
7 b m Oscar(IRE) Lady Rolfe (IRE) (Alzao (USA))
(41) 811[10] 1201[3] 1284[3] (1541) (1660) 1818[3] 2371[6]

Emirate Isle *Chris Grant* 66h 48c
10 b g Cois Na Tine(IRE) Emmajoun (Emarati (USA))
5360[7]

Emiratesdotcom *Milton Bradley* 19h
8 b g Pivotal Teggiano (IRE) (Mujtahid (USA))
2886[11] 4904[P]

Emma Soda *Paul Davies* 103h 108c
9 b m Milan Ms Trude (IRE) (Montelimar (USA))
3111[2] 3836[P] (4630)

Emperor Of Rome (IRE) *Tim Fitzgerald* 94h
6 b g Antonius Pius(USA) Fire Flower (Sri Pekan (USA))
798[F] 1078[6] 1206[4]

Emperor's Choice (IRE) *Venetia Williams* 115h 143c
7 b g Flemensfirth(USA) House-Of-Hearts (IRE) (Broken Hearted)
2537[6] 3205[P] 3655[7] (4026)
4270[2] 4821[P] 5571[P]

Empire Levant (USA) *Paul Nicholls* 128h 121c
7 gr g Empire Maker(USA) Orellana (USA) (With Approval (CAN))
3088[8] 3459[3] *4020[5] 4497[2]* 4805[P]

Empire Of Dirt (IRE) *C A Murphy* 144h
7 b g Westerner Rose Of Inchiquin (IRE) (Roselier (FR))
2706a[5] 4456a[4] (4708a) 5201a[5]

Empresario (IRE) *Denis Gerard Hogan* 119h
5 ch g Hurricane Run(IRE) La Stravaganza (USA) (Rainbow Quest (USA))
3516[5]

Emral Silk *Sue Smith* 118h
6 b g Revoque(IRE) Silk Stockings (FR) (Trempolino (USA))
2037[3] 2426[7] (3448)

Emrani (USA) *Donald McCain* 101h
7 b g Rahy(USA) Ebaza (IRE) (Sinndar (IRE))
1108[4]

Enchanted Forest (IRE) *Michael Hourigan* 130h
6 b g Galileo(IRE) Halland Park Lass (IRE) (Spectrum (IRE))
2533[14]

Enchanted Garden *Malcolm Jefferson* 134h
6 ch g Sulamani(IRE) Calachuchi (Martinmas)
(3735) 4576[2] 5534[3]

Enchanting Smile (FR) *Mark Gillard* 97h 92c
7 b m Rakti A Thousand Smiles (IRE) (Sadler's Wells (USA))
2474[10]
2726[5] 3687[3] 4416[U] 4633[4] 4802[F] 5304[2] ◆ (5393)

Encore Un Fois *Henry Hogarth* 66h
6 br g Val Royal(FR) Factice (USA) (Known Fact (USA))
75[P]

Endear *Martin Keighley*
10 ch m Pivotal Enchant (Lion Cavern (USA))
1176[P]

Endeavor *Dianne Sayer* 105h 113c
9 ch g Selkirk(USA) Midnight Mambo (USA) (Kingmambo (USA))
(171) **(403)**
◆ **882[4] 1160[2]** 1544[3]
1666[3] 1785[3] 1979[P] **2222[7] 2793[2] 2996[5] 3395[3]**
3758[9] 3937[3] 4222[4] 4616[4] 5207[P] 5532[9]

Endofdiscusion (IRE) *Paul Webber* 100h 105c
7 b g Flemensfirth(USA) Fake Tan (IRE) (Eagle Eyed (USA))
2313[P] 2825[2] 3281[7]

Engai (GER) *David Bridgwater* 110h 112c
8 b g Noroit(GER) Enigma (GER) (Sharp Victor (USA))
521[2] 605[2] 808[2] (948) 1048[2] **(1301)**
1478[5] 4241[4] 5141[4] 5487[5]

Enter Milan (IRE) *John Flint* 80h
9 b g Milan Eva Fay (IRE) (Fayruz)
144[P]

Entertain Me *Robin Dickin* 100h 128c
10 b m Kadastrof(FR) Just The Ticket (IRE) (Jolly Jake (NZ))
738[3] **3113[2]**
3391[6] **4908[6]**
(5176)
5543[2]

Epee Celeste (FR) *Michael Chapman* 88h 105c
8 ch m Spadoun(FR) Juste Ciel (USA) (Septieme Ciel (USA))
508[4] 1283[5] 1396[2] 1598[5] 3150[4] 3267[P] 3502[6]
3730[P] 3852[4]
4066[5] (4309)
4481[3] 4740[15] 5191[5] (5405)

Epic Storm (IRE) *Martin Keighley* 101h
6 b g Montjeu(IRE) Jaya (USA) (Ela-Mana-Mou)
856^{5} 1152^{7} 3568^{5} 3821^{7} 4371^{6}

Erdeli (IRE) *Kevin Bishop* 109h 57c
10 b g Desert Prince(IRE) Edabiya (IRE) (Rainbow Quest (USA))
191^{4} 691^{10}

Ereyna *Renee Robeson* 103h
5 gr m Erhaab(USA) Tereyna (Terimon)
36^{6} 2600^{8} 3159^{13} 3438^{6} 4760^{5}

Ergo Sum *Robin Mathew* 95h
7 bl g Fair Mix(IRE) Idiot's Lady (Idiots Delight)
1991^{9} 2893^{5} 3427^{5} 3871^{2} 4527^{B} 4866^{4}

Erica Starprincess *George Moore* 90h
4 b f Bollin Eric Presidium Star (Presidium)
2168^{3}

Ericht (IRE) *Nicky Henderson* 125h 146c
8 b g Alderbrook Lady Orla (IRE) (Satco (FR))
2782^{2} 3259^{5} (4055)
4742^{P}

Ernest Speak (IRE) *Martin Hill* 95h
5 b g Jeremy(USA) Mijouter (IRE) (Coquelin (USA))
2011^{11} 2280^{F} 5140^{5} 5236^{5} 5490^{12}

Errol Flynn (IRE) *Tony Carroll* 67h
8 bb g Danehill Dancer(IRE) Warusha (GER) (Shareef Dancer (USA))
2083^{12} 2467^{13} 2770^{11} 2891^{6}

Escape Artist *David Thompson* 70h
7 gr g Act One Free At Last (Shirley Heights)
72^{5} 799^{P}

Escape To The West *Joanne Foster* 76h
6 b g Westerner Makeabreak (IRE) (Anshan)
2738^{9} 3350^{9} 4476^{6} 5448^{3}

Escardo (GER) *David Bridgwater* 78h 91c
11 b g Silvano(GER) Epik (GER) (Selkirk (USA))
602^{4} 749^{2} 807^{6} 1057^{2} 1328^{5} 1547^{4}

Escort'men (FR) *Ian Williams* 123h 127c
8 ch g Robin Des Champs(FR) Escortee (FR) (Cadoudal (FR))
1520^{8} 1699^{4} 1889^{2} 2087^{7} 2366^{9} *4020^{13}*

Escudero (IRE) *Paul Nicholls* 124h 119c
9 ch g Snurge What A Breeze (IRE) (Naheez (USA))
921^{2}

Eseej (USA) *Geoffrey Deacon* 89h
9 ch g Aljabr(USA) Jinaan (USA) (Mr Prospector (USA))
2013^{9} *4327^{10}*

Esme Rides A Gaine *Christopher Wilson* 32h 81c
12 gr m Doubletour(USA) Silver Penny (Silly Prices)
74^{P} 2735^{4} (3022)
3834^{4} 4775^{3} 5104^{4}

Esporao (IRE) *Rob Summers* 124h 124c
8 b g Hawk Wing(USA) Roman Love (IRE) (Perugino (USA))
(1158)
1426^{P} 1821^{6}

Essteepee *Tim Vaughan* 70b
5 b g Double Trigger(IRE) Lamper's Light (Idiots Delight)
4177^{3} 4844^{11}

Estates Recovery (IRE) *Luke Dace* 52h 76c
9 b g Luso Jendam (IRE) (Fourstars Allstar (USA))
4021^{13} **4402^{P} 4661^{F}** 4906^{7}
5344^{P}

Esteem *David Evans* 100h 97c
11 b g Mark Of Esteem(IRE) Please (Kris)
43^{6}

Estinaad (USA) *Brian Ellison* 93h
4 b f Street Sense(USA) Dawla (Alhaarth (IRE))
(1658) 1786^{2}

Estoril (FR) *G Cherel* 109h 121c
7 b g Enrique Estremadura (GER) (Konigsstuhl (GER))
5425a^{12}

E Street Boy *David Pipe* 117h 108c
8 b g Kayf Tara Eau De Vie (Terimon)
244^{8}

Etania *Ian Williams* 81h
6 b m King's Theatre(IRE) Linnet (GER) (Dr Fong (USA))
2602^{9} 2824^{F} 3163^{12} 4091^{5} 4703^{7} 5405^{4}

Eternal Vine *Malcolm Jefferson* 59b
5 gr m Grape Tree Road Altogether Now (IRE) (Step Together I (USA))
2885^{6} 3898^{9}

Ethelred (IRE) *Jamie Snowden* 78b
6 b g Alflora(IRE) Navale (FR) (Baryshnikov (AUS))
4844^{6}

Etheridge Annie *Hugo Froud* 98b
5 b m Leander Lady Harriet (Sir Harry Lewis (USA))
4135^{2} 4540^{2} 4916^{5}

Ethics Girl (IRE) *John Berry* 97h
8 b m Hernando(FR) Palinisa (FR) (Night Shift (USA))
593^{2}

Eton Dorney (USA) *John Ferguson* 106b
5 b g Medaglia d'Oro(USA) Sweet And Firm (USA) (Peteski (CAN))
1261^{2} 1499^{6}

Eton Rambler (USA) *George Baker* 86h
4 bb g Hard Spun(USA) Brightbraveandgood (USA) (Smart Strike (CAN))
1920^{5} 2248^{5}

Etxalar (FR) *Lucinda Russell* 95h 119c
11 b g Kingsalsa(USA) Tender To Love (Old Vic)
1666^{5} 1872^{3} 2416^{3} (3107)
3526^{P} (4086)
4669^{3} 5218^{3}

Eudemis (FR) *David Rees* 106h 99c
6 b m Martaline Anazeem (IRE) (Irish River (FR))
765^{15}

Euro Farmer (IRE) *Barry Brennan* 95c
14 b g Eurobus Small Iron (General Ironside)
1010^{P}

Europe (IRE) *Sara Ender* 37b
5 ch g Manduro(GER) Twiggy's Sister (IRE) (Flying Spur (AUS))
4582^{8}

Euro Trash (IRE) *Nigel Twiston-Davies* 81h
8 b g Anshan Euroblend (IRE) (The Parson)
201^{8}

Eurourmrlucky (IRE) *Gordon Elliott* 80b
7 b g Classic Cliche(IRE) Lasca Creek (IRE) (Desert King (IRE))
1292^{4}

Evella (IRE) *Neil King* 127h 104c
10 ch m Beneficial Drimadrian (Gildoran)
378^{P}

Even If *Jonjo O'Neill* 111h
6 b g King's Theatre(IRE) Melody Maid (Strong Gale)
1856^{4} 2083^{9} 2272^{4} 2689^{3} 3094^{7} 3390^{4} 4933^{3} 5351^{4}

Everaard (USA) *Philip Kirby* 115h 117c
8 ch g Lion Heart(USA) Via Gras (USA) (Montbrook (USA))
18^{4} 958^{P}
2884^{5} 3478^{5} (4105)
4190^{2} 4894^{2} (5299)

Everdon Brook (IRE) *David Thompson* 115h
9 br g Laveron Shean Rose (IRE) (Roselier (FR))
4957^{P}

Ever Fortune (USA) *Brian Ellison* 103h
5 ch g El Corredor(USA) Beyond Price (USA) (King Of Kings (IRE))
3034^{7} 3330^{9} 4796^{3} 5231^{7}

Evergreen Forest (IRE) *Natalie Lloyd-Beavis* 82h
6 ch g Haafhd Inaaq (Lammtarra (USA))
1625^{7} 1794^{11} 1946^{6}

Everkingly *Anna Brooks* 77h
8 b g Bollin Eric Pink Mosaic (Safawan)
729^{8} 1106^{9}

Everreadyneddy *Maurice Barnes*
4 ch g Ad Valorem(USA) Maugwenna (Danehill (USA))
2154^{P} 2733^{P}

Everylasting (IRE) *Rose Dobbin* 61h 84c
7 b g Millenary All French (IRE) (Lepanto (GER))
74^{4} 555^{3} 802^{P}

Ewe Are Joking *Ferdy Murphy* 71h
6 b g Midnight Legend Ewe Beauty (FR) (Phantom Breeze)
471^{15}

Exclusion (USA) *Noel Quinlan* 68h
4 bb f Include(USA) Long Silence (USA) (Alleged (USA))
1813^{7}

Exclusive Dancer *George Moore* 96h
5 gr m Notnowcato Exclusive Approval (USA) (With Approval (CAN))
1305^{4} 1496^{F} 1713^{5} 2226^{9} 2514^{4}

Exclusive Rights *Charlie Longsdon* 91b
6 b m Fair Mix(IRE) Rosie Ring (IRE) (Phardante (FR))
33^{P} 186^{P}

Exclusive Waters (IRE) *Gary Moore* 74h
4 b g Elusive City(USA) Pelican Waters (IRE) (Key Of Luck (USA))
1985^{5}

Executive's Hall (IRE) *Ben Haslam* 94h 93c
10 b g Saddlers' Hall(IRE) Overtime (IRE) (Executive Perk)
17^{3} 471^{3} 804^{3} (1073) 1188^{4} 1374^{8} 1506^{4} 5298^{10}

Exemplary *Alexandra Dunn* 107h
7 b g Sulamani(IRE) Epitome (IRE) (Nashwan (USA))
1632^{3} 1864^{6} 2474^{12} 3157^{3} (3290) *4324^{7}* 5034^{13} 5526^{4}

Exiles Return (IRE) *Jacqueline Retter* 81h
12 b g Needle Gun(IRE) Moores Girl (IRE) (Mandalus)
37^{2} 456^{6} 846^{8} 925^{8} 1479^{4} 1645^{P} 1700^{P}

Exitas (IRE) *Oliver Sherwood* 102b
6 b g Exit To Nowhere(USA) Suntas (IRE) (Riberetto)
4473^{3} 5028^{5} 5454^{4}

Exit To Freedom *John Wainwright* 85h
8 ch g Exit To Nowhere(USA) Bobanvi (Timeless Times (USA))
19^{5} 564^{3} 902^{5} 1205^{5} 1631^{4} 3265^{P} 3636^{8} (5298)

Exmoor Challenge *Jeremy Scott* 53h
5 b g Thank Heavens Bullys Maid (Button Bright (USA))
4175^{8} 4391^{6}

Exmoor Mist *Victor Dartnall* 93h
6 gr g Kayf Tara Chita's Flora (Alflora (IRE))
2940^{8} 3357^{10} 3956^{9} 4599^{6}

Exning Halt *John Quinn* 88h
5 b g Rail Link Phi Phi (IRE) (Fasliyev (USA))
475^{5}

Exotic Flower (FR) *Robert Collet* 120h
6 b g Poliglote Desert's Flower (FR) (Highest Honor (FR))
863a^{0}

Exotic Man (FR) *John Wade* 111h 118c
9 ch g Arvico(FR) Northine (FR) (Northern Treat (USA))
583^{2}

Expanding Universe (IRE) *Tony Carroll* 122h
7 b g Galileo(IRE) Uliana (USA) (Darshaan)
2286^{5} 2492^{16} 3249^{7} 3740^{5} 4510^{5} 4760^{10}

Experimentalist *Tim Vaughan* 119h
6 b g Monsieur Bond(IRE) Floppie (FR) (Law Society (USA))
(706) 928^{2} 956^{3} 1337^{3} (1496) 1625^{2} 1766^{4} 2949^{11} 3263^{4} 4277^{7}

Explained (IRE) *Tim Vaughan* 115h 121c
7 b g Exit To Nowhere(USA) All Told (IRE) (Valanjou (FR))
251^{2} 3249^{P} 5040^{2}
(5451)

Extra Bold *Miss A Goschen* 69h 103c
12 b g Overbury(IRE) Tellicherry (Strong Gale)
297^{2} 655^{4}

Extreme Cara (FR) *G Cherel* 130h 133c
5 b g Hurricane Cat(USA) Magic Cara (FR) (Akarad (FR))
1983a^{8} 2414a^{P}

Extreme Impact *Evan Williams* 120h 74c
8 b g Rock Of Gibraltar(IRE) Soviet Moon (IRE) (Sadler's Wells (USA))
(3775) 4271^{8} 4489^{6} 5183^{4}

Extremely So *Chris Down* 109h
8 ch m Kyllachy Antigua (Selkirk (USA))
3420^{4} 3959^{3}

Extreme Sud (FR) *N Bertran De Balanda* 125h 140c
6 b g Enrique Fac Simile (FR) (Kaldoun (FR))
5425a^{5}

Eyeline *Andrew Hollinshead* 82h
4 b g Needwood Blade Waterline Twenty (IRE) (Indian Danehill (IRE))
1182^{4} 2038^{4} 2559^{7} 3014^{7}

Eyre Apparent (IRE) *Lucinda Russell* 120h 120c
9 ch g Turgeon(USA) Miss Poutine (FR) (Chamberlin (FR))
341^{6} 1666^{8}

Eyre Square (IRE) *John Wade* 71h 77c
11 b g Publisher(USA) Eyre Eile (IRE) (Miner's Lamp)
5164^{3}

Fabrika *Nicky Henderson* 121h
6 b m Presenting Daprika (FR) (Epervier Bleu)
2801^{2} (4917)

Face To Face *David Pipe* 43b
5 b g Kayf Tara Monsignorita (IRE) (Classic Cliche (IRE))
4445^{3}

Factor Fifty (IRE) *Philip Kirby* 99h
5 b g Definite Article Sun Screen (Caerleon (USA))
207^{2} ◆ (699) 1792^{4} 2104^{5} *4018^{8}* 4772^{3}

Fago (FR) *Paul Nicholls* 111h 155c
6 bb g Balko(FR) Merciki (FR) (Villez (USA))
2281^{6} (2656)
3320^{5} 4414^{4} 5156^{F}

Faha (IRE) *Andy Turnell* 98h 44c
8 b m Catcher In The Rye(IRE) Tarayib (Hamas (IRE))
237^{9}

Fair Bramble *Oliver Sherwood* 103h 110c
8 b m Fair Mix(IRE) Briery Ann (Anshan)
268^{3} **2007^{6}**
2424^{3} 3171^{2} 3769^{5} 4337^{3} 5009^{3} (5246)
5453^{F}

Fair Breeze *Richard Phillips* 82h
7 b m Trade Fair Soft Touch (IRE) (Petorius)
540^{3} 977^{6} 1267^{10} 1700^{3} 2679^{3} 3009^{7}

Fair Dilemma (IRE) *Paul Henderson* 122h 127c
9 b g Dr Massini(IRE) Midnight Dilemma (IRE) (Eagle Eyed (USA))
(5458)

Fair Dolly *Sophie Leech*
6 b m Fair Mix(IRE) Bay Fair (Arctic Lord)
1064^{7}

Fair Dreamer *Harry Fry* 111h
6 gr g Fair Mix(IRE) Emma's Dream (Karinga Bay)
(2912) 4102^{9} 4988^{2} 5303^{5}

Fair Funny (IRE) *Edward U Hales* 104h
6 b m King's Theatre(IRE) Dainty Daisy (IRE) (Buckskin (FR))
3804a^{5}

Fair Gun Lady *Michael Scudamore* 47h
6 gr m Fair Mix(IRE) Persistent Gunner (Gunner B)
1814^{7}

Fair Loch *K R Burke* 124h
6 gr g Fair Mix(IRE) Ardentinny (Ardross)
3350^{2} 4103^{3} 4807^{2} 5251^{5}

Fair Trade *Alan King* 129h
7 ch g Trade Fair Ballet (Sharrood (USA))
15^{U} (235)
2227^{U} 2519^{12}

Fairview Sue *Claire Dyson* 62h
10 gr m Alflora(IRE) Tall Story (Arzanni)
1495^{7}

Fairweather Friend *Jennie Candlish* 101h
5 gr m Fair Mix(IRE) Lucylou (IRE) (Bob Back (USA))
1935^{6} 2444^{F} 2600^{4} 3159^{6} 3920^{4} 4381^{4}

Fairwood Massini (IRE) *Tim Vaughan* 116h 121c
9 b g Dr Massini(IRE) Supreme Sirene (IRE) (Supreme Leader)
(641) **778^{3}**
958^{4} (1161) 1286^{2} **(1361)**
(1521) 1636^{3} 2197^{3}
2389^{P}

Fairwood Present (IRE) *John Buxton* 78h 67c
16 ch g Presenting Ladys Wager (Girandole)
335^{5} 655^{P}

Fairy Alisha *Trevor Wall* 112h
6 ch m Doyen(IRE) Regal Fairy (IRE) (Desert King (IRE))
333^{F} 729^{3}

Fairy Bay *Pam Ford* 25h
7 b m Fair Mix(IRE) Jack It In (Derrylin)
1318^{6} 1671^{10} 2317^{14}

Fairyinthewind (IRE) *Brendan Powell* 109h 118c
5 ch m Indian Haven Blue Daze (Danzero (AUS))
(46) 292^{6} (947) 1258^{2} 1697^{P} 2763^{4} 5518^{4}

Fairymount (IRE) *G D Hanmer*
9 b g Ashkalani(IRE) Last Century (IRE) (Glacial Storm (USA))
4658^{P}

Fairy Rath (IRE) *Nick Gifford* 113h 132c
8 ch g Accordion Killoughey Fairy (IRE) (Torus)
(217) **2212^{F}**
2816^{7} 3287^{3}

Fairytale Theatre (IRE) *Paul Nicholls* 119h
7 b m King's Theatre(IRE) Bay Dove (Alderbrook)
2506^{12} 2907^{2} (4331) (4500) 4961^{6} 5370^{14}

Faith Jicaro (IRE) *James Unett* 96h
7 b m One Cool Cat(USA) Wings To Soar (USA) (Woodman (USA))
505^{5} 812^{5} (1043) 1173^{U} 1729^{5} 2084^{7} 2888^{5}

Faith Keeper (IRE) *Fergal O'Brien* 96h 112c
9 ch g Beneficial Witney Girl (Le Bavard (FR))
2701^{4}
(3033) 3176^{U} 3836^{4} 4481^{6} 4759^{2} 5032^{4} 5334^{S}

Falcarragh (IRE) *Tim Vaughan* 125h 113c
7 ch g Alderbrook Magherareagh Lady (IRE) (Old Vic)
(1255) (1431) (1483) 1685^{11} 2492^{P}

Falcon Island *Colin Tizzard* 74h 141c
9 b g Turtle Island(IRE) Dolly Sparks (IRE) (Electric)
81^{6} 1746^{8} 2072^{P} 2925^{5} 3294^{4} 3742^{P} 4991^{6}

Falcon's Ginger *John Weymes* 65b
4 ch f Grape Tree Road Sheriff's Falcon (IRE) (Presenting)
2160^{8} 3214^{9}

Falcon's Legend *John Weymes* 76b
4 ch f Midnight Legend Bling Noir (FR) (Moscow Society (USA))
4749^{4} 5063^{8}

Falcon's Present *John Weymes* 74h
6 br m Presenting Mini Mandy (Petoski)
(187) 2885^{5} 3329^{3} 4743^{4} 5494^{10}

False Economy (IRE) *Michael Hourigan* 145h 121c
9 b g Orpen(USA) Ashanti Dancer (IRE) (Dancing Dissident (USA))
1801a^{3} 5420a^{3}

Family Motto *Chris Gordon* 97b
5 b g Tobougg(IRE) Be My Mot (IRE) (Be My Native (USA))
4498^{4} 5028^{7}

Famousandfearless (IRE) *David Pipe* 89h
6 b g Presenting Clandestine (Saddlers' Hall (IRE))
2197^{4} 2476^{11} ◆ 2761^{8}

Fanjos Luck (IRE) *Alan Jones* 55h
7 b g Oscar(IRE) Dr Bernish Lass (IRE) (Dr Massini (IRE))
407^{P} **518^{F}**

Fanny Fantastic *Miss Imogen Pickard*
5 b m Alflora(IRE) Court Champagne (Batshoof)
1318^{8} 2022^{12}

Fantastic Gold *M O Cullinane* 111h 124c
8 ch m Fantastic Light(USA) Spain Lane (USA) (Seeking The Gold (USA))
3403a^{P}

Fantasy King *James Moffatt* 124h
8 b g Acclamation Fantasy Ridge (Indian Ridge)
4736^{18} 5296^{2}

Faolan (IRE) *Robin Bastiman* 28b
4 b g Amadeus Wolf Sudden Interest (FR) (Highest Honor (FR))
2960^{13}

Farasi Kubwa *Venetia Williams* 90h
6 b g Millenary Lily Grey (FR) (Kadalko (FR))
3225^{5} 4175^{5} 5426^{6}

Far Away So Close (IRE) *Paul Nolan* 129h 140c
9 b g Norwich Ballyknock Lass (IRE) (Electric)
(1896a)

Farbreaga (IRE) *Jamie Poulton* 103h 125c
8 b g Shernazar Gleann Alainn (Teenoso (USA))
31^{6} **2437^{2}**
3176^{F} (4067)
(4537) 4934^{7}

Farewellatmidnight *Alex Hales* 93h 108c
8 b m Midnight Legend Fond Farewell (IRE) (Phardante (FR))
64^{P}

Farley's Risk (IRE) *Michael McElhone* 95h 75c
7 ch g Marignan(USA) Cormac Lady (IRE) (Simply Great (FR))
783^{9}

Farlow Des Mottes (FR) *F Nicolle* 143c
6 b g Maresca Sorrento(FR) Jolie Redaely (FR) (Diamond Prospect (USA))
1902a^{3}

Farmer Frank *Nick Kent* 95c
11 b g Cotation Carly-J (Cruise Missile)
388^{2} 757^{10} 1089^{4} 1202^{5} 1300^{2} 1534^{2} 1800^{6}

Farmer Matt (IRE) *Fergal O'Brien* 111h 124c
8 bb g Zagreb(USA) Ashville Native (IRE) (Be My Native (USA))
2922^{2} (4602)
5089^{4}

Farmer's Friend *John Mackie* 88b
5 b g Passing Glance Flawspar (Montjoy (USA))
76^{5} 291^{5}

Farm Pixie (IRE) *Ann Hamilton* 101h 103c
8 b g Snurge Blue Bobby (IRE) (Flemensfirth (USA))
168^{4} **2591^{3}**
2870^{2} 3394^{3} 4082^{2} 4606^{4} 5104^{5} 5356^{7}

Farragon (IRE) *Lucinda Russell* 85b
4 b g Marienbard(IRE) Oath Of Allegiance (IRE) (Supreme Leader)
4043^{7}

Far West (FR) *Paul Nicholls* 153h
5 b g Poliglote Far Away Girl (FR) (Cadoudal (FR))
2372^{2} 2669^{4} 4147^{F} 4752^{21}

Fascino Rustico *Paul Nicholls* 129h
6 b g Milan Rustic Charm (IRE) (Charnwood Forest (IRE))
2802^{5} 3258^{2} 4281^{F} 4503^{5} 5251^{F}

Fashion Faux Pas (IRE) *Paul Henderson* 97h 80c
7 b m Beneficial Supreme Designer (IRE) (Supreme Leader)
2663^{9}
3033^{P} 4067^{6}

Fashion Week *Sue Gardner* 72h 54c
9 gr g Linamix(FR) Picture Princess (Sadler's Wells (USA))
42^{5} **247^{5}**
597^{U} (Dead)

Fa'Side Castle (IRE) *Maurice Barnes*
5 b g Dylan Thomas(IRE) Keyaki (IRE) (Shinko Forest (IRE))
5479^{13}

Fast Exit (IRE) *Noel C Kelly* 97h 75c
7 b g Exit To Nowhere(USA) Gift Token (Batshoof)
471^{6} **749^{5}**
873^{8}

Father Arthur *Richard Rowe* 75h
6 gr g Silver Patriarch(IRE) Amber Starlight (Binary Star (USA))
2432^{11} 2858^{11}

Father Edward (IRE) *John Ferguson* 105b
5 b g Flemensfirth(USA) Native Side (IRE) (Be My Native (USA))
(544) 2254^{6}

Father Shine (IRE) *Shaun Harris* 99h 115c
11 bb g Supreme Leader Shean Hill (IRE) (Bar Dexter (USA))
341[2] 606[2] 902[F] **1397[4] 1636[8] 2346[2] 2873[2] 3113[3] 4862[5] 5516[6]**

Faugheen (IRE) *W P Mullins* 159h
6 b g Germany(USA) Miss Pickering (IRE) (Accordion)
(3380a) ◆ (4750) ◆

Faultless Feelings (IRE) *Martin Keighley* 123h 134c
8 b g Milan Duchess Of Cork (IRE) (Satco (FR))
1091[3]
(1563) 1957[6] 2889[P] 3366[2]

Faustina Pius (IRE) *Matt Sheppard* 115h 103c
6 b m Antonius Pius(USA) Out In The Sun (USA) (It's Freezing (USA))
2888[6]

Favorite Girl (GER) *Michael Appleby* 106h
6 b m Shirocco(GER) Favorite (GER) (Montjeu (IRE))
2397[2] (2848) 3391[4] 3736[3] 5291[3]

Favourable Fellow (IRE) *Geoffrey Harker* 89h
5 b g Beneficial Magic Moonbeam (IRE) (Decent Fellow)
2347[8] 2871[4] 3388[10] 3614[P]

Favoured Nation (IRE) *Jonjo O'Neill* 89h 121c
7 b g Milan Bless Of Honour (IRE) (Shardari)
394[P] (930) ◆ 1361[F]

Fayette County (IRE) *Tim Vaughan* 130h
7 b g Golden Lariat(USA) Midsyn Lady (IRE) (Sharp Victor (USA))
2030[2] (4514) (5015) ◆

Fear Glic (IRE) *Jackie Du Plessis* 127h
8 b g Dr Massini(IRE) Graineuaile (IRE) (Orchestra)
409[4] (5429)

Fearless Leader *David Bridgwater* 81h 88c
7 b g Dr Fong(USA) Queen's Dancer (Groom Dancer (USA))
806[4] 1049[P] 1202[8] (1629)
1767[5] 2177[5]

Fearless Tunes (IRE) *Donald McCain* 100h
6 b g Shantou(USA) Miss Snapdragon (IRE) (Topanoora)
4492[2] 4958[6] 5479[3]

Feast Of Fire (IRE) *Mike Sowersby* 104h
7 ch g St Jovite(USA) Bellagrana (Belmez (USA))
368[2] 933[4] **1083[P]** 1205[9] 4108[4] 4478[3] (4893)

Featherintheattic (IRE) *Warren Greatrex* 124h 105c
9 b g Bahri(USA) Silk Feather (USA) (Silver Hawk (USA))
1053[3] 1184[3] 1315[4] 1577[8]

Feeling (IRE) *Dai Burchell* 86h
10 b g Sadler's Wells(USA) La Pitie (USA) (Devil's Bag (USA))
376[4] 651[11]

Feeling Peckish (USA) *Michael Chapman* 77h 78c
10 ch g Point Given(USA) Sunday Bazaar (USA) (Nureyev (USA))
1172[8] 2047[P]

Feenakilmeedy (IRE) *C Byrnes* 122h
6 b m Alflora(IRE) Nun Better (IRE) (Presenting)
5200a[P]

Feisty Lass (IRE) *Gordon Elliott* 95h 66c
8 ch m Flemensfirth(USA) Back The Queen (IRE) (Bob Back (USA))
(868) 958[2]
1147[6]

Felix Yonger (IRE) *W P Mullins* 153h 160c
8 b g Oscar(IRE) Marble Sound (IRE) (Be My Native (USA))
(2550a)
3314a[2] 3928a[2] 4764[4]

Femme D'Espere *Trevor Wall* 65h
8 b m Celts Espere Drummer's Dream (IRE) (Drumalis)
2876[10] 3728[13] 4379[5] 5072[11] 5283[5]

Fennell Bay (IRE) *John Ferguson* 126h
5 b g Dubawi(IRE) Woodrising (Nomination)
(3469) (4221) 4750[12]

Fennis Moll (IRE) *John Joseph Hanlon* 79h 95c
5 b m Presenting No Moore Bills (Nicholas Bill)
567[10]

Fentara *Mark Walford* 125h 138c
9 b m Kayf Tara Miss Fencote (Phardante (FR))
2805[P] 3725[2] 4104[2] 4430[3] 4669[P] 4953[2] (5210) 5386[3]

Fereni *Kevin Bishop* 42b
5 gr m Tamayaz(CAN) Clotted Cream (USA) (Eagle Eyed (USA))
298[7] 675[10]

Fergall (IRE) *Seamus Mullins* 140h
7 br g Norwich Gaybrook Girl (IRE) (Alderbrook)
(174) (3031) 3322[6] 4550[2] (5399)

Fergal Mael Duin *David Bridgwater* 117h
6 gr g Tikkanen(USA) Fad Amach (IRE) (Flemensfirth (USA))
2178[3] 3427[2] 3735[2]

Ferndale *Ann Duffield* 78h
5 b m Royal Applause Carradale (Pursuit Of Love)
471[13]

Ferney Boy *Chris Fairhurst* 52h
8 b g Courteous Jendorcet (Grey Ghost)
2340[5] 2732[10]

Festival Bound (IRE) *Caroline Fryer* 72h 99c
8 b g Insan(USA) Copper Hill (IRE) (Zaffaran (USA))
162[F] 595[3] 710[P] 965[2]

Festival Folklore (IRE) *Henry Oliver*
6 b m Dr Massini(IRE) Corsican Pine (IRE) (Executive Perk)
3961[12]

Festive Affair (IRE) *Jonjo O'Neill* 130c
6 br g Presenting Merry Batim (IRE) (Alphabatim (USA))
3057[P] 3368[3] (3715)
4742[9]

Festive Felon (IRE) *Noel Meade* 140h
7 b g Gold Well Takara (IRE) (Shernazar)
5200a[10]

Fev Rover (IRE) *Simon West* 68b
7 br g Zagreb(USA) Mrs Pharback (IRE) (Presenting)
2738[7] 3002[9]

Fiachra (IRE) *Natalie Lloyd-Beavis* 60h
4 b g Elnadim(USA) Nesaah's Princess (Sinndar (IRE))
1524[5] 1624[6] 1743[7]

Fiddleesticks (IRE) *William Kinsey* 96h
6 b g Heron Island(IRE) Dawn Native (IRE) (Be My Native (USA))
1935[8] 4579[4] 5282[2]

Fiddler Onthe Hoof (IRE) *Martin Todhunter* 51h
5 b g Librettist(USA) Venus Rising (Observatory (USA))
2030[8]

Fiddlers Bid *Fergal O'Brien* 109h 124c
7 b g Sulamani(IRE) Charitini (GER) (Winged Love (IRE))
2662[P] 2875[3]

Fiddler's Flight (IRE) *John Norton* 65h
8 b g Convinced Carole's Dove (Manhal)
2049[5] 5300[F]

Fiddlers Reel *Jane Clark* 115h 128c
11 ch g Karinga Bay Festival Fancy (Le Coq D'Or)
340[3] 2841[5] 3111[4] 4236[7] 4551[2] (4894) ◆
5210[U] 5513[2]

Fidelor (FR) *Alex Hales* 94h 51c
8 b g Sagacity(FR) Fille Fidele (FR) (Lost World (IRE))
1797[7] 3503[2] 3692[4] 4071[P] 4447[5] (4783) 5069[10]

Fiendish Flame (IRE) *Jennie Candlish* 125h 150c
10 ch g Beneficial Deenish (IRE) (Callernish)
(11) 204[2]
5142[F]

Fiftyfive Degrees (IRE) *Ms Jackie Williamson* 29h 56c
13 b g Presenting Streets (Furry Glen)
535[4]

Fiftyonefiftyone (IRE) *John Cornwall* 103h 125c
10 b g Oscar(IRE) Great Dante (IRE) (Phardante (FR))
(98) (411)
520[U] 735[4] 1077[2] 1470[7] 1537[3] 1780[P] 4861[5]
5290[7] 5517[4]

Figaro *Tim Vaughan* 125h
6 ch g Medicean Chorist (Pivotal)
2341[5] 2900[2] 3390[2] (4224) 4426[P] 5353[3]

Fight Away Boys (IRE) *Lucinda Russell* 103h
6 ch g Vertical Speed(FR) Say Ya Love Me (IRE) (Presenting)
4958[7] 5479[4]

Fight Commander (IRE) *Oliver Sherwood* 104h
5 b g Oscar(IRE) Creidim (IRE) (Erins Isle)
3994[3] 4664[3] 5088[11]

Fighter Jet *Alan King* 128h
6 b g Oasis Dream Totality (Dancing Brave (USA))
1007[7] (1176) (1440) 1867[5] 2655[2]

Filatore (IRE) *Bernard Llewellyn* 118h
5 ch g Teofilo(IRE) Dragnet (IRE) (Rainbow Quest (USA))
1793[8] 2285[4] 3128[2] 4024[2] 4332[4]

Filbert (IRE) *Philip Hobbs* 119h 140c
8 b g Oscar(IRE) Coca's Well (IRE) (Religiously (USA))
2212[4] ◆ (2816) ◆ 3660[4] 4032[5]

Filbert Fox (IRE) *Alistair Whillans* 90h 80c
8 b g Snurge Shean Storm (IRE) (Glacial Storm (USA))
3022[5] 3824[P] 4577[P] **4775[2] 5104[P] 5321[6]**

Fill The Power (IRE) *Sue Smith* 130h 144c
8 b g Subtle Power(IRE) Our Alma (IRE) (Be My Native (USA))
3776[4] 4104[4] ◆ (4339)
4821[7] 5276[P]

Fil's Glory (FR) *D Cadot*
10 b g French Glory Fill Oriane (FR) (Fill My Hopes (FR))
200a[F]

Filun *Anthony Middleton* 77h
9 b g Montjeu(IRE) Sispre (FR) (Master Willie)
1275[13] 1442[P]

Finaghy Ayr (IRE) *Ian Duncan* 101h
6 ch g Lahib(USA) Ali Ankah (IRE) (Insan (USA))
2217[6] 3495[5] 3829[3] (4649) 5256[11]

Final Assault (IRE) *Lucinda Russell* 113h
5 bb g Beneficial Last Campaign (IRE) (Saddlers' Hall (IRE))
1792[5] 2217[4] 2823[4] 3516[2] (3935) 4369[5] 4667[2] 5272[2]

Final Flyer (IRE) *Nikki Evans* 62h
10 br g Beneficial Highways Daughter (IRE) (Phardante (FR))
3062[P] 4972[P] 5001[4]

Final Nudge (IRE) *David Dennis* 109b
5 br g Kayf Tara Another Shot (IRE) (Master Willie)
3433[2]

Final Pass (IRE) *Donald McCain* 101h
6 b g Gamut(IRE) Final Peace (IRE) (Satco (FR))
5286[2] 5554[2]

Financial Climate (IRE) *Oliver Sherwood* 116h 138c
7 b g Exit To Nowhere(USA) Claudia's Pearl (Deploy)
(294) 2177[F]
3006[3] (3366)
3717[3] 4427[P] 5178[3] (5495)

Finbin (IRE) *Henry Hogarth* 75h 78c
12 b g Presenting More Dash (IRE) (Strong Gale)
444[8] **5321[7]**

Finch Flyer (IRE) *Aytach Sadik* 100h 79c
7 ch g Indian Ridge Imelda (USA) (Manila (USA))
377[5] 674[5] 714[4] 968[4]
1014[5] 1395[3] 1547[3] 1669[3] 1710[6] 2044[2] 2349[2] 2562[8] 5144[2]
5361[6]

Finding Your Feet (IRE) *Jonjo O'Neill* 110h
6 bb g Heron Island(IRE) Silvretta (IRE) (Tirol)
1273[6] 1391[6] 1887[2] (2034) 2510[3] 3013[6]

Findlay's Find (IRE) *Mrs Myfanwy Miles* 112c
8 ch g Medicean Lady Pahia (IRE) (Pivotal)
(94) 413[6]
658[5] 4915[8]

Fine Jewellery *Tom Gretton* 43h
5 b g Epalo(GER) Lola Lolita (FR) (Dom Alco (FR))
4980[6] 5288[6]

Fine Kingdom *Brian Ellison* 106h
5 b g King's Best(USA) Eurolink Sundance (Night Shift (USA))
1009[5]

Fine Lily *Venetia Williams* 68b
5 gr m Fair Mix(IRE) Lily Grey (FR) (Kadalko (FR))
1919[8]

Fine Moment *Kevin Frost* 110h
6 b m Pivotal Evasive Quality (FR) (Highest Honor (FR))
2513[P] 2981[3] 3438[5] 3818[3] 4074[2] 4698[2] (5245) 5405[2]

Fine Parchment (IRE) *Charlie Mann* 101h 137c
11 b g Presenting Run For Cover (IRE) (Lafontaine (USA))
(508)
(2367) (2931)
4034[5] 4769[P] 5092[P]

Fine Resolve *Adrian Wintle* 94h
5 b g Refuse To Bend(IRE) Papillon De Bronze (IRE) (Marju (IRE))
289[10] 669[10]

Fine Rightly (IRE) *S R B Crawford* 135h
6 b g Alflora(IRE) Bealtaine (IRE) (Zaffaran (USA))
(3126a) (3494) 4200[2] (4340) 5277[5]

Fine Words *Alan King* 109h
6 b g Alflora(IRE) Gospel (IRE) (Le Bavard (FR))
2266[2] ◆ 3166[7] 4535[4]

Fingal Bay (IRE) *Philip Hobbs* 154h 149c
8 b g King's Theatre(IRE) Lady Marguerrite (Blakeney)
(4174) ◆ (4765)

Finger Onthe Pulse (IRE) *Jonjo O'Neill* 129h 135c
13 b g Accordion Quinnsboro Ice (IRE) (Glacial Storm (USA))
204[11] 587[8] (859)
1047[3] 1302[2] 1686[8] 1969[9] 2448[P] 2785[P] 3065[12]

Fingers Crossed (IRE) *Paul Webber* 84b
4 b g Bach(IRE) Awesome Miracle (IRE) (Supreme Leader)
4909[5]

Finian's Rainbow (IRE) *Nicky Henderson* 137h 164c
11 b g Tiraaz(USA) Trinity Gale (IRE) (Strong Gale)
2503[P]

Finlodex *Murty McGrath*
7 ch g Pastoral Pursuits Ela Aphrodite (Halling (USA))
2272[P]

Finmerello *Kim Bailey* 95h
8 b m Definite Article Belle Magello (FR) (Exit To Nowhere (USA))
2[3] 293[2] 640[11] 1321[7] 2353[3] 2679[5] 3871[6]

Finnegan Paddy (IRE) *Tim Vaughan* 116h 67c
8 ch g Moscow Society(USA) Holy Easter (IRE) (Persian Mews)
1769[F]

Fintan *Laura Young* 92h 116c
11 ch g Generous(IRE) Seeker (Rainbow Quest (USA))
432[5] 674[6] 1012[6] 1122[6] 1551[9] 2051[8] **3164[3]**
3431[4] 3799[F] 4486[4] 4734[F] 5143[5] 5243[5]

Fiorella (FR) *P Lenogue* 92h
4 b f Della Francesca(USA) Flower Of Freedom (FR) (Sadler's Wells (USA))
130a[10]

Firebird Flyer (IRE) *Evan Williams* 128h 136c
7 b g Winged Love(IRE) Kiora Lady (IRE) (King's Ride)
2388[6] 2798[19] 3028[10]
3424[4] 4026[2] (4509)
5383[3]

Fireside Dreams *Geoffrey Harker* 11b
5 b g Boogie Street Champagne N Dreams (Rambo Dancer (CAN))
2885[8]

Firethorn (IRE) *C A McBratney* 102h
5 gr g Dalakhani(IRE) Liege (IRE) (Night Shift (USA))
1661[9]

Fire Tower *Richard Phillips* 103b
6 ch m Firebreak Lamper's Light (Idiots Delight)
324[4] 2892[7]

Fireweld *Patricia Shaw* 73b
7 b m Weld Bella Astra (Daring March)
1353[4] 1445[4] 1861[12]

Firm Order (IRE) *Paul Webber* 110h 135c
9 b g Winged Love(IRE) Fairylodge Scarlet (IRE) (Mister Lord (USA))
120[2] 431[2] (1988)
2367[4] 3006[2] 4344[3] 4741[P]

Firmount Beech (IRE) *Mrs E Scott* 74b 85c
10 b g Anshan Tinkers Lady (IRE) (Sheer Grit)
5553[9]

First Avenue *Laura Mongan* 125h
9 b g Montjeu(IRE) Marciala (IRE) (Machiavellian (USA))
1520[P] 3648[8] 4682[12] 5345[6]

First Fandango *Tim Vaughan* 143h 129c
7 b g Hernando(FR) First Fantasy (Be My Chief (USA))
215[14] 2100[6] *4303[10]* 4765[21]
5232[5]

First In The Queue (IRE) *Nicky Henderson* 143h
7 b g Azamour(IRE) Irina (IRE) (Polar Falcon (USA))
(734) 901[2] 1045[3] 1564[3] (1960) (2064)

First Lad *Nicholas Pomfret* 26h 17c
7 ch g First Trump Intrepid Gal (Terimon)
3602[10]
4484[P] 4793[U] 5362[3]

First Lieutenant (IRE) *M F Morris* 151h 170c
9 ch g Presenting Fourstargale (IRE) (Fourstars Allstar (USA))
1951a[3] 2234a[4] 3376a[2] 4183a[3] 5133[4]

First Mohican *Alan King* 128h
6 ch g Tobougg(IRE) Mohican Girl (Dancing Brave (USA))
(4103) 4421[4] 4807[4]

First Morning (IRE) *Michael Blake* 98h 87c
9 b g Tamayaz(CAN) Emily's Pride (Shirley Heights)
536[6] 635[3] 833[8] (977) 1110[8] **1175[P] 1274[U] 1549[5]**

First Of Never (IRE) *Lynn Siddall* 73h
8 b g Systematic Never Promise (FR) (Cadeaux Genereux)
223[6] 2596[P] 2701[8] 3014[8] 3265[P] *4496[5]* 4823[4] 5052[3] ◆

First Page *Paul Cowley* 80b
4 b f Definite Article Campannello (Saddlers' Hall (IRE))
4867[6]

First Spirit *Sarah Robinson* 64h
8 ch m First Trump Flaming Spirt (Blushing Flame (USA))
686[8] 1153[7]

Firth Of Bavard *Robert Goldie* 29h
7 b g Flemensfirth(USA) Ice Bavard (Le Bavard (FR))
4665[P] 5508[11]

Firth Of The Clyde *Malcolm Jefferson* 111h 139c
9 b g Flemensfirth(USA) Miss Nel (Denel (FR))
2159[2] (2751)
(3738) 4235[3] 4768[10]

Fisher *John Quinn* 133h
5 br g Jeremy(USA) Elfin Laughter (Alzao (USA))
4224[10] 4813[2]

Fishing Bridge (IRE) *David Rees* 122h
9 ch g Definite Article Rith Ar Aghaidh (IRE) (Phardante (FR))
3798[P] 4028[5] 4841[7] 5186[P]

Fistral Beach (IRE) *Paul Nicholls* 125h 149c
11 b g Definite Article Empress Of Light (Emperor Jones (USA))
204[9]

Fitandproperjob *Anthony Middleton* 88h 95c
8 b g Helissio(FR) Talkasha (IRE) (Doyoun)
267[10] (384) 564[U] 661[9] 764[5] 902[P]
1834[5] 2044[4] 2335[2] 2576[3] 3027[2] 3439[5] (3817)
4004[4] 4486[7]
4992[3] 5437[U]

Fitobust (IRE) *Lawney Hill* 89h 62c
8 b g Classic Cliche(IRE) Noan Rose (IRE) (Roselier (FR))
326[P] 1010[5] 1172[7] (1406) 1538[2]

Fitz Volonte *Andrew J Martin* 96h 95c
7 br g Passing Glance Swordella (Broadsword (USA))
302[P] 500[4]

Fitzwilly *Mick Channon* 118h
4 b g Sixties Icon Canadian Capers (Ballacashtal (CAN))
(1044) 4419[6] 4807[3] ◆ 4963[4] 5568[13]

Five In A Row (IRE) *Brian Ellison* 119h
6 ch g Blueprint(IRE) Ela Plaisir (IRE) (Grand Plaisir (IRE))
(2037) 2819[4] 3453[2] *(4297)* 4697[7]

Five Out Of Five (IRE) *Evan Williams* 105h 102c
10 b g Saddlers' Hall(IRE) Grangemills (Strong Gale)
(926)
(1172) 1502[3]

Five Rivers (IRE) *Susan Corbett* 76h 115c
8 ch g Accordion Native Country (IRE) (Be My Native (USA))
5218[P] 5484[5]

Five Star Wilsham (IRE) *Nigel Twiston-Davies* 115h 121c
10 b g Bob's Return(IRE) Riverpauper (IRE) (Over The River (FR))
358[13] 659[4] **923[P]** 1155[6]
1959[2] 3730[U] 4601[U] 5558[P]

Five To Five *Lynsey Kendall*
6 b g Librettist(USA) Fiveofive (IRE) (Fairy King (USA))
2968[P]

Fix It Right (IRE) *Emma Lavelle* 116h 88c
6 br g Vinnie Roe(IRE) Rock Cottage Lady (IRE) (Phardante (FR))
1707[3] 2284[6] (2786) 3085[7] 4933[10] **5525[3]**

Flag Flier *Mike Sowersby* 68h
11 ch m Alflora(IRE) Glenn's Slipper (Furry Glen)
222[P] 444[11]

Flame And Flower (IRE) *Conor O'Dwyer* 90h
5 b g Scorpion(IRE) Gilt Benefit (IRE) (Beneficial)
2995a[5] (Dead)

Flamenco Lad *Martin Hill* 98b
4 b g Tamure(IRE) Monda (Danzig Connection (USA))
2015[2] 2926[2] *4296[3]* 5021[3]

Flame Of Dixie (IRE) *Jennie Candlish* 89h
8 b m Beneficial Deenish (IRE) (Callernish)
29[6]

Flame Of The Glen *Barry Brennan* 55h
8 ch g Deploy Furry Queen (Furry Glen)
367[8]

Flaming Arrow (IRE) *Kevin Ryan* 116h
6 b g Sadler's Wells(USA) Pescia (IRE) (Darshaan)
344[3] 850[7] 1020[4]

Flaming Charmer (IRE) *Colin Tizzard* 111h 128c
6 ch g Flemensfirth(USA) Kates Charm (IRE) (Glacial Storm (USA))
2012[F] (2287)
2811[3] 3745[F] 4373[3] 4885[4]

Flaming Gorge (IRE) *Fleur Hawes* 123h 137c
9 ch g Alderbrook Solmus (IRE) (Sexton Blake)
238[4] 3150[3] 3738[2] 4418[8] 4685[7] 5230[4] (5444)

Flaming King *Marc Barber* 26b
6 b g King O' The Mana(IRE) Flaming Katey (Tigerwood)
4728[13]

Flaming Thistle (IRE) *N W Alexander*
10 b g Flemensfirth(USA) Native Thistle (IRE) (Ovac (ITY))
172[4] 580[P]

Flamin June *Kevin Morgan*
8 ch m Karinga Bay Nessfield (Tumble Wind I)
1090[P] 1305[10] 2252[P]
Flanagan (IRE) *Peter Bowen* 112h 95c
10 b g Old Vic Fosterandallen (IRE) (Petoski)
141[2] 481[6] 641[5] 692[2] 942[P]
Flan The Man (IRE) *Miss S Randell*
8 ch g Well Chosen Lucynor (IRE) (Norwich)
4274[P]
Flash Harriet *John Mackie* 91h
10 ch m Classic Cliche(IRE) Harry's Bride (Sir Harry Lewis (USA))
376[6] 423[5]
Flash Jackson *Mme L Audon* 104h 99c
6 b g Turgeon(USA) Katoune (FR) (Snurge)
863a[8]
Flash Tommie (IRE) *Michael Appleby* 96h
6 b g City Honours(USA) African Keys (IRE) (Quws)
2681[6] 3177[P] 4693[3] 4796[4] 5366[10]
Flashyfrank *David Elsworth* 92b
5 b g Franklins Gardens White Flash (Sure Blade (USA))
2254[5] 2667[6] 2912[2]
Flashy Star *Paul Henderson* 88h
5 ch m Mr Greeley(USA) Galileo's Star (IRE) (Galileo (IRE))
46[2] 427[6] 1270[4] 1438[6] 1630[4] 2271[4] 4504[9]
Flatfoot Boogie (FR) *N F Glynn* 137h
9 b g King's Theatre(IRE) Cure The Blues (IRE) (Phardante (FR))
849[4] 5157[11]
Flawless Filly (IRE) *Rose Dobbin* 78h
4 gr f Clodovil(IRE) Min Asl Wafi (IRE) (Octagonal (NZ))
3613[P] 4614[3] 4811[5] 5206[P]
Flaxen Flare (IRE) *Gordon Elliott* 152h
5 ch g Windsor Knot(IRE) Golden Angel (USA) (Slew O'Gold (USA))
2206a[3] 2533[4] 3200[3] 3910a[2] 4785[5] 5274[6]
Flaybay *Chris Grant*
6 b m Grape Tree Road I'll Skin Them (IRE) (Buckskin (FR))
1980[P]
Fleet Dawn *Brian Ellison* 130h
8 b g Polish Precedent(USA) Wychnor Dawn (IRE) (Broken Hearted)
2758[4]
Fleet Fox *N W Alexander* 62b
7 b g Alflora(IRE) Minora (IRE) (Cataldi)
1980[P]
Flemengo (IRE) *Jonjo O'Neill* 78h
5 gr m Flemensfirth(USA) Roosca Rock (IRE) (Roselier (FR))
1863[7] 2579[4] 3010[13]
Flemensmix *Kim Bailey* 109h
6 gr g Flemensfirth(USA) Perfect Mix (FR) (Sagamix (FR))
2507[5] 3838[5] 4281[4] 4491[3]
Flemenson (IRE) *Jonjo O'Neill* 132h
5 b g Flemensfirth(USA) Andrea Cova (IRE) (Strong Gale)
(1937) 2279[2] (4038) 4271[P]
Flemenstar (IRE) *A J Martin* 128h 164c
9 b g Flemensfirth(USA) Different Dee (IRE) (Beau Sher)
(2410a)
Flementime (IRE) *Martin Keighley* 125h
6 ch m Flemensfirth(USA) Funny Times (Silver Patriarch (IRE))
3010[2] 3649[5] (4068) 4392[2] 5427[P]
Flemi Two Toes (IRE) *Sarah Humphrey* 104h 110c
8 b g Flemensfirth(USA) Silva Venture (IRE) (Mandalus)
1917[6] 2253[2] **2722[2] 3033[3] (3502)** 3691[P] **4354[4] 4792[P]**
Fletchers Flyer (IRE) *Harry Fry* 119b
6 b g Winged Love(IRE) Crystal Chord (IRE) (Accordion)
4824[2]
Flew The Nest (IRE) *Jonjo O'Neill* 92h
6 b m King's Theatre(IRE) Full Of Birds (FR) (Epervier Bleu)
450[4] 717[4] 947[8] 1084[4] 1275[F] 1320[12]
Flexi Time (IRE) *Stephen Hughes* 27h
10 b g Environment Friend Princess Perk (IRE) (Executive Perk)
854[P] 1706[11] 2723[5]
Flichity (IRE) *John Cornwall* 99h 83c
9 br g Turtle Island(IRE) Chancy Gal (Al Sirat)
117[P] 285[2] 597[P] 2425[P] 2574[2] 3033[P] 3266[U] 3881[3] 4067[5] 4248[3]
4484[5] 4984[4]
5192[4] 5362[2]
Flicka Williams (IRE) *Tony Coyle* 133h
7 b g Broadway Flyer(USA) Millies Girl (IRE) (Millfontaine)
(1582) (1797) (2516) 3081[5] 3430[2] 4144[P]
Flight Control (IRE) *Peter Croke* 94h 95c
9 b g Lahib(USA) Theredandthegreen (IRE) (Bob Back (USA))
891a[7]
Fling Me (IRE) *Rose Dobbin* 89h
7 b g Definite Article Seductive Dance (Groom Dancer (USA))
1851[0] 494[5] 1791[U] 1982[P] 2997[P] 4746[7]
Flinstone (IRE) *Jonjo O'Neill* 98h
5 b g Presenting Sweet Liss (IRE) (Saddlers' Hall (IRE))
4177[6] 4903[P] 5341[F]
Flintham *Mark Bradstock* 100h
5 b g Kayf Tara Plaid Maid (IRE) (Executive Perk)
270[11] 2181[3] 2768[3] 4535[3]
Flobury *Barry Leavy* 91h
6 b m Overbury(IRE) Miss Flora (Alflora (IRE))
3863[11] 4310[10] 4758[13] 4950[P] 5245[3]
Flogarose (FR) *Lucy Normile* 89h
5 ch m Bonbon Rose(FR) Rosala (FR) (Lashkari)
1665[7] 1979[P] 3212[5] 3518[6] 4770[P] 5532[3]
Florabury *Sarah-Jayne Davies* 65b
5 b m Alflora(IRE) Emerald Project (IRE) (Project Manager)
842[8] 4916[13]

Florafern *Oliver Sherwood* 129h
9 b m Alflora(IRE) Mossy Fern (Le Moss)
2663[3] 3457[3]
Flora Lea *Andrew Price* 89h
7 b m Alflora(IRE) Castanet (Pennekamp (USA))
2289[P] 2770[7] **3729[P]** 4717[6] 5116[13]
Floral Spinner *Bill Turner* 107h 79c
7 b m Alflora(IRE) Dawn Spinner (Arctic Lord)
70[2] 1946[2] 3840[2] 4090[4] 4356[4]
4918[4] 5246[7]
Florida Beat *Dai Burchell* 98h
4 br g Passing Glance Florida Heart (First Trump)
5064[7] 5403[7]
Florida Quays (IRE) *David Dennis* 97h
6 b g Craigsteel Florida Bay (IRE) (Florida Son)
4091[6] 4604[4] 4972[3] 5366[2] 5523[5]
Florishwells D'Ete (FR) *W P Mullins* 124h
4 b f Irish Wells(FR) Florilla (GER) (Big Shuffle (USA))
5199a[7] 5470a[7]
Flowerbud *Jim Best* 33h 23c
9 b m Fantastic Light(USA) Maidment (Insan (USA))
687[3]
Flow Jo (IRE) *Karen George*
6 b m Intikhab(USA) Pespita (IRE) (Desert King (IRE))
856[P]
Flugzeug *Seamus Mullins* 88h 90c
6 gr g Silver Patriarch(IRE) Telmar Flyer (Neltino)
242[P] 2082[2] 2290[6] 2540[F] 2765[2] 3688[2] 4720[2] 5113[3] (5401)
Flute Bowl *Gary Moore* 111h
4 b f Black Sam Bellamy(IRE) Queen's Dancer (Groom Dancer (USA))
3167[9] 3719[4] (4730) 5057[4] (5455)
Fluter Phil *Roger Ingram* 85h
7 b g Piccolo Figura (Rudimentary (USA))
31[7]
Fly By Knight *Tim Walford* 84h
5 b g Desert King(IRE) Lox Lane (IRE) (Presenting)
1793[9] 3872[12]
Fly Home Harry *Alan Swinbank* 114b
5 b g Sir Harry Lewis(USA) Fly Home (Skyliner)
(2223) (2871) 3276[2] 4763[2] 5173[17]
Flying Award (IRE) *Sue Gardner* 108h 137c
10 br g Oscar(IRE) Kate's Machine (IRE) (Farhaan)
2537[7] (3743)
4026[P] (4601)
5348[P]
Flying Bandit (IRE) *Fergal O'Brien* 98h
5 b g Bandari(IRE) Pegus Love (IRE) (Executive Perk)
5547[3]
Flying Doctor *Alistair Whillans* 107h 107c
11 b g Mark Of Esteem(IRE) Vice Vixen (CAN) (Vice Regent (CAN))
1161[5] 1284[6] 1374[2] 1565[6] **1756[6]** 1874[3] 2333[P]
2497[8] 2789[F]
Flying Eagle (IRE) *Peter Bowen* 130h
6 b g Oscar(IRE) Fille D'Argent (IRE) (Desert Style (IRE))
1819[2] 2368[2] (2654) 4370[2] 4838[U] (5036) 5510[4]
Flying Native (IRE) *Nicky Henderson* 70b
5 b g Winged Love(IRE) Native Success (IRE) (Be My Native (USA))
250[7] 675[7]
Flying Phoenix *Michael Blake* 112h
6 b m Phoenix Reach(IRE) Rasmalai (Sadler's Wells (USA))
2513[1] 1173[6] 2084[4] 2698[2] (2888)
Flying Quest *Linda Blackford* 81b
5 b g Rainbow High Dinkies Quest (Sergeant Drummer (USA))
298[6] 483[9] 588[7]
Flying Squad (UAE) *Rose Dobbin* 88h 117c
10 b g Jade Robbery(USA) Sandova (IRE) (Green Desert (USA))
25[P] 220[P] 555[P]
Focail Maith *Neil King* 116h
6 b g Oratorio(IRE) Glittering Image (IRE) (Sadler's Wells (USA))
3034[5] 3269[8] 3469[4] 4573[5] 4796[2] 4988[5] (5443)
Foggy's Wall (IRE) *Paul Nicholls* 126h
6 b g Golan(IRE) Mrs Masters (IRE) (Un Desperado (FR))
2924[3] 3422[2] *4297[9]* 4731[2] 4937[F] (5548)
Fog Patches (IRE) *Lucinda Russell* 89h 104c
8 br g Oscar(IRE) Flash Parade (Boreen (FR))
3019[7] 3394[4] 3936[F] 4220[P] 5321[9]
Foildubh (IRE) *John Patrick Ryan* 151h 154c
10 b g Woods Of Windsor(USA) Bushey Glen (IRE) (Roselier (FR))
1801a[6]
2483a[4] 2985a[F] 3376a[6] 5197a[3]
Folie A Deux (IRE) *William Kinsey* 100h 108c
12 b g Anshan Flynn's Girl (IRE) (Mandalus)
64[3]
Following Dreams (IRE) *Alastair Ralph*
7 b g Beneficial Follow Mama (IRE) (Saddlers' Hall (IRE))
58[U]
Follow The Master *Brian Forsey* 95h
8 b g Alflora(IRE) Daisy May (In The Wings)
2689[10] 5016[8] 5177[3]
Follow The Tracks (IRE) *Brian Barr* 79h
6 bb g Milan Charming Mo (IRE) (Callernish)
1056[5] 1255[6] 1270[8] 1337[5] 1890[P]
Folly Farm (IRE) *Richard Woollacott* 50h
6 gr g Definite Article West Hill Rose (IRE) (Roselier (FR))
3694[9]
Folsom Blue (IRE) *Conor O'Dwyer* 154h 145c
7 b g Old Vic Spirit Leader (IRE) (Supreme Leader)
4455a[2] 5099a[3] 5474a[5]
Fond Memory (IRE) *Nigel Twiston-Davies* 115h
6 b g Dr Massini(IRE) Glacier Lilly (IRE) (Glacial Storm (USA))
2912[1] 2181[9] 2644[4] 3070[7] 4538[2] 5030[8] (5554)

Font *Lawney Hill* 111h 111c
11 b g Sadler's Wells(USA) River Saint (USA) (Irish River (FR))
832[2] 1060[4] (1444)
1748[2] 1959[10]
Foolsandorses (IRE) *W De Best-Turner* 67h
6 b g Beneficial All Honey (IRE) (Fourstars Allstar (USA))
2534[13] 2912[6] 5070[14] 5308[7] 5524[8]
Foot The Bill *Patrick Holmes* 94h 108c
9 b g Generous(IRE) Proudfoot (IRE) (Shareef Dancer (USA))
(206) **789[2]**
2310[4] 2498[4] 3876[P] 4816[3] 5494[6]
Forced Family Fun *John Quinn* 115h
4 b g Refuse To Bend(IRE) Juniper Girl (IRE) (Revoque (IRE))
(2592) 2881[U] 3127[2] (3599) 4224[5] 4722[3]
Force Of Habit *Joanne Foster* 118h 87c
8 gr g Dalakhani(IRE) Bedside Story (Mtoto)
2558[4] 2880[F] 3451[P] 4107[9] **4616[2] 4748[5]**
Force To Spend *Lisa Day*
7 b m Reset(AUS) Mon Petit Diamant (Hector Protector (USA))
808[F]
Forest Rhythm (IRE) *Seamus Mullins* 76h 61c
10 b g Great Palm(USA) Eurythmic (Pharly (FR))
489[8] 687[4]
Forestside (IRE) *Barry Murtagh* 79h 81c
9 br g Zagreb(USA) Silver Sunset (Arzanni)
1147[3] 1377[5] 1756[7] 2036[P] 2308[3] 2880[3] 3143[2] 3449[3] 3517[5] 4203[3]
4748[4] 5107[4]
Forest Walker (IRE) *Dan Skelton* 131c
7 b g Morozov(USA) Queen Polly (IRE) (Pollerton)
58[6] (2194)
2293[4] 3321[6] 3742[2] 4089[P] 5385[2]
Foreverbest (IRE) *Roger Teal* 30b
5 b m Kalanisi(IRE) Clerhane Belle (IRE) (Astarabad (USA))
1871[3] 5367[11]
Forever My Friend (IRE) *Peter Bowen* 92h 118c
7 b g King's Theatre(IRE) Kazan Lady (IRE) (Petardia)
(478) **(639)**
◆ 689[2] 871[4] (1012)
1039[F] 1361[2] 1425[2]
Forever Present (IRE) *Nicky Henderson* 103h
7 br m Presenting Sidalcea (IRE) (Oscar (IRE))
2720[2] 3195[8]
Foreverpresenting (IRE) *Malcolm Jefferson* 118c
10 ch g Presenting Cash It In (IRE) (Kemal (FR))
(899) **1184[2]**
Forever Waining (IRE) *Peter Bowen* 95h
8 b g Choisir(AUS) Dahoar (Charnwood Forest (IRE))
503[4] 854[8] 1675[11]
Forgeon (FR) *T Civel* 97h 107c
5 b g Turgeon(USA) Fortigna (FR) (Petit Loup (USA))
1742a[9]
Forget And Forgive (IRE) *Anthony Middleton* 80h
6 b g Clouseau(DEN) Mollunde (IRE) (Un Desperado (FR))
874[5] 2083[10] 2369[11] 2564[9] 2906[12] 4823[3]
Forgivienne *Evan Williams* 107h
7 b m Alflora(IRE) Always Forgiving (Commanche Run)
2043[2] 2471[8] 3159[2] 3733[P] 4491[P]
Forgotten Gold (IRE) *Tom George* 134h 145c
8 b g Dr Massini(IRE) Ardnataggle (IRE) (Aristocracy)
2065[U] 2939[8] 3990[F] 4509[2] 5068[4] 5371[2]
Forgotten Promise *Brian Barr* 34h
7 b m Revoque(IRE) Ivory's Promise (Pursuit Of Love)
2463[9] 2766[14] 3699[P]
Forgotten Symphony (IRE) *Brian Ellison*
10 b g Bach(IRE) Ethans Rose (IRE) (Roselier (FR))
2046[U] 2155[P]
For Instance (IRE) *Tony Coyle* 100b
4 b g Milan Justamemory (IRE) (Zaffaran (USA))
5219[3]
Formal Bid (IRE) *Gordon Elliott* 118h
7 bb g Oratorio(IRE) Sharamaine (IRE) (King Charlemagne (USA))
(1656) 2085[6]
Formedable (IRE) *Violet M Jordan* 59h 63c
12 ch g Moonax(IRE) Castle Flame (IRE) (Carlingford Castle)
710[4] **861[P]**
1104[2] 1272[P] 5262[P]
Formulation (IRE) *Rebecca Menzies* 105h
7 b g Danehill Dancer(IRE) Formal Approval (USA) (Kingmambo (USA))
1848[8] 2597[3] 2904[5] 3021[4] 3274[5]
Forpadydeplasterer (IRE) *Thomas Cooper* 129h 149c
12 b g Moscow Society(USA) Run Artiste (Deep Run)
1604a[9] 1613a[2] 1897a[8]
Forrardon Xmoor *Miss Jessica Westwood* 74h
5 gr g Fair Mix(IRE) The Nuns Song (Sir Harry Lewis (USA))
2614[9] 2761[9] 3136[9] 3434[P]
Forresters Folly *Alan King* 123h 116c
8 b g Bollin Eric Miss Wyandotte (Henbit (USA))
80[2] 2106[4] **2475[F] 3004[P]** 5333[P]
For Sahkey Moony (IRE) *Cathy Hamilton* 56h 65c
9 b g Welsh Lion(IRE) Dromhale Lady (IRE) (Roselier (FR))
926[P]
Forsocks D'Ycy (FR) *G Cherel* 108h 76c
4 b g Hurricane Cat(USA) Sagane Des Mottes (FR) (Abdonski (FR))
262a[8]
Forster Street (IRE) *James Moffatt* 94h
5 b g Acclamation Easy To Thrill (Soviet Star (USA))
1419[3]

Fort Canning *William Amos* 33b
5 b g Barathea(IRE) Cream Tease (Pursuit Of Love)
5109[7]
Forthefunofit (IRE) *Jonjo O'Neill* 121h
5 b g Flemensfirth(USA) Sommer Sonnet (IRE) (Taipan (IRE))
2354[2] 2773[2] (3144)
For The Staff (IRE) *Jackie Du Plessis* 137h 107c
10 br g Tamayaz(CAN) Shanes Bay (IRE) (Henbit (USA))
175[4]
Fortification (USA) *Stephen Hughes* 100h 89c
11 gr g With Approval(CAN) Palisade (USA) (Gone West (USA))
5122[P]
Fortuna Rose *Julian Smith* 107h
8 b m Sir Harry Lewis(USA) Swiss Rose (Michelozzo (USA))
606[P] 3566[2]
For Two (FR) *Paul Nicholls* 127h
5 gr g Act One Forcat (FR) (Bering)
1866[3] 1960[4] 5353[6] ◆
Fort Worth (IRE) *Jonjo O'Neill* 114b
5 b g Presenting Victorine (IRE) (Un Desperado (FR))
(2681)
Forty Crown (IRE) *John Wade* 115h 98c
8 b g Court Cave(IRE) Forty Quid (IRE) (Exhibitioner)
2516[5]
2882[8] 2959[F] 3922[3] 4338[3] **4771[4]** (5319)
Forward Flight (IRE) *Sue Smith* 118h
8 b g Dilshaan Too Advanced (USA) (Nijinsky (CAN))
3270[3] 3659[3] ◆ (4579) (4670) 5256[4]
Foryourinformation *Rebecca Curtis* 120b
5 b g Kayf Tara Sleepless Eye (Supreme Leader)
2456[2] (4030)
Forzy Origny (FR) *Martin Todhunter* 111h 109c
12 gr g Sleeping Car(FR) Forza Malta (FR) (Royal Charter (FR))
113[7]
Fosters Cross (IRE) *Thomas Mullins* 149h 144c
12 b g Dr Massini(IRE) Francie's Treble (Quayside)
1067a[3]
1168a[7] 1801a[5]
3806a[8] 3910a[16]
Foundation Man (IRE) *Jonjo O'Neill* 99h 128c
7 b g Presenting Function Dream (IRE) (Strong Gale)
1939[2] ◆ (2270)
2928[3] 5060[2] 5573[6]
Foundry Square (IRE) *S Flook* 129h 132c
8 br g Oscar(IRE) Moon Approach (IRE) (Shernazar)
1375[2] 1518[3] 1728[2] 1976[F] (3720)
4092[P] 4348[2] 4788[P] 5232[2] (5491)
Fountains Blossom *Lawney Hill* 80b
5 b m Passing Glance Fountain Crumble (Dr Massini (IRE))
1317[7]
Fountains Flypast *Anthony Honeyball* 104h
10 b g Broadway Flyer(USA) Miss Flower Girl (Petoski)
3028[6] 5128[14] 5526[P]
Fountains Mary *Anthony Honeyball* 105h
6 gr m Midnight Legend Carswell Mayfly VII (Damsire Unregistered)
2273[2] 2697[4] (3044) 3566[3] 4933[15] 5112[7]
Four Nations (USA) *George Baker* 103h
6 ch g Langfuhr(CAN) Kiswahili (Selkirk (USA))
(240) 671[4] 995[4] 1414[4]
Fourovakind *Harry Whittington* 136h 125c
9 b g Sir Harry Lewis(USA) Four M'S (Majestic Maharaj)
2798[9]
3279[4] 3881[U] 4412[3] 4704[P]
Four Shuck Men (IRE) *Tim Vaughan* 99h
6 b g Spartacus(IRE) Shed (Halling (USA))
72[3] 499[5]
Fourth Act (IRE) *Colin Tizzard* 106h
5 b g King's Theatre(IRE) Erintante (IRE) (Denel (FR))
1861[7] 4130[4] 4993[7]
Fourth Estate (IRE) *Nicky Henderson* 124h
8 b g Fantastic Light(USA) Papering (IRE) (Shaadi (USA))
2717[2] 4682[P] 5251[7]
Fourth In Line (IRE) *Mrs L Braithwaite* 106b 85c
10 b g Flemensfirth(USA) Lantern Line (The Parson)
58[7] 424[4]
Fox Appeal (IRE) *Emma Lavelle* 152h 155c
7 b g Brian Boru Lady Appeal (IRE) (Phardante (FR))
215[5] **2019[2]**
2374[2] ◆ (3185)
3893[3] 4420[3] 5137[4]
Foxcub (IRE) *Tom Symonds* 134h
6 b g Bahri(USA) Foxglove (Hernando (FR))
49[4] (184) 581[2] 756[3] (1745) 1960[3] 2630[F] (3028)
3646[6] 4264[8] 4752[23] 5142[6]
Foxes Bridge *Colin Tizzard* 104h
6 b g Tamure(IRE) Risky May (Petoski)
306[2] 2474[P] 4132[P]
Fox Norton (FR) *Nick Williams* 140h
4 b g Lando(GER) Natt Musik (FR) (Kendor (FR))
262a[4] 1684[2] (3089) 5132[6]
Foxrock (IRE) *T M Walsh* 131h 146c
6 b g Flemensfirth(USA) Midnight Light (IRE) (Roselier (FR))
3404a[3] (3791a)
(4315a) ◆ 4741[9]
Fox Run (IRE) *Paul Nicholls* 131h
6 b g Shantou(USA) Viola Crown (IRE) (King's Theatre (IRE))
1867[F]
Foxtail Hill (IRE) *Rebecca Curtis* 66h
5 b g Dr Massini(IRE) Flynn's Girl (IRE) (Mandalus)
2788[7] 3734[5] 4535[5]

Fozy Moss *Stuart Coltherd* 76h 88c
8 b g And Beyond(IRE) Peggy Sioux (IRE) (Little Bighorn)
3161[13]
2155[7] 2445[5] 2591[2] 3022[2] ◆ 3497[7] 3936[P] (4082) 4220[7]
4630[P] 4773[P]

Frampton (IRE) *Charlie Longsdon* 107b
5 b g Presenting Drumavish Lass (IRE) (Oscar (IRE))
2905[3] 5028[3]

Franciscan *Donald McCain* 137h
6 b g Medicean Frangy (Sadler's Wells (USA))
(1389) (2341) 2657[3] 3088[7] 4056[F] 4550[10] (5160) (5353)

Francis Du Mesnil (FR) *Liam Corcoran* 100h 105c
12 b g Saint Preuil(FR) Franciscaine (FR) (Legend Of France (USA))
44[5] 305[P]

Francly Flora *James Payne*
13 b m Alflora(IRE) Si-Gaoith (Strong Gale)
4604[P]

Franco Is My Name *Peter Hedger*
8 b g Namid Veronica Franco (Darshaan)
4987[P] 5400[P]

Frangipani Lady *Nick Williams* 72b
5 b m Milan Rachel C (IRE) (Phardante (FR))
3728[8] 3570[P]

Frankie Falco *Giuseppe Fierro* 75h
8 br h Bollin Eric Marsh Marigold (Tina's Pet)
1266[P]

Frankie Four Feet *Michael Mullineaux* 91h
6 br g Proclamation(IRE) Miss Holly (Makbul)
1690[3] 2053[4] 5190[8]

Frankie's Promise (IRE) *N W Alexander* 122h
6 ch g Fruits Of Love(USA) According To Molly (IRE) (Accordion)
1975[U] 2217[3] 2838[2] 3495[2] 4364[U] (4609) (5320)

Franklino (FR) *Chris Gordon* 104h 110c
7 ch g Gold Away(IRE) Amour Fatal (IRE) (Rainbows For Life (CAN))
710[3] (1275) 1434[2] **1765[2]**

Franklin Roosevelt (IRE) *David Pipe* 102h 127c
8 b g Beneficial Glen's Gale (IRE) (Strong Gale)
(242)
(2110) 2367[3] ◆ 2953[8] 3858[4]

Frank N Fair *Zoe Davison* 71h
6 br m Trade Fair Frankfurt (GER) (Celtic Swing)
2022[5] 2570[6] 2745[4] 3153[6]

Frank The Slink *Micky Hammond* 80h 118c
8 b g Central Park(IRE) Kadari (Commanche Run)
18[P] 2036[4] 2498[2] 2841[4] 3287[P] (4606)
(5215)

Freckle Face *Bill Turner* 99h 136c
7 br g Septieme Ciel(USA) Wavet (Pursuit Of Love)
2467[9]
2719[3] 2887[5] 3180[U] (3799)
(4448) (4885)

Fred Bojangals (IRE) *Barbara Butterworth* 89h 117c
12 b g Scribano Southern Princess (Black Minstrel)
78[3] 282[4] 445[4]
864[6] 879[10]
2421[P] 2868[7]
3107[4] 3637[4] 3924[5]
4477[F]

Freddie Brown *George Charlton* 108h 115c
10 b g Missed Flight Some Shiela (Remainder Man)
23[2] 493[P]

Freddie Mael Duin *David Bridgwater* 42h
5 gr g Fair Mix(IRE) Fad Amach (IRE) (Flemensfirth (USA))
4971[6]

Freddies Return (IRE) *P York* 48h 119c
13 b g Flemensfirth(USA) Rachael's Dawn (Rakaposhi King)
62[9] 328[3]

Freddy Q (IRE) *Roger Teal* 95h
5 ch g Iffraaj Barnabas (ITY) (Slip Anchor)
2644[6] 3686[5] 4467[4]

Freddy's Star (IRE) *Martin Hill* 108h 98c
12 ch g Kris Kutaisi (IRE) (Soviet Star (USA))
193[3] 429[5] 829[5] 1106[3]

Fred Kennet *Paul Fitzsimons* 94h
9 ch g Kadastrof(FR) Evaporate (Insan (USA))
503[13]

Fred Le Macon (FR) *Alan King* 109h
5 b g Passing Sale(FR) Princess Leyla (Teenoso (USA))
207[4] 2759[3] 3282[4] *4495[4]* 4959[4]

Fredo (IRE) *Ian Williams* 128h 128c
10 ch g Lomitas Felina (GER) (Acatenango (GER))
1959[5] 2487[6] 2979[7] *4303[11]* **4402[5] (4663)**
4725[2] 5092[3] 5348[3]

Fred Willetts (IRE) *David Evans* 81h
6 b g Noverre(USA) Intaglia (GER) (Lomitas)
729[P]

Free Advice (IRE) *Marc Barber* 88h
7 b g Milan Coco Opera (IRE) (Lafontaine (USA))
1188[P]

Freedom Flying *Lee James* 63h 47c
11 b m Kalanisi(IRE) Free Spirit (IRE) (Caerleon (USA))
2449[7] 3141[7]

Free Falling *Alastair Lidderdale* 78h 47c
8 ch m Selkirk(USA) Free Flying (Groom Dancer (USA))
2470[5] 2690[6] 3009[5] 3699[5] 4071[3] 4472[5] 5143[P]

Free Of Charge (IRE) *Philip Hobbs* 91h
5 ch g Stowaway Sweetasanu (IRE) (Sri Pekan (USA))
3295[5] 4810[10] 5305[3]

Free Thinking *Nicky Henderson* 122h
6 b m Hernando(FR) Liberthine (FR) (Chamberlin (FR))
(2467) 2810[6] 4528[2] 5368[7]

Free To Dream (IRE) *Venetia Williams* 140h
7 b g Heron Island(IRE) Southsea Lady (IRE) (Kemal (FR))
2490[5] ◆ (2624) 2798[13]

Free World (FR) *Lady Susan Brooke* 82h 124c
10 b g Lost World(IRE) Fautine (FR) (Fast Topaze (USA))
98[3] 853[4] 2721[4] 2890[5] 3156[3] (3439)
3662[2] ◆ 4089[4] 4352[4] 4908[4] 5058[2]
5290[8]

French Canadian (FR) *Mrs C J Robinson* 68c
8 b g Spadoun(FR) Floresca (FR) (Hellios (USA))
424[3]

French Opera *Nicky Henderson* 139h 160c
11 b g Bering On Fair Stage (IRE) (Sadler's Wells (USA))
2664[2] 3080[2] *4020[10]* **4790[5] 5155[9] 5570[5]**

French Seventyfive *Miss Gill Boanas*
7 b g Pursuit Of Love Miss Tun (Komaite (USA))
4617[F]

French Ties (IRE) *Jennie Candlish* 110h 123c
12 ch g John French No Ties (IRE) (General View)
355[11] 1085[3] 1204[3] 1326[2]

Freneys Well *E Bolger* 82h 106c
14 b g Primitive Rising(USA) Betrothed (Aglojo)
1905a[F]

Fresh Air And Fun (IRE) *Alastair Ralph* 97h 116c
11 bb g Trans Island Executive Ellie (IRE) (Executive Perk)
63[7] 335[3] 4355[3] 5135[U]

Fresh Princess (FR) *R Chotard* 121h
8 b m Dai Jin Alpha City (Unfuwain (USA))
263a[10]

Friendly Society (IRE) *Noel Williams* 98h 121c
9 ch g Moscow Society(USA) Friendly Breeze (Strong Gale)
3065[7] 3958[P] 5307[5]

Frith (IRE) *Lucy Normile* 45h 71c
12 b g Benny The Dip(USA) Melodist (USA) (The Minstrel (CAN))
281[6] 749[6] 1715[5]

Frizzo (FR) *Alan King* 110h 112c
7 ch g Ballingarry(IRE) Floridene (FR) (Saumarez)
2362[7] 3028[7] 4556[5] 5059[11]

Fromthetop (IRE) *Michael Scudamore* 85h 83c
8 b g Windsor Castle Rose Of Solway (IRE) (Derring Rose)
478[3] 690[6] 969[2] (1267) 1406[4]
1548[4]

Frontier Boy (IRE) *James Ewart* 100h 93c
10 b g New Frontier(IRE) Mary Bridie (IRE) (Meneval (USA))
74[2]

Frontier Dancer (IRE) *Lawney Hill* 96h 117c
10 b g New Frontier(IRE) All The Gear (IRE) (Nashamaa)
38[6] 606[3]

Frontier Spirit (IRE) *Nigel Twiston-Davies* 99h 120c
10 b g New Frontier(IRE) Psalmist (Mystiko (USA))
2199[6] 2939[P] 3362[P] 3742[P] 4027[2] 4572[P] 5385[4]

Frontier Vic *Nigel Twiston-Davies* 108h
7 b g Old Vic Right On Target (IRE) (Presenting)
338[4] 417[9] 716[3] (1664) 1887[5] 2241[3] 2723[2]
5007[3] 5523[2]

Frosty Dawn *Mike Sowersby* 44h
6 b m Desideratum Frosty Petal (Silver Patriarch (IRE))
3116[P] 3453[P] 3735[8] 4479[7] 4891[6] 5161[12] 5521[P]

Frosty Lad (IRE) *Lawney Hill*
10 b g Moscow Society(USA) Johnston's Crest (IRE) (Be My Native (USA))
2739[P]

Frozen Over *Chris Down* 105h
6 b g Iceman Pearly River (Elegant Air)
1832[6] 2476[9] 3163[7] 3650[10] 5005[2] 5238[2] ◆
5490[3]

Fruit Fayre *Mrs Sheila Crow* 106c
7 b m Sir Harry Lewis(USA) Fruity Farm (Weld)
61[P] (5485)

Fruity Bun *Keiran Burke* 81h
4 b f Dr Fong(USA) Little Conker (Red Ransom (USA))
3641[6] 4513[3] 4882[2] 5029[3] 5071[9]

Fruity O'Rooney *Gary Moore* 125h 139c
11 b g Kahyasi Recipe (Bustino)
1746[6] 2070[5] 4035[5] 4346[7] 4738[11] 5068[U] (5261)

Fujin Dancer (FR) *Brian Ellison* 124h
9 ch g Storming Home Badaayer (USA) (Silver Hawk (USA))
93[5] (4794) 5231[3]

Full Jack (FR) *Pauline Robson* 113h 123c
7 b g Kahyasi Full Contact (FR) (Cadoudal (FR))
1788[3]
1976[3] 2800[9] 3476[6] 4665[3]

Full Of Joy (IRE) *Jonjo O'Neill* 118h 126c
9 b g King's Theatre(IRE) Penny Brae (IRE) (Montelimar (USA))
(542) **670[3]**
1040[5] 1316[2] (1579)
1709[6] 2157[4] 2451[P]

Full Of Mischief (IRE) *K F Clutterbuck* 94b
6 ch m Classic Cliche(IRE) Drama Chick (Riverwise (USA))
5440[10]

Full Ov Beans *Michael Gates* 93h 105c
10 ch g Midnight Legend Scarlet Baroness (Baron Blakeney)
43[5] 252[7]
674[2] 898[6] 1018[7]
1835[4] 2025[6] 2576[2] 2739[U] 3139[3] (3470)
(3855) 4250[U]
4486[P] 5066[4]
(5437)

Full Shift (FR) *Nicky Henderson* 139h
5 b g Ballingarry(IRE) Dansia (GER) (Lavirco (GER))
(2823) 3716[2] (4423) 4789[11]

Full Speed (GER) *Philip Kirby* 116h
9 b g Sholokhov(IRE) Flagny (FR) (Kaldoun (FR))
201[2]

Full Throttle (IRE) *Jonjo O'Neill* 109h
5 b g Scorpion(IRE) Hot Bunny (IRE) (Distinctly North (USA))
359[5] 768[2] 2252[F] 2621[2]

Funky Munky *Alistair Whillans* 103h
9 b g Talaash(IRE) Chilibang Bang (Chilibang)
2245[2] 2597[4] 2879[5] 3398[7] 4553[6] 4957[2] (5217)

Funny Star (FR) *Paul Nicholls* 125h 144c
6 ch g Tot Ou Tard(IRE) Funny Miss (FR) (Bering)
2012[3] 2565[2] (2782)
(3045) 4055[3] 5091[8]

Furie Glory (IRE) *Denis Coakley* 67b
6 gr m Oscar(IRE) Ma Furie (FR) (Balleroy (USA))
1719[7]

Furmagiatt *J Cole* 85b 62c
10 b g In The Wings Sumingasefa (Danehill (USA))
5337[P]

Furrows *Oliver Sherwood* 107h 124c
9 b g Alflora(IRE) See More Furrows (Seymour Hicks (FR))
286[2]

Further More (IRE) *Emma Lavelle* 76h 93c
7 gr g Hasten To Add(USA) Cottage Lass (IRE) (Roselier (FR))
2088[4] 2861[4] 3048[2] 3687[P]

Fuse Wire *Dai Burchell* 94h 98c
7 b g Tamayaz(CAN) Zaffaranni (IRE) (Zaffaran (USA))
4281[10] 4569[6] 4838[4] 5177[4] **5551[3]**

Fushicho *Brendan Powell*
5 ch g Phoenix Reach(IRE) Rasmalai (Sadler's Wells (USA))
1200[P] 1519[P]

Fuzzy Logic (IRE) *Bernard Llewellyn* 111h
5 b g Dylan Thomas(IRE) Gates Of Eden (USA) (Kingmambo (USA))
(482) 4887[5] 5040[6]

Gabbys Star *Shaun Lycett*
7 b m Denounce Jims Sister (Welsh Captain)
1523[P] 1539[5]

Gabrial The Great (IRE) *Donald McCain* 127h
5 b g Montjeu(IRE) Bayourida (USA) (Slew O'Gold (USA))
2933[2]

Gabriella Rose *Alan King* 95b
4 b f Kayf Tara Elaine Tully (IRE) (Persian Bold)
5077[6] 5374[7]

Gadreel (IRE) *Anthony Middleton*
5 b g Dark Angel(IRE) Borsalino (USA) (Trempolino (USA))
856[U]

Gaelic Myth *Kim Bailey* 96b
4 b g Midnight Legend Shannon Native (IRE) (Be My Native (USA))
(5492) ◆

Gaiety Star *John O'Neill*
5 b m Zafeen(FR) Little Miss Prim (Gildoran)
4296[P]

Gaillimh A Chroi (IRE) *John Queally* 116b
5 b m Flemensfirth(USA) Burnt Out (IRE) (Anshan)
(4683)

Gainsborough's Art (IRE) *Harry Chisman* 52h 46c
9 ch g Desert Prince(IRE) Cathy Garcia (IRE) (Be My Guest (USA))
117[P] 285[6] 602[5] 964[P] 1331[9] 2051[7] 2427[P] 4783[3]
5066[P] **5404[P]**

Gair Leat (IRE) *Liam Corcoran* 70h
10 ch g Oscar Schindler(IRE) Valsdaughter (IRE) (Executive Perk)
4838[5] 5258[8] 5550[4]

Gaitway *Nicky Henderson* 125b
4 b g Medicean Milliegait (Tobougg (IRE))
(4964)

Galant Nuit (FR) *Mrs R Burt*
10 b g Comte Du Bourg(FR) Little Blue (FR) (Reve Bleu (FR))
4079[U]

Galaxy Rock (IRE) *Jonjo O'Neill* 119h 133c
10 b g Heron Island(IRE) Blue Pool (Saddlers' Hall (IRE))
851[4] 1047[F] (Dead)

Galbally King (IRE) *A Pennock* 65h 97c
9 ch g Beneficial Carney Hill (IRE) (Doubletour (USA))
424[2]

Gale Force Oscar (IRE) *L M Power* 115c
9 br g Oscar(IRE) Distant Gale (IRE) (Strong Gale)
4788[P] (5545)

Galiotto (IRE) *Gary Moore* 99h
8 b g Galileo(IRE) Welsh Motto (USA) (Mtoto)
3140[8] 5116[2]

Gallaflynn (IRE) *M Barber* 102h 31c
9 b g Winged Love(IRE) Cockney Rainbow (IRE) (Rainbows For Life (CAN))
4727[9]

Gallant Oscar (IRE) *A J Martin* 114h 134c
8 b g Oscar(IRE) Park Wave (IRE) (Supreme Leader)
5474a[U]

Gallant Tipp (IRE) *E J O'Grady* 137h 115c
6 b g Definite Article Noble Delight (IRE) (Saddlers' Hall (IRE))
3931a[5] 4523a[2] 5200a[9]

Gallery Exhibition (IRE) *Kim Bailey* 100h
7 b g Portrait Gallery(IRE) Good Hearted (IRE) (Broken Hearted)
1991[7] ◆ (2471) 3166[6] 5343[5]

Galley Slave (IRE) *Michael Chapman* 81h 60c
9 b g Spartacus(IRE) Cimeterre (IRE) (Arazi (USA))
384[6] 564[2] 1073[3] 1205[10] 1374[3] 1689[5] 1917[8]
4327[9] 4981[3] 5242[10]

Gallic Warrior (FR) *Fergal O'Brien* 117h
7 b g Nononito(FR) Rosa Gallica (Sula Bula)
1915[6] 2280[4] 2695[4] 3728[4] 4599[2] 5088[9] 5335[11]

Gallox Bridge *Tim Vaughan* 120h 140c
9 b g Kayf Tara Explorer (Krisinsky (USA))
249[5] (1990)
2645[4] 4089[P] 4768[F]

Galway Jack (IRE) *Caroline Bailey* 139c
9 b g Witness Box(USA) Cooldalus (IRE) (Mandalus)
6[4] 392[8] 2785[4] 3211[5] 3853[2] (4593)
(5053) 5430[4]

Gamain (IRE) *Ben Case* 104b
5 b g Gamut(IRE) Glass Curtain (IRE) (Old Vic)
5014[3]

Gambling Girl (IRE) *Mrs John Harrington* 125h
5 ch m Hawk Wing(USA) Gambling Spirit (Mister Baileys)
(2205a) 2852a[10] 3339a[P] 5368[9]

Gambo (IRE) *Evan Williams* 115h 121c
8 b g Oscar(IRE) River Thyne (IRE) (Good Thyne (USA))
12[3] **334[2]**
5488[P]

Game Dorabella *Laura Hurley* 16b
6 ch m Avonbridge Ground Game (Gildoran)
675[13] 2981[9] 3160[6]

Ganbei *Mrs Stephanie Easterby* 123c
8 ch g Lomitas Native Ring (FR) (Bering)
4788[F]

Gandalfe (FR) *David Arbuthnot* 84h 114c
9 bb g Laveron Goldville (FR) (Gold And Steel (FR))
245[4] (2251)
2762[5] 4031[4]

Gansey (IRE) *Sue Smith* 128h 136c
12 br g Anshan Ebony Jane (Roselier (FR))
2072[5] 2939[4] 3414[2] 4204[5] 4430[5] 4900[4]

Gap Of Dunloe (IRE) *Peter Bowen* 109h
6 b g Hurricane Run(IRE) Karri Valley (USA) (Storm Bird (CAN))
503[14] (925) 1363[5] 1707[11] 5183[3]

Gardefort (FR) *Venetia Williams* 110h 123c
5 bb g Agent Bleu(FR) La Fresnaie (FR) (Exit To Nowhere (USA))
4273[P] ◆ 4742[F] 5230[6]

Garde Fou (FR) *Paul Henderson* 118h 101c
8 b g Kapgarde(FR) Harpyes (FR) (Quart De Vin (FR))
3092[6] 3643[4] 4161[7] (5037) 5186[P]

Garde La Victoire (FR) *Philip Hobbs* 140h
5 b g Kapgarde(FR) Next Victory (FR) (Akarad (FR))
(2075) (2602) 3070[2] 3644[4] 4736[14] (5140) (5347)

Garden's Rose (FR) *F-M Cottin* 89h
5 gr g Walk In The Park(IRE) Oyez Oyez (FR) (Nombre Premier)
703a[11]

Garde Ville (FR) *Lisa Williamson* 104h
4 ch g Kapgarde(FR) Ville Eagle (FR) (Villez (USA))
262a[5] 3028[8] 3245[4] 3781[4] 4073[4] 4629[4] ◆
5112[10]

Garlands Quest *Richenda Ford* 10b
5 b m Relief Pitcher Coolers Quest (Saddlers' Hall (IRE))
1531[7] 2022[13]

Garleton (IRE) *Maurice Barnes* 91h 145c
13 b g Anshan Another Grouse (Pragmatic)
170[4] 448[4] 680[P] 1978[6] 2358[6] 2972[4] 5482[5]

Garnock (IRE) *David Bridgwater* 99h
6 b m Craigsteel Sister Stephanie (IRE) (Phardante (FR))
(1523) 1823[4] 2027[7]

Garrahalish (IRE) *Robin Dickin* 125h
6 b g Presenting Savu Sea (IRE) (Slip Anchor)
2052[4] 2826[3] (3278) 3654[P] 4266[4] 4510[6] (4901)
5387[8]

Garryleigh (IRE) *David Pipe* 122h
7 b g Statue Of Liberty(USA) Hunter's Valley (Nicolotte)
140[2] ◆ 417[2] (592) 878[3]

Garryowen Oscar (IRE) *Joanne Foster* 77h 61c
8 b g Oscar(IRE) Austocon (IRE) (Be My Native (USA))
727[5] **964[F]**

Gartan Boy *Anabel K Murphy*
6 ch g Denounce Killmacrennan Lady (IRE) (Gladden)
4498[7] 5524[P]

Garth (IRE) *Lucinda Russell* 78h
6 b g Sayadaw(FR) Zaffaran Express (IRE) (Zaffaran (USA))
4631[2] 5102[9]

Garth Mountain *Hugh Burns* 100h
7 b g Rock Of Gibraltar(IRE) One Of The Family (Alzao (USA))
678[6] 788[8] 2169[6]

Garton Star (IRE) *Harry Fry* 80h
5 bl g Presenting Suir Decision (IRE) (Boyne Valley)
4102[8] 4950[5] 5140[10]

Gas Line Boy (IRE) *Philip Hobbs* 126h 137c
8 b g Blueprint(IRE) Jervia (Affirmed (USA))
1709[3] (2283)
2674[3] 3162[4] 4769[8] 5362[U]

Gassin Golf *Richard Lee* 130h
5 b g Montjeu(IRE) Miss Riviera Golf (Hernando (FR))
1706[3] 1970[4] 2225[3] 2813[5] 4682[2] 5088[3]

Gate Please (IRE) *Rebecca Curtis* 117h
9 b g Rashar(USA) Linda Babe (IRE) (Lancastrian)
1764[2] 2147[2] 2740[4] 3130[4] 4024[4] 4838[2]

Gauvain (GER) *Philip Hobbs* 138h 141c
12 b g Sternkoenig(IRE) Gamina (GER) (Dominion)
1485[9] 1867[4] 2100[2] 2504[6] **3082[7] 3414[5] 5092[4]**
5371[7]

Gavi *Karen George* 74h
8 b g Danehill Dancer(IRE) Lydia Maria (Dancing Brave (USA))
843[5] 1008[5] 1152[9] 1269[3] 1633[7]

Gavroche Gaugain (FR) *Dan Skelton* 49h 101c
10 b g Varese(FR) Jobereine (FR) (Joberan (FR))
109[3] 1442[7]

Gaye Memories *Dan Skelton* 110h
6 b m Overbury(IRE) Gaye Memory (Buckskin (FR))
2298[13] 2600[11] 4903[16] (4971) 5291[5] ◆

Gay Sloane (IRE) *Richard Woollacott* 132h 108c
10 b g Anabaa(USA) Seattle's Wood (USA) (Woodman (USA))
539[3] 781[F]

G'Dai Sydney *Peter Bowen* 102b
6 b g Choisir(AUS) Silly Mid-On (Midyan (USA))
338[5] (862) (1016)

Geanie Mac (IRE) *Linda Perratt* 81h
5 ch m Needwood Blade Dixie Evans (Efisio)
2309[5] 2792[P]

Gemini June (IRE) *M Foley* 76h
10 b m Alflora(IRE) Miss Jamielou (IRE) (Be My Native (USA))
61[P]

Geminus (IRE) *Tim Vaughan* 108h
6 b g Choisir(AUS) Macca Luna (IRE) (Kahyasi)
503[12] 966[6] 1306[P]

Gemix (FR) *N Bertran De Balanda* 165h
6 ch h Carlotamix(FR) Ges (FR) (Hours After (USA))
(685a) 2240a[3] 3084[4] 5577a[4]

General Barton (IRE) *Paul W Flynn* 98h
8 gr g Presenting Fille D'Argent (IRE) (Desert Style (IRE))
828[3]

General Girling *Caroline Keevil* 78h
7 b g General Gambul Gold Charm (Imperial Fling (USA))
156[P] 519[8] 711[3] 876[7] 3009[3] 3699[7] 3955[4] 4275[4] 4636[4] 4883[8] **5309[P]**

General Hardi *John Wade* 108h 119c
13 b g In Command(IRE) Hardiprincess (Keen)
169[7] (470) 747[5]
4057[5]

Generalise *Venetia Williams* 65h 76c
8 br g Generous(IRE) Polarise (Arctic Lord)
247[U]

General Miller *Nicky Henderson* 140h 137c
9 b g Karinga Bay Millers Action (Fearless Action (USA))
562[3] 787[5] (1049)
1204[P] (1581)

General Ross (IRE) *Colin Tizzard* 89h 95c
7 b g Generous(IRE) Rossmore Girl (IRE) (Scenic)
(4989)
5237[4] 5394[9]

General Tete Jaune (FR) *Y Fertillet* 90h
10 ch g Rochesson(FR) Kirzinnia (FR) (Zino)
1424a[F]

General Tiberius *K R Burke* 61b
5 b g Selkirk(USA) Eminencia (Sadler's Wells (USA))
3276[5] 4226[10]

Generous Bob *Seamus Mullins* 82b
7 ch g Generous(IRE) Bob's Finesse (Gran Alba (USA))
4504[P] 4911[14] 5402[P]

Generous Chief (IRE) *Chris Grant* 98h
6 b g Generous(IRE) Yosna (FR) (Sicyos (USA))
1980[7] 3018[F] 3829[4] 4186[3] 4461[3] 5161[3] 5359[3]

Generous Helpings (IRE) *Gary Moore* 108h
5 ch g Generous(IRE) Saffron Pride (IRE) (Be My Native (USA))
4808[3] ◆ 5257[4]

Generous June (IRE) *Paddy Butler* 80b
6 ch m Generous(IRE) Outo'Theblue (IRE) (Grand Lodge (USA))
4495[5]

Generous Ransom (IRE) *Nick Gifford* 126h
6 ch g Generous(IRE) Penneyrose Bay (Karinga Bay)
2018[5] 3166[5] 3880[3] *4301[6]* (4888) (5128) 5384[3]

Generous Spender *Heather Cobb* 94h
8 b g Spendent Molly Dreamer (Rushmere)
4527[8] 4760[14]

Genes Quest *Michael Appleby* 64h
7 b m Rainbow High Polly Tino (Neltino)
1007[6] 1176[7]

Genetic Code *Karen Tutty* 83b
6 ch g Generous(IRE) Seems So Easy (USA) (Palmister (USA))
76[6]

Genny Wren *Renee Robeson* 99h 99c
8 ch m Generous(IRE) Wren Warbler (Relkino)
122[5] 1768[5] **2722[U] 3502[5] 4354[P]**

Genson *Richard Woollacott* 95h
5 b g Generous(IRE) Gaynor (Almoojid)
3133[8] 3697[7] 4280[P] 4987[F] 5548[3]

Genstone Trail *Alan King* 94h 104c
8 b m Generous(IRE) Stoney Path (Petoski)
2691[10] 3227[4] 4108[5] 4308[5] **5246[2]**

Gentle Bob (IRE) *Tom George* 102h 116c
9 b g Bob's Return(IRE) Maraniza (IRE) (Akarad (FR))
3859[4] 4372[2] 5076[4]

Gentleman Anshan (IRE) *Rosemary Gasson* 39h 137c
10 b g Anshan Second Violin (IRE) (Cataldi)
204[3] (392)
672[U] 900[3] 1047[10] 1576[5]

Gentleman Jon *Colin Tizzard* 117h
6 b g Beat All(USA) Sudden Spirit (FR) (Esprit Du Nord (USA))
1974[8] 2457[5] (4632) 5153[9]

Gentlemans Token *Clive Mulhall* 8b
6 b g Gentleman's Deal(IRE) Bella Mary (Derrylin)
4349[10]

Genuine Art *Lucy Jones* 61h
7 b m Generosity Impulsive Bid (IRE) (Orpen (USA))
2385[F] 2648[8] 3128[P] 4972[9] 5143[12]

Geordie Boy *Sheena West* 87h
5 bb g Araafa(IRE) Entail (USA) (Riverman (USA))
758[9] 1059[3]

Georgea (IRE) *Gary Moore* 78h
5 ch m Generous(IRE) Newbay Lady (Terimon)
101[3] 2022[6] *2442[4]* 2824[6] 3783[8]

George Almighty *Maurice Barnes* 20b
6 b g Denounce Etching (USA) (Groom Dancer (USA))
173[12]

George Arthur *Nick Gifford* 89b
6 ch g Croco Rouge(IRE) Belmarita (IRE) (Belmez (USA))
5130[6]

George Fernbeck *Brian Ellison* 104h
6 ch g Java Gold(USA) Burmese Days (Montjeu (IRE))
5161[4] (5359) ◆ (5520)

George My Friend *Simon Waugh* 80h
8 b g River Falls Mystical Madam (Teenoso (USA))
750[P]

George Nympton (IRE) *Dominic Ffrench Davis* 120h 125c
8 br g Alderbrook Countess Camilla (Bob's Return (IRE))
1464a[5] 1623a[7] 2025[5] 2293[6] 2977[4] (3431)
3652[P] 4278[P]
4861[2] 5176[6] 5549[U]

George Woolf *Tim Vaughan* 111h 72c
6 b g Iceman Beading (Polish Precedent (USA))
486[9] 767[4] 1020[5]
1175[4] 1287[4] 1751[5]

Georgian Firebird *Alan Swinbank* 98b
4 b f Firebreak Skovshoved (IRE) (Danetime (IRE))
3663[4] (4191) 4618[2] 4944[2]

Georgian King *Martin Keighley* 114h 99c
11 b g Overbury(IRE) Roslin (Roscoe Blake)
2691[2] 3263[2] *4021[11]* 4700[10] 5074[10] 5333[10]

Georgie Lad (IRE) *Philip Hobbs* 98h
6 b g Gold Well Top Step (IRE) (Step Together I (USA))
2181[P] 4397[6]

Gerdago (IRE) *K J Condon* 131h
4 b g Aussie Rules(USA) Touchy Feelings (IRE) (Ashkalani (IRE))
2851a[4] 4432a[3] ◆ 4755[8] 5470a[8]

Germany Calling (IRE) *Charlie Longsdon* 124h
5 b g Germany(USA) Markir (IRE) (Flemensfirth (USA))
1671[3] 1958[2] 4421[5] ◆ 4736[17]

Gers Benefit (IRE) *Tommy Morgan* 20h 90c
10 b m Beneficial Sara's Pinkie (IRE) (Roselier (FR))
5062[4]

Gershwinner (IRE) *Ms Emma Oliver* 32h 94c
11 b g Classic Cliche(IRE) Dalton Lady (Roscoe Blake)
180[4]

Getabuzz *Tim Easterby* 131h
6 b g Beat Hollow Ailincala (IRE) (Pursuit Of Love)
2075[5] 2493[8] 2998[3] 3284[2] (3614) (3920) ◆ 4428[F] (4941) 5384[14]

Getaway Car *Gerard Butler* 75h
4 ch g Medicean Lomapamar (Nashwan (USA))
1536[6]

Get Back In Line (IRE) *Jonjo O'Neill* 127h
6 b g Milan Daraheen Diamond (IRE) (Husyan (USA))
2758[U] 3771[6] 5067[5] 5452[5]

Get Going *Paul Cowley*
4 b g Motivator Good Girl (IRE) (College Chapel)
1624[P]

Get Home Now *Peter Bowen* 124h
6 b g Diktat Swiftly (Cadeaux Genereux)
42[3] 253[2] 556[2] (767) 877[8] (1203) 1350[2] 1485[4] 1972[11] 2102[9]

Get It On (IRE) *Evan Williams* 104h 135c
9 b g King's Theatre(IRE) Keshia (Buckskin (FR))
(2078)
(2149) 3362[5] 3957[5]
4414[6] 4675[3]

Get Me Out Of Here (IRE) *Jonjo O'Neill* 154h
10 b g Accordion Home At Last (IRE) (Mandalus)
2213[12] 2533[8] 4752[2] 5471a[2]

Geton Xmoor (IRE) *Miss Jessica Westwood* 79h
7 b g Heron Island(IRE) Get On With It (IRE) (Old Vic)
5524[5]

Get Ready To Go (IRE) *Richard Ford* 101h 83c
10 b g Turtle Island(IRE) Buckalong (IRE) (Buckskin (FR))
162[3] 4220[4] 4905[2] 5460[3]

Get The Papers *Pauline Robson* 62h 78c
7 b g Kayf Tara Smart Topsy (Oats)
2308[5] 3041[6]

Getting Ready (IRE) *Nigel Twiston-Davies* 118h 98c
7 b g Westerner Last Campaign (IRE) (Saddlers' Hall (IRE))
3183[P] 4399[P]

Getyouractttogether (IRE) *C R Willes*
10 b g Odyle(USA) Eyre Eile (IRE) (Miner's Lamp)
57[P]

Gevrey Chambertin (FR) *David Pipe* 149h 119c
6 gr g Dom Alco(FR) Fee Magic (FR) (Phantom Breeze)
(2672)
4262[P] 4751[9]

Ghaabesh (IRE) *Barry Leavy* 99h
7 b g Alhaarth(IRE) Alyakkh (IRE) (Sadler's Wells (USA))
501[2] 727[4] 852[11] 1206[7] 1331[7] 3264[3] 3353[5] 4447[P] 5072[5] 5298[11]

Ghizao (GER) *Paul Nicholls* 137h 160c
10 b g Tiger Hill(IRE) Glorosia (FR) (Bering)
3032[6] 3645[P]

Ghost Of A Smile (IRE) *Ian Williams* 106h 115c
6 b g Oscar(IRE) Dix Huit Brumaire (FR) (General Assembly (USA))
1795[9] 2286[8] 2802[7] 3070[6] 3390[8] 3878[4] (4571) 4760[6] 5233[6]

Giant Hercules (IRE) *Phil McEntee* 97h
7 b g Val Royal(FR) Mistle Thrush (USA) (Storm Bird (CAN))
4[8] 246[7] 897[5] 1201[5] 1404[4] 1783[7] 2062[7]

Giantofaman (IRE) *D T Hughes* 140h
6 b g Stowaway Anno Mundi (USA) (Red Ransom (USA))
(4523a) 5157[12]

Giant O Murchu (IRE) *Lawney Hill* 108h 116c
10 b g Carroll House Centralspires Best (Nishapour (FR))
705[P] 859[4] ◆ 999[5] 1441[3] (1522)
1767[6] 1990[6]

Giant Sequoia (USA) *Sophie Leech* 75h
10 ch g Giant's Causeway(USA) Beware Of The Cat (USA) (Caveat (USA))
4636[P]

Gibb River (IRE) *Nicky Henderson* 141h
8 ch g Mr Greeley(USA) Laurentine (USA) (Private Account (USA))
2213[5] 2813[9] 4147[14]

Gibbstown (IRE) *Paul Stafford* 98h 97c
8 b m Bob Back(USA) Kitty Maher (IRE) (Posen (USA))
1038[P] 1376[6] 3755[2] (4652)
4812[3] (5104)
5321[4]

Gifted Leader (USA) *Ian Williams* 124h
9 b g Diesis Zaghruta (USA) (Gone West (USA))
4302[7] 5067[2] (5452)

Gift Of Dgab (IRE) *A J Martin* 132h 132c
10 b g Winged Love(IRE) Creative Princess (IRE) (Creative Plan (USA))
1604a[6] ◆ 2503[P]

Gigondas *Gary Moore* 105h
5 ch g Grape Tree Road Queen's Dancer (Groom Dancer (USA))
858[7] 1436[3] 2006[5] (2760) 3025[3] 4724[3]

Gilanto (IRE) *Michael Blake* 85h
7 b g Milan Topham Gale (IRE) (Topanoora)
2106[6] 2457[11] 2840[6] 3569[P] 4760[13]

Gilded Age *Mandy Rowland* 95h 80c
8 b g Cape Cross(IRE) Sweet Folly (IRE) (Singspiel (IRE))
2545 543[6] 1429[7] 1538[7] 1824[7] 2877[10] 3432[P]

Gilded Article (IRE) *A J Martin* 63b
6 b m Definite Article Springfield Gilda (IRE) (Gildoran)
842[11]

Giles Cross (IRE) *Victor Dartnall*
12 b g Saddlers' Hall(IRE) Mystockings (Idiots Delight)
4732[P]

Gilgamboa (IRE) *E Bolger* 143h
6 b g Westerner Hi Native (IRE) (Be My Native (USA))
(3910a) ◆ 4736[13]

Gilly's Filly *Bill Turner* 31b
4 b f With The Flow(USA) True Dove (Kayf Tara)
2318[10] *2731[7]*

Gilnockie *James Ewart* 105b
6 b g Kayf Tara Eloquent Lawyer (Law Society (USA))
2223[4] 3042[2] 3500[2] 5063[5]

Gilt Shadow (IRE) *S R B Crawford* 138h
6 b g Beneficial Baile An Droichid (IRE) (King's Ride)
2852a[8] 3931a[3] ◆

Gilzean (IRE) *Alex Hales* 93h
8 b g Flemensfirth(USA) Sheknowso (Teenoso (USA))
476[8]

Gin Cobbler *Victor Thompson* 84h 108c
8 b g Beneficial Cassia (Be My Native (USA))
114[3] 279[2] 493[4] 4554[10] 5164[6]

Ginger B *Maurice Barnes* 32b
5 ch m Needwood Blade Milladella (FR) (Nureyev (USA))
5500[9]

Ginger Fizz *Ben Case* 108h
7 ch m Haafhd Valagalore (Generous (IRE))
3600[6] *4493[2]* (4910) 5295[2]

Ginger Mac *John Mackie* 75b
6 ch g Needwood Blade Impish Jude (Imp Society (USA))
699[8] 768[9]

Ginger's Lad *Michael Easterby* 67h 92c
10 ch g Elmaamul(USA) Chadwick's Ginger (Crofthall)
20[4] 281[3] 600[2] 749[3] 964[5] 1089[P] 1417[4] 1577[P]

Gingers Reflection *Carroll Gray* 91h 70c
8 ch g Alflora(IRE) Trassey Bridge (Strong Gale)
2460[5] 2765[6]

Ginja Ninja *Rob Summers* 70b
6 ch m Vinnie Roe(IRE) Mrs Ritchie (Teenoso (USA))
5249[9]

Giorgio Quercus (FR) *Nicky Henderson* 116h 141c
9 b g Starborough Winter Breeze (FR) (Kaldoun (FR))
6[7] 334[3] (2714)
4768[6] 5156[F]

Gitane Du Berlais (FR) *W P Mullins* 130h
4 b f Balko(FR) Boheme Du Berlais (FR) (Simon Du Desert (FR))
(2934) (3804a)

Give Me The Remote (IRE) *Graeme McPherson* 40h
6 br g Asian Heights Ali-Kin (Strong Gale)
944[8] 1118[9] 1176[9]

Gizzit (IRE) *Karen George* 100h 98c
8 b g Son Of Sharp Shot(IRE) Suez Canal (FR) (Exit To Nowhere (USA))
322[4] 1710[4] 2315[6] 2696[6]
3048[F] 4504[8] 5522[8]

Glaced Over *Donald McCain* 91h
9 br m Overbury(IRE) Brun Bess (IRE) (Glacial Storm (USA))
316[11] 868[6] 1379[6]

Glacial Roes (IRE) *Sarah-Jayne Davies* 43h
6 ch m Vinnie Roe(IRE) Glacial Field (IRE) (Glacial Storm (USA))
2026[13] 3159[9] 4917[6] 5229[7]

Gladstone (IRE) *Polly Gundry* 16h
6 b g Dansili Rockerlong (Deploy)
3092[10] 3422[11]

Glamorous Gg *John Bryan Groucott* 76h 68c
9 ch m Classic Cliche(IRE) Glamour Game (Nashwan (USA))
94[5] 473[U]

Glamorous Sister (IRE) *Robert Stephens* 93b
4 b f Jeremy(USA) Glamorous Air (IRE) (Air Express (IRE))
4561[5] 5077[4] 5374[14]

Glasson Lad (IRE) *Ferdy Murphy* 78h 86c
7 b g Quws Glasson House (IRE) (Supreme Leader)
168[3] 476[7] 752[6]

Glazig Du Graglan (FR) *Christian Le Galliard* 83c
9 b g Mad Tax(USA) Botanica (FR) (Ajdayt (USA))
1623a[4]

Gleannacreim (IRE) *Carroll Gray* 80h 70c
11 ch g Old Vic Rosie Brook (IRE) (Be My Native (USA))
79[4] 295[4] 522[8]

Gleann Na Ndochais (IRE) *Alistair Whillans* 106h 109c
8 b g Zagreb(USA) Nissereen (USA) (Septieme Ciel (USA))
341[4] 2595[P] 3213[5] 4940[4] 5216[2]

Glenarm *Seamus Mullins* 96b
5 b m Kayf Tara Rumbled (Halling (USA))
5195[4]

Glen Beg (IRE) *Miss Elizabeth Doyle* 128h 80c
7 br m Norwich Welsh Ana (IRE) (Welsh Term)
5172[3]

Glenconkeyne (IRE) *Noel C Kelly* 121h
7 b g Minashki(IRE) Slan Duff (IRE) (Shinko Forest (IRE))
727[2] 3937[5]

Glen Countess (IRE) *Brendan Powell* 98h 122c
7 b m Pilsudski(IRE) Countessdee (IRE) (Arctic Lord)
(472) (789)
871[3] 1015[4] 2348[3] (2749)
(3058) 3365[2]

Glencree (IRE) *John Wade* 115h 126c
10 b g Presenting Hidden Ability (IRE) (Alphabatim (USA))
384[2] 681[8] (1785) 2198[8] 3066[9]

Glendaars Best (IRE) *G T Lynch* 90h
5 b g King's Best(USA) Tomanivi (Caerleon (USA))
891a[6]

Glen Lord *Mrs N C Neill* 90c
11 ch g Anshan Furry Queen (Furry Glen)
28[P] 1663[P] 1876[4] 4225[F]

Glenquest (IRE) *Terence O'Brien* 110h 133c
11 b g Turtle Island(IRE) Solar Quest (IRE) (King's Ride)
2708a[11]

Glens Boy (IRE) *Jonjo O'Neill* 58h 89c
10 b g Dushyantor(USA) Glens Lady (IRE) (Mister Lord (USA))
3325[5] 3603[6]

Glens Melody (IRE) *W P Mullins* 146h
6 b m King's Theatre(IRE) Glens Music (IRE) (Orchestra)
3084[3] (3649) (4158) 4740[2]

Glenwood Present (IRE) *Bob Buckler* 74h
7 ch g Presenting Chancy Lass (IRE) (Religiously (USA))
293[F] 640[6] 997[P]

Glenwood Prince (IRE) *Jeremy Scott* 95h 106c
8 b g King's Theatre(IRE) Moll Bawn (IRE) (Presenting)
1707[4]
1942[3] 2313[3] (2619)
3137[2] 3688[3] 4843[P]

Glidewell *A N Dalton* 91c
12 b g Gildoran Throw In Your Hand (Niniski (USA))
94[4] 4485[P]

Global Bonus (IRE) *Caroline Bailey* 78b
5 b g Heron Island(IRE) That's The Bonus (IRE) (Executive Perk)
5014[13] 5447[8]

Global Flyer *Caroline Bailey* 102h 110c
10 b g Sir Harry Lewis(USA) Flicker (Unfuwain (USA))
7[4] 693[8]

Global Power (IRE) *Oliver Sherwood* 136h 131c
8 b g Subtle Power(IRE) Bartelko (IRE) (The Bart (USA))
(2246)

Global Recovery (IRE) *Des Donovan* 76h
7 b g El Corredor(USA) Altarejos (IRE) (Vettori (IRE))
161[4]

Global Warming (IRE) *Emma Lavelle* 102h 105c
10 b g King's Theatre(IRE) Croi Na Greine (IRE) (Broken Hearted)
2110[3] 2578[P] 3603[P]

Gloshen (IRE) *Philip Kirby* 52h
8 b h Fath(USA) Olivia Jane (IRE) (Ela-Mana-Mou)
1794[F] 1975[P] 2196[10] 2420[8]

Glowinginthedark (IRE) *Charlie Longsdon* 117h
6 b g Dr Massini(IRE) Autumn Beauty (IRE) (Darnay)
1861[4] 2243[3] 2826[4] 3841[2] 4574[2] 5280[4]

Goal (IRE) *Gordon Elliott* 119h 126c
6 b g Mujadil(USA) Classic Lin (FR) (Linamix (FR))
732[2] (959)

Go All The Way (IRE) *J T R Dreaper* 128h 147c
9 b g Milan Kings Rose (IRE) (King's Ride)
1001a[3] 1897a[10]

Go Amwell *J R Jenkins* 101h 74c
11 b g Kayf Tara Daarat Alayaam (IRE) (Reference Point)
241[5] 428[3] 1121[6] (1405) (1538) 1917[3] 2253[P] 2680[7] 3151[6] 4906[9]

Go Annie *Jo Davis* 92h 51c
6 gr m Proclamation(IRE) Bright Spangle (IRE) (General Monash (USA))
1321[8] 1711[8] 2148[4]
2348[4] 3687[F]

Goat Castle (IRE) *Nigel Twiston-Davies* 88h 69c
10 b g Goldmark(USA) Rolands Girl (IRE) (Soughaan (USA))
267[9] 640[7] 1120[8] (1575) 1674[9]

Go Conquer (IRE) *Donald McCain* 116b
5 b g Arcadio(GER) Ballinamona Wish (IRE) (Kotashaan (FR))
(5219)

God's County (FR) *Sophie Leech* 122h
9 gr g Verglas(IRE) Toujours Elle (USA) (Lyphard (USA))
800[10] 1019[6]

Godsmejudge (IRE) *Alan King* 122h 153c
8 b g Witness Box(USA) Eliza Everett (IRE) (Meneval (USA))
2502[5] 2953[P] 4544[P] 5276[2] 5571[3]

God's Own (IRE) *Tom George* 135h 159c
6 b g Oscar(IRE) Dantes Term (IRE) (Phardante (FR))
1867[U] (2268) 2490[14] **3386[2] 3893[4] 4420[2]**

Godwit *Eugene Stanford* 106h
6 b m Noverre(USA) Hen Harrier (Polar Falcon (USA))
(383) 696[6] 848[3] 1043[8] 1400[5] 1783[4]

Gogeo (IRE) *Alan Swinbank* 103h
7 b g Val Royal(FR) Steal 'Em (Efisio)
(4327)

Going Concern (IRE) *Evan Williams* 112h
7 b g Overbury(IRE) Scorpio Girl (Scorpio (FR))
2385[6] (2614) 3225[P] 4674[3] 5040[4]

Going Nowhere Fast (IRE) *Bernard Llewellyn* 90h
9 b g Exit To Nowhere(USA) Sister Gabrielle (IRE) (Buckskin (FR))
2474[6] 2766[10] 3062[4] 3426[5] 4733[7] 4972[U]

Going Twice *Steve Woodman* 75h
9 b g Josr Algarhoud(IRE) Its Your Bid (Dilum (USA))
307[5] 484[6] 1275[11]

Going Wrong *Dan Skelton* 99h 114c
11 b g Bob Back(USA) Lucy Glitters (Ardross)
2624[5] 2956[P] 3324[2] 3593[4]

Golanova *Gary Moore* 113h
6 b g Golan(IRE) Larkbarrow (Kahyasi)
1270[2] 1404[3] (1625) 1941[3] 2729[3] 3741[12] 4937[4]

Golans Choice (IRE) *Rose Dobbin* 27b
5 b g Golan(IRE) Sea Voyager (IRE) (High Roller (IRE))
4958[10]

Golan Silk *Anthony Honeyball* 94b
4 b g Golan(IRE) Silk Daisy (Barathea (IRE))
5264[3]

Golan Sun (IRE) *Paul Stafford* 83h
6 b g Golan(IRE) Shandarr (IRE) (John French)
4647[6] 4811[6]

Golantilla (IRE) *A J Martin* 131b
6 br g Golan(IRE) Scintilla (Sir Harry Lewis (USA))
4756[11]

Golan Way *Tim Vaughan* 130h 145c
10 b g Golan(IRE) Silk Daisy (Barathea (IRE))
4225[U] (4706)
5171[F] 5364[LFT]

Goldan Jess (IRE) *Philip Kirby* 120h
10 b g Golan(IRE) Bendis (GER) (Danehill (USA))
(565) (1398)

Gold Carrot *Gary Moore* 89h
6 b g Beat All(USA) Emma-Lyne (Emarati (USA))
3994[9] *4297[6]* 4807[12] 4959[7] 5258[6]

Gold Chain (IRE) *Dianne Sayer* 89h
4 b f Authorized(IRE) Mountain Chain (USA) (Royal Academy (USA))
2307[2] 4614[2]

Gold Cygnet (IRE) *Theresa Gibson* 48h 45c
9 b g Beneficial Windy Bee (IRE) (Aristocracy)
2031[P] 4628[P]

Golden Acorn (IRE) *Jamie Snowden* 85h
5 b m Ad Valorem(USA) Golden Heart (Salse (USA))
1934 (391) 765[9] 1018[9]

Golden Calf (IRE) *Peter Bowen* 102h
7 b g Gold Well Cherry In A Hurry (IRE) (Be My Native (USA))
1854[5] 2296[4] 2874[4] 3227[2] 4070[7]

Golden Call (IRE) *Jennie Candlish* 137h 139c
10 b g Goldmark(USA) Call Me Countess (IRE) (Aristocracy)
1923[6] 2452[P] 2785[6] 3717[5] (4104)
4544[4]

Golden Chieftain (IRE) *Colin Tizzard* 119h 148c
9 b g Tikkanen(USA) Golden Flower (GER) (Highland Chieftain)
4279[5]
4738[15] 5170[5] 5371[6]

Golden Firth (IRE) *A J Martin* 112h
7 b m Flemensfirth(USA) Golden Flower (GER) (Highland Chieftain)
3021[P]

Golden Future *Peter Niven* 91h
11 b g Muhtarram(USA) Nazca (Zilzal (USA))
2519[11] 2794[7]

Golden Gael *Jeremy Scott* 74h
8 ch m Generous(IRE) Gaelic Gold (IRE) (Good Thyne (USA))
2084[P]
2632[P] 2948[11] *4303[9]* 5030[14]

Golden Games (IRE) *Daniel O'Brien* 88h
8 b m Montjeu(IRE) Ski For Gold (Shirley Heights)
2862[6]

Golden Hoof (IRE) *Nicky Henderson* 130h 133c
6 b g Oscar(IRE) Nuovo Style (IRE) (Be My Native (USA))
2668[11] 4805[13] 5158[8]

Golden Jubilee (USA) *Nigel Twiston-Davies* 82h
5 bb g Zavata(USA) Love Play (USA) (Friendly Lover (USA))
8[6]

Golden Milan (IRE) *Rebecca Curtis* 108h
6 b g Milan Belle Provence (FR) (Phantom Breeze)
4267[6] 5071[6]

Golden Orchid (IRE) *Miss Clare Louise Cannon*
5 b m Arcadio(GER) Midnight Orchid (IRE) (Petardia)
5109[8]

Golden Plan (IRE) *Mark Fahey* 127h
8 b g Goldmark(USA) Graphic Artist (IRE) (Accordion)
4051[8]

Golden Sparkle (IRE) *Ian Duncan* 121h
8 ch m Samraan(USA) Bye For Now (Abednego)
2345[6] 3499[5] 4058[4] 4668[2] 5255[3] ◆ (5509)

Golden Squirell (IRE) *Brendan Powell* 81h 82c
7 ch g Oscar Schindler(IRE) Coppeen Storm (IRE) (Glacial Storm (USA))
878[6] 1154[4] 1191[7]
1338[2] 1528[2] 1701[2]

Golden View (IRE) *Karen McLintock* 105b 107c
9 b g Goldmark(USA) In Grace's View (IRE) (Shardari)
113[8] 566[3] 1039[P]

Golden Wonder (IRE) *D T Hughes* 125h 147c
8 b g Goldmark(USA) Polyploid (IRE) (Pollerton)
2258a[5] 5474a[2]

Gold Futures (IRE) *Nicky Richards* 130h
5 b g Gold Well Don't Discount Her (IRE) (Millfontaine)
1977[4] 2393[4]

Goldie Horn *Nigel Twiston-Davies* 90h
6 ch m Where Or When(IRE) Gulshan (Batshoof)
715[14] 3733[7] 4569[2] 4910[6]

Gold Ingot *Alan King* 110h
7 ch g Best Of The Bests(IRE) Realms Of Gold (USA) (Gulch (USA))
(233) 1991[10] 4991[2] 5285[10]

Gold Opera (IRE) *N W Alexander* 109b
5 b g Gold Well Flute Opera (IRE) (Sharifabad (IRE))
4205[3]

Goldray *Richard Lee* 74h
8 ch m Central Park(IRE) Go Mary (Raga Navarro (ITY))
4910[10]

Gold Show *Edwin Tuer* 106h
5 gr m Sir Percy Pearl Bright (FR) (Kaldoun (FR))
2493[7] 2883[3] 3329[8] 3614[2] 4187[7] 4531[6]

Goldslic (FR) *Robert Collet* 121h 67c
8 b g Slickly(FR) Goldaka (FR) (Goldneyev (USA))
263a[7]

Gonalston Cloud (IRE) *Nick Kent* 98h
7 br g Cloudings(IRE) Roseoengus (IRE) (Roselier (FR))
1732[5] 2189[6] 2507[7] 2748[10] 3842[2] 4070[5]

Gone Forever *Brian Ellison* 102b
4 b g Quest For Fame Erudite (Generous (IRE))
2160[3] 2830[2] (3619) 4310[2]

Goneinaglance *Andrew J Martin* 94b
5 b m Passing Glance It's Missy Imp (Fearless Action (USA))
4135[3] 4403[8] 5014[14] 5528[5]

Gone Too Far *Alan King* 124h
6 b g Kayf Tara Major Hoolihan (Soldier Rose)
(239) (2225) 2602[2] 4102[3] 4680[9] 5445[2]

Goochypoochyprader *Nick Lampard* 100h 49c
7 ch m Karinga Bay Mrs Ritchie (Teenoso (USA))
2568[11] 2896[7] 3692[2] 3821[4] 4444[P] 4717[3] **5246[11]**

Goodacres Garden (IRE) *Shaun Lycett* 87h
7 b g Oscar(IRE) Living A Dream (IRE) (Heavenly Manna)
2417[3] 2999[6] 3432[P] 4371[8] 4733[11]

Good As New *Denis Quinn*
4 b f Araafa(IRE) New Design (IRE) (Bluebird (USA))
3468[P]

Good Boy Jackson *R Mike Smith* 107h
6 b g Firebreak Fisher Island (IRE) (Sri Pekan (USA))
2306[10]

Go Odee Go (IRE) *Dan Skelton* 110b
6 b g Alkaadhem Go Franky (IRE) (Hollow Hand)
3049[2] ◆ *4016[5]* 4728[4] 5028[2]

Good Egg (IRE) *Mrs Lorna Fowler* 118c
11 b g Exit To Nowhere(USA) Full Of Surprises (IRE) (Be My Native (USA))
1666[4] 2450[6]

Goodgoshmsmolly *Helen Nelmes* 62b
5 b m Amrak Ajeeb(IRE) Larry's Law (IRE) (Law Society (USA))
2398 2745[8]

Goodlukin Lucy *Keith Dalgleish* 82h
7 ch m Supreme Sound Suka Ramai (Nashwan (USA))
879[8] 5302[5]

Good Of Luck *Warren Greatrex* 103h
5 b g Authorized(IRE) Oops Pettie (Machiavellian (USA))
848[4] 1183[P] 1270[7] 1475[3] 1567[6] 3062[3] (4703)
4866[2] 4937[F] 5436[P]

Good Order *Tom George* 101h 129c
9 b g Alflora(IRE) Twinnings Grove (IRE) (Lord Americo)
(3325)
3647[P] 5513[8]

Goodtime Boy (IRE) *Alex Hales* 118h
6 b g Catcher In The Rye(IRE) Tour At Dawn (IRE) (Shernazar)
2598[7]

Goodtoknow *Richard Lee* 111h 132c
6 b g Presenting Atlantic Jane (Tamure (IRE))
289[P] **2315[U]**
2518[2] 2749[2] (3223)
4412[P] 5299[3]

Goodwood Mirage (IRE) *Jonjo O'Neill* 122h
4 b g Jeremy(USA) Phantom Waters (Pharly (FR))
(3641) 3885[6] 4419[5] ◆ 4755[B]

Goohar (IRE) *Henry Daly* 117h
5 b g Street Cry(IRE) Reem Three (Mark Of Esteem (IRE))
2453[3] 3061[2] ◆ (3415) 4680[7]

Go On Arch (IRE) *Nigel Twiston-Davies* 95h 98c
8 b g Oscar(IRE) Good Aim (IRE) (Priolo (USA))
1547[7] 1673[5]

Goonyella (IRE) *J T R Dreaper* 145h 145c
7 br g Presenting Miss Fresher (FR) (Pampabird)
2708a[5] 3361[8] 4386a[2]
5474a[7]

Gores Island (IRE) *Gary Moore* 123h 119c
8 b g Beneficial Just Leader (IRE) (Supreme Leader)
2447 1783[8] (2362) 2742[3] 3646[P] **4885[2] 5031[2]**
5336[F]

Gorey Lane (IRE) *John Norton* 100h 95c
8 b g Oscar(IRE) Supremely Deep (IRE) (Supreme Leader)
2626[P] 2818[F] 3335[3] 3824[9] 4308[3] 4553[2] 5069[3]

Gorgehous Lliege (FR) *Venetia Williams* 83h 117c
8 b g Lavirco(GER) Charme D'Estruval (FR) (Mistigri)
2367[2] ◆ 2670[9] (3178)

Gorhams Gift *Jamie Poulton* 73h
6 b g Double Trigger(IRE) Linden Grace (USA) (Mister Baileys)
95[8] **2825[F]**
3033[P]

Goring One (IRE) *Anna Newton-Smith* 95h 120c
9 b g Broadway Flyer(USA) Brigette's Secret (Good Thyne (USA))
(1944)
2646[3] 2909[4] 3853[3] 4681[4] 4886[P]

Goring Two (IRE) *Anna Newton-Smith* 12h 100c
9 br g Needle Gun(IRE) Kam Slave (Kambalda)
2441[2] 3139[P] 3687[5] 3855[F] 4109[P] 4720[P]

Gorsky Island *Tom George* 109h 116c
6 b g Turtle Island(IRE) Belle Magello (FR) (Exit To Nowhere (USA))
2654[4] 3116[2] 4029[3]
5031[4]

Gospel Preacher *Richard Woollacott* 111b
9 b g Kayf Tara Gospel (IRE) (Le Bavard (FR))
2275[P] 3129[P]

Gosser Time *P Ponting* 65c
11 gr g Silver Patriarch(IRE) Run Tiger (IRE) (Commanche Run)
3993[5]

Gotadime (IRE) *P J Rothwell* 79h
5 b g Gamut(IRE) Grangeclare Lark (IRE) (Old Vic)
5424a[9]

Got Attitude (IRE) *Tony Carroll* 112h 112c
11 ch g Beneficial Ilderton Road (Noalto)
2450[P] 3164[6] 3855[2] 4486[6] 5247[3] 5442[3]

Go Teescomponents *Keith Reveley* 31h 24c
7 b g Septieme Ciel(USA) Linea-G (Keen)
67[9] **2791[0]**
580[P]

Gotham City (IRE) *David Pipe* 90b
5 b g September Storm(GER) Open Miss (Dracula (AUS))
2634[5]

Gotoyourplay (IRE) *Venetia Williams* 97h 131c
10 ch g Definite Article Johnston's Flyer (IRE) (Orchestra)
(4732)
5119[4] 5558[F]

Got The Nac (IRE) *S R B Crawford* 114h
5 br g Beneficial Hey Jude (IRE) (Mandalus)
2499[10] 4647[4]

Goulanes (IRE) *David Pipe* 133h 152c
8 b g Mr Combustible(IRE) Rebolgiane (IRE) (Red Sunset)
2502[10] 3361[P] (4821)

Go West (IRE) *A Hamilton* 113h 91c
13 b g Flemensfirth(USA) Roaming (IRE) (Be My Native (USA))
496[7] 535[2]

Go West Young Man (IRE) *Henry Daly* 110h
6 b g Westerner Last Of Her Line (Silver Patriarch (IRE))
3034[12] 4546[3] 5075[0] 5191[2]

Graasp The Nettle *Harry Whittington* 55b
4 br g Araafa(IRE) Beacon Silver (Belmez (USA))
4452[3]

Grab The Glory (IRE) *Gary Moore* 123h 94c
8 b g Accordion Full Of Surprises (IRE) (Be My Native (USA))
1986[5]

Gracchus (USA) *Richard Price* 99h 114c
8 b g Black Minnaloushe(USA) Montessa (USA) (Montbrook (USA))
236[5] 674[8] 929[3]
4921[P] 5179[8]

Grace And Beauty (IRE) *Paul Henderson* 71h
6 b m Diamond Green(FR) Balliamo (IRE) (Royal Academy (USA))
1771[0]

Grace And Fortune *Richard Rowe* 108h
7 b m Grape Tree Road Nouveau Cheval (Picea)
2566[3] 2860[5] 4719[4] 5351[15]

Grace A Toi Enki (FR) *A Chaille-Chaille* 122h
5 ch g Agent Bleu(FR) Cadiane (FR) (Cadoudal (FR))
703a[3]

Graceful Descent (FR) *Karen Tutty* 96h
9 b m Hawk Wing(USA) Itab (USA) (Dayjur (USA))
966[2] 1506[11]

Graduation Night *Jamie Snowden* 98h 130c
8 br g Kayf Tara Jadidh (Touching Wood (USA))
393[C]

Graffiti Art *Brendan Powell* 101b
5 b m Kayf Tara Art Affair (GER) (Germany (USA))
4016[4] 4683[7] 5077[12]

Grafty Girl *Roger Curtis* 55b
7 b m Gamut(IRE) Mirador (Town And Country)
1[P]

Grams And Ounces *Tony Newcombe* 104h 101c
7 b g Royal Applause Ashdown Princess (IRE) (King's Theatre (IRE))
3031[8] 3744[14] 4353[6] 5067[9] 5335[6]

Granaruid (IRE) *Alison Hamilton* 123h 123c
11 br g Alderbrook Lady Lorraine (IRE) (Oscar (IRE))
342[5] 511[2] (752) 804[5] 958[5] 2172[5] (2844)
3398[10] (4625) (4834) 5272[9]

Grandad Mac *Alan Coogan* 55h
6 b g Invincible Spirit(IRE) No Rehearsal (FR) (Baillamont (USA))
2563[10] 2728[3]

Grandads Horse *Charlie Longsdon* 133h 141c
8 bb g Bollin Eric Solid Land (FR) (Solid Illusion (USA))
(562) ◆ 786[2] (963)
1686[7] (1923)
2365[3] 4742[12] 4960[8]

Grand Article (IRE) *Paul Cowley* 95h 81c
10 ch g Definite Article Grand Morning (IRE) (King Of Clubs)
1824[3] 3856[2] 5012[9]
(5404)

Grand Charly (FR) *T Civel* 120h 131c
7 b g Le Triton(USA) Sherkane (FR) (Lesotho (USA))
838a[8]

Grande Antarctique (FR) *Jennie Candlish* 110b
4 b g Antarctique(IRE) Puerta Grande (FR) (Lesotho (USA))
5063[2] 5499[2]

Grand Fella (IRE) *Ken Wingrove* 73h 39c
9 ch g Raise A Grand(IRE) Mummys Best (Bustino)
43[9] 1314[P] 1547[8]

Grand Gigolo (FR) *Ian Williams* 98h
5 b g Enrique Belle D'Ecajeul (FR) (Le Nain Jaune (FR))
1919[7] 2602[12] 3061[13] 3602[7] 4533[3] 4906[5]

Grand Gold *Seamus Durack* 118h 111c
5 b g Librettist(USA) Night Symphonie (Cloudings (IRE))
5030[5]

Grandiloquent *Brian Ellison* 70h
5 b g Rail Link High Praise (USA) (Quest For Fame)
5160[4] 5479[8]

Grandinas (FR) *X Betron* 95h
5 bb m Kaldou Star Ygrande (FR) (Subotica (FR))
703a[12]

Grand Introduction (IRE) *Fergal O'Brien* 87b
4 b g Robin Des Pres(FR) What A Breeze (IRE) (Naheez (USA))
5070[7]

Grandioso (IRE) *Paul Nicholls* 123h 155c
7 b g Westerner Champagne Warrior (IRE) (Waajib)
2800[3] 3082[P] 3772[2] 4422[10]

Grand Lad (IRE) *Grant Cann* 62b
6 br g Beneficial Shanann Lady (IRE) (Anshan)
4638[7]

Grand March *Kim Bailey* 100h
5 b g Beat All(USA) Bora Bora (Bairn (USA))
1138[3] 1599[3] 1935[9] 2265[9] 3163[6] 4703[3] 5282[3]

Grandma Smith *Kim Bailey* 88b
6 b m Tobougg(IRE) Grandma Lily (IRE) (Bigstone (IRE))
5195[8]

Grandouet (FR) *Nicky Henderson* 157h 157c
7 bb g Al Namix(FR) Virginia River (FR) (Indian River (FR))
2363[U] 2950[2] 3318[2] 4737[6] 5134[7]

Grands Crus (FR) *David Pipe* 152h 168c
9 gr g Dom Alco(FR) Fee Magic (FR) (Phantom Breeze)
2268[5]

Grand Vintage (IRE) *Evelyn Slack* 96h
8 gr g Basanta(IRE) Rivers Town Rosie (IRE) (Roselier (FR))
3271[5] 3924[3] 4475[7] 5357[2] ◆

Grand Vision (IRE) *Colin Tizzard* 143h
8 gr g Old Vic West Hill Rose (IRE) (Roselier (FR))
3457[P] 3653[2] 4025[3] 4765[20] 5158[7]

Grange Boy (IRE) *J T R Dreaper* 93h
6 b g Turtle Island(IRE) Hackler Poitin (IRE) (Little Bighorn)
71[4]

Granny Blackwood *Martin Todhunter*
6 b m Nayef(USA) Aunt Rita (IRE) (Grand Lodge (USA))
278[P]

Gran Torino (IRE) *Evan Williams* 88h 88c
9 b g Milan Miss Greinton (GER) (Greinton)
2284[9] 2598[14] 3007[7]
4354[P]

Granville Island (IRE) *Jennie Candlish* 129h 131c
7 b g Flemensfirth(USA) Fox Glen (Furry Glen)
1921[4] 2448[3] 2751[5] (3204)
3652[7] (4007)
4532[5] 4900[3]

Granwood *Tim Walford* 108h
8 ch m Midnight Legend Half Each (Weld)
67[5] 222[2] (444) 751[2] 2786[6]

Grapetree *David Evans*
4 b g Bertolini(USA) Lambadora (Suave Dancer (USA))
2026[14]

Grape Tree Flame *Peter Bowen* 97h
6 ch m Grape Tree Road Althrey Flame (IRE) (Torus)
874[3] 1138[5] 2773[4] 3189[6] 3840[P]

Grate Fella (IRE) *Sue Smith* 113h
6 b g King's Best(USA) Moonlight Paradise (USA) (Irish River (FR))
2848[C] (3451) 4070[0] 4426[C] 4745[4]

Gratia Plena (FR) *B De Watrigant* 126h
8 b m Solid Illusion(USA) Mea Maxima Culpa (FR) (Holst (USA))
406a[P]

Gravitate *Paul Webber* 67h
5 ch g Pivotal Spacecraft (USA) (Distant View (USA))
671[6] 857[P] 2893[6]

Gray Beck *Seamus Durack* 69b
6 ch g Alflora(IRE) Spot The Dot (Silver Patriarch (IRE))
3295[7]

Graylyn Amber *Robert Eddery* 67b
9 b m Nomadic Way(USA) State Lady (IRE) (Strong Statement (USA))
2825[P] 3570[P] 4757[U]

Graylyn Ruby (FR) *Robin Dickin* 70h
9 b g Limnos(JPN) Nandi (IRE) (Mujadil (USA))
2292[7] 2787[12]

Great Choice (IRE) *David Pipe* 110h
5 b g Westerner Granuale (IRE) (Seamanship)
3194[2] 3920[5] 4514[3] 5236[U]

Greatday Allweek (IRE) *Seamus Mullins*
5 ch m Kutub(IRE) Correct And Right (IRE) (Great Commotion (USA))
2442[5] 2907[P]

Great Demeanor (USA) *Dianne Sayer* 52h
4 b g Bernstein(USA) Hangin Withmy Buds (USA) (Roar (USA))
3872[U] 4003[5] 4234[11] 4307[8]

Great Hero *Richard Phillips* 102h 110c
9 ch g Arkadian Hero(USA) Great Tern (Simply Great (FR))
428^{P}

Great Kicker (IRE) *Richard Woollacott* 79h 67c
9 b g Great Palm(USA) Keep The Change (IRE) (Castle Keep)
191^{3}

Great Link *Tony Carroll* 112h
5 b g Rail Link The Strand (Gone West (USA))
1915^{8} 2563^{5} (2886) (4369) 4659^{5} 4781^{4} 5294^{7}

Great Oak (IRE) *Tim Vaughan* 109h 133c
8 b m Dushyantor(USA) Reginella (IRE) (Supreme Leader)
(748) ◆ 1347^{2} 1731^{3}
2101^{6} 3153^{3}
3738^{P}

Great Ocean Road (IRE) *David Thompson* 86h 79c
11 ch g Shernazar Princess Breda (IRE) (Long Pond)
3115^{5} 2339^{P} (2735)
3022^{P}

Greatown (IRE) *William Kinsey* 89h
7 gr g Great Palm(USA) Townhall (IRE) (Roselier (FR))
67^{P}

Great's Autrechene (FR) *Charlie Longsdon* 111c
7 b g Great Pretender(IRE) Daynag Royale (FR) (Royal Charter (FR))
245^{P}

Great Try (IRE) *Paul Nicholls*
5 b g Scorpion(IRE) Cherry Pie (FR) (Dolpour)
(4329) ◆

Great Value (IRE) *Graeme McPherson* 120h 133c
9 b g Revoque(IRE) Dame De L'Oise (USA) (Riverman (USA))
2230^{P} 2848^{2} 3599^{6}
(4862) 5230^{U}

Greek Fire *Dave Morris* 83b
5 b g Sinndar(IRE) Grecian Slipper (Sadler's Wells (USA))
675^{8} 944^{5}

Green And White (ITY) *Dave Roberts* 93h
4 b g Denon(USA) Sequita (GER) (Lomitas)
1934^{4} 2098^{4} 2455^{2}

Greenaway's Eye (FR) *James Frost* 66h
5 b h Catcher In The Rye(IRE) Alma Thomas (IRE) (Orpen (USA))
517^{9}

Green Bank (IRE) *Charlie Longsdon* 113h 124c
8 b g Morozov(USA) Queen Polly (IRE) (Pollerton)
393^{7} 690^{3} **806^{P} (1088)** (1205)
1469^{2} 1637^{3} 1988^{10} 5180^{3} 5406^{2}

Green Belt Elite (FR) *Venetia Williams* 85h 94c
10 b g Astarabad(USA) Vallee Bleue (FR) (Tip Moss (FR))
520^{5} 3362^{P} 4027^{P} *4302^{13}* 4599^{4} 5544^{P}

Green Dragon (FR) *A J Martin* 126h
5 b g Green Tune(USA) Bocanegra (FR) (Night Shift (USA))
1139a^{7}

Green Du Ciel (FR) *I M Mason* 105h 75c
9 gr g Smadoun(FR) Sucre Blanc (FR) (Green Tune (USA))
287^{P}

Green Flag (IRE) *Lucinda Russell* 136h 147c
7 b g Milan Erin Go Brea (IRE) (Un Desperado (FR))
(1976) ◆ **(2220) (2817)**
3260^{2} 4041^{U} 4738^{4} 5276^{6}

Green Hackle (IRE) *Oliver Sherwood*
9 b g Stowaway Honey Mustard (IRE) (Roselier (FR))
3959^{P} **5407^{P}**

Greenlaw *Charlie Longsdon* 120h 107c
8 b g Helissio(FR) Juris Prudence (IRE) (Law Society (USA))
2395^{3}

Green Lightning (IRE) *Peter Bowen* 108h
7 b g Montjeu(IRE) Angelic Song (CAN) (Halo (USA))
49^{3} 184^{5} 651^{2} 686^{3} (829) (881) 958^{P}

Greensalt (IRE) *Donald McCain* 118h
6 b g Milan Garden City (IRE) (Shernazar)
2420^{2} 3208^{2} 3781^{3} 4776^{2}

Green Special (ITY) *Dave Roberts* 66h
4 ch g Denon(USA) Groove (ITY) (Dashing Blade)
1920^{10} 3768^{6}

Green To Gold (IRE) *Don Cantillon* 100h 122c
9 gr g Daylami(IRE) Alonsa (IRE) (Trempolino (USA))
1050^{6} 1634^{8}

Green Winter (IRE) *Henry Oliver* 92b
6 ch g Well Made(GER) Assistine (IRE) (Oscar (IRE))
5492^{4}

Green Wizard (IRE) *Sue Smith* 120h 129c
8 b g Wizard King Ajo Green (IRE) (Moscow Society (USA))
(121) **(322)**
(553) 2199^{5}
2395^{P} 2817^{2} 3617^{P} 3825^{P} 4593^{F} 4819^{7} 5297^{F}

Grenoli (FR) *John Cornwall* 47h 55c
13 b g Garde Royale Pietrosella (FR) (Alias Smith (USA))
965^{P}

Grethel (IRE) *Alan Berry* 84h
10 b m Fruits Of Love(USA) Stay Sharpe (USA) (Sharpen Up)
17^{5} 506^{5} 532^{3} 1043^{4} 1073^{5} 1379^{4} 1399^{F}

Grey Area (IRE) *Tristan Davidson* 108h
9 gr g Portrait Gallery(IRE) Queen's Run (IRE) (Deep Run)
3525^{F} 3938^{6} 4338^{9} 5556^{9}

Grey Blue (IRE) *Nicky Henderson* 100h
4 gr g Verglas(IRE) Zut Alors (IRE) (Pivotal)
3641^{3} *4300^{4}* 5190^{5}

Greybougg *Nigel Hawke* 73b
5 gr g Tobougg(IRE) Kildee Lass (Morpeth)
2513^{6} *4017^{9}* 5016^{8}

Grey Command (USA) *Philip Kirby* 82h
9 gr g Daylami(IRE) Shmoose (IRE) (Caerleon (USA))
221^{3} 561^{7}

Grey Earl *Richard Lee* 102h
7 gr g Karinga Bay Forever Grey (IRE) (Celio Rufo)
2703^{3} 3194^{9} 3796^{3} 4411^{6} 4945^{6}

Greyfriars Drummer *Charlie Mann* 130h
6 ch g Where Or When(IRE) Loveleaves (Polar Falcon (USA))
2624^{P}

Grey Gold (IRE) *Richard Lee* 133h 153c
9 gr g Strategic Choice(USA) Grouse-N-Heather (Grey Desire)
2244^{3} 3197^{3} 3660^{2} (4032)
4414^{2}

Grey Life *Malcolm Jefferson* 88h 116c
8 gr g Terimon More To Life (Northern Tempest (USA))
(5355) ◆

Grey Missile *Jeremy Scott* 113h 110c
9 gr g Terimon Bonne Anniversaire (Alflora (IRE))
(237) 486^{5}

Grey Shadow (IRE) *John Wade* 52c
8 gr g Tikkanen(USA) Prospect Lady (IRE) (Boreen (FR))
2224^{P} 3037^{5}

Grey Soldier (IRE) *Sophie Leech* 122h 125c
9 gr g Galileo(IRE) Crusch Alva (FR) (Unfuwain (USA))
(474) ◆ **798^{4} 1047^{P} 1076^{4} 1194^{6} 1441^{4}**
1484^{3} 1750^{4} 2041^{4} 2287^{8} 2618^{P}

Greywell Boy *Nick Williams* 107h 130c
7 gr g Fair Mix(IRE) Rakajack (Rakaposhi King)
2212^{3} 2645^{6} 2816^{3} 3080^{7} 4400^{2} (4660)
4960^{6}

Grey Wulff (IRE) *Emma Lavelle* 16h 42c
9 gr g Oscar(IRE) Only A Rose (Glint Of Gold)
3820^{5} 5342^{P}

Grilyne (FR) *Tom Symonds* 76h
5 b g Kapgarde(FR) Marie De Valois (FR) (Moulin)
2026^{7} 2296^{6}

Grimley Girl *Sarah-Jayne Davies* 102h
8 b m Sir Harry Lewis(USA) Grimley Gale (IRE) (Strong Gale)
166^{2} 561^{P} 717^{7} 811^{P}

Groody Hill (IRE) *C Roche* 96h 123c
8 gr g Alderbrook Secret Leave (Long Leave)
3868a^{P}

Groomed (IRE) *Sue Smith* 111h 120c
6 b g Acclamation Enamoured (Groom Dancer (USA))
479^{2} **864^{5}**
967^{4} 3599^{8} 3758^{7} (4533)
5058^{3} 5453^{2}

Groovy Dancer *Rose Dobbin* 97h
7 ch m Groom Dancer(USA) Cita Verda (FR) (Take Risks (FR))
491^{2} 626^{6} 881^{4} 1161^{2}

Ground Ginger *James Bethell* 80h
4 ch g Byron Hoh Hedsor (Singspiel (IRE))
2881^{5}

Grouse Lodge (IRE) *Donald McCain* 128h 135c
8 b g Well Chosen Arctic Jane (IRE) (Dayeem (USA))
2517^{5} 3287^{P}

Grouse Mountain (IRE) *Charlie Longsdon* 70b
5 b g Craigsteel Black Manipulator (IRE) (Glacial Storm (USA))
647^{5}

Grovemere (IRE) *Debra Hamer* 96h 109c
9 bb g Beneficial Holly Grove Lass (Le Moss)
89^{P} 254^{2} 436^{4} 643^{P} **805^{P}**

Grove Pride *Henry Daly* 123h 136c
9 b g Double Trigger(IRE) Dara's Pride (IRE) (Darazari (IRE))
2646^{7}

Grove Silver (IRE) *Jennie Candlish* 115b
5 gr g Gamut(IRE) Cobbler's Well (IRE) (Wood Chanter)
(4431) 4902^{4}

Grumeti *Alan King* 151h 139c
6 b g Sakhee(USA) Tetravella (IRE) (Groom Dancer (USA))
2821^{3} 3261^{5} 4279^{3} 4739^{8} 5134^{5}

Gtaab *Sophie Leech* 35h
8 b g Cape Cross(IRE) Nabadhaat (USA) (Mr Prospector (USA))
253^{P} 319^{RR}

Guanciale *Brendan Powell* 98h 107c
7 b g Exit To Nowhere(USA) Thenford Lass (IRE) (Anshan)
2582^{6} 3281^{2} 3785^{P} 4067^{4} *4326^{6}*

Guardi (IRE) *Dean Ivory*
5 gr g Dalakhani(IRE) Grizel (Lion Cavern (USA))
3163^{P}

Guards Chapel *Gary Moore* 120h
6 b g Motivator Intaaj (IRE) (Machiavellian (USA))
97^{7} 421^{6} (1273) 1527^{3} 1627^{6}

Gud Day (IRE) *Fergal O'Brien* 118h 124c
6 gr g Aussie Rules(USA) Queen Al Andalous (IRE) (King's Best (USA))
371^{2} 697^{3} 850^{U} 924^{7} **1133^{2}** ◆ **1263^{3} 1326^{3}**
1549^{2} (1657)
1973^{4} 2890^{U} *4300^{13}* 5020^{4}
5511^{3}

Guess Again (IRE) *David Pipe* 113h 133c
9 b g Milan Guess Twice (IRE) (Deep Run)
(2297)
2475^{6} 3059^{P}

Guest Of Honour (FR) *Renee Robeson* 105b
6 b g Hurricane Run(IRE) Pats Martini (USA) (Red Ransom (USA))
160^{5} 1771^{8} 2252^{P} 2720^{P}

Guitar Pete (IRE) *D T Hughes* 141h
4 br g Dark Angel(IRE) Innishmore (IRE) (Lear Fan (USA))
2500^{2} (3305a) (4178a) 4784^{3} (5132)

Gulfport *Donald McCain* 77h
5 b m Three Valleys(USA) Biloxi (Caerleon (USA))
1^{4} 375^{3} 506^{7} 765^{14}

Gulf Punch *Donald McCain* 112h
7 b m Dubawi(IRE) Fruit Punch (IRE) (Barathea (IRE))
111^{5} 476^{6} 1084^{2} 1818^{7} (2843) (3145) 3566^{P}
4381^{2} 4625^{2} 5255^{8}

Gullible Gordon (IRE) *Peter Bowen* 126h 136c
11 ch g Anshan Cronohill (IRE) (Mister Lord (USA))
3557 509^{2} (733)
(787) 1362^{9} 2491^{F} 2937^{13}

Gullinbursti (IRE) *Emma Lavelle* 140h 150c
8 b g Milan D'Ygrande (IRE) (Good Thyne (USA))
(2395) 2672^{5} **3165^{3} 3897^{P} 4953^{3} 5170^{3} 5569^{2}**

Gunmoney (IRE) *G T H Bailey* 122c
9 br g High Roller(IRE) Tenpence Princess (IRE) (Prince Bee)
60^{2} 3801^{2} 4113^{2} (4485)
4706^{2}

Gunna Be A Devil (IRE) *Jeremy Scott* 120h 120c
10 b g Alflora(IRE) Gunna Be Precious (Gunner B)
(3435)
5525^{2}

Gunner Fifteen (IRE) *Fergal O'Brien* 110h
6 b g Westerner Grandy Hall (IRE) (Saddlers' Hall (IRE))
(2513) 2940^{3} 3501^{P}

Gunner Lindley (IRE) *Stuart Coltherd* 103h
7 ch g Medicean Lasso (Indian Ridge)
2970^{9} 3937^{6} 4817^{9}

Gunpoint (IRE) *Richard Drake* 40h
10 b g Rainbow Quest(USA) Sharp Point (IRE) (Royal Academy (USA))
4615^{11} 4981^{P}

Guns At Midnight *Tim Walford* 68b
6 ch g Midnight Legend Smokey Diva (IRE) (Orchestra)
3619^{7}

Gun Shy (IRE) *Gary Moore* 123h
6 b g Norwich Debbies Scud (IRE) (Roselier (FR))
1764^{3} 4807^{7} (5257) 5396^{2}

Guns Of Love (IRE) *Robin Dickin* 35h 60c
12 b g Lord Of Appeal Golden Seekers (Manado)
84^{7} 183^{5} 1105^{12} 1280^{P} **1548^{F} 2044^{9}** 2175^{P}

Gurkha Brave (IRE) *Karen McLintock* 104h
6 b g Old Vic Honeyed (IRE) (Persian Mews)
2499^{4} 3002^{2} 3760^{U} 4460^{2}

Gus Macrae (IRE) *Rebecca Curtis* 122h 135c
10 b g Accordion Full Of Surprises (IRE) (Be My Native (USA))
1730^{4} 2212^{5} 2488^{7} 2812^{10} 3197^{2} 3772^{7} 4414^{P}
5136^{5}

Gwendoliner (IRE) *Tom Symonds* 88b
5 b m Flemensfirth(USA) Clandestine (Saddlers' Hall (IRE))
4598^{2} 5077^{9}

Gwili Spar *Peter Bowen* 83h
6 ch g Generosity Lady Of Mine (Cruise Missile)
1401^{5} 482^{3} 640^{2} ◆ 783^{7} 1364^{3} 1582^{3} 1820^{4}

Gwladys Street (IRE) *William Kinsey* 109h 107c
7 b g Portrait Gallery(IRE) Native Ocean (IRE) (Be My Native (USA))
2155^{F} 2805^{2} 3223^{3} 3526^{4} 3827^{7} 4382^{2}

Gwyre (IRE) *Mrs Sarah Easterby*
8 b m Mull Of Kintyre(USA) Boadicea (Celtic Swing)
5062^{P}

Gymdoli *Rayson Nixon* 107h
7 br g Endoli(USA) Split The Wind (Strong Gale)
24^{P}

Haar *Andy Turnell* 107h 120c
10 ch g Selkirk(USA) Chilly Start (IRE) (Caerleon (USA))
(5) (96)
1060^{11}

Haatefina *Mark Usher* 101h
4 b f Haatef(USA) Felona (Caerleon (USA))
2975^{3} 3385^{2} 3857^{2} 4401^{2} 4730^{5}

Habbie Simpson *Miss J M Furness* 116h 116c
9 b g Elmaamul(USA) Hamanaka (USA) (Conquistador Cielo (USA))
(557)
(4225)

Hada Men (USA) *Venetia Williams* 135h
9 b g Dynaformer(USA) Catchy (USA) (Storm Cat (USA))
205^{2} 2454^{6} 2807^{7} 3207^{6} 3775^{4}

Hades Des Mottes (FR) *E Lecoiffier* 98c
9 b g Rifapour(IRE) Hell Des Mottes (FR) (Hellios (USA))
1532a^{8}

Hadrian's Approach (IRE) *Nicky Henderson* 130h 155c
7 b g High Chaparral(IRE) Gifted Approach (IRE) (Roselier (FR))
2269^{2} 2815^{U} (3165)
4738^{14} (5571)

Hadron Collider (FR) *Chris Nenadich* 70h
9 ch g Dubai Destination(USA) Liver De Saron (USA) (Mt. Livermore (USA))
650^{14} 829^{16} 1428^{8} 1837^{P}

Hail The Brave (IRE) *Philip Kirby* 106b
5 ch g Lahib(USA) Parverb (IRE) (Parliament)
3112^{2} 4205^{5}

Hail Tiberius *Martin Keighley* 92h
7 b g Iktibas Untidy Daughter (Sabrehill (USA))
2671^{3} 5031^{0} 1674^{11} (1711) (1799) 1822^{3} 3264^{7}
4377^{2}

Haliana *John Upson* 1b
5 ch m Sakhee(USA) Boojum (Mujtahid (USA))
141^{3} 589^{9} 2043^{P}

Halifax (IRE) *Tony Newcombe* 119h
6 ch g Halling(USA) Lady Zonda (Lion Cavern (USA))
72^{2} (201) 449^{4} 2630^{6} 3031^{6} 3741^{P} 4533^{6}
4969^{2} 5179^{4}

Haling Park (UAE) *Clarissa Caroe* 73h
8 b m Halling(USA) Friendly (USA) (Lear Fan (USA))
67^{4} 711^{7} 2176^{6} 2535^{7} 2894^{P} 3119^{P} 3434^{P}

Haljaferia (UAE) *Mike Sowersby* 84h
8 ch g Halling(USA) Melisendra (FR) (Highest Honor (FR))
2017

Halkirk (IRE) *Alan Swinbank* 79b
5 b g Nayef(USA) Sil Sila (IRE) (Marju (IRE))
3835^{6}

Halley (FR) *Tom George* 118h 141c
7 b g Loup Solitaire(USA) Moon Glow (FR) (Solar One (FR))
1902a^{P} 2264a^{P} 3191^{3}
3554^{P}

Hallings Comet *Adrian Wintle* 125h 125c
5 ch g Halling(USA) Landinium (ITY) (Lando (GER))
1152^{2} (1553) 1987^{5}

Halling's Wish *Gary Moore* 107h
4 br g Halling(USA) Fair View (GER) (Dashing Blade)
(1743) 2098^{2}

Hallmark Star *Lucinda Russell* 113h 108c
5 b g Nayef(USA) Spring (Sadler's Wells (USA))
1661^{4} 1979^{4} 2217^{7} 3284^{P} 4085^{2} 4629^{2} 5214^{4}

Hallssio *P Lenogue* 113h 88c
6 b g Halling(USA) Elayoon (USA) (Danzig (USA))
131a^{P}

Halogen *Donald McCain* 116h
5 b g Halling(USA) Trompette (USA) (Bahri (USA))
563^{8} 784^{5}

Halo Moon *Donald McCain* 107h
6 br g Kayf Tara Fragrant Rose (Alflora (IRE))
1937^{7} 2444^{3}

Halucha (IRE) *Paul Webber* 104h 79c
9 b g Luso Rose Basket (IRE) (Roselier (FR))
(460) **789^{4}**
1825^{P} 2314^{4} (2473) 2715^{7} 3044^{3} *4299^{10}* 4449^{3}
5191^{P} 5489^{P}

Hamble *Julia Feilden* 99h
5 b g Librettist(USA) Time For Tea (IRE) (Imperial Frontier (USA))
3118^{3}

Hameldown Tor *E Walker* 74h 116c
10 b g Kayf Tara Priscilla (Teenoso (USA))
59^{3} 523^{3} 658^{2} 5337^{3}

Hamilton Hill *Bernard Llewellyn* 77h
7 b g Groom Dancer(USA) Loriner's Lass (Saddlers' Hall (IRE))
1672^{11}

Hammer *Mike Sowersby* 83h
9 b g Beat Hollow Tranquil Moon (Deploy)
1306^{10} 1495^{8}

Hammersly Lake (FR) *Nicky Henderson* 133h
6 b g Kapgarde(FR) Loin De Moi (FR) (Loup Solitaire (USA))
2647^{F}

Hand Act Or Part (IRE) *Lady Susan Watson*
8 b g Wizard King Caislean Beg (IRE) (Rising)
510^{P}

Handazan (IRE) *Alan King* 135h 127c
5 b g Nayef(USA) Handaza (IRE) (Be My Guest (USA))
(1866) 1970^{3} 2490^{15}

Handford Henry (IRE) *Michael Appleby* 85h
8 b g Brian Boru Second Violin (IRE) (Cataldi)
320^{5} 669^{5} 965^{P} 1121^{F}

Handiwork *Steve Gollings* 120h
4 ch g Motivator Spinning Top (Alzao (USA))
(2899) (3332) 3768^{2} 4268^{4} 4755^{9} 5132^{13}

Handmaid *Peter Bowen* 110h
5 b m King's Theatre(IRE) Hand Inn Glove (Alflora (IRE))
372^{2} (841) 1539^{2} 2506^{15}

Hand On Bach (IRE) *Warren Greatrex* 97h 90c
6 b g Bach(IRE) Deise Blues (IRE) (Flemensfirth (USA))
2210^{10}
2437^{7} 3015^{5} 4865^{5} 5234^{3}

Handsome Buddy (IRE) *Michael Gates* 92h 105c
7 br g Presenting Moya's Magic (IRE) (Phardante (FR))
(44) 248^{6}
646^{2} 763^{5} 972^{4} 1174^{8} 1673^{4}
2023^{4} 4481^{4} 4704^{3} (4905)
5293^{F} 5407^{5}

Handsome Horace (IRE) *Philip Hobbs* 92b
4 br g Presenting Paumafi (IRE) (Shardari)
5339^{4}

Handsome Stranger (IRE) *Alan Bailey* 97h
4 ch g Tamayuz Just Special (Cadeaux Genereux)
1985^{4} 2294^{4}

Handy Andy (IRE) *Colin Tizzard* 127h 132c
8 b g Beneficial Maslam (IRE) (Robellino (USA))
1959^{4} (2487)
2812^{P} 3455^{7} 3717^{P} 4886^{6} 5348^{4}

Hanga Roa (IRE) *Gary Moore* 105h
4 b g Hannouma(IRE) Fine And Mellow (FR) (Lando (GER))
785^{2} 1044^{2} (1271) 1536^{4} (1781) 2038^{3} 2932^{15}
3154^{2}

Hannah Just Hannah *Alastair Lidderdale* 97b
5 gr m Proclamation(IRE) Evaporate (Insan (USA))
3160^{5}

Hannah's Princess (IRE) *Warren Greatrex* 108h
5 b m Kalanisi(IRE) Donna's Princess (IRE) (Supreme Leader)
(1472) *(2442)* 5159^{6}

Hannibal The Great (IRE) *Charlie Longsdon* 134h
6 b g Milan Town Gossip (IRE) (Indian Ridge)
239^{2} (1764) 2252^{F} (2875)

Hansupfordetroit (IRE) *Bernard Llewellyn* 122h 138c
9 b g Zagreb(USA) Golden Needle (IRE) (Prince Of Birds (USA))
1698^{U} 1888^{2} 2389^{3} 2651^{2} (3358)
3745^{2} 4035^{U}

Happy River (IRE) *Lucinda Russell* 71h
7 b g Pierre Breezy River (IRE) (Over The River (FR))
3495^{7}

Harangue (IRE) *Paul John Gilligan* 117h 90c
6 br g Street Cry(IRE) Splendeur (FR) (Desert King (IRE))
(1266) (1306)

Harbour Court *Alan Hill* 127c
8 ch g Karinga Bay Royal Squeeze (IRE) (King's Ride)
(58) **(658)**
4239[U] 4788[5] ◆

Hard House *Mark Gillard* 74b
7 ch g Trade Fair Tuppenny Blue (Pennekamp (USA))
994[0] 1107[P]

Hard To Tell (IRE) *Bill Turner* 65b
8 b g Presenting Superior Dawn (IRE) (Mandalus)
30[P]

Hardwick Bay *Michael Appleby* 75h
8 ch m Karinga Bay Silver Madam (Broadsword (USA))
1008[7] 1688[7]

Hare In A Round (IRE) *Rebecca Curtis* 94h
6 b g Craigsteel Killone Brae (King's Ride)
1671[7] 2009[5] 2471[9] 2720[11]

Hargeisa (FR) *D Bernier*
11 b m Robin Des Pres(FR) Face A La Pente (FR) (Un Numide (FR))
200a[P]

Harlequins Gleams *Anna Newton-Smith* 49h
6 b g Gleaming(IRE) Harlequin Walk (IRE) (Pennine Walk)
3686[8] 4467[P] 5110[P] 5400[U]

Harleys Max *Susan Corbett* 39b
5 b g Winged Love(IRE) Researcher (Cosmonaut)
2738[11] 3042[14]

Harouet (FR) *Peter Bowen* 118h 134c
9 ch g Vertical Speed(FR) Lairna (FR) (Beaudelaire (USA))
(1852)
2841[6] 3361[P]

Harpsy Cord (IRE) *Henry De Bromhead* 100h 123c
8 b g Accordion Pitalina's Return (IRE) (Bob's Return (IRE))
3806a[6]

Harriet's Ark *Julian Smith* 37h
7 ch m Sir Harry Lewis(USA) Brush The Ark (Brush Aside (USA))
85[5] 412[5] 5229[6] 5524[10]

Harris (IRE) *William Kinsey* 110h 115c
7 b g Beneficial Porter Tastes Nice (IRE) (Dry Dock)
554[P] 2035[P] (3145)
4188[2] (4613)
4896[P] 5489[10]

Harris Garden (IRE) *Paul Cowley* 92h 99c
7 b g Pilsudski(IRE) Bay Pearl (FR) (Broadway Flyer (USA))
122[P] 661[7] 844[4]
1119[4] 1416[3] 1668[3] 1800[4] 5263[3]

Harris Hawk *John Wade* 113h 117c
9 b g Karinga Bay Harristown Lady (Muscatite)
3823[3] 4339[2] 4894[3] 5210[3]

Harrison's Cave *Chris Grant* 65h
6 b g Galileo(IRE) Sitara (Salse (USA))
1714[5]

Harristown *Charlie Longsdon* 122h
4 ch g Bering New Abbey (Sadler's Wells (USA))
(1855) 2294[3] 2899[3] (4111) 4682[11]

Harry Dore *Richard Price*
8 ch g Sir Harry Lewis(USA) Gladie (Arzanni)
716[P] 1107[8]

Harry Flashman *Greg Aitken* 108h 111c
13 ch g Minster Son Youandi (Silver Season)
315[2] 496[4] 5135[16]

Harry Hunt *Graeme McPherson* 129h 128c
7 b g Bertolini(USA) Qasirah (IRE) (Machiavellian (USA))
118[2] (394)
603[3] 2180[3] 2757[5] *4494[3]* **4793[F]** 5345[5]

Harry Partridge *Sue Gardner* 24b
5 ch g With The Flow(USA) Bizimki (Ardross)
4177[4] 5241[P]

Harry's Choice *Raymond York* 50b
6 b g Sir Harry Lewis(USA) Chosen (IRE) (Glacial Storm (USA))
1770[6]

Harry's Farewell *Polly Gundry* 121h
7 b g Sir Harry Lewis(USA) Golden Mile (IRE) (King's Ride)
2536[3] 3643[3] (4132)

Harrys Whim *Maurice Barnes* 103h 98c
9 b m Sir Harry Lewis(USA) Whimbrel (Dara Monarch)
67[7] **562[P]**
759[4] 1104[4] 2789[9]
3209[F] 3921[5] 4202[U] 5211[U]

Harry The Viking *Paul Nicholls* 116h 139c
9 ch g Sir Harry Lewis(USA) Viking Flame (Viking (USA))
3091[7] 4104[3] ◆ 4544[P] 5430[5]

Harry Topper *Kim Bailey* 139h 170c
7 b g Sir Harry Lewis(USA) Indeed To Goodness (IRE) (Welsh Term)
(2229)
2930[3] 3888[3] (4145)
4821[P]

Hartforth *Donald Whillans* 115h
6 ch g Haafhd St Edith (IRE) (Desert King (IRE))
(1873) 2218[2] 2842[2] (3520) (4006) 4545[4] 5252[3]

Harting Hill *Violet M Jordan* 71h
9 b g Mujahid(USA) Mossy Rose (King Of Spain)
635[P] 856[F]

Hartside (GER) *Peter Winks* 118h
5 b g Montjeu(IRE) Helvellyn (USA) (Gone West (USA))
1729[7] 1913[4] (2198) 2519[5] 2848[3] 3201[2] 3328[3] 3599[7] 3891[10] 4187[3] 4573[2] 4893[4] 5061[4] 5365[F]

Hassadin *Michael Blake* 43h
8 ch g Reset(AUS) Crocolat (Croco Rouge (IRE))
845[P] 933[10] 1134[P] 1488[5] 1645[6] 1890[6] 3959[P] 4334[P] 5069[P]

Hatters River (IRE) *Ali Brewer* 114h 124c
7 b g Milan Curzon Ridge (IRE) (Indian Ridge)
2475[4] 2955[F] 3158[4] 4696[2]

Haughtons Bridge (IRE) *J J Lambe* 85h 108c
6 gr g Cloudings(IRE) Miss Badsworth (IRE) (Gunner B)
3935[4] 5272[P]

Haveumistim *Bernard Llewellyn* 77h
8 ch g Umistim Willmoss (Le Moss)
155[7] 434[5] 477[5] 686[9] 1137[F]

Have You Had Yours (IRE) *Jane Walton* 82h 91c
8 br g Whitmore's Conn(USA) Mandys Moynavely (IRE) (Semillon)
449[6] **625[6]**
1038[P] 1851[7] (2338)
2591[4] (4890) ◆ 5483[3]

Have You Seen Me (IRE) *Nigel Twiston-Davies* 113h 134c
11 b g Beneficial Silent Supreme (IRE) (Supreme Leader)
587[3] 2488[16] 3065[11] 3859[2] 4244[4]

Havingotascoobydo (IRE) *Martin Keighley* 111h 131c
9 b g Witness Box(USA) In Blue (IRE) (Executive Perk)
1766[P]
2086[6] 2488[11] 2909[F] 2943[P] 3389[P] 5290[P]

Hawaii Five Nil (IRE) *Jonjo O'Neill* 118h
6 b g Gold Well Polish Rhythm (IRE) (Polish Patriot (USA))
1958[4] 2711[3] 3070[8] (4187)

Hawaii Klass *Donald Whillans* 117h 120c
9 ch g Classic Cliche(IRE) Youandi (Silver Season)
(341) **677[4]**
883[2] 1162[P] 4086[3] 4464[U] 5218[4] 5533[P]

Hawker *John Ferguson* 101h
4 ch g Street Cry(IRE) Dunnes River (USA) (Danzig (USA))
4054[5]

Hawkes Point *Paul Nicholls* 138h 146c
9 b g Kayf Tara Mandys Native (IRE) (Be My Native (USA))
2943[4] 3361[2] 4270[6] 5171[18]

Hawkeye Native (IRE) *M Barber* 122c
8 b g Pilsudski(IRE) Native Tango (IRE) (Be My Native (USA))
(329) **658[3]**

Hawk Gold (IRE) *Michelle Bryant* 82h
10 ch g Tendulkar(USA) Heiress Of Meath (IRE) (Imperial Frontier (USA))
(243) 540[4] 1000[2] 1438[2] 1630[3]

Hawk High (IRE) *Tim Easterby* 128h
4 b g High Chaparral(IRE) Septembers Hawk (IRE) (Machiavellian (USA))
(2098) 2733[2] (3857) 4268[6] (4755) 5132[10]

Hawkhill (IRE) *Tim Vaughan* 132h
8 b g Hawk Wing(USA) Crimphill (IRE) (Sadler's Wells (USA))
1290[6] 1520[2] 1627[8] 1685[8] (2366) 2668[S] 3083[6] 4799[6]

Hawk Moth (IRE) *John Spearing* 52h
6 b g Hawk Wing(USA) Sasimoto (USA) (Saratoga Six (USA))
390[8]

Hayjack *Charlie Longsdon* 124h 132c
9 b g Karinga Bay Celtic Native (IRE) (Be My Native (USA))
2020[U]
2177[U] 3059[5]

Hazel Brook *Mary Hambro* 97b
5 b m High Chaparral(IRE) Didbrook (Alzao (USA))
970[2] 1353[3] (1531) 1861[6]

Hazeldene *Martin Hill* 85h 80c
12 ch g Dancing High Gaelic Charm (IRE) (Deep Run)
1057[6] 1336[5]

Hazy Dawn *Richard Woollacott* 97h 89c
9 b m Cloudings(IRE) Quiet Dawn (Lighter)
32[6] 248[P]

Hazy Tom (IRE) *Charlie Longsdon* 87h 142c
8 b g Heron Island(IRE) The Wounded Cook (IRE) (Muroto)
(1730)
2244[5] 2800[U] 3090[7] *4020[3] (4328)* 4789[19] 5158[U] **5517[3]**

Hazza The Jazza *Richard Guest* 84h
4 br g Jeremy(USA) Zagaleta (Sri Pekan (USA))
1786[6] 1920[4] 2200[7]

Head Hunted *Jim Best* 59h
7 b g Dubai Destination(USA) Tropical Breeze (IRE) (Kris)
1258[P] 1890[P] 2008[9]

Heading To First *Paddy Butler* 84h
7 b g Sulamani(IRE) Bahirah (Ashkalani (IRE))
2002[11] 2272[11] 5400[5]

Headly's Bridge (IRE) *Simon Earle* 121h 136c
8 b g Tillerman Brockton Flame (Emarati (USA))
2271[3] 3169[3] 3328[2] 3802[4] 4278[2]
(4560) (4780)
5253[3]

Head Of The Class (IRE) *Brian Ellison* 101h
5 ch g Flemensfirth(USA) Dinner At One (IRE) (Marignan (USA))
4547[5] 4958[5] 5300[3]

Head Rush *Warren Greatrex* 72b
6 b g Exit To Nowhere(USA) Petale De Rose (IRE) (Roselier (FR))
2667[9]

Head Spin (IRE) *Seamus Mullins* 99h 99c
6 b g Beneficial Who Tells Jan (Royal Fountain)
2535[5] 2877[F] 3119[3]
3551[3] 3687[4]

Health Is Wealth (IRE) *Colin Tizzard* 77h 109c
9 br g Anshan Cherry Black (IRE) (Roselier (FR))
245[6] 632[6] 757[3] 972[6] (1349)
1626[3] 1830[7] 5390[P]

Heaney (IRE) *T J Taaffe* 136h 135c
7 b g Flemensfirth(USA) The Red Wench (IRE) (Aahsaylad)
1897a[5] 5474a[6]

Hearditbefore (IRE) *Matt Sheppard* 68b
6 b m Sendawar(IRE) Princess Breda (IRE) (Long Pond)
1712[13] 2009[P]

Heart Dancer (FR) *Simon Shirley-Beavan* 97h
8 b g Dark Moondancer Petite Emilie (FR) (Mtoto)
1977[5] 2355[4] 2840[2]
3213[F]

Heart O Annandale (IRE) *Alistair Whillans* 83h 72c
7 b g Winged Love(IRE) She's All Heart (Broken Hearted)
491[P] **798[P]**
4652[P] 5107[P] 5514[P]

Heart O' The West (IRE) *Alistair Whillans* 83h
10 b g Tamayaz(CAN) She's All Heart (Broken Hearted)
222[P] **340[P]**

Heath Hunter (IRE) *David Pipe* 131h
7 b g Shantou(USA) Deep Supreme (IRE) (Supreme Leader)
2369[2] (2732) (3270) 4264[4] 5384[2]

Heathyards Flyer *Nick Lampard* 100b 82c
11 b g Beat All(USA) Heathyards Gem (Governor General)
4442[P]

Heaven Ball (FR) *F Nicolle*
4 ch g Ballingarry(IRE) Heaven Guest (USA) (Giant's Causeway (USA))
614a[F]

Heavenstown (IRE) *John Spearing* 121h 97c
8 ch g Bienamado(USA) Little Bliss (IRE) (Beau Sher)
12[9] 2510[10] 2771[10] (4070) 4338[2] 4677[4] 4841[2] (4949) 5186[5] 5372[14]

Hector's Choice (FR) *Richard Lee* 115h 138c
10 bb g Grey Risk(FR) The Voice (FR) (Ski Chief (USA))
2365[7] 2812[12] (5126)

Hector's House *Nikki Evans* 73h 69c
8 b g Tobougg(IRE) Thrasher (Hector Protector (USA))
2175[3]
2615[2] 3799[U] 4416[U] 4636[6] 5431[5]

Heels Overhead *John Bryan Groucott*
8 ch m Karinga Bay Killatty Player (IRE) (The Noble Player (USA))
94[P] 717[U] 878[P]

Heez A Cracker (FR) *Tom George* 124h 131c
8 b g Goldneyev(USA) Jolly Harbour (Rudimentary (USA))
217[P]

Heezagrey (IRE) *James Evans* 75h
11 gr g Naheez(USA) Silver Belle (IRE) (Roselier (FR))
248[11] 601[6] 965[3] 1188[3] 1405[6] 1538[3] 1784[7]
2047[P]

Heez A Steel (IRE) *Jane Walton* 92h 105c
13 b g Naheez(USA) Ari's Fashion (Aristocracy)
580[F] 2497[3]
2735[2] 3022[6] 4238[4] 4577[4]
(4942) 5358[6] 5558[U]

Heliopsis (IRE) *Lucinda Russell* 104h 75c
9 b g Beneficial Bright Note (Buckskin (FR))
5213[6]

Helium (FR) *Alexandra Dunn* 118h 114c
9 b g Dream Well(FR) Sure Harbour (SWI) (Surumu (GER))
202[4] (3957) 4333[3] 4634[3] 4781[2] 5233[8]

He'llberemembered (IRE) *P G Fahey* 149h 147c
11 ch g Blue Ocean(USA) Remember Rob (IRE) (Deep Society)
1604a[12] 5156[8]

Hellesbelles (IRE) *Tim Vaughan* 91h
6 b m Helissio(FR) Madame Luso (IRE) (Luso)
2309[4] 2865[4] 3274[7] *4328[4]* 5012[6]

Hello George (IRE) *Philip Hobbs* 116b
5 b g Westerner Top Ar Aghaidh (IRE) (Topanoora)
359[3] 1869[2] (2368)

Hello Mr Kelly (IRE) *Mrs K M Diggle*
9 b g Wizard King Van Castle (IRE) (Corrouge (USA))
58[P]

Hellorboston (IRE) *Donald McCain* 122h
6 b g Court Cave(IRE) Helorhiwater (IRE) (Aristocracy)
2103[6] 3018[2] 3392[2] 3938[2] (4491) 4954[6] 5559[3]

Helloutofdodge (IRE) *R P Rath* 98b
8 b g Ashkalani(IRE) Eskimo Kiss (IRE) (Distinctly North (USA))
538[7]

Hell's Bay (FR) *Keiran Burke* 124h 132c
12 b g Supreme Leader Queen's Flagship (IRE) (Accordion)
(432) **672[6]**
780[3] **923[P]**

Hell's Spirit (IRE) *David Dennis* 113h
6 b g Oscar(IRE) Last Century (IRE) (Glacial Storm (USA))
4280[P]

Helpston *Pam Sly* 93h 107c
10 b g Sir Harry Lewis(USA) Chichell's Hurst (Oats)
659[8] **851[P]**

Hel Tara *Nicky Henderson* 100b
5 b m Kayf Tara Heltornic (IRE) (Zaffaran (USA))
(5249)

Hendry Trigger *Bernard Llewellyn*
5 ch g Double Trigger(IRE) Denise Best (IRE) (Goldmark (USA))
2614[F]

Henllan Harri (IRE) *Peter Bowen* 118h
6 br g King's Theatre(IRE) Told You So (IRE) (Glacial Storm (USA))
(962) 2946[3] 3734[3] 5070[2]

Henok (FR) *David Pipe* 103h 108c
8 ch g Kapgarde(FR) Harkosa (FR) (Nikos)
34[6]

Henri De Boistron (FR) *Tom George* 81h
4 b g Enrique Highness Royale (FR) (Garde Royale)
2015[8] 2455[5] 2750[8] 3161[12]

Henrio (IRE) *Fergal O'Brien* 80b
6 ch g Golan(IRE) Sarahall (IRE) (Saddlers' Hall (IRE))
1138[9] **1262[P]**

Henri Parry Morgan *Peter Bowen* 125h
6 b g Brian Boru Queen Of Thedaises (Over The River (FR))
140[5] (499)

Henrybrowneyes (IRE) *Ian Williams* 105b
5 ch g Goldmark(USA) The Vine Browne (IRE) (Torus)
4017[5] ◆ 4728[10] 5181[7]

Henry Higgins (IRE) *Charles O'Brien* 125h
4 b g Jeremy(USA) Moonchild (GER) (Acatenango (GER))
3305a[3] 4178a[5] 4432a[5]

Henry Hook (IRE) *Mark Gillard* 128h 126c
10 ch g Presenting Swing The Lead (IRE) (Good Thyne (USA))
411[P]

Henry Hurst (IRE) *Jimmy Fox* 95h 67c
8 b g Bob's Return(IRE) Proper Primitive (Primitive Rising (USA))
176[10] 650[9] 809[3] 1106[4] 1267[4] 1320[3] **2313[7]**

Henry Jenkins *Malcolm Jefferson* 30h
7 gr g Fair Mix(IRE) Altogether Now (IRE) (Step Together I (USA))
4038[5] 4891[8]

Henry King (IRE) *Victor Dartnall* 100h 127c
10 gr g Great Palm(USA) Presenting Shares (IRE) (Presenting)
2508[3] ◆ 3093[2] 4110[6]

Henry San (IRE) *Alan King* 117h 125c
7 ch g Exceed And Excel(AUS) Esclava (USA) (Nureyev (USA))
457[3] 1012[4] (1197)
1302[3] 1521[2]

Henryville *Harry Fry* 131h
6 b g Generous(IRE) Aquavita (Kalaglow)
2569[2] 3387[8] *4299[3]* (4801) 5030[2] 5128[2] 5574[7]

Henwood (IRE) *Colin Tizzard* 95h
6 ch g Old Vic Katty Barry (IRE) (Alderbrook)
544[8] 2109[6] 2369[9] 3956[5] 4275[8] 4883[7] 5143[8]

Herbalist *Ben Pauling* 79h
4 ch g Haafhd Puya (Kris)
2038[6] 2276[6]

Herdsman (IRE) *Sue Smith* 96h 138c
9 b g Flemensfirth(USA) My Sunny South (Strong Gale)
2171[5] (2451)
2841[2] 3416[6] (4190)
4741[P]

Here Comes Moss *John Flint* 81h
7 b g Karinga Bay Madam Mosso (Le Moss)
1695[3]

Herecomesthebride *Philip Hobbs* 45b
4 br f Midnight Legend This Side (IRE) (Dr Massini (IRE))
3167[10]

Herecomesthehollow (IRE) *Nigel Twiston-Davies* 99h
8 ch g Flemensfirth(USA) Drumcay Polly (IRE) (Le Bavard (FR))
4506[5] 4959[6] 5177[9]

Herecomesthetruth (IRE) *Chris Gordon* 124h 120c
12 ch g Presenting Beagan Rose (IRE) (Roselier (FR))
331[4]

Herecomestrouble *Malcolm Jefferson* 113h
7 b g Gentleman's Deal(IRE) Owenreagh (IRE) (Glacial Storm (USA))
699[9] 1094[2] 3147[4] 3657[4] 5190[2]

Here I Am (IRE) *Diana Grissell* 97h
7 br g Presenting The Last Bank (IRE) (Phardante (FR))
2266[P] 4807[8] 5366[12]

Heres Action Man *John Holt* 86b
6 b g Nomadic Way(USA) Jesmund (Bishop Of Cashel)
2701[0]

Here's Henry *David Brace* 57b
5 b g Needle Gun(IRE) Holly Oak (Cruise Missile)
675[9]

Here's Herbie *Sue Gardner* 123h
6 b g Classic Cliche(IRE) Tyre Hill Lilly (Jupiter Island)
2028[6] 2280[9] 2536[5] 3694[5] 4334[2] (4599) (5030) 5351[6]

Heresmynumber (IRE) *Henry Daly* 75b
4 b g Kalanisi(IRE) Broken Rein (IRE) (Orchestra)
4951[4]

Here's To Harry *N W Alexander* 54h
7 b g Helissio(FR) Harrietfield (Nicholas Bill)
313[11] 3017[9]

Heritage Way *S R B Crawford* 116b
5 b g Tamayaz(CAN) Morning Caller (IRE) (Zaffaran (USA))
(4205)

Herminella *Ali Brewer* 88h
6 b m Lucky Story(USA) Herminoe (Rainbow Quest (USA))
1018[11]

Hermosa Vaquera (IRE) *Anna Newton-Smith* 91h
4 b f High Chaparral(IRE) Sundown (Polish Precedent (USA))
2577[5] 3003[7] 3686[4] 5026[7] 5262[2] 5459[5]

Herod The Great *Alan King* 125h
4 ch g Sakhee's Secret Pella (Hector Protector (USA))
1727[2] (1934) (2294) 2500[6]

Heronry (IRE) *Nicky Henderson* 137h
6 b g Heron Island(IRE) In A Tizzy (Sizzling Melody)
205[U] **2019[P]**
3060[2] *4021[3]* (5093) 5372[9]

Heronshaw (IRE) *Henry Daly* 124h
7 b g Heron Island(IRE) Cool Merenda (IRE) (Glacial Storm (USA))
2288[2] 2807[3]

Herons Heir (IRE) *Dan Skelton* 78h
6 b g Heron Island(IRE) Kyle Lamp (IRE) (Miner's Lamp)
3187[7] 3716[5]

Heron's Mill (IRE) *James Ewart* 106h
6 b g Heron Island(IRE) Princess Vic (IRE) (Old Vic)
2202[5] 2497[5] 2997[U] 5056[2]

Hero's Call *Julian Smith* 85h 74c
9 b m Arkadian Hero(USA) Sense Of Value (Trojan Fen)
320^{3} 482^{10} **3015^{2} 5498^{P}**

Herostatus *Jason Ward* 102h
7 ch g Dalakhani(IRE) Desired (Rainbow Quest (USA))
1924^{4} 2172^{P} 2746^{6}

Herr Larry Hewis *Sarah-Jayne Davies* 66b
6 b g Sir Harry Lewis(USA) Avenches (GER) (Dashing Blade)
4728^{12} 5492^{9}

Herschel (IRE) *Gary Moore* 89h
8 br g Dr Fong(USA) Rafting (IRE) (Darshaan)
31^{9}

He's A Bully (IRE) *Polly Gundry* 105b
5 b g Westerner Kitty Maher (IRE) (Posen (USA))
5264^{2}

He's A Gentleman *Michael Easterby* 53b
7 b g Gentleman's Deal(IRE) Lady Confess (Backchat (USA))
3147^{8} 3567^{P}

He's A Hawker (IRE) *Michael Mullineaux* 111h 87c
9 ch g Fourstars Allstar(USA) Dromin Deel (IRE) (Lanfranco)
933^{12} (1087) (1391) 1634^{P} 2050^{P}

Hes Our Lad (IRE) *Anthony Honeyball* 134h 135c
8 b g Rudimentary(USA) Polyzar (IRE) (Shernazar)
1860^{F}

He's Our Man (IRE) *Ross O'Sullivan* 129h 133c
9 b g Statue Of Liberty(USA) She's Our Mare (IRE) (Commanche Run)
$1178a^{4}$ $1702a^{6}$

He's The Daddy *Nigel Twiston-Davies* 110h 102c
7 b g Generous(IRE) Brambly Hedge (Teenoso (USA))
393^{9} 2616^{2} 2944^{3} (3280) 4161^{P} **5004^{5} 5390^{P}**

Heston *Robert Stephens* 85b
5 ch g Halling(USA) Friend For Life (Lahib (USA))
4598^{3}

Heurtevent (FR) *Tony Carroll* 114h 72c
5 bb g Hold That Tiger(USA) Sybilia (GER) (Spectrum (IRE))
2087^{14} 2561^{10} 2848^{10} 3328^{7} 4366^{P} 5072^{14}
5522^{4}

Hever Road (IRE) *David Pearson* 95c
15 ch g Anshan The Little Bag (True Song)
555^{P}

Hey Big Spender (IRE) *Colin Tizzard* 109h 149c
11 b g Rudimentary(USA) Jim's Monkey (Monksfield)
2070^{4} (2822)
3361^{P} 3655^{P} 4754^{11} (5092)
5383^{5}

Hi Bob *Lucinda Egerton* 76h
6 b g Bollin Eric Leading Line (Leading Man)
4582^{7} 4944^{7} 5300^{P} 5354^{6}

Hi Bronco *John Ryall* 73h
7 b g Emperor Fountain Win A Hand (Nearly A Hand)
2912^{11} 5117^{14} 5548^{4}

Hi Candy (IRE) *Ben Haslam* 83h
4 b f Diamond Green(FR) Dancing Steps (Zafonic (USA))
582^{3} (1394) 1684^{P} 3212^{6} 3828^{4} 4595^{8} 5298^{13}

Hi Dancer *Ben Haslam* 109h 96c
11 b g Medicean Sea Music (Inchinor)
1046^{9} 1378^{9} 1504^{6} 2198^{13} 2597^{10} 2868^{6}
3659^{10} 4336^{10}

Hidden Cyclone (IRE) *John Joseph Hanlon* 148h 166c
9 b g Stowaway Hurricane Debbie (IRE) (Shahanndeh)
$1157a^{2}$ (1613a)
2503^{3} $3338a^{2}$ 3773^{2} 4766^{2}

Hidden Future (IRE) *C A McBratney* 108h 130c
8 b g Akbar(IRE) Lisheen Lady (IRE) (Broken Hearted)
864^{4} 883^{U} 1162^{5}

Hidden Horizons (IRE) *S R B Crawford* 102h 126c
8 b m Winged Love(IRE) Dansana (IRE) (Insan (USA))
310^{3} **4337^{U}**
4626^{3} 5558^{2}

Hidden Identity (IRE) *Tim Vaughan* 139h
8 b m Beneficial Swanbrook Leader (IRE) (Supreme Leader)
(1867) (2433) 3649^{3} 4158^{4} 4740^{4} 5370^{P}

Hidden Justice (IRE) *John Quinn* 131h
5 b g Lawman(FR) Uncharted Haven (Turtle Island (IRE))
3477^{13} 3892^{10} 4423^{7} (4897)

Hidden Link *Tom Symonds* 72h
4 b g Rail Link Gloved Hand (Royal Applause)
3641^{7} 4307^{7} 4722^{9}

Hide The Evidence (IRE) *Michael McElhone* 118h 109c
13 ch g Carroll House Andarta (Ballymore)
1656^{4}

Hi George *Malcolm Jefferson* 120h 131c
6 b g Doyen(IRE) Our Ethel (Be My Chief (USA))
563^{4} 801^{3} **(2882)**

Higgsy *Martin Hill* 87b
6 ch g Generous(IRE) Carmel's Joy (IRE) (Carlingford Castle)
160^{8}

High Aspirations (IRE) *Michael Blake* 86h
6 b g Dr Massini(IRE) Divining (IRE) (Dowsing (USA))
2509^{6} 3326^{6} 3567^{P} 5007^{6} 5234^{9}

Highbury High (IRE) *Paul Henderson* 118h 111c
7 gr g Salford Express(IRE) Betseale (IRE) (Step Together I (USA))
921^{5} 1870^{2} (2633)
2784^{U} 3150^{8} (4696)

Highest Red *Natalie Lloyd-Beavis*
5 ch g Byron Honor Rouge (IRE) (Highest Honor (FR))
1059^{P}

High Fair *Sandy Forster* 84h
8 b m Grape Tree Road Miss Tango (Batshoof)
3393^{2} 3723^{7} 4770^{5} 5494^{8}

Highfields Dancer *Gary Moore* 27b
6 b g Silver Patriarch(IRE) Linguistic Dancer (Aragon)
862^{10} *4019^{7}*

High Holloa *Caroline Bailey* 68h
5 ch m Distant Music(USA) Elmside Katie (Lord David S (USA))
462^{6} 715^{13} 4069^{6} 4487^{6} 4863^{P} 5244^{P}

High Hoylander *Sue Smith* 76h
8 b g Aljabr(USA) Ma-Arif (IRE) (Alzao (USA))
2736^{6}

High Kite (IRE) *Warren Greatrex* 107h 114c
8 bb g High-Rise(IRE) Sister Rose (IRE) (Roselier (FR))
4299^{8} 4760^{2} 5059^{2} 5520^{7}

Highland Cathedral *James Walton* 91h 121c
10 ch g Minster Son Celtic Waters (Celtic Cone)
5161^{2}

Highlander Ted *Mark Walford* 90h
6 b g Midnight Legend Half Each (Weld)
2596^{P} 3520^{4} 4461^{2} 5056^{3}

Highland Lodge (IRE) *Emma Lavelle* 137h 150c
8 b g Flemensfirth(USA) Supreme Von Pres (IRE) (Presenting)
2108^{2} 2815^{4} ◆ **3361^{P} 4263^{6} 4962^{8}**

Highland Love *Jedd O'Keeffe* 102h 92c
9 b g Fruits Of Love(USA) Diabaig (Precocious)
283^{3}

Highland Rain *Jennie Candlish* 86h 77c
6 ch g Sir Harry Lewis(USA) Scottish Clover (Scottish Reel)
565^{6} **759^{5}**
930^{3} 1038^{8} 1188^{10}

Highland Retreat *Harry Fry* 147h
7 b m Exit To Nowhere(USA) St Kilda (Past Glories)
(2371) (2713) (3770) 4740^{8}

Highland River *Dave Roberts* 88h 93c
8 b g Indian Creek Bee One (IRE) (Catrail (USA))
29^{7} 264^{4} 1121^{7}
1186^{4} 1314^{3} 1675^{5} 3192^{4} 3353^{4} 3593^{6} **3799^{2}**
4243^{8} *4325^{6}*

Highlife Dancer *Mick Channon* 80h
6 br g Imperial Dancer Wrong Bride (Reprimand)
1348^{6}

High On A Hill (IRE) *Iain Jardine* 81h
7 b g Val Royal(FR) Blue Kestrel (IRE) (Bluebird (USA))
1288^{4} 1675^{P} 1824^{4}

Highpower (IRE) *Jonjo O'Neill* 111h
5 b g Flemensfirth(USA) Holly Grove Lass (Le Moss)
2602^{6} 3061^{7} 3415^{3}

Highrate (IRE) *Kim Bailey* 102h 115c
8 b g Presenting Hollygrove Cliche (Classic Cliche (IRE))
(113) **1988^{P}**

High Ron *Caroline Bailey* 129c
9 b g Rainbow High Sunny Heights (Golden Heights)
459^{2} 839^{7} 1119^{2} 1303^{3} 1403^{5} 2700^{6} (3565)
(3836) 4448^{4} 4704^{6} (5515)

High Storm (IRE) *Bernard Llewellyn* 120h 126c
7 b g High Chaparral(IRE) Lady Storm (IRE) (Mujadil (USA))
806^{6} (1133) 1485^{12}

High Stratos *John Joseph Hanlon* 97h
5 b g Montjeu(IRE) Hyabella (Shirley Heights)
(14) 589^{4}

Hightown (IRE) *Alison Batchelor* 91h 78c
7 b g King's Theatre(IRE) Faucon (Polar Falcon (USA))
5^{5} 1625^{4} 1822^{F}

High Ville (IRE) *David Pipe* 124h
8 b g Beneficial Brenny's Pearl (IRE) (Good Thyne (USA))
(42) 201^{P} 767^{3} (933) 1011^{2} 1304^{2}

Highway Code (USA) *Richard Lee* 125h 133c
8 b g Street Cry(IRE) Fairy Heights (IRE) (Fairy King (USA))
634^{2} 859^{3} 1053^{2} 1425^{3} 2461^{3}
(2797) 4768^{17} 4921^{4} 5230^{3}

Highway Joe *Ian Williams* 29b
7 b m Central Park(IRE) Fringe Benefit (IRE) (Executive Perk)
5427^{P}

Hilden *William Muir* 94h
5 b m Dansili Singleton (Singspiel (IRE))
483^{8}

Hillbilly Boy (IRE) *Bill Turner*
4 b g Haafhd Erreur (IRE) (Desert King (IRE))
3154^{P}

Hill Forts Gloria (IRE) *Lawney Hill* 95h 41c
9 b m King's Theatre(IRE) Ad Gloria (IRE) (Shernazar)
490^{8} 1188^{8} 1405^{3} 1538^{P}

Hill Forts Harry *Seamus Mullins* 84b
5 ch g Arkadian Hero(USA) Queen Of The Suir (IRE) (Carlingford Castle)
2912^{4}

Hilltime (IRE) *Clive Mulhall* 69h 76c
14 b g Danetime(IRE) Ceannanas (IRE) (Magical Wonder (USA))
968^{6} 1206^{P}

Hilton Du Berlais (FR) *A Chaille-Chaille* 124h
4 b f Saint Des Saints(FR) Anais Du Berlais (FR) (Dom Pasquini (FR))
$2262a^{4}$

Himalayan Express *Mrs David Plunkett* 56h 121c
10 b g Rakaposhi King Street Magic (IRE) (Jolly Jake (NZ))
(57) **4131^{10}**
655^{9} 3720^{P} 4658^{7} 5135^{8}

Himayna *Christopher Kellett* 96h 90c
10 b m Generous(IRE) Himaya (IRE) (Mouktar)
248^{P}

Himrayn *Anabel K Murphy* 92h 113c
11 b g Generous(IRE) Himaya (IRE) (Mouktar)
833^{4} 1109^{F} 1351^{2} 1479^{2} 1582^{8}
1668^{5}

Hi Note *Sheena West* 133h 121c
6 b m Acclamation Top Tune (Victory Note (USA))
304^{5} 1745^{2} 1766^{2}
2249^{2} 2565^{3} 3096^{4}

Hinterland (FR) *Paul Nicholls* 143h 157c
6 b g Poliglote Queen Place (FR) (Diamond Prospect (USA))
(2363)
(2950) 4753^{U} 5168^{7}

Hint Of Mint *Nick Williams* 133h
5 b g Passing Glance Juno Mint (Sula Bula)
2476^{10} 2906^{3} (3592) 4173^{4} (5003) (5239) ◆

Hinton Indiana *Dan Skelton* 125h 88c
9 b g Kayf Tara Hinton Grace (Vital Season)
94^{P} 1914^{P} 2110^{4} 5401^{2}

Hinton Magic *Jonjo O'Neill* 43h
5 b m Revoque(IRE) Miss Quickly (IRE) (Anshan)
4403^{6} 5071^{7}

Hippomene (FR) *J-P Gallorini* 132h
4 b g Dream Well(FR) Dindounas (FR) (Astarabad (USA))
(2262a)

Hired Hand (IRE) *Jonjo O'Neill* 110h
8 b g High Chaparral(IRE) Piffle (Shirley Heights)
488^{4} 812^{8} 1087^{P}

His Excellency (IRE) *David Pipe* 134h 151c
6 ch g King's Best(USA) Road Harbour (USA) (Rodrigo De Triano (USA))
2532^{7} 2952^{8} 3333^{F} 3660^{6} 4053^{2} 4790^{14} 5275^{4}
5535^{4}

History Lesson *Alan Jones* 52h
8 ch g Golan(IRE) Once Upon A Time (Teenoso (USA))
536^{P} 788^{P}

Hi Tide (IRE) *J R Jenkins* 107h 107c
10 br g Idris(IRE) High Glider (High Top)
289^{4} 605^{3} 846^{6} 1093^{P} 1495^{2} 1551^{3} (1840)
5365^{B}

Hitman Harry *Tina Jackson* 104b
6 b g Sir Harry Lewis(USA) Bonnie Buttons (Lord Bud)
2738^{2} 4895^{5}

Hit The Headlines (IRE) *Caroline Fryer* 133h 133c
8 b g Flemensfirth(USA) Heather Breeze (IRE) (Lord Americo)
3065^{2} 4685^{8} 4792^{4}

Hit The Road Jack (IRE) *S R B Crawford* 83h
8 b g Kadeed(IRE) Durgams Delight (IRE) (Durgam (USA))
1164^{7}

Hit The Switch *Michael Mullineaux* 102h 56c
8 b g Reset(AUS) Scenic Venture (IRE) (Desert King (IRE))
1083^{6} 1325^{P}

Hit The Top (IRE) *Sue Smith* 129h
7 b g Gold Well Smooth Leader (IRE) (Supreme Leader)
848^{7} 1037^{3} 1418^{2} 3271^{3} (3618) 3832^{2} 4550^{3}
4833^{F} 4941^{2} 5277^{4}

Hittin'The Skids (IRE) *Mandy Rowland*
6 ch m Fruits Of Love(USA) Hush Deal (Tipsy Creek (USA))
2190^{P}

H M S Intrepid *Anthony Honeyball* 74h
6 b g Intikhab(USA) Lakatoi (Saddlers' Hall (IRE))
1124^{2} ◆ 1264^{6} 1429^{8}

Hoare Abbey (IRE) *Tom George* 106h 107c
8 ch g Definite Article Tourist Attraction (IRE) (Pollerton)
1135^{P}

Hoar Frost *Karen Tutty* 61h
9 b m Fraam Natalie Jay (Ballacashtal (CAN))
17^{7} 1841^{11}

Hobb's Dream (IRE) *Neil Mulholland* 58h 92c
10 br m Winged Love(IRE) La-Greine (Strong Gale)
778^{7} 1300^{P} 1701^{B} 5122^{4}
5546^{3}

Hobsons Bay (IRE) *Sheena Walton* 43h
9 b g Flemensfirth(USA) Ou La La (IRE) (Be My Native (USA))
536^{9} 630^{10} 2844^{P} 2869^{P}

Hodgson (IRE) *Sarah Humphrey* 112h 118c
9 gr g Oscar(IRE) Gairha Grey (IRE) (Norwich)
(370) **504^{4}**
(781) **960^{5}**
1498^{3} **1687^{3}**
2149^{2} 2873^{4}

Hold Court (IRE) *Evan Williams* 125h 129c
7 br g Court Cave(IRE) Tipsy Miss (IRE) (Orchestra)
2080^{8} 2490^{18} 2944^{13} 3419^{7} 4353^{4} (5233)
5384^{16}

Hold Em Cowboy (IRE) *Gordon Elliott* 126h 128c
10 b g Moscow Society(USA) One To Two (IRE) (Astronef)
1543^{2}

Holden Caulfield (IRE) *Nick Ayliffe* 76h
9 b g Catcher In The Rye(IRE) God Speed Her (Pas De Seul)
517^{7} 833^{P} 1643^{P}

Hold On Julio (IRE) *Alan King* 132h 152c
11 br g Blueprint(IRE) Eileens Native (IRE) (Be My Native (USA))
1968^{P}

Hold The Bucks (USA) *Daniel Steele* 97h
8 b g Hold That Tiger(USA) Buck's Lady (USA) (Alleged (USA))
2274^{2} 2770^{P} 3140^{5} 3249^{5} 3556^{2} (4469) (4721)
5118^{2} 5457^{P}

Hollins *Tony Forbes* 103h 111c
10 b g Lost Soldier(USA) Cutting Reef (IRE) (Kris)
698^{4} 1581^{4} 1634^{5} 1797^{9} **1939^{9} 2194^{3} 2512^{2}**
2772^{2} (3190)
4822^{4} 5076^{3}

Hollow Blue Sky (FR) *Nigel Twiston-Davies* 110h 124c
7 gr g Turgeon(USA) Run For Laborie (FR) (Lesotho (USA))
(2155)
2749^{4} ◆ **3172^{3} 3879^{4} (4372)**
5385^{3} 5533^{2}

Hollow Heartbeat (IRE) *Brendan Powell* 82h 36c
7 b g Flemensfirth(USA) Polly's Joy (IRE) (Oscar (IRE))
122^{P} 997^{9}

Hollow Penny *Alan King* 120h
6 b g Beat Hollow Lomapamar (Nashwan (USA))
2050^{U} 2314^{7} 5030^{3} 5457^{3}

Hollow Tree *Donald McCain* 126h
6 b g Beat Hollow Hesperia (Slip Anchor)
215^{13} *4327^{5}* 4814^{6} 5482^{4}

Hollywood All Star (IRE) *Graeme McPherson* 101h
5 b g Kheleyf(USA) Camassina (IRE) (Taufan (USA))
2783^{12} 3128^{7} 3592^{P} 5008^{6} 5490^{6}

Holmwood Legend *Neil Mulholland* 89h 140c
13 b g Midnight Legend West-Hatch-Spirit (Forzando)
6^{P}

Hologram *David Elsworth* 110b
5 b g Teofilo(IRE) Love Divine (Diesis)
(298)

Holy Veil *Alexandra Dunn* 97b
5 b m Kayf Tara Holy Smoke (Statoblest)
2583^{4} 4735^{5}

Holywell (IRE) *Jonjo O'Neill* 157h 165c
7 b g Gold Well Hillcrest (IRE) (Thatching)
2242^{3} 2882^{2} 3291^{U} (3831)
(4344) (4738)
(5154)

Home Farm (IRE) *A L T Moore* 121h 149c
7 b g Presenting Tynelucy (IRE) (Good Thyne (USA))
$5474a^{P}$

Home For Tea *Tom Symonds* 95h
5 b g Westerner Wolnai (Cloudings (IRE))
3160^{4} 3728^{9} 4091^{8} 4467^{P} 4988^{4} 5242^{13}

Home Girl (IRE) *Susan Johnson* 64h
6 br m Milan Homebird (IRE) (Be My Native (USA))
187^{12} 1885^{11} 2147^{8} 2453^{7} 2886^{7} 4071^{P}

Homer Run (IRE) *Simon Earle* 110h
7 b g Classic Cliche(IRE) Suir Native (IRE) (Be My Native (USA))
264^{8} 852^{6} (2877) (3192) 5345^{3}

Home Run (GER) *David Pipe* 135h
6 ch g Motivator Hold Off (IRE) (Bering)
718^{7} (2529) 2671^{4} 2949^{2} 3646^{7} 4025^{5} 4805^{17}

Honest And True (IRE) *Alistair Whillans* 44h 76c
7 b g Desert Prince(IRE) Highly Respected (IRE) (High Estate)
627^{4} 749^{10} 868^{7}

Honest John *Steve Gollings* 131h 121c
10 b g Alzao(USA) Tintera (IRE) (King's Theatre (IRE))
2394^{U} 3019^{6} 3603^{3} 3874^{6} 4078^{P} 4695^{P}

Honey Bach (IRE) *B R Hamilton* 120h
7 b m Bach(IRE) Lough Lein Leader (IRE) (Supreme Leader)
$1802a^{7}$ $2205a^{6}$ $3804a^{6}$

Honey Of A Kitten (USA) *David Evans* 91h
6 b g Kitten's Joy(USA) Sweet Baby Jane (USA) (Kingmambo (USA))
333^{4} 730^{11}

Honourable Emperor (IRE) *Noel Meade* 124h
5 b g Holy Roman Emperor(IRE) Belle Of Honour (USA) (Honour And Glory (USA))
$1139a^{3}$

Honourable Gent *Rose Dobbin* 91h
6 b g Gentleman's Deal(IRE) Gudasmum (Primitive Rising (USA))
218^{8} 494^{6} 1540^{6} (1790) 2169^{3} (3038)

Honour A Promise *Paul Webber* 89h 59c
6 b m Norse Dancer(IRE) Motcombe (IRE) (Carroll House)
2053^{8} 2824^{4} 3159^{11}

Honour System (IRE) *John Ferguson* 118h
7 ch g King's Best(USA) Rawabi (Sadler's Wells (USA))
73^{U} (517) 2668^{8} 3648^{9} 4224^{6} 5294^{6}

Honour The King (IRE) *John Bryan Groucott* 5h
8 bb g Insan(USA) Cassies Girl (IRE) (Mandalus)
2509^{11} 2768^{4}

Honour The World (IRE) *Shaun Lycett* 79h 89c
9 b g Tobougg(IRE) Sewards Folly (Rudimentary (USA))
503^{11} 1136^{P}

Hopatina (IRE) *Neil Mulholland* 115h
8 b m Flemensfirth(USA) Bonny Lass (Bonny Scot (IRE))
(2008) (2620) (3566) 4070^{4}

Hopeand *Charles Pogson* 98h 109c
9 b m King's Theatre(IRE) Land Of Glory (Supreme Leader)
1090^{3} 1305^{3} 1428^{7} 2190^{5} **(2349)**
2626^{2} (3152)
3268^{2} 3837^{4} 5363^{5}

Hope For Glory *Jason Ward* 39h
5 b g Proclamation(IRE) Aissa (Dr Devious (IRE))
2104^{6} 4476^{8} 4939^{8}

Hopefull *R Mike Smith* 69b
4 bl f Overbury(IRE) Maryscross (IRE) (Presenting)
3663^{7} 4205^{6}

Hope Point *Mark Usher* 85h
6 b m Overbury(IRE) East Rose (Keen)
5522^{10}

Hope Royal *Lawney Hill* 64b
7 ch m Karinga Bay Royal Squeeze (IRE) (King's Ride)
4^{9} 270^{9} 945^{6}

Hopping Hare *Neil Mulholland* 87b
6 b g Loup Sauvage(USA) Rio Pops (Broadsword (USA))
433^{7}

Hopstrings *Charlie Brooks* 116h
6 ch m Sulamani(IRE) Hop Fair (Gildoran)
878^{8} 1090^{2} 1187^{2} (1387) 1432^{2} 1635^{2} 1829^{P}
5427^{2}

Horace *Harry Fry* 95h
6 b g Hernando(FR) Ancora (IRE) (Accordion)
2740^{6}

Horace Hazel *Anthony Honeyball* 101b
5 b g Sir Harry Lewis(USA) Kaream (Karinga Bay)
5130^4

Horatio Caine (FR) *Mrs Julie Mansell*
7 b g Assessor(IRE) Red Flower (USA) (Trempolino (USA))
3801^U

Horatio Hornblower (IRE) *Nick Williams* 132h
6 bb g Presenting Countess Camilla (Bob's Return (IRE))
(4024) 4271^P (4937) 5387^2

Horendus Hulabaloo (IRE) *M F Morris* 134h
5 b g Beneficial Renvyle Society (IRE) (Moscow Society (USA))
2256a^2 4523a^5

Horizontal Speed (IRE) *Philip Hobbs* 138h
6 b g Vertical Speed(FR) Rockababy (IRE) (King's Ride)
(2011) 2461^2 2808^2 (3422) (3782) 4680^{13} (5387) ◆

Horny Devil *Marc Barber*
7 b g Dreams End Killy Lass (IRE) (Buckskin (FR))
638^P

Horsted Valley *Warren Greatrex* 106b
4 gr g Fair Mix(IRE) Kullu Valley (Turgeon (USA))
(5367)

Hortense Mancini *Lucy Wadham* 72h
5 ch m King's Best(USA) Have Fun (Indian Ridge)
36^4 *4499^6* 4796^8

Horton *Barry Murtagh* 57b
6 b g Beat All(USA) Fen Terrier (Emarati (USA))
2795^6

Hotgrove Boy *Stuart Coltherd* 86h 103c
7 b g Tobougg(IRE) Tanwir (Unfuwain (USA))
3040^5 3525^P **3831^F 4004^2 4203^P (4748)**
4890^P 5483^2

Hot Pepper *Chris Down* 78h
6 gr g Tikkanen(USA) Copper Valley (Nearly A Hand)
3363^{10} 4171^{11} 4391^7 5015^F

Hot Spice *Michael Easterby* 103h
6 b g Kodiac Harlestone Lady (Shaamit (IRE))
267^7 756^5

Hot Whiskey (IRE) *Brendan Powell* 109h 111c
6 ch g Flemensfirth(USA) Fair Gina (IRE) (Long Pond)
2107^U 2450^4 2847^P 3435^6 4132^P *4299^7* 4760^3
5114^2 5307^3

Hot Whiskey N Ice (IRE) *Noel Williams* 122h
5 b g Milan Fair Gina (IRE) (Long Pond)
(2773) 4130^2 (4442)

Houblon Des Obeaux (FR) *Venetia Williams* 145h 166c
7 b g Panoramic Harkosa (FR) (Nikos)
(2214)
2815^6 (3199)
3888^4 4263^3 4787^9 5133^6 5571^U

Houndscourt (IRE) *Jamie Snowden* 121h 106c
7 b g Court Cave(IRE) Broken Rein (IRE) (Orchestra)
140^6 (2429)
2955^4 5257^6

Houseparty *Zoe Davison* 109h
6 b g Invincible Spirit(IRE) Amusing Time (IRE) (Sadler's Wells (USA))
384^8 947^2 968^3 3148^3 *4023^{12} 4324^6* 4573^7
5012^8 5459^9

Houston Dynimo (IRE) *Nicky Richards* 114h 75c
9 b g Rock Of Gibraltar(IRE) Quiet Mouse (USA) (Quiet American (USA))
752^3 2158^4

Howaboutnever (IRE) *Donald McCain* 85h
6 b g Shantou(USA) Sarah's Cottage (IRE) (Topanoora)
2456^3 4431^5

Howaboutnow (IRE) *Donald McCain* 124h
7 ch g Shantou(USA) Sarah's Cottage (IRE) (Topanoora)
(2621) 3417^F

Howard's Legacy (IRE) *Venetia Williams* 122h 136c
8 b g Generous(IRE) Ismene (FR) (Bad Conduct (USA))
2072^P 2438^2 3366^4 4104^P 4681^6 5430^2

Howareyougoingon (IRE) *G D Hanmer* 41c
10 b g Rock Hopper Kilternan Norwich (IRE) (Norwich)
535^5

Howizee *Maurice Barnes* 129h 112c
8 gr g Baryshnikov(AUS) Sendai (Le Moss)
358^2 **625^3**
1926^7 2170^5 2807^4 3108^P 5256^F 5379^2

Howlett (IRE) *Derek Frankland* 67h
6 b g Ishiguru(USA) Royal Show (IRE) (Sadler's Wells (USA))
76^3 599^4 944^4 2893^9

Howlin Moon *Michael Attwater*
6 ch m Zamindar(USA) Steppin Out (First Trump)
3098^7 3230^4

Howlongisafoot (IRE) *Paul Nicholls* 124h
5 b g Beneficial Miss Vic (IRE) (Old Vic)
1991^{11} 3086^3 4175^2 4442^2 5093^4 (5389)

How's D Strawboss (IRE) *Aytach Sadik*
9 gr g Environment Friend Taken For A Ride (IRE) (King's Ride)
2872^P

How's My Friend *Grant Cann* 111h 115c
9 b g Karinga Bay Friendly Lady (New Member)
62^{11} 766^4 5131^2 5287^2

Howwoulduno (IRE) *Liam Lennon* 123h 129c
6 b g Desert King(IRE) Whadouno (IRE) (Abednego)
(800) 1148^2 (1159) 1415^2 5320^4

Howwrongcanyoube *Alan King* 104b
5 b g Kayf Tara Diva (Exit To Nowhere (USA))
5388^5

Howya Buddy (IRE) *Adrian Wintle* 113h
9 b g Heron Island(IRE) Boccachera (IRE) (Phardante (FR))
650^{10} 925^{14}

Hubood *Zoe Davison* 64h
6 b m Refuse To Bend(IRE) Shuheb (Nashwan (USA))
383^4 671^{11} 2004^{12}

Hudson Gunner (IRE) *Francesca Nimmo* 58b
7 b g Milan Hudson Hope (IRE) (Topanoora)
4936^U

Huff And Puff *Venetia Williams* 126h
7 b g Azamour(IRE) Coyote (Indian Ridge)
3728^5 4103^2 ◆ 4959^2

Hughesie (IRE) *Evan Williams* 98b
5 b g Indian Danehill(IRE) Collatrim Choice (IRE) (Saddlers' Hall (IRE))
3160^2 5042^2

Hugo Drax (IRE) *David Pipe* 70h
7 b g Bienamado(USA) Young Love (FR) (Jeune Homme (USA))
174^6 686^5 829^{13} 1018^P

Humbel Ben (IRE) *Alan Jones* 75h 114c
11 br g Humbel(USA) Donegans Daughter (Auction Ring (USA))
371^P 756^8 1580^9
1696^3 2014^5 2618^P 3172^P 3693^P 4352^P

Humbie (IRE) *Pauline Robson* 108h 132c
10 b g Karinga Bay South Queen Lady (IRE) (King's Ride)
512^5 **2199^2**

Humphrey Bee (IRE) *N W Alexander* 114c
11 br g Oscar Schindler(IRE) Gladriels Jem (IRE) (Mister Lord (USA))
120^9 504^F 5533^4

Hung Parliament (FR) *Alan King* 100h
6 b g Numerous(USA) Sensational Mover (USA) (Theatrical (IRE))
2644^5 4807^{14} 5445^4

Hunky Dorey *Alexandra Dunn* 55h
8 b g Clan Of Roses Somethingaboutmary (IRE) (Fayruz)
2147^9 2286^{14} 3128^P 4334^P

Hunt Ball (IRE) *Nicky Henderson* 48h 163c
9 b g Winged Love(IRE) La Fandango (IRE) (Taufan (USA))
4265^3 4766^4 5171^{17} 5569^3

Hunters Belt (IRE) *George Bewley* 121h 101c
10 b g Intikhab(USA) Three Stars (Star Appeal)
1378^6
2839^5 3142^F 4002^2 4625^4 (5212) 5357^3

Hunters Hoof (IRE) *Nicky Henderson* 115b
5 b g Flemensfirth(USA) Madgehil (IRE) (Anshan)
2216^6 2788^2 5173^{12}

Hunters Lodge (IRE) *Nigel Twiston-Davies* 113h 131c
8 ch g Subtle Power(IRE) Native Orchid (IRE) (Be My Native (USA))
642^6 1396^4 (1959)
2487^3 2953^6 3416^5 4026^P

Hunting Party (IRE) *D T Hughes* 136h 135c
8 b g City Honours(USA) Highland May (IRE) (Commanche Run)
3868a^{11} 4769^P

Hunting Tower *Tim Vaughan* 133h 124c
10 b g Sadler's Wells(USA) Fictitious (Machiavellian (USA))
1054^2 1268^2 **1851^3 2574^3**

Hurakan (IRE) *Richard Price* 114h
8 gr g Daylami(IRE) Gothic Dream (IRE) (Nashwan (USA))
1672^2

Hurraboru (IRE) *David Thompson* 116h
7 b g Brian Boru Fastlass (Celtic Cone)
114^F 4893^5 5059^{10} 5438^P

Hurricane Carter (IRE) *Natalie Lloyd-Beavis* 91c
14 ch g Zaffaran(USA) Persian Argument (IRE) (Persian Mews)
165^3 323^2 597^3 728^6

Hurricane Fly (IRE) *W P Mullins* 173h
10 b g Montjeu(IRE) Scandisk (IRE) (Kenmare (FR))
(2552a) (3402a) (3930a) 4739^4

Hurricane Herbie (IRE) *Nick Williams* 99h
6 b g Erhaab(USA) Rocheflamme (FR) (Snurge)
47^P

Hurricane Hollow *Keith Dalgleish* 114b
4 b g Beat Hollow Veenwouden (Desert Prince (IRE))
(2160) 4226^2 4561^6 5173^7

Hurricane Ivan (IRE) *Fergal O'Brien* 104h
6 b g Golden Tornado(IRE) Woodram Delight (Idiots Delight)
2076^5 2316^7 2875^4 3425^P 5012^5

Hurricane John (IRE) *Venetia Williams* 73h
4 b g Hurricane Run(IRE) Top Lady (IRE) (Shirley Heights)
3714^7 4073^6 4401^{10}

Hurricane's Girl *Jonjo O'Neill* 79b
5 b m Hurricane Run(IRE) Wise Little Girl (Singspiel (IRE))
2354^6

Hurricane Vic *Alan King* 92b
4 b g Mount Nelson Fountains Abbey (USA) (Giant's Causeway (USA))
4424^4 4964^3

Hurry On Lil (IRE) *Patrick Holmes* 55b
5 ch m Hurricane Run(IRE) Foreign Relation (IRE) (Distant Relative)
173^8

Hydrant *Richard Guest* 40h
8 b g Haafhd Spring (Sadler's Wells (USA))
3838^8 5302^P

Hyperlink (IRE) *John Ferguson* 100h
5 b g Cape Cross(IRE) Surf The Web (IRE) (Ela-Mana-Mou)
8^4 808^4

I Am Colin *Nigel Twiston-Davies* 107h
5 b g Zafeen(FR) Dd's Glenalla (IRE) (Be My Native (USA))
1863^4 2189^3 2755^{13} 4933^{12}

Ibiza Sunset (IRE) *Brendan Powell* 97h
6 b g Chineur(FR) Romanylei (IRE) (Blues Traveller (IRE))
758^6 1641^4 2568^8 2980^{13}

Icanmotor *Claire Dyson* 85h
7 b m Midnight Legend Lochnagold (Lochnager)
368^4 765^6 2980^3 3192^8 4823^2 5282^4

I Can Run Can You (IRE) *Jonjo O'Neill* 91h 70c
8 ch g Old Vic Merry Batim (IRE) (Alphabatim (USA))
71^9 **478^P**
637^7 **1038^U**

Ice Cool Benny (IRE) *Andy Hobbs* 110c
10 br g Beneficial Mahon Rose (IRE) (Roselier (FR))
430^2 689^P

Ice Cool Curler *Ali Brewer* 77b
5 br g Kayf Tara Frosty Mistress (Arctic Lord)
5028^6 5541^P

Ice Ice Baby *John C McConnell* 100h
5 b m Iceman Evasive Quality (FR) (Highest Honor (FR))
891a^2 1185^5

Ice 'N' Easy (IRE) *Charlie Longsdon* 100h 131c
8 b g Dushyantor(USA) Glacial Valley (IRE) (Glacial Storm (USA))
3642^2 4039^4 4685^5 5074^9
(5516)

Ice Nelly (IRE) *Stuart Kittow* 82h
6 b m Iceman Dancing Nelly (Shareef Dancer (USA))
3289^P 5175^5 5393^5

Iconic Rose *Pam Sly* 107h
7 ch m Sir Harry Lewis(USA) Standing Bloom (Presidium)
122^P 2253^6 2680^2 (3119)

Icy Colt (ARG) *Paul Webber* 41h 63c
8 br g Colonial Affair(USA) Icy Desert (USA) (Desert Secret (IRE))
1687^P 2397^{11}

Ide No Idea (IRE) *Caroline Fryer* 60h 71c
10 b g Anshan Gales Wager (Strong Gale)
461^P 4376^4

Ifan (IRE) *Tim Vaughan* 72h
6 b g Ivan Denisovich(IRE) Montana Miss (IRE) (Earl Of Barking (IRE))
994^3

Ifandbutwhynot (IRE) *David O'Meara* 142h
8 b g Raise A Grand(IRE) Cockney Ground (IRE) (Common Grounds)
2069^3 ◆ 2533^{10} (2758) 3477^2 3779^5 4752^{15}
5274^5

If And When *Mrs V J Morse* 49h 17c
6 ch g Where Or When(IRE) Pardon Moi (First Trump)
4246^8

If I Had Him (IRE) *George Baker* 94h
10 b g City Honours(USA) Our Valentine (IRE) (Be My Native (USA))
(993a) (1250a) (1827a)

If In Doubt (IRE) *Philip Hobbs* 143h
6 b g Heron Island(IRE) Catchers Day (IRE) (Catcher In The Rye (IRE))
(2828) 3646^2 4174^2 4765^9

Ifits A Fiddle *Richard Phillips* 82h
5 b m Kalanisi(IRE) Fiddling Again (Hernando (FR))
2266^P 3602^8 5002^8

If I Were A Boy (IRE) *Dominic Ffrench Davis* 100h 103c
7 b m Invincible Spirit(IRE) Attymon Lill (IRE) (Marju (IRE))
1640^3

Ifonlyalfie *Chris Bealby* 83h 100c
9 b g Alflora(IRE) Ifni Du Luc (FR) (Chamberlin (FR))
206^2 597^5 1202^7 1936^8 2313^5 5193^5

Ifonlywecud (IRE) *Clive Mulhall* 91b
5 b g Celtic Swing Mrs Dalloway (IRE) (Key Of Luck (USA))
389^6 1499^3 5500^5

Ifyousayso (IRE) *Tom George* 114h 136c
7 ch g Definite Article Rosato (IRE) (Roselier (FR))
2451^4 (2897)
(3603) 4934^2 5373^P

Ifyouthinkso *Lucy Jones* 104h 70c
7 b g Hernando(FR) Evriza (IRE) (Kahyasi)
1829^P 2150^2 2620^2 2827^7 4070^P 5037^3 5432^3

If You Wish (IRE) *Tim Easterby* 77b
6 ch g Zerpour(IRE) Bu Hagab (IRE) (Royal Academy (USA))
76^9

I Got Power *Keith Reveley* 117h
5 ch g Grape Tree Road I Got Rhythm (Lycius (USA))
173^2 3147^6 3602^4 3872^2 4546^4 4889^F 5445^3

Iguacu *Richard Price* 88h
10 b g Desert Prince(IRE) Gay Gallanta (USA) (Woodman (USA))
1519^3 1795^{10} 2265^{16} 2886^4 5238^7

I Hear A Symphony (IRE) *J J Lambe* 130h 140c
12 b g Accordion Annilogs Daughter (IRE) (Yashgan)
356^{15}

Iheardu *Neil Mulholland* 92h 107c
8 b g Overbury(IRE) Tina Gee (Orchestra)
175^6 669^8 829^9 **976^3**

Ihtikar (USA) *Lucy Normile* 20h
4 b g Invasor(ARG) Ranin (Unfuwain (USA))
1786^9 4772^P

I Know The Code (IRE) *Lynn Siddall* 104h 84c
9 b g Viking Ruler(AUS) Gentle Papoose (Commanche Run)
2510^8 2771^5 3191^8
4451^3 4778^P 5107^3

Ikorodu Road *Matt Sheppard* 126h 143c
11 b g Double Trigger(IRE) Cerisier (IRE) (Roselier (FR))
(2086)
2937^{16}

Iktiview *Philip Kirby* 93h
6 ch g Iktibas Eastview Princess (J B Quick)
(75) 2169^{11} 2449^{11} 3141^3 3264^6 4223^5 4981^4
5359^4

Ilewinbrittania *Gary Brown*
5 br g Lahib(USA) Ilewin Janine (IRE) (Soughaan (USA))
4452^P

Ilewindelilah *Gary Brown* 70h
6 b m Grape Tree Road Bridepark Rose (IRE) (Kemal (FR))
842^5 1064^4 4758^8 5064^{11} 5236^9

Ilewin For Hannah *Gary Brown* 82h 60c
7 b g Generous(IRE) Ilewin Janine (IRE) (Soughaan (USA))
5237^7

Ilewin Kim *Gary Brown* 73h 76c
8 b g Grape Tree Road Bridepark Rose (IRE) (Kemal (FR))
1105^5 1266^7 **3015^U 4416^8 4762^F**

Il Fenomeno (ITY) *Noel Meade* 145h 125c
8 b g Denon(USA) Fabulous Charm (ITY) (Fabulous Dancer (USA))
3806a^5 3910a^{14}

Ilion (POL) *J Vana Jr*
10 b g Jape(USA) Isaura (POL) (Demon Club (POL))
1683a^6

I'Ll Be Frank *Maurice Barnes* 102h
9 b g Fraam Miss Opulence (IRE) (Kylian (USA))
17^2 219^2 444^9 556^4 801^2 884^P (1874) 2843^U
3145^6 4957^8

I'Lldoit *Michael Scudamore* 61h
7 br g Tamayaz(CAN) Club Oasis (Forzando)
33^9 649^P

Illegale (IRE) *Nikki Evans* 75h
8 b m Poliglote Pinkai (IRE) (Caerleon (USA))
89^P 407^4 1000^3 1351^5 1479^3 2568^P

Illicit Illusion (IRE) *T Lacey* 97c
6 b g Heron Island(IRE) Nether The Lady (IRE) (Montelimar (USA))
4485^4

Illico Macias (FR) *P Leblanc* 103h 96c
4 b g Jeremy(USA) Trapiche (Vettori (IRE))
614a^2

Illysantachristina *Rebecca Curtis* 105h
11 b m Parthian Springs Arian Spirit (IRE) (High Estate)
1153^6

Il Presidente (GER) *Ian Williams* 107h
7 ch g Royal Dragon(USA) Independent Miss (GER) (Polar Falcon (USA))
1794^3

Il Testone (FR) *Chris Grant* 100h
5 b g Laveron Gaelic Music (FR) (Poliglote)
389^5 3522^4 4605^3 5206^6

Imagine The Chat *Rebecca Curtis* 100b
5 b g Kayf Tara Be My Bird (Be My Chief (USA))
(3133) 4149^7

I'm A Joker *Sarah Humphrey* 96b
5 ch g Erhaab(USA) Yota (FR) (Galetto (FR))
3508^3

I'm A Rocker (IRE) *Donald McCain* 90h
5 b g Gold Well Over Slyguff (IRE) (Over The River (FR))
4081^5 4397^4 4945^8

Imjoeking (IRE) *Lucinda Russell* 119h 130c
7 b g Amilynx(FR) Go Franky (IRE) (Hollow Hand)
2515^2 2957^6 4646^2 4955^4

I'm Not Telling (IRE) *Grant Cann* 103b 32c
6 ch g Definite Article Incognito (FR) (Apple Tree (FR))
589^3 768^5

Impact Zone *I M Mason* 82h 107c
10 br g Erhaab(USA) Stormy Gal (IRE) (Strong Gale)
288^2 657^3

Imperial Circus (IRE) *Philip Hobbs* 124h 131c
8 b g Beneficial Aunty Dawn (IRE) (Strong Gale)
(1815)
2487^8 3068^4 4886^7 5371^4

Imperial Commander (IRE) *Nigel Twiston-Davies* 112h 159c
13 b g Flemensfirth(USA) Ballinlovane (Le Moss)
2815^P

Imperial Cru *Diana Grissell*
6 b g Imperial Dancer Miss Fizz (Charmer)
246^8

Imperial Elegance *Sheena West* 72h
5 b m Imperial Dancer Canadian Capers (Ballacashtal (CAN))
308^8

Imperial Leader (IRE) *Nigel Twiston-Davies* 132h
6 b g Flemensfirth(USA) Glamorous Leader (IRE) (Supreme Leader)
2813^{13} 3771^2 4174^3 4805^{15} 5372^6

Imperial Legacy *Jo Davis* 46h
6 b g Imperial Dancer Miss Muffett (IRE) (Hero's Honor (USA))
647^3 874^7 1007^8 1270^{10}

Imperial Prince (IRE) *Michael Smith* 89b
5 b g Subtle Power(IRE) Satco Rose (IRE) (Satco (FR))
4611^4 5500^4

Imperial Royale (IRE) *Patrick Clinton* 83h
13 ch g Ali-Royal(IRE) God Speed Her (Pas De Seul)
558^P

Imperial Shabra (IRE) *Patrick O Brady* 128h 133c
10 b g Imperial Ballet(IRE) Jane Digby (IRE) (Magical Strike (USA))
1168a^{19} (Dead)

Imperial Stargazer *Sheena West* 104h
5 gr g Imperial Dancer Sky Light Dreams (Dreams To Reality (USA))
240^6 671^2 856^3 1176^4 1625^3 (2085) 2538^4
2932^{14}

Imperial Vic (IRE) *Michael Smith* 121h 140c
9 bb g Old Vic Satco Rose (IRE) (Satco (FR))
(340) **1976^2**
◆ **2419^3 2971^3 3725^3 4953^4 5495^2**

Impertinent *Noel Quinlan* 50h
4 b f Halling(USA) Incarnation (IRE) (Samum (GER))
3469^6

I'm So Lucky *Mrs S E Busby* 77h 94c
12 b g Zilzal(USA) City Of Angels (Woodman (USA))
4658^5

I'm So Special (IRE) *Susan Johnson* 82h
8 b m Milan Hudson Hope (IRE) (Topanoora)
3871[11] 4595[3] 4883[10]

I'm The Article (IRE) *Harry Fry* 108h
8 ch g Definite Article Our Sioux (IRE) (Jolly Jake (NZ))
(79) 435[3]

In A Heartbeat *Martin Keighley* 90b
5 b m Beat All(USA) La Folichonne (FR) (Useful (FR))
1523[2] 1599[5] 1826[6]

Inandover *John Mackie* 88h 100c
9 b g Dover Patrol(IRE) Inspirational (IRE) (Lahib (USA))
1494[3] 1668[9] 1825[F] (2047)
2425[F]

Inarticulate (IRE) *Seamus Mullins* 89h
6 b m Definite Article Bun Doite (IRE) (Old Vic)
970[3] 1264[2]

In By Midnight *Tom George* 108h 102c
6 ch m Midnight Legend Moyliscar (Terimon)
1[3] (2027) 2352[2] 2948[9] 3391[3] 5291[2] 5509[3]

Inca Dove *Renee Robeson* 78b
5 ch m Sleeping Indian Stock Dove (Deploy)
4253[2]

Incendo *Ian Williams* 101h
8 ch g King's Best(USA) Kindle (Selkirk (USA))
671[3] 857[4]

Incentivise (IRE) *Richard Lee* 84h 124c
11 ch g Snurge Festive Isle (IRE) (Erins Isle)
509[5] 2157[3] 2670[4] 2923[6] 3858[5] 4490[2]

Incher Rose (IRE) *Johnny Farrelly* 64b
6 ch m Golan(IRE) Dun Dun (IRE) (Saddlers' Hall (IRE))
2978[F]

Inch Manor (IRE) *Philip Kirby* 72h
6 b g Fruits Of Love(USA) Erald-De-Mo (IRE) (Erdelistan (FR))
564[7] 1073[P]

Indepub *Martin Todhunter* 100h
5 b g Indesatchel(IRE) Champenoise (Forzando)
1378[8] 1504[5] 1665[4] 2034[P] 4667[4] 4943[7] 5217[4]
5556[F]

Indevan *W P Mullins* 143h
6 b g Indesatchel(IRE) Be Most Welcome (Most Welcome)
(1893a) 2256a[F] 2505[4] 4752[P]

Indiana Bay (IRE) *Mrs Jill Dennis* 109c
7 ch g Indian River(FR) Easter Saturday (IRE) (Grand Plaisir (IRE))
58[2] 5337[4]

Indiana Oscar *Carroll Gray* 51h
6 b g Oscar(IRE) Indian Miss (Idiots Delight)
3956[11] 4281[9] 4988[9]

Indian Castle (IRE) *Donald McCain* 129h 146c
6 b g Dr Massini(IRE) Indian Legend (IRE) (Phardante (FR))
(339) **(2747)**
◆ 3331[2] (3886)
4769[7]

Indian Citizen (IRE) *Arthur Whiting* 91h 74c
7 ch m Indian River(FR) Curra Citizen (IRE) (Phardante (FR))
(320) 590[6]
779[6] 1936[7]

Indian Daudaie (FR) *Sarah Humphrey* 115h 122c
7 ch g Nicobar Aldounia (FR) (Kaldoun (FR))
4820[11]

Indian Groom (IRE) *John Wade* 94h 128c
9 gr g High Chaparral(IRE) Taatof (IRE) (Lahib (USA))
508[7] 734[8]

Indian Icon (FR) *D T Hughes* 129h
4 b c Indian Rocket Playing Star (FR) (Starborough)
5470a[6]

Indian Print (IRE) *Victor Thompson* 88c
10 ch g Blueprint(IRE) Commanche Glen (IRE) (Commanche Run)
28[P]

Indian Ruler (IRE) *Philip Kirby*
9 ch g Rainwatch Tothemanorborn (IRE) (Royal Abjar (USA))
1118[P] 1418[P]

Indian Stream *Peter Bowen* 101h
5 ch m Generous(IRE) Zaffarimbi (IRE) (Zaffaran (USA))
(1671) 1885[2]

Indian Voyage (IRE) *Maurice Barnes* 94h 130c
6 b g Indian Haven Voyage Of Dreams (USA) (Riverman (USA))
279[5] 579[2] 3107[2] 3528[4] (4080)
4367[4] 4833[2] (5058)
(5218)

Indian Winter (IRE) *Stephen Francis Magee* 95b
7 b g Indian Ridge Chill Seeking (USA) (Theatrical (IRE))
1546[2]

Indiefront *Jo Davis* 81h
5 b m Indesatchel(IRE) Jonchee (FR) (Le Thuit Signol (FR))
462[3] 2286[12] 5244[7] 5403[8]

Indigo Island (IRE) *Robert Bewley* 89h 87c
5 b g Trans Island Go Indigo (IRE) (Cyrano De Bergerac)
2347[12] 2732[S] 2866[4] 3106[5] 3639[5] 3924[2] 4475[5]
4616[3] 4940[2] 5107[P] 5556[3]

Indigo Rock (IRE) *Malcolm Jefferson* 122h 116c
8 b g Pierre Thethirstyscholars (IRE) (Be My Native (USA))
449[2] (747) 1755[3] **2494[4] 3397[3] 5060[3] 5558[5]**

Indispensabelle *Linda Jewell* 21b
5 b m Passing Glance Belle Largesse (Largesse)
309[7]

Indubitably *Noel C Kelly* 94h
8 b g Tobougg(IRE) Margaret's Gift (Beveled (USA))
1379[13] 1982[6]

I Need A Hero (IRE) *Sarah Humphrey* 88h 117c
9 b g Oscar Schindler(IRE) Old Fontaine (IRE) (Millfontaine)
670[2] 766[8]

I Need Gold (IRE) *Donald McCain* 138h
6 b g Gold Well Coola Cross (IRE) (Be My Native (USA))
2513[2] 2954[3] (3453) 4186[2] (4665)

In Fairness (IRE) *Nicky Henderson* 105h
5 b g Oscar(IRE) Dix Huit Brumaire (FR) (General Assembly (USA))
239[4] 2802[6] 3166[9] (4664)

Inisheer Boy (IRE) *Ronald O'Leary* 77b
7 b g Presenting Cara Crown (IRE) (Rainbows For Life (CAN))
862[5]

Inishrush (IRE) *Bill Turner* 29h 107c
13 br g Presenting Ballyknock Lass (IRE) (Electric)
636[2] 1055[P]

Inner Drive (IRE) *Alan King* 114b
6 b g Heron Island(IRE) Hingis (IRE) (Shernazar)
2375[2] ◆ *4498[2]*

Inner Steel (IRE) *Lydia Richards* 103h 111c
9 b g Zagreb(USA) Mrs McClintock (IRE) (Arctic Lord)
305[F] 541[3] (712)

Inniscastle Boy *Jim Goldie* 87h
5 b g Sir Percy Galapagar (USA) (Miswaki (USA))
2217[12] 2341[8] 2792[6] 3518[7]

Innis Shannon (IRE) *George Bewley* 86b
4 b f Stowaway Put On Hold (IRE) (Lord Americo)
2247[3]

Innocent Girl (IRE) *Lucinda Russell* 82h
5 b m King's Theatre(IRE) Belle Innocence (FR) (Turgeon (USA))
1667[6] 1974[14] 2514[9] 2998[4] 3393[4]

Innoko (FR) *Tony Carroll* 85h
4 gr g Carlotamix(FR) Chalana (Ashkalani (IRE))
1934[5] 2364[3] 2975[9]

Innsbruck *John Quinn* 96h
4 b g Tiger Hill(IRE) Lille Hammer (Sadler's Wells (USA))
2168[6] 2899[4]

Inoogoo (IRE) *Brian Ellison* 116h 116c
9 b g Great Palm(USA) Ballindante (IRE) (Phardante (FR))
2350[3] 2793[4] 4549[3] ◆ 4815[3] (5555)

Inside Dealer (IRE) *Colin Tizzard* 90h 125c
10 b g Presenting Sea Gale (IRE) (Strong Gale)
1642[2] 1815[3] 2108[3] 2468[6] 2909[3] 5334[6]

Inside Knowledge (USA) *Garry Woodward* 98h
8 rg g Mizzen Mast(USA) Kithira (Danehill (USA))
266[4] 429[4] 561[5] (730) 854[4] 1136[7] 1320[6] 1467[3]
1799[6] 1940[4] 2787[8] 4107[4] 4447[6] 5298[3]

Inside Out *Anthony Honeyball* 48h
4 ch f Presenting On The Outside (IRE) (Anshan)
4735[7] 5195[9] 5524[P]

Instagramher *Charlie Brooks* 74h
4 b f Beat All(USA) Follow My Leader (IRE) (Supreme Leader)
2318[6] 2604[P] 3167[6]

Instinctual *Brendan Powell* 100h
4 ch g Observatory(USA) Be Glad (Selkirk (USA))
1439[2] 1743[2] 1934[2]

Intac (IRE) *Sarah-Jayne Davies* 72h 97c
12 b g Dr Massini(IRE) Nicat (Wolver Hollow)
335[4] 655[8] 1326[6] 1429[9]

Intent (IRE) *Chris Bealby* 92h
5 b m Jeremy(USA) Cant Hurry Love (Desert Prince (IRE))
3469[P]

Interior Minister *Jonjo O'Neill* 91h
4 b g Nayef(USA) Sister Maria (USA) (Kingmambo (USA))
3714[6] 4073[5] 4401[8] 4889[12]

Interpleader *Mrs S W Lewis* 81h 79c
9 b g Luso Braceys Girl (IRE) (Be My Native (USA))
692[6] 832[P] 4915[7]

In The Binyanis (IRE) *Jonjo O'Neill* 73h
7 b g Waky Nao Black Ouzel (IRE) (Taipan (IRE))
435[5]

In The Crowd (IRE) *Richard Price* 102h
5 ch g Haafhd Eliza Gilbert (Noverre (USA))
1866[5] 1970[5] 2474[11]

In The Gate (IRE) *Charlie Longsdon* 102h
6 b g King's Theatre(IRE) The Distaff Spy (Seymour Hicks (FR))
2621[9] 2850[6] 3115[5] 3740[3] 4132[P] 4699[P]

In The Haven (IRE) *Joanne Foster* 111h 99c
11 ch g Topanoora Cafe Matisse (IRE) (Le Moss)
418[7] (534)
1075[6] 1300[P] 1376[8] 1982[11]

Inthelineoffire (IRE) *David Rees* 96b 57c
9 b g Bach(IRE) Jensalee (IRE) (Supreme Leader)
1343[4]

In The Rough (IRE) *Jonjo O'Neill* 113h
5 b g Scorpion(IRE) Sounds Charming (IRE) (Presenting)
2254[3] 2627[3] 3175[3] 4343[5] ◆ 5190[3]

Into The Wind *Jim Best* 64h
7 ch m Piccolo In The Stocks (Reprimand)
1958[10] 2272[10] 2893[7] 3175[12]

Investissement *Charlie Longsdon* 99h
8 b g Singspiel(IRE) Underwater (USA) (Theatrical (IRE))
1674[4] 2051[4]

Investment Expert (IRE) *Brian Ellison* 95h
4 b g Tamayuz Kindling (Dr Fong (USA))
3822[4] 4054[7]

Invicta Lake (IRE) *Suzy Smith* 117h
7 b g Dr Massini(IRE) Classic Material (Classic Cliche (IRE))
2376 1745[F] (2105) (2569) 2798[7] 3186[4] *4023[7]*
4300[9] 4697[3] 5128[8] 5457[2]

Invictus (IRE) *Alan King* 111h 139c
8 b g Flemensfirth(USA) Clashwilliam Girl (IRE) (Seymour Hicks (FR))
2815[11]

Invincible Hero (IRE) *Declan Carroll* 69h
7 b g Invincible Spirit(IRE) Bridelina (FR) (Linamix (FR))
2876[9]

Invisible Touch *Martin Smith*
4 gr f Act One Zarma (FR) (Machiavellian (USA))
2436[10]

Iolith (GER) *Alan King* 120h
9 b g Monsun(GER) Indian Jewel (GER) (Local Suitor (USA))
386[P]

Iona Days (IRE) *Julian Smith* 103h 124c
9 br g Epistolaire(IRE) Miss Best (FR) (Grand Tresor (FR))
508[2] 923[5]

Iouascore (IRE) *Lady Susan Brooke* 64h
7 br g Craigsteel Dottie Digger (IRE) (Catrail (USA))
1891[4] 2153[6] 3063[5] 3728[10]

Ipsos Du Berlais (FR) *Noel Meade* 147h 144c
8 gr g Poliglote Isis Du Berlais (FR) (Cadoudal (FR))
3791a[5] 3868a[8]

Irish Buccaneer (IRE) *Philip Hobbs* 128h
7 b g Milan Supreme Serenade (IRE) (Supreme Leader)
4820[5] ◆ 5345[F]

Irish By Name (IRE) *John Wade* 79h 36c
8 ch g Definite Article Rosies All The Way (Robellino (USA))
2156[12] 3335[P] **5216[7]**

Irish Cavalier (IRE) *Rebecca Curtis* 133h
5 rg g Aussie Rules(USA) Tracker (Bustino)
(433) (2178) (2453) 4261[4] (4945) 5153[7]

Irish Guard *John O'Neill* 76h 87c
13 b g Infantry I Sharp Practice (Broadsword (USA))
2396[P] 2699[P]

Irish Octave (IRE) *Rosemary Gasson* 80b
4 b g Gamut(IRE) Fairytaleofnewyork (IRE) (Zaffaran (USA))
5014[11]

Irish Rebel (IRE) *Miss Clare Hobson* 83c
10 b g Tel Quel(FR) Never On Sunday (IRE) (Religiously (USA))
327[7] 5435[4]

Irish Saint (FR) *Paul Nicholls* 152h
5 bb g Saint Des Saints(FR) Minirose (FR) (Mansonnien (FR))
2758[F] 3200[12] (3771) 4147[3] 5134[6]

Irish Thistle (IRE) *H Rogers* 130h 140c
7 b g Luso Which Thistle (IRE) (Saddlers' Hall (IRE))
3928a[6] 4314a[F]

Iris Nobile (FR) *D Guillemin* 86c
4 b g Della Francesca(USA) Bella Ciao (IRE) (Entrepreneur)
262a[P]

Iron Butterfly *James Eustace* 113h
5 b m Shirocco(GER) Coh Sho No (Old Vic)
2435[5] 3012[6] (3391) 4907[3]

Iron Chancellor (IRE) *Mrs Sue Popham* 100h 115c
9 b g Alderbrook Masriyna (IRE) (Shahrastani (USA))
5131[3]

Iron Duke *Liam Corcoran* 109h 73c
8 gr g Refuse To Bend(IRE) Arinaga (Warning)
637[9]

Ironic (FR) *Tom George* 107h 77c
6 b g Califet(FR) Iron Lassie (USA) (Deputy Minister (CAN))
2845[P] 3429[P]

Ironical (IRE) *Shaun Lycett* 103h
10 b g Bob's Return(IRE) Cheryls Pet (IRE) (General Ironside)
2526 719[7] (1062) 1391[4] 1597[6] 2292[6] 2598[11]

Ironically (IRE) *Neil King* 105h
5 b m Refuse To Bend(IRE) Dutch Auction (USA) (Mr Greeley (USA))
2445 (Dead)

Irving *Paul Nicholls* 149h
6 b g Singspiel(IRE) Indigo Girl (GER) (Sternkoenig (IRE))
(2476) ◆ (2644) (3184) (4421) ◆ 4736[9]

Isaacstown Lad (IRE) *William Amos* 104h 99c
7 b g Milan Friends Of Friends (IRE) (Phardante (FR))
3921[3] ◆ 4460[5] 4776[7] 5106[F]

Isdaal *Kevin Morgan* 74h
7 ch m Dubawi(IRE) Faydah (USA) (Bahri (USA))
3034[15] 4796[6]

Ishusharella *J R Jenkins* 90b
5 b m Doyen(IRE) Emily-Mou (IRE) (Cadeaux Genereux)
5195[6] 5440[5]

Iskrabob *Philip Hide* 15b
4 ch g Tobougg(IRE) Honour Bolton (Past Glories)
3719[10]

Island Confusion (IRE) *Lucinda Russell* 103h
6 b g Heron Island(IRE) Anshan Gail (IRE) (Anshan)
218[2]

Island Cruise (IRE) *Pat Murphy* 110h
6 b g Turtle Island(IRE) Chuckawalla (IRE) (Buckskin (FR))
3177[P] 4093[3] ◆ 4356[2] 4702[3] 5037[2]

Island Heights (IRE) *Lucinda Russell* 117h
5 b g Heron Island(IRE) La Reina (IRE) (Executive Perk)
3826[9] 4234[4] 4429[2] (4648) 4834[2]

Island Life (IRE) *S Flook* 114h 111c
11 b g Turtle Island(IRE) Life Support (IRE) (High Estate)
4511[2] 4655[P] 5135[12] 5287[4]

Islandmagee (IRE) *Evan Williams* 107h 110c
7 b g Heron Island(IRE) Sakanda (IRE) (Vayrann)
10[10] 480[8] 2617[3]
3596[8] 4087[2]
4633[3] 5017[3] 5428[2]

Island Whisper (IRE) *Ben Case* 72b
7 b m Turtle Island(IRE) Whistles Dream (IRE) (Presenting)
2052[6] 2354[11]

Isla Pearl Fisher *N W Alexander* 103h 130c
11 br g Supreme Sound Salem Beach (Strong Gale)
2841[7] (3521)
4238[3] 4953[P] 5481[2]

Isobar (GER) *Donald McCain*
8 b g Monsun(GER) Ice Dream (GER) (Mondrian (GER))
1183[P]

Isola Bella *Jonathan Portman* 89h
5 ch m Sleeping Indian Tetravella (IRE) (Groom Dancer (USA))
1443[4] 1517[2] 2176[2] 2470[P] 2628[P]

Isthereadifference (IRE) *Neil Mulholland* 95h 95c
7 gr g Amilynx(FR) Jennys Grove (IRE) (Strong Gale)
408[5] 641[P] 844[11] (1364) 2008[6] **2478[3]** 5395[10]

Italian Master (IRE) *Dan Skelton* 126h 135c
8 bb g Milan Augusta Brook (IRE) (Over The River (FR))
431[3] (2394)

Italian Symphony (IRE) *Brendan Powell* 75h
4 b f Galileo(IRE) Tea Break (Daylami (IRE))
4016[11] 5140[7] 5305[6] 5547[6]

Itmakessense *Charlie Longsdon* 95h
7 ch g Trade Fair Giant Leap (Giant's Causeway (USA))
1016[3] 1256[4] 1404[5] 1466[4]

Itoldyou (IRE) *Linda Jewell* 102h 119c
8 ch g Salford Express(IRE) Adisadel (IRE) (Petardia)
5[6] 2437[4] (2863)
3137[3] 3690[4] 4249[U]
(4440) (4798)
5344[3]

I Told You So (IRE) *Donald McCain* 73h
5 b m Oscar(IRE) My Twist (IRE) (Flemensfirth (USA))
1132[5] 1731[5] 2559[6]

It's A Doddle (IRE) *Jonjo O'Neill* 118h
6 b g Oscar(IRE) Nic An Ree (IRE) (King's Ride)
2507[3] ◆ 2806[3] (3128) 3802[2] 4161[F] 5387[F]

It's A Gimme (IRE) *Jonjo O'Neill* 138h 132c
7 b g Beneficial Sorcera (GER) (Zilzal (USA))
2227[2]

It's All An Act (IRE) *John Joseph Hanlon* 87h
6 br g Presenting Royal Lucy (IRE) (King's Ride)
(1546) (1667) 2534[10]

Its A Long Road *Tim Dennis* 97b
6 b g Grape Tree Road Blue Shannon (IRE) (Be My Native (USA))
1712[6]

It's A Mans World *Brian Ellison* 124h
8 b g Kyllachy Exhibitor (USA) (Royal Academy (USA))
(1399) (1540) 1656[3] 2068[2] 4745[5] 5067[4] (5251)

Its A Mistake (IRE) *Milton Bradley* 62h
7 b g Aboo Hom Creative Princess (IRE) (Creative Plan (USA))
592[8]

It's A New Day *Jonjo O'Neill* 97h
6 br g Kayf Tara One Of Those Days (Soviet Lad (USA))
376[9]

Its April *Robert Walford* 71h
6 b m Pasternak Lorgnette (Emperor Fountain)
2463[6] 2907[10] 3289[8]

Its A Sting (IRE) *Tony Coyle* 107b
5 b g Scorpion(IRE) Wyndham Sweetmarie (IRE) (Mister Lord (USA))
4329[2] (4986)

Its A Story *Mairi Wilson*
7 ch m Lucky Story(USA) Inchmore (Captain Maverick (USA))
4889[P]

It's High Time (IRE) *Lucinda Russell* 119b
6 b g Kalanisi(IRE) Windsor Dancer (IRE) (Woods Of Windsor (USA))
2347[2] (3002) 5173[8]

It's Me And You *Michael Easterby* 81h 90c
6 b g Dubai Destination(USA) Time Crystal (IRE) (Sadler's Wells (USA))
750[4] **786[5]**
873[7]

It's Only Business *Jim Best* 110h
4 ch g Haafhd Noble Plum (IRE) (King's Best (USA))
(725) (785) 975[2] 1044[4]

It's Oscar (IRE) *James Evans* 112h
7 b g Oscar(IRE) Lady Bramble (IRE) (Be My Native (USA))
318[4] 948[4] **1184[F]** 5542[5]

Its Ruby *Robert Walford* 82h
8 b m Midnight Legend Lorgnette (Emperor Fountain)
5395[7]

Itstimeforapint (IRE) *Lucinda Russell* 99h
6 b g Portrait Gallery(IRE) Executive Pearl (IRE) (Executive Perk)
4043[6] 4364[3] 4647[5] 5050[2] ◆

It's Time To Dance (FR) *Tim Easterby* 39b
4 b f Country Reel(USA) Just Dance Me (FR) (Linamix (FR))
4749[5]

Itsuptoyou (IRE) *Arthur Whiting* 116h 129c
10 b g Dr Massini(IRE) I Blame Theparents (Celtic Cone)
3787[5] 4515[4] 4822[P] (5237)
(5527)

Its Who You Are (IRE) *Jeffrey Ian Mulhern* 96b
5 b m Flemensfirth(USA) Playwaki (USA) (Miswaki (USA))
3866a[P]

It'syourdeal (IRE) *Nick Ayliffe*
9 b m Milan Native Gift (IRE) (Be My Native (USA))
922[P] 1052[P]

Ittirad (USA) *John Ferguson* 119h
6 b g Dubai Destination(USA) Noushkey (Polish Precedent (USA))
857[2] 1255[2] ◆ (1466) 1685[7] 2064[3]

Itzacliche (IRE) *Nicky Richards* 87h 111c
14 b g Classic Cliche(IRE) Ower (IRE) (Lomond (USA))
25[P] 496[6]

Ivan Boru (IRE) *Keith Reveley* 124h
6 b g Brian Boru Miranda's Lace (IRE) (Bach (IRE))
(22) (2444) 2936[9]

Ivan Grozny (FR) *W P Mullins* 134h
4 b g Turtle Bowl(IRE) Behnesa (IRE) (Suave Dancer (USA))
4178a[4] 4755[12] (5470a)

Ivanhoe *Michael Blanshard* 102h
4 b c Haafhd Marysienka (Primo Dominie)
2466[4] (3127) 3714[5] 5034[6]

Ivanka (IRE) *Noel C Kelly* 103h
6 b m Acclamation Evidence (Machiavellian (USA))
3639[7] 5532[11]

Ivans Back (IRE) *Nick Kent* 83h
9 b g Soviet Star(USA) Better Back Off (IRE) (Bob Back (USA))
852[8] 1120[5] 2679[4] 3038[4] 3265[5] 4309[3] 4527[2]

Ivan Vasilevich (IRE) *John Quinn* 120h
6 b g Ivan Denisovich(IRE) Delisha (Salse (USA))
858[3]

Ivebeenthinking *Tom Symonds* 83h
6 b m One More Tiger Moonlight Saunter (USA) (Woodman (USA))
46[7] 423[6] 651[12] 765[12] (1938) 2004[3] 2291[3]

Ivor's King (IRE) *Colin Tizzard* 98h 135c
7 b g King's Theatre(IRE) Christelle (IRE) (Revoque (IRE))
(1698)
1857[4] (2211)

Ivor's Queen (IRE) *Colin Tizzard* 98b
5 b m King's Theatre(IRE) Sonnerschien (IRE) (Be My Native (USA))
2479[2] 3961[4]

Ivy Gate (IRE) *Jonjo O'Neill* 117h
6 b g Westerner Key Partner (Law Society (USA))
3173[3] 3800[3] 4428[2] 4949[5]

Ixora (IRE) *Jamie Snowden* 119h 119c
8 gr m Milan Tucacas (FR) (Highest Honor (FR))
587[9] 1304[4] 1581[5] 1972[4] 2226[8]

Izza Diva *John Holt* 36h
6 b m Nomadic Way(USA) Pebbles Moonlight (IRE) (Asir)
3469[P] 4102[10] 4528[5] 4950[P]

Izzini (IRE) *S R B Crawford* 112h
6 b m Dr Massini(IRE) Cistercian (IRE) (Anshan)
4756[18]

Izzy Piccolina (IRE) *Geoffrey Deacon* 88b
6 b m Morozov(USA) Chloara (IRE) (Flemensfirth (USA))
3656[7] 4540[4] 5014[10]

Jabus (IRE) *A Oliver* 116h
8 b g Bob Back(USA) Salsita (FR) (Fijar Tango (FR))
891a[13]

Jacaranda Star *Geoffrey Harker*
6 b g Grape Tree Road Chantilly Rose (Primitive Rising (USA))
4958[11] 5499[P]

Jack Albert (IRE) *Dianne Sayer* 105h 73c
7 gr g Cloudings(IRE) Lisdoylelady (IRE) (Glacial Storm (USA))
117[5] 2591[7] (2997) 3396[5] 4223[2] (4981) (5075) 5191[F]

Jack Bene (IRE) *Miss Louise Allan* 122h 122c
8 gr g Beneficial Securon Rose (IRE) (Roselier (FR))
(4252)
4661[7] 5127[3] 5439[5]

Jack By The Hedge *Caroline Keevil* 112h
5 b g Overbury(IRE) Bluebell Path (Classic Cliche (IRE))
(307) 2011[5] 2266[3] *4018[5]*

Jackies Solitaire *Anthony Honeyball* 107h 128c
6 ch m Generous(IRE) Bond Solitaire (Atraf)
4418[7] 5030[15] 5186[4] ◆

Jack Kane *Josie Ross*
7 ch g Ishiguru(USA) Armada Grove (Fleetwood (IRE))
1288[P]

Jackofhearts *Jean McGregor* 61b
6 b g Beat Hollow Boutique (Selkirk (USA))
3500[7]

Jacks Grey *Fergal O'Brien* 108h 98c
9 gr g Karinga Bay Arctic Chick (Henbit (USA))
(48) 604[3]
931[6]

Jacks Island (IRE) *J P Kenny* 104h 128c
11 br g Turtle Island(IRE) Good Thyne Mary (IRE) (Good Thyne (USA))
3068[S]

Jacksonslady (IRE) *J P Dempsey* 133h 142c
9 b m Jackson's Drift(USA) Leinster Lady (IRE) (Lord Chancellor (USA))
1168a[3] 1604a[11]

Jack's The Lad (IRE) *Mrs Alice Campbell* 86c
10 b g Aahsaylad Kate Ross (Salluceva)
5364[2]

Jack The Gent (IRE) *George Moore* 115h 128c
10 b g Anshan Asidewager (IRE) (Brush Aside (USA))
(167) **(446)**
735[5] 1782[P] 1921[10] 2785[5] 3323[4] 3738[6] *4325[4]*
4532[2] 5517[P]

Jackthejourneyman (IRE) *Tom Gretton* 102h
5 b g Beneficial Maslam (IRE) (Robellino (USA))
14[4] 359[9] 4758[10]

Jacobella *Jonathan Portman* 70h
4 b f Rob Roy(USA) Veni Bidi Vici (Horse Chestnut (SAF))
2066[5]

Jacqueline Hyde *Nigel Dunger* 63b
5 b m Beat All(USA) Kansas City (FR) (Lute Antique (FR))
239[7] 462[10]

Jac The Legend *Steve Gollings* 101h
5 b g Midnight Legend Sky Burst (Gunner B)
2627[7] 2878[2] 3271[4] 4693[5] 4980[4] 5514[P]

Jaja De Jau *Anthony Honeyball* 94h
5 br m Sakhee(USA) Jadidh (Touching Wood (USA))
488[7] 648[4] 765[2] 924[8] 3692[3] 4721[6] 5072[2]

Jakeys Girl *Pat Phelan* 63h
7 b m Dubai Destination(USA) Rosewood Belle (USA) (Woodman (USA))
307[6]

Jakherphi D'Art (FR) *C Plisson* 110h 87c
6 b g Khalkevi(IRE) Faena d'Artagnan (FR) (Marignan (USA))
198a[3] 863a[9]

Jambobo *Chris Down* 79h
5 b g Acclamation Hovering (IRE) (In The Wings)
407[12] 635[P] 3426[P] 3788[P]

Jameel (USA) *John Ferguson* 119h
6 b g Monsun(GER) Maids Causeway (IRE) (Giant's Causeway (USA))
(31)

James Pine (IRE) *Mrs Annabel Brook* 97c
15 b g Jamesmead Princess Astrid (IRE) (Mandalus)
62[10]

James Pollard (IRE) *Bernard Llewellyn* 109h
9 ch g Indian Ridge Manuetti (IRE) (Sadler's Wells (USA))
(1342) 1627[7] 1889[4] 2698[6] 2760[2] 5179[10]

Jamesson (IRE) *Jamie Snowden* 85h 96c
9 b g Bishop Of Cashel Native Belle (IRE) (Be My Native (USA))
303[3] 639[2] 759[P] 1104[P]

Jammy (IRE) *Lawney Hill* 81b
5 b g Oscar(IRE) Tabachines (FR) (Art Francais (USA))
2667[8]

Jamsie Hall (IRE) *Gordon Elliott* 121h 143c
11 b g Saddlers' Hall(IRE) Elegant Kate (IRE) (Good Thyne (USA))
1168a[13] 1545[6] 1604a[8] 1897a[3] (2070)
2708a[10] 5474a[4]

Janaab (IRE) *Tim Easterby*
4 ch g Nayef(USA) Mood Indigo (IRE) (Indian Ridge)
3332[P] 3616[P]

Jan Jandura (IRE) *William Amos* 63h 59c
9 b g Flemensfirth(USA) Friends Of Friends (IRE) (Phardante (FR))
2310[P] 2870[5]

Janmat (FR) *A Mesnil*
14 b g Perugino(USA) Lead Cora (FR) (Lead On Time (USA))
1279a[F]

Jan Smuts (IRE) *Wilf Storey* 67h
6 b g Johannesburg(USA) Choice House (USA) (Chester House (USA))
2360[8] 3040[13]

Jasani *Alan Brown* 67h
6 b g Gentleman's Deal(IRE) Bred For Pleasure (Niniski (USA))
5108[8] 5354[7]

Jaslinga (FR) *M Nigge* 109h
5 b m Ballingarry(IRE) Jasla (FR) (Highest Honor (FR))
1199a[6]

Jasper Massini (IRE) *Philip Kirby* 89h
9 b g Dr Massini(IRE) Graigue Lass (IRE) (Phardante (FR))
3723[4] 4816[6]

Jat Punjabi *Jo Hughes* 109h 125c
10 b g Karinga Bay Balmoral Princess (Thethingaboutitis (USA))
114[5] 2508[7] 3190[5] 3836[5]

Jaunty Dove *Miss Imogen Pickard* 80b
12 b m Atraf Flossy Dove (Le Moss)
4981[P]

Jaunty Inflight *Brian Eckley* 86h
5 b g Busy Flight Jaunty Walk (Overbury (IRE))
250[10] 4417[7] 4672[P]

Jaunty Journey *Nigel Twiston-Davies* 110h 122c
11 ch g Karinga Bay Jaunty June (Primitive Rising (USA))
(321) **509[B]**
2246[5] 2670[8] 3366[5] 3836[U] 4070[U] 4489[2] **4704[2]**
(5122)
5334[P] 5559[2]

Java Rose *Charlie Longsdon* 112h
5 b m Ishiguru(USA) Mighty Splash (Cape Cross (IRE))
101[2] 3153[4] 4903[2]

Jawaab (IRE) *Philip Kirby* 98h
10 ch g King's Best(USA) Canis Star (Wolfhound (USA))
202[9] 933[6] 4981[9]

Jawahal Du Mathan (FR) *Arthur Whitehead* 81h
6 b g Smadoun(FR) Stone's Glow (USA) (Arctic Tern (USA))
1700[P] 2886[8] 3226[6]

Jawhary *Robert Walford* 108h 107c
7 bb g Pivotal Moon's Whisper (USA) (Storm Cat (USA))
37[F]

Jawinski (IRE) *David Evans* 64h
4 b g Jeremy(USA) Karinski (USA) (Palace Music (USA))
725[5]

Jayandbee (IRE) *Philip Hobbs* 103h 116c
7 b g Presenting Christines Gale (IRE) (Strong Gale)
(1474)
1626[F] 1859[2] 2110[2] (2468)
2923[3] 4990[2] 5334[3]

Jay Are (IRE) *Gary Moore* 86h
5 b g Heron Island(IRE) Vulpalm (IRE) (Great Palm (USA))
5088[10]

Jayjay Joules *Lisa Williamson* 57b
6 b m Overbury(IRE) Pearly Bay (Karinga Bay)
372[14] 768[11]

Jayjayrumi (IRE) *Ms N M Hugo* 102b
6 b g Heron Island(IRE) Rumi (Nishapour (FR))
1392[3]

Jazz City *Michael Blanshard* 109h
14 br g Rock City Hullo Mary Doll (Lidhame)
1700[P] 1860[P]

Jazz Man (IRE) *Mark Rimell* 97h
7 ch g Beneficial Slaney Jazz (Orchestra)
174[11] 1915[P] 2850[8] 2954[6] 3284[P] 5022[5] 5402[4]

Jazz Thyme (IRE) *Bernard Llewellyn* 85b
5 b m Helissio(FR) Thyne Square (IRE) (Good Thyne (USA))
1318[2] 2654[5] 2892[6]

Jd Rockefeller *Paul D'Arcy* 16h
4 ch g Sakhee(USA) Perle D'Or (IRE) (Entrepreneur)
975[P] 1044[5]

Jean D'Angely (FR) *F Danloux*
11 ch g Pelder(IRE) Jaune Et Or (FR) (Le Nain Jaune (FR))
559a[7]

Jean De Florette (IRE) *Nigel Twiston-Davies* 115h
7 b h Helissio(FR) Ismene (FR) (Bad Conduct (USA))
(2285) 2728[P]

Jean Fleming (IRE) *Jamie Snowden* 119h 115c
7 b m Flemensfirth(USA) Dromhale Lady (IRE) (Roselier (FR))
2029[2] **2769[3]**

Jeano De Toulouse (FR) *Oliver Sherwood* 117h
7 b g Lavirco(GER) Indecidable (FR) (Gay Minstrel (FR))
33[4] 1941[7] (3249)

Jeanry (FR) *Arthur Whitehead* 97h 107c
11 b g Marathon(USA) Envergure (Kenmare (FR))
49[5] 1582[2] 2289[3]
(4416) 4488[2] 5176[7] 5549[P] (Dead)

Jeans Lady *Martin Keighley* 64b
5 b m Milan Indian Miss (Idiots Delight)
3656[8] *4329[8]*

Jebulani *Barry Murtagh* 83h
4 b g Jelani(IRE) Susan's Dowry (Efisio)
1786[8] 2154[6] 2733[4] 3636[6]

Jennies Jewel (IRE) *Jarlath P Fahey* 143h
7 b m Flemensfirth(USA) Fishin Joella (IRE) (Gone Fishin)
3403a[3] 3790a[2] 4312a[4] 4740[11]

Jennys Melody (IRE) *B Arthey* 113b
5 b m Gamut(IRE) Pharaway Stream (IRE) (Phardante (FR))
(4749) 5381[2]

Jennys Surprise (IRE) *Fergal O'Brien* 102b
6 b m Hawk Wing(USA) Winning Jenny (IRE) (Leading Counsel (USA))
3181[3] 4403[2]

Jepeck (IRE) *Karen Tutty* 93b
5 b g Westerner Jenny's Jewel (IRE) (Be My Native (USA))
5219[6]

Jerry Lee (IRE) *Violet M Jordan* 85h 73c
11 b g Orpen(USA) Vinicky (USA) (Kingmambo (USA))
1272[U]

Jessica Valentine (IRE) *Keith Reveley* 96b
7 b m King's Theatre(IRE) Jessica One (IRE) (Supreme Leader)
2809[3]

Je T'Aime (IRE) *Donald McCain* 95h
5 b m Heron Island(IRE) J'y Reste (FR) (Freedom Cry)
35[3] 717[2] 1007[2] 1286[5] 1373[2] 2312[2]

Jet Master (IRE) *N W Alexander* 128h 139c
8 b g Brian Boru Whats The Reason (IRE) (Strong Gale)
1849[U] 2031[U] 2359[2] 3109[3] 3519[2] (4549)
(4955)

Jetnova (IRE) *Alan King* 123h 110c
9 b g Luso Yamashina (IRE) (Kahyasi)
119[7] 2630[4] 3892[9]

Jetson (IRE) *Mrs John Harrington* 158h 130c
9 b g Oscar(IRE) La Noire (IRE) (Phardante (FR))
215[2] 2408a[5] 3866a[3] 4765[5] 5138[4]

Jeu De Roseau (IRE) *Chris Grant* 120h
10 b g Montjeu(IRE) Roseau (Nashwan (USA))
1398[6] 1660[7] 2170[2]

Jewel In The Sun (IRE) *Ben Haslam* 108h 111c
9 b g Milan Savanagh (IRE) (Brush Aside (USA))
(698) 767[5] 1205[11] **1397[5] 2749[7]**

Jewelled Dagger (IRE) *Sharon Watt* 58h
10 b g Daggers Drawn(USA) Cappadoce (IRE) (General Monash (USA))
1506[10]

Jewellery (IRE) *Kevin Bishop* 98h
7 bb m King's Best(USA) Eilean Shona (Suave Dancer (USA))
254[P] 522[9] 765[8] 829[4] 1051[4]

Jezki (IRE) *Mrs John Harrington* 173h
6 b g Milan La Noire (IRE) (Phardante (FR))
(2206a) (2855a) 3402a[2] 3930a[4] (4739)

Jezza *Karen George* 68h
8 br g Pentire Lara (GER) (Sharpo)
293[8] 521[9]

Jigsaw Financial (IRE) *Laura Young* 87h
8 b g Brian Boru Ardcolm Cailin (IRE) (Beneficial)
522[7] 637[5] (1018) (1109) 1267[2] 1339[2] 1488[6]
4887[7] 5242[3]

Jigsaw Puzzle (IRE) *David Pipe* 97h 42c
8 b g Presenting Star Child (GER) (Neshad (USA))
2018[12]
3176[7]

Jimbill (IRE) *Tim Vaughan* 134h 124c
8 br g Flying Legend(USA) Ah Gowan (IRE) (High Estate)
(1518) ◆ **1728[4] 2716[F]**

Jim Bowie (IRE) *J J Lambe* 112h 103c
9 b g Dushyantor(USA) Delibonne (IRE) (Erdelistan (FR))
3939[F] 5256[3]

Jim Job Jones *Neil Mulholland* 58h 75c
10 b g Tipsy Creek(USA) Sulapuff (Sula Bula)
431[P] 2423[2] 2619[F] 3472[R] 3635[2] 4843[6]

Jimmie Brown (USA) *Andrew Crook* 110h 94c
6 b g Street Cry(IRE) Vid Kid (CAN) (Pleasant Colony (USA))
2356[8] 2515[5] 2955[P] 3213[P]

Jimmy The Hat (IRE) *Gordon Elliott* 123h 132c
8 b g Accordion Pride 'N' Joy (IRE) (Lashkari)
(1286) 1541[3]
(4651)

Jimmy The Jetplane (IRE) *Kim Bailey* 116h
6 b g Jimble(FR) C'Est Cool (IRE) (Roi Guillaume (FR))
584[2] 3877[5] 4694[4] 4931[6] (5307)

Jim Tango (FR) *Karen McLintock* 82h 94c
10 bb g Jimble(FR) Fitanga (FR) (Fijar Tango (FR))
864[7] 1075[5] 1876[6] (2361)
2737[2] 3143[5] 3517[4]

Jim Will Fix It (IRE) *Seamus Roche* 131h 138c
9 b g Lord Of Appeal North County Lady (IRE) (Roselier (FR))
2550a[P] 3314a[U]

Jive Master (IRE) *Tim Vaughan* 113h 101c
9 b g Marignan(USA) Ardkilly Jive (Noble Patriarch)
472[5] 709[3] 964[4] 1344[P]

Joaci (IRE) *Patricia Shaw* 52h 85c
14 b g Presenting Miss Sarajevo (IRE) (Brush Aside (USA))
692[P] 1859[6]

Joanne One (IRE) *Jamie Snowden* 122h
6 ch m Vinnie Roe(IRE) Bobs Star (IRE) (Bob Back (USA))
(1885) (2463) 3737[2] *4298[6]* 4961[11]

Jock Des Mottes (FR) *Elizabeth Juckes* 45b
7 b g Maresca Sorrento(FR) Jolie Redaely (FR) (Diamond Prospect (USA))
1124[8] **1262[P]**

Joe Bugg (IRE) *Roy Brotherton* 75h
5 b g Presenting Four Fields (IRE) (Fourstars Allstar (USA))
1869[15] 2602[15]

Joeluke *Philip Kirby* 62h
4 br g Cockney Rebel(IRE) Enthralled (Zafonic (USA))
1501[3]

Joe The Rogue (IRE) *Paul Henderson* 73h 106c
7 gr g Amilynx(FR) Roco-Bridge (IRE) (Lord Americo)
856[10]
1150[4] 1272[5] (1528) ◆ **1598[3] 1859[4]**

Joffrey (IRE) *Nicky Richards* 113b
5 b g Brian Boru Ballyknock Present (IRE) (Presenting)
5219[2] ◆

Johanna Fosie (IRE) *W T Reed*
5 ch m Peintre Celebre(USA) Yding (IRE) (Danehill (USA))
2495[P]

John Louis *Venetia Williams* 108h
6 ch g Bertolini(USA) Native Ring (FR) (Bering)
3956[4] 4450[7] 5064[4] ◆

John Mor *S R B Crawford* 94h
5 b g Flemensfirth(USA) Storm In Front (IRE) (Fourstars Allstar (USA))
4370[4]

Johnny Og *Martin Keighley* 110h
5 b g Flemensfirth(USA) Mrs Roberts (Bob Back (USA))
239[6] 1712[10] 2079[6] 2285[2] 2593[6] 3614[5] 5353[P]

Johnnys Legacy (IRE) *Conor Dore* 96h 100c
7 b g Ecton Park(USA) Lexy May (USA) (Lear Fan (USA))
2250[6] 2510[11] 2770[4] 3264[4] 3353[3]
3876[3] *4324[5]* **4482[8] 4723[3] 4985[2] 5111[U] 5263[2]**
5442[6]

Johnny's Way *G B Foot*
10 b g Nomadic Way(USA) Miss Marigold (Norwick (USA))
4936[P]

John Reel (FR) *Dan Skelton* 123h
5 b g Country Reel(USA) John Quatz (FR) (Johann Quatz (FR))
1935[3] (2426) 2893[2]

John's Gem *Zoe Davison* 99h
9 ch g Silver Patriarch(IRE) Hollow Legs (Alflora (IRE))
4906[8] 5260[P]

Johns Luck (IRE) *Neil Mulholland* 72h
5 b g Turtle Island(IRE) Jemima Yorke (Be My Guest (USA))
4417[6] 5070[12] 5541[10]

John's Ruby *William Young Jnr*
4 b f Sixties Icon Sakaka (Tobougg (IRE))
3214[11]

Johns Spirit (IRE) *Jonjo O'Neill* 134h 150c
7 b g Gold Well Gilt Ridden (IRE) (Heron Island (IRE))
(1060)
(2503) 3082[5] 4768[4] 5170[10]

Join The Clan (IRE) *Jonjo O'Neill* 134h
5 b g Milan Millicent Bridge (IRE) (Over The River (FR))
2265[15] 2563[4] 2858[5] 3390[6] (4308) 4449[P] 5333[2]

Join The Navy *Kate Buckett* 102h 98c
9 b g Sea Freedom Join The Parade (Elmaamul (USA))
2580[U] 2739[3] 3196[F] 3687[P] (4334) 4519[2] 5238[5]

Join Together (IRE) *Paul Nicholls* 111h 154c
9 b g Old Vic Open Cry (IRE) (Montelimar (USA))
1868[9] 2264a[6] 2937[14]

Jojabean (IRE) *Alan King* 113h
7 b g Milan Garden City (IRE) (Shernazar)
185[4] (538) 2755[6] 5074[12] 5333[12]

Joker Choker (IRE) *Nicky Henderson* 126h 122c
9 b g Oscar(IRE) Stormy Lady (IRE) (Glacial Storm (USA))
204[4]

Jokers And Rogues (IRE) *John Wade* 104h
6 b g Beneficial Ashfield Girl (IRE) (Beau Sher)
1924[6] 2520[7] 3144[0] 3618[3] 4189[5]

Jolipoulinderuins (FR) *F Cheyer* 121h
5 b g Subotica(FR) Corbelle (FR) (Air Du Nord (USA))
1983a[6]

Jollyallan *Harry Fry* 120b
5 b g Rocamadour Life Line (Exit To Nowhere (USA))
(5130) ◆

Jolly Boys Outing (IRE) *Rosemary Gasson* 85c
11 b g Glacial Storm(USA) St Carol (IRE) (Orchestra)
32[P] 2700[U] 2923[5] 3178[4] 3277[P] 5011[6] 5406[4]

Jolly Roger (IRE) *Tony Carroll* 124h 121c
7 b g Oratorio(IRE) Chalice Wells (Sadler's Wells (USA))
734[5] 831[5] 973[5] 1342[4] 1729[2] 1889[5]

Jolly's Cracked It (FR) *Harry Fry* 112b
5 b g Astarabad(USA) Jolly Harbour (Rudimentary (USA))
(3994)

Jolly Valentine *Neil King* 94h
6 b g Sakhee(USA) Violet (IRE) (Mukaddamah (USA))
3034[9] 3501[3] 3872[8] 4533[8]

Jomade (IRE) *Andy Hobbs* 66h 61c
8 b g Definite Article Culmore Native (IRE) (Be My Native (USA))
248[P]

Jon (IRE) *Alistair Whillans* 46b
6 ch g Refuse To Bend(IRE) Calgarth (IRE) (Efisio)
2422[7]

Jonnie Skull (IRE) *Phil McEntee* 115h
8 b g Pyrus(USA) Sovereign Touch (IRE) (Pennine Walk)
(1519) 1779[7] 2064[7]

Jonny Delta *Jim Goldie* 118h
7 ch g Sulamani(IRE) Send Me An Angel (IRE) (Lycius (USA))
344[2]

Jonny Rye (IRE) *Michael Appleby* 104h 88c
10 ch g Anshan Claudia Electric (IRE) (Electric)
322[3] 596[7] 670[P]

Jonsfella *Susan Corbett* 78b
6 gr g Silver Patriarch(IRE) Piracy (Jupiter Island)
584[9] 682[5] 880[P]

Jordans Day *Susan Corbett* 24h
9 gr m Baryshnikov(AUS) Magical Day (Halling (USA))
1751[P] 1871[3] 2309[F]

Joseph Mercer (IRE) *Tina Jackson* 106h
7 b g Court Cave(IRE) Vikki's Dream (IRE) (Kahyasi)
121[9] 2516[4] 2956[4] 3191[6]

Joshua Lane (IRE) *Edward P Harty* 135b
5 b g Gamut(IRE) Teffia Native (IRE) (Kotashaan (FR))
3187[2] 4756[3]

Josie's Dream (IRE) *Jo Hughes* 20h
6 b g Tau Ceti Gallery Breeze (Zamindar (USA))
1706[12]

Josies Orders (IRE) *Jonjo O'Neill* 131h
6 b g Milan Silent Orders (IRE) (Bob Back (USA))
1634[7] (2073) 2956[3] (3195) (3882) 4765[22] 5138[15] 5544[8]

Josses Hill (IRE) *Nicky Henderson* 150h
6 b g Winged Love(IRE) Credora Storm (IRE) (Glacial Storm (USA))
(2667) (3163) 3644[2] 4736[2] (5153)

J R Hawk (IRE) *William Reed* 65b
6 bb g Hawk Wing(USA) Miss Shivvy (IRE) (Montjeu (IRE))
1861[10]

Jubilee Games *Richard Fahey* 82h
4 b g Pastoral Pursuits Jane Jubilee (IRE) (Mister Baileys)
1684[6]

Judiciary (IRE) *Rebecca Curtis* 116h
7 b g Invincible Spirit(IRE) Theory Of Law (Generous (IRE))
1551[2] ◆ 1634[9] 1840[7]

Juicy Legend *Chris Gordon* 77h
7 b g Midnight Legend Juicy Lucy (Bonny Scot (IRE))
95[11] 3251[3] 3788[4] 4721[4] 5262[3] 5459[3]

Jukebox Melody (IRE) *John Wade* 109h 84c
8 b g Brian Boru Carmels Cottage (IRE) (Riberetto)
24[P] 289[3] 563[7]
2155[U] 2882[7] 3019[P] 3451[F] 3659[11] 4076[P]

Julie Prince (IRE) *Brendan Powell* 107h 107c
8 b g Desert Prince(IRE) Daniella Ridge (IRE) (Indian Ridge)
1133[5] 1274[3] (1401)
1596[5] 1835[3] 2039[S] 2251[5]

Jumbo John (IRE) *Mrs Lorna Fowler* 114h
8 b g Presenting Hazel's Glory (IRE) (Mister Lord (USA))
(313)

Jumeirah Liberty *Zoe Davison* 76h
6 ch g Proclamation(IRE) Gleam Of Light (IRE) (Danehill (USA))
235[8] 1625[8]

Jump City (FR) *Paul Nicholls* 133h 139c
8 b g Muhtathir Just Fizzy (Efisio)
(1944)
2714[3] 2925[4] 3647[2] 4035[6] 4422[9] 5126[3]

Jumps Road *Colin Tizzard* 138h 123c
7 b g Clerkenwell(USA) Diletia (Dilum (USA))
2213[10] 2647[6] (2910) 3083[3] 3779[3] 4147[10] (4558) 4785[16] 5172[13]

Jump Up *Peter Bowen* 101h 78c
8 b g Carnival Dancer Taylor Green (USA) (Green Dancer (USA))
(1890) 2691[8]
3836[3] 4354[5] 4843[5] 5185[4] 5433[10]

Junction Fourteen (IRE) *Emma Lavelle* 137h
5 b g King's Theatre(IRE) Chevet Girl (IRE) (Roselier (FR))
2279[3] (2740) (3263) 3646[F] 4789[13]

June French (FR) *Kevin Tork* 74h 85c
6 b m Jimble(FR) Sunbelt Broker (Lahib (USA))
368[3] 765[5] 932[F] 2312[8] 3434[5] 3955[P] **5342[U] 5398[2]**

Junior *David Pipe* 133h 161c
11 ch g Singspiel(IRE) For More (FR) (Sanglamore (USA))
6[2] 448[5] 2937[P] 3285[4] 3698[3] 4026[4] 4427[8] 4821[9] 5092[6]

Junior Jack *Jennifer Mason* 88h 88c
9 b g Kayf Tara O My Love (Idiots Delight)
713[4] 1089[3] 1174[P]

Juno The Muffinman (IRE) *Tim Vaughan* 110h
5 b g Holy Roman Emperor(IRE) Mackenzie's Friend (Selkirk (USA))
47[4] 501[F] 3118[2] 4351[R]

Just A Gin *Iain Jardine* 40b
6 ch m Grape Tree Road Just A Diamond (Primitive Rising (USA))
1877[11]

Just Annie *Lucy Normile* 77b
6 b m Revoque(IRE) Carbery Spirit (IRE) (Glacial Storm (USA))
4240[7]

Justanother Muddle *Sheena West* 117b
5 gr g Kayf Tara Spatham Rose (Environment Friend)
246[4] (3363) 4149[4] (5028)

Just A Par (IRE) *Paul Nicholls* 145h 155c
7 b g Island House(IRE) Thebrownhen (IRE) (Henbit (USA))
2077[2] (2756)
3260[4] 4751[7] 5154[6]

Just Archie (USA) *Lady Herries* 95h
6 b g Arch(USA) Copper Rose (USA) (Unbridled (USA))
246[2] 544[9] 1107[5] 1270[6] 1552[F] 1749[4]

Just Awake *Mrs A M Thomson* 103c
7 b g Prince Daniel(USA) Katinka (Rymer)
629[U] 747[P] **5209[2]**

Just A Whisper *Keiran Burke* 76h
8 b m Talkin Man(CAN) T'Be Sure (IRE) (Doubletour (USA))
46[5] 1269[P]

Just Bee (IRE) *Rayson Nixon*
5 b m Zerpour(IRE) Miss Jamielou (IRE) (Be My Native (USA))
5381[11]

Just Benny (IRE) *Richard Phillips* 99h 78c
9 b g Beneficial Artic Squaw (IRE) (Buckskin (FR))
122[2] 3503[3] 4275[P]
4884[5]

Just Beware *Zoe Davison* 78h
12 b m Makbul Bewails (IRE) (Caerleon (USA))
243[6] 2090[7] 2274[5] 2581[8] 2862[7] 3140[9] 4721[7] 5116[12]

Just Bridget (IRE) *Miss C M E Haydon* 82c
8 b m Dushyantor(USA) Ganpati (IRE) (Over The River (FR))
327[5]

Justcallhimbilly *Shaun Harris* 71b
4 ch g Phoenix Reach(IRE) Rainbows Guest (IRE) (Indian Lodge (IRE))
5367[7]

Just Cameron *Philip Kirby* 124h
7 b g Kayf Tara Miss Fencote (Phardante (FR))
(367) 737[5] 2954[F] 3110[3] 3724[5] (4629) 5251[2] 5512[4]

Just Chilly *Lucinda Russell* 91h
5 b m Kayf Tara Your Punishment (IRE) (Montelimar (USA))
2752[13] 4614[4] 4956[3]

Just Cloudy *Robert Walford* 100h
10 b g Cloudings(IRE) Tycoon Tina (Tina's Pet)
(686) 2008[3] 2430[2] 2620[4] 4444[P]

Just Fabulous *George Moore* 84h
5 b m Sakhee(USA) Tipsy Me (Selkirk (USA))
560[F] 748[3] 897[3]

Just Fee *Nick Mitchell* 94h
7 b m Emperor Fountain Mabel's Memory (IRE) (Over The River (FR))
2463[3] 3168[5] 3697[8]

Just For Pleasure (IRE) *Lucinda Russell* 91b
4 b f Kayf Tara Heltornic (IRE) (Zaffaran (USA))
(3727) ◆

Just Gets Better (IRE) *Sean Curran*
5 gr g Bertolini(USA) Fun Loving (IRE) (Selkirk (USA))
4904[P]

Just Got Lucky *Emma Lavelle* 49h
6 ch m Definite Article Single Handed (Cloudings (IRE))
715[8] 841[6] 970[9] 1265[6]

Justification *Gary Moore* 130h
6 b g Montjeu(IRE) Colorspin (FR) (High Top)
4143[4]

Justjoe (IRE) *Micky Hammond* 82h 98c
8 b g Carroll House Made Of Marble (IRE) (Norwich)
109[4] 224[3] 763[7]

Just Lewis *Nikki Evans*
7 ch g Sir Harry Lewis(USA) Mcmahon's River (Over The River (FR))
1891[P] 2471[13]

Just Like Beth *Giuseppe Fierro* 21b
6 b m Proclamation(IRE) Just Beth (Carlingford Castle)
3863[13] 4114[5]

Just Maddie *Rayson Nixon* 55h 53c
10 gr m Supreme Sound Delightfool (Idiots Delight)
172[P] 578[4]
625[P]

Just Once Up *Kevin Hunter*
5 b g Dutch Art Mac Rhapsody (Night Shift (USA))
284[P] 584[P]

Just Poppy (IRE) *Iain Jardine* 12h
5 ch m Ad Valorem(USA) Nebulae (IRE) (Unfuwain (USA))
1853[13]

Just Satisfaction *Nick Lampard*
5 b m Trade Fair Bathwick Fancy (IRE) (Desert Sun)
2442[7] 5244[P]

Just Spot *Kevin Bishop* 100h
7 ch m Baryshnikov(AUS) Just Jasmine (Nicholas Bill)
2029[P] 3788[3] 4172[3] 4504[5]

Just Stripe *Rayson Nixon* 58h
7 gr m Supreme Sound Delightfool (Idiots Delight)
2309[7]

Just The Job (IRE) *Neil Mulholland* 48h 108c
10 b g Religiously(USA) Fashions Side (Quayside)
482[9]

Just Tyn (IRE) *Martin Todhunter* 74h
7 b g Westerner Christian Cullen (IRE) (Supreme Leader)
1754[8] 1853[10] 2202[P]

Just Watch Ollie (IRE) *John Coombe* 86b
8 b g Indian Danehill(IRE) Westgate Run (Emperor Jones (USA))
2920[9] 3425[P]

Just When *Patrick Chamings* 121h
5 b g Dalakhani(IRE) Cape Grace (IRE) (Priolo (USA))
235[5] (2004) 2492[12] 3169[7]

Kaafel (IRE) *Peter Hedger* 97h
5 b g Nayef(USA) Tafaani (IRE) (Green Desert (USA))
1779[4] 2018[7]

Kadalkin (FR) *Nigel Hawke* 107h
8 b g Robin Des Champs(FR) Kadalma (FR) (Cadoudal (FR))
233[2] 649[8] 1281[F]

Kadella (FR) *E Lecoiffier*
5 b g Della Francesca(USA) Luarca (Robellino (USA))
1465a[P]

Kagouillot (FR) *Reginald Brown* 95h
5 gr g Kaldounevees(FR) Espoir De Mazere (IRE) (Hawk Wing (USA))
4024[8] 4350[9] 5001[3]

Kai Broon (IRE) *Lucinda Russell* 99h 119c
7 b g Marju(IRE) Restiv Star (FR) (Soviet Star (USA))
343[2] 583[5]

Kaid De Lonray (FR) *A Le Clerc* 99c
12 b g Kaid Pous(FR) Turkish Lady (FR) (Baby Turk)
199a[7] 855a[F]

Kaikias (IRE) *Jonjo O'Neill* 108h
7 b g Flemensfirth(USA) Special Case (IRE) (Be My Native (USA))
2942[5] 3800[5] 4029[5]

Kajun Thunder (IRE) *B Arthey* 53b
5 ch g Trans Island Love Me Please (IRE) (Darshaan)
225[5]

Kaki De La Pree (FR) *Tom Symonds* 135h
7 b g Kapgarde(FR) Kica (FR) (Noir Et Or)
1749[2] ◆ (2076) (3108) 3367[5] 4272[2]

Kaki Island (IRE) *Chris Gordon* 103h
6 b g Heron Island(IRE) Arctic Banner (IRE) (Arctic Lord)
2368[6] 2711[4] 3175[6] 3550[5] 4444[5] 4674[2] 5118[F]

Kalamill (IRE) *Shaun Lycett* 98h
7 b g Kalanisi(IRE) Desert Pageant (IRE) (Desert King (IRE))
1674[7] 2274[3] 2616[5] 3044[U] 3955[5]

Kalanessa *Jim Goldie* 75b
5 br m Kalanisi(IRE) Vanessa Bell (IRE) (Lahib (USA))
1792[11]

Kalani King (IRE) *Anthony Honeyball* 95h
7 b g Ashkalani(IRE) Supreme Kellycarra (IRE) (Supreme Leader)
140[8]

Kalann (IRE) *Sabrina J Harty* 125h
7 b g Barathea(IRE) Karkiyla (IRE) (Darshaan)
2533[13]

Kalevala (FR) *R Chotard* 104h
4 gr f Big Shuffle(USA) Gute Zeit (GER) (Platini (GER))
130a[8]

Kalico Kim (IRE) *John Patrick Ryan* 107h 112c
10 b m King's Theatre(IRE) Witney (IRE) (Strong Gale)
2484a[5] 2986a[P]

Kalimantan (IRE) *Tim Vaughan* 57h
4 b c Azamour(IRE) Kalamba (IRE) (Green Dancer (USA))
2899[7] 3127[5] 3245[6]

Kallina (IRE) *Liam Grassick* 44b
6 b m Kalanisi(IRE) Ballerina Babe (IRE) (Spectrum (IRE))
841[11] 1064[6]

Kalmbeforethestorm *Helen Nelmes* 115h
6 ch g Storming Home Miss Honeypenny (IRE) (Old Vic)
233[9] 920[2] 1191[2] 1828[3] 2210[5] 5128[3]

Kalucci (IRE) *Barry Brennan* 99h
5 b g Kalanisi(IRE) Anno Luce (Old Vic)
4[4] 318[2]

Kambis *Gary Moore* 128h 73c
6 b g Tobougg(IRE) Queen Tomyra (IRE) (Montjeu (IRE))
304[3] **425[7]**

Kamiro D'Or (FR) *E Leray* 92h 80c
5 b h Agnes Kamikaze(JPN) Lili Turgeon (FR) (Turgeon (USA))
2464a[6]

Kangaroo Court (IRE) *Emma Lavelle* 143h 153c
10 b g Lahib(USA) Tombazaan (IRE) (Good Thyne (USA))
(1485) ◆ (1858)

Kanturk (IRE) *Peter Bowen* 115h
8 b g Wareed(IRE) Kanturk Belle (IRE) (King's Ride)
336[3] (643) ◆ 782[2]

Kaolak (USA) *Jim Goldie* 116h
8 bb h Action This Day(USA) Cerita (USA) (Magesterial (USA))
(578) **882[F]**

Kapga De Cerisy (FR) *Venetia Williams* 126h 152c
6 ch g Kapgarde(FR) Non Liquet (Kendor (FR))
(2365)

Kapricorne (FR) *Sophie Leech* 82h
7 b g Kapgarde(FR) Colombe Royale (FR) (Passing Sale (FR))
4021[12] 4176[4] 4636[5] 4803[3] 5431[3]

Kap West (FR) *Laura Young* 97c
9 b g Kapgarde(FR) Themis Eria (FR) (Signe Divin (USA))
84[3] 378[3] 639[3] 2023[2]

Karasakal (IRE) *Mrs Kim Sly* 94b
11 b g Kahyasi Karasta (IRE) (Lake Coniston (IRE))
4782[P]

Karazhan *Nicky Henderson* 129h
6 b g Dr Fong(USA) Karasta (IRE) (Lake Coniston (IRE))
3031[4] 4899[7]

Karinga Dancer *Harry Fry* 143h 151c
8 b g Karinga Bay Miss Flora (Alflora (IRE))
(2069) 2372[5]
(3087) 3601[3] 5352[3]

Karinga Dandy (IRE) *Sue Smith* 112h 93c
8 b g Karinga Bay Well Then Now Then (IRE) (Supreme Leader)
2073[6] 2357[3] **2747[F]** 5074[2]
(5362)

Karinga Queen (IRE) *Gordon Elliott* 86h 109c
10 ch m Karinga Bay Ceolbridgequeen (IRE) (Executive Perk)
960[4]

Karingo *Lucy Normile* 98h
7 ch g Karinga Bay Wild Happening (GER) (Mondrian (GER))
313[10] 676[3] 880[U] 1664[6] 4223[P]

Karisma King *Sue Smith* 105b
5 br g Supreme Sound Hollybush (IRE) (Ali-Royal (IRE))
5063[4] 5367[9]

Karl Marx (IRE) *Mark Gillard* 98h
4 b g Red Clubs(IRE) Brillano (FR) (Desert King (IRE))
1193[F] 1271[3] 1335[3] 1473[2] 1743[5] 1855[4] 2276[4] 2920[8] 3788[8] 4504[4] (4882) 5125[10] 5522[2]

Karmine (GER) *F Nicolle* 95h
5 ch m Sholokhov(IRE) Karuma (GER) (Surumu (GER))
703a[10]

Kartanian (IRE) *Philip Hobbs* 107h
8 br g Kalanisi(IRE) Katiykha (IRE) (Darshaan)
2020[F] 2087[13] 2908[8] 3420[9] 3959[P]

Kasbadali (FR) *Oliver Sherwood* 139h 136c
9 b g Kahyasi Nikalie (FR) (Nikos)
(2692)
4681[2]

Kasban *Jim Best* 100h
10 b g Kingmambo(USA) Ebaraya (IRE) (Sadler's Wells (USA))
690[7] 1121[5]

Kashmir Peak (IRE) *John Quinn* 129h
5 b g Tiger Hill(IRE) Elhareer (IRE) (Selkirk (USA))
2533[15] 5172[12]

Kasim (CZE) *Premek Kejzlar*
9 b g Magnus(POL) Kasira (CZE) (Paico)
1905a[4]

Kastani Beach (IRE) *Seamus Mullins* 101h 110c
8 br g Alderbrook Atomic View (IRE) (Old Vic)
2009[4]
2582[3] 3137[P] 4242[5] 4659[2]
(5111) 5456[4]

Kastela Stari *Tim Fitzgerald* 83b
7 b m Beat Hollow Campaspe (Dominion)
2347[10] 3529[3]

Katachenko (IRE) *Donald McCain* 132h
5 b g Kutub(IRE) Karalee (IRE) (Arokar (FR))
3002[3] 3516[3] (4460) (5205) 5531[2]

Katenko (FR) *Venetia Williams* 125h 163c
8 b g Laveron Katiana (FR) (Villez (USA))
2815[F] 2938[4] 3780[4] 4145[3] 4787[11]

Kates Benefit (IRE) *David Kenneth Budds* 127h 130c
8 b m Beneficial Greenflag Princess (IRE) (Executive Perk)
2986a[2] 3750a[4] 5197a[4] 5475a[P]

Katgary (FR) *Paul Nicholls* 130h
4 b g Ballingarry(IRE) Kotkira (FR) (Subotica (FR))
4755[2] 5172[6]

Kathlatino *Micky Hammond* 81h
7 b m Danbird(AUS) Silver Rhythm (Silver Patriarch (IRE))
2169[9] 2449[8] 2736[5] 3284[3] 3636[4] 4189[6] 4607[8]

Kathleen Frances *Ali Brewer* 119h
7 b m Sakhee(USA) Trew Class (Inchinor)
1814[5] 3010[5] 3391[9] 3854[4]

Katies Choice (IRE) *R Mike Smith* 69h
6 gr g Croco Rouge(IRE) Rosetown Girl (IRE) (Roselier (FR))
2422[4] 2998[6]

Katie's Massini (IRE) *Henry Oliver* 82h 60c
6 b m Dr Massini(IRE) Our Lucky Supreme (IRE) (Supreme Leader)
589[6] 1671[9] 1823[5] 2317[12] 4807[17] 5177[8] 5298[7]

Katie T (IRE) *Kevin Prendergast* 135h
5 b m Beneficial Long Acre (Mark Of Esteem (IRE))
(4846a)

Katika Kapanga *Mandy Rowland* 17h
7 b g Helissio(FR) Masouri Sana (IRE) (Broken Hearted)
878[P]

Katnap (FR) *D Sourdeau De Beauregard* 110h 135c
7 br g Sleeping Car(FR) Kittygale (IRE) (Strong Gale)
455a[8]

Katnapping *Robert Waley-Cohen* 99h
6 br m Sleeping Car(FR) Karolina (FR) (Pistolet Bleu (IRE))
417[6] 669[11] 2191[3] 2470[P]

Katys Girl (IRE) *Mrs Gillian Callaghan* 122h 122c
8 b m Pyrus(USA) River Dance (GER) (Lomitas)
2343[2]

Kauto Alcazar (FR) *Sue Smith* 102h
6 b g Priolo(USA) Kauto Karolyna (FR) (Village Star (FR))
168[10]

Kauto D'Aloes (FR) *Ferdy Murphy*
5 ch g Byzantium(FR) Kauto Karolyna (FR) (Village Star (FR))
5530a[7]

Kauto Stone (FR) *Paul Nicholls* 126h 166c
8 ch g With The Flow(USA) Kauto Relka (FR) (Port Etienne (FR))
2234a[5] 2952[5] 3773[3] 4265[5] 4766[9] 5156[U] 5570[6]

Kauto Sweety (FR) *J Bertran De Balanda* 102h 115c
7 ch g Bonbon Rose(FR) Kauto Relstar (FR) (Art Bleu)
(1464a)
Kauto The Roc (FR) *Anabel K Murphy* 90h 105c
10 ch g With The Flow(USA) Kauto Of Realm (FR) (Signe Divin (USA))
7[2] 566[7] 2428[5]
2699[4]
Kayaan *Pam Sly* 127h
7 br g Marju(IRE) Raheefa (USA) (Riverman (USA))
(563) 901[5] 1203[3] 3028[4] 3892[11] 4306[3] 4897[4]
Kayalar (IRE) *Evan Williams* 102h 93c
6 b g Noverre(USA) Katiykha (IRE) (Darshaan)
333[5] 678[5] 924[6] 1487[2] 2449[6] 2764[5] 3119[P]
4488[3] 5487[3]
Kaycee (IRE) *Roger Curtis* 54h 75c
9 ch g King Charlemagne(USA) Bollicina (USA) (Woodman (USA))
285[4] 541[4] 969[7]
Kayef (GER) *Michael Scudamore* 104h
7 ch g Nayef(USA) Kassna (IRE) (Ashkalani (IRE))
2691[5]
Kayf Aramis *Nigel Twiston-Davies* 125h
12 b g Kayf Tara Ara (Birthright)
144[5]
Kayf Blanco *Graeme McPherson* 104b
5 b g Kayf Tara Land Of Glory (Supreme Leader)
4810[4]
Kayf Charmer *Stuart Howe* 59b
4 b f Kayf Tara Silver Charmer (Charmer)
2015[10] 4735[10] 5389[F]
Kayf Hampshire (IRE) *W J Burke* 107b
5 b m Kayf Tara Hamshire Gale (IRE) (Strong Gale)
5159[9]
Kayfleur *Henry Daly* 116h
5 b m Kayf Tara Combe Florey (Alflora (IRE))
(2298) 2675[2] (3159) 3782[2]
Kayf Moss *John Flint* 144h
6 b g Kayf Tara Madam Mosso (Le Moss)
2648[5] 3116[6] 3357[8] (3821) (4028) (4441) 5167[8]
Kayfrou *Brian Ellison* 90h 69c
9 b g Kayf Tara Roufontaine (Rousillon (USA))
188[8] 521[5] 730[4] 925[3] 1121[9]
1433[3] (3062) 3451[5] 4699[3]
Kayfton Pete *Charles Pogson* 111h 108c
8 b g Kayf Tara Jonchee (FR) (Le Thuit Signol (FR))
65[2] 418[6] 600[4] 898[7] 1134[2] 1400[8] 1938[2] 2051[2]
2698[8] 3149[2] 3597[4]
Kaylif Aramis *Nigel Twiston-Davies* 141h
7 b g Kayf Tara Ara (Birthright)
2080[3] 2490[F] 3200[6] 3646[5] (4264) 4752[F] 5138[2]
5574[P]
Kaysersberg (FR) *Neil King* 133h
7 b g Khalkevi(IRE) Alliance Royale (FR) (Turgeon (USA))
358[4] 2624[6] (3875) 4347[3] (4697) 5372[P]
Kazlian (FR) *Johnny Farrelly* 138h
6 b g Sinndar(IRE) Quiet Splendor (USA) (Unbridled (USA))
3369[5]
Kealigolane (IRE) *Barry Murtagh* 124h 133c
10 gr g Beneficial Leone Des Pres (FR) (Tip Moss (FR))
1921[6] 2222[5] (3001)
3476[P] 4669[P] 5210[P]
Kealshore Again (IRE) *Danielle McCormick* 111h
5 br g Exit To Nowhere(USA) Sinnaja (Sinndar (IRE))
1171[8] 1378[P]
Keel Haul (IRE) *Henry Oliver* 125h
6 br g Classic Cliche(IRE) Tara Hall (Saddlers' Hall (IRE))
768[4] 945[2] 1108[3] 1256[3] (2292) 2936[3] 3269[2]
(4157) ◆ (4503) 5384[11]
Keel Road (IRE) *Mrs Kim Smyly* 79h 15c
12 b m Luso Wiltreo (IRE) (Insan (USA))
61[P]
Keenan's Future (IRE) *S Rea* 49h 106c
13 ch g Safety Catch(USA) The Singer (IRE) (Accordion)
62[5] 357[3] 660[8] 4348[P] 5135[13]
Keeneland (IRE) *Donald McCain* 122h
7 b g Westerner Delphinium (IRE) (Dr Massini (IRE))
4579[6] (4952) (5484)
Keenes Day (FR) *Sophie Leech* 111h
9 gr g Daylami(IRE) Key Academy (Royal Academy (USA))
358[20] 719[P]
Keen Eye (IRE) *Jonjo O'Neill* 84h
5 b g Milan Jolivia (FR) (Dernier Empereur (USA))
1935[12] 2089[6] 2280[7] 2696[12] 3062[9]
Keen's Token *Clive Mulhall* 37b
8 b g Keen Bella Mary (Derrylin)
290[P] 761[P]
Keep Hope Alive *Michael O'Hare* 102h
5 b g Exit To Nowhere(USA) Baily Mist (IRE) (Zaffaran (USA))
2174[8]
Keep Kicking (IRE) *Jonjo O'Neill* 36h
7 b g Tiger Hill(IRE) Dalannda (IRE) (Hernando (FR))
643[P]
Keep On Track (IRE) *E Bolger* 74h 132c
7 ch g Rudimentary(USA) Corries Rein (IRE) (Anshan)
3068[6]
Keep Presenting (IRE) *Rebecca Curtis* 101b
5 b g Presenting Keep The Change (IRE) (Castle Keep)
3363[3] 4349[5] 5021[9]
Keep The Cash (IRE) *David Pipe* 101h
6 b g Oscar(IRE) Waterloo Ball (IRE) (Where To Dance (USA))
390[3] 517[11] 1306[7] 4733[6] 5007[7] 5234[12] 5523[9]
Keki Buku (FR) *Philip Hobbs* 139h 136c
11 b g Kadalko(FR) Bigouden (What A Guest)
236[3] (840)

Kells Belle (IRE) *Nicky Henderson* 140h
8 b m Alflora(IRE) Clandestine (Saddlers' Hall (IRE))
215[19]
Kellys Brow (IRE) *Ben Pauling* 123h 90c
7 b g Golan(IRE) Eyebright (IRE) (Zaffaran (USA))
205[6] **534[3]**
2490[13]
Kelpie Blitz (IRE) *Paul Morgan* 69h
5 gr g Verglas(IRE) Summer Spice (IRE) (Key Of Luck (USA))
5064[12]
Keltic Crisis (IRE) *Sophie Leech* 106h 93c
10 b g Needle Gun(IRE) Catch Ball (Prince Sabo)
2722[F] 3279[U] 3696[F] 5247[10]
Keltic Rhythm (IRE) *Neil King* 113h 123c
7 b g Milan Ballinaroone Girl (IRE) (Carroll House)
4[2] 389[3] 1632[2] 1794[2] 2296[5] 2908[3] 3186[P] 4105[5]
(4484)
4725[4] (5023)
5450[2]
Keltus (FR) *Paul Nicholls* 124h
4 gr g Keltos(FR) Regina D'Orthe (FR) (R B Chesne)
(1862) 2200[4] 3031[2] 4755[4] 5568[4]
Kelvingrove (IRE) *Jonjo O'Neill* 116h
4 b g Hurricane Run(IRE) Silversword (FR) (Highest Honor (FR))
(5064) 5448[2]
Kemaliste (FR) *Y-M Porzier* 127h 102c
5 b g Shirocco(GER) Anacapri (FR) (Anabaa (USA))
1199a[5] 1983a[7] 2414a[9]
Kenasie (FR) *J-P Gallorini* 108h
4 b g Kendargent(FR) Maille Asie (FR) (Kahyasi)
1741a[5]
Kentford Grey Lady *Emma Lavelle* 142h 128c
8 gr m Silver Patriarch(IRE) Kentford Grebe (Teenoso (USA))
2010[2] 2769[4]
Kentford Heiress *Seamus Mullins* 75h
4 b f Midnight Legend Kentford Duchess (Jupiter Island)
2436[8]
Kentford Legend *Seamus Mullins* 99h 128c
7 b g Midnight Legend Quistaquay (El Conquistador)
(156) 2105[15]
2712[3] 3368[4] (4243)
(4657) (4990)
5278[3]
Kentford Myth *Seamus Mullins* 98h
4 b f Midnight Legend Quistaquay (El Conquistador)
3167[5] 3961[9] 5002[6]
Kent Street (IRE) *Sue Smith* 97h 92c
9 ch g Flemensfirth(USA) Fernhill (IRE) (Good Thyne (USA))
24[F] 2158[5] 2516[7] 4596[3] 4893[8] 5059[12] 5319[4]
Kentucky Hyden (IRE) *Nicky Henderson* 141h
4 ch g Kentucky Dynamite(USA) Cap Serena (FR) (Highest Honor (FR))
(2364) ◆ 3078[2] 3360[2] 3885[2] 4784[2]
Keppel Isle (IRE) *Laura Mongan* 55h
5 b g Heron Island(IRE) Wadi Khaled (FR) (Bering)
1523[3] 1764[9] *4018[11] 4493[9]*
Kept *Alison Batchelor* 83h
5 ch g Pivotal Possessed (Desert Prince (IRE))
5117[7]
Kerry Maur *Chris Gordon* 75b
5 b g Kayf Tara Eau De Vie (Terimon)
5130[10]
Keshi Pearl *Henry Daly* 121h
6 b m Kayf Tara Pearly-B (IRE) (Gunner B)
(324) (2600) 3203[3]
Kettlewell *Warren Greatrex* 112h
5 ch g Auction House(USA) Angel Chimes (Most Welcome)
(599) 760[2] 994[F] 1082[2] (1256) (1595) 1913[6]
4023[5] 5125[9]
Kevin Fancy (IRE) *John Upson* 64b 63c
8 b m Zagreb(USA) Top Flight Travel (IRE) (Buckskin (FR))
1825[P] 2277[F] 2425[U] 2849[6] 3595[P]
Keychain (IRE) *Brendan Powell* 101h
4 b g Key Of Luck(USA) Sarifa (IRE) (Kahyasi)
1855[3] 2248[4] (2577) 2932[10] 4963[9] 5335[10]
Key Cutter (FR) *Paul Webber* 116h 120c
10 b g Alderbrook Two Roads (Boreen (FR))
190[2] 504[P]
Keyhole Kate *Polly Gundry*
5 b m Kheleyf(USA) Striking Pose (IRE) (Darshaan)
1348[U]
Key To Milan *Chris Down* 101h
8 b g Milan Key West (FR) (Highest Honor (FR))
1833[2] 2105[13] **2460[P]** 5143[4]
Key To The West (IRE) *David Dennis* 127h
7 b g Westerner Monte Solaro (IRE) (Key Of Luck (USA))
2049[F] (2351) (2728) (2806) 3096[P]
Khahyalista (FR) *Mlle N Pfohl*
4 b f Khalkevi(IRE) Perlista (FR) (Varese (FR))
2781a[P]
Khazium (IRE) *Claire Dyson* 101h
5 br g Kheleyf(USA) Hazium (IRE) (In The Wings)
505[7] 604[7] 1402[5] 2271[8] 2696[10] 2980[6] **3876[F]**
Khelac *Micky Hammond* 80h
4 b g Kheleyf(USA) Miss Lacey (IRE) (Diktat)
3332[6] 3616[4] 3822[6] 4476[5] 4889[11]
Kiama Bay (IRE) *Jim Best* 88h
8 b g Fraam La Panthere (USA) (Pine Bluff (USA))
4959[10] 5064[9] 5174[5]
Kian's Delight *Peter Bowen* 127h 132c
6 b g Whipper(USA) Desert Royalty (IRE) (Alhaarth (IRE))
356[5] **(594)**
830[3] (957)
1476[6] 1686[3] 1971[7] 5170[4] ◆ 5383[8]
Kian's Joy *Jedd O'Keeffe* 88h
5 b g Mind Games Lunasa (IRE) (Don't Forget Me)
171[6]

Kibo *Kim Bailey* 87b
4 b g Lucarno(USA) Fantastisch (IRE) (Fantastic Light (USA))
2436[3] 2926[6] 5447[6]
Kicking Time (IRE) *Sarah Humphrey* 38h
8 b g Luso Fairy Dawn (IRE) (Old Vic)
3[P] 1281[7] 1915[9]
Kick On (FR) *T Clout* 108h
5 b g Poliglote Kilda (IRE) (Night Shift (USA))
1199a[P]
Kick On Boss (IRE) *W McCreery* 126h
8 b g Rudimentary(USA) Cherry Tops (IRE) (Top Of The World)
4708a[10]
Kicks Milan (IRE) *Tony Carroll* 56b
7 b m Milan Honor Kicks (FR) (Highest Honor (FR))
187[11]
Kid Cassidy (IRE) *Nicky Henderson* 145h 162c
8 b g Beneficial Shuil Na Lee (IRE) (Phardante (FR))
(2532)
3338a[7] 4753[7]
Kid Wizzard (USA) *David Pipe* 82b
5 b g Lemon Drop Kid(USA) Dear Daughter (Polish Precedent (USA))
483[7]
Kie (IRE) *Donald McCain* 121h 141c
6 b g Old Vic Asura (GER) (Surumu (GER))
2666[7] 4053[3] 4955[U] (5306)
Kiestown Chief (IRE) *R C Garton* 101c
11 b g Exit To Nowhere(USA) Golden Native (IRE) (Be My Native (USA))
4246[4] 4485[8]
Kigreat De La Pree (FR) *G Mousnier* 76c
6 b m Great Pretender(IRE) Kica (FR) (Noir Et Or)
1214a[F] 1623a[3]
Kijivu *Alastair Lidderdale* 95h
9 gr m Erhaab(USA) Alsiba (Northfields (USA))
540[7]
Kikili *Nick Gifford* 56b
6 b g Cotation Dawn Frolics (Silver Patriarch (IRE))
2864[5] 4715[P]
Kikos (FR) *Mrs K Lee* 74h 104c
12 ch g Nikos Balgarde (FR) (Garde Royale)
331[3] 655[6]
Kilavalley (IRE) *Hugo Froud* 121h 108c
7 b g City Honours(USA) Cry In The Dark (Godswalk (USA))
3094[9] 3802[6] 4172[2]
Kilbarry Beauty (IRE) *John E Kiely* 124h
7 br m Saffron Walden(FR) Molly Maguire (IRE) (Supreme Leader)
2205a[9] 3380a[P]
Kilbree Chief (IRE) *Lucinda Russell* 126h
6 b g Dr Massini(IRE) Lame Excuse (IRE) (Presenting)
345[3] 1924[2] (2337) 2819[5] 4040[2] 4670[3] 5103[3]
5252[6]
Kilbree Kid (IRE) *Tom George* 124h 124c
7 b g Cloudings(IRE) Bustingoutallover (USA) (Trempolino (USA))
828[2] (1052) (1337) (1662) 1968[4] 5510[5]
Kilcascan *Rosemary Gasson* 94c
10 b g Alflora(IRE) Peasedown Tofana (Teenoso (USA))
1798[4] 1936[3] 2829[6] 3193[6] 5546[4]
Kilcaskin Star (IRE) *Karen Tutty* 100h
8 b g Zagreb(USA) Kentucky Key (IRE) (Key Of Luck (USA))
19[4] 280[5]
Kilcolman Wizard (IRE) *Liam Corcoran* 84h
8 b g Wizard King Ouch (IRE) (Anshan)
1525[U] 1672[9] 1824[P] 2105[16] 2470[12]
Kilcommon Pride (IRE) *Roger Curtis* 69h 111c
9 br g Catcher In The Rye(IRE) Ballyhookeen Lass (IRE) (Balla Cove)
321[3]
Kilcooley (IRE) *Charlie Longsdon* 131h
5 b g Stowaway Bealaha Essie (IRE) (Denel (FR))
1854[2] (2627) (4307) ◆ (4693) 5167[10]
Kilcrea Asla (IRE) *Graeme McPherson* 108h 129c
13 b g Oscar(IRE) Alottalady (IRE) (Mandalus)
508[8] 2812[13] (3414)
4675[4] 5386[4]
Kilcullen Article (IRE) *Michael Scudamore* 88h
6 b g Definite Article Mood I'm In (GER) (Saddlers' Hall (IRE))
5015[4]
Kilderry Dean (IRE) *James Frost* 87h
7 b g Croco Rouge(IRE) Perkalette (IRE) (Executive Perk)
691[6] 844[6] 997[3]
Kilfinichen Bay (IRE) *Violet M Jordan* 86h
6 b g Westerner Cailin Deas (IRE) (Pistolet Bleu (IRE))
380[4] 2513[9] 3422[P] 3598[7] 5227[8]
Kilflora *Claire Dyson* 108h 110c
11 b g Alflora(IRE) Stac-Pollaidh (Tina's Pet)
2510[P] 2903[3] **3190[P]** (3269) 3597[7] 4533[9] 4969[P]
Kilgefin Star (IRE) *Michael Smith* 129h
6 b g Saddlers' Hall(IRE) High Church Annie (IRE) (Bustomi)
(1980) 2355[3] 3036[4] 4694[2] (4956) 5387[4]
Kilkenny Kim (IRE) *Jennie Candlish* 93b
5 b m Beneficial Benbradagh Vard (IRE) (Le Bavard (FR))
1919[5] 2422[3] 2809[5]
Kilkishen (IRE) *John Joseph Hanlon* 95b
4 b g Oscar(IRE) Coming Home (FR) (Exit To Nowhere (USA))
5424a[6]
Killackey's Pub (IRE) *Paul Davies* 42b
6 b m Publisher(USA) Mrs Killackey (IRE) (Oscar (IRE))
1317[10]
Killala Quay *Charlie Longsdon* 149h
7 b g Karinga Bay Madam Bijou (Atraf)
(737) ◆ (1863) ◆ 2490[7] (2929) 3654[P] 4750[4]
5157[5]

Killary Bay (IRE) *Mrs T Corrigan* 105h 105c
10 b g Accordion Kindly Light (IRE) (Supreme Leader)
557[2] 4042[P]
Killegney *Michael Gates* 90h 87c
10 b m Tel Quel(FR) The Distaff Spy (Seymour Hicks (FR))
2575[3] 2744[4] 3179[P]
3472[F] 3817[P] 4242[F] 4447[8] 5069[2] 5436[U]
Killfinnan Castle (IRE) *Violet M Jordan* 51h 80c
11 br g Arctic Lord Golden Seekers (Manado)
4243[5] 4486[9] 4982[6] 5263[8]
Killshannon (IRE) *David Bridgwater* 75b
5 ch g Royal Anthem(USA) Fortune And Favour (IRE) (Homo Sapien)
4473[6] 4728[7]
Killtilane Rose (IRE) *W Harney* 108h 110c
9 ch m Flemensfirth(USA) Miss Rose (IRE) (Phardante (FR))
4848a[5]
Killultagh Vic (IRE) *W P Mullins* 138h
5 b g Old Vic Killultagh Dawn (IRE) (Phardante (FR))
4756[6]
Kill Van Kull (IRE) *Marc Barber* 68h
5 b g Johannesburg(USA) Stephanootz (USA) (Afternoon Deelites (USA))
2089[8] 2286[10] 2648[7] 4733[P]
Killyglass (IRE) *Emma Lavelle* 126b
7 b g Heron Island(IRE) Grande Solitaire (FR) (Loup Solitaire (USA))
1595[P]
Kilmacowen (IRE) *Fergal O'Brien* 95h 101c
8 b g Flemensfirth(USA) Baunfaun Run (IRE) (Roselier (FR))
1956[17]
2446[4]
Kilmurvy (IRE) *Jeremy Scott* 126h
6 b g Shantou(USA) Spagna (IRE) (Definite Article)
2087[3] 2362[0] 2798[5] 3186[3] 3741[2] 4144[4] 5345[2]
Kilquiggan (IRE) *Sandy Thomson* 93b
6 gr g Vinnie Roe(IRE) Irene's Call (IRE) (Cardinal Flower)
2499[11]
Kilronan High (IRE) *Nigel Twiston-Davies* 100b
5 b m Mountain High(IRE) Broadcast (Broadsword (USA))
5374[P]
Kilrush (IRE) *Neil Mulholland* 119h 105c
8 gr g Dilshaan Pride Of Passion (IRE) (Daylami (IRE))
(254) 1917[5]
2582[5] (2744) 3435[2] 3741[7] 4161[P]
Kilrye (IRE) *David Pipe* 84h
7 b g Catcher In The Rye(IRE) Kiladante (IRE) (Phardante (FR))
640[8] 852[2] 2910[7] 3288[8] 3420[5] 3699[P]
Kilshanna (IRE) *Bernard Llewellyn* 45h 60c
9 b g Bach(IRE) Mugazine (Kemal (FR))
759[7] 997[8]
Kilvergan Boy (IRE) *Nigel Twiston-Davies* 84h 82c
10 br g Zagreb(USA) Brigante (IRE) (Grand Lodge (USA))
248[10] 1344[5] (1655)
1859[3] 2152[3] 2603[4] 2829[8] 3114[2] 3277[2] 3797[F]
Kimora (IRE) *Marc Barber* 96h
8 b m Bach(IRE) Blue Gale (IRE) (Be My Native (USA))
777[6] 948[3] 1017[2] 1176[2] 1329[3] 1497[4] 1885[8]
2148[7] 2291[9] 3264[2] 3604[5]
Kims Firebud *Debra Hamer* 87h
7 b g Firebreak Kims Pearl (IRE) (Jurado (USA))
671[12] 777[P] 1595[7] 2718[10]
Kim Tian Road (IRE) *Martin Hill* 119h
8 b m King's Theatre(IRE) Shaunies Lady (IRE) (Don't Forget Me)
688[P] 2371[13] 3043[8] 3744[P]
Kincora Fort (IRE) *Noel Williams* 106b
5 b g Brian Boru Glenview Rose (IRE) (Roselier (FR))
4016[9] 5339[3]
Kindly Note *Emma Lavelle* 115h 104c
7 ch m Generous(IRE) Vent D'Aout (IRE) (Imp Society (USA))
379[3] 811[11] **1594[3] 2632[F]**
Kind Of Easy (IRE) *Emma Lavelle* 110h 130c
8 b g Kalanisi(IRE) Specifiedrisk (IRE) (Turtle Island (IRE))
(2017)
2283[8] 3092[5] 3691[P]
Kingaroo (IRE) *Garry Woodward* 80h
8 b g King Charlemagne(USA) Lady Naomi (USA) (Distant View (USA))
1137[3] 1306[6] 1938[11] 2051[P]
King Boru (IRE) *Emma Lavelle* 123h
6 b g Brian Boru Final Instalment (IRE) (Insan (USA))
233[6] 538[4] 1552[2] ◆ 1797[3] (2764) ◆ 5333[6]
King Brex (DEN) *N W Alexander* 95h 91c
11 b g Primatico(USA) Moon Shine (DEN) (Shining Steel)
1143[5] 1158[3] 1374[9]
King Caractacus *Lawney Hill* 94h
9 b g Fleetwood(IRE) Go Tally-Ho (Gorytus (USA))
538[6] 767[7]
King Chop (FR) *F Nicolle* 127h 70c
4 b g Indian Rocket Mahitica (FR) (Solicitor I (FR))
(262a)
Kingcora (FR) *Venetia Williams* 110h 124c
6 b g King's Theatre(IRE) Coralisse Royale (FR) (Tip Moss (FR))
1745[8] 2366[6] 2529[14]
3155[5] 3693[2] 3769[4] 4440[U] 4822[5] (5284)
King Diamond (FR) *J R Goss* 87c
13 b g Exit To Nowhere(USA) Diamona (FR) (Diamond Shoal)
287[6]
Kingdom Of Munster (IRE) *Richard Ford* 98h 92c
7 b g Danehill Dancer(IRE) Kitty O'Shea (Sadler's Wells (USA))
511[6] **625[5]**
759[9] 942[8] 1073[8]

King Edmund *Chris Gordon* 118h 144c
11 b g Roi De Rome(USA) Cadbury Castle (Midyan (USA))
1746[2] 2212[6] 2666[5] 2890[3] 3197[8] (3642) 4034[3] 4768[14] 5156[U] 5524[2]

King Fingal (IRE) *John Quinn* 111h
9 b g King's Best(USA) Llia (Shirley Heights)
419[2]

Kingfisher Creek *Colin Tizzard* 92b
4 b g Kayf Tara Symbiosis (Bien Bien (USA))
2926[3]

King Fontaine (IRE) *J J O'Shea* 94h 121c
11 b g King's Theatre(IRE) Kerfontaine (Lafontaine (USA))
4057[U] 4348[5] (5287)

King Helissio (IRE) *Neil Mulholland* 103h 109c
6 b g Helissio(FR) Banner Buzz (IRE) (King's Ride)
2050[4] 2529[11] 5019[6] ◆

King Kalium (IRE) *Donald Whillans* 80h 57c
8 b g Kayf Tara Hannah Park (IRE) (Lycius (USA))
311[P]

King Kayf *Noel Williams* 63b
5 b g Kayf Tara Firecracker Lady (IRE) (Supreme Leader)
4824[8]

King Kurt (IRE) *Kevin Ryan* 95h
6 b g Holy Roman Emperor(IRE) Rutledge (IRE) (Entrepreneur)
1540[4] 2520[8]

King Mak *Marjorie Fife* 87h 128c
12 gr g Makbul Miss Nova (Ra Nova)
67[6] 565[4] 1073[6] 1419[4] 1580[P]

King Massini (IRE) *Evan Williams* 98h 133c
8 b g Dr Massini(IRE) King's Linnet (IRE) (King's Ride)
(2722)
2887[2] (3065)
(3158) 4738[F] 5385[10] ◆

King Muro *Fergal O'Brien* 88h
4 b g Halling(USA) Ushindi (IRE) (Montjeu (IRE))
4722[4] 4987[U] 5403[6]

King Of Alcatraz (IRE) *N Harris* 117c
8 gr g Great Palm(USA) Foxy Flame (IRE) (Tremblant)
(159) **658[7]**
5035[2] 5346[U]

King Of Dubai *Tim Vaughan* 91b
9 b g Dubai Destination(USA) Pearl Barley (IRE) (Polish Precedent (USA))
5186[P] ◆

King Of Forces *Denis Quinn* 84h
5 b g Halling(USA) Group Force (IRE) (Montjeu (IRE))
1152[5] 1255[8]

King Of Glory *Venetia Williams* 107h
6 b g Kayf Tara Glory Be (Gunner B)
1749[6] 4332[2] 5036[4]

King Of Jazz (IRE) *Peter Bowen* 69h
6 b g Acclamation Grand Slam Maria (FR) (Anabaa (USA))
5036[7] 5182[3]

King Of Strings (IRE) *Mark Walford* 107h
5 b g Desert King(IRE) Lemon Cello (IRE) (Accordion)
2660[5] 2968[2] 3516[4] 5212[4] 5452[3]

King Of The Night (GER) *Malcolm Jefferson* 158h 132c
10 b g Lomitas Kaiserlerche (GER) (Subotica (FR))
217[8] 1686[6] 2063[3]

King Of The Picts (IRE) *John Patrick Shanahan* 138h
5 ch g Rock Of Gibraltar(IRE) Belle Rebelle (IRE) (In The Wings)
1139a[5] (1802a) 2407a[3] 3339a[2] 4180a[3] 5153[3]

King Of The Road *Mrs Janet Ackner* 80c
12 ch g Romany Rye Queen's Cross (Kinglet)
62[14]

King Of The Wolds (IRE) *Malcolm Jefferson* 118h 136c
7 b g Presenting Azaban (IRE) (Be My Native (USA))
(2171)
(2574) 3333[2] 3894[4] 4532[4] 5278[2]

King Of Wing (IRE) *Phil McEntee* 91h
5 b g Hawk Wing(USA) Miss Shivvy (IRE) (Montjeu (IRE))
1535[3] 1633[P]

King Ozzy (IRE) *Lawney Hill* 97h 96c
10 b g King Charlemagne(USA) Kingpin Delight (Emarati (USA))
1783[P] 2569[4] 2760[7] 3151[5] **3470[U] 3883[5] 4633[2] 4795[2] 5115[7] 5442[5]**

King Rolfe (IRE) *Tim Vaughan* 109h
6 b g King's Theatre(IRE) Lady Rolfe (IRE) (Alzao (USA))
(2083) 2657[5] 3448[5] *4324[2]* 4674[4] 5391[7]

Kings Apollo *Tom Symonds* 95h
5 b g King's Theatre(IRE) Temple Dancer (Magic Ring (IRE))
(2470) 2701[2] (2827) 3174[4] 4351[8] 4883[4] **5309[U]**

Kings Bandit (IRE) *Donald McCain* 135h
6 b g King's Theatre(IRE) Gentle Lady (IRE) (Strong Gale)
3194[4] (4506) (5295) (5524)

Kings Bayonet *Alan King* 113h
7 ch g Needwood Blade Retaliator (Rudimentary (USA))
4555[3] 5128[13]

King's Chase (IRE) *N W Padfield* 97h 77c
12 b g Zaffaran(USA) Sister Nora (IRE) (The Parson)
327[6]

King's Chorister *Barry Murtagh* 93h
8 ch g King's Best(USA) Chorist (Pivotal)
342[3] 730[14] 884[P]
1870[F] 2335[P] 2791[U] 2999[4] 3639[F] 4366[6] 4615[7] (5556)

King's Ciel *Sean Curran* 90h
5 ch g Septieme Ciel(USA) King's Jewel (King's Signet (USA))
4632[8] 5305[4]

Kingscombe (USA) *Linda Jewell* 60h
5 rg g Mizzen Mast(USA) Gombeen (USA) (Private Account (USA))
2876[P] 3880[8]

Kings Destiny *Nicky Henderson* 109h
8 b g Dubai Destination(USA) Jalousie (IRE) (Barathea (IRE))
8[3] 1093[5]

Kings Flagship *Chris Down*
9 b g Lahib(USA) Queen's Flagship (IRE) (Accordion)
2469[U]

Kingsfold Flare *Gary Moore* 86h
7 ch m Central Park(IRE) Kingsfold Blaze (Mazilier (USA))
3556[4] 4760[8] 5143[3] 5402[2]

Kings Folly (IRE) *Lucinda Russell* 87h
6 b g Dushyantor(USA) Beltane Queen (IRE) (Strong Gale)
4043[9] 4772[4] 5102[P] 5479[10]

King's Grace *Donald McCain* 127h 135c
8 b g King's Theatre(IRE) Beauchamp Grace (Ardross)
203[3] (3275)
4464[2] (4948)
(5281)

Kings Grey (IRE) *Keith Reveley* 108h 139c
10 gr g King's Theatre(IRE) Grey Mo (IRE) (Roselier (FR))
(66) **249[6]**
2101[3] 2783[3]
3090[5] 4543[4] 5136[11] (5517)

Kings Lad (IRE) *Colin Tizzard* 127h
7 b g King's Theatre(IRE) Festival Leader (IRE) (Supreme Leader)
4935[2]

King's Legacy (IRE) *Alan Hill* 103h 121c
10 b g King's Theatre(IRE) Kotton (FR) (Cyborg (FR))
1047[7] 1283[P] 5346[5]

Kings Lodge *Nicky Henderson* 98h 125c
8 b g King's Theatre(IRE) Mardello (Supreme Leader)
(1744)
2107[6] 2468[5] 3085[8]

Kingsmere *Henry Daly* 133h 143c
9 b g King's Theatre(IRE) Lady Emily (Alflora (IRE))
1969[13] 2529[6] (5372) 5489[2]

Kingsmoss (IRE) *J J Lambe* 110h 110c
9 b g Luso Galamear (Strong Gale)
355[12]

Kings Music (IRE) *Philip Hobbs* 104h
8 b g Bach(IRE) Kings Rose (IRE) (King's Ride)
2040[14]

King's Odyssey (IRE) *Denis Coakley* 110b
5 b g King's Theatre(IRE) Ma Furie (FR) (Balleroy (USA))
3863[2] ◆

King's Opus (IRE) *Kim Bailey* 91h
5 b g King's Theatre(IRE) Kahysera (Kahyasi)
389[4] 4980[5] 5227[4] 5547[10]

Kings Palace (IRE) *David Pipe* 154h
6 b g King's Theatre(IRE) Sarahs Quay (IRE) (Witness Box (USA))
(1749) (1968) (3081) ◆ 4786[F]

Kingspark Boy (IRE) *E R Clough* 69h 69c
7 b g Tillerman Malacca (USA) (Danzig (USA))
5041[4]

King Spirit (IRE) *Brendan Powell* 112h 127c
6 b g Fruits Of Love(USA) Tariana (IRE) (Revoque (IRE))
(118) **3551[2]**

Kings River (FR) *Venetia Williams* 74b
5 bb g Lost World(IRE) Si Parfaite (FR) (Solon (GER))
2773[6]

King's Tempest *Nigel Twiston-Davies* 107b
5 b g Act One Queen Of Spades (IRE) (Strong Gale)
(4909)

King's Warrior (FR) *Tom George* 100h
7 b g King's Best(USA) Save Me The Waltz (FR) (Halling (USA))
3728[8] 3988[4] 4569[4] 5005[4]

Kingswell Theatre *Lucinda Russell* 101b
5 b g King's Theatre(IRE) Cresswell Native (IRE) (Be My Native (USA))
4671[4]

King Vahe (IRE) *Robert Johnson* 56h
5 b g One Cool Cat(USA) Tethkar (Machiavellian (USA))
4364[P] 4612[6]

King Vuvuzela (IRE) *Paul Nolan* 126h 134c
7 b g Flemensfirth(USA) Coolgavney Girl (IRE) (Good Thyne (USA))
4742[10]

King William (IRE) *David Martin Kelly* 124h
6 b g Trans Island Orador Sur Glane (IRE) (Shernazar)
3215a[2] (Dead)

King Zeal (IRE) *Barry Leavy* 106h
10 b g King's Best(USA) Manureva (USA) (Nureyev (USA))
10[9] 505[4] 2198[12] 2561[8] (2904) 3012[P] 3740[4] 4157[2] 4305[F] 5075[6]

Kipour'son (FR) *M Seror* 113h 125c
6 b g Daliapour(IRE) Kirkla (FR) (Bikala)
838a[3] 5425a[10]

Kirbys Glen (IRE) *Keiran Burke* 76h 93c
12 b g Charente River(IRE) Silence To Silence (IRE) (Salmon Leap (USA))
2633[3] 3281[P] 4734[4]

Kirkaig *Alistair Whillans* 86h
9 b g Best Of The Bests(IRE) Screen Idol (IRE) (Sadler's Wells (USA))
1158[4] 1979[5]

Kirkhammerton (IRE) *Barry Leavy* 75h 97c
12 ch g Grand Lodge(USA) Nawara (Welsh Pageant)
17[9]

Kirkleigh *R B Chanin* 127c
9 b g Kirkwall Memoranda (Husyan (USA))
60[3]

K Island (IRE) *Richard Price* 82h
6 b m Fruits Of Love(USA) Indiana Princess (Warrshan (USA))
471[14]

Kitchapoly (FR) *Donald McCain* 113h
4 b g Poliglote Kotkicha (FR) (Mansonnien (FR))
1394[2] 1536[3] 1684[5] (1786) 2200[6] 4224[9] 5090[6]

Kitegen (IRE) *Robin Dickin* 116h 130c
8 b g Milan Keen Gale (IRE) (Strong Gale)
1867[7]
(4804) ◆ **5089[3] 5382[2] 5573[4]**

Kitnkaboodle (IRE) *Stuart Coltherd* 2h
9 ch m Karinga Bay Sacre Du Printemps (IRE) (Old Vic)
1654[P] 1788[5]

Kitten Rock (FR) *E J O'Grady* 138h
4 b g Laverock(IRE) The Cat Eater (FR) (Tagel (USA))
5470a[2]

Kitts Delight (IRE) *M O Quigley* 94h 45c
7 b m Kris Kin(USA) Claranete Princess (IRE) (Princely Heir (IRE))
891a[9]

Kiwayu *Philip Kirby* 82h
5 b g Medicean Kibara (Sadler's Wells (USA))
2493[14]

Klaus (POL) *Cestmir Olehla* 82c
9 b g Jape(USA) Klara (POL) (Who Knows)
1905a[3]

Klepht (IRE) *Thomas Mullins* 113h 144c
9 b g Great Palm(USA) What A Mewsment (IRE) (Persian Mews)
1168a[6]

Knapp Bridge Boy *James Payne* 65h 71c
14 b g Wimbleball Toll Bridge (New Member)
40[5] 3172[P]

Knave Of Clubs (IRE) *Jeremy Scott* 89h
5 b g Red Clubs(IRE) Royal Bounty (IRE) (Generous (IRE))
4987[2] 5235[9]

Knight Blaze *David Brace* 71h 54c
7 b m Bach(IRE) Braceys Girl (IRE) (Be My Native (USA))
657[8]

Knight Flight *Anna Newton-Smith* 79b
9 b m Sir Harry Lewis(USA) Punnett's Town (Sulaafah (USA))
3195[F]

Knight In Purple *John Mackie* 130h
10 b g Sir Harry Lewis(USA) Cerise Bleue (FR) (Port Lyautey (FR))
82[4] (447) 591[10] 850[2] 1041[4] 1185[6] 1922[2]

Knightly Escapade *Brian Ellison* 107h
6 ch g Sakhee(USA) Queen Of Iceni (Erhaab (USA))
1415[3] 2156[2] 2493[2] 2840[5] *(4301)* 4941[F]

Knight Of Noir (IRE) *David Pipe* 135h
5 b g Winged Love(IRE) At Dawn (IRE) (Lashkari)
270[2] 2631[F] (3695) (4280) ◆ 4680[14]

Knight Of Pleasure *Gary Moore* 134h
5 ch g Exit To Nowhere(USA) Kim Fontenail (FR) (Kaldounevees (FR))
(2538) 3096[2] 3771[7] 4682[P]

Knight ofthe Realm *Caroline Keevil* 98h
5 b g Kayf Tara Flow (Over The River (FR))
3049[5] 3994[11] 5016[5]

Knighton Combe *Jamie Snowden* 107h 135c
14 b g Midnight Legend Cindercombe (Ra Nova)
393[8]

Knight Pass (IRE) *David Pipe* 121h
8 b g Accordion Toulon Pass (IRE) (Toulon)
2171[P]

Knight's Reward *Tim Vaughan* 83b
4 b g Sir Percy Wardeh (Zafonic (USA))
3049[4] *4017[11]* 4964[8]

Knight Valliant *Barbara Butterworth* 101h
11 gr g Dansili Aristocratique (Cadeaux Genereux)
444[F] 2844[3] 3141[5] 3618[4] 3940[4] 4957[3] 5217[P]

Knight Woodsman *R Mike Smith* 85h 92c
10 ch g Sir Harry Lewis(USA) Jowoody (Gunner B)
20[7] 169[6] 1655[5] 1789[6] 2310[3] 2789[8] 5514[11]

Knock A Hand (IRE) *Richard Lee* 136h 143c
9 br g Lend A Hand Knockcross (IRE) (Lake Coniston (IRE))
2242[2] 2672[11]
(3109) 3361[P] 3777[3] (4245)
4819[2]

Knockanarrigan (IRE) *John Joseph Hanlon* 115h 129c
6 b g Shantou(USA) Ruby Thewes (IRE) (Anshan)
565[5] 1660[8]

Knockanrawley (IRE) *Kim Bailey* 129h 128c
6 gr g Portrait Gallery(IRE) Hot Lips (IRE) (Good Thyne (USA))
(2826) 3177[2] 3800[2] 4272[P] (4839)

Knockara Beau (IRE) *George Charlton* 154h 154c
11 b g Leading Counsel(USA) Clairabell (IRE) (Buckskin (FR))
863a[5]
(1978) 2502[2] 3067[5] (3890)
4238[2] 4787[7]

Knock Boy (IRE) *Linda Jewell*
12 b g Pistolet Bleu(IRE) Past Times (IRE) (Un Desperado (FR))
1534[P]

Knockcairn (IRE) *Ian Duncan*
7 ch m Lahib(USA) Knockcairn Express (IRE) (Lafontaine (USA))
2217[P] 4199[P] 4832[5]

Knockgraffon King (IRE) *Donald McCain* 131h 129c
9 ch g Beneficial Kilternan Gale (IRE) (Good Thyne (USA))
3019[5] (3526) ◆ **4368[P]**

Knockgraffon Lad (USA) *Brendan Powell* 99h
7 b g Forestry(USA) Miss Dahlia (USA) (Strawberry Road (AUS))
947[3] 1269[2] 1582[9] 1674[3] 1822[2] 1938[5] 5490[5]

Knock House (IRE) *Mick Channon* 131h
5 ch g Old Vic Lady's Gesture (IRE) (Anshan)
(4) 2642[3] (3136) 3774[2] 4750[13]

Knocklayde Express (IRE) *S R B Crawford* 104b
5 b m Scorpion(IRE) Aupora (IRE) (Bob Back (USA))
(4240)

Knocklayde Vic (IRE) *Gordon Elliott* 111h
10 ch g Old Vic Laughing Lesa (IRE) (Bob Back (USA))
681[10]

Knockraheen (IRE) *Jonjo O'Neill* 117h 110c
6 b g Heron Island(IRE) Nancy's Stile (IRE) (Mandalus)
289[2] 2158[6] 2936[5] 3435[5] 4070[6]
4602[3] 5032[5] 5515[P]

Knockturnal (IRE) *Malcolm Jefferson* 83h
6 ch m Refuse To Bend(IRE) Knocktartan (IRE) (King's Ride)
682[4] 2342[5] 2675[6] 2865[5] 3518[3] 3871[F]

Know More Oats (IRE) *Victor Dartnall* 100h
6 b g Sanglamore(USA) Greenacre Mandalay (IRE) (Mandalus)
2946[5] 3695[6] 4163[4] 4391[U] 5074[11]

Know No Fear *Alastair Lidderdale* 103h
9 b g Primo Valentino(IRE) Alustar (Emarati (USA))
2432[4] 2718[6] 3163[9]

Knox Overstreet *Martin Hill* 99h
6 b g Indesatchel(IRE) Charlie Girl (Puissance)
1345[P]

Kodicil (IRE) *Mark Walford* 116h
6 b g Kodiac Miss Caoimhe (IRE) (Barathea (IRE))
1754[3] 2444[2] 2956[8] 3451[4] (3740) 3851[3] 4306[5] 4596[6]

Kolonel Kirkup *Michael Dods* 96h
4 b g Dr Fong(USA) Strawberry Lolly (Lomitas)
3332[4] 4003[2] 4476[2] 4939[6]

Koolala (IRE) *Paul Webber* 126h
6 b m Kayf Tara Squaw Talk (USA) (Gulch (USA))
2467[2] (2767) *4300[8]* 4531[2] (5124) 5370[4]

Koralsdarling (IRE) *Alan Jones* 64h
10 b g Witness Box(USA) Jenny's Jewel (IRE) (Be My Native (USA))
1475[4]

Kosta Brava (FR) *Michael Smith* 101h 110c
10 ch g Nikos Tamana (USA) (Northern Baby (CAN))
883[4] 1077[P]

Kotkieglote (FR) *J-P Gallorini* 100h 132c
7 b m Poliglote Katiana (FR) (Villez (USA))
2264a[P] 2415a[P]

Kotkiri (FR) *Alan King* 88b
5 b g Ballingarry(IRE) Kakira (FR) (Cadoudal (FR))
2667[7]

Kotmaille (FR) *F Leralle*
9 ch g Maille Pistol(FR) Kotine (FR) (Phantom Breeze)
2465a[11]

Koultas King (IRE) *Tim Vaughan* 112h
7 b g Exit To Nowhere(USA) Carrigmoorna Style (IRE) (Dr Massini (IRE))
(1341) (1533) 2006[P] 2624[4]

Kozmina Bay *Bernard Llewellyn* 86h
5 b m Notnowcato Kozmina (IRE) (Sadler's Wells (USA))
2898[9] (3188) 5139[5]

Krackatoa King *Noel Williams* 93b
6 b g Kayf Tara Firecracker Lady (IRE) (Supreme Leader)
4638[6] 5014[9]

Krasnodar (IRE) *Malcolm Jefferson* 65b
4 gr g Medaaly Azyouare (IRE) (Classic Cliche (IRE))
5454[6]

Kris Cross (IRE) *Lucinda Russell* 126h 131c
7 ch g Kris Kin(USA) Perfidia (Perpendicular)
340[4] 625[2] 1787[3] 2246[3] (2662)
3521[2] (4464)
4819[P] 5348[U]

Kris Magic (IRE) *Colin Heard* 77b
7 b m Kris Kin(USA) Insan Magic (IRE) (Insan (USA))
412[7] 3991[P]

Kris Spin (IRE) *Richard Lee* 147h
6 br g Kris Kin(USA) Auditing Empress (IRE) (Accordion)
2316[2] 2942[2] (3860) 4415[2] 5093[2] 5550[2]

Kriss William (FR) *E Turner* 40h 60c
8 b g Califet(FR) Pretty William (FR) (Bojador (FR))
165[4]

Kristallo (GER) *Dai Burchell* 78h 79c
9 ch g Lando(GER) Key West (GER) (In The Wings)
730[10] 1364[10]

Kruseman *Richard Woollacott* 90h
7 b g Doyen(IRE) Polar Charge (Polar Falcon (USA))
42[8] 635[7] 686[P] 5522[7]

Kruzhlinin (GER) *Donald McCain* 122h 153c
7 ch g Sholokhov(IRE) Karuma (GER) (Surumu (GER))
355[4] 2072[4] (2358)
(2972) 3897[7] 4552[3] 5171[10]

Kublai (FR) *Philip Hobbs* 87h
4 b g Laveron Java Dawn (IRE) (Fleetwood (IRE))
4638[3] 5145[7]

Kuda Huraa (IRE) *Alan King* 120h
6 b g Montjeu(IRE) Healing Music (FR) (Bering)
4558[2] 4935[6]

Kudu Country (IRE) *Tom Tate* 126h 123c
8 gr g Captain Rio Nirvavita (FR) (Highest Honor (FR))
3648[4] 4426[6] (4899)

Kudu Shine *Richard Woollacott* 114h
8 b g Karinga Bay Flora Bright (Alflora (IRE))
3697[4] 4175[9] 4993[4] 5351[5]

Kuilsriver (IRE) *Nick Gifford* 124h 93c
7 b g Cape Cross(IRE) Ripple Of Pride (IRE) (Sadler's Wells (USA))
3096[U] *4020[12]* 4264[P]

Kukurudu (IRE) *Simon West* 93h
7 b g Tikkanen(USA) Tullyfoyle (IRE) (Montelimar (USA))
737[7] 847[4] 897[8] 2999[7] 5285[U]

Kumbeshwar *Alan King* 133h 159c
7 b g Doyen(IRE) Camp Fire (IRE) (Lahib (USA))
1969[10] 2281[4] 2503[10] 3458[3] 3887[9] 4032[7] 5350[5]

Kusadasi (IRE) *Marc Barber* 118b 100c
9 b g Beneficial Otorum (IRE) (Muroto)
(854) **926[2]**
1344[6] 1887[10]

Kwo Neshe (IRE) *Malcolm Jefferson* 94b
4 bb g Fruits Of Love(USA) Bonny River (IRE) (Exit To Nowhere (USA))
5388[7]

Kykate *William Kinsey* 108h 122c
8 b m Hamas(IRE) Coleham (Saddlers' Hall (IRE))
(26) **181[F]**
2159[3] 3287[4] 3823[U] 4007[5] 4668[4]
5162[2]

Kylenoe Fairy (IRE) *Paul Henderson* 113h 115c
10 ch m Anshan Supreme Stroke (IRE) (Supreme Leader)
409[7] 831[7] **(996)**
1197[4] 1485[P]

Kyles Faith (IRE) *Martin Keighley* 101h 105c
6 b g Court Cave(IRE) Littleton Liberty (Royal Applause)
270[7] 1672[6] 2085[5] 2296[3] 2691[12] 3029[8] *4023[8]*
4398[4] 4475[2] **4723[P] 5065[3] 5293[P]**

Kylestyle (IRE) *F Flood* 129h
5 b g Oscar(IRE) Bobs Star (IRE) (Bob Back (USA))
4456a[5] 5420a[F]

La Bacouetteuse (FR) *Iain Jardine* 80h
9 b g Miesque's Son(USA) Toryka (Vettori (IRE))
1664[5] 1873[9]

La Belle Sauvage *Kim Bailey* 95h
7 ch m Old Vic Lady Rebecca (Rolfe (USA))
2432[8] 2767[5] 3188[3] 4823[9] 5033[5]

Lac Fontana (FR) *Paul Nicholls* 149h
5 b g Shirocco(GER) Fontaine Riant (FR) (Josr Algarhoud (IRE))
(1958) 2530[4] (3891) ◆ (4785) (5167)

Lachlan Bridge (GER) *A Chaille-Chaille* 132h 124c
6 b g Dubawi(IRE) Lady Zorreghuietta (FR) (Anabaa (USA))
1583a[3]

Lachlan Mor *Stuart Coltherd* 86h
5 b g Josr Algarhoud(IRE) Miss Campanella (Bal Harbour)
2738[6] 3522[6] 4776[11] 5050[4] 5354[11]

Lackamon *Sue Smith* 131h 141c
9 b g Fleetwood(IRE) Pearlossa (Teenoso (USA))
4651[F] 4814[2] 4954[3] **5276[8]**

Lacocodanza *George Moore* 23h
5 b m Tamure(IRE) Miss Petronella (Petoski)
1420[5] 1719[3] 2037[5] 2752[9] 3329[F] 4083[5] 4476[7]
4889[P]

Lac Sacre (FR) *John Flint* 127h
5 b g Bering Lady Glorieuse (FR) (Le Glorieux)
2087[11] 2559[2] 2846[3] (3118) 3756[2] 4512[2] 4612[2]
(5040) 5239[3]

Lacunae (IRE) *Seamus Mullins* 66h
6 b m Definite Article Maig Mandy (IRE) (Mandalus)
35[5] 462[5] 1823[6] 2273[4]

Ladeka (FR) *Mlle T Puitg* 116h
4 b f Linda's Lad Madeka (FR) (Kadalko (FR))
130a[5]

Ladfromhighworth *Mrs Camilla Scott* 100c
9 b g Kier Park(IRE) Cavisoir (Afzal)
5123[6] 5553[8]

Ladies Dancing *Chris Down* 109h
8 b g Royal Applause Queen Of Dance (IRE) (Sadler's Wells (USA))
10[3] 304[7] 1828[4] 2111[5] 2474[7] 3043[4] 5125[7]
5335[2]

Lady Barastar (IRE) *Amanda Perrett* 48h
6 b m Barathea(IRE) Stariya (IRE) (Soviet Star (USA))
1270[13]

Lady Bonanova (IRE) *J R Jenkins*
4 b f Haatef(USA) Lady Express (IRE) (Soviet Star (USA))
1934[U]

Lady Boru (IRE) *Dan Skelton* 90h
6 b m Brian Boru Roaming (IRE) (Be My Native (USA))
2579[3] 3010[9]

Lady Bridget *Mark Gillard* 88h 70c
6 b m Hawk Wing(USA) Change Partners (IRE) (Hernando (FR))
83[2] 293[3] 2696[7] 3043[5] 3692[8] 3959[6] 4604[2]
4885[6] 5551[4]

Lady Busanda *George Moore* 86b
4 b f Fair Mix(IRE) Spirit Of Ecstacy (Val Royal (FR))
4191[4] 4618[7]

Lady Buttons *Philip Kirby* 110b
4 b f Beneficial Lady Chapp (IRE) (High Chaparral (IRE))
(2960) 3460[7] (4342) 5159[2]

Lady Charisma *Philip Hobbs* 106h
5 b m Presenting Lady Cad (FR) (Cadoudal (FR))
2317[5] (2824) 3988[F] 5018[4]

Lady Cliche *Roger Curtis* 39b
5 b m Kirkwall Madam Cliche (Classic Cliche (IRE))
4[12] 715[11]

Lady De Crusse (FR) *E Leenders* 102c
9 b m Bedawin(FR) Sarpevale (FR) (Sarpedon I (FR))
2384a[3]

Lady Fingers *Nigel Twiston-Davies* 100h
6 b m Kirkwall Wellfield (Primitive Rising (USA))
2317[9] 2767[6] 3010[8] 3566[4] 5034[8] 5177[2] 5395[4]

Lady From Geneva *Brendan Powell* 95h 71c
7 ch m Generous(IRE) Schizo-Phonic (Gildoran)
99[6] 3425[8] *4299[5]* 4595[4]
4884[6]

Lady Gargoyle *Jim Goldie* 87h
6 br m Lucky Story(USA) Gargoyle Girl (Be My Chief (USA))
880[2] 1161[P] 1664[P] 2309[9]

Lady Garvagh *Richard Woollacott* 73h
4 b f Lucarno(USA) Dedrunknmunky (IRE) (Rashar (USA))
4730[6] 5244[F]

Lady Kathleen *Paul Webber* 114h
7 b m Hernando(FR) Lady Of Fortune (IRE) (Sovereign Water (FR))
2663[4] 2948[5] 3319[P] 4907[5]

Lady Lectra *John Flint* 92h
5 b m Multiplex Coronation Queen (Pivotal)
519[2] 828[4] 920[4] 1519[4]

Lady Myfanwy *Mrs Myfanwy Miles* 19c
13 b m Sir Harry Lewis(USA) Orange Princess (Cruise Missile)
(13) **413[5]**
657[4] 872[5] 972[3] 1055[4] 1344[P] 4655[P]

Lady Oaksey *Bob Buckler* 30h
8 b m Tobougg(IRE) Silk Law (IRE) (Barathea (IRE))
1749[U] 2009[F] 2463[10] 3046[5]

Lady Of Provence *Nicky Henderson* 90b
5 gr m Fair Mix(IRE) Rosa Canina (Bustino)
567[5] 4240[4]

Lady Of Verona (IRE) *Lucinda Russell* 92h 98c
7 b m Old Vic Innovate (IRE) (Posen (USA))
1664[7] 2333[3] 2974[4]
4337[F] 4551[3] (4771)
(5211)

Lady Sinatra *Oliver Sherwood* 80h
6 b m Where Or When(IRE) Kythia (IRE) (Kahyasi)
188[P] 540[8]

Lady Valtas *Martin Bosley* 68h
6 b m Val Royal(FR) Phantasmagoria (Fraam)
561[10]

Ladyvie (FR) *David Pipe* 86h 101c
7 b m Vic Toto(FR) Ladykish (FR) (Comte Du Bourg (FR))
637[4] **1197[9]**

Laganbank (IRE) *W P Mullins* 140h 147c
8 b g Norwich Listen Up (Good Thyne (USA))
1168a[8] 1776a[4] 2123a[4]

Lagan Canal (IRE) *A J Martin* 125h
7 b g Heron Island(IRE) Trumpster's Gale (IRE) (Strong Gale)
498[3] (682)

Lagan Katie *Bill Turner* 81h
8 b m Kayf Tara Bichette (Lidhame)
4018[12]

La Garde Royale (FR) *J Ortet* 121c
5 b m Kapgarde(FR) Latran (FR) (Pistolet Bleu (IRE))
2263a[7]

Laidback Leo *Robin Dickin* 30h
6 ch g Golden Snake(USA) Rockstine (IRE) (Ballad Rock)
2[11]

Laird Of Monksford (IRE) *Donald McCain* 79h
5 b g Shantou(USA) Back Log (IRE) (Bob Back (USA))
3433[5] 4384[5] 5295[5]

Lajidaal (USA) *Gary Moore* 95h 97c
7 b g Dynaformer(USA) Tayibah (IRE) (Sadler's Wells (USA))
100[3] 242[4] 305[3] 485[7] (707)

Lakefield Rebel (IRE) *Henry Hogarth* 95h
8 bb g Presenting River Mousa (IRE) (Over The River (FR))
1850[3] 2197[5] 2621[8] 2974[5]

Lake World (FR) *Mlle M-L Mortier* 88h 109c
11 b g Lost World(IRE) Lac Tamaris (FR) (Mansonnien (FR))
131a[7]

Lakota Ghost (USA) *Seamus Durack* 56h
6 b g Rockport Harbor(USA) Political Alert (USA) (Giant's Causeway (USA))
184[P]

La Madonnina (IRE) *Caroline Keevil* 89h
6 b m Milan Supreme Nova (Supreme Leader)
306[6] 519[4] 708[8] 828[5] 969[5] 4472[3] 4887[8] 5235[4]

Lamblord (IRE) *Carroll Gray* 105h
7 b g Brian Boru Princess Symphony (IRE) (Lashkari)
2369[7] ◆ (2696)

Lamb Or Cod (IRE) *Philip Hobbs* 130h 146c
7 ch g Old Vic Princess Lizzie (IRE) (Homo Sapien)
2080[2] 2504[13] 2935[5]
3291[2] 4439[3] 4819[3] (5373)

Lamboro Lad (IRE) *Peter Bowen* 125h 131c
9 b g Milan Orchard Spray (IRE) (Supreme Leader)
39[2] 1730[2] 2373[8] 4509[P] 4886[2] 5184[2] (5513)

Lambro (IRE) *W P Mullins* 137h 140c
9 b g Milan Beautiful Tune (FR) (Green Tune (USA))
1168a[9] 1604a[P]

Lamb's Cross *Mark Gillard* 110h 112c
8 b g Rainbow High Angie Marinie (Sabrehill (USA))
(2653)
3135[U] 3170[3] 4989[3] 5176[P]

Lamego (FR) *Mme P Butel* 142h 116c
7 b g Ski Chief(USA) Bal De Foire (FR) (Always Fair (USA))
406a[12] 685a[12] 1901a[7] 2240a[4] 5577a[7]

L'Amiral David (FR) *Alan King* 91b
4 bb g My Risk(FR) Mme La Vicomtesse (FR) (Baroud D'Honneur (FR))
4561[4] 4964[4] 5447[7]

L'Ami Serge (IRE) *G Macaire* 131h
4 b g King's Theatre(IRE) La Zingarella (IRE) (Phardante (FR))
1741a[2]

Lamool (GER) *Tim Vaughan* 120h 127c
7 b g Mamool(IRE) Linara (GER) (Windwurf (GER))
455a[7]
(5228) ◆

Lamps *Michael Blake* 133h
7 b g Dynaformer(USA) Conspiring (USA) (Grand Slam (USA))
3359[7] (3737) 4277[5] 4517[3] (4724) (4864)

Lanarkshire (IRE) *Jennifer Mason* 61h
5 ch g Iffraaj Voyage Of Dreams (USA) (Riverman (USA))
188[P]

Lancetto (FR) *Evan Williams* 118h 150c
9 b g Dubai Destination(USA) Lanciana (IRE) (Acatenango (GER))
1960[8]
2212[2] 2666[4] 2890[2] (3197)
3773[6] 4790[15] 5570[4]

Lancing *A J Martin* 111h
5 b g Dansili Montare (IRE) (Montjeu (IRE))
678[3]

Landecker (IRE) *N W Alexander* 121h
6 br g Craigsteel Winsome Breeze (IRE) (Glacial Storm (USA))
2037[4] 2823[5] 3516[9] (4234) 4550[7] (5206) 5510[P]

Landenstown Pearl (IRE) *Sarah Humphrey* 85h
8 b m Definite Article Golden Moment (IRE) (Roselier (FR))
3434[2] 3852[5] 4309[5] 4595[10] 5069[8] (5461)

Landenstown Star (IRE) *Mark Gillard* 93h 87c
9 ch g Bob's Return(IRE) Slieve Bernagh (IRE) (Phardante (FR))
1275[14] 1488[8] 1645[7] 2148[2] 2278[3]
2765[5] 3227[5] 4071[P] 4330[6] 4733[8]

Landerbee (IRE) *Seamus Mullins* 83h
7 b g Exit To Nowhere(USA) Ithastobedone (IRE) (Be My Native (USA))
2536[7] 3434[P] 3692[7] 4471[P] 4636[2] 5116[7]

Landmarque *Tony Coyle* 105b
5 b g Milan M N L Lady (Polar Falcon (USA))
3619[3] (4480)

Land Of Soprani (FR) *F-M Cottin* 88h 103c
9 ch m Lando(GER) Sopran Biro (IRE) (Roi Danzig (USA))
1464a[2]

Land Of Vic *Peter Bowen* 133h
6 b m Old Vic Land Of Glory (Supreme Leader)
2298[5] 2506[11] 2907[5] 3388[5] (3733) (4090) 4542[5]
(5255)

Landolino (FR) *Mrs J L Le Brocq* 115h
9 b g Trempolino(USA) Champagne Sorbet (FR) (Kaldounevees (FR))
993a[2] 1250a[2] 1827a[4]

Landscape (FR) *Venetia Williams* 137h
6 b g Lando(GER) Universelle (USA) (Miswaki (USA))
3200[P]

Landulph Lass *Jackie Du Plessis* 75h
7 b m Thank Heavens Easter Again (Shaab)
3168[10] 3697[12]

Langarve Lady (IRE) *Neil Mulholland* 100h
6 b m Oscar(IRE) Fashions Monty (IRE) (Montelimar (USA))
187[7] 2053[6] 2317[13] 2718[P] 3005[11] 3289[5] 3955[P]
4595[5] 4883[3]

Langarve Lass (IRE) *Neil Mulholland* 74h
5 b m Oscar(IRE) Fashions Monty (IRE) (Montelimar (USA))
187[10] 3872[15] 4467[6] 4910[11]

Langham Lily (USA) *Sarah Humphrey* 80h
5 bb m Badge Of Silver(USA) Silver Frau (USA) (Silver Charm (USA))
2514[11] 5257[8]

Langley *Tim Vaughan* 93h
7 b g Trempolino(USA) Late Night (GER) (Groom Dancer (USA))
1342[7] 2085[4] 2698[7]

Langley House (IRE) *Dianne Sayer* 75h
7 b m Milan No Moore Bills (Nicholas Bill)
73[5] 278[3] 1373[U]

Lang Shining (IRE) *Lady Blandford*
10 ch g Dr Fong(USA) Dragnet (IRE) (Rainbow Quest (USA))
4252[R]

Lansdowne Princess *Johnny Farrelly* 78h 86c
12 b m Cloudings(IRE) Premier Princess (Hard Fought)
2312[5] 2690[5]

Lanta's Legacy *Jeremy Scott* 41b
4 ch f Central Park(IRE) Purple Patch (Afzal)
5130[12]

Lapin Garou (FR) *Colin Tizzard* 75h 75c
7 gr g Martaline Bella Grande (FR) (Villez (USA))
248[9] 687[5]

Lap Of Honour (IRE) *Ferdy Murphy* 103h
10 b g Danehill Dancer(IRE) Kingsridge (IRE) (King's Theatre (IRE))
870[P] 1143[F] 1280[6]

Lapworth (IRE) *Michael Appleby* 22h
7 b g Alflora(IRE) La Bella Villa (Relkino)
2905[5] 4546[9]

Larabelle (FR) *Mlle T Puitg* 109h
4 b f Linda's Lad Orabelle (FR) (Freedom Cry)
130a[4]

Lara Dora (IRE) *Laura Hurley* 66b
8 b m Pasternak Remember Dora (IRE) (Classic Memory)
2176[P] 2535[P]

Laraghcon Boy (IRE) *Tony Carroll* 92b
5 ch g Stowaway Hannah Mooney (IRE) (Shahanndeh)
3734[4] *4329[3]* ◆

Larkhall *Mike Sowersby* 55h 28c
7 b g Saddlers' Hall(IRE) Larkbarrow (Kahyasi)
786[F] 1260[9] 1416[F] 1497[P] 1718[7] 1873[8]

Larks Lad (IRE) *M Foley* 109b 120c
10 b g Bob Back(USA) Higher Again (IRE) (Strong Gale)
432[2] 757[9] 1566[2] 1972[13]
4936[F]

Larks Rising *Caroline Keevil* 68h
6 b g Relief Pitcher Black A Brook (IRE) (Good Thyne (USA))
588[6] 2570[8] (2745) 2981[6] 3422[8] 3747[6]

Larteta (FR) *Sarah Humphrey* 108h
5 b g Enrique Ariel (IRE) (Caerleon (USA))
1255[5] 1418[3] 1565[7] ◆ 1714[4] 2771[2] 3029[2] ◆
3473[4]

Lascaux *Luke Dace* 75h
5 ch m Pivotal Tora Bora (Grand Lodge (USA))
1749[P]

La Segnora (FR) *R Le Gal* 140h 127c
8 gr m Turgeon(USA) Sentosa (FR) (Kaldounevees (FR))
(455a)

Laser Blazer *Alan King* 115h
6 b g Zafeen(FR) Sashay (Bishop Of Cashel)
4959[3]

Lashonara (FR) *H Billot*
4 b f Night Tango(GER) Paranda (FR) (Jeune Homme (USA))
615a[P]

Laskaline (FR) *G Cherel* 121h 124c
5 b m Martaline Laskadya (FR) (Lashkari)
1983a[P]

Lastchanceforlisa (IRE) *John Flint* 103h
8 b m Old Vic Montelisa (IRE) (Montelimar (USA))
2193[7] 2894[S]

Last Chance Ranch *Derek Shaw* 80h
4 b g Manduro(GER) Rakata (USA) (Quiet American (USA))
2392[4] 2899[6] 3592[7]

Last Instalment (IRE) *Philip Fenton* 137h 168c
9 ch g Anshan Final Instalment (IRE) (Insan (USA))
3751a[3] (4183a)
4787[U]

Last Lulu (FR) *D Grandin*
6 b g Lost World(IRE) Lady Daisy (FR) (Amthaal (USA))
559a[9]

Lastoftheleaders (IRE) *A J Martin* 136h 146c
11 b g Supreme Leader Heather Breeze (IRE) (Lord Americo)
1168a[P] 3806a[3] (Dead)

Last Shadow *Jonjo O'Neill* 110h
5 b g Notnowcato Fairy Queen (IRE) (Fairy King (USA))
1551[6]

Last Shot (FR) *Venetia Williams* 104h 135c
7 b g Le Fou(IRE) Lucky Shot (FR) (Corporate Report (USA))
370[4] (2462)
2721[2] 2873[5] (3156)
3294[2] 3894[3] 4036[4] 4414[7] 4800[2] 4921[U] 5136[P]

Last Time D'Albain (FR) *Liam P Cusack* 98h 143c
10 b g Sassanian(USA) Lightim (FR) (Lightning (FR))
5171[U]

Latelo *Charlie Mann* 85b
6 b g Shirocco(GER) Laurencia (Shirley Heights)
3863[9]

Latest Fashion (IRE) *Christopher Wilson* 84h
8 ch m Ashkalani(IRE) Musical Bramble (IRE) (Accordion)
552[4] 3144[6] 3451[P] 4615[P]

Latest Trend (IRE) *S Penny* 108h 96c
8 b g Moscow Society(USA) Wall-Nut Grove (IRE) (Satco (FR))
97[2] **179[4]**
693[7] 870[4] 1009[4] **4505[3] 5131[P]**

Latin Connection (IRE) *S R B Crawford* 117h 113c
8 b g Soviet Star(USA) Via Verbano (IRE) (Caerleon (USA))
24[6] 342[4] 681[11]

Lauberhorn *Evan Williams* 111h 111c
7 b g Dubai Destination(USA) Ski Run (Petoski)
47[2] 332[U] 375[2]
779[5] 931[4] (1153)
1192[2] 1282[3] 1537[4] 1708[5]

Laudatory *Nicky Henderson* 135h
8 b g Royal Applause Copy-Cat (Lion Cavern (USA))
82[P] 673[6] 831[6] (1258) (1520) 1685[5] 1960[6]

Laughing Game *Laura Hurley* 44h 49c
10 b m Classic Cliche(IRE) Ground Game (Gildoran)
2023[P] 2175[5] 2541[7]

Laughton Park *Suzy Smith* 107h
9 ch g Karinga Bay Brass Castle (IRE) (Carlingford Castle)
89[5] 4760[4] (5112)

L'Aumance Girl (FR) *A Adeline De Boisbrunet*
6 b m Astarabad(USA) L'Aumance (FR) (Mont Basile (FR))
703a[P]

Launchpad *Kevin Hunter* 124h 109c
7 ch g Starcraft(NZ) Revival (Sadler's Wells (USA))
75[F]

Laurens Ruby (IRE) *John Flint* 91h
5 b m Kalanisi(IRE) Double Dream (IRE) (Double Eclipse (IRE))
483[3] 842[3] 1056[2] 1578[4] 1672[7] 1814[6] 2292[9]

Laustra Bad (FR) *David Pipe* 127h 102c
11 b g Astarabad(USA) Love Crazy (FR) (Loup Solitaire (USA))
158[6] 486[6] 764[3] 1020[6] 1123[5]

Lava Lamp (GER) *Evan Williams* 130h 116c
7 b g Shamardal(USA) La Felicita (Shareef Dancer (USA))
409[3] (512) 782[5] 1042[8]
1343[3] (1817)
2468[P] 3730[9] 4413[6] 4841[8] 5186[6] 5429[6]

Lavella Wells *Sue Smith* 83b
6 b m Alflora(IRE) Jazzy Refrain (IRE) (Jareer (USA))
970[7]

Lawsons Thorns (IRE) *Dan Skelton* 103b
5 b g Presenting Ardnurcher (IRE) (King's Ride)
1690[2] 3760[3] 4772[F]

Laybach (IRE) *Jim Goldie* 76h 82c
10 br g Bach(IRE) River Breeze (IRE) (Sharifabad (IRE))
316[5] **533[3]**
866[3] 1163[P] 1567[5] 1791[5] **2219[F] 2361[U]** 2794[P]

Layla Joan (IRE) *Gordon Elliott* 140h 99c
6 b m Oscar(IRE) Ericas Charm (Alderbrook)
(3934) (4200) 4542[U] 5199a[U]

Layline (IRE) *Gay Kelleway* 78h
7 b g King's Best(USA) Belle Reine (King Of Kings (IRE))
2876[8]

Leader Of The Gang *David Pipe* 120h
8 b g Karinga Bay Material Girl (Busted)
5075[3] 5260[2]

Leader Of The Land (IRE) *Robert Stephens* 105h
7 ch g Halling(USA) Cheerleader (Singspiel (IRE))
1152[F] (1348)

Lead Kindly Light (IRE) *Sean Byrne* 117h 137c
10 ch m Beneficial Shining Spear (Commanche Run)
2985a[2]

Lead The Way *Jonathan Portman*
4 b f Indian Haven Way To The Stars (Dansili)
3167[14]

Leah Claire (IRE) *W McCreery* 136h
8 ch m Tomba Kate Emily (IRE) (Priolo (USA))
3910a[11]

Leahnor (IRE) *John Flint* 70b
5 gr m Flemensfirth(USA) Silver Pursuit (Rainbow Quest (USA))
2298[16] 3035[5]

Lean Araig (IRE) *Oliver McKiernan* 116b
5 ch g Old Vic Glens Music (IRE) (Orchestra)
2995a[4]

Lean Burn (USA) *Barry Leavy* 92h
8 b g Johannesburg(USA) Anthelion (USA) (Stop The Music (USA))
21[4] 5037[7] 2511[4] 3062[7] 3428[2] (4107) (4336)

Leap In The Dark *John Mackie*
8 b m Midnight Legend Spring Collection (Tina's Pet)
2189[P] 2429[P]

Leath Acra Mor (IRE) *Ian Williams* 121h
8 b g King's Theatre(IRE) Happy Native (IRE) (Be My Native (USA))
(650) 845[11] 1045[2] 1304[5]

Leave It Be (IRE) *Johnny Farrelly* 113h
7 gr g High-Rise(IRE) Farh Quest (IRE) (Farhaan)
2280[2]

Le Bacardy (FR) *Tony Carroll* 123h 137c
8 b g Bahhare(USA) La Balagna (Kris)
(234) **2211[6]**
2465a[10] 2845[4] 3323[5] 4861[4] (5013)
(5141) 5254[2] (5275)

Lebanna *Tim Easterby* 87h
4 br f Bollin Eric Bollin Annabel (King's Theatre (IRE))
2160[2] 2604[4] 2960[6] 3613[4] 3826[8] 4037[3] 4746[2] 4938[2] 5161[8] 5494[7]

Le Bec (FR) *Emma Lavelle* 125h 158c
6 ch g Smadoun(FR) La Pelode (FR) (Dress Parade)
(1796)
(2501) 3079[2] 4751[F]

Le Bel Anjou (FR) *F-M Cottin* 129h 133c
6 b g Malinas(GER) Epsibelle (IRE) (Darshaan)
(838a)
2264a[P]

Lecale Lad (IRE) *Tim Vaughan* 94h
7 b g Revoque(IRE) Thyngreesa (Classic Cliche (IRE))
2393[9] 3115[7] 3567[3] 5177[7]

Le Commencement (IRE) *I Heaney* 115h 115c
12 b g Beneficial Ballyduggan Queen (IRE) (King Luthier)
329[P]

Ledbury Star (IRE) *Matt Sheppard* 82h
8 b g Mr Combustible(IRE) Sapien Dame (IRE) (Homo Sapien)
1837[P]

Leeroar (IRE) *Jo Davis* 100h 94c
6 b g Let The Lion Roar Leane (IRE) (Good Thyne (USA))
2150[4] 2766[8] 4334[7]
(4654) 5401[3]

Le Fin Bois (FR) *Tim Vaughan* 120h
4 b g Poliglote La Mache (FR) (Morespeed)
4755[19]

Legacy Gold (IRE) *David Pipe* 138h
6 b m Gold Well Durgams Delight (IRE) (Durgam (USA))
2506[3] ◆ (3010) (3818) (4394) 4805[4]

Legendary Hop *Chris Bealby* 105h 104c
8 b m Midnight Legend Hopping Mad (Puget (USA))
(2396)
3739[U] 4078[P] (4337)
5246[10]

Legend Erry (IRE) *Venetia Williams* 91h 91c
10 b g Act One Azure Lake (USA) (Lac Ouimet (USA))
247[3]

Leg Iron (IRE) *Sheena West* 105h 118c
9 b g Snurge Southern Skies (IRE) (Dr Massini (IRE))
242[2] 712[5] (2979)
3554[F] 4704[9] 5373[4]

Le Grand Chene (FR) *Sophie Leech* 84h 102c
8 b g Turgeon(USA) Faitiche D'Aubry (FR) (Le Nain Jaune (FR))
(378) **749[9]**
832[9] 1104[3] 2615[P] 3048[4] (3281)
3730[4] 4354[7] 4932[7] 5187[4] 5433[3]

Le Grand Luce (FR) *J-P Gallorini* 152h
5 b g Dream Well(FR) Reaction Rapide (FR) (Bering)
683a[3] 1983a[2] 2414a[2] 5577a[2]

Leish Oscar (IRE) *Neil McKnight* 109h 123c
8 b m Oscar(IRE) Blackwater Valley (IRE) (Crash Course)
111[4]

Leith Hill Legasi *Charlie Longsdon* 85h
5 b m Kahyasi Leith Hill Star (Comme L'Etoile)
2298[8] 2864[2] 3438[4] 4068[5] 4375[4] 4803[6] 5402[P]

L'Eldorado (FR) *Chris Bealby* 117h 130c
9 b g Urban Ocean(FR) Little Warden (IRE) (Bellman (FR))
204[10]

L'Eminence Grise (IRE) *Maurice Barnes* 101h
7 gr g Kahyasi Belle Innocence (FR) (Turgeon (USA))
2355[9] 2838[3]

Lemon Drop Red (USA) *Paul Webber* 118h 120c
6 b g Lemon Drop Kid(USA) Skipper's Mate (USA) (Skip Away (USA))
10[5] **234[U]**
634[3] 899[U] 1282[4]

Lemon Grove *Martin Bosley* 71h
4 b f Compton Place Lemon Tree (USA) (Zilzal (USA))
4730[7] 5244[8]

Lemon's Gent *Paul Webber* 108h 113c
7 br g Generous(IRE) Lemon's Mill (USA) (Roberto (USA))
(117) **2270[4]**
2895[F] 5342[2]

Lemons Ground *Jamie Snowden* 104h
5 ch g Generous(IRE) Misty Move (IRE) (Saddlers' Hall (IRE))
(309) 2368[8] 3134[6] 3747[5] 4694[6] 5033[F]

Lemony Bay *Oliver Sherwood* 117h
5 b g Overbury(IRE) Lemon's Mill (USA) (Roberto (USA))
(338) 2225[6] 2783[2] 3388[14] 4808[6] 5341[P]

Lenderking (IRE) *Michael Chapman* 20b
6 b g Sleeping Indian Roses From Ridey (IRE) (Petorius)
2078 2916 4758

Leney Cottage (IRE) *Alison Thorpe* 104b
7 b g Witness Box(USA) Fleur De Tal (Primitive Rising (USA))
2422[2]

Lennie The Laugh (IRE) *Martin Bosley* 81b
7 b g Frenchmans Bay(FR) Silent Memory (IRE) (Danehill (USA))
433[5]

Lennoxwood (IRE) *Mark Usher*
6 rg g Verglas(IRE) Sigonella (IRE) (Priolo (USA))
2432[P]

Leo Luna *Gary Moore* 133h
5 b g Galileo(IRE) Eva Luna (USA) (Alleged (USA))
1970[6] 4264[3] 4789[15] 5574[5]

Le Pergolese (FR) *Nigel Hawke* 68h 84c
8 b g Sagacity(FR) Rasinixa (FR) (Linamix (FR))
3134[P] 3956[8] 4514[7]
4984[P] 5301[4] 5407[2]

Le Reve (IRE) *Lucy Wadham* 133h 135c
6 br g Milan Open Cry (IRE) (Montelimar (USA))
2063[U] (2249)
2756[U] 3079[3] 3594[4] 4270[P] 4661[2]

Le Rocher (FR) *Nick Williams* 149h
4 b g Saint Des Saints(FR) Belle Du Roi (FR) (Adieu Au Roi (IRE))
(614a) (1741a) 2262a[7] (3360) (3885)

Leroy Parker (IRE) *Barry Murtagh* 94h 94c
6 ch g Titus Livius(FR) Jameela (IRE) (Danehill (USA))
1665[9]
2159[6] 2356[P] 2418[3] 3041[8] 3527[P]

Le Seychellois (FR) *Richard Ford* 79h 98c
14 ch g Mansonnien(FR) Adjirah (FR) (Sicyos (USA))
566[4] 871[P] 1103[2] 1202[P] 1377[6] 1784[P]

Less Time (IRE) *Jonjo O'Neill* 105h
5 br g Oscar(IRE) Woodville Princess (IRE) (Torus)
4135[5] 4598[4] 4904[7]

Letbeso (IRE) *Peter Bowen* 116h
6 ch g Vinnie Roe(IRE) Go Hunting (IRE) (Abednego)
649[2] 878[2]

Letemgo (IRE) *Giles Smyly* 112h
6 b g Brian Boru Leteminletemout (IRE) (Be My Native (USA))
317[4] (1941) 2210[3] 2764[3] 2908[4] 5191[6] 5542[4]

Le Temujin (IRE) *J-Y Artu* 118h
6 b g Hawk Wing(USA) La Paja (IRE) (Galileo (IRE))
263a[2]

Letmespeak (IRE) *Victor Dartnall* 13h
9 b g Tikkanen(USA) Ithastobesaid (IRE) (Lanfranco)
3697[9]

Le Tranquille (FR) *M Rolland* 142h 128c
7 b g Reste Tranquille(FR) Kaer Gwell (FR) (Garde Royale)
406a[P]

Letsby Avenue *Alan King* 138h
6 b g Tikkanen(USA) Peel Me A Grape (Gunner B)
19[2] 374[2] (847) (1201) (1597)

Lets Get Cracking (FR) *Alan Jones* 69h
10 gr g Anabaa Blue Queenhood (FR) (Linamix (FR))
1700[4]

Lets Get Serious (IRE) *James Ewart* 131h 135c
8 b g Overbury(IRE) Vendimia (Dominion)
170[3] 495[6]

Letter Of Credit (IRE) *James Joseph Mangan* 125h 145c
9 br g Bob Back(USA) Common Verse (IRE) (Common Grounds)
4709a[2] 5099a[2] 5474a[15]

Letterofthelaw (IRE) *Rebecca Curtis* 81h
5 b g Old Vic Darrens Lass (IRE) (Montelimar (USA))
2472[4] 2978[12]

Letterpress (IRE) *John Wade* 96h
10 b g King's Theatre(IRE) Empress Of Light (Emperor Jones (USA))
1848[6]

Le Vent D'Antan (FR) *Miss Elizabeth Doyle* 143h
5 b g Martaline Leeloo (JPN) (Dr Devious (IRE))
5200a[2]

Leviathan *Venetia Williams* 131h
7 b g Dubawi(IRE) Gipsy Moth (Efisio)
1960[P] 3012[4] (3201) 4333[F] (4726) 5172[21] 5399[6]

Leviche *Alan King* 87b
4 ch g Shirocco(GER) Alla Prima (IRE) (In The Wings)
2015[4] 2391[3] *2731[5]*

Lewis *David Thompson* 101b
5 b g Kayf Tara Island Of Memories (IRE) (Beneficial)
5499[6]

Lewlaur Supreme (IRE) *William Young Jnr* 80h
11 b g Supreme Leader Dark Dame (IRE) (Norwich)
110[5] 219[5] 536[7] 803[P] 868[11] 1158[5]

Lexicon Lad (IRE) *Tom George* 108h 130c
9 ch g Presenting Hazel's Glory (IRE) (Mister Lord (USA))
(355)

Lexington Blue *Seamus Mullins*
4 b g Bertolini(USA) Jasmine Breeze (Saddlers' Hall (IRE))
5400[F]

Lexi's Boy (IRE) *Donald McCain* 133h
6 gr g Verglas(IRE) Jazan (IRE) (Danehill (USA))
2958[7] 3648[3] ◆ 3891[8]

Leyland (IRE) *Lawney Hill* 90h
5 b g Peintre Celebre(USA) Lasting Chance (USA) (American Chance (USA))
1169[F] 1259[P] 1567[9]

Leyla's Gift *Lydia Richards* 30b
5 b m Milan Leyaaly (Night Shift (USA))
5441[2]

L Frank Baum (IRE) *Bernard Llewellyn* 95h
7 b g Sinndar(IRE) Rainbow City (IRE) (Rainbow Quest (USA))
1595[2] 2011[12]

Liars Poker (IRE) *Oliver Sherwood* 98h
7 b g Beneficial Strong Willed (Strong Gale)
4091[4] 4863[4]

Libation *John Flint*
5 ch m Doyen(IRE) Cream Jug (IRE) (Spectrum (IRE))
1531[U]

Libaute (FR) *M Rolland* 138h
7 gr m High Yield(USA) Libellule (FR) (Highest Honor (FR))
406a[10]

Liberty Court (IRE) *Tim Vaughan* 123h
7 b g Court Cave(IRE) Miss Vikki (IRE) (Needle Gun (IRE))
2949[15] (5235)

Liberty One (IRE) *Richard Woollacott* 126h
8 b g Milan Same Old Story (IRE) (Welsh Term)
3956[2] ◆ (4391) (4820)

Liberty's Gift (IRE) *Paul W Flynn* 133h 122c
6 b g Statue Of Liberty(USA) Raheefa's Mix (IRE) (Linamix (FR))
2069[6]

Lidar (FR) *Alan King* 117h 144c
9 ch g Take Risks(FR) Light Wave (FR) (Marignan (USA))
3170[2] *4020[8]* **4543[9] 5392[4]**

Lie Forrit (IRE) *Lucinda Russell* 141h 129c
10 b g Subtle Power(IRE) Ben Roseler (IRE) (Beneficial)
(1926) 2672[3] ◆ 3108[6] (4954)
5276[P]

Lienosus (IRE) *Evan Williams* 140h 100c
8 b g Old Vic Red Supporter (Priolo (USA))
2079[3] 3060[4] (3784) 4269[7]
4946[3]

Lie To Me (FR) *E Lellouche*
4 b g Slickly(FR) Lady Carole (FR) (Subotica (FR))
1741a[P]

Lieutenant Colonel *D T Hughes* 151h
5 br g Kayf Tara Agnese (Abou Zouz (USA))
4750[6] (5200a) ◆

Lieutenant Miller *Nicky Henderson* 123h
8 b g Beat All(USA) Still Runs Deep (Karinga Bay)
2529[4] 2935[4] 5256[P]

Life And Soul (IRE) *Donald McCain* 132h
7 b g Azamour(IRE) Way For Life (GER) (Platini (GER))
(15) (354) (494) 688[2] (1041) 1350[3] 1987[2]

Life And Times (USA) *John Ferguson* 77h
6 bb g Medaglia d'Oro(USA) Sur Ma Vie (USA) (Fusaichi Pegasus (USA))
383[3]

Life In Bars *Dave Roberts* 16b
4 b f Denounce Judy The Drinker (Snurge)
2318[11]

Life Long (IRE) *Anabel K Murphy* 89h
10 b g Old Vic Be My Rainbow (IRE) (Be My Native (USA))
590[7] 751[P]

Life Of A Luso (IRE) *Paul Henderson* 112h 135c
10 b g Luso Life Of A Lady (IRE) (Insan (USA))
158[P] 3933 **851[14] 1476[9] (1642)**
1971[10]

Life Of Laughter (USA) *Willie Musson* 83h
6 b g Elusive Quality(USA) Country Garden (Selkirk (USA))
427[F]

Lifetime (IRE) *Brian Ellison* 110h
6 b g Shamardal(USA) La Vita E Bella (IRE) (Definite Article)
22[3] 491[4] 967[3] 1922[11] 2198[3] ◆ 2519[3] 2932[12] 3284[4]

Lightening Rod *Michael Easterby* 126h 140c
9 b g Storming Home Bolero (Rainbow Quest (USA))
2064[6] 2519[10] 2958[5] 3088[4]

Lightentertainment (IRE) *Chris Gordon* 101h
6 b g King's Theatre(IRE) Dochas Supreme (IRE) (Supreme Leader)
1864[7] 2272[7] 2711[6] 3434[4]

Lightning Bill *Caroline Bailey*
6 gr g Silver Patriarch(IRE) Lightning Fork (IRE) (Common Grounds)
945[P] 1154[7]

Lightning Moley (IRE) *Tracey Watkins* 77h
11 ch g Lord Of Appeal Arabella Bee (Abednego)
4535[9] 4838[7] 5177[10] 5432[4]

Lightning Strike (GER) *Paul Webber* 118h 145c
11 ch g Danehill Dancer(IRE) La Capilla (Machiavellian (USA))
659[5]

Lights Of Broadway (IRE) *Bernard Llewellyn* 102h 98c
8 b m Broadway Flyer(USA) Supreme Call (IRE) (Supreme Leader)
2663[8] 2896[2] 3420[7] 4676[2] 5037[P]

Light The City (IRE) *Ruth Carr* 111h
7 b g Fantastic Light(USA) Marine City (JPN) (Carnegie (IRE))
2225[7] 2393[6] 2520[5] (2869) 3021[2] (3274) 4608[3]

Light The World (FR) *Kevin Frost* 94h
6 b g Layman(USA) Lignite (IRE) (Priolo (USA))
2013[11] 2877[9] 3047[4] 3426[10]

Like A Diamond (IRE) *Evan Williams* 93h
4 b g Antonius Pius(USA) Silk Law (IRE) (Barathea (IRE))
2881[3]

Likearollingstone (IRE) *Sean Curran* 124h 97c
9 ch g Definite Article Bannow Girl (IRE) (Glacial Storm (USA))
48[5] **431[F]**

Like Clockwork *Mark H Tompkins* 86h
5 b g Rail Link Tenpence (Bob Back (USA))
2783[8]

Like Minded *Dan Skelton* 140h 124c
10 b g Kayf Tara Sun Dante (IRE) (Phardante (FR))
2268[2] (2935) 3646[3] 4264[7] 5158[16]

Like Your Style (IRE) *Edward P Harty* 128h 142c
10 b g Flemensfirth(USA) Alpha Style (GER) (Saddlers' Hall (IRE))
1604a[10]

Lilac Belle *Alex Hales* 90h
8 b m Robellino(USA) Lilac Dreams (Second Set (IRE))
2191[7] 2679[6] 3149[5] 3856[P]

Lillioftheballet (IRE) *Jim Goldie* 101h 43c
7 b m Rakti Lillibits (USA) (Kingmambo (USA))
1544[6] 1785[12] 2306[6] 2794[6] **3519[4] 4815[P]**

Lillybrook (IRE) *Nigel Twiston-Davies* 93h
8 br m Alderbrook Lilly Bolero (Fearless Action (USA))
268[6] 391[2] 738[6]

Lilly's Legend *Mark Walford* 73h
4 ch f Midnight Legend Dalticia (FR) (Cadoudal (FR))
3214[4] 3727[3] 4074[9] 4776[10] 5320[8]

Lily Little Legs (IRE) *Ian Williams* 95h
5 gr m Westerner Silvers Promise (IRE) (Presenting)
3898[6] 4797[5] (5408)

Lily Marie *Mike Hammond*
5 b m Overbury(IRE) Rose Marie (IRE) (Executive Perk)
1499[7]

Lily Mars (IRE) *Neil Mulholland* 72h
7 br m Presenting Tiffany Jazz (IRE) (Good Thyne (USA))
3295[2] *4297[4]* 5026[9] 5308[5] 5547[9]

Lily Potts *Chris Down* 73h
5 gr m Proclamation(IRE) Jucinda (Midyan (USA))
1348[F] 1483[F] 1832[5] 2463[8]

Lily Waugh (IRE) *Anthony Honeyball* 120h
7 b m King's Theatre(IRE) Killultagh Dawn (IRE) (Phardante (FR))
146[2] (1771) 2506[2] 3005[3] 3570[2] (4698) 4961[3] 5370[8]

Lilywhite Gesture (IRE) *Fergal O'Brien* 98b
5 b m Presenting Loyal Gesture (IRE) (Darazari (IRE))
1719[2] *2583[6]*

Limnara (FR) *Mlle D Schnepp*
5 ch m Limnos(JPN) La Clara (FR) (Mansonnien (FR))
703a[P]

Lindengrove *Dave Roberts* 73h 4c
9 ch g Executive Perk Lady Blakeney (Baron Blakeney)
534[7]

Lindenhurst (IRE) *John C McConnell* 135h
4 b g Captain Marvelous(IRE) Royal Jubilee (IRE) (King's Theatre (IRE))
582[2] ◆ (1182) 4784[9] 5470a[3]

Linden Rose *Steph Hollinshead*
5 b m Striking Ambition Inchtina (Inchinor)
3508[7]

Lindsay's Dream *Zoe Davison* 105h 100c
8 b m Montjeu(IRE) Lady Lindsay (IRE) (Danehill Dancer (IRE))
384[4] 2084[6] 2435[4]
3135[2] 3318[U] 4717[5] 5018[3] 5116[9]

Line D'Aois (IRE) *Michael Scudamore* 108b
6 b g Craigsteel Old Line (IRE) (Old Vic)
225[2] (1877)

Lion Na Bearnai (IRE) *Thomas Gibney* 109h 141c
12 b g New Frontier(IRE) Polly Plum (IRE) (Pollerton)
4435a[4] 5171[P] 5474a[11]

Lion On The Prowl (IRE) *Alexandra Dunn* 92h 82c
10 b g Sadler's Wells(USA) Ballerina (IRE) (Dancing Brave (USA))
5435[F]

Lisahane Bog *Peter Hedger* 32h
7 b g Royal Applause Veronica Franco (Darshaan)
177[11] 5402[P]

Lisbon (IRE) *Patrick Griffin* 127h
6 b g Cape Cross(IRE) Caraiyma (IRE) (Shahrastani (USA))
27[2] (475) (870) 1148[4] 1159[3] 1504[2]

Lisdonagh House (IRE) *Lynn Siddall* 98h
12 b g Little Bighorn Lifinsa Barina (IRE) (Un Desperado (FR))
2430[7] 2770[10] 3192[7] 4615[P]

Lisheen Hill (IRE) *Richard Phillips* 105h 55c
8 b g Witness Box(USA) Lady Lamb (IRE) (Executive Perk)
2598[9] 3044[P] 4906[3] 5285[7]

Lisrose (IRE) *Ms Alice Curran* 119h 120c
9 b m Beneficial Clara Rose (IRE) (Good Thyne (USA))
4848a[7]

Listen And Learn (IRE) *Jonjo O'Neill* 121h
6 b g Presenting Loyal Gesture (IRE) (Darazari (IRE))
708[P] 925[4] (1259) 1345[2] (1645) 2050[3] 2764[2]

Listen Boy (IRE) *Nigel Twiston-Davies* 120h 123c
8 ch g Presenting Buckalong (IRE) (Buckskin (FR))
2179[3]

Little Bit Lively (IRE) *Sarah Humphrey* 14h
5 br g Flemensfirth(USA) Miranda's Lace (IRE) (Bach (IRE))
1013[5] 1261[5] 1770[7] 2176[9]

Little Boy Boru (IRE) *S R B Crawford* 110h
6 b g Brian Boru How Is Things (IRE) (Norwich)
3495[3] 3938[5] 4365[3] 4625[3]

Little Carmela *Violet M Jordan* 96h
10 gr m Beat Hollow Carmela Owen (Owington)
320[4] 460[4] 811[8]

Little Chip (IRE) *Charlie Longsdon* 99h 129c
7 b g Dushyantor(USA) Aunt Chris (IRE) (Moscow Society (USA))
(1687)
1748[3] 2394[4] (3026)
5068[P] 5444[5]

Little Cornham (IRE) *Mrs C Fear* 99c
7 b g Moscow Society(USA) Benrue Supreme (IRE) (Supreme Leader)
58[F] 5123[2]

Littledean Jimmy (IRE) *John O'Shea* 43h
9 b g Indian Danehill(IRE) Gold Stamp (Golden Act (USA))
4700[P] 5019[12]

Little Dotty *Giuseppe Fierro* 85b
5 br m Erhaab(USA) Marsh Marigold (Tina's Pet)
372[10] (647)

Little Eaglet (IRE) *Colin Heard* 95h 96c
10 br g Dushyantor(USA) Bagatelle (IRE) (Strong Gale)
42[4] 295[2] (690) 925[13] 1477[P] 4733[5] 5033[4]

Little Fleur (IRE) *Johnny Farrelly* 64b
6 b m Westerner Fleur (GER) (Perugino (USA))
1261[6]

Little Glenshee (IRE) *N W Alexander* 121h 121c
8 gr m Terimon Harrietfield (Nicholas Bill)
2418[2] 2969[2] 3395[F] 3823[F] (4367) 4668[3] **5213[3]**

Little Jimmy *Tom Gretton* 68h 94c
7 br g Passing Glance Sementina (USA) (Silver Charm (USA))
2727[4] 4241[F] 4477[2] 4570[2] 4815[2] (5065)
5437[2]

Little Jon *Nigel Twiston-Davies* 129h
6 b g Pasternak Jowoody (Gunner B)
270[6] 1712[4] 2153[3] 2875[2] 3357[7] 4143[2] 4682[6]
5158[15]

Little King Robin (IRE) *Colin Bowe* 132h 111c
6 b m King's Theatre(IRE) Regle D'Or (FR) (Robin Des Champs (FR))
1893a[3] 1948a[2] 2205a[4] 4740[9] 5199a[4]

Little Legend *Miss C M E Haydon* 122c
10 b g Midnight Legend Amber Bright (Little Wolf)
(165)
(3862) ◆ 4655[4] 5292[4]

Little Louie *Gary Moore* 102b
5 ch g Nomadic Way(USA) Lillie Lou (Tomba)
4296[4] 4473[7] 5264[P]

Little Miss Monty *Mrs S M Farr* 55c
13 b m Silver Owl Miss Montgomery (IRE) (Montekin)
657[7]

Little Pop *Nigel Twiston-Davies* 109h
6 b g Pasternak Flagship Daisy May (IRE) (Kahyasi)
1578[2] (1935) 2492[17] 3390[9]

Little Posh (IRE) *Peter Niven* 88b
5 br m Winged Love(IRE) Lady Oakwell (IRE) (King's Ride)
5381[3]

Little Pudding *Mary Hambro* 33b
6 b m Sleeping Indian Neptunalia (Slip Anchor)
1919[9]

Little Roxy (IRE) *Anna Newton-Smith* 80h
9 b m Dilshaan Brunswick (Warning)
2581[4] 3692[5] 4469[3] 4721[2] 5116[11] 5402[P]

Littleton Lad (IRE) *Zoe Davison* 79b
6 bb g Close Conflict(USA) Knockraha Star (IRE) (Marignan (USA))
4017[16] 4135[7] 4575[7]

Little Windsor *Peter Hiatt* 59b
5 b m Central Park(IRE) Sonderborg (Great Dane (IRE))
1318[7] 1445[5] 1671[11]

Lively Baron (IRE) *Donald McCain* 116h 130c
9 b g Presenting Greavesfind (The Parson)
1852[2] 2246[7] 2670[6] 3521[4] 4572[2] 5215[2]

Living Next Door (IRE) *A J Martin* 120h 135c
8 b g Beneficial Except Alice (IRE) (Orchestra)
2708a[F] 4741[5] ◆

Liz's D'Estruval (IRE) *John Joseph Murphy* 121c
6 b m Presenting Mega D'Estruval (FR) (Garde Royale)
2484a[F] 4848a[6] 5415a[5]

Ll Cool Horse *Tom Gretton* 66b
5 b g Lavirco(GER) Jaxelle (FR) (Lights Out (FR))
395[6] 2507[12] 3816[P]

Local Hero (GER) *Steve Gollings* 143h
7 b g Lomitas Lolli Pop (GER) (Cagliostro (GER))
216[3] 1046[8] 3477[3] 4056[2] 4789[7] 5399[P]

Local Present (IRE) *James Turner* 73h 85c
11 ch g Presenting Local Issue (IRE) (Phardante (FR))
(1876)
2338[P]

Loch Ba (IRE) *Mick Channon* 103h 140c
8 b g Craigsteel Lenmore Lisa (IRE) (Phardante (FR))
2452[2] 2815[14] 3205[2] 3655[4] 4270[3] 4821[P]

Lochnagar (GER) *Venetia Williams* 109h
5 b g Sholokhov(IRE) Lindenblute (Surumu (GER))
4350[3] 4632[4]

Lochnell (IRE) *Brian Ellison* 88b
5 b m Winged Love(IRE) Nothing For Ever (IRE) (Tikkanen (USA))
3727[5] 4240[5] 4647[P]

Lochore (IRE) *William Amos* 79h
8 b g Morozov(USA) Fulgina (FR) (Double Bed (FR))
114[P] 311[6]

Lodgician (IRE) *Nigel Twiston-Davies* 98h 95c
12 b g Grand Lodge(USA) Dundel (IRE) (Machiavellian (USA))
(1078) 1137[5] 1429[3] 1816[3]
1939[7] 2849[2] 3015[P] 4072[6] 4911[12]

Logans Run (IRE) *Mrs S E Busby* 117b 25c
11 b g Shernazar Toposki (FR) (Top Ville)
4922[8]

Logical Approach (IRE) *David Thompson* 102h
7 b g Tikkanen(USA) Anntella (IRE) (Phardante (FR))
(536) 1041[5] 1143[3] 2169[5] 2511[3] 3149[6] 3451[3]
3830[F]

Loin D'Etre Sage (FR) *F Nicolle* 107h 103c
4 b f Sageburg(IRE) Lointaine (USA) (Lyphard's Wish (FR))
(615a)

Loire (CZE) *Pavel Slozil*
6 b m Rainbows For Life(CAN) Lucydara (CZE) (Dara Monarch)
1904a[10]

Lola *Michael Dods* 74b
4 b f Rob Roy(USA) Seamill (IRE) (Lafontaine (USA))
2960[8] 3663[6]

Lola Galli *David Pipe* 97b
6 br m Old Vic Tahoe (IRE) (Marju (IRE))
483[6] 715[3] 1445[2] *2583[3]*

Lombardy Boy (IRE) *Michael Banks* 91h
9 b g Milan Horner Water (IRE) (Over The River (FR))
29[3] 460[7] 1917[7] 2253[P]

Lombok *Gary Moore* 74h
8 b g Hernando(FR) Miss Rinjani (Shirley Heights)
429[9] 1438[7] 1643[5]

London Skolar *James Eustace* 49h
4 b g Tobougg(IRE) Coh Sho No (Old Vic)
4401[F] 4903[15]

Lone Foot Laddie (IRE) *Lucinda Russell* 109h
5 b g Red Clubs(IRE) Alexander Phantom (IRE) (Soviet Star (USA))
344[U] 494[3] 2970[F] 4463[3] 4813[6] (5377)

Lone Ranger (FR) *Venetia Williams* 103h
6 b h Muhtathir L'Etoile De Mer (FR) (Caerleon (USA))
2040[12] 2492[18] 3195[P]

Long Distance (FR) *Lucinda Russell* 104h 90c
9 bb g Storming Home Lovers Luck (IRE) (Anabaa (USA))
17[10]

Long John *Jackie Du Plessis* 104h
7 gr g Silver Patriarch(IRE) Magic Valentine (Magic Ring (IRE))
2691[7]

Long Lunch *Charlie Longsdon* 122h
5 b g Kayf Tara Royal Keel (Long Leave)
(1690) (2002) 3184[F] 3838[2] 4904[2] 5257[2]

Long Run (FR) *Nicky Henderson* 132h 174c
9 b g Cadoudal(FR) Libertina (FR) (Balsamo (FR))
2229[5] 2673[4] 3262[U] (4238)
5171[F]

Long Wave (IRE) *Charlie Longsdon* 108h 113c
7 b g Milan Mrs Avery (IRE) (Supreme Leader)
854[3] (1121) 1565[3] **2046[3] 2431[4] 2722[3] (4759)**
5515[3]

Longwood Lad (IRE) *Carole Ikin* 82b
12 br g Bob's Return(IRE) Longwood Lass (IRE) (Lahiq (USA))
1426[U] 1547[P]

Look For Love *Sue Gardner* 119h
6 b g Pursuit Of Love Look Here's May (Revoque (IRE))
2630[9] 3169[8] 3744[11] 4333[P] 5019[4] 5391[3]

Looking For Mick *Victor Dartnall* 60b
5 ch g Milk It Mick Seeker (Rainbow Quest (USA))
5145[8]

Looking Glass *Tim Easterby* 57h
5 b m Westerner Reflective Way (Mirror Boy)
4749[3] 5354[10]

Looking Hopeful (IRE) *Nicky Henderson* 116h
8 b g Heron Island(IRE) Mahaasin (Bellypha)
186[3] 517[5]

Looking On *Steve Gollings* 118h
6 b g Observatory(USA) Dove Tree (FR) (Charnwood Forest (IRE))
4745[3] 5061[3]

Looking Tanned *Michael Appleby* 80b
5 b g Passing Glance Tanning (Atraf)
1690[4] 2053[9]

Looking Well (IRE) *Nicky Richards* 104b
5 b g Gold Well Different Level (IRE) (Topanoora)
(5560)

Lookout Mountain (IRE) *Jonjo O'Neill* 125h 111c
6 b g Flemensfirth(USA) Thegoodwans Sister (IRE) (Executive Perk)
1388[4] 2202[4] (2253) 2516[2] 2944[4] 3359[8] 4347[5]
4934[5] 5215[4]

Lookoutnow (IRE) *Eoin Doyle* 139h 129c
9 b g Beneficial Rose Ana (IRE) (Roselier (FR))
3868a[12]

Looks Like Magic *Neil King* 96b
5 gr g Fair Mix(IRE) Cirrious (Cloudings (IRE))
1261[4]

Looks Like Power (IRE) *Debra Hamer* 96b
4 ch g Spadoun(FR) Martovic (IRE) (Old Vic)
2015[3] 3460[5]

Lookslikerainted (IRE) *Rebecca Curtis* 130h
7 b g Milan Kilcrea Gale (IRE) (Strong Gale)
5036[2] (5182) 5347[7]

Looks Like Slim *Ben De Haan* 101h 110c
7 b g Passing Glance Slims Lady (Theatrical Charmer)
251[8] 2271[7] **2677[4] 3152[2] 3268[3] 4989[2] 5398[5]**

Loose Chips *Charlie Longsdon* 144h 144c
8 b g Sir Harry Lewis(USA) Worlaby Rose (Afif)
2005[3] 2539[2] (3259)
(3881) 4420[5]

Looselipssinkships (IRE) *William Kinsey* 84b
7 ch g Talkin Man(CAN) Seaward (Slip Anchor)
862[9] 1124[6]

Loose Preformer (IRE) *Michael Hawker* 89h 107c
8 b g Luso Out Performer (IRE) (Persian Bold)
115[4] (449) 554[2] 747[4] 967[2] 1134[4]
3862[2] 4079[P] 5164[P]

Lorain (CZE) *Stepanka Sedlackova*
7 ch h Rainbows For Life(CAN) Lodgia (IRE) (Grand Lodge (USA))
1904a[F]

Lord Aldervale (IRE) *Steve Woodman* 68h
7 br g Alderbrook Monavale (IRE) (Strong Gale)
3138[P] 5258[F]

Lord Bellamy (IRE) *Martin Wilesmith*
12 b g Lord Americo Paean Express (IRE) (Paean)
4511[P]

Lord Brendy *Robert Johnson* 113h
6 gr g Portrait Gallery(IRE) Hervey Bay (Primitive Rising (USA))
1975[6] 2197[7] 2593[2] 3017[4] 4081[4] 4379[3] 5206[2]
(5479)

Lord Carrigross (IRE) *Linda Blackford* 41h
7 b g Gold Well Carrig Ross (Lord Ha Ha)
5016[P] 5117[13] 5389[3]

Lord De Beaufai (FR) *J J Lambe* 96b
6 b g Epalo(GER) Perle De Beaufai (FR) (Epervier Bleu)
1792[2]

Lordenshaws (IRE) *Robert Johnson* 80h
7 bz g Cloudings(IRE) Slaney Rose (IRE) (Roselier (FR))
284[8] 584[8] 2443[5] 4429[P] 4605[5] 4943[8]

Lord Farquaad *Robin Dickin* 24b
5 b g Royal Applause Monkey Madge (Cape Cross (IRE))
1712[14]

Lord Fendale (IRE) *S Donohoe* 98b
5 ch g Erewhon(USA) Upton Lady (IRE) (Lord Upton (IRE))
3002[8] 4226[6]

Lord Fox (IRE) *Shaun Harris* 67h 95c
7 b g Alflora(IRE) Foxfire (Lord Americo)
339[5] 554[3] 2649[5]
2959[4] 3283[U] 3497[2] 3936[5] 4243[6] (4482)
(4795) 5038[4] 5301[9]

Lord Gale (IRE) *John Bryan Groucott* 125h 42c
8 ch g Bach(IRE) Wire Lady (IRE) (Second Set (IRE))
604[8] 808[11]

Lord Grantham (IRE) *Henry Daly* 126h
7 b g Definite Article Last Of Her Line (Silver Patriarch (IRE))
119[2] (479) (777) 1042[P] **3155[F]**

Lord Kennedy (IRE) *Alex Hales* 99h 94c
9 b g Saddlers' Hall(IRE) Minstrel Madame (IRE) (Black Minstrel)
2437[P] 2825[4] 3015[8]

Lord Landen (IRE) *Fergal O'Brien* 98h 112c
9 br g Beneficial Agua Caliente (IRE) (Old Vic)
2427[2]
2825[3] 3595[4] *4301[7]* **(4486)**
4654[U] 4865[9]
(5394)

Lord Lescribaa (FR) *Philip Hobbs* 85h 106c
11 b g Ungaro(GER) Manon Lescribaa (FR) (Trebrook (FR))
522[4] **(692)**
778[8] (1055)
1486[P] 1642[5] 1798[6] 2017[6] 2297[6]

Lord Lir (IRE) *Tim Vaughan* 48h 118c
8 b g Oscar Schindler(IRE) Milford Woman (IRE) (Taipan (IRE))
5112[12]

Lord Louis *P A Jones*
13 b g Sir Harry Lewis(USA) Cute Pam (Pamroy)
94[P]

Lord Luso (IRE) *Philip Kirby* 108h
8 b g Luso Sweet Carol (IRE) (Carroll House)
68[U] 280[3] 512[9]

Lord Navits (IRE) *David Bridgwater* 91h 124c
6 b g Golan(IRE) Nanavits (IRE) (Lord Americo)
122[F] 590[5] 730[8]
(4242) (4488)
(4592) 4919[4]

Lord Of Drums (IRE) *Lucinda Russell* 91h 112c
8 b g Beat Of Drums Treat A Lady (IRE) (Lord Americo)
(882) **1147[2]**
1287[3] (2996)
3143[3] 3478[6] 4222[3] 4822[7] 5318[3] 5666[4]

Lord Of House (GER) *Charlie Mann* 125h 140c
6 ch g Lord Of England(GER) Lake House (IRE) (Be My Guest (USA))
2282[3] 2643[4] 3057[3] (3294)
3429[2] (3732)
4159[4] 4515[3]

Lord Of Scotland (FR) *Alan King* 125h
5 gr g Lord Du Sud(FR) Etoile Rose (IRE) (Montjeu (IRE))
4307[3] 4805[P]

Lord Of The Dunes *Colin Tizzard* 107h 107c
6 b g Desert King(IRE) Dame Fonteyn (Suave Dancer (USA))
(83) 521[4]
3690[5] 3960[2] 4372[P] 5126[9] 5304[8]

Lordofthehouse (IRE) *Tom George* 126h
6 ch g Danehill Dancer(IRE) Bordighera (USA) (Alysheba (USA))
1889[R] 2758[P]

Lord Prestige (FR) *M Rolland* 156h 123c
7 b g Kapgarde(FR) Prestige Girl (FR) (Prestigieux (FR))
406a[2] 685a[5] 1901a[4] 2240a[2] 5577a[6]

Lord Protector (IRE) *Philip Hobbs* 127h
7 b g Oscar(IRE) Warts And All (IRE) (Commanche Run)
(2932) 3661[5] (4413) 4805[9] 5384[13]

Lord Redsgirth (IRE) *Lucy Normile* 97h 102c
9 ch g Flemensfirth(USA) Wisebuy (IRE) (Mister Lord (USA))
341[5] 883[9] 3939[P] 4222[P]

Lordship (IRE) *Tom Gretton* 82h 71c
10 b g King's Best(USA) Rahika Rose (Unfuwain (USA))
1519[2] 1633[8] 2090[2]
2677[5]

Lord Usher (IRE) *George Charlton* 104h
7 b g Lord Americo Beet Five (IRE) (Seclude (USA))
3392[4] 4234[3] 4550[8]

Lord Westhead (IRE) *Danielle McCormick* 60b
5 b g Bach(IRE) Dawning Day (IRE) (Shernazar)
2981[8] 3415[7]

Lord Wheathill *Lisa Williamson*
7 b g Tobougg(IRE) Classic Quartet (Classic Cliche (IRE))
807[F]

Lord Windermere (IRE) *J H Culloty* 139h 170c
8 b g Oscar(IRE) Satellite Dancer (IRE) (Satco (FR))
2815[8] 3376a[7] 4183a[6] (4787)

Lorikarad (FR) *Miss C C Jones*
10 b g Roakarad Loriana (FR) (Welkin (CAN))
3801[7] 4511[P]

Los Amigos (IRE) *J T R Dreaper* 129h 137c
7 br g Overbury(IRE) Lady Shackleton (IRE) (Zaffaran (USA))
3868a[2] ◆

Los Nadis (GER) *Jim Goldie* 120h 96c
10 ch g Hernando(FR) La Estrella (GER) (Desert King (IRE))
1289[4] 1541[4] 2345[4]
2996[4] 3475[2] 4058[5] 4650[P] 5559[7]

Lost Arca (FR) *Robin Mathew* 95h
8 b g Lost World(IRE) Luarca (Robellino (USA))
730[9] 1051[3] 1405[9] 2181[2]

Lost Glory (NZ) *Jonjo O'Neill* 118h 145c
9 b g Montjeu(IRE) Joie De Vivre (NZ) (Zabeel (NZ))
(448) **851[3]**
1971[15] 3091[P] 4769[P]

Lost In Newyork (IRE) *Nick Kent* 97h
7 b g Arakan(USA) Lace Flower (Old Vic)
1170[3] 1379[9] 1820[F] 2191[4] 2787[9] (2898) 3328[6]
3650[5] 4398[2]

Lost Legend (IRE) *Jonjo O'Neill* 112h 137c
7 b g Winged Love(IRE) Well Orchestrated (IRE) (King's Ride)
(45) **(656)**
900[4] 1076[3] 1195[U] (1330) 1581[6] **2714[4] 4418[6]**
(4806) ◆ 5156[P] 5385[7]

Lots Of Memories (IRE) *P G Fahey* 154h
7 b g Jammaal Remember Rob (IRE) (Deep Society)
1893a[2] (2256a) 2706a[4] 2983a[3] 3380a[P]

Lotus Pond (IRE) *Alan King* 100h
6 b g Beneficial Capard Lady (IRE) (Supreme Leader)
2426[4] 2876[6] 4904[9]

Loudmouth (IRE) *Charlie Longsdon* 121h 118c
7 br g Milan Grandy Invader (IRE) (Presenting)
1916[2] ◆

Loughalder (IRE) *Matt Sheppard* 93h 128c
8 ch g Alderbrook Lough Lein Leader (IRE) (Supreme Leader)
2290[3] 2578[2] 2979[6] (4402)
(4704) 4962[11]

Lough Coi (IRE) *Anthony Middleton* 104h 107c
8 b g Insatiable(IRE) Roisin Dove (IRE) (Grand Plaisir (IRE))
2078[4] 2194[2] 2367[6] 2727[6] 2804[P] 3325[4] 3635[4]
4109[2] 4354[2] 4481[2]
4657[2] 4968[5]
5453[3]

Lough Derg Way (IRE) *Jamie Snowden* 116h 124c
8 b g Dushyantor(USA) Lotschberg Express (Rymer)
(179) **(636)**
◆ 859[6] 1579[P] 5284[4]

Lough Kent *Nicky Henderson* 130h 118c
5 b g Barathea(IRE) King's Doll (IRE) (King's Best (USA))
4264[P] 4785[20]

Louis Ludwig (IRE) *Tim Vaughan* 104h 93c
9 b g Mull Of Kintyre(USA) Fantastic Bid (USA) (Auction Ring (USA))
489[4] 650[13]
1014[2] 1328[3] 2062[6]

Louis Pasteur (IRE) *D L Drake* 98h 86c
9 b g Luso Aokay (IRE) (Roselier (FR))
571[10] 413[8]

Louis Phillipe (IRE) *Linda Blackford* 85h 88c
7 ch g Croco Rouge(IRE) Presenting's Wager (IRE) (Presenting)
174[9] 479[5] **2599[3]**

Loukhaar (IRE) *Jonathan Geake* 85b
6 b g Westerner Gold Air (Sri Pekan (USA))
5310[6]

Lovcen (GER) *Alan King* 109h 129c
9 b g Tiger Hill(IRE) Lady Hawk (GER) (Grand Lodge (USA))
2100[3] 2672[12]

Lovely As (FR) *Emmanuel Clayeux* 100h
5 b m Assessor(IRE) Line Lovely (FR) (Mansonnien (FR))
703a[9]

Lovely Muck *Nigel Twiston-Davies* 95h
9 b m Alflora(IRE) Madam Muck (Gunner B)
1364[8] 1700[7]

Love Marmalade (IRE) *Alistair Whillans* 94h
4 ch g Duke Of Marmalade(IRE) Green Castle (IRE) (Indian Ridge)
3474[4] 3781[6] 4199[P] 4647[3]

Love On Top (IRE) *John J Walsh* 124h
6 b m Westerner Supreme Eile (IRE) (Supreme Leader)
4846a[4] ◆

Love Rory (IRE) *E Bolger* 139h 128c
6 b g Winged Love(IRE) Lonely Teardrop (IRE) (Spanish Place (USA))
4754[10]

Loves Blind (IRE) *Pat Murphy* 86b
5 b g Fruits Of Love(USA) Naughty Marietta (IRE) (Good Thyne (USA))
4810[8] 5181[9]

Lovey Dovey (IRE) *Simon West* 115h
10 b m Winged Love(IRE) Dansana (IRE) (Insan (USA))
(932) (1634) 5370[P]

Low Gales (IRE) *Charlie Mann* 105h
8 b g Dr Massini(IRE) Glorious Gale (IRE) (Strong Gale)
2468[P] 2786[4] 3044[7] 4545[P]

Loxlade (FR) *F Nicolle* 130h 118c
4 b f Sholokhov(IRE) Minesota (FR) (Danehill (USA))
130a[2]

Loxley Mezile *Simon Earle* 49h
5 br m Strategic Prince Haiti Dancer (Josr Algarhoud (IRE))
4988[11] 5245[9]

Loyaute (FR) *Chris Down* 134h
7 ch m Green Tune(USA) Iles Marquises (IRE) (Unfuwain (USA))
353[3] 2084[5] 2371[7] 3117[2] (4129) 4392[4] (4920)
5370[3]

L Stig *Henry Daly* 81h
4 b g Striking Ambition Look Here's May (Revoque (IRE))
2926[7] 4904[F]

Lua De Itapoan *Malcolm Jefferson* 110h
9 gr m Silver Patriarch(IRE) Gotogeton (Le Moss)
(4381) 5059[4]

Lucanor (IRE) *Paul Webber* 91h
6 b g Indian Danehill(IRE) Persian Avenue (IRE) (Persian Mews)
185[9] 2393[10]

Lucas Pitt *Michael Scudamore* 72h
7 b g Kyllachy Bardot (Efisio)
2285[8] 2614[13] 3605[P]

Lucax (FR) *M Seror*
4 b f Lugny(FR) Calyx (FR) (Irish River (FR))
2781a[P]

Lucematic *Chris Grant* 112h
8 b m Systematic Soldier's Song (Infantry I)
310[7]

Lucette *Richard Woollacott* 53h
6 b m Overbury(IRE) Winnow (Oats)
46[8] 292[0] 458[4] 592[10] 1479[P]

Lucette Annie *S J Partridge* 111c
10 ch m Alflora(IRE) Running For Annie (Gunner B)
61[4] 4788[11]

Luci Di Mezzanotte *Oliver Sherwood* 120h 118c
6 ch m Sulamani(IRE) Dissolve (Sharrood (USA))
85[2] (450) 706[2] 2675[3] 4542[4] 4961[9] 5370[7]

Luckster *David Evans* 73h
4 b g Lucky Story(USA) Bisaat (USA) (Bahri (USA))
3161[14] 4450[5] 4569[8] 4883[9]

Luckwell Bridge *Kevin Bishop*
9 b g Baryshnikov(AUS) Good Skills (Bustino)
2011[U] 2280[P]

Lucky Cody (IRE) *Brian Ellison* 97h
5 b g Blueprint(IRE) Ware Vic (IRE) (Old Vic)
2347[7] 2621[4] 2954[P] 4428[P] **5192[F]**

Lucky Emily *John Mackie* 82b
5 b m Central Park(IRE) Father's Pride (Karinga Bay)
3016[5] 4895[8]

Lucky G (IRE) *Keith Dalgleish* 84b
5 b m Celtic Swing Deemeh (IRE) (Brief Truce (USA))
682[3]

Lucky Landing (IRE) *Tony Coyle* 118h 135c
8 bb g Well Chosen Melville Rose (IRE) (Phardante (FR))
787[3] 900[5] 1204[4] (1285)
(1390) 1470[2] 1730[3] (1921)
4543[7] 4790[8] 5156[16] 5378[4]

Lucky Lane (IRE) *Jane Clark* 86c
9 b g Saddlers' Hall(IRE) Zuhal (Busted)
510[3]

Lucky Lukey *Jennie Candlish* 100h 87c
8 gr g Cape Town(IRE) Imprevue (IRE) (Priolo (USA))
322[5] 503[2]

Lucky Prince *Brian Eckley* 102h
7 b g Lucky Owners(NZ) Sun Bonnet (Grand Lodge (USA))
3428[6] 5282[6]

Lucky Sovereign (IRE) *Rebecca Curtis* 84b
5 b g Kayf Tara Chakoss (FR) (Nikos)
250[5]

Lucky Sun *Philip Kirby* 103h
8 b g Lucky Owners(NZ) Sun Bonnet (Grand Lodge (USA))
145[P] 1791[3] 2596[5] 2974[9]

Lucky Sunny (IRE) *Venetia Williams* 102h 118c
11 b g Pasternak Flying Fur (IRE) (Elbio)
3414[P] 3833[3] 4131[F] 4352[2] 4477[U] 5118[3]
5549[P]

Lucky Thirteen *Richard Phillips* 51h
6 b g Passing Glance Lingua Franca (Formidable (USA))
1016[2] 2745[3] 4904[10]

Lucky To Be Alive (IRE) *Peter Bowen* 90h
7 bb g Presenting Praisethepreacher (IRE) (Sharifabad (IRE))
145[6] 1169[4] 1565[5] 1631[F] 1917[4]
2088[P]

Lucky Vic (IRE) *Barry Brennan* 39h 89c
8 b g Old Vic Graphic Lady (IRE) (Phardante (FR))
45[4] 585[9] 1134[P]

Luctor Emergo (IRE) *Keith Dalgleish* 109h
5 b g Amadeus Wolf Batilde (IRE) (Victory Piper (USA))
2596[P] (2999) 5059[8]

Lucys Girl (IRE) *Jamie Snowden* 89h
7 b m Portrait Gallery(IRE) Bubbleover (IRE) (Hubbly Bubbly (USA))
755[6] 1017[U] 1090[F] (1432) 1529[6] 1824[5] 5242[14]

Lucy's Legend (IRE) *Paul Henderson* 94h 106c
8 b m Norwich Townhall (IRE) (Roselier (FR))
236[7] 632[5] 832[3] 1197[5] 1767[4] 2270[P] 2629[5]

Luggers Hall (IRE) *Tony Carroll* 95h
6 b g Cape Cross(IRE) Saabga (USA) (Woodman (USA))
1378[10] 2292[F]

Luimneach Abu (IRE) *J P Broderick* 120h
6 b g High Chaparral(IRE) Mamlakah (IRE) (Unfuwain (USA))
(891a)

Lukey Luke *James Turner* 86h 100c
11 b g Kayf Tara Skiddaw Samba (Viking (USA))
(20) **(224)**
555[P] 2334[4] 2784[3] 3107[F] 4078[P]

Lukeys Luck *Jennie Candlish* 112h 114c
8 b g Cape Town(IRE) Vitelucy (Vettori (IRE))
566[6] 726[2] 859[7] 1012[3] 1135[3] 1327[4]

Lulu's Gift (IRE) *Michael Mullineaux* 76h
8 gr m Lahib(USA) She's A Gift (Bob's Return (IRE))
376[10] 810[5] 927[9] 1265[7]

Lumpys Gold *Paul Nicholls* 116h
6 b g Tikkanen(USA) Elegant Accord (IRE) (Accordion)
2009[2] 2631[2] 2908[2] 5391[8]

Lunar Legend *Lucinda Russell* 38h
5 b m Generous(IRE) Reivers Moon (Midnight Legend)
4958[12] 5206[P]

Lundy Sky *Tony Newcombe* 118h
9 b g Zaha(CAN) Rosina Mae (Rousillon (USA))
4393[2] 5074[8]

L'Unique (FR) *Alan King* 147h
5 b m Reefscape Sans Tune (FR) (Green Tune (USA))
2226[6] 2533[12] 4158[3] 4740[3] 5370[2] (5574)

Lupita (IRE) *Derrick Scott* 85h 74c
10 ch m Intikhab(USA) Sarah (IRE) (Hernando (FR))
461[6] 2290[P] 4884[9] 5433[7]

Lusiad (IRE) *Karl Thornton* 47c
12 b g Luso Black Dale (IRE) (Burslem)
866[7]

Luv U Whatever *Jo Hughes* 51h
4 b g Needwood Blade Lady Suesanne (IRE) (Cape Cross (IRE))
582[5]

Lydon House *Barry T Murphy* 111c
15 ch g Lancastrian The Mount (Le Moss)
509[P]

Lymm Grey *Jo Davis* 77b
5 gr m Fair Mix(IRE) Ellie Bee (Primitive Rising (USA))
1869[14] 2752[11] 3228[3] *4296[13]*

Lypharez *Y-M Porzier* 109h
7 b g Doyen(IRE) Lumiere D'Espoir (FR) (Saumarez)
263a[P]

Lyreen Legend (IRE) *D T Hughes* 148h 165c
7 b g Saint Des Saints(FR) Bint Bladi (FR) (Garde Royale)
3376a[5] 4183a[5] 4787[6]

Lyric Street (IRE) *Donald McCain* 118h
6 b g Hurricane Run(IRE) Elle Danzig (GER) (Roi Danzig (USA))
3735[3] 4103[8] 4429[F]

Lysino (GER) *Chris Grant* 103h
5 ch g Medicean Lysuna (GER) (Monsun (GER))
2169[4] 2449[3] 2794[5] 3210[2] 3527[4] 4187[6]

Lyssio (GER) *Jim Best* 116h
7 b g Motivator Lysuna (GER) (Monsun (GER))
(593) 848[2] (994) 1107[2] 1627[P]

Lyvius *Nicky Henderson* 140h 125c
6 b g Paolini(GER) Lysuna (GER) (Monsun (GER))
2211[4] 3066[2] (3648) 4056[4] 4785[8] 5158[17]

Mabel Tasman *Neil Mulholland* 112h 112c
8 ch m Midnight Legend West Coast (Forty Niner (USA))
481[7]

Mac Aeda *Malcolm Jefferson* 123h 133c
10 gr g Kayf Tara Altogether Now (IRE) (Step Together I (USA))
2199[3] 2674[F]

Macarthur *David Rees* 113h
10 b g Montjeu(IRE) Out West (USA) (Gone West (USA))
140[10] 517[4] 691[2] 783[8] 856[2] 1072[3] 2045[3]
2467[10] 3007[6]

Mac Beattie *Evan Williams* 59h 71c
8 b g Beat All(USA) Macnance (IRE) (Mandalus)
145[F] 854[7] **921[8] 1174[6] 1314[4]**

Mac Bertie *Evan Williams* 73h
5 b g Beat All(USA) Macnance (IRE) (Mandalus)
4844[8]

Macbeth (IRE) *Tim Vaughan* 107h
5 b g Acclamation Filandre (Cadeaux Genereux)
2002[3]

Maccabees *Roger Curtis* 63h
5 b g Motivator Takarna (IRE) (Mark Of Esteem (IRE))
2581[6] 3009[8] 3692[6] 4471[4] 4721[9] 4967[8] 5402[6]

Macgillycuddy *Harriet Graham* 48h
5 b g And Beyond(IRE) Tofino Swell (Primitive Rising (USA))
2223[6]

Macgregor's Ace *N W Alexander* 71b
5 ch g Tobougg(IRE) Bridge Pal (First Trump)
497[7]

Mackeson *Chris Bealby* 22h
5 gr g Baryshnikov(AUS) Travelling Lady (Almoojid)
2602[18] 3735[U] 4075[P]

Macklycuddy (USA) *Rebecca Menzies* 97h 73c
8 b g Monashee Mountain(USA) Exellensea (USA) (Exbourne (USA))
2202[P] 2333[P] 2596[6]

Mac Le Couteau *Evan Williams* 66h
6 b g Overbury(IRE) Macnance (IRE) (Mandalus)
477[8] 1176[10] 1341[7]

Macra Na Feirme (IRE) *Debra Hamer* 81b
11 br g Exit To Nowhere(USA) De Derri (IRE) (Denel (FR))
2148[9] **2887[P]**

Ma Cranky (IRE) *Chris Grant* 34h
6 b m Flemensfirth(USA) Northern Mill (IRE) (Distinctly North (USA))
2973[7]

Mac's Grey (IRE) *Zoe Davison* 72h 79c
7 gr g Great Palm(USA) Gypsy Kelly (IRE) (Roselier (FR))
95[9] 484[7] 2008[12] 2573[5] *4019[10]* **4890[4] 5398[U]**

Mac's Return (IRE) *Paul Nicholls* 59h
7 b g Flemensfirth(USA) Dark Mist (IRE) (Mister Lord (USA))
3182[P]

Mac Steamy (IRE) *William Kinsey* 108h
8 ch g Bienamado(USA) Aroseforclare (Royal Vulcan)
68[F] 4161[P] **4399[P]**

Madame De Guise (FR) *Nicky Henderson* 110h
5 b m Le Balafre(FR) Paradana (FR) (Dress Parade)
2089[4] 2600[7] (5018) 5191[P]

Madame Flirt *Dianne Sayer* 34b
5 b m Generous(IRE) Parisienne Gale (IRE) (Lapierre)
2871[5] 3529[7]

Madame Jasmine *Suzy Smith* 118h 85c
9 gr m Karinga Bay Roslin (Roscoe Blake)
302[P]

Madam Lilibet (IRE) *Sharon Watt* 95h
5 b m Authorized(IRE) Foxilla (IRE) (Foxhound (USA))
2516[F] 2842[7] 3192[5] 3525[2] 4201[3] 4478[4] 4577[P]

Madam Noso *Richard King* 80h
10 ch m Riverwise(USA) Lady Noso (Teenoso (USA))
99[10] 2473[9] 3174[P]

Mad Brian (IRE) *Mrs Gillian Callaghan* 141h 150c
8 b g Brian Boru Needle Doll (IRE) (Needle Gun (IRE))
2708a[2] 3404a[6]

Made In Time (IRE) *Rebecca Curtis* 125h 131c
9 bb g Zagreb(USA) No Easy Way (IRE) (Mandalus)
4092[2] (4355)
4788[F]

Madeira Girl (IRE) *Jonjo O'Neill* 97h
5 b m Bachelor Duke(USA) Last Cry (FR) (Peintre Celebre (USA))
49[P] 391[7] 2896[P]

Mad Jack Mytton (IRE) *Jonjo O'Neill* 91b
4 b g Arcadio(GER) Gilt Ridden (IRE) (Heron Island (IRE))
2436[2] 5338[4]

Mad Moose (IRE) *Nigel Twiston-Davies* 119h 156c
10 ch g Presenting Sheshollystar (IRE) (Fourstars Allstar (USA))
2532[6] 2952[P]

Madness Light (FR) *Warren Greatrex* 130h 120c
5 b g Satri(IRE) Majestic Lady (FR) (Octagonal (NZ))
2695[2] (3092) (3430) 3889[P] 4786[P]

Madox (FR) *J Bertran De Balanda* 101h 131c
10 b g Trempolino(USA) Musareva (FR) (Turgeon (USA))
863a[10]

Mad Professor (IRE) *John Cornwall* 81h 76c
11 b g Mull Of Kintyre(USA) Fancy Theory (USA) (Quest For Fame)
65[5] 183[2] 378[2] 694[3] 807[7] 964[2] 1149[6] 2349[4]
2576[4] 2849[5] 4247[P] 4762[4]
5442[P]

Ma Du Fou (FR) *Warren Greatrex* 107b
4 bb g Le Fou(IRE) Belle Du Ma (FR) (Zamindar (USA))
(5500)

Maestro Royal *Nicky Henderson* 109b
5 b g Doyen(IRE) Close Harmony (Bustino)
2759[2] 4986[4]

Ma Filleule (FR) *Nicky Henderson* 136h 164c
6 gr m Turgeon(USA) Kadaina (FR) (Kadalko (FR))
2713[3]
3082[P] (3321)
4738[2] (5156)

Maften (IRE) *Victor Thompson* 41h 39c
11 b g City Honours(USA) Mafiosa (Miami Springs)
28[6]

Maggie Aron *James Hughes* 82h
8 gr m Generous(IRE) Pems Gift (Environment Friend)
145[3] 844[13] 932[4] 1000[5]

Maggie Blue (IRE) *Harriet Graham* 99h 48c
6 b m Beneficial Top Ar Aghaidh (IRE) (Topanoora)
27[9] 1790[8] (2497) 2842[3] 2974[6] **4771[5]**

Maggio (FR) *Patrick Griffin* 131h 144c
9 b g Trempolino(USA) La Musardiere (FR) (Cadoudal (FR))
1545[5] 1752[4] (1788)
2358[2] 3759[7] 3776[2] (4552)
5569[5]

Maghero (FR) *P Peltier* 137h
5 b g Poliglote Madragoa (FR) (Kaldoun (FR))
683a[P]

Magical Island *Sarah Kerswell* 77h
11 gr g Thowra(FR) Alice's Mirror (Magic Mirror)
1051[6]

Magical Legend *Sarah Kerswell* 55h 52c
13 gr m Midnight Legend Alice's Mirror (Magic Mirror)
757[U] 1197[P]

Magical Treasure *Sarah Kerswell* 87h 91c
10 gr g Riverwise(USA) Alice's Mirror (Magic Mirror)
1320[9]
1644[3] 1701[R] 1837[P]

Magic Guest (FR) *B Jollivet* 99h
6 ch g Red Guest(IRE) L'Astree (FR) (Tropular)
455a[10]

Magic Money *Kim Bailey* 113h
6 b m Midnight Legend Sticky Money (Relkino)
41[5] (1814) 2476[3] 2764[P] (5229) 5486[3]

Magic Present *Malcolm Jefferson* 104h 80c
7 b g Presenting Magic Bloom (Full Of Hope)
(497) 790[4] 2355[5] 2866[2] 3208[3] 3726[5] 4553[12]
5559[8]

Magic Skyline (IRE) *Brian Ellison* 110h
4 b f Refuse To Bend(IRE) Grecian Air (FR) (King's Best (USA))
2557[4] (2733) 3474[5] (3613) 4305[6] 4466[2]

Magna Cartor *Nicky Henderson*
4 b g Motivator Hora (Hernando (FR))
3229[2]

Magnifique Etoile *Charlie Longsdon* 152h
7 b g Kayf Tara Star Diva (IRE) (Toulon)
(2087) ◆ 2665[F] 4752[16]

Magnum Too (IRE) *Beth Roberts*
5 b g Westerner Glenair Lucy (IRE) (Luso)
4030[9]

Mahab El Shamaal *Alan Jessop*
6 b g Motivator Soliza (IRE) (Intikhab (USA))
2783[P]

Mahican (IRE) *John Ferguson* 109h
4 b g Cape Cross(IRE) Dark Indian (IRE) (Indian Ridge)
(2975) 3857[P] 4345[5]

Mahogany Blaze (FR) *Nigel Twiston-Davies* 69h 117c
12 b g Kahyasi Mahogany River (Irish River (FR))
392[7] 2646[F] 3882[9]

Mahrajaan (USA) *C Byrnes* 121h 127c
11 b g Machiavellian(USA) Karen S (USA) (Kris S (USA))
1001a[4]

Maid Of Might (IRE) *Laura Young* 85b
6 b m Flemensfirth(USA) Kestral Heights (IRE) (Eagle Eyed (USA))
85[8] 588[8]

Maid Of Silk (IRE) *Neil Mulholland* 101h 103c
8 b m Blueprint(IRE) Silk Style (Polish Precedent (USA))
248[3] 942[4] (1336)
1437[P] 1942[4]

Mail De Bievre (FR) *Tom George* 127h 140c
9 b g Cadoudal(FR) Coyote Davis (IRE) (Kaldoun (FR))
2415a[4] 3362[3] ◆

Main Reason (IRE) *Evan Williams* 73b
6 b m Golan(IRE) Regents Dream (Deep Run)
2892[8]

Ma'Ire Rua (IRE) *Alan Jones* 84h
7 ch g Presenting Long Acre (Mark Of Esteem (IRE))
1974[12] 2711[0] 2906[11] 3988[5] 4987[3]

Maisiefantaisie *Tom Symonds* 63b
7 b m Zafeen(FR) Cumbrian Concerto (Petong)
338[6]

Maison De Ville (GER) *Brian Ellison* 115h
6 b m Sholokhov(IRE) Morbidezza (GER) (Lecroix (GER))
2883[6] 3757[3] (4304) (4743)

Maison Royale *Seamus Durack* 82h
6 b g Val Royal(FR) Rock Villa (Class Distinction)
99[11] 637[P]

Maizy Missile (IRE) *Mary Evans* 96h 96c
12 b m Executive Perk Landsker Missile (Cruise Missile)
43[8] 377[3] 632[10] (1086)
1186[2] 1638[4]

Majaales (USA) *Tom George* 117h
11 b g Diesis Roseate Tern (Blakeney)
263a[11] 734[6]

Majala (FR) *Tom George* 135h 146c
8 b g Lavirco(GER) Majae (FR) (Dom Pasquini (FR))
2081[2] ◆ **3333[F] 3806a[P] 4160[5] 4559[7] (5535)**

Majaresca (FR) *E Lecoiffier*
9 b g Maresca Sorrento(FR) Majamone (FR) (Carmont (FR))
2384a[F]

Majestic Bull (USA) *Sue Gardner* 96h
8 bb g Holy Bull(USA) Croissant (USA) (Lycius (USA))
17[F] 178[3] 640[12] 829[12]

Majestic Concorde (IRE) *D K Weld* 141h 160c
11 b g Definite Article Talina's Law (IRE) (Law Society (USA))
1168a[15]

Major Dolois (FR) *Patrice Quinton* 90h 105c
8 gr g Majorien Ruaha River (FR) (Villez (USA))
1214a[3] 1532a[P] 2384a[P]

Majorica King (FR) *Oliver Sherwood* 96h 121c
8 b g Kahyasi Majorica Queen (FR) (Kaldoun (FR))
(30) **369[F]**
2797[7] 3325[2] 4077[4] 5068[3] 5497[F]

Major Ivan (IRE) *Malcolm Jefferson* 105b
5 b g Fruits Of Love(USA) Martinstown Queen (IRE) (Saddlers' Hall (IRE))
4958[2] 5560[2]

Major Malarkey (IRE) *Nigel Twiston-Davies* 112h 133c
11 b g Supreme Leader Valley (IRE) (Flemensfirth (USA))
355[5] 509[F] 2487[10] (2923)
3655[P] 4962[7] 5348[2]

Major Martin (IRE) *Gary Moore* 93h
5 b g Flemensfirth(USA) Miss Emer (IRE) (Be My Native (USA))
1712[11] 2316[U] 2520[6] 2826[6] 5116[14] 5459[6]

Major Milborne *Jamie Snowden* 112h
6 ch g Exit To Nowhere(USA) Motown Melody (IRE) (Detroit Sam (FR))
2728[2] 3175[2] 3697[3] 4715[6]

Major Parkes *Donald McCain* 75h
4 gr g Fair Mix(IRE) My Melody Parkes (Teenoso (USA))
1813[6] 2154[4] 5227[9]

Major Ridge (IRE) *Robert Bewley* 91b
5 b g Indian Danehill(IRE) Native Novel (IRE) (Be My Native (USA))
4671[5] 5109[5] 5324[8]

Makadamia *David Pipe* 109h
5 b m Kahyasi Makounji (FR) (Tip Moss (FR))
2298[2] 2752[8] 3961[5] 4910[4] 5124[4]
Makari *Nicky Henderson* 136h 131c
7 b g Makbul Seraphim (FR) (Lashkari)
(1913) ◆ (2045) 2213[7] (3088) 4785[17]
Makbullet *Michael Smith* 125h 110c
7 gr g Makbul Gold Belt (IRE) (Bellypha)
4549[5]
Make A Fuss *Gerry Enright* 33h
5 gr m Proclamation(IRE) Fustaan (IRE) (Royal Applause)
5400[7]
Make A Track (IRE) *C F Swan* 142h 156c
8 ch g Hernando(FR) Tracker (Bustino)
4435a[P] 5474a[P]
Makellys Blackpool *Richard Ford* 68h
5 b m Sir Harry Lewis(USA) Pondimari (FR) (Marignan (USA))
531[4] 2559[8] 2767[12] 3334[5]
Make Me A Fortune (IRE) *Steve Gollings* 111h
6 bb g Heron Island(IRE) Biora Queen (IRE) (Old Vic)
(389) 1919[4] 2426[2] 2621[7] 3270[2] 3851[2] 4347[9] 5075[P]
Makethe Mostofnow (IRE) *Evan Williams* 119h 130c
9 b g Milan Pass The Leader (IRE) (Supreme Leader)
2080[9] 2652[4] 3130[3] 3359[9] 4028[3]
(4490) 5184[4] 5430[6]
Makhzoon (USA) *N W Alexander* 119h 82c
10 bb g Dynaformer(USA) Boubskaia (Niniski (USA))
1656[7] 2158[P] (2746) 2844[4] 3499[2] (4002) 4365[2] 5208[6] 5534[7]
Mala Beach (IRE) *Gordon Elliott* 156h
6 b g Beneficial Peppardstown (IRE) (Old Vic)
2408a[2] 3374a[3] (3866a)
Maldivian Reef (IRE) *Alan King* 98b
6 ch g Reefscape Spirited Soul (IRE) (Luso)
3049[3]
Malibu Rock *Suzy Smith* 105h
6 b g Tiger Hill(IRE) High Straits (Bering)
2864[4] *4296[10]* 4993[5] 5257[5]
Malibu Sun *Ben Pauling* 106h 121c
7 ch g Needwood Blade Lambadora (Suave Dancer (USA))
2599[P] 3008[2] 3876[4] 4723[5] (5027)
(5144)
Malin Bay (IRE) *Nicky Richards* 127h
9 b g Milan Mirror Of Flowers (Artaius (USA))
681[3] (867) 1042[5] 1430[4] 1660[3] 2100[P]
Maljimar (IRE) *Nick Williams* 67h 125c
14 b g Un Desperado(FR) Marble Miller (IRE) (Mister Lord (USA))
199a[3] 1214a[5] 1683a[3] (2384a)
Maller Tree *David Dennis* 124h 88c
7 b g Karinga Bay Annaberg (IRE) (Tirol)
1594[6] 2538[7] 2944[10] (3471) 3646[P]
4027[P] 4517[4] 4864[3] 5183[2] (5434) (5493)
Mallowney (IRE) *Timothy Doyle* 135h 152c
8 br g Oscar(IRE) Silkaway (IRE) (Buckskin (FR))
3928a[F] 4314a[2] ◆
Mallusk (IRE) *Shaun Lycett* 86h 104c
9 b g Exit To Nowhere(USA) Saucy Nun (IRE) (Orchestra)
1797[8]
2194[4] 2700[P] 3281[6] 3696[P] 3883[6]
Malt Master (IRE) *Nicky Henderson* 126h 136c
7 b g Milan Dantes Profit (IRE) (Phardante (FR))
1969[12] 2452[P] 2949[10] 4051[9]
Mam Ratagan *Heather Main* 63h 104c
13 b g Mtoto Nika Nesgoda (Suave Dancer (USA))
2440[4] 2977[7]
Manadam (FR) *Ian Williams* 88h 88c
11 b g Mansonnien(FR) Cadoudame (FR) (Cadoudal (FR))
601[4] 690[8]
Manaus Opera (FR) *E Lecoiffier* 99h 92c
7 gr g Kendor(FR) Garota Da Ipanema (FR) (Sillery (USA))
198a[F]
Manballandall (IRE) *Fergal O'Brien* 123h
6 b g Flemensfirth(USA) Omas Lady (IRE) (Be My Native (USA))
2288[4]
Mandarin Sunset (IRE) *James Ewart* 112h 123c
7 ch g Presenting Danatello (FR) (Dress Parade)
22[7] 313[2] 676[2] (2792)
3142[4] 5480[2]
Mandy's Boy (IRE) *Ian Williams* 108h
4 b g Kyllachy African Queen (IRE) (Cadeaux Genereux)
2750[4] 2927[6] 2975[2] 3768[4] 4345[7] 4722[2] 5090[7]
Man From Moscow *Mrs H Norman* 63c
11 b g Gleaming(IRE) Mosta (IRE) (Moscow Society (USA))
325[P] 4443[3]
Manger Hanagment (IRE) *Barry Brennan* 120h 126c
9 br g Heron Island(IRE) Island Religion (IRE) (Religiously (USA))
78[4] 596[5] 996[6] 1194[4] 1352[3] 1493[5]
Mangonel *Jo Davis* 92h 65c
10 ch m Beckett(IRE) Apachee Flower (Formidable (USA))
264[6] 650[7] 829[10]
Manhattan Mead *Michael Madgwick* 65h
4 ch g Central Park(IRE) Honey Nut (Entrepreneur)
3719[6] 4810[9] 5341[4]
Manics Man *Helen Nelmes* 84h
9 ch g Double Trigger(IRE) No Near Miss (Nearly A Hand)
9[P]
Man In Black (FR) *Nick Williams* 102h
5 gr g Turgeon(USA) Mimosa De Wasa (FR) (Roakarad)
1937[5]
Mannered *John Wade* 82h 95c
9 b g Alflora(IRE) Manettia (IRE) (Mandalus)
555[5] 2201[4] 3635[P] 3834[3] 4380[U] 4577[7]
5104[6] 5321[3]
Mannish Boy (FR) *F-M Cottin* 111h
4 b g Poliglote Polissena (FR) (Midyan (USA))
1741a[3]
Man Of Leisure *Anthony Honeyball* 139h
10 b g Karinga Bay Girl Of Pleasure (IRE) (Namaqualand (USA))
(640) ◆ (669) (719) 812[2] (1045) (1155)
1343[F] 1433[U] 1564[2] 1954[6] 2433[6]
Man Of Principles (IRE) *Stuart Coltherd* 45h 37c
11 bb g Bob Back(USA) Shuil Le Gaoth (IRE) (Strong Gale)
311[P] 630[8] 1379[11] **1655[P]**
Man Of Steel (IRE) *Peter Bowen* 107h
5 b g Craigsteel Knappogue Honey (IRE) (Anshan)
14[6] (483) (768) (1013) 1856[5] 2049[4] 2285[3] 2648[3]
Manogue Supreme (IRE) *Neil Mulholland* 97h 96c
8 b m Oscar(IRE) Dunmanogue (IRE) (Supreme Leader)
4795[4] 5498[P]
Manor Brook (IRE) *Charlie Longsdon* 73b
6 b m Westerner Fey Macha (IRE) (Phardante (FR))
4043[11]
Manshoor (IRE) *Lucy Wadham* 98h
9 gr g Linamix(FR) Lady Wells (IRE) (Sadler's Wells (USA))
598[3] 902[7]
Mansonien L'As (FR) *Donald McCain* 83h 107c
8 b g Mansonnien(FR) Star Des As (FR) (Kaldou Star)
2619[3] (3277)
3797[3] 4382[5] 4773[2]
Mantles Heath (IRE) *Paul Cowley* 55b
6 br g Beneficial Bobs Lass (IRE) (Bob's Return (IRE))
14[10] 270[12]
Man With Van (IRE) *S R B Crawford* 136h 125c
8 b g Milan Delibonne (IRE) (Erdelistan (FR))
4670[2]
Many Clouds (IRE) *Oliver Sherwood* 139h 157c
7 br g Cloudings(IRE) Bobbing Back (IRE) (Bob Back (USA))
(2242)
2658[2] (3331)
4262[2] 4751[8] 5154[4]
Many Levels *John Quinn* 79h
4 br g Nayef(USA) Polygueza (FR) (Be My Guest (USA))
1439[5]
Manyriverstocross (IRE) *Alan King* 139h 148c
9 b g Cape Cross(IRE) Alexandra S (IRE) (Sadler's Wells (USA))
(2282)
2950[6] 4033[2] 4742[7] (5091)
5275[5]
Manyshadesofblack (IRE) *Tina Jackson* 58h
6 b m Tikkanen(USA) Wynyard Dancer (Minster Son)
2885[7] 3110[P] 4479[P] 5354[9]
Many Stars (IRE) *Dan Skelton* 113h
6 b g Oscar(IRE) Tempest Belle (IRE) (Glacial Storm (USA))
2181[7] 2874[2] (4761) 5256[8]
Maoi Chinn Tire (IRE) *Jennie Candlish* 119h 104c
7 b g Mull Of Kintyre(USA) Primrose And Rose (Primo Dominie)
(505) 812[7] 973[4] 1042[11]
1503[F] 1780[P]
Maple Valley Gale (IRE) *Liam Lennon* 86h 96c
10 b m Winged Love(IRE) Deerpark Gale (IRE) (Strong Gale)
802[U]
Maple Valley Gold (IRE) *Liam Lennon* 109h
6 b m Generous(IRE) Deerpark Gale (IRE) (Strong Gale)
5379[8]
Ma Pretention (FR) *Robert Collet* 112h
6 b m Great Pretender(IRE) Makaldoun (FR) (Kaldounevees (FR))
863a[0]
1583a[P]
Maraased *Stephen Hughes* 93h
9 b g Alhaarth(IRE) Fleeting Rainbow (Rainbow Quest (USA))
648[5] 852[3]
Maraweh (IRE) *Lucinda Russell* 93h
4 b g Muhtathir Itqaan (USA) (Danzig (USA))
5205[4] 5531[5]
Marble Walk (IRE) *Richard Rowe* 97h 58c
9 b g Oscar(IRE) Clowater Lassie (IRE) (Phardante (FR))
2430[P]
2741[3] 3138[P]
4716[6]
March Seventeenth (IRE) *Brian Ellison* 78h
6 br g Flemensfirth(USA) Palesa Accord (IRE) (Accordion)
3831[P] 4546[7] 4772[7] 4956[9]
Marcilhac (FR) *Venetia Williams* 134h 124c
5 b g Smadoun(FR) One Way (FR) (Exit To Nowhere (USA))
3136[2] ◆ (3552) 4805[2] ◆
Marcomax (FR) *J Planque* 86h 86c
8 b g Ballingarry(IRE) Rose Beryl (FR) (Lost World (IRE))
1623a[2]
Marcus Antonius *Jim Boyle* 119h 118c
7 b g Mark Of Esteem(IRE) Star Of The Course (USA) (Theatrical (IRE))
97[3] (488) 1665[6] **2726[2] 3183[6] 3551[U] 3690[P] 5340[6]**
Mardood *P Wilson*
9 b g Oasis Dream Gaelic Swan (IRE) (Nashwan (USA))
4837[P]
Marfleet *Mrs D Walton* 45h 71c
14 b g Prince Daniel(USA) Gay Broad (Gay Fandango (USA))
112[P]
Margaret Baker *Ronald Harris* 64b
4 b f Windsor Castle Daisy Leigh (Crested Lark)
4916[10]
Margh Arhansek (IRE) *Tony Newcombe*
7 gr g Heron Island(IRE) Molls Rose (IRE) (Coquelin (USA))
4632[P]
Maria's Choice (IRE) *Jim Best* 88h
5 b g Oratorio(IRE) Amathusia (Selkirk (USA))
5008[7] 5175[9]
Marico (FR) *Tom Symonds* 87h 90c
6 bb g Lavirco(GER) Mary Bay (FR) (Tel Quel (FR))
(241) 460[6] 969[P] **1150[5] 1300[P]** (1635) 1820[6]
Ma Ridge *Sarah-Jayne Davies*
10 ch g Tumbleweed Ridge Ma Barnicle (IRE) (Al Hareb (USA))
1487[P]
Marie Deja La (FR) *Chris Gordon* 101h
8 b m Daliapour(IRE) Comedie Divine (FR) (Lesotho (USA))
490[5] 543[3] (711) 925[7] 1436[4] 1645[4] 1945[9] 2312[6] 2715[3] 4472[6] 4676[3] 5260[3] 5402[3]
Marie Des Anges (FR) *Anthony Honeyball* 80h 118c
6 b m Ballingarry(IRE) No Coincidence (IRE) (Indian Ridge)
2194[P] 3742[5] 4392[P]
4948[4]
Mariet *Suzy Smith* 87h
5 ch m Dr Fong(USA) Medway (IRE) (Shernazar)
2265[12] 2564[5] 2858[8] 3140[6] *4493[7]* 5116[6] 5402[7]
Marina Blue *Dave Roberts* 51b
5 b m Norse Dancer(IRE) Davana Blue (FR) (Epervier Bleu)
1094[5]
Marine Band *Sue Smith* 68h
8 b g Bandmaster(USA) Darakah (Doulab (USA))
3017[10]
Marishi Ten (IRE) *Jo Davis* 21h
4 b f Invincible Spirit(IRE) Scripture (IRE) (Sadler's Wells (USA))
5393[9]
Marito (GER) *W P Mullins* 153h 156c
8 b g Alkalde(GER) Maratea (USA) (Fast Play (USA))
2552a[2]
Marju King (IRE) *Phil Middleton* 106h 79c
8 b g Marju(IRE) Blue Reema (IRE) (Bluebird (USA))
1597[3] 1783[3] **3729[P]** *4020[7]* **4970[9]** 5066[6] 5402[P]
Marju's Quest (IRE) *David Dennis* 105h
4 b g Marju(IRE) Queen's Quest (Rainbow Quest (USA))
2455[4] 2750[6] 3161[8] 5365[5] 5552[7]
Markadam *Dianne Sayer* 105h 122c
8 b g Mark Of Esteem(IRE) Elucidate (Elmaamul (USA))
169[3] 4835[2]
Markami (FR) *Johnny Farrelly* 55h
4 ch g Medicean Marque Royale (Royal Academy (USA))
4722[8] 4987[5] 5117[12]
Markem (IRE) *Rose Dobbin* 111h
7 ch g Beneficial Dummy Run (IRE) (Glacial Storm (USA))
2035[P] 2245[5] (3639) (3922) 4338[10] 4957[6]
Market Option (IRE) *Venetia Williams* 101h 106c
8 b g Lord Americo Ticklepenny (IRE) (In The Wings)
2314[14] 3013[7] 3821[5] 4351[5] **4970[4] 5309[3]**
Markttag *Jonjo O'Neill* 86h
4 b g Manduro(GER) Makhsusah (IRE) (Darshaan)
4307[5] 4807[10]
Mark Twain (IRE) *Kim Bailey* 111h 116c
7 b g Rock Of Gibraltar(IRE) Lady Windermere (IRE) (Lake Coniston (IRE))
12[5] 698[5]
Marky Bob (IRE) *Hugo Froud* 115h 122c
9 b g Turtle Island(IRE) Bobomy (IRE) (Bob Back (USA))
57[2] 287[3] 655[2] 3093[P] 3431[6] 5458[4]
Marlborough House *Chris Grant* 93h
4 b g Dylan Thomas(IRE) Eurolink Raindance (IRE) (Alzao (USA))
2168[5] 2750[7] 4003[3] 4460[4] 4941[7] 5163[7]
Marlee Massie (IRE) *N W Alexander* 63h
5 b g Dr Massini(IRE) Meadstown Miss (IRE) (Flemensfirth (USA))
682[7] 2037[13] 2337[8] 3392[8] 4038[4] 4774[P] 5556[6]
Marlee Mourinho (IRE) *N W Alexander* 81h
8 br g Pushkin(IRE) Spur Of The Moment (Montelimar (USA))
2968[10] 3495[8] 3935[5] 4607[3]
Marleno (GER) *Anthony Middleton* 101h 97c
8 b g Lecroix(GER) Mondalita (GER) (Alkalde (GER))
4072[7]
4723[2] 4970[6] 5243[U] 5380[4]
Marley Roca (IRE) *Paul Webber* 112h 129c
10 bb g Tamayaz(CAN) Gaye Gordon (Scottish Reel)
93[6] **392[5]**
2785[3] 3065[6] *4303[12]* **4661[5] 5127[U] 5290[5]**
Marlpit Oak *J H Young* 68c
9 b m Midnight Legend Lonicera (Sulaafah (USA))
326[4]
Marmalade Man *Seamus Mullins* 94h
8 ch g Karinga Bay Kentford Duchess (Jupiter Island)
2641[2] 2908[7] 3553[3] 4071[4] 4803[2] 5022[6]
Marmas *John Mackie* 108h
5 ch g Sir Percy Kitabaat (IRE) (Halling (USA))
449[3] (897) 1391[7] (1689) 2345[5]
Marodima (FR) *Jamie Snowden* 143h 143c
11 b g Robin Des Pres(FR) Balbeyssac (FR) (Beyssac (FR))
419[5]
Marrakech Trader (NZ) *Rose Dobbin* 89h
7 ch g Pentire Eastern Bazaar (IRE) (King Persian)
2037[U] 2422[5] 3935[3] 4364[F] 5102[6]
Martalin (FR) *Patrice Quinton* 103h
8 b g Martaline Stanelme (FR) (Kashtan (FR))
(1424a)
Martello Tower (IRE) *Ms Margaret Mullins* 128h
6 b g Milan Johnsalice (IRE) (Zaffaran (USA))
4708a[4]
Martial Law (IRE) *David Pipe* 18h
8 ch g Galileo(IRE) Tree Tops (Grand Lodge (USA))
3989[12]
Martin Cash (IRE) *Paul Henderson* 99h 105c
8 b g Oscar(IRE) Native Singer (IRE) (Be My Native (USA))
(4633)
4795[3] 5342[5]
Martin Chuzzlewit (IRE) *Martin Todhunter* 77h
5 ch g Galileo(IRE) Alta Anna (FR) (Anabaa (USA))
4221[6] 4889[P]
Mart Lane (IRE) *Dr Richard Newland* 135h 146c
9 br g Stowaway Western Whisper (IRE) (Supreme Leader)
(2180)
2365[6] 3091[3] (3389)
3897[P] 4544[9] 5156[P] 5383[P]
Martys Mission (IRE) *Miss Becky Furber* 106h 116c
12 b g Zaffaran(USA) Parson's Lodge (IRE) (The Parson)
3993[F] 4355[2] (4518)
5094[4]
Marufo (IRE) *Tracey L Bailey* 90h 113c
12 b g Presenting Bucks Cregg (IRE) (Buckskin (FR))
4057[7] 4348[7] 5131[5]
Mary May *Susan Corbett*
6 b m Ferrule(IRE) Leighten Lass (IRE) (Henbit (USA))
885[9]
Mary Milan (IRE) *Malcolm Jefferson* 104h
7 b m Milan Pristina (IRE) (Mandalus)
2447[6]
Masked Man (IRE) *Charlie Mann* 58h 116c
11 ch g Alhaarth(IRE) Misbegotten (IRE) (Baillamont (USA))
387[P]
Masquerade (IRE) *Warren Greatrex* 116h
5 b g Fruits Of Love(USA) Beechill Dancer (IRE) (Darnay)
2053[2] *2439[3]* (3061) 3920[3] 4808[5] 5057[3] 5426[3]
Masquerading (IRE) *Jonjo O'Neill* 81h
4 b g Singspiel(IRE) Moonlight Dance (USA) (Alysheba (USA))
3768[5]
Massachusetts *Rob Summers* 77h
7 ch g Singspiel(IRE) Royal Passion (Ahonoora)
264[F] 903[4] 1105[F] 1171[6]
Massannie (IRE) *David Pipe* 127h
6 b m Dr Massini(IRE) Bathwick Annie (Sula Bula)
(502) (755) (922) 1045[F] 3689[2] 4600[2] 4961[P]
Massena (IRE) *Venetia Williams* 118h 143c
7 b g Marju(IRE) Mayara (IRE) (Ashkalani (IRE))
247[4] (2628)
2797[2] 3431[2] (3596)
(4241) (4341)
4515[2] 5003[2] 5064[2] **5306[3] 5573[8]**
Massini Lotto (IRE) *John Quinn* 120h
7 b g Dr Massini(IRE) Our Lot (IRE) (Phardante (FR))
164[F]
Massinimoss (IRE) *Ross O'Sullivan* 68h
9 b g Dr Massini(IRE) Collybrook Lady (IRE) (Mandalus)
881[5]
Massini's Maguire (IRE) *Tim Vaughan* 121h 129c
13 b g Dr Massini(IRE) Molly Maguire (IRE) (Supreme Leader)
4346[10] 4732[3] 5156[13]
Massini's Trap (IRE) *J A Nash* 136h
5 b g Dr Massini(IRE) Sparrow's Trap (IRE) (Magical Wonder (USA))
2206a[4] 3184[4] 3910a[8] 5172[19]
Master Benjamin *Jeremy Scott* 120h
7 b g Fair Mix(IRE) Morning Flight (IRE) (Supreme Leader)
1991[3]
Master Bud *Susan Corbett* 75h
9 b g Endoli(USA) Future Romance (Distant Relative)
115[P] 1281[6] 4776[6] 5056[P] 5494[11]
Master Butcher (IRE) *Rebecca Curtis* 112h
7 b g Court Cave(IRE) Carleen Gold (Carlingford Castle)
1712[3] 2279[6] 2808[3] 4356[3] 5285[8]
Master Cardor Visa (IRE) *Emma Baker* 94h
9 br g Alderbrook Princess Moodyshoe (Jalmood (USA))
99[2] 254[3] 1945[10] 2470[8] 2690[10] 4275[10]
Master Conor (IRE) *Henry Hogarth*
8 b g Classic Cliche(IRE) Shuil Iontach (IRE) (Oscar (IRE))
4775[P]
Master Cynk *Tom George* 100h
7 ch g Diableneyev(USA) Model View (USA) (Distant View (USA))
3189[7] 3716[6] 3872[11] 4132[P] 5556[4]
Master Dee (IRE) *Donald McCain* 116h
5 b g King's Theatre(IRE) Miss Lauren Dee (IRE) (Montelimar (USA))
3147[2] (3640) 4343[3] 5008[3]
Master Dennis *Dan Skelton* 91b
5 b g Fair Mix(IRE) Rose Alto (Adonijah)
1523[5]
Masterful Act (USA) *Alan McCabe* 85h
7 ch g Pleasantly Perfect(USA) Catnip (USA) (Flying Paster (USA))
1443[3] *4328[2]*
Masterleaderman (IRE) *Michael Smith* 113h
6 b g Beneficial Atagirl (IRE) (Supreme Leader)
2342[3] (3392) 4814[4] 5256[10]
Master Malt *Jonjo O'Neill* 117h
6 b g Milan Mrs Malt (IRE) (Presenting)
4343[8] 4693[8] 5403[4]
Master Mariner (IRE) *Paul Henderson* 100c
10 ch g Safety Catch(USA) Mariners Flow (IRE) (Lanfranco)
5551[2]

Master Max *Jeremy Scott* 39h
7 b g Reset(AUS) Folly Finnesse (Joligeneration)
4171[10]
Master Medic (IRE) *Mrs S Alner* 71h 118c
13 b g Dr Massini(IRE) Name A Reason (IRE) (Buckskin (FR))
(297)
Master Milan (IRE) *Jonjo O'Neill* 114h 127c
8 b g Milan English Clover (Tina's Pet)
378[P]
Master Murphy (IRE) *Jane Walton* 96h 45c
9 b g Flemensfirth(USA) Awbeg Beauty (IRE) (Supreme Leader)
2336[4] 2819[6] 3210[3] 4553[7] 4774[3] (5106)
Master Neo (FR) *Nigel Hawke* 63h 121c
8 gr g Turgeon(USA) Really Royale (FR) (Garde Royale)
3097[4] 3858[F] 4678[4] (5180)
5299[5]
Master Of The Game (IRE) *Nicky Henderson* 138h 138c
8 ch g Bob's Return(IRE) Lady Monilousha (IRE) (Montelimar (USA))
2813[17] (3892) 4785[25]
Master Of The Hall (IRE) *Micky Hammond* 108h 91c
10 b g Saddlers' Hall(IRE) Frankly Native (IRE) (Be My Native (USA))
2229[F] 2822[8] 3285[P] 4040[5] 4670[4] 4897[8] 5105[4]
5379[9]
Master Of The Sea (IRE) *Nigel Twiston-Davies* 144h
7 b g Misternando Sea Gale (IRE) (Strong Gale)
2672[P]
Master Overseer (IRE) *David Pipe* 131h 146c
11 b g Old Vic Crogeen Lass (Strong Gale)
3655[P] 4557[5]
Master Rajeem (USA) *Nigel Twiston-Davies* 99h
5 bb g Street Cry(IRE) Rajeem (Diktat)
2197[6] 2471[2] 2874[7] 5036[P]
Master Red (IRE) *Donald McCain* 125h
5 b g Red Clubs(IRE) Glory Days (GER) (Tiger Hill (IRE))
2453[2] 2806[F] 4234[F] (4811) (5296)
Masters Hill (IRE) *Colin Tizzard* 136h 136c
8 gr g Tikkanen(USA) Leitrim Bridge (IRE) (Earl Of Barking (IRE))
(2009)
2373[P] 3081[2] 3654[2] 4786[5]
Master Spider (IRE) *Susan Corbett* 61b
5 b g Scorpion(IRE) Penteli (Double Trigger (IRE))
4611[12]
Master T (USA) *Peter Bull* 85h 85c
15 b g Trempolino(USA) Our Little C (USA) (Marquetry (USA))
328[F]
Master Ted (IRE) *Jennie Candlish* 79h
8 b g Overbury(IRE) Romantic Gesture (IRE) (Mister Lord (USA))
317[P] 558[4] 729[7]
Master Todd (IRE) *Grant Cann* 115h 115c
9 ch g Dream Well(FR) Falika (FR) (Hero's Honor (USA))
4395[P] 4672[3] 4903[3] 5550[3]
Master Vintage *Richard Phillips* 94b
6 b g Kayf Tara What A Vintage (IRE) (Un Desperado (FR))
4824[5] ◆ 5181[8]
Master Wells (IRE) *James Frost* 80h
13 b g Sadler's Wells(USA) Eljazzi (Artaius (USA))
407[6] 522[2] 1105[8]
Master Wickham (IRE) *Paul Webber* 97h
5 b g Darsi(FR) Beechberry (IRE) (Shernazar)
2724[7] 4343[9] 4971[4]
Master Workman (IRE) *David Kemp* 107c
8 b g Posidonas Bobbie Magee (IRE) (Buckskin (FR))
5435[2]
Matako (FR) *Caroline Keevil* 102h 109c
11 b g Nikos Verabatim (FR) (Pampabird)
1699[7] 1940[8] 2690[3] 2980[5] 3425[2]
Material Boy *Barry Leavy* 74h 83c
7 b g Karinga Bay Material Girl (Busted)
1886[4] 2633[4] 2979[P] 4822[6] 5185[F]
Materiana (IRE) *Andrew Hollinshead* 23b
6 bb m Presenting Jay Lo (IRE) (Glacial Storm (USA))
2298[15] 2724[10] 3733[8]
Matmata De Tendron (FR) *Andrew Crook* 89h 87c
14 gr g Badolato(USA) Cora Des Tamarix (FR) (Iron Duke (FR))
(2339)
2594[3] 3022[7]
Ma Toolan (IRE) *John Mackie* 103h
7 b m Presenting Killoughey Fairy (IRE) (Torus)
1575[P]
Matripajo (IRE) *Jonjo O'Neill* 87h
5 br g Westerner Una Juna (IRE) (Good Thyne (USA))
1869[11] 3163[13] 4535[P] 4959[8] 5341[5]
Matrow's Lady (IRE) *Neil Mulholland* 122h
7 b m Cloudings(IRE) I'm Maggy (NZ) (Danseur Etoile (FR))
2099[P]
Matthew Riley (IRE) *Philip Kirby* 131h
7 b g Dr Massini(IRE) Helorhiwater (IRE) (Aristocracy)
2671[10] 3207[2] 4347[2]
Mattie's Passion (IRE) *Jennie Candlish* 74h
7 b g Helissio(FR) Backrow Passion (IRE) (Commanche Run)
1793[12] 1935[11]
Mauricetheathlete (IRE) *Martin Keighley* 92h 97c
11 b g Sayarshan(FR) Ardagh Princess (Proverb)
358[19] 1797[10] 2288[12]
2867[3] 3730[8] *4326[5]* **4678[F]** 4913[7] 5520[10]
Maurisca (FR) *Richard J Bandey* 85h 106c
9 b g Maresca Sorrento(FR) Maurise (FR) (April Night (FR))
4936[3]
Mawaakef (IRE) *J R Jenkins* 85h
6 b g Azamour(IRE) Al Euro (FR) (Mujtahid (USA))
593[7]
Max Bygraves *Kim Bailey* 95h 123c
11 ch g Midnight Legend Smokey Diva (IRE) (Orchestra)
3065[3] 4886[3] 5092[9]
Maxdelas (FR) *Roy Brotherton* 95h
8 ch g Sabrehill(USA) Quendora (FR) (Kendor (FR))
661[4] 854[5] 1938[13] 2679[F] 3047[10] 3428[5] 4703[6]
5522[3]
Maxed Out King (IRE) *Sue Smith* 113h
6 ch g Desert King(IRE) Lady Max (IRE) (Mandalus)
3640[4] 3920[2] ◆ 4075[6] 5354[P]
Maxford Lady (IRE) *Jamie Snowden* 67h
5 b m Presenting Berkeley House (IRE) (Beneficial)
5077[11] 5393[6]
Maxi Chop (FR) *Paul Nicholls* 125h
6 b g Muhaymin(USA) Scotch Mockery (FR) (Persifleur (USA))
2111[2] 2492[4] 3066[8]
Maxilian (IRE) *Emma Lavelle* 29h
5 b g Milan Super Size (IRE) (Shernazar)
3016[4] 5071[8] 5541[P]
Maxi Mac (IRE) *Trevor Wall* 91h
4 ch g Thousand Words Crimada (IRE) (Mukaddamah (USA))
1813[4] 2466[9] 4722[10] 5238[8] 5490[10]
Maxim Gorky (IRE) *Noel Meade* 137h
7 b g Montjeu(IRE) Altruiste (USA) (Diesis)
3910a[7]
Maxi's Lady (IRE) *David Rees* 67h
7 b m Gold Well Macs Belle (IRE) (Topanoora)
1706[8] 1885[9] 2312[P] 2620[5]
Max Laurie (FR) *Michael Banks* 68h
9 bl g Ungaro(GER) Laurie Mercurialle (FR) (Dom Pasquini (FR))
2877[8]
Max The Minister *Hughie Morrison* 94b
4 bl g Pastoral Pursuits Franciscaine (FR) (Legend Of France (USA))
4909[2] 5264[4]
Max Ward (IRE) *Charlie Brooks* 124h
5 b g Milan Made Easy (IRE) (Rudimentary (USA))
1599[6] 1819[5] 4594[4] 4931[8] (5236) ◆
Mayan Flight (IRE) *Tony Carroll* 90h
6 b g Hawk Wing(USA) Balimaya (IRE) (Barathea (IRE))
758[3] 857[5] 1152[12]
Maybe I Wont *James Moffatt* 117h
9 b g Kyllachy Surprise Surprise (Robellino (USA))
2420[3] 2958[6] (3271) 3832[3] 4550[9] 4941[5] 5379[7]
May Be Some Time *Stuart Kittow* 112h
6 ch g Iceman Let Alone (Warning)
3034[6] 4758[3] 5174[2]
Mayfair Music (IRE) *Nicky Henderson* 136h
5 br m Presenting Native Bid (IRE) (Be My Native (USA))
2506[5] (2907) ◆ (4542)
Maygo's Joy *Suzy Smith*
4 b g Josr Algarhoud(IRE) Nikki Bea (IRE) (Titus Livius (FR))
5190[P]
May Hay *Anthony Carson* 91b
4 b f Dubai Destination(USA) Trounce (Barathea (IRE))
2318[3] 3167[2] 3663[2] 4561[3]
Maypole Joe (IRE) *Raymond York*
4 b g Iffraaj Spanish Needle (Green Desert (USA))
1743[P]
Maypole Lass *Renee Robeson* 98h
4 ch f Halling(USA) Maigold Lass (Mark Of Esteem (IRE))
2557[3] 2934[4] 3385[4] 4531[7] 4917[2] 5229[3]
May's Boy *James Moffatt* 104h
6 gr h Proclamation(IRE) Sweet Portia (IRE) (Pennekamp (USA))
2340[4] 2998[2] 5377[3]
Mazuelo (FR) *G Cherel* 137h 128c
6 b g Poliglote Jolie Mome (FR) (Art Francais (USA))
406a[8] 685a[10]
Mazurati (IRE) *Ben Case* 100b
5 b g Definite Article Mazuma (IRE) (Mazaad)
5070[4] 5447[5]
Mazuri Cowboy (IRE) *Eoin Doyle* 136h 130c
9 b g Pilsudski(IRE) Kabale (IRE) (Ikdam)
3866a[7]
McCabe Creek (IRE) *Alan King* 103b
4 b g Robin Des Pres(FR) Kick And Run (IRE) (Presenting)
4561[2] 5173[15]
Mccauley (IRE) *Robert Walford* 99h 125c
11 b g Vettori(IRE) Tintinara (Selkirk (USA))
31[10] 264[17]
McIlhatton (IRE) *Paul Nicholls* 130h
6 b g Fruits Of Love(USA) Penny Haven (IRE) (Camden Town)
(3) 410[2] 3263[6] 3892[2] (5258)
Mclovin (IRE) *S R B Crawford* 116h
8 b g Winged Love(IRE) Clive's Choice (IRE) (Executive Perk)
3495[4] 3935[2]
Mcmonagle (USA) *Alan Brown*
6 ch g Mizzen Mast(USA) Dippers (USA) (Polish Numbers (USA))
5295[P]
Mcmurrough (IRE) *Malcolm Jefferson* 131h 144c
10 b g Spectrum(IRE) Sensitive (IRE) (Posen (USA))
2671[5] 3661[3] **4039[U] 4346[3] 5276[P]**
Mcnulty Wray (IRE) *Ferdy Murphy*
6 b g Westerner Lyphard Abu (IRE) (Lyphard's Special (USA))
584[13]
Mcvicar *Alan King* 124h 114c
5 b g Tobougg(IRE) Aries (GER) (Big Shuffle (USA))
2366[3] 2910[4] **5031[9]**
Meadowcroft Boy *Alistair Whillans* 122h
5 b g Kayf Tara Blackbriery Thyne (IRE) (Good Thyne (USA))
(2840) 3778[3]
Meadstown (IRE) *Mark Shears*
6 gr g Talkin Man(CAN) Little Rose (IRE) (Roselier (FR))
2858[13]
Me And Ben (IRE) *Fergal O'Brien* 100h 115c
7 b m Revoque(IRE) Rare Gesture (IRE) (Shalford (IRE))
765[4] 932[3] ◆ 1043[2] 1321[2] (1373) 1529[2] 1731[2]
3030[4] 3203[6]
4482[2] 4966[3] 5246[4] (5369)
Medal Of Valour (JPN) *Mark Gillard* 60h
6 b g Medaglia d'Oro(USA) Tres Tres Joli (USA) (Gone West (USA))
3956[P] 4988[8]
Medburn Cutler *George Baker* 59b
4 ch g Zafeen(FR) Tiegs (IRE) (Desert Prince (IRE))
4267[8] 4561[8]
Medermit (FR) *Alan King* 145h 157c
10 gr g Medaaly Miss D'Hermite (FR) (Solicitor (FR))
4265[4] 4766[8]
Medieval Chapel (FR) *Nicky Henderson* 124h
6 gr g Ballingarry(IRE) Best Ever (FR) (Kaldoun (FR))
3182[4] 4052[3]
Medinas (FR) *Alan King* 156h
7 bb g Malinas(GER) Medicis (FR) (Sicyos (USA))
2228[2] 2814[2] 4767[7] 5572[5]
Meet Henry *Rayson Nixon* 56b
5 b g Common World(USA) Tyspane (Zilzal (USA))
4958[9] 5324[7]
Meetings Man (IRE) *Ali Brewer* 122h
7 gr g Footstepsinthesand Missella (IRE) (Danehill (USA))
(784)
Meetmeatthemoon (IRE) *Philip Hobbs* 102b
5 gr m Flemensfirth(USA) Valleya (FR) (Linamix (FR))
3656[2] 4403[4] (4916)
Meet The Critics (IRE) *Jonjo O'Neill* 110h 111c
11 b g Rashar(USA) Rose Basket (IRE) (Roselier (FR))
265[P]
Meglio Ancora *Richard Ford* 77h
7 ch g Best Of The Bests(IRE) May Fox (Zilzal (USA))
184[6]
Meilyr *Mrs C Lawrence* 96c
11 b g Relief Pitcher Cahermone Lady (IRE) (Cardinal Flower)
4518[3] 4915[F] 5131[P]
Meirig's Dream (IRE) *Philip Hobbs* 78h 78c
8 b g Golan(IRE) Women In Love (IRE) (Danehill (USA))
2004[2] 2291[4] **3015[3] 3595[P] 5027[7]**
Meister Eckhart (IRE) *Alan King* 150h 139c
8 bb g Flemensfirth(USA) Carrabawn (Buckskin (FR))
2374[P] 4441[2] 4752[13] 5138[3]
Melancholy Hill (FR) *Yannick Fouin* 93h 81c
4 b f My Risk(FR) Rouge Pivoine (FR) (Lost World (IRE))
615a[5]
Melbourne Lady *P Fegan* 94b
6 b m Hawkeye(IRE) Red Barons Lady (IRE) (Electric)
5560[4]
Mellow Manner (IRE) *A J McNamara* 58h
6 b m Iffraaj Prince's Passion (Brief Truce (USA))
891a[11]
Melodic Rendezvous *Jeremy Scott* 157h
8 ch g Where Or When(IRE) Vic Melody (FR) (Old Vic)
(2372) 2821[5] (3779) (4279) 4739[7] 5169[7]
Melua Maid (IRE) *Mrs B Ewart*
12 b m Flemensfirth(USA) Chatty Lookalike (IRE) (Good Thyne (USA))
172[P] 4042[P] 5062[P]
Memberof (FR) *Alan King* 98h
4 bb g Khalkevi(IRE) Former Member (USA) (Dynaformer (USA))
2098[P] 4111[8] 5426[4]
Memorabilia *John Ferguson* 100h 130c
6 b g Dansili Sentimental Value (USA) (Diesis)
(4861)
Memory Cloth *Brian Ellison* 113h
7 b g Cape Cross(IRE) Gossamer (Sadler's Wells (USA))
2089[3] 2340[F] 2718[4] 3274[3] 3659[6]
Mendip Express (IRE) *Harry Fry* 106h 156c
8 bb g King's Theatre(IRE) Mulberry (IRE) (Denel (FR))
(2224)
(2803) (3455)
4148[3] 5276[P]
Menorah (IRE) *Philip Hobbs* 165h 172c
9 b g King's Theatre(IRE) Maid For Adventure (IRE) (Strong Gale)
3262[P] 4766[10] 5133[5] (5569)
Mentalist (FR) *Venetia Williams* 106h 122c
6 b g Westerner Lady Carole (FR) (Subotica (FR))
2714[P] 3093[4] 3504[2] 3820[2] 3958[U] 4448[3] 4725[P]
Mercers Court (IRE) *Neil King* 125h
6 b g Court Cave(IRE) Vikki's Dream (IRE) (Kahyasi)
3194[8] 4473[2] 4761[4] 5110[4]
Merchant Of Dubai *Jim Goldie* 113h
9 b g Dubai Destination(USA) Chameleon (Green Desert (USA))
2311[2] 3000[4] 3475[6]
Merchant Of Milan *Brendan Powell* 100h 107c
6 b g Milan Repunzel (Carlingford Castle)
1712[9] 2106[5] 2457[9] 2874[3] 3280[4]
3715[4]
Mercury Bay (IRE) *Evan Williams* 57h
9 ch g Karinga Bay Jolie Landaise (FR) (Beaudelaire (USA))
141[P]
Merehead (FR) *Paul Nicholls* 123h
8 gr g Al Namix(FR) Moneda (FR) (Cadoudal (FR))
2362[P]
Meridiem *Caroline Fryer* 94h
10 b g Tamure(IRE) Anatomic (Deerhound (USA))
31[4] 264[5] 456[7]
Merlin's Wish *Martin Keighley* 132c
9 gr g Terimon Sendai (Le Moss)
321[2] 2290[2] ◆ (2594)
(3267) 3617[2] 4741[F]
Merrion Square (IRE) *Paul Nicholls* 120h 137c
8 b g Kotashaan(FR) Parverb (IRE) (Parliament)
(238) **680[3]**
1868[11] 2931[2] 3321[F] 4681[F] 5344[6]
Merrydown (IRE) *Nicky Richards* 119h
11 b g Oscar(IRE) Euro Coin Lady (IRE) (Phardante (FR))
24[3] 4814[5] 5256[7]
Merrydown Vintage (IRE) *S R B Crawford* 89h 79c
7 ch g Ballingarry(IRE) Cure The Blues (IRE) (Phardante (FR))
1038[3] 1344[4] 3145[4] 4461[5] 5559[P]
Merry King (IRE) *Jonjo O'Neill* 120h 147c
7 ch g Old Vic Merry Queen (IRE) (Anshan)
2214[2] 2815[5] 3361[5] 3780[3] 4270[P] 5276[4] ◆
Merry Minster *James Walton* 93h 87c
7 b m Minster Son Merry Tina (Tina's Pet)
112[F] 506[6] 747[6] 804[P]
1160[3] 1287[2]
Messina Straights *George Bewley* 34h
6 br g Blueprint(IRE) Calabria (Neltino)
4431[9] 5103[P]
Mexican Mick *Charlie Longsdon* 34h
5 ch g Atraf Artic Bliss (Fraam)
4569[10]
Mezarat (ITY) *Michael Gates* 83h 79c
9 ch g Dream Well(FR) Dayara (GER) (Kornado)
30[U] 807[5] 3799[P] 4243[P]
Mezzanisi (IRE) *Peter Bowen* 103h
9 b g Kalanisi(IRE) Mezzanine (Sadler's Wells (USA))
2147[6] 2385[3] 2696[2]
Mia Matriarch *Donald Whillans* 88h 35c
8 ch m Silver Patriarch(IRE) Youandi (Silver Season)
20[P]
Mia's Anthem (IRE) *Noel C Kelly* 93h 78c
6 ch g Royal Anthem(USA) Windmill View (IRE) (Glacial Storm (USA))
1109[4] (1631) 1982[4] **2591[6]** 2974[10]
Mia's Vic (IRE) *Edward Creighton* 115h 107c
9 b g Old Vic Mill Lane Flyer (IRE) (Un Desperado (FR))
799[4] 1751[4] **3637[2] 4716[2] 5111[2] 5342[3]**
Mibleu (FR) *Colin Tizzard* 48h 116c
14 b g Agent Bleu(FR) Eauseille (FR) (Un Numide (FR))
236[4] 520[4] (853)
999[3] 1263[6] 1352[2] 1478[4] 1921[8]
Mic Aubin (FR) *Jennifer Mason* 89h 100c
11 b g Broadway Flyer(USA) Patney (FR) (Hasty Tudor (USA))
542[4] ◆ 4275[5]
4637[2] 4809[2] 5129[F] 5546[P]
Michael Michael *Mick Channon* 48h
8 ch g Kadastrof(FR) Mrs M (Royal Vulcan)
706[7]
Micheal Flips (IRE) *Andy Turnell* 148h 154c
10 b g Kayf Tara Pianissimo (IRE) (Shernazar)
204[6]
Michel Le Bon (FR) *Chris Gordon* 109h 149c
11 b g Villez(USA) Rosacotte (FR) (Rose Laurel)
2953[P]
Michigan Assassin (IRE) *Debra Hamer* 89h 106c
12 b g King's Theatre(IRE) Shuil Ar Aghaidh (The Parson)
832[8] 1135[P] 1260[4] (1344)
1577[6] 2041[3]
Mick Duggan *Simon Hodgson*
4 ch g Pivotal Poppy Carew (IRE) (Danehill (USA))
1743[P]
Mickelson (IRE) *Jonjo O'Neill* 140h 125c
8 b g Old Vic Life Support (IRE) (High Estate)
1203[P]
Mickie *Henry Daly* 146h
6 gr m Kayf Tara Island Mist (Jupiter Island)
1972[U] 2371[5] (2798) (3319) 3770[3] 4269[2]
4765[12] 5255[4]
Mick Staraco (FR) *Mme E Siavy-Julien* 96h 87c
4 b g Gallo's Wells(IRE) Septieme Element (FR) (Bering)
1741a[9]
Micky Fingers *Philip Kirby* 66h
5 b g Grape Tree Road Lissadell (IRE) (Zaffaran (USA))
5219[9]
Micquus (IRE) *Jonathan Geake* 92h
5 b g High Chaparral(IRE) My Potters (USA) (Irish River (FR))
1625[5] 1946[4] 2536[11] 4132[P]
Micro Mission (IRE) *Chris Grant* 119h 111c
8 b m Flemensfirth(USA) Micro Villa (IRE) (Electric)
1978[F] 2193[4] 2357[6] 3726[3] 4338[5] 4650[2] 5255[5]
Mic's Delight (IRE) *Victor Dartnall* 120h 124c
10 b g Witness Box(USA) Warrior Princess (IRE) (Mister Lord (USA))
2288[10]
3424[2] 3742[3] 4418[3] 4932[9] 5006[3] 5336[3]
Mid Div And Creep *Alan Hill* 125c
14 b m Sovereign Water(FR) Knightsbridge Bred (Montelimar (USA))
(61)
Midlothian (IRE) *John Ferguson* 99h
6 b g Monsun(GER) Sunray Superstar (Nashwan (USA))
69[2]

Midnight Appeal *Alan King* 128h 146c
9 b g Midnight Legend Lac Marmot (FR) (Marju (IRE))
215[17]
(2452) 2939[10] 4134[2] 4422[4] 5276[F] 5571[13]

Midnight Belle *Tom Symonds* 121h
7 b m Midnight Legend Cherry Alley (IRE) (Persian Mews)
(2029) (2352) 3117[3] 3731[2] (4392)

Midnight Cataria *Alan King* 117h
5 b m Midnight Legend Calamintha (Mtoto)
187[4] (2043) 2801[5] 3159[3] (4508) 4961[5] 5489[8]

Midnight Charmer *Emma Baker* 66h 101c
8 b g Midnight Legend Dickies Girl (Saxon Farm)
141[3] (1800)
(2067) 2518[3] (3008)
3439[3] 3855[F] 4759[7]

Midnight Choice *James Evans* 77h
9 b g Midnight Legend Pearl's Choice (IRE) (Deep Run)
710[P] 2427[3] 2766[5]
4507[U] 4981[P]

Midnight Chorister *Alex Hales* 97b
6 b g Midnight Legend Royal Musical (Royal Abjar (USA))
395[4] 2905[4]

Midnight Dove *Andrew Price* 97h 91c
9 ch g Karinga Bay Flighty Dove (Cruise Missile)
385[4]

Midnight Game *W P Mullins* 147h 104c
7 b g Montjeu(IRE) Midnight Angel (GER) (Acatenango (GER))
1067a[4] 1801a[2] 2552a[4] 4285a[2] 5420a[12]

Midnight Gold *Julian Smith*
14 ch g Midnight Legend Yamrah (Milford)
713[P] 942[P]

Midnight Jazz *Ben Case* 107b
4 b f Midnight Legend Ring Back (IRE) (Bob Back (USA))
3167[7] (4403) 5159[18]

Midnight Lira *Caroline Keevil* 93h 108c
7 ch m Midnight Legend Bally Lira (Lir)
421[4] **634[7]**
1629[5] (1769)
2462[4] 2765[F] (3171)
3785[P] *4299[9]* **(5336)**

Midnight Macarena *Lucy Wadham* 110h 110c
9 ch m Midnight Legend Royal Tango (Petoski)
(70) 379[5]
693[3] (2424)
2572[F] 2874[8]
3325[P] *4021[9]* **4354[6] 4809[6] 5065[5] 5433[F]**

Midnight Memories *Steph Hollinshead* 77b
4 ch f Midnight Legend Bajan Blue (Lycius (USA))
3656[6] 4310[8] 4951[7]

Midnight Minx *Anthony Honeyball* 111h
7 b m Midnight Legend Phar Breeze (IRE) (Phardante (FR))
1885[5] 5026[3]

Midnight Monkey *Lady Anne Connell* 30b
6 ch g Midnight Legend Teeton Glaive (Broadsword (USA))
544[13]

Midnight Mustang *Andrew J Martin* 85h 87c
7 b g Midnight Legend Mustang Molly (Soldier Rose)
1387[4] 1578[5] 1784[2] 2076[6] 2470[4] 2690[7] 3425[3]
4484[3] 4946[P] 5523[6]

Midnight Oscar (IRE) *Kim Bailey* 123h
7 br g Oscar(IRE) Midnight Light (IRE) (Roselier (FR))
2107[U] 2267[F] 3085[4] 3387[5] 4913[2] 5285[4]

Midnight Pearl (USA) *Mark Bradstock* 29h
11 bb m Woodman(USA) Elegant Ridge (IRE) (Indian Ridge)
46[11]

Midnight Poet *James Given*
4 ch g Byron Molly Pitcher (IRE) (Halling (USA))
785[P]

Midnight Prayer *Alan King* 121h 146c
9 b g Midnight Legend Onawing Andaprayer (Energist)
358[6] **(2177)**
2941[U] 3162[2] (4162) ◆ (4741)

Midnight Request *Tom Symonds* 100h
5 b g Midnight Legend Friendly Request (Environment Friend)
1935[10] 2286[6] 2614[11] 3188[6] 3821[2] 3959[2]
4309[7] 5019[5]

Midnight Return (IRE) *Richard Ford* 44h
8 b m Midnight Legend By Return (IRE) (Bob's Return (IRE))
2563[11] 3432[P]

Midnight Sail *Alan King* 138h 141c
11 b g Midnight Legend Mayina (Idiots Delight)
2714[6] (4685)
5385[6]

Midnight Sequel *Neil Mulholland* 60h
5 b m Midnight Legend Silver Sequel (Silver Patriarch (IRE))
4529[8]

Midnight Spin *Philip Hobbs* 86b
4 b g Midnight Legend Bobbie Dee (Blakeney)
4964[7] 5492[5]

Midnight Streaker *B Arthey* 84h
5 ch m Midnight Legend Grandma Griffiths (Eagle Eyed (USA))
3934[4] 4743[2] 5322[5]

Midnight Thomas *Martin Keighley* 77h
5 b g Midnight Legend Vivacious Lass (IRE) (Common Grounds)
458[3] 1519[7] 1595[6] 2004[8] 5522[6]

Midnight Thunder (IRE) *Colin Tizzard* 112h
5 ch g Beneficial Peppardstown (IRE) (Old Vic)
1974[17] 2940[6] 3370[2] 3746[2] 4503[3] 4750[15]

Midnight Tuesday (FR) *Dan Skelton* 123h 122c
9 b g Kapgarde(FR) Deat Heat (FR) (Volochine (IRE))
12[6] **432[4]**
1549[3] 1780[2] 2025[3] 4727[12]

Midnight Whisper *Richard Woollacott* 107h
8 ch g Midnight Legend Spread The Word (Deploy)
122[F] **713[P]**

Miel Cafe (FR) *Mme C Baron-Losfeld*
6 ch g Denham Red(FR) Istrie (FR) (Estephe Du Moulin (FR))
198a[P]

Mieuxmix (IRE) *Peter Niven* 36h
5 gr m Fair Mix(IRE) Mille Et Une Nuits (FR) (Ecologist)
187[8] 1719[5] 2309[8]

Might As Well *Seamus Mullins* 103h 98c
11 gr g Terimon Might Be (Gunner B)
100[2] 461[5] 692[4] 2047[5] 2478[P]

Mightavago *Tim Walford* 72h
5 b g Sir Harry Lewis(USA) Cashel Dancer (Bishop Of Cashel)
429[7]

Mighty Clarets (IRE) *Peter Bowen* 112h
7 br g Whipper(USA) Collected (IRE) (Taufan (USA))
140[12] 479[6] 661[3] 788[2] (846) 876[5] 1041[6]

Mighty Cliche (IRE) *Dianne Sayer* 83h
5 b g Classic Cliche(IRE) Mighty Mandy (IRE) (Mandalus)
4611[14] 4889[9] 5057[U] 5102[8] 5320[10]

Mighty Leader (IRE) *Michael O'Hare* 75h
6 b g Milan Madam Leader (IRE) (Supreme Leader)
1138[8]

Mighty Mambo *Lawney Hill* 95h
7 b g Fantastic Light(USA) Mambo's Melody (Kingmambo (USA))
2016[3] 2568[4] 2862[13] 3434[6] (5262)

Mighty Minnie *Henry Daly* 98b
5 b m Sir Harry Lewis(USA) Vanina II (FR) (Italic (FR))
2809[2] ◆ 4867[3]

Mighty Mobb (IRE) *Seamus Mullins* 105h 121c
7 b g Accordion Dusty Lane (IRE) (Electric)
3176[2] 3827[4] 4399[2] 5180[2]

Mighty Monty *Victor Dartnall* 107h
9 br g Overbury(IRE) Ruby Star (IRE) (Grand Plaisir (IRE))
37[5] 833[P]

Mighty Snazy *Tim Vaughan* 108h 115c
10 b g Overbury(IRE) Come To Tea (IRE) (Be My Guest (USA))
849[2] (1048) 1285[6] 1500[3]

Mighty Thor *Lydia Richards*
4 b g Norse Dancer(IRE) Leyaaly (Night Shift (USA))
1743[U] 2276[P]

Mighty Whitey (IRE) *Noel C Kelly* 120h
8 b g Sesaro(USA) Deeco Valley (IRE) (Satco (FR))
875[3] (929)

Mijhaar *John Ferguson* 136h
6 b g Shirocco(GER) Jathaabeh (Nashwan (USA))
(2783) ◆ 3501[F] 5153[5]

Mikael D'Haguenet (FR) *W P Mullins* 152h 153c
10 b g Lavirco(GER) Fleur D'Haguenet (FR) (Dark Stone (FR))
2483a[5] 2552a[3]

Mike McCann (IRE) *Michael O'Hare* 111b
6 b g Helissio(FR) Inzamaam (IRE) (Zaffaran (USA))
(885) 4547[11]

Milan Bound (IRE) *Jonjo O'Neill* 132h
6 b g Milan Bonnie And Bright (IRE) (Topanoora)
(2030) (2768) 3081[4] 3882[5] 4277[P]

Milaneen *Tim Vaughan* 80h
8 b m Milan Kosheen (IRE) (Supreme Leader)
477[6] 961[2] 1331[10]

Milanese (IRE) *Emma Lavelle* 115h
6 b g Milan Elma Joyce (IRE) (Anshan)
2279[8] 2942[F] 5015[F] 5332[5]

Milan Flyer (IRE) *Noel C Kelly* 90h
8 b g Milan Flying Jennie (Burslem)
1977[6] 2337[6] 3525[5] 4649[5]

Milan Of Hope (IRE) *Charles Pogson* 84h
7 b g Milan Miss Bertaine (IRE) (Denel (FR))
207[3] 584[6] 2426[8] 2874[5] 3086[6] 3605[5] 3842[P]

Milano Magic (IRE) *N W Alexander* 111h 83c
8 b g Milan Magical Mist (IRE) (Be My Native (USA))
1875[2] 2073[3] 2655[10]
3041[U] 4040[3]
4551[P] 5514[2]

Milano Supremo (IRE) *Chris Grant* 112h
9 b g Milan Lucy Popp (IRE) (Supreme Leader)
(110) 445[F]

Milan Royale *Kevin Hunter* 90h 98c
9 b g Milan Ciroyalta (FR) (Royal Charter (FR))
1870[7] 2219[3] (2880)
3352[6]

Milans Cross (IRE) *Jennie Candlish* 93h
6 b g Milan Fair Enough (IRE) (Phardante (FR))
3428[8] 3723[9]

Milans Well (IRE) *Brendan Powell* 107h 104c
8 b g Milan Panoora Queen (IRE) (Topanoora)
1205[7] 3691[P] **4840[P]** (5234)

Milarrow (IRE) *Colin Tizzard* 116h 120c
7 b g Milan Fleeting Arrow (IRE) (Commanche Run)
2014[6] 2754[5] 2931[F] 3693[4] 4109[4] 4933[11]

Milborough (IRE) *Tim Vaughan* 137h 136c
8 b g Milan Fox Burrow (IRE) (Supreme Leader)
2490[12]
(3011) 3496[F] 4041[2] 4741[8] 5192[2]

Milburn *Gail Haywood*
8 ch g First Trump Baroness Rose (Roselier (FR))
5182[P]

Miles Of Sunshine *Ron Hodges* 86h
9 b g Thowra(FR) Rainbow Nation (Rainbow Quest (USA))
2689[8] 2886[10] 3046[3] 3195[9] 3426[7] 3788[9] 4883[P]

Miles To Memphis (IRE) *Alan King* 118b
5 b g Old Vic Phillis Hill (Karinga Bay)
(4810) ◆ (5279) ◆

Miley Shah (IRE) *J P Kenny* 144h 139c
9 b g City Honours(USA) Mazovia (FR) (Taufan (USA))
1801a[7]
5273[P]

Milgen Bay *Oliver Sherwood* 109h 118c
8 br g Generous(IRE) Lemon's Mill (USA) (Roberto (USA))
853[5] 1050[4] 1186[3] 1767[3] 1988[6] 5346[4]

Military Call *R Mike Smith* 85h
7 b g Royal Applause Trump Street (First Trump)
1661[6] 2217[17] 2998[P]

Military Precision (IRE) *David Pipe* 83h
8 b g Exit To Nowhere(USA) Devil Leader (USA) (Diesis)
49[12]

Millanisi Boy *Richard Woollacott* 95b
5 b g Kalanisi(IRE) Millennium Rose (IRE) (Roselier (FR))
3994[7] 4335[3] 5188[2]

Mill Bay *S R B Crawford* 97h
7 b g Karinga Bay Lacounsel (FR) (Leading Counsel (USA))
881[3]

Millenary Magic (IRE) *David Rees* 90h
7 b g Millenary Petted Slave (Sandalay)
2147[5] 2386[4] 2648[P]

Millenarys Lady (IRE) *David Rees* 100h 31c
7 b m Millenary Poachers Run (IRE) (Executive Perk)
1364[6] 1517[B] 2535[6]
2741[5]

Miller's Maverick *Grant Cann* 87h
6 b g Millkom Gables Girl (Sousa)
14[5] 298[4] 4281[12] 4632[17] 4959[F] 5117[10] 5283[4]

Millers Pudsey *David Bridgwater* 59h
8 b g Pasternak Gables Girl (Sousa)
5288[5]

Millers Reef (IRE) *Keith Dalgleish* 103h 106c
8 b g Bob Back(USA) Silent Supreme (IRE) (Supreme Leader)
171[5] **627[U]**
752[4] 1419[5] 1656[5] 1785[10] (3334) 3842[S] 4201[8]
4446[2] 4774[7] **5107[P]**

Millicent Silver *Nigel Twiston-Davies* 103b
5 gr m Overbury(IRE) Common Girl (IRE) (Roselier (FR))
(3656) 4342[2] 5159[13]

Millie O'Brien *Philip Hobbs* 79h
6 b m Milan Mrs Philip (Puissance)
178[6] (522) 1051[8] 1675[10]

Milly Malone (IRE) *Adrian Wintle* 101h 71c
8 b m Milan Sharp Single (IRE) (Supreme Leader)
833[12] **1800[5]**

Milo Man (IRE) *Evan Williams* 133h
6 b g Milan Rilmount (IRE) (Roselier (FR))
(2420) 3592[3] (3956)

Milo Milan (IRE) *Richard Lee* 110h 120c
9 b g Milan Simply Divine (IRE) (Be My Native (USA))
2179[5] 3874[P] 4913[3]

Milord (GER) *Kim Bailey* 125h
5 br g Monsun(GER) Montserrat (GER) (Zilzal (USA))
1793[F] 2189[2] 2647[3] ◆ 2951[8] 3322[F] 3796[F]
4022[P] 5088[4]

Milor De La Borie (FR) *David Pipe* 87h
5 gr g Turgeon(USA) Trop Tard (FR) (Fabulous Dancer (USA))
174[5] 390[4] 4604[3] 5177[6] 5234[8]

Milord Thomas (FR) *D Bressou* 133h 127c
5 b g Kapgarde(FR) Star D'Avril (FR) (Phantom Breeze)
(1465a)
(1742a) (2263a)

Milosam (IRE) *Philip Hobbs* 78h 109c
7 b g Milan Lady Sam (IRE) (Topanoora)
89[4] **1942[P]**
(2478)
(2765) (3421)
3958[2] 4354[P] (5004)
5240[2]

Milton D'Or (FR) *E Leray* 82c
5 bb g Great Journey(JPN) Love Love Kate (FR) (Saint Andrews (FR))
2464a[5]

Minden Dawn *Peter Maddison* 26h
8 gr m Baryshnikov(AUS) Minden Rose (Lord Bud)
3826[14]

Minden March *Peter Maddison* 49h
9 b m Baryshnikov(AUS) Minden Rose (Lord Bud)
3329[5] 3605[6] 3924[6]

Minella (IRE) *W M Wanless* 97b
10 b g Moscow Society(USA) Castlefarm Leader (IRE) (Supreme Leader)
430[P]

Minella Bliss (IRE) *Nikki Evans* 98h 85c
9 gr g Old Vic Carraigrose (IRE) (Roselier (FR))
254[4] 690[4] 933[3] 1121[4] **1349[3] 1474[6]** 1784[6]

Minella Definitely (IRE) *Neil Mulholland* 118h 116c
7 br g Definite Article West Along (Crash Course)
2211[F] 2565[F] 2941[5] 3874[7] 4555[6] 4731[3] 5125[8]

Minella Duchess (IRE) *Grace Harris* 12h
7 b m Oscar(IRE) Minella Lass (IRE) (Buckskin (FR))
4917[7]

Minella Fifty (IRE) *Jonjo O'Neill* 98h 110c
6 b g King's Theatre(IRE) Burnt Out (IRE) (Anshan)
179[7] 385[F] 641[2] 789[P] 1136[5]

Minella Fiveo (IRE) *John Butler* 116h
6 b g Westerner Autumn Sky (IRE) (Roselier (FR))
1968[6]

Minella Forfitness (IRE) *Nicky Henderson* 147h
7 b g Westerner Ring Of Water (USA) (Northern Baby (CAN))
3771[8]

Minellaforleisure (IRE) *Alex Hales* 126h
6 br g King's Theatre(IRE) Dame Foraine (FR) (Raintrap)
(2109) 2530[3]

Minellaforlunch (IRE) *Henry Oliver* 101h 104c
7 b g King's Theatre(IRE) Loughaderra (IRE) (Strong Gale)
3[F] 185[5] 1706[S] 1937[6] 2210[12]
2897[6] 3439[4] 5404[3]

Minellaformarriage (IRE) *Neville Thomas* 68b
8 bb g Bob Back(USA) Frog Street (IRE) (Orchestra)
5545[P]

Minella For Party (IRE) *Dan Skelton* 113h 106c
7 b g Flemensfirth(USA) Dame Foraine (FR) (Raintrap)
237[3] **2315[4]**
2599[8]

Minella For Steak (IRE) *Jonjo O'Neill* 125h
7 b g King's Theatre(IRE) Preview Days (IRE) (Supreme Leader)
45[F] 1468[2] 1565[8] 1917[2] (2150) (2288) 2798[8]

Minella Foru (IRE) *Edward P Harty* 142h
5 b g King's Theatre(IRE) Shannon Rose (IRE) (Topanoora)
(2407a) 2852a[7] 4456a[3] 4785[6]

Minella For Value (IRE) *John Butler* 119h 138c
8 br g Old Vic Nightngale Express (IRE) (Strong Gale)
1957[4] 5170[7]

Minella Friend (IRE) *Evan Williams* 123h
5 b g King's Theatre(IRE) Don't Waste It (IRE) (Mister Lord (USA))
2011[2] 2457[3] 3598[2] 4546[5]

Minella Gathering (IRE) *Paul Henderson* 95h
5 b g Old Vic A Plus Ma Puce (FR) (Turgeon (USA))
4132[4] 4501[3] 5033[9]

Minellahalfcentury (IRE) *Paul Nicholls* 126h
6 b g Westerner Shanakill River (IRE) (Anshan)
2288[6] 3741[4] (4277) 5372[8]

Minella Hero (IRE) *Sarah Humphrey* 88h
6 b g Old Vic Shannon Rose (IRE) (Topanoora)
(1124) 1794[8] 2732[6] 5071[P]

Minella On Line (IRE) *Rebecca Curtis* 127h
5 b g King's Theatre(IRE) Bally Bolshoi (IRE) (Bob Back (USA))
1869[5] ◆ 2667[3] 3357[3] 3643[2] 4423[3] (4677)

Minella Present (IRE) *Neil Mulholland* 120b
5 b g Presenting Dabaya (IRE) (In The Wings)
3035[3] (5021) 5499[3]

Minella Ranger (IRE) *Paul Henderson* 79h 93c
8 ch g Beneficial Minella Lass (IRE) (Buckskin (FR))
636[P] 1055[P] 1349[4] 1474[U] 2575[4]
3470[2]

Minella Reception (IRE) *Nigel Twiston-Davies* 117h
8 b g King's Theatre(IRE) Cadourova (FR) (Cadoudal (FR))
3128[5] (4091) 4538[3] 5512[2]

Minella Scamp (IRE) *David Pipe* 98b
5 b g King's Theatre(IRE) Forgotten Star (IRE) (Don't Forget Me)
1869[6] 2479[3]

Minella Special (IRE) *Paul Henderson* 117h
8 b g King's Theatre(IRE) Della Wee (IRE) (Fidel)
3989[10] 4423[5] 4969[P] 5260[9]

Minella Stars (IRE) *Guy Henderson* 121h 126c
9 b g Accordion V'Soske Gale (IRE) (Strong Gale)
4788[6]

Minella Theatre (IRE) *Alan Hill* 87h 106c
11 b g King's Theatre(IRE) Ring Of Water (USA) (Northern Baby (CAN))
3720[4] 3993[4]

Miner Distraction *Jeremy Scott* 107h
6 b m Desert King(IRE) Miner Yours (Miner's Lamp)
3168[13] 3423[5] 3991[3] 4392[3] 5307[P]

Minerfortyniner (IRE) *Giles Smyly* 62h
5 br g Catcher In The Rye(IRE) Hungry Eyes (IRE) (Old Vic)
5088[13]

Mingun Bell (USA) *Ed de Giles* 43h
7 b g Mingun(USA) Miss Tippins (USA) (Squadron Leader (USA))
290[7]

Mini Island (IRE) *Richard Hawker*
5 b m Heron Island(IRE) Our Prima Donna (IRE) (Be My Native (USA))
3961[13]

Minimee *Phil McEntee*
4 b g Dubai Destination(USA) Malaaq (Green Desert (USA))
1781[P]

Mini Muck *Nigel Twiston-Davies* 118h
8 b m Kayf Tara Madam Muck (Gunner B)
1373[4] (1731) 2084[F] (2896) (2980) 3731[5] 4508[4]
5233[4]

Minister Of Mayhem *Nick Mitchell* 30h
4 ch g Sakhee's Secret First Fantasy (Be My Chief (USA))
1985[9] 2466[P] 5524[9]

Mini The Minx (IRE) *Donald Whillans* 82h
8 br m Accordion Gypsy Run (Nomadic Way (USA))
2843[7] 3824[11]

Mini Vic (IRE) *Miss Elizabeth Doyle* 122h 109c
10 b m Old Vic River Of Peace (IRE) (Over The River (FR))
3750a[9]

Minkie Moon (IRE) *Mark Campion* 76h 80c
6 b g Danehill Dancer(IRE) Minkova (IRE) (Sadler's Wells (USA))
449[P] **3024[2]**

Minneapolis *Alison Batchelor* 90h
9 b g Sadler's Wells(USA) Teggiano (IRE) (Mujtahid (USA))
2292[8] 2828[10]

Minnie Mustang *Andrew J Martin* 65b
6 b m Midnight Legend Mustang Molly (Soldier Rose)
4824[10] 5410[5]

Minority Interest *Daniel O'Brien* 110h
5 ch g Galileo(IRE) Minority (Generous (IRE))
3134[2] ◆ 3686[U] 4467[7]

Minsky Mine (IRE) *Michael Appleby* 80h
7 b g Montjeu(IRE) Summer Trysting (USA) (Alleged (USA))
3599[11] 3839[8] 4699[7] 4791[4]

Minstalad *Karen Tutty* 74h 86c
10 ch g Minster Son Denby Wood (Lord Bud)
444^{2} **(492)**
601^{2} 965^{P}
1202^{2}

Minstrel Lad *Jonjo O'Neill* 70h
6 ch g Where Or When(IRE) Teal Flower (Pivotal)
290^{9}

Minx Of The Lamp *Alan King* 29b
5 gr m Fair Mix(IRE) Lamp's Return (Bob's Return (IRE))
4499^{5}

Miracle Cure (IRE) *Venetia Williams* 86h
5 b g Whipper(USA) Bring Back Matron (IRE) (Rock Of Gibraltar (IRE))
4807^{11}

Miracle House (IRE) *Tim Vaughan* 115h 101c
10 b g Carroll House Mum's Miracle (IRE) (Luso)
921^{9} 1325^{3} 1687^{P}

Miranour *Liam Lennon* 112h 105c
9 b g Mujahid(USA) Mirana (IRE) (Ela-Mana-Mou)
1178a^{6} 1418^{P} (Dead)

Mischievous Milly (IRE) *Oliver Sherwood* 140h
6 b m Old Vic Jennifers Diary (IRE) (Supreme Leader)
2226^{4} 2813^{6} 3649^{2} 4158^{2}

Mishrif (USA) *J R Jenkins* 59h
8 bb g Arch(USA) Peppy Priscilla (USA) (Latin American (USA))
1779^{9}

Misirlou (FR) *Tim Vaughan* 59b
4 bb g Limnos(JPN) Other Salsa (FR) (Kingsalsa (USA))
4498^{6} 5492^{10}

Miss Ballantyne *Nicky Henderson* 120h 127c
7 br m Definite Article Gardana (FR) (Garde Royale)
2928^{7} 4701^{3} (5344)

Miss Beattie *Andrew Price* 69b
7 b m Beat All(USA) Scratch The Dove (Henbit (USA))
1578^{F}

Miss Bella Rose *Richard Guest* 56b
7 gr m Silver Patriarch(IRE) City Rose (Tragic Role (USA))
2878^{7}

Miss Biscotti *Martin Bosley* 95h
6 ch m Emperor Fountain Bellacaccia (IRE) (Beau Sher)
2600^{13} (3153)

Miss Chatterbox *C Dawson* 76h 77c
9 b m Dapper Clohamon Gossip (IRE) (Lord Americo)
510^{4}

Miss Dimples (IRE) *Sarah-Jayne Davies* 65h
5 gr m Tikkanen(USA) Scolboa House (IRE) (Bob's Return (IRE))
372^{13} 841^{10} 3159^{10} 4074^{8} 5002^{9}

Miss Duffy *William Kinsey* 90h
6 ch m Sir Harry Lewis(USA) Dolly Duff (Alflora (IRE))
1^{5} 552^{3} 2808^{P}

Miss Estela (IRE) *Warren Greatrex* 121b
4 b f Tobougg(IRE) Simply Divine (IRE) (Be My Native (USA))
(4735) (5374)

Miss Fortywinks *Seamus Mullins* 86h
5 gr m Act One Andromache (Hector Protector (USA))
3854^{F} 4394^{F} 5026^{8} 5393^{3}

Miss H Lewiss *Nigel Twiston-Davies* 73h
6 b m Sir Harry Lewis(USA) Broadbrook Lass (Broadsword (USA))
433^{3} 768^{7} 1280^{5}

Missing The Craic *Sean Curran* 61h
8 b g Josr Algarhoud(IRE) Missed Again (High Top)
317^{P}

Missionaire (USA) *Tony Carroll* 93h 98c
7 bb g El Corredor(USA) Fapindy (USA) (A.P. Indy (USA))
810^{4} **1939^{4}**
2615^{F} 5013^{3} 5243^{7}

Mission Complete (IRE) *Jonjo O'Neill* 122h 112c
8 b g Milan Kilmington Breeze (IRE) (Roselier (FR))
321^{P} 1055^{P} 1155^{2} (1284) 1363^{2} 1956^{12} 2655^{12} 3013^{8} 3435^{4}

Mission To Mars (IRE) *Nigel Twiston-Davies* 105h 96c
5 b g Presenting Nivalf (Gildoran)
1891^{3} 2178^{P} 2802^{8} 4069^{3} 4573^{3} 4937^{8} **5289^{3}**

Miss Lamorna (IRE) *Sue Gardner* 72b
5 br m Presenting Paumafi (IRE) (Shardari)
2892^{9}

Miss Lilly Lewis *Richard Phillips* 105b
6 b m Sir Harry Lewis(USA) Theme Arena (Tragic Role (USA))
1531^{5}

Miss Lucky Penny *Ian Williams* 104h
8 ch m Karinga Bay Singing Cottage (Greensmith)
3189^{9} 3872^{16} 4700^{2} 5075^{2} 5351^{7}

Miss Macnamara (IRE) *Martin Todhunter* 81h
5 b m Dylan Thomas(IRE) Kincob (USA) (Kingmambo (USA))
15^{5} 223^{3} 1043^{6}

Miss Mayfair (IRE) *Lawney Hill* 86h
7 b m Indian Danehill(IRE) Cocktail Party (USA) (Arctic Tern (USA))
1281^{5} 1552^{3} 2541^{4} 2827^{6} 3251^{2} 4446^{5} 5022^{2}

Miss Milborne *Jamie Snowden* 120h 91c
8 b m Tamure(IRE) Motown Melody (IRE) (Detroit Sam (FR))
3718^{3} 4484^{2} 5010^{3}

Miss Mohawk (IRE) *Alan Brown* 81h
5 ch m Hawk Wing(USA) Karmafair (IRE) (Always Fair (USA))
4479^{2} 4743^{3} 5102^{P} 5449^{P}

Miss Morn (IRE) *Robin Dickin*
8 b m Loup Sauvage(USA) Frosty Morn (Cruise Missile)
4018^{13}

Miss Overbury (IRE) *Anthony Middleton* 25h
8 br m Overbury(IRE) Chickabiddy (Henbit (USA))
116^{P}

Miss Overdrive *Oliver Sherwood* 114h
10 b m Overbury(IRE) Free Travel (Royalty)
121^{4}

Miss Palm (IRE) *D Deacon* 113h 114c
10 gr m Great Palm(USA) Miss Lurgan (IRE) (Euphemism)
3750a^{8}

Miss Pheebs *Colin Teague* 69b
5 b m Multiplex Fluoree (FR) (Xaar)
754^{7}

Miss Probus *Nick Williams* 90b
5 b m Erhaab(USA) Probus Lady (Good Times (ITY))
841^{4} 2907^{13}

Miss Redbrook (IRE) *Sarah-Jayne Davies* 55b
7 b m Alderbrook Too Red (IRE) (Un Desperado (FR))
1879^{9} 715^{12}

Miss Saffron *Sue Gardner* 89h 103c
11 br m Access Ski Saffron Lake (Shaab)
657^{6} 2029^{3}
2390^{3} 2700^{3} 3797^{P} (5032)
5334^{U}

Miss Sassypants *Seamus Mullins* 89h
5 ch m Hernando(FR) Serraval (FR) (Sanglamore (USA))
(1064) (1317) 5159^{10}

Miss Siskin *James Frost* 82h
5 b m Morpeth Miss Grace (Atticus (USA))
5393^{P}

Miss Sunflower *Tina Jackson* 69h 73c
12 ch m Keen Ellfiedick (Alfie Dickins)
532^{4} 628^{7} **753^{3} 1089^{2} 4220^{5} 4890^{6} 4982^{7} 5301^{5}**
5498^{P}

Miss Tenacious *Ron Hodges* 117h 125c
7 b m Refuse To Bend(IRE) Very Speed (USA) (Silver Hawk (USA))
(191) **411^{3}**
(2629)
3294^{5} 4502^{5} 5126^{8} 5527^{2}

Miss Tilly Dove *Andrew Price* 50h
6 b m Overbury(IRE) Scratch The Dove (Henbit (USA))
2286^{13} 2767^{13}

Miss Tilly Oscar (IRE) *David Evans* 93h
8 b m Oscar(IRE) Whisky Chaser (Never So Bold)
2470^{P} 2888^{3} 3157^{4}

Miss Tinks *Richard Woollacott* 70h 40c
8 ch m Exit To Nowhere(USA) Miss O'Grady (IRE) (Over The River (FR))
637^{10} 3047^{9} 3425^{P} 3699^{11}

Miss Tique (FR) *Venetia Williams* 110h 69c
6 b m Network(GER) Berthevine (FR) (Singasinga (FR))
3884^{6} 4353^{7} 4717^{F}
5246^{8}

Miss Treacle *Bernard Llewellyn* 43b
7 ch m Dreams End Miss Montgomery (IRE) (Montekin)
842^{10}

Miss Twiggs *Barry Leavy* 44b
5 b m Helissio(FR) Seviot (Seymour Hicks (FR))
3063^{7}

Miss Twiggy *Brian Ellison* 23b
6 b m Alflora(IRE) Gee Tee Supermodel (Terimon)
2422^{8} 4038^{P}

Mistariva (IRE) *Venetia Williams* 65h
7 b g Kris Kin(USA) Mrs Battleaxe (IRE) (Supreme Leader)
3282^{3} 4340^{5}

Misteray *Bill Turner* 76h
4 ch g Singspiel(IRE) Hannda (IRE) (Dr Devious (IRE))
2466^{6} 3003^{8}

Mister Bricolage (IRE) *Fergal O'Brien* 113h 107c
7 br g Oscar(IRE) Almost Trumps (Nearly A Hand)
1924^{8} 2492^{14} **3027^{5}**

Mister Carrot *George Baker*
4 b g Elusive City(USA) It's Twilight Time (Royal Applause)
2830^{11}

Mister Carter (IRE) *Ian Williams* 92h
7 b g Antonius Pius(USA) Kotdiji (Mtoto)
1708^{6}

Mister Chairman (IRE) *Nicky Henderson* 85b
6 b g Shantou(USA) Out Of Trouble (IRE) (Mandalus)
4575^{5} 5021^{7}

Mister Chancer (IRE) *Richard J Bandey* 119h 114c
9 b g Craigsteel Cluain Chaoin (IRE) (Phardante (FR))
4252^{2} 4727^{10}

Mister D (IRE) *George Bewley* 98h 60c
8 ch g Anshan Eleanors Joy (Sheer Grit)
1654^{4} 1980^{4} 2245^{6} 4223^{11} **5355^{5}**

Mister Dillon *Nicky Henderson* 143h 128c
7 b g Sulamani(IRE) Kabayil (Dancing Brave (USA))
718^{2} 845^{8} 3069^{5} (3387) 4051^{2} 4765^{7} 5372^{3}

Mister Fantastic *Dai Burchell* 91h
8 ch g Green Tune(USA) Lomapamar (Nashwan (USA))
2176^{U} 3157^{10} 4911^{10} (5118)

Mister First (FR) *Robert Alan Hennessy* 123h 128c
8 b g Trempolino(USA) Queen Running (FR) (Cadoudal (FR))
3759^{3} 4204^{4}

Mister Frosty (IRE) *Michael Squance* 93h
8 gr g Verglas(IRE) La Chinampina (FR) (Darshaan)
4450^{3} 4791^{3} 5072^{8}

Mister Grez (FR) *Dan Skelton* 106h 129c
8 gr g Turgeon(USA) Yoruba (FR) (Cyborg (FR))
(1886)
1971^{4} 2365^{8} 3287^{5} 4725^{3} 5176^{2} 5516^{4}

Mister Happy (FR) *Mme C De La Soudiere-Niault* 96h
4 b g Great Journey(JPN) Lyric Melody (FR) (Lyphard's Wish (FR))
614a^{8}

Mister Hendre *Anthony Honeyball* 73h
6 gr g Fair Mix(IRE) Bonne Anniversaire (Alflora (IRE))
141^{P}

Mister Hotelier (IRE) *C A Murphy* 133h
7 b g Beneficial Accordian Lady (IRE) (Accordion)
5158^{11}

Mister Hyde (IRE) *Jonjo O'Neill* 126h 142c
9 b g Beneficial Solar Quest (IRE) (King's Ride)
358^{14} 591^{7} 845^{5}

Mister Jones *Sue Smith* 98h
6 b g Val Royal(FR) Madame Jones (IRE) (Lycius (USA))
284^{4} (584) 2738^{4} 3144^{5} 3872^{10} 4005^{3} 4553^{13} 4746^{5} 5298^{P}

Mister Marker (IRE) *Nicky Richards* 121h 143c
10 ch g Beneficial Bavards Girl (IRE) (Le Bavard (FR))
2246^{2} 2822^{P} 3617^{P} (4236)
4651^{2} 5276^{P}

Mister Matt (IRE) *Tom Symonds* 78h 132c
11 b g Alflora(IRE) Swing Quartet (IRE) (Orchestra)
520^{3} 1001a^{6} 1746^{5} 2081^{6} 5353^{11}

Mister Moonax (IRE) *Chris Down* 92h 98c
14 ch g Moonax(IRE) Edna Cottage (The Parson)
1052^{5}
1262^{3} 1477^{3}
1830^{U}

Mister Newby (IRE) *Richard Phillips* 118h
8 b g Oscar(IRE) Sallie's Girl (IRE) (Un Desperado (FR))
185^{2} ◆ 1972^{14} 2954^{5} 3600^{4} (4933) 5351^{11}

Mister Nibbles (IRE) *S R B Crawford* 126h
6 br g Kalanisi(IRE) Miss Best (FR) (Grand Tresor (FR))
2493^{6} 4550^{5} 5250^{U}

Mister Philson (IRE) *S R B Crawford* 99h 116c
9 b g Saddlers' Hall(IRE) Molo River (IRE) (Fourstars Allstar (USA))
2670^{P} 3019^{4} 3638^{6}
4368^{2} (4669)
5558^{4}

Mister Snowball (FR) *Chris Down* 109h 103c
7 ch g Ballingarry(IRE) No Coincidence (IRE) (Indian Ridge)
2107^{5} 2370^{6} 3642^{P} 3784^{P} 5019^{3} 5285^{5}

Mister Stickler (IRE) *Chris Grant* 33h 53c
10 b g Alflora(IRE) Almost Trumps (Nearly A Hand)
2222^{P} 4477^{3} 4892^{4}

Mister Teddy *F A Hutsby* 101b 107c
9 b g Tamure(IRE) Thamesdown Tootsie (Comedy Star (USA))
4246^{F} 4485^{5}

Mister Wall Street (FR) *Rebecca Menzies* 103h 97c
9 br g Take Risks(FR) Miss Breezy (FR) (Sicyos (USA))
2996^{6} 4341^{4} 4748^{3} 5193^{6}

Mister Wiseman *Nigel Hawke* 92h 92c
12 gr g Bal Harbour Genie Spirit (Nishapour (FR))
117^{6} 378^{4} 632^{7} (898)
1050^{5} 1086^{3} 1174^{P} 2021^{2} 2277^{2} 2396^{S} (2739)
2861^{2} 3139^{P}
4416^{3} 4578^{5}
4985^{6}

Mistic Academy (IRE) *Jim Best* 42h 48c
9 ch m Royal Academy(USA) Mistic Sun (Dashing Blade)
1668^{7}

Mistral Reine *Lucy Wadham* 108h
5 b m King's Theatre(IRE) Classic Gale (USA) (Classic Cliche (IRE))
2435^{3} 2663^{5} (3151) 3473^{2} 3860^{4} (4249) 5010^{P} 5438^{P}

Mistress Mole (IRE) *Paul Nicholls* 103b
5 br m Definite Article Emmylou Du Berlais (FR) (Kadalko (FR))
4735^{2} 5374^{11}

Mist The Boat *Tim Vaughan* 103h
6 b g Generous(IRE) Baily Mist (IRE) (Zaffaran (USA))
945^{4} 1281^{4} 1580^{2} 1673^{7} 5283^{F}

Misty Mornin *Zoe Davison* 56h
6 gr m Central Park(IRE) Belle Rose (IRE) (Roselier (FR))
2273^{P} 2579^{5} 2725^{6}
4793^{2}

Mitchell *David Thompson* 47h
4 ch g Haafhd Maid To Matter (Pivotal)
2881^{6}

Mitchell's Way *Alan Swinbank* 125h 134c
7 ch g Needwood Blade Ghana (GER) (Bigstone (IRE))
2519^{13}
3658^{4} 4188^{4} *(4326)* **(4578)**
(4833) 5053^{3} 5376^{2}

Mitt'N'Marg *Trevor Wall* 54b
6 b g Sulamani(IRE) Margarets Wish (Cloudings (IRE))
1016^{8} 1819^{P}

Mixboy (FR) *James Ewart* 81b
4 gr g Fragrant Mix(IRE) Leston Girl (FR) (Lesotho (USA))
5560^{6}

Mixed Blend *Alistair Whillans* 80b
5 gr g Fair Mix(IRE) Proper Posh (Rakaposhi King)
498^{P}

Mixed Meaning (IRE) *Stuart Howe* 60h
6 gr g Fair Mix(IRE) Connotation (Mujahid (USA))
80^{4} 156^{4} 407^{14} 2284^{F}

Mixed Message (IRE) *Brian Ellison* 98h
4 b f Kodiac Berenica (IRE) (College Chapel)
(1920) 5531^{3}

Mixologist *Warren Greatrex* 118h
7 gr g Fair Mix(IRE) Matchboard Again (IRE) (Supreme Leader)
3007^{2} 3169^{2} 3922^{6} *4300^{5}*

Mlyn (CZE) *F Kovacik*
8 b g Minds Music(USA) Millenia (CZE) (Lincoln (CZE))
1904a^{U}

Mm Dazzler (IRE) *Adrian Maguire* 114b
6 b g Fruits Of Love(USA) Harristown Peach (IRE) (Mister Mat (FR))
(3230)

Moaning Butcher *Dave Roberts* 74h
4 b g Lucarno(USA) Musical Chimes (Josr Algarhoud (IRE))
1727^{4} 2455^{6} 3224^{4} *4327^{6}*

Mobaasher (USA) *Patricia Shaw* 104h 87c
11 ch g Rahy(USA) Balistroika (USA) (Nijinsky (CAN))
998^{P} 4501^{2} 4677^{3} 5022^{8}

Mobane Ali *Susan Corbett* 66h
6 b m Ferrule(IRE) Penteli (Double Trigger (IRE))
110^{P}

Modeligo (IRE) *Matt Sheppard* 74h
5 b g Indian Danehill(IRE) Glens Lady (IRE) (Mister Lord (USA))
2026^{12} 2453^{6} 3070^{9} 4093^{6}

Module (FR) *Tom George* 141h 166c
7 b g Panoramic Before Royale (FR) (Dauphin Du Bourg (FR))
2281^{2} 3032^{4} (4146)
4753^{3}

Modus *Robert Stephens* 123b
4 ch g Motivator Alessandra (Generous (IRE))
(2015) (3460) 4756^{8} ◆ 5173^{11}

Moel Famau *Nicky Henderson* 10b
5 b m Flemensfirth(USA) Daprika (FR) (Epervier Bleu)
3063^{8}

Mohanad (IRE) *Philip Hide* 102h
8 b g Invincible Spirit(IRE) Irish Design (IRE) (Alhaarth (IRE))
304^{9}

Mohawk Ridge *James Moffatt* 123h
8 b g Storming Home Ipsa Loquitur (Unfuwain (USA))
3351^{5} 3614^{3} (4081) 4548^{2} (5102)

Moheebb (IRE) *Robert Johnson* 88h
10 b g Machiavellian(USA) Rockerlong (Deploy)
1754^{9} 2840^{7} 3756^{4} 4612^{7} 4811^{8}

Mohi Rahrere (IRE) *Barry Leavy* 108h 112c
11 b g New Frontier(IRE) Collinstown Lady (IRE) (Welsh Term)
321^{4} 2157^{F} 3059^{4} 3267^{4} 5074^{4}

Mojeek (IRE) *Gary Moore*
6 b g High-Rise(IRE) Beardie's Dream (IRE) (Luso)
2711^{F}

Mojolika *Tim Easterby* 124h
6 ch g Motivator Kalandika (Diesis)
901^{4} 2198^{4} 2519^{8} 3000^{6} 3599^{2} 3892^{3} 4426^{2} 5384^{5}

Moka De L'Isle (FR) *Mrs S A Bramall* 73h 109c
14 ch g Video Rock(FR) Ceres De L'Isle (FR) (Bad Conduct (USA))
200a^{P}

Molaise Lad (IRE) *Barry Brennan* 116h
8 b g Morozov(USA) Artic Annie (IRE) (Torus)
(319) 503^{9}

Moleskin (IRE) *Victor Dartnall* 110h 116c
11 b g Saddlers' Hall(IRE) Magic Gale (IRE) (Strong Gale)
1988^{3} 2462^{2} 3172^{6} 4109^{3} 5247^{5}

Molko Jack (FR) *Michael Mullineaux* 122h 100c
10 bb g Lavirco(GER) Line As (FR) (Cadoudal (FR))
1800^{7} (2048)
2396^{2} (2626)
3015^{7} 3272^{3} 4241^{P}

Molly Beag (IRE) *Adrian Maguire*
4 b f Marienbard(IRE) Sister Phoebe (IRE) (Germany (USA))
3229^{6}

Molly Cat *Alan Swinbank* 105b
4 ch f Dylan Thomas(IRE) Pentatonic (Giant's Causeway (USA))
(3663) ◆ *4017^{2}* 5159^{12}

Molly Maid (IRE) *Dominic Ffrench Davis* 93h
6 b m Oscar(IRE) Maid For Adventure (IRE) (Strong Gale)
4114^{3} 4600^{3}

Molly Milan *Jim Goldie* 94h
6 b m Milan Dolly Sparks (IRE) (Electric)
2217^{14} 2495^{4} 5250^{3}

Mollyow (IRE) *Eugene Stanford* 107h
6 ch m Iceman Corryvreckan (IRE) (Night Shift (USA))
1043^{5}

Molly's A Diva *Kim Bailey* 118h
7 ch m Midnight Legend Smokey Diva (IRE) (Orchestra)
2600^{9} 3168^{9} (3438) 4276^{3} 4508^{5} 4961^{4} 5427^{4}

Molo *David Pipe* 100b
4 b f Kalanisi(IRE) Belle Magello (FR) (Exit To Nowhere (USA))
(5077)

Molon Labe (IRE) *David Rees* 109h
7 ch g Footstepsinthesand Pillars Of Society (IRE) (Caerleon (USA))
(266) (375) 503^{6} 1429^{2}

Molten Brown *Miss C Marshall* 91c
9 b g Needle Gun(IRE) Molten (Ore)
(510) **4225^{6}**
4554^{P}

Momkinzain (USA) *Lucinda Russell* 103h
7 b g Rahy(USA) Fait Accompli (USA) (Louis Quatorze (USA))
(316) (678) 961^{3} 1161^{3} 1848^{2} 2997^{6} 5532^{5}

Mona Agnes (IRE) *Fergal O'Brien* 98b
6 b m Westerner Ben's Turn (IRE) (Saddlers' Hall (IRE))
2809^{P}

Monarch's Way *John Ferguson* 116h 120c
7 b g King's Best(USA) La Bayadere (Sadler's Wells (USA))
78^{2} 411^{4} 596^{F} 757^{P}

Monart Diamond *Tim Vaughan* 42b
5 gr g Presenting Line White (FR) (Pitchounet (FR))
2472^{9} 3433^{6} 5016^{F}

Monashee (IRE) *George Charlton* 86h
9 bb g Monashee Mountain(USA) On The Bridle (IRE) (Mandalus)
75[P]

Monasterevin (IRE) *Noel Quinlan* 91b
6 ch g Danroad(AUS) Alpathar (IRE) (Simply Great (FR))
1671[6] 1826[7]

Monbeg (IRE) *Martin Todhunter* 92h 90c
7 b g Revoque(IRE) Dikler Gale (IRE) (Strong Gale)
19[6] 339[3] 470[6] 1873[7] 2172[4]
2591[8] (2734)
2870[6] 3275[7] 3528[3] 3925[4] 4626[4]

Monbeg Dude (IRE) *Michael Scudamore* 126h 151c
9 b g Witness Box(USA) Ten Dollar Bill (IRE) (Accordion)
1968[3]
2502[4] ◆ (3067)
4544[5] 5171[7]

Monbeg Theatre (IRE) *Jamie Snowden* 110b
5 b g King's Theatre(IRE) Amberina (IRE) (Bob Back (USA))
2472[3] 3440[2] (4310)

Moncarno *David Pipe* 27b
4 b g Lucarno(USA) Sparkling Jewel (Bijou D'Inde)
3133[10]

Mon Chevalier (IRE) *Carroll Gray* 90h 116c
11 b g Montjeu(IRE) Kumta (IRE) (Priolo (USA))
2629[3] 3960[5] 4637[4] 5017[2] 5363[4]

Monderon (FR) *Richard Hawker* 101h
7 bb g Laveron Lomonde (FR) (Great Lakes)
2934 (2701) 2980[7] 4599[7] 4883[6]

Mondo Cane (IRE) *Charles Pogson* 106h 106c
7 b g Beneficial La Vita E Bella (FR) (Le Nain Jaune (FR))
3921[2] 4248[U] 4594[2] 5157[13]

Monetaire (FR) *J Bertran De Balanda* 119h 119c
8 b g Anabaa(USA) Monitrice (FR) (Groom Dancer (USA))
1984a[P]

Monetary Fund (USA) *Venetia Williams* 132h
8 b g Montjeu(IRE) Maddie G (USA) (Blush Rambler (USA))
215[7] 1956[10] 2345[3] 2504[7] 2672[7] 3882[6] 4051[F]
4489[5] 5093[6] ◆ 5544[6]

Money For Nothing *Alan King* 108h
5 b g Kayf Tara Top Of The Dee (Rakaposhi King)
2369[4] 2947[7] 4931[7] 5335[5]

Money Maid (IRE) *Simon Earle* 86h
6 ch m Blueprint(IRE) Maid Of Music (IRE) (Orchestra)
4008[4] 4331[P] 4945[7] 5124[6] ◆ 5244[4] 5343[4]

Moneymix *Ali Brewer* 78h 80c
7 gr g Fair Mix(IRE) Sticky Money (Relkino)
182[P] 878[9] 2954[9] 3788[5] 4334[4] 4519[4] 5139[2]
5397[2]

Money Money Money *Jim Best* 63h
8 b m Generous(IRE) Shi Shi (Alnasr Alwasheek)
1432[4] 1672[13] 1915[P] 2536[10]

Money Talks *Michael Madgwick* 109h
4 br g Motivator Movie Mogul (Sakhee (USA))
4807[9] 5455[2]

Mongress Boy (IRE) *Andy Hobbs* 109h 65c
9 gr g Beneficial Securon Rose (IRE) (Roselier (FR))
265[P] 435[2] 649[6] 799[P]

Mon Homme *Mark Rimell* 81h
7 br g Loup Sauvage(USA) Mistinguett (IRE) (Doyoun)
761[7] 847[6] 2571[7]

Moniques Gift *Chris Down*
6 b m Grape Tree Road Dalticia (FR) (Cadoudal (FR))
4394 [P]

Monita Bonita *Tim Easterby* 88h
5 b m King's Theatre(IRE) Monita Des Bois (FR) (Snurge)
(970) 2495[5] 2865[2] 3270[4] 3871[9] 5494[16]

Monkerty Tunkerty *Miss Jessica Westwood* 65b 137c
11 b g Silver Patriarch(IRE) Orphan Annie (Gunner B)
851[11] 2931[4] ◆ 3554[3] 3743[P]

Monkey Kingdom *Rebecca Curtis* 134h
6 b g King's Theatre(IRE) Blast Freeze (IRE) (Lafontaine (USA))
(4411) (4950) 5167[9]

Monkey Milan (IRE) *Philip Kirby* 125h
8 b g Milan Beech Lodge (IRE) (Supreme Leader)
1680[6]

Monksgold (IRE) *Alan King* 108h
6 b g Gold Well Opium (Polish Precedent (USA))
4546[6] 4993[3] 5541[3]

Mon Nickson (FR) *G Macaire* 115h 117c
4 b g Nickname(FR) Linaving (FR) (Linamix (FR))
262a[P]

Monogram *Victor Thompson* 105h 106c
10 ch g Karinga Bay Dusky Dante (IRE) (Phardante (FR))
579[0]

Mon Parrain (FR) *Paul Nicholls* 145c
8 b g Trempolino(USA) Kadaina (FR) (Kadalko (FR))
2199[P] 4544[8] (5371)

Monpilou (FR) *G Macaire* 149h 132c
7 b g Saint Des Saints(FR) Gavotte De Brejoux (FR) (Iris Noir (FR))
406a[P] 1901a[5]

Mon Reve *Violet M Jordan* 86h
6 br m Fair Mix(IRE) Song For Jess (IRE) (Accordion)
637[P] 860[11]

Monroe Park (IRE) *Alan Blackmore* 100h 87c
9 b g Spectrum(IRE) Paloma Bay (IRE) (Alzao (USA))
162[F] 490[F] 2062[4] 2571[2] 2894[8] 3468[3] 3852[6]
4791[2] 5066[8]

Monsamou (IRE) *P Chevillard* 137h 122c
5 b g Bienamado(USA) Alphadite (IRE) (Alphabatim (USA))
2263a[4]

Monsieur Cadou (FR) *Tom George* 115h 128c
9 b g Cadoudal(FR) Dame De Trefles (FR) (Antheus (USA))
2246[8] 3416[P]

Monsoon Music (IRE) *Lucinda Russell* 60h 77c
10 b g Dushyantor(USA) Stormey Tune (IRE) (Glacial Storm (USA))
20[P] 311[P]

Montana Belle (IRE) *John Butler* 98b
4 b f High Chaparral(IRE) Stiletta (Dancing Brave (USA))
2604[3] (3167)

Montbazon (FR) *Alan King* 148h
7 bb g Alberto Giacometti(IRE) Duchesse Pierji (FR) (Cadoudal (FR))
4147[16] 4785[3] 5274[7]

Monte Cavallo (SAF) *Rebecca Curtis* 132h 127c
9 b g Saumarez Mufski (SAF) (Al Mufti (USA))
(369) 673[8] **1175[2] 1426[3]**

Montefeltro *John Ferguson* 119h
6 ch g Medicean Bustling (Danehill (USA))
(306) 581[3] 756[7]

Monte Kaolino (IRE) *Nick Gifford* 41h
6 ch g Sandmason Direct Pursuit (IRE) (Hubbly Bubbly (USA))
189[P] 233[P]

Monthly Medal *Wilf Storey* 59h
11 b g Danehill Dancer(IRE) Sovereign Abbey (IRE) (Royal Academy (USA))
2449[9] 3830[P]

Montjen (IRE) *Karen Tutty* 77b
4 b f Montjeu(IRE) Nuriva (USA) (Woodman (USA))
3167[4] 3663[5]

Montoya's Son (IRE) *Tim Vaughan* 94h 123c
9 ch g Flemensfirth(USA) Over The Grand (IRE) (Over The River (FR))
66[2] 282[5]

Montpellier (FR) *Mme L Audon* 126h 120c
8 b g Della Francesca(USA) What Cheeky (FR) (Cadoudal (FR))
2465a[6]

Mont Royale *Jonjo O'Neill* 90h
6 b g Hurricane Run(IRE) Wild Academy (IRE) (Royal Academy (USA))
(1792) 4349[7] 5409[2]

Montys Cash *Heather Cobb* 86b
8 b g Spendent Satcotino (IRE) (Satco (FR))
4761[P] 5024[P]

Monty's Revenge (IRE) *Martin Keighley* 89h 103c
9 b g Bob's Return(IRE) Native Bavard (IRE) (Be My Native (USA))
265[5] 1015[P] 1349[2]

Monzino (USA) *Michael Chapman* 51b
6 bb g More Than Ready(USA) Tasso's Magic Roo (USA) (Tasso (USA))
383[6] 5190[P]

Moon Devil (IRE) *Peter Bowen* 111h
7 b g Muhtarram(USA) Mandys Moynavely (IRE) (Semillon)
337[4] 638[2] 845[10] 1341[2]

Moon Dice (IRE) *Paul W Flynn* 140h 132c
9 b g Norwich Ella Come Back (IRE) (Bob Back (USA))
1801a[4] 2102[8]

Mooney's Cottage (IRE) *Michael O'Hare* 77h
9 b g Quws De Lourde (IRE) (Roselier (FR))
4553[15]

Moonlight Drive (IRE) *Jonjo O'Neill* 125h 129c
8 b g Oscar(IRE) Perspex Queen (IRE) (Presenting)
119[P]

Moonlight Maggie *Tom George* 73h 85c
7 b m Pasternak Moyliscar (Terimon)
2825[5] 3352[2] 3883[F] 4462[5]

Moonlit Bay *Venetia Williams*
4 b f Midnight Legend Newton Mo (Homo Sapien)
2781a[2]

Moonlit Orchard (FR) *Michael Blake*
4 b f Apple Tree(FR) Last Eclipse (FR) (Alleged (USA))
1624[7]

Moonlone Lane (IRE) *Paul Stafford* 100h 94c
7 b g Oscar(IRE) Shandarr (IRE) (John French)
879[3] 1379[10] 1544[2]
1876[5]

Moon Melody (GER) *Mike Sowersby* 82h 93c
11 b g Montjeu(IRE) Midnight Fever (IRE) (Sure Blade (USA))
74[3] 444[5]
601[7] 751[6] (965) 1121[2] 1565[11] 1874[5] **2902[3]**
3114[4]

Moon Over Miami (GER) *D Holmes* 96h 114c
13 b g Dashing Blade Miss Esther (GER) (Alkalde (GER))
(287) **655[7]**
4554[8] 4705[5]

Moon Prince (IRE) *Michael Winters* 102h
12 ch g Moonax(IRE) Spanish Ryham (IRE) (Spanish Place (USA))
1945[6]

Moon Racer (IRE) *Michael Ronayne* 118b
5 b g Saffron Walden(FR) Angel's Folly (Wesaam (USA))
(5424a)

Moonshine Lad (IRE) *Gordon Elliott* 140h
6 b g Milan Parsons Term (IRE) (The Parson)
3931a[2] 4386a[P] 4665[2] 5200a[8]

Moon Trip *John Ferguson* 100h
5 b g Cape Cross(IRE) Fading Light (King's Best (USA))
1200[4] 1533[2] 1754[4] 2051[6]

Moonunderwater (IRE) *R Donohoe* 56h
7 br g Norwich Roseaustin (IRE) (Roselier (FR))
3215a[6]

Moorlands George *Jeremy Scott* 82h
6 b g Grape Tree Road Sandford Springs (USA) (Robellino (USA))
1712[7] 3697[10] 4175[10] 4903[12]

Moorlands Jack *Jeremy Scott* 94h 108c
9 b g Cloudings(IRE) Sandford Springs (USA) (Robellino (USA))
860[4] ◆ 1136[6] 1267[5]
(1549) 1834[U] 2007[2] 2462[3] 2873[F] 3596[4]

Moorlands Mist *Philip Hobbs* 136h
7 gr g Fair Mix(IRE) Sandford Springs (USA) (Robellino (USA))
2458[4] (2944) 3359[5] 4144[7] 5093[9]

Moorland Sunset *Caroline Keevil* 113h 112c
7 b g Pasternak Lady Harriet Luis (Sir Harry Lewis (USA))
2046[2] 2462[7] 3421[P]

Moorway (IRE) *Andrew Hollinshead*
4 b g Dylan Thomas(IRE) Cordelia (Green Desert (USA))
725[7]

Mootabar (IRE) *Chris Fairhurst* 85h
7 gr g Verglas(IRE) Melanzane (Arazi (USA))
3828[8] 4478[2] 4816[5] 5106[2] 5359[11]

Moratab (IRE) *Keiran Burke* 91h
5 b g Dubai Destination(USA) Bahr (Generous (IRE))
2215[7] 3163[14] 3550[6] 3788[13]

More Buck'S (IRE) *Paul Nicholls* 95b
4 ch g Presenting Buck's Blue (FR) (Epervier Bleu) (5339)

Morebutwhen *Richard King* 105b
7 b m Morpeth Lady Noso (Teenoso (USA))
2946[7] 4411[P] 5120[P]

More Equity *Dianne Sayer* 105h 114c
12 b m Classic Cliche(IRE) Sillymore (Silly Prices)
172[5] 492[4] 566[U] 802[P] 1039[3] 1163[4] (1377)
(1469) 1659[4] 1978[3] (2310)
2971[4] 3394[5]
3874[5] 4236[5] 4461[10] 4773[4]

More Glory (IRE) *Keith Goldsworthy* 73h
6 b g Morozov(USA) Motility (IRE) (Yashgan)
79[5] 479[B] 592[9]

More Like Mum *Tina Jackson*
8 br m Rock City Carole's Delight (Idiots Delight)
800[P]

Morello Mist *Richard Drake* 36h
9 gr m Cloudings(IRE) Cherry Dee (Ardross)
1874[7] 2333[P] **2734[P]** 2974[7]

Morello Royale (IRE) *Colin Tizzard* 78b
4 b f King's Theatre(IRE) Mystic Cherry (IRE) (Alderbrook)
3167[3] 3719[5] 4403[7] 5374[10]

More Of That (IRE) *Jonjo O'Neill* 172h
6 b g Beneficial Guigone (FR) (Esprit Du Nord (USA))
(2230) (2671) ◆ (3084) ◆ (4767)

Morestead (IRE) *Brendan Powell* 86h 96c
9 ch g Traditionally(USA) Itsy Bitsy Betsy (USA) (Beau Genius (CAN))
98[4] 305[5] (489)
705[3] 846[5]
1272[6] 1435[4] 1534[5] 1675[6]
1769[3] 2021[3] 2278[P]
2540[2] 2727[2]
3248[2] 3564[4]
4802[3] 5027[2]
5263[7] 5442[2]

More Tricks *James Frost* 61h
6 b m Morpeth Supreme Daughter (Supreme Leader)
3049[9] 3168[14] 3422[9] 3695[9] 4330[4]

Morgana *Simon Hodgson*
6 b m Norse Dancer(IRE) En Vacances (IRE) (Old Vic)
5393[11]

Morgan's Bay *Tom George* 14h 115c
9 b g Karinga Bay Dubai Dolly (IRE) (Law Society (USA))
2450[5] 2895[P] 3431[5] (4483)
4653[2] 5336[5]

Morgans Rock (IRE) *Sarah Dawson* 23b
6 b g Beneficial Ivory Queen (Teenoso (USA))
5166[5]

Morito Du Berlais (FR) *Paul Nicholls* 100h
5 b g Turgeon(USA) Chica Du Berlais (FR) (Cadoudal (FR))
2940[5] 5236[6]

Morning Assembly (IRE) *P A Fahy* 151h 156c
7 b g Shantou(USA) Barrack Village (IRE) (Montelimar (USA))
(2551a)
3404a[2] 4751[3] ◆

Morning Moment *Caroline Bailey* 122c
12 b g Killer Instinct Golf World (IRE) (Mandalus)
504[P]

Morning Reggie *Oliver Sherwood* 107h
5 gr g Turgeon(USA) Nile Cristale (FR) (Northern Crystal)
2375[5] 2947[5] 4343[6] 5174[3] (5547)

Morning Royalty (IRE) *James Moffatt* 136h
7 b g King's Theatre(IRE) Portryan Native (IRE) (Be My Native (USA))
2221[2] 2669[5] 3206[3] 3779[4] 4785[15] 5158[P]

Morning Time (IRE) *Lucinda Russell* 103h 95c
8 b g Hawk Wing(USA) Desert Trail (IRE) (Desert Style (IRE))
314[3] (630) (803) (879) 1143[2] 1379[8] **1876[3]**
(2336) 2597[5] 5105[P]

Morning With Ivan (IRE) *Martin Todhunter* 106h
4 b f Ivan Denisovich(IRE) Grinneas (IRE) (Barathea (IRE))
2881[2] 3385[3] 3757[2] (4466) (4614)

Moroman (IRE) *David Kemp* 115c
7 b g Morozov(USA) Emma's Love (IRE) (Witness Box (USA))
5439[U]

Mo Rouge (IRE) *Mrs Jackie Stephen* 108h
6 b g Croco Rouge(IRE) Just A Mo (IRE) (Supreme Leader)
225[6] 676[4] 1980[5] 2342[P] 5508[2]

Morpet *Ron Hodges* 76b
5 b g Morpeth Kathies Pet (Tina's Pet)
412[6]

Mortimers Cross *John Needham* 104h 131c
13 b g Cloudings(IRE) Leinthall Doe (Oats)
3223[4] 3554[4] 4086[5]

Mortlestown (IRE) *Martin Keighley* 106h
6 b g Milan Pima (IRE) (Commanche Run)
1632[7] 3357[9] 4594[3]

Moscow In April (IRE) *Pat Murphy* 92h
7 ch m Moscow Society(USA) Muharib Lady (IRE) (Muharib (USA))
(122) 590[2] 946[P] 1170[P]

Moscow Mannon (IRE) *Henry De Bromhead* 142h 158c
8 b g Moscow Society(USA) Unfaithful Thought (Mind Games)
5168[4]

Moscow Me (IRE) *Henry Oliver* 107h
7 b g Moscow Society(USA) Just Trust Me (IRE) (Warcraft (USA))
971[2] 1152[6] 1255[7] 1374[6] (1674) (2051) 2676[6]
2891[3] 3157[5] 4899[8]

Moscow Menace (IRE) *Miss K Scott* 114c
7 b g Moscow Society(USA) Sky Flagship (FR) (Sky Lawyer (FR))
4239[2] 4554[2] 4837[2] 5536[3]

Moscow Mule *Laura Hurley* 98c
11 b g Moscow Society(USA) Madam Advocate (Avocat)
32[P] (269)
418[2] 600[P] *4021[14]* **5404[P]**

Moscow Presents (IRE) *Philip Kirby* 120h
6 b g Presenting Moscow Madame (IRE) (Moscow Society (USA))
2314[12] 2844[6] (3413) 3638[3] 4006[3] 4814[P]

Moscow Red (IRE) *Matt Sheppard* 46h
8 ch g Moscow Society(USA) Chirouble (IRE) (High Roller (IRE))
848[10] 1256[P]

Moskovskaya (FR) *H Billot*
5 b m Astarabad(USA) Malandra (Mtoto)
1199a[P]

Moss Cloud (IRE) *Donald McCain* 115h
7 bb g Cloudings(IRE) Adare Moss (IRE) (Le Moss)
(2493) 2838[4] 5214[3] 5537[P]

Mossey Joe (IRE) *E Bolger* 112h 125c
11 ch g Moscow Society(USA) Delmiano (IRE) (Henbit (USA))
(660) **5135[3]**

Moss On The Mill *Ben Case* 118h
6 br g Overbury(IRE) Mimis Bonnet (FR) (Bonnet Rouge (FR))
2720[5] 3173[4] (3850) 4969[8]

Mosspark (IRE) *Emma Lavelle* 141h
6 b g Flemensfirth(USA) Patio Rose (Petoski)
(2457) (3326) (4374) ◆ 4786[P]

Moss Street *Gordon Elliott* 114h
4 b g Moss Vale(IRE) Street Style (IRE) (Rock Of Gibraltar (IRE))
4199[P]

Mosstown (IRE) *Liam Corcoran* 125h 92c
8 b g Dilshaan Tavildara (IRE) (Kahyasi)
966[P] **1550[5]**
1699[P]

Most Eligible *David Pipe* 64h
7 b g Pursuit Of Love Danzig's Heiress (Danzig Connection (USA))
(588) 874[2] 1329[4]

Most Honourable *Michael Smith* 104h
4 b g Halling(USA) Her Ladyship (Polish Precedent (USA))
1658[4] 2154[2] 2592[U] (2881) 3448[4] 4054[6] 4834[6]

Mostly Bob (IRE) *Sophie Leech* 119h 130c
11 b g Bob Back(USA) Town Gossip (IRE) (Indian Ridge)
249[8] 509[P] 851[9] (1060)
1579[4] 1868[P]

Motorhead *Bob Buckler* 78b
5 ch h Motivator Duchcov (Caerleon (USA))
1539[4]

Motou (FR) *Richard Phillips* 107h
9 b g Astarabad(USA) Picoletta (FR) (Galetto (FR))
(2427) 2891[2] 3191[9]

Motown Bob (IRE) *Henry De Bromhead* 99b
4 br g Presenting Silent Orders (IRE) (Bob Back (USA))
5424a[5]

Moufatango (FR) *Nicky Richards* 113h
8 bb g Sagacity(FR) Bold-E-Be (Persian Bold)
(1751) (2035)

Moujik Borget (FR) *Venetia Williams* 125h
6 ch g Layman(USA) Fancy Tune (FR) (Green Tune (USA))
(2668) 3648[10] 3957[3] 4634[6] 5239[5]

Moula (CZE) *J Uhl*
6 b g Magnus(POL) Miss Mistery (CZE) (Manhattan Project)
1904a[F]

Moulin De La Croix *Oliver Sherwood* 87h 109c
10 b m Muhtarram(USA) Brambly Hedge (Teenoso (USA))
1886[P] 3058[7] 3248[3] 4352[3] 5027[3]

Moulin Tour (FR) *Henry Oliver* 68h 83c
8 ch g Majorien Queen Of Kenda (FR) (Kendor (FR))
269[6]

Mountain Cliche (IRE) *Jo Hughes*
7 b g Classic Cliche(IRE) Quarry Girl (IRE) (Lord Americo)
4029[P]

Mountaineer (FR) *Gary Moore* 106h 107c
9 b g Saint Des Saints(FR) Mistica (FR) (Subotica (FR))
1594[P] 1765[4] 2013[2]

Mountain King *Philip Hobbs* 130h
5 b g Definite Article Belle Magello (FR) (Exit To Nowhere (USA))
(2981) (3728) (4266) 4664[2]

Mountain Of Mourne (IRE) *Linda Blackford* 117b
5 ch g Mountain High(IRE) Katies Native (IRE) (Be My Native (USA))
433[2] (3295) 4149[3] 4756[21]

Mountainous (IRE) *Richard Lee* 127h 147c
9 b g Milan Mullaghcloga (IRE) (Glacial Storm (USA))
2452[3] 2943[3] (3361)
4026[5] 5171[F]

Mountain Tunes (IRE) *Jonjo O'Neill* 131h
5 br g Mountain High(IRE) Art Lover (IRE) (Over The River (FR))
(2316) (3177)

Mount Benbulben (IRE) *Gordon Elliott* 148h 165c
9 b g Beneficial Dramatic Dame (IRE) (Buckskin (FR))
2234a[U] 3262[4] 4435a[2]

Mount Gunnery *Robert Walford* 116h 106c
6 b g Kayf Tara Bobs Bay (IRE) (Bob's Return (IRE))
2469[7]

Mount Hope (IRE) *Donald McCain* 106h
7 ch g Albano(IRE) Quiet Sovereign (Supreme Leader)
475[7] 727[3]

Mount Odell *Gary Moore* 98h
6 b g Motivator Oscars Vision (IRE) (Oscar Schindler (IRE))
731[5] 1764[6] 2018[6] 2215[5] 2696[9] 3420[P]

Mount Sandel (IRE) *Mrs Alison Hickman* 120h 98c
13 b g Supreme Leader Droichidin (Good Thyne (USA))
329[P]

Mount Sion (IRE) *E Bolger* 93h 108c
8 b g Beneficial Miss Di (IRE) (Phardante (FR))
1905a[F]

Mount Vesuvius (IRE) *Paul Henderson* 107h
6 b g Spartacus(IRE) Parker's Cove (USA) (Woodman (USA))
178[2] 407[3] ◆ 686[2] 764[2] 924[5] 1273[2] (1443) (1504) 1699[3] 1943[3] 4937[9]

Mount Welcome (IRE) *Martin Weston* 111h 108c
10 b g Bach(IRE) Be My Vixen (IRE) (Be My Native (USA))
(43) **183[3]**
536[4] **(687)**
852[P] 1106[7]

Mourad (IRE) *W P Mullins* 137h
9 ch g Sinndar(IRE) Mouramara (IRE) (Kahyasi)
3790a[6] 5471a[5]

Mourne Paddy (IRE) *S R B Crawford* 110c
10 b g Winged Love(IRE) Mourne Miner (IRE) (Miner's Lamp)
679[3] 1147[5]

Moveable Asset (IRE) *Roger Curtis* 128h
6 b g Trans Island Mica Male (ITY) (Law Society (USA))
4897[6] 5231[11]

Move Along *Anthony Honeyball* 20b
7 ch m Grape Tree Road What A Mover (Jupiter Island)
1770[8] *2583[5]*

Moyaliff (IRE) *Sarah Humphrey* 123h
7 b g King's Theatre(IRE) Instant Queen (IRE) (Executive Perk)
119[P]

Moyle Park (IRE) *W P Mullins* 137h
6 ch g Flemensfirth(USA) Lovely Present (IRE) (Presenting)
3339a[3]

Moyne Nineoseven (IRE) *Noel Quinlan* 97h
8 b g Milan Laprida (IRE) (Executive Perk)
421[7] 669[7] 844[9] 946[3] 1275[6] 1405[2] 1538[5]

Moyode Wood *Brian Ellison* 112c
9 b g Overbury(IRE) Country Choice (IRE) (Paean)
2033[P] 2334[2] 2820[P]

Moyvic (IRE) *A J Martin* 99h
5 b g Old Vic Moydrum Castle (IRE) (Arctic Lord)
5537[6]

Mozoltov *W P Mullins* 145h 154c
8 b g Kayf Tara Fairmead Princess (Rudimentary (USA))
3928a[3] (4455a)
4764[F] 5422a[U]

Mr Bachster (IRE) *Richard Lee* 95h 93c
9 b g Bach(IRE) Warrior Princess (IRE) (Mister Lord (USA))
1169[7] 1331[5] 1580[6] 1838[2] **(2044)**
(2562) 5361[5]

Mr Beatle *Keith Reveley* 95b
5 br g Beat All(USA) Northern Native (IRE) (Be My Native (USA))
5447[3]

Mr Blue Nose *Karen George*
4 b g Tobougg(IRE) Cape Siren (Warning)
725[6]

Mr Bolt (IRE) *Michael O'Hare* 86h
9 br g Akbar(IRE) Keep The Pace (IRE) (Shardari)
2172[6] 2770[8]

Mr Bridger *Paul Nicholls* 107h
5 ch g Shirocco(GER) Diamant Noir (Sir Harry Lewis (USA))
2479[4] 3388[6]

Mr Burbidge *Neil Mulholland* 60b
6 b g Midnight Legend Twin Time (Syrtos)
354[U]

Mr Cardle (IRE) *Oliver Sherwood* 102h
5 b g Golan(IRE) Leave Me Be (IRE) (Be My Native (USA))
76[2] 2254[2] 2720[4]

Mr Chippy (IRE) *Donald McCain* 70h 86c
10 b g Laveron Lady Denel (IRE) (Denel (FR))
3528[P] 5104[3]

Mr Cracker (IRE) *Tim Vaughan* 93b
9 ch g Anshan Sesame Cracker (Derrylin)
1168a[18] 4160[P] 4768[P]

Mr Duffy (IRE) *D T Hughes* 107h 90c
12 br g Presenting Senorita Bonita (IRE) (Strong Gale)
1377[2] 1789[5]

Mr Fickle (IRE) *Gary Moore* 111h
5 b g Jeremy(USA) Mamara Reef (Salse (USA))
2265[7] 2906[8] 3034[10] 4371[7] 4703[2] 5238[3]

Mr Fiftyone (IRE) *Mrs John Harrington* 133h
5 b g Jeremy(USA) Maka (USA) (Diesis)
2377a[2] 2852a[6] 3667a[3] 3931a[6]

Mr Fitzroy (IRE) *Jo Davis* 92h
4 ch g Kyllachy Reputable (Medicean)
3161[10] 5175[4]

Mr Gardner (IRE) *Polly Gundry* 131h 131c
11 b g Deploy Lady Padivor (IRE) (Zaffaran (USA))
2283[6] 2812[9] 4104[6]

Mr Gee Jay *Nigel Twiston-Davies* 61h 96c
8 bl h Beat All(USA) Riverbank Rose (Lighter)
(141) ◆ 639[P]

Mr Goofy (IRE) *Michael Scudamore* 89c
13 b g Rock Hopper Jamie's Lady (Ashmore (FR))
1314[P] 5361[2]

Mr Grey (IRE) *Ben Case* 88h
6 gr g Great Palm(USA) Presenting Shares (IRE) (Presenting)
2266[6]

Mr Hudson (IRE) *Paul Nicholls* 83h 92c
9 b g Old Vic Esbeggi (Sabrehill (USA))
39[5] 587[12]

Mr Jay Dee (IRE) *Claire Dyson* 21h 89c
9 b g Lord Americo Emmas Flyer (IRE) (Beneficial)
181[5] 763[P] 1266[8]

Mr Kealshore *George Moore* 46h
5 b g Beat All(USA) Breeze Lie (FR) (Phantom Breeze)
1877[9] 2196[9]

Mr Lando *Tony Carroll* 109h
5 b g Shirocco(GER) Capitana (GER) (Lando (GER))
1913[P]

Mr Lennygreengrass (IRE) *Fergal O'Brien* 46h
7 b g Millenary Grassed (Busted)
2660[10] *4297[10]* 4702[6] 5288[P]

Mr Lover Lover (IRE) *John Butler*
5 b g Catcher In The Rye(IRE) Lovingit (IRE) (Fasliyev (USA))
599[P]

Mr Mansson (IRE) *Lucy Normile* 81h
7 b g Millenary Supreme Dare (IRE) (Supreme Leader)
3038[9] 3392[9] 5554[5]

Mr Maybe (IRE) *John Whyte*
9 b g Exit To Nowhere(USA) Miss Mayberry (IRE) (Bob Back (USA))
4252[RR]

Mr Maynard *Renee Robeson* 97h
5 ch g Notnowcato Crystal Cavern (USA) (Be My Guest (USA))
4529[5] 5057[6] 5403[5]

Mr Mistopheles (IRE) *Philip Kirby* 74h
6 b g Presenting Supreme Touch (IRE) (Supreme Leader)
747[P] 1419[2] 1790[6] 2169[10] 2497[9]

Mr Mole (IRE) *Paul Nicholls* 148h 144c
6 br g Great Pretender(IRE) Emmylou Du Berlais (FR) (Kadalko (FR))
216[2] **(2976)**
3185[3] 4101[2] 4790[F] (5551)

Mr Moonshine (IRE) *Sue Smith* 139h 156c
10 b g Double Eclipse(IRE) Kinross (Nearly A Hand)
2071[4] 2359[5] 2674[7] 2937[3] (3476)
(4160) ◆ 4552[2] 5171[15]

Mr Moss (IRE) *Evan Williams* 104h 142c
9 b g Moscow Society(USA) Yesterdays Gorby (IRE) (Strong Gale)
1991[5]
2487[5] 2822[6]

Mr Muddle *Sheena West* 102h 124c
7 gr g Imperial Dancer Spatham Rose (Environment Friend)
2977[2] 3164[4] 3859[5] 4539[3] 5112[6]

Mr Plod *J R Jenkins* 81h
9 ch g Silver Patriarch(IRE) Emily-Mou (IRE) (Cadeaux Genereux)
251[7] **786[F]**

Mr Robinson (FR) *Rob Summers* 72h 81c
7 b g Robin Des Pres(FR) Alberade (FR) (Un Desperado (FR))
2[5] **425[6]**
759[2] 926[6] 2152[4] 5404[6]

Mr Satco (IRE) *Donald McCain* 120h
6 b g Mr Combustible(IRE) Satlin (IRE) (Satco (FR))
(498) 731[3] 885[4] (1037) 1393[5]

Mrs Burbidge *Neil Mulholland* 61h
4 b f Pasternak Twin Time (Syrtos)
5303[6] 5541[8]

Mrs Eff *Philip Kirby* 110h 114c
8 b m Tamure(IRE) Roman Uproar (Primitive Rising (USA))
(111) 476[3] 3145[P] 3724[P]
4337[2]

Mr Selby *Nicky Richards* 85b
5 b g Terimon Bee-A-Scally (Scallywag)
1792[7] 2840[P]

Mrs Grass *Jonathan Haynes* 80h
7 ch m And Beyond(IRE) Tempted (IRE) (Invited (USA))
218[5] 1418[5] 1790[10] 2336[3] 2736[3] 3110[5] 3636[7] 3940[P] 4201[5] 4465[6] 4776[5] 5056[6] 5322[6]

Mr Shahady (IRE) *Victor Thompson* 11h 66c
9 b g Xaar Shunaire (USA) (Woodman (USA))
510[7]

Mr Shantu (IRE) *Jonjo O'Neill* 117h
5 b g Shantou(USA) Close To Shore (IRE) (Bob Back (USA))
2708[4] 2368[5] 2885[2] *4017[3]* 4450[4] 4807[15] 5117[U] 5235[6]

Mrs Jordan (IRE) *Venetia Williams* 101h
6 b m King's Theatre(IRE) Regents Dancer (IRE) (Flemensfirth (USA))
(1599) 2089[5] 2600[5] 3168[3] 3438[3] 4090[6] 5016[3] 5235[7]

Mrs Mac Veale (IRE) *Robert Murphy* 125h
9 b m Karinga Bay Carrigmorna Flyer (IRE) (Bob Back (USA))
2706a[6]

Mrs Peachey (IRE) *Kim Bailey* 132h
7 b m Brian Boru Maracana (IRE) (Glacial Storm (USA))
(268) (552) 738[4] (1783) 2371[2] 2948[4] 3319[5] 4961[12] 5370[13]

Mrs Peacock (IRE) *N J Edwards*
9 b m Dushyantor(USA) Peacock Feather (Bustino)
4518[P]

Mr Spiggott (IRE) *Gary Moore* 96h
5 b g Intikhab(USA) Green Green Grass (Green Desert (USA))
2564[3] 2858[P]

Mrs Rooney *Sue Gardner* 76b
7 b m Morpeth Lucky Mo (Zambrano)
1196[4]

Mr Supreme (IRE) *Keith Reveley* 117h 119c
9 b g Beneficial Ardfallon (IRE) (Supreme Leader)
2498[3] 3283[P] 3603[8] 3874[2] 4606[3] (5055)
(5481)

Mrs Winchester (IRE) *Caroline Keevil* 54h
5 b m Scorpion(IRE) Supreme Nova (Supreme Leader)
3049[8] 3961[11] 4540[6] 5236[8] 5389[P]

Mr Syntax (IRE) *Tim Fitzgerald* 100h 126c
10 b g King's Theatre(IRE) Smile Awhile (USA) (Woodman (USA))
2355[7] 3036[5] **3389[3] 4606[2] 5497[2]**

Mr Toy Boy *Helen Nelmes*
4 b g Phoenix Reach(IRE) Toy Girl (IRE) (Cadeaux Genereux)
4177[P]

Mr Trilby (IRE) *David Pipe* 80h
7 b g Millenary Bamji (IRE) (Dr Massini (IRE))
146[4] 499[3] 828[9] 1832[9]

Mr Utah *Henry Hogarth* 126h
7 b g Presenting Raphuca (IRE) (Be My Native (USA))
2172[2] (2866) (3396) 4347[8] 4834[3] (5379)

Mr Vendman (IRE) *Ian Williams* 95h
4 b g Whipper(USA) So Precious (IRE) (Batshoof)
3224[2] 4345[6] 4401[6] 4679[6] 5494[9]

Mr Watson (IRE) *Jonjo O'Neill* 139h 111c
7 b g Gold Well Risk And Reward (IRE) (Topanoora)
1640[4] 1973[3] 2976[4] 4190[P] 5336[P]

Mt Kintyre (IRE) *J Tickle*
8 b g Mull Of Kintyre(USA) Nihonpillow Mirai (IRE) (Zamindar (USA))
5123[P]

Mubrook (USA) *Brian Ellison* 118h
9 b g Alhaarth(IRE) Zomaradah (Deploy)
4306[7] 4697[6] 5061[6] 5272[4] 5484[6]

Much A Doo *Paul Henderson* 73b
6 gr g Act One Cos I Do (IRE) (Double Schwartz)
760[8] 862[7] 3295[6]

Muckle Roe (IRE) *Nigel Twiston-Davies* 114h
5 b g Westerner Island Crest (Jupiter Island)
1667[3] 1974[18] 2876[5] 3728[2] ◆ 5347[6]

Mudita Moment (IRE) *Venetia Williams* 121h
9 b g Heron Island(IRE) Woodville Leader (IRE) (Supreme Leader)
(3434) (3553) (4108) 4491[2] 4834[5]

Muharrer *Michael Dods* 105h
5 b g Shamardal(USA) Shawahid (USA) (A.P. Indy (USA))
2968[4]

Muhtaris (IRE) *John Ferguson* 114h
4 b g Teofilo(IRE) Fann (USA) (Diesis)
(3003) 4111[7] 4401[5]

Muirhead (IRE) *Noel Meade* 127h 139c
11 b g Flemensfirth(USA) Silaoce (FR) (Nikos)
1168a[4] 1604a[3] 1897a[13] 2708a[P]

Mukonzi Has (FR) *M Rolland* 85h 119c
6 b g Turgeon(USA) Miss Benedicte (FR) (Baby Turk)
1984a[P]

Muldoon's Picnic (IRE) *Kim Bailey* 132h 140c
8 b g King's Theatre(IRE) Going My Way (Henbit (USA))
(16) **(603)**
(1918)
3594[3] 4738[P] 5344[F]

Mullaghanoe River (IRE) *Noel Meade* 130h 142c
6 b g Beneficial Wahiba Hall (IRE) (Saddlers' Hall (IRE))
3908a[3] 4709a[U] 5474a[F]

Mulligan's Man (IRE) *Donald McCain* 125h 118c
7 b g Morozov(USA) Rashmulligan (IRE) (Rashar (USA))
234[U] 369[2] 679[2] 899[3] 1144[2] 1390[3] 1753[2] 2496[4]
3272[U] 3736[5]

Mullinavat (IRE) *Tom George* 49b
5 b g Beneficial Kilfane (IRE) (Hollow Hand)
2026[11]

Multilicious *Mark Walford* 73h
4 b f Multiplex Ryan's Quest (IRE) (Mukaddamah (USA))
1920[0] 2154[3] 2592[6] 3385[8] 4309[6]

Multitude Of Sins *Colin Tizzard* 120h
7 b g Lucky Owners(NZ) Lady Turk (FR) (Baby Turk)
847[8] 920[3] 1052[4] 1337[4] (1697) 1943[6] 2461[9]

Multiview *Tom Symonds* 84h
5 b m Multiplex Lacounsel (FR) (Leading Counsel (USA))
1264[4] 1427[6] 5244[5]

Mumbles Bay (IRE) *Peter Bowen* 41h
8 b g Oscar(IRE) Klipperstreet (IRE) (Supreme Leader)
1364[9] 3605[P]

Mumbles Head (IRE) *Peter Bowen* 134h 139c
13 ch g Flemensfirth(USA) Extra Mile (Torus)
355[9] 680[8] (1146)
4769[P]

Mumbles Pier (IRE) *Peter Bowen* 86h 114c
9 b g Definite Article Golden Jorden (IRE) (Cadeaux Genereux)
241[2] ◆ 436[3]

Mumgos Debut (IRE) *Lucinda Russell* 99h 99c
6 b g Royal Anthem(USA) Black Queen (IRE) (Bob Back (USA))
313[12] 865[5] 1159[4] 1543[5] 1791[8]
3213[2] 3722[2] 4203[P]

Mungo Park *Sophie Leech* 97h
6 b g Selkirk(USA) Key Academy (Royal Academy (USA))
1171[7]

Munlochy Bay *Matt Sheppard* 102h
10 b m Karinga Bay Meghdoot (Celestial Storm (USA))
393[6] 719[6] 811[7] 1266[B] 1391[5] 1917[10]

Munsaab (IRE) *Charlie Longsdon* 122h 118c
8 b g Alhaarth(IRE) Claustra (FR) (Green Desert (USA))
2102[5] 2538[3] 2935[7]
3429[3] 3738[4] 4696[3] 5076[2] 5385[11]

Murcar *Liam Corcoran* 110h
9 ch g Medicean In Luck (In The Wings)
604[2] 767[6] 2314[9] 5260[6]

Murfreesboro *Raymond York* 97h
11 b g Bahamian Bounty Merry Rous (Rousillon (USA))
29[P] 903[12]

Murrayana (IRE) *Colin Tizzard* 92b
4 b g King's Theatre(IRE) Royalrova (FR) (Garde Royale)
4424[6] 5241[4]

Murray Mount (IRE) *Charlie Mann* 64b
4 b g Trans Island Ash (Salse (USA))
4964[14]

Murtys Delight (IRE) *Dr Richard Newland* 108h
7 b g Bach(IRE) Valley Supreme (IRE) (Supreme Leader)
2189[P] 2471[7] 2748[5] 3061[6] 3740[2] 3884[P] 4351[4] 4893[6]

Musical Wedge *Claire Dyson* 87h 116c
10 ch g Sir Harry Lewis(USA) Wedge Musical (What A Guest)
2253[8]
(2700) 3267[2] 3743[5] 4402[7] 4601[5] 4990[P]

Music In The Air *Robin Dickin* 77h
10 ch m Kadastrof(FR) Makin Whoopee (IRE) (Air Display (USA))
71[6] 460[2]

Music Of The Morn *Mrs Julie Mansell* 58c
7 b m Alflora(IRE) Magical Molly (Henbit (USA))
4922[6] 5248[U]

Musnad (USA) *Brian Ellison* 116h 97c
6 ch g Mr Greeley(USA) Jadarah (USA) (Red Ransom (USA))
171[2] **474[3]**

Musselwick Bay *Marc Barber*
6 b m Dreams End Midnight May (Mister Lord (USA))
1445[6]

Mut'Ab (USA) *Mark Gillard* 104h 81c
9 b g Alhaarth(IRE) Mistle Song (Nashwan (USA))
926[5]

Mutanawwer *Andrew Crook* 108b
5 br g Red Ransom(USA) Nasheed (USA) (Riverman (USA))
389[2] ◆ 885[3] 1138[2] (1420)

Mutashabek (USA) *Caroline Keevil* 86h
4 b g Arch(USA) Siyadah (USA) (Mr Prospector (USA))
5305[8]

Muwalla *Chris Grant* 104h 109c
7 b g Bahri(USA) Easy Sunshine (IRE) (Sadler's Wells (USA))
202[3] **446[F]**
882[5] 1206[5] 1280[2] **1417[2] (1503)**
2173[7] 2791[4] 5357[6]

Muzey's Princess *Michael Mullineaux* 71b
8 b m Grape Tree Road Premier Princess (Hard Fought)
1266[P]

Mwaleshi *Sue Smith* 141h 143c
9 b g Oscar(IRE) Roxy River (Ardross)
2069[9]
(2515) 2839[2] (3202)
3386[U]

My Best Man *Tony Carroll* 5h
8 b g Forzando Victoria Sioux (Ron's Victory (USA))
1779[11] 2089[10]

My Boy George (IRE) *John O'Shea* 96b
6 b g Artan(IRE) Gold Stamp (Golden Act (USA))
1836[2]

My Boy Ginger *Chris Gordon* 76h
5 ch g Byron Lady Chef (Double Trigger (IRE))
243[9] 308[6]

My Boy Paddy (IRE) *Nigel Twiston-Davies* 106h 123c
10 ch g Accordion Securon Rose (IRE) (Roselier (FR))
2157[2] 3858[6] 5119[P] 5284[3]

My Brother Sylvest *David Pipe* 125h 138c
8 b g Bach(IRE) Senna Da Silva (Prince Of Birds (USA))
806[5] (1346) 1485[5] **(1782)** 1943[2] **2212[13] 2531[5]**

My Dads Horse *Evan Williams* 113c
8 ch g Exit To Nowhere(USA) Fruity Farm (Weld)
2643[3] 3601[5] 4541[3] 4946[5]

My Dancing Angel (IRE) *Mrs Rosemary Rooney* 79h
5 b m St Jovite(USA) My Friend Annie (IRE) (Supreme Leader)
2995a[10]

My Destination (IRE) *Declan Carroll* 78h
5 b g Dubai Destination(USA) Gossamer (Sadler's Wells (USA))
2874[6] 3208[P] 3600[8] 3877[14]

Myetta *Lydia Richards* 47h
6 gr m Silver Patriarch(IRE) Henrietta Holmes (IRE) (Persian Bold)
268[8]

My Fella (IRE) *Andrew Quick* 109h 85c
11 gr g Insatiable(IRE) Deep Impact (Deep Run)
58[9] 4518[P]

My Flora *Dan Skelton* 87h 129c
10 b m Alflora(IRE) Bishop's Folly (Weld)
77[2] 596[4] 3058[5] 3603[4] (4966)
5211[3]

My Friend George *Dianne Sayer* 82h 96c
8 ch g Alflora(IRE) Snowgirl (IRE) (Mazaad)
473[3] ◆ 881[P]
1798[P]

My Friend Riquet (FR) *Dave Roberts* 65h
7 b g Laveron Brave Chartreuse (FR) (Villez (USA))
946[6] 1121[11] 1631[6] 1673[8] **1728[P] 3635[U]** *4325[5]*

My Guardian Angel *Mark H Tompkins* 120h
5 b g Araafa(IRE) Angels Guard You (Bahamian Bounty)
2068[4] (2718) 2932[6] 4794[2] 5399[5]

My Idea *Maurice Barnes* 106h 112c
8 b g Golan(IRE) Ghana (GER) (Bigstone (IRE))
1674[4] 493[U] 583[3] 1665[2]
1981[3] 2031[5] 2356[6] (2791)
2996[3] 3658[2] 4055[5] (5060)
5297[B]

My Lad Percy *Rebecca Curtis* 108h 95c
6 b g Central Park(IRE) Only Millie (Prince Daniel (USA))
145[2] (253) (503) 767[U] 877[12]
1083[4] 1257[F]

My Legal Lady *Stuart Howe* 109h
9 b m Sir Harry Lewis(USA) Clifton Mist (Lyphento (USA))
144[3] 3604[4] 4599[5] 5391[2]

My Lil Ledge (IRE) *Mrs Julie Mansell* 78c
9 b m Oscar Schindler(IRE) Old Mother Hubbard (IRE) (Strong Gale)
61[P]

Mylittlemouse (IRE) *Helen Nelmes* 70b
6 b m Turtle Island(IRE) Ballybeg Rose (IRE) (Roselier (FR))
5130[8]

My Lord *Luke Dace* 110h
6 br g Ishiguru(USA) Lady Smith (Greensmith)
691[5] 846[2] (927) 1173[5] (1551) 1840[6]

Mylord Collonges (FR) *Susan Nock* 81h 117c
14 bl g Video Rock(FR) Diane Collonges (FR) (El Badr)
92[6]

My Lucky Flame (IRE) *Sean Curran* 119h
7 b m Flemensfirth(USA) My Friend Annie (IRE) (Supreme Leader)
317[2] 502[2] (649) (878) (1084) 1330[4] 1818[6]
2150[P]

My Maj (FR) *Yannick Fouin* 136h 136c
5 ch g Majorien Janemarie (FR) (Cricket Ball (USA))
683a[5] 1983a[3] 2414a[5]

My Manikato *Richard Phillips* 69h
7 ch g Starcraft(NZ) Rainbow Queen (FR) (Spectrum (IRE))
671[8]

My Mate Jake (IRE) *James Given* 105h
6 ch g Captain Rio Jam (IRE) (Arazi (USA))
560[6]

My Mate Paddy *Ms N M Hugo* 82h
7 b g Deploy City Times (IRE) (Last Tycoon)
19[P]

My Mate Vinnie (IRE) *Jonjo O'Neill* 119h 118c
7 ch g Vinnie Roe(IRE) A Rare One (IRE) (Mandalus)
(461) **713[2]**
1049[4] 1257[4] 1486[2] 2099[P]

My Miss Lucy *Charlie Longsdon* 108h
8 b m Alflora(IRE) Corn Lily (Aragon)
2317[3] (3005)

My Moment (IRE) *David Thompson* 105h 113c
11 ch g Presenting Golden Moment (IRE) (Roselier (FR))
1076[5] 1396[3]

My Murphy (IRE) *W J Burke* 142h 147c
8 b g Presenting Fine De Claire (Teenoso (USA))
3404a[4] 4315a[2] 5474a[P]

My Nosy Rosy *Ben Case* 92h
6 b m Alflora(IRE) Quiz Night (Kayf Tara)
1938[U] 2191[2] 2679[8]

My Oh Mount Brown (IRE) *Alan McCabe* 125h
7 b g Millenary My O Mio (IRE) (Norwich)
1495[5] (1718) (1820) 2202[2] (2771) 3286[P] (4596)

My Old Lady (IRE) *Denis Gerard Hogan* 83h
9 ch m Old Vic Kendilstown Lady (IRE) (Phardante (FR))
5302[4]

My Silver Lilly *Clive Drew* 67h 82c
7 b m Silver Patriarch(IRE) Myumi (Charmer)
2698[P] 3014[P] **4110[5] 4481[7] 4778[P]**

My Son Harry (IRE) *Victor Dartnall* 59b
6 b g Heron Island(IRE) Carraigbyrne (IRE) (Over The River (FR))
412[10] 1525[4]

My Space *Fiona Shaw* 73h
8 b m Pasternak Eatons (Daring March)
4632[13] 4910[12]

Mysteree (IRE) *Lucinda Russell* 124h
6 b g Gold Well Hillside Native (IRE) (Be My Native (USA))
(1054) 1980[2] 2355[2] 2954[1] 4200[3] (4050) 5093[10]

Mystery Drama *Alan King* 113h
4 b f Hernando(FR) Mystery Lot (IRE) (Revoque (IRE))
(2557) 2934[2] 5455[3]

Mystical Dreamer (IRE) *Ronald O'Leary* 83h
5 ch g Flemensfirth(USA) Voodoo Magic (GER) (Platini (GER))
(2738)

Mystical Flame (IRE) *David Pipe* 63b
5 b m Flemensfirth(USA) Lizzie Bathwick (IRE) (Glacial Storm (USA))
5021[8] 5241[8]

Mystic Appeal (IRE) *Jeremy Scott* 110h
8 br g Alderbrook Piseog (IRE) (Pistolet Bleu (IRE))
4172[5] 4501[4] 5022[7]

Mystifiable *Fergal O'Brien* 117h 72c
6 gr g Kayf Tara Royal Keel (Long Leave)
1795[4] 1958[5] 2602[3] 3012[2] **4077[5]**

Mystified (IRE) *Alan Berry* 89h 84c
11 b g Raise A Grand(IRE) Sunrise (IRE) (Sri Pekan (USA))
474[4] 534[5] 1074[4]

Mysula *Claire Dyson* 29h
7 b m Sulamani(IRE) Air Of Affection (Air Express (IRE))
369[U] 4595[P] 4823[6] 5234[13]

Mytara *Clive Drew* 72b
9 br m Kayf Tara Myumi (Charmer)
2679[P]

My Tent Or Yours (IRE) *Nicky Henderson* 173h
7 b g Desert Prince(IRE) Spartan Girl (IRE) (Ela-Mana-Mou)
(2821) (3261) *(4302)* 4739[2] 5274[3]

My Wigwam Or Yours (IRE) *Nicky Henderson* 139h
5 b g Beneficial Midnight Pond (IRE) (Long Pond)
14[2] 338[3] 1974[4] 2432[2] 2808[F] 3278[3] (4931)
5347[4]

Nadiya De La Vega (FR) *Nicky Henderson* 148c
8 bb m Lost World(IRE) Shinobie (FR) (Le Nain Jaune (FR))
2503[13] 3090[3] 3647[7] 4768[P] 5475a[2]

Nagpur (FR) *Venetia Williams* 137h 133c
8 b g Byzantium(FR) Bel'Cris (FR) (Cricket Ball (USA))
(182) ◆ **394[3]**

Nahneh (IRE) *John Wade* 45h
8 b g Beneficial Arusha Rose (IRE) (Supreme Leader)
556[7] 678[9]

Nail 'M (IRE) *Nigel Hawke* 101h 119c
6 b g Milan Honor Kicks (FR) (Highest Honor (FR))
185[8] 592[5] 2616[3]
2922[U] 3176[4] (4451)
(4580) 4835[4] 5334[4]

Naledi *Richard Price* 87h
10 b g Indian Ridge Red Carnation (IRE) (Polar Falcon (USA))
49[6] 253[7] 648[6] 809[6] (1106) 1269[5] 1428[5] 1633[4]
1799[13]

Nalim (IRE) *W A Bethell* 83h 69c
8 b g Milan Hati Roy (IRE) (Lafontaine (USA))
3801[5]

Namibian (IRE) *John Ferguson* 98h
6 b g Cape Cross(IRE) Disco Volante (Sadler's Wells (USA))
3034[8] 3598[P]

Nampour (FR) *Colin Tizzard* 126h
9 gr g Daylami(IRE) Nadira (FR) (Green Desert (USA))
82[8]

Napoletano (ITY) *Michael Scudamore* 63h
8 b g Kyllachy Nationality (Nashwan (USA))
71[10]

Narcissist (IRE) *Michael Easterby* 109h
5 b g Dylan Thomas(IRE) Gabare (FR) (Galileo (IRE))
2225[10] 2520[3] 2732[8] 5496[4]

Naschador (FR) *E Leray*
10 b g Nashamaa Orielle (FR) (Pharly (FR))
1532a[P]

Nash Point (IRE) *Tim Vaughan* 84h
5 ch g Kris Kin(USA) Ten Dollar Bill (IRE) (Accordion)
2266[7] 2471[11] 3357[15] 4729[4] 5234[7]

Nataani (IRE) *Jo Davis* 107h 136c
11 br g Presenting Clahada Rose (IRE) (Roselier (FR))
845[9] **1579[3]**
1868[8] 4662[7]
5344[7]

Nataraja *Tony Coyle* 84b
5 b g Norse Dancer(IRE) Floral Rhapsody (Alflora (IRE))
790[8] 1013[7]

Nathans Pride (IRE) *Tim Vaughan* 103h
6 ch g Definite Article Tricias Pride (IRE) (Broken Hearted)
3187[8] 4226[4]

National Petition (IRE) *Miss Victoria Easterby* 84h 110c
12 b g King's Theatre(IRE) Retinue (IRE) (Mister Lord (USA))
557[P]

Native Brian (IRE) *Alexandra Dunn* 97h
8 b g Brian Boru Gentle Native (IRE) (Be My Native (USA))
1672[8] 1864[8] 2009[7] 2628[3] 2908[F] 3174[P]

Native Colony *John O'Shea* 111h
6 b g St Jovite(USA) Self Esteem (Suave Dancer (USA))
163[4] 977[2] 1258[F] 1483[2]

Native Court (IRE) *Mark Michael McNiff* 98h
8 b g Court Cave(IRE) Native Lier (IRE) (Be My Native (USA))
747[7] 2596[P]

Native Explorer *John Gallagher* 76b
5 b m Kayf Tara Explorer (Krisinsky (USA))
5528[11]

Native Gallery (IRE) *Ben De Haan* 147h 131c
9 gr g Portrait Gallery(IRE) Native Bev (IRE) (Be My Native (USA))
356[8] 2454[4] 2813[12]
3647[3] 3897[P]

Native Optimist (IRE) *Sheena Walton* 83h
7 b g Broadway Flyer(USA) Native Orchid (IRE) (Be My Native (USA))
2355[P] 2838[6] 3634[4] 3824[4] 4461[7] 5161[11] 5359[8]

Native Princess *Renee Robeson* 21b
4 b f Tobougg(IRE) Forest Pride (IRE) (Be My Native (USA))
4403[9]

Native Spa (IRE) *Michael Smith* 103h
6 b g Norwich Thethirstyscholars (IRE) (Be My Native (USA))
3042[6] 3829[5] 4609[3] 4891[5]

Natural High (IRE) *Sean Curran* 115h
9 b g Sadler's Wells(USA) Cool Clarity (IRE) (Indian Ridge)
1729[8]

Nautical Approach (IRE) *S G Allen* 91h 113c
11 b g Oscar(IRE) Creative Approach (IRE) (Toulon)
297[P]

Nautical Twilight *Malcolm Jefferson* 96h
4 gr f Proclamation(IRE) Anabranch (Kind Of Hush)
2168[4] 2733[3] 3212[2] 3527[6] 4531[8]

Nearest The Pin (IRE) *John Joseph Hanlon* 134h 146c
9 b g Court Cave(IRE) Carnbelle (IRE) (Electric)
4806[2]

Nearly May *Donald Whillans* 98b
6 b m Winged Love(IRE) Lindajane (IRE) (Erin's Hope)
885[6] 3727[2] 4240[11]

Nearly Normal (IRE) *David Dennis* 46h
5 b g Scorpion(IRE) Lakeshore Lodge (IRE) (Taipan (IRE))
2354[10] 2978[15]

Near The Water (IRE) *R J Harraway* 104h 90c
10 b g Oscar(IRE) The Dark One (IRE) (Mandalus)
297[4] 430[F]

Nebula Storm (IRE) *Gary Moore* 93h
7 b g Galileo(IRE) Epping (Charnwood Forest (IRE))
708[5] 1275[12] 1428[6] 1630[5] 2062[3]

Neck Or Nothing (GER) *Philip Hobbs* 123b
5 b g Intikhab(USA) Nova (GER) (Winged Love (IRE))
2534[8] 4756[12] 5310[2]

Ned Buntline *Noel Meade* 138h 146c
6 b g Refuse To Bend(IRE) Intrum Morshaan (IRE) (Darshaan)
4790[2]

Ned Stark (IRE) *Alan King* 119h
6 b g Wolfe Tone(IRE) Last Moon (IRE) (Montelimar (USA))
2457[2] (5541)

Ned The Post (IRE) *E Walker* 99c
10 b g Riberetto Legal Tour (IRE) (Legal Circles (USA))
658[4] 5337[P]

Ned The Vet (IRE) *S J Mahon* 73h
7 b g Xaar Fritillary (Vettori (IRE))
1331[12]

Nedzer's Return (IRE) *Gordon Elliott* 92h 113c
12 b g Bob's Return(IRE) Moydanganrye (IRE) (Over The River (FR))
680[P] (Dead)

Needwood Park *Ray Craggs* 86h
6 br g Needwood Blade Waterpark (Namaqualand (USA))
283[P] 3274[8] 3636[9]

Nefyn Bay *Donald McCain* 90h
5 b g Overbury(IRE) So Cloudy (Cloudings (IRE))
367[5] 732[6] 843[4]

Neighbourhood (USA) *James Evans* 108h
6 bb g Street Cry(IRE) Miznah (IRE) (Sadler's Wells (USA))
2280[6] 4450[2] 4904[8]

Neighbours Lady *Patrick J Hanly* 86b
7 b m Karinga Bay Mulloch Brae (Sunyboy)
4485[P]

Nellie Forbush *Sophie Leech* 88h
4 b f Phoenix Reach(IRE) Santa Isobel (Nashwan (USA))
1727[3] 1920[2] (2066) 5518[3]

Nell's Nan (IRE) *John C McConnell* 96h
6 b m Shantou(USA) Bobnval (IRE) (Bob Back (USA))
1187[5] (Dead)

Nelson Du Ronceray (FR) *Jean McGregor*
13 b g Lute Antique(FR) Trieste (FR) (Quart De Vin (FR))
5514[P]

Nelson's Bay *Noel Quinlan* 84h
5 b g Needwood Blade In Good Faith (USA) (Dynaformer (USA))
427[5]

Neltara *Claire Dyson* 129h
10 b g Kayf Tara Lucia Forte (Neltino)
1968[5]

Nemo Spirit (IRE) *Jim Best* 100h
9 gr g Daylami(IRE) La Bayadere (Sadler's Wells (USA))
2004[11]

Neptune Equester *Sandy Thomson* 118h 113c
11 b g Sovereign Water(FR) All Things Nice (Sweet Monday)
509[3] 2428[2] 2746[2] 3108[5] 3505[3] **4661[6]** 4954[2]
5558[P]

Nesterenko (GER) *Nicky Henderson* 128h
5 b g Doyen(IRE) Nordwahl (GER) (Waajib)
2467[3] 2858[4] (3390) ◆ 3599[4] 3891[4] (5057)
5172[4]

Neston Grace *Simon Hodgson* 111h
6 b m Kayf Tara Politely (Tragic Role (USA))
(519) 1639[3] 1941[11] (2695) 2932[9] 3423[6] *4298[3]*

Netherby *Gary Moore* 122h 108c
8 b g Fair Mix(IRE) Lissadell (IRE) (Zaffaran (USA))
1782[3]

Nether Stream (IRE) *David Dennis* 97h
10 b g Blueprint(IRE) Shuil Ub (Le Moss)
2045[7] 2292[5] 2598[8] 3420[11] 3788[10] 5191[P]

Netminder (IRE) *Sandy Thomson* 129h 130c
8 b g Insatiable(IRE) Princess Douglas (Bishop Of Orange)
1976[P] 2822[5]

Never Another (USA) *Julia Feilden*
5 b g Manduro(GER) Discuss (USA) (Danzig (USA))
1690[P]

Never Enough Time (IRE) *Thomas Foley* 150h
6 b g Oscar(IRE) Ou La La (IRE) (Be My Native (USA))
4785[24]

Never Never (IRE) *Donald McCain* 111h
4 b g Jeremy(USA) Argus Gal (IRE) (Alzao (USA))
(5109)

Neverownup (IRE) *K F Clutterbuck* 105h 119c
9 b g Quws Cobble (IRE) (Bigstone (IRE))
1018[3] 1153[4] **1303[2] 1534[3] 1668[P]** 5434[2]

Never Says Never *Bob Buckler* 110h
6 b g Tamure(IRE) Quick Exit (Exit To Nowhere (USA))
458[2] 638[4] 1946[5] 2286[3] 2755[9]

Neville *Philip Hobbs* 104h
6 b g Revoque(IRE) Dudeen (IRE) (Anshan)
(731) 2028[3] 2457[F]

Neville Woods *J L Gledson* 110h
7 b g Alflora(IRE) Angie Marinie (Sabrehill (USA))
359[10] 3002[6] 4548[7] 4956[4] 5206[4]

New Academy *John Wade* 44h
6 ch g Zamindar(USA) New Abbey (Sadler's Wells (USA))
2341[9]

New Christmas (USA) *Chris Down* 112h
7 rg g Smoke Glacken(USA) Occhi Verdi (IRE) (Mujtahid (USA))
2280[F]

Newdane Dancer (IRE) *Dianne Sayer* 96h 82c
7 b m Golan(IRE) Flagofconvienience (IRE) (Old Vic)
1716[4] 1870[6] 2035[F] 2306[7] (3353) 3830[3] (4465)
4615[2] 4957[5] 5302[6]

Newforge House (IRE) *Brendan Powell* 96h
6 b g High-Rise(IRE) Treasure Island (Rainbow Quest (USA))
1826[4] 2681[2] 3278[5] 3783[6]

Newmans Boy *Neil Mulholland* 45h
7 ch g Loup Sauvage(USA) Newman's Conquest (El Conquistador)
809[9] 997[P]

New Phase (IRE) *A J McNamara* 141h 117c
10 b g Spectrum(IRE) South Of Heaven (IRE) (Fairy King (USA))
1896a[2] (Dead)

New Shuil (IRE) *John Wade* 85b
10 b g New Frontier(IRE) Shuil Ura (IRE) (Phardante (FR))
4222[P] 5060[P]

Newspage (IRE) *John Wade* 32h 75c
8 b g Blueprint(IRE) Newlineview (IRE) (Saddlers' Hall (IRE))
2155[5] 2818[8] 3275[6]

New Spirit (FR) *F Nicolle* 109h
4 ch g Soave(GER) Accademia (FR) (Exit To Nowhere (USA))
262a[F]

Newton Thistle *Ben Pauling* 91h 42c
7 b g Erhaab(USA) Newton Venture (Petoski)
3873[7] 4243[F] (4446) 4779[P] 5114[8]

New Vic (IRE) *Nicky Richards*
8 ch g Old Vic Innovate (IRE) (Posen (USA))
339[4]

New Year's Eve *John Ferguson* 130h
6 b g Motivator Midnight Angel (GER) (Acatenango (GER))
1256[2] 1404[2] (1839) 3477[8] (3880) (4306) ◆
4682[10]

Newyearsresolution (IRE) *Simon Waugh* 97h 78c
10 b g Mr Combustible(IRE) That's Magic (IRE) (Lord Americo)
112[6] 4042[6] 4617[5]

New Zafeen (IRE) *Rebecca Menzies* 72b
4 b g Zafeen(FR) Modelliste (Machiavellian (USA))
3214[10] 4895[11] 5108[6]

Nexius (IRE) *Keith Dalgleish* 117h
5 b g Catcher In The Rye(IRE) Nicolaia (GER) (Alkalde (GER))
3144[10] 3616[3] 3872[13] (4816) (5375) ◆

Next Edition (IRE) *Philip Kirby* 107h
6 b g Antonius Pius(USA) Starfish (IRE) (Galileo (IRE))
927[2] 1785[7]

Next Exit (IRE) *John Cornwall* 77h 116c
9 b g Exit To Nowhere(USA) Pilgrim Star (IRE) (Marju (IRE))
779[4] 1494[4] 1916[P] 2063[U] 5067[10]
5446[3]

Next Hight (IRE) *Sue Smith* 105h
7 b g High Chaparral(IRE) Night Petticoat (GER) (Petoski)
2156[10] 2225[8] 2869[2] 3040[11] (3636) 4085[P] 4612[4]

Next Oasis (IRE) *Paul Henderson* 97h 118c
8 b g Classic Cliche(IRE) Clearwater Glen (Furry Glen)
235[6] **634[5]**
◆ (832)
1192[P] 1636[F] 2370[P] 5352[4]

Next Sensation (IRE) *Michael Scudamore* 106h 150c
7 b g Brian Boru Road Trip (IRE) (Anshan)
1553[3]
(2007) (2496)
2816[U] (3386)
4790[4] ◆ 5168[5]

Next To Nowhere (IRE) *Christopher Kellett* 47h 44c
9 ch g Exit To Nowhere(USA) Zarote (IRE) (Mandalus)
3141[12]

Nez Rouge (FR) *Nigel Twiston-Davies* 99h 96c
13 gr g April Night(FR) Gracieuse Des Bois (FR) (Panoramic)
719[3] 860[3] 1073[2] 1707[9] **1886[5] 2721[8]**

Niceboy (IRE) *Daniel Steele* 52b
10 br g Environment Friend Take The Catch (Relief Pitcher)
3138[P] 3251[P] *4298[13]* **4439[P]**

Nicene Creed *Sophie Leech* 107h 25c
9 b g Hernando(FR) First Fantasy (Be My Chief (USA))
1940[3] 2458[2] 2842[4] 3413[5] 3699[9]
4884[10] 5187[P]

Niceonefrankie *Venetia Williams* 113h 150c
8 b g Ishiguru(USA) Chesnut Ripple (Cosmonaut)
6[5] (2645)
2800[5] 3897[5] 4422[6] 4962[6] 5261[5] 5383[P]

Nicki's Nipper *Shaun Lycett* 59b
6 b m Denounce Mistress Star (Soldier Rose)
2026[10]

Nicknack (FR) *P Peltier*
4 b f Nickname(FR) Villa Joyeuse (FR) (Kahyasi)
615a[P]

Nicks Power (IRE) *Robin Dickin* 109h 104c
8 b g Luso Shii-Take's Girl (Deploy)
812[12]
1550[4] 1834[4] 2048[3]

Nick The Dove (IRE) *Chris Nenadich* 55b
6 b g Tamure(IRE) Sovereign Dove (Sovereign Water (FR))
141[2] 874[10] 1427[7]

Nicky Nutjob (GER) *John O'Shea* 102h
8 b g Fasliyev(USA) Natalie Too (USA) (Irish River (FR))
17[8] 266[5] 429[2] (543) 640[5] 801[4] 1018[5] 1188[2] 1363[3] (1436) 1538[6] 1887[3] 2020[2] 2388[4] 3060[5] 4700[8] 5019[10] 5262[12]

Nicky Tam (IRE) *Henry Hogarth* 58h 80c
12 bb g Presenting Wigmore (IRE) (Denel (FR))
172[6] 580[8] (1038)
1163[6]

Nicolas Chauvin (IRE) *Nicky Henderson* 102b
6 b g Saffron Walden(FR) Kenzie (IRE) (Presenting)
5492[3] ◆

Night Alliance (IRE) *Dr Richard Newland* 105h 139c
9 ch g Pierre Next Venture (IRE) (Zaffaran (USA))
1887[6] 2253[3] **(2390)**
(2646) 2972[F] (3205)
3780[P] 4769[P]

Night In Milan (IRE) *Keith Reveley* 124h 149c
8 b g Milan Chione (IRE) (Mandalus)
355[2] 2170[3] 2672[14] **(3091)**
3897[P] (4544)

Nightline *Henry Daly* 100b
4 b g Midnight Legend Whichway Girl (Jupiter Island)
2830[4] 5021[2]

Night Of Passion (IRE) *Jeremy Scott* 109h
6 b m Winged Love(IRE) Miss Dundee (FR) (Esprit Du Nord (USA))
849[U] 922[4] 1132[4] 2004[9] 2312[3] 2690[2] (3138) (3227) 3691[2] 4161[P] 5033[2]

Night Safe (IRE) *Nigel Twiston-Davies* 101h 109c
13 b g Safety Catch(USA) Rock All Night (IRE) (Orchestra)
4354[P] 4843[2] 5185[5] 5546[P]

Nikas (CZE) *S Popelka Jr*
9 b g Scater(POL) Nika (CZE) (Chiavari (IRE))
1905a[2]

Niki Royal (FR) *Jamie Snowden* 110h 96c
9 b m Nikos Balgarde (FR) (Garde Royale)
179[6] 2021[4] 2312[11] 2698[5] **3058[4]** 4472[4]

Nikita Du Berlais (FR) *Robert Collet* 145h
7 b m Poliglote Chica Du Berlais (FR) (Cadoudal (FR))
406a[6] 685a[P]

Niknad *Brian Ellison* 55h
4 b f Zafeen(FR) Eau Rouge (Grand Lodge (USA))
1394[P] 1501[4]

Nils (IRE) *P Favero*
8 b g Kheleyf(USA) Bu Hagab (IRE) (Royal Academy (USA))
1683a[2]

Nimbus Gale (IRE) *Oliver Sherwood* 93b
5 b g Cloudings(IRE) Barton Gale (IRE) (Strong Gale)
2660[6] 4575[4] 5249[11]

Ninepointsixthree *John O'Shea* 101h
4 b g Bertolini(USA) Armada Grove (Fleetwood (IRE))
2577[2] 3245[7] 4401[3] 4534[4]

Nine Stories (IRE) *Chris Grant* 127h 130c
9 b g Catcher In The Rye(IRE) Irinatinvidio (Rudimentary (USA))
2344[9]
2793[P] 2894[3] 3000[P]

Ninetieth Minute (IRE) *J J O'Shea* 109b 133c
11 b g Old Vic Myown (IRE) (Le Bavard (FR))
3720[F] 4274[P]

Ninetynine (IRE) *Maurice Barnes*
7 b m Exit To Nowhere(USA) Sparkling Jess (Alderbrook)
885[8] 1420[7]

Ninfea (IRE) *Neil King* 86h 94c
6 b m Le Vie Dei Colori Attymon Lill (IRE) (Marju (IRE))
166[5] **645[U]**
931[2] 1063[4] 1192[5] 2424[4] 2632[U] 2896[4]
3152[U] 3472[P]

Ninive (FR) *F Nicolle* 115h
7 b m Sinndar(IRE) Narcose (FR) (Valanour (IRE))
863a[3]

Nipper John (IRE) *L M Power* 85h 95c
13 b g Luso Triswell (IRE) (Rashar (USA))
4915[5]

Nippy Des Mottes (FR) *Mrs Jackie Brooke* 131h 93c
13 b g Useful(FR) Julie Des Mottes (FR) (Puma Des Mottes (FR))
557[5]

Nisaal (IRE) *Sandy Forster* 84h
9 b g Indian Ridge Kahalah (IRE) (Darshaan)
222[6] 628[6]

Nishay (IRE) *David Rees* 33h
7 bb g Classic Cliche(IRE) Winged Victory (IRE) (Dancing Brave (USA))
267[14] 729[P] 1266[P]

Noakarad De Verzee (FR) *Giles Smyly* 91c
13 b g Roakarad Taratata (FR) (Prove It Baby (USA))
2394[7] 2730[6]

Noble Bacchus (IRE) *Fergal O'Brien* 28h
4 b g Acclamation Vintage Tipple (IRE) (Entrepreneur)
1044[U] 1271[6]

Noble Bell *Lucinda Russell* 19b
4 ch g Ad Valorem(USA) Mindanao (Most Welcome)
5219[10]

Noble Ben (IRE) *Mrs H S M Ridley* 91h 100c
12 ch g Beneficial I'm Happy Now (IRE) (Torus)
57[7] 4511[P] 5035[4]

Noble Chic *James Frost* 105h 80c
9 ch g Generous(IRE) Chicodove (In The Wings)
(178) **636[U]**
998[6]

Noble Friend (IRE) *Chris Gordon* 100h 85c
6 b g Presenting Laragh (IRE) (Oscar (IRE))
2002[4] 2272[5] 2642[9] *4494[2]* 5005[6] 5304[9]

Noble Inn (FR) *W P Mullins* 130h
4 b g Sinndar(IRE) Nataliana (Surumu (GER))
2851a[2] 4755[11]

Noble Jack (IRE) *Richard Ford* 73h
8 b g Elusive City(USA) Begine (IRE) (Germany (USA))
21[7]

Noble Legend *Caroline Bailey* 139c
7 b g Midnight Legend Elmside Katie (Lord David S (USA))
2199[11] 2674[P] (3287)
3655[P] 4244[2] 4681[P] 4900[5] 5350[P]

Noble Perk *Adrian Wintle* 90h
9 ch g Executive Perk Far From Perfect (IRE) (Phardante (FR))
4883[2] 5432[P]

Noble Prince (GER) *Paul Nolan* 137h 144c
10 b g Montjeu(IRE) Noble Pearl (GER) (Dashing Blade)
1951a[4] 4752[7]
5415a[2]

Noble Witness (IRE) *Charles Pogson* 88h 113c
11 b g Witness Box(USA) Jennas Pride (IRE) (Kambalda)
(265) 646[6]
872[4] 1917[11] 2428[4] **2884[4] 3193[4] 3502[7] 4066[4]**
4243[7]

Nobunaga *Venetia Williams* 113h 126c
9 ch g Beat Hollow Absolute Precision (USA) (Irish River (FR))
735[3] 859[5]

No Buts *David Bridgwater* 115h 137c
6 b g Kayf Tara Wontcostalotbut (Nicholas Bill)
163[2] **2508[2]**
3004[3] (3690) ◆ **3861[2] 4160[3]**

Noche De Reyes (FR) *Tom George* 113h 131c
5 bb g Early March Cochinchine (IRE) (Namaqualand (USA))
2492[11] 2848[4] **3202[4] 3787[3] 4804[5] (4919)**
5091[7]

No Compromise *Richard Phillips* 71h
5 b m Avonbridge Highly Liquid (Entrepreneur)
243[P] 810[10]

Nodda High Kid *Donald Whillans* 93h
8 ch g Sir Harry Lewis(USA) Lindajane (IRE) (Erin's Hope)
2245[3] 3396[7]

Nodebateaboutit *Tom George* 101h 118c
9 b g Alflora(IRE) Mystere (IRE) (Montelimar (USA))
3413[4]
3743[4] 4396[2] 5032[P] 5558[P]

Nodform Richard *Donald McCain* 116h 126c
8 b g Groom Dancer(USA) Shayzara (IRE) (Turtle Island (IRE))
495[7] (2884)
5299[F] 5481[3]

Nodforms Violet (IRE) *Karen McLintock* 99h 109c
10 ch g Rashar(USA) Whose Yer Wan (IRE) (Remainder Man)
115[2] 1037[4]

No Dice (IRE) *David Pipe* 117b
5 ch g Presenting Roxbury (Overbury (IRE))
4267[3]

Nodividendsagain *Evan Williams* 96h
6 b g Kayf Tara Catherine's Run (IRE) (Kotashaan (FR))
140[7] 761[4]

No Duffer *Henry Daly* 102h 122c
7 ch g Karinga Bay Dolly Duff (Alflora (IRE))
2087[5]
2599[P] 3418[3] (4399)
5284[P]

No Ifs No Buts *David Bridgwater* 76h
5 b m Kayf Tara Wontcostalotbut (Nicholas Bill)
1317[8] 1519[6] 1625[9] 1823[7] 2016[4] 2291[6] 2862[8] 3179[P]

Noir Et Vert (FR) *N W Alexander* 65h 88c
13 b g Silver Rainbow Danse Verte (FR) (Brezzo (FR))
4239[4]

Noir Girl *Philip Kirby* 90b
5 b m Beat All(USA) Forever Shineing (Glint Of Gold)
970[6] (1318)

No Likey (IRE) *Philip Hobbs* 114h
7 b g Helissio(FR) Money Galore (IRE) (Monksfield)
5034[9]

No Loose Change (IRE) *Paul Nicholls* 124h 153c
9 b g Bob Back(USA) Quit The Noise (IRE) (Un Desperado (FR))
6[8] 633[2]
(923) 1362[6] (1552)

Nomadic Dreamer *Sophie Leech* 108h 116c
11 ch g Nomadic Way(USA) Nunsdream (Derrylin)
203[2] 585[4] 899[2] 1133[6] 1192[6] 1709[7] 2428[P]

Nomadic Storm *David Bridgwater* 70h 108c
8 b g Nomadic Way(USA) Cateel Bay (Most Welcome)
91[F] 374[6] 3265[P] 4865[8] **5398[3]**

Nom De D'La (FR) *J-P Gallorini* 126h 135c
8 b h Lost World(IRE) Newness (IRE) (Simply Great (FR))
1984a[6] 2415a[6]

Nom De Guerre (IRE) *Ben De Haan* 108h 111c
12 b g Presenting Asklynn (IRE) (Beau Sher)
2560[2] 2847[3] 4990[P]

No More Whispers (IRE) *Marc Barber* 79c
9 b g Kahyasi Dizzy's Whisper (IRE) (Supreme Leader)
4654[F] 4843[P]

No No Bingo (IRE) *Charlie Longsdon* 113h 116c
8 b g Craigsteel Little Anna (IRE) (Lord Americo)
(3419) 3884[5] 4801[P]

No No Cardinal (IRE) *Mark Gillard* 82h 90c
5 ch g Touch Of Land(FR) Four Moons (IRE) (Cardinal Flower)
410[7] 1152[P] 1348[8] 1487[U] 1643[8] 3988[12] 4281[P]
4989[U] 5237[3]

No No Charlie (IRE) *Charlie Longsdon* 103h
7 b g Croco Rouge(IRE) Dianeme (Primo Dominie)
1915[7] 2426[6] 4143[5] 4573[F] 4866[5] 5179[5]

No No Mac (IRE) *Charlie Longsdon* 126h
5 b g Oscar(IRE) Whatdoyouthinkmac (IRE) (Supreme Leader)
1795[2] 2215[3] 2932[4] (3567) (4694) 5384[12]

No No Romeo (IRE) *Charlie Longsdon* 124h
5 b g Scorpion(IRE) Penny Brae (IRE) (Montelimar (USA))
250[2] ◆ (2354) 4575[2] 5167[7]

Nonotnow *Tim Easterby* 90h
4 ch g Notnowcato Get Jealous (IRE) (Intikhab (USA))
2392[2]

No Planning *Sue Smith* 122h 148c
7 b g Kayf Tara Poor Celt (Impecunious)
1923[3] (2517)
2972[2] 3205[3] (4039)
4400[4] 4953[6] (5383)

No Principles *Julian Smith* 116h 121c
11 b g Overbury(IRE) Selective Rose (Derring Rose)
512[P] 845[3] **2693[P] 3137[P]** 5074[P]

No Pushover *Nicky Henderson* 97b
5 b m Scorpion(IRE) Poussetiere Deux (FR) (Garde Royale)
36[3] 3181[2] (4540) 5159[20]

Norberix (FR) *G Cherel* 94h
4 gr g Al Namix(FR) Liganberry (FR) (Turgeon (USA))
262a[P]

Nordic Affair *S Arthur* 65h
10 b g Halling(USA) Affair Of State (IRE) (Tate Gallery (USA))
993a[3] 1250a[3] 1827a[5]

Nordic Nymph *Henry Daly* 73h
5 b m Norse Dancer(IRE) Silken Pearls (Leading Counsel (USA))
2892[5] 4910[13]

Nordic Quest (IRE) *Nicky Henderson* 128h
5 b g Montjeu(IRE) Nordtanzerin (GER) (Danehill Dancer (IRE))
3034[3] 3598[3] 4947[3] (5303)

No Reason Why (IRE) *Andrew Leyshon* 12c
10 b m Saddlers' Hall(IRE) Stormy Miss (IRE) (Glacial Storm (USA))
180[6]

No Regrets (FR) *Angela Clarke* 88h 116c
13 b g Nononito(FR) Betty Royale (FR) (Royal Charter (FR))
1673[P] 1837[P]

Norfolk Sky *Brian Barr* 117h
5 ch m Haafhd Cayman Sound (Turtle Island (IRE))
2265[8] 4632[6] (5026) 5368[4]

Normandy Landings *Neil Mulholland* 92h 74c
11 gr g Alflora(IRE) Hinemoa (IRE) (Mandalus)
248[P] 489[6]

No Routine (IRE) *Jonjo O'Neill* 89h
5 gr g Beneficial Mixwayda (FR) (Linamix (FR))
1935[13] 2178[6] 2265[11] 2770[9] 3140[10]

Norse Of Corse *Malcolm Jefferson*
4 b g Norse Dancer(IRE) Hot Classic (Classic Cliche (IRE))
5499[P]

Norse Wren *Renee Robeson* 98h
6 ch g Norse Dancer(IRE) Wren Warbler (Relkino)
1783[6]

Northern Acres *N W Alexander* 96h
8 b g Mtoto Bunting (Shaadi (USA))
2034[5] 2497[6] 3040[6] 3525[F] 3940[6] 4816[7] 5106[P] (5532)

Northern Executive (IRE) *Karen McLintock* 103h
6 b g Milan Letterwoman (IRE) (Fourstars Allstar (USA))
19[3] 223[F] 629[4]

Northern Meeting (IRE) *Robert Stephens* 92h
4 b f Dylan Thomas(IRE) Scottish Stage (IRE) (Selkirk (USA))
4910[2] 5393[2]

Northern Oscar (IRE) *Mark Walford* 106h
6 b g Oscar(IRE) Cailin's Princess (IRE) (Luso)
116[7] 2230[P] 3269[4] 3724[P] 4533[5] 4957[7] 5272[7] 5520[P]

Northern Warrior *Hugh Burns* 70b
6 b g Tamure(IRE) Rail Cat (Catrail (USA))
313[P] 494[7] 2443[U]

North London *James Frost* 85h
7 b g Morpeth Miss Grace (Atticus (USA))
(1700) 2690[13]

Northwest Du Lys (FR) *J-L Guillochon* 98h 132c
9 bl g Medaaly Shailann (FR) (Gaspard De La Nuit (FR))
1984a[2]

No Secrets (IRE) *David Pipe* 134h 137c
10 b g King's Theatre(IRE) Happy Native (IRE) (Be My Native (USA))
2812[4] ◆ **3424[5] 4962[2]**

Nosey Box (IRE) *Noel C Kelly* 106h
8 b m Witness Box(USA) Cautious Leader (Supreme Leader)
3523[2] 3934[2] 5322[2]

No Substitute (IRE) *Alan King* 104h 126c
9 b g Definite Article Kindly Light (IRE) (Supreme Leader)
3388[7] 4130[P] **5456[2]**

No Such Number *Julia Feilden* 115h
6 b g King's Best(USA) Return (USA) (Sadler's Wells (USA))
(2876) 4807[16]

Notabotheronme (IRE) *Dai Burchell* 67h 84c
12 bb g Religiously(USA) Kylogue's Delight (Strong Gale)
461[9] 2082[3] 2290[P] 2702[F] 3193[P]

Not A Doctor (IRE) *Polly Gundry* 63h
11 b g Rashar(USA) Kilmalum Daisy (IRE) (Spanish Place (USA))
1169[5] 1339[6] 1497[P]

Not Another Monday (IRE) *George Moore* 51h
6 bb g Great Palm(USA) Americo Rescue (IRE) (Lord Americo)
790[9] 2443[4] 2783[11] 3735[7] 5521[9]

Notarfbad (IRE) *Jeremy Scott* 124h 132c
8 b g Alderbrook Angels Flame (IRE) (Un Desperado (FR))
342[2] **779[3]**
1133[3] (1857)
2212[10] 2694[3] 3992[2] 4131[3] 4279[4]

Notario Has (FR) *P Peltier* 115h 121c
5 gr g Turgeon(USA) Noria Des Bordes (FR) (Epervier Bleu)
1742a[3]

Notcantdoit (IRE) *Polly Gundry* 74h
7 ch g Classic Cliche(IRE) Tanya Thyne (IRE) (Good Thyne (USA))
295[P] 436[7] 590[12]

Nothingbutthetruth (IRE) *Richard Woollacott* 91h 102c
10 b g Witness Box(USA) Named And Shamed (IRE) (Electric)
293[7] **485[2]**
639[4] 1103[7] 1260[7] 1437[4] (1526)
1644[4]

Nothing Is Forever (IRE) *Chris Down* 99h
10 b g Daylami(IRE) Bequeath (USA) (Lyphard (USA))
(193) 521[10] 977[7] 5304[3]

Nothing Personal *Karen George* 68h
7 b g Double Trigger(IRE) Nothings Forever (Oats)
174[8] 318[6] 519[9] 1517[3]

No Through Road *Michael Scudamore* 94h 83c
7 b g Grape Tree Road Pendil's Delight (Scorpio (FR))
4482[4] 5038[2] 5433[P]

Notimetowaste (IRE) *Donald McCain* 89b
7 b m Revoque(IRE) Supreme Blend (IRE) (Supreme Leader)
372[7] 532[P]

Not Many Know That (IRE) *Marc Barber* 44h
8 b g Winged Love(IRE) The Cree River (IRE) (Glacial Storm (USA))
1497[P] 1632[8]

Notnowivorheadache *Paul Webber* 102b
5 b m Notnowcato Inchcoonan (Emperor Jones (USA))
1671[2] 3507[8]

Notonebuttwo (IRE) *Chris Grant* 90h
7 b g Dushyantor(USA) Daiquiri (IRE) (Houmayoun (FR))
2334[P] 2818[P] 3022[P] 3525[4] 3824[6] 4553[5]
5055[P]

No To Trident *John Flint* 108h
9 b g Zilzal(USA) Charmante Femme (Bin Ajwaad (IRE))
37[3] 480[3] 783[3]

Not Til Monday (IRE) *J R Jenkins* 123h
8 b g Spartacus(IRE) Halomix (Linamix (FR))
(161) 501[3] 727[P] 1913[5] 2250[2]

Notus De La Tour (FR) *David Pipe* 119h 124c
8 b g Kutub(IRE) Ridiyla (IRE) (Akarad (FR))
2080[10] 2813[16] 3430[3] 3661[4]

Nouailhas *Andrew Hollinshead* 56h 85c
8 b g Mark Of Esteem(IRE) Barachois Princess (USA) (Barachois (CAN))
1137[6]
1301[3] 1547[6] 1668[2] 1914[P] 2044[3]

Novel Dancer *Lydia Richards* 83h
6 b g Dansili Fictitious (Machiavellian (USA))
95[6] 706[8]

Novikov *Sophie Leech* 84h 84c
10 ch g Danehill Dancer(IRE) Ardisia (USA) (Affirmed (USA))
377[6] 472[6] 694[P] 873[9] 1174[7] 1401[2] 1530[7] 1643[P]

Now Ben (IRE) *Nicky Henderson* 59h
6 ch g Beneficial Bannow Beach (IRE) (Saddlers' Hall (IRE))
2375[8] 5088[14]

Nowdoro *Julie Camacho* 108h
5 ch g Notnowcato Salydora (FR) (Peintre Celebre (USA))
3115[P]

Now I Win Again (IRE) *S R B Crawford* 114b
6 b m Flemensfirth(USA) Divine Accord (IRE) (Accordion)
880[P]

Now Listen To Me *Charles Whittaker* 56h 63c
11 br g Slip Anchor Calendula (Be My Guest (USA))
3421[3]

No Woman No Cry *Colin Tizzard* 86h
9 b g Kayf Tara Motown Melody (IRE) (Detroit Sam (FR))
854[10] 925[5] 1051[7] 1339[3] 1351[3]
1474[P] 1643[6]

Now Then Charlie (IRE) *John Ferguson* 110h 126c
9 b g Definite Article Katie's Cracker (Rambo Dancer (CAN))
3[2] (695)
963[3] 1197[P]

Now This Is It (IRE) *S R B Crawford* 140h 119c
10 ch g Accordion Leitrim Bridge (IRE) (Earl Of Barking (IRE))
356[7] **677[U]**
1290[2]

Nowurhurlin (IRE) *Mrs S J Stilgoe* 115h 122c
7 b g Saddlers' Hall(IRE) Pint Taken (IRE) (Needle Gun (IRE))
(90) 4079[2]
4705[3] (5094)
5491[5]

Nowweareseven *Nigel Twiston-Davies* 76h
7 b m Court Cave(IRE) Migsy Malone (Afzal)
4350[10] 5002[7] 5174[F] 5524[4]

Nozic (FR) *Zoe Davison* 60h 130c
13 b g Port Lyautey(FR) Grizilh (FR) (Spoleto)
236[9] 2365[P] 2567[P] 3093[5] 3652[4] 4131[4] (4718)
5017[5] 5458[P]

Nudge And Nurdle (IRE) *Nigel Twiston-Davies* 123h 115c
13 b g Shernazar Firey Comet (IRE) (Buckskin (FR))
44[8]

Nudge The Nugget *Nigel Hawke* 34h
6 br g Grape Tree Road Furry Dance (USA) (Nureyev (USA))
897[6] 1329[5] 1348[U] 1483[P]

Nulera (FR) *T Castanheira* 100h 60c
4 b f Poliglote Loup The Loup (FR) (Loup Solitaire (USA))
615a[7]

Numbercruncher (IRE) *Michael Hawke* 90h 111c
8 b g Beneficial Josie's Turn (IRE) (Kambalda)
778[F] 873[6] (1104)
1172[2] 1325[5] 5553[5]

Numen (IRE) *Barry Brennan* 99h 103c
10 b g Fath(USA) Hawala (IRE) (Warning)
456[8] 852[7] 1273[5] 1443[6] 1495[F]

Numide (FR) *G Chambers* 121h 108c
11 b g Highest Honor(FR) Numidie (FR) (Baillamont (USA))
523[P]

Nurse Brace *David Brace* 78h
5 b m Milan Bajan Girl (FR) (Emperor Jones (USA))
292[5] 2353[P]

Nurse Ratched (IRE) *Fergal O'Brien* 77h
5 b m Presenting Mascareigne (FR) (Subotica (FR))
(160) 699[2] 857[7] 1017[7] 1265[5] 1718[4] 1820[8]

Nutin Fancy (IRE) *Philip Hobbs* 110h
8 br g Oscar(IRE) Ennel Lady (IRE) (Erin's Hope)
2691[14] 3435[7]

Nuts N Bolts *Lucinda Russell* 131h 145c
8 b g Marju(IRE) Anniversary (Salse (USA))
(2670)
3285[P] 4270[4] 5276[P]

Oaklands Bobby *R G Russ* 92c
12 b g Busy Flight Bonnie Buttons (Lord Bud)
4225[4] 4617[6]

Oakmoss (IRE) *Mark Michael McNiff* 13h
8 b g Rudimentary(USA) Sindys Gale (Strong Gale)
290[10]

Oakwell (IRE) *Sally Hall* 95h
6 b g Antonius Pius(USA) Cindy's Star (IRE) (Dancing Dissident (USA))
800[6] 968[5]

Oak Wood (IRE) *John Upson* 75h
6 ch g Bienamado(USA) Oakum (IRE) (Danehill Dancer (IRE))
1937[8] 2189[7] 2509[4] 2827[P] 3605[9] *4326[7]* 4446[7]

Obispo (IRE) *C A McBratney* 104h 96c
8 br g Bishop Of Cashel Supreme Sensation (IRE) (Supreme Leader)
881[F] 1544[5]

Obistar (FR) *David Pipe* 67h
4 b g Astarabad(USA) Vallee Du Luy (FR) (Oblat (FR))
4030[2] 4632[10] 5003[7] 5235[10]

Obscurity (IRE) *Jonathan Portman* 81h
6 ch g Exit To Nowhere(USA) Lady Cadia (FR) (Cadoudal (FR))
79[6]

O'Callaghan Strand (AUS) *Jonjo O'Neill* 105h 122c
8 ch g Galileo(IRE) New Gold Dream (AUS) (Alzao (USA))
2014[3] 2370[5] 2884[2] *4302[11]* **4696[4] 5176[5] 5516[5]**

Ocarina (FR) *N W Alexander* 62h 111c
12 b g Bulington(FR) Alconea (FR) (Brezzo (FR))
5323[5]

Occasionally Yours (IRE) *Alan Blackmore* 116h
10 b g Moscow Society(USA) Kristina's Lady (IRE) (Lafontaine (USA))
486[2] 2064[5] 2362[8]
2574[F] 3471[P] 4794[5] 4969[5] 5260[5] 5443[3]

Oceana Gold *Emma Lavelle* 132h 134c
10 ch g Primo Valentino(IRE) Silken Dalliance (Rambo Dancer (CAN))
840[3] 974[6] (1151)

Ocean Applause *John Ryan* 81h
4 b g Royal Applause Aldora (Magic Ring (IRE))
1813[5]

Ocean Club *Brian Ellison* 124h 75c
7 ch g Storming Home Strictly Cool (USA) (Bering)
956[2] (1393) 1576[3] 1662[2] 2337[3] **2817[4] 2901[P]**

Ocean Waves (IRE) *Jedd O'Keeffe* 39h
5 b g Milan Myown (IRE) (Le Bavard (FR))
(1854) 3657[5] 4776[P]

Ockey De Neulliac (FR) *N Mechie* 112h 133c
12 ch g Cyborg(FR) Graine De Neulliac (FR) (Le Nain Jaune (FR))
(4274)
4788[U]

O Crotaigh (IRE) *Alan Brown* 124h 125c
10 b g Beneficial Jerpoint Rose (IRE) (Roselier (FR))
201[9] **448[8]**
508[9] 1204[2] 1470[6] 1542[4] 1687[2]

Oculi (FR) *A Adeline De Boisbrunet* 116c
10 b g Denham Red(FR) Ottolina (FR) (Saint Cyrien (FR))
2415a[5]

Oculist *Ben De Haan* 106h
6 b g Dr Fong(USA) Eyes Wide Open (Fraam)
1118[4] 1561[2]

Oddjob (IRE) *David Pipe* 101h 109c
10 b g Bob's Return(IRE) Bettyhill (Ardross)
120[7] 641[4] 778[2]

Oddsmaker (IRE) *Maurice Barnes* 58h
13 b g Barathea(IRE) Archipova (IRE) (Ela-Mana-Mou)
1754[10]

Odin (IRE) *Don Cantillon* 116h
6 b g Norse Dancer(IRE) Dimelight (Fantastic Light (USA))
477[4] (671) 758[2] 1258[3] 1466[2] 1535[2] 1688[4]

Oedipe (FR) *Mrs N Sheppard* 121h 88c
12 ch g Chamberlin(FR) Massada (FR) (Smadoun (FR))
62[7]

O'Faolains Boy (IRE) *Rebecca Curtis* 136h 163c
7 b g Oscar(IRE) Lisa's Storm (IRE) (Glacial Storm (USA))
3196[2] 3777[P] (4262)
(4751) 5154[5]

Offherocker *Claire Dyson* 57h
7 b m Generosity Houston Heiress (USA) (Houston (USA))
4450[8] 4569[9] 4758[11]

Officially Modern (IRE) *Fergal O'Brien* 94h 77c
7 ch g Beneficial Musical Millie (IRE) (Orchestra)
290[2] 484[8] **806[9] 1063[P]** 1306[9]
2441[F] 3157[9]

Offshore Account (IRE) *Tracey L Bailey* 82h 132c
14 b g Oscar(IRE) Park Breeze (IRE) (Strong Gale)
3720[3] 4936[4] 5127[P]

Off The Ground (IRE) *Emma Lavelle* 127h 151c
8 b g Oscar(IRE) Kaysel (IRE) (Torus)
2267[3] (2785)
(3090) 4764[8] 5136[14]

Off The Wall (IRE) *David Pipe* 110h 118c
7 ch g Presenting Ginger Bar (IRE) (Ashmolean (USA))
3129[3] 3565[P] 5032[2] 5129[P]

Oficial Ben (IRE) *Jonjo O'Neill* 75b
5 b g Beneficial Up A Dee (IRE) (Executive Perk)
4810[11]

Ogee *Renee Robeson* 137h 137c
11 ch g Generous(IRE) Aethra (USA) (Trempolino (USA))
205[3] 659[3] (1091) (1430)

Oh Crick (FR) *Alan King* 105h 135c
11 ch g Nikos Other Crik (FR) (Bigstone (IRE))
1990[5] 2488[13] 2694[4] 4106[7]

Oh Dear Oh Dear *Ron Hodges* 81h
6 b m Pasternak Post It (Thowra (FR))
177[7] 755[5]

Ohio Gold (IRE) *Colin Tizzard* 136h 140c
8 b g Flemensfirth(USA) Kiniohio (FR) (Script Ohio (USA))
2019[3] 2460[4] 3259[2] 3886[4] 4742[P] (5073)
5178[2]

Oh Right (IRE) *Dianne Sayer* 77h 90c
10 b g Zagreb(USA) Conna Bride Lady (IRE) (Phardante (FR))
1376[2] 1655[3] 1800[8] 2333[P]
2445[4] 2870[4] 3356[4]
(3755) (3876)
4462[3] 4984[2] 5556[7]

Oh So Charming *Mark Gillard* 68h
5 b g Kayf Tara Charmatic (IRE) (Charnwood Forest (IRE))
2016[F]

Oh So High (IRE) *Liam Corcoran*
5 ch m Mountain High(IRE) Oh So Breezy (IRE) (Be My Native (USA))
2566[P]

Oh Toodles (IRE) *Mrs C J Robinson* 101c
7 b g Milan Be My Granny (Needle Gun (IRE))
13[2]

Oil Burner *William Amos* 102h 114c
9 b g Sir Harry Lewis(USA) Quick Quote (Oats)
113[5] 2421[5] 3019[P] 3498[3] (3936)
4368[3] 5513[7]

Oiseau De Nuit (FR) *Colin Tizzard* 109h 158c
12 b g Evening World(FR) Idylle Du Marais (FR) (Panoramic)
2071[5] 2532[4] 2952[4] 3320[2] 3773[5] 4790[F] 5136[6]
5392[3]

Oklahoma Seven (FR) *J-L Gay* 126h 128c
7 b m Saint Des Saints(FR) Quick Ville (FR) (Villez (USA))
2465a[5]

Old Dreams (IRE) *Nick Gifford* 97h 114c
8 b m Old Vic I Can Imagine (IRE) (Husyan (USA))
242[6] 541[5] 709[2] 1272[F] 1529[P]
(1626) 1744[P]

Oldeddietherebel (IRE) *Barry T Murphy* 88b
5 ch g Old Vic Quinnsboro Guest (IRE) (Be My Guest (USA))
1016[4]

Old Kilcash (IRE) *John Joseph Hanlon* 126h
6 ch g Urban Ocean(FR) Brierfield Lady (IRE) (Montelimar (USA))
2256a[5]

Old Magic (IRE) *Sophie Leech* 96h
9 b g Old Vic Maeve's Magic (IRE) (Mandalus)
1711[10] 2045[5] 2291[5] 2862[12]

Old Pals Act (IRE) *Jonjo O'Neill* 106h 112c
6 ch g Presenting Golden Bay (Karinga Bay)
145[4] 543[2] 730[2] 1109[2] **1175[P] 1577[3]**

Old Tricks (IRE) *Colin Tizzard* 126h 100c
7 br g Flemensfirth(USA) Cabin Glory (The Parson)
2288[11]
2629[P] 3292[2] 3741[9] 3989[6] 4174[6] 4393[3] 4991[5]
5121[3] 5309[4]

Old Way (IRE) *Venetia Williams* 103h
8 b g Gold Away(IRE) Brooklyn's Dance (FR) (Shirley Heights)
2105[U] 2430[6] **3565[P]** (4659)

Oleohneh (IRE) *Malcolm Jefferson* 77h
6 b m Flemensfirth(USA) Dewasentah (IRE) (Supreme Leader)
(3529) 4008[3] 4431[7] (4944) 5159[14]

Olive Grove *Alan Mactaggart* 31b
8 ch m Central Park(IRE) Olive Branch (Le Moss)
2495[P]

Oliver's Gold *Mark Walford* 111h
6 b g Danehill Dancer(IRE) Gemini Gold (IRE) (King's Best (USA))
(1120) (1206) 1378[7] (5496)

Oliver's Hill (IRE) *Charlie Longsdon* 122h
5 b g Shantou(USA) River Rouge (IRE) (Croco Rouge (IRE))
(4889) 5258[3]

Ollie G *Chris Grant* 107h
6 b g Denounce Silver Rosa (Silver Patriarch (IRE))
173[3] 2795[2] 4221[2]

Ollisu Lad (IRE) *Tim Vaughan*
5 b g Westerner Nick's Jule (IRE) (Perugino (USA))
4445[5] 5140[P] 5548[P]

Olofi (FR) *Tom George* 142h 126c
8 gr g Slickly(FR) Dona Bella (FR) (Highest Honor (FR))
16[U]

Olympian Boy (IRE) *Sophie Leech* 98h 118c
10 b g Flemensfirth(USA) Notanissue (IRE) (Buckskin (FR))
1596[2] 1746[4] 2212[14] 3039[6] 4965[4] 5176[4] 5543[5]

Olynard (IRE) *Michael Mullineaux*
8 b g Exceed And Excel(AUS) Reddening (Blushing Flame (USA))
4476[10]

Omaruru (IRE) *Renee Robeson* 106h 94c
7 b g Cape Cross(IRE) Monturani (IRE) (Indian Ridge)
2599[6]

Omid *Evelyn Slack* 96h
6 b g Dubawi(IRE) Mille Couleurs (FR) (Spectrum (IRE))
1713[7] 2030[6] 2444[4] (2842) 5217[2]

On Alert *Seamus Durack* 82h
6 b g Deploy Morina (USA) (Lyphard (USA))
188[P] 965[P]

On Broadway (IRE) *Lucinda Russell* 113h 117c
8 b g Broadway Flyer(USA) Snap Out Of It (IRE) (Strong Gale)
224[P] 2155[P] 2594[2]

Onderun (IRE) *Emma Lavelle* 119b
5 b g Flemensfirth(USA) Warts And All (IRE) (Commanche Run)
4267[2]

One Act *Michael Easterby* 63b
5 gr m Act One Fujakka (IRE) (Vettori (IRE))
4618[8] 4895[12]

One Big Love *Keiran Burke* 100b
6 b m Tamure(IRE) Sound Appeal (Robellino (USA))
4735[4] 5077[3] 5374[6]

One Call (IRE) *C N Nimmo* 97h 72c
10 b g Topanoora Open Call (IRE) (Montelimar (USA))
510[5]

One Conemara (IRE) *Nicky Henderson* 125h 86c
6 b g Milan Rose Of Kerry (IRE) (Roselier (FR))
2490[F] 4105[P] 5489[3] ◆

Onedin Line *Venetia Williams* 87h 87c
6 ch g Pivotal One So Wonderful (Nashwan (USA))
376[7] **830[6]**

One Fine Day (IRE) *Mrs John Harrington* 134h
5 b m Choisir(AUS) Night Eyes (IRE) (Night Shift (USA))
1802a[8]

One For Arthur (IRE) *Lucinda Russell* 119h
5 b g Milan Nonnetia (FR) (Trempolino (USA))
4431[2] 4956[2] ◆

One For Harry (IRE) *Nicky Richards* 124h
6 b g Generous(IRE) Strawberry Fool (FR) (Tel Quel (FR))
2032[3] 2447[4] 3191[2] 3499[P] (5105) 5534[2]

One For Hocky (IRE) *Nicky Richards* 74h
6 b g Brian Boru Wire Lady (IRE) (Second Set (IRE))
3270[6]

One For Joules (IRE) *John Flint* 130h
7 b m Choisir(AUS) Stuttgart (Groom Dancer (USA))
1889[P]

One For The Boss (IRE) *Dai Burchell* 87h 93c
7 b g Garuda(IRE) Tell Nothing (IRE) (Classic Secret (USA))
254[P] **707[P]**
2044[6] 2416[P] 2772[3] 4970[7] 5243[8]

Onefortheboyz *Sean Curran* 51b
4 gr g Zafeen(FR) Molly Malone (Formidable (USA))
3719[8]

One For The Guv'Nr (IRE) *Nicky Henderson* 112b
5 b g Oscar(IRE) Wintry Day (IRE) (Presenting)
(4016) 4495[2] (5241)

One In A Milan (IRE) *Evan Williams* 107h 139c
9 b g Milan Kitty Star (IRE) (Montelimar (USA))
2170[F] 2652[3] **2889[P] 3361[4]** 4415[6] 4677[5] **5171[F]**

One In A Row (IRE) *Andrew Crook* 82h 90c
7 ch g Saffron Walden(FR) Rostarr (IRE) (Roselier (FR))
3270[9] 3639[6] 3824[10]
4530[3] 4744[2] 4890[5] 5301[7]

One Lucky Lady *Nicky Henderson* 137h 115c
6 b m Lucky Story(USA) One For Philip (Blushing Flame (USA))
(119) 591[4] 877[2] *(4494)* 4789[5] 5370[11]

One Million *Rose Dobbin* 78h
5 b g Dubai Destination(USA) Talwin (IRE) (Alhaarth (IRE))
75[0]

One More Dinar *John Bryan Groucott* 46h 100c
11 b g Kayf Tara One More Dime (IRE) (Mandalus)
32[4] 2297[P] 2678[P] 2872[P]

Onenightinvienna (IRE) *Philip Hobbs* 109h
5 b g Oscar(IRE) Be My Granny (Needle Gun (IRE))
3016[3] 3734[2] (4335) 5036[3]

Oneofapear (IRE) *Mike Sowersby* 108h
8 b g Pyrus(USA) Whitegate Way (Greensmith)
897[2] 1281[3] 1875[5] 2625[4] 2903[5]

One Term (IRE) *Rebecca Curtis* 123h 130c
7 b g Beneficial One Edge (IRE) (Welsh Term)
356[3] 591[8] **(1083)**
(1184) (1550)

One Track Mind (IRE) *Warren Greatrex* 118b
4 b g Flemensfirth(USA) Lady Petit (IRE) (Beneficial)
(5499)

Onetwobeat *Mrs T R Kinsey* 64b 100c
9 b m Beat All(USA) Angel Falling (Scottish Reel)
4274[3]

Ongenstown Lad (IRE) *Mrs Gillian Callaghan* 142h 109c
10 b g Bach(IRE) Lantern Logic (IRE) (Royal Fountain)
2345[P]

On Gossamer Wings (IRE) *Ferdy Murphy* 93c
10 b g Winged Love(IRE) Katie Parson (The Parson)
117[F]

On His Own (IRE) *W P Mullins* 147h 170c
10 b g Presenting Shuil Na Mhuire (IRE) (Roselier (FR))
685a[7]
2937[6] (3868a)
(4435a) 4787[2]

Online *Tracy Waggott*
4 b g Rail Link Fairy Steps (Rainbow Quest (USA))
582[P]

Only Exception (IRE) *M C Grassick* 106h
5 b m Jeremy(USA) Misaayef (USA) (Swain (IRE))
2205a[8]

Only Hope *Andy Hobbs* 93h
10 b m Marju(IRE) Sellette (IRE) (Selkirk (USA))
252[12]

Only Witness (IRE) *Brendan Powell* 102h 126c
9 b g Witness Box(USA) Shiny Button (Bob's Return (IRE))
3044[5] **3858[P]**

On The Bridge (IRE) *Jeremy Scott* 144h 143c
9 b g Milan Bay Dove (Alderbrook)
(845) (877)
943[2] 1195[3] 1956[4] 4765[6] 5138[7]

On The Buckle *Rose Dobbin* 84h
6 b g Overbury(IRE) Arctic Revel (Arctic Lord)
(101) 1661[8] 2217[16] 2783[9] 5360[9]

On The Case *Tom George* 63h 90c
6 ch g Generous(IRE) Tulipa (POL) (Jape (USA))
140[14]
3876[P] 5243[2]

On The Cusp (IRE) *Violet M Jordan* 72h
7 b g Footstepsinthesand Roman Love (IRE) (Perugino (USA))
948[7]

On The Feather *Jim Best* 98h
8 br m Josr Algarhoud(IRE) Fotheringhay (Loup Sauvage (USA))
540[5] 903[2] 1428[3] (1517) 1822[7]

On The Fringe (IRE) *E Bolger* 144c
9 b g Exit To Nowhere(USA) Love And Porter (IRE) (Sheer Grit)
4788[3]

On The Move *Anthony Honeyball* 94h
6 b m Sir Harry Lewis(USA) What A Mover (Jupiter Island)
246[3] 717[9] 920[13] 3686[7] (5007) 5523[3]

On The Off Chance *Jonjo O'Neill* 107h
6 b m Presenting Winnowing (IRE) (Strong Gale)
166[4] 423[3] 811[4] 932[2] 1321[6]

On The Raz *Jacqueline Retter* 57b
7 b m Rakaposhi King Trillow (Pitpan)
1671[12]

On The Record (IRE) *Jonjo O'Neill* 104h
6 br g Presenting Diva Antonia (IRE) (King's Theatre (IRE))
2511[8] 4865[3] (5177)

Ontheslate (IRE) *Neil King* 86h 77c
8 b g Beneficial Florida (IRE) (Sri Pekan (USA))
32[3] 206[4] 541[P] 763[P]

On The Way Home (IRE) *Jonjo O'Neill* 48h
5 b m Flemensfirth(USA) Home At Last (IRE) (Mandalus)
46[9] 3676[6]

On Tour (IRE) *Evan Williams* 122b
6 b g Croco Rouge(IRE) Galant Tour (IRE) (Riberetto)
(1819) 2472[2] (2885) 3187[3]

On Trend (IRE) *Nick Gifford* 113h 140c
8 b g Jammaal Comrun (IRE) (Commanche Run)
2214[8] 2502[7] 3006[4] 3321[P] 3647[4] 4035[7] (4886)

On Vacation (IRE) *John Joseph Hanlon* 63b
6 b g Kahyasi Lurane (FR) (Royal Charter (FR))
3835[7]

Onwards'N'Upwards *Christine Dunnett* 46h
6 b g Diktat Lunar Goddess (Royal Applause)
595[5]

Oorayvic (IRE) *Sue Smith* 92h
7 ch g Snurge Miss Murtle (IRE) (Old Vic)
173[4] 699[5] 847[9] 3330[P] 3826[7] 4005[5] 4336[8]
4615[3] 5366[6]

Ooson (IRE) *Mrs O C Jackson*
7 gr g Tikkanen(USA) Miss Bobby Bennett (Kings Lake (USA))
4658[P]

Opaleo (FR) *F-M Cottin* 96h 110c
5 b g Assessor(IRE) Jolie Puce (FR) (General Assembly (USA))
703a[7]

Open Day (IRE) *Jonjo O'Neill* 135h
8 b g Oscar(IRE) Shaping (IRE) (Deep Run)
1867[2] 4271[5] 4789[P]

Open Hearted *Nicky Henderson* 140h 135c
7 b g Generous(IRE) Romantic Dream (Bustino)
(3057)
3368[2]

Opening Batsman (IRE) *Harry Fry* 82h 151c
8 b g Morozov(USA) Jolly Signal (IRE) (Torus)
2214[P] 2815[F] 3387[11]
4552[5] 5571[12]

Opera Og (IRE) *Venetia Williams* 85h 127c
8 b g Oscar(IRE) Maspaloma (IRE) (Camden Town)
2450[3] 2812[F] 4502[3]

Operateur (IRE) *Ben Haslam* 89h
6 b g Oratorio(IRE) Kassariya (IRE) (Be My Guest (USA))
2169[7] 2449[10] 3038[3] 3210[F]

Operatic Heights (IRE) *Alan McCabe* 103h
5 b g Golan(IRE) Opera Lover (IRE) (Sadler's Wells (USA))
1690[5] 2252[P] 3388[8] 3841[4] *4327[4]*

Ophelia's Kiss *Brendan Powell* 89h
7 b m Karinga Bay Baileys Baby (Puissance)
691[11] 977[5]

Optical High *Sue Smith* 77h
5 b g Rainbow High Forsweets (Forzando)
73[3] 449[8] 629[10] 2169[12] 2360[10] 2596[8] 2877[4]
3334[3]

Orabora *Philip Hobbs* 125h 113c
8 b g Alflora(IRE) Magic Orb (Primo Dominie)
2538[6]
3183[5] 5179[12]

Oracle (GER) *F-M Cottin* 94h 113c
10 b g Poliglote Old Beino (FR) (Highest Honor (FR))
263a[9]

Orangeaday *Ben Case* 125h
7 b g Kayf Tara One Of Those Days (Soviet Lad (USA))
3286[5] (5542)

Orange Gizmo (IRE) *Venetia Williams* 16h
10 ch m Exit To Nowhere(USA) Dark Princess (IRE) (Good Thyne (USA))
1580[11]

Orange Nassau (FR) *Charlie Longsdon* 100h 128c
8 gr g Martaline Vilaya (FR) (Cadoudal (FR))
(1859)
(2201) 2979[2] 3267[3] (4695)
5334[P]

Oranger (FR) *Andrew J Martin* 45h 98c
12 b g Antarctique(IRE) True Beauty (Sun Prince)
34[7] 248[7] 504[6] 805[6] 4079[F]

Orang Outan (FR) *Laura Hurley* 103h 103c
12 b g Baby Turk Ellapampa (FR) (Pampabird)
418[3] (600)
4762[3] 5247[U]

Orby's Man (IRE) *Charlie Longsdon* 99b
5 b g Arcadio(GER) Gleann Oisin (IRE) (Le Bavard (FR))
4310[4] 4895[6]

Orcenhac (FR) *C Scandella*
4 bb g Smadoun(FR) One Way (FR) (Exit To Nowhere (USA))
1741a[P]

Orchard Mist *Bernard Llewellyn* 83b
5 b m Sakhee(USA) Haladiya (IRE) (Darshaan)
4417[5] 4735[9]

Orchard Road (USA) *Lucinda Russell* 106h
7 b g Street Cry(IRE) Aunt Mottz (USA) (Honey Jay (USA))
1667[7] 1977[3] 2493[10]

Orcus (FR) *M Seror* 124h
5 b h Russian Blue(IRE) Perfidie (IRE) (Monsun (GER))
1983a[P]

Or De Grugy (FR) *N W Alexander* 105h 122c
12 b g April Night(FR) Girlish (FR) (Passing Sale (FR))
25[5] 1852[5] (3394)
4236[2] 5210[P]

Ordo Ab Chao (IRE) *Alan King* 124b
5 b g Heron Island(IRE) Houldyurwhist (IRE) (Supreme Leader)
(4575) 5173[4] ◆

Or D'Oudairies (FR) *Ferdy Murphy* 101h 109c
12 b g April Night(FR) Belle Truval (FR) (Rose Laurel)
(220) **(566)**
757[8]

Orfeo Conti (FR) *Miss Rose Grissell* 64h 96c
12 ch g Bulington(FR) Gazelle Lulu (FR) (Altayan)
328[2] 597[4] 4782[5] 5135[15]

Organization (IRE) *Sarah-Jayne Davies*
6 b g Beneficial Johnstown Lass (IRE) (Oscar (IRE))
862[11]

Orgilgo Bay (IRE) *John C McConnell* 122h
4 b g Lawman(FR) Third Dimension (FR) (Suave Dancer (USA))
3224[3] 4178a[6] 4755[3] ◆

Oriel Bank (IRE) *I M Mason* 79b 61c
9 b m Definite Article Miss Congeniality (IRE) (Un Desperado (FR))
58[10]

Oriental Cat *Venetia Williams* 61h
7 b g Tiger Hill(IRE) Sentimental Value (USA) (Diesis)
2191[6]

Oriental Love (GER) *F-X De Chevigny* 84h
4 b f Doyen(IRE) Oriental Lane (GER) (Seattle Dancer (USA))
2781a[P]

Origan Joly (FR) *Mme A-D Lefeuvre* 75c
12 gr g April Night(FR) Fortune Jolie (FR) (Un Numide (FR))
200a[7]

Original Star (IRE) *Derek Frankland* 102h 54c
9 b g Rashar(USA) Hogan Stand (Buckskin (FR))
48[7] 254[P] 2470[6]
2897[7]

Orion Express *Sue Gardner* 103h 100c
13 b g Bahhare(USA) Kaprisky (IRE) (Red Sunset)
637[F]

Orion Star (IRE) *Seamus Mullins* 89b 30c
12 ch g Fourstars Allstar(USA) Rosies Sister (IRE) (Deep Run)
485[8] 942[P] 1437[P]

Orla's Rainbow (IRE) *Gary Moore* 87h
4 b g Oratorio(IRE) Red Ray (Pivotal)
(1624)

Orlittlebylittle *Donald McCain* 81h 30c
8 b g Bollin Eric Davana Blue (FR) (Epervier Bleu)
3639[8]
4383[P] 4475[6] 4757[6] 5072[15] 5431[9]

Orphee Des Blins (FR) *G Wroblewski* 143c
12 b m Lute Antique(FR) Ving's Road (FR) (King's Road (FR))
(1905a)

Orsippus (USA) *Michael Smith* 135h 127c
8 bb g Sunday Break(JPN) Mirror Dancing (USA) (Caveat (USA))
215[8] 2100[4] 4056[8] 5384[15]

Orsm *Laura Mongan* 96h
7 b g Erhaab(USA) Royal Roulette (Risk Me (FR))
428[6] 710[7] 946[4] 1275[4] 1784[5]

Ortax De Maesax (FR) *C Macault*
12 b g Mad Tax(USA) Fad'Or (FR) (Saint Preuil (FR))
200a[10]

Orthodox Lad *Dr Richard Newland* 114h
6 ch g Monsieur Bond(IRE) Ashantiana (Ashkalani (IRE))
808[3] 948[2] 1041[3] (1152) 1319[2] 1400[3] (1525) 1627[2] 1685[2] 1745[5]

Ortolan (GER) *Donald McCain* 94h
9 ch g Next Desert(IRE) Optik (GER) (Monsun (GER))
3721[4] **4488[P]**

Orvita (FR) *Helen Nelmes* 97h 79c
12 b g Lute Antique(FR) Ulvita (FR) (Spoleto)
2275[P] (2541)

Orzare (IRE) *Philip Hide* 107h 62c
8 b g Montjeu(IRE) Contare (Shirley Heights)
2019[U] 2211[7] 2538[5] 3096[3]

Oscar Baby (IRE) *Diana Grissell* 73h 59c
8 b m Oscar(IRE) Snowbaby (IRE) (Be My Native (USA))
2008[14]
2712[4]

Oscar Chimes (IRE) *M T O'Donovan* 120h
7 b g Oscar(IRE) Heather Belle (IRE) (Executive Perk)
2983a[6]

Oscar Close (IRE) *David Bridgwater* 110h 114c
9 br g Oscar(IRE) Upham Close (Oats)
98[6] (426) 650[2] **871[5]** 1108[P]

Oscar Davy (IRE) *Philip Hobbs* 120h 125c
8 b g Oscar(IRE) Galtee Castle (IRE) (Be My Native (USA))
1959[F] 2662[F]

Oscar Delta (IRE) *James Joseph Mangan* 148c
11 b g Oscar(IRE) Timerry (IRE) (Alphabatim (USA))
4788[10]

Oscar Fortune (IRE) *Jonjo O'Neill* 129h
6 b g Oscar(IRE) Platin Run (IRE) (Strong Gale)
(1915) (2243) 2929[4] 3653[6]

Oscargo (IRE) *Paul Nicholls* 141h 134c
10 b g Oscar(IRE) Broken Rein (IRE) (Orchestra)
9[3] 296[2] 1338[F] 1957[5]

Oscar Hill (IRE) *David Bridgwater* 135h 147c
8 b g Oscar(IRE) Elizabeth Tudor (IRE) (Supreme Leader)
204[12] 1990[4] (2694)
(2890) 3660[8] 4032[6]

Oscar Hoof (IRE) *Nicky Henderson* 135h
6 b g Oscar(IRE) New Legislation (IRE) (Dominion Royale)
2657[2] (3388) (4807) ◆ 5167[F]

Oscar Jane (IRE) *Johnny Farrelly* 93h
7 b m Oscar(IRE) Turrill House (Charmer)
691[S] 2013[7] 2696[4] 2980[12]

Oscar Lateen (IRE) *Sandy Thomson* 92h
6 b g Oscar(IRE) Storm Call (Celestial Storm (USA))
22[10] 1980[6] 2417[4] 3040[P]

Oscar Leney (IRE) *J T R Dreaper* 98c
8 b g Oscar(IRE) Sound Case (IRE) (Husyan (USA))
580[5]

Oscar Magic (IRE) *Nigel Twiston-Davies* 130h
7 bb g Oscar(IRE) Just An Illusion (IRE) (Shernazar)
(1695) 1968[P] 2949[7] **3259[P]** 4028[4]

Oscar O'Scar (IRE) *Philip Kirby* 104h
6 b g Oscar(IRE) Shining Lights (IRE) (Moscow Society (USA))
1123[6] 1634[4] ◆

Oscar Prairie (IRE) *Warren Greatrex* 131h 114c
9 b g Oscar(IRE) Silver Prairie (IRE) (Common Grounds)
481[10] 1943[5] 2366[4] 2949[9] 3292[4] (3798) 4277[3] 5333[9]

Oscar Rainbow *Tracey Barfoot-Saunt* 78h 44c
8 b g Oscar(IRE) Fionnula's Rainbow (IRE) (Rainbows For Life (CAN))
71[2] 252[4] 4911[F]
4970[10]

Oscar Rock (IRE) *Malcolm Jefferson* 141h
6 b g Oscar(IRE) Cash And New (IRE) (Supreme Leader)
(2196) 2819[2] 3367[3] 4272[3] 5510[2]

Oscars Business (IRE) *Robert Tyner* 103h 129c
10 b m Oscar Schindler(IRE) Mens Buisiness (IRE) (Buckskin (FR))
3868a[3]

Oscars Den (IRE) *Tim Vaughan* 133h
6 b g Oscar(IRE) Lyre Hill (IRE) (Strong Gale)
(2507) (3110) 5347[2]

Oscarsfriend (IRE) *C J Lawson*
10 b g Oscar(IRE) Native Woodfire (IRE) (Mister Majestic)
325[P]

Oscarslad (IRE) *Harry Fry* 110h 123c
8 b g Oscar(IRE) Velvet Huxley (IRE) (Fourstars Allstar (USA))
4884[3] 5309[2]

Oscars Law *Matt Sheppard* 67h
7 b g Emperor Fountain Miss K C (Roviris)
116[10] 436[10]

Oscar's Passion (IRE) *David Harry Kelly* 106h
5 gr m Oscar(IRE) Passiflora (FR) (April Night (FR))
1948a[6]

Oscar's Pet (IRE) *Tom Symonds* 96h
6 b m Oscar(IRE) Kilcoleman Lady (IRE) (Presenting)
187[5] 462[4] 2027[3] 2801[6] 4093[5] 4472[7] 4823[P]

Oscar's Secret (IRE) *Kim Bailey* 111h
7 b g Oscar(IRE) Black Flora (IRE) (Alflora (IRE))
336[8]

Oscar Stanley (IRE) *Rose Dobbin* 71h
7 b g Oscar(IRE) Mujavail (IRE) (Mujadil (USA))
1664[P]

Oscar Sunset (IRE) *Evan Williams* 131h
7 b g Oscar(IRE) Derravarra Sunset (IRE) (Supreme Leader)
336[4]

Oscars Way (IRE) *Don Cantillon* 65h
6 b g Oscar(IRE) Derrigra Sublime (IRE) (Flemensfirth (USA))
483[2] 644[2] 2978[13]

Oscars Well (IRE) *A J Martin* 143h 149c
9 bb g Oscar(IRE) Placid Willow (IRE) (Convinced)
2141a[2] 2235a[4] 4752[18]
5474a[P]

Oscar Tanner (IRE) *Martin Todhunter* 122h
6 br g Oscar(IRE) Rose Tanner (IRE) (Roselier (FR))
(629) 747[3] 2732[3] 3273[2] 4941[3]

Oscarteea (IRE) *Anthony Honeyball* 125b
5 b g Oscar(IRE) Miss Arteea (IRE) (Flemensfirth (USA))
359[2] (1869) 3187[5] 4756[10]

Oscar The Myth (IRE) *Jeremy Scott* 70h 80c
8 b g Oscar(IRE) Have A Myth (IRE) (Roselier (FR))
3114[F] 4481[P]

Oscar Too (IRE) *Sandy Thomson* 46b
5 b g Oscar(IRE) Biddy Earley (IRE) (Black Minstrel)
1792[12]

Oscar Whisky (IRE) *Nicky Henderson* 156h 162c
9 b g Oscar(IRE) Ash Baloo (IRE) (Phardante (FR))
2489[2] (3064)
(3456) (4033)
4764[F] 5137[2]

Oscar Zulu (IRE) *Philip Hobbs* 103h
7 b g Oscar(IRE) The Gullett (IRE) (Shernazar)
116[12]

Oscatara (IRE) *Donald McCain* 120h 104c
7 bb g Oscar(IRE) Nethertara (Netherkelly)
3430[P]
4530[2] 4898[P]

Osgood *Gary Moore* 96h
7 b g Danehill Dancer(IRE) Sabreon (Caerleon (USA))
4469[6] (4967) 5242[9]

Osmosia (FR) *Chris Gordon* 98h 101c
9 b m Mansonnien(FR) Osmose (FR) (Cricket Ball (USA))
166[7] 540[11] 977[4] 1273[7] 1438[3]
1530[2] 1630[7] 1822[5] **2003[3]** 2278[4] 2581[3] (3009)
3164[2] *4303[13]* **4762[5]** 5116[4]

Osorios Trial *Anthony Middleton* 98h
7 ch g Osorio(GER) Skytrial (USA) (Sky Classic (CAN))
857[3] 1059[2] 1258[4] 1348[2] 1475[P]

Osric (IRE) *Laura Young* 111h 116c
11 b g Mister Mat(FR) Miss Ondee (FR) (Dress Parade)
719[5] 875[2] 1634[11]

Ossie's Dancer *Martin Smith* 116h
5 ch g Osorio(GER) Nina Ballerina (Kahyasi)
3469[5] 3838[3] 4411[4] 4818[F] (5179)

Osso Bello (FR) *F-M Cottin* 104h 104c
6 b g Corri Piano(FR) Sweet Valrose (FR) (Cadoudal (FR))
1740a[4]

Ostland (GER) *Charlie Longsdon* 127h 143c
9 b g Lando(GER) Ost Tycoon (GER) (Last Tycoon)
204[13]

Otago Trail (IRE) *Venetia Williams* 120b
6 b g Heron Island(IRE) Cool Chic (IRE) (Roselier (FR))
3863[3] (4445) 4951[2]

Otatou (FR) *F Lagarde* 113c
12 b g Robin Des Pres(FR) Canlastou (FR) (Tanlas (FR))
1279a[2]

Otto Nicolai *Sean Curran* 26h
5 gr g Singspiel(IRE) Majoune (FR) (Take Risks (FR))
185[12] 435[6]

Otto The Great (FR) *Mrs Antonia Bealby* 93h 129c
6 gr g Turgeon(USA) Hunorisk (FR) (Mansonnien (FR))
233[3] (633) 1142[2] **5439[3]**

Our Bomber Harris *Harry Fry* 117h 138c
10 b g Saddlers' Hall(IRE) Gaye Fame (Ardross)
659[9]

Our Boy Ben *Malcolm Jefferson* 110h
5 b g Revoque(IRE) Magic Bloom (Full Of Hope)
1599[8] 2174[5] (2593) 3017[6] 3920[6] 4957[4] ◆ 5537[4]

Our Cat (IRE) *Fergal O'Brien* 102h
6 b m Royal Anthem(USA) Run Cat (IRE) (Lord Americo)
4114[4] 4777[3] 5124[F] 5427[5]

Our Chief (IRE) *David Pipe* 101h
5 b g Old Vic Torsha (IRE) (Torus)
4638[4] 5042[7]

Our Choice (IRE) *Nick Kent* 124h 116c
12 b g Indian Danehill(IRE) Spring Daffodil (Pharly (FR))
1093[P] 1206[P]

Our Conor (IRE) *D T Hughes* 164h
5 b g Jeremy(USA) Flamands (IRE) (Sadler's Wells (USA))
3402a[3] 3930a[2] 4739[F] (Dead)

Our Crusade *Michael Easterby* 47h
7 ch g Rainbow Quest(USA) Angeleno (IRE) (Belong To Me (USA))
944[3] 1420[4] 1578[8]

Our Dawn *Michael Mullineaux*
6 b m Overbury(IRE) Dawn's Della (Scottish Reel)
1732[7]

Our Differences (IRE) *M Barber* 30c
7 b g Kaieteur(USA) Helen's Sisters (IRE) (Welsh Term)
5545[6]

Our Father (IRE) *David Pipe* 137h 154c
8 gr g Shantou(USA) Rosepan (IRE) (Taipan (IRE))
2815[7] 4270[5] 4769[9] 5171[U]

Our Guardian Angel (IRE) *Christopher Kellett* 94b
10 b m Dushyantor(USA) Hearth (IRE) (King's Ride)
1443[8]

Our Island (IRE) *Tim Vaughan* 121h 125c
9 b g Turtle Island(IRE) Linda's Leader (IRE) (Supreme Leader)
1959[7] 2670[5] 3455[4] 4427[9] 4842[2] 5039[4]

Our Joey (IRE) *George Bewley* 122h
6 b g Wareed(IRE) Put On Hold (IRE) (Lord Americo)
1788[2] 2655[4] 3108[4]

Our Kaempfer (IRE) *Charlie Longsdon* 123b
5 b g Oscar(IRE) Gra-Bri (IRE) (Rashar (USA))
(1836) 2534[3] 4756[17] 5173[5]

Our Katie (IRE) *Garrett Ahern* 131h
7 gr m Dr Massini(IRE) Tara The Grey (IRE) (Supreme Leader)
3203[4]

Our Maimie (IRE) *R McGlinchey* 77h
8 b m Luso Cormac Lady (IRE) (Simply Great (FR))
777[2] 1561[6]

Ourmanmassini (IRE) *Suzy Smith* 117h
6 b g Dr Massini(IRE) Aunty Dawn (IRE) (Strong Gale)
2210[7] 2561[4] 3263[P] *4018[2] 4298[2] 4496[2]* 4799[2] 5239[4]

Our Mick *Donald McCain* 110h 152c
8 gr g Karinga Bay Dawn's Della (Scottish Reel)
2452[P] 2938[3] 3887[P] 5170[6] 5383[P]

Our Ollie (IRE) *Paul John Gilligan* 104h 93c
8 b g Court Cave(IRE) Vikki's Dream (IRE) (Kahyasi)
4793[F]

Our Phylli Vera (IRE) *Alan King* 107h
5 b m Motivator With Colour (Rainbow Quest (USA))
2568[3] (3140) (4717) 5018[5]

Our Play (IRE) *Lydia Richards* 8h
6 b g Oratorio(IRE) Red Shoe (Selkirk (USA))
306[P]

Our Pollyanna (IRE) *Alan King* 108h
7 b m Flemensfirth(USA) Polly Anthus (Kahyasi)
2600[2] 4261[3] 4931[4] 5427[6]

Our Princess Ellie (USA) *Derek Shaw* 8h
6 ch m Borrego(USA) Dear Abigail (USA) (Dehere (USA))
560[7]

Outback (IRE) *Neil King* 103h 76c
5 b g Kodiac Florida City (IRE) (Pennekamp (USA))
202[5] 1468[3] 1634[P]
1765[6] 2067[3] 2251[P]

Outlaw Tom (IRE) *Lucinda Russell* 105h 112c
10 b g Luso Timely Approach (IRE) (Good Thyne (USA))
2516[8]
3019[P] 3413[9]
4368[4] 4773[3] (5321)

Out Of Nothing *Dai Burchell* 84h
11 br m Perryston View Loves To Dare (IRE) (Desert King (IRE))
2291[P] 3047[6] 4911[6]

Outrageous Request *William Stone* 120h 79c
8 ch g Rainbow Quest(USA) La Sorrela (IRE) (Cadeaux Genereux)
870[6] (1148) 1290[4] 1544[4] 1656[2] **1849[5]** 2221[7] (2846)

Overafrica (IRE) *Donald McCain* 99h 96c
8 b g Overbury(IRE) Siberiansdaughter (IRE) (Strong Gale)
221[10]

Over And Above (IRE) *Henry Hogarth* 102h 81c
8 b g Overbury(IRE) Rose Gold (IRE) (Nucleon (USA))
64[6] 473[2] 601[5] 753[8] 2047[P] 2445[P] 2735[7] (3834)
4066[P] 4613[4] 4982[3]
5358[4]

Overclear *Victor Dartnall* 109h 121c
12 b g Overbury(IRE) Callope (USA) (Recitation (USA))
2180[P] 3065[5] 4131[2] 4685[6] 5141[2] 5340[P]

Overdante *Charlie Longsdon* 97h
7 b m Overbury(IRE) Mrs Wumpkins (IRE) (Phardante (FR))
2[2]

Overlaw *Stuart Coltherd* 58h 97c
12 br g Overbury(IRE) Reprieve (Riberetto)
2361[6] 2737[4] 3517[6]

Overlay *Lawney Hill* 82h
10 br m Overbury(IRE) Lay It Off (IRE) (Strong Gale)
543[9] 969[4]

Overlut (FR) *S L Bevan* 123h 113c
12 bl g Discover D'Auteuil(FR) Lutsine (FR) (Zino)
(655)

Over My Head *Claire Dyson* 89h
6 gr g Overbury(IRE) Altesse De Sou (FR) (Saint Preuil (FR))
367[U] 2178[8] 2252[4] 2509[7] 3014[4] (3432) 3824[3] 4330[2] 4729[6]

Overnight Fame (IRE) *Tom George* 106h 111c
10 b m Kayf Tara Best Of The Girls (IRE) (Supreme Leader)
370[3] 2618[2] 3058[2] 3555[2] (4912)

Overpresently *Simon Waugh*
6 b m Overbury(IRE) Coole Presence (IRE) (Presenting)
5205[P]

Overpriced *Maurice Barnes* 116h
8 b m Chocolat De Meguro(USA) One Stop (Silly Prices)
111[2] (342) 581[5] 681[13] 1785[8] 2032[U] 3212[7] 4952[2] 5251[3]

Over The Air *John Spearing* 70h
6 br m Overbury(IRE) Moonlight Air (Bold Owl)
3961[10] 4867[7] 5427[F]

Over The Bridge *Mark Gillard* 42b
4 b g Multiplex Do It On Dani (Weld)
5145[10] 5492[11]

Over The Thyme *Karen McLintock* 69b
6 b g Overbury(IRE) Griselina (IRE) (Mandalus)
768[8] 885[5]

Overton Lad *Peter Pritchard* 55h 73c
13 gr g Overbury(IRE) Safe Arrival (USA) (Shadeed (USA))
32[7] 1825[6] 2313[4] 2603[3] 2829[3] 3114[P] 5011[P]

Overtoyoulou *Chris Grant* 70b
6 b m Overbury(IRE) Champagne Lou Lou (Supreme Leader)
5381[6]

Over To You Ruby (IRE) *Alistair Whillans* 58b
7 b m Blueprint(IRE) Supreme Madam (IRE) (Supreme Leader)
629^{P}

Ovilia (IRE) *Donald McCain* 90b
5 gr m Clodovil(IRE) Five Of Wands (Caerleon (USA))
1317^{4} 1531^{3} 1719^{6}

Ovthenight (IRE) *Roger Curtis* 86h 89c
9 b g Noverre(USA) Night Beauty (King Of Kings (IRE))
5069^{P} **5433^{5}**

Owega Star (IRE) *Peter Fahey* 136h 140c
7 br g Basanta(IRE) Los Monteros (IRE) (College Chapel)
1804a^{2} 4709a^{3}

Owenacurra (IRE) *Miss Rose Grissell* 103c
9 b g Windsor Castle Husstar (IRE) (Husyan (USA))
325^{4}

Owen Glendower (IRE) *Sophie Leech* 123h 138c
9 br g Anshan Native Success (IRE) (Be My Native (USA))
900^{2} 1146^{3} 1686^{12} 1923^{5} 2373^{9} 3065^{10} 3158^{5}

Owen Na View (IRE) *Fergal O'Brien* 108h
6 bb g Presenting Lady Zephyr (IRE) (Toulon)
1667^{2} 1991^{8} 2471^{3} 3023^{F} 4075^{5} 4726^{5} 5537^{P}

Owner Occupier *Chris Gordon* 15h 29c
9 ch g Foxhound(USA) Miss Beverley (Beveled (USA))
34^{5} 305^{4} 490^{7}

Oyster Shell *Henry Daly* 121h 132c
7 br g Bollin Eric Pearly-B (IRE) (Gunner B)
(116) 560^{3} 1688^{2} **2042^{3} (2469)**
4921^{2} 5091^{5} 5382^{3}

Ozamo (FR) *P Peltier* 133h 137c
7 b g Alamo Bay(USA) Ozee (FR) (Robin Des Champs (FR))
1902a^{6} 2264a^{P}

Pacha D'Oudairies (FR) *Michael Blake* 95h 96c
11 b g Ungaro(GER) Forlane V (FR) (Quart De Vin (FR))
141^{5} 692^{3}

Pacha Du Polder (FR) *Paul Nicholls* 124h 151c
7 b g Muhtathir Ambri Piotta (FR) (Caerwent)
392^{6} 4738^{10} 5350^{6}

Paddleyourowncanoe (IRE) *Emma Baker* 92h
13 b g Saddlers' Hall(IRE) Little Paddle (IRE) (Remainder Man)
145^{5} 407^{10}

Paddocks Lounge (IRE) *Jim Best* 88h
7 b g Oscar(IRE) Sister Rosza (IRE) (Roselier (FR))
4450^{6} 4569^{7} 4632^{7} 4931^{10}

Paddy Curry (IRE) *Mrs E Watson* 109h 27c
12 bb g Pistolet Bleu(IRE) Sterna Star (Corvaro (USA))
315^{5}

Paddy Mulligan (IRE) *John Ferguson* 81b
5 b g Presenting Laragh (IRE) (Oscar (IRE))
2354^{8}

Paddy Partridge *Tim Vaughan* 106h 94c
8 b g Pivotal Treble Heights (IRE) (Unfuwain (USA))
266^{2} 445^{2} 1134^{P} 1342^{2}

Paddysparks (IRE) *Henry Oliver* 83h 72c
10 b g Beneficial Polar Charm (IRE) (Supreme Leader)
802^{5} 1103^{3} 1376^{7} 1548^{3} 1837^{6}

Paddy's Saltantes (IRE) *Alex Hales* 75h
4 b g Redback Shall We Tell (Intikhab (USA))
5064^{10} 5519^{6}

Paddy The Hare (IRE) *Dr Richard Newland* 114h 135c
9 ch g Old Vic Boragh Thyme (IRE) (Simply Great (FR))
500^{3} (726)
(900) 1047^{8}

Paddy The Oscar (IRE) *Grace Harris* 96h 120c
11 b g Oscar(IRE) Parsonage (The Parson)
4175^{4} 4393^{4} 4677^{P} 5183^{5}

Paddy The Plumber (IRE) *Simon Waugh* 24c
8 b g Dr Massini(IRE) Heather Ville (IRE) (Yashgan)
625^{9}

Paddy The Stout (IRE) *Paul Henderson* 63h 111c
9 b g Oscar Schindler(IRE) Misty Silks (Scottish Reel)
2729^{7}
3093^{P} 3294^{3} 3742^{4} (4131)
4560^{3}

Padge (IRE) *Evan Williams* 105b
5 b g Flemensfirth(USA) Mona Vic (IRE) (Old Vic)
3194^{3}

Padre Tito (IRE) *Emma Lavelle* 120h
6 b g Milan Augusta Brook (IRE) (Over The River (FR))
2106^{2} 2648^{2} 3173^{5}

Page One Two Nine (IRE) *Miss J Luton* 98b 33c
11 b g Luso Corvally (Corvaro (USA))
5323^{F}

Pagham Belle *Nigel Hawke* 85h
6 b m Brian Boru Sambara (IRE) (Shardari)
1017^{5} 1305^{6} 1639^{4} 1799^{8} 2291^{2} 2511^{F} 2921^{U}
3140^{4} 3788^{6} 4072^{2} 4398^{6}

Paintball (IRE) *Charlie Longsdon* 132h
7 b g Le Vie Dei Colori Camassina (IRE) (Taufan (USA))
182^{F}

Painted Gold *Sarah-Jayne Davies* 80h
8 ch m Central Park(IRE) Iron Pyrites (Blaze O'Gold (USA))
3733^{4} 4375^{5}

Painted Sky *Iain Jardine* 24h
11 ch g Rainbow Quest(USA) Emplane (USA) (Irish River (FR))
476^{9} 751^{P} 884^{P} 1073^{10} 1673^{10}

Painted Tail (IRE) *Alan Swinbank* 83h
7 b m Mark Of Esteem(IRE) Bronwen (IRE) (King's Best (USA))
3274^{4}

Paint The Clouds *Warren Greatrex* 130h 139c
9 b g Muhtarram(USA) Preening (Persian Bold)
(4936)
(5292)

Pairc Na Gcapall (IRE) *Neil King* 60h 84c
12 b g Taipan(IRE) Ballindante (IRE) (Phardante (FR))
(597) **766^{3}**
972^{5}

Pairc Na Leasa (IRE) *Martin Todhunter* 101h
8 b g Beat All(USA) Seymour Roses (Seymour Hicks (FR))
4223^{9} 4465^{7} 4774^{10}

Pair Of Jacks (IRE) *Malcolm Jefferson* 124h
6 ch g Presenting Halona (Pollerton)
2104^{4} 2823^{3} 4693^{4} 4889^{3} (5357) ◆

Palace Jester *David Pipe* 138h 123c
9 b g King's Theatre(IRE) Jessolle (Scallywag)
39^{4} 294^{2} 518^{4} 766^{P} 1316^{P}

Paladin (IRE) *John Ferguson* 102h
5 b g Dubawi(IRE) Palwina (FR) (Unfuwain (USA))
2252^{3}

Palanour (FR) *Sue Gardner*
6 ch g Valanour(IRE) Palala River (Colmore Row)
517^{P}

Palermo Don *Donald McCain* 106b
4 b g Beat Hollow Kristal Bridge (Kris)
3719^{3} ◆ (4902)

Palio Square (USA) *John Flint* 102h
7 bb g Harlan's Holiday(USA) Teewee's Hope (CAN) (Defrere (USA))
253^{P} 521^{6} 686^{10}

Palmarrick (IRE) *Nick Kent* 38h
7 b g Great Palm(USA) Lynrick Lady (IRE) (Un Desperado (FR))
2174^{4} 2627^{6} 3115^{8}

Palm Grey (IRE) *Sue Smith* 105b
6 gr g Great Palm(USA) Lucy Cooper (IRE) (Roselier (FR))
4480^{3} 4944^{3}

Palmyra (IRE) *Martin Hill* 67h
5 ch m Haafhd Tasjeel (USA) (Aljabr (USA))
155^{5} 407^{13}

Palos Conti (FR) *Brian Ellison* 113h 119c
11 ch g Robin Des Champs(FR) Dona Mirande (FR) (Pebble (FR))
1659^{7} 2201^{3} 2820^{2} 3759^{5} 4695^{2} 5193^{7}

Palus San Marco (IRE) *Charlie Longsdon* 105h
5 b g Holy Roman Emperor(IRE) Kylemore (IRE) (Sadler's Wells (USA))
475^{4} 671^{5} 2051^{11} 2794^{P}

Palypso De Creek (FR) *Mrs J Dawson* 111h 126c
11 b g Brier Creek(USA) Belgheera (FR) (Vorias (USA))
63^{2} (4042)
(4348)

Pamak D'Airy (FR) *Henry Hogarth* 105h 110c
11 b g Cadoubel(FR) Gamaska D'Airy (FR) (Marasali)
2338^{2} 2737^{3} 3020^{2} (3637)
4080^{6} 4341^{3} (4815)
5318^{2}

Pamela Lewis *Pam Sly* 82b
7 b m Sir Harry Lewis(USA) Worlaby Rose (Afif)
567^{6} 790^{7}

Pampanito *Donald McCain* 49h
8 b g Bollin Eric Seamill (IRE) (Lafontaine (USA))
1575^{8} 1940^{P} 2869^{8}

Pampelonne (IRE) *Charlie Longsdon* 105h 106c
8 b m Oscar(IRE) Bondi Storm (IRE) (Glacial Storm (USA))
2678 708^{2}

Pamplona Run (IRE) *Harry Fry*
6 b g Flemensfirth(USA) Bilboa (FR) (Phantom Breeze)
2942^{P}

Panache *Angela Clarke* 98h
9 b g King's Best(USA) Exclusive (Polar Falcon (USA))
8^{U} 192^{3} 434^{2} 716^{5} 1674^{8}

Panama Canal (IRE) *S Robinson* 55h 81c
9 b g Accordion Maltese Lady (IRE) (Viking (USA))
4485^{7}

Panama Petrus (IRE) *Venetia Williams* 126h
6 b g Alflora(IRE) Pride 'N' Joy (IRE) (Lashkari)
2316^{3} (4075) 4428^{3} 4680^{10}

Pandorica *Bernard Llewellyn* 77h
6 b m Indesatchel(IRE) Hope Chest (Kris)
1639^{5}

Pandy *George Baker* 103h
5 b m Sakhee(USA) Ceiriog Valley (In The Wings)
2809^{4} 3159^{P} 5229^{2} ◆

Pandy Wells *Graeme McPherson* 24h
5 b m Kayf Tara Alina Rheinberg (GER) (Waky Nao)
2513^{7} 3181^{6} 5124^{10} 5427^{7}

Panther Claw (IRE) *Paul Nolan* 142c
8 gr g Old Vic Rose Of Inchiquin (IRE) (Roselier (FR))
2708a^{8} 3868a^{7} (Dead)

Panthers Run *Jonathan Haynes* 72h 65c
14 b g Jendali(USA) Dorado Beach (Lugana Beach)
109^{5} 627^{6} 802^{P} 1876^{8} 2338^{3} 3107^{6} 3637^{3} 3799^{3}
4203^{4} 4581^{4}
5107^{P}

Pantxoa (FR) *Alan King* 128h 146c
7 b g Daliapour(IRE) Palmeria (FR) (Great Palm (USA))
238^{F} 562^{2} 839^{3} (1257)
(1362) (1709)
1957^{2} 2373^{P} (5352)

Paolozzi (IRE) *Seamus Durack* 74b
5 b g Oscar(IRE) Miss Eurolink I (Touching Wood (USA))
3160^{3}

Papa Caruso *Sue Smith* 112h 121c
10 b g Kayf Tara Madonna Da Rossi (Mtoto)
220^{3} 495^{5} (1076)

Papamoa *N W Alexander* 108h 120c
9 gr g Terimon Larksmore (Royal Fountain)
(2157)
3111^{P}

Papradon *Nigel Twiston-Davies* 89h 130c
10 b g Tobougg(IRE) Salvezza (IRE) (Superpower)
(457) **714^{P}**
(1135)
(1327) 1425^{5}

Paradise Expected *Mark Gillard* 40h 45c
11 ch m North Briton Phenomenon (Unfuwain (USA))
1349^{P} 1800^{9} 2023^{P}

Paradise Valley (IRE) *Mick Channon* 126h
5 b g Presenting Native Wood (IRE) (Be My Native (USA))
3035^{2} ◆ 3841^{3} (5305) (5445) ◆

Parazar (FR) *D Summersby* 98h 73c
9 b g Kutub(IRE) Paraja (IRE) (Doyoun)
57^{8} 180^{P}

Parc Des Princes (USA) *Nicky Richards* 105h
8 bb g Ten Most Wanted(USA) Miss Orah (Unfuwain (USA))
12^{8} 4533^{11} 4893^{2} 5482^{3}

Pareto (CZE) *Cestmir Olehla*
7 ch g Rainbows For Life(CAN) Pulnoc (CZE) (Shy Groom (USA))
1683a^{5}

Parigny (FR) *F-M Cottin* 114h 132c
8 b g Tagula(IRE) Romilly (FR) (Subotica (FR))
1902a^{7} 2264a^{U} 2415a^{2}

Paris Clermont (FR) *H Despont* 103h
5 b g Voix Du Nord(FR) Ania De Clermont (FR) (Ungaro (GER))
703a^{2}

Parkam Jack *Richard Woollacott* 114h 104c
8 b g Grape Tree Road Rakajack (Rakaposhi King)
180^{3} 763^{4}

Parkham Gent (IRE) *Laura Young* 43h
7 gr g Luso Solo Rose (Roselier (FR))
828^{12}

Park House *Ray Craggs* 87b
5 b g Tillerman Rasin Luck (Primitive Rising (USA))
284^{6} 699^{7}

Park Lane *Noel Quinlan* 99h 108c
8 b g Royal Applause Kazeem (Darshaan)
1493^{3}

Parsnip Pete *Tom George* 117h 145c
8 b g Pasternak Bella Coola (Northern State (USA))
(2049)
2488^{10} 2816^{2} 3080^{4} 4921^{6} (5136)

Parson's Punch *Lucy Normile* 109h
9 b g Beat Hollow Ordained (Mtoto)
344^{5} 681^{14} 884^{P} (961) 1289^{S}

Parting Way (IRE) *Tim Vaughan* 87h
6 b g Golan(IRE) Best Mother (IRE) (King's Theatre (IRE))
3187^{9} 3838^{4} 4664^{5} ◆ 4807^{13}

Party Girls (FR) *David Pipe* 52h
6 b m Astarabad(USA) Canadiane (FR) (Nikos)
2022^{7} 2761^{U} 2906^{15} 3168^{11} 3733^{P} 3991^{F}
4600^{P} 5235^{12}

Party Palace *Stuart Howe* 105h
10 b m Auction House(USA) Lady-Love (Pursuit Of Love)
(37) (521) (691) 924^{3} (995) 1828^{6}

Party Pictures (IRE) *Miss Jessica Westwood* 85b 108c
11 b g Exit To Nowhere(USA) Beccemma (IRE) (Over The River (FR))
57^{9} 159^{3} 413^{U} 632^{9}

Party Rock (IRE) *Jennie Candlish* 145h
7 b g Vinnie Roe(IRE) Garryduff Eile (IRE) (Oscar (IRE))
(356) 2102^{7} 2671^{7} 2935^{2} 3292^{6} 3646^{P} 4112^{6}
4752^{P} 5158^{F}

Pas De Blabla (FR) *A Lefeuvre*
4 bl f Ultimately Lucky(IRE) Blabliramic (FR) (Panoramic)
2781a^{6}

Paskalis *Emma Lavelle* 73b
5 b g Kayf Tara Easter Comet (Gunner B)
4824^{6}

Pasquini Rouge (FR) *Patrice Quinton* 103h 135c
6 b g Passing Sale(FR) Scevollia (FR) (Dom Pasquini (FR))
3068^{3}

Passage Vendome (FR) *W P Mullins* 135h 137c
8 b g Polish Summer Herodiade (FR) (Starborough)
2550a^{3} 4790^{F} 5420a^{15}

Passato (GER) *Jo Davis* 103h 127c
10 b g Lando(GER) Passata (FR) (Polar Falcon (USA))
01^{6} 392^{0} 072^{P} 1740^{7} 2080^{C} 2894^{0} 4725^{F}

Pass Friend *Martin Bosley* 55h
6 b m Passing Glance Miss Traxdata (Absalom)
567^{11} 857^{10} 1058^{6}

Passing Fiesta *Sarah-Jayne Davies* 62h
5 b m Passing Glance Clarice Starling (Saddlers' Hall (IRE))
324^{8} 715^{P} 3956^{7} 4350^{7}

Passing Through *Gordon Elliott* 117h 93c
10 b g Exit To Nowhere(USA) Island Hopper (Be My Native (USA))
883^{10}

Pass Muster *Philip Kirby* 109h
7 b g Theatrical(IRE) Morning Pride (IRE) (Machiavellian (USA))
(2794) ◆ 2921^{2} 3518^{2} *(4023)* ◆ 4794^{8}

Pass The Hat *A L T Moore* 126h 133c
7 ch g Karinga Bay Moor Spring (Primitive Rising (USA))
2708a^{6}

Pass The Time *Neil Mulholland* 132h
5 b m Passing Glance Twin Time (Syrtos)
353^{5} 1084^{3} 2477^{2} (2763) 3895^{4} (4531) 4740^{7}
5158^{9}

Pastek (FR) *Dr Jeremy Naylor* 78b
11 b g Ungaro(GER) Capsolane (FR) (Son Of Silver)
328^{F} 871^{8}

Pastoral *Tony Coyle* 87b
5 b m Rail Link Cut Corn (King's Theatre (IRE))
1472^{3}

Pas Trop Tard (FR) *Maurice Barnes* 134h
7 b g Caballo Raptor(CAN) This Melody (FR) (Saint Preuil (FR))
1922^{4} 2230^{P} 2958^{2} 3273^{3} 3892^{6} 4056^{3} 4224^{3}
5512^{3}

Pasture Bay (IRE) *Fergal O'Brien* 111h
8 b g Flemensfirth(USA) Silver Oak (IRE) (Anshan)
(1200) 1350^{5}
1916^{P} 3183^{P} 5030^{P}

Patavium (IRE) *Edwin Tuer* 98h
11 b g Titus Livius(FR) Arcevia (IRE) (Archway (IRE))
3618^{7} 4189^{4} (4615) 4938^{4} 5484^{4}

Pateese (FR) *Philip Hobbs* 144h 128c
9 b g Priolo(USA) Flyer (FR) (Highest Honor (FR))
215^{18}
1484^{2} 1594^{5} 2268^{3} 2798^{2} 3369^{2} 4144^{8} 4765^{13}
5138^{11} 5544^{3}

Pathian Prince *E R Clough* 82h 109c
11 b g Parthian Springs Smilingatstrangers (Macmillion)
335^{2} 4092^{P} 4915^{U}

Patricktom Boru (IRE) *R W J Willcox* 91h 95c
7 b g Brian Boru Brehon Law (IRE) (Alphabatim (USA))
540^{9} 637^{U} 829^{11} 1110^{7} **4485^{6} 5545^{4}**

Patriot (IRE) *Barry Murtagh* 55h 28c
10 b g Sadler's Wells(USA) Sweeten Up (Shirley Heights)
4465^{5} 4774^{P} 5161^{9}

Pats Preference (IRE) *Victor Thompson* 40c
8 bb g Tamayaz(CAN) Kissangel (IRE) (Namaqualand (USA))
28^{5}

Patsy Finnegan *Alan King* 127h 127c
12 b g Sir Harry Lewis(USA) Bampton Fair (Free Boy)
(120) **642^{U}**

Patsys Castle (IRE) *Kim Bailey* 117h
7 ch g Windsor Castle Annienoora (IRE) (Topanoora)
1915^{4} 2296^{2} 3195^{P} 5128^{9} 5351^{P}

Pattara *Noel Williams* 79b
5 b m Kayf Tara Fortunes Course (IRE) (Crash Course)
2298^{10} 2946^{8}

Paudi The Punter (IRE) *Gordon Elliott* 121h 87c
8 b g Classic Cliche(IRE) La Golondrina (IRE) (Carroll House)
3936^{P}

Paupers Present (IRE) *Jeremy Scott* 83h
6 b m Presenting Paumafi (IRE) (Shardari)
1936^{6} 637^{8}

Pause And Clause (IRE) *N W Alexander* 103b
10 b g Saddlers' Hall(IRE) Silver Glen (IRE) (Roselier (FR))
2220^{F}

Pay The King (IRE) *Paul Nicholls* 116h
7 b g King's Theatre(IRE) Knocktartan (IRE) (King's Ride)
2529^{5} 4051^{6} 5351^{8}

Peaceful Gardens *Jeremy Scott* 51h
5 b m Franklins Gardens So Peaceful (Prince Of Peace)
3168^{12}

Peachey Moment (USA) *Nicky Richards* 78h 112c
9 bb g Stormin Fever(USA) Given Moment (USA) (Diesis)
387^{2} 680^{5} 869^{3} 1085^{5} 2820^{3} 3272^{2} 4080^{5} 4551^{5}
4985^{P}

Peak Seasons (IRE) *Michael Chapman* 76h 94c
11 ch g Raise A Grand(IRE) Teresian Girl (IRE) (Glenstal (USA))
(34) **162^{2}**
285^{3} 472^{2} 597^{U} 693^{2} 1039^{6} 1075^{2} 1174^{2} 1202^{4}
1260^{6}
1377^{4} 1715^{U}
1914^{5} 2067^{5}
2396^{3} 2562^{6}
3180^{P}

Peaks Of Fire (IRE) *Joanne Foster* 111h 114c
7 b g High Chaparral(IRE) Crimson Glory (Lycius (USA))
90^{U} 446^{3} 555^{7} 726^{P} 1981^{4} 2349^{F}

Peak Storm *John O'Shea* 99h
5 b g Sleeping Indian Jitterbug (IRE) (Marju (IRE))
2467^{8} 2614^{7} 2753^{3} 3157^{7}

Pearl (IRE) *Ron Hodges* 90h
10 b m Daylami(IRE) Briery (IRE) (Salse (USA))
2690^{9} 2760^{4} 5234^{14}

Pearl Castle (IRE) *John Quinn* 138h
4 b g Montjeu(IRE) Ghurra (USA) (War Chant (USA))
3332^{3} (3872) ◆ (4345) 4784^{7}

Pearls Legend *John Spearing* 122h 124c
7 b g Midnight Legend Pearl's Choice (IRE) (Deep Run)
826 **2469^{3}**
2976^{3} 3156^{2} 3769^{F} 4007^{2} 4418^{5} 4861^{3} 5552^{3}

Pearly Legend *Neil Mulholland* 91b
6 b m Midnight Legend Sea Pearl (Derring Rose)
4296^{7} 4735^{8}

Pearlysteps *Henry Daly* 116h 140c
11 ch g Alflora(IRE) Pearly-B (IRE) (Gunner B)
(3801)
(4092) 4788^{4}

Pearse (FR) *Louisa Carberry* 113h 128c
10 ch g River Bay(USA) Little Rocket (Bustino)
5425a^{3}

Peckhamecho (IRE) *Rebecca Curtis* 145h 137c
8 b g Beneficial Nolans Pride (IRE) (Good Thyne (USA))
1766^{6} 2080^{7}

Pectora (IRE) *Oliver Sherwood* 101b
5 b m Kalanisi(IRE) Nerissa (IRE) (Great Palm (USA))
567^{3} (842) 4683^{6}

Pedrow (IRE) *Brian Barr*
6 b g Pierre Promalady (IRE) (Homo Sapien)
1056^{8}

Pegase Du Carcaud (FR) *F Lagarde* 110c
11 b g Dear Doctor(FR) Aureole De Monts (FR) (Nellio (FR))
1279a^3

Pegasus Prince (USA) *Brian Storey* 82h 107c
10 b g Fusaichi Pegasus(USA) Avian Eden (USA) (Storm Bird (CAN))
471^{12} 750^P

Pegasus Walk (IRE) *Rose Dobbin* 63b
5 b g Beneficial Porter Tastes Nice (IRE) (Dry Dock)
4944^6 5324^9

Peggy's Legend *Tony Carroll*
6 b m Midnight Legend Babs Wheal (Petoski)
2892^{11}

Peintre Abstrait (IRE) *R Holcak*
8 ch g Peintre Celebre(USA) Prairie Runner (IRE) (Arazi (USA))
1905a^5

Pelcomb Bridge *Marc Barber*
9 b g King O' The Mana(IRE) Flaming Katey (Tigerwood)
4838^P

Pelennor (FR) *Stephen Hughes* 81h
10 b g River Bay(USA) Alidami (GER) (Damister (USA))
783^6 946^P

Pelican Rock (IRE) *David Thompson*
5 b g Amadeus Wolf Darby Shaw (IRE) (Kris)
3350^P

Pelmanism *Brian Ellison* 78h
7 b g Piccolo Card Games (First Trump)
2753^4

Pembroke House *Sarah-Jayne Davies* 106h
7 gr g Terimon Bon Coeur (Gunner B)
14^7 395^5 2467^4 2720^8 2978^6 4596^5 5112^3 5490^8

Pena Dorada (IRE) *Alan J Brown* 113h 113c
7 b g Key Of Luck(USA) Uluwatu (IRE) (Unfuwain (USA))
113^4 4225^2 (4554)
4837^4 5536^4

Pendra (IRE) *Charlie Longsdon* 140h 143c
6 ch g Old Vic Mariah Rollins (IRE) (Over The River (FR))
(2031)
(2726) 3197^7 4742^3 5474a^{10}

Pen Gwen (FR) *Philip Kirby* 35h 82c
11 b g Le Balafre(FR) Dans Dro (FR) (Spoleto)
5107^P 5323^P 5514^{10}

Penmore Mill (IRE) *F A Hutsby* 129c
9 b g Shernazar Stephens Street (IRE) (Kahyasi)
(288) **4057^4**
◆ (4782)
4922^3

Pennant Dancer *Debra Hamer* 86h
7 b g Grape Tree Road Pennant Princess (Alflora (IRE))
71^8 407^F 1631^P 1708^8 1837^5 2571^3 2886^3 3426^6 4911^8 (5432)

Pennies And Pounds *Julian Smith* 65h
7 b m Sir Harry Lewis(USA) Sense Of Value (Trojan Fen)
324^7 3010^{11} 5036^8

Pennine Josie *James Moffatt* 75h
5 b m Josr Algarhoud(IRE) Pennine Star (IRE) (Pennine Walk)
3147^5 3616^P 4234^7 5057^8

Pennys Tune (IRE) *Matthew J Smith* 112h
7 b m Montjeu(IRE) Diarshana (GER) (Darshaan)
891a^3

Pension Plan *Peter Bowen* 140h
10 b g Alflora(IRE) Dalbeattie (Phardante (FR))
(144) (2388) 3207^P

Pensnett Bay *Shaun Lycett* 59h 123c
9 ch g Karinga Bay Balmoral Princess (Thethingaboutitis (USA))
113^P 2512^5 3113^4 4448^2 4822^3

Pentiffic (NZ) *Venetia Williams* 130c
11 br g Pentire Sailing High (NZ) (Yachtie (AUS))
238^7 4057^U 4274^6 (4705)
5135^U 5232^3

Penyfan Dawn (IRE) *Polly Gundry* 114h 98c
10 ch g Bach(IRE) Aillwee Dawn (Deep Run)
643^P

Pepite Rose (FR) *Venetia Williams* 113h 154c
7 bb m Bonbon Rose(FR) Sambre (FR) (Turgeon (USA))
2047 392^4 (3333)
3645^4 4032^8 (4960)
5155^6 5570^2

Peplum (FR) *Mrs Tina Cook* 65h 65c
11 b g Subotica(FR) Great Filly (FR) (Murmure (FR))
657^9

Peqeno Diablo (IRE) *Claire Dyson* 70h
9 br g Alexius(IRE) Miss Huro (IRE) (Mandalus)
2191^8 2427^4 2770^3 3009^4 (3251) 3569^7 4447^9 5283^U

Perfect Candidate (IRE) *Fergal O'Brien* 113h 123c
7 b g Winged Love(IRE) Dansana (IRE) (Insan (USA))
1863^2
3873^4 4537^4 5559^5

Perfect Focus (IRE) *P M Quinlan* 94h
7 ch g Basanta(IRE) Yellow Bog Common (IRE) (Common Grounds)
891a^{10}

Perfectly Willing (IRE) *T F Sage* 111c
8 b g Luso Dark Nightingale (Strong Gale)
5337^5

Perfect Poison (IRE) *Donald McCain* 88h
6 b g Vinnie Roe(IRE) Noddys Confusion (IRE) (Supreme Leader)
380^3 629^7 848^8

Perfect Promise (IRE) *James Joseph Mangan* 104b
6 b m Presenting Snape (IRE) (Strong Gale)
3126a^4

Perfect Romance *Patrick Chamings* 97b
5 ch m Singspiel(IRE) Flamjica (USA) (Real Quiet (USA))
1599^2 2022^9

Perfect Shot (IRE) *Sarah-Jayne Davies* 56h
8 b g High Chaparral(IRE) Zoom Lens (IRE) (Caerleon (USA))
3598^8 3728^{12} *4327^{11}*

Perfect Smile (IRE) *Noel Meade* 140h 137c
9 bb g Anshan Mambo Music (FR) (Rusticaro (FR))
3806a^7

Perfect Timing *Johnny Farrelly* 96h 114c
6 b g Shantou(USA) Winnetka Gal (IRE) (Phardante (FR))
29^{13} 1364^4 1631^2 1718^2 1945^3 5177^{14}

Pericoloso (IRE) *Ms A E Embiricos* 118c
8 b g Heron Island(IRE) Phills Serenade (IRE) (Lancastrian)
5435^P

Periquest *Alex Hales* 90b
5 b g Overbury(IRE) Rippling Brook (Phardante (FR))
4310^6 4824^7 5249^7

Persian Fox (IRE) *Stephen Hughes* 64h
10 b g King Charlemagne(USA) Persian Mistress (IRE) (Persian Bold)
843^6 948^8

Persian Herald *Sue Smith* 111h 100c
6 gr g Proclamation(IRE) Persian Fortune (Forzando)
2^6 376^2 593^4 788^7 1058^3 1134^3 1402^3 1633^{10} (2062) 2176^3 (2559) (2573) 2846^4 3149^4 3324^P 3468^4 (3839) 4187^4 4378^3 4608^2 5105^2

Persian Peril *Alan Swinbank* 62h
10 br g Erhaab(USA) Brush Away (Ahonoora)
3350^6

Persian Snow (IRE) *Philip Hobbs* 132h 142c
8 b g Anshan Alpine Message (Tirol)
2211^3 2714^5 3436^2 (3861)
4160^2 ◆ (4400)
4742^6 5350^7

Personal Shopper *H Smyth* 93h 89c
7 b m King's Theatre(IRE) Island Hopper (Be My Native (USA))
4770^P

Pertemps Heights *M Foley* 69c
7 b g North Col(IRE) Hera (Thethingaboutitis (USA))
59^5

Pertemps Networks *Michael Easterby* 118h 99c
10 b g Golden Snake(USA) Society Girl (Shavian)
2958^9 3201^6 3527^5 4943^P

Pertinent (FR) *Charles Whittaker* 115h 121c
11 b g Sleeping Car(FR) Jamais De La Vie (FR) (Saint Preuil (FR))
2908^5 3290^2 (5033) 5307^2

Pertuis (IRE) *Micky Hammond* 105h
8 gr g Verglas(IRE) Lady Killeen (IRE) (Marju (IRE))
2198^2 2519^6 3288^3 3659^4

Pestal And Mortar (IRE) *F G Hand* 103h 116c
9 b m Tamayaz(CAN) Lady Meargan (IRE) (Yashgan)
5475a^7

Pete *Barry Murtagh* 99h 99c
11 b g Overbury(IRE) Fen Terrier (Emarati (USA))
109^U 283^5 536^2 803^P 1078^4 (1374)
1395^F 1580^4 2035^2

Peter *Paul Webber* 93b
6 b g Kayf Tara Tisho (Sir Harry Lewis (USA))
270^4

Peterbrown (IRE) *Nick Gifford* 107h
6 b g Shantou(USA) Grove Juliet (IRE) (Moscow Society (USA))
163^3 3473^P 4700^3 5438^P

Peter Muck *Nigel Twiston-Davies* 78h
11 b g Alflora(IRE) Madam Muck (Gunner B)
1706^7 1860^5 2535^F

Pete The Feat (IRE) *Charlie Longsdon* 91h 149c
10 b g King's Theatre(IRE) Tourist Attraction (IRE) (Pollerton)
1868^F 2452^P (3006)
3416^3 4035^F 4557^U 4821^F

Petie McSweetie (IRE) *Richard Woollacott* 93h 88c
7 b g Accordion Crafty Rule (IRE) (Warcraft (USA))
540^{10} **632^8**

Peti Kap (FR) *L Viel* 125c
5 b g Kapgarde(FR) La Petite Angevine (FR) (Sandhurst Prince)
2263a^P

Petit Bob (FR) *G Macaire*
11 ro g April Night(FR) Princesse De Mars (FR) (Jolie Mars (FR))
1279a^P

Petit Ecuyer (FR) *Barry Brennan* 98h 104c
8 b g Equerry(USA) Petite Majeste (FR) (Riverquest (FR))
98^7 4372^4 4658^8 5115^8 5301^6

Petit Fleur *Julian Smith* 79h
12 b m Nomadic Way(USA) Sense Of Value (Trojan Fen)
738^7 2691^{13} 3117^4 5069^P

Petit Hibou *Sean Curran* 51b
6 b g Lahib(USA) Madam Killeshandra (Jurado (USA))
1056^6

Petit Robin (FR) *Nicky Henderson* 160h 154c
11 b g Robin Des Pres(FR) Joie De Cotte (FR) (Lute Antique (FR))
3080^9

Petomic (IRE) *Paul John Gilligan* 66h
9 ch g Dubai Destination(USA) Petomi (Presidium)
517^P

Petrarchick (USA) *Emma Baker* 79h 63c
7 b m Arch(USA) Tustin (USA) (Conquistador Cielo (USA))
408^3 485^6 759^P 2423^P 2690^{11} 3009^6

Petrocelli *Tim Vaughan* 74h
7 b g Piccolo Sarcita (Primo Dominie)
640^9 1137^8 1269^P 1331^6 2004^6 2862^{11}

Petroupetrov (FR) *Tim Vaughan* 91h 96c
11 br g Ungaro(GER) Harlem (FR) (Garde Royale)
141^4 478^2 692^P 872^3 1103^4

Pettifour (IRE) *Nigel Twiston-Davies* 113h 124c
12 b g Supreme Leader Queen Of Natives (IRE) (Be My Native (USA))
1978^4 2537^8

Peut Etre Sivola (FR) *Johnny Farrelly*
11 b g Robin Des Champs(FR) Largentiere (FR) (Antheus (USA))
2290^P

Phakos (FR) *P Cottin* 123c
11 b g Robin Des Champs(FR) Tipperary II (FR) (Chamberlin (FR))
199a^2 1532a^7

Phantom Prince (IRE) *Brendan Powell* 124h
5 b g Jeremy(USA) Phantom Waters (Pharly (FR))
95^2 3094^3 3599^F (4799) 5142^2 5574^F

Phantom Ranch *Alastair Lidderdale*
5 b g Act One Highbrook (USA) (Alphabatim (USA))
1552^P

Pharaon De Touzaine (FR) *John O'Shea* 53h 63c
11 b g Subotica(FR) Diana De Vonnas (FR) (El Badr)
669^9 946^7 **1055^P**

Phar Away Island (IRE) *Graeme McPherson* 90h
6 br g Heron Island(IRE) Phar From Men (IRE) (Phardante (FR))
29^P 163^5 444^{10} 2016^5 2278^2 2535^4 5359^2

Phare Isle (IRE) *Ben Case* 124h 116c
9 b g Turtle Island(IRE) Pharenna (IRE) (Phardante (FR))
336^5 718^6 2314^8 2529^{15} 2903^2 3505^F 3798^3 4076^U 4308^2 4697^4 5128^5 5489^5

Pharly De Kerser (FR) *Patrice Quinton* 126h 131c
11 gr g Medaaly Riuscita (FR) (Vacarme (USA))
1984a^7

Phase Shift *Brian Ellison* 118h 116c
6 b m Iceman Silent Waters (Polish Precedent (USA))
506^2 2084^2 **2515^4 3354^2 3831^3 4483^4** 4698^3
5228^7

Philchezski (IRE) *Andrew Crook* 24h
7 ch g Pilsudski(IRE) Springfield Gilda (IRE) (Gildoran)
76^{10} 695^4

Philharmonic Hall *Marc Barber*
6 b g Victory Note(USA) Lambast (Relkino)
4398^F

Philosofy *David O'Meara* 95b
4 ch f Barathea(IRE) Idealistic (IRE) (Unfuwain (USA))
3835^3 (4008)

Phoenix Des Mottes (FR) *John Cornwall* 79h 79c
11 b g Useful(FR) Camille Des Mottes (FR) (Abdonski (FR))
429^{11} 969^P **2560^4 2772^5 2872^3 (3114)**
3595^P 3855^3 4486^P 4759^4 (4982)
5065^2 5193^2
5293^5

Phoenix Eye *Michael Mullineaux* 80h 92c
13 b g Tragic Role(USA) Eye Sight (Roscoe Blake)
903^7 969^6 1267^8 1442^5 1689^7 2397^{10}

Phoenix Flight (IRE) *James Evans* 114h
9 b g Hawk Wing(USA) Firecrest (IRE) (Darshaan)
1972^5 5030^{10} 5520^2

Phoenix Returns (IRE) *Alan Swinbank* 113h
6 br g Phoenix Reach(IRE) Oscar's Lady (IRE) (Oscar (IRE))
2032^6 2454^U 2970^8

Phone Home (IRE) *Nick Mitchell* 117h 120c
7 bb g Heron Island(IRE) Ancestral Voices (IRE) (Strong Gale)
38^2 **2107^7**
2459^5 3004^P 3421^P 4411^3 4662^2 5030^P 5351^{12}

Photogenique (FR) *Rob Summers* 74h 63c
11 b m Cyborg(FR) Colombia (FR) (Le Riverain (FR))
248^F 765^{13} 932^P 1280^4 1718^5 3188^9 3842^P 4398^{11} 4783^4

Piano Concerto (USA) *Sophie Leech* 101h
7 b g Red Ransom(USA) Storm Song (USA) (Summer Squall (USA))
1176^3

Pibrac (FR) *F-M Cottin* 139h 144c
10 ch g Spadoun(FR) Palissandre (FR) (Phantom Breeze)
2264a^5

Picabo Kid (USA) *Miss S L Klug* 59h 77c
11 b g Lemon Drop Kid(USA) Picabo Street (USA) (Deputy Minister (CAN))
5439^4

Picaroon *Alexandra Dunn* 96h 112c
10 b g Jade Robbery(USA) Anaam (Caerleon (USA))
4021^8 4326^3 **4505^2 4912^3 5336^2**

Piccadilly Circus *David Pipe* 82b
5 b g King's Theatre(IRE) Disallowed (IRE) (Distinctly North (USA))
4575^6

Pickamus (FR) *Henry Daly* 116h 139c
11 gr g April Night(FR) Duchesse Du Cochet (FR) (Native Guile (USA))
1971^8 (2889)
3458^4 4769^6 5092^P

Picklegend *Richard Woollacott* 33h
8 b g Midnight Legend Miss Pickle VII (Damsire Unregistered)
193^P

Picks Milan (IRE) *Philip Kirby* 108h 60c
8 b g Milan Butchies Girl (IRE) (Alphabatim (USA))
556^P 3724^P **5216^6 5376^4**

Picodean *Robert Stephens* 94b
6 b g Tikkanen(USA) Gipsy Girl (Motivate)
3133^4 4030^6 5310^3

Picsoudu Bredeloup (FR) *Guy Denuault*
8 b g Baroud D'Honneur(FR) Roza Du Bredeloup (FR) (Sinjar (FR))
199a^F

Picture Post (USA) *Nicky Henderson* 86h
7 b g Mr Greeley(USA) Cherokee (USA) (Storm Cat (USA))
116^5

Piece Of Magic *Michael Easterby* 73h
9 b m Alflora(IRE) Madame Illusion (FR) (Solid Illusion (USA))
1105^4

Pied Du Roi (IRE) *Charlie Longsdon* 99b
4 b g Robin Des Pres(FR) Long Acre (Mark Of Esteem (IRE))
4902^2

Pierrers Bounty (IRE) *Henry Hogarth* 113h
7 b g Pierre Willow Stream (IRE) (Corrouge (USA))
2823^6 3189^8 3618^8 3922^5 4478^7 (4774) 5059^9

Pierrot Bay (FR) *T Trapenard* 125h 127c
7 b g Martaline Peace Bay (FR) (Alamo Bay (USA))
406a^P
5425a^9

Pigeon Island *Nigel Twiston-Davies* 142h 139c
11 gr g Daylami(IRE) Morina (USA) (Lyphard (USA))
448^3 680^7 2070^2 2674^5 3067^3 3455^P 3888^7
4557^3 5513^5

Pilgreen (FR) *Robert Walford* 116h
9 ch g Green Tune(USA) Galinetta (FR) (Galetto (FR))
4129^5 4555^2 (5019)

Pimbury (IRE) *Fiona Shaw* 50h 18c
12 b g Pistolet Bleu(IRE) Duchess Of Kinsale (IRE) (Montelimar (USA))
4275^9 4803^5

Piment D'Estruval (FR) *Tim Vaughan* 114h 125c
11 bb g Sheyrann(IRE) Gabika De Keroger (FR) (Shafoun (FR))
142^3 578^2
(999)

Pinamar *Paul Webber* 89b
4 ch f Shirocco(GER) Highland Ceilidh (IRE) (Scottish Reel)
4916^6

Pindar (GER) *Joanne Foster* 86h 90c
10 b g Tertullian(USA) Pierette (GER) (Local Suitor (USA))
(1331) 1428^4 1643^3 2062^2 3038^8 **3352^3 3635^F**

Pineau De Re (FR) *Dr Richard Newland* 146h 157c
11 b g Maresca Sorrento(FR) Elfe Du Perche (FR) (Abdonski (FR))
851^6 1047^{12} 1283^2 1362^3 2504^5
2937^F 3108^2 3207^7 **(3698)** 4765^3 **(5171)**

Pine Creek *John Ferguson* 139h
6 b g Doyen(IRE) Valley Of Gold (FR) (Shirley Heights)
(2213) 2533^6 3200^7

Pinerolo *Sue Smith* 105h 136c
8 b g Milan Hollybush (IRE) (Ali-Royal (IRE))
2868^4
3037^4 3331^3 (4188)
(4425) 4819^P 5278^P

Pink Gin *Jim Old* 112h
6 ch g Alflora(IRE) Miss Mailmit (Rakaposhi King)
2534^{12} 2940^{10} 3175^4 (3796) 4397^2 4535^6

Pink Hat (IRE) *W P Mullins* 130h
6 b m Presenting Victorine (IRE) (Un Desperado (FR))
4708a^9

Pink Mischief *Andrew Crook* 78h
4 gr f Holy Roman Emperor(IRE) Feather (USA) (Unbridled's Song (USA))
3757^7 4037^4 4476^4 5163^{11}

Pinkneys Prince *Nick Williams* 103h 113c
7 b g Fair Mix(IRE) Cool Run (Deep Run)
(1939)

Pinnacle Ofpassion (IRE) *Nick Lampard* 54h
6 b m Presenting Olives Hall (IRE) (Saddlers' Hall (IRE))
36^8 484^{11} 706^6 755^P

Pinotage *Peter Niven* 103h
6 br g Danbird(AUS) Keen Melody (USA) (Sharpen Up)
2904^6 3390^5 3830^4

Pipe Banner *Anthony Middleton* 115h 85c
10 b g Silver Patriarch(IRE) Bella Macrae (Bustino)
118^7 242^7

Piper Hill (IRE) *Tony Coyle* 120h
6 b g Hawk Wing(USA) Mini Dane (IRE) (Danehill (USA))
1007^3 1118^3 1201^4 (1388) (1498) 2050^P

Pippa Greene *Nicky Henderson* 114h
10 b g Galileo(IRE) Funny Girl (IRE) (Darshaan)
1729^4 2198^{10} 2717^4 5365^9

Pirans Car *Nigel Hawke* 91h
8 b g Sleeping Car(FR) Karolina (FR) (Pistolet Bleu (IRE))
179^U 408^F 590^P 876^8 1110^2 1275^7 **1426^F** 1552^5 1711^5 2013^4 2289^2

Pirates Cay *Alan King* 103h
7 b g Black Sam Bellamy(IRE) Mistic World (Monsun (GER))
4574^4

Pistol (IRE) *Philip Hobbs* 123h 99c
5 b g High Chaparral(IRE) Alinea (USA) (Kingmambo (USA))
1866^4
2922^3 3658^3 4031^5 4537^6 5032^8

Pistol Basc (FR) *Rebecca Menzies* 96c
10 ch g Maille Pistol(FR) Moldane (FR) (Sicyos (USA))
20^6 1163^3 1300^P (2445)
2870^3 (3352)
4222^P 5301^8

Pistolet Noir (FR) *Richard Woollacott* 98h 87c
8 b g Maille Pistol(FR) Black Et Or (FR) (Noir Et Or)
1436^P 3132^6 5242^7

Pistolet Time (IRE) *Mrs Caroline Crow* 87h 123c
12 b g Pistolet Bleu(IRE) Piscean Ode (IRE) (Phardante (FR))
496^P

Pistol Jack (IRE) *S McParlan* 96h 98c
12 bb g Pistolet Bleu(IRE) Burren Gale (IRE) (Strong Gale)
883^5

Pithivier (FR) *Peter Niven* 99b
4 b g Poliglote Kelbelange (FR) (Ganges (USA))
4043^3 ◆ 4431^3 5324^2

Pitter Patter *Fergal O'Brien* 112b
4 b f Nayef(USA) Pixie Ring (Pivotal)
(2318) (3719) 4683^8

Pixie Cut (IRE) *Alistair Whillans* 95h
4 b f Chineur(FR) Fantastic Cee (IRE) (Noverre (USA))
3385^7 3613^2 3934^P 4364^2 4770^6

Plain Sailing (IRE) *John Ferguson* 111h
5 b g Manduro(GER) Ocean Silk (USA) (Dynaformer (USA))
(675) 790^3 (944) (1191) 1270^5

Plan Again (IRE) *Donald McCain* 113h
7 b g Gamut(IRE) Niamh's Leader (IRE) (Supreme Leader)
(1975) 4221^3 4956^8

Planet Of Sound *Philip Hobbs* 124h 152c
12 b g Kayf Tara Herald The Dawn (Dubassoff (USA))
(3647)
4422^7

Planetoid (IRE) *Jim Best* 111h
6 b g Galileo(IRE) Palmeraie (USA) (Lear Fan (USA))
(635) ◆ (729) 1816^2

Played Away *Caroline Fryer* 72h
6 b g Squared Away Fleet Amour (USA) (Afleet (CAN))
417^8 593^{10} 860^P

Playhara (IRE) *Nicky Henderson* 105h
5 b m King's Theatre(IRE) Harringay (Sir Harry Lewis (USA))
372^9 *2442^2* *2583^2* *3098^2* 3570^U 4917^5 5140^6 5244^9

Playing (FR) *Thomas Foley* 118h 131c
11 b g Astarabad(USA) Jouable (FR) (Garde Royale)
3868a^{10}

Playing The Field (IRE) *Mrs Alison Christmas* 104h 109c
9 b g Deploy Gaelic Buccaneer (IRE) (Un Desperado (FR))
288^3 4042^P 5164^5

Playing With Fire (IRE) *Robin Dickin* 89h 91c
10 gr m Witness Box(USA) Smokey Path (IRE) (Scallywag)
4653^P 4861^7 5247^9

Pleasant Company (IRE) *David Pipe* 120h
6 b g Presenting Katie Flame (IRE) (Alderbrook)
(2216) 3182^3 4391^4

Please Talk (IRE) *Noel Meade* 132h 131c
8 b g Beneficial Fresh Partner (IRE) (Yashgan)
2708a^P

Plein Pouvoir (FR) *Venetia Williams* 110h 133c
11 b g Maresca Sorrento(FR) Dellerie (FR) (Le Pontet (FR))
294^4 (2370)
2939^F

Plenty Of Chat (IRE) *Peter Winks* 68h 93c
10 b g Oscar(IRE) Ollatrim Lady (Strong Gale)
737^6

Plinth (IRE) *A P O'Brien* 141h
4 b g Montjeu(IRE) Crazy Volume (IRE) (Machiavellian (USA))
4178a^3 4784^{12} 5470a^5

Pliny (IRE) *Peter Bowen* 71h 76c
10 bb g Accordion American Chick (IRE) (Lord Americo)
461^4 1038^7

Plougala (FR) *Y-M Porzier* 124h 130c
5 b g Plouescop(FR) Danse Cantilienne (FR) (Danehill Dancer (IRE))
2263a^8

Plug In Baby *Nick Mitchell* 77h
6 b m Xaar Medinaceli (IRE) (Grand Lodge (USA))
686^6 876^4 997^6 1266^F 1339^8 1631^5

Plum Pudding (FR) *David Bridgwater* 86h 108c
11 b g Fado(FR) Tale (FR) (Sillery (USA))
1914^2 2067^2 2567^5 2911^3 3739^3

Plum Stone *Charlie Mann* 111b
5 b m Loup Sauvage(USA) Stoney Path (Petoski)
(2583) 5159^{19}

Plus Fours (USA) *Michael Appleby* 17h
5 rg g Mizzen Mast(USA) Quick To Please (USA) (Danzig (USA))
593^U 671^{13}

Plus Jamais (FR) *Jim Goldie* 111h
7 b g Caballo Raptor(CAN) Branceilles (FR) (Satin Wood)
22^5 2218^5 2936^6 3398^6 (3937) ◆ (4667) 5251^4 5537^F ◆

Pobs Trophy *Richard Guest* 87h
7 b g Umistim Admonish (Warning)
75^2 184^2 429^6 651^4 (903)

Pod *Caroline Keevil* 63h 80c
6 b g Tikkanen(USA) Opal'Lou (FR) (Garde Royale)
42^9 **2088^3**
2478^2 ◆ 2825^P 3421^P 5263^6

Podium Dancer *Nick Lampard* 12b
7 b m Revoque(IRE) Mille Et Une Nuits (FR) (Ecologist)
755^P

Poet *Clive Cox* 127h
9 b g Pivotal Hyabella (Shirley Heights)
2717^8 3744^6 4147^{12}

Poetic Power (IRE) *Claire Dyson* 94h
5 b g Dylan Thomas(IRE) Chalice Wells (Sadler's Wells (USA))
1120^6 1400^F 1799^9 (2511) 2679^2 3062^5 3149^8 4597^5 4818^6 5238^4 5459^8

Poetic Presence (IRE) *Adrian Wintle* 67b
4 b f Presenting Johnston's Crest (IRE) (Be My Native (USA))
4916^9 5492^7

Poetic Star *Ben Haslam*
4 b g Byron Balwarah (IRE) (Soviet Star (USA))
3822^P

Poetic Verse *John Quinn* 108h
4 gr f Byron Nina Fontenail (FR) (Kaldounevees (FR))
2557^2 2934^3 3154^3

Point Blank (IRE) *Jonjo O'Neill* 29h 124c
8 b g Oscar(IRE) High Ace (IRE) (Good Thyne (USA))
334^F 718^5

Point Guard (IRE) *Don Cantillon* 100b
6 b g Westerner Holly'sreturn (IRE) (Bob's Return (IRE))
3863^4

Point Of Attack (IRE) *Robin Dickin* 52h
5 ch g Beneficial Aimees Princess (IRE) (Good Thyne (USA))
4909^8 5426^7

Point Proven (IRE) *J T B Hunt* 106c
12 ch g Old Vic Any Old Music (IRE) (Montelimar (USA))
288^P

Points Of View *Kim Bailey* 116h 113c
9 b g Galileo(IRE) On Point (Kris)
386^4 659^7 1011^4
1493^2 1687^P 2895^P

Point The Toes (IRE) *Mark Fahey* 119h
9 b m Atraf Fern Fields (IRE) (Be My Native (USA))
5370^P

Point West (IRE) *Johnny Farrelly* 75h 69c
10 b g Tamayaz(CAN) Coming Home (FR) (Exit To Nowhere (USA))
1135^5 1344^P

Polamco (IRE) *Harry Fry* 110b
5 b g Old Vic Shanesia (IRE) (Erins Isle)
2216^9 4728^5 (5145)

Polarbrook (IRE) *Donald McCain* 104h 120c
7 br g Alderbrook Frozen Cello (IRE) (Arctic Lord)
47^3 499^2 **806^3 1015^3 (1147)** 1388^3 **1750^6 2201^F**
2805^3 3394^2 4448^P

Polden Prince *James Frost* 18b
7 b g Superior Premium Maid Of Mischief (Be My Chief (USA))
874^{11} 1196^6

Polid'Ajonc (FR) *G Macaire* 111h
4 b f Poliglote Fleur D'Ajonc (FR) (April Night (FR))
130a^3

Polidam (FR) *A Chaille-Chaille* 121h 135c
5 b g Trempolino(USA) Eladame (FR) (Snurge)
2263a^2

Poligrouas (FR) *P Peltier* 110h
4 b f Poliglote Tarah Rederie (FR) (Cadoudal (FR))
2781a^4

Polisky (FR) *Paul Nicholls* 131h 128c
7 b g Poliglote Dusky Royale (FR) (Double Bed (FR))
996^7 1709^4 2107^F 2662^2 2754^3 3321^5 *4299^2*
4661^4

Politelysed *Robert Johnson* 84h
8 ch m Courteous Allegedly Red (Sabrehill (USA))
3040^P 3639^{10} 4336^5 4615^4 4770^2 5161^5

Politeness (FR) *Rose Dobbin* 98h
5 b g Poliglote Martiniquaise (FR) (Anabaa (USA))
1853^4 2420^7 4221^5 4615^{13} 5163^{10}

Politeo (FR) *Nick Williams* 91h 94c
8 ch g Lando(GER) Italienne (USA) (Distant View (USA))
1424a^8 1740a^6

Political Paddy *Rayson Nixon* 88h 103c
12 b g Vitus Political Mill (Politico (USA))
221^6

Polly Hopper *Nigel Twiston-Davies* 117h
8 b m Generous(IRE) Brambly Hedge (Teenoso (USA))
268^2 532^2 755^3 (1134) 1265^3

Polly Peachum (IRE) *Nicky Henderson* 145h
6 b m Shantou(USA) Miss Denman (IRE) (Presenting)
3186^5 (4907) (5370) 5572^2

Polly's Rose *Ian Semple*
5 b m Bahamian Bounty Tiana (Diktat)
3529^8

Pollystone (IRE) *Martin Keighley* 99h
8 b m High-Rise(IRE) Miss Pollerton (IRE) (Pollerton)
1^2 450^7 876^{11} (1567) 1633^6

Polly Wiggle *Caroline Fryer* 82b
5 ch m Generous(IRE) Single Handed (Cloudings (IRE))
4867^{10} 5440^9

Pol O'Murchu *Ferdy Murphy* 89b
7 gr g Fair Mix(IRE) La Folichonne (FR) (Useful (FR))
359^7

Polo Springs *Graeme McPherson* 95h
7 gr m Baryshnikov(AUS) Cristal Springs (Dance Of Life (USA))
3605^{11} 4972^2 (5282) (5395)

Polstar (FR) *Harry Whittington* 113h
5 b g Poliglote Star Dancing (Danehill Dancer (IRE))
3469^3 3796^5 4103^{10} (4527) 4943^5 (5238)

Polvere D'Oro *Michael Mullineaux* 79h
4 b g Revoque(IRE) Dusty Anne (IRE) (Dushyantor (USA))
4722^5

Pomegranate *Tracey Barfoot-Saunt* 71b
6 b m Proclamation(IRE) Granita (CHI) (Roy (USA))
4499^9 4735^{11}

Poncho *Mark Rimell* 97h
5 b m Cape Cross(IRE) Pixie Ring (Pivotal)
3329^2

Ponte Di Rosa *Simon Hodgson* 54h
6 b m Avonbridge Ridgewood Ruby (IRE) (Indian Ridge)
2176^7 2473^{10}

Poole Master *David Pipe* 134h 147c
9 ch g Fleetwood(IRE) Juste Belle (FR) (Mansonnien (FR))
217^4 2939^7 3362^4 (4027)
(4414) 5156^{12}

Popaway *Mrs Pauline Harkin* 112c
9 b m Nomadic Way(USA) Sea Poppy (Baron Blakeney)
61^3

Pop Island (FR) *A Chaille-Chaille* 101c
11 b g Mansonnien(FR) Island Du Frene (FR) (Useful (FR))
1424a^2

Poppies Milan (IRE) *Ferdy Murphy* 72b
5 b g Milan Second Best (IRE) (Supreme Leader)
173^{10} 498^5

Poppy Gregg *Dr Jeremy Naylor* 77h 82c
9 b m Tamure(IRE) Opalette (Sharrood (USA))
2743^U 3179^P 4729^P

Population *John Ferguson* 124h
7 ch g Noverre(USA) Ville D'Amore (USA) (Irish River (FR))
2344^3 2647^4 (2998)

Porgy *Brian Ellison* 120h 120c
9 b g Dansili Light Ballet (Sadler's Wells (USA))
2171^U 2496^5

Port And Ward (IRE) *John O'Shea* 78b
5 ch m Captain Rio Gold Stamp (Golden Act (USA))
675^5 1013^4

Porters War (IRE) *Jeremy Scott* 107h 112c
12 ch g Flemensfirth(USA) Grainne Geal (General Ironside)
426^P 1988^8 2270^5 (2861)

Port Hill *Liam Corcoran* 98h
7 ch g Deportivo Hill Farm Dancer (Gunner B)
307^2 688^3 920^7

Portmeade *Elizabeth Scott* 79h
12 b g Thowra(FR) Oneninefive (Sayyaf)
79^3 241^U 690^9 829^8 1105^{10}

Port Melon (IRE) *Paul Nicholls* 134h
6 br g Presenting Omyn Supreme (IRE) (Supreme Leader)
2505^3 ◆ 5157^{10}

Portofino Wasp (IRE) *Jonjo O'Neill* 97h
5 b g Milan Kiniohio (FR) (Script Ohio (USA))
848^6 (971) 1107^3 2980^4 ◆

Port Of The Oak (IRE) *Philip M Byrne* 84h
6 b g Indian River(FR) Princess Alannah (IRE) (Un Desperado (FR))
1009^P

Porto Prince (IRE) *Mrs Belinda Clarke*
8 b g Court Cave(IRE) Green Formation (Green Desert (USA))
335^P

Portrait Gale (IRE) *Marc Barber* 39b
7 gr g Portrait Gallery(IRE) Classy Gale (IRE) (Needle Gun (IRE))
141^{11} 944^{11}

Portway Flyer (IRE) *Ian Williams* 132h
6 br g King's Theatre(IRE) Next Best Thing (IRE) (Taipan (IRE))
1348^5 1632^6 (2787) (2891) (2921) 4102^2 4805^3 5252^5

Posh Bird (IRE) *Peter Niven* 115h 129c
11 b m Winged Love(IRE) Lady Oakwell (IRE) (King's Ride)
169^8 (509)

Posh Millie (IRE) *Ron Hodges* 46b
4 b f Relief Pitcher Rainbow Nation (Rainbow Quest (USA))
5145^9

Posilox (FR) *W Menuet* 123c
8 b g Loxias(FR) Positronique (FR) (Pigeon Voyageur (IRE))
199a^5 1532a^6

Positano Sud (FR) *M Rolland* 122h
4 ch g Linda's Lad Amalfitana (FR) (Pistolet Bleu (IRE))
2262a^P

Possibly Flora *Richard Woollacott* 81h 112c
9 b m Rakaposhi King Calling Flora (Alflora (IRE))
1265^4 1552^6 1731^4 2312^F **3015^P 3421^2 3785^3**
4482^3 5004^3 (5187)
5369^2

Possol (FR) *Henry Daly* 124h 105c
11 b g Robin Des Pres(FR) Alberade (FR) (Un Desperado (FR))
336^7 659^2 1195^7 1581^3 1956^{16}

Potkettleblack *Chris Bealby* 69b
5 b m Westerner Bin It (IRE) (Supreme Leader)
35^9 699^6

Potomac (IRE) *Rose Dobbin* 111h
6 b g Shamardal(USA) Pippas Song (Reference Point)
22^6 494^2 732^4 865^7

Potters Cross *Rebecca Curtis* 130h
7 b g Alflora(IRE) Teeno Nell (Teenoso (USA))
1864^3 ◆ 2079^2 ◆ (2649) 3081^3 3654^4 4347^P

Potters Dream (IRE) *Fergal O'Brien* 68h 65c
8 b g Oscar(IRE) Mona Curra Gale (IRE) (Strong Gale)
1188^5 1406^7 **1594^7 1716^5** 1837^7

Potts Bridge (IRE) *Paul Stafford* 85h 34c
8 b g Tamayaz(CAN) Silverbridge (IRE) (Peacock (FR))
280^6

Pouchki De Somoza (FR) *Y Gourraud* 119h 119c
11 ch g Discover D'Auteuil(FR) Planete D'O (FR) (Son Of Silver)
616a^P

Poungach (FR) *Paul Nicholls* 150h 148c
8 b g Daliapour(IRE) Shalaine (FR) (Double Bed (FR))
2373^4 3165^4 3457^P
4732^2 5571^8

Pour Changer (FR) *Stephen Hughes* 91h 116c
9 b g Daliapour(IRE) Chop And Change (FR) (Double Bed (FR))
407^P (810) 947^7 1106^{10} 1711^P

Pour Toi Georges (FR) *E Leenders* 106h 115c
5 b m Michel Georges Morosa (USA) (Theatrical (IRE))
1742a^4

Powderonthebonnet (IRE) *Richard Phillips* 101h
6 b g Definite Article Zuhal (Busted)
173^U 498^2 2614^F

Powerful Action (IRE) *Philip Hobbs* 92h
6 b g Tau Ceti Abbey The Leader (IRE) (Supreme Leader)
1712^5 2978^{11} 3422^5 3694^6

Powerful Ambition (IRE) *Brian Ellison* 118h
8 b g Bob Back(USA) Native Shore (IRE) (Be My Native (USA))
2099^U

Power Of God (IRE) *Tim Vaughan* 97h
6 b g Heron Island(IRE) Aruba Dam (IRE) (Be My Native (USA))
3046^4 3782^7 4068^7 5431^2

Power Pack Jack (IRE) *Nigel Twiston-Davies* 85h 118c
11 b g Rudimentary(USA) Monas Jem (IRE) (Be My Native (USA))
(778)
1060^{10} 2390^P

Powerstown Dreams (IRE) *Steve Gollings* 121h
5 b g Brian Boru Our Idol (IRE) (Mandalus)
2354^3 (2788) 3388^3 ◆ 4052^4

Powertakeoff (IRE) *Henry Oliver* 93h 74c
6 b g Court Cave(IRE) Diminished (IRE) (Alphabatim (USA))
866^8 879^5 2898^7 3434^7 (4247) 4597^3 5072^9
5237^5

Praetura (IRE) *Paul Nicholls* 62b
4 b g Flemensfirth(USA) Native Side (IRE) (Be My Native (USA))
5130^{11}

Prairie Lad *Sandy Thomson* 88h
6 b g Alflora(IRE) An Bothar Dubh (Strong Gale)
2838^5 3392^7 4901^P

Prasina Russata (IRE) *David Pipe* 98h
7 b g Accordion Henrietta (IRE) (Hushang (IRE))
2761^5 2906^7 3163^F 4501^P

Preacher's Belle *Philip Kirby* 95b
5 ch m Courteous Moonshine Malt (Superlative)
4191^5

Precentors Court (IRE) *Brian Rothwell* 75b
7 b g Bienamado(USA) Buck On (Royal Vulcan)
2738^{10} 2871^6

Precious Ground *Kevin Bishop* 85b
4 b g Helissio(FR) Wild Ground (IRE) (Simply Great (FR))
5339^6

Precision Strike *Richard Guest* 63h
4 b g Multiplex Dockside Strike (Docksider (USA))
582^4 785^6 1394^3 1790^9 2787^P

Predateur (FR) *J J Lambe* 95h 117c
11 b g Nikos Fia Rosa (FR) (Royal Charter (FR))
77^6

Premier Portrait (IRE) *Kim Bailey* 112h
7 b g Portrait Gallery(IRE) Shesnotthelast (IRE) (Mandalus)
(2028) 2316^4 3013^5 4161^4 4555^5 4933^6

Premier Sagas (FR) *Nicky Richards* 107h 129c
10 b g Sagacity(FR) Estampe (FR) (Balleroy (USA))
170^9 677^5

Presence Felt (IRE) *Jonjo O'Neill* 116h 118c
6 br g Heron Island(IRE) Faeroe Isle (IRE) (Erins Isle)
2598^2 2755^{11} 3085^9
3418^4 3739^4 4490^3

Present Accepted *Nerys Dutfield* 93h
7 b g Presenting Kwaheri (Efisio)
155^2 293^6 686^7

Presentandcorrect (IRE) *T F Sage* 82h 118c
13 ch g Presenting Friston (IRE) (Roselier (FR))
63^U 413^2 660^7

Presented (IRE) *Brian Ellison* 101h 119c
7 ch g Presenting Rustic Court (IRE) (Quayside)
2339^2 (2818)
3478^2 (3853)
4427^6 4896^2 5278^P

Present Flight (IRE) *Lucinda Russell* 102b
5 ch g Presenting Grangeclare Flight (IRE) (Old Vic)
5109^2

Presenting Arms (IRE) *Harry Fry* 115h
7 b g Presenting Banningham Blaze (Averti (IRE))
(4300) 4726^{10} 5335^4

Presenting Dr T (IRE) *Harry Chisman* 69h 27c
8 b g Luso Halfway Home (Presenting)
1837^P 2008^5

Presenting Junior (IRE) *Martin Todhunter* 89h 98c
7 b g Presenting Dr Alice (IRE) (Dr Massini (IRE))
21^6 **279^4**
580^4 (753)
(1376) 1789^2 2036^F 4940^6 5356^3 ◆

Presenting Juno (IRE) *Martin Todhunter* 66b
7 ch m Presenting Elegant City (Scallywag)
15^{11}

Presenting Me (IRE) *Evan Williams* 97h
6 ch m Presenting She's Our Native (IRE) (Be My Native (USA))
41^3 502^4 932^U 1118^6 1273^3 1347^3 1639^2 1814^3

Presenting Newmill (IRE) *Harry Whittington* 101b
6 b m Presenting Madam Newmill (IRE) (Taipan (IRE))
5374^5

Presenting Paddy (IRE) *Sarah Humphrey* 108h 80c
6 b g Presenting Bula Beag (IRE) (Brush Aside (USA))
121^{11} **839^5**

Presenting Pricila (IRE) *Charlie Longsdon* 37b
5 b m Presenting Inishbeg House (IRE) (Glacial Storm (USA))
2195^7

Presenting Ruby (IRE) *Neil Mulholland* 86h
9 b m Presenting Thyne And Shine (IRE) (Good Thyne (USA))
1265^2 1529^7 1675^7

Presentings Return (IRE) *Jonjo O'Neill* 70h
5 br g Presenting Gales Return (IRE) (Bob's Return (IRE))
2660^8 2933^F 3163^{18} 3388^{18} 4069^7

Presenting The Way *Harry Fry* 110h
7 ch g Presenting Euphorie (GER) (Feenpark (GER))
2254^4 2761^4 4903^6 5308^2

Present Lodger (IRE) *Lucinda Russell* 95h
6 b g Presenting Hannigan's Lodger (IRE) (Be My Native (USA))
4901^4 5320^9

Present Potential (IRE) *N W Alexander* 110h 110c
7 b g Presenting Calbrooke (IRE) (Beneficial)
(5209)
5485[2]

Present To You (IRE) *David Bridgwater* 108h 120c
9 ch g Presenting Charm Of Toulon (IRE) (Toulon)
2468[7] 2700[2] 3858[3] 4470[2] 4678[P] 5390[4]

Present Trend (IRE) *Charlie Longsdon* 86h
5 br m Presenting Trendy Attire (IRE) (Luso)
2298[9] 3181[5] 3689[4] 5245[5] 5393[7]

Present View *Jamie Snowden* 116h 146c
6 b g Presenting Carry Me (IRE) (Lafontaine (USA))
1915[3]
2267[2] (2623)
3059[2] (4418) ◆ (4742)

Presidential Lady (IRE) *Chris Grant* 85b
5 b m Hurricane Run(IRE) Sheer Glamour (IRE) (Peintre Celebre (USA))
3529[5] 3727[6] 4342[3]

President Jose (FR) *Robert Collet* 118h
8 b g Slickly(FR) Old Beino (FR) (Highest Honor (FR))
455a[4]

Pressies Girl (IRE) *Paul Nicholls* 114h
6 b m Presenting Leader's Hall (IRE) (Saddlers' Hall (IRE))
4335[2] 4683[5] 5124[2] ◆ (5427)

Pret A Thou (FR) *John Bryan Groucott* 110h 123c
11 ch g Funny Baby(FR) Va Thou Line (FR) (El Badr)
(537) 2292[11]
2618[4]

Prettyasapicture *Alan King* 94h
5 b m King's Theatre(IRE) Fortune's Girl (Ardross)
4499[3] 5196[2] 5528[4]

Priceless Art (IRE) *Tommy Morgan* 93h 121c
9 b g Anabaa(USA) My Ballerina (USA) (Sir Ivor (USA))
646[4] 859[P] 1020[8] 1429[4] 1565[13]
4782[4]

Prickles *Richard Woollacott* 100h 56c
9 ch m Karinga Bay Squeaky (Infantry I)
1567[8] 1938[10] **2039[S] 2562[7] 3048[U]** 3428[7]

Pride Of The Artic (IRE) *Peter Fahey* 121h 138c
9 b g Definite Article Tricias Pride (IRE) (Broken Hearted)
1168a[17]

Prideofthecastle (IRE) *David Pipe* 132h
7 b g Waky Nao Park's Pet (IRE) (Bob Back (USA))
(395) 2316[6] (2924) 3695[3] (4112) 4805[12]

Priest Island (IRE) *Tom George* 103h
8 b g Heron Island(IRE) Chapel Field (IRE) (Sayaarr (USA))
562[P]

Primacy (IRE) *Neil Mulholland*
5 br m Primary(USA) Seaborne (Slip Anchor)
290[P]

Prima Porta *Evan Williams* 137h 136c
8 b m American Post Porta Marzia (CHI) (Roy (USA))
2226[2] 3649[4] 3770[4]
(4918)

Prime Contender *Jennie Candlish* 108h
12 b g Efisio Gecko Rouge (Rousillon (USA))
456[2] 3451[6] 3839[6] 4533[10] 5012[10]

Prime Location *David Pipe* 117h
8 b g Generous(IRE) Sovereignsflagship (IRE) (Supreme Leader)
1019[2] 1340[6] 1645[5]

Primitive Dancing *Caroline Bailey* 23h
5 b g Bello Carattere Primitive Dancer (Primitive Rising (USA))
874[8] 1118[10] 1329[6]

Primitive Sam *Chris Bealby* 37b
6 b g Samraan(USA) Jeanann (Primitive Rising (USA))
4598[6] 5014[16]

Primo Blue *Noel Williams* 82b
4 b g Primo Valentino(IRE) Flintwood (Gunner B)
5264[7]

Primo Milano *Evan Williams* 62h
5 b g Milan She's Our Native (IRE) (Be My Native (USA))
3734[6] 5341[6] 5548[P]

Primroseandblue (IRE) *W P Mullins* 133h 96c
10 b g Shernazar Karlybelle (FR) (Sandhurst Prince)
3910a[21]

Primrose Time *Lucy Normile* 90h 115c
11 gr m Alflora(IRE) The Whirlie Weevil (Scallywag)
23[P]

Prince Blackthorn (IRE) *William Amos* 100h 90c
8 b g Desert Prince(IRE) Notable Dear (ITY) (Last Tycoon)
279[8] 2338[4] (2870)
(3925) 4747[P]

Prince De Beauchene (FR) *W P Mullins* 154h 158c
11 b g French Glory Chipie D'Angron (FR) (Grand Tresor (FR))
2234a[3] 2815[13] 3376a[9] 3751a[4] 5171[16]

Prince Du Seuil (FR) *Richard Phillips* 80h 77c
11 b g Lucky Dream(FR) Hermione III (FR) (Pebble (FR))
5076[5]

Prince Freddie *Roy Brotherton* 78h
6 b g Red Ransom(USA) Pitcroy (Unfuwain (USA))
1152[8] 1331[11] 2191[5] 2511[2] 2770[2] 3188[5] 4334[P] 5072[7] 5242[4]

Princeful (FR) *Milton Bradley* 91h 91c
11 b g Useful(FR) Spinner's Mate (FR) (Miller's Mate)
45[F] 394[6] 585[7]

Prince Khurram *Donald McCain* 114h
4 b c Nayef(USA) Saree (Barathea (IRE))
3714[3] ◆ 4379[2]

Princely Conn (IRE) *Thomas Mullins* 112b
5 b g Whitmore's Conn(USA) High Priestess (IRE) (Priolo (USA))
2995a[3]

Princely Hero (IRE) *Chris Gordon* 99h 100c
10 b g Royal Applause Dalu (IRE) (Dancing Brave (USA))
(305) 485[3]
709[P] 871[6] 1272[3] 1437[2] 1528[3] 2017[5] 2540[3]
(2603)
3008[5] 3250[4] 4441[6] 4798[3]
5025[5] 5460[2]

Princely Player (IRE) *Philip Hobbs* 138h 131c
7 b g King's Theatre(IRE) Temptation (FR) (Lando (GER))
(1766) 1972[3]
2343[F] (2719)
3087[2] 4789[9]

Prince Massini (IRE) *Ian Prichard* 105h 105c
13 b g Dr Massini(IRE) Persian Desert (IRE) (Persian Mews)
180[2]

Prince Of Dreams *Ed de Giles* 112h 136c
7 b g Sadler's Wells(USA) Questina (FR) (Rainbow Quest (USA))
3323[3] 3652[U] 3833[2] 4543[8] (4965)
5306[5]

Prince Of Fire (GER) *C F Swan* 137h 137c
9 b g Waky Nao Pacaya (GER) (Acatenango (GER))
(1001a)

Prince Of Pirates (IRE) *Nicky Henderson* 120h 146c
9 b g Milan Call Kate (IRE) (Lord Americo)
3067[4]

Princeofthedesert *Garry Woodward* 91h
8 b g Nayef(USA) Twilight Sonnet (Exit To Nowhere (USA))
2900[5] 3872[14] 4068[9]

Prince Oui Oui (FR) *P Peltier* 137h 116c
8 gr g Poliglote Cobee De Liniers (FR) (Dom Pasquini (FR))
1901a[2] 2240a[6]

Prince Pippin (IRE) *Lucy Jones* 103h
8 b g King Charlemagne(USA) Staploy (Deploy)
(264) 421[3] 783[4] 1345[4] 1887[4] 5307[P]

Prince Siegfried (FR) *John Ferguson* 140h
8 b g Royal Applause Intrum Morshaan (IRE) (Darshaan)
2068[5] (2432) 3184[F] 3644[6] 4786[P]

Princess Annabelle *Rod Millman* 88h
5 ch m Sworn In(USA) Marybelle (Double Trigger (IRE))
174[10] 410[3] 717[10]

Princess Bella (IRE) *Fergal O'Brien* 98h
5 b m Presenting Miss Cozzene (FR) (Solid Illusion (USA))
85[U] 3228[5] 3877[15] 4594[7] 4917[4] 5366[7]

Princess Caetani (IRE) *David Dennis* 113h
5 b m Dylan Thomas(IRE) Caladira (IRE) (Darshaan)
2514[5] 2767[2] 3010[3] 3733[2] 4375[3]

Princesse Fleur *Michael Scudamore* 97h
6 b m Grape Tree Road Princesse Grec (FR) (Grand Tresor (FR))
(252) 436[2] 844[2] 932[5] 1675[2]

Princesse Kap (FR) *J-P Gallorini* 131h 129c
6 b m Kapgarde(FR) Princesse Turgeon (FR) (Turgeon (USA))
838a[7] 1902a[9]

Princesse Katie (IRE) *James Bennett* 76h
8 b m Presenting Another Shot (IRE) (Master Willie)
368[8] 1635[5] 1784[3] (2723)

Princess Tara (IRE) *Peter Bowen* 103h
4 b f Kayf Tara Oscars Vision (IRE) (Oscar Schindler (IRE))
2391[2] (4844) 5159[8]

Prince Tam *Harriet Graham* 76h 96c
10 gr g Terimon Princess Maxine (IRE) (Horage)
(23) 1753[4]
1876[2] 2496[2] 3039[7] 3395[5] 3722[5] 5207[5] 5483[4]

Prince Tartare (FR) *Robert Collet* 103h 117c
5 b g Equerry(USA) Nuance Tartare (FR) (Nononito (FR))
1199a[10]

Prince Tom *Alexandra Dunn* 104h 138c
10 b g King's Theatre(IRE) Cresswell Native (IRE) (Be My Native (USA))
851[5] 4936[P]

Princeton Plains (IRE) *Edward P Harty* 134h 95c
8 b g Tagula(IRE) Lightstorm (IRE) (Darshaan)
3910a[20]

Princeton Royale (IRE) *Neil King* 96b
5 bb g Royal Anthem(USA) Shelikesitstraight (IRE) (Rising)
3035[4]

Printing Press (IRE) *Joanne Foster*
8 ch g Blueprint(IRE) Fairpark (IRE) (Shardari)
967[P]

Print Night (FR) *P Chemin*
11 ch g April Night(FR) Grande Folle (FR) (Highlanders (FR))
616a[P]

Print Shiraz (IRE) *Rose Dobbin* 63h
6 b g Bahri(USA) Cherry Hills (IRE) (Anabaa (USA))
1875[7] 2355[P] 3036[P]

Prio Royal (FR) *Y-M Porzier* 112c
6 b g Priolo(USA) Royale Babies (FR) (Jimble (FR))
1740a[8]

Priors Gold *Laura Mongan* 115h
7 ch g Sakhee(USA) Complimentary Pass (Danehill (USA))
1319[4] 1783[2]

Private Equity (FR) *Nicky Henderson* 132c
6 b g High Yield(USA) Annette Girl (IRE) (Mtoto)
164[2]

Private Jones *Miss Imogen Pickard* 47h
5 br g Trade Fair Dafne (Nashwan (USA))
1539[3] 5227[10]

Private Malone (IRE) *A J Kennedy* 106b
5 b g Darsi(FR) Native Artist (IRE) (Be My Native (USA))
944[2]

Prize Fighter (IRE) *Lynn Siddall* 80h
12 b g Desert Sun Papal (Selkirk (USA))
283[P]

Probably Not (IRE) *H Smyth* 68h
7 b g Marignan(USA) Quiver Tree (Lion Cavern (USA))
4776[12]

Problema Tic (FR) *David Pipe* 116h 140c
8 b g Kapgarde(FR) Atreide (FR) (Son Of Silver)
358[17] **587[5]**
(680) 851[12]
1047[11] 2674[P] 2949[14]
3199[5] 4769[10] 5256[6]
5513[4]

Professeur Emery (FR) *Warren Greatrex* 119h 127c
7 b g Officiel(FR) Karmadeine (FR) (Kaldoun (FR))
(856) (1059)
(1175)

Prolinx (IRE) *Charlie Mann* 94h 132c
9 b g Oscar(IRE) Winter Break (IRE) (Executive Perk)
(286) 672[3]

Promanco *Charlie Longsdon* 102b
5 b m Kayf Tara Shelayly (IRE) (Zaffaran (USA))
4114[2]

Promised Wings (GER) *Chris Gordon* 121h 104c
7 ch g Monsun(GER) Panagia (USA) (Diesis)
2288[9] 2742[5] 3505[5] 4161[5] 4556[4] 4933[14]

Prompter *Jonjo O'Neill* 128h
7 b g Motivator Penny Cross (Efisio)
1685[3] 2910[2] 3031[3] 4147[P] *4302[8]* 4820[12]

Proper Job *Polly Gundry* 15h
6 b g Rainbow High Merlin Cider (Un Desperado (FR))
2479[8] 2912[7] 3363[9] 3782[9]

Proper Villan (IRE) *Geoffrey Deacon* 111h
9 bb g Naheez(USA) Nativa Negra (IRE) (Be My Native (USA))
233[4] 1945[2]

Prophete De Guye (FR) *James Evans* 114h 129c
11 b g Apple Tree(FR) Kasibelle De Guye (FR) (Scooter Bleu (IRE))
334[6] 1527[P]

Prosecco (IRE) *Lucinda Russell* 104h 127c
12 b g Perpendicular Bay Gale (IRE) (Abednego)
2222[6] 3395[4] 4204[P] (4628)
5207[4]

Prospect Wells (FR) *Paul Nicholls* 150h 142c
9 b g Sadler's Wells(USA) Brooklyn's Dance (FR) (Shirley Heights)
539[2] (779)
861[2]

Proud Jack *Ann Hamilton* 46h
6 br g Generous(IRE) Miss Royello (Royal Fountain)
225[3] 497[3] 4631[4] 4956[10]

Proud Times (USA) *Ali Brewer* 118h 120c
8 bb g Proud Citizen(USA) Laura's Pistolette (USA) (Big Pistol (USA))
141[7] (2278) (2581) (2770) 2932[7]
(4004) 4444[4]
4862[2] 5121[P]

Prouts Pub (IRE) *Nick Gifford* 113h
5 b g Catcher In The Rye(IRE) A Woman In Love (Muhtarram (USA))
(2439) 5064[3] 5305[P]

Provo (IRE) *Paul Nicholls* 135h 135c
7 br g Presenting Pairtree (Double Trigger (IRE))
3291[F]

Pru *Mary Evans* 63h
6 br m Weld Floranz (Afzal)
477[7] 857[P] 1082[5] 5036[P]

Psi (USA) *Gary Moore* 99h 97c
9 b g Hernando(FR) Visions Of Clarity (IRE) (Sadler's Wells (USA))
99[7] **709[5]**

Ptit Zig (FR) *Paul Nicholls* 160h
5 b g Great Pretender(IRE) Red Rym (FR) (Denham Red (FR))
683a[2] (2414a) 3200[2] 3779[2] 4739[6] 5134[4]

Ptolomeos *Sean Regan*
11 b g Kayf Tara Lucy Tufty (Vin St Benet)
3353[P]

Pudsey House *John Wade* 118h
7 b g Double Trigger(IRE) Dara's Pride (IRE) (Darazari (IRE))
168[6] 2397[5] 2789[3] 3145[3] (3356) 4006[F] 4347[6]

Puerto Azul (IRE) *Bernard Scriven* 86h
10 ch g Beneficial Droichidin (Good Thyne (USA))
1864[9] 2011[9] 2280[12] 2473[F] 2764[7] 2920[P] 5523[7]

Puffin Billy (IRE) *Oliver Sherwood* 150h
6 b g Heron Island(IRE) Downtown Train (IRE) (Glacial Storm (USA))
2758[5]

Puisque Tu Pars (FR) *Gary Moore* 112b
4 b g Walk In The Park(IRE) Pierre Azuree (FR) (Le Glorieux)
(4561) 5173[10]

Pullmen *Paul Henderson* 77h
6 gr g Silver Patriarch(IRE) Moon Spinner (Elmaamul (USA))
1764[7] 2644[F] 3697[13] 5139[7]

Pulpitarian (USA) *Lucinda Russell* 116h
6 b g Pulpit(USA) Bedanken (USA) (Geri (USA))
2075[3] ◆ 2341[6] 2968[3] 3330[P] 4952[6]

Pumboo (FR) *James Moffatt* 96h 97c
11 gr g Dadarissime(FR) Contessina (FR) (Mistigri)
627[2] ◆ 749[8]

Puncho (FR) *Patrice Quinton* 109c
11 gr g Medaaly Fast Valley (FR) (Tel Quel (FR))
1214a[2] 1424a[7]

Punjabi *David Pipe* 131h
11 b g Komaite(USA) Competa (Hernando (FR))
2813[8]

Purcell's Bridge (FR) *Rose Dobbin* 118h 115c
7 b g Trempolino(USA) Theatrical Lady (USA) (Theatrical (IRE))
24[F] 1926[2] 2158[8]
2955[P] 3823[4] 4580[4] 4896[4]

Pur De Sivola (FR) *Nick Lampard*
11 b g Robin Des Champs(FR) Gamine D'Ici (FR) (Cadoudal (FR))
1314[P]

Pure Anticipation (IRE) *Tim Vaughan* 103h 101c
9 gr m Old Vic Lady Of Gortmerron (IRE) (Orchestra)
726[4] 930[2] 1010[3] 1260[11] 1548[8]

Pure Faith (IRE) *Peter Bowen* 135h 144c
10 b g Anshan Bolaney Girl (IRE) (Amazing Bust)
66[3] 157[4] (587)
672[2] 851[2] 1195[5] (1304) 1956[15] **2071[10] 5276[P]**

Pure Oxygen (IRE) *Harry Fry* 102h
6 br g Presenting Katday (FR) (Miller's Mate)
3388[9]

Pure Poteen (IRE) *Neil Mulholland* 103h 85c
6 ch g Flemensfirth(USA) Taking My Time (IRE) (High Roller (IRE))
2745[7] 3422[6] 3694[7]
3861[4] 4175[11]

Pure Science (IRE) *Nigel Twiston-Davies* 127h
6 ch g Galileo(IRE) Rebelline (IRE) (Robellino (USA))
1954[4] 2505[5] 2850[3] 3359[4] 3798[5] 4024[3] (4512) 5534[4]

Pure Style (IRE) *Charlie Longsdon* 115h
6 b g Desert Style(IRE) Pure Fiction (Zilzal (USA))
(4818)

Purple Bay (IRE) *John Ferguson* 137h
5 b g Dubawi(IRE) Velvet Lady (Nashwan (USA))
1919[2] (2089) (2340) 2657[4] 3088[2] 5239[2]

Purple Harry *Tina Jackson* 90h
6 gr g Sir Harry Lewis(USA) Ellfiedick (Alfie Dickins)
3112[6] 4431[6] 5102[7] 5320[6]

Purple 'n Gold (IRE) *David Pipe* 115h
5 b g Strategic Prince Golden Dew (IRE) (Montjeu (IRE))
(1008) 1389[3] 1627[3] 1697[2] 5239[9] 5490[2]

Pur Style (FR) *E J O'Grady* 96h 106c
6 ch m Turgeon(USA) Cayras Style (FR) (Trempolino (USA))
3750a[7]

Pursuitofhappiness (IRE) *Neil Mulholland* 53b
6 b g Classic Cliche(IRE) Lake Tour (IRE) (Aristocracy)
1771[7]

Push Me (IRE) *Iain Jardine* 95h
7 gr m Verglas(IRE) Gilda Lilly (USA) (War Chant (USA))
(1791) 1979[8] 2794[4] 3141[6]

Push The Trigger *Caroline Keevil* 89h 85c
7 b g Double Trigger(IRE) Pushing Gold (Gold Dust)
5428[3]

Puyol (IRE) *Lisa Williamson* 84h 108c
12 bb g Zaffaran(USA) Star Mover (Move Off)
90[3]

Puzzle Time *Giles Bravery* 94b
4 b f Araafa(IRE) Puzzling (Peintre Celebre (USA))
2318[2] (2604) 3460[10]

Pyjama Game (IRE) *Rose Dobbin* 105h 115c
8 b g Hernando(FR) Princess Claudia (IRE) (Kahyasi)
(74) 222[7] **866[6] 1088[3] (1505)**
(1756) 2033[4] 2594[F]

Pyleigh Lass *Martin Keighley* 116h
8 gr m Silver Patriarch(IRE) Lady Callernish (Callernish)
3361[10] 2013[8] 2458[12] *4023[11]* 4393[5] (4676) 5010[5] 5333[13] 5542[F]

Pyracantha *Jennie Candlish* 106h 114c
9 b g Muhtarram(USA) Forsythia (Most Welcome)
972[2] 1202[6]

Pyrardini (USA) *J-L Guillochon* 104h 105c
5 b g Bernardini(USA) Pyramid Lake (USA) (Broad Brush (USA))
703a[6]

Pyrshan (IRE) *Graeme McPherson* 62b
5 b g Pyrus(USA) Runshangale (IRE) (Anshan)
5286[6]

Qalinas (FR) *David Pipe* 125h 112c
7 gr g Malinas(GER) Tabletiere (FR) (Kaldounevees (FR))
2288[3] 2652[6]

Qaspal (FR) *Philip Hobbs* 138h 120c
10 b g Subotica(FR) Une Du Chatelier (FR) (Quart De Vin (FR))
1444[2] 1659[U]

Qasser (IRE) *Harry Whittington* 93h
5 b g Intikhab(USA) Surrender To Me (USA) (Royal Anthem (USA))
1578[7] 2083[8] 2265[14] 3140[3] 3353[2] 4371[2] 4721[3]

Qianshan Leader (IRE) *Emma Lavelle* 95h 129c
10 b g Anshan Gaelic Leader (IRE) (Supreme Leader)
39[3] 1642[P] 1830[2] 2693[7] 2923[U] 4886[4] 5306[4]

Qoubilai (FR) *Tony Coyle* 98h 120c
10 b g Passing Sale(FR) Varcady (FR) (Imyar)
192[2] 519[3] **960[2]** 1200[2] 1840[4] **2149[4] 4007[4]**
4327[2] 4478[5]

Qrackers (FR) *Miss V Collins* 130h 130c
10 b g Lahint(USA) Babolna (FR) (Tropular)
331[5] (4511)

Quacity (FR) *Lucinda Russell* 88h 112c
10 b g Sagacity(FR) Desert Show (IRE) (Desert Style (IRE))
881[2]

Quaddick Lake (IRE) *Richard Woollacott* 110h 76c
11 br g Blueprint(IRE) Wondermac (IRE) (Jeu De Paille (FR))
1989[3] 2080[6] 2461[7] 3130[2] 3263[7] 3744[10] 3989[9] 4278[U] 4634[5] 5030[9] 5335[9]

Quadou Ville (FR) *G Lecomte*
10 b g Nashamaa Jadoudy Ville (FR) (Cadoudal (FR))
200a[9]

Quadrato (GER) *Tim Vaughan* 105h
7 br g Sholokhov(IRE) Quadrata (GER) (Big Shuffle (USA))
1506[2] 1641[2] **1834[F]**

Quadriller (FR) *Philip Hobbs* 107h 110c
7 b g Lando(GER) Tabachines (FR) (Art Francais (USA))
808[5] (1058) 1171[3] 1475[2] 1697[3] **2007[4]**

Qualitee *Claire Dyson* 87h 106c
9 b m Superior Premium Coco Loco (Bin Ajwaad (IRE))
64[7] 590[11]

Qualviro (FR) *Tim Vaughan* 122h 122c
10 b g Lavirco(GER) French County (FR) (Cyborg (FR))
393[2] 659[6] 998[5]
(4079) 4376[3] 5041[3]

Qualypso D'Allier (FR) *Richard Woollacott* 88h 89c
10 b g Dark Moondancer Miss Akarad (FR) (Akarad (FR))
4661[P] 5127[U] 5240[4]

Quantique (FR) *Venetia Williams*
10 gr m Lavirco(GER) Griffee (FR) (Royal Charter (FR))
1575[7]
2039[F] 2348[F]

Quantitativeeasing (IRE) *E Bolger* 98h 149c
9 ch g Anshan Mazuma (IRE) (Mazaad)
1168a[2] 1604a[16] 4754[13]

Quantum Theory (IRE) *G D Hanmer* 110b
10 b g Luso Lady Renowned (IRE) (Lord Americo)
4485[P]

Quart Monde (FR) *F Nicolle* 113h 139c
10 ch g Network(GER) In Extremis (FR) (Quart De Vin (FR))
1902a[2] 2264a[3]

Quarton (IRE) *Evan Williams* 113h 111c
7 b g Peintre Celebre(USA) Marjie (IRE) (Desert Style (IRE))
501[4] **931[5]**
1149[4] (1315)
1401[4]

Quartz De Thaix (FR) *Venetia Williams* 145h 125c
10 b g Ragmar(FR) Une Amie (FR) (Prove It Baby (USA))
2452[5] 2943[P] 3457[2] 3890[5] 4174[4] 4269[6] 4765[18]
5371[P]

Quatuor Collonges (FR) *C R Willes* 61h 91c
10 ch g Video Rock(FR) Elegante Collonges (FR) (Quart De Vin (FR))
58[4] 430[3]

Quayside Court (IRE) *Claire Dyson* 54h 82c
10 ch g Anshan Rustic Court (IRE) (Quayside)
100[4] 601[8] 1103[P] 1202[3] 1548[P] 1825[3] 2478[4]
(2829)
(2872) 4982[5] 5460[P]

Quedillac (FR) *S Penny* 111h 103c
10 b g Clerkenwell(USA) Esmidanne (FR) (Dastaan (FR))
297[3]

Queen Alphabet (IRE) *Peter Fahey* 128h
5 b m King's Theatre(IRE) A-To-Z (IRE) (Ahonoora)
5159[5]

Queen Avalon *Lucy Wadham*
5 b m Overbury(IRE) Newton Mo (Homo Sapien)
1770[10]

Queen Of Epirus *Brian Rothwell* 93h
6 ch m Kirkwall Andromache (Hector Protector (USA))
932[10] 2449[4] 2736[2] 3141[8] 3353[7]

Queen Of Mantua (IRE) *Fergal O'Brien* 91h 109c
8 b m Old Vic Papoose (IRE) (Little Bighorn)
265[2] 641[6] 972[U] 1174[3]

Queen Of The Stage (IRE) *Robin Dickin* 86b
4 b f King's Theatre(IRE) Supreme Du Casse (IRE) (Supreme Leader)
5409[5]

Queen Of The West (IRE) *Jamie Snowden* 99h 83c
7 b m Vinnie Roe(IRE) Slow Starter (IRE) (Dr Massini (IRE))
303[P]

Queen Olivia *Caroline Bailey* 107h
6 b m King's Theatre(IRE) Queen's Leader (Supreme Leader)
2317[6] 2824[5] 4901[5] 5365[2] (5518)

Queen's Bay *Jamie Snowden* 112h 116c
8 b m Karinga Bay Minibelle (Macmillion)
4966[4] 5369[5]

Queens Grove *Kevin Bishop* 133h
8 gr m Baryshnikov(AUS) Just Jasmine (Nicholas Bill)
3649[U]

Queen Spud *Henry Daly* 109h
5 b m Multiplex Hurtebise (FR) (Groom Dancer (USA))
46[6] 1578[6] 1824[8] 2470[3] 2891[5] 3391[2] 3604[2]
4907[6] (5291)

Queens Regatta (IRE) *Bruce Mactaggart* 50b
5 b m King's Theatre(IRE) Friendly Craic (IRE) (Mister Lord (USA))
4240[10] 4631[5] 5560[12]

Queen's Star *Andrew Balding* 110h
5 ch m With Approval(CAN) Memsahib (Alzao (USA))
3005[6] 4411[2]

Queenswood Bay *David Dennis* 55h
8 b m Karinga Bay Forest Maze (Arzanni)
4398[10] 4595[P]

Queenys King (IRE) *David Dennis* 37h
6 b g Desert King(IRE) Midway (IRE) (Warcraft (USA))
2456[4] 2940[14]

Queiros Bleu (FR) *Henry De Bromhead* 127h 130c
10 b g Ungaro(GER) Guibolle Bleue (FR) (Ghost Buster'S (FR))
1971[6]

Quel Ballistic *Peter Bowen* 90h 120c
10 b g Kayf Tara Herballistic (Rolfe (USA))
120[8] (541)
(646) 869[2] 1135[P]

Quel Bruere (FR) *John Upson* 88h 106c
10 gr g Sassanian(USA) Housseliere (FR) (April Night (FR))
805[2] 873[2]

Quel Elite (FR) *James Moffatt* 114h
10 b g Subotica(FR) Jeenly (FR) (Kadalko (FR))
24[P] 512[8] 3013[4] ◆ 3396[2] 3638[4] 3775[2] 4271[4]
4489[3] 4954[4]

Quelle Chance (IRE) *John Wade* 100h 83c
8 ch g Old Vic Iona Flyer (IRE) (Montelimar (USA))
534[6] 763[9]

Quentin Collonges (FR) *Henry Daly* 135h 145c
10 gr g Dom Alco(FR) Grace Collonges (FR) (Bayolidaan (FR))
2502[U] 3067[7]

Que Pasa (IRE) *David Harry Kelly* 140h
6 b m Loup Solitaire(USA) Tinopasa (FR) (No Pass No Sale)
1802a[2] 2205a[5] 4846a[3]

Quercy Du Manoir (FR) *Jean-Paul Gasnier* 46c
10 b g Freedom Cry Hue Du Manoir (FR) (Iron Duke (FR))
616a[4] 2384a[U] 3068[8]

Querido (GER) *Paddy Butler* 34h
10 b g Acatenango(GER) Quest Of Fire (FR) (Rainbow Quest (USA))
2858[12]

Quernstone (USA) *Harry Whittington* 62h
5 b g Smart Strike(CAN) Sluice (USA) (Seeking The Gold (USA))
1553[5] 1625[11] 1764[11]

Quest For Caviar *Anna Newton-Smith* 44b
4 b g Air Quest Itsinthepost (Risk Me (FR))
5264[11]

Questions Answered (IRE) *E McNamara* 128h 138c
9 ch g Old Vic Sleetmore Gale (IRE) (Strong Gale)
1604a[4] 1897a[F]

Quest Magic (IRE) *John Wade* 103h
8 ch g Fantastic Quest(IRE) Magic Sign (IRE) (The Parson)
218[4] 511[5]

Quetzal (IRE) *Martin Todhunter* 97h 104c
9 b g Mr Combustible(IRE) Auction Piece (IRE) (Auction Ring (USA))
341[P] 728[3] 869[P] 1163[7]

Quevega (FR) *W P Mullins* 162h
10 b m Robin Des Champs(FR) Vega IV (FR) (Cap Martin (FR))
(4740)

Quickasyoucan (IRE) *C A McBratney* 119h
6 b g Beneficial Nativebaltic (IRE) (Be My Native (USA))
5252[2]

Quick Baby (FR) *J Follain* 135c
10 b g Le Balafre(FR) Good Day Sunshine (FR) (Hellios (USA))
1532a[2]

Quick Brew *Maurice Barnes* 111h
6 b g Denounce Darjeeling (IRE) (Presenting)
1667[12] 1975[U] 2156[3] 2732[5] 3017[5] 3274[6] 4832[2]
5057[5] 5377[5]

Quick Decisson (IRE) *Philip Hobbs* 124h
6 b g Azamour(IRE) Fleet River (USA) (Riverman (USA))
2668[9] 3430[4] (3744) 3891[6] 4278[8] 5030[7] 5353[7]

Quick Gold (FR) *E Leray*
10 ch g Goldneyev(USA) Darra (FR) (Jefferson I)
2384a[P]

Quick Jack (IRE) *A J Martin* 129h
5 ch g Footstepsinthesand Miss Polaris (Polar Falcon (USA))
(2492) ◆ 3910a[3]

Quick N' Easy (IRE) *Sue Gardner* 79b
4 ch g Vertical Speed(FR) Tarmons Duchess (IRE) (The Parson)
5181[11]

Quickpick Vic (IRE) *A J Martin* 145h
7 b g Old Vic Anotherfling (IRE) (Mandalus)
4180a[4] 4708a[U] 5201a[7]

Quietude *Nigel Twiston-Davies* 54b
4 ch g Three Valleys(USA) Ataraxy (Zamindar (USA))
5560[11]

Quiet Whisper (IRE) *Kim Bailey* 97h 61c
8 b g Quiet American(USA) Relish (IRE) (Sadler's Wells (USA))
31[8] 762[6]

Quil Est Beau (FR) *Mrs Jo Sleep*
10 b g Ungaro(GER) Histoire Vraie (FR) (Panoramic)
4518[P]

Quincy Des Pictons (FR) *Alan Jones* 95h 145c
10 b g Kadalko(FR) Izabel Des Pictons (FR) (Bayolidaan (FR))
2074[U] 2939[F] 4209[6]
4675[2] 5535[10]

Quinder Spring (FR) *Lucinda Russell* 92h 103c
10 gr g Chef De Clan(FR) Virginia Spring (FR) (Beaudelaire (USA))
169[5] 492[8] 1655[2] 1936[6] 2310[5] 2818[7] 3755[6]

Quinlandio (IRE) *Brendan Powell* 94b
4 b g Thousand Words La Shalak (IRE) (Shalford (IRE))
4844[2] 5070[6]

Quinola Des Obeaux (FR) *Rob Summers* 70h
10 b g Useful(FR) Zaouia (FR) (Cyborg (FR))
3692[9] 4072[8] 5072[12]

Quinsman *Caroline Bailey*
8 b g Singspiel(IRE) Penny Cross (Efisio)
119[P] 505[8] 877[11] 1093[4] 1203[5] 1391[3] 1783[5]

Quintos (FR) *Guy Denuault*
10 gr g Rifapour(IRE) Mission Speciale (FR) (Mendez (FR))
1424a[5]

Quinz (FR) *Philip Hobbs* 120h 145c
10 b g Robin Des Champs(FR) Altesse Du Mou (FR) (Tin Soldier (FR))
2214[P] 2800[8] 3455[5] 4769[12]

Quiscover Fontaine (FR) *E Bolger* 107h 134c
10 b g Antarctique(IRE) Blanche Fontaine (FR) (Oakland (FR))
2491[9] 4754[9]

Quite By Chance *Colin Tizzard* 117h
5 b g Midnight Legend Hop Fair (Gildoran)
160[3] 1695[2] 2011[3] 2492[15] 3744[9] 4444[2] ◆ 5005[7]

Quito De La Roque (FR) *C A Murphy* 140h 164c
10 b g Saint Des Saints(FR) Moody Cloud (FR) (Cyborg (FR))
1776a[F] 3751a[7] 4435a[P] 5171[P]

Quito Du Tresor (FR) *Lucinda Russell* 116h 132c
10 b g Jeune Homme(USA) Itiga (FR) (Djarvis (FR))
677[3] 1146[2] 1291[3] 1545[4] 1659[8] (2346)
2793[3] 3476[7] 4053[5] 5253[2]

Quix *Miss G E J Anderson* 99b
8 gr g Fair Mix(IRE) Teeno Nell (Teenoso (USA))
4225[P]

Qulinton (FR) *Johnny Farrelly* 125h 132c
10 b g Bulington(FR) Klef Du Bonheur (FR) (Lights Out (FR))
591[3] 845[6] 998[2] 1195[9] **1642[F]** 1956[19]
3068[P]

Quoquoalco (FR) *E Lecoiffier* 108c
10 b g Nononito(FR) Jaboise (FR) (Passing Sale (FR))
(616a)
1532a[F]

Raajih *Gordon Elliott* 117h 138c
6 gr g Dalakhani(IRE) Thakafaat (IRE) (Unfuwain (USA))
(1659)
1663[3] 1957[8]

Racey Lacey *Nigel Twiston-Davies* 97h
7 b m Loup Sauvage(USA) La Feuillarde (FR) (Nikos)
669[6]

Rachael's Ruby *Roger Teal* 92h
7 b m Joe Bear(IRE) Fajjoura (IRE) (Fairy King (USA))
240[3] 708[6] 1627[P] 2004[P] 2271[5]

Racing Europe (IRE) *Brian Ellison* 108b
5 b g Kayf Tara Titanic Quarter (IRE) (Turgeon (USA))
3760[2] 4349[4]

Racing Pulse (IRE) *John Quinn* 142h
5 b g Garuda(IRE) Jacks Sister (IRE) (Entitled (IRE))
(3036) 3454[3] 4052[2] 5157[6]

Racoleur (FR) *D Delorme* 120c
9 ch g Fragrant Mix(IRE) Gracieuse D'Aron (FR) (Video Rock (FR))
855a[2] 1532a[F]

Radetsky March (IRE) *Geoffrey Deacon* 51h 120c
11 b g Taipan(IRE) Jane Jones (IRE) (Beau Sher)
323[P] 4274[P] 4443[4] 5432[P]

Radharc Nahabhainn (IRE) *Fergal O'Brien* 102b
6 b g Saddlers' Hall(IRE) Mills Moss (IRE) (Bob Back (USA))
862[2] 1712[8] 1974[16] 2720[P]

Radharc Na Mara (IRE) *Miss H Harper* 104c
10 b m Balla Cove Poor Reception (IRE) (Mandalus)
(5062)
5164[4] 5323[6]

Radical Bay *Nicholas Pomfret* 86h
10 b g Karinga Bay Radical Lady (Radical)
969[3] 1406[6] 1497[P]

Radical Impact (IRE) *Venetia Williams* 70h
6 ch g Beneficial Shean Alainn (IRE) (Le Moss)
2289[4] 3227[P] 4729[5] 5007[P]

Radio Nowhere (IRE) *Donald McCain* 106h 106c
6 b g Beneficial Creidim (IRE) (Erins Isle)
19[10] 1937[10] 2417[6] 2787[4] **3041[2] 4222[P] 4613[3]**

Radmores Express *John O'Shea* 93b
5 b g Primo Valentino(IRE) Emma Lilley (USA) (Theatrical (IRE))
14[3] 225[4] 1819[3]

Radmores Jewel *John O'Shea* 73b
4 ch f Primo Valentino(IRE) Emma Lilley (USA) (Theatrical (IRE))
4561[7] 4867[11]

Radmores Return *John O'Shea* 64b
6 b m Overbury(IRE) Harvey's Sister (Le Moss)
372[12]

Radmores Revenge *Sophie Leech* 122h
11 b g Overbury(IRE) Harvey's Sister (Le Moss)
(219) (2617) 2951[11] 3201[7] 4028[8] 5179[2] 5429[3]

Radmores Surprise *John O'Shea*
5 b m Revoque(IRE) Harvey's Sister (Le Moss)
2809[6]

Radsoc De Sivola (FR) *John Cornwall* 101h 66c
9 bl g Video Rock(FR) Kerrana (FR) (Cadoudal (FR))
64[5] 286[P] 426[6] 759[P] 1563[P] 1638[6] 1782[4] 2048[4]
3152[4] 3268[5]
4592[4] 4723[P]

Raduis Bleu (FR) *Lady Susan Brooke* 116h 119c
9 gr g Dadarissime(FR) Regence Bleue (FR) (Porto Rafti (FR))
(143) 2041[2]
2468[4] 2650[3] 2889[5] 4842[3] 5039[5] 5488[3]

Rafafie *Sue Gardner* 105h
6 b g Kayf Tara Florie (Alflora (IRE))
2659[8] 2940[13] 3697[6] 4391[5] 5034[3]

Rafale Precieux (FR) *Mme M Desvaux* 125h 123c
9 b g Le Balafre(FR) Djerba De Champfeu (FR) (El Badr)
1583a[4] 2465a[7]

Raggios Boy *Barry Murtagh* 77h
8 ch g Karinga Bay Fen Terrier (Emarati (USA))
222[5] 630[4]

Rag Tiger (GER) *J Bertran De Balanda* 113h 107c
8 b g Pentire Rosarium (GER) (Zinaad)
559a[5]

Ragtime Lady *Steven Dixon*
6 b m General Gambul Pink Lady (El Conquistador)
1531[8] 5028[8]

Raid Stane (IRE) *Miss K Scott*
8 b g Morozov(USA) Rashhattan (IRE) (Rashar (USA))
5209[P]

Raifteiri (IRE) *William Young Jnr* 71h 69c
7 b g Galileo(IRE) Naziriya (FR) (Darshaan)
534[4] 802[3] 866[4] 1038[F] 1163[P] 5209[6] 5536[5]

Railway Dillon (IRE) *Donald McCain* 108h 131c
9 b g Witness Box(USA) Laura's Native (IRE) (Be My Native (USA))
(3059)
3717[P] 4204[P] 4669[P]

Railway Vic (IRE) *James Frost* 117h 53c
7 b g Old Vic Penny Apples (IRE) (Jolly Jake (NZ))
2921[4] 3174[3] 4334[8]
5237[6]

Railway Zira (IRE) *David Harry Kelly* 124h
6 b m Westerner Mill Emerald (Old Vic)
4386a[P] 4846a[7]

Rainbow Beauty *Tom George* 79h
4 ch f Manduro(GER) Just Like A Woman (Observatory (USA))
5393[4]

Rainbow Haze *Mrs K M Dando* 102b
8 b g Rainbow High Kristal Haze (Krisinsky (USA))
49[P] 482[4] 844[5]
5545[P]

Rainbow Peak (IRE) *John Ferguson* 140h
8 b g Hernando(FR) Celtic Fling (Lion Cavern (USA))
3350[4] (3877) 4234[2] 4785[12] 5172[2] ◆

Rainbow Trout (IRE) *Mrs Z Smith*
8 ch m Snurge Lucky Trout (Beau Charmeur (FR))
430[P]

Rain Down (FR) *Donald McCain* 82b
5 b g Sassanian(USA) Royale Floriane (FR) (Cyborg (FR))
5286[5]

Rain Mac *Donald McCain* 104h
6 b g Beat Hollow Quenched (Dansili)
561[2] 678[8]

Rainy City (IRE) *Paul Nicholls* 91b
4 b g Kalanisi(IRE) Erintante (IRE) (Denel (FR))
4296[5] 4964[5]

Raise A Spark *Donald McCain* 85b
4 b g Multiplex Reem Two (Mtoto)
4951[5]

Rajamand (FR) *Miss Chloe Roddick* 113c
8 gr g Linamix(FR) Ridafa (IRE) (Darshaan)
5[4] 5553[F]

Rajdhani Express *Nicky Henderson* 134h 162c
7 br g Presenting Violet Express (FR) (Cadoudal (FR))
2503[5] 4766[3] 5155[7]

Rajnagan (IRE) *Paul Webber* 133h 141c
10 ch g Muhtarram(USA) Rajnagara (IRE) (Darshaan)
82[2] **249[3]**
672[4] 974[3]

Rakane Rouge (FR) *P Cottin*
6 b m Arakan(USA) Prompt (Old Vic)
198a[F]

Raktiman (IRE) *Michael Appleby* 107h
7 ch g Rakti Wish List (IRE) (Mujadil (USA))
(967) 1284[7] 1414[2]

Rally *Nicky Henderson* 120h
5 b g Rail Link Waki Music (USA) (Miswaki (USA))
1794[5] (2197) 2505[8] 3130[8]

Rally The Troops (IRE) *Jonjo O'Neill* 54h
7 b g Flemensfirth(USA) Roaming (IRE) (Be My Native (USA))
847[7] 1019[5]

Ramona Chase *Jim Best* 39h
9 b g High Chaparral(IRE) Audacieuse (Rainbow Quest (USA))
3047[13]

Rampant Ronnie (USA) *Nikki Evans* 101h
9 b g Honor Glide(USA) Jalfrezi (Jalmood (USA))
49[P] 661[12] 965[7]

Rancher (IRE) *Tony Carroll* 73h
4 b g High Chaparral(IRE) Shot Of Redemption (Shirley Heights)
1781[3]

Randall *Martin Bosley*
6 b g Superior Premium Wilderness Bay (IRE) (Fasliyev (USA))
3734[10] 4796[10] 5227[P]

Randalls Mill (IRE) *M P Sunderland* 83b
6 b g Gold Well Darnadulce (IRE) (Darnay)
3002[7]

Rangitoto (IRE) *Charles Whittaker* 132h
9 b g Old Vic Kendos Dream (IRE) (Presenting)
2798[P] (Dead)

Ranjaan (FR) *Paul Nicholls* 133h
6 b g Dubai Destination(USA) Ridafa (IRE) (Darshaan)
(2717) 3088[6] *4022[2] 4302[2]*

Raphy De La Roche (FR) *Yannick Fouin* 128h 128c
9 gr g Dom Alco(FR) Casaque Du Perche (FR) (Abdonski (FR))
5530a[F]

Rapid Heat Lad (IRE) *Andrew Hollinshead* 115h
5 b g Aussie Rules(USA) Alwiyda (USA) (Trempolino (USA))
3060[P]

Rapidolyte De Ladalka (FR) *Simon Shirley-Beavan* 130c
9 b g Network(GER) Emeraude Du Moulin (FR) (Djarvis (FR))
1978[5] 3059[P] 4382[4]

Rare Bob (IRE) *D T Hughes* 121h 150c
12 bb g Bob Back(USA) Cut Ahead (Kalaglow)
1956[7]

Rare Coincidence *Alan Berry* 89h
13 ch g Atraf Green Seed (IRE) (Lead On Time (USA))
21[P] 471[8] 537[5] 799[6] 1078[2] 1374[7] 4475[P]

Rare Legend (IRE) *John Joseph Hanlon* 118h
7 b g Stowaway Shambala (IRE) (Imperial Ballet (IRE))
3829[2]

Rascal (IRE) *Dan Skelton* 103h
5 b g Milan Montagues Lady (IRE) (Montelimar (USA))
3440[7] 4776[3] 5227[2]

Rasheed *Lucy Wadham* 105h 83c
6 b g Oasis Dream Alexandrine (IRE) (Nashwan (USA))
3^4 2598^{12} 2904^2
3596^7 *4020^4* 4781^3
5194^F

Rash Move (IRE) *F A Hutsby* 124c
13 bb g Rashar(USA) Lady Tarsel (Tarqogan)
57^3 287^2 557^3

Rasteau (IRE) *Tom Keddy* 65h
6 b g Barathea(IRE) Mistra (IRE) (Rainbow Quest (USA))
184^U

Rathcor *S Rea* 126h 112c
12 b g Overbury(IRE) Brenig (Horage)
657^P

Rather Curious (IRE) *David Phelan* 110h 106c
10 b g Corrouge(USA) Imlistening (IRE) (Tremblant)
325^3

Rathlin *M F Morris* 146h 158c
9 b g Kayf Tara Princess Timon (Terimon)
(1157a) 3790a^5 **4062a^3 4766^7 5155^5**

Rathmoyle House (IRE) *Gordon Elliott* 89h 93c
8 br g Anshan Secluded Eclipse (IRE) (Seclude (USA))
867^7 **1542^F**

Rathnaroughy (IRE) *Malcolm Jefferson* 106h 85c
10 b g Bach(IRE) Lee Valley Lady (IRE) (Boyne Valley)
798^B 1039^4

Rathvawn Belle (IRE) *Lucinda Russell* 98h
7 b m Luso Duck 'N' Dive (IRE) (Accordion)
1871^2 2309^2 2973^6 3757^5

Rathvinden (IRE) *W P Mullins* 149h
6 b g Heron Island(IRE) Peggy Cullen (IRE) (Presenting)
3654^F 3889^2 4750^3

Ratify *Dai Burchell* 93h 126c
10 br g Rakaposhi King Sea Sky (Oats)
206^3 485^4 2090^3
(2699) 3190^2 (4570)
(4992) (5543)

Rattleandrun (IRE) *Brendan Powell* 85h
6 b g Bienamado(USA) Whitesmith Beauty (IRE) (Lord Americo)
4135^6 4664^7 4863^8 5140^4 5441^5

Rattlin *Sue Smith* 122h 81c
6 b m Bollin Eric Parslin (The Parson)
15^4 (223) (626) 2158^P 2352^3
2734^5 (2956) 3286^2 4040^6 4668^5 5075^4 (5449)

Ravensbill (IRE) *William Amos* 47b
12 b g Sea Raven(IRE) Two Hills Folly (IRE) (Pollerton)
2445^P

Ravens Brook (IRE) *Richard Lee* 96h 116c
8 br g Alderbrook Triple Triumph (IRE) (Welsh Term)
2390^4 (3222)
3662^P 4744^5

Ravensdale Lady (IRE) *Mark Michael McNiff* 104c
8 b m Flemensfirth(USA) Sure Quest (Sure Blade (USA))
5321^8

Ravens Nest *Ben Pauling* 83h
4 b g Piccolo Emouna (Cadeaux Genereux)
1781^4 1920^6 3592^8

Ravens Secret *Tracey Barfoot-Saunt* 106h 34c
9 br g Overbury(IRE) Secret Pearl (IRE) (Alphabatim (USA))
3605^{10} *4326^8* **4484^6 4885^7**

Raven's Tower (USA) *Ben Pauling* 126h
4 b g Raven's Pass(USA) Tizdubai (USA) (Cee's Tizzy (USA))
1624^2 1813^2 (2274) ◆ 2970^F 3317^3 3686^2 (4401) 4755^6 (5090) 5568^7

Ravethebrave (IRE) *Alan Hill* 129c
10 b g Rashar(USA) Mrs Blobby (IRE) (Rontino)
60^P 4788^P

Raving Renee *Lucy Jones* 44b
6 b m Overbury(IRE) Chartridge Hill (Crested Lark)
3133^9

Ravi River (IRE) *Alistair Whillans* 76h
10 ch g Barathea(IRE) Echo River (USA) (Irish River (FR))
316^6 630^7 (1379) 1575^6 2336^P 2869^5

Ravissante Du Rheu (FR) *T Trapenard* 96h 104c
4 b f Antarctique(IRE) Venus Du Rheu (FR) (Bricassar (USA))
130a^0 615a^3

Rawnaq (IRE) *Matthew J Smith* 143h
7 b g Azamour(IRE) Sharemata (IRE) (Doyoun)
2533^3

Rayadour (IRE) *Micky Hammond* 98h
5 b g Azamour(IRE) Rayyana (IRE) (Rainbow Quest (USA))
1924^{13} 2030^9 2336^P 4336^7 (5161) (5302) (5494)

Rayak (IRE) *Jonjo O'Neill* 107h
4 b g Invincible Spirit(IRE) Rayyana (IRE) (Rainbow Quest (USA))
2455^3 2975^7 3161^2 3822^2 4679^5 5061^F

Raya Star (IRE) *Alan King* 139h 154c
8 b g Milan Garden City (IRE) (Shernazar)
(2192)
2531^2 3185^2 4146^3 4790^F

Ray Diamond *Jackie Du Plessis* 105h 109c
9 ch g Medicean Musical Twist (USA) (Woodman (USA))
98^5 542^7 1833^3 (2013) 2828^2 **3172^2 3693^3**
5019^8 **5394^6**

Rayhani (USA) *J A Nash* 114h 114c
11 b g Theatrical(IRE) Bahr Alsalaam (USA) (Riverman (USA))
1342^3

Raynell *Noel Quinlan* 56h
6 b g Araafa(IRE) Milly-M (Cadeaux Genereux)
182^P

Rayvin Black *Oliver Sherwood* 122h
5 b g Halling(USA) Optimistic (Reprimand)
(8) 560^2 (1832) 2213^6

Raz De Maree (FR) *D T Hughes* 119h 153c
9 ch g Shaanmer(IRE) Diyala III (FR) (Quart De Vin (FR))
2708a^P 5171^8

Razzle Dazzle 'Em *Shaun Harris* 89h
5 b g Phoenix Reach(IRE) Rasmani (Medicean)
1399^U 1496^3 1632^9 1793^6 2051^{10}

Reach Out *Mrs A Malzard* 74h
6 ch g Phoenix Reach(IRE) Cocorica (IRE) (Croco Rouge (IRE))
5478a^2

Reach The Beach *Brendan Powell* 94h
5 ch m Phoenix Reach(IRE) Comtesse Noire (CAN) (Woodman (USA))
3005^{10} 3289^7

Ready Token (IRE) *Charlie Longsdon* 117h
6 gr g Flemensfirth(USA) Ceol Tire (IRE) (Roselier (FR))
3735^F 4163^F 4863^3 5300^2

Real Milan (IRE) *Donald McCain* 127h 131c
9 b g Milan The Real Athlete (IRE) (Presenting)
3389^4 3825^2 4544^P 4900^2 5350^3

Real Steel (IRE) *Philip Fenton* 147h
6 br g Old Vic Grangeclare Dancer (IRE) (Top Of The World)
(4456a) 5201a^2

Realt Ag Leimt (IRE) *M R Peters* 109h 100c
8 b g Beneficial Edwarda (Safawan)
(424)

Realta Mo Croi (IRE) *Neil Mulholland* 102h
6 b m Westerner Solar Quest (IRE) (King's Ride)
(710) 2312^4 2723^3 3119^P

Realt Dubh (IRE) *Noel Meade* 134h 157c
10 b g Beneficial Suez Canal (FR) (Exit To Nowhere (USA))
2985a^5 3751a^5

Realt Mor (IRE) *Gordon Elliott* 123h 157c
9 b g Beneficial Suez Canal (FR) (Exit To Nowhere (USA))
2141a^3 2410a^3

Reaping The Reward (IRE) *Lucinda Russell* 122h 111c
10 b g Sylvan Express Zamaine (IRE) (Zaffaran (USA))
342^P (884)
3519^3 4055^P 4900^F 5273^4

Rearrange *Chris Bealby* 69h
5 b m Rail Link New Order (Singspiel (IRE))
897^P 1595^5 1938^{14} 2883^9

Reasonable Force *Keith Reveley* 104h 88c
8 b g Forzando Noreasonatall (Lord David S (USA))
65^6 600^P

Rebeccas Choice (IRE) *Dai Burchell* 115h 129c
11 b g Religiously(USA) Carolin Lass (IRE) (Carlingford Castle)
1868^7 2419^5 2979^3 4914^3 (5348)

Rebel Alliance (IRE) *Richard A Thomas* 86h 108c
9 b g Lord Of Appeal Pandoras Hope (IRE) (Carefree Dancer (USA))
(335) **655^P**
4355^P 4705^6 5491^3

Rebel Brunel (FR) *J-L Guillochon*
9 b g Clerkenwell(USA) Italika (FR) (Roi De Rome (USA))
2384a^F

Rebel Chief (IRE) *Richard A Thomas* 112b
13 b g Oscar(IRE) Limavady (IRE) (Executive Perk)
5491^P

Rebel Du Maquis (FR) *Paul Nicholls* 94h 123c
9 b g Brier Creek(USA) Jade De Chalamont (FR) (Royal Charter (FR))
(63) **672^7**

Rebel Fitz (FR) *Michael Winters* 160h 157c
9 b g Agent Bleu(FR) Gesse Parade (FR) (Dress Parade)
(1178a)
(1804a) 1955^2 (5422a)

Rebel Flag (IRE) *Chris Bealby* 79h
7 br g Statue Of Liberty(USA) Ibiza (GER) (Linamix (FR))
182^P

Rebel High (IRE) *Derek Frankland* 96h 98c
10 ch g Hymns On High Celia's Fountain (IRE) (Royal Fountain)
30^4 269^4 2295^5 2562^3 2895^3 5243^4

Rebel Island (IRE) *John Panvert* 55h
5 b m Heron Island(IRE) Rebel Rebel (FR) (Pebble (FR))
5339^7

Rebel Rebellion (IRE) *Paul Nicholls* 131h 153c
9 b g Lord Americo Tourmaline Girl (IRE) (Toulon)
2081^5 2365^4 (2939)
4032^3 4559^2 5156^{15}

Rebel Swing *Joanne Foster* 99h 115c
8 b g Robellino(USA) Ninia (USA) (Affirmed (USA))
420^2 492^7

Reblis (FR) *Gary Moore* 110h 132c
9 b g Assessor(IRE) Silbere (FR) (Silver Rainbow)
2567^6 (3137)
(3554) 4962^{12} 5348^5

Recession Proof (FR) *John Quinn* 123h
8 ch g Rock Of Gibraltar(IRE) Elevate (Ela-Mana-Mou)
2504^{12} 3200^F 4147^{15} 4517^P

Reckless Romeo (IRE) *Richard Ford* 87h
5 b g Heliostatic(IRE) Ballerina Babe (IRE) (Spectrum (IRE))
471^{11} 751^5 881^6 1105^3 1405^4 2842^P 3335^P

Record Breaker (IRE) *Donald McCain* 94h
10 b g In The Wings Overruled (IRE) (Last Tycoon)
592^4 849^5 1110^5 1391^P

Recway Lass *Des Donovan* 77h
6 ch m Doyen(IRE) Zarma (FR) (Machiavellian (USA))
1^6 1305^5 1496^2 1630^6 5116^3

Red Admirable (IRE) *Graeme McPherson* 120h
8 b g Shantou(USA) Eimears Pet (IRE) (Lord Americo)
48^6 737^4 (2510) 2828^{11} 3269^5 4726^4 5429^5

Red Anchor (IRE) *Linda Jewell* 88h 100c
10 ch g Snurge Clonartic (IRE) (Be My Native (USA))
2438^P 2861^P 4718^4 5023^F 5263^{11}

Red Devil Lads (IRE) *Rebecca Curtis* 112h
5 b g Beneficial Welsh Sitara (IRE) (Welsh Term)
2153^2 2759^4 3166^3 4029^2 4555^4 4937^5

Red Eight (USA) *John Butler* 76h
4 bb g Gone West(USA) Katherine Seymour (Green Desert (USA))
785^3 975^6 1044^P

Redera (IRE) *A J Martin* 134h 116c
8 b g Chevalier(IRE) Lady Redera (IRE) (Inzar (USA))
2533^{11}

Red Eyes *Chris Grant* 106h
6 b g Beat Hollow Kardelle (Kalaglow)
1200^3 1399^3 (1500) 1654^6 2311^7

Red Four *George Baker* 99h
4 ch f Singspiel(IRE) Protectorate (Hector Protector (USA))
(3385) 3857^3 4730^3

Red Hott Robbie *Giuseppe Fierro* 89b
5 b g Revoque(IRE) Abbiejo (IRE) (Blues Traveller (IRE))
4763^7 4902^6 5249^{10}

Red Inca *Brian Ellison* 129h
6 ch g Pivotal Magicalmysterykate (USA) (Woodman (USA))
216^5

Redinga *Linda Jewell* 52h
8 ch m Karinga Bay Medway Queen (Pitpan)
4298^{12} 4797^F 5024^P

Red Jade *Keiran Burke* 120h
9 ch g Dubai Destination(USA) Red Slippers (USA) (Nureyev (USA))
697^6

Red Joker (IRE) *Andrew Crook* 72h
4 br g Red Clubs(IRE) Lady Singspiel (IRE) (Singspiel (IRE))
4889^8 5295^6

Redkalani (IRE) *Keith Reveley* 101b
6 b g Ashkalani(IRE) La Femme En Rouge (Slip Anchor)
3042^3 4431^4 5108^2

Red Legacy *Sean Regan*
6 ch m Distant Music(USA) Emma May (Nicholas Bill)
5500^{13}

Red Legend *Zoe Davison* 51b
6 ch m Midnight Legend Haliguen Bay (Karinga Bay)
4916^{15}

Red Lion Rock (IRE) *J J Lambe* 105b
4 b c Rock Of Gibraltar(IRE) Royal Bounty (IRE) (Generous (IRE))
(2247)

Redlynch Rock (IRE) *Bob Buckler* 87h 103c
6 b g Brian Boru College Ground (IRE) (College Chapel)
634^6 830^4 1831^3 2110^P 3955^P 4888^3 **5144^4**
5395^5

Red Myst (IRE) *Victor Thompson* 41h 56c
9 ch g Beneficial That's Not Fair (IRE) (Supreme Leader)
510^F 625^8

Red Mystique (IRE) *Maurice Barnes* 21h
5 b g Red Clubs(IRE) Sacred Love (IRE) (Barathea (IRE))
3^7 306^8 3516^P

Red Name (FR) *P Peltier* 120h 129c
4 ch g Nickname(FR) Fidelety (FR) (Villez (USA))
2262a^8

Red Not Blue (IRE) *Simon Earle* 133h 133c
11 b g Blueprint(IRE) Silent Valley (Forzando)
851^P 1091^2 1268^4 1430^3 1747^4 1972^9 2504^8 2798^3 3069^7 4949^8 5372^{11}

Redoubtablefighter (IRE) *Anthony Middleton*
8 b g Kayf Tara La Brigantine (IRE) (Montelimar (USA))
2181^P

Redoute Star (AUS) *Paul D'Arcy* 97h
8 b g Redoute's Choice(AUS) Significant Moment (AUS) (Bletchingly (AUS))
696^3

Redpender (IRE) *James Moffatt* 109h 106c
8 gr g Great Palm(USA) Josie Murphy (IRE) (Orchestra)
1875^4 (2217) 2970^5 3618^5 4553^3

Red Riverman *Nigel Twiston-Davies* 120h 128c
6 b g Haafhd Mocca (IRE) (Sri Pekan (USA))
(1343)
1782^2 (2012)
2287^7 2694^5 3064^3 3318^4 4279^6

Red Rocco (IRE) *Nigel Twiston-Davies* 114h 136c
7 ch g Croco Rouge(IRE) Youbetido (IRE) (Eurobus)
2670^2 3361^P 3743^P 4270^U 4821^5 5386^P

Red Rock (FR) *Emma Lavelle* 99h 110c
9 b g Saint Cyrien(FR) Ariloba De Brize (FR) (Roymel (FR))
1629^3 1710^5 (2021)
2741^2 3729^P 5027^6

Red Rosso *Rob Summers* 92h 91c
9 ch g Executive Perk Secret Whisper (Infantry)
33^6 651^{14} 1120^9
1550^6 1835^6 2699^R

Red Rouble (IRE) *Nigel Twiston-Davies* 102h 112c
9 ch g Moscow Society(USA) Chirouble (IRE) (High Roller (IRE))
420^5

Red Seventy *David Pipe* 125h
5 b g Sakhee(USA) Dimakya (USA) (Dayjur (USA))
2476^5 2906^2 3728^3 (4634) 5067^3 5231^4

Red Sherlock *David Pipe* 148h
5 ch g Shirocco(GER) Lady Cricket (FR) (Cricket Ball (USA))
(2534) (3115) (3657) ◆ (3889) 4750^9

Red Skipper (IRE) *John O'Shea* 122h 104c
9 ch g Captain Rio Speed To Lead (IRE) (Darshaan)
10^4 4726^6 4947^4 5260^{11}

Red Tortue (IRE) *Tony Coyle* 74h
5 b g Turtle Island(IRE) Howrwedoin (IRE) (Flemensfirth (USA))
897^F

Red Watch (IRE) *L Price*
12 b g Woods Of Windsor(USA) Maxi Miss (IRE) (Orchestra)
5041^P

Red Whisper *Rob Summers* 92h 102c
10 ch g Midnight Legend Secret Whisper (Infantry)
193^5 456^3 927^5
1175^U 5289^4

Reef Dancer (IRE) *Robert Johnson* 85c
11 b g Pasternak Shareef Walk (Shareef Dancer (USA))
1375^4 1563^5 1851^6 2173^8

Reelwill (FR) *Derek Shaw* 39h 36c
9 gr m Dom Alco(FR) Jeep Will (FR) (Royal Charter (FR))
3113^P 3740^7 3878^P

Refer *Phil Middleton* 119h
4 b g Rail Link Trellis Bay (Sadler's Wells (USA))
(1439) 1781^2 1862^4 2466^5 2932^5 4963^3 5353^2

Refusal *Caroline Bailey* 95h 113c
6 b g Teofilio(IRE) Frankie Fair (IRE) (Red Sunset)
5^2 426^4

Refuse To Mambo *Andrew Hollinshead*
4 ch g Refuse To Bend(IRE) Sovereign's Honour (USA) (Kingmambo (USA))
725^P

Regal Approach (IRE) *Kim Bailey* 99h 125c
11 b g Bob Back(USA) Crash Approach (Crash Course)
89^3

Regal County (IRE) *Alexandra Dunn* 99h
8 b g King's Theatre(IRE) County Kerry (FR) (Comrade In Arms)
318^5 521^{12}

Regal D'Estruval (FR) *Dr Richard Newland* 115h 111c
9 b g Panoramic Haie D'Estruval (FR) (Cyborg (FR))
81^4 282^8 4036^6 (4791) 5001^2
5194^F 5434^P

Regal Diamond (IRE) *Peter Bowen* 129h
6 b h Vinnie Roe(IRE) Paper Money (IRE) (Supreme Leader)
(359) 1974^6 2286^2 2933^4 3454^2 3889^4 4356^P 4786^P

Regal Encore (IRE) *Anthony Honeyball* 132h
6 b g King's Theatre(IRE) Go On Eileen (IRE) (Bob Back (USA))
2075^2 (2564) 3017^2 4682^4

Regal Flow *Caroline Keevil* 98h
7 b g Erhaab(USA) Flow (Over The River (FR))
2105^7 2473^2 2827^8 5262^7

Regal One (IRE) *David Bridgwater* 115h 115c
6 b g Antonius Pius(USA) Regal Dancer (IRE) (Dancing Dissident (USA))
2287^4 ◆ 2845^F 3429^4 4031^P 4469^5 5066^7 **5398^4**

Regal Park (IRE) *Gary Moore* 93h 85c
7 b g Montjeu(IRE) Classic Park (Robellino (USA))
2016^6 2278^P **2726^4 3250^P 3883^2 4734^P**

Regal Presence (IRE) *Victor Dartnall* 115h 120c
7 ch g Presenting Lucy Lodge (IRE) (Moscow Society (USA))
422^3 2283^4 3389^P 4884^2 5129^P 5334^P

Regal Ramirez *Chris Grant* 90h
6 gr g Needwood Blade Beverley Hills (IRE) (Mozart (IRE))
22^9 558^{10} 788^5 4817^7

Regal Reform (IRE) *Richard A Thomas*
9 b g Endeavour(USA) Lady Muscadet (IRE) (Muscatite)
5491^P

Regal Rumpus *L Jefford* 109h 120c
12 br g Rakaposhi King Avena (Oats)
413^7

Regal Swain (IRE) *Alan Swinbank* 102h
6 b g Ivan Denisovich(IRE) Targhyb (IRE) (Unfuwain (USA))
2493^5 2968^5

Reggie Parrot *Sue Smith* 64b
7 ch g Soviet Star(USA) Jazzy Refrain (IRE) (Jareer (USA))
2174^6

Reggie Perrin *Pat Phelan* 107h
6 ch g Storming Home Tecktal (FR) (Pivotal)
304^6 2271^6 3094^4 3249^3 5304^6

Reglis Brunel (FR) *E Lecoiffier* 108h 136c
9 b g Ungaro(GER) Lady Du Rocher (FR) (Goldneyev (USA))
1902a^4 2264a^U

Reg's Ruby *David Bridgwater* 68h 73c
8 b m Pursuit Of Love Sweets (IRE) (Persian Heights)
600^6 805^7

Reign Silver (IRE) *Lee Carter* 81b
6 gr m Cloudings(IRE) Charlies Rising (IRE) (Rising)
391^P

Reillys Daughter *Richard Mitchell* 96h
6 b m Diktat Compose (Anabaa (USA))
2907^{12} 4910^3 5175^7 5393^P

Reizovic (IRE) *John E Kiely* 124h
9 b g Catcher In The Rye(IRE) Naivity (IRE) (Auction Ring (USA))
3910a^F

Reland (FR) *Mrs Jackie Stephen* 91b
9 ch g Shaanmer(IRE) Falkland III (FR) (Video Rock (FR))
4465^P **4775^P**

Relax (FR) *Venetia Williams* 144c
9 b g Fragrant Mix(IRE) Magik (FR) (Kadalko (FR))
2674^P (3131)
3647^5 (4035)
4427^P

Relentless (IRE) *Jim Best* 75h
4 b g Dylan Thomas(IRE) Karamiyna (IRE) (Shernazar)
1335[4]

Relentless Dreamer (IRE) *Rebecca Curtis* 106b
5 br g Kayf Tara Full Of Elegance (FR) (Cadoudal (FR))
1891[F] 3016[2] 4824[3]

Reliable Richie (IRE) *R G Chapman* 79h 57c
8 b g Sunshine Street(USA) Chance Eile (IRE) (Camden Town)
5123[P]

Relic Rock (IRE) *Steve Gollings* 129b
6 b g Bienamado(USA) Nighty Bless (IRE) (Executive Perk)
(4043) 4349[2] (4824) 5173[2] ◆

Remedio (IRE) *Andrew Crook* 83b
4 b g Ramonti(FR) Cant Hurry Love (Desert Prince (IRE))
5063[7] 5454[7]

Remember Rose (IRE) *Y-M Porzier* 122h 128c
11 b g Insatiable(IRE) Couture Rose (IRE) (Ajraas (USA))
838a[5] 1902a[P] 2264a[P]

Remiluc (FR) *Paul Nicholls* 102h
5 b g Mister Sacha(FR) Markene De Durtal (FR) (Sharken (FR))
5117[4]

Renagisha (IRE) *Jim Best* 61h
8 b m Luso Slaney Rose (IRE) (Roselier (FR))
595[4] 1259[6] 1538[P] 2008[7]

Renard (FR) *Venetia Williams* 148c
9 bb g Discover D'Auteuil(FR) Kirmelia (FR) (Chamberlin (FR))
1969[7] 2488[8] (2945)
(3362) 3772[4] 3887[7] 4544[3] 4738[9] 5170[11]

Renard D'Irlande (FR) *Venetia Williams* 127h 131c
9 gr g April Night(FR) Isati'S (FR) (Chamberlin (FR))
(2508)
2757[4] 3594[U] 3886[3] 4245[3] 4819[6] 5068[F]

Rendezvous Peak *Lucy Wadham* 102h
5 b g High-Rise(IRE) Jurado Park (IRE) (Jurado (USA))
2439[2] 2788[6] 4069[4] 4891[3] ◆ 5408[3]

Rendl Beach (IRE) *Rebecca Curtis* 130h 90c
7 b g Milan Erins Emblem (IRE) (Erins Isle)
2010[F] 2539[4] 2812[P]

Renegotiate *Dr Richard Newland* 95h
5 ch g Trade Fair L'Extra Honor (USA) (Hero's Honor (USA))
843[3] 928[4] 1052[6]

Rene Le Roi (FR) *Tim Easterby* 89h
5 b g King O' The Mana(IRE) Madonna Da Rossi (Mtoto)
284[3] 560[5] 2197[9] 2621[10]

Renko (FR) *X-L Le Stang*
9 b g Winning Smile(FR) Eccica (FR) (Pure Hasard (FR))
1623a[P]

Renne Du Houx (FR) *J Merienne* 90c
9 b m Silver Rainbow Dyane Du Houx (FR) (King's Road (FR))
1464a[7]

Renneti (FR) *W P Mullins* 142h
5 b g Irish Wells(FR) Caprice Meill (FR) (French Glory)
2852a[2] 5200a[RR]

Renoyr (FR) *Malcolm Jefferson* 119h
9 b g Kalmoss(FR) Idee De Valeur (FR) (Roi De Rome (USA))
93[4] 1203[6]

Renta Gallery (IRE) *Richard A Thomas*
8 ch m Portrait Gallery(IRE) Renty (IRE) (Carlingford Castle)
5545[P]

Representingceltic (IRE) *Pat Phelan* 81h 117c
9 ch g Presenting Nobull (IRE) (Torus)
238[2] 426[2] 1527[5]

Requin (FR) *Victor Dartnall* 72h 120c
9 bb g Video Rock(FR) Funkia (FR) (Royal Charter (FR))
3662[5] 3990[6] 4678[7] 5180[5]

Residence And Spa (IRE) *Helen Rees* 85h
6 b g Dubai Destination(USA) Toffee Nosed (Selkirk (USA))
177[6] 1833[S] 2696[11] 2920[5] (3425) 3699[3]

Res Ipsa Loquitur (IRE) *J F Levins* 78h
6 b m Beneficial Calomeria (Groom Dancer (USA))
2499[0]

Resistencia (FR) *E Vagne* 116c
9 gr m Kapgarde(FR) Belfaster (FR) (Royal Charter (FR))
704a[2] 1532a[P]

Resourceful Miss *Paul Webber* 88h
5 b m Dubai Destination(USA) Resourceful (IRE) (Entrepreneur)
186[4] 1779[10] 3153[5]

Respectueux (FR) *David Brace* 108h 105c
8 b g Robin Des Pres(FR) Rouge Folie (FR) (Agent Bleu (FR))
846[7] 1018[8]

Ressurection Bay *Paul Webber* 104b
6 b g Helissio(FR) Coccinelle (IRE) (Great Marquess)
874[4] ◆

Rest And Be (IRE) *Alan Jones* 101b
7 bb m Vinnie Roe(IRE) Bobs Star (IRE) (Bob Back (USA))
(1196) 1489[2]

Restezen D'Armor (FR) *Mrs O C Jackson* 60h 93c
9 b g Grand Tresor(FR) Lafrizen D'Armor (FR) (Africanus (FR))
331[P] 4505[4] 5035[6]

Restless Harry *Robin Dickin* 116h 154c
10 b g Sir Harry Lewis(USA) Restless Native (IRE) (Be My Native (USA))
1956[20] 2672[10] **3366[U] 3455[U] (3717)**
3888[5] (4263)
4738[12] 5571[4]

Retrieve (AUS) *John Ferguson* 107h
7 b g Rahy(USA) Hold To Ransom (USA) (Red Ransom (USA))
3330[4] 4103[6]

Retrieve The Stick *Malcolm Jefferson* 104h
5 b m Revoque(IRE) Anabranch (Kind Of Hush)
567[2] 754[2] 970[5] 1472[2] 2309[3] 2883[5] (3393) (3523)

Retroson (IRE) *Michael Scudamore* 67b
6 b g Lahib(USA) Retro's Girl (IRE) (Zaffaran (USA))
1819[6] 2472[6] 3115[F]

Return Spring (IRE) *Philip Hobbs* 142h
7 b g Vinnie Roe(IRE) Bettys Daughter (IRE) (Supreme Leader)
(2504) 3069[2] (3457) 4174[10] 5138[21]

Revaader *Mark Gillard* 113h
6 b m Revoque(IRE) Wave Rider (Zaffaran (USA))
292[2] 631[5] 2725[5] 3289[3] 3747[2] 4173[3] 4394[2] 4604[F] 5117[3] 5303[3]

Revani *Johnny Farrelly* 124h
7 b g Sulamani(IRE) Clotted Cream (USA) (Eagle Eyed (USA))
4888[7] (5335)

Revanna *Peter Niven* 84b
5 b m Revoque(IRE) Kingennie (Dunbeath (USA))
2347[9] 3760[7]

Reve De Kerza (FR) *A Le Clerc* 97c
9 ch g Secret Singer(FR) Reverie Du Pontet (FR) (Le Pontet (FR))
200a[3]

Reve De Sivola (FR) *Nick Williams* 164h 143c
9 b g Assessor(IRE) Eva De Chalamont (FR) (Iron Duke (FR))
685a[11] (2240a) 2814[3] (3198) 3890[4] 4767[8]

Reverb *Nicky Henderson* 117h
5 b g Tiger Hill(IRE) Gemini Gold (IRE) (King's Best (USA))
270[3] 699[4] 2266[4] 2614[2] 2932[3] 5179[6]

Reverend Green (IRE) *Chris Down* 57h
8 b g Tagula(IRE) Red Letter (Sri Pekan (USA))
2282[4] 3163[15]

Reves D'Amour (IRE) *Jamie Snowden* 103h
5 ch m Midnight Legend Poppy Maroon (Supreme Leader)
(462) 1823[2] 2317[2] (2865)

Rev It Up (IRE) *Tim Vaughan* 126h 126c
8 b g Revoque(IRE) Von Carty (IRE) (Supreme Leader)
2077[5] 2867[2] 4347[7] 5186[2]

Revocation *Lucinda Russell* 115h
6 b g Revoque(IRE) Fenella (Phardante (FR))
(1754) 2103[3] 2655[5]

Revolution (FR) *J J Lambe* 70h
5 gr m Dutch Art Restless Rixa (FR) (Linamix (FR))
2205a[10]

Revouge *Jim Old* 73h
5 b g Revoque(IRE) Eva's Edge (IRE) (Good Thyne (USA))
380[8] 2703[8] 5008[10] 5120[6] 5408[6]

Revupclover (IRE) *Polly Gundry* 41h
7 gr g Revoque(IRE) Kingsfield Clover (Terimon)
716[9] 828[13] 920[12]

Rev Up Ruby *George Bewley* 107h
6 b m Revoque(IRE) Kingennie (Dunbeath (USA))
173[5] 754[3] 1661[10] 1853[8] 1975[7] (2495) 2973[3] 5509[5]

Rexmehead (IRE) *Andrew Wilson* 56h 53c
13 b g Fort Morgan(USA) Moon Rose (IRE) (Imperial Frontier (USA))
5298[9]

Reyes Magos (IRE) *Seamus Durack* 106h
8 b g Indian Danehill(IRE) Cincuenta (IRE) (Bob Back (USA))
1832[3] 2787[3]

Reyno *Renee Robeson* 104h
6 b g Sleeping Indian Tereyna (Terimon)
2314[13] 3280[P] 4700[11]

Rhamnus *Ben Pauling* 102h
4 b g Sakhee's Secret Happy Lady (FR) (Cadeaux Genereux)
5132[14]

Rhapando *Paul Webber* 115h
5 b g Hernando(FR) Rhapsody Rose (Unfuwain (USA))
2216[2] 2947[4] 4343[4] 5008[4]

Rhinestone Rebel (IRE) *Peter Hiatt* 103b
8 ch g Rashar(USA) Flute Opera (IRE) (Sharifabad (IRE))
5490[P]

Rhum (FR) *Nigel Twiston-Davies* 112h 123c
9 ch g Dark Moondancer Ireland (FR) (Kadalko (FR))
1346[6] 1521[3] 1659[2] 1748[U] 2246[4] 2678[4] 2923[P]
(3730)

Rhymers Ha' *Lucinda Russell* 122h 119c
7 br g Kasakov Salu (Ardross)
167[2] 798[U] 1144[3] 1753[3] 2359[4] 2751[6] 3398[11]
4235[6] 4952[5] 5208[7]

Rhymers Stone *Lucinda Russell* 110h
6 b g Desideratum Salu (Ardross)
1790[5] 2360[3] 2794[P] (3210) 3937[2] (4608)

Rhythm Star *Jamie Snowden* 102b
4 b f Beat All(USA) Star Award (IRE) (Oscar (IRE))
(3961) (5264)

Rhyton (IRE) *Lucy Normile*
7 b g Rainbow Quest(USA) Sea Picture (IRE) (Royal Academy (USA))
2999[P]

Ricardo's Girl (IRE) *Steve Gollings*
5 b m Westerner Precious Lady (Exit To Nowhere (USA))
567[P] 4253[5]

Richard's Sundance (IRE) *Victor Dartnall* 148h 140c
12 b g Saddlers' Hall(IRE) Celestial Rose (IRE) (Roselier (FR))
3698[P] 3993[2] (4443)
5135[7]

Rich Buddy *Richard Phillips* 120h
8 b g Kayf Tara Silver Gyre (IRE) (Silver Hawk (USA))
121[5] 606[5] 2715[4] 4913[5] 5333[8]

Rich Forever (IRE) *James Bethell*
4 b g Camacho Sixfields Flyer (IRE) (Desert Style (IRE))
2098[P]

Rich Lord *Ferdy Murphy* 114h 130c
10 b g Zamindar(USA) Al Corniche (IRE) (Bluebird (USA))
18[5]

Richmond (FR) *Venetia Williams* 115h 129c
9 b g Assessor(IRE) Hirondel De Serley (FR) (Royal Charter (FR))
(2437)
2633[2] 3065[8]

Richo *Shaun Harris* 87h 99c
8 ch g Bertolini(USA) Noble Water (FR) (Noblequest (FR))
34[2] 314[6] 903[8]
1089[LFT]

Rich Revival (IRE) *Miss Elizabeth Doyle* 126h 137c
10 b g Turtle Island(IRE) Rich Desire (Grey Desire)
3868a[P]

Rick (FR) *John Ferguson* 142h 126c
10 b g Astarabad(USA) Catty Jolie (FR) (Mansonnien (FR))
2395[4] 2955[3] 3142[3]

Ricketyrock *Nick Mitchell* 68h
8 b g Riverwise(USA) Apatura Cherry (All Fair)
951[2] 2628[0] 2862[9] 3138[P] 4823[11] 5262[9]

Riddleofthesands (IRE) *Nigel Twiston-Davies* 101h 108c
10 bb g Oscar(IRE) Flaxen Pride (IRE) (Pips Pride)
(2615)
2699[2] 3156[4] (4352)
4723[4] 5065[6] 5487[6]

Riddlestown (IRE) *Caroline Fryer* 103h 114c
7 b g Cloudings(IRE) Gandi's Dream (IRE) (Commanche Run)
1061[5] 1306[4] **1518[5] 1629[4] (1914)**
2067[F] 2431[2] 2897[3] 3151[4] 3473[5] **4109[P] 4482[7]**
4759[3] ◆ (5009) (5247)
5515[2]

Ride The Range (IRE) *Chris Grant* 114h
5 bb g High Chaparral(IRE) Jade River (FR) (Indian River (FR))
2499[5] 3042[4] 3619[4] 4429[3] 4811[2] 5160[2]

Rifleman (IRE) *Richard Lee* 84h 82c
14 ch g Starborough En Garde (USA) (Irish River (FR))
248[5] 522[5] 690[11] **1103[6] 1344[2] 1548[6] 1825[2] 2702[3]**

Rifle Shot (IRE) *Donald McCain* 106h 72c
7 bb g Indian River(FR) Ravaleen (IRE) (Executive Perk)
808[8] **1133[9]**
1315[P]

Rigadin De Beauchene (FR) *Venetia Williams* 103h 150c
9 bb g Visionary(FR) Chipie D'Angron (FR) (Grand Tresor (FR))
(4270)
5276[P] 5571[P]

Rightdownthemiddle (IRE) *Michael Mulvany* 129h
6 b g Oscar(IRE) Alternative Route (IRE) (Needle Gun (IRE))
5200a[5]

Rightonthyme *Tom Symonds* 53h
7 b m Milan Four Thyme (Idiots Delight)
2190[10] 2536[8]

Right Step *Pat Phelan* 113h
7 b g Xaar Maid To Dance (Pyramus (USA))
1943[4] 3322[5] 3648[5] 4726[3] 5067[7]

Right Stuff (FR) *Gary Moore* 114h
11 bb g Dansili Specificity (USA) (Alleged (USA))
419[4]

Right To Rule (IRE) *Donald McCain* 98h
5 b g Rock Of Gibraltar(IRE) Epistoliere (IRE) (Alzao (USA))
3288[10] 3659[5] 4189[P] 4817[3] 5282[7]

Rigid *Tony Carroll* 94h
7 ch g Refuse To Bend(IRE) Supersonic (Shirley Heights)
505[F] 1058[4] 2090[6] 2291[11] 2898[8]

Rigidity *Tim Vaughan* 117h 116c
7 b g Indian Ridge Alakananda (Hernando (FR))
77[P] 762[4]

Rigolo Ville (FR) *Richard Hobson* 101h
9 gr g Visionary(FR) Imperatrice Ville (FR) (Seurat)
1580[7] 2105[5] 2353[4] (2690) 2980[8]

Riguez Dancer *Donald McCain* 105h 122c
10 b g Dansili Tricoteuse (Kris)
1923[7] 2421[7] 2820[6] 3478[4] 4696[5] 5356[8]

Rime Avec Gentil (FR) *Bernard Llewellyn* 101h 108c
9 b g Kapgarde(FR) Quenice (FR) (Quart De Vin (FR))
(251) (371) 756[4] 831[4] 973[2] 1173[3] 1345[5]
1596[4]

Ringa Bay *David Bridgwater* 124c
9 ch g Karinga Bay Redgrave Wolf (Little Wolf)
2041[5] 2394[6] 2512[3] (3504)
3717[4] 4026[P] 4396[U] 4798[P]

Ring Bo Ree (IRE) *Tom George* 100h 109c
11 b g Topanoora La Ronde (Common Grounds)
1666[P] 1886[3] 2194[5] 2911[2] 4109[P] 5394[5]

Ring Eye (IRE) *John O'Shea* 100h
6 b g Definite Article Erins Lass (IRE) (Erins Isle)
5140[8]

Rinnagree Rosie *Lucy Normile* 98h
8 gr m Silver Patriarch(IRE) Gretton (Terimon)
3208[4] (3495) 3934[3] 4649[6]

Rio De Sivola (FR) *Nick Williams* 100h 123c
5 bl g Caballo Raptor(CAN) Pierrebrune (FR) (Cadoudal (FR))
1465a[5] 1742[8] (2601)
3183[2] 3732[3]

Rio Milan (IRE) *Fergal O'Brien* 113h 104c
8 b g Milan Lady Medina (IRE) (Be My Native (USA))
1937[3] 2768[2] 3189[4]
3436[3] 4596[4] 4903[9] **5032[7]**

Rior (IRE) *Paul Henderson* 105h
7 b g King's Theatre(IRE) Sara's Gold (IRE) (Ashkalani (IRE))
563[6] 1941[6] 2314[3] (2908) 3186[F] 4538[5] 5128[10] 5457[4]

Rio Tinto (FR) *J Follain* 104c
9 b g Le Balafre(FR) Ikeya Des Salines (FR) (Le Nain Jaune (FR))
855a[5]

Riptide *Michael Scudamore* 104h 87c
8 b g Val Royal(FR) Glittering Image (IRE) (Sadler's Wells (USA))
2902[P]

Riquet The King (FR) *Alan Brown* 81b
5 b g Laveron Brave Chartreuse (FR) (Villez (USA))
4895[10] 5166[3]

Rise Before Dawn (IRE) *M Kehoe*
7 b g Millenary Valparisa (FR) (Priolo (USA))
5248[P]

Rise To Glory (IRE) *Shaun Harris*
6 b h King's Best(USA) Lady At War (Warning)
1399[P]

Rising Teal *Lucy Wadham* 103h
5 b m Phoenix Reach(IRE) Tealby (Efisio)
35[8] 2317[4] 2697[2] 3247[3] 4074[3] 4472[P] 5245[4]

Risk (IRE) *Miss A Goschen* 18h 109c
11 ch g Acatenango(GER) Belua (GER) (Lomitas)
481[4] 656[6] 4727[11]

Riskier *John Wade* 104h 132c
9 gr g Kier Park(IRE) Risky Girl (Risk Me (FR))
(282)
(1753) 2448[6] 2972[5] 3634[3] 4627[2] 4941[6]

Rival D'Estruval (FR) *Pauline Robson* 135h 149c
9 b g Khalkevi(IRE) Kermesse d'Estruval (FR) (Cadoudal (FR))
3776[5]

Rivaliste (FR) *M Rolland* 99h 127c
9 b g Robin Des Champs(FR) Idomale (FR) (Dom Alco (FR))
838a[9] 5530a[3]

River Bollin *Tim Easterby* 88h
4 b g Bollin Eric Bollin Roberta (Bob's Return (IRE))
2160[4] 2960[5] 3721[3] 4005[2]

River Choice (FR) *Yannick Fouin* 116h 140c
11 ch g River Mist(USA) Noraca (FR) (Akarad (FR))
(1740a)
1984a[5] 2264a[4]

River Clare (IRE) *John O'Shea* 93h
6 br g Indian River(FR) Lakyle Lady (IRE) (Bob Back (USA))
3063[4] 3778[6] 4350[6] 4945[4]

River Dancing (IRE) *Andy Turnell* 95h
7 b g Muhtarram(USA) Peacefull River (IRE) (Over The River (FR))
631[10] 2906[5] 3290[5] 3959[P] 5034[7] 5395[9]

River Deep (IRE) *Philip Hobbs* 116h
5 ch g Mountain High(IRE) Testaway (IRE) (Commanche Run)
2375[3] (3508) 4763[5]

River D'Or (FR) *Sophie Leech* 106h 110c
9 b g Saint Preuil(FR) Une Pomme D'Or (FR) (Pot D'Or (FR))
265[4] 712[P] 871[7] 1959[6] 2290[5] 2923[P] 3277[4]

River Exit (IRE) *Nigel Twiston-Davies* 80h
7 b g Exit To Nowhere(USA) Kilbricken Sunset (IRE) (Over The River (FR))
116[9]

River Maigue (IRE) *Nicky Henderson* 140h
7 b g Zagreb(USA) Minor Tantrum (IRE) (Executive Perk)
2951[3] 3646[P]

Rivermouth *Laura Mongan* 71b
9 ch g Karinga Bay Rippling Brook (Phardante (FR))
5023[F]

River Purple *John Mackie* 105h 112c
7 b g Bollin Eric Cerise Bleue (FR) (Port Lyautey (FR))
201[4] 503[3] 730[7] 933[9] **2046[F]** 2787[5]
(3015) 3352[4] 4985[5] ◆ (5301)
5498[2]

River Rat *John Holt* 64h
7 bl m Erhaab(USA) River Ness (Buckskin (FR))
945[P]

River Sava (IRE) *Jamie Poulton* 84h
7 b g Zagreb(USA) Running Board (IRE) (Deep Run)
306[5]

Riverside Theatre *Nicky Henderson* 137h 164c
10 b g King's Theatre(IRE) Disallowed (IRE) (Distinctly North (USA))
(3032)
3262[U] 4265[6] 5138[9]

Road Show *Keith Goldsworthy* 64h
7 b g Sadler's Wells(USA) Danilova (USA) (Lyphard (USA))
140[13]

Road To Freedom *Lucy Wadham* 102h
5 b g Revoque(IRE) Go Classic (Classic Cliche (IRE))
4349[8] 4808[7] 5288[3]

Road To Riches (IRE) *Noel Meade* 110h 155c
7 b g Gamut(IRE) Bellora (IRE) (Over The River (FR))
2853a[3] ◆ 3308a[P] 3908a[4]

Roalco De Farges (FR) *Philip Hobbs* 119h 139c
9 gr g Dom Alco(FR) Vonaria (FR) (Vorias (USA))
4035[P] 4509[3] (4962)
5276[P] 5571[7]

Robbers Roost (IRE) *Tim Vaughan* 112h
6 b g Flemensfirth(USA) Chapel Queen (IRE) (Jolly Jake (NZ))
284[2] 2864[3] 3271[6] 4251[2] ◆ (4672) 5288[P]

Robber Stone *Debra Hamer* 83h
6 gr g Proclamation(IRE) Amiata (Pennekamp (USA))
631[P] 948[5] 1107[6] 1269[6] 1351[9]

Robbie *Keith Reveley* 133h 134c
10 b g Robellino(USA) Corn Lily (Aragon)
167[3] (425)
(2343) 3088[3]
3386[6] 3892[8]
4532[3] 4899[F] 5054[2] 5557[3]

Rob Conti (FR) *Philip Hobbs* 115h 136c
9 bb g Network(GER) Initiale Royale (FR) (Video Rock (FR))
11[5] 587[7] 996[8] 1201[2] 1337[2] 1476[2] 1686[2] 1969[2]
4355[4] 4705[4] 5094[2]
5346[7]

Roberto Goldback (IRE) *Nicky Henderson* 141h 156c
12 b g Bob Back(USA) Mandysway (IRE) (Mandalus)
2214[4] 2937[12] 3897[6] 4769[3] 5276[P]

Roberto Pegasus (USA) *Alan King* 120h
8 bb g Fusaichi Pegasus(USA) Louju (USA) (Silver Hawk (USA))
2492[6] 3031[7] 5003[4]

Robert's Well (FR) *J Planque*
9 b g Roman Saddle(IRE) Idole De Pont Kerlo (FR) (Quitte Et Passe I (FR))
855a[F]

Robin Brook (IRE) *Pam Sly* 22b
4 b f Robin Des Pres(FR) Gaybrook Girl (IRE) (Alderbrook)
4763[8]

Robin's Command (IRE) *Rose Dobbin* 86h 98c
7 gr g Tikkanen(USA) Marian's Wish (IRE) (Phardante (FR))
1982[10]
2356[5] 2737[5] 3020[5] 5355[2] (5483)

Robinsfirth (IRE) *Colin Tizzard* 114b
5 b g Flemensfirth(USA) Phardester (IRE) (Phardante (FR))
2216[4]

Robin The Rich (IRE) *Richard Guest* 71b
4 b g Robin Des Pres(FR) Maid Of Music (IRE) (Orchestra)
2960[10] 4986[9]

Robin Will (FR) *Richard Woollacott* 111h 104c
9 bl g Dark Moondancer Gleep Will (FR) (Laniste)
323[U] 1959[11] 2650[F] 3191[5] 3784[6] 5032[6] 5334[P]

Robobar (FR) *Jim Best* 108c
9 b g Passing Sale(FR) Carvine D'Or (FR) (Pot D'Or (FR))
(1300)
1336[4]

Roby De Cimbre (FR) *S Robinson* 118h 116c
11 gr g Myrakalu(FR) Belle De Liziere (FR) (Bojador (FR))
287[P]

Roc D'Apsis (FR) *Tom George* 115h 124c
5 gr g Apsis Rocapina (FR) (Solon (GER))
2295[3] 2601[2] (3113)
5511[2]

Roc De Guye (FR) *James Evans* 35h 119c
9 b g Video Rock(FR) Kasibelle De Guye (FR) (Scooter Bleu (IRE))
65[4] 489[3] 600[5] 805[3] (1260)
(1577) (1798)
2067[4] 2895[2] (5193)
(5450)

Roc De Prince *James Ewart* 102h
5 b g Shirocco(GER) Louella (USA) (El Gran Senor (USA))
(732) 2968[7] 4234[9] 5212[P]

Rockabilly Riot (IRE) *Martin Todhunter* 102h
4 br g Footstepsinthesand Zawariq (IRE) (Marju (IRE))
(3516) 4548[5] 4939[3]

Rock A Doodle Doo (IRE) *Sally Hall* 121h
7 b g Oratorio(IRE) Nousaiyra (IRE) (Be My Guest (USA))
732[3] 1924[7] 2225[4] ◆ 3390[10] 4476[3] 4889[2] 5061[2]

Rockawango (FR) *James Ewart* 128h 130c
8 b g Okawango(USA) Janou La Belle (FR) (Shining Steel)
(2418)
3202[5] 4235[F] 4367[P] 4833[4] 4955[P] 5210[F]

Rockchasebullett (IRE) *Fergal O'Brien* 108h 121c
6 b g Catcher In The Rye(IRE) Last Chance Lady (IRE) (Mister Lord (USA))
1664[4]
1939[11] (2293)
2599[4] 4908[2] 5533[P]

Rock Climber (IRE) *Y-M Porzier* 97c
6 b g Poliglote Hidden Silver (Anabaa (USA))
559a[8]

Rock Diamond (IRE) *Brendan Powell* 16h
4 b f Rock Of Gibraltar(IRE) Yaky Romani (IRE) (Victory Note (USA))
3857[6]

Rockers Field (IRE) *B A Furnival* 40h 34c
12 bb g Insatiable(IRE) Princess Douglas (Bishop Of Orange)
3862[P] 4922[7]

Rocket Scientist *Colin Tizzard* 90h
5 gr g Proclamation(IRE) Motown Melody (IRE) (Detroit Sam (FR))
3363[8] *4017*[12] 4988[6] 5305[9]

Rocking Blues (FR) *Rose Dobbin* 112h 116c
9 b g Lavirco(GER) Herbe De La Roque (FR) (Courtroom (FR))
2034[2]
2446[F] 3039[4] 3395[2] 4080[3] (4551)
4898[P]

Rockingtimes (IRE) *Henry Oliver* 45h
6 b g Golan(IRE) Native Wonder (IRE) (Good Thyne (USA))
716[7] 1019[7]

Rockiteer (IRE) *Henry Daly* 125h 140c
11 b g Rudimentary(USA) Party Woman (IRE) (Sexton Blake)
334[4] 757[2] 1060[6] (1470)
1815[2] (4922)
(5232)

Rock Me Zippo (IRE) *Sean Curran* 79h
6 b g Millenary Babylonia (IRE) (Be My Guest (USA))
5288[4] 5541[6]

Rock On Bollinski *Tim Fitzgerald* 97b
4 b g Bollin Eric Bred For Pleasure (Niniski (USA))
3214[2] 4043[5] 4986[5]

Rock On Rocky *Matt Sheppard* 116h
6 b g Overbury(IRE) Tachometer (IRE) (Jurado (USA))
4030[5] 4417[4] 4728[9] 5016[4] 5175[2] 5547[2]

Rock On Ruby (IRE) *Harry Fry* 170h 152c
9 b g Oscar(IRE) Stony View (IRE) (Tirol)
1989[2]
(3135) (4101)
4737[8] 5134[2]

Rock Peak (IRE) *Bernard Llewellyn* 70h
9 b g Dalakhani(IRE) Convenience (IRE) (Ela-Mana-Mou)
1700[8] 2090[5]

Rock Relief (IRE) *Chris Grant* 124h
8 gr g Daylami(IRE) Sheer Bliss (IRE) (Sadler's Wells (USA))
2230[P] 2821[8] 3108[7] 3724[2] 4670[5] 5054[3]

Rockshandy (IRE) *Patrick Neville* 122h 123c
8 b g Anshan Gaelic Leader (IRE) (Supreme Leader)
1959[U]

Rock The Kasbah (IRE) *Philip Hobbs* 97b
4 ch g Shirocco(GER) Impudent (IRE) (In The Wings)
5181[2]

Rock This Town (IRE) *Brendan W Duke* 36b
5 b g Kutub(IRE) Davis Rock (Rock City)
5424a[10]

Rockweiller *Steve Gollings* 64h
7 b g Rock Of Gibraltar(IRE) Ballerina Suprema (IRE) (Sadler's Wells (USA))
3469[P]

Rockyaboya (IRE) *W P Mullins* 137h 137c
10 ch g Rock Hopper Motility (IRE) (Yashgan)
2708a[4]

Rocky Bender (IRE) *Venetia Williams* 96h 111c
9 b g Saddlers' Hall(IRE) Silver Spirit (IRE) (Parliament)
2041[6] 2691[6]
3193[3] 3691[P] 4176[2] 4678[6] 5004[2] 5129[2] 5515[5]

Rocky Creek (IRE) *Paul Nicholls* 142h 164c
8 b g Dr Massini(IRE) Kissantell (IRE) (Broken Hearted)
2815[2] 3888[2] 5171[5]

Rocky Elsom (USA) *David Arbuthnot* 110h 99c
7 b g Rock Of Gibraltar(IRE) Bowstring (IRE) (Sadler's Wells (USA))
2007[7] 2469[8] 3152[P]

Rocky Island (IRE) *Jennie Candlish* 88h 85c
6 b g Heron Island(IRE) Loury The Louse (IRE) (Hollow Hand)
1924[11] 2189[10] 2493[11] 5191[P] 5515[4]

Rocky Rebel *Chris Bealby* 108h 56c
6 b g Norse Dancer(IRE) Gulchina (USA) (Gulch (USA))
202[8] 786[4]
898[9] 1092[2]

Rocky Ryan (IRE) *Jim Best* 99h
11 b g Even Top(IRE) The Dara Queen (IRE) (Dara Monarch)
241[F] 965[P]

Rocky Stone (IRE) *Donald McCain* 99h 13c
6 b g Cloudings(IRE) Crandon Park (Sir Harry Lewis (USA))
2422[6] 2866[3] 3061[9] 3330[3] (3824) 4461[8] 4774[9]
(5283)

Rocky Wednesday (IRE) *Gordon Elliott* 133h 94c
7 b g Rock Of Gibraltar(IRE) Tuesday Morning (Sadler's Wells (USA))
3910a[22] 5172[15]

Rody (FR) *Tom George* 118h 143c
9 ch g Colonel Collins(USA) Hamelie II (FR) (Dress Parade)
2816[4] ◆ 3660[P] 3894[P] 4414[8] 5120[3] 5389[F]

Roger Beantown (IRE) *Zoe Davison* 111h 133c
9 b g Indian Danehill(IRE) Best Wait (IRE) (Insan (USA))
394[4] (806) ◆ 1049[2] 2287[5] 2928[2] 3259[6]
4036[3] 4684[3] 5456[5]

Rogue Angel (IRE) *M F Morris* 135h 143c
6 b g Presenting Carrigeen Kohleria (IRE) (Luso)
2258a[3] 3791a[4] 4741[7] 5099a[4] 5474a[16]

Rogue Dancer (FR) *Michael Banks* 51h
9 b g Dark Moondancer Esperanza IV (FR) (Quart De Vin (FR))
30[P] 265[P]

Roi De Garde (FR) *Chris Bealby* 85h 106c
8 b g Kapgarde(FR) Belle Du Roi (FR) (Adieu Au Roi (IRE))
32[8]

Roi Du Mee (FR) *Gordon Elliott* 145h 164c
9 b g Lavirco(GER) British Nellerie (FR) (Le Pontet (FR))
1776a[F] 1951a[2] (2234a)
2673[P] 4183a[7] 4435a[P] 5082a[4]

Roi Du Tango (FR) *J Bigot*
8 b g My Risk(FR) Faine (FR) (Fijar Tango (FR))
1740a[P] 2384a[P]

Roisini Bay (IRE) *Richenda Ford*
10 b g Saddlers' Hall(IRE) Zuhal (Busted)
485[P] 1701[P] 2619[F]

Roja Dove (IRE) *Neil King* 122h
5 b m Jeremy(USA) Knight's Place (IRE) (Hamas (IRE))
2205a[2] 3005[5] 3423[7] 4531[F] 5368[8]

Rojo Vivo *Henry Hogarth* 112h 68c
8 b g Deploy Shareef Walk (Shareef Dancer (USA))
4082[5] 4773[U]

Rolanta (FR) *James Frost* 78h
9 b m Maresca Sorrento(FR) Gazelle De Sou (FR) (Ajdayt (USA))
635[5] ◆ 1106[F]

Rolecarr (IRE) *Ann Hamilton* 119h 137c
11 b g Tragic Role(USA) Nuit D'Ete (USA) (Super Concorde (USA))
170[6] 448[7] 2358[5] 2972[3] 3526[2] 3725[4]

Rolling Aces (IRE) *Paul Nicholls* 130h 157c
8 b g Whitmore's Conn(USA) Pay Roll (IRE) (Roselier (FR))
(2235a)
2930[2] 4265[P] 5155[2] 5569[4]

Rolling Dough (IRE) *Sophie Leech* 84h
6 b m Indian Danehill(IRE) High Dough (IRE) (High Roller (IRE))
187[6] 717[11] 1731[P] 2886[2] (3157) 5490[3]

Rolling Maul (IRE) *Peter Bowen* 128h
6 b g Oscar(IRE) Water Sports (IRE) (Marju (IRE))
(146) (644) ◆ 1863[5] 2103[4] 2385[2] 2806[2] 3130[5]

Rolling Star (FR) *Nicky Henderson* 153h
5 b g Smadoun(FR) Lyli Rose (FR) (Lyphard's Wish (FR))
(2669) 3200[11] 4147[17]

Roll On Has (FR) *J-P Gallorini* 139h
4 b f Policy Maker(IRE) Royale Lombok (FR) (Villez (USA))
2262a[3]

Roll On Ruby (IRE) *Alan Phillips* 101b
6 ch m Definite Article Barichara (FR) (Exit To Nowhere (USA))
(250) 5159[16]

Roll The Dice (IRE) *Philip Hobbs* 102h 116c
8 b g Oscar(IRE) Sallowglen Gale (IRE) (Strong Gale)
4502[4] 5121[P]

Roman Conquest *Seamus Mullins* 114h 120c
10 b g Roi De Rome(USA) Kellys Conquest (El Conquistador)
2460[P]

Roman Cruise *Peter Dowson* 84h 69c
11 ch g Roi De Rome(USA) Fair Cruise (Cruise Missile)
510[6]

Romanesco (FR) *Gordon Elliott* 104h 140c
9 b g Epistolaire(IRE) Kadrige (FR) (Video Rock (FR))
1168a[14] 1604a[14]

Roman Flight (IRE) *David Dennis* 135h
6 b g Antonius Pius(USA) Flight Sequence (Polar Falcon (USA))
1046[3] 2717[3] 2910[F] 4224[2] 4558[U] 4899[3] 5172[7]
5452[2]

Romantic Fashion (IRE) *Mrs Prunella Dobbs* 117h
7 b m Milan Valentine Gale (IRE) (Strong Gale)
3804a[3] 4365[4] (4668) 5255[6]

Romany Quest *Linda Blackford* 91h
7 b g Nomadic Way(USA) Dinkies Quest (Sergeant Drummer (USA))
3697[5] ◆ 4411[8] 5395[P]

Romany Ryme *George Bewley* 116h 88c
8 ch g Nomadic Way(USA) Rakaposhi Ryme (IRE) (Rakaposhi King)
2034[4] 2337[2] 3018[3] 3396[8] 3726[2] 4006[F] 4428[F]
5105[3] 5300[4]

Romney Marsh *Roger Curtis* 89h 83c
13 br m Glacial Storm(USA) Mirador (Town And Country)
478[4] 2008[11] 2312[13] 2896[5] 3553[0] 5069[P]

Ron *Jonjo O'Neill* 87h
6 ch g Dubai Destination(USA) Trew Class (Inchinor)
49[8] 252[8] 375[4]

Ronald Gee (IRE) *Jim Goldie* 82b
7 ch g Garuda(IRE) Panache Lady (IRE) (Cyrano De Bergerac)
1792[9]

Ronaldinho (IRE) *Alan King* 119h
4 b g Jeremy(USA) Spring Glory (Dr Fong (USA))
3364[4] ◆ 3885[5] 4345[3] 5090[3] 5568[8]

Ronaldo Des Mottes (FR) *David Pipe* 142h
9 b g Rifapour(IRE) Gemma (FR) (Djarvis (FR))
2951[9] 3200[5]

Ronnie Lawson (IRE) *John Ferguson* 98h
5 b g King's Theatre(IRE) Sarahs Quay (IRE) (Witness Box (USA))
2347[3] 2602[7] 4102[6]

Ronnie Rockcake *Ben Pauling* 65h
4 b g Tiger Hill(IRE) Vitesse (IRE) (Royal Academy (USA))
2436[4] 2830[7] *4296*[12] 4506[6] 4722[7] 5174[7]

Rons Dream *Peter Bowen* 95b
4 b f Kayf Tara Empress Of Light (Emperor Jones (USA))
3133[2] 3619[2] (4253) 4986[6]

Ron Waverly (IRE) *Pat Phelan* 78h
4 ch g Haatef(USA) Mermaid Beach (Slew O'Gold (USA))
1524[F] 1985[7]

Rooftop Rainbow (IRE) *Linda Blackford* 71h 97c
10 b g Lord Americo Rulleena (IRE) (Boreen (FR))
1320[P]

Roparta Avenue *Diana Grissell* 84h 93c
7 b g Nomadic Way(USA) Miss Fizz (Charmer)
308[U] 2582[4]
4451[P] 4716[4] 5113[4]

Rory's Brother (IRE) *Denis Gerard Hogan* 107h 109c
7 b g Rudimentary(USA) Dunany Star (IRE) (Salluceva)
5297[2]

Rosa Fleet (IRE) *Venetia Williams* 117h
6 b m Alflora(IRE) Crimond (IRE) (Zaffaran (USA))
2513[5] 3010[12] 3746[4] (4074) 4487[2] (4777) 5229[4]

Rosa Imperialis *Robert Walford* 72h
5 ch m Imperial Dancer Motcombe (IRE) (Carroll House)
3289[F] *4496*[4] 5002[4]

Ros Castle (IRE) *Rose Dobbin* 109h 125c
8 ch g Flemensfirth(USA) Castlehaven (IRE) (Erins Isle)
2421[2] 2971[5] 3498[4] 4236[4] 4900[P]

Roseini (IRE) *Tony Carroll* 89h 84c
8 b m Dr Massini(IRE) Deise Rose (IRE) (Glacial Storm (USA))
29[4] 264[13] 1582[6] 2312[12] 2699[3]

Roselaine (FR) *G Chaignon* 83c
9 b m Sleeping Car(FR) Solaine (FR) (Pot D'Or (FR))
2384a[4]

Roseneath (IRE) *Alex Hales* 70h 103c
10 b g Saddlers' Hall(IRE) Vital Approach (IRE) (Mandalus)
7[3] 461[7] 942[5] (1103)
2578[3] 2902[2] 3437[2] 3696[5] 4657[3] 5113[5]

Rose Of Marron (IRE) *John Upson* 65h
7 b g Dilshaan Sunset Park (IRE) (Red Sunset)
383[P] 1794[14] 2316[P] 2850[P] *4327*[8]

Rose Of The Moon (IRE) *David O'Meara* 130h 142c
9 gr g Moonax(IRE) Little Rose (IRE) (Roselier (FR))
2937[10] (3825)
5171[F] 5571[P]

Rose Of The World (IRE) *Jo Davis* 100b
6 ch m Vinnie Roe(IRE) Frankly Native (IRE) (Be My Native (USA))
2026[3] 3507[7]

Rose Pageant *Dan Skelton* 45b
5 ch m Loup Sauvage(USA) Realms Of Roses (Mister Baileys)
3181[9]

Rose Red *Rob Summers* 92h
7 ch m Weld Secret Whisper (Infantry)
268[7] 761[6] 1132[3] 1331[2] 1567[7] 2511[5] 2787[7]
3636[2]

Roses Legend *Reginald Brown* 87h 103c
9 b g Midnight Legend Graig Hill Rose (Rustingo)
175[5] 393[4]
646[3] 806[10] 965[5]
1172[10]

Roseville Cottage (IRE) *John Wade* 98h 99c
7 b g Kris Kin(USA) Johnny's Idea (IRE) (Woodborough (USA))
3824[8]
4940[3] 5301[P]

Rosewood Lad *J S Moore* 42h
7 ch g Needwood Blade Meandering Rose (USA) (Irish River (FR))
233[8]

Rosie Du Berlais (IRE) *Philip Kirby* 95c
8 ch m Beneficial Marina Du Berlais (FR) (Mister Sicy (FR))
(4617)
5062[F] 5164[U] 5485[4]

Rosie Probert *Nicky Henderson* 124h
5 b m Dylan Thomas(IRE) Corsican Sunset (USA) (Thunder Gulch (USA))
(477) 696[2] (1107) (1132) (2084) 2492[9] 2810[4]
3203[5]

Rosies Peacock *D H Llewellyn* 60b 108c
11 b g Peacock Jewel Final Rose (Derring Rose)
660[4]

Roskeen Boy (IRE) *Miss Louise Allan*
9 b g Oscar(IRE) Peptic Lady (IRE) (Royal Fountain)
3801[P]

Roslin Moss *Donald Whillans* 70h
8 ch g Loup Sauvage(USA) Etourdie (USA) (Arctic Tern (USA))
222[P]

Rosoff (IRE) *Laura Mongan* 82h 99c
12 b g New Frontier(IRE) Annida (IRE) (Torus)
489[7] 2568[6]
2727[5] 3139[P] 3692[10]

Rosquero (FR) *Robert Johnson* 86h 110c
9 ch g Blushing Flame(USA) Kingsgirl (FR) (Dom Alco (FR))
2444[P] 2736[7] 2869[6] 3270[5] 3723[3] (4366) 4836[5]
5213[5]

Rossa Parks (IRE) *Neil Mulholland* 113h 113c
8 b m Anshan Alshou (IRE) (Alzao (USA))
2424[2] (2632)
3033[4] 4637[5] 4840[P] 5437[3]

Rossbrin (IRE) *Anna Brooks* 78h 98c
9 b g Flemensfirth(USA) Mustard Mor (IRE) (Norwich)
7[8] 420[3] 713[5] 1538[9]
1798[P]

Rossington *John Wainwright* 70b
5 b g Gentleman's Deal(IRE) Ettrbee (IRE) (Lujain (USA))
1690[6] 2788[8] 3640[8]

Rossini's Dancer *N W Alexander* 95h 134c
9 b g Rossini(USA) Bint Alhabib (Nashwan (USA))
1654[5]
(1872) (2072)
2972[6] 3521[3] 4039[3] 5053[P] 5513[10]

Rosslyn Castle *Jonjo O'Neill* 111h
5 ch g Selkirk(USA) Margarula (IRE) (Doyoun)
507[3] 631[2] ◆ 856[P] 3163[11] 3802[7] 4305[4] (4674)
◆ 4818[3] 5217[3] 5493[2]

Rossmore Lad (IRE) *Charlie Longsdon* 120h 130c
9 bb g Beneficial Celestial Rose (IRE) (Roselier (FR))
190[3] 566[8] (763)

Rossoneri (IRE) *Nigel Twiston-Davies* 108h
7 b g Milan Native Crystal (IRE) (Be My Native (USA))
2393[2] 4574[6] 5408[P]

Rothman (FR) *Paul Nicholls* 65h
4 b g Michel Georges Bravecentadj (FR) (True Brave (USA))
5120[5]

Rotterdan (FR) *T Boivin*
9 b g Ultimately Lucky(IRE) Cowley Manor (USA) (Irish River (FR))
855a[F]

Roudoudou Ville (FR) *Victor Dartnall* 99h 145c
9 bb g Winning Smile(FR) Jadoudy Ville (FR) (Cadoudal (FR))
2940[4] 3786[P] 4674[P]
5261[4] 5535[2]

Rouge Et Blanc (FR) *Oliver Sherwood* 105h 134c
9 ch g Mansonnien(FR) Fidelety (FR) (Villez (USA))
2180[P] 2694[2] 2957[3] 3990[2] 4160[4] 4509[6]

Rough Fighter (USA) *Neil Mulholland* 103b
5 b g Mizzen Mast(USA) Louis D'Or (USA) (Mr Prospector (USA))
2724[3] *4017*[7] 5145[4]

Rough King (IRE) *Jennie Candlish* 35h
5 b g King's Theatre(IRE) Ringzar (IRE) (Shernazar)
4384[6]

Round The Horn (IRE) *Jim Old* 74h 52c
14 ch g Master Willie Gaye Fame (Ardross)
3798[P] 4779[5]

Round Tom (FR) *R Barber* 127h 117c
9 br g Sleeping Car(FR) Mamie Bleue (FR) (Air Du Nord (USA))
(180) **373[4]**

Rouquine Sauvage *Anthony Honeyball* 80h
6 ch m Loup Sauvage(USA) No Need For Alarm (Romany Rye)
(2022) 2745[2] 3507[6] 4467[P] 5547[11]

Roving Lad (IRE) *Paul John Gilligan* 84h 121c
7 b g Vinnie Roe(IRE) Pellerossa (IRE) (Good Thyne (USA))
1303[F] 4792[3]

Rowanna (IRE) *Colin Tizzard* 71h
6 b m Vinnie Roe(IRE) Baytrix (IRE) (Carroll House)
80[3] 522[11]

Rowan Road *Mrs D Walton* 85h 73c
10 gr m Minster Son Yemaail (IRE) (Shaadi (USA))
5062[3]

Rowlestone Lad *John Flint* 118h
7 b g Sulamani(IRE) Charmante Femme (Bin Ajwaad (IRE))
2085[2] 2698[3]

Roxy Beat *John Quinn* 70h
6 b m Beat All(USA) Roxy River (Ardross)
73[4]

Roxyfet (FR) *G Cherel* 110h 104c
4 b g Califet(FR) Roxalamour (FR) (Valanour (IRE))
262a[2]

Roxy Madam *Mandy Rowland* 54b
5 br m Generous(IRE) Masouri Sana (IRE) (Broken Hearted)
567[12] 2681[5]

Royal And Ancient (IRE) *David Thompson* 72h 91c
7 b g Danehill Dancer(IRE) Champaka (IRE) (Caerleon (USA))
17[P] **114[P]**

Royal Boy (FR) *Nicky Henderson* 150h 111c
7 bb g Lavirco(GER) Quintanilla (FR) (Royal Charter (FR))
2716[3] (3182) (3644)

Royal Caper *John Ryan* 45h
4 b g Royal Applause Ukraine (IRE) (Cape Cross (IRE))
1781[6]

Royal Caviar (IRE) *W P Mullins* 127b
6 b g Vinnie Roe(IRE) Blackwater Babe (IRE) (Arctic Lord)
3126a[2]

Royal Chatelier (FR) *Michael Blake* 99h 115c
9 b g Video Rock(FR) Attualita (FR) (Master Thatch)
2110[5] 2290[4] (2578)
2979[P] 3827[3] (3958)
4396[7] 4719[3]

Royal Deal *Michael Easterby* 104h
7 b g Gentleman's Deal(IRE) Royal Distant (USA) (Distant View (USA))
606[P] 876[10]

Royal Defence (IRE) *Mick Quinn* 98h
8 b g Refuse To Bend(IRE) Alessia (GER) (Warning)
266[U] 1269[4] 1533[3] 1913[2] 2430[P] 2581[7]

Royale Knight *Dr Richard Newland* 91h 133c
8 b g King's Theatre(IRE) Gardana (FR) (Garde Royale)
(248) **(495)**
◆ **642[3] 923[2] 1040[2] 1396[7]** 2458[9]
(2971) 3655[3] 4427[7] 4968[2] 5558[3]

Royale's Charter *Nick Williams* 119h 137c
8 ch g Karinga Bay Royale De Vassy (FR) (Royal Charter (FR))
1047[14] 1476[10] 1670[2] 2461[6]

Royal Fou (FR) *Patrice Quinton*
9 b g Le Balafre(FR) Grande Folie (FR) (Highlanders (FR))
1424a[3]

Royal Gig *Tim Etherington*
5 br m Val Royal(FR) Sainte Gig (FR) (Saint Cyrien (FR))
450[P]

Royal Guardsman (IRE) *Ali Brewer* 124h 127c
7 b g King's Theatre(IRE) Lisa Du Chenet (FR) (Garde Royale)
2434[2] 2928[4] ◆ **3386[4] 4806[U] 4932[3]**

Royal Irish Hussar (IRE) *Nicky Henderson* 138h
4 b c Galileo(IRE) Adjalisa (IRE) (Darshaan)
(1684) (2200) (2500) 3089[3] 4784[6]

Royal Kicks (FR) *Suzy Smith* 94h 112c
13 b g Garde Royale Al Kicks (FR) (Al Nasr (FR))
1768[F]

Royal Macnab (IRE) *Jamie Snowden* 108h
6 b g Beneficial Tina McBride (IRE) (Oscar (IRE))
47 2195[6] 2900[3] 4693[7] **5281[P]**

Royal Mile (IRE) *David Pipe* 76h 90c
10 br g Bob's Return(IRE) Country Style (Town And Country)
692[P]

Royal Moll (IRE) *W P Mullins* 109h
7 b m King's Theatre(IRE) Moll Bawn (IRE) (Presenting)
3380a[4]

Royal Native (IRE) *Anthony Honeyball* 116h
6 b g King's Theatre(IRE) Hollygrove Native (IRE) (Be My Native (USA))
1747[2] (2284) 2458[F] 2944[5] 3691[4]

Royal Opera *Stephen Hughes* 115h
6 b g Acclamation Desert Gold (IRE) (Desert Prince (IRE))
505[3] 784[2] 4599[P]

Royal Palladium (FR) *Venetia Williams* 102h
6 gr g King's Theatre(IRE) Dent Sucree (FR) (Turgeon (USA))
2189[4] 2509[5] 2808[4] 3061[8] 4761[2] 4933[7]

Royal Peak (IRE) *David Pipe* 101h
7 b g Bach(IRE) Dante's Ville (IRE) (Phardante (FR))
407[9] 924[9] (1170) 1259[2] (1320) 1339[4] 1631[7] 1829[5]

Royal Player *Philip Hobbs* 131h
5 b g King's Theatre(IRE) Kaydee Queen (IRE) (Bob's Return (IRE))
(3697) (4163) ◆ 4423[4] 5333[4]

Royalracket (IRE) *Paul Webber* 85h
6 b g Royal Anthem(USA) Allaracket (IRE) (The Parson)
2602[10] 3163[P] 4758[9] 5069[6]

Royalraise (IRE) *Oliver Sherwood* 90b
5 b g Royal Anthem(USA) Raise The Issue (IRE) (Galileo (IRE))
3863[7]

Royal Rationale (IRE) *David Pipe* 89h
10 b g Desert Prince(IRE) Logic (Slip Anchor)
176[11]

Royal Regatta (IRE) *Philip Hobbs* 130h
6 b g King's Theatre(IRE) Friendly Craic (IRE) (Mister Lord (USA))
(2103) ◆ (2850) 3454[5] 4789[10] 5349[P]

Royal Ripple (IRE) *Paul Henderson* 101h
6 ch g Royal Anthem(USA) Sparkling Opera (Orchestra)
1877[2] 2375[7] 2788[4] *4017[6]* 4808[4] 5257[7]

Royal Riviera *Nigel Twiston-Davies* 98h 113c
8 b g Nayef(USA) Miss Cap Ferrat (Darshaan)
1363[6] 1660[6] **1981[2] 2149[3] 2730[2] 3129[4] 3693[5]**
4067[2] 4486[8] (5039)

Royal Rojo *Chris Grant* 76b
5 ch g Prince Daniel(USA) Micklow Magic (Farfelu)
4976 790[13]

Royal Roo *Mark Rimell* 67b
5 b m Overbury(IRE) Royal Roxy (IRE) (Exit To Nowhere (USA))
3898[7] 5454[5]

Royal Salute *Anthony Honeyball* 45b
4 br g Flemensfirth(USA) Loxhill Lady (Supreme Leader)
5188[4]

Royal Sam (IRE) *Martin Todhunter* 82h 122c
9 ch g Bach(IRE) Dereenavurrig (IRE) (Lancastrian)
2224[4] 2517[4] 2971[P] 3283[4] 4086[4] 4771[3] 5299[P]

Royal Skies (IRE) *John Ferguson* 114h
4 b g Dubawi(IRE) Kalana (FR) (Rainbow Quest (USA))
3332[2] 4111[3]

Royal Supreme (IRE) *Alex Hales* 100b
4 br g Royal Anthem(USA) Supreme Baloo (IRE) (Supreme Leader)
(3926) 5173[18]

Royal Swain (IRE) *Anthony Honeyball* 48h
8 b g Val Royal(FR) Targhyb (IRE) (Unfuwain (USA))
849[6]

Royal Trooper (IRE) *Jim Best* 99h
8 b g Hawk Wing(USA) Strawberry Roan (IRE) (Sadler's Wells (USA))
1106[2] 1137[2] 1567[3] 2004[7]

Royal Vacation (IRE) *Colin Tizzard* 117b
4 b g King's Theatre(IRE) Summer Break (IRE) (Foxhound (USA))
4267[4] 4756[9]

Royaume Bleu (FR) *Alex Hales* 80h 106c
9 ch g Kapgarde(FR) Dear Blue (FR) (Cyborg (FR))
2023[3] 2829[F] 3277[3] (3688)
4066[3] 4471[U]
5011[9]

Roybuoy *Derrick Scott*
7 b g Royal Applause Wavy Up (IRE) (Brustolon)
175[P] 2478[P]

Roycano *Michael Easterby* 78h
4 ch g Lucarno(USA) Royal Distant (USA) (Distant View (USA))
2168[8] 2592[2]

Rozener (IRE) *Henry Hogarth* 92h
8 b g Moscow Society(USA) David's Lass (IRE) (Arctic Lord)
2520[4] 2748[8] 3600[9] 3828[P] 4938[5] 5494[15]

Rozolenn (FR) *Venetia Williams* 104h 91c
9 gr g Kaktoz D'Armor(FR) Belle Indifference (FR) (Kendor (FR))
1939[6] 2540[F] 2765[4]

Ruacana *John Ferguson* 139h 125c
5 b g Cape Cross(IRE) Farrfesheena (USA) (Rahy (USA))
2102[11] 2951[4] 3891[5] 4789[12]

Ruapehu (IRE) *Charles Whittaker* 115c
8 b g Presenting Silver Prayer (IRE) (Roselier (FR))
58[U] 2726[3] 3291[3] (5309)
(5390)

Ruaraidh Hugh (IRE) *Chris Bealby* 67h
5 b g Craigsteel Decent Shower (Decent Fellow)
4329[5] 5367[6]

Rubayat (IRE) *Yannick Fouin* 104h 75c
5 b g Kahyasi Operam (Kris)
2464a[7]

Rubber Bullet *Tim Etherington* 70b
6 b m Tikkanen(USA) Indiarubber (Barrys Gamble)
2841[0] 1499[P]

Ruben Cotter (IRE) *Paul Nicholls* 116h 141c
8 b g Beneficial Bonnie Thynes (IRE) (Good Thyne (USA))
2487[9] 2812[3] ◆

Ruberslaw *Iain Jardine*
8 b g Beat All(USA) Plus Tu Mets (FR) (Roi De Rome (USA))
3018[P] 3392[10] 3829[P] 4200[P]

Rubert (IRE) *Denis W Cullen* 96h 124c
11 b g Rudimentary(USA) Pharaway Stream (IRE) (Phardante (FR))
2410a[4]

Rubi Ball (FR) *W P Mullins* 141h 162c
9 ch g Network(GER) Hygie (FR) (Lute Antique (FR))
3376a[3]

Rubi Light (FR) *Robert Alan Hennessy* 130h 158c
9 b g Network(GER) Genny Lights (FR) (Lights Out (FR))
1776a[3] 2483a[6] 2991a[2] 3338a[6]

Rubin (CZE) *Martina Ruzickova*
12 b g Laten(CZE) Rubi (CZE) (Amyndas)
1904a[2]

Rubis D'Albain (FR) *Patrice Quinton*
9 b g Ragmar(FR) Celia De Toury (FR) (Royal Charter (FR))
199a[P]

Rubis De Reve (FR) *Robert Collet* 107h 98c
4 ch f Dream Well(FR) Rubilite (FR) (Indian River (FR))
615a[2]

Rubis Du Rheu (FR) *T Trapenard* 92c
5 b g Sin Kiang(FR) Venus Du Rheu (FR) (Bricassar (USA))
2464a[4]

Rubis Sur Ongle (FR) *G Cherel* 116h 140c
9 ch g Robin Des Champs(FR) Birgonde (FR) (Quart De Vin (FR))
1902a[P]

Rubrics (IRE) *Donald McCain*
5 gr g High Chaparral(IRE) Inner Strength (FR) (Take Risks (FR))
647[P]

Ruby Bay (IRE) *Tim Walford* 91h 99c
9 ch g Beneficial Ruby Supreme (IRE) (Supreme Leader)
2877[2] 3040[2] **3275[3]**

Ruby Crown *Kim Bailey* 107h
12 b m Rakaposhi King Suilven (Teenoso (USA)) (423)

Ruby Glow *Seamus Mullins* 108h
6 b m Septieme Ciel(USA) Ruby Too (El Conquistador)
2463[2] 3117[P] 5018[2] 5427[3]

Ruby Haze *Phillip Dando*
7 ch m Dreams End Kristal Haze (Krisinsky (USA))
841[12]

Ruby Mac (IRE) *Tony Carroll* 30h
6 b m Flemensfirth(USA) Macaw-Bay (IRE) (Strong Gale)
2981[7] 3818[5]

Rubyminx *Lynn Siddall*
8 b m Grape Tree Road Windfola (Sovereign Water (FR))
4743[P] 5103[P]

Ruby's From Milan (IRE) *Mark Shears* 77b
6 b m Milan Rubita (IRE) (Good Thyne (USA))
842[6] 1016[7] 5029[P]

Ruby Valentine (FR) *Jim Wilson* 77h 58c
11 b m Kayf Tara A Ma Valentine (FR) (Caerwent)
188[7] 925[11] 1860[3] (2571) 4972[6] 5282[8]

Rudemeister (IRE) *Lucinda Russell* 118h 126c
8 b g Rudimentary(USA) Boardroom Belle (IRE) (Executive Perk)
312[3] 579[F] (1750)
1923[4] 3759[P] 4900[6] 5497[P]

Rudigreen (IRE) *Noel Quinlan* 123h 120c
11 b g Rudimentary(USA) Green Avenue (IRE) (Satco (FR))
(77) **709[4]**
873[3] 930[5] (1174)
(1274) 1325[2] 1403[3] 1549[6]

Rudinero (IRE) *Barry Brennan* 20h 23c
12 gr g Rudimentary(USA) Cash Chase (IRE) (Sexton Blake)
100[5] 4759[P]

Ruff Luck *Seamus Mullins* 49h
4 b f Lucarno(USA) Ruffie (IRE) (Medicean)
1271[5] 1439[U] 1524[6]

Rufino (IRE) *P J Rothwell* 103h
4 ch g Presenting Hushaby (IRE) (Eurobus)
5424a[7]

Rugged Jack (FR) *Victor Dartnall* 114h
7 b g Bonbon Rose(FR) A Plus Ma Puce (FR) (Turgeon (USA))
2509[3] 3173[7] 3783[2] (4604) 4760[12] (4887) 5033[3] 5335[7] 5537[2]

Rule Of Thumb *Paul Henderson* 106h
6 b g Tobougg(IRE) Carreamia (Weldnaas (USA))
1749[7] 2109[5] 2573[4] (3029)

Ruler Of All (IRE) *Peter Winks* 133h 101c
8 b g Sadler's Wells(USA) Shabby Chic (USA) (Red Ransom (USA))
216[11] 447[2] 480[2] 734[3] 850[5] 2102[6] 2372[6] 2668[2] 3088[10]

Rule The World *M F Morris* 163h
7 b g Sulamani(IRE) Elaine Tully (IRE) (Persian Bold)
2855a[4] 3374a[2] (3790a) 4767[6]

Rum And Butter (IRE) *Jonjo O'Neill* 145h 138c
6 b g Milan Silent Valley (Forzando)
486[4] 719[2] (1054) (1350) 1485[2] 1954[2] 4789[23]

Rumbavu (IRE) *Robert Waley-Cohen* 102c
8 br g Overbury(IRE) Strong Swimmer (IRE) (Black Minstrel)
658[12]

Rumble Of Thunder (IRE) *Philip Kirby* 133h
8 b g Fath(USA) Honey Storm (IRE) (Mujadil (USA))
216[4] 901[U] 3477[12] 3832[5] (4058) 4306[2] 4897[2] 5277[2]

Rumbury Grey *S Flook* 127c
11 gr g Overbury(IRE) Polly Buckrum (Buckley)
(59) **357[2]**
660[5]

Rum Ginney *K F Clutterbuck* 59h
6 b m Carnival Dancer Silent Gem (Bijou D'Inde)
319[3] 593[8]

Rumpleteazer (IRE) *Shaun Harris* 77h
6 b g Oscar(IRE) Fleeting Arrow (IRE) (Commanche Run)
828[11] 1393[3]

Run Along Boy *Miss H Cumbley* 113h 118c
9 b g Beat All(USA) Gunner Be Good (Gunner B)
286[4] 714[2] 871[P] 1153[3] 1306[3] (1860)
5346[P]

Run Brave Run (IRE) *Martin Todhunter* 47h
6 b g Generous(IRE) Running Wild (IRE) (Anshan)
584[10] 1853[11]

Rundell *D T Hughes* 119h
4 b g Notnowcato Shardette (IRE) (Darshaan)
5470a[10]

Running Brook (IRE) *R Mike Smith* 26b
7 b g Alderbrook May As Well (Kemal (FR))
2420[P]

Running Bull (IRE) *Linda Jewell*
4 b g Papal Bull Miss Barbados (IRE) (Hawk Wing (USA))
1271[P]

Running On Faith *Garry Woodward*
6 b g Phoenix Reach(IRE) Amazing Grace Mary (Dancing Spree (USA))
2432[P]

Run On Sterling *Paul Webber* 104h
5 b g Dr Fong(USA) Dansara (Dancing Brave (USA))
2759[6] 4810[2] ◆ (5447)

Run Rabbit Run *Tim McCarthy* 71h
6 b g Hurricane Run(IRE) Triple Gold (IRE) (Goldmark (USA))
4758[14] 5236[P]

Run Ructions Run (IRE) *Tim Easterby* 131h
5 b m Westerner Perfect Prospect (IRE) (Golan (IRE))
324[2] 2196[2] (2514) 2883[2] (3329) 3818[2] (4305) (4961) 5368[5]

Runswick Days (IRE) *John Wade* 88h 86c
7 b g Presenting Miss Lauren Dee (IRE) (Montelimar (USA))
173[11] 1792[10] 2030[7] 2823[7] 3826[10] 4223[3] 4461[6]
4940[5]

Runswick Relax *John Wade* 84h 75c
8 ch g Generous(IRE) Zany Lady (Arzanni)
473[7] 2339[P] 3925[6] 5055[P]

Runswick Royal (IRE) *Ann Hamilton* 144h 137c
5 ch g Excellent Art Renada (Sinndar (IRE))
2344[6] 2669[3] 3088[9] 3477[4] 4056[F] (4237) 4785[P]

Run With The Wind (IRE) *Michael Hourigan* 136h 128c
8 b g Sadler's Wells(USA) Race The Wild Wind (USA) (Sunny's Halo (CAN))
1804a[5]

Ruperra Tom *Sophie Leech* 95b
6 b g Kayf Tara Cathy's Dream (IRE) (Husyan (USA))
1138[6] 1353[5]

Rupert Bear *James Walton* 114h 112c
8 b g Rambling Bear Glittering Stone (Dancing High)
2159[5] ◆ **3039[5] 3524[4] 4084[4]** 4836[6]

Ruse Des Planches (FR) *P Chemin* 132c
9 b g Goldneyev(USA) Boute Selle (FR) (Alycos (FR))
131a[3]

Russborough (FR) *Venetia Williams* 107h 92c
5 b g Turgeon(USA) Heritage River (FR) (Kaldounevees (FR))
4832[3] 5486[5]

Russe Blanc (FR) *Richard Lee* 98h 113c
7 wh g Machiavellian Tsar(FR) Fleur De Mad (FR) (Maiymad)
2155[3] (2772)
3190[3] 3785[P] 4626[2] 5247[2]

Russett Star *Charlie Longsdon*
6 ch m Midnight Legend Apple Anthem (True Song)
3840[P]

Russian Conquest *Seamus Mullins* 54h 98c
8 gr g Baryshnikov(AUS) Kellys Conquest (El Conquistador)
175[7] 632[4] 807[4]

Russian George (IRE) *Steve Gollings* 63h
8 ch g Sendawar(IRE) Mannsara (IRE) (Royal Academy (USA))
2903[6]

Russian Song (IRE) *Fiona Shaw* 105h 71c
10 b g Moscow Society(USA) Sweet Charm (IRE) (Glacial Storm (USA))
518[6] 690[12] 4275[11] 4729[9] 4933[9]

Russian War (IRE) *Gordon Elliott* 144h 128c
11 b g Moscow Society(USA) Oneofmegirls (IRE) (Supreme Leader)
733[2] 869[4]

Russie With Love *Chris Down* 108h
8 b m Alflora(IRE) Vieille Russie (Kenmare (FR))
12[4] 379[4] 811[6] 2477[3] 3731[P] 5391[P]

Rustic John *H Edward Haynes* 30c
14 ch g Afzal Spartiquick (Spartan General)
63[U] 976[P] 1104[6]

Rusty Nail (IRE) *James Frost* 58h 76c
9 b g Tikkanen(USA) Aoki (IRE) (Roselier (FR))
631[11] 875[7] **921[6]** 1191[8]
1644[2] 2441[4] 3048[3] 5394[7]

Rutherglen *John Quinn* 132h
4 b g Tiger Hill(IRE) Hanella (IRE) (Galileo (IRE))
(2750) ◆ (3224) (3474) 4784[5]

Ruttan Lake (IRE) *Tim Vaughan* 81h 100c
11 b g Winged Love(IRE) Crossmacahilly (IRE) (Executive Perk)
868[4]

Rydalis (FR) *Venetia Williams* 109h 127c
9 b m Kapgarde(FR) Fleurissa (FR) (Dress Parade)
2283[2] 2468[2] 3158[2] 3293[4] 3730[3] (4244)
4572[3]

Ryde By Knight *Nicky Henderson* 88b
6 b g Grape Tree Road Knight Ryde (Broadsword (USA))
4810[7]

Rydon Pynes *Martin Hill* 132h
6 b g Beat All(USA) Persian Smoke (Persian Bold)
(2279) 4144[2] 4786[F] 5333[3] (5544)

Rye Tangle (IRE) *Sophie Leech* 92b
6 br g Catcher In The Rye(IRE) Kadarassa (IRE) (Warning)
944[10] 1264[5] 1595[P]

Ryton Runner (IRE) *Lucinda Russell* 104h
6 b g Sadler's Wells(USA) Love For Ever (IRE) (Darshaan)
310[8] 867[6] 958[3] 1164[5] 3520[3] (4461) 4814[3] 5514[9] 5559[6]

Ryvalo Des Brosses (FR) *Jean-Paul Gasnier* 100c
9 b g Passing Sale(FR) Idole Des Brosses (FR) (Port Etienne (FR))
855a[6]

Sablazo (FR) *Andy Turnell* 77h 87c
8 b g Ragmar(FR) Daytona II (FR) (Video Rock (FR))
1121[P]
(2727) 3248[U] 3687[2] 4416[2] 5027[5] 5115[3]

Sab Le Beau (FR) *Alan Brown* 39h
5 b g Sabiango(GER) La Peliniere (FR) (Mansonnien (FR))
389[8] 5448[4]

Sable Des Ongrais (FR) *P Chemin* 131h 127c
10 b g Marchand De Sable(USA) Krasnoyarsk (FR) (Zilzal (USA))
2465a[2]

Sacramento King (IRE) *Jonathan Geake* 100h
5 gr g Desert King(IRE) Kindle Ball (FR) (Kaldounevees (FR))
3182[6] 5088[7] 5486[4]

Sacred Mountain *James Walton* 27h 103c
13 b g Primitive Rising(USA) Gone Astray (The Parson)
4239[5] 4837[5] (5164)

Sacre Toi (FR) *James Ewart* 96h 131c
8 b g Network(GER) Magicielle (FR) (Video Rock (FR))
2751[4] 3021[5] 3398[9]

Saddle Pack (IRE) *James Walton* 88h 104c
11 b g Saddlers' Hall(IRE) Zuhal (Busted)
583[6] 2597[7]
3833[P] 4080[7]

Saddlers Deal (IRE) *Chris Grant* 85h 94c
9 b g Saddlers' Hall(IRE) Native Deal (IRE) (Be My Native (USA))
343[6] 864[8] 1075[3]

Saddlers Encore (IRE) *Philip Hobbs* 126h
5 br g Presenting Saddlers Leader (IRE) (Saddlers' Hall (IRE))
2667[5] 3863[8] 4280[P] (4993) (5332)

Saddlers Mot *Karen Tutty* 100h 87c
10 b m Saddlers' Hall(IRE) Be My Mot (IRE) (Be My Native (USA))
(17) 222[4] 750[2] 1205[3] 1506[7] 1874[2] 2596[2] 4938[6] 5106[5] 5298[2]

Sadler'Sflaure (FR) *N Bertran De Balanda* 128c
8 b g Ballingarry(IRE) Flaurella (FR) (Rose Laurel)
1902a[8]

Sadler's Risk (IRE) *Henry De Bromhead* 150h 150c
6 b g Sadler's Wells(USA) Riskaverse (USA) (Dynaformer (USA))
4752[17]

Sadler's Star (GER) *Michael Blake* 107h 108c
11 b g Alwuhush(USA) Sadlerella (IRE) (King's Theatre (IRE))
44[7] 238[6] 636[5] 778[5] 976[5] 1272[2] 1548[2] (1644) 1798[3] 1988[5]

Sadma *John Ferguson* 95h
5 gr g Street Cry(IRE) Blue Dress (USA) (Danzig (USA))
2858[6] 3134[9]

Sadyjaune (FR) *E Lecoiffier* 103c
8 b m Califet(FR) Ladyjaune (FR) (Turgeon (USA))
1464a[4] 1984a[10] 2415a[P]

Safari Adventures (IRE) *Richard A Thomas* 99b
12 b g King's Theatre(IRE) Persian Walk (FR) (Persian Bold)
4355[P]

Safari Journey (USA) *Lucinda Egerton* 113h 113c
10 ch g Johannesburg(USA) Alvernia (USA) (Alydar (USA))
4579[2]
5058[5] 5357[4]

Safe Home (IRE) *John Quinn* 75h
4 ch g Danehill Dancer(IRE) In Safe Hands (IRE) (Intikhab (USA))
4772[5]

Safe Investment (USA) *Lawney Hill* 95h 95c
10 b g Gone West(USA) Fully Invested (USA) (Irish River (FR))
1103[5] 1274[2] (1435)
1530[4] 1629[P] 2067[6] 3468[P]

Safferano (IRE) *Tim Vaughan* 92h
8 b g Saffron Walden(FR) Paryiana (IRE) (Shernazar)
1339[5] (1824) 2016[9] (2575) 5432[P]

Saffron Park *Anna Newton-Smith* 48h
5 ch g Compton Place Beacon Silver (Belmez (USA))
308[P]

Saffron Prince *David Bridgwater* 108h
6 b g Kayf Tara Jan's Dream (IRE) (Executive Perk)
2083[5] 2564[2] 2858[3] *4018[7]* 4350[4] 4801[B]

Saffron Wells (IRE) *Neil King* 133h
6 b g Saffron Walden(FR) Angel's Folly (Wesaam (USA))
1771[6] 3148[2] 3816[2] ◆ (4076) 4251[3] 4680[2]

Safran De Cotte (FR) *Henry Daly* 129h 131c
8 gr g Dom Alco(FR) Vanille De Cotte (FR) (Italic (FR))
2841[3] 3205[P] 3655[6] 4427[4]

Saga De Tercey (FR) *Donald McCain* 123h
9 b g Sagacity(FR) Fanciulla Del West (USA) (Manila (USA))
110[4] 503[5] 804[6] 1018[P]

Saga Mome (FR) *L Viel* 100h 103c
8 b m Indian River(FR) Belle Momme (FR) (Grand Tresor (FR))
838a[P]

Sagliere *John Wade* 66b
9 gr g Sagamix(FR) D'Egliere (FR) (Port Etienne (FR))
1976[P]

Sagredo (USA) *Jonjo O'Neill* 114h 120c
10 b g Diesis Eternity (Suave Dancer (USA))
902[2] 1062[6] **1346[5] 1503[2] 1670[6] 1886[P]**

Sahrati *Michael Blake* 102h 102c
10 ch g In The Wings Shimna (Mr Prospector (USA))
650[6] 1109[5] 1275[10]

Sail And Return *Phil Middleton* 123h 117c
10 b g Kayf Tara Maidwell (Broadsword (USA))
121[2] (393) (659) 780[6] **861[F] 963[2] 1594[4]** 1628[6]
1916[3] 3603[10] 4968[4] 5373[3]

Sail By The Sea (IRE) *David Pipe* 138h
6 b g Heron Island(IRE) Trajectus (Homo Sapien)
(5117)

Sailors Warn (IRE) *E J O'Grady* 136h
7 b g Redback Coral Dawn (IRE) (Trempolino (USA))
3910a[12] 5420a[9]

Saindor (FR) *R Chotard* 140h 146c
10 b g Saint Des Saints(FR) Fleche D'Or (FR) (Saint Cyrien (FR))
406a[P]
(1583a)

Sainglend *Sean Curran* 128h 105c
9 b g Galileo(IRE) Verbal Intrigue (USA) (Dahar (USA))
718[8] 845[12] 1042[10]

Saint Are (FR) *Tim Vaughan* 137h 145c
8 bb g Network(GER) Fortanea (FR) (Video Rock (FR))
2071[8] 2674[4] 4769[P] 5170[F]

Saint Breiz (FR) *Carroll Gray* 115h
8 bb g Saint Des Saints(FR) Balladina (FR) (Saint Cyrien (FR))
4171[P] (4281) 4603[2] 4993[6] 5541[2]

Saint Brieuc (FR) *Simon West* 89h
5 bb g Saint Des Saints(FR) Merci Alkmene (FR) (Exit To Nowhere (USA))
3417[4]

Saint Charles (FR) *Nicky Henderson* 86b
4 b g Manduro(GER) Tropical Barth (IRE) (Peintre Celebre (USA))
5279[11]

Saint Du Chenet (FR) *M Rolland* 151h 136c
8 b g Poliglote Tchela (FR) (Le Nain Jaune (FR))
685a[4] 1901a[F] 2240a[5] 5577a[3]

Saint Firmin (FR) *Robert Collet* 132h 127c
5 bb g Saint Des Saints(FR) Fleur Des Villes (FR) (Villez (USA))
2263a[P] 2414a[6]

Saint Gervais (IRE) *John E Kiely* 138h 135c
9 b g Revoque(IRE) Just Precious (Ela-Mana-Mou)
1950a[U]

Saint Guru *Barry Brennan* 63b
7 b g Ishiguru(USA) St James's Antigua (IRE) (Law Society (USA))
412[9]

Saint Helena (IRE) *Jim Best* 46h
6 b m Holy Roman Emperor(IRE) Tafseer (IRE) (Grand Lodge (USA))
3422[P] 3550[P] 3686[9] 4467[P] 5117[11] 5303[8]

Saint Jerome (IRE) *Jamie Osborne* 131h
4 b g Jeremy(USA) Eminence Gift (Cadeaux Genereux)
1813[3] (2466) (4904) (5227) 5568[3]

Saint John Henry (FR) *David Pipe* 86h
4 b g Saint Des Saints(FR) Noceane (FR) (Pistolet Bleu (IRE))
4569[5] 4904[11] 5236[4]

Saint Palois (FR) *J Ortet* 118h 139c
6 b g Saint Des Saints(FR) Toutevoie (FR) (Sillery (USA))
(1902a)
2264a[2]

Saint Peray (FR) *Bob Buckler* 72h 61c
8 b g Fragrant Mix(IRE) Gintonique (FR) (Royal Charter (FR))
2473[5] 3044[6] **3785[P]**

Saint Roque (FR) *Paul Nicholls* 146h 137c
8 b g Lavirco(GER) Moody Cloud (FR) (Cyborg (FR))
(486) (591) (688) (1954) 2929[3] 3081[F] *4019[3]* 4786[P] **5352[2]**

Saints And Sinners (IRE) *Michael Easterby* 123h 119c
6 b g Gold Well How Provincial (IRE) (Be My Native (USA))
3028[9]
3418[5] 3859[6] 4077[2] 4894[F] 5385[5]

Saint Thomas (IRE) *John Mackie* 121h
7 b g Alhaarth(IRE) Aguilas Perla (IRE) (Indian Ridge)
1389[2] (1578) (1713) 2344[8]

Saint Val (FR) *J Bertran De Balanda* 119h 116c
5 b g Saint Des Saints(FR) Vallee Du Luy (FR) (Oblat (FR))
5425a[F]

Sakhee's Alround *K F Clutterbuck* 42h
4 ch f Sakhee's Secret Regal Run (USA) (Deputy Minister (CAN))
5245[10]

Sakhees Romance *Philip Kirby*
4 b f Sakhee(USA) Chance For Romance (Entrepreneur)
1501[P]

Sakina (FR) *G Brillet* 110h
4 b f Spirit One(FR) Talena (Zafonic (USA))
130a[6]

Salamix (FR) *Mme I Pacault* 90h 88c
8 gr g Al Namix(FR) Kadalka (FR) (Kadalko (FR))
1464a[6]

Salford Lady *Philip Hobbs* 4b
5 b m Zafeen(FR) She's The Lady (Unfuwain (USA))
2022[11] 3010[P]

Salmanazar *Alan King* 133h
6 b g Classic Cliche(IRE) Leroy's Sister (FR) (Phantom Breeze)
2433[P] 2949[13]

Salmonliv *Noel Wilson*
7 gr g Kayf Tara Tactix (Nearly A Hand)
4428[P]

Salpierre (IRE) *Jonjo O'Neill* 120h
9 b g Pierre Promalady (IRE) (Homo Sapien)
(428) (1011) 1155[4]

Salsify (IRE) *Rodger Sweeney* 113h 152c
9 b g Beneficial Our Deadly (IRE) (Phardante (FR))
660[3]

Saltagioo (ITY) *Anthony Middleton* 87h
10 b g Dr Devious(IRE) Sces (Kris)
977[U] 1331[4]

Salto Chisco (IRE) *Donald McCain* 115h
6 b g Presenting Dato Fairy (IRE) (Accordion)
2075[6] 2443[2]

Salubrious (IRE) *Paul Nicholls* 156h
7 b g Beneficial Who Tells Jan (Royal Fountain)
2504[2] 3084[2] 3198[2] 4767[9] 5169[5]

Salut Flo (FR) *David Pipe*
9 b g Saint Des Saints(FR) Royale Marie (FR) (Garde Royale)
3082[P]

Salut Honore (FR) *Alex Hales* 88h 105c
8 b g Lost World(IRE) Kadalkote (FR) (Kadalko (FR))
472[4] (2313)
2700[5] 3281[5] 3834[6] 4759[6]

Salut L'As (FR) *Sue Gardner* 80h
8 ch g Kaldou Star Kayas (FR) (Solido (FR))
2011[U] 2289[5] **2922[P]**

Samandy *Susan Corbett* 53b
5 ch m Septieme Ciel(USA) Magical Day (Halling (USA))
498[7]

Samarkand (IRE) *Neil King* 80h
6 b g Sadler's Wells(USA) Romantic Venture (IRE) (Indian Ridge)
307[7]

Sambelucky (IRE) *Keith Reveley* 88h 88c
9 b g Barathea(IRE) Kalimar (IRE) (Bigstone (IRE))
2445[2] 2880[4] 5051[3] 5442[4]

Sambulando (FR) *Richard Hobson* 106h 106c
11 gr g Kouroun(FR) Somnambula (IRE) (Petoski)
4703[5] 5072[3] 5552[4]

Same Difference (IRE) *Nigel Twiston-Davies* 140h 151c
8 b g Mr Combustible(IRE) Sarahs Reprive (IRE) (Yashgan)
2214[11] 2815[10] 3655[P] 4769[5] 5571[P]

Samedi Soir *Keith Reveley* 92b
4 b f Black Sam Bellamy(IRE) Bonne Anniversaire (Alflora (IRE))
5077[5]

Samenerve (FR) *Stuart Morris* 118c
7 br g Protektor(GER) Sweetberry (FR) (Limnos (JPN))
7[P] 4782[P]

Sametegal (FR) *Paul Nicholls* 149h
5 b g Saint Des Saints(FR) Loya Lescribaa (FR) (Robin Des Champs (FR))
(1970) 2533[2] 3261[3] 4056[5] 4752[8]

Samingarry (FR) *Nigel Hawke* 108h 141c
7 ch g Ballingarry(IRE) Samansonnienne (FR) (Mansonnien (FR))
289[5] 1887[7] **(2099)**
2275[3] (2693)
(2941) 3886[5] 4751[P] 4962[3] (5178)

Samizdat (FR) *John Upson* 70h 42c
11 b g Soviet Star(USA) Secret Account (FR) (Bering)
21[2] 264[10] 598[U] 903[11] 1940[P] 2679[P] 5302[7]

Sam Lord *James Moffatt* 107h 121c
10 ch g Observatory(USA) My Mariam (Salse (USA))
27[5] 2169[2] 2447[2] 3012[7] 3274[2] (3527) 3922[7] 4085[3] 4648[2] 5319[6]

Sammy Blade *Alan Phillips* 35b
6 ch g Needwood Blade Aspen Ridge (IRE) (Namid)
3734[9] 4728[11] 5227[P]

Sammyman *Michael Blanshard* 83h
7 b g Tamure(IRE) Bajan Rose (Dashing Blade)
2695[7] 3128[9] 4971[P]

Sammy Spiderman *Miss K Scott* 13h 86c
11 b g Karinga Bay Thorterdykes Lass (IRE) (Zaffaran (USA))
4239[R] 4837[8]

Sam Patch *Donald Whillans* 93h 83c
11 ch g Weldnaas(USA) Youandi (Silver Season)
172[P] 3936[4] 4380[2] 4775[F]

Samson Collonges (FR) *Rebecca Menzies* 82c
8 gr g Fragrant Mix(IRE) Idole Collonges (FR) (Brezzo (FR))
473[8] 2335[5] 2735[8] 3022[P] 3528[2] 3797[2] 3936[P]
4652[U] (4775)
5104[2]

Samstown *Alistair Whillans* 112h 136c
7 b g Kingsalsa(USA) Red Peony (Montjeu (IRE))
2155[4] ◆ (2901)
3205[4] 3743[2] 4669[2] (5278)

Samtheman *Micky Hammond* 104h 97c
9 b g Dancing Spree(USA) Sisterly (Brotherly (USA))
2591[9] 3015[4] 3925[5] 4380[6] 4747[2] (4940) ◆

Samtomjones (IRE) *John Norton* 53b
6 ch g Presenting She's All That (IRE) (Bob Back (USA))
2174[9]

Samurai Way *Venetia Williams* 94h 112c
12 b g Darshaan Truly Special (Caerleon (USA))
2730[3] 3223[2] 3437[3]

Sam Winner (FR) *Paul Nicholls* 144h 153c
7 b g Okawango(USA) Noche (IRE) (Night Shift (USA))
2501[3] ◆ (3079)
4148[2] 4751[5] 5276[P]

Sanctioned *Robert Stephens*
5 b g Authorized(IRE) Kazeem (Darshaan)
5548[P]

Sanctuary *Kim Bailey* 48h
8 ch g Dr Fong(USA) Wondrous Maid (GER) (Mondrian (GER))
1495[6]

Sandanski (IRE) *Tom Gretton* 114h
6 b g Definite Article Castle Hope (IRE) (Old Vic)
435[4] **2024[P]**
5037[4] **5180[P]**

Sand Artist (IRE) *Venetia Williams* 70h
6 b g Sandmason Belon Breeze (IRE) (Strong Gale)
2720[9] 3326[5] 3716[8] 4391[U] 5003[9]

Sandra Mia (FR) *Mlle J Legatte* 113h
5 b m Enrique Sandra Maria (FR) (Homme De Loi (IRE))
1199a[2]

Sands Cove (IRE) *Charlie Mann* 125h 128c
7 b g Flemensfirth(USA) Lillies Bordello (IRE) (Danehill Dancer (IRE))
2287[3] 2694[F] 3045[4] 3418[6] 3787[4] 4660[3] 4965[2] 5340[2]

Sandy Beach *Colin Tizzard* 78b
4 b g Notnowcato Picacho (IRE) (Sinndar (IRE))
3460[9] 4964[15]

Sandy Cay (FR) *P Lenogue* 120h 95c
7 b g Hernando(FR) Sierra (FR) (Anabaa (USA))
263a[5]

Sandynow (IRE) *Peter Bowen* 63h 111c
9 ch g Old Vic Kasterlee (FR) (Stay For Lunch (USA))
778[9] 1055[P] 2290[P] 2458[13] 3119[P]

Sandy's Double *Jamie Snowden* 106h 117c
8 ch g Double Trigger(IRE) Skipcarl (IRE) (Carlingford Castle)
2008[2]

Sangfroid *Andrew Quick* 92h 84c
10 gr g With Approval(CAN) Affaire D'Amour (Hernando (FR))
1110[3] 1267[11] **5123[5]**

Sankyouplease (IRE) *Michael Scudamore* 78h
6 b g Golan(IRE) Special Case (IRE) (Be My Native (USA))
1875[P]

Sanouva (FR) *J-P Gallorini* 111h 96c
5 b m Muhtathir Dindounas (FR) (Astarabad (USA))
1742a[6]

Sanpor (IRE) *R P Rath* 82b
11 b g Taipan(IRE) Not A Bother Tohim (IRE) (Abednego)
1486[P]

San Siro (IRE) *Philip Mitchell*
8 b g Milan Foxtail (IRE) (Be My Native (USA))
4297[14]

Santayana (GER) *David Evans* 92h
5 ch m Manduro(GER) Saderlina (IRE) (Sadler's Wells (USA))
2718[9]

San Telm (IRE) *Renee Robeson* 126h 130c
9 b g Oscar(IRE) Magical Mist (IRE) (Be My Native (USA))
2020[4]
2508[8] (3150)
3594[U] 3882[3] 4271[6] 4662[3] 5093[P]

Santera (IRE) *John Spearing* 98h
10 br m Gold Away(IRE) Sainte Gig (FR) (Saint Cyrien (FR))
811[P] 1284[9] 1699[P]

Santiag (FR) *G Lecomte* 100h 100c
8 b g Diableneyev(USA) Idria Des Bois (FR) (Saint Estephe (FR))
200a[4]

Santo De Lune (FR) *Dan Skelton* 93h
4 gr g Saint Des Saints(FR) Tikidoun (FR) (Kaldoun (FR))
2975[4] ◆

Santo Thomas (FR) *Venetia Williams* 110h
8 gr g Chichicastenango(FR) European Style (FR) (Ezzoud (IRE))
2561[9] 3132[2] 3597[2] 3839[2] 4129[3] 4512[4] 5040[3]

Saoirse Dun (IRE) *P J Rothwell* 96b 141c
8 b g Flemensfirth(USA) Dorrha Rose (IRE) (Carroll House)
5474a[3]

Saphir Des Bois (FR) *F Lloyd* 77h 115c
10 b g Saint Des Saints(FR) Studieuse (FR) (Snurge)
655[P] 1085[P]

Saphir Des Monts (FR) *P Chemin*
8 b g Le Balafre(FR) Daizy De Lancray (FR) (Royal Charter (FR))
616a[P]

Saphir Du Rheu (FR) *Paul Nicholls* 162h
5 gr g Al Namix(FR) Dona Du Rheu (FR) (Dom Pasquini (FR))
2366[5] 2813[4] ◆ (2949) (3646) ◆ (4025) 4441[4]

Saphir River (FR) *Lucinda Russell* 150h 133c
8 gr g Slickly(FR) Miss Bio (FR) (River Mist (USA))
356[13] 2221[5] (3286) 3775[5] 4820[6]

Sapphire Moon *Alan King* 96h
7 b m Alflora(IRE) Be My Valentine (IRE) (Be My Native (USA))
5026[5]

Sapphire Rouge (IRE) *Seamus Mullins* 96h 53c
8 ch m Alderbrook Emerald Express (Bigstone (IRE))
(99) 1340[4] 1529[4] 1768[4] 2312[7] 2701[5]
2863[4]

Sarahs Doll *Dai Burchell* 65h
6 b m Tatters The Robe (Robellino (USA))
3128[P] 4091[9] 4350[12] 4988[7] 5522[13]

Sarando *Alex Hales* 103h 102c
9 b g Hernando(FR) Dansara (Dancing Brave (USA))
39[U] 158[R]
2646[P] 2944[8] 3435[3] 3691[3] 4571[P]

Sarasola *Alistair Whillans*
7 b g Helissio(FR) Researcher (Cosmonaut)
747[P]

Sardinia (IRE) *Paul Nolan* 119h
4 b g Galileo(IRE) Shouk (Shirley Heights)
5470a[11]

Sarenice (FR) *James Frost* 100h
8 gr g April Night(FR) Delice Du Soleil (FR) (Altayan)
177[4] (1000) (3426)

Sarika (FR) *Nick Williams* 77h 114c
8 b g Grand Tresor(FR) Arika (FR) (Le Riverain (FR))
616a^{U} 855a^{7} 1486^{5} 1683a^{7} (1904a)
2384a^{2} 5334^{5}

Sarjinsky (IRE) *Mlle C Comte* 101h
4 ch g Raven's Pass(USA) Dinka Raja (USA) (Woodman (USA))
1741a^{P}

Saroque (IRE) *Venetia Williams* 105h 130c
7 b g Revoque(IRE) Sarakin (IRE) (Buckskin (FR))
2828^{5}
3129^{2} (3365)
3690^{3} (4031)
4395^{2} 5178^{5}

Sarraco (IRE) *Richard Lee* 108h
8 ch g Old Vic Harelda (Hector Protector (USA))
370^{P}

Sarsari (IRE) *Alan Jarvis* 89b
6 ch g Redback Annahala (IRE) (Ridgewood Ben)
760^{6}

Sash Of Honour (IRE) *Tim Vaughan* 112h
5 ch h Galileo(IRE) Adoration (USA) (Honor Grades (USA))
1764^{4} 2271^{9} 2904^{7}

Sassanova (FR) *Charlie Longsdon* 78b
4 b f Sassanian(USA) Anglaise (IRE) (Darshaan)
4964^{6}

Sassy Wren *Chris Down* 77h
9 ch m Best Of The Bests(IRE) Times Of Times (IRE) (Distinctly North (USA))
155^{4} 517^{6} 765^{10} 1000^{8} 1269^{7} 1479^{P}

Sa Suffit (FR) *Jim Goldie* 116h 129c
11 b g Dolpour(IRE) Branceilles (FR) (Satin Wood)
2358^{4}

Satanic Beat (IRE) *Jedd O'Keeffe* 121h
5 br g Dark Angel(IRE) Slow Jazz (USA) (Chief's Crown (USA))
1713^{4} 2225^{5} 2493^{9} 2868^{2} (4813)

Satou (FR) *Philip Hobbs* 65h 121c
8 gr g Fragrant Mix(IRE) Jonquiere (FR) (Trebrook (FR))
(766) **923^{6}**
1396^{6}

Saudi Pearl (IRE) *Nigel Twiston-Davies* 82h
6 br g Rakti Cheeky Weeky (Cadeaux Genereux)
1662^{5} 2011^{10} 2178^{7}
2825^{F} 5009^{P}

Sausalito Sunrise (IRE) *Philip Hobbs* 143h
6 b g Gold Well Villaflor (IRE) (Religiously (USA))
2529^{3} ◆ (2942) (3207) 3896^{5} 4786^{6} (5280) (5510) ◆

Sava Bridge (IRE) *Paul Henderson* 62h
7 b g Zagreb(USA) Myglass (IRE) (Strong Gale)
1016^{5} 1599^{7} 1732^{4} 2009^{8}

Savanas (FR) *Yannick Fouin* 100h 109c
4 gr g Davidoff(GER) Dedale (FR) (Turgeon (USA))
1741a^{8}

Savant Bleu (FR) *Kim Bailey* 106h 133c
8 ch g Agent Bleu(FR) Avane III (FR) (Quart De Vin (FR))
(18) **1815^{4}**
2108^{P} 2931^{6} 3389^{6} 4932^{2} (5127)
(5430)

Saved By John (IRE) *Tim Vaughan* 123h 138c
9 b g Revoque(IRE) Lady Appeal (IRE) (Phardante (FR))
2072^{2} 2666^{2} 3080^{5} 4414^{5} 4806^{6} 5392^{F}

Savello (IRE) *A J Martin* 144h 157c
8 ch g Anshan Fontaine Frances (IRE) (Lafontaine (USA))
2985a^{4} 3806a^{9} (4790)

Save My Blushes *Denis Gerard Hogan* 109h 123c
8 ch g Tobougg(IRE) American Rouge (IRE) (Grand Lodge (USA))
2721^{6} 3068^{10}

Save The Bees *Declan Carroll* 98h
6 b g Royal Applause Rock Concert (Bishop Of Cashel)
3144^{4} 3598^{F} 3877^{17}

Savigne (FR) *Mali Droueche* 49h 76c
9 b g Miesque's Son(USA) Touvoie (FR) (Anabaa (USA))
5425a^{P}

Sawago (FR) *Miss E Rodney*
8 bb g Gold Away(IRE) Maikawa (FR) (Green Tune (USA))
4355^{P}

Say When *Alan King* 96h
6 b g Fair Mix(IRE) Miss Wyandotte (Henbit (USA))
389^{7} 2878^{6} 4909^{6} 5547^{F}

Scales (IRE) *Richard Lee* 108h
8 b g Bob Back(USA) Mrs Avery (IRE) (Supreme Leader)
42^{10} 650^{11} (1887) 2314^{10} 3013^{2} 3157^{2} 4028^{6} 4969^{4} 5233^{5}

Scampi Boy (IRE) *Paul Webber* 112h 106c
10 b g Flemensfirth(USA) Loch Lomond (IRE) (Dry Dock)
286^{3} 2599^{P} 3190^{P}

Scarlet Fire (IRE) *Nicky Richards* 121h 74c
7 b g Helissio(FR) Ross Dana (IRE) (Topanoora)
2490^{10}
2882^{9}

Scarlett Lady *Ali Brewer* 89b
6 bb m Kayf Tara Frosty Mistress (Arctic Lord)
4810^{6} 5440^{3}

Scarlet Whispers *Pam Sly* 90h
5 b m Sir Percy Hieroglyph (Green Desert (USA))
1017^{3} 1176^{5} 1305^{7}

Scenic Route (IRE) *Giles Smyly* 67h
8 b g Hamairi(IRE) What A Scene (IRE) (Scenic)
1062^{7}

Scepticism (USA) *Charlie Mann* 63h
4 b g Elusive Quality(USA) Never Is A Promise (USA) (Capote (USA))
975^{8} 1193^{4} 1624^{5}

Scheherazadesdream *Jennie Candlish* 66h
7 ch m Stage Pass Ambitious Annie (Most Welcome)
71^{7} 1109^{P}

Schelm (GER) *Ronald O'Leary* 116h 116c
12 b g Alwuhush(USA) Shoba (GER) (Local Suitor (USA))
1572a^{2} 1613a^{P}

Schindler's Prince (IRE) *Mrs H S M Ridley* 109c
9 ch g Oscar Schindler(IRE) Coppeen Storm (IRE) (Glacial Storm (USA))
335^{7} 658^{P} 3862^{4} 4348^{3} 4706^{3}

Schinken Otto (IRE) *Malcolm Jefferson* 69h 101c
13 ch g Shinko Forest(IRE) Athassel Rose (IRE) (Reasonable (FR))
23^{7} 281^{7} 1638^{2} 2306^{9}

Scholastica *Tom Symonds* 126h
7 b m Old Vic La Perrotine (FR) (Northern Crystal)
(2663) 2948^{3} 3319^{6} 4144^{6}

Scimon Templar (FR) *Pauline Robson* 97h 95c
6 bb g Saint Des Saints(FR) Made In Law (FR) (Northern Crystal)
3723^{2} 4201^{4} 4366^{2} 4667^{3} 5212^{3} 5556^{U}

Scoglio *Dave Roberts* 119h
6 b g Monsieur Bond(IRE) Ex Mill Lady (Bishop Of Cashel)
(10) 304^{2} 850^{6} 1185^{2}

Scolt Head Island *Caroline Bailey* 44h
8 ch m Alflora(IRE) Auchendinny Jay (Primitive Rising (USA))
1823^{8} 2675^{7} 3854^{P} 4247^{P}

Scommettitrice (IRE) *Mark Gillard* 41h
6 b m Le Vie Dei Colori Hard To Lay (IRE) (Dolphin Street (FR))
1017^{8} 1132^{P} 1305^{9}

Scooter Boy *Alex Hales* 105b
5 b g Revoque(IRE) Always Forgiving (Commanche Run)
5014^{2}

Score Card (IRE) *Henry Daly* 87b
4 b g Scorpion(IRE) Auditing Empress (IRE) (Accordion)
4923^{3}

Scorer (IRE) *Jonjo O'Neill* 69h
6 b g Oscar(IRE) Mandysway (IRE) (Mandalus)
174^{7} 640^{4} 809^{5}

Scorpions Sting (IRE) *James Ewart* 85h
5 b g Scorpion(IRE) Strong Wishes (IRE) (Strong Gale)
2217^{5} 4364^{5}

Scotch Warrior *R Mike Smith* 71b 135c
10 ch g Karinga Bay Tarda (Absalom)
(343)
(1162) 1291^{2} (1545)
1659^{6} (5253)
5535^{7}

Scoter Fontaine (FR) *Rebecca Curtis* 125h 124c
8 b g Sleeping Car(FR) Blanche Fontaine (FR) (Oakland (FR))
91^{2} 358^{10} 638^{3} (945) 1154^{2}

Scotsbrook Legend *Shaun Lycett* 110h
6 b m Midnight Legend Scots Brook Terror (Terimon)
(3597) (4573)

Scots Gaelic (IRE) *John Quinn* 125h
7 ch g Tomba Harmonic (USA) (Shadeed (USA))
2102^{4} 2655^{7} 3000^{3} 3471^{P} 4058^{3} 4726^{U} (4781) 5172^{14}

Scotswell *Harriet Graham* 127h 130c
8 b g Endoli(USA) Tofino Swell (Primitive Rising (USA))
24^{2} ◆ 358^{18} 512^{4} 1042^{6} 1398^{5}
2220^{2} 2517^{3} 2817^{3} 2971^{2} 4552^{4} (4953) ◆
5278^{6}

Scottish Boogie (IRE) *Seamus Durack* 98h
7 b g Tobougg(IRE) Scottish Spice (Selkirk (USA))
1123^{3} **1939^{P}**

Screaming Brave *Sheena West* 119h
8 br g Hunting Lion(IRE) Hana Dee (Cadeaux Genereux)
673^{F} 858^{4} 1092^{5} (1171)

Scribe (IRE) *David Evans* 97h
6 b g Montjeu(IRE) Crafty Example (USA) (Crafty Prospector (USA))
2718^{14} 4350^{5} 4724^{2} 4882^{P}

Scrum V *Mrs N Naughton* 92h 97c
10 b g Sonus(IRE) Miss The Post (Bustino)
4617^{2} 5536^{2}

Scuderia (IRE) *Jamie Snowden* 87h 81c
7 b g Kris Kin(USA) Class Society (IRE) (Lahib (USA))
2316^{P} 3880^{4} **4716^{5} 5185^{P}**

Scutsisland (IRE) *Rosemary Gasson* 90h
5 br g Heron Island(IRE) Soviet Princess (IRE) (Soviet Lad (USA))
4986^{7} 5547^{5}

Seabougg *James Eustace* 77b
6 ch g Tobougg(IRE) Sea Jade (IRE) (Mujadil (USA))
309^{4} 1200^{P}

Seabreeze D'Ho (FR) *Christian Le Galliard* 129h
8 b g Enrique Peutiot (FR) (Valanour (IRE))
3083^{F}

Sea Cadet *Laura Mongan* 80h 94c
12 gr g Slip Anchor Stormy Gal (IRE) (Strong Gale)
242^{3} 712^{6} 1437^{3} 1548^{7} 1768^{2} 2744^{3} 3138^{4} (5022) 5461^{5}

Sea Claria (FR) *Venetia Williams* 98h
4 b f Sinndar(IRE) Triclaria (GER) (Surumu (GER))
4268^{P} 4730^{2}

Sea Cliff (IRE) *Andrew Crook* 78h 53c
10 b g Golan(IRE) Prosaic Star (IRE) (Common Grounds)
2596^{P} 4938^{7} 5359^{12}

Seacon Beg (IRE) *Nigel Twiston-Davies* 91b
5 b g Generous(IRE) Moon Storm (IRE) (Strong Gale)
5409^{3}

Sea Island Pearl *Philip Hobbs* 85h
5 b m Revoque(IRE) What A Gem (Karinga Bay)
1639^{RR} 1832^{2} 2280^{F} 2695^{8} 5522^{P}

Sea Light (IRE) *C Byrnes* 123h
6 b g Brian Boru Matinee Show (IRE) (Carroll House)
3910a^{4}

Sea Lord (IRE) *John Ferguson* 149h
7 b g Cape Cross(IRE) First Fleet (USA) (Woodman (USA))
15^{2} (186) ◆ (427) (812) (1046) (1290) (1987) 2530^{2} 5167^{6}

Sealous Scout (IRE) *Donald McCain* 118h
6 b g Old Vic Hirayna (Doyoun)
2196^{5} 3110^{2} 3614^{4} 4510^{3} (5208)

Seamus Rua (IRE) *Charlie Longsdon* 15h
6 ch g Indian River(FR) Chance Eile (IRE) (Camden Town)
1599^{4} 1826^{5} 2089^{9}

Sean Airgead (IRE) *Mark Michael McNiff* 110h 130c
9 ch g Scribano Ryleen Lady (IRE) (Lashkari)
(1397)
2972^{U}

Seancill Oir (IRE) *S Donohoe* 108h
9 b m King's Theatre(IRE) Carey's Lodge (IRE) (Bob Back (USA))
4223^{10}

Seaquel *Tony Carroll* 95h
8 b m Kyllachy Broughton Singer (IRE) (Common Grounds)
266^{U} 578^{3}

Sea Rocket (IRE) *Dominic Ffrench Davis* 119h
6 b m Shantou(USA) Ghillie's Bay (IRE) (King's Ride)
5366^{P}

Searree *Mrs Pauline Geering* 69h 30c
9 b m Daylami(IRE) Magongo (Be My Chief (USA))
523^{P}

Sea Saffron *Sue Gardner* 105h 132c
13 b g Sea Raven(IRE) Saffron Lake (Shaab)
509^{7}

Seaside Rock (IRE) *Keith Dalgleish* 90h
4 b g Oratorio(IRE) Miss Sacha (IRE) (Last Tycoon)
2307^{3} 2790^{3} 3127^{4} 3390^{F} 3830^{P}

Seaside Shuffle (IRE) *Sophie Leech* 92h 80c
9 bb g Wizard King Leaden Sky (IRE) (Roselier (FR))
812^{13} 1206^{9} 1351^{6} 1711^{6} 1938^{4} 2877^{5} (3047)

Seas Of Green *Paul Cowley* 90h
7 ch m Karinga Bay Emerald Project (IRE) (Project Manager)
2824^{7} 3005^{4} 3326^{4} 3854^{P} 4823^{7} 5291^{4}

Seas The Moment (IRE) *Chris Gordon* 84h
5 b m Westerner Meursault (IRE) (Salt Dome (USA))
3230^{3} 4499^{7} 5264^{8}

Sea Tiger *Alan King* 84b
4 b g Tiger Hill(IRE) Possessive Artiste (Shareef Dancer (USA))
2926^{4} *4296^{11}*

Seattle Drive (IRE) *David Pipe* 111h
6 b g Motivator Seattle Ribbon (USA) (Seattle Dancer (USA))
1979^{P} 2250^{P}

Sea Wall (FR) *Paul Nicholls* 91h
6 b g Turgeon(USA) Si Parfaite (FR) (Solon (GER))
2279^{7} 5235^{5}

Sea Wall *C Storey* 121h 125c
12 b g Giant's Causeway(USA) Spout (Salse (USA))
315^{U}

Sebastians Charm (IRE) *Warren Greatrex* 101b
6 b g Kris Kin(USA) Redeemagain (IRE) (Royal Fountain)
1138^{7} (1489)

Secret Beau *David Evans* 69h
4 gr g Sakhee's Secret Belle Reine (King Of Kings (IRE))
4722^{6}

Secret Dancer (IRE) *Alan Jones* 111h
9 b g Sadler's Wells(USA) Discreet Brief (IRE) (Darshaan)
556^{6}

Secret Desert *Rebecca Menzies*
8 b g Dubai Destination(USA) Lady Bankes (IRE) (Alzao (USA))
5298^{P}

Secret Edge *Alan King* 125h 97c
6 b g Tobougg(IRE) Burton Ash (Diktat)
182^{4} 3884^{3}

Secrete Stream (IRE) *Malcolm Jefferson* 128h
5 ch g Fruits Of Love(USA) Bonny River (IRE) (Exit To Nowhere (USA))
(173) 1667^{5} 2748^{2} (3330) ◆ 3826^{2} 4550^{4}

Secret Island *Anthony Day* 32h
5 b m Alflora(IRE) Precious Island (Jupiter Island)
389^{P} 841^{9} 3115^{P} 3226^{8} 3469^{P} 4980^{7}

Secure Investment *Oliver Sherwood* 79h
6 b g Alflora(IRE) Ivy Edith (Blakeney)
2354^{9} 2978^{14} 3728^{7} 4340^{4}

Sedano (FR) *Sara Ender* 88h
8 bb g Dark Moondancer Kadalville (FR) (Kadalko (FR))
948^{6} 4693^{6} 4980^{F} 5320^{12}

Sedgemoor Express (IRE) *Nigel Hawke* 106h
6 bb g Presenting Pretty Native (IRE) (Be My Native (USA))
290^{6} 517^{7} 686^{4} 833^{7} 1087^{5} 1351^{4} (1479) (1633) 1674^{6} 1941^{U} 2045^{2} 2210^{4}

Sedgemoor Top Bid (IRE) *Nigel Hawke* 91h
6 b g Marignan(USA) Hazy Fiddler (IRE) (Orchestra)
828^{10} 2457^{14} 2689^{5}
3176^{F} 3959^{8} 4172^{7} 4513^{4} 4882^{4} 5029^{4} 5298^{14}

Seebright *Victor Dartnall* 129h 142c
7 b g Milan Aranga (IRE) (Supreme Leader)
(2742) 3292^{5} 4277^{4} **4885^{3} (5259)**
(5533)

Seedless *Donald McCain* 112h 112c
9 br m Mtoto Unseeded (Unfuwain (USA))
1084^{5} **1390^{P}**

Seedling *Charles Egerton* 125h
5 b g Cockney Rebel(IRE) Unseeded (Unfuwain (USA))
(1770) 2265^{10} 2802^{2} ◆ 4143^{3}

See Double You (IRE) *Ronan M P McNally* 125h 123c
11 b g Saddlers' Hall(IRE) Mandy's Treasure (IRE) (Mandalus)
3939^{2} (4666) 5256^{2}

Seedsman *Charles Egerton* 124h
7 ch g Sulamani(IRE) Unseeded (Unfuwain (USA))
2446^{P}

Seefood (IRE) *D T Hughes* 149h 120c
7 b g Kahyasi Anne Theatre (Saddlers' Hall (IRE))
4765^{14} 5138^{17}

See More Power (IRE) *Paul Henderson* 59h
9 ch g Fleetwood(IRE) Joan Of Arc (Supreme Leader)
3550^{7} 4070^{P} 4275^{14}
4716^{F}

See The Legend *Sandy Forster* 85h
9 b m Midnight Legend Amys Delight (Idiots Delight)
2843^{4} 3940^{3} 4201^{7} 4553^{8}

See What Happens (IRE) *Martin Todhunter* 114h 120c
8 b g Tikkanen(USA) Fontanalia (FR) (Rex Magna (FR))
2171^{3} 2450^{8} 2820^{4} 4578^{F} 5297^{P}

Seeyouallincoppers (IRE) *Paul W Flynn* 112h
4 b g Saffron Walden(FR) Millenium Love (IRE) (Great Commotion (USA))
4963^{5}

Seeyouatmidnight *Sandy Thomson* 154h
6 b g Midnight Legend Morsky Baloo (Morpeth)
(3017) (4052) (4269) 5157^{3}

See You Jack *Caroline Bailey* 101h 42c
9 b g Dolpour(IRE) Layston Pinzal (Afzal)
2^{4}

Sego Success (IRE) *Alan King* 123h
6 b g Beneficial The West Road (IRE) (Mister Lord (USA))
2252^{8} (2874) 4272^{4} 5332^{F}

Seigneur Des Bois (FR) *D Buckett* 116c
8 b g Ballingarry(IRE) Studieuse (FR) (Snurge)
312^{7} 3720^{2} 3993^{F} 4518^{5} 4936^{2}

Seize *James Moffatt* 75h 77c
12 gr g Silver Patriarch(IRE) Sleepline Princess (Royal Palace)
222^{P} **566^{11}**
802^{6} 1038^{9}

Seldom Inn *Sandy Thomson* 109b
6 ch g Double Trigger(IRE) Portland Row (IRE) (Zaffaran (USA))
(3042) 4671^{3} 5279^{14}

Send For Tim (IRE) *Mrs Gaye Williams* 58h 13c
11 b g Corrouge(USA) Duneavey (IRE) (Mandalus)
4246^{9} 4485^{P}

Sendiym (FR) *Dianne Sayer* 92h 99c
7 b g Rainbow Quest(USA) Seraya (FR) (Danehill (USA))
17^{6} **(281)**
536^{3} **627^{5}**
1075^{4} 1395^{2} (1716) 1790^{2} **(1981)**
2173^{F} 2361^{5} 4581^{2} 5483^{6}

Senor Alco (FR) *Victor Thompson* 95h 94c
8 gr g Dom Alco(FR) Alconea (FR) (Brezzo (FR))
28^{3} 112^{P} 496^{5} 5209^{4}

Seondeok (IRE) *David Rees* 63b
6 br m Shantou(USA) Retinue (IRE) (Mister Lord (USA))
715^{10}

Separate Shadows (FR) *Donald McCain* 111h
6 ch g Bernebeau(FR) Chagrin D'Amour (IRE) (Last Tycoon)
367^{2} (716) 1048^{3} 1183^{2} 1414^{6}

September Blaze *Paul Webber* 101h 104c
7 b m Exit To Nowhere(USA) Mid Day Chaser (IRE) (Homo Sapien)
2477^{6} 3391^{8} **4242^{7} 4918^{2}**

Septenarius (USA) *Brian Baugh* 26b
5 b g Empire Maker(USA) Reams Of Verse (USA) (Nureyev (USA))
1427^{8} 1671^{14}

Sequoia Forest *Martin Keighley* 30b
5 gr g Proclamation(IRE) Armada Grove (Fleetwood (IRE))
3049^{10}

Serenity Now (IRE) *Brian Ellison* 113h
6 b g Key Of Luck(USA) Imdina (IRE) (Soviet Star (USA))
2174^{2} 2499^{6} 4480^{2} 4945^{F} 5064^{5} 5205^{3}

Sergeant Dick (IRE) *Barry Brennan* 115h 128c
9 b g Lord Of Appeal Darawadda (IRE) (Kasmayo)
2107^{S} (2389)
2757^{3} 3642^{5} 4273^{3} 4560^{6} 5516^{P}

Sergeant Mattie (IRE) *Charlie Longsdon* 134h
6 b g Naheez(USA) Glyde Lady (IRE) (Shardari)
(1853) (4715) 5110^{2}

Sergeant Pink (IRE) *Dianne Sayer* 120h 130c
8 b g Fasliyev(USA) Ring Pink (USA) (Bering)
220^{2} (533) 801^{6} **(864)**
(1077) 1162^{4} (1291)
1545^{2} (1636)
1852^{3} 2199^{7} 2939^{9} 4610^{3} 4953^{U}
5218^{5}

Sergeant Thunder *Paul Nicholls* 126h
5 ch g Halling(USA) Dissolve (Sharrood (USA))
3877^{9}

Serienschock (GER) *F-M Cottin* 123h 122c
6 b g Sholokhov(IRE) Saldenehre (GER) (Highest Honor (FR))
685a^{P}
1583a^{6} 2465a^{3}

Serious Mixture *Hilary Parrott* 91h 99c
7 b g Fair Mix(IRE) Bonne Anniversaire (Alflora (IRE))
19^{P} 3388^{17} 4838^{6}
5259^{3}

Sertao (FR) *Milton Bradley* 73h
8 b g Passing Sale(FR) Etoile Bleu (FR) (Ghost Buster'S (FR))
49^{13}

Seskinane (IRE) *Brian M McMahon* 141h 124c
8 b g Imperial Ballet(IRE) Three For The Road (IRE) (Buckskin (FR))
4386a^3

Seslost (CZE) *Z Matysik*
10 gr m Mill Pond(FR) Sandra (CZE) (Sharp End)
1905a^P

Settledoutofcourt (IRE) *Lucinda Russell* 91h 120c
8 b g Court Cave(IRE) Ardagh Princess (Proverb)
(310) 556^5
1925^3 (2335)
(2498) 2959^3 (3397)
3939^P 4894^4

Seven Belle *Dai Burchell* 34b
4 b f Septieme Ciel(USA) Auction Belle (Auction House (USA))
2318^9 2830^9

Seven Nation Army (IRE) *David Pipe* 125b
5 gr g Rock Of Gibraltar(IRE) Crepe Ginger (IRE) (Sadler's Wells (USA))
(3187) 4149^5

Seven Summits (IRE) *Sophie Leech* 107h
7 b g Danehill Dancer(IRE) Mandavilla (IRE) (Sadler's Wells (USA))
708^3 (3830) 5125^3 5542^8

Seventeen Black (IRE) *David Rees* 69b
6 b g Subtle Power(IRE) Snowbaby (IRE) (Be My Native (USA))
731^7

Seventh Hussar *Alison Batchelor* 85h 98c
8 b g Alflora(IRE) Shuil Do (IRE) (Be My Native (USA))
(2441)
(2580) 3246^4

Seventh Sign *Alan King* 138h
5 b g Pivotal Rahayeb (Arazi (USA))
2268^4 2798^{16} 3359^6 (4347) 4805^6 5544^9

Seventh Sky (GER) *Charlie Mann* 128h 122c
7 b g King's Best(USA) Sacarina (Old Vic)
235^2 2951^{10} 3322^8 4278^3 4558^F 4794^{10} 5067^6
5452^4

Seven Woods (IRE) *Tom George* 124h 132c
8 b g Milan Charlotte's Moss (Le Moss)
(296) **553^2**
2108^4 2438^3 3358^2 3882^8
4427^5 5119^2

Sew On Target (IRE) *Colin Tizzard* 113h 136c
9 b g Needle Gun(IRE) Ballykea (IRE) (Montelimar (USA))
157^2 1969^3 2488^2 3082^4 3652^6 3887^4 (4036)
4768^{16} 5136^{10}

Seymour Eric *Martin Keighley* 138h 126c
9 b g Bollin Eric Seymour Chance (Seymour Hicks (FR))
2459^3 2747^2 3131^P 3653^P 3882^7 4264^6 4820^9
5093^{14}

Seymour Legend *Jim Wilson* 82h
8 b g Midnight Legend Rosehall (Ardross)
368^6 5242^{11} 5541^9

Sgt Bull Berry *Peter Maddison* 29h
7 b g Alflora(IRE) Cede Nullis (Primitive Rising (USA))
1094^4 3036^7 3208^P

Sgt Reckless *Mick Channon* 150h
7 b g Imperial Dancer Lakaam (Danzero (AUS))
2369^3 (2711) 3258^3 *(4022)* 4736^4 ◆ 5153^2

Shabra Charity (IRE) *Patrick O Brady* 91h 121c
9 ch m Rudimentary(USA) Leighlinbridge (IRE) (Montelimar (USA))
1951a^5

Shadarpour (IRE) *Gary Moore* 108h
5 b g Dr Fong(USA) Shamadara (IRE) (Kahyasi)
267^{12} 1822^4 (2862) 3029^3 4888^9

Shaddaii (FR) *Caroline Keevil* 80h
8 gr g April Night(FR) Gypsie D'Artois (FR) (Mistigri)
42^6 (490) 876^3 *4493^3* 5143^7

Shades Of Autumn (IRE) *Linda Blackford* 101h 94c
9 ch g Anshan Be Right (IRE) (Be My Native (USA))
2470^P 2766^6 **3421^P 5394^2**

Shades Of Midnight *Donald Whillans* 99b
4 b g Midnight Legend Hannah Park (IRE) (Lycius (USA))
4958^3 (5324)

Shadesofnavy *Peter Pritchard* 74h
8 ch g Fleetwood(IRE) Safe Arrival (USA) (Shadeed (USA))
417^7 649^P

Shadow Boxer *Donald Whillans* 79b 92c
9 gr g Makbul Shadows Of Silver (Carwhite)
3022^P 4652^P 5055^P

Shadow Catcher *Gordon Elliott* 138h
6 ch g Haafhd Unchain My Heart (Pursuit Of Love)
1290^3

Shadow Cruise (IRE) *Bernard Llewellyn* 90b
5 ro g Touch Of Land(FR) Rosafi (IRE) (Roselier (FR))
3363^6 4030^S

Shadow Eile (IRE) *Mrs D A Love* 137h 122c
9 b m Beneficial Rubys Shadow (IRE) (Supreme Leader)
1067a^7
1702a^8 2116a^4

Shadow Of The Day *Lee James* 19b
7 b g Sugarfoot She Who Dares Wins (Atraf)
2052^7

Shadows Lengthen *Michael Easterby* 118h 134c
8 b g Dansili Bay Shade (USA) (Sharpen Up)
2198^9
2488^{12} 3287^F ◆ 4106^6 (4532)
(4900) 5535^{12}

Shadrack (IRE) *Keith Reveley* 106h 126c
10 gr g Tamayaz(CAN) Alba Dancer (Gran Alba (USA))
2496^3 3039^2 4543^5 4861^6 5207^3

Shady Glen (IRE) *Graeme McPherson* 71h
5 br g Dr Massini(IRE) Poppins (IRE) (Invited (USA))
5182^P 5541^7

Shady Lane *Alan King* 108h 100c
7 b m Alflora(IRE) Stoney Path (Petoski)
41^4 353^4 2292^2 2598^6 **4989^F**

Shady Sadie (IRE) *Rose Dobbin* 83h 74c
7 b m Dushyantor(USA) Beltane Queen (IRE) (Strong Gale)
168^5 3040^P **3876^P**

Shakalakaboomboom (IRE) *Nicky Henderson* 54h 78c
10 b g Anshan Tia Maria (IRE) (Supreme Leader)
4021^6 4347^P
4738^{17} 5171^P

Shaker Style (USA) *Barry Murtagh* 82h
8 ch g Gulch(USA) Carr Shaker (USA) (Carr De Naskra (USA))
75^3 316^4 558^2

Shakespeare Dancer *James Evans*
5 b m Norse Dancer(IRE) Sharbasia (IRE) (King's Best (USA))
2280^P

Shake The Barley (IRE) *Tom George* 91h 116c
11 ch g Marignan(USA) Glengarra Princess (Cardinal Flower)
294^U 600^7 965^4

Shaking Hands (IRE) *David Pipe* 130c
10 b g Bach(IRE) Picton Lass (Rymer)
3131^P 3366^F 3698^P 4396^8

Shalamiyr (FR) *Sarah-Jayne Davies* 107h 103c
9 gr g Linamix(FR) Shamanara (IRE) (Danehill (USA))
(1547)
1835^2 2039^3 (2423)
2615^P 3439^P

Shales Rock *Mrs C J Robinson* 121c
8 b g Karinga Bay Home Talk (IRE) (Euphemism)
(4727)
(5165) 5346^8

Shalianzi (IRE) *Gary Moore* 96h
4 b g Azamour(IRE) Shalama (IRE) (Kahyasi)
2364^U 2796^7 3003^5 3245^3 4963^{11}

Shalimar Fromentro (FR) *Nick Williams* 109h 131c
8 gr g Martaline Miss Des Ormeaux (FR) (Glaieul (USA))
199a^4 855a^4 1532a^5 1905a^U 2384a^F 3068^5 3730^2

Shalone *Adrian Wintle* 125h
10 ch g Tobougg(IRE) Let Alone (Warning)
2807^P 4897^9 5285^U

Shamar (FR) *W P Mullins* 138h
6 br g Dr Fong(USA) Shamalana (IRE) (Sinndar (IRE))
1802a^3

Shammick Boy (IRE) *Victor Dartnall* 133h 123c
9 b g Craigsteel Dulcet Music (IRE) (Topanoora)
176^8 (2080) 3169^6 3957^4 4935^4 5142^7 5429^4

Shanaderry Kin (IRE) *Simon Earle* 101h
5 b g Kris Kin(USA) Sweet Innocence (IRE) (King's Ride)
5042^5 5258^5

Shanahan's Turn (IRE) *Henry De Bromhead* 140h
6 b g Indian Danehill(IRE) Chanson Indienne (FR) (Indian River (FR))
4750^8

Shanann Star (IRE) *Gordon Edwards* 31h 90c
8 br m Anshan Baile An Droichid (IRE) (King's Ride)
5553^7

Shanen (IRE) *Pauline Robson* 111h
8 b g Tikkanen(USA) Ursha (IRE) (Shardari)
1980^3 3832^6

Shanendou (IRE) *Tom George* 92h
5 br m Turtle Island(IRE) Portobello Sunrise (IRE) (Broken Hearted)
2752^2 3727^8 4331^3 5244^3

Shaneshill (IRE) *W P Mullins* 137b
5 b g King's Theatre(IRE) Darabaka (IRE) (Doyoun)
4756^2 ◆

Shangani (USA) *Venetia Williams* 122h 144c
8 b g Giant's Causeway(USA) Tanzania (IRE) (Alzao (USA))
2656^3 2939^P 3642^3 3887^5 4133^2 (4559)
4768^{11} 5385^P

Shankhouse Wells (IRE) *George Charlton* 91b
6 b m Milan Norwood Cross (IRE) (Anshan)
173^6 2752^4

Shanks A Lot *Lucy Jones* 103h
7 b g Beat All(USA) Florida Fact (Factual (USA))
1154^6

Shanksforamillion *David Rees*
5 b g Needle Gun(IRE) Cool Connie (IRE) (Commanche Run)
1341^8 1561^P

Shannina *David Thompson* 82h
9 b g Shaanmer(IRE) Jannina (FR) (Useful (FR))
628^9

Shannon Rock (FR) *J-P Gallorini* 132h 159c
8 b g Turgeon(USA) Shannondore (FR) (Nashamaa)
1902a^5 (2264a)

Shannon Spirit (IRE) *Paul Henderson* 114h 102c
9 b g Snurge Spirit Of The Nile (FR) (Generous (IRE))
179^F 2742^P
3152^3 3472^F 4482^P

Shanpallas (IRE) *C Byrnes* 135h 142c
6 b g Golan(IRE) Evnelu (IRE) (Old Vic)
3886^8

Shanroe Boru (IRE) *J J Lambe* 101b
5 b g Brian Boru Strong Tide (IRE) (Strong Gale)
2223^5

Shanroe Santos (IRE) *J J Lambe* 103b
5 b g Definite Article Jane Hall (IRE) (Saddlers' Hall (IRE))
5279^7

Shanroe Secret (IRE) *J J Lambe* 92h
7 b g Zagreb(USA) Honey Bank (IRE) (Capitano)
72^P

Shanroe Society (IRE) *J J Lambe* 112h
8 b g Definite Article Wensum Dancer (Shareef Dancer (USA))
3937^4

Shantou Breeze (IRE) *Michael Madgwick* 100h 97c
7 b m Shantou(USA) Homersmare (IRE) (Shardari)
303^2 485^P (805) 1270^3 1432^3
5009^P 5263^5 (5397)

Shantou Ed (IRE) *P A Fahy* 129h
5 ch g Shantou(USA) Fair Maid Marion (IRE) (Executive Perk)
4386a^5 4708a^5

Shantou Magic (IRE) *Charlie Longsdon* 137h
7 b g Shantou(USA) Supreme Magical (Supreme Leader)
(2018) (2393) 3367^4 3989^4 4789^{14}

Shantou Tiger (IRE) *Donald McCain* 113h
5 b g Shantou(USA) Opus One (Slip Anchor)
1732^6 2724^5 4480^4 4950^3 5300^U

Shanty Town (IRE) *Suzy Smith* 94h
5 b g Zagreb(USA) Rapsan (IRE) (Insan (USA))
5241^6

Shan Valley (IRE) *Stuart Coltherd* 87h 59c
8 ch m Shantou(USA) Statim (Marju (IRE))
2306^3 ◆ 3518^4 4336^2 4465^2 4607^5
5355^4

Sharadiyn *Clive Mulhall* 62h
11 b g Generous(IRE) Sharadiya (IRE) (Akarad (FR))
1301^P

Shareni (IRE) *Paul Nicholls* 106h
5 b g Azamour(IRE) Sharesha (IRE) (Ashkalani (IRE))
2906^4

Share Option *Tony Carroll* 100h 106c
12 b g Polish Precedent(USA) Quota (Rainbow Quest (USA))
89^7 **418^4**

Share The Dosh *J R Jenkins* 36h
6 ch m Doyen(IRE) Lady Starlight (IRE) (Almutawakel)
291^7 971^3 1265^P

Sharivarry (FR) *Victor Thompson* 102h 98c
8 ch g Ballingarry(IRE) Sharsala (IRE) (Shahrastani (USA))
30^5 281^5 5165^P

Sharlene's Quest (IRE) *James Hughes* 85h
8 b m Revoque(IRE) Sanka (IRE) (Standiford (USA))
590^3 860^6 946^5 1320^5

Sharney Sike *Stuart Coltherd* 99h 115c
8 ch g And Beyond(IRE) Squeeze Box (IRE) (Accordion)
(3041)
(3823) 4430^4 4551^4 (4812)
5216^5

Sharon *Edward U Hales* 92b
5 b m Shirocco(GER) Ancora (IRE) (Accordion)
483^4

Sharp *Donald McCain* 86b
5 b g Haafhd Brightest (Rainbow Quest (USA))
1546^3

Sharp Suit (IRE) *Seamus Mullins* 91h 124c
7 bb g Milan True Blade (Sabrehill (USA))
241^3

Shays River (IRE) *Evan Williams* 44h 82c
9 b g Heron Island(IRE) Miss Flic (Kinglet)
8^P 4024^P **4088^3** 4350^P 4632^{14} 4945^0

Sheilas Lady *Andrew Crook* 101h
6 b m Tamure(IRE) Ladies From Leeds (Primitive Rising (USA))
2752^5 3112^4 3727^4 4776^4 5322^4

She Is A Cracker (FR) *Mrs C M Gorman* 86h
9 b m Cadoudal(FR) Douchka (FR) (Fijar Tango (FR))
1320^2 1406^2

Shelford (IRE) *Dan Skelton* 127h
5 b g Galileo(IRE) Lyrical (Shirley Heights)
477^2 5088^2

She Ranks Me (IRE) *Donald McCain* 133h 126c
7 gr m Golan(IRE) Rosealainn (IRE) (Roselier (FR))
2763^2 3206^4 **4202^F (4468)**
4918^3 5369^6

Sheriff Hutton (IRE) *Martin Hill* 133h 126c
11 b g Rudimentary(USA) Will She What (IRE) (Lafontaine (USA))
845^2 ◆ **923^3** (1195) 1485^8
4932^{10} 5119^P

Shernando *Nicky Henderson* 135h
7 b g Hernando(FR) Shimmering Sea (Slip Anchor)
3^3

Sherreb (IRE) *Anna Newton-Smith*
8 b g Zagreb(USA) Sherberry (IRE) (Shernazar)
3093^P 4716^P

She's Humble (IRE) *Linda Jewell* 75h 90c
12 ch m Humbel(USA) She's No Tourist (IRE) (Doubletour (USA))
707^5 1089^5 1272^4 1530^5 2003^P 2441^P

She's Late *Jonjo O'Neill* 110h
4 ch g Pivotal Courting (Pursuit Of Love)
4345^4 4959^5

She's Noble *Suzy Smith* 88h
7 b m Karinga Bay Alta (Arctic Lord)
3136^6 4797^F 5124^{11} (5402)

Shesnotforturning (IRE) *Ben Haslam*
4 b f Refuse To Bend(IRE) Diplomats Daughter (Unfuwain (USA))
1684^8

Shimla Dawn (IRE) *Mark Walford* 130h
6 b g Indian Danehill(IRE) Tina Thyne (IRE) (Good Thyne (USA))
1875^3 (2903) ◆ 3661^2 4075^2

Shine A Diamond (IRE) *Lucinda Russell* 96h 82c
6 gr g St Jovite(USA) Mossy Grey (IRE) (Step Together I (USA))
1877^5 2420^4 2748^9 3516^7 **3876^7 4616^5**

Shine In Time (IRE) *Laura Mongan* 91h
6 b m Definite Article Time To Shine (Pivotal)
4797^3 5114^P

Shining Cross (IRE) *Richard Woollacott*
4 b g Cape Cross(IRE) Shining Debut (IRE) (In The Wings)
5003^{10}

Shinko Moon *Jamie Snowden* 87h
7 b g Shinko Forest(IRE) Silver Moon (Environment Friend)
188^4 436^{11} 635^6 927^8

Shinooki (IRE) *Alex Hales* 92h
7 br g Blueprint(IRE) Rapid Response (IRE) (Be My Native (USA))
2181^5 2850^7 3735^9 4865^{11}

Shinrock Beat *Barry Brennan* 65h 51c
7 b g Beat All(USA) Alice Jones (IRE) (King's Ride)
969^P 1176^P

Shipton *Brendan Powell* 89h
5 b g Nayef(USA) Silk Road (Dansili)
1937^P 2457^7 2808^5 3166^{11} 3878^8

Shirls Son Sam *Chris Fairhurst* 21h
6 b g Rambling Bear Shirl (Shirley Heights)
1754^F 2420^U 4081^6

Shivalric (IRE) *Nicky Richards* 74h
6 b g Fruits Of Love(USA) Shamaiyla (FR) (Sendawar (IRE))
316^8 678^7 879^9

Shivsingh *Martin Hill* 101h
5 b g Montjeu(IRE) Vistaria (USA) (Distant View (USA))
2474^P 3043^7

Shoal Bay Dreamer *Dianne Sayer* 70h 87c
8 b m Central Park(IRE) Ninfa (IRE) (The Parson)
2219^2 2416^2 2818^3

Shockingtimes (IRE) *Charlie Mann* 107h 125c
7 b g Wareed(IRE) Jolly Lady (IRE) (Jolly Jake (NZ))
(2046)
2662^U 2909^F 3266^2 4932^5 5228^6

Shock N Freaney (IRE) *Anthony Middleton* 85c
7 ch g Clouseau(DEN) Iliner (IRE) (Fresh Breeze (USA))
1052^P
1262^5 1440^P
1528^4 1572a^4 1629^U 1825^5 2047^2

Shoegazer (IRE) *David Pipe* 137h 151c
9 b g Bach(IRE) American Native (IRE) (Lord Americo)
1195^6 **1476^3**

Shooters Wood (IRE) *Paul Nicholls* 96h 144c
10 b g Needle Gun(IRE) Talbot's Hollow (IRE) (Strong Statement (USA))
3080^{10} 3894^P *4495^3* **4790^{16} 5392^5**

Shooting Times *Lucinda Russell* 101h 96c
9 b g Commanche Run Rainbow Times (IRE) (Jareer (USA))
(311) **492^6**
866^P 1789^P 2497^4 3525^7 4223^6 (5514)

Shoreacres (IRE) *Ms Gillian Jones* 114h 114c
11 b g Turtle Island(IRE) Call Me Dara (IRE) (Arapahos (FR))
5346^2

Short Takes (USA) *Donald McCain* 116h
6 ch g Lemon Drop Kid(USA) Gabriellina Giof (Ashkalani (IRE))
2904^8 3451^7 4187^2 ◆ (4378) 4533^2 (4836)
5319^5

Shotavodka (IRE) *David Pipe* 144h 149c
8 ch g Alderbrook Another Vodka (IRE) (Moscow Society (USA))
2213^9 2454^2 2813^2 3200^8 **3831^2 (4373)**
5073^3 5383^2

Shot From The Hip (GER) *E J O'Grady* 150h 145c
10 b g Monsun(GER) Sopran Biro (IRE) (Roi Danzig (USA))
1604a^5 1897a^4 ◆ 2708a^{13}

Shotgun Paddy (IRE) *Emma Lavelle* 127h 158c
7 b g Brian Boru Awesome Miracle (IRE) (Supreme Leader)
(2077) ◆ 2658^3 3095^2 (3655)
4741^2

Shot In The Dark (IRE) *Jonathan Geake* 91h
5 ch g Dr Fong(USA) Highland Shot (Selkirk (USA))
295^7 711^4 946^8 2278^P

Shouldavboughtgold (IRE) *William Kinsey* 103h 116c
7 b g Classic Cliche(IRE) Sancta Miria (IRE) (Toulon)
556^F 2073^7 2655^9
2959^2 3283^2 3565^2

Should I Stay (FR) *Gary Moore* 115h 95c
6 b g Muhtathir Dusky Royale (FR) (Double Bed (FR))
2007^F 2025^P 3249^4 3959^4 (4377) 4659^3 4937^2
(5441)

Shout It Aloud *Tim Vaughan* 62b
5 b g Proclamation(IRE) Party Charmer (Charmer)
4016^2 ◆ 4547^9

Showman (IRE) *M S Dilworth*
11 ch g Carroll House Bettys The Act (IRE) (Mister Lord (USA))
325^P

Showmehow *Ray Craggs* 18h
6 b m Grape Tree Road Rasin Luck (Primitive Rising (USA))
278^5

Show Public (FR) *Simon Shirley-Beavan* 74h 115c
8 b g Network(GER) Grageline (FR) (Hellios (USA))
(112) **1976^U**

Shrapnel (IRE) *Gordon Elliott* 144h 140c
8 bb g Flemensfirth(USA) Victoria Theatre (IRE) (Old Vic)
(2116a)
2550a^4 3314a^6 3806a^P 4314a^3

Shrewd Investment *Miss L Thomas* 108h 123c
8 ch g Beauchamp King Zaffarimbi (IRE) (Zaffaran (USA))
287^4 523^5 4705^2 (5035)
5491^2

Shubaat *John Ferguson* 123h
7 ch g Monsun(GER) Zaynaat (Unfuwain (USA))
3506^P 4758^4 (5071) 5258^2

Shuh Shuh Gah (IRE) *David Bridgwater* 116h
7 ch g Accordion Hannigan's Lodger (IRE) (Be My Native (USA))
185[3] 538[5]
Shuil Gealach (IRE) *Paul Webber* 100h
6 b m Flemensfirth(USA) Rith Ar Aghaidh (IRE) (Phardante (FR))
324[3] (715) 4487[3] 4797[2]
Shuil Royale (IRE) *David Arbuthnot* 124h 130c
9 b g King's Theatre(IRE) Shuil Na Lee (IRE) (Phardante (FR))
1944[5] 2367[5] 3097[2] ◆ 3293[5] 4134[5]
Shutthefrontdoor (IRE) *Jonjo O'Neill* 148h 155c
7 bb g Accordion Hurricane Girl (IRE) (Strong Gale)
(2074) ◆ 2501[2] 3079[4] 4741[6] (5474a)
Shy John *P W Mason* 130c
8 b g Kier Park(IRE) Shy Lizzie (Buzzards Bay)
(3993)
(4246) 4788[8] 5131[4]
Siberian Tiger (IRE) *Evan Williams* 127h 125c
9 b g Xaar Flying Millie (IRE) (Flying Spur (AUS))
508[3] 780[2]
851[8] 1040[3] 1362[5] 1815[P]
Si Bien (FR) *Ali Brewer* 42h 47c
9 b g Solon(GER) Secret Gold (GER) (Lemhi Gold (USA))
631[6] 810[6] 1000[6] 1860[P] 4721[10]
5144[P]
Si C'Etait Vrai (FR) *D T Hughes* 140h 140c
8 b g Robin Des Champs(FR) Bleu Perle (FR) (Pistolet Bleu (IRE))
2551a[4]
Sid *Mark Gillard* 68h
6 ch g Needwood Blade Easter Moon (FR) (Easter Sun)
192[4] 517[13] 808[7] 1000[7]
Sidbury Hill *Seamus Mullins* 112h
6 ch g Midnight Legend Flora Macdonald (Alflora (IRE))
(2026) 2667[2] 5181[3]
Side Step *Nicky Henderson* 109b
5 b m Norse Dancer(IRE) Magic Score (Shambo)
2892[3] (3898) 4683[9]
Sidi Bouknadel (FR) *J-L Guillochon* 117h 149c
6 gr g Blackdoun(FR) Essaouira (FR) (Solid Illusion (USA))
5425a[2]
Sidney Melbourne (USA) *Paul Nicholls* 129h
7 ch g Lemon Drop Kid(USA) Tolltally Light (USA) (Majestic Light (USA))
(192) 673[2] 831[2] 1041[2]
Sid's Topper (FR) *Tom George*
4 bb g Anabaa Blue Last Sicyos (FR) (Sicyos (USA))
5021[P]
Sierra Victor (IRE) *Rose Dobbin* 70b 102c
11 b g Blueprint(IRE) An Charraig Mhor (IRE) (Tremblant)
492[5] (802)
1377[U] 1505[3]
Signalman *Sandy Thomson* 98h 121c
10 gr g Silver Patriarch(IRE) Kairine (IRE) (Kahyasi)
342[P]
Signed Request (IRE) *Henry Oliver* 102h
7 b g Fantastic Quest(IRE) Magic Sign (IRE) (The Parson)
244[9]
Sign Of A Victory (IRE) *Nicky Henderson* 137h
5 b g Kayf Tara Irish Wedding (IRE) (Bob Back (USA))
359[4] (2472) ◆ 2802[4] *(4019)* ◆ (4529) (4959)
5250[2]
Siksika (IRE) *Dan Skelton* 90h
6 b m Golan(IRE) Native Delight (IRE) (Be My Native (USA))
2027[4] 2317[10] 2602[17] 4981[8] 5282[P]
Silas Mariner (IRE) *Mandy Rowland* 127h 114c
7 b g Indian Danehill(IRE) Fancy Boots (IRE) (Salt Dome (USA))
64[2] 206[6]
Silent Cliche (IRE) *Ms N M Hugo* 92h 94c
10 b g Classic Cliche(IRE) Mini Moo Min (Ardross)
112[P] 5431[4]
Silent Knight (IRE) *Warren Greatrex* 87h
5 b g Pierre Aristocracy Lass (IRE) (Aristocracy)
3567[5] 3796[8] 4506[7] 4888[6]
Silent Owner *Paddy Butler*
6 b m Norse Dancer(IRE) Popsleebobross (IRE) (Revuque (IRE))
1625[P] **1744[P]**
Silent Snow (IRE) *W T Reed* 86b
9 ch g Moscow Society(USA) Miss Ogan (IRE) (Supreme Leader)
4225[U]
Silk And Roses *Mrs Wendy Hamilton* 66h 70c
11 gr m Roi De Rome(USA) Joetta (IRE) (Roselier (FR))
4617[3] 5209[5]
Silk Hall (UAE) *J J Lambe* 140h 54c
9 b g Halling(USA) Velour (Mtoto)
216[7] (1067a) 5274[10] 5471a[7]
Silk Sky *Phil McEntee* 29b
8 ch m Shahrastani(USA) Insulate (Sula Bula)
1[P] 3116[P] 4074[P]
Silsol (GER) *Paul Nicholls* 140h
5 b g Soldier Hollow Silveria (GER) (Groom Dancer (USA))
2075[4] 3023[2] 3989[2] *4300[2]* (5272) ◆ (5550)
Silver B *Mark Brisbourne*
6 gr m Silver Patriarch(IRE) Hill Farm Dancer (Gunner B)
1599[13]
Silver By Nature *Lucinda Russell* 103h 152c
12 gr g Silver Patriarch(IRE) Gale (Strong Gale)
2674[2] (Dead)
Silver Chop (FR) *F Nicolle* 134h 121c
5 b g Soave(GER) Free Track (FR) (Solid Illusion (USA))
1742a[5]
Silver Commander *Victor Dartnall* 114h 130c
7 gr g Silver Patriarch(IRE) New Dawn (Rakaposhi King)
9[2] 302[2] 1831[2] 2107[3] 2928[5]
Silver Concorde *D K Weld* 140b
6 b g Dansili Sacred Pearl (IRE) (Daylami (IRE))
(4756)
Silver Crossing *John Wade* 93b
5 b g Avonbridge Silver Purse (Interrex (CAN))
4611[11] 5063[6] 5500[7]
Silver Dragon *Tony Coyle* 102h
6 gr g Silver Patriarch(IRE) Gotogeton (Le Moss)
1467[4] 1873[2] (1940) 2202[3] 3265[P] *4326[4]* 4461[9] (4823) 5366[5]
Silver Eagle (IRE) *Kim Bailey* 136h
6 gr g Presenting Lady Lincon (IRE) (Great Palm (USA))
(19) (317) 1972[2] 2504[11] 2826[2] 3086[5] 5093[10]
Silver Gent (IRE) *Donald McCain* 108h
6 gr g Milan All's Rosey (IRE) (Roselier (FR))
3926[2] 4574[5] 5071[5] (5508)
Silvergrove *Richard Woollacott* 103h
6 b g Old Vic Classic Gale (USA) (Classic Cliche (IRE))
3173[9] 3695[5] 4171[5] 4514[6] 5005[8]
Silver Marizah (IRE) *Roger Ingram* 56h
5 b m Manduro(GER) Maharani (USA) (Red Ransom (USA))
2272[8]
Silver Regent (USA) *J Vana Jr*
9 b g Silver Deputy(CAN) Alexine (ARG) (Runaway Groom (CAN))
1904a[6]
Silver Roque (FR) *Fergal O'Brien* 106h 148c
8 b g Laveron Bible Gun (FR) (Pistolet Bleu (IRE))
(2448)
3082[P] 5535[6]
Silver Songstress *John Weymes* 82b
4 b f Singspiel(IRE) Composing (IRE) (Noverre (USA))
2731[4] 5381[10]
Silver Sophfire *Sue Smith* 86h
8 gr m Silver Patriarch(IRE) Princess Timon (Terimon)
218[6] 450[5] 629[9] 2333[P]
Silver Steel (FR) *Richard Ford* 42h 100c
11 b g Robin Des Pres(FR) Oliver's Queen (FR) (King Cyrus I (USA))
172[2] 707[P] 3755[7] 4570[3] 5442[P]
Silver Storm *Tristan Davidson* 81b
6 gr m Tikkanen(USA) Ifni Du Luc (FR) (Chamberlin (FR))
2752[10] 3042[8] 3529[4] 4429[P]
Silver Tassie (IRE) *Noel Meade* 132h
6 b g Shantou(USA) Silver Castor (IRE) (Indian Ridge)
1893a[4] 2256a[4]
Silver Token *David Brace* 108h 118c
9 gr g Silver Patriarch(IRE) Commanche Token (IRE) (Commanche Run)
(5041)
5165[2] 5553[3]
Silverton *Lucy Normile* 96h
7 gr m Silver Patriarch(IRE) Gretton (Terimon)
316[12] 2217[2] 3210[6]
Silver Vogue *Sue Smith* 83h
6 gr g Revoque(IRE) Pusslin (Gran Alba (USA))
4384[3] 4605[4] 5050[5] 5296[6]
Silver Whisper (FR) *A Le Clerc*
10 gr g Baroud D'Honneur(FR) Madame Flibuste (FR) (Rahotep I (FR))
199a[P]
Silver Wren *Renee Robeson* 111h
7 gr m Silver Patriarch(IRE) Wren Warbler (Relkino)
2193[2] 4070[3] 4508[P]
Silviniaco Conti (FR) *Paul Nicholls* 164h 179c
8 ch g Dom Alco(FR) Gazelle Lulu (FR) (Altayan)
2673[3] (3262)
4787[4] (5133)
Simarian (IRE) *Evan Williams* 134h 95c
9 b g Kalanisi(IRE) Sinnariya (IRE) (Persian Bold)
158[4] **680[F]**
Simarthur *Lucinda Russell* 117h 66c
7 gr g Erhaab(USA) Dusty Too (Terimon)
1755[2] 2030[5] (3018) 3726[4]
4530[4] 5481[P]
Simmi's Tiger *Anthony Carson* 50b
4 b g Tiger Hill(IRE) Simacota (GER) (Acatenango (GER))
2830[6] *3229[5]*
Simmons *Alastair Lidderdale* 86h
6 b m Spartacus(IRE) One For Me (Tragic Role (USA))
2978[P] 5245[6]
Simmply Sam *Marjorie Fife* 74h
7 b m Nomadic Way(USA) Priceless Sam (Silly Prices)
4479[6] 4743[5]
Simonet (FR) *E Leenders*
11 b g Simon Du Desert(FR) La Star (FR) (Arctic Tern (USA))
200a[P]
Simon Squirrel (IRE) *Charlie Brooks* 102b
4 b g Robin Des Champs(FR) Misty Heather (IRE) (Oscar (IRE))
(5181)
Simplified *Michael Chapman* 71h
11 b m Lend A Hand Houston Heiress (USA) (Houston (USA))
161[6] 4796[9] 5189[U]
Simply A Legend *Alan King* 127h
5 b g Midnight Legend Disco Danehill (IRE) (Danehill Dancer (IRE))
146[3] 2018[2] 2471[5] 3034[2] *4019[6]* 4506[2] (5088)
Simply Charles (IRE) *Hilary Parrott* 89b 90c
7 ch g Blueprint(IRE) Stormy Sea (IRE) (Strong Gale)
2719[5] 3011[6] 4885[5] 5263[4] 5433[4]
Simply Ned (IRE) *Nicky Richards* 135h 157c
7 ch g Fruits Of Love(USA) Bishops Lass (IRE) (Marju (IRE))
1849[F] (2222)
2656[2] 3037[2] (3894)
4543[3] 5168[2]
Simply Wings (IRE) *Richard Lee* 120h 134c
10 b g Winged Love(IRE) Simply Deep (IRE) (Simply Great (FR))
2180[2] 2645[3] 3362[P] 4675[5]
Simson (FR) *T Boivin* 93h 93c
8 ch g Ragmar(FR) Ulmeta II (FR) (Olmeto)
(1623a)
Sinbad The Sailor *George Baker* 121h
9 b g Cape Cross(IRE) Sinead (USA) (Irish River (FR))
(1707) 1956[9] 3186[8] 4801[3] 5128[7]
Sin Bin (IRE) *Paul Nicholls* 119h 120c
8 b g Presenting Navaro (IRE) (Be My Native (USA))
2073[2]
2475[P] *4326[2]* **5006[2]**
Sing Alone *Christopher Kellett*
8 ch g Band On The Run Remalone (Remezzo)
5071[P]
Singaminnie (FR) *H Billot* 98h
4 b f Davidoff(GER) Singapore Lady (FR) (Goldmark (USA))
615a[6]
Singapore Gold (FR) *P Cottin*
7 b g Sagacity(FR) Icaressa (Anabaa (USA))
1214a[F]
Singapore Sky (FR) *Yannick Fouin* 102h 125c
7 b g Sagacity(FR) Desert Threat (IRE) (Desert Prince (IRE))
455a[0]
Singapore Sling (FR) *A Bonin* 140h 104c
5 ch g Muhtathir Spinning Secretary (USA) (Spinning World (USA))
1983a[5] 2414a[4]
Singapore Story (FR) *Neil King* 66b
5 bb g Sagacity(FR) Vettorina (FR) (Vettori (IRE))
4310[9] 5447[10]
Singh Is King *Marc Barber* 89b
6 b g Fair Mix(IRE) Leading Lady (Fraam)
5070[8] 5310[5]
Sin Miedo (IRE) *Mrs John Harrington* 114h
4 br g Intikhab(USA) Xaviera (IRE) (Xaar)
2851a[5]
Sin Palo (IRE) *W P Mullins* 116b 133c
10 b g Dushyantor(USA) Platinum Gold (Proverb)
1572a[5] 1897a[7] 4754[P]
Sir Benfro *Keith Goldsworthy* 76h
8 b g Runyon(IRE) Dunrowan (Dunbeath (USA))
482[6] 590[13]
Sir Bruno (FR) *Tim Vaughan*
7 ch g Hernando(FR) Moon Tree (FR) (Groom Dancer (USA))
994[U]
Sir Des Champs (FR) *W P Mullins* 143h 174c
8 b g Robin Des Champs(FR) Liste En Tete (FR) (Video Rock (FR))
2991a[F] 3376a[4]
Sir Du Bearn (FR) *Peter Bowen* 53h 137c
8 bb g Passing Sale(FR) Girl Du Bearn (FR) (Sarpedon (FR))
2086[5] 2269[U] 2812[11] 3131[2] 3416[4] 4026[P] 5170[9]
5276[P]
Sir Dylan *Ronald Harris* 104h
5 b g Dylan Thomas(IRE) Monteleone (IRE) (Montjeu (IRE))
80[F] 994[2] 1525[2] 4513[P]
Sire Collonges (FR) *Paul Nicholls* 124h 149c
8 gr g Dom Alco(FR) Idylle Collonges (FR) (Quart De Vin (FR))
1971[9] 2491[6] (3068)
4754[8] 5371[3]
Sire De Grugy (FR) *Gary Moore* 149h 174c
8 ch g My Risk(FR) Hirlish (FR) (Passing Sale (FR))
(2081) ◆ 2532[2] (2952)
(3320) (3773)
(4753) (5570)
Sirene D'Ainay (FR) *Emmanuel Clayeux* 143h 126c
8 b m Dom Alco(FR) Evermine (FR) (Perrault)
4740[F]
Sir Frank (IRE) *David Pipe* 121h 127c
9 b g Old Vic Leave Me Be (IRE) (Be My Native (USA))
1636[6] 1797[5] 2458[3] (2691) 3085[6]
Sir Frodlot (IRE) *Brondan Powoll* 115h
5 b g Choisir(AUS) Wurfklinge (GER) (Acatenango (GER))
244[3] 591[6]
Sir Harry Hotspur *John Mackie* 88h
6 gr g Tikkanen(USA) Harry's Bride (Sir Harry Lewis (USA))
589[7] 2954[10] 3388[U] 3598[9] 4945[5] 5366[11]
Sir Hubert *Richard Rowe* 66b
4 b g Multiplex Lacounsel (FR) (Leading Counsel (USA))
5264[10]
Sir Ivan *Harry Fry* 97b
4 b g Midnight Legend Tisho (Sir Harry Lewis (USA))
5241[3]
Sir John *Suzy Smith* 74h
8 ch g Sir Harry Lewis(USA) Jenga (Minster Son)
1105[F]
Sir Kezbaah (IRE) *Richard Woollacott* 113h 81c
10 b g Oscar(IRE) Madam Chloe (Dalsaan)
3172[P] 5333[7]
Sir Lynx (IRE) *Chris Bealby* 118h 100c
7 gr g Amilynx(FR) Minilus (IRE) (Luso)
2599[7] 3823[U] 4250[2] 4482[6] 5498[4]
Sir Mangan (IRE) *Donald McCain* 127h
6 b g Darsi(FR) Lady Pep (IRE) (Cajetano (USA))
2104[3] 2520[2] 3036[2] (3634) 4038[2] 4489[4] 5280[3]
Sir Mattie (IRE) *David Rees* 111h 120c
9 bb g Moscow Society(USA) Manhattan Catch (IRE) (Safety Catch (USA))
481[3] 642[2] 766[6]
Sirnita *Richard Guest* 7b
5 br m Striking Ambition Zenita (IRE) (Zieten (USA))
4867[14]
Siro Demur (FR) *Philip Rowley* 117c
8 ch g Murmure(FR) Jourenuit (FR) (Chamberlin (FR))
557[6] (4658)
5035[P] (5346)
Sirop De Menthe (FR) *Miss Jessica Westwood* 104h
4 ch g Discover D'Auteuil(FR) Jolie Menthe (FR) (Bateau Rouge)
725[4] (975) 1182[2] 2927[5] 3134[5] 3802[U]
Sir Pitt *John Bryan Groucott* 115h
7 b g Tiger Hill(IRE) Rebecca Sharp (Machiavellian (USA))
3128[4] 3600[2] 4224[8] 5071[2] 5353[9]
Sirrah Star (IRE) *Neil Mulholland* 95b
6 gr m Great Palm(USA) Simply Deep (IRE) (Simply Great (FR))
2634[2] *4016[15]* 5440[8]
Sir Rowan (FR) *J Planque* 110c
8 b g Kapgarde(FR) Idole De Pont Kerlo (FR) (Quitte Et Passe I (FR))
199a[8]
Sir Safir *Peter Niven* 86b
4 b g Croco Rouge(IRE) Angela's Ashes (Common Grounds)
3619[5] 4310[7]
Sir Scorpion (IRE) *Thomas Mullins* 111b
5 b g Scorpion(IRE) Lady Goldilocks (IRE) (Mister Lord (USA))
5424a[2]
Sir Tantallus Hawk *Alistair Whillans* 92h 92c
10 b g Overbury(IRE) Mobile Miss (IRE) (Classic Secret (USA))
5251[6]
Sir Tommy *Maurice Barnes* 85b
5 ch g Sir Harry Lewis(USA) Rose Of Overbury (Overbury (IRE))
4205[8] 4944[4] 5499[9]
Sir Trevor (IRE) *John Bryan Groucott* 42h
5 b g Refuse To Bend(IRE) Joyfullness (USA) (Dixieland Band (USA))
8[9] 857[11]
Sir Tyto (IRE) *Ali Brewer* 94b
6 b g Fruits Of Love(USA) Sophie May (Glint Of Gold)
412[4] 768[6]
Sir Valentino (FR) *Tom George* 115h 129c
5 b g Early March Valentine (FR) (Double Bed (FR))
2083[2] 2876[3] **3354[F] 3732[2] 4536[F]** (5519)
Sir Vinski (IRE) *Nicky Richards* 112b
5 ch g Vinnie Roe(IRE) Mill Emerald (Old Vic)
(4958)
Sisterbrooke (IRE) *John Panvert*
5 ch m Trans Island Cool Merenda (IRE) (Glacial Storm (USA))
2583[8]
Sister Guru *Peter Hedger*
5 b m Ishiguru(USA) Ulysses Daughter (IRE) (College Chapel)
2265[R]
Sitting Back (IRE) *Ms G Howell*
10 b g Flying Legend(USA) Double Pearl (IRE) (Doubletour (USA))
4485[P]
Sivola De Sivola (FR) *Tom George* 120h 139c
8 gr g Martaline Kerrana (FR) (Cadoudal (FR))
340[2] (736)
(1888) 2220[3] 3387[9]
4962[13]
Six Des Champs (FR) *A Lacombe* 130c
10 b g Robin Des Champs(FR) Balle Six (FR) (Balsamo (FR))
131a[2]
Six One Away (IRE) *Paul Webber* 90h
5 gr g Tikkanen(USA) Surfing France (FR) (Art Francais (USA))
2040[6] 2453[5] 3061[5] 5075[P]
Six Stone Ned (IRE) *Noel Meade* 128h 132c
8 gr g Great Palm(USA) Ashfield Rosie (IRE) (Roselier (FR))
1950a[2] 2116a[3] 2550a[7]
Sixty Something (FR) *Paul Webber* 127h 140c
8 gr g Dom Alco(FR) Jaunas (FR) (Lute Antique (FR))
2221[F] 2672[13]
3011[2] 3327[3] 4273[2] (4946)
5373[2]
Sizing America (IRE) *Miss S Randell* 54h 115c
13 b g Lord Americo Annfield Lady (IRE) (Furry Glen)
5135[10]
Sizing Australia (IRE) *Henry De Bromhead* 118h 134c
12 b g New Frontier(IRE) All The Gear (IRE) (Nashamaa)
2937[U] 4754[5]
Sizing Codelco (IRE) *Henry De Bromhead* 135h
5 b g Flemensfirth(USA) La Zingarella (IRE) (Phardante (FR))
4708a[3]
Sizing Europe (IRE) *Henry De Bromhead* [illegible]5h 173c
12 b g Pistolet Bleu(IRE) Jennie Dun (IRE) (Mandalus)
(1776a)
2234a[2] 3338a[4] 4753[4]
Sizing France (FR) *J Bertran De Balanda* [illegible]5h 130c
6 b g Astarabad(USA) Miss Academy (FR) (Video Rock (FR))
(454a)
Sizing Gold (IRE) *Henry De Bromhead* 105h 145c
7 b g Flemensfirth(USA) Mandys Gold (IRE) (Mandalus)
3791a[2] 4764[6]
Sizing Italy (IRE) *Henry De Bromhead* 126h 140c
7 b g Milan Julias Love (IRE) (Mister Lord (USA))
1178a[2] 1973[2]

Sizing Machine (IRE) *Henry De Bromhead* 138h 132c
6 b g King's Theatre(IRE) Sno-Cat Lady (IRE) (Executive Perk)
2550a[6]

Sizing Rio (IRE) *Henry De Bromhead* 141h 148c
6 b g Heron Island(IRE) Shyanne (IRE) (Mandalus)
(2258a) ◆ 2853a[4] 3404a[P] (Dead)

Sizing Symphony (IRE) *Henry De Bromhead* 144h 129c
8 b g Sadler's Wells(USA) Amberina (IRE) (Bob Back (USA))
1957[7]

Skating Home (IRE) *P Ponting*
8 b g Luso Wintry Day (IRE) (Presenting)
5545[P]

Ski Guide *Lucinda Russell* 57b
4 b g Three Valleys(USA) Dansara (Dancing Brave (USA))
2247[5]

Skint *Ali Brewer* 122h 126c
8 b g King's Theatre(IRE) No More Money (Alflora (IRE))
591[5] ◆ 782[3] 877[6]
1050[2] 1194[2] 1302[6] 2958[3] 4682[9] 5496[3]

Ski Sunday *Tim Vaughan* 145h 121c
9 b g King's Best(USA) Lille Hammer (Sadler's Wells (USA))
1343[2] 1744[2] 2078[P] *4325[3]* **4915[3] 5287[3]**

Sky Calling *Martin Keighley* 101h 113c
11 b m Bal Harbour Curlew Calling (IRE) (Pennine Walk)
251[5] 858[8]

Sky Flyer (FR) *J-C Baudoin* 91h 65c
6 b g Great Pretender(IRE) Themis Eria (FR) (Signe Divin (USA))
198a[9]

Sky Khan *Richard Guest* 130h
5 b g Cape Cross(IRE) Starlit Sky (Galileo (IRE))
354[2] 673[5] (928) 1139a[2] ◆ (1418) 3758[5] 4736[16]

Sky Run (FR) *C Lerner* 93h
4 b f Astarabad(USA) Sky Dance i (FR) (Sky Lawyer (FR))
130a[9]

Sky Watch (IRE) *Warren Greatrex* 116h
7 b g Flemensfirth(USA) The Shining Force (IRE) (Strong Gale)
2689[2] 3136[3] 3695[4] 4175[3] 4596[2] 4969[6]

Slam *Tom George* 57h
9 b g Beat Hollow House Hunting (Zafonic (USA))
1269[9]

Slaney Star (IRE) *Jim Best* 105h
6 b g Cloudings(IRE) Slaney Rose (IRE) (Roselier (FR))
599[3] 862[3] 1632[4] 1749[5] 2002[7] 2272[0] 2564[6] 2740[8] 4247[2] 4447[2] 4636[8] 4882[F] 5029[0]

Sleep In First (FR) *James Ewart* 110h 128c
8 bb g Sleeping Car(FR) First Union (FR) (Shafoun (FR))
26[3] (583) 678[4] **2793[F]** 2970[7]
3476[5] 4224[7] 4746[3] 5214[5]

Sleeping City (FR) *Victor Dartnall* 104h
7 bb g Sleeping Car(FR) City Prospect (FR) (Diamond Prospect (USA))
116[F] 2111[7] 2910[5] 3390[11]

Sleepy (FR) *Sophie Leech* 22h
8 b g Sleeping Car(FR) Haida IV (FR) (Passing Sale (FR))
4018[9] 4350[11] 4931[P]

Sleepy Eye (IRE) *Jedd O'Keeffe* 78h
5 b g Catcher In The Rye(IRE) Lithica (IRE) (Orpen (USA))
3330[8]

Sleepy Haven (IRE) *Jennie Candlish* 120h
4 b g Indian Haven High Society Girl (IRE) (Key Of Luck (USA))
725[3] 2098[3] (2455) 2927[2] 3364[3] 4081[2] 4899[5] 5190[4] 5568[2]

Slick Operator (IRE) *D J Dickenson*
8 b g Flemensfirth(USA) Glacier Lilly (IRE) (Glacial Storm (USA))
5485[F]

Slipper Satin (IRE) *Noel Quinlan* 105h
4 b f Excellent Art In The Ribbons (In The Wings)
2577[3] (3854) 4037[U] 4307[4] 4576[3]

Slow Game (FR) *G Cherel* 122h 119c
8 b g Al Namix(FR) Jouable (FR) (Garde Royale)
131a[6]

Slow Train Coming (IRE) *Evan Williams* 112h
7 b g Sanglamore(USA) Donegal House (IRE) (Overbury (IRE))
1341[3] 1697[P]

Smad Place (FR) *Alan King* 161h 163c
7 gr g Smadoun(FR) Bienna Star (FR) (Village Star (FR))
2249[U] (2459)
(4148) 4751[2]

Smadynium (FR) *Philip Hobbs* 119h 125c
6 gr g Smadoun(FR) Sea Music (FR) (Bering)
371[4] 1729[6] 2032[4] 2668[3] (2879) 3201[4]
3615[2] 4549[2] 5290[6]

Smalib Monterg (FR) *Dr Richard Newland* 130h
8 b g Smadoun(FR) Liberty'S (FR) (Chamberlin (FR))
356[2] (409) 901[F]

Smart Catch (IRE) *Tony Carroll* 118h 110c
8 b g Pivotal Zafaraniya (IRE) (Doyoun)
202[7] 833[9] **1939[8] (2560)**
2897[U] 4482[5] (4984)
5450[3]

Smart Exit (IRE) *Renee Robeson* 107h 110c
7 b g Exit To Nowhere(USA) Navaro (IRE) (Be My Native (USA))
2275[2] 2678[3] 3178[2] (3797)
4451[4] 5025[4]

Smart Freddy *Ben Pauling* 121h
8 b g Groom Dancer(USA) Smart Topsy (Oats)
2742[2]

Smart Money (IRE) *Venetia Williams* 115h 110c
7 br g Spadoun(FR) Victoria Day (Reference Point)
2729[2] 3094[2] 3802[3]
4560[2]

Smart Motive *Alan King* 77h
4 b g Motivator Santana Lady (IRE) (Blakeney)
2436[5] 4349[6] 5305[7]

Smart Ruler (IRE) *James Moffatt* 118h
8 ch g Viking Ruler(AUS) Celebrated Smile (IRE) (Cadeaux Genereux)
1713 475[2] (1072) (1415) 1540[2] 2344[U] 3758[3] 4899[6] 5295[3]

Smart Story *Fergal O'Brien*
7 b g Iktibas Clever Nora (IRE) (Topanoora)
4298[8] 4535[P]

Smashing (FR) *W P Mullins* 145h 118c
5 gr g Smadoun(FR) Faragreen (FR) (Green Tune (USA))
4147[9] 4752[4]

Smiles For Miles (IRE) *David Pipe* 114h
6 b g Oscar(IRE) Native Kin (IRE) (Be My Native (USA))
2195[4] 3116[3] 3600[5] 3694[4] ◆ 4132[2] 4516[3]

Smiling Lady (IRE) *David Rees* 102h 94c
8 ch m Kris Kin(USA) Band Of Colour (IRE) (Spectrum (IRE))
142[4] 269[5] 419[6]

Smoking Aces (IRE) *Jonjo O'Neill* 142h 136c
10 b g Old Vic Callmartel (IRE) (Montelimar (USA))
2945[6] 3554[2] 4026[3] 4427[2]

Smooth Classic (IRE) *David Pipe* 118h 112c
10 b g Luso Noan Rose (IRE) (Roselier (FR))
117[2] 420[6] 689[3]

Smooth Handle *Danielle McCormick*
4 ch g Dutch Art Naomi Wildman (USA) (Kingmambo (USA))
1394[P]

Smooth Stepper *Sue Smith* 99b
5 b g Alflora(IRE) Jazzy Refrain (IRE) (Jareer (USA))
5108[3]

Snake Eyes (IRE) *Nicky Henderson* 121h
6 b g Oscar(IRE) Be My Belle (IRE) (Be My Native (USA))
2178[4] 3910a[6]

Snapchat (IRE) *Seamus Durack* 105h
7 b g Shantou(USA) Kelly's Native (IRE) (Be My Native (USA))
1013[2] ◆ 1261[3] 1427[5] 1793[4] 2002[5] 2272[6] 2718[12] 3149[3] 3878[F] 4275[P]

Snapping Turtle (IRE) *Donald Whillans* 94h 94c
9 b g Turtle Island(IRE) Rachael's Dawn (Rakaposhi King)
(3040) 3726[6]

Snap Tie (IRE) *Philip Hobbs* 153h 141c
12 b g Pistolet Bleu(IRE) Aries Girl (Valiyar (IRE))
356[P]

Snippetydoodah *Michael Roberts* 88b
6 b m King's Theatre(IRE) Kimpour (FR) (Hawker's News (IRE))
2570[4]

Snooze (FR) *F Nicolle* 134c
8 br g Sleeping Car(FR) Kittygale (IRE) (Strong Gale)
1984a[P]

Snooze N You Lose *Jean McGregor* 30c
9 b g Helissio(FR) Utmost (IRE) (Most Welcome)
314[7] 627[8] 1147[7] 1789[P] 5483[P]

Snoqualmie Chief *Gordon Elliott* 93h
4 b g Montjeu(IRE) Seattle Ribbon (USA) (Seattle Dancer (USA))
1658[F]

Snow Alert *John Norton* 86h
8 ch g Where Or When(IRE) Ela Aphrodite (Halling (USA))
15[6] 283[7] 852[5] 1306[5] 1635[4] 2787[P] 4865[P] 5300[7]

Snowball (IRE) *David Arbuthnot* 63h
7 gr g Alderbrook Rosafi (IRE) (Roselier (FR))
517[P] 971[F]

Snowed In (IRE) *Barbara Butterworth* 101h
5 gr g Dark Angel(IRE) Spinning Gold (Spinning World (USA))
1939[F] 2155[P] 2241[6] 2904[3] 3288[6] 3569[6] 4836[3] (5214) 5375[3]

Snuker *James Ewart* 80h 103c
7 b g Snurge Briar Rose (IRE) (Roselier (FR))
30[7] 311[2] 492[2] (2416)
(2591) 2974[3]
3497[F] 4382[3] (4626)
4942[3]

So Bazaar (IRE) *Andrew Wilson* 72h
7 b g Xaar Nature Girl (USA) (Green Dancer (USA))
3353[P] 3871[8] 4817[8] 5360[3]

So Cheeky *Richard Guest* 86h
5 ch m Fantastic View(USA) Fallujah (Dr Fong (USA))
552[2] 1400[9] 2679[7] 2877[15] 3264[P]

Social Overdrive (IRE) *Emma Baker* 93h
8 b g Alderbrook La Grande Duchesse (IRE) (Accordion)
3850[3]
4344[P] 4883[P]

Social Realism (IRE) *Jonjo O'Neill* 123h
6 b m Pivotal Russian Revolution (Dubai Millennium)
2673 (651) (738) 1043[3] (1347) 1564[7]

Society Shares (IRE) *Graeme McPherson* 115h
9 ch g Moscow Society(USA) Presenting Shares (IRE) (Presenting)
(3130) 3661[8]

Soeur Blanche (IRE) *Roy Brotherton* 88h
8 b m Oscar(IRE) Sunset Leader (IRE) (Supreme Leader)
367[9]

So Fine (IRE) *Philip Hobbs* 136h 135c
8 bb g Definite Article Not So Green (IRE) (Roselier (FR))
358[15] 1430[2] 1628[4] (1747) 1956[3] 2345[7] 3069[3] 4765[16] 5093[7]

Softsong (FR) *James Evans* 132h
6 b g Singspiel(IRE) Soft Gold (USA) (Gulch (USA))
(3598) 5349[P]

Sohappyharry *Jane Mathias* 73h
8 ch g Sir Harry Lewis(USA) Sohapara (Arapahos (FR))
718[4] 1011[3] 1284[8] 1488[7]

Sohcahtoa (IRE) *Andrew Crook* 87h
8 b g Val Royal(FR) Stroke Of Six (IRE) (Woodborough (USA))
1714[3] 2034[6] 2869[4] 3145[8]

So It Will Be (IRE) *Miss G E J Anderson* 65c
10 b m Publisher(USA) Beccemma (IRE) (Over The River (FR))
557[P]

Solaras Exhibition (IRE) *Tim Vaughan* 135h 64c
6 b g Great Exhibition(USA) Solara (GER) (Danehill (USA))
850[3] (973) 1685[10] 2344[5]

Solar Impulse (FR) *Paul Nicholls* 128h
4 b g Westerner Moon Glow (FR) (Solar One (FR))
3360[4] 4419[3] 4755[7] 5142[5] (5426)

Solar Sky *David Elsworth* 111h
6 ch g Galileo(IRE) La Sky (IRE) (Law Society (USA))
4807[5] ◆ 5236[3]

Soledad De Monnaie (FR) *P Journiac* 111c
8 b g Maresca Sorrento(FR) Calola (FR) (En Calcat (FR))
131a[5]

Soleil D'Avril (FR) *Mrs Sarah Easterby* 107h 86c
8 bb g Laveron Melanie Du Chenet (FR) (Nikos)
112[5]

Sole Survivor (FR) *Paul Webber* 100h
7 gr g Smadoun(FR) Sellaginella (Konigsstuhl (GER))
3419[5] **3876[P]**

Sole Witness (IRE) *C A McBratney* 98h 138c
10 b g Witness Box(USA) Deeco Valley (IRE) (Satco (FR))
2708a[7] 3868a[6] 5276[P]

Solidago (IRE) *S R B Crawford* 103h
7 b g Vinnie Roe(IRE) Native Belle (IRE) (Be My Native (USA))
2997[3] 3520[2] 4460[3] 5537[3]

Solid Concrete (IRE) *Neil Mulholland* 50h 101c
8 b m Insatiable(IRE) Official Secret (Polish Patriot (USA))
3092[9] 3357[12] 4176[7]

Solis (GER) *Dianne Sayer* 107h 100c
11 ch g In The Wings Seringa (GER) (Acatenango (GER))
221[2] (750) 867[9] 3938[P] 4553[9] **4771[2]** 5559[F]

Solitairy Girl *Harry Dunlop* 77h
5 b m Loup Solitaire(USA) Aphrodisias (FR) (Double Bed (FR))
3194[7] 4923[4]

Solitary Palm (IRE) *Brian Forsey* 93h 90c
11 gr g Great Palm(USA) Grande Solitaire (FR) (Loup Solitaire (USA))
84[4] (408)
1336[6] 1474[3] 1701[F]

Soliwery (FR) *David Pipe* 92h
6 b g Equerry(USA) Solimade (FR) (Loup Solitaire (USA))
1794[7] 2111[10]

Solix (FR) *Ian Williams* 119h 133c
8 bb g Al Namix(FR) Solimade (FR) (Loup Solitaire (USA))
1901a[8]
2269[4] 2812[6] ◆ 3205[5] 3897[4] 4661[3] 4738[16] 5253[P]

Solkap (FR) *G Chaignon* 117c
8 b g Kapgarde(FR) Solaine (FR) (Pot D'Or (FR))
559a[3]

Soll *Jo Hughes* 110h 144c
9 ch g Presenting Montelfolene (IRE) (Montelimar (USA))
2953[5] 4035[4] 4270[7] 4681[5] 5156[11]

Solo Jugadores *Richard Guest* 92h
6 b g Central Park(IRE) Billie Holiday (Fairy King (USA))
146[5] 648[7] 1007[4] 1072[5] 1506[3] 1575[5]

Solstice Dawn *Peter Winks* 93h
6 b m Lyphento(USA) Ryders Hill (Zaffaran (USA))
2196[7] 2514[10] 2850[5]

Solstice Son *Anthony Honeyball* 119h
5 b g Haafhd Karasta (IRE) (Lake Coniston (IRE))
(1891) 2216[7] 2602[13] 3034[14] 3226[5] (4719) (4803) (4913) 5074[3]

Solstice Star *Anthony Honeyball* 107b
4 b g Kayf Tara Clover Green (IRE) (Presenting)
3460[3]

Solway Bay *Lisa Harrison* 104h 104c
12 b g Cloudings(IRE) No Problem Jac (Safawan)
169[9] 495[3] 867[4] (958) 1164[3] 1304[P]
1469[P] 1798[7] 1982[5]

Solway Dandy *Lisa Harrison* 104h
7 b g Danroad(AUS) Solway Rose (Minster Son)
316[2] 884[F] 5532[2] ◆

Solway Dornal *Lisa Harrison* 83h 85c
9 b g Alflora(IRE) Solway Donal (IRE) (Celio Rufo)
172[3] 311[3] 444[6]
(473) 580[3] 628[3] 868[3] **1038[5]** 1073[4]
1163[2] 1300[3] 1377[3] 1416[2]
1505[2] 1655[4]
1789[U] 4607[2]
(4747) (4938)
4982[2] 5052[2]
5358[5] 5514[7]

Solway Legend *Lisa Harrison* 62h
7 ch g And Beyond(IRE) Spicey Cut (Cut Above)
3161[4] 4607[P] 5056[5] 5359[7]

Solway Sam *Lisa Harrison* 94h 100c
11 b g Double Trigger(IRE) Some Gale (Strong Gale)
312[4] 763[3] 1163[5] 1542[U] 1660[5] 2218[3] 4981[6] 5514[4]

Solway Silver *Lisa Harrison* 45h
8 gr g Silver Patriarch(IRE) Solway Rose (Minster Son)
1982[8]

Solway Star *Lisa Harrison* 62h
11 ch g Zaha(CAN) Cuddle Bunny (IRE) (Statoblest)
1073[P]

Solway Summer *Lisa Harrison* 62b
5 b m Double Trigger(IRE) Solway Donal (IRE) (Celio Rufo)
5560[10]

Solwhit (FR) *C Byrnes* 166h
10 b g Solon(GER) Toowhit Towhee (USA) (Lucky North (USA))
685a[2]

Somchine *Seamus Mullins* 110h
6 b g Volochine(IRE) Seem Of Gold (Gold Dust)
240[2] 484[U] 716[2] 1052[3]

Some Buckle (IRE) *Tom George* 106b
5 b g Milan Miss Moppit (IRE) (Torus)
4349[3]

Some Lad (IRE) *Alison Hamilton* 94h 97c
9 b g Beneficial Some News (IRE) (Be My Native (USA))
316[3] **493[2]**
4223[P] (4817)
5051[2] 5212[P]

Somemothersdohavem *Venetia Williams* 125h
5 ch g Avonbridge Show Off (Efisio)
3322[P] 3892[7] ◆ 4157[6] 4413[2] 4517[2] 4682[8] 5231[5]

Some Officer (IRE) *T Hogan* 133h
7 b g Court Cave(IRE) Commanche Blake (IRE) (Commanche Run)
2983a[7]

Some Plan (IRE) *Tom George* 115b
6 b g Winged Love(IRE) Lough Hyne (Classic Cliche (IRE))
4824[4]

Somerby (IRE) *Richenda Ford* 96c
11 b g Sadler's Wells(USA) Oriental Mystique (Kris)
(2082)
2441[3] 3797[4] 4066[2] 4601[P]

Somersby (IRE) *Mick Channon* 145h 167c
10 b g Second Empire(IRE) Back To Roost (IRE) (Presenting)
(2281)
2952[2] 3773[U] 4753[2]

Somerset Island (IRE) *Michael Smith* 96h
6 b g Barathea(IRE) Art Work (Zafonic (USA))
475[6]

Somerset Jem *Kevin Bishop* 98b
5 b g Sir Harry Lewis(USA) Monger Lane (Karinga Bay)
4638[5]

Somerset Lias (IRE) *Bob Buckler* 113h
6 b g Golan(IRE) Presenting Gayle (IRE) (Presenting)
2011[7] 2631[F] 4281[3] 5235[8]

Some Slam (IRE) *Mrs J Bright* 72h
9 b g Orpen(USA) Diva Aldante (IRE) (Phardante (FR))
523[P]

Somethingwonderful (IRE) *D T Hughes* 135h
6 bb g Viking Ruler(AUS) Innishmore (IRE) (Lear Fan (USA))
2852a[9] 5172[11]

Some Tikket (IRE) *D T Hughes* 139h 146c
7 b g Tikkanen(USA) Ally Rose (IRE) (Roselier (FR))
4314a[U]

Sommersturm (GER) *David Evans* 54h
10 b g Tiger Hill(IRE) Sommernacht (GER) (Monsun (GER))
436[8]

Sona Sasta (IRE) *S J Gilmore* 132c
11 b g Sonus(IRE) Derry Lark (IRE) (Lancastrian)
4706[P]

Song Of Pride (GER) *Mandy Rowland* 60h
10 ch g Platini(GER) Song Of Peace (GER) (Zampano (GER))
1799[11] 1940[F] 3014[U] 3119[5] 3569[P]

Songsmith *Lucy Wadham* 127h
6 b g Librettist(USA) Venus Rising (Observatory (USA))
4423[2] 4820[3] 5384[4]

Sonic Weld *Andrew J Martin* 18b
5 b m Zafeen(FR) Jamadast Roma (Doubletour (USA))
2472[12] *3230[5]*

Sonny Jim *John Mackie* 80h
6 b g Needwood Blade Sonderborg (Great Dane (IRE))
116[11] 434[4] 696[5] 927[11] 1799[14]

Sonny The One *Colin Tizzard* 89b
4 ch g Tobougg(IRE) Annie Fleetwood (Anshan)
5021[4] 5338[5]

Sonny Thyne *Lucinda Russell* 92b
5 b g Overbury(IRE) This Thyne (Good Thyne (USA))
3760[6] 4370[5]

Sonofagun (FR) *Ian Williams* 106h 131c
8 b g Turgeon(USA) Detonante (FR) (Cardoun (FR))
661[5] 844[3] (966) 1062[4]
2599[2] 3164[5] *4298[10]* **(4723)**
(4921) 5392[5] 5517[2]

Son Of Flicka *Tony Coyle* 129h 128c
10 b g Groom Dancer(USA) Calendula (Be My Guest (USA))
1728[P] 2882[4] 3450[2] 4346[4] 4752[11]
5192[U] 5362[U]

Son Of Suzie *Fergal O'Brien* 122h
6 gr g Midnight Legend Suzie Cream Cheese (IRE) (Royal Charter (FR))
270[5] 2773[3] (3194) (4450) 5008[5] 5510[6]

Sonoftheking (IRE) *Philip Hobbs* 93h
6 b g King's Theatre(IRE) Nikadora (FR) (Nikos)
233[7] 1595[4] 1828[7] 2105[10] 2690[14]

Sonofvic (IRE) *Paul Nicholls* 141h 147c
9 ch g Old Vic Prudent View (IRE) (Supreme Leader)
(2010)
2692[4]

Sonoran Sands (IRE) *Brendan Powell* 100h
6 b g Footstepsinthesand Atishoo (IRE) (Revoque (IRE))
4022[11] 4726[B] 5239[8]

Son Vida (IRE) *Alan Bailey*
6 b g Titus Livius(FR) Sombreffe (Polish Precedent (USA))
427[P]

Sooley *Michael Appleby* 49b
7 ch m Shahrastani(USA) Capponicus (IRE) (Woodborough (USA))
970[12]

So Oscar (IRE) *Lawney Hill* 103b
6 b g Oscar(IRE) So Proper (IRE) (Topanoora)
(2703) 5014[6]

Sophonie (FR) *Tom George* 110h 108c
8 b m Kapgarde(FR) Kore Des Obeaux (FR) (Saint Cyrien (FR))
343[5]

Sortina (CZE) *J Votava*
7 gr m Mill Pond(FR) Sorah (CZE) (House Rules I (USA))
1904a[9]

So Sudden *Mark Rimell* 48b
5 b m Needwood Blade Sudden Spirit (FR) (Esprit Du Nord (USA))
3863[12]

Sotovik (IRE) *Miss D V Carter*
13 gr g Aahsaylad Moenzi (IRE) (Paris House)
4554[P]

Soudain (FR) *Steve Gollings* 117h 129c
8 ch g Dom Alco(FR) Ebene D'Avril (FR) (Video Rock (FR))
(2678)
2971[P]

Soul Angel *Sandy Forster* 83h 82c
10 ch g Tipsy Creek(USA) Over Keen (Keen)
2818[5] 3107[5] 4203[2] 4220[3] 4462[4] 4652[2] 4775[4]
5358[3]

Soulard (USA) *Sophie Leech*
11 b g Arch(USA) Bourbon Blues (USA) (Seeking The Gold (USA))
63[9] 413[9]

Soul Magic (IRE) *Harriet Graham* 82h 102c
12 b g Flemensfirth(USA) Indian Legend (IRE) (Phardante (FR))
23[3] 533[4] (1075)
(1395) 5483[5]

Sound Investment (IRE) *Paul Nicholls* 124h 145c
6 b g Dr Massini(IRE) Drumcay Polly (IRE) (Le Bavard (FR))
2630[5] 2935[6] **3386[5] 3787[2] (4515)**
(4684) 5136[13] 5573[3]

Sound Stage *Miss S Berry* 79h 114c
11 b g Saddlers' Hall(IRE) Re-Release (Baptism)
40[3] 542[3] 636[3] 832[5] 5035[5]

Sous Officier (FR) *G Cherel* 109h 117c
8 b g Alberto Giacometti(IRE) Graine De Beaute (FR) (Conquistador I (FR))
1464a[P] 1740a[2]

Souter Point (USA) *William Kinsey* 94h
8 bb g Giant's Causeway(USA) Wires Crossed (USA) (Caller I.D. (USA))
563[9] 1848[5] 2397[8]

South Circle (IRE) *Liam Lennon* 78h
6 ch m Desert King(IRE) Bonnybridge (IRE) (Zaffaran (USA))
5381[9]

Southfield Belle (IRE) *Caroline Keevil* 68b
5 b m Presenting Laureldean Belle (IRE) (Supreme Leader)
5310[10]

Southfield Theatre (IRE) *Paul Nicholls* 152h
6 b g King's Theatre(IRE) Chamoss Royale (FR) (Garde Royale)
(2106) 2504[3] 3069[4] 3292[3] *4021[5]* 4765[2] (5572)

Southfield Vic (IRE) *Paul Nicholls* 119h
5 ch g Old Vic Chamoss Royale (FR) (Garde Royale)
1712[2] 2534[5] *4016[7]* 4993[2]

Southfork *Brendan Powell* 98h
5 ch g Nayef(USA) New Choice (IRE) (Barathea (IRE))
293[P]

Southsea Island (IRE) *Rebecca Curtis* 105b
6 b g Heron Island(IRE) Southsea Lady (IRE) (Kemal (FR))
4030[4] 4728[6]

South Stack *Kim Bailey* 116h 116c
9 b g Alflora(IRE) Mandy Chat (IRE) (Mandalus)
322[2] 2025[4] 4893[9] 5191[4]

Southway Queen *Sue Gardner* 95h
10 b m Morpeth Nearly A Score (Nearly A Hand)
590[9] 1051[2] 1340[2] 1477[4] (1784) 2473[6]

Southway Star *Sue Gardner* 91h 92c
9 b m Morpeth Nearly A Score (Nearly A Hand)
5004[P] 5240[8]

Sovereigns Legacy *John Panvert* 21h
7 b g Helissio(FR) Sovereign (Interrex (CAN))
1768[6] 1945[12]

Sovereign Spirit (IRE) *Michael Blake* 92h
12 b g Desert Prince(IRE) Sheer Spirit (IRE) (Caerleon (USA))
178[4] 829[3] (1105)

Sovinnie (IRE) *Jane Mathias* 81b
5 ch g Vinnie Roe(IRE) Sohapara (Arapahos (FR))
1489[5]

Soweheard (IRE) *Gordon Elliott* 125h
7 ch g Accordion Go Get Her (IRE) (Shardari)
747[2] 1037[2]

So Young (FR) *W P Mullins* 158h
8 b g Lavirco(GER) Honey (FR) (Highlanders (FR))
406a[9]

Spabreaksdotcom (IRE) *Liam Corcoran*
9 b m Desert Prince(IRE) Adirika (IRE) (Miswaki (USA))
1946[7]

Spaceman *Martin Bosley* 88h
11 b g In The Wings Souk (IRE) (Ahonoora)
444[3]

Space Ship *Robert Alan Hennessy* 114h
4 ch g Galileo(IRE) Angara (Alzao (USA))
4054[4] ◆

Spagetti Western (IRE) *David Bridgwater* 78h
7 b g Luso Shes Sharp (IRE) (Sharp Charter)
2602[14]

Spanish Arch (IRE) *Charlie Longsdon* 109h 121c
7 b g Westerner Piepowder (In The Wings)
2024[3] 2623[4] (3266)
4031[3]

Spanish Cruise (IRE) *Lucinda Egerton* 68h 60c
10 gr g Daylami(IRE) Baldemara (FR) (Sanglamore (USA))
4699[P] 4938[9]

Spanish Fleet *John Wade* 100h
6 b g Cadeaux Genereux Santisima Trinidad (IRE) (Definite Article)
1875[8] 2748[7] 3106[3] 3527[3] 3871[3] 4465[4]

Spanish Fork (IRE) *Sheena West* 95h
5 br g Trans Island Wings Awarded (Shareef Dancer (USA))
99[4] 295[8] 710[P] 1275[8] 1538[4] 1784[4] 2541[5]

Spanish Optimist (IRE) *Tim Vaughan* 124h 84c
8 b g Indian Danehill(IRE) La Traviata (Spectrum (IRE))
1796[6] 2901[P] 5004[P] 5450[4]

Spanish Trail *Christopher Kellett* 58h
5 b m Rail Link La Coruna (Deploy)
1132[6] 1305[8]

Spanish Treasure (GER) *Andy Turnell* 124h
8 b g Black Sam Bellamy(IRE) Santa Zinaada (GER) (Zinaad)
4023[9] 5345[P]

Sparkle (FR) *D Sourdeau De Beauregard* 110h
8 ch m Turgeon(USA) Belisama (FR) (Mansonnien (FR))
616a[5]

Sparkling Hand *Peter Atkinson* 102h
8 b m Lend A Hand Sparkling Yasmin (Derring Rose)
626[7] 2879[8] (3212) 3391[5] 3724[P] 4531[5] 4770[7]

Sparkling Tara *Sue Smith* 101h 112c
9 b g Kayf Tara Sparkling Yasmin (Derring Rose)
282[3] 566[P] (799)
1088[4]

Sparrow Hills (IRE) *Steven Dixon* 87h 70c
10 b g Moscow Society(USA) Glenstal Forest (IRE) (Glenstal (USA))
4496[6]

Spartaculous *W De Best-Turner* 73b
6 b m Spartacus(IRE) Sachiko (Celtic Swing)
841[8]

Spartan Angel (IRE) *Nicky Henderson* 97h
6 b m Beneficial Greek Melody (IRE) (Trojan Fort)
(5195)

Spartilla *Daniel O'Brien* 86h
5 b h Teofilo(IRE) Wunders Dream (IRE) (Averti (IRE))
2858[9] 3134[7] 3686[6] 4467[8] 5400[4]

Sparville (IRE) *Kim Bailey* 94h 119c
8 ch g Docksider(USA) Play The Queen (IRE) (King Of Clubs)
142[F] 585[F] 5227[3]

Spead Du Valon (FR) *F Nicolle* 104c
8 b g Kapgarde(FR) Image Du Valon (FR) (The Wonder (FR))
1279a[4]

Special Account (IRE) *Jeremy Scott* 125h 123c
9 b g Luso Thegirlfromslane (IRE) (Mandalus)
409[5] **645[2]**
839[4] 1150[3] 1316[5] (2014)
2508[4] 2945[5] 3172[P] 4914[P] (5121)
5385[12]

Specialagent Alfie *Nick Gifford* 131h
8 b g Alflora(IRE) Oso Special (Teenoso (USA))
216[F] 2213[11] 2647[2] ◆ 2951[7] 3322[7] 5399[P]

Special Boru (IRE) *Sarah Kerswell* 74h 74c
8 b g Brian Boru Green Angerton (Alderbrook)
295[3] 661[F] 828[8]
1053[4]

Special Catch (IRE) *Keith Reveley* 137h
7 b g Catcher In The Rye(IRE) Top Quality (Simply Great (FR))
2069[4] 2671[3] ◆ (3206) 4237[3] 4805[14]

Special Mix *Michael Easterby* 111h
6 b g Proclamation(IRE) Flaming Spirt (Blushing Flame (USA))
857[6]

Special Occasion *Miss S L Gould* 102b
10 b g Inchinor Special Beat (Bustino)
657[P] 5131[P]

Special Portrait (IRE) *Mark Hughes* 122c
10 gr g Portrait Gallery(IRE) Goin Home (IRE) (Warcraft (USA))
62[2] 315[U] (535)
4057[6] 4554[P] 5164[2] 5323[P]

Special Report (IRE) *Neil Mulholland* 87h
4 b g Mujadil(USA) Ellistown Lady (IRE) (Red Sunset)
2168[9] 2577[4] 3003[10] 5118[P] 5395[12]

Special Robon (FR) *Venetia Williams* 108h 108c
6 b g Robin Des Champs(FR) Spinage (FR) (Village Star (FR))
203[P]

Special Tiara *Henry De Bromhead* 122h 161c
7 b g Kayf Tara Special Choice (IRE) (Bob Back (USA))
2141a[U] 2532[3] 4062a[4] 4753[6] 5570[3]

Special Vintage *Graeme McPherson* 22h
8 br g Grape Tree Road Special Beat (Bustino)
2296[8] 3177[P] 3326[P]

Special Wells *Sue Smith* 108b
5 ch g Alflora(IRE) Oso Special (Teenoso (USA))
4895[4] 5279[4] ◆

Speckled Door *Caroline Bailey* 105h
6 b g Brian Boru Monte Mayor Golf (IRE) (Case Law)
2429[2] 2826[P] 3850[4] (4865) 5520[9]

Speed Master (IRE) *Nigel Twiston-Davies* 131h 136c
8 b g King's Theatre(IRE) Handy Lass (Nicholas Bill)
2389[5] 2797[8] (4908)
5228[2] 5373[P]

Speed Steed (IRE) *Tim Vaughan* 103h 115c
7 b g One Cool Cat(USA) Dhakhirah (IRE) (Sadler's Wells (USA))
57[6] 764[6]

Speedy Bruere (FR) *David Bridgwater* 113h 126c
8 gr g Turgeon(USA) Divine Bruere (FR) (Son Of Silver)
3023[3]
3424[P] 3738[5] 4036[2] 4448[P] 4800[3] 5013[2] 5336[4]

Speedy Tunes (IRE) *Nicky Henderson* 123h
7 b g Heron Island(IRE) Art Lover (IRE) (Over The River (FR))
(4758) 5233[2]

Spencer Lea *Andrew Price* 119h
6 b g Overbury(IRE) Castanet (Pennekamp (USA))
2648[4] 3225[2] 3643[5] (4510) 4662[6]

Spencers Lad *Michael Easterby* 78h
4 b g Sixties Icon Black Opal (Machiavellian (USA))
3214[6] 3822[7] 4003[4] 4612[8]

Spending Time *Colin Tizzard* 87h
5 b g King's Theatre(IRE) Karello Bay (Kahyasi)
1869[8] 2375[10] 3782[3] 4029[P]

Speranza (CZE) *Jaroslav Pechacek*
9 b g Magnus(POL) Sussex (CZE) (Beldale Ball (USA))
1905a[U]

Sphinx (FR) *Edwin Tuer* 113h
16 b g Snurge Egyptale (Crystal Glitters (USA))
3413[8] 3726[P]

Spice Hill (IRE) *Nick Ayliffe* 88h 77c
8 b g Indian Danehill(IRE) Histologie (FR) (Quart De Vin (FR))
1018[2] 1170[2] **1314[5]** 1635[6] 2760[8] 3174[P]

Spiculas (IRE) *Keith Reveley* 109h
5 ch g Beneficial Alicia's Charm (IRE) (Executive Perk)
2426[3] ◆ 4343[P] 4901[3]

Spiekeroog *Alan Brown* 92h 79c
8 ch g Lomitas Special (Polar Falcon (USA))
1751[2] 2879[6] 4478[6] 4981[7] 5359[9]

Spike Mac (IRE) *Richard Harper* 26h
9 b g Glacial Storm(USA) Edionda (IRE) (Magical Strike (USA))
1838[3] 3800[6] **4162[3] 4248[U]** 4702[P]

Spin Cast *Brian Ellison* 111h
6 b g Marju(IRE) Some Diva (Dr Fong (USA))
1754[2] 2718[2] 3351[3] 3756[3] 5365[8] 5496[9]

Spinning Away *N W Alexander* 89b
6 ch m Alflora(IRE) Minora (IRE) (Cataldi)
2752[7]

Spinning Scooter *Hilary Parrott* 74b
4 b g Sleeping Indian Spinning Coin (Mujahid (USA))
4923[5]

Spinning Waters *Dai Burchell* 93h
8 b g Vettori(IRE) Secret Waters (Pharly (FR))
456[4] 783[5] 927[7] 1018[4] 1331[3] 3047[2]

Spin The Beat *Marc Barber* 49b
4 b g Beat All(USA) Little Red Spider (Bustino)
2391[5]

Spirit Minded *Giles Smyly* 21h
6 b m Silver Patriarch(IRE) Dickies Girl (Saxon Farm)
2479[9] 3568[6] 3796[P]

Spiritofchartwell *Nick Gifford* 93h
6 ch g Clerkenwell(USA) Rollin Rock (Rock Hopper)
246[6] 706[RR] 761[5]

Spirit Of Lake (IRE) *Karen George* 58h 84c
12 b g Sheer Danzig(IRE) Rosheen (IRE) (Brush Aside (USA))
84[8] 408[2] 1260[5]

Spirit Of Shankly *Charlie Longsdon* 138h
6 ch g Sulamani(IRE) Lago D'Oro (Slip Anchor)
(1688) 2103[2] (2659) 3646[4] ◆ *4018[4]* 4374[2]
5138[8]

Spirit Of Xaar (IRE) *Linda Jewell* 95h
8 b g Xaar Jet Cat (IRE) (Catrail (USA))
427[4] 1625[12]

Spirit Oscar (IRE) *Oliver Sherwood* 123h 123c
6 b m Oscar(IRE) Grange Classic (IRE) (Jurado (USA))
(2579) (3247) 3552[3]
4248[2] 4701[2] 5124[3]

Spirit River (FR) *Dave Roberts* 103h 86c
9 b g Poliglote Love River (FR) (Epervier Bleu)
9[5] 3798[6] 4087[4]

Spitfire Ace (IRE) *Donald McCain* 91h 95c
6 b g Zagreb(USA) Coolafancy (IRE) (Accordion)
1387[3] 1561[8] **1870[4] 2219[U] 2518[4]**

Spithead *Mike Sowersby* 58h
4 b g Tiger Hill(IRE) Cyclone Connie (Dr Devious (IRE))
2899[5]

Spitz (FR) *Rose Dobbin* 105h
6 b g Enrique Spezzia (FR) (Snurge)
1975[3] 4234[5] 4548[6] 4952[3] ◆

Splash Of Ginge *Nigel Twiston-Davies* 146h
6 b g Oscar(IRE) Land Of Honour (Supreme Leader)
1576[4] 1706[2] 2243[4] (2933) 3184[3] 3654[3] (4147)
4736[15] 5167[2]

Spock (FR) *Alexandra Dunn* 92h 125c
9 b g Lost World(IRE) Quark Top (FR) (Perrault)
11[4] 642[5] 943[5] 1197[3] 1326[4] 1493[P] (1670)
1921[5] 5035[7] 5306[2]

Spoil Me (IRE) *Jonjo O'Neill* 100h 111c
7 b g Presenting Akayid (Old Vic)
121[F] 1575[3] 1674[5]
2887[3] *4023[6] 4299[6] 4496[3]* **4985[3] 5237[U] 5487[F]**

Spookydooky (IRE) *Jonjo O'Neill* 110h
6 b g Winged Love(IRE) Kiora Lady (IRE) (King's Ride)
1864[5] ◆ 2156[4] 3735[5] 4075[4]

Sporting Boy (IRE) *Johnny Farrelly* 126h 117c
6 b g Barathea(IRE) Sportsticketing (IRE) (Spectrum (IRE))
118[4] 234[F] 594[2] 781[5] 1012[5] 1122[3] 1263[5] (1699)
5142[P]

Sporting Club Girl *Jim Best* 63h
4 b f Kyllachy Validate (Alhaarth (IRE))
2577[8] 3003[9] 3245[5] 3692[11] 4330[7]

Sports Model (IRE) *Valerie Jackson* 43h
8 ch g Presenting Belmarita (IRE) (Belmez (USA))
22[P]

Sportsreport (IRE) *Seamus Mullins* 74h 87c
6 b g Coroner(IRE) Goforthetape (IRE) (Gothland (FR))
160[4] 519[7] 920[10]
1053[5] 3550[F] 4068[6] 4371[9]
4718[3] 5115[2] 5397[4]

Spot The Ball (IRE) *Jonjo O'Neill* 108h 106c
9 b g Oscar(IRE) Sudden Inspiration (IRE) (Good Thyne (USA))
555[4]

Spotthestripe *G J Tarry* 101c
9 b m Cloudings(IRE) Teeton Bubbley (Neltino)
4246[2] 5062[2]

Spring Back *Edwin Tuer* 80b
6 b m Silver Patriarch(IRE) Danceback (IRE) (Bob Back (USA))
2738[5] 3351[F]

Springboks (IRE) *Alan King* 68b
4 b g Flemensfirth(USA) Roaming (IRE) (Be My Native (USA))
4964[12]

Spring Heeled (IRE) *J H Culloty* 135h 151c
7 b g Old Vic Central Arch (Dilum (USA))
1613a[3] 1897a[2] 2502[8] (4769)
5571[5]

Springhill Boy *Geoffrey Deacon* 58b
7 b g Kayf Tara Gemma Day (Le Bavard (FR))
862[8]

Springhill Lad *Geoffrey Deacon* 48h
7 b g Kayf Tara Anouska (Interrex (CAN))
544[2] 3694[U] 3988[11]

Springinherstep (IRE) *Nicky Henderson* 122h
7 b m Saddlers' Hall(IRE) Lady Lamb (IRE) (Executive Perk)
292[3] 2477[5] 3031[5] 4920[2] 5231[2]

Spring Over (IRE) *Ian Duncan* 97h
8 ch m Samraan(USA) Superswap (IRE) (Gone Fishin)
2217[11] 2495[3] 2973[4] 4083[3] 4668[6]

Spring Secret *Tim Vaughan*
8 b g Reset(AUS) Miss Brooks (Bishop Of Cashel)
994[P]

Spring Steel (IRE) *Ben Pauling* 113h
5 b g Dushyantor(USA) Fieldtown (IRE) (Anshan)
483[5] 3872[4] 5088[P]

Spring Wolf *John Ryall* 101b
6 br g Loup Sauvage(USA) Spring Grass (Pardigras)
5339[2]

Sprinter Sacre (FR) *Nicky Henderson* 151h 190c
8 bb g Network(GER) Fatima III (FR) (Bayolidaan (FR))
3320[P]

Sprogzilla *Alan Phillips* 29b
5 gr m Fair Mix(IRE) Gentle Approach (Rakaposhi King)
4867[13]

Spunky *Marc Barber* 78h
5 b g Invincible Spirit(IRE) Passe Passe (USA) (Lear Fan (USA))
2083[11] 2291[13] 4398[7] 4733[10] 5139[6]

Spyder *Lucy Wadham* 122h
6 b g Resplendent Glory(IRE) Collect (Vettori (IRE))
4068[2] ◆ (5008) 5257[F] 5541[4]

Square Beaujon (FR) *D Windrif* 121h 125c
5 b g Satri(IRE) Bella Giaconda (GER) (Goofalik (USA))
2263a[3]

Squealy Keely *James Turner* 28h
6 b m Kahyasi Granny Shona (IRE) (Nashwan (USA))
15[9] 4576[5] 4743[P]

Squeeze Me *Peter Bowen* 101h
7 b m Grape Tree Road Ask Me Not (IRE) (Shernazar)
(874) 2153[4] 2513[3] 2768[F] 3116[4]

Squinch *Mrs David Plunkett* 94b
10 b g Kayf Tara Alta (Arctic Lord)
4727[13]

Squire Trelawney *Dan Skelton* 114h
8 b g Domedriver(IRE) Crockadore (USA) (Nijinsky (CAN))
2314[2] 2755[5] 2936[4] 4700[5] 4906[2] 5351[13]

Sraid Padraig (IRE) *A J Martin* 115b 139c
8 b g Revoque(IRE) Loughaneala (IRE) (Be My Native (USA))
4768[8] 5474a[13]

Staccato Valtat (FR) *John O'Shea* 116h
8 gr g Fragrant Mix(IRE) Harmonie De Valtat (FR) (Video Rock (FR))
5542[9]

Stack The Deck (IRE) *P A Fahy* 121b
5 ch g Beneficial Allaboveboard (IRE) (Alphabatim (USA))
4756[P] (Dead)

Stadium Of Light (IRE) *Shaun Harris* 94h
7 b g Fantactic Light(USA) Troblo Sovon (UCA) (Fusaichi Pegasus (USA))
605[7] 730[12] 788[6] 1379[7] 1633[5] 1791[6] (2176)
2427[P] 2787[11] 3118[4] 3141[9]

Stafford Charlie *John O'Shea* 93h 78c
8 ch g Silver Patriarch(IRE) Miss Roberto (IRE) (Don Roberto (USA))
1057[4] 1149[2] 1328[4]

Stagecoach Jasper *Sue Smith* 95h 118c
8 b g Sir Harry Lewis(USA) Flintwood (Gunner B)
114[P] 224[F] 2155[8] 2334[5] 2818[F] 4067[F] 4380[5] 4626[6]

Stagecoach Pearl *Sue Smith* 105h 137c
10 gr g Classic Cliche(IRE) Linwood (Ardross)
1921[2] 2101[7] 2448[5] 2957[5] 4955[5] 5378[2]

Stage King *Warren Greatrex* 97h
8 b g King's Theatre(IRE) Blue Dante (IRE) (Phardante (FR))
2631[3] 2978[10] 3434[P]

Stag Hill (IRE) *Bernard Llewellyn* 90h
5 ch g Redback Counting Blessings (Compton Place)
1795[7] 2040[11] 2385[5] 2886[5] 3188[4] 4757[7] 4967[6]

Staigue Fort *Emma Lavelle* 127h 94c
6 b g Kirkwall Mulberry Wine (Benny The Dip (USA))
33[3] 517[3] 808[9] 1020[3] 1255[3] (1488) 1597[4]
(1828) *4022[6] 4300[7]* 5093[12]
5451[4]

Stand Clear *David Thompson* 88h 91c
9 b m Sir Harry Lewis(USA) Clair Valley (Ardross)
(445) 626[5] 801[10] 932[7] 1043[9] 1143[P] 1506[5]
1717[B] 1751[3] 5298[4] 5434[4]

Standing Ovation (IRE) *David Pipe* 83h 136c
7 b g Presenting Glittering Star (IRE) (Good Thyne (USA))
645[5] 832[4] 1637[F] (1830) (1942) (2108) (2373) 2487[7] 4422[8] 4738[6] 5156[U]

Standing Strong (IRE) *Zoe Davison*
6 b g Green Desert(USA) Alexander Three D (IRE) (Pennekamp (USA))
2018[13]

Standintheband (IRE) *N W Alexander* 105h 88c
7 b g Old Vic Superior Dawn (IRE) (Mandalus)
1850[5] **2969[5]**

Stand 'N' Boogie *Pam Sly* 87b
4 ch f Tobougg(IRE) Standing Bloom (Presidium)
4867[4] 5196[6]

Stand To Reason (IRE) *Nicky Henderson* 133h
6 ch g Danehill Dancer(IRE) Ho Hi The Moon (IRE) (Be My Guest (USA))
(2906) (3370) 3778[4]

Stanley Bridge *Barry Murtagh* 102h
7 b g Avonbridge Antonia's Folly (Music Boy)
27[7] 537[2] 801[9] 1979[9] 2597[8] 3038[5] 3830[5] (4943) 5360[2]

Stantastic *Mark Campion* 75b
6 b g Holy Roman Emperor(IRE) Ghita (IRE) (Zilzal (USA))
790[11] 1124[7]

Star Belucky *Roy Brotherton* 39b
6 b m Overbury(IRE) Herecomespapin (IRE) (Naheez (USA))
768[10]

Starburst Diamond (IRE) *Charles Whittaker* 67h 64c
12 ro g Old Vic Camlin Rose (IRE) (Roselier (FR))
2911[4] 5240[P]

Star Date (IRE) *Oliver Sherwood* 111h
5 b g Galileo(IRE) Play Misty For Me (IRE) (Danehill Dancer (IRE))
3501[4] 5117[2] 5519[2]

Star D'Authie (FR) *Y Gourraud*
4 bl f Protektor(GER) Star Kal (FR) (Kaldoun (FR))
615a[P]

Star Des Planches (FR) *P Chemin* 109c
8 b g Le Balafre(FR) Boute Selle (FR) (Alycos (FR))
(1214a)

Star Flight (FR) *A Chaille-Chaille* 125h 103c
5 b m Poliglote Marly Flight (FR) (Mansonnien (FR))
1465a[2]

Star For Life (USA) *Eoin Doyle* 108h
5 b g Giant's Causeway(USA) Clerical Etoile (ARG) (The Watcher (USA))
1139a[11]

Star Galaxy (IRE) *John Flint* 80h 104c
14 b g Fourstars Allstar(USA) Raven Night (IRE) (Mandalus)
411[2] 533[5] 781[R]

Star Hill *Alan King*
7 b m Starcraft(NZ) Mistress Bankes (IRE) (Petardia)
240[P]

Star In Flight *Donald McCain* 133h 115c
7 b g Mtoto Star Entry (In The Wings)
1849[4] 2882[6] *4020[6]* **5380[3]**

Starlet Mandy (IRE) *Nigel Twiston-Davies* 71h
11 br m Presenting Actress Mandy (IRE) (Mandalus)
423[4] 765[11] 1121[8]

Starlife (FR) *David Pipe* 100h
5 b m Saint Des Saints(FR) Presidence (FR) (Nikos)
178[P]

Starlight Air *John Spearing* 90h
11 ch m Karinga Bay Moonlight Air (Bold Owl)
(71) 252[9] 730[3] 1364[12] 1565[14]

Starlight Sonata *Emma Lavelle* 79b
4 b f Tagula(IRE) Starlight Express (FR) (Air Express (IRE))
5130[3] 5528[8]

Star Lily (IRE) *Keith Reveley* 105h
5 b m King's Theatre(IRE) Mrs Battleaxe (IRE) (Supreme Leader)
(2752) 4191[3] 5499[7]

Starluck (IRE) *David Arbuthnot* 145h 142c
9 gr g Key Of Luck(USA) Sarifa (IRE) (Kahyasi)
216[6]

Star Neuville (FR) *E Bolger* 132h 130c
8 br g East Of Heaven(IRE) Danystar (FR) (Alycos (FR))
4754[12]

Star Of Aragon (IRE) *J A Nash* 130h
8 b g Saffron Walden(FR) Delicacy (IRE) (Danehill Dancer (IRE))
2069[8]

Star Of Boru (IRE) *Paul John Gilligan* 103h
7 b g Brian Boru Divine Bloo (IRE) (Pistolet Bleu (IRE))
367[4]

Star Of Massini (IRE) *Seamus Mullins* 100h 102c
7 b g Dr Massini(IRE) Star Of The Orient (IRE) (Moscow Society (USA))
293[5] **539[4] 709[P]**

Star Of Mayfair (USA) *Alan Jarvis* 87h
4 ch g Tale Of The Cat(USA) Kinsale Lass (USA) (Royal Academy (USA))
2796[8]

Star Of Salford *David Pipe* 79b
5 b m Hernando(FR) City Of Angels (Woodman (USA))
3898[8]

Starplex *Lucinda Russell* 94b
4 b g Multiplex Turtle Bay (Dr Fong (USA))
(3214) 4384[4]

Star Presenter (IRE) *Paul Webber* 93h 102c
6 b g Presenting Star Councel (IRE) (Leading Counsel (USA))
8[5] 1783[9] 2848[7] **4242[P] 5115[5]**

Star Ride *Mark Bradstock* 82b
5 b g Kayf Tara Star Diva (IRE) (Toulon)
101[7]

Starship Trouper *Neil Mulholland* 66b
6 b g First Trump Bay Of Plenty (Teenoso (USA))
2375[12] 3782[P] 4987[P]

Starsky Des Mottes (FR) *Victor Dartnall* 105h 112c
8 b g Useful(FR) Camille Des Mottes (FR) (Abdonski (FR))
179[3] 712[8]

Start Royal (FR) *Alan Hill* 89h 119c
10 b g Starborough Marie Des Epeires (FR) (Rose Laurel)
329[3]

State Department *Philip Hobbs* 85h
7 b g Doyen(IRE) Time For Tea (IRE) (Imperial Frontier (USA))
1056[3] 1427[4] 1695[4] 1795[12] 2002[9]

State The Blend *Sue Gardner* 80b
4 ch f Proclamation(IRE) Darjeeling (IRE) (Presenting)
2015[7] 5492[6]

Station Closed (IRE) *Mrs Lorna Fowler* 91h
6 b m Kutub(IRE) Laser Supreme (IRE) (Supreme Leader)
1654[3]

Status Quo (CZE) *Miroslav Sevcik*
8 ch g Exaltation(IRE) Surprice (CZE) (Sharp End)
1905a[U]

Stay In My Heart (IRE) *Laura Mongan* 104h
5 ch m Medicean Christmas Cracker (FR) (Alhaarth (IRE))
3007[4] *4023[14]* 4801[F] 5112[5] 5402[5]

St Dominick (IRE) *Jackie Du Plessis* 103h
7 b g Oscar(IRE) Kilcrea Breeze (IRE) (Fresh Breeze (USA))
2946[4] 5120[2] ◆

Steady Girlfriend *Anthony Honeyball* 106h 106c
9 ch m Classic Cliche(IRE) Dame Fonteyn (Suave Dancer (USA))
2632[F]

Steady Progress (IRE) *Richard Ford* 79h 87c
6 b g Flemensfirth(USA) Creaking Step (IRE) (Shernazar)
5354[5]

Steel A Look *Fergal O'Brien* 62b
5 b m Passing Glance Cutting Edge (Golden Heights)
842[9]

Steel Away J (IRE) *Christopher Kellett* 70b
7 b g Craigsteel Celtic Fox (IRE) (Strong Gale)
699[11] 1016[6]

Steel City *Seamus Mullins* 120h
6 gr g Act One Serraval (FR) (Sanglamore (USA))
2924[2] (3501) 3694[3] 4680[P]

Steel Summit (IRE) *David Dennis* 100h
5 b g Craigsteel B Greenhill (Gunner B)
246[5] 3388[13] 3728[6] 3988[2] 4937[7] 5128[12] 5436[4]

Steepleofcopper (IRE) *Alan Jessop* 101h 75c
8 ch g Classic Cliche(IRE) Tanya Thyne (IRE) (Good Thyne (USA))
2536[9] 3850[F] 4715[P]
5192[3]

Stella Marris *Christopher Wilson*
7 br m Danroad(AUS) Riyoom (USA) (Vaguely Noble)
73[U]

Stellar Notion (IRE) *Tom George* 131h
6 bb g Presenting Green Star (FR) (Green Tune (USA))
(3063) (3721) ◆ 4343[2]

Stella's Fella *Giles Smyly* 113h
6 b g Septieme Ciel(USA) Gaspaisie (FR) (Beyssac (FR))
250[11] 1770[3] 2393[7] 4931[9] 5140[0] 5303[2]

Stephanie Frances (IRE) *Dan Skelton* 105h
6 b m King's Theatre(IRE) Brownlow Castle (IRE) (Supreme Leader)
2876[4] 3757[6]

Stephen Hero (IRE) *Dan Skelton* 108h
4 br g Celtic Swing Albaiyda (IRE) (Brief Truce (USA))
2750[2] 3317[2] 3599[5] 5568[12]

Steps To Freedom (IRE) *Mrs John Harrington* 149h 138c
8 b g Statue Of Liberty(USA) Dhakhirah (IRE) (Sadler's Wells (USA))
1067a[2] 5420a[11]

Sterling Bill (IRE) *Neil Mulholland* 38h
6 gr m Cloudings(IRE) Coolgarry Girl (IRE) (Supreme Leader)
711[P]

Sterling Gent (IRE) *Liam Corcoran* 101h
7 gr g Cloudings(IRE) Company Credit (IRE) (Anshan)
631[4] 849[3] 1118[7] 2210[6] 2908[9] 5069[4] 5366[3]

Steviekey (IRE) *John Joseph Hanlon* 15h
8 b g Zagreb(USA) Zuni Socialite (IRE) (Up And At 'Em)
1664[P]

Stevie Thunder *Ian Williams* 109h
9 ch g Storming Home Social Storm (USA) (Future Storm (USA))
5294[3] 5490[9]

St Gregory (IRE) *Nicky Richards* 78h 40c
6 ch m Presenting Ardrom (Ardross)
340[P] 1873[10] 2497[2] 2974[2] 5514[P]

Stickers *Alan Jessop* 74h
7 b g Generous(IRE) Dunsfold Duchess (IRE) (Bustino)
2028[P] 2296[7]

Stickleback *Micky Hammond* 92h
5 ch m Manduro(GER) The Stick (Singspiel (IRE))
2596[3] 3335[2] 4338[8] 4774[6]

Stiff Upper Lip (IRE) *Oliver Sherwood* 114h
4 b c Sakhee's Secret Just In Love (FR) (Highest Honor (FR))
3857[4] (4534) 4963[6] (5403) 5568[9]

St Ignatius *Alan Bailey* 104h
7 b g Ishiguru(USA) Branston Berry (IRE) (Mukaddamah (USA))
2432[6] 4794[3] 5443[8]

Still Believing (IRE) *Evan Williams* 121h
6 ch m Blueprint(IRE) Im A Believer (IRE) (Erins Isle)
2388[3]
3129[P] 3729[P] 4090[3] (4351) 4508[7] 4841[5]

Stitched In Time (IRE) *Rose Dobbin* 96h 100c
7 b g Needle Gun(IRE) Broken Pockets (IRE) (Broken Hearted)
2202[P] (2789) 2999[5] 3520[P]

St Nicolas D'Acy (FR) *Robert Collet* 126h
8 b g Laveron Desert's Flower (FR) (Highest Honor (FR))
455a[2]

Stocktons Wing (IRE) *Charles O'Brien* 140h
5 b g Jeremy(USA) Jumilla (USA) (El Gran Senor (USA))
5420a[5]

Stodini (FR) *Mme V Seignoux* 130h
8 ch g Lesotho(USA) Kaberdini (FR) (Chamberlin (FR))
863a[2]

Stone (IRE) *Miss E Alvis* 115c
8 b g Lahib(USA) Stone Beck (Lapierre)
(430)

Stonebrook (IRE) *Donald McCain* 127h
6 b g Flemensfirth(USA) Boberelle (IRE) (Bob Back (USA))
(2422) (3112) 3826[3] ◆ (4199) (4605) 5158[14]

Stone Light (FR) *Venetia Williams* 114h 125c
6 ch m Ballingarry(IRE) Yellow Light (FR) (Lightning (FR))
2763[3]
3171[3] 4536[2] (4701)

Stonemadforspeed (IRE) *Sirrell Griffiths* 103h
6 b g Fruits Of Love(USA) Diamond Forever (Teenoso (USA))
4844[5]

Stonethrower (IRE) *Tim Vaughan* 114h 135c
9 b g Dushyantor(USA) Ciaras Charm (IRE) (Phardante (FR))
4782[2] (5230)

Stoney Silence *Charlie Mann* 85h
6 b g Generous(IRE) Stoney Path (Petoski)
2279[10] 2900[6]

Stony Road (IRE) *John Flint* 106h
7 b g Hubbly Bubbly(USA) Laur's Melody (IRE) (Meneval (USA))
38[7]

Stopped Out *Philip Kirby* 144h 124c
9 gr g Montjoy(USA) Kiomi (Niniski (USA))
(2454) 3369[3] 4264[P]

Storey Hill (USA) *Richard Guest* 66h
9 bb g Richter Scale(USA) Crafty Nan (USA) (Crafty Prospector (USA))
1688[6]

Storm Alert *Sue Gardner* 116h
7 ch g Karinga Bay Rash-Gale (IRE) (Rashar (USA))
2284[3] 2655[6] (4393) 5333[5] 5489[6]

Stormbay Bomber (IRE) *Rebecca Curtis* 90b
5 bb g September Storm(GER) Top Tottie (IRE) (Alzao (USA))
1819[4]

Storm Brig *Alistair Whillans* 120b
9 b g Heron Island(IRE) The Storm Bell (IRE) (Glacial Storm (USA))
3206[P]

Stormhoek (IRE) *Nigel Twiston-Davies* 107h 115c
9 ch g Alderbrook Auntie Honnie (IRE) (Radical)
3190[4] 3837[2] 4241[3] 4490[P] 4968[P]

Storminator (FR) *J-P Gallorini* 133h 111c
5 gr g Stormy River(FR) Becquarette (FR) (Nombre Premier)
1983a[4] 2414a[7]

Stormin Exit (IRE) *Jim Goldie* 117h 129c
11 b g Exit To Nowhere(USA) Stormin Norma (IRE) (Runnett)
24[4] **2222[2]**
2939[5] 3498[7] (3756)
4053[4] 4369[4]
4651[3] 4955[3] 5253[5]

Storming Gale (IRE) *Donald McCain* 120h 132c
8 b g Revoque(IRE) Dikler Gale (IRE) (Strong Gale)
25[4] 508[6] 3001[2] 3759[F] 4610[4] 5378[5]

Storming Strumpet *Tom George* 71b
4 b f Kayf Tara Rosita Bay (Hernando (FR))
4964[9]

Stormion (IRE) *Lucinda Russell* 100h 81c
9 b g Flemensfirth(USA) El Moss (IRE) (Le Moss)
1874[P]
2339[4] 3022[P]

Storm Of Saintly (FR) *G Macaire* 126h 155c
5 bb g Saint Des Saints(FR) The Storm (FR) (Garde Royale)
2263a[F]

Storm Of Swords (IRE) *Dan Skelton* 110h
6 ch g Beneficial Crossbar Lady (IRE) (Flemensfirth (USA))
2534[9] 3061[F] 4904[4] 5175[3]

Storm Quest *Robin Dickin* 19h
7 ch m Storming Home Recherchee (Rainbow Quest (USA))
1794[12]

Storm Survivor (IRE) *Jonjo O'Neill* 127h 138c
8 b g Milan Lindas Present (IRE) (Presenting)
238[3] 718[3]
(851) 1868[3] 2937[F] 3199[6] 4104[5] 4544[2]

Storm To Pass *Caroline Fryer* 100h
6 b g Overbury(IRE) Silver Peak (FR) (Sillery (USA))
67[3] 320[2] (598) 5438[5]

Stormyisland Ahead *Evan Williams* 91h 108c
9 b g Turtle Island(IRE) Queen's Banquet (Glacial Storm (USA))
84[5] 481[5] 641[8] 930[7] 1344[3] (2290)
3131[P]

Stormy Oscar (IRE) *Jamie Snowden* 111h 98c
7 b g Oscar(IRE) So Proper (IRE) (Topanoora)
247[2] 585[U] 705[5] 931[7] 1149[5] 1435[5]

Stormy Weather (FR) *Brian Ellison* 129h 135c
8 gr g Highest Honor(FR) Stormy Moud (USA) (Storm Bird (CAN))
1378[5] 1504[3] 1685[6] (1922) 2821[7] 3758[8] *4497[4]* 4813[5] **5275[P]**

Stow *Michael Blake* 126h
9 ch g Selkirk(USA) Spry (Suave Dancer (USA))
2024[8] 2512[P] 2894[2] (3324) (3468) 3593[2] (4513) (5001) 5066[3]

Straidnahanna (IRE) *Sue Smith* 122h
5 gr g Medaaly Sue's Song (Alflora (IRE))
2196[4] 2659[4] 3036[3] 3781[2] ◆ 4272[P] 4901[2] 5252[4]

Straits Of Messina (IRE) *Tom Symonds* 102h
5 b g Mountain High(IRE) Scylla (Rock City)
160[2] 1793[10] 2040[13] 2189[9] 2351[5] (3856) 4107[F] 4305[2] 4911[3] 5143[9]

Strandfield Bay (IRE) *Sharon Watt* 91h
8 b m Wizard King Stylish Chic (IRE) (Arazi (USA))
881[8] 1137[7] 2169[8] 3038[10]

Strange Bird (IRE) *Richard Rowe* 98h
9 b m Revoque(IRE) Ethel's Bay (IRE) (Strong Gale)
2744[5] 3553[4] (4471) 4803[7]

Strangelittlegirl *Patrick Gilligan* 91h
6 b m Shirocco(GER) Cephalonia (Slip Anchor)
70[3] 502[P]

Strategic Exit *James Frost* 61h
6 ch g Exit To Nowhere(USA) Penny's Crown (Reprimand)
2906[13] 3128[P] 5140[11] 5235[11] 5523[10]

Strathaird (IRE) *Andrew Crook* 72h 67c
10 b g Medicean Heed My Warning (IRE) (Second Set (IRE))
21[9] **183[P]**
602[3] 694[4] 1086[4] 1328[9] 1876[9] 2737[7] 3564[5] 3722[4]
4203[5]

Strathcal *Tom Symonds* 104h 100c
8 b g Beat Hollow Shall We Run (Hotfoot I)
30[6] 269[3] 583[4]

Strawberry Hill (IRE) *Caroline Keevil* 90h 114c
8 b g Winged Love(IRE) Icydora (FR) (Cyborg (FR))
1939[3] 2251[4] (2741)
3504[U]

Streams Of Whiskey (IRE) *Nicky Richards* 97h 130c
7 br g Spadoun(FR) Cherry Tops (IRE) (Top Of The World)
340[P] (1870)
2220[F] 2817[F] 4105[6]
4572[4] (5385)

Streedagh Lady (IRE) *Mark Michael McNiff* 90b 91c
10 ch m Anshan Proper Decision (IRE) (Old Vic)
285[5]

Street Dance (IRE) *Keith Goldsworthy* 98h 84c
8 b g Beneficial Zvezda (IRE) (Soviet Lad (USA))
84[P]

Street Entertainer (IRE) *David Pipe* 122h
7 br g Danehill Dancer(IRE) Opera Ridge (FR) (Indian Ridge)
216[8] 1046[8] 1485[10] 1745[4]

Street Name (FR) *G Cherel* 129h
4 b g Al Namix(FR) Acland Street (FR) (Zabeel (NZ))
2262a[5]

Street Runner *Karl Thornton* 109h
8 b g Rainbow Quest(USA) Dansara (Dancing Brave (USA))
1164[6] 1565[2]

Streets Of Newyork *Brian Ellison* 113h
7 b g Dalakhani(IRE) Minute Waltz (Sadler's Wells (USA))
2970[4] 3477[5]

Strictly Cissbury *Brendan Powell* 61h
5 b g Sakhee(USA) Distant Music (Darshaan)
951[0] 3692[P] 4636[P]

Strictly The One (IRE) *Neil Mulholland* 75b
4 b g Robin Des Pres(FR) Rita's Charm (IRE) (Arctic Lord)
5130[7]

Strike Fast (IRE) *William Kinsey* 110h 36c
9 gr g Portrait Gallery(IRE) Street Rose (IRE) (Roselier (FR))
4041[3] 4425[4] 4673[P] 5103[2]

Strobe *Lucy Normile* 109h 107c
10 ch g Fantastic Light(USA) Sadaka (USA) (Kingmambo (USA))
282[6] 583[7] 753[4] (883)
(960) 1291[P] (1666)
1872[6] 2346[3] 5555[6]

Strollawaynow (IRE) *David Arbuthnot* 126h
7 b g Oscar(IRE) Rose Of Salome (IRE) (Roselier (FR))
2178[2] 2467[6] ◆ 3092[2] (3694) 4130[3] 4680[8] 5110[3] 5332[3]

Strongbows Legend *Charlie Longsdon* 92h 124c
9 ch g Midnight Legend Miss Crabapple (Sunyboy)
44[3] 420[4] (693)
757[7] 1918[F]

Strong Conviction *Simon Hodgson* 75h
4 ch g Piccolo Keeping The Faith (IRE) (Ajraas (USA))
3857[5] 4281[8] 4534[2]

Strongly Suggested *Jonjo O'Neill* 119h 107c
7 b g Kayf Tara Branston Lily (Cadeaux Genereux)
(561) 846[3] (1061) 1285[2] (1471) 1922[10]
2469[P] 4919[7] 5527[4]

Strongpoint (IRE) *S R B Crawford* 140h 125c
10 br g Bob Back(USA) Ceo Draiochta (IRE) (Erins Isle)
681[2] 884[2] **1162[2]** (3000) (3477) 4785[19] 5172[5] (5512)

Strong Survivor (USA) *Evelyn England* 28h
11 b g Kingmambo(USA) Summer Solstice (IRE) (Caerleon (USA))
1106[8] 1170[P]

Strumble Head (IRE) *Peter Bowen* 115h 117c
9 b g Anshan Milan Moss (Le Moss)
143[5] 642[4] 1060[5] (1283)
1642[6] 2623[P]

Studfarmer *John Panvert*
4 b g Multiplex Samadilla (IRE) (Mujadil (USA))
1473[P] 4882[P]

Style Setter *Donald McCain* 64h
4 b f Beat Hollow Wooden Doll (USA) (Woodman (USA))
785[4] 1044[3]

Stylish Chap (IRE) *John Quinn* 92b
4 b g New South Wales Curragh Bawn Lass (IRE) (Supreme Leader)
5500[3]

Sublime Talent (IRE) *Evan Williams* 47h 124c
8 b g Sadler's Wells(USA) Summer Trysting (USA) (Alleged (USA))
81[3] 411[P] 2448[4] 2977[6] 3324[5] 4087[5]

Subordinate (GER) *Andy Turnell*
5 b g Echo Of Light Suborneuse (USA) (Diesis)
3098[3]

Suburban Bay *Alan King* 120h 123c
9 ch g Karinga Bay Orchid House (Town And Country)
757[5] 1088[P] 1326[5] 1577[2] 1988[2] (2431) 2623[P]

Such A Legend *Kim Bailey* 126h
6 ch g Midnight Legend Mrs Fizziwig (Petoski)
3182[7] 4693[2] 5008[2] (5175) (5531)

Sucker Punch (IRE) *Noel Meade* 101b
5 b g Scorpion(IRE) Lemonfield Lady (IRE) (Presenting)
2995a[6]

Sudden Light (IRE) *Jim Best* 78h
8 b m Presenting Coolshamrock (IRE) (Buckskin (FR))
3138[P] 3425[P]

Sudden Wish (IRE) *Gary Moore* 92h
5 b m Jeremy(USA) Fun Time (Fraam)
2564[4] 2725[3] 3153[2]

Sud Pacifique (IRE) *Donald McCain* 125h
6 b g Montjeu(IRE) Anestasia (IRE) (Anabaa (USA))
176[5] 447[3] 673[4] 850[11] 1173[4] 1378[3] 1960[10] 2970[3] 3758[4] 4058[2] 4745[P]

Sudski Star (IRE) *Patrick Griffin* 92h 113c
6 b g Pilsudski(IRE) Mogen's Star (IRE) (Be My Native (USA))
2998[5] 3494[3] 3516[8] 4223[12] **4367[5] 4628[3] (5207) (5318)**

Suerte Al Salto (IRE) *Chris Gordon* 122h 125c
7 b g Old Vic The Great O'Malley (IRE) (Mandalus)
(539) **1857[3]**
2469[6] 2977[3] (5456)

Suffice (IRE) *Laura Young* 66h
5 b g Iffraaj Shallat (IRE) (Pennekamp (USA))
5003[8]

Sugar Hiccup (IRE) *Jim Best* 111h
6 b m Refuse To Bend(IRE) Raysiza (IRE) (Alzao (USA))
(1351) (1438) (1495) 1941[4] 2616[4]

Sugar Sensation (IRE) *Alan J Brown*
8 b g Sugarfoot Star Sensation (IRE) (Sri Pekan (USA))
112[P]

Sukiyaki (IRE) *Charlie Longsdon* 99h
5 b g Dubawi(IRE) Sukeena (IRE) (Brief Truce (USA))
3061[4] 3258[6] 3427[4] *4019[4]* 4903[7] 5395[6]

Sullane Chief (IRE) *P C O'Connor* 143h
6 b g Exit To Nowhere(USA) Fortuna Favente (IRE) (Supreme Leader)
3910a[19]

Sulon (FR) *Patrice Quinton* 100h 110c
8 b g Passing Sale(FR) Fest Noz (FR) (Port Etienne (FR))
199a[P] 855a[3]

Sultana Belle (IRE) *S R B Crawford* 108h 125c
6 b m Black Sam Bellamy(IRE) Sultana (GER) (Law Society (USA))
868[2] 1145[3] 1718[3] (1871) 2205a[7] 2883[4]

Sultan Silk (FR) *T Doumen* 102h
4 b g Sulamani(IRE) Taffetas (FR) (Nikos)
1741a[7]

Sumkindasuprstar (IRE) *John O Clifford* 116h 133c
10 b g Gulland Rockababy (IRE) (King's Ride)
1776a[6] 1897a[12]

Sum Laff (IRE) *Karl Thornton* 101h 97c
10 ch g Publisher(USA) Tiergarten (IRE) (Brief Truce (USA))
883[7]

Summer Echo *Andi Brown* 40b
4 b f Echo Of Light Summer Cry (USA) (Street Cry (IRE))
3167[13]

Summerlea (IRE) *Micky Hammond* 106h
8 ch g Alhaarth(IRE) Verbania (IRE) (In The Wings)
3141[2] 3451[2] 3618[2] (4475) 4893[7]

Summer Sounds (IRE) *Tom Symonds* 97b
5 bb g Definite Article Marble Sound (IRE) (Be My Native (USA))
4135[4]

Summer Star (IRE) *T M Walsh* 123h 110c
6 b m Medicean Summer Stage (In The Wings)
4455a[3]

Summer Storm (FR) *Guy Denuault* 104h
5 ch m Go Between(FR) Orageuse (Bering)
1199a[8]

Summertime Lady *Colin Tizzard* 85h
6 b m Desert King(IRE) Shelayly (IRE) (Zaffaran (USA))
85[4] 2463[5] 2907[9] 3289[4] ◆

Summery Justice (IRE) *Venetia Williams* 112h 137c
10 b g Witness Box(USA) Kinsella's Rose (IRE) (Roselier (FR))
2646[P] 3059[3] 4134[4] (4557) 4821[4] 5276[5] 5571[6]

Sumner (IRE) *William Davies* 60h 77c
10 b g Xaar Black Jack Girl (IRE) (Ridgewood Ben)
1668[P] 1835[5]

Sunarri (IRE) *Jane Walton* 36h 105c
10 b g Sonus(IRE) Rosearro (IRE) (Roselier (FR))
75[8]

Sunblazer (IRE) *Kim Bailey* 101h
4 gr g Dark Angel(IRE) Damask Rose (IRE) (Dr Devious (IRE))
4889[10]

Sun Cloud (IRE) *Malcolm Jefferson* 118h 140c
7 b g Cloudings(IRE) Miss Melrose (Bob Back (USA))
553[U] 1660[10]
2157[F] 2446[3] (3019) (3617) 4427[F] 4821[8] 5513[3]

Sundahia (FR) *J-D Marion* 134c
7 b g Sunshack Aida D'Erios (FR) (Art Bleu)
1984a[9] 2415a[P] 5425a[F]

Sunday Serenade (IRE) *Peter Fahey* 120h
6 b m Flemensfirth(USA) Ariels Serenade (IRE) (Presenting)
2506[9] 4846a[6]

Sun Dream *Geoffrey Deacon* 22h
7 b m Desert Sun I Have A Dream (SWE) (Mango Express)
1265[8] 1519[P]

Sundream (GER) *G Macaire* 139h 133c
6 b g Lomitas Salista (GER) (Heraldiste (USA))
5425a[6]

Sunglasses (IRE) *Nicky Henderson* 92b
7 b g Fruits Of Love(USA) Penny Haven (IRE) (Camden Town)
899[U] 1088[P]

Sun Lady (FR) *Jane Walton* 77h
8 b m Rifapour(IRE) Vousseliere (FR) (Tourangeau (FR))
444[P] 629[8]

Sunnyhillboy (IRE) *Jonjo O'Neill* 132h 142c
11 b g Old Vic Sizzle (High Line)
2504[10] (3069)

Sunny Ledgend *Andrew J Martin* 127h 134c
9 b g Midnight Legend Swordella (Broadsword (USA))
3798[2]
4265[P] 4418[F] 4820[8] 4949[6] **5385[14]**

Sun Quest *Steven Dixon* 100h
10 b g Groom Dancer(USA) Icaressa (Anabaa (USA))
267[6] 691[3] 1273[8] 1699[9] 4334[P] 5012[4] 5522[11]

Sunsational Girl *Brian Eckley* 1b
5 ch m Byron Sun Bonnet (Grand Lodge (USA))
2809[7] 3433[7]

Sunset Song *Theresa Gibson* 15h
10 b m Supreme Sound Cudder Or Shudder (IRE) (The Parson)
73[7] 218[P]

Sunsetten (IRE) *Hugh Burns* 102b
10 b g Tendulkar(USA) Rosy Affair (IRE) (Red Sunset)
4696[P]

Sunshine Buddy *Chris Down* 81h
7 b m Reel Buddy(USA) Bullion (Sabrehill (USA))
2771[8] 3192[6]

Sun Sky Blue (FR) *G Mousnier* 108c
7 gr g Urgent Request(IRE) Middle East (FR) (Akarad (FR))
1214a[6]

Suntiep (FR) *W P Mullins* 138h 138c
8 b g Ungaro(GER) Galostiepy (FR) (Laostic (FR))
4741[3] ◆

Sun Tzu (IRE) *Peter Bowen* 106h 130c
10 br g Definite Article Told You So (IRE) (Glacial Storm (USA))
334[7]

Sun Wild Life (FR) *Robert Walford* 112h
4 b g Antarctique(IRE) Nidelia (FR) (Sleeping Car (FR))
262a[6] 3003[2] 3641[4] 4391[2] 5030[11]

Supari *Sarah-Jayne Davies* 79b
5 b g Beat All(USA) Susie Bury (Overbury (IRE))
3295[4] *4016[12] 4329[4]* 4694[P]

Supasundae *Tim Fitzgerald* 105b
4 b g Galileo(IRE) Distinctive Look (IRE) (Danehill (USA))
(4895) ◆

Super Ally (IRE) *Andrew Parker* 104h 116c
9 b g Flemensfirth(USA) Strong Tide (IRE) (Strong Gale)
25[2]

Superciliary *Chris Gordon* 114h
5 b g Dansili Supereva (IRE) (Sadler's Wells (USA))
1711[3] 2568[2] 3007[3] 3420[2] 3569[3] 4599[8] (5005) (5125) 5353[P]

Super Collider *Susan Corbett* 115h
7 b g Montjeu(IRE) Astorg (USA) (Lear Fan (USA))
(93) 480[3] (648) 812[3] 1048[4] 1148[6] 1285[5] 1544[7] 5377[2]

Super Cookie *Noel Quinlan* 80h
4 b f Dylan Thomas(IRE) Dance Lesson (In The Wings)
2750[5] 3385[9] 4722[11]

Super De Sivola (FR) *T Trapenard* 115h 121c
8 b g Robin Des Champs(FR) Superbia (FR) (Leading Counsel (USA))
2465a[8]

Super Duplex *Pat Phelan* 100h
7 b g Footstepsinthesand Penelope Tree (IRE) (Desert Prince (IRE))
708[9] 1697[5]

Super Duty (IRE) *Donald McCain* 142h 155c
8 b g Shantou(USA) Sarah's Cottage (IRE) (Topanoora)
2815[P] 3165[2]

Superior Command (IRE) *Lucinda Russell* 94h
5 b g Lahib(USA) Decent Dime (IRE) (Insan (USA))
5279[9]

Superior Fire (IRE) *Charlie Longsdon* 92b
4 b g Arcadio(GER) Take Aim (Gunner B)
3656[3] 5070[5]

Superior Quality (IRE) *Charlie Longsdon* 109h 132c
9 br g Winged Love(IRE) Unknown Quality (Sabrehill (USA))
1851[2] 2249[4] 3737[6]
5089[2]

Super Lunar (IRE) *Alan King* 102h
5 b g Super Celebre(FR) Kapricia Speed (FR) (Vertical Speed (FR))
4397[3] 4863[6] 5343[3]

Superman De La Rue (FR) *David Rees* 121h 94c
8 b g Akhdari(USA) Impala De La Rue (FR) (Brugnon (FR))
3004[6] 3431[P]

Supermightyfine *Jo Hughes* 80h 66c
7 b g Slip Anchor Wordy's Wonder (Welsh Captain)
122[6] **422[6]**
641[7]

Supernoverre (IRE) *Alan Jones* 53h
8 b g Noverre(USA) Caviare (Cadeaux Genereux)
1643[11] 3426[11] 4519[P]

Super Pipo (FR) *H Billot* 95h
5 b g Soave(GER) Roannaise (FR) (Octagonal (NZ))
703a[8]

Super Sam *John Spearing* 104b
5 gr g Overbury(IRE) Gaye Sophie (Environment Friend)
4951[3]

Supersticion *Michael Madgwick* 86h
5 b m Red Ransom(USA) Go Supersonic (Zafonic (USA))
490[10] 1764[5] 2016[8] 2907[6] 5262[10]

Super Villan *Mark Bradstock* 119h 123c
9 ch g Alflora(IRE) Country House (Town And Country)
358[21]
2267[P] (2651)
2979[P] 3886[9] 4602[4] 4932[8] 5333[11]

Supralunary *Robin Mathew* 59b
8 b g Midnight Legend Heresy (IRE) (Black Minstrel)
839[P] 930[P] 1055[P]

Supreme Asset (IRE) *Donald McCain* 115h 131c
6 b g Beneficial Hollygrove Supreme (IRE) (Supreme Leader)
2515[3] 3037[3] 3418[2] (4084) 5213[2]

Supreme Bailerina (IRE) *W P Mullins* 110h
6 b m Norse Dancer(IRE) Second Best (IRE) (Supreme Leader)
2506[6]

Supreme Bob (IRE) *Lucy Jones* 102h 103c
8 b g Bob's Return(IRE) Suprememories (IRE) (Supreme Leader)
2598[5]
3729[6] 4172[4]
4396[4] 4840[3] 5187[2] 5428[U]

Supreme Builder *Miss G E J Anderson* 102b
13 b g Supreme Leader Osocool (Teenoso (USA))
4554[P]

Supreme Doc (IRE) *M T O'Donovan* 135h 138c
9 b g Dr Massini(IRE) Castlehill Lady (IRE) (Supreme Leader)
1168a[5] 5135[U] 5415a[6]

Supreme Duke (IRE) *Philip Hobbs* 90h 112c
12 br g Supreme Leader Shelikesitstraight (IRE) (Rising)
1397[2]

Supreme Luxury (IRE) *Dan Skelton*
5 b m Iffraaj Stay Hernanda (Hernando (FR))
2467[F]

Supreme Present *Kim Bailey* 110h
6 b m Presenting Deep Sunset (IRE) (Supreme Leader)
2495[P] *4019[2] 4297[2] (4495)*

Supreme Regime (IRE) *Miss Katy Jane Price* 99c
8 b g Old Vic Shampooed (IRE) (Law Society (USA))
5545[2]

Suprise Vendor (IRE) *Stuart Coltherd* 114h 125c
8 ch g Fath(USA) Dispol Jazz (Alhijaz)
23[4] (109)
493[6] 2356[2] (2595)
(2804) 3354[F] 3615[5] 4084[U] (4235) 4549[8] 5557[5]

Surely Try (FR) *Mme I Pacault* 90h 105c
4 b g Prince Kirk(FR) Carmen Tonic (FR) (Double Bed (FR))
262a[7] 614a[6]

Surenaga (IRE) *Philip Rowley* 112h 123c
12 b g Arctic Lord Surely Madam (Torenaga)
60[U] 373[2] 660[P]

Sureness (IRE) *Charlie Mann* 79h
4 ch f Hurricane Run(IRE) Silk Dress (IRE) (Gulch (USA))
4730[8]

Sure Reef (IRE) *W P Mullins* 139h
5 ch g Choisir(AUS) Cutting Reef (IRE) (Kris)
(3931a) ◆

Sure Thing (FR) *Henry Daly* 110h 121c
8 b g Ragmar(FR) Harpe (FR) (Bayolidaan (FR))
(29) 482[2] 833[2] **4970[2] 5031[8]**

Surf And Turf (IRE) *Kevin Frost* 116h 127c
8 ch g Beneficial Clear Top Waltz (IRE) (Topanoora)
585[8] (714)
781[2] 999[4] 1063[3] (1326)
1470[5] 2013[10] 2447[8] (5521)

Surging Seas (IRE) *Tony Coyle* 105b
5 b g Tiger Hill(IRE) Musardiere (Montjeu (IRE))
2499[3] 3863[5] 4384[2]

Surprise Us *Richard Hambleton*
7 b g Indian Ridge Pingus (Polish Precedent (USA))
5041[U]

Susquehanna River (IRE) *Nigel Twiston-Davies* 109h 120c
7 b g Indian River(FR) Calistoga (IRE) (Mujadil (USA))
336[2] **(1925)**
2099[3] 2754[2] 3389[5] 5032[3] 5348[8]

Sustainability (IRE) *Venetia Williams* 116h 131c
9 ch g Old Vic Over The Glen (IRE) (Over The River (FR))
3786[2] **4430[6]**

Sutes *Alan Jones* 80b
6 b g Kahyasi Misleain (IRE) (Un Desperado (FR))
1861[8] 2479[S] 2912[8]

Sutton Sid *Chris Gordon* 81h
4 ch g Dutch Art Drastic Measure (Pivotal)
1271[2] 2038[5]

Swaledale Lad (IRE) *Richard Ford* 130h 137c
7 b g Arakan(USA) Tadjnama (USA) (Exceller (USA))
1083[3] 1550[3] 1849[2] ◆ **2159[7] 5281[2]** ◆

Swallows Delight (IRE) *Mrs Julie Mansell* 108c
9 br g Tamayaz(CAN) Windmill Star (IRE) (Orchestra)
57[4] 4246[3] 4658[3] 5135[9]

Swallowshide *Emma Lavelle* 127h
5 b g Hernando(FR) Kentford Grebe (Teenoso (USA))
239[3] (2631) 3388[4] 3774[6]

Swampfire (IRE) *Gary Moore* 125h
6 b g Anabaa(USA) Moonfire (Sadler's Wells (USA))
901[3] 1045[4] 2366[13] 3094[10]

Swanage Bay (IRE) *Anthony Middleton* 49b
7 b g Dilshaan Special Mention (IRE) (Nashwan (USA))
1826[8]

Swansbrook (IRE) *Mrs Sue Popham* 97h 98c
11 b g Alderbrook Bobsyourdad (IRE) (Bob's Return (IRE))
4518[2] 4915[4]

Swatow Typhoon (IRE) *Donald McCain* 123h 135c
7 b g Shantou(USA) Oscar Leader (IRE) (Supreme Leader)
2803[3] (3209)
(3496) 3921[4] 4427[P]

Sweeney Tunes *Paul Nolan* 123h 146c
8 ch g Karinga Bay Nan (Buckley)
2123a[3]

Sweeps Hill (NZ) *Jonjo O'Neill* 130b
10 b g Montjeu(IRE) Windfield Dancer (NZ) (Zabeel (NZ))
3798[P]

Sweet Boy Vic (IRE) *Chris Gordon* 87h
6 b g Old Vic Sweet Second (IRE) (Second Set (IRE))
2564[8] 2947[U] 3138[5] 3553[2] 3878[2] 4275[2] 4700[9]

Sweet Deal (IRE) *Nicky Henderson* 102h
4 gr g Verglas(IRE) Compromise (FR) (Fasliyev (USA))
2927[4]

Sweet Louise (IRE) *Barry Brennan* 45h
4 b f Azamour(IRE) Maria Luisa (IRE) (King's Best (USA))
2557[9]

Sweet My Lord (FR) *W P Mullins* 142h 141c
8 b g Johann Quatz(FR) Hasta Manana (FR) (Useful (FR))
1604a[13] 2708a[P]

Sweet Prince (IRE) *Jonjo O'Neill* 86h
7 b g Court Cave(IRE) Simply Sweep (IRE) (Simply Great (FR))
590[10]

Swift Arrow (IRE) *Donald McCain* 94h 138c
8 b g Overbury(IRE) Clover Run (IRE) (Deep Run)
1850[4]
(2359) 2793[P] (4053)
4543[6] 5156[P]

Swift Blade (IRE) *Lady Herries* 80h
6 ch g Exceed And Excel(AUS) Gold Strike (IRE) (Rainbow Quest (USA))
8[7]

Swift Counsel (IRE) *Mrs D Williams* 98h 111c
13 b g Leading Counsel(USA) Small Iron (General Ironside)
657[2]

Swift Escape *Tim Vaughan* 103h
7 b g Exit To Nowhere(USA) Vivre Aimer Rire (FR) (Cyborg (FR))
1152[3] 1387[2] 1561[5] 1938[12]

Swiftly Done (IRE) *Declan Carroll*
7 b g Whipper(USA) Ziffany (Taufan (USA))
3330[P]

Swincombe Rock *David Bridgwater* 113h 139c
9 ch g Double Trigger(IRE) Soloism (Sulaafah (USA))
2108[U] 2537[3]

Swincombe Star *Robert Walford* 98b
5 b g With The Flow(USA) Lady Felix (Batshoof)
2634[3] *4296[6]* 5145[5]

Swincombe Stone *Anthony Honeyball* 91h 42c
7 ch g Best Of The Bests(IRE) Soloism (Sulaafah (USA))
2315[U] 2633[U] 3007[5]
3693[8]

Swincomb Silvalady *Robert Walford* 00h
6 b m Silver Patriarch(IRE) Lady Felix (Batshoof)
970[13] 2907[7] 3168[7]

Swindy *Sue Smith* 69h
6 b g Hurricane Run(IRE) Red Passion (USA) (Seeking The Gold (USA))
22[11]

Swing Bill (FR) *David Pipe* 118h 147c
13 gr g Grey Risk(FR) Melodie Royale (FR) (Garde Royale)
2937[5] 4769[11] 5171[9]

Swing Bowler *David Pipe* 146h
7 b m Galileo(IRE) Lady Cricket (FR) (Cricket Ball (USA))
4147[5] 4682[7] 5274[4]

Swingbridge (IRE) *Chris Grant* 94h 106c
6 b g Milan Creative Approach (IRE) (Toulon)
4613[F] 4984[3] 5515[P]

Swing De Balme (FR) *Mlle N Pfohl*
8 b g Cachet Noir(USA) Cyclosporine (FR) (Mansonnien (FR))
131a[P]

Swing Hard (IRE) *Sue Smith* 107h 122c
6 br g Zagreb(USA) Hurricane Jane (IRE) (Strong Gale)
80[4] 1072[2] ◆ 1393[2] 1752[5] 2073[8]
2356[3] (2820)
3211[4] (3478)

Swinging Hawk (GER) *Ian Williams* 121h
8 ch g Hawk Wing(USA) Saldenschwinge (GER) (In The Wings)
(2598) (2755)

Swing State *Tom Gretton* 78h
9 b g Overbury(IRE) Peg's Permission (Ra Nova)
1793^{11} 3192^{9} 4309^{2} 4823^{8}

Swiss Art (IRE) *Sue Smith* 112h 85c
8 b g One Cool Cat(USA) Alpine Park (IRE) (Barathea (IRE))
2051^{9} **2349^{F}**

Switched Off *Kevin Frost* 120h
9 b g Catcher In The Rye(IRE) Button Hole Flower (IRE) (Fairy King (USA))
512^{3} 4157^{8} 5019^{9}

Swnymor (IRE) *Rebecca Curtis* 133h
5 b g Dylan Thomas(IRE) Propaganda (IRE) (Sadler's Wells (USA))
1866^{F} 3648^{7} 4025^{6} 4413^{5} 4820^{2} 5172^{10} 5349^{9}

Sybarite (FR) *Nigel Twiston-Davies* 125h 128c
8 bb g Dark Moondancer Haida III (FR) (Video Rock (FR))
2642^{6} 3195^{2} 3800^{4} (4356) (5559)

Sycho Fred (IRE) *Mike Sowersby* 76h 82c
13 b g Buster King Rebecca Steel (IRE) (Arapahos (FR))
206^{8} 601^{3} 753^{7} (1089)
1202^{P} 1300^{P} 1715^{4} 2396^{4} 2872^{P} 3355^{P}

Sydney Paget (IRE) *Donald McCain* 131h 149c
7 b g Flemensfirth(USA) Shuil Aoibhinn (IRE) (Phardante (FR))
(2674) ◆ 3285^{P} 3780^{5} 4953^{P}

Sylvan Legend *Caroline Keevil* 81h
6 b g Midnight Legend Sylvan Warbler (USA) (Blushing Groom (FR))
1764^{8} (2766) 2920^{7} 3426^{12} 5262^{11}

Symphonick (FR) *Tim Fitzgerald* 107h 105c
8 b g Passing Sale(FR) Cymphonie (FR) (Djarvis (FR))
800^{2} 1008^{6} 1674^{10} 1873^{3} 2034^{3} 2596^{7}

Symphonie D'Anjou (FR) *A Chaille-Chaille* 122h 127c
6 gr m Turgeon(USA) Grande Or Rose (FR) (Rose Laurel)
1984a^{8}

Synthe Davis (FR) *Laura Mongan* 116h 121c
9 b m Saint Des Saints(FR) Trumpet Davis (FR) (Rose Laurel)
45^{3} 234^{2} (705)
943^{4} 1522^{3} 1767^{2} 2270^{6} 2948^{10}

Syrian *Barry Murtagh*
7 b g Hawk Wing(USA) Lady Lahar (Fraam)
4811^{P} 5206^{P}

Taaresh (IRE) *Kevin Morgan* 116h
9 b g Sakhee(USA) Tanaghum (Darshaan)
480^{6} 1093^{3} (1319) 1685^{4} 1922^{7} 2717^{5} 3031^{9} 4794^{7} 5365^{3}

Tabhachtach (IRE) *S Slevin* 131h 133c
7 b g Quws Erin Anam Cara (IRE) (Exit To Nowhere (USA))
4769^{U}

Table Bluff (IRE) *John Spearing* 93h
5 ch g Indian Haven Double Deal (Keen)
2602^{11} 2893^{3} 3175^{9} 5072^{10} 5519^{5}

Tackler (IRE) *Jonjo O'Neill* 102h
6 br g Presenting Merry Queen (IRE) (Anshan)
68^{3}

Tadabeer *Ian Williams* 86h
6 b g Green Desert(USA) Perfect Plum (IRE) (Darshaan)
651^{3} 852^{4}

Tae Kwon Do (USA) *Tim Vaughan* 94h 117c
8 b g Thunder Gulch(USA) Judy's Magic (USA) (Wavering Monarch (USA))
83^{6} 407^{7} 1675^{8} 1945^{5}

Taffy Dare (IRE) *Alan King* 83h
5 b m Court Cave(IRE) Three More (USA) (Sanglamore (USA))
2675^{5} 4487^{5} 4910^{8}

Taffy Thomas *Peter Bowen* 100h 110c
10 b g Alflora(IRE) Tui (Tina's Pet)
1886^{2} 2370^{4} 3730^{6} 4078^{U} 4250^{3} 4656^{4} 5193^{4}

Tafika *Paul Webber* 97h 117c
10 b g Kayf Tara Shiwa (Bustino)
321^{P} 2847^{5} 3325^{6} 4663^{2}

Taggia (FR) *Alison Batchelor* 103h
7 b m Great Pretender(IRE) Ecossaise II (FR) (Useful (FR))
5257^{3}

Tagrita (IRE) *Paul Nicholls* 135h
6 b m King's Theatre(IRE) Double Dream (IRE) (Double Eclipse (IRE))
2801^{3} (3173) (3991) (4276) 5157^{8}

Tahiti Pearl (IRE) *Sue Smith* 98h 140c
10 b g Winged Love(IRE) Clara's Dream (IRE) (Phardante (FR))
77^{4} 2448^{2} 2751^{2} 3090^{2} 3287^{2} (3923)
5156^{U} 5253^{P}

Taiga Des Chambres (FR) *Patrice Quinton* 113c
7 b m Network(GER) Hermes Rochelaise (FR) (Boston Two Step (USA))
3068^{P}

Taigan (FR) *Giles Smyly* 126h
7 b g Panoramic Lazary (FR) (Bobinski)
(289) (604) 1042^{2} 3892^{5}

Taikun Tino (FR) *Yannick Fouin* 117h 123c
7 b g Lost World(IRE) Cometina (FR) (Arctic Tern (USA))
(2465a)

Tail Of The Bank (IRE) *Laura Young* 97h 106c
11 b g Flemensfirth(USA) Dear Money (IRE) (Buckskin (FR))
37^{7}

Takaatuf (IRE) *John Wade* 101h 95c
8 b g Dubai Destination(USA) Karlaka (IRE) (Barathea (IRE))
201^{6} **679^{4}**
1715^{3} 1981^{P}

Take A Bow *Nicky Henderson* 117h
5 b g Norse Dancer(IRE) Madame Illusion (FR) (Solid Illusion (USA))
(1712) ◆ 2850^{4}

Take Of Shoc'S (IRE) *Sophie Leech* 93h 107c
10 ch g Beneficial Dear Dunleer (IRE) (Montelimar (USA))
(1710)
(2387) 2977^{8} 5247^{P} 5487^{8}

Takeroc (FR) *Alexandra Dunn* 111h 133c
11 gr g Take Risks(FR) Rochambelle (FR) (Truculent (USA))
236^{10} 520^{P} 1670^{5} 2078^{5} ◆ 2440^{2} 2721^{3} 3156^{P}
5141^{5} 5527^{5}

Takestan (IRE) *Patrick O Brady* 96h
11 b g Selkirk(USA) Takariya (IRE) (Arazi (USA))
1950a^{F}

Take The Cash (IRE) *Donald McCain* 132h
5 b g Cloudings(IRE) Taking My Time (IRE) (High Roller (IRE))
3835^{4} (4576) 4950^{4}

Take The Crown *Henry Oliver* 97h
5 gr g Fair Mix(IRE) Miss Wizadora (Gildoran)
760^{9} 948^{U} 1107^{4} 1183^{4} 1400^{10} 4504^{7} (4911) (5012) 5335^{3}

Take The Mick *Venetia Williams* 92h 125c
7 b g Ishiguru(USA) Michaelmas Daizy (Michelozzo (USA))
2510^{7} 2891^{4} **3729^{2} ◆ 3876^{2} (4354)**
4451^{2} 4490^{P} 5039^{3} 5488^{P}

Takeyourcapoff (IRE) *Mrs John Harrington* 131h
9 b m King's Theatre(IRE) Masriyna's Article (IRE) (Definite Article)
1948a^{3}

Talented Kid *John Ferguson* 97b
5 b g Teofilo(IRE) See You Later (Emarati (USA))
412^{2} 599^{2}

Talisasoto (FR) *T Boivin*
7 b m Timboroa La Patronne (FR) (Hamas (IRE))
1623a^{F}

Talkin Sence (IRE) *Stuart Coltherd* 123h 110c
9 b g Heron Island(IRE) Catatonia (IRE) (Cataldi)
2158^{2} (2357)
2969^{4} 3499^{4}

Talkin Thomas (IRE) *Nicky Richards* 112h 117c
8 b g Talkin Man(CAN) Keerou Lady (IRE) (Be My Native (USA))
1785^{6}
2173^{3} 2623^{P} 3041^{3} 4744^{3} 5356^{4}

Talk Of Saafend (IRE) *Dianne Sayer* 90h
9 b m Barathea(IRE) Sopran Marida (IRE) (Darshaan)
21^{3} 868^{10}

Talkonthestreet (IRE) *Philip Hobbs* 104h 133c
7 b g Milan Super Size (IRE) (Shernazar)
2655^{11}
2889^{4} 3424^{3} (4968)
5488^{2}

Tallanstown Boy (IRE) *Mrs Rose Partridge* 89c
9 b g Winged Love(IRE) Tallanstown (IRE) (King's Ride)
180^{P}

Tallevu (IRE) *Noel Chance* 68h
5 ch g Stormy River(FR) Pascarina (FR) (Exit To Nowhere (USA))
161^{5}

Tallulah Mai *Alastair Lidderdale* 90h 86c
7 b m Kayf Tara Al Awaalah (Mukaddamah (USA))
1391^{11}
3876^{5} *4303^{8}* **4482^{F}** 4967^{5} 5242^{15}

Tamarillo Grove (IRE) *Sophie Leech* 113h
7 b g Cape Cross(IRE) Tamarillo (Daylami (IRE))
521^{7} 697^{5} (924) 1173^{2} 1203^{7} 1400^{7} 5552^{6}

Tamarton Tansy *Fergal O'Brien* 57h
7 b m Tamure(IRE) Killerton Clover (High Season)
85^{6} 5002^{11} 5332^{P}

Tambalong *Caroline Keevil* 54b
6 b m Tamure(IRE) Baie D'Along (FR) (Tel Quel (FR))
2298^{17} 2745^{6}

Tamberma (FR) *P Journiac*
7 b g
5530a^{5}

Tambour Major (FR) *Simon Shirley-Beavan* 53h
7 b g Myrakalu(FR) Joaillere (FR) (Silver Rainbow)
5508^{9}

Tambura *G C Maundrell* 80b
4 b f Tamure(IRE) Singing Cottage (Greensmith)
4916^{8}

Taming The Tweet *J R Jenkins* 79h
4 b f Act One Pants (Pivotal)
2066^{4} 2557^{8}

Tammys Hill (IRE) *Liam Lennon* 106h 141c
9 b g Tamayaz(CAN) Hillside Lass (Troy Fair)
660^{6} (4788) ◆

Tanerko Emery (FR) *David Pipe* 149h 135c
8 b g Lavirco(GER) Frequence (FR) (Panoramic)
2192^{2} 2533^{5} ◆ **2799^{F}**

Tango In The Night *Chris Bealby* 43h
7 b g Fleetwood(IRE) Secret Dance (Sadler's Wells (USA))
963^{P}

Tangolan (IRE) *Phil Middleton* 120h
6 ch g Golan(IRE) Classic Note (IRE) (Classic Secret (USA))
1535^{5} 1840^{U}

Tang Royal (FR) *Richard Rowe* 83h
7 ch g Epalo(GER) Bea De Forme (FR) (Sleeping Car (FR))
95^{7} 538^{P} 706^{4} 2473^{8} 3009^{10}

Tanks For That (IRE) *Nicky Henderson* 114h 152c
11 br g Beneficial Lady Jurado (IRE) (Jurado (USA))
1969^{P} 3080^{6} *(4303)* **4790^{9} 5156^{F}**

Tanner Bet *Polly Gundry* 56b
6 b m Thank Heavens Vercheny (Petoski)
1056^{7} 1196^{5}

Tanner Hill (IRE) *James Evans* 58h
6 b g Milan Carlingford Leader (IRE) (Supreme Leader)
2878^{5} 3440^{11}

Tantalized *Dave Roberts* 75h
5 b m Authorized(IRE) Tarabela (CHI) (Hussonet (USA))
506^{3} *4328^{U}*

Tantamount *Lucinda Russell* 121h
5 b g Observatory(USA) Cantanta (Top Ville)
531^{5} 865^{4} (1145) ◆ 1286^{3} 1664^{2} (2936) 3479^{2}

Tante Sissi (FR) *Alan King* 116h 122c
7 b m Lesotho(USA) Kadjara (FR) (Silver Rainbow)
2632^{P} 2948^{8}
4804^{7} 5228^{3}

Tapaidh Frankie (IRE) *Simon West* 89b
5 br m Waveney(UAE) Corravilla (IRE) (Yashgan)
5196^{4} 5424a^{12}

Tap Night (USA) *Lucinda Russell* 130h 153c
7 ch g Pleasant Tap(USA) Day Mate (USA) (Dayjur (USA))
2244^{2} 2503^{8} 3082^{8} 3887^{3} ◆ 4768^{P} 5253^{4} 5535^{9}

Taqaat (USA) *Stephen Hughes* 92h
6 b g Forestry(USA) Alrayihah (IRE) (Nashwan (USA))
177^{8} 436^{6}

Taquin Du Seuil (FR) *Jonjo O'Neill* 143h 164c
7 bb g Voix Du Nord(FR) Sweet Laly (FR) (Marchand De Sable (USA))
(2151)
(2489) 2950^{3} 3456^{2} (3777)
(4764)

Taraakum (FR) *Andrew Crook* 69b
4 gr g Clodovil(IRE) Lockup (IRE) (Inchinor)
2960^{11}

Tarabela *Johnny Farrelly* 115h 106c
11 b m Kayf Tara Rocky Revival (Roc Imp)
3281^{4} 3688^{F} (4176) (4275)

Tara Bridge *Chris Gordon* 67b
6 b g Kayf Tara Annie Greenlaw (Petoski)
4473^{5}

Tara Dancer *Renee Robeson* 34h
6 b m Kayf Tara Suave Shot (Suave Dancer (USA))
1090^{6}

Tara Dee (IRE) *Andrew Wilson* 65b
5 b m Golan(IRE) Liberwoman (IRE) (Among Men (USA))
5381^{4}

Tara Dove *Michael Appleby* 42b
6 gr m Kayf Tara Kildee Lass (Morpeth)
324^{11} 675^{11}

Taradrewe *Anthony Honeyball* 117h
7 b m Kayf Tara Kaream (Karinga Bay)
1^{U} 140^{9} 484^{3} 932^{8} 3569^{4} 5007^{4} (5114) ◆ (5260)

Tara For Lilly *Sue Gardner* 96b
5 b m Kayf Tara Tyre Hill Lilly (Jupiter Island)
4735^{6}

Tara Mac *Keith Dalgleish* 104b
5 b m Kayf Tara Macklette (IRE) (Buckskin (FR))
4240^{2} 4582^{3} 5159^{11}

Tara Mist *Henry Daly* 115b
5 gr m Kayf Tara Island Mist (Jupiter Island)
(2892) 3507^{2} 4683^{2} 5159^{3}

Tara Muck *Nigel Twiston-Davies* 102h
7 b m Kayf Tara Madam Muck (Gunner B)
(1499) 1885^{6} 2190^{0} 2824^{3} 3391^{7}

Taranis (FR) *Charles Whittaker* 135h 150c
13 ch g Mansonnien(FR) Vikosa (FR) (Nikos)
63^{U}

Tarantelle *John Spearing* 62b
5 br m Kayf Tara Suave Shot (Suave Dancer (USA))
4296^{15} 4867^{12}

Tara Point *Paul Nicholls* 119b
5 gr m Kayf Tara Poppet (Terimon)
(5528)

Tara Road *Rebecca Curtis* 113h
6 b g Kayf Tara Sparkling Jewel (Bijou D'Inde)
2368^{3} (2946) 3182^{5} 4093^{2} 5088^{5}

Tara Rose *Nigel Twiston-Davies* 106h 128c
9 br m Kayf Tara True Rose (IRE) (Roselier (FR))
1923^{2} ◆ 2371^{8}
2925^{6} 4559^{4} 4960^{7} 5230^{5}

Tara Royal *P York* 79b
9 b g Kayf Tara Poussetiere Deux (FR) (Garde Royale)
4355^{P}

Tara Springs *Barry Murtagh* 38h
5 b m Kayf Tara Moor Spring (Primitive Rising (USA))
4240^{9} 4605^{6} 4939^{P} 5322^{P}

Tara Tavey (IRE) *Kevin Bishop* 95h 84c
9 gr m Kayf Tara Slieve League (IRE) (Roselier (FR))
2619^{4} 3250^{P} 4176^{6} 5007^{2} 5234^{6} 5432^{6}

Tara Warrior (IRE) *Tim Vaughan* 92h 69c
8 b g Dilshaan Dungeon Princess (IRE) (Danehill (USA))
1306^{P} 1582^{7} 1799^{5} 2090^{P} 2470^{11}

Tarla (FR) *W P Mullins* 150h 140c
8 b m Lavirco(GER) Targerine (FR) (Gairloch)
5475a^{8}

Tarmac Girl *Tim Vaughan* 79h
6 b m Alflora(IRE) Cool Spice (Karinga Bay)
8^{U} 391^{6} 477^{3} 640^{13}

Taroum (IRE) *Tony Carroll* 108h
7 b g Refuse To Bend(IRE) Taraza (IRE) (Darshaan)
812^{6} 947^{4} (1400) 1442^{2} 1506^{6} 1840^{5} 2292^{10} 2617^{5}

Tarquinius (FR) *Gordon Elliott* 88h 111c
11 gr g Turgeon(USA) Shannon Bells (FR) (Nashamaa)
2822^{7} 3868a^{P} 4427^{P}

Tarraco (FR) *Venetia Williams* 91h 118c
7 b g Sassanian(USA) Marie Esther (FR) (Chamberlin (FR))
321^{P} 1748^{U} 2578^{4} 3502^{2} (4720)
4843^{4} (5025)
5558^{P}

Tartak (FR) *Victor Dartnall* 98h 135c
11 b g Akhdari(USA) Tartamuda (FR) (Tyrnavos)
1969^{4} 3205^{P} 4768^{12}

Tartan Snow *Stuart Coltherd* 126h 126c
14 b g Valseur(USA) Whitemoss Leader (IRE) (Supreme Leader)
3825^{P} (4239)
4554^{3} 4837^{6} 5135^{2} 5535^{11}

Tartan Tiger (IRE) *John Quinn* 108h
8 ch g Flemensfirth(USA) River Clyde (IRE) (Presenting)
5379^{5}

Taruma (FR) *Simon West* 119h 120c
6 gr g Martaline Vie De Reine (FR) (Mansonnien (FR))
734^{7} 867^{5} (1164)

Tarvini (IRE) *Jonjo O'Neill* 115h 106c
9 b g Kalanisi(IRE) Tarwila (IRE) (In The Wings)
690^{5} ◆ 965^{6} (1188) 1267^{3} (1477) 1707^{2} 2284^{2} 2715^{8}

Tasheba *Sophie Leech* 118h 90c
9 ch g Dubai Destination(USA) Tatanka (IRE) (Lear Fan (USA))
181^{4} 508^{11} 728^{P} 799^{5}

Tashkaldou (FR) *Dan Skelton* 91h
5 b g Kaldou Star Tashka (FR) (Cricket Ball (USA))
2254^{10} 2718^{13} 3175^{8} 3568^{3}

Tastes Like More (IRE) *Mrs A R Hewitt* 58b
12 b m Close Conflict(USA) Fly Your Kite (IRE) (Silver Kite (USA))
535^{P}

Taste The Wine (IRE) *Bernard Llewellyn* 110h
8 gr g Verglas(IRE) Azia (IRE) (Desert Story (IRE))
(304) 480^{4} 831^{3} 5005^{5} 5179^{9}

Tataniano (FR) *Richard Rowe* 129h 148c
10 b g Sassanian(USA) Rosa Carola (FR) (Rose Laurel)
2532^{5} 2952^{7} 3320^{4} 3645^{P}

Tatenen (FR) *Richard Rowe* 123h 142c
10 b g Lost World(IRE) Tamaziya (IRE) (Law Society (USA))
(2812)
4034^{2} 4768^{3} 5156^{4}

Tatispout (FR) *R Chotard* 100h 132c
7 b m Califet(FR) Larmonie (FR) (Great Palm (USA))
863a^{P}

Tatting *Chris Dwyer* 69h
5 ch g Street Cry(IRE) Needlecraft (IRE) (Mark Of Esteem (IRE))
696^{7}

Taupin Rochelais (FR) *Patrice Quinton* 103h 95c
7 b g Al Namix(FR) Katia Rochelaise (FR) (Panoramic)
2384a^{F}

Tavenger (FR) *A Gregoire* 102c
7 b g Reste Tranquille(FR) Scavenger (FR) (Nashamaa)
200a^{2}

Taxi Des Obeaux (FR) *Philip Kirby* 78h
7 bb g Maresca Sorrento(FR) Madrilene (FR) (Subotica (FR))
5102^{10} 5493^{4}

Taxiformissbyron *Iain Jardine*
4 b f Byron Miss Respect (Mark Of Esteem (IRE))
4956^{P}

Tayarat (IRE) *Michael Chapman* 118h 100c
9 b g Noverre(USA) Sincere (IRE) (Bahhare (USA))
3856^{5} 4305^{5} 4699^{P} 4791^{6} **5073^{4} (5194)**
(5363)

Taylor (IRE) *Nicky Henderson* 111b
5 b m Presenting Britway Lady (IRE) (Norwich)
5374^{3} ◆

Taylors Secret *Patricia Rigby* 75b
8 b g Indian Haven Top Tune (Victory Note (USA))
1374^{P}

Tchang Goon (FR) *Zoe Davison* 105h 77c
10 b g Marathon(USA) Royal Hostess (IRE) (Be My Guest (USA))
2441^{5} 2727^{7} 3139^{7} 3551^{4} 3715^{5} 3819^{4} 4034^{4}
4159^{5} 4420^{P} 4795^{U}
5113^{P} 5263^{P}

Tchatchaco Ya Ya *Nicky Richards* 50h
7 b g Equerry(USA) Tchatchacoya (FR) (Sin Kiang (FR))
1977^{P} 2340^{6} 2840^{P}

Teaatreids (IRE) *Brian Ellison* 75h
6 ch m Royal Anthem(USA) Orchard Lass (On Your Mark)
2823^{10} 3270^{P} 4466^{4} 4889^{13} 5360^{10}

Tea Caddy *Jamie Snowden* 106h 109c
8 b m Kadastrof(FR) Little Tern (IRE) (Terimon)
268^{5} **645^{4}**
2348^{2} (2572)
3058^{8} 4337^{4} 5010^{4}
5369^{7}

Teaforthree (IRE) *Rebecca Curtis* 136h 158c
10 b g Oscar(IRE) Ethel's Bay (IRE) (Strong Gale)
3361^{9} 4263^{2} 4787^{8} 5171^{U}

Tea For Two *Nick Williams* 134b
5 b g Kayf Tara One For Me (Tragic Role (USA))
4149^{2} ◆ 4964^{2} (5338)

Tea In Marrakech (IRE) *William Kinsey* 54b
6 b g Spadoun(FR) Bagatelle (IRE) (Strong Gale)
2195^{8} 4951^{6}

Teak (IRE) *Ian Williams* 111h
7 b g Barathea(IRE) Szabo (IRE) (Anabaa (USA))
850^{9} 1398^{2} 1485^{3} 1564^{5} 1972^{12}

Tealissio *Lucy Wadham* 119h
8 b g Helissio(FR) Tealby (Efisio)
2050^{6} 2561^{3} (2729) 3249^{6} *4023^{4}* 4469^{4} 5365^{P}

Teals Star *C I Ratcliffe* 70h
10 b g Gods Solution Morcat (Morston (FR))
184^{9} 1137^{P} 1633^{P}

Tears From Heaven (USA) *Chris Grant* 94h 90c
8 bb g Street Cry(IRE) Heavenly Aura (USA) (St Jovite (USA))
2789^{5}
3755^{3} (4220)
4652^{3} 4942^{P} 5358^{8}

Ted Dolly (IRE) *Tom Symonds* 108h 107c
10 bb g Bob's Return(IRE) Little Pearl (IRE) (Bigstone (IRE))
1067a^{6}
2116a^{5} 4131^{5} 4919^{5}

Teddy Tee (IRE) *Nicky Richards* 80b
5 b g Mountain High(IRE) Knocksouna Lady (IRE) (Oscar (IRE))
4611[7]

Tedeum De Chamirey (FR) *F-X De Chevigny*
7 b g Dom Alco(FR) Dielette (FR) (El Badr)
863a[P]

Tedney Express (IRE) *Evan Williams* 23b
7 b g Presenting Persian Argument (IRE) (Persian Mews)
4091[10]

Ted Spread *Suzy Smith* 130h
7 b g Beat Hollow Highbrook (USA) (Alphabatim (USA))
82[3] 3088[5] 4935[3] 5399[F]

Ted Veale (IRE) *A J Martin* 146h 153c
7 b g Revoque(IRE) Rose Tanner (IRE) (Roselier (FR))
2531[3] 3308a[5] 3928a[4] ◆ 4737[F] 5168[6]

Teeiygee *Mike Sowersby* 47h
6 b g Bollin Eric Paxford Lady (Alflora (IRE))
283[P] 788[9]

Teejay Flying (FR) *T Trapenard* 114h 121c
6 b g Tiger Groom Flora Florette (FR) (Goldneyev (USA))
838a[P]

Teenage Dream (IRE) *Derek Shaw* 95h 102c
6 b g Antonius Pius(USA) Lucayan Star (IRE) (First Trump)
2353[P] 2676[P] 2787[10]
2976[5] 3564[U] 4890[2]

Teenage Idol (IRE) *Evelyn Slack* 132h
10 bb g Sadler's Wells(USA) Kaaba (Darshaan)
119[6]

Teenage Kicks (IRE) *Polly Gundry* 55h 114c
9 ch g Giant's Causeway(USA) Ruissec (USA) (Woodman (USA))
38[8] 244[P]

Teerie Express *George Bewley* 102h 99c
13 b g Sir Harry Lewis(USA) Trecento (Precious Metal)
222[P] 471[5]

Teescomponents Max *Keith Reveley* 86h
5 b g Grape Tree Road Our Tees Component (IRE) (Saddlers' Hall (IRE))
4349[9] 4895[7] 5295[8]

Teeton Blackvelvet *Caroline Bailey*
5 gr m Fair Mix(IRE) Teeton Priceless (Broadsword (USA))
4487[P] 4777[P] 5245[8]

Tegenaria Atrica (USA) *Sara Ender*
8 b g Toccet(USA) Sochi (USA) (Prized (USA))
288[P] 557[P]

Teide Mistress (USA) *Alistair Whillans* 38b
4 bb f Medaglia d'Oro(USA) Chandelle No. Five (USA) (Yes It's True (USA))
2247[4]

Tell Everyone (FR) *G Cherel* 96h 96c
5 b g Califet(FR) La Curamalal (IRE) (Rainbow Quest (USA))
1742a[P] (2464a)

Tell Me Y (IRE) *Jonjo O'Neill* 119h
7 ch g Kris Kin(USA) Ebony Jane (Roselier (FR))
144[4]

Tel Pere Tel Fils (FR) *G Macaire* 113c
7 ch g Robin Des Champs(FR) Nocha (FR) (Zino)
1464a[3]

Temair Feis *Miss H Watson*
11 b g Kayf Tara Bay Fair (Arctic Lord)
430[U]

Temoin Du Calif (FR) *Mme I Pacault*
7 b g Califet(FR) Basilia (FR) (Mont Basile (FR))
1740a[7]

Tempest River (IRE) *Ben Case* 131h 130c
8 b m Old Vic Dee-One-O-One (Slip Anchor)
358[9] **(2434)**
3030[3] 3886[7] 4685[2] 5369[4] ◆

Templebraden (IRE) *Henry Oliver* 122h
7 b g Brian Boru Baunfaun Run (IRE) (Roselier (FR))
3440[5] (3841) 4340[2] 4594[5] 4949[3]

Temple Lord (FR) *Jonjo O'Neill* 138h 128c
8 gr g Califet(FR) Temple Queen (GER) (Local Suitor (USA))
92[4] 508[5] 840[P] 996[4] (1263)
1441[2] 1746[3] 1921[3] 2212[8]

Tempoline (FR) *D Sourdeau De Beauregard* 116h
6 b m Martaline Miss Mendha (FR) (Mister Sicy (FR))
(263a)

Tempuran *David Bridgwater* 103h
5 rg g Unbridled's Song(USA) Tenderly (IRE) (Danehill (USA))
1152[4] 1795[5] 2040[3] 2628[5] 3650[9] 4398[8] 4703[4]

Tenacious Spring (FR) *F Nicolle* 123h
7 ch g Tertullian(USA) Classic Spring (GER) (Winged Love (IRE))
455a[P]

Ten Bob (IRE) *Jonjo O'Neill*
8 b g Oscar(IRE) Ariann's Pride (IRE) (Presenting)
4157[P]

Tenby Jewel (IRE) *Mark Gillard* 106h
9 ch g Pilsudski(IRE) Supreme Delight (IRE) (Supreme Leader)
3784[P] 4377[4] 4677[6] 4911[2] **5428[P]**

Tender Surprise *Neil King* 90h
5 b m Doyen(IRE) Spring Surprise (Hector Protector (USA))
2432[5]

Tenmoku *Jonjo O'Neill* 104h
5 b m Westerner Blast Freeze (IRE) (Lafontaine (USA))
1885[3] 2190[8] 2600[6] 5191[9] 5449[5]

Ten More (IRE) *Bill Turner* 77h
10 b g Old Vic Tenterden (IRE) (Tenby)
100[U] 241[P]

Tennessee Bird *Mike Sowersby* 80h
6 b g Danbird(AUS) Tennessee Star (Teenoso (USA))
661[8] 803[2] 903[5] 1120[3] 1259[5]

Tenor De Guerre (FR) *Fergal O'Brien* 88b
7 b g Epalo(GER) Hache De Guerre (FR) (Royal Charter (FR))
433[6]

Teochew (IRE) *Warren Greatrex* 123h
6 b m Shantou(USA) Papal Princess (IRE) (Revoque (IRE))
2029[5] 2948[2] 3419[4] 3649[6] 5010[7] 5285[2] ◆

Teo Vivo (FR) *Pauline Robson* 114h 107c
7 gr g Great Pretender(IRE) Ifranne (FR) (April Night (FR))
2308[F] 2356[P] 2791[2] 3041[7] 4744[P] 5494[4]

Terfel's Toscar (IRE) *Tim Vaughan* 104h 106c
9 b g Oscar(IRE) Jill's Girl (IRE) (Be My Native (USA))
789[P] (1163)
1316[3] 1486[4] 1798[5] 2155[P]

Ter Mill (CZE) *Antonin Novak*
8 ro g Mill Pond(FR) Tereza (CZE) (Ludovico (GER))
1904a[3]

Terminal (FR) *W P Mullins* 134h 149c
7 b g Passing Sale(FR) Durendal (FR) (Clafouti (FR))
1168a[10] 1604a[P] 2815[9]

Terntheothercheek *Jennie Candlish* 79h
5 b m Multiplex My Tern (IRE) (Glacial Storm (USA))
755[4] 945[3] 1110[P] 1169[P] 2701[7] 2896[6] 3062[6] 3432[P]

Terpsichore *Barry Brennan* 32h
4 ch f Beat Hollow Effie (Royal Academy (USA))
3613[5]

Terra Firma *Brendan Powell* 69b
4 b g Lucarno(USA) Solid Land (FR) (Solid Illusion (USA))
4017[14] 4964[11]

Terry Tibbs (IRE) *J T R Dreaper* 41c
9 b g Tikkanen(USA) Poor Reception (IRE) (Mandalus)
1728[5] 2339[P]

Teshali (IRE) *Anthony Middleton* 118h 108c
8 bg g Anabaa(USA) Tashiriya (IRE) (Kenmare (FR))
191[2] 419[3] 673[3] 762[5] 973[6] 1054[7]

Tetlami (IRE) *Nicky Henderson* 142h 140c
8 ch g Daylami(IRE) Tetou (IRE) (Peintre Celebre (USA))
2816[9]

Tetralogy (IRE) *Tom Gretton* 49h
5 b g Old Vic Quadrennial (IRE) (Un Desperado (FR))
5182[2]

Texas Jack (IRE) *Noel Meade* 143h 159c
8 b g Curtain Time(IRE) Sailors Run (IRE) (Roselier (FR))
2235a[3] 2483a[3] (3751a)
4183a[4]

Texas Rose (IRE) *Rebecca Menzies* 105h
7 b m Beneficial Dusty Melody (IRE) (Taipan (IRE))
1940[2] 1982[3] 2495[2] 3393[3]

Texit To Nowhere (IRE) *Ian Duncan* 29b
7 b m Exit To Nowhere(USA) Leader Of Fashion (IRE) (Supreme Leader)
584[11]

Thanks For Coming *Nicky Henderson* 127h 137c
8 b g Helissio(FR) Kyle Rhea (In The Wings)
(422) 733[P]
1155[3] **(4934)**

Tharaya *Claire Dyson* 61h
9 b m Choisir(AUS) Karlaska (Lashkari)
3604[6] 3828[P]

Thatchers Gold (IRE) *Dave Roberts* 117h
6 b g Gold Well Chesterfield Lady (IRE) (Taipan (IRE))
647[2] 3734[8]

Thatildee (IRE) *Chris Grant* 91h
6 b g Heron Island(IRE) Good Thyne Mary (IRE) (Good Thyne (USA))
1877[7] 2499[7] 3036[P] 4005[6] 4576[4] 5494[3]

Thatlldoforus *Alistair Whillans* 49b
6 b m Double Trigger(IRE) Bantel Bargain (Silly Prices)
3727[9]

That'll Do Nicely (IRE) *Nicky Richards* 95h 79c
11 b g Bahhare(USA) Return Again (IRE) (Top Ville)
110[2] 219[3] 879[7] 3756[RR]

Thats Ben (IRE) *Tom Gretton* 29c
9 b g Beneficial Classy Dancer (IRE) (Alphabatim (USA))
2179[P] 2560[5] 4470[P] 4942[4]

That's Exactly (IRE) *Neil Mulholland* 89b
5 ch m Bach(IRE) Maracana (IRE) (Glacial Storm (USA))
588[5] 675[6]

Thatsmylot (IRE) *Stuart Coltherd* 71b
5 ch g Rudimentary(USA) Yellow Soil Star (IRE) (Perugino (USA))
4205[7] 4548[P] 5479[12]

That's Rhythm (FR) *Miss Sally Duckett* 110h 137c
14 b g Pistolet Bleu(IRE) Madame Jean (FR) (Cricket Ball (USA))
(373) (657)
(4057)
4788[P]

That's The Deal (IRE) *John Cornwall* 72h 111c
10 bb g Turtle Island(IRE) Sister Swing (Arctic Lord)
181[2] 355[3] (596)
733[3] 1493[4] 1636[5] 2065[F] 2350[4] 2873[P] 3150[2]
3853[P]
4725[5] 4862[3]
5361[P]

Thats Yer Man (IRE) *Linda Blackford* 84h
6 ch g Marignan(USA) Glengarra Princess (Cardinal Flower)
2912[3] 3994[8] 4417[9] 5303[4]

Thatwasthepension (IRE) *Brian Storey* 45h
8 b g Milan Biondo (IRE) (College Chapel)
803[P]

The Absent Mare *Robin Dickin* 63h 89c
6 gr m Fair Mix(IRE) Precious Lucy (FR) (Kadrou (FR))
809[10] **899[F]**
2039[6] 2349[3] 5246[9]

Theatrebar *Tom Symonds* 121h
6 b g King's Theatre(IRE) Ardenbar (Ardross)
2195[3] (2720) 3225[3] 3884[2] 4308[4] 4680[11]

Theatre Bird (IRE) *Sean Thomas Doyle* 137h
6 b m King's Theatre(IRE) Hallaniya (IRE) (Doyoun)
(3403a) 3804a[P]

Theatre Evening (IRE) *Fergal O'Brien* 111h
6 b g King's Theatre(IRE) Waydale Hill (Minster Son)
(410)

Theatre Guide (IRE) *Colin Tizzard* 127h 158c
7 b g King's Theatre(IRE) Erintante (IRE) (Denel (FR))
2269[3] 2815[3] 3067[2]

Theatre King'S (IRE) *S J Mahon* 84b
5 br m Presenting Lizzy Langtry (IRE) (King's Theatre (IRE))
1318[4]

Theatrelands *Charlie Longsdon* 110h 101c
6 ch g Beat Hollow Dance Dress (USA) (Nureyev (USA))
201[10] 1633[9] (1822) (2111) 2676[5]
(3024)

Theatre One (IRE) *Sarah Dawson* 64b
5 b g King's Theatre(IRE) Jessica One (IRE) (Supreme Leader)
4958[13]

Theatrical Star *Colin Tizzard* 118h 143c
8 b g King's Theatre(IRE) Lucy Glitters (Ardross)
1868[12] 2081[3] 2488[9] 2800[U] (3424)
3772[3] 4035[3]

Theatrical Style (IRE) *Donald McCain* 106b
5 b g Alhaarth(IRE) Little Theatre (IRE) (Old Vic)
(2347)

The Backup Plan (IRE) *Donald McCain* 99h
5 ch g Presenting Jay Lo (IRE) (Glacial Storm (USA))
2627[5] 3448[2] 4761[5] 5354[3]

The Bailiff (IRE) *David Pipe*
5 br g Definite Article Snipe Hunt (IRE) (Stalker)
4296[8]

The Bard O Tully (IRE) *B Arthey* 94h
6 b g Publisher(USA) Hess O Tully (IRE) (Leading Counsel (USA))
221[9]

The Bay Bandit *Neil Mulholland* 110h
7 b g Highest Honor(FR) Pescara (IRE) (Common Grounds)
(390) 631[7] 1058[2] 1827a[2] 1551[4] 1816[5] (5478a)

The Bear Trap (IRE) *Rebecca Curtis* 116h 54c
7 b g Westerner Calendula (Be My Guest (USA))
2362[3] 2813[11] **5281[3]**

The Bells O Peover *Donald McCain* 39h
6 b g Selkirk(USA) Bay Tree (IRE) (Daylami (IRE))
186[7]

The Big Apple (IRE) *C Roche* 102h
4 b g Presenting Bannow Girl (IRE) (Glacial Storm (USA))
4708a[8]

The Big Freeze (IRE) *Tim Vaughan* 112h 115c
8 b g Beneficial Kilfane (IRE) (Hollow Hand)
1959[3] 2594[P]

The Black Baron (IRE) *Lucy Wadham* 115h 124c
12 br g Lord Americo Royal Nora (IRE) (Dromod Hill)
(181) 596[2]

The Black Lion (IRE) *Nick Kent* 89h 86c
13 b g Un Desperado(FR) Satrouse (IRE) (Satco (FR))
65[P]

The Bogman's Ball *Grace Harris* 89h
8 gr g Silver Patriarch(IRE) Monica's Story (Arzanni)
4411[7] 4672[4] 5015[6] 5431[7]

The Bold Lord (IRE) *Alan Swinbank* 93h
6 ch g Bachelor Duke(USA) Bold Nora (IRE) (Persian Bold)
800[7] 958[P]

The Boogeyman (IRE) *Anthony Middleton* 53h
8 br g King's Theatre(IRE) Market Lass (IRE) (Orchestra)
4703[8] 4972[10]

The Boozy Bishop (IRE) *Sheena Walton* 78h
9 b g Bishop Of Cashel Ann's River (IRE) (Over The River (FR))
3828[6] 4465[8] 4612[5] 4774[P] 5163[8] 5360[8]

The Bull Hayes (IRE) *Michael Appleby* 115h 103c
8 b g Sadler's Wells(USA) No Review (USA) (Nodouble (USA))
1268[3] 2064[4] 2519[7] 2729[5] (3025)

The Chazer (IRE) *Richard Lee* 105h 132c
9 gr g Witness Box(USA) Saffron Holly (IRE) (Roselier (FR))
587[11] 2086[7] 2529[12]
2945[4] 3325[3] 4027[3]

The Chief Villain *S R B Crawford* 105h
6 b g Doyen(IRE) Vilany (Never So Bold)
584[4] 885[7] 4548[3] ◆

The Cider Maker *Colin Tizzard* 95b
4 b g Kayf Tara Dame Fonteyn (Suave Dancer (USA))
4016[8] 4638[2] 5310[7]

The Clock Leary (IRE) *Venetia Williams* 118h
6 b g Helissio(FR) Kiwi Babe (Karinga Bay)
3092[4] 3567[4] (4189) 4841[6]

The Clyda Rover (IRE) *Helen Nelmes* 92h 113c
10 ch g Moonax(IRE) Pampered Molly (IRE) (Roselier (FR))
2108[P] 2537[P] 4968[P]

The Cockney Mackem (IRE) *Nigel Twiston-Davies* 121h 136c
8 b g Milan Divine Prospect (IRE) (Namaqualand (USA))
337[3] 1046[4] 1281[2]
(1426) 1550[2] 1661[2]
1973[F] 2489[4] 2531[4] 3197[F] 4806[F]

The Cookie Jar (IRE) *C A Murphy* 118h
7 b m Alderbrook Garrylough (IRE) (Monksfield)
2205a[3] 4846a[8] 5199a[5]

Thecornishwren (IRE) *John Ryan*
5 ch m Medecis Coulisse (IRE) (In The Wings)
1779[P]

The Crafty Butcher (IRE) *Michael Hourigan* 140h 123c
7 b g Vinnie Roe(IRE) Ivy Queen (IRE) (Green Desert (USA))
2268[6]

The Darling Boy *David Pipe* 100h 115c
9 b g Medicean Silver Top Hat (USA) (Silver Hawk (USA))
3062[2] (4519) 5034[10]

Thedeboftheyear *Chris Down* 96h 50c
10 b m Sir Harry Lewis(USA) Juste Belle (FR) (Mansonnien (FR))
1917[9] 2284[8] 3425[5] 4176[3] (4501) 5007[9]

The Debtor (IRE) *Anthony Middleton* 66b
7 b g Dr Massini(IRE) Congeniality (USA) (Katowice (USA))
944[9]

Thedfactor (IRE) *Jane Walton* 64b
5 b g Kalanisi(IRE) Insan Magic (IRE) (Insan (USA))
5219[7]

The Disengager (IRE) *Philip Hobbs* 71h 155c
10 b g Snurge The Doctors Wife (IRE) (Mandalus)
204[5] (672)
1168a[20] (1476)
1686[4] 4789[22]

The Dodgy Dealer *Nigel Hawke*
5 gr g With Approval(CAN) Annishirani (Shaamit (IRE))
4016[10]

Thedreamstillalive (IRE) *Jim Old* 53h 85c
14 ch g Houmayoun(FR) State Of Dream (IRE) (Carmelite House (USA))
2462[6] 3595[2] 3817[2] (4656)

Thedrinkymeister (IRE) *Kim Bailey* 99h
5 b g Heron Island(IRE) Keel Row (Relkino)
5014[5]

The Druids Nephew (IRE) *Andy Turnell* 137h 145c
7 b g King's Theatre(IRE) Gifted (Shareef Dancer (USA))
2180[4] 2812[F] 2943[2] 3897[P]

The Ferick (IRE) *Alan Swinbank* 77h
8 b g Kris Kin(USA) Minaun Heights (Doyoun)
630[3]

The Finger Post (IRE) *Helen Nelmes* 116h
7 b g Zagreb(USA) Mystic Madam (IRE) (Lafontaine (USA))
768[3] 1483[F]

The Flaming Matron (IRE) *N W Alexander* 102h 86c
8 b m Flemensfirth(USA) The Mighty Matron (IRE) (Montelimar (USA))
(532) 2218[P] 2973[5] 3212[4] 3523[3] **4337[P] 5211[2]**

The Folkes Choice *Henry De Bromhead* 110h 116c
8 b m King's Theatre(IRE) Mammy's Choice (IRE) (Mandalus)
1702a[5]

The Fonz *Renee Robeson* 117h
8 b g Oasis Dream Crystal Cavern (USA) (Be My Guest (USA))
336[9] 718[9]

The Four Elms (IRE) *John J Walsh* 120h
6 b g Desert Style(IRE) Flying Freedom (IRE) (Archway (IRE))
4285a[4]

The Fox's Decree *Martin Keighley* 100h 100c
10 br g Diktat Foxie Lady (Wolfhound (USA))
264[3] 860[5] 902[4]
1057[5]

The Friary (IRE) *Lucinda Russell* 96h 122c
7 b g Kris Kin(USA) Native Design (IRE) (Be My Native (USA))
1756[3] 2033[3] (2334)
3111[3] (4368)
4835[P]

Thefriendlygremlin *John Upson* 81h
6 b g Vinnie Roe(IRE) Queen's Fantasy (Grand Lodge (USA))
91[8] 417[4] 460[11] 1820[5] 2701[11]

The Game Changer (IRE) *C F Swan* 143h
5 b g Arcadio(GER) Gilt Ridden (IRE) (Heron Island (IRE))
3339a[6] 3910a[17] 4708a[2] 5153[8]

The Game Is A Foot (IRE) *Gary Moore* 107h
7 b g Oscar(IRE) Cooksgrove Rosie (IRE) (Mandalus)
1888 (2568) 2670[F] 2766[4] 3660[4] 4111[3] 4700[7]

Thegaygardener *Evan Williams* 114h
6 b g Sulamani(IRE) Lady Blade (IRE) (Daggers Drawn (USA))
767[2] 850[10] 1058[5]

The General Lee (IRE) *Lady Susan Brooke* 85b 116c
12 bb g Accordion Catrionas Castle (IRE) (Orchestra)
59[P] 4092[3] 4355[P]

The Giant Bolster *David Bridgwater* 102h 170c
9 b g Black Sam Bellamy(IRE) Divisa (GER) (Lomitas)
2673[7] 2938[U] 3457[5]
(3888) 4787[3]

The Ginger Man (IRE) *Michael Scudamore* 48h 79c
13 ch g Carroll House Diminished (IRE) (Alphabatim (USA))
1105[11]

The Goldmeister (IRE) *Charlie Longsdon* 91h 90c
7 b g Craigsteel M C A River (Tina's Pet)
926[3] 1701[3] 2088[P]

The Good Guy (IRE) *Graeme McPherson* 104h 101c
11 b g Lord Americo Lady Farnham (IRE) (Farhaan)
178[0] (471)
(759) 930[P] 1172[4] 1376[4] 1945[7] 5391[5]

The Govaness *Fergal O'Brien* 116b
5 b m Kayf Tara Just Kate (Bob's Return (IRE))
(36) 1974[5] (2506) 5159[4]

The Green Ogre *Gary Moore* 121h
4 b g Dubai Destination(USA) Takegawa (Giant's Causeway (USA))
3161^{13} 3641^{2} 4268^{3} 4632^{2} 5090^{2} 5399^{2}

The Grey One (IRE) *Milton Bradley* 62h 60c
11 gr g Dansili Marie Dora (FR) (Kendor (FR))
43^{P} 183^{6} 602^{8} 694^{P} 898^{8} 1328^{8} 1435^{3} 1530^{6} 1710^{F} 1835^{6}

The Grey Taylor (IRE) *Steve Gollings* 105b
5 gr g Royal Anthem(USA) Penny Tan (IRE) (Roselier (FR))
3276^{4} 4547^{2} 4986^{2} 5367^{4}

The Halfway Bar (IRE) *Miss Gill Boanas* 130h 94c
13 b g Leading Counsel(USA) Le Sept (Le Bavard (FR))
315^{3}

The Happy Warrior *Bob Buckler* 111h
6 b g Luso Martomick (Montelimar (USA))
174^{4} 519^{6} 1945^{11} 2920^{3} (3420) 3569^{2} (4172) 4334^{3} 4733^{3} (5143) 5234^{2}

The Hardy Boy *Miss N Worley* 23h 60c
14 br g Overbury(IRE) Miss Nero (Crozier)
331^{P}

The Hollinwell *Eugene M O'Sullivan* 26h 107c
11 b g Classic Cliche(IRE) Action De Balle (FR) (Cricket Ball (USA))
4788^{14}

Thehoodlum *Jean McGregor* 8b
7 b g Fraam Trilby (In The Wings)
962^{5}

Thehookybooky (IRE) *Miss G E J Anderson* 69c
8 ch g Environment Friend Mahira (IRE) (Be My Native (USA))
112^{P}

Thehorsemaytalk (IRE) *Mark Shears* 83c
9 gr g Old Vic Rosealainn (IRE) (Roselier (FR))
518^{5} 921^{P} 1303^{5} 1701^{P} 2290^{P}

The Housekeeper (IRE) *David Harry Kelly* 132h 115c
7 b m Heron Island(IRE) The Wounded Cook (IRE) (Muroto)
3380a^{U}

The Ice Factor *S R B Crawford* 114h
6 b g Iceman Kiruna (Northern Park (USA))
870^{2} 1148^{5}

The Informant *Seamus Mullins* 84h 90c
8 gr g Central Park(IRE) Belle Rose (IRE) (Roselier (FR))
95^{5} **2275^{P}**
2619^{P} 3139^{P} (3564)
4416^{5} 4802^{4} (5115)
(5398)

Theionlady (IRE) *Richard Woollacott* 80h
4 gr f Presenting Valleya (FR) (Linamix (FR))
4534^{3} 5124^{9}

The Irish Tig (IRE) *Graeme McPherson*
9 br g Muroto Saffron Spirit (Town And Country)
839^{P}

The Iron Curtain (IRE) *Sean Curran*
8 b g Soviet Star(USA) Isla (IRE) (Turtle Island (IRE))
367^{P}

The Iron Maiden *Jo Davis* 69b
5 gr m Proclamation(IRE) Bright Spangle (IRE) (General Monash (USA))
3181^{7}

The Italian Yob (IRE) *Nick Williams* 98h 139c
6 b g Milan The Rebel Lady (IRE) (Mister Lord (USA))
2012^{2} 2460^{2} (2928)
3886^{P} 4395^{P} 5089^{P}

The Job Is Right *Michael Hourigan* 139h
6 gr g With Approval(CAN) Common Request (USA) (Lear Fan (USA))
(2983a) 3380a^{2} 4386a^{P} 4786^{P}

The Jugopolist (IRE) *John Cornwall* 114h 88c
7 b g Oscar(IRE) Chance My Native (IRE) (Be My Native (USA))
500^{P} 2510^{5} 2894^{5} 3419^{2} (3593) 3737^{5} 4070^{P}

The Ketchup Kid (IRE) *David Phelan* 94c
6 b g Fruits Of Love(USA) Junga Connection (Danzig Connection (USA))
327^{4}

The Kings Assassin (IRE) *Chris Gordon* 92h
6 bb g King's Theatre(IRE) Assidua (IRE) (Anshan)
874^{6} 1007^{P} 1270^{9} 1525^{U} 1625^{6} 5307^{7}

The Knoxs (IRE) *Sandy Thomson* 135h 130c
11 b g Close Conflict(USA) Nicola Marie (IRE) (Cardinal Flower)
2228^{P} 2672^{P} 3273^{4}
3414^{P} 3759^{4} 4271^{P} 4897^{3} 5169^{6}

The Kvilleken *Martin Keighley* 94h
6 b g Fair Mix(IRE) Wannaplantatree (Niniski (USA))
1974^{11} 2476^{6} 3388^{11} 3782^{5}

The Lady Maggi (FR) *Lucinda Russell* 74b
4 b f Robin Des Champs(FR) Miss Poutine (FR) (Chamberlin (FR))
4902^{7}

The Last Bridge *Susan Johnson* 87h 98c
7 b g Milan Celtic Bridge (Celtic Cone)
2148^{8} 3227^{6} **(4066)**
4243^{4} (4729)
5185^{2} 5433^{2} 5546^{2}

The Last Bullit *Marc Barber*
8 br g Tamayaz(CAN) Flat Shoes (IRE) (Parthian Springs)
1553^{P}

The Last Leg (IRE) *Karen McLintock* 95b
5 b g Old Vic Raphuca (IRE) (Be My Native (USA))
4611^{8}

The Last Night (FR) *Emma Lavelle* 102h 119c
7 ch g April Night(FR) La Pelode (FR) (Dress Parade)
(3027)
(5340)

The Last Samuri (IRE) *Donald McCain* 132h
6 ch g Flemensfirth(USA) Howaboutthis (IRE) (Oscar (IRE))
2037^{2} (2355) (2808) (3829) 5157^{9}

The Liquidator *David Pipe* 145h
6 b g Overbury(IRE) Alikat (IRE) (Alhaarth (IRE))
(2156) ◆ (2530) 3644^{5} 4736^{11}

Thelobstercatcher *Tim Vaughan* 135h 123c
10 gr g Silver Patriarch(IRE) Everything's Rosy (Ardross)
62^{4} 481^{9}

The Lodge Road (IRE) *Martin Todhunter* 96h
6 b g Holy Roman Emperor(IRE) Golden Coral (USA) (Slew O'Gold (USA))
1008^{4} 1415^{4} 1713^{6} 2306^{8}

The Mad Robertson (IRE) *Jonjo O'Neill* 113h 130c
7 b g Accordion Quinnsboro Ice (IRE) (Glacial Storm (USA))
5^{3} 1012^{2} 1197^{2} 1327^{F}

The Magherally Man (IRE) *T P Eades* 85c
10 b g Winged Love(IRE) Prospect Lady (IRE) (Boreen (FR))
430^{P}

The Magic Bishop *Malcolm Jefferson* 110h 115c
9 b g Bishop Of Cashel Magic Bloom (Full Of Hope)
169^{10} 2394^{2} 2623^{3} 3478^{3} 3827^{P} 4580^{P} 5299^{2}

Themanfromcork *Brendan Powell* 69h
7 b g Overbury(IRE) Country Choice (IRE) (Paean)
847^{5}

Themanfrom Minella (IRE) *Ben Case* 124h
5 b g Shantou(USA) Bobomy (IRE) (Bob Back (USA))
3187^{6} 3602^{3} (4574) 5157^{P}

The Master Remover (IRE) *Chris Gordon* 94h
5 ch g Royal Anthem(USA) Kit Kat Kate (IRE) (Moscow Society (USA))
1770^{5} 2467^{11} 2753^{2} 3175^{10} 3851^{P} 5457^{6}

The Mighty Milan (IRE) *T J Nagle Jr* 129h
7 b g Milan The Mighty Matron (IRE) (Montelimar (USA))
1802a^{4}

Themilanhorse (IRE) *John Ferguson* 140h 128c
8 b g Milan Sports Leader (IRE) (Supreme Leader)
(164) **487^{5}**
1040^{4} 4057^{F}

The Minack (IRE) *Paul Nicholls*
10 b g King's Theatre(IRE) Ebony Jane (Roselier (FR))
3780^{F}

The Mobb (IRE) *Dave Roberts* 79h
6 b g Westerner Marlogan (IRE) (Presenting)
4091^{7} *4326^{9}*

The Mongolian (IRE) *Martin Todhunter* 78h
6 b m Presenting Elegant City (Scallywag)
880^{4}

The Mumper (IRE) *Alan King* 95h 114c
7 br g Craigsteel Na Moilltear (IRE) (Miner's Lamp)
289^{6} **2475^{3}**
2784^{4} 5176^{3}

The Musical Guy (IRE) *Nigel Twiston-Davies* 119h 129c
8 b g Lahib(USA) Orchestral Sport (IRE) (Orchestra)
422^{2} 733^{4} 2700^{F} 3026^{4} 4914^{4} 5180^{P}

The Nephew (IRE) *Jonjo O'Neill* 96h 122c
6 b g Indian River(FR) Charlottine (IRE) (Spectrum (IRE))
1364^{5} ◆ 1479^{P} **1550^{7} (1638) ◆ (1668)**
1710^{3} 2155^{2} *4303^{6} 4493^{5}* **4908^{3} (5549)**

The New One (IRE) *Nigel Twiston-Davies* 173h
6 b g King's Theatre(IRE) Thuringe (FR) (Turgeon (USA))
(1989) ◆ (3083) ◆ 3261^{2} 4739^{3} ◆ (5134)

Theodore Lamb *Paul Webber* 96h 96c
9 b g Lahib(USA) Our Leader (IRE) (Supreme Leader)
806^{8}

Theologist (IRE) *Dr Richard Newland* 123h
8 b g Galileo(IRE) Medina (IRE) (Pennekamp (USA))
1747^{3}

Theology *Steve Gollings* 32h
7 b g Galileo(IRE) Biographie (Mtoto)
2393^{8}

Theophrastus (IRE) *Nick Gifford* 74h 114c
12 b g Overbury(IRE) Over The Glen (IRE) (Over The River (FR))
265^{P} 766^{P}

The Orange Rogue (IRE) *N W Alexander* 110h
7 b g Alderbrook Classic Enough (Classic Cliche (IRE))
3112^{3} 3494^{2} 3935^{F} 4199^{5} 5208^{3}

The Ould Lad (IRE) *Tom George* 109h 94c
6 b g Heron Island(IRE) Badger Hammel (IRE) (Insan (USA))
3166^{4} 3716^{4} **4560^{4}**

The Outlaw (IRE) *Paul Nicholls* 98b
4 b g Presenting Bonnie Parker (IRE) (Un Desperado (FR))
5241^{2} ◆

Theoystercatcher (IRE) *Tim Vaughan* 94h
8 b m Presenting The Strongest Link (IRE) (Executive Perk)
42^{7} 543^{5} 829^{2} 997^{2} 1169^{3} 1339^{7} 3425^{P}

The Package *David Pipe* 137h 148c
11 br g Kayf Tara Ardent Bride (Ardross)
4738^{3} 5171^{12}

The Paddy Premium (IRE) *N W Alexander* 111h 101c
14 b g Glacial Storm(USA) Miss Cripps (IRE) (Lafontaine (USA))
864^{3} (1160)
1395^{4} 1666^{7}

The Panama Kid (IRE) *Malcolm Jefferson* 109h 129c
10 b g Presenting Mrs Jodi (Yaheeb (USA))
282^{9} 566^{5} (3355)
(3874) 4236^{6} 4953^{5}

The Paparrazi Kid (IRE) *W P Mullins* 138h 146c
7 b g Milan Banbury Cross (IRE) (Supreme Leader)
(3314a)

The Perfect Crime (IRE) *Ian Williams* 94h
5 b g Oscar(IRE) Gimme Peace (IRE) (Aristocracy)
2104^{7} 3175^{P} 3877^{11} 4529^{3} 4818^{5} 5366^{9}

The Pier (IRE) *Anna Brooks* 126h
8 ch g Alhaarth(IRE) Cois Cuain (IRE) (Night Shift (USA))
2742^{6} 3028^{11} 4157^{7} 4512^{3} 4947^{2} 5365^{4}

The Pirate's Queen (IRE) *Alan King* 132h
5 b m King's Theatre(IRE) Shivermetimber (IRE) (Arctic Lord)
(85) 2190^{2} 2810^{2} 4276^{4} 4961^{2} 5368^{3}

The Potting Shed (IRE) *Emma Lavelle* 99h 124c
7 br g Presenting Barracree Rose (IRE) (Roselier (FR))
606^{4} **(1834)**
2293^{2} 2847^{2} ◆ 5373^{P}

The Pounds (IRE) *Thomas Foley* 127h
8 b g Shantou(USA) November Rain (IRE) (Be My Native (USA))
4523a^{4} 4708a^{6}

The Presidents Man (IRE) *Barry Brennan* 63h
7 b g Presenting Damoiselle (Sir Harry Lewis (USA))
595^{6} 686^{11}

The Purchaser (IRE) *Chris Bealby* 88h
6 b g Definite Article Cash Customer (IRE) (Bob Back (USA))
4102^{7} 4891^{7} 5408^{4}

The Quantum Kid *Peter Hiatt* 89h 91c
10 b g Desert Prince(IRE) Al Hasnaa (Zafonic (USA))
1206^{8}
1401^{P} 1630^{2} 1824^{6}

The Rainbow Hunter *Kim Bailey* 123h 148c
10 b g Rainbow High Sobranie (High Top)
2065^{2} ◆ 2674^{6} (3897) ◆ 5171^{U}

The Ramblin Kid *Micky Hammond* 125h
6 b g Westerner Disallowed (IRE) (Distinctly North (USA))
3657^{3} (4428) 5103^{4}

The Rattler Obrien (IRE) *Martin Hill* 108h 119c
8 b g Beneficial Clonea Lady (IRE) (Lord Ha Ha)
326^{2} (1945) 3044^{2} 4172^{P} (5391)

The Reader (FR) *J-P Gallorini* 135c
5 b g Lando(GER) Shadline (FR) (Septieme Ciel (USA))
1742a^{2}

Therealmick (IRE) *Martin J Hogan* 102b
5 b g Gamut(IRE) Verlinden (IRE) (Doubletour (USA))
2995a^{S}

Theredballoon *David Elsworth* 95h
8 ch g Sulamani(IRE) Sovana (FR) (Kadounor (FR))
4493^{4} 5072^{6} 5521^{4}

The Red Laird *Neil King* 106h
11 b g Kayf Tara Sekhmet (Gunner B)
3191^{P} 3691^{P}

There Is No Point (IRE) *Jonjo O'Neill* 107h
5 b m Galileo(IRE) Akilana (IRE) (Mark Of Esteem (IRE))
4016^{3} 5195^{2}

There's No Panic (IRE) *Paul Nicholls* 134h 133c
9 ch g Presenting Out Ranking (FR) (Le Glorieux)
2214^{P} 2646^{5} (2953)
4769^{P}

There's No Rules *Richard Guest* 88h
5 br g Authorized(IRE) Excellent (Grand Lodge (USA))
184^{10} 252^{5} 376^{5} 558^{7}

There You Are *Jonjo O'Neill* 68h
5 b g Beat All(USA) Mandys Native (IRE) (Be My Native (USA))
2602^{16} 2893^{10} 3796^{9}

The Road Ahead *Peter Bowen* 103h
7 b m Grape Tree Road Althrey Flame (IRE) (Torus)
395^{2} (567) 847^{2} 1814^{4} 2510^{6} 2860^{4}

Theroadtocroker (IRE) *Denis Paul Murphy* 62b 124c
10 bb g Witness Box(USA) Shuil Aoibhinn (IRE) (Phardante (FR))
(200a)
2123a^{5} 2491^{7}

Theroadtogorey (IRE) *Sarah Robinson* 86h 63c
8 b g Revoque(IRE) Shannon Mor (IRE) (Zaffaran (USA))
188^{P} **921^{7}**
1701^{P}

The Rockies (IRE) *Evan Williams* 100h 105c
7 b g Oscar(IRE) Calling Classy (IRE) (Good Thyne (USA))
1887^{8} **2041^{P}**

The Romford Pele (IRE) *Rebecca Curtis* 127h 144c
7 b g Accordion Back And Fore (IRE) (Bob Back (USA))
1865^{2} 2489^{3} ◆ 2799^{3} 4088^{2} 4806^{4} 5349^{6}

The Rubber Man (IRE) *Patrick J Hanly* 96c
10 ch g Goldmark(USA) Allmosa (Alleging (USA))
62^{16} 4727^{7}

The Scarlett Woman *Kim Bailey* 66b
5 b m Kayf Tara Double Red (IRE) (Thatching)
5374^{12}

The Selector *Chris Gordon* 60h
5 b m Crosspeace(IRE) Lojo (Pivotal)
842^{7} *2442^{3}* 2906^{14} 4758^{15} 5026^{P} 5258^{U} 5396^{3}

The Shrimp (IRE) *Sandy Thomson* 85h 91c
7 gr g Indian Danehill(IRE) Rheban Lass (IRE) (Eurobus)
1870^{8} 2339^{P} 3755^{5} 3936^{3} 4220^{2} 4630^{4} 5358^{9}

The Shy Man (IRE) *George Moore* 70h 123c
11 b g Grand Plaisir(IRE) Black Betty (Furry Glen)
606^{P}

The Skyfarmer *Philip Hobbs* 138h
6 br g Presenting Koral Bay (FR) (Cadoudal (FR))
(1856) (2761) (3066) 3771^{5} 4789^{16}

The Snappy Poet *Jeremy Scott* 98h
5 ch g Byron Runaway Star (Superlative)
2634^{4} 2946^{6} *4017^{8}* 5117^{6} 5524^{3}

The Sneezer (IRE) *Alexandra Dunn* 106h 123c
11 br g Topanoora Bel Azur (IRE) (Electric)
236^{6} 520^{6} 833^{11}
900^{P} 3197^{P} 3431^{3} 3693^{6} 3960^{P} 4757^{5}

The Society Man (IRE) *Michael Chapman* 82h 97c
7 ch g Moscow Society(USA) Redruth (IRE) (Sri Pekan (USA))
5521^{P}

The Squinty Bridge *Lucinda Russell* 93b
6 b g Heron Island(IRE) The Storm Bell (IRE) (Glacial Storm (USA))
2222^{3} 3500^{6}

The Starboard Bow *Lucinda Russell* 90h
7 b g Observatory(USA) Overboard (IRE) (Rainbow Quest (USA))
3518^{9} 3940^{5} 4366^{7}

The Stig (FR) *Nick Littmoden* 110h
6 b g Panoramic Statyra (FR) (Double Bed (FR))
101^{5} 1779^{3} (2068) 2676^{3} 3134^{8} *4493^{6}* 4794^{4}

The Sweetener (IRE) *Richard Woollacott* 93h
5 b g Kris Kin(USA) Sheila's Pet (IRE) (Welsh Term)
14^{9} 2479^{6} 3194^{6}

The Thirsty Bricky (IRE) *David Thompson* 103h 124c
12 b g Saddlers' Hall(IRE) Splendid Choice (IRE) (The Parson)
113^{3} 312^{6} 2512^{4} 2749^{3} 3019^{2} 3150^{F} 3617^{3}

The Tiddly Tadpole *Simon West* 122h
9 b g Tipsy Creek(USA) Froglet (Shaamit (IRE))
697^{F}

The Tracey Shuffle *Brian Ellison* 126h 95c
8 br g Kapgarde(FR) Gaspaisie (FR) (Beyssac (FR))
780^{8} 1289^{3} 1527^{4} 4648^{P}

The Tullow Tank (IRE) *Philip Fenton* 148h
6 b g Oscar(IRE) Bobbing Back (IRE) (Bob Back (USA))
(2852a) (3339a) 4180a^{2}

Theunnamedsoldier *Nigel Hawke* 102b
6 b g Revoque(IRE) Miss Tango (Batshoof)
4417^{2} 5021^{6}

The Unsub (IRE) *Gordon Elliott* 116b
6 b g Flemensfirth(USA) Simply Joyful (Idiots Delight)
4205^{2} (4671) 5279^{2}

The Vicar (IRE) *David Rees* 125h 101c
11 b g Bob Back(USA) Moon Storm (IRE) (Strong Gale)
461^{3}

The Village (IRE) *Lucinda Russell* 51h
5 b g Lahib(USA) Melisande (Slip Anchor)
284^{5} 4199^{6} 4548^{9} 4832^{6}

The Walnut Tree (IRE) *David Lewis* 12h 66c
13 b g Mister Lord(USA) Janet's Girl (IRE) (Mandalus)
430^{P}

The Way It Works (IRE) *Lucinda Russell* 89b
4 b f Kalanisi(IRE) Hamari Gold (IRE) (Priolo (USA))
5560^{3}

The Wealerdealer (IRE) *David Pipe* 107h
7 b g Vinnie Roe(IRE) Lantern Liz (IRE) (Montelimar (USA))
2279^{5} 2476^{7} ◆ 2761^{6} 4275^{3} 4699^{2} 5307^{6}

The Weatherman (IRE) *Donald McCain* 104h
7 b g Definite Article Stateable Case (IRE) (Be My Native (USA))
119^{P} 581^{7} 870^{5} 1087^{U} 1285^{7} 1729^{3} 2245^{4} 3802^{F} 4085^{5} 4615^{P}

The Wee Lass *Arthur Whiting* 85h
7 b m Act One Fragrant Rose (Alflora (IRE))
1890^{7}

The Wee Midget *Arthur Whiting* 84h
9 b g Mtoto Fragrant Rose (Alflora (IRE))
460^{10} 637^{3} **942^{P}** 1051^{P}

The Western Hill (IRE) *Tom Symonds* 57b
5 b g Westerner Marie The (FR) (Exit To Nowhere (USA))
4^{10}

The Wexfordian (IRE) *Martin Keighley* 113b
5 b g Shantou(USA) Going My Way (Henbit (USA))
4267^{5} 4728^{2}

The Wicked Kipper *Martin Keighley* 95h
6 b m King's Theatre(IRE) Wicked Crack (IRE) (King's Ride)
449^{5} 1561^{3} 1631^{3}

The Wife's Sister *James Evans* 8c
13 b m Classic Cliche(IRE) Hard Love (Rambo Dancer (CAN))
713^{7} 942^{10}

The Winged Assasin (USA) *Shaun Lycett* 79h
8 b g Fusaichi Pegasus(USA) Gran Dama (USA) (Rahy (USA))
650^{8} 756^{10} 1442^{6}

The Winking Prawn (IRE) *Kim Bailey* 105b
7 b g Beneficial Rocamadoura (Roi Danzig (USA))
1138^{4} ◆

The Winkler (IRE) *Eoin Doyle* 123h
5 gr g Medaaly Osirixa (FR) (Linamix (FR))
4386a^{6}

The Wonga Coup (IRE) *Pat Phelan*
7 b g Northern Afleet(USA) Quichesterbahn (USA) (Broad Brush (USA))
427^{F} 5305^{U}

The Yank *Richard Lee* 87h
5 b g Trade Fair Silver Gyre (IRE) (Silver Hawk (USA))
2563^{U} 4904^{6} 5300^{6}

The Young Master *Neil Mulholland* 119h
5 b g Echo Of Light Fine Frenzy (IRE) (Great Commotion (USA))
1711^{9} 2353^{2} (2535) 2690^{F} (3473) (3638)

Thinger Licht (FR) *Tony Carroll* 101h 93c
5 b g Clety(FR) Family Saga (FR) (Caerwent)
2314^{16}
2464a^{8} 3012^{9} 3324^{6} 4353^{5} 4607^{6} 4783^{2} 5242^{5}

Things Change (IRE) *John Quinn* 113h
6 b g Old Vic Northwood May (Teenoso (USA))
22^{4} (531) 800^{3}

Think *Clive Mulhall* 81h
7 ch g Sulamani(IRE) Natalie Jay (Ballacashtal (CAN))
5581^{11} 2787^{14}

Think Its All Over (USA) *Evan Williams* 90h 104c
7 b g Tiznow(USA) A P Petal (USA) (A.P. Indy (USA))
2039^{2} 2173^{2} 3222^{F} 4352^{5} 4734^{5}

Think Out Loud *Jonjo O'Neill* 95h
5 b g Kalanisi(IRE) Campannello (Sadlers' Hall (IRE))
2621^{14}

Third Act (IRE) *Colin Tizzard* 88h
5 b g King's Theatre(IRE) Starry Lady (IRE) (Marju (IRE))
1771^{2} (4135) 4756^{20} 5303^{U}

Third Half *Tim Vaughan* 108h
5 b g Haafhd Treble Heights (IRE) (Unfuwain (USA))
1058^{7} 1280^{P}

Third Intention (IRE) *Colin Tizzard* 151h 156c
7 b g Azamour(IRE) Third Dimension (FR) (Suave Dancer (USA))
(1955)
2374^{3} 2756^{2} 3260^{3} 4262^{3} 4768^{5}

Third Of The Third *David Pipe* 116h 107c
7 bb g Presenting Gavotte Du Cochet (FR) (Urbain Minotiere (FR))
140^{3} ◆ 479^{F} 777^{F}

This Thyne Jude *Lucinda Russell* 76h
6 gr m Silver Patriarch(IRE) This Thyne (Good Thyne (USA))
1292^{2} 1792^{8} 5554^{4}

Thistlecrack *Colin Tizzard* 106b
6 b g Kayf Tara Ardstown (Ardross)
(5310)

Thistle Stikk *Lucy Jones* 56h
7 b g Selkirk(USA) Tamso (USA) (Seeking The Gold (USA))
777^{7}

Thomas Bell (IRE) *John O'Shea* 79h
10 b g Moscow Society(USA) Cottage Girl (IRE) (Actinium (FR))
1266^{3} 1364^{2} 1434^{4} 1582^{5} 1837^{4} 2090^{4}

Thomas Brown *Harry Fry* 122b
5 b g Sir Harry Lewis(USA) Tentsmuir (Arctic Lord)
1869^{4} (2759) 4149^{8} (4951)

Thomas Crapper *Robin Dickin* 141h
7 b g Tamure(IRE) Mollycarrs Gambul (General Gambul)
(1972) (2490) 3069^{8} 3771^{4} 4789^{2} 5349^{10}

Thomas Edison (IRE) *A J Martin* 140h
7 b g Danehill Dancer(IRE) Bright Bank (IRE) (Sadler's Wells (USA))
2533^{8} 4785^{13}

Thomas Junior (FR) *David Pipe* 114h
5 b g Dylan Thomas(IRE) Smiling (Sadler's Wells (USA))
2654^{3} 3598^{4} 3956^{3} 4571^{2} 4933^{4} ◆ 5182^{P}

Thomastown (IRE) *Ian Williams*
7 ch g Stowaway Bealaha Essie (IRE) (Denel (FR))
4298^{11} 4838^{P}

Thomas Wild *Philip Hobbs* 105h 121c
9 ch g Muhtarram(USA) Bisque (Inchinor)
294^{3} (4396)
4635^{2} 5180^{4}

Thom Thumb (IRE) *Paul Webber* 78h
8 ch g Flemensfirth(USA) Ardlea Dawn (IRE) (Glacial Storm (USA))
3796^{7}

Thoresby (IRE) *Ben Case* 106h 98c
8 b g Milan I Remember It Well (IRE) (Don't Forget Me)
(421) 1565^{12} 2314^{6} 3029^{5} 5441^{2}

Thorlak (FR) *James Ewart* 91h 99c
7 b h Caballo Raptor(CAN) Temara (FR) (Rex Magna (FR))
2341^{7} 3036^{6} 3392^{5} 4201^{P} 5056^{4}
5480^{5}

Thorncliffer *Derek Shaw* 62h 85c
10 ch g Generous(IRE) Recipe (Bustino)
2772^{4} 2902^{P} 3595^{U} 3817^{P} 4759^{8} 5009^{5}

Thornleigh Ben (IRE) *N R W Wright* 39b 115c
9 bb g Anshan Kings Belle (IRE) (King's Ride)
(5439)

Thornton Alice *Richard Phillips* 102h
9 b m Kayf Tara Lindrick Lady (IRE) (Broken Hearted)
(68) 811^{3} 1136^{4} 1266^{2} 1477^{2} 1707^{5} 5441^{4}

Thorpe (IRE) *Lucinda Russell* 114h
4 b g Danehill Dancer(IRE) Minkova (IRE) (Sadler's Wells (USA))
2790^{2} 3474^{2} 4054^{3}

Thousand Stars (FR) *W P Mullins* 162h
10 gr g Grey Risk(FR) Livaniana (FR) (Saint Estephe (FR))
406a^{4} 685a^{9} 3402a^{5} 5169^{3} (5471a)

Thouva (FR) *Tristan Davidson* 110h 126c
7 b g Raglmai(FR) Lady Thou (FR) (Kadalko (FR))
3204^{P}

Three Chords (IRE) *Caroline Bailey* 60h 116c
10 b g Winged Love(IRE) Crystal Chord (IRE) (Accordion)
728^{P} 872^{2}

Three Kingdoms (IRE) *John Ferguson* 144h
5 ch g Street Cry(IRE) Chan Tong (BRZ) (Hampstead (URU))
(1924) 2492^{3} ◆ (2893) (3322) 4736^{12}

Three White Socks (IRE) *Brian Ellison* 114h
7 b g Whipper(USA) Halesia (USA) (Chief's Crown (USA))
3271^{7} 3659^{8}

Throthethatch (IRE) *Lucinda Russell* 76b
5 b g Beneficial Castletownroche (IRE) (Saddlers' Hall (IRE))
3500^{5}

Thunder Child *N K Allin* 46h 100c
14 gr g Cloudings(IRE) Double Dutch (Nicholas Bill)
335^{P}

Thundering Home *Richard Mitchell* 108h
7 gr g Storming Home Citrine Spirit (IRE) (Soviet Star (USA))
2617^{4} 2910^{8} 4573^{4} 5019^{7}

Thunder Sheik (IRE) *Fergal O'Brien* 121h 98c
6 b h Green Tune(USA) Realy Queen (USA) (Thunder Gulch (USA))
30^{P} 631^{3} (808) (848) 1008^{3} (1173)

Thunderstorm (IRE) *Philip Hobbs* 133h 126c
9 b g Milan Elizabeth Tudor (IRE) (Supreme Leader)
2211^{5} 2945^{3} 3259^{4} 4106^{4}

Thurnham *Stuart Coltherd* 72h
8 b g Tobougg(IRE) Nobratinetta (FR) (Celtic Swing)
2493^{16} 2875^{5} 3605^{P} 5056^{P}

Thyflori (FR) *R Le Gal* 128h 118c
6 b m Apsis Tuffslolyloly (FR) (Double Bed (FR))
2240a^{P}

Thymeandthymeagain *Hugo Froud* 41b
5 b m Alflora(IRE) Four Thyme (Idiots Delight)
3181^{10} 4335^{6}

Thyne Gale (IRE) *Graeme McPherson*
4 b f Arcadio(GER) Kilternan Gale (IRE) (Good Thyne (USA))
2436^{9} 2830^{10}

Thyne River (IRE) *Bernard Llewellyn*
4 b f Indian River(FR) Thyne Square (IRE) (Good Thyne (USA))
4417^{8}

Tibberton Tara *Martin Weston*
6 b m Kayf Tara Give Me Strength (IRE) (Flemensfirth (USA))
185^{P}

Ticinese *Heather Main* 46b
4 b g Lucarno(USA) Maidwell (Broadsword (USA))
4561^{10} 4964^{17}

Tickatack (IRE) *Graeme McPherson* 111h 108c
9 gr g Tikkanen(USA) Theflyingcannister (IRE) (Little Bighorn)
2046^{5} 2431^{3} 2784^{2} 3603^{7} 5390^{2}

Ticket *Jennie Candlish* 14h
5 b m Revoque(IRE) Raffles (FR) (Turgeon (USA))
14^{8} 3721^{11} 2190^{13} 2697^{P}

Tickity Bleue *Alan King* 111h
6 gr m Tikkanen(USA) Cerise Bleue (FR) (Port Lyautey (FR))
2767^{4} (3438)

Tick Tocker (IRE) *Donald McCain* 121h
6 b g Beat Hollow Cortona (IRE) (Caerleon (USA))
(91) 470^{2}

Tidal Bay (IRE) *Paul Nicholls* 156h 174c
13 b g Flemensfirth(USA) June's Bride (IRE) (Le Moss)
(2228)
2673^{5} 3361^{3} 4183a^{2} 5171^{U} 5276^{7}

Tidal Dance (IRE) *Venetia Williams* 130h
7 b g Craigsteel Musical Waves (IRE) (Orchestra)
3653^{F} (3800) 3860^{2} 4280^{3} 4415^{5} 4839^{3}

Tidal Way (IRE) *Charlie Longsdon* 126h
5 gr g Red Clubs(IRE) Taatof (IRE) (Lahib (USA))
93^{7} (1729) 2198^{5} 2668^{5} 3322^{3} *4023^{10}* 4306^{6}
4726^{8} 5260^{12}

Tidara Angel (IRE) *D Windrif* 143h
7 b m Oratorio(IRE) Tidal Reach (USA) (Kris S (USA))
406a^{3} 685a^{8}

Tide Runner *Liam Corcoran* 75h
8 b g Selkirk(USA) Robellino Miss (USA) (Robellino (USA))
5003^{6}

Tiermore (IRE) *R E Luke* 85h 112c
10 br g Bob's Return(IRE) Billmar (Kambalda)
4133^{3} ◆ (523)
996^{2} 1197^{6} 1444^{3} 1521^{4} 4922^{4} 5491^{P}

Tiger Billy (IRE) *Wilf Storey* 71h 36c
12 ch g Accordion Lady Leona (Leander)
112^{P} 753^{P}

Tiger Feat *Alan King* 72b
4 b g Tiger Hill(IRE) Hannah's Dream (IRE) (King's Best (USA))
4824^{9}

Tiger O'Toole (IRE) *Evan Williams* 94h 92c
9 gr g King's Theatre(IRE) Memsahib Ofesteem (Neltino)
3786^{4} 4413^{7} 5231^{9}

Tiger Roll (IRE) *Gordon Elliott* 144h
4 b g Authorized(IRE) Swiss Roll (IRE) (Entrepreneur)
(2392) 4178a^{2} (4784)

Tiger's Jacey (IRE) *James Hughes* 83h
7 b m Milan Shes Elite (IRE) (Supreme Leader)
2^{9} 4071^{1} 925^{P}

Tignello (IRE) *Emma Baker* 77h
9 b g Kendor(FR) La Genereuse (Generous (IRE))
875^{6} 1018^{P}

Tigre D'Aron (FR) *Chris Gordon* 76h 71c
7 gr g Dom Alco(FR) Fleche Noir II (FR) (Quart De Vin (FR))
1918^{2}

Tigresse Bleue *Jonjo O'Neill* 125h
6 b m Bachelor Duke(USA) Tigresse Africaine (FR) (Tiger Hill (IRE))
379^{6} (2430) (2616) 2948^{P}

Tigridia (IRE) *Sarah Wall* 76h
7 br m Brian Boru Indian Legend (IRE) (Phardante (FR))
417^{3} 706^{5} 2566^{P} 4715^{P} 5110^{5} 5262^{U} 5396^{4}

Tijori (IRE) *Bernard Llewellyn* 119h
6 b g Kyllachy Polish Belle (Polish Precedent (USA))
1706^{4} (1864) 2742^{7}

Tikkandemickey (IRE) *Raymond Shiels* 123h
8 gr g Tikkanen(USA) Miss Vikki (IRE) (Needle Gun (IRE))
(2597) 3017^{3} 3499^{3} 3724^{4} (4772) 5102^{2} 5320^{3}

Tikketoride *Peter Pritchard* 40b
6 gr g Tikkanen(USA) Safe Arrival (USA) (Shadeed (USA))
2703^{9}

Tiller Belle *Nicky Henderson* 94h
6 b m Revoque(IRE) Farmer's Pet (Sharrood (USA))
36^{5} 1873 ◆ 5446 3816^{P} 4761^{3} 5026^{4} 5307^{S}
5432^{8}

Tillernoora (IRE) *Patrick Griffin* 88h
7 b m Tillerman Native Topsy (IRE) (Topanoora)
1292^{6} 1373^{3} 1500^{4}

Tilt Du Chatelier (FR) *Robin Dickin* 23b
7 ch g Arnaqueur(USA) Une Du Chatelier (FR) (Quart De Vin (FR))
1794^{13} 2028^{P}

Timarello (IRE) *G J Tarry* 65b
11 br m Turtle Island(IRE) Marello (Supreme Leader)
4485^{P}

Timber King *Marjorie Fife* 77b
5 b g Desideratum Chanteuse (Rudimentary (USA))
284^{9}

Time And Again (FR) *Tim Vaughan* 40b
4 b g Sassanian(USA) Petillante Royale (FR) (Vertical Speed (FR))
4452^{4}

Time Book (IRE) *Colin Tizzard* 93h 93c
8 b g Galileo(IRE) Pocket Book (IRE) (Reference Point)
(303) 489^{5}
1765^{5} 2007^{5} 2478^{5} 2766^{7}

Time Do (FR) *Caroline Keevil* 113h 110c
7 ch g Grand Tresor(FR) Demoiselle Do (FR) (Le Pontet (FR))
(32)

Time For Action (IRE) *David Wachman* 94h
4 ch g Dylan Thomas(IRE) Celtic Heroine (IRE) (Hernando (FR))
5470a^{13}

Timeforarun (IRE) *David Thompson* 29b
6 b g Luso Timely Run (IRE) (Deep Run)
284^{11}

Time For Rupert (IRE) *Paul Webber* 110h 150c
10 ch g Flemensfirth(USA) Bell Walks Run (IRE) (Commanche Run)
3198^{4}
3897^{8} 4346^{2} 4738^{18} 5092^{2} 5371^{8}

Time For Spring (IRE) *Charlie Longsdon* 106h 132c
10 b g Snurge Burksie (IRE) (Supreme Leader)
18^{6} 1852^{4} 2367^{P} 2715^{6} 3029^{7}

Time Gentlemen *G D Hanmer* 103c
9 ch g Karinga Bay Mrs Muffet (Roselier (FR))
94^{2} 658^{9}

Time Of My Life (IRE) *Patrick Holmes* 101h
5 b g Galileo(IRE) In My Life (IRE) (Rainbow Quest (USA))
3350^{5} 3872^{7} 4529^{6}

Timesawastin (IRE) *Evan Williams* 137h 132c
8 b g Curtain Time(IRE) Innocent Approach (IRE) (Dry Dock)
182^{3} 2171^{4} 2945^{2} 3456^{4} 3886^{F}

Timesishard (IRE) *Graeme McPherson* 132h
7 b g Misternando Smokey Flavour (IRE) (Aahsaylad)
2529^{9} 2944^{11} (3085) 4814^{7} 5372^{10}

Timesremembered (IRE) *Emma Lavelle* 146h
6 bb g Akbar(IRE) Native Hope (IRE) (Be My Native (USA))
(1795) (2079) ◆ 2505^{2} 3367^{2} 3896^{6} 4752^{6}

Time To Think *Seamus Mullins* 95h 125c
9 b m Alflora(IRE) Shuil Do (IRE) (Be My Native (USA))
3093^{3} (3859)
4502^{2} 4992^{2} 5543^{4}

Timpo (FR) *Henry Daly* 112h 101c
11 ch g Baby Turk Faensa (FR) (Fabulous Dancer (USA))
461^{2} 2297^{5} 3114^{3} 5293^{P}

Tim's Approach (IRE) *William Young Jnr* 66h
9 b g Luso Creative Approach (IRE) (Toulon)
676^{6} 959^{3} 1145^{7} 1286^{6} 1379^{5} 1506^{8} 1543^{4}
1664^{F} 1718^{6} 2217^{15} 2449^{F}

Tim The Chair (IRE) *Emma Lavelle* 64h 86c
9 b g Pierre Dinah B (IRE) (Yashgan)
2297^{P}

Tina's Gift *Seamus Mullins* 47b
4 b f Catcher In The Rye(IRE) Rose Tina (Tina's Pet)
2318^{8}

Tinctoria *Kevin Ryan* 83h
4 b f Oratorio(IRE) Blue Indigo (FR) (Pistolet Bleu (IRE))
1501^{2} 1658^{P} 1920^{3}

Tindaro (FR) *Paul Webber* 112h 140c
7 gr g Kingsalsa(USA) Star's Mixa (FR) (Linamix (FR))
(236) 447^{4} **840^{2} 974^{2} (1746)**
2488^{P} 2890^{4}

Tinelyra (IRE) *Fergal O'Brien* 86h 99c
8 b g Mr Combustible(IRE) Ladyogan (IRE) (Torus)
189^{F} 592^{7} 1320^{4}
1518^{4} 1800^{3} 2039^{4} 2562^{2} 3277^{F} 3502^{4} 3817^{P}
4970^{8} (5243)
5404^{2}

Tinker Time (IRE) *Bob Buckler* 124h
6 b g Turtle Island(IRE) Gypsys Girl (IRE) (Husyan (USA))
2079^{5} 2386^{5} 2661^{4} 3697^{2} 4277^{6} 5030^{6} (5351)

Tinos Tank (IRE) *Hilary Parrott* 86b
5 b g Flemensfirth(USA) Tinopasa (FR) (No Pass No Sale)
4547^{10} 4844^{7} 5070^{9}

Tinotara *R Chotard*
4 b f Kayf Tara Tinovala (FR) (Valanour (IRE))
130a^{P}

Tin Pot Man (IRE) *Evan Williams* 107h 100c
8 br g Tillerman White-Wash (Final Straw)
481^{8} 597^{6} 1837^{2}
2619^{2} 3958^{3} 4729^{8}
5038^{5} 5433^{6}

Tinseltown *Brian Rothwell* 113h
8 b g Sadler's Wells(USA) Peony (Lion Cavern (USA))
(605) 697^{2} 968^{2} 1378^{4} 1922^{6} 2198^{15}

Tiny Dancer (IRE) *Alan Swinbank* 100h 119c
6 b g Darsi(FR) Taipans Girl (IRE) (Taipan (IRE))
218^{3} 2030^{4} 2360^{5} 2843^{2} **(4202)**
4613^{2} (4744)
5058^{4}

Tiny Tenor (IRE) *David Dennis* 119h 110c
8 b g Indian Danehill(IRE) Blue Infanta (Chief Singer)
1535^{6}
1640^{2} 1916^{P}

Tiot Cas (FR) *P Chemin* 107h 128c
7 b g Dark Moondancer Legende Sacree (FR) (Hawker's News (IRE))
(2415a)

Tip Dancer (FR) *Robert Collet* 95h 99c
8 b g Chichicastenango(FR) Dancer Lady (FR) (Pink (FR))
455a^{0}

Tipsy Gypsy (IRE) *Tim Vaughan* 80h
7 b g Milan Montanara (IRE) (Montelimar (USA))
5036^{5}

Tiptoeaway (IRE) *Tim Easterby* 62h 89c
9 b g Insan(USA) My Blackbird (IRE) (Mandalus)
4418^{P} 4900^{7} 5385^{F}

Tiptop Ville (FR) *L Viel* 121h 131c
7 b g East Of Heaven(IRE) Jadoudy Ville (FR) (Cadoudal (FR))
838a^{4}

Tiqris *Philip Hobbs* 136h
6 ch g Midnight Legend Calamintha (Mtoto)
2802^{3} ◆ 3163^{3} (3826) 4173^{2} 4558^{B} 4991^{F}

Tiquer (FR) *Alan Jones* 14h 105c
6 b g Equerry(USA) Tirenna (FR) (Sleeping Car (FR))
1598^{P} 3015^{6} 4822^{2}

Tiradia (FR) *J R Jenkins* 116h
7 bb g Without Connexion(IRE) Jimanji (FR) (Kadalko (FR))
49^{5} 184^{8} 429^{3} 788^{3} 1400^{2} 5341^{2} (5522)

Tir Au But (FR) *G Cherel* 138h 132c
7 b g Trempolino(USA) Maitresse de Maison (FR) (Video Rock (FR))
5577a^{5}

Tire Larigot (FR) *Tom George*
7 b g Muhtathir Rhaetia (IRE) (Priolo (USA))
3388^{P}

Tirley Bay *Julian Smith* 31h
10 b m Karinga Bay Tirley Pop Eye (Cruise Missile)
3159^{12}

Tisfreetdream (IRE) *Peter Pritchard* 89h 78c
13 b g Oscar(IRE) Gayley Gale (IRE) (Strong Gale)
117^{F} 601^{F} 764^{8} 860^{10} 2470^{7} 2877^{3} 3324^{4}
4447^{P} 4865^{7}

Tistory (FR) *Nicky Henderson* 130h
7 ch g Epalo(GER) History (FR) (Alesso (USA))
(458) 3166^{2} (4546) 5157^{P}

Titanesque (FR) *J Bertran De Balanda*
7 b g Sassanian(USA) Sadlerfarala (FR) (Dress Parade)
1583a^{P}

Titans Approach (IRE) *Graeme McPherson* 90b
5 b g High Chaparral(IRE) Armelles Approach (IRE) (Definite Article)
5188^{3} 5492^{8}

Titch Strider (IRE) *John Panvert* 96h
9 b m Milan Just Little (Mtoto)
(295) 633^{3}

Titchwood (IRE) *Jonjo O'Neill* 123h 135c
6 b g Flemensfirth(USA) Aker Wood (Bin Ajwaad (IRE))
2643^{2} 3131^{4} 4245^{2} 4842^{U} 5184^{P}

Tito Dela Barriere (FR) *E Lecoiffier* 119h 125c
7 b g April Night(FR) Road Movie (FR) (Exit To Nowhere (USA))
(1984a)
5425a^{11}

Titus Bolt (IRE) *Jim Goldie* 123h
5 b g Titus Livius(FR) Megan's Bay (Muhtarram (USA))
2221^{3} 2970^{2} 3477^{6} 3758^{2} 4199^{3} (4364) 4647^{2}
5272^{3} (5534)

Tiumen (POL) *J Vana Jr* 143c
13 b g Beaconsfield Toskanella (POL) (Demon Club (POL))
1905a^{U}

Toarmandowithlove (IRE) *Susan Corbett* 95b
6 ch m Choisir(AUS) Deadly Buzz (IRE) (Darshaan)
5109^{2} 5381^{5}

Toby Lerone (IRE) *Dan Skelton* 113h 131c
7 b g Old Vic Dawn's Double (IRE) (King's Ride)
2177^{4} (2350)
(2438) 2939^{F} 3642^{4} 4031^{2} 4819^{5} 5031^{5}

To Choose (IRE) *Thomas Gibney* 117h
5 b g Choisir(AUS) Jannadav (IRE) (Barathea (IRE))
5420a^{10}

Todareistodo *Jim Old* 92h 113c
8 gr g Fair Mix(IRE) Its Meant To Be (Gunner B)
2291^{10}
2618^{3} 3439^{2} 4372^{3} 5009^{2}

Todoistodare *Brendan Powell* 1h
4 b f Tobougg(IRE) Misrepresented (IRE) (Presenting)
2318^{5} 3167^{12} *4329^{10}* 4534^{5} 5026^{P}

Toe To Toe (IRE) *Lucy Jones* 105h
6 br g Presenting Tavildara (IRE) (Kahyasi)
1341^{4}
4482^{P} 5395^{13}

Tofino Bay (IRE) *D T Hughes* 150h 155c
11 br g Bishop Of Cashel Boyne View (IRE) (Buckskin (FR))
2235a^{F} 2708a^{P}

Togiak (IRE) *David Pipe* 101h
7 b g Azamour(IRE) Hawksbill Special (IRE) (Taufan (USA))
2696^{3}

Tokyo Javilex (FR) *Nigel Hawke* 95h 115c
7 b g Sleeping Car(FR) Etoile Du Lion (FR) (New Target)
2510^{9} 2920^{4} 3839^{3}
4242^{2} ◆ (4581)
(5017) (5428)

Toledo Gold (IRE) *Maurice Barnes* 104h 115c
8 ch g Needwood Blade Eman's Joy (Lion Cavern (USA))
(679) **798[3]**
882[3] 1144[4] 1378[12]
1657[4] 1849[6] 2173[P]

To Live (FR) *Nick Gifford* 109h 126c
7 ch g Brier Creek(USA) Obrigada (FR) (Roi De Rome (USA))
(162) **763[2]**
(972) **1060[3]**
1628[5]

Tolkeins Tango (IRE) *Victor Dartnall* 111h 116c
6 ch g Beneficial Aule (FR) (Vaguely Pleasant (FR))
2284[11] 3013[3] 3741[11]
4412[5] (4637)
5020[3] 5121[2]

Tomahawk Wood *Donald Whillans* 87b
5 ch g Courteous Meda's Song (Master Willie)
345[5]

Tom Bach (IRE) *Hywel Evans* 99c
10 ch g Bach(IRE) Fiovefontaine (IRE) (Lafontaine (USA))
1859[P] (2152)
2619[U] 2829[4] (4843)
(5038) (5185)

Tom Horn (IRE) *Noel Meade* 110h 134c
8 ch g Beneficial Lady Shackleton (IRE) (Zaffaran (USA))
1897a[9] 2708a[12]

Tomibola (IRE) *Harry Whittington* 95h
6 b g Definite Article Cebola (FR) (Bigstone (IRE))
116[6] 417[12] 2018[8] 2920[2]

Tomis (CZE) *Antonin Novak* 70c
13 b g Manhattan Project Tereza (HUN) (Nagyvezer (HUN))
1905a[U]

Tom Lamb *Sally Hall* 106b
4 ch g Central Park(IRE) Lucinda Lamb (Kayf Tara) (4384)

Tommy O'Dwyer (IRE) *John Ferguson* 89b
5 b g Milan Always Present (IRE) (Presenting)
4480[5]

Tommysteel (IRE) *Victor Thompson* 85c
9 br g Craigsteel Sarahs Music (IRE) (Orchestra)
4554[7]

Tomorrow Night *Jennifer Mason* 16h
4 b f Kayf Tara Whizz Back (IRE) (Bob Back (USA))
3049[7] 4632[16] 5124[12]

Tomorrow's Legend *George Moore* 76b
4 b g Midnight Legend Colvada (North Col (IRE))
4895[9] 5499[8]

Tom O'Tara *Robin Dickin* 83h 91c
10 b g Kayf Tara Mrs May (Carlingford Castle)
43[7] 269[2] 418[5] 687[2] 898[4]

Tom Sang (FR) *Jamie Snowden* 89h 84c
7 b g Dom Alco(FR) Idee (FR) (Lute Antique (FR))
264[11] 640[10] 2862[4] 3140[7] 4336[6]
4890[3] 5111[7]

Tom's Pride (IRE) *Victor Thompson* 71c
11 br g Witness Box(USA) Proverb's Way (Proverb)
625[7]

Tom Wade (IRE) *Shaun Harris* 115h
7 b g Rakti Plutonia (Sadler's Wells (USA))
511[P] (696) 729[2] (850) 1046[6] 1173[7] 4058[6]
4302[10] 4463[5] 4947[5] 5365[6]

Toner D'Oudairies (FR) *Gordon Elliott* 145h 154c
7 b g Polish Summer Iroise D'Oudairies (FR) (Passing Sale (FR))
(1951a)
2235a[2] 2483a[2] 4062a[2] 4457a[2] 5155[4] (5415a)

Tonvadosa *Donald McCain* 125h
6 b m Flemensfirth(USA) Sleepless Eye (Supreme Leader)
(2973) 3203[7] (5103) 5510[3]

Tony Dinozzo (FR) *Peter Bowen* 105h 114c
7 b g Lavirco(GER) Arika (FR) (Le Riverain (FR))
237[F] **500[F]**
756[6] 1581[2] 1645[3]
2293[5] 2599[P] 3026[2] (3472)
3853[F] 4089[5] 4657[4] 5121[F] 5290[4]

Tony Star (FR) *Philip Hobbs* 140h 142c
7 b g Lone Bid(FR) Effet De Star (FR) (Grand Tresor (FR))
217[3] 1796[3] 1969[8] 4742[8] 4960[2] 5278[5]

Too Cool To Fool (IRE) *Jim Goldie* 97h 112c
11 b g Bob Back(USA) Mandysway (IRE) (Mandalus)
3497[3] 3936[2] (4203) (4365)
4666[3] 4957[9]
(5254) 5511[5]

Too Generous *David Pipe* 122h
6 b m Generous(IRE) Little Feat (Terimon)
3731[4] 4076[2]

Toohighforme (IRE) *Nick Gifford*
5 b g Mountain High(IRE) Summertime Girl (IRE) (Glacial Storm (USA))
4445[4]

Toola Boola *Philip Kirby* 92b
4 b f Tobougg(IRE) Forsythia (Most Welcome)
4618[4] 5195[3]

Too Much Too Soon (IRE) *Paul Webber* 107b
5 b g Craigsteel Zara Rose (IRE) (Zaffaran (USA))
3440[6] 4575[3]

Toon River (IRE) *Miss Mary Louise Hallahan* 125h 139c
9 b g Witness Box(USA) Melody Thyne (IRE) (Good Thyne (USA))
5474a[P]

Toostrong (FR) *W P Mullins* 124h 130c
7 ch g Network(GER) Fleurissa (FR) (Dress Parade)
1702a[7] 1804a[P]

Too Trigger Happy *Dr Jeremy Naylor* 80b
5 b m Double Trigger(IRE) Hilarious (IRE) (Petorius)
462[9] 715[9] 1013[3]

Toowoomba (IRE) *Philip Hobbs* 108h
6 b g Milan Lillies Bordello (IRE) (Danehill Dancer (IRE))
2109[2] 2718[3] 3597[3]

Topaze Collonges (FR) *Charlie Longsdon* 89h 115c
7 gr g Dom Alco(FR) Flicka Collonges (FR) (Trebrook (FR))
2078[3] 2440[5] 3093[6] 3439[7] 4440[3] 4762[2] 5111[6]

Top Benefit (IRE) *Richard Harper* 89h 85c
12 gr g Beneficial Cottage Lass (IRE) (Roselier (FR))
(100) **461[P]**
1784[P] **2044[5]**
2313[6] 2702[0] 2829[7] 3180[4] 3797[5] 4243[P] 4778[4]

Top Billing *Nicky Richards* 102h 66c
5 br g Monsun(GER) La Gandilie (FR) (Highest Honor (FR))
368[7] 1791[4] 1982[2] 2417[7] 3040[4] (3605) 4105[7]
4933[13] 5520[8]

Top Chief *Mark Rimell* 89h
6 b g Doyen(IRE) For More (FR) (Sanglamore (USA))
101[6] 544[11] 2002[8] 2564[7] 2954[7] 3280[P] 5143[13]
5523[8]

Top Dancer (FR) *Warren Greatrex* 113h 126c
7 b g Dark Moondancer Latitude (FR) (Kadalko (FR))
2297[4] ◆ (2754)
2931[5]

Top Gamble (IRE) *David Pipe* 130h
6 ch g Presenting Zeferina (IRE) (Sadler's Wells (USA))
2490[9] 4174[F] 4897[F]

Topinambour (FR) *David Greenwood* 74c
14 gr g Turgeon(USA) La Deviniere (IRE) (Nashamaa)
557[7]

Topless (IRE) *C W Loggin* 99h 81c
13 gr m Presenting Tara The Grey (IRE) (Supreme Leader)
61[5] 330[2]

Top Lune (FR) *J Delaunay*
4 bb f Roli Abi(FR) Top Fleur (FR) (Mansonnien (FR))
2781a[P]

Top Madam (IRE) *Donal Coffey* 147h
8 ch m Beneficial Supreme Madam (IRE) (Supreme Leader)
1948a[4]

Top Of The Range (IRE) *Nicky Henderson* 142h 131c
7 br g Presenting Brenny's Pearl (IRE) (Good Thyne (USA))
(2643)
4055[U] 4344[4] 4806[5]

Topo Gigio (FR) *Robert Bewley* 71b 80c
10 b g Even Top(IRE) Chateau Lina (IRE) (Paris House)
110[3] 316[10]

Topolski (IRE) *David Arbuthnot* 128h
8 b g Peintre Celebre(USA) Witching Hour (IRE) (Alzao (USA))
205[4] 1597[8]

Top Show *Dean Ivory* 78h
5 b g Sakhee(USA) Rose Show (Belmez (USA))
2254[11] 4135[9] *4297[13]* 4424[7] 4903[14] 5408[5]

Top Smart *Seamus Mullins* 117h 133c
8 b g Karinga Bay Clover Dove (Overbury (IRE))
(39) **2108[6]**
2953[11] 5348[6]

Topthorn *Martin Bosley* 21h 104c
8 gr g Silver Patriarch(IRE) Miss Traxdata (Absalom)
411[5] 674[4] 2251[F] 2721[7] 2977[9] 5487[7]

Top Totti *Henry Daly* 134h
6 b m Sir Harry Lewis(USA) Jannina (FR) (Useful (FR))
337[2] 738[5] (1639) 2084[3] 2663[2] 2948[6] (3731)
4090[2] 4740[6] 5370[12]

Top Wood (FR) *David Pipe* 138h 120c
7 ch g Kotky Bleu(FR) Heure Bleu (FR) (Grand Tresor (FR))
(4271) 4765[19] 5544[4]

Torero *Diana Grissell* 109h
5 b g Hernando(FR) After You (Pursuit Of Love)
2858[7] 3134[3] 3550[4] 4555[P] 5112[4] 5260[7] 5457[5]

Torgamah Lad (IRE) *Venetia Williams* 100h
6 b g High-Rise(IRE) Brook Forte (Alderbrook)
2467[7] 3061[11] 3226[4] 4107[7] 4334[5] 4636[P] 5012[11]

Tornade D'Estruval (FR) *Sarah Humphrey* 71h 87c
7 b m Network(GER) Onde D'Estruval (FR) (Art Bleu)
697[7] 5365[11]

Tornade Precieuse (FR) *Mme M Desvaux* 127h 127c
7 b m Network(GER) Kerfournoise (FR) (Funny Baby (FR))
(5530a)

Tornado Bob (IRE) *Donald McCain* 140h 102c
9 bb g Bob Back(USA) Double Glazed (IRE) (Glacial Storm (USA))
24[5] (718) 1042[4] 3875[P]

Tornado In Milan (IRE) *Evan Williams* 125h 126c
8 b g Milan Julika (GER) (Nebos (GER))
2042[4] 3156[F] 3204[5] (3787) 4333[2] **4515[P]**

Torphichen *E J O'Grady* 143h 148c
9 ch g Alhaarth(IRE) Genoa (Zafonic (USA))
3806a[4]

Torran Sound *Lawney Hill* 101h
7 b g Tobougg(IRE) Velvet Waters (Unfuwain (USA))
565[3] 860[8] 1275[3] 1580[5] 1824[2] 3852[3] 4471[3]
5234[4]

Torrential Raine *Michael Blake* 104h
6 b g Storming Home La Riveraine (USA) (Riverman (USA))
2105[8] 2842[5] 3473[3]

Torrento City (FR) *Y-M Porzier*
7 b g Marescs Sorrento(FR) Jolly City (FR) (Argument (FR))
455a[P]

Torrington Deal *Malcolm Jefferson* 58h
6 b m Gentleman's Deal(IRE) Miss Danbys (Charmer)
1690[7] 2354[12] 2883[7] 3350[7]

Total Assets *Simon Waugh* 115h
6 b m Alflora(IRE) Maid Equal (Pragmatic)
313[8] 629[5] 1717[F] 2447[7] 2999[2] (3525) 4038[3]
(4553)

Totalize *Brian Ellison* 137h
5 b g Authorized(IRE) You Too (Monsun (GER))
3200[P] 3891[2] 4147[11]

Totem Flow (FR) *G Cherel* 91h 103c
7 b g With The Flow(USA) Kalinca De Thaix (FR) (Lights Out (FR))
838a[F]

Tothemoonandback (IRE) *Gary Moore* 109h 112c
6 gr g Dr Massini(IRE) Mrs Jones (FR) (Saint Preuil (FR))
30[3] 1942[2]

To The Sky (IRE) *John O'Shea* 103h
6 b g Saffron Walden(FR) Tara Tara (IRE) (Fayruz)
(1487) 1697[4] 2474[5] 2717[7] 2886[6] 4882[3] 5139[3]

Toubab (FR) *Dan Skelton* 121h 133c
8 gr g Martaline Tabachines (FR) (Art Francais (USA))
2161[0]
1194[3] 1346[4] 1476[11] 1889[3] 2087[10] 4726[7] 5231[8]

Toubeera *Venetia Williams* 136h
8 b m Tobougg(IRE) Efizia (Efisio)
(1) (374) 2505[7] 2801[4] (3689) (4175) (4272)
4542[3] 4961[8] 5157[P]

Touch Back (IRE) *Jonjo O'Neill* 125h 103c
8 b g Shantou(USA) Back Log (IRE) (Bob Back (USA))
2087[9] 2362[6] 2828[7] 3328[8] (3884) 5186[P]

Touching History (IRE) *Tim Etherington*
5 b g Titus Livius(FR) Lady Naryana (IRE) (Val Royal (FR))
1713[P]

Touch Judge (IRE) *Jonjo O'Neill* 44h
5 b g Westerner Royal Thimble (IRE) (Prince Rupert (FR))
3016[7]

Touch Of Steel (IRE) *James Ewart* 77b
5 b g Craigsteel Tourmaline Girl (IRE) (Toulon)
3500[4] 4958[8]

Touch The Eden (FR) *W P Mullins* 134h 149c
7 b g Malinas(GER) Loika (FR) (Sleeping Car (FR))
(5099a)
5474a[P]

Tough Cookie (IRE) *Michael Gates* 86b 62c
11 b g Rashar(USA) Vam Cas (IRE) (Carlingford Castle)
269[P]

Toughness Danon *Ian Williams* 111h
8 b g Tiger Hill(IRE) Templerin (GER) (Acatenango (GER))
(1561) 1634[LFT] 2529[RR]

Tough Talkin Man (IRE) *Peter Bowen* 109h 100c
10 ch g Bob's Return(IRE) Ashby Hill (IRE) (Executive Perk)
1049[3] 1577[4] 1834[2] 2046[4]

Tough Trade *Chris Grant* 120h
5 b g Trade Fair Cesana (IRE) (Desert Prince (IRE))
2493[13] (2968) 3826[4] 4550[6] 4956[F] 5531[U]

Tour D'Argent (FR) *Donald McCain* 122h 123c
7 b g Martaline Keep Well (FR) (Agent Bleu (FR))
2176 2031[4] 2957[4] 4235[5] 5031[7] 5480[4]

Tour Des Champs (FR) *Nigel Twiston-Davies* 120h 146c
7 bb g Robin Des Champs(FR) Massada I (FR) (Kashtan (FR))
1971[2] 2502[6] 3361[P] 4422[3] 4738[5]

Tourist Board (IRE) *Mrs Ali Sherwin* 93c
11 b g Presenting Glen Of Erin (Furry Glen)
523[P]

Tourtiere *George Moore* 103h
6 b g Act One Kindle (Selkirk (USA))
1853[3] 2156[9] 2341[4] 2879[P]

Toutancarmont (FR) *Mme I Pacault* 105h 124c
7 gr g Al Namix(FR) Furie De Carmont (FR) (Carmont (FR))
(199a)

Town Mouse *Neil King* 118h
4 ch g Sakhee(USA) Megdale (IRE) (Waajib)
975[P] 1044[U] (1536) 1684[3] 1985[2] (2248) 4224[11]
4794[9] 5090[4] 5452[6]

Toye Native (IRE) *C A McBratney* 130h
6 ch m Presenting Lorna's Lady (IRE) (Be My Native (USA))
1148[3] (1289) 1541[2]

Trackanais (FR) *Simon Shirley-Beavan* 31h
7 b g Milford Track(IRE) Havanaise (FR) (Vorias (USA))
2795[5] 3147[3] 5479[11]

Tracking Time *Andrew J Martin* 106h
7 b g Central Park(IRE) E Minor (IRE) (Blushing Flame (USA))
384[3] ◆ 966[5] 3650[3] 4075[3] 4132[5] 4371[3] 4818[4]
5033[10] 5403[2]

Trackmate *James Evans* 138h
8 b g Muhtarram(USA) Cruz Santa (Lord Bud)
(358) (1956) ◆

Tradewinds (FR) *Nicky Henderson* 105h
6 b g Kapgarde(FR) Royale Floriane (FR) (Cyborg (FR))
2644[3]

Traditional Bob (IRE) *Evan Williams* 86h 86c
9 b g Saddlers' Hall(IRE) Portia's Delight (IRE) (The Parson)
4805[16]
5230[F]

Trafalgar (FR) *Nigel Twiston-Davies* 121h 130c
7 b g Laveron Dzaoudzie (FR) (El Badr)
(2024) ◆ 2693[5]

Trafficker (IRE) *Graeme McPherson* 87h
7 b g Flemensfirth(USA) Sulawesi (IRE) (In The Wings)
5280[5]

Trafords Hero *Tony Coyle* 96h
6 b g Parthian Springs Be My Shuile (IRE) (Be My Native (USA))
3880[6] 4446[P] 5059[3]

Train Of Thought (IRE) *Evan Williams* 126h 91c
6 b g Sadler's Wells(USA) Cool Clarity (IRE) (Indian Ridge)
1550[F] 1867[10] 2461[P] **4660[6]**

Trakeur (FR) *Simon Hodgson* 83h 52c
7 b g Myrakalu(FR) Nataly (FR) (Ragmar (FR))
79[7] 1431[4] 1553[4]
1834[6] 2175[F] 2690[12]

Tranquil Sea (IRE) *Warren Greatrex* 133h 149c
12 b g Sea Raven(IRE) Silver Valley (IRE) (Henbit (USA))
1001a[5] 1168a[12] 3362[2] 3923[3] (4346)
4769[P] 5170[12]

Transfer *Richard Price* 90h
9 br g Trans Island Sankaty Light (USA) (Summer Squall (USA))
49[7] 252[3] 1675[4] (1837) 2473[B] 2877[6]

Transient Bay (IRE) *Philip Kirby* 93b
4 b g Trans Island Boarding Pass (IRE) (Accordion)
4582[4] 5109[4]

Trapper Peak (IRE) *Caroline Bailey* 104h
5 b g Westerner Banningham Blaze (Averti (IRE))
2703[2] 3440[4] 4598[5] 5519[4]

Travis County (IRE) *Brian Ellison* 110h
5 b g Jeremy(USA) Manchaca (FR) (Highest Honor (FR))
475[3] 2198[7] 2561[5] (2868)

Treacle Moon *Mrs Sarah L Dent* 73b
11 b m Kayf Tara Monica's Story (Arzanni)
5209[P]

Treelara *Miss Imogen Pickard* 31b
7 ch m Grape Tree Road Leamlara Rose (IRE) (Le Moss)
1064[5] 1265[P]

Tree Of Life *Paul Fitzsimons* 86b
4 ch f Medicean Antebellum (FR) (Anabaa (USA))
2604[5]

Tregaro (FR) *Mike Sowersby* 89h 103c
8 b g Phantom Breeze Touques (FR) (Tip Moss (FR))
564[8] **693[6]**
898[5] 1260[8] 1470[4] (1566)
1636[F] 1872[5] 2394[5] 2873[3] 3113[B]

Treliver Manor (IRE) *Emma Lavelle* 107b
6 b g Flemensfirth(USA) Loch Lomond (IRE) (Dry Dock)
4839[P]

Trempolin (FR) *F-M Cottin* 126h 117c
7 ch g Trempolino(USA) Cate Bleue (FR) (Katowice (FR))
2465a[9]

Trend Is My Friend (USA) *Donald McCain* 108h
5 bb g Lemon Drop Kid(USA) Silva (FR) (Anabaa (USA))
171[4] 865[3] 1159[2] 1466[3]

Trentside William *Mike Sowersby*
7 b g Bollin William Aunt Gladys (IRE) (Glacial Storm (USA))
747[P] 847[F] 967[P]

Tresor De Bontee (FR) *Richard Lee* 111h 123c
7 b g Grand Seigneur(FR) Bontee (FR) (Le Pontet (FR))
(3429)
3992[3] 4560[P] 5228[5]

Tresor De La Vie (FR) *Victor Dartnall* 81h 86c
7 gr g Epalo(GER) Joie De La Vie (FR) (Quart De Vin (FR))
2106[7] 4171[8] 4514[4]
5004[4] 5237[8]

Tresor De L'Isle (FR) *James Ewart* 84h 103c
7 br g Dark Moondancer Ad Vitam Eternam (FR) (Cap Martin (FR))
30[8] 555[6] (2219)
2518[F] 3107[3] 3528[7]

Trevaylor Boy (IRE) *Sue Gardner* 105b
7 b g Lahib(USA) Blue Glass (Ardkinglass)
1869[3] 2368[4]

Trezor (POL) *Hana Kabelkova* 87c
10 b g In Camera(IRE) Trebia (POL) (Special Power (IRE))
1905a[F]

Triangular (USA) *Harry Fry* 112h 131c
9 b g Diesis Salchow (USA) (Nijinsky (CAN))
587[6] 3603[2] (4134)

Tribal Dance (IRE) *John O'Shea* 97h 90c
8 br g Flemensfirth(USA) Native Sparkle (IRE) (Be My Native (USA))
5[7] 269[7] 804[4] 929[5] 1267[9] (1580) 1890[3] 2470[2]
2571[5] 4398[5]
4663[4] 5283[7]

Tribes And Banner (IRE) *C F Swan* 132h 142c
10 br g Bob's Return(IRE) Kaysdante (IRE) (Phardante (FR))
1613a[4] 1776a[5]

Tribu D'Estruval (FR) *Tom George* 79h
7 bb m Sleeping Car(FR) Mome D'Estruval (FR) (Cyborg (FR))
2190[7] 2767[8] 3117[P]

Tribulation (IRE) *Robert Walford* 110h
6 br g Diktat Royal York (Bustino)
2286[4] ◆ 2940[9] 3695[8]

Trickaway (IRE) *Philip Hobbs* 108h
6 b g Stowaway Rosie's Trix (IRE) (Luso)
1974[9] (4177) 5181[4] 5508[3]

Trifolium (FR) *C Byrnes* 147h 158c
7 b g Goldneyev(USA) Opium Des Mottes (FR) (April Night (FR))
3308a[2] (3928a) ◆ 4737[3] 5168[3]

Trifollet *Andrew J Martin* 58h 80c
9 b m Kirkwall St Doughla'S (IRE) (Phardante (FR))
291[0] **4759[5]**
5011[7] 5546[7]

Triggerman *Philip Hobbs* 115h 132c
12 b g Double Trigger(IRE) Carrikins (Buckskin (FR))
355[8] 509[F] 2070[R] 2693[4] 3698[4] 4190[3]

Trigger The Light *Alan King* 114h 130c
13 ch g Double Trigger(IRE) Lamper's Light (Idiots Delight)
4402[P] 4704[5]

Trillerin Minella (IRE) *Graeme McPherson* 105h
6 b g King's Theatre(IRE) Eva Fay (IRE) (Fayruz)
1869[12] 2695[5] 3175[11] 3602[5] 4887[2] 5285[9]

Tri Nations (UAE) *Anthony Middleton* 116h 105c
9 ch g Halling(USA) Six Nations (USA) (Danzig (USA))
565^8 691^9 833^6 903^6 **(1063)**
1192^3 1274^4 1441^5 1522^4 1638^5 1822^6

Triolo D'Alene (FR) *Nicky Henderson* 102h 164c
7 ch g Epalo(GER) Joliette D'Alene (FR) (Garde Royale)
(6) **2214^3**
(2815)
4787^{10} 5171^P

Triple Brandy *Karen George* 77b
5 br g Double Trigger(IRE) Aquavita (Kalaglow)
298^8 412^8 731^8

Triple Eight (IRE) *Philip Kirby* 95h
6 b g Royal Applause Hidden Charm (IRE) (Big Shuffle (USA))
3872^9 4103^{12} 4529^7 4817^6

Trip The Light *Phil Middleton* 112h
9 b g Fantastic Light(USA) Jumaireyah (Fairy King (USA))
119^4 267^4 503^8 697^4 756^P

Triptico (FR) *Evan Williams* 114h 134c
8 gr g Turgeon(USA) Al Kicks (FR) (Al Nasr (FR))
2199^4 2943^5 3205^P 4027^4

Trois Huit (FR) *E Leenders*
7 b g Shaanmer(IRE) Insoumise (FR) (Royal Charter (FR))
855a^F 1532a^F

Trois Vallees (USA) *Lucinda Russell* 105h
5 bb g Elusive Quality(USA) Chamrousse (USA) (Peaks And Valleys (USA))
1661^5 1958^8 2340^F

Trojan Sun *Tom Symonds* 104h 115c
8 bb g Kayf Tara Sun Dante (IRE) (Phardante (FR))
2350^2 3113^F (3879)
4372^P 4990^3 5129^4

Trooper Clarence *Evan Williams* 79h 116c
10 b g Trempolino(USA) Ten To Six (Night Shift (USA))
249^7 840^4 1151^2 1352^4 1696^4 2293^8

Trooper Royal *Sue Smith* 65b
4 b g Zafeen(FR) Faithful Beauty (IRE) (Last Tycoon)
3214^8 4480^7

Troopingthecolour *Steve Gollings* 49h
8 b g Nayef(USA) Hyperspectra (Rainbow Quest (USA))
4022^{10}

Tropenfeuer (FR) *James Moffatt* 88h
7 b m Banyumanik(IRE) Tropensonne (GER) (Konigsstuhl (GER))
536^8

Trop Fort (FR) *Tim Vaughan* 100h 117c
7 b g Bernebeau(FR) Violeta (FR) (Rhapsodien)
1133^4 1282^2 1563^3

Tropical Sky (IRE) *Michael Chapman*
6 b g Librettist(USA) Tropical Breeze (IRE) (Kris)
599^6 699^{12} 1690^U 3148^P 3829^P

Tropical Three (IRE) *Michael Hourigan* 118h
6 gr m Portrait Gallery(IRE) Tropical Ocean (IRE) (Anshan)
1893a^5 2801^P

Tropic De Brion (FR) *Pavel Vitek*
7 b g Network(GER) Milka De Brion (FR) (Cadoudal (FR))
1905a^6

Trouble Digger *T Lacey* 47h 115c
9 ch g Double Trigger(IRE) Inesdela (Wolver Hollow)
59^P

Troubled Waters *Jason Ward* 90b
5 b m Kayf Tara Air Of Affection (Air Express (IRE))
3042^5

Trouble In Paris (IRE) *Barry Murtagh* 93h 79c
7 ch g Great Palm(USA) Ten Dollar Bill (IRE) (Accordion)
168^P **2155^6**
2416^7 3355^4 4775^5 5301^2 5498^3

Troubletimestwo (FR) *Tony Carroll* 80h
8 gr g Linamix(FR) Time Of Trouble (FR) (Warning)
237^7

Troufion (FR) *Caroline Fryer* 102h
5 gr g Smadoun(FR) La Troussardiere (FR) (Maresca Sorrento (FR))
2028^5
2251^U 4863^2 5088^{12} 5521^{10}

Troyan (IRE) *Robin Dickin* 111h
7 b g King's Theatre(IRE) Talk The Talk (Terimon)
2981^4 4506^3 4863^5

Trozulon (FR) *Venetia Williams* 102h 91c
7 b g Roli Abi(FR) Manza (FR) (Bobinski)
3280^3 3740^6 **4067^P 4488^4 5009^6 5433^9**

Truckers Benefit (IRE) *Tim Vaughan* 94h 99c
9 b g Beneficial Lady Jurado (IRE) (Jurado (USA))
694^P 1376^5

Truckers Darling (IRE) *Don Cantillon* 113h
7 b m Flemensfirth(USA) Nicat's Daughter (IRE) (Oscar (IRE))
2725^2 3034^{11} 3278^9 (3840) (4083) 4381^3 4717^4 5010^6

Truckers First *Richard Phillips* 81b
6 b m Kayf Tara Cheeky Trucker (Atraf)
842^4

Truckers Highway (IRE) *John Bryan Groucott* 103b
5 b g Rudimentary(USA) Countessdee (IRE) (Arctic Lord)
5249^2

Truckers Steel (IRE) *Tom George* 110h
6 b g Craigsteel Frantesa (Red Sunset)
(2052) ◆ 3115^3

Trucking Along (IRE) *S R B Crawford* 134h 116c
8 br g Zagreb(USA) Pegus Gold (Strong Gale)
356^{14} 1398^4 1752^7 1926^4 (2221) 2671^8 3201^3 (3499) 4369^2

True Blue (IRE) *Nigel Twiston-Davies* 108h 125c
7 ch g Blueprint(IRE) Fontaine Frances (IRE) (Lafontaine (USA))
142^2 (585)
781^F

True Gold *Michael Mullineaux* 11b
4 b f Beat All(USA) Jackie Jarvis (IRE) (Alphabatim (USA))
4480^8

True Pleasure (IRE) *James Bethell*
7 b m Choisir(AUS) Absolute Pleasure (Polar Falcon (USA))
506^8

Trumix *Kim Bailey* 107h
6 b g Fair Mix(IRE) Indeed To Goodness (IRE) (Welsh Term)
91^4 374^4 1887^P 2598^{13} 4887^9 5029^P

Trustan Times (IRE) *Tim Easterby* 150h 148c
8 b g Heron Island(IRE) Ballytrustan Maid (IRE) (Orchestra)
2228^4 2672^8 3108^3
3776^3 4765^4
5276^3

Trust Me Boy *John E Long* 75h
6 gr g Avonbridge Eastern Lyric (Petong)
5403^P

Trust Thomas *Ann Hamilton* 110h
6 ch g Erhaab(USA) Yota (FR) (Galetto (FR))
280^4 1717^3 2360^2 2868^5 3398^3 3659^2 4224^4 4952^7 5212^2

Try Catch Me (IRE) *Alison Batchelor* 21h 107c
9 b g Commander Collins(IRE) Misty River (IRE) (Over The River (FR))
98^2 705^2 898^P 1435^U 1522^5 1767^U

Tsar Alexandre (FR) *Warren Greatrex* 115h
7 b g Robin Des Champs(FR) Bertrange (FR) (Torvay (FR))
4297^7 4546^2 4931^5

Tuffstuff *Brian Barr* 105b
6 b g Generous(IRE) Life Line (Exit To Nowhere (USA))
5014^8 5181^6

Tukitinyasok (IRE) *Clive Mulhall* 79h
7 b g Fath(USA) Mevlana (IRE) (Red Sunset)
15^7

Tulipe De Ballon (FR) *D Retif* 123h 101c
8 b m Turgeon(USA) Tel Muze (FR) (Tel Quel (FR))
863a^4

Tulla Emerald (IRE) *Natalie Lloyd-Beavis* 11h 66c
9 b g Beneficial Kilfane (IRE) (Hollow Hand)
594^F 687^P 805^4 1010^P 1149^F 1328^7

Tullamore Dew (IRE) *Nick Gifford* 127h 136c
12 ch g Pistolet Bleu(IRE) Heather Point (Pollerton)
1971^3 3285^2 3698^2 4263^5 4557^4 5092^7

Tullintain (IRE) *Robert Tyner* 86h 131c
11 b g Oscar(IRE) Daradante (IRE) (Phardante (FR))
2983a^8

Tullyesker Hill (IRE) *David Pipe* 128h
5 b g Shantou(USA) Couture Daisy (IRE) (Desse Zenny (USA))
(2570) ◆ 2978^4 3357^4 3694^2 (4161) ◆ 4415^8 5186^P

Tullyraine (IRE) *Nigel Twiston-Davies* 124h 129c
10 b g Winged Love(IRE) Struell Princess (Avocat)
358^7 **2024^4**
2451^2 3717^8 4245^5 (4842)
5184^5

Tunnel Vision (IRE) *Nikki Evans* 55b
7 bb g Craigsteel Mill Top Lady (IRE) (Topanoora)
1124^9 1891^5

Tunza The Lion *Richard Ford*
7 b g Trade Fair Bella Helena (Balidar)
1074^P

Turban (FR) *W P Mullins* 141h 155c
7 b g Dom Alco(FR) Indianabelle (FR) (Useful (FR))
(3806a)
4283a^2 5197a^F

Turbo Du Ranch (FR) *Warren Greatrex* 117h 129c
7 gr g Useful(FR) Zoumba Du Ranch (FR) (Smadoun (FR))
164^3 (504)
646^7 878^5
1257^3 1440^4

Turbulance (IRE) *Bernard Llewellyn* 47h 52c
12 gr g Snurge Full Deck (IRE) (Roselier (FR))
478^5

Turcagua (FR) *W P Mullins* 97b
4 gr g Turgeon(USA) Acancagua (FR) (Subotica (FR))
5424a^3

Turf Trivia *George Moore* 96h 101c
7 gr g Alhaarth(IRE) Exclusive Approval (USA) (With Approval (CAN))
109^U 281^2 602^F (694)
798^U 1716^3 2048^2 2173^6 2737^6 3143^4 3722^3 (4383) 4477^F 4890^7 5355^3

Turkey Creek (IRE) *Paul Webber* 95b
5 b g Scorpion(IRE) Emesions Lady (IRE) (Bigstone (IRE))
2479^5 4923^2

Turned To Gold (IRE) *Robert Johnson*
5 ch g Teofilo(IRE) Silver Bracelet (Machiavellian (USA))
507^P

Turn Over Sivola (FR) *Alan King* 129h 144c
7 b g Assessor(IRE) Notting Hill (FR) (Garde Royale)
216^{14}
1986^2 2363^2 2716^2 3386^3 4543^2 5136^2

Turn The Tide *Natalie Lloyd-Beavis* 82h
6 b m Footstepsinthesand Syrian Dancer (IRE) (Groom Dancer (USA))
391^3 648^{10} 729^9 809^{11}

Turoyal (FR) *Laura Hurley* 97h
6 gr g Turgeon(USA) Quelle Est Belle (FR) (Tel Quel (FR))
3863^{10} 5408^7

Turtle Cask (IRE) *Alistair Whillans* 101b
5 b g Turtle Island(IRE) Sayce (IRE) (Supreme Leader)
3500^3

Turtlethomas (IRE) *Lawney Hill* 102h
8 br g Turtle Island(IRE) Makingyourmindup (IRE) (Good Thyne (USA))
121^6 764^P

Turtle Tim (IRE) *Miss S L Pidsley* 100c
10 b g Turtle Island(IRE) Acumen (IRE) (Phardante (FR))
5553^4

Turtle Watch *Jim Goldie* 116h
6 b g Where Or When(IRE) Cita Verda (FR) (Take Risks (FR))
494^4 676^5 880^5 1785^{11} (1979) (2241)

Tuscan Gold *Laura Mongan* 120h
7 ch g Medicean Louella (USA) (El Gran Senor (USA))
48^2 237^4 *4022^7* 4799^3

Tuskar (USA) *Alan Jones* 52b
8 ch g Mr Greeley(USA) Maria Donna (USA) (With Approval (CAN))
687^P

Tuskar Rock (FR) *Venetia Williams* 99h 100c
11 gr g Turgeon(USA) Shannondore (FR) (Nashamaa)
1579^5 3696^2 4396^5 4840^2 5023^3 5240^P

Tutchec (FR) *Nicky Richards* 99h 135c
7 gr g Turgeon(USA) Pocahontas (FR) (Nikos)
113^6 (2036)
(2421) (2841)
(3725) 4835^3

Tweedle Dee *Noel Quinlan* 83h
5 b m Araafa(IRE) Sismique (Warning)
1795^6 2083^{13}

Tweedledrum *Tom Symonds* 122h
7 b m Beat Hollow Tweed Mill (Selkirk (USA))
1956^{18} 2713^4 (2860) 3198^3 3770^6 4040^F 4174^8

Tweedo Paradiso (NZ) *Rose Dobbin* 93h
7 br g Golan(IRE) Buzz (NZ) (Dedicated Rullah (USA))
283^4 558^9 (1848) 2306^4 2787^6 3141^4 4223^8 4817^4 ◆

Tweety Kash (FR) *F-M Cottin* 60h 68c
5 b m Bonbon Rose(FR) Sainte Kash (FR) (Saint Preuil (FR))
2464a^F

Twelve Roses *Kim Bailey* 142h
6 ch g Midnight Legend Miniature Rose (Anshan)
33^2 (417) 1828^2 2230^2 2798^4 ◆ 3263^9 4750^5

Twentypoundluck (IRE) *Patrick Griffin* 103h 120c
9 ch g Beneficial Guitane Lady (IRE) (Commanche Run)
282^7 882^2 (1144)
1750^3 1849^3

Twice Lucky *Sue Smith* 80h 100c
10 b g Mtoto Foehn Gale (IRE) (Strong Gale)
2036^3 2335^4 2518^5 2818^2 3355^2 3755^4 5358^2

Twice Returned (IRE) *Dan Skelton* 124h 87c
8 b g Old Vic Almost Regal (IRE) (Jurado (USA))
1863^3 2458^{14} **4934^6 5194^5** 5548^2

Twice Shy (IRE) *Mike Hammond*
6 b m Winged Love(IRE) Juno Beach (Jupiter Island)
1599^{12}

Twill Stand To Us (IRE) *Brian Ellison* 106h 111c
7 b g Beneficial Guitane Lady (IRE) (Commanche Run)
470^4 ◆ 629^3 **798^2 960^3 1417^3 1666^6** 2342^4

Twin Barrels *Sarah-Jayne Davies* 111h
7 ch g Double Trigger(IRE) Caballe (USA) (Opening Verse (USA))
140^4

Twin Bud *Anna Newton-Smith* 97h
9 b m Double Trigger(IRE) Little Bud (Lord Bud)
99^5 379^2 1565^9 2006^7

Twinlight (FR) *W P Mullins* 143h 161c
7 b g Muhtathir Fairlight (GER) (Big Shuffle (USA))
(2141a)
(2985a) 3645^3 4457a^3 5197a^2

Twin Plan (IRE) *J J Lambe* 124h 124c
9 ch m Beneficial Valley (IRE) (Flemensfirth (USA))
5255^7
5475a^4

Twirling Magnet (IRE) *Jonjo O'Neill* 123h 147c
8 b g Imperial Ballet(IRE) Molly Maguire (IRE) (Supreme Leader)
18^2 839^F (1085)
1362^2 1476^5 1686^{14} (1957)
2214^7 4769^U 5171^F

Two Jabs *Mark Brisbourne* 101b
4 b g Teofilo(IRE) Red Bravo (USA) (Red Ransom (USA))
(2436) 2830^3 5264^9

Twojayslad *Ian Williams*
5 b g Kayf Tara Fulwell Hill (Anshan)
4296^9

Two Mile Bridge (IRE) *Paul Henderson* 80h
8 b m Dushyantor(USA) Serengeti Plains (IRE) (Toulon)
2286^9 2740^7 3290^7 4500^4 5007^{11}

Two Oscars (IRE) *Andrew Crook* 82h
8 b g Oscar(IRE) Coumeenoole Lady (The Parson)
72^4 558^6 803^P 969^P 1320^F 2333^P 3353^6 4746^6

Twopoundsofbutter (IRE) *Tim Vaughan* 96h 81c
7 bb g Beneficial Jezel (IRE) (Accordion)
2648^6 2940^7 3357^{14} 4471^2 5461^P

Two Rockers (IRE) *Alan King* 145h
7 b g Milan Foxhall Blue (IRE) (Pistolet Bleu (IRE))
2672^9 4264^F 5138^{14}

Two Shades Of Blue *Beth Roberts* 59h
7 b m Advise(FR) Smilingatstrangers (Macmillion)
1341^6 1706^{10} 1885^{10}

Two Sugars *Laura Mongan* 69h
6 b g Val Royal(FR) Princess Galadriel (Magic Ring (IRE))
2272^9 2564^{10}

Twoways (IRE) *Mark Rimell* 126h 109c
8 br g Bob's Return(IRE) Braw Lass (Alflora (IRE))
761^8 1913^7 **2677^3 2977^5** 3288^4 (3802) (4085) 4503^2 4820^4 5172^P

Twyford *William Reed* 98h 78c
7 b g Bach(IRE) Commanche Token (IRE) (Commanche Run)
177^2 651^8 828^6 1061^6

Tycoon Prince (IRE) *P M J Doyle* 97b
4 b g Trans Island Downtown Train (IRE) (Glacial Storm (USA))
5424a^4

Typhon De Guye (FR) *Martin Keighley* 98h 108c
7 ch g Dom Alco(FR) Mascotte De Guye (FR) (Video Rock (FR))
254^7 2473^4 3179^2
(5407)

Typical Oscar (IRE) *Michael Blake* 80c
7 b g Oscar(IRE) Kachina (IRE) (Mandalus)
2028^P
2459^6 2756^U 3011^7

Tyquaveron (FR) *J Planque* 75c
7 b g Laveron Tyquabella (FR) (Lute Antique (FR))
1424a^F

Tyre Hill Lady *David Dennis* 94b
5 b m Midnight Legend Springbrook Girl (Alderbrook)
4540^3 5195^{10} 5440^4

Tyriac (FR) *J-P Gallorini* 53h
4 b g Agent Bleu(FR) Ua Uka (FR) (Turgeon (USA))
1741a^{10}

Tyrur Ted *Frank Sheridan* 93h 45c
9 b g Val Royal(FR) Spanish Serenade (Nashwan (USA))
1938^6
2315^7 3062^8

Tyup Pompey (IRE) *Ann Price* 81h 62c
13 ch g Docksider(USA) Cindy's Baby (Bairn (USA))
13^4

Tzar's Dancer (FR) *E Leenders* 105h 149c
6 b g Tzar Rodney(FR) Steel Dancer (FR) (Kaldounevees (FR))
(5425a)

Tzora *Martin Hill* 136h
9 b g Sakhee(USA) Lucky Arrow (Indian Ridge)
(176) (831) 1046^F *4303^2* 4785^{21}

Ubaldo Des Menhies (FR) *Jonjo O'Neill* 130h
6 bb g Network(GER) Ker Marie (FR) (Esprit Du Nord (USA))
2366^{12} 2668^{10} 3132^5 3832^7 4278^P 4726^9 5040^5

Ubaltique (FR) *Donald McCain* 137h 117c
6 b g Balko(FR) Ode Antique (FR) (Subotica (FR))
118^5 534^2 2221^P (3398) (3832) 4426^3 5172^{18}

Ucocotte (FR) *Guy Denuault* 103h 105c
6 b m Califet(FR) Paresca (FR) (Maresca Sorrento (FR))
454a^4

Uddy (FR) *Alain Couetil* 144h
6 b m Voix Du Nord(FR) Idy (FR) (Quart De Vin (FR))
4740^{10}

Ueueteotl (FR) *James Ewart* 125h
6 gr g Tikkanen(USA) Azturk (FR) (Baby Turk)
22^2 1977^2 (2311) ◆ 3000^7

Uganda Glory (USA) *George Baker* 88h
4 br f Hat Trick(JPN) Febrile (USA) (Trempolino (USA))
2557^5

Ugly Bug *Seamus Mullins* 125h
8 b g Runyon(IRE) Mutual Decision (IRE) (Supreme Leader)
2944^6 3359^2 3775^3 4415^P 5093^{15} 5544^7

Ugo (USA) *Evan Williams* 122h 104c
6 b g Street Cry(IRE) Min Elreeh (USA) (Danzig (USA))
82^7 **594^F**
781^F

Ugolin De Beaumont (FR) *Bob Buckler* 96b
6 b g Alberto Giacometti(IRE) Okarina De Beaumont (FR) (Ragmar (FR))
3994^6

Uhlan Bute (FR) *Venetia Williams* 127h
6 ch g Brier Creek(USA) Jonquiere (FR) (Trebrook (FR))
(290) 2932^2 ◆ 3066^7 3592^2 (3686) 3989^7 4799^7

Uiop *David Bridgwater* 49h
6 b g Caballo Raptor(CAN) Qwertyze (FR) (Maresca Sorrento (FR))
1016^0 1124^5

Ukrainian Star (IRE) *Martin Keighley* 99h 112c
11 ch g Carrowkeel(IRE) Gemmasdelemma (IRE) (Red Sunset)
121^7

Ulck Du Lin (FR) *Paul Nicholls* 114h 137c
6 b g Sassanian(USA) Miss Fast (FR) (Prince Fast (FR))
2212^9 2816^8 3197^5 3887^8 4559^5 4960^4 5458^2

Ulex (FR) *Alain Couetil* 113c
6 b g Maresca Sorrento(FR) Baladine Des Pres (FR) (Sharken (FR))
454a^F

Ulis De Vassy (FR) *Nick Williams* 114h 123c
6 b g Voix Du Nord(FR) Helathou (FR) (Video Rock (FR))
559a^6 1175^3 (1441) ◆ **1857^5**

Ullswater (IRE) *Andy Turnell* 102h
6 b g Singspiel(IRE) Uluwatu (IRE) (Unfuwain (USA))
49^2 243^2 ◆ (456) 1061^2 1799^4 2013^6

Ulrick (FR) *C Dubourg* 90c
6 b g Denham Red(FR) Irish Lane (FR) (Cyborg (FR))
198a^4 454a^8

Ultiep (FR) *Karen McLintock* 63h
6 gr g Ragmar(FR) Naltiepy (FR) (Dom Alco (FR))
2037^8 2355^8 3018^6

Ultimate *Brian Ellison* 125h 144c
8 b g Anabaa(USA) Nirvana (Marju (IRE))
677^2 ◆ **(2199)**
2822^4 3477^7
4039^R 5384^6

Ultimatum Du Roy (FR) *Alex Hales* 96h 122c
6 b g Brier Creek(USA) La Fleur Du Roy (FR) (Sleeping Car (FR))
2887^4 3365^3 (3739)
4110^3 4537^3 5385^8

Ultra Du Chatelet (FR) *Lucinda Russell* 97h 116c
6 b g Network(GER) Grandeur Royale (FR) (Royal Charter (FR))
1540^{3}
1872^{4} 2157^{U} 2749^{5} 3498^{5} 5218^{2}

Ultragold (FR) *Colin Tizzard* 94h 130c
6 bb g Kapgarde(FR) Hot D'Or (FR) (Shafoun (FR))
1957^{9} 2107^{4} 2693^{2} 3097^{3} 3990^{5} 4131^{P}

Ultra Klass (FR) *Jamie Snowden* 92h 89c
6 b g Ungaro(GER) Leathou (FR) (Lute Antique (FR))
3278^{6} 3880^{5} **4242^{6} 4663^{5} 5011^{5} 5407^{4}**

Ultranet (FR) *G Chaignon* 97h 111c
6 b g Network(GER) First Union (FR) (Shafoun (FR))
454a^{F}

Ultravox (USA) *Jeremy Scott* 120h 114c
7 b g Lemon Drop Kid(USA) Lynnwood Chase (USA) (Horse Chestnut (SAF))
2111^{8}

Ulys Du Charmil (FR) *Alan King* 123h
6 b g Malinas(GER) Jest In Ball (FR) (Perrault)
82^{5}

Ulysse Collonges (FR) *Chris Grant* 129h 137c
6 b g Voix Du Nord(FR) Kapucine Collonges (FR) (Dom Alco (FR))
217^{F}

Ulzana's Raid (IRE) *Alan King* 133h
5 ch g Bach(IRE) Peace Time Beauty (IRE) (Saddlers' Hall (IRE))
(270) 2375^{6} 2978^{3} (4903) (5252)

Umberto D'Olivate (FR) *Robert Walford* 115h 136c
6 b g Alberto Giacometti(IRE) Komunion (FR) (Luchiroverte (IRE))
2111^{4}
(2618) 3172^{5} (3693)
(4536) (4800)

Umoristic (FR) *Reginald Brown* 88h
6 gr g Baroud D'Honneur(FR) Canlastou (FR) (Tanlas (FR))
390^{5} 651^{13} 716^{8}

Umustbejoking (FR) *Michael Blake* 100h 97c
6 b m Lavirco(GER) Arika (FR) (Le Riverain (FR))
521^{8} 651^{7} 765^{3} 927^{6} **1149^{7} 5363^{2}**

Un Ace (FR) *Kim Bailey* 145h
6 b g Voix Du Nord(FR) First Ball (FR) (Beyssac (FR))
(4343) 4736^{8} ◆ 5167^{P}

Un Ami (FR) *Nick Williams* 123h 98c
6 gr g Dom Alco(FR) Immage (FR) (Bad Conduct (USA))
198a^{5} 454a^{7} 2009^{U}

Unanime *A Adeline De Boisbrunet* 94h 104c
6 b m Epalo(GER) Behariya (IRE) (Sadler's Wells (USA))
198a^{2}

Un Anjou (FR) *David Dennis* 95h 124c
6 bb g Panoramic Idee D'Estruval (FR) (Port Etienne (FR))
454a^{P} 2007^{3} 2251^{2} 2618^{6} (2977)
3027^{3} 3596^{2} 4036^{5} 5194^{2} 5340^{4}

Un Beau Matin (IRE) *Gordon Elliott* 142h
6 gr g Sagamix(FR) Millesimee (FR) (Video Rock (FR))
2408a^{4} 3866a^{2} 4312a^{3} 5471a^{4}

Un Beau Roman (FR) *W P Mullins* 142h
6 br g Roman Saddle(IRE) Koukie (FR) (Lute Antique (FR))
1802a^{6}

Un Bleu A L'Aam (FR) *Victor Dartnall* 99h
6 b g Shaanmer(IRE) Bleu Perle (FR) (Pistolet Bleu (IRE))
2507^{6} 3163^{8} 3747^{7} 4504^{6} 5072^{4}

Un Bon P'Tit Gars (FR) *Nick Williams* 120h 128c
6 b g Robin Des Champs(FR) Nee A Saint Voir (FR) (Pistolet Bleu (IRE))
455a^{P}
2287^{2} 2811^{2} 3362^{P} 4560^{5} 5382^{4}

Uncle Jimmy (IRE) *Philip Hobbs* 142h
7 bb g Alderbrook Carrabawn (Buckskin (FR))
1858^{2} 2102^{3} ◆ 2490^{4} (3653) 4765^{17} 5138^{20}

Uncle Junior (IRE) *W P Mullins* 129h 155c
13 b g Saddlers' Hall(IRE) Caslain Nua (Seymour Hicks (FR))
2491^{2} 3868a^{P} 4754^{7}

Uncle Muf (USA) *Ali Brewer* 13b
4 b g Curlin(USA) Peak Maria's Way (USA) (Pyramid Peak (USA))
(2731) (3229) 5173^{19}

Uncle Pelder (IRE) *K F Clutterbuck* 86b 108c
7 b g Pelder(IRE) Aunt Annie (IRE) (Synefos (USA))
425^{2} 594^{3} 898^{3} 1122^{4} (1325)

Uncle Pettit (IRE) *Jonathan Portman* 86h 77c
6 bb g Heron Island(IRE) Special Ballot (IRE) (Perugino (USA))
2631^{4} 3138^{3} 3955^{P}
4884^{7} 5113^{7} 5394^{3}

Uncle Roger (IRE) *Eve Johnson Houghton* 89h
5 b g Camacho Felin Gruvy (IRE) (Tagula (IRE))
177^{5}

Uncle Tom Cobley (IRE) *Michael Scudamore* 136c
10 b g King's Theatre(IRE) Platinum Leader (IRE) (Supreme Leader)
5517^{P}

Uncle Tone (IRE) *David A Kiely* 102b
5 b g Pelder(IRE) Daisy A Day (IRE) (Asir)
2153^{5}

Uncut Stone (IRE) *Peter Niven* 103h
6 b g Awesome Again(CAN) Suitably Discreet (USA) (Mr Prospector (USA))
168^{8} 933^{5}

Under (FR) *F-M Cottin* 89h 118c
6 b m Le Malemortois(FR) Juventus II (FR) (Lute Antique (FR))
454a^{6}

Underlay Underlay *Ron Hodges* 43h
6 b g Namid Rainbow Nation (Rainbow Quest (USA))
193^{8}

Undertheboardwalk (IRE) *A J Martin* 128h 133c
8 b g Dr Massini(IRE) Bemyhostess (IRE) (Bob Back (USA))
2529^{8}

Underwood (FR) *Michael Roberts* 66h
6 b g Assessor(IRE) Attualita (FR) (Master Thatch)
3136^{7} 3552^{5} 4442^{P}

Un De Sceaux (FR) *W P Mullins* 164h
6 b g Denham Red(FR) Hotesse De Sceaux (FR) (April Night (FR))
(4285a) ◆ (5577a)

Une Artiste (FR) *Nicky Henderson* 135h 138c
6 b m Alberto Giacometti(IRE) Castagnette III (FR) (Tin Soldier (FR))
2226^{7}
2859^{2} (3030)
3750a^{2} (4133) 4789^{8} **(5475a)**

Une Bonne Fois (FR) *M Rolland* 116h 101c
6 b m Muhtathir Escomptee (FR) (Roi De Rome (USA))
559a^{4}

Une Des Bieffes (FR) *Michael Scudamore* 78h
6 b m Le Fou(IRE) Belle D'Ecajeul (FR) (Le Nain Jaune (FR))
70^{5} 241^{P} 690^{F} 1320^{10} 2541^{P}

Unefille De Guye (FR) *Victor Dartnall* 79h
6 bb m Voix Du Nord(FR) Mascotte De Guye (FR) (Video Rock (FR))
35^{4} 462^{7} 2022^{2} 2463^{U} 2689^{7} 2906^{9} 5177^{13}

Unekaina (FR) *E Lecoiffier* 76c
6 b m Lost World(IRE) Little County (FR) (Art Francais (USA))
198a^{6}

Une Vague (FR) *E Leenders* 125h 126c
6 b m Voix Du Nord(FR) Nouvelle Vague (FR) (Ragmar (FR))
1901a^{6}

Unex Canaletto *James Ewart* 99h
5 b g Motivator Logic (Slip Anchor)
(168) 2936^{7} 3475^{4}

Unex Modigliani (IRE) *Dan Skelton* 112h
5 ch g Hurricane Run(IRE) Chronicle (Observatory (USA))
4758^{2} 5400^{3}

Unexpected *Donald McCain* 23b
6 ch g Cat Daddy Updown (Sir Harry Lewis (USA))
1392^{4}

Unex Picasso *Barry Murtagh* 103h
6 b g Galileo(IRE) Ruff Shod (USA) (Storm Boot (USA))
(476)

Unforgettable (IRE) *Robin Dickin* 124h 125c
11 b g Norwich Miss Lulu (IRE) (King Luthier)
236^{2} 520^{2} 735^{6}

Un Guet Apens (FR) *James Ewart* 118h 135c
6 b g Enrique Belisama (FR) (Mansonnien (FR))
2222^{3} 3204^{3} (3272)
4833^{3} 4955^{2} (5213)
5557^{4}

Unidexter (IRE) *Sheena West* 89h
4 br g Footstepsinthesand Run To Jane (IRE) (Doyoun)
1624^{3} 1743^{3} 2276^{3} 2577^{6}

Unik De Nougi (FR) *Tom George* 83h 91c
6 b g Califet(FR) Gracieuse De Nouji (FR) (Port Etienne (FR))
1939^{10}

Union Du Chenet (FR) *Nicky Henderson* 95h 104c
6 b g Kahyasi Tchela (FR) (Le Nain Jaune (FR))
417^{5} 2755^{12} 4105^{P}

Unioniste (FR) *Paul Nicholls* 117h 161c
6 gr g Dom Alco(FR) Gleep Will (FR) (Laniste)
2229^{3} (2938)
3376a^{8} 3897^{3} 5170^{8}

Union Jack D'Ycy (FR) *Venetia Williams* 104h 127c
6 b g Bonnet Rouge(FR) Jacady (FR) (Fill My Hopes (FR))
2889^{P} (3858)
4190^{U} 4402^{3} 4704^{7} 5184^{U}

Union Saint (FR) *James Frost* 130h
6 b g Saint Des Saints(FR) Us Et Coutumes (FR) (Shining Steel)
(336) 409^{2} 1195^{4} 2630^{10} 3130^{P} 3744^{7} 3989^{8}

Unique D'Ainay (FR) *F-M Cottin* 106h 112c
6 b m Assessor(IRE) Nuit Noire (FR) (Sleeping Car (FR))
263a^{4} **454a^{2}**

United Park (FR) *G Macaire* 126h 133c
6 b g Antarctique(IRE) Goldoulyssa (FR) (Cadoudal (FR))
838a^{2} 1984a^{4} 2415a^{P}

Universe Of Gracie (GER) *Petr Juranek*
9 b g Pentire Ulanowa (GER) (Kamiros (IRE))
1904a^{4}

Un Jour D Ete (FR) *Nick Littmoden* 57h
6 b m Dano-Mast Hasta Manana (FR) (Useful (FR))
2190^{9} 2978^{P}

Unknown Legend (IRE) *Anthony Middleton* 101h
7 b g Heron Island(IRE) Late Call (IRE) (Callernish)
2197^{8} 2659^{7} 3225^{4} 4700^{12} 5069^{P} 5242^{8} 5436^{3}

Unknown Rebel (IRE) *Donald McCain* 131h
6 b g Night Shift(USA) Crystalline Stream (FR) (Polish Precedent (USA))
1148^{7}

Unmoothaj *Pam Sly* 50h
4 b g Green Desert(USA) Sundus (USA) (Sadler's Wells (USA))
1781^{5}

Un Noble (FR) *Nicky Richards* 85b
4 gr g Near Honor(GER) Noble Gary (FR) (Loup Solitaire (USA))
5219^{5}

Uno Valoroso (FR) *Mark Walford* 61h
6 b g Voix Du Nord(FR) Danse D'Avril (FR) (Quart De Vin (FR))
221^{P} 5521^{7}

Unowhatimeanharry *Helen Nelmes* 114h
6 b g Sir Harry Lewis(USA) Red Nose Lady (Teenoso (USA))
2272^{3} 2740^{3} 4171^{3} 4441^{5} 4969^{3}

Un Reve Du Granval (FR) *D Sourdeau De Beauregard*
6 ch g Malinas(GER) Apple Mille (FR) (Apple Tree (FR))
198a^{P}

Unrykikipeu (FR) *J Thibault*
6 ch g East Of Heaven(IRE) Voltige A L'Ouest (FR) (El Condor (FR))
454a^{P}

Unsist (FR) *Nick Gifford* 68h 41c
6 bb g Shaanmer(IRE) Niqita (FR) (Subotica (FR))
1270^{14} 1525^{3} 1625^{10} 2008^{8} **2741^{4} 3048^{P}**

Un Temps Pour Tout (IRE) *David Pipe* 156h
5 b g Robin Des Champs(FR) Rougedespoir (FR) (Bonnet Rouge (FR))
2414a^{3} 3778^{2} (4261)

Untilla Legend *Alex Hales* 69b
6 ch g Midnight Legend Tilla (Bin Ajwaad (IRE))
2254^{9}

Until Midnight (IRE) *Alexandra Dunn*
4 b g Moss Vale(IRE) Emma's Star (ITY) (Darshaan)
1624^{P} 1855^{P}

Until The Man (IRE) *Natalie Lloyd-Beavis* 69h
7 b g Tillerman Canoe Cove (IRE) (Grand Lodge (USA))
264^{16} 852^{10} 927^{12} 2105^{11} 5143^{2}

Unzing (FR) *F Nicolle* 119h 122c
6 b g Voix Du Nord(FR) Magik (FR) (Kadalko (FR))
454a^{5}

Up And Go (FR) *Donald McCain* 147h 118c
6 ch g Martaline Santoria (FR) (Limnos (JPN))
2658^{4} 3057^{4} 4367^{2} 4833^{5}

Up And Go Banbou (FR) *Mme V Seignoux* 88h
6 b g Robin Des Pres(FR) Lady Banbou (FR) (Useful (FR))
455a^{P}

Upazo (FR) *W P Mullins* 145h
6 b g Enrique Honey (FR) (Highlanders (FR))
3644^{3} 4785^{22} 5200a^{P}

Upbeat Cobbler (FR) *Henry Daly* 102h 90c
6 gr m Brier Creek(USA) Jade De Chalamont (FR) (Royal Charter (FR))
(2193) 2663^{7} 3413^{7} 4508^{6}
5246^{5}

Upepito (FR) *Venetia Williams* 110h 122c
6 b g Khalkevi(IRE) Friandise II (FR) (Mistigri)
3738^{3} 4053^{6} 5530a^{2}

Up For An Oscar (IRE) *Kim Bailey* 123h 134c
7 b g Oscar(IRE) Queen Of Harts (IRE) (Phardante (FR))
(185) 606^{F} 1398^{8} 1634^{2} (1752) 1956^{5} ◆ 5372^{P}

Upham Atom *Kate Buckett* 102h 131c
11 b g Silver Patriarch(IRE) Upham Lady (Bustino)
2798^{15}
2909^{F} 4516^{4}
4962^{9} (5334)

Upham Running (IRE) *Kate Buckett* 79h
6 b g Definite Article Tara Brooch (IRE) (Supreme Leader)
298^{5} 3092^{F} 3988^{7} 4535^{P} 4959^{9} 5262^{13}

Up In Flames (IRE) *Martin Keighley* 40h
5 b g Red Clubs(IRE) Flames (Blushing Flame (USA))
47^{5} 266^{6}

Uppercut De L'Orne (FR) *Donald McCain* 92h 90c
6 ch g Kapgarde(FR) Murcie (FR) (Epervier Bleu)
345^{4} 2337^{4} 2732^{7} 3278^{7} **4082^{7} 4744^{4}**

Upper Deck (IRE) *Richard Phillips* 80h 67c
9 b g Beckett(IRE) Princess Accord (USA) (D'Accord (USA))
692^{5} 965^{P} 1405^{5} **1548^{5} 1701^{4} 2082^{P}**

Uppertown Cave (IRE) *Donald McCain* 114b
5 b g Court Cave(IRE) Newtown Charlie (IRE) (Welsh Term)
(3500) 4205^{4} 4832^{F}

Uppingham *Malcolm Jefferson* 120h
5 ch g Doyen(IRE) Karakul (IRE) (Persian Bold)
731^{4} 2627^{2} 3063^{3} 3602^{2} 3877^{3}

Upsala Collonges (FR) *G Cherel* 119c
6 gr g Dom Alco(FR) Ivresse Collonges (FR) (Video Rock (FR))
454a^{3} 1984a^{P}

Upsie (FR) *W P Mullins* 147h
6 b m Le Balafre(FR) Medjie (FR) (Cyborg (FR))
3403a^{4} 3790a^{4} 5471a^{3}

Upsilon Bleu (FR) *Pauline Robson* 144h 145c
6 b g Panoramic Glycine Bleue (FR) (Le Nain Jaune (FR))
2359^{3} 2800^{4} 3476^{4} 3894^{2} 4237^{2}
5275^{3}

Upswing (IRE) *Jonjo O'Neill* 133h
6 b g Beneficial Native Country (IRE) (Be My Native (USA))
(2032) 2490^{6} 2949^{4} 3292^{F} (4144)

Up The Ante (IRE) *Fergal O'Brien*
6 b g Royal Anthem(USA) Mags Benefit (IRE) (Beneficial)
2659^{P}

Up The Bees *Philip Kirby* 106b
4 b g Kayf Tara West River (USA) (Gone West (USA))
(5063)

Up To (FR) *T Poche* 92h 74c
6 ch g Acambaro(GER) Cate Bleue (FR) (Katowice (FR))
454a^{P}

Up To Al (IRE) *John Wainwright* 67b
6 b g Heron Island(IRE) Pretonic (Precocious)
1690^{8} 1877^{8}

Upton Mead (IRE) *Kevin Tork* 72h 110c
7 b g Jimble(FR) Inchinnan (Inchinor)
7^{6} 245^{5} 305^{2} 489^{2} 542^{2} 1526^{P} (2003)
2270^{2} 2370^{3} 2567^{4} 2911^{5}
3246^{2} 3470^{R}
(3555) 3730^{7}

Upton Oaks *Chris Down* 88h
8 b g Sir Harry Lewis(USA) Copper Valley (Nearly A Hand)
156^{2} 410^{6} (Dead)

Upton Wood *Chris Down* 106h
8 ch g Fleetwood(IRE) Miss Counsel (Leading Counsel (USA))
1941^{2} 3044^{4} 4132^{P} 5179^{P}

Up To Something (FR) *Charlie Longsdon* 132h 142c
6 b g Brier Creek(USA) Evane (FR) (Lute Antique (FR))
(1849)
2211^{2} 2799^{2} 3185^{4} 3873^{5} 4742^{11}

Up To The Mark *Miss V Collins* 73b 120c
9 b g Mark Of Esteem(IRE) Villella (Sadler's Wells (USA))
92^{5} 674^{9} 1108^{2} 1319^{6} **1577^{5} 5491^{P}**

Upwelling (FR) *J-P Gallorini* 112h 134c
6 b g Robin Des Pres(FR) Idylle Du Marais (FR) (Panoramic)
1984a^{3}

Up Your Game (IRE) *Seamus Mullins* 63h
6 b g Milan Katie Snurge (IRE) (Snurge)
79^{P}

Uramazin (IRE) *Philip Hide* 92h
8 ch g Danehill Dancer(IRE) Uriah (GER) (Acatenango (GER))
1779^{6} 2215^{6}

Urano (FR) *W P Mullins* 132h
6 b g Enrique Neiland (FR) (Cyborg (FR))
4523a^{6} 5200a^{7}

Urbain De Sivola (FR) *Paul Nicholls* 142h 142c
6 ch g Le Fou(IRE) Neva De Sivola (FR) (Blushing Flame (USA))
2951^{2}
3259^{3} ◆ 4789^{4}

Urban Hymn (FR) *Malcolm Jefferson* 141h
6 b g Robin Des Champs(FR) Betty Brune (FR) (Dark Stone (FR))
(2254) ◆ 2659^{2} (3417) ◆ (3896) 4786^{7}

Urban Kode (IRE) *Lucinda Russell* 102h
6 b g Kodiac Urbanize (USA) (Chester House (USA))
342^{F} 681^{5}

Urcalin (FR) *David Arbuthnot* 118h
6 b g Network(GER) Caline So (FR) (Port Etienne (FR))
82^{F} 2828^{8} 3648^{6} 5030^{F}

Uriah Heep (FR) *Alan King* 116h
5 b g Danehill Dancer(IRE) Canasita (Zafonic (USA))
1779^{2} 2271^{2} 2474^{P}

Urkashe (FR) *E Lecoiffier* 95h 127c
6 b m Clety(FR) Meralda (FR) (Baby Turk)
5425a^{4}

Urlanie (FR) *Mme A-E Gareau*
6 b m Turbo Jet(FR) Melanie Du Chenet (FR) (Nikos)
131a^{P}

Urticaire (FR) *W P Mullins* 136h
6 b m Mister Sacha(FR) Opium Des Mottes (FR) (April Night (FR))
3403a^{5} 4846a^{2} 5199a^{3}

Ussee (FR) *Ben Case* 106h
6 gr m Vangelis(USA) Duchesse Pierji (FR) (Cadoudal (FR))
4377^{3} 4698^{5} 5112^{2} 5449^{P}

Ustica (IRE) *Philip Kirby* 107b
4 b g Trans Island Shady's Wish (IRE) (Lancastrian)
(4611)

Utaly (FR) *Michael Roberts* 45b
6 b g Shaanmer(IRE) Nataly (FR) (Ragmar (FR))
1771^{9}

Ute Antique (FR) *Ferdy Murphy* 27h
6 b m Robin Des Pres(FR) Joie De Cotte (FR) (Lute Antique (FR))
803^{P}

Ut Majeur Aulmes (FR) *Victor Dartnall* 123h 128c
6 ch g Northern Park(USA) My Wish Aulmes (FR) (Lyphard's Wish (FR))
2366^{8} (3012) 3744^{3} 4278^{9}
5073^{2} (5511)

Utopian (FR) *David Dunsdon* 118h 125c
6 ch g Kapgarde(FR) Djeti (FR) (Boyatino (FR))
(5435)

Utopian *Rose Dobbin* 102h
5 b g Rock Of Gibraltar(IRE) Idealistic (IRE) (Unfuwain (USA))
1854^{4} 2499^{9} 3330^{6} 4548^{4} 4811^{4} 5357^{7}

Utopie Des Bordes (FR) *Nicky Henderson* 143h 118c
6 b m Antarctique(IRE) Miss Berry (FR) (Cadoudal (FR))
2371^{4} 2672^{2} ◆ 2949^{5} 3319^{4} 3770^{5} 4765^{11}
5138^{5}

Uxizandre (FR) *Alan King* 133h 162c
6 ch g Fragrant Mix(IRE) Jolisandre (FR) (Dear Doctor (FR))
(2005)
(2565) 4400^{5} 4764^{2} (5137)

Vacario (GER) *Brian Barr* 36h
10 br g Acatenango(GER) Vaillance (GER) (Dashing Blade)
193^{P}

Vagner (FR) *Tom George* 38b
5 b g Voix Du Nord(FR) Evane (FR) (Lute Antique (FR))
3656^{9}

Vaihau (FR) *Jonjo O'Neill* 113h
5 br g Lavirco(GER) Niponne (FR) (Funny Baby (FR))
4421^{6} ◆

Vaillant Creek (FR) *Alex Hales* 67h
5 b g Brier Creek(USA) Ker Marie (FR) (Esprit Du Nord (USA))
3872^{17} 4863^{7}

Valantino Oyster (IRE) *Tracy Waggott* 71h
7 b g Pearl Of Love(IRE) Mishor (Slip Anchor)
1419^{P}

Valco De Touzaine (FR) *Paul Nicholls* 128h 135c
5 gr g Dom Alco(FR) Narcisse De Touzaine (FR) (Roi De Rome (USA))
1698^2 (2227)
(2558) 3202^2 4159^3 5275^F

Val D'Allier (FR) *Jim Old* 110h
5 b g Special Kaldoun(IRE) Exlilie (FR) (Royal Charter (FR))
1820^2 4377^6 4906^P

Val D'Arc (FR) *Philip Hobbs* 114h 125c
5 b g Le Balafre(FR) Lextrienne (FR) (Neustrien (FR))
5382^5

Valdez *Alan King* 141h 159c
7 ch g Doyen(IRE) Skew (Niniski (USA))
(2460)
(2811) ◆ (3893) ◆ 4737^5 5273^2

Valeur Ajoutee (FR) *E Leenders* 70c
6 ch m Polish Summer Grande Souveraine (FR) (Sillery (USA))
198a^7

Valid Point (IRE) *Jim Old* 121h 121c
8 b g Val Royal(FR) Ricadonna (Kris)
(2314)
3011^5 4780^2 5121^4

Valid Reason *Dean Ivory* 126h
7 b g Observatory(USA) Real Trust (USA) (Danzig (USA))
2366^2 2798^{11} 3186^9 *4302^5* 4423^P 4662^P

Valkov *Tony Carroll* 81h
7 b m Val Royal(FR) Petrikov (IRE) (In The Wings)
592^6

Vallani (IRE) *Lucinda Russell* 80h
9 ch m Vettori(IRE) Hecuba (Hector Protector (USA))
628^P 1874^6 2789^4 2999^3 3520^P 4461^{11}

Valleyofmilan (IRE) *Donald McCain* 119h 109c
7 b g Milan Ikdam Valley (IRE) (Ikdam)
(280) 737^3 902^6 **(1074)**
1291^P 1549^4

Valley Road *Tim Dennis* 26b
6 b m Grape Tree Road Vallingale (IRE) (Strong Gale)
324^9 3289^R

Valnamixe Du Mee (FR) *Robert Johnson* 65b
5 b g Al Namix(FR) Kateline Du Mee (FR) (Panoramic)
4611^{13} 5324^6

Valona Star *Nick Ayliffe*
6 b m Man Among Men(IRE) Valona Valley (IRE) (Reprimand)
3049^{11}

Valoroso *Richard Woollacott* 96b 135c
9 b g Laveron Millennium Rose (IRE) (Roselier (FR))
2812^5 ◆ 3321^2 3780^6

Valrene *Robin Dickin* 106h
8 b m Grape Tree Road Across The Water (Slip Anchor)
4157^P 4508^P 4865^6 5283^2

Valseur Du Granval (FR) *Tom George* 83h
5 b g Della Francesca(USA) La Grande Vallee (FR) (Chef De Clan (FR))
2053^7 3034^{13}

Valseur Lido (FR) *W P Mullins* 145h
5 b g Anzillero(GER) Libido Rock (FR) (Video Rock (FR))
(3215a) 4736^{10} ◆ (5201a)

Val Sugana (IRE) *P Favero*
7 b m King's Theatre(IRE) Alaska Star (IRE) (Danehill (USA))
1683a^F

Value At Risk *Philip Fenton* 132b
5 b g Kayf Tara Miss Orchestra (IRE) (Orchestra)
4756^{13}

Van Diemens Land (USA) *Charlie Mann* 112h
7 b g Arch(USA) Trylko (USA) (Diesis)
289^8 488^3 852^9 997^7 1203^8

Vandross (IRE) *Neil King* 114h
4 b g Iffraaj Mrs Kanning (Distant View (USA))
3003^3 (3245) 3768^3 4112^3 4755^{14} 5090^U 5455^4

Vaniteux (FR) *Nicky Henderson* 150h
5 br g Voix Du Nord(FR) Expoville (FR) (Video Rock (FR))
(2947) 3258^4 (4102) ◆ 4736^3

Van Mildert (IRE) *Evelyn Slack* 51h
5 b m Observatory(USA) Vanilla Delight (IRE) (Orpen (USA))
75^B

Vapiano (IRE) *David Pipe* 107h 120c
8 b g Cape Cross(IRE) Nasij (USA) (Elusive Quality (USA))
1087^4 1551^P

Vardas Supreme (IRE) *Richard Drake* 70c
11 b g Beneficial Mrs Supreme (IRE) (Supreme Leader)
1876^7 2048^P 2338^6 2518^6 3020^6 3180^5 3528^5

Varene De Vauzelle (FR) *James Ewart* 90h
5 b g Assessor(IRE) Laureine (FR) (Sleeping Car (FR))
2795^3 4902^5 5205^F 5554^6

Varom (FR) *Paul Nicholls* 115h
5 gr g Charming Groom(FR) Morava (FR) (Perrault)
2225^2 2659^5 3872^5

Vasco Du Mee (FR) *Gordon Elliott* 115h 110c
5 b g Goldneyev(USA) British Nellerie (FR) (Le Pontet (FR))
790^5 **4202^2**

Vasco Du Ronceray (FR) *Nicky Henderson* 140h
5 gr g Al Namix(FR) Landza De Ronceray (FR) (Chamberlin (FR))
5172^8 5574^4

Vasco D'Ycy (FR) *Sarah Humphrey* 114h
5 b g Equerry(USA) Ingrid Des Mottes (FR) (Useful (FR))
2230^4 2671^{12} 3471^4 4579^3 5059^P

Vasco Pierji (FR) *Donald McCain* 98h
5 b g Sleeping Car(FR) Angelina (FR) (Brezzo (FR))
682^2 2871^3 3495^6 3781^8 4081^3 4834^7

Vauban Du Seuil (FR) *Harry Fry* 85h
5 b g Epalo(GER) Parika Du Seuil (FR) (Blushing Flame (USA))
3783^P 4987^4 5305^5

Vauban Laugil (FR) *C Aubert* 109h 91c
5 b g Tirwanako(FR) Capucine De Baudan (FR) (Italic (FR))
2464a^2

Vautour (FR) *W P Mullins* 158h
5 b g Robin Des Champs(FR) Gazelle De Mai (FR) (Dom Pasquini (FR))
(3667a) (4180a) ◆ (4736) ◆

Va'Vite (IRE) *Anthony Middleton* 126h
7 b m Vinnie Roe(IRE) Presenting Shares (IRE) (Presenting)
244^2 (353) 386^2 (901) 1045^5 1818^4 1956^{11} 2371^{12}

Vaxalco (FR) *J H Culloty* 117h
5 gr g Dom Alco(FR) Galaxie I (FR) (Useful (FR))
5574^6

Vazaro Delafayette (FR) *David Pipe* 96h
5 bl g Robin Des Champs(FR) Etoile Du Merze (FR) (If De Merze (FR))
1974^3 2375^4 2802^9 3166^8

Veauce De Sivola (FR) *Nick Williams* 125h
5 b g Assessor(IRE) Eva De Chalamont (FR) (Iron Duke (FR))
703a^5 2087^{12} **3615^F** 3989^5 (4516) ◆

Vedani (IRE) *Tony Carroll* 112h
5 b g Dalakhani(IRE) Velandia (IRE) (Sadler's Wells (USA))
2210^8 2492^8 3597^5 5294^P

Veinard De Ballon (FR) *D Retif* 109h 87c
6 gr g Clety(FR) Trysquel (FR) (Tel Quel (FR))
455a^6
5530a^6

Velator *Anthony Honeyball* 119h 133c
7 b g Old Vic Jupiter's Message (Jupiter Island)
296^P 1944^6 5126^P

Veloce (IRE) *Donald McCain* 117h 100c
6 b g Hurricane Run(IRE) Kiftsgate Rose (FR) (Nashwan (USA))
3328^5
3819^3 5251^8

Velvet Vic (IRE) *Richard Guest* 82h
8 b g Old Vic Elleena Rose (IRE) (Roselier (FR))
71^3 253^8 **601^P** 750^P

Venceremos *Charlie Longsdon* 100h
7 b m Generous(IRE) Miss Orchestra (IRE) (Orchestra)
91^F 502^5 2028^2 2663^{10} 4076^4

Vendor (FR) *Alan King* 139h 118c
6 gr g Kendor(FR) Village Rainbow (FR) (Village Star (FR))
356^{11} (2813) 4147^8 4752^{10} 5277^6

Vendredi Trois (FR) *Emma Lavelle* 69h
5 b g Shaanmer(IRE) Legende Sacree (FR) (Hawker's News (IRE))
239^5 2018^9 3166^{10}

Venetian Lad *Lydia Richards* 97h 115c
9 ro g Midnight Legend Henrietta Holmes (IRE) (Persian Bold)
96^U 542^P 2017^3 2567^2 4440^5 4809^3 5023^2

Venez Horace (FR) *Giles Smyly* 15h
5 b g Polish Summer Fripperie (FR) (Bojador (FR))
2026^9 2703^5 3716^9

Venir Rouge *Harry Whittington* 81h 102c
10 ch g Dancing Spree(USA) Al Awaalah (Mukaddamah (USA))
188^6

Vent Sombre (FR) *G Cherel* 124h 127c
5 b g Network(GER) Ode Rock (FR) (Video Rock (FR))
1742a^7 5425a^7

Venture To War (IRE) *Tony Coyle* 89h 95c
8 ch m Wareed(IRE) Wayward Venture (IRE) (Mister Mat (FR))
17^P 110^6

Verano (GER) *Charlie Mann* 110h
5 ch g Lord Of England(GER) Vive La Vie (GER) (Big Shuffle (USA))
4529^4 4988^3

Vera's Article (IRE) *Raymond York* 94b
6 b m Definite Article Nut Eile (IRE) (Torus)
5374^8 ◆

Veratan (FR) *Venetia Williams* 94h
7 b g Sinndar(IRE) Vermentina (IRE) (Darshaan)
2040^7 2507^{10} 2614^{10} 3157^6 3420^{10} 4071^2

Verdasco (FR) *Donald McCain* 84h
5 b g Sassanian(USA) Babolna (FR) (Tropular)
4043^{10} 5296^9 5479^7

Vergality Ridge (IRE) *Ronald Harris* 70h
4 gr g Verglas(IRE) Phoenix Factor (IRE) (Indian Ridge)
1335^2 1439^6 1743^6

Verko (FR) *Micky Hammond* 81h
5 br g Lavirco(GER) Lady Vernizy (FR) (Video Rock (FR))
5296^7 5354^4 ◆

Vermouth Bleu (FR) *Jonjo O'Neill* 111h
5 b g Network(GER) Jacinthe Bleue (FR) (Ghost Buster'S (FR))
2900^4 3175^7 3602^6 4350^2 4838^8

Vertueux (FR) *Tony Carroll* 91h 50c
9 gr g Verglas(IRE) Shahrazad (FR) (Bering)
852^P 1816^4 **2039^7 2562^5** 2898^6 5189^3

Verve Argent (FR) *Paul Webber* 84b
5 gr g Fragrant Mix(IRE) Devise II (FR) (Djarvis (FR))
4909^7 5409^7

Very Heaven (FR) *G Cherel* 93h 122c
5 b g Khalkevi(IRE) Hawai De Vonnas (FR) (Cadoudal (FR))
5425a^8

Very Noble (FR) *Paul Nicholls* 116h
5 b g Martaline Isati'S (FR) (Chamberlin (FR))
309^3 1869^9 2369^5 2761^7 *(4493)* 5003^3 5305^2 5526^2

Very Stylish (IRE) *Jonjo O'Neill* 88h 93c
10 b g Winged Love(IRE) Native Craft (IRE) (Be My Native (USA))
481^{11} 766^5 972^P 2179^6 2394^9 2902^P 5293^6

Very Wood (FR) *Noel Meade* 153h
5 b g Martaline Ball Of Wood (FR) (Cadoudal (FR))
2407a^2 2852a^5 3559a^3 (4786)

Vesperal Dream (FR) *Paul Nicholls* 113h 103c
5 bl g Network(GER) Pampanilla (FR) (April Night (FR))
1857^6 2287^6 5140^2
5573^7

Vesper Bell (IRE) *W P Mullins* 141h 148c
8 b g Beneficial Fair Choice (IRE) (Zaffaran (USA))
2937^F 3655^U 3868a^9 5171^{13}

Vesuvhill (FR) *Ben Case* 94b
5 ch g Sabrehill(USA) L'Orchidee (FR) (Gunboat Diplomacy (FR))
3863^6 4473^4

Vexillum (IRE) *Simon Hodgson* 103h
5 br g Mujadil(USA) Common Cause (Polish Patriot (USA))
8^2 ◆ (155) 631^8 858^9 1429^5 2250^5 2628^4 3290^6 5143^{10}

Veyranno (FR) *Tom George* 64h
5 bb g Anzillero(GER) Nheyranne (FR) (Sheyrann (IRE))
2773^5 3166^{12} 3838^7 4758^{12}

Via Archimede (USA) *Lucinda Russell* 96h 86c
9 ch g Hussonet(USA) Azarina (IRE) (Kenmare (FR))
750^3 799^3 868^5
1163^8

Viacometti (FR) *Tom George* 87h
5 gr g Alberto Giacometti(IRE) L'Epi (FR) (Great Palm (USA))
(345) 2354^5 2933^6 3163^{17} 3602^9 5016^9

Via Sundown (FR) *Gary Moore* 109h 144c
6 ch g Until Sundown(USA) Via Fratina (FR) (Mansonnien (FR))
2267^F (2730)
(3097) 3651^4 (4439)

Vibrato Valtat (FR) *Paul Nicholls* 140h
5 gr g Voix Du Nord(FR) La Tosca Valtat (FR) (Dom Alco (FR))
174^2 2492^5 2947^2 3322^2 (4173) 4682^3 (5250)

Vicator *Anthony Honeyball* 69h
6 b g Old Vic Jupiter's Message (Jupiter Island)
140^{16} 5114^3

Vice Et Vertu (FR) *Henry Daly* 130h
5 b g Network(GER) Duchesse Du Cochet (FR) (Native Guile (USA))
(2286) (3106) 4005^4 4680^{12}

Vicente (FR) *Paul Nicholls* 133h
5 b g Dom Alco(FR) Ireland (FR) (Kadalko (FR))
2109^4 4514^2 (4991) 5252^P

Vicenzo Mio (FR) *Paul Nicholls* 137h
4 b c Corri Piano(FR) Sweet Valrose (FR) (Cadoudal (FR))
3078^4 (3317) 3885^3

Vicky De L'Oasis (FR) *W P Mullins* 137h
5 b m Ultimately Lucky(IRE) Japonaise III (FR) (Signe Divin (USA))
2810^3 3804a^2 4456a^2

Vicky's Charm (IRE) *Barry Brennan* 103b
5 b m Old Vic Sweet Charm (IRE) (Glacial Storm (USA))
5077^2

Vicky Valentine *Alistair Whillans* 61h
4 b f Rock Of Gibraltar(IRE) Silcasue (Selkirk (USA))
2592^4

Vico (IRE) *Ali Brewer* 107h 118c
10 b g Old Vic Over The Glen (IRE) (Over The River (FR))
2755^{10} 4700^6 (5436)

Vicpol (ITY) *Tom Gretton* 63h
8 b g Poliglote Vehota Vic (Old Vic)
253^9 1170^P 1635^7

Vics Canvas (IRE) *Dermot Anthony McLoughlin* 145h
11 b g Old Vic Oilpainting (IRE) (Welsh Term)
4765^F

Vic's Moll (IRE) *Polly Gundry* 39h
8 b m Old Vic Winning Molly (IRE) (Maramouresh (IRE))
717^{12} 828^U

Victor Hewgo *Keith Reveley* 129h 143c
9 b g Old Vic Pennys Pride (IRE) (Pips Pride)
3601^2 (3873)
4344^2 (4541)
5170^P

Victoria Rose (IRE) *Richard Woollacott* 5h 20c
9 b m Old Vic West Hill Rose (IRE) (Roselier (FR))
248^4

Victor Leudorum (IRE) *Charlie Mann* 115h 130c
7 b g Wareed(IRE) Rock Garden (IRE) (Bigstone (IRE))
9^4 1085^2 (1262)
1425^4 2065^P

Victor Lynch (IRE) *Philip Kirby* 111h
8 b g Old Vic Jmember (IRE) (Jurado (USA))
556^P

Victors Serenade (IRE) *Anthony Honeyball* 121h 147c
9 b g Old Vic Dantes Serenade (IRE) (Phardante (FR))
2388^2 **3655^P**

Victory Gunner (IRE) *Richard Lee* 122h 120c
16 ch g Old Vic Gunner B Sharp (Gunner B)
3730^{10} 4396^3 4678^3 5039^2

Victrix Gale (IRE) *A J Martin* 136h 135c
8 b m Presenting Ballyclough Gale (IRE) (Strong Gale)
851^7 2487^4

Vic Venturi (IRE) *Adrian Wintle* 101h 123c
14 ch g Old Vic Carmen Lady (Torus)
(323) **660^P**
2033^2

Vide Cave (FR) *Paul Nicholls* 106h
5 b g Secret Singer(FR) Kenna (FR) (Epervier Bleu)
2196^6

Vieux Lion Rouge (FR) *David Pipe* 141h
5 ch g Sabiango(GER) Indecise (FR) (Cyborg (FR))
(3747) (3988) (4379) 4789^{21} 5347^3

Vieux Morvan (FR) *G Cherel* 119h 127c
5 b g Voix Du Nord(FR) Moskoville (FR) (Kadalko (FR))
2263a^6

Vif Argent (FR) *David Pipe* 126h 129c
5 b g Dom Alco(FR) Formosa (FR) (Royal Charter (FR))
1971^{12} 2694^P 3065^{15} 3362^P (4502)
5126^5 5385^F

Vigil (IRE) *D K Weld* 134b
5 b g Dansili Magnolia Lane (IRE) (Sadler's Wells (USA))
4756^5

Vikekhal (FR) *Gary Moore* 111h
5 b g Khalkevi(IRE) Gesse Parade (FR) (Dress Parade)
1770^4 2216^{10} 2642^7 (3134) 4069^5 5125^4

Viking Blond (FR) *Sophie Leech* 110h 110c
9 ch g Varese(FR) Sweet Jaune (FR) (Le Nain Jaune (FR))
1956^{14}
2491^U 2943^6 4271^P 5066^5 (5183)

Viking Chief (IRE) *John Wade* 91h
7 b g Westerner Diamond Sal (Bob Back (USA))
4811^U 5050^3 5295^4

Viking Mistress *Martin Keighley* 39h
6 b m Bollin Eric Mistress Caramore (IRE) (Moscow Society (USA))
462^8 2368^7 2752^6 5300^9

Viking Rebel (IRE) *W T Reed* 118h 111c
12 b g Taipan(IRE) Clodagh's Dream (Whistling Deer)
4042^7 (4837)

Viking Splash (IRE) *David Kemp* 95b 103c
11 b g Stowaway Honey Mustard (IRE) (Roselier (FR))
3801^3

Vilja (IRE) *David Pipe* 98h
5 ch m Bach(IRE) Dapples (IRE) (Accordion)
2506^{13} 2907^4

Village Secret *Brian Barr* 10b
8 ch g Pasternak Daphne Odora (Elmaamul (USA))
2280^P 2457^P

Village Vic (IRE) *Philip Hobbs* 136h
7 b g Old Vic Etoile Margot (FR) (Garde Royale)
(1672)

Villa Royale *David O'Meara* 93h
5 b m Val Royal(FR) Villa Carlotta (Rainbow Quest (USA))
2514^6 2767^U

Villoresi (IRE) *John Quinn* 119h
5 b g Clodovil(IRE) Villafranca (IRE) (In The Wings)
2933^3 5057^2

Vimiero (USA) *Jonjo O'Neill* 113h
7 bb g Dynaformer(USA) Merrymaker (ARG) (Rainbow Corner)
(1475) 1562^3 1708^4 1860^2

Vinaigrette *Richard Phillips* 72b
5 b m Kayf Tara What A Vintage (IRE) (Un Desperado (FR))
5196^7

Vincitore (FR) *Miss C V Hart* 94h 102c
8 b g Starborough Viva Vodka (FR) (Crystal Glitters (USA))
(4915)

Vineman *David Bridgwater* 88b
7 b g Grape Tree Road Great Ovation (FR) (Boston Two Step (USA))
3194^5 4397^U 4513^P

Vinnie My Boy (IRE) *Peter Bowen* 128h
6 ch g Vinnie Roe(IRE) Copper Magic (IRE) (Zaffaran (USA))
511^3 669^2 (860) 933^8 1205^{12} 1597^7

Vinnie Red (IRE) *Evan Williams* 101b
5 ch g Vinnie Roe(IRE) Conzara (IRE) (Mandalus)
4547^3

Vinnie's Girl (IRE) *Martin Bosley* 85h
7 b m Vinnie Roe(IRE) Keralba (USA) (Sheikh Albadou)
29^P 598^4 860^{12}

Vinnieslittle Lamb (IRE) *David Bridgwater* 102h 94c
6 b m Vinnie Roe(IRE) Polar Lamb (IRE) (Brush Aside (USA))
1935^2 2193^3 2697^3 3010^6 3878^5
5246^3

Vinnie The Fish (IRE) *Brendan Powell* 121h
6 br g Vinnie Roe(IRE) Darwin Angel (IRE) (Presenting)
1255^{11} 1330^3 (1497) 1968^P

Vinnie The Pooh (IRE) *Nick Gifford* 98b
6 b g Vinnie Roe(IRE) Ministerial Model (IRE) (Shalford (IRE))
4810^5 ◆

Vinny Gambini (IRE) *Rose Dobbin* 117h
7 b g Vinnie Roe(IRE) Red Velvet (So Factual (USA))
(1977) (2838) 3286^P 4365^5 4834^8

Vino Griego (FR) *Gary Moore* 140h 158c
9 b g Kahyasi Vie De Reine (FR) (Mansonnien (FR))
1969^U 2503^F (2930)
3780^P 4145^P 4738^{13} 5170^2 ◆

Vinomore *Dianne Sayer* 44h 19c
8 b m Grape Tree Road Sillymore (Silly Prices)
4836^7 5189^4

Vinstar (FR) *Donald McCain* 110h
5 b g Charming Groom(FR) Kali Star (FR) (Tagel (USA))
22^8 1793^7 2156^5 2783^4 4102^4 (4980) 5377^4

Vintage Class (IRE) *Mrs Kayley Woollacott* 108c
11 b g Hernando(FR) Native Bid (IRE) (Be My Native (USA))
5127^P

Vintage Mag (FR) *F Nicolle* 106c
5 b g Polish Summer Fabuville (FR) (Fabulous Dancer (USA))
1465a^4

Vintage Red *Chris Bealby* 84h 51c
6 ch g Grape Tree Road Simply Stunning (Primitive Rising (USA))
183^7

Vintage Star (IRE) *Sue Smith* 130h 148c
8 b g Presenting Rare Vintage (IRE) (Germany (USA))
(2419)
2822[2] 3361[6] 3780[2] 4738[F] 5171[P]

Vintage Tea *Richard Woollacott* 96h 87c
7 b g Beat All(USA) Come To Tea (IRE) (Be My Guest (USA))
767[8] **2651[F]**
3176[6] 3696[P]

Vintage Vixon (IRE) *Tim Vaughan* 80h
7 b m Moscow Society(USA) Bar Un'que (IRE) (Un Desperado (FR))
2701[P] 5282[5]

Violet Dancer *Gary Moore* 124h
4 b g Bertolini(USA) Another Secret (Efisio)
(2276) (2927) 3360[3] 4111[4] 4755[10] 5132[9]

Violets Boy (IRE) *Brendan Powell* 113h 118c
7 br g King's Theatre(IRE) Sunshine Rays (Alflora (IRE))
698[2] 902[3] 1203[4]
(1282) 1470[3] 1636[4] 1830[6] 2270[3] 2762[6]

Violin Davis (FR) *Harry Fry* 110h 137c
8 b m Turgeon(USA) Trumpet Davis (FR) (Rose Laurel)
2244[4] 2812[8]

Virak (FR) *Paul Nicholls* 149h 107c
5 b g Bernebeau(FR) Nosika D'Airy (FR) (Oblat (FR))
2080[11]
434[7]
2601[3] (3786) (4333) 4789[6] 5349[4]

Virginia Ash (IRE) *Colin Tizzard* 113h
6 ch g Definite Article Peace Time Girl (IRE) (Buckskin (FR))
1744[U] 1831[P] 2288[7] 2458[7] 2798[10] 2944[7] (3691) 4144[5] 4393[7]

Virtuel D'Oudon (FR) *David Pipe* 124h
5 b g Network(GER) La Belle Illusion (FR) (Turgeon (USA))
(4473) (5024) 5332[2]

Vision De La Vie (FR) *Pauline Robson* 77h
4 ch g Sin Kiang(FR) Vidahermosa (FR) (Kahyasi)
3214[7] 4811[7] 5190[9] 5554[3]

Vision Des Champs (FR) *Gary Moore* 103h 105c
5 b g Saint Des Saints(FR) Manita Des Champs (FR) (Fabulous Dancer (USA))
4799[5]
5091[9] 5340[5] 5458[3]

Vision Of Judgment *Ollie Pears* 16h
4 b g Byron Glorious Colours (Spectrum (IRE))
785[7]

Vision Of Lights (IRE) *Bernard Llewellyn* 52h
9 b g Fantastic Light(USA) Kadassa (IRE) (Shardari)
434[7]

Vito De Beauchene (FR) *F Flood* 86h 86c
5 gr g Visionary(FR) Iranica De Laulne (FR) (Panoramic)
1139a[13]

Vittachi *Alistair Whillans* 76h
7 b g Bertolini(USA) Miss Lorilaw (FR) (Homme De Loi (IRE))
2360[6] 2794[3]

Vivaccio (FR) *Venetia Williams* 116h
5 b g Antarctique(IRE) Cybelle (FR) (Saint Cyrien (FR))
(703a) 3023[P] 4069[2] 4820[7] 5537[P]

Vivacissimo (IRE) *Yannick Fouin* 129h 108c
7 ch g Muhtathir Valley Orchard (FR) (Zilzal (USA))
263a[6]
559a[2] 1984a[P]

Viva Colonia (IRE) *Brian Ellison* 139h 147c
9 ch g Traditionally(USA) Ansariya (USA) (Shahrastani (USA))
1047[13] 2071[3] 2666[6] 2952[6] 3476[2] 4790[11] 5156[U] 5253[7]

Vivaldi Collonges (FR) *Paul Nicholls* 132h
5 b g Dom Alco(FR) Diane Collonges (FR) (El Badr)
2197[2] 3454[6] 4163[3] (5256) ◆

Viva Steve (IRE) *Mick Channon* 124h 112c
6 b g Flemensfirth(USA) Eluna (Unfuwain (USA))
2508[6] 3004[7] 4105[2] 4415[4]

Vivona Hill *Nicky Richards* 73h
10 b g Overbury(IRE) Lets Go Dutch (Nicholas Bill)
1145[6] 1797[P]

V Neck (IRE) *Paul Nicholls* 124h
5 b g Sir Harry Lewis(USA) Swift Settlement (King's Ride)
2566[2] 3173[2] 5128[4]

Vodka Moon *Sharon Watt* 87b
5 gr g Beat All(USA) Auntie Kathleen (Terimon)
1854[8]

Vodka 'n Tonic (IRE) *Nicky Henderson* 96h
5 b g Presenting Ballagh Dawn (IRE) (Buckskin (FR))
207[6] *2439[4]* *(4498)*

Vodkaontherocks (IRE) *Philip Hobbs* 67b
6 b g Oscar(IRE) My Native (IRE) (Be My Native (USA))
4844[9]

Vodka Red (IRE) *Robert Johnson* 99h
6 b g Ivan Denisovich(IRE) Begine (IRE) (Germany (USA))
21[5] 558[3] 1790[4] 2360[7] 3038[7] 3210[8] 4187[5] 4527[B] 4817[2] (5052)

Vodka Wells (FR) *Brian Ellison* 101h
4 b g Irish Wells(FR) Kahipiroska (FR) (Mansonnien (FR))
5568[11]

Voice From Above (IRE) *Patrick Holmes* 84h
5 b m Strategic Prince Basin Street Blues (IRE) (Dolphin Street (FR))
2309[6] 2514[8] 2883[8]

Voiladenuo (FR) *Guy Denuault* 133h 126c
5 b h Network(GER) Paresca (FR) (Maresca Sorrento (FR))
1983a[P] 2414a[8]

Volare (FR) *M Rolland* 104h 104c
5 b g Enrique Belle Attente (FR) (Cadoudal (FR))
703a[4] 1199a[12] **1465a[3]**

Volcan D'Oudairies (FR) *G Cherel*
5 gr g Madoun(FR) Java D'Oudairies (FR) (Cyborg (FR))
2464a[P]

Volcanic (FR) *Donald McCain* 125h 116c
5 b g Al Namix(FR) Queen Of Rock (FR) (Video Rock (FR))
(4627) 5102[5]

Volcanic Jack (IRE) *Michael Chapman* 85h
6 b g Kodiac Rosaria Panatta (IRE) (Mujtahid (USA))
1393[4] 1595[3] 1688[5] 1958[6] 2432[P] 2573[3] 2904[4] 3157[8]

Volcan Surprise (FR) *Caroline Fryer* 78h 118c
6 b g Dom Alco(FR) Invitee Surprise (FR) (April Night (FR))
387[5] 5435[3]

Volio Vincente (FR) *Carroll Gray* 62h 78c
7 bb g Corri Piano(FR) Vollore (FR) (Cadoudal (FR))
156[3] 519[10] 649[9]
1338[3] 1474[5] (1701)
2082[4] 2603[5] (2743) 4446[6] **4905[4] 5401[5]**

Volnay De Thaix (FR) *Nicky Henderson* 143h
5 ch g Secret Singer(FR) Mange De Thaix (FR) (Mont Basile (FR))
(2265) ◆ (2753) 3184[2] (4935) 5167[5]

Volo Mio *Chris Grant* 88h
7 b g Endoli(USA) Carol's Flight (Missed Flight)
2355[6]

Voltchesko (FR) *Robert Walford* 109h
5 b g Della Francesca(USA) Mass Media (FR) (Agent Bleu (FR))
2581[2] 2898[2] 4703[B]

Volt Face (FR) *David Pipe* 114h
5 ch g Kapgarde(FR) Jourenuit (FR) (Chamberlin (FR))
2667[4] 3175[5] 4632[5] (5120) 5349[11]

Von Galen (IRE) *Michael Scudamore* 103h 85c
13 b g Germany(USA) Castle Carrig (IRE) (Le Bavard (FR))
32[5] 692[P] (1825)
2313[P] 2702[2] 2829[5]

Vortex Star *Michael Chapman* 47b
5 gr g Dalakhani(IRE) Spinning The Yarn (Barathea (IRE))
3835[9] *4329[11]*

Vosges (FR) *James Ewart* 113h 119c
7 b g Turgeon(USA) Vanilla Sky (FR) (Kaldounevees (FR))
34[4] 314[5]

Vote For Doodle (IRE) *Liam Corcoran* 77h
9 ch g Subtle Power(IRE) Shuil Ash (IRE) (Norwich)
637[6] 1121[P]

Votez Pour Moi (FR) *G Macaire* 92h 130c
5 gr g Sacro Saint(FR) Biblique (FR) (Saint Cyrien (FR))
2263a[P]

Voyage A New York (FR) *Lucinda Russell* 118h
5 b g Kapgarde(FR) Pennsylvanie (FR) (Dadarissime (FR))
2037[9] 3781[5] 4199[2] (4832) 5354[2]

Vrombel (FR) *Jonjo O'Neill* 70b
5 b g Laveron Ombrelle (FR) (Octagonal (NZ))
1499[4]

Vujiyama (FR) *Jonjo O'Neill* 112h
5 br g Voix Du Nord(FR) Ili Dancer (FR) (Missolonghi (USA))
1793[3] 2189[8] 2614[4] 3012[5]

Vukovar (FR) *Harry Fry* 125h 148c
5 b g Voix Du Nord(FR) Noraland (FR) (Homme De Loi (IRE))
2976[2] ◆ (3368)
4764[7]

Vulcanite (IRE) *Charlie Longsdon* 140h 145c
7 b g Dubawi(IRE) Daraliya (IRE) (Kahyasi)
1969[11] 2433[5] 2951[13] 3200[15] (5067)

Vuvuzela *Rebecca Menzies* 107h
8 ch g Sir Harry Lewis(USA) Clair Valley (Ardross)
5319[3]

Waaheb (USA) *D K Weld* 146h
7 b g Elusive Quality(USA) Nafisah (IRE) (Lahib (USA))
4752[20]

Wabanaki Legend *Malcolm Jefferson* 57h
5 b m Fair Mix(IRE) Wuchowsen (IRE) (King's Ride)
3619[8] 5367[10]

Wacket Willie *J M B Cookson* 74c
8 b g Supreme Sound Pyewacket (Belfort (FR))
5165[R]

Waddingstown (IRE) *Lucinda Russell* 104b
5 ch g Presenting Ebony Queen (Classic Cliche (IRE))
4671[2] 5057[P]

Waddingtown Hero (IRE) *L M Power*
7 b g Subtle Power(IRE) Miss Liz (IRE) (Beneficial)
5123[U]

Wadham Hill *William Reed* 49h
12 b m Bandmaster(USA) Sport Of Fools (IRE) (Trojan Fen)
637[F] 1351[10]

Wadswick Court (IRE) *Charlie Longsdon* 135h
6 b g Court Cave(IRE) Tarasandy (IRE) (Arapahos (FR))
(1919) 2534[7] (3034) (3568) 4266[2]

Wagga Dee Dee (FR) *P-O Robert*
10 b g Wagon Master(FR) Diana Dee (Blakeney)
200a[8]

Wah Wah Taysee (IRE) *David Bridgwater* 87h 77c
7 b g Saddlers' Hall(IRE) Slieve Bernagh (IRE) (Phardante (FR))
2002[6] 2432[7] 2893[4]
4482[P] 4723[6] 5144[F] 5401[4]

Wait No More (IRE) *Neil Mulholland* 66h 105c
9 ch g Strategic Choice(USA) Tearaway Lady (IRE) (Tidaro (USA))
117[4] (689)
832[6] 1039[5] 1361[3] 1626[7] 4633[5] 4992[4] 5394[4]

Wakanda (IRE) *Sue Smith* 117h
5 b g Westerner Chanson Indienne (FR) (Indian River (FR))
1713[2] 2103[7] 3086[4] 3875[2]

Wak A Turtle (IRE) *Richard Woollacott* 76h 86c
6 b g Turtle Island(IRE) Playwaki (USA) (Miswaki (USA))
254[8] **1433[2]**
1530[3]

Wake Your Dreams (IRE) *Jennie Candlish* 123h
6 b g Oscar(IRE) Rose Karanja (Terimon)
(337) 563[2] 801[5] (1281) (1467) 5387[3]

Walcot Lathyrus *Richard Lee* 103h 109c
9 b g Alflora(IRE) Strong Cloth (IRE) (Strong Gale)
585[5] 763[P] 873[10] (1835)
2387[F]

Walden (IRE) *I R Ferguson* 126c
7 b g Winged Love(IRE) Huncheon Siss (IRE) (Phardante (FR))
4057[2] 4837[3]

Walden Prince (IRE) *Richard Lee* 106h 90c
7 b g Saffron Walden(FR) Kahyasi Princess (IRE) (Kahyasi)
251[P] **425[4]**
687[F] ◆ 1063[2] 5017[4] ◆

Waldorf Salad *Venetia Williams* 128h
6 b g Millenary Ismene (FR) (Bad Conduct (USA))
2210[15] 3420[3] (3878) (3955) 4662[4] 5252[P]

Waldsee (GER) *Paul Morgan*
9 b g Xaar Wurftaube (GER) (Acatenango (GER))
3174[P]

Walkabout Creek (IRE) *Steve Gollings* 133h 130c
7 b g Alderbrook La Mouette (USA) (Hawkster (USA))
2242[4] 2622[3] 3601[4] 5451[5]

Walkon (FR) *Alan King* 155h 155c
9 gr g Take Risks(FR) La Tirana (FR) (Akarad (FR))
2071[U] 4145[4] 5171[P]

Walk On Al (IRE) *Dan Skelton* 129h
6 b g Alflora(IRE) Wave Back (IRE) (Bob Back (USA))
2316[5] (3116) 3896[4] 4702[2] 5157[7]

Walk Sibo (FR) *D Windrif* 119h 132c
6 b g Balko(FR) Walk Sibir (FR) (Simon Du Desert (FR))
263a[P]

Walls Way *Tracey Barfoot-Saunt* 69h 85c
10 ch g Karinga Bay Wilming (Komaite (USA))
84[P] 1442[3]
1577[7] 1668[6]

Walser (IRE) *John Wade* 108h
7 b g Milan Brass Neck (IRE) (Supreme Leader)
2597[2] 3273[6] 3724[3] 5208[4] 5484[7]

Walter De La Mare (IRE) *Anabel K Murphy* 98h
7 b g Barathea(IRE) Banutan (IRE) (Charnwood Forest (IRE))
193[7] 903[10] (3264) 3856[4] 4107[3] 4398[3] 4597[2] 5012[3] 5302[3] 5459[P]

Walter Wallace (IRE) *S Flook* 95b
9 b g Chevalier(IRE) Ishaam (Selkirk (USA))
4355[P]

Walter White (IRE) *Philip Hobbs* 111h
4 b g Dark Angel(IRE) Fun Time (Fraam)
785[5] 975[5] (1193) (1473) 1536[2]

Waltham Abbey *Lynsey Kendall* 89h 77c
13 b g Relief Pitcher Flash-By (Ilium)
75[7] 803[3] 1073[7]

Waltz Darling (IRE) *Keith Reveley* 121h
6 b g Iffraaj Aljafliyah (Halling (USA))
27[4] 1009[3] 1158[2] 1289[5] (2447) 2786[P] (4612) 4864[2] 5443[5]

Waltzing Tornado (IRE) *Neil Mulholland* 100h 113c
10 ch g Golden Tornado(IRE) Lady Dante (IRE) (Phardante (FR))
44[4] 248[2] 504[3] 713[6] (2425)
(2540) (2702)
3097[5] 3293[2]

Waltz Legend (IRE) *Liam Lennon* 109h 109c
8 b m Flying Legend(USA) Vienna Waltz (IRE) (Orchestra)
5322[3]

Wan (FR) *P Favero*
7 b g Tagula(IRE) Wana Doo (USA) (Grand Slam (USA))
(1683a)

Wanaba (FR) *Mme P Butel* 133h 96c
5 b g Anabaa(USA) Willamina (IRE) (Sadler's Wells (USA))
683a[6] 2414a[P]

Wansbeck *James Frost* 64h
6 b g Morpeth Adalie (Absalom)
3746[P] 5548[6]

Warden Hill (IRE) *Mick Channon* 134h
6 br g Presenting Moon Storm (IRE) (Strong Gale)
(1991) 2490[8] (3086) 3896[3] 4949[2]

War Lord (IRE) *Philip Kirby* 99h
4 b g Aussie Rules(USA) Carn Lady (IRE) (Woodman (USA))
1934[3] (2168) 4952[9]

Warne (IRE) *B R Hamilton* 145h 138c
10 b g Bob Back(USA) Dusky Diva (IRE) (Be My Native (USA))
(5135)

War Of The World (FR) *Chris Bealby* 94b 72c
8 b g Lost World(IRE) Folklorique (FR) (Groom Dancer (USA))
899[4] 1133[8]

War On (IRE) *Chris Grant* 112h 116c
7 br g Presenting Alannico (Overbury (IRE))
27[P] **553[4]**
2494[3] 3209[2] 3526[3] 4427[P] 4812[6] 5321[P]

War On The Rocks (IRE) *Fergal O'Brien* 94b
5 b g Wareed(IRE) Rock Garden (IRE) (Bigstone (IRE))
5014[7]

Warrant Officer *Sheena West* 94h
4 gr g Misu Bond(IRE) Kilmovee (Inchinor)
2975[6] 3134[F] 3550[3] *4022[12]* 4469[U] 4758[6]

Warrantor (IRE) *Warren Greatrex* 109b
5 b g Turtle Island(IRE) Pixie Dust (IRE) (Desert King (IRE))
(5409)

Warrior Conquest *Jamie Snowden* 83h
9 b g Alhaarth(IRE) Eilean Shona (Suave Dancer (USA))
4632[9]

Warriors Tale *Nicky Richards* 103b
5 b g Midnight Legend Samandara (FR) (Kris)
2223[2] 3760[4] 5109[6]

Warsaw Pact (IRE) *Steven Dixon* 92h 57c
11 b g Polish Precedent(USA) Always Friendly (High Line)
490[9] 924[10] 1443[5] 1700[9] 4275[12] (4636) (4779) 5114[4] 5431[6]

War Singer (USA) *David Pipe* 125h
7 b g War Chant(USA) Sister Marilyn (USA) (Saint Ballado (CAN))
1046[12]

War Treaty (IRE) *Mark Shears* 83h
6 b g Wareed(IRE) Via Viaduct (IRE) (Febrino)
2479[7] 2864[6] 5029[U] 5332[P] 5550[5]

Warwickshire (IRE) *A Pennock* 35h 114c
7 b g Westerner Emeranna (IRE) (Dr Massini (IRE))
4727[3] (5248)
5491[4]

Wasabi (IRE) *John Berry* 82h
5 b m Tiger Hill(IRE) Quinzey (JPN) (Carnegie (IRE))
3854[3] 4467[9] 5008[9]

Was My Valentine *Jo Davis* 103h
7 b m Best Of The Bests(IRE) Eleonor Sympson (Cadeaux Genereux)
717[6] 2210[13] 3094[5] 3503[P] 4332[3] 4717[2]

Watch House (IRE) *Michael Gates* 89h 106c
9 ch g Deploy Derby Affair (Teenoso (USA))
420[P] 656[7] 759[3] 942[P] 1014[4] 1105[2] 1169[2] 1320[7]
(1548) (1637)
1798[F] 1959[12]

Watchmego *Maurice Barnes* 68b
6 b m Supreme Sound One Stop (Silly Prices)
450[P]

Watchmetail (IRE) *John Panvert* 71h
8 bb g Amilynx(FR) Ellie Anna (IRE) (Bravefoot)
2476[12] 2766[11] 3047[11]

Watered Silk *Lucy Wadham* 120h
6 gr g Encosta De Lago(AUS) Tussah (Daylami (IRE))
1685[9] 2490[17]

Waterford Star (IRE) *Tom George* 116h
6 b g Oratorio(IRE) Robin (Slip Anchor)
479[3] (849)

Water Garden (FR) *David Pipe* 134h 112c
8 gr g Turgeon(USA) Queenstown (FR) (Cadoudal (FR))
158[3]

Watergate (IRE) *Richard Rowe* 94h 95c
8 gr g Verglas(IRE) Moy Water (IRE) (Tirol)
542[5] 1528[P] 2003[4]

Watergate Bay (IRE) *Paul Nicholls* 96h
8 b g Definite Article Empress Of Light (Emperor Jones (USA))
780[7]

Waterside Road *Iain Jardine* 44b
5 b g Generous(IRE) Miss Morelli (IRE) (Beneficial)
2795[7] 3144[P]

Waterski *Jean McGregor* 59h 81c
13 b g Petoski Celtic Waters (Celtic Cone)
315[4] 496[P]

Waterunder (IRE) *David Pipe* 135h
7 br g Vinnie Roe(IRE) Be My Katie (IRE) (Be My Native (USA))
(480) 782[4] 1054[6] (2461) 2951[5] 3200[10] 3891[7]

Water Wagtail *Emma Lavelle* 105h 116c
7 b g Kahyasi Kentford Grebe (Teenoso (USA))
2150[3] 2691[4] **3785[2] 4399[6] (5129)**

Watledge (FR) *Tom George* 91h 81c
7 b g Lando(GER) Flower Of Freedom (FR) (Sadler's Wells (USA))
20[8]

Watt Broderick (IRE) *Ian Williams* 117h
5 ch g Hawk Wing(USA) Kingsridge (IRE) (King's Theatre (IRE))
1319[7] 2292[F] 2573[2] *4301[2]* (4972) 5005[3] (5061)

Watts Up Son *Declan Carroll* 61h
6 b g Diktat Local Fancy (Bahamian Bounty)
2507[11] 2846[P]

Wave Breaker (IRE) *Robert Johnson* 78h 81c
7 b g Moscow Society(USA) Lily Langtry (IRE) (Duky)
473[6] 628[8] 2336[5] **3925[3] 4380[4] 4775[6]** 5298[12]

Wave The Grapes *Peter Bowen* 94b
7 br m Grape Tree Road Wave Back (IRE) (Bob Back (USA))
970[11] 1445[3] 1523[4]

Waving *Tony Carroll* 92h
5 b g High Chaparral(IRE) Pretty Davis (USA) (Trempolino (USA))
1779[8] 2085[3] 5238[F]

Waxies Dargle *Noel Meade* 138h
5 b g Sakhee(USA) Cup Of Love (USA) (Behrens (USA))
5201a[P]

Wayne Manor (IRE) *Lucinda Russell* 102h
5 br g Cape Cross(IRE) Inchmahome (Galileo (IRE))
1286[P] 1664[P] 3525[3] 4201[6] 4823[10] 5494[2]

Way Up In The Air (IRE) *Robert Tyner* 133h 131c
7 ch m Rock Of Gibraltar(IRE) Gold Flair (Tap On Wood)
2986a[7] 3910a[P]

Wayward Glance *Keith Dalgleish* 129h 128c
6 b g Sadler's Wells(USA) Daring Aim (Daylami (IRE))
518[3] 1119[3] (1429) 1708[3] 2516[3] **(3111)**
3223[F] 4449[2] (4814)

Wayward Prince *Hilary Parrott* 104h 156c
10 b g Alflora(IRE) Bellino Spirit (IRE) (Robellino (USA))
18585
22292 2938P 45447 5171F

Waywood Princess *John Bryan Groucott* 77h 58c
9 b m Sir Harry Lewis(USA) First Bee (Gunner B)
26206 33354 3824P
4066F

Weather Babe *David Pipe* 119h
6 b m Storming Home Bathwick Babe (IRE) (Sri Pekan (USA))
26711 (2477) 27132 374110 49074

Weather The Storm *Oliver Sherwood* 74b
6 b m Zafeen(FR) Top Gale (IRE) (Topanoora)
55006

Webberys Dream *Jeremy Scott* 80h 126c
11 b g Bandmaster(USA) Sheilas Dream (Inca Chief (USA))
39907 4396P 46373 4992F

Webbswood (IRE) *Sean Curran* 97h
5 b g Catcher In The Rye(IRE) Victory Run (IRE) (Old Vic)
401613 50648 53083

Wedger Pardy (IRE) *Kim Bailey* 108c
13 b g Zaffaran(USA) Raise The Bells (Belfalas)
1279aP

Wee Giant (USA) *Tony Coyle* 73h
8 ch g Giant's Causeway(USA) Christmas In Aiken (USA) (Affirmed (USA))
2596P 287711

Weekend Millionair (IRE) *David Pipe* 132h 110c
7 ch g Arakan(USA) Almi Ad (USA) (Silver Hawk (USA))
21512 **839F**

Weetfromthechaff *Maurice Barnes* 95h
9 gr g Weet-A-Minute(IRE) Weet Ees Girl (IRE) (Common Grounds)
75P

Weeumba *Sandy Forster* 45h
9 ch m And Beyond(IRE) Weejumpawud (Jumbo Hirt (USA))
5526 880P

Weigh It Up (IRE) *Charlie Longsdon* 102b
6 ch g Flemensfirth(USA) Uppermost (Montjeu (IRE))
3177P

Weird Al (IRE) *Donald McCain* 61h 166c
11 b g Accordion Bucks Gift (IRE) (Buckley)
85113

Welcometothejungle *Keiran Burke* 104h
6 b m Lucky Story(USA) Kasamba (Salse (USA))
853 250610 32899

Well Connected *Emma Lavelle* 85b
5 b m Presenting Lisa Du Chenet (FR) (Garde Royale)
38985 50778

Wellforth (IRE) *Barry Brennan* 113h 135c
10 b g New Frontier(IRE) Faitch's Lady (IRE) (Dock Leaf)
25104 28076 **34162 36174 4270F**

Well Hello There (IRE) *Jonjo O'Neill* 104h 129c
8 b g Oscar(IRE) Bird Of Passage (Shambo)
162 (642) ◆ 1888F 22835 2889P

Well Mett (IRE) *Fergal O'Brien* 109h 126c
7 b g Gold Well Beit Millat (USA) (Alleged (USA))
(47) (89) 1582
5182 6704 9214 1195P
(5536)

Well Refreshed *Gary Moore* 101h 150c
10 b g Nikos Cool Spring (IRE) (Zaffaran (USA))
197114 29533 3361P 4270P 4732F 5092P

Well Regarded (IRE) *Emma Lavelle* 133h 133c
9 b g Dr Massini(IRE) Glenelly Valley (IRE) (Presenting)
168611

Well Related *Henry Hogarth* 62h
7 ch g Prince Daniel(USA) Wynyard Lady (Say Primula)
58412 2049P 382612 4005P 44769 5359P

Well Rewarded (IRE) *Emma Lavelle* 93b
4 b g Beneficial Lady Fancy (IRE) (Taipan (IRE))
50703 ◆

Welsh Bard (IRE) *Donald McCain* 116h
5 ch g Dylan Thomas(IRE) Delphinium (IRE) (Dr Massini (IRE))
(72) ◆ 1689 36186 39224 44789 52856

Werenearlyoutofit (IRE) *Graeme McPherson* 115h
6 b g Asian Heights Ballerina Laura (IRE) (Riot Helmet)
197413 24323

Wessex King (IRE) *Henry Daly* 121h 128c
10 b g Second Empire(IRE) Winchester Queen (IRE) (Persian Bold)
4327 27976 3323P 49085 51943 (5453)

Westaway (IRE) *David Arbuthnot* 122h
7 bb g Westerner I'llaway (IRE) (Heron Island (IRE))
5383 2316P 25362 294412 31955 37416 (4555) 46625

West Bay Hoolie *Helen Nelmes* 64h 80c
8 b g Nomadic Way(USA) West Bay Breeze (Town And Country)
1336P 30084 5027P

West Brit (IRE) *R Mike Smith* 119h
6 b g High Chaparral(IRE) Aldburgh (Bluebird (USA))
8129 9953 (1535) 3499P

Westbrooke (IRE) *Charlie Mann* 62b
4 b g Duke Of Marmalade(IRE) Stylist (IRE) (Sadler's Wells (USA))
507011

West Cork Flash (IRE) *Paul Henderson* 90h 114c
10 ch g Windsor Castle Galley Flash (IRE) (Phardante (FR))
325U 44402 47982 51293

West End (IRE) *Kim Bailey* 99h 96c
7 b g Westerner Brown Bess (IRE) (Definite Article)
17949 19355 21785
28974 49376 54383

West End Classic (IRE) *Tracey Watkins* 99h
7 br g Westerner Classic Mix (IRE) (Classic Secret (USA))
47P 6494 7774 8766 10193 45015

West End Rocker (IRE) *Alan King* 113h 142c
12 bb g Grand Plaisir(IRE) Slyguff Lord (IRE) (Lord Americo)
48213

Westend Theatre (IRE) *Jane Walton* 82h
5 b g Darsi(FR) Ballyvelig Lady (IRE) (Project Manager)
18547 25935 42348 47768

Westerly Breeze (IRE) *Martin Keighley* 105h
6 b g Westerner Sup A Whiskey (IRE) (Commanche Run)
27203 35063 41616 46772 50338 54413

Western Approaches *Ian Williams* 109h
7 b m Westerner Bayariyka (IRE) (Slip Anchor)
20456 27635 28882 (3043) 3756F

Western Bound (IRE) *Barbara Butterworth* 117h 71c
13 ch g Presenting Mid West Girl (IRE) (Commanche Run)
2218 8689 13744
17893 249710
2870F 47474 535910

Western Boy (IRE) *P A Fahy* 146h
5 b g Antonius Pius(USA) Skala (IRE) (Hernando (FR))
3667a2 47367

Western Diva (IRE) *David Pipe* 117h
5 b m Westerner Duck 'N' Dive (IRE) (Accordion)
352 39612 4403S 50144 (5448)

Western Dolly *Caroline Fryer*
5 b m Westerner Dolly Sparks (IRE) (Electric)
41146 42534 4863U

Western Dream *Dai Burchell* 45b
6 b g Westerner Simiola (Shaamit (IRE))
5889

Western Gale (IRE) *Martin Todhunter* 102h 105c
11 br g Presenting Kate Gale (IRE) (Strong Gale)
183 766P

Western High *Jim Best* 103h
9 b g Rainbow High Western Ploy (Deploy)
966P

Western Island (IRE) *Edward Cawley* 76h 87c
11 b g Turtle Island(IRE) Lady Of The West (IRE) (Mister Lord (USA))
1666P

Western Jo (IRE) *Philip Hobbs* 128h
6 b g Westerner Jenny's Jewel (IRE) (Be My Native (USA))
2807P 33872 37756

Western Kate (IRE) *John Flint* 105h
7 b m Westerner Golden Odyssey (IRE) (Barathea (IRE))
2911 (637) 8112

Western King (IRE) *Charlie Mann* 123h 125c
7 b g Definite Article Western Road (GER) (King's Theatre (IRE))
1433 4874 972P 11352 13166 (1486)
16423 (2041)
24755

Western Movie *Philip Hobbs* 95h
6 b g Westerner Fortune's Girl (Ardross)
21895 27115 306112 463212 5016B 51178

Western Prize *Tim Vaughan* 105h
6 br g High Chaparral(IRE) Spot Prize (USA) (Seattle Dancer (USA))
2404 11185 15614 17172 18292

Western Warhorse (IRE) *David Pipe* 130h 161c
6 b g Westerner An Banog (IRE) (Anshan)
25292 ◆ 27986 **(3601)**
(4737) 51373

Western Way (IRE) *Don Cantillon* 118b
5 b g Westerner Faucon (Polar Falcon (USA))
10943 12643 14272 (1539)

Western Xpress (IRE) *Peter Bowen* 102b
6 b g Westerner Lockersleybay (IRE) (Orchestra)
7902

Wester Ross (IRE) *Evan Williams* 114h 126c
10 b g Fruits Of Love(USA) Diabaig (Precocious)
(632) 7054
9433 (1186)
13462 14782

West Of The Road (IRE) *Mrs L Braithwaite* 91c
8 b g Wareed(IRE) Chatty Di (Le Bavard (FR))
3263

Weston Lodge (IRE) *Christopher Kellett* 79h 67c
8 b g Aahsaylad Slip Me Fippence (Royal Applause)
2626P 27845 32223 486512
5065P

Westward Point *Warren Greatrex* 126h 129c
7 ch g Karinga Bay Hottentot (Sula Bula)
21514 (2955)

Westwire Toby (IRE) *Lynn Siddall* 77h
12 ch g Anshan Ware It Well (IRE) (Torus)
1224 2215 4608 6285

West With The Wind *Evan Williams* 117h 148c
9 b g Fasliyev(USA) Midnight Angel (GER) (Acatenango (GER))
(157) 68010
9744 1194F

West Wizard (FR) *Nicky Henderson* 134h
5 bb g King's Theatre(IRE) Queen's Diamond (GER) (Konigsstuhl (GER))
27112

Wetak (FR) *David Pipe* 109h 135c
7 b g Antarctique(IRE) Rhapsodie (FR) (Saint Cyrien (FR))
838a6 4263F 47689 ◆ 5170P 53508

Weybridge Light *David Thompson* 104h
9 b g Fantastic Light(USA) Nuryana (Nureyev (USA))
2217 7522 8844 14143 (1717) 20513 23115 54965

Whadaurmeddlewimei *Alistair Whillans* 93b
4 b g Central Park(IRE) Thorterdykes Lass (IRE) (Zaffaran (USA))
46112

Whatagoa (IRE) *Richard Rowe* 75h
7 b m Bishop Of Cashel Gotta Goa (IRE) (Publisher (USA))
3689P 4467P 472111 511610

What A Good Night (IRE) *Nigel Twiston-Davies* 93h 111c
6 br g Westerner Southern Skies (IRE) (Dr Massini (IRE))
1457 15803 16753
(2088) 2722F 3193U 35653 4066P 49705 5433P

What A Joke (IRE) *William Reed* 37h
7 b g Vinnie Roe(IRE) Shaping (IRE) (Deep Run)
13532 14893 18566

What A Laugh *G D Hanmer* 103h 125c
9 b g Kayf Tara Just For A Laugh (Idiots Delight)
(357) 6609
42745 4655P

What An Oscar (IRE) *Nigel Twiston-Davies* 126h 119c
9 b g Oscar(IRE) Katie Buckers (IRE) (Yashgan)
845P **16692**
18883 2177P 2895U 3113U 45558 5183P

What A Steel (IRE) *Alistair Whillans* 116h
10 b g Craigsteel Sonya's Pearl (IRE) (Conquering Hero (USA))
5126 8018 11644 13983 16604

What A Warrior (IRE) *Nigel Twiston-Davies* 117h 139c
7 b g Westerner Be Right (IRE) (Be My Native (USA))
18682 24524 28127 31993 37725 44006 49625
5488P

What Er Say *Mrs O Bush* 115h 95c
9 b g Karinga Bay Spread The Word (Deploy)
55536

What Of It (IRE) *Mrs Sarah Ward* 113c
11 bb g Tel Quel(FR) Whats The Trouble (IRE) (Alphabatim (USA))
575 (331)
54916

Whatsabillion (IRE) *Anabel K Murphy* 90h 86c
12 bb g Lahib(USA) Outstanding Order (IRE) (College Chapel)
5223 7505 8297 11056

What's For Tea *Paddy Butler* 74h 44c
9 b m Beat All(USA) Come To Tea (IRE) (Be My Guest (USA))
3083 14385 163010
17657 2003P 3009P

Whats Goin On (IRE) *Jonjo O'Neill* 34h
5 b g Trade Fair Beckerson (IRE) (Alzao (USA))
4346

Whats Happening (IRE) *Tom George* 135h 141c
7 b g Lahib(USA) Rebeccas Star (IRE) (Camden Town)
27572 ◆ 31625 35942 442212 51784

Whatsupjack (IRE) *Shaun Harris* 101h
7 b g Catcher In The Rye(IRE) Riverstown Girl (IRE) (Buckskin (FR))
179U 7844 8769 287712 3119P

Whats Up Woody (IRE) *John Wade* 111h 120c
9 b g Beneficial Lady Noellel (IRE) (Step Together I (USA))
24214 3211F 36624 45782 52186

Whatuthink (IRE) *Oliver McKiernan* 150h 113c
12 ch g Presenting Glen's Encore (IRE) (Orchestra)
3374a4

Whatwillwedonext (IRE) *Martin Hill* 74h
8 b g Brian Boru Pigeon Rock (IRE) (Jurado (USA))
317310 53958

Wheelavher *Claire Dyson* 78h 75c
8 br m Fair Mix(IRE) True Rose (IRE) (Roselier (FR))
1227 **3226**
601F 24234 36058 48235 **50654 52409 53525**

Wheelavim *Claire Dyson* 82h
6 b g Beat All(USA) Plus Tu Mets (FR) (Roi De Rome (USA))
272012 34155 37467 41075 45276

Wheelavit (IRE) *Claire Dyson* 63h
11 b g Elnadim(USA) Storm River (USA) (Riverman (USA))
3847 66111 1206P 13517 179912

When Ben When (IRE) *Colin Tizzard* 98h
5 b g Beneficial Almnadia (IRE) (Alhaarth (IRE))
247210 40913 50166

Whenever *Richard Phillips* 110h
10 ch g Medicean Alessandra (Generous (IRE))
430110 490913

When I'm Sixtyfour (IRE) *Jonjo O'Neill* 102b
5 b g Oscar(IRE) Warmley's Gem (IRE) (Phardante (FR))
3802 7312

Whenindoubtdoit (IRE) *David Arbuthnot* 112h
7 ch g Shantou(USA) Warning Cry (IRE) (Over The River (FR))
18511 **3785P**

When In Roam (IRE) *John O'Shea* 67h
5 b m Flemensfirth(USA) Roaming (IRE) (Be My Native (USA))
5445 10643 (1392) 17323 32474

Where's Malachy (IRE) *Rose Dobbin* 95h
6 ch g Muhtarram(USA) County Classic (Noble Patriarch)
53205 5554F

Wheres The Hare (IRE) *Jonjo O'Neill* 115h 99c
7 b g Flemensfirth(USA) Knocknabrogue (IRE) (Afzal)
118P 5045

Wheyaye *Valerie Jackson* 98h
12 ch m Midnight Legend Sayin Nowt (Nicholas Bill)
3145P

Whichever *Richard Phillips* 100b
8 ch m Where Or When(IRE) Pip's Way (IRE) (Pips Pride)
3788P 4823F

Whichwaytobougie *Keith Reveley* 83h
5 b g Tobougg(IRE) Whichway Girl (Jupiter Island)
27885 31447 338812 36007

Whileaway (USA) *Neil Mulholland* 94h
5 b g Mizzen Mast(USA) Routine (USA) (Empire Maker (USA))
25636 34277 530411

While You Wait (IRE) *Gary Moore* 118h
5 b g Whipper(USA) Azra (IRE) (Danehill (USA))
26287 (5029) 52624 (5459)

Whinstone Dani (IRE) *Miss Clare Louise Cannon* 97h 61c
7 gr m Tikkanen(USA) Deemiss (IRE) (Buckskin (FR))
30178

Whinstone Dee (IRE) *Miss Clare Louise Cannon* 94h
6 ch g Desert King(IRE) Deemiss (IRE) (Buckskin (FR))
15405 17547 30185

Whipcrackaway (IRE) *Peter Hedger* 115h
5 b g Whipper(USA) Former Drama (USA) (Dynaformer (USA))
236611 27424 3263P

Whiskey And Red (IRE) *Colin Bowe* 115h 110c
9 b g Craigsteel Old Line (IRE) (Old Vic)
8327 2390P

Whiskey Chaser (IRE) *Donald McCain* 93h
6 br g Flemensfirth(USA) Cregane Lass (IRE) (Oscar (IRE))
3282U 38165 52065

Whiskey Ridge (IRE) *Sue Smith* 94h 112c
8 b g High-Rise(IRE) Little Chartridge (Anshan)
3852 ◆ (555)
2749F 2959P 32835 4082P (4380)
45783 48922 (5497)

Whisky Yankee (IRE) *Jonjo O'Neill* 130h
7 br g Presenting Southcoast Gale (IRE) (Strong Gale)
21511 293510 31867 37418 40287

Whisper (FR) *Nicky Henderson* 159h
6 b g Astarabad(USA) Belle Yepa (FR) (Mansonnien (FR))
24903 29493 (3369) 40252 (4752) (5169)

Whispering Bob (IRE) *Charlie Longsdon* 100h 54c
7 b g Presenting Baden's Queen (IRE) (Bob Back (USA))
20834 23698 **47167**

Whispering Boy (IRE) *David Bridgwater* 72h
7 b g Talkin Man(CAN) Dolphins View (IRE) (Dolphin Street (FR))
7588 8787 1019U 11188 13208

Whispering Gallery *John Ferguson* 143h
8 b g Daylami(IRE) Echoes In Eternity (IRE) (Spinning World (USA))
34574 ◆

Whispering Harry *Henry Oliver* 110h
5 b g Sir Harry Lewis(USA) Welsh Whisper (Overbury (IRE))
1865 179910 (2090) 25117 287713 34263 37882 (4072) 43533 (4538)

Whispering Jack *Keiran Burke* 75h 126c
9 b g Beat All(USA) Ski Shot (Petoski)
442 (481)
6465 8598 923P 29457 37436 *402110* **4732P 4809P**

Whistling Senator (IRE) *Jonjo O'Neill* 103h 127c
7 b g Presenting Merry Batim (IRE) (Alphabatim (USA))
77 709P (942)
(1015) (1425)
16372 18303 22972 29232 5373P

Whitby Jack *Gary Moore* 130h
7 b g Bering Sablonne (USA) (Silver Hawk (USA))
26478 295112

White Diamond *Nigel Twiston-Davies* 99h
7 b m Bertolini(USA) Diamond White (Robellino (USA))
20515 (3149)

White Singer (FR) *A Le Clerc* 80c
8 ch g Secret Singer(FR) Bergatta (FR) (Don Roberto (USA))
1623a5

White Star Line (IRE) *D T Hughes* 117h 141c
10 b g Saddlers' Hall(IRE) Fairly Deep (Deep Run)
(1604a) ◆ 25016

Who Am I *Debra Hamer* 95h
8 bb g Tamayaz(CAN) Short Fuse (IRE) (Zaffaran (USA))
115210 13292 1342F 47039 5143P

Whodoyouthink (IRE) *Oliver McKiernan* 126h 126c
9 b g Court Cave(IRE) Glen's Encore (IRE) (Orchestra)
1897a11 281515

Who Owns Me (IRE) *Charlie Mann* 133h 110c
8 b g Milan Top Lassie (IRE) (Topanoora)
21776 25393 3178F 36537 (4040) 45562 4954P 5544P

Who's Cross (IRE) *Nicky Henderson* 122h
6 b g Runyon(IRE) Mystery Escort (Sir Harry Lewis (USA))
1769 20874 27179

Who's Emma *Chris Fairhurst*
4 b f Rob Roy(USA) Autumn Bloom (IRE) (Fantastic Light (USA))
4008P

Who's Jeff (IRE) *Philip Hobbs* 109h
6 b g Westerner Kitty Maher (IRE) (Posen (USA))
5172 1816F 22924 28488 36506 43516 55525

Who'Slaughingnow (IRE) *D D Ockenden* 77c
7 gr g Portrait Gallery(IRE) Solar Lady (IRE) (Shahrastani (USA))
112F

Why Always Me (IRE) *Chris Bealby* 49h
6 b g Milan Cool Supreme (IRE) (Supreme Leader)
20496 25755

Wicked Spice (IRE) *Nicky Richards* 100h
5 b g Old Vic Afdala (IRE) (Hernando (FR))
46119 55086

Wicklewood *Mark Gillard* 89h 97c
8 b g Mujahid(USA) Pinini (Pivotal)
1517U 16439 19409 24768 30475 40247 **4373F**
47342 50274 51443 5394P

Wicklow Brave *W P Mullins* 149h
5 b g Beat Hollow Moraine (Rainbow Quest (USA))
47366 5201a6

Wicklow Lad *N W Alexander* 124h 132c
10 gr g Silver Patriarch(IRE) Marina Bird (Julio Mariner)
1978[P] 2421[3] 3205[6] (3498)
3825[3] 4204[2] (4430)
4651[4]

Wiesentraum (GER) *Lucy Wadham* 116h 137c
8 ch g Next Desert(IRE) Wiesenblute (GER) (Big Shuffle (USA))
1204[5] (1302)
1686[10] (2065)
2646[P] 4792[2] 5170[P]

Wiffy Chatsby (IRE) *Paul Nicholls* 125h 128c
7 br g Presenting Star Child (GER) (Neshad (USA))
(645)

Wigsy (IRE) *Gary Brown*
5 br g Craigsteel Newlineview (IRE) (Saddlers' Hall (IRE))
671[F]

Wilcos Mo Chara (IRE) *Donald McCain* 115b
6 b g Oscar(IRE) She's A Venture (IRE) (Supreme Leader)
(2795)

Wild At Midnight *Fergal O'Brien* 88b
5 b m Midnight Legend Wild Dream (Derrylin)
4867[9] 5249[4]

Wild Card *Donald McCain* 115h
7 b g First Trump Vanina II (FR) (Italic (FR))
(33) 1924[3] 4609[2] 5320[2]

Wild Desert (FR) *Tony Carroll* 69h 97c
9 bb g Desert Prince(IRE) Sallivera (IRE) (Sillery (USA))
1378[13] 1689[8]

Wild Diamond (IRE) *Tim Vaughan* 77h
4 b f Hernando(FR) Step With Style (USA) (Gulch (USA))
582[6] 975[4] 1193[3] 1335[5] 2307[4]

Wilde And Willing (IRE) *Seamus Mullins* 69h
6 b g Oscar(IRE) Turtlena (IRE) (Turtle Island (IRE))
4171[7] 5110[6]

Wilde Blue Yonder (IRE) *Alan King* 148h
5 b g Oscar(IRE) Blue Gallery (IRE) (Bluebird (USA))
(2195) (2802) ◆ 3370[F] 4266[F] 4736[5] 5167[4]

Wilde Pastures (IRE) *James Ewart* 107h 119c
9 gr g Oscar(IRE) Kingsfield Clover (Terimon)
2359[6] 3333[P] 4772[2] 5163[3] **5555[5]**

Wilde Ruby (IRE) *Seamus Mullins* 115h
7 b m Oscar(IRE) Ruby Thewes (IRE) (Anshan)
38[3] 393[10]

Wildest Dreams (IRE) *Jane Walton* 93b
5 b g Flemensfirth(USA) Suspicious Minds (Anabaa (USA))
2499[12] 3640[6]

Wild Geese (IRE) *Lucinda Russell* 111h 126c
7 br g Cape Cross(IRE) Intrepidity (Sadler's Wells (USA))
(312) **680[9]**
869[P] 1542[2] 1659[F] 5558[P]

Wild Legend (IRE) *Richard Rowe* 67b
5 ch m Flying Legend(USA) Burren View (IRE) (Mazaad)
544[10] *4017[13]*

Wild Tonto (IRE) *Nigel Twiston-Davies* 83h 110c
11 b g Saddlers' Hall(IRE) Shipping News (IRE) (Glacial Storm (USA))
37[6] 289[9] 829[15]

Wild West (IRE) *Jonjo O'Neill* 96h
6 ch g Galileo(IRE) Monumental Gesture (Head For Heights)
650[12] 876[P]

William Butler (IRE) *Mrs Libby Lawson* 103h 78c
14 b g Safety Catch(USA) Rosie Josie (Trombone)
329[P]

William Hogarth *Keith Goldsworthy* 79h 68c
9 b g High Chaparral(IRE) Mountain Holly (Shirley Heights)
643[3] 1109[6]

William Money (IRE) *Chris Grant* 112b 126c
7 b g Cloudings(IRE) All Of A Kind (IRE) (Orchestra)
170[7]

William Percival (IRE) *Mark Gillard* 79h
8 b g Presenting Soy Alegre (IRE) (Night Shift (USA))
997[5] 1267[6] (1339) 1477[6]

William's Wishes (IRE) *Evan Williams* 131h 157c
9 b g Oscar(IRE) Strong Wishes (IRE) (Strong Gale)
2281[5]

William Wild *Tina Jackson* 69b
6 b g Bollin Eric Winnie Wild (Primitive Rising (USA))
5063[9] 5500[8]

Willie Hall *William Amos* 88h 95c
10 b g Alflora(IRE) G'Ime A Buzz (Electric)
77[5] 2596[4] 3040[7] 3639[3] (3924) 4223[7]

Willoughby Hedge *Alan King* 124h
7 b g King's Theatre(IRE) Mini Mandy (Petoski)
(554) (2296)

Willow Island (IRE) *David Evans* 98h
5 b g Dark Angel(IRE) Cidaris (IRE) (Persian Bold)
4971[3] 5236[2]

Willow's Saviour *Dan Skelton* 142h
7 ch g Septieme Ciel(USA) Willow Gale (Strong Gale)
(2210) (2344) (3200)

Willpower (IRE) *Nicky Henderson* 95h
5 b g Montjeu(IRE) Noble Pearl (GER) (Dashing Blade)
2471[10] 3023[4] 4664[6] 5059[7] 5366[8]

Wilton Milan (IRE) *Paul Nicholls* 126h 111c
6 b g Milan Biondo (IRE) (College Chapel)
1858[U]
2941[P] 3745[F] 4395[5] 5259[2]

Wily Fox *James Eustace* 119h
7 ch g Observatory(USA) Kamkova (USA) (Northern Dancer (CAN))
(2397) 2625[3] 3328[4] 3786[3] 4306[4] (4700) 5075[5]
5384[8]

Wind Echo *Rayson Nixon* 28b
6 br g Supreme Sound Split The Wind (Strong Gale)
1877[12] 2037[12] 2355[P] 2968[P] 4956[P]

Windpfeil (IRE) *Dominic Ffrench Davis* 92h
8 bl g Indian Ridge Flying Kiss (IRE) (Sadler's Wells (USA))
(540) 810[3] 3650[P] 5262[8]

Winds And Waves (IRE) *Henry Daly* 121h 123c
8 b g Alflora(IRE) Sail By The Stars (Celtic Cone)
2024[2] 2451[P] 3717[6] 4704[8]

Wind Shuffle (GER) *Lucinda Russell* 74h 127c
11 b g Big Shuffle(USA) Wiesensturmerin (GER) (Lagunas)
1656[6]

Windsor Brook (IRE) *L Buyl*
7 ch g Alderbrook Windsor Breeze (IRE) (Windsor Castle)
1464a[P]

Windwood Lad *Michael O'Hare* 82h
9 b g Mtoto Amadella (Minshaanshu Amad (USA))
884[5] 1136[8]

Winged Crusader (IRE) *Nigel Twiston-Davies* 117h
6 b g Winged Love(IRE) Reine Berengere (FR) (Esprit Du Nord (USA))
2720[6] 3177[5] 3747[3] (4371) (4906) 5351[P]

Winged Farasi *Joanne Foster* 96h 86c
10 b g Desert Style(IRE) Clara Vale (IRE) (In The Wings)
965[P] **1074[3]**
1375[P]

Wing Mira (IRE) *Venetia Williams* 87h
6 b g Winged Love(IRE) Miraflores (IRE) (Montelimar (USA))
2285[7] 2806[4] 4506[4] ◆ 4945[9] 5117[9] 5542[7]

Wings Of Smoke (IRE) *Tim Vaughan* 117h 139c
9 gr g King's Theatre(IRE) Grey Mo (IRE) (Roselier (FR))
1670[4] 2797[4] 3204[2] 4660[5] 5290[2]

Winneys Boy *Shaun Lycett* 60b
6 b g Mr Kalandi(IRE) Winneys Folly (Tigani)
4575[8] 5014[15]

Winning Spark (USA) *Jackie Du Plessis* 103h
7 b g Theatrical(IRE) Spark Sept (FR) (Septieme Ciel (USA))
97[8] 4888[4]

Winston Churchill (IRE) *Sophie Leech* 112h 104c
8 b g Presenting Star Councel (IRE) (Leading Counsel (USA))
117[3] 641[3] 802[P] 873[5]

Winstone (IRE) *George Charlton* 92h
9 b g Pierre Cushenstown Best (IRE) (Gallic Heir)
5484[3]

Winter Alchemy (IRE) *Nicky Richards* 97h 97c
9 b g Fruits Of Love(USA) Native Land (Be My Native (USA))
1164[2] 1468[P] **1789[4] 4982[4]** 5514[8]

Wintered Well (IRE) *Jennie Candlish* 116h
6 b g Milan Stratosphere (Selkirk (USA))
338[2] 848[U] 897[4] 1082[4] 1183[6] 2787[2] (3014)
3192[2] (5072) (5163) 5349[P]

Wise Hawk *Jackie Du Plessis* 99h 65c
9 b g Hawk Wing(USA) Dombeya (IRE) (Danehill (USA))
540[2] **2460[6]**
3426[4] 4504[F]

Wise Oscar (IRE) *D T Hughes* 130h 133c
10 b g Oscar(IRE) Mona Curra Gale (IRE) (Strong Gale)
1604a[7] 1897a[6]

Wishes And Stars (IRE) *Tim Dennis* 106h 97c
8 b m Old Vic She's No Trouble (IRE) (Zaffaran (USA))
317[3] **5428[5]**

Wishes Or Watches (IRE) *John Upson* 95h 66c
14 br g Bravefoot Shadya's Amal (Shaadi (USA))
898[P] 1172[P]

Wishfull Dancer (IRE) *John Mackie* 26h
6 br g Hawk Wing(USA) Sun Slash (IRE) (Entrepreneur)
790[12] 1599[9] 1795[14]

Wishfull Thinking *Philip Hobbs* 138h 162c
11 ch g Alflora(IRE) Poussetiere Deux (FR) (Garde Royale)
2071[6] 2503[6] 2938[2] (3887)
4753[5] 5155[8]

Wish In A Well (IRE) *S R B Crawford* 105b
5 b g Gamut(IRE) Lady Bellingham (IRE) (Montelimar (USA))
5279[5] 5560[5]

Wistari Rocks (IRE) *Tim Vaughan* 99b
5 b g Heron Island(IRE) Hi Honey (IRE) (Persian Mews)
1671[5]

Wiston Dreamer *R E Luke*
8 b g Dreams End Daisy's Choice (Tigerwood)
4355[P]

Witchesintune *Helen Nelmes* 72h
7 b m Beat Hollow Music Park (IRE) (Common Grounds)
521[11] 3009[9] **4716[P]**

Witch One *Ashley Dodgson* 38h
11 b m Silver Patriarch(IRE) Catton Lady (Chas Sawyer)
19[P]

Witch's Hat (IRE) *Jim Old* 85h 90c
11 br g Hubbly Bubbly(USA) Bold Shilling (IRE) (Meneval (USA))
117[7] 3180[3] 4486[5] 4778[2] 5394[8]

Witch Way *Ashley Dodgson* 40h
9 gr m Silver Patriarch(IRE) Catton Lady (Chas Sawyer)
72[P]

Wither Yenot (IRE) *Ben Case* 117h
7 b g Tikkanen(USA) Acacia Bloom (IRE) (Old Vic)
2009[3] (2566) 3151[3] 3471[5]

With Hindsight (IRE) *Alan Jones*
6 ch g Ad Valorem(USA) Lady From Limerick (IRE) (Rainbows For Life (CAN))
1946[P]

Withoutdefavourite (IRE) *Henry Oliver* 105h
6 b g Oscar(IRE) Camden Confusion (IRE) (Camden Town)
4304[5] 4535[8] 4808[2] 5191[3] 5351[P]

Withy Mills *Kevin Bishop* 91h 75c
9 gr m Baryshnikov(AUS) Gipsy Rose (Nicholas Bill)
2628[U] 2766[9] 3047[8] (3788) 3959[5] 4334[P] (5034)
5125[5]

Witness (FR) *H Billot* 112h
5 b g Astarabad(USA) Belle Yepa (FR) (Mansonnien (FR))
1199a[11]

Witness In Court (IRE) *Donald McCain* 115h 145c
7 b g Witness Box(USA) Inter Alia (IRE) (Dr Massini (IRE))
1976[P] (3519) ◆ 4055[4] 4684[2] 5091[6] 5289[2]
(5382)

Wogan *Mrs Dawn Woolf* 81h 98c
14 b g Presenting Fall About (Comedy Star (USA))
4915[6]

Wojciech *Warren Greatrex* 91b
4 b f Lucarno(USA) Pondimari (FR) (Marignan (USA))
2604[6] 3167[11]

Wolfe Mountain (IRE) *Linda Blackford* 68h
5 b g Mountain High(IRE) Rachel's Choice (IRE) (Ela-Mana-Mou)
3133[7] 4177[5] 5389[4]

Wolf Hall (IRE) *Violet M Jordan* 92b
7 br g Presenting Water Rock (El Conquistador)
2006[P] **2722[P]**

Wolf Shield (IRE) *George Moore* 116h 118c
7 b g King's Theatre(IRE) Garlucy (IRE) (Un Desperado (FR))
(115) ◆ 512[2] 1752[6] 2050[5] 2516[9] 3085[5] (3726)
4271[3] 4954[7]

Wolf Sword (IRE) *George Moore* 106b
5 b g Flemensfirth(USA) Dame O'Neill (IRE) (Dr Massini (IRE))
2660[4] ◆ (3276) 4958[4]

Wolftrap (IRE) *Laura Young* 97b
5 b g Mountain High(IRE) Dear Money (IRE) (Buckskin (FR))
3656[5] 3994[10] 5338[8]

Wolmar *John Mackie* 67b
5 b m Beat All(USA) Kadari (Commanche Run)
731[9] 790[10] 1013[8]

Wom *Neil King* 103h
6 b g Tiger Hill(IRE) Vayavaig (Damister (USA))
161[3] (429) 784[3] 927[4] 1058[U] 1400[6] 1567[2]
1799[2] 1938[3] 2397[9] 4972[5] 5072[13] 5443[7]

Wonderful Charm (FR) *Paul Nicholls* 134h 159c
6 b g Poliglote Victoria Royale (FR) (Garde Royale)
(2063) ◆ (2374) ◆ (2799)
3064[2] 4764[5] 5154[3]

Woodbank *Dan Skelton* 118h 133c
7 br g Needwood Blade Potter's Gale (IRE) (Strong Gale)
1817[U] 2042[2] 2785[2] ◆ 3087[F] (5446) ◆

Woodford County *Philip Hobbs* 123h 128c
7 b g Sonus(IRE) Moylena (Bustomi)
2288[13] 2715[5] (3191) 3784[5]
4110[4] (4412)
4886[5] 5386[2]

Woodland Walk *Emma Lavelle* 121h
6 ch m Generous(IRE) Duchess Of Kinsale (IRE) (Montelimar (USA))
(2675) 3168[4] 4276[5] 4907[2] 5449[2]

Woodpole Academy (IRE) *Philip Kirby* 130h
7 b g Beneficial Midday Caller (IRE) (Miner's Lamp)
2935[11] 3430[P]

Woodstock (IRE) *Ann Hamilton* 92h
4 b g High Chaparral(IRE) Woodwin (IRE) (Woodman (USA))
5296[8] 5479[5]

Wood Yer (IRE) *Nigel Twiston-Davies* 93h 123c
8 ch g Anshan Glenasheen (IRE) (Presenting)
2458[15]
2931[7] (3437)
(3820) 4339[4] 5385[F]

Woody Waller *Sophie Leech* 85h 114c
9 ch g Lomitas Reamzafonic (Grand Lodge (USA))
1151[4] 1666[2] 2014[4] 2618[P] 3324[3]

Woolcombe Folly (IRE) *Paul Nicholls* 131h 158c
11 bb g Presenting Strong Gara (IRE) (Strong Gale)
249[2] 392[2] 1047[2] 1157a[3] 1969[6] 2503[9]

Wooly Bully *Alan King* 105h
4 b g Sixties Icon Baycliffe Rose (Karinga Bay)
1439[4] (1524) 1862[2] 3003[6] 4332[P]

Wooly Tom (IRE) *Patrick Mooney* 128h
10 bb g Alexius(IRE) Jordans Pet (IRE) (Vision (USA))
5420a[13]

Word Of Warning *Philip Kirby* 97h 109c
10 gr g War Chant(USA) Frosty Welcome (USA) (With Approval (CAN))
581[6] 751[P] 1374[5] 1675[9] 1940[10]

Wordy's Boy *Charles Pogson* 111h
9 b g Kayf Tara Wordy's Wonder (Welsh Captain)
3659[P] 3839[7] (4597)

Workbench (FR) *Dan Skelton* 114h 126c
6 b g Network(GER) Danhelis (FR) (Hellios (USA))
(2762)
3045[3] 3787[P] 4592[3] 5141[3]

Work Boy *Richard Drake* 88h 114c
13 b g Nomadic Way(USA) Swift Reward (Kinglet)
4578[4] (4892)
5060[U] 5162[3] 5497[U]

Wor Lass *Iain Jardine* 89h
6 br m And Beyond(IRE) Patience Please (King Of Spain)
5479[9]

Worth A Go (IRE) *Liam Corcoran* 101b
7 gr g Hasten To Add(USA) Love Or Porter (IRE) (Saddlers' Hall (IRE))
1124[3] 1489[4]

Worth A King'S *Philip Kirby* 89h 41c
8 b g Red Ransom(USA) Top Romance (IRE) (Entrepreneur)
471[2]

Worthy Award (IRE) *Jonjo O'Neill* 112h
6 b g Presenting Take Ine (FR) (Take Risks (FR))
4904[3]

Wosayu *Colin Tizzard* 67h 85c
8 b g Central Park(IRE) Waltz On Air (Doc Marten)
84[6] 408[4]

Wot A Shot (IRE) *C A McBratney* 103h 67c
5 b g Refuse To Bend(IRE) Ashdali (IRE) (Grand Lodge (USA))
865[2] 1661[7]

Wotsthecatch (IRE) *Michael Scudamore* 63b
6 b g Fruits Of Love(USA) Miss Perky (IRE) (Creative Plan (USA))
1138[10] 1499[5] 1937[P]

Wounded Warrior (IRE) *Noel Meade* 134h
5 b g Shantou(USA) Sparkling Sword (Broadsword (USA))
3931a[4]

Wrecking Ball (IRE) *Amy Weaver*
4 b g Royal Applause Shatarah (Gulch (USA))
3469[P]

Writers Block (IRE) *John Joseph Hanlon* 15h 25c
11 b g Lil's Boy(USA) Nordic Pageant (IRE) (Nordico (USA))
1320[13]

Wrong Turn (IRE) *A J Martin* 129c
8 b g Well Chosen Friendly Spirit (Nicholas Bill)
4738[P]

W Six Times *Alistair Whillans* 91h
8 b m Double Trigger(IRE) Be My Mot (IRE) (Be My Native (USA))
2596[F] 3210[7] 3636[3] 3940[2] (4201) 5056[7]

Wuff (IRE) *Tom George* 130h
6 b g Beneficial Dummy Run (IRE) (Glacial Storm (USA))
2660[2] ◆ (3189) (3781) 4272[6]

Wunfurlez *Diana Grissell* 87h
6 b g Kayf Tara Fairlead (Slip Anchor)
2368[9] 3136[10] 3552[4] 4715[4] 5436[7]

Wychwoods Brook *Evan Williams* 123h 149c
8 b g Midnight Legend Miss Millbrook (Meadowbrook)
2389[2] 2651[F] (3093)
(3780) 4270[F]

Wychwoods Mist *Claire Dyson* 56h
7 b m Umistim Blackchurch Lass (IRE) (Taum Go Leor (IRE))
2029[6] 2473[7] 2723[7]

Wyck Hill (IRE) *David Bridgwater* 110h 148c
10 b g Pierre Willow Rose (IRE) (Roselier (FR))
2214[9] 2937[9] 3361[P] (4427)
4821[6]

Wyfield Rose *Jamie Snowden* 102h
5 b m Kayf Tara Miniature Rose (Anshan)
(1826) 2506[8] 3005[7] 4528[3] 4917[3]

Wylder (FR) *Mlle V Crozetiere-Roulet* 89h 103c
10 b g Mister Tullio(FR) Miss Geralde (FR) (Carmarthen (FR))
704a[4]

Wymeswold *Michael Mullineaux* 86h
7 b m Alflora(IRE) Dominie Breeze (Primo Dominie)
324[10] 567[8] 715[6] (1719) 3010[10] 3270[8] 4980[3]
5291[P]

Wynn Darwi (IRE) *Debra Hamer* 83h
9 bb g Anshan Noughtynova (Petoski)
777[5] 1863[9] 2147[7] 2648[9]

Wyoyo (IRE) *Tim Vaughan*
4 b g Moss Vale(IRE) Jersey Lillie (IRE) (Hector Protector (USA))
4987[P]

Wyse Hill Teabags *Jim Goldie* 134h
9 b g Theatrical Charmer Mrs Tea (First Trump)
3477[10] (4051) 5277[3]

Xaarcet (IRE) *Colin Tizzard* 120h 102c
7 b g Xaar Anoukit (Green Desert (USA))
2389[4] 2928[8] 3358[P] 3741[13] 4129[4] 4278[7] 4888[8]

Xclaim *Micky Hammond* 46h
6 ch g Proclamation(IRE) Tahara (IRE) (Caerleon (USA))
15[8] 383[5]

Xenophon *Michael Chapman* 103h 81c
6 b g Phoenix Reach(IRE) Comtesse Noire (CAN) (Woodman (USA))
203[4] 385[5] 565[7] 2062[5] 2253[5] 2430[P] 2903[4]
3119[4] **5193[3] 5361[3] 5407[3]**

Yabadabadoo *Emma Lavelle* 103h
6 b g Doyen(IRE) Kabayil (Dancing Brave (USA))
2252[2] 4904[5] 5341[3]

Y A Bon (IRE) *Martin Hill* 94h
6 b g Black Sam Bellamy(IRE) Tarte Fine (FR) (Goldneyev (USA))
160[6] 412[3] 3782[6] 4171[6] 4514[8] 5029[2]

Yabora (FR) *Alexandra Dunn* 65h 66c
9 b g Timboroa Hyacinthe (FR) (Epervier Bleu)
178[P] *444[P]*

Ya Hafed *Sheena West* 108h 108c
6 ch g Haafhd Rule Britannia (Night Shift (USA))
538[2] **3033[2]**
3879[P] *4494[4]*

Yajber (USA) *Sheena West*
5 rg g Aljabr(USA) Futuh (USA) (Diesis)
5110[P]

Yankee Hill (FR) *Mlle T Puitg* 130h
5 b g Muhtathir Luna Hill (FR) (Danehill (USA))
(1983a)

Yanky Sundown (FR) *M Nicolau* 123c
9 b g Until Sundown(USA) Yanky Panky (USA) (Allen's Prospect (USA))
(704a)
2384a[F]

Yasir (USA) *Conor Dore* 111h
6 b g Dynaformer(USA) Khazayin (USA) (Bahri (USA))
4304[3] 5071[3] 5260[10]

Yazdi (IRE) *Henry Oliver* 100h
5 b g Galileo(IRE) Lucky Spin (Pivotal)
185[7] 1087[3] 1388[5] 2980[9] 3265[2] 4070[P] 4309[4]
4969[7] 5179[3] 5542[6]

Ybarra (FR) *D Bressou* 97h
4 ch f Ballingarry(IRE) Fille Formidable (USA) (Trempolino (USA))
615a[8]

Yellow Ball (FR) *Venetia Williams* 106h 126c
6 ch m Ballingarry(IRE) Louve Antique (FR) (Loup Solitaire (USA))
3097^{6} 3389^{P} 3743^{3} 4161^{3}
4635^{3} 5425a^{F}

Yellow Duke (FR) *Charles Pogson* 85h
7 ch g Robin Des Champs(FR) Miss Cadouline (FR) (Nikos)
648^{P} 847^{P}

Yes Daddy (IRE) *Tim Vaughan* 109h
6 b g Golan(IRE) Hollygrove Samba (IRE) (Accordion)
383^{2} 879^{4} 3420^{6} (4866) 5353^{10}

Yes I Will *Charlie Longsdon* 97h
5 b g Kahyasi Flinders (Henbit (USA))
2254^{7} 2602^{5} 2858^{10} 3163^{5}

Yes Tom (IRE) *S R B Crawford* 96h 143c
9 gr g Tikkanen(USA) Ammieanne (IRE) (Zaffaran (USA))
5276^{9}

Yesyoucan (IRE) *Brian Ellison* 147h 142c
9 b g Beneficial Except Alice (IRE) (Orchestra)
2074^{4} (2494)
2839^{3} (3658)
3881^{2} 4752^{P} 5158^{18}

Y O Me *Sirrell Griffiths* 69h
7 ch m Alflora(IRE) Yo Kiri-B (Night Shift (USA))
717^{8}

Yoneti (FR) *E Leenders* 88c
5 b g Irish Wells(FR) Aulne River (FR) (River Mist (USA))
2464a^{3}

Yorkist (IRE) *Brian Ellison* 136h
6 ch g Urban Ocean(FR) Kilbarry Demon (IRE) (Bob's Return (IRE))
2032^{5} 2241^{4} (3350) (3616) (3736) 4056^{6} (4426) 5172^{9}

You Know Yourself (IRE) *Sue Smith* 102h 127c
11 b g Dr Massini(IRE) Gift Of The Gab (IRE) (Orchestra)
(25) **170^{5}**
4338^{U} **4835^{5}**
5053^{5} 5299^{P}

Youmaysee *Mick Channon* 84h
4 b f Authorized(IRE) Purple Vision (Rainbow Quest (USA))
2557^{6} 2796^{9}

Youm Jamil (USA) *Tony Carroll* 74h 73c
7 rg g Mizzen Mast(USA) Millie's Choice (IRE) (Taufan (USA))
183^{P} 1014^{F} 1331^{8}

You Must Know Me (IRE) *Henry De Bromhead* 132h 145c
8 ch g Snurge Waterloo Park (IRE) (Alphabatim (USA))
2939^{3} 5156^{6}

Young Cheddar (IRE) *Polly Gundry* 91h
7 b m Croco Rouge(IRE) Sin Ceist Eile (IRE) (Simply Great (FR))
4331^{2} 4500^{2}

Youngdocgallagher (IRE) *Michael Mullineaux* 91b
5 b g Zagreb(USA) Too Back (IRE) (Toulon)
5410^{4}

Young Hurricane (IRE) *Dr Richard Newland* 109h 119c
8 b g Oscar(IRE) Georgia On My Mind (FR) (Belmez (USA))
2105^{4}
(2582) 2901^{3} 3293^{P} 3820^{3} 4537^{5} 5284^{2} 5356^{2}
5516^{P}

Young Jay *Andrew Crook* 81h
4 b g Josr Algarhoud(IRE) Young Sue (Local Suitor (USA))
3351^{7} 3822^{5} 4345^{8} 5375^{4}

Young Lou *Robin Dickin* 78h
5 b m Kadastrof(FR) Wanna Shout (Missed Flight)
2040^{10} 2312^{9} 2598^{10} 3188^{8} 3434^{3} 4398^{9}
5494^{14}

Young Sparky (IRE) *Pauline Robson* 73h
7 bb g Oscar(IRE) Our Dream (IRE) (Bob Back (USA))
2360^{9}

Your Busy (IRE) *J A Nash* 127h 134c
11 b g Anshan Springfort Society (IRE) (Moscow Society (USA))
1362^{4} (1572a)
2070^{6} 2939^{2} 5156^{14}

You'resomedreamer (IRE) *Lucinda Russell* 85h 110c
6 bb g Cloudings(IRE) Criaire Nouveau (IRE) (Darnay)
1877^{3} 2337^{7} 2593^{7} 3494^{4} **4367^{3}**

Yourholidayisover (IRE) *Patrick Holmes* 105h
7 ch g Sulamani(IRE) Whitehaven (Top Ville)
2792^{3} 3516^{6} 3877^{7}

Yourlookinathim (IRE) *Jim Goldie* 92h
8 b g Flemensfirth(USA) Christmas River (IRE) (Be My Native (USA))
310^{9} 4711^{10} 3520^{5}

You Too Pet (IRE) *Fergal O'Brien* 80h
6 b g Norwich Pollys Pet (IRE) (Little Bighorn)
1869^{13} 2076^{7}

Yukon Delta (IRE) *Robert Johnson* 88h 92c
7 ch g Old Vic Red Fern (IRE) (Mister Lord (USA))
19^{8} 554^{4} 2843^{5}
3209^{4} 3635^{U} 4186^{4} 4461^{4} 4774^{5}
5301^{3} (5498)

Zabana (IRE) *Andrew Lynch* 137h
5 ch g Halling(USA) Gandia (IRE) (Danehill (USA))
1139a^{10} 5158^{5}

Zacharova (IRE) *Mrs Jo Messenger* 64h 103c
11 b g Lil's Boy(USA) Voronova (IRE) (Sadler's Wells (USA))
62^{R}

Zafaraban (IRE) *Aytach Sadik* 102h
7 gr g Dalakhani(IRE) Zafaraniya (IRE) (Doyoun)
808^{6} 1061^{3} 1136^{2} 3029^{6} 3195^{11} 4249^{3} 4471^{5}
5362^{R} 5489^{R}

Zaffaran Rain (IRE) *K F Clutterbuck*
5 ch m Presenting Borleagh Blonde (IRE) (Zaffaran (USA))
2579^{P} 3506^{6} 3840^{P}

Zafranagar (IRE) *Ian Williams* 114h 104c
9 b g Cape Cross(IRE) Zafaraniya (IRE) (Doyoun)
2198^{6} 2519^{2} (2561) 3066^{4} 4278^{6} 5231^{6}

Zaidpour (FR) *W P Mullins* 164h
8 b g Red Ransom(USA) Zainta (IRE) (Kahyasi)
406a^{7} 685a^{3} 2855a^{2} (3374a) 3866a^{6} 4312a^{2}

Zakatal *Simon Earle* 116h
8 gr g Kalanisi(IRE) Zankara (FR) (Linamix (FR))
4327^{7} 4571^{6}

Zalgarry (FR) *Arthur Whitehead* 120h
7 b g Ballingarry(IRE) Spleen (FR) (Sillery (USA))
1020^{2} 1363^{4} 1699^{2} 3028^{2}

Zama Zama *Evan Williams* 80h 116c
7 b g Sakhee(USA) Insinuation (IRE) (Danehill (USA))
144^{8} **369^{3}**
596^{6} 781^{3} 995^{5}
1151^{3} 1274^{P} 1478^{3}

Zambezi Tiger (IRE) *Patrick Griffin* 89h
5 b g Tiger Hill(IRE) Johannesburg Cat (USA) (Johannesburg (USA))
1288^{3} 1785^{9}

Zamdy Man *Venetia Williams* 150h
5 b g Authorized(IRE) Lauderdale (GER) (Nebos (GER))
(2215) (2657) (3778)

Zamoyski *Steve Gollings* 116h
4 ch g Dutch Art Speech (Red Ransom (USA))
2200^{3} 2392^{3} 4345^{2} ◆ 5090^{11} 5296^{4}

Zanir (FR) *Graeme McPherson* 100h
10 b g Munir Shahmy (USA) (Lear Fan (USA))
3593^{3}

Zanstra (IRE) *Colin Tizzard* 70b
4 b g Morozov(USA) Enistar (IRE) (Synefos (USA))
5130^{9}

Zaplamation (IRE) *John Quinn* 121h
9 b g Acclamation Zapatista (Rainbow Quest (USA))
(2519) (2958) 3477^{U}

Zarkandar (IRE) *Paul Nicholls* 165h
7 b g Azamour(IRE) Zarkasha (IRE) (Kahyasi)
2665^{2} 3083^{2} 3459^{2} 4279^{2} 4767^{4} 5169^{4}

Zaru (FR) *James Ewart* 124h 137c
8 bb g Laveron Zianini (FR) (Dom Pasquini (FR))
2421^{6} (3039)
3211^{2} 5053^{U} (5482)

Zarzal (IRE) *Evan Williams* 129h 139c
6 b g Dr Fong(USA) Zarwala (IRE) (Polish Precedent (USA))
1046^{5} 1520^{3} **1698^{3} 2151^{3} (2721)** 3132^{4} **3732^{F}**
4507^{3} 4921^{5} 5399^{4}

Zava River (IRE) *Jamie Snowden* 105h 55c
7 b g Zagreb(USA) Great Accord (IRE) (Accordion)
1942^{5}

Zayfire Aramis *Nigel Twiston-Davies* 50h
5 ch g Zafeen(FR) Kaylifa Aramis (Kayf Tara)
2940^{12}

Zazamix (FR) *Andrew Crook* 90h 91c
9 b g Sagamix(FR) Ombre Bleue (FR) (Agent Bleu (FR))
109^{2} ◆ **281^{4}**

Zelos Diktator *Sean Curran* 90h
8 br g Diktat Chanterelle (IRE) (Indian Ridge)
29^{9} 436^{5} 2430^{P} 3119^{P} 3553^{P} 4760^{9} **5011^{P}**

Zenax Des Brosses (FR) *J Bigot* 111c
11 gr g Mad Tax(USA) Karenzed (FR) (Synefos (USA))
616a^{6}

Zen Factor *Jonathan Portman* 103h 93c
9 b g Josr Algarhoud(IRE) Zabelina (USA) (Diesis)
2251^{P} 2727^{3} 3687^{P} 4416^{7}

Zermatt (IRE) *John Quinn* 107h
5 ch g Strategic Prince Await (IRE) (Peintre Celebre (USA))
2196^{3}

Zeroeshadesofgrey (IRE) *Neil King* 120b
5 gr g Portrait Gallery(IRE) Hazy Rose (IRE) (Roselier (FR))
3508^{2} (3835) (4349) 4756^{15}

Zest For Life (IRE) *E Bolger* 96h 119c
10 b g Lord Americo Lucky To Live (IRE) (Salluceva)
1905a^{U} 2491^{8} 3068^{9}

Zhukov (IRE) *Kevin Tork* 95h 96c
12 b g Saddlers' Hall(IRE) Tamasriya (IRE) (Doyoun)
2727^{8} 3008^{6} (3248)
3470^{3} 3817^{5} 4718^{5} 4802^{2} 5115^{4}

Ziga Boy (FR) *Alan King* 111h 121c
5 gr g Califet(FR) Our Ziga (FR) (Linamix (FR))
4535^{2}
4932^{4} ◆

Ziggerson Hill *Jackie Du Plessis*
7 ch m Kadastrof(FR) Tregale (Chukaroo)
3694^{F}

Ziggie (IRE) *Donald McCain* 102h 97c
7 b g Dilshaan Like A Caterpillar (IRE) (Supreme Leader)
(225) 676^{F} 880^{6} 2874^{9} 4546^{8} **4984^{F} 5376^{3}**

Zigzaga (IRE) *Lydia Richards* 34h 84c
8 b g Zagreb(USA) Mrs McClintock (IRE) (Arctic Lord)
5259^{4} 5401^{P}

Zinnia Des Obeaux (FR) *N Devilder* 97c
7 b m Panoramic Zaouia (FR) (Cyborg (FR))
200a^{5}

Zipit (IRE) *Mrs Laura Gretton* 91c
9 b g Zagreb(USA) Pollys Rock (IRE) (Rock Hopper)
247^{6} 726^{P} 4727^{P}

Zip Wire (IRE) *Donald McCain* 110h
5 b g Oratorio(IRE) Jaya (USA) (Ela-Mana-Mou)
3351^{4} *4300^{6}*

Zorro's Blade *Michael Mullineaux* 38b
6 b g Needwood Blade Beechy Bank (IRE) (Shareef Dancer (USA))
675^{12}

Zouti (FR) *Gary Moore* 84h
6 b g Kahyasi Reine De Sabot (FR) (Homme De Loi (IRE))
3788^{12}

Zuider Zee (GER) *John Ferguson* 140h
7 b g Sakhee(USA) Zephyrine (IRE) (Highest Honor (FR))
2433^{2} 2671^{11}

Zuileka *James Moffatt* 79h
5 b m Observatory(USA) Cashema (IRE) (Cape Cross (IRE))
1737 2347^{11} 3835^{5} 4234^{10} 4487^{4} 5102^{11}

Zulu Oscar *Harry Fry* 118b
5 b g Oscar(IRE) Loxhill Lady (Supreme Leader)
298^{2} (2375) *(4298)*

Zulu Principle *Helen Nelmes* 88h
7 b g Tiger Hill(IRE) Tu Eres Mi Amore (IRE) (Sadler's Wells (USA))
37^{8} 3087 924^{P}

Top Trainers – British Jumps 2013–2014

NAME	*WINS–RUNS*	*%*	*2ND*	*3RD*	*4TH*	*WIN PRIZE*	*TOTAL PRIZE*	*£1 STAKE*
Paul Nicholls	118–587	20%	107	70	59	£1,383,758	£2,469,893	-134.23
Nicky Henderson	124–514	24%	77	56	48	£1,357,750	£2,019,936	-17.27
Philip Hobbs	106–542	20%	74	52	55	£977,475	£1,583,308	+21.37
Jonjo O'Neill	135–810	17%	105	95	81	£1,148,965	£1,572,505	-174.99
David Pipe	90–591	15%	64	58	68	£1,019,595	£1,433,119	-85.14
Nigel Twiston-Davies	77–559	14%	83	71	52	£702,181	£1,166,345	-101.52
Alan King	75–444	17%	64	49	57	£645,228	£1,112,823	-29.41
Venetia Williams	86–574	15%	73	72	53	£739,013	£1,110,493	-142.64
Donald McCain	142–775	18%	116	110	86	£665,421	£964,606	-135.22
Dr Richard Newland	38–167	23%	22	24	9	£821,179	£929,129	+10.23
W P Mullins	11–68	16%	8	8	8	£452,543	£855,396	-29.09
Gary Moore	45–315	14%	35	47	35	£677,659	£825,381	-14.91
Peter Bowen	69–356	19%	62	36	49	£441,890	£598,397	+57.06
Sue Smith	61–395	15%	57	45	47	£378,551	£598,180	-33.77
Evan Williams	55–419	13%	52	59	57	£383,280	£597,808	-58.64
Colin Tizzard	26–310	8%	30	43	42	£270,447	£564,336	-149.81
Emma Lavelle	41–233	18%	37	40	19	£306,888	£519,836	-24.35
Lucinda Russell	66–521	13%	65	84	64	£296,800	£503,244	-124.13
Charlie Longsdon	78–387	20%	48	53	38	£343,364	£496,742	-86.51
Tom George	40–288	14%	47	25	39	£270,628	£448,344	-91.26
Tim Vaughan	59–505	12%	78	57	66	£244,615	£423,480	-153.41
Rebecca Curtis	38–236	16%	39	37	26	£231,807	£413,100	-94.57
J H Culloty	2–7	29%	0	0	0	£363,302	£367,670	+27.00
John Ferguson	50–218	23%	35	22	27	£247,347	£365,546	-37.02
Fergal O'Brien	47–317	15%	34	37	49	£221,455	£357,764	+19.15
Kim Bailey	35–265	13%	28	33	36	£248,889	£346,854	-47.23
Dan Skelton	27–171	16%	26	22	20	£230,525	£327,272	-17.66
Nick Williams	23–129	18%	19	10	17	£200,999	£309,875	+43.68
Harry Fry	34–117	29%	17	10	10	£217,365	£302,748	+56.19
David Bridgwater	21–213	10%	28	28	28	£175,031	£300,295	-46.64
Oliver Sherwood	34–185	18%	35	29	24	£167,396	£297,965	-57.83
Gordon Elliott	19–79	24%	19	8	7	£148,750	£293,271	+16.50
Brian Ellison	39–279	14%	42	41	31	£173,250	£287,804	-27.43
Nicky Richards	25–166	15%	25	18	18	£173,251	£253,353	-18.47
Warren Greatrex	43–192	22%	26	27	18	£161,419	£251,100	+33.02
Mrs John Harrington	1–7	14%	1	0	1	£238,051	£248,672	+3.00
Jeremy Scott	23–202	11%	18	27	19	£186,347	£248,173	-48.72
Mick Channon	11–62	18%	10	13	8	£74,459	£247,465	-12.34
Henry Daly	35–180	19%	30	21	14	£154,905	£245,715	-7.80
Martin Keighley	21–216	10%	33	17	15	£132,194	£235,559	-98.40
Ian Williams	30–205	15%	29	24	17	£137,201	£235,461	-49.43
Richard Lee	17–155	11%	28	29	12	£137,249	£233,564	-37.15
Malcolm Jefferson	30–187	16%	25	29	20	£128,588	£227,453	-20.82
Paul Webber	16–211	8%	31	21	26	£117,820	£223,991	-119.13
Keith Reveley	19–134	14%	18	34	11	£134,066	£187,318	-29.33
John Quinn	18–85	21%	12	15	6	£117,083	£177,645	+2.90
Seamus Mullins	24–214	11%	25	24	29	£114,266	£176,575	-26.82
Tim Easterby	13–101	13%	17	12	10	£111,191	£169,656	-17.40
N W Alexander	24–181	13%	22	25	15	£110,714	£166,184	+45.54
Neil Mulholland	31–251	12%	26	27	29	£115,881	£162,210	-56.24

Top Jockeys – British Jumps 2013–2014

NAME	WINS–RUNS	%	2ND	3RD	4TH	WIN PRIZE	TOTAL PRIZE	£1 STAKE
A P McCoy	218–903	24%	149	119	111	£1,386,424	£2,250,140	-138.63
Richard Johnson	155–831	19%	126	119	98	£1,202,081	£1,880,985	-13.21
Jason Maguire	130–662	20%	108	86	73	£623,299	£899,185	-107.53
Noel Fehily	127–596	21%	73	79	59	£870,911	£1,315,414	-9.92
Sam Twiston-Davies	115–774	15%	112	99	81	£924,027	£1,550,269	-157.57
Tom Scudamore	100–629	16%	91	68	68	£1,078,602	£1,587,004	-70.92
Aidan Coleman	97–647	15%	97	80	62	£678,832	£1,113,027	-139.58
Brian Hughes	86–617	14%	97	99	70	£402,337	£678,359	-52.24
Paddy Brennan	77–527	15%	77	60	72	£385,092	£636,526	-79.88
Tom O'Brien	74–528	14%	75	53	59	£478,608	£723,084	-8.77
Daryl Jacob	70–361	19%	67	41	39	£618,879	£1,179,133	-75.48
Leighton Aspell	65–402	16%	61	41	44	£952,483	£1,176,513	-44.56
Denis O'Regan	64–445	14%	62	54	55	£302,137	£481,466	-153.92
Nick Scholfield	60–530	11%	55	55	57	£454,514	£665,057	-228.90
Jamie Moore	60–480	13%	67	69	49	£816,628	£1,030,321	-123.59
Barry Geraghty	57–238	24%	32	31	24	£1,318,633	£1,671,482	+0.24
Wayne Hutchinson	54–325	17%	31	35	33	£382,609	£533,623	+10.88
Ryan Mania	53–339	16%	46	38	52	£347,335	£533,044	+52.95
Paul Moloney	52–515	10%	51	63	67	£382,843	£606,652	-94.27
Gavin Sheehan	50–325	15%	44	41	32	£189,437	£323,099	-36.78
Peter Buchanan	47–345	14%	43	47	43	£245,092	£392,688	-34.33
Wilson Renwick	46–369	12%	46	49	45	£211,757	£343,786	-61.63
Liam Treadwell	42–292	14%	26	37	22	£253,710	£374,638	+76.78
Brendan Powell	41–390	11%	33	44	47	£242,233	£406,384	-80.58
James Reveley	41–254	16%	35	56	24	£235,601	£345,128	-47.19
Robert Thornton	37–295	13%	47	32	35	£227,441	£560,106	-131.22
Brian Harding	36–337	11%	35	31	45	£204,769	£308,639	-85.67
Michael Byrne	34–248	14%	23	19	27	£128,296	£182,265	-38.33
Dougie Costello	32–431	7%	45	53	56	£161,037	£268,665	-209.40
Felix De Giles	30–247	12%	31	21	27	£132,763	£206,590	-51.23
Henry Brooke	29–281	10%	25	29	28	£126,955	£198,432	+11.32
Andrew Tinkler	29–233	12%	34	23	26	£127,247	£250,229	-25.48
Trevor Whelan	29–188	15%	23	28	23	£103,342	£150,985	+83.65
Adam Wedge	27–260	10%	25	34	34	£145,104	£245,895	-31.25
Nico de Boinville	27–151	18%	12	16	14	£149,770	£226,675	+103.75
David Bass	26–213	12%	19	18	19	£117,683	£197,268	-68.24
Conor Shoemark	26–209	12%	32	21	16	£111,310	£162,051	-69.71
Harry Skelton	26–198	13%	28	28	23	£219,330	£326,444	-51.78
Tom Cannon	25–364	7%	42	44	34	£137,258	£241,219	-164.65
James Best	25–211	10%	23	23	24	£115,596	£188,050	-43.05
Richie McLernon	24–299	8%	29	32	27	£306,429	£428,488	-106.96
Ian Popham	24–281	9%	35	23	20	£196,231	£309,223	-96.12
Jake Greenall	24–220	11%	22	26	25	£94,404	£166,590	-91.01
Donal Devereux	24–164	15%	9	10	20	£136,108	£168,531	-29.77
Andrew Thornton	23–350	7%	36	37	52	£106,767	£219,348	-168.22
Joshua Moore	23–221	10%	27	35	22	£159,741	£261,858	-35.25
Kielan Woods	23–194	12%	22	30	20	£86,085	£137,266	+52.96
Lucy Alexander	22–220	10%	20	24	20	£113,739	£167,056	-1.75
Jonathan England	22–196	11%	24	20	18	£120,318	£199,751	-65.25
Tony Kelly	22–179	12%	19	34	11	£66,652	£109,997	-8.30

Top Owners – British Jumps 2013–2014

NAME	WINS–RUNS	%	2ND	3RD	4TH	WIN PRIZE	TOTAL PRIZE
John P McManus	121–610	20%	91	73	52	£1,294,384	£2,052,076
J A Provan	5–18	28%	2	2	0	£579,086	£596,828
The Preston Family & Friends Ltd	6–7	86%	1	0	0	£468,613	£483,572
Dr R Lambe	3–7	43%	0	0	0	£397,472	£401,840
Andrea & Graham Wylie	8–55	15%	8	5	9	£173,452	£397,015
R S Brookhouse	29–93	31%	10	8	15	£318,341	£377,261
Bloomfields	49–213	23%	34	21	26	£245,398	£360,141
Potensis Limited & Chris Giles	5–13	38%	4	1	3	£213,744	£352,606
Gigginstown House Stud	4–31	13%	4	2	4	£219,215	£330,360
Mrs Diana L Whateley	25–68	37%	9	7	7	£265,074	£328,615
Mrs S Ricci	5–16	31%	2	0	2	£225,584	£326,001
The Brushmakers	4–9	44%	1	1	0	£90,712	£303,682
Mrs S Such	7–14	50%	4	1	0	£220,876	£292,383
Trevor Hemmings	18–137	13%	26	10	21	£126,299	£252,321
Walters Plant Hire Ltd	10–46	22%	6	7	4	£195,586	£238,429
A J White	1–4	25%	2	0	0	£156,613	£236,806
Mrs T P Radford	10–40	25%	10	8	3	£70,560	£231,002
Mrs Gay Smith	16–80	20%	10	5	8	£181,590	£209,485
Mrs Jean R Bishop	3–19	16%	3	5	3	£117,186	£200,397
The Stewart Family	8–41	20%	4	4	8	£134,830	£192,939
Simon Munir	5–28	18%	6	4	1	£114,365	£189,739
Mr & Mrs R Kelvin-Hughes	8–25	32%	2	2	2	£154,588	£172,298
P J Martin	15–87	17%	19	12	12	£94,847	£156,453
F Lloyd	6–37	16%	6	5	6	£140,282	£154,678
Masterson Holdings Limited	10–34	29%	2	2	5	£137,543	£147,611
Paul & Clare Rooney	24–103	23%	22	11	13	£100,666	£140,638
Mrs S Smith	19–161	12%	17	24	15	£89,757	£139,918
Mr & Mrs William Rucker	7–52	13%	5	10	10	£56,128	£132,502
Options O Syndicate	4–16	25%	3	3	0	£96,974	£131,933
N A Twiston-Davies	19–107	18%	17	11	13	£65,681	£131,090
Christopher W T Johnston	2–5	40%	0	0	1	£122,400	£129,877
Potensis Limited	5–10	50%	1	0	1	£125,925	£129,772
Mr & Mrs Sandy Orr	2–8	25%	0	2	0	£113,739	£124,806
The Johnson & Stewart Families	1–16	6%	5	0	1	£4,106	£124,672
Simon Munir & Isaac Souede	7–38	18%	7	2	6	£46,994	£121,897
Favourites Racing	10–68	15%	10	9	5	£40,319	£121,772
T G Leslie	23–95	24%	14	12	12	£84,805	£119,392
Simon Hunt & Gary Lambton	1–2	50%	0	1	0	£56,950	£118,449
J Hales	3–21	14%	3	4	1	£52,519	£118,402
Mrs P Sloan	1–19	5%	1	6	3	£56,270	£116,682
J D Neild	2–9	22%	2	2	2	£92,047	£115,572
Cash For Honours	3–6	50%	0	0	0	£111,254	£114,706
The Bellamy Partnership	5–26	19%	3	3	0	£88,492	£114,589
R J H Geffen	10–33	30%	3	3	0	£63,803	£114,454
Martin Broughton & Friends 1	4–6	67%	1	1	0	£103,312	£114,431
Tim Syder	11–37	30%	9	4	1	£71,689	£113,967
Mr And Mrs J D Cotton	7–26	27%	6	4	0	£57,266	£112,712
Trembath, Hyde, Outhart & Hill	2–5	40%	1	0	0	£103,517	£110,916
Mrs Janet Davies	8–63	13%	4	12	8	£65,917	£109,604

Raceform Top Rated Chasers and Hurdlers 2013–2014

Chasers

Cue Card	180
Silviniaco Conti	179
Captain Chris	176
Dynaste	175
Sire De Grugy	174
Tidal Bay	172
Harry Topper	170
Lord Windermere	170
On His Own	170
The Giant Bolster	170

Hurdlers

Jezki	173
My Tent Or Yours	173
The New One	173
More Of That	172
Hurricane Fly	170
At Fishers Cross	166
Celestial Halo	165
Diakali	165
Rock On Ruby	165
Zarkandar	165

Novice Chasers

Holywell	165
Taquin Du Seuil	164
O'Faolains Boy	163
Smad Place	163
Balder Success	162
Oscar Whisky	162
Uxizandre	162
Champagne Fever	161
Dodging Bullets	161
Western Warhorse	161

Novice Hurdlers

Beat That	159
Faugheen	159
Vautour	158
Kings Palace	154
Seeyouatmidnight	154
Don Poli	153
Very Wood	153
Clondaw Court	152
Cole Harden	152
Deputy Dan	151

Raceform Jumps Record Times 2013–2014

AINTREE

Distance	Time	Age	Weight	Going	Horse	Date
2m C	3m 45.2	9	10-7	Firm	Nohalmdun	Apr 7 ,1990
2m 1f H	4m 8.3	5	11-5	Gd to firm	Rumble Of Thunder (IRE)	Oct 22, 2011
2m 4f C	4m 47.5	8	11-6	Gd to firm	Wind Force	Apr 2 ,1993
2m 4f H	4m 37.1	5	10-11	Gd to firm	Gallateen	Apr 2 ,1993
2m 5f 110y C	5m 19.3	10	10-4	Good	Always Waining	Apr 8 , 2011
3m 110y H	5m 50.6	6	10-2	Gd to firm	Andrew's First	Apr 1 ,1993
3m 1f C	6m 3.4	7	11-3	Gd to firm	Cab on Target	Apr 2 ,1993
4m 4f NC	8m 47.8	11	10-6	Firm	Mr Frisk	Apr 7 ,1990

ASCOT

Distance	Time	Age	Weight	Going	Horse	Date
2m H	3m 33.3	4	10-8	Good	Brampour	Oct 29, 2011
2m 1f C	4m 3.0	8	11-12	Gd to firm	Crossbow Creek	Oct 28, 2006
2m 3f C	4m 38.65	8	11-11	Good	Master Minded (FR)	Nov 19, 2011
2m 3f 110y H	4m 30.8	7	11-0	Good	Overturn	Nov 19, 2011
2m 5f 110y C	5m 12.6	9	10-13	Good	Kew Jumper (IRE)	Apr 11, 2008
3m H	5m 34.1	6	11-2	Good	Heronry	Mar 30, 2014
3m C	5m 49.6	9	10-10	Good	Exmoor Ranger	Oct 29, 2011
3m 1f H	5m 57.3	7	11-7	Gd to firm	Lough Derg	Dec 22, 2007

AYR

Distance	Time	Age	Weight	Going	Horse	Date
2m H	3m 27.4	6	10-7	Firm	Secret Ballot	Apr 19,1980
2m C	3m 38.7	6	11-0	Gd to firm	Clay County	Oct 12,1991
2m 4f C	4m 44.1	8	12-2	Firm	Chandigar	May 15,1972
2m 4f H	4m 35.0	8	9-10	Firm	Moss Royal	Apr 19,1974
2m 5f 110y H	5m 4.7	7	10-13	Good	Cucumber Run	Apr 21, 2012
3m 110y H	5m 42.0	13	10-11	Firm	Nautical Lad	Apr 6 ,1964
3m 1f C	5m 57.7	9	11-0	Gd to firm	Top 'N' Tale	May 12,1982
4m1f C	7m 55.1	8	9-9	Gd to firm	Hot Weld	Apr 21, 2007

BANGOR-ON-DEE

Distance	Time	Age	Weight	Going	Horse	Date
2m 1f H	3m 44.5	9	10-2	Firm	Andy Rew	Apr 24, 1982
2m 1f 110y C	4m 5.0	6	11-11	Gd to firm	Beherayn	Jul 31, 2009
2m 4f H	4m 34.1	5	11-13	Good	Smithy's Choice	Apr 25, 1987
2m 4f 110y C	4m 49.7	8	10-12	Good	The Disengager (IRE)	Jul 24, 2012
3m H	5m 34.0	5	11-2	Gd to firm	General Pershing	Apr 20, 1991
3m 110y C	5m 50.6	8	11-3	Gd to firm	He's The Gaffer (IRE)	Aug 16, 2008
3m 6f C	7m 34.1	6	12-0	Good	Kaki Crazy (FR)	May 23, 2001
4m 1f C	8m 50.7	6	10-11	Gd to soft	Nazzaro	Dec 3, 1995

CARLISLE

Distance	Time	Age	Weight	Going	Horse	Date
2m C	3m 54.5	5	11-5	Good	Up To Something	Oct 11, 2013
2m 1f H	4m 10.9	6	11-5	Good	Houston Dynimo (IRE)	Oct 7, 2011
2m 3f 110y H	4m 45.1	5	11-11	Good	Nexius	Apr 19, 2014
2m 5f C	5m 24.1	6	10-13	Gd to soft	Frank The Slink	Mar 22, 2012
3m 110y C	6m 0.7	8	10-13	Gd to firm	Ripalong Lad (IRE)	Oct 9, 2009
3m 1f H	6m 13.5	5	11-0	Good	Mr Preacher Man	Oct 25, 2007
3m 2f C	6m 40.4	8	11-3	Good	Lady of Gortmerron (IRE)	Oct 6, 2000

CARTMEL

Distance	Time	Age	Weight	Going	Horse	Date
2m 1f 110yH	3m 56.2	5	10-9	Gd to firm	Lisbon	May 25, 2013
2m 1f 110yC	4m 7.5	12	11-13	Hard	Clever Folly	May 27, 1992
2m 5f 110y C	5m 6.1	10	10-10	Firm	Corrarder	May 30, 1994
2m 6f H	5m 13.7	10	11-12	Gd to firm	The Good Guy	May 25, 2013
3m 2f C	6m 21.3	12	11-12	Good	Better Times Ahead	Aug 29, 1998
3m 2f H	5m 57.9	10	11-3	Firm	Portonia	May 30, 1994
3m6f C	7m12.0	10	11-4	Good	Chabrimal Minster	May 26, 2007

CATTERICK

Distance	Time	Age	Weight	Going	Horse	Date
2m C	3m 44.6	6	10-0	Firm	Preston Deal	Dec 18, 1971
2m H	3m 36.5	7	11-3	Firm	Lunar Wind	Apr 22, 1982
2m 3f C	4m 38.5	5	11-0	Good	Hi George	Dec 4, 2013
2m 3f H	4m 31.5	5	11-6	Good	Smadynium (FR)	Dec 4, 2013
3m 1f 110y C	6m 14.0	10	10-1	Gd to firm	Clever General	Nov 7 , 1981
3m 1f 110y H	6m 3.8	6	10-9	Gd to firm	Seamus O'Flynn	Nov 7 , 1981
3m 6f C	7m 41.8	10	10-11	Gd to soft	General Hardi	Nov 13, 2011

CHELTENHAM

Distance	Time	Age	Weight	Going	Horse	Date
2m OldC		3m 44.6		8	12-0	Good
Edredon Bleu (FR)		Mar 15, 2000				
2m110y OldH	3m 45.25	6	11-10	Gd to soft	Jezki	Mar 11, 2014
2m110y NwC	3m 52.4	7	10-11	Gd to firm	Samakaan (IRE)	Mar 16, 2000
2m 1f NwH	3m 51.2	5	11-2	Gd to firm	Moody Man	Mar 15, 1990
2m1f NewH	3m 51.2	4	11-0	Good	Detroit City (USA)	Mar 17, 2006
2m4f110yNH	4m 45.0	6	10-4	Gd to firm	Sir Dante (IRE)	Apr 15, 1997
2m4f110yOC	4m 49.6	9	10-3	Good	Dark Stranger (FR)	Mar 15, 2000
2m 5f OldH	4m 52.0	6	11-7	Good	Monsignor (IRE)	Mar 15, 2000
2m 5f NwC	5m 1.6	9	11-10	Gd to firm	Barnbrook Again	Apr 18, 1990
2m 5f110yNH	4m 53.6	4	10-9	Good	Fashion House	Spt 19, 1968
3m 110yNwH	5m 36.6	6	11-10	Gd to firm	Bacchanal (IRE)	Mar 16, 2000
3m 1f OldC	5m 59.7	8	10-3	Good	Marlborough (IRE)	Mar 14, 2000
3m 1f110yNC	6m 13.4	9	10-11	Gd to firm	Bigsun	Mar 15, 1990
3m 1f110yOH	6m 3.4	9	11-2	Good	Rubhahunish (IRE)	Mar 14, 2000
3m 2f110yNC	6m 29.7	6	11-10	Good	Long Run (FR)	Mar 18, 2011
3m 3f110yOC	7m 1.0	6	10-2	Good	Shardam (IRE)	Nov 15, 2003
3m 7f XCC	7m 51.70	8	10-9	Gd to firm	Balthazar King (IRE)	Mar 13, 2012
4m 1f NwC	8m 33.2	7	11-11	Good	Hot Weld	Mar 16, 2006

CHEPSTOW

Distance	Time	Age	Weight	Going	Horse	Date
2m 110y H	3m 43.2	4	10-1	Firm	Tingle Bell	Oct 4 , 1986
2m 110y C	3m 54.1	8	12-0	Firm	Panto Prince	May 9 , 1989
2m 3f 110y C	4m 42.5	5	11-4	Good	Balder Success (FR)	Oct 12, 2013
2m 4f 110y H	4m 36.2	9	11-3	Firm	Aileen's Cacador	Apr 23 , 1957
3m H	5m 33.5	10	10-0	Firm	Chucklestone	May 11 , 1993
3m C	5m 47.9	9	10-11	Firm	Broadheath	Oct 4 , 1986
3m 2f 110y C	6m 39.4	7	12-0	Firm	Jaunty Jane	May 26, 1975
3m 5f 110y C	7m 24.0	9	10-5	Firm	Creeola	Apr 23 , 1957

DONCASTER

Distance	Time	Age	Weight	Going	Horse	Date
2m 110y H	3m 46.6	6	10-0	Gd to firm	Good for a Loan	Feb 24, 1993
2m 110y C	3m 51.9	12	10-9	Gd to firm	Itsgottabealright	Jan 28, 1989
2m 3f C	4m 36.9	7	11-0	Good	Off The Ground (IRE)	Nov 29, 2013
2m 3f 110y H	4m 33.0	4	10-12	Good	Bobby Ewing (IRE)	Dec 11, 2009
3m C	5m 52.4	7	11-7	Good	Beneficial Reform	Mar 3, 2012
3m 110yH	5m 43.2	6	11-10	Good	Allthekingshorses	Feb 22, 2012
3m 2f C	6m 11.8	9	10-10	Good	Always Right	Mar 5, 2011

EXETER

Distance	Time	Age	Weight	Going	Horse	Date
2m 1f H	3m 52.2	4	10-10	Gd to firm	Made In France (FR)	Sep 28, 2004
2m 1f 110y C	3m 58.1	7	11-7	Firm	Bushwacker	May 3, 2011
2m 3f H	4m 14.7	5	10.13	Firm	My Brother Sylvest	Oct 18, 2011
2m 3f 110y C	4m 27.9	8	11-11	Gd to firm	West With The Wind	May 7, 2013
2m 5f 110y H	5m 5.7	7	10-6	Gd to firm	Cruising Bye	Oct 10, 2013
2m 6f 110y H	5m 18.5	7	11-10	Gd to firm	Presenting Express	Oct 4, 2006
2m 7f 110y H	5m 26.2	8	10-11	Gd to firm	Very Cool	May 4, 2010
2m 7f 110yC	5m 30.1	7	11-4	Gd to firm	Mister Gloss	May 14, 2008
3m C	5m 42.8	8	10-5	Gd to firm	Dennis The Legend	May 5, 2009
3m 110y H	5m 42.3	5	11-7	Firm	Il Capitano	Oct 1 , 2002
3m 1f 110yC	6m 3.0	8	11-4	Gd to firm	Radnor Lad	May 14, 2008
4m C	8m 9.3	10	11-5	Good	Major Malarkey	Dec 6, 2013

FAKENHAM

Distance	Time	Age	Weight	Going	Horse	Date
2m H	3m 45.7	5	10-9	Gd to firm	Cobbet (CZE)	May 9, 2001
2m 110y C	3m 44.9	11	12-4	Firm	Cheekio Ora	Apr 23, 1984
2m 4f H	4m 41.1	4	10-8	Gd to firm	Ayem (IRE)	May 16, 1999
2m 5f 110yC	5m 10.1	13	12-2	Gd to firm	Skipping Tim	May 25, 1992
2m 7f 110yH	5m 37.1	6	11-3	Good	Laughing Gas (IRE)	May 20, 1995
3m 110y C	5m 57.0	7	11-1	Gd to firm	Specialize	May 16, 1999

FFOS LAS

Distance	Time	Age	Weight	Going	Horse	Date
2m C	3m 45.25	6	11-12	Gd To firm	West With The Wind	Aug 25, 2011
2m H	3m 33.60	6	10-11	Good	Valain (IRE)	Aug 28, 2009
2m 3f 110y C	4m 37.34	7	10-12	Firm	Cold Harbour	May 31, 2011
2m 4f H	4m 39.40	6	10-9	Good	Plunkett (IRE)	Jun 18, 2009
2m 5f C	5m 9.70	8	11-11	Gd to firm	Putney Bridge	Jun 17, 2010
2m 6f H	5m 15.4	6	11-0	Good	Koultas King	Aug 22, 2013
3m C	5m 49.60	7	11-7	Good	Sea Wall	Jun 18, 2009
3m H	5m 41.50	5	11-9	Good	Quattrocento (FR)	Jun 18, 2009
3m 1f 110y C	6m 7.10	7	10-1	Good	Backstage (FR)	Aug 28, 2009

FONTWELL

Distance	Time	Age	Weight	Going	Horse	Date
2m 2f C	4m 14.5	12	10-1	Gd to firm	A Thousand Dreams (IRE)	Jun 3 , 2002
2m 2f 110y H	4m 6.8	7	10-2	Gd to firm	Hyperion du Moulin II (FR)	Jun 3 , 2002
2m 6f C	5m 13.9	10	10-0	Gd to firm	Contes (IRE)	Jun 3, 2002
2m 6f 110y H	5m 6.7	7	10-1	Gd to firm	Mister Pickwick (IRE)	Jun 3, 2002
3m 2f 110y C	6m 24.3	5	10-2	Gd to firm	Il Capitano	May 6, 2002
3m 3f H	6m 21.6	5	11-2	Gd to firm	Lord Of The Track (IRE)	Aug 18, 2003
3m 4f C	7m 11.1	8	10-6	Good	Strolling Vagabond (IRE)	Mar 18, 2007

HAYDOCK

Distance	Time	Age	Weight	Going	Horse	Date
2m C	3m 52.3	7	11-7	Good	Witness In Court (IRE)	Apr 19, 2014
2m H (Inr)	3m 44.3	5	11-5	Good	Perpetually (IRE)	Oct 26, 2011
2m 4f H (Inr)	4m 32.1	5	11-2	Good	My Brother Sylvest	Oct 26, 2011
2m 4f H	4m 33.0	7	10-11	Good	Carlton Jack	Apr 19, 2014
2m 4f H (Fxd)	4m 32.1	6	11-12	Good	Horizontal Speed	Apr 20, 2014
2m 4f C	4m 49.9	6	11-7	Good	Etxalar (FR)	Oct 28, 2009
3m H (Inr)	5m 33.7	8	10-9	Good	Liberate	May 7, 2011
3m H (Fxd)	5m 37.6	5	10-13	Gd to soft	Dynaste	Nov 19, 2011
3m C	5m 41.5	7	10-6	Good	No Planning	Apr 19, 2014
3m 4f C	7m 7.7	9	10-8	Good	Blenheim Brook	Apr 19, 2014

HEXHAM

Distance	Time	Age	Weight	Going	Horse	Date
2m 110y H	3m 57.8	8	11-7	Gd to firm	Francies Fancy (IRE)	Jun 19, 2005
2m 110y C	3m 53.6	9	11-9	Gd to firm	Adamatic	Jun 17, 2000
2m 4f 110y H	4m 31.5	6	11-0	Gd to firm	Pappa Charlie (USA)	May 27, 1997
2m 4f 110y C	4m 55.4	8	9-11	Firm	Mr Laggan	Spt 14, 2003
3m H	5m 45.4	7	9-9	Firm	Fingers Crossed	Apr 29, 1991
3m 1f C	6m 7.6	9	9-11	Gd to firm	Silent Snipe	Jun 1, 2002
4m C	8m 34.0	10	10-12	Good	Simply Smashing (IRE)	Mar 18, 2010

HUNTINGDON

Distance	Time	Age	Weight	Going	Horse	Date
2m 110y H	3m 32.7	5	11-11	Gd to firm	Weather Front	Aug 31, 2009
2m 110y C	3m 53.3	5	10-0	Gd to firm	No Greater Love (FR)	May 23, 2007
2m 4f 110y C	4m 46.4	10	10-13	Gd to firm	Peccadillo	Sep 26, 2004
2m 4f 110y H	4m 32.9	6	10-12	Gd to firm	Richie's Delight (IRE)	Aug 30, 1999
2m 5f 110y H	4m 45.8	6	11-5	Firm	Sound of Laughter	Apr 14, 1984
3m C	5m 44.3	7	11-9	Gd to firm	Ozzie Jones	Spt 18, 1998
3m 2f H	5m 50.2	8	11-12	Gd to firm	Orchard King (IRE)	Aug 31, 2009
3m 6f 110y C	8m 2.7	9	10-4	Gd to soft	Kinnahalla (IRE)	Nov 24, 2001

KELSO

Distance	Time	Age	Weight	Going	Horse	Date
2m 110y H	3m 38.9	6	11-12	Gd to firm	Life And Soul	May 26, 2013
2m 1f C	4m 2.6	8	11-9	Firm	Mr Coggy	May 2 , 1984
2m 2f H	4m 8.7	6	11-7	Gd to firm	Croco Bay	May 26, 2013
2m 6f 110y H	5m 12.2	4	11-3	Firm	Hit The Canvas (USA)	Sep 30, 1995
2m 6f 110y C	5m 29.6	10	10-13	Good	Bas De Laine (FR)	Nov 13, 1996
3m 1f C	6m 1.2	13	12-0	Gd to firm	Mcgregor The Third	Sept 19, 1999
3m 3f H	6m 10.1	8	11-5	Firm	Ambergate	Oct 21, 1989
3m 4f C	7m 2.3	7	10-6	Good	Seven Towers (IRE)	Dec 2 , 1996
4m C	8m 7.4	8	10-0	Good	Seven Towers	Jan 17, 1997

KEMPTON

Distance	Time	Age	Weight	Going	Horse	Date
2m C	3m 48.3	6	10-9	Good	Hoo La Baloo (FR)	Oct 21, 2007
2m H	3m 40.40	7	11-8	Good	Australia Day (IRE)	Oct 17, 2010
2m 4f 110y C	5m 7.0	9	11-4	Good	Au Courant (IRE)	Apr 20, 2009
2m 5f H	5m 2.5	7	11-12	Good	Dover's Hill	Apr 20, 2009
3m C	5m 57.4	8	11-10	Good	Kauto Star (FR)	Dec 26, 2008
3m 110y H	6m 6.50	5	11-9	Good	Dreamsoftheatre	Nov 25, 2013

LEICESTER

Distance	Time	Age	Weight	Going	Horse	Date
2m H	3m 39.6	6	10-11	Gd to firm	Ryde Again	Nov 20, 1989
2m C	3m 54.5	5	11-7	Good	William's Wishes (IRE)	Nov 15, 2010
2m 4f 110y C	5m 22.6	5	11-2	Gd to firm	Theatrelands	Dec 11, 2013
2m 4f 110y H	4m 45.5	4	11-7	Gd to firm	Prince of Rheims	Dec 5, 1989
2m 7f 110y C	5m 44.8	6	11-10	Gd to firm	Little Chip	Dec 11, 2013

LINGFIELD

Distance	Time	Age	Weight	Going	Horse	Date
2m C	3m 48.7	9	11-2	Gd to firm	Rapide Plaisir (IRE)	Sep 28, 2007
2m 110y H	3m 47.2	5	11-0	Firm	Va Utu	Mar 19, 1993
2m 3f 110y H	4m 37.4	6	10-3	Firm	Bellezza	Mar 20, 1993
2m 4f 110y C	5m 4.0	8	11-7	Good	Copsale Lad	Oct 29, 2005
2m 7f H	5m 31.9	8	11-6	Gd to firm	Herecomestanley	Sep 28, 2007
3m C	5m 58.4	6	11-3	Firm	Mighty Frolic	Mar 19, 1993

LUDLOW

Distance	Time	Age	Weight	Going	Horse	Date
2m C	3m 47.3	5	11-7	Gd to firm	Pearl King (IRE)	Apr 5, 2007
2m H	3m 35.9	10	11-10	Good	Alwaystheoptimist	Oct 9, 2013
2m 4f C	4m 47.3	10	11-8	Gd to firm	Handy Money	Apr 5, 2007
2m 5f H	4m 54.7	8	11-0	Gd to firm	Willy Willy	Oct 11, 2001
3m H	5m 33.3	5	9-11	Good	Dark Spirit	Oct 9, 2013
3m C	5m 48.4	9	10-12	Firm	Bold Perk	Oct 5, 2011

MARKET RASEN

Distance	Time	Age	Weight	Going	Horse	Date
2m 1f 110yH	3m 57.4	7	11-5	Good	Australia Day (IRE)	Jul 17, 2010
2m 2f C	4m 13.6	11	10-2	Gd to firm	Mister Wiseman	Jul 7, 2013
2m 3f H	4m 26.1	6	11-9	Gd to soft	Attaglance	Feb 19, 2012
2m 4f C	4m 41.4	8	11-1	Good	Bocciani	May 10, 2013
2m 5f H	5m 3.7	7	11-3	Gd to soft	Fiulin	Feb 19, 2012
2m 6f 110yC	5m 18.3	8	10-12	Gd to firm	Paddy The Hare (IRE)	Jul 7, 2013
3m H	5m 38.8	6	12-5	Firm	Trustful	May 21, 1977
3m 1f C	6m 1.0	7	11-8	Gd to firm	Allerlea	May 1, 1985
3m 4f 110y C	7m 17.5	10	11-1	Good	Fin Bec (FR)	Nov 20, 2003

MUSSELBURGH

Distance	Time	Age	Weight	Going	Horse	Date
2m H	3m 35.9	3	10-7	Gd to firm	Joe Bumpas	Dec 11, 1989
2m C	3m 48.1	8	10-12	Gd to firm	Sonsie Mo	Dec 6, 1993
2m 4f C	4m 44.5	7	11-9	Gd to firm	Bohemian Spirit (IRE)	Dec 18, 2005
2m 4f H	4m 34.7	9	11-7	Good	Strongpoint (IRE)	Dec 9, 2013
3m C	5m 47.7	7	11-10	Firm	Snowy (IRE)	Dec 18, 2005
3m 110y H	5m 36.2	6	11-1	Soft	Seeyouatmidnight	Feb 2, 2014

NEWBURY

Distance	Time	Age	Weight	Going	Horse	Date
2m 110y H	3m 45.2	5	10-2	Gd to firm	Dhofar	Oct 25, 1985
2m 1f C	3m 57.34	6	11-5	Good	Valdez	Nov 30, 2013
2m 2f 110y C	4m 31.87	7	11-9	Gd to soft	Highway Code (IRE)	Nov 29, 2013
2m 3f H	4m 26.7	4	11-0	Good	Songsmith	Mar 24, 2012
2m 4f C	4m 47.9	8	11-12	Gd to firm	Espy	Oct 25, 1991
2m 5f H	4m 48.63	6	11-0	Good	Argento Luna	Mar 21, 2009
2m 6f 110y C	5m 28.93	5	11-10	Good	Pepite Rose (FR)	Mar 24, 2012
3m C	5m 42.53	7	11-10	Gd to soft	Long Run (FR)	Feb 17, 2012
3m 110y H	5m 45.4	8	10-9	Good	Lansdowne	Oct 25, 1996
3m 2f 110y C	6m 22.86	9	10-8	Good	Ikorodu Road	Mar 23, 2012

NEWCASTLE

Distance	Time	Age	Weight	Going	Horse	Date
2m H	3m 40.7	7	10-10	Good	Padre Mio	Nov 25, 1995
2m 110y C	3m 56.7	7	11-12	Firm	Greenheart	May 7, 1990
2m 4f C	4m 46.7	7	9-13	Firm	Snow Blessed	May 19, 1984
2m 4f H	4m 42.0	4	10-10	Hard	Mils Mij	May 13, 1989
3m C	5m 48.1	8	10-4	Firm	Even Swell	Oct 30, 1975
3m H	5m 40.1	4	10-5	Gd to firm	Withy Bank	Nov 29, 1986
3m 6f C	7m 30.0	8	12-0	Good	Charlie Potheen	Apr 28, 1973
4m 1f C	8m 30.4	7	10-0	Good	Domaine de Pron (FR)	Feb 21, 1998

NEWTON ABBOT

Distance	Time	Age	Weight	Going	Horse	Date
2m 110y C	3m 53.2	8	11-3	Gd to firm	Norborne Bandit (IRE)	Aug 22, 2009
2m 1f H	3m 45.0	5	11-0	Firm	Windbound Lass	Aug 1, 1988
2m 3f H	4m 15.2	5	10-8	Gd to firm	Rum And Butter	Aug 22, 2013
2m 5f 110y C	5m 2.1	7	11-0	Good	Mhilu (IRE)	Jul 13, 2009
2m 6f H	4m 55.4	7	10-0	Firm	Virbian	Jun 30, 1983
3m 2f 110y C	6m 9.5	8	11-7	Gd to firm	No Loose Change	Jul 8, 2013
3m 3f H	6m 16.7	8	10-13	Gd to firm	Celebrity Call (IRE)	Jun 4, 2009

PERTH

Distance	Time	Age	Weight	Going	Horse	Date
2m C	3m 44.6	7	10-7	Gd to firm	Sergeant Pink (IRE)	Jul 3, 2013
2m 110y H	3m 38.2	5	11-6	Gd to firm	Lisbon (IRE)	Jul 3, 2013
2m 4f 110y H	4m 41.2	8	10-2	Firm	Valiant Dash	May 19, 1994
2m 4f 110y C	4m 53.0	8	11-12	Gd to firm	Abragante (IRE)	Jul 2, 2009
3m C	5m 46.2	7	10-12	Gd to firm	Problema Tic	Jun 9, 2013
3m 110y H	5m 41.6	10	11-1	Gd to firm	Imtihan (IRE)	Jul 2, 2009

PLUMPTON

Distance	Time	Age	Weight	Going	Horse	Date
2m H	3m 31.0	3	11-1	Firm	Royal Derbi	Sep 19, 1988
2m 1f C	4m 5.00	7	11-12	Good	Gauvain (GER)	Apr 13, 2009
2m 4f C	4m 42.8	6	11-0	Gd to firm	Dead Or Alive (IRE)	May 10, 2009
2m 5f H	4m 46.8	4	11-2	Gd to firm	Urban Warrior	Sep 21, 2008
3m 1f 110y H	5m 57.6	10	11-12	Good	Take The Stand	Oct 16, 2006
3m 2f C	6m 23.5	9	9-7	Gd to firm	Sunday Habits	Apr 19, 2003
3m 5f C	7m 19.8	6	11-7	Gd to firm	Ecuyer Du Roi (FR)	Apr 15, 2002

SANDOWN

Distance	Time	Age	Weight	Going	Horse	Date
2m C	3m 43.4	9	11-6	Gd to firm	Dempsey (IRE)	Apr 28, 2007
2m 110yH	3m 42.0	6	10-0	Firm	Olympian	Mar 13, 1993
2m 4f 110y C	4m 57.2	8	11-7	Gd to firm	Coulton	Apr 29, 1995
2m 4f 110y H	4m 35.7	5	11-3	Gd to firm	Oslot (FR)	Apr 28, 2007
2m 6f H	5m 5.6	8	11-3	Firm	Kintbury	Nov 5, 1983
3m H	5m 39.1	6	11-5	Gd to firm	Rostropovich	Apr 27, 2002
3m 110y C	5m 59.0	8	12-7	Good	Arkle	Nov 6, 1965
3m 5f 110y C	7m 9.1	9	10-0	Gd to firm	Cache Fleur (FR)	Apr 29, 1995

SEDGEFIELD

Distance	Time	Age	Weight	Going	Horse	Date
2m 110y C	3m 53.6	7	10-1	Good	Sheepclose (IRE)	Jul 15, 2012
2m 1f H	3m 45.7	6	10-5	Gd to firm	Country Orchid	Sep 5, 1997
2m 4f H	4m 38.3	7	11-4	Gd to firm	Ad Murum (IRE)	Aug 11, 2006
2m 4f C	4m 45.5	9	11-12	Good	Tahiti Pearl	Apr 24, 2013
2m 5f C	4m 59.2	8	11-10	Gd to firm	Pennybridge	Spt 30, 1997
2m 5f 110y H	4m 46.3	7	10-0	Gd to firm	Palm House	Spt 4, 1992
3m 3f C	6m 29.3	7	11-8	Gd to firm	The Gallopin' Major	Sept 14, 1996
3m 3f 110y H	6m 19.7	7	9-13	Firm	Pikestaff (USA)	Jul 25, 2005

SOUTHWELL

Distance	Time	Age	Weight	Going	Horse	Date
2m C	3m 54.6	6	11-7	Good	Memorabilia	Mar 17, 2014
2m H	3m 45.1	6	11-12	Good	Fair Gale	May 25, 2011
2m 4f 110y C	5m 6.6	7	10-13	Good	Gentleman Anshan (IRE)	May 17, 2011
2m 4f 110y H	4m 57.3	8	11-3	Good	Red Not Blue (IRE)	May 17, 2011
3m 110y H	6m 2.8	6	11-10	Good	Wiesentraum (GER)	Feb 29, 2012
3m 110y C	6m 15.2	6	10-7	Good	Ambrose Princess	May 25, 2011
3m 2f H	6m 10.2	6	10-7	Good	Super Ross (IRE)	Aug 16, 2009

STRATFORD

Distance	Time	Age	Weight	Going	Horse	Date
2m 110y H	3m 40.4	6	11-12	Hard	Chusan	May 7, 1956
2m 110y C	3m 56.7	6	11-0	Gd to firm	Professeur Emery	Aug 1, 2013
2m 3f H	4m 19.7	7	9-11	Gd to firm	Mister Ermyn	Jul 29, 2000
2m 4f C	4m 35.4	9	10-0	Gd to soft	Gentleman Anshan	May 19, 2013
2m 5f 110y C	4m 56.5	6	9-10	Gd to firm	Spare Change (IRE)	Sep 16, 2007
2m 6f 110y H	5m 6.8	6	11-0	Firm	Broken Wing	May 31, 1986
2m 7f C	5m 23.8	9	11-4	Gd to firm	Five Out Of Five	Aug 1, 2013
3m 3f H	6m 13.1	7	10-8	Gd to firm	Burren Moonshine (IRE)	Jun 11, 2006
3m 4f C	6m 38.3	10	12-0	Good	Mossey Joe (IRE)	Jun 7, 2013

TAUNTON

Distance	Time	Age	Weight	Going	Horse	Date
2m 110y C	3m 49.5	8	10-9	Firm	I Have Him	Apr 28, 1995
2m 1f H	3m 39.5	4	12-0	Hard	Indian Jockey	Oct 3, 1996
2m 3f C	4m 24.9	7	11-3	Firm	Wait No More	Mar 28, 2012
2m 3f 110y H	4m 19.7	5	10-6	Firm	Prairie Spirit	Apr 2, 2009
2m 7f 110y C	5m 39.80	7	11-10	Firm	Glacial Delight (IRE)	Apr 24, 2006
3m 110y H	5m 30.4	7	10-4	Firm	On My Toes	Oct 15, 1998
3m 3f C	6m 40.1	8	11-8	Firm	Fourpointone	Mar 21, 2009
4m2f 110y C	8m 59.0	9	11-9	Good	Cold Mountain	Mar 29, 2011

TOWCESTER

Distance	Time	Age	Weight	Going	Horse	Date
2m H	3m 39.5	4	10-0	Firm	Nascracker (USA)	May 22, 1987
2m 110y C	3m 52.4	12	10-3	Good	Crack At Dawn	May 21, 2013
2m 3f 110y C	4m 53.5	6	11-0	Gd to firm	Home	May 20, 2011
2m 3f 110y H	4m 39.0	7	11-2	Gd to firm	Bathwick Man	May 22, 2012
2m 5f H	5m 0.9	7	11-2	Gd to firm	Mailcom	May 3, 1993
2m 6f C	5m 21.0	6	11-5	Gd to firm	Paint The Clouds	May 17, 2011
3m H	5m 44.0	9	9-10	Firm	Dropshot	May 25, 1984
3m 110y C	5m 52.6	10	10-13	Gd to firm	Lucky Luk (FR)	May 29, 2009

UTTOXETER

Distance	Time	Age	Weight	Going	Horse	Date
2m H	3m 37.2	4	10-9	Gd to firm	Flying Eagle	Jun 11, 1995
2m C	3m 41.5	6	11-0	Good	Tapageur	Aug 8, 1991
2m 4f 110y H	4m 39.1	8	10-9	Gd to firm	Chicago's Best	Jun 11, 1995
2m 5f C	4m 54.2	8	11-8	Firm	McKenzie	Apr 27, 1974
2m 6f 110y H	5m 6.8	8	11-8	Gd to firm	Fealing Real (IRE)	Jun 27, 2010
2m 6f 110y C	5m 35.6	6	11-0	Good	Brassick	Jul 26, 2013
3m C	5m 56.8	6	11-2	Good	Always Waining (IRE)	May 5, 2007
3m H	5m 32.3	8	10-12	Gd to firm	Painted Sky	Oct 2, 2011
3m 2f C	6m 23.5	10	11-13	Gd to firm	Mcgregor the Third	Oct 5, 1996
4m 1f 110y C	8m 41.3	8	10-3	Gd to soft	Goulanes (IRE)	Mar 15, 2014

WARWICK

Distance	Time	Age	Weight	Going	Horse	Date
2m H	3m 34.6	5	11-4	Gd to firm	Arabian Bold	May 22, 1993
2m 110y C	3m 46.3	6	11-0	Gd to firm	Bambi De L'Orme (FR)	May 7, 2005
2m 3f H	4m 14.9	6	11-7	Gd to firm	Runaway Pete	Nov 2, 1996
2m 4f 110y C	4m 53.3	9	9-12	Gd to firm	Dudie	May 16, 1987
2m 5f H	4m 43.6	5	10-10	Firm	Three Eagles (USA)	May 11, 2002
3m 110y Ch	6m 0.2	7	11-8	Good	Shining Gale (IRE)	Mar 18, 2009
3m 1f H	5m 53.5	7	11-0	Gd to firm	City Poser	Apr 2, 2002
3m 2f C	6m 16.1	12	10-12	Gd to firm	Castle Warden	May 6, 1989
3m 5f C	7m 12.09	12	11-7	Good	Arnold Layne (IRE)	Mar 23, 2011

WETHERBY

Distance	Time	Age	Weight	Going	Horse	Date
2m C	3m 43.3	8	10-9	Gd to soft	Mwaleshi	Nov 16, 2013
2m 110y H	3m 43.9	8	10-7	Gd to firm	Olivino (GER)	Apr 26, 2009
2m 4f H	4m 42.0	6	11-7	Gd to firm	Lady Wright (IRE)	Apr 26, 2009
2m 4f 110y C	4m 47.8	7	10-12	Good	Drever Route (IRE)	Oct 13, 2010
2m 6f H	5m 5.7	7	11-0	Gd to firm	San Deng	Apr 26, 2009
2m 6f H	5m 5.7	6	11-0	Gd to firm	Oscar Barton (IRE)	Apr 17, 2011
2m 6f 110y C	5m 24.9	6	11-3	Good	Pistol Basc (FR)	Oct 13, 2010
3m 1f C	5m 52.1	9	11-0	Good	Nacarat (FR)	Oct 30, 2010
3m 1f H	5m 51.6	11	11-9	Good	Garleton	May 24, 2012

WINCANTON

Distance	Time	Age	Weight	Going	Horse	Date
2m H	3m 25.8	6	10-5	Good	Nearby	Nov 6, 2010
2m C	3m 37.9	6	11-11	Good	Kie	Apr 13, 2014
2m 4f H	4m 29.46	7	10-4	Gd to firm	Uffa Fox (IRE)	Oct 14, 2010
2m 5f C	4m 59.2	11	11-10	Firm	Edredon Bleu (FR)	Oct 26, 2003
2m 6f H	4m 57.0	6	10-0	Good	Santera (IRE)	Nov 6, 2010
3m 1f 110yC	6m 9.7	11	11-6	Gd to firm	Swansea Bay	Nov 8, 2003
3m 3f 110yC	6m 37.2	7	11-8	Good	Gullible Gordon (IRE)	Oct 24, 2010

WORCESTER

Distance	Time	Age	Weight	Going	Horse	Date
2m H	3m 33.4	10	11-5	Good	Chilbury Hill	Aug 28, 2013
2m 110y C	3m 52.5	9	11-7	Good	Oceana Gold	Jul 30, 2013
2m 4f H	4m 28.7	7	10-4	Gd to firm	Jigsaw Financial	Jul 17, 2013
2m 4f C	4m 38.2	8	10-5	Good	Moorlands Jack	Sep 10, 2013
2m 7f C	5m 29.7	6	10-2	Good	Whistling Senator	Aug 28, 2013
3m H	5m 23.5	7	11-5	Good	Saticon	Jun 27, 2012

SPLIT SECOND SPEED RATINGS

The following list shows the fastest performances of chasers and hurdlers which have recorded a speed figure of 105 or over during the 2013-2014 season. Additional information in parentheses following the speed figure shows the distance of the race in furlongs, course, state of going and the date on which the figure was achieved.

CHASING

A Stray Shot 105 (31f,Chl,GS,Mar 12)
Aachen 108 (24f,Don,GS,Feb 19)
Able Deputy 108 (17f,Asc,G,Mar 30)
Acapulco Gold 105 (20f,Str,G,Jun 7)
According To Trev 108 (24 1/2f,Chl,G,Oct 18)
Ackertac 108 (24 1/2f,Chl,GS,Mar 11)
Adrenalin Flight 108 (24f,Kem,HY,Feb 7)
Ahyaknowyerself 105 (20 1/2f,Chl,GS,Mar 11)
Aikideau 106 (26 1/2f,Nab,GF,Jly 21)
Al Alfa 111 (16 1/2f,Chp,HY,Feb 22)
Al Co 110 (22 1/2f,Mar,G,Sep 28)
Al Ferof 120 (21f,Chl,G,Mar 13)
Alasi 112 (20 1/2f,Hun,GS,Dec 12)
Alderbrook Lad 106 (16f,Cat,HY,Jan 9)
Alfie Sherrin 108 (24 1/2f,Chl,GS,Mar 11)
Alfie Spinner 109 (25 1/2f,Wcn,GS,Nov 9)
Alpha Victor 107 (33 1/2f,Utt,GS,Mar 15)
Alvarado 113 (35 1/2f,Ain,GS,Apr 5)
American Spin 109 (26 1/2f,Nab,G,May 28)
Amuse Me 106 (22f,Sed,GF,Sep 5)
Anay Turge 111 (16f,Chl,G,Nov 15)
And The Man 105 (20f,Ayr,HY,Jan 2)
Aneyeforaneye 105 (24f,Per,GF,Jun 9)
Annacotty 111 (24f,Chp,GS,Dec 7)
Another Flutter 105 (16 1/2f,Wor,S,Oct 23)
Anquetta 112 (16 1/2f,Wor,G,May 12)
Any Currency 112 (31f,Chl,GS,Mar 12)
Ardkilly Witness 111 (24f,Kem,S,Feb 22)
Argocat 112 (25f,Ain,G,Apr 3)
Arkose 106 (24 1/2f,Tow,G,Apr 20)
Arnaud 110 (16 1/2f,Don,GS,Jan 25)
Art Of Logistics 107 (17f,Leo,S,Dec 26)
Arvika Ligeonniere 113 (17f,Leo,S,Dec 27)
Astracad 114 (20f,Ain,G,Oct 26)
Atlanta Falcon 109 (20f,Wor,G,Jly 10)
Attaglance 112 (20 1/2f,Chl,G,Nov 16)
Attycran 105 (20f,Sed,G,May 14)
Australia Day 109 (16 1/2f,Tau,GF,May 2)
Avoca Promise 107 (20 1/2f,Hun,S,Oct 15)

Baby Mix 112 (16 1/2f,Nab,G,Jun 25)
Baby Shine 109 (22f,Tow,HY,Dec 26)
Badger Foot 107 (20f,Ncs,S,Mar 28)
Baile Anrai 112 (24f,Don,S,Jan 25)
Baileys Concerto 108 (16f,Crl,G,Apr 19)
Balder Succes 120 (19 1/2f,Chp,G,Oct 12)
Balding Banker 106 (20 1/2f,Hex,G,Oct 4)
Ballincurrig 108 (20f,Str,G,Apr 13)
Ballinvarrig 106 (19 1/2f,Exe,S,Dec 19)
Bally Legend 113 (24f,Kem,S,Feb 22)
Bally Sands 105 (26f,War,S,Jan 23)
Ballybough Gorta 107 (26f,Crt,G,Aug 26)
Ballycasey 114 (24 1/2f,Chl,G,Mar 12)
Ballygarvey 108 (16f,Chl,G,Nov 15)
Ballylifen 105 (20f,Utt,GS,Mar 29)
Ballynagour 113 (20f,Chl,G,Mar 13)
Ballyoliver 108 (26f,Crl,GS,Mar 16)
Ballypatrick 110 (33f,Ncs,HY,Feb 22)
Ballytober 110 (24f,Chp,GS,Dec 7)
Ballywatt 106 (19 1/2f,Chp,GS,Apr 25)
Balthazar King 115 (35 1/2f,Ain,GS,Apr 5)
Balzaccio 107 (20 1/2f,Sth,S,Mar 3)
Bar De Ligne 109 (20f,Mus,GS,Jan 17)
Barlow 106 (24f,Chp,G,Mar 20)
Barrakilla 110 (20 1/2f,War,S,Dec 31)
Be My Deputy 105 (20 1/2f,Wet,S,Jan 21)
Bear's Affair 107 (21 1/2f,Fak,G,Oct 25)
Becauseicouldntsee 105 (25f,Fai,S,Apr 6)
Beforeall 108 (25 1/2f,Ffo,HY,Apr 6)
Beggar's Velvet 106 (23f,Str,GF,Jly 21)
Bellenos 110 (17f,Asc,G,Mar 30)
Benbens 109 (23f,Str,GS,Mar 29)
Bendant 105 (19 1/2f,Exe,GS,Oct 22)
Benefficient 114 (17f,Leo,S,Dec 27)
Beneficial Reform 109 (23 1/2f,Kel,G,May 8)
Benefit Cut 107 (20f,Mar,S,Feb 4)
Bennys Mist 112 (21 1/2f,Ain,G,Apr 4)
Bennys Quest 106 (16 1/2f,Nab,GF,Aug 22)
Benvolio 110 (24f,Nby,GS,Dec 18)
Bertie Boru 107 (19 1/2f,Exe,G,Dec 6)
Best Boy Barney 107 (23 1/2f,Tau,G,Apr 10)
Big Fella Thanks 108 (24f,Don,GS,Feb 19)
Big Shu 112 (31f,Chl,GS,Mar 12)
Big Talk 106 (23f,Str,S,Sep 17)
Billie Magern 111 (24f,Hun,G,Apr 28)
Billy Cuckoo 105 (20 1/2f,Sth,G,Dec 3)
Bincombe 107 (20f,Hay,G,Mar 19)
Bit Of A Jig 107 (20f,Ncs,G,Nov 15)
Black Thunder 111 (24f,Lin,S,Dec 14)
Blackwater King 105 (16f,Crl,G,Apr 19)
Bob Ford 108 (24 1/2f,Ban,S,Nov 30)
Bobcatbilly 109 (21f,Hay,HY,Feb 15)
Bobowen 113 (22 1/2f,Mar,GF,Jly 20)
Bobs Worth 115 (26 1/2f,Chl,G,Mar 14)
Bocamix 105 (17f,Kel,G,Apr 29)
Bocciani 111 (20f,Mar,G,May 10)
Bold Chief 111 (24f,Hay,G,Apr 19)
Bold Perk 109 (26 1/2f,Fon,GF,May 26)
Boston Bob 119 (21f,Chl,G,Mar 13)
Bouggler 115 (22 1/2f,Mar,G,Sep 28)
Bradley 107 (24 1/2f,Chl,G,Oct 19)
Brass Tax 108 (24f,Kem,G,Apr 15)
Brassick 114 (22 1/2f,Utt,G,Jly 26)
Brick Red 109 (17f,Asc,G,Mar 30)
Bright New Dawn 113 (21f,Leo,S,Jan 25)
Bringewood Belle 105 (24f,Chp,G,Apr 21)
Brunswick Gold 105 (22 1/2f,Mar,G,May 19)
Buck Mulligan 111 (20f,Str,GS,May 19)
Buck's Bond 107 (25 1/2f,Wcn,G,Dec 5)
Buckers Bridge 109 (25f,Fai,SH,Feb 22)
Bucking The Trend 108 (22f,Fon,GS,Dec 10)
Bullet Street 106 (16f,San,S,Mar 7)
Burn And Turn 107 (20f,Fai,GY,Apr 21)
Burton Port 112 (29 1/2f,San,GS,Apr 26)
Bury Parade 115 (21 1/2f,Asc,HY,Jan 18)
Buthelezi 109 (16f,Lei,GF,Nov 18)
Buywise 111 (21f,Chl,G,Apr 16)
Bygones Of Brid 105 (16 1/2f,Hex,G,Jun 23)

Cairdin 109 (17f,Leo,S,Dec 26)
Camden 108 (26 1/2f,Nab,S,Apr 1)
Canaly 106 (24 1/2f,Leo,S,Dec 27)
Cantlow 112 (20f,Nby,GS,Nov 29)
Caolaneoin 107 (19f,Leo,YS,Dec 28)
Cap Elorn 106 (16 1/2f,Hun,G,Sep 9)
Cape Dutch 108 (16 1/2f,Tau,G,Dec 12)
Cape Tribulation 108 (25f,Wet,S,Dec 26)
Captain Chris 117 (21 1/2f,Asc,S,Feb 15)
Captain Conan 112 (16f,San,G,Dec 7)
Captain Kelly 105 (26 1/2f,Nab,GF,Sep 24)
Captain Sully 106 (20f,Str,G,Jly 2)
Cara Court 106 (20f,Sed,S,Apr 4)
Cardigan Island 107 (21f,Wcn,G,Oct 17)
Carlingford Lough 113 (24 1/2f,Chl,G,Mar 12)
Carlito Brigante 108 (20f,Crl,G,Apr 19)
Carrickboy 105 (21f,Wcn,HY,Jan 30)
Carrigmorna King 108 (22 1/2f,Nby,G,Nov 30)
Carruthers 105 (29 1/2f,San,GS,Apr 26)
Carry Each Other 107 (25f,Fai,S,Apr 6)
Castlelawn 105 (16f,Per,GF,Jly 3)
Catch Tammy 105 (17 1/2f,Str,S,Sep 17)
Categorical 107 (20f,Ncs,S,Mar 4)
Caulfields Venture 109 (22f,Fon,G,Apr 11)
Cause Of Causes 110 (24 1/2f,Leo,S,Dec 27)
Cedre Bleu 107 (21f,Chl,S,Jan 1)
Champagne Fever 113 (16f,Chl,GS,Mar 11)
Champion Court 116 (20 1/2f,Hun,GS,Dec 12)
Chance Du Roy 112 (35 1/2f,Ain,GS,Apr 5)
Chandlers Cross 106 (24f,Utt,GF,Jly 17)
Changing The Guard 116 (16 1/2f,Nab,G,Jun 25)
Chapolimoss 107 (24f,Hun,S,Mar 2)
Chartreux 109 (24 1/2f,San,GS,Mar 8)
Chicago Grey 110 (31f,Chl,G,Nov 15)
Christopher Wren 107 (16f,Lei,GF,Dec 1)
Ciceron 105 (22 1/2f,Mar,G,Jun 21)
Citrus Mark 107 (18f,Mar,GF,Jly 7)
Claragh Native 109 (16f,Mus,G,Nov 29)
Claret Cloak 116 (16f,San,G,Dec 7)
Clondaw Flicka 107 (25f,Wet,S,Dec 26)
Clondaw Hero 106 (20f,Crl,G,Apr 19)
Cloudy Bob 106 (24f,Kem,GS,Mar 15)
Cloudy Joker 107 (16f,Cat,S,Jan 22)
Cloudy Too 113 (25f,Wet,S,Dec 26)
Cnoc Seoda 105 (24f,Kem,S,Dec 27)
Coeur De Fou 106 (16f,Per,S,Apr 25)
Colbert Station 105 (21f,Leo,S,Jan 25)
Colebrooke 109 (22f,Fon,HY,Nov 17)
Colour Squadron 114 (20 1/2f,Chl,G,Nov 16)
Conquisto 115 (20f,Ain,G,Oct 26)
Consigliere 110 (19 1/2f,Chp,S,Mar 8)
Coole River 107 (23 1/2f,Tau,G,Nov 14)
Corrin Wood 107 (24 1/2f,War,HY,Jan 11)
Count Guido Deiro 107 (25 1/2f,Wcn,HY,Dec 26)
Counting House 107 (24f,Chp,GS,Dec 7)
Court By Surprise 108 (25 1/2f,Wcn,GS,Nov 9)
Coverholder 109 (21f,Hay,HY,Jan 18)
Cowards Close 107 (23 1/2f,Tau,G,Apr 23)
Croco Bay 107 (16f,Cat,S,Dec 28)
Cry Of Freedom 105 (16f,Wet,G,May 23)
Cue Card 119 (24f,Kem,S,Dec 26)
Current Event 109 (20 1/2f,Per,GF,Jun 9)

Dare Me 111 (20 1/2f,Per,S,Apr 24)
Dare To Endeavour 109 (24f,Exe,S,Feb 21)
Daring Article 111 (21f,Leo,S,Jan 25)
Dark Energy 108 (20 1/2f,Per,G,Sep 9)
Dark Lover 108 (20 1/2f,Kem,S,Feb 22)
Dashing George 107 (21 1/2f,Fak,HY,Feb 14)
Daymar Bay 107 (19 1/2f,Exe,GS,Mar 26)
De Blacksmith 109 (20f,Plu,S,Oct 21)
De Boitron 112 (25f,Wet,G,May 23)
De Faoithesdream 110 (16 1/2f,Nab,GF,Aug 3)
De La Bech 111 (24f,Chp,GS,Dec 7)
Decade Player 106 (17f,Leo,S,Dec 26)
Decent Lord 107 (16 1/2f,Ncs,HY,Jan 15)
Defy Logic 117 (17f,Leo,S,Dec 26)
Deireadh Re 107 (22f,Fon,GS,May 15)
Deise Dynamo 106 (20f,Sed,GS,Oct 31)
Delphi Mountain 105 (16 1/2f,Nab,G,Apr 25)
Desert Cry 112 (16f,Ayr,GS,Apr 12)
Destroyer Deployed 107 (24 1/2f,Fak,HY,Feb 14)
Diamond Harry 110 (31f,Chl,G,Nov 15)
Dineur 108 (22 1/2f,Mar,GF,Jly 20)
Diocles 107 (19f,Cat,G,Dec 17)
Djakadam 115 (21f,Leo,S,Jan 25)
Doctor Foxtrot 106 (24f,Kem,G,Apr 15)
Dodging Bullets 114 (16f,Kem,S,Dec 27)
Doeslessthanme 107 (16 1/2f,Don,G,Mar 1)
Dolatulo 110 (23f,Str,GS,Mar 29)
Domtaline 107 (19 1/2f,Exe,G,Dec 6)
Don Cossack 110 (21f,Leo,SH,Feb 9)
Donnas Palm 105 (22 1/2f,Mar,GF,Jly 20)
Dorset Naga 105 (20f,Fon,G,Oct 5)
Double Chocolate 105 (26 1/2f,Fon,GF,May 26)
Double Handful 107 (20f,Wor,G,Jun 23)
Double Ross 117 (20f,Chl,G,Mar 13)
Double Seven 115 (35 1/2f,Ain,GS,Apr 5)
Doubletoilntrouble 105 (28f,Str,G,Apr 13)
Doynosaur 113 (16 1/2f,Ncs,G,Dec 12)
Drumlang 106 (20f,Mus,GS,Jan 17)
Drumshambo 114 (17f,Asc,GS,Nov 2)
Duke Of Lucca 113 (25f,Ain,G,Apr 5)
Duneen Point 106 (23 1/2f,Tau,G,Mar 24)
Dungeel 106 (25 1/2f,Cat,S,Jan 1)
Dunlough Bay 105 (22f,Tow,HY,Dec 26)
Dursey Sound 110 (20 1/2f,Ban,GS,Oct 3)
Dynaste 123 (21f,Chl,G,Mar 13)

Easily Pleased 105 (16 1/2f,Nab,G,Oct 11)
Easter Day 110 (19 1/2f,Chp,G,Oct 12)
Easter Meteor 111 (20f,Nby,GS,Nov 29)
Eastlake 111 (16 1/2f,Chl,G,Dec 14)
Edmund Kean 110 (23 1/2f,Lei,S,Jan 7)
Eduard 108 (16f,Crl,GS,Dec 1)
Eleazar 108 (26 1/2f,Fon,GF,May 26)
Elenika 107 (17f,Asc,S,Dec 21)
Ely Brown 107 (23 1/2f,Lei,GS,Dec 27)
Emperor's Choice 111 (28f,Ffo,HY,Feb 1)
Endeavor 106 (16f,Mus,G,Nov 29)
Entertain Me 111 (19 1/2f,Chp,GS,Apr 5)
Ericht 109 (20f,Mus,S,Feb 2)
Etxalar 106 (25f,Ayr,HY,Mar 8)

Fair Dilemma 108 (17f,Plu,GS,Apr 21)
Fairwood Massini 107 (23f,Str,GF,Sep 7)
Fairy Rath 111 (20f,Hay,G,May 11)
Farbreaga 107 (22 1/2f,Nby,HY,Feb 28)
Farmer Matt 107 (24f,Exe,HY,Mar 4)
Father Shine 105 (20f,Mus,G,Nov 8)
Faultless Feelings 106 (24 1/2f,Chl,G,Oct 18)
Felix Yonger 114 (20f,Chl,G,Mar 13)
Fentara 107 (24f,Don,GS,Feb 6)
Fiddlers Reel 106 (25f,Wet,G,Mar 18)
Fiendish Flame 110 (20f,Mar,G,May 10)
Fiftyonefiftyone 106 (16 1/2f,Nab,GF,May 20)
Filbert 109 (17f,Asc,GS,Nov 2)
Fill The Power 105 (24f,Don,GS,Feb 6)
Financial Climate 111 (25f,Wet,GS,Apr 22)
Fine Parchment 107 (21 1/2f,Crt,S,May 27)
Finger Onthe Pulse 110 (20 1/2f,Sth,G,Aug 18)
Firebird Flyer 112 (24f,Hay,G,Apr 19)
Firm Order 108 (26 1/2f,Fon,GS,Dec 10)
First Lieutenant 114 (24f,Leo,SH,Feb 9)
Firth Of The Clyde 108 (18f,Mar,HY,Jan 16)
Flaming Charmer 107 (16 1/2f,Chp,HY,Nov 6)
Flaming Gorge 107 (24f,Hun,G,Apr 21)
Flanagan 105 (24f,Ffo,G,May 9)
Flying Award 105 (30 1/2f,Exe,HY,Mar 4)
Folsom Blue 105 (29f,Fai,GY,Apr 21)
Font 105 (23f,Str,GF,Jly 21)
Forest Walker 106 (20f,Utt,S,Nov 1)
Forever My Friend 105 (20f,Utt,GF,Jly 17)
Forgotten Gold 108 (24f,Lud,S,Feb 27)
Foundation Man 106 (22 1/2f,Wet,GS,Mar 28)
Foundry Square 109 (20 1/2f,Ban,GS,Oct 3)
Fox Appeal 115 (20 1/2f,Kem,S,Feb 22)
Foxrock 108 (24f,Leo,YS,Dec 29)

Freckle Face 106 (19½f,Tow,HY,Feb 23)
Fredo 106 (23f,Str,S,Mar 10)
French Opera 112 (16½f,Chl,G,Mar 14)
Fruity O'Rooney 110 (22f,Fon,G,Apr 11)
Full Of Joy 109 (24½f,Ban,G,Sep 13)
Funny Star 109 (16½f,Tau,G,Dec 12)

Galaxy Rock 109 (26f,Utt,G,Jun 30)
Galway Jack 109 (24f,Hun,G,Apr 28)
Gansey 107 (21½f,Ain,S,Dec 7)
Garleton 111 (25f,Wet,G,May 23)
General Miller 106 (20f,Mar,G,May 31)
Gentleman Anshan 113 (20f,Str,GS,May 19)
Gentleman Duke 106 (17f,Leo,S,Dec 26)
Get It On 106 (19½f,Ffo,HY,Oct 29)
Ghizao 112 (20½f,Hun,GS,Dec 12)
Giorgio Quercus 106 (20f,Chl,G,Mar 13)
Glen Countess 105 (22½f,Mar,G,Jun 21)
Glenquest 109 (21f,Leo,S,Jan 25)
God's Own 115 (20½f,Kem,S,Feb 22)
Godsmejudge 112 (29½f,San,GS,Apr 26)
Golden Call 109 (24f,Don,GS,Feb 6)
Golden Chieftain 108 (25f,Ain,G,Apr 5)
Golden Wonder 107 (25f,Fai,S,Apr 6)
Good Order 106 (20½f,Lei,GS,Dec 27)
Goodtoknow 107 (24½f,Ban,HY,Dec 22)
Gorgehous Lliege 106 (24½f,Tow,S,Dec 19)
Goring One 108 (21f,Wcn,G,Oct 17)
Goulanes 108 (33½f,Utt,GS,Mar 15)
Grandads Horse 112 (20f,Mar,G,May 31)
Grandioso 113 (21½f,Asc,HY,Jan 18)
Grandouet 121 (16f,San,G,Dec 7)
Granville Island 105 (16f,Wet,G,Oct 16)
Green Bank 105 (24½f,Tow,G,Apr 20)
Green Flag 111 (23½f,Kel,GS,Oct 19)
Green Wizard 107 (24f,Ncs,G,Nov 30)
Grey Gold 112 (16f,San,HY,Feb 1)
Greywell Boy 109 (17f,Asc,GS,Nov 2)
Gud Day 107 (16f,Per,GS,Sep 25)
Gullible Gordon 110 (22½f,Mar,G,Jun 21)
Gullinbursti 110 (22½f,Mar,S,Nov 10)
Gus Macrae 113 (17f,Asc,S,Dec 21)

Haar 107 (20½f,Hun,G,Apr 28)
Hadrian's Approach 113 (29½f,San,GS,Apr 26)
Hansupfordetroit 106 (19½f,Ffo,HY,Nov 10)
Harry Hunt 105 (20f,Str,S,Oct 31)
Harry The Viking 106 (24f,Don,GS,Feb 6)
Harry Topper 117 (24f,Nby,HY,Feb 8)
Hatters River 105 (23½f,Tau,G,Nov 14)
Hawaii Klass 105 (20½f,Per,GF,Jun 9)
Hawkes Point 108 (24f,Chp,GS,Dec 7)
Hazy Tom 109 (20½f,Ban,GS,Oct 3)
He'llberemembered 112 (21f,Leo,S,Jan 25)
Headly's Bridge 109 (20f,Ayr,GS,Apr 11)
Hector's Choice 108 (21f,Wcn,GS,Apr 2)
Hell's Bay 108 (20f,Wor,G,May 22)
Henry King 105 (20f,Utt,S,Nov 16)
Henry San 110 (20½f,Sth,G,Aug 18)
Herdsman 107 (26f,Crl,GS,Dec 1)
Hey Big Spender 110 (24f,Hay,G,Apr 19)
Hi George 107 (19f,Cat,G,Dec 4)
Hi Note 108 (20½f,Hun,GS,Nov 3)
Hidden Cyclone 122 (21f,Chl,G,Mar 13)
High Ron 108 (22½f,Utt,G,Jly 26)
Highland Lodge 109 (26½f,Nby,G,Nov 30)
Highrate 105 (23f,Hex,G,May 4)
Highway Code 108 (16½f,Nab,GF,Jun 5)
Hinterland 122 (16f,San,G,Dec 7)
His Excellency 109 (20½f,Per,S,Apr 24)
Hit The Headlines 106 (21f,Chl,G,Dec 13)
Hodgson 105 (20½f,Ban,G,May 18)
Hollins 105 (20f,Utt,HY,Dec 20)
Hollow Blue Sky 106 (20f,Crl,S,Oct 30)
Holywell 114 (25f,Ain,G,Apr 4)
Home Farm 108 (24½f,Leo,S,Dec 27)
Houblon Des Obeaux 109 (26½f,Chl,G,Mar 14)
Howard's Legacy 108 (24f,Chp,G,Apr 21)
Humbie 110 (20½f,Wet,GS,Nov 1)
Hunt Ball 120 (21f,Chl,G,Mar 13)

Ice 'N' Easy 108 (20½f,Kem,S,Jan 11)
Ifyousayso 106 (24f,Don,GS,Jan 8)
Ikorodu Road 109 (20f,Str,S,Oct 26)
Imjoeking 108 (16f,Wet,GS,Nov 16)
Imperial Circus 109 (31f,Chl,G,Dec 13)
Imperial Vic 110 (23½f,Kel,GS,Oct 19)
Indian Castle 111 (21f,Chl,HY,Jan 25)
Inoogoo 107 (16f,Per,S,Apr 25)
Inside Dealer 109 (26½f,Nab,GF,Sep 24)
Invictus 105 (26½f,Nby,G,Nov 30)
Iona Days 106 (21½f,Crt,S,May 27)
Ipsos Du Berlais 110 (24½f,Leo,S,Dec 27)
Is Herself About 108 (17f,Leo,S,Mar 2)
Islandmagee 105 (19½f,Chp,G,Apr 21)
It's A Gimme 108 (16f,Wet,GS,Nov 2)
Italian Master 105 (25f,Mar,S,Nov 10)
Itoldyou 106 (24f,Kem,G,Apr 15)
Ivor's King 107 (16½f,Nab,GS,Sep 30)

Jack The Gent 107 (16f,Wet,G,May 23)
Jamsie Hall 105 (29f,Fai,GY,Apr 21)
Jayandbee 105 (32f,Exe,G,Dec 6)
Jet Master 109 (17f,Kel,G,Mar 22)
Jimbill 107 (20f,Str,GF,Sep 7)
Jimmy The Hat 110 (20f,Ayr,HY,Mar 7)
Johns Spirit 115 (20f,Chl,G,Oct 19)
Joker Choker 106 (20f,Mar,G,May 10)
Jump City 108 (21f,Wcn,G,Oct 17)
Junior 111 (24f,Hun,G,Apr 28)
Jupitor 109 (25f,Fai,S,Apr 6)
Just A Par 116 (24f,Nby,GS,Nov 28)

Kapga De Cerisy 111 (20½f,San,S,Nov 9)
Kasbadali 107 (24f,Exe,G,Nov 24)
Katenko 112 (25f,Hay,HY,Jan 18)
Katnap 107 (19f,Leo,YS,Dec 28)
Kauto Stone 107 (16f,San,G,Dec 7)
Keki Buku 109 (16½f,Wor,GF,Jun 26)
Keltic Rhythm 107 (23½f,Lei,GS,Feb 25)
Kentford Legend 105 (25½f,Wcn,GS,Mar 23)
Kian's Delight 110 (22½f,Mar,G,Sep 28)
Kid Cassidy 111 (16f,Chl,G,Nov 17)
Kie 109 (16f,Wcn,G,Apr 13)
Kind Of Easy 105 (22f,Fon,S,Oct 23)
King Edmund 109 (20½f,Kem,S,Jan 11)
King Massini 107 (21f,Chl,G,Dec 13)
King Of The Night 110 (22½f,Mar,G,Sep 28)
King Of The Wolds 110 (21½f,Fak,GS,Nov 19)
King Vuvuzela 111 (17f,Leo,S,Dec 26)
King's Grace 109 (20½f,Ban,GS,Apr 12)
Kingcora 106 (24½f,Ban,GS,Apr 12)
Kings Grey 108 (16f,Ain,G,Oct 27)
Knock A Hand 109 (21f,Crl,HY,Dec 15)
Knockara Beau 111 (26½f,Chl,G,Mar 14)
Knockgraffon King 107 (24f,Ncs,HY,Jan 4)
Kris Cross 107 (24f,Mus,S,Feb 24)
Kruzhlinin 110 (23½f,Kel,GS,Nov 9)
Kumbeshwar 106 (20½f,Chl,G,Nov 16)
Kykate 106 (17f,Kel,G,Apr 29)
Kylecrue 110 (21f,Leo,S,Mar 2)

Lamb Or Cod 109 (25½f,Chl,G,Apr 17)
Lamboro Lad 107 (24f,Exe,G,Mar 18)
Lamool 107 (20f,Lud,G,Apr 10)
Lancetto 114 (17f,Asc,S,Dec 21)
Last Instalment 117 (24f,Leo,SH,Feb 9)
Last Shot 107 (16f,Lud,GS,Dec 18)
Lauberhorn 109 (16½f,Nab,GF,Aug 3)
Lava Lamp 108 (20f,Lud,G,Oct 9)
Le Bacardy 113 (16f,Ayr,GS,Apr 12)
Le Bec 118 (25½f,Chl,G,Dec 14)
Le Reve 111 (25½f,Chl,G,Dec 14)
Lets Get Serious 108 (23½f,Kel,G,May 8)
Lexicon Lad 109 (25f,Ain,G,May 17)
Life Of A Luso 110 (26½f,Nab,GF,Sep 24)
Little Glenshee 109 (16f,Ayr,HY,Feb 20)
Loch Ba 109 (24½f,Ban,HY,Nov 13)
Loose Chips 110 (20½f,Kem,S,Dec 26)
Lord Lescribaa 107 (26½f,Nab,GF,Jly 21)
Lord Navits 110 (16f,Lei,S,Feb 13)
Lord Of Drums 105 (16f,Per,G,Jly 4)
Lord Of House 106 (16f,Utt,HY,Dec 31)
Lord Windermere 117 (26½f,Chl,G,Mar 14)
Lost Glory 113 (25f,Wet,G,May 23)
Lost Legend 109 (20½f,Kem,GS,Mar 15)
Loudmouth 106 (20½f,Hun,S,Oct 15)
Lough Derg Way 105 (21½f,Nab,GF,Jun 5)
Lucky Landing 109 (16f,Wet,G,Oct 16)
Lyreen Legend 114 (26½f,Chl,G,Mar 14)

Ma Filleule 115 (21½f,Ain,G,Apr 4)
Mac Aeda 108 (20½f,Wet,GS,Nov 1)
Maggio 115 (23½f,Kel,GS,Mar 1)
Majala 112 (20½f,Per,S,Apr 24)
Major Malarkey 106 (32f,Exe,G,Dec 6)
Majorica King 109 (23f,Str,GS,Mar 29)
Make A Track 109 (21f,Leo,S,Jan 25)
Mallowney 115 (17f,Leo,S,Mar 2)
Many Clouds 110 (20½f,Wet,S,Dec 27)
Manyriverstocross 111 (17f,Asc,G,Mar 30)
Marcus Antonius 105 (16f,Lin,HY,Nov 26)
Markadam 107 (26f,Crl,GS,Mar 16)
Mart Lane 109 (24f,Don,GS,Dec 29)
Massena 108 (16f,Lei,S,Jan 7)
Master Neo 105 (24f,Chp,S,Apr 5)
Mcmurrough 110 (24f,Don,GS,Feb 19)
Medermit 113 (21f,Chl,G,Mar 13)
Memorabilia 106 (16f,Sth,G,Mar 17)
Mendip Express 110 (26½f,Chl,S,Jan 1)
Menorah 108 (25f,Ain,G,Apr 3)
Merlin's Wish 106 (32f,Hex,HY,Nov 20)
Merrion Square 108 (24f,Kem,G,May 12)
Merry King 112 (25f,Hay,HY,Jan 18)
Micheal Flips 106 (20f,Mar,G,May 10)
Midnight Appeal 112 (24f,Kem,S,Feb 22)
Midnight Lira 106 (19½f,Exe,G,Apr 15)
Midnight Prayer 109 (24f,Nby,GS,Dec 18)
Midnight Sail 109 (20½f,San,GS,Mar 8)
Milborough 106 (24f,Utt,S,Dec 10)
Milosam 108 (23½f,Tau,G,Nov 28)
Minella For Value 107 (24½f,Chl,G,Oct 18)
Minsk 112 (19f,Leo,YS,Dec 28)
Minstalad 105 (26f,Kel,GF,May 26)
Miss Ballantyne 109 (24f,Kem,G,Apr 15)
Miss Tenacious 106 (16f,Wcn,G,Nov 21)
Mister First 105 (20f,Mus,GS,Jan 17)
Mister Grez 108 (24½f,Chl,G,Oct 19)
Mister Marker 109 (23½f,Kel,GS,Feb 13)
Mister Philson 108 (25f,Ayr,HY,Mar 8)
Mister Wiseman 108 (18f,Mar,GF,Jly 7)
Mitchell's Way 106 (20f,Ncs,S,Mar 28)
Mitebeall Forluck 108 (17f,Leo,S,Dec 26)
Module 113 (20½f,Hun,GS,Dec 12)
Mon Parrain 107 (25½f,Chl,G,Apr 17)
Monbeg Dude 112 (25½f,Chl,G,Dec 13)
Moorlands Jack 105 (20f,Wor,G,Sep 10)
More Equity 105 (25f,Mar,G,Aug 31)
Morning Assembly 114 (24½f,Chl,G,Mar 12)
Moscow Mannon 116 (17f,Leo,S,Mar 2)
Mostly Bob 107 (23f,Str,GF,Jly 21)
Mount Benbulben 115 (24f,Kem,S,Dec 26)
Mount Colah 117 (17f,Leo,S,Mar 2)
Mountainous 108 (24f,Chp,GS,Dec 7)
Mozoltov 109 (17f,Leo,HY,Jan 26)
Mr Gee Jay 108 (24f,Ffo,G,May 6)
Mr Moonshine 113 (23½f,Kel,GS,Mar 1)
Mr Muddle 105 (16f,War,GS,Dec 8)
Mr Syntax 106 (24f,Don,GS,Dec 29)
Muldoon's Picnic 108 (23½f,Lei,S,Jan 7)
Mullaghanoe River 107 (21f,Leo,S,Jan 25)
Musical Wedge 106 (24½f,Tow,GS,Nov 24)
Mwaleshi 110 (16f,Wet,GS,Nov 16)
My Flora 106 (20f,Sed,G,May 2)
My Idea 107 (22½f,Wet,GS,Mar 28)
My Murphy 105 (24f,Leo,YS,Dec 29)

Nadiya De La Vega 108 (20f,Fai,GY,Apr 21)
Nagpur 108 (20½f,Sth,G,May 9)
Nataani 105 (24½f,Ban,G,Sep 13)
Nearest The Pin 108 (20½f,Kem,GS,Mar 15)
Ned Buntline 114 (16½f,Chl,G,Mar 14)
Next Sensation 114 (16½f,Chl,G,Mar 14)
Niceonefrankie 119 (19f,Asc,GS,Nov 22)
Night Alliance 109 (24f,Asc,GS,Nov 22)
Night In Milan 113 (26f,Don,G,Mar 1)
No Buts 107 (20½f,War,HY,Feb 8)
No Duffer 105 (20f,Hay,HY,Dec 30)
No Loose Change 109 (26½f,Nab,GF,Jly 8)
No Planning 115 (24f,Hay,G,Apr 19)
No Secrets 110 (26½f,Nby,GS,Mar 22)
Noble Legend 108 (20½f,Wet,S,Dec 26)
Noche De Reyes 105 (17f,Asc,G,Mar 30)
Nodform Richard 106 (25½f,Cat,G,Dec 4)
Notarfbad 107 (16½f,Nab,G,Oct 11)

O'Faolains Boy 117 (24½f,Chl,G,Mar 12)
Oceana Gold 107 (16½f,Wor,G,Jly 30)
Off The Ground 108 (19f,Don,G,Nov 29)
Ohio Gold 109 (20½f,Kem,S,Dec 26)
Oiseau De Nuit 107 (20f,Ain,G,Oct 26)
Olympian Boy 105 (19½f,Chp,GS,Apr 25)
On His Own 116 (26½f,Chl,G,Mar 14)
On The Bridge 108 (20f,Wor,G,Jly 10)
On The Way Out 107 (17f,Leo,S,Dec 26)
On Trend 108 (24f,Exe,G,Mar 18)
One Term 105 (20½f,Ban,GF,Jly 23)
Or De Grugy 108 (23½f,Kel,GS,Feb 13)
Orange Nassau 105 (25f,Mar,GS,Mar 9)
Oscar Hill 108 (17½f,Exe,G,Nov 24)
Oscar Whisky 115 (21f,Chl,G,Dec 13)
Oscargo 106 (24½f,Chl,G,Oct 18)
Our Father 107 (26½f,Nby,G,Nov 30)
Our Island 107 (26½f,Chl,S,Jan 1)
Our Mick 108 (25f,Ain,G,Apr 5)
Owen Glendower 106 (20½f,Wet,GS,Oct 16)
Oyster Shell 107 (16f,Lud,G,Nov 14)

Pacha Du Polder 108 (24½f,Chl,GS,Mar 11)
Paddy The Hare 109 (22½f,Mar,GF,Jly 7)
Palos Conti 105 (20f,Ncs,G,Nov 30)
Pantxoa 111 (25½f,Ffo,G,Aug 23)
Papradon 105 (24f,Utt,S,Jly 29)
Parsnip Pete 113 (16f,Ain,G,Apr 3)
Pasquini Rouge 109 (31f,Chl,G,Dec 13)
Pass The Hat 111 (21f,Leo,S,Mar 2)
Passato 107 (20f,Str,S,Oct 26)
Peachey Moment 105 (24f,Per,GF,Jun 9)
Pendra 107 (16f,Crl,GS,Oct 24)
Pepite Rose 114 (16f,San,GS,Apr 26)
Persian Snow 113 (20½f,War,S,Feb 21)
Pete The Feat 109 (26½f,Fon,GS,Dec 10)
Picaroon 105 (19½f,Exe,G,Apr 15)
Pigeon Island 111 (25f,Wet,G,May 23)
Piment D'Estruval 106 (16½f,Nab,GF,Jly 15)
Pineau De Re 117 (35½f,Ain,GS,Apr 5)
Pinerolo 109 (16½f,Ncs,G,Dec 12)
Planet Of Sound 107 (24f,Kem,S,Feb 22)
Plein Pouvoir 106 (21f,Wcn,GS,Nov 9)
Poole Master 113 (16½f,Chp,HY,Feb 22)
Posh Bird 107 (30f,Crt,S,May 27)
Poungach 107 (25½f,Wcn,GS,Nov 9)
Power Pack Jack 105 (24f,Ffo,G,Jun 20)
Present To You 105 (24½f,Tow,GS,Nov 24)
Present View 108 (24½f,Ban,S,Dec 13)
Presented 107 (24½f,Fak,HY,Jan 23)
Prince Of Pirates 106 (25½f,Chl,G,Dec 13)
Prince Tom 109 (26f,Utt,G,Jun 30)
Princely Player 107 (20f,Lud,GS,Nov 25)
Problema Tic 111 (24f,Per,GF,Jun 9)
Prolinx 105 (21½f,Str,GF,Jun 8)
Prospect Wells 108 (23f,Str,G,Jly 2)
Pure Faith 112 (26f,Utt,G,Jun 30)

Qianshan Leader 105 (24f,Exe,GF,Oct 10)
Qoubilai 105 (20 1/2f,Per,GF,Jly 14)
Queiros Bleu 105 (24 1/2f,Chl,G,Oct 19)
Quincy Des Pictons 106 (20 1/2f,Per,S,Apr 24)
Quito Du Tresor 110 (20f,Ayr,GS,Apr 11)

Raajih 105 (20 1/2f,Per,GS,Sep 26)
Raduis Bleu 105 (21f,Ffo,G,May 6)
Railway Dillon 109 (24 1/2f,Ban,S,Dec 13)
Rajdhani Express 121 (21f,Chl,G,Mar 13)
Rajnagan 110 (16 1/2f,Wor,G,May 12)
Rathlin 114 (21f,Chl,G,Mar 13)
Ratify 107 (19 1/2f,Chp,GS,Apr 25)
Ray Diamond 105 (19 1/2f,Exe,S,Dec 19)
Raya Star 106 (19f,Asc,S,Dec 20)
Raz De Maree 108 (35 1/2f,Ain,GS,Apr 5)
Real Milan 105 (24f,Don,GS,Dec 29)
Rebel Rebellion 110 (21 1/2f,Ain,S,Dec 7)
Reblis 108 (29f,Plu,HY,Jan 5)
Refusal 106 (20 1/2f,Hun,G,Apr 28)
Relax 111 (24 1/2f,San,HY,Feb 1)
Renard 111 (26f,Don,G,Mar 1)
Renard D'Irlande 109 (21f,Chl,HY,Jan 25)
Representingceltic 107 (24f,Kem,G,May 12)
Restless Harry 112 (29 1/2f,San,GS,Apr 26)
Rio De Sivola 111 (16f,War,GS,Nov 20)
Riskier 106 (20f,Sed,G,May 14)
River Purple 107 (20 1/2f,Wet,GS,Apr 13)
Riverside Theatre 117 (20 1/2f,Hun,GS,Dec 12)
Roalco De Farges 111 (26 1/2f,Nby,GS,Mar 22)
Rob Conti 113 (22 1/2f,Mar,G,Sep 28)
Robbie 105 (19f,Don,G,Feb 28)
Roberto Goldback 107 (24f,Don,S,Jan 25)
Robin's Command 106 (17f,Kel,G,Apr 22)
Roc D'Apsis 107 (16f,War,GS,Nov 20)
Rocky Creek 112 (26 1/2f,Nby,G,Nov 30)
Rockyaboya 111 (24 1/2f,Leo,S,Dec 27)
Roger Beantown 109 (20f,Wor,G,Jun 23)
Rolecarr 106 (24f,Ncs,HY,Jan 4)
Rossa Parks 107 (21f,Wcn,G,Nov 21)
Rossini's Dancer 106 (20 1/2f,Hex,G,Oct 12)
Roudoudou Ville 111 (20 1/2f,Per,S,Apr 24)
Rouge Et Blanc 108 (21f,Wcn,HY,Jan 30)
Royale Knight 109 (32f,Kel,GS,Dec 8)
Ruapehu 108 (26 1/2f,Nab,G,Apr 19)
Ruben Cotter 107 (22 1/2f,Nby,G,Nov 30)
Rudemeister 107 (20 1/2f,Hex,G,Oct 4)
Rudigreen 107 (20f,Sed,G,May 2)

Safran De Cotte 108 (33f,Ncs,HY,Feb 22)
Sam Winner 120 (25 1/2f,Chl,G,Dec 14)
Same Difference 106 (26 1/2f,Nby,G,Nov 30)
Samingarry 112 (24f,Chp,GS,Dec 7)
Samstown 107 (25f,Ayr,HY,Mar 8)
San Telm 108 (21 1/2f,Fak,GS,Dec 17)
Sands Cove 105 (16 1/2f,Tau,G,Dec 12)
Saoirse Dun 106 (29f,Fai,GY,Apr 21)
Saroque 108 (24f,Exe,S,Feb 21)
Savant Bleu 109 (24f,Chp,G,Apr 21)
Saved By John 110 (17f,Asc,GS,Nov 23)
Savello 115 (16 1/2f,Chl,G,Mar 14)
Scotch Warrior 111 (20f,Ayr,GS,Apr 11)
Scotswell 108 (25f,Ayr,S,Nov 2)
Seebright 106 (24f,Per,S,Apr 24)
Sergeant Dick 107 (19 1/2f,Ffo,HY,Nov 10)
Sergeant Pink 108 (17 1/2f,Crt,GF,Jly 22)
Settledoutofcourt 106 (23 1/2f,Kel,S,Dec 29)
Seven Woods 108 (33f,Ncs,HY,Feb 22)
Sew On Target 113 (20f,Chl,G,Oct 19)
Shadows Lengthen 109 (19f,Don,G,Feb 28)
Shalimar Fromentro 107 (31f,Chl,G,Dec 13)
Shamiran 105 (17f,Fai,S,Apr 6)
Shangani 111 (20 1/2f,Kem,HY,Feb 7)
Shanpallas 107 (17f,Leo,S,Dec 26)
Sharney Sike 106 (20 1/2f,Wet,S,Jan 21)
She Ranks Me 106 (20f,Plu,S,Apr 5)
Shoegazer 109 (21 1/2f,Nab,G,Aug 31)
Shooting Times 106 (20 1/2f,Per,G,May 15)
Shotavodka 114 (24f,Hay,G,Apr 19)
Shotgun Paddy 110 (24f,Lin,S,Dec 14)
Shouldavboughtgold 106 (25f,Wet,S,Dec 26)
Shrapnel 109 (16f,Fai,GF,Oct 12)
Shuil Royale 105 (24f,Lin,S,Dec 14)
Shutthefrontdoor 110 (24 1/2f,Chl,G,Nov 16)
Si C'Etait Vrai 112 (19f,Leo,YS,Dec 28)
Siberian Tiger 107 (25 1/2f,Ffo,G,Aug 23)
Silver Commander 106 (22f,Fon,GS,May 15)
Silver Roque 109 (20f,Sed,S,Nov 12)
Silviniaco Conti 121 (24f,Kem,S,Dec 26)
Simply Ned 115 (16f,Ain,G,Apr 5)
Simply Wings 108 (19f,Asc,GS,Nov 22)
Sin Bin 105 (23 1/2f,Tau,G,Mar 24)
Sir Du Bearn 108 (25 1/2f,Ffo,HY,Dec 16)
Sir Mattie 106 (24f,Ffo,G,Jun 6)
Sire Collonges 110 (31f,Chl,G,Nov 15)
Sire De Grugy 116 (16f,San,G,Dec 7)
Sixty Something 108 (24 1/2f,Ban,GS,Mar 22)
Sizing Australia 106 (31f,Chl,GS,Mar 12)
Sizing Europe 107 (16f,Chl,G,Mar 12)
Sizing Gold 108 (20f,Chl,G,Mar 13)
Sizing Symphony 106 (24 1/2f,Chl,G,Oct 18)
Skint 106 (16 1/2f,Nab,GF,Aug 3)
Sleep In First 106 (16 1/2f,Hex,GF,Jun 1)
Smad Place 116 (24 1/2f,Chl,G,Mar 12)
Smadynium 105 (16f,Cat,HY,Jan 9)
Smart Exit 105 (24 1/2f,Tow,S,Dec 19)
Smoking Aces 110 (33f,Ncs,HY,Feb 22)
Snuker 105 (20 1/2f,Per,G,May 15)
Solix 108 (24f,Don,S,Jan 25)
Soll 105 (29 1/2f,San,G,Dec 7)
Some Tikket 108 (17f,Fai,S,Apr 6)
Somersby 114 (16f,San,G,Dec 7)
Son Of Flicka 109 (24f,Don,GS,Feb 19)
Sonofagun 110 (16 1/2f,Nab,G,Apr 19)
Soudain 106 (30 1/2f,Hun,S,Nov 23)
Sound Investment 110 (16 1/2f,Tau,HY,Feb 27)
Special Account 106 (19 1/2f,Exe,GS,Oct 22)
Special Tiara 113 (16f,San,GS,Apr 26)
Speed Master 106 (20 1/2f,War,G,Mar 19)
Spirit Oscar 105 (20 1/2f,War,S,Mar 9)
Spock 107 (16f,Wcn,G,Apr 13)
Spring Heeled 108 (25 1/2f,Chl,G,Mar 13)
Sraid Padraig 105 (20f,Chl,G,Mar 13)
Stagecoach Pearl 107 (16f,Wet,G,Oct 16)
Standing Ovation 111 (25 1/2f,Wcn,GS,Nov 9)
Stone Light 106 (20 1/2f,War,S,Mar 9)
Stonethrower 105 (20f,Lud,G,Apr 10)
Storm Survivor 113 (26f,Utt,G,Jun 30)
Stormin Exit 106 (20f,Ayr,HY,Mar 7)
Strobe 106 (20 1/2f,Per,GF,Jly 14)
Strumble Head 109 (25f,Mar,G,Aug 17)
Summery Justice 113 (26 1/2f,Nby,HY,Mar 1)
Super Duty 108 (24f,Nby,GS,Dec 18)
Super Villan 107 (21f,Ffo,S,Nov 22)
Supreme Asset 109 (16 1/2f,Ncs,G,Dec 12)
Swaledale Lad 108 (16f,Crl,G,Oct 11)
Swatow Typhoon 107 (24 1/2f,Ban,S,Nov 30)
Sweeney Tunes 107 (24 1/2f,Leo,S,Dec 27)
Swing Bill 108 (35 1/2f,Ain,GS,Apr 5)
Swing Hard 107 (20f,Ncs,G,Nov 30)
Sydney Paget 110 (25f,Hay,HY,Jan 18)
Synthe Davis 105 (20f,Wor,G,Jly 10)

Tahiti Pearl 110 (20f,Sed,HY,Jan 26)
Talbot Road 109 (21f,Leo,S,Jan 25)
Tap Night 107 (20 1/2f,Chl,G,Nov 16)
Taquin Du Seuil 118 (20f,Chl,G,Mar 13)
Tara Rose 108 (20 1/2f,Wet,GS,Oct 16)
Tartak 113 (20f,Chl,G,Oct 19)
Tartan Snow 105 (20 1/2f,Per,S,Apr 24)
Tatenen 111 (22 1/2f,Nby,G,Nov 30)
Tayarat 105 (18f,Mar,G,Apr 6)
Teaforthree 110 (26 1/2f,Chl,G,Mar 14)
Ted Veale 106 (16f,Ain,G,Apr 5)
Temple Lord 107 (16f,Wet,G,Oct 16)
Terminal 106 (26 1/2f,Nby,G,Nov 30)
Texas Jack 113 (24f,Leo,SH,Feb 9)
Thanks For Coming 107 (22f,Tow,G,May 21)
That's The Deal 107 (21 1/2f,Fak,G,Jun 2)
The Black Baron 106 (21 1/2f,Fak,G,Jun 2)
The Cockney Mackem 106 (16 1/2f,Wor,G,Aug 28)
The Disengager 111 (21 1/2f,Nab,G,Aug 31)
The Druids Nephew 110 (24f,Chp,GS,Dec 7)
The Giant Bolster 116 (26 1/2f,Chl,G,Mar 14)
The Italian Yob 107 (20 1/2f,San,G,Dec 6)
The Mumper 106 (23 1/2f,Tau,G,Nov 14)
The Musical Guy 105 (22f,Tow,G,May 21)
The Nephew 106 (16 1/2f,Nab,G,Apr 25)
The Package 110 (24 1/2f,Chl,GS,Mar 11)
The Panama Kid 106 (24f,Don,GS,Jan 24)
The Rainbow Hunter 113 (24f,Don,S,Jan 25)
The Romford Pele 119 (19 1/2f,Chp,G,Oct 12)
Theatre Guide 111 (26 1/2f,Nby,G,Nov 30)
Theatrical Star 111 (21 1/2f,Asc,HY,Jan 18)
There's No Panic 107 (29 1/2f,San,G,Dec 7)
Theroadtocroker 107 (31f,Chl,G,Nov 15)
Third Intention 111 (24f,Nby,GS,Nov 28)
Thomas Wild 107 (25 1/2f,Wcn,S,Mar 6)
Tidal Bay 114 (24f,Leo,SH,Feb 9)
Time For Rupert 110 (24f,Don,GS,Feb 19)
Time To Think 105 (19 1/2f,Chp,GS,Apr 25)
Tindaro 105 (16 1/2f,Wor,GF,Jun 26)
Titchwood 106 (19f,Asc,GS,Nov 22)
To Live 106 (23f,Str,GF,Jly 21)
Toby Lerone 108 (20f,Lin,HY,Nov 12)
Tokyo Javilex 106 (19 1/2f,Chp,G,Apr 21)
Tony Star 109 (20f,Hay,G,May 11)
Too Cool To Fool 108 (16f,Ayr,GS,Apr 11)
Top Of The Range 107 (19f,Asc,GS,Nov 22)
Tornado In Milan 107 (16 1/2f,Tau,HY,Jan 18)
Tour Des Champs 112 (24f,Kem,S,Feb 22)
Tranquil Sea 111 (24f,Don,GS,Feb 19)
Tresor De Bontee 107 (16f,Utt,HY,Dec 31)
Triangular 110 (24f,Kem,HY,Feb 7)
Trifolium 115 (17f,Leo,S,Dec 26)
Triolo D'Alene 113 (24f,Hun,G,Apr 28)
Triptico 105 (20 1/2f,Wet,GS,Nov 1)
Trouble In Paris 105 (20 1/2f,Wet,GS,Apr 13)
True Blue 105 (16 1/2f,Wor,G,Jun 1)
Trustan Times 107 (21f,Hay,HY,Jan 18)
Tullamore Dew 109 (25f,Wet,S,Dec 26)
Turbo Du Ranch 105 (24f,Utt,G,May 26)
Turn Over Sivola 112 (16f,Ain,G,Apr 3)
Tutchec 108 (26f,Crl,GS,Dec 1)
Twentypoundluck 105 (16f,Per,GS,Jly 30)
Twin Plan 105 (20f,Fai,GY,Apr 21)
Twinlight 108 (17f,Fai,S,Apr 6)
Twirling Magnet 111 (24 1/2f,Chl,G,Oct 18)
Ulck Du Lin 107 (17f,Asc,S,Dec 21)
Ultimate 111 (20 1/2f,Wet,GS,Nov 1)
Ultimatum Du Roy 105 (22 1/2f,Nby,S,Dec 28)
Umberto D'Olivate 108 (18f,Fon,GS,Mar 15)
Un Anjou 107 (16f,Lei,S,Jan 7)
Un Guet Apens 108 (17f,Kel,G,Mar 22)
Uncle Junior 112 (31f,Chl,G,Nov 15)
Uncle Pelder 106 (18f,Mar,GF,Jly 7)
Undertheboardwalk 110 (21f,Leo,S,Jan 25)
Une Artiste 113 (20 1/2f,Kem,HY,Feb 7)
Union Jack D'Ycy 106 (26f,War,S,Jan 23)
Unioniste 113 (25f,Ain,GS,Dec 7)
Up And Go 108 (16f,Ayr,HY,Feb 20)
Up To Something 110 (16f,Crl,G,Oct 11)
Upsilon Bleu 112 (16 1/2f,Don,GS,Jan 25)
Urbain De Sivola 109 (20 1/2f,Kem,S,Dec 26)
Usa 108 (16f,Fai,GF,Oct 12)
Ut Majeur Aulmes 106 (16f,Per,GS,Apr 23)
Uxizandre 117 (20f,Chl,G,Mar 13)

Valco De Touzaine 114 (16f,Wet,GS,Nov 2)
Valdez 112 (16 1/2f,Don,GS,Jan 25)
Valoroso 106 (22 1/2f,Nby,G,Nov 30)
Via Sundown 110 (22f,Fon,HY,Feb 23)
Victor Hewgo 109 (24f,Don,GS,Feb 19)
Victrix Gale 109 (24 1/2f,Leo,S,Dec 27)
Vif Argent 107 (21f,Wcn,HY,Feb 26)
Vino Griego 112 (25f,Ain,G,Apr 5)
Vintage Star 112 (25f,Hay,HY,Jan 18)
Violin Davis 105 (22 1/2f,Nby,G,Nov 30)
Viva Colonia 114 (20f,Ain,G,Oct 26)

Waltzing Tornado 106 (25 1/2f,Wcn,HY,Dec 26)
War On 105 (20f,Ncs,G,Nov 15)
Watch House 107 (24f,Utt,G,Sep 22)
Wayward Glance 108 (22 1/2f,Utt,G,Jly 26)
Wayward Prince 111 (25f,Wet,GS,Nov 2)
Well Hello There 107 (24f,Ffo,G,Jun 6)
Well Mett 106 (26 1/2f,Nab,G,May 28)
Well Refreshed 106 (29 1/2f,San,G,Dec 7)
Wessex King 105 (20f,Mar,G,Apr 21)
West With The Wind 109 (19 1/2f,Exe,GF,May 7)
Wester Ross 107 (20f,Wor,G,Jly 10)
Western King 108 (26 1/2f,Nab,GF,Sep 24)
Western Warhorse 114 (16f,Chl,GS,Mar 11)
Wetak 105 (20f,Chl,G,Mar 13)
What A Warrior 107 (26 1/2f,Nby,GS,Mar 22)
Whats Happening 109 (23 1/2f,Lei,S,Jan 7)
Whispering Jack 106 (24f,Ffo,G,May 25)
Whistling Senator 105 (32f,Exe,G,Dec 6)
Who Owns Me 105 (22f,Fon,HY,Nov 17)
Wicklow Lad 110 (20f,Ncs,HY,Feb 22)
Wiesentraum 111 (20 1/2f,Sth,G,Aug 18)
Wiffy Chatsby 109 (20f,Wor,G,Jun 6)
Wings Of Smoke 107 (20f,Str,G,Apr 13)
Wishfull Thinking 110 (20 1/2f,Chl,G,Nov 16)
Witness In Court 108 (16f,Mus,S,Jan 3)
Wonderful Charm 114 (21f,Chl,G,Dec 13)
Wood Yer 105 (23 1/2f,Lei,S,Jan 21)
Woodbank 105 (19f,Don,G,Nov 29)
Woolcombe Folly 112 (20f,Str,GS,May 19)
Workbench 107 (16 1/2f,Tau,G,Nov 28)
Wrong Turn 105 (21f,Leo,YS,Dec 29)
Wychwoods Brook 113 (25f,Hay,HY,Jan 18)
Wyck Hill 111 (33f,Ncs,HY,Feb 22)

Yesyoucan 111 (20f,Ncs,G,Nov 15)
You Must Know Me 110 (21 1/2f,Ain,G,Apr 4)
Your Busy 109 (21 1/2f,Ain,S,Dec 7)

Zaru 106 (16 1/2f,Ncs,G,Dec 12)
Zarzal 107 (16f,Lud,GS,Nov 25)

HURDLES

Aazif 113 (17f,Ban,GF,Jly 23)
Abbyssial 111 (16f,Fai,SH,Feb 22)
Abracadabra Sivola 112 (16f,Hay,HY,Feb 15)
Accordingtojodie 105 (17f,Ban,G,May 18)
Act Alone 106 (19 1/2f,Don,GS,Jan 8)
Act Of Kalanisi 109 (16f,Ffo,HY,Dec 16)
Activial 110 (16f,Kem,S,Feb 22)
Adelar 108 (17f,Ban,G,Aug 2)
Adriana Des Mottes 110 (16f,Fai,SH,Feb 22)
Agent Archie 105 (17f,Ban,G,Aug 2)
Aglaophonos 110 (16f,Lud,G,Oct 24)
Ahyaknowyerself 110 (16f,Wcn,GS,Nov 9)
Akdam 106 (20f,Fak,S,Jan 23)
Al Co 106 (24f,Mar,S,Nov 21)
Alaivan 112 (17f,Chl,G,Mar 14)
Alasi 106 (16 1/2f,Don,GS,Jan 25)
Albert Bridge 106 (16f,Plu,S,Feb 24)
Alcala 105 (16f,Kem,S,Feb 22)
Alder Mairi 110 (20f,Wcn,HY,Jan 30)
Aldopicgros 107 (16f,Kem,G,Oct 20)
Algernon Pazham 112 (20 1/2f,Lei,GS,Dec 11)
All That Remains 108 (16f,Fak,G,Oct 25)
Allez Cool 105 (16 1/2f,Hex,HY,Nov 20)
Allow Dallow 109 (20 1/2f,Utt,HY,Dec 20)

Allow Me 105 (20½f,Kel,G,Apr 22)
Alpha Victor 105 (24f,Ban,HY,Feb 26)
Alsadaa 107 (19f,Str,GS,Mar 29)
Always Archie 107 (21f,Lud,G,Apr 22)
Alwaystheoptimist 108 (16f,Wcn,G,Oct 17)
Amore Alato 111 (16f,Kem,S,Feb 22)
Ampleforth 109 (20½f,Sth,HY,Jan 6)
Anay Turge 106 (17f,Nab,GF,Jun 5)
Andy Kelly 107 (22f,Asc,S,Dec 20)
Angles Hill 109 (21f,Chl,G,Nov 15)
Annelko 105 (16f,Utt,G,Jly 26)
Annie Power 117 (16½f,Don,GS,Jan 25)
Another Hero 105 (20½f,Chl,G,Apr 16)
Another Mattie 108 (16f,Ayr,HY,Feb 20)
Anteros 107 (16½f,Chp,G,Apr 21)
Any Given Moment 109 (24½f,Mus,S,Feb 2)
Apache Stronghold 105 (20f,Fai,S,Apr 6)
Araldur 106 (20f,Chp,S,Oct 26)
Arctic Court 111 (24½f,Mus,G,Nov 8)
Arctic Fire 117 (17f,Chl,G,Mar 14)
Area Access 106 (22½f,Str,GS,Mar 29)
Argaum 110 (17f,Nab,GF,Sep 24)
Arrayan 107 (16f,Lud,HY,Feb 5)
Art Of Payroll 109 (16f,Leo,S,Mar 2)
Art Professor 109 (20½f,Hun,S,Feb 6)
As I Am 114 (16½f,Nby,S,Nov 30)
Ashbrittle 109 (20f,Fon,G,Oct 5)
Ashdown Lad 109 (16f,Lud,G,Oct 24)
Ashes House 105 (20½f,Utt,GS,Oct 17)
Ashford Wood 111 (20f,Ffo,S,Mar 16)
Astigos 105 (24f,Hay,HY,Feb 15)
At Fishers Cross 111 (24½f,Ain,GS,Apr 5)
Attaglance 108 (24½f,Mus,S,Feb 2)
Attwaal 108 (16½f,Don,GS,Feb 6)
Aubusson 111 (20f,Chp,GS,Dec 7)
August Hill 107 (16f,Wcn,HY,Dec 26)
Auld Sthock 106 (21f,Plu,GS,Apr 21)
Aurore D'Estruval 111 (16f,Hay,HY,Feb 15)
Australia Day 107 (16f,Mus,G,Nov 8)
Avidity 105 (16f,Ayr,HY,Mar 7)
Azorian 106 (20f,Fai,S,Apr 6)
Azure Fly 105 (24f,Asc,G,Mar 30)

Baccalaureate 107 (16f,Utt,G,Jun 30)
Ballincurrig 105 (16½f,Hun,S,Nov 23)
Bally Legend 108 (22½f,Fon,S,Oct 23)
Ballyalton 118 (21f,Chl,G,Mar 12)
Ballyculla 107 (24f,Chl,G,Apr 17)
Ballyglasheen 111 (16f,Lud,G,Oct 24)
Ballyheigue Bay 108 (21f,Plu,S,Mar 10)
Ballythomas 108 (22f,Wet,GS,Apr 13)
Baltimore Rock 110 (16½f,San,S,Mar 8)
Baradari 105 (16½f,Chl,G,Mar 12)
Barizan 112 (17f,Chl,G,Mar 14)
Battle Group 105 (24f,Hay,G,May 11)
Batu Ferringhi 105 (16f,Ffo,HY,Nov 10)
Bayan 112 (21f,Chl,G,Mar 12)
Bazart 109 (17f,Nab,GF,Sep 24)
Beachfire 108 (20½f,Hun,S,Oct 15)
Beat That 115 (24½f,Ain,GS,Apr 4)
Ben Cee Pee M 105 (21f,Mar,G,Apr 6)
Benbane Head 109 (27f,Nab,GF,Aug 3)
Benbecula 112 (16f,Wcn,GS,Mar 23)
Benefit Of Youth 106 (22½f,Str,G,Aug 29)
Benzanno 112 (16f,Cat,GS,Feb 25)
Berkeley Barron 108 (22f,San,S,Mar 7)
Bernardelli 106 (16½f,Hun,S,Nov 23)
Beyeh 106 (20½f,Sth,GS,Dec 15)
Big Buck's 108 (24f,Chl,G,Mar 13)
Big Casino 106 (20f,Crl,S,Oct 30)
Big Hands Harry 109 (21f,Nby,HY,Feb 28)
Big Time Billy 107 (23½f,Exe,GF,May 7)
Big Water 106 (16½f,Wet,GS,Oct 16)
Billy Biscuit 105 (24f,Ban,GS,Apr 12)
Billy Twyford 105 (24f,Asc,G,Mar 30)
Bishops Heir 108 (27f,Kel,GS,Nov 9)
Bishopslough 107 (16f,Leo,S,Mar 2)
Blacklough 107 (16f,Leo,SH,Feb 9)
Blake Dean 108 (16f,Ncs,HY,Jan 15)
Blakemount 114 (20f,Wet,GS,Nov 16)
Blue Buttons 108 (17f,Tau,HY,Dec 30)
Bob's Legend 108 (19f,Str,GS,Mar 29)
Bob's World 105 (17f,Sed,GS,Mar 11)
Bobble Boru 108 (16f,Wcn,HY,Dec 26)
Bollin Judith 107 (17f,Tau,G,Nov 28)
Bombadero 108 (16f,Ffo,GS,Oct 13)
Bonnet's Vino 107 (19f,Mar,S,Nov 21)
Bourne 105 (22f,San,GS,Dec 7)
Bow Badger 107 (16½f,Per,G,May 16)
Bowie 105 (19f,Mar,S,Dec 26)
Brave Vic 109 (21f,Plu,HY,Jan 5)
Breaking Bits 108 (18½f,Fon,GF,Aug 15)
Bright Abbey 105 (19f,Nab,GF,Jly 21)
Bright Applause 105 (16½f,Kel,G,Oct 6)
Brinestine 106 (17f,Tau,G,Nov 14)
Broadway Buffalo 111 (24f,Chl,G,Mar 13)
Brother Brian 109 (19f,Nby,S,Jan 15)
Brother Du Berlais 105 (21½f,Ayr,GS,Apr 12)
Broughton 106 (16½f,Don,G,Dec 14)
Brunello 106 (20f,Sed,S,Nov 26)
Buckhorn Tom 106 (22f,Nab,GF,Sep 24)
Bull And Bush 112 (20f,Fon,GS,Dec 10)
Busted Tycoon 109 (20½f,Per,GF,Jun 9)
Busty Brown 109 (18f,Leo,S,Mar 2)
By The Boardwalk 106 (22f,Asc,GS,Nov 23)
Bygones Of Brid 110 (16f,Ncs,S,Mar 28)
Bygones Sovereign 108 (22f,Asc,S,Dec 20)

Cadeau George 107 (24f,Tow,HY,Feb 23)
Caid Du Berlais 108 (20½f,Chl,G,Mar 14)
Calaf 106 (16½f,Str,G,Apr 13)
Calculated Risk 110 (20f,Sed,S,Dec 26)
Calipto 111 (17f,Ain,G,Apr 3)
Call A Truce 105 (16f,Utt,S,May 15)
Call Box 106 (20½f,Hex,GS,Oct 4)
Call Me Vic 106 (19½f,Don,GS,Jan 24)
Call The Cops 111 (16f,Sth,S,Nov 8)
Canadian Diamond 106 (18½f,Fon,GS,May 15)
Cannon Fodder 106 (24½f,Kem,S,Dec 27)
Canuspotit 108 (20½f,Sth,G,Dec 15)
Capellanus 110 (24½f,Mus,G,Nov 8)
Captain Cee Bee 116 (16½f,Chl,GS,Mar 11)
Captain Clayton 105 (22f,Wet,HY,Feb 18)
Captain Cutter 113 (21f,Nby,HY,Dec 28)
Cara's Oscar 110 (22f,Fai,GY,Apr 21)
Cardigan Island 105 (20f,Wor,G,Jly 3)
Carlton Jack 105 (20½f,Utt,G,Oct 6)
Carole's Destrier 112 (21½f,Hun,HY,Jan 2)
Carole's Spirit 110 (24f,Asc,HY,Jan 18)
Carraig Mor 117 (20½f,Utt,S,Nov 1)
Carrigmorna King 109 (20f,Wcn,G,Nov 21)
Carters Rest 106 (16½f,Wet,GS,Apr 13)
Cash And Go 111 (17f,Chl,G,Mar 14)
Castlemorris King 107 (16f,Lud,G,Apr 10)
Cawdor House Bert 107 (20f,Ffo,S,Mar 16)
Ceasar Milan 109 (19½f,Tau,HY,Feb 27)
Celestial Halo 110 (24f,Hay,HY,Feb 15)
Celtic Monarch 107 (17½f,Crt,S,May 27)
Centasia 108 (16f,Utt,S,Nov 1)
Chalk It Down 105 (17f,Nab,GS,Apr 25)
Champagne At Tara 110 (16½f,San,GS,Dec 7)
Champagne West 117 (21f,War,GS,Dec 8)
Chase The Spud 106 (16f,Utt,S,Nov 16)
Chase The Wind 110 (16f,Plu,GS,Dec 16)
Chatterbox 108 (16½f,Nby,GS,Nov 28)
Chavoy 106 (24½f,Ayr,HY,Jan 27)
Cheltenian 114 (16f,Utt,HY,Dec 31)
Chesil Beach Boy 108 (17f,Tau,HY,Jan 28)
Chilworth Screamer 106 (20f,Fon,G,Sep 8)
Chris Pea Green 114 (20f,Fon,HY,Feb 23)
Churchtown Love 108 (17f,Ban,HY,Feb 26)
Citizenship 109 (17f,Exe,S,Dec 19)
Civil Unrest 111 (16f,Mus,G,Nov 7)
Civil War 108 (16½f,Don,GS,Feb 6)
Clan William 107 (16f,Utt,S,May 15)
Clarcam 112 (17f,Ain,G,Apr 3)
Clerk's Choice 108 (21f,Chl,G,Mar 12)
Clever Cookie 108 (16f,Mus,GS,Jan 17)
Clondaw Draft 108 (16f,Wor,GF,Aug 20)
Clondaw Hero 105 (24½f,Mus,G,Nov 8)
Clondaw Kaempfer 108 (21f,Chl,G,Mar 12)
Cloud Brook 110 (20f,Ffo,S,Nov 22)
Cloud Creeper 114 (20f,Fon,GS,Nov 27)
Cloudy Bob 106 (21f,Mar,S,Nov 21)
Cobajayisland 105 (20½f,Per,GS,Apr 23)
Cockney Sparrow 117 (16f,Ayr,GS,Apr 12)
Cocktails At Dawn 108 (21f,Kem,G,Apr 15)
Coffee 110 (16½f,Str,GF,Jun 8)
Cogry 107 (20½f,Utt,HY,Dec 20)
Cole Harden 114 (21f,Chl,G,Mar 12)
Come On Laurie 106 (16f,Tow,HY,Dec 26)
Comedinewithme 106 (20f,Fon,HY,Dec 26)
Comical Red 107 (24½f,Tau,HY,Jan 28)
Commissioned 110 (17f,Ain,G,Apr 3)
Communicator 106 (16½f,Nby,S,Dec 18)
Coronea Lilly 105 (24f,Mar,G,Aug 31)
Cotton Mill 113 (16f,Ncs,G,Nov 30)
Count Danilo 107 (20f,Fak,GS,Dec 17)
Coup De Grace 105 (20f,Fon,GS,Mar 15)
Courage 110 (24f,Leo,S,Dec 28)
Court Minstrel 115 (16f,Ayr,GS,Apr 12)
Cove 109 (21f,Plu,S,Mar 10)
Creepy 111 (21f,Chl,G,Nov 16)
Croco Bay 105 (17f,Sed,G,May 14)
Cross Kennon 110 (24f,Chl,G,Mar 13)
Crowning Jewel 111 (20f,Ain,G,Oct 27)
Cry Of Freedom 109 (17f,Tau,GF,May 2)
Cup Final 109 (16f,Kem,S,Feb 22)
Curzon Line 111 (16f,Lud,G,Oct 24)
Cyrien Star 109 (24f,Ban,GS,Dec 13)

Damascus Steel 111 (16½f,Hex,G,May 11)
Dan Breen 108 (16f,Plu,GS,Apr 20)
Dare To Endeavour 106 (20½f,Utt,HY,Dec 20)
Dartford Warbler 109 (20½f,Utt,G,Sep 11)
Dazinski 106 (22½f,Str,G,Aug 29)
Decimus 106 (22½f,Str,G,Mar 22)
Decoy 107 (20½f,Hex,GS,Oct 4)
Deep Trouble 113 (17f,Chl,G,Mar 14)
Deepsand 105 (16½f,Wet,GS,Dec 7)
Definitely Glad 109 (16½f,Wet,G,May 23)
Dell' Arca 116 (20f,Ain,GS,Apr 5)
Della Sun 106 (20½f,Utt,G,Jly 26)
Deputy Dan 116 (21f,War,GS,Dec 8)
Descaro 105 (16f,Utt,G,Jun 13)
Desoto County 110 (16f,Hay,S,Dec 30)
Detroit Red 105 (20f,Chp,GS,Apr 25)
Dhaular Dhar 106 (16½f,Per,G,Sep 9)
Diakali 115 (17f,Chl,G,Mar 14)
Diamond King 113 (17f,Ban,GS,Dec 13)
Dildar 106 (16f,Asc,GS,Nov 2)
Discovery Bay 109 (16f,Mus,G,Nov 8)
Dispour 109 (16½f,San,GS,Apr 26)
Doctor Harper 108 (17f,Exe,GS,Nov 5)
Doing Fine 107 (22f,Asc,GS,Nov 23)
Dolatulo 107 (18½f,Fon,HY,Nov 17)
Dolores Delightful 106 (16½f,San,GS,Apr 26)
Don Poli 111 (20½f,Chl,G,Mar 14)
Don't Be Late 110 (20f,Wor,G,Aug 13)
Dooney Rock 106 (20½f,Utt,G,Sep 11)
Double Double 105 (17f,Chl,G,Apr 16)
Double Irish 106 (16f,Leo,S,Dec 27)
Dovils Date 106 (17f,Tau,S,Mar 10)
Down Ace 110 (16f,Tow,GS,Nov 7)
Downtown Boy 111 (20f,Sed,S,Nov 26)
Doyly Carte 109 (16½f,Don,GS,Jan 25)
Doynosaur 106 (16½f,Wet,GS,Nov 16)
Dragon's Den 107 (16f,Wcn,S,Mar 6)
Dream Deal 106 (16½f,Chp,HY,Nov 21)
Dream Flyer 105 (22f,Wet,GS,Dec 7)
Dreamsoftheatre 105 (27f,Nab,GF,Jly 21)
Dresden 105 (16½f,Str,GF,Jun 18)
Drop Out Joe 107 (20f,Crl,G,Oct 11)
Drum Valley 110 (20f,Ain,G,Oct 27)
Dubawi Island 107 (17f,Ban,S,Dec 22)
Duke Of Navan 110 (16f,Ncs,G,Nov 30)
Dumbarton 107 (16½f,Wet,GS,Oct 16)
Dunraven Storm 109 (17f,Chl,G,Mar 14)
Duroble Man 109 (16f,Kem,G,Oct 20)

Early Applause 106 (16½f,Per,GF,Jun 9)
Edgardo Sol 109 (21f,Chl,G,Mar 12)
Edlomond 106 (16f,Tow,GS,Nov 24)
Ellnando Queen 114 (21f,Plu,G,Mar 31)
Embsay Crag 107 (22½f,Kel,G,Apr 22)
Emily Gray 108 (17f,Chl,G,Apr 17)
Emily's Flyer 105 (24½f,Per,G,Sep 9)
Emral Silk 105 (19f,Cat,S,Jan 1)
Enchanted Garden 107 (19f,Mar,HY,Jan 16)
Enchanting Smile 110 (17f,Nab,G,Apr 19)
Endeavor 105 (16½f,Kel,G,May 8)
Esporao 108 (16½f,Per,GS,Jly 31)
Ethics Girl 105 (16f,Fak,G,Jun 2)
Experimentalist 108 (20f,Fon,G,Oct 5)

Fair Dreamer 110 (16f,Wcn,GS,Mar 23)
Fair Loch 109 (16½f,Don,GS,Feb 6)
Fair Trade 108 (16f,Kem,G,May 12)
Far West 112 (16f,Wcn,GS,Nov 9)
Fascino Rustico 106 (16f,Kem,S,Dec 26)
Faugheen 120 (21f,Chl,G,Mar 12)
Fayette County 109 (20f,Crl,GS,Oct 24)
Fergal Mael Duin 110 (16f,Utt,HY,Dec 31)
Fergall 111 (16f,Plu,GS,Apr 20)
Figaro 109 (19f,Mar,GS,Dec 5)
Fighter Jet 107 (22½f,Str,G,Aug 29)
Filatore 107 (16f,Ffo,HY,Dec 16)
Final Assault 108 (16f,Ayr,S,Nov 2)
Fine Rightly 108 (16f,Ayr,HY,Jan 2)
Fingal Bay 113 (24f,Chl,G,Mar 13)
First In The Queue 109 (16f,Fak,G,Oct 25)
First Mohican 112 (16½f,Don,GS,Feb 6)
Fisher 107 (16f,Ncs,G,Mar 15)
Fitandproperjob 105 (17f,Mar,G,May 19)
Flaxen Flare 114 (17f,Chl,G,Mar 14)
Fleet Dawn 106 (16½f,Nby,GS,Nov 28)
Flemenson 106 (20½f,Utt,GS,Oct 17)
Flementime 109 (20½f,Sth,HY,Feb 3)
Flicka Williams 107 (20½f,Utt,HY,Dec 31)
Flute Bowl 106 (17f,Tau,S,Mar 10)
Flying Doctor 106 (22f,Crt,G,Aug 24)
Focail Maith 106 (16½f,Hun,G,Apr 21)
Foggy's Wall 105 (19f,Nab,G,Apr 25)
Followmeuptocarlow 105 (24f,Leo,S,Dec 28)
Fond Memory 105 (16½f,Per,S,Apr 25)
For Two 105 (17f,Chl,G,Apr 16)
Forced Family Fun 106 (16½f,Don,GS,Jan 8)
Forever Present 108 (21f,Lud,GS,Nov 25)
Formal Bid 108 (16½f,Per,GS,Sep 25)
Forward Flight 106 (20f,Sed,S,Mar 2)
Fox Norton 108 (17f,Ain,G,Apr 3)
Foxcub 109 (20½f,Lei,GS,Dec 11)
Franciscan 110 (17f,Chl,G,Apr 16)
Frankie's Promise 109 (16f,Ayr,S,Nov 2)
Free Thinking 108 (16f,Lud,G,Nov 14)
Free To Dream 109 (24f,Mar,S,Nov 21)
Fujin Dancer 107 (16f,Fak,G,Mar 14)
Full Shift 109 (19f,Nby,S,Jan 15)
Full Throttle 108 (19f,Mar,S,Nov 21)

Garde La Victoire 110 (16½f,Chl,GS,Mar 11)
Garrahalish 107 (16f,Tow,HY,Dec 26)
Gassin Golf 109 (16½f,San,S,Mar 8)
Gate Please 110 (20f,Ffo,S,Mar 16)
George Fernbeck 105 (24½f,Sth,G,Apr 23)
Gerdago 109 (16f,Fai,SH,Feb 22)
Germany Calling 107 (16f,Kem,S,Feb 22)
Get Home Now 107 (19f,Mar,G,Aug 4)
Get Me Out Of Here 112 (21f,Chl,G,Mar 12)
Ghost Of A Smile 105 (21½f,Hun,S,Mar 2)
Gift Of Dgab 107 (16f,Leo,S,Mar 2)
Gifted Leader 108 (17f,Mar,G,Apr 21)
Gigondas 111 (17f,Tau,G,Nov 28)
Gilgamboa 111 (16f,Leo,S,Jan 25)
Ginger Fizz 109 (16½f,Wet,GS,Apr 13)
Gitane Du Berlais 112 (17f,Ain,S,Dec 7)
Glen Beg 110 (16½f,Ain,GS,Apr 5)

Glencree 106 (16 1/2f,Kel,G,Oct 6)
Glowinginthedark 105 (20 1/2f,Hun,S,Mar 2)
Go West Young Man 105 (19 1/2f,Don,G,Mar 1)
God's Own 107 (21f,Kem,GS,Nov 4)
Going Concern 109 (16 1/2f,Chp,HY,Nov 21)
Golanova 107 (18 1/2f,Fon,GF,Aug 15)
Gold Patrol 107 (24f,Leo,S,Dec 28)
Goldan Jess 107 (22f,Crt,G,Aug 26)
Goodwood Mirage 105 (16f,Kem,S,Feb 22)
Goohar 114 (17f,Ban,GS,Dec 13)
Gores Island 105 (20f,Fon,GS,Nov 27)
Granaruid 106 (19 1/2f,Crl,GS,Mar 16)
Great Link 109 (16f,Ayr,HY,Feb 20)
Grumeti 114 (16f,Ncs,G,Nov 30)
Guards Chapel 105 (20f,Fon,G,Sep 8)
Guitar Pete 113 (17f,Ain,G,Apr 3)

Haatefina 106 (16f,War,S,Jan 23)
Halifax 105 (19f,Mar,G,May 10)
Handazan 110 (16 1/2f,Chp,G,Oct 12)
Handsome Stranger 105 (16f,Kem,G,Oct 20)
Hanga Roa 105 (16f,Lud,G,Oct 24)
Hannibal The Great 105 (20f,Fon,G,Oct 5)
Harristown 116 (17f,Nab,G,Oct 11)
Hartforth 107 (25 1/2f,Cat,HY,Jan 31)
Hartside 106 (16f,Hay,S,Dec 21)
Hawaii Five Nil 105 (16f,Cat,HY,Feb 10)
Hawk High 108 (16 1/2f,Chl,G,Mar 12)
Hawkhill 108 (16 1/2f,San,HY,Nov 9)
Head Of The Class 105 (22f,Wet,GS,Apr 13)
Headly's Bridge 106 (17f,Exe,S,Dec 19)
Heath Hunter 112 (20f,Sed,S,Nov 26)
Heavenstown 108 (24f,Ban,GS,Mar 22)
Helium 109 (17f,Tau,HY,Jan 28)
Henri Parry Morgan 109 (24f,Utt,GF,May 26)
Henry Higgins 105 (16f,Leo,SH,Feb 9)
Henryville 106 (20f,Fon,GS,Mar 15)
Here's Herbie 107 (19f,Exe,GS,Mar 26)
Heronry 109 (24f,Asc,G,Mar 30)
Hi Note 110 (20f,Fon,G,Oct 5)
Hi Tide 105 (16f,Wor,G,Oct 10)
Hidden Identity 111 (20 1/2f,Hun,S,Nov 12)
Hide The Evidence 105 (16 1/2f,Per,GS,Sep 25)
Highland Retreat 111 (24f,Asc,HY,Jan 18)
Highpower 109 (16f,Hay,S,Dec 30)
Highway Code 106 (17f,Exe,S,Nov 13)
Hint Of Mint 112 (16f,Lei,HY,Jan 7)
Hold Court 106 (21f,Lud,G,Apr 10)
Hold The Bucks 105 (16f,Plu,S,Feb 24)
Hollow Tree 105 (22 1/2f,Kel,G,Apr 22)
Home Run 108 (22f,San,GS,Dec 7)
Homer Run 106 (21f,Kem,G,Apr 15)
Horatio Hornblower 106 (16f,Ffo,HY,Feb 1)
Horizontal Speed 111 (17f,Exe,GS,Oct 22)
Howaboutnow 110 (19f,Mar,S,Nov 21)
Howlongisafoot 105 (24f,Asc,G,Mar 30)
Howwoulduno 106 (16 1/2f,Hex,G,Jun 23)
Huff And Puff 111 (16 1/2f,Don,GS,Feb 6)
Hunting Tower 109 (20f,Wor,G,Aug 13)
Hurricane Fly 119 (16 1/2f,Chl,GS,Mar 11)

I Need Gold 105 (24 1/2f,Ayr,HY,Mar 8)
I'Ll Be Frank 105 (16 1/2f,Hex,G,May 11)
If In Doubt 110 (23 1/2f,Exe,HY,Feb 9)
Ifandbutwhynot 111 (16 1/2f,Nby,GS,Nov 28)
Imperial Leader 107 (23 1/2f,Exe,HY,Feb 9)
In By Midnight 106 (20 1/2f,Sth,S,Nov 8)
In The Rough 105 (16f,Tow,S,Dec 19)
Indevan 107 (21f,Chl,G,Nov 16)
Indigo Rock 107 (24f,Hex,G,Jun 15)
Irish Buccaneer 106 (20 1/2f,Utt,GS,Mar 15)
Irish Cavalier 109 (16 1/2f,Str,S,Oct 31)
Irish Saint 112 (16 1/2f,Nby,HY,Feb 8)
Ironical 105 (22 1/2f,Str,GF,Jly 21)
Irving 114 (16f,Kem,S,Feb 22)
Island Confusion 110 (16 1/2f,Hex,G,May 11)
Island Heights 105 (19 1/2f,Crl,GS,Mar 16)
It's A Doddle 108 (16f,Ffo,HY,Dec 16)
It's A Mans World 109 (16 1/2f,Per,G,Sep 9)
Ittirad 107 (16f,Fak,G,Oct 25)
Ivan Grozny 108 (16f,Leo,SH,Feb 9)

Jack By The Hedge 105 (17f,Exe,GS,Oct 22)
James Pollard 109 (17f,Tau,G,Nov 28)
Jaunty Journey 105 (27f,Per,S,Apr 25)
Jetson 112 (24f,Chl,G,Mar 13)
Jezki 122 (16 1/2f,Chl,GS,Mar 11)
Jojabean 107 (20 1/2f,Sth,G,May 9)
Josies Orders 105 (24 1/2f,Ain,GS,Oct 26)
Josses Hill 116 (16 1/2f,Chl,GS,Mar 11)
Joxer 106 (18f,Leo,S,Mar 2)
Jumps Road 109 (16 1/2f,Nby,HY,Mar 1)
Junction Fourteen 115 (20f,Fon,GS,Nov 27)
Just Cameron 109 (17f,Ban,G,May 18)

Kaki De La Pree 111 (25f,Crl,S,Dec 15)
Kaki Island 107 (16 1/2f,Chp,S,Mar 8)
Kalucci 106 (16f,Utt,S,May 15)
Kambis 106 (18 1/2f,Fon,GS,May 15)
Kangaroo Court 110 (22f,Nab,GF,Sep 1)
Karinga Dancer 111 (17f,Ain,GS,Oct 26)
Karinga Dandy 107 (27f,Kel,GS,Nov 9)
Kashmir Peak 105 (16 1/2f,Ain,GS,Apr 5)
Katgary 109 (16 1/2f,Ain,GS,Apr 5)
Kayaan 107 (19f,Mar,G,May 31)
Kayf Moss 115 (20f,Fon,HY,Feb 23)
Kaylif Aramis 111 (19 1/2f,Asc,S,Feb 15)
Kaysersberg 105 (24 1/2f,Don,GS,Feb 19)
Keel Haul 107 (16f,Wcn,HY,Feb 26)
Keeneland 106 (20 1/2f,Kel,G,Apr 22)
Keltus 107 (16 1/2f,Hun,GS,Dec 12)
Kelvingrove 105 (16 1/2f,Str,GS,Mar 29)
Kentucky Hyden 112 (17f,Chl,HY,Jan 25)
Key To The West 113 (16f,Sth,S,Nov 8)
Keychain 107 (17f,Nab,G,Oct 11)
Kian's Delight 105 (20f,Ain,G,May 17)
Kilbree Chief 105 (24f,Hex,S,Mar 31)
Kilflora 106 (19f,Mar,S,Dec 26)
Kilgefin Star 107 (19f,Mar,GS,Mar 9)
Killala Quay 117 (21f,Chl,G,Mar 12)
Killegney 105 (22 1/2f,Str,GS,Mar 29)
Kilmurvy 106 (21f,Kem,G,Apr 15)
King Edmund 106 (19 1/2f,Tau,G,Apr 23)
King Of Strings 105 (17f,Mar,G,Apr 21)
King Of The Picts 112 (16f,Leo,S,Dec 27)
King Shabra 107 (20f,Fai,GF,Oct 12)
Kings Bandit 110 (16 1/2f,Wet,GS,Apr 13)
Kings Lad 108 (16 1/2f,Nby,G,Mar 21)
Kings Palace 108 (22 1/2f,Fon,G,Oct 4)
Kingsmere 111 (24f,Chl,G,Apr 17)
Knight In Purple 109 (16 1/2f,Wet,G,May 23)
Knight Of Pleasure 109 (18 1/2f,Fon,HY,Nov 17)
Knock House 107 (21f,Plu,S,Dec 16)
Knockara Beau 108 (24f,Chl,HY,Jan 25)
Koolala 110 (22f,Wcn,GS,Apr 2)
Koultas King 108 (20 1/2f,Hun,G,Sep 9)
Kris Spin 108 (24f,Asc,G,Mar 30)
Kuda Huraa 108 (16 1/2f,Nby,HY,Mar 1)
Kudu Country 108 (16f,Hay,G,Mar 19)
Kusadasi 105 (20 1/2f,Utt,G,Jun 30)

Lac Fontana 118 (17f,Chl,G,Mar 14)
Lac Sacre 106 (16f,Ffo,S,Mar 27)
Lackamon 109 (27f,Kel,G,Mar 22)
Lamb Or Cod 109 (20f,Chp,S,Oct 26)
Lancing 106 (16 1/2f,Per,GF,Jun 9)
Lastoftheleaders 105 (16f,Leo,S,Dec 27)
Laudatory 110 (16 1/2f,Str,GF,Sep 7)
Laughton Park 105 (21f,Plu,G,Mar 31)
Lava Lamp 109 (22f,Crt,S,May 27)
Le Rocher 117 (17f,Chl,HY,Jan 25)
Le Vent D'Antan 109 (20f,Fai,S,Apr 6)
Legacy Gold 109 (17f,Exe,S,Feb 21)
Lemons Ground 105 (16f,Plu,GS,Dec 16)
Leo Luna 106 (19 1/2f,Asc,S,Feb 15)
Letsby Avenue 108 (22 1/2f,Str,GS,Sep 17)
Leviathan 107 (16f,Hay,S,Dec 21)
Liberty One 108 (20 1/2f,Utt,GS,Mar 15)
Lie Forrit 110 (27f,Kel,G,Mar 22)
Lienosus 105 (20f,Chp,S,Oct 26)
Lieutenant Colonel 114 (21f,Chl,G,Mar 12)
Lieutenant Miller 106 (20f,Ain,S,Dec 7)
Life And Soul 108 (16 1/2f,Kel,GF,May 26)
Lifetime 106 (16 1/2f,Wet,GS,Nov 16)
Lightening Rod 107 (16 1/2f,Don,G,Dec 14)
Like Minded 108 (20f,Ain,S,Dec 7)
Lily Waugh 112 (20f,Fon,GS,Dec 10)
Lisbon 109 (17 1/2f,Crt,GF,May 25)
Listen And Learn 108 (22f,Nab,GF,Sep 24)
Little Jon 107 (16 1/2f,Nby,HY,Feb 8)
Local Hero 106 (16f,Mus,S,Jan 1)
Long Lunch 110 (16f,War,G,Mar 19)
Lookout Mountain 106 (26f,Hun,GS,Nov 3)
Lord Brendy 110 (16 1/2f,Hex,HY,Nov 20)
Lord Grantham 106 (20 1/2f,Utt,G,May 4)
Lord Protector 108 (16 1/2f,Chp,HY,Feb 22)
Los Nadis 110 (24 1/2f,Mus,G,Nov 8)
Loyaute 106 (16f,Lud,G,Mar 20)
Luci Di Mezzanotte 112 (16 1/2f,Wet,G,May 23)
Lucky Landing 105 (19f,Mar,G,Aug 17)
Luctor Emergo 105 (24 1/2f,Mus,G,Dec 9)
Lyssio 109 (16f,Fak,G,Jun 2)
Lyvius 119 (17f,Chl,G,Dec 13)

Madness Light 108 (20 1/2f,Utt,HY,Dec 31)
Magic Money 107 (21f,Lud,G,Apr 10)
Magnifique Etoile 108 (19f,Str,S,Oct 26)
Major Milborne 107 (16f,Tow,S,Dec 19)
Makadamia 106 (22f,Wcn,GS,Apr 2)
Makari 111 (16 1/2f,Don,G,Dec 14)
Makhzoon 109 (22f,Wet,GS,Nov 27)
Maller Tree 107 (20f,Fak,S,Jan 1)
Man Of Leisure 108 (20 1/2f,Utt,G,Sep 11)
Marcilhac 110 (21f,Plu,HY,Jan 5)
Markem 105 (20f,Sed,HY,Jan 26)
Marmas 106 (24 1/2f,Mus,G,Nov 8)
Masquerade 115 (17f,Ban,GS,Dec 13)
Massena 110 (17f,Tau,G,Mar 24)
Master Dee 110 (16 1/2f,Don,GS,Feb 19)
Master Of The Game 113 (19 1/2f,Don,GS,Jan 25)
Master Red 108 (16 1/2f,Wet,GS,Apr 13)
Masters Hill 106 (23 1/2f,Exe,GS,Oct 22)
Matthew Riley 106 (24 1/2f,Don,GS,Feb 19)
Mcllhatton 107 (22f,Nab,GF,May 20)
Medieval Chapel 106 (24 1/2f,Mus,S,Feb 2)
Medinas 107 (24f,Chl,G,Mar 13)
Meetings Man 108 (17f,Mar,G,Jun 21)
Meister Eckhart 114 (20f,Fon,HY,Feb 23)
Melodic Rendezvous 113 (16f,Wcn,GS,Nov 9)
Mercers Court 109 (21f,Plu,G,Mar 31)
Mickie 114 (24f,Hay,HY,Feb 15)
Midnight Belle 107 (20 1/2f,Sth,S,Nov 8)
Midnight Cataria 105 (21f,Nby,GS,Mar 22)
Mighty Clarets 109 (16f,Wor,GF,Jun 26)
Milan Bound 110 (20f,Crl,GS,Oct 24)
Milano Supremo 105 (16 1/2f,Hex,G,May 4)
Milo Man 108 (16f,Lei,HY,Jan 7)
Milord 107 (20 1/2f,Utt,S,Nov 1)
Minella Foru 114 (17f,Chl,G,Mar 14)
Minella Friend 110 (17f,Exe,GS,Oct 22)
Minella Reception 108 (16 1/2f,Per,GS,Apr 23)
Minority Interest 111 (16f,Plu,GS,Dec 16)
Miss Fortywinks 105 (17f,Nab,G,Apr 19)
Mister Dillon 111 (24f,Chl,G,Mar 13)
Mister Newby 108 (20 1/2f,Sth,G,May 9)
Mixologist 107 (17f,Exe,S,Dec 19)
Mo Rouge 107 (20 1/2f,Per,GS,Apr 23)
Mohawk Ridge 111 (17f,Crl,HY,Feb 5)
Mojolika 109 (16f,Ncs,HY,Feb 22)
Molly's A Diva 107 (21f,Nby,GS,Mar 22)
Momkinzain 108 (16 1/2f,Per,GF,Jun 9)
Mondo Cane 105 (20 1/2f,Sth,S,Mar 3)
Monetary Fund 110 (24 1/2f,Mus,G,Nov 8)
Montbazon 117 (17f,Chl,G,Mar 14)
Montefeltro 105 (18 1/2f,Fon,GS,May 15)
More Of That 113 (24f,Chl,G,Mar 13)
Morning Royalty 108 (17f,Chl,G,Mar 14)
Mortlestown 105 (20 1/2f,Sth,S,Mar 3)
Moss Cloud 105 (16f,Ncs,G,Nov 15)
Moss On The Mill 105 (21f,Lud,GS,Nov 25)
Mosspark 113 (20 1/2f,Hun,S,Feb 20)
Mount Vesuvius 108 (17f,Sed,GF,Sep 5)
Mountain King 111 (16f,Lud,HY,Jan 16)
Moyle Park 110 (16f,Leo,S,Dec 27)
Mr Cardle 105 (21f,Lud,GS,Nov 25)
Mr Mole 110 (16f,Hay,G,May 11)
Mr Utah 105 (19 1/2f,Crl,GS,Mar 16)
Mrs Eff 105 (20 1/2f,Hex,G,May 4)
Mrs Peachey 105 (20 1/2f,Hun,G,Oct 6)
Muckle Roe 105 (16f,Lud,HY,Jan 16)
Muhtaris 108 (18 1/2f,Fon,GS,Dec 10)
Multitude Of Sins 107 (17f,Nab,GS,Sep 30)
Munsaab 108 (20f,Ain,G,Oct 27)
My Brother Sylvest 106 (16f,Wcn,G,Oct 17)
My Guardian Angel 106 (16f,Fak,G,Mar 14)
My Miss Lucy 113 (20f,Fon,GS,Dec 10)
My Tent Or Yours 121 (16 1/2f,Chl,GS,Mar 11)
My Wigwam Or Yours 107 (21f,Nby,G,Mar 21)
Mysteree 106 (24 1/2f,Ayr,HY,Mar 7)
Mystery Drama 108 (17f,Ain,S,Dec 7)

Narcissist 109 (20f,Wet,GS,Nov 16)
Nautical Twilight 105 (16f,Ncs,S,Dec 21)
Neighbourhood 105 (16f,Tow,HY,Feb 23)
Neptune Equester 109 (27f,Kel,G,Mar 22)
Nesterenko 110 (16 1/2f,Ain,GS,Apr 5)
Never Enough Time 109 (16f,Leo,SH,Feb 9)
New Year's Eve 109 (19f,Mar,S,Feb 16)
Nexius 106 (20f,Ncs,G,Mar 15)
No Loose Change 106 (22f,Nab,GF,Jun 5)
No No Mac 110 (20 1/2f,Sth,HY,Jan 6)
No No Romeo 106 (20f,Ain,GS,Apr 5)
No Such Number 106 (16f,Sth,G,Dec 3)
No To Trident 105 (16f,Ffo,G,May 25)
Noble Prince 110 (21f,Chl,G,Mar 12)
Northern Meeting 108 (17f,Nab,G,Apr 19)
Northern Oscar 105 (19f,Mar,S,Dec 26)
Now This Is It 110 (16 1/2f,Per,G,Aug 17)

Ocean Club 108 (22f,Crt,G,Aug 26)
Old Tricks 107 (22f,Wcn,HY,Dec 26)
Old Way 106 (16 1/2f,San,S,Mar 7)
Oliver's Gold 106 (16f,Utt,G,Jly 26)
Oliver's Hill 105 (16 1/2f,Wet,G,Mar 18)
On The Bridge 111 (24f,Chl,G,Mar 13)
One For Harry 106 (20 1/2f,Hex,S,Mar 31)
One Lucky Lady 107 (20 1/2f,Utt,G,May 4)
One Term 108 (20f,Ain,G,May 17)
Orangeaday 106 (20f,Chp,GS,Apr 25)
Orgilgo Bay 106 (16 1/2f,Chl,G,Mar 12)
Oscar Fortune 109 (20 1/2f,Hun,S,Oct 15)
Oscar Hoof 107 (16f,Kem,GS,Mar 15)
Oscar Magic 105 (22f,San,GS,Dec 7)
Oscar Rock 111 (20f,Wet,GS,Nov 1)
Oscar Tanner 109 (20f,Sed,S,Dec 26)
Oscars Den 109 (16f,Utt,S,Nov 16)
Ossie's Dancer 108 (16 1/2f,Chp,S,Apr 5)
Otto The Great 108 (22f,Nab,GF,Jun 5)
Our Boy Ben 112 (16 1/2f,Hex,HY,Nov 20)
Our Conor 114 (16f,Leo,S,Dec 29)
Outrageous Request 108 (16f,Lei,GS,Dec 1)

Padre Tito 107 (20f,Ffo,S,Nov 22)
Pandy 105 (21f,Lud,G,Apr 10)
Paradise Valley 105 (16 1/2f,Hun,G,Apr 21)
Parc Des Princes 106 (22 1/2f,Kel,G,Apr 22)
Parson's Punch 105 (16 1/2f,Per,GF,Jly 14)
Party Palace 105 (17f,Nab,GF,Jly 15)
Party Rock 113 (20f,Ain,G,May 17)
Pas Trop Tard 106 (16 1/2f,Wet,GS,Oct 16)
Pass The Time 109 (17f,Tau,G,Nov 28)

Pateese 109 (24f,Chl,G,Mar 13)
Patsys Castle 105 (20 1/2f,Hun,S,Oct 15)
Pearl 107 (17f,Tau,G,Nov 28)
Pearl Castle 110 (16 1/2f,Don,GS,Jan 24)
Peckhamecho 105 (20f,Chp,S,Oct 26)
Pension Plan 107 (24f,Ffo,G,May 6)
Persian Herald 105 (20 1/2f,Hex,S,Mar 31)
Pertuis 105 (16 1/2f,Wet,GS,Nov 16)
Pete 107 (22f,Crt,G,Aug 24)
Phase Shift 106 (16 1/2f,Str,S,Oct 26)
Phone Home 105 (22f,San,S,Mar 7)
Pilgreen 105 (20f,Chp,S,Mar 25)
Pindar 108 (17f,Nab,GF,Sep 24)
Pine Creek 109 (16f,Asc,GS,Nov 2)
Pineau De Re 112 (24f,Chl,G,Mar 13)
Pink Gin 106 (16f,Tow,HY,Jan 19)
Pixie Cut 105 (16f,Ayr,HY,Feb 20)
Plinth 109 (16f,Leo,SH,Feb 9)
Population 107 (16f,Mus,G,Nov 8)
Port Melon 109 (21f,Chl,G,Nov 16)
Portway Flyer 108 (21f,Kem,GS,Mar 15)
Potomac 106 (16 1/2f,Kel,GF,May 26)
Potters Cross 108 (20f,Chp,S,Oct 26)
Present View 105 (20 1/2f,Hun,S,Oct 15)
Pressies Girl 108 (22f,Wcn,GS,Apr 2)
Prideofthecastle 111 (20 1/2f,Hun,S,Feb 6)
Prima Porta 108 (24f,Asc,HY,Jan 18)
Prince Rudi 106 (22f,Fai,GY,Apr 21)
Prince Siegfried 107 (16 1/2f,Hun,S,Nov 12)
Princely Player 111 (20f,Fon,G,Oct 5)
Princess Annabelle 105 (22f,Nab,GF,May 20)
Prompter 107 (16 1/2f,Hun,GS,Dec 12)
Ptit Zig 115 (16 1/2f,Chl,GS,Mar 11)
Purcell's Bridge 106 (22f,Wet,GS,Oct 16)
Pure Faith 108 (27f,Nab,GF,Aug 3)
Pure Science 105 (21f,Chl,G,Nov 16)
Purple Bay 110 (16 1/2f,Don,G,Dec 14)

Quaddick Lake 105 (20f,Chp,S,Oct 26)
Quadriller 106 (16 1/2f,Str,GF,Jly 21)
Quartz De Thaix 109 (24f,Chl,S,Jan 1)
Queen Olivia 106 (16f,Sth,G,Apr 23)
Quel Elite 107 (27f,Kel,G,Mar 22)
Quest Magic 105 (16 1/2f,Hex,G,May 11)
Quick Brew 107 (17f,Crl,GS,Mar 16)
Quick Decisson 108 (16f,Wcn,HY,Jan 16)
Quick Jack 109 (16f,Leo,S,Jan 25)
Quickpick Vic 111 (16f,Leo,SH,Jan 26)
Quite By Chance 109 (17f,Exe,GS,Oct 22)

Racing Pulse 111 (24 1/2f,Mus,S,Feb 2)
Radmores Revenge 108 (16 1/2f,Hex,G,May 11)
Rainbow Peak 112 (16 1/2f,Ain,GS,Apr 5)
Rajnagan 107 (17f,Tau,GF,May 2)
Raktiman 105 (20 1/2f,Sth,G,Jly 14)
Rally 107 (20f,Wet,GS,Nov 1)
Ranjaan 106 (16 1/2f,Don,G,Dec 14)
Rare Bob 106 (24f,Chl,G,Oct 18)
Rathvinden 118 (21f,Chl,G,Mar 12)
Rattlin 107 (24f,Mar,G,Apr 21)
Raven's Tower 106 (16 1/2f,San,GS,Apr 26)
Rawnaq 112 (16 1/2f,Chl,G,Nov 17)
Ray Diamond 105 (19 1/2f,Tow,GS,Nov 30)
Rayadour 108 (16 1/2f,Wet,GS,Apr 13)
Rayvin Black 106 (17f,Exe,GF,Oct 10)
Ready Token 107 (22f,Wet,GS,Apr 13)
Real Steel 112 (16f,Fai,S,Apr 6)
Reaping The Reward 106 (20 1/2f,Per,G,Jly 4)
Red Admirable 105 (19f,Mar,S,Dec 26)
Red Seventy 108 (16f,Wcn,S,Mar 6)
Red Sherlock 114 (20 1/2f,Sth,G,Dec 15)
Redera 106 (16 1/2f,Chl,G,Nov 17)
Redpender 112 (16f,Ayr,S,Nov 2)
Refer 108 (17f,Chl,G,Apr 16)
Regal D'Estruval 106 (16f,Fak,G,Mar 14)
Regal Encore 108 (16 1/2f,Hex,S,Dec 11)
Return Spring 111 (24f,Chl,S,Jan 1)
Revaader 108 (17f,Exe,S,Feb 21)
Revani 105 (17f,Exe,G,Apr 15)
Reve De Sivola 115 (25f,Asc,S,Dec 21)
Reverb 107 (16 1/2f,Chp,HY,Nov 21)
Reves D'Amour 109 (16f,Tow,GS,Nov 7)
Revocation 108 (16 1/2f,Hex,GS,Oct 4)
Rhapando 110 (16 1/2f,Don,GS,Feb 19)
Rime Avec Gentil 105 (17f,Ban,G,May 18)
Rio Milan 106 (20 1/2f,Utt,HY,Dec 20)
Rior 105 (22f,Wcn,G,Dec 5)
Robbie 109 (16 1/2f,Don,G,Dec 14)
Roberto Pegasus 107 (17f,Tau,G,Mar 24)
Rock On Rocky 105 (16 1/2f,Chp,GS,Apr 5)
Rock On Ruby 117 (16f,Kem,GS,Oct 20)
Rock Relief 107 (16f,Ncs,S,Mar 28)
Rocky Wednesday 107 (16f,Leo,S,Dec 27)
Roman Flight 108 (16 1/2f,Ain,GS,Apr 5)
Romany Ryme 105 (22f,Wet,GS,Apr 13)
Ronaldinho 105 (17f,Chl,HY,Jan 25)
Ronaldo Des Mottes 106 (16f,Asc,S,Dec 21)
Rosa Fleet 106 (17f,Ban,HY,Feb 26)
Rosie Probert 108 (16 1/2f,Str,S,Oct 26)
Rosquero 106 (16f,Ayr,HY,Feb 20)
Rosslyn Castle 108 (16 1/2f,Chp,S,Mar 8)
Royal Boy 111 (16f,Kem,S,Jan 11)
Royal Irish Hussar 112 (16 1/2f,Chl,G,Nov 16)
Royal Macnab 107 (19f,Mar,GS,Dec 5)
Royal Opera 106 (17f,Mar,G,Jun 21)
Royal Player 109 (21f,War,S,Feb 8)
Royal Regatta 109 (20 1/2f,Lei,GS,Dec 1)
Rugged Jack 105 (20 1/2f,Per,S,Apr 24)
Rule The World 108 (24f,Chl,G,Mar 13)
Ruler Of All 107 (16 1/2f,Wet,G,May 23)
Rum And Butter 109 (19f,Nab,GF,Aug 22)
Rumble Of Thunder 107 (19f,Mar,S,Feb 16)
Run Along Boy 108 (19f,Nab,G,Oct 11)
Run Ructions Run 111 (21f,Nby,GS,Mar 22)
Runswick Royal 111 (18f,Kel,GS,Feb 13)
Russborough 106 (17f,Crl,GS,Mar 16)
Rutherglen 109 (17f,Ban,S,Dec 22)

Saffron Wells 106 (21f,Mar,S,Feb 4)
Sail And Return 105 (27f,Str,G,May 19)
Sailors Warn 111 (18f,Leo,S,Mar 2)
Saint Jerome 113 (16f,War,G,Mar 19)
Saint Roque 109 (20f,Wor,G,Jun 1)
Saint Thomas 109 (17f,Sed,GF,Oct 1)
Salubrious 111 (25f,Asc,S,Dec 21)
Sam Lord 105 (16f,Ncs,HY,Jan 4)
Sametegal 112 (16 1/2f,Chl,G,Nov 17)
Sammy Black 107 (22f,Fai,GY,Apr 21)
Saphir Du Rheu 111 (22f,San,GS,Dec 7)
Saphir River 107 (22f,Wet,S,Dec 26)
Satanic Beat 108 (16f,Ncs,G,Mar 15)
Sausalito Sunrise 109 (24f,Ban,GS,Apr 12)
Scholastica 107 (22f,Asc,GS,Nov 23)
Scimon Templar 107 (16f,Ncs,HY,Jan 15)
Scoglio 108 (18 1/2f,Fon,GS,May 15)
Scots Gaelic 109 (20f,Ain,G,Oct 27)
Scotsbrook Legend 106 (16 1/2f,Hun,S,Mar 2)
Scotswell 106 (22 1/2f,Kel,G,Apr 29)
Sea Lord 111 (17f,Mar,G,Jly 20)
Sealous Scout 106 (22 1/2f,Kel,S,Apr 7)
Seas Of Green 106 (20f,Fon,GS,Dec 10)
Secrete Stream 107 (16 1/2f,Wet,S,Jan 21)
Seebright 107 (20f,Fon,GS,Nov 27)
Seedling 110 (16 1/2f,Nby,GS,Nov 29)
Seefood 109 (24f,Leo,S,Dec 28)
Seeyouatmidnight 115 (24f,Hay,HY,Feb 15)
Separate Shadows 108 (17f,Ban,G,May 18)
Sergeant Mattie 113 (21f,Plu,G,Mar 31)
Settledoutofcourt 105 (24 1/2f,Per,G,May 15)
Seventh Sign 108 (24 1/2f,Don,GS,Feb 19)
Seventh Sky 107 (16f,Kem,G,May 12)
Sgt Reckless 115 (16 1/2f,Chl,GS,Mar 11)
Shadow Catcher 109 (16 1/2f,Per,G,Aug 17)
Shammick Boy 110 (20f,Chp,S,Oct 26)
Shanahan's Turn 113 (21f,Chl,G,Mar 12)
Shantou Magic 110 (19f,Mar,S,Nov 10)
Sheriff Hutton 110 (27f,Nab,GF,Aug 3)
Shoegazer 107 (27f,Nab,GF,Aug 3)
Shooting Times 106 (24 1/2f,Per,GS,Apr 23)
Shuh Shuh Gah 108 (20 1/2f,Sth,G,May 9)
Sidney Melbourne 108 (16 1/2f,Str,GF,Jun 8)
Sign Of A Victory 107 (16 1/2f,Nby,GS,Nov 29)
Silsol 110 (20 1/2f,Lei,GS,Dec 11)
Silver Gent 108 (20 1/2f,Per,GS,Apr 23)
Silverton 110 (16f,Ayr,S,Nov 2)
Sinbad The Sailor 105 (24f,Chl,G,Oct 18)
Sir Mangan 111 (20f,Wet,GS,Nov 16)
Sir Pitt 106 (16f,Ffo,HY,Dec 16)
Sirop De Menthe 108 (16f,Plu,GS,Dec 16)
Skint 105 (16 1/2f,Wet,GS,Dec 7)
Sky Khan 106 (16 1/2f,Str,GF,Jun 8)
Sleep In First 106 (16 1/2f,Per,GF,Jun 9)
Sleepy Haven 108 (16 1/2f,San,GS,Apr 26)
Smalib Monterg 111 (20f,Ain,G,May 17)
Smart Freddy 106 (20f,Fon,GS,Nov 27)
Smart Ruler 108 (17 1/2f,Crt,GF,Jly 22)
Smashing 111 (21f,Chl,G,Mar 12)
So Fine 109 (24f,Chl,G,Oct 18)
Softsong 106 (19 1/2f,Don,GS,Jan 8)
Solar Impulse 109 (16 1/2f,Chp,G,Apr 21)
Solaras Exhibition 107 (16f,Utt,G,Jun 30)
Solway Bay 105 (24 1/2f,Per,GF,Jly 14)
Somchine 106 (16f,Wor,G,Jun 11)
Somemothersdohavem 108 (19 1/2f,Tau,HY,Feb 27)
Somethingwonderful 105 (16 1/2f,Ain,GS,Apr 5)
Son Of Flicka 108 (21f,Chl,G,Mar 12)
Son Of Suzie 106 (16f,Tow,HY,Feb 23)
Songsmith 107 (20 1/2f,Utt,GS,Mar 15)
Southfield Theatre 112 (24f,Chl,G,Mar 13)
Soweheard 105 (24f,Hex,G,Jun 15)
Sparkling Hand 106 (16f,Ncs,S,Dec 21)
Special Catch 107 (18f,Kel,GS,Feb 13)
Speedy Tunes 105 (21f,Lud,G,Apr 10)
Spirit Of Shankly 111 (20 1/2f,Hun,S,Feb 20)
Spirit Oscar 110 (20f,Fon,HY,Dec 26)
Splash Of Ginge 116 (20f,Ain,GS,Apr 5)
Sporting Boy 105 (19f,Nab,GS,Sep 30)
Springinherstep 106 (16f,Lud,G,Apr 10)
Spyder 108 (20 1/2f,Sth,HY,Feb 3)
St Ignatius 106 (16f,Fak,G,Mar 14)
Star Of Aragon 105 (16f,Leo,SH,Feb 9)
Steel City 106 (16 1/2f,Hun,HY,Jan 2)
Stellar Notion 111 (16 1/2f,Don,GS,Feb 19)
Stevie Thunder 105 (16 1/2f,Str,G,Apr 13)
Stiff Upper Lip 106 (16f,Tow,G,Apr 20)
Stonebrook 107 (16f,Ayr,HY,Feb 11)
Storm Of Swords 107 (16f,War,G,Mar 19)
Stormin Exit 107 (16f,Ayr,HY,Feb 20)
Stormy Weather 109 (16 1/2f,Wet,GS,Oct 16)
Stow 107 (17f,Tau,G,Mar 24)
Streets Of Newyork 105 (16f,Mus,S,Jan 1)
Strike Fast 105 (24f,Hex,S,Mar 31)
Strollawaynow 109 (21f,Plu,G,Mar 31)
Strongpoint 110 (16f,Mus,S,Jan 1)
Stuccodor 106 (16f,Leo,SH,Jan 26)
Such A Legend 106 (16 1/2f,Chp,GS,Apr 5)
Sud Pacifique 106 (16 1/2f,Str,GF,Jun 8)
Sun Wild Life 107 (18 1/2f,Fon,GS,Dec 10)
Super Collider 105 (17f,Ban,G,May 3)
Superciliary 105 (16f,Wcn,GS,Apr 2)
Supreme Carolina 107 (24f,Leo,S,Dec 28)
Swallowshide 105 (22f,Wcn,G,Nov 21)
Swampfire 106 (19f,Mar,GF,Jly 7)
Swing Bowler 113 (16f,Ayr,GS,Apr 12)
Swing Hard 106 (17 1/2f,Crt,GF,Jly 22)
Swinging Hawk 105 (19f,War,GS,Nov 20)
Switched Off 105 (22f,Crt,S,May 27)
Swnymor 107 (20 1/2f,Utt,GS,Mar 15)
Sybarite 107 (27f,Per,S,Apr 25)
Symphonick 105 (16 1/2f,Hex,G,Jun 23)

Taaresh 106 (16f,Wor,G,Aug 19)
Tagrita 105 (23 1/2f,Exe,S,Dec 19)
Taigan 106 (20 1/2f,Sth,G,Jun 2)
Talkin Sence 109 (27f,Kel,GS,Nov 9)
Tanerko Emery 109 (16 1/2f,Chl,G,Nov 17)
Tantamount 105 (20f,Ain,S,Dec 7)
Taradrewe 106 (20f,Fon,G,Apr 11)
Taste The Wine 109 (18 1/2f,Fon,GS,May 15)
Teak 106 (22f,Nab,GF,Sep 1)
Tealissio 105 (16f,Lei,GS,Nov 18)
Ted Spread 107 (16 1/2f,Don,G,Dec 14)
Templebraden 106 (24f,Ban,GS,Mar 22)
Tempuran 106 (16f,Lud,G,Oct 24)
Teshali 107 (16 1/2f,Str,GF,Jun 8)
The Bay Bandit 105 (16 1/2f,Str,GF,Jly 21)
The Bull Hayes 105 (16 1/2f,Wet,GS,Nov 16)
The Green Ogre 108 (16f,Plu,GS,Apr 20)
The Knoxs 105 (24 1/2f,Ain,GS,Apr 5)
The Liquidator 113 (16 1/2f,Chl,GS,Mar 11)
The Mighty Milan 105 (16f,Leo,SH,Feb 9)
The New One 122 (16f,Kem,GS,Oct 20)
The Orange Rogue 107 (16f,Ayr,HY,Jan 2)
The Pirate's Queen 110 (21f,Nby,GS,Mar 22)
The Rattler Obrien 105 (22f,Nab,G,Apr 19)
The Skyfarmer 121 (17f,Chl,G,Dec 13)
The Tullow Tank 116 (16f,Leo,S,Dec 27)
Theatre Evening 109 (22f,Nab,GF,May 20)
Theatrebar 110 (21f,Lud,GS,Nov 25)
Themanfrom Minella 107 (20 1/2f,Hun,S,Mar 2)
Things Change 108 (17 1/2f,Crt,S,May 29)
Thomas Crapper 110 (21f,Chl,G,Nov 15)
Thomas Edison 110 (17f,Chl,G,Mar 14)
Thoresby 105 (19 1/2f,Tow,G,May 21)
Thousand Stars 114 (20f,Fai,GY,Apr 21)
Three Kingdoms 113 (16 1/2f,Chl,GS,Mar 11)
Thunder Sheik 106 (16 1/2f,Str,GF,Aug 1)
Tiger Roll 112 (17f,Chl,G,Mar 14)
Tikkandemickey 105 (16 1/2f,Hex,S,Dec 11)
Timesremembered 111 (20f,Chp,S,Oct 26)
Tinker Time 105 (24f,Chl,G,Apr 16)
Tiny Dancer 105 (16 1/2f,Hex,G,May 11)
Tiqris 110 (16 1/2f,Nby,GS,Nov 29)
Tiradia 106 (17f,Tau,G,Apr 23)
Tistory 109 (19 1/2f,Don,G,Mar 1)
Titus Bolt 108 (20 1/2f,Per,S,Apr 24)
Tom Wade 108 (16f,Utt,G,Jun 30)
Tonvadosa 108 (24f,Hex,S,Mar 31)
Tony Dinozzo 105 (22f,Nab,GF,Sep 24)
Top Totti 106 (22f,Asc,GS,Nov 23)
Top Wood 106 (24f,Hay,HY,Feb 15)
Torero 110 (16f,Plu,GS,Dec 16)
Tornado In Milan 106 (17f,Tau,HY,Feb 18)
Totalize 107 (17f,Chl,HY,Jan 25)
Toubeera 111 (20 1/2f,Utt,GS,May 18)
Town Mouse 108 (16f,Kem,G,Oct 20)
Trackmate 110 (24f,Chl,G,Oct 18)
Travis County 105 (17f,Sed,GS,Dec 3)
Trickaway 107 (20 1/2f,Per,GS,Apr 23)
Truckers Steel 106 (20 1/2f,Sth,G,Dec 15)
Trucking Along 108 (16f,Ayr,HY,Feb 20)
Trustan Times 112 (24f,Chl,G,Mar 13)
Tsar Alexandre 106 (19 1/2f,Don,G,Mar 1)
Tullyesker Hill 105 (21f,War,GS,Dec 8)
Turtle Watch 105 (16 1/2f,Kel,GS,Oct 19)
Twelve Roses 116 (21f,Chl,G,Mar 12)
Twoways 106 (16f,Wcn,HY,Feb 26)
Tzora 109 (17f,Nab,G,Jun 25)

Ubaltique 106 (18f,Kel,S,Dec 29)
Uhlan Bute 109 (16f,Lei,HY,Jan 7)
Ulzana's Raid 108 (21f,War,GS,Dec 8)
Un Ace 115 (16 1/2f,Don,GS,Feb 19)
Un Beau Matin 108 (20f,Fai,GY,Apr 21)
Un Temps Pour Tout 110 (16f,Hay,HY,Jan 18)
Uncle Jimmy 110 (20f,Ain,G,Oct 27)
Unex Picasso 105 (26f,Crt,GF,May 25)
Union Saint 108 (27f,Nab,GF,Aug 3)
Unowhatimeanharry 108 (20f,Fon,GS,Nov 27)
Up For An Oscar 109 (20 1/2f,Sth,G,May 9)
Upazo 105 (16f,Kem,S,Jan 11)
Upsie 109 (20f,Fai,GY,Apr 21)
Upsilon Bleu 110 (18f,Kel,GS,Feb 13)
Upswing 107 (22f,San,GS,Dec 7)
Urbain De Sivola 108 (20 1/2f,Chl,G,Mar 14)
Urban Hymn 105 (20f,Hay,HY,Dec 30)
Ut Majeur Aulmes 106 (16f,Utt,GS,Dec 10)
Utopie Des Bordes 109 (24f,Chl,G,Mar 13)

Va'Vite 108 (19f,Mar,GF,Jly 7)
Valid Reason 105 (16½f,San,HY,Nov 9)
Valmy Baie 105 (20f,Fai,SH,Feb 22)
Valseur Lido 115 (16f,Fai,S,Apr 6)
Vandross 107 (18½f,Fon,GS,Dec 10)
Vaniteux 115 (16½f,Chl,GS,Mar 11)
Vasco Du Ronceray 107 (16½f,Ain,GS,Apr 5)
Vautour 119 (16½f,Chl,GS,Mar 11)
Vendor 109 (16½f,Nby,HY,Feb 8)
Very Noble 109 (17f,Tau,G,Mar 24)
Very Wood 105 (24f,Chl,G,Mar 14)
Vibrato Valtat 113 (16½f,San,GS,Dec 7)
Vicente 108 (20f,Wcn,GS,Mar 23)
Vicenzo Mio 112 (16f,Kem,S,Dec 27)
Vicky De L'Oasis 109 (16½f,Nby,S,Nov 30)
Vieux Lion Rouge 106 (16f,Wcn,HY,Jan 16)
Vikekhal 112 (16f,Plu,GS,Dec 16)
Vimiero 107 (17f,Nab,G,Aug 31)
Vinny Gambini 107 (19½f,Crl,S,Dec 1)
Vinstar 105 (17f,Mar,G,Mar 23)
Violet Dancer 111 (16f,Plu,S,Nov 4)
Virak 110 (17f,Tau,HY,Feb 18)
Virtuel D'Oudon 107 (22½f,Fon,GS,Mar 25)
Vivaldi Collonges 107 (24½f,Ayr,GS,Apr 11)
Volnay De Thaix 114 (20f,Ain,GS,Apr 5)
Voyage A New York 108 (17f,Crl,GS,Mar 16)
Vujiyama 105 (16½f,Chp,HY,Nov 21)
Vulcanite 108 (16½f,Str,GS,Mar 29)

Wakanda 107 (17f,Sed,GF,Oct 1)
Wake Your Dreams 105 (21f,Lud,G,May 16)
Waldorf Salad 109 (24½f,Tau,HY,Jan 28)
Waltz Darling 107 (16½f,Per,GS,Jly 31)
Warden Hill 107 (24f,Ban,GS,Mar 22)
Waterunder 108 (17f,Exe,S,Nov 13)
Wayward Glance 106 (24f,Ncs,G,Mar 15)
Well Mett 106 (23½f,Exe,GF,May 7)
Welsh Bard 108 (21½f,Sed,G,May 2)
Werenearlyoutofit 106 (16½f,Hun,S,Nov 12)
West Brit 105 (16½f,Hun,G,Sep 9)
West Wizard 109 (16f,Kem,G,Nov 25)
Westaway 106 (21f,Nby,HY,Mar 1)
Westerly Breeze 106 (21f,Lud,GS,Nov 25)
Western Boy 114 (16½f,Chl,GS,Mar 11)
Whisper 113 (21f,Chl,G,Mar 12)
Wicklow Brave 114 (16½f,Chl,GS,Mar 11)
Wilde Blue Yonder 116 (20f,Ain,GS,Apr 5)
Willow's Saviour 114 (16f,Asc,S,Dec 21)
Wily Fox 105 (19f,Mar,S,Nov 10)
Wolf Shield 105 (22f,Crt,S,May 27)
Woodford County 105 (24f,Utt,HY,Dec 20)
Woodland Walk 106 (24f,Mar,G,Apr 21)
Worthy Award 108 (16f,War,G,Mar 19)
Wuff 110 (20½f,Utt,HY,Dec 20)
Wyse Hill Teabags 111 (24½f,Mus,S,Feb 2)

Yazdi 107 (16½f,Chp,S,Apr 5)
Yorkist 110 (16f,Ncs,HY,Feb 22)

Zafranagar 107 (16½f,Wet,GS,Nov 16)
Zalgarry 107 (20½f,Lei,GS,Dec 11)
Zamdy Man 111 (16f,Hay,HY,Jan 18)
Zamoyski 106 (16½f,Don,GS,Feb 19)
Zaplamation 108 (16½f,Wet,GS,Nov 16)
Zarkandar 112 (20½f,Chl,S,Jan 1)
Zaru 108 (22½f,Kel,G,Apr 22)
Zarzal 106 (16f,Plu,GS,Apr 20)
Ziga Boy 105 (21f,Nby,HY,Feb 28)
Zuider Zee 109 (20½f,Hun,S,Nov 12)